Garzanti

comprehensive

italian-english   *english-italian*

dictionary

Garzanti
comprehensive
italian-english   english-italian
dictionary

edited by Mario Hazon

McGraw-Hill Book Company, Inc.
New York   Toronto   London

Garzanti comprehensive italian-english english-italian dictionary

© *Copyright 1961 by Garzanti Editore.*
Printed in Italy
All rights reserved. This book or parts thereof
may not be reproduced in any form without
written permission of the publishers

Library of Congress Catalog Card Number: 62-20508

22920

Publisher's Foreword

Intended to be the richest, most authoritative one-volume work in the field, this is the first comprehensive Italian-English, English-Italian dictionary realized in the postwar period. Professor Mario Hazon, a distinguished scholar in both Italian and English literature, has directed the work of many noted persons in preparation of this exceptional instrument.

The significance of the dictionary to those in the English-speaking world lies in its presenting detailed information for those who employ Italian in intellectual pursuits while, at the same time, meeting the needs of those who use Italian in everyday life.

The terminology of scholarship, literature, science and technology, art, and economics and commerce are presented with thoroughness. Contemporary colloquialisms are presented along with the standard language of contemporary social life. Idioms are given careful attention.

There are approximately 120,000 entries. In a typical entry the various meanings are listed with indication of the field where each is found and with examples showing the correct use of the word in context. Accent marks accompany each word in the Italian-English section.

The publishers wish to convey sincere thanks to Giovanna Foa of the Universita Commerciale Luigi Bocconi of Milan, who gave valuable advice to both Professor Hazon and the publishers. Thanks also go to the Professors Joseph W. Binns, Dennis A. Chamberlin, Anna Carveri, Giorgio Cusatelli, Vittorio Gozzer, Eleanora Heger Vita, and Liliana Zaccarelli, who have contributed generously.

How To Use the Dictionary

In the Italian-English section each term is supplied with an accent mark to aid in more accurate pronunciation. Entries of identical graphic aspects but of different etymological derivation are treated separately and are identified by an Arabic numeral placed immediately after each one. Within each entry the basic meanings taken on by a single term are identified by Arabic numerals placed immediately before each meaning. A list of initials and abbreviations used in Italy can be found in the appendix to the Italian-English section.

In the English-Italian section complex nouns and similar semantic associations are placed at the bottom of the entry to which they are related and are identified by an asterisk. Changes taken on by a term following a double consonant as well as the irregular plural forms are listed. Basic forms of the paradigm of irregular verbs have also been given. Verbs requiring specific construction bear a Roman numeral that refers to the corresponding paragraph of the table "Costruzioni del verbo inglese" (page viii). In the appendix to the English-Italian section are a list of proper nouns identical in both languages, a list of initials and abbreviations used in the English-speaking countries, and tables of weights and measures and monetary systems of Anglo-Saxon countries.

v

LETTERE E SIMBOLI

USATI PER LA TRASCRIZIONE FONETICA

(International Phonetic Association)

VOCALI

[i:] come in *see* [si:], *police* [pə'li:s], *clean* [kli:n]
[i] come in *six* [siks], *live* [liv], *money* ['mʌni]
[e] come in *yes* [jes], *bed* [bed], *head* [hed]
[æ] come in *cat* [kæt], *man* [mæn], *tax* [tæks]
[ɑ:] come in *car* [kɑ:*], *bath* [bɑ:θ], *yard* [jɑ:d]
[ɔ] come in *not* [nɔt], *dog* [dɔg], *cotton* ['kɔtn]

[ɔ:] come in *nor* [nɔ:*], *George* [dʒɔ:dʒ], *door* [dɔ:*]
[u] come in *put* [put], *good* [gud], *would* [wud]
[u:] come in *goose* [gu:s], *shoe* [ʃu:], *blue* [blu:]
[ʌ] come in *cut* [kʌt], *love* [lʌv], *country* ['kʌntri]
[ə:] come in *bird* [bə:d], *learn* [lə:n], *nurse* [nə:s]
[ə] come in *away* [ə'wei], *over* ['ouvə*], *centre* ['sentə*]

SEMIVOCALI

[w] come in *war* [wɔ:*], *well* [wel], *one* [wʌn]

[j] come in *yet* [jet], *yield* [ji:ld], *young* [jʌŋ]

DITTONGHI

[ei] come in *may* [mei], *made* [meid], *they* [ðei]
[ou] come in *home* [houm], *know* [nou], *coat* [kout]
[ai] come in *dine* [dain], *kind* [kaind], *right* [rait]
[au] come in *out* [aut], *house* [haus], *town* [taun]

[ɔi] come in *oil* [ɔil], *boy* [bɔi], *loyal* ['lɔiəl]
[iə] come in *ear* [iə*], *idea* [ai'diə], *beer* [biə*]
[ɛə] come in *air* [ɛə*], *there* [ðɛə*], *care* [kɛə*]
[uə] come in *sure* [ʃuə*], *tour* [tuə*], *mature* [mə'tjuə*]

CONSONANTI

[b] come in *baby* ['beibi], *book* [buk], *able* ['eibl]
[d] come in *dear* [diə*], *loud* [laud], *garden* ['gɑ:dn]
[f] come in *fall* [fɔ:l], *free* [fri:], *off* [ɔ:f]
[g] come in *game* [geim], *big* [big], *exam* [ig'zæm]
[h] come in *he* [hi:], *hot* [hɔt], *who* [hu:]
[k] come in *cooking* ['kukiŋ], *fact* [fækt], *Christmas* ['krisməs]
[l] come in *let* [let], *Alps* [ælps], *shall* [ʃæl]
[l] come in *colonel* ['kə:nl], *conventional* [kən'venʃənl], *flannelly* ['flænli]
[m] come in *mark* [mɑ:k], *mother* ['mʌðə*], *Tom* [tɔm]
[n] come in *no* [nou], *nice* [nais], *sun* [sʌn]
[ŋ] come in *nationally* ['næʃnəli], *seasonable* ['si:znəbl], *twopenny* ['tʌpni]
[p] come in *pencil* ['pensl], *spend* [spend], *lip* [lip]

[r] come in *rose* [rouz], *great* [greit], *merry* ['meri]
[s] come in *sea* [si:], *school* [sku:l], *kiss* [kis]
[t] come in *time* [taim], *tea* [ti:], *water* ['wɔ:tə*]
[v] come in *very* ['veri], *give* [giv], *glove* [glʌv]
[z] come in *amuse* [ə'mju:z], *passes* ['pɑ:siz], *zone* [zoun]
[ŋ] come in *long* [lɔŋ], *bringing* ['briŋiŋ], *king* [kiŋ]
[s] come in *dash* [dæʃ], *sugar* ['ʃugə*], *ocean* ['ouʃən]
[tʃ] come in *church* [tʃə:tʃ], *child* [tʃaild], *each* [i:tʃ]
[ʒ] come in *measure* ['meʒə*], *pleasure* ['pleʒə*], *rouge* [ru:ʒ]
[dʒ] come in *gem* [dʒem], *job* [dʒɔb], *page* [peidʒ]
[θ] come in *thanks* [θæŋks], *three* [θri:], *north* [nɔ:θ]
[ð] come in *this* [ðis], *those* [ðouz], *father* ['fɑ:ðə*]

ALTRI SEGNI

* in fine di parola indica [r], che normalmente si pronuncia solo se la parola che segue inizia con suono vocalico: *farther off* ['fɑ:ðərɔ:f]

' è l'accento tonico principale e precede la sillaba su cui posa maggiormente la voce: *brother* ['brʌðə*]

, è l'accento tonico secondario e precede la sillaba su cui la voce posa più brevemente; si ha soltanto nei polisillabi: *communication* [kə,mju:ni'keiʃən]

- sta ad indicare che le due lettere tra cui è collocato si devono pronunciare separatamente: *outskirt* ['aut-skə:t]

: dopo vocale, ne indica l'allungamento

(:) dopo vocale, indica che l'allungamento di questa è facoltativo

Le lettere in corsivo possono essere pronunciate od omesse.

COSTRUZIONI DEL VERBO INGLESE

(I)   Verbi e locuzioni seguiti dal gerundio o dal participio presente:

I shall avoid seeing him,	Eviterò di vederlo.
Is it worth while going?	Vale la pena di andare?
I saw him running,	Lo vidi correre.

N.B. - I verbi di percezione reggono il participio presente quando l'azione espressa dall'infinito italiano è continuata e viene compiuta dall'oggetto del verbo di percezione.

(II) Verbi seguiti dall'infinito o dal gerundio:

He began to read (o *reading*),	Cominciò a leggere.

(III) Verbi reggenti l'accusativo, anzichè il dativo come i corrispondenti italiani:

I answered him,	Gli risposi.
I ordered him to go,	Gli ordinai di andare.
He permitted me to go,	Permise che andassi.

(IV) Verbi reggenti l'accusativo e l'infinito:

He wants me to go for him,	Vuole che io vada per lui.
He can't bear you to be unhappy,	Non può sopportare che tu sia infelice.

(V)   Verbi reggenti l'infinito senza *to*:

I made him go,	Lo costrinsi ad andare.
You had better write to him,	Faresti meglio a scrivergli.
I saw him fall into the river,	Lo vidi cadere nel fiume.

N.B. - I verbi di percezione reggono l'infinito senza *to* quando l'azione espressa dall'infinito italiano viene percepita in tutto il suo svolgersi e compiuta dall'oggetto del verbo di percezione.

(VI) Verbi seguiti dall'accusativo e dal participio passato:

I heard him called by his mother,	Lo udii chiamare da sua madre.
I saw him saved by a sailor,	Lo vidi salvare da un marinaio.
I had my coat cleaned,	Feci pulire a secco il mio soprabito.

N.B. - I verbi di percezione reggono l'accusativo e il participio passato quando l'azione espressa dall'infinito italiano viene subita dall'oggetto del verbo di percezione. Prendono questa costruzione anche i verbi *to have* e *to get* nei significati corrispondenti all'italiano *fare* seguito da infinito e complemento diretto.

Abbreviations

abbr.	= abbreviazione. abbreviation		*contr.*	= contrazione. contraction
acc.	= accusativo. accusative		*(cuc.)*	= cucina. kitchen
(acu.)	= acustica. acoustics.		*dat.*	= dativo. dative
(acr.)	= aeronautica. aeronautics		*(dial.)*	= dialettale. dialect
ag.	= aggettivo. adjective		*dif.*	= difettivo. defective
(agr.)	= agricoltura. agriculture		*dim.*	= diminutivo. diminutive
(alg.)	= algebra. algebra		*(dir.)*	= diritto. law
(amer.)	= americano, inglese degli		*distrib.*	= distributivo. distributive
	Stati Uniti d'America.		*ecc.*	= eccetera. et cetera
	American English		*(eccl.)*	= ecclesiastico. ecclesiastical
(amm.)	= amministrazione.		*(econ.)*	= economia. economics
	administration		*(edil.)*	= edilizia. building trades
(anat.)	= anatomia. anatomy		*(elett.)*	= elettrologia, elettricità.
(ang.-in.)	= anglo-indiano			electricity
	Anglo-Indian		*(entom.)*	= entomologia. entomology
(arald.)	= araldica. heraldry		*etc.*	= *et cetera* (eccetera)
(arc.)	= arcaico. archaic		*f.*	= femminile. feminine
(arch.)	= architettura. architecture		*(fam.)*	= familiare. familiar
(archeol.)	= archeologia. archeology		*(farm.)*	= farmacia. pharmacy
(arit.)	= aritmetica. arithmetic		*(ferr.)*	= ferrovie. railroading
(art.)	= arti. the arts		*fig.*	= figurato. figurative
art.	= articolo. article		*(fil.)*	= filosofia. philosophy
(artig.)	= artigianato, artigianale.		*(fis.)*	= fisica. physics
	vocational arts		*(fisiol.)*	= fisiologia. physiology
(artigl.)	= artiglieria. artillery		*(fonet.)*	= fonetica. phonetics
(astr.)	= astronomia. astronomy		*(foto.)*	= fotografia. photography
att.	= attributo. attribute		*gener.*	= generalmente. generally
(austral.)	= austaliano. Australian		*(geog.)*	= geografia. geography
(aut.)	= automobile, automobilismo.		*(geol.)*	= geologia. geology
	automobile		*(geom.)*	= geometria. geometry
av.	= avverbio. adverb		*ger.*	= gerundio. gerund
(biol.)	= biologia. biology		*(gr.)*	= greco, grecismo. Greek
(bot.)	= botanica. botany		*(gram.)*	= grammatica. grammar
c.	= comune (di genere comune).		*i.*	= intransitivo. intransitive
	common gender		*(idiot.)*	= idiotismo. idiom
card.	= cardinale. cardinal number		*imp.*	= impersonale. impersonal
(chim.)	= chimica. chemistry		*imperat.*	= imperativo. imperative
(chir.)	= chirurgia. surgery		*(ind.)*	= industria. industry
(cine.)	= cinematografia.		*indef.*	= indefinito. indefinite
	cinematography		*indic.*	= indicativo. indicative
co.	= cosa. thing		*inf.*	= infinito. infinative
(col.)	= coloniale, inglese coloniale.		*(ing.)*	= ingegneria. engineering
	colonial, British colonial		*inter.*	= interiezione. interjection
coll.	= collettivo. collective		*interr.*	= interrogativo. interrogative
(comm.)	= commercio, finanza.		*(irl.)*	= irlandese. Irish
	commerce, finance		*(iron.)*	= ironico. ironical
comp.	= comparativo. comparative		*irr.*	= irregolare. irregular
compl.	= complemento. complement		*(ittiol.)*	= ittiologia. icthyology
condiz.	= condizionale. conditional			
cong.	= congiunzione. conjunction			
congiunt.	= congiuntivo. conjunctive			

(lat.)	=	latino, latinismo. Latin, Latinism
l. av.	=	locuzione con valore di avverbio. locution used adverbally
l. cong.	=	locuzione con valore di congiunzione. locution used as a conjunction
l. prep.	=	locuzione con valore di preposizione. locution used as a preposition
(lett.)	=	letteratura. literature
(letter.)	=	letterario. literary
(letteral.)	=	letteralmente. literally
(log.)	=	logica. logic
m.	=	maschile. masculine
(mar.)	=	marina. navy
(mat.)	=	matematica. mathematics
(mec.)	=	meccanica. mechanics
(med.)	=	medicina. medicine
(metal.)	=	metallurgia. metallurgy.
(mil.)	=	militare. military
(min.)	=	mineralogia. mineralogy
(miner.)	=	minerario. mining
(mit.)	=	mitologia. mythology
(mus.)	=	musica. music
n.	=	neutro. neuter
(neol.)	=	neologismo. neologism
no.	=	nome. noun
nom.	=	nominativo. nominative
num.	=	numerale. numeral
ord.	=	ordinale. ordinal
(ornit.)	=	ornitologia. ornithology
(ott.)	=	ottica. optics
p.	=	participio. participle
(paleont.)	=	paleontologia. paleontology
pass.	=	passato, tempo passato. past tense, past
(patol.)	=	patologia. pathology
p.e.	=	per esempio. for example
pers.	=	personale. personal
(pitt.)	=	pittura. painting
pl.	=	plurale. plural
(poes.)	=	poesia. poetry
(poet.)	=	poetico. poetic
(pol.)	=	politica. politics
(pop.)	=	popolare. popular
poss.	=	possessivo. possessive
p.p.	=	participio passato. past participle
p.pr.	=	participio presente. present participle
pr.	=	proprio. proper

pred.	=	predicato. predicate
prep.	=	preposizione. preposition
pres.	=	presente, tempo presente. present, present tense
pron.	=	pronome. pronoun
prov.	=	proverbio. proverb
ql.co.	=	qualche cosa. something
qlcu.	=	qualcuno. someone
r.	=	riflessivo. reflexive
(rad.)	=	radiofonia. radio
(rar.)	=	raro. rare
reg.	=	regolare. regular
rel.	=	relativo. relative
(relig.)	=	religione. religion
rem.	=	remoto. remote
(ret.)	=	retorica. rhetoric
s.	=	sostantivo. noun
(scherz.)	=	scherzoso. humorous
(scient.)	=	scientifico. scientific
(scoz.)	=	scozzese. Scottish
(scult.)	=	scultura. sculpture
sing.	=	singolare. singular
(sl.)	=	slang (gergo)
s.o.	=	someone (quarcuno)
sogg.	=	soggetto. subject
(sott.)	=	sottinteso. implied
spec.	=	specialmente. especially
(spor.)	=	sport, sportivo. sport
(spreg.)	=	spregiativo. especially
(st.)	=	storia, storico. history—historic
sthg.	=	something (qualche cosa)
(strum.)	=	strumento. instrument
superl.	=	superlativo. superlative
t.	=	transitivo. transitive
(teat.)	=	teatro. theatrical
(tec.)	=	tecnico. technical
(tel.)	=	telefonia, telegrafia. telephone
(teol.)	=	teologia. theology
(tip.)	=	tipografia. typography
(tv.)	=	televisione. television
v.	=	verbo. verb
V.	=	vedi. see
(vet.)	=	veterinaria. veterinary
(volg.)	=	volgare. vulgar
(zool.)	=	zoologia. zoology

ITALIAN - ENGLISH

A

a^1, *s.f.m.* (*prima lettera dell'alfabeto italiano*) a (*pl.* as, a's) ‖ *dall'—* *alla zeta, fig.* completely (*o* thoroughly *o* from beginning to end); *essere all'—, fig.* to be at the beginning ‖ *— come Ancona,* (*tel.*) a for Andrew.

a^2, **ad**, *prep.* **1.** (*termine*) **to:** *dallo a me,* give it to me; *raccontalo a chi vuoi!,* (*fam.*) tell it to the (horse-) marines! **2.** (*stato in luogo*) **at** (*riferito a città piccole,* con home e negli indirizzi); **in** (*riferito a città grandi*): *è a casa quasi tutto il giorno,* she is at home most of the day; *è nato a Roma, ma abita a Milano,* he was born in Rome, but he lives in Milan; *la vidi a Como,* I saw her at Como; *il Primo Ministro abita al 10 di Downing Street,* the Prime Minister lives at 10, Downing Street **3.** (*moto a luogo*) **to;** (*con* to arrive) **at, in;** (*con* home *non si traduce*): *il battello arriva a Dover alle 11 antimeridiane,* the boat arrives at Dover at 11 a.m.; *il treno arriva a Londra alle 17,05,* the train arrives in (*o* at) London at 5.05 p.m.; *va' a casa!,* go home!; *vado a Torino,* I am going to Turin **4.** (*tempo determinato*) **at:** *alla 1, alle 3, alle 3,55,* at one o' clock, at three o' clock, at three fifty-five; *a mezzanotte,* at midnight ‖ *fino a domani,* till to-morrow **5.** (*frequenza, prezzo, costo*) **a, an:** *due volte al giorno,* twice a day; *duecento lire al chilo,* two hundred lire a kilo; *tre pasti al giorno,* three meals a day **6.** (*modo*) **at, in, after:** *a caso,* at random; *a modo suo,* in his own way; *alla moda francese,* after the French fashion **7.** (*distributivo*) **by:** *due a due,* two by two; *vendere a dozzine,* to sell by the dozen **8.** (**Fraseologia**): *a bordo,* on board; *a cavallo,* on horseback; *a piedi,* on foot.

àbaco, *s.m.* (*arch.*) abacus (*pl.* abaci).

abàte, *s.m.* (*rettore di abbazia*) abbot; (*ecclesiastico senza ufficio determinato*) abbé.

abazìa, *s.f.* **1.** abbey **2.** (*dignità di abate*) abbacy.

abbacchiàre, *v.t.* **1.** to beat (fruit) down **2.** (*vendere a poco prezzo*) to sell cheap.

abbacchiàto, *ag. fig.* dejected, disheartened, dispirited.

abbacchiatúra, *s.f.* beating down (of fruit).

abbàcchio, *s.m.* (*dial.*) lamb, spring lamb.

abbachìsta, *s.c.* abacist.

abbacinaménto, *s.m.* **1.** (*accecamento*) blinding **2.** (*abbagliamento*) dazzling.

abbacinàre, *v.t.* **1.** (*accecare*) to blind **2.** (*abbagliare*) to dazzle (anche *fig.*) **3.** (*arch.*) to discolour.

abbacinatóre, *ag.* dazzling ‖ *s.m.* dazzler.

àbbaco, *s.m.* **1.** (*arte di fare i conti*) art of computing **2.** (*elementare libro di aritmetica*) elementary arithmetic book **3.** (*arch.*) abacus (*pl.* abaci).

abbacóne, *s.m.* day-dreamer.

abbadàre, *v.i.* (*badare*) to mind (s.o., sthg.), to take care of (s.o., sthg.), to pay attention; to look after (s.o., sthg.).

abbadéssa, *s.f.* abbess.

abbagliaménto, *s.m.* dazzling.

abbagliànte, *ag.* dazzling: *luce —,* (*aut.*) driving beam; (*amer.*) upper beam.

abbagliàre, *v.t.* to dazzle; to blind (with a light): *una bellezza che abbaglia,* a dazzling beauty.

abbàglio, *s.m.* **1.** (*abbagliamento*) dazzling **2.** (*errore, sbaglio*) mistake, blunder: *prendere —,* to be mistaken, to misunderstand, to make a blunder.

abbaiaménto, *s.m.***1.** barking; (*latrato*) howling **2.** (*minacce, insulti*) threats (*pl.*), insults (*pl.*).

abbaiàre, *v.i.* **1.** to bark; (*di cane da caccia*) to bay (*latrare*) to howl ‖ *— alla luna,* to bark (*o* to bay) at the moon ‖ *can che abbaia non morde, prov.* his bark is worse than his bite **2.** (*minacciare, insultare*) to bark (at s.o.), to threaten (s.o.), to insult (s.o.) **3.** (*cantar male*) to bellow (out).

abbaiàta, *s.f.* **1.** bark, barking; (*di cani da caccia*) bay, baying **2.** (*sgridata*) scolding.

abbaiatóre, *s.m.* barker.

abbaíno, *s.m.* **1.** (*finestrino*) dormer (-window) **2.** (*soffitta*) garret.

abbàio, *s.m.* bark, barking: *conosco il mio cane dal suo —,* I know my dog by his bark.

abbaióne, *s.m.* **1.** great barker **2.** (*chiacchierone*) babbler.

abballàre, *v.t.* to bale, to pack (goods) into bales ‖ *abballarne grosse,* to tell tall stories.

abballottàre, *v.t.* to handle roughly.

abbandonàre, *v.t.* **1.** (*una persona*) to forsake, to abandon, to leave: *lo abbandonarono su un'isola deserta,* they forsook (*o* left) him on a desert island (*o* they marooned him); *— un amico nel bisogno,* to forsake a friend in need **2.** (*contravvenendo a una legge*) to desert: *— moglie e figli,* to desert one's wife and children; *— il proprio posto,* to desert one's post **3.** (*un luogo*) to leave, to quit, to flee from (a place): *aveva abbandonato il paese natio,* she had fled from (*o* left *o* quitted) her native country **4.** (*trascurare*) to neglect: *— un giardino,* to neglect a garden **5.** (*rinunciare a*) to give up, to drop, to renounce: *— il mondo,* to renounce the world; *— un progetto,* to give up (*o* to drop) a scheme; *— un tentativo,* to give up (*o* to renounce) an attempt **6.** (*lasciar cadere*): *— con sconforto il capo sul petto,* to hang down one's head ‖ **abbandonàrsi**, *v.r.* **1.** (*alle passioni, al dolore, ecc.*) to give oneself up, to give free course; (*a vizi, fantasie*) to indulge in (sthg.) **2.** (*perder coraggio*) to lose heart, courage **3.** (*rilassarsi*) to relax; (*sdraiarsi*) to lie down; (*lasciarsi cadere*) to drop: *si abbandonò su una sedia,* he dropped on a chair.

abbandonataménte, *av.* unreservedly.

abbandonàto, *ag.* **1.** (*trascurato*) neglected: *un giardino —,* a neglected garden **2.** (*di casa*) deserted **3.** (*fuori uso, di parola, ecc.*) obsolete ‖ *s.m.* (*trovatello*) foundling.

abbandóno, *s.m.* **1.** (*rinuncia*) giving up, renouncing **2.** (*di persona*) forsaking, abandonment **3.** (*isolamento*) isolation **4.** (*incuria*) carelessness: *lasciare nell'—,* to neglect: *lasciava nell'— il suo giardino,* he let his garden run wild **5.** *dichiarazione di —,* (*dir.*) abandonment notice.

abbarbagliaménto, *s.m.* dazzling.

abbarbagliàre, *v.t.* to dazzle.

abbarbàre, *v.i.* to take root; to strike roots ‖ **abbarbàrsi, abbarbicàrsi**, *v.r.* to cling (anche *fig.*).

abbaruffaménto, *s.m.* scuffle; quarrel, dispute.

abbaruffàre, *v.t.* (*arruffare*) to ruffle; to rumple ‖ **abbaruffàrsi**, *v.r.* to scuffle; to quarrel.

abbaruffàta, *s.f.* scuffle; tumult.

abbaruffìo, *s.m.* confusion; (*baruffa*) scuffle.

abbassalíngua, *s.m.* (*med.*) tongue depressor.

abbassaménto, *s.m.* **1.** lowering; sinking: *— di temperatura,* fall in temperature **2.** *fig.* lowering, humiliation, abasement.

abbassàre, *v.t.* **1.** to lower; to pull down; to let down: — *il capo,* to lower (*o* to bend down) one's head; (*con sconforto*) to hang down one's head; — *il finestrino,* to let the window down; — *una leva,* to pull down a lever (*o* a lever down); — *gli occhi,* to lower one's eyes; — *una saracinesca,* to pull down a rolling shutter (*o* to let a shutter down); — *il sipario,* to drop the curtain; — *la voce,* to lower (*o* to drop) one's voice ‖ — *le armi,* to lay down one's arms ‖ — *la cresta, fig.* to swallow one's pride ‖ — *il livello,* to lower the standard; — *i prezzi,* to lower (*o* to reduce) prices **2.** (*umiliare*) to lower; to humble; to abase: *Dio abbassa i superbi,* God humbles the proud ‖ **abbassàrsi,** *v.r.* **1.** (*chinarsi*) to stoop down; to bend down **2.** (*diminuire*) to diminish; to lower; to abate **3.** (*calare, ridursi*): (*di prezzo*) to go down; (*di acque*) to subside; (*di vento*) to drop; (*di temperatura*) to fall **4.** (*umiliarsi, avvilirsi*) to humble oneself, to stoop, to debase oneself.

abbàsso, *av.* below; down; downstairs ‖ *inter.* down!, down with!: — *il tiranno!,* down with the tyrant!.

abbastànza, *av.* **1.** (*sufficientemente, a sufficienza*) enough, sufficiently: — *bene, buono,* well enough, good enough; *avete carne* —?, have you got enough meat (*o* meat enough)? ‖ *ne ho avuto* — *di lui,* I have had enough of him **2.** (*discretamente*) fairly: *sei* — *accurato nel tuo lavoro, però potresti fare meglio,* you are fairly accurate in your work, still you could do better **3.** (*piuttosto*) rather: *è* — *caro, qui, il vino!,* wine is rather dear here! **4.** (*fam.*) pretty: *sono* — *stanco,* I am pretty tired.

abbastàre, *V.* **bastàre.**

abbàttere, *v.t.* **1.** to pull down; to demolish; (*atterrare*) to knock down; (*alberi*) to fell, to cut down **2.** (*animali*) to slaughter **3.** (*aer.*) to shoot down (planes); (*amer.*) to down: *tre aerei furono abbattuti,* three planes were downed **4.** (*mar.*) to cast **5.** (*scoraggiare*) to dishearten; (*spossare*) to depress, to pull down ‖ **abbàttersi,** *v.r.* **1.** (*imbattersi*) to meet (s.o.) by chance; to happen to meet (s.o.), to run into (s.o.) **2.** *fig.* to be discouraged, to be disheartened, to lose heart.

abbattifièno, *s.m.* trap-door (in a hay-loft).

abbattiménto, *s.m.* **1.** throwing down, knocking down, pulling down; demolition; (*di alberi*) felling **2.** (*di animali*) slaughter **3.** (*depressione morale*) dejectedness, dejection; (*prostrazione fisica*) seediness, lack of energy **4.** (*miner.*) mining, winning; (*con esplosione*) blasting.

abbattitóre, *s.m.* **1.** destroyer **2.** (*di animali*) slaughterer **3.** (*di piante*) feller.

abbattùta, *s.f.* **1.** (*di alberi*) felling, clearing **2.** (*mar.*) turn: — *in carena,* careening **3.** (*mil.*) abatis.

abbatuffolàre, *v.t.* to wind into a ball ‖ **abbatuffolàrsi,** *v.r.* (*azzuffarsi*) to quarrel.

abbazìa, *s.f.* **1.** abbey **2.** (*dignità di abate*) abbacy.

abbaziàle, *ag.* abbatial.

abbecedàrio, *s.m.* primer; spelling-book.

abbelliménto, *s.m.* **1.** embellishment, ornament **2.** *pl.* (*mus.*) grace-notes.

abbellìre, *v.t.* to embellish, to adorn, to beautify ‖ **abbellìrsi,** *v.r.* to adorn oneself.

abbellìto, *ag.* embellished, adorned.

abbellitóre, *s.m.,* **abbellitríce,** *s.f.* adorner.

abbellitùra, *V.* **abbelliménto.**

abbenché, (*arc.*) per **benché.**

abbeveràre, *v.t.* to water (anche *mar.*) **2.** (*irrigare*) to irrigate, to water ‖ **abbeveràrsi,** *v.r.* (*di persone*) to drink; (*di animali*) to water.

abbeveratóio, *s.m.* watering place; trough.

abbiadàre, *v.t.* to feed on oats.

abbicàre, *v.t.* (*agr.*) to stack.

abbicci, *s.m.* **1.** alphabet **2.** (*principi elementari*) primer ‖ *esser all'*—, *fig.* to be at the very beginning.

abbiènte, *ag.* wealthy, well-to-do, well off ‖ *gli abbienti,* wealthy people.

abbiètto, *e derivati, V.* **abìetto,** *e derivati.*

abbigliaménto, *s.m.* (suit of) clothes; dress; (*letter.*) apparel, attire: *industria dell'*—, clothing industry.

abbigliàre, *v.t.* to dress ‖ **abbigliàrsi,** *v.r.* to dress (oneself), to adorn oneself.

abbigliatùra, *s.f.* **1.** (*atto di abbigliare*) dressing **2.** (*modo di vestire*) dress, clothes (*pl.*).

abbinaménto, *s.m.* coupling.

abbinàre, *v.t.* to couple, to link together.

abbindolaménto, *s.m.* cheat, trick, deception.

abbindolàre, *v.t.* **1.** to reel, to spool **2.** *fig.* to cheat, to outwit, to dupe, to deceive ‖ **abbindolàrsi,** *v.r.* (*di fili*) to get entangled.

abbindolatóre, *s.m.,* **abbindolatríce,** *s.f.* cheater, deceiver, duper.

abbindolatùra, *s.f.* cheat, trick, deception.

abbiosciàre, *v.t.* to knock down ‖ **abbiosciàrsi,** *v.r.* to lose courage; (*fam.*) to give in.

abbisciàre, *v.t.* (*mar.*) to jag, to range.

abbisognàre, *v.i.* to need (s.o., sthg.); to want (s.o., sthg.); to require (sthg.); to be necessary: *che vi abbisogna?,* what do you need?; *il muro abbisogna di riparazioni,* the wall needs repairings.

abbittàre, *v.t.* (*mar.*) to bitt, to secure to a bitt.

abbitumàre, *v.t.* to bituminize.

abboccaménto, *s.m.* **1.** interview, talk, conversation: *ebbi un* — *col Presidente,* I had an interview with the President; *riferendoci al nostro* — *col vostro rappresentante,* referring to our conversation with your representative **2.** (*anat.*) anastomosis **3.** (*di condotti*) buttjoining (of two pipes).

abboccàre, *v.i.* (*di pesci*) to bite: — *all'amo,* to bite at the hook; *fig.* to be taken by bait (*o* to be taken in *o* to be deceived) ‖ *v.t.* **1.** (*afferrare*) to catch, to snap up **2.** (*riempire*) to fill (to the brim): — *le botti,* to fill barrels **3.** (*congiungere*) to join: — *due condotti,* to join up two pipes ‖ **abboccàrsi,** *v.r.* to have an interview, to meet (s.o.).

abboccàto, *ag.* **1.** (*di vino*) palatable: *vino* —, palatable wine **2.** (*pieno sino all'orlo*) brimful, full to the brim **3.** (*di buona bocca*) of good appetite.

abboccatói, *s.m.* (*di fornace*) mouth (of a furnace).

abboccatùra, *s.f.* **1.** (*l'afferrare con la bocca*) snapping **2.** (*di pesci*) biting **3.** (*bocca di vaso, ecc.*) opening, mouth.

abbomínio, *e derivati, V.* **abomínio,** *e derivati.*

abbonacciaménto, *s.m.* (*mar.*) calm.

abbonacciàre, *v.t.* **1.** (*mar.*) to calm **2.** *fig.* to calm, to soothe, to appease; to quiet down ‖ **abbonacciàrsi,** *v.r.* (*di vento*) to drop; (*di mare*) to smooth down.

abbonaménto, *s.m.* (*a giornale, rivista*) subscription; (*ferroviario*) season-ticket: *fare l'*— *a una rivista,* to subscribe to a magazine.

abbonàre, *v.t.* **1.** to make (s.o.) a subscriber: *ti ho abbonato al «Times»,* I have made you a subscriber to "The Times" **2.** (*defalcare*) to deduct: *l'albergatore ci ha abbonato parte del conto,* the innkeeper has made us a reduction in the bill **3.** (*approvare*) to approve: — *un conto,* to approve an account ‖ **abbonàrsi,** *v.r.* to subscribe: — *a un giornale,* to subscribe to a newspaper.

abbonàto, *s.m.* (*a giornale, rivista*) subscriber; (*ferroviario*) season-ticket holder, (*amer.*) commuter.

abbondànte, *ag.* **1.** abundant, plentiful: *un raccolto* —, a plentiful crop **2.** (*ricco*) rich (in sthg.); abounding (in sthg.): *una terra* — *di minerali,* a land rich in minerals.

abbondanteménte, *av.* abundantly, plentifully.

abbondànza, *s.f.* abundance, plenty; copiousness: — *di tempo, tempo in* —, plenty of time ‖ *il corno dell'*—, the horn of plenty ‖ *nuotare nell'*—, to roll in wealth.

abbondàre, *v.i.* (*avere in abbondanza*) to have plenty (of sthg.), to abound (in sthg.), to be rich (in sthg.); to teem (with sthg.); (*essere abbondante*) to be plentiful, to teem: *la nostra campagna ha sempre abbondato di viti,* our country has always abounded in grapes; *il pesce è sempre abbondato in queste acque,* fish have always teemed in these waters.

abbonıménto, *s.m.* **1.** calming, appeasing **2.** (*di terreno*) improving.

abboníre, *v.t.* **1.** to calm, to appease, to soothe **2.** (*terreno*) to reclaim, to improve ‖ **abbonírsi,** *v.r.* to grow calm, to be appeased.

abbordàbile, *ag.* accessible; approachable.

abbordàggio, *s.m.* (*mar.*) boarding.

abbordàre, *v.t.* **1.** (*mar.*) to board **2.** (*mar.*) (*attaccare*) to grapple with (a ship); to attack **3.** (*una persona*) to accost, to open conversation with (s.o.); (*un argomento*) to broach.

abbordatóre, *s.m.* (*mar.*) boarder.

abbórdo, *s.m.* access, approach: *un uomo di facile* —, *fig.* an affable (*o* approachable) man.

abborracciaménto, *s.m.* bungling; botching.

abborracciàre, *v.t.* to bungle, to botch: *il lavoro fu abborracciato,* the work was botched.

abborracciataménte, *av.* carelessly, botchily.

abborracciatóre, *s.m.* botcher, bungler.

abborracciatúra, *s.f.* bungling; botching.

abborraccióne, *s.m.* botcher, bungler.

abbottàrsi, *v.r.* to cram oneself (with sthg.); to get stuffed (with sthg.).

abbottonàre, *v.t.* to button (up) ‖ **abbottonàrsi,** *v.r.* to button one's clothes (up).

abbottonàto, *ag.* (*cauto, riservato*) reserved, reticent.

abbottonatúra, *s.f.* **1.** button-holes (*pl.*); (*bottoniera*) row of buttons **2.** (*l'abbottonare*) buttoning.

abbozzacchiàre, *v.t.* to sketch roughly (anche *fig.*).

abbozzàre¹, *v.t.* to sketch (anche *fig.*): — *un sorriso,* to smile faintly (*o* to give the shadow of a smile) **2.** (*statua*) to rough-hew **3.** (*pitt.*) to sketch, to crayon (out), to outline.

abbozzàre², *v.i.* (*aver pazienza*) to be patient.

abbozzàre³, *v.t.* (*mar.*) to stopper.

abbozzàta, *s.f.* sketching.

abbozzatíccio, abbozzàto, *ag.* sketchy.

abbozzatóre, *s.m.,* **abbozzatríce,** *s.f.* sketcher; (*art.*) hewer.

abbòzzo, *s.m.* **1.** sketch, outline; (*scult.*) rough cast, rough-draft; (*pitt.*) drawing, sketch **2.** (*fam.*) (*persona malformata*) manikin, shrimp.

abbozzolàrsi, *v.r.* **1.** (*di bachi*) to cocoon, to form a cocoon **2.** (*di farina che si raggruma*) to form lumps, to lump.

abbracciabòschi, *s.m.* (*bot. pop.*) honeysuckle.

abbracciaménto, *s.m.* (*abbraccio*) embrace; (*l'abbracciare*) embracing, hugging; (*sl.amer.*) necking.

abbracciàre, *v.t.* **1.** to embrace, to hug; (*sl. amer.*) to neck; (*avvinghiare*) to clasp in one's arms: *la bimba abbracciava teneramente la bambula,* the girl was hugging her doll; *l'edera abbraccia la quercia,* the ivy twines round the oak ‖ *chi troppo abbraccia nulla stringe, prov.* grasp all, lose all **2.** (*seguire, accettare*) to embrace; to adopt, to espouse, to take up: — *una carriera,* to take up (*o* to embrace) a career; — *una causa, un partito,* to espouse a cause, a party; — *una risoluzione,* to adopt a resolution **3.** (*racchiudere, comprendere*) to enclose, to include, to comprise; *fig.* to span: *le fortificazioni abbracciano un vasto terreno,* the fortifications enclose a vast area; *un Impero che abbraccia dodici nazioni,* an Empire that includes (*o* comprises) twelve nations; *la sua vita abbraccia mezzo secolo,* his life spans half century **4.** (*afferrare*) to grasp: *la mente non può* — *troppe cose insieme,* the mind cannot grasp too many things at the same time **5.** (*con lo sguardo*) to take in: *da qui l'occhio abbraccia tutta la valle,* from here the eye takes in the whole valley ‖ **abbracciàrsi,** *v.r.* to embrace (s.o., sthg.): — *a una colonna,* to embrace a column ‖ *v.r. reciproco* to embrace each other (one another).

abbracciàta, *s.f.* embrace, hug.

abbracciatútto, *s.m.* (*pop.*) Jack of all trades.

abbràccio¹, *s.m.* embrace, hug: *un forte* —, a big hug.

abbràccio², *s.m.* embracing.

abbraccióna, *s.f.,* **abbraccióne,** *s.m.* (*ficcanaso*) busybody, meddler.

abbraccióni, *av.* (in the act of) embracing.

abbracciucchiàre, *v.t.* to hug repeatedly.

abbrancàre¹, *v.t.* to grasp, to clutch, to grip; (*afferrare*) to seize ‖ **abbrancàrsi,** *v.r.* to catch hold (of s.o., sthg.), to clasp (at s.o., sthg.).

abbrancàre², *v.t.* (*mettere in branco*) to put (an animal) in a herd ‖ **abbrancàrsi,** *v.r.* to join the herd.

abbreviaménto, *s.m.* abbreviation; (*compendio*) abridg(e)ment; epitome.

abbreviàre, *v.t.* to shorten, to cut short, to curtail; (*compendiare*) to abridge; (*una parola*) to abbreviate (a word): — *un discorso, le vacanze,* to curtail a speech, one's holidays ‖ *abbreviate, vi prego,* please, be brief.

abbreviataménte, *av.* (*in breve*) briefly, in brief; (*in compendio*) in abridged, in abbreviated form.

abbreviatívo, *ag.* abbreviating.

abbreviatóre, *s.m.* abridger, abbreviator.

abbreviatúra, abbreviazióne, *s.f.* abridg(e)ment, abbreviation.

abbriccàgnolo, *s.m.* **1.** (*ornit. pop.*) tree creeper **2.** *fig.* (*cavillo*) cavil.

abbrivàre, *v.t.* (*mar.*) to get (a ship) under way ‖ *v.i.* to pull away, to start off; to make headway.

abbrividíre, *v.i.* to shudder, to quiver.

abbrívo, *s.m.* (*mar. aer.*) freshway: — *in avanti,* headway; — *indietro,* sternway; *prendere l'*—, to make headway (*o* to begin to move on).

abbronzaménto, *s.m.* **1.** (*dato dal sole*) tanning, bronzing **2.** (*artig.*) bronzing.

abbronzàre, *v.t.* **1.** to bronze **2.** (*al sole*) to tan, to make brown, to bronze **3.** (*torrefare, abbrustolire*) to roast (brown), to toast **4.** (*abbruciacchiare*) to scorch ‖ **abbronzàrsi,** *v.r.* (*al sole*) to get sunburnt, to get tanned.

abbronzatúra, *s.f.* **1.** (*atto*) burning, tanning, browning, sunburn; (*effetto*) tan **2.** (*artig.*) bronzing.

abbruciacchiaménto, *s.m.* scorching, singeing.

abbruciacchiàre, *v.t.* to scorch, to singe.

abbruciàre, *e derivati,* *V.* **bruciàre,** *e derivati.*

abbrumàre, *v.i.* (*mar.*) to be eaten away by sea-moss; to rot.

abbrunàre, *v.t.* **1.** (*rendere scuro*) to brown, to darken **2.** (*parare a lutto*) to hang with black: — *le bandiere,* (*issarle a mezz'asta*) to hang flags at half-mast ‖ **abbrunàrsi,** *v.r.* **1.** (*diventare scuro*) to grow dark **2.** (*mettersi il lutto*) to put on mourning.

abbrunàto, *ag.* **1.** (*parato a lutto*) hung with black **2.** (*issato a mezz'asta*) hung at half-mast **3.** (*vestito a lutto*) wearing mourning.

abbrunire, *v.t.* to darken ‖ *v.i.* **1.** to grow dark, to grow brown **2.** (*di pelle*) to become tanned.

abbrustiàre, *v.t.* (*rar.*) to scorch, to singe.

abbrustolàre, *V.* **abbrustolíre.**

abbrustoliménto, *s.m.* broiling; toasting; roasting.

abbrustolíre, *v.t.* (*carne*) to broil, to roast; (*caffè*) to roast; (*pane*) to toast: *pane abbrustolito,* toast.

abbrutiménto, *s.m.* **1.** (*l'abbrutirsi*) brutalization **2.** (*stato di abbrutimento*) brutishness **3.** (*avvilimento*) dejection.

abbrutíre, *v.t.* to brutalize, to make brutal ‖ **abbrutírsi,** *v.r.* to become brutal; (*degradarsi*) to abase oneself.

abbruttíre, *V.* **imbruttíre.**

abbuiaménto, *s.m.* darkening; (*oscurità*) obscurity.

abbuiàre, *v.t.* **1.** to darken, to obscure **2.** (*nascondere*) to conceal, to hide; *fig.* to obscure ‖ **abbuiàrsi,** *v.r.* **1.** to get dark, to grow dark, to grow dim **2.** (*rannuvolarsi*) to become cloudy **3.** *fig.* to grow sad.

abbuòno, *s.m.* **1.** (*comm.*) allowance, discount: — *per ammanco,* allowance for shortage; — *per avaria,* allowance for average (*o* damage); — *per corpi estranei,* draft allowance; — *per deficienza di peso,* allowance for short weight; *concedere un* —, to make an allowance **2.** (*spor.*) handicap.

abburattaménto, *s.m.* sifting.

abburattàre, *v.t.* **1.** (*separare dalla crusca*) to sift flour) **2.** (*discutere, ventilare*) to ventilate; to discuss **3.** (*malmenare, scuotere*) to maltreat, to misuse, to bully ‖ *v.i.* (*parlare forbito*) to pick one's words ‖ **abburattàrsi**, *v.r.* (*dibattersi*) to rave, to toss about.

abburattatóre, *s.m.*, **abburattatríce**, *s.f.* sifter, bolter.

abburattatúra, *s.f.* sifting, bolting.

abburattóne, *s.m.* tiresome talker, chatterbox.

abdicàre, *v.i.* to abdicate (sthg.): — *alla corona*, to abdicate the crown ‖ *v.t.* to resign, to renounce, to surrender: — *i propri diritti*, to surrender one's rights.

abdicatàrio, *ag.* abdicating.

abdicazióne, *s.f.* abdication.

abduttóre, *ag.* (*anat.*) abducent: *muscolo* —, abducent muscle (*o abductor*) ‖ *s.m.* (*anat.*) abductor.

abduzióne, *s.f.* (*fisiol.*) abduction.

Abèle, *no.pr.m.* Abel.

aberràre, *v.i.* to stray, to go astray.

aberrazióne, *s.f.* **1.** aberration: *in un momento di* —, in a moment of aberration **2.** (*astr. fis. ott.*) aberration: — *di sfericità*, spherical aberration.

abetàia, *s.f.* fir-wood, fir plantation.

abéte, *s.m.* **1.** (*albero*) fir(-tree) **2.** (*legno*) fir-wood.

abetèlla, *s.f.* (*edil.*) circular section wooden pole.

abetína, *s.f.* fir-wood; fir plantation.

abiàtico, *ag.* ancestral ‖ *s.m.* (*dial.*) grandchild (*pl.* grandchildren).

abiettaménte, *av.* abjectly, basely.

abiettézza, *s.f.* abjectness, vileness, baseness.

abiètto, *ag.* abject, base, vile, contemptible.

abiezióne, *s.f.* abasement, abjection.

Abigail, *no.pr.f.* (*Bibbia*) Abigail.

abigeàto, *s.m.* (*dir.*) cattle-stealing; (*amer.*) rustling.

abígeo, *s.m.* (*dir.*) cattle-stealer; (*amer.*) rustler.

àbile, *ag.* **1.** able, capable **2.** (*esperto*) experienced; clever, skilful: — *in un mestiere*, clever at a trade; — *in tutte le arti*, skilled in all the arts; — *a fare ql.co.*, clever at doing sthg.; *adulatore* —, adroit flatterer; *mani abili*, skilled hands **3.** (*dir.*) legally qualified **4.** (*mil.*) fit: — *al servizio militare*, fit for military service; *dichiarare* —, to report fit 1... service.

abilità, *s.f.* **1.** ability, capacity **2.** (*perizia*) cleverness, skill, dexterity: — *manuale*, manual dexterity; — *nel fare ql.co.*, skill in (o cleverness at) doing sthg.; *vincere qlcu. in* —, to outwit s.o.

abilitàre, *v.t.* **1.** to qualify: — *all'insegnamento*, to qualify for teaching; *essere abilitato dottore*, to qualify as (a) doctor **2.** (*dir.*) to empower, to entitle.

abilitazióne, *s.f.* qualification: *esame di* —, qualifying examination; *conseguire l'* — *all'insegnamento dell'inglese in una scuola media*, to qualify as an English teacher in a secondary school.

abilménte, *av.* skilfully.

abiogènesi, *s.f.* (*scient.*) abiogenesis.

abissàle, *ag.* abysmal, profound, bottomless; (*incommensurabile*) measureless, unfathomable.

Abissínia, *no.pr.f.* (*geog.*) Abyssinia.

abissíno, *ag.s.m.* Abyssinian.

abísso, *s.m.* **1.** abyss, gulf, chasm: *fra te e me c'è di mezzo un* —, there is a gulf between us; *i profondi abissi dell'oceano*, the unfathomed deep ‖ *essere sull'orlo dell'* —, to be on the verge of ruin **2.** (*inferno*) hell **3.** (*subisso*) great quantity.

abitàbile, *ag.* inhabitable, habitable.

abitabilità, *s.f.* habitability, habitableness.

abitàcolo, *s.m.* **1.** (*mar.*) binnacle; (*aer.*) cockpit **2.** (*abituro*) slum dwelling, hovel.

abitànte, *ag.* living, dwelling ‖ *s.c.* inhabitant, resident: *gli abitanti della foresta*, the denizens of the forest; — *di città*, townsman, townswoman (*pl.* townsfolk); — *di villaggio*, villager; *questa città ha tre milioni di abitanti*, this city has three million inhabitants.

abitàre, *v.t.* to inhabit, to dwell in (a place), to live in (a place): — *un castello*, to inhabit (o to dwell in) a castle;

— *una piccola casa*, to live in a small house ‖ *v.i.* to live, to reside, to dwell: — *in campagna*, to live in the country.

abitàto, *ag.* inhabited, peopled ‖ *s.m.* (*luogo abitato*) inhabited place, built-up area.

abitatóre, *s.m.*, **abitatríce**, *s.f.* inhabitant, dweller.

abitazióne, *s.f.* habitation; dwelling (place), residence; house: *problema dell'* —, housing problem; *questo appartamento non è adatto come* —, this flat is not fit for habitation; *la tua* — *è molto comoda*, your house is very comfortable.

abitíno, *s.m.* **1.** pretty dress **2.** (*scapolare*) scapular.

àbito, *s.m.* **1.** (*da uomo*) suit; (*da donna*) dress, frock: — *a coda* (*di rondine*), tail-coat; — *da cerimonia*, dress-coat; — *da lutto*, mourning; *abiti fatti*, ready-made clothes; (*fam. amer.*) hand-me-down clothes; *abiti su misura*, clothes made to measure; *abiti vecchi* old clothes; (*amer.*) hand-out; *taglio d'* —, dress-length ‖ *quest'* — *ti sta a pennello*, this dress fits you very well ‖ *farsi fare un* —, to have a suit, a dress made; *togliersi gli abiti*, to take off one's clothes (o to undress) **2.** (*di sacerdote*) cassock, gown; (*di frate*) frock, habit: *vestire l'* —, to take the habit (o to enter a religious order) ‖ *l'* — *non fa il monaco*, *prov.* it is not the cowl that makes the monk **3.** (*di animale*) coat **4.** (*disposizione dell'animo*) habit: — *mentale*, habit of mind **5.** *V.* **abitúdine 6.** (*med.*) habit: — *apoplettico*, apoplectic habit; — *astenico*, asthenic habit.

abituàle, *ag.* habitual, usual, customary, wonted, regular: *con la sua* — *gentilezza*, with her wonted kindness; *un male* —, a customary evil.

abitualménte, *av.* habitually, usually, regularly.

abituàre, *v.t.* to accustom, to inure ‖ **abituàrsi**, *v.r.* to accustom oneself, to get used, to get accustomed: *ci siamo abituati a|non badare alle lamentele*, we have accustomed ourselves to ignoring (o to ignore) complaints (o we have got used to not minding complaints).

abituàto, *ag.* accustomed (to sthg., to do sthg. o to doing sthg.); (*avvezzo, allenato*) inured (to sthg., to do sthg.); (*solito*) wont (to do sthg.): *com'era* — *a fare*, as he was wont to do; *è* — *al freddo*, he is inured to cold; *era* — *a venire ogni giorno*, he used to come every day; *sono* — *a fare un sonnellino pomeridiano*, I am accustomed to having a short nap in the afternoon.

abitudinàrio, *ag.* following a routine ‖ *s.m.* routinist.

abitúdine, *s.f.* habit, practice; (*usanza*) custom, use: *come d'* —, as usual; *d'* —, as a rule; *secondo l'* —, according to the custom; *come è* — *fra i grandi*, as is the practice among the great; *ormai ho l'* — *di alzarmi presto*, now I am used to getting up early; *avere l'* — *di fare ql.co.*, to be in the habit of doing sthg.; *prendere una brutta* —, to fall into a bad habit.

abitúro, *s.m.* slum dwelling, humble dwelling, hovel; (*poet.*) abode.

abiúra, *s.f.* abjuration.

abiuràre, *v.t.* to abjure: — *un'eresia*, to abjure a heresy.

ablatívo, *ag.s.m.* (*gram.*) ablative ‖ *essere ridotto all'* —, *fig.* to be hard up.

ablazióne, *s.f.* (*chir. geol.*) ablation.

ablegàto, *s.m.* (*eccl.*) ablegate.

abluzióne, *s.f.* ablution.

abnegàre, *v.t.* to abnegate.

abnegazióne, *s.f.* abnegation, self-denial.

abnòrme, *ag.* abnormal.

abolíre, *v.t.* to abolish, to suppress: — *una legge*, to repeal an act.

abolítivo, *ag.* of annulment.

abolizióne, *s.f.* abolition, abolishment, suppression; (*di decreti, leggi, ecc.*) repeal, rescission, annulment, abrogation.

abolizionísmo, *s.m.* abolitionism.

abolizionísta, *s.c.* abolitionist.

abomàso, *s.m.* (*anat. zool.*) abomasus, abomasum.

abominàbile, abominàndo, *ag.* abominable, loathsome.

abominàre, *v.t.* to abominate, to loathe, to abhor.

abominazióne, *s.f.* abomination, loathing, abhorrence.

abominévole, *ag.* abominable, loathsome.

abomínio, *s.m.* abomination, loathing, abhorrence.

aborígeno, *ag. s.m.* native, aboriginal: *gli aborigeni*, the natives, the aborigines.

aborriménto, *s.m.* abhorrency, hatred, horror, loathing, abomination.

aborríre, *v.t.* to abhor, to loathe, to abominate; to hate.

abortíre, *v.i.* 1. to abort, to miscarry: *fare — qlcu.*, to procure s.o.'s abortion 2. *fig.* to fail, to miscarry.

abortívo, *ag.* abortive || *s.m.* (*med.*) abortifacient.

abòrto, *s.m.* 1. (*med.*) abortion, miscarriage 2. (*il feto*) fetus 3. *fig.* (*di opera mal riuscita*) failure, abortion; (*di persona*) abortion; shrimp.

abràdere, *v.t.* to abrade; to scrape off.

Abràmo, *no.pr.m.* Abraham.

abrasióne, *s.f.* 1. abrasion (anche *med.*); scraping off 2. (*escoriazione*) abrasion, lesion of the skin, excoriation.

abrasívo, *ag. s.m.* abrasive.

abrogàre, *v.t.* (*dir.*) to abrogate, to cancel, to annul, to rescind, to revoke, to repeal: — *una legge*, to repeal an Act.

abrogatòrio, *ag.* (*dir.*) abrogative, annulling, rescinding.

abrogazióne, *s.f.* (*dir.*) abrogation, annulment, repeal, rescission.

abròstine, *s.m.* (*bot.*) wild grapes (*pl.*).

abròtano, *s.m.* (*bot.*) wormwood.

abrupto, ex, *l. av.* (*lat.*) suddenly.

abruzzése, *ag.* living in the Abruzzi; (coming from) Abruzzi: *vino —*, wine from the Abruzzi (*o* Abruzzi wine) || *s.c.* inhabitant of the Abruzzi.

Abrúzzi e Molíse, *no.pr.m.pl.* (*geog.*) Abruzzi e Molise.

àbside, *s.f.* 1. (*arch.*) apse 2. (*geom. astr.*) apsis (*pl.* apsides).

abulía, *s.f.* (*patol.*) aboulia; *fig.* lack of will-power.

abúlico, *ag.* (*patol.*) aboulic; *fig.* lacking in will-power.

abúna, *s.m.* (*patriarca della Chiesa abissina*) Abune.

abusàre, *v.i.* 1. (*usare malamente*) to abuse (sthg.), to misuse (sthg.): *abusi della tua salute*, you abuse your health; *il vino vi fa bene, ma non dovete abusarne*, wine is good for you, but you must not drink too much of it 2. (*approfittare*) to abuse (sthg.), to take (undue) advantage: *non voglio — della tua fiducia*, I do not want to take advantage of your confidence; — *della bontà di qlcu.*, to trespass on s.o.'s kindness; — *di un privilegio*, to abuse a privilege || **abusàrsi**, *v.r.* (*fam.*) to take advantage.

abusivaménte, *av.* abusively.

abusívo, *ag.* abusive.

abúso, *s.m.* 1. (*cattivo uso*) abuse, misuse: — *di potere*, (*dir.*) abuse of power 2. (*uso eccessivo*) abuse, excessive use: *non fate — di tranquillanti*, don't make excessive use of tranquilizers.

acàcia, *s.f.* (*bot.*) acacia.

acagiú, *s.m.* (*bot.*) mahogany.

Acàia, *no.pr.f.* (*geog. st.*) Achaia.

acànto, *s.m.* (*bot. arch.*) acanthus.

àcaro, *s.m.* (*zool.*) acarus (*pl.* acari).

acàrpo, *ag.* (*bot.*) acarpous.

acatalessía, *s.f.* (*fil.*) acatalepsy.

acatalèttico, *ag.* (*poes.*) acatalectic.

acattòlico, *ag.* non-Catholic.

àcca, *s.f.* letter H || *non ne capimmo un'—*, we could not make head or tail of it; *non ne sapeva un'—*, he knew nothing about it; *non vale un'—*, it isn't worth a fig.

accadèmia, *s.f.* 1. academy: — *di musica*, school of music; — *di scherma*, fencing school 2. (*trattenimento musicale*) (*pubblico*) public musical entertainment; (*privato*) private musical entertainment 3. (*scuola superiore*) academy 4. (*discorsi inutili*): *fare dell'—*, *fig.* to split hairs (*o* to talk theoretically).

accademicaménte, *av.* 1. academically 2. (*in astratto*) abstractly, theoretically.

accadèmico, *ag.* academical || *s.m.* academician.

accadére, *v.i.* to happen, to chance, to occur; (*di disgrazia*) to befall: *ciò accadde a me*, this occurred to me; *mi accadde di vederlo*, I happened (*o* chanced) to see him.

accadiménto, *s.m.* (*rar.*) happening, occurrence.

accadúto, *s.m.* happening, event: *egli è molto spiacente dell'—*, he is very sorry for what happened.

accagionàre, *v.t.* to accuse, to blame, to charge, to impute: — *qlcu. di ql.co.*, to accuse s.o. of sthg. (*o* to blame s.o. for sthg. *o* to charge s.o. with sthg. *o* to impute sthg. to s.o.).

accagliaménto, *s.m.* curdling.

accagliàre, *v.i.*, **accagliàrsi**, *v.r.* to curdle, to coagulate.

accagliatúra, *s.f.* curdling.

accalappiacàni, *s.m.* dog-catcher.

accalappiaménto, *s.m.* 1. catching 2. *fig.* seduction.

accalappiàre, *v.t.* 1. to catch 2. *fig.* to dupe, to ensnare, to allure, to entrap || **accalappiàrsi**, *v.r.* to get mixed up.

accalappiatóre, *s.m.* deceiver, ensnarer.

accalappiatúra, *s.f.* ensnaring.

accalcàre, *v.t.* to crowd || **accalcàrsi**, *v.r.* to crowd, to throng; to press together.

accaldàrsi, *v.r.* 1. to get heated 2. *fig.* to get excited.

accaldàto, *ag.* hot.

accaloraménto, *s.m.* excitement; heat.

accaloràre, *v.t.* to excite, to animate, to rouse || **accaloràrsi**, *v.r.* to get excited.

accampaménto, *s.m.* (*mil.*) encampment, camp (anche *spor.*).

accampàre, *v.t.* 1. to encamp, to camp 2. *fig.* to allege: — *diritti*, to lay claims; — *pretesti*, to bring forward excuses; — *ragioni*, to allege motives (for sthg.) || *v.i.*, **accampàrsi**, *v.r.* (*mil.*) to encamp; to camp (anche *spor.*).

accampionaménto, *s.m.* (*comm. amm.*) entry in an official register, registration.

accampionàre, *v.t.* 1. (*registrare al campione*) to register, to record 2. (*stadera*) to stamp as correct.

accaniménto, *s.m.* 1. (*furia*) ra᭺ ᎐᎐ness, fury, rage; (*odio*) obstinate hatred 2. (*tenacia*) intense application, ruthless obstinacy, tenacity.

accanírsi, *v.r.* 1. (*infierire*) to rage, to be pitiless 2. (*ostinarsi*) to persist, to insist (on sthg., on doing sthg.), to concentrate doggedly (on sthg, on doing sthg.).

accanitaménte, *av.* 1. furiously 2. (*ostinatamente*) doggedly.

accaníto, *ag.* 1. (*spietato*) pitiless, ruthless, relentless, fierce: *odio —*, fierce hatred 2. (*ostinato*) obstinate, keen, dogged: *fumatore —*, inveterate smoker.

accannellaménto, *s.m.* (*ind.*) winding, spooling.

accannellàre, *v.t.* (*ind.*) to wind, to spool.

accànto, *av.* beside, near, by || *prep.* by, at the side of, near, beside, close to: — *al tavolo vi era una poltrona*, beside the table there was an armchair; *era — a me*, he was near me (*o* beside me *o* at my side); *stava in piedi — a lui*, she was standing near him.

accantonaménto, *s.m.* 1. (*mil.*) cantonment, billets (*pl.*) 2. (*comm.*) reserve funds (*pl.*).

accantonàre, *v.t.* 1. (*mil.*) to billet, to provide with quarters 2. (*comm.*) to set aside, to put in reserve.

accantonàto, *ag.* (*arch.*) angular.

accaparraménto, *s.m.* (*comm.*) buying up, forestalling, monopolising, cornering.

accaparràre, *v.t.* 1. (*comm.*) to buy up, to forestall, to monopolize, to corner 2. (*prenotare*) to book; to secure: *voleva — un posto*, he wanted to secure a place.

accaparratóre, *s.m.* buyer up, monopolizer, monopolist; hoarder; (*spreg.*) profiteer, shark.

accapigliaménto, *s.m.* scuffle, brawl.

accapigliàrsi, *v.r.* 1. to scuffle, to come to blows 2. (*litigare*) to quarrel.

accappatóio, *s.m.* bath-gown, bath-wrap; (*amer.*) bath-robe.

accappiàre, *v.t.* to loop, to noose.

accapponàre, *v.t.* to caponize ‖ *v.i.* to creep: *vi farò — la pelle,* I'll make your flesh creep ‖ **accapponàrsi,** *v.r.* to get goose-flesh: *mi si accapponò la pelle,* I went all goose-flesh (*o* I got goose-flesh).

accappucciàre, *v.t.* to put a hood, a cowl on (s.o., sthg.) ‖ **accappucciàrsi,** *v.r.* to put on a hood, a cowl; to wrap up one's head.

accappucciàto, *ag.* hooded.

accarezzaménto, *s.m.* caressing, fondling; petting.

accarezzàre, *v.t.* 1. to caress, to fondle; (*fam.*) to pet ‖ — *le spalle di qlcu.,* (*fam.*) to thrash s.o. soundly 2. (*un animale*) to stroke: *accarezzò il gatto,* he stroked his cat 3. (*adulare*) to flatter 4. (*vagheggiare*) to cherish, to entertain: — *un progetto,* to entertain a project; — *una speranza,* to cherish a hope.

accartocciaménto, *s.m.* 1. wrapping (in paper) 2. (*di foglie, carta, ecc.*) curling up, crumpling up 3. (*arch.*) cartouche.

accartocciàre, *v.t.* 1. (*avvolgere in carta*) to wrap up (in paper) 2. (*spiegazzare*) to curl up, to crumple up ‖ **accartocciàrsi,** *v.r.* to curl up, to crumple up.

accartocciatúra, *s.f.* curling up, crumpling up.

accasaménto, *s.m.* marriage.

accasàre, *v.t.* to marry, to give in marriage ‖ **accasàrsi,** *v.r.* 1. to marry, to get married 2. (*metter su casa*) to settle down.

accasciaménto, *s.m.* depression; dejection.

accasciàre, *v.t.* to depress: *la notizia li accasciò,* they were overwhelmed at (*o* crushed by) the news ‖ **accasciàrsi,** *v.r.* to lose heart, to become utterly discouraged.

accasermàre, *v.t.* (*mil.*) to barrack.

accastellaménto, *s.m* 1. (*mar.*) forecastle and quarterdeck 2. (*mucchio*) heap.

accastellàre, *v.t.* 1. (*mil.*) to fortify 2. (*ammucchiare*) to heap up, to pile up.

accastellàto, *ag.* 1. (*mar.*) with forecastle and quarterdeck 2. (*ammucchiato*) heaped up, piled up.

accatastaménto, *s.m.* 1. pile, heap, mass 2. (*l'accatastare*) piling up, heaping up, stacking 3. (*registrazione di beni al catasto*) registration of real property.

accatastàre, *v.t.* 1. to heap up, to pile up, to stack 2. (*registrare al catasto*) to register at the registry office.

accatastatóre, *s.m.* (*ind.*) stacker.

accattabríghe, *s.c.* 1. quarrelsome person 2. (*faccendone*) busybody.

accattafièno, *s.m.* (*agr.*) hay-maker, tedder.

accattaménto, *s.m.* 1. begging 2. (*prestito*) borrowing.

accattàre, *v.t.* 1. to beg 2. (*chiedere in prestito*) to borrow: *ho dovuto — mille lire,* I had to borrow one thousand liras 3. *fig.* to fish for (sthg.): — *complimenti,* to fish for compliments.

accattatòzzi, *s.m.* (*mendicante*) beggar.

accàtto, *s.m.* 1. begging 2. (*elemosina*) alms 3. *sapere d'—,* second-hand knowledge.

accattóna, *s.f.* beggar, mendicant.

accattonàggio, *s.m.* begging, mendicity.

accattóne, *s.m.* beggar, mendicant.

accavalcàre, *v.t.* 1. to climb over 2. (*stare a cavalcioni su*) to bestride.

accavalciàre, *v.t.* 1. to be astride (sthg.), to sit astride (sthg.), to straddle 2. (*di ponte*) to span.

accavalcióne, accavalcióni, *av.* astride, astraddle: *Tommaso era seduto — sulle ginocchia di suo padre,* Tom was sitting astride his father's knee; *porsi gli occhiali — sul naso,* to put one's spectacles on one's nose.

accavallaménto, *s.m.* overlapping; (*ammonticchiamento*) crossing.

accavallàre, *v.t.* 1. (*sovrapporre*) to overlap 2. (*incrociare*) to cross: — *le gambe,* to cross one's legs 3. (*am-*

mucchiare) to pile up ‖ **accavallàrsi,** *v.r.* to overlap: *le onde si accavallavano,* the waves poured forward breaking one against the crest of the other.

accavigliàre, *v.t.* (*artig.*) to wind (thread) on pegs.

accecaménto, *s.m.* 1. blinding 2. *fig.* derangement of mind, lack of perception 3. (*intasamento*) obstruction, stoppage.

accecàre, *v.t.* 1. to blind 2. *fig.* to blind, to dim the mind of (s.o.): *era accecato dalla passione,* he was blinded with passion 3. (*intasare*) to stop, to obstruct 4. (*mec.*) to countersink ‖ *v.i.,* **accecàrsi,** *v.r.* to become blind.

accecatóio, *s.m.* (*mec.*) countersink, fraise: — *cilindrico,* counterbore.

accecatúra, *s.f.* 1. blinding 2. (*mec.*) countersink.

accèdere, *v.i.* 1. (*avvicinarsi*) to approach (s.o., sthg.) 2. (*entrare*) to enter (a place) 3. *fig.* to enter (upon an office); to join (a party); to assent (to an opinion, a policy) 4. — *ad un luogo,* (*dir.*) to make an inquest on the spot 5. — *a una proposta,* (*comm.*) to comply with a request (*o* to accede to a proposal).

acceleraménto, *s.m.* acceleration.

acceleràre, *v.t.* to quicken, to hasten, to speed up; to accelerate (anche *mec.*): — *il lavoro,* to speed up the work; — *il passo,* to quicken one's steps; — *il traffico,* to speed up the traffic; — *la velocità,* to accelerate (to increase the speed).

acceleratívo, *ag.* accelerating, quickening.

acceleràto, *ag.* quick; (*mec. fis.*) accelerated ‖ *s.m.* slow train; (*fam. amer.*) whistle train.

acceleratóre, *s.m.* (*chim. fis. mec.*) accelerator.

accelerazióne, *s.f.* 1. (*fis.*) acceleration: — *centripeta,* centripetal acceleration; — *di gravità,* acceleration of gravity; — *media,* average acceleration 2. (*aut.*) pick-up.

accèndere, *v.t.* 1. to light: *accese la pipa,* he lit his pipe; — *un fiammifero,* to strike a match; — *il gas,* to turn on the gas (*o* the gas on); — *la radio, la luce,* to switch on (*o* to put on) the radio, the light 2. *fig.* to inflame, to kindle, to excite, to stir up 3. (*chim.*) to ignite 4. (*aut.*) to hit 5. — *un conto,* (*comm.*) to open an account ‖ **accèndersi,** *v.r.* 1. to light (up) 2. (*prender fuoco*) to take fire, to catch fire 3. *fig.* to kindle, to light up, to become excited: *i suoi occhi si accesero,* her eyes lit up; — *in volto,* to blush 4. *fig.* (*innamorarsi*) to fall in love (with s.o.).

accendíbile, *ag.* inflammable.

accendiménto, *s.m.* lighting.

accendisígaro, *s.m.* (cigarette-) lighter.

accenditóio, *s.m.* lighting-stick.

accenditóre, *s.m.* 1. lighter: — *automatico,* (cigarette-) lighter 2. (*mec.*) igniter.

accennàre, *v.i.* 1. to make a sign, to beckon; (*col capo*) to nod: *gli accennò di sì col capo,* he nodded to him 2. *fig.* to allude; to hint at (sthg.); to mention (sthg.), to refer: *come già accennato,* as already mentioned ‖ *v.t.* 1. to point to (s.o., sthg.) ‖ — *coppe e dar denari, fig.* to promise one thing and give another 2. (*pitt.*) to sketch, to outline 3. — *un motivo,* (*mus.*) to sing a few notes, to play a few notes (of a tune).

accénno, *s.m.* 1. sign, slight indication; (*col capo*) nod 2. *fig.* hint, allusion; mention: *fece — alla sua audacia,* he hinted at his boldness; *in quel libro vi è un — al Petrarca,* Petrarch is mentioned in that book.

accensíbile, *ag.* 1. inflammable 2. *fig.* easily excited.

accensióne, *s.f.* 1. lighting 2. (*mec. aut.*) ignition; (*di caldaia*) starting: — *a batteria,* battery ignition; — *a scintilla,* spark ignition; — *a spinterogeno,* coil ignition; — *difettosa,* faulty ignition; *chiavetta d'—,* ignition-key.

accentàre, *v.t.* 1. to accent, to stress 2. (*dare risalto a*) to accentuate, to stress, to emphasize.

accentatúra, *s.f.* accentuation, stressing.

accènto, *s.m.* 1. accent; (*tonico*) stress 2. (*pronuncia*) accent, pronunciation 3. (*voce, parola*) word 4. (*mus.*) accent.

accentoríno, *s.m.* (*ornit.*) accentor.

accentramént o, *s.m.* centralization.

accentràre, *v.t.* to centralize; to concentrate ‖ **accentràrsi,** *v.r.* to gather, to assemble.

accentratóre, *ag.* centralizing ‖ *s.m.,* **accentratríce,** *s.f.* centralizer.

accentuàre, *v.t.* **1.** to accentuate, to lay the stress on (sthg.) **2.** (*dare risalto a*) to stress, to emphasize.

accentuataménte, *av.* **1.** (*notevolmente*) remarkably **2.** (*enfaticamente*) emphatically.

accentuazióne, *s.f.* accentuation.

acceppàre, *v.t.* (*mar.*) to block (the anchor).

accerchiaménto, *s.m.* encircling, surrounding.

accerchiàre, *v.t.* to encircle, to surround: *il nemico fu accerchiato,* the enemy was surrounded.

accercinàre, *v.t.* to roll up.

accertàbile, *ag.* ascertainable, verifiable.

accertaménto, *s.m.* **1.** assurance, ascertainment; (*verifica*) verification, control **2.** (*comm.*): — *di un conto,* settlement of an account; *giorno di* —, settling day; *fare un* — *di cassa,* to make a cash inventory.

accertàre, *v.t.* **1.** (*assicurare*) to assure; (*verificare*) to verify, to ascertain, to control **2.** (*comm.*) to settle: — *un conto,* to settle an account ‖ **accertàrsi,** *v.r.* **1.** to make sure **2.** (*comm.*) to ascertain (sthg.), to see (sthg.).

accertataménte, *av.* assuredly.

accéso, *ag.* **1.** alight, lit up **2.** (*in volto*) blushing, flushed **3.** — *d'indignazione,* highly indignant; — *d'ira,* in a temper, in a rage **4.** (*pitt.*) very vivid, bright: *rosso* —, bright red **5.** (*comm.*) unpaid: *conto* —, unpaid (*o* outstanding) account.

accessíbile, *ag.* **1.** accessible, within the reach of (s.o.); open to (s.o.) **2.** (*di persona*) approachable: *è difficilmente* —, he is difficult to approach (*o* to get at).

accessibilità, *s.f.* accessibility.

accessióne, *s.f.* **1.** accession **2.** (*consenso*) assent, agreement **3.** (*pol.*) adhesion **4.** (*dir.*) improvement of property, natural growth of property **5.** (*astr.*) new moon.

accèsso, *s.m.* **1.** access, admission, admittance: — *libero,* free admittance; *viale d'*—, avenue of approach ‖ *uomo di facile* —, *fig.* easily approachable man **2.** (*assalto impetuoso di una passione*) fit: — *d'ira,* fit of anger **3.** (*patol.*) fit, attack, access: — *isterico,* hysterical fit (*o* fit of hysterics).

accessoriaménte, *av.* accessorily, additionally.

accessòrio, *ag.* accessory, additional ‖ *s.m.* accessory, fitting (anche *mec.*); (*di abbigliamento*) outfit.

accestiménto, *s.m.* (*bot.*) shooting, sprouting.

accestíre, *v.i.* (*bot.*) to shoot out; to sprout.

accétta, *s.f.* hatchet ‖ *fatto con l'*—, *fig.* rough-hewn ‖ *darsi l'* — *sui piedi,* *fig.* to injure oneself.

accettàbile, *ag.* acceptable (anche *comm.*).

accettabilità, *s.f.* acceptability (anche *comm.*).

accettabilménte, *av.* acceptably.

accettànte, *s.c.* (*comm.*) acceptor.

accettàre, *v.t.* **1.** to accept, to consent to (sthg.), to agree to (sthg.): — *la presidenza,* to consent to be (*o* to being) president; — *una proposta,* to accept an offer (*o* to agree to a proposal); — *di fare ql.co.,* to agree to do sthg. **2.** (*comm.*) to accept: — *una cambiale, un ordine,* to accept a bill, an order.

accettàta, *s.f.* blow with a hatchet.

accettatóre, *s.m.,* **accettatríce,** *s.f.* accepter.

accettazióne, *s.f.* acceptance (anche *comm.*): — *condizionata,* conditional (*o* qualified) acceptance; — *in bianco,* blank acceptance; — *incondizionata,* general acceptance; — *per intervento,* acceptance for honour ‖ *in caso di mancata* —, in case of non-acceptance; *per* — *immediata,* subject to immediate acceptance; *rifiuto di* —, refusal of acceptance ‖ *curare l'*—, to provide for acceptance; *dare l'*—, to comply with acceptance.

accettevolménte, *av.* acceptably.

accettilazióne, *s.f.* (*dir.*) acceptilation.

accètto, *ag.* **1.** received with pleasure; (*caro*) dear:

ben —, welcome: *ella era ben accetta a tutti,* she enjoyed universal favour **2.** (*comm.*) honoured, accepted.

accezióne, *s.f.* acceptation, meaning.

acchetàre, acchetàrsi, *V.* **acquietàre, acquietàrsi.**

acchiappacàni, *s.m.* (*rar.*) dog-catcher.

acchiappamósche, *s.m.* **1.** fly-catcher (anche *bot.*) **2.** (*fannullone*) idler.

acchiappanúvole, *s.m.* dreamer of dreams, wool-gatherer.

acchiappàre, *v.t.* **1.** to catch, to seize: *il poliziotto acchiappò il ladro,* the policeman caught the thief **2.** (*sorprendere*) to catch: *vi ho acchiappato sul fatto,* I caught you red-handed **3.** (*intrappolare*) to trap.

acchiappatóio, *s.m.* trap, snare (anche *fig.*).

acchiocciolaménto, *s.m.* winding up, coiling up.

acchiocciolàre, *v.t.* to wind (up), to coil (up) ‖ **acchiocciolàrsi,** *v.r.* to coil up.

acchitàrsi, *v.r.* (*biliardo*) to lead off.

acchíto, *s.m.* (*biliardo*) lead-off ‖ *di primo* —, *fig.* (*a prima vista*) at first sight; (*immediatamente*) at once.

acchiúdere, *V.* **acclúdere.**

àccia, *s.f.* **1.** coarse thread **2.** (*rar.*) (*capecchio*) tow.

acciabattaménto, *s.m.* **1.** botching, cobbling **2.** (*lavoro malfatto*) botch.

acciabattàre, *v.t.* to botch, to cobble.

acciabattatúra, *s.f.* botching.

acciabattóne, *s.m.* botcher, bungler.

acciaccaménto, *s.m.* crushing, bruising.

acciaccàre, *v.t.* **1.** to crush, to bruise **2.** *fig.* to enfeeble, to weaken.

acciaccàto, *ag.* **1.** (*ammaccato*) bruised **2.** (*abbattuto*) broken-down **3.** (*ammalato*) ailing, feeble.

acciaccatúra, *s.f.* **1.** bruise **2.** (*mus.*) acciaccatura.

acciàcco, *s.m.* **1.** (chronic) infirmity, ailment, disease **2.** (*danno*) damage.

acciaccóso, *ag.* sickly, mawkish.

acciaiàre, *v.t.* **1.** to convert (iron) into steel **2.** (*rinforzare con acciaio*) to steel.

acciaiatúra, *s.f.* steeling.

acciaieria, *s.f.* steel-works, steel-mill, steel-plant.

acciaíno, *s.m.* sharpener, sharpening steel.

acciàio, *s.m.* **1.** steel: — *dolce,* mild (*o* soft) steel; — *duro,* hard steel; — *forgiato, fucinato,* forged steel; — *grezzo, naturale,* raw steel; — *in lingotti,* ingot steel; — *inossidabile,* stainless steel; — *laminato,* rolled steel; — *legato, speciale,* alloy (*o* compound) steel; — *malleabile,* flange steel; — *semiduro,* medium steel; — *stampato,* pressed steel; — *temperabile,* hardenable steel; — *temperato,* hardened steel ‖ *blu* —, steel blue; *lamiera di* —, sheet steel; *lana d'*—, steel wool; *profilati d'*—, structural steel; *rivestito in* —, steel-clad; *struttura d'*—, steel work **2.** *fig.* steel: *cuore d'*—, heart of steel **3.** (*poet.*) (*spada*) sword; (*armatura*) armour.

acciaiuòla, *s.f.* hobnail.

acciaiuòlo, *s.m.* sharpener, sharpening steel.

acciambellàre, *v.t.,* **acciambellàrsi,** *v.r.* to curl up, to coil up: *il cane si acciambellò sul tappeto,* the dog curled up on the carpet.

acciaríno, *s.m.* **1.** steel (of tinder-box), flint-lock **2.** (*di fucile*) gun-lock **3.** (*mec.*) (*di ruota*) linchpin **4.** — *ad inerzia,* (*mar.*) inertia pistol.

acciàro, *s.m.* **1.** steel **2.** (*poet.*) (*spada*) sword.

acciarpaménto, *s.m.* botching, bungling.

acciarpàre, *v.t.* to botch, to bungle.

acciarpataménte, *av.* carelessly, clumsily.

acciarpatóre, *s.m.,* **acciarpatríce,** *s.f.* botcher, bungler.

acciarpío, *s.m.* botching, bungling.

accidèmpoli, *inter.* (*fam.*) the deuce!, good heavens!.

accidentàle, *ag.* **1.** casual, accidental, fortuitous **2.** (*non essenziale*) non-essential, accessory, additional **3.** (*mus.*) accidental.

accidentalità, *s.f.* casualness.

accidentalménte, *av.* accidentally, casually, by chance.

accidentàto, *ag.* **1.** (*paralitico*) paralyzed **2.** (*di terreno*) uneven, irregular.

accidènte, *s.m.* **1.** (*caso non previsto*) chance, accident, mishap ‖ *per —,* by chance ‖ *non mi importa un —!,* I don't care a dash (*o a damn*)! **2.** (*colpo apoplettico*) apoplectic fit **3.** (*persona brutta*) *fig.* ugly person; (*persona cattiva*) bad person: *quella donna è un —,* that woman is awful **4.** *fig.* (*ragazzo vivace*) imp, mischievous child; lively child **5.** (*fil.*) accident **6.** (*mus.*) accidental.

accidènti, *inter.* dash!, dash it!, damn!.

accidia, *s.f.* sloth, sluggishness, indolence, laziness.

accidiosaménte, *av.* slothfully, lazily.

accidióso, *ag.* slothful, indolent, lazy.

accigliaménto, *s.m.* frown; stern look.

accigliàrsi, *v.r.* to frown; *fig.* to look angry, sullen.

accigliataménte, *av.* frowningly.

accigliàto, *ag.* frowning; *fig.* sullen, gloomy.

accigliatúra, *s.f.* **1.** (*cipiglio*) frown, frowning **2.** (*spazio tra le sopracciglia*) space between the eyebrows **3.** (*forma delle sopracciglia*) shape of the eyebrows.

accíngersi, *v.r.* to set about (sthg., doing sthg.); to get ready, to prepare oneself; to be on the point of (doing sthg.): *bisogna che mi accinga a fare i bagagli,* I must set about my packing.

acciocché, *cong.* in order that, so that, that: *l'ho invitata — tu la veda,* I have invited her in order that you may see her.

acciocchíre, *v.t.* to make sleep like a log; (*rendere sonnolento*) to make drowsy ‖ *v.i.* to sleep like a log.

acciocchíto, *ag.* sleepy, drowsy; (*immerso nel sonno*) sound asleep.

acciottolàre, *v.t.* **1.** to cobble **2.** (*far cozzare piatti, ecc.*) to clatter.

acciottolàto, *s.m.* cobbled paving.

acciottolatúra, *s.f.* cobbled paving.

acciottolío, *s.m.* clatter.

accipigliàrsi, *v.r.* to frown; *fig.* to get angry.

acciucchíre, *v.t.* to bewilder, to amaze.

acciuffàre, *v.t.* **1.** to seize by the hair **2.** (*prendere, arrestare*) to seize; to catch: *acciuffò l'involto e fuggì,* he seized the bundle and ran away; *il poliziotto acciuffò il ladro,* the policeman caught the thief ‖ **acciuffàrsi,** *v.r.* **1.** to seize each other by the hair **2.** to come to blows, to scuffle.

acciúga, *s.f.* **1.** anchovy: *pasta d'acciughe,* anchovy paste ‖ *pigiati, stretti come acciughe,* packed like sardines **2.** *fig.* (*donna magra*) very thin woman **3.** (*bot. pop.*) wild marjoram.

acciugàio, *s.m.* seller of salted anchovies.

acciugàta, *s.f.* anchovy sauce.

accivettàre, *v.t.* **1.** to decoy, to allure (birds) by means of an owl **2.** (*rendere cauti*) to render cautious **3.** *fig.* (*attirare*) to allure, to entice.

accivettàto, *ag.* **1.** (*cauto*) experienced; cautious **2.** (*smaliziato*) crafty; cunning.

acclamàre, *v.t.* **1.** (*applaudire*) to acclaim; to cheer; to applaud: *l'oratore fu acclamato rumorosamente,* the speaker was loudly cheered **2.** (*eleggere con grida di consenso*) to acclaim; to hail; to elect by acclamation: *lo acclamarono re,* they hailed him (as) king ‖ *v.i.* (*inneggiare*) to cheer; to shout: *la folla acclamò per la vittoria dell'imperatore,* the crowd shouted for the emperor's victory.

acclamatóre, *s.m.,* **acclamatríce,** *s.f.* applauder, acclaimer, shouter.

acclamazióne, *s.f.* acclamation, applause, ovation, cheer: *per —,* by acclamation.

acclimàre, acclimatàre, *v.t.* to acclimatize, to acclimate ‖ **acclimàrsi, acclimatàrsi,** *v.r.* to get acclimatized, to become acclimatized; to acclimatize (oneself).

acclimatazióne, acclimazióne, *s.f.* acclimatization, acclimation.

acclíne, *ag.* sloping, slanting; inclined (anche *fig.*).

acclíve, *ag.* steep, sheer.

acclúdere, *v.t.* to enclose, to inclose: *vi accludiamo...,*

(*comm.*) please find herewith enclosed... (*o enclosed please find...*); — *ql.co. in una lettera,* to enclose sthg. in a letter.

acclúsa, *s.f.* enclosed letter.

acclúso, *ag.* enclosed ‖ — *alla presente, qui —,* (*comm.*) herewith enclosed; *come da acclusa fattura,* (*comm.*) as per enclosed invoice.

accoccàre, *v.t.* **1.** (*artig.*) to fasten to the notch of the spindle **2.** (*una freccia*) to nock, to notch **3.** (*un colpo*) to strike (a blow) **4.** *fig.* (*giocare un tiro a*) to take in, to dupe.

accoccolàrsi, *v.r.* to squat (down), to crouch (down).

accodaménto, *s.m.* filing; queuing (up).

accodàre, *v.t.* to put in line, to arrange one behind the other; to place in the rear: — *animali,* to put animals head to tail ‖ **accodàrsi,** *v.r.* **1.** to take the rear (of s.o., sthg.); to follow (s.o., sthg.); to tail (after s.o., sthg.) **2.** (*far la coda*) to queue (up).

accogliènza, *s.f.* reception; welcome: *fare buona — a qlcu.,* to give s.o. a hearty reception (*o* to welcome s.o. *o* to greet s.o. *o* to make s.o. welcome).

accògliere, *v.t.* **1.** to receive; (*far buona accoglienza a*) to welcome: — *qlcu. a braccia aperte,* to receive s.o. with open arms **2.** (*esaudire*) to grant: — *una richiesta,* to grant (*o* to accede to) a request **3.** (*approvare*) to consent to (sthg.): — *una proposta,* to consent to a proposal.

accogliménto, *s.m.* reception.

accogliticcio, *ag.* mustered at random; picked up haphazard.

accolitàto, *s.m.* (*eccl.*) order of the acolytes.

accòlito, *s.m.* **1.** acolyte; (*turiferario*) thurifer **2.** *fig.* (*seguace*) follower.

accollacciàto, *ag.* **1.** wearing-high-necked dress **2.** (*di vestito*) high-necked.

accollaménto, *s.m.* **1.** (*a sè*) taking upon oneself; (*ad altri*) laying on to others **2.** *V.* **accòllo.**

accollàre, *v.t.* **1.** to put round the neck **2.** (*mettere al giogo*) to yoke **3.** (*caricar troppo*) to burden **4.** *fig.* to saddle, to charge: — *un compito a qlcu.,* to saddle (*o* to charge) s.o. with a task; — *una responsabilità a qlcu.,* to saddle s.o. with a responsibility (*o* to lay a responsibility on s.o.) **5.** (*dare in appalto*) to assign ‖ **accollàrsi,** *v.r.* to take upon oneself, to undertake: — *tutti i debiti,* to take all the debts upon oneself.

accollàta, *s.f.* (*st.*) accolade.

accollatàrio, *s.m.* (*dir.*) contractor.

accollàto, *ag.* high-necked: *abito —,* high-necked dress.

accollatóre, *s.m.,* **accollatríce,** *s.f.* tendering party.

accollatúra, *s.f.* neckline.

accòllo, *s.m.* **1.** overload, burden **2.** (*comm.*) tender, contract **3.** (*arch.*) corbel, projection **4.** (*mil.*) projection of main wall of fort.

accòlta, *s.f.* meeting, gathering; assembly.

accoltellàre, *v.t.* to stab, to knife.

accoltellàto, *s.m.* (*edil.*) edge course.

accoltellatóre, *s.m.* stabber.

accomandànte, *s.m.* (*comm.*) limited partner.

accomandàre, *v.t.* **1.** (*raccomandare*) to recommend; (*affidare*) to entrust **2.** (*comm.*) to entrust with working capital **3.** (*assicurare legando*) to make fast.

accomandatàrio, *s.m.* (*comm.*) acting partner, general partner.

accomàndita, *s.f.* (*comm.*) limited partnership.

accomiatàre, *v.t.* **1.** (*congedare*) to give (s.o.) leave **2.** (*licenziare*) to dismiss ‖ **accomiatàrsi,** *v.r.* to take leave (of s.o.), to say good-bye (to s.o.).

accomodàbile, *ag.* **1.** (*che si può riparare*) repairable **2.** (*adattabile*) adjustable, adaptable.

accomodaménto, *s.m.* **1.** adjustment, settlement, arrangement **2.** (*conciliazione*) conciliation.

accomodànte, *ag.* yielding.

accomodàre, *v.t.* **1.** (*riparare*) to repair, to mend; (*mettere in ordine*) to set in order; (*correggere*) to correct **2.** (*sistemare*) to settle, to arrange: — *un conto*, to settle an account; — *la faccenda*, to settle the matter || — *qlcu. per le feste*, (*fam.*) to give s.o. a thrashing || *v.i.* (*fare comodo*): *non mi accomoda*, it does not suit me at all || **accomodàrsi**, *v.r.* **1.** (*sedersi*) to sit down, to take a seat: *si accomodi!*, take a seat! **2.** (*mettersi a proprio agio*) to make oneself at home **3.** (*servirsi*) to help oneself.

accomodataménte, *av.* conveniently, opportunely.

accomodatìccio, *s.m.* botched repair.

accomodàto, *ag.* opportune, suitable, convenient.

accomodatúra, *s.f.* **1.** (*riparazione*) mending, repairing **2.** (*adattamento*) adjustment, accommodation **3.** (*compromesso*) accommodation, settlement.

accomodazióne, *s.f.* (*fisiol.*) accommodation.

accòmodo, *s.m.* compromise; conciliation.

accompagnàbile, *ag.* that can be accompanied; (*accoppiabile*) that can be coupled; (*di cose*) matchable.

accompagnaménto, *s.m.* **1.** accompanying **2.** (*seguito*) retinue, train of attendants, suite **3.** (*mus.*) accompaniment.

accompagnàre, *v.t.* **1.** to accompany: — *un fanciullo a scuola*, to take a boy to school; — *qlcu. a casa*, to see s.o. home; — *qlcu. alla stazione*, to see s.o. to the station (*o* to see s.o. off); — *una signora*, to escort a lady; — *una sposa all'altare*, to give a bride away || — *con l'occhio*, to follow with one's eyes || — *l'uscio*, to close the door gently (*o* without slamming it) **2.** (*accoppiare*) to couple || *Dio li fa e poi li accompagna*, *prov.* birds of a feather flock together **3.** (*fare armonizzare*) to match **4.** (*mus.*) to accompany || **accompagnàrsi**, *v.r.* **1.** to keep company **2.** (*accoppiarsi*) to couple **3.** (*armonizzare con*) to match (*sthg.*): *i guanti dovrebbero — al vestito*, the gloves should match the dress.

accompagnatóre, *s.m.*, **accompagnatríce**, *s.f.* **1.** (*chi accompagna*) companion **2.** (*mus.*) accompanist.

accomunàbile, *ag.* that may be joined, united.

accomunaménto, *s.m.* communing; sharing.

accomunàre, *v.t.* (*unire*) to join, to unite; (*associare*) to associate; (*mettere in comune*) to share || **accomunàrsi**, *v.r.* **1.** (*mescolarsi*) to mix, to mingle **2.** *fig.* (*fraternizzare*) to commune, to fraternize.

acconcézza, *s.f.* (*rar.*) suitability; convenience.

acconciàbile, *ag.* adjustable; suitable.

acconciaménte, *av.* properly, suitably, conveniently.

acconciaménto, *s.m.* adaptation; arrangement.

acconciàre, *v.t.* to adjust, to arrange; to adorn; (*capelli*) to dress || — *l'animo a ql.co.*, to prepare one's mind to sthg. || — *per le feste*, (*fam.*) to give s.o. a thrashing || **acconciàrsi**, *v.r.* **1.** (*ornarsi*) to adorn oneself, to dress up; (*vestirsi*) to dress oneself, to attire oneself: — *i capelli*, to do one's hair **2.** (*adattarsi*) to submit.

acconciataménte, *av.* properly, suitably, conveniently.

acconciatóre, *s.m.*, **acconciatrice**, *s.f.* hairdresser.

acconciatúra, *s.f.* hair-style; (*fam.*) hair-do.

accòncio, *ag.* (*adatto*) fit, proper; (*opportuno*) convenient: *venire, cadere in —*, to happen opportunely (*o* at the right moment).

accondiscendènte, *ag.* (*cortese*) obliging; (*compiacente*) yielding; (*che si degna*) condescending.

accondiscendènza, *V.* **condiscendènza**.

accondiscéndere, *v.i.* **1.** (*acconsentire*) to consent, to agree, to comply (with sthg.): *accondiscese a una riduzione di prezzo*, he consented to a reduction in price (*o* to reduce the price); *siamo pronti ad — ai vostri desideri*, we are ready to comply with your wishes **2.** (*essere accondiscendente*) to condescend: *il Primo Ministro accondiscese a ricevere i giornalisti*, the Prime Minister condescended to receive the journalists.

acconigliàre, *v.t.* (*mar.*) to ship (the oars).

acconsentiménto, *s.m.* consent, approval.

acconsentíre, *v.i.* **1.** to consent, to agree: *egli acconsentì ad andare a casa*, he consented to go home;

essi acconsentirono a rinunciare ai loro diritti, they agreed to abandon their rights || *chi tace acconsente*, *prov.* silence gives consent **2.** (*annuire*) to nod assent, to assent **3.** (*mar.*) to spring, to crack || *v.t.* (*rar.*) to allow: *il medico gli acconsente il vino*, the doctor allows him to drink some wine.

acconsenziènte, *ag.* consenting, consentient.

accontentàre, *v.t.* to satisfy, to please, to content || **accontentàrsi**, *v.r.* to be satisfied (with sthg.), to be pleased (with sthg.), to be content (with sthg.): *ci accontentiamo di molto poco*, we are content with very little.

accónto, *s.m.* payment on account, partial payment: *in —*, in partial payment (*o* on account); *ricevere un —*, to receive money on account.

accoppàre, *v.t.* to kill, to do to death.

accoppiàbile, *ag.* matchable, that may be coupled.

accoppiaménto, *s.m.* **1.** coupling, pairing, matching **2.** (*di buoi al giogo*) yoking, pairing **3.** (*mec.*) connection, coupling.

accoppiàre, *v.t.* **1.** to couple; (*appaiare*) to pair; (*aggiogare*) to yoke **2.** *fig.* (*armonizzare*) to match **3.** (*unire*) to join, to unite, to bring together || **accoppiàrsi**, *v.r.* to couple, to mate; (*sposarsi*) to get married.

accoppiatóio, *s.m.* double leash.

accoppiatóre, *s.m.*, **accoppiatríce**, *s.f.* matchmaker.

accoppiatúra, *s.f.* coupling, pairing.

accoraménto, *s.m.* grief, sorrow, heart-ache.

accoràre, *v.t.* to grieve, to cause grief (to s.o.): — *qlcu.*, to break s.o.'s heart || **accoràrsi**, *v.r.* to grieve: *ella s'accorò per la morte di quel buon uomo*, she grieved at (*o* for) the death of that good man.

accorataménte, *av.* sadly, mournfully.

accoràto, *ag.* sad, sorrowful, mournful.

accoratóio, *s.m.* sharp knife for slaughtering pigs.

accorciàbile, *ag.* reducible, shortening.

accorciaménto, *s.m.* shortening.

accorciàre, *v.t.* to shorten, to make shorter: — *un discorso*, to cut a speech short || **accorciàrsi**, *v.r.* to shorten, to become short(er): *le giornate cominciano ad —*, days are getting shorter.

accorciataménte, *av.* in short, briefly.

accorciatívo, *ag.* shortening || *s.m.* (*gram.*) diminutive: *Gianni è l' — di Giovanni*, Gianni is short for Giovanni.

accorciatóia, *s.f.* short cut.

accorciatóio, *ag.* shortening: *un sentiero —*, a short cut.

accorciatóre, *s.m.*, **accorciatríce**, *s.f.* shortener.

accorciatúra, *s.f.* shortening.

accordàbile, *ag.* allowable, grantable.

accordabilménte, *av.* compatibly.

accordaménto, *s.m.* **1.** (*accordo*) agreement **2.** (*mus.*) tuning up.

accordàre, *v.t.* **1.** (*concedere*) to grant, to concede **2.** (*mus.*) to tune **3.** (*armonizzare*) to harmonize, to match **4.** (*gram.*) to make agree: — *in genere e numero*, to make agree in gender and number **5.** (*conciliare*) to bring together, to conciliate || **accordàrsi**, *v.r.* to agree; to come to an agreement, to an understanding.

accordàta, *s.f.* (*rough*) tuning.

accordataménte, *av.* **1.** in agreement, concordantly **2.** (*mus.*) in tune.

accordatóre, *s.m.*, **accordatrice**, *s.f.* tuner: — *di pianoforte*, piano tuner.

accordatúra, *s.f.* (*mus.*) tuning.

accordellàre, *v.t.* to twist.

accordellàto, *s.m.* (*ind. tessile*) corduroy.

accòrdo, *s.m.* **1.** arrangement, agreement, consent, (*anche comm.*); concordance, accord: *come d'—*, as agreed; *d'—*, granted (*o* agreed); *di comune —*, by mutual (*o* common) consent; *in — con ql.co.*, in accordance with sthg.; *in base agli accordi presi*, by the terms of our agreement; *salvo — in contrario*, except agreement to the contrary; *non siamo ancora d'— sul prezzo*, we have not yet agreed upon the price; *siamo d'—!*, it is a deal!; *addivenire ad un —,* to come to an arrangement (*o* to enter into an arrangement); *agire d'—,* to act in accordance; *andare d'— con qlcu.,* to get along well with s.o.; *essere, trovarsi d'—,* to agree: *sono d'— con voi che la merce è di ottima qualità,* I agree with you that the goods are of excellent quality; *non andare d'—,* to disagree; *mettersi d'—,* to come to an understanding; *stare, attenersi agli accordi,* to stand by (*o* to keep to) the agreement ‖ *d'amore e d'—,* in full agreement 2. (*mus.*) chord; (*armonia, consonanza*) tune, pitch: *— arpeggiato,* broken chord; *essere in —,* to be in tune 3. *fig.* harmony, accord, concordance: *l'— dei colori in questo quadro,* the harmony of colours in this picture.

accòrgersi, *v.r.* (*percepire*) to perceive (sthg.); (*divenire consapevole*) to become aware (of sthg.), to notice (sthg.); (*rendersi conto*) to realize (sthg.): *non me ne sono mai accorto,* I have never noticed it; *non mi ero accorto che pioveva,* I was not aware it was raining; *si accorse di essere osservato,* he perceived that he was being watched; *ti sei accorto che stavi commettendo un errore?,* did you realize that you were making a mistake?; *senza —,* (*inavvertitamente*) inadvertently; (*con facilità*) with the greatest ease.

accorgimento, *s.m.* 1. (*sagacia*) sagacity, shrewdness 2. (*stratagemma*) trick, ingenious contrivance, clever device, expedient.

accorpàto, *ag.* (*di animale*) pregnant.

accórrere, *v.i.* to run, to hasten, to rush: *accorrerete a rassicurarlo,* you will hasten to reassure him; *molti accorsero a sentirlo,* many people flocked to hear him; *— in aiuto di qlcu.,* to rush to the help of s.o.

accorruòmo, *inter.* (*rar.*) help!.

accortaménte, *av.* adroitly, shrewdly.

accortézza, *s.f.* 1. (*sagacia*) sagacity, shrewdness 2. (*astuzia*) cunning.

accòrto, *ag.* 1. (*sagace*) shrewd, sagacious 2. (*saggio*) wise 3. (*informato*): *fare — qlcu.,* to warn (*o* to caution) s.o.

accosciàrsi, *v.r.* to squat (down).

accostàbile, *ag.* approachable, accessible.

accostaménto, *s.m.* 1. approach, approaching: *manovra d'—,* (*mar.*) hauling (*o* haulage) 2. (*combinazione di colori, ecc.*) combination.

accostàre, *v.t.* 1. to approach, to draw near, to put near: *accosta la sedia al muro,* draw the chair near the wall 2. (*porte, finestre, ecc.*) to set ajar: *accostate la porta,* set the door ajar 3. (*frequentare*) to frequent: *è tanto sciocca che nessuno l'accosterà mai,* she is so silly that nobody will ever have anything to do with her ‖ *v.i.* 1. (*aer. mar.*) to haul, to tack: *— a dritta,* to haul (*o* to tack) to starboard; *— a sinistra,* to haul (*o* to tack) to port 2. (*aut.*) to go alongside ‖ **accostàrsi,** *v.r.* 1. to come near (s.o., sthg.), to go near (s.o., sthg.) ‖ *— all'Eucarestia,* to receive Holy Communion 2. (*aderire*) to join (sthg.): *— a un partito,* to join a party 3. (*assomigliare*) to resemble (s.o., sthg.); to be like (s.o., sthg.).

accostévole, *ag.* approachable, accessible; (*affabile*) affable.

accòsto, *ag.* (*rar.*) near: *la scala è accosta al muro,* the ladder is leaning against the wall ‖ *av. prep.* near (at hand), close to, near by: *— —,* very near; *la casa —,* the next-door house; *stagli —,* keep close to him.

accostolàre, *v.t.* (*mar.*) to rib (a ship).

accostolatúra, *s.f.* (*ind. tessile*) wrinkle (in pressed cloth).

accostumàbile, *ag.* adaptable; apt, easy to get accustomed, apt to get trained.

accostumàre, *v.t.* (*rar.*) to accustom ‖ **accostumàrsi,** *v.r.* to become accustomed, to get accustomed, to get used.

accostumàto, *ag.* used, accustomed.

accotonàre, *v.t.* 1. (*ind. tessile*) to raise 2. (*imbot-*

tire) to stuff with cotton 3. (*neol.*) (*capelli*) to back-comb.

accotonatóre, *s.m.* (*ind. tessile*) raiser.

accotonatúra, *s.f.* 1. (*ind. tessile*) raising 2. (*neol.*) (*di capelli*) back-combing.

accottimàre, *v.t.* to give as piece-work.

accovacciàrsi, *v.r.* to crouch (down), to squat (down): *la tigre s'accovacciò prima di balzare sulla preda,* the tiger crouched before pouncing upon its prey.

accovacciolàrsi, *v.r.* to squat (down).

accovonàre, *v.t.* (*agr.*) to sheaf, to sheave.

accozzàglia, *s.f.* huddle, medley, disorderly mass: *un'— di gente,* a motley crowd.

accozzaménto, *s.m.* muddle, huddle.

accozzàre, *v.t.* to muddle, to huddle, to mix together ‖ *non — il pranzo con la cena, fig.* to be unable to make both ends meet ‖ **accozzàrsi,** *v.r.* 1. to huddle, to get together 2. (*cozzare*) to butt.

accòzzo, *s.m.* huddle, medley, confusion.

accreditàbile, *ag.* creditable, trustworthy.

accreditaménto, *s.m.* (*comm.*) credit, crediting.

accreditàre, *v.t.* 1. to credit: *— una somma a qlcu.,* to credit s.o. with an amount (*o* to credit an amount to s.o.) 2. (*valorizzare*) to credit, to give credit to (s.o., sthg.) 3. (*confermare*) to confirm, to make credible 4. (*pol.*) to accredit, to supply with credentials ‖ **accreditàrsi,** *v.r.* to obtain credit, esteem; to gain credit.

accreditàto, *ag.* 1. (*di persona*) qualified (for sthg.); accredited 2. (*di somma*) credited.

accréscere, *v.t.* to augment, to increase, to enlarge ‖ **accréscersi,** *v.r.* to increase, to grow; (*moltiplicarsi*) to multiply.

accrescimento, *s.m.* (*crescita*) increase, growth; (*l'accrescersi*) increasing.

accrescitivo, *ag.* augmentative ‖ *s.m.* (*gram.*) augmentative: *riccone è — di ricco,* "riccone" ("very rich man") is an augmentative of "ricco" (rich man).

accrespàre, *v.t.* (*viso*) to wrinkle, to pucker; (*stoffa*) to ruffle; (*acqua*) to ripple, to ruffle; (*carta*) to crumple; (*capelli*) to fuzz, to friz, to crisp.

accrespatúra, *s.f.* (*di viso*) wrinkling, puckering; (*di stoffa*) ruffling; (*di acqua*) rippling, ruffling; (*di carta*) crumpling; (*di capelli*) fuzziness, frizziness.

accrezióne, *s.f.* (*dir.*) accretion.

accúbito, *s.m.* 1. recumbency 2. (*letto conviviale*) triclinium (*pl.* triclinia).

accucciàrsi, *v.r.* to curl (oneself) up.

accudíre, *v.i.* to attend, to look (after s.o., sthg.): *— alla bottega,* to mind the shop; *— alle faccende domestiche, alla casa,* to do the housework, to do the housekeeping.

acculàre, *v.t.* to move back, backwards; (*un cavallo*) to rein back, to back: *— il carro al muro,* to back the cart against the wall ‖ **acculàrsi,** *v.r.* (*di animali*) to squat on the haunches; to sit on the hind legs.

accuiattàre, *v.t.* 1. to bump down ‖ *— le panche,* to sit idle 2. (*un libro*) to board.

accumulàbile, *ag.* accumulative, cumulative.

accumulaménto, *s.m.* accumulation.

accumulàre, *v.t.* to amass, to store up, to heap up, to hoard ‖ *interessi accumulati,* accrued interests ‖ **accumulàrsi,** *v.r.* to accumulate, to pile up.

accumulatóre, *s.m.* 1. hoarder, accumulator 2. (*elett.*) accumulator, (storage) battery 3. *— d'aria,* (*mar.*) accumulator, compressed air tank.

accumulatríce, *s.f.* hoarder, accumulator.

accumulazióne, *s.f.* 1. (*l'accumulare*) accumulating, hoarding 2. (*cumulo*) accumulation, pile, hoard.

accuratamente, *av.* accurately, carefully, precisely.

accuratézza, *s.f.* accuracy, care, precision, exactness.

accuràto, *ag.* accurate, careful, precise, exact.

accúsa, *s.f.* 1. accusation, charge: *fare delle accuse contro qlcu.,* to make charges against s.o. 2. (*dir.*) indictment, charge, arraignment; (*per alto tradimento*) impeachment: *atto d'*—, (bill of) indictment; *capo d'*—, count of indictment; *sotto l'*— *di,* under the charge of; *muovere un'*— *contro qlcu.,* to bring a charge against s.o.

accusàbile, *ag.* chargeable (with sthg.), indictable (for sthg.).

accusabilità, *s.f.* chargeability.

accusàre, *v.t.* **1.** to accuse, to charge; to censure, to inculpate: *l'accusò di negligenza,* he charged her with negligence; — *il destino, fig.* to blame fate **2.** *(dir.)* to indict, to accuse, to prosecute; *(di alto tradimento)* to impeach: *fu accusato di tradimento,* he was indicted as a traitor **3.** *(manifestare)* to show up, to bring out: *parole che accusano una grande ignoranza,* words that betray (o show) great ignorance **4.** *(sentire)* to feel: — *un dolore,* to feel a pain **5.** *(comm.)* to acknowledge: — *ricevuta di,* to acknowledge receipt of **6.** *(carte)* to declare ‖ **accusàrsi,** *v.r.* to accuse oneself.

accusàta, *s.f. (carte)* declaration.

accusatìvo, *ag.s.m. (gram.)* accusative.

accusàto, *s.m. (dir.)* accused; defendant, prisoner (at the bar).

accusatóre, *ag.* accusing, accusative ‖ **accusatóre,** *s.m.,* **accusatrìce,** *s.f.* accuser, prosecutor: *pubblico* —, *(dir.)* public prosecutor.

accusatòrio, *ag.* accusatory.

acedìa, *s.f.* acedia; accidie; sloth.

acèfali, *s.m. pl. (zool.)* Acephala.

acefalìa, *s.f. (teratologia)* acephalia, acephalism.

acèfalo, *ag. (zool.)* acephalous.

aceràia, *s.f.* maple wood.

acerbaménte, *av.* **1.** *(aspramente)* sharply **2.** *(prematuramente)* prematurely.

acerbétto, *ag.* rather unripe; *(acidulo)* sourish.

acerbézza, *s.f.* **1.** *(immaturità)* unripeness **2.** *(sapore agro)* sourness **3.** *fig. (asprezza)* sharpness.

acerbità, *s.f.* **1.** *(immaturità)* unripeness **2.** *fig. (asprezza, durezza)* sharpness.

acèrbo, *ag.* **1.** unripe, green (anche *fig.*): *essere* — *per certi studi,* to be unripe for certain studies **2.** *(prematuro)* premature: *è* — *discutere questo affare,* it is premature to discuss this business **3.** *(acido, agro)* sour: *gusto* —, sour taste **4.** *fig. (aspro, duro)* sharp.

aceréta, *s.f.* maple wood.

àcero, *s.m. (bot.)* maple.

acerrimaménte, *av.* fiercely.

acèrrimo, *ag. superl.* (very) fierce, implacable, most bitter: *odio* —, most bitter (o fierce) hatred.

acèrvo, *s.m. (mucchio)* heap.

acescènte, *ag. (rar.)* turning sour.

acetàbolo, *s.m.* **1.** *(archeol.)* vinegar bottle **2.** *(bossolo dei giocolieri)* dice box.

acetàre, *v.t.* to season with vinegar, to pickle.

acetàto, *ag.* smelling of vinegar; seasoned with vinegar ‖ *s.m. (chim.)* acetate: — *di piombo,* lead acetate.

acetèlla, *s.f.* **1.** water mixed with vinegar **2.** *(bot.)* sorrel.

acètico, *ag. (chim.)* acetic.

acetificazióne, *s.f. (chim.)* acetification.

acetilène, *s.m.* acetylene.

acetìre, *v.i.* to turn sour.

acéto, *s.m.* vinegar: — *cosmetico,* toilet vinegar; *dei sette ladri,* aromatic vinegar; *verdura sotto* —, pickles; *pigliare d'*—, to turn sour.

acetolièra, *s.f.* cruet.

acetòmetro, *s.m.* acetometer.

acetóne, *s.m. (chim.)* acetone.

acetósa, *s.f. (bot.)* sorrel.

acetosèlla, *s.f. (bot.)* wild sorrel.

acetosità, *s.f.* acidity, sourness.

acetóso, *ag.* vinegary, vinegarish; acetous, sour.

acetùme, *s.m.* pickles (*pl.*).

achènio, *s.m. (bot.)* achene, akene.

achèo, *ag.s.m. (st.)* Achaean ‖ *gli Achei,* the Achaei.

Acherónte, *no.pr.m. (geog. mit.)* Acheron.

acherontèo, *ag. (mit.)* Acherontean, infernal.

acheròntico, *ag. (mit.)* Acherontic; funereal.

Achille, *no.pr.m.* Achilles.

achillèa, *s.f. (bot.)* yarrow.

achirànto, *s.m. (bot.)* amaranthus, amaranth.

acianoblepsìa, *s.f. (patol.)* acyanoblepsia, acyanopsia.

acicolàre, *ag. (min. bot.)* needle-shaped.

acidificàre, *v.t.* to acidify.

acidificazióne, *s.f.* acidification.

acidìmetro, *s.m.* acidimeter.

acidità, *s.f.* **1.** acidity, sourness, tartness **2.** *(di stomaco)* hyperchlorhydria.

àcido, *ag.* **1.** acid, sour **2.** *fig.* sharp ‖ *s.m. (chim.)* acid.

acidòsi, *s.f. (patol.)* acidosis.

acidulàre, *v.t.* to acidulate, to make slightly acid.

acìdulo, *ag.* acidulous, slightly acid.

acidùme, *s.m.* **1.** acid matter **2.** *(sapore acido)* sour taste, sourness.

acinesìa, *s.f. (med.)* akinesia, akinesis.

acinètico, *ag. (farm.)* akinesic.

acinifórme, *ag.* aciniform (anche *anat.*); berry-like.

àcino, *s.m.* **1.** *(seme)* acinus **2.** *(chicco)* grape, berry **3.** *(anat.)* acinus (*pl.* acini).

acinóso, *ag.* **1.** acinaceous **2.** *(aciniforme)* aciniform (anche *anat.*).

acloridrìa, *s.f. (patol.)* achlorhydria.

àcme, *s.f.* **1.** acme; *(ret.)* climax **2.** *(di malattia)* crisis (*pl.* crises).

àcne, *s.m. (med.)* acne.

aconitìna, *s.f. (chim.)* aconitine.

acònito, *s.m. (bot.)* aconite.

acotilèdone, *ag. (bot.)* acotyledonous ‖ *s.f.* acotyledon.

àcqua, *s.f.* **1.** water: — *ammoniacale,* gas liquor; — *di Colonia,* eau-de-Cologne; — *distillata,* distilled water; — *di seltz,* soda water; — *dolce,* fresh water; — *dura,* hard water; — *ferma,* stagnant water; — *gassosa,* aerated water; — *leggera,* soft water; — *lustrale, santa,* holy water; — *marina,* sea water; — *minerale,* mineral water; — *ossigenata, (chim.)* hydrogen peroxide (o oxygenated water); — *piovana,* rain water; — *potabile,* drinking water; — *ragia, (chim.)* turpentine, oil (o spirit) of turpentine; — *regia,* aqua regia; — *salata,* salt water; — *salmastra,* brackish water; — *sorgiva,* spring water; — *termale,* hot spring (o thermal) water; — *vegeto-minerale,* vegeto-mineral water ‖ *corso d'*—, stream (o waterway); *filo d'*—, trickle of water; *getto d'*—, fountain; *giuochi d'*—, fountains (playing); *specchio d'*—, expanse of water ‖ — *cheta, fig. ...*, *person; (fam.)* sly boots: *l'*— *cheta rovina i ponti,* still waters run deep ‖ — *in bocca!,* keep it under your hat! ‖ *diamante della più bella,* diamond of the first water ‖ *un pesce fuor d'*—, a fish out of water ‖ *tempesta in un bicchier d'*—, a storm in a tea-cup ‖ *affogare in un bicchier d'*—, to lose one's head over nothing ‖ *assomigliarsi come due gocce d'*—, to be as like as two peas ‖ *avere l'*— *alla gola,* to be on the brink of disaster ‖ *fare* —, to leak (o to take on water) ‖ *fare un buco nell'*—, to beat the air (o to work without any result) ‖ *lavorare sott'*—, to act in an underhand way ‖ *lasciar correre l'*— *per la sua china,* to let matters take their course (o to refrain from interfering) ‖ *mettere* — *sul fuoco,* to damp s.o.'s enthusiasm (o to pour oil on troubled waters) ‖ *navigare in cattive acque,* to be hard up ‖ *pestare l'*— *nel mortaio,* to work uselessly ‖ *tirare l'*— *al proprio mulino,* to bring grist to one's mill ‖ — *passata non macina più, prov.* let bygones be bygones **2.** *(pioggia)* rain: — *a catinelle,* heavy rain; *rovescio d'*—, shower (o downpour o cloud-burst) ‖ *prendere dell'*—,' to get soaked.

acquacedràta, *s.f.* citron-water.

acquacedratàio, *s.m.* seller of soft drinks.

acquafòrte, *s.f.* **1.** *(art.)* etching **2.** *(chim.)* nitric acid.

acquafortìsta, *s.m.* etcher, aquafortist.

acquàio, *s.m.* (kitchen) sink.

acquaiòlo, *s.m.* water-carrier; seller of water.

acquamaníle, *s.m.* (*eccl.*) ewer.
acquamarína, *s.f.* (*min.*) aquamarine.
acquaplàno, *s.m.* **1.** (*idroscivolante con motore*) hydroplane **2.** (*spor.*) aquaplane.
acquàre, *v.t.* (*rar.*) to water ‖ *v.i.* (*far provvista d'acqua*) to take on water.
acquartieraménto, *s.m.* (*mil.*) quartering, billet.
acquartieràre, *v.t.* to quarter ‖ **acquartieràrsi,** *v.r.* to be quartered, to be billeted.
acquarzènte, *s.f.* brandy.
acquasantièra, *s.f.* (holy water) stoup.
acquàta, *s.f.* **1.** downpour **2.** (*luogo di rifornimento*) watering-place.
acquàtico, *ag.* aquatic: *sport* —, aquatic sport.
acquattàre, *v.t.* to hide ‖ **acquattàrsi,** *v.r.* **1.** to crouch, to squat (down): *la tigre si acquattò prima di balzare,* the tiger crouched before springing; *la vecchia si acquattò al fuoco,* the old woman squatted by the fire **2.** (*nascondersi*) to hide oneself (by squatting, crouching).
acquavíte, *s.f.* brandy.
acquazzóne, *s.m.* (heavy) shower, downpour, cloudburst: *che — torrenziale!,* what a downpour!.
acquedótto, *s.m.* aqueduct.
àcqueo, *ag.* watery, aqueous: *vapor* —, steam (o water vapour); *umor* —, (*anat.*) aqueous humour.
acquerellàre, *v.t.* to paint in water-colours.
acquerellísta, *s.c.* water-colourist.
acquerèllo, *s.m.* **1.** (*colore stemperato, dipinto*) water-colour **2.** (*vinello*) light wine.
acquerúgiola, *s.f.* drizzle.
acquidernatúra, *s.f.* (*artig.*) quiring, binding sheets of paper into quires.
acquidóccio, *s.m.* drain.
acquiescènte, *ag.* acquiescent.
acquiescènza, *s.f.* acquiescence, submission.
acquietàbile, *ag.* appeasable.
acquietaménto, *s.m.* appeasement, quieting.
acquietàre, *v.t.* to appease, to calm (down); to pacify; (*liti*) to settle; (*creditori*) to satisfy ‖ **acquietàrsi,** *v.r.* to become appeased, to quieten down, to subside, to still: *il temporale si è acquietato,* the storm has passed away.
acquirènte, *s.c.* buyer, purchaser.
acquisíre, *v.t.* to acquire, to obtain: — *un'abitudine, una reputazione,* to acquire a habit, a reputation.
acquisitívo, *ag.* acquisitive.
acquisíto, *ag.* acquired: *un diritto* —, an acquired right; *gusto* —, acquired taste.
acquisitóre, *s.m.* acquirer.
acquisizióne, *s.f.* acquisition.
acquistàbile, *ag.* buyable, purchasable; (*ottenibile*) obtainable, available.
acquistàre, *v.t.* **1.** (*comprare*) to buy, to purchase: *ho acquistato questo soprabito a buon mercato,* I bought this coat cheap; — *la libertà a prezzo della vita,* to purchase freedom with one's blood **2.** (*ottenere*) to acquire, to get, to obtain: *egli acquistò una bella eredità,* he acquired a handsome inheritance; — *fama di,* to obtain a reputation for **3.** *fig.* (*guadagnare*) to gain: — *tempo,* to gain time (o to defer a matter); — *terreno,* to make progress ‖ *il vino acquista con gli anni,* wine improves with age ‖ **acquistàrsi,** *v.r.* to gain, to win: *si è acquistato molti amici con la sua bontà,* his goodness gained him many friends; — *la fiducia di qlcu.,* to win s.o.'s confidence.
acquísto, *s.m.* **1.** purchase; (*amer.*) buy: *potere d'*—, purchasing power; *fare degli acquisti,* to go shopping; (*comm.*) to make purchases **2.** (*acquisizione*) acquisition **3.** (*conquista*) conquest; (*annessione*) annexation.
acquitríno, *s.m.* marsh, swamp, bog.
acquitrinóso, *ag.* marshy, swampy, boggy.
acquolína, *s.f.* **1.** drizzle **2.** *far venire l'*— *in bocca a qlcu.,* to make s.o.'s mouth water.
acquosità, *s.f.* wateriness, aquosity.

acquóso, *ag.* watery, soggy, sodden.
àcre, *ag.* pungent, acrid, sharp; *fig.* acrimonious, sarcastic; (*acido*) sour, tart: *fumo* —, pungent smoke; *osservazione* —, cutting (o sarcastic) remark; *suono* —, piercing sound; *vino* —, sour wine.
acrèdine, *s.f.* acridity; *fig.* acrimony, bitterness; (*acidità*) sourness, tartness.
acreménte, *av.* pungently, acridly, sharply; *fig.* acrimoniously, sarcastically, harshly.
acrídio, *s.m.* (*entom.*) locust.
acrílico, *ag.* (*chim.*) acrylic: *resine acriliche,* acrylic resins.
acrimònia, *s.f.* acrimony, pungency, acerbity.
acrimonióso, *ag.* acrimonious, pungent, harsh.
acrisía, *s.f.* (*fil. patol.*) acrisy, acrisia.
àcro, *s.m.* (*agr.*) acre (*misura di superficie* = a 40,468).
acroamàtico, *ag.* (*fil.*) acroamatic, esoteric.
acròbata, *s.c.* acrobat, funambulist, tumbler.
acrobàtico, *ag.* acrobatic.
acrobatísmo, *s.m.* acrobatism.
acrobazía, *s.f.* acrobatics (*pl.*): *fare delle acrobazie, fig.* to perform stunts.
acrocòro, *s.m.* **1.** plateau **2.** (*vetta*) summit.
acromàtico, *ag.* (*fis.*) achromatic.
acromatísmo, *s.m.* (*fis.*) achromatism.
acromatopsía, *s.f.* (*patol.*) daltonism.
acromegalía, *s.f.* (*patol.*) acromegaly.
acrònico, *ag.* (*astr.*) acronical, acronycal.
acrònimo, *s.m.* acronym.
acròpoli, *s.f.* acropolis.
acròstico, *ag.s.m.* acrostic.
acrotèrio, *s.m.* (*arch.*) acroteriòn, acroterium (*pl.* acroteria).
acuíre, *v.t.* to sharpen, to stimulate, to whet (anche *fig.*): — *l'interesse,* to stimulate interest.
aculeàto, *ag.* **1.** (*zool. bot.*) aculeate, aculeated **2.** (*appuntito*) pointed.
acúleo, *s.m.* **1.** (*bot.*) aculeus (*pl.* aculei), prickle, thorn **2.** (*zool.*) aculeus (*pl.* aculei), sting; (*dell'istrice*) quill **3.** *fig.* incentive, stimulus (*pl.* stimuli).
acúme, *s.m.* **1.** acumen, acuteness, insight, perspicacity: *egli ha un grande — critico,* he has a deep critical insight **2.** (*stimolo*) stimulus (*pl.* stimuli).
acuminàre, *v.t.* to sharpen to whet, to edge.
acústica, *s.f.* acoustics.
acústico, *ag.* acoustic: *assorbimento* —, (*fis.*) sound absorption; *cornetto* —, ear-trumpet.
acutaménte, *av.* acutely, sharply.
acutàngolo, *ag.* (*geom.*) acute-angled.
acutézza, *s.f.* **1.** acuteness, sharpness **2.** (*di mente*) acumen, perspicacity.
acutizzàre, *v.t.* to make acute ‖ **acutizzàrsi,** *v.r.* to become, to grow acute: *la crisi si acutizzò improvvisamente,* the crisis suddenly became very serious.
acúto, *ag.* **1.** acute, pointed, sharp: *angolo* —, (*geom.*) acute angle; *arco* —, (*arch.*) lancet (o pointed) arch **2.** (*violento, intenso*) intense, acute: *desiderio* —, strong desire; *freddo* —, intense (o piercing) cold; *malattia acuta,* acute illness **3.** (*perspicace*) sharp, subtle, perspicacious, acute: *mente acuta,* subtle mind **4.** (*aspro*) shrill: *nota acuta,* shrill note; *suono* —, shrill (o piercing) sound **5.** *nota acuta,* (*mus.*) high note **6.** *accento* —, (*fonet.*) acute accent.
ad, *V.* a².
Àda, *no.pr.f.* Ada(h).
adacquaménto, *s.m.* watering, sprinkling.
adacquàre, *v.t.* to water, to sprinkle.
adacquatúra, *s.f.* watering, sprinkling.
adagiaménto, *s.m.* placing, setting, laying.
adagiàre, *v.t.* to lay down with care, to put down with care ‖ **adagiàrsi,** *v.r.* to lie down, to subside: *si adagiò nella poltrona,* he subsided into an arm-chair.
adagíno, *av.* gently, slowly, softly.

adàgio[1], *av.* **1.** (*lentamente*) slowly; (*fam.*) slow: *il suo cuore batte più* —, his heart is beating slower; *andare* —, to go slow(ly) **2.** (*senza fretta*) in a leisurely way **3.** (*cautamente*) cautiously: *andare* — (*o cautamente*), *fig.* to go slow(ly) **4.** (*con delicatezza*) gently, softly ‖ *s.m.* (*mus.*) adagio.

adàgio[2], *s.m.* (*proverbio*) saw, adage, proverb, saying.

adamànte, *s.m.* (*poet.*) adamant, diamond.

adamantíno, *ag.* **1.** adamantine (anche *fig.*): *coscienza adamantina*, righteous conscience **2.** (*di stile*) terse, lucid.

adamítico, *ag.* Adamic(al): *usanze adamitiche*, primitive customs; *in costume* —, in one's birthday suit (*o* naked).

Adàmo, *no.pr.m.* Adam ‖ *pomo d'* —, Adam's apple.

adattàbile, *ag.* adaptable.

adattabilità, *s.f.* adaptability.

adattaménte, *av.* conveniently, suitably.

adattaménto, *s.m.* **1.** adaptation, adaption (anche *med.*) **2.** (*assestamento*) adjustment.

adattàre, *v.t.* to adapt, to fit, to adjust, to modify: — *un romanzo per il teatro*, to adapt a novel for the stage; — *un vestito a qlcu.*, to fit a garment on s.o. ‖ **adattàrsi**, *v.r.* **1.** to adapt oneself, to fit oneself, to adjust oneself: — *a un nuovo ambiente*, to adjust oneself to a new surrounding; — *alle circostanze*, to adapt oneself to circumstances **2.** (*rassegnarsi*) to put up with (sthg.), to resign oneself: *dobbiamo adattarci*, we must make the best of things (*o* circumstances) **3.** (*andar bene*) to fit (s.o., sthg.): *quest'abito ti si adatta alla perfezione*, this dress fits you perfectly **4.** (*convenire*) to suit (s.o., sthg.): *questo lavoro si adatta ai miei gusti*, this job suits my tastes.

adattàto, adàtto, *ag.* **1.** fit, suited; proper, right: *non è adatto per queste parti*, he is ill-suited to these parts; *scegli il momento adatto*, choose the right time **2.** (*qualificato, che va bene*) qualified, suitable: *vestito adatto alle circostanze*, dress suitable for (*o* to) circumstances.

addàrsi, *v.r.* (*letter.*) **1.** (*accorgersi*) to perceive (s.o., sthg.), to notice (s.o., sthg.) **2.** (*dedicarsi*) to devote oneself.

addaziàre, *v.t.* to impose duty on (sthg.), to make dutiable.

addebitàre, *v.t.* to debit: — *un conto a qlcu.*, to charge an account to s.o. (*o* to debit s.o. with an account).

addébito, *s.m.* **1.** debit **2.** (*accusa*) charge, accusation, imputation: *fare un* — *a qlcu. per ql.co.*, to charge s.o. with sthg.

addèndo, *s.m.* (*arit.*) addendum (*pl.* addenda).

addensaménto, *s.m.* **1.** thickening, condensation **2.** (*di persone*) crowd, gathering **3.** (*ind. tessile*) beating up.

addensàre, *v.t.* to thicken ‖ **addensàrsi**, *v.r.* **1.** to thicken **2.** (*affollarsi*) to gather, to throng, to crowd.

addensatóre, *s.m.* (*miner.*) densifier, thickener.

addentàre, *v.t.* **1.** to seize with one's teeth, to bite, to snap at (sthg.) **2.** (*afferrare*) to catch **3.** *fig.* to censure **4.** (*mec.*) to cog.

addentatúra, *s.f.* **1.** bite **2.** (*mec.*) cogging.

addentellàre, *v.t.* (*arch.*) to leave toothings at (wall corners).

addentellàto, *s.m.* **1.** clue, connexion **2.** (*arch.*) toothing.

addentellatúra, *s.f.* (*arch.*) toothing.

addentràrsi, *v.r.* to penetrate; to go (into sthg.): — *in una questione*, *fig.* to probe a question.

addéntro, *av.* inside, within: *è molto* — *nella faccenda*, he is very well acquainted with the matter.

addestràbile, *ag.* trainable.

addestraménto, *s.m.* training; (*mil.*) drilling: — *fisico*, physical training; *essere senza* —, to be out of training.

addestràre, *v.t.* to train; (*mil.*) to drill ‖ **addestràrsi**, *v.r.* to train, to practise.

addestratóre, *s.m.* trainer.

addétto, *ag.* employed (in sthg.), attached: *ufficiale* — *allo Stato Maggiore come interprete*, officer attached to the Staff as interpreter ‖ *s.m.* attaché: — *militare*, military attaché.

addí, *av.* on the (day) of: — *25 maggio*, on the 25th of May.

addiacciàre, *v.t.* **1.** to freeze **2.** (*le greggi*) to fold, to pen up ‖ **addiacciàrsi**, *v.r.* to freeze.

addiàccio, *s.m.* pen, sheep-fold; (*mil.*) bivouac: *dormire all'* —, to sleep in the open.

addiètro, *av.* **1.** (*di spazio*) behind (anche *fig.*): *dare* —, to draw back (*o* to recoil); *lasciare qlcu.* —, to leave s.o. behind; *restare* — *negli studi*, to lag (*o* to remain) behind with one's studies ‖ — *!*, stand back! **2.** (*di tempo*) before, ago: *in* —, *per l'* —, in the past; *tre mesi* —, three months ago; *era arrivato due anni* —, he had arrived two years before ‖ *continuare come* —, to go on as before; *volgersi* —, to think of the past.

addiètro, *s.m.* (*mar.*) stern.

addimandàre, *v.t.* (*rar.*) to ask.

addío[2], *s.m.* **1.** good-bye: *dire* — *a qlcu.*, to say good-bye to s.o. ‖ *andarsene senza dire* —, to leave abruptly (*o* to take French leave) **2.** (*poet.*) farewell: *un discorso d'* —, a farewell speech; *dare l'ultimo* — *a qlcu.*, to bid the last farewell to s.o.

addío, *inter.* **1.** good-bye; (*fam.*) bye-bye, ta-ta **2.** (*arrivederci*) so long, see you soon, see you later **3.** (*poet.*) farewell, adieu: — *per sempre!*, farewell, adieu!.

addíre, *v.t.* (*poet.*) to inscribe ‖ **addírsi**, *v.r.* to become (s.o.), to suit (s.o.): *quest'abito non mi si addice*, this dress does not suit me ‖ *« Il lutto si addice ad Elettra »*, "Mourning Becomes Electra".

addirittúra, *av.* **1.** (*completamente, del tutto*) quite **2.** (*direttamente*) directly: *egli venne* —, he came directly **3.** (*nelle esclamazioni*) really!.

addirizzàre, *v.t.* to straighten; *fig.* to correct, to amend ‖ **addirizzàrsi**, *v.r.* **1.** (*volgere al bello*) to clear up **2.** (*dirigersi*) to go (towards s.o., sthg.).

addirizzatúra, *s.f.* **1.** straightening; *fig.* amending **2.** (*scriminatura*) parting.

additaménto, *s.m.* indication.

additàre, *v.t.* to point at, to (s.o., sthg.), to point out; (*mostrare*) to show: *additò l'uomo che stava passando*, he pointed at the man who was passing by; *tutto lo addita come il solo colpevole*, everything points to him as the only culprit; — *il cammino a qlcu.*, to show s.o. the way.

addiveníre, *v.i.* **1.** (*divenire*) to become **2.** (*accadere*) to happen, to chance **3.** (*venire*): — *ad un accordo*, to come to an understanding (*o* to an agreement).

addizionàle, *ag.* additional, supplementary ‖ *s.f.* supplementary tax.

addizionàre, *v.t.* to add up, to sum up: *addiziona queste cifre*, add these figures up.

addizionatríce, *s.f.* adder, adding-machine.

addizióne, *s.f.* addition, adding up.

addobbaménto, *s.m.* **1.** decoration, ornament **2.** (*cuc.*) dressing **3.** (*concia*) tanning, dressing.

addobbàre, *v.t.* **1.** to adorn, to deck, to decorate: *i muri erano decorati con...*, the walls were adorned with... ‖ *essere addobbato come un albero di Natale*, to be all decked out **2.** (*conciare*) to tan, to dress (skins) **3.** (*armare cavaliere*) to dub (s.o.) a knight.

addobbatóre, *s.m.* decorator.

addòbbo, *s.m.* **1.** decoration; hangings (*pl.*) **2.** (*eccl.*) sacred ornaments (*pl.*) **3.** (*truogolo per concia*) tan-pit, tan-vat.

addocilíre, *v.t.* **1.** to tame **2.** (*pelli*) to soften.

addogàre, *v.t.* **1.** to stave **2.** (*arald.*) to divide into vertical bands.

addolciménto, *s.m.* **1.** sweetening **2.** *fig.* softening; mitigation.

addolcíre, *v.t.* **1.** to sweeten: — *una bibita*, to sweeten a drink **2.** *fig.* to soften: *cerca di* — *i tuoi modi*, try to be more gentle in your manners; *solo gli anni po-*

trebbero — il suo carattere, only age could soften his character **3.** (*calmare, lenire*) to soothe, to relieve, to alleviate; to appease: — *la collera di qlcu.*, to soothe s.o.'s anger; — *una pena*, to soothe (o to relieve) a pain **4.** (*metalli*) to soften ‖ **addolcírsi**, *v.r.* **1.** *fig.* to soften, to become, to grow mild(er), to become soft(er); to grow gentle: *il clima si è addolcito*, the climate has grown milder; *il suo sguardo si addolcì*, his look became softer **2.** (*lenirsi*) to soften, to relent, to calm down.

addolcitívo, *ag.* **1.** sweetening **2.** (*lenitivo*) soothing‖ *s.m.* (*farm.*) (*lenitivo*) lenitive.

addoloràre, *v.t.* to grieve, to pain, to give pain to (s.o.), to distress: *l'avete addolorata*, you have hurt her feelings; *m'addolora sapere che...*, it grieves me (o it makes me sad o it pains me) to know that...; *queste notizie lo hanno addolorato*, he was grieved at the news; *le sue parole mi hanno profondamente addolorato*, his words have deeply distressed me ‖ **addoloràrsi**, *v.r.* to grieve, to be grieved (at sthg.); (*essere spiacente*) to be sorry, to regret: *si addolora nel vederlo in miseria*, he grieves to see him in want; *si addolorava di non poter andare*, she was very sorry (o she regretted) she couldn't go.

addoloràto, *ag.* grieved; sorrowful; sorry: *uno sguardo —*, a sorrowful look; *ne sono molto —*, I am very sorry; *siamo addolorati di apprendere che...*, we are grieved (o distressed) to hear that....

Addoloràta (l'), *s.f.* Our Lady of Sorrows.

addomandàre, *V.* **domandàre**.

addòme, *s.m.* (*anat.*) abdomen.

addomesticàbile, *ag.* tamable.

addomesticaménto, *s.m.* domestication, taming.

addomesticàre, *v.t.* **1.** to domesticate, to tame; *fig.* to tame, to subdue; to make gentle, to make sociable, tractable **2.** (*assuefare*) to accustom; (*piante*) to acclimatize **3.** (*agr.*) (*terreno*) to reclaim ‖ **addomesticàrsi**, *v.r.* **1.** to become tame, domesticated; (*di persona*) to grow, to become more sociable **2.** (*divenir familiare*) to get accustomed; to grow familiar with (sthg.).

addomesticàto, *ag.* tame, domesticated ‖ *giuoco —*, rigged game; *rivoluzione addomesticata*, sham revolution.

addomesticatóre, *s.m.*, **addomesticatríce**, *s.f.* tamer.

addomesticatúra, *s.f.* (*di piante*) culture, growing.

addomestichévole, *ag.* easily domesticated, easily tamable.

addomestichevolézza, *s.f.* tamability.

addominàle, *ag.* (*anat.*) abdominal.

addoppiaménto, *s.m.* doubling.

addoppiàre, *v.t.* to double.

addoppiatóio, *s.m.* (*ind. tessile*) doubler.

addormentàre, *v.t.***1.**to put to sleep, to send to sleep: — *cullando*, to lull (o to rock) to sleep **2.** (*attutire*) to deaden, to allay: *questa medicina addormenta il dolore*, this medicine allays pain **3.** (*annoiare*) to send to sleep, to bore: *libri del genere mi addormentano*, books of that kind send me to sleep **4.** (*med.*) to anaesthetize, to give an anaesthetic to (s.o.): *fu addormentato*, he was given an anaesthetic **5.** (*intorpidire*) to benumb **6.** (*boxe*) to knock out ‖ **addormentàrsi**, *v.r.* **1.** to fall asleep, to go to sleep: — *profondamente*, to fall into a sound sleep; *riuscire ad —*, to get to sleep **2.** (*intorpidirsi*) to go to sleep: *mi si è addormentata la gamba*, my leg has gone to sleep **3.** *fig.* to sleep: *non addormentarti sui libri*, don't sleep over your books ‖ — *nel Signore*, to die peacefully ‖ — *sugli allori*, to rest on one's laurels.

addormentatívo, *ag.* soporific, soporiferous.

addormentàto, *ag.* **1.** asleep, sleeping ‖ *la Bella Addormentata*, the Sleeping Beauty **2.** (*assonnato, sonnolento*) sleepy, drowsy: *sguardo —*, sleepy look; *aver l'aria addormentata*, to look half asleep; *fig.* to have no life in one (o to be a slow coach) **3.** *fig.* slow; stupid ‖ *è un —*, he is a sleepy-head **4.** (*intorpidito*) benumbed, numb **5.** (*con anestetico*) anaesthetized **6.** (*di passione*) dormant.

addormírsi, *v.r.* (*poet.*) to fall asleep.

addossaménto, *s.m.* **1.** (*l'addossarsi*) taking on, undertaking **2.** (*l'addossare*) laying on.

addossàre, *v.t.* **1.** (*appoggiare*) to lean: — *una scala a un muro*, to lean a ladder against a wall **2.** (*attribuire*) to lay (sthg.) on (s.o.), to saddle (s.o.) with (sthg.); (*imputare*) to charge (s.o.) with (sthg.): — *una colpa a qlcu.*, to lay (o to throw) the blame on s.o.; — *una responsabilità a qlcu.*, to lay the responsibility on s.o. (o to saddle s.o. with a responsibility) **3.** (*gravare*) to burden (s.o.) with (sthg.) **4.** (*affidare*) to entrust (s.o.) with (sthg.): *gli addossò un lavoro*, he entrusted him with a job ‖ **addossàrsi**, *v.r.* **1.** (*appoggiarsi*) to lean **2.** (*affollarsi*) to crowd, to throng (together) **3.** *fig.* (*prendere su di sè*) to take upon oneself, to saddle oneself with (sthg.), to undertake, to shoulder: — *la colpa*, to take the blame; — *un peso*, to shoulder a burden; — *la responsabilità*, to take the responsibility upon oneself.

addossàto, *ag.* **1.** leaning (against sthg) **2.** (*arald.*) addorsed.

addòsso, *av.prep.* **1.** on, upon: *non ho denari —*, I have no money on me; *quella donna porta — un patrimonio*, that woman is wearing a fortune; *mettersi ql.co. —*, to put sthg. on (o to put on sthg.); *avere — una malattia*, to suffer from (o to have) a disease ‖ *d'—*, off: *gli cascavano i panni d'—*, he was wearing baggy clothes; *levarsi ql.co. d'—*, to take off sthg.; *non gli toglieva gli occhi d'—*, he could not take his eyes off him ‖ *avere il diavolo —*, to be possessed; *fig.* to be restless **2.** (*vicino*) close: *la casa è — alla chiesa*, the house is close to the church; *stare — a qlcu.*, to press (o to urge) s.o. **3.** (*contro*): *dare — a qlcu.*, to assault (o to attack) s.o.; *fig.* to contradict s.o.; (*biasimare*) to blame (o to speak ill of) s.o.

addótto, *ag.* adduced; (*citato*) quoted; (*allegato*) alleged.

addottoraménto, *s.m.* (*conseguimento di laurea*) graduation; (*conferimento di laurea*) graduation, conferring of a university degree.

addottoràre, *v.t.* to graduate, to confer a university degree on (s.o.) ‖ **addottoràrsi**, *v.r.* to become a doctor, to take a university degree, to graduate.

addottoràto, *ag.* graduated.

addottrinaménto, *s.m.* teaching, instruction.

addottrinàre, *v.t.* to instruct, to teach ‖ **addottrinàrsi**, *v.r.* to acquire knowledge, to become learned.

addottrinàto, *ag.* learned.

addrizzàre, *V.* **addirizzàre**.

adducíbile, *ag.* pleadable, adducible.

addúrre, *v.t.* to adduce, to advance, to bring forward, to put forward, to produce: (*allegare*) to allege; (*citare*) to quote, to cite; (*come scusa*) to plead: *adduse come scusa l'ignoranza*, he pleaded ignorance; — *delle buone ragioni*, to give (o to put forward o to produce) good arguments; — *un pretesto*, to advance a pretext; — *una prova*, to put forward a proof; — *qlcu. ad esempio*, to quote s.o. as an example.

adduttóre, *ag.* (*anat.*) adducent.

adduzióne, *s.f.* (*fisiol.*) adduction.

adeguàbile, *ag.* **1.** proportionable, adjustable **2.** conformable, adaptable.

adeguaménto, *s.m.* **1.** equalization, proportioning, adjustment; — *dei prezzi*, adjustment of prices **2.** (*adattamento*) adaptation.

adeguàre, *v.t.* **1.** (*pareggiare*) to equalize, to proportionate, to adjust **2.** (*adattare*) to conform, to adapt, to fit, to suit ‖ **adeguàrsi**, *v.r.* to conform oneself, to adapt oneself: — *alle circostanze*, to adapt oneself (o to rise) to the circumstances.

adeguataménte, *av.* **1.** adequately, proportionately **2.** (*in modo conveniente*) suitably, fitly **3.** (*in modo giusto*) fairly.

adeguàto, *ag.* **1.** adequate, proportionate **2.** (*adatto*) suitable, convenient, fit **3.** (*giusto*) right, fair.

Adelàide, *no.pr.f.* Adelaide.

Adèle, *no.pr.f.* Adela.

adempíbile, *ag.* accomplishable, that may be fulfilled; (*eseguibile*) executable, performable.

adémpiere, *V.* **adempíre.**

adempiménto, *s.m.* fulfilment, accomplishment; (*esecuzione*) execution, carrying out, performance.

adempíre, *v.t.* (*compiere*) to fulfil, to accomplish; (*eseguire*) to execute, to carry out, to perform: *ciò gli impedì di — il suo compito,* that prevented him from accomplishing his task; *egli adempì i suoi ordini,* he carried out his orders; — *i desideri di qlcu.,* to meet (o to fulfil) s.o.'s wishes; — *un obbligo,* to meet (o to fulfil) an obligation; — *una promessa,* to keep a promise; — *i propri doveri,* to fulfil (o to perform) one's duties ‖ **adempírsi,** *v.r.* to come true, to be fulfilled: *la profezia si adempì,* the prophecy came true.

adeníte, *s.f.* (*patol.*) adenitis.

adenòidi, *s.f. pl.* (*anat.*) adenoids.

adenoidísmo, *s.m.* (*patol.*) adenoidism.

adenoidíte, *s.f.* (*patol.*) adenoiditis.

adenología, *s.f.* adenology.

adenòma, *s.m.* (*patol.*) adenoma.

adenopatía, *s.f.* (*patol.*) adenopathy.

adenotomía, *s.f.* (*chir.*) adenotomy.

adèpto, *s.m.* 1. adept, initiate 2. (*seguace*) follower, adherent.

adequazióne, *s.f.* adequacy.

aderènte, *ag.* 1. sticking, adherent, adhering: — *al costume democratico,* in harmony with democratic usage; *parole aderenti al testo,* words sticking to the text 2. (*di abito*) tight, close-fitting: *abito — in vita,* dress close-fitting round the waist ‖ *s.m.* supporter, follower, partisan, adherent.

aderènza, *s.f.* 1. adhesion, adherence 2. (*med.*) adhesion 3. *pl.* (*relazioni*) (high) connections, relations, supporters.

adèrgere, *v.t.* to raise ‖ **adèrgersi,** *v.r.* to rise.

aderíre, *v.i.* 1. (*stare attaccato*) to adhere, to stick (anche *fig.*): *questo cerotto non aderisce,* this plaster doesn't stick; *gli aderiva alle spalle,* it stuck to his back; — *ai fatti,* to stick to the facts; — *a un'opinione,* to stick to an opinion 2. (*acconsentire, accondiscendere*) to agree, to assent, to give assent; to comply with (sthg.); to yield: — *ai desideri di qlcu.,* to comply with (o to yield to) s.o.'s wishes; — *a una proposta,* to agree to a proposal; — *a una richiesta,* to comply with a request 3. (*parteggiare per*) to join (sthg.): — *a un partito,* to join a party.

adescaménto, *s.m.* 1. enticement, allurement; (*seduzione*) seduction 2. (*idraulica*) priming.

adescàre, *v.t.* 1. to lure, to allure, to entice; (*sedurre*) to seduce 2. (*idraulica*) to prime.

adescatóre, *s.m.,* **adescatríce,** *s.f.* enticer; allurer; seducer.

adesióne, *s.f.* 1. adhesion; adherence 2. (*consenso*) adhesion, assent: *dar la propria — a un partito,* to join a party; *dare la propria — a una proposta,* to give one's support (o assent) to a proposal; *ritirare la propria — da un partito,* to leave a party (o to stop supporting a party) 3. (*fis.*) adhesion.

adesívo, *ag.* adhesive: *nastro —,* adhesive tape ‖ *s.m.* adhesive.

adèspoto, *ag.* (*di testo letterario*) anonymous.

adèsso, *av.* now, at present; (*al giorno d'oggi*) nowadays; (*or ora*) just now ‖ *fino —,* till now; *per —,* for the present (o for the time being).

adiacènte, *ag.* adjacent, adjoining; contiguous; next: *angoli adiacenti,* (*geom.*) adjacent angles; *la casa —,* the adjoining house.

adiacènza, *s.f.* 1. adjacency, contiguity: *l'— di due angoli,* (*geom.*) the adjacency of two angles 2. (*vicinanza*) nearness, vicinity 3. *gener. pl.* (*luoghi adiacenti*) neighbourhood (*sing.*), environs (*pl.*), surroundings (*pl.*).

adiànto, *s.m.* (*bot.*) adiantum; (*capelvenere*) maidenhair.

adibíre, *v.t.* to use (sthg.) as, for (sthg.) ;to assign: — *ad uso di,* to use as.

adinamía, *s.f.* (*patol.*) adynamia; weakness: — *cardiaca,* cardiac adynamia.

àdipe, *s.m.* fat, fatness.

adipocèra, *s.f.* (*grasso cadaverico*) adipocere.

adiposità, *s.f.* adiposity; (*patol.*) adiposis.

adipóso, *ag.* adipose, fat(ty): *tessuto —,* adipose tissue.

adiraménto, *s.m.* (*rar.*) anger; wrathfulness.

adiràre, *v.t.* (*muovere ad ira*) to anger, to irritate, to make (s.o.) angry, to enrage: — *qlcu.,* to get s.o.'s temper up ‖ **adiràrsi,** *v.r.* to get angry, to get enraged, to fret and fume, to lose one's temper, to flare up, to fly into a passion.

adirataménte, *av.* angrily; wrathfully.

adiràto, *ag.* angry; irritated; out of temper.

adíre, *v.i.* (*dir.*) to present oneself ‖ *v.t.* (*dir.*): — *un'eredità,* to take possession of an inheritance; — *le vie legali,* to take legal steps (o to start legal proceedings).

àdito, *s.m.* 1. entry, entrance, access 2. *fig.*: *dare — to give rise; to give cause (for sthg.): dare — a chiacchiere,* to give cause for gossip; *non dare — a speranze,* to allow no hope.

adiutatóre, adiutóre, *s.m.* 1. assistant, help(er) 2. (*dir.*) assistant magistrate.

adiuvànte, *ag.* 1. adjuvant, auxiliary 2. (*farm.*) adjuvant.

adocchiaménto, *s.m.* ogling, glance.

adocchiàre, *v.t.* 1. to eye, to glance at (s.o., sthg.) 2. (*con desiderio*) to ogle; to covet 3. (*scorgere*) to perceive, to see, to catch a glimpse of (s.o., sthg.): — *la preda,* to catch sight of the prey.

adolescènte, *ag.* adolescent, teen-aged ‖ *s.m.* adolescent, teen-ager, youth, stripling ‖ *s.f.* adolescent, teen-ager, young girl.

adolescènza, *s.f.* adolescence, youth; (*fam.*) teens.

Adòlfo, *no.pr.m.* Adolph.

adombràbile, *ag.* 1. suspicious, touchy, umbrageous 2. (*di cavallo, ecc.*) shy, skittish.

adombraménto, *s.m.* 1. shading, shade 2. *fig.* suspicion 3. (*cenno*) suggestion 4. (*simbolo*) symbol.

adombràre, *v.t.* 1. to shade 2. (*celare*) to hide, to conceal: — *le proprie cattive intenzioni,* to conceal one's evil intentions 3. (*simboleggiare*) to symbolize: *questa immagine adombra la Divinità,* this image symbolizes God 4. (*abbozzare*) to outline: *ho appena adombrato il mio progetto,* I have only outlined my plan ‖ **adombràrsi,** *v.r.* 1. (*di cavallo, ecc.*) to shy, to get skittish 2. (*farsi ombroso*) to get suspicious 3. (*impermalirsi*) to resent (sthg.), to take offence (at sthg.), to feel hurt.

Adóne, *no.pr.m.* (*mit.*) Adonis ‖ **adóne,** *s.m.* dandy, beau: *non è un —,* he is anything but handsome.

adonestàre, *v.t.* to give the appearance of honesty to (sthg.).

adònide, *s.m.* (*bot.*) adonis.

adònio, *s.m.* (*poes.*) Adonic (verse).

adontàre, *v.t.* to affront, to offend ‖ **adontàrsi,** *v.r.* to be offended (at, by sthg.), to take offence (at sthg.), to feel hurt.

adoperàbile, *ag.* employable, us(e)able.

adoperàre, adopràre, *v.t.* to employ, to use ‖ **adoperàrsi, adopràrsi,** *v.r.* to endeavour, to strive (after sthg.), to do one's utmost: *mi adoprerò per accontentarti,* I'll endeavour to satisfy you; — *molto per fare ql.co.,* to take a lot of trouble to do sthg.

adoràbile, *ag.* adorable; charming.

adorabilità, *s.f.* adorableness.

adorabilménte, *av.* adorably, charmingly.

adoràre, *v.t.* 1. to adore, to worship: — *Dio,* to worship God 2. (*fam.*) to adore, to love passionately.

adoratóre, *s.m.,* **adoratríce,** *s.f.* 1. adorer, worshipper 2. (*ammiratore*) ardent admirer; (*corteggiatore*) lover.

adorazióne, *s.f.* adoration, worship.

adornàbile, *ag.* capable of embellishment.

adornaménto, *s.m.* ornament, adornment, embellishment; (*di abiti, ecc.*) trimming.

adornàre, *v.t.* **1.** to adorn, to deck; (*vestiti*) to trim **2.** (*abbellire*) to beautify, to embellish (anche *fig.*): *le virtù adornano l'animo,* virtues beautify the soul ‖ **adornàrsi,** *v.r.* to adorn oneself; (*fam.*) to dress up, to deck oneself out.

adornataménte, *av.* **1.** ornately **2.** (*con ricercatezza*) elegantly, gracefully.

adórno, *ag.* adorned, embellished; (*bello per natura*) naturally beautiful.

adottàbile, *ag.* adoptable; acceptable.

adottaménto, *s.m.* adoption.

adottànte, *s.c.* adopter.

adottàre, *v.t.*‖ **1.** (*dir.*) to adopt **2.** *fig.* to adopt, to accept: — *una dottrina,* to accept a doctrine; — *un nome,* to adopt (*o* to take *o* to assume) a name; — *un progetto di legge,* to pass (*o* to carry) a bill.

adottatóre, *s.m.,* **adottatríce,** *s.f.* adopter.

adottívo, *ag.* adoptive: *figlio* —, adoptive son.

adozióne, *s.f.* adoption: *il mio paese di* —, my adopted country.

adrenalína, *s.f.* (*chim. farm.*) adrenalin.

Adriàno, *no.pr.m.* Adrian; (*st.*) Hadrian.

adriàtico, *ag.* Adriatic ‖ **Adriàtico (l'),** *no.pr.m.* (*geog.*) the Adriatic.

aduggiaménto, *s.m.* **1.** overshadowing (anche *fig.*) **2.** (*noia*) dullness; (*tristezza*) sadness; (*oppressione*) oppressiveness.

aduggiàre, *v.t.* **1.** to overshadow (anche *fig.*) **2.** (*intristire*) to sadden; (*opprimere*) to oppress, to weigh.

adulàre, *v.t.* to flatter, to adulate, to fawn upon (s.o.): — *sfacciatamente qlcu.,* to flatter s.o. shamelessly.

adulatóre, *s.m.,* **adulatríce,** *s.f.* flatterer, cajoler, wheedler, adulator; sycophant.

adulatòrio, *ag.* adulatory, flattering, sycophantic.

adulazióne, *s.f.* adulation, flattery, cajolery: — *grossolana,* gross (*o* base) flattery.

adúltera, *s.f.* adulteress.

adulteràbile, *ag.* liable to adulteration.

adulteraménto, *s.m.* adulteration, sophistication, falsification.

adulteràre, *v.t.* **1.** to adulterate, to debase **2.** (*documenti, ecc.*) to falsify, to tamper with (sthg.).

adulteratóre, *ag.* adulterating ‖ *s.m.,* **adulteratríce,** *s.f.* adulterator, falsifier.

adulterazióne, *V.* **adulteraménto.**

adulteríno, *ag.* adulterine.

adultèrio, *s.m.* adultery.

adúltero, *ag.* adulterous ‖ *s.m.* adulterer.

adúlto, *ag.* adult, grown-up ‖ *s.m.* grown-up (person); (*amer.*) oldster: *gli adulti,* grown-up people.

adunaménto, *s.m.* gathering, assembling: — *di persone,* gathering (*o* assemblage) of people.

adunànza, *s.f.* assembly, meeting: — *di famiglia,* family gathering; *indire un'*—, to call a meeting.

adunàre, *v.t.* to assemble, to gather, to collect; (*mil.*) to muster: — *ricchezze,* to amass riches ‖ **adunàrsi,** *v.r.* to assemble, to meet, to gather.

adunàta, *s.f.* **1.** (*mil.*) muster; parade: —!, fall in! (*o* form up!); *suonare l'*—, to sound the fall-in (call) **2.** (*riunione*) assembly.

aduncàre, aduncinàre, *v.t.* to hook.

adúnco, *ag.* hooked: *naso* —, hooked nose.

adunghiàre, *v.t.* to clutch, to claw, to seize, to grasp.

adúnque, *cong.* then, therefore, so.

adusàre, *v.t.* (*rar.*) to accustom ‖ **adusàrsi,** *v.r.* to accustom oneself, to get accustomed.

adusàto, *ag.* accustomed.

adústo, *ag.* **1.** sunburnt **2.** (*bruciacchiato*) scorched.

aèdo, *s.m.* (*cantore*) singer; (*poeta*) poet.

aeràre, *v.t.* **1.** to air, to ventilate **2.** (*chim.*) to aerate.

aeràto, *ag.* **1.** well-aired, airy, ventilated **2.** (*chim.*) aerated.

aeratóre, *s.m.* (*ind.*) aerator.

aerazióne, *s.f.* **1.** airing, ventilation **2.** (*chim.*) aeration.

àere, *s.m.* (*poet.*) air.

aereàre, *v.t.* **1.** to air, to ventilate **2.** (*chim.*) to aerate.

aereàto, *ag.* **1.** airy, ventilated **2.** (*chim.*) aerated.

aèreo, *ag.* **1.** aerial, airy, of the air, air (*attributivo*): *difesa aerea,* air defence; *ferrovia aerea,* air railway; *forze aeree,* air-force; *linea aerea,* air-line ‖ *per via aerea,* by air; *posta aerea,* air-mail (*o* air-post) **2.** (*etereo*) ethereal, aerial **3.** *fig.* vain: *speranze aeree,* vain hopes **4.** *prospettiva aerea,* (*pitt.*) aerial perspective ‖ *s.m.* **1.** *V.* **aeroplàno 2.** (*rad.*) (*antenna*) aerial, antenna.

aerificazióne, *s.f.* (*chim.*) aerification.

aerifórme, *ag.* (*fis.*) aeriform, gaseous ‖ *s.m.* aeriform substance: *meccanica degli aeriformi,* pneumatics.

aerocartògrafo, *s.m.* aerocartograph.

aerocistèrna, *s.m.* (*aer.*) air tanker.

aerodína, *s.m.* (*aer.*) aerodyne.

aerodinàmica, *s.f.* (*fis.*) aerodynamics.

aerodinàmico, *ag.* **1.** (*fis.*) aerodynamic: *tunnel* —, wind tunnel **2.** (*di linea affusolata*) stream-lined: *carrozzeria aerodinamica,* stream-lined coachwork.

aeròdromo, *s.m.* aerodrome, airport; (*amer.*) airdrome: — *galleggiante,* seadrome (*o* floating aerodrome).

aerofagía, *s.f.* (*med.*) aerophagia.

aerofàro, *s.m.* (*aer.*) (air-)beacon.

aerofobía, *s.f.* (*patol.*) aerophobia.

aeròfono, *s.m.* (*aer. mil.*) aerophone, sound locator.

aerofotocartografía, *s.f.* aerophotocartography.

aerofotografía, *s.f.* aerophotography.

aerofotogrammetría, *s.f.* aerophotogrammetry.

aerògrafo, *s.m.* **1.** (*tec.*) spray-gun **2.** (*foto.*) airgraph.

aerolínea, *s.f.* (*aer.*) airline.

aerolíto, *s.m.* (*geol.*) aerolite, aerolith.

aerología, *s.f.* (*meteorologia*) aerology.

aerometría, *s.f.* aerometry.

aeròmetro, *s.m.* (*fis.*) aerometer.

aeromèzzo, aeromòbile, *s.m.* aircraft.

aeromodellísmo, *s.m.* (*aer. spor.*) model aeronautics.

aeromodèllo, *s.m.* (*aer. spor.*) model aircraft.

aeronàuta, *s.m.* pilot; (*di aerostato*) aeronaut, pilot, balloonist.

aeronàutica, *s.f.* aeronautics ‖ *Aeronautica Militare,* Air Force; *Ministero dell'Aeronautica,* Air Ministry.

aeronàutico, *ag.* aeronautic(al): *ingegneria* —, aeronautical engineering.

aeronàve, *s.f.* airship.

aeropàrco, *s.m.* airplane park.

aeroplàno, *s.m.* aircraft, (aereo)plane; (*amer.*) airplane: — *a energia atomica,* atom-powered aeroplane; — *a grande autonomia,* long-range aircraft; — *a pattini,* aeroplane on skis; — *a razzo,* rocket plane; — *a reazione, a turbogetto,* jet plane (*o* turbo jet); — *anfibio,* amphibian (aeroplane); — *bimotore,* twin-engined aircraft; — *da bombardamento,* bomber (plane); — *da caccia,* fighter (*o* pursuit) plane; — *da combattimento,* battle plane; — *da corsa,* racing plane; — *da passeggeri,* passenger plane; — *da ricognizione,* scout (*o* reconnaissance) plane; — *da trasporto,* transport plane (*o* freighter); — *di linea,* airliner; — *di linea a reazione,* jet-airliner; — *di portaerei,* carrier-based plane; — *militare,* war-plane; — *monomotore, multimotore,* single -engined aircraft, multi-engined aircraft; — *per volo radente,* hedge hopping plane; — *per volo supersonico,* supersonic plane; — *quadrimotore,* four-engined aircraft; — *senza coda, senza elica,* tailless, propellerless plane; — *senza pilota,* pilotless plane.

aeropòrto, *s.m.* airport, aerodrome: — *galleggiante,* seadrome (*o* floating aerodrome).

aeroscàlo, *s.m.* aerodrome.

aerosilurànte, *s.m.* torpedo-bomber.

aerosòl, *s.m.* (*chim.*) aerosol.
aerostàtica, *s.f.* aerostatics.
aerostàtico, *ag.* aerostatic.
aeròstato, *s.m.* aerostat, balloon.
aerostière, *s.m.* aeronaut, balloonist.
aeroterapía, *s.f.* (*med.*) aerotherapeutics.
aerotèrmico, *ag.* aerothermic.
aerotrasportàto, *ag.* air-borne.
àfa, *s.f.* **1.** sultriness; stuffiness, closeness: *che —!*, what sultry weather! **2.** (*noia, fastidio*) tedium, boredom **3.** (*nausea*) sickness.
afasía, *s.f.* (*patol.*) aphasia.
afàto, *ag.* **1.** (*di frutto*) withered; stunted **2.** (*di persona*) sickly, puny.
afèlio, *s.m.* (*astr.*) aphelion (*pl.* aphelia).
afèresi, *s.f.* (*gram.*) apheresis, aphaeresis.
affàbile, *ag.* affable, amiable, obliging.
affabilità, *s.f.* affability, courtesy, kindness.
affabilménte, *av.* affably, kindly.
affaccendaménto, *s.m.* bustle, fuss.
affaccendàrsi, *v.r.* to bustle about, to busy oneself.
affaccendàto, *ag.* bustling, busy.
affaccettàre, *v.t.* to facet.
affacchinaménto, *s.m.* drudgery, fag.
affacchinàrsi, *v.r.* to drudge, to fag, to toil.
affacciàre, *v.t.* **1.** (*mostrare*) to show, to present **2.** to point out: *— dubbi*, to raise doubts; *— un'ipotesi*, to propound (o to put forward) a hypothesis ‖ **affacciàrsi**, *v.r.* **1.** to show oneself: *— alla finestra*, to put one's head (o to lean) out of the window; (*farsi vedere senza sporgersi*) to appear at the window; (*far capolino*) to peep out **2.** (*presentarsi alla mente*) to occur (to s.o.): *mi si affacciò un'idea*, an idea struck me **3.** (*di malattia*) to manifest itself **4.** to face (a place): *quella casa si affaccia sulla piazza*, that house faces the square.
affagottàre, *v.t.* to bundle up, to wrap (sthg.) up in a bundle ‖ **affagottàrsi**, *v.r.* to dress clumsily, to muffle oneself up.
affagottàto, *ag.* clumsily dressed.
affaldàre, *v.t.* to fold up.
affamàre, *v.t.* to starve (out); to reduce to starvation: *— una città, una guarnigione*, to starve out a town, a garrison ‖ *v.i.* to starve.
affamàto, *ag.* **1.** hungry, starving **2.** *fig.* eager.
affannaménto, *s.m.* anxiety, worry, agitation.
affannàre, *v.t.* to trouble, to vex, to worry ‖ **affannàrsi**, *v.r.* **1.** (*provare affanno*) to worry oneself, to be anxious **2.** (*affaccendarsi*) to busy oneself, to bustle about.
affannàto, *ag.* **1.** breathless, panting **2.** (*turbato*) worrying.
affànno, *s.m.* **1.** breathlessness **2.** (*travaglio*) labour, toil **3.** (*pena*) worry, trouble, pain; (*angoscia*) anxiety, anguish: *prendersi —*, to worry.
affannóne, *s.m.* (*scherz.*) busybody.
affannosaménte, *av.* **1.** breathlessly **2.** (*ansiosamente*) anxiously; painfully.
affannóso, *ag.* **1.** breathless, gasping: *lavoro —*, *fig.* feverish work; *respiro —*, difficult breathing **2.** anxious; painful.
affaràccio, *s.m.* bad affair.
affardellàre, *v.t.* **1.** to bundle up: *— lo zaino*, (*mil.*) to pack up one's kit **2.** (*mettere insieme alla rinfusa*) to heap up.
affàre, *s.m.* **1.** affair, matter, business: *— di cuore*, (love) affair; *questo è — tuo*, this is your (own) business; *questo è un altro —*, that is another question; *questo è un brutto —*, this is a bad business ‖ *affari di stato*, affairs of state; *affari esteri*, foreign affairs; *affari pubblici*, public affairs; *il Ministero degli Affari Esteri*, (*in Gran Bretagna*) the Foreign Office; (*negli Stati Uniti*) the State Department ‖ *un — d'oro*, a golden opportunity (o the chance of a lifetime) ‖ *donna di mal —*, woman of bad reputation; *persona di mal —*,

disreputable person ‖ *è un affare di un attimo*, it won't take a minute ‖ *non è un affare di stato!*, it is no great matter! **2.** (*comm.*) business; (*contratto, acquisto vantaggioso*) bargain: *hai fatto un —*, you got a real bargain; *qual è il suo genere di affari?*, what is his line of business?; *questo è un vero —*, this is a real bargain; *i suoi affari vanno a gonfie vele*, his business is thriving ‖ *essere in affari*, to be in business; *fare affari*, to do business; *fare affari con qlcu.*, to transact business with s.o.; *fare un cattivo —*, to make a bad bargain; *introdurre qlcu. negli affari*, to set s.o. up in business; *parlare d'affari*, to talk business; (*fam.*) to talk shop; *viaggiare per affari*, to travel on business ‖ *uomo d'affari*, business-man ‖ *è un — fatto!*, that's settled! (o done!) ‖ *gli affari sono affari*, business is business.
affarétto, affaríno, *s.m.* **1.** trifling business **2.** (*cosa da nulla*) trifle.
affarísmo, *s.m.* speculation.
affarísta, *s.m.* speculator.
affaróne, *s.m.* bargain, very good business.
affarúccio, affarúcolo, *s.m.* petty business.
affascinaménto, *s.m.* (*rar.*) enchantment, fascination, glamour.
affascinànte, *ag.* enchanting, charming, fascinating, glamorous.
affascinàre[1], *v.t.* **1.** to fascinate, to charm **2.** (*stregare*) to enchant, to bewitch.
affascinàre[2], *v.t.* (*riunire in fascine*) to fagot, to bundle up, to make (sthg.) into a fag(g)ot, a bundle.
affascinatóre, *s.m.* enchanter, charmer, seducer.
affascinatríce, *s.f.* enchantress, charmer.
affastellaménto, *s.m.* **1.** fag(g)oting, tying in bundles **2.** (*mucchio*) bundle, heap **3.** *fig.* confusion.
affastellàre, *v.t.* **1.** (*legare in fastelli*) to bundle up, to tie into bundles **2.** (*ammucchiare*) to hoard, to heap (up), to pile (up) **3.** *fig.* to make a mess of (sthg.), to bundle up confusedly.
affastèllio, *s.m.* **1.** bundling up **2.** *fig.* mess.
affaticaménto, *s.m.* **1.** fatiguing, tiring out **2.** (*fatica*) weariness, fatigue.
affaticàre, *v.t.* **1.** to fatigue, to tire, to (make) weary, to fag: *quel lavoro lo affaticò*, that work tired him; *— gli occhi*, to strain one's eyes **2.** (*impoverire*) to exhaust: *— un terreno*, to exhaust (o to impoverish) a piece of ground **3.** (*molestare*) to harass: *il capitano affaticò il nemico con frequenti attacchi*, the captain harassed the enemy by frequent attacks ‖ **affaticàrsi**, *v.r.* **1.** to tire, to get tired, to get strained, to be jaded: *— a furia di parlare*, to talk oneself tired; *— nel fare ql.co.*, to tire oneself doing sthg. **2.** (*adoperarsi*) to strive **3.** (*lavorare accanitamente*) to work hard, to fag: *quell'uomo si affaticò per tutta la vita*, that man worked hard all his life.
affàtto, *av.* **1.** entirely, quite, completely, absolutely: *è rovinato —*, he is completely ruined **2.** (*in frasi negative*) at all: *niente —*, not at all (o nothing at all); *con ciò non ne seppe — di più*, he was none the wiser for it.
affattucchiàre, *V.* **affatturàre**.
affatturaménto, *s.m.* **1.** enchantment, spell; sorcery, witchcraft **2.** (*adulteramento*) adulteration, sophistication.
affatturàre, *v.t.* **1.** to bewitch, to charm, to put under a spell **2.** (*adulterare*) to sophisticate, to adulterate.
affatturatóre, *s.m.* **1.** sorcerer; wizard **2.** (*manipolatore*) adulterator.
affatturatríce, *s.f.* sorceress; witch.
affazzonàre, *v.t.* to patch up; to arrange.
affé, *inter.* really!; indeed!; (in) faith!.
affermàbile, *ag.* affirmable.
affermàre, *v.t.* **1.** to affirm, to declare, to assert, to maintain, to aver, to state positively: *— ql.co. sotto giuramento*, to state sthg. on oath **2.** (*confermare*) to assert: *— un diritto*, to assert a right; *— la propria*

autorità, to make one's authority felt (*o* to assert oneself) ‖ **affermàrsi**, *v.r.* to assert one's authority, to assert oneself; (*farsi un nome*) to make a name for oneself.

affermatíva, *s.f.* affirmative.

affermativaménte, *av.* affirmatively.

affermatívo, *ag.* affirmative: *in caso* —, if it is possible.

affermazióne, *s.f.* **1.** affirmation, statement, assertion; assurance: — *dei propri diritti*, self-assertion; *fare un' — arrischiata*, to make a bold statement **2.** (*successo*) achievement; performance.

afferraménto, *s.m.* clutch, grasp; clutching, grasping.

afferràre, *v.t.* **1.** to seize, to get hold of (s.o., sthg.), to grasp, to clutch, to catch: *se lo vedete, afferratelo*, if you see him, get hold of him; — *qlcu. per il braccio*, to catch s.o. by the arm **2.** *fig.* to seize, to grasp: *non so se afferri l'idea*, I don't know if you understand; — *un'idea*, to grasp an idea; — *un'occasione*, to seize an opportunity ‖ **afferràrsi**, *v.r.* to grasp at (s.o., sthg.) to clutch at (s.o., sthg.) to seize (s.o., sthg.): *il nuotatore cercava di — al remo*, the swimmer tried to clutch at the oar; *si afferrò alla ringhiera*, she held tight to the handrail; — *ad una persona*, to clutch at a person.

affertilíre, *v.t.* (*rar.*) to fertilize.

affettàre[1], *v.t.* (*tagliare a fette*) to slice ‖ **affettàrsi**, *v.r.*: — *un dito*, to cut one's finger.

affettàre[2], *v.t.* (*ostentare, fingere*) to affect, to pretend, to feign, to simulate: — *un'aria disinvolta*, to simulate indifference.

affettataménte, *av.* affectedly, ostentatiously.

affettàto[1], *s.m.* sliced ham; sliced salame: *compra un po' d'*—, buy some sliced ham.

affettàto[2], *ag.* (*ostentato*) affected; snobbish; prim: *modi affettati*, prim manners.

affettatóre, *ag.* slicing.

affettatríce, *s.f.* slicing machine, slicer.

affettatúra, *s.f.* cutting into slices; slicing up.

affettazióne, *s.f.* (*ostentazione*) affectation, pretence; ostentation; show.

affettíbile, *ag.* **1.** easily affected; impressionable **2.** (*modificabile*) modifiable.

affettività, *s.f.* affectivity.

affettívo, *ag.* affective; emotional.

affètto[1], *ag.* affected (with sthg.); afflicted (with sthg.); suffering (from sthg.): *era — da mania di persecuzione*, he was suffering from persecution mania ‖ *beni affetti da ipoteca*, (*dir.*) mortgaged property.

affètto[2], *s.m.* affection; fondness; love: *con* —, (*nella chiusa di una lettera*) with love; *era il mio unico* —, he was my only love; *portare — a qlcu.*, to set one's affection (up)on s.o.

affettuosaménte, *av.* lovingly; tenderly; affectionately.

affettuosità, *s.f.* affection; affectionateness; tenderness; fondness.

affettuóso, *ag.* tender, loving, affectionate; fond: *saluti affettuosi da Giorgio*, love from George; *mostrarsi — verso qlcu.*, to behave affectionately towards s.o.

affezionàbile, *ag.* disposed to feel affection, disposed to become affectionate.

affezionaménto, *s.m.* fondness; attachment.

affezionàre, *v.t.* to inspire with affection, to endear ‖ **affezionàrsi**, *v.r.* to grow, to become fond of (s.o., sthg.) ‖ *v.r. reciproco* to grow, to become fond of each other (one another).

affezionàto, *ag.* affectionate, loving; fond: *è molto — al suo lavoro*, he is very fond of his work.

affezióne, *s.f.* **1.** affection, attachment; fondness ‖ *prezzo d'*—, fancy price **2.** (*patol.*) affection, disease: — *nervosa*, nervous disease.

affiancàre, *v.t.* **1.** (*mil.*) to flank **2.** (*mettere vicino*) to place side by side **3.** (*aiutare*) to help, to support ‖ **affiancàrsi**, *v.r.* **1.** (*mil.*) to march side by side **2.** (*avvi-*

cinarsi) to come up by the side of (s.o., sthg.) **3.** *fig.* (*collaborare con*) to co-operate (with s.o., sthg.), to support (s.o., sthg.).

affiancàto, *ag.* **1.** (*mil.*) flanked: — *a*, at the side of; *marciare affiancati*, to march side by side **2.** (*aiutato*) supported, helped, seconded.

affiataménto, *s.m.* **1.** concord, harmony **2.** (*comprensione*) understanding.

affiatàre, *v.t.* **1.** to bring together **2.** (*mus.*) to harmonize, to tune ‖ **affiatàrsi**, *v.r.* to come to an understanding, to agree; (*familiarizzarsi*) to befriend (s.o.), to become familiar; (*andar molto d'accordo*) to get on (well) together ‖ **affiatàrsi**, *v.r. reciproco* to become familiar with each other (one another).

affibbiàre, *v.t.* **1.** to buckle, to clasp **2.** *fig.* to burden (s.o.) with (sthg.), to saddle (s.o.) with (sthg.), to shift: *affibbiò la responsabilità di quel delitto al suo complice*, he shifted the responsibility of that crime upon his partner; *mi hanno affibbiato un biglietto falso*, they passed off on me a counterfeit banknote; — *a qlcu. i propri misfatti*, to saddle s.o. with one's misdeeds **3.** (*ingiurie, botte*) to give, to lodge: *gli affibbiai uno schiaffo*, I gave him a slap in the face; — *una pedata a qlcu.*, to kick s.o.

affibbiatúra, *s.f.* buckling, fastening; clasp.

affidaménto, *s.m.* **1.** trust, confidence: *non dà* —, he inspires no confidence **2.** (*assicurazione*) assurance: *mi diede — che*, he gave me assurance that... (*o* he assured me that...); *dare formale* —, to give positive assurance.

affidàre, *v.t.* **1.** to entrust, to confide: *ella sapeva che poteva affidargli la propria vita*, she knew she could entrust her life to him; — *una somma, un compito, un dovere a qlcu.*, to entrust s.o. with a sum, a task, a duty (*o* to entrust a sum, a task, a duty to s.o.) **2.** (*confidare*) to confide: — *un segreto*, to confide a secret **3.** (*consegnare*) to commit: — *alla memoria, a uno scritto*, to commit to memory, to writing; — *l'anima a Dio*, to commit one's soul to God **4.** (*dir.*) to grant: — *la custodia di un bambino alla madre*, to grant custody of a child to its mother ‖ **affidàrsi**, *v.r.* to rely (up)on (s.o., sthg.): to depend upon (s.o., sthg.), to trust to (s.o., sthg.): *affidati alle tue forze e non al caso*, trust to your own strength, not to chance; *mi affido a voi*, I rely (*o* I am depending) (up)on you; *mi affido al vostro buon senso*, I trust your common sense.

affidàvit, *s.m.* (*dir.*) affidavit.

affienàre, *v.t.* to feed on hay.

affieníre, *v.i.* to grow stunted.

affievoliménto, *s.m.* **1.** weakening, attenuation, diminution **2.** (*rad.*) fading.

affievolíre, *v.t.* to weaken, to enfeeble ‖ **affievolírsi**, *v.r.* to weaken, to grow weak: *la sua voce si affievoliva*, his voice was growing faint (*o* weak); *il suono si affievolì*, the sound grew faint.

affíggere, *v.t.* **1.** to post up, to stick up, to affix, to placard: — *un manifesto*, to put up a poster **2.** (*fissare*) to fix: — *lo sguardo su qlco., qlcu.*, to fix one's eyes on sthg., on s.o. ‖ **affíggersi**, *v.r.* to gaze at (s.o., sthg.), to stare at (s.o., sthg.).

affilaménto, *s.m.* sharpening; whetting.

affilàre[1], *v.t.* (*dare il filo a*) to sharpen, to whet, to give an edge to (sthg.), to put an edge on (sthg.); (*sul cuoio*) to strop; (*sulla mola*) to grind; (*sulla pietra*) to hone: *quel rasoio ha bisogno di essere affilato*, that razor wants sharpening; — *una lama*, to put an edge on a blade; — *un rasoio*, to strop a razor ‖ *ha una lingua affilata*, *fig.* she has a sharp tongue ‖ — *le armi*, *fig.* to get ready for a fight ‖ **affilàrsi**, *v.r.* to get thin, to get lean: *gli si è affilato il viso*, he got (*o* grew) thinner in the face (*o* his face grew thinner).

affilàre[2], *v.t.* (*agr.*) (*piantare in fila*) to plant in a row ‖ **affilàrsi**, *v.r.* (*porsi in fila*) to queue (up).

affilàta, *s.f.* (slight) sharpening; touch of the strop.

affilàto, *ag.* **1.** sharp (anche *fig.*): *coltello* —, sharp knife; *lingua affilata*, sharp tongue **2.** thin: *naso, viso* —, thin nose, face.

affilatóio, *s.m.* sharpener.

affilatúra, *s.f.* sharpening, whetting.

affilettàre, *v.t.* **1.** to knot the mesh of (nets) **2.** (*edil.*) to point (brickwork).

affiliàre, *v.t.* to affiliate, to associate || **affiliàrsi,** *v.r.* to become associated (with sthg.), to become a member (of sthg.), to join (sthg.).

affiliàto, *s.m.* (affiliated) member; associate.

affiliazióne, *s.f.* affiliation.

affinàggio, *s.m.* (*metal.*) refining.

affinaménto, *s.m.* **1.** refining, refinement: — *dell'intelligenza*, *fig.* sharpening of the intelligence **2.** (*carpenteria*) thinning **3.** (*metal.*) refining, fining: — *di minerali ferrosi*, smelting of iron ores.

affinàto, *ag.* refined (anche *metal.*): — *e temprato*, refined and hardened.

affinàre, *v.t.* **1.** (*perfezionare*) to improve, to refine: — *il proprio gusto*, to refine (*o* to improve) one's taste **2.** (*aguzzare*) to sharpen; (*assottigliare*) to (make) thin **3.** (*metal.*) to refine || **affinàrsi,** *v.r.* **1.** (*diventare migliore*) to improve, to refine, to get refined **2.** (*aguzzarsi*) to become sharp(er); (*assottigliarsi*) to become thin, thinner **3.** (*metal.*) to get refined.

affinatóio, *s.m.* (*metal.*) (fining-) forge.

affinatóre, *ag.* (*spec. metal.*) refining || *s.m.* (*spec. metal.*) refiner.

affinatúra, *V.* **affinaménto.**

affinché, *cong.* so that, in order that, that: *avvicinatevi,* — *vi senta meglio*, come nearer, so that I can hear you better.

affíne, *ag.* analogous, like, akin (*predicativo*); similar; (*di origine comune*) akin (*predicativo*); kindred: *lingue affini*, kindred languages; *prodotti affini*, similar goods; *queste due parole sono affini*, these two words are akin (*o* have a common stem) || *s.m.* relative, relation, kinsman (*pl.* kinsmen) || *s.f.* relative, relation, kinswoman (*pl.* kinswomen).

affíne di, *l. cong.* to, in order to, so as to: *egli studiò molto* — *di ottenere un bel voto*, he studied hard in order to obtain good marks.

affinità, *s.f.* **1.** affinity, relationship **2.** *fig.* affinity, resemblance, similarity of character: — *spirituale*, spiritual affinity **3.** (*attrazione*) affinity, liking, attraction **4.** (*chim.*) affinity.

affiocaménto, affiochiménto, *s.m.* hoarseness.

affiocàre, affiochíre, *v.i.* to become hoarse; (*diluce*) to grow dim, to fade || **affiocàrsi, affiochìrsi,** *v.r.* (*di voce, suono, ecc.*) to grow weak, to faint; (*di luce*) to grow dim.

affioraménto, *s.m.* **1.** cropping up **2.** (*miner. geol.*) outcrop.

affioràre, *v.i.* **1.** to appear on the surface, to surface **2.** (*miner. geol.*) to outcrop.

affissàre, *v.t.* **1.** (*poet.*) per **fissàre 2.** || **affissàrsi,** *v.r.* (*poet.*) per **fissàre 1.**

affissàre, *V.* **fissàre,** *v.t.* **1. 2.**

affissióne, *s.f.* bill-posting, bill-sticking, placarding: *è vietata l'*—, post no bills; *ordinare l'* — *di un discorso*, to order a speech to be placarded.

affísso, *s.m.* **1.** (*avviso*) bill; (*cartello*) placard; (*manifesto*) poster **2.** (*gram.*) affix.

affittàbile, *ag.* to (be) let (*predicativo*); (*da noleggio*) for hire (*predicativo*).

affittacàmere, *s.m.* landlord || *s.f.* landlady.

affittànza, *s.f.* **1.** (*pigione*) rent **2.** (*contratto*) lease.

affittàre, *v.t.* **1.** (*dare in affitto*) to let, to lease, to rent: *casa da* —, house to let; *ho affittato la mia casa ad un amico*, I have let my house to a friend **2.** (*prendere in affitto*) to rent **3.** (*prendere a noleggio*) to hire; (*dare a noleggio*) to hire (out).

affittíre, *v.t.i.*, **affittírsi,** *v.r.* to thicken.

affítto, *s.m.* rent; rental: — *alto*, heavy (*o* high) rent; *camere in* —, rented rooms; *contratto d'*—, (*comm.*)

lease contract; *essere in debito di tre mesi di* —, to owe three months' rent.

affittuàle, affittuàrio, *s.m.* tenant; (*a lunga scadenza*) lease-holder.

afflàto, *s.m.* **1.** breath **2.** (*ispirazione*) afflatus.

affliggènte, *ag.* depressing, distressing; troublesome.

affliggere, *v.t.* to afflict, to distress, to vex; (*tormentare*) to trouble: *la sua lettera mi ha profondamente afflitto*, his letter has deeply distressed me; *essere afflitto dai reumatismi*, to be afflicted with rheumatism || **affliggersi,** *v.r.* to grieve; (*tormentarsi*) to worry: *non hai motivo di affliggerti*, you have no cause to worry; *si afflissero tutti per la morte di tante persone*, they all grieved at (*o* for *o* over) the death of so many people.

afflittívo, *ag.* afflicting || *pena afflittiva*, corporal punishment.

afflítto, *ag.* sad, sorrowful, distressed || *gli afflitti*, the afflicted.

afflizióne, *s.f.* affliction, distress; (*flagello*) calamity: *le afflizioni della vecchiaia*, the afflictions of old age; *la guerra è una grande* —, war is a great calamity.

afflosciàre, afflosceíre, *v.i.*, **afflosciàrsi, affloscéirsi,** *v.r.* **1.** to become flabby **2.** *fig.* to weaken.

affluènte, *ag.* affluent || *s.m.* affluent, tributary (stream).

affluènza, *s.f.* **1.** (*di acque*) flow, flowing, flood; (*di persone*) crowd, multitude, concourse **2.** (*abbondanza*) affluence, abundance, plenty.

affluíre, *v.i.* (*di acque*) to flow; (*di persone*) to crowd, to flock, to throng; (*di cose*) to pour in.

afflussionàto, *ag.* (*patol.*) suffering from a cold: *essere* —, to have a cold.

afflússo, *s.m.* (*fisiol.*) afflux.

affocàre, *v.t.* **1.** (*arroventare*) to heat, to inflame (anche *fig.*) **2.** (*appiccare il fuoco a*) to ignite, to set on fire || **affocàrsi,** *v.r.* (*prendere fuoco*) to take fire, to catch fire; *fig.* to flare up.

affocàto, *ag.* **1.** fiery (anche *fig.*) **2.** (*color fuoco*) fiery, blazing-red.

affogaménto, *s.m.* drowning.

affogàre, *v.t.* to drown; *fig.* to smother, to stifle: *affogò i gattini nel lago*, he drowned the kittens in the lake; — *qlcu. di complimenti*, to smother s.o. with kindness || *v.i.* to be drowned: *cadde nell'acqua e affogò*, he fell into the water and was drowned || *affogo in questo cappello*, this hat is much too large for me || — *dal caldo*, to be stifled with heat || — *in un bicchiere d'acqua*, to make mountains out of molehills || — *nei debiti*, to be overburdened with debts (*o* to be up to one's eyes in debt) || *o bere o* —, to be between the devil and the deep blue sea || **affogàrsi,** *v.r.* to drown oneself; *fig.* to ruin oneself.

affogàto, *ag.* **1.** drowned; *fig.* oppressed (with sthg.); overwhelmed (with sthg.) || *stanza affogata*, stuffy room **2.** *uova affogate*, (*cuc.*) poached eggs || *s.m.* a drowned man.

affollaménto, *s.m.* (*l'affollarsi*) crowding; (*folla*) over-crowding, throng, concourse.

affollàre, *v.t.* **1.** to crowd, to throng **2.** *fig.* to overwhelm || **affollàrsi,** *v.r.* to throng, to crowd (together), to huddle together, to press (up): *la gente si affollava intorno a lui*, people pressed round him.

affollàto, *ag.* **1.** crowded **2.** (*sopraffatto*) overwhelmed (with sthg.).

affondaménto, *s.m.* sinking; foundering.

affondàre, *v.t.* **1.** (*sommergere*) to sink, to submerge **2.** (*immergere*) to plunge, to dip: — *la penna nel calamaio*, to dip one's pen into the inkpot || — *l'ancora*, (*mar.*) to cast anchor **3.** (*far più profondo*) to deepen: — *un fosso*, to deepen a ditch || *v.i.* to sink: *la nave affondò*, the ship sank || **affondàrsi,** *v.r.* to sink, to go to the bottom, to founder, to subside.

affondatóre, *s.m.* sinker.

affondatúra, *s.f.* deepening.

afforcàre, *v.i.,* **afforcàrsi,** *v.r.* (*mar.*) to moor (with both anchors).

affórco, *s.m.* (*mar.*) second anchor, spare anchor.

afforzaménto, *s.m.* **1.** reinforcement **2.** (*mil.*) fortification.

afforzàre, *v.t.* to strengthen; to fortify (anche *mil.*) ‖ **afforzàrsi,** *v.r.* **1.** to strengthen **2.** (*mil.*) (*per attacco*) to muster sufficient troops for attack; (*per difesa*) to muster sufficient troops for defence.

affoscàre, *v.t.* (*rar.*) to dim, to obscure.

affossaménto, *s.m.* **1.** ditching **2.** (*fosso*) ditch.

affossàre, *v.t.* to ditch ‖ **affossàrsi,** *v.r.* to become hollow: *gli si affossarono le guance*, his cheeks became hollow.

affossàto, *ag.* **1.** entrenched; surrounded by ditches **2.** (*incavato*) hollow: *occhi affossati*, hollow (*o* deepsunk) eyes.

affossatúra, *s.f.* **1.** ditching **2.** (*fossa*) ditch.

affralíre, *v.t.* (*poet.*) to enfeeble, to weaken ‖ **affralírsi,** *v.r.* (*rar.*) to become frail, to grow feeble.

affrancàbile, *ag.* releasable.

affrancaménto, *s.m.* release, deliverance, liberation.

affrancàre, *v.t.* **1.** to release, to set free, to liberate, to free: — *uno schiavo*, to free a slave **2.** (*lettera, pacco, ecc.*) to stamp **3.** (*dir.*) to remit **4.** (*dar vigore a*) to strengthen ‖ **affrancàrsi,** *v.r.* **1.** to free oneself **2.** (*rinfrancarsi*) to take courage, to become confident.

affrancàto, *ag.* **1.** (*liberato*) free **2.** (*munito di francobollo*) stamped.

affrancatúra, *s.f.* (*posta*) postage.

affrancazióne, *s.f.* **1.** (*posta*) stamping **2.** (*dir.*) enfranchisement; exemption.

affrànto, *ag.* **1.** (*dal dolore*) broken-hearted; dismayed **2.** (*stanchissimo*) worn out, tired out, exhausted.

affratellaménto, *s.m.* **1.** fraternization **2.** (*cameratismo*) fellowship; intimacy.

affratellàre, *v.t.* to get to fraternize ‖ **affratellàrsi,** *v.r.* to fraternize.

affrescàre, *v.t.* (*pitt.*) to fresco.

affrésco, *s.m.* (*pitt.*) fresco (*pl.* frescos, frescoes): *dipingere ad* —, to paint in fresco.

affrettaménto, *s.m.* hurrying, hastening.

affrettàre, *v.t.* **1.** to hasten, to hurry: — *il passo*, to quicken one's pace **2.** (*anticipare*) to anticipate: — *le nozze*, to anticipate the date of the marriage ‖ **affrettàrsi,** *v.r.* to hasten, to hurry, to hurry up, to make haste: *affrettatevi, per favore*, hurry up, please; *mi affretto a dirvi*, I hasten to tell you.

affrettataménte, *av.* hastily, in haste; (*in gran fretta*) in a hurry, hurriedly.

affrettàto, *ag.* **1.** hasty, hurried: *un pasto* —, a hurried meal **2.** (*trascurato*) careless, done in haste: *un lavoro* —, a careless work.

àffrico, *s.m.* south west wind.

affrittellàre, *v.t.* to fry (eggs).

affrontàbile, *ag.* that may be faced.

affrontàre, *v.t.* **1.** to face, to confront: *per voi affronterei la morte*, I would face death for you; *un uomo coraggioso affronta il pericolo senza paura*, a bold man confronts danger without fear; — *battaglia*, to engage battle **2.** *fig.* to deal with (s.o., sthg.): — *un argomento difficile*, to deal with (*o* to tackle) a difficult subject; — *un problema*, to tackle (*o* to discuss) a problem **3.** (*confrontare*) to compare ‖ **affrontàrsi,** *v.r.* (*offendersi*) to take offence (at sthg.), to take umbrage (at sthg.): *egli si affronta di nulla*, he takes offence at (*o* exception to) the least thing ‖ *v.r. reciproco* **1.** to meet hostilely; (*venire alle mani*) to come to blows; to begin to fight **2.** to face each other (one another); (*essere di fronte*) to be opposite to each other (one another).

affrónto, *s.m.* affront, insult, outrage, slight, snub: *fare un* — *a qlcu.*, to offer an affront to s.o. (*o* to slight s.o. *o* to insult s.o.); *infliggere un* — *a qlcu.*, to snub (*o* to slight) s.o.; *subire un* — *da parte di qlcu.*, to suffer an affront at the hands of s.o.

affumicaménto, *s.m.* **1.** smoking **2.** (*annerimento da fumo*) blackening with smoke **3.** (*di carne, di pesce, ecc.*) smoking, smoke-curing; (*di aringhe*) bloating, curing, kippering.

affumicàre, *v.t.* **1.** to fill with smoke **2.** (*annerire col fumo*) to stain with smoke, to blacken **3.** (*carne, pesce, ecc.*) to smoke, to smoke-cure; (*aringhe*) to bloat, to cure, to kipper.

affumicàto, *ag.* **1.** blackened by smoke **2.** (*di carne, pesce, ecc.*) cured, smoked; (*di aringhe*) kippered, cured, bloated **3.** *lenti affumicate*, sun-glasses.

affusàre, *v.t.* to taper.

affusàto, *ag.* tapered, tapering.

affusióne, *s.f.* (*chim.*) affusion, pouring on.

affusolàre, *v.t.* to taper.

affusolàto, *ag.* tapered, tapering: *colonna affusolata*, tapered column; *dita affusolate*, tapering fingers.

affústo, *s.m.* (*mil.*) gun-carriage: — *a scomparsa*, disappearing carriage; — *ferroviario*, railway mount.

àfidi, *s.m.pl.* (*entom.*) aphides; (*pop.*) plant-lice.

àfnio, *s.m.* (*chim.*) hafnium.

afonía, *s.f.* (*patol.*) aphonia.

àfono, *ag.* voiceless; (*patol.*) aphonic, aphonous.

aforísma, aforísmo, *s.m.* aphorism.

aforisticaménte, *av.* aphoristically.

aforístico, *ag.* aphoristic.

afóso, *ag.* sultry, sweltering, oppressive: *tempo* —, sultry weather.

afrézza, *s.f.* sour taste.

Àfrica, *no.pr.f.* (*geog.*) Africa: — *del Sud*, South Africa.

africàno, *ag. s.m.* African.

àfrico, *s.m.* south-west wind.

àfro, *ag.* sour, acid.

afrodisíaco, *ag. s.m.* aphrodisiac.

Afrodíte, *no.pr.f.* (*mit.*) Aphrodite.

afronítro, *s.m.* (*chim.*) saltpetre.

afróre, *s.m.* stink, reek, stench.

àfta, *s.f.* (*patol.*) aphtha: — *epizootica*, (*vet.*) epizootic aphtha.

Agamènnone, *no.pr.m.* (*lett.*) Agamemnon.

agamía, *s.f.* (*biol.*) agamo-genesis.

agàmico, *ag.* (*biol.*) agamic.

àgape, *s.f.* agape.

àgar àgar, *s.m.* (*chim.*) agar-agar.

agàrico, *s.m.* (*bot.*) agaric.

àgata[1], *s.f.* (*min.*) agate.

Àgata[2], *no.pr.f.* Agatha.

àgave, *s.f.* (*bot.*) agave.

agèmina, *s.f.* (*artig.*) damascening (steel).

ageminàre, *v.t.* (*artig.*) to damascene, to damaskeen.

agènda, *s.f.* note-book, memorandum book, agenda: — *tascabile*, pocket note-book.

agènte, *s.m.* **1.** agent, broker, representative: — *commissionario*, commission agent; — *compratore*, buying agent; — *delle tasse*, tax collector; — *di assicurazioni*, insurance agent; — *di cambio*, stock-broker; — *di campagna*, factor; — *di polizia*, policeman; — *di spedizioni*, shipping agent; — *di vendite*, selling agent; — *diplomatico*, diplomatic agent; — *esclusivo*, sole agent; — *immobiliare*, estate (*o* land) agent; (*amer.*) relator; — *investigativo*, detective; — *letterario*, literary agent; — *provocatore*, (*pol.*) "agent provocateur"; — *pubblicitario*, press agent; — *segreto*, secret agent **2.** (*fis. chim.*) agent: — *chimico*, chemical agent; — *fisico*, physical agent; — *terapeutico*, therapeutical agent **3.** (*gram.*) agent.

agenzía, *s.f.* agency: — *d'informazioni*, information bureau (*o* enquiry-office); — *di pubblicità*, advertising agency; — *di trasporti*, forwarding agency; — *di viaggi*, travel agency (*o* travel bureau).

Agesilào, *no.pr.m.* (*st.*) Agesilaus.

agevolaménto, *s.m.* facilitation.

agevolàre, *v.t.* to facilitate, to make easy, to help forward.

agevolazióne, s.f. facilitation, facility: *offrire agevolazioni di pagamento*, to offer facilities of payment.

agévole, ag. **1.** easy, handy, comfortable; (*di strada*) smooth **2.** (*di prezzo*) reasonable.

agevolézza, s.f. **1.** facilitation, facility: — *di pagamento*, easy terms **2.** (*comodità*) comfort.

agevolménte, av. easily; smoothly; comfortably.

aggallàre, v.i. (*mar.*) to rise to the surface, to come up to the surface.

aggallàto, s.m. marshy ground, floating ground.

agganciaménto, s.m. **1.** hooking, clasping **2.** (*allacciamento*) linking, linkage.

agganciàre, v.t. **1.** to hook, to clasp **2.** (*ferr.*) to couple (up): — *la locomotiva*, to couple up the engine.

aggangheràre, v.t. to hinge ‖ **aggangheràrsi,** v.r. **1.** (*allacciarsi*) to fasten; to clasp **2.** (*tenersi stretti, uniti*) to keep together.

aggarbàre, v.t. (*rar.*) to give a good shape to (sthg.) ‖ v.i. (*rar.*) to suit (s.o.).

aggattigliàrsi, v.r. to wrangle (about).

aggattonàre, v.i. to creep, to crawl.

aggavignàre, v.t. (*rar.*) to clutch, to lay hold of (sthg.).

aggeggiàre, v.t. (*rar.*) to arrange.

aggéggio, s.m. gadget, device, contrivance.

aggelàre, v.t., **aggelàrsi,** v.r. to freeze, to congeal.

aggentilíre, v.t., **aggentilírsi,** v.r. to refine.

aggettàre, v.i. (*arch.*) to jut (out), to project.

aggettivaménte, av. (*gram.*) adjectivally.

aggettivàre, v.t. **1.** (*gram.*) to turn (sthg.) into an adjective; to use (sthg.) as an adjective **2.** to put adjectives.

aggettivazióne, s.f. (*gram.*) adjectivation.

aggettívo, s.m. (*gram.*) adjective: — *attributivo*, attributive adjective.

aggètto, s.m. **1.** (*arch.*) projection, overhang **2.** (*aer.*) overhang **3.** (*mec.*) boss, lug.

aggheronàto, ag. gusseted (anche *arald.*).

agghiacciaménto, s.m. congelation, congealment; frosting.

agghiacciàre, v.t. to congeal; to freeze (anche *fig.*): *la notizia mi agghiacciò il cuore*, the news chilled me (o the news struck me dumb) ‖ v.i., **agghiacciàrsi,** v.r. to freeze, to congeal; to turn to ice; to become cold.

agghiàccio, s.m. (*mar.*) steering-gear; compensating -gear.

agghiaiàre, v.t. to gravel; to strew with gravel.

agghindaménto, s.m. bedizenment, dressing up; showy dressing.

agghindàre, v.t. to dress smartly, to trim, to bedizen, to deck out ‖ **agghindàrsi,** v.r. to dress (oneself) up.

aggiaccàre, v.t. (*rar.*) to rumple.

aggiàccio, V. **agghiàccio.**

aggiardinàre, v.t. to transform (sthg.) into a garden.

àggio, s.m. (*comm.*) agio, premium: — *sull'oro*, agio on gold; *fare* —, to be at a premium.

aggiogàbile, ag. fit for harness.

aggiogaménto, s.m. yoking.

aggiogàre, v.t. **1.** to yoke; to join in pairs **2.** (*soggiogare*) to subjugate.

aggiornaménto, s.m. **1.** (*rinvio*) adjournment, postponement **2.** (*di un libro*) revision; (*di un impianto*) modernization, renovation: — *tecnico*, technical modernization.

aggiornàre, v.t. **1.** (*rinviare*) to adjourn, to postpone **2.** (*mettere al corrente*) to bring up-to-date ‖ v.i. (*farsi giorno*) to dawn ‖ **aggiornàrsi,** v.r. to brush up one's knowledge, to get fresh information.

aggiornàto, ag. up-to-date: *essere* — *nel progresso tecnico*, to be abreast of technical progress.

aggiotàggio, s.m. (*comm.*) agiotage; stock-jobbing.

aggiotatóre, s.m. (*comm.*) stock-jobber.

aggiraménto, s.m. **1.** turning, encirclement **2.** (*mil.*) outflanking **3.** (*inganno*) deception, circumvention.

aggiràre, v.t. **1.** to go round (sthg.): — *un ostacolo*, to avoid an obstacle **2.** (*mil.*) to outflank **3.** (*raggirare, ingannare*) to deceive, to cheat, to dupe ‖ **aggiràrsi,** v.r. **1.** to wander about, to go about, to roam (about), to rove (a place): *si aggirava per le vie*, he roved the streets; — *nei boschi, per le strade*, to wander through the woods, about the streets; — *per le colline*, to roam over the hills ‖ *il prezzo si aggirava sulle cinque sterline, fig.* the price was around five pounds **2.** (*trattarsi di*) to handle, to deal with (sthg.): *il sermone si aggira su questi argomenti*, the sermon deals with (o runs upon) these subjects.

aggiràta, s.f. turning round, encirclement.

aggiratóre, s.m., **aggiratríce,** s.f. trickster, deceiver.

aggiudicàbile, ag. awardable.

aggiudicànte, s.m. **1.** awarder **2.** (*dir.*) adjudger.

aggiudicàre, v.t. **1.** to award **2.** (*dir.*) to adjudge.

aggiudicatàrio, s.m. **1.** (*dir.*) person to whom sthg. has been adjudged **2.** (*ad un'asta*) highest bidder.

aggiudicatívo, ag. (*dir.*) adjudicative.

aggiudicazióne, s.f. **1.** award **2.** (*dir.*) adjudgement, adjudication.

aggiúngere, v.t. to add: — *delle note marginali*, to append marginal notes ‖ **aggiúngersi,** v.r. (*di persona*) to join (s.o.); (*di cosa*) to be added.

aggiungiménto, s.m. adding, addition.

aggiúnta, s.f. addition; (*dir. comm.*) rider.

aggiuntàre, v.t. to join, to bind, to fasten; to piece.

aggiuntatúra, s.f. **1.** joining together; piecing up **2.** (*punto di aggiuntatura*) joint, juncture.

aggiuntívo, ag. **1.** additional **2.** (*gram.*) adjective.

aggiúnto, ag. added, joined ‖ s.m. **1.** (*gram.*) adjective, epithet **2.** (*assistente*) assistant.

aggiunzióne, s.f. adjunction, addition.

aggiustàbile, ag. adjustable, arrangeable (anche *fig.*); mendable, repairable.

aggiustàggio, s.m. (*mec.*) adjustment, fitting.

aggiustaménto, s.m. repairing, mending; *fig.* settlement, arrangement.

aggiustàre, v.t. **1.** to adjust, to adapt: — *la musica alle parole*, to adapt the music to the words **2.** (*sistemare*) to arrange: — *le cose*, to arrange (o to settle) matters ‖ — *qlcu.*, to pay s.o. his due ‖ — *qlcu. per il dì delle feste*, to give s.o. a sound thrashing **3.** (*mettere in ordine*) to put in order: — *i conti*, to settle accounts **4.** (*riparare*) to mend, to repair: — *le scarpe*, to mend shoes ‖ **aggiustàrsi,** v.r. (*venire ad un accordo*) to come to an agreement, to come to an understanding.

aggiustatézza, s.f. precision, accuracy, exactness.

aggiustatóre, s.m. **1.** adjuster **2.** (*mec.*) fitter: — *di modelli*, pattern setter.

aggiustatúra, s.f. repair, mending.

agglobàre, v.t. to conglobate, to conglobe.

agglomeraménto, s.m. agglomeration; (*di persone*) crowding.

agglomeràre, v.t. to agglomerate, to accumulate, to bring together ‖ **agglomeràrsi,** v.r. to agglomerate, to bind.

agglomeràto, ag. agglomerate; thick ‖ s.m. agglomerate (anche *geol.*).

agglomerazióne, s.f. agglomeration.

agglutinaménto, s.m. agglutination.

agglutinànte, ag. **1.** agglutinant, adhesive: *sostanze agglutinanti*, agglutinants (o agglutinant substances) **2.** (*glottologia*) agglutinative: *lingue agglutinanti*, agglutinative languages.

agglutinàre, v.t. to glue together; to agglutinate ‖ **agglutinàrsi,** v.r. to agglutinate.

agglutinatívo, ag. agglutinative.

agglutinazióne, s.f. agglutination.

agglutiníne, s.f.pl. (*chim.*) agglutinins.

aggobbíre, v.t. to crook ‖ v.i., **aggobbírsi,** v.r. to crook, to become crooked.

aggomitolàre, *v.t.* to wind up, to wind (sthg.) into a ball ‖ **aggomitolàrsi**, *v.r.* to roll oneself up, to curl up, to huddle up.

aggomitolatóre, *s.m.* winder.

aggomitolatúra, *s.f.* winding into a ball.

aggottaménto, *s.m.* (*mar.*) bailing out.

aggottàre, *v.t.* (*mar.*) to bail out, to pump out: — *una barca*, to bail (out) a boat (*o* to bail the water out of a boat).

aggottatóio, *s.m.* scoop.

aggottatúra, *s.f.* (*mar.*) bailing out.

aggradàre, *v.i.* (*vivo solo nella 3ª persona sing. del pres.indic.*) to like (sthg.): *come vi aggrada*, as you like (*o* as you please); *se ciò non vi aggrada...*, if you don't like it....

aggradévole, *ag.* agreeable, pleasant; charming.

aggradevolménte, *av.* agreeably, pleasantly; charmingly.

aggradiménto, *s.m.* enjoying, liking; preference, predilection.

aggradíre, *v.t.* to like, to enjoy, to appreciate; (*cibo*) to relish ‖ *v.i.* to like (sthg.): *questo non mi aggradisce*, I don't like it.

aggraffàre, *v.t.* to claw; to seize, to clutch, to grasp ‖ **aggraffàrsi**, *v.r.* to hold tight (to sthg.); to cling (to sthg.).

aggraffignàre, *v.t.* **1.** to claw; to clutch, to grasp **2.** (*fam.*) (*rubacchiare*) to steal, to pilfer.

aggranchiàre, aggranchíre, *v.t.* to benumb ‖ **aggranchiàrsi, aggranchírsi**, *v.r.* to become numb; to get stiff.

aggranchíto, *ag.* benumbed (with sthg.); stiff (with sthg.): — *dal freddo*, numbed with cold.

aggrancíre, *v.t.* to clutch, to seize, to catch.

aggrandiménto, *s.m.* enlargement.

aggrandíre, *v.t.* to enlarge (anche *fig.*); to increase; to extend; (*esagerare*) to exaggerate ‖ *v.i.* to become larger, to become bigger ‖ **aggrandírsi**, *v.r.* to grow bigger, to grow larger; to grow more powerful; to increase.

aggranfiàre, *v.t.* to claw; to seize; to clutch, to grasp.

aggrappàre, *v.t.* **1.** to seize, to grapple **2.** (*mar.*) to bite, to hold ‖ **aggrappàrsi**, *v.r.* (*attaccarsi*) to get hold of (sthg.); (*stare attaccato*) to cling ‖ — *a un fuscello*, *fig.* to catch at a straw.

aggràppo, *s.m.* act of catching, act of grappling.

aggrappolàrsi, *v.r.* to cluster.

aggrappàto, *ag.* clinging: *stare* — *a ql.co.*, to cling to sthg.

aggrappolàto, *ag.* clustered.

aggraticciàre, *v.t.* to twist ‖ **aggraticciàrsi**, *v.r.* to wind round; to intertwine; to cling.

aggravànte, *ag.* aggravating ‖ *s.f.* (*dir.*) aggravating circumstance.

aggravàre, *v.t.* **1.** to overburden, to aggravate (anche *fig.*): — *qlcu. oltre ogni limite*, to overburden s.o. beyond endurance **2.** (*peggiorare*) to make worse: *voi non fate che* — *le cose*, you are only making things worse **3.** (*punire*) to punish severely ‖ **aggravàrsi**, *v.r.* **1.** (*posarsi, premere*) to rest **2.** (*di malattia*) to grow worse, to become worse, to worsen **3.** (*mangiare troppo*) to overburden one's stomach, to overeat.

aggravàto, *ag.* **1.** (*oppresso*) overburdened (with sthg.) **2.** (*peggiorato*) worse **3.** (*incolpato*) charged (with sthg.).

aggràvio, *s.m.* **1.** (*peso, incomodo, danno*) burden; inconvenience; damage: — *di coscienza*, *fig.* guilty conscience **2.** (*onere*) burden; (*imposta*) tax: — *di spese*, considerable outlay (*o* heavier outlay) **3.** (*imputazione*) charge.

aggraziàre, *v.t.* to make graceful, to render pleasant ‖ **aggraziàrsi**, *v.r.* **1.** (*diventare aggraziato*) to grow graceful **2.** (*ingraziarsi*) to win s.o.'s favour.

aggraziataménte, *av.* gracefully.

aggraziàto, *ag.* graceful, gentle-mannered.

aggredíre, *v.t.* to assault, to assail, to attack.

aggregàbile, *ag.* addable.

aggregaménto, *s.m.* aggregation.

aggregàre, *v.t.* **1.** (*aggiungere al numero*) to add to a number **2.** (*ammettere a una compagnia*) to aggregate, to associate, to admit ‖ **aggregàrsi**, *v.r.* to aggregate; to unite with (sthg.), to join (sthg.), to be admitted to (sthg.), to become a member of (sthg.).

aggregatívo, *ag.* aggregative.

aggregàto, *ag.* **1.** (*unito*) united: *forze aggregate*, united (*o* joint) forces **2.** (*sostituto*) substitutive, supplementary, associated ‖ *s.m.* **1.** (*unione*) aggregate, aggregation: *la città è un* — *di famiglie*, a town is an aggregation of families **2.** (*impiegato aggiunto*) temporary clerk; (*di dottore*) locum(-tenens) **3.** (*geol.*) aggregate.

aggregazióne, *s.f.* aggregation; union.

aggreggiàre, *v.i.* to gather in a flock ‖ **aggreggiàrsi**, *v.r.* (*spreg.*) to troop together, to crowd (together).

aggressióne, *s.f.* assault, aggression, attack: — *a mano armata*, armed assault; *essere vittima di un'*—, to be assaulted.

aggressívo, *ag.* aggressive ‖ *s.* (*chim. mil.*) chemical agent used in warfare.

aggressóre, *s.m.* aggressor, attacker; assailant.

aggrevàre, *v.t.* to aggravate; to overload.

aggricciàre, *v.t.* to chill, to freeze ‖ **aggricciàrsi**, *v.r.* (*di freddo*) to shiver with cold, to shudder with cold; (*di paura*) to shiver with fear, to shudder with fear.

aggrinzàre, aggrinzíre, *v.t.* to wrinkle (up) ‖ **aggrinzàrsi, aggrinzírsi**, *v.r.* to wrinkle, to shrivel (up): *mi si aggrinza la pelle*, my skin is wrinkling.

aggrondàre, *V.* aggrottàre.

aggrondatúra, *s.* frowning.

aggroppaménto, *s.* **1.** knotting **2.** (*ammassamento*) gathering.

aggroppàre¹, *v.t.* **1.** to knot **2.** (*avvolgere*) to wind; to coil **3.** (*ammassare*) to amass.

aggroppàre², *v.t.* (*curvare*) to hump, to hunch.

aggroppatúra, *s.f.* knot.

aggrottàre, *v.t.*: — *le ciglia*, to frown, to knit one's brows.

aggrovigliaménto, *s.m.* entanglement.

aggrovigliàre, *v.t.* to wind; to entangle ‖ **aggrovigliàrsi**, *v.r.* to kink; to get entangled (anche *fig.*).

aggrovigliatúra, *s.f.* **1.** winding-up; entanglement **2.** (*scompiglio*) disorder.

aggrumàre, *v.i.*, **aggrumàrsi**, *v.r.* to coagulate, to clot; to curdle.

aggrumolàre, *v.i.*, **aggrumolàrsi**, *v.r.* to heart (up), to form a head, to loaf.

aggruppaménto, *s.m.* grouping, gathering.

aggruppàre, *v.t.* to group, to assemble; to arrange in groups ‖ **aggruppàrsi**, *v.r.* to group, to form into groups; (*riunirsi*) to assemble, to gather.

aggruzzolàre, *v.t.* to hoard, to scrape up (money).

agguagliàbile, *ag.* **1.** capable of being made equal **2.** (*paragonabile*) comparable.

agguagliaménto, *s.m.* **1.** equalization, levelling **2.** (*paragone*) comparison.

agguagliàre, *v.t.* **1.** to equalize; to place on the same level, to level; to balance **2.** (*paragonare*) to compare **3.** (*spianare*) to plane, to smooth, to make smooth ‖ **agguagliàrsi**, *v.r.* **1.** to become equal to (s.o., sthg.); to place oneself on the same footing as (s.o.) **2.** (*paragonarsi*) to compare oneself to (s.o.).

agguàglio, *s.m.* comparison.

agguantàre, *v.t.* **1.** to catch, to grasp, to seize **2.** (*mar.*) to hold on (sthg.) **3.** — *al vento*, (*mar.*) to get the weather-gauge.

agguàto, *s.m.* ambush, ambuscade; (*trappola*) snare: *cadere in* —, to fall into an ambush (*o* to be caught in a snare); *stare in* —, to lie in wait (*o* to be on the look-out); *tendere un* —, to make (*o* to lay) an ambush (*o* to waylay *o* to ambush); *fig.* to lay a snare (for s.o.).

agguattàre, *v.t.* to hide ‖ **agguattàrsi,** *v.r.* to hide (oneself).

agguerriménto, *s.m.* 1. battle-training 2. *fig.* inuring, inurement.

agguerríre, *v.t.* 1. to train (s.o.) for warfare, to inure (s.o.) to war 2. *fig.* to inure: — *alle privazioni,* to inure to hardship ‖ **agguerrírsi,** *v.r.* 1. to train oneself for warfare 2. *fig.* to harden, to become inured: — *alla fatica,* to become inured to fatigue.

agguerríto, *ag.* seasoned; battle-trained.

agguindolàre, *v.t.* 1. (*ind. tessile*) to wind on a reel 2. *fig.* to swindle.

aghétto, *s.m.* 1. (*puntale di stringa*) tag, aglet 2. (*stringa*) (tagged) lace; (*di scarpe*) (boot-) lace.

aghifórme, *ag.* needle-shaped.

agiataménte, *av.* in ease and comfort: *vivere —,* to live in plenty (*o* to be comfortably off).

agiatézza, *s.f.* comfort, ease: *ella vive nell'—,* she is well-off.

agiàto, *ag.* well-off, well-to-do; in easy circumstances.

agíbile, *ag.* feasible, practicable.

àgile, *ag.* agile, nimble, quick (anche *fig.*); (*di mano*) deft.

agilità, *s.f.* agility, nimbleness, quickness (anche *fig.*).

agilménte, *av.* nimbly, with agility; (*con destrezza*) deftly.

àgio, *s.m.* 1. comfort; (*comodo*) ease, leisure: *gli agi della vita,* the comforts of life; *lo farò a mio —,* I shall do it at my leisure; *sentirsi a proprio —,* to feel at one's ease ‖ *a bell' —,* at one's leisure (*o* without haste) 2. (*opportunità*) time; opportunity: *era tardi e non ebbi — di risentirlo,* it was late and I had no time to hear it again; *non ebbe — di dirmene il perchè,* he had no opportunity to tell me why 3. (*ferr.*) expansion joint.

agiografía, *s.f.* hagiography.

agiogràfico, *ag.* hagiographic(al).

agiògrafo, *s.m.* hagiographer.

agíre, *v.i.* 1. to act, to operate: *il veleno agisce lentamente,* poison operates slowly; — *nell'interesse di qlcu.,* to act in the interest(s) of (*o* on behalf of) s.o.; — *per conto proprio,* to act on one's own account; — *su qlcu.,* *fig.* to influence s.o. 2. (*comportarsi*) to behave: *questo non è modo di —,* this is not the way to behave 3. (*funzionare*) to work: *la molla non agisce,* the spring does not work 4. (*dir.*) to institute legal proceedings (against s.o.); to proceed (against s.o.).

agitàbile, *ag.* 1. shakable 2. (*di persona*) excitable.

agitaménto, *s.m.* 1. shaking 2. (*di persona*) excitement.

agitàre, *v.t.* 1. to agitate; (*scuotere*) to shake, to stir; (*scuotere violentemente*) to toss: — *la mano,* to wave one's hand ‖ — *prima dell'uso,* shake well before using 2. (*commuovere*) to stir, to excite 3. (*discutere*) to discuss, to debate: — *un problema,* to bring forward a question ‖ **agitàrsi,** *v.r.* 1. to be agitated: *il mare si agita,* the sea is rising; *ql.co. si agita nell'acqua,* sthg. is bobbing on the water; — *nel sonno,* to toss in one's sleep 2. (*darsi d'attorno*) to bustle (about) 3. (*emozionarsi, eccitarsi*) to get excited, to become upset 4. (*pol.*) to agitate; to clamour.

agitàto, *ag.* 1. agitated; troubled; excited; (*irrequieto*) restless ‖ *mare —,* rough sea 2. (*mus.*) agitato.

agitatóre, *s.m.* 1. agitator (anche *pol.*); (*pol.*) ringleader 2. (*mec.*) stirrer; mixer.

agitazióne, *s.f.* 1. agitation 2. (*tumulto*) tumult, rebellion, riot, public commotion: — *operaia,* labour unrest 3. (*eccitazione*) excitement.

agliàceo, *ag.* garlic-smelling; garlic-tasting.

agliàio, *s.m.* garlic field.

agliàro, *s.m.* seller of garlic.

agliàta, *s.f.* (*cuc.*) garlic sauce.

agliétto, *s.m.* 1. (*bot.*) fresh garlic 2. *fig.* trifle.

àglio, *s.m.* garlic: *testa d'—,* clove (*o* pig) of garlic ‖ *roder, mangiar l'—,* *fig.* to eat one's heart out (*o* to fume *o* to rage in silence).

agnatízio, *ag.* (*dir.*) agnatic.

agnàto, *s.m.* (*dir.*) agnate.

agnazióne, *s.f.* (*dir.*) agnation.

agnèlla, *s.f.* ewe-lamb.

agnellàio, *s.m.* lamb butcher.

agnellatúra, *s.f.* lambing.

agnellíno, *s.m.* lambkin ‖ — *di Persia,* Persian lamb.

agnèllo, *s.m.* 1. lamb: *costoletta di —,* lamb cutlet ‖ *l'Agnello di Dio,* (*Bibbia*) the Lamb of God ‖ *un lupo in veste di —,* a wolf in lamb's clothing 2. *fig.* meek person.

agnellòtti, *V.* agnolòtti.

agnellòtto, *s.m.* 1. young sheep (*invariato al pl.*) 2. *fig.* simpleton, booby, fat-head.

Agnèse, *no.pr.f.* Agnes.

agnína, *s.f.* sheepskin.

agnizióne, *s.f.* recognition.

agnocàsto, *s.m.* (*bot.*) chaste tree.

Àgnolo, *no.pr.m.* (*arc.*) Angel.

agnolòtti, *s.m.* (*cuc.*) «agnolotti» (sort of ravioli filled with forcemeat).

agnosticísmo, *s.m.* agnosticism.

agnòstico, *ag.* agnostic.

agnusdèi, *s.m.* Agnus Dei.

àgo, *s.m.* 1. needle: — *da calza,* knitting-needle; — *da rammendo,* darning-needle; *cruna dell'—,* eye of the needle; *lavoro ad —,* needlework; *infilar l'—,* to thread a needle 2. (*di bilancia*) tongue, index 3. (*mec.*) needle, tongue: — *dello scambio,* (*ferr.*) switch blade (*o* tongue); — *d'inclinazione magnetica,* dipping needle; — *magnetico,* magnetic needle 4. (*chim.*) (long thin) crystal.

agognànte, *ag.* eager, desirous.

agognàre, *v.t.* to desire eagerly, to long for (sthg.), to crave for (sthg.), to hanker after (sthg.).

agognàto, *ag.* coveted, longed for.

agonàle, *ag.* (*letter.*) agonistic.

agóne[1], *s.m.* 1. athletic contest; contest 2. (*arena*) sports ground; field; arena: *scendere nell'—,* to enter the lists 3. (*poet.*) combat.

agóne[2], *s.m.* (*ittiol.*) alose, allice.

agonía, *s.f.* 1. pangs of death (*pl.*); agony: *è in —,* he is in the throes of death (*o* he is in his last agony) 2. (*ansietà, tormento*) agony, anxiety, anguish.

agonísta, *s.m.* athlete.

agonística, *s.f.* 1. athletics; agonistics 2. (*arte di addestrare il corpo*) athletic training 3. (*attitudine combattiva nelle gare*) athletic spirit.

agonístico, *ag.* agonistic; athletic.

agonizzànte, *ag.* dying, agonizing.

agonizzàre, *v.i.* to be in one's death agony, to be in the throes of death.

àgora, *s.f.* agora.

agorafobía, *s.f.* (*patol.*) agoraphobia.

agoràio, *s.m.* 1. needle-case 2. (*chi fabbrica aghi*) needlemaker.

agostàno, *ag.* August (*attributivo*): *fieno —,* August hay.

agostiniàno, *ag.* Augustinian ‖ *s.m.* Augustinian, Austin friar.

agostíno[1], *ag.* 1. born in August 2. (*che matura in agosto*) ripening in August: *uva agostina,* August grapes.

Agostíno[2], *no.pr.m.* Augustin(e), Austin: *Sant'—,* Saint Augustine.

agósto, *s.m.* August: *in —,* in August.

agrafía, *s.f.* (*patol.*) agraphia.

agraménte, *av.* sourly; harshly.

agrammatísmo, *s.m.* (*patol.*) agrammatism.

agrària, *s.f.* agriculture.

agràrio, *ag.* agrarian ‖ *s.m.* 1. (*proprietario terriero*) land-owner 2. (*pol.*) agrarian.

agrèste, *ag.* agrestic, rural, rustic.

agrestíno, *ag.* sourish.

agrèsto, *s.m.* 1. unripe grapes 2. (*succo*) verjuice 3. (*profitto*) rake-off.

agrestóso, *ag.* sourish.

agrestúme, *s.m.* sourness.

agrétto, *ag.* sourish.

agrézza, *s.f.* sourness; acidity.

agrícola, *s.m.* (*letter.*) agriculturist, farmer.

agrícolo, *ag.* agricultural: *mostra agricola,* agricultural show.

agricoltóre, *s.m.* farmer, agriculturist.

agricoltúra, *s.f.* agriculture, farming.

agrifòglio, *s.m.* (*bot.*) holly.

agrígno, *ag.* sourish; *fig.* sharp.

agrimensóre, *s.m.* land-surveyor.

agrimensúra, *s.f.* land-surveying.

Agríppa, *no.pr.m.* (*st.*) Agrippa.

Agrippína, *no.pr.f.* (*st.*) Agrippina ‖ **agrippína,** *s.f.* sofa, couch with one arm only.

àgro[1]**,** *s.m.* field; territory; country surrounding a town ‖ *l'Agro Pontino,* the Pontine plain.

àgro[2]**,** *ag.* **1.** sour, acid **2.** *fig.* sharp, harsh, pungent ‖ *s.m.* **1.** (*agrezza*) sourness **2.** (*bevanda*) citrus juice.

agrodólce, *ag.* **1.** bitter-sweet; sourish **2.** *fig.* cattish.

agrología, *s.f.* agrology.

agronomía, *s.f.* agronomy.

agronòmico, *ag.* agronomical.

agrònomo, *s.m.* agronomist.

agróre, *s.m.* sourness.

agrúme, *s.m.* sourness; acidity.

agruméto, *s.m.* citrus plantation, citrus orchard.

agrúmi, *s.m.pl.* citrus fruit (*sing.*).

agúcchia, *s.f.* (knitting-) needle.

agucchiàre, *v.i.* **1.** (*cucire*) to stitch, to sew **2.** (*lavorare a maglia*) to knit.

agúglia, *s.f.* **1.** (*di chiesa*) spire **2.** (*obelisco*) obelisk **3.** (*ittiol.*) needle-fish, garfish **4.** (*di bussola*) compass needle **5.** (*mar.*) rapping needle.

agugliàta, *s.f.* needleful.

agugliòtto, *s.m.* (*arc. ornit.*) eaglet.

aguzzaménto, *s.m.* sharpening; whetting.

aguzzàre, *v.t.* to sharpen, to point, to whet (anche *fig.*); *fig.* to excite, to stimulate ‖ — *l'appetito a qlcu.,* to whet s.o.'s appetite ‖ — *l'ingegno, la mente di qlcu.,* to sharpen s.o.'s wits ‖ *il bisogno aguzza l'ingegno, prov.* necessity is the mother of invention.

aguzzatóre, *s.m.,* **aguzzatríce,** *s.f.* sharpener.

aguzzatúra, *s.f.* sharpening.

aguzzíno, *s.m.* **1.** (*st.*) galley-sergeant **2.** (*carceriere*) jailor, jailer, gaoler **3.** *fig.* tyrant, torturer.

agúzzo, *ag.* sharp; pointed.

ah, *inter.* ah!; ah ah!; aha!.

ahi, *inter.* ah!.

ahimè, *inter.* alas!; (*povero me*) dear me!.

àia, *s.f.* threshing-floor ‖ *menare il can per l'—, fig.* to beat about the bush.

Aiàce, *no.pr.m.* (*lett.*) Ajax.

Aída, *no.pr.f.* Aïda.

Amedèo, *no.pr.m.* Amadeus.

aigrette, *s.f.* **1.** (*ornit.*) osprey **2.** (*pennacchio*) egret.

àio, *s.m.* tutor.

aire, *s.m.* swing, impulse; turn: *dar l'— a ql.co., a qlcu.,* to set sthg. going, to start s.o. off; *prendere l'—,* to get going (o to start off).

airóne, *s.m.* (*ornit.*) heron.

aíta, *s.f.* (*poet.*) help!.

aitànte, *ag.* **1.** strong, vigorous, sturdy **2.** (*valoroso*) brave.

aitàre, (*poet.*) per **aiutàre.**

aiuòla, *s.f.* flower-bed.

aiutànte, *ag.* aiding, helping ‖ *s.m.* **1.** assistant; helper **2.** (*mil.*) adjutant: — *di campo,* aide-de-camp.

aiutàre, *v.t.* to help, to aid, to lend (s.o.) a hand; to co-operate with (s.o.); (*soccorrere*) to succour, to assist; to relieve; (*la memoria*) to stimulate: *mi sono fatto — da mia sorella,* I got my sister to help me; — *qlcu. a mettere il cappotto,* to help s.o. on with his overcoat; — *qlcu. a fare un lavoro,* to cooperate with s.o. in a work; — *qlcu. a uscire (da un veicolo),* to help s.o. out ‖ **aiutàrsi,** *v.r.* to help oneself, to do on'es best ‖ *aiutati che Dio t'aiuta, prov.* God helps those who help themselves ‖ **aiutàrsi,** *v.r. reciproco* to help each other (one another).

aiutatóre, *s.m.,* **aiutatríce,** *s.f.* helper; succourer.

aiúto, *s.m.* **1.** help, aid, relief: —*!,* help!; — *ai poveri,* poor relief; *chiamare, chiedere —,* to call for help; *gridare —,* to call out for help **2.** (*chi aiuta*) helper; assistant: — *giardiniere,* under gardener **3.** *pl.* (*mil.*) reinforcements.

aizzaménto, *s.m.* instigation, provocation.

aizzàre, *v.t.* to instigate, to provoke; to enrage; (*incitare*) to incite: — *un cane contro qlcu.,* to set a dog on s.o.

aizzatóre, *s.m.* instigator; inciter.

à jour, *s.m.* (*ricamo*) hem-stitch: *fare l'— a un fazzoletto,* to hem-stitch a handkerchief.

àla, *s.f.* **1.** wing; (*di pinguino*) flipper: *l'uccello batteva le ali,* the bird beat (o fluttered) its wings ‖ *la paura gli metteva le ali ai piedi, fig.* fear lent him wings; *abbassare le ali, fig.* to yield (o to surrender); *essere sotto le ali di qlcu., fig.* to be under s.o.'s wing; *spiegare le ali,* to spread one's wings; *tarpare le ali,* to pinion; to clip the wings (anche *fig.*) **2.** (*arch. mec. aer.*) wing; (*di elica*) blade; (*di chiesa*) aisle: *l'— destra del palazzo,* the right wing of the palace **3.** (*mil.*) wing, flank; (*spor.*) wing: — *destra, sinistra,* (*calcio*) right wing, left wing; *mezz'— destra, sinistra,* (*calcio*) inside right, inside left; *la cavalleria era ammassata all'— sinistra,* (*mil.*) the cavalry were massed on the left wing **4.** (*lato*) side ‖ *far —,* to form a double hedge.

alabàmio, *s.m.* (*chim.*) alabamine.

alabandína, *s.f.* (*min.*) alabandine.

alabàrda, *s.f.* halberd.

alabardière, *s.m.* halberdier.

alabastràio, *s.m.* worker in alabaster.

alabastríno, *ag.* alabaster (*attributivo*); alabastrine (anche *fig.*).

alabastríte, *s.f.* imitation alabaster.

alabàstro, *s.m.* alabaster.

àlacre, *ag.* active; brisk; (*laborioso*) industrious; (*sollecito*) ready.

alaceménte, *av.* actively; briskly; (*con sollecitudine*) readily.

alacrità, *s.f.* alacrity; briskness; (*laboriosità*) laboriousness; (*sollecitudine*) promptitude.

alàggio, *s.m.* (*mar.*) haulage; towage; (*aer.*) beaching.

alalà, *s.m.* (*grido di guerra greco*) alalà.

alalía, *s.f.* (*patol.*) alalia.

alamànno, *ag.s.m.* German.

alamàro, *s.m.* frog.

alambícco, *s.m.* alembic; still.

Alàno[1]**,** *no.pr.m.* Alan.

alàno[2]**,** *s.m.* (*cane*) Great Dane.

alàre[1]**,** *s.m.* andiron, firedog.

alàre[2]**,** *v.t.* **1.** (*una rete*) to haul in **2.** (*una barca*) to tow.

alàre[3]**,** *ag.* alar, alary: *apertura —,* (*aer.*) wing span.

Alaríco, *no.pr.m.* (*st.*) Alaric.

alàrio, *ag.*: *truppe alarie,* auxiliary troops ‖ *s.m.* **1.** Roman soldier fighting on the wings **2.** (*ausiliario*) auxiliary soldier.

alàta, *s.f.* wing-stroke.

alàto, *ag.* **1.** winged ‖ *gli alati,* birds **2.** (*elevato*) lofty: *poesia alata,* lofty poetry.

Alàsca, *no.pr.f.* (*geog.*) Alaska.

àlba, *s.f.* **1.** dawn, daybreak: *all'—,* at dawn (o at daybreak) **2.** *fig.* beginning, dawn, dawning **3.** (*mus.*) aubade.

albagía, *s.f.* haughtiness.

albagióso, *ag.* haughty.

albàna, *s.m.* "Albana" (kind of Italian wine).

albanèlla, *s.f.* (*ornit.*) hen-harrier.

albanése, *ag.s.m.* Albanian ‖ *far l'—,* (*fam.*) to pretend not to understand.

Albanía, *no.pr.f.* (*geog.*) Albania.

albarèllo, àlbaro, *s.m.* (*bot.*) abele.

albaspína, *s.f.* (*bot.*) hawthorn.

àlbatro[1], *s.m.* (*bot.*) arbutus.
àlbatro[2], *s.m.* (*ornit.*) albatross.
albèdine, *s.f.* (*colore biancastro*) whitish colour.
albeggiaménto, *s.m.* dawning.
albeggiàre, *v.i.* 1. *imp.* to dawn (anche *fig.*) 2. (*biancheggiare*) to be white; to verge on white.
alberàre, *v.t.* 1. to plant (sthg.) with trees 2. (*mar.*) to mast (a ship); to step a mast 3. (*inalberare*) to hoist.
alberàto, *ag.* planted with trees.
alberatúra, *s.f.* 1. tree-plantation 2. (*mar.*) masts (*pl.*), masting; (*legname per alberi di nave*) timber for masts.
alberèlla, *s.f.* (*bot.*) asp, aspen tree.
alberèllo[1], *s.m.* 1. sapling 2. (*pioppo bianco*) abete.
alberèllo[2], *s.m.* (*barattolo*) pot; (*per il sale*) salt-box.
alberése, *s.m.* (*min.*) limestone.
alberéta, *s.f.*, **alberéto**, *s.m.* 1. plantation 2. (*bosco di pioppi*) poplar plantation.
alberétto, *s.m.* (*mar.*) mast.
albergàre, *v.t.* 1. to lodge; (*dare asilo a*) to shelter 2. *fig.* to cherish, to harbour || *v.i.* to lodge, to dwell.
albergatóre, *s.m.*, **albergatríce**, *s.f.* hotel-keeper.
alberghería, *s.f.* 1. hotel; inn 2. common lodging-house.
alberghièro, *ag.* hotel (*attributivo*): *industria alberghiera*, hotel trade.
albèrgo, *s.m.* hotel: *scese all'—*, he put up at the hotel.
Albéríco, *no.pr.m.* Aubrey; (*st.*) Alberich.
àlbero, *s.m.* 1. tree: *— da frutto*, fruit-tree; *— della gomma*, rubber plant; *— di legno dolce, duro*, soft, hard timber tree || *— della libertà*, tree of liberty || *— di Natale*, Christmas tree || *— genealogico*, genealogical tree || *al primo colpo non cade l'—*, *prov.* Rome was not built in one day || *si conosce l'— dal frutto*, *prov.* by their fruits ye shall know them 2. (*mar.*) mast: *— da carico*, derrick; *— di bompresso*, bowsprit; *— di contromezzana*, mizzen-topmast; *— di gabbia*, main-topmast; *— di mezzana*, mizzenmast; *— di parrocchetto*, fore-topmast; *— di prua*, fore mast; *— di trinchetto*, fore (mast); *— maestro*, mainmast; *— maggiore*, lower mast; *attrezzatura dell'—*, mast rigging; *picco d'—*, peak; *testa dell'—*, mast-head 3. (*mec.*) shaft: *— a camme*, camshaft; *— a gomiti*, crank shaft; *— base*, standard shaft; *— cavo*, quill; *— del cambio di velocità*, gear shaft; *— dell'elica*, tail shaft; *— della turbina*, turbine shaft; *— di propulsione*, propeller shaft; *— di trasmissione*, propeller (*o* transmission) shaft; *— motore*, driving shaft.
Albèrta, *no.pr.f.* Alberta.
Albèrto, *no.pr.m.* Albert.
albicòca, *s.f.* apricot.
albicòcco, *s.m.* apricot(-tree).
albigése, *ag.* (*st. relig.*) Albigensian || *s.m.pl.* (*st. relig.*) Albigenses.
albína, *s.f.* albiness.
albinàggio, *s.m.* (*dir.*) escheat.
albinísmo, *s.m.* albinism.
albíno, *ag.* whitish || *s.m.* albino (*pl.* albinos).
albíte, *s.f.* (*min.*) albite.
àlbo, *s.m.* 1. roll, list: *— degli avvocati*, Law List; *— d'onore*, roll of honour; *essere radiato dall'—*, to be struck off the roll 2. (*per fotografie, ecc.*) album 3. (*tavola per l'affissione di avvisi*) notice-board.
Alboíno, *no.pr.m.* (*st.*) Alboin.
albóre, *s.m.* 1. dawn, dawning (anche *fig.*): *gli albori della civiltà*, the dawning of civilization; *ai primi albori*, at dawn 2. (*luce biancheggiante*) whitish light 3. (*poet.*) (*biancore*) whiteness.
albúgine, *s.f.* 1. (*patol.*) albugo 2. (*bot.*) albugo.
albugíneo, *ag.* albuginean, albugineous.
àlbum, *s.m.* album.
albúme, *s.m.* 1. albumen 2. (*bot.*) albumen.
albumína, *s.f.* (*chim. biol.*) albumin.
albuminàre, *v.t.* (*ind.*) to albumenize.
albuminàto, *s.m.* (*chim.*) albuminate.

albuminòide, *s.m.* (*chim.*) albuminoid.
albuminúria, *s.f.* (*patol.*) albuminuria.
albúrno, *s.m.* (*bot.*) alburnum, sap-wood.
àlca, *s.f.* (*ornit.*) auk.
àlcade, *s.m.* alcalde.
alcàico, *ag.* (*poes.*) Alcaic.
alcalescènte, *ag.* (*chim.*) alkalescent.
alcalescènza, *s.f.* (*chim.*) alkalescence, alkalescency.
àlcali, *s.m.* (*chim.*) alkali (*pl.* alkalis, alkalies).
alcàlico, *ag.* (*chim.*) alkaline.
alcalígeno, *ag.* (*chim.*) alkaligenous.
alcalimetría, *s.f.* (*chim.*) alkalimetry.
alcalímetro, *s.m.* (*chim.*) alkalimeter.
alcalinità, *s.f.* (*chim.*) alkalinity.
alcalíno, *ag.* (*chim.*) alkaline: *—terroso*, alkaline-earth.
alcalizzàre, *v.t.* (*chim.*) to alkalify, to alkalize.
alcalòide, *s.m.* (*chim.*) alkaloid.
alcànna, *s.f.* (*bot.*) alkanet, henna.
àlce, *s.m.* (*zool.*) elk.
Alcèo, *no.pr.m.* (*st. lett.*) Alcaeus.
alchechèngi, *s.m.* (*bot.*) winter-cherry.
alchèrmes, *s.m.* alkermes.
alchímia, *s.f.* alchemy.
alchimísta, *s.m.* alchemist.
alchimístico, *ag.* alchemistic(al), alchemic(al).
alchimizzàre, *v.t.* 1. to alchemize 2. *fig.* to falsify || *v.i.* to practise alchemy.
Alcibíade, *no.pr.m.* (*st.*) Alcibiades.
Alcíde, *no.pr.m.* (*mit.*) Alcides.
alcióne[1], *s.m.* (*ornit.*) kingfisher.
Alcióne[2], *no.pr.f.* (*mit.*) Alcyone.
alciònio, *ag.* (*astr.*) of the winter solstice.
àlcole, **àlcool**, *s.m.* alcohol: *— denaturato*, denatured alcohol; *— etilico*, ethyl alcohol; *— metilico*, methyl alcohol; *— puro*, absolute alcohol || *darsi all'—*, to take to drink.
alcoòlico, *ag.* alcoholic.
alcoolísmo, *s.m.* alcoholism.
alcoolizzàre, *v.t.* to alcoholize.
alcoolizzàto, *ag.s.m.* alcoholic.
alcoolòmetro, *s.m.* (*chim.*) alcoholometer.
Alcoràno, *s.m.* Alkoran.
alcòva, *s.f.* alcove || *i segreti dell'—*, the privacies of the bed-chamber.
Alcuíno, *no.pr.m.* (*st.*) Alcuin.
alcún, **alcúno**, *ag.indef.* 1. *pl.* (*in proposizioni affermative o interrogative da cui si attenda risposta affermativa*) some; a few: *alcuni anni fa*, some years ago; *disse alcune parole di saluto*, he said a few words of greeting; *gradiresti alcuni biscotti?*, will you have some biscuits? 2. (*in proposizioni negative*) any; (*usandosi nell'inglese la forma affermativa*) no: *senza — dubbio*, without any doubt; *non aveva — nemico*, he had no enemies; *non aveva alcuna notizia da una settimana*, he had had no (*o* he hadn't had any) news for a week || *pron. indef.* 1. (*in proposizioni interrogative, dubitative, condizionali*) anybody, anyone (*riferiti a persona*); any (*riferito a cose e con partitivo*): *non hai incontrato —?*, haven't you met anybody?; *se — ti dicesse...*, if anyone were to tell you... 2. (*in proposizioni negative di forma non interrogativa*) anybody, anyone (*riferito a persone*); any (*riferito a cose*); (*accompagnato da un partitivo*) any (*riferito a persone e a cose*); (*usandosi nell'inglese la forma affermativa*) nobody, no one (*riferiti a persone*); none; (*accompagnato da un partitivo*) none: « *Hai dei libri inglesi?* », « *Non ne ho —* », "Have you got any English book?", "I have none (*o* I haven't any)"; *non vidi —*, I saw no one (*o* I didn't see anyone); *non vidi — di voi*, I didn't see any of you (*o* I saw none of you) 3. (*in proposizioni affermative*) somebody, someone; *pl.* some people (*solo riferito a persone*); some; a few; (*accompagnato da un partitivo*) some, a few: *alcuni di loro si lamentarono di aver sete*, some (*o* a few) of them complained of being thirsty; *alcuni lo approvano, altri*

no, some (people) approve of it, some don't; — *mi disse che...*, someone told me that...; *ne vendette alcuni*, he sold a few.

alcunché, *pron. indef.* **1.** (*in proposizioni interrogative, dubitative, condizionali*) **anything 2.** (*in proposizioni negative di forma non interrogativa*) **anything**; (*usandosi nell'inglese la forma affermativa*) **nothing 3.** (*in proposizioni affermative*) **something.**

aldèide, *s.f.* (*chim.*) aldehyde: — *formica*, formic aldehyde (*o* formaldehyde *o* methanal).

aldíno, *ag.* (*tip.*) Aldine.

Àldo, *no.pr.m.* Aldous.

àlea, *s.f.* chance, risk, hazard ‖ *correre l'—*, to run the risk.

aleatòrio, *ag.* aleatory; depending on contingencies; problematical, hazardous, risky.

aleggiàre, *v.i.* to flutter, to flap; *fig.* to hover (about).

alemànno, *ag.s.m.* German.

alenàre, *v.i.* (*ansare*) to pant.

aleríone, *s.m.* (*arald.*) a(l)lerion.

aleróne, *s.m.* (*aer.*) aileron.

alesàggio, *s.m.* **1.** (*mec.*) bore **2.** (*alesatura*) (*a mano*) reaming; (*su alesatrice*) boring.

alesàre, *v.t.* (*mec.*) (*a mano*) to ream; (*su alesatrice*) to bore; (*al tornio*) to lathe-bore.

alesatóre, *s.m.* **1.** (*strumento*) reamer, rhymer: — *cilindrico, conico*, straight, taper reamer; — *fisso*, solid reamer; — *sferico*, ball reamer **2.** (*operaio*) borer.

alesatríce, *s.f.* (*mec.*) boring-machine.

alesatúra, *s.f.* (*mec.*) (*a mano*) reaming; (*su alesatrice*) boring: — *sferica*, spherical boring; — *su tornio*, lathe-boring.

Alessàndra, *no.pr.f.* Alexandra ‖ *dim.* Sandra.

Alessàndria, *no.pr.f.* (*geog.*) Alexandria (in Egypt).

alessandríno, *ag.* Alexandrian, Alexandrine: *la scuola alessandrina*, the Alexandrian School; *verso —*, Alexandrine (line) ‖ *s.m.* (*poes.*) Alexandrine.

Alessàndro, *no.pr.m.* Alexander ‖ *dim.* Alec(k), Alex, Sandy.

alessía, *s.f.* (*patol.*) alexia.

alessifàrmaco, *s.m.* (*farm.*) alexipharmic.

alessitèrio, *s.m.* (*farm.*) alexiteric.

Alèssio, *no.pr.m.* Alexis; (*st.*) Alexius.

alétta, *s.f.* **1.** (*pinna*) fin **2.** (*mec.*) tongue; (*di raffreddamento*) fin; (*di fuso*) flyer **3.** (*aer.*) tab: — *comandabile*, controlled tab **4.** (*mar.*) rolling chock, bilge keel, bilge piece.

alettàre, *v.t.* (*mec.*) to fin.

alettatúra, *s.f.* (*mec.*) finning.

Alètto, *no.pr.f.* (*mit.*) Alecto.

alettóne, *s.m.* (*aer.*) aileron, balancing flap: — *compensato*, balanced aileron.

aleuróne, *s.m.* (*chim.*) aleurone.

àlfa, *s.f.* **1.** (*prima lettera dell'alfabeto greco*) alpha ‖ *particella —*, (*fis.*) alpha particle; *raggi —*, (*fis.*) alpha rays **2.** *fig.* beginning: *dall'— all'omega*, from A to Z (*o* from beginning to end) **3.** (*bot.*) esparto.

alfabèta, *s.c.* literate.

alfabeticaménte, *av.* alphabetically.

alfabètico, *ag.* alphabetic(al): *per ordine —*, alphabetically (*o* in alphabetical order).

alfabèto, *s.m.* **1.** alphabet: — *Morse*, Morse alphabet (*o* code) **2.** (*primi rudimenti*) alphabet; primer: *questo libro contiene l'— della medicina*, this book contains the A B C of medicine; *stiamo studiando l'— della matematica*, we are just studying the first steps of mathematics.

alfàna, *s.f.* (*arc.*) powerful and spirited horse.

alfière, *s.m.* **1.** (*mil.*) ensign; standard bearer **2.** (*scacchi*) bishop.

alfíne, *av.* (*finalmente*) at last.

Alfònso, *no.pr.m.* Alphonso.

Alfrèdo, *no.pr.m.* Alfred ‖ *dim.* Alf, Alfie.

àlga, *s.f.* (*bot.*) seaweed, alga (*pl.* algae).

àlgebra, *s.f.* algebra.

algebricaménte, *av.* algebraically.

algèbrico, *ag.* algebraic(al).

algebrísta, *s.m.* algebr(a)ist.

algènte, *ag.* (*poet.*) algid.

Algería, *no.pr.f.* (*geog.*) Algeria.

Algèri, *no.pr.f.* (*geog.*) Algiers.

algeríno, *ag.s.m.* Algerian, Algerine.

algesimetría, *s.f.* (*med.*) algesimetry.

algesímetro, *s.m.* (*med.*) algesimeter.

algidità, *s.f.* (*patol.*) algidity.

àlgido, *ag.* (*poet. patol.*) algid.

algofilía, *s.f.* (*patol.*) algophily.

algolagnía, *s.f.* (*patol.*) algolagnia.

algometría, *s.f.* (*med.*) algesimetry.

algòmetro, *s.m.* (*med.*) algesimeter.

algonchiàno, *ag.* (*geol.*) Algonkian.

algóre, *s.m.* **1.** (*poet.*) intense cold **2.** (*patol.*) algor.

aliànte, *s.m.* (*aer.*) glider, gliding machine: — *rimorchiato*, towed glider; — *veleggiatore*, sailplane; *lancio di un —*, casting off of a glider.

aliàre, *v.i* (*aleggiare*) to flutter; (*volare*) to fly.

àlias, *av.* (*lat.*) alias, otherwise.

alibattènte, *s.m.* (*aer.*) ornithopter.

àlibi, *s.m.* (*dir.*) alibi.

alicànte, *s.m.* (*vino*) alicant(e).

alice[1], *s.f.* (*ittiol.*) anchovy.

Alice[2], *no.pr.f.* Alice ‖ « — *nel paese delle meraviglie* », "Alice in Wonderland" ‖ *dim.* Allie, Ellie, Elsie.

alicòrno, *s.m.* (*poet.*) unicorn.

alidàda, *s.f.* alidad(e).

alidaménte, *av.* dryly, aridly.

alidézza, *s.f.* dryness, aridity, drought.

alidíre, *v.t.* to dry, to parch ‖ *v.i.* to dry up, to parch ‖ **alidírsi**, *v.r.* to dry up; (*di pianta*) to wither (up, away).

àlido, *ag.* dry, arid; (*di pianta*) withered ‖ *s.m.* dryness, aridity; (*stagione alida*) drought.

alidóre, *s.m.* dryness, aridity; (*stagione alida*) drought.

alienàbile, *ag.* (*dir.*) alienable, transferable.

alienabilità, *s.f.* (*dir.*) alienability.

alienaménto, *V.* **alienazióne.**

alienànte, *s.m.* (*dir.*) alienator.

alienàre, *v.t.* **1.** (*dir.*) to alienate, to part with (sthg.), to transfer **2.** *fig.* to alienate, to estrange: *questa azione gli alienò l'animo di tutti*, this action alienated all hearts from him; — *l'affetto, la stima di qlcu.*, to estrange s.o. ‖ **alienàrsi**, *v.r.* to estrange oneself, to become estranged (from s.o., sthg.), to become a stranger (to s.o., sthg.).

alienatàrio, *s.m.* (*dir.*) alienee.

alienàto, *ag.* lunatic, mad, insane ‖ *s.m.* lunatic, madman (*pl.* madmen): *casa, asilo per alienati*, lunatic asylum (*o* madhouse).

alienazióne, *s.f.* **1.** (*dir.*) alienation, transfer **2.** (*allontanamento dell'animo*) alienation, estrangement **3.** (*pazzia*) mental alienation, derangement, insanity, madness.

alienísta, *s.m.* alienist.

alièno, *ag.* **1.** averse (to sthg., to doing), opposed (to sthg., to doing), adverse (to sthg., to doing): *sono — dai sotterfugi*, I am opposed to subterfuges **2.** (*rilutante*) loath (*predicativo*); reluctant, unwilling, disinclined: *era — dal prestare denaro agli amici*, he was loath to lend money to his friends; *non era — dal godere dei piaceri della vita*, he was not unwilling to enjoy the pleasures of life **3.** (*straniero*) alien, foreign.

aliétta, *s.f.* (*pinna*) fin.

alifàtico, *ag.* (*chim.*) aliphatic.

alígero, *ag.* (*poet.*) **1.** (*alato*) winged **2.** (*veloce*) fast.

alighièro, *s.m.* (*mar.*) boat-hook.

alimentàre, *ag.* **1.** alimentary: *generi alimentari*, foodstuffs; *regime —*, diet **2.** (*mec.*) feed(ing).

alimentàre, *v.t.* **1.** to feed, to nourish (*anche fig.*): *i ruscelli che alimentano un fiume*, the streams that feed a river **2.** (*dir.*) to provide maintenance, alimony for (s.o.) **3.** (*approvvigionare*) to supply with food **4.** (*caldaie*) to feed, to stoke ‖ **alimentàrsi**, *v.r.* to feed (on sthg.).

alimentàrio, *ag.* alimentary (*anche dir.*).

alimentatóre, *s.m.* **1.** nourisher **2.** (*mec.*) feeder.

alimentazióne, *s.f.* **1.** nourishment, feeding **2.** (*cibo*) food **3.** (*dieta*) diet **4.** (*mec.*) feeding; (*ferr.*) (*rifornimento*) provisionment, supply.

alimentízio, *ag.* alimentary.

aliménto, *s.m.* **1.** food, aliment, nutriment ‖ *gli alimenti dei poveri,* (*amm.*) the maintenance of the poor **2.** *pl.* (*dir.*) alimony (*sing.*), maintenance (*sing.*): *provvedere gli alimenti alla propria moglie,* to provide alimony for one's wife.

alimònia, *s.f.* (*dir.*) alimony.

alínea, *s.f.* (*tip.*) (new) paragraph.

aliòsso, *s.m.* (*anat.*) astragalus (*pl.* astragali).

alípede, *ag.* (*poet.*) wing-footed.

alíquota, *s.f.* aliquot (part), rate.

alisèo, *s.m.* trade-wind.

alitàre, *v.i.* to breathe; (*di vento*) to blow gently.

àlito, *s.m.* **1.** breath: — *cattivo,* halitosis **2.** (*respiro*) respiration, breathing **3.** (*venticello*) breeze.

allacciaménto, *s.m.* **1.** lacing, tying **2.** (*collegamento*) inking, link: — *ferroviario,* railway-junction.

allacciàre, *v.t.* **1.** to lace, to tie, to bind: — *una vena,* (*chir.*) to tie a vein **2.** (*abbottonare*) to fasten, to button up: *allacciò il cappotto e se ne andò,* he buttoned up his coat and went away **3.** *fig.* to establish; to open up: — *relazioni d'affari con qlcu.,* to establish business connections with s.o. **4.** (*collegare*) to connect, to link up: — *due linee ferroviarie,* to connect two railway lines **5.** (*elett. mec.*) to connect.

allacciatúra, *s.f.* **1.** lacing, tying, fastening **2.** (*di bottoni*) buttoning, fastening.

allagaménto, *s.m.* flood, overflowing, inundation.

allagàre, *v.t.* to inundate, to flood; *fig.* to spread all over (sthg.) ‖ **allagàrsi,** *v.r.* to be flooded.

Allàh, *no. pr. m.* (*relig. maomettana*) Allah.

allampanàre, *v.i.* to become thin, to become lean.

allampanàto, *ag.* lanky, lean, thin.

allappàre, *V.* **allegàre²** **1.**

allargaménto, *s.m.* **1.** widening, broadening; (*ampliamento*) enlargement **2.** (*aumento*) increase.

allargàre, *v.t.* **1.** to widen, to broaden; (*ampliare*) to enlarge, to increase (*anche fig.*): *quell'attore ha allargato il suo repertorio,* that actor has broadened his repertoire; — *la cerchia dei propri affari,* to enlarge one's sphere of activity **2.** (*estendere*) to extend, to spread; (*aprire*) to open: *il pavone allargò la coda,* the peacock spread its tail; — *le braccia,* to open one's arms; — *la mano,* to open one's hand; *fig.* to be generous **3.** (*abiti*) to let out, (*scarpe*) to stretch **4.** (*attenuare*) to release: — *il freno,* to release the brake; *fig.* to give more freedom (*o* to allow more liberty) **5.** — *il tempo,* (*mus.*) to slacken the tempo ‖ **allargàrsi,** *v.r.* **1.** to become wide, to widen out; (*ampliarsi*) to become larger **2.** (*estendersi*) to extend, to spread (out) ‖ *mi si allargò il cuore, fig.* my heart lightened.

allargatúra, *s.f.* widening; enlargement.

allarmànte, *ag.* alarming: *in modo* —, alarmingly; *sintomi allarmanti,* alarming symptoms.

allarmàre, *v.t.* to alarm, to frighten; to terrify: *la notizia non mi allarmò,* the news did not frighten me ‖ **allarmàrsi,** *v.r.* to take alarm, to take fright.

allàrme, *s.m.* **1.** alarm, warning, alert: *cessato* —, all clear; *segnale d'* —, alarm signal; *segnale d'* — *aereo,* air-raid warning; *sirena d'* —, siren **2.** *fig.* fear; agitation; sudden apprehension: *la polizia fu tenuta in stato d'* — *per settimane,* the police were kept on the alert for weeks ‖ *falso* —, false alarm.

allarmísta, *s.m.* alarmist, scaremonger.

allascàre, *v.t.* (*mar.*) to loosen, to let go.

allàto, a làto, *av.* near, close by, beside, at the side of: *egli mi camminava* — *al lato,* he walked beside me.

allattaménto, *s.m.* suckling, nursing: — *artificiale,* bottle-feeding.

allattàre, *v.t.* **1.** to suckle, to nurse, to give (a child) suck **2.** (*nutrire*) to nourish.

allattatríce, *s.f.* wet-nurse, suckler.

allattatúra, *s.f.* suckling, nursing.

alleànza, *s.f.* alliance: *stringere* — *con qlcu.,* to form an alliance with s.o. ‖ *la Santa Alleanza,* the Holy Alliance.

alleàrsi, *v.r.* to form an alliance, to ally oneself, to enter into an alliance.

alleàto, *ag.* allied (to s.o.) ‖ *s.m.* ally: *gli alleati,* the allies.

allegàbile, *ag.* allegeable.

allegagióne, *s.f.* (*agr.*) setting.

allegaménto, *s.m.* **1.** (*agr.*) setting **2.** (*dei denti*) setting on edge (of the teeth).

Allègani (gli), *no.pr.m.pl.* (*geog.*) the Alleghenies.

allegàre¹, *v.t.* **1.** to allege, to plead as an excuse, to give as a reason **2.** (*accludere*) to enclose: *allego i documenti richiesti,* I enclose herewith the required documents.

allegàre², *v.t.* **1.** (*i denti*) to set on edge: — *i denti a qlcu.,* to set s.o.'s teeth on edge **2.** (*metal.*) to alloy ‖ *v.i.* (*agr.*) (*attecchire*) to take root; to set.

allegàto, *s.m.* (*comm.*) enclosure: *avete dimenticato di unire gli allegati,* you have forgotten to insert the enclosures.

allegazióne¹, *s.f.* allegation.

allegazióne², *s.f.* (*di denti*) setting on edge (of the teeth).

alleggeriménto, *s.m.* **1.** lightening **2.** *fig.* alleviation, mitigation, relief.

alleggeríre, *v.t.* **1.** to lighten, to unburden: — *una nave,* to lighten a ship **2.** *fig.* to relieve, to ease, to alleviate: *fui alleggerito da quella grave preoccupazione,* I was relieved of that great worry; *lo alleggerirono del portafoglio,* (*scherz.*) they relieved him of his wallet ‖ **alleggerírsi,** *v.r.* **1.** to become lighter **2.** (*liberarsi*) to relieve oneself (*anche fig.*): — *di un carico,* to relieve oneself of a load **3.** (*negli abiti*) to put on lighter clothes.

alleggiaménto, *V.* **alleggeriménto.**

alleggiàre, *V.* **alleggeríre.**

allèggio, *s.m.* **1.** (*mar.*) lighter, barge **2.** (*valvola di scarico di imbarcazione*) boat-plug.

allegoría, *s.f.* allegory.

allegoricaménte, *av.* allegorically.

allegòrico, *ag.* allegoric(al).

allegorísta, *s.m.* (*rar.*) allegorist.

allegorizzàre, *v.t.* (*rar.*) to allegorize.

allegraménte, *av.* merrily, cheerfully, gaily: *prenderla allegramente,* (*fam.*) take it with a smile.

allegràre, *v.t.* (*rar.*) to gladden, to cheer (up) ‖ **allegràrsi,** *v.r.* to rejoice, to cheer up.

allegrétto, *s.m.* (*mus.*) allegretto.

allegrézza, *s.f.* cheerfulness, joyfulness, mirth, gaiety: *questi costumi aggiungono* — *allo spettacolo,* these costumes add to the gaiety of the scene.

allegría, *s.f.* mirth, fun, jollity, cheerfulness: — *rumorosa,* merriment.

allégro, *ag.* **1.** merry, cheerful, gay, jolly; good-humoured: *stare* —, to be merry **2.** (*di colore*) bright **3.** (*di luogo*) pleasant **4.** (*scherz.*) (*alticcio*) tipsy, tight ‖ *s.m.* (*mus.*) allegro.

allegróne, *s.m.* cheerful fellow, jolly fellow.

allelúia, *s.m.* hallelujah, halleluiah, alleluia.

allenaménto, *s.m.* training (*anche spor.*); (*di squadre*) coaching: *essere in* —, to be in training.

allenàre, *v.t.* to train (*anche spor.*); to exercise; (*squadre*) to coach ‖ **allenàrsi,** *v.r.* to train, to make oneself fit.

allenatóre, *s.m.* (*spor.*) trainer; (*di squadre*) coach; (*di corridori*) pace-maker, pacer.

alleníre, *v.t.* to soften, to alleviate.

allentaménto, *s.m.* **1.** (*di velocità*) slackening, slowing down **2.** (*di tensione*) loosening, slackening, relaxation (*anche fig.*) **3.** (*mec.*) release: — *del freno,* release of the brake.

allentàre, *v.t.* **1.** to slacken, to loosen, to relax (anche *fig.*): — *la disciplina,* to slacken the discipline; — *le redini,* to loosen (*o* to slacken) the reins; — *la stretta,* to relax one's hold; — *un vestito,* to unlace a dress **2.** (*mec.*): — *il freno,* to release the brake; — *una vite,* to loosen a screw **3.** (*rallentare*) to slacken, to slow down: — *il passo,* to slacken one's pace ‖ *v.i.,* **allentàrsi,** *v.r.* **1.** to slacken, to loosen, to become slack; (*di ingranaggio*) to work loose **2.** (*patol.*) to rupture.

allentatúra, *s.f.* (*patol.*) hernia, rupture.

allergía, *s.f.* (*patol.*) allergy.

allèrgico, *ag.* allergic: — *al fumo, ai gatti,* allergic to smoke, to cats.

allessàre, *v.t.* to boil.

allésso, *ag.* boiled ‖ *chi la vuole* — *e chi arrosto, fig.* some want it one way and some another ‖ *s.m.* boiled meat.

allestiménto, *s.m.* **1.** preparation, getting ready: — *delle vetrine,* window-dressing; — *scenico,* (*teat.*) staging **2.** (*mar.*) rigging, fitting out.

allestíre, *v.t.* **1.** to prepare, to make ready: — *il pranzo,* to prepare dinner **2.** (*mar.*) to rig out, to fit out; to arm ‖ **allestírsi,** *v.r.* to prepare oneself, to get ready.

alletamàre, *v.t.* (*agr.*) to manure.

allettaménto, *s.m.* **1.** allurement, enticement **2.** (*attrazione*) attraction; charm, fascination.

allettànte, *ag.* **1.** alluring **2.** (*attraente*) attractive, charming.

allettàre[1], *v.t.* **1.** to allure, to entice **2.** (*affascinare*) to attract; to charme, to fascinate **3.** (*uccelli*) to decoy, to charm.

allettàre[2], *v.t.* (*agr.*) to beat down: *il vento ha allettato il grano,* the wind has beaten down (*o* laid *o* lodged) the wheat ‖ **allettàrsi,** *v.r.* **1.** (*agr.*) to lie down, to become flattened **2.** (*mettersi, essere costretto a letto*) to take to one's bed, to keep one's bed.

allettatíva, *V.* **allettaménto.**

allettatóre, *s.m.,* **allettatríce,** *s.f.* enticer, charmer.

allettévole, *ag.* **1.** alluring, enticing **2.** (*attraente*) inviting, attractive.

allevaménto, *s.m.* **1.** (*di bambino*) bringing up; rearing **2.** (*di animali*) rearing, breeding: — *di bestiame,* cattle-breeding; — *di cavalli,* horse-breeding; — *di pecore,* sheep-breeding **3.** (*luogo di allevamento*) farm: — *di cavalli,* stud-farm; — *di pecore,* sheep-farm (*o* austral. sheep-station).

allevàre, *v.t.* **1.** (*bambini*) to bring up; to rear, to nurse; (*allattare*) to suckle **2.** (*bestiame*) to breed, to rear.

allevàta, *V.* **allevaménto 2.**

allevatóre, *s.m.,* **allevatríce,** *s.f.* breeder.

allevatúra, *V.* **allevaménto.**

alleviaménto, *s.m.* relief; alleviation; mitigation.

alleviàre, *v.t.* to relieve; to alleviate; to mitigate.

allibíre, *v.i.* **1.** (*impallidire di paura*) to turn pale with fear **2.** (*restare sbigottito*) to be dismayed.

allibraménto, *s.m.* registration.

allibràre, *v.t.* to book, to register, to record.

allibratóre, *s.m.* bookmaker.

allicciàre, *v.t.* **1.** (*ind. tessile*) to heddle **2.** — *una sega,* (*falegnameria*) to set the teeth of a saw.

allietàre, *v.t.* to gladden, to cheer ‖ **allietàrsi,** *v.r.* to rejoice (in, at sthg.), to become cheerful.

alliève, *s.f.* **1.** pupil, schoolgirl; (*studentessa*) student **2.** (*apprendista*) apprentice.

alliève[1], *s.m.* **1.** pupil, schoolboy; (*studente*) student **2.** (*apprendista*) apprentice **3.** (*mil.*) cadet: — *di marina,* naval cadet **4.** (*animale da allevare*) suckling.

alliève[2], *s.m.* (*valvola di scarico di imbarcazione*) boat-plug.

alligatóre, *s.m.* (*zool.*) alligator.

alligazióne, *s.f.* (*comm.*) alligation.

allignàre, *v.i.* **1.** to take root; to thrive **2.** *fig.* to grow.

allindàre, *v.t.* **1.** to make spruce, to make tidy **2.** *fig.* to polish ‖ **allindàrsi,** *v.r.* to tidy up.

allineaménto, *s.m.* **1.** alignment, ranging, setting in a row; laying out (of sthg.): — *di caratteri,* (*tip.*) ranging

of characters; — *di case,* laying out of houses **2.** (*mil.*) dressing **3.** (*mar.*) leading mark.

allineàre, *v.t.* **1.** to line up, to align, to set in a row, to bring into line, to lay out: — *gli alberi,* to lay out trees (in a line); — *i caratteri,* to range (*o* to align) characters; — *delle cifre,* to tabulate figures (*o* to go into figures) **2.** (*mil.*) to dress, to draw up: — *i soldati,* to dress a line of soldiers ‖ **allineàrsi,** *v.r.* **1.** to fall into line **2.** (*mil.*) to dress: — *a destra!,* right dress!.

allitterazióne, *s.f.* alliteration.

allivellàre, *v.t.* to level.

allividíre, *v.i.* to turn pale.

Allòbrogi, *no.pr.m.pl.* Allobroges.

allocazióne, *s.f.* (*ippica*) prize-money.

allocchería, *s.f.* stupidity.

allòcco, *s.m.* **1.** (*zool.*) owl **2.** *fig.* dunce, fool, booby, ninny: *far l'*—, to play the fool.

allocròico, *ag.* (*rar.*) shot.

allocutóre, *s.m.,* **allocutríce,** *s.f.* speaker.

allocuzióne, *s.f.* allocution; (*eccl. dir.*) charge: *fare un'*—, to deliver an authoritative address (*o* an allocution).

allodiàle, *ag.* (*dir.*) allodial, freehold: *beni allodiali,* allodial (*o* freehold) estate; *proprietario di beni allodiali,* freeholder.

allodialità, *s.f.* (*dir.*) allodiality.

allòdio, *s.m.* (*dir.*) allodium.

allòdola, *s.f.* skylark, lark.

allogagióne, *s.f.* **1.** letting, leasing **2.** assignment (of work).

allogaménto, *s.m.* **1.** placing, location; (*di denaro*) investing, investment **2.** (*contratto d'affitto*) lease.

allogàre, *v.t.* **1.** to place conveniently: *ha una figlia da* —, she has a daughter to marry off; — *qlcu.,* to find employment for s.o. **2.** (*investire*) to invest **3.** (*dare in affitto*) to lease ‖ **allogàrsi,** *v.r.* to find employment (with s.o.).

allogatóre, *s.m.,* **allogatríce,** *s.f.* **1.** lessor **2.** (*appaltatore*) contractor.

allogazióne, *s.f.* **1.** placing; location **2.** (*contratto d'affitto*) lease.

allògeno, *ag. s.m.* alien.

alloggiaménto, *s.m.* **1.** lodging, housing, accomodation: *cercò un* — *per la notte,* he looked for a night's lodging **2.** (*mil.*) (*in caserma*) quartering, quarters (*pl.*); (*in casa privata*) billet, billeting; (*accampamento*) encampment, camp **3.** (*mec.*) housing slot: — *per chiavetta,* keyway, spline, slot; — *per molla,* spring holder.

alloggiàre, *v.t.* **1.** to lodge, to accomodate, to house, to give (s.o.) lodgings: *ti posso* — *per la notte,* I can put you up for the night **2.** (*mil.*) (*in caserma*) to quarter; (*in casa privata*) to billet; (*in accampamento*) to camp ‖ *v.i.* **1.** to lodge, to live, to stay, to take lodgings **2.** (*mil.*) (*in caserma*) to be quartered; (*in casa privata*) to be billeted.

alloggiatóre, *s.m.* landlord.

alloggiatríce, *s.f.* landlady.

allòggio, *s.m.* **1.** lodging; (*appartamento*) flat; (*stanze*) lodgings (*pl.*): — *ammobiliato,* furnished flat; *indennità di* —, living-out allowance; *vitto e* —, board and lodging **2.** (*mil. mar.*) quarters (*pl.*): *maresciallo d'*—, quartermaster.

allontanaménto, *s.m.* **1.** removal, removing, sending away; (*estraniamento*) estrangement **2.** (*licenziamento*) dismissal.

allontanàre, *v.t.* **1.** to remove, to get (s.o., sthg.) out of the way; (*cacciar via*) to drive away, to turn away; to banish; *fig.* to put away, to avert: *allontanò la sedia dal tavolo,* he moved the chair away from the table; — *un pericolo,* to avert a danger; — *qlcu. da un'idea,* to deter s.o. from an idea; — *le zanzare dal viso di un bambino,* to drive the mosquitoes away from a child's face **2.** (*licenziare*) to dismiss, to turn out, to remove ‖ **allontanàrsi,** *v.r.* **1.** to go away, to depart: *si allontanò senza dire una parola,* she departed without saying a word; — *da qlcu.*, to leave s.o. 2. (*deviare*) to swerve, to deviate: — *dalla virtù, fig.* to deviate from virtue.

allopatía, *s.f* (*med.*) allopathy.

allopaticaménte, *av.* (*med.*) allopathically.

allopàtico, *ag.* (*med.*) allopathic.

alloppiaménto, *s.m.* drugging with opium.

alloppiàre, *v.t.* to drug with ópium.

allòppio, *s.m.* (*rar.*) opium.

allóra, *av.* 1. (*in quel tempo*) then, at that time, in that time: *d'— in poi,* since then on (*o* from that time); *il Primo Ministro di —,* the then Prime Minister; *proprio —,* just then; *sino —,* until then ‖ *— —,* just: *era uscito — —,* he had just gone out 2. (*in tal caso*) then, well then, in that case, such being the case: *—, cosa avete intenzione di fare?,* well then, what are you going to do? 3. (*quindi*) therefore, so: *disse che non c'era, — tornai indietro,* he said she was not there, so I went back again.

allorché, *cong.* when.

alloritmía, *s.f.* (*patol.*) allorhythmia.

allòro, *s.m.* laurel (anche *fig.*): *incoronare di —,* to crown with laurels; *riposare sugli allori,* to rest on one's laurels ‖ *incoronato di —,* laureate (*o* laurelled).

allorquàndo, *cong.* when.

allotropía, *s.f.* (*chim.*) allotropy.

allotròpico, *ag.* (*chim.*) allotropic(al).

allòtropo, *s.m.* (*chim.*) allotrope.

allottàre, *v.t.* to raffle (off).

allucchettàre, *v.t.* to lock up.

allucciolàre, *v.i.* to sparkle, to glitter.

àlluce, *s.m.* (*anat.*) big toe.

alluciàre, *v.t.* to look at (s.o., sthg.) eagerly, to gaze at, on (s.o., sthg.); (*adocchiare*) to eye.

allucidàre, *v.t.* to polish.

allucignolàre, *v.t.* 1. to twist 2. (*sgualcire*) to crumple, to crush.

allucinàre, *v.t.* 1. (*abbagliare*) to dazzle 2. (*dare allucinazioni a*) to hallucinate; to bewitch ‖ **allucinàrsi,** *v.r.* to deceive oneself.

allucinàto, *ag.* (*di sguardo*) hallucinated; (*di persona*) entranced.

allucinazióne, *s.f.* hallucination: *soffrire di allucinazioni,* to be subject to hallucinations.

allúda, *s.f.* (*conceria*) soft leather, kid, chamois.

allúdere, *v.i.* to allude, to refer; to hint (at sthg.): *a questo si alludeva durante la discussione,* this was alluded to during the debate.

allumàre[1], *v.t.* 1. (*illuminare*) to lighten 2. (*arc.*) (*accendere*) to light (up).

allumàre[2], *v.t.* (*ind. tessile*) to alum, to treat with alum.

allumatúra, *s.f.* (*ind. tessile*) steeping in alum-water.

allúme, *s.m.* (*chim.*) alum.

allumína, *s.f.* (*chim.*) alumina.

alluminàre, *v.t.* to illuminate.

alluminatóre, *s.m.* illuminator.

allumínio, *s.m.* (*chim.*) aluminium: *eliminazione dell'—,* (*metal.*) de-aluminizing.

alluminóso, *ag.* (*chim.*) aluminous.

allunàre, *v.i.* (*neol.*) to moon.

allunàto, *ag.* crescent-shaped.

allungàbile, *ag.* extensible.

allungaménto, *s.m.* 1. lengthening, extension; prolongation; (*fonet.*) lengthening 2. (*mec. fis.*) elongation, extension, stretching, stretch: — *alla trazione,* stretch (*o* elongation); — *percentuale,* percentage elongation.

allungàre, *v.t.* 1. to lengthen, to extend: — *un vestito,* to lengthen a dress; — *una vocale,* to lengthen a vowel ‖ — *il passo,* to quicken one's steps ‖ — *la strada,* to go the long way round 2. (*stendere*) to stretch (out): — *il collo,* to stretch one's neck; — *le mani,* to stretch out one's hands: — *le mani su q1.co., fig.* to lay hands on sthg.; — *il muso,* to pull a long face; — *gli orecchi,* to strain one's ears ‖ — *una pedata,* to lodge a kick ‖ **allungàrsi,** *v.r.* 1. to lengthen, to grow long(er); (*crescere*) to grow tall: *i giorni si allungano,* the

days are drawing out 2. (*stirarsi*) to stretch.

allungatúra, *s.f.* lengthening; prolongation.

allúngo, *s.m.* 1. lengthening-piece 2. (*comm.*) allonge, rider.

allupàre, *v.i.* to be as hungry as a hunter.

allupàto, *ag.* as hungry as a hunter.

allusióne, *s.f.* allusion, hint: *non si fece — all'argomento,* no allusion was made to the subject.

allusívo, *ag.* allusive.

alluviàle, *ag.* (*geol.*) alluvial.

alluvionàle, *ag.* alluvial.

alluvionàto, *ag.* damaged by floods ‖ *s.m.* flood victim.

alluvióne, *s.f.* 1. flood; (*geol.*) alluvium 2. (*dir.*) alluvion.

àlma[1], *s.f.* (*poet.*) soul.

Àlma[2], *no.pr.f.* Alma.

almagèsto, *s.m.* almagest.

almanaccàre, *v.i.* 1. (*fantasticare*) to dream (of, about s.o., sthg.); to build castles in the air, in Spain; (*congetturare*) to muse (on, upon s.o., sthg.) 2. (*sforzarsi di capire*) to puzzle (about, over sthg.).

almanàcco, *s.m.* almanac, calendar: — *astronomico,* ephemeris; — *di Gotha,* Almanach de Gotha.

almàneo, *av.* (*letter.*) at least.

almèa, *s.f.* alma(h).

alméno, *av.* at least.

àlmo, *ag.* (*poet.*) 1. vivifying 2. (*immortale*) immortal, divine.

àlno, *s.m.* (*bot.*) alder-tree.

àloe, *s.m.* (*bot.*) aloe.

alògeno, *s.m.* (*chim.*) halogen.

alogenúro, alòide, *s.m.* (*chim.*) haloid.

alóne, *s.m.* (*astr.*) halo.

alopecía, *s.f.* (*patol.*) alopecia.

alpàca, *s.m.* (*zool.*) alpaca ‖ *s.f.* (*lana, tessuto*) alpaca.

alpàcca, *s.f.* (*metal.*) nickel silver, German silver.

àlpe, *s.f.* alp.

alpéggio, *s.m.* mountain summer pasture (for cattle).

alpèstre, *ag.* 1. (*alpino*) alpine 2. (*montagnoso*) mountainous 3. (*ripido*) steep.

Àlpi (le), *no.pr.f.pl.* (*geog.*) the Alps.

alpigiàno, *s.m.* mountaineer.

alpinísmo, *s.m.* (*spor.*) alpinism, (mountain-)climbing, mountaineering.

alpinísta, *s.m.* alpinist, (mountain-)climber, mountaineer.

alpíno, *ag.* Alpine ‖ *s.m.* "alpino" (*pl.* "alpini").

alquànto, *ag.* 1. some, a certain amount of: *aveva — denaro con sè,* he had a certain amount of money with him; *aveva — timore di suo zio,* he went in some awe of his uncle 2. *pl.* several, a few, a number of: *alquanti amici,* several (*o* a few) friends; *non posso farlo per alquante ragioni,* I can't do it for a number of reasons ‖ *pron.* 1. some, a certain amount of: *ne presi —,* I took some (*o* I took a certain amount of it) 2. *pl.* some, several: *c'erano molti libri e ne comprai alquanti,* there were a great many books and I bought some (*o* several) ‖ *av.* somewhat, a little, a bit, rather: *era — irrequieto,* he was somewhat restless; *era — ubriaco,* he was a bit (*o* a little) tipsy; *sono — stanco,* I am rather tired.

Alsàzia, *no.pr.f.* (*geog.*) Alsatia.

alsaziàno, *ag.* Alsatian: *cane —,* Alsatian dog (*o* wolf) ‖ *s.m.* Alsatian ‖ **alsaziàna,** *s.f.* Alsatian.

altaléna, *s.f.* 1. (*appesa a due funi*) swing; (*palo, tavola messi in bilico*) see-saw: *giocare all'—,* to play on a see-saw 2. *fig.* ups and downs (*pl.*): *l'— della vita,* the ups and downs of life 3. *fig.* (*indecisione*) indecision, wavering.

altalenàre, *v.i.,* **altalenàrsi,** *v.r.* 1. (*su funi*) to swing; (*su tavole*) to see-saw 2. *fig.* (*essere indeciso*) to waver.

altaménte, *av.* highly; (*con voce verbale*) very much: — *stimato,* highly esteemed; *lo stimo —,* I esteem him very much.

altàna, *s.f.* roof-terrace.

altàre, *s.m.* altar: — *maggiore,* high altar; *tovaglia d'* —, altar-cloth ‖ *sacrificio dell'* —, Mass ‖ *condurre all'* —, to lead to the altar ‖ *porre qlcu. sugli altari,* to hero-worship s.o. ‖ *scoprire gli altarini,* (*scherz.*) to discover s.o.'s secrets (o to clear up a mystery).

altèa, *s.f.* (*bot.*) althaea, althea: — *rosea,* holly-hock.

alteràbile, *ag.* **1.** alterable, changeable **2.** (*adulterabile*) liable to adulteration, liable to deterioration **3.** (*falsificabile*) falsifiable, forgeable.

alterabilità, *s.f.* **1.** alterability, changeableness **2.** (*adulterabilità*) liability to adulteration, to deterioration.

alteraménte, *av.* proudly; haughtily, loftily.

alteràre, *v.t.* **1.** to alter, to change; (*cibo*) to adulterate; (*salute*) to impair, to affect; (*lineamenti*) to disfigure; (*mus.*) to inflect: *questo altera le cose,* that alters matters **2.** (*falsificare*) to falsify, to counterfeit: — *fatti,* to misrepresent (o to distort o to mis-state) facts; — *una firma,* to forge a signature; — *una moneta,* to counterfeit a coin; — *un testo,* to falsify a text; — *la verità,* to twist the truth ‖ **alteràrsi,** *v.r.* **1.** (*mutarsi*) to alter, to change; (*andare a male*) (*di cibo*) to go bad; (*di latte, burro*) to go sour; (*di merci*) to deteriorate, to perish **2.** (*turbarsi*) to be affected; (*arrabbiarsi*) to get angry: *si altera facilmente,* he is easily annoyed; *la sua voce si alterò,* his voice faltered (o broke); *il suo viso si alterò quando mi vide,* his face dropped when he saw me.

alteràto, *ag.* **1.** (*adulterato*) adulterated; (*guasto*) (gone) bad **2.** (*falsificato*) forged **3.** (*turbato*) upset, unsettled; (*irato*) angry: *voce alterata,* faltering (o broken) voice ‖ *polso* —, quick pulse ‖ *essere* — *dal vino,* to be drunk.

alterazióne, *s.f.* **1.** (*mutamento*) alteration, change **2.** (*deteriorazione*) deterioration; (*di cibo*) adulteration; (*di merci*) perishing; (*della salute*) impairment **3.** (*falsificazione*) forgery, falsification, counterfeiting, forging **4.** (*turbamento*) emotion; (*eccitazione*) excitement; (*della voce*) faltering, breaking **5.** (*di rocce*) weathering (of rocks) **6.** (*mus.*) inflecting (of note).

altercàre, *v.i.* to quarrel, to wrangle, to dispute.

altercazióne, *s.f.,* **altèrco,** *s.m.* quarrel, wrangle, altercation, dispute.

alterègo, *s.m.* alter ego.

alterézza, *s.f.* **1.** (*dignità*) dignity **2.** (*orgoglio*) pride.

alterígia, *s.f.* haughtiness, arrogance, loftiness.

alternaménte, *V.* **alternativaménte.**

alternàre, *v.t.* **1.** to alternate: *alternava il riso con le lacrime,* she alternated laughter with tears **2.** (*agr.*) to rotate (crops) ‖ **alternàrsi,** *v.r.* **1.** to alternate **2.** (*accadere alternamente*) to happen by turns.

alternativa, *s.f.* **1.** (*l'alternarsi*) alternation: — *di timori e speranze,* alternation of fear and hope **2.** (*scelta*) alternative, choice, option: *non c'è* —, there is no alternative; *questo fatto non ci lascia alcuna* —, this fact leaves us no choice (o option).

alternativaménte, *av.* **1.** alternately, by turns, in turn, one after the other **2.** alternatively, otherwise.

alternatívo, *ag.* **1.** alternative **2.** (*mec.*) reciprocating.

alternàto, *ag.* **1.** alternate ‖ *coltivazione alternata,* (*agr.*) rotation of crops **2.** (*elett.*) alternating: *corrente alternata,* alternating current.

alternatóre, *s.m.* (*elett.*) alternator.

alternazióne, *s.f.* alternation.

altèrno, *ag.* alternate: *angoli alterni,* (*geom.*) alternate angles; *venire a giorni alterni,* to come on alternate days.

altèro, *ag.* **1.** (*dignitoso*) dignified **2.** (*orgoglioso*) proud **3.** (*altezzoso*) haughty, arrogant, lofty.

altézza, *s.f.* **1.** height: — *sul livello del mare,* height above sea level; *lo lasciò cadere da un'* — *di dieci metri,* he dropped it from a height of ten metres ‖ *l'automobile si fermò all'* — *del numero sette,* the car stopped opposite number seven ‖ *la nave era all'* — *di Capo Horn,* the ship was off Cape Horn **2.** (*statura*) tallness **3.** (*pro-*

fondità) depth: — *d'un pozzo,* depth o₁ a well **4.** (*di tessuto*) width **5.** (*di suono*) loudness **6.** *fig.* (*di carattere*) nobility, loftiness, grandeur; (*di pensiero, sentimenti*) loftiness ‖ *non era all'* — *di trattare l'argomento,* he was not up to the task of dealing with the subject ‖ *essere all'* — *di un compito,* to be equal to a task ‖ *essere all'* — *dei tempi,* to be up-to-date (o to be abreast of the times) ‖ *essere all'* — *di una situazione,* to be able to face a situation (o to be equal to a situation) **7.** (*titolo*) Highness: *Sua Altezza Reale il Principe di Galles,* His Royal Highness the Prince of Wales; *Vostra Altezza,* Your Highness **8.** (*astr.*) altitude: — *del Sole,* altitude of the sun.

altezzosaménte, *av.* haughtily, proudly.

altezzóso, *ag.* haughty, arrogant, lofty.

altíccio, *ag.* tipsy, tight.

altimetría, *s.f.* altimetry.

altimètrico, *ag.* altimetrical.

altímetro, *s.m.* altimeter.

altipiàno, *s.m.* plateau, tableland.

altisonànte, *ag.* high-sounding, resounding.

altíssimo, *ag. superl.* very high ‖ *l'Altissimo,* the Most High.

altitonànte, *ag.* loud-thundering.

altitúdine, *s.f.* (*geog.*) altitude, height.

àlto[1], *ag.* **1.** tall; high: *un uomo* —, a tall man; *quella torre è molto alta,* that tower is very high; *questo monte è* — *2114 metri,* this mountain is 2114 metres high **2.** *fig.* high, excellent, great; (*generoso*) generous; (*nobile*) noble: *alta direzione,* top management; *l'alta finanza,* high finance; *l'alta matematica,* higher mathematics; — *funzionario,* high-placed official; — *tradimento,* high treason; *le classi alte,* the upper classes; *un uomo di* — *ingegno,* a man of high intellect ‖ *andare a testa alta,* to carry (o to hold) one's head high **3.** (*di suono*) loud: *ad alta voce,* in a loud voice (o loudly) **4.** (*di tessuto*) wide **5.** (*profondo*) deep: — *silenzio,* profound silence; *acqua alta,* deep water **6.** (*geog.*) northern, upper: *Alta Italia,* Northern Italy; *Alta Lombardia,* Upper Lombardy **7.** (*st.*) early: — *Medioevo,* early Middle Ages **8.** (*di tempo*) late: *la Pasqua è alta quest'anno,* Easter is late this year ‖ *la stagione alta,* the height of the season **9.** (*difficile*) difficult: *questo problema è troppo* — *per me,* this problem is too difficult for me ‖ *s.m.* **1.** height ‖ *gli alti e i bassi della vita,* the ups and downs of life (o the vicissitudes of life) ‖ *un ordine venuto dall'* —, an order from high quarters ‖ *far cadere una cosa dall'* —, to exaggerate the value of what one gives ‖ *guardare qlcu. dall'* — *in basso,* to look down on s.o. (o to look at s.o. contemptuously) **2.** (*cielo*) heaven: *un'ispirazione venuta dall'* —, an inspiration from heaven.

àlto[1], *av.* **1.** high; above, up: *mani in* —*!,* hands up!; *mirare* —, to aim high **2.** (*ad alta voce*) aloud, loudly: *proclamare* — *che...,* to proclaim loudly that....

àlto[2], *s.m.* stop: —*!,* halt! (o stop!); *fare* —, to stop.

altofórno, *s.m.* (*metal.*) smelting furnace; blast-furnace.

altolocàto, *ag.* high-ranking, important.

altomàre, *s.m.* high seas (*pl.*); open sea.

altoparlànte, *s.m.* loud-speaker.

altorilièvo, *s.m.* (*art.*) high-relief, alto-relievo.

altostràto, *s.m.* (*metereologia*) alto-stratus.

altresí, *av.* also, too; likewise.

altrettàle, *ag.* such, similar; equal.

altrettànto, *ag. correlativo* **1.** (*in espressioni affermative*) as much (...as); *pl.* as many (...as): *ho due penne e altrettante matite,* I have got two pens and as many pencils **2.** (*in espressioni negative*) so much (...as); *pl.* so many (...as): *non ci sono altrettanti uomini quante donne,* there are not so many gentlemen as ladies ‖ *pron. correlativo* **1.** (*in espressioni affermative*) as much (...as); *pl.* as many (...as): *ho tre pere e tu ne hai altrettante,* I have got three pears and you have as many **2.** (*in espressioni negative*) so much

(...as); *pl.* **so many** (...as): *ho due fratelli, ma tu non ne hai altrettanti*, I have two brothers, but you don't have so many **3.** (*la medesima cosa*) **the same**: «*Buona fortuna!*», «*Altrettanto a voi!*», "Good luck!", "The same to you!"; *egli si alzò ed io feci* —, he got up and I did the same || *av.* correlativo **1.** (*con ag. e av., in espressioni affermative*) **as** (...as), **equally** (...as): *due volte* —, twice as much; *ella era* — *gentile quanto te*, she was as kind (*o* equally kind) as you **2.** (*con ag. e av., in espressioni negative*) **so** (...as), **equally** (...as): *non lo vidi* — *bene*, I could not see him so (*o* equally) well **3.** (*con verbi, in espressioni affermative*) **as much** (as); (*in espressioni negative*) **so much** (as): *egli non studia* —, he doesn't study as much; *egli studia molto e lavora* —, he studies hard and works as much; *mangiammo avidamente e bevemmo* —, we ate ravenously and drank accordingly.

àltri, *pron.indef.sing.* **someone else; another person**: — *continuerà l'opera più degnamente di me*, someone else will continue the work more worthily than I did; — *dirà chi di noi ha ragione*, someone else will say which of us is right; *non l'ho detto ad* — *che a te*, I have told no one but you.

altrièri, *av.* the day before yesterday.

altriménti, *av.* **otherwise**; but for that || *cong.* (*in caso contrario*) **or else, otherwise**.

àltro, *ag.* **1. other; another**: *un'altra volta*, another time; *ci sono altre cose che devi sapere*, there are other things you must know; *hai altri amici a Milano?*, have you any other friends in Milan? **2.** (*diverso*) **different**: *ci arrivarono per un'altra strada*, they got there by a different route || *è un* — *par di maniche*, *fig.* it is quite a different kettle of fish **3.** (*con pronomi interrogativi, indefiniti e avverbi composti con* where) **else**: *chi* —?, who else?; *in qualche* — *luogo*, somewhere else; *nessun* —, no one else; *poc'* —, little else **4.** (*in più, ancora, ulteriore*) **more; further**: *lesse due altri capitoli*, he read two more chapters; *non aveva altre ragioni per rifiutare*, he had no further reason to refuse; *ripetilo un'altra volta*, say it once more; *vuoi dell'* — *tè?*, will you have some more tea? **5.** (*in espressioni di tempo passato*) **other**; (*con significato di* penultimo) **before last**: *l'* — *giorno*, the day before last (*o* two days ago); *soltanto l'* — *giorno mi diceva che...*, only the other day he was telling me that... **6.** (*in espressioni di tempo futuro*) **next**: *verrò quest'altra settimana*, I'll come next week **7.** (*con i pronomi* noi, voi): *noi altri*, we; *voi altri*, you people || *pron.* **1. another** (one); *pl.* **others, other people**: *ho finito questo libro, puoi darmene un* — ?, I have read this book through, can you give me another? (*o* another one?); *una persona ben educata cerca di non dar fastidio agli altri*, a well-behaved person tries not to inconvenience other people; *se non volete fare questo lavoro, ci sono altri che lo faranno*, if you will not do this job, there are others who will **2.** (*nei pronomi reciproci* l'un l'altro, gli uni gli altri) (*tra due*) **each other**; (*tra molti*) **one another**: *i due fratelli si aiutano l'un l'* —, the two brothers help each other; *i suoi alunni cominciarono ad accusarsi l'un l'* —, his pupils began to accuse one another **3.** (*in correlazione con i pronomi* uno, uni, alcuni): *alcuni... altri...*, **some... some...**: *alcuni ridevano, altri piangevano*, some were laughing, some were crying; *l'uno e l'* —, both; *nè l'uno nè l'* —, neither; *o l'uno o l'* —, either **4.** (*ancora qualcosa, qualcosa in più*) **more**: *farò questo ed* —, (*in senso buono*) I'll do that and much more; (*minaccia*) I'll do that and worse; *ha sofferto molto, ma ha da soffrire dell'* —, he has suffered a good deal, but more is coming to him; *non ho finito, c'è dell'* —, I haven't done yet, there is more to come || *ci vuol* —, it takes much more than that! **5.** (**Fraseologia**): — *che!*, certainly!: «*Vi sentite di andare?*», «*Altro che!*», "Do you feel like going?", "Certainly!" || *da un giorno all'* —, from day to day; *un giorno o l'* —, one of these

days || *non* — *che*, nothing but: *non fate* — *che giocare*, you do nothing but play || *se non* —, at least: *se non* —, *è una ragazza di buon senso*, at least she is a sensible girl || *senz'* —, certainly (*o* by all means *o* of course *o* presently): *hai senz'* — *ragione*, of course you are right; *verrò senz'* —, I'll certainly come (*o* I will come immediately *o* presently) || *tutt'* —!, not at all!: «*Sei stanco?*», «*Tutt'* —!», "Are you tired?", "Not at all!" || *tutt'* — *che*, anything but: *è tutt'* — *che bella*, she is anything but beautiful.

altrónde, *av.* **1.** (*di luogo*) **from elsewhere 2.** *d'* —, **besides; on the other hand; however**.

altróve, *av.* **elsewhere, somewhere else**.

altrúi, *ag.* **other people's, one's neighbour's, someone else's**: *non denigrare la merce* —, do not disparage other people's goods; *non invidiare la fortuna* —, don't be envious of your neighbour's good fortune; *si trovò per errore in casa* —, he found himself by mistake in someone else's house || *pron. obliquo* **others, other people, one's neighbour, someone else**: *la cosa importante è non nuocere* —, the important thing is not to harm others; *giovare* — *è una grande gioia*, to help others (*o* other people *o* one's neighbour) is a great joy || *s.m.* (*l'altrui, la roba d'altri*) **the property of others**: *chi dell'* — *prende*, he who takes the property of others.

altruísmo, *s.m.* **altruism, unselfishness**.

altruísta, *s.c.* **altruist, unselfish person**.

altruisticaménte, *av.* **altruistically, unselfishly**.

altruístico, *ag.* **altruistic, unselfish**.

altúra, *s.f.* **1. height, elevation 2.** *fig.* **haughtiness**.

alúnna, *s.f.* **pupil; schoolgirl**.

alunnàto, *s.m.* **apprenticeship**.

alúnno, *s.m.* **1. pupil; schoolboy**; (*discepolo*) **disciple 2.** (*apprendista*) **apprentice**.

alveàre, *s.m.* **beehive**.

àlveo, *s.m.* **1. river-bed 2.** (*canale*) **canal**.

alveolàre, *ag.* **1. alveolate, cell-like, cellular 2.** (*anat.*) **alveolar 3.** (*fonet.*) **alveolar**.

alveolíte, *s.f.* (*patol.*) **alveolitis**.

alvéolo, *s.m.* **alveolus** (*pl.* alveoli): — *di dente*, **alveolus** (*o* tooth-socket).

Alvèrnia, *no.pr.f.* (*geog.*) **Auvergne**.

alvíno, *ag.* (*anat.*) **alvine**.

Alvíse, *no.pr.m.* **Lewis**.

àlvo, *s.m.* **belly; abdomen; womb**.

alzàia, *s.f.* **1. tow(ing-)line; hawser, hauling; warping (line) 2.** (*strada*) **towing-path**.

alzaménto, *s.m.* **lifting, raising, heaving**.

alzàna, *V.* alzàia **1.**

alzàre, *v.t.* **1. to lift** (up), **to raise**; (*a fatica*) **to heave**: — *le carte*, to cut cards; — *le mani al cielo*, to lift up one's hands; — *gli occhi*, to raise one's eyes (*o* to look up); — *pesi*, to lift (*o* to heave) weights; — *un prezzo*, to raise (*o* to increase) a price; — *il sipario*, to raise the curtain; — *la voce*, to raise one's voice; — *la voce contro qlcu.*, to scold s.o. || — *il gomito*, to drink heavily || — *le mani su qlcu.*, to threaten (*o* to beat) s.o. || — *le spalle*, to shrug one's shoulders || — *il tacco*, to skedaddle (*o* to scurry) **2.** (*costruire*) **to build**; (*erigere*) **to erect**: — *un muro*, to build a wall; — *una statua*, to erect a statue **3.** (*rialzare*) **to heighten**: — *il tetto di una casa*, to heighten the roof of a house **4.** (*mar.*) **to hoist**: — *la bandiera*, to hoist the flag; — *le vele*, to hoist the sails; (*salpare*) to set sails || **alzàrsi**, *v.r.* **1.** (*di vento, sole*) **to rise**: *ora il sole si alza alle quattro*, now the sun rises at four; *il vento si alza*, the wind is rising (*o* the wind begins to blow) **2.** (*in piedi*) **to stand up. to rise to one's feet**: *il pubblico si alzò in piedi*, the audience rose to their feet **3.** (*dal letto*) **to get up**: *a che ora ti alzi di solito?*, at what time do you get up as a rule? **4.** (*crescere in altezza*) **to grow tall**: *il tuo ragazzo si è alzato*, your son has grown tall.

alzàta, *s.f.* **1.** (*l'alzare*) **lifting up, raising**; (*l'alzarsi*) **rise, rising**: *l'* — *del sole*, the rising of the sun || — *d'ingegno*, *fig.* **brain-wave** || — *di scudi*, *fig.* **revolt, rising** ||

— *di spalle,* shrug of the shoulders ‖ *votare per — e seduta,* to vote by rising or remaining seated 2. (*argine*) embankment; river-bank 3. (*arch.*) elevation 4. (*di carte*) cut 5. (*centro tavola*) epergne, centre-piece 6. (*mec.*) (*della valvola*) lift.

alzàto, *ag.* up, out of bed: *la finestra è alzata,* the (sash-)window is up; *non è ancora alzata,* she is not up yet (*o* she is still in bed).

alzatóre, *s.m.* riser.

alzàvola, *s.f.* (*ornit.*) teal (*pl.* teal, teals).

àlzo, *s.m.* (*di fucile*) rear sight, back sight; (*di cannone*) elevating arc.

amàbile, *ag.* 1. amiable, lovable 2. (*di bevanda*) sweet: *vino* —, sweet wine.

amabilità, *s.f.* amiability, lovableness.

amabilménte, *ag.* amiably, kindly.

amàca, *s.f.* hammock.

Amadígi, *no.pr.m.* (*lett.*) Amadis.

amadríade, *s.f.* (*mit. zool.*) hamadryad.

amàlgama, *s.m.* 1. (*chim.*) amalgam 2. amalgamation.

amalgamàre, *v.t.* 1. (*chim.*) to amalgamate 2. to mix; to amalgamate; to combine.

Amàlia, *no.pr.f.* Amalia, Amelia ‖ *dim.* Millie.

amànte, *ag.* loving, fond, keen: — *della pesca,* fond of fishing; *non è molto* — *della musica,* she is not very keen on music ‖ *s.m.* lover ‖ *s.f.* mistress, lover.

amanuènse, *s.m.* amanuensis (*pl.* amanuenses); copyist, scribe.

amàraco, *s.m.* (*bot.*) sweet marjoram.

amaraménte, *av.* bitterly: *pentirsi* —, to repent bitterly; *piangere* —, to shed bitter tears.

amarantíno, *ag.* amaranthine.

amarànto, *ag.* amaranth ‖ *s.m.* (*bot.*) amaranth.

amaràsca, *s.f.* (*bot.*) egriot.

amarascàto, *ag.* (*di vino*) flavoured with egriot juice.

amaraschíno, *s.m.* maraschino.

amaràsco, *s.m.* (*bot.*) wild-cherry tree.

amàre, *v.t.* 1. to love, to be in love with (s.o.): *l'ama alla follia,* he loves her to distraction; *farsi — da qlcu.,* to win s.o.'s love (*o* affection) 2. to be fond of (s.o., sthg.); to like; to care for (s.o., sthg.): *amo molto la musica,* I am very fond of (*o* I like *o* I delight in) music; — *fare ql.co.,* to like to do sthg. (*o* doing sthg.) 3. (*richiedere*) to require: *quest'albero ama il terreno sassoso,* this tree requires a stony soil.

amareggiàre, *v.t.* 1. to make bitter; *fig.* to embitter 2. (*rattristare*) to sadden, to grieve ‖ **amareggiàrsi,** *v.r.* 1. (*addolorarsi*) to grieve 2. (*torturarsi*) to fret.

amarèna, *s.f.* (*bot.*) sour black cherry.

amarèno, *s.m.* (*bot.*) black cherry tree.

amarétto, *s.m.* rather bitter ‖ *s.m.* (*biscotto*) macaroon.

amarézza, *s.f.* 1. bitterness; *fig.* bitterness, embitterment 2. (*dolore*) sorrow, sadness 3. (*risentimento*) resentment.

amaríccio, *ag.* bitterish.

amàrico, *s.m.* Amharic.

amarílli, *s.f.* (*bot.*) amaryllis ‖ **Amarílli,** *no.pr.f.* (*poes.*) Amaryllis.

amaritúdine, *s.f.* (*letter.*) bitterness.

amàro, *ag.* bitter; *fig.* bitter, painful: — *come il veleno,* as bitter as hell; *amare lacrime,* bitter tears; *boccone* —, bitter pill; *ironia amara,* biting irony; *avere la bocca amara,* to have a bitter taste in one's mouth ‖ *s.m.* 1. bitter taste 2. (*rancore*) grudge, resentment 3. (*liquore*) bitters (*pl.*).

amarógnolo, *ag.* bitterish.

amàrra, *s.f.* (*mar.*) moorings (*pl.*), hawser.

amarràre, *v.t.* (*mar.*) to moor.

amarúme, *s.m.* 1. bitter matter 2. *fig.* (*animosità, malanimo*) animosity, ill-will, grudge.

amàta, *s.f.* darling, beloved, sweetheart.

amàto, *ag.* beloved‖ *s.m.* darling, beloved, sweetheart.

amatóre, *s.m.* 1. lover 2. (*chi si occupa d'arte per diletto*) amateur; (*chi si occupa d'arte superficialmente*) dilettante (*pl.* dilettanti).

amatòrio, *ag.* amatory.

amatríce, *s.f.* lover.

amauròsi, *s.f.* (*patol.*) amaurosis.

amauròtico, *ag.* (*patol.*) amaurotic.

amàzzone, *s.f.* 1. (*mit.*) Amazon 2. (*donna che cavalca*) lady rider 3. *fig.* masculine woman, amazon 4. (*costume femminile per equitazione*) (lady's) riding-habit.

amazzònio, *ag.* Amazonian.

ambàgi, *s.f.pl.* circomlocutions, ambages: *senza* —, plainly.

ambascería, *s.f.* 1. embassy 2. (*missione diplomatica*) diplomatic mission.

ambàscia, *s.f.* 1. breathlessness 2. (*gravissima afflizione*) anguish, pain, agony.

ambasciàta, *s.f.* 1. (*ufficio e sede di ambasciatore*) embassy 2. (*messaggio*) message: *fare un'*—, to bring (*o* to give) a message.

ambasciatóre, *s.m.* 1. ambassador 2. (*messaggero*) messenger ‖ — *non porta pena, prov.* don't blame the announcer of bad news.

ambasciatòrio, *ag.* ambassadorial.

ambasciatríce, *s.f.* ambassadress.

ambedúe, *ag.pron.* **both:** *vi vidi* —, I saw both of you (*o* you both).

ambiàre, *v.i.* (*ippica*) to amble.

ambiatúra, *s.f.* (*ippica*) amble.

ambidèstro, *ag.* 1. ambidextrous, ambidexter 2. *fig.* (*astuto, scaltro*) sly, cunning.

ambientàle, *ag.* ambient: *condizioni ambientali,* environment conditions; *mutamenti ambientali,* changes in environment.

ambientàre, *v.t.* 1. to acclimatize, to adapt 2. (*personaggio, fatto, ecc.*) to place: *cercare di* — *il luogo in cui Cesare morì,* to try to place the spot where Caesar died ‖ **ambientàrsi,** *v.t.* to get used to the place, to grow accustomed to the place.

ambiènte, *ag.* ambient: *temperatura* —, ambient (*o* room) temperature ‖ *s.m.* 1. ambient 2. *fig.* environment; milieu; sphere; surroundings (*pl.*); (*influenze ambientali*) ambience: — *storico,* historical milieu; *fuori del suo* — *è come un pesce fuor d'acqua,* out of his environment (*o* sphere) he is like a fish out of water 3. (*stanza*) room; (*luogo*) place.

ambiguaménte, *av.* ambiguously, equivocally.

ambiguità, *s.f.* ambiguousness, ambiguity, equivocalness.

ambíguo, *ag.* 1. (*di persona*) queer, shady 2. (*di discorso, linguaggio*) ambiguous, equivocal, obscure.

àmbio, *s.m.* (*ippica*) amble.

ambíre, *v.t.i.* to desire (sthg.); to long for (sthg., to do), to be longing for (sthg.), to aim at (sthg.), to lust for (sthg.).

àmbito, *s.m.* 1. (*spazio circoscritto*) ambit, precincts (*pl.*) 2. *fig.* sphere, ambit 3. (*limiti*) limits (*pl.*): *entro l'*— *della legge,* within the limits of the law.

ambivalènte, *ag.* ambivalent.

ambivalènza, *s.* ambivalence.

ambizióne, *s.f.* ambition: *l'*— *di brillare,* the ambition to shine; — *di popolarità,* hankering after popularity; *divorato dall'*—, eaten up with ambition; *senza* —, unambitious(ly); *egli aveva delle grandi ambizioni,* he had great ambitions.

ambiziosàggine, *s.f.* foolish ambition.

ambiziosaménte, *av.* ambitiously.

ambizióso, *ag.* ambitious.

àmbo, *ag.pron.* **both:** — *i sessi,* both sexes.

àmbo, *s.m.* "ambo" (two numbers drawn at a lottery) ‖ *che bell'*—*!, fig.* what a nice couple!.

ambóne, *s.m.* (*arch.*) ambo (*pl.* ambos, ambones).

àmbra, *s.f.* 1. amber ‖ *chiaro come l'*—, *fig.* as clear as daylight 2. — *grigia,* ambergris.

ambracàne, *s.m.* ambergris.

ambràto, *ag.* 1. amber-coloured 2. (*odoroso d'ambra*) amber-scented.

Ambrògio, *no.pr.m.* Ambrose.

ambròsia, *s.f.* ambrosia.

ambrosiàno, *ag.* **1.** (*eccl.*) Ambrosian: *inno* —, Ambrosian chant **2.** (*milanese*) Milanese ‖ *s.m.* Milanese.

ambròsio, *ag.* ambrosial; divinely fragrant; divine.

ambulàcro, *s.m.* ambulatory.

ambulànte, *ag.* strolling, itinerant: *fruttivendolo, pescivendolo* —, coster, costermonger; *suonatore* —, street -musician; *venditore* —, pedlar (*o* huckster *o* hawker) (*o amer.* pitchman) ‖ *biblioteca* —, *fig.* walking encyclopaedia; *cadavere* —, *fig.* walking ghost ‖ *s.m.* (*vagone postale*) mail-coach.

ambulànza, *s.f.* **1.** (*mil.*) ambulance **2.** (*ambulatorio*) casualty department; surgery; first aid station **3.** (*autoambulanza*) ambulance (car).

ambulatòrio, *ag.* deambulatory ‖ *s.m.* **1.** (*luogo dove si passeggia*) ambulatory, deambulatory **2.** (*ambulanza*) casualty department; surgery; first aid station.

Ambúrgo, *no.pr.f.* (*geog.*) Hamburg.

amèba, *s.f.* (*biol.*) amoeba (*pl.* amoebas, amoebae).

amebèo, *ag.* (*poes.*) amoebæan, amebean.

amebíasi, *s.f.* (*patol.*) amoebiasis, amebism.

ameboìde, *ag.* amoeboid, amoebic.

Amedèo, *no.pr.m.* Amadeus.

Amèlia, *no.pr.f.* Amelia ‖ *dim.* Millie.

àmen, *s.m.* amen ‖ *in un* —, in a tick.

amenaménte, *av.* agreeably, pleasantly, amusingly.

amenità, *s.f.* **1.** pleasantness, agreeableness, amenity **2.** (*facezia*) pleasantry, joke.

amèno, *ag.* **1.** pleasant, pleasing, agreeable, delightful: *luogo* —, pleasant spot **2.** (*divertente*) amusing, funny: *tipo* —, (*scherz.*) funny chap.

amenorrèa, *s.f.* (*patol.*) amenorrhoea.

amentàceo, *ag.* (*bot.*) amentaceous.

amènto, *s.m.* (*bot.*) amentum (*pl.* amenta); ament.

amènza, *s.f.* (*patol.*) amentia, dementia.

americàna, *s.f.* (*spor.*) cycle relay-race.

americanàta, *s.f.* show-off.

americanísmo, *s.m.* Americanism.

americanizzàrsi, *v.r.* to Americanize.

americàno, *ag.* American ‖ *s.m.* **1.** American; U.S. citizen **2.** (*aperitivo*) kind of vermouth.

amerício, *s.m.* (*chim.*) americium.

Amerígo, *no.pr.m.* Amerigo.

ametìsta, *s.f.* (*min.*) amethyst.

ametistína, *s.f.* (*bot.*) amethystine.

ametistíno, *ag.* amethystine.

amfíbolo, *V.* **anfíbolo.**

amiànto, *s.f.*◦(*min.*) amiant(h)us, asbestos.

amíca, *s.f.* friend; woman friend; lady friend; girl friend: *invita tutte le tue amiche al nostro tè*, ask all your girl friends to our tea-party.

amicaménte, *av.* in a friendly way.

amicàrsi, *v.r.* (*diventare amico di*) to make friends with (s.o.), to become friends with (s.o.): — *qlcu.*, to gain s.o.'s friendship.

amichévole, *ag.* friendly: *accoglienza* —, friendly welcome (*o* friendly reception) ‖ *all'*—, without ceremony (*o* in a friendly way).

amichevolménte, *av.* in a friendly way, friendly.

amicízia, *s.f.* **1.** friendship; amity: *coltivare un'*—, to cultivate a friendship; *dire ql.co. in* —, to tell sthg. in confidence; *fare* — *con qlcu.*, to make friends with s.o.; *guastare un'*—, to spoil a friendship ‖ *patti chiari* — *lunga*, *prov.* clear understanding breeds long friendship **2.** *pl.* (*amici*) friends: *hai molte amicizie?*, have you many friends?

amíco, *ag.* **1.** friendly; (*affezionato*) devoted: *famiglia amica*, friendly family; *nazione amica*, friendly nation **2.** (*propizio*) favourable, propitious: *le stelle non erano amiche*, the planets were not propitious.

amíco, *s.m.* friend, man friend; boy friend: — *del cuore*, bosom-friend; — *di casa*, old friend; — *di famiglia*, family friend; *siamo grandi amici*, (*fam.*) we are great pals; *agire da* —, to act as a friend; *diventare* — *di qlcu.*, to make friends with s.o.; *essere* —

della lettura, to be fond of reading; *essere* — *dell'ordine*, to be a lover of order; *fingersi* —, to feign friendship ‖ *l'*—, (*scherz.*) that fellow (*o* our fellow) ‖ *l'* — *di tutti non è* — *di nessuno*, *prov.* everybody's friend is nobody's friend ‖ *gli amici si riconoscono nelle avversità*, *prov.* a friend in need is a friend indeed.

amicóne, *s.m.* chum, pal; (*amer.*) buddy.

amidàceo, *ag.* starchy.

àmido, *s.m.* starch: — *di riso*, rice starch ‖ *colla d'*—, starch paste.

amígdala, *s.f.* (*anat.*) tonsil.

amigdalíte, *s.f.* (*patol.*) tonsillitis.

Amílcare, *no.pr.m.* (*st.*) Hamilcar.

amilopsína, *s.f.* (*chim.*) amylopsin.

aminoàcido, *s.m.* (*chim.*) amino-acid.

amissíbile, *ag.* amissible, liable to be lost.

amistà, *s.f.* (*poet.*) friendship; amity.

amítto, *s.m.* (*eccl.*) amice.

Amlèto, *no.pr.m.* (*lett.*) Hamlet.

ammaccaménto, *V.* **ammaccatúra.**

ammaccàre, *v.t.* to bruise, to contuse; (*acciaccare*) to bruise; to dent; to crush.

ammaccatúra, *s.f.* bruise; (*acciaccamento*) crush.

ammaestràbile, *ag.* **1.** trainable **2.** (*di animale feroce*) tamable.

ammaestraménto, *s.m.* **1.** (*addestramento*) training **2.**(*insegnamento*)teaching **3.**(*di animali feroci*) taming.

ammaestràre, *v.t.* **1.** (*addestrare*) to train **2.** (*insegnare a*) to teach, to instruct **3.** (*animali feroci*) to tame.

ammaestratívo, *ag.* instructive.

ammaestràto, *ag.* **1.** trained: *cane* —, trained dog **2.** (*di animale feroce*) tame: *leone* —, tame lion.

ammaestratóre, *s.m.* **1.** trainer **2.** (*domatore*) tamer.

ammagliàre, *v.t.* to cord, to bind up as by netting.

ammainàre, *v.t.* **1.** to lower, to strike, to furl: — *la bandiera*, to lower (*o* to haul down) the flag; — *le vele*, to strike the sails **2.** *fig.* (*desistere da*) to give up, to withdraw from (sthg.), to renounce.

ammalàre, *v.i.*, **ammalàrsi**, *v.r.* to fall ill, to be taken ill: *ella si ammalò seriamente*, she was taken seriously ill.

ammalàto, *ag.* ill (*gener. predicativo*); sick (*gener. attributivo*); diseased (anche *fig.*): *bimbo* —, sick child; *organi ammalati*, diseased organs; *è* — *di corpo e di spirito*, he is diseased in body and mind; *sei* —?, are you ill? ‖ *s.m.* **1.** sick person: *curare un* —, to nurse a sick man **2.** (*cliente di medico*) patient.

ammalazzàre, *v.i.*, **ammalazzàrsi**, *v.r.* to get sickly.

ammaliàre, *v.t.* to bewitch; to charm; to fascinate.

ammaliatóre, *ag.* charming; fascinating; bewitching: *modi ammaliatori*, fascinating manners; *occhi ammaliatori*, bewitching eyes; *sorriso* —, charming smile ‖ *s.m.* charmer, fascinating man; seducer.

ammaliatríce, *s.f.* fascinating woman; bewitcher.

ammalinconíre, *v.t.* to make melancholy ‖ **ammalinconírsi**, *v.r.* to become sad, to become melancholy.

ammaliziàre, *V.* **ammalizzíre.**

ammaliziàto, *ag.* cunning, artful.

ammalizzíre, *v.t.* to make cunning ‖ *v.i.* to grow cunning, to become artful, to sharpen one's wits.

ammaltàre, *v.t.* to mortar.

ammàmmolàto, *ag.* sleepy; drowsy.

ammànco, *s.m.* (*comm.*) shortage: — *di cassa*, deficit; — *di peso*, shortage of weight; *colmare un* —, to refund a deficit.

ammandorlàto, *ag.* lozenged, lozenge-shaped.

ammanettàre, *v.t.* to handcuff.

ammanieràre, *v.t.* to embellish, to ornament.

ammanieràto, *ag.* affected, artificial; mannered.

ammannàre, *v.t.* (*agr.*) to sheave; to bind in sheaves.

ammannellàre, *v.t.* to wind into skeins.

ammanniménto, *s.m.* preparation; (*cuc.*) dressing.

ammanníre, *v.t.* to prepare; (*cuc.*) to dress: — *il pranzo*, to get dinner ready.

ammansàre, **ammansíre**, *v.t.* **1.** (*addomesticare*) to domesticate, to tame **2.** *fig.* to calm, to appease, to placate ‖ **ammansàrsi, ammansírsi**, *v.r.* **1.** to become tame **2.** *fig.* to calm down, to become calm, to be appeased.

ammantàre, *v.t.* **1.** to mantle; to cover **2.** *fig.* to conceal, to cloak, to disguise, to wrap up ‖ **ammantàrsi**, *v.r.* to put on a mantle, to be covered (with sthg.): *i prati si ammantano di fiori*, meadows are covering with flowers.

ammantatúra, *s.f.* **1.** covering **2.** (*letter.*) mantle, cloak.

ammantellàre, *v.t.* **1.** to cloak, to cast a cloak over (s.o., sthg.) **2.** *fig.* to disguise, to shield.

ammànto, *s.m.* (*letter.*) mantle, cloak.

ammaràggio, *s.m.* (*aer.*) alighting on water.

ammaràre, *v.i.* (*aer.*) to alight on water.

ammarezzàre, *v.t.* to water; to mottle.

ammarezzatúra, *s.f.* **1.** (*atto*) watering **2.** (*effetto*) watered effect; moiré.

ammarinàre, *v.t.* to man (a ship).

ammassaménto, *s.m.* heap, mass, accumulation.

ammassàre, *v.t.* **1.** to amass, to heap, to hoard up **2.** (*accumulare*) to accumulate ‖ **ammassàrsi**, *v.r.* **1.** (*affollarsi*) to crowd together **2.** (*accumularsi*) to accumulate.

ammassicciàre, *v.t.* **1.** to make solid and compact **2.** (*strada, ecc.*) to ballast ‖ **ammassicciàrsi**, *v.r.* to become solid, to become massive.

ammassicciàto, *s.m.* ballasting.

ammàsso, *s.m.* **1.** heap, mass, pile, hoard (of goods): — *del grano*, corn pool **2.** (*amm.*) government pool.

ammatassàre, *v.t.* to wind into skeins.

ammattàre, *v.t.* (*gergo mar.*) to rig, to equip.

ammattiménto, *s.m.* *fig.* trouble, annoyance; nuisance.

ammattíre, *v.i.* **1.** to go mad: *non farmi* —*!*, don't drive me mad! **2.** (*stillarsi il cervello*) to puzzle one's brains; to rack one's brains.

ammattonaménto, *s.m* brick paving.

ammattonàre, *v.t.* to pave with bricks.

ammattonàto, *s.m.* brick floor, brick pavement.

ammattonatúra, *s.f.* brick paving.

ammazzaménto, *s.m.* killing; murder; slaughter.

ammazzàre, *v.t.* **1.** to kill (anche *fig.*); (*assassinare*) to slaughter, to murder: *egli ammazzò il suo nemico*, he killed his enemy; *l'emozione lo ha ammazzato*, the shock killed him ‖ — *il tempo*, to kill time **2.** (*mortificare*) to mortify; (*opprimere*) to overpower, to overwhelm: *il caldo mi ammazza*, heat overpowers me; *certi metodi d'insegnamento ammazzano l'ingegno*, some teaching methods mortify the intellect ‖ **ammazzàrsi**, *v.r.* **1.** (*suicidarsi*) to kill oneself, to commit suicide ‖ — *di lavoro*, *fig.* to overwork, to work oneself to death **2.** (*rimanere ucciso*) to get killed: *si ammazzò in uno scontro*, he got killed in a crash.

ammazzasètte, *s.m.* braggart; bully.

ammazzatóio, *s.m.* slaughter-house; shambles (*pl.*).

ammazzatóre, *s.m.* killer, slaughterer, murderer.

ammazzolàre, *v.t.* to make bunches of (sthg.); to make bouquets of (sthg.).

ammelmàre, *v.t.* to bespatter with mud ‖ **ammelmàrsi**, *v.r.* to bespatter oneself with mud.

ammenàre, *v.t.* to strike, to hit.

ammencíre, *v.t.* to make flabby ‖ **ammencírsi**, *v.r.* to become flabby.

ammènda, *s.f.* **1.** (*riparazione*) amends (*pl.*): *fare* — *di ql.co.*, to make amends for sthg. **2.** (*dir.*) reparation, compensation **3.** (*multa*) fine, penalty.

ammendaménto, *s.m.* amendment, correction.

ammendàre, *v.t.* to amend, to correct ‖ **ammendàrsi**, *v.r.* to amend oneself, to correct oneself.

ammennicolo, *s.m.* **1.** (*aggeggio*) gadget, jigger **2.** (*fronzolo*) trinket, gewgaw **3.** (*cavillo*) cavil; (*pretesto*) pretext; (*inezia*) trifle **4.** (*dir.*) adminicle.

amméttere, *v.t.* **1.** (*introdurre, lasciar entrare*) to admit, to receive: — *in società*, (*comm.*) to take into partnership; — *qlcu. a corte*, to receive s.o. at Court; — *qlcu. nella Chiesa*, to receive s.o. into the Church; *essere ammesso all'accademia, in un club*, to be admitted to the Academy, to a club ‖ *i cani, i bambini, non sono ammessi*, dogs, children, not admitted **2.** (*accettare*) to admit, to grant: *ammesso ciò*, granting this (*o* in that case); *la tua domanda è stata ammessa*, your request has been granted (*o* accepted) **3.** (*concedere, supporre*) to admit, to concede, to grant, to acknowledge, to suppose: *ammesso che...*, suppose (*o* in the case) that...; *ammettendo che egli non parta subito*, supposing he should not leave at once; *ammettiamo pure che tu abbia ragione*, let us grant you are right; *ammetto che fu una buona idea*, I admit it was a good idea; *lo ammetto*, I admit it **4.** (*tollerare*) to allow, to suffer: *non* — *interruzioni*, to suffer no interruptions.

ammezzaménto, *s.m.* halving.

ammezzàre, *v.t.* **1.** to halve: — *una bottiglia*, (*riempirla a metà*) to fill half a bottle; (*vuotarla a metà*) to empty half a bottle **2.** (*pronunziare male*) to half utter; to stop in the middle of (a word).

ammezzàto, *s.m.* (*arch.*) mezzanine.

ammezzíre, *v.i.*, **ammezzírsi**, *v.r.* to become over-ripe.

ammiceàre, *v.i.* to wink (at s.o.).

ammíceo, *s.m.* wink.

ammídi, *s.f.pl.* (*chim.*) amides.

ammína, *s.f.* (*chim.*) amine.

amminícolo *V.* **ammennícolo.**,

amministràre, *v.t.* **1.** to manage, to direct: — *una azienda*, to manage a business (*o fam.* to run a business); — *un paese*, to run a country; — *una scuola*, to run a school **2.** (*dir. eccl.*) to administer: — *la giustizia* to administer justice; — *i Sacramenti*, to administer the Sacraments.

amministrativaménte, *av.* administratively.

amministratívo, *ag.* administrative: *anno* —, financial year; *dettagli d'ordine* —, administrative details; *divisione amministrativa* (*dello Stato*), administrative division (of the State).

amministratóre, *s.m.* **1.** manager, director: — *delegato*, managing director **2.** (*di beni privati*) administrator.

amministratríce, *s.f.* **1.** manageress **2.** administratrix (*pl.* administratrices).

amministrazióne, *s.f.* administration, management: *cattiva* —, mismanagement; *consiglio d'*—, board of directors; *entrare nell'*— *civile*, to enter the civil service (*o* to become a civil servant).

amminoàcidi, *s.m.pl.* (*chim.*) amino-acids.

ammiràbile, *ag.* admirable, wonderful.

ammirabilménte, *av.* admirably, wonderfully.

ammiràglia, *ag.* (*mar.*) admiral ‖ *s.f.* (*mar.*) admiral (-ship); flag-ship.

ammiragliàto, *s.m.* **1.** Admiralty **2.** (*ufficio di ammiraglio*) admiralship.

ammiràglio, *s.m.* admiral: — *d'Armata*, Admiral of the Fleet; *l'*— *Nelson*, Admiral Nelson; *contr'*—, Rear-Admiral; *grande* —, Chief (*o* High) Admiral; *vice* —, Vice-Admiral.

ammiràndo, *ag.* admirable.

ammiràre, *v.t.* to admire: *perfino i suoi nemici lo ammirano*, even his enemies admire him.

ammirativaménte, *av.* admiringly.

ammiratívo, *ag.* admiring.

ammiratóre, *s.m.*, **ammiratríce**, *s.f.* admirer; lover; (*di attore, cantante, campione sportivo, ecc.*) fan: *corrispondenza inviata dagli ammiratori*, fan mail.

ammirazióne, *s.f.* admiration.

ammirévole, *ag.* admirable: *contegno* — *per la sua dignità*, behaviour admirable for its dignity.

ammiseríre, *v.t.* to impoverish.

ammissíbile, *ag.* admissible; allowable.

ammissibilità, *s.f.* admissibility.

ammissióne, *s.f.* **1.** admission, admittance: *esame di* —, entrance examination: *esame di* — *all'università*, university entrance examination; *norme per l'*—, conditions for admittance; *tassa di* —, entrance fee **2.** (*dir.*) acknowledgment, admission **3.** (*mec.*) admission, induction: *tubo di* —, induction pipe.

ammobiliaménto, *s.m.* furnishing; (*mobilio*) furniture.

ammobiliàre, *v.t.* to furnish.

ammobiliàto, *ag.* furnished: *camere ammobiliate,* furnished rooms.

ammodernaménto, *s.m.* modernization, modernizing.

ammodernàre, *v.t.* to modernize.

ammodíno, *av.* (*con garbo*) gently, nicely; properly; (*con cura*) with care.

ammòdo, *ag.* (*garbato*) nice, well-bred; proper; (*discreto*) prudent, discreet; (*onesto*) honest ǁ *av.* (*con garbo*) gently, nicely; properly; (*con cura*) with care.

ammogliàre, *v.t.* to give a wife to (s.o.), to match ǁ **ammogliàrsi,** *v.r.* to marry, to get married (to s.o.).

ammogliàto, *ag.* married ǁ *s.m.* married man.

ammoinàre, *v.t.* to cajole.

ammollaménto, *s.f.* drenching, soaking.

ammollàre, *v.t.* **1.** (*inzuppare*) to drench, to soak **2.** (*ammorbidire*) to soften **3.** (*allentare*) to slack, to slacken ǁ — *uno schiaffo a qlcu.,* to slap s.o.'s face ǁ **ammollàrsi,** *v.r.* **1.** (*inzupparsi*) to get soaked **2.** (*ammorbidirsi*) to become soft **3.** (*allentarsi*) to slacken.

ammolliènte, *ag. s.m.* (*farm.*) emollient.

ammolliménto, *s.m.* softening.

ammollíre, *v.t.* **1.** to soften **2.** *fig.* to appease, to soothe, to soften, to mollify ǁ **ammollírsi,** *v.r.* to mellow, to soften (anche *fig.*).

ammoníaca, *s.f.* (*chim.*) ammonia.

ammoniacàle, *ag.* (*chim.*) ammoniacal.

ammoniacàto, *ag.* (*chim.*) ammoniated.

ammoníaco, *ag.* (*chim.*) ammoniac.

ammoniménto, *s.m.* admonition, admonishment; (*rimprovero*) reproof; (*avvertimento, consiglio*) warning; (*esortazione*) exhortation: *questo ti serva di* —, may this be a warning (*o* a lesson) to you.

ammònio, *s.m.* (*chim.*) ammonium: *carbonato d'*—, ammonium carbonate; *solfato d'*—, ammonium sulphate.

ammoníre, *v.t.* to admonish; (*avvertire*) to warn; (*esortare*) to exhort.

ammoníte, *s.f.* (*paleont.*) ammonite.

ammonitóre, *s.m.,* **ammonitríce,** *s.f.* warner.

ammonizióne, *s.f.* admonition; (*rimprovero*) reproof; (*avvertimento*) warning.

ammontaménto, *s.m.* heaping up.

ammontàre, *s.m.* (*comm.*) amount: — *esatto,* exact amount; — *lordo,* gross amount; — *presunto,* amount expected; *per l'* — *netto,* for net amount.

ammontàre, *v.t.* to heap ǁ *v.i.* to amount: *a quanto ammonta il mio debito?,* how much does my debt amount to? ǁ **ammontàrsi,** *v.r.* to gather, to collect.

ammonticchiàre, *v.t.* to heap up, to pile up ǁ **ammonticchiàrsi,** *v.r.* **1.** to pile up **2.** (*affollarsi*) to crowd (together), to crowd up.

ammorbaménto, ¦*s.m.* infection, infecting, tainting.

ammorbàre, *v.t.* **1.** to infect, to taint **2.** (*corrompere*) to corrupt, to taint **3.** (*aria, ecc.*) to make (sthg.) stink ǁ *v.i.* (*ammalarsi*) to get ill, to fall sick.

ammorbidiménto, *s.m.* softening.

ammorbidíre, *v.t.* to soften (anche *fig.*) ǁ **ammorbidírsi,** *v.r.* to grow soft, to soften.

ammorchiàto, *ag.* dreggy, slimy.

ammorsàre, *v.t.* **1.** (*stringere con una morsa*) to vice **2.** (*mordere*) to bite.

ammorsàto, *ag.* (*arch.*) toothing (*attributivo*).

ammorsatúra, *s.f.* (*arch.*) toothing-stone.

ammorsellàto, *s.m.* (*cuc.*) meat-hash.

ammortaménto, *s.m.* (*comm.*) amortization, redemption; depreciation: — *di un debito,* redemption (*o* extinction) of a debt; *fondo di* —, sinking-fund; *quota di* —, depreciation allowance.

ammortàre, *v.t.* **1.** to deaden, to mortify **2.** (*comm.*) to amortize, to redeem, to pay off.

ammortiménto, *s.m.* **1.** complete numbness, deadening **2.** (*mortificazione*) mortification.

ammortíre, *v.t.* **1.** to numb, to deaden; (*indebolire* to weaken **2.** (*smorzare, attutire*) to soothe: — *la ca‾duta,* to break the fall.

ammortizzàbile, *ag.* (*comm.*) amortizable, redeemable.

ammortizzaménto, *V.* **ammortaménto.**

ammortizzàre, *V.* **ammortàre 2.**

ammortizzatóre, *s.m.* (*mec.*) shock-absorber.

ammortizzazióne, *V.* **ammortaménto.**

ammorzaménto, *s.m.* (*di luce, calore, energia*) weakening, diminishing; extinction.

ammorzàre, *v.t.* **1.** to weaken; (*luce*) to dim; to extinguish **2.** *fig.* to calm, to allay.

ammosciàre, ammoscíre, *v.i.* to become flabby, to droop; (*avvizzire*) to wither (up).

ammostàre, *v.t.* to press (grapes) ǁ *v.i.* to yield must.

ammostatóre, *s.m.* wine-presser.

ammostatúra, *s.f.* pressing of grapes.

ammucchiaménto, *s.m.* **1.** (*mucchio*) mound, heap; pile **2.** (*l'ammucchiare*) heaping, piling up.

ammucchiàre, *v.t.* to heap; (*con ordine*) to pile up ǁ **ammucchiàrsi,** *v.r.* to pile up; (*affollarsi*) to throng (together), to crowd (together).

ammuffíre, *v.i.* to grow musty, to get mouldy ǁ — *in casa, fig.* to languish at home (*o* to live in seclusion).

ammulinàre, *v.t.* to revolve rapidly, to whirl ǁ *v.i.* to whirl.

ammutinaménto, *s.m.* mutiny.

ammutinàre, *v.t.* to cause to mutiny, to incite to mutiny ǁ **ammutinàrsi,** *v.r.* to mutiny, to revolt, to break into mutiny, to rise in arms.

ammutinàto, *ag.* mutinous.

ammutinatóre, *s.m.* mutineer.

ammutíre, ammutolíre, *v.i.* to become dumb; (*essere ridotto al silenzio*) to be struck dumb ǁ *v.t.* to strike dumb, to dumbfound; (*far tacere*) to silence, to hush.

amnesía, *s.f.* amnesia, loss of memory.

àmnio, *s.m.* (*biol.*) amnion (*pl.* amnia).

amnistía, *s.f.* amnesty: *legge di* —, act of oblivion.

amnistiàre, *v.t.* to amnesty, to give amnesty to (s.o.).

amnistiàto, *s.m.* person included in an amnesty.

àmo, *s.m.* **1.** fish-hook: *abboccare, mordere all'*—, to bite at the hook (anche *fig.*); *prendere all'* —, to hook: *prendere all'* — *un marito, fig.* to hook a husband **2.** (*esca*) bait; (*inganno*) deceit.

amoèrre, amoèrro, *s.m.* moire.

amòmo, *s.m.* (*bot.*) amomum.

amoràle, *ag.* amoral.

amoràzzo, *s.m.* love-affair, intrigue, amour.

amóre, *s.m.* **1.** love; tenderness, devotion: — *platonico,* Platonic love; *il fare all'*—, love-making; *la sposò per* —, he married her for love; *fare all'* — *con qlcu.,* to make love to s.o. (*o* to court s.o.); *soffrire di mal d'*—, to be love-sick ǁ — *di sè,* selfishness; — *proprio,* self-respect (*o* self-esteem) ǁ *Amore, (mit.)* Cupid **2.** (*carità*) charity **3.** (*cosa, persona amata*) beloved, darling; sweetheart: — *mio,* my beloved (*o* my darling) **4.** (*cosa, persona graziosa*) darling: *quel bambino è un* —, that child is a darling; *quel quadro è un* —, that painting is a beauty **5.** (*zelo*) enthusiasm; zeal: *con* —, heartily (*o* willingly): *egli studia con* —, he studies with enthusiasm **6.** *per* — *di,* for the sake of: *per* — *di brevità,* for the sake of brevity; *per* — *di Dio,* for God's sake; *per* — *mio,* for my sake ǁ *per* — *o per forza,* willy-nilly (*o* by hook or by crook).

amoreggiaménto, *s.m.* love-making, flirtation.

amoreggiàre, *v.i.* to flirt: — *con qlcu.,* to flirt with s.o.

amorétto, *s.m.* flirtation, amourette, passing fancy.

amorévole, *ag.* loving.

amorevolézza, *s.f.* **1.** lovingness; (*gentilezza*) loving-kindness **2.** (*dono in segno d'affetto*) love-token.

amorevolménte, *av.* lovingly.

amorfía, *s.f.* (*scient.*) amorphousness, amorphism.

amòrfo, *ag.* amorphous.

amoríno, *s.m.* 1. (*Cupido*) Cupid 2. (*bambino grazioso*) little darling 3. (*bot.*) mignonette 4. (*divano fatto a S*) S-shaped couch.

amorósa, *s.f.* 1. lover, sweetheart 2. (*teat.*) amorosa.

amorosaménte, *av.* lovingly.

amoróso, *ag.* 1. (*che vuol bene*) loving, affectionate, amorous: *figlio* —, affectionate (*o loving*) son 2. (*d'amore*) amorous: *poesia amorosa,* amorous verse 3. (*mus.*) amoroso ‖ *s.m.* 1. lover, gallant, beau (*pl.* beaux), sweetheart 2. (*teat.*) amoroso.

Àmos, *no.pr.m.* (*Bibbia*) Amos.

amoscíno, *s.m.* (*bot.*) damson.

amovíbile, *ag.* 1. movable, removable 2. (*di funzionario, ecc.*) transferable.

amovibilità, *s.f.* 1. movability, removability 2. (*di funzionario, ecc.*) transferability.

ampelidèe, *s.f.pl.* (*bot.*) Ampelidaceae.

amperàggio, *s.m.* (*elett.*) amperage.

ampère, *s.m.* (*elett.*) ampere.

amperòmetro, *s.m.* (*elett.*) amperometer, ammeter.

ampiaménte, *av.* 1. amply, widely, extensively 2. (*diffusamente*) diffusely.

ampiézza, *s.f.* 1. (*larghezza*) width, wideness; (*di ambiente*) roominess: — *di pensiero,* *fig.* breadth of thought 2. (*abbondanza*) ampleness, abundance, fullness, copiousness 3. (*fis. elett.*) amplitude.

àmpio, *ag.* 1. wide, ample, large; (*spazioso*) spacious, roomy: *un* — *teatro,* a wide theatre 2. (*di abito*) comfortable 3. (*di stile*) copious, abundant, diffuse.

amplessicàule, *ag.* (*bot.*) amplexicaul.

amplèsso, *s.m.* embrace.

ampliaménto, *s.m.* amplification, enlargement; (*aumento*) increase.

ampliàre, *v.t.* 1. to amplify, to enlarge, to extend, to dilate 2. (*aumentare*) to increase ‖ **ampliàrsi,** *v.r.* to become larger, to extend.

ampliatívo, *V.* **amplificatívo.**

amplificàre, *v.t.* 1. to enlarge, to broaden, to expand, to extend; (*fis.*) to amplify 2. (*magnificare con parole*) to amplify; to enhance; to exaggerate.

amplificatívo, *ag.* ampliative, amplifying; (*amer.*) amplificatory: *stile* —, *fig.* diffuse (*o pompous*) style.

amplificatóre, *s.m.* (*rad.*) amplifier: — *di alta frequenza,* high-frequency amplifier; — *di bassa frequenza,* low-frequency amplifier; — *per grammofono,* phonograph-type amplifier.

amplificazióne, *s.f.* 1. (*rad.*) amplification, gain: — *totale,* over-all amplification (*o gain*); *coefficiente di* —, amplification factor 2. development, expansion.

àmplio, *V.* **àmpio.**

amplíssimo, *ag. superl.* very ample, very wide, very large.

amplitúdine, *s.f.* amplitude.

ampólla, *s.f.* 1. phial 2. (*per olio, aceto*) cruet 3. (*eccl.*) ampulla (*pl.* ampullæ) 4. (*elett.*) bulb.

ampollièra, *s.f.* cruet-stand; cruet.

ampollína, *s.f.* (*eccl.*) ampulla (*pl.* ampullæ).

ampollosaménte, *av.* bombastically.

ampollosità, *s.f.* pomposity; exaggeration.

ampollóso, *ag.* enflated, pompous, pretentious; bombastic: *stile* —, bombastic style.

amputàre, *v.t.* (*chir.*) to amputate.

amputazióne, *s.f.* (*chir.*) amputation.

amulèto, *s.m.* amulet; talisman; charm.

anàbasi, *s.f.* (*med.*) anabasis ‖ « *L'Anabasi* », (*lett.*) " The Anabasis ".

anabattísta, *s.m.* (*st. relig.*) Anabaptist.

anabolísmo, *s.m.* (*fisiol.*) anabolism.

anacàrdo, *s.m.* (*bot.*) cashew-tree; cashew-nut.

ànace, *s.f.* (*bot.*) anise: *seme d'*—, aniseed.

anaciàto, *ag.* flavoured with aniseed.

anacíno, *s.m.* aniseed drop.

Anaclèto, *no.pr.m.* Anaclete.

anacolúto, *s.m.* (*gram.*) anacoluthon (*pl.* anacolutha).

anacònda, *s.m.* (*zool.*) anaconda.

anacorèta, *s.m.* anchoret, anchorite; hermit (anche *fig.*).

anacorètico, *ag.* anchoretic; *fig.* solitary.

Anacreónte, *no.pr.m.* (*st. lett.*) Anacreon.

anacreòntica, *s.f.* (*poes.*) Anacreontic (poem).

anacreòntico, *ag.* (*poes.*) Anacreontic.

anacronísmo, *s.m.* anachronism.

anacronístico, *ag.* anachronistic, anachronous.

anacrúsi, *s.f.* (*poes. mus.*) anacrusis (*pl.* anacruses).

anadiomène, *ag.* Anadyomene (*attributivo*).

anadiplòsi, *s.f.* (*ret.*) anadiplosis.

anafilàssi, *s.f.* (*med.*) anaphylaxis.

anàfora, *s.f.* (*ret.*) anaphora.

anagàllide, *s.f.* (*bot.*) scarlet pimpernel.

anàglifo, *s.m.* (*art.*) anaglyph.

anaglíptica, *s.f.* anaglyptics.

anagogía, *s.f.* (*teol.*) anagoge.

anagogicaménte, *av.* (*teol.*) anagogically.

anagògico, *ag.* (*teol.*) anagogic(al).

anàgrafe, *s.f.* registry office, registrar's office ‖ *Ufficio Anagrafe,* General Registry Office.

anagràmma, *s.m.* anagram.

anagrammàre, *v.t.* to anagrammatize.

anagrammaticaménte, *av.* anagrammatically.

anagrammàtico, *ag.* anagrammatic(al).

anagrammísta, *s.c.* anagrammatist.

anagrammatizzàre, *v.t.* to anagrammatize.

analcoòlico, *ag.* soft: *bibita analcoolica,* soft drink.

anàle, *ag.* (*anat.*) anal.

analèttico, *ag.s.m.* (*farm.*) analeptic.

analfabèta, *ag.s.c.* illiterate.

analfabetísmo, *s.m.* illiteracy.

analgesía, *s.f.* (*med.*) analgesia.

analgèsico, *ag.s.m.* (*farm.*) analgetic, analgesic.

anàlisi, *s.f.* 1. analysis (*pl.* analyses); testing: — *del sangue,* blood test ‖ *in ultima* —, after all 2. (*gram.*) parsing; analysis (*pl.* analyses): — *logica,* sentence-analysis; *fare l'*— *di una frase,* to analyse a sentence.

analísta, *s.c.* analyst.

analiticaménte, *av.* analytically.

analítico, *ag.* analytical: *chimica analitica,* analytical chemistry; *lingua analitica,* analytical language.

analizzàre, *v.t.* to analyse (anche *gram.*): — *una frase,* to parse (*o* to analyse) a sentence.

analizzatóre, *s.m.* (*chim.*) analyst; (*mec.*) analyser.

analogaménte, *av.* analogously; likewise.

analogía, *s.f.* analogy: — *con, tra,* analogy with, between; *per* — *con...,* on the analogy of...; *ragionare per* —, to argue from analogy.

analogicaménte, *av.* analogically.

analògico, *ag.* analogic(al).

analogísmo, *s.m.* argument by analogy; analogy.

anàlogo, *ag.* analogous, similar, parallel.

anamnèsi, *s.f.* (*med.*) anamnesis.

anamnèstico, *ag.* (*med.*) anamnestic.

ananàsso, *s.m.* (*bot.*) pine-apple.

anapèstico, *ag.* (*poes.*) anapaestic.

anapèsto, *s.m.* (*poes.*) anapaest.

anaplastía, anaplàstica, *s.f.* (*chir.*) anaplasty.

anarchía, *s.f.* anarchy.

anarchicaménte, *av.* anarchically.

anàrchico, *ag.* anarchic(al), anarchistic ‖ *s.m* anarchist.

anarchísmo, *s.m.* anarchism.

anarcòide, *s.m.* anarchist.

anasàrca, *s.m.* (*patol.*) anasarca.

Anassàgora, *no.pr.m.* (*st. fil.*) Anaxagoras.

Anassimàndro, *no.pr.m.* (*st. fil.*) Anaximander.

Anassímene, *no.pr.m.* (*st. fil.*) Anaximenes.

Anastàsia, *no.pr.f.* Anastasia.

Anastàsio, *no.pr.m.* (*st.*) Anastasius.

anastàtico, *ag.* (*tip.*) anastatic.

anastigmàtico, *ag.* (*ott.*) anastigmatic.

anastomizzàre, *v.i.* (*chir.*) to anastomose.

anastomòsi, *s.f.* (*anat. chir.*) anastomosis (*pl.* anastomoses).

anàstrofe, *s.f.* (*gram.*) anastrophe.

anatèma, *s.m.* anathema.

anatematizzàre, anatemizzàre, *v.t.* to anathematize; to excommunicate.

Anatòlia, *no.pr.f.* (*geog.*) Anatolia.

anatomìa, *s.f.* anatomy (anche *fig.*): — *comparata,* comparative anatomy; — *vegetale,* vegetable anatomy (*o* phytotomy); — *zoologica,* animal anatomy (*o* zootomy) ‖ *pezzo di* —, anatomical specimen (*o rar.* anatomy); *fig.* skeleton, mummy.

anatomicaménte, *av.* anatomically.

anatòmico, *ag.* anatomic(al): *teatro* —, anatomical theatre ‖ *s.m.* anatomist.

anatomìsta, *s.m.* anatomist.

anatomizzàre, *v.t.* to anatomize; *fig.* to analyse.

ànatra, *s.f.* duck; (*maschio*) drake.

anatràia, *s.f.* duck-pond.

anatrèlla, *s.f.* small duck; young duck.

anatròccolo, anatròtto, *s.m.* duckling.

ànca, *s.f.* 1. hip, haunch: *menar l'*—, to waddle 2. (*anat.*) ilium (*pl.* ilia) 3. (*mar.*) quarter.

ancèlla, *s.f.* maid-servant, maid.

ancestràle, *ag.* ancestral.

ànche, *av.* 1. (*pure*) also, too, as well; (*in frasi negative*) either: — *noi lo vedemmo,* we also saw him (*o* we saw him too); — *Giovanni non beve,* John does not drink either; « *Lo vidi ieri* », « *Anch'io* », "I saw him yesterday", "So did I" 2. (*davanti ai comp.*) even, still: — *meglio,* even (*o* still) better 3. (*perfino*) even ‖ *cong.*:— *a, se, quand'*—, even if (*o* though): — *a dirglielo farà di sua testa,* even if you tell him, he'll have his own way.

ancheggiàre, *v.i.* to waddle.

anchilosàto, *ag.* ankylosed.

anchilòsi, *s.f.* (*patol.*) ankylosis.

anchilostòma, *s.m.* (*zool.*) hookworm.

anchilostomiàsi, *s.f.* (*patol.*) ankylostomiasis.

anchìna, *s.f.* (*tela di cotone*) nankeen.

Anchìse, *no.pr.m.* (*lett.*) Anchises.

ància, *s.f.* reed; (*di oboe, clarinetto*) tongue.

ancillàre, *ag.* ancillary.

ancìpite, *ag.* 1. ancipital, two-headed 2. (*bot.*) ancipital, two-edged 3. *fig.* (*dubbio*) uncertain, dubious.

àneo, (*rar.*) per **ànche.**

ancóna[1], *s.f.* 1. (*tavola di altare*) altar-piece 2. (*arch.*) ancon; (*nicchia*) niche 3. (*immagine votiva*) votive picture, votivo tablet.

Ancóna[2], *no.pr.f.* (*geog.*) Ancona.

ancóne, *s.m.* (*anat.*) ancon, elbow.

àncora[1], *s.f.* 1. (*mar.*) anchor: — *ad una marra,* one-armed anchor; — *a picco,* anchor apeak; — *a tazza,* mushroom anchor; — *da terra,* shore anchor; — *di ormeggio,* mooring anchor; — *di poppa,* stern anchor; — *di posta,* bower (anchor); — *flottante,* drogue (*o* drag anchor); — *impigliata,* foul anchor; *gettare l'*—, to cast (*o* to drop) anchor; *levar l'*—, to weigh anchor; *stare all'*—, to be (*o* to lie *o* to ride) at anchor 2. *fig.* hope: — *di salvezza,* last hope 3. (*elett.*) keeper 4. (*di orologio*) anchor: *orologio ad* —, lever-watch.

ancóra[2], *av.* 1. (*tuttora*) still: *sei* — *qui?,* are you still here? 2. (*finora, nelle frasi negative*) yet: *non sono* — *arrivati,* they have not yet arrived (*o* they haven't arrived yet) 3. (*di nuovo*) again: *sono certo che ci vedremo* —, I am sure we shall meet again 4. (*davanti ai comparativi*) still, even: — *più difficile,* still (*o* even) more difficult (*o* more difficult still) 5. (*con pronomi ed aggettivi quantitativi*) more: — *molti libri,* many more books; — *un po',* a little more 6. (*di più di, nelle frasi affermative*) some more; (*nelle frasi negative e dubitative*) any more: *ne vuoi* —?, will you have some more?; (*dubitativo*) will you have any more?; *vorrei* — *del pane,* I should like some more bread 7. (*più a lungo*) longer: *restate* — *un po',* stay a little longer.

ancoraché, *cong.* even if, though.

ancoràggio, *s.m.* (*mar.*) anchorage, berth: *diritti di* —, anchorage (dues).

ancoràre, *v.t.,* **ancoràrsi,** *v.r.* to anchor.

ancoràto, *ag.* 1. riding at anchor 2. (*a forma di ancora*) anchor-shaped.

ancorché, *cong.* even if, though.

ancoréssa, *s.f.* (*mar.*) one-armed anchor; buoy type single arm anchor.

Andalusìa, *no.pr.f.* (*geog.*) Andalusia.

andalùso, *ag.s.m.* Andalusian.

andaménto, *s.m.* 1. (*tendenza*) trend; (*corso*) course, state; (*procedimento*) proceeding; (*movimento*) movement, progress; (*comportamento*) behaviour: — *degli affari, del mercato,* state of business, of the market; — *di casa,* housewifery; *l'*— *del pensiero romantico è alieno dal materialismo,* the trend of romantic thought is away from materialism; *riferire sull'*— *delle cose,* to report on the state of affairs 2. (*andatura*) gait.

andàna, *s.f.* 1. rope-walk 2. (*mar.*) tier: *ormeggiarsi all'*—, to anchor by the stem.

andànte, *ag.* 1. (*scadente*) plain, common; cheap: *articolo* —, cheap article; *cibo* —, poor food 2. (*comm.*) current, instant: *anno, mese* —, current year, month; *come vi scrissi il 6* —, as I wrote (to) you on the 6th inst. 3. (*continuo*) continuous: *muro* —, continuous wall 4. (*di stile*) plain ‖ *s.m.* (*mus.*) andante.

andeménte, *av.* usually.

andantézza, *s.f.* 1. (*correntezza*) ease 2. affability.

andantíno, *s.m.* (*mus.*) andantino.

andàre, *v.i.* 1. to go (anche *fig.*): *Anna va a scuola ogni giorno,* Anne goes to school every day; — *a caccia,* to go shooting; (*a cavallo*) to go hunting; — *a cavallo,* to go on horseback (*o* to ride); — *a far compere,* to go shopping; — *a grandi passi,* to walk very fast (*o* to stride); — *a letto,* to go to bed; — *alla deriva,* (*mar.*) to go adrift; *fig.* to drift with the tide; — *a nozze,* (*come invitato*) to go to a wedding; (*sposarsi*) to get married; — *a picco, a fondo,* (*di nave*) to sink; — *a piedi,* to go on foot (*o* to walk); — *a spasso,* to go for a walk; — *a tentoni,* to grope (about); — *a tre cilindri,* (*aut.*) to run on three cylinders; — *a velocità eccessiva,* (*in automobile*) to speed; — *a zonzo,* to lounge about; — *e venire,* to come and go; — *fuori strada,* to run off; *fig.* to go astray; — *in automobile, to go by car* (*o* to motor); — *in barca,* to go by boat; — *in bicicletta,* to ride a bicycle (*o* to cycle); — *in retromarcia,* (*aut.*) to go in reverse; — *in treno,* to go by train ‖ *chi va là?,* who is there? ‖ *come va?, how are you? ‖ va da sè che,* it goes without saying (*o* it stands to reason *o* it is a matter of course) *that* ‖ — *a fondo in una questione,* to examine a problem thoroughly ‖ — *a gambe all'aria,* to tumble ‖ — *allo sbaraglio,* to run great risks (*o* to face great dangers) boldly ‖ — *a male,* to go bad (*o* to rotten) ‖ — *a monte,* to fail ‖ — *a tempo,* (*mus.*) to keep time ‖ — *fino in fondo,* to carry on to the end ‖ — *in cerca di guai,* to look for troubles ‖ — *in pezzi,* to go to pieces ‖ — *in rovina,* to get ruined ‖ — *lontano,* to go far (*o* to distinguish oneself) ‖ — *per i fatti propri,* to go one's own way (*o* to mind one's own business) ‖ — *sul sicuro,* to play on velvet ‖ *lasciare* —, to take no notice (*o* to let go) 2. (*di orologio*) *l'orologio va avanti, indietro,* the clock is fast, is slow; *l'orologio va bene, male,* the clock is right, is wrong 3. (*di nave*) to be bound for (a place) 4. (*procedere*) to proceed; (*procedere bene*) to prosper, to thrive; (*procedere male*) to go badly: *gli affari vanno bene, male,* business is brisk, slack ‖ — *di bene in meglio,* to go better and better; — *di male in peggio,* to go from bad to worse ‖ *così va il mondo!,* such is the way of the world! 5. (*finire*) to end: *credo che andrà così,* I suppose it will end in that way (*o* that will be the issue of the matter) 6. (*fare visita*) to call on (s.o.), to visit (s.o.): *andai da lui sabato scorso,* I called on him on Saturday last 7. (*essere molto venduto*) to sell, to be in demand: *la birra va molto,* beer sells well ‖ — *a ruba*, to sell like hot cakes **8.** (*aver corso legale*) **to be legal tender**: *questa moneta non va più*, this coin is no longer legal tender **9.** (*essere di moda*) **to be fashionable, to be in fashion**: *la seta va sempre, ma quest'anno il cotone non va più*, silk is always in (fashion), but cotton this year is out (of fashion) **10.** (*convenire, confarsi*) **to suit** (s.o.); (*di indumento*) **to fit** (s.o.): *quest'abito ti va bene*, this dress fits you; *questo colore non ti va bene*, this colour does not suit you; *il treno delle cinque ci andrebbe bene*, the five o' clock train would suit us **11.** (*piacere, gradire*) **to like** (*costruzione pers.*): *questa faccenda non mi va* (*a genio*), I don't like (o I dislike) this affair; *non mi va di uscire stasera*, I don't feel inclined to go (o I don't feel like going) out to-night **12.** (*succedere*) **to happen**: *vada come vada!*, happen what may! **13.** (*occorrere*) **to be required**: *per un abito ci vanno quattro metri di stoffa*, for a dress four metres of material are required; *per comperare quel quadro mi ci sono andati tanti soldi*, I had to put down a great deal of money for that painting **14.** (*seguito da p.p. nel senso di* dovere) V. **dovére 15.** (*usato al posto di* essere come ausiliare) V. **èssere 16.** (*seguito da ger. nel senso di* stare) V. **stàre 17.** (*Fraseologia*): *andiamo, coraggio!*, cheer up!; *va' al diavolo!*, (*fam.*) to hell with you!; *va' a morire ammazzato!*, (*fam.*) go and do yourself in!; *va' in malora!*, (*fam.*) go to the devil!; *vallo a contare al Kaiser!*, (*fam.*) tell it to the marines!; — *a Canossa*, to eat humble pie; — *di corpo*, to clear one's bowels; — *in brodo di giuggiole*, to be thrilled (o to be extremely pleased); — *in visibilio per ql.co.*, to rave about sthg. ‖ **andàrsene**, *v.r.* **1. to go away; to leave** (a place): *andiamocene*, let's go (o let's be off); *andatevene*, go away; *devo andarmene*, I must be going; *finalmente se ne andò*, at last he went away (o he left) ‖ — *in fumo*, to end in smoke **2.** (*morire*) **to die 3.** (*sparire*) (*di macchie*) **to come off**.

andàre, *s.m.* **1.** (*andatura*) gait; walk; carriage **2.**: *all'— di, sull'— di*, after the manner of **3.** *a lungo —*, in the long run ‖ *a tutt'—*, without ceasing (anche *fig.*) ‖ *con l'— del tempo*, with the passing of time.

andàta, *s.f.* **1.** going: — *e ritorno*, (going) there and back; *biglietto di —*, single ticket; *biglietto di — e ritorno*, return ticket; *viaggio di —*, outward journey; *viaggio di — e ritorno*, journey there and back; (*mar.*) voyage out and home **2.** (*partenza*) start: *dare l'—*, to give the start **3.** (*andatura*) gait; walk; carriage.

andàto, *ag.* **1.** (*trascorso*) gone (by), elapsed, passed: *in tempi andati*, in times gone by **2.** *essere bell'e —*, to be ruined; (*di persona*) to be done for; (*di cosa*) to be worn out; (*molto ammalato*) to be in poor health (o run down).

andatúra, *s.f.* **1.** (*modo di camminare*) walk; gait; carriage; bearing: — *marziale*, soldierly bearing; — *sciolta*, free (o easy) carriage; *riconoscere qlcu. dall'—*, to know s.o. by his walk (o gait) **2.** (*velocità; lunghezza del passo*) pace: — *di un cavallo*, pace of a horse; *la macchina correva a tutta —*, the car was going at top speed; *camminare ad — sostenuta*, to walk at a brisk pace ‖ *fare l'—*, (*spor.*) to set the pace (o to make the running) **3.** (*mar.*) point of sailing; (*velocità di navigazione*) rate: *all'— di venti nodi*, at the rate of twenty knots.

andàzzo, *s.m.* **1.** custom of the moment, fashion of the moment **2.** (*cattiva abitudine*) bad custom **3.** (*cattivo andamento*) bad trend.

Ànde (le), *no.pr.f.pl.* (*geog.*) the Andes.

andesítico, *ag.* (*geol.*) andesitic.

andicappàre, *v.t.* (*gener. spor.*) to handicap.

andirivièni, *s.m.* **1.** coming and going **2.** (*intrico*) maze, labyrinth (anche *fig.*) **3.** (*confusione*) bustle.

àndito, *s.m.* **1.** passage **2.** (*ingresso*) vestibule.

Andòrra, *no.pr.f.* (*geog.*) Andorra.

Andrèa, *no.pr.m.* Andrew ‖ *dim.* Andy, Dandy.

androcèo, *s.m.* (*bot.*) androecium (*pl.* androecia).

androginía, *s.f.* (*bot. biol.*) androgyny.

androgínico, *ag.* (*bot. biol.*) androgynous.

andrògino, *ag.* (*bot. biol.*) androgynous; hermaphroditic(al) ‖ *s.m.* (*bot. biol.*) androgyne; hermaphrodite.

Andròmaca, *no.pr.f.* (*lett.*) Andromache.

Andròmeda, *no.pr.f.* (*mit. astr.*) Andromeda.

andróne, *s.m.* lobby, (entrance-)hall, corridor.

aneddòtica, *s.f.* anecdotage.

aneddòtico, *ag.* anecdotic(al), anecdotal.

anèddoto, *s.m.* anecdote.

anelànte, *ag.* **1.** panting, breathless **2.** *fig.* eager (for sthg., to do), longing (for sthg.).

anelanteménte, *av.* **1.** pantingly, breathlessly **2.** *fig.* eagerly.

anelàre, *v.i.* **1.** to gasp, to pant **2.** *fig.* to long (for sthg.), to yearn (for, after sthg.): *il suo cuore anelava alla partenza*, her heart yearned for departure.

anèlito, *s.m.* **1.** gasp, panting: *l'estremo —*, the last breath **2.** *fig.* yearning (for, after sthg.), longing (for sthg.).

anèllide, *s.m.* (*zool.*) annelid ‖ *gli anellidi*, Annelida.

anèllo, *s.m.* **1.** ring: — *di fidanzamento*, engagement ring; — *di matrimonio*, wedding ring ‖ *dare, prendere l'—*, to get married **2.** (*ditale*) thimble **3.** (*cerchio di metallo*) ring; link: *gli anelli*, (*ginnastica*) the rings; — *da tovagliolo*, napkin-ring; *anelli di catena*, links of a chain; — *di una chiave*, bow of a key; — *di guarnizione*, (*mec.*) packing ring; *anelli d'ormeggio*, (*mar.*) mooring rings (o ballards); — *di strappamento*, (*aer.*) rip link; — *di tenuta*, (*mec.*) gas ring; — *di trazione*, shackle; — *distanziatore*, spacer ring; — *plastico di tenuta*, (*artigl.*) gas-check ring (o gas-check pad); — *portamiccia di una spoletta*, time ring **4.** (*arch.*) listel **5.** (*ricciolo*) curl **6.** (*intermediario*) link, intermediary: — *di congiunzione*, intermediary (o link); — *mancante*, missing link.

anellóso, *ag.* annulate, annulose.

anèlo, *ag.* (*poet.*) **1.** breathless, panting **2.** (*pieno di desiderio*) longing (for sthg.), yearning (for, after sthg.).

anemía, *s.f.* (*patol.*) anaemia: — *perniciosa*, pernicious anaemia.

anèmico, *ag.* anaemic.

anemòfilo, *ag.* (*bot.*) anemophilous.

anemògrafo, *s.m.* anemograph.

anemología, *s.f.* anemology.

anemòmetro, *s.m.* anemometer.

anèmone, *s.m.* (*bot.*) anemone: — *di mare*, (*zool.*) sea anemone.

anemoscòpio, *s.m.* anemoscope.

aneròbio, *s.m.* anaerobe; anaerobium (*pl.* anaerobia).

aneròide, *ag.* (*fis.*) aneroid.

anestesía, *s.f.* (*med.*) anaesthesia.

anestesímetro, *s.m.* (*med.*) anaesthesimeter.

anestesísta, *s.c.* anaesthetist.

anestètico, *ag.s.m.* (*med.*) anaesthetic.

anestetizzàre, *v.t.* (*med.*) to anaesthetize.

anéto, *s.m.* (*bot.*) dill.

aneurísma, *s.m.* (*patol.*) aneurysm.

aneurismàtico, *ag.* aneurysmal.

anfanàre, *v.i.* **1.** to move about aimlessly, to bustle about, to stroll about **2.** (*farneticare*) to rave, to talk incoherently.

anfanatóre, *s.m.*, **anfanatríce**, *s.f.* chatterer.

anfesibèna, *s.f.* (*mit. zool.*) amphisbaena.

anfiartròsi, *s.f.* (*anat.*) amphiarthrosis.

anfíbio, *ag.* amphibious ‖ *s.m.* **1.** (*zool.*) amphibian **2.** (*mil. aer.*) amphibian; (*per operazioni di sbarco*) amphibious landing-craft; (*amer.*) amtrack.

anfíbolo, *ag.* **1.** (*min.*) amphibole **2.** (*ret. fil.*) amphibolic, ambiguous.

anfibología, *s.f.* (*ret. fil.*) amphibology, ambiguity.

anfibologicaménte, *av.* (*ret. fil.*) amphibologically, ambiguously.

anfibològico, *ag.* (*ret. fil.*) amphibolic.

anfíbraco, *s.m.* (*poet.*) amphibrach.

anfiòsso, *s.m.* (*zool.*) amphioxus (*pl.* amphioxi); lancelet.

anfiteatràle, *ag.* amphitheatrical.

anfiteàtro, *s.m.* amphitheatre; (*amer.*) amphitheater.

Anfitrióne, *no.pr.m.* (*mit.*) Amphitryon ‖ **anfitrióne,** *s.m.* amphitryon, host.

anfizióne, *s.m.* (*st. greca*) amphictyon.

anfizionía, *s.f.* (*st. greca*) amphictyony.

anfiziònico, anfiziònio, *ag.* (*st. greca*) amphictyonic.

ànfora, *s.f.* amphora (*pl.* amphorae).

anfràtto, *s.m.* ravine, gorge.

anfrattuosità, *s.f.* anfractuosity (anche *anat.*): *le del cervello,* the anfractuosities of the brain.

anfrattuóso, *ag.* anfractuous; winding.

angariàre, *v.t.* to vex, to oppress; (*con tasse, balzelli*) to overtax.

angariatóre, *s.m.,* **angariatríce,** *s.f.* oppressor;| (*tiranno*) tyrant; (*prepotente*) overbearing person.

angarieggiàre, *v.t.* to vex; to annoy, to molest.

àngela, *s.f.* angel; *fig.* pure, noble and beautiful woman ‖ **Àngela,** *no.pr.f.* Angela.

Angèlica, *no.pr.f.* Angelica.

angelicàle, *ag.* (*letter.*) angelic.

angelicaménte, *av.* angelically.

angelicàto, *ag.* angel-like: *la donna angelicata,* the angel-like woman (*o* the woman-angel).

angèlico, *ag.* angelic(al) ‖ *L'Angelico, il Beato Angelico,* Fra' Angelico ‖ *il Dottore Angelico,* the Angelic Doctor ‖ *la Salutazione Angelica,* (*eccl.*) the Angelic Salutation.

àngelo, *s.m.* angel: *— custode,* guardian angel; (*scherz.*) policeman; *l'— delle tenebre,* the angel of darkness ‖ **Àngelo,** *no.pr.m.* Angel.

anghería, *s.f.* vexation, imposition; (*tassa esosa*) exaction, extortion.

anghière, *s.m.* (*mar.*) boat-hook.

angína, *s.f.* (*patol.*) angina; quinsy: *— pectoris,* angina pectoris.

anginóso, *ag.* anginous, anginal ‖ *s.m.* person suffering from angina.

angiocolíte, *s.f.* (*patol.*) angiocholitis.

angioíno, *ag.s.m.* (*st.*) Angevin.

angioíte, *s.f.* (*patol.*) angiitis.

àngiolo, *s.m.* angel.

angiología, *s.f.* (*med.*) angiology.

angiòma, *s.f.* (*patol.*) angioma.

angiospèrma, *ag.* (*bot.*) angiospermous, angiospermal.

angiospèrme, *s.f.pl.* (*bot.*) angiosperms.

angiòtribo, *s.m.* (*chir.*) angiotribe.

angipòrto, *s.m.* (*vicolo cieco*) blind alley; (*stradetta angusta*) narrow lane.

anglicanísmo, *s.m.* (*st. relig.*) Anglicanism.

anglicàno, *ag.s.m.* (*st. relig.*) Anglican.

anglicísmo, *s.m.* Anglicism.

angleizzàre, *v.t.* to Anglicize.

ànglico, *ag.* English.

ànglo-, (*prefisso*) Anglo-: *— americano,* Anglo-American.

anglofilía, *s.f.* Anglophilism.

anglòfilo, *ag.s.m.* Anglophil(e).

anglofobía, *s.f.* Anglophobia.

anglòfobo, *ag.s.m.* Anglophobe.

anglòmane, *ag.s.c.* Anglomaniac.

anglomanía, *s.f.* Anglomania.

anglosàssone, *ag.s.c.* Anglo-Saxon ‖ *s.m.* (*lingua*) Old-English, Anglo-Saxon, the Anglo-Saxon language.

angolàre, *ag.* angular: *pietra —,* (*arch.*) corner-stone (*o* headstone) (anche *fig.*) ‖ *s.m.: grande —,* (*foto.*) aplanatic lens (*o* euryscope).

angolarità, *s.f.* angularity.

angolarménte, *av.* angularly.

angolàto, *ag.* angled.

angolazióne, *s.f.* (*cine.*) angle-shot: *— dal basso,* low-shot.

àngolo, *s.m.* 1. corner: *— di strada,* street-corner; *calcio d'—,* (*spor.*) corner-kick; *casa d'—,* corner house;

posto d'—, corner seat; *gira l'—,* go round the corner; *cercare ql.co. in ogni —,* to look for sthg. high and low (*o* in every corner); *mettere un bambino nell'—,* to put a child in the corner ‖ *un — appartato,* a retired spot (*o* place *o* nook) ‖ *giocare ai quattro angoli,* to play (at) puss in the corner 2. (*fis. geom. mil., ecc.*) angle: *— acuto,* (*geom.*) acute (*o* oblique) angle; *— assiale,* (*miner.*) axial angle; *— azimutale,* (*astr. aer. mar.*) azimuth angle; *— di attacco,* (*artigl.*) firing angle; *— di atterraggio,* (*aer.*) landing angle; *— di beccheggio,* (*aer.*) angle of pitch; *— di caduta,* (*artigl.*) angle of fall; *— di curvatura,* bending angle; *— di deviazione, di incidenza,* (*fis.*) angle of deviation, of incidence; *— di direzione,* (*artigl.*) bearing; *— di emergenza,* (*ott.*) angle of emergence; *— di inclinazione,* angle of elevation, inclination; *— di mira,* (*mil.*) angle of sighting; *— di osservazione,* (*mil.*) angle at the target (*o* observation angle); *— di rifrazione* (*ott.*) refraction angle; *— di salita,* (*aer.*) angle of climb; *— di tiro,* (*mil.*) angle of fire; *— giro,* (*geom.*) round angle; *— limite,* (*ott.*) critical angle; *— morto,* (*mil.*) dead (*o* blind) angle; *— ottuso,* (*geom.*) obtuse angle; *— piano,* (*geom.*) plane angle; *— piatto,* (*geom.*) straight angle; *— retto,* (*geom.*) right angle: *ad — retto con,* at right angle to; *— visivo,* (*mil.*) visual angle.

angolosità, *s.f.* angularity.

angolóso, *ag.* angular (anche *fig.*); sharp-cornered: *carattere —,* angular disposition; *donna angolosa,* bony woman; *viso —,* bony face.

Angora, *no.pr.f.* (*geog.*) Angora: *coniglio d'—,* Angora rabbit; *gatto d'—,* Angora cat; *lana d'—,* Angora wool.

angòscia, *s.f.* anguish, woe, distress.

angosciàre, *v.t.* to afflict, to aggrieve, to anguish, to distress, to grieve ‖ **angosciàrsi,** *v.r.* to worry (about sthg.), to be distressed (about sthg.), to grieve (over sthg.).

angosciàto, *ag.* anguished, distressed.

angosciosaménte, *av.* painfully, distressingly.

angoscióso, *ag.* 1. (*che dà angoscia*) distressing, painful 2. (*che è pieno di angoscia*) full of anguish.

angostúra, *s.f.* angostura.

àngue, *s.m.* (*poet.*) snake, serpent.

anguílla, *s.f.* 1. (*ittiol.*) eel: *— marinata,* soused eel 2. (*persona sfuggente, infida*) unreliable person, slippery person, elusive person: *che —!,* what a slippery eel!; *ella è sfuggente come un'—,* she is as slippery as an eel 3. (*persona agile*) nimble person, quick person, agile person 4. (*mar.*) carling; *pl.* (*per ponti*) deck girders.

anguillàia, *s.f.* eel-pond, eel-preserve.

anguinàia, *s.f.* (*anat.*) groin.

angúria, *s.f.* water-melon.

angustaménte, *av.* 1. narrowly 2. (*meschinamente*) meanly, niggardly, pettily, stingily.

angústia, *s.f.* 1. (*strettezza di spazio*) straitness, narrowness 2. (*ristrettezza di tempo*) limited time, want of time 3. (*affanno, tribolazione*) anguish, distress, pain: *essere nelle angustie,* to be in distress (*o* in difficulties) 4. (*grettezza*) meanness, niggardliness, pettiness.

angustiàre, *v.t.* to afflict, to distress, to harass, to torment ‖ **angustiàrsi,** *v.r.* to worry (about sthg.), to fret (over sthg.), to be distressed (about sthg.), to be afflicted (at sthg.).

angústo, *ag.* 1. strait, narrow 2. *fig.* mean, petty, stingy; narrow-minded, small-minded.

ànice, *s.m.* (*bot.*) anise: *seme d'—,* aniseed.

anidríde, *s.f.* (*chim.*) anhydride: *— carbonica,* carbonic anhydride (*o* carbon dioxide).

anidríte, *s.f.* (*min.*) anhydrite.

anídro, *ag.* (*chim.*) anhydrous.

aníle, *s.m.* (*bot.*) anil, indigo shrub.

anilína, *s.f.* (*chim.*) aniline.

ànima, *s.f.* 1. soul: *le anime dannate,* lost souls; *gridare come un'— dannata,* to cry out like a lost soul; *le anime dei defunti,* the departed souls; *le anime purganti,* the souls in Purgatory; *aver cura delle anime,* *(di sacerdote)* to have cure of souls; *pregare per l'— di qlcu.,* to pray for s.o.'s soul; *raccomandare l'— a Dio,* to commend one's soul to God *(o* to trust to God) || *— mia!,* my beloved (one)! || *in corpo e —,* in body and soul; *appartenere a qlcu. — e corpo,* to belong to s.o. body and soul || *darei l'— per saperlo,* I'd give my life to know (it) || *avere ql.co. sull'—,* to be heavy-hearted || *darsi — e corpo a ql.co.,* to give oneself body and soul to sthg. *(o* to throw oneself heart and soul into sthg. *o* to throw one's whole soul into sthg.) || *darsi all'—,* to turn to religion || *esalare l'—,* to die *(o* to give up the ghost *o* to breathe one's last) || *essere l'— dannata di qlcu.,* to be s.o.'s accomplice; *(il cattivo consigliere)* to be s.o.'s evil angel || *evocare l'— di qlcu.,* to call up the spirit of s.o. || *far dannare l'— a qlcu., (fam.)* to torment s.o. *(o* to drive s.o. mad) || *giocarsi l'—,* to stake everything || *reggere l'— coi denti,* to be very ill || *rompere l'— a qlcu., (volg.)* to bother *(o* to worry) s.o. || *vendere l'— a caro prezzo,* to sell one's life dearly **2.** *(parte centrale; nerbo; elemento vivificatore; energia spirituale)* soul, moving spirit, heart; *(di arma da fuoco)* bore; *(di cannone)* tube; *(di rotaia)* web; *(di timone)* rudderpost, rudderstock; *(metal.)* core: *l'— del legno,* the heart of wood; *l'— del violino,* the sound-post of a violin; *l'— di una corda,* the heart *(o* core *o* central strand) of a rope; *senz'—,* soulless *(o* spiritless) || *ci ho messo tutta l'—,* I have set my whole heart upon it || *il denaro è l'— della guerra,* money is the soul of war || *dare — allo stile,* to enliven the style || *esser l'— di ql.co.,* to be the life and soul *(o* the moving spirit *o* the prime mover) of sthg. **3.** *(cuore, sentimento)* heart, feeling: *mi congratulo con te con tutta l'—,* I congratulate you from the bottom of my heart; *arrivare all'—, (commuovere)* to stir s.o.'s heart; *desiderare ql.co. con tutta l'—,* to desire sthg. with all one's heart *(o* ardently); *mettere dell'— nel fare ql.co.,* to do sthg. with feeling; *non avere —,* to have no feelings **4.** *(persona): Napoli conta oltre un milione di anime,* Naples has over one million inhabitants *(o* souls *o* people); *non conosceva — viva,* he didn't know a single soul *(o* person); *non dirlo ad — viva,* don't tell a living soul *(o* anybody).

animalàccio, *s.m. fig.* brute, beast.

animàle, *ag.* **1.** animal: *regno —,* animal kingdom **2.** *fig.* animal, sensual, brutal || *s.m.* **1.** animal: *gentile con gli animali,* kind to dumb beasts *(o* animals) || *Società protettrice degli animali,* Society for Prevention of Cruelty to Animals **2.** *fig.* brute, beast.

animalería, *s.f.* **1.** bestial action, bestiality **2.** *(insieme di animali)* menagerie.

animalescaménte, *av.* in a bestial way.

animaléseo, *ag.* bestial, beastly.

animalità, *s.f.* animality, animal nature.

animalóne, *s.m. fig.* brute, beast.

animàre, *v.t.* **1.** to animate, to give life to (s.o., sthg.), to endow with life, to enliven, to vivify (anche *fig.*): *lo spirito che anima le sue opere,* the spirit that breathes through his works; *— una conversazione,* to enliven *(o* to quicken) a conversation || *essere animato da buoni sentimenti verso qlcu.,* to entertain good feelings for s.o. **2.** *(incoraggiare)* to encourage: *— i soldati,* to encourage the soldiers || **animàrsi,** *v.r.* **1.** *(divenire più animato)* to become animated, to become livelier: *la discussione si animava,* the debate was becoming livelier *(o* was waxing hot); *il suo viso si animò,* his face lit *(o* brightened) up **2.** *(prendere coraggio)* to take courage **3.** *(rallegrarsi)* to brighten, to cheer up **4.** *(agitarsi)* to get excited.

animataménte, *av.* animatedly.

animatívo, *ag.* vivifying, enlivening, inspiriting.

animàto, *ag.* **1.** *(vivente)* alive, living: *esseri animati, living beings* || *cartoni animati,* (animated) cartoons **2.** *(vivace)* animated, lively, vivacious; brisk: *descrizione, discussione animata,* animated description, discussion; *mercato —, (comm.)* animated *(o* brisk *o* buoyant) market; *la conversazione era animatissima,* the con-

versation had reached a high pitch; *la tua commedia è animata, (fam.)* your comedy has go.

animatóre, *ag.* animating, enlivening, quickening || *s.m.,* **animatríce,** *s.f.* animator, enlivener, quickener.

animazióne, *s.f.* **1.** animation; liveliness; briskness: *l'— del mercato, (comm.)* the buoyancy *(o* briskness) of the market; *l'— delle strade,* the bustle in the streets; *commedia che manca di —,* play that lacks animation **2.** *(cine.)* animation.

animèlla, *s.f.* sweetbread.

animísmo, *s.m. (st. fil.)* animism.

ànimo, *s.m.* **1.** *(mente, pensiero)* mind; heart: *ho in — di andare a Roma,* I have a (good) mind *(o* it is my intention) to go to Rome; *mi nasce nell'— un sospetto,* there is a suspicion springing up in my mind; *aprire l'— a qlcu.,* to open one's heart to s.o.; *avere l'— altrove,* to have other intentions *(o* to focus one's attention on sthg. else); *leggere nell'— di qlcu.,* to read s.o.'s heart; *tener ql.co. nell'—,* to keep *(o* to have) sthg. in mind || *con tutto l'— mio,* with all my heart **2.** *(coraggio)* courage, heart, daring: *non ho l'—, non mi regge l'—, non mi basta l'— di fare ql.co.,* I haven't the heart to do sthg. *(o* I don't feel equal to doing sthg.); *farsi —,* to take *(o* to pluck up) heart *(o* courage) *perdersi d'—,* to lose heart *(o* one's daring) || *—!,* cheer up! *(o* courage! *o* come on!) **3.** *(inclinazione, disposizione)* disposition: *con mal —,* with malevolence *(o* with an evil intention); *di mal —,* reluctantly; *stato d'—,* mood: *non sono nello stato d'— adatto per ciò,* I am in no mood for that; *sono nello stato d'— d'andare a teatro,* I am in the mood *(o* I feel inclined) to go to the theatre; *era d'— gentile,* she was of a kind disposition; *alienare l'— di qlcu.,* to alienate s.o. (from oneself, from s.o.) || *lo feci di buon —,* I did it willingly; *star di buon —,* to be cheerful **4.** *(parere, opinione)* mind, opinion: *questo è l'— mio,* this is my opinion.

animosaménte, *av.* **1.** *(con coraggio)* courageously, daringly, bravely **2.** *(con rancore)* grudgingly, with animosity.

animosità, *s.f.* **1.** *(mal animo)* animosity, animus, spite; hatred: *agire per —,* to act out of spite; *nutrire dell'— verso qlcu.,* to bear a grudge against s.o. **2.** *(rar.)* courage.

animóso, *ag.* **1.** brave, bold, courageous, spirited || *un pugno di animosi,* a small number *(o* a handful) of bold men **2.** *(ostile)* malevolent, spiteful.

anióne, *s.m. (elett. chim.)* anion.

anisétta, *s.f.* anisette.

anisocoría, *s.f. (patol.)* anisocoria.

anisóne, *s.f.* anisette.

anisotropía, *s.f. (fis.)* anisotropy, aeolotropy.

anisòtropo, *ag. (fis.)* anisotropic.

Aníta, *no.pr.f.* Anita.

ànitra, *s.f.* duck; *(maschio)* drake.

Ànkara, *no.pr.f. (geog.)* Ankara.

Ànna, *no.pr.f.* Anna, Anne, Ann || *dim.* Annie, Nancy.

Annabèlla, *no.pr.f.* Annabel(le).

annacquaménto, *s.m.* watering; diluting (anche *fig.*).

annacquàre, *v.t.* **1.** to water, to dilute **2.** *fig.* to moderate, to mitigate: *annacquò il suo entusiasmo,* he moderated his enthusiasm.

annacquàto, *ag.* **1.** watered, diluted: *vino —,* diluted wine **2.** *fig.* watered; *(di stile)* weak; *(di colore)* washed-out, pale, faded.

annaffiaménto, *s.m.* watering, sprinkling, sprinkle.

annaffiàre, *v.t.* to water, to sprinkle, to bedew.

annaffiàta, *s.f.* watering, sprinkling, sprinkle.

annaffiatóio, *s.m.* sprinkle, watering-can, watering -pot.

annaffiatríce, *s.f.* water-cart, watering vehicle, road sprinkler.

annaffiatúra, *s.f.* watering, sprinkling, sprinkle.

annàli, *s.m. pl.* annals.

annalísta, *s.m.* annalist.

annasàre, *V.* **annusàre.**

annaspàre, *v.t.* to reel, to wind (thread) on reels, to spool ‖ *v.i.* **1.** to grope **2.** *fig.* to grope, to bustle about aimlessly; to strive without any result ‖ — *nel buio,* to grope about.

annaspicàre, *v.i.* to falter, to stutter.

annaspío, *s.m.* groping, bustling.

annàta, *s.f.* **1.** year: — *di intensi affari,* active year; *movimento di affari nell'*—, yearly turnover; *gli devo un'*— *d'affitto,* I owe him one year's rent **2.** *(raccolto)* crop: *una cattiva* —, a poor crop.

annebbiaménto, *s.m.* **1.** fogginess **2.** *(offuscamento)* dimness: — *della vista,* dimming of the eyesight.

annebbiàre, *v.t.* **1.** to fog; to dim, to obscure: *occhi annebbiati dalle lacrime,* eyes dimmed with tears **2.** *fig.* to dull: *i vizi annebbiano l'intelletto,* vices dull the brain ‖ *v.i. imp.* to get foggy, to become misty: *quando ci andai, annebbiava,* when I went there, it was getting (*o* turning) foggy ‖ **annebbiàrsi,** *v.r.* **1.** *(diventar nebbioso)* to become, to grow foggy **2.** *(offuscarsi)* to grow dim.

annegaménto, *s.m.* **1.** drowning **2.** *fig.* ruin.

annegàre, *v.t.* to drown ‖ *v.i.* to drown, to get drowned, to be drowned: *egli annegò,* he was drowned; *poco mancava che annegasse,* he was nearly drowned ‖ **annegàrsi,** *v.r.* to drown oneself.

annegàto, *ag.* drowned ‖ *s.m.* drowned person.

anneghittiménto, *s.m.* idleness; laziness.

anneghittíre, *v.t.* to make lazy, to make indolent ‖ *v.i.,* **anneghittírsi,** *v.r.* to grow lazy, to become indolent; *(fam.)* to laze.

anneràre, *v.t.* to blacken ‖ *v.i. imp. (farsi buio)* to darken, to get dark, to get dim.

anneriménto, *s.m.* blackening.

anneríre, *v.t.* to blacken ‖ **annerírsi,** *v.r.* to blacken, to darken, to grow dark: *il cielo si annerisce,* the sky is growing dark (*o* is overcast).

annerìto, *ag.* blackened; black; dark.

anneritúra, *s.f.* blackening, blackness.

annessióne, *s.f.* annexation.

annèsso, *ag.* **1.** connected, joined **2.** *(di documenti, ecc.)* attached, appended; annexed: *(comm.) (accluso,* enclosed*)*: *articoli annessi al contratto di società,* (comm.) articles of co-partnership ‖ *s.m.* **1.** *(edificio aggiunto)* annex(e), out-building, outlying building **2.** *(documento aggiunto)* appendage, annex(e); *(comm.) (allegato)* enclosure **3.** *annèssi e connèssi,* appendages.

annestàre, *v.t.* to graft.

annèttere, *v.t.* **1.** to annex: — *politicamente un paese ad un altro,* to annex a country to another ‖ — *importanza a ql.co.,* to attach importance to sthg. **2.** *(documenti, ecc.)* to annex, to join, to append, to attach; *(comm.) (accludere)* to enclose.

Anníbale, *no.pr.m.* Hannibal.

annichilaménto, *s.m.,* annihilation.

annichilàre, *v.t.* **1.** to annihilate, to destroy **2.** *fig.* to crush, to stupefy ‖ **annichilàrsi,** *v.r.* to abase oneself, to lower oneself; *(fam.)* to eat humble pie.

annichilazióne, *s.f.* annihilation.

annichilíre, *V.* **annichilàre.**

annidàre, *v.t.* **1.** to nest **2.** *fig.* to nurse in one's bosom ‖ **annidàrsi,** *v.r.* **1.** *(fare il nido)* to nest, to build a nest **2.** *(starsene seminascosto in un luogo)* to nestle; *(nascondersi)* to hide.

annientaménto, *s.m.* **1.** annihilation, destruction **2.** *(di desideri, speranze, ecc.)* frustration.

annientàre, *v.t.* to annihilate, to destroy ‖ **annientàrsi,** *v.r.* **1.** to come to nothing **2.** *fig.* to humiliate oneself, to abase oneself; *(fam.)* to eat humble pie.

anniversàrio, *ag.s.m.* anniversary: *è l'*— *del mio matrimonio,* it is the anniversary of my marriage; *è il suo* —, it is his birthday.

ànno, *s.m.* **1.** year: — *amministrativo, finanziario,* financial (*o* fiscal) year; — *bisestile,* leap-year; *(astr.)* bissextile year; — *civile,* civil year; — *corrente, in*

corso, present (*o* running) year; — *giuridico,* legal year; — *luce,* (astr.) light-year; — *lunare,* (astr.) lunar year; *l'*— *prossimo, venturo,* next year (*o* the year to come); — *scolastico, accademico,* school year; *l'*— *scorso,* last year; — *sidereo,* (astr.) sidereal year; — *solare,* (astr.) solar (*o* calendar) year ‖ — *di grazia,* year of your grace (*o* of our Lord) ‖ *un* — *dopo l'altro,* year in year out (*o* year after year *o* year by year); *col passare degli anni,* as years go by; *di* — *in* —, from year to year; *due volte all'* —, twice a year; *durante tutto l'* —, all year round; *in capo all'* —, at the end of the year; *per molti anni di fila,* for several years on end; *per un certo numero di anni,* for a term of years; *tutti gli anni,* every year ‖ *Anno Santo,* (eccl.) Jubilee Year ‖ *capo d'* —, New Year's Day ‖ *carico d'anni,* stricken in years ‖ *i migliori anni della nostra vita,* the best years (*o* the prime) of our lives; *nel fiore degli anni,* in the prime of life; *i verd'anni,* early years ‖ *studente del terzo* —, student in his third year ‖ *è stato un* — *in novembre,* a year last November; *sarà un* — *in ottobre,* a year in (*o* next) October ‖ *aspettare l'*— *nuovo,* to see the New Year in; *augurare a qlcu. il buon* —, to wish s.o. a happy New Year ‖ *essere avanti negli anni,* to be on in years; *finire, compiere gli anni,* to have one's birthday; *levarsi gli anni,* to knock a few years off one's age; *portare bene gli anni,* not to look one's age ‖ *lavorare tredici mesi all'* —, to work hard **3.** *(periodo di tempo lungo ed indeterminato)* a long time: *cent'anni, mill'anni,* a very long (*o* undefined) time: *sono cent'anni che non vi vedo,* I have not seen you for ever so long (*o* for such a long time); *(sl. amer.)* for a month of Sundays (*o* it is donkey's years since I saw you *o* I haven't seen you for donkey's years); *è un* — *che lo aspetto,* I have been waiting for him a long time **3.** *(nelle indicazioni di età):* età *tra i tredici e i diciannove anni,* teen-age: *ragazzo fra i tredici e i diciannove anni,* teen-ager (*o* teen-age boy); *poteva essere tra i quaranta e i cinquant'anni,* he may have been any age between forty and fifty; *«Quanti anni hai?» «Ho vent'anni»,* "How old are you?" "I am twenty (years old)"; *avere poco più di trent'anni,* to be in one's early thirties; *essere nel tredicesimo* —, to be in one's thirteenth year; *essere tra i tredici e i diciannove anni,* to be in one's teens.

annobiliménto, *s.m. (di azione)* ennoblement; *(di spirito, ecc.)* elevation, uplifting.

annobilíre, *v.t.* **1.** to ennoble; to elevate, to uplift **2.** *(abbellire)* to embellish, to adorn ‖ *v.i.* to be annobled.

annoccàre, *v.t. (agr.)* to layer.

annodaménto, *s.m.* knotting, tying.

annodàre, *v.t.* to knot, to tie in a knot, to tie in knots ‖ — *amicizie,* to make friends ‖ **annodàrsi,** *v.r.* to become knotted, to form a knot; *(aggrovigliarsi)* to kink ‖ *gli si annodò la lingua in bocca,* he became tongue-tied.

annodatóre, *s.m.,* **annodatríce,** *s.f.* knotter.

annodatúra, *s.f.* **1.** knotting **2.** *(anat.)* joint.

annoiaménto, *s.m. (fastidio)* annoyance; *(tedio)* weariness, tediousness; boredom.

annoiàre, *v.t. (infastidire)* to annoy; *(stancare)* to bore, to weary, to tire ‖ **annoiàrsi,** *v.r.* to grow weary, to be bored: — *a morte,* to be bored to death; *(fam.)* to be fed up.

annoiàto, *ag.* bored, weary, tired; *(fam.)* fed up.

annoiatóre, *s.m.,* **annoiatríce,** *s.f.* tiresome person; *(fam.)* bore.

annòna, *s.f.* provisions *(pl.),* food supplies *(pl.).*

annonàrio, *ag.* pertaining to provisions: *carta annonaria,* ration-card; *leggi annonarie,* food rationing laws.

annóso, *ag.* old: *albero* —, old (*o* ancient) tree.

annotàre, *v.t. (corredare di note)* to annotate; *(prender nota di)* to make a note of (sthg.), to take a note of (sthg.), to jot down.

annotariàre, *v.t.* to appoint notary.

annotazióne, *s.f.* annotation, note.

annottàre, *v.i. imp.* to grow dark, to get dark, to darken.

annottolàre, *v.t.* to latch.

annoveraménto, *s.m.* numbering; enumeration.

annoveràre, *v.t.* to enumerate; to number, to count.

annuàle, *ag.* annual, yearly ‖ *s.m.* anniversary.

annualità, *s.f.* annuity; (*reddito annuo*) yearly income; (*rata annuale*) yearly instalment.

annualménte, *av.* **1.** annually, yearly **2.** (*d'anno in anno*) from year to year.

annuàrio, *ag.* (*rar.*) yearly ‖ *s.m.* year-book: — *commerciale*, trade directory.

annuíre, *v.i.* **1.** (*col capo*) to nod (in assent) **2.** (*acconsentire*) to consent, to assent.

annullaménto, *s.m.* annulment; cancellation: — *di una legge*, repeal; — *di un ordine*, (*comm.*) cancelling of an order.

annullàre, *v.t.* to annul, to make void; to annihilate; (*comm.*) to cancel; (*una legge*) to repeal: — *gli effetti di ql.co.*, to undo the effects of sthg.; — *un matrimonio*, to annul a marriage; — *un ordine*, (*comm.*) to cancel an order ‖ **annullàrsi**, *v.r.* to humble oneself.

annunciàre, *v.t.* **1.** to announce, to herald, to give notice of (sthg.): *chi devo — ?*, what name shall I say? ‖ *farsi — presso qlcu.*, to send in one's name to s.o. (o to give in one's name) **2.** (*predire*) to foretell: *il cielo annunzia bel tempo*, the sky foretells fine weather.

annunciatóre, *s.m.*, **annunciatríce**, *s.f.* announcer (anche della radio).

annunciazióne, *s.f.* annunciation ‖ (*festa dell'*)*Annunciazione*, (*eccl.*) the Annunciation (o Lady Day).

annunziàre, *V.* **annunciàre**.

Annunzíàta, *s.f.* the Virgin Mary ‖ *no.pr.f.* Annunziata.

annunziatóre, **annunziatríce**, *V.* **annunciatóre**, **annunciatríce**.

annunziazióne, *V.* **annunciazióne**.

annúnzio, *s.m.* **1.** announcement, notification, notice: — *mortuario*, obituary (notice); — *pubblicitario*, advertisement: *mettere un — pubblicitario sui giornali del mattino*, to put an advertisement in the morning papers; *fare un —*, to make an announcement **2.** (*presagio*) presage.

ànnuo, *ag.* annual, yearly: *abbonamento —*, yearly subscription.

annusàre, *v.t.* **1.** to smell; (*rumorosamente, specialmente di animali*) to sniff: — *tabacco*, to take snuff **2.** *fig.* to smell out, to discover: — *ql.co. di losco*, to smell a rat.

annusàta, *s.f.* sniff.

annuvolaménto, *s.m.* darkening; cloudiness.

annuvolàre, *v.t.* to cloud (anche *fig.*) ‖ **annuvolàrsi**, *v.r.* to get cloudy, to grow cloudy, to cloud; to get overcast, to become overcast, to become gloomy (anche *fig.*): *il cielo si è annuvolato*, the sky has become overcast (with clouds).

annuvolàto, *ag.* cloudy; overcast, gloomy (anche *fig.*).

àno, *s.m.* (*anat.*) anus.

anòbio, *s.m.* (*entom.*) anobium.

anodíno, *ag.* **1.** (*farm.*) anodyne, soothing **2.** (*insignificante*) irrelevant; plain ‖ *s.m.* (*farm.*) anodyne.

ànodo, *s.m.* (*elett.*) anode.

anòfele, *s.f.* (*entom.*) anopheles.

anomalía, *s.f.* anomaly.

anòmalo, *ag.* anomalous.

anònima, *s.f.* (*comm.*) joint-stock company.

anònimo, *ag.* anonymous: *una lettera anonima*, an anonymous letter ‖ *s.m.* anonym.

anoplotèrio, *s.m.* (*paleont.*) anoplothere.

anoressía, *s.m.* (*patol.*) anorexy.

anormàle, *ag.* abnormal; anomalous.

anormalità, *s.f.* abnormality.

ànsa, *s.f.* **1.** (*manico*) handle **2.** *fig.* (*pretesto*) pretext, opportunity: *dare —*, to offer an opportunity **3.** (*insenatura*) cove, creek; (*di fiume*) bend **4.** (*anat.*) ansa.

ansaménto, *s.m.* panting.

ansànte, *ag.* panting.

ansàre, *v.i.* to pant.

anseàtico, *ag.* (*st.*) Hanseatic: *lega anseatica*, Hanseatic League (o Hanse).

Ansèlmo, *no.pr.m.* Anselm.

anseríno, *ag.* (*patol.*) auserine: *pelle anserina*, anserine skin.

ànsia, *s.f.* **1.** anxiety, anxiousness: *pieno d'—*, full of anxiety; *stare in —*, to be anguished (o to feel great anxiety) **2.** (*bramosia*) eagerness, anxiousness.

ansietà, *V.* **ànsia 1.**

ànsima, *s.f.* shortness of breath; breathlessness; panting.

ansimàre, *v.i.* to pant.

ànsimo, *V.* **ànsima**.

ansiosaménte, *av.* **1.** anxiously **2.** (*con desiderio vivo*) eagerly.

ansióso, *ag.* **1.** anxious **2.** (*desideroso*) eager, anxious: *essere — d'imparare l'inglese*, to be eager to learn English.

ànsito, *s.m.* panting.

ànta, *s.f.* shutter; (*di armadio*) door.

antagonísmo, *s.m.* antagonism.

antagonísta, *s.c.* antagonist, opponent ‖ *s.* (*anat.*) antagonist.

Antàres, *no.pr.f.* (*astr.*) Antares.

antàrtico, *ag.* Antarctic: *Circolo Polare Antartico*, Antarctic Circle; *Polo Antartico*, Antarctic Pole.

antecedènte, *ag.* antecedent, previous, preceding, prior, foregoing ‖ *s.m.* **1.** (*gram. fil. mat.*) antecedent **2.** *pl.* (*avvenimenti*) antecedents.

antecedenteménte, *av.* previously, before.

antecedènza, *s.f.* (*di tempo*) antecedence, priority, precedence; (*di posizione*) anteriority, precedence.

antecèdere, *v.t.i.* to precede.

antecessóre, *s.m.* predecessor, antecessor.

antedétto, *ag.* aforesaid.

antefàtto, *s.m.* antecedent fact: *mi narrò l'—*, he told me what had happened before.

antefíssa, *s.f.* (*arch.*) antefix.

anteguèrra, *ag.* pre-war ‖ *s.m.* pre-war times (*pl.*): *prezzi d'—*, pre-war prices.

antèlio, *s.m.* (*astr.*) anthelion.

antelmíntico, *ag.s.m.* (*farm.*) anthelmintic.

antelucàno, *ag.* antelucan, before dawn; before the break of day: *vento —*, wind blowing just before dawn.

antelunàre, *ag.* **1.** before the new moon: *giorni antelunari*, the first three days of the new moon **2.** created before the moon.

antemuràle, *s.m.* **1.** defence wall, rampart **2.** (*mar.*) breakwater **3.** *fig.* defence, protection.

antenàto, *s.m.* ancestor, forefather.

antènna, *s.f.* **1.** (*mar.*) lateen yard **2.** (*palo*) pole **3.** (*zool.*) antenna (*pl.* antennæ) **4.** (*rad.*) aerial, antenna (*pl.* antennas): — *antidisturbo*, antistatic aerial; — *trasmittente*, transmitting antenna (o radiator).

antennàle, *s.m.* (*mar.*) head of a sail.

antepórre, *v.t.* **1.** to place before, to put before: *al piacere egli antepone il dovere*, he puts duty before pleasure **2.** (*preferire*) to prefer ‖ **antepórsi**, *v.r.* to consider oneself superior.

antepríma, *s.f.* (*cine.*) preview.

antèra, *s.f.* (*bot.*) anther.

anterióre, *ag.* **1.** (*nello spazio*) fore; (*rar.*) anterior: *i fari anteriori*, (*aut.*) the front lights; *zampe anteriori*, fore legs **2.** (*nel tempo*) previous, preceding; former; (*rar.*) anterior: *in una vita —*, in a former life.

anteriorità, *s.f.* **1.** priority, anteriority **2.** (*preminenza*) precedence.

anteriorménte, *av.* previously, before: — *alla promulgazione della legge*, (*dir.*) prior to the promulgation of the law.

antesignàno, *s.m.* **1.** (*st.*) standard-bearer **2.** *fig.* (*capo*) leader **3.** (*precursore*) forerunner, precursor.

antiabbagliànte, *ag.* anti-dazzle.

antiàcido, *ag.s.m.* (*chim.*) antacid.

antiaèreo, *ag.* anti-aircraft: *cannone* —, anti-aircraft gun; *fuoco* —, anti-aircraft fire.

antialcalíno, *ag.* (*chim.*) antialkaline.

antialcoòlico, *ag.* teetotal, antialcoholic: *lega antialcoolica,* antialcohol league.

antibattèrico, *ag.* (*farm.*) antibacteriai.

antibilióso, *ag.* (*farm.*) antibilious.

antibiòtico, *ag. s.m.* (*farm.*) antibiotic.

antibràccio, *s.m.* (*anat.*) forearm.

anticàglia, *s.f.* **1.** (*spreg.*) worthless old stuff, worthless antique **2.** (*oggetto antico*) antique, old curiosity: *negozio di anticaglie,* old curiosity shop **3.** (*persona vecchia, antiquata*) (old) fogey; old-fashioned person.

anticaménte, *av.* in times past, in times gone by, formerly; (*letter.*) of yore.

anticàmera, *s.f.* **1.** anteroom, antechamber; lobby || *fare* —, to be kept waiting; *far fare* — *a qlcu.,* to keep s.o. waiting **2.** (*servi addetti al servizio di un signore*) attendance.

anticàrro, *ag.* (*mil.*) anti-tank.

anticattòlico, *ag.* anticatholic.

anticheggiàre, *v.i.* to affect old-fashioned manners.

antichità, *s.f.* **1.** antiquity, ancientness, ancientry: *l'*— *di una tradizione,* the antiquity of a tradition **2.** (*tempo antico*) antiquity; ancient times (*pl.*) **3.** *pl.* (*oggetti antichi*) antiques, antiquities, old curiosities: *negozio di* —, antique-shop.

anticiclóne, *s.m.* (*meteorologia*) anticyclone.

anticiclònico, *ag.* (*meteorologia*) anticyclonic.

anticipàre, *v.t.* to anticipate, to forestall; (*denaro*) to pay in advance, to advance || *v.i.* to come earlier, to happen earlier: *quest'anno il caldo ha anticipato,* this year warm weather has come earlier.

anticipataménte, *av.* in advance, beforehand, in anticipation: *ringraziare, pagare* —, to thank, to pay in advance.

anticipàto, *ag.* advanced: *pagamento* —, (*comm.*) payment in advance, prepayment.

anticipazióne, *s.f.* anticipation; (*comm.*) advance: — *in conto corrente,* (*comm.*) advance on current account; *concedere un'*—, (*comm.*) to grant an advance.

antícipo, *s.m.* **1.** advance; (*caparra*) earnest: *dare un* —, to give an earnest || *in* —, in advance (*o* before time); *essere in* —, to be before time; *pagare in* —, to pay in advance **2.** (*aut.*) spark advance, spark lead.

anticlericàle, *ag.s.m.* anticlerical.

anticlericalísmo, *s.m.* anticlericalism.

antíco, *ag.* ancient: *greco* —, ancient Greek; *il mondo* —, the ancient world; *monumento* —, ancient monument; *storia antica,* ancient history; *i tempi più antichi,* the earliest times || *gli antichi,* the ancients || *l'Antico Testamento,* the Old Testament || *all'antica,* old-fashioned, out of date: *siamo un tantino all'antica,* we are a bit old-fashioned.

anticolèrico, *ag.* (*farm.*) anticholeric.

anticomunísta, *ag.s.c.* anti-communist.

anticongelànte, *s.m.* (*aut.*) anti-freeze, anti-freezing mixture.

anticonoscènza, *s.f.* (*fil.*) foreknowledge, prescience.

anticonóscere, *v.t.* to foreknow, to forebode.

anticòrpo, *s.m.* (*fisiol.*) antibody.

anticorrosivo, *ag.* anticorrosive, corrosion-proofing || *s.m.* anticorrosion, anticorrosive.

anticórte, *s.f.* forecourt.

anticostituzionàle, *ag.* anticonstitutional.

antícresi, *s.m.* (*dir.*) antichresis.

anticristiàno, *ag.* antichristian.

anticrísto, *s.m.* Antichrist.

anticrittogàmico, *ag.s.m.* (*agr.*) anticryptogamic; fungicide.

antidàta, *s.f.* antedate, foredate.

antidatàre, *v.t.* to antedate, to foredate.

antidemocràtico, *ag.* antidemocratic.

antidiftèrico, *ag.* (*farm.*) antidiphtheric.

antidiluviàno, *ag.s.m.* antediluvian (anche *fig.*).

antidinàstico, *ag.* antidynastic.

antídoto, *s.m.* (*farm.*) antidote.

antiemètico, *ag.* (*farm.*) antiemetic.

antiestètico, *ag.* antiæsthetic, unæsthetic.

antifascísmo, *s.m.* antifascism.

antifascísta, *ag.s.c.* antifascist.

antifebbríle, *ag.* (*farm.*) febrifugal, antifebrile || *s.m.* (*farm.*) febrifuge.

antiflogístico, *ag.* (*farm.*) antiphlogistic.

antífona, *s.f.* (*mus. eccl.*) antiphon, antiphony || *capire l'*—, *fig.* to take a hint || *ripetere la stessa* —, *fig.* to be always harping on the same string.

antifonàrio, *s.m.* (*mus. eccl.*) antiphonary.

antífrasi, *s.f.* (*ret.*) antiphrasis.

antifràstico, *ag.* (*ret.*) antiphrastic.

antifrizióne, *s.f.* antifriction: *metallo* —, babbitt.

antifúrto, *ag.s.m.* antitheft: *dispositivo* —, antitheft device.

antigàs, *ag.* anti-gas, gas-proof: *maschera* —, gas-mask.

antígene, *s.* (*farm.*) antigen.

Antígone, *no.pr.f.* (*mit.*) Antigone.

Antílle (le), *no.pr.f.pl.* (*geogr.*) the Antilles.

antilogía, *s.f.* antilogy.

antílope, *s.m.* (*zool.*) antelope.

antimalàrico, *ag.* (*farm.*) antimalarial.

antimatèria, *s.f.* (*fis.*) anti-matter.

antimeridiàno, *ag.* antemeridian; ante meridiem (*abbr.* a. m.): *erano le sette antimeridiane,* it was seven a. m. (o seven in the morning).

antimilitarísmo, *s.m.* antimilitarism.

antimilitarísta, *s.c.* antimilitarist; pacifist.

antimilitarístico, *ag.* antimilitaristic.

antimonàrchico, *ag.* antimonarchic(al).

antimoniàle, *ag.* (*chim.*) antimonial.

antimònico, *ag.* (*chim.*) antimonic.

antimònio, *s.m.* (*chim.*) antimony: [*solfuro di* —, antimony sulfide.

antimonióso, *ag.* (*chim.*) antimonious.

antinazionàle, *ag.* antinational.

antinefrítico, *ag.* (*farm.*) antinephritic.

antineuròtico, *ag.* (*farm.*) antineurotic.

antineutróne, *s.m.* (*fis.*) antineutron.

antinevràlgico, *ag.* (*farm.*) antinevralgic.

antinomía, *s.f.* antinomy.

Antiòchia, *no.pr.f.* (*geog.*) Antioch.

Antíoco, *no.pr.m.* (*st.*) Antiochus.

antiofídico, *ag.* (*farm.*) antiophidic: *siero* —, antiophidic serum.

antipàpa, *s.m.* antipope.

antipàsto, *s.m.* hors-d'œuvre.

antipatía, *s.f.* antipathy, dislike, aversion: *provammo subito un'*— *reciproca,* we at once felt a mutual dislike; *avere* — *per qlcu., ql.co.,* to have an aversion to (*o* for) s.o., sthg.

antipaticaménte, *av.* disagreeably; unpleasantly.

antipàtico, *ag.* disagreeable; unpleasant: *come sei* — *oggi!,* how disagreeable you are to-day!; *mi è* —, I dislike him (*o* I feel a dislike for him).

antipenúltimo, *ag.* last but two.

antiperistàlsi, *s.f.* (*fisiol.*) antiperistalsis.

antiperistàltico, *ag.* (*fisiol.*) antiperistaltic.

antipirètico, *ag.* (*farm.*) antipyretic.

antipirína, *s.f.* (*farm.*) antipyrin.

antípodi, *s.m.pl.* antipodes || *essere agli* —, *fig.* to be poles apart (*o* to differ greatly).

antipolítico, *ag.* ill-advised.

antipòrta, *s.f.* **1.** outer door **2.** fortification in front of town gate **3.** (*tip.*) blank page before half-title.

antipòrto, *s.m.* outer port.

antiprotóne, *s.m.* (*fis.*) antiproton.

antiquària, *s.f.* antiquarianism; archeology.

antiquariàto, *s.m.* antique-trade.

antiquàrio, *ag.* antiquarian: *libreria antiquaria,* antiquarian bookshop ‖ *s.m.* **1.** antiquary; antique dealer **2.** (*studioso d'antichità*) archaelogist.

antiquàto, *ag.* **1.** antiquated: *persona, scrittura antiquata,* antiquated person, writing **2.** (*fuori moda*) old-fashioned, out of date: *termine* —, obsolete word.

antiràbbico, *ag.* (*farm.*) antirabic.

antireligióso, *ag.* antireligious.

antireumàtico, *ag.* (*farm.*) antirheumatic.

antirivoluzionàrio, *ag.* antirevolutionary ‖ *s.m.* antirevolutionist.

antirúggine, *ag.* anti-rust (*attributivo*); rust-proof, rust-resistant: *vernice* —, anti-rust paint.

antisàla, *s.f.* antechamber.

antischiavismo, *s.m.* antislavery.

antiscorbútico, *ag.* (*farm.*) antiscorbutic.

antisdrucciolévole, *ag.* anti-slip (*attributivo*); (*aut.*) anti-skid (*attributivo*), non-skid (*attributivo*).

antisemíta, *s.c.* anti-Semite.

antisemitismo, *s.m.* anti-Semitism.

antisèpsi, *s.f.* (*med.*) antisepsis.

antisèttico, *ag.* (*farm.*) antiseptic: *medicazione* —, antiseptic dressing.

antisociàle, *ag.* antisocial.

antispasmòdico, *ag.* (*farm.*) antispasmodic.

antistamína, *s.f.* (*farm.*) antihistamine.

antistànte, *ag.* before, in front of: *il giardino* — *la casa,* the garden before the house.

antistèrico, *ag.* (*farm.*) antihysteric.

antístite, *s.m.* (*eccl.*) antistes (*pl.* antistites).

antístrofe, *s.f.* (*poes.*) antistrophe.

antítesi, *s.f.* antithesis (*pl.* antitheses).

antitetànico, *ag.* (*farm.*) antitetanic: *siero* —, antitetanic serum.

antiteticaménte, *av.* antithetically.

antitètico, *ag.* antithetic(al).

antitossína, *s.f.* (*chim. biol.*) antitoxin.

antivedére, *v.t.* to foresee.

antiveggènte, *ag.* foreseeing.

antiveggènza, *s.f.* foresight; foreknowledge.

antivenèreo, *s.m.* (*farm.*) antivenereal remedy.

antiveníre, *v.t.* to forestall, to anticipate.

antivigília, *s.f.* the day before the eve: *l'* — *di Natale,* two days before Christmas.

antología, *s.f.* anthology.

antològico, *ag.* anthological.

Antònia, *no.pr.f.* Antonia ‖ *dim.* Antoniette, Netty.

Antònio, *no.pr.m.* Ant(h)ony; (*st.*) Antonius ‖ *dim.* Tony, Nanty.

antonomàsia, *s.f.* (*ret.*) antonomasia.

antonomasticaménte, *av.* (*ret.*) antonomastically.

antonomàstico, *ag.* (*ret.*) antonomastic.

antràce, *s.m.* (*patol.*) anthrax.

antracène, *s.f.* (*chim.*) anthracene.

antracíte, *s.f.* (*min.*) anthracite.

àntro, *s.m.* **1.** (*caverna*) cave, cavern; grotto **2.** (*tana*) den (anche *fig.*) **3.** (*anat.*) antrum; cavity: — *pilorico,* antrum pyloricum.

antropocèntrico, *ag.* (*fil.*) anthropocentric.

antropofagía, *s.f.* anthropophagy.

antropòfago, *ag.* anthropophagous ‖ *s.m.* cannibal.

antropòide, *ag. s.m.* (*zool.*) anthropoid.

antropología, *s.f.* anthropology.

antropològico, *ag.* anthropological.

antropòlogo, *s.m.* anthropologist.

antropometría, *s.f.* anthropometry.

antropomètrico, *ag.* anthropometric(al): *ufficio* —, criminal anthropometry department.

antropomòrfe, *s.f.pl.* (*zool.*) anthropoids.

antropomorfísmo, *s.m.* anthropomorphism.

antropomorfíta, *s.m.* anthropomorphite.

antropomòrfo, *ag.* anthropomorphous, anthropoid.

anulàre, *ag.* annular; ring-like ‖ *eclisse* —, (*astr.*) annular eclipse ‖ *s.m.* ring-finger.

anurèsi, *s.f.* (*patol.*) anury.

anúri, *s.m.pl.* (*zool.*) Anoura.

ànzi, *cong.* **1.** (*di più*) nay; and even; and more than that: *un amico,* — *un fratello,* a friend, nay a brother; *sto bene,* — *benissimo,* I am well, indeed, very well **2.** (*al contrario*) **on the contrary:** *non è stupido,* — *è intelligente,* he is not silly, on the contrary, he is intelligent **3.** — *che,* **rather than 4.** — *che no,* rather: *sei sciocchino* — *che no,* you are rather silly.

ànzi, *prep.* **before:** *voi arrivate* — *tempo,* you arrive before time.

anzianità, *s.f.* seniority: *diritto di* —, right of seniority; *per* —, in order of seniority; *ha venti anni di* —, he has been 20 years in office (on the rolls); *avanzare per* —, to be promoted by (order of) seniority.

anziàno, *ag.* **1.** (*avanti negli anni*) elderly; (*vecchio*) old **2.** (*che è stato nominato prima, che ha occupato per primo un posto*) senior: *il socio* —, the senior partner ‖ *s.m.* **1.** (*st.*) (*magistrato delle repubbliche italiane nel Medioevo*) elder **2.** (*decano*) doyen.

anzianòtto, *ag.* elderly, getting old.

anziché, *cong.* **1.** (*piuttosto che*) **rather than 2.** (*invece di*) **instead of** (sthg., doing).

anzidétto, *ag.* aforesaid, aforenamed, above-mentioned, aforecited.

anzitèmpo, *av.* before time.

anzitútto, *av.* first of all, in the first place.

aònio, *ag.* (*mit.*) Aonian.

aorísto, *s.m.* (*gram.*) aorist.

aòrta, *s.f.* (*anat.*) aorta.

aortíte, *s.f.* (*patol.*) aortitis.

apache, *s.m.* **1.** (*pellerossa*) Apache **2.** (*teppista*) apache.

apagogía, *s.f.* (*fil.*) apagoge.

apatía, *s.f.* apathy, indifference, listlessness: *uscire da uno stato di* —, to rouse oneself.

apaticaménte, *av.* apathetically, listlessly.

apàtico, *ag.* apathetic(al), listless.

apatíte, *s.f.* (*min.*) apatite.

àpe, *s.f.* bee; (*maschio*) drone: — *operaia,* working bee (o worker); — *regina,* queen bee; *nido di api,* honeycomb; (*ricamo*) smocking.

apepsía, *s.f.* (*patol.*) apepsy.

aperitívo, *s.m.* aperitif; appetizer.

apèrta, *s.f.* opening ‖ *all'* —, frankly.

apertaménte, *av.* openly, plainly, frankly.

apèrto, *ag.* **1.** open: — *al pubblico,* open to the public; — *tutta la notte,* open all night; *chi ha lasciato la porta aperta?,* who has left the door open? ‖ *a braccia aperte,* with open arms; *a cuore* —, with open heart; *a mani aperte,* with open hands ‖ *ad occhi aperti,* with open eyes (o open-eyed): *sognare ad occhi aperti,* to day-dream ‖ *faccia aperta,* fig. open face; *uomo di mente aperta,* fig. open-minded man; *a viso* —, frankly **2.** fig. open: *aperta campagna,* the open country; *all'aria aperta,* in the open air (o in the open); *giuochi all'aria aperta,* outdoor games; *mare* —, open sea **3.** (*manifesto*) open: *guerra aperta,* open hostilities; *nemico* — *del governo,* open enemy of the government **4.** (*comm.*): *credito* —, open credit; *tenere un conto* — *in banca,* to keep one's account open at the bank **5.** (*fonet.*) open: *vocale aperta,* open vowel ‖ *s.m.* open place, open air: *all'* —, in the open air: *cura all'* —, open air treatment; *una scuola all'* —, an open air school.

apèrto, *av.* plainly; frankly: *parlare* —, to speak frankly.

apertúra, *s.f.* **1.** opening: — *di una porta, di un museo,* opening of a door, of a Museum; — *di un testamento,* reading of a will ‖ *ore di* —, (*di negozio, ecc.*) business hours; (*di museo*) visiting hours **2.** (*inizio, inaugurazione*) opening, beginning: — *del Parlamento,* opening of Parliament; *l'* — *della caccia,* the first day of the shooting season; — *di ostilità,* outbreak of hostilities; *conferenza, cerimonia, discorso di* —, opening lecture, ceremony, speech **3.** (*spacco, foro*) opening, aperture; (*di una grotta*) mouth; (*in una siepe*) gap, break; (*di macchina automatica*) slot: *praticare un'—nella porta*, to cut a hole in the door **4.** (*di mente*) broad-mindedness **5.** (*comm.*) opening: — *di conto*, opening of an account; — *di credito*, cash credit (*o* opening of a credit); — *di fallimento*, docket opening; *corso di —*, opening rate **6.** (*ampiezza di un arco*) width, span; (*di un compasso*) spread of compass-legs **7.** (*mus.*) ouverture **8.** (*foto.*) aperture.

apètalo, *ag.* (*bot.*) apetalous.

apiàlo, *V.* **apicoltóre**.

apiària, *s.f.* bee-keeping, apiculture.

apiàrio, *s.m.* **1.** apiary **2.** (*alveare*) beehive.

àpice, *s.m.* **1.** (*mat.*) apex (*pl.* apices, apexes) **2.** (*rar.*) (*cima*) top, summit **3.** *fig.* acme, height, apex; climax: *l'— della gloria*, the height (*o* apex) of glory **4.** (*anat.*) apex (*pl.* apices, apexes): — *del cuore*, apex of the heart.

apicíte, *s.f.* (*patol.*) apicitis.

apicoltóre, *s.m.* bee-master, bee-keeper; apiarist, apiculturist.

apicoltúra, *s.f.* bee-keeping, apiculture.

àpio, *s.m.* (*bot.*) celery.

apiressía, *s.f.* (*med.*) apyrexy.

apirètico, *ag.* (*med.*) apyretic.

apístico, *ag.* apiarian.

aplanàtico, *ag.* (*ott.*) aplanatic.

aplomb, *s.m.* self-assurance, self-possession: *perdere l'—*, to loose one's self-possession.

apnèa, *s.f.* (*patol.*) apnoea, apnea.

apocalísse, *s.f.* apocalypse || *cavallo dell'—*, (*scherz.*) jade, sorry hack.

apocalíttico, *ag.* apocalyptic(al).

apocopàre, *v.t.* (*gram.*) to apocopate.

apòcope, *s.f.* (*gram.*) apocope.

apocrifo, *ag.* apocryphal || *libri apocrifi*, apocrypha.

apocromàtico, *ag.* (*ott.*) apochromatic.

apodíttico, *ag.* (*fil.*) apodictic(al), apodeictic.

àpodo, *ag.* (*zool.*) apodal || *s.m.* (*zool.*) apod.

apòdosi, *s.f.* (*gram.*) apodosis.

apòfisi, *s.f.* (*anat.*) apophysis.

apoftègma, *s.m.* apophthegm.

apogèo, *s.m.* (*astr.*) apogee (anche *fig.*): *la sua gloria ha raggiunto l'—*, his glory is at its apogee (*o* he is at the height of his glory).

apògrafo, *s.m.* apograph.

apòlide, *ag.s.c.* stateless (person).

apoliticità, *s.f.* **1.** unconcern for politics **2.** (*non attinenza con la politica*) want of political character.

apolítico, *ag.* non-political.

Apollinàre, *no.pr.m.* (*st.*) Apollinaris.

apollíneo, *ag.* **1.** Apollonian **2.** (*bellissimo*) handsome, of perfect beauty.

Apòllo, *no.pr.m.* (*mit.*) Apollo || *è un —*, *fig.* he is an Apollo.

apologètica, *s.f.* (*teol.*) apologetics.

apologètico, *ag.* apologetic(al).

apología, *s.f.* apologia.

apologísta, *s.m.* apologist.

apologizzàre, *v.i.* to apologize.

apòlogo, *s.m.* apologue.

aponeuròsi, *s.f.* (*anat.*) aponeurosis.

aponeuròtico, *ag.* (*anat.*) aponeurotic.

apoplessía, *s.f.* apoplexy.

apoplèttico, *ag.* apoplectic: *colpo —*, apoplectic fit (*o* stroke) || *s.* apoplectic.

a pòsta, *V.* **appòsta**.

apostasía, *s.f.* apostasy.

apòstata, *ag.s.c.* apostate.

apostatàre, *v.i.* to apostatize.

apostàtico, *ag.* apostatical.

apostèma, *s.m.* (*patol.*) apostem(a), abscess.

apostemàre, *v.i.* (*patol.*) to apostemate, to suppurate.

apostolàto, *s.m.* apostolate, apostleship.

apostolicaménte, *av.* apostolically.

apostòlico, *ag.* apostolic; (*papale*) papal: *benedizione apostolica*, apostolic benediction (*o* papal blessing); *legato —*, papal legate; *successione apostolica*, apostolic succession || *Chiesa apostolica romana*, Roman Catholic Church || *Sede apostolica*, Apostolic See || *simbolo —*, Apostles' Creed.

apòstolo, *s.m.* apostle: *il principe degli apostoli*, the Prince of the Apostles.

apostrofàre[1], *v.t.* (*gram.*) to apostrophize.

apostrofàre[2], *v.t.* (*ret.*) to apostrophize: — *qlcu.*, to address s.o.

apòstrofe, *s.f.* (*ret.*) apostrophe.

apòstrofo, *s.m.* (*gram.*) apostrophe.

apotèma, *s.f.* (*geom.*) apothem.

apoteòsi, *s.f.* apotheosis, deification || *fare l' — di qlcu.*, *fig.* to sing the praises of s.o.

appaceàre, *v.t.* to pack (up).

appacchettàre, *v.t.* to do up into a parcel; to parcel (up).

appaciaménto, *s.m.* appeasement.

appaciàre, **appacificàre**, *v.t.* to pacify, to appease || **appaciàrsi**, **appacificàrsi**, *v.r.* to be reconciled, to make peace; (*fam.*) to make it up.

appadiglionàre, *v.t.* to dispose as a pavilion || **appadiglionàrsi**, *v.r.* to pitch one's tent.

appagàbile, *ag.* satisfiable, that may (*o* can) be satisfied (*o* gratified): *la tua è una curiosità —*, yours is a curiosity that can be gratified.

appagaménto, *s.m.* satisfaction, gratification.

appagàre, *v.t.* to satisfy, to gratify, to please: *niente lo appaga*, nothing pleases him; — *il desiderio di qlcu.*, to gratify (*o* to meet *o* to grant) s.o.'s wish; — *la propria curiosità*, to gratify (*o* to satisfy) one's own curiosity; — *la sete*, to quench one's thirst || **appagàrsi**, *v.r.* to be satisfied (with sthg.), to be content (with sthg.): *mi appago di ciò che possiedo*, I am content with what I have.

appaiaménto, *s.m.* **1.** pairing, coupling **2.** (*di colori*) matching.

appaiàre, *v.t.* **1.** to couple, to pair **2.** (*armonizzare colori*, *capi di vestiario*) to match **3.** (*aggiogare buoi in coppia*) to yoke; (*apparigliare cavalli*) to match || **appaiàrsi**, *v.r.* **1.** to pair; (*di animali*) to mate **2.** (*armonizzare*) to match.

appaiàto, *ag.* **1.** coupled: *appaiati*, in pairs (*o* in couples): *lavorare appaiati*, to work in couples **2.** (*di capi di vestiario*, *colori*) matched.

Appalàchi (**gli**), *no.pr.m.pl.* (*geog.*) the Appalachians.

appallottàre, **appallottolàre**, *v.t.* to roll into a ball, to make into balls || **appallottàrsi**, **appallottolàrsi**, *v.r.* **1.** to form into a ball, into balls **2.** (*avvolgersi su se stesso*) to coil up.

appaltàre, *v.t.* to give (sthg.) out by contract.

appaltatóre, *s.m.*, **appaltatríce**, *s.f.* undertaker, bidder, contractor: *aspirante —*, tenderer.

appàlto, *s.m.* contract, bid, undertaking contract: *in —*, by contract: *lavoro in —*, contract work; *offerta di —*, tender; *concorrere per l'— di ql.co.*, to make a tender for sthg.; *dare in —*, to give out by contract; *mettere ql.co. in —*, to put out sthg. to contract; *prendere in —*, to take by contract.

appannàggio, *s.m.* apanage, appanage.

appannaménto, *s.m.* **1.** (*di metalli*) tarnishing; (*di vetri*, *specchi*) clouding, dimming, tarnishing **2.** (*della vista*) dimming.

appannàre, *v.t.* **1.** (*metalli*) to tarnish; (*vetri*, *specchi*) to cloud, to dim, to tarnish, to dull: — *uno specchio*, to tarnish (*o* to cloud) a mirror **2.** (*la vista*) to dim, to cloud: *occhi appannati di lacrime*, eyes dimmed (*o* clouded) with tears || **appannàrsi**, *v.r.* **1.** (*di vetri*, *specchi*) to tarnish **2.** (*della vista*) to grow dim.

appannàto, *ag.* **1.** (*di specchi*, *vetri*, *metalli*) tarnished **2.** (*di vista*) dim **3.** (*di voce*) veiled, husky: *voce appannata*, veiled (*o* husky) voice.

appannatúra, *s.f.* tarnishing, tarnish.

apparàto, *s.m.* **1.** (*apparecchio, apprestamento*) apparatus; (*mec.*) contrivance: — *chirurgico*, surgical apparatus; — *di guerra*, apparatus of war ‖ — *critico*, (*lett.*) apparatus criticus **2.** (*decorazione*) decoration, ornament **3.** (*spiegamento, mostra*) display, show; (*pompa*) pomp **4.** (*teat.*) scenery **5.** (*anat.*) apparatus: — *digerente*, digestive apparatus.

apparatóre, *s.m.*, **apparatríce**, *s.f.* decorator.

apparecchiaménto, *s.m.* preparation.

apparecchiàre, *v.t.* **1.** (*preparare*) to prepare: — *la tavola*, to lay the table (*o* the cloth) **2.** (*ind. tessile*) to dress: — *tessuti*, to dress textile fàbrics ‖ **apparecchiàrsi**, *v.r.* to get ready, to make oneself ready.

apparecchiàto, *ag.* ready, prepared.

apparecchiatóre, *s.m.* **apparecchiatríce**, *s.f.* decorator.

apparecchiatúra, *s.f.* **1.** (*preparazione*) preparation **2.** (*ind. tessile*) dressing.

apparécchio, *s.m.* **1.** apparatus, set; (*congegno*) device, appliance: — *compensatore*, (*ferr.*) compensating device; — *di ascolto*, listening apparatus; — *di illuminazione*, lighting apparatus; — *fotografico*, camera; — *per alta frequenza*, (*elett.*) high-frequency apparatus; — *radio*, radio set (*o* wireless); — *radiografico*, radiographic apparatus; — *ricevente*, receiving set; — *telefonico*, telephone (apparatus); — *telegrafico*, telegraph set; — *televisivo*, television set; — *trasmittente*, sender ‖ *resti all'*—!, (*tel.*) hold the line! **2.** (*aeroplano*) aeroplane, plane: — *da bombardamento*, bomber; — *da combattimento*, fighter; — *da ricognizione*, scouting plane; — *di linea*, airliner.

apparentaménto, *s.m.* alliance (anche *pol.*); connection.

apparentàrsi, *v.r.* to become related (to s.o.) by marriage: — *con una famiglia*, to marry into a family.

apparentàto, *ag.* related: *essere* — *con qlcu.*, to be related to s.o.

apparènte, *ag.* **1.** (*illusorio*) seeming, apparent: *morte* —, (*med.*) catalepsy **2.** (*evidente, chiaro*) apparent, evident, obvious, clear, plain.

apparenteménte, *av.* apparently, seemingly.

apparènza, *s.f.* **1.** appearance: *in* —, seemingly, apparently; *giudicando dalle apparenze*, to all appearance; *secondo le apparenze, dice il vero*, there is every indication of his speaking the truth; *giudicare dalle apparenze*, to judge from (*o* by) appearances; *introdursi presso qlcu. sotto falsa* —, to force one's way in under false pretences; *salvare l'*—, to save appearances (*o* to keep up appearances *o* to save one's face) ‖ *l'* — *inganna*, all is not gold that glitters **2.** (*aspetto*) appearance, aspect, look: *di bella* —, of good appearance (*o* good-looking) **3.** (*pompa*) ostentation, show: *per* —, ostentatiously; *un dono di molta* —, a showy present.

apparigliàre, *v.t.* to pair; to match, to couple.

apparíre, *v.i.* **1.** (*mostrarsi*) to appear, to become visible, to come into sight: *gli apparve un fantasma*, a ghost appeared to him; *un sorriso apparve sulle sue labbra*, a smile came to his lips ‖ — *nella nebbia, all'orizzonte*, to loom out of the fog, to loom upon the horizon **2.** (*aver l'aspetto*) to look, to seem: *vuole* — *elegante*, she wants to look elegant **3.** (*risultare*) to appear, to result: *da questi documenti appare che tu sbagli*, from these documents it appears (*o* results) you are wrong.

appariscènte, *ag.* **1.** (*che colpisce*) striking, conspicuous, remarkable **2.** (*vistoso*) gaudy, showy; ostentatious.

appariscènza, *s.f.* **1.** appearance, look **2.** (*vistosità*) showiness, gaudiness.

apparitóre, *s.m.* (*st.*) apparitor.

apparizióne, *s.f.* apparition.

appartaménto, *s.m.* flat, suite of rooms; (*amer.*) apartment: — *ammobiliato*, furnished flat; — *da affittare*, flat to let; — *senza ascensore*, (*amer.*) walk-up apartment.

appartàre, *v.t.* to set apart; (*separare*) to separate ‖ **appartàrsi**, *v.r.* to withdraw, to seclude oneself, to retire (anche *fig.*): — *nella propria stanza*, to retire to one's room.

appartataménte, *av.* apart, in seclusion, separately.

appartàto, *ag.* secluded, remote, set apart, lonely, solitary: *rimanere* —, to keep (oneself) to oneself; *vivere* —, to live in seclusion.

appartenènte, *ag.* belonging, pertaining.

appartenènza, *s.f.* **1.** belongings (*pl.*) **2.** (*annesso*) appurtenance, appendage.

appartenére, *v.i.* **1.** to belong, to appertain: *terre appartenenti allo Stato*, lands belonging to the State **2.** (*essere parente, amico, ecc.*) to be related **3.** (*essere iscritto a una società*) to be a member (of sthg.) **4.** (*convenire*) to lie within one's competence ‖ **appartenérsi**, *v.r.* to lie within one's competence.

appassiménto, *s.m.* withering, fading.

appassionaménto, *s.m.* passion, ardour, fervour.

appassionàre, *v.t.* to impassion, to excite with passion ‖ **appassionàrsi**, *v.r.* to become fond of (sthg.), to become impassioned of (sthg.), to conceive a passion for (sthg.).

appassionataménte, *av.* passionately.

appassionàto, *ag.* **1.** impassioned, passionate **2.** (*che ha passione per ql.co.*) keen (on sthg.): — *per la musica*, keen on music **2.** (*parziale*) partial, one-sided, biased ‖ *s.m.* fan: — *del calcio*, foot-ball fan.

appassíre, *v.t.i.* to wither, to fade; to dry up ‖ *fare* —, to wither *o v.i.*, **appassírsi**, *v.r.* to wither, to fade (anche *fig.*).

appassíto, *ag.* withered, faded; dried up.

appassitúra, *s.f.* withering, fading.

appastàrsi, *v.r.* to thicken to a paste.

appellàbile, *ag.* (*dir.*) appealable.

appellabilità, *s.f.* (*dir.*) power, right of appeal.

appellànte, *ag.* (*dir.*) appellant, appealing: *la parte* —, the appealing party ‖ *s.c.* (*dir.*) appellant.

appellàre, *v.t.* to name, to denominate, to call ‖ *v.i.*, **appellàrsi**, *v.r.* to appeal (anche *dir.*): *mi appello al vostro buon senso*, I appeal to your common sense; — *a un'altra corte*, to appeal to another court.

appellatívo, *ag.s.m.* appellative.

appellazióne, *s.f.* **1.** (*dir.*) appellation **2.** (*denominazione*) name.

appèllo, *s.m.* **1.** (*dir.*) appeal: *giudizio senza* —, final appeal; *senza* —, not appealable: *la decisione di questa corte è senza* —, there is no appeal from this court; *fare* — (*a un tribunale*) *contro una decisione*, to appeal (to a court) against a decision; *interporre* — *contro qlcu.*, to bring an appeal against s.o.; *respingere una sentenza in* —, to quash a sentence on appeal; *ricorrere in* —, to appeal ‖ *Corte d'*—, Court of Appeal **2.** (*chiamata, rassegna*) call, roll-call, muster: *fare l'*—, to call (over) the roll; *mancare all'*—, to be absent; *rispondere all'*—, to answer the roll-call **3.** (*esortazione, invocazione*) appeal, call: *il suo caldo* — *fu ascoltato*, his warm appeal was listened to; *fare* — *a qlcu.*, to appeal to s.o. (*o* to call upon s.o.'s help) ‖ *fare* — *a tutto il proprio coraggio*, to summon up (*o* to call on) all one's courage.

appéna, *av.* **1.** (*a fatica*) scarcely, hardly, with difficulty: *potevo* — *capirlo*, I could hardly understand him **2.** (*pochissimo*) very little, scantily **3.** (*da poco*) just; scarcely, hardly: — *uscito*, (*di pubblicazione*) just out; *eravamo* — *arrivati*, we had just arrived ‖ *morì* — *diciottenne*, she died when only eighteen **4.** (*correlativo*) hardly...(when); as soon as, no sooner...than: *era* — *entrato quando squillò il telefono*, he had hardly come in when the telephone rang; *eravamo* — *usciti quando incominciò a piovere*, hardly had we gone out when the rain began; (*non*) — *arrivai lo vidi*, as soon as I arrived I saw him (*o* no sooner did I arrive than I saw him).

appenàre, *v.t.* (*rar.*) to distress, to afflict.

appèndere, *v.t.* **1.** to hang (up): *dobbiamo — i quadri alle pareti*, we must hang the pictures on the walls **2.** (*impiccare*) to hang.

appendíce, *s.f.* **1.** (*aggiunta*) appendix (*pl.* appendixes, appendices), appendage **2.** (*di libro, giornale*) appendix (*pl.* appendixes, appendices); supplement ‖ *romanzo d'—*, serial (story) **3.** (*anat.*) appendix (*pl.* appendixes, appendices), appendage: — *caudale*, caudal appendage; — *vermicolare*, vermiform appendix.

appendicíte, *s.f.* (*patol.*) appendicitis.

appendicolàre, *ag.* (*anat.*) appendicular.

appenditóre, *s.m.* hanger.

appendízie, *s.f.pl.* payment in kind (*sing.*).

appennecchiàre, *v.t.* to fill (a distaff) with (wool, flax, etc.).

appennellàre, *v.t.* (*mar.*) to back.

Appennini (gli), *no.pr.m.pl.* (*geog.*) the Apennines.

appercezióne, *s.f.* (*fil.*) apperception.

appesantíre, *v.t.* to make heavy, to weigh down; *fig.* to make dull: *occhi appesantiti dal sonno*, eyes heavy with sleep; *troppi particolari appesantiscono questo romanzo*, too many details make this novel dull reading ‖ **appesantírsi,** *v.r.* to become heavier, to get heavier, to grow heavier.

appéso, *ag.* hanging, suspended: *un lampadario — al soffitto*, an electric lamp hanging from the ceiling; *un quadro — a una parete*, a picture hanging on a wall.

appestàre, *v.t.* **1.** (*infettare*) to infect; to taint, to plague **2.** (*impuzzire*) to stink ‖ **3.** *fig.* to taint; to corrupt ‖ *v.i.* (*puzzare fieramente*) to stink.

appestàto, *ag.* **1.** infected (with the plague), plague-stricken; tainted (anche *fig.*) **2.** (*fetido*) stinking ‖ *s.m.* person infected with the plague; plague-stricken person.

appetènte, *ag.* **1.** (*appetitoso*) appetizing **2.** (*desiderabile*) desirable, tempting, alluring, enticing.

appetènza, *s.f.* **1.** (*appetito*) appetite **2.** (*desiderio*) appetency, appetence, longing for (sthg.).

appetíbile, *ag.* desirable, pleasing, attractive.

appetibilità, *s.f.* desirability, attractiveness.

appetíre, *v.t.* (*desiderare*) to desire eagerly, greatly; to crave for, after (sthg.) ‖ *v.i.* (*destare l'appetito*) to stimulate the appetite, to whet the appetite: *quel cibo appetisce poco*, that food is not very appetizing.

appetitívo, *ag.* appetitive, appetizing.

appetíto, *s.m.* appetite; *fig.* appetite, desire; lust: *un buon —*, a good appetite; *mancanza di —*, loss of appetite; *mangiare con —*, to eat with (an) appetite; *mortificare gli appetiti*, to mortify carnal lusts; *riacquistare l'—*, to recover one's appetite; *rovinare l'— a qlcu.*, to spoil (*o* to take away) s.o.'s appetite; *stuzzicare l'—*, to whet the appetite ‖ *l'— viene mangiando*, *prov.* the appetite grows with what it feeds on.

appetitosaménte, *av.* **1.** with appetite **2.** (*in modo da stimolare l'appetito*) appetizingly.

appetitóso, *ag.* appetizing; *fig.* tempting, attractive.

appètto a, *prep.* **1.** (*dirimpetto*) opposite, facing **2.** (*in confronto*) in comparison (with s.o., sthg.) **3.** (*contro*) against ‖ *stare — a qlcu.*, to stand face to face with s.o.

appezzaménto, *s.m.* plot of land, piece of ground.

appezzàre, *v.t.* **1.** (*mettere insieme*) to piece together **2.** (*dividere in pezzi*) to divide, to separate into pieces.

appezzatúra, *s.f.* **1.** piecing, repairing, patching **2.** (*punto di congiunzione*) join.

appiacevolíre, *v.t.* to make pleasant, to make agreeable.

appianàbile, *ag.* **1.** that may be levelled; that may be smoothed over (anche *fig.*) **2.** (*che può essere risolto*) that may be settled.

appianaménto, *s.m.* **1.** levelling, smoothing **2.** settling, removal.

appianàre, *v.t.* **1.** to level, to flatten, to plane, to smooth: — *una strada*, to level a road **2.** *fig.* to smooth away; to remove; to settle: — *una difficoltà*, to smooth

over (*o* away) a difficulty (*o* to remove a difficulty); — *una questione*, to settle a question.

appianatóia, *s.f.* (*strum. artig.*) float.

appianatóio, *s.m.* roller; steam roller.

appiastràre, *v.t.* **1.** to plaster **2.** (*appiccicare*) to stick.

appiastratúra, *s.f.* **1.** plastering **2.** (*appiccicatura*) sticking.

appiastricciàre, *V.* **appiccicàre.**

appiattaménto, *s.m.* **1.** crouching **2.** (*occultamento*) hiding; concealment.

appiattàre, *v.t.* **1.** (*appiattire*) to flatten **2.** (*mettere di piatto*) to lay flat **3.** (*nascondere*) to hide, to conceal ‖ **appiattàrsi,** *v.r.* **1.** (*nascondersi*) to conceal oneself, to hide oneself, to be in hiding **2.** (*stare in agguato*) to lie in wait **3.** (*rannicchiarsi*) to crouch.

appiattiménto, *s.m.* flattening; levelling.

appiattíre, *v.t.* **1.** to flatten, to make flat; to level **2.** (*avvilire*) to humble; to degrade ‖ **appiattírsi,** *v.r.* to become flat, to flatten; (*di pneumatici*) to become deflated.

appiàtto, (*rar.*) per **appiattaménto.**

appiccàgnolo, *s.m.* **1.** hook, peg **2.** *fig.* pretext, cavil.

appiccaménto, *s.m.* hanging.

appiccàre, *v.t.* **1.** (*congiungere*) to join **2.** (*appendere*) to hang (up): *egli appiccò il cappello a un gancio*, he hung his hat on a peg **3.** (*impiccare*) to hang **4.** — *il fuoco a*, to set fire to **5.** (*cominciare*) to start: — *battaglia*, to give battle **6.** (*contagiare*) to infect, to contaminate ‖ **appiccàrsi,** *v.r.* **1.** (*attaccarsi*) to fasten on, to cling **2.** (*impiccarsi*) to hang oneself **3.** (*comunicarsi, di contagio*) to get affected.

appiccatíccio, *ag.* sticky (anche *fig.*); gluey.

appiccatúra, *s.f.* joining.

appiccicànte, *ag.* adhesive; sticky; gluey.

appiccicàre, *v.t.* **1.** to stick; (*attaccare*) to attach, to join; (*con colla liquida*) to glue; (*con colla in pasta*) to paste **2.** *fig.* (*appioppare*) to palm off, to fob off, to foist: *mi appiccicarono una moneta falsa*, they palmed off a bad coin on me ‖ — *uno schiaffo a qlcu.*, to slap (*o* to smack) s.o.'s face ‖ *v.i.* to be sticky, gluey ‖ **appiccicàrsi,** *v.r.* to stick, to adhere; *fig.* to hang on, to stick: *egli è sempre appiccicato alle gonne della mamma*, he is always hanging on to his mother.

appiccicatíccio, *ag.* sticky (anche *fig.*); gluey ‖ *s.m.* patchwork, jumble.

appiccicatúra, *s.f.* **1.** sticking, gumming **2.** (*unione malfatta*) patching.

appiccichíno, *s.m.* sticker, hanger-on.

appiccicóso, *ag.* sticky, gluey.

appicciníre, appicciolíre, *v.t.* to make smaller, to belittle.

appícco, *s.m.* *fig.* pretext, peg, cavil.

appiccolíre, *v.t.* to make smaller, to belittle.

appiè, a piè, *prep.* below, at the bottom, at the foot: — *del letto, del monte*, at the foot of the bed, of the mountain; — *delle scale*, downstairs; — *di pagina*, at the foot of the page ‖ *av.* below, at the foot.

appiedàre, *v.t.* to dismount.

appièno, *av.* fully; quite; thoroughly.

appigionaménto, *s.m.* letting; renting.

appigionàre, *v.t.* **1.** (*dare a pigione*) to let, to lease (out) ‖ *appigionasi*, house to let **2.** (*prendere a pigione*) to rent, to lease.

appigliàrsi, *v.r.* **1.** to get hold (of sthg.), to hold on, to cling **2.** *fig.* to follow (sthg.): — *a un pretesto*, to take a pretext.

appíglio, *s.m.* pretext, cavil: *dare — alle critiche*, to give occasion (*o* a pretext) to censure.

appinzàre, *v.t.* to prick; (*di insetti*) to sting; to bite.

appinzatúra, *s.f.* pricking; (*di insetti*) bite; sting.

àppio, *s.m.* (*bot.*) celery.

appiómbo, *av.* perpendicularly ‖ *s.m.* **1.** perpendicularity: *prendere l'— di un muro*, to take the plumb of a wall **2.** *fig.* self-assurance, self-possession: *perdere l'—*, to lose one's self-possession (*o* one's nerve).

appioppàre, *v.t.* **1.** to give: — *un calcio a qlcu.*, to give s.o. a kick; — *uno schiaffo a qlcu.*, to slap (*o* to smack) s.o.'s face **2.** (*affibbiare*) to palm off, to fob off, to foist, to pass off: — *un diamante falso a qlcu.*, to fob off (*o* to palm off) an imitation diamond on s.o. **3.** (*piantare a pioppi*) to plant with poplars.

appisolàrsi, *v.r.* to doze off, to drop asleep.

applacidíre, *v.t.* to appease, to abate || **applacidírsi,** *v.r.* to become appeased, to calm down.

applaudíre, *v.t.* **1.** to applaud; (*con la voce*) to cheer; (*con le mani*) to clap **2.** *fig.* to applaud, to praise, to approve, to commend || *v.i.* to clap one's hands.

applauditóre, *s.m.*, **applauditríce,** *s.f.* applauder.

applàuso, *s.m.* **1.** applause (*solo sing.*); (*a gran voce*) cheers (*pl.*): *applausi prolungati*, great applause (*o* loud cheers) **2.** *fig.* praise, approval.

applicàbile, *ag.* applicable: *questa regola è — a tutti i casi*, this rule applies to all cases.

applicabilità, *s.f.* applicability.

applicàre, *v.t.* **1.** to apply, to lay: — *un linimento, un cataplasma*, to apply a liniment, a poultice; — *ql.co. a qlcu.*, to apply (*o* to lay) sthg. on (*o* to) s.o. || — *uno schiaffo alla faccia di qlcu.*, to slap (*o* to smack) s.o.'s face **2.** (*dir.*) to carry out, to enforce, to administer: — *la legge*, to bring (*o* to put) the law into operation (*o* to enforce the law); — *una legge a un caso particolare*, to apply a law to a special case; — *una multa*, to impose a fine **3.** (*accostare*) to set: — *una tromba alle (proprie) labbra*, to set a bugle to one's lips **4.** (*rivolgere, dedicare*) to apply: — *la mente a ql.co.*, to apply (*o* to turn *o* to bend) one's mind to sthg.; — *il proprio sapere*, to apply one's knowledge **5.** (*assegnare, un ufficio*) to appoint, to nominate || **applicàrsi,** *v.r.* to apply oneself, to devote oneself: *quello scolaro si applica molto*, that schoolboy studies very hard.

applicatamént e, *av.* carefully, diligently.

applicàto, *ag.* **1.** applied: *arte applicata*, applied (*o* industrial) art **2.** *fig.* studious, diligent || *s.m.* clerk (in an inferior position).

applicazióne, *s.f.* **1.** application: — *di ghiaccio sulla fronte*, application of ice to the forehead || *scuola d'—*, school of instruction **2.** *fig.* (close) attention, care, diligence; intense study; steadiness **3.** (*guarnizione*) trimming **4.** (*dir.*) enforcement || *in — della legge*, in pursuance of the law **5.** (*ind.*) appliance: *applicazioni industriali*, industrial appliances.

appoderaménto, *s.m.* turning into farm-land.

appoderàre, *v.t.* to turn into farm-land || **appoderàrsi,** *v.r.* to settle on a farm.

appoderàto, *ag.* cultivated, under crop.

appoderazióne, *s.f.* turning into farm-land.

appoggiacàpo, *s.m.* **1.** head-rest **2.** (*copripoltrona*) antimacassar; (*amer.*) tidy.

appoggiamàno, *s.m.* **1.** hand-rest **2.** (*pitt.*) maulstick.

appoggiaménto, *s.m.* supporting.

appoggiàre, *v.t.* **1.** to lean; (*posare*) to lay, to put; to rest: *ecco il piatto, appoggialo sul tavolo*, here is the plate, lay it on the table; — *una scala al muro*, to lean a ladder against the wall; — *la testa su un cuscino*, to rest one's head on a pillow **2.** *fig.* to back, to support: — *una mozione*, to second a motion; — *una petizione*, to support a petition; — *qlcu. in una richiesta*, to support (*o* to back up) s.o. in a request **3.** (*mus.*) to dwell on (a note), to sustain (a note) || **appoggiàrsi,** *v.r.* **1.** to lean: *voleva — al mio braccio*, he wanted to lean on my arm; — *al muro*, to lean against the wall **2.** *fig.* to rely (on s.o., sthg.), to depend (on s.o., sthg.) || — *sull'autorità di qlcu.*, to found upon (*o* to take one's stand on) s.o.'s authority **3.** (*di uccello*) to perch, to roost.

appoggiàta, *V.* **appoggiatúra 1.**

appoggiatèsta, *V.* **appoggiacàpo.**

appoggiatóio, *s.m.* **1.** support, rest **2.** (*spalliera*) back **3.** (*ringhiera di scala*) stair-rail, banisters.

appoggiatúra, *s.f.* **1.** (*l'appoggiare*) supporting; (*l'appoggiarsi*) leaning, resting **2.** (*mus.*) appoggiatura.

appòggio, *s.m.* **1.** support: *muro d'—*, supporting (*o* retaining *o* bearing) wall; *piano di —*, (*mec.*) face; *punto di —*, (*mec.*) fulcrum **2.** *fig.* assistance, support, backing: — *a un candidato*, backing (up) of a candidate; *dare il proprio — a qlcu.*, to back s.o. up; *essere senza alcun —*, to be unprotected **3.** (*persona che appoggia*) supporter **4.** (*comm.*) (*comprova*) voucher: *documenti all'—*, proofs and illustrations; *documento d'—*, voucher.

appollaiàrsi, *v.r.* to roost, to perch.

appoppàto, *ag.* (*mar.*) tail-heavy, stern-heavy, down by the stern; (*aer.*) tail-heavy.

appórre, *v.t.* **1.** to affix: — *la propria firma*, to affix one's signature; — *il proprio sigillo*, to affix one's seal; — *i sigilli*, to affix (*o* to place) the seals **2.** (*una clausola*) to insert, to append: — *una clausola ad un atto*, to insert a clause in (*o* to add a clause to) an act **3.** (*attribuire, imputare*) to ascribe, to impute || **appórsi,** *v.r.* to guess, to hit the mark: *se mal non mi appongo*, if I am not mistaken.

apportàre, *v.t.* **1.** to bring: — *delle notizie a qlcu.*, to bring news to s.o. **2.** (*produrre*) to produce, to yield, to bring in: *il commercio apporta benessere*, trade produces prosperity **3.** (*causare*) to cause, to occasion: *la guerra apporta carestia*, war causes famine **4.** (*comm.*) to contribute.

apportatóre, *s.m.*, **apportatríce,** *s.f.* messenger; bearer; — *di pace*, messenger of peace.

appòrto, *s.m.* **1.** (*comm.*) contribution: — *di capitale*, contribution (*o* increase) of capital **2.** (*spiritismo*) apport.

appositaménte, *av.* on purpose, purposely, deliberately, intentionally.

appositívo, *ag.* (*gram.*) appositive, in apposition, appositional.

appositízio, *ag.* artificial, feigned.

appòsito, *ag.* **1.** (*speciale*) special: *con — manifesto saranno indicati il giorno e l'ora di partenza*, the date and time of departure will be announced by special notices **2.** (*adatto*) suitable, fitting, proper: *luogo —*, proper place.

apposizióne, *s.f.* **1.** affixing: — *del sigillo*, affixing of the seal **2.** (*gram.*) apposition.

appòsta, *av.* **1.** (*di proposito*) on purpose; wilfully, intentionally: *sono certo che l'ha fatto —*, I am sure he did it on purpose **2.** (*con scopo preciso*) specially, for a special purpose, designedly.

appostaménto, *s.m.* **1.** (*agguato*) ambush: *truppe in —*, troops in ambush **2.** (*postazione*) emplacement.

appostàre, *v.t.* **1.** to lie in wait for (s.o., sthg.); to waylay **2.** (*adocchiare*) to watch || **appostàrsi,** *v.r.* to lie in wait, to lurk.

appozzàre, *v.t.* to make puddles in (sthg.) || **appozzàrsi,** *v.r.*: — *lo stomaco*, to make oneself sick with water.

appratiménto, *s.m.* turning into pasture-land.

appratíre, *v.t.i.*, **appratírsi,** *v.r.* to turn into pasture-land.

apprèndere, *v.t.* (*imparare*) to learn; (*venire a sapere*) to learn, to hear; to come to know of (sthg.); (*insegnare*) to teach: *ho appreso che...*, I have heard that... (*o* it has come to my knowledge that...); *l'ho appreso da buona fonte*, I have it on good authority; — *facilmente*, to be a quick learner || **apprèndersi,** *v.r.* to take hold (of sthg.), to cling (to sthg.).

apprendiménto, *s.m.* learning.

apprendísta, *s.c.* apprentice, beginner; (*in ufficio*) junior clerk: *mettere qlcu. come — presso qlcu.*, to apprentice s.o. to s.o. (*o* to bind s.o. as an apprentice to s.o.).

apprendistàto, *s.m.* apprenticeship: *fare l'— presso qlcu.*, to serve one's apprenticeship with s.o.

apprensióne, *s.f.* **1.** (*preoccupazione*) concern, anxiety; (*paura*) fear: *nutrire apprensioni sulla sorte di qlcu.,* to be uneasy about s.o.'s fate **2.** (*l'apprendere*) apprehension, learning **3.** (*comprensione*) understanding.

apprensíva, *s.f.* apprehension; understanding.

apprensívo, *ag.* **1.** (*ansioso*) uneasy, apprehensive; (*pauroso*) fearful **2.** (*atto ad apprendere*) quick, intelligent, receptive.

appressaménto, *s.m.* approach, drawing near.

appressàre, *v.t.* to bring (sthg.) near, to draw (sthg.) near ‖ **appressàrsi,** *v.r.* to approach (s.o., sthg.), to draw near (s.o., sthg.): *allora mi si appressò,* then he approached me (*o* drew near me).

apprèsso, *av.* near, close by; (*poi*) then ‖ *il giorno* —, the next day ‖ *come* —, as below (*o* as follows) ‖ *prep.* near, by, close to; (*dopo*) after; (*dietro*) behind; (*in confronto*) in comparison (with sthg.).

apprestaménto, *s.m.* preparation.

apprestàre, *v.t.* to prepare, to get ready; (*allestire*) to fit, to equip ‖ **apprestàrsi,** *v.r.* to prepare (oneself), to get ready: — *a fare ql.co.,* to prepare to do sthg.

apprettàre, *v.t.* (*ind. tessile*) to dress, to size.

apprettatúra, *s.f.* (*ind. tessile*) dressing, sizing.

apprètto, *s.m.* (*ind. tessile*) dressing: *dare l'* —, to size.

apprezzàbile, *ag.* appreciable, perceptible, appraisable; valuable.

apprezzaménto, *s.m.* **1.** appreciation, estimation; valuation **2.** (*valutazione, di terreno, ecc.*) evaluation **3.** (*giudizio*) opinion: *fece apprezzamenti sfavorevoli sulla tua condotta,* he expressed an unfavourable opinion on your behaviour.

apprezzàre, *v.t.* **1.** to appreciate; to esteem: *apprezzo il fatto che...,* I do not deny (*o* I quite realize *o* I am sensible of) the fact that...; *essere apprezzato,* to be appreciated (*o* to be held in repute) **2.** (*valutare*) to value, to appraise, to estimate.

approcciàrsi, *v.r.* (*arc.*) to approach (s.o., sthg.): *gli assedianti si approcciarono alla piazzaforte,* the besiegers approached the stronghold.

approccio, *s.m.* approach (anche *fig.*).

approdàre[1], *v.i.* (*riuscire*) to reach (sthg.): *a che approderete dopo questo?,* what will you come to, after this?; *non — a nulla,* to be (of) no avail: *questa discussione non approda a nulla,* this discussion is of no avail.

approdàre[2], *v.i.* (*mar.*) to land; to get ashore: *la nave approdò a New York,* the ship landed at New York; *non poterono* —, they could not get ashore.

approdàre[3], *v.t.* (*agr.*) to plant (sthg.) along the edges of a field.

apprôdo, *s.m.* (*mar.*) **1.** (*l'approdare*) landing **2.** (*luogo d'approdo*) landing-place.

approfittàre, *v.i.* to profit (by s.o., sthg.), to benefit (by s.o., sthg.); to gain (from s.o., sthg.) ‖ **approfittàrsi,** *v.r.* **1.** (*avvantaggiarsi, valersi*) to take advantage; to avail oneself: — *dell'occasione,* to avail oneself of the opportunity **2.** (*abusare*) to take undue advantage.

approfondaménto, *s.m.* **1.** deepening **2.** *fig.* search; probing.

approfondàre, *v.t.* **1.** to make deeper, to deepen **2.** *fig.* (*esaminare*) to examine closely, to probe into (sthg.), to search into (sthg.), to go deep into (sthg.) — *una questione,* to probe (*o* to go deep into) a question ‖ **approfondàrsi,** *v.r.* **1.** to become deeper **2.** *fig.* to learn thoroughly: *vorrebbe* — *nello studio dell'inglese,* he would like to get a deeper knowledge of English.

approfondimento, *V.* **approfondamónto.**

approfondíre, *V.* **approfondàre.**

approntàre, *v.t.* to make ready; to prepare.

appropinquàrsi, *v.r.* (*arc.*) to approach (s.o., sthg.): *appropinquati,* come nearer.

appropriàbile, *ag.* assumable; appropriable.

appropriàre, *v.t.* (*adattare*) to suit, to adapt, to arrange; to fit: — *il linguaggio alle circostanze,* to adapt one's language to the circumstances ‖ **appropriàrsi,**

v.r. **1.** to take possession of (sthg.), to take to oneself, to appropriate: — *indebitamente denaro,* to embezzle money **2.** (*assimilare*) to assimilate.

appropriataménte, *av.* appropriately; suitably.

appropriàto, *ag.* appropriate; suitable (for s.o., sthg.); (*opportuno*) convenient (for s.o., sthg.): — *all'occasione,* appropriate to the occasion; — *a questo uso,* suitable for (*o* to) this use; *un vocabolo* —, a proper word.

appropriazióne, *s.f.* appropriation, usurpation: — *fraudolenta,* fraudulent conversion; — *indebita,* embezzlement.

approssimàre, *v.t.* to bring (sthg.) near ‖ **approssimàrsi,** *v.r.* **1.** (*avvicinarsi*) to approach, to come near(er); (*di tempo*) to draw near: *l'inverno si approssima,* winter is drawing near **2.** *fig.* to approximate; to come near: *una bellezza che si approssima al sublime,* a beauty that approximates to the sublime (*o* a beauty that comes near to the sublime).

approssimativaménte, *av.* approximately; nearly.

approssimatívo, *ag.* approximative; approximate; rough: *ammontare* —, (*comm.*) approximate amount; *calcolo* —, rough estimate; *non è che una cifra approssimativa,* it is but a rough figure.

approssimazióne, *s.f.* approximation: *per* —, approximately, roughly.

approvàbile, *ag.* approvable; deserving approval.

approvaménto, *V.* **approvazióne.**

approvàre, *v.t.* **1.** to approve of (sthg., s.o.'s doing): *mio padre non approva affatto che noi mariniamo la scuola,* my father does not approve at all of our playing truant **2.** (*promuovere*) to pass: *essere approvato agli esami,* to pass one's examinations **3.** (*accettare ufficialmente*) to approve, to sanction: — *una legge,* to pass a bill **4.** (*acconsentire a*) to assent to (sthg.): — *una teoria,* to assent to a theory.

approvativo, *ag.* approbatory.

approvazióne, *s.f.* **1.** approval, approbation: *ottenere l'* — *di qlcu.,* to obtain s.o.'s approval **2.** (*sanzione*) sanction **3.** (*consenso*) assent.

approvvigionaménto, *s.m.* **1.** (*l'approvvigionare*) victualling, supplying: *l'* — *viveri di una nave,* the victualling of a ship **2.** *pl.* (*provviste*) provisions, supplies: *fonte di* —, source of supply **3.** (*armamento*) armament.

approvvigionàre, *v.t.* to provision, to supply provisions to (s.o., sthg.), to supply: — *di cibo,* to victual; — *di combustibile,* to supply with fuel.

approvvisionaménto, *V.* **approvvigionaménto.**

approvvisionàre, *V.* **approvvigionàre.**

appruàto, *ag.* (*mar.*) bow-heavy, down by the bow; (*aer.*) nose-heavy.

appúlso, *s.m.* (*astr.*) appulse.

appuntàbile, *ag.* imputable; blamable.

appuntaménto, *s.m.* **1.** rendezvous; (*professionale*) appointment; (*fam. amer.*) date: *luogo di* —, meeting-place; *ho un* — *col dentista,* I have an appointment with my dentist; *fissare un* — *con qlcu.,* to make a date with s.o.; *mancare a un* —, to break an appointment; *mantenere un* —, to keep an appointment **2.** (*incontro*) meeting: *il nostro* — *riuscì,* our meeting was successful **3.** (*arc.*) (*regolamento*) rule, regulation **4.** (*arc.*) (*accordo*) pact, agreement.

appuntàre. *v.t.* **1.** (*rendere appuntito*) to sharpen, to point **2.** (*dirigere, puntare*) to point; (*gli occhi*) to turn: — *il fucile contro qlcu.,* to point the gun at s.o.; — *gli occhi su ql.co.,* to turn one's eyes on sthg.; — *lo sguardo,* to look hard at sthg.) **3.** (*annotare*) to note (down), to make a note of (sthg.) **4.** (*censurare*) to blame, to censure **5.** (*fissare, stabilire*) to point out, to establish **6.** (*con spilli*) to pin (up): — *uno spillo su ql.co.,* to stick a pin into sthg. **7.** (*mec.*) (*saldare*) to tack-weld ‖ **appuntàrsi,** *v.r.* **1.** (*diventare appuntito*) to sharpen **2.** (*arrestarsi*) to stop **3.** (*essere rivolto*) to be pointed (at s.o., sthg.), to be turned: *il suo sguardo si appuntò su di me,* his look turned on me.

appuntàto, *ag.* 1. (*registrato*) registered, noted 2. (*preciso*) accurate, precise: *un uomo* —, an accurate man 3. (*aguzzo*) pointed, sharpened ‖ *s.m.* (*mil.*) lance -corporal (of the " Carabinieri ").

appuntàto, *av.* affectedly: *parlare* —, to talk in an affected manner.

appuntatóre, *s.m.* (*artig.*) glass-blower.

appuntatúra, *s.f.* 1. sharpening, pointing 2. *fig.* censure, blame.

appuntellàre, *v.t.* 1. to prop; to stay; to shore up 2. *fig.* to back, to support.

appuntellatúra, *s.f.* 1. propping 2. *fig.* support.

appuntíno, *av.* nicely, precisely: *cotto* —, done to a turn.

appuntíssimo, *av.* most exactly, most precisely.

appuntíto, *ag.* pointed; sharpened.

appúnto[1], *s.m.* 1. (*annotazione*) note, record; (*osservazione*) remark: *fare un* —, to make a note; *prendere appunti*, to take notes 2. (*critica*) blame, criticism, censure: *muovere un* — *a qlcu.*, to blame s.o.

appúnto[2], *av.* exactly, precisely; (*proprio*) just: *per l'*—, that's (o just) so; that's it.

appuràre, *v.t.* 1. (*verificare*) to verify 2. (*chiarire*) to make clear 3. (*accertare*) to ascertain 4. — *un patrimonio*, (*comm.*) to clear an estate of debts.

appuzzàre, *v.t.* to stink; (*ammorbare*) to infect, to taint.

aprìco, *ag.* sunny; warmed by the sun.

Aprìle, *s.m.* April ‖ *pesce d'*—*!*, April fool!; *un pesce d'*—, trick played on April Fool's Day: *fare un pesce d'*— *a qlcu.*, to make an April-fool of s.o.; *primo d'*—, All Fools' Day (o April Fools' Day).

a priòri, *ag.* presumptive ‖ *av.* a priori, presumptively.

apriorísmo, *s.m.* apriorism.

apriorístico, *ag.* aprioristic.

aprìre, *v.t.* 1. to open: *aprì la porta con un calcio*, he kicked the door open; — *la bocca*, to open one's mouth; — *bruscamente una finestra*, to fling a window open; — *il gas*, to turn on the gas; — *una porta (chiusa a chiave)*, to unlock a door ‖ *aprì una nuova succursale*, (*comm.*) he established a new agency ‖ *egli aprìva il corteo*, he was leading the procession ‖ *egli aprì il suo animo all'amico*, he opened his mind to his friend ‖ — *le braccia a qlcu.*, to welcome s.o. ‖ — *un conto*, (*comm.*) to open an account ‖ — *una lettera (suggellata)*, to unseal a letter ‖ — *gli occhi su*, to become aware of; — *gli occhi a qlcu. su ql.co.*, to enlighten s.o. as to sthg. ‖ — *le porte al nemico*, to surrender ‖ *apriti cielo!*, (*fam.*) good gracious! (o good heavens! o goodness gracious!) 2. (*spaccare*) to split, to crack 3. (*sezionare*) to section, to dissect 4. (*scavare*) to dig: *aprì una fossa nel campo*, he dug a ditch in the field 5. (*incominciare*) to begin, to open: *aprì la serie*, he began the series; — *il discorso*, to begin to speak 6. (*dichiarare*) to declare, to reveal ‖ **aprìrsi**, *v.r.* 1. to open; (*con violenza*) to burst open: *le finestre della nostra casa si aprivano su un parco*, the windows of our house opened on a park; *lentamente la porta si aprì*, the door slowly opened ‖ — *un varco tra la folla*, to cut (o to push) one's way through the crowd 2. (*fendersi*) to crack, to split 3. (*sbocciare*) to bloom 4. (*confidarsi*) to open one's mind (to s.o.), to unbosom oneself (to s.o.) 5. (*rasserenarsi, di tempo*) to clear up.

apriscàtole, *s.m.* tin-opener; (*amer.*) can-opener.

a prónti, *l. av.*: *pagamento* —, (*comm.*) cash-payment.

àptero, *ag.* (*entom.*) apterous, wingless ‖ *s.* (*entom.*) apteran.

apuàno, *ag.* of the Apuanian Mountains.

Apúlia, *no.pr.f.* (*geog. st.*) Apulia.

àpulo, *ag.s.m.* Apulian.

aquàrio, *s.m.* aquarium (*pl.* aquariums, aquaria) ‖ *Aquario*, (*astr.*) Aquarius, Water-bearer.

aquàtico, *ag.* aquatic.

àquila, *s.f.* 1. (*ornit.*) eagle: — *di mare*, sea-eagle; *dagli occhi d'*—, *fig.* eagle-eyed (o sharp-sighted);

---

sguardo d'—, *fig.* keen (o penetrating) glance ‖ *Aquila*, (*astr.*) Aquila 2. (*arald.*) eagle: — *bicipite*, double-headed eagle (o *amer.* double-eagle) 3. (*mil.*) eagle, standard: *l'*— *nera di Prussia*, the black eagle of Prussia; *le aquile romane*, the Roman eagles 4. *fig.* genius, master-mind, man of outstanding intelligence: *non è un'*—, he is no genius.

aquilàstro, *s.m.* (*ornit.*) erne.

aquilègia, *s.f.* (*bot.*) columbine.

aquilìfero, *s.m.* (*st. romana*) eagle-bearer.

aquilìno, *ag.* aquiline: *naso* —, aquiline nose.

aquilonàre, *ag.* northern (*attributivo*).

aquilóne, *s.m.* 1. (*vento del nord*) north wind 2. (*giocattolo*) kite: *far volare un* —, to fly a kite.

aquilòtto, *s.m.* (*ornit.*) young eagle, eaglet.

Aquisgràna, *no.pr.f.* (*geog.*) Aachen.

Aquitània, *no.pr.f.* (*geog. st.*) Aquitaine.

àra[1], *s.f.* 1. pagan altar 2. (*letter.*) altar 3. (*astr.*) halo.

àra[2], (*agr.*) are (*misura di superficie* = 119.6 sq. yd).

àra[3], (*ornit.*) macaw.

Arabèlla, *no.pr.f.* Arabella.

arabescàre, *v.t.* to decorate with arabesques; to doodle.

arabésco, *s.m.* arabesque.

Aràbia, *no.pr.f.* (*geog.*) Arabia ‖ — *Saudita*, Saudi Arabia.

aràbico, *ag.* Arabic, Arabian: *cifre arabiche*, Arabic numerals; *Golfo* —, Arabian Sea; *gomma arabica*, gum -arabic.

aràbile, *ag.* arable, ploughable.

arabísta, *s.c.* Arabist.

àrabo, *ag.* (*persone, cavalli*) Arab; (*tradizioni, costumi*), Arabian: *cavallo* —, Arab horse ‖ *araba fenice*, Arabian bird (o phoenix) ‖ *s.m.* 1. Arab; (*rar.*) Arabian 2. (*lingua*) Arabic ‖ *questo è* — *per me*, this is Greek to me (o this is beyond my comprehension) ‖ **àraba**, *s.f.* Arab; (*rar.*) Arabian.

aràchide, *s.f.* (*bot.*) peanut, groundnut: *burro di* —, peanut butter; *olio di* —, peanut oil.

aràcnide, *s.m.* (*entom.*) arachnid.

aracnòide, *s.f.* (*anat.*) arachnoid (membrane).

aracnoidíte, *s.f.* (*patol.*) arachnitis, arachnoiditis.

Aragóna, *no.pr.f.* (*geog.*) Aragon.

aragonése, *ag.s.c.* Aragonese.

aragoníte, *s.f.* (*min.*) aragonite.

aragósta, *s.f.* sea crayfish, crawfish; (*fam.*) lobster; langouste.

aràldica, *s.f.* heraldry.

aràldico, *ag.* heraldic: *consulta araldica*, Heralds' College.

aràldo, *s.m.* herald.

aramàico, *ag.s.m.* Aramaic.

araménto, *s.m.* ploughing, tilling.

arancéto, *s.m.* orange-grove.

arància, *s.f.* orange.

aranciàio, *s.m.* orange-seller.

aranciàta, *s.f.* orange squash; (*succo d'arancia*) orange juice.

aranciàto, *ag.* orange-coloured.

arancièra, *s.f.* orangery.

arancíno, *ag.* orange (*attributivo*); (*che ha sapore d'arancia*) tasting of orange ‖ *s.m.* small orange.

aràncio, *s.m.* 1. (*albero*) orange(-tree): *fiori d'*—, orange blossoms 2. (*colore*) orange.

arancióne, *ag.* orange(-coloured) ‖ *s.m.* bright orange.

aràre, *v.t.* 1. to plough; to furrow; (*amer.*) to plow ‖ — *diritto*, *fig.* to behave well 2. (*mar.*) to drag.

aratívo, *ag.* ploughable, tillable, arable.

aratóre, *ag.* ploughing ‖ *s.m.* ploughman (*pl.* ploughmen); (*amer.*) plowman (*pl.* plowmen).

aratríce, *s.f.* motor-plough.

aràtro, *s.m.* plough; (*amer.*) plow: — *assolcatore*, lister; — *bivomere*, two-bottom plough (o two-furrow plough); — *da trattore*, sulky plough; — *multiplo* (*per trattrici*), gang plough.

aratúra, *s.f.* 1. ploughing 2. (*tempo dell'aratura*) ploughing-time.

araucària, *s.f.* (*bot.*) araucaria.

arazzería, *s.f.* 1. tapestry- factory 2. (*arazzi*) tapestry.

arazzière, *s.m.* 1. (*chi fa arazzi*) tapestry-weaver, tapestry-maker 2. (*chi vende arazzi*) tapestry seller.

aràzzo, *s.m.* arras, piece of tapestry: *la sala era adorna di arazzi*, the hall was hung with tapestry.

arbitràggio, *s.m.* 1. (*comm.*) arbitrage 2. (*spor.*) umpirage, umpireship.

arbitràle, *ag.* arbitral.

arbitràre, *v.t.* 1. to arbitrate 2. (*spor.*) to umpire; (*calcio, boxe*) to referee ‖ *v.i.* to arbitrate, to act as arbitrator; to make an award ‖ **arbitràrsi**, *v.r.* to take the liberty (to do, of doing).

arbitrariaménte, *av.* arbitrarily.

arbitràrio, *ag.* arbitrary.

arbitràto, *s.m.* arbitration: *decidere per —*, to decide by arbitration; *ricorrere a un —*, to have recourse to an arbitration; *sottoporre una controversia ad —*, to submit a claim to arbitration.

arbìtrio, *s.m.* 1. will ‖ *libero —*, (*fil.*) free will 2. (*potere assoluto*) absolute power 3. (*atto arbitrario*) arbitrary act ‖ *ad —*, arbitrarily.

àrbitro, *s.m.* 1. (*dir.*) arbitrator 2. (*spor.*) umpire; (*calcio, boxe*) referee: *fare da — in una partita di calcio*, to referee (o to act as referee in) a football match 3. *fig.* arbiter: *— dell'eleganza*, arbiter of taste.

àrbore, *s.m.* (*poet.*) tree.

arbòreo, *ag.* arboreous; arboreal.

arborescènte, *ag.* arborescent.

arborescènza, *s.f.* arborescence.

arboréto, *s.m.* arboretum (*pl.* arboreta).

arboricoltóre, *s.m.* arboriculturist.

arboricoltúra, *s.f.* arboriculture.

arborifórme, *ag.* tree-shaped.

arborizzàto, *ag.* (*min.*) arborized.

arboscèllo, *s.m.* young tree.

arbústo, *s.m.* shrub.

arbúto, *s.m.* (*bot.*) arbutus, arbute.

àrea, *s.f.* 1. ark ‖ *— dell'Alleanza*, (*Bibbia*) Ark of the Covenant ‖ *— di Noè*, Noah's ark (anche *fig.*): *vecchio quanto l' — di Noè*, as old as the hills ‖ *— di scienza*, *fig.* eminent scholar (o *fam.* walking encyclopedia o mine of information) 2. (*sarcofago*) sarcophagus; tomb.

arcàccia, *s.f.* (*mar.*) stern-frame.

àrcade, *ag.* Arcadian ‖ *s.m.* 1. (*st. lett.*) Arcadian 2. *fig.* empty, rhetorical writer.

Arcàdia, *no.pr.f.* 1. (*geog. st.*) Arcady; Arcadia (anche *fig.*) 2. (*st. lett.*) Arcadia.

arcàdico, *ag.* (*st. lett.*) Arcadian.

arcaicità, *s.f.* antiquity, ancientness.

arcàico, *ag.* archaic; (*di parole, stile*) obsolete.

arcaísmo, *s.m.* archaism.

arcàle, *s.m.* (*di porta*) arch; (*di tetto*) rafter.

arcanaménte, *av.* mysteriously; occultly.

arcàngelo, *s.m.* archangel.

arcàno, *ag.* arcane; mysterious, enigmatic ‖ *s.m.* mystery, arcanum (*pl.* arcana).

arcaréccio, *s.m.* (*edil.*) purlin, purline.

arcàta, *s.f.* 1. (*arco*) arch; (*serie di archi*) arcade; (*passaggio ad arco*) archway: *— cieca*, (*arch.*) blind arcade 2. (*luce, vano di arco*) span 3. (*anat.*) arch, arcus: *— dentale*, dental arch; *— orbitale*, orbital arch 4. (*mus.*) bowing 5. (*spazio pari al tiro di un arco*) bowshot 6. (*mil.*) trajectory (of a projectile) ‖ *tirare in —*, to shoot blind; *fig.* to make a shot in the dark.

arcàto, *ag.* arched.

arcàvola, *s.f.* great-great-grandmother.

arcàvolo, *s.m.* great-great-grandfather.

àrce, *s.f.* 1. (*fortezza*) fortress, citadel 2. (*vetta*) summit, top.

archeggiàre, *v.t.* (*rar.*) to bow ‖ *v.i.* (*mus.*) to bow (on a violin, etc.).

archéggio, *s.m.* (*mus.*) bow.

archeología, *s.f.* archaeology.

archeologicaménte, *av.* archaeologically.

archeològico, *ag.* archaeologic(al).

archeòlogo, *s.m.* archaeologist.

archètipo, *ag.* (*fil.*) archetypal ‖ *s.m.* archetype; original model; prototype.

archétto, *s.m.* 1. small arch 2. (*per catturare uccelli*) gin, snare 3. (*mus.*) bow.

archiacúto, *ag.* (*arch.*) gothic, ogived, ogival.

archiàtro, *s.m.* archiater.

archibugière, *s.m.* (*st.*) (h)arquebusier.

archibúgio, *s.m.* (*st.*) (h)arquebus.

archibusièra, *s.f.* range of loop-holes.

archiginnàsio, *s.m.* "Archiginnasio" (name given to the Universities of Bologna and Rome).

archilòchio, *ag.s.m.* (*poes.*) Archilochian.

archimandrìta, *s.m.* archimandrite.

Archimède, *no.pr.m.* (*st.*) Archimedes.

archipèndolo, archipènzolo, *s.m.* plumb-line, plumb-rule.

architettaménto, *s.m.* 1. planning 2. *fig.* plot, machination.

architettàre, *v.t.* 1. to draw the plan of (sthg.); to lay out plans of (sthg.) 2. *fig.* to plot; to contrive, to devise: *— inganni*, to devise stratagems.

architétto, *s.m.* architect.

architettonicaménte, *av.* architecturally.

architettònico, *ag.* architectonic, architectural.

architettóre, *s.m.* 1. planner 2. *fig.* plotter, contriver.

architettúra, *s.f.* architecture.

architravàta, *s.f.* (*arch.*) trabeation; arrangement of architraves.

architravàto, *ag.* architraved.

architravatúra, *V.* architravàta.

architràve, *s.m.* (*arch.*) architrave.

archiviàre, *v.t.* to register in the archives; to place in the archives; (*comm.*) to file, to place on file: *la vostra pratica è stata archiviata*, your papers have been placed on file.

archiviatúra, *s.f.* recording; (*comm.*) filing.

archívio, *s.m.* archives (*pl.*); (*comm.*) file ‖ *Archivio di Stato*, Record Office.

archivìsta, *s.m.* archivist.

archivòlto, *s.m.* (*arch.*) archivolt.

Arcibàldo, *no.pr.m.* Archibald ‖ *dim.* Arch, Archie, Baldie.

arcibeàto, *ag.* very happy, extremely happy.

arciconfratèrnita, *s.f.* main confraternity.

arciconsolàto, *s.m.* (*st.*) degree and office of the President of the Crusca Academy.

arcicònsolo, *s.m.* (*st.*) the President of the Crusca Academy.

arcicontènto, *ag.* very glad, extremely glad.

arcidiaconàto, *s.m.* (*eccl.*) archdeaconry; archdeaconship.

arcidiàcono, *s.m.* (*eccl.*) archdeacon.

arcidiàvolo, *s.m.* arch-fiend.

arcidiòcesi, *s.f.* (*eccl.*) archdiocese.

arcidúca, *s.m.* archduke.

arciducàle, *ag.* archducal.

arciducàto, *s.m.* 1. (*titolo*) archdukedom 2. (*territorio*) archduchy.

arciduchéssa, *s.f.* archduchess.

arcière, *s.m.* archer, bowman (*pl.* bowmen).

arcignaménte, *av.* gruffly, surlily; sulkily; sourly.

arcígno, *ag.* gruff, surly; (*imbronciato*) sullen, sulky.

arcimiliardàrio, *ag.* enormously rich; (*amer.*) worth more than a billion ‖ *s.m.* multimillionaire; (*amer.*) billionaire.

arcimilionàrio, *ag.* very rich; (*amer.*) worth more than a million ‖ *s.m.* multimillionaire.

arcióne, *s.m.* 1. saddle-bow; (*sella*) saddle: *montare in —*, to get on horseback 2. (*arch.*) rib 3. (*di culla*) rocker.

arcipèlago, *s.m.* archipelago (*pl.* archipelagos).

arciprète, *s.m.* (*eccl.*) archpriest, dean.

arcipretúra, *s.f.* **1.** (*dignità di arciprete*) deanship, deanery **2.** (*prebenda di arciprete*) prebend of a dean.

arcispedàle, *s.m.* main hospital.

arcivescovàdo, arcivescovàto, *s.m.* archbishopric.

arcivescovíle, *ag.* archiepiscopal.

arcivéscovo, *s.m.* archbishop.

àrco, *s.m.* **1.** (*arma*) bow: *corda dell'*—, bow-string; *tiro d'*—, bow-shot; *tendere l'*—, to bend (*o* to draw *o* to string) the bow **2.** (*geom.*) arc **3.** (*arch.*) arch: — *a sesto acuto*, ogive (*o* gothic) arch; — *a tutto sesto*, round arch; — *trionfale*, triumphal arch **4.** (*mus.*) bow: *quartetto d'archi*, string quartet; *strumenti ad*—, the strings **5.** (*violinista*) violinist; fiddler **6.** (*elett.*) arc: — *voltaico*, electric arc; *lampada ad* —, arc-lamp **7.** (*anat.*) arch: — *del piede*, arch of the foot.

arcobaléno, *s.m.* rainbow.

arcolàio, *s.m.* **1.** wool-winder; skein-winder; reel-winder ‖ *girare come un* —, *fig.* to bustle about **2.** (*persona bizzarra*) odd, fantastic person **3.** (*ghiribizzo*) whim; fancy.

arcontàto, *s.m.* (*st. greca*) archonship.

arcónte, *s.m.* (*st. greca*) archon.

arcuàre, *v.t.* to arch, to curve; (*piegare*) to bend.

arcuàto, *ag.* arched, arcuated; (*piegato*) bent: *dalle gambe arcuate*, bow-legged (*o* bandy-legged).

ardènte, *ag.* **1.** (*che brucia*) burning, scorching; (*infuocato*) hot, red hot, blazing: *carboni ardenti*, burning coals; *sole* —, scorching sun **2.** *fig.* burning; fervent; ardent; passionate; fiery: *amore* —, passionate love; *cavallo* —, fiery (*o* high-mettled) horse; *occhi ardenti*, burning eyes; *preghiera* —, fervent prayer; *temperamento* —, fiery temper **3.** (*di colore*) bright, brilliant: *colore* —, bright colour; *rosso* —, fiery red **4.** *camera* —, funeral chamber; *cappella* —, mortuary chapel.

ardenteménte, *av.* ardently; passionately; fervently; eagerly.

ardènza, *V.* ardóre.

àrdere, *v.t.* **1.** (*bruciare*) to burn, to scorch ‖ *spirito da* —, (*chim.*) methylated spirit **2.** (*inaridire, seccare*) to dry (up), to wither, to shrivel: *il sole le ha arso i capelli*, the sun has dried up her hair; *terra arsa dal sole*, sun-scorched earth **3.** *fig.* (*infiammare*) to inflame; to burn; to set ablaze ‖ *v.i.* **1.** to burn, to be on fire: *ardono i lumi*, the lights are burning (*o* the lights are shining); *la casa arde*, the house is burning (*o* the house is on fire) **2.** *fig.* to glow (with sthg.), to burn (with sthg.): *ardeva di collera*, she was burning with rage; — *di curiosità*, to be aflame with curiosity; — *di sete*, to be dying with thirst (*o* to have a burning thirst).

ardèsia, *s.f.* slate: *cava di* —, slate quarry; *lavoro (di copertura) con* —, (*arch.*) slating.

ardiglióne, *s.m.* tongue of a buckle.

ardiménto, *V.* ardíre.

ardimentosaménte, *av.* **1.** boldly, daringly; bravely; fearlessly **2.** (*temerariamente*) recklessly; (*sfacciatamente*) impudently.

ardimentóso, *ag.* **1.** bold, daring; brave; fearless **2.** (*temerario*) reckless; (*sfacciato*) impudent.

ardíre, *s.m.* **1.** boldness; daring **2.** (*temerità*) temerity; audacity; (*sfacciataggine*) impudence: *ebbe l'*— *di continuare a mentire*, he had the impudence to go on lying.

ardíre, *v.i.* to dare; to venture: *non ardì parlare*, he dared (*o* durst) not speak (*o* he had not the courage of speaking); *quel ragazzo ardì insultare mia sorella*, that boy had the impudence to offend my sister.

arditaménte, *av.* boldly, daringly.

arditézza, *s.f.* courage; boldness, daring; (*audacia*) audacity; forwardness: — *delle linee di un quadro*, boldness of outline in a picture; *egli ha avuto l'*— *di scrivermi*, he has had the audacity (*o* cheek) to write to me.

ardíto, *ag.* **1.** (*coraggioso, audace*) bold, hardy, daring: *egli è molto* — *con le donne*, he is very bold with women; *egli ha dei concetti arditi*, he has advanced ideas; *avere il pennello* —, to wield a bold brush ‖ *farsi* —, to make bold: *mi faccio* — *di chiederle un favore*, may I make so bold as to ask you a favour? **2.** (*che presenta rischi*) risky; hazardous; dangerous: *impresa ardita*, risky undertaking **3.** (*ripido*) steep: *salita ardita*, steep ascent ‖ *s.m.* (*mil.*) « ardito » (*pl.* « arditi ») (Italian assault soldier, 1915-18).

ardóre, *s.m.* **1.** fierce heat **2.** *fig.* ardour; passion; keen desire; mettle; (*fervore*) fervour: *cavallo pieno di* —, high-spirited (*o* high-mettled) horse; *fare ql.co. con* —, to do sthg. fervently (*o* with zeal).

arduaménte, *av.* arduously; laboriously.

arduità, *s.f.* arduousness; hardness.

àrduo, *ag.* **1.** arduous, hard, difficult; laborious: *uno sport molto* —, a very strenuous sport; *questo è un* — *compito*, this is a difficult (*o* hard) task **2.** (*erto*) arduous, steep.

àrea, *s.f.* **1.** area: — *fabbricabile*, building ground ‖ — *di rigore*, (*spor.*) penalty area **2.** (*geom.*) area, surface **3.** (*sfera d'azione*) range, sphere.

areàto, *ag.* **1.** aired; ventilated **2.** (*scient.*) aerated.

areazióne, *s.f.* **1.** airing **2.** (*scient.*) aeration.

arèca, *s.f.* (*bot.*) **1.** areca **2.** (*noce di betel*) areca-nut.

àrem, *s.m.* harem.

arèna, *s.f.* **1.** (*sabbia*) sand **2.** (*arch.*) arena (anche *fig.*): *l'*— *politica*, *fig.* the arena of politics.

arenàceo, *ag.* sandy, arenaceous.

arenàio, *s.m.* sand-pit.

arenaménto, *V.* arrenaménto.

arenàre, *V.* arrenàre.

arenària, *s.f.* (*min.*) sandstone.

arenàrio, *ag.* sandy, arenaceous: *pietra arenaria*, sandstone ‖ *cimiteri arenari*, catacombs ‖ *s.m.* gladiator.

arengàrio, *s.m.* tribune.

arèngo, *s.m.* (*st.*) **1.** (*assemblea*) assembly **2.** (*luogo di raduno*) meeting-place.

areníle, *s.m.* sandy shore.

arenóso, *ag.* sandy, arenaceous.

arèola, *s.f.* (*rar.*) **1.** small area, areola (*pl.* areolae) **2.** flower-bed.

areòmetro, *s.m.* (*fis.*) aerometer.

areonàuta, *V.* aeronàuta.

areopagíta, *s.m.* Areopagite.

areopàgo, *s.m.* Areopagus.

areoplàno, *V.* aeroplàno.

areostàtico, *ag.* aerostatic.

areòstato, *s.m.* balloon, aerostat.

Aretúsa, *no.pr.f.* (*mit.*) Arethusa.

arfasàtto, *s.m.* (*rar.*) mean fellow; (*raggiratore*) swindler.

àrgano, *s.m.* **1.** (*mar.*) capstan **2.** (*mec.*) windlass, winch ‖ *a forza d'argani*, *fig.* with great difficulty (*o* with great effort).

argentàre, *v.t.* to silver, to silver-plate, to plate with silver.

argentàto, *ag.* **1.** (*color argento*) silvery, silver: *volpe argentata*, silver-fox **2.** (*coperto d'argento*) silver-plated.

argentatóre, *s.m.* silver plater.

argentatúra, *s.f.* silver-plating: — *galvanica*, electro-plating.

argènteo, *ag.* silvery, silver: *capelli argentei*, silver hair; *il chiarore* — *della luna*, the silvery light of the moon.

argentería, *s.f.* silver, silver-plate, silver ware.

argentièra, *s.f.* silver mine.

argentière, *s.m.* silversmith.

argentífero, *ag.* argentiferous.

Argentína, *no.pr.f.* (*geog.*) Argentina.

argentíno[1]**,** *ag.* silvery, argentine: *voce argentina*, silvery voice.

argentíno[2]**,** *ag.s.m.* Argentine.

argènto, *s.m.* **1.** silver (anche *fig.*): — *battuto*, wrought silver; — *dorato*, silver gilt; *bromuro d'*—, (*chim.*) silver bromide; *capelli d'*—, *fig.* silver hair;

cloruro d'—, (*chim.*) silver chloride; *lega d'—*, (*metal.*) sterling silver; *nitrato d'—*, (*chim.*) silver nitrate ‖ *— vivo*, (*chim.*) quicksilver, mercury: *avere addosso l'— vivo, fig.* to be restless ‖ *bianco d'—*, (*pitt.*) white lead ‖ *età dell'—*, silver age ‖ *nozze d'—*, silver wedding ‖ *la parola è d'—, il silenzio è d'oro, prov.* speech is silver, silence is gold 2. *pl.* (*argenteria*) silver, silver -plate, silver ware (*solo sing.*) 3. *pl.* (*monete d'argento*) silver coins.

argentóne, *s.m.* German silver, nickel silver.

argílla, *s.f.* 1. clay (anche *fig.*): *— grassa,* rich clay; *pensa di essere fatto di un'altra —,* (*fam.*) he thinks he is formed of another clay 2. (*per vasai*) argil, clay.

argillàceo, *ag.* clayey, argillaceous.

argillóso, *ag.* clayey.

arginàle, *ag.* embankment (*attributivo*) ‖ *s.m.* (*rar.*) long dyke.

arginaménto, *s.m.* 1. embanking; damming up; stemming 2. (*pol.*) containment: *tattica di —,* containment policy.

arginàre, *v.t.* 1. to embank; to dam; to dyke, to stem 2. *fig.* to stem: *— una passione,* to stem a passion.

arginatúra, arginazióne, *V.* **arginaménto.**

àrgine, *s.m.* embankment; bank; (*diga*) dyke ‖ *far — a ql.co., fig.* to oppose sthg.; *porre — a ql.co., fig.* to stem sthg.

argívo, *ag.s.m.* Argive.

Àrgo, *no.pr.m.* 1. (*mit.*) Argus ‖ *dagli occhi d'—, fig.* Argus-eyed 2. (*astr.*) Argo.

Àrgo, *no.pr.f.* (*geog.*) Argos.

àrgo, *s.m.* (*chim.*) argon.

argomentàre, *v.t.* to infer, to deduce: *lo argomentò dalle sue parole,* he deduced it from his words ‖ *v.i.* to argue, to discuss: *— con qlcu. di ql.co.,* to argue with s.o. about sthg. ‖ **argomentàrsi,** *v.r.* (*ingegnarsi*) to exert oneself, to endeavour.

argomentatóre, *ag.* argumentative ‖ *s.m.,* **argomentatrìce,** *s.f.* arguer, reasoner.

argomentazióne, *s.f.* 1. reasoning, argumentation 2. (*ret.*) argumentation.

argoménto, *s.m.* 1. subject; topic; subject-matter; matter: *questo non è — per una conversazione piacevole,* this is no topic for a pleasant conversation; *ritorneremo sull'—,* we'll come back to the matter; *il vostro libro tratta ampiamente l'—,* your book deals extensively with the subject; *confutare un —,* to refute an argument ‖ *— cornuto,* dilemma 2. (*prova a sostegno*) argument: *— portato a favore di ql.co.,* argument advanced in favour of sthg. 3. (*indizio, segno*) proof: *il silenzio è — di colpa,* silence is a proof of guilt 4. (*cagione*) occasion: *le buone azioni sono — di lode,* good actions are occasion for praise 5. (*sommario*) summary; synopsis.

àrgon, *s.m.* (*chim.*) argon.

argonàuta, *s.m.* 1. (*mit.*) Argonaut 2. *fig.* daring navigator 3. (*zool.*) argonaut, paper nautilus.

argot, *s.m.* slang.

arguìre, *v.t.* 1. (*dedurre*) to deduce, to infer 2. (*indovinare*) to guess.

argutaménte, *av.* 1. acutely, keenly; shrewdly 2. (*facetamente*) wittily.

argutézza, *s.f.* 1. acuteness, keenness; shrewdness 2. (*l'essere faceto*) wittiness.

argúto, *ag.* 1. (*acuto*) acute, sharp, keen; (*sottile*) subtle, shrewd 2. (*faceto*) witty 3. (*di suono*) melodious; harmonious; (*argentino*) silvery; (*squillante*) shrill, acute 4. (*di sguardo*) keen, sharp.

argúzia, *s.f.* 1. (*di spirito*) wit; humour 2. (*detto arguto*) witty remark.

ària, *s.f.* 1. air: *— aperta,* open air: *giuochi all'— aperta,* outdoor games; *— compressa,* compressed air; *— condizionata,* conditioned air; *— ferma,* still air; *— liquida,* (*fis.*) liquid air; *— mefitica,* foul air; *— secca,* dry air; *— viziata,* stale (*o* stuffy) air; *cambiamento d'—,* change of air; *colpo d'—,* chill; *condizionamento*

dell'—, air conditioning; *corrente d'—,* draught; *in linea d'—,* as the crow flies; *per via d'—,* by air; *spostamento d'—,* windage; *vuoto d'—,* (*aer.*) air hole (*o* air pocket *o* air pit); *dare — ad una stanza,* to air (*o* to ventilate) a room; *prendere (una boccata d')—,* to go out for a short walk (*o* a breather) ‖ *camera d'—,* (*tec.*) inner tube; *filtro dell'—,* (*aut.*) air cleaner; *presa d'—,* (*aut.*) air intake (*o* air inlet) ‖ *c'è ql.co. in —,* there is sthg. in the air ‖ *andare all'—, fig.* to fail (*o* to fall through) ‖ *buttar tutto all'—, fig.* to throw up everything ‖ *campar d'—,* to live on air (*o* upon nothing) ‖ *capire ql.co. per —,* to grasp sthg. at once ‖ *dire ql.co. a mezz'—,* to hint at sthg. ‖ *fare castelli in —, fig.* to build castles in Spain (*o* in the air) ‖ *mandare all'—,* to cause to fail ‖ *mettere tutto in —,* to throw everything into confusion ‖ *mutare —,* to move (*o* to change one's residence) ‖ *gli stracci vanno all'—, prov.* the poor always get the worst of it (*o* beggars can't be choosers) 2. (*aspetto*) appearance, look; mien: *— di famiglia,* family likeness; *la città prende un'— di festa,* the town assumes a holiday appearance; *ha l'— di galantuomo,* he looks a trustworthy person; *ha un'— molto dolce,* she looks very gentle; *mi venne incontro con — triste,* he came to meet me with a sad countenance ‖ *darsi delle arie,* to give oneself airs (*o* to put on a high-and-mighty manner) 3. (*mus.*) tune, air, melody; (*di opera*) aria: *vecchia canzone su un'— nuova,* old song to a new tune.

arianésimo, arianísmo, *s.m.* (*st. relig.*) Arianism.

Ariànna, *no.pr.f.* (*mit.*) Ariadne.

ariàno[1]**,** *ag.s.m.* (*seguace di Ario*) Arian.

ariàno[2]**,** *ag.s.m.* (*indoeuropeo*) Aryan.

aridaménte, *av.* aridly, drily, dryly.

aridità, *s.f.* (*di terreno, mente, argomento*) aridity; barrenness; aridness; (*di cuore*) lack of feeling.

àrido, *ag.* (*di terreno, mente, argomento*) arid; dry; barren; (*di cuore*) lacking feeling.

àridi, *s.m.pl.* dry substances.

arieggiàre, *v.t.* 1. (*dare aria a*) to air, to ventilate: *— una stanza,* to air a room 2. (*somigliare a*) to resemble, to look like: *il figlio arieggia il padre,* the son looks like his father ‖ *v.i.* (*somigliare*) to resemble (s.o., sthg.), to look like (s.o., sthg.); (*imitare*) to imitate (s.o., sthg.): *questo pittore arieggia a Goya,* this painter imitates Goya; *— a gran dama,* to put on the airs of a great lady.

arieggiàto, *ag.* aired.

Arièle, *no.pr.m.* (*lett.*) Ariel.

ariéte, *s.m.* 1. (*zool.*) ram ‖ *Ariete,* (*astr.*) Aries, the Ram 2. (*mil.*) battering-ram.

ariétta, *s.f.* light tune; (*di opera*) arietta.

aríllo, *s.m.* (*bot.*) aril, seed-coat.

arínga, *s.f.* herring: *— affumicata,* kippered herring (*o* kipper *o* bloater); *— salata,* salted herring.

Àrio, *no.pr.m.* (*st. relig.*) Arius ‖ **àrio,** *ag.s.m.* Aryan.

arióso, *ag.* 1. airy 2. (*mus.*) ariose.

ariostésco, *ag.* 1. (*lett.*) of Ariosto; in Ariosto's style 2. (*fantastico*) fantastic.

arìsta[1]**,** *s.f.* (*cuc.*) (roast) saddle of pork.

arísta[2]**,** *s.f.* (*bot.*) arista, awn.

Aristàrco, *no.pr.m.* (*st. lett.*) Aristarchus ‖ **aristàrco,** *s.m.* severe critic.

Arístide, *no.pr.m.* (*st.*) Aristides.

aristòcrate, *s.m.* aristocrat.

aristocraticaménte, *av.* aristocratically.

aristocràtico, *ag.* aristocratic(al) ‖ *s.m.* aristocrat.

aristocrazía, *s.f.* 1. aristocracy (anche *fig.*) 2. (*contegno altezzoso*) haughtiness.

Aristòfane, *no.pr.m.* (*st. lett.*) Aristophanes.

aristofanésco, *ag.* (*lett.*) Aristophanic.

àriston, *s.m.* (*mus.*) barrel-organ.

Aristòtele, *no.pr.m.* (*st. fil.*) Aristotle.

aristotèlico, *ag.* (*fil.*) Aristotelian.

aritenòide, *ag.* (*anat.*) arytenoid.

aritmètica, *s.f.* arithmetic.

aritmeticaménte, *av.* arithmetically.

aritmètico, *ag.* arithmetical: *progressione aritmetica,* arithmetical progression ‖ *s.m.* arithmetician.

aritmía, *s.f.* (*patol.*) arrhythmy, arrhytmia.

arítmico, *ag.* arrhythmic(al).

arlecchinàta, *s.f.* **1.** harlequinade **2.** (*buffonata*) (piece of) buffoonery.

arlecchinésco, *ag.* **1.** clownish **2.** (*a tanti colori*) motley.

arlecchíno, *s.m.* **1.** harlequin **2.** *fig.* buffoon; inconsequent person; weathercock.

ariòtto, *s.m.* **1.** (*persona sciatta*) sloven **2.** (*mangione*) glutton.

àrma, *s.f.* **1.** weapon, arm: — *a ripetizione,* repeater; — *atomica,* atomic weapon; *armi bianche,* sidearms: *combattere all'— bianca,* to fight with cold steel; *armi corte, portatili,* small arms; *armi da fuoco,* fire-arms; *armi subacquee,* submarine weapons; *fatto d'armi,* passage of arms (o fight); *galleria d'armi,* armoury; *gente d'arme,* soldiers; *maestro d'arme,* fencing-master; *una nuova —,* a new weapon; *piazza d'armi,* parade ground; *porto d'armi,* license to carry fire-arms; *uomo d'armi,* man at arms ‖ *abbassare le armi, fig.* to surrender; *caricare un'— da fuoco,* to load (o to shot); *chiamare alle armi,* to call to arms; *correre alle armi,* to fly (o to rush) to arms (o to prepare for battle); *deporre le armi,* to cease hostilities; *essere sotto le armi,* to serve the colours (o to serve in the army o to be doing military service); *levarsi in armi contro qlcu.,* to rise up in arms against s.o.; *passare qlcu. per le armi,* to shoot s.o.; *prendere le armi,* to begin hostilities (o to take up arms); *presentare le armi,* to present arms; *spianare l'— contro qlcu.,* to level one's gun at s.o. ‖ *all'armi!,* to arms! ‖ *essere alle prime armi, fig.* to be still a novice **2.** (*mil.*) force: — *azzurra,* air force; — *di fanteria,* infantry **3.** (*arald.*) coat of arms.

armacòllo, ad, *l.av.* baldric-wise.

armadiétto, *s.m.* **1.** (*farmaceutico*) first-aid outfit, medicine-closet, medicine-chest **2.** (*per ufficio, spogliatoio*) (clothes-)locker **3.** (*per strumenti tecnici, medici*) cabinet.

armadíllo, *s.m.* (*zool.*) armadillo.

armàdio, *s.m.* **1.** (*per abiti*) wardrobe: — *a muro,* built-in wardrobe; — *a specchio,* mirror-wardrobe **2.** (*per stoviglie*) cupboard; china-closet **3.** (*per strumenti tecnici, medici*) cabinet.

armaiuòlo, *s.m.* armourer, gunsmith.

armamentàrio, *s.m.* **1.** (*strumenti*) instruments (*pl.*), implements (*pl.*) **2.** (*accessori*) paraphernalia (*pl.*); outfit **3.** (*armeria*) armoury.

armaménto, *s.m.* **1.** arming, providing with arms; armament **2.** (*mar.*) apparel, equipment, fitting-out, rigging: — *di lancia,* crew of a launch ‖ *in —,* on commission **3.** (*ferr.*) superstructure, unballasted permanent way: *posa dell'—,* laying of the superstructure **4.** (*miner.*) timbering.

Armàndo, *no.pr.m.* Herman(n).

armàre, *v.t.* **1.** to arm; to provide with arms: *armò i suoi uomini,* he armed his men ‖ — *qlcu. cavaliere,* (*st.*) to dub s.o. knight **2.** (*mar.*) to equip, to rig, to fit out: — *un argano,* to rig (o to man) a capstan; — *una barca,* to man a boat; — *i remi,* to lay on oars **3.** (*armi*) to cock, to load: — *un fucile,* to cock a gun **4.** (*edil.*) to reinforce **5.** — *la chiave,* (*mus.*) to put the key-signature (to a piece of music) **6.** (*fortificare*) to fortify, to strengthen, to brace ‖ *v.i.* (*prepararsi per la guerra*) to arm, to prepare for war ‖ **armàrsi,** *v.r.* to arm oneself (with sthg.) ‖ — *di coraggio,* to summon up all one's courage (o to brace oneself to a task o to man oneself) ‖ — *di pazienza,* to take patience.

armàta, *s.f.* **1.** army: *un'— di ventimila uomini,* an army twenty thousand strong; *corpo d'—,* army corps **2.** (*mar.*) fleet ‖ *l'Invincibile Armata,* (*st.*) the Invincible Armada.

armàto, *ag.* **1.** armed (anche *fig.*): — *di pazienza, di coraggio,* armed with patience, with courage ‖ *a mano*

armata, by force of arms: *rapina a mano armata,* hold-up (o armed) robbery **2.** (*fornito*) provided, equipped, furnished: — *degli strumenti adatti,* provided (o equipped) with the right instruments; — *di artigli,* armed with claws **3.** (*mar.*) manned **4.** (*elett.*) armored: *cavo —,* armored cable **5.** (*edil.*) reinforced ‖ *s.m.* armed man.

armatóre, *s.m.* **1.** (*chi allestisce una nave*) fitter-out; shipbuilder **2.** (*chi possiede una nave*) shipowner.

armatúra, *s.f.* **1.** armour: *una vecchia —,* an old armour **2.** (*telaio*) framework; (*impalcatura edile*) scaffolding; (*intelaiatura di ferro*) reinforcement **3.** (*elett.*) (*di cavo*) armor; (*di magnete*) armature **4.** (*rad.*) (*di condensatore variabile*) plate **5.** (*ind. tessile*) weave: — *semplice,* plain weave.

àrme, *V.* **àrma** **1.** **3.**

armeggiaménto, *s.m.* **1.**(*manovre*) manoeuvring **2.***fig.* (*l'affaccendarsi*) bustling, bustle; (*il tramare*) manoeuvring **3.** (*st.*) (*torneamento*) joust, tournament.

armeggiàre, *v.i.* **1.** (*maneggiare armi*) to handle arms **2.** (*manovrare*) to manoeuvre **3.** *fig.* (*darsi da fare*) to bustle, to busy oneself; (*tramare*) to manoeuvre **4.** (*st.*) (*torneare*) to joust, to tourney.

armeggío, *s.m.* **1.** (*maneggio d'armi*) handling of arms **2.** (*l'affaccendarsi*) bustling; (*intrigo*) manoeuvre **3.** (*movimento di congegni*) intricate movement of machinery.

armeggióna, *s.f.,* **armeggióne,** *s.m.* **1.** (*chi fa imbrogli*) swindler **2.** (*intrigante*) busybody.

Armènia, *no.pr.f.* (*geog.*) Armenia.

armèno, *ag.s.m.* Armenian.

armentàrio, *ag.* of a herd ‖ *s.m.* herdsman (*pl.* herdsmen).

arménto, *s.m.* herd.

armería, *s.f.* armoury.

Armída, *no.pr.f.* (*lett.*) Armida.

armière, *s.m.* gunsmith.

armígero, *ag.* armed; *fig.*bellicose, bold ‖ *s.m.* **1.**(*guerriero*) warrior **2.** (*scudiero*) armiger; squire.

armílla, *s.f.* **1.** armlet **2.** (*braccialetto*) bracelet.

armillàre, *ag.* armillary: *sfera —,* (*astr.*) armillary sphere.

Armínio, *no.pr.m.* (*st.*) Arminius.

armistízio, *s.m.* armistice: *chiedere l'—,* to ask for an armistice ‖ *anniversario dell'—,* Armistice Day.

armonía, *s.f.* harmony; consonance; accord; agreement (anche *fig.*): *in —,* in harmony: *quest'affermazione non è in — con i tuoi principi,* this statement is not in keeping with your principles; *il tuo abito e le tue scarpe sono in perfetta —,* your dress and shoes match perfectly.

armònica, *s.f.* (*mus.*) harmonica: — *a bocca,* mouth-organ.

armonicaménte, *av.* harmonically.

armònico, *ag.* harmonic, harmonious: *cassa armonica,* (*mus.*) sound-box; *frequenza armonica,* (*elett.*) harmonic frequency; *serie armonica,* (*mat.*) harmonic series.

armònio, *s.m.* (*mus.*) harmonium.

armoniosaménte, *av.* harmoniously.

armonióso, *ag.* harmonious.

armonísta, *s.m.* (*mus.*) harmonist.

armonizzàre, *v.t.* **1.** (*mus.*) to harmonize; to attune **2.** *fig.* (*mettere in armonia*) to bring into harmony; to harmonize; to attune ‖ *v.i.* **1.** (*essere in armonia*) to harmonize **2.** (*di colori, abiti*) to match.

armoricàno, *ag.s.m.* Armorican.

Arnàldo, *no.pr.m.* Arnold.

arnése, *s.m.* **1.** (*strumento*) tool, implement; (*specialmente da cucina*) utensil: *arnesi da giardino,* garden (o gardening) tools **2.** (*aggeggio*) gadget, contrivance; (*fam.*) contraption **3.** *cattivo —, fig.* crook (o nasty piece of work o disreputable type) **4.** *male in —, in cattivo —,* shabbily (o sadly) dressed (o shabby).

àrnia, *s.f.* (bee)hive.

àrnica, *s.f.* (*bot.*) arnica.

arnióne, *s.m.* kidney.

Arnòldo, *no.pr.m.* Arnold.

àro, *s.m.* (*bot.*) arum.

Aròldo, *no.pr.m.* Harold.

aròma, *s.m.* aroma, flavour ‖ *sale e aromi*, salt and spices.

aromàtico, *ag.* 1. aromatic 2. (*aromatizzato*) spicy.

aromatizzàre, *v.t.* to make aromatic, to aromatize, to flavour.

àrpa, *s.f.* (*mus.*) harp: — *eolia*, Aeolian harp; *suonare l'—*, to play the harp.

arpagóne, *s.m.* 1. (*mar.*) (*rostro*) grapnel, grappling iron 2. *fig.* (*avaro*) miser, stingy man.

arpeggiaménto, *s.m.* (*mus.*) arpeggio (*pl.* arpeggios).

arpeggiàre, *v.i.* (*mus.*) 1. to harp, to play the harp 2. (*fare arpeggi*) to arpeggio, to play arpeggios.

arpéggio, *s.m.* (*mus.*) arpeggio (*pl.* arpeggios).

arpése, *s.m.* (*edil.*) cramp(-iron).

arpía, *s.f.* 1. (*mit.*) harpy (anche *fig.*) 2. (*ornit.*) harpy -eagle.

arpicòrdo, *s.m.* (*mus.*) harpsichord.

arpióne, *s.m.* 1. (*da baleniere*) harpoon 2. (*uncino*) hook, grapnel 3. (*cardine*) hinge 4. (*ferr.*) spike.

arpionismo, *s.m.* (*mec.*) ratchet gear.

arpísta, *s.c.* (*mus.*) harpist.

àrra, *s.f.* 1. (*comm.*) earnest (money) 2. *fig.* (*pegno*) pledge, token: — *d'amicizia*, token of friendship.

arrabattàrsi, *v.r.* (*darsi da fare*) to bestir oneself, to muddle; (*fare tentativi*) to strive, to endeavour.

arrabbiaménto, *s.m.* rage.

arrabbiàre, *v.i.* 1. (*di cane*) to become affected with rabies; (*di persona*) to become angry 2. (*agr.*) to suffer through excessive heat, fog ‖ **arrabbiàrsi,** *v.r.* to get angry, to madden; to fly into a temper, to fly into a passion: *egli si arrabbiò con il figlio*, he got angry with his son ‖ *non t'—!*, take it easy! (*o* keep cool!).

arrabbiataménte, *av.* angrily.

arrabbiàto, *ag.* 1. (*di cane*) rabid, mad; (*di persona*) angry, enraged ‖ « *i giovani arrabbiati* », (*neol.*) "angry young men" 2. (*entusiasta*) enthusiastic; keen: *pescatore* —, enthusiastic angler; *sportivo* —, keen sportsman.

arrabbiatúra, *s.f.* rage: *prendersi un'—*, to fly into a passion (*o* to have a fit of anger).

arraffàre, *v.t.* to grasp, to seize; to snatch at (sthg.).

arramacciàre, *V.* abborracciàre.

arrampicàrsi, *v.r.* 1. to climb, to shin; (*con difficoltà*) to clamber: — *sulle montagne*, to climb mountains; — *su un albero*, to climb up a tree; — *su una scala*, *su un muro*, to climb up (*o* to shin up) a ladder, a wall ‖ — *sui vetri*, *fig.* to try to defend an untenable opinion 2. (*di piante*) to creep, to climb, to trail.

arrampicàta, *s.f.* climb, climbing.

arrampicatóre, *s.m.*, **arrampicatríce,** *s.f.* mountain climber.

arrancàre, *v.i.* 1. (*camminare zoppicando*) to limp, to waddle; (*camminare a fatica*) to plod along, to trudge 2. *fig.* to strive hard 3. (*mar.*) to row vigorously, to pull (at the oars): *arranca!*, pull away!.

arrandellàre, *v.t.* 1. (*colpire con un randello*) to cudgel 2. (*scaraventare*) to throw, to fling; (*gettar via*) to throw away 3. (*vendere a prezzo bassissimo*) to sell for next to nothing, to undersell; (*fam.*) to sell for a song.

arrangiàre, *v.t.* to arrange, to settle ‖ **arrangiàrsi,** *v.r.* 1. (*cavarsela alla meglio*) to make shift; to manage; to do the best one can, to fix things as best one can ‖ *arrangiatevi!*, do the best you can!; *che si arrangi!*, that's his own look-out! 2. (*accordarsi*) to come to an agreement: *arrangiatevi tra voi*, settle it amongst yourselves.

arrangolàrsi, *v.r.* 1. (*affannarsi*) to take great pains 2. (*arrovellarsi*) to worry (oneself).

arrapinàrsi, *v.r.* 1. (*stizzirsi*) to get furious 2. (*arrabattarsi*) to exert oneself.

arrappàre, *v.t.* (*arraffare*) to snatch at (sthg.).

arrecàre, *v.t.* 1. (*portare*) to bring 2. (*causare*) to cause: — *dolore*, to cause sorrow; — *piacere*, to give pleasure.

arredaménto, *s.m.* 1. (*allestimento*) fitting out 2 furnishings (*pl.*); (*mobilia*) furniture.

arredàre, *v.t.* 1. (*ammobiliare*) to furnish; (*allestire*) to fit out, to fit up 2. (*mil.*) (*equipaggiare*) to equip.

arredatóre, *s.m.*, **arredatríce,** *s.f.* 1. internal decorator 2. (*cine.*) set dresser.

arrèdo, *s.m.* 1. (piece of) furniture 2. *pl.* furniture (*sing.*); furnishings; fittings ‖ *arredi sacri*, vestments and vessels (for church ceremonies).

arrembàggio, *s.m.* (*mar.*) boarding.

arrembàre[1], *v.t.i.* (*mar.*) (*abbordare*) to board.

arrembàre[2], *v.i.*, **arrembàrsi,** *v.r.* (*camminare a fatica*) to trudge, to trail.

arrembàto, *ag.* 1. dead tired, worn out; (*di cavallo*) jaded 2. *fig.* in a bad financial position.

arrenaménto, *s.m.* (*mar.*) running aground, stranding.

arrenàre, *v.i.*, **arrenàrsi,** *v.r.* (*mar.*) to run aground, to strand (anche *fig.*).

arrèndersi, *v.r.* 1. to surrender (oneself), to give oneself up; to submit: — *a condizioni onorevoli*, to surrender on honourable terms 2. *fig.* to give it up, to yield: — *al destino*, to yield to fate.

arrendévole, *ag.* 1. pliant, flexible, supple 2. *fig.* yielding, docile, compliant.

arrendevolézza, *s.f.* 1. pliability, flexibility, suppleness 2. *fig.* docility.

arrendevolménte, *av.* submissively; compliantly.

arrestàre, *v.t.* 1. (*fermare*) to stop: — *un motore*, to stop an engine; — *il progresso*, to stop progress 2. (*trarre in arresto*) to arrest, to capture, to seize: *l'assassino non è ancora stato arrestato*, the murderer is still at large; *lo arrestarono per furto*, they arrested him for theft ‖ **arrestàrsi,** *v.r.* 1. (*fermarsi*) to stop: *quell'orologio si arrestò alle cinque*, that watch stopped at five; *il treno si arrestò*, the train came to a stand 2. (*fare una pausa*) to pause, to linger: *si arrestò qualche secondo, poi aggiunse...*, he paused for a short while, then he added....

arrèsto, *s.m.* 1. (*cattura*) arrest, capture; (*mil.*) arrest: — *di rigore*, close arrest; — *semplice*, open arrest; *in* — (*o agli arresti*), under arrest: *mettere un ufficiale agli arresti*, to put an officer under arrest; *mandato di* —, warrant: *spiccare un mandato di* —, to issue a warrant 2. (*fermata*) stop, arrest (of motion), stopping: *segnale d'—*, stop signal 3. *fig.* standstill, stoppage: *gli affari hanno subìto un* —, business has come to a standstill 4. (*pausa*) pause, interval 5. (*mec.*) stop, catch: — *di emergenza*, emergency stop; — *di sicurezza*, safety catch; *valvola d'—*, cut off valve; *vite d'—*, stop screw.

arretàre, *v.t.* (*rar.*) to ensnare; to entrap.

arretràre, *v.t.* to pull back; (*ritirare*) to withdraw: *arretrarono, fecero* — *le loro truppe*, they withdrew their troops ‖ *v.i.*, **arretràrsi,** *v.r.* to draw back, to move back, to step back: *arretrò spaventato*, he drew back in a fright.

arretràto, *ag.* 1. backward; behindhand (*predicativo*): *è un paese* —, it is a backward country 2. (*comm.*) in arrears, outstanding: *interessi arretrati*, outstanding interests; *pagamento* —, outstanding (*o* overdue) payment ‖ *s.m.* 1. arrear(s): *essere in* — *con ql.co.*, to be in arrear(s) with sthg. (*o* to be behindhand with sthg.) 2. *pl.* (*comm.*) arrears: *arretrati di pigione*, *di salario*, arrears of rent, of wages; *liquidare gli arretrati*, to pay arrears.

àrri, *inter.* gee-ho!, gee-(h)up!.

arricchiménto, *s.m.* enrichment, enriching.

arricchíre, *v.t.* to enrich, to make rich, to make wealthy (anche *fig.*): — *la mente di cognizioni*, to enrich one's mind with knowledge ‖ *v.i.*, **arricchírsi,**

v.r. to become rich, to grow rich; to add to one's wealth: *la lingua si arricchisce continuamente di parole nuove*, the language is always adding to its wealth of words; — *a spese altrui*, to grow rich at the expense of others.

arricchíto, *s.m.* profiteer; nouveau riche: — *di guerra*, war profiteer.

arricciaménto, *s.m.* 1. (*di capelli*) curling 2. (*accartocciamento*) crumpling.

arricciàre, *v.t.* 1. to curl ‖ — *il naso*, to turn up one's nose 2. (*accartocciare*) to crumple (up) 3. (*muri*) to lime-wash (before whitewashing) ‖ **arricciàrsi**, *v.r.* to curl one's hair, to bristle up; (*diventar riccio*) to become curly.

arricciàto, *ag.* curled, curly.

arricciatúra, *s.f.* 1. (*di capelli*) hair curling 2. (*secondo strato d'intonaco*) floating coat, floated coat.

arríccio, *V.* **arricciatúra** 2.

arricciolaménto, *s.m.* hair-curling.

arricciolàre, *v.t.*, **arricciolàrsi**, *v.r.* to form into small curls.

arridàre, *v.t.* (*mar.*) to set up.

arrídere, *v.i.* to be favourable, to be propitious, to favour (s.o.), to assist (s.o.); to smile on (s.o.): *se vi arride la fortuna*, if fortune smiles on you.

Arrígo, *no.pr.m.* Henry.

arrínga, *s.f.* harangue, address; (*dir.*) pleading, defense.

arringàre, *v.t.i.* to harangue.

arringatóre, *s.m.*, **arringatríce**, *s.f.* haranguer; (*spreg.*) soap-box orator.

arríngo, *s.m.* 1. (*arengo*) assembly 2. (*gara*) lists (*pl.*): *scendere nell'* —, to enter the lists (*o* to take part in a competition *o* to join in a fight).

arrischiàre, *v.t.* to risk, to venture: *arrischiò la vita per lui*, he risked his life for him ‖ **arrischiàrsi**, *v.r.* to venture, to risk, to dare: — *un poco*, to run a few risks (*o* a slight risk).

arrischiataménte, *av.* 1. hazardously, riskily 2. (*imprudentemente*) rashly.

arrischiàto, *ag.* 1. risky, venturesome 2. (*imprudente*) rash.

arrisicàre, (*fam.*) per **arrischiàre**.

arríva, *av.* (*mar.*) aloft.

arrivàre, *v.i.* 1. to come (to a place), to arrive (at a place), to reach (a place), to get (to a place): *arrivammo a Londra sani e salvi*, we reached London safe and sound; *arriverà domani*, he will arrive (*o* get) to-morrow; *arrivò in ritardo per il pranzo*, he turned up late for dinner; *gli arrivarono altri libri*, he received other books; *le loro voci ci arrivarono attraverso il lago*, their voices reached us across the lake ‖ *chi tardi arriva, male alloggia*, prov. first come, first served 2. *fig.* to attain (sthg.), to achieve (sthg.), to get at (sthg.), to arrive (at sthg.): *col coraggio si arriva ovunque*, with courage one can get anywhere; *è arrivato all'impossibile*, he has achieved the impossible; — *al proprio scopo*, to attain (*o* to achieve) one's ends; — *alla verità*, to arrive (*o* to get) at the truth 3. (*riuscire*) to manage (to do); to succeed (in doing): *non arrivo a capirlo*, I can't make him out 4. (*capitare*) to happen: *qualunque cosa arrivi*, whatever happens ‖ *le disgrazie non arrivano mai sole*, prov. it never rains but it pours 5. (*aver successo*) to attain success: *il suo scopo è* —, he aims at success 6. (*essere ridotto a*) to be reduced to (sthg., doing): *arrivò a chiedere l'elemosina*, he was reduced to begging 7. (*capire*) to understand (sthg.), to make out (sthg.): *non ci arrivo*, I can't make it out 8. (*di abiti*) to fit (s.o.): *questa giacca non mi arriva*, this coat does not fit me.

arrivàto, *ag.* 1. successful: *è un uomo d'affari* —, he is a successful businessman 2. *ben* —!, welcome! ‖ *s.m.* successful man, made man.

arrivedérci, *inter.* goodbye; (*fam.*) so long; see you soon: — *giovedì*, goodbye till (*o* see you on *o* see you next) Thursday.

arrivísmo, *s.m.* pushfulness; social climbing.

arrivísta, *s.c.* careerist; thruster, social climber; pushing fellow; (*sl. amer.*) go-getter.

arrívo, *s.m.* arrival: *arrivi e partenze*, arrivals and departures; *il mio* — *a Milano*, my arrival in Milan; *all'albergo vi sono nuovi arrivi*, there are new arrivals at the hotel; *attendiamo nuovi arrivi di merce*, (*comm.*) we are expecting fresh supplies.

arroccaménto, *s.m.* 1. (*scacchi*) castling 2. *linea d'* —, (*mil.*) line of communication.

arroccàre[1], *v.t.* 1. (*scacchi*) to castle 2. (*mil.*) to protect, to defend ‖ **arroccàrsi**, *v.r.* (*scacchi*) to castle.

arroccàre[2], *v.t.* to fill the distaff with (sthg.).

arrocchiàre, *v.t.* 1. to roll up, to make rolls of (sthg.), to make (sthg.) into rolls 2. (*abborracciare*) to bungle.

arrochiménto, *s.m.* hoarseness.

arrochíre, *v.t.* to hoarsen, to make hoarse ‖ *v.i.*, **arrochírsi**, *v.r.* (*farsi rauco*) to hoarsen, to become hoarse, to grow hoarse.

arrogànte, *ag.* arrogant, haughty, presumptuous.

arroganteménte, *av.* arrogantly, haughtily, presumptuously.

arrogànza, *s.f.* arrogance, haughtiness, presumption.

arrogàre, *v.t.* (*dir.*) to adopt ‖ **arrogàrsi**, *v.r.* to arrogate to oneself; to claim unduly.

arrogazióne, *s.f.* (*dir.*) adoption.

arrolaménto, *s.m.* (*mil.*) enlistment, enrolment.

arrolàre, *v.t.* to enlist, to enrol, to call up ‖ **arrolàrsi**, *v.r.* (*mil.*) to join up, to be called up, to enlist; (*volontariamente*) to volunteer.

arrolàto, *s.m.* (*mil.*) recruit.

arrolatóre, *s.m.* (*mil.*) recruiting sergeant.

arroncigliàre, *v.t.* to hook ‖ **arroncigliàrsi**, *v.r.* to curl up, to coil up.

arronzàrsi, **arronzinàrsi**, *v.r.* to bestir oneself; to strive hard.

arrossaménto, *s.m.* reddening; blushing.

arrossàre, *v.t.* to redden; (*tinger di rosso*) to dye red ‖ *v.i.*, **arrossàrsi**, *v.r.* (*diventar rosso*) to become red, to redden; to blush.

arrossiménto, *s.m.* blushing; reddening.

arrossíre, *v.i.* 1. to blush, to turn red 2. (*vergognarsi*) to be ashamed.

arrostiménto, *s.m.* roasting.

arrostíre, *v.t.* to roast; (*sulla graticola*) to grill, to broil: — *il pane*, to toast bread ‖ **arrostírsi**, *v.r.* to roast, to get roasted: — *al sole*, to broil in the sun.

arrostíto, *ag.* roasted, roast, grilled, broiled; *carne arrostita*, roast meat; *castagne arrostite*, roasted (*o* roast) chestnuts.

arrostitúra, *s.f.* roasting.

arròsto, *ag.* roast ‖ *s.m.* roast: — *di maiale*, roast pork; — *di manzo*, roast beef; — *di vitello*, roast veal ‖ *molto fumo e poco* —, *fig.* much show and little behind it.

arrotaménto, *s.m.* whetting, sharpening; grinding.

arrotàre, *v.t.* 1. (*affilare*) to whet, to sharpen; to grind ‖ — *i denti*, to grind one's teeth 2. (*levigare*) to smooth 3. (*investire*) to run over 4. (*st.*) (*sottoporre al supplizio della ruota*) to break on the wheel ‖ **arrotàrsi**, *v.r.* to be restless; to work hard.

arrotatúra, *s.f.* whetting, sharpening; grinding.

arrotíno, *s.m.* knife-grinder.

arrotolàre, *v.t.* to roll up.

arrotondàre, *v.t.* to round, to make round: — *una cifra*, *fig.* to make a round figure; — *il proprio stipendio*, *fig.* to add to one's salary; — *lo stipendio di qlcu.*, *fig.* to raise s.o.'s salary ‖ **arrotondàrsi**, *v.r.* to become round; (*diventar grassottello*) to become plump.

arrovellàrsi, *v.r.* 1. (*stizzirsi*) to get enraged 2. (*angustiarsi*) to worry oneself, to bother 3. (*darsi molto da fare*) to strive.

arroventaménto, *s.m.* (*l'arroventare*) making red-hot.

arroventàre, *v.t.* to make red-hot ‖ **arroventàrsi**, *v.r.* to become red-hot.

arroventàto, *ag.* red-hot.

arroventatúra, *s.f.* red-heat.

arroventíre, *V.* **arroventàre.**

arrovesciaménto, *s.m.* upsetting, overturning, reversal; turning upside down.

arrovesciàre, *v.t.* **1.** (*capovolgere*) to overturn, to turn over, to upset **2.** (*rivoltare*) to turn out, to turn inside out: *arrovesciò le tasche,* he turned his pockets inside out ‖ **arrovesciàrsi,** *v.r.* to turn upside down, to be overturned, to capsize, to overturn.

arrovèscio, a rovèscio, *av.* (*capovolto*) upside down ‖ *andare —, fig.* to go from bad to worse; *capire —,* to misunderstand.

arrozzíre, *v.t.* to make coarse, to make rough ‖ *v.i.* to become coarse, to become rough.

arruffamatàsse, *s.c.* swindler; intriguer; marplot.

arruffaménto, *s.m.* ruffling; entangling, entanglement.

arruffapòpoli, *s.m.* agitator; demagogue; ringleader.

arruffàre, *v.t.* **1.** (*intricare*) to entangle **2.** (*scarmigliare*) to ruffle: — *i capelli a qlcu.,* to ruffle s.o.'s hair; — *le penne,* to ruffle (up) one's feathers **3.** (*intricare*) to entangle ‖ **arruffàrsi,** *v.r.* **1.** (*di capelli, peli*) to ruffle (up), to bristle (up): *gli si arruffò il pelo,* its hair bristled **2.** (*intricarsi*) to get entangled (anche *fig.*).

arruffataménte, *av.* untidily, in disorder.

arruffàto, *ag.* **1.** (*scompigliato*) ruffled, dishevelled, untidy **2.** (*complicato, intricato*) entangled, intricate, involved.

arruffianàre, *v.t.* to patch up.

arruffío, *s.m.* confusion, disorder, entanglement.

arruffóne, *s.m.* muddler, bungler.

arrugginíre, *v.t.* to rust, to make rusty, to cover with rust ‖ *v.i.,* **arrugginírsi,** *v.r.* **1.** to rust, to get rusty, to grow rusty **2.** *fig.* to become dull, to become rusty: *la mente si arrugginisce nell'ozio,* mind rusts in idleness.

arrugginíto, *ag.* rusty.

arruvidíre, *v.t.* to make rough, to roughen ‖ *v.i.,* **arruvidírsi,** *v.r.* to become rough, to grow rough.

arsèlla, *s.f.* (zool.) mussel.

arsenàle, *s.m.* **1.** (*cantiere*) ship-yard **2.** (*fabbrica, deposito di armi*) arsenal **3.** (*fam.*) (*ripostiglio*) lumber-room.

arsenalòtto, *s.m.* ship-yard worker.

arseniàto, *s.m.* (chim.) arsenate.

arsenicàle, *ag.* (chim.) arsenical.

arsenicàto, *ag.* (chim.) arsenical; (*contenente arsenico pentavalente*) arsenic.

arsènico, *s.m.* (chim.) arsenic.

arsenióso, *ag.* (chim.) arsenious.

àrsi, *s.f.* (prosodia, mus.) arsis.

arsicciàre, *v.t.* to singe, to scorch.

arsíccio, *ag.* singed, scorched; (*riarso*) parched: *ho la gola arsiccia per la sete,* I am parched with thirst.

arsióne, *s.f.* **1.** burning **2.** (*eccessivo calore*) excessive heat **3.** (*arsura da sete*) parching thirst **4.** (*calore febbrile*) temperature.

àrso, *ag.* **1.** (*bruciato*) burnt **2.** (*riarso, secco*) dry, dried up.

arsúra, *s.f.* **1.** burning **2.** (*siccità*) drought **3.** (*da sete*) parching thirst **4.** (*da febbre*) feverish thirst.

artataménte, *av.* (*rar.*) artfully; craftily; deceitfully.

àrte, *s.f.* **1.** art: — *applicata,* applied art; *arti belle,* fine arts; — *decorativa,* decorative art; *l'— di fare ql.co.,* the art of doing sthg.; — *plastica e figurativa,* painting and sculpture; *opera d'—,* work of art ‖ *l'— per l'—,* art for art's sake **2.** (*complesso di regole*) art: *l'— della guerra,* warcraft; *l'— di governare,* statesmanship; *l'— oratoria,* oratory **3.** (*corporazione*) corporation, guild: *l'— della lana,* the wool guild **4.** (*abilità*) skill, talent: *l'— con cui è stato fatto questo vaso,* the craftsmanship displayed in this vase; *fatto con molta —,* made with great skill (o very skillfully made) ‖ *l'— del Michelaccio,* laziness ‖ *l'— di godersi la vita,* the art of enjoying life **5.** (*artifizio, astuzia*) art, artifice, cunning: *quell'uomo è pieno di arti,* that man is full of cunning ‖ *ad —,* on purpose.

artefàre, *v.t.* to adulterate.

artefàtto, *ag.* adulterated; not genuine; faked: *vino —,* adulterated wine.

artéfice, *s.m.* **1.** artificer, maker, craftsman (*pl.* craftsmen) **2.** *fig.* author, creator ‖ *il Sommo Artefice,* the Almighty (o the Creator).

Artèmide, *no.pr.f.* (mit.) Artemis.

Artemísia, *no.pr.f.* (mit.) Artemisia ‖ **artemísia,** *s.f.* (bot.) artemisia.

artèria, *s.f.* (anat.) artery (anche *fig.*): — *commerciale,* artery of commerce; — *di traffico,* thorough-fare; — *ferroviaria,* arterial railway.

arteriàle, *ag.* (anat.) arterial.

arteriología, *s.f.* arteriology.

arterioscleròsi, *s.f.* (patol.) arteriosclerosis.

arterioscleròtico, *ag.* (patol.) arteriosclerotic.

arterióso, *ag.* (anat.) arterial.

arteriotomía, *s.f.* (chir.) arteriotomy.

arteríte, *s.f.* (patol.) arteritis.

artesiàno, *ag.* artesian: *pozzo —,* artesian well.

àrtico, *ag.* arctic ‖ *Circolo Polare Artico,* Arctic Circle ‖ *Polo Artico,* Arctic (o North) Pole.

articolàre, *ag.* articular: *dolori articolari,* pains in the joints.

articolàre, *v.t.* **1.** to articulate **2.** (*pronunciare bene*) to articulate, to pronounce distinctly **3.** (*proferire*) to utter: *non potè — parola,* he could not utter a single word ‖ **articolàrsi,** *v.r.* to articulate.

articolataménte, *av.* distinctly.

articolàto, *ag.* **1.** articulate: *suoni articolati,* articulate sounds **2.** (*gram.*) contracted: *preposizioni articolate,* contracted prepositions **3.** (*fatto di parti movibili*) jointed, hinged.

articolazióne, *s.f.* **1.** (anat.) articulation **2.** (*punto di giuntura*) joint, connection, link **3.** (*l'articolare le parole*) articulation; utterance.

articolísta, *s.c.* columnist.

artícolo, *s.m.* **1.** (gram.) article: — *determinativo,* indeterminativo, definite, indefinite article **2.** (*di giornale*) article: — *di fondo,* editorial (o leading article o leader); — *di prima pagina,* front page article **3.** (comm.) article; (*insieme di articoli trattati*) line: — *aggiunto,* side-line; *articoli da caccia, da pesca,* hunting, fishing implements; — *di lusso,* luxury article; — *di moda,* fashionable article; — *principale,* stock article; *questo non è il mio —,* this is not my line; *essere ben fornito di un —,* to be well stocked with an article; *essere sprovvisto di un —,* to be out of an article **4.** (comm.) (*voce di contratto, ecc.*) item: — *numero uno,* item (number) one **5.** (teol.) article: — *di fede,* article of faith; *in — di morte,* in the article of death (o at the point of death).

artière, *s.m.* **1.** handicraftsman (*pl.* handicraftsmen), mechanic, artisan **2.** (*mil.*) sapper.

artificiàle, *ag.* artificial.

artificialménte, *av.* artificially.

artificière, *s.m.* **1.** (*mil.*) artillery artificer; (*amer.*) artificer; (*mar.*) gunner **2.** (*pirotecnico*) pyrotechnist.

artifício, *s.m.* **1.** artifice, contrivance, device: *gli artifici per mezzo dei quali le orchidee vengono fertilizzate,* the contrivances by which orchids are fertilized ‖ *fuochi d'—,* fireworks **2.** (*astuzia*) cunning, slyness, craftiness: *uomo pieno d'—,* man full of cunning **3.** *pl.* (*mil.*) artifices; (*per segnalazioni*) light and smoke devices, flares and light signals.

artificiosaménte, *av.* artfully, cunningly, slyly.

artificiosità, *s.f.* artfulness, cunning, slyness.

artificióso, *ag.* artful, sly, cunning.

artifiziàre, *v.t.* to adulterate, to falsify, to counterfeit.

artifiziàto, *ag.* adulterate, fictitious, counterfeit; (*amer.*) bogus.

artifízio, *e derivati, V.* **artifício,** *e derivati.*

artigianàto, *s.m.* **1.** (*arte manuale*) handicraft **2.** (*piccola industria*) small industry **3.** (*classe artigiana*) craftsmen (*pl.*), the artisan class.

artigianésco, *ag.* pertaining to handicraft.

artigiàno, *ag.* artisan ‖ *s.m.* craftsman (*pl.* craftsmen), artisan, handicraftsman (*pl.* handicraftsmen).

artigliàre, *v.t.* (*rar.*) **1.** to claw, to scratch **2.** (*aggrapparsi a*) to clutch.

artigliàto, *as.* clawed.

artiglière, *s.m.* (*mil.*) artilleryman (*pl.* artillerymen), artillerist; gunner (anche *mar.*).

artiglieria, *s.f.* artillery, ordnance: — *da campagna*, field artillery; — *di marina*, naval armament; — *pesante*, heavy artillery; *parco d'*—, artillery-park; *pezzo d'*—, piece of ordnance.

artíglio, *s.m.* **1.** claw; (*di uccelli rapaci*) talon: *colpo d'*—, scratch **2.** *fig.* clutch: *l'*— *dello strozzino*, the usurer's clutch.

artimóne, *s.m.* (*mar.*) mizzen(-sail).

artiodàttilo, *s.m.* (*zool.*) artiodactyl (*pl.* artiodactyla).

artísta, *s.c.* artist; (*scultore*) sculptor; (*pittore*) painter: — *di canto*, singer (o artiste); — *di danza*, dancer (o artiste); — *drammatico*, actor.

artisticaménte, *av.* artistically.

artístico, *ag.* artistic(al): *senso* —, artistry; *non c'è niente di* — *in quell'opera*, there is nothing artistic in that work.

àrto, *s.m.* (*anat.*) limb: — *artificiale*, artificial limb; *arti inferiori*, lower limbs; *arti superiori*, upper limbs.

artríte, *s.f.* (*patol.*) arthritis: — *deformante*, rheumatoid arthritis.

artrítico, *ag.* (*patol.*) arthritic: *dolori artritici*, pain in the joints (o arthritis).

artrodía, *s.f.* (*anat.*) arthrodia.

artrología, *s.f.* arthrology.

artròpodo, *s.m.* (*zool.*) arthropod.

Artú, *no.pr.m.* (*lett.*) Arthur.

Artúro, *no.pr.m.* **1.** Arthur **2.** (*astr.*) Arcturus.

aruspicàre, *v.t.* (*rar.*) to augur; to forebode.

arúspice, *s.m.* (*st. romana*) haruspex (*pl.* haruspices).

aruspicína, *s.f.* (*st. romana*) haruspicy.

arvàlo, *s.m.* (*st. romana*) Arval Brother (*pl.* Arval Brethren).

arvícola, *s.m.* (*zool.*) field-mouse (*pl.* field-mice); harvest-mouse (*pl.* harvest-mice).

arzàgola, *s.f.* (*ornit.*) teal (*invariato al pl.*).

arzènte, *ag.* (*arc.*) burning: *acqua* —, aqua vitæ ‖ *s.m.* brandy.

arzigogolàre, *v.i.* **1.** (*fantasticare*) to fancy (sthg.), to day-dream **2.** (*sottilizzare*) to cavil (at sthg.).

arzigògolo, *s.m.* **1.** (*cavillo*) cavil, subtlety **2.** (*ghiribizzo, fantasia*) whim **3.** (*giro tortuoso di parole*) roundabout expression.

arzigogolóne, *s.m.* caviller.

arzíllo, *ag.* sprightly, lively, brisk; animated: *un vecchietto* —, a brisk old man; *un vino* —, a brisk wine.

asbèsto, *s.m.* (*min.*) asbestos.

Ascànio, *no.pr.m.* (*lett.*) Ascanius.

ascàride, *s.m.* (*zool.*) ascarid; (*fam.*) roundworm.

àscaro, *s.m.* (*mil.*) askari (*invariato al pl.*).

ascèlla, *s.f.* **1.** (*anat.*) armpit ‖ *sotto-ascelle*, dress-shields ‖ *stare con le mani sotto le ascelle, fig.* to stand by in idleness **2.** (*bot.*) axil.

ascellàre, *ag.* axillary.

ascendentàle, *ag.* of the ascendants.

ascendènte, *ag.* ascendent, ascendant, rising, upward: *scala* —, (*mus.*) ascending scale; *volo* —, (*aer.*) climbing flight ‖ *s.m.* **1.** (*prestigio, influenza*) ascendancy, ascendency, influence: *avere* — *su qlcu.*, to have ascendancy over s.o. **2.** (*astr.*) ascendant **3.** (*antenato*) ascendant, ascendent, ancestor.

ascendènza, *s.f.* (*antenati*) ancestors (*pl.*), lineal ascendants (*pl.*).

ascéndere, *v.i.* **1.** to ascend, to rise (anche *fig.*): —

a grandi onori, to ascend to great honours; — *al trono*, to ascend the throne **2.** (*ammontare*) to amount: *le spese ascendono a ventimila lire*, expenses amount to twenty thousand lire ‖ *v.t.* (*rar.*) to ascend, to go up (sthg.), to climb: — *un monte*, to climb a mountain.

ascensionàle, *ag.* ascensional, upward: *forza* —, (*aer.*) lifting (o elevating) power.

ascensióne, *s.f.* ascension; (*scalata*) climb; (*aer.*) climb, ascent: — *retta*, (*astr.*) right ascension ‖ *l'Ascensione*, (*eccl.*) Ascension-day.

ascensionísta, *s.m.* climber, alpinist, ascensionist.

ascensóre, *s.m.* lift; (*amer.*) elevator.

ascensorísta, *s.m.* lift attendant, lift boy.

ascésa, *s.f.* **1.** ascent **2.** (*al trono*) accession.

ascèsi, *s.f.* mystical practice.

ascèsso, *s.m.* (*patol.*) abscess; gathering: — *al dito*, gathered finger; — *alla gengiva*, gumboil; *vuotare un* —, to drain an abscess.

ascèta, *s.c.* ascetic: *vivere da* —, to lead an austere life.

ascètica, *s.f.* (*teol.*) ascetics.

asceticaménte, *av.* ascetically.

ascètico, *ag.* ascetic(al).

ascetísmo, *s.m.* asceticism.

àscia, *s.f.* axe; (*accetta*) hatchet: *fatto con l'*—, rough-hewn; *fig.* clumsily made ‖ *maestro d'*—, (*mar.*) carpenter.

asciàre, *v.t.* to rough-hew; to chop.

asciàta, *s.f.* axe stroke.

asciòlvere, *v.i.* to breakfast.

asciòlvere, *s.m.* breakfast: *all'*—, at breakfast.

ascíssa, *s.f.* (*mat.*) abscissa (*pl.* abscissæ, abscissas), absciss(e) (*pl.* abscisses).

ascíte, *s.f.* (*patol.*) ascites; (*fam.*) dropsy.

ascítico, *ag.* (*patol.*) ascitic(al); (*fam.*) dropsical.

ascitízio, *ag.* **1.** alien **2.** (*preso a prestito*) borrowed **3.** (*accessorio*) accessory, additional.

asciugacapélli, *s.m.* hair-drier.

asciugamàno, *s.m.* towel.

asciugaménto, *s.m.* drying; wiping.

asciugàre, *v.t.* to dry (up); (*tergere con un panno, con una mano*) to wipe (off) ‖ — *una bottiglia*, to drink up a (whole) bottle ‖ — *le tasche di qlcu.*, to drain s.o.'s pockets ‖ *v.i.* to dry (up), to get dry: *ho messo i panni ad* — *e ora stanno asciugando*, I've put the linen to dry and now it's getting dry ‖ **asciugàrsi**, *v.r.* (*un panno*) to wipe oneself: *asciugati le mani*, wipe your hands; — *le lagrime*, to wipe one's tears.

asciugatóio, *s.m.* **1.** towel: — *da bagno*, bath towel **2.** (*mec.*) drier, dryer.

asciugatúra, *s.f.* drying; wiping.

asciuttaménte, *av.* drily, dryly; *fig.* sharply.

asciuttézza, *s.f.* dryness; aridity (anche *fig.*); sterility.

asciútto, *ag.* **1.** dry (anche *fig.*): *un discorso* —, *una risposta asciutta*, a dry speech, a dry reply; *tempo, regione, vento* —, dry weather, country, wind; *da tenere in luogo* —, to be kept dry; *indossai vestiti asciutti*, I put on dry clothing ‖ *balia asciutta*, dry nurse ‖ *pane* —, (*senza companatico*) dry bread ‖ *pasta asciutta*, cheese macaroni ‖ *rimanere a bocca asciutta, a denti asciutti, fig.* to be disappointed **2.** (*senza lacrime*) dry, tearless: *a ciglio* —, tearless; *occhi asciutti*, dry eyes **3.** (*magro*) thin, lean: *un viso* —, a thin face **4.** (*di vino, secco*) dry: *vino* —, dry wine **5.** (*privo di denaro*) penniless ‖ *s.m.* dry place: *essere all'*—, to be out of the rain (o under cover) ‖ *restare all'*—, *fig.* to be penniless (o to have run out of money o to be hard up).

asciútto, *av.* drily, dryly; *fig.* sharply.

asciuttóre, *s.m.* drought, dryness.

asclepiadèo, *ag.* Asclepiadean ‖ *s.m.* (*poes.*) Asclepiad.

ascoltàre, *v.t.* **1.** to listen to (s.o., sthg.); to hear: *ascoltami!*, listen to me! (o look here!); *ascoltate attentamente!*, pay attention!; *ascoltatemi fino in fondo*, hear me out; — *cantare gli uccelli*, to listen to the birds singing; — *con tutte e due le orecchie*, to listen with both ears (*o* to be all ears); — *da un solo orecchio*, to be only half listening (*o* to pay little attention); — *la radio*, to listen in (*o* to listen to the radio): — *radio Milano*, to listen in to Milan **2**. (*dar retta a*) to pay attention to (s.o., sthg.); to listen to (s.o., sthg.): *non ascolta nessuno*, he pays attention to no one; *non avete voluto ascoltarmi*, you would not listen to me; *se mi avessero ascoltato!*, if I had been listened to!; — *il consiglio di qlcu.*, to take s.o.'s advice **3**. (*med.*) to auscultate **4**. (*assistere a*) to attend: — *le lezioni*, to attend classes; — *la Messa*, to hear (*o* to attend) Mass || *v.i.* **1**. (*origliare*) to eavesdrop **2**. (*mettersi in ascolto, prestare orecchio*) to lend an ear.

ascoltatóre, *s.m.*, **ascoltatrice**, *s.f.* **1**. listener; hearer **2**. *pl.* (*uditorio*) audience (*sing.*).

ascoltazióne, *s.f.* **1**. listening **2**. (*med.*) auscultation.

ascólto, *s.m.* listening (anche *rad.*), hearing: *sono in* —, I am listening; *dare* — *a*, to listen to || *al primo* —, at first hearing.

ascóndere, *v.t.* (*poet.*) to hide || **ascóndersi**, *v.r.* to hide; to conceal oneself.

ascóso, *ag.* (*poet.*) hidden.

ascrèo, *ag.* (*letter.*) of Ascra; Hesiodic || *i canti ascrei*, didactic poems.

ascrívere, *v.t.* **1**. (*annoverare*) to count, to register **2**. (*attribuire*) to impute, to ascribe: *gli fu ascritto a merito, a biasimo, il fatto di essersi opposto*, he got the praise, the blame, for opposing.

asèpsi, *s.f.* (*med.*) asepsis.

asessuàle, *ag.* (*biol.*) asexual.

asèttico, *ag.* (*med.*) aseptic.

asfaltàre, *v.t.* to asphalt.

asfàlto, *s.m.* asphalt.

asfissía, *s.f.* asphyxia, asphyxy; suffocation; (*da gas*) gassing.

asfissiànte, *ag.* asphyxiating; suffocating: *gas* —, poison-gas.

asfissiàre, *v.t.* to asphyxiate; to suffocate; (*con gas venefici*) to gas || *v.i.* to suffocate; to die of asphyxia || **asfissiàrsi**, *v.r.* to asphyxiate oneself; (*col gas*) to gas oneself.

asfissiàto, asfíttico, *ag.* asphyxiated; (*da gas*) gassed: *morire* —, to die of asphyxia.

asfodèlo, *s.m.* (*bot.*) asphodel.

Àsia, *no.pr.f.* (*geog.*) Asia.

asiàtico, *ag.s.m.* Asiatic, Asian: *influenza asiatica*, (*patol.*) Asian 'flu; *lusso* —, oriental splendour; *morbo* —, (*patol.*) cholera.

asílo, *s.m.* **1**. (*rifugio*) refuge, shelter, retreat: *luogo di* —, (place of) refuge; *senza* —, homeless; *cercare* —, to seek refuge; *dare* — *a qlcu.*, to harbour (*o* to shelter) s.o. || *diritto d'*—, (*dir.*) right of sanctuary **2**. (*ricovero, scuola*): — *infantile*, kindergarten (*o* infant school); — *notturno*, night shelter; — *per i poveri*, workhouse.

asimmetría, *s.f.* asymmetry.

asimmètrico, *ag.* asymmetrical, unsymmetrical.

àsina, *s.f.* she-ass: *latte d'*—, ass's milk.

asinàggine, *s.f.* **1**. asininity, stupidity; ignorance **2**. (*asinata*) foolish act; foolish remark.

asinàio, *s.m.* **1**. (*guidatore d'asini*) ass-driver **2**. (*allevatore d'asini*) ass-breeder **3**. (*negoziante d'asini*) ass-dealer.

asinàta, *s.f.* foolish action; foolish remark.

asincronísmo, *s.m.* (*scient.*) asynchronism.

asíncrono, *ag.* (*scient.*) asynchronous.

asíndeto, *s.m.* (*ret.*) asyndeton.

asinèllo, *s.m.* **1**. (*asino piccolo*) small donkey **2**. (*asino giovane*) ass's foal, ass's colt.

asinería, *s.f.* **1**. asininity, stupidity; (*grande ignoranza*) gross ignorance **2**. (*asinata*) foolish act; foolish remark: *non dire asinerie!*, don't talk nonsense!; *questa è una bella* —*!*, this is sheer nonsense!.

asinescaménte, *av.* stupidly, foolishly.

asinésco, *ag.* asinine, stupid, foolish.

asiníno, *ag.* asinine || *tosse asinina*, hooping cough.

asinità, *s.f.* stupidity, asininity.

àsino, *s.m.* **1**. ass, donkey: — *maschio*, jackass || — *risalito, bardato*, *fig.* upstart || *la bellezza dell'*—, the passing beauty of youth || *strada a schiena d'*—, cambered road || *testardo come un* —, as stubborn as an ass || *trotto dell'*—, a flash in the pan: *il suo entusiasmo per imparare l'inglese si è mostrato un trotto dell'*—, his enthusiasm to learn English proved to be a flash in the pan || *è inutile lavare la testa all'*—, there is no washing a blackmoor white || *credere che un* — *voli*, to swallow anything || *fare come l'*— *di Buridano*, to be unable to make a choice || *legare l'*— *dove vuole il padrone*, to do as one's master wishes **2**. *fig.* ass, jackass, goof, blockhead, dolt: — *che non sei altro!*, you fool! (*o* you jackass!) || *pezzo d'*—*!*, you big fool! || *qui casca l'*—, there is the rub || *ponte dell'*—, Asses' bridge (*o* Pons Asinorum) || *meglio un* — *vivo che un dottore morto*, *prov.* a live dog is better than a dead lion || *raglio d'*— *non sale al cielo*, *prov.* a fool's talk carries no weight.

asíntote, *s.f.* (*geom.*) asymptote.

asintòtico, *ag.* (*geom.*) asymptotic(al).

asísmico, *ag.* earthquake-proof.

àsma, *s.f.* (*patol.*) asthma: *soffriva d'*— *bronchiale*, he suffered from bronchial asthma.

asmàtico, *ag.* **1**. asthmatic(al) **2**. *fig.* (*di stile*) jerky.

àsola, *s.f.* buttonhole.

asolàre, *v.i.* **1**. (*alitare, spirare, di brezza*) to blow gently: *il vento asolava*, there was a gentle breeze blowing **2**. (*rigirare intorno ad un luogo*) to go round and round **3**. (*andare a prendere l'aria*) to go out for a breath of air || **asolàrsi**, *v.r.* (*prender aria*) to take the air.

àsolo, *s.m.* gentle breeze, light breeze, breath of wind || *pigliar* —, to take a breath of fresh air.

asparagéto, *s.m.*, **asparagiàia**, *s.f.* asparagus-bed.

asparagína, *s.f.* (*chim.*) asparagine.

aspàrago, *s.m.* (*bot.*) asparagus.

Aspàsia, *no.pr.f.* (*st. greca*) Aspasia.

àspe, *s.m.* (*mar.*) capstan bar.

asperèlla, *s.f.* (*bot.*) horse-tail.

aspèrgere, *v.t.* to besprinkle, to sprinkle: — *d'acqua santa*, to sprinkle with holy water.

aspèrge(s), *s.m.* (*eccl.*) aspergillum, sprinkler || *dare* — to give a blessing with holy-water.

aspèrgine, *s.f.* aspersion, sprinkling.

aspergitóre, *s.m.*, **aspergitrice**, *s.f.* sprinkler.

asperità, *s.f.* **1**. asperity **2**. (*di superficie*) unevenness; ruggedness; roughness **3**. (*di carattere*) harshness, sharpness **4**. (*di stile*) crabbedness.

aspersióne, *s.f.* sprinkling, aspersion.

aspersòrio, *s.m.* (*eccl.*) aspergillum.

aspettànza, *s.f.* expectation; anticipation.

aspettàre, *v.t.* **1**. to wait for (s.o., sthg.); (*con desiderio*) to look for (s.o., sthg.); (*con timore*) to apprehend: *aspetta che arrivi il treno*, wait for the train to arrive; *aspettami*, wait for me; *i tuoi progressi si fanno* —, your progress is slow in coming; *non correre, aspetta un momento*, don't run, wait a moment; *aspetta che ti accomodo io!*, you'll catch it! || *aspettalo!*, start waiting, then! || *me l'aspettavo*, just as I expected || *qui vi aspettavo*, now we'll see what you can do || — *la palla al balzo*, to wait for a favourable opportunity || *farsi* — *da qlcu.*, *far* — *qlcu.*, to keep s.o. waiting || *aspetta cavallo che l'erba cresca*, *prov.* while the grass is growing the horse starveth || *chi ha tempo non aspetti tempo*, *prov.* a stitch in time saves nine || *chi la fa l'aspetti*, *prov.* we reap as we sow **2**. (*comm.*) to await: *aspettando cortese risposta...*, awaiting your kind reply... || **aspettàrsi**, *v.r.* to expect; (*con desiderio*) to look forward to (sthg.), to anticipate; (*con timore*) to apprehend: *non mi aspettavo che tu arrivassi subito*, I did not expect you to arrive at once; *si aspettano troppo da me*, they expect too much of me.

aspettatíva, *s.f.* **1.** expectation; hope; anticipation: *contrariamente ad ogni —*, contrary to all expectation(s); *corrispondere all'—*, to come up to s.o.'s expectation(s) **2.** (*esonero temporaneo*) temporary retirement: *essere in —*, to be temporarily relieved of one's work.

aspettazióne, *s.f.* expectation; anticipation.

aspètto[1], *s.m.* **1.** appearance; aspect; look: *la città ha un — europeo*, the town has a European look ‖ *a primo —*, at first sight **2.** (*di persona*) appearance; looks (*pl.*); mien: *un giovane di bell'—*, a good-looking young man; *che — ha?*, what does he look like?; *ha l'— di un pazzo*, he looks like a lunatic; *ha un — triste*, he looks sad; *il suo — smentisce le sue parole*, his looks belie his words; *cambiare —*, to change appearance **3.** (*lato*) side; aspect: *sotto questo —*, from this point of view; *avete considerato ogni — del problema?*, ·have you considered every aspect of the question? **4.** (*astr.*) aspect.

aspètto[2], *s.m.* **1.** wait; (*l'aspettare*) waiting: *sala d'—*, waiting-room **2.** (*mus.*) pause.

àspide, *s.m.* **1.** (*zool.*) asp **2.** *fig.* wicked person, evil-doer **3.** (*arc. artigl.*) aspic.

aspirànte, *ag.* **1.** aspirant, aspiring, aiming (at sthg.) **2.** (*mec.*) sucking: *pompa —*, suction pump ‖ *s.m.* aspirant; applicant; (*candidato*) candidate: *— ad un impiego*, applicant for a position (*o* situation).

aspirapólvere, *s.m.* vacuum cleaner; (*fam.*) vac.

aspiràre, *v.t.* **1.** to inspire, to breathe in, to inhale: *— l'aria pura*, to breathe in the pure air; *— il fumo*, to inhale the smoke **2.** (*mec.*) to suck, to intake **3.** (*fonet.*) to aspirate: *non — le h*, to drop one's h's ‖ *v.i.* (*desiderare di ottenere*) to aspire; to aim (at sthg., doing): *— alla mano di qlcu.*, to seek s.o. in marriage; *— al potere assoluto*, to aim at absolute power.

aspiratóre, *s.m.* **1.** aspirator, exhauster, exhaust fan: *— a pale*, vane aspirator; *— centrifugo*, centrifugal fan **2.** (*chir.*) aspirator.

aspirazióne, *s.f.* **1.** aspiration; yearning (after, for sthg.) **2.** (*mec.*) suction, intake: *— della polvere*, dust suction; *lavoro di —*, intake work; *valvola di —*, suction-valve (*o* air-inlet) **3.** (*fonet.*) aspiration.

aspirína, *s.f.* (*farm.*) aspirin.

àspo, *s.m.* (*strum. artig.*) swift, reel.

asportàbile, *ag.* removable.

asportàre, *v.t.* **1.** to remove **2.** (*chir.*) to extirpate.

asportazióne, *s.f.* **1.** removal **2.** (*chir.*) extirpation.

aspraménte, *av.* harshly, sharply; rudely.

aspreggiàre, *v.t. fig.* to treat harshly.

asprétto, *ag.* sourish, tart ‖ *s.m.* sour taste.

asprézza, *s.f.* **1.** sourness **2.** (*ruvidezza*) roughness **3.** *fig.* harshness, rudeness.

asprí, *s.m.* aigrette, spray.

asprígno, *ag.* sourish, tartish ‖ *s.m.* sour taste.

àspro, *ag.* **1.** (*acido*) sour, tart **2.** (*ruvido*) rough **3.** *fig.* harsh, sharp; (*sgarbato*) rude, rough: *modi aspri*, rough manners; *parole aspre*, harsh words **4.** (*di clima*) hard, severe, rigorous: *inverno —*, hard winter **5.** (*arduo*) hard: *un — compito*, a hard task; *un'aspra salita*, a steep ascent; *combattimento —*, fierce (*o* hard) fight.

assaettaménto, *s.m.* annoyance; irritation.

assaettànte, *ag.* **1.** darting to and fro **2.** (*pungente*) pungent; annoying.

assaettàre, *v.t.* **1.** to dart **2.** (*molestare*) to annoy, to irritate; to be exceedingly unpleasant with (s.o.): *un puzzo che assaetta*, an overpowering smell ‖ **assaettàrsi**, *v.r.* **1.** (*arrabbiarsi*) to get angry **2.** (*affaticarsi*) to toil, to work hard.

assafètida, *s.f.* (*farm.*) asafoetida.

assaggiàre, *v.t.* **1.** to taste: *non vuole — nulla*, he doesn't want to taste food ‖ *— la frusta*, *fig.* to

have a taste of the whip **2.** (*provare*) to attempt; to try **3.** (*metalli*) to assay.

assaggiatóre, *s.m.*, **assaggiatríce**, *s.f.* taster.

assaggiatúra, *s.f.* **1.** tasting **2.** (*miner.*) assaying.

assàggio, *s.m.* **1.** tasting **2.** (*campione*) sample **3.** (*piccola quantità*) small quantity **4.** (*miner.*) assay: *— esplorativo di petrolio*, (*sl. amer.*) wild cat.

assài, *ag.* (*molto*) much, plenty of, a good deal of, a lot of; (*molti*) many; (*moltissimi*) a good many: *c'era — gente*, there were a good many people; «*Hai libri inglesi?*», «*Ne ho —*», "Have you got any English books?", "I have a good many".

assài, *av.* **1.** (*molto*) very, much: *— bello*, very fine; *— meglio*, much better; *— volentieri*, very willingly; *ho dormito —*, I have slept a long time **2.** (*abbastanza*) enough: *hai parlato —*, you have said enough.

assàle, *s.m.* axle; *— anteriore, posteriore*, front, rear axle; *— motore*, (*mec.*) driving-axle.

assalíre, *v.t.* **1.** to assail, to attack: *ci assalirono a colpi di pietra*, they assailed us with a volley of stones; *i nemici assalirono il nostro accampamento*, the enemy attacked our camp **2.** *fig.* to seize, to assail: *fu assalito dai dubbi*, he was assailed with doubts; *fu assalito dalla paura*, he was seized with fear **3.** (*di malattia*) to strike down, to attack, to affect: *l'assalì una febbre violenta*, he was struck down by a violent fever **4.** (*di temporale, ecc.*) to catch: *fummo assaliti dal temporale*, we were caught in the storm.

assalitóre, *ag.* assailing, attacking ‖ *s.m.*, **assalitríce**, *s.f.* assailer, assailant; (*attaccante*) attacker.

Assalònne, *no.pr.m.* Absalom.

assaltàbile, *ag.* assaultable.

assaltàre, *v.t.* to assault, to attack.

assaltatóre, *s.m.* assaulter.

assàlto, *s.m.* assault, attack (*anche fig.*): *un — di febbre*, *fig.* an attack of fever; *muovere all'—*, to make (*o* to give) assault; *pigliare d'—*, to take (*o* to carry) by assault; *respingere un —*, to repel an assault ‖ *di primo —*, *fig.* at first.

assaporaménto, *s.m.* tasting.

assaporàre, *v.t.* **1.** to savour; to taste, to relish **2.** *fig.* to enjoy, to relish.

assaporíre, *v.t.* to season, to spice; (*dare un gusto speciale a*) to flavour.

assassinaménto, *s.m.* murder, assassination.

assassinàre, *v.t.* **1.** to assassinate, to murder **2.** *fig.* to murder: *gli attori hanno assassinato la mia commedia*, the actors have murdered my play.

assassínio, *s.m.* murder ‖ *quel libro è un vero —*, *fig.* that book is a complete failure.

assassíno, *ag.* murderous ‖ *occhi assassini*, *fig.* killing eyes ‖ *s.m.* **1.** murderer, assassin: *quel medico è un —*, *fig.* that doctor is a killer **2.** *fig.* (*mascalzone*) evil-doer.

àsse[1], *s.f.* (*tavola di legno*) board; plank: *— da stiro*, ironing-board.

àsse[2], *s.m.* **1.** (*geom.*) axis (*pl.* axes): *— di rotazione*, rotation axis; *— terrestre*, (*geog.*) polar axis **2.** (*perno di ruota, assale*) axle: *— fisso, mobile*, rigid, turning axle **3.** (*aer.*): *— di resistenza*, drag axis; *— longitudinale*, rolling axis; *— principale*, zerolift axis; *— trasversale*, pitching axis **4.** *— montato normale*, (*ferr.*) standard wheel set; *— motore*, (*aut.*) driving axle.

àsse[3], *s.m.* **1.** (*moneta romana*) as **2.** (*dir.*): *— demaniale*, the whole of the real estate owned by the State; *— ecclesiastico*, Church estate (annexed to the Italian State before the "Conciliazione"); *— ereditario*, hereditament; *— patrimoniale*, the whole patrimony.

asseechíre, *v.i.* to thin, to become thin, to grow thin.

assecondàre, *v.t.* **1.** (*favorire*) to favour: *devo — i suoi piani?*, shall I help him on with his plans? **2.** (*esaudire*) to comply with (sthg.): *assecondai il suo desiderio*, I complied with his wish.

assediànte, *ag.* besieging ‖ *s.m.* besieger.

assediàre, *v.t.* **1.** to besiege **2.** *fig.* (*non dar pace a*) to besiege, to beset; to pester: *lo assediarono di richieste*, they beset him with requests **3.** (*circondare in folla*) to surround; to crowd round (s.o., sthg.); to throng round (s.o., sthg.): *essi assediarono la porta*, they thronged round the door.

assediàto, *ag.* besieged || *gli assediati*, the besieged.

assediatóre, *s.m.* besieger.

assèdio, *s.m.* **1.** siege: *stato d'*—, state of emergency; *levare l'*—, to raise the siege; *proclamare lo stato di* —, to proclaim martial law; *stringere d'*— *una città*, to lay siege to (o.to besiege) a town **2.** *fig.* importunity; pestering.

assegnàbile, *ag.* assignable.

assegnaménto, *s.m.* **1.** assignment, allotment **2.** (*somma assegnata*) sum allotted **3.** (*affidamento*) reliance: *fare* — *su qlcu.*, (o *ql.co.*), to rely on s.o., on sthg.

assegnàre, *v.t.* **1.** (*dare, destinare*) to assign, to allot **2.** (*concedere*) to grant, to award: *il primo premio è stato assegnato a lui*, the first prize has been awarded to him **3.** (*fissare*) to fix: *è stato assegnato il tempo per questo lavoro*, the time-limit for this job has been fixed.

assegnataménte, *av.* **1.** particularly, determinately **2.** (*con parsimonia*) thriftily.

assegnatàrio, *s.m.* (*dir.*) assignee; allottee, grantee: — *di una rendita vitalizia*, grantee of a life-annuity.

assegnàto, *ag.* **1.** (*comm.*) unpaid: *porto* —, carriage-forward **2.** (*parco*) thrifty || *s.m.* (*st.*) assignat.

assegnazióne, *s.f.* assignation, assignment; allotment: — *dei profitti*, (*comm.*) allocation of profits.

asségno, *s.m.* **1.** allowance: *assegni familiari*, family allowances **2.** (*comm.*) cheque; (*amer.*) check: — *al portatore*, cheque to bearer; — *circolare*, bank draft; — *in bianco*, blank cheque; — *sbarrato*, crossed cheque; *libretto di assegni*, cheque-book; *emettere un* —, to issue (o to draw) a cheque || *contro* —, cash on delivery (*abbr.* C. O. D.).

assemblèa, *s.f.* **1.** meeting: — *di famiglia*, family reunion; — *generale degli azionisti*, general meeting of shareholders **2.** (*corpo deliberante*) assembly: — *legislativa*, legislative assembly **3.** (*mar. mil.*) muster.

assembraménto, *s.m.* **1.** concourse of people; assemblage: *divieto di* —, ban (put) on meetings (o assembly) **2.** (*folla*) throng, mob.

assembràre, *v.t.* to assemble; to gather || **assembràrsi**, *v.r.* to assemble; to meet; to gather.

assennataménte, *av.* wisely; judiciously; (*prudentemente*) prudently.

assennatézza, *s.f.* common sense; wisdom; (*prudenza*) prudence.

assennàto, *ag.* sensible; judicious; wise; (*prudente*) prudent.

assènso, *s.m.* assent; approval; sanction.

assentàrsi, *v.r.* **1.** to absent oneself **2.** (*partire*) to leave (a place), to go away.

assènte, *ag.* absent; away from: *è* — *da casa da un anno*, he has been away from home for a whole year; *il suo spirito è* —, his thoughts are far away || *s.c.* absentee: *lista degli assenti*, absentees' list; *gli assenti hanno sempre torto*, the absent are always in the wrong.

assenteísmo, *s.m.* **1.** absenteeism **2.** (*disinteresse*) indifference: *fu deplorato l'*— *delle classi dirigenti*, the indifference of the ruling classes was deplored.

assentiménto, *s.m.* assent; consent; approval.

assentíre, *v.i.* to assent, to consent; to approve (sthg.), to acquiesce (in sthg): — *col capo*, to nod in assent.

assentitaménte, *av.* cautiously; sensibly, wisely.

assentíto, *ag.* cautious; sensible; judicious.

assènza, *s.f.* **1.** absence: — *da scuola*, non-attendance at school; — *dal lavoro*, absence from work; *durante la mia* —, in (o during) my absence; *quante assenze hai fatto?*, how often have you been absent? || *brillare per l'*—, to be conspicuous by one's absence **2.** (*mancanza*) lack; want: — *di gusto*, lack of taste; — *di immaginazione*, want of imagination; *senti-*

re l'— *di qlcu.*, to miss s.o. **3.** (*dir.*): *dichiarazione d'*—, assumption of death; *presunzione d'*—, presumed death.

assenziènte, *ag.* consentient, assenting || *s.c.* assentient.

assènzio, *s.m.* **1.** (*bot.*) absinth(e), wormwood **2.** (*liquore*) absinth(e) **3.** *fig.* bitterness, acridity; (*dispiacere*) trouble, affliction.

àssere, *s.m.* (*mar.*) ram.

asserèlla, *s.f.* small board.

asserènte, *ag.* affirming, asserting.

asseríbile, *ag.* assertable.

asseríre, *v.t.* **1.** (*affermare*) to affirm, to assert: — *un diritto*, to assert a right; — *la propria innocenza*, to affirm one's innocence **2.** (*sostenere*) to maintain, to declare, to claim: *asserisco che la colpa era tua*, I maintain that it was your fault.

asseritóre, *s.m.* assertor.

àssero, *s.m.* (*mar.*) ram.

asserpolàrsi, *v.r.* (*rar.*) to writhe, to squirm; to wriggle; to coil up like a snake.

asserragliaménto, *s.m.* **1.** blocking up **2.** (*sbarramento*) obstruction, obstacle, impediment **3.** (*barriera*) barricade, barrier.

asserragliàre, *v.t.* to block; to hinder, to barricade || **asserragliàrsi**, *v.r.* to barricade oneself.

assertíva, *s.f.* assertion, declaration.

assertivaménte, *av.* assertively, affirmatively.

assertívo, *ag.* assertive, affirmative.

assèrto, *s.m.* assertion, affirmation; positive statement.

assertóre, *s.m.* **1.** assertor **2.** (*difensore*) defender; advocate, champion: — *dei diritti dei popoli*, champion of peoples' rights.

assertòrio, *ag.* assertive.

asserviménto, *s.m.* enslavement, enthralment.

asservíre, *v.t.* to enslave, to subdue, to subject, to reduce (s.o.) to slavery: — *le proprie passioni*, to subdue one's passions || **asservírsi**, *v.r.* to submit, to become a slave.

asserzióne, *s.f.* assertion; statement; affirmation: — *gratuita*, gratuitous remark.

assessoràto, *s.m.* assessorship; aldermanship.

assessóre, *s.m.* (*alle imposte*) assessor; (*municipale, in Gran Bretagna*) alderman (*pl.* aldermen): — *comunale, regionale*, councillor responsible for a municipal, regional department.

assestaménto, *s.m.* arrangement, adjustement; (*sistemazione definitiva*) settlement: — *del bilancio*, (*amm.*) balance of the budget; — *del terreno*, (*edil.*) ground settling; *piano di* —, (*geol.*) bed plane.

assestàre, *v.t.* **1.** to arrange; to settle: — *una faccenda*, to settle a matter **2.** — *un colpo*, to deal a blow || **assestàrsi**, *v.r.* to settle (down).

assestataménte, *av.* **1.** in good order, tidily **2.** (*assennatamente*) sensibly.

assestatézza, *s.f.* **1.** order, exactness **2.** (*senno*) common sense.

assestàto, *ag.* **1.** (*in ordine*) well arranged; (*di persona*) tidy **2.** (*assennato*) sensibile.

assèsto, *s.m.* settlement.

assetàre, *v.t.* to make thirsty; *fig.* to excite.

assetàto, *ag.* **1.** thirsty; *fig.* (*bramoso*) eager (for sthg): *è* — *di gloria*, he thirsts for (o after) glory; *essere* —, to be thirsty || *dar da bere agli assetati*, to give drink to the thirsty **2.** (*di terreno, riarso*) parched, dry, thirsty.

assettaménto, *s.m.* **1.** arrangement; settlement **2.** (*edil.*) setting of building on ground.

assettàre, *v.t.* **1.** to arrange, to trim, to put in order **2.** (*pettinare*) to comb **3.** (*adornare*) to adorn || **assettàrsi**, *v.r.* (*mettersi in ordine*) to tidy up; (*mettersi gli abiti migliori*) to spruce up **2.** (*sedersi*) to sit down **3.** (*edil.*) to set.

assettataménte, *av.* in good order, nicely, tidily.

assettàto, *ag.* **1.** well arranged, adjusted; (*in ordine*) in good order; tidy **2.** (*adorno*) trimmed.

assettatúra, *s.f.* arrangement, adjustment; settlement.

assètto, *s.m.* **1.** good order: *in —,* in trim; *mettere in —,* to put in order ‖ *in — di guerra,* in fighting trim **2.** (*mar. aer.*) trim: *una nave in —,* a ship in (good) trim **3.** (*edil.*) bond.

asseveraménto, *s.m.,* asseveration.

asseverànza, *s.f.* assuredness; certainty.

asseveràre, *v.t.* to asseverate, to assert, to affirm; to proclaim.

asseverataménte, *av.* with certainty.

asseveratìvo, *ag.* affirmative; positive.

asseveratóre, *s.m.* assertor; affirmer.

asseverazióne, *s.m.* asseveration.

assiàle, *ag.* (*mat.*) axial: *gioco —,* (*mec.*) end float.

assicèlla, *s.f.* small board, small plank.

assicìna, *s.f.* (*ind. tessile*) batten.

assicuràbile, *ag.* insurable.

assicuràre, *v.t.* **1.** (*fissare, legare*) to fasten, to secure; (*con una corda*) to tie (up) **2.** (*procurare definitivamente*) to secure: *voglio assicurarti una vecchiaia serena,* I want to secure a peaceful old age for you **3.** (*promettere*) to assure, to give assurance of (sthg.): *mi assicurò che avrebbe parlato,* he assured me he would speak **4.** (*affermare*) to affirm; (*dichiarare*) to declare **5.** (*comm.*) to insure, to assure: *voglio — la casa contro gli incendi,* I want to insure my house against fire; *— la vita,* to assure one's life **6.** (*posta*) to register: *— una lettera, un pacco,* to register a letter, a parcel ‖ **assicùrarsi,** *v.r.* **1.** (*reggersi*) to hold on; (*legarsi*) to fasten oneself: *— ad una fune,* to fasten oneself to a rope **2.** (*procurarsi*) to secure; to get: *voglio assicurarmi una copia del tuo ultimo libro,* I want to secure a copy of your latest book **3.** (*accertarsi*) to make sure: *desiderano — della tua onestà,* they wish to make sure of your honesty; *mi sono assicurato che non vi è pericolo,* I have made sure (o I am satisfied) there is no danger **4.** (*comm.*) to insure oneself, to effect an insurance: *— contro i furti,* to insure oneself against theft; *— sulla vita,* to effect a life insurance (o to take out a life insurance policy).

assicuràta, *s.f.* registered letter.

assicuràto, *ag.* **1.** assured **2.** (*comm.*) insured, assured ‖ *s.m.* the insured, the insurant.

assicuratóre, *ag.* insurance (*attributivo*): *società assicuratrice,* insurance company ‖ *s.m.* insurer, assurer; (*spec. mar.*) underwriter.

assicurazióne, *s.f.* **1.** (*dichiarazione, affermazione*) assurance: *mi diede — di ciò,* he gave me assurance of this **2.** (*comm.*) insurance, assurance: *— contro la disoccupazione,* unemployment insurance; *— contro gli incendi,* fire insurance; *— contro gli incidenti sul lavoro,* employer's liability insurance; *— contro l'invalidità,* sickness and disablement insurance; *— contro i rischi di guerra,* war risk insurance; *— contro terzi,* third party insurance; *— marittima,* marine insurance; *— mista,* endowment insurance; *— sulla vita,* life assurance; *agente d'—,* insurance broker; *compagnia d'—,* insurance company; *polizza d'—,* insurance policy; *premio d'—,* insurance premium.

assideraménto, *s.m.* frost-bite: *morire d'—,* to freeze to death.

assideràre, *v.t.* to chill, to benumb: *il gelo aveva assiderato i suoi piedi,* his feet were benumbed by (o with) cold ‖ *v.i.* **assideràrsi,** *v.r.* to get chilled; to get congealed.

assideràto, *ag.* frost-bitten; frozen to death: *sono —,* (*fam.*) I'm just freezing.

assiderazióne, *s.f.* frost-bite.

assìdersi, *v.r.* to sit down; to take one's seat: *il re si assise sul trono,* the king took his seat on the throne.

assiduaménte, *av.* **1.** assiduously **2.** (*diligentemente*) sedulously: *vi sta lavorando —,* he is hard at work on it.

assiduità, *s.f.* **1.** assiduousness, assiduity **2.** (*costanza*) sedulousness, steadiness: *— al lavoro,* devotion to work; *— allo studio,* close application to study; *— nel*

fare ql.co., steadiness in doing sthg. **3.** (*frequenza*) regular attendance: *l'— a questi corsi non diminuisce mai,* the attendance at these classes never drops off.

assìduo, *ag.* **1.** assiduous, sedulous, diligent; persevering; steady: *— al proprio lavoro,* devoted to his work; *lavoratore —,* hard-worker; *sforzi assidui,* untiring efforts **2.** (*di visitatore, cliente*) regular, constant: *è un — frequentatore di questo ristorante,* he is a regular customer of this restaurant.

assième, *V.* insiéme.

assiepaménto, *s.m.* **1.** (*il circondare con siepe*) hedging **2.** (*affollamento*) crowding.

assiepàre, *v.t.* (*circondare con siepe*) to hedge (in), to fence (in); to enclose with a hedge ‖ **assiepàrsi,** *v.r.* (*affollarsi*) to crowd (round sthg.).

assillàre, *v.t.* to urge, to goad, to spur on; (*tormentare*) to worry, to harass: *il pensiero della sua famiglia lo assillava,* the thought of his family spurred him on.

assìllo, *s.m.* **1.** (*entom.*) horse-fly, gadfly **2.** *fig.* (*incitamento*) urge, spur; goad: *sotto l'— della miseria,* goaded by need **3.** *fig.* (*tormento*) worry; (*pensiero tormentoso*) harassing thought.

assimilàbile, *ag.* **1.** assimilable **2.** (*paragonabile*) comparable.

assimilabilità, *s.f.* assimilability.

assimilàre, *v.t.* to assimilate, to absorb (anche *fig.*) ‖ **assimilàrsi,** *v.r.* to assimilate.

assimilatìvo, *ag.* assimilative.

assimilatóre, *s.m.,* **assimilatríce,** *s.f.* assimilator.

assimilazióne, *s.f.* assimilation.

assiòlo, *s.m.* (*ornit.*) horned owl.

assiòma, *s.m.* axiom.

assiomaticaménte, *av.* axiomatically.

assiomàtico, *ag.* axiomatic(al).

assiòmetro, *s.m.* (*mar.*) telltale, rudder indicator.

Assìria, *no.pr.f.* (*geog. st.*) Assyria.

assìro, *ag.s.m.* Assyrian.

assìsa, *s.f.* **1.** uniform **2.** (*tassa*) excise; duty.

assìse, *s.f.pl.* assizes ‖ *Corte d'Assise,* Court of Assizes.

assìso, *ag.* **1.** seated **2.** (*situato*) situated.

assistentàto, *s.m.* assistantship.

assistènte, *ag.s.c.* assistant: *— chirurgo,* assistant surgeon; *— di laboratorio,* laboratory assistant; *— di volo,* hostess; *— universitario,* assistant-professor.

assistènza, *s.f.* **1.** presence, attendance **2.** (*aiuto*) assistance, aid, help: *— alla navigazione,* navigational aids; *— legale,* legal aid; *— visuale,* (*aer.*) visual aids; *prestare — a qlcu.,* to assist s.o. **3.** (*beneficenza*) welfare: *opera di —,* welfare institution; *reparto —,* welfare section; *vivere di — pubblica,* to live on public relief (o on the dole) **4.** (*comm.*) service.

assistenziàle, *ag.* charitable: *centro —,* welfare centre; *opera —,* charitable institution.

assìstere, *v.t.* **1.** to assist, to support, to help, to favour: *se la fortuna vi assiste,* if fortune favours you; *ti assisterò come posso,* I'll give you all the assistance I can **2.** (*curare*) to nurse, to cure, to tend: *— gli ammalati,* to nurse (o to cure o to look after) the sick ‖ *v.i.* to be present (at sthg.); to attend (sthg.); (*essere testimone*) to witness (sthg.), to be a witness: *— ad una cerimonia,* to be present at a ceremony; *— ad un incidente stradale,* to be a witness to a road accident; *— ad una lezione,* to attend (o to go to) a lesson; *— ad una partita di calcio,* to watch a football match.

assitàre, *v.t.* (*rar.*) **1.** (*di cane*) to scent **2.** to know (a person) well.

assìto, *s.m.* **1.** wooden partition; (*pavimento di assi*) floor boards (*pl.*), wooden flooring; plank floor **2.** (*steccato*) stockade.

assiuòlo, *s.m.* (*ornit.*) horned owl.

àsso, *s.m.* **1.** (*carte, dadi, ecc.*) ace: *l'— di picche,* the ace of spades **2.** (*spor.*) ace, champion: *— dell'aviazione:* air-ace (o ace-pilot); *— del volante,* crack racing-driver; — *del pugilato*, champion boxer **3.** *piantare in* —, to leave in the lurch.

associaménto, *s.m.* lease of cattle on fifty-fifty terms.

assocciàre, *v.t.* (*dare bestiame a soccida*) to lease out (cattle).

associàbile, *ag.* associable.

associabilità, *s.f.* associability.

associaménto, *s.m.* association.

associàre, *v.t.* **1.** to associate, to unite, to join: — *idee, concetti*, to associate (*o* to connect *o* to put together) ideas, concepts **2.** (*prendere come socio*) to take into partnership: *lo associai al nostro circolo*, I made him a member of our club ‖ **associàrsi**, *v.r.* **1.** to join: *mi associo a loro nel ringraziarti*, I join (with) them in thanking you; *si associarono nell'impresa*, they joined (together) in the enterprise **2.** (*divenire membro*) to become a member (of sthg.): — *a un circolo*, to become a member of (*o* to join) a club **3.** (*abbonarsi*) to subscribe: — *ad un giornale*, to subscribe to a newspaper.

associatívo, *ag.* associative: *proprietà associativa*, (*mat.*) associative property.

associàto, *s.m.* **1.** associate, member **2.** (*comm.*) partner **3.** (*abbonato*) subscriber.

associatóre, *s.m.* collector of subscriptions.

associazióne, *s.f.* **1.** association: — *di idee*, association of ideas ‖ — *a delinquere*, (*dir.*) criminal association **2.** (*comm.*) association, society, company; (*sindacale*) combination; (*società in nome collettivo*) partnership: — *commerciale*, trading association; — *di operai, lavoratori*, trade-union; — *riconosciuta*, incorporated association; *entrare* — *con qlcu.*, to enter into partnership with s.o.

associazionísmo, *s.m.* (*psicologia*) associationism.

assodaménto, *s.m.* **1.** (*consolidamento*) consolidation; (*indurimento*) hardening **2.** (*accertamento*) ascertainment.

assodàre, *v.t.* **1.** (*consolidare*) to consolidate; (*indurire*) to harden **2.** (*accertare*) to ascertain, to make (sthg.) sure ‖ **assodàrsi**, *v.r.* **1.** (*diventare sodo*) to become compact, firm **2.** (*indurirsi*) to grow hard, to harden.

assodàto, *ag.* **1.** (*accertato, stabilito*) ascertained, certain **2.** (*rassodato, indurito*) hardened, compact.

assoggettàbile, *ag.* subduable.

assoggettaménto, *s.m.* **1.** (*stato di soggezione*) subjection **2.** (*l'assoggettare*) subduing, subjugation.

assoggettàre, *v.t.* to subject, to subjugate, to subdue (anche *fig.*): — *le passioni*, to subdue one's passions ‖ **assoggettàrsi**, *v.r.* to submit oneself.

assolàre[1], *v.t.* (*mettere a strati*) to set in layers.

assolàre[2], *v.t.* (*soleggiare*) to expose to the sun.

assolàto, assolàto, *ag.* sunny.

assolcàre, *v.t.* (*agr.*) to furrow.

assoldaménto, *s.m.* recruiting, enlistment.

assoldàre, *v.t.* **1.** (*reclutare*) to recruit; to enlist **2.** (*mercenari per servizi*) to engage, to hire ‖ **assoldàrsi**, *v.r.* (*arruolarsi*) to enlist, to join the colours.

assòlo, *s.m.* (*mus.*) solo (*pl.* solos, soli).

assòlto, *ag.* **1.** (*teol.*) absolved **2.** (*dir.*) acquitted.

assolutaménte, *av.* **1.** absolutely **2.** (*senza dubbio*) undoubtedly **3.** (*in generale*) generically: — *parlando*, generically speaking (*o* on the whole).

assolutézza, *s.f.* absoluteness.

assolutísmo, *s.m.* (*pol.*) absolutism.

assolutísta, *s.c.* (*pol.*) absolutist.

assolúto, *ag.* absolute: *ablativo* —, (*gram.*) ablative absolute; *ente* —, (*fil.*) the absolute; *maggioranza assoluta*, absolute (*o* clear) majority; *padrone* —, absolute (*o* despotic) master; *potere* —, absolute (*o* unrestricted) power; *temperatura assoluta*, (*fis.*) absolute (*o* abs.) temperature; *verità assoluta*, absolute truth; *vuoto* —, (*fis.*) absolute vacuum; *zero* —, (*fis. chim.*) absolute zero **1** *s.m.*: *l'* —, (*fil.*) the Absolute.

assolutóre, *s.m.* absolvent, absolver.

assolutòrio, *ag.* absolutory.

assoluzióne, *s.f.* **1.** (*teol.*) absolution **2.** (*dir.*) acquittal, discharge.

assòlvere, *v.t.* **1.** (*teol.*) to absolve **2.** (*dir.*) to acquit, to discharge **3.** (*adempiere*) to accomplish: — *un compito*, to accomplish a task.

assomiglànza, *s.f.* resemblance, likeness.

assomiglànte, *ag.* like, alike: *è* — *a suo padre*, he is like his father; *è difficile trovare due persone perfettamente assomiglianti*, it is difficult to find two persons alike; *quel tuo ritratto non è* —, that portrait of yours is not like you.

assomigliàre, *v.t.* (*paragonare*) to compare ‖ *v.i.* to be like (s.o.), to look like (s.o.); to resemble (s.o.): *assomiglia a suo padre*, he is like his father (o he takes after his father); *a che cosa assomiglia?*, what is it like?; *a chi assomiglia?*, whom does he resemble? ‖ **assomigliàrsi**, *v.r. reciproco* to resemble each other (one another); to be alike: *questi due fratelli non si assomigliano*, these two brothers do not resemble each other (o are not alike); *si assomigliano come due gocce d'acqua*, they are as alike as two peas.

assommàre[1], *v.t.* **1.** to add (together, up) **2.** (*riunire in sè*) to combine.

assommàre[2], *v.i.* (*venire a galla*) to emerge.

assonànte, *ag.* assonant.

assonànza, *s.f.* assonance.

assonàre, *v.i.* to assonate.

assonnacchiàto, *ag.* half-asleep, drowsy.

assonnàre, *v.t.* to put to sleep ‖ *v.i.*, **assonnàrsi**, *v.r.* to fall asleep; to drop off to sleep.

assonnàto, assonníto, *ag.* sleepy, drowsy.

assopiménto, *s.m.* drowsiness, dozing, doziness.

assopíre, *v.t.* **1.** to drowse, to make drowsy, sleepy, dozy **2.** (*calmare*) to appease ‖ **assopírsi**, *v.r.* **1.** to doze off, to grow sleepy, to grow drowsy, to drop off to sleep **2.** (*calmarsi*) to be appeased.

assopíto, *ag.* drowsy, dozing.

assorbènte, *ag.* absorbing, absorbent: *carta* —, blotting-paper ‖ *s.m.* absorbent: — *acustico*, (*edil.*) deadening (*o* sound-proofing); — *igienico*, sanitary towel; — *metallico*, (*rad.*) getter.

assorbiménto, *s.m.* absorption: — *delle riserve*, using up of reserves; — *di energia elettrica*, electrical input; *coefficiente di* —, (*chim.*) absorption coefficient; *misuratore di* —, (*fis.*) absorptionmeter.

assorbíre, *v.t.* **1.** to absorb; (*liquidi*) to soak; (*gas*) to occlude: *le spugne assorbono l'acqua*, sponges absorb (o soak *o* soak up) water **2.** *fig.* to absorb, to take up, to engross: *l'Impero assorbì tutti i piccoli stati*, the Empire absorbed all the lesser states; — *l'attenzione, il tempo di qlcu.*, to engross s.o.'s attention, time; — *le energie*, to absorb (o to take up) energies.

assorbitóre, *ag.* absorbent ‖ *s.m.* absorber.

assordàggine, *s.f.* **assordaménto**, *s.m.* deafening; deafness.

assordànte, *ag.* deafening.

assordàre, *v.t.* to deafen; (*stordire*) to stun: *mi stai assordando*, you are deafening me.

assordàto, *ag.* deafened, deaf; (*stordito*) stunned.

assordiménto, *s.m.* deafening; deafness.

assordíre, *v.t.* (*rendere sordo*) to deafen ‖ *v.i.* (*diventare sordo*) to become deaf.

assórgere, *v.i.* to rise, to stand up, to get up.

assortiménto, *s.m.* assortment (anche *fig.*); selection, stock, choice: — *di campioni*, (*comm.*) set of samples; — *limitato, variato*, limited, varied choice; *ricco* —, large (o extensive *o* rich) choice; *esaurire, rinnovare l'*—, to exhaust, to renew the stock.

assortíre, *v.t.* **1.** to stock, to furnish: — *un negozio*, to stock a shop **2.** *fig.* to (as)sort, to match: *i colori di quel vestito sono bene assortiti*, the colours of that dress are well matched.

assortíto, *ag.* **1.** assorted, sorted: *bene assortiti*, well-assorted; *male assortiti*, ill-assorted **2.** (*fornito*) stocked, supplied: *negozio bene* —, well-stocked (*o* well-supplied) shop **3.** (*che armonizza*) matched: *colori bene assortiti*, well-matched colours.

assòrto, *ag.* absorbed: — *nella preghiera*, absorbed in prayer.

assottigliaménto, *s.m.* **1.** thinning **2.** (*diminuzione*) diminution; reduction.

assottigliàre, *v.t.* **1.** (*rendere sottile*) to thin, to make thin **2.** (*aguzzare*) to sharpen: — *la mente di qlcu.*, to sharpen s.o.'s wits **3.** (*diminuire*) to diminish; to reduce: — *il patrimonio*, to diminish (*o* to reduce) one's possessions ‖ **assottigliàrsi,** *v.r.* (*diventar sottile, più sottile*) to grow thin, thinner: *il suo viso si assottigliava sempre più*, her face grew thinner and thinner.

assottigliàta, *s.f.* thinning.

assottigliatúra, *V.* **assottigliaménto.**

Assuàn, *no.pr.f.* (*geog.*) Aswan, Assuan.

assuefàre, *v.t.* to accustom, to habituate, to inure ‖ **assuefàrsi,** *v.r.* to get accustomed, to become accustomed, to get inured; to accustom oneself, to inure oneself: *egli si assuefece al cibo cattivo*, he became inured to bad food.

assuefazióne, *s.f.* custom; habit.

Assuèro, *no.pr.m.* (*Bibbia*) Ahasuerus.

assúmere, *v.t.* **1.** to assume: — *un'aria di protezione*, to assume (*o* to put on) a patronizing air; — *una carica*, to enter upon (*o* to undertake) an office; — *un impegno*, to assume an engagement; — *informazioni su qlcu.*, *ql.co.*, to make inquiries about s.o., sthg.; — *uno pseudonimo*, to assume a pseudonym; — *una responsabilità*, to take on (*o* to take upon oneself *o* to assume) a responsibility (*o* to make oneself responsible) **2.** (*in servizio*) to engage, to employ: — *un impiegato*, to engage a clerk (*o* to employ s.o. as a clerk) **3.** (*intraprendere*) to undertake **4.** (*innalzare a dignità*) to raise: *assunto al Pontificato*, raised to the Papacy ‖ *essere assunto in Cielo*, to ascend to Heaven ‖ **assúmersi,** *v.r.* to undertake; to assume, to take upon oneself: — *a carico*, to take (*o* to assume) upon oneself; — *un incarico*, to take upon oneself an appointment; — *tutti i rischi*, to assume all risks.

Assúnta, *s.f.* Our Lady, the Virgin Mary received into Heaven ‖ (*festa dell'*) —, Assumption Day (*o* Feast of the Assumption) ‖ *no.pr.f.* Assunta.

assuntívo, *ag.* assumptive: *armi assuntive*, (*arald.*) assumptive arms; *giudizio* —, assumptive judgment.

assúnto, *s.m.* **1.** (*impresa*) undertaking; (*compito*) task **2.** (*fil.*) assumption.

assunzióne, *s.f.* **1.** (*ascesa*) accession: *l'* — *al trono*, the accession to the throne **2.** *Assunzione*, (*teol.*) Assumption: *festa dell'Assunzione*, Assumption Day **3.** (*impiego*) engagement; hiring **4.** (*fil.*) assumption.

assunzionísta, *s.m.* (*eccl.*) Assumptionist.

assurdaménte, *av.* absurdly.

assurdità, *s.f.* absurdity: *l'* — *di una simile situazione*, the absurdity of such a situation; *è il colmo dell'*—, it is the height of absurdity; *dire delle* —, to talk nonsense.

assúrdo, *ag.* absurd, preposterous: *conclusione assurda*, absurd conclusion; *rivendicazione assurda*, preposterous claim ‖ *s.m.* absurdity: *l'*— *di questa ipotesi*, the absurdity of this hypothesis; *dimostrazione per* —, proof ab absurdo.

assúrgere, *v.i.* to rise: — *ad alta carica*, to rise to high office (*o* dignity).

àsta, *s.f.* **1.** pole: — *del compasso*, compass leg; *della bilancia*, arm of a balance; — *di bandiera*, flagstaff; *salto con l'*—, (*spor.*) pole-jumping **2.** (*lancia*) lance, spear **3.** (*primo segno di scrittura*) pothook; (*segno diritto*) straight stroke: *fare le aste*, to draw (*o* to make) pothooks **4.** (*comm.*) auction: *banditore d'*—, auctioneer; *vendita all'*—, auction sale; *vendere all'*—, to sell by auction **5.** (*mar.*) boom; (*di timone*) stock: — *di controfiocco*, flying jib-boom; — *di fiocco*, jib-boom; — *di posta*, lower (*o* swinging) boom **6.** (*tec.*)

rod: — *articolata*, (*mec.*) trace; — *del cambio*, (*aut.*) gear selector rod; — *del parafulmine*, lightening rod; — *di collegamento*, (*mec.*) connecting rod (*o* amer. pitman); — *di comando*, (*mec.*) push rod; — *di guida*, (*mec.*) slide bar; — *di presa* (*di tram, ecc.*), trolley; — *di stantuffo*, (*mec.*) piston rod.

àstaco, *s.m.* (*zool.*) crayfish.

astàute, *ag.* present: *medico* —, doctor on duty ‖ *s.m.* (*spettatore*) on-looker, looker-on, bystander.

astantería, *s.f.* casualty-ward.

astàta, *s.f.* stroke of lance.

astàto, *ag.* armed with a lance ‖ *s.m.* (*st. romana*) Roman lance.

asteggiàre, *v.i.* to draw pothooks.

astèmio, *ag.* abstemious: *sono* —, I do not take any alcoholic drink ‖ *s.m.* teetotaller; abstainer.

astenérsi, *v.r.* to abstain, to refrain, to forbear: *dovrebbe* — *dal divulgare chiacchiere*, he ought to refrain (*o* he ought to forbear) from spreading gossip; *mi astenni dall'interrogarla*, I kept myself from questioning her; — *dall'alcool*, to abstain from alcoholic drinks ‖ *nel dubbio, astienti*, when in doubt, forbear.

astenía, *s.f.* asthenia.

astènico, *ag.* asthenic.

astenopía, *s.f.* (*patol.*) asthenopia.

astensióne, *s.f.* abstention: — *dal voto*, abstention.

astensionísmo, *s.m.* (*pol.*) abstention.

astensionísta, *s.c.* (*pol.*) abstentionist.

astèrgere, *v.t.* to wipe; to absterge; to cleanse.

astèria, *s.f.* **1.** (*zool.*) asteroid, starfish **2.** (*min.*) asteriated corundum.

asteríseo, *s.m.* asterisk.

asterísmo, *s.m.* **1.** (*astr.*) constellation, asterism **2.** (*min.*) asterism.

asteròide, *s.m.* (*astr.*) asteroid.

asteròmetro, *s.m.* (*astr.*) asterometer.

astersióne, *s.f.* cleansing, abstersion.

astersívo, *ag.* cleansing, abstersive.

Astianàtte, *no.pr.m.* (*lett.*) Astyanax.

asticciuòla, *s.f.* **1.** (*piccola asta*) pothook **2.** (*di penna*) penholder.

astigmàtico, *ag.* astigmatic.

astigmatísmo, *s.m.* astigmatism.

àstile, *ag.* (*arch.*) astylar.

astinènte, *ag.* abstinent, temperate, sober, abstemious.

astinènza, *s.f.* **1.** (*l'atto di astenersi*) abstinence, abstention **2.** (*abitudine di astenersi*) abstemiousness, abstinency.

àstio, *s.m.* (*odio*) bitter hatred; (*rancore*) resentment, rancour; (*invidia*) envy; (*fam.*) grudge: *perchè hai* — *contro di me?*, why do you bear me a grudge?.

astiosaménte, *av.* rancorously, resentfully; (*malevolmente*) spitefully.

astiosità, *s.f.* rancour, resentfulness; (*malevolenza*) spitefulness.

astióso, *ag.* rancorous, resentful; (*malevolo*) spiteful.

astóre, *s.m.* (*ornit.*) goshawk.

astracàn, *s.m.* astrakhan.

astràgalo, *s.m.* **1.** (*anat. bot.*) astragalus (*pl.* astragali*) **2.** (*arch.*) astragal.

astràle, *ag.* astral: *corpo* —, (*teosofia*) astral body; *lampada* —, astral lamp.

astràrre, *v.t.* to abstract, to consider apart, to separate ‖ *v.i.* to leave (sthg.) out of consideration ‖ **astràrsi,** *v.r.* to think about sthg. else; not to pay attention: *mentre egli parlava, io mi astraevo*, while he was talking, my mind wandered.

astràttàggine, *s.f.* **1.** absence of mind, absent-mindedness, abstractedness **2.** (*sbadataggine*) inattention, carelessness.

astrattaménte, *av.* **1.** abstractly: — *parlando*, speaking in the abstract **2.** (*distrattamente*) abstractedly; absent-mindedly.

astrattézza, *s.f.* **1.** abstractness **2.** (*distrazione*) absent-mindedness, abstractedness.

astrattísmo, *s.m.* **1.** abstractness **2.** (*art.*) abstractionism.

astrattísta, *s.m.* (*art.*) abstractionist.

astràtto, *ag.* **1.** abstract: *nome* —, (*gram.*) abstract noun; *quadro* —, abstract picture **2.** (*distratto*) abstracted, absent-minded ‖ *s.m.* abstract ‖ *in* —, in the abstract: *la virtù in* —, virtue in the abstract.

astrazióne, *s.f.* **1.** abstraction: *fatta* — *da ciò*, apart from that; *fare* — *da ql.co.*, to leave sthg. out of consideration (*o* to disregard sthg.) **2.** (*concetto astratto*) abstraction, abstract conception **3.** (*distrazione*) abstractedness, absence of mind, absent-mindedness.

Astrèa, *no.pr.f.* (*mit.*) Astraea ‖ **astrèa,** *s.f.* (*zool.*) astraeid.

astrétto, *ag.* **1.** (*legato*) astricted **2.** (*costretto*) compelled.

astringènte, *ag.s.m.* astringent.

astríngere, *v.t.* **1.** (*letter.*) to compel, to force **2.** (*costipare*) to constipate.

àstro, *s.m.* **1.** star; (*pianeta*) planet **2.** (*bot.*) aster.

astrodinàmica, *s.f.* astrodynamics.

astrofísica, *s.f.* astrophysics.

astrografía, *s.f.* astrography.

astrolàbio, *s.m.* (*st. astr.*) astrolabe.

astrolatría, *s.f.* star-worship, astrolatry.

astrologàre, *v.i.* **1.** to practise astrology; to astrologize **2.** (*fantasticare*) to build castles in the air.

astrología, *s.f.* astrology: — *giudiziaria*, judicial astrology; — *naturale*, natural astrology.

astrològico, *ag.* astrologic(al).

astròlogo, *s.m.* astrologer; (*fam.*) star-gazer ‖ *crepi l'* —!, God (*o* Heaven) forbid!.

astrometeorología, *s.f.* astrometeorology.

astròmetro, *s.m.* (*astr.*) astrometer.

astronàuta, *s.m.* (*neol.*) astronaut.

astronàutica, *s.f.* (*neol.*) astronautics.

astronàve, *s.f.* (*neol.*) space-ship.

astronomía, *s.f.* astronomy.

astronomicaménte, *av.* astronomically.

astronòmico, *ag.* astronomic(al): *anno* —, sideral year.

astrònomo, *s.m.* astronomer.

astrusàggine, *V.* **astruseria.**

astrusaménte, *av.* abstrusely.

astruseria, astrusità, *s.f.* abstruseness; (*cosa, discorso astruso*) intricacy.

astrúso, *ag.* abstruse, hidden, recondite, obscure.

astucciàio, *s.m.* **1.** (*chi fabbrica astucci*) case-maker **2.** (*chi vende astucci*) case-seller.

astúccio, *s.m.* case, box; container, holder; (*fodero*) sheath: — *da lavoro*, housewife (*o fam.* hussy); — *di cuoio*, leather case; — *metallico*, metallic sheath; — *per gioielli*, jewel case; — *per occhiali*, spectacle-case; — *porta-aghi*, neddle-case.

Astúrie (le), *no.pr.f.pl.* (*geog.*) the Asturias.

astutaménte, *av.* astutely; cunningly.

astutézza, *s.f.* astuteness; cunning.

astúto, *ag.* astute; cunning; shrewd, sagacious.

astúzia, *s.f.* **1.** (*qualità*) astuteness, cunning **2.** (*atto*) artifice, trick.

Atanàsio, *no.pr.m.* (*st.*) Athanasius.

atarassía, *s.f.* (*fil.*) ataraxy, ataraxia.

atassía, *s.f.* (*patol.*) ataxy.

atàssico, *ag.* (*patol.*) ataxic.

atàvico, *ag.* atavic.

atavísmo, *s.m.* atavism.

àtavo, *s.m.* ancestor.

ateísmo, *s.m.* atheism.

ateísta, *s.c.* atheist.

ateístico, *ag.* atheistic.

atelier, *s.m.* atelier; (*sartoria*) workroom.

atellàna, *ag.s.f.* (*st. teat.*) Atellan.

Atène, *no.pr.f.* (*geog.*) Athens.

atenèo, *s.m.* **1.** (*archeol.*) athenaeum **2.** (*accademia*) academy **3.** (*università*) university.

ateniése, *ag.s.m.* Athenian.

àteo, *ag.* atheistic ‖ *s.m.* atheist.

atermàno, *ag.* (*fis.*) athermanous.

ateròma, *s.m.* (*patol.*) atheroma.

ateromatóso, *ag.* (*patol.*) atheromatous: *degenerazione ateromatosa*, atheromatous degeneration.

atesíno, *ag.* of the river Adige ‖ *s.m.* inhabitant of the region of the upper Adige.

atípico, *ag.* atypic(al) (anche *patol.*).

Atlànte, *no.pr.m.* (*mit.*) Atlas ‖ **atlànte,** *s.m.* **1.** atlas **2.** (*anat.*) atlas **3.** (*entom.*) atlas moth.

atlàntico, *ag.* **1.** *fig.* huge, gigantic: *fatica atlantica*, huge (*o* gigantic) effort **2.** (*geog.*) Atlantic ‖ *Carta Atlantica*, (*pol.*) Atlantic Charter; *Patto Atlàntico*, (*pol.*) North Atlantic Treaty (*o* Pact) ‖ **Atlàntico,** *no.pr.m.* (*geog.*) the Atlantic.

Atlàntide, *no.pr.f.* (*geog. mit.*) Atlantis.

atlèta, *s.c.* **1.** athlete **2.** *fig.* champion.

atlètica, *s.f.* athletics.

atleticaménte, *av.* athletically.

atlètico, *ag.* athletic.

atmosfèra, *s.f.* atmosphere.

atmosfèrico, *ag.* atmospheric: *pressione atmosferica*, (*fis.*) atmospheric pressure.

atòllo, *s.m.* (*geog.*) atoll.

atòmico, *ag.* atomic: *bomba atomica*, atom(ic) bomb; *energia atomica*, atomic energy; *massa atomica*, atomic mass; *peso* —, atomic weight.

atomísmo, *s.m.* (*st. fil.*) atomism.

atomísta, *s.m.* (*st. fil.*) atomist.

atomística, *s.f.* (*fis.*) atomic theory.

atomístico, *ag.* (*fis.*) atomistic.

atòmium, *s.m.* atomium.

àtomo, *s.m.* atom (anche *fig.*): *frantumatore dell'* —, (*fis.*) atom smasher; *grammo* —, (*fis.*) gram atom.

atonàle, *ag.* (*mus.*) atonal.

atonía, *s.f.* (*med.*) atony.

àtono, *ag.* (*fonet.*) atonic.

atout, *s.m.* (*delle carte*) trump: *giocare degli atouts*, to trump.

atrabíle, *s.f.* black bile, atrabiliousness; *fig.* melancholy, acrimony, gloominess.

atrabiliàre, *ag.* atrabilious; *fig.* gloomy, melancholy, hypochondriac, acrimonious.

Atrèo, *no.pr.m.* (*mit.*) Atreus.

atrepsía, *s.f.* (*patol.*) atrepsy, atrepsia.

atresía, *s.f.* (*patol.*) atresia.

atrichía, *s.f.* (*patol.*) atrichia, atricosis.

atricomía, *s.f.* (*patol.*) alopecia.

atriènse, *s.m.* (*in Roma antica*) door-keeper.

àtrio, *s.m.* **1.** (*vestibolo*) (entrance-)hall **2.** (*archeol.*) atrium (*pl.* atriums, atria) **3.** (*anat.*) auricle.

àtro, *ag.* **1.** black; dark **2.** *fig.* horrid; gloomy.

atróce, *ag.* atrocious, dreadful, terrible, cruel.

atroceménte, *av.* atrociously, dreadfully, terribly.

atrocità, *s.f.* atrociousness; atrocity.

atrofía, *s.f.* (*patol.*) atrophy.

atròfico, *ag.* (*patol.*) atrophic.

atrofizzàre, *v.t.* (*patol.*) to atrophy ‖ **atrofizzàrsi,** *v.r.* to atrophy; to wither, to waste away (anche *fig.*).

atrofizzàto, *ag.* (*patol.*) atrophic.

atropína, *s.f.* (*chim.*) atropine.

atropísmo, *s.m.* (*patol.*) atropism.

Àtropo, *no.pr.f.* (*mit.*) Atropos ‖ **àtropo,** *s.f.* (*entom.*) death's-head moth.

attaccàbile, *ag.* **1.** attachable **2.** (*assalibile*) assailable.

attaccabottóni, *s.c. fig.* buttonholer; chatterbox.

attaccabríghe, *s.m.* wrangler, quarrelsome fellow.

attaccàgnolo, *s.m.* **1.** peg; hook **2.** *fig.* cavil.

attaccalíte, *s.m.* wrangler, quarrelsome fellow.

attaccaménto, *s.m.* **1.** attachment, attaching; fastening **2.** *fig.* attachment, affection: *avere dell'* — *per qlcu.*, to entertain an attachment for s.o..

attaccapànni, *s.m.* **1.** (*mobile*) cloak-stand; hat-stand **2.** (*gruccia*) hanger; (clothes-)peg; clothes-hook.

attaccàre, *v.t.* **1.** (*unire*) to attach, to bind, to fasten, to tie: *attaccale insieme*, fasten (o tie) them together ‖ *egli è ancora attaccato alle gonnelle di sua madre*, he is still tied to his mother's apron-strings **2.** (*cucire*) to sew on ‖ — *bottone con qlcu.*, *fig.* to buttonhole s.o. **3.** (*appiccicare*) to stick; (*con colla*) to glue, to paste: — *un manifesto*, to stick (o to post) up a bill **4.** (*bestie da tiro*) to harness: *attaccò i cavalli alla carrozza*, he harnessed the horses to the carriage **5.** (*appendere*) to hang: *attaccò il quadro alla parete*, he hung the picture on the wall **6.** (*assalire*) to attack (anche *fig.*): *le nazioni che attaccarono la Francia*, the countries that attacked France; — *le opinioni di qlcu.*, to attack s.o.'s opinions **7.** (*iniziare*) to begin; (*mus.*) to open: — *discorso con qlcu.*, to begin to talk to s.o.; — *lite*, to begin quarrelling **8.** (*malattia*) to infect: *gli attaccò il morbillo*, he infected him with measles **9.** (*chim.*) to attack, to dissolve; (*metallografia*) to etch ‖ *v.i.* **1.** (*essere appiccicoso*) to be sticky **2.** (*attecchire*) to take root, *fig.* to find favour; to find followers; to be successful: *i suoi scherzi non attaccarono*, his jokes were not successful; *la pianta attacca*, the plant is taking root; *questa moda attacca davvero*, this fashion finds many followers (o finds favour) indeed ‖ *non attacca!*, that won't do! **3.** (*essere contagioso*) to be contagious ‖ **attacàrsi,** *v.r.* **1.** (*appigliarsi*) to cling **2.** (*affezionarsi*) to become fond of (s.o., sthg.); to become attached to (s.o., sthg.) **3.** (*fam.*) (*di cibi*) to stick (on the bottom of the pan) **4.** (*rar.*) (*azzuffarsi*) to fight.

attaccatíccio, *ag.* **1.** sticky **2.** (*di persona*) boring, sticky **3.** (*med.*) contagious ‖ *s.m.* burnt taste.

attaccàto, *ag.* **1.** *fig.* attached, devoted: *le era profondamente* —, he was deeply attached to her; *sono molto attaccati*, they are very much bound up in each other **2.** (*avaro, avido*) stingy, niggardly.

attaccatúra, *s.f.* junction, union: — *della manica*, arm-hole.

attacchíno, *s.m.* **1.** bill-poster, bill-sticker **2.** *fig.* quarrelsome fellow.

attàcco, *s.m.* **1.** (*mil.*) attack, assault: — *aereo*, air attack; — *di sorpresa*, surprise attack: *sferrammo un — di sorpresa*, we made a surprise attack; *formazione d'*—, attack formation; *precipitarsi all'*—, to start an attack; *ritornare all'*—, to return to the attack **2.** (*patol.*) attack; fit: — *di cuore*, heart attack; — *di fegato*, liver attack; — *di tosse*, fit of coughing **3.** (*punto di unione*) juncture **4.** (*mec.*) connection: — *di un tubo*, pipe connection; — *elettrico*, connecting plug **5.** (*metallografia*) etching **6.** (*ferr.*) coupling **7.** (*insieme di animali da tiro*) team ‖ — *a due*, carriage and pair **8.** (*per sci*) ski fastening.

attaché, *s.m.* (*pol.*) attaché.

attagliàrsi, *v.r.* to suit (s.o.), to fit (s.o.): *questo mi si attaglia*, this suits (o fits) me.

attanagliàre, *v.t.* to pincer.

attapinàrsi, *v.r.* **1.** (*arrabattarsi*) to worry oneself; to worry along **2.** (*lamentarsi*) to complain.

attardàrsi, *v.r.* **1.** (*indugiarsi*) to delay, to loiter **2.** (*essere in ritardo*) to be late.

attastàre, *v.t.* to touch; to feel.

attecchiménto, *s.m.* (*agr.*) taking root, sprouting; flourishing (anche *fig.*).

attecchíre, *v.i.* **1.** (*agr.*) to take root, to strike root, to sprout; to flourish (anche *fig.*) **2.** (*aver fortuna*) to find favour, to catch on: *la nuova rivista ha attecchito subito*, the new magazine caught on at once.

attediàre, *v.t.* to weary, to annoy ‖ **attediàrsi,** *v.i.* to become tired (of s.o., sthg.), to become disgusted (with s.o., sthg.).

atteggiaménto, *s.m.* attitude: — *ostile*, hostile attitude; — *politico*, political attitude.

atteggiàre, *v.t.* **1.** to give an attitude to (sthg.), to give an expression to (sthg.): *atteggiò il viso a com-*

passione, he assumed a sympathetic expression **2.** (*modellare*) to shape ‖ **atteggiàrsi,** *v.r.* **1.** to assume an attitude, to assume an expression **2.** (*posare a*) to pose as: *si atteggiava ad artista*, he posed as an artist.

attempàrsi, *v.r.* to grow old.

attempàto, *ag.* elderly, aged.

attendaménto, *s.m.* (*mil.*) encampment; (*spor.*) camp, camping.

attendàrsi, *v.r.* (*mil.*) to encamp, to pitch tents; (*spor.*) to camp (out).

attendènte, *s.m.* (*mil.*) orderly; (*nell'esercito britannico*) batman (*pl.* batmen).

attèndere, *v.t.* **1.** to wait for (s.o., sthg.), to await: *attendiamo pronta risposta*, (*comm.*) we await a prompt reply; *che cosa attendete?*, what are you waiting for?; — *che qlcu. faccia ql.co.*, to wait for s.o. to do sthg.: *non attese che noi arrivassimo*, he did not wait for us to arrive; — *febbrilmente ql.co.*, to be on the tiptoe of expectation; *andare ad — qlcu. alla stazione*, to meet s.o. at the station **2.** (*aspettare, aspettarsi, prevedere*) to expect: *era da* —, it was to be expected; *non so che cosa mi attende*, I do not know what to expect; *si attende che arrivi da un momento all'altro*, he is expected (o we expect him) at any moment ‖ *v.i.* **1.** (*aspettare*) to wait: *attendi un momento*, wait a moment **2.** (*applicarsi, dedicarsi, prestare attenzione*) to attend, to apply oneself, to devote oneself: — *agli affari*, to attend to one's business **3.** (*accudire*) to attend, to look after (s.o., sthg.): — *a un bambino*, to look after a child.

attendíbile, *ag.* reliable, trustworthy.

attendibilità, *s.f.* reliability, trustworthiness.

attenènte, *V.* **attinènte.**

attenènza, *s.f.* **1.** appurtenance **2.** (*parentela*) relationship; kinship.

attenére, *v.i.* **1.** (*concernere*) to concern (sthg.), to regard (sthg.): *per ciò che attiene al fatto*, as regards the matter **2.** (*appartenere*) to belong, to pertain ‖ *v.t.* to keep, to maintain ‖ **attenérsi,** *v.r.* **1.** to cling (on, to sthg.), to hold (on, to sthg.): *egli si attiene alla sua idea*, he clings to his idea; — *ad un prezzo*, to keep to a price **2.** (*seguire*) to follow (sthg.), to conform: *dovete attenervi alle regole*, you must conform to the rules; — *ai consigli di qlcu.*, to follow s.o.'s advice; — *alle istruzioni di qlcu.*, (*comm.*) to follow s.o.'s instructions **3.** (*limitarsi*) to stick: — *ai cibi semplici*, to stick to plain food.

attentaménte, *av.* attentively; (*con cura*) carefully.

attentàre, *v.i.* to attempt (sthg.): — *alla vita di qlcu.*, to attempt s.o.'s life ‖ **attentàrsi,** *v.r.* (*osare*) to dare; to venture: *egli non si attenta a parlarne a suo padre*, he dare not speak of it to his father.

attentàto, *s.m.* attempt, outrage: — *alla moralità*, indecent behaviour; *commettere un — alla vita di qlcu.*, to make an attempt on s.o.'s life.

attentatóre, *s.m.* attempter.

attentatòrio, *ag.* criminal.

attentatríce, *s.f.* attempter.

attènto, *ag.* attentive; heedful; careful; diligent: —*!*, take care! (o look out!); *attenti al cane*, beware of the dog; — *al gradino*, mind the step; *un — esame*, a careful examination; *sta' —!*, be careful!: *sta' — alla tua salute*, be careful of your health; *sta' attento a ciò che dico*, pay attention to what I'm saying; *stammi — al bambino*, look after (o mind) the child for me ‖ *attenti!*, (*mil.*) attention!; *mettersi sull'attenti*, to come to attention; *stare sull'attenti*, to stand at attention.

attenuaménto, *s.m.* attenuation; mitigation; (*di colpa*) extenuation.

attenuànte, *ag.* (*dir.*) extenuating, extenuatory: *circostanze attenuanti*, extenuating circumstances ‖ *s.f.* (*dir.*) extenuating circumstance, extenuating proof.

attenuàre, *v.t.* to attenuate, to subdue; to tone down; (*diminuire la gravità di*) to extenuate: *nulla può — la sua colpa*, nothing can extenuate his guilt.

attenuataménte, *av.* in a subdued way.

attenuàto, *ag.* attenuate, subdued.

attenuazióne, *s.f.* attenuation, subduing, toning down; (*di colpa*) extenuation.

attenzióne, *s.f.* **1.** attention, care: *fate —!*, take care! (*o* have care! *o* be careful!); *maneggiare con —!*, handle with care!; *mi permetto di richiamare la vostra cortese — su ciò*, (*comm.*) I beg to call your kind attention to this; *non fateci —*, take no heed (*o* notice); *rivolgeremo tutta la nostra — all'esecuzione dei vostri ordini*, (*comm.*) we shall devote our best attention to the execution of your orders; *fare —*, to take care (*o* to be careful *o* to look out): *fare — alla propria salute*, to take care of one's health; *prestare — a qlcu.*, *a ql.co.*, to pay attention to s.o., to sthg.; *richiamare, attirare l'— di qlcu. su ql.co.*, to call (*o* to draw) s.o.'s attention to a fact (*o* to point out a fact to s.o. *o* to bring a fact before s.o.) **2.** (*cortesia*) regard, kindness.

attepidíre, *v.t.* to cool ‖ *v.i.*, **attepidírsi**, *v.r.* to cool (down).

attergàre, *v.t.* to endorse ‖ **attergàrsi**, *v.r.* to place oneself behind (s.o.).

attergàto, *s.m.* (*comm.*) docket; endorsment.

àttero, *ag.* (*di insetto*) apterous; wingless.

atterràggio, *s.m.* (*aer.*) landing: *— cieco*, blind landing; *— di coda*, tail landing; *— di fortuna, forzato*, emergency landing; *— radioguidato, strumentale*, blind, instrument landing; *carrello di —*, landing gear; *operazione di —*, landing procedure; *pista di —*, landing strip (*o* runway); *terreno d'—*, landing ground.

atterraménto, *s.m.* **1.** knocking down **2.** V. **atterràggio**.

atterràre, *v.t.* to knock down, to fell; *fig.* to prostrate, to humiliate: *— un albero*, to fell (*o* to cut down) a tree ‖ *v.i.* (*aer.*) to land, to alight: *— con carrello rientrato*, to bellyland; *— con urto*, to crash; *— corto*, to undershoot; *— lungo*, to overshoot ‖ **atterràrsi**, *v.r.* (*arc.*) to become disheartened, to become discouraged.

atterriménto, *s.m.* frightening; fright.

atterríre, *v.t.* to terrify, to strike with terror; to frighten ‖ **atterrírsi**, *v.r.* to become terrified.

attésa, *s.f.* **1.** (*periodo d'attesa*) wait; (*l'attendere*) waiting: *in — di una vostra risposta*, (*comm.*) awaiting your reply; *una lunga —*, a long wait; *l'— è spesso penosa*, waiting is often painful; *essere in — di qlcu.*, to be waiting for s.o. **2.** (*aspettazione, speranza*) expectation **3.** (*sospensione*) suspense: *fu lasciato in —*, he was kept in suspense.

attéso, *ag.* **1.** waited for **2.** (*desiderato, sperato*) expected, longed for: *abbiamo finalmente ricevuto la notizia tanto attesa*, we have at last received the longed for news.

attesoché, attéso che, *cong.* seeing that, considering that: *— tuo padre era già partito*, considering that your father had already left.

attestàre[1], *v.t.* (*certificare*) to attest, to certify; (*testimoniare*) to attest, to bear witness to (sthg.); (*asserire, dichiarare*) to state, to testify.

attestàre[2], *v.t.* **1.** (*artig.*) to join **2.** (*mec.*) to abut ‖ **attestàrsi**, *v.r.* (*mil.*) **1.** (*serrare i ranghi*) to close ranks **2.** (*formare una testa di ponte*) to establish a bridge-head.

attestàto, *s.m.* **1.** (*certificato*) certificate; (*comm.*) testimonial **2.** (*prova*) proof, demonstration; (*segno*) token: *accettate questo in — della mia amicizia*, accept this as a token of my friendship.

attestatúra, *s.f.* junction, joint.

attestazióne, *s.f.* **1.** attestation **2.** (*dimostrazione*) demonstration; (*segno*) sign; token.

Àttica, *no.pr.f.* (*geog.*) Attica.

atticaménte *av.* after, in the Attic style.

atticciàto, *ag.* sturdy, stout, thickset, stocky.

atticísmo, *s.m.* atticism.

atticísta, *s.m.* atticist.

atticizzàre, *v.i.* to atticize.

àttico, *ag.* Attic: *sali attici*, *fig.* Attic salt (*o* Attic wit *o* refined wit) ‖ *s.m.* (*arch.*) attic.

attiepidíre, attiepidírsi, V. **attepidíre, attepidírsi**.

attiguità *s.f.* contiguity; adjacency.

attíguo, *ag.* contiguous; adjoining; adjacent.

Àttila, *no.pr.m.* (*st.*) Attila.

attillàre, *v.t.* to fit close to the body ‖ **attillàrsi**, *v.r.* to dress oneself in close-fitting clothes; to spruce oneself up.

attillataménte, *av.* elegantly, smartly.

attillatézza, *s.f.* **1.** (*di vestiti*) tightness **2.** (*di persona*) affected elegance.

attillàto, *ag.* **1.** close-fitting; tight: *abito —*, close-fitting (*o* tight) dress **2.** (*azzimato*) dressed up.

attillatúra, *s.f.* smartness; dressing up.

Attília, *no.pr.f.* Attilia.

Attílio, *no.pr.m.* Attilio.

àttimo, *s.m.* moment, instant: *in un —*, in a moment.

attinènte, *ag.* pertaining, belonging, relating: *la vostra risposta non è — all'argomento*, your reply is not pertaining to the subject.

attinènza, *s.f.* relation, connection: *ciò non ha alcuna — con l'argomento in questione*, this bears no relation at all with (*o* to) the matter in hand.

attíngere, *v.t.* **1.** (*raggiungere*) to reach, to attain: *attinse la più alta vetta dell'arte*, he attained the highest summit of art **2.** (*trarre*) to draw: *— acqua da un pozzo*, to draw water from a well; *— denaro da qlcu.*, *fig.* to draw on s.o. for money (*o* to sponge on s.o.) **3.** (*procurarsi*) to get: *— informazioni da qlcu.*, to get (*o* to obtain) information from s.o.

attingitóio, *s.m.* pail; bucket.

attingitóre, *ag.* drawing ‖ *s.m.*, **attingitríce**, *s.f.* drawer.

attínia, *s.f.* (*zool.*) actinia (*pl.* actiniae, actinias), sea-anemone.

attinicità, *s.f.* (*chim. foto. fis.*) actinism.

attínico, *ag.* (*chim. foto. fis.*) actinic.

attínio, *s.m.* (*chim.*) actinium.

attinografía, *s.f.* (*med.*) X-ray photography.

attinògrafo, *s.m.* (*foto.*) actinograph, actinometer.

attinometría, *s.f.* (*meteorologia*) actinometry.

attinòmetro, *s.m.* (*meteorologia*) actinometer, exposure meter.

attinoterapía, *s.f.* (*med.*) actinotherapy.

attiràre, *v.t.* to attract, to draw (*anche fig.*): *il magnete attira il ferro*, a magnet attracts iron; *la sua commedia attira un gran pubblico*, his play is a great draw; *— l'attenzione di qlcu.*, to draw (*o* to attract) s.o.'s attention; *— ql.co. su qlcu.*, to draw (*o* to bring) sthg. on s.o.: *ciò attirò su di lui l'odio dei suoi amici*, that drew upon him the hatred of his friends; *questa azione attirò su di lui la collera di suo padre*, this action brought down his father's wrath on him; *— lo sguardo di qlcu.*, to draw s.o.'s eye **2.** (*adescare*) to allure, to entice: *— qlcu. con promesse*, to entice s.o. with promises ‖ **attiràrsi**, *v.r.* to draw upon oneself, to bring upon oneself; to win: *mi sono attirato tutto il biasimo*, I have drawn all the blame upon myself; *— l'affetto di qlcu.*, to win s.o.'s affection; *— delle critiche*, to come in for criticism.

attitúdine[1], *s.f.* turn; disposition, aptitude; bent: *— per la musica*, natural bent for music; *ha molte attitudini*, he is naturally gifted; *avere (molta) — per le lingue*, to have a (real) turn for languages.

attitúdine[2], *s.f.* attitude; posture: *prendere un'— istrionica*, to strike a theatrical attitude.

attivaménte, *av.* actively, industriously.

attivàre, *v.t.* to activate, to make active; (*mettere in attività*) to put in action, in activity; to bring into action: *— il fuoco*, to stir up the fire; *— una macchina*, to start an engine.

attivatóri, *s.m.pl.* (*chim.*) activators.

attivazióne, *s.f.* (*chim. fis. atomica*) activation: *ener-*

gia di —, (*chim.*) activation energy ‖ *linea in* —, (*ferr.*) line working.

attivísmo, *s.m.* **1.** (*st. fil.*) activism **2.** (*pol.*) activism, militancy.

attivísta, *s.c.* **1.** (*st. fil.*) activist **2.** (*pol.*) activist, militant.

attivístico, *ag.* **1.** (*fil. pol.*) activist(ic) **2.** (*attivo*) active.

attività, *s.f.* **1.** activity: — *industriale*, industrial activity; — *negli affari*, animation in business; *campo di* —, sphere of activity (*o* of action); *in* —, in activity (*o* in action *o* at work); *è un momento di grande* —, this is a very busy time; *entrare in* —, (*di vulcano*) to become active; *mantenere in* — *un'industria*, to keep an industry going **2.** (*operosità*) activity; industry; briskness; dispatch: *la sua* — *è sorprendente*, his activity is surprising **3.** (*comm.*) credit account; profit: — *e passività*, assets and liabilities **4.** (*fis. atomica*) activity.

attívo, *ag.* **1.** active: *collaborazione attiva*, active collaboration; *commercio* —, brisk trade; *in servizio* —, (*mil.*) on the active list; *vulcano* —, active volcano **2.** (*operoso*) active, industrious; (*di scolaro*) diligent: *uomo* —, active (*o* industrious *o* energetic) man; *vita attiva*, active life **3.** (*gram.*) active: *verbo* —, active verb **4.** (*comm.*) active, profitable, productive, bearing interest; (*esigibile*) receivable: *cambiali attive*, receivable bills; *conti attivi*, receivable accounts; *interessi attivi*, (*incassati*) received interest; (*da incassare*) receivable interest **5.** (*chim.*) activated ‖ *s.m.* **1.** (*comm.*) assets (*pl.*); credit balance: — *disponibile, indisponibile*, assets in hand, unavailable assets; — *e passivo*, assets and liabilities; — *fallimentare*, debtor's assets; — *immobilizzato*, fixed assets; — *mobiliare, immobiliare*, personal, real assets; *ammontare dell'* —, amount of assets; *prospetto dell'* — *e del passivo*, statement of assets and liabilities ‖ *accertare l'* —, to ascertain (*o* to find out) assets; *avere ql.co. al proprio* —, to have sthg. to one's credit (anche *fig.*); *mettere ql.co. all'* — *di qlcu.*, to credit s.o. with sthg. (anche *fig.*) **2.** (*gram.*) active form; (*di verbo*) active voice: *verbo all'* —, verb in the active voice.

attizzaménto, *s.m.* poking; stirring up (anche *fig.*); (*aizzamento*) incitement, instigation.

attizzàre, *v.t.* **1.** to poke, to stir up **2.** *fig.* (*eccitare*) to stir up; to excite; to arouse; (*aizzare*) to incite, to instigate, to urge.

attizzatóio, *s.m.* poker.

attizzatóre, *ag.* stirring (up) ‖ *s.m.*, **attizzatrìce**, *s.f.* stirrer (up); *fig.* inciter, instigator, urger.

attizzíno, *s.m.* inciter, instigator.

àtto¹, *s.m.* **1.** act; (*azione*) action; (*fatto*) deed: — *di coraggio*, brave deed; *un* — *generoso*, a generous deed **2.** (*teol.*) act: — *di fede, di contrizione*, act of faith, of contrition **3.** (*atteggiamento*) attitude; (*gesto*) gesture **4.** (*teat.*) act: *commedia in tre atti*, three-act play **5.** (*attestato, certificato*) certificate: — *di morte, nascita*, certificate of death, of birth (*o* death, birth certificate) **6.** (*trattato*) treaty: — *di pace*, peace treaty **7.** (*dir.*) deed; (*comm.*) bill: — *apocrifo, autentico*, forged, original deed; — *di accusa*, indictment; — *di compravendita*, contract of purchase; — *di vendita*, bill of sale; *legalizzazione di un* —, certification (*o* authentication) of a deed; *registrazione di un* —, record (*o* recording) of a deed; *rilascio di un* —, delivery of a deed; *sottoscrizione di un* —, signature of a deed; *trascrizione di un* —, transcription of a deed; *annullare, autenticare, legalizzare, redigere un* —, to cancel, to authenticate, to certify, to draw a deed; *registrare un* —, to record a deed; *rilasciare un* —, to deliver (*o* to issue) a deed **8.** *pl.* (*dir.*) legal proceedings: *fare gli atti a qlcu.*, to institute (*o* to take) legal proceedings against s.o.; *mettere agli atti*, to record in the journals; *passare agli atti*, to file (documents) (*o* to register in the archives) **9.** *pl.* (*di un'assemblea, società, ecc.*) proceedings; (*transazioni*) transactions: *gli atti di un'assemblea*, the proceedings of a meeting; *mettere agli atti*,

to record in the minutes **10.** *pl.* (*verbale*) records (of proceedings); transactions ‖ *Atti del Parlamento*, Official Records of Parliamentary Proceedings; (*del parlamento inglese*) Hansard **11.**(**Fraseologia**): *all'* — *del carico, dello scarico*, on loading, on unloading; *all'* — *della consegna*, on delivery; *all'* — *delle dimissioni*, on resignation (*o* resigning); *all'* — *dell'ordinazione*, when ordering (*o* when placing the order); *all'* — *del pagamento*, on payment; *all'* — *della partenza*, (*per mare*) on sailing ‖ *all'* — *pratico*, in practice ‖ *in* — *di stima*, as a mark of esteem ‖ *inflazione in* —, inflation in progress ‖ *dare* — *di ql.co.*, to acknowledge sthg.; (*comm.*) to acknowledge receipt of sthg. ‖ *fare* — *di presenza*, to put in an appearance ‖ *mettere in* — *ql.co.*, to carry out sthg. (*o* to put sthg. into action): *il nostro programma è già in* —, our programme is already being carried out ‖ *prendere* — *di ql.co.*, to take note of sthg. (*o* to note sthg. *o* to record sthg.).

àtto², *ag.* **1.** (*adatto, idoneo*) fit, fitted; suitable; qualified (for sthg., to do sthg.) **2.** (*capace*) capable, able.

attonànte, *s.m.* (*farm.*) tonic, corroborant.

attonàre, *v.t.* (*med.*) to strengthen; to invigorate.

attondàre, *v.t.* to round, to make round.

attonitaménte, *av.* astonishingly; amazingly; astoundingly; amazedly, in amazement.

attònito, *ag.* astonished; amazed; astounded.

attórcere, *v.t.* to twist; (*con forza*) to wring ‖ **attòrcersi**, *v.r.* to twist; to writhe, to squirm.

attorcigliaménto, *s.m.* twisting; twining.

attorcigliàre, *v.t.* to twist; to twine: — *ql.co. intorno a ql.co.*, to twist (*o* to twine *o* to entwist) sthg. round sthg. ‖ **attorcigliàrsi**, *v.r.* to wind, to twine; (*di serpente*) to coil: *l'edera si attorciglia* (*intorno*) *alla quercia*, ivy twines round the oak; *il serpente si attorcigliò intorno alla sua preda*, the serpent coiled (itself) round its prey.

attóre, *s.m.* **1.** actor (anche *fig.*); (*spreg.*) play-actor: — *cinematografico*, screen actor; *attori girovaghi*, strolling players; *primo* —, leading actor (*o* man); *fu il principale* — *di quell'avvenimento*, *fig.* he was the chief actor in that event; *diventare* —, to become an actor (*o* to go on the stage) **2.** (*dir.*) plaintiff.

attorniaménto, *s.m.* **1.** surrounding; encircling; besiegement **2.** *fig.* besiegement.

attorniàre, *v.t.* **1.** to surround, to encircle; (*assediare*) to besiege **2.** *fig.* to besiege; to pester: *l'attorniava* (*insistentemente*) *per ottenere del denaro*, he was always pestering him for money ‖ **attorniàrsi**, *v.r.* to surround oneself (with s.o., sthg.).

attórno, *av.* about, around, round, roundabout: *per dieci miglia* —, for ten miles (a)round; *tutt'* —, all around; *non c'era nessuno* —, there was nobody about; *vivono qui* —, they live hereabout; *andare* —, to stroll about ‖ *darsi d'* —, to get busy ‖ *levarsi d'* —, to get out of the way ‖ *levarsi qlcu. d'* —, (*liberarsene*) to get rid of s.o. ‖ *prep.* **about, around, round, roundabout:** — *alla tavola*, round the table; *le colline* — *alla città*, the hills around the town; *ciò che accadde* — *a noi*, what took place roundabout (*o* round) us; *la Terra gira* — *al Sole*, the earth goes round the sun; *radunarsi* — *al fuoco*, to gather about the fire ‖ *girare* — *ad un problema*, (*fam.*) to beat about the bush ‖ *stare* — *a qlcu.* (*per ottenere ql.co.*), to besiege (*o* to pester) s.o. (for sthg.).

attorràre, *v.t.* to stack, to pile up.

attortigliaménto, *s.m.* twisting; twining.

attortigliàre, attortigliàrsi, *V.* **attorcigliàre, attorcigliàrsi**.

attossicaménto, *s.m.* poisoning.

attossicàre, *v.t.* **1.** to poison **2.** (*appestare*) to pollute: — *l'aria*, to pollute the air **3.** *fig.* (*amareggiare*) to embitter; (*corrompere*) to corrupt; (*rovinare*) to spoil; to poison.

attrabaccàre, *v.i.* (*arc. mil.*) to encamp under canvas.

attraccàggio, *s.m.* (*mar.*) mooring; (*alla banchina*) docking.

attraccàre, *v.t.* (*mar.*) to moor; (*allabanchina*) to dock.

attraènte, *ag.* attractive; charming, fascinating; (*allettante*) alluring; (*simpatico*) engaging: *modi attraenti,* charming manners; *sorriso* —, engaging (*o* fetching) smile; *è poco* —, she is unattractive.

attrappíre, *V.* **rattrappíre.**

attrappíto, *V.* **rattrappíto.**

attràrre, *v.t.* to attract, to draw (anche *fig.*); (*allettare*) to allure: *questo progetto non lo attrae,* this plan does not attract him; *lasciarsi* — *da qlco., da qlcu.,* to fall for sthg., s.o.: *piccole cose da cui gli uomini si lasciano* —, little things (that) men fall for; *sentirsi attratto verso qlcu.,* to feel drawn to s.o.

attrattíva, *s.f.* attraction; (*seduzione*) allurement; (*fascino*) charm: *l'— di un buon piatto,* the attraction of a good dish; *le attrattive di una donna,* the charms of a woman; *la grande — del giorno,* the great attraction of the day; *esercitare una — su qlcu.,* to attract s.o.

attrattivaménte, *av.* attractively.

attrattívo, *ag.* attractive; (*seducente*) alluring, enticing.

attraversaménto, *s.m.* crossing.

attraversàre, *v.t.* 1. to cross; to pass through (a place): *il ponte attraversa il fiume,* the bridge crosses (*o* spans) the river; *quel pensiero mi attraversò la mente,* that thought crossed my mind; — *a nuoto un fiume,* to swim across a river; — *un bosco,* to walk through a wood; — *una città,* to go (*o* to pass) through a town; — *di corsa una strada,* to run across a road; — *in aereo,* to fly across; — *in bicicletta, in automobile, a cavallo un paese,* to cycle, to drive, to ride through a country; — *un prato,* to walk across a meadow; — *una strada,* to cross (*o* to go across *o* to step across) a road 2. (*ostacolare*) to thwart, to frustrate: — *il cammino di qlcu.,* to get in s.o.'s way (*o* to cross *o* to thwart s.o.'s plans) 3. — *l'ancora,* (*mar.*) to fish the anchor 4. — *con un arco,* (*arch.*) to span.

attravèrso (a), *prep.* 1. (*di luogo*) **across; through:** — *al bosco,* through the wood; — *il fiume,* across the river 2. (*di tempo*) **through:** — *un lungo periodo,* through a long period ‖ *av.* (*rar.*) across; *fig.* **wrong:** *tu intendi* —, you've got it wrong.

attrazióne, *s.f.* attraction: — *magnetica,* (*fis.*) magnetic attraction; — *molecolare,* (*fis.*) molecular (*o* adhesive) attraction (*o* cohesive force).

attrazzàre, *v.t.* (*mar.*) to rig.

attràzzo, *s.m.* 1. (*mar.*) rig 2. *pl.* (*arnesi*) tools, implements.

attrezzaménto, *s.m.* 1. equipping; fitting out 2. (*attrezzi*) fittings (*pl.*).

attrezzàre, *v.t.* 1. (*equipaggiare*) to equip; (*arredare*) to fit out; (*rifornire di attrezzi*) to supply with tools 2. (*mar.*) to rig.

attrezzatúra, *s.f.* 1. equipment, outfit: *l'— di una fabbrica,* the equipment of a factory; *attrezzature produttive,* productive plants; — *turistica,* tourist organization 2. (*mar.*) rigging.

attrezzísta, *s.m.* (*teat.*) property-man (*pl.* property-men), property-master, scene-shifter.

attrézzo, *s.m.* tool, implement.

attribuíbile, *ag.* attributable.

attribuíre, *v.t.* 1. to attribute, to ascribe: *attribuimmo la sua ira ad un malinteso,* we attributed his anger to a misunderstanding; *non vi attribuimmo importanza,* we attached no importance to it 2. (*assegnare*) to assign, to award ‖ **attribuírsi,** *v.r.* to arrogate, to arrogate to oneself; to claim; to ascribe to oneself.

attributívo, *ag.* attributive.

attribúto, *s.m.* 1. attribute 2. (*gram.*) attribute, attributive.

attribuzióne, *s.f.* attribution: *le attribuzioni del sindaco,* the attributions of a mayor.

attríce, *s.f.* actress: — *cinematografica,* screen (*o* film) actress (*o* star).

attristaménto, *s.m.* saddening, sorrow, sadness.

attristàre, *v.t.* to sadden.

attristíre, *v.i.,* **attristírsi,** *v.r.* 1. to become sad, to sadden 2. (*perdere le forze*) to grow thin; to lose strength, to weaken.

attríto, *ag.* 1. (*consumato*) worn out; attrited 2. (*teol.*) feeling attrition, attrite ‖ *s.m.* 1. friction, attrition 2. *fig.* disagreement, dissension.

attrizióne, *s.f.* 1. (*teol.*) attrition 2. (*mec.*) friction; (*fis.*) abrasion.

attruppaménto, *s.m.* 1. trooping 2. (*folla*) crowd, throng; (*spreg.*) mob.

attruppàrsi, *v.r.* to troop (together); to crowd, to throng.

attuàbile, *ag.* feasible; practicable, possible.

attuàle, *ag.* 1. (*del momento*) present: *l'indirizzo* —, the present address; *il valore* —, the present value 2. (*in atto*) actual: *grazia* —, (*teol.*) actual grace 3. (*reale*) real.

attualísmo, *s.m.* (*st. fil.*) actualism.

attualità, *s.f.* 1. (*il momento presente*) the moment 2. (*cosa d'attualità*) topical question, topical subject: *è un argomento di* —, it is a topical subject; *essere di grande* —, to be of great interest 3. (*modernità*) up-to-dateness 4. (*esistenza di atto*) actuality 5. (*realtà*) reality.

attualménte, *av.* 1. (*al momento*) at present, at the present time, now 2. (*effettivamente, in atto*) actually, really.

attuàre, *v.t.* to carry into effect, to carry out, to put in practice; to accomplish ‖ **attuàrsi,** *v.r.* (*realizzarsi*) to come true, to prove true; (*avvenire*) to come to pass.

attuariàle, *ag.* (*mat. finanziaria*) actuarial.

attuàrio, *s.m.* 1. (*mat. finanziaria*) actuary 2. (*dir.*) registrar.

attuazióne, *s.f.* 1. putting into effect, carrying out 2. (*realizzazione*) accomplishment; fulfilment.

attuffaménto, *s.m.* plunging; diving.

attuffàre, *v.t.* to plunge; to dive; (*intingere*) to dip ‖ **attuffàrsi,** *v.r.* to plunge; to dive.

attutíre, *v.t.* to mitigate, to moderate, to soothe, to appease: — *un rumore,* to deaden a noise ‖ **attutírsi,** *v.r.* to calm down, to become appeased, to become deadened.

attutíto, *ag.* deadened, soothed.

aucúpio, *s.m.* (*arc.*) bird-liming.

audàce, *ag.* bold, audacious, fearless, daring.

audaceménte, *av.* boldly, audaciously, daringly.

audàcia, *s.f.* 1. boldness, audacity, daring 2. (*sfrontatezza*) audacity, impudence: *avete l'— di dirmi questo!,* you have the face to tell me that!.

àudio, *s.m.* (*tv.*) sound.

audiòmetro, *s.m.* (*med. fis.*) audiometer.

auditóre, *s.m.* 1. listener, hearer 2. (*dir.*) junior judge.

auditòrio, *s.m.* 1. (*luogo dove si dà udienza*) audience chamber; auditorium 2. (*sala per concerti*) concert-hall, auditorium 3. (*pubblico*) audience.

audizióne, *s.f.* 1. (*fisiol.*) hearing 2. (*teat.*) audition; performance 3. (*dir.*) examination of witnesses.

àuge, *s.m.* 1. (*astr.*) apogee 2. *fig.* summit, highest point: *essere in* —, *fig.* to enjoy great favour.

augèllo, (*poet.*) per **uccèllo.**

augnàre, *v.t.* 1. (*dial.*) (*adunghiare*) to claw 2. (*carpenteria*) to mitre.

augnatúra, *s.f.* (*carpenteria*) mitre-joint.

auguràle, *ag.* 1. (*st. romana*) augural 2. (*di augurio*) auspicious; of good wish: *espressioni augurali,* well wishing expressions (*o* wishes).

auguràre, *v.t.* 1. to wish: *gli augurai la buona notte e poi me ne andai a letto,* I bid him good-night and then went to bed; *gli auguro gioia,* I wish him joy; *gli auguro la morte,* I wish him to die (*o* I hope he will die) 2. (*predire*) to predict, to forebode ‖ **auguràrsi**, *v.r.* to hope, to wish, to look forward to (sthg., doing).

auguràto, *ag.*: *bene* —, fortunate, happy; *male* —, unfortunate (*o* unhappy) ‖ *s.m.* (*st. romana*) augurship.

àugure, *s.m.* (*st. romana*) augur.

augúrio, *s.m.* **1.** wish: *auguri di Natale e Capodanno*, season's greetings; *con i migliori auguri*, wishing you all the best **2.** (*presagio*) omen; presage: *ritenere ql.co. di buon* —, to take sthg. as a good omen ‖ *uccello di buon* —, bird of good omen; *uccello di mal* —, bird of ill omen (*o* Jonah).

auguróso, *ag.* ominous.

Augústa, *no.pr.f.* Augusta.

augustàle, *ag.* imperial.

augustèo, *ag.* **1.** Augustan: *l'età augustea*, the Augustan Age **2.** (*imperiale*) imperial.

augústo, *ag.* august, majestic ‖ *s.m.* (*titolo dato agli imperatori romani*) Augustus ‖ **Augústo**, *no.pr.m.* Augustus.

àula, *s.f.* hall; room: — *di scuola*, school-room; — *di tribunale*, Court-room; — *magna*, public hall (of a University); — *universitaria*, lecture-hall.

aulicaménte, *av.* in a courtly style; pompously.

àulico, *ag.* **1.** (*di corte*) aulic, courtly **2.** (*pomposo*) pompous.

aumentàbile, *ag.* increasable, augmentable.

aumentàre, *v.t.* to increase; to enlarge; to augment; (*fam. amer.*) to up; (*elevare*) to raise: *aumentò la velocità*, he increased speed; — *i prezzi*, to raise prices; — *la produzione*, to increase production; — *uno stipendio*, to raise a salary ‖ *v.i.* to increase, to grow, to enlarge; (*salire*) to rise: *la febbre gli aumenta*, his temperature is rising; *il prezzo della carne aumenta*, the price of meat is rising; *simili casi andavano aumentando*, such cases were on the increase (*o* were increasing in number); *le spese aumentano*, expenses are going up; — *di peso*, to increase in weight (*o* to put on weight).

auménto, *s.m.* **1.** increase; augmentation; addition: — *di capitale*, increase of capital; — *di stipendio*, increase in salary (*o* amer. raise); *il continuo* — *delle nostre vendite*, the steady increase of our sales; *essere in* —, to be on the increase; *portare un notevole* — *di capitale*, to bring a large addition of capital **2.** (*rialzo*) rise: *un* — *di prezzi, di valore, di temperatura*, a rise of prices, of value, in temperature.

àuna, *s.f.* aune (*antica misura di lunghezza corrispondente all'inglese* ell = m. 1,143).

aunghiàre, *v.t.* (*rar.*) to clutch, to claw.

àura, *s.f.* **1.** breeze ‖ — *popolare*, *fig.* popular favour **2.** (*patol.*) aura.

auràto, *ag.* (*poet.*) **1.** golden **2.** *fig.* brilliant, sparkling.

Aurèlia, *no.pr.f.* Aurelia.

Aureliàno, *no.pr.m.* (*st.*) Aurelian.

Aurèlio, *no.pr.m.* Aurelius.

àureo, *ag.* **1.** (*d'oro*) gold: *un* — *bracciale*, a gold bracelet **2.** (*dorato*) golden: *aurei capelli, auree chiome*, golden hair **3.** *fig.* golden, valuable, excellent: *l'età aurea della nostra poesia*, the golden age of our poetry ‖ *numero* —, (*astr.*) golden number; *regola aurea*, (*arit.*) rule of three.

aurèola, *s.f.* **1.** aureola, aureole, halo **2.** *fig.* glory; halo.

aureomicína, *s.f.* (*farm.*) aureomycin.

àurico, *ag.* (*mar.*): *vela aurica*, fore-and-aft sail.

auricolàre, *ag.* auricular: *confessione* —, (*eccl.*) auricular confession; *testimone* —, (*dir.*) auricular witness ‖ *s.m.* (*mignolo*) little finger.

aurífero, *ag.* auriferous, gold-bearing: *terreno* —, gold-field.

auríga, *s.m.* charioteer ‖ *Auriga*, (*astr.*) Auriga.

auròra, *s.f.* **1.** dawn, daybreak, break of day: — *australe*, aurora australis; — *boreale*, aurora borealis; *prima dell'*—, before dawn **2.** *fig.* dawn; beginning,

rise: *l'*— *di una civiltà*, the dawn of a civilization ‖ **Auròra**, *no. pr. f.* Aurora.

auroràle, *ag.* auroral.

auscultàre, *v.t.i.* (*med.*) to auscultate.

auscultazióne, *s.f.* (*med.*) auscultation.

ausiliàre, *ag.* **1.** (*gram.*) auxiliary **2.** *V.* **ausiliàrio**.

ausiliària, *s.f.* (*mil.*) member of the Women's Army Auxiliary Corps.

ausiliàrio, *ag.* auxiliary; subsidiary: *macchina ausiliaria*, auxiliary engine; *truppe ausiliarie*, subsidiary troops (*o* auxiliaries); *ufficiale* —, reserve officer.

ausiliatóre, *s.m.*, **ausiliatríce**, *s.f.* helper.

ausilio, *s.m.* **1.** (*letter.*) help, aid **2.** (*difesa*) defence.

ausònio, *ag.* (*letter.*) Italic.

auspicàbile, *ag.* desirable.

auspicàle, *ag.* auspicious ‖ *pietra* —, corner-stone.

auspicàre, *v.t.* to augur; to forebode.

auspicàto, *ag.* (*letter.*) auspicate; fortunate.

àuspice, *s.m.* **1.** (*st. romana*) augur **2.** (*protettore*) patron: — *il principe*, under the patronage (*o* under the auspices) of the Prince.

auspício, *s.m.* **1.** (*st. romana*) auspice, omen: *di buon, cattivo* —, of good, ill omen **2.** (*augurio*) wish **3.** (*protezione*) protection, favour: *sotto gli auspici di qlcu.*, under the patronage of s.o.

austeraménte, *av.* austerely, sternly, strictly.

austerità, *s.f.* austerity, sternness; strictness.

austèro, *ag.* austere, stern, severe, strict; (*disadorno*) unadorned: *fare una vita austera*, to lead an austere life.

austràle, *ag.* austral, southern: *vento* —, south wind ‖ *Polo Australe*, South Pole.

Austràlia, *no.pr.f.* (*geog.*) Australia.

australiàna, *s.f.* (*spor.*) pursuit cycle race on track.

australiàno, *ag.s.m.* (*geog.*) Australian.

Àustria, *no.pr.f.* (*geog.*) Austria.

austríaco, *ag.s.m.* Austrian ‖ **austríaca**, *s.f.* Austrian.

àustro, *s.m.* **1.** (*Sud*) South **2.** (*vento*) Auster.

àustro-ungàrico, *ag.* (*st.*) Austro-Hungarian.

aut-aut, *cong.* (*lat.*) this or that; yes or no ‖ *s.m.* dilemma: *gli pose un* —, he put him in(to) a dilemma.

autarchìa, *s.f.* economic self-sufficiency; autarchy; (*pol.*) political independence.

autàrchico, *ag.* self-sufficient: *prodotto* —, home product.

autèntica, *s.f.* **1.** (*amm.*) (*approvazione*) authoritative approval **2.** (*dir.*) authentication **3.** *le Autentiche*, (*leggi di Giustiniano*) the Authentics.

autenticaménte, *av.* authentically.

autenticàre, *v.t.* to authenticate, to legalize; to certify.

autenticàto, *ag.* (*amm.*) certified: *copia autenticata*, certified copy (*o* probate).

autenticazióne, *s.f.* authentication.

autenticità, *s.f.* authenticity, genuineness: *mettere in dubbio l'*—, to question the genuineness.

autèntico, *ag.* **1.** authentic: *atto* —, authentic act; *testo* —, authentic text **2.** (*vero*) true; (*genuino*) genuine, pure: *racconto* —, true story.

autière, *s.m.* (*mil.*) transport corps orderly.

autísmo, *s.m.* (*patol.*) autism.

autísta, *s.m.* driver, motor-car driver: — *di piazza*, taxi-driver (*o* cabman).

àuto, *abbr.* di **automòbile**.

autoambulànza, *s.f.* motor-ambulance.

auto-attrézzi, *s.f.* (*aut.*) breakdown-lorry.

autobiografía, *s.f.* autobiography.

autobiogràfico, *ag.* autobiographic(al).

autobiògrafo, *s.m.* autobiographer.

autoblínda, **autoblindàta**, *s.f.* (*mil.*) armoured car.

autobótte, *s.f.* (*aut.*) tank truck.

autobrúceo, *s.m.* **1.** (*mil.*) (*carro armato*) tank **2.** (*trattore su cingoli*) caterpillar tractor.

àutobus, *s.m.* (motor-)bus (*pl.* buses); (*per lunghi viaggi*) (motor-)coach: — *a due piani*, double-decker.

autocarovàna, *s.f.* motor-convoy; party of cars.

autocàrro, *s.m.* (motor-)lorry; (*amer.*) truck.

autoclàve, *s.f.* (*med.*) autoclave; sterilizer.

autocommutatóre, *s.m.* (*tel.*) automatic telephone switch.

autocorrièra, *s.f.* (motor-)coach.

autòcrata, **autòcrate**, *s.m.* autocrat; despot; *fig.* despotic person.

autocraticaménte, *av.* autocratically; despotically.

autocràtico, *ag.* autocratic; despotical, despotic.

autocrazía, *s.f.* autocracy.

autocromía, *s.f.* (*foto.*) autochromy.

autòctono, *ag.* autochthonous ‖ *s.m.* autochthon (*pl.* autochthones, autochthons); aboriginal, native.

autodafé, *s.m.* **1.** (*st.*) auto-da-fé (*pl.* autos-da-fé), auto-de-fé (*pl.* autos-de-fé) **2.** (*rogo*) pyre.

autodecisióne, *s.f.* self-determination.

autodidàtta, *s.m.* autodidact; self-taught man ‖ *s.f.* autodidact; self-taught woman.

autodifésa, *s.f.* self-defence.

autodomínio, *s.m.* self-control.

autòdromo, *s.m.* autodrome; motordrome; (*amer.*) motor-racing track.

autofecondazióne, *s.f.* (*biol. bot.*) self-fertilization; autogamy.

autofurgóne, *s.m.* van.

autogenía, *s.f.* (*biol.*) autogeny, autogenesis.

autògeno, *ag.* autogenous: *saldatura autogena*, (*mec.*) autogenous welding; *vaccino* —, (*med.*) autogenous vaccine.

autogíro, *s.m.* (*aer.*) autogyro.

autografàre, *v.t.* to autograph.

autografía, *s.f.* autography.

autogràfico, *ag.* autographic(al).

autògrafo, *ag.* autographic(al): *una lettera autografa di Keats*, a letter in Keats's own hand ‖ *s.m.* autograph.

autoinduzióne, *s.f.* (*elett.*) self-induction.

autointossicazióne, *s.f.* (*patol.*) auto-intoxication.

autoipnòsi, *s.f.* autosuggestion.

autolatría, *s.f.* self-worship; narcissism.

autolesióne, *s.f.* **1.** (*patol.*) autolesion **2.** (*lesione a scopo doloso*) self-injury.

autolesionísta, *s.c.* **1.** (*patol.*) autolesionist **2.** (*chi cagiona a se stesso lesione a scopo doloso*) self-injurer.

autolettíga, *s.f.* (motor-)ambulance.

autòma, *s.m.* automaton (*pl.* automatons, automata) (anche *fig.*); robot.

automaticaménte, *av.* automatically.

automaticità, *s.f.* automaticity.

automàtico, *ag.* **1.** automatic: *distributore* —, slot machine (o automatic machine); *pistola, fucile* —, automatic pistol, gun; *ristorante* —, automat **2.** *fig.* automatic: *azione automatica*, automatic action ‖ *s.m.* (*bottone*) —, press botton; (*fam. amer.*) snapper.

automatísmo, *s.m.* automatism.

automazióne, *s.f.* (*neol.*) automation.

automedónte, *s.m.* (*poet.*) charioteer; (*scherz.*) (*automobilista*) driver Jehu.

automèzzo, *s.m.* motor-vehicle.

automòbile, *ag.* (*che si muove da sè*) self-moving; self-propelling; (*amer.*) automotive ‖ *s.f.* motor-car, car, automobile: — *aperta*, open car (o cabriolet); — *da corsa*, racing car; — *di serie*, production-model car (o *amer.* stock car); — *fuori serie*, special-body car; *salone dell'*—, motor show; *faremo una bella gita in* —, we are going for a pleasant drive; *andare in* — *in un luogo*, to motor to a place; *guidare l'*—, to drive a car.

automobilísmo, *s.m.* motoring.

automobilísta, *s.c.* motorist.

automobilístico, *ag.* motor (*attributivo*): *corsa automobilistica*, motor-race.

automotóre, *s.m.* self-propelling engine.

automotríce, *s.f.* (*ferr.*) rail-car; motor-coach.

autonomía, *s.f.* **1.** autonomy, self-government **2.** (*aer. aut.*) range; fuel distance: — *di volo*, (*aer.*) maximum duration.

autonomísta, *s.c.* autonomist.

autònomo, *ag.* **1.** autonomous, self-governing **2.** (*mec.*) self-contained.

autoparchéggio, *s.m.* car-park; parking.

autopàrco, *s.m.* **1.** car-park; parking **2.** (*mil.*) military car-park.

autoplàstica, *s.f.* (*chir.*) autoplasty.

autoplàstico, *ag.* (*chir.*) autoplastic.

autopómpa, *s.f.* (motor) fire-engine.

autopsía, *s.f.* autopsy.

autopúbblica, *s.f.* taxi, cab, taxi-cab.

autopúllman, *s.m.* (motor-)coach.

autóre, *s.m.* **1.** author; maker; originator; promoter: *l'* — *di un delitto*, perpetrator of a crime; *essere l'* — *della rovina di qlcu.*, to be the cause of s.o.'s downfall ‖ *gli autori dei nostri giorni*, (*letter.*) (*i nostri genitori*) our progenitors **2.** (*di libri*) author, writer; (*di musica*) composer; (*di quadri*) painter; (*di sculture*) sculptor: *quadro d'* — *antico*, old master's painting ‖ *diritti d'*—, copyright **3.** (*dir.*) original owner.

autorespiratóre, *s.m.* aqualung.

autorévole, *ag.* authoritative.

autorevolézza, *s.f.* authoritativeness.

autorevolménte, *av.* authoritatively.

autoriméssa, *s.f.* garage.

autorità, *s.f.* authority: — *costituita*, legai authority; *le* — *della città*, the town authorities; *le* — *militari*, the military authorities; — *paterna*, parental authority; *è una persona di grande* —, he is a very influential man; *l'«Oxford English Dictionary»* è *la maggior* — *per la lingua inglese*, the "Oxford English Dictionary" is the best authority on the English language; *sei davvero un'*— *in questo campo*, you are really an authority on (o a connoisseur in) this subject; *agire con piena* —, to act with full powers; *avere* — *su qlcu.*, to have authority over s.o.

autoritariaménte, *av.* authoritatively; imperiously.

autoritàrio, *ag.* authoritative; dictatorial.

autoritràtto, *s.m.* self-portrait.

autorizzàbile, *ag.* authorizable.

autorizzàre, *v.t.* **1.** (*dare autorità a*) to authorize, to empower **2.** (*permettere a*) to authorize, to permit, to allow: *la pesca è autorizzata*, fishing is free **3.** (*dare diritto a*) to entitle; to justify: *queste scoperte autorizzano a pensare che...*, these discoveries entitle us to believe that....

autorizzazióne, *s.f.* **1.** authorization; warrant; (*permesso*) permission; (*licenza*) licence; (*consenso*) consent: *con l'*— *dell'autore*, under licence from the author; *avere l'*— *per la vendita di ql.co.*, to be licensed to sell sthg. **2.** (*documento*) permit.

autorotazióne, *s.f.* (*aer.*) autorotation.

autoscàfo, *s.m.* (*mar.*) motor-boat.

autoscàtto, *s.m.* (*foto.*) automatic release.

autoscuòla, *s.f.* driving school.

autostèllo, *s.m.* (*neol.*) motel.

autostòp, *s.m.* (*neol.*) hitch-hiking: *fare l'*—, *viaggiare con l'*—, to hitch-hike (o *amer.* to thumb).

autostoppísta, *s.c.* (*neol.*) hitch-hiker.

autostràda, *s.f.* motor-way, speedway; (*amer.*) superhighway: — *a quattro corsie*, four-lane superhighway.

autosuggestióne, *s.f.* autosuggestion.

autotelàio, *s.m.* (*aut.*) chassis.

autotipía, *s.f.* (*tip.*) autotypography.

autotrèno, *s.m.* motor-lorry; (*amer.*) truck.

autovaccíno, *s.m.* (*med.*) autovaccine.

autoveícolo, *s.m.* motor-vehicle.

autovettúra, *s.f.* motor-car, car, automobile.

autoviràfte, *ag.* (*foto.*) self-towing.

autríce, *s.f.* authoress, author: *ella era* — *di parecchi romanzi*, she was the author of several novels.

autunnàle, *ag.* autumnal.

autúnno, *s.m.* autumn; (*amer.*) fall ‖ *l'*— *della vita*, the autumn of life.

àva, *s.f.* **1.** (*nonna*) grandmother **2.** (*antenata*) ancestress.

avallànte, *s.m.* (*comm.*) guarantor.

avallàre, *v.t.* to guarantee, to guaranty (anche *fig.*): — *una cambiale*, (*comm.*) to back a bill.

avallàto, *ag.* (*comm.*) backed ‖ *s.m.* (*dir.*) guarantee.

avàllo, *s.m.* (*comm.*) guaranty, guarantee (anche *fig.*).

avambràccio, *s.m.* forearm.

avampòrto, *s.m.* outer port.

avampósto, *s.m.* (*mil.*) outpost.

Avàna, *no.pr.f.* (*geog.*) Havana ‖ **avàna**, *s.m.* (*sigaro*) Havana (cigar) ‖ *ag.* (*di colore*) light brown.

avancòrpo, *s.m.* forepart.

avanguàrdia, *s.f.* van, vanguard (anche *fig.*): *artisti, letteratura d'—*, vanguard (o advanced) artists, literature; *essere all'—*, to be in the van: *è all'— della moda*, she is in the van of fashion.

avanía, *s.f.* **1.** (*st.*) avania **2.** (*sopruso*) abuse of authority; bullying; intimidation.

avannòtto, *s.m.* (*ittiol.*) fry.

avanscopèrta, *s.f.* (*mil.*) scouting party: *andare in —*, to reconnoitre (o to make a reconnaissance o to scout).

avanspettàcolo, *s.m.* (*teat.*) introductory variety turn.

avànti, *av.* **1.** (*tempo*) **before**; **forward**: *d'ora in —*, from now forward ‖ *il tuo orologio è — di dieci minuti*, your watch is ten minutes fast ‖ *essere — in un lavoro*, to be well ahead with (o to have made good progress in) one's work ‖ *essere — negli anni*, to be elderly (o to be well on in years) **2.** (*spazio*) **forward**: *andare —*, to move forward (o to proceed); *fare due passi —*, to advance two steps; *farsi —*, to step forward; *fig.* to push oneself forward; *piegarsi in —*, to lean forward ‖ *—!*, (*entrate!*) come in!; (*andate avanti!*) go ahead!; (*mil.*) forward! ‖ *— a tutto vapore*, (*mar.*) full steam ahead ‖ *numeri dispari tre passi —*, odd numbers three paces to the front ‖ *tirare —*, to run along: *riusciamo appena appena a tirare —*, we just manage to run along ‖ *— che*, *l.cong.* **before**; **rather than** (do): *— che rivolgermi a lui voglio tentare ogni altro mezzo*, before applying (o rather than apply) to him I want to try all other means ‖ *prep.* **1.** (*tempo*) **before**: *— alla chiusura*, before closing time; *— Cristo*, before Christ (*abbr.* B.C.); *venire — mezzogiorno*, to come before lunchtime **2.** (*spazio*) **before**, **in the presence of**, **in front of**: *— all'uscio*, before the door; *guardate — a voi*, look in front of you.

avantièri, *av.* the day before yesterday.

avantrèno, *s.m.* **1.** (*artigl.*) limber **2.** (*aut.*) forecarriage.

avanzaménto, *s.m.* **1.** advancing, putting forward **2.** (*progresso*) advancement, advance, progress **3.** (*promozione*) promotion.

avanzàre, *v.t.* **1.** to advance; *fig.* to put forward, to put forth: *— un piede*, to put one foot forward; *— pretese*, to lay claims (o to claim); *— una proposta, una teoria*, to put forward a proposal, a theory **2.** (*superare*) to surpass; to exceed: *egli mi avanzava di una testa*, he was a head taller than I **3.** (*promuovere*) to promote: *egli fu avanzato dal suo principale*, he was promoted by his boss **4.** (*essere creditore di*) to be creditor for (sthg.): *avanzo mille lire da mio fratello*, my brother owes me one thousand liras; *— diecimila lire da qlcu.*, to be s.o.'s creditor for ten thousand liras **5.** (*risparmiare*) to set money by, to save money: *ho avanzato ql.co. per la vecchiaia*, I have saved some money for my old age ‖ *v.i.* **1.** to move forward, to go forward, to go on, to proceed, to advance: *avanzammo nel bosco*, we advanced into the wood; *non potevamo —*, we couldn't proceed (o go farther); *— a grandi passi*, to stride forward ‖ *il vostro lavoro avanza assai*, your work is going forward ‖ *— negli anni*, to go (o to get) on in years (o to grow old) ‖ *fare — le truppe*, to advance the troops (o to move the troops forward) **2.** (*essere d'avanzo*) to be left: *quando avrò pagato tutti i debiti, non mi avanzerà nulla*, when

I have paid all my debts there will be nothing left; *avanzarono due pagnotte*, two loaves were left over ‖ **avanzàrsi**, *v.r.* (*farsi innanzi, inoltrarsi*) to get on, to advance: *l'estate si avanza*, summer is coming; *una lingua di terra si avanza nel mare*, a strip of land runs out into the sea; *il nemico si avanza*, the enemy are advancing.

avanzàta, *s.f.* (*mil.*) advance.

avanzatíccio, *s.m.* remnant, scrap.

avanzàto, *ag.* advanced: *— negli anni*, elderly (o advanced in years); *ad un'ora avanzata della notte*, at a late hour of (o in) the night (o late in the night); *in età avanzata*, well on in years; *posizione avanzata*, (*mil.*) advanced post; *teorie avanzate*, advanced theories.

avànzo, *s.m.* **1.** remnant, remainder, residue; scrap: *— di cibo*, remnant of food; *— di stoffa*, scrap of cloth; *divisione senza —*, division with no remainder ‖ *— di cassa*, (*comm.*) cash on hand ‖ *— galera*, gallows-bird (o jail-bird) ‖ *— utili indivisi*, (*comm.*) unpaid profit brought forward **2.** *pl.* remains, ruins: *avanzi di un tempio*, remains of a temple **3.** *d'—*, more than enough; even too much: *ne ho d'—*, I have quite enough.

avanzúme, *s.m.* scraps (*pl.*); offal; garbage.

avaràccio, *s.m.* miser, mean fellow.

avaraménte, *av.* avariciously, stingily, niggardly.

avaría, *s.f.* **1.** (*mar.*) damage: *la merce ha sofferto una grave —*, the goods have been seriously damaged **2.** (*comm.*) average: *— generale*, general average; *— semplice*, particular average; *liquidatore d'—*, average adjuster; *indennizzare un'—*, to make good an average.

avariàre, *v.t.* (*mar.*) to cause damage to (sthg.), to damage.

avariàto, *ag.* **1.** (*mar.*) damaged **2.** (*marcio*) spoiled, decayed, rotten.

avarízia, *s.f.* avarice; stinginess, niggardliness.

avàro, *ag.* avaricious; stingy, niggardly; tight-fisted ‖ *s.m.* miser; niggard.

àve, *inter.* hail!, welcome!.

Àve, *s.f.* (*preghiera*) Hail Mary ‖ *in men di un'—*, in a twinkling of an eye (o in no time).

avellàna, *s.f.* (*bot.*) filbert; hazel-nut.

avèllo, *s.m.* sepulchre, tomb, grave.

avemaría, avemmaría, *s.f.* **1.** (*preghiera*) Hail Mary: *dieci avemmarie*, ten Hail-Marys; *quando suona l'—*, when the ave-bell rings **2.** (*grano del rosario*) ave.

avéna, *s.f.* **1.** oats (*pl.*) **2.** (*zampogna*) oat.

avére, *v.t.* **1.** (*in funzione ausiliaria con i verbi transitivi e molti intransitivi*) **to have**: *il cane ha abbaiato tutta notte*, the dog has barked all the night long; *ho letto il tuo libro*, I have read that book of yours **2.** (*in senso generale*) **to have**: *egli ha molti amici*, he has many friends; *ha gli occhi azzurri*, he has blue eyes; *ha spesso il raffreddore*, she often has colds; *— il diritto di fare ql.co.*, to have a (o the) right to do sthg. (o to have the right of doing sthg.) ‖ *— a cuore*, to have at heart ‖ *— da fare, a che fare con qlcu., ql.co.*, to have sthg. to do with s.o., sthg. ‖ *avercela con qlcu.*, to have a grudge against s.o. (o to be angry with s.o.) **3.** (*possedere*) **to own**, **to possess**, **to have** (**got**): *aveva una grande tenuta*, he had (o owned) a big estate **4.** (*ottenere*) **to get**, **to obtain**: *ha avuto un buon impiego*, he has got a good job; *vedrò se posso averlo*, I'll see if I can get it; *— ql.co. a poco prezzo*, to get sthg. cheap **5.** (*indossare*) **to have on**, **to wear**: *aveva (indosso) il cappotto nuovo*, he had on (o was wearing) his new coat **6.** *— da*, (*dovere*) **to have to** (do sthg.): *ho da andar via presto*, I have to leave early **7.** (**Fraseologia**): *che hai?*, what's the matter with you?; *«Quanti anni hai?»*, *«Ho sedici anni»*, "How old are you?", "I am sixteen (years old)"; *— bisogno di qlcu., ql.co.*, to need s.o., sthg.; *— caldo*, to be (o to feel) hot; *— compassione di*, to be (o to feel) sorry for; *— da fare*, to be busy; *— fame, freddo*, to be hungry, cold; — *in animo di fare ql.co.*, to intend to do sthg.; — *in odio*, to hate; — *in pregio*, to esteem; — *per regola*, to make it a rule; — *probabilità di*, to stand a chance of; — *qlcu. al proprio servizio*, to keep s.o. at one's service; — *ragione, torto*, to be right, wrong; — *sentore di ql.co.*, to get wind of sthg.; — *sete*, to be thirsty; — *sonno*, to be sleepy; — *vergogna*, to be (*o* to feel) ashamed; *aversela a male*, to take offence.

avére, *s.m.* **1.** (*patrimonio*) property, possession; estate; riches (*pl.*) **2.** (*comm.*) credit: *a vostro* —, to your credit; *dare e* —, debit and credit; *il vostro* — *ammonta a quaranta sterline*, your credit amounts to forty pounds; *quant'è il vostro* —?, how much do I owe you?.

avèrla, *s.f.* (*ornit.*) shrike.

avernàle, avèrno, *ag.* avernal; infernal.

Avèrno, *no.pr.m.* (*geog. mit.*) Avernus.

Averroè, *no.pr.m.* (*st. fil.*) Averroes.

aviàrio, *s.m.* aviary.

aviatóre, *s.m.* aviator, airman (*pl.* airmen), flyer; pilot.

aviatòrio, *ag.* aircraft (*attributivo*), aviation (*attributivo*).

aviatríce, *s.f.* airwoman (*pl.* airwomen), aviatress, aviatrix.

aviazióne, *s.f.* aviation; (*arma*) Air Force: *campo d'* —, airfield; *scuola d'* —, aviation school; *ufficiale d'* —, flying officer.

avicoltóre, *s.m.* aviculturist, bird-fancier.

avicoltúra, *s.f.* aviculture; bird-rearing; bird-fancying.

avicultóre, *s.m.* aviculturist, bird-fancier.

avidaménte, *av.* avidly; greedily; eagerly.

avidità, *s.f.* avidity; (*ingordigia*) greed; (*brama*) eagerness (for sthg., to do).

àvido, *ag.* avid; (*ingordo*) greedy; (*desideroso*) eager (for sthg., to do): — *d'imparare*, eager to learn.

avière, *s.m.* (*mil.*) airman (*pl.* airmen).

avifàuna, *s.f.* avifauna.

Avignóne, *no.pr. f.* (*geog.*) Avignon.

aviogètto, *s.m.* (*aer.*) jet, jet-plane, jet-aircraft.

aviolínea, *s.f.* (*aer.*) air line, airway.

avioràzzo, *s.m.* (*aer.*) rocket plane.

avioriméssa, *s.f.* (*aer.*) hangar; airplane shed.

aviotrasportàto, *ag.* (*aer.*) air-borne.

avitaminósi, *s.f.* (*patol.*) avitaminosis.

avíto, *ag.* ancestral.

àvo, *s.m.* **1.** grandfather **2.** *pl.* ancestors, forefathers, forebears.

avocàre, *v.t.* (*dir.*) to remove (a law suit) to a higher court ‖ — *a sè*, to take it upon oneself.

avocazióne, *s.f.* (*dir.*) removing to a higher court.

àvola, *s.f.* grandmother.

àvolo, *s.m.* **1.** grandfather **2.** *pl.* ancestors, forefathers, forebears.

avòrio, *s.m.* ivory: — *vegetale*, vegetable ivory; *collezione di avori*, a collection of ivories; *mercante d'* —, ivory dealer ‖ — *nero*, (*gli schiavi*) black ivory ‖ *Costa d'Avorio*, (*geog.*) Ivory Coast.

avúlso, *ag.* (*sradicato*) uprooted; (*strappato via*) torn away, torn off.

avúta, *s.f.* (*vincita al giuoco*) win: *tre avute*, three wins.

avvalérsi, *v.r.* to avail oneself.

avvallaménto, *s.m.* sinking; depression, hollow.

avvallàre, *v.t.* to lower, to turn downwards ‖ *v.i.*, **avvallàrsi,** *v.r.* to sink.

avvallatúra, *s.f.* depression, hollow.

avvaloraménto, *s.m.* strengthening.

avvaloràre, *v.t.* **1.** to give value to (sthg.); (*accrescere il valore di*) to enhance **2.** (*rafforzare*) to strengthen ‖ **avvaloràrsi,** *v.r.* to increase in strength; to become stronger.

avvampaménto, *s.m.* flare; flash.

avvampànte, *ag.* flaring up.

avvampàre, *v.i.* to flare up, to blaze up (anche *fig.*): *avvampò di collera*, he flared up in a temper ‖ *v.t.* (*ardere*) to burn; to scorch.

avvantaggiàre, *v.t.* to advantage; to further; to improve, to better ‖ **avvantaggiàrsi,** *v.r.* to draw advantage from (sthg.), to improve, to profit by (sthg.): *la mia salute se ne è avvantaggiata*, my health has improved.

avvantaggiàto, *ag.* over-measure (*attributivo*); improved: *un miglio* —, a good mile.

avvedérsi, *v.r.* to perceive (s.o., sthg.), to notice (s.o., sthg.); to become aware: *mi ferì senza avvedersene*, he hurt my feelings unwillingly; *si avvide di ciò*, he became aware of it (*o* noticed it *o* perceived it).

avvediménto, *s.m.* wisdom; sagacity; shrewdness.

avvedutaménte, *av.* **1.** (*accortamente*) prudently, shrewdly; cannily; cleverly; (*sagacemente*) sagaciously **2.** (*intenzionalmente*) purposely.

avvedutézza, *s.f.* (*accortezza*) shrewdness, canniness, cleverness; (*sagacia*) sagacity; (*prudenza*) wariness.

avvedúto, *ag.* (*accorto*) shrewd, canny; (*sagace*) sagacious; (*prudente*) wary, cautious.

avvelenaménto, *s.m.* poisoning.

avvelenàre, *v.t.* **1.** to poison **2.** (*amareggiare*) to poison, to embitter: *gli avvelenò l'esistenza*, she poisoned his life **3.** (*corrompere*) to empoison; *fig.* to corrupt ‖ **avvelenàrsi,** *v.r.* to poison oneself.

avvelenàto, *ag.* **1.** poisoned: *morire* —, to die from poisoning **2.** (*velenoso*) poisonous **3.** (*amareggiato*) embittered **4.** (*corrotto*) empoisoned.

avvelenatóre, *s.m.*, **avvelenatríce,** *s.f.* poisoner.

avveleníre, *v.t.* (*rar.*) to poison.

avvenènte, *ag.* charming; pretty; lovely.

avvenenteménte, *av.* charmingly; pleasantly.

avvenènza, *s.f.* charm; loveliness; grace.

avvenévole, *ag.* (*rar.*) charming; pretty; lovely.

avvenevolézza, *s.f.* (*rar.*) charm; loveliness; grace.

avvenevolménte, *av.* (*rar.*) charmingly; pleasantly.

avveniménto, *s.m.* **1.** event; occurrence: *avvenimenti di grande importanza*, pregnant events; *un romanzo pieno di avvenimenti*, a novel full of incident(s) **2.** (*al trono*) accession.

avveníre[1], *s.m.* future ‖ *in* —, in future ‖ *giovane di grande* —, youth of great promise.

avveníre[2], *v.i.* to happen, to occur, to come to pass; (*aver luogo*) to take place: *checchè avvenga*, whatever may happen; *come avvenne che lo incontraste?*, how did you happen to meet him? ‖ **avvenírsi,** *v.r.* **1.** (*addirsi*) to suit (s.o.), to become (s.o.) **2.** (*imbattersi*) to happen to meet (s.o.), to come across (s.o.).

avventàre, *v.t.* **1.** to hurl **2.** *fig.* to pour out ‖ *v.i.* (*essere troppo vistoso*) to be gaudy, to be showy: *quel rosso avventa troppo*, that red is too gaudy (*o* showy) ‖ **avventàrsi,** *v.r.* to throw oneself, to rush; to hurl oneself; (*dall'alto*) to swoop down: *l'aquila si avventò sulla sua preda*, the eagle swooped down on its prey; *il gatto s'avventò contro il ragazzo*, the cat rushed upon the boy; *si avventò sul nemico*, he hurled himself at the enemy.

avventàggine, *V.* avventatézza.

avventataménte, *av.* rashly, inconsiderately.

avventatézza, *s.f.* rashness, recklessness, inconsiderateness.

avventàto, *ag.* rash, reckless, inconsiderate: *giudizio* —, rash judgment; *parole avventate*, rash words.

avventísmo, *s.m.* (*st. relig.*) Adventism.

avventísta, *s.m.* (*st. relig.*) Adventist.

avventízio, *ag.* **1.** (*temporaneo*) temporary **2.** (*dir.*) adventitious: *beni avventizi*, adventitious property ‖ *s.m.* temporary clerk; day-labourer.

avvènto, *s.m.* **1.** (*eccl.*) Advent **2.** (*arrivo*) coming; arrival: *l'* — *di una nuova era*, the coming (*o* the beginning) of a new age **3.** (*assunzione al trono*) accession.

avventóre, *s.m.* customer; patron.

avventúra, *s.f.* **1.** adventure **2.** (*caso*) chance: *per* —, perhaps (*o arc.* peradventure) ‖ (*per caso*) by chance.

avventuràre, *v.t.*, **avventuràrsi,** *v.r.* to venture: *avventurò la vita*, he ventured his life; *ci avventurammo in un viaggio pericoloso*, we ventured on a perilous journey.

avventuraté, ** *av.* **1. (*fortunatamente*) luckily, fortunately **2.** (*alla ventura*) at random.

avventuràto, *ag.* **1.** lucky, fortunate **2.** (*arrischiato*) risky.

avventurièra, *s.f.* adventuress.

avventurière, avventurièro, *s.m.* adventurer.

avventurína, *s.f.* (*min.*) aventurine.

avventurosaménte, *av.* **1.** adventurously **2.** (*felicemente*) prosperously.

avventuróso, *ag.* **1.** adventurous, venturesome, enterprising **2.** (*fortunato*) lucky, fortunate: *giorno —,* auspicious day.

avveraménto, *s.m.* fulfillment, accomplishment, realization.

avveràre, *v.t.* **1.** to fulfil, to realize **2.** (*verificare*) to verify ‖ **avveràrsi,** *v.r.* to come true, to be realized; to prove true: *i miei sogni si sono avverati,* my dreams have come true; *la sua profezia si avverò presto,* his prophecy soon proved true.

avverbiàle, *ag.* (*gram.*) adverbial.

avverbialménte, *av.* (*gram.*) adverbially.

avvèrbio, *s.m.* (*gram.*) adverb.

avverdíre, *v.t.* to make green, to green; (*dipingere in verde*) to paint green ‖ *v.i.* to turn green, to green.

avversaménte, *av.* adversely.

avversàre, *v.t.* (*opporsi a*) to oppose; (*ostacolare*) to thwart, to cross, to hinder.

avversàrio, *ag.* contrary, opposing; (*ostile*) hostile ‖ *s.m.* opponent, adversary, antagonist; (*nemico*) enemy.

avversatívo, *ag.* (*gram.*) adversative.

avversatóre, *s.m.* opposer; (*avversario*) opponent, antagonist.

avversióne, *s.f.* aversion, dislike, antipathy; (*ripugnanza*) loathing: *alcuni ragazzi provano — per il latte,* some boys have a loathing for milk; *sentire una grande — per qlcu.,* to feel a strong dislike for s.o.

avversità, *s.f.* adversity; misfortune.

avvèrso, *ag.* **1.** (*sfavorevole*) adverse, unfavourable; (*ostile*) adverse, hostile, contrary: *— al governo democratico,* adverse (*o* hostile) to a democratic government; *circostanze avverse,* adverse (*o* unfavourable) circumstances ‖ *la parte avversa,* (*dir.*) the opposing party **2.** (*che sente avversione*) averse: *essere — a qualsiasi novità,* to be averse to any novelty ‖ *prep.* (*rar.*) against: *reclamare — una decisione,* to claim against a decision.

avvertènza, *s.f.* **1.** (*consideratezza*) considerateness **2.** (*attenzione, cura*) attention, care: *avere l'— di fare qlco.,* to take care to do sthg. **3.** (*avvertimento*) warning **4.** (*osservazione*) notice, remark **5.** (*prefazione*) preface, introduction, foreword.

avvertíbile, *ag.* noticeable, perceptible.

avvertiménto, *s.m.* **1.** (*informazione*) notice **2.** (*ammonimento*) warning, admonition.

avvertíre, *v.t.* **1.** (*avvisare, informare*) to inform, to let (s.o.) know **2.** (*mettere in guardia*) to advise **3.** to warn, to caution **3.** (*percepire, osservare*) to notice, to observe: *— un dolore,* to feel a pain ‖ *v.i.* (*avere l'avvertenza*) to take heed, to take care.

avvertitaménte, *av.* advisedly, thoughtfully.

avvertíto, *ag.* (*avveduto*) shrewd, (*sagace*) sagacious.

avvezzàre, *v.t.* to accustom: *è un bambino male avvezzato,* he is a spoilt child; *— qlcu. a fare qlco.,* to accustom s.o. to do (*o* to doing) sthg. ‖ **avvezzàrsi,** *v.r.* to accustom oneself, to get accustomed.

avvézzo, *ag.* accustomed; used: *— a fare qlco.,* accustomed to do (*o* to doing) sthg.

avviaménto, *s.m.* **1.** starting, start, beginning; (*introduzione*) introduction ‖ *scuola d'— al lavoro,* vocational training school; *scuola d'— commerciale,* commercial school; *scuola d'— industriale,* technical school **2.** (*comm.*) goodwill **3.** (*mec.*) (*azione*) starting, setting in motion; (*meccanismo*) starting device: *— automatico,* self-starting; *— elettrico,* electric starting; *manovella d'—,* starting handle.

avviàre, *v.t.* **1.** to start, to set in motion; to set going; to set on foot: *— una macchina, un motore,* to start (up) a machine, an engine **2.** (*iniziare*) to begin, to start; *fig.* to initiate, to start: *— una conversazione,* to start a conversation; *— qlcu. a un mestiere,* to start s.o. to a trade; *— qlcu. negli affari,* to start s.o. in business; *— trattative,* to start dealings ‖ *— il fuoco,* to start (*o* to kindle) a fire ‖ *— la maglia,* to cast on stitches ‖ **avviàrsi,** *v.r.* to set out; to draw toward (sthg.): *la commedia si avvia alla fine,* the comedy draws toward the end; *— a scuola,* to set out for school.

avviàto, *ag.* **1.** initiated: *essere — in una scienza, in un'arte,* to be initiated in a science, in an art; *essere bene —,* to be on the straight path; *essere male —,* to be on the wrong path (*o* to be going astray) **2.** (*comm.*) introduced, thriving: *azienda avviata,* thriving business; *quel commerciante è molto bene —,* that business man is doing extremely well.

avviatóre, *s.m.* starter: *— a combustione interna,* internal-combustion starter; *— automatico,* self-starter; *— elettrico,* electric starter.

avviatúra, *s.f.* **1.** (*avviamento*) start, starting **2.** (*di lavoro a maglia*) first row of stitches **3.** (*di fuoco*) kindling.

avvicendaménto, *s.m.* **1.** alternation **2.** (*agr.*) rotation, course, shift (of crops).

avvicendàre, *v.t.* **1.** to alternate **2.** (*agr.*) to rotate, to vary (crops) ‖ **avvicendàrsi,** *v.r.* to alternate; to follow each other (one another) in turns.

avvicinaménto, *s.m.* approaching, approach.

avvicinàre, *v.t.* **1.** to approach, to draw near(er), to bring near(er): *avvicina la sedia,* draw up your chair; *i mezzi di comunicazione avvicinano i popoli,* means of communication draw peoples together; *— ql.co. a qlcu., a ql.co.,* to bring (*o* to draw) sthg. near (*o* to) s.o., sthg. **2.** (*frequentare*): *— una persona,* to be on familiar terms with a person; *donna difficile da —,* woman of difficult access (*o* approach) ‖ **avvicinàrsi,** *v.r.* **1.** to approach (s.o.), to get near (s.o., sthg): *la fine si avvicina,* the end is approaching; *la notte si avvicina,* night is drawing on; *l'ora si avvicina,* the hour is drawing near (*o* is at hand); *quell'uomo mi si avvicina,* that man approaches me (*o* comes near me) ‖ *— al vero,* to make a good guess **2.** (*somigliare*) to be similar: *l'oro si avvicina all'ottone per il colore,* gold is similar in colour to brass.

avvilíménto, *s.m.* **1.** (*scoraggiamento*) dejection **2.** (*degradazione*) debasement **3.** (*umiliazione*) humiliation.

avvilíre, *v.t.* **1.** (*scoraggiare*) to dishearten, to dispirit **2.** (*degradare*) to degrade, to abase, to lower **3.** (*umiliare*) to humiliate **4.** (*svilire, deprezzare*) to depreciate, to lower, to bring down ‖ **avvilírsi,** *v.r.* **1.** (*scoraggiarsi*) to get disheartened, to lose heart: *non ti avvilire al primo insuccesso,* don't be disheartened by a single failure **2.** (*degradarsi*) to degrade oneself, to lower oneself **3.** (*umiliarsi*) to humble oneself, to mortify oneself.

avvilíto, *ag.* **1.** (*scoraggiato*) downcast, dispirited, dejected, discouraged **2.** (*degradato*) degraded, abased **3.** (*umiliato*) humbled, mortified.

avviluppaménto, *s.m.* **1.** (*avvolgimento*) envelopment, wrapping up **2.** (*intrico*) entanglement **3.** (*confusione*) jumble.

avviluppàre, *v.t.* **1.** (*avvolgere*) to envelop, to wrap up **2.** (*aggrovigliare*) to entangle **3.** (*imbrogliare*) to dupe, to cheat ‖ **avviluppàrsi,** *v.r.* **1.** (*avvolgersi*) to wrap oneself up **2.** (*aggrovigliarsi*) to get entangled.

avviluppataménte, *av.* confusedly.

avvinàre, *v.t.* to season (casks) ‖ *— un bicchiere,* to rinse a glass with wine.

avvinàto, *ag.* **1.** ruby **2.** (*avvinazzato*) tipsy.

avvinazzàre, *v.t.* to make drunk ‖ **avvinazzàrsi,** *v.r.* to get drunk, to become tipsy.

avvinazzàto, *ag.* tipsy.

avvincènte, *ag.* engaging, fascinating, charming: *modi avvincenti,* engaging manners; *un racconto —,* an exciting story (*o fam.* a thriller); *un sorriso —,* a winning smile.

avvíncere, *v.t.* **1.** to bind, to tie up **2.** (*attrarre*) to attract, to fascinate, to charm, to enthral: *essere avvinto dalla bellezza di una donna,* to be enthralled by a woman's beauty.

avvincigliàre, *v.t.* to bind tightly.

avvinghiàre, *v.t.* to clutch, to clinch ‖ **avvinghiàrsi,** *v.r.* to cling: *mi si avvinghiò,* she clung to me.

avvínto, *ag.* **1.** bound, tied up **2.** (*attratto*) fascinated, charmed.

avvío, *s.m.* start: *dare, prendere l'—,* to start, to start off.

avvisàglia, *s.f.* **1.** (*scaramuccia*) skirmish **2.** (*primo segno*) foreshadowing.

avvisàre, *v.t.* **1.** to inform, to let know: *ci pregiamo di avvisarvi,* (*comm.*) we beg to inform you (*o* to let you know); *non fummo avvisati a tempo debito,* we were not advised (*o* informed) in due time **2.** (*dir.*) to give notice to (s.o.), to send notice to (s.o.) **3.** (*mettere in guardia*) to warn: *avreste dovuto avvisarlo del pericolo,* you ought to have warned him of the danger ‖ *v.i.* (*giudicare*) to judge; (*pensare*) to think.

avvisataménte, *av.* judiciously; cautiously.

avvisàto, *ag.* judicious, well-advised; cautious, prudent ‖ *uomo —, mezzo salvato, prov.* forewarned is forearmed.

avvisatóre, *s.m.* **1.** messenger; (*teat.*) call-boy **2.** (*strumento d'allarme*) warning signal, call-bell, alarm.

avvíso, *s.m.* **1.** (*annunzio*) announcement, notice, advice: *— al lettore,* foreword (*o* prefatory note); *— al pubblico,* notice to the public; *— di consegna,* (*comm.*) delivery note; *— di incasso,* notice of collection; *— di pagamento,* notice (*o* advice) of payment; *— di spedizione,* (*comm.*) shipping notice (*o* notice of dispatch); *— pubblicitario,* (*sui giornali*) advertisement; *quando sua madre morì, mise un —sul giornale,* when his mother died, he put an obituary in the newspaper; *dare —,* to give notice: *dare — formale a qlcu.,* (*dir.*) to serve a notice on s.o. ‖ *come d'—,* as advised **2.** (*consiglio*) warning: *ciò ti sia d'—,* let this be a warning to you **3.** (*manifesto*) poster, placard **4.** (*opinione*) opinion, judgment: *a mio —,* in my opinion; *sono dello stesso —,* I am of the same opinion (*o* mind); *mutare d'—,* to change one's mind **5.** *star sull'—,* to be watchful.

avvíso-scòrta, *s.m.* **1.** (*mec.*) screwing **2.** (*mar. mil.*) escort vessel.

avvistàre, *v.t.* to sight, to get sight of (s.o., sthg.): *— una nave, la terra,* to sight a ship, land.

avvistàto, *ag.* (*avveduto*) shrewd, judicious.

avvitaménto, *s.m.* (*aer.*) spin.

avvitàre, *v.t.* (*mec.*) to screw (down) ‖ *v.i.* (*aer.*) to spin, to corkscrew ‖ **avvitàrsi,** *v.r.* (*aer.*) to fall in a spin.

avvitatríce, *s.f.* (*mec.*) screwer.

avviticchiaménto, *s.m.* twining, twisting, interlacing.

avviticchiàre, *v.t.* to twine ‖ **avviticchiàrsi,** *v.r.* to twine (round s.o., sthg.), to twist (round s.o., sthg.), to wind (round s.o., sthg.); *fig.* to cling: *l'edera si avviticchia al tronco,* ivy twines round the trunk.

avviticciàre, *v.t.* to twine, to wind ‖ **avviticciàrsi,** *v.r.* to twist (round sthg.).

avvitíre, *v.t.* (*agr.*) to set (a piece of land) with vines.

avvivaménto, *s.m.* enlivening, animation, vivification.

avvivàre, *v.t.* **1.** to enliven, to quicken, to animate, to vivify; (*di colori*) to brighten **2.** (*oreficeria*) to burnish ‖ **avvivàrsi,** *v.r.* to be enlivened; (*diventare animato*) to become lively; (*di fuoco*) to rekindle (anche *fig.*).

avvivatóio, *s.m.* burnisher.

avvivatóre, *ag.* vivifying, enlivening ‖ *s.m.,* **avvivatríce,** *s.f.* enlivener, animator.

avvizziménto, *s.m.* withering; fading.

avvizzíre, *v.i.* **1.** to wither; (*perdere freschezza e colori*) to fade **2.** (*languire*) to droop, to wilt.

avvizzíto, *ag.* withered; faded.

avvocàta, *s.f.* (*patrona*) protectress ‖ *Avvocata,* (*la Madonna*) Mediatrix.

avvocatésco, *ag.* (*spreg.*) pettifoggish.

avvocatéssa, *s.f.* **1.** lady lawyer **2.** (*iron.*) talkative woman.

avvocàto, *s.m.* **1.** (*genericamente*) lawyer; counsel; (*amer.*) counsellor: *rivolgersi ad un —,* to apply to a lawyer **2.** (*in Gran Bretagna*) solicitor; (*arc. pop.*) attorney-at-law (*con facoltà di discutere cause presso le Corti di grado inferiore*); barrister (*con facoltà di discutere cause presso le Corti di grado superiore*) ‖ *Albo degli Avvocati,* Law-List ‖ *Ordine degli Avvocati,* Law Society **3.** (*negli Stati Uniti*) attorney(-at-law) **4.** (*consulente legale*) legal adviser **5.** (*difensore*) counsel for the defence, defending counsel **6.** *fig.* advocate, pleader, intercessor ‖ *— del diavolo,* devil's advocate; *— delle cause perse,* defender of lost causes.

avvocatúra, *s.f.* legal profession; (*funzione di avvocato*) advocacy: *esercitare l'—,* to carry on legal practice.

avvòlgere, *v.t.* **1.** to wrap (up): *— ql.co. nella carta, in un panno,* to wrap (up) sthg. in paper, in a cloth **2.** (*arrotolare*) to wind; to roll up: *— filo, spago,* to wind thread, string; *— un tappeto,* to roll up a carpet **3.** *fig.* to wrap: *egli avvolge i suoi discorsi nel mistero,* he wraps his speeches in mystery; *la notte ci avvolse,* darkness closed in upon us ‖ *— con uno sguardo,* to sweep one's eyes over s.o. ‖ **avvòlgersi,** *v.r.* **1.** (*avvilupparsi*) to wrap oneself up **2.** (*attorcigliarsi*) to twine (round sthg.), to wind (round sthg.).

avvolgíbile, *ag.* that may be rolled up, that may be twined round ‖ *s.m.* (*rolling*) blind; (*saracinesca*) (*rolling*) shutter.

avvolgiménto, *s.m.* **1.** winding, rolling up; (*di pacchi*) wrapping up **2.** (*elett.*) winding **3.** (*di molla*) coiling.

avvolgitóre, *s.m.,* **avvolgitríce,** *s.f.* **1.** (*ind. tessile*) lap-machine; (*di lana*) beamer **2.** (*cine.*) take up.

avvoltàre, *V.* **avvòlgere.**

avvolticchiàre, *v.t.* **1.** to wind round and round **2.** (*ingarbugliare*) to entangle ‖ **avvolticchiàrsi,** *v.r.* (*attorcigliarsi*) to twine (round sthg.).

avvòlto, *ag.* **1.** wrapped (up) (anche *fig.*): *l'affare era — nel più fitto mistero,* the affair was wrapped in the thickest mystery **2.** (*arrotolato*) rolled (up); (*piegato*) folded (up).

avvoltóio, *s.m.* vulture (anche *fig.*).

avvoltolàre, *v.t.* **1.** to wrap roughly **2.** (*arrotolare*) to roll up ‖ **avvoltolàrsi,** *v.r.* to roll up; to wallow: *— nel fango,* to wallow in the mud.

azalèa, *s.f.* (*bot.*) azalea.

aziènda, *s.f.* business, firm, concern; shop; factory: *— agricola,* farm; *— industriale,* manufacturing concern; *— privata,* private undertaking.

aziendàle, *ag.* firm (*attributivo*); business (*attributivo*), concern (*attributivo*): *spaccio —,* works canteen.

àzimut, *s.m.* (*astr.*) azimuth.

azimutàle, *ag.* (*astr.*) azimuthal.

azionaménto, *s.m.* working, actuation: *dispositivo d'—,* (*mec.*) driving gear.

azionàre, *v.t.* to set in action, to set in motion, to operate, to drive, to work, to run, to set going: *— i freni,* to work (*o* to put on) the brakes; *— una leva,* to move a lever; *— una macchina,* to set a machine going: *essere azionato da una molla,* to be moved by a spring; *essere azionato dal vapore,* to be steam-driven.

azionàrio, *ag.* (*comm.*) share (*attributivo*): *capitale —,* share capital (*o* capital stock).

azióne, *s.f.* **1.** action, act: *mettere in —,* to put in action: *mettere in — un principio,* to put a principle in action (*o* to carry a principle into action) **2.** (*operazione*) action, deed: *fare una buona —,* to do a good action (*o* a good deed) **3.** (*efficacia*) action, fact; (*scient.*) action, effect: *— dell'acqua,* agency (*o* effect) of water; *— di un acido,* action of an acid; *— e reazione,* action and reaction; *— reciproca,* interaction **4.** (*gesto*) gesture **5.** (*prontezza ed assiduità nell'operare*) action: *uomo d'*—, man of action **6.** (*dir.*) action; lawsuit; trial: — *di risarcimento*, action for damages; — *penale*, penal action (o criminal prosecution); — *pubblica*, prosecution; *intentare un'*— *contro qlcu.*, to bring an action against s.o. **7.** (*teat.*) action; (*di commedia, romanzo*) plot: *scena che ritarda l'*—, scene that delays the action **8.** (*mil.*) action, deed, exploit, fight, engagement: *un'*—*brillante*, a brilliant feat of arms **9.** (*comm.*) share: — *al portatore*, transferable share (o share payable to bearer); — *differita*, deferred share; *azioni a matrice*, unissued shares (o *amer.* stock); —*nominativa*, registered share; — *ordinaria*, common (o ordinary) share; — *preferenziale*, preference share; — *interamente pagata*, paid up share; *sottoscrivere un'*—, to subscribe (o to pay up fully) a share.

azionísta, *s.m.* (*comm.*) shareholder; (*amer.*) stockholder: *l'assemblea degli azionisti*, the shareholders' meeting.

azòico, *ag.* (*geol.*) azoic.

azotàre, *v.t.* (*chim.*) to azotize.

azotàto, *ag.* (*chim.*) azotic, nitric, nitrogenous.

azotemía, *s.f.* (*patol.*) azotemia.

azòtico, *ag.* (*chim.*) azotic.

azòto, *s.m.* (*chim.*) azote, nitrogen.

azoturía, *s.f.* (*patol.*) azoturia.

aztèco, *ag.* Aztec, Aztecan ‖ *s.m.* Aztec.

àzza, *s.f.* battle-axe.

azzampàto, *ag.* with legs: *bene* —, with well-shaped legs.

azzannaménto, *s.m.* bite.

azzannàre, *v.t.* to fang; (*mordere*) to bite.

azzannatúra, *s.f.* bite.

azzardàre, *v.t.* to hazard, to risk, to venture: — *una supposizione*, to venture a guess ‖ **azzardàrsi**, *v.r.* to venture, to dare: *non mi azzarderei ad uscire con questo tempo*, I wouldn't risk going out in such weather.

azzardàto, *ag.* risky, hazardous; bold, daring; (*precipitoso*) rash: *una risposta azzardata*, a rash answer.

azzàrdo, *s.m.* hazard, risk; peril; danger: *giocatore d'*—, gambler; *giuoco d'*—, game of chance; *mettersi a un* —, to venture (o to run a risk).

azzardóso, *ag.* risky, hazardous; (*di persona*) bold.

azzeccagarbúgli, *s.m.* (*spreg.*) pettifogger; pettifogging lawyer.

azzeccàre, *v.t.* **1.** (*appioppare*) to hit, to strike: — *un colpo*, to strike a blow **2.** (*indovinare*) to guess ‖ *azzeccarla*, to hit the mark (o *fam.* to hit the nail on the head) ‖ *non azzeccarne una*, to miss every time **3.** (*riuscire*): *s'è messo a fare il sarto e l'ha azzeccata*, he set up as a tailor and did very well.

azzeruòla, *s.f.* (*bot.*) azarole.

azzeruòlo, *s.m.* (*bot.*) azarole-tree.

àzzima, *s.f.* unleavened dough.

azzimàre, *v.t.* to dress smartly, to dress up, to deck ‖ **azzimàrsi**, *v.r.* to deck oneself out.

azzimàto, *ag.* dressed up, smartly dressed.

azzimèlla, *s.f.* unleavened bread.

àzzimo, *ag.* unleavened: *pane* —, unleavened bread.

azzittàre, azzittíre, *v.t.* to silence, to hush ‖ **azzittàrsi, azzittírsi**, *v.r.* to become silent.

azzoppàre, *v.t.* to lame ‖ *v.i.*, **azzoppàrsi**, *v.r.* to become lame.

azzoppiménto, *s.m.* **1.** making lame **2.** (*divenire zoppo*) becoming lame.

Azzòrre (le), *no.pr.f.pl.* (*geog.*) the Azores.

azzuffaménto, *s.m.* scuffle, affray; fray.

azzuffàrsi, *v.r.* to come to blows; to quarrel.

azzurràto, *ag.* bluish.

azzurreggiàre, *v.i.* to be bluish, to be of a bluish colour.

azzurríccio, azzurrígno, *ag.* light blue.

azzurríno, *ag.* clear blue.

azzúrro, *ag.* blue, sky-blue, azure: — *cupo*, dark blue; *dagli occhi azzurri e dai capelli d'oro*, with blue eyes and golden hair (o blue-eyed and golden-haired) ‖ *l'arma azzurra*, (*l'Aviazione italiana*) the Italian Air Force ‖ *Principe* —, (*fam.*) Prince Charming ‖ *s.m* azure, sky-blue ‖. *l'*—, (*il cielo*) the azure (o the sky).

azzurrògnolo, *ag.* bluish.

B

b, *s.f.m.* **1.** (*seconda lettera dell'alfabeto italiano*) b (*pl.* bs, b's) ‖ — *come Bologna*, (*tel.*) b for Benjamin **2.** (*mus.*) si.
Bàal, *no.pr.m.* (*divinità fenicia*) Baal (*pl.* Baalim).
babà, *s.m.* (*cuc.*) "baba" (sponge-cake steeped in rum syrup).
babàu, *s.m.* bugbear, bogey, bugaboo.
babbàccio, *ag.* simple-minded, foolish.
babbaccióne, *s.m.* booby, simpleton.
babbalèo, babbalòcco, (*rar.*) per **babbèo**.
babbèo, *ag.* foolish, stupid ‖ *s.m.* simpleton, blockhead, fool, booby.
babbíno, *s.m.* (*fam.*) daddy.
babbióne, *s.m.* simpleton, blockhead, fool, booby.
bàbbo, *s.m.* father; (*fam.*) dad, daddy; (*amer.*) pop: —, *dove sei?*, Father, where are you? (o where are you, daddy?).
babbuàggine, *s.f.* stupidity.
babbuàsso, (*rar.*) per **babbèo**.
babbúccia, *s.f.* slipper; (*orientale*) babouche.
babbuíno, *s.m.* **1.** (*zool.*) baboon **2.** *fig.* fool, dolt.
Babèle, *no.pr.f.* (*geog. st.*) Babel ‖ *torre di* —, tower of Babel ‖ **babèle**, *s.f.* (*confusione*) babel, disorder, confusion: *è una vera* —, it is an absolute babel (o it's pandemonium).
babèlico, *ag.* **1.** pertaining to Babel **2.** (*confuso*) confused, discordant: *confusione babelica*, babel.
babilonése, *ag.s.m.* Babylonian.
Babilònia, *no.pr.f.* (*geog. st.*) (*città*) Babylon; (*impero*) Babylonia ‖ **bilabònia**, *s.f.* (*confusione*) great disorder, babel.
babilònico, *ag.* Babylonian.
babirússa, *s.m.* (*zool.*) babiroussa, babirussa.
babórdo, *s.m.* (*mar.*) port; larboard.
bacàio, *s.m.* silk-worm breeder.
bacàre, *v.i.*, **bacàrsi**, *v.r.* to get worm-eaten; (*marcire*) to go rotten, to rot.
bacaticcio, *ag.* rather maggoty; rottenish.
bacatíno, *ag.* (*di bimbo malaticcio*) sickly.
bacàto, *ag.* **1.** worm-eaten, maggoty; (*marcio*) rotten **2.** *fig.* rotten, morally corrupt.
bàcca, *s.f.* berry.
baccalà, *s.m.* **1.** stockfish, dried cod **2.** (*persona allampanata*) tall thin person, telephone pole; (*persona sciocca*) booby.
baccalaureàto, *s.m.* baccalaureate.
baccanàle, *s.m.* Bacchanal.
baccàno, *s.m.* uproar, din, hubbub.
baccànte, *s.f.* Bacchante.
baccarà[1], *s.m.* (*giuoco d'azzardo*) baccarat.
baccarà[2], *s.m.* (*cristallo*) Baccarat glass, Baccarat crystal.
baccellieràto, *s.m.* bachelorship, baccalaureate.
baccellière, *s.m.* bachelor.
baccèllo, *s.m.* **1.** (*bot.*) pod **2.** *fig.* fool, simpleton.
bacchétta, *s.f.* **1.** rod, stick; (*del direttore d'orchestra*) baton; (*di tamburo*) drumstick; (*del pittore*) maulstick: — *divinatoria*, divining rod; — *magica*, magic wand ‖ *comandare a* —, to rule with an iron hand (o to rule with a rod of iron) **2.** (*ind. tessile*) faller.
bacchettàre, *v.t.* **1.** to flog, to beat with a rod **2.** (*svendere*) to sell cheap.
bacchettàta, *s.f.* rod stroke.
bacchétto, *s.m.* **1.** short stick **2.** (*manico della frusta*) whip-handle.

bacchettóna, *s.f.*, **bacchettóne**, *s.m.* bigot.
bacchettonería, *s.f.* bigotry.
bacchiàre, *v.t.* to beat (fruit) down.
bacchiàta, *s.f.* **1.** pole stroke **2.** *V.* **batòsta 2.**
bacchiatúra, *s.f.* **1.** beating (fruit) down **2.** (*periodo*) the period of beating (fruit) down.
bàcchico, *ag.* Bacchic.
bàcchio, *s.m.* long pole.
Bàcco, *no.pr.m.* (*mit.*) Bacchus ‖ *devoto a* —, (*iron.*) devotee of Bacchus; *effetti di* —, effects of drinking ‖ *per* —!, by Jove!.
bachèca, *s.f.* show-case.
bachelite, *s.f.* (*chim. ind.*) bakelite.
bacheròzzo, bacheròzzolo, *s.m.* **1.** (*bruco*) maggot, grub; (*verme*) worm **2.** (*scarafaggio*) cockroach, bug.
bachicoltóre, *s.m.* silk-worm breeder.
bachicoltúra, *s.f.* silk-worm breeding.
baciamàno, *s.m.* **1.** hand-kissing **2.** (*bacio mandato con la mano*) kiss-blowing.
baciapíle, *s.c.* bigot.
baciapólvere, *s.m.* bigot.
baciàre, *v.t.* **1.** to kiss: — *la pantofola al papa*, to kiss the Pope's toe; — *qlcu. sulla guancia*, to kiss s.o. on the cheek; — *la terra sotto i piedi di qlcu.*, *fig.* to worship the ground under s.o.'s feet ‖ *vi bacio le mani*, (*epistolare*) my kindest regards ‖ — *basso*, (*umiliarsi*) to kiss the dust **2.** (*toccare*) to touch; (*lambire*) to lap ‖ **baciàrsi**, *v.r. reciproco* to kiss each other.
bacile, *s.m.* (*letter.*) wash-hand-basin.
bacillàre, *ag.* (*biol.*) bacillary.
bacíllo, *s.m.* (*biol.*) bacillus (*pl.* bacilli).
bacinèlla, *s.f.* **1.** (small) basin **2.** (*foto.*) tray.
bacinèllo, bacinétto, *s.m.* (*elmo*) basinet, basnet.
bacíno, *s.m.* **1.** (*bacinella*) basin: *lavati le mani nel* —, wash your hands in the basin **2.** (*metal.*) basin: — *di colata*, sprue basin (o sprue pot); — *di raccolta*, catch basin **3.** (*anat.*) pelvis **4.** (*geog.*) basin: *il* — *del Po*, the Po basin; — *idrografico*, catchment basin **5.** (*mar.*) dock, wet dock: — *di carenaggio*, dry dock; — *di costruzione navale*, shipbuilding dock; — *di marea*, tidal dock (o tidal basin); — *di raddobbo*, graving (o dry) dock; — *di ripulsa*, flushing basin (o dock); — *galleggiante*, floating dock; *diritti di* —, dockage; *prova in* —, dock trial; *far entrare una nave in* —, to dock a ship **6.** (*geol.*) field: — *carbonifero*, coal field.
bàcio[1], *s.m.* kiss: — *d'addio*, parting kiss; *ella gli diede il* — *della buona notte*, she kissed him good-night ‖ — *di Giuda*, Judas kiss ‖ *mangiare qlcu. di baci*, to smother s.o. with kisses ‖ *morire nel* — *del Signore*, to die peacefully.
bacio[2], *ag.* facing north ‖ *s.m.* shady site facing north ‖ *a* —, facing north.
baciòzzo, *s.m.* (*scherz.*) hearty kiss, smack.
baciucchiaménto, *s.m.* (*rar.*) repeated kissing; fondling; billing; (*sl. amer.*) necking.
baciucchiàre, *v.t.* to kiss repeatedly; to fondle ‖ **baciucchiàrsi**, *v.r. reciproco* to kiss (each other) repeatedly, to go on kissing (each other); to fondle each other; to bill; (*sl. amer.*) to neck.
bàco, *s.m.* worm: — *da seta*, silkworm; — *del formaggio*, cheese-hopper.
bàcolo, *s.m.* (*eccl.*) cross staff.
bacología, *s.f.* sericulture, silkworm-breeding.
bacològico, *ag.* sericultural.

bacòlogo, *s.m.* sericulturist.

Bacóne, *no.pr.m.* (*st. fil.*) Bacon.

baconiàno, *ag.* (*fil.*) Baconian.

bactèrio, *s.m.* bacterium (*pl.* bacteria).

bàda, *s.f.*: *tenere a — qlcu.*, to hold s.o. at bay.

badalóne, *s.m.* 1. big simpleton; (*vagabondo*) tramp, vagrant; gadabout 2. (*leggio da chiesa*) lectern.

badùre, *v.i.* 1. (*fare attenzione*) to mind (s.o., sthg.): *bada al gradino!*, mind the step! 2. (*dare peso, occuparsi*) to mind (s.o., sthg.), to mark (s.o., sthg.): *bada alle mie parole!*, mark my words!; *badate ai fatti vostri!*, mind your own business!; *non badategli, è un beone!*, do not mind him, he is an inveterate drunkard! 3. (*stare attento, preoccuparsi*) to be careful (of sthg.): *egli bada alla sua salute*, he is very careful of his health; *non — al proprio interesse*, to disregard one's own interest; *senza — a spese*, regardless of expense 4. (*prendersi cura*) to take care (of s.o., sthg.), to look after (s.o., sthg.): *badate ai bambini!*, take care of the children! (o look after the children!) 5. (*continuare con ostinazione*) to continue obstinately, to insist (on doing): *egli bada a giocare d'azzardo*, he continues obstinately to gamble (o he insists on gambling) ‖ **badàrsi**, *v.r.* to look out: *badatevi, viene un'automobile!*, look out, there is a car coming!.

badèrna, *s.f.* (*mar.*) pudd(en)ing.

badéssa, *s.f.* abbess.

badía, *s.f.* 1. abbey 2. (*dignità di abate*) abbacy.

badiàle, *ag.* prosperous; large, spacious ‖ *una bugia —*, a whopping lie.

badilànte, *s.m.* navvy.

badíle, *s.m.* shovel.

bàffo, *s.m.* 1. moustache (*gener. invariato al pl.*): *baffi corti, a spazzola*, short, clipped moustache; *portare i baffi*, to wear a moustache ‖ *farla sotto i baffi a qlcu.*, to do sthg. under s.o.'s nose ‖ *farsene un —*, not to care a rap (about it) ‖ *leccarsi i baffi*, to lick one's lips: *manicaretto da leccarsi i baffi*, very tasty dish ‖ *ridere sotto i baffi*, to laugh in one's sleeve 2. (*di animali*) whisker 3. (*sgorbio, macchia*) smear: *un — d'inchiostro sulla carta*, a smear of ink on the paper 4. (*mar.*) bow wave.

baffúto, *ag.* moustached; with a moustache.

bagagliàio, *s.m.* luggage van, luggage car; (*amer.*) baggage car.

bagàglio, *s.m.* 1. luggage (*solo sing.*); (*amer.*) baggage (*solo sing.*): *— a mano*, light luggage; *— registrato*, registered luggage (o *amer.* checked baggage); *deposito —*, left-luggage office (o *amer.* baggage-room o check-room); *scontrino del —*, luggage check (o *amer.* baggage check); *fare i bagagli*, to pack (up); *disfare i bagagli*, to unpack 2. (*mil.*) accoutrements (*pl.*).

bagarinàggio, *s.m.* corner, cornering; (*amer.*) scalping.

bagaríno, *s.m.* corner man; (*amer.*) scalper.

bagàscia, *s.f.* (*volg.*) harlot, whore.

bagàssa, *s.f.* (*ind. zucchero*) bagasse.

bagattèlla, *s.f.* 1. trifle; bagatelle: *è una —!*, it's a mere trifle! 2. (*mus.*) bagatelle.

bagattíno, *s.m.* 1. "bagattino" (old Venetian coin) 2. *fig.* (*uomo da nulla*) worthless man.

Bagdàd, *no.pr.f.* (*geog.*) Bag(h)dad.

baggèo, (*rar.*) per **babbèo**.

baggiàna, *s.f.* (*bot.*) broad bean.

baggianàta, *s.f.* foolish action; piece of foolery.

baggiàno, *ag.* stupid, foolish ‖ *s.m.* fool; simpleton, booby.

bàglio, *s.m.* (*mar.*) beam: *— del ponte*, deck beam; *— di boccaporto*, hatch beam; *— maestro*, midship beam; *— mobile*, shifting beam.

baglióre, *s.m.* 1. dazzle; ray, flash (anche *fig.*): *— di speranza*, ray (o flash) of hope 2. (*patol.*) flare.

bagnaiuòla, **bagnaiuòlo**, *V.* **bagnína**, **bagníno**.

bagnànte, *s.c.* bather.

bagnàre, *v.t.* 1. to wet; (*immergere*) to dip; (*inzuppare*) to steep, to soak; (*inumidire*) to damp(en), to

moist(en); (*spruzzare*) to sprinkle, to water: *la pioggia mi bagnò fino alle ossa*, I was soaked through (in the rain); *— i fiori*, to water flowers; *— i piedi nel ruscello*, to dip one's feet in the stream; *— una spugna*, to soak (o to wet) a sponge ‖ *— i galloni, le spalline*, to celebrate a promotion 2. (*di mare, fiume, ecc.*) to wash: *la città è bagnata dal mare*, the town is washed by the sea; *il fiume bagna la città*, the river flows through the town ‖ **bagnàrsi**, *v.r.* 1. to get wet 2. (*prendere un bagno*) (*in luogo aperto*) to bathe; (*nella vasca*) to take a bath.

bagnaròla, *s.f.* bath (-tub): *— di zinco*, zinc bath.

bagnasciúga, *s.f.* (*mar.*) wind and water line.

bagnàta, *s.f.* soaking.

bagnàto, *ag.* wet: *come un pulcino*, as wet as a drowned rat; *— fino alle ossa, fradicio*, wet to the skin (o wet through o soaked through).

bagnatúra, *s.f.* 1. bathe; bathing 2. (*cura*) medical bathing 3. (*ind. tessile*) steeping 4. *pl.* (*arc.*) bathing (season) (*sing.*).

bagnína, *s.f.*, **bagníno**, *s.m.* bathing attendant.

bàgno, *s.m.* 1. bath: *accappatoio da —*, bath-robe; *stanza da —*, bath-room; *vasca da —*, bath-tub; *fare un —*, to take a bath (o to have a bath) ‖ *— di fango*, mud-bath; *— di sole*, sun-bath; *— turco*, Turkish bath ‖ *bagni pubblici*, public baths (o bathing establishment) ‖ *Ordine del Bagno*, (*st.*) Order of the Bath ‖ *essere in un — di sudore*, to perspire profusely 2. (*in luogo aperto*) bathe: *costume da —*, bathing-costume (o bathing-suit); *cuffia da —*, bathing cap; *stagione dei bagni*, bathing season; *ti piacciono i bagni di mare?*, do you like sea-bathing?; *andare ai bagni di mare*, to go to the sea-side; *fare il —*, to bathe (o to swim) 3. *pl.* (*luogo dove si fanno i bagni*) baths; watering-place (*sing.*) 4. (*chim.*) bath 5. (*foto.*) bath: *— d'annerimento*, blackening bath; *— d'arresto*, shortstop bath; *— d'inversione*, reversing bath; *— rallentatore*, restraining bath 6. (*metal.*) bath: *— di sale per alte temperature*, highheat salt bath; *— di tempra*, quenching bath (o hardening medium) 7. *— penale*, penitentiary (o convict prison).

bagnomaría, **a**, *l. av.* in bain-marie: *cuocere a —*, to cook in bain-marie ‖ *s.f.* (*ind. chim.*) water bath.

bagnuòlo, *s.m.* (*med.*) fomentation.

bagordàre, *v.i.* to revel, to carouse.

bagórdo, *s.m.* revelry, carousal.

Bahàma (le), *no.pr.f.pl.* (*geog.*) the Bahamas.

bài, *s.*: *nè ai nè —*, nothing: *uscì senza dire nè ai nè —*, he went out without uttering a single word.

bàia[1], *s.f.* (*scherzo*) joke; drollery; prank; jest; (*chiassata per schernire una persona*) hooting: *dare la — a qlcu.*, to make fun of s.o.

bàia[2], *s.f.* (*geog.*) bay, bight: *la — di Hudson*, Hudson Bay.

baiadèra, *s.f.* bayadère.

baiàta, *s.f.* shouting; uproar; (*chiassata per schernire una persona*) hooting.

baícolo, *s.m.* "baicolo" (thin dry Venetian biscuit).

bailàmme, *s.m.* (*baccano*) uproar, hubbub.

bàio, *ag.s.m.* bay.

baiòcco, *s.m.* "baiocco" (copper coin of the old Papal States) ‖ *non vale un —*, *fig.* it is not worth a (brass) farthing.

baionétta, *s.f.* bayonet: *assalto alla —*, bayonet-charge; *inastare la —*, to fix bayonets.

baionettàta, *s.f.* 1. (*colpo di baionetta*) bayonet thrust 2. (*ferita da baionetta*) bayonet wound.

bàita, *s.f.* "baita" (Alpine hut).

Balaclàva, *no.pr.f.* (*geog.*) Balaklava.

balalàica, *s.f.* (*mus.*) balalaika.

balàscio, *s.m.* (*min.*) balas(-ruby).

balaustràta, *s.f.* (*arch.*) balustrade.

balaustràto, *ag.* balustraded.

balaustríno, *s.m.* (*compasso di precisione*) bow-compasses (*pl.*).

balaústro, *s.m.* (*arch.*) baluster.

balbettaménto, *s.m.* stammering, stuttering.

balbettàre, *v.i.* to stammer, to stutter; (*del bambino che impara a parlare*) to lisp ‖ *v.t.* to falter: *lo scolaro balbettò la sua lezione*, the school-boy faltered out his lesson; *Tommaso balbetta un po' di tedesco*, Thomas speaks broken German; — *una scusa*, to mumble an excuse.

balbettío, *s.m.* stammering, stuttering.

balbettóne, *s.m.* (*rar.*) stammerer, stutterer.

bàlbo, *ag.* (*arc.*) stammering, stuttering.

balbutíre, (*arc.*) per **balbettàre.**

balbúzie, *s.f.* stammering, stammer, stuttering, stutter.

balbuziènte, *ag.* stammering, stuttering ‖ *s.c.* stammerer, stutterer.

Balcàni (i), *no.pr.m.pl.* (*geog.*) 1. the Balkans, the Balkan States 2. *i* (*Monti*) —, the Balkan Mountains.

balcànico, *ag.* Balkan.

bàlco, *s.m.* (*poet.*) balcony.

balconàta, *s.f.* 1. balcony 2. (*di teatro*) dress-circle, balcony.

balcóne, *s.m.* balcony.

baldacchíno, *s.m.* canopy, baldachin; (*del letto*) tester.

baldànza, *s.f.* boldness; (*sicurezza di sè*) (self-)assurance, self-confidence.

baldanzeggiàre, *v.i.* to display boldness.

baldanzosaménte, *av.* boldly.

baldanzóso, *ag.* daring, bold; (*sicuro di sè*) self-confident.

Baldassàrre, *no.pr.m.* 1. Balthazar 2. (*Bibbia*) Belshazzar.

baldézza, (*arc.*) per **baldànza.**

bàldo, *ag.* daring, bold, fearless.

baldòria, *s.f.* 1. (*fuoco d'allegria*) bonfire 2. (*festa*) merrymaking, festivity, spree: *far* —, to make merry.

Baldovíno, *no.pr.m.* Baldwin.

baldràcca, *s.f.* (*volg.*) harlot, whore.

Baleàri (le), *no.pr.f.pl.* (*geog.*) the Balearic Islands.

baléna, *s.f.* 1. whale: *caccia alla* —, whaling; *stecca di* —, whalebone 2. *fig.* (*persona grossa e goffa*) fat clumsy person.

balenaménto, *s.m.* (*rar.*) lightning.

balenàre, *v.i.* 1. *imp.* to lighten: *balenò tutta la notte*, it lightened all night long ‖ *in men che non balena*, in the twinkling of an eye 2. *fig.* to flash: *un'idea mi balenò nella mente*, an idea flashed through my mind.

balenièra, *s.f.* (*mar.*) whaler, whale-boat.

balenière, *s.m.* whaler, whaleman (*pl.* whalemen).

balenío, *s.m.* lightning; (*folgorio*) flashing, flashes of light (*pl.*): *il — delle spade*, the flashing of the swords.

baléno, *s.m.* lightning; (*folgorio*) flash ‖ *in men di un* —, in the twinkling of an eye (*o* in a flash).

balenòttera, *s.f.* (*zool.*) rorqual.

balenòtto, *s.m.* (*zool.*) whale-calf (*pl.* whale-calves).

balèstra, *s.f.* 1. crossbow, arblast, arbalest ‖ *dare il pane con la* —, *fig.* to do a kind deed with bad grace 2. (*mec.*) half-elliptic spring, leaf spring 3. (*tip.*) galley.

balestràio, *s.m.* 1. (*chi fabbrica balestre*) crossbow maker 2. (*chi vende balestre*) crossbow-seller.

balestràre, *v.t.* 1. to shoot with a crossbow 2. *fig.* (*mandare da un posto all'altro*) to send from pillar to post; (*mandar lontano*) to send far away.

balestràta, *s.f.* crossbow shot.

balestrièra, *s.f.* (*fortificazioni*) loophole.

balestrière, *s.m.* arbalester, crossbowman (*pl.* crossbowmen).

balestrúccio, *s.m.* (*ornit.*) house-martin.

balì, *s.m.* (*st.*) bailiff.

bàlia[1], *s.f.* 1. wet-nurse: — *asciutta*, dry-nurse; *suo figlio è a* —, her child is at nurse; *dare a* —, to put out to nurse ‖ *tener ql.co. a* —, (*tenere presso di sè a lungo*) to keep sthg. a long time 2. (*aer.*) (*dirigibile*) nurse balloon.

balía[2], *s.f.*: *in — delle onde*, at the mercy of the waves; *in — di se stesso*, without any help or control; *darsi in — ai piaceri*, to give oneself up to pleasure; *essere in — di qlcu.*, to be at s.o.'s mercy.

baliàtico, *s.m.* 1. nursing 2. (*retribuzione della balia*) wet-nurse's wages (*pl.*) 3. (*bimbo a balia*) nurs(e)ling; foster-child (*pl.* foster-children).

bàlio, *s.m.* foster-father.

balipèdio, *s.m.* (*mil.*) firing-range.

balísta, *s.f.* ballista (*pl.* ballistae).

balística, *s.f.* ballistics.

balístico, *ag.* ballistic.

balistíte, *s.f.* (*esplosivo*) ballistite.

bàlla, *s.f.* 1. (*di lana, cotone, ecc.*) bale: *comprimere in balle*, to press in bales 2. *fig.* (*mucchio*) heap; lot: *una — di bugie*, a pack of lies 3. (*volg.*) (*fandonia*) fib: *questa è una* —, this is a fib 4. *pigliar la* —, (*fam.*) (*prendere la sbornia*) to get drunk.

ballàbile, *ag.* dance (*attributivo*): *musica* —, dance music ‖ *s.m.* (*mus.*) dance music.

ballàre, *v.t.i.* to dance: *balla come un orso*, he dances very clumsily; — *dalla gioia*, to dance for joy; — *un valzer*, to dance a waltz (*o* to waltz) ‖ *far — i denti*, (*mangiare*) to eat ‖ *fare — qlcu. su un quattrino*, to keep s.o. in check ‖ *quando non c'è la gatta i sorci ballano*, prov. when the cat's away the mice will play.

ballàta, *s.f.* 1. (*poes.*) ballad, ballade; (*ballata popolare*) ballad 2. (*mus.*) ballade.

ballatóio, *s.m.* 1. gallery 2. (*di gabbia di uccello*) perch.

ballerína, *s.f.* 1. (*classica*) ballerina (*pl.* ballerine, ballerinas); ballet-dancer, professional dancer; (*di rivista*) chorus-girl ‖ — *sulla corda*, rope-dancer 2. (*donna che balla bene*) good dancer; (*in una coppia, la dama*) partner: *dov'è la mia* —?, where is my partner? 3. (*ornit.*) wagtail.

balleríno, *s.m.* 1. (*classico*) ballet-dancer, professional dancer 2. (*uomo che balla bene*) good dancer; (*in una coppia, il cavaliere*) partner.

ballettàre, *v.i.* to hop; to skip, to jump (about).

ballétto, *s.m.* (*teat.*) ballet.

ballísta, *s.m.* (*volg.*) fibber.

bàllo, *s.m.* 1. dance; (*il ballare*) dancing; (*giro di danza*) dance: *corpo di* —, (*teat.*) troupe of ballet-dancers; *maestro di* —, dancing-master; *musica da* —, dance music; *scuola di* —, dancing-school; *fare un* —, to have a dance ‖ *essere in* —, *fig.* to be engaged in sthg.; *tirare in* —, *fig.* to call into question (*o* to bring up); *venire in* —, *fig.* to come up for discussion ‖ *quando si è in — bisogna ballare*, prov. once one has put one's hand to the plough there is no turning back 2. (*festa da ballo*) ball: *in maschera*, fancy-dress ball; — *studentesco*, hop 3. *canzone a* —, (*ballata*) ballade 4. — *di San Vito*, (*patol.*) St. Vitus's dance.

ballonzolàre, *v.i.* (*saltellare*) to trip (along).

ballòtta[1], *s.f.* unpeeled boiled chestnut.

ballòtta[2], *s.f.* (*pallottola usata nelle votazioni*) ballot.

ballottàggio, *s.m.* second ballot, ballotage.

ballottaménto, *s.m.* (*mar.*) tossing.

ballottàre, *v.t.* 1. (*arc.*) to ballot 2. (*sballottare*) to toss.

balneàre, balneàrio, *ag.* bathing (*attributivo*): *stabilimento* —, bathing establishment; *stagione* —, bathing season; *stazione* —, seaside resort.

baloccàre, *v.t.* to amuse with toys: — *qlcu.*, *fig.* (*farsi giuoco di qlcu.*) to trifle with s.o. ‖ **baloccàrsi,** *v.r.* 1. to toy; to play with toys 2. *fig.* (*gingillarsi*) to waste time, to trifle.

balòcco, *s.m.* toy; play-thing (anche *fig.*): *non era che un — nelle sue mani*, he was but a play-thing in her hands.

baloccóne, *s.m.* trifler; (*perditempo*) idle fellow, idler, loafer.

balògio, *ag.* unwell; (*indisposto*) out of sorts, indisposed; (*malaticcio*) sickly-looking ‖ *tempo* —, unsettled *o* uncertain weather.

balordàggine, *s.f.* 1. stupidity; dullness 2. (*atto da* *balordo*) foolish action; stupid act; (*detto da balordo*) nonsense: *dire delle balordaggini*, to talk nonsense.

balordaménte, *av.* stupidly; foolishly.

balórdo, *ag.* **1.** stupid, slow-witted, dull-witted: *discorso* —, senseless talk ‖ *sentirsi* —, (*non sentirsi bene di salute*) to feel out of sorts (*o* to be under the weather) **2.** (*mediocre, scadente*) bad: *affare* —, bad business ‖ *s.m.* fool, fat-head, blockhead; lumpish person.

balsamèlla, *s.f.* (*cuc.*) bechamel.

balsàmico, *ag.* balsamic; (*salubre*) balmy.

bàlsamo, *s.m.* balm; balsam.

bàlta, *s.f.* overturning; capsizing; upset ‖ *gli ha dato di — il cervello*, he has gone off his head ‖ *dar la — a un patrimonio*, (*sperperarlo*) to squander a fortune.

bàlteo, *s.m.* baldric.

bàltico, *ag.* Baltic ‖ **Bàltico (il)**, *no.pr.m.* (*geog.*) the Baltic.

Baltimòra, *no.pr.f.* (*geog.*) Baltimore.

baluàrdo, *s.m.* rampart, bulwark (anche *fig.*): *il — della libertà*, the bulwark of liberty.

baluginàre, *v.i.* to flicker; to blink.

bàlza, *s.f.* **1.** cliff; crag **2.** (*di abito*) flounce.

balzàna, *s.f.* white streak (on horse's foot).

balzàno, *ag.* **1.** white-footed: *cavallo* —, white-footed horse **2.** (*stravagante*) queer, odd, eccentric: *cervello* —, queer fellow.

balzàre, *v.i.* **1.** to jump, to leap, to spring; to bounce, to start: *balzò nella stanza*, he bounced into the room; *le balzò il cuore*, her heart gave a leap; — *a cavallo*, to mount one's horse; — *a terra*, to jump down (*o* to alight *o* to dismount); — *dal letto*, to leap out of bed; — *di gioia*, to jump (*o* to leap) for joy; — *in avanti*, to jump forward; — *in piedi*, to jump to one's feet; — *su ql.co.*, to spring at (*o* to pounce on) sthg. **2.** *fig.* (*emergere*) to stand out: *dall'esame del testimonio balzò la verità*, the truth stood out from the examination of the witness ‖ *v.t.* (*sbalzare*) to throw: *il cavallo lo balzò di sella*, the horse threw him from the saddle.

balzellàre, *v.i.* to skip, to hop ‖ *v.t.* (*appostare*) to watch, to lie in wait for (s.o., sthg.), to hop.

balzèllo, *s.m.* **1.** skip **2.** (*tassa*) heavy tax.

balzellóne, *s.m.* leap, sudden jump: *andare avanti a balzelloni*, to proceed by sudden jumps; *parlare a balzelloni*, to talk at random.

bàlzo[1], *s.m.* bound, jump, leap: *fare un* —, to make a leap ‖ *aspettare la palla al* —, *fig.* to wait for a favourable opportunity; *cogliere la palla al* —, *fig.* to seize an opportunity.

bàlzo[2], *s.m.* (*di monte*) cliff, crag: *campo a balzi*, terrace.

bambàgia, *s.f.* **1.** (*ovatta*) cotton-wool ‖ *salute di* —, delicate health ‖ *tenere nella* —, *fig.* to keep with great care (*o* to keep in cotton-wool *o* to pamper) **2.** (*cascame*) cotton-waste.

bambagíno, *ag.* woolly.

bambagióso, *ag.* as soft as cotton-wool; woolly.

Bambèrga, *no.pr.f.* (*geog.*) Bamberg.

bambìna, *s.f.* child (*pl.* children); (*in fasce*) baby; (*ragazzina*) little girl.

bambinàggine, *s.f.* **1.** childishness **2.** (*atto da bambino*) childish action.

bambinàia, *s.f.* nurse, nursemaid; (*fam.*) nanny.

bambinàta, *s.f.* childish action.

bambineggiàre, *v.i.* to behave like a child.

bambinería, *V.* **bambinàggine**.

bambinésco, *ag.* childish.

bambinétta, *s.f.*, **bambinétto**, *s.m.* child (*pl.* children), tot; (*sl.*) kid; (*fam. amer.*) moppet, tyke.

bambìno, *s.m.* child (*pl.* children); (*sl.*) kid; (*in fasce*) baby; (*ragazzetto*) little boy: *racconti per bambini*, nursery tales; *sorveglianza di bambini*, baby-sitting; *bada ai bambini!*, look after the children!; *dare alla luce un* —, to bring forth a child (*o* to give

birth to a child) ‖ *il Bambino Gesù*, the Infant Jesus.

bàmbo, *ag.* **1.** foolish, stupid, silly **2.** (*puerile*) puerile, childish.

bamboccería, *s.f.* **1.** childishness **2.** (*atto da bamboccio, da sciocco*) silly action.

bambocciàta[1], *s.f.* **1.** childishness **2.** (*atto da bamboccio, da sciocco*) silly action.

bambocciàta[2], *s.f.* (*pitt.*) bambocciade.

bambòccio, *s.m.* **1.** plump child **2.** (*bambola di cenci*) rag-doll **3.** (*sciocco*) silly man, simpleton: *non fare il* —!, don't be silly!.

bàmbola, *s.f.* **1.** doll; puppet: *giocare alle bambole*, to play with dolls **2.** *fig.* (*ragazza graziosa ma insignificante*) doll.

bamboleggiaménto, *s.m.* childish behaviour.

bamboleggiàre, *v.i.* (*parlare da bambino*) to talk like a child; (*agire da bambino*) to act like a child, to behave childishly.

bambolóne, **bambolòtto**, *s.m.* plump baby, chubby child.

bambú, *s.m.* (*bot.*) bamboo ‖ *cortina di* —, (*neol. pol.*) bamboo curtain.

banàle, *ag.* banal, commonplace (*attributivo*).

banalità, *s.f.* banality, triviality, commonplace; (*volgarità*) vulgarity: *questa è una pura* —, this is a mere banality.

banàna, *s.f.* banana.

bananéto, *s.m.* banana-plantation.

bananièra, *s.f.* banana boat.

banàno, *s.m.* banana(-tree).

banàto, *s.m.* (*dignità di bano*) banate.

bànca, *s.f.* bank: — *agricola*, land bank; — *di credito*, credit bank; — *di emissione*, bank of issue; *la Banca di Inghilterra*, the Bank of England; *affari di* —, banking business; *biglietto di* —, banknote; *libretto di* —, bank-book (*o* pass-book); *succursale di una* —, bank-branch; *avere depositi in* —, to have money deposited with a bank; *fare operazioni di* —, to bank.

bancàbile, *ag.* bankable, current.

bancarèlla, *s.f.* stall, booth; (*di libri*) bookstall.

bancarellísta, *s.c.* bookstall keeper; (*venditore di libri usati*) bouquiniste.

bancàrio, *ag.* banking (*attributivo*), bank (*attributivo*): *assegno* —, cheque (*o amer.* check); *casa bancaria*, banking house; *credito* —, bank credit; *operazione bancaria*, banking (*o* bank) transaction; *riserva bancaria*, bank reserve.

bancarótta, *s.f.* bankruptcy: — *fraudolenta*, fraudulent bankruptcy; *fare* —, to go bankrupt; *mandare in* —, to bankrupt.

bancarottière, *s.m.* bankrupt.

banchettànte, *s.c.* banqueter; feaster.

banchettàre, *v.i.* to banquet; to feast.

banchétto, *s.m.* banquet; feast: *sala dei banchetti*, banqueting-hall ‖ *il — celeste*, *fig.* the heavenly banquet.

banchière, *s.m.* banker.

banchíglia, *s.f.* ice-bank.

banchína, *s.f.* **1.** (*molo*) quay, wharf, dock; pier: — *di carico*, (*mar.*) loading dock; — *di scarico*, (*mar.*) unloading (*o* discharging) wharf; *diritto di* —, wharfage (*o* quayage); *franco* —, (*comm.*) free on quay (*o* free on wharf) **2.** (*lungomare*) waterfront **3.** (*piattaforma*) platform **4.** (*terrapieno*) bank **5.** (*per pedoni, ciclisti*) banquette, sidewalk.

banchísa, *s.f.* ice-pack.

bànco[1], *s.m.* **1.** bench, seat: — *degli accusati*, dock; — *dei magistrati*, magistrate's bench; — *della giuria*, jury box; — *di chiesa*, pew (*o* stall); — *di scuola*, school bench (*o* form); — *dei testimoni*, witness box; — *di vendita*, counter; — *ministeriale*, treasury bench; — *per rematori*, (*mar.*) thwart ‖ *sotto* —, *fig.* on the sly **2.** (*tavolo*) bench: — *di collaudo*, (*tec.*) test stand (*o* test bench); — *di controllo*, (*tec.*) inspection table — *di taratura*, (*tec.*) calibrating table **3.** (*ind. tessile*) — *a fusi*, fly frame (*o* spindle frame); — *del pettine* hackling bench; — *per stoppino*, rowing frame **4.** (*di giuoco*) bank: *far saltare il* —, to break the bank; *tenere il* —, to hold the bank **5.** (*banca*) bank: *Banco di Napoli*, Bank of Naples **6.** (*massa, raggruppamento*): — *di carbone*, (*miner.*) seam of coal; — *di coralli*, coral-reef; — *di ghiaccio*, ice-field (*o* ice-floe); — *di nebbia*, fog-bank; — *di ostriche*, oyster-bed; — *di rocce*, (*geol.*) reef; — *di sabbia*, sand-bank (*o* sand-bar) **7.** — *del lotto*, lottery office.

Bànco², *no.pr.m.* (*lett.*) Banquo.

bancogíro, *s.m.* (*comm.*) clearing.

banconòta, *s.f.* banknote.

bànda¹, *s.f.* **1.** side || *da* — *a* —, from side to side; *dall'altra* —, (*stato*) on the other side; (*moto a*) to the other side; (*moto da*) from the other side || *lasciar da* —, to leave aside **2.** (*mar.*) side: *la nave va alla* —, the ship has a list.

banda², *s.f.* **1.** (*arald.*) bend **2.** (*striscia di stoffa di colore differente*) band.

banda³, *s.f.* **1.** (*mil.*) company of soldiers **2.** (*masnada di delinquenti*) gang **3.** (*di sonatori*) band: *direttore, maestro di* —, band-master.

bandèlla, *s.f.* **1.** (*di porta*) hinge **2.** (*elett.*) bus bar **3.** (*metal.*) strap.

banderàio, *s.m.* **1.** (*chi fabbrica bandiere*) flag manufacturer, flag-maker **2.** (*porta-bandiera*) standard-bearer.

banderuòla, *s.f.* **1.** weathercock (anche *fig.*); (wind) vane: *sei una* —, you are a weathercock **2.** (*di nave*) banderol(e).

bandièra, *s.f.* flag; colours (*pl.*); banner; ensign: *l'alza* —, the hoistering of the flag; *porta-* —, ensign; *ammainare la* —, to lower the flag; *battere* — *inglese*, to fly the Union Jack; *issare la* —, to hoist the flag; *issare la* — *a mezz'asta*, to hoist the flag at half-mast; *spiegare una* —, to unfurl a flag || — *di convenienza*, (*neol.*) flag of convenience || *a bandiere spiegate*, with flying colours || *andare sotto le bandiere*, to join the colours; *essere sotto le bandiere*, to serve with the colours || *mutar* —, *fig.* to be a weathercock.

bandinèlla, *s.f.* roller-towel.

bandíre, *v.t.* **1.** to announce publicly, to proclaim **2.** (*esiliare*) to banish, to exile: — *una persona*, to banish a person **3.** (*mettere da parte*) to put aside: — *i complimenti*, to put aside ceremony.

bandísta, *s.m.* bandsman (*pl.* bandsmen).

bandíta, *s.f.* preserve: — *di caccia*, game preserve.

bandíto¹, *V.* **imbandíto**.

bandíto², *s.m.* **1.** bandit, brigand, highwayman (*pl.* highwaymen); outlaw, gangster **2.** (*esiliato*) exile.

banditóre, *s.m.* **1.** town-crier **2.** (*di aste pubbliche*) auctioneer.

bàndo, *s.m.* **1.** ban: *essere al* —, to be under a ban (*o* to be forbidden); *mettere al* —, to ban || — *alle cerimonie!*, don't stand on ceremony!; — *alle sciocchezze!*, no more nonsense! **2.** (*esilio*) banishment: *essere al* —, to be banished **3.** (*annunzio pubblico*) announcement, proclamation: — *di concorso*, announcement of competition.

bandolièra, *s.f.* bandoleer, cross-belt || *a* —, baldric-wise.

bàndolo, *s.m.* end of skein || *perdere il* —, *fig.* to get mixed up.

bandóne, *s.m.* corrugated iron.

bàngio, *s.m.* (*mus.*) banjo.

bàno, *s.m.* (*governatore, in Ungheria*) ban.

baobàb, *s.m.* (*bot.*) baobab.

bar¹, *s.m.* **1.** (*mescita*) bar: — *con tavola calda*, snack-bar **2.** (*mobiletto*) bar.

bar², *s.m.* (*fis.*) bar.

bàra, *s.f.* coffin.

Baràbba, *no.pr.m.* (*Bibbia*) Barabas || **baràbba**, *s.m.* (*briccone*) scoundrel, villain, rascal.

baracàno, *s.m.* barracan.

baràcca, *s.f.* **1.** hut, barrack; booth || *piantare* — *e burattini*, to give it up || *stentare a mandare avanti la* —,

to have difficulty in making both ends meet **2.** *fig.* (*cosa, faccenda instabile*) unsteady thing **3.** *fare* —, (*gozzovigliare*) to revel.

baraccaménto, *s.m.* (*mil.*) barracks (*pl.*); hutments (*pl.*).

baracchíno, *s.m.* small shed, small hut.

baraccóne, *s.m.* **1.** large shed; booth: *i baracconi della fiera*, showmen's booths **2.** (*carrozzone di zingari*) caravan.

baraónda, *s.f.* babel, chaos.

baràre, *v.i.* to cheat: — *alle carte*, to cheat at cards.

bàratro, *s.m.* **1.** chasm, abyss (anche *fig.*): *c'è un* — *fra noi*, there is an abyss between us **2.** (*inferno*) hell.

barattaménto, *s.m.* barter; (*scambio*) exchange.

barattàre, *v.t.* to barter; (*scambiare*) to exchange: — *una parola con qlcu.*, to exchange a few words with s.o.; — *le parole*, *fig.* (*non mantenere una promesssa*) to be insincere (*o* not to keep a promise); — *saluti*, to exchange greetings.

barattatóre, *s.m.*, **barattatríce**, *s.f.* barterer; chafferer.

barattería, *s.f.* **1.** fraud; deception; trickery **2.** (*mar.*) barratry.

barattière, *s.m.* **1.** (*imbroglione*) cheat; swindler **2.** (*dir.*) barrator.

baràtto, *s.m.* barter; (*scambio*) exchange.

baràttolo, *s.m.* **1.** pot, jar **2.** (*di metallo*) tin; (*amer.*) can.

bàrba, *s.f.* **1.** beard: — *a punta*, pointed beard; — *lunga*, long beard; *sapone da* —, shaving soap; *servizio di* — *e capelli*, shave and haircut; *quanto prendete per la* —?, how much do you charge for a shave?; *far la* — *a qlcu.*, to shave s.o.; *farsi la* —, to shave (*o* to have a shave) || *alla* — *di qlcu.*, at the expense of s.o. || *in* — *a*, in spite of (*o* notwithstanding) || *farla in* — *a qlcu.*, to do sthg. to s.o.'s face || *far la* — *di stoppa a qlcu.*, to play a trick (*o* a joke) on s.o. || *servire qlcu. di* — *e capelli*, *fig.* to teach s.o. a lesson **2.** (*di animale*) beard; (*di pesce*) barbel, wattle; (*di uccello*) beard, wattle **3.** (*bot.*) beard; (*radici*) rootlets (*pl.*): *mettere la* —, to take (*o* to strike) root **4.** (*fam.*) (*noia*) bore: *che* —!, what a bore! **5.** (*di libro intonso*) deckle-edge.

barbabiètola, *s.f.* (red) beet, beet-root: — *da zucchero*, sugar beet (*o* white-beet).

barbacàne, *s.m.* (*edil.*) buttress; (*edil. mil.*) barbican.

barbagiànni, *s.m.* **1.** (*ornit.*) barn owl, white owl **2.** (*sciocco*) stupid fellow; dolt; blockhead.

barbàglio, *s.m.* dazzle; glare; glitter.

barbalòceo, *s.m.* (*buono a nulla*) good-for-nothing.

Bàrbara, *no.pr.f.* Barbara || *dim.* Bab, Babs, Babbie.

barbaraménte, *av.* barbarously; ferociously.

barbàre, *v.i.* to take root, to strike root, to root.

barbareggiàre, *v.i.* **1.** to act barbarously **2.** (*usare barbarismi*) to barbarize one's language.

barbarescaménte, *av.* barbarically.

barbarésco, *ag.* **1.** barbaric **2.** (*della Barberia*) Barbaresque || *s.m.* (*abitante della Barberia*) Barbaresque, Barbarian.

barbaricaménte, *av.* barbarically.

barbàrico, *ag.* barbaric.

barbàrie, *s.f.* **1.** barbarousness **2.** (*crudeltà*) cruelty; ferocity; barbarity **3.** (*nel linguaggio*) barbarism.

barbarísmo, *s.m.* **1.** (*nel linguaggio*) barbarism **2.** (*atto barbaro*) barbarity, cruelty.

bàrbaro, *ag.* **1.** barbarian, barbarous **2.** (*crudele*) ferocious; barbaric, cruel; uncouth || *s.m.* barbarian.

barbassòro, *s.m.* **1.** (*valvassore*) vavasour **2.** (*iron.*) (*sapientone*) wiseacre; know-all.

barbàta, *s.f.* (*bot.*) mass of roots; roots (*pl.*).

barbàto, *ag.* **1.** bearded **2.** (*bot.*) barbate.

barbazzàle, *s.m.* curb.

barbèra, *s.m.* "barbera" (kind of Italian red wine).

bàrbero, *ag.* Berber || *s.m.* (*cavallo*) barb.

barbétta, *s.f.* **1.** small beard, short beard: — *a punta,* pointed beard; (*fam.*) goatee: *quel signore ha la — a punta,* that gentleman wears a pointed beard **2.** (*piattaforma nelle corazzate*) turret **3.** (*fortificazioni*) barbette **4.** (*ciuffo di peli sul garretto del cavallo*) fetlock.

barbicaménto, *s.m.* rooting.

barbicàre, *v.i.,* **barbicàrsi,** *v.r.* **1.** to strike root, to take root **2.** *fig.* (*prender piede*) to find followers; to take root.

barbière, *s.m.* **1.** barber: *negozio di —,* barber's shop **2.** (*parrucchiere*) hairdresser.

barbiería, *s.f.* barber's shop.

barbificàre, *v.i.* **1.** to take root, to strike root **2.** (*fam. scherz.*) (*annoiare*) to bore, to weary.

barbíno, *ag.* (*fam.*) badly done: *fare una figura barbina,* to cut a very poor figure ‖ *s.m.* razor-wipe.

bàrbio, *s.m.* (*ittiol.*) barbel.

barbitonsóre, *s.m.* (*scherz.*) barber.

barbitúrico, *ag.* (*farm.*) barbituric ‖ *s.m.* (*farm.*) barbiturate.

bàrbo, *s.m.* (*ittiol.*) barbel.

barbògio, *ag.* doting; senile ‖ *s.m.* dotard.

barbóne, *s.m.* **1.** long beard **2.** (*uomo barbuto*) long-bearded man **3.** (*straccione*) tramp; ragamuffin, tatterdemalion **4.** (*specie di cane*) poodle.

barbóso, *ag.* (*fam.*) tedious; tiresome, boring.

barbòzza, *s.f.* **1.** lower jaw of horse **2.** (*parte dell'elmo*) chin-guard.

barbugliaménto, *s.m.* mumbling; stammering; lisping.

barbugliàre, *v.i.* to mumble; to stammer; to lisp; to stutter.

barbuglióne, *s.m.* mumbler, stammerer, lisper; stutterer.

barbúta, *s.f.* (*parte dell'elmo*) chin-guard.

barbúto, *ag.* bearded.

bàrca, *s.f.* boat: — *a remi,* rowing-boat; — *a vapore,* steamboat; — *a vela,* sailing-boat; — *da pesca,* fishing-boat; — *di salvataggio,* life-boat; *arrivammo in —,* we came by boat; *andare in —,* to go by boat (*o* to go boating) ‖ *siamo tutti nella stessa —, fig.* we are all in the same boat ‖ *reggere la —, fig.* to be an accomplice in a fraud ‖ *spingere la —, fig.* to help the business along.

barcàccia, *s.f.* **1.** (*vecchia barca*) old boat; tub **2.** (*teat.*) stage-box.

barcaiuòlo, *s.m.* boatman (*pl.* boatmen); waterman (*pl.* watermen); (*di traghetto*) ferryman (*pl.* ferrymen).

barcamenàrsi, *v.r.* (*destreggiarsi*) to wangle; to manage things cleverly; (*tenere il piede in due staffe*) to keep in with both sides, to run with the hare and hunt with the hounds.

barcarízzo, *s.m.* (*mar.*) gangway, gangplank.

barcaròla, *s.f.* (*mus.*) barcarole, barcarolle.

barcàta, *s.f.* boat-load.

barcheggiàre, *v.i.* to go boating; (*in barca a vela*) to go sailing ‖ **barcheggiàrsi,** *V.* **barcamenàrsi.**

barchéggio, *s.m.* plying to and fro (of boats).

barchétta, *s.f.* small boat; dinghy, dingey, dingy.

barchétto, *s.m.* very small boat; small dinghy.

barcollaménto, *s.m.* staggering, swaying, tottering.

barcollàre, *v.i.* **1.** to stagger, to sway, to totter, to vacillate **2.** *fig.* (*tentennare*) to hesitate, to waver.

barcollío, *s.m.* staggering, tottering, swaying.

barcollóne, barcollóni, *av.: entrò —,* he staggered into the room; *andare —,* to stagger along.

barcóne, *s.m.* long boat.

bàrda, *s.f.* horse-armour.

bardaménto, *s.m.* **1.** (*il bardare*) harnessing **2.** (*bardatura, finimenti*) harness; trappings (*pl.*).

bardàre, *v.t.* **1.** to harness **2.** (*scherz.*) to dress up; to trim ‖ **bardàrsi,** *v.r.* (*scherz.*) to dress up: *si bardò per il ballo,* she dressed up for the ball.

bardàssa, *s.m.* urchin; little rascal.

bardatúra, *s.f.* harness; trappings (*pl.*).

bardèlla, *s.f.* rough heavy saddle.

bardellóne, *s.m.* large saddle (for breaking in young horses).

bardíglio, *s.m.* (*min.*) bardiglio.

bàrdo, *s.m.* (*st.*) bard.

bardolíno, *s.m.* " bardolino " (kind of Italian red wine).

bardòsso, a, *l.av.* bare-back: *cavalcare a —,* to ride bare-back.

bardòtto, *s.m.* **1.** (*zool.*) hinny **2.** (*cavalcatura del buttero*) cattle-driver's mount **3.** (*chi tira l'alzaia*) tower **4.** (*apprendista*) apprentice.

barèlla, *s.f.* **1.** (*per feriti*) stretcher, litter: *portare qlcu. su una —,* to carry s.o. on a stretcher **2.** (*per sassi, sabbia, ecc.*) barrow, hand-barrow.

barellàre, *v.t.* to carry on a stretcher ‖ *v.i.* (*barcollare*) to stagger, to totter, to sway.

barellàta, *s.f.* barrowful, barrow-load.

barèna, *s.f.* shoal, shelf, sandbank (left dry at low tide in a lagoon).

bàrgia, *s.f.* dewlap.

bargíglio, *s.m.* wattle.

bargigliúto, *ag.* wattled.

baricèntrico, *ag.* (*fis.*) barycentric.

baricèntro, *s.m.* (*fis.*) barycentre.

bàrico, *ag.* (*chim.*) baric.

bariglióne, *s.m.* barrel.

barilàio, *s.m.* cooper.

baríle, *s.m.* barrel, cask ‖ *fare a scarica barili,* to put the blame on others (*o* to shift off responsibilities).

barilòtto, barilòzzo, *s.m.* **1.** keg, small cask **2.** (*centro del bersaglio*) bull's eye: *fare —, fig.* to score a bull's eye.

bàrio, *s.m.* (*chim.*) barium.

barisfèra, *s.f.* (*geofisica*) barysphere.

barísta, *s.m.* **1.** barman (*pl.* barmen); (*amer.*) bar-tender **2.** (*chi possiede, conduce un bar*) barkeeper; (*amer.*) barkeep ‖ *s.f.* barmaid.

baríte, *s.f.* (*chim. min.*) baryta.

baritína, *s.f.* (*min.*) barytes, barite, heavy spar.

baritonàle, *ag.* baritone (*attributivo*); barytone (*attributivo*): *voce —,* baritone voice.

baritoneggiàre, *v.i.* to sing like a baritone.

baritono, *s.m.* baritone, barytone.

barlàccio, *ag.* **1.** addled **2.** (*di persona*) sickly.

barlétta, *s.f.* small barrel; pocket-flask.

barlétto, *s.m.* **1.** small barrel **2.** (*morsa da falegname*) carpenter's wooden vice, bench stop.

barlúme, *s.m.* **1.** dim light, glimmer, glim **2.** *fig.* glimpse, faint idea: *un — di speranza,* a gleam of hope **3.** (*conoscenza superficiale*) superficial knowledge.

Bàrnaba, *no.pr.m.* Barnabas.

barnabíta, *s.m.* (*eccl.*) Barnabite.

bàro, *s.m.* card-sharper, cheat; trickster.

barocchísmo, *s.m.* **1.** tendency to baroque **2.** (*ampollosità*) bombast.

barocciàio, *s.m.* carter.

barocciàta, *s.f.* cart-load.

baroccíno, *s.m.* light two-wheeled cart; (*calessino*) gig.

baròccio, *s.m.* **1.** cart **2.** *fig.* (a) great deal, (a) lot.

baròcco, *ag.* **1.** baroque **2.** (*ampolloso*) bombastic **3.** (*strano, bizzarro*) odd, bizarre, quaint ‖ *s.m.* baroque.

barògrafo, *s.m.* (*fis.*) barograph, altigraph.

baròlo, *s.m.* " barolo " (kind of Italian red wine).

barometría, *s.f.* (*fis.*) barometry.

baromètrico, *ag.* (*fis.*) barometric(al).

baròmetro, *s.m.* (*fis.*) barometer: *il — si abbassa, sale,* the barometer is falling, rising.

baronàle, *ag.* baronial.

baronàta, *s.f.* (*bricconata*) roguery; knavery; trickery.

baroncíno, *s.m.* young baron; baron's son.

baróne[1]**,** *s.m.* baron.

baróne[2]**,** *s.m.* (*arc.*) (*briccone*) rogue.

baronésco[1], *ag.* baronial.

baronésco[2], *ag.* (*arc.*) (*di, da briccone*) roguish.

baronéssa, *s.f.* baroness.

baronétto, *s.m.* baronet (*abbr.* Bart.); (*davanti al nome*) Sir; (*facoltativo dopo il cognome*) Bart.: *il — James Brown*, Sir James Brown, Bart.; *il — Lawrence* (*Olivier*), Sir Lawrence (Olivier).

baronía, *s.f.* 1. baronage 2. (*dominio di barone*) barony.

baroscòpio, *s.m.* (*fis.*) baroscope.

bàrra, *s.f.* 1. bar: *andare alla —*, to plead at the bar (*o* to plead in Court) 2. (*mar.*) tiller, helm 3. (*banco di sabbia*) sand bar 4.(*di metalli*) bar: — *d'oro*, bar of gold; *oro in barre*, gold in bars 5. (*di morso di cavallo*) bar.

barracàno, *s.m.* barracan.

barricàre, *v.t.* to barricade, to block ‖ **barricàrsi**, *v.r.* to barricade oneself: *si barricò dietro un mucchio di bugie*, he took refuge behind a pack of lies.

barricàta, *s.f.* barricade.

barrièra, *s.f.* 1. barrier: *la — del suono*, the sound barrier; — *di calore*, heat barrier; — *naturale*, natural barrier 2. (*cancello, steccato*) gate, fence; railing; palisade 3. *fig.* (*ostacolo*) barrier; obstacle; hindrance: *la poca salute e la mancanza di denaro possono essere entrambe — all'istruzione*, poor health and lack of money may both be barriers to education 4. (*geol.*) bar.

barríre, *v.i.* to trumpet.

barríto, *s.m.* trumpeting.

barròccio, *e derivati*, *V.* **baròccio**, *e derivati*.

Bàrtolo, *no.pr.m.* *dim.* di **Bartolomèo**.

Bartolomèo, *no.pr.m.* Bartholomew ‖ *dim.* Bart, Bat.

barúffa, *s.f.* quarrel; brawl, scuffle: *far —*, to quarrel (*o* to brawl *o* to scuffle).

barzellétta, *s.f.* joke; funny story ‖ *prendere in — ql.co.*, to make jest of sth.

barzellettàre, *v.i.* to crack jokes, to tell jokes; to tell funny stories.

basàlte, *s.m.* (*min.*) basalt.

basàltico, *ag.* (*min.*) basaltic.

basàlto, *s.m.* (*min.*) basalt.

basaménto, *s.m.* 1. base, pedestal; (*di colonna*) plinth: *il — di una statua*, the base of a statue 2. (*zoccolo di pareti*) skirting board 3. (*zoccolo di muro esterno*) footing.

basàre, *v.t.* to found, to base ‖ **basàrsi**, *v.r.* to base oneself: *non devi basarti sulle prime impressioni!*, you must not base yourself on first impressions!.

bàsco, *ag.* Basque ‖ *s.m.* 1. Basque 2. (*berretto*) beret.

bàscula, **basculla**, *s.f.* weighing-machine: — *automatica*, slot weghing-machine.

bàse, *s.f.* 1. base: — *di un triangolo*, base of a triangle 2. (*fondamento*) basis (*pl.* bases), foundation, ground: *la — delle ricerche*, the basis for research -work ‖ *in — a ciò*, on this ground; *in — a ql.co.*, on the ground of sth.; *senza —*, groundless 2.(*arch.*) base, basement 4.(*edil.*) (*fondazione*) sill 5.(*econ.*) standard: — *oro*, gold standard 6.(*mil.*) base: — *aerea, navale*, air, naval base; *ritorno alla —*, (*aer.*) return to base 7. (*chim.*) base 8. — *comune*, (*mec.*) common bedplate.

basétta, *s.f.* side-whisker.

bàsico, *ag.* (*chim.*) basic.

basilàre, *ag.* 1. foundamental, basal 2. (*anat.*) basilar: *arteria —*, basilar artery.

Basilèa, *no.pr.f.* (*geog.*) Basel, Basle, Bâle.

basílica, *s.f.* basilica.

basilicàle, *ag.* basilican.

basílico, *s.m.* (*bot.*) basil.

Basílio, *no.pr.m.* Basil.

basilíseo, *s.m.* 1. (*mit.*) basilisk ‖ *sguardo da —*, basilisk-glance 2. (*zool.*) basilisk.

basilíssa, *s.f.* (*st.*) Byzantine empress.

basíre, *v.i.* to swoon, to faint: — *dal freddo*, to faint with cold.

bassaménte, *av.* 1. meanly, basely 2. (*a bassa voce*) in a low voice, softly.

bassétta, *s.f.* (*giuoco di carte*) basset.

bassétto, *s.m.* (*mus.*) bassette, bassetto.

bassézza, *s.f.* 1. baseness, meanness 2. (*azione meschina*) mean action.

basso, *ag.* 1. low; (*di statura*) short; (*di acque*) shallow; (*di suoni*) low, soft: *bassa marea*, low tide; *acqua bassa*, shallow water: *trovarsi in basse acque*, *fig.* to be in low water (*o* to be in financial difficulties); *fronte bassa*, low forehead; *prezzo —*, low price; *stanza bassa*, low room; *statura bassa*, low stature; *un uomo —*, a short man; *voce bassa*, low voice ‖ *le Basse Alpi*, (*geog.*) the Lower Alps; *la Bassa Alsazia*, (*geog.*) Lower Alsace; *il Basso Egitto*, (*geog.*) Lower Egypt; *i Paesi Bassi*, (*geog.*) the Low Countries ‖ — *latino*, Low Latin ‖ *altare —*, (*eccl.*) low altar; *messa bassa*, (*eccl.*) low mass ‖ *far man bassa*, to sack (*o* to plunder) 2. (*inferiore*) low, inferior: *bassa qualità*, (*comm.*) inferior quality 3. (*st.*) late: — *Medioevo*, late Middle Ages 4. (*abietto*) base, vile: *una bassa calunnia*, a base calumny ‖ *s.m.* 1. lower part, bottom ‖ *gli alti e bassi della vita*, the ups and downs of life ‖ *cadere in —*, to lose one's reputation (*o* one's social standing) 2. (*mus.*) bass ‖ *chiave di —*, bass clef.

bassofóndo, *s.m.* 1. (*geog.*) shallow; shallow water 2. (*strato inferiore della società*) the underworld: *i bassifondi sociali*, the scum of society.

bassopiàno, *s.m.* lowland.

bassorilièvo, *s.m.* bas(s)-relief.

bassòtto, *ag.* thickset: *quel tuo amico —*, that thickset friend of yours ‖ *s.m.* (*cane*) dachshund; (*fam.*) sausage-dog.

bassúra, *s.f.* lowland.

bàsta, *s.f.* 1. (*imbastitura*) basting, tacking 2. (*orlo*) tuck.

bastànte, *ag.* sufficient, enough.

bastanteménte, *av.* sufficiently, enough.

bastàrda, *s.f.* 1. illegitimate daughter 2. (*lima*) bastard file.

bastàrdo, *ag.* 1. bastard, illegitimate 2. (*di animale, pianta*) crossbred, mongrel 3. *fig.* false, spurious ‖ *s.m.* 1. bastard, illegitimate son 2. (*di animale*) mongrel 3. (*tip.*) slanting writing.

bastàre, *v.i.* 1. to be enough, to be sufficient, to suffice (s.o.): *bastò una parola per persuaderlo*, one word was enough to persuade him; *basti dire che...*, it is enough (*o* suffice it) to say that...; *gli bastò la mia parola*, he was satisfied with my word; *mi bastano mille lire*, one thousand lire will be enough for me ‖ *basta!*, enough! (*o* stop it! *o mar.* avast!): *basta con i dittatori!*, away with dictators!; *basta con queste chiacchiere!*, enough of this idle talk! ‖ *non mi basta l'animo* (*di fare ql.co.*), I have no courage (to do sth.) ‖ — *a se stesso*, to have no need for others (*o* to be self-sufficient) 2. (*durare*) to last: *questo vestito mi deve — tutto l'anno*, this suit must last me the whole year.

bastévole, *ag.* sufficient, enough.

bastevolménte, *av.* sufficiently.

bàstia[1], *V.* **bàsta**.

bastia[2], *s.f.* (*mil.*) fortification, rampart, stockade.

bastíglia, *s.f.* bastille, fortress ‖ *la Bastiglia*, the Bastille.

bastiménto, *s.m.* ship, vessel; (*nave da carico*) cargo -boat; (*mercantile*) merchant ship.

bastingàggio, *s.m.* (*mar.*) topgallant bulwarks (*pl.*).

bastionàre, *v.t.* to rampart, to fortify with ramparts.

bastionàta, *s.f.* fortification, ramparts (*pl.*).

bastióne, *s.m.* rampart, bastion.

bàsto, *s.m.* 1. pack-saddle: *cavallo da —*, pack horse ‖ *essere da — e da sella*, *fig.* to be able to turn one's hand to anything ‖ *mettere il — a qlcu.*, *fig.* to subjugate s.o. 2. — *rovescio*, culvert.

bastonàre, *v.t.* 1. to beat; to cane; (*randellare*) to drub, to cudgel: *lo bastonarono a sangue*, they beat him until they drew blood ‖ *ha l'aria di un cane bastonato*, *fig.* he looks beaten (*o* crestfallen) 2. (*fig. rar.*) to censure

bastonàta, *s.f.* blow with a stick, blow with a cane; (*randellata*) blow with a cudgel ‖ *bastonate da orbi*, furious caning.

bastonatóre, *s.m.* beater; (*con randello*) drubber.

bastonatúra, *s.f.* beating; caning; (*con randello*) drubbing, cudgelling.

bastóne, *s.m.* 1. stick; cane; staff; baton; (*randello*) cudgel, club: — *da passeggio*, walking-stick; — *di maresciallo*, field-marshal's baton ‖ *mettere il — tra le ruote a qlcu.*, *fig.* to put a spoke in s.o.'s wheel (o to thwart s.o.) 2. (*forma di pane*) long loaf 3. *fig.* (*sostegno*) staff, support: *il — della sua vecchiaia*, the staff of his old age 4. *pl.* (*a carte*) the suit in Italian (playing) cards corresponding to clubs.

batacchiàre, *v.t.* to beat with a clapper.

batacchiàta, *s.f.* blow with a clapper.

batàcchio, *s.m.* clapper.

batimetría, *s.f.* bathymetry.

batimètrico, *ag.* bathymetric.

batímetro, *s.m.* bathometer.

batiscàfo, *s.m.* (*mar.*) bathyscaph(e).

batisfèra, *s.f.* 1. bathysphere 2. (*abisso marino*) abyss.

batisfèrio, *s.m.* bathysphere.

batísta, *s.f.* (*tela*) batiste, cambric.

batòcchio, *s.m.* clapper.

batometría, *e derivati*, *V.* **batimetría**, *e derivati*.

batòsta, *s.f.* 1. (*percossa*) blow 2. *fig.* blow; accident, misfortune; (*perdita finanziaria*) financial loss; (*sconfitta*) defeat: *subire una —*, to suffer defeat.

batràce, *s.m.* (*zool.*) batrachian.

batracomiomachìa, *s.f.* 1. (*lett.*) batrachomyomachy 2. *fig.* futile, polemic, ridiculous controversy.

battàglia, *s.f.* 1. battle, fight: — *campale*, pitched battle; — *navale*, sea fight; *campo di —*, battle-field; *finta —*, mock battle; *fronte di —*, line of battle; *ordine di —*, battle order (o *letter.* battle array); *esercito schierato in —*, army drawn up in battle array (o in battle order); *dare — a qlcu.*, to give battle to s.o. (o to join battle with s.o.); *rifiutare, accettare —*, to refuse, to accept battle; *vincere una —*, to win a battle ‖ *cavallo da —*, war-horse (o charger) ‖ *cavallo di —*, *fig.* favourite subject (o favourite piece o *fam.* pet subject): *è il suo cavallo di —*, he rides this subject to death 2. (*pitt.*) battle-piece 3. (*conflitto*) conflict, struggle: — *di interessi*, conflict of interests.

battagliàre, *v.i.* 1. to battle, to fight, to struggle 2. *fig.* (*disputare*) to argue, to dispute.

battaglièro, *ag.* warlike, bellicose: *avversario —*, *fig.* fierce opponent.

battàglio, *s.m.* clapper.

battaglióne, *s.m.* (*mil.*) battalion.

battàna, *s.f.* 1. (*imbarcazione*) punt 2. (*remo corto*) scull.

battellàta, *s.f.* boat-load.

battellière, *s.m.* boatman (*pl.* boatmen).

battèllo, *s.m.* 1. boat: — *a remi*, rowing-boat; — *a vela*, sailing-boat; — *da pesca*, fishing-boat; — *di salvataggio*, life-boat; *venni in —*, I came by boat; *andare in —*, to go boating (o to boat) 2. (*piccolo piroscafo*) steamboat, steamer.

battènte, *s.m.* 1. (*di porta*) leaf; wing; (*di finestra*) shutter: *porta a due battenti*, double-door (o folding -door) 2. (*di boccaporto*) washboard 3. (*picchiotto di porta*) knocker 4. (*idraulica*) head 5. (*artigl.*) hurter 6. (*ind. tessile*) batten, sley 7. (*di orologio*) hammer.

bàttere, *v.t.* 1. to beat; to strike, to hit: *battendogli una mano sulla spalla*, clapping him on the back; *egli mi battè*, he gave me a blow; *la notizia gli fece — il cuore*, the news thrilled him (o made his heart beat stronger); *l'orologio battè le quattro*, the clock struck four; — *le ali*, to flutter; — *le mani*, to clap hands; — *il pallone*, to kick the ball; — *i piedi*, to stamp (one's feet); — *il tamburo*, to beat the drum; — *il tempo*, to beat time; — *l'acqua nel mortaio*, *fig.* to plough the sands ‖ — *il chiodo*, *fig.* to insist ‖ — *i denti*, to chatter: *batteva i denti per il freddo*, his teeth were chattering

with cold ‖ *in un batter d'occhio*, in the twinkling of an eye ‖ — *il naso in qlcu.*, *fig.* to run (o to bump) into s.o. ‖ — *il tacco*, *fig.* to take to one's heels ‖ *non sapere dove — il capo*, *fig.* to be at a loss ‖ *senza — ciglio*, without batting an eyelid 2. (*sconfiggere*) to overcome, to defeat, to overpower; (*spor.*) to beat: — *qlcu. in ql.co.*, to beat s.o. in sthg. (o at sthg.) 3. (*metal.*) to hammer; (*coniare*) to mint: *ferro battuto*, hammered (o wrought) iron; — *il ferro a freddo*, to cold-hammer iron; — *moneta*, to mint coin ‖ — *il ferro finché è caldo*, *fig.* to strike while the iron is hot (o to make hay while the sun shines) 4. (*trebbiare*) to thrash, to thresh: — *il grano*, to thresh corn 5. (*percorrere*) to scour: — *la campagna*, to scour the country; — *un sentiero*, to beat a path 6. (*scrivere a macchina*) to type (write) 7. (*mar. mil.*) to fly: — *bandiera nera*, to fly a black flag 8. (*tennis*) to serve ‖ *v.i.* 1. (*dare colpi*) to beat, to tap, to knock: *battè piano alla sua finestra*, he tapped at her window; — *alla porta*, to knock at the door ‖ — *in ritirata*, to beat a hasty retreat ‖ — *in testa*, (*di motore*) to knock ‖ *la lingua batte dove il dente duole*, *prov.* the tongue ever turns to the aching tooth 2. (*di cuore, di polso*) to throb, to pulsate: *il cuore gli batteva*, his heart was beating (o was going pit-a-pat); *il cuore gli batteva da scoppiare*, his heart was throbbing violently ‖ **bàttersi**, *v.r.* 1. to beat oneself: — *il petto*, to beat one's breast; *fig.* to repent ‖ *battersela*, to run away (o to beat it) 2. (*combattere*) to fight ‖ *v.r. reciproco* (*duellare*) to duel.

batterìa, *s.f.* 1. (*mil.*) battery: — *a cavallo*, horse battery; — *contraerea*, antiaircraft battery; — *costiera*, coastal battery; — *da campo*, field battery; — *di artiglieria*, battery of artillery; — *di grosso calibro*, heavy battery; *fuoco di —*, battery fire 2. (*elett.*) (electric) battery: — *di accumulatori*, storage battery; — *di ricambio*, refill for electric torch 3. (*mus.*) battery 4. (*mar.*) battery deck 5. — *da cucina*, kitchen utensils (*pl.*) 6. (*spor.*) heat 7. (*di orologio*) striking mechanism.

battèrico, *ag.* bacterial.

battèrio, *s.m.* bacterium (*pl.* bacteria).

batteriología, *s.f.* bacteriology.

batteriològico, *ag.* bacteriological.

batteriòlogo, *s.m.* bacteriologist.

batterioterapìa, *s.f.* bacteriotherapy.

batterìsta, *s.m.* (*mus.*) ~~battery man~~ *drummer*

battesimàle, *ag.* baptismal.

battésimo, *s.m.* 1. (*relig.*) baptism, christening: *certificato di —*, certificate of baptism; *nome di —*, Christian (o first o baptismal) name; *registro dei battesimi*, register of baptisms; *dare il — a qlcu.*, to baptize s.o.; *ricevere il —*, to receive baptism (o to be baptized); *tenere a — un bambino*, (*di padrino*) to stand (as) godfather to a child; (*di madrina*) to stand (as) godmother to a child 2. *fig.* baptism: — *dell'aria*, first flight; — *del fuoco*, baptism of fire: — *della linea*, ducking on crossing the line; — *di sangue*, baptism of blood 3. (*di campane, navi*) baptism, blessing.

battezzàndo, *s.m.* (*relig.*) person to be christened.

battezzàre, *v.t.* 1. (*relig.*) to baptize, to christen: *è stato battezzato cattolico*, he was baptized a Roman Catholic; — *un bambino con il nome di Carlo*, to christen a child Charles 2. *fig.* (*dare il nome*) to christen, to nickname; to dub: *battezzò la pazienza codardia*, he baptized patience cowardice; *essi lo avevano battezzato « il Negro »*, they had christened (o dubbed) him "the Nigger" 3. (*campane, navi*) to baptize 4. (*annacquare*) to water down: — *il vino*, to water down one's wine ‖ **battezzàrsi**, *v.r.* (*autoproclamarsi*) to baptize oneself: *egli si battezzò da sè un grande uomo*, he baptized himself a great man.

battezzatóre, *s.m.* baptizer.

battezzatòrio, *s.m.* baptismal font.

battibaléno, *s.m.*: *in un —*, in a twinkling (o in the twinkling of an eye o *fam.* in a jiffy).

battibécco, *s.m.* squabble, petty quarrel, bickering: *battibecchi in famiglia,* family squabbles.

batticàrne, *s.m.* meat pounder, meat pestle.

batticóda, *s.m.* (*ornit.*) wagtail.

batticòffa, *s.m.* (*mar.*) top-lining.

batticuòre, *s.m.* 1. heart-throb, throbbing, palpitation 2. (*apprensione*) anxiety; (*timore*) fear.

battifiànco, *s.m.* stable cross-bar.

battifrédo, *s.m.* watch-tower.

battígia, *s.f.* shore-line, water-edge.

battilàno, *s.m.* woolcomber.

battilàstra, *s.m.* panel beater, sheet metal worker.

battilòro, *s.m.* gold-beater.

battimàno, *s.m.* clapping (of hands); (*applauso*) applause.

battimàzza, *s.m.* blacksmith's assistant.

battiménto, *s.m.* 1. (*acu.*) beat 2. (*mec.*) striking.

battipàlo, *s.m.* (*mec.*) pile engine, pile-driver.

battipànni, *s.m.* carpet-beater.

battiscàrpa, a, *l.av.* 1. (*in fretta*) in haste 2. (*in piedi*) standing.

battísta, *s.m.* baptist || **Battísta,** *no.pr.m.* Baptist || *Giovanni il —,* John the Baptist.

battistèro, *s.m.* baptist(e)ry.

battistràda, *s.m.* 1. (*chi precede*) outrider: *fare da —,* to lead the way 2. (*di pneumatico*) tread, track: *— applicato,* cap; *— liscio,* smooth tread; *— scolpito,* engraved tread; *applicare un nuovo —,* to cap; *ricostruire il —,* to retread.

bàttito, *s.m.* 1. heart-beat, palpitation 2. *fig.* anxiety, care 3. (*mec.*) pant; (*anormale*) rattle; (*di biella, punteria, ecc.*) knock, knocking: *— dello stantuffo,* piston slap; *— in testa,* spark knock (*o* spark ping).

battitóia, *s.f.* (*tip.*) planer.

battitóio, *s.m.* 1. (*ind. tessile*) willow; (*per lino, canapa*) stencher, beater 2. (*battente di porta*) door-knocker.

battitóre, *s.m.* 1. (*tennis*) server; (*cricket, baseball*) batsman (*pl.* batsmen), striker; (*caccia*) beater 2. (*mec.*) (*di trebbiatrice*) awner; (*di macchina tessile*) beater 3. (*arc. mil.*) scout.

battitúra, *s.f.* 1. beating; (*fam.*) thrashing 2. (*agr.*) threshing.

bàttola, *s.f.* clapper.

battología, *s.f.* (*ret.*) battology.

battològico, *ag.* (*ret.*) battological.

battúta, *s.f.* 1. beat, beating: *— di mani,* clapping (of hands); *— di piedi,* stamping (of feet); *dare una — a qlcu.,* (*fam.*) to give s.o. a beating || *— di caccia,* beating; *— di polizia,* round-up 2. (*osservazione*) remark: *— di spirito,* witty remark 3. (*mus.*) bar, measure: *— d'aspetto,* rest 4. (*tennis*) service 5. (*teat.*) cue: *dare la — a qlcu.,* to give s.o. his cue; *perdere la —,* to miss one's cue.

battúto, *ag.* 1. beaten, struck: *isola battuta dai flutti,* sea-girt isle || *a spron —,* at full speed 2. *fig.* (*affranto*) crushed, tired out, worn out 3. (*di metallo*) hammered, beaten; (*lavorato a martello*) wrought: *ferro —,* wrought-iron; *oro —,* beaten gold 4. (*coniato*) coined, minted 5. (*di strada*) beaten, trodden, frequented: *un sentiero —,* a beaten path || *s.m.* 1. (*di carne*) hash, hashed meat 2. (*di erbe*) minced herbs (*pl.*) 3. (*lardo tritato con cipolle*) dressing made of minced bacon and onions.

batùffolo, batúfolo, *s.m.* flock: *un — di cotone,* a cotton flock.

bàu, (*voce onomatopeica riproducente un abbaio*) bowwow: *far —,* to bowwow.

Bàuci, *no.pr.f.* (*mit.*) Baucis.

baúle, *s.m.* trunk: *— armadio,* wardrobe trunk; *disfare i bauli,* to unpack; *fare i bauli,* to pack up; (*prepararsi a partire*) to prepare for a journey || *viaggiare come un —,* to travel without learning anything.

baussíte, *s.f.* (*min.*) bauxite.

baútta, *s.f.* domino (*pl.* dominoes).

bauxíte, *s.f.* (*min.*) bauxite.

bàva, *s.f.* 1. slaver, slobber; (*di bambini*) dribble: *far la —,* to slaver; (*di rabbia*) to foam; *fig.* (*arrabbiarsi*) to get angry 2. (*di lumache*) slime 3. (*di vento*) light breeze 4. (*di seta*) silk filament 5. (*metal.*) flash.

bavaglíno, *s.m.* bib.

bavàglio, *s.m.* gag: *metter il — a qlcu.,* to gag s.o. || *mettere altrui il —,* *fig.* (*impedirgli di parlare*) to prevent s.o. from speaking.

bavarése, *ag. s.m.* Bavarian.

bavèlla, *s.f.* 1. floss 2. (*tessuto*) floss-silk.

bàvera, *s.f.* tippet, cape, muffler.

baverína, *s.f.* collarette, collar.

bàvero, *s.m.* collar: *— di pelliccia,* fur collar || *prendere qlcu. per il —,* to seize s.o. by the scruff of his neck; *fig.* (*turlupinarlo*) to dupe s.o.

bavétta, *s.f.* (*metal.*) burr.

Bavièra, *no.pr.f.* (*geog.*) Bavaria.

bavóso, *ag.* slavering, slobbery.

bazàr, *s.m.* 1. department store 2. (*mercato orientale*) bazaar.

bazooka, *s.m.* (*mil.*) bazooka.

bàzza¹, *s.f.* good luck: *che —!,* what luck!.

bàzza², *s.f.* (*mento sporgente*) slipper-chin.

bazzàna, *s.f.* basan.

bazzècola, *s.f.* trifle.

bàzzica, *s.f.* (*giuoco di carte*) bezique; (*giuoco di biliardo*) pool.

bazzicàre, *v.t.* to frequent: *egli bazzica sempre lo stesso luogo,* he always frequents the same place || *v.i.* to frequent (a place); to resort (to a place): *non bazzica più nei bar,* he no longer resorts to bars.

bazzòffia, *s.f.* 1. (*brodaglia*) slops (*pl.*) 2. *fig.* hash, botch, bungle.

bazzòtto, *ag.* 1. soft-boiled: *uova bazzotte,* soft-boiled eggs 2. (*grassoccio*) plump, stout.

be', *inter.* (*apocope di* bene) well.

bè, (*voce onomatopeica riproducente un belato*) baa.

beàre, *v.t.* to make glad, to make happy || **beàrsi,** *v.r.* to rejoice (at, in sthg.), to delight (in sthg.).

beataménte, *av.* blissfully; happily.

beatificàre, *v.t.* to beatify: *fu beatificato subito dopo la morte,* he was beatified soon after death.

beatificazióne, *s.f.* beatification.

beatífico, *ag.* beatific(al).

beatitúdine, *s.f.* 1. beatitude; blessedness || *le Beatitudini del Discorso della Montagna,* the Beatitudes of the Sermon on the Mount || *Sua Beatitudine,* His Holiness (the Pope) 2. (*felicità terrena*) happiness, bliss.

beàto, *ag.* 1. happy, glad; blissful: *vita —,* happy life || *— lui!,* (*fam.*) lucky fellow! 2. (*relig.*) blessed || *beati i poveri di spirito,* blessed are the poor in spirit || *s.m.* (*relig.*) blessed soul, soul in bliss.

Beatríce, *no.pr.f.* Beatrice, Beatrix || *dim.* Bee, Trix.

bebè, *s.m.* baby, infant.

béca, *s.f.* vulgar country-woman (*pl.* -women).

bécca, *s.f.* (*cocca di fazzoletto*) corner (of a handkerchief).

beccàccia, *s.f.* (*ornit.*) woodcock.

beccaccíno, *s.m.* (*ornit.*) snipe.

beccafíco, *s.m.* (*ornit.*) beccafico.

beccàio, *s.m.* butcher.

beccamòrti, *s.m.* grave-digger, sexton.

beccàre, *v.t.* 1. to peck; to pick up (with the beak) 2. (*ferire col becco*) to peck: *— a morte,* to peck to death 3. (*scherz.*) (*mangiare*) to eat 4. *fig.* (*stuzzicare*) to tease 5. (*guadagnare*) to win, to get 6. (*prendere, acchiappare*) to catch: *ho beccato un raffreddore,* I have caught a cold; *non mi beccherai!,* you won't catch me doing that! || **beccàrsi,** *v.r.* 1. (*procurarsi*) to win, to get: *mi sono beccato mille lire,* I have won a thousand lire 2. *— il cervello,* to rack one's brains || *v.r. reciproco* 1. (*di uccelli*) to peck each other (one another) 2. *fig.* (*litigare*) to quarrel, to wrangle.

beccàre, *s.m.* 1. (*becchime*) birdseed 2. (*scherz.*) (*cibo*) food.

beccàta, *s.f.* **1.** (*colpo di becco*) peck **2.** (*quantità afferrata col becco*) beakful.

beccatèllo, *s.m.* **1.** (*edil.*) bracket, corbel **2.** (*piuolo*) peg.

beccatóio, *s.m.* seed-trough (of a bird-cage).

beccatúra, *s.f.* pecking.

beccheggiàre, *v.i.* (*mar.*) to pitch.

becchéggio, *s.m.* (*mar.*) pitch, pitching.

becchería, *s.f.* butcher's shop.

becchíme, *s.m.* **1.** birdseed **2.** (*scherz.*) (*cibo*) food.

becchíno, *s.m.* grave-digger, sexton.

bécco[1], *s.m.* **1.** beak, bill; (*scherz.*) (*bocca*) mouth ‖ *non ha il —, d'un quattrino*, he is penniless ‖ *bagnarsi il —*, to drink ‖ *dar di —*, to bite ‖ *mettere il — in*, to interfere with (*o* to poke one's nose into) ‖ *ecco fatto il — all'oca!*, there you are! (*o* now that's done!) **2.** (*cosa fatta a forma di becco*): — *del gas*, gas-burner; *il — di una penna*, the nib of a pen ‖ — *Bunsen*, (*chim.*) Bunsen burner **3.** (*mar.*) bow, prow.

bécco[2], *s.m.* **1.** (*zool.*) billy-goat **2.** (*marito tradito*) cuckold ‖ *essere — e bastonato*, to have insult added to injury.

beccolàre, *v.t.* to eat slowly, to peck.

beccúccio, *s.m.* **1.** small beak **2.** (*di ampolla*) neck; (*di teiera, caffettiera, ecc.*) spout.

beccúto, *ag.* beaked, billed.

beceràta, *s.f.* (*dial.*) caddish trick.

bécero, *s.m.* (*dial.*) cad; boor.

becerúme, *s.m. coll.* cads (*pl.*).

bedína, *s.f.* trawl, trawl-net.

beduína, *s.f.* (*mantello con cappuccio*) hooded cloak.

beduíno, *ag.s.m.* Bedouin ‖ *i beduini*, the Bedouins.

bee, (*voce onomatopeica riproducente un belato*) baa.

befàna, *s.f.* **1.** (*Epifania*) Epiphany **2.** "befana" (old fairy bringing toys to children) **3.** (*strenna*) gift, present **4.** (*donna brutta*) ugly (old) woman, harridan.

bèffa, *s.f.* mockery, derision; jest; hoax: *farsi beffe di qlcu.*, to make a fool of s.o.; (*deriderlo, dileggiarlo*) to laugh at s.o. (*o* to sneer at s.o.) ‖ *avere il danno e le beffe*, to have insult added to injury.

beffardaménte, *av.* scoffingly; mockingly.

beffàrdo, *ag.* scoffing; mocking: *riso —*, derisive laughter ‖ *s.m.* scoffer; mocker.

beffàre, *v.t.* to mock, to deride; to banter; to hoax; to gibe at (s.o.) ‖ **beffàrsi**, *v.r.* to scoff (at s.o., sthg.), to laugh at (s.o., sthg.): *si beffa di tutto e di tutti*, (*fam.*) he does not care a hang for anybody or anything.

beffatóre, *s.m.*, **beffatríce**, *s.f.* scoffer, mocker.

beffeggiàre, *v.t.* to flout; to jeer at (s.o., sthg.), to gibe at (s.o., sthg.), to taunt.

beffeggiatóre, *s.m.*, **beffeggiatríce**, *s.f.* giber, taunter.

bèga, *s.f.* **1.** quarrel, altercation; dispute **2.** (*affare intricato*) entangled affair.

begàrdo, *s.m.* (*st. relig.*) beghard.

beghína, *s.f.* **1.** (*st. relig.*) beguine **2.** (*bigotta*) bigot.

beghinàggio, *s.m.* (*st. relig.*) beguinage.

beghíno, *s.m.* **1.** (*st. relig.*) beghard **2.** (*bigotto*) bigot.

begliuòmini, *s.m.* (*bot.*) balsam.

begònia, *s.f.* (*bot.*) begonia.

bei, *s.m.* bey.

beige, *ag.s.m.* beige.

beilicàto, *s.m.* (*grado di bei, distretto governato dal bei*) beylic.

belàre, *v.i.* **1.** to bleat **2.** (*piagnucolare*) to whine.

belàto, *s.m.* bleat, bleating.

bèlga, *ag.s.m.* Belgian.

Bèlgio, *no. pr.m.* (*geog.*) Belgium.

Belgràdo, *no.pr.f.* (*geog.*) Belgrade.

Belínda, *no.pr.f.* Belinda.

belinogràmma, *s.m.* telephotography.

belío, *s.m.* **1.** continual bleating **2.** (*piagnucolio*) whimpering, whining.

Belisàrio, *no.pr.m.* (*st.*) Belisarius.

bèlla, *s.f.* **1.** beauty, belle: *la — del villaggio, del ballo*, the belle of the village, of the ball ‖ *la Bella Addormentata*, the Sleeping Beauty ‖ *la Bella e la*

Bestia, Beauty and the Beast **2.** (*innamorata*) sweet-heart; fiancée; (*fam.*) girl (-friend) **3.** (*spor.*) final **4.** (*a carte*) final game **5.** (*bot.*) marvel of Peru.

belladònna, *s.f.* (*bot. farm.*) belladonna.

bellaménte, *av.* **1.** (*in bel modo*) nicely; (*con bella maniera*) politely; gracefully **2.** (*abilmente*) skilfully; adroitly.

bellétta, *s.f.* slime, slush, mud; mire.

bellétto, *s.m.* rouge; (*trucco*) make-up.

bellézza, *s.f.* **1.** beauty; loveliness; (*di uomo*) handsomeness: *apparve in tutta la sua —*, she appeared in all her beauty; *era orgogliosa della sua —*, she was proud of her good looks; *questo quadro è una —*, this picture is a beauty; *tua sorella è una vera —*, your sister is a real beauty; *conservare, perdere la propria —*, to preserve, to lose one's beauty ‖ *canta che è una —*, she sings beautifully ‖ *istituto di —*, beauty parlour; *prodotti di —*, beauty preparations (*o* aids to beauty); *trattamento di —*, beauty treatment **2.** (*bella donna*) beauty, beautiful woman: *vi erano tutte le bellezze della città*, all the beauty of the town was there ‖ *vieni qua, — mia*, come here, (my) darling **3.** *pl.*: *le bellezze della natura*, the beauties of nature; *le bellezze della campagna*, the amenities of the country **4.** *la — di un anno*, a whole year; *ho speso la — di mille lire*, I have spent a cool thousand lire.

bèllico[1], *ag.* (*del tempo di guerra*) wartime (*attributivo*); military, martial; war (*attributivo*): *materiale —*, war material; *ordine —*, martial array.

bèllico[2], *s.m.* (*pop.*) navel.

bellicóso, *ag.* warlike; bellicose; martial; pugnacious.

belligeràne, *ag.* belligerent; rival ‖ *s.c.* belligerent.

belligerànza, *s.f.* belligerency, belligerence.

bellígero, *ag.* warlike; bellicose; martial; pugnacious.

bellimbústo, *s.m.* dandy; fop; beau (*pl.* beaux); coxcomb: *fare il —*, to play the dandy.

bellíno, *ag.* pretty, nice ‖ *con le belle belline*, with nice manners (*o* coaxingly) ‖ *ne ho sentite di belline sul tuo conto!*, (*iron.*) I have heard some pretty tales about you!.

bèllo, *ag.* **1.** fine, beautiful; (*di uomo*) handsome: *una bella donna*, a beautiful woman; *belle gambe*, shapely legs; *un bell'uomo*, a handsome man ‖ *le belle arti*, the fine arts; *le belle lettere*, literature ‖ *la bella età*, (the days of) youth; *ai sui bei giorni*, in his palmy days ‖ *una bella occasione*, a fine opportunity ‖ *il bel sesso*, the fair sex ‖ — *spirito*, pretty wit: *un — spirito*, a wit ‖ *avere un bel giuoco*, (*a carte*) to have good cards (*o* fair play) ‖ *Filippo il Bello*, (*st.*) Philip the Fair **2.** (*elegante*) smart, spruce: *il bel mondo*, the fashionable set; *il mio abito —*, (*di donna*) my best (*o* my party) frock ‖ *come sei —!*, you do look smart! ‖ *farsi —*, to smarten oneself up; (*vantarsi*) to blow one's trumpet **3.** (*nobile*) fine, noble: *una bella anima*, a noble (*o* generous) soul; *un bel nome*, an honoured (*o* a glorious) name; *bei sentimenti*, fine (*o* noble) feelings **4.** (*gentile*) kind, fine: *belle maniere*, refined manners **5.** (*sereno*) fine: *un bel cielo*, a clear sky; *una bella giornata*, a fine day; *fa —*, it is fair (*o* fine) weather **6.** (*importante*) fine; important: *ha un bel posto*, he has an important position; *farsi un bel nome*, to make a name for oneself **7.** (*piacevole*) nice, pleasant: *un bel carattere*, a pleasant character **8.** (**Fraseologia**): *bel —*, gently (*o* slowly): *sta venendo bel —*, he is coming slowly ‖ *bell'e morto*, as dead as a door nail ‖ *una bella età*, a ripe old age ‖ *un bel mascalzone, un mascalzone — e buono*, a thorough rascal ‖ *una bella paura*, an awful fright ‖ *a bella posta*, on purpose ‖ *che bel vantaggio!*, (*scherz.*) a fine advantage indeed! ‖ *nel bel mezzo*, right in the middle ‖ *avete un bel correre, non lo prenderete mai*, run as you may you won't catch him; *avete un bel parlare*, you may talk till all's blue (*o* till you are blue in the face); *aveva un bel dire*, in spite of his assertions; *ebbi un bel cercare, ma non trovai niente*, search as I might, I found nothing ‖

ne ha fatte delle belle!, pretty things he has been up to! || *questa è bella!*, that's a funny (o queer) story! || *raccontarne delle belle su qlcu.*, to spread nice reports about s.o. || *scamparsela bella*, to have a narrow escape (o a close shave) || *tutto questo è molto —, ma...*, that's all very fine, but....

bèllo, *s.m.* **1.** the beautiful, beauty: *il — della vita*, the beauty of life || *il — piace a tutti*, everybody likes what's nice **2.** (*innamorato*) sweetheart, lover; (*fam.*) boy(-friend) **3.** (**Fraseologia**): *sul più —*, at the right moment; (*iron.*) at the most awkward time || *che si fa di —?*, what are we going to do? || *ci volle del — e del buono per convincerlo*, it took a lot (of trouble) to persuade him || *il tempo si mette al —*, it is clearing up || *ora viene il —*, now you'll hear the best of it; (*iron.*) now the fat is in the fire.

bellòcchio, *s.m.* (*min.*) cat's eye.

bellòccio, *ag.* goodish-looking: *una ragazza belloccia e prosperosa*, a buxom wench.

bellospírito, *s.m.* character, wit, witty person, wag: *è proprio un —*, he is a character.

belluíno, *ag.* bestial, brutal, beastly.

bellumóre, *s.m.* character, wag, wit, witty person.

bellúria, *s.f.* (*fam.*) outward beauty.

beltà, *s.f.* (*poet.*) beauty.

bélva, *s.f.* **1.** wild animal, wild beast **2.** (*bruto*) brute.

belvedére, *s.m.* **1.** (*arch.*) belvedere **2.** (*mar.*) mizzen-topgallant sail **3.** (*ferr.*) observation end: *vettura —*, observation car.

belzebú, *s.m.* Beelzebub; (*fam. scherz.*) Old Nick.

belzuíno, *s.m.* (*bot. chim.*) benzoin.

bembè, *inter.* (*fam.*) well!.

benaccètto, *ag.* welcome.

benaffètto, *ag.* **1.** (*assai stimato*) highly esteemed **2.** (*molto affezionato*) very fond (of s.o., sthg.).

benallevàto, *ag.* well-bred.

benalzàto, *inter.* good morning!.

benamàto, *ag.* beloved, cherished; darling.

benànche, *cong.* (*fam.*) even if, though.

benandàta, *s.f.* **1.** (*mancia*) tip, gratuity **2.** (*buonuscita*) indemnity, key-money.

benarrivàto, *inter.* welcome! || *s.m.* welcome: *dare il — a qlcu.*, to welcome s.o.

beneauguràto, *ag.* (*letter.*) auspicious; happy; desired.

benavvedúto, *ag.* shrewd, wise, sagacious.

benavventuràto, *ag.* **1.** lucky, fortunate **2.** (*prospero*) prosperous; (*felice*) happy.

benché, *cong.* although, though; (*per quanto*) however: *— ascoltassi con attenzione, non riuscii a capire*, however closely I listened, I could not understand; *— tardi, continuò a lavorare*, though it was late, he went on working || *non avevo il — minimo sospetto*, I did not have even the slightest suspicion.

bènda, *s.f.* **1.** bandage; band: *gli tolse le bende*, he took off (o removed) his bandages || *le sacre bende*, the holy bands; (*veli di monaca*) nun's veils || *gli tolsi la — dagli occhi*, *fig.* I undeceived him; *quando gli cadde la — dagli occhi*, *fig.* when he perceived the truth (o when truth dawned upon him); *avere le bende agli occhi*, *fig.* to be blinded **2.** *— di terzarolo*, (*mar.*) reef-band.

bendàggio, *s.m.* **1.** (*boxe*) handwraps (*pl.*) **2.** *V.* **bendatúra.**

bendàre, *v.t.* to bandage, to bind up, to dress; to wrap up: *la sua mano era bendata*, his hand was bandaged; *— una ferita*, to dress a wound || *— gli occhi a qlcu.*, *fig.* to blindfold s.o.

bendatúra, *s.f.* **1.** bandaging **2.** (*fasciatura*) bandage.

bendóne, *s.m.* (*eccl.*) mitre-band.

bène, *s.m.* **1.** good: *questo ti farà —*, this will do you good; *augurare del — a qlcu.*, to wish s.o. well; *dire — di qlcu.*, to speak well of s.o.; *fare del —*, to engage in good works || *a fin di —*, to a good purpose || *ogni ben di Dio*, *fig.* all sorts of good things || *per il tuo —*, (*per amor tuo*) for your sake || *Sommo Bene*, (*Dio*)

Summum Bonum || *voler — a qlcu.*, to love (o to be fond of) s.o. **2.** (*persona amata*) beloved person, darling; (*innamorato, innamorata*) sweetheart: *mio —*, (my) darling (o my sweetheart o my love) **3.** (*vantaggio*) advantage: *per il — del popolo*, for the welfare of the people; *per il tuo —*, to your advantage **4.** (*dono*) gift; blessing: *la salute è il più grande dei beni*, health is the greatest of blessings **5.** *pl.* property (*sing.*), possession (*sing.*): *beni di consumo*, consumer goods; *beni immobili*, real estate; *beni mobili*, personal property (o movables o goods and chattels); *beni strumentali*, stock-in-trade || *avere dei beni al sole*, to be a man of property.

bène, *av.* **1.** well: *abbastanza —*, fairly well (o tolerably well); *quell'abito non mi va —*, that dress does not fit me; *questo soprabito non mi sta —*, this overcoat does not suit me; *va —!*, all right!; *star —*, to be well (o to be in good health) || *di — in meglio*, better and better || *nè — nè male*, so so (o *sl. amer.* fifty-fifty) || *persona per —*, (*onesta*) honest (o trustworthy) person; (*educata*) well-bred person || *lo credo —!*, I can well believe it! || *lo sgridai ben —*, I scolded him severely || *vi sta — —!*, it serves you right! || *star — a denari*, to have plenty of money (o to be well off) **2.** (*molto*) very, quite: *il dono fu ben accetto*, the gift was very welcome; *saremo ben lieti se...*, we shall be very pleased if...; *essere ben stanco*, to be very tired (o to be tired out) **3.** (*nientemeno*) **no less than; as much as;** (*pl.*) **as many as:** *ho scritto ben venti pagine*, I have written no less than twenty pages; *mi costerà ben duecento dollari*, it will cost me a good two hundred dollars.

benedettíno, *ag.* (*eccl.*) Benedictine || *s.* **1.** (*eccl.*) Benedictine || *pazienza da —*, patience of a saint **2.** (*liquore*) benedictine.

benedétto, *ag.* **1.** blessed: *memoria benedetta*, blessed (o dear) memory || *Benedetto Iddio!*, Good Lord! || *è un — uomo*, he is a queer fellow **2.** (*consacrato*) consecrated, blessed; holy: *acqua benedetta*, holy water; *pane —*, consecrated bread **3.** (*agognato*) much desired; much wished-for: *il dì — della vittoria*, the much wished-for day of our victory.

Benedétto, *no.pr.m.* Benedict, Bennet.

benedícite, *s.m.* benedicite; (*fam.*) grace: *recitare il —*, to say grace.

benedíre, *v.t.* **1.** to bless: *benedirò sempre il giorno che ti conobbi*, I shall always bless the day I met you; *Dio vi benedica!*, God bless you!; *il padre benedisse i figli*, the father blessed his sons; *il sacerdote benedisse la casa*, the priest blessed the house || *va' a farti —!*, (*fam.*) go to hell! (o go to Jericho!); *mandare a farvi —*, (*fam.*) to send to hell **2.** (*consacrare*) to consecrate, to bless.

benedizióne, *s.f.* **1.** blessing; (*alla fine delle funzioni*) benediction: *il Papa diede la Sua — ai pellegrini*, the Pope gave the pilgrims His blessing **2.** (*consacrazione*) consecration **3.** *fig.* blessing: *questa pioggia è una — per la campagna*, this rain is a blessing for the country; *la tua venuta è una vera — per noi*, your coming is a real blessing for us.

beneducàto, *ag.* well-mannered.

benefattóre, *s.m.* benefactor.

benefattríce, *s.f.* benefactress.

beneficàre, *v.t.* to benefit; to aid; to help: *fu lui a — quella famiglia*, he was the one who helped that family.

beneficènza, *s.f.* charity; beneficence: *istituto di —*, charitable institution; *recita di —*, benefit performance.

beneficiàle, *ag.* (*dir. eccl.*) beneficed.

beneficiàre, *v.t.* to benefit; to offer advantage to (s.o., sthg.) || *v.i.* to benefit (by sthg.): *egli beneficiò di un'amnistia*, he benefited by an act of pardon.

beneficiàrio, *ag.* (*dir.*) beneficiary || *s.m.* **1.** (*dir.*) beneficiary **2.** (*dir. eccl.*) incumbent **3.** (*comm.*) payee.

beneficiàta, *s.f.* (*teat.*) benefit, benefit night.

beneficiàto, *ag.* (*dir. eccl.*) beneficed || *s.m.* **1.** (*dir.*) beneficiary **2.** (*dir. eccl.*) incumbent.

benefício, *s.m.* **1.** benefit: *a — di qlcu.*, for the benefit of s.o. **2.** (*vantaggio*) advantage: *almeno ha il — di una buona salute*, at least he has the advantage of good health; *trarre — da ql.co.*, to profit by (o of) sthg. **3.** (*comm.*) gain, profit: *— lordo, netto,* gross, net gain; *margine di — dell'8%*, 8% profit margin (o margin of profit) || *accettare col — di inventario*, to accept with benefit of inventory; *fig.* to accept (an opinion) for what it is worth **4.** (*dir. eccl.*) benefice **5.** (*evacuazione*) evacuation (of the bowels).

benèfico, *ag.* **1.** beneficent; charitable **2.** (*vantaggioso*) beneficial: *pioggia benefica*, beneficial rain.

benefízio, *e derivati,* V. **benefício,** *e derivati.*

benemerènte, *ag.* (*letter.*) well deserving; meritorious.

benemerènza, *s.f.* merit || *in —,* as a reward.

benemèrito, *ag.* well deserving: *è un uomo — della sua patria,* he is a man well deserving (o he is a man that has deserved well) of his country || *la Benemerita,* "the Carabinieri" (o the Italian Carabineers).

beneplàcito, *s.m.* **1.** (*consenso*) consent; (*approvazione*) approval **2.** (*arbitrio*) will: *a tuo —,* at your pleasure (o as you like).

benespésso, *av.* very often.

benèssere, *s.m.* **1.** (*di salute*) well-being, comfort; welfare **2.** (*prosperità*) prosperity, welfare: *lavorare per il — della famiglia,* to work for the welfare of one's family.

benestànte, *ag.* well-off, of independent means || *s.m.* well-to-do person.

benestàre, *s.m.* **1.** assent, approval, sanction; (*sl. amer.*) okay: *dare il — di un conto,* (*comm.*) to acknowledge the correctness of an account; *dare il — per ql.co.,* to give one's approval of sthg. (o to okay sthg.) **2.** (*benessere*) comfortable living.

benevolènte, *ag.* benevolent; (*gentile*) kind.

benevolènza, *s.f.* benevolence; favour: *vi preghiamo di conservarci la vostra —,* (*comm.*) we beg to continue your favour to us.

benevolménte, *av.* benevolently; kindly.

benèvolo, *ag.* benevolent, well-disposed; (*gentile*) kind: *parole benevole,* kind words.

benfàre, *s.m.* (*letter.*) well-making; well-doing.

benfàtto, *ag.* **1.** well-made; (*bello*) handsome; (*proporzionato*) well-proportioned, well-shaped **2.** (*buono d'animo*) obliging.

Bengàla, *no.pr.m.* (*geog.*) Bengal || **bengàla,** *s.m.* Bengal light.

bengalése, *ag.s.m.* Bengali, Bengalese.

bengàli, *s.m.* Bengali.

bengalína, *s.f.* (*stoffa*) bengaline.

bengalíno, *s.m.* (*ornit.*) bengali.

Bengòdi, *s.m.*: *il paese di —,* land of plenty, land of milk and honey; Cockaigne.

Beniamíno, *no.pr.m.* Benjamin || *dim.* Ben, Benny || **beniamíno,** *s.m.* darling, favourite child: *— della fortuna,* Fortune's darling (o Fortune's minion).

benignaménte, *av.* benignly, benignantly.

benignità, *s.f.* **1.** benignity; kindness of heart **2.** (*di clima*) mildness.

benígno, *ag.* **1.** benign (anche *med.*); benignant: *stelle benigne,* benignant stars; *tumore —,* benign tumour **2.** (*di clima*) mild.

beníno, *av.* fairly well, pretty well || *per —,* properly: *far le cose per —,* to do things properly (o accurately).

benintenzionàto, *ag.* well-meaning.

benintéso, *av.* of course, naturally: *verrai con noi, —,* you will come with us, of course.

beníssimo, *av.* very well, perfectly well, all right; (*amer.*) okay (*abbr.* O.K.): *egli sta —,* he is very well (o okay).

Beníto, *no.pr.m.* Bennet(t).

bènna, *s.f.* (*mec.*) bucket: *— a gabbia,* skeleton bucket; *— a quattro valve,* orange-peel bucket; *— a valve,* grapple bucket (o grab).

bennàto, *ag.* **1.** well-born **2.** (*beneducato*) well-bred.

benóne, *av.* very well; (*amer.*) okay (*abbr.* O.K.).

benparlànte, *s.m.* correct speaker.

benpensànte, *ag.* sensibile, judicious, reasonable, moderate || *s.m.* orthodox person, right-minded person || *i benpensanti,* the right-thinking.

benportànte, *ag.* hale || *è —,* she carries her years well.

benservíto, *s.m.* testimonial: *dare il — a qlcu.,* to give s.o. a testimonial; (*licenziarlo*) to dismiss s.o. (o to sack s.o. o to give s.o. the sack).

bensí, *cong.* **but;** (*ma piuttosto*) **rather:** *io non c'ero, c'era — mio fratello,* I was not there, but my brother was; *non voglio la morte del peccatore, — che si converta e viva,* I do not desire the death of the sinner, rather that he should be converted and live.

bentornàto, *inter.* welcome!: *— a casa!,* welcome home!; *— in Italia!,* welcome back to Italy! || *ag. s.m.* welcome: *dare il — a qlcu.,* to welcome s.o.'s return.

benuscíta, *s.f.* (*comm.*) key-money, premium.

benvedúto, *ag.* agreeable, well-accepted.

benvenúto, *inter.* welcome! || *ag.s.m.* welcome: *uu cordiale —,* a hearty welcome; *dare il — a qlcu.,* to welcome s.o.

benvísto, *ag.* agreeable, well-accepted.

benvolére, *s.m.* (*rar.*) benevolence.

benvolére, *v.t.* to like: *farsi —,* to make oneself liked; *prendere a — qlcu.,* to take a liking to s.o.

benvolúto, *ag.* well-liked, dear, beloved.

benzína, *s.f.* petrol; (*amer.*) gasoline, gas; (*per smacchiare*) benzine, benzoline: *fare il pieno di —,* to fill up.

benzoàto, *s.m.* (*chim.*) benzoate.

benzoè, *s.m.* (*chim.*) benzoin.

benzofenóne, *s.m.* (*chim.*) benzophenone.

benzòico, *ag.* (*chim.*) benzoic.

benzoíno, *s.m.* (*bot. chim.*) benzoin.

benzòlo, *s.m.* (*chim.*) benzole, benzol.

benzonaftòlo, *s.m.* (*farm.*) naphtholbenzoate.

benzopirène, *s.m.* (*chim.*) benzpyrene.

beóne, *s.m.* drunkard, hard drinker; (*sl.*) boozer.

beòta, *ag.s.m.* Bœotian (anche *fig.*).

Bèppe, *no.pr.m. dim.* di **Giusèppe.**

bequàdro, *s.m.* (*mus.*) natural.

bèrbero, *ag.* Berber || *s.m.* **1.** Berber **2.** (*bot.*) barberry.

berceuse, *s.f.* (*mus.*) berceuse; lullaby.

berciàre, *v.i.* to bawl (out).

bèrcio, *s.m.* bawl.

bercióne, *s.m.* bawler.

bére, *v.t.* **1.** to drink: *egli beve molto latte,* he drinks a lot of milk; *beve volentieri,* he likes wine; *questo vino si lascia —,* this wine goes down well (o is palatable) || *beviamoci su!,* let us forget it! (o let bygones be bygones!) || *— a centellini,* to sip; *— a garganella,* to drink at a draught (o at one gulp); *— a lunghi sorsi,* to drink long draughts; *— a sazietà,* to drink to satiety; *alla salute di qlcu.,* to drink (to) s.o.'s health; *— come una spugna, come un otre,* to drink like a fish (o to drink to excess); *— fino all'ultima goccia,* to drain a glass || *— un uovo,* to suck an egg || *— cogli occhi, fig.* to look at s.o. with rapture; *— grosso, fig.* to believe anything; *— le parole di qlcu., fig.* to drink in s.o.'s tales; *darla a —, fig.* to tell tall stories (o lies o fibs) **2.** (*assorbire*) to absorbe, to imbibe, to soak up, to suck in: *la terra arida bevve tutta l'acqua,* the parched land absorbed all the water.

bére, *s.m.* **1.** (*bevanda*) drink: *questo vino è un bel —,* this wine is a nice drink **2.** (*atto del bere*) drinking: *il — in fretta ti fa male,* drinking in a hurry is bad for you; *è portato al —,* he is addicted to drinking.

Berengàrio, *no.pr.m.* (*st.*) Berengarius.

Berenice, *no.pr.f.* Berenice.

bergamòtta, *ag.*: *pera —,* (*bot.*) bergamot pear || *s.f.* (*bot.*) bergamot.

bergamòtto, *s.m.* **1.** (*bot.*) bergamot **2.** (*essenza*) bergamot.

bergère, s.f. 1. (*pastorella*) shepherdess 2. (*poltrona*) easy-chair.

Bergsoniàno, ag. (*st. fil.*) Bergsonian.

beribèri, s.m. (*patol.*) beriberi.

beríllio, s.m. (*chim.*) beryllium.

beríllo, s.m. (*min.*) beryl.

beriuòlo, s.m. (bird-cage) trough.

berlíeche, s.m. (*scherz.*) devil || *far — e berlocche,* (*fam.*) to play fast and loose.

berlína[1], s.f. (*gogna*) pillory: *essere alla —,* to stand in the pillory; *fig.* to be exposed to ridicule; *mettere alla —,* to put in the pillory (*o* to pillory); *fig.* to pillory (*o* to expose to ridicule).

berlína[2], s.f. 1. (*carrozza*) berlin, gala carriage 2. (*automobile*) limousine; sedan.

berlinése, ag. Berlinese || s.c. Berliner.

berlingàccio, s.m. Thursday before Lent.

berlingòzzo, s.m. « berlingozzo » (kind of Italian cake).

Berlíno, no.pr.f. (*geog.*) Berlin.

Bermúde (the), no.pr.f.pl. (*geog.*) the Bermudas.

Bèrna, no.pr.f. (*geog.*) Berne.

Bernardína, no.pr.f. Bernardine.

Bernardíno, no.pr.m. dim. di **Bernàrdo.**

Bernàrdo, no.pr.m. Bernard || dim. Bernardine.

berneggiàre, v.i. 1. to write in Berni's style 2. (*scrivere in tono burlesco*) to write in a burlesque style.

bernésco, ag. 1. (*lett.*) of Berni; in Berni's style 2. (*scherzoso, giocoso*) burlesque.

bernése, ag. s.c. Bernese.

bernòccolo, s.m. bump (anche *fig.*); (*gonfiore*) swelling || *avere il — della medicina,* to have the bump of (*o* to have a turn for) medicine.

bernoccolúto, ag. bumpy.

berrétta, s.f. 1. cap: *— da notte,* night-cap 2. (*eccl.*) biretta: *— cardinalizia,* Cardinal's biretta.

berrettàio, berrettinàio, s.m. 1. (*chi fa berretti*) cap-maker 2. (*chi vende berretti*) cap-seller.

berrétto, s.m. cap: *— basco,* beret; *— con visiera,* peaked cap || *— frigio,* (*st.*) Phrygian cap.

bersagliàre, v.t. 1. (*sparare contro*) to shoot at (s.o., sthg.) 2. (*tormentare*) to torment, to harass, to vex.

bersaglière, s.m. "bersagliere" (*pl.* "bersaglieri") || *alla bersagliera,* boldly (*o* bravely): *procedere alla bersagliera,* to go on at full speed.

bersàglio, s.m. target; butt (anche *fig.*): *un difficile —,* a difficult target; *tiro al —,* target-shooting; *divenne il — di tutte le nostre burle,* he became the butt of all our practical jokes; *colpire il —,* to hit the mark.

bersò, s.m. bower; pergola.

Bèrta[1], no.pr.f. Bertha || *la grossa —,* (*st. mil.*) Big Bertha || *non è più il tempo che — filava,* the good old times are gone.

bèrta[2], s.f. joke, raillery, mockery: *dar la — a qlcu.,* to mock s.o. (*o* to make fun of s.o.).

bèrta[3], s.f. (*battipalo*) ram, rammer.

bèrta[4], s.f. (*ornit.*) magpie.

berteggiàre, v.t. to mock, to rally; (*schernire*) to rail at (s.o.).

bertésca, s.f. (*fortificazione*) bartizan.

Bertòldo, no.pr.m. Berthold || **bertòldo,** s.m. (*balordo*) blockhead, dolt.

Bertràndo, no.pr.m. Bertrand, Bertram || dim. Bert(ie).

bertúccia, s.f. 1. (*zool.*) Barbary ape 2. *fig.* (*donna brutta*) ugly woman 3. *pigliar la —, fig.* (*ubriacarsi*) to get drunk.

bertuccióne, s.m. 1. (*zool.*) baboon 2. *fig.* (*uomo brutto*) ugly fellow.

bestémmia, s.f. 1. oath, curse, swear: *una litania di bestemmie,* a volley of oaths; *tirar bestemmie,* to swear 2. (*empietà*) blasphemy: *la tua teoria è una vera —,* your theory is true blasphemy 3. (*discorso sciocco*) nonsense: *non dire bestemmie!,* (*fam.*) don't talk nonsense!.

bestemmiàre, v.i. 1. to curse, to swear 2. (*parlare empiamente*) to blaspheme 3. (*parlare scioccamente*) to talk nonsense || *v.t.* (*parlare in modo scorretto*) to jabber, to mangle (a language): *bestemmia un po' d'inglese,* he speaks broken English.

bestemmiatóre, s.m., **bestemmiatríce,** s.f. 1. swearer 2. (*chi parla empiamente*) blasphemer.

bestemmióne, s.m. habitual swearer.

béstia, s.f. 1. beast, animal: *— da soma,* beast of burden; *— da tiro,* draught-animal; *le bestie,* (*il bestiame*) cattle || *lavoro da —,* drudgery || *conoscere l'umore della —, fig.* to know s.o.'s whims || *fare una vita da —,* to lead a dog's life (*o* a hard life) || *montare in —,* to lose one's temper (*o* to fly into a passion) 2. *fig.* (*uomo sciocco*) fool, blockhead: *parla da —,* he talks nonsense 3. (*uomo brutale*) brute.

bestiàle, ag. 1. bestial, beastlike, beastly 2. (*terribile*) awful, beastly: *stanchezza —,* awful tiredness.

bestialità, s.f. 1. bestiality; beastliness 2. *fig.* foolishness || *non dire —!,* (*fam.*) don't talk nonsense!; *fare delle —,* to make blunders.

bestialménte, av. bestially; in a beastly manner.

bestiàme, s.m. cattle: *— grosso,* cattle (*o* heavy beasts); *— minuto,* smaller live-stock (*o* light beasts); *adunata del — per la marcatura,* round-up; *cento capi di —,* a hundred head of cattle; *allevare del —,* to breed cattle.

bestiàrio, s.m. 1. (*gladiatore*) bestiary 2. (*st. lett.*) bestiary.

bestióne, s.m. 1. big beast 2. (*uomo sciocco e brutale*) brute, beast 3. (*stupido*) blockhead.

bèta, s.f. (*seconda lettera dell'alfabeto greco*) beta.

betatróne, s.m. (*fis.*) betatron.

bètel, s.m. (*bot.*) betel.

Betlèmme, no.pr.f. (*geog. st.*) Bethlehem.

betònica, V. **bettònica.**

betonièra, s.f. (*edil.*) cement mixer; mortar mixing machine.

bétta, s.f. (*mar.*) barge.

Bétta, no.pr.f. dim. di **Elisabètta.**

béttola, s.f. tavern; public-house, pub: *contegno da —,* vulgar behaviour; *discorsi da —,* vulgar talk.

bettolànte, s.m. pub customer; (*fam.*) pub crawler.

bettolière, s.m. pub-keeper, inn-keeper, publican.

bettolína, s.f. (*mar.*) lighter; barge.

bettolíno, s.m. (*mil.*) canteen.

bettònica, s.f. (*bot.*) betony || *essere più noto della —,* to be very well known (*o* to be well known everywhere).

betúlla, s.f. (*bot.*) birch.

bevànda, s.f. drink; beverage: *— alcoolica,* intoxicating drink; *— analcoolica,* soft drink.

bevatróne, s.m. (*fis. atomica*) bevatron.

beveràggio, s.m. 1. beverage; (*per animali*) mash 2. (*pozione*) potion.

beveratóio, s.m. (drinking-)trough.

beveréccio, ag. (*gradevole a bersi*) nice to drink.

beveríno, s.m. bird-cage trough.

beveróne, s.m. 1. mash 2. long drink.

bevíbile, ag. 1. (*potabile*) drinkable 2. (*gradevole a bersi*) nice to drink.

bevitóre, s.m., **bevitríce,** s.f. drinker: *— abituale,* habitual drinker; *forte —,* hard (*o* heavy) drinker.

bevóne, s.m. (*rar.*) drunkard.

bevúta, s.f. 1. (*sorso*) draught 2. (*atto del bere*) drinking.

bèy, s.m. bey.

beylicàto, s.m. beylic.

bezzicàre, v.t. 1. (*beccare*) to peck: *— a morte,* to peck to death 2. *fig.* (*punzecchiare*) to tease.

bezzicàta, s.f. 1. peck 2. *fig.* teasing.

bezzicatúra, s.f. 1. peck 2. *fig.* teasing.

bèzzo, s.m. 1. (*moneta antica*) "bezzo" (old Venetian coin) 2. money: *ha molti bezzi,* he has a lot of money (*o* he is well off).

bi, s.f. letter B.

biàcca, *s.f.* ceruse, white lead.

biàcco, *s.m.* 1. (*zool.*) coluber 2. *fig.* (*codardo*) coward.

biàda, *s.f.* 1. forage; fodder 2. *pl.* (*messi*) crops.

biadaiuòlo, *s.m.* corn-dealer.

biadàre, *v.t.* to feed, to fodder.

biàdo, *ag.s.m.* (*colore*) light blue.

Blàgio, *no.pr.m.* Blaise.

Biànca, *no.pr.f.* Blanche.

biancàna, *s.f.* (*terreno brullo*) waste land, barren land.

Biancanéve, *no.pr.f.* Snowwhite.

biancàstro, *ag.* whitish.

biancheggiaménto, *s.m.* 1. (*l'imbianchire*) whitening 2. (*biancore*) whiteness.

biancheggiàre, *v.i.* (*essere bianco*) to be white; (*diventare bianco*) to whiten, to grow white: *i campi biancheggiano di neve*, the fields are white with snow; *il cielo biancheggia*, the sky is white; *i miei capelli cominciano a* —, my hair is growing hoary (*o* is turning white).

biancheria, *s.f.* linen: — *da letto*, bed-linen; — *da tavola*, table-linen; — *personale*, underwear (*o* underclothes *o* underlinen); *corda per stendere la* —, clothes-line.

bianchétto, *s.m.* 1. (*biacca cosmetica*) ceruse 2. (*lisciva*) lye 3. (*intonaco*) whitewash 4. *pl.* (*ittiol.*) white-bait (*sing.*).

bianchézza, *s.f.* whiteness.

bianchíccio, *ag.* whitish.

bianchiménto, *s.m.* 1. whitening; bleaching 2. (*di metalli preziosi*) scouring, dipping.

bianchíre, *v.t.* 1. to whiten; (*zucchero, sale, ecc.*) to bleach 2. (*metalli*) to polish; to scour.

biànco, *ag.* white: *carnagione bianca*, fair complexion; *foglio* —, (*non scritto*) blank sheet; *era* — *come un cencio, come un panno lavato*, he was as white as a sheet ‖ *arma bianca*, cold steel ‖ *arte bianca*, (*arte del fornaio*) bakery ‖ *la Casa Bianca*, the White House ‖ *carbone* —, hydro-electric power ‖ *il Mar Bianco*, the White Sea ‖ *il Monte Bianco*, Mont Blanc ‖ *notte bianca*, sleepless night ‖ *la razza bianca*, the white race ‖ *voci bianche*, children's voices ‖ *dare a qlcu. carta bianca*, to give s.o. unlimited power to act (*o* to give carte blanche to s.o.) ‖ *fare i capelli bianchi in un lavoro*, to get old in a job ‖ *fare il viso* —, to turn pale.

biànco, *s.m.* 1. white: *il* — *dell'occhio*, the white of the eye (*o* cornea); *un* — *d'uovo*, the white of an egg: *tre bianchi d'uovo*, three whites of eggs ‖ *i bianchi*, the whites ‖ — *e nero*, (*pitt.*) black and white ‖ *cucitrice di* —, seamstress ‖ *di punto in* —, all of a sudden ‖ *pesce in* —, boiled fish ‖ *tratta delle bianche*, white-slave traffic ‖ *far vedere* — *per nero a qlcu.*, *fig.* to deceive s.o. (*o* to take s.o. in) 2. (*spazio bianco in un testo*) blank: *gli spazi in* — *devono essere riempiti*, the blanks should be filled in; *lasciare uno spazio in* —, to leave a blank ‖ *in* —, blank: *assegno in* —, (*comm.*) blank cheque; *cambiale in* —, (*comm.*) undated bill; *girata in* —, (*comm.*) blank endorsement ‖ *passaporto in* —, blank passport ‖ *mettere, porre nero su* —, *fig.* to put down in writing 3. (*bianco di calce per opere in muratura*) whitewash: *dare il* — *ad una stanza*, to whitewash a room.

biancomangiàre, *s.m.* (*cuc.*) blancmange.

biancóne, *ag.* pasty ‖ *s.m.* (*ornit.*) harrier eagle.

biancóre, *s.m.* (*poet.*) whiteness.

biancospíno, *s.m.* (*bot.*) hawthorn.

biancúme, *s.m.* (*spreg.*) 1. whitish colour 2. (*insieme di cose bianche*) white mass.

biàscia, *s.f.* slaver.

biasciaménto, *s.m.* mumbling.

biasciàre, *V.* **biascicàre.**

biascicapaternòstri, *s.m.* bigot; devotee.

biascicàre, *v.t.* to mumble (anche *fig.*): — *preghiere, parole*, to mumble prayers, words.

biascicatúra, *s.f.* mumbling.

biascicóne, *s.m.* mumbler.

biasimàbile, *ag.* blam(e)able, blameworthy.

biasimàre, *v.t.* to blame; to censure; to reprove: *biasimò se stesso per non essere stato gentile*, he blamed himself for not having been kind; *dovete* — *solo voi stessi!*, you have only yourself to blame!.

biasimatóre, *s.m.,* **biasimatrice,** *s.f.* blamer; reprover.

biasimévole, *ag.* blam(e)able, blameworthy.

biasimevolménte, *av.* blam(e)ably.

biàsimo, *s.m.* blame; censure; reproof: *degno di* —, blameworthy.

biàvo, *ag.s.m.* (*colore*) pale blue.

bibàce, *ag.* (*rar.*) bibulous; absorbing.

bibàsico, *ag.* (*chim.*) bibasic, dibasic.

bíbbia, *s.f.* Bible.

biberon, *s.m.* feeding-bottle: *nutrire un bambino con il* —, to bring up a child on the bottle.

bíbita, *s.f.* drink, beverage: — *analcoolica*, soft drink ‖ *bibite*, (*rinfreschi*) refreshments.

bíblico, *ag.* biblical.

bibliofilía, *s.f.* bibliophilism, bibliophily.

bibliòfilo, *s.m.* bibliophil(e); book-lover.

bibliografía, *s.f.* bibliography.

bibliogràfico, *ag.* bibliographic(al).

bibliògrafo, *s.m.* bibliographer.

biblioiàtrica, *s.f.* (*neol.*) art of book-restoring.

bibliolatría, *s.f.* bibliolatry.

bibliología, *s.f.* bibliology.

bibliòlogo, *s.m.* bibliologist.

bibliòmane, *s.m.* bibliomaniac.

bibliomanía, *s.f.* bibliomania.

bibliomanzía, *s.f.* bibliomancy.

bibliotèca, *s.f.* 1. library: — *circolante*, circulating library ‖ — *ambulante*, (*scherz.*) (*persona erudita*) walking encyclopædia (*o* library) 2. (*scaffale per libri*) bookcase, bookshelf.

bibliotecària, *s.f.,* **bibliotecàrio,** *s.m.* librarian.

biblística, *s.f.* science of the Bible.

bíbulo, *ag.* (*rar.*) bibulous; absorbing.

bíca, *s.f.* 1. stack 2. *fig.* (*mucchio, massa*) heap; pile.

bicamerale, *ag.* (*pol.*) bicameral.

bicarbonàto, *s.m.* (*chim.*) bicarbonate: — *di sodio*, sodium bicarbonate.

bicchieràio, *s.m.* 1. (*chi fabbrica bicchieri*) drinking-glass maker 2. (*chi vende bicchieri*) drinking-glass seller.

bicchieràta, *s.f.* 1. drink; drinking-party: *la* — *finì in una rissa*, the drinking-party finished in a riot; *ha fatto una* — *con gli amici per festeggiare la laurea*, he got together with his friends for a drink to celebrate his degree 2. (*contenuto di un bicchiere*) glassful.

bicchière, *s.m.* 1. glass: — *per l'acqua*, water-glass; — *per il vino*, wine-glass 2. (*contenuto*) glassful, glass: *un* — *di acqua, vino*, a glass of water, of wine; *il* — *trabocca*, the glass is running over ‖ *il* — *della staffa*, the stirrup-cup ‖ *una tempesta in un* — *d'acqua*, a storm in a tea-cup ‖ *affogare in un* — *d'acqua*, to lose one's head about nothing.

Bíce, *no.pr.f. dim.* di **Beatríce.**

bicèfalo, *ag.* bicephalous, two-headed.

bicentenàrio, *ag.s.m.* bicentenary.

biciclétta, *s.f.* bicycle; (*fam.*) bike: — *a motore*, motor-bicycle; — *da corsa*, racing bicycle; — *da strada*, roadster; *andare in* —, to ride a bicycle (*o* to cycle); *recarsi in un luogo in* —, to cycle to a place; *viaggiare l'Italia in* —, to cycle round Italy.

bicíclo, *s.m.* velocipede ‖ (*fam.*) penny-farthing.

bicimotóre, *s.m.* motor-bicycle.

bicípite, *ag.* two-headed: *l'aquila* —, the two-headed eagle ‖ *s.m.* (*anat.*) biceps (*pl.* bicepses).

bieloríuro, *s.m.* (*chim.*) bichloride.

bicòcca, *s.f.* 1. hill-top castle 2. (*casupola*) hut; hovel; poky little house; shanty.

bicolóre, *ag.* two-coloured, bicoloured.

bicòncavo, *ag.* (*ott.*) biconcave.
biconvèsso, *ag.* (*ott.*) biconvex.
bicòrne, *ag.* **1.** two-horned ‖ *argomento* —, dilemma **2.** (*biforcuto*) forked.
bicòrnia, *s.f.* two-beaked anvil.
bicòrno, *ag.* **1.** two-horned **2.** (*biforcuto*) forked ‖ *s.m.* two-cornered hat.
bicornúto, *V.* **bicòrne**.
bicromàto, *s.m.* (*chim.*) bichromate.
bicuspidàle, *ag.* bicuspidate.
bicúspide, *ag.* bicuspid.
bidè, *s.m.* bidet.
bidèlla, *s.f.* janitrix, janitress, portress.
bidèllo, *s.m.* janitor; porter: — *di scuola, di università*, school, university porter.
bidènte, *s.m.* (*agr.*) bident; pitchfork; two-pronged -fork.
bidet, *s.m.* bidet.
bidóne, *s.m.* **1.** can, tank: — *per l'olio*, oil-can **2.** (*fam.*) (*tiro mancino*) nasty trick.
biecaménte, *av.* **1.** (*obliquamente*) asquint, askew, askance **2.** (*torvamente*) sullenly; (*malvagiamente*)wickedly, perversely.
bièco, *ag.* **1.** (*obliquo*) askew, asquint (*predicativi*) **2.** (*torvo*) sullen, sinister; (*malvagio*) wicked.
bièlla, *s.f.* (*mec.*) connecting rod: — *accoppiata*, (*ferr.*) side rod; — *d'accoppiamento*, drag link; — *laterale*, side beam; — *madre*, master (connecting) rod ‖ *occhio di* —, connecting rod small end; *testa di* —, big end of the connecting rod.
biennàle, *ag.* biennial ‖ *la Biennale* (*di Venezia*), the Biennial Exhibition (of Modern Art in Venice).
biennalménte, *av.* biennially.
b[i]ènne, *ag.* biennial.
biènnio, *s.m.* biennium (*pl.* biennia).
biètola, *s.f.* (*bot.*) beet, beetroot.
bietolàggine, *s.f.* stupidity, silliness, credulity.
bietolóne, *s.m.* simpleton, fool.
biètta, *s.f.* **1.** locking bar, set bar: — *trasversale*, (*mec.*) cotter **2.** (*bazza*) slipper-chin.
bifàse, *ag.* (*elett.*) two-phase (*attributivo*): *alternatore* —, two-phase generator.
biffa, *s.f.* (*topografia*) sighting stake: — *da misura*, surveyor's rod; — *scorrevole*, levelling rod.
bìfido, *ag.* bifid: *lingua bifida*, forked tongue.
bifilàre, *ag.* **1.** bifilar **2.** (*elett.*) double-wire (*attributivo*).
bifocàle, *ag.* (*ott.*) bifocal: *lente* —, bifocal lens.
bifólco, *s.m.* **1.** ploughman (*pl.* ploughmen); farm labourer **2.** (*persona rozza*) boor; uncouth man, yokel.
bifora, *s.f.* (*arch.*) mullioned window.
biforcaménto, *s.m.* bifurcation.
biforcàrsi, *v.r.* to fork, to bifurcate.
biforcatúra, *s.f.* bifurcation.
biforcazióne, *s.f.* **1.** bifurcation, fork, branching **2.** (*ferr.*) branching off, bifurcation.
biforcúto, *ag.* bifurcate, biforked, forked: *barba biforcuta*, forked beard.
bifórme, *ag.* biform.
bifrónte, *ag.* **1.** two-faced: *Giano* —, two-faced Janus **2.** (*insincero*) double-faced: *uomo* —, opportunist.
biga[1], *s.f.* (*cocchio romano*) biga.
biga[2], *s.f.* (*mar.*) shears (*pl.*).
bigamìa, *s.f.* bigamy.
bìgamo, *ag.* bigamous ‖ *s.m.* bigamist.
bigattièra, *s.f.* silkworm nursery.
bigàtto, *s.m.* silkworm.
bigèllo, *s.m.* coarse grey cloth.
bigeminàto, *ag.* bigeminal.
bighellàre, *v.i.* to lounge; to loaf; to saunter.
bighellóna, *s.f.*, **bighellóne**, *s.m.* lounger; loafer; saunterer.
bighellonàre, *v.i.* to lounge; to loaf; to saunter.
bigherìno, *s.m.* thread-lace.

bigìno, *s.m.* crib; (*amer.*) pony.
bìgio, *ag.* **1.** grey; (*amer.*) gray: *filo* —, grey thread; *pan* —, brown bread **2.** *fig.* plain; dull ‖ *s.m.* grey; (*amer.*) gray.
bigiògnolo, *ag.* greyish; (*amer.*) grayish.
bigiotteria, *s.f.* trinkets shop.
bigiottière, *s.m.* dealer in trinkets.
biglia, *V.* **bìlia**.
bigliàrdo, *V.* **biliàrdo**.
bigliettàrio, *s.m.* (*sui tram, autobus*) conductor; (*sui treni*) ticket-collector; (*di stazione*) booking-clerk; (*di teatro*) box-office attendant.
bigliettería, *s.f.* (*di stazione*) booking-office; (*amer.*) ticket office; (*botteghino di teatro*) box-office; (*di campo sportivo*) gate.
bigliétto, *s.m.* **1.** (*breve scritto*) note; short letter: — *galante*, love-letter; *mandagli un* — *per informarlo*, drop him a note to inform him **2.** (*cartoncino*) card: — *da visita*, visiting-card; — *di invito*, invitation card; — *di Natale*, Christmas-card; —, *postale*, letter-card; *eccovi il mio* —, here is my card **3.** (*contrassegno d'un prezzo pagato*) ticket: — *a prezzo ridotto*, cheap ticket; — *circolare*, tourist (*o circular*) ticket; — *di abbonamento*, season ticket; — *di andata e ritorno*, return ticket; (*amer.*) round-trip ticket; — *di andata semplice*, single ticket; (*amer.*) one-way ticket; — *di favore*, complimentary ticket; — *di ingresso*, (*in stazione*) (platform) ticket; — *di prenotazione*, (*di un posto*) reserved-seat ticket; — *ferroviario*, railway ticket; — *festivo*, week-end ticket; — *supplementare*, extra ticket; *mezzo* —, half-fare ticket; *sportello biglietti*, booking-office; *il* — *vale sino alla fine del mese*, the ticket is valid until the end of the month; *essere munito di* —, to be provided with ticket **4.** (*banconota*) banknote: — *da mille lire*, a thousand lire (bank)note; — *di banca*, (bank) note; *emissione di biglietti di banca*, issue of banknotes **5.** (*comm.*) note: — *all'ordine*, promissory note (*o* note of hand).
bignè, *s.m.* cream puff.
bigodíno, *s.m.* (hair-)curler.
bigóncia, *s.f.* **1.** pannier ‖ *a bigonce*, in great quantity: *piove a bigonce*, it is raining cats and dogs **2.** (*rar.*) chair, pulpit: *salire in* —, to ascend the pulpit (*o* to pose as a learned person).
bigóncio, *s.m.* tub, bucket.
bigòtta[1], *s.f.* bigot, devotee, bigoted woman: *una vecchia* —, a bigoted (*o* sanctimonious) old woman.
bigòtta[2], *s.f.* (*mar.*) dead eye.
bigottería, *s.f.*, **bigottísmo**, *s.m.* bigotry.
bigòtto, *ag.* over-devout, bigoted ‖ *s.m.* bigot, devotee, bigoted man.
bikíni, *s.m.* bikini.
bilabiàto, *ag.* (*bot.*) bilabiate.
bilància, *s.f.* **1.** balance, scale(s): — *a bilico*, platform scale; — *a indice*, dial balance; — *a molla*, spring balance; — *a ponte*, weigh bridge; — *automatica*, automatic weighing machine; — *d'assaggio*, (*per orefici*) assay balance; — *di precisione*, precision balance; — *elettrica*, electric balance; — *galvanoplastica*, plating balance; — *idrostatica*, hydrostatic balance; — *pesa bambini*, baby scales; — *romana*, (*stadera*) steelyard; *piatto della* —, scale ‖ *la Bilancia*, (*astr.*) the Scales ‖ *dare il tratto, il tracollo alla* —, to weigh down the scales ‖ *far pendere la* — *da una parte*, to turn the scale (anche *fig.*) ‖ *porre due cose sulla* —, *fig.* to weigh two things one against the other ‖ *tenere in pari la* —, to hold scales even **2.** (*comm.*) balance: — *commerciale*, balance of trade; — *delle importazioni e esportazioni*, balance of import and export; *la* — *del commercio ci è favorevole*, we have a favourable balance of trade; *la* — *del commercio ci è sfavorevole*, the balance of trade is unfavourable to us **3.** (*rete da pesca*) trawl(-net) **4.** (*traversa di carrozza, carro*) whipple tree, swingletree **5.** (*d'orologio*) balance.
bilanciàio, *s.m.* scale maker.

bilanciaménto, *s.m.* balance, balancing.

bilanciàre, *v.t.* **1.** to balance: *sei capace di* — *un bastone sulla punta del naso?,* can you balance a stick on the tip of your nose? **2.** (*ponderare*) to weigh, to consider carefully: — *le parole,* to weigh one's words; — *il pro e il contro,* to weigh the pros and cons **3.** (*equivalere a*) to balance: *il profitto non bilancia le perdite,* the profit does not balance the loss ‖ **bilanciàrsi,** *v.r.* (*stare in equilibrio*) to balance ‖ *v.r. reciproco* to be equivalent, to balance.

bilanciaménte, *av.* in equilibrium.

bilanciatóre, *ag.* balancing ‖ *s.m.,* **bilanciatríce,** *s.f.* balancer.

bilancière, *s.m.* **1.** (*di orologio*) balance-wheel, swing-wheel: *asse del* —, verge; *molla del* —, hairspring (*o* balance spring) **2.** (*mec.*) equalizer, compensator; (*pressa a mano*) fly press **3.** (*conio*) coining press.

bilancíno, *s.m.* **1.** (*di carrozza*) splinter-bar ‖ — *compensazione molle,* (*aut.*) spring equalizing rocker arm **2.** (*cavallo di rinforzo*) trace-horse.

bilàncio, *s.m.* budget; (*comm.*) balance sheet: — *consuntivo,* appropriation account; — *di previsione,* estimate; — *di verifica,* trial balance; — *fallimentare,* statement of affairs; — *generale dei conti,* balance of payments; *progetto di* —, draft balance; *il nostro* — *personale è abbastanza soddisfacente,* our family budget is fairly satisfactory; *approvare il* —, to pass the budget; *chiudere, fare il* —, to strike the balance; (*pesare i pro e i contro*) to weigh the pros and cons; *mettere in* —, to estimate; *presentare il* —, to present the budget; *stanziare in* —, to appropriate in the balance; *votare il* —, to vote expenditures.

bilaterále, *ag.* bilateral: *contratto* —, (*dir.*) indenture; *paralisi* —, (*patol.*) bilateral paralysis.

bilateralità, *s.f.* bilaterality.

bíle, *s.f.* **1.** (*fisiol.*) bile: — *sparsa,* (*itterizia*) jaundice; *spargimento di* —, bilious attack **2.** *fig.* (*collera*) bile, bad temper, ill-humour: *far rodere qlcu. dalla* —, to rouse s.o.'s anger (*o sl.* to rile s.o.); *riversare la propria* — *contro qlcu.,* to rail at s.o.; *sentirsi rodere dalla* — *per ql.co.,* to fret (*o* to worry) about sthg.: *a forza di rodersi dalla* — *si fece venire la febbre,* he fretted so much that he developed a temperature.

bilèneo, *V.* **sbilèneo.**

bília, *s.f.* **1.** (*al biliardo*) (*buca*) pocket: *fare* —, to hole a ball **2.** (*pallina di vetro, ecc. usata nei giuochi infantili*) marble: *giocare alle bilie,* to play marbles.

biliardàio, *s.m.* **1.** (*chi fabbrica biliardi*) billiard-maker **2.** (*chi vende biliardi*) billiard-seller.

biliàrdo, *s.m.* billiards (*pl.*): *stecca da* —, billiard-cue; *tavolo da* —, billiard-table; *panno del* —, billiard-cloth; *stanza del* —, billiard-room; *giocare a* —, to play billiards.

biliàre, *ag.* (*fisiol.*) biliary: *calcolo* —, (*patol.*) bile-stone (*o* gall-stone); *colica* —, (*patol.*) biliary colic.

bílico, *s.m.* **1.** equipoise, equilibrium, balance; *fig.* (*incertezza, dubbio*) uncertainty, suspense, doubt: *mettere in* —, to poise (*o* to balance); *stare in* —, to be balanced (*o* to be in equilibrium) **2.** (*perno*) pivot.

bilíngue, *ag.* **1.** bilingual **2.** (*insincero*) insincere, double-faced.

bilióne, *s.m.* **1.** (*un milione di milioni*) billion **2.** (*miliardo*) one thousand millions, milliard; (*amer.*) billion.

bilióso, *ag.* **1.** bilious **2.** *fig.* peevish, irascible.

bilirubína, *s.f.* (*chim. biol.*) bilirubin.

bilobàto, *ag.* (*bot.*) bilobate.

bilústre, *ag.* ten years old (*predicativo*); ten years long (*predicativo*); ten-year-old (*attributivo*).

bímane, *ag.* bimanal, bimanous.

bímani, *s.m.pl.* Bimana.

bímano, *ag.* two-handed.

bímba, *s.f.,* **bímbo,** *s.m.* child (*pl.* children); baby.

bimèmbre, *ag.* two-membered.

bimensíle, *ag.* fortnightly; (*spec. amer.*) semimonthly ‖ *s.m.* semimonthly.

bimestràle, *ag.* **1.** (*che ricorre ogni due mesi*) bimonthly **2.** (*che dura due mesi*) bimestrial.

bimèstre, *s.m.* (period of) two months.

bimetàllico, *ag.* (*econ.*) bimetallic.

bimetallísmo, *s.m.* (*econ.*) bimetallism.

bimetallísta, *s.m.* (*econ.*) bimetallist.

bimotóre, *ag.* (*aer.*) twin-engined plane, bimotor.

binàrio, *ag.* (*arit. chim.*) binary: *scala binaria,* binary scale ‖ *s.m.* railway line, track; (*amer.*) railroad: — *a scartamento ridotto,* narrow gauge line; — *cieco,* dead-end siding; — *di carico,* loading siding; — *di raccordo,* connecting line; — *morto,* dead-end track; — *unico,* single line (*o* single track); *doppio* —, double line (*o* double track); *biglietto di accesso ai binari,* platform ticket; *incrocio di binari,* crossing of lines; *rete di binari,* network of lines.

bináto, *ag.* binate (anche *bot.*); in pairs, coupled: *colonne binate,* (*arch.*) twin columns.

bínda, *s.f.* (*mec.*) (lifting) jack: — *a cremagliera,* ratchet jack; — *a vite,* jackscrew.

bíndolo, *s.m.* **1.** (*strum. artig.*) winder **2.** (*ruota per attingere acqua*) water-wheel **3.** (*pretesto*) pretext; (*cavillo*) cavil; (*aggiramento*) circumvention **4.** (*imbroglione*) swindler, cheat.

binòc(c)olo, *s.m.* binoculars (*pl.*); (*da teatro*) opera-glass; (*da campagna*) field-glass.

binoculàre, *ag.* binocular.

binòmio, *s.m.* (*alg.*) binomial.

binucleàre, *ag.* (*fis.*) binucleate, binuclear.

biòccolo, *s.m.* (*di lana*) flock; (*di cotone*) lump; (*di candela*), candledrip; (*di neve*), snow-flake.

bioccolúto, *ag.* flocky, flocculent, floccose.

biochímica, *s.f.* (*chim.*) biochemistry.

biòdo, *s.m.* (*bot.*) club-rush, bulrush.

biofilía, *s.f.* instinct of self-preservation.

biogènesi, *s.f.* biogenesis.

biogenètico, *ag.* biogenetic.

biogenía, *s.f.* biogeny.

biografía, *s.f.* biography: — *romanzata,* biographical novel.

biograficaménte, *av.* biographically.

biogràfico, *ag.* biographic(al).

biògrafo, *s.m.* biographer.

biòleo, *V.* **bifòleo.**

biología, *s.f.* biology.

biologicaménte, *av.* biologically.

biològico, *ag.* biologic(al).

biòlogo, *s.m.* biologist.

biometeorología, *s.f.* biometeorology.

biónda[1]**,** *s.f.* **1.** blonde, fair (-haired) woman: — *incendiaria,* (*fam.*) stunning blonde **2.** (*tintura*) hair-dye.

biónda[2]**,** *s.f.* (*merletto*) blonde (lace).

biondàstro, *ag.* blondish; fairish.

biondeggiànte, *ag.* yellowing.

biondeggiàre, *v.i.* to turn yellow, to turn golden.

biondézza, *s.f.* fairness.

biondíccio, *ag.* blondish; fairish.

biondína, *s.f.* fair-haired girl; (*bambina bionda*) fair-haired little girl.

biondíno, *s.m.* fair-haired boy.

bióndo, *ag.* fair, flaxen; (*di uomo*) blond, fair-haired; (*di donna*) blonde, fair-haired: *le bionde spighe,* the golden (*o* yellow) ears ‖ *s.m.* **1.** (*colore*) flaxen, fair colour: — *cenere,* ash-blond; — *platino,* platinum blond; *capelli di un* — *dorato,* golden hair **2.** (*uomo biondo*) fair-haired man, blond.

bioplàsma, *s.m.* (*biol.*) bioplasm.

biopsía, *s.f.* (*med.*) biopsy.

biòscia, *s.f.* (*rar.*) **1.** slush **2.** (*broda*) slop.

biòssido, *s.m.* (*chim.*) dioxide: — *di manganese,* black oxide of manganese.

biòtto, *ag.* (*dial.*) **1.** naked, undressed **2.** *fig.* wretched, miserable.

bipartíre, *v.t.* to halve; to cut in two ‖ **bipartírsi,** *v.r.* to fork; to branch off, to divide, to bifurcate.

bipartíto, *ag.* bipartite.

bipartizióne, *s.f.* **1.** bipartition **2.** (*punto di divisione*) bifurcation.

bípede, *ag.* biped(al), two-footed ‖ *s.m.* biped.

bipènne, *s.f.* two-edged hatchet.

biplàno, *s.m.* (*aer.*) biplane.

bipolàre, *ag.* (*elett.*) bipolar.

bipósto, *s.m.* (*aer.*) two-seater.

biquadràto, *ag.* (*mat.*) biquadratic.

bírba, *s.m.* **1.** hare-brained youngster; scapegrace **2.** (*furfante*) scoundrel, rogue, rascal, scamp.

birbantàggine, *s.f.* roguery, knavery, rascality.

birbànte, *s.m.* **1.** scoundrel, rogue, rascal; (*sl.*) rotter: *ah, —, ti ho preso!*, (*scherz.*) little rogue, I've caught you! **2.** (*furbacchione*) sly-boots.

birbanteggiàre, *v.i.* to act in a villainous way.

birbantería, *s.f.* villainous action; nasty trick; knavery, rascality: *questa è una —*, this is a nasty trick.

birbantésco, *ag.* roguish, knavish.

birbàta, birbería, *V.* **birbantería.**

birbésco, *ag.* **1.** knavish **2.** (*furbo*) sly: *modi birbeschi*, sly manners.

bírbo, *V.* **bírba.**

birbonàta, *s.f.* knavish action; knavery; nasty trick, dirty trick ‖ *quella statua è una vera —, fig.* that statue is a real disgrace.

birbóne, *ag.: ebbi una paura birbona*, I was scared stiff (*o sl.* I was in a blue funk); *fa un freddo —*, it is bitterly cold ‖ *s.m.* scoundrel, rogue, rascal, trickster.

birboneggiàre, *v.i.* to act roguishly.

birbonería, *V.* **birbantería.**

birboneseaménte, *av.* roguishly, knavishly.

birbonésco, *ag.* roguish, knavish.

bírcio, *ag.* **1.** (*miope*) short-sighted **2.** (*che guarda di traverso*) squint-eyed.

bireattóre, *s.m.* (*aer.*) two-engined jet.

birème, *s.f.* (*mar.*) bireme.

biribíssi, *s.m.* **1.** « biribissi » (a game of chance played with counters) **2.** (*piccola trottola*) small spinning top.

birichinàta, *s.f.* prank; mischievous trick, roguish trick.

birichíno, *ag.* cheeky, naughty ‖ *s.m.* urchin, mischievous boy, cheeky youngster.

birifrangènte, *ag.* (*ott.*) birefringent.

birifrangènza, *s.f.* (*ott.*) birefringence.

birignào, *s.m.* (*teal.*) drawl.

birillo, *s.m.* skittle, skittle-pin, ninepin: *giuoco dei birilli*, (game of) skittles; *giocare ai birilli*, (*con una palla*) to play at ninepins; (*con un disco di legno*) to play at skittles.

Birmània, *no.pr.f.* (*geog.*) Burma.

birmàno, *ag.s.m.* Burmese, Burman.

bíro, *s.f.* biro, ball (point) pen.

biroccíno, *s.m.* cabriolet.

biròccio, *s.m.* cart.

bírra, *s.f.* beer; (*chiara, bionda*) ale; (*scura*) porter: *— alla spina*, draught beer; *— leggera*, weak (*o* small) beer; *— molto forte*, stout; *un boccale di —*, a tankard of beer; *fabbricare —*, to brew beer.

birràio, *s.m.* **1.** (*fabbricante di birra*) brewer **2.** (*venditore di birra*) publican; bar-keeper.

birrería, *s.f.* **1.** beer-house, ale-house; bar **2.** (*fabbrica di birra*) brewery.

bírro, *s.m.* (*spreg.*) bogy; copper; flatfoot.

birróne, *s.m.* stout.

bís, *s.* (*a teatro*) encore: *chiedere il — a un cantante*, to encore a singer; *chiedere il — di una canzone*, to encore a song ‖ (*treno*) —, (*ferr.*) relief (train).

bisàccia, *s.f.* packsaddle; (*zaino*) knapsack, haversack.

bisànte, *s.m.* **1.** (*moneta antica*) bezant **2.** (*arch.*) bezant.

Bisànzio, *no.pr.f.* (*geog. st.*) Byzantium.

bisareàvola, *s.f.* great-great-grandmother.

bisareàvolo, *s.m.* great-great-grandfather.

bisàva, bisàvola, *s.f.* great-grandmother.

bisàvo, bisàvolo, *s.m.* great-grandfather.

bisbeticaménte, *av.* cantankerously, crabbedly, irritably; (*di donna*) waspishly, shrewishly.

bisbètico, *ag.* **1.** cantankerous, crabbed, irritable; (*di donna*) waspish, shrewish ‖ «*La bisbetica domata*», "The Taming of the Shrew" **2.** (*stravagante*) eccentric; odd; peculiar.

bisbigliaménto, *s.m.* whispering.

bisbigliàre, *v.t.i.* to whisper (anche *fig.*): *egli le bisbigliò delle gentili parole*, he whispered some kind words to her ‖ *si bisbiglia un po' sul tuo conto!*, there has been some gossip about you! (*o* people have been talking about you!).

bisbigliatóre, *s.m.*, **bisbigliatríce**, *s.f.* whisperer.

bisbíglio, *s.m.* **1.** whisper: *in un —*, in a whisper **2.** (*rad.*) (*interferenza*) monkey chatter.

bisbíglio, *s.m.* whispering.

bisbiglióna, *s.f.*, **bisbiglióne**, *s.m.* inveterate whisperer: *quella vecchia è una gran —*, that old woman is a great gossip.

bisbòccia, *s.f.* feast, carousal; (*fam.*) spree: *fare —*, to feast (*o fam.* to go on the spree).

bisbocciàre, *v.i.* to feast, to revel; (*fam.*) to have a spree, to go on the spree.

bisboccióne, *s.m.* reveller, carouser; merry maker.

bísca, *s.f.* gambling-house; gaming-den.

Biscàglia, *no.pr.f.* (*geog.*) Biscay: *Golfo di —*, Bay of Biscay.

biscaglína, *s.f.* (*mar.*) Jacob's-ladder.

biscaglíno, *ag.s.m.* Biscayan.

biscaiuòlo, *s.m.* gambler.

biscànto, *s.m.* **1.** bisected angle **2.** *fig.* (*luogo appartato*) nook.

biscazzàre, *v.t.* to gamble away ‖ *v.i.* to frequent gambling-houses.

biscazzière, *s.m.* **1.** (*chi tiene bisca*) gambling-house-keeper **2.** (*chi segna i punti al giuoco del biliardo*) marker **3.** (*chi frequenta le bische*) gambler.

bíschero, *s.m.* (*mus.*) tuning-peg, tuning-pin.

bischétto, *s.m.* cobbler's desk.

bíscia, *s.f.* snake: *— acquaiola*, water snake ‖ *procedere a —*, to zigzag (*o* to move in a zigzag line).

biscottàre, *v.t.* to bake twice over (*o* over again); (*tostare*) to toast.

biscottería, *s.f.* **1.** (*fabbrica*) biscuit factory **2.** (*negozio*) biscuit shop **3.** (*biscotti*) biscuits (*pl.*).

biscottifício, *s.m.* biscuit factory.

biscottíno[1], *s.m.* **1.** small biscuit **2.** (*buffetto*) fillip.

biscottíno[2], *s.m.* (*aut.*) link, shackle.

biscòtto, *s.m.* **1.** biscuit; (*amer.*) cookie: *— da tè*, tea-cake; *pane —*, ship('s)-biscuit (*o* sea-biscuit); *— salato*, water-biscuit **2.** (*ceramica*) bisque, biscuit-ware.

biseròma, *s.f.* (*mus.*) demisemiquaver.

biseugína, *s.f.*, **biseugíno**, *s.m.* second cousin.

bisdòsso, a, *l.av.* bare-back: *cavalcare a —*, to ride bare-back.

bisdrúcciolo, *ag.* (*gram.*) having an accent on the third syllable before the last.

bisecànte, *ag.* (*geom.*) bisecting.

bisecàre, *v.t.* (*geom.*) to bisect.

biségolo, *s.m.* (*strum. artig.*) polisher.

Bisèrta, *no.pr.f.* (*geog.*) Bizerte.

bisessuàle, *ag.* (*bot.*) bisexual.

bisestíle, bisèsto, *ag.* bissextile: *anno —*, leap-year.

bisettimanàle, *ag.* bi-weekly.

bisettríce, *s.f.* (*geom.*) bisector, bisecting line.

bisezióne, *s.f.* (*geom.*) bisection.

bisíllabo, *ag.* disyllabic ‖ *s.m.* disyllable.

bislaccheería, *s.f.* oddness.

bislàcco, *ag.* odd, queer: *è una testa bislacca*, he is an odd fellow (*o* a queer fellow); *mi diede una risposta bislacca*, he gave me a strange reply.

bislúngo, *ag.* oblong.

bismúto, *s.m.* (*min.*) bismuth: *minerali di —*, bismuth ores.

bisnipóte, *s.c.* **1.** (*di nonni*) great-grandchild (*pl.* grandchildren); (*maschio*) great-grandson; (*femmina*) great-granddaughter **2.** (*di zii*) (*maschio*) great-nephew; (*femmina*) great-niece.

bisnònna, *s.f.* great-grandmother.

bisnònno, *s.m.* **1.** great-grandfather **2.** *pl.* (*antenati*) ancestors.

bisógna, *s.f.* **1.** (*affare, caso*) affair, business **2.** (*necessità*) necessity, need: *servire alla —*, to answer the need.

bisognàre, *v.i.* **1.** *imp.* (*essere necessario*) to be necessary; (*con costruzione pers.*): to have (to do); must; ought (to do); to be forced; to be compelled: *bisogna che partiate subito*, you must leave at once (*o it is necessary for you to leave at once*); *bisogna che sia sempre bene informato*, it is necessary for me always to be well informed; *bisognava che voi lo vedeste!*, you ought to have seen it!; *bisogna diffidare*, you must be on your guard; *bisogna proprio dire che si è comportato bene*, I am bound to say he behaved well; *bisognerà strappare quel dente*, that tooth will have to come out; *credo che bisogna lavorare sodo per riuscire*, I think one must work hard to be successful; *non c'è treno, bisognerà percorrere il tragitto a piedi*, there is no train, so we must needs walk ‖ *bisogna vedere quanti soldati sono arrivati!*, you should see how many soldiers have come here! **2.** (*aver bisogno*) (*con costruzione pers.*) to want (sthg.), to need (sthg.); (*mancare di*) to lack (sthg.), to be in lack of (sthg.): *bisognano di capitali*, they lack capital; *gli bisognavano diecimila lire*, he wanted ten thousand lire; *mi bisogna il vostro consiglio*, I need your advice.

bisognévole, *ag.* necessary ‖ *s.m.* the needful; (*l'indispensabile per vivere*) the necessaries of life (*pl.*).

bisógno, *s.m.* **1.** (*necessità*) necessity, need; (*mancanza*) want, shortage: *in caso di —*, in case of need; *in caso di, al — rivolgersi a...*, (*comm.*) in case of need apply to...; *non c'è — di dire che*, it goes without saying that; *non ci fu — di dirglielo due volte*, there was no need to tell him so twice; *avere — di ql.co.*, to want (*o to need o to be in need of o to be short of*) sthg.: *ha urgente — del vostro aiuto*, he is in urgent need of your help; *ha urgente — di denaro*, he is hard pressed for money (*o he is hard up*) **2.** (*povertà*) poverty, necessity ‖ *il — aguzza l'ingegno*, necessity is the mother of invention **3.** (*esigenza*) needs (*pl.*); requirements (*pl.*): *i miei bisogni sono pochi*, my needs are few **4.** (*bisogno fisiologico*): *avere un —*, to want to go to the lavatory (*o to the W. C. o fam.* to want to spend a penny).

bisognosaménte, *av.* poorly.

bisognóso, *ag.* needy, poor: *un fratello — di aiuto dev'essere aiutato*, a brother in need of help must be helped ‖ *i bisognosi*, the poor (*o the needy*).

bisolfàto, *s.m.* (*chim.*) bisulphate.

bisolfíto, *s.m.* (*chim.*) bisulphite.

bisolfúro, *s.m.* (*chim.*) bisulphide.

bisónte, *s.m.* (*zool.*) bison.

bissàre, *v.t.* (*teat.*) to give an encore of (sthg.).

bísso, *s.m.* byssus (*pl.* bysses, byssi) (*anche zool.*).

bissóna, *s.f.* "bissona" (eight-oar gala gondola).

bistécca, *s.f.* beefsteak: *— al sangue*, underdone beefsteak; (*amer.*) rare beefsteak; *— ben cotta*, well -done beefsteak; *— di filetto*, rump-steak.

bisticciaménto, *s.m.* tiff, squabble; quarrel; (*il bisticciare*) quarrelling.

bisticciàre, *v.i.*, **bisticciàrsi**, *v.r.* to have a tiff, to squabble, to bicker; to quarrel.

bistíccio, *s.m.* **1.** (*litigio*) tiff, squabble, bicker; quarrel **2.** (*giuoco di parole*) quibble, pun.

bistíccio, *s.m.* quarrelling.

bistóndo, *ag.* roundish.

bistòrto, *ag.* crooked, twisted.

bistràto, *ag.* bistred: *occhi bistrati*, bistred eyes.

bistrattàre, *v.t.* to ill-treat, to maltreat, to bully.

bístro, *s.m.* bistre.

bísturi, **bisturí**, *s.m.* (*chir.*) lancet, bistoury.

bisúlco, *ag.* (*zool.*) bisulcate.

bisúnto, *ag.* greasy, oily: *unto e —*, filthy.

Bitínia, *no.pr.f.* (*geog. st.*) Bithynia.

bitòrzolo, *s.m.* **1.** pimple; lump, swelling **2.** (*bot.*) knot.

bitorzolúto, *ag.* pimply, pimpled.

bítta, *s.f.* (*mar.*) bollard, bitt: *prove alla —*, bollard test; *trazione alla —*, bollard pull; *volta di —*, bitter.

bitter, *s.m.* (*aperitivo*) bitters (*pl.*); appetizer.

bitumàre, *v.t.* to bituminize.

bitúme, *s.m.* bitumen.

bituminàre, *v.t.* to bituminize.

bituminóso, *ag.* bituminous.

biúta, *s.f.* **1.** (*cuc.*) icing **2.** (*belletto*) rouge.

bivaccàre, *v.i.* to bivouac.

bivàcco, *s.m.* bivouac.

bivalènte, *ag.* (*chim.*) bivalent, divalent.

bivalènza, *s.f.* (*chim.*) bivalence.

bivàlve, *ag.* (*zool.*) bivalve, bivalvular ‖ *s.m.* (*zool.*) bivalve.

bívio, *s.m.* **1.** cross-road(s); forking; junction; parting of the ways **2.** *fig.* alternative; uncertainty: *l'Inghilterra è giunta a un — molto importante*, Britain is facing a very momentous decision.

bizantineggiàre, *v.i.* (*ragionare con eccessivo spirito analitico*) to split hairs.

bizantinísmo, *s.m.* Byzantinism, hairsplitting.

bizantíno, *ag.* **1.** Byzantine **2.** *fig.* (*eccessivamente analitico*) subtle; minute ‖ *s.m.* Byzantine.

bízza, *s.f.* caprice; freak; whim: *fare le bizze*, to be peevish (*o wayward*); (*di bambini*) to be naughty.

bizzarraménte, *av.* oddly; strangely; whimsically.

bizzarría, *s.f.* **1.** peculiarity; oddness **2.** (*atto, detto bizzarro*) extravagance; eccentricity; oddity; whimsicalness: *gli si perdonano le sue bizzarrie*, people forgive his whimsies **3.** (*cosa bizzarra*) freak, curiosity.

bizzàrro, *ag.* **1.** strange; odd; whimsical; eccentric; (*grottesco*) bizarre: *cervello —*, strange mind (*o ideas o outlook*); *opinioni bizzarre*, odd opinions; *tipo —*, queer fish; *conosceva tutta gente bizzarra*, all the people he knew were eccentric; *egli fa le cose più bizzarre*, he does the strangest things; *questo è —,!* well, that's odd! **2.** (*di cavallo*) high spirited.

bizzèffe, **a**, *l.av.* in great quantity, plentifully, abundantly, galore: *denaro a —*, money galore (*o lots of money*); *aver denaro a —*, to have money to burn.

bizzòco, **bizzòchero**, *s.m.* bigot.

bizzosaménte, *av.* (*in modo irascibile*) irritably; (*capricciosamente*) waywardly, freakishly.

bizzóso, *ag.* (*irascibile*) irritable; irascible; (*capriccioso*) wayward, freakish.

blandaménte, *ag.* blandly, mildly, gently.

blandiménto, *s.m.* blandishment; cajolery.

blandíre, *v.t.* to blandish; to cajole; to soothe; to coax; (*adulare*) to flatter.

blandízie, *s.f.pl.* (*moine*) blandishments; cajolery (*sing.*); caresses; (*adulazione*) flattery (*sing.*); (*lusinga*) allurement (*sing.*).

blàndo, *ag.* (*mite*) bland, soft, mild; (*carezzevole*) soothing, caressing; (*delicato*) delicate, gentle: *una cura blanda*, a bland (*o mild*) treatment; *dieta blanda*, bland diet; *punizione blanda*, mild punishment.

blasfemàre, *v.i.* (*rar.*) to blaspheme.

blasfèmo, *ag.* blasphemous; profane: *una parola blasfema*, a blasphemous word ‖ *s.m.* blasphemer.

blasonàto, *ag.* blazoned; (*nobile*) noble.

blasóne, *s.m.* **1.** blazon; coat of arms: *insozzare il proprio —*, to sully (*o to besmirch*) one's escutcheon; *ridare prestigio al proprio —*, to restore the fortunes of one's house **2.** *fig.* (*nobile origine*) nobility, noble birth, noble rank.

blasonísta, *s.m.* blazoner, herald.

blastèma, *s.f.* (*biol. bot.*) blastema.

blateràre, *v.i.* to blab; to prate; (*chiacchierare*) to chatter: — *come una gazza,* to chatter like a magpie; — *di politica,* to prate about politics.

blateróne, *s.m.* chatterbox; blabber, prater: *è un* —, he is a chatterbox.

blàtta, *s.f.* (*scarafaggio*) cockroach, bug.

blefaríte, *s.f.* (*patol.*) blepharitis.

blefarofimòsi, *s.f.* (*patol.*) blepharophimosis.

blefaroplegía, *s.f.* (*patol.*) blepharoplegia.

blefaroptòsi, *s.f.* (*patol.*) blepharoptosis.

blefarospàsmo, *s.m.* (*patol.*) blepharospasm.

blefaròstato, *s.m.* (*chir.*) blepharostat.

blènda, *s.f.*(*min.*) blende;(*pop.*) black-jack, mock-lead.

blenorragía, *s.f.*(*patol.*)blennorrhoea, blennorrhagia.

blèso, *ag.* lisping: *pronuncia blesa,* lisp ‖ *s.m.* lisper.

blínda, *s.f.* (*mil.*) armour-plate.

blindaménto, *s.m.* (*mil.*) blindage, armour-plating.

blindàre, *v.t.* (*mil.*) to blind; to armour; to protect with armour-plates.

blindàto, *ag.* armoured, armour-plated: *treno* —, armoured train.

blindatúra, *s.f.* 1. (*mil.*) blindage, armour-plating 2. (*aer.*) (*di elica di legno*) metal edging.

bloccàre, *v.t.* 1. (*chiudere, interrompere*) to block (up); (*arrestare*) to stop: *porto bloccato dai ghiacci,* harbour blocked by ice; *strada bloccata,* road blocked; — *la palla,* to stop the ball; — *il traffico,* to block the traffic ‖ — *una legge,* (*pol.*) to block a bill 2. (*mil.*) to blockade 3. (*isolare*) to close, to isolate 4. (*mec.*) to stall; to lock: *ql.co. bloccò il motore,* sthg. stalled the engine (o the motor); — *i comandi,* to lock the controls 5. (*comm.*) to freeze; to peg: — *un assegno,* to stop a cheque; — *il mercato, gli affitti, i prezzi,* to peg the market, rents, prices ‖ **bloccàrsi,** *v.r.* to jam, to stick: *l'ascensore si è bloccato,* the lift has jammed; *la sua automobile si bloccò nel fango,* his car stuck in the mud.

blòcco¹, *s.m.* 1. (*mil.*) blockade: *forzare, rompere il* —, to run the blockade; *togliere il* —, to raise the blockade ‖ *il Blocco Continentale,* (*st.*) the Continental System 2. (*su strade, ferrovie*) block; (*amer.*) stall: *cabina di* —, signal-box; *posto di* —, road block; *segnale di* —, block-signal 3. *fare un* — (*biliardo*) to hole a ball 4. (*patol.*) block 5. — *dei fitti,* rent-control; — *dei licenziamenti,* veto on dismissals.

blòcco², *s.m.* 1. block: — *di marmo,* block of marble 2. (*comm.*) bulk, lump, lot: *comprare in* —, to buy in bulk: *li compreremo in* —, we'll buy up the whole lot 3. (*pol.*) bloc, coalition: — *di centro,* centre parties 4. (*di carta*) pad: — *di carta da lettere,* writing-pad; — *per appunti,* note-book.

blónda, *s.f.* (*merletto*) blonde (lace).

blu, *ag.* blue ‖ *sangue* —, blue blood ‖ *mi ha fatto una fifa* —, (*fam.*) it put me in a blue funk ‖ *s.m.* blue: — *di Prussia,* Prussian blue.

bluàstro, *ag.* bluish.

blúsa, *s.f.* 1. blouse 2. (*camiciotto per uomo*) smock -frock.

bòa¹, *s.m.* 1. (*serpente*) boa 2. (*striscia di piume, di pelliccia, per signore*) boa.

bòa², *s.f.* (*mar.*) buoy: — *con campana,* bell-buoy; — *luminosa,* light buoy.

boàrio, *ag.* cattle (*attributivo*): *foro, mercato* —, cattle market.

boàro, *s.m.* cowherd, cowboy.

boàto, *s.m.* rumble; bellow; roar: *il* — *del terremoto,* the rumble of the earthquake.

bob, *s.m.* (*guidoslitta*) bobsleigh, bobsled: *pratica del* —, bob-sleighing.

bobína, *s.f.* 1. (*rocchetto*) reel, spool, bobbin 2. (*elett.*) coil, bobbin.

bobinatrice, *s.f.* 1. (*elett.*) winding machine, coil winder 2. (*ind. tessile*) winding frame.

bobísta, *s.m.* (*spor.*) bobsleigh rider, bobsled rider.

bócca, *s.f.* 1. mouth: *aveva la* — *piena,* he had his mouth full; *non osò aprir* —, he dared not open his mouth ‖ *a* —, by word of mouth ‖ *acqua in* —!, hush! ‖ *in* — *al lupo!,* good luck! ‖ *è la* — *della verità,* he is truth itself ‖ *avere la* — *buona,* to have a pleasant taste in one's mouth ‖ *cavare ql.co. di* — *a qlcu., fig.* to get s.o. to tell sthg. ‖ *dire a mezza* —, to say half -heartedly (o by hints o in a vaguely allusive manner) ‖ *dire ciò che viene in* —, to say whatever comes into one's mind ‖ *essere di buona* —, to be easily satisfied ‖ *essere sulla* — *di tutti,* to be the talk of the town (o to be the common topic); (*essere criticato*) to be criticized by everyone ‖ *fare la* — *a qlcu.,* to acquire a taste for sthg. ‖ *far venire l'acquolina in* — *a qlcu.,* to make s.o.'s mouth water ‖ *levare il pane di* — *a qlcu., fig.* to take the bread out of s.o.'s mouth; *levarsi il pan di* — *per qlcu., fig.* to starve oneself for s.o.'s sake ‖ *mettere un discorso in* — *a qlcu.,* to put a speech into s.o.'s mouth ‖ *pendere dalla* — *di qlcu., fig.* to hang on s.o.'s lips (o to listen attentively to s.o.) ‖ *restare a* — *aperta, fig.* to be astonished (o to stand gaping o to stand open-mouthed) ‖ *restare a* — *asciutta, fig.* to have no share in a gain (o in the enjoyment of sthg.) ‖ *tappare, chiudere la* — *a qlcu.,* to silence s.o. 2. (*apertura*) opening, mouth: — *d'acqua,* hydrant; — *di alto forno,* throat; — *da fuoco,* gun; — *da incendio,* fire-plug; — *dello stomaco,* pit of the stomach; — *di una caverna,* mouth of a cave; — *di forno,* stoke-hole; — *di un sacco,* mouth of a bag; — *di un vaso,* mouth of a jar 3. (*di fiume*) mouth 4. — *di leone,* (*bot.*) snap-dragon.

boccaccésco, *ag.* 1. (*lett.*) of Boccaccio; in the style of Boccaccio 2. (*licenzioso*) licentious; lascivious.

boccaccévole, *ag.* 1. (*spreg.*) after the style of Boccaccio 2. (*licenzioso*) licentious; lascivious.

boccàccia, *s.f.* 1. grimace: *fare una* —, to make a wry face (o a grimace); *far le boccacce a qlcu.,* to pull (o to make) faces at s.o. 2. (*persona sboccata*) foul -mouthed person: *essere una* —, *fig.* to be calumnious.

boccadilúpo, *s.f.* mantrap.

boccadòpera, *s.f.* (*teat.*) proscenium.

boccadòro, *ag.* talkative, loquacious ‖ *s.m.* wiseacre.

boccàglio, *s.m.* (*mec.*) nozzle; (*tubo di efflusso*) nosepiece.

boccalàio, *s.m.* 1. (*chi fabbrica boccali*) jug maker 2. (*chi vende boccali*) jug seller.

boccàle, *s.m.* jug; (*di metallo*) tankard: — *di birra,* tankard of beer.

boccalíno, *s.m.* small jug; pannikin.

boccapòrto, *s.m.* (*mar.*) hatchway, hatch.

boccascèna, *s.f.* (*teat.*) proscenium.

boccàta, *s.f.* mouthful ‖ *prendere una* — *d'aria,* to take an airing.

boccétta, *s.f.* small bottle.

boccheggiaménto, *s.m.* gasping.

boccheggiànte, *ag.* gasping; (*morente*) dying: *giacque* —, he lay gasping.

boccheggiàre, *v.i.* to gasp: *boccheggiava per mancanza d'aria,* he was gasping for air.

bocchèllo, *s.m.* (*metal.*) gate.

bocchétta, *s.f.* 1. small opening 2. (*di strumento musicale*) mouth-piece 3. (*di serratura*) plate; selvage 4. (*di scarpe*) tongue.

bocchíno, *s.m.* small mouth, pretty mouth ‖ *fare il* —, to screw up one's mouth 2. (*per fumatori*) holder, mouth-piece: — *di pipa,* pipe mouth-piece; — *per sigarette,* cigarette-holder; — *per sigari,* cigar-holder 3. (*di strumento musicale*) mouth-piece.

bòccia, *s.f.* 1. bowl; (*per l'acqua*) jug, bottle; (*per il vino*) decanter 2. (*spor.*) bowl: *il giuoco delle bocce,* bowling; *campo per il giuoco delle bocce,* bowling alley; (*erboso*) bowling-green; *fare una partita alle bocce,* to play a game of bowls; *giocare alle bocce,* to play bowls (o to bowl) 3. (*scherz.*) (*testa*) pate 4. (*boccio*) bud 5. *pl.* (*bolle di sapone*) soap-bubbles.

bocciàre, *v.t.* **1.** (*respingere*) to reject: *la mozione fu bocciata*, the motion was rejected; — *un progetto di legge*, to reject (*o* to throw) a bill **2.** (*agli esami*) to fail; (*fam.*) to plough, to pluck: *essere bocciato*, *farsi* —, to fail (at an examination) (*o fam.* to get plucked *o* ploughed) **3.** (*alle bocce*) to hit.

boccíno, *s.m.* **1.** (*bocciuolino*) tiny bud: — *di rosa*, rosebud **2.** (*alle bocce*) jack **3.** (*scherz.*) (*testa*) pate.

bòccio, *s.m.* bud: *essere in* —, to be in bud.

bocciuòlo, *s.m.* **1.** bud **2.** (*di candeliere*) socket **3.** (*di pipa*) stem **4.** (*di canna*) internode.

bóccola, *s.f.* **1.** (*orecchino*) ear-ring **2.** (*mec.*) bushing, bush, ferrule: *mettere una* —, to bush **3.** (*ferr.*) axle box.

bóccolo, *s.m.* curl, lock.

bocconcèllo, *s.m.* morsel, bit.

bocconcíno, *s.m.* **1.** morsel ‖ *a bocconcini*, in tiny pieces (*o* little by little) **2.** (*boccone squisito*) titbit, dainty, choice morsel, delicacy **3.** (*persona, cosa desiderabile*) desirable person, desirable thing.

boccóne, *s.m.* **1.** bit, morsel: *un* — *di pane*, a morsel of bread; *dammene un* —*!*, give me a bit!; *mangiamo un* — *e poi partiamo*, let us have a quick snack and then leave ‖ — *amaro*, *fig.* bitter pill ‖ *a pezzi e a bocconi*, a bit at a time ‖ — *ghiotto*, dainty ‖ *non è* — *per i vostri denti!*, it is out of your reach! **2.** (*boccata*) mouthful: *in un* —, in a mouthful: *mangiàre in un* — to gulp down **3.** (*esca*) bait (anche *fig.*): *prendere uno al* —, *fig.* to bait s.o.

boccóni, *av.* pronely, lying face downwards: *cadere* —, to fall flat on one's face; *giacere* —, to lie face downwards (*o* to lie on one's face).

boccúccia, *s.f.* **1.** small mouth: *bella* —, pretty little mouth ‖ *fare* —, (*storcere il naso dinanzi a ql.co.*) to turn up one's nose **2.** (*persona fastidiosa*) fastidious person.

boche, *s.m.* (*spreg.*) boche.

bodíno, *V.* budíno.

bodoniàno, *ag.* (*tip.*) in Bodoni's style, in Bodoni's manner: *carattere* —, Bodoni type; *rilegato alla bodoniana*, bound in boards.

Boèmia, *no.pr.f.* (*geog.*) Bohemia.

boèmo, *ag.s.m.* Bohemian.

boèro, *ag.* Boer ‖ *s.m.* **1.** Boer **2.** (*dolce*) chocolate-coated liqueur cherry.

Boèzio, *no.pr.m.* (*st. fil.*) Boethius.

bòffice, *ag.* **1.** (*soffice*) soft **2.** (*grassoccio*) plump.

bofonchiàre, *v.i.* to grumble.

bofónchio, *s.m.* (*entom.*) bumble-bee.

Bogotà, *no.pr.f.* (*geog.*) Bogotá.

bohème, *s.f.* (*vita di bohème*) bohemianism: *fare una vita da* —, to lead a Bohemian (*o* an unconventional) life.

bohémien, *ag.s.m.* Bohemian.

bòia, *s.m.* **1.** executioner; (*addetto all'impiccagione*) hang-man (*pl.* hang-men); (*addetto alla decapitazione*) headsman (*pl.* headsmen) **2.** (*malandrino*) rascal.

boiàcca, *s.f.* (*edil.*) cement grout.

boiàrdo, *s.m.* boyar(d).

boiàta, *s.f.* **1.** rubbish: *quel film era una* —, that film was rubbish **2.** (*cattiva azione*) nasty trick.

boicottàggio, *s.m.* boycott, boycotting: — *parlamentare*, (*amer.*) filibustering.

boicottàre, *v.t.* to boycott: *mi boicottarono per far fallire i miei piani*, they boycotted me to undo my plans.

boldróne, *s.m.* fleece (of a sheep).

Bolèna, *no.pr.f.* (*st.*) Boleyn.

bolèro, *s.m.* **1.** (*musica, danza*) bolero **2.** (*giacchettina per signora*) bolero.

bolèto, *s.m.* (*bot.*) boletus.

bòlgia, *s.f.* **1.** (*fossa dell'Inferno dantesco*) pit (of hell) **2.** (*luogo in cui regna confusione*) bedlam, babel **3.** (*borsa, sacca*) bag.

bòlide, *s.m.* **1.** (*astr.*) bolide **2.** (*automobile da corsa*) racing-car ‖ *arrivò come un* —, he dashed in.

bolína, *s.f.* (*mar.*) bowline: *andar di* —, to sail on a bowline.

Bolívia, *no.pr.f.* (*geog.*) Bolivia.

boliviàno, *ag.s.m.* Bolivian.

bólla[1], *s.f.* **1.** bubble: — *d'aria*, air bubble (*o* gas pocket); *fare bolle di sapone*, to blow bubbles **2.** (*vescica*) blister; (*pustola*) pimple.

bólla[2], *s.f.* **1.** (*eccl.*) (Papal) bull **2.** (*comm.*) *V.* bollétta 1.

bollandísta, *s.m.* (*st.*) Bollandist.

bollàre, *v.t.* **1.** to stamp: *far* — *una lettera*, to get a letter stamped **2.** (*con marchio a fuoco*) to brand (anche *fig.*): *il suo delitto lo bollò per sempre*, his crime branded him for ever.

bollàrio, *s.m.* (*eccl.*) collection of Papal bulls.

bollàto, *ag.* **1.** stamped: *carta bollata*, stamped paper **2.** (*con marchio a fuoco*) branded (anche *fig.*): *bestiame* —, branded cattle.

bollatúra, *s.f.* **1.** stamping **2.** (*con marchio a fuoco*) branding (anche *fig.*).

bollènte, *ag.* boiling; (*molto caldo*) hot; (*rovente*) burning, fiery (anche *fig.*): *acqua* —, boiling water.

bollétta, *s.f.* **1.** (*comm.*) bill; (*ricevuta*) receipt, voucher: — *d'entrata*, bill of entry; — *di consegna*, delivery note; — *di imbarco*, shipping bill; — *di transito*, transit bill; — *doganale*, customs certificate **2.** (*tec.*) tack **3.** *trovarsi, essere in* —, (*fam.*) to be penniless (*o* to be on one's uppers *o* to be hard up).

bollettàrio, *s.m.* (*comm.*) counterfoil-book.

bollettíno, *s.m.* **1.** (*di notizie*) bulletin: — *di guerra*, war bulletin **2.** (*pubblicazione periodica*) gazette: — *ufficiale*, official gazette **3.** (*comm.*) note, list: — *dei cambi*, exchange list; — *dei prezzi*, price list; — *di consegna*, delivery note; — *di ordinazione*, order sheet; — *di spedizione*, forwarding note.

bollíre, *v.i.* **1.** to boil: *la minestra già bolle*, the soup is already boiling ‖ *cominciare a* —, to come to the boil ‖ — *di collera*, *fig.* to boil with anger **2.** (*sentir molto caldo*) to feel hot: *oggi si bolle dal caldo*, to day it's boiling hot **3.** (*fermentare*) to brew (anche *fig.*): *qualcosa bolle in pentola*, there is something brewing ‖ *un bolli bolli*, (*una gran confusione*) a turmoil ‖ *v.t.* (*fare bollire*) to boil: *hai* — *la carne per oggi?*, have you boiled the meat for today?.

bollíta, *s.f.* boiling: *dare una* — *a ql.co.*, to bring sthg. to the boil.

bollitíccio, *s.m.* sediment.

bollíto, *ag.* boiled ‖ *s.m.* boiled meat: *è pronto il* —*?*, is the boiled meat ready?.

bollitóre, *s.m.* boiler; kettle: — *elettrico*, electric kettle.

bollitúra, *s.f.* **1.** boiling **2.** (*decotto*) decoction.

bóllo, *s.m.* **1.** stamp: *un* — *da tre pence*, a threepenny stamp; — *di circolazione*, (*aut.*) license tag; *carta da* —, stamped paper; *diritti di* —, stamp duty; *marca da* —, revenue stamp; *abbonarsi al* —, to compound for stamp duty **2.** (*sigillo*) seal: — *a secco*, embossed seal **3.** (*bernoccolo*) bump **4.** (*cicatrice*) scar **5.** (*marchio*) brand.

bollóne, *s.m.* (*mec.*) bolt; large nail.

bollóre, *s.m.* **1.** boil, boiling, ebullition: *dare il* — *a ql.co.*, to bring sthg. to the boil; *levare, alzare il* —, to come to the boil **2.** (*caldo eccessivo*) excessive heat **3.** (*ardore*) excitement, ardour.

bollóso, *ag.* pimply.

bòlo, *s.m.* **1.** (*terra argillosa*) bole **2.** (*pillola*) pill; (*grossa pillola*) bolus **3.** — *alimentare*, chewed food.

Bológna, *no.pr.f.* (*geog.*) Bologna.

bolognése, *ag.s.c.* Bolognese.

bolsàggine, *s.f.* **1.** (*di cavallo*) heaves (*pl.*), broken-wind **2.** (*debolezza*) weakness.

bolscevíco, *ag.s.m.* Bolshevik, Bolshevist.

bolscevísmo, *s.m.* Bolshevism.

bolscevizzàre, *v.t.* to Bolshevize.

bólso, *ag.* **1.** (*di cavallo*) broken-winded **2.** (*debole*) weak.

bolzonàre, *v.t.* **1.** (*st.*) to ram **2.** to punch.

bolzóne, *s.m.* 1. (*ariete*) ram 2. (*freccia per balestra*) blunt arrow 3. (*punzone*) punch.

bóma, *s.f.* (*mar.*) boom.

bómba[1], *s.f.* 1. bomb: — *a gas*, chemical bomb; — *a mano*, hand grenade; — *antisommergibili, di profondità*, depth charge; — *a scoppio ritardato*, time bomb; — *atomica*, atomic bomb; — *incendiaria*, incendiary bomb; *gettar bombe*, to drop bombs ‖ *a prova di —*, bomb-proof 2. (*grossa sorpresa*) sensation, sensational event: *ora scoppia la —!*, now the fat is in the fire! 3. — *di riso*, (*cuc.*) rice pudding 4. (*bombetta*) bowler-hat.

bómba[2], *s.m.* (*giuoco di bambini*) base ‖ *tornare a —*, to get back to the point.

bombàrda, *s.f.* 1. (*mortaio*) mortar 2. (*st. mil.*) bombard 3. (*mar.*) two-mast sailing-ship 4. (*mus.*) bombardone.

bombardaménto, *s.m.* bombardment, bombing; (*cannoneggiamento*) shelling: — *catodico*, (*fis.*) cathodic bombardment; — *pesante*, (*sl.*) strafe; *aeroplano da —*, bomber.

bombardàre, *v.t.* 1. to bomb; (*cannoneggiare*) to shell; (*sl.*) (*pesantemente*) to strafe: — *in picchiata*, to dive bomb 2. (*fis.*) to bombard.

bombardàta, *s.f.* bombardment; bombing.

bombardièra, *s.f.* 1. (*mil.*) embrasure 2. (*mar.*) bomb-vessel.

bombardière, *s.m.* 1. (*soldato addetto alle bombarde*) bombardier 2. (*aer.*) bomber.

bombardíno, *s.m.* (*mus.*) euphonium.

bombardóne, *s.m.* (*mus.*) saxtuba, bombardon(e).

bombé, *ag.* convex, curved, bulging.

bombétta, *s.f.* bowler-hat, bowler; (*amer.*) derby.

bómbice, *s.m.* (*entom.*) silk-worm; bombyx.

bómbo, *s.m.* 1. (*rimbombo*) roar 2. (*ronzio*) buzzing.

bómbola, *s.f.* 1. cylinder, bottle, bomb: — *d'ossigeno*, oxygen bottle; — *per gas*, gas cylinder (*o* gas bottle); — *per nebulizzazione*, aerosol bomb 2. (*per lampada al kerosene*) glass-globe.

bombolóne, *s.m.* (*cuc.*) cream-puff.

bombonièra, *s.f.* bonbonnière; candy-box.

bomprèsso, *s.m.* (*mar.*) bowsprit.

bonàccia, *s.f.* 1. dead calm, lull: *essere in —*, to be becalmed 2. *fig.* tranquillity, ease.

bonàccio, *ag.* good-natured, simple and kind-hearted.

bonaccióne, *ag.* good-natured ‖ *s.m.* good-natured person, simple and kind-hearted man.

bonalàna, *s.m.* (*scherz.*) rascal, rogue, scoundrel.

bonamàno, *s.f.* tip.

bonapartísmo, *s.m.* (*st.*) Bonapartism.

bonapartísta, *s.c.* (*st.*) Bonapartist.

bonariaménte, *av.* good-naturedly, kind-heartedly; in a friendly manner.

bonarietà, *s.f.* good nature; kindness, kindly disposition, friendliness.

bonàrio, *ag.* good-natured, friendly, kind, kind-hearted, affable, simple.

Bonaventúra, *no.pr.m.* Bonaventura.

bonbon, *s.m.* " bon-bon ", sweetmeat; (*amer.*) candy.

boncuóre, *s.m.* warm-heartedness.

bondiòla, *s.f.* "bondiola" (big round pork sausage).

bongiórno, *s.m.* good morning: *dare il —*, to say good morning.

bongustàio, *s.m.* gourmet.

bongústo, *s.m.* (good) taste: *avere —*, to have good taste.

Bonifàcio, *no.pr.m.* Boniface.

bonífica, *s.f.*, **bonificaménto,** *s.m.* 1. (land) reclamation; drainage: — *isotermica*, austempering 2. (*luogo bonificato*) reclaimed land 3. — *chimica*, (*mil.*) (*degassificazione*) degassing.

bonificàre, *v.t.* 1. to reclaim, to improve 2. (*mil.*) (*degassificare*) to degas 3. (*comm.*) to allow a discount of (*sthg.*); to grant an allowance of (*sthg.*): *gli bonificarono il 5 %*, they granted him an allowance of 5 %.

bonificazióne, *s.f.* 1. (land) reclamation; improvement, amelioration (of land) 2. (*luogo bonificato*) reclaimed land 3. (*mil.*) (*degassificazione*) degassing 4. (*comm.*) abatement, allowance, reduction: — *per pagamento a pronti*, cash discount; *concedere una — del 2 %*, to grant a discount of 2 %; *domandare una —*, to ask for an allowance.

bonífico, *s.m.* (*comm.*) allowance, discount, rebate: *ordine di —*, transfer order.

bon mot, *s.m.* "bon mot" (*pl.* "bons mots"); witty remark, witticism.

bonne, *s.f.* 1. (*cameriera*) maid (servant) 2. (*bambinaia*) nursemaid.

bonomía, *s.f.* good nature, simple-heartedness, bonhomie: *con —*, good-naturedly.

bonsènso, *s.m.* (common) sense; (*fam. amer.*) horse sense: *una persona di —*, a sensible person.

bontà, *s.f.* 1. (*di cosa*) goodness, good quality, excellence: *la — dei nostri prodotti è insuperata*, the quality of our products is unequalled 2. (*di persona*) goodness, kindness, benignancy: — *di cuore*, goodness of heart; *abbiate la — di ascoltarmi*, will you be so kind as to listen to me? (*o* will you have the goodness to listen to me?); (*più perentorio*) have the kindness to listen to me 3. *pl.* (*arc.*) gifts, qualities, merits: *quel tale crede di possedere tutte le bontà!*, that fellow pretends he possesses all qualities!.

bontempóne, *s.m.* jolly dog, merry fellow.

bon ton, *s.m.* "bon-ton"; good breeding.

bonuòmo, *s.m.* simple man, good-natured man.

bonuscíta, *s.f.* (*comm.*) key-money, premium.

bónzo, *s.m.* bonze.

Bòoz, *no.pr.m.* (*Bibbia*) Boaz.

bòra, *s.f.* bora.

boràce, *s.m.* (*chim.*) borax.

boràcico, *ag.* (*chim.*) boracic, boric.

boracífero, *ag.* (*min.*) boraciferous.

boracíte, *s.f.* (*min.*) boracite.

boràto, *s.m.* (*chim.*) borate.

borbogliaménto, *s.m.* 1. (*gorgogliamento*) rumbling, gurgling 2. (*borbottio*) grumbling, mumbling.

borbogliàre, *v.i.* 1. (*gorgogliare*) to rumble 2. (*borbottare*) to grumble, to mumble.

borboglío, *s.m.* 1. (*gorgoglio*) rumbling 2. (*borbottio*) grumbling.

Borbóne, *o.m.* (*st.*) Bourbon.

borbònico, *ag.* (*st.*) Bourbon (*attributivo*) ‖ *s.m.* (*fautore dei Borboni*) Bourbonist.

borborígmo, borborísmo, *s.m.* (*fisiol.*) borborygm.

borbottaménto, *s.m.* grumbling, mumbling.

borbottàre, *v.i.* to grumble, to mumble, to mutter.

borbottatóre, *s.m.* grumbler, mumbler.

borbottío, *s.m.* grumbling, mumbling.

borbottóna, *s.f.*, **borbottóne,** *s.m.* grumbler.

bòrchia, *s.f.* stud, boss, knob; (*da tappezziere*) upholsterer's nail.

bordàglia, *s.f.* (*marmaglia*) mob, rabble.

bordàme, *s.m.* (*mar.*) foot of sail.

bordàre, *v.t.* 1. (*orlare*) to hem; to border 2. (*cerchiare*) to rim; (*mec.*) to bead 3. (*mar.*) (*fasciare*) to plank; (*spiegare, le vele*) to flatten (in) (sail) 4. (*colpire*) to knock, to strike ‖ *v.i.* (*mar.*) (*bordeggiare*) to tack.

bordàta, *s.f.* (*mar.*) 1. (*di cannoni*) broadside 2. (*navigazione obliqua*) tacking: *prendere una —*, to tack 3. (*ciascuno dei tratti percorsi nel bordeggiare*) beat.

bordatíno, bordàto, *s.m.* (*stoffa rigata*) ticking.

bordatríce, *s.f.* (*mec.*) beading machine, flanging machine, curling machine, flanging press.

bordatúra, *s.f.* 1. rim, border; (*orlatura*) hemming 2. (*mec.*) lag; beading 3. (*modanatura*) swage.

bordeaux, *s.m.* 1. (*vino*) "Bordeaux" (kind of French claret) 2. (*colore*) claret red.

bordeggiàre, *v.i.* 1. (*mar.*) to tack 2. *fig.* to contend with difficulties.

bordéggio, *s.m.* (*mar.*) tacking (about).

bordèllo, *s.m.* **1.** (*schiamazzo*) uproar; noise **2.** (*postribolo*) brothel, bawdyhouse.

borderò, *s.m.* bordereau, memorandum (*pl.* memorandums, memoranda); (detailed) statement; docket: — *dei prezzi,* price-list; — *di spedizione,* (*comm.*) dispatch note.

bordíno, *s.m.* **1.** (*ferr.*) (wheel) flange **2.** (*mec.*) flat band **3.** (*arch.*) molding.

bórdo, *s.m.* **1.** edge: *il — della strada,* the edge of the road **2.** (*bordatura*) border **3.** (*mec.*) rim: — *della ruota,* wheel rim **4.** *persona d'alto —, fig.* person of high rank **5.** (*mar.*) board: *giornale di —,* log-book; *andare a —,* to go on board (o aboard); *essere a —,* to be on board; *gettare fuori —,* to throw overboard; *virare di —,* to tack about (anche *fig.*) ‖ *fuori —,* outboard motor-boat ‖ *prendere qlcu. a —,* (*in automobile*) to give s.o. a lift **6.** *franco —,* (*comm.*) free on board (*abbr.* f.o.b.).

bordò, *s.m.* **1.** (*vino*) "Bordeaux" (kind of French claret) **2.** (*colore*) claret red.

bordonàle, *s.m.* (*arch.*) main beam.

bordóne[1], *s.m.* pilgrim's staff; (*arc.*) burdoun.

bordóne[2], *s.m.* (*mus.*) low undersong to a melody; (*di organo, piva*) bourdon, drone ‖ *tener — a qlcu., fig.* to aid and abet s.o. (o to be s.o.'s accomplice).

bordóne[3], *s.m.* (*ornit.*) plumule, down-feather ‖ *venire, rizzarsi i bordoni,* (*fam.*) to have one's hair stand on end.

bordúra, *s.f.* **1.** (*orlatura*) hem; border; fringe; rim **2.** (*arald.*) bordure.

bòrea, *s.m.* **1.** North **2.** (*vento del nord*) Boreas ‖ **Bòrea,** *no.pr.m.* (*mit.*) Boreas.

boreàle, *ag.* northern, boreal: *aurora —,* aurora borealis.

borgàta, *s.f.* village.

borghése, *ag.* **1.** bourgeois, middle-class: *morale —,* bourgeois (o middle-class) morals **2.** (*civile*) civilian: *abito —,* civilian dress ‖ *in —,* (*mil.*) in mufti (o in civilian dress); *poliziotto in —,* plainclothes -detective (o man); *mettersi in —,* to put on mufti (o to change into civilian dress) **3.** (*comune, volgare*) plain, common: *gusti borghesi,* plain tastes; *vita —,* ordinary life ‖ *s.m.* middle-class person; (*leggermente spreg.*) bourgeois: *piccolo —,* lower middle-class person.

borghesía, *s.f.* middle class(es): *l'alta —,* the upper middle class(es); *la piccola —,* the lower middle class(es) ‖ *di buona —,* of good social standing.

borghigiàno, *s.m.* peasant; villager.

bórgo, *s.m.* **1.** village **2.** (*sobborgo*) suburb.

Borgógna, *no.pr.f.* (*geog.*) Burgundy: *vino di —,* Burgundy (wine).

borgognóne, *ag. s.m.* Burgundian.

borgomàstro, *s.m.* burgomaster.

bòria, *s.f.* haughtiness, arrogance; ostentation: *è un uomo pieno di —,* he is a (self-)conceited man (o he is an arrogant man); *metter su —,* to become arrogant.

boriàrsi, *v.r.* to boast (about sthg.); (*fam.*) to show off (sthg.): *di che si boria quell'uomo?,* what is that man boasting about?.

bòrico, *ag.* (*chim.*) boracic, boric: *acido —,* boric o boracic) acid.

borióne, *s.m.* (*tipo borioso*) conceited fellow.

boriosaménte, *av.* haughtily, arrogantly.

borióso, *ag.* haughty, arrogant, conceited.

boriúccia, *s.f.* petty pride.

bòrni, *s.m.pl.* (*arch.*) (*pietre sporgenti*) kerb-stones.

bòro, *s.m.* (*chim.*) boron.

borotàlco, *s.m.* talcum powder.

bórra, *s.f.* **1.** (*scarti di lana per imbottiture*) waste wool; flocks (*pl.*) **2.** (*imbottitura*) stuffing **3.** (*ind. laniera*) dropping **4.** *fig.* (*robaccia*) rubbish, trash.

borràccia, *s.f.* water-bottle, flask; (*mil.*) canteen.

borraccína, *s.f.* (*bot.*) moss.

borràggine, borràna, *s.f.* (*bot.*) borage.

bórro, *s.m.* gully; ravine.

bórsa[1], *s.f.* **1.** purse, money purse; (*borsetta*) bag, hand-bag; (*tasca*) pouch (anche *fig.*): — *per documenti,* brief case; — *da lavoro,* work-bag; — *da tabacco,* tobacco pouch; — *per l'acqua calda,* hot-water bottle ‖ — *di studio,* scholarship ‖ *l'ho comprato di mia —,* I bought it with my own money; *allentare, stringere i cordoni della —,* to loosen (o to tighten) the purse -strings; *far — comune,* to share expenses; *tenere i cordoni della —,* to hold the purse-strings ‖ *la — o la vita!,* your money or your life! ‖ *avere le borse agli occhi,* to have bags under one's eyes **2.** (*anat.*) bursa **3.** (*eccl.*) burse.

bórsa[2], *s.f.* (*Borsa valori*) Stock Exchange: *giuoco di —,* speculating in shares (o *spreg.* stock-jobbing o stock-jobbery); *listino di —,* stock-list.

borsai(u)òlo, *s.m.* pickpocket; bag-snatcher.

borsanéra, *s.f.* black market.

borsanerísta, *s.c.* blackmarketeer.

borsàta, *s.f.* bagful.

borseggiàre, *v.t.* to pick (s.o.'s) pockets.

borséggio, *s.m.* pocket-picking.

borsellíno, *s.m.* purse; money-bag.

borsétta, *s.f.* hand-bag, bag.

borsísta[1], *s.m.* (*chi giuoca in Borsa*) stock-broker.

borsísta[2], *s.m.* (*chi gode di una borsa di studio*) scholarship holder.

Bòrtolo, *no.pr.m.* Bart.

borzacchíno, *s.m.* blucher boot.

boscàglia, *s.f.* brushwood, underwood.

boscaiòlo, *s.m.* **1.** woodsman (*pl.* woodsmen), wood -cutter **2.** (*guardaboschi*) forester.

boscàta, *s.f.* boscage.

boscàto, *ag.* woody.

boscheréccio, *ag.* woody; (*letter.*) sylvan; woodland (*attributivo*): *poesia boschereccia,* sylvan poetry.

boschétto, *s.m.* thicket, grove: — *di aranci,* orange grove.

boschívo, *ag.* woody: *terreno —,* woodland.

bòsco, *s.m.* **1.** wood, forest: — *ceduo,* coppice; *attraversare un —,* to go through a wood ‖ *uomo da — e da riviera,* jack of all trades ‖ *essere uccel di —, fig.* to be free ‖ *un — di capelli,* a head of hair ‖ *portare legna al —,* to carry coals to Newcastle **2.** (*in bachicoltura*) cocoonery.

boscóso, *ag.* woody, wooded.

Bòsforo, *no.pr.m.* (*geog.*) Bosphorus.

Bòsnia, *no.pr.f.* (*geog. st.*) Bosnia.

bosníaco, *ag.s.m.* Bosnian, Bosniac.

bòsso, *s.m.* **1.** (*bot.*) box **2.** (*legno*) boxwood.

bòssolo, *s.m.* **1.** (*rar.*) (*scatoletta di legno*) small wooden box **2.** (*di cartuccia*) cartridge-case.

bostoniàno, *ag.* Bostonian.

botànica, *s.f.* botany.

botanicaménte, *av.* botanically.

botànico, *ag.* botanical; (*arc.*) botanic ‖ *s.m.* botanist.

Bòtnia, *no.pr.f.* (*geog.*) Bothnia.

bòtola, *s.f.* trap-door.

bòtolo, *s.m.* **1.** (*cane*) cur: — *ringhioso,* snarling cur (o dog) **2.** (*persona ringhiosa*) snarling fellow.

botrioterapía, *s.f.* (*med.*) botryotherapy.

bòtta[1], *s.f.* **1.** (*colpo*) blow, stroke; (*fam.*) whack: *dare un sacco di botte a qlcu.,* to whack s.o. (o to give s.o. a thorough thrashing); *menar botte da orbi,* to deal a volley of blows **2.** (*rumore sordo*) thud **3.** (*d'arma da fuoco*) report, shot **4.** (*scherma*) pass, thrust, lunge **5.** (*battuta*) sarcastic remark, witty retort: *spettacolo di — e risposta,* (*rad. tv.*) quiz programme (o give-away show) **6.** *fig.* blow: *fu una terribile —,* it was a terrible blow (o shock) ‖ *a — calda,* on the spur of the moment.

bòtta[2], *s.f.* (*rospo*) toad.

bottàccio, *s.m.* **1.** (*barile*) barrel **2.** (*stagno di mulino*) mill-pond.

bottàglie, *s.f. pl.* jack boots.

bottàio, *s.m.* cooper.

bottàme, *s.m.* casks (*pl.*), barrels (*pl.*).

bottàrga, *s.f.* (*cuc.*) botargo.

bottàta, *s.f.* gibe, retort, quip.

bótte, *s.f.* **1.** barrel; (*specialmente per liquidi*) cask: *mettere in —,* to barrel (*o* to cask) || *dare un colpo al cerchio e uno alla —, fig.* to run with the hare and hunt with the hounds || *essere in una — di ferro, fig.* to be on the safe side || *non si può avere la — piena e la moglie ubriaca, prov.* you cannot have your cake and eat it || *la — dà il vino che ha, prov.* what is bred in the bone comes out in the flesh **2.** (*arch.*): *volta a —,* barrel vault; *volta a mezza —,* semicircular vault.

bottéga, *s.f.* shop: *ragazzo di —,* shop-boy; *vetrina di —,* shop-window; *aprire una —,* to open a shop; *mettere a —,* to apprentice; *metter su —,* to set up shop; *tenere una —,* to keep a shop || *ferro di —, fig.* spy (*o* informer) || *far — degli ideali, fig.* to betray one's ideals.

bottegàio, *ag.* venal: *arte bottegaia,* mercenary art || *s.m.* shop-keeper; (*amer.*) store-keeper.

bottegànte, *s.m.* shop-keeper; (*amer.*) store-keeper.

botteghíno, *s.m.* **1.** (*piccola bottega*) small shop **2.** (*biglietteria di teatro*) box-office **3.** (*ricevitoria del lotto*) lottery betting shop.

bottèllo, *s.m.* (*etichetta*) label.

botticíno, *s.m.* "botticino" (kind of marble).

bottíglia, *s.f.* bottle: *— da vino,* wine-bottle; *una — di vino,* a bottle of wine; *bottiglie vuote,* (*sulla tavola di un convito*) dead-men (*o* marines); *collo di —,* bottle-neck; *viro di —,* select wine; *mettere vino in —,* to bottle wine || *— di Leyda,* (*fis.*) Leyden jar || *verde —,* bottle-green.

bottigliería, *s.f.* **1.** wine shop; wine-lodge **2.** (*cantina*) cellar.

bottíno[1], *s.m.* booty, loot, spoil(s), prey, plunder: *i ladri si divisero il —,* the thieves shared the spoil(s); *mettere una città a —,* to plunder (*o* to pillage *o* to loot *o* to sack) a town.

bottíno[2], *s.m.* (*fogna*) cesspool.

bòtto, *s.m.* **1.** blow **2.** (*di campana*) stroke; toll **3.** *di —,* (*improvvisamente*) suddenly; (*subito*) at once || *in un —,* in a tick (*o* in the twinkling of an eye): *tutto in un —,* all of a sudden || *tutti in un —,* altogether.

bottonàio, *s.m.* **1.** (*chi fabbrica bottoni*) button-manufacturer, button-maker **2.** (*chi vende bottoni*) button-seller.

bottoncíno, *s.m.* **1.** small button; (*di camicia*) stud **2.** (*bocciuolo*) bud: *— di rosa,* rose-bud; *fig.* pretty girl **3.** (*bitorzoletto*) pimple **4.** (*di fioretto*) button **5.** (*elett.*) (*pulsante*) button.

bottóne, *s.m.* **1.** button: *— automatico,* press-button; *— del colletto,* collar-stud; *bottoni gemelli,* cuff-links; *allacciare un —,* to fasten a button; *attaccare un — (a un abito, ecc.),* to sew a button (on a dress, etc.) || *attaccare un — a qlcu., fig.* to buttonhole s.o. **2.** (*bocciuolo*) bud: *— di rosa,* rose-bud **3.** (*elett.*) (*pulsante*) button; (*mec.*) (*di manovella*) pin; (*ott.*) knob.

bottonièra, *s.f.* row of buttons.

botulísmo, *s.m.* (*patol.*) botulism.

boutade, *s.f.* flash of wit.

bovàro, *s.m.* cowherd, cattle-driver, cowboy.

bòve, *V.* búe.

bovíndo, *s.m.* (*arch.*) bow-window, bay (-window).

bovíno, *ag.* bovine.

bovíni, *s.m.pl.* cattle (*sing.*).

bòvolo, *s.m.* (*mec.*) conical spiral spring.

box, *s.m.* **1.** (*recinto per cavalli*) box **2.** (*aut. spor.*) pit **3.** (*autorimessa*) lock-up garage.

boxe, *s.f.* (*pugilato*) boxing.

boxeur, *s.m.* (*pugilatore*) boxer.

bòzza, *s.f.* **1.** (*arch.*) (*bugna*) ashlar **2.** (*bernoccolo, gonfiore*) bump, swelling; *— frontale,* (*anat.*) frontal eminence **3.** (*tip.*) proof: *— finale,* press-proof; *— impaginata,* page-proof; *— in colonna,* galley-proof; *correttore, revisore di bozze,* proof-reader; *correzione di*

bozze, proof-reading (*o* proof-correction); *prima —,* foul (*o* flat) proof; *seconda —,* revise; *terza —,* second revise; *correggere le bozze,* to proof-read (*o* to proof-correct); *tirare una —,* to pull a proof **4.** (*di contratti, lettere, ecc.*) draft; (*abbozzo, brutta copia*) rough draft, rough copy **5.** (*mar.*) stopper; (*spezzone di cavo*) guy, rope: *nodo di —,* stopper knot.

bozzacchióne, *s.m.* withered plum.

bozzacchiúto, *ag.* misshapen, ill-shaped.

bozzàto, *ag.* (*arch.*) embossed.

bozzèllo, *s.m.* (*mar.*) block: *— a braccio,* brace block; *— a coda,* tail block; *— a molinello,* swivel block; *— apribile,* snatch block; *— da fune,* rope block.

bozzétto, *s.m.* **1.** sketch, outline **2.** (*breve componimento narrativo*) novelette.

bòzzima, *s.f.* **1.** (*ind. tessile*) size **2.** (*pastone per i polli*) mash.

bozzimàre, *v.t.* (*ind. tessile*) to size.

bozzolàio, *s.m.* cocoon-seller.

bòzzolo, *s.m.* **1.** cocoon **2.** (*groppo di farina, crema, ecc.*) lump, knot.

bozzolóso, bozzolúto, *ag.* lumpy, knotty.

Brabànte, *no.pr.m.* (*geog.*) Brabant.

bràca, *s.f.* **1.** (*corda, catena per sollevare travi, botti, ecc.*) sling: *— a ganci,* can hook **2.** (*ciascuna delle due parti che formano i calzoni*) trouser-leg **3.** *pl.* (*mutande*) drawers; (*calzoni*) trousers || *gli cascarono le brache,* (*fig. volg.*) he lost courage; *calar(si) le brache,* (*fig. volg.*) to give in (*o* to yield).

bracalóne, *s.m.* **1.** sloven; untidy person **2.** (*persona negligente*) careless fellow.

braccàre, *v.t.* **1.** (*una preda*) to hound, to chase, to hunt **2.** (*una persona*) to hunt down: *il fuggiasco era braccato dalla polizia,* the fugitive was hunted down by the police **3.** (*onori, lodi, guadagni, ecc.*) to hunt after, for (*sthg.*), to seek for (*sthg.*), to pursue.

braccétto, a, *l.av.* arm-in-arm: *camminavano a —,* they walked arm-in-arm.

braccheggiàre, *v.t.* **1.** (*spiare*) to spy upon (s.o.) **2.** *V.* **braccàre.**

bracchéggio, *s.m.* searching; scenting (of hounds).

bracchière, *s.m.* (*caccia*) whipper-in, huntsman (*pl.* huntsmen).

bracciàle, *s.m.* **1.** (*braccialetto*) armlet, bangle, bracelet: *— in cuoio,* (*per orologio*) wrist-watch strap **2.** (*fascia portata al braccio come segno distintivo*) arm-band **3.** (*armatura del braccio*) armlet.

braccialétto, *s.m.* bracelet, armlet.

bracciànte, *s.m.* labourer, day-labourer: *— agricolo,* farm-labourer; (*amer.*) farm-hand.

bracciàre, *v.t.* (*mar.*) to brace: *— di punta,* to brace up; *— in croce,* to brace in (*o* to).

bracciàta, *s.f.* **1.** armful: *una — di fiori,* an armful of flowers || *a bracciate,* in great quantity **2.** (*nuoto*) stroke: *attraversò il canale a lunghe bracciate,* with long strokes he crossed the canal.

bracciatèlla, *s.f.* **1.** small armful **2.** (*ciambella*) bun.

bracciatúra, *s.f.* measuring by arm's length.

braccière, *s.m.* lady's escort.

bràccio, *s.m.; pl.f.* **bràccia** (*nei sensi 1. 2. 3.*); *pl.m.* **bràcci** (*negli altri sensi*) **1.** arm: *a braccia,* by hand (*o* by strength of arms); *con le braccia in croce,* (with) his arms folded across his breast; *con le braccia tese,* with outstretched arms; *lo prese in —,* she took him in her arms; *lo prese per un —,* he seized him by the arm; *avere qlcu. al —,* to have s.o. on one's arm; *essere in — a qlcu.,* to be in s.o.'s arms; *incrociare le braccia,* to fold one's arms; *fig.* to go on strike; *offrire il — a una signora per andare nella sala da pranzo,* to take a lady in to dinner; *portare qlcu. in —,* to carry s.o. in one's arms || *il — secolare,* (*st.*) the secular arm || *dagli un dito e si prenderà un —,* give him an inch and he'll take a yard || *accogliere qlcu. a braccia aperte, fig.* to welcome s.o. with open arms (*o* with great cordiality) || *avere le braccia legate, fig.* to have one's hands tied || *avere le* *braccia lunghe*, *fig.* to be very influential (*o* to have a wide influence) ‖ *avere qlcu. sulle braccia*, *fig.* to have s.o. in one's charge (*o* on one's hands) ‖ *essere il — destro di qlcu.*, to be s.o.'s right hand ‖ *essere in — alla disperazione*, to be a prey to (*o* to be overcome with) despair ‖ *fare un discorso a —*, to make an impromptu speech ‖ *sentirsi cascar le braccia*, to lose courage: *quando udii la sua risposta, mi cascarono le braccia*, when I heard his reply I lost all courage ‖ *tendere le braccia a qlcu.*, *fig.* to ask for s.o.'s help 2. *pl.* (*braccianti*) labourers, hands: *la vostra fattoria ha bisogno di altre braccia*, your farm needs more hands 3. "braccio" (*pl.* "braccia") (*misura di lunghezza variabile*); (*mar.*) fathom (*misura di profondità* = m. 1,829) 4. (*arch.*) wing 5. (*mar.*) (*di ancora*) arm; (*di remo*) web; (*per orientare i pennoni*) brace 6. (*di croce*) limb 7. (*di fiume*) arm; (*di mare*) sound, strait 8. (*mec.*) arm; (*di bilancia, stadera*) beam, bar; (*di grammofono*) pick -up: — *di leva*, lever arm; — *di manovella*, crank arm (*o* crank throw *o* crank web); — *mobile*, (*di gru*) (adjustable) jib; (*di sestante*) index bar; — *portante*, supporting arm.

bracciuòlo, *s.m.* 1. arm: *sedia a bracciuoli*, arm -chair 2. (*appoggiatoio di scala*) banisters (*pl.*) 3. (*mar.*) bracket plate, knee plate.

bràcco, *s.m.* 1. (*cane*) hound 2. (*investigatore*) detective; (*fam.*) sleuth.

bracconière, *s.m.* poacher.

bràce, *s.f.* embers (*pl.*); live charcoal: *farsi di —*, *fig.* to blush ‖ *cadere dalla padella nella —*, to fall out of the frying-pan into the fire.

brachétta, *s.f.* trouser-flap.

brachiàle, *ag.* (*anat.*) brachial.

brachicardìa, *s.f.* (*med.*) brachycardia, bradycardia.

brachicefalìa, *s.f.* (*anat.*) brachycephaly.

brachicèfalo, *ag.* (*anat.*) brachycephalic, brachycephalous ‖ *s.m.* brachycephal (*pl.* brachycephales).

brachigrafìa, *s.f.* brachygraphy.

brachilogìa, *s.f.* (*ret.*) brachylogy.

bràcia, *V.* **bràce**.

bracière, *s.m.* brazier.

braciòla, *s.f.* 1. chop: — *di maiale*, pork chop; — *di montone*, mutton chop ‖ *fare braciole di qlcu.*, (*scherz.*) (*farlo a pezzi*) to make mincemeat of s.o. 2. (*costoletta*) cutlet 3. (*bistecca*) steak.

bràdipo, *s.m.* (*zool.*) sloth.

bradisìsmo, *s.m.* (*geol.*) bradyseism.

bràdo, *ag.* untamed, wild: *bestiame —*, wild cattle.

bràga, braghétta, *V.* **bràca, brachétta**.

bràgia, *V.* **bràce**.

bràgo, *s.m.* (*letter.*) mire, mud.

bragòzzo, *s.m.* (*mar.*) "bragozzo" (two-mast fishing boat in the Adriatic).

Brahma, *no.pr.m.* (*relig. indù*) Brahma.

Brahmapútra, *no.pr.m.* (*geog.*) Brahmaputra.

braille, *s.m.* (*sistema di scrittura per ciechi*) braille.

bràma, *s.f.* longing; covetousness; avidity, greed.

bramàbile, *ag.* desirable, covetable.

bramànico, *ag.* (*st. relig.*) Brahmanic(al), Brahminio(al).

bramanésimo, bramanìsmo, *s.m.* (*st. relig.*) Brahmanism, Brahminism.

bramàno, *s.m.* (*st. relig.*) Brahman, Brahmin.

bramàre, *v.t.* to long for (s.o., sthg.), to desire, to crave for, after (sthg.), to covet: *bramava di ritornare in patria*, he longed to go back to his country; *bramo la solitudine*, I am longing for solitude.

bramína, *s.f.* (*st. relig.*) Brahminee, Brahmani.

bramíno, *s.m.* (*st. relig.*) Brahmin, Brahmaṅ.

bramíre, *v.i.* to roar; to bellow; (*di cervo*) to bell.

bramíto, *s.m.* roar, roaring; bellow, bellowing; (*di cervo*) bell.

bramosaménte, *av.* longingly, covetously.

bramosìa, bramosità, *s.f.* longing, covetousness, avidity, greed.

bramóso, *ag.* desirous; eager (for sthg., to do); thirsting (for sthg.); greedy.

b12ca, *s.f.* 1. *branche della tenaglia*, jaws of pliers 2. (*zampa, artiglio*) claw; *fig.* (*mano protesa ad afferrare*) clutching hand, grasping hand: *cadere nelle branche di qlcu.*, to fall into s.o.'s claws 3. (*sezione, settore*) branch: *una — della scienza*, a branch of science 4. — *di scale*, flight of stairs.

brancàta, *s.f.* 1. handful 2. (*zampata*) blow with a claw.

brànchia, *s.f.* gill, branchia (*pl.* branchiæ).

branchiàle, *ag.* (*zool.*) branchial.

branchiàti, *s.m. pl.* (*zool.*) Branchiata.

branchìfero, *ag.* branchiferous.

branchifórme, *ag.* branchiform.

brancicaménto, *s.m.* handling, feeling, fingering.

brancicàre, *v.t.* 1. to handle, to feel, to finger 2. (*stazzonare*) to paw.

brancicatúra, *s.f.* handling, feeling, fingering.

brànco, *s.m.* 1. (*mandria*) herd; (*di lupi*) pack; (*di pecore, di uccelli*) flock; (*di pesci*) shoal, school 2. (*spreg.*) (*folla di persone*) herd, pack: *un — di sciocchi*, a pack of fools ‖ *a branchi*, in droves, in numbers.

brancolaménto, *s.m.* groping.

brancolàre, *v.i.* to grope (one's way), to proceed tentatively (anche *fig.*): *brancolando uscì dalla cella*, he groped his way out of the cell; *brancolava nel buio*, he groped in the dark.

brancolóni, *av.* gropingly.

brànda, *s.f.* 1. camp-bed, folding bed 2. (*su navi*) hammock.

Brandebúrgo, *no.pr.m.* (*geog.*) Brandenburg.

brandeggiàre, *v.t.* (*mar. artigl.*) to train.

brandéggio, *s.m.* (*mar. artigl.*) training.

brandèllo, *s.m.* 1. shred, rag, tatter: *con gli abiti a brandelli*, in rags (*o* in tatters); *fare a brandelli*, to tear to pieces (*o* to tear up) 2. (*pezzetto*) bit.

brandiménto, *s.m.* brandishing.

brandíre, *v.t.* to brandish.

bràndo, *s.m.* (*poet.*) sword.

bràno, *s.m.* 1. piece, shred ‖ *a brani*, in small pieces: *cadere a brani*, to fall to pieces; *fare a brani*, to tear to pieces 2. (*passo di un testo*) passage, extract: *egli ha imparato questo — a memoria*, he has learned this passage by heart.

branzíno, *s.m.* (*ittiol.*) bass (fish).

brasàre, *v.t.* (*cuc.*) to braise.

brasàto, *ag.* (*cuc.*) braised: *manzo —*, braised beef.

brasatúra, *s.f.* (*mec.*) brazing: — *ad arco*, arc-brazing.

bràsca, *s.f.* (*metal.*) dross.

Brasíle, *no.pr.m.* (*geog.*) Brazil, Brasil ‖ **brasíle**, *s.m.* (*legno*) Brazil-wood.

Brasília, *no.pr.f.* (*geog.*) Brazilia.

brasiliàno, *ag.s.m.* Brazilian.

bràttea, *s.f.* (*bot.*) bract.

bratteàto, *ag.* (*bot.*) bracteate.

bràtteola, *s.f.* (*bot.*) bracteole, bractlet.

bravàccio, *s.m.* 1. (*prepotente*) bully, swashbuckler 2. (*spaccone*) braggart, swaggerer: *non fare il —!*, don't swagger so much! (*o* stop boasting! *o* stop bragging!).

bravaménte, *av.* 1. (*risolutamente*) bravely 2. (*con abilità*) cleverly.

bravàre, *v.t.* 1. (*minacciare*) to threaten 2. (*provocare, sfidare*) to provoke, to be defiant to (s.o., sthg.): — *qlcu. con insolenza*, to defy s.o. insolently ‖ *v.i.* (*fare il gradasso*) to brag, to boast, to swagger.

bravàta, bravazzàta, *s.f.* 1. (*azione audace*) bravado, bluster 2. (*millanteria*) boasting, brag.

braveggiàre, *v.i.* to swagger, to boast.

bràvo, *ag.* 1. (*abile, capace*) clever; skilful; good (at sthg.); (*esperto*) expert; (*ricco di esperienza*) experienced: *è un — operaio*, he is a skilled workman; *è una brava insegnante*, she is an experienced teacher; *mio fratello è — in matematica*, my brother is good at mathematics ‖ —!, bravo! (*o* very well! *o* well done!) || *alla brava*, skilfully, cleverly 2. (*buono*) good; (*egregio*) very good; (*degno di stima*) worthy, honest: *è una brava persona*, he is an honest person; *è un — uomo*, he is a worthy fellow || *da — !, su, da — !*, (*fam.*) be a good boy! (*o there's a good boy! o* there's a darling!) 3. (*ardito*) brave, courageous: *un — soldato*, a brave soldier || *fare il —*, to swagger (*o* to boast) 4. (*enfatico*): *ci vorrà il suo — tempo*, it will take a good deal of time || *s.m.* (*scherano*) bravo (*pl.* bravoes, bravos).

bravúra, *s.f.* 1. (*abilità*) cleverness, skill 2. (*ardimento*) bravery, courage 3. (*mus.*) bravura: *pezzo di —*, bravura.

bréccia[1], *s.f.* breach: *aprire, fare una —*, to open a breach; *battere in —*, (*mil.*) to shell one point; *essere sulla —*, to stand in the breach (anche *fig.*); *far —*, *fig.* to make a good impression.

bréccia[2], *s.f.* 1. (*brecciame per coprire strade*) crushed stone, road metal 2. (*ghiaia*) gravel 3. (*geol.*) breccia.

brecciàme, *s.m.* (*per coprire strade*) road metal.

breccióso, *ag.* 1. (*coperto con brecciame*) gravelly, metalled: *strada brecciosa*, metalled road 2. (*geol.*) brecciated.

brefotròfio, *s.m.* foundling hospital.

brègma, *s.m.* (*anat.*) bregma (*pl.* bregmata).

Brèma, *no.pr.f.* (*geog.*) Bremen.

brénna, *s.f.* (*ronzino*) jade; hack.

brènta, *s.f.* 1. (*bigoncia*) wine cask 2. "brenta" (*misura di capacità variabile*).

Breslàvia, *no.pr.f.* (*geog.*) Breslau.

Bretàgna, *no.pr.f.* (*geog.*) Brittany; Bretagne || *Gran —*, Great Britain; (*fam.*) Britain.

bretèlle, *s.f. pl.* braces; (*amer.*) suspenders.

brètone, *ag.* 1. (*della Britannia*) British: *il ciclo —*, (*st. lett.*) the British cycle 2. (*della Bretagna*) Breton || *s.m.* 1. (*della Britannia*) Briton 2. (*della Bretagna*) Breton.

brève[1], *ag.* 1. (*di durata, estensione*) short, brief; (*conciso*) concise: *— discorso*, brief speech; *— distanza*, short distance; *— intervallo*, brief interval; *— soggiorno*, brief stay; *andare per la strada più —*, to go the shortest way || *nel più — termine*, (*comm.*) in the shortest time (*o* as soon as possible) || *in —*, in short (*o* summing up); *tra —*, shortly (*o* in a short time) 2. (*fonet.*) short || *s.f.* 1. (*fonet.*) short syllable, breve 2. (*mus.*) breve.

brève[2], *s.f.* (*lettera papale*) breve, brief.

breveménte, *av.* 1. briefly, shortly 2. (*in breve*) in short, summing up, in conclusion.

brevettàbile, *ag.* patentable.

brevettàre, *v.t.* (*fornire del brevetto di invenzione*) to patent.

brevettàto, *ag.* patent, patented.

brevétto, *s.m.* 1. (*letters*) patent: *— di invenzione*, patent of invention; *attestato di —*, letters patent; *detentore di —*, patentee; *presentare la domanda di —*, to file a patent; *rilasciare un —*, to issue a letters patent (*o amer.* to deliver a letters patent) || *Ufficio Brevetti*, Patent Office 2. (*patente*) patent; (*di pilota aeronautico*) licence: *prendere un —*, to take out a patent; *rilasciare un —*, to issue a patent 3. (*mil.*) commission: *— di ufficiale*, officer's commission.

brevlàrio, *s.m.* 1. (*eccl.*) breviary 2. (*compendio*) compendium (*pl.* compendiums, compendia).

brevilíneo, *ag.* short-statured.

breviloquènte, *ag.* concise; (*rar.*) breviloquent; laconic.

breviloquènza, *s.f.* conciseness, concision; (*rar.*) breviloquence; laconism.

brevità, *s.f.* brevity, shortness; (*concisione*) conciseness: *per —*, for the sake of brevity.

brézza, *s.f.* breeze: *una leggera —*, a gentle breeze.

briàco, *ag.* drunk, drunken; intoxicated: *è — fradicio*, he is dead drunk || *s.m.* drunk, drunken man.

briacóna, *s.f.*, **briacóne**, *s.m.* drunkard; toper.

Briarèo, *no.pr.m.* (*mit.*) Briareus.

bríceo, *s.m.* kettle; pot; jug: *— del caffè*, coffee-pot; *— del latte*, milk-jug; *— del tè*, tea-kettle.

bríccola, *s.f.* (*st. mil.*) catapult.

bricconàggine, *s.f.* roguery; knavery.

bricconàta, *s.f.* roguish trick, knavish action.

bricconcèllo, *s.m.* (*scherz.*) little rogue.

briccóne, *s.m.* rogue; rascal; knave.

bricconeggiàre, *v.i.* to rogue; to cheat; to swindle.

bricconería, *s.f.* 1. roguery, knavery 2. (*azione da briccone*) knavish trick, rascally action.

bricconésco, *ag.* knavish; rascally.

brícíola, *s.f.* crumb: *non ne ha lasciato una —*, he did not leave a crumb || *tirar su uno a briciole di pane*, (*allevarlo con cure infinite*) to bring up s.o. with loving care.

brícíolo, *s.m.* bit, tiny bit; morsel: *fare in briccioli*, to tear to bits || *non hai un — di criterio!*, you have no sense at all!.

bricòlla, *s.f.* smuggler's bag.

bridgísta, *s.c.* bridge-player.

bríga, *s.f.* 1. trouble, care: *prendersi, darsi la — di fare ql.co.*, to take the trouble to do sthg. 2. (*lite*) quarrel: *attaccar — con qlcu.*, to pick a quarrel with s.o.

brigadière, *s.m.* (*mil.*) 1. (*nell'Esercito Britannico, generale di brigata*) brigadier; (*negli Stati Uniti*) brigadier general 2. (*sottufficiale dei Carabinieri*) "brigadiere" (rank corresponding to a sergeant in the army).

brigantàggio, *s.m.* brigandage; highway robbery.

brigànte, *s.m.* 1. brigand, bandit, robber, highwayman (*pl.* highwaymen) 2. (*fam.*) (*cattivo soggetto*) bad egg 3. (*scherz.*) rogue, rascal.

brigantésco, *ag.* brigandish.

brigantína, *s.f.* (*mar.*) spanker.

brigantíno, *s.m.* (*mar.*) brig, brigantine: *— a palo*, bark (*o* barque); *— goletta*, hermaphrodite brig.

brigàre, *v.t.* to intrigue for (sthg.): *ha brigato la nomina di sindaco*, he intrigued for his election as mayor || *v.i.* to intrigue.

brigàta, *s.f.* 1. party; company || *poca — vita beata*, the fewer the better 2. (*mil.*) brigade.

Brighèlla, *no.pr.m.* (*st. teat.*) Brighella || **brighèlla**, *s.m.* (*burattino, pagliaccio*) buffoon, clown.

Brígida, *no.pr.f.* Bridget, Brigid || *dim.* Biddy.

bríglia, *s.f.* 1. bridle; (*redine*) rein: *a — sciolta*, hell for leather (*o* at full gallop *o* at full speed); *abbandonare la —*, to drop the reins (anche *fig.*); *allentare la —*, to slacken the reins (anche *fig.*); *dar la — a un cavallo*, to give a horse free rein (*o* to give a horse the rein); *mettere la — a un cavallo*, to bridle (*o* to put a bridle on) a horse; *reggere, tenere le briglie*, to hold the reins; *fig.* to hold (*o* to assume) the reins; *tirare la —*, to draw rein (anche *fig.*) || *lasciare la — sul collo a qlcu.*, *fig.* to give s.o. a free rein || *tenere in —*, *fig.* (*una passione, la lingua, ecc.*) to bridle (*o* to curb *o* to put a bridle on): *tenere in — qlcu.*, to keep s.o. in check 2. (*mar.*) bobstay 3. (*idraulica*) dam 4. (*mec.*) bridle; (*di tornio*) dog.

bríll a, *s.f.* (*agr.*) hulling-machine.

brillaménto, *s.m.* 1. glitter, glare 2. (*di mina*) blasting, shooting, firing, explosion.

brillantàre, *v.t.* 1. (*mec.*) to buff, to polish 2. (*falegnameria*) to polish, to furbish 3. (*sfaccettare*) to cut facets on (a precious stone) 4. (*cuc.*) (*glassare*) to ice, to frost: *— un dolce*, to frost (*o* to ice) a cake.

brillànte, *ag.* 1. brilliant, witty: *un — risultato*, a brilliant (*o* striking) result; *conversazione, ingegno —*, sparkling conversation, wit; *idea —*, brilliant idea; *uno scrittore —*, a brilliant writer; *è d'intelligenza —*, he is brilliant (*o* very smart) 2. (*scintillante*) sparkling, brilliant; (*splendente*) shining, bright || *s.m.* 1. (*gemma*) brilliant 2. (*teat.*) comic actor.

brillanteménte, *av.* brilliantly: *superò l'esame —*, he passed his exam with flying colours.

brillantína, *s.f.* brilliantine.

brillàre[1], *v.i.* 1. (*splendere*) to shine; (*specialmente* *di stelle*) to twinkle; (*scintillare*) to sparkle; (*di luce fredda, metallica*) to glitter, to gleam: *gli occhi del gatto brillano al buio*, a cat's eyes shine (*o* gleam) in the dark; *l'oro brilla*, gold gleams (*o* glitters); *il suo viso brillò di contentezza*, happiness shone in his face (*o* his face shone with happiness); *i suoi occhi brillarono di gioia*, her eyes sparkled with joy 2. *fig.* to shine, to distinguish oneself: *non brilla nella conversazione*, he does not shine in conversation; — *per ql.co.*, to stand out for sthg. || *brilla per la sua assenza*, (*scherz.*) he is conspicuous by his absence 3. (*di vino*) to sparkle || *v.t.* (*far brillare*): — *una mina*, to blast (*o* to fire) a mine.

brillàre², *v.t.* to hull, to husk, to polish: — *il riso, l'orzo*, to hull (*o* to husk) rice, barley.

brillatóio, *s.m.* 1. (*macchina*) polisher 2. (*luogo*) rice-mill.

brillatúra, *s.f.* (*del riso*) hulling, husking, polishing.

brillo, *ag.* tipsy, slightly drunk.

brína, *s.f.* 1. (white) frost, hoar-frost; (*poet.*) rime 2. (*canizie incipiente*) hoariness.

brinàre, *v.i.imp.*: *ha brinato*, there has been a (hoar-) frost; *stanotte brinerà*, there will be a frost to-night.

brinàta, *s.f.* frost, hoar-frost.

brinàto, *ag.* 1. covered with frost, covered with hoar-frost; (*poet.*) rimy 2. (*che sta incanutendo*) hoary.

brindàre, *v.i.* to toast (s.o.), to drink a toast: — *a qlcu.*, to toast s.o. (*o* to drink a toast to s.o.): — *alla salute di qlcu.*, to drink s.o.'s health; — *con qlcu.*, to touch glasses with s.o.

brindèllo, *s.m.* tatter, rag, shred.

brindellóna, *s.f.*, **brindellóne**, *s.m.* slovenly person.

bríndisi, *s.m.* toast: *fare un* — *a qlcu.*, to drink a toast (*o* a health) to s.o.

brío, *s.m.* 1. vivacity, spirit, animation, liveliness, sprightliness; (*fam.*) go: *persona piena di* —, sprightly person; *parlare con* —, to talk animatedly; *essere pieno di* —, to be full of go 2. (*mus.*) brio.

brioche, *s.f.* brioche.

briosaménte, *av.* vivaciously, spiritedly, lively.

briosità, *s.f.* vivaciousness, good spirits (*pl.*).

brióso, *ag.* vivacious, spirited, lively, sprightly.

bríscola, *s.f.* 1. (*giuoco di carte*) "briscola" 2. (*carta importante*) trump (anche *fig.*) || *contare come il due di* —, *fig.* to count for nothing 3. *pl.* (*busse*) blows.

Brisèlde, *no.pr.f.* (*lett.*) Briseis.

Britànnia, *no.pr.f.* (*geog. st.*) Britain.

britànnico, *ag.* British; Britannic: *Sua Maestà Britannica*, Her Britannic Majesty.

britànno, *s.m.* Briton.

brividío, *s.m.* shivering; shuddering.

brívido, *s.m.* shiver; (*di paura, di orrore*) shudder; (*fam.*) creeps (*pl.*): *ascoltarlo mi faceva venire i brividi*, it made me shudder (*o* it gave me the shivers *o* it gave me the creeps) to listen to him; *aveva brividi di febbre, di freddo*, she was shivering with fever, with cold.

brizzolàto, *ag.* 1. (*macchiettato*) speckled 2. (*di capelli*) grizzled; (*di persona*) grey-haired: *mio padre è un po'* —, my father is getting grey.

brizzolatúra, *s.f.* 1. (*macchiettatura*) speckledness 2. (*canizie*) grizzling.

bròcca¹, *s.f.* 1. jug; (*anfora*) pitcher, ewer: *una* — *di latte*, a jug of milk 2. (*contenuto di una brocca*) jugful.

bròcca², *s.f.* 1. (*germoglio*) shoot, sprout, bud 2. (*centro del bersaglio*) target-centre, bull 3. (*chiodo ornamentale*) stud.

broccàio¹, *s.m.* (*chi fabbrica, vende brocche*) potter.

broccàio², *s.m.* (*strum. artig.*) punch.

broccàrdo, *s.m.* (*st. dir.*) brocard.

broccatèllo, *s.m.* 1. (*tessuto*) brocatel(le) 2. (*marmo*) brocatello.

broccàto, *s.m.* brocade: — *d'oro*, gold brocade.

brocchière, *s.m.* (*st.*) buckler.

bròcco¹, *s.m.* 1. (*ramoscello*) stick; (*germoglio*) shoot, sprout 2. (*centro del bersaglio*) target-centre, bull 3. (*riccio in rilievo di alcuni tessuti*) curl.

bròcco², *s.m.* 1. (*ronzino*) jade; worn-out horse 2. (*persona inetta*) beast: *egli è un* —, he is a perfect (*o* regular) beast.

bròccolo, *s.m.* broc(c)oli.

brochure, *s.f.* 1. brochure, pamphlet 2. *en* —, paper-bound.

bròda, *s.f.* 1. (*acqua sudicia*) dish-water, slops (*pl.*) 2. (*brodo lungo*) thin broth; (*minestra lunga*) thin soup, slop; (*caffè lungo*) weak coffee || *andare in* — *di giuggiole*, *fig.* to be extremely pleased 3. *fig.* (*discorso prolisso*) lot of wind.

brodàglia, *s.f.* slops (*pl.*).

brodétto, *s.m.* 1. broth with beaten eggs and lemon juice 2. (*brodo lungo*) thin broth 3. (*zuppa di pesce*) fish soup || *antico come il* —, as old as the hills.

brodícchio, *s.m.* 1. (*brodo lungo*) thin broth 2. (*fango*) mud.

brodíglia, *s.f.* (*fanghiglia*) muddy water; mud.

bròdo, *s.m.* broth: — *di pollo*, chicken broth; — *lungo*, thin broth; — *ristretto*, consommé (*o* beef-tea); *minestra di* — *di pollo*, chicken soup; *tagliatelle, fettuccine in* —, noodle soup; *prendere un* —, to take a cup of broth || *andare in* — *di giuggiole*, *fig.* to be extremely pleased || *lasciar cuocere qlcu. nel suo* —, to let s.o. stew in his own juice (*o* to take no notice of s.o.).

brodolóna, *s.f.*, **brodolóne**, *s.m.* 1. sloppy eater 2. (*persona sciatta*) slovenly person, sloven; (*di donna*) slattern, slut.

brodóso, *ag.* watery; (*fam.*) wishy-washy: *minestra brodosa*, thin soup.

brogliàccio, *s.m.* waste-book.

brogliàre, *v.i.* to intrigue.

brogliàsso, **brogliàzzo**, *s.m.* waste-book.

bròglio, *s.m.* intrigue: — *elettorale*, (*pol.*) corruption at elections.

brolétto, *s.m.* (*st.*) "Broletto" (Court of Justice in the Lombard communes).

bròlo, *s.m.* (*arc.*) 1. (*giardino*) garden 2. (*frutteto*) orchard 3. (*orto*) vegetable garden, kitchen-garden.

bromàto, *s.m.* (*chim.*) bromate.

bromatología, *s.f.* bromatology.

bròmico, *ag.* (*chim.*) bromic: *acido* —, bromic acid.

bromísmo, *s.m.* (*med.*) bromism.

bròmo, *s.m.* (*chim.*) bromine.

bromòlio, *s.m.* (*foto.*) bromoil process.

bromúro, *s.m.* (*chim.*) bromide: — *d'argento*, silver bromide.

bronchiàle, *ag.* (*anat.*) bronchial.

bronchíte, *s.f.* (*patol.*) bronchitis.

bronchiuòlo, *s.m.* (*anat.*) bronchiole.

bróncio, *s.m.* 1. (*dispetto infantile*) pout: *avere, fare, mettere il* —, to pout 2. (*cipiglio, viso scuro*) sulkiness: *gli tengo il* —, I have a grudge against him; *avere il* —, to be sulky (with s.o.); *fare, mettere il* —, to sulk.

brónco, *s.m.* 1. (*tronco nodoso*) knotty trunk; (*ceppo*) stump; (*sterpo*) scrub 2. (*anat.*) bronchus (*pl.* bronchi, bronchia).

broncóne, *s.m.* 1. (*grosso tronco*) large stump 2. (*palo per sostenere le viti*) vine-prop.

broncopleuríte, *s.f.* (*patol.*) broncho-pleuritis.

broncopolmoníte, *s.f.* (*patol.*) broncho-pneumonia.

broncostenòsi, *s.f.* (*patol.*) bronchostenosis.

brontofobía, *s.f.* (*patol.*) brontophobia.

brontolaménto, *s.m.* 1. grumbling; (*borbottio*) muttering, murmuring, mumbling 2. (*del tuono*) rumble, roar.

brontolàre, *v.i.* 1. to grumble; (*borbottare*) to mutter, to mumble, to murmur 2. (*del tuono*) to rumble, to roar.

brontolío, *s.m.* 1. grumbling, murmuring; (*borbottio*) muttering, murmuring, mumbling 2. (*del tuono*) rumble, roar.

brontolóna, *s.f.*, **brontolóne**, *s.m.* grumbler.

brontosàuro, *s.m.* (*paleont.*) brontosaurus.

brontotèrio, *s.m.* (*paleont.*) brontothere.

bronzàre, *v.t.* to bronze.

bronzatúra, *s.f.* bronzing.

brónzeo, *ag.* 1. bronze (*attributivo*): *di color —,* bronze 2. (*simile a bronzo*) bronzy.

bronzína, *s.f.* (*mec.*) 1. bushing, bush, brass 2. (*cuscinetto*) bearing.

bronzíno, *ag.* bronze ‖ *s.m.* bell on horse's collar.

bronzísta, *s.m.* worker in bronze.

brónzo, *s.m.* 1. bronze: *un vaso di —,* a bronze vase ‖ *un cuore di —,* (*ardito*) a heart-of-oak; (*duro*) a hard-hearted person; *una faccia di —,* a brazen-faced person 2. (*statua*) bronze: *una collezione di bronzi e di avori,* a collection of bronzes and ivories 3. *pl.* (*campane*) bells: *suonano i sacri bronzi,* the church bells are ringing 4. *pl.* (*cannoni*) guns: *lasciamo parlare bronzi,* let the guns speak (out).

bròscia, *s.f.* slops (*pl.*).

brossúra, *s.f.* paper-back binding: *in —,* paper-bound.

brucàre, *v.t.* 1. to browse on (sthg.); to nibble at (sthg.) 2. (*sfrondare*) to strip off (leaves).

brucatúra, *s.f.* 1. browsing; nibbling 2. stripping off (leaves from a plant).

bruciacchiàre, *v.t.* 1. (*bruciare in superficie*) to scorch, to sear; (*strinare*) to singe 2. (*del gelo*) to nip, to frost: *è bruciacchiato dal gelo,* it is frost-nipped.

bruciacchiatúra, *s.f.* scorching; singeing.

bruciaménto, *s.m.* burning.

bruciapélo, a, *l.av.* 1. (*improvvisamente*) suddenly, unexpectedly, point-blank 2. (*vicino*) point-blank: *colpo a —,* point-blank shot; *sparare a — a qlcu.,* to fire point-blank at s.o.

bruciàre, *v.t.* 1. to burn; (*incendiare*) to burn down, to set fire to (sthg.); (*del gelo*) to frost, to nip; (*del calore*) to scorch: *quel pazzo bruciò la propria casa,* that lunatic set fire to his own house ‖ *— le cervella a qlcu.,* to blow s.o.'s brains out ‖ *— la scuola, fig.* to play truant ‖ *le tappe, fig.* to shoot ahead ‖ *— il paglione, fig.* to fail to keep a promise 2. (*med.*) (*cauterizzare*) to cauterize ‖ *v.i.* 1. to burn; (*fiammeggiare*) to blaze: *il fuoco brucia allegramente,* the fire is gaily blazing; *il granaio brucia,* the barn is on fire 2. (*essere infiammato*) to smart: *ti bruciano gli occhi?,* are your eyes smarting? 3. *fig.* (*ardere*) to burn: *— dalla curiosità,* to be aflame with curiosity; *— dalla sete,* to be very thirsty (*o* to have a burning thirst); *— di passione per qlcu.,* to be consumed (*o* to burn) with passion for s.o. ‖ **bruciàrsi,** *v.r.* to burn oneself: *mi sono bruciato un dito,* I have burnt my finger; *— le ali,* to burn one's wings.

bruciàta, *s.f.* roast chestnut.

bruciatàio, *s.m.* chestnut vendor.

bruciatíccio, *s.m.* 1. burnt residue 2. (*odore di bruciato*) smell of burning 3. (*sapore di bruciato*) burnt taste: *questa crema sa di —,* this custard tastes burnt.

bruciàto, *ag.* 1. burnt; (*dal gelo*) nipped; (*dal calore*) scorched: *— dal sole,* sunburnt; *germoglio — dal gelo,* bud nipped by frost ‖ *gioventù bruciata,* (*gergo*) beat generation ‖ *ore bruciate,* hot hours ‖ *uomo —,* broken man 2. (*di colore*) maroon ‖ *s.m.* smell of burning: *sapere di —,* to taste burnt.

bruciatóre, *s.m.* 1. burner: *— di gas,* gas burner 2. (*cannello*) torch.

bruciatúra, *s.f.* 1. burning 2. (*scottatura*) burn; scald.

brucióre, *s.m.* burning; sore; smart (anche *fig.*): *— di stomaco,* heartburn.

brúco, *s.m.* (*entom.*) caterpillar; grub; (*baco*) maggot ‖ *ignudo —, fig.* in dire straits (*o* extremely poor).

brughièra, *s.f.* heath; moor.

brûlé, *ag.* burnt: *latte —,* caramel custard; *vino —,* mulled wine.

brulicàme, *s.m.* swarm, swarming.

brulicànte, *ag.* swarming (with s.o., sthg.): *carogna — di vermi,* carrion swarming with maggots.

brulicàre, *v.i.* to swarm (with s.o., sthg.); to seethe (with sthg.) (anche *fig.*): *la strada brulicava di soldati,* the street was swarming with soldiers; *la sua testa*

brulicava di idee, his head was seething with ideas (*o* he was bursting with ideas).

brulichío, *s.m.* swarming, swarm.

brúllo, *ag.* 1. bare, naked; (*sterile*) barren: *un albero —,* a naked tree; *una distesa di brulle colline,* a stretch of bare hills 2. *fig.* (*spoglio, privo*) destitute.

brulòtto, *s.m.* (*mar.*) fire ship.

brúma¹, *s.f.* 1. (*foschia*) mist; haze 2. (*vecchiaia*) old age.

brúma², *s.f.* (*zool.*) teredo; ship-worm.

brumàio, *s.m.* (*st. francese*) Brumaire.

brumàle, *ag.* 1. (*invernale*) wintery 2. (*nebbioso*) misty; hazy.

brumísta, *s.m.* (*dial.*) coachman (*pl.* coachmen): cabby.

brumóso, *ag.* misty, hazy.

brúna, *s.f.* dark-haired woman; brunette.

brunàstro, *ag.* brownish.

brunézza, *s.f.* brownness.

Brunílde, *no.pr.f.* (*lett.*) Brunhild, Brünnhilde, Brynhild.

bruniménto, *s.m.* burnishing; polishing.

bruníre, *v.t.* to burnish, to polish; to blue.

brunìto, *ag.* burnished, polished; blued.

brunitóio, *s.m.* (*strum. artig.*) burnisher.

brunitóre, *s.m.* burnisher, polisher.

brunitúra, *s.f.* polishing, burnishing.

brúno, *ag.* brown, dusky: *— di capelli,* brown- (*o* dark-) haired; *— di pelle, di carnagione,* swarthy ‖ *s.m.* 1. (*colore*) brown 2. (*uomo bruno*) dark-haired man 3. (*lutto*) mourning.

Brúno, *no.pr.m.* Bruno.

brúsca, *s.f.* horse-brush.

bruscaménte, *av.* rudely, roughly; bluntly.

bruscàre, *v.t.* to prune.

bruschinàre, *v.t.* to brush.

bruschíno, *s.m.* scrubbing brush.

brúsco, *ag.* 1. (*di sapore aspro*) sharp; sourish: *vino —,* sharp wine 2. (*aspro, rozzo, crudo*) sharp, harsh, rough, brusque: *modi bruschi,* rude manners; *un risveglio —,* an unpleasant awakening; *tempo —,* stormy weather; *tempi bruschi, fig.* hard times ‖ *con le brusche,* with rough (*o* brusque) manners ‖ *s.m.* sourish taste.

brúscolo, *s.m.* speck; mote: *ho un — nell'occhio,* I have a speck in my eye.

brusío, *s.m.* buzz, buzzing, humming; whispering 2. (*gran quantità*) lots (*pl.*); heaps (*pl.*).

brusíre, *v.i.* to buzz; to whisper.

brutàle, *ag.* 1. (*animalesco*) brutish 2. (*violento*) brutal: *hanno un padre —,* they have a brute of a father.

brutalità, *s.f.* 1. (*natura bruta*) brutishness 2. (*violenza*) brutality.

brutalménte, *av.* 1. (*animalescamente*) brutishly 2. (*violentemente*) brutally.

brúto, *ag.* 1. brute: *forza bruta,* brute force; *materia bruta,* brute matter 2. (*violento*) brutal ‖ *s.m.* 1. brute; beast 2. (*persona bestiale*) brute.

Brúto, *no.pr.m.* (*st.*) Brutus.

bruttaménte, *av.* uglily.

bruttàre, *v.t.* to soil, to dirty, to sully (anche *fig.*): *quel gesto bruttò per sempre la sua fama,* that action sullied his fame for ever.

bruttézza, *s.f.* ugliness.

brútto, *ag.* 1. ugly: *che brutta statua!,* what an ugly statue!; *quel ragazzo è più — di quanto credessi,* that boy is worse-looking (*o* uglier) than I thought ‖ *— come il peccato,* as ugly as sin 2. (*scialbo, insignificante*) plain: *un volto piuttosto —,* a rather plain face 3. (*di aspetto malsano*) ill-looking; sick; bad: *aver brutta cera,* to look sick 4. (*cattivo*) bad: *una brutta azione,* a bad action; *brutte notizie,* bad news; *— segno,* bad omen; *— tempo,* bad weather; *— voto,* bad mark; *avere un — raffreddore,* to have a bad cold; *fare brutta* *figura*, to cut a bad (*o* a poor) figure || *alle brutte*, if the worst happens (*o* if the worst comes to the worst): *venire alle brutte*, (*scendere ai fatti*) to come to blows **5.** (*biasimevole*) mean, low-down; (*sconveniente*) unseemly: *un — comportamento*, an unseemly behaviour; *un — tiro*, a mean trick.

bruttúra, *s.f.* **1.** ugly thing **2.** (*azione turpe*) base action.

brúzzico, brúzzolo, *s.m.* daybreak, dawn: *si levò a —*, he got up at daybreak.

Bruxelles, *no.pr.f.* (*geog.*) Brussels || *cavolini di —*, Brussels sprouts.

búa, *s.f.* (*voce infantile*) sore, hurt; pain.

buàccio, *s.m.* fool, blockhead; dolt.

buàggine, *s.f.* stupidity, foolishness.

búbbola¹, *s.f.* (*frottola*) tale, story; (*bugia*) lie, fib.

búbbola², *s.f.* (*ornit.*) hoopoe.

bubbolàre, *v.i.* **1.** (*del tuono*) to rumble; to roll **2.** (*tremare*) to quake, to shiver || *v.t.* **1.** (*defraudare con l'inganno*) to cheat **2.** (*scialacquare*) to squander, to dissipate.

bubbolàta, *s.f.* nonsense (*solo sing.*).

bubbolièra, *s.f.* collar of bells.

búbbolo, *s.m.* sleigh-bell; harness bell.

bubbóne, *s.m.* bubo (*pl.* buboes).

bubbònico, *ag.* (*patol.*) bubonic: *peste bubbonica*, the plague (*o* bubonic plague).

búca, *s.f.* **1.** pit; hole; (*cavità*) hollow, cavity: *— cieca*, pit fall; *— delle lettere*, letter-box; *— del suggeritore*, (*teat.*) prompter's box; *scavare una —*, to dig a hole (*o* a pit) || *— del biliardo*, billiard pocket: *far —*, to pocket (a ball) || *— del golf*, golf-hole; *far —*, to hole a ball **2.** (*tomba*) grave.

bucacchiàre, *v.t.* to riddle.

bucanéve, *s.f.* (*bot.*) snow-drop.

bucanière, *s.m.* (*st.*) buccaneer; filibuster.

bucàre, *v.t.* to hole; to pierce; (*trivellare*) to bore; to perforate; (*pungere*) to prick: *— biglietti*, to punch tickets; *un grido da — gli orecchi*, an earsplitting scream || *v.i.* (*di pneumatico*) to puncture: *ho bucato*, I have got a puncture || **bucàrsi**, *v.r.* **1.** (*di calze, ecc.*) to hole **2.** (*pungersi*): *mi sono bucata un dito con un ago*, I pricked my finger with a needle.

Búcarest, *no.pr.f.* (*geog.*) Bucharest.

bucatàio, *s.m.* laundryman (*pl.* laundrymen).

bucàto¹, *ag.* pierced, perforated || *avere le mani bucate*, *fig.* to be a spend-thrift.

bucàto², *s.m.* **1.** (*lavatura*) washing: *giorno del —*, washing-day; *fare il —*, to do the washing || *di —*, white (*o* clean): *lenzuolo di —*, fresh-laundered sheet **2.** (*panni messi in bucato*) laundry.

bucatúra, *s.f.* **1.** (*azione del bucare*) piercing, boring; (*di pneumatico*) puncturing **2.** (*buco*) hole; (*di pneumatico*) puncture.

búcchero, *s.m.* (*archeol.*) bucchero, bucaro.

búccia, *s.f.* (*di frutto*) peel, skin, rind; (*di legume*) hull; (*di albero*) cortex, skin, bark: *— d'arancia*, orange-peel || *avere la — dura*, *fig.* to stand hard work; *essere della stessa —*, to be of the same bad sort || *rivedere le bucce a qlcu.*, (*criticarlo severamente*) to criticize s.o. severely (*o* to find fault with s.o.).

búccina, *s.f.* bugle-horn.

buccinàre, *v.t.* to divulge || *v.i.* to blow the bugle-horn.

buccinatòrio, *ag.*: *muscolo —*, (*anat.*) buccinator.

búccola, *s.f.* ear-ring.

búccolo, *s.m.* curl.

Bucèfalo, *no.pr.m.* (*mit.*) Bucephalus || **bucèfalo**, *s.m.* (*scherz.*) (*cavallo di poco pregio*) jade, worn-out horse.

bucherellàre, *v.t.* to riddle.

bucherellàto, *ag.* riddled.

bucinàre, *v.t.* to whisper: *si bucina che...*, it is rumoured that....

búcine, *s.m.* (*tipo di rete*) tunnel-net.

bucintòro, *s.m.* (*st.*) bucentaur.

búco, *s.m.* hole; (*apertura*) orifice, aperture: *— della chiave*, key-hole; *questa camera è un —*, *fig.* this room is very small; *chiudere, tappare un —*, to stop a hole; *fig.* to pay off a debt; *fare un — in ql.co.*, to make a hole in sthg.: *fare un — in una cassa*, *fig.* to embezzle money || *fare un — nell'acqua*, to beat the air (*o* to fail) || *non cavare un ragno da un —*, to obtain no result.

bucòlica, *s.f.* (*poes.*) bucolic.

bucòlico, *ag.* bucolic, pastoral (*anche poes.*).

bucrànio, *s.m.* (*arch.*) bucrane; bucranium (*pl.* bucrania).

Búdda, *no.pr.m.* (*st. relig.*) Buddha.

buddísmo, *s.m.* (*st. relig.*) Buddhism.

buddísta, *s.m.* (*st. relig.*) Buddhist.

buddístico, *ag.* (*st. relig.*) Buddhistic(al).

budellàme, *s.m.* entrails (*pl.*), bowels (*pl.*).

budèllo, *s.m.*; *pl.f.* **budèlla, budèlle** (*nei sensi* 1. 2.); *pl.m.* **budèlli** (*nei sensi* 3. 4.) **1.** bowel, intestine, gut: *budella*, bowels (*o* intestines *o fam.* guts) **2.** (*materiale per corde di violino, ecc.*) catgut: *corde di —*, catgut strings **3.** *fig.* (*passaggio, strada stretta*) alley **4.** (*tubo*) narrow tube: *un — di gomma*, a narrow rubber tube.

budíno, *s.m.* pudding.

budrière, *s.m.* sword-belt.

búe, *s.m.* **1.** ox (*pl.* oxen); *— muschiato*, musk-ox; *— selvatico*, bison (*o* wild ox); *carne di —*, beef || *occhio di —*, (*arch.*) bull's eye || *sangue di —*, (*colore*) dark-red || *mettere il carro innanzi ai buoi*, *fig.* to put the cart before the horse **2.** *fig.* (*persona stolta*) dull fellow; dunce; dolt.

búfalo, *s.m.* (*zool.*) buffalo: *pelle di —*, buff.

bufèra, *s.f.* storm: *— di neve*, snow-storm (*o* blizzard); *— di vento*, gale.

búffa, *s.f.* **1.** (*cappuccio*) cowl, hood **2.** (*visiera di elmo*) visor.

buffàre, *v.i.* to puff, to blow || *v.t.* (*giuoco della dama*) to huff.

buffàta, *s.f.* gust.

buffet, *s.m.* **1.** (*mobile*) cupboard, sideboard **2.** (*tavola per rinfreschi*) buffet, refreshment bar **3.** (*bar della stazione*) buffet, refreshment room.

buffettería, *s.f.* (*mil.*) accoutrements (*pl.*).

buffétto, *s.m.* fillip: *dare un — a qlcu.*, to fillip s.o. on the cheek.

búffo¹, *ag.* **1.** (*divertente*) droll, funny, comical **2.** (*strano*) funny, odd, queer: *questa è buffa!*, this is funny! **3.** (*teat.*) buffo, comic: *opera buffa*, comic opera || *s.m.* (*teat.*) buffo.

búffo², *s.m.* gust; puff, breath.

buffonàta, *s.f.* buffoonery, prank, jest.

buffóne, *s.m.* **1.** buffoon, clown, fool: *— di corte*, court jester (*o* fool); *è un —*, he is a wag; *è il — della compagnia*, he is the laughing-stock of the company; *smettila di fare il —!*, stop playing the clown! (*o* the buffoon!) **2.** *fig.* (*persona di scarsa serietà*) unreliable person.

buffoneggiàre, *v.i.* **1.** (*fare il buffone*) to play the buffoon **2.** (*scherzare*) to jest, to joke.

buffonería, *s.f.* buffoonery; tomfoolery.

buffonescaménte, *av.* jestingly, jokingly.

buffonésco, *ag.* **1.** (*da buffone*) clownish **2.** (*comico*) funny, comical.

buganvíllea, *s.f.* (*bot.*) bougainvillaea, bougainvilia.

buggeràre, *v.t.* (*volg.*) to deceive, to cheat.

bugía¹, *s.f.* lie; (*falsità*) falsehood: *— innocente, innocua*, fib; *— pietosa*, white lie; *dire bugie*, to tell lies || *le bugie hanno le gambe corte*, *prov.* truth will out.

bugía², *s.f.* flat candlestick.

bugiardaménte, *av.* falsely.

bugiàrdo, *ag.* **1.** false || *far — qlcu.*, to prove s.o. a liar **2.** (*ingannevole*) deceiving, deceitful || *s.m.* liar.

bugigàttolo, *s.m.* **1.** (*stanzino*) small room **2.** (*ripostiglio*) lumber-room.

bugióne, *s.m.* **1.** (*grossa bugia*) big lie **2.** (*bugiardo incallito*) inveterate liar.

bugliuòlo, *s.m.* bucket.

búgna, *s.f.* 1. (*arch.*) ashlar 2. (*mar.*) clew, clue.

bugnàto, *s.m.* (*arch.*) ashlar(-work).

búgno, *s.m.* beehive.

búgnola, *s.f.* 1. (*paniere*) wicker basket 2. (*cassetta dei maniscalchi*) farrier's box 3. (*scherz.*) (*pulpito*) pulpit.

búio, *ag.* dark: *luogo* —, dark place; *tempo* —, cloudy weather; *la stanza era quasi buia*, the room was almost in darkness ‖ *s.m.* 1. (*oscurità*) dark, darkness: — *pesto*, pitch dark; *essere al* —, to be in the dark (*o* in darkness) ‖ *c'è del* — *in questo*, there is sthg. suspicious in this ‖ *essere* (*completamente*) *al* — *di ql.co.*, to be (quite) ignorant of sthg. (*o* in the dark about sthg.); *tenere qlcu. al* — *di ql.co.*, to conceal sthg. from s.o. (*o* to keep s.o. in ignorance of sthg.) ‖ *mettere qlcu. al* —, (*in prigione*) to put s.o. in prison (*o* to imprison s.o.) 2. (*l'imbrunire*) nightfall: *sarò qui a* —, I'll be here at nightfall.

bulbàre, *ag.* (*anat.*) bulbar.

bulbífero, *ag.* bulbiferous.

bulbifórme, *ag.* bulbiform.

bulbíllo, *s.m.* (*bot.*) bulbil.

búlbo, *s.m.* 1. (*bot.*) bulb 2. (*di capello*) bulb 3. (*dell'occhio*) globe; eyeball 4. (*di termometro*) bulb.

bulbocastàno, *s.m.* (*bot.*) pig-nut tree, earth-nut tree.

bulbóso, *ag.* bulbous.

Bulgaría, *no.pr.f.* (*geog.*) Bulgaria.

búlgaro, *àg.* Bulgarian ‖ *s.m.* 1. Bulgarian 2. (*cuoio*) Russia leather.

bulimía, *s.f.* (*med.*) bulimia, bulimy.

bulinàre, *v.t.* to engrave.

bulíno, *s.m.* 1. (*strum. artig.*) burin, graver 2. *fig.* (*incisore*) burinist, engraver.

bullétta[1], *s.f.* (*bolletta, ricevuta*) bill; receipt.

bullétta[2], *s.f.* (*chiodo*) (tin-)tack; tingle; nail; (*di scarpe*) hobnail.

bullettíno, *s.m.* bulletin.

bullóne, *s.m.* (*mec.*) bolt, screw bolt: — *a chiavetta*, cotter bolt; — *ad U*, U bolt; *dado del* —, nut; *gambo del* —, body (*o* shank); *testa del* —, bolthead.

buonamàno, *s.f.* tip.

buongiórno, *V.* **bongiórno**.

buongustàio, *s.m.* gourmet.

buongústo, *V.* **bongústo**.

buòno, *ag.* 1. good: *un buon coltello*, a good knife; *un buon dizionario*, a good dictionary; *una buona madre*, a good mother; *una buona strada*, a good road; *sii* —!, be a good boy!; *essere un buon cristiano*, to be a good Christian ‖ — *come il pane*, as good as gold ‖ *un buon diavolo*, a well-meaning fellow ‖ *un uomo* — *tre volte*, (*fam.*) a simpleton 2. (*prevegole, di buona qualità*) good; first rate (*attributivo*): *in quel museo si conserva un buon quadro del Tintoretto*, they have a very good Tintoretto in that museum ‖ *il salotto* —, the front room; *l'abito* —, one's best suit 3. (*foriero di sensazioni piacevoli*) good; nice; lovely: *un buon vino*, a good wine; *che buon profumo hanno questi fiori!*, what a lovely scent these flowers have! (*o* don't these flowers smell lovely?); *come è buona questa minestra!*, very good (*o* nice) soup this! 4. (*genuino*) good, genuine: *moneta buona*, good (*o* genuine) money 5. (*sano*) good, wholesome: *un buon vitto*, a wholesome food 6. (*di tempo*) fine: *tempo* —, fine weather 7. (*abbondante*) abundant; (*grande*) large; (*lungo*) long: *una buona dose*, a good strong dose; *un buon lasso di tempo*, quite a long while; *un buon pezzo di pane*, a large piece of bread; *un'ora buona*, a full hour: *lo aspettai un'ora buona*, I waited for him more than an hour 8. (*divertente*) good, amusing: *una buona commedia*, a good (*o* amusing) play 9. (*propizio, vantaggioso*) good, profitable, advantageous: *un buon investimento*, a good (*o* advantageous) investment; *una buona occasione*, a favourable opportunity; *una buona stella*, a lucky star ‖ *a buon prezzo*, cheap 10. (*adatto*) good, fit, suitable: — *da mangiare*, fit to eat 11. (*abile*)

good, clever, skilful: *un buon chirurgo*, a skilful surgeon; *un buon musicista*, a fine musician; *un buon scolaro*, a clever pupil ‖ — *a nulla*, good-for-nothing 12. (*gentile, generoso, umano*) kind, benevolent, gracious, friendly: *buone parole*, kind words; *un buon ragazzo*, a good-natured boy; *una buona signora*, a kind-hearted lady; *persona di buon cuore*, good-hearted person; *sii tanto* — *da ascoltarmi*, be so kind (*o* so good) as to listen to me 13. (*onesto, rispettabile*) good, honest, virtuous, upright: *un buon cittadino*, an honest citizen; *di buona famiglia*, of good family (*o* with a good background) ‖ *buona società*, high society 14. (*in formule di cortesia*) good, happy: *buona fortuna!*, good luck!; *buona notte!*, good night!; *buon viaggio!*, a pleasant journey! 15. (**Fraseologia**): *buon'anima*, late lamented ‖ *buon pro vi faccia!*, much good may it do you! ‖ *alla buona*, informal: *una persona alla buona*, a free and easy person; *una riunione alla buona*, an informal party; *era vestito molto alla buona*, he was dressed very plainly; *facciamo alla buona*, let us do without ceremony ‖ *a buon diritto*, by right ‖ *con le buone*, with persuasion (*o* without constraint) ‖ *di buon grado*, with pleasure ‖ *di buon'ora*, early (in the morning) ‖ *di buon passo*, briskly ‖ *di buona voglia*, willingly ‖ *Dio ce la mandi buona!*, God help us! ‖ *darsi buon tempo*, to have a good time ‖ *essere di buona bocca*, to eat everything and anything; *fig.* to be easily pleased ‖ *essere in buona*, to be in a good mood; (*essere in buoni rapporti con qlcu.*) to be on good terms with s.o. ‖ *essere, parlare in buona fede*, to be, to speak in good faith ‖ *far buon viso a cattivo giuoco*, to put a good face on it ‖ *guardare qlcu. di buon occhio*, to look kindly on s.o. ‖ *menar* —, to bring good luck ‖ *tornare in buona con qlcu.*, to make it up with s.o.

buòno[1], *s.m.* 1. good: *c'è del* — *in ciò*, there is something in it ‖ *buon per te!*, luckily for you! ‖ *ci volle del bello e del* — *per convincerlo!*, it took a lot to convince him! ‖ *è un poco di* —, he is a nasty piece of work ‖ *il tempo si mette al* —, the weather is clearing up ‖ *faticare a* —, to work hard ‖ *piovere a* —, to rain hard (*o* heavily) ‖ *saper di* —, to smell fine (*o* to have a nice smell) 2. (*persona*) good person: *i buoni*, good people; *i buoni e i cattivi*, the good and the wicked; *fare il* —, to be good (*o* to keep quiet); *fa' il* —!, keep quiet!.

buòno[2], *s.m.* 1. (*comm.*) bond; bill: — *di consegna*, delivery order; — *del Tesoro*, Treasury bond; — *d'incasso*, money-order 2. (*tagliando*) coupon.

buonsènso, *V.* **bonsènso**.

buontempóne, *V.* **bontempóne**.

buonuscíta, *V.* **bonuscíta**.

burattàre, *v.t.* to bolt; to sift (anche *fig.*).

burattinàio, *s.m.* puppet showman; Punch and Judy showman.

burattinàta, *s.f.* 1. puppet-show 2. *fig.* puppetlike action.

burattíno, *s.m.* 1. puppet; marionette: *spettacolo di burattini*, puppet-show (*o* puppet-play *o* Punch and Judy show); *teatro dei burattini*, puppet (*o* marionette) theatre 2. (*persona vana e incostante*) puppet.

buràtto, *s.m.* sieve; (*per mulino*) sifter, bolter.

burbànza, *s.f.* haughtiness; arrogance.

burbanzosaménte, *av.* haughtily; arrogantly.

burbanzóso, *ag.* haughty; arrogant.

búrbera, *s.f.* (*mec.*) windlass.

búrbero, *ag.* grumpy, surly; brusque, rough; gruff: *un aspetto* —, a forbidding countenance; *un'indole burbera*, a surly disposition; *una risposta burbera*, a rough reply; *voce burbera*, gruff voice ‖ *un* — *benefico*, *fig.* a rough diamond.

burchiellésco, *ag.* (*lett.*) of Burchiello; in Burchiello's style.

burchièllo, *s.m.* (*mar.*) wherry.

búrchio, *s.m.* (*mar.*) lighter, barge.

búre, *s.f.* (*agr.*) plough beam.

bureau, *s.m.* bureau.

burétta, *s.f.* (*chim.*) burette, buret.

burgràvio, *s.m.* (*st.*) burgrave.

buriàna, *s.f.* **1.** thunder-storm; (*tempesta di neve*) snow-storm **2.** (*mar.*) gale **3.** (*trambusto*) confusion.

buríeco, *s.m.* (*rar.*) jack-ass.

burína, *V.* **bolína.**

búrla, *s.f.* trick, prank; (*scherzo*) joke; practical joke; (*beffa*) hoax: *mi fecero una bella* —, they played (o served) me a fine trick (o they played a fine trick on me) || *da, per* —, just for fun (o in fun o in jest) || *non mettere in* — *le mie parole!*, don't make light of my words! || *mettere in* — *ogni cosa*, to make a joke of everything || *mettere in* — *qlcu.*, to make fun of s.o.

burlàre, *v.t.* (*fare una burla a*) to play a trick on (s.o.); to play (s.o.) a prank; to make a fool of (s.o.) || *v.i.* (*parlare per giuoco*) to joke; to banter, to talk jestingly: *non burlo*, I am not pulling your leg (o I am not joking) || **burlàrsi,** *v.r.* **1.** (*prendersi giuoco*) to make fun of (s.o.), to laugh at (s.o.), to mock (s.o. o at s.o.); (*farsi beffe*) to jeer (at s.o.); to flout (s.o.): — *di qlcu.*, to make fun of s.o. (o *fam.* to pull s.o.'s leg) **2.** (*tenere in nessun conto*) to make light of (s.o., sthg.); to take (s.o., sthg.) into no account.

burlescaménte, *av.* comically, jokingly.

burléseo, *ag.* farcical, comical.

burlétta, *s.f.* jest; joke: *far la* —, to be jesting; *mettere qlcu. in* —, to poke fun at s.o.

burlevolménte, *av.* jokingly; humorously.

burlévole, *ag.* **1.** (*che suscita riso*) laughable **2.** (*burlesco*) comical, farcical; (*giocoso*) humorous, playful.

burlóne, *s.m.* teaser, joker, jester.

burnús, *s.m.* (*mantello arabo*) burnous(e).

buròcrate, *s.m.* bureaucrat; (*specialmente in Gran Bretagna*) Civil Servant; red-tapist.

burocraticaménte, *av.* bureaucratically.

burocràtico, *ag.* bureaucratic; red-tape (*attributivo*): *linguaggio* —, Civil Service language.

burocratísmo, *s.m.* bureaucracy; red-tapism.

burocrazía, *s.f.* **1.** bureaucracy; (*specialmente in Gran Bretagna*) Civil Service; red-tape **2.** (*pedanteria burocratica*) red-tape.

burràio, *s.m.* dairyman (*pl.* dairymen).

burràsca, *s.f.* **1.** storm, tempest, squall: *il mare è in* —, the sea is very rough **2.** (*disgrazia*) misfortune.

burrascosaménte, *av.* stormily; violently.

burrascóso, *ag.* stormy (anche *fig.*): *discussione burrascosa*, stormy discussion; *mare* —, stormy sea.

burràto[1], *ag.* (*imburrato*) buttered.

burràto[2], *s.m.* (*letter.*) (*burrone*) ravine, gorge.

burrifício, *s.m.* dairy.

búrro, *s.m.* butter: — *fuso*, melted butter; — *vegetale*, margarine; *uova al* —, fried eggs || — *di cacao*, lipsalve (o cocoa-butter).

burróna, *ag.*: *pera* —, butter-pear.

burróne, *s.m.* ravine, gorge.

burróso, *ag.* buttery, fat.

búsca, *s.f.* quest: *andare in* — *di ql.co.*, to go in quest of sthg. || *andare alla* —, to go in search of adventure; (*mar.*) to load goods for an unknown destination.

buscàre, *v.t.*, **buseàrsi,** *v.r.* to get: *mi sono buscato un raffreddoraccio*, I have caught a bad cold || *buscarle, buscarne*, to get a beating; *buscarne di sode*, to get a thrashing (o a good hiding).

buscheràre, *v.t.* (*volg.*) **1.** (*ingannare*) to deceive; (*truffare*) to swindle **2.** (*sciupare*) to spoil.

buscheràta, *s.f.* (*volg.*) **1.** (*inganno*) deception; (*truffa*) swindle **2.** (*sproposito*) mistake, blunder; (*sciocchezza*) nonsense.

buscherío, *s.m.* **1.** (*trambusto*) hubbub **2.** (*gran quantità*) a great deal, a lot, lots (*pl.*).

busécca, *s.f.* (*dial.*) tripe.

busécchia, *s.f.* gut.

busíllis, *s.m.*: *qui sta il* —, (*fam.*) there is the stumbling-block (o the rub o the snag).

bússa, *s.f.* blow: *prender le busse*, to get a thrashing.

bussàre, *v.t.* to knock: *si prega di* — (*alla porta*), please knock (at the door) || — *a quattrini*, (*fam.*) to ask for money.

bussàta, *s.f.* knock.

bussétto, *s.m.* (*strum. artig.*) sleeking stick, sleeker.

hússo, *s.m.* (*bot.*) box.

bússola[1], *s.f.* compass: — *azimutale*, azimuth compass; — *di rotta*, steering compass; *ago della* —, compass needle: *inclinazione magnetica dell'ago della* —, dip of compass needle; *rosa della* —, compass card (o rose) || *perdere la* —, (*perdere la testa*) to lose one's bearings (o to lose one's head).

bússola[2], *s.f.* **1.** (*controporta*) inner door **2.** (*portantina*) sedan (-chair) **3.** (*paravento*) screen.

bussolànte, *s.m.* (*eccl.*) Pope's attendant.

bussolòtto, *s.m.* **1.** (*per giocare ai dadi*) dice-box; (*del prestigiatore*) juggler's box: *giocatore di bussolotti*, juggler (o prestidigitator); (*imbroglione*) cheater (o trickster o impostor) **2.** (*barattolo*) can, tin.

bústa, *s.f.* **1.** envelope: — *affrancata e cón indirizzo*, stamped and addressed envelope; — *lacerata, strappata*, torn envelope; — *paga*, pay-envelope; *lettera in* — *aperta*, unsealed letter (o letter in unsealed envelope); *chiudi bene la* —!, seal the envelope well! || *in* — *a parte*, under separate cover **2.** (*astuccio*) case.

bustàia, *s.f.* corset-maker, stay-maker.

bustarèlla, *s.f.* (*gergo*) bribe; (*sl. amer.*) payola.

bustína, *s.f.* **1.** small envelope **2.** (*mil.*) service cap.

bústo, *s.m.* **1.** (*anat. scult.*) bust **2.** (*indumento femminile*) corset; stays (*pl.*).

butadiène, *s.m.* (*chim.*) butadiene.

butàno, *s.m.* (*chim.*) butane.

butíle, *s.m.* (*chim.*) butyl.

butilène, *s.m.* (*chim.*) butylene.

butírro, *s.m.* butter.

butirróso, *ag.* buttery.

buttafuòri, *s.m.* **1.** (*teat.*) call-boy **2.** (*mar.*) outrigger.

buttàre, *v.t.* **1.** to throw, to fling, to cast: — *ql.co. dalla finestra*, to throw sthg. out of the window; — *qlcu. in prigione*, to throw (o to cast) s.o. into prison; — *sassi contro un cane*, to throw stones at a dog; — *via*, to throw (o to cast) away (o to discard) || — *all'aria*, to upset (anche *fig.*) || — *giù*, (*demolire*) to demolish (o to knock down); (*di vento*) to blow down; *fig.* (*screditare*) to discredit; (*scoraggiare*) to discourage: — *giù un articolo*, *fig.* to throw off an article || — *in faccia a qlcu.*, to fling in s.o.'s teeth (o to reproach s.o. openly) **2.** (*sprecare*) to waste: — *il tempo*, to waste time || — *via il proprio denaro dalla finestra*, to play ducks and drakes with one's money **3.** (*mandare fuori, emettere*) to send forth, to send out: *la fontana butta poco oggi*, the fountain is not playing to-day; *la sua ferita butta sangue*, his wound is bleeding **4.** (*metal.*) to cast || *v.i.* (*germogliare*) to shoot forth, to sprout || **buttàrsi,** *v.r.* (*gettarsi*) to throw oneself: *l'aquila si buttò sull'agnello*, the eagle pounced on the lamb; *egli si buttò ai miei piedi*, he threw himself at my feet; *si buttò in mare*, he jumped into the sea; — *col paracadute*, to parachute (o to bale out) || *mi sono buttato a bere*, I have taken to drinking || *il tempo si butta al bello*, the weather is clearing || — *giù*, (*sdraiarsi*) to lie down; *fig.* (*avvilirsi*) to lose courage.

buttasèlla, *s.m.* (*mil.*) doot-and-saddle.

buttàta, *s.f.* **1.** throw **2.** (*germoglio*) shoot, sprout.

butteràre, *v.t.* (*metal. med.*) to pit.

butteràto, *ag.* (*metal. med.*) pitted.

butteratúra, *s.f.* (*metal. med.*) pitting.

búttero, *s.m.* cowherd of the Maremma.

búzzo, *ag.* (*rar.*) (*nuvoloso*) cloud; *fig.* gloomy || *s.m.* paunch, belly; (*grosso ventre*) pot-belly: *empirsi il* —, to eat much; *metter su* —, to get fat || *di* — *buono*, very eagerly (o with great enthusiasm).

buzzúrro, *s.m.* **1.** (*zoticone*) boor **2.** (*venditore di caldarroste*) chestnut seller.

byroniàno, *ag.* (*lett.*) Byronic.

C

c, *s.f.m.* **1.** (*terza lettera dell'alfabeto italiano*) c (*pl.* cs, c's) ‖ — come Como, (*tel.*) c for Charlie **2.** *C*, (*numero romano equivalente a 100*) C (one hundred).

ca', *abbr.* di **càsa.**

càbala, *s.f.* **1.** (*st. fil.*) cab(b)ala **2.** (*occultismo*) cab(b)ala **3.** (*nel lotto*) art of foretelling lottery numbers **4.** (*intrigo*) cabal, secret intrigue, underhand plot: *far cabale,* to cabal (*o* to intrigue *o* to plot).

cabalétta, *s.f.* (*mus.*) cabaletta.

cabalísta, *s.m.* **1.** (*occultista*) cabalist **2.** (*nel lotto*) foreteller of lottery numbers.

cabalístico, *ag.* cabalistic(al).

cabalóna, *s.f.,* **cabalóne,** *s.m.* (*intrigante*) intriguer, plotter.

cabanèlla, *s.f.* (*mar.*) «cabanella» (rowing-boat used in tunny fishing).

càbbala, *s.f.* (*st. fil.*) cab(b)ala.

cabestàno, *s.m.* (*mar.*) capstan.

cabíla, *s.f.* Kabyle.

cabína, *s.f.* **1.** box, hut: — *balneare,* bathing-hut; — *elettorale,* polling-booth; — *telefonica,* telephone-box (*o* telephone-booth) **2.** (*mar. aer.*) cabin: — *a due cuccette,* two-berth cabin; — *di coperta,* deckhouse; — *di lusso,* luxury cabin; — *di navigazione,* charthouse; (*aer.*) navigator compartment; — *di poppa,* after cabin; — *passeggeri,* (*aer.*) passenger compartment; — *piloti,* cockpit (*o* pilot's compartment); — *pressurizzata,* pressure cabin; *cameriere di* —, cabin steward; *classe* —, cabin class **3.** (*ferr.*) cab; (*elett.*) cabin: — *comando segnali,* signal box; — *di blocco,* railway signal box; — *di comando,* engineer's cab; — *di trasformazione,* (*elett.*) transformer room.

cablogràmma, *s.m.* cablegram, cable: *per* —, by cable.

cabotàggio, *s.m.* (*mar.*) cabotage, coasting trade: *nave di piccolo* —, coasting vessel.

cabotière, *s.m.* (*mar.*) coaster.

cabotièro, *ag.* (*mar.*) coasting ‖ *s.m.* coaster, coasting vessel.

Cabòto, *no.pr.* (*st.*) Cabot.

cabràre, *v.i.* (*aer.*) to pull up; (*sl.*) to zoom.

cabràta, *s.f.* (*aer.*) pull-up; (*sl.*) zoom.

cacadùbbi, *s.c.* (*volg.*) irresolute, wavering person.

cacào, *s.m.* **1.** (*bot.*) cacao (-tree): *burro di* —, cacao -butter (*o* cocoa-butter *o* cocoa-fat); *semi di* —, cacao -seeds (*o* cacao-beans) **2.** (*polvere, bevanda*) cocoa: *fabbrica di* —, cocoa-mill; *una tazza di* —, a cup of cocoa.

cacàre, *v.i.* (*volg.*) to evacuate one's bowels.

cacarèlla, *s.f.* (*volg.*) diarrhœa.

cacasénno, *s.m.* (*pop.*) wiseacre.

cacatòa, cacatúa, *s.m.* (*ornit.*) cockatoo.

cacatúra, *s.f.* dirt, ordure: — *di mosche,* fly-dirt.

càcca, *s.f.* **1.** human excrement, ordure **2.** (*sudiciume*) dirt.

cacchióne, *s.m.* **1.** (*larva di ape*) bee-larva (*pl.* bee -larvae) **2.** *pl.* (*uova di mosca*) flyblow (*sing.*); fly-eggs.

càccia¹, *s.f.* hunt; hunting; (*arc.*) chase: — *grossa,* big game hunting; (*i capi abbattuti nel corso di questa*) big game; *cane da* —, sporting dog; *capanno di* —, hunting-box; *corno da* —, hunting-horn; *fucile da* —, (*per uccelli*) shot gun; *licenza di* —, game-licence; *pallini da* —, small shot; *una riserva di* —, a game-preserve: *stagione di* —, shooting season; (*alla volpe*) hunting season; *partecipammo a una* — *alla volpe,* we joined in a fox-hunt; *ti piace la* — *alla volpe?,*

do you like fox-hunting?; *andare a* —, to go hunting; (*di uccelli*) to go shooting; *fig.* to hunt (for sthg.).

càccia², *s.m.* **1.** (*aer.*) fighter: — *a reazione,* jet -fighter **2.** *abbr.* di **cacciatorpedinière.**

cacciabombardière, *s.m.* (*aer.*) fighter-bomber.

cacciachiòdo, *s.m.* (*strum.*) nail-driver.

cacciagióne, *s.f.* **1.** game **2.** (*caccia*) hunt(ing).

cacciamósche, *s.m.* fly-swatter, fly-whisk.

cacciapàssere, *s.m.* scarecrow.

cacciàre, *v.t.* **1.** to hunt; (*uccelli*) to shoot: — *uccelli,* to fowl; — *la volpe,* to go fox-hunting **2.** (*mar. mil.*) to chase **3.** (*scacciare*) to drive out, to expel, to chase: *lo cacciò di casa,* he chased him out of his house; *riuscì a cacciarglielo dalla mente,* he succeeded in driving it out of his head; — *un ragazzo da scuola,* to expel a boy from school **4.** (*ficcare, spinger dentro*) to drive in, to thrust: — *il naso negli affari altrui,* to poke one's nose into other people's business **5.** (*mettere*) to put: *dove ho cacciato il mio ombrello?,* where did I put my umbrella? **6.** (*emettere*) to utter: — *un grido,* to utter a cry ‖ *v.i.* to go hunting; (*uccelli*) to go shooting, to fowl ‖ **cacciàrsi,** *v.r.* **1.** (*introdursi*) to thrust oneself **2.** — *in testa ql.co.,* to drive sthg. into one's head.

cacciasommergíbili, *s.m.* (*mar. mil.*) submarine chaser.

cacciàta, *s.f.* **1.** (*partita di caccia*) shooting-party **2.** (*lo scacciare*) expulsion: *la* — *di Adamo ed Eva dal Paradiso Terrestre,* the expulsion of Adam and Eve from the Garden of Eden.

cacciatóra, *s.f.* **1.** (*giacca*) shooting-jacket **2.** *pollo alla* —, (*cuc.*) stewed chicken.

cacciatóre, *s.m.* **1.** hunter (*anche fig.*); shooter, sportsman (*pl.* sportsmen); (*di caccia grossa*) huntsman (*pl.* huntsmen): — *di dote,* fortune-hunter; — *di frodo,* poacher; *cacciatori di teste,* scalp-hunters **2.** (*mil.*) rifleman (*pl.* riflemen): *cacciatori a cavallo,* light cavalry **3.** (*servo in livrea*) lackey, footman (*pl.* footmen).

cacciatorpedinière, *s.m.* (*mar. mil.*) torpedo-boat destroyer.

cacciatríce, *s.f.* huntress; sportswoman (*pl.* sportswomen).

cacciavíte, *s.m.* screwdriver.

cacciú, *s.m.* (*farm.*) cachou.

cacciúcco, *s.m.* (*dial.*) "cacciucco", fish-soup.

càccola, *s.f.* (*volg.*) **1.** eye-gum **2.** (*moccio*) snivel, mucus **3.** (*sudiciume nella lana delle pecore*) dirt.

cacherèllo, *s.m.* dung (of goat, sheep, etc.).

cacheróso, *ag.* affected; lackadaisical, mawkish.

cachessía, *s.f.* (*med.*) cachexia, cachexy.

cachèttico, *ag.* (*med.*) cachectic(al).

càchi¹, *ag.* khaki: *color* —, khaki (colour); *divisa* —. khaki uniform.

càchi², *s.m.* **1.** (*albero*) persimmon(-tree) **2.** (*frutto*) persimmon.

cachínno, *s.m.* (*letter.*) cachinnation.

caciàia, *s.f.* cheese room.

caciàio, *s.m.* **1.** (*chi fabbrica formaggio*) cheese-maker **2.** (*chi vende formaggio*) cheese-monger.

cacíco, *s.m.* (*capo messicano*) cacique.

càcio, *s.m.* cheese: *crosta di* —, cheese-rind; *una forma di* —, a (whole) cheese ‖ *cascare come il* — *sui maccheroni, fig.* to happen (*o* to come *o* to turn up) at the right moment ‖ *essere alto come un soldo di* —, to

107

be very short; (di bambino) to be a tiny tot ‖ essere pane e — con qlcu., fig. to be hand in glove with s.o.

caciocavàllo, s.m. "caciocavallo" (very savoury oblong-shaped cheese of Southern Italy).

cacióso, ag. cheesy.

caciòtta, caciuòla, s.f. "caciotta" (small Italian cheese).

Càco, no.pr.m. (mit.) Cacus.

cacofonìa, s.f. cacophony.

cacofònico, ag. cacophonous, ill-sounding.

cacografìa, s.f. cacography.

cactèa, s.f., **càceto**, s.m. (bot.) cactus (pl. cacti, cactuses).

cacúme, s.m. (arc.) top, summit.

cadaúno, pron. (specialmente usato nel linguaggio burocratico) each: ebbero due biglietti —, they were given two tickets each (o each of them was given two tickets).

cadàvere, s.m. 1. corpse ‖ è un — ambulante, he is a living corpse (o skeleton) 2. fig. (persona macilenta) ghost, skeleton.

cadavèrico, ag. cadaverous, corpse-like; (med.) cadaveric; (mortalmente pallido) deadly pale; ghastly: rigidità cadaverica, (med.) rigor mortis.

cadènte, ag. falling; (di astri) setting: foglie cadenti, falling leaves; il sole —, the setting sun; stella —, shooting star ‖ età —, decrepit old age.

cadènza, s.f. 1. cadence; (ritmo) rhythm; (mus.) cadenza: in —, rhythmically; battere la —, to beat time 2. (accento) accent: parla con — milanese, he speaks with a Milanese accent.

cadenzàre, v.t. 1. to give rhythm to (sthg.) 2. (mus.) to lead (sthg.) up to a cadence.

cadenzàto, ag. rhythmical: passo —, rhythmical step.

cadére, v.i. 1. to fall (down): gli sono caduti i capelli, he has lost his hair; la neve cade fitta, the snow is falling thick; la pioggia cadeva a torrenti, the rain fell in torrents; — a capofitto, to fall headlong (o head first); — ai piedi di qlcu., to fall at s.o.'s feet; — a terra, to fall to the ground; — bocconi, to fall flat on one's face; — dalle scale, to tumble down the stairs; — di mano, to drop from one's hand; — in ginocchio, to fall on one's knees; — in mare, (da un'imbarcazione) to fall overboard; — in piedi, to fall on one's feet (o legs) (anche fig.); — supino, to fall on one's back ‖ mi caddero le braccia, fig. my spirits fell (o I felt disheartened) ‖ — addormentato, to fall asleep ‖ — ammalato, to fall ill (o to be taken ill) ‖ — a proposito, (venire al momento giusto) to come in the nick of time (o at the right moment); (venir comodo) to come in handy ‖ — dalla padella nella brace, (fam.) to fall out of the frying-pan into the fire ‖ — dalle nuvole, fig. to be taken aback ‖ — dal sonno, to be overcome by sleep; — di mente, to slip from one's mind ‖ — in contraddizione, to contradict oneself ‖ — in deliquio, to faint ‖ — in disgrazia, to fall into disgrace (o to lose s.o.'s favour) ‖ — in un'imboscata, to fall into an ambush ‖ — in miseria, to fall into poverty ‖ — in peccato, to fall into sin (o to sin o to commit sin) ‖ — in pezzi, to fall to pieces ‖ — nell'errore, to fall into error ‖ — nel volgare, to lapse into vulgarity ‖ — sotto una regola, to come within a rule ‖ far —, to knock down; fig. to bring about the fall of : fecero — il governo, they brought about the fall of the Government ‖ lasciar —, to drop: lasciar — un argomento, to let a matter drop; lasciarsi — su una poltrona, to sink into an arm-chair 2. (capitolare) to fall: il forte cadde dopo molti attacchi, the fortress fell after many attacks 3. (morire in battaglia) to fall, to be killed: molti soldati caddero in quella battaglia, many soldiers fell (o were killed) in that battle 4. (ricorrere) to fall: Pasqua cade tardi quest'anno, Easter falls late this year 5. (comm.) (di prezzi) to fall 6. (tramontare, di astri) to set 7. (calare) to drop: il vento cade, the wind is dropping 8. (far fiasco) to fail: la commedia cadde, the play failed; egli cadde agli esami, he failed (o was plough-

ed) at his examinations 9. (di stoffe, abiti) to hang: un abito che cade bene, a dress that hangs (o fits) well.

cadére, s.m.: al — del giorno, at the close of day; al — della notte, at nightfall; al — del sole, at sunset.

cadétto, ag. cadet (attributivo) ‖ s.m. 1. cadet: era il — di un'antica famiglia, he was the cadet of an old family 2. (mil.) cadet 3. (mar.) midshipman (pl. midshipmen) (abbr. middy).

cadì, s.m. (magistrato musulmano) cadì.

Càdice, no.pr.f. (geog.) Cadiz.

caditóia, s.f. 1. (di torre) embrasure 2. (botola) trap, trap-door.

càdmio, s.m. (chim.) cadmium.

caducaménte, av. transiently; fleetingly.

caducèo, s.m. (mit. st.) caduceus (pl. caducei).

caducità, s.f. 1. caducity; perishableness, frailness; (il rapido passare) transiency 2. (dir.) caducity, lapse.

cadúco, ag. 1. perishable, frail; (che passa) fleeting, transient; (cadente) decaying: età caduca, declining age 2. (biol.) caducous, deciduous: denti caduchi, milk teeth; foglie caduche, caducous leaves 3. mal —, (arc.) falling sickness (o epilepsy).

cadúta, s.f. 1. fall, falling: — d'acqua, waterfall; la — delle foglie, the fall of the leaves 2. fig. fall, downfall; ruin, failure: — dei prezzi, (comm.) fall in prices; — delle quotazioni, (comm.) drop in market -prices; la — del ministero, the fall of the government ‖ la — dell'uomo, (Bibbia) the Fall (of man) 3. (fis.) fall; drop: — di potenziale, (elett.) potential drop (o fall of potential); — di pressione, pressure drop; — di temperatura, drop in temperature; — di tensione, (elett.) voltage drop; — termica, heat drop 4. (mar.) (di vela quadra) leech.

cadúto, ag. 1. fallen 2. fig. (rovinato) ruined; (vinto) vanquished 3. (morto in battaglia) fallen ‖ i caduti, the fallen: monumento ai caduti, war memorial.

caffè, ag. coffee-coloured: abito —, coffee-coloured suit ‖ s.m. 1. coffee: — e latte, café au lait (o white coffee); — leggero, weak coffee; — macinato, ground coffee; — nero, black coffee; — tostato, roasted coffee; chicco di —, coffee-bean; fondi di —, coffee grounds; macinino da —, coffee-mill; piantagione di —, coffee plantation; tazza da —, coffee-cup; macinare il —, to grind coffee 2. (luogo pubblico) coffee-house; (di tipo italiano, francese) café: — della stazione, refreshment room 3. (colore) coffee colour.

caffè-concèrto, s.m. café-chantant.

caffeìna, s.f. (chim.) caffeine.

caffelàtte, s.m. white coffee, coffee and milk; (fam.) milk with a dash of coffee.

caffettàno, s.m. caftan, kaftan.

caffettièra, s.f. 1. coffee-pot 2. (scherz.) (locomotiva, automobile malandata) rickety vehicle, shandrydan.

caffettière, s.m. coffee-house keeper.

càffo, s.m. (numero dispari) odd number: giuocare a pari e —, to play at odds and evens.

cafóne, s.m. (dial.) 1. Southern Italian peasant 2. fig. (zoticone) boor.

càfro, ag. e s.m. Kafir.

cagionàre, v.t. (causare) to cause; (dare occasione a) to occasion; (dare origine a) to give rise to (sthg.): che cosa ha cagionato il tuo ritardo?, what caused you to be late?.

cagióne, s.f. (causa) cause; (motivo) reason, motive: a — di, owing to (o because of o on account of); trovar —, to find a pretext.

cagionévole, ag. sickly, weak, delicate: salute —, delicate health.

cagionevolézza, s.f. sickliness.

cagionóso, ag. sickly, weak, delicate.

cagliàre, v.i., **cagliàrsi**, v.r. to curdle.

càglio, s.m. rennet.

càgna, s.f. 1. bitch 2. (spreg.) (donna di facili costumi) bitch 3. (spreg.) (pessima attrice) bad actress; (pessima cantante) bad singer 4. (ferr.) jim-crow.

cagnàccio, s.m. cur.

cagnàra, *s.f.* **1.** furious barking (of several dogs together) **2.** (*clamore*) brawling, uproar, clamour **3.** (*trambusto*) fuss; hubbub.

cagnésco, *ag.*: *in —*, surlily: *guardare qlcu. in —*, to scowl at s.o. (*o* to cast a surly look upon s.o.); *guardarsi in —*, to scowl at each other.

cagnolíno, *s.m.* **1.** (*cucciolo*) puppy **2.** (*cane piccolo*) small dog **3.** (*cane da salotto*) lap-dog.

cagnòtto, *s.m.* **1.** (*sicario*) hired ruffian; (*bravaccio*) hired bully **2.** (*seguace servile*) hanger-on (*pl.* hangers-on).

caícco, *s.m.* (*mar.*) caique.

caimàno, *s.m.* (*zool.*) cayman.

Caíno, *no.pr.m.* (*Bibbia*) Cain || **caíno,** *s.m.* **1.** fratricide; (*assassino*) murderer **2.** (*traditore*) traitor.

Càio, *no.pr.m.* (*st.*) Caius.

càla, *s.f.* **1.** (*geog.*) cove, creek **2.** (*mar.*) hold.

calabrése, *ag.s.c.* Calabrian.

Calàbria, *no.pr.* (*geog.*) Calabria.

calabróne, *s.m.* (*entom.*) hornet.

calafatàre, *v.t.* (*mar.*) to caulk.

calafàto, *s.m.* (*mar.*) caulker.

calamàio, *s.m.* **1.** ink-stand, ink-pot **2.** (*zool.*) calamary.

calamarétto, calamàro, *s.m.* (*zool.*) calamary.

calamína, *s.f.* (*min.*) calamine.

calamíta[1], *s.f.* magnet, loadstone (anche *fig.*): *— artificiale,* artificial magnet; *elettro- —,* electromagnet.

calamità[2], *s.f.* calamity, misfortune, disaster.

calamitàre, *v.t.* to magnetize (anche *fig.*).

calamitàto, *ag.* magnetic.

calamitóso, *ag.* calamitous, disastrous.

càlamo, *s.m.* **1.** (*bot.*) calamus (*pl.* calami): *— aromatico,* sweet calamus **2.** (*canna*) reed **3.** (*asta di freccia*) arrow-shaft **4.** (*fusto di penna*) calamus (*pl.* calami); quill.

calàndra[1], *s.f.* (*ornit.*) wood-lark.

calàndra[2], *s.f.*: *— del grano,* (*entom.*) weevil.

calàndra[3], *s.f.* (*mec.*) calender: *— a tre rulli,* three-roller calender; *— a vapore,* rotary steam press.

calandràre, *v.t.* (*ind.*) to calender.

calandríno[1], *s.m.* simpleton.

calandríno[2], *s.m.* (*strum. artig.*) bevel rule.

calàndro[1], *s.m.* (*ornit.*) titlark, meadow pipit.

calàndro[2], *s.m.* (*strum. artig.*) folding rule.

calànte, *ag.* **1.** falling, sinking; (*di astri*) setting: *sole —,* setting sun **2.** (*decrescente*) decreasing: *luna —,* waning moon; *marea —,* ebb-tide **3.** (*declinante*) declining: *fama —,* declining fame **4.** *moneta —,* (*comm.*) light weight coin.

calàppio, *s.m.* **1.** (*laccio*) snare **2.** (*inganno*) trap; deceit.

calaprànzi, *s.m.* service lift (from kitchen to dining-room).

calàre, *v.t.* **1.** (*abbassare*) to lower, to let down; to drop: *ella calò un cestino,* she let down a small basket; *— una imbarcazione,* to lower a boat; *— i prezzi,* to lower prices || *cala la tela,* (*teat.*) curtain drops || *— un fendente,* to strike a cleaving blow **2.** (*ammainare*) to strike; to take in || *v.i.* **1.** (*discendere*) to descend, to go down: *— su di un paese,* to invade a country **2.** (*tramontare, di astri*) to set **3.** (*accorciarsi*) to grow shorter: *i giorni stanno calando,* the days are shortening (*o* are growing shorter *o* are drawing in) **4.** (*abbassarsi*) (*di febbre*) to abate; (*della marea*) to ebb; (*di acqua*) to decrease, to shoal, to shallow; (*di vento, temperatura*) to drop: *il vento cala,* the wind is dropping **5.** (*comm.*) (*di prezzi, valori*) to fall, to come down: *le azioni stanno calando,* the stocks are falling; *la merce cala di prezzo,* the goods are cheapening **6.** (*divenir fioco*) to lower, to sink **7.** (*diminuire di peso*) to lose weight: *sono calato due chili,* I have lost two kilos **8.** (*mus.*) to drop in pitch || **calàrsi,** *v.r.* to let oneself down.

calàre, *s.m.*: *al — della notte,* at nightfall; *al — del sole,* at sunset.

calàta, *s.f.* **1.** (*discesa*) descent: *la prima — dei Visigoti in Italia,* the first descent of the Visigoths upon Italy (*o* the first Visigothic invasion of Italy) **2.** (*banchina*) quay **3.** (*abbassamento*) fall: *— del sipario,* (*teat.*) fall of the curtain.

càlca, *s.f.* crowd, throng: *fendere la —,* to force one's way (*o* to squeeze) through the crowd.

calcafògli, *s.m.* paper-weight.

calcagnàta, *s.f.*: *dare una — a ql.co.,* to put one's heel on sthg.; *schiacciare ql.co. con una —,* to crush sthg. with one's heel: *schiacciò lo scorpione con una —,* he crushed the scorpion with his heel.

calcàgno, *s.m.* heel || *menar le calcagna,* to run away (*o* to take to one's heels) || *stare alle calcagna di qlcu.,* to follow s.o. closely; (*pedinarlo*) to shadow s.o.

calcagnuòlo, *s.m.* (*mar.*) heel, skeg.

calcaléttere, *s.m.* paper-weight.

Calcànte, *no.pr.m.* (*mit.*) Calchas.

calcàra, *s.f.* calcar.

calcàre[1], *ag.* (*min.*) calcareous || *s.m.* (*min.*) limestone: *— fondente,* (*metal.*) flux.

calcàre[2], *v.t.* **1.** to tread: *— le orme di qlcu.,* to tread in s.o.'s footsteps || *— le scene,* (*teat.*) to tread the boards (*o* the stage) **2.** (*premere con forza*) to press down || *— l'accento su ql.co.,* to lay stress upon (*o* to stress *o* to emphasize) sthg. || *— la mano,* (*esagerare*) to exaggerate || *— la mano su qlcu.,* (*vessarlo*) to lay a heavy hand on (*o* to oppress) s.o. **3.** (*ricalcare*) to calk: *— un disegno,* to calk a drawing.

calcàreo, *ag.* calcareous.

calcàta, *s.f.* trampling; pressure.

càlce[1], *s.f.* lime: *— aerea,* common lime; *— idraulica,* water (*o* hydraulic) lime; *— spenta,* slaked lime (*o* lime paste); *— viva,* caustic lime (*o* quicklime); *acqua di —,* lime-water; *bianco di —,* whitewash.

càlce[2], in, *l. av.* at the foot, at the bottom: *in — alla presente,* (*comm.*) here at foot (*o* below).

Calcedònia, *no.pr.f.* (*geog.st.*) Chalcedon.

calcedònio, *s.m.* (*min.*) chalcedony.

calceolària, *s.f.* (*bot.*) Calceolaria.

calcése, *s.m.* (*mar.*) top of a lateen mast: *albero a —,* lateen mast.

calcestrúzzo, *s.m.* concrete, beton.

calciàre, *v.t.* to kick: *— in porta,* (*spor.*) to kick at goal.

calciatóre, *s.m.* (*spor.*) footballer.

càlcico, *ag.* (*chim.*) calcic.

Calcídica, *no.pr.f.* (*geog.*) Chalcidice.

calcificazióne, *s.f.* (*med.*) calcification.

calcína, *s.f.* lime, mortar: *— grassa,* fat lime; *— viva,* caustic lime (*o* quicklime).

calcinàccio, *s.m.* **1.** flake of dry plaster **2.** *pl.* rubble (*sing.*); debris (*sing.*).

calcinàio, *s.m.* lime-pit.

calcinàre, *v.t.* **1.** (*chim.*) to calcine **2.** (*metal.*) to oxidize, to roast **3.** (*agr.*) to lime, to dress with lime.

calcinatúra, *s.f.,* **calcinazióne,** *s.f.* **1.** calcination **2.** (*agr.*) liming.

calcíno, *s.m.* (*vet.*) muscardine.

calcinòsi, *s.f.* (*patol.*) calcinosis.

calcinóso, *ag.* limy.

càlcio[1], *s.m.* **1.** kick: *— d'angolo,* (*spor.*) corner; *— d'inizio,* (*spor.*) kick-off; *— di punizione,* (*spor.*) free kick; *— di rigore,* (*spor.*) penalty; *lo mandai fuori a calci,* I kicked him out; *prender a calci qlcu.,* to kick s.o. || *dare un — alla fortuna,* to turn one's back on fortune || *fare a calci,* fig. to clash: *questi due mobili fanno a calci tra loro,* these two pieces of furniture clash || *ricevere il — dell'asino,* to be hurt in return for a kindness **2.** (*giuoco del calcio*) football; (*fam.*) soccer: *giocare al —,* to play football **3.** (*di arma da fuoco*) butt: *— di fucile,* rifle butt (*o* rifle stock).

càlcio[2], *s.m.* (*chim.*) calcium.

calciocianamíde, *s.f.* (*chim.*) calcium cyanamide.

calcístico, *ag.* (*spor.*) football (*attributivo*): *incontro —,* football match; *società calcistica,* football club.

calcíte, *s.f.* (*min.*) calcite.

càlco, *s.m.* **1.** drawing, tracing **2.** (*copia esatta*) close copy **3.** (*scult.*) cast.

calcografía, *s.f.* chalcography.

calcogràfico, *ag.* chalcographic(al).

caleògrafo, *s.m.* chalcographer.

càlcola, *s.f.* (*ind. tessile*) (loom) treadle.

calcolàbile, *ag.* calculable, computable.

calcolàre, *v.t.* **1.** to calculate, to compute, to reckon **2.** (*prevedere col raziocinio, l'effetto di una cosa*) to calculate, to estimate, to value, to consider, to think of (sthg.): *senza — i vostri vantaggi*, without considering (*o* thinking of *o* mentioning) your advantages ‖ *v.i.* to calculate, to reckon.

calcolatóre, *ag.* calculating: *macchina calcolatrice*, calculator (*o* calculating machine) ‖ *s.m.* **1.** reckoner, computer **2.** *fig.* shrewd fellow, clever selfish man ‖ **calcolatríce**, *s.f.* **1.** reckoner, computer **2.** *fig.* shrewd woman, clever selfish woman **3.** (*mec.*) calculator, calculating machine.

càlcolo, *s.m.* **1.** calculation, reckoning, computation; (*mat.*) calculus (*pl.* calculi): — *approssimativo*, approximate calculation (*o* rough estimate); — *delle probabilità*, theory (*o* calculus) of probability; — *differenziale*, differential calculus; — *integrale*, integral calculus; *essere svelto, bravo nei calcoli*, to be quick (*o* a good hand) at figures; *fare calcoli*, to make calculations (*o* to calculate): *fare i propri calcoli*, *fig.* to make one's plans; *tener — di ql.co.*, to take sthg. into consideration **2.** (*patol.*) calculus (*pl.* calculi); stone: — *biliare*, gall-stone; — *renale*, renal calculus.

calcolóso, *ag.* (*patol.*) calculous.

calcomanía, *s.f.* transfer.

calcopiríte, *s.f.* (*min.*) chalcopyrite.

calcotipía, *s.f.* etching; copperplate engraving.

caldàia, *s.f.* **1.** (*per riscaldamento di liquidi*) kier **2.** (*per produzione di vapore*) boiler: — *a nafta*, oil-fired boiler; — *a vapore*, steam boiler; — *elettrica*, electric boiler.

caldàio, *s.m.* cauldron.

caldalléssa, *s.f.* boiled chestnut.

caldaménte, *av.* warmly; hotly (anche *fig.*).

caldàna, *s.f.* **1.** (*calura*) heat; stuffiness **2.** (*scalmana*) sudden flush ‖ *prendere una —*, (*innamorarsi perdutamente*) to fall head over heel in love.

caldàno, *s.m.* brazier.

caldarròsta, *s.f.* roast chestnut.

caldarostàio, *s.m.* roast chestnut vendor.

Caldèa, *no.pr.* (*geog.st.*) Chaldea.

caldeggiàre, *v.t.* to favour, to support warmly; to back (up).

caldeggiàto, *ag.* favoured, supported.

caldeggiatóre, *s.m.* supporter.

caldèo, *ag.s.m.* Chaldean, Chaldee.

calderàio, *s.m.* coppersmith; (*stagnino*) tinker.

calderóne, *s.m.* **1.** cauldron **2.** *fig.* (*gran quantità di cose disordinate*) medley, hotchpotch.

càldo, *s.m.* **1.** warm; (*molto caldo*) hot: *acqua calda*, hot water: *bottiglia dell'acqua calda*, hot-water bottle; *una tazza di tè ben —*, a cup of hot tea ‖ *battere il ferro finché è —*, *fig.* to strike while the iron is hot (*o* to make hay while the sun shines) ‖ *piangere a calde lacrime*, to weep bitterly **2.** *fig.* ardent, fervent, warm, passionate: *un — appello*, a warm appeal; *una calda preghiera*, a fervent prayer; *una calda raccomandazione*, a warm recommendation ‖ *a sangue —*, in warm blood ‖ *testa calda*, hot-headed person ‖ *avere il sangue — della gioventù*, to have the hot blood of youth ‖ *pigliarsela calda per ql.co.*, to take sthg. to heart (*o* to put one's best into sthg.) **3.** (*di colore*) warm: *un colore —*, a warm colour; *tinte calde*, warm tints **4.** (*recente*) hot, fresh, recent: *notizie calde calde*, latest news ‖ *s. m.* **1.** heat: — *soffocante*, stifling (*o* oppressive) heat; *ondata di —*, heat-wave; *avete —?*, are you warm (*o* hot)?; *fa più — oggi*, it is warmer to-day; *il mio nuovo cappotto tiene molto —*, my new coat is very

warm; *tenere un piatto in —*, to keep a dish hot ‖ *non fare nè — nè freddo*, *fig.* to make no difference **2.** *fig.* (*fervore*) fervour; eagerness.

caldúra, *s.f.* heat.

calèdone, *ag.s.m.* Caledonian.

calefazióne, *s.f.* (*fis.*) calefaction.

caleidoscòpio, *s.m.* kaleidoscope.

calèmma, *s.f.* (*mar.*) high-tidal wave.

calendàrio, *s.m.* **1.** (*modo di computare il tempo*) calendar: — *Gregoriano*, Gregorian calendar **2.** (*taccuino*) calendar, almanac: — *a fogli mobili*, tear-off calendar; — *da tavolo*, desk calendar.

calènde, *s.f.pl.* kalends, calends ‖ *alle — greche*, on (*o* at) the Greek calends: *rimandare ql.co. alle — greche*, to put off sthg. (*o* to put sthg. off) till doomsday.

calendimàggio, *s.m.* **1.** May-day: *a —*, on May-day (*o* on May 1st) **2.** (*festeggiamenti del primo di maggio*) May-day festivities (*pl.*).

calenzuòlo, *s.m.* (*ornit.*) greenfinch.

calepíno, *s.m.* (*arc.*) vocabulary.

calére, *v.imp.dif.* (*rar.*) to matter: *di ciò non mi cale*, that does not matter to me (*o* I do not care about that) ‖ *mettere ql.co. in non cale*, to disregard (*o* to attach no importance to *o* to care nothing about) sthg.

calèsse, *s.m.* gig; calash, cabriolet.

calessíno, *s.m.* gig.

calétta, *s.f.* (*artig.*) mortise, mortice; (*a coda di rondine*) dovetail.

calettàre, *v.t.* to mortise; (*mec.*) to key: — *a caldo*, to shrink on; — *con chiavetta a cuneo*, to key by wedge ‖ *v.i.* to tally, to fit closely.

calettatúra, *s.f.* **1.** mortising; (*mec.*) keying; (*a coda di rondine*) dovetailing **2.** (*incastro*) dap joint.

calía, *s.f.* **1.** (*limatura d'oro*) gold filing **2.** (*anticaglia*) worthless old thing; old stuff.

calibràre, *v.t.* to calibrate; to calliper; to gauge.

calibratóio, *s.m.* (*mec.*) calibrator.

calibratúra, *s.f.* (*mec.*) calibration; gauging.

càlibro, *s.m.* **1.** (*diametro interno*) caliber, calibre; bore, gauge: *di grosso, medio, piccolo —*, (*artigl.*) large-, medium-, small-caliber; *fucile di — dodici*, twelve-gauge gun; *grossi calibri*, (*artigl.*) heavy guns **2.** (*strumento per misurare tale diametro*) callipers (*pl.*); gauge **3.** *fig.* (*importanza*) calibre, caliber; standing; importance: *un grosso —*, (*un uomo importante*) a V.I.P. (*abbr. di* Very Important Person) ‖ *sono tutti dello stesso —*, they are all of the same calibre.

calieànto, *s.m.* (*bot.*) calycanthus.

càlice¹, *s.m.* **1.** goblet; chalice, drinking-cup: *un amaro —*, a bitter cup; *bicchiere a —*, goblet; *bere il — fino alla feccia*, to drain the cup to its dregs **2.** (*eccl.*) chalice.

càlice², *s.m.* (*bot.*) calyx (*pl.* calyces, calyxes); flower-cup.

calicò, *s.m.* (*ind. tessile*) calico.

calidàrio, *s.m.* (*archeol.*) calidarium (*pl.* calidaria).

califfàto, *s.m.* caliphate.

califfo, *s.m.* caliph, calif.

californiàno, *ag.s.m.* Californian.

càliga, *s.f.* caliga (*pl.* caligae).

calígine, *s.f.* **1.** thick fog; (*nebbia unita a fumo*) smog **2.** (*poet.*) (*oscurità*) darkness **3.** (*offuscamento della vista*) dimness.

caliginóso, *ag.* **1.** foggy **2.** (*oscuro*) dark.

Calígola, *no.pr.m.* (*st. romana*) Caligula.

Calípso, *no.pr.f.* (*mit.*) Calypso.

callàia, *s.f.* **1.** opening (through a hedge) **2.** (*viottolo*) path.

càlle, *s.m.* (*poet.*) path ‖ *s.f.* "calle" (narrow street in Venice).

callífugo, *s.m.* corn-plaster, corn-cure.

calligrafía, *s.f.* **1.** (*scrittura*) handwriting, hand: *avere una bella, brutta —*, to write a good, a bad hand **2.** (*arte di scrivere bene*) penmanship **3.** (*rar.*) (*bella scrittura*) calligraphy; beautiful handwriting.

calligraficaménte, *av.* calligraphically.
calligràfico, *ag.* calligraphic.
callígrafo, *s.m.* calligrapher, calligraphist: *perito* —, handwriting expert.
Callimaco, *no.pr.m.* (*st. lett.*) Callimachus.
Callíope, *no.pr.f.* (*mit.*) Calliope.
callista, *s.m.* chiropodist; pedicure.
càllo, *s.m.* corn: *mi ha pestato i calli,* he has trod on my corns (anche *fig.*) ‖ *fare il — a ql.co.,* *fig.* to get accustomed (*o* inured) to sthg.
callosità, *s.f.* callosity.
callóso, *ag.* 1. callous; horny; (*ruvido*) rough: *mani callose,* rough hands 2. *fig.* (*insensibile*) callous: *coscienza callosa,* callous conscience.
càlma, *s.f.* 1. calm, tranquillity, quiet, quietness; (*immobilità e silenzio*) stillness: *non perdete la* —!, (*non adiratevi!*) keep your temper! (*o fam.* keep your hair on!); (*non perdete la testa!*) keep cool!; *agire con* —, to act coolly (*o* with composure) 2. (*bonaccia*) calm 3. (*comm.*) dullness.
calmànte, *ag.* calming; soothing, sedative, calmative ‖ *s.m.* (*farm.*) sedative, calmative.
calmàre, *v.t.* 1. to calm, to quiet, to pacify 2. (*placare*) to appease, to tranquillize 3. (*lenire*) to soothe, to relieve ‖ **calmàrsi,** *v.r.* 1. to calm down, to become calm, to compose one's mind: *calmati!,* calm (*o* compose) yourself! 2. (*placarsi*) to be appeased 3. (*diminuire di violenza*) to abate: *la tempesta si calmò,* the storm abated (*o* blew over); *il vento si calma,* the wind is dropping (*o* abating).
calmieràre, *v.t.* to control the price of (sthg.) officially.
calmière, *s.m.* official price-list.
càlmo, *ag.* 1. calm, quiet, still 2. (*di persona che non perde la calma*) composed, cool, self-collected 3. (*del mare*) calm, smooth 4. (*comm.*) dull, slack.
calmùcco, *ag.s.m.* 1. Kalmuck, Kalmyk 2. (*ind. tessile*) kalmuck, kalmyk ‖ **calmùcca,** *s.f.* Kalmuck, Kalmyk.
càlo, *s.m.* 1. (*diminuzione*) shrinkage, diminution: — *di fusione,* (*metal.*) melting loss 2. (*comm.*) shrinkage, wastage; (*di prezzi*) abatement.
calòcchia, *s.f.* (*agr.*) flail staff.
calomelàno, *s.m.* (*farm.*) calomel.
calóre, *s.m.* 1. (*forte*) heat; (*moderato*) warmth: — *differenziale,* (*aer.*) superheat; — *residuo,* (*fis.*) afterheat; — *specifico,* (*fis.*) specific heat; *colpo di* —, heat-stroke (*o* heat-apoplexy); *produrre* —, (*fis.*) to generate heat 2. *fig.* warmth, heat; eagerness, ardour, fervour: *nel — della discussione,* in the heat of the argument; *nel — della mischia,* in the heat of the fight; *il — della sua accoglienza ci commosse,* the warmth of his welcome (*o* his warm welcome) affected us; *accettò la nostra proposta con* —, he eagerly agreed to our proposal 3. (*patol.*) skin eruption, rash, inflammation; (*fam.*) skin-spots (*pl.*) 4. *in* —, (*di animale*) on (*o* in) heat.
caloría, *s.f.* (*fis.*) calory, calorie: *grande* —, great (*o* large) calorie; *piccola* —, small calorie.
calòrico, *ag.* (*fis.*) caloric, heat (*attributivo*).
calorífero, *s.m.* heating apparatus, radiator: *impianto centrale di caloriferi,* central heating.
calorífico, *ag.* calorific.
calorimetría, *s.f.* (*fis.*) calorimetry.
calorimètrico, *ag.* (*fis.*) calorimetric(al).
calorímetro, *s.m.* (*fis.*) calorimeter.
calorizzàre, *v.t.* (*metal.*) to calorize.
calorizzàto, *ag.* (*metal.*) calorized.
calorizzazióne, *s.f.* (*metal.*) calorizing.
calórna, *s.f.* (*mar.*) winding tackle.
calorosaménte, *av.* warmly, heartily; eagerly.
calorosità, *s.f.* warmth, heat.
caloróso, *ag.* 1. (*animato*) warm: *discussione calorosa,* warm discussion 2. (*cordiale*) hearty 3. (*che non sente il freddo*) not feeling the cold.
calòscia, *s.f.* golosh, galosh, overshoe: *dove sono le mie calosce?,* where are my galoshes?.

calòtta, *s.f.* 1. cap: — *cranica,* (*anat.*) skull-cap; — *polare,* (*geog.*) ice-cap; — *sferica,* (*geom.*) spherical bowl 2. (*papalina*) skull-cap; (*eccl.*) calotte 3. (*mec.*) cap; (*coperchio*) cover: — *coprimorsetti,* (*elett.*) terminal board guard; — *di orologio,* back of a watch; — *di protezione,* cover 4. (*aer.*) (*di paracadute*) canopy.
calpestaménto, *s.m.* trampling down.
calpestàre, *v.t.* 1. to trample on (sthg.), to tread heavily on (sthg.), to crush under foot ‖ *è vietato — l'erba,* keep off the grass 2. *fig.* (*non rispettare*) to trample on (sthg.); (*opprimere*) to oppress: *non puoi — i diritti altrui,* you cannot trample on other people's rights.
calpestío, *s.m.* 1. (*scalpiccio*) trampling of feet, pattering of feet 2. (*il calpestare*) trampling.
calúggine, calúgine, *s.f.* down.
calumàre, *v.t.* (*mar.*) to lay out (a chain, a cable).
càlumet, caluméto, *s.m.* (*pipa dei pellerossa*) calumet.
calúnnia, *s.f.* slander, slanderous report; false charge; calumny: *spargere calunnie,* to spread slander.
calunniàre, *v.t.* to slander, to calumniate, to backbite.
calunniatóre, *s.m.,* **calunniatríce,** *s.f.* slanderer, calumniator.
calunniosaménte, *av.* slanderously, calumniously.
calunnióso, *ag.* slanderous, calumnious, calumniatory.
calúra, *s.f.* heat.
Calvàrio, *no.pr.m.* (*geog. st.*) Calvary ‖ **calvàrio,** *s.m.* long suffering, series of troubles.
calvinísmo, *s.m.* (*st. relig.*) Calvinism.
calvinísta, *s.c.* (*st. relig.*) Calvinist.
calvinístico, *ag.* (*st. relig.*) Calvinistic(al).
Calvíno, *no.pr.* (*st. relig.*) Calvin.
calvízie, *s.f.* baldness.
càlvo, *ag.* bald ‖ *s.m.* bald(-headed) person; (*fam.*) baldhead, baldpate.
càlza, *s.f.* 1. (*corta, da uomo*) sock; (*da donna*) stocking: — *di lana,* worsted sock; — *elastica,* (*med.*) elastic stocking; — *fatta a mano,* hand-knitted stocking; *un paio di calze di nailon,* a pair of nylon stockings; *venditore di calze,* hosier ‖ *si fece tirare le calze,* *fig.* it took a lot to persuade him ‖ *fare le calze a qlcu.,* *fig.* to give a bad report on s.o. 2. (*lavoro a maglia*) knitting: *ferro da* —, knitting-needle; *fare la* —, to knit.
calzamàglia, *s.f.* tights (*pl.*).
calzànte *ag.* suitable, appropriate, fitting.
calzàre[1], *s.m.* (*poet.*) boot.
calzàre[2], *v.t.* 1. (*mettere ai piedi, indossare*) to put on ‖ — *il coturno,* *fig.* (*scrivere tragedie*) to write tragedise. (*interpretarle*) to act tragedies 2. (*avere ai piedi, in, dosso, portare*) to wear: *che numero (di scarpe) calzi?;* what size (of shoes) do you wear? 3. (*fornire di scarpe*) to provide with shoes 4. — *un carro,* to wedge up a cart ‖ *v.i.* (*andar bene*) to fit (s.o., sthg.): *ti calza come un guanto,* it fits you like a glove; *l'esempio calza a perfezione,* the example is quite suitable (*o* appropriate)-
calzàto, *ag.* shod: *ben* —, well shod ‖ *sei un asino — e vestito,* you are a perfect ass (*o* fool).
calzatóia, *s.f.* (*mec. aut.*) chock, chuck, wedge.
calzatóio, *s.m.* shoehorn.
calzatúra, *s.f.* footwear; (*scarpa*) shoe; (*scarpa alta, stivale*) boot: *negozio di calzature,* boot (*o* shoe) shop.
calzaturifìcio, *s.m.* boot factory, shoe factory.
calzeròtto, *s.m.* sock.
calzettàio, *s.m.* 1. (*chi fabbrica calze*) hose-maker 2. (*chi vende calze*) hosier.
calzettóni, *s.m.pl.* heavy socks, thick socks.
calzíno, *s.m.* sock.
calzolàio, *s.m.* shoemaker, bootmaker.
calzolería, *s.f.* 1. shoemaker's shop 2. (*negozio di calzature*) boot-shop.
calzoncíni, *s.m.pl.* shorts.
calzóni, *s.m.pl.* trousers; (*fam.*) pants; (*per donna*)

slacks: — *a righe*, striped trousers; — *alla zuava*, knicker-bockers; — *corti*, shorts; — *da golf*, plus-fours; — *di flanella*, flannel trousers ‖ *farsela nei* —, (*volg.*) to be in a blue funk (*o* to have one's heart in one's boots) ‖ *portare i* —, *fig.* (*di donna che si impone all'uomo*) to wear the trousers.

Càm, *no.pr.m.* (*Bibbia*) Ham.

camàglio, *s.m.* (*di armatura*) camail.

camaldolése, *ag.s.m.* (*eccl.*) Camaldolite.

camaleónte, *s.m.* chameleon (anche *fig.*).

camarílla, *s.f.* clique, cabal, camarilla.

camàuro, *s.m.* (*eccl.*) "camauro" (red velvet cap, bordered with ermine, worn by the Pope).

cambellòtto, *s.m.* camlet.

cambiàbile, *ag.* changeable.

cambiadísco, *s.m.* (automatic) record-changer.

cambiàle, *s.f.* (*comm.*) bill of exchange, bill: — *a breve scadenza*, short-dated bill; — *a lunga scadenza*, long-dated bill; — *a vista*, bill at sight (*o* sight draft); — *di comodo*, accomodation bill; — *falsa, falsificata*, forged bill; — *fittizia*, fictitious bill; — *in bianco*, blank bill; — *in circolazione*, outstanding bill; — *in sofferenza*, unpaid bill; — *pagabile all'estero*, foreign bill; — *pagabile all'interno*, inland bill; — *pagabile su piazza*, local bill; — *pagherò*, promissory note (*o* note of hand); — *tratta*, draft; *duplicato di una* —, duplicate of a bill; *emissione di una* —, issue of a bill; *questa* — *scade il 20 corr.*, this bill falls due on the 20th inst.; *avallare una* —, to back a bill; *emettere una* —, to issue a bill; *girare una* —, to endorse a bill; *incassare una* —, to cash (*o* to collect) a bill; *non pagare una* —, to dishonour a bill; *pagare una* —, to pay (*o* to honour) a bill; *protestare una* —, (*con protesto preliminare*) to note a bill; (*con protesto definitivo*) to protest a bill; *rinnovare una* —, to renew a bill; *scontare una* —, to discount a bill.

cambiaménto, *s.m.* change; (*modifica*) alteration: — *di marea*, turn of the tide; — *di rotta*, (*mar.*) alteration of course; — *di vento*, shift of wind; — *in meglio, in peggio*, change for the better, for the worse; *brusco* — *di temperatura*, sudden change in temperature; *c'è stato un* — *di proprietario*, the property has changed hands; *ella fece alcuni cambiamenti al suo vestito*, she made a few alterations to her dress; *un gran* — *s'è operato in lui*, a great change has come over him; *hai fatto un gran* —, you have changed very much; *hai fatto un gran* — *in meglio*, you have greatly improved; *noi avremmo bisogno di un* —, (*d'aria, di lavoro*) we need a change; *apportare un* — *a una clausola*, to make a change (*o* an alteration) in a clause; *fare un* —, to bring about a change.

cambiamonéte, *s.m.* money-changer.

cambiàre, *v.t.* **1.** to change: *cambiamo discorso*, let us drop the subject; *cambia tono !*, mend your manners !; *questo ha cambiato le mie idee*, this has changed my ideas; — *abito*, to change one's dress (*o* clothes); — *casa*, to move; — *colore*, to change colour; (*impallidire*) to turn pale; — *direzione*, to change one's direction (*o* to alter one's course); — *indirizzo*, to change one's address; — *marcia*, (*aut.*) to change gear; — *passo*, (*mil.*) to change step; — *le penne*, (*di uccelli*) to moult; — *posto*, to change one's seat: *posto con qlcu.*, to change seats with s.o.; — *il proprio modo di vivere*, to change one's way of living; — *strada*, to take another road; — *treno*, to change trains; — *vita*, to turn over a new leaf ‖ — *le carte in tavola*, *fig.* to change one's (*o* to sing another) tune **2.** (*denaro, valuta*) to change: *puoi cambiarmi queste mille lire?*, can you change this thousand lire note? ‖ *v.i.* to change: *il tempo sta cambiando*, the weather is going to change; *tutto cambia nel mondo*, everything changes in this world; *il vento cambia*, the wind is shifting ‖ *tanto per* —, just for a change ‖ **cambiàrsi**, *v.r.* **1.** to change: *non ti sei cambiato affatto*, you have not changed at all **2.** (*d'abito*) to change: *non ho nulla per cambiarmi*,

I have nothing to change into **3.** (*mutarsi*) to turn (into s.o., sthg.): *la pioggia si è cambiata in neve*, the rain has turned into snow.

cambiàrio, *ag.* (*comm.*) exchange (*attributivo*); of exchange: *agente* —, stock-broker; *effetto* —, bill of exchange.

cambiavalúte, *s.m.* money-changer.

càmbio, *s.m.* **1.** change; (*modifica*) alteration; (*scambio*) exchange: — *d'abiti*, change of clothes; — *dei cavalli*, change of horses; — *della guardia*, (*mil.*) changing of the guard; — *di biancheria*, change of linen ‖ *in* — *di*, in exchange for; (*invece di*) instead of ‖ *prendere in* — *qlcu.*, to mistake one person for another **2.** (*cosa avuta, data in cambio*) exchange **3.** (*econ.*) exchange: — *alto, basso, favorevole, sfavorevole*, high, low, favourable, unfavourable exchange; — *effettivo*, real exchange; — *su Londra*, exchange on London; *agente di* —, stock-broker; *controllo del* —, exchange control; *corso del* —, rate of exchange: *corso del* — *del giorno*, current rate of exchange; *lettera di* —, bill of exchange; *operazioni di* —, operation in foreign exchange; *oscillazioni del* —, fluctuation (in the rate) of exchange; *parità di* —, par of exchange; *rialzo, ribasso del* —, rise, fall in the rate of exchange; *ufficio di* —, foreign exchange office ‖ *guadagnare al* —, to gain on (*o* by) the exchange **4.** (*cambio di una moneta in spiccioli*) change: *fare il* —, to get the change **5.** (*spiccioli*) (small) change: *mi spiace, ma non ho* —, sorry, I haven't any change **6.** (*mec.*) change gear, change-speed gear, speed gear: — *a preselettore*, preselecting gear-box; — *a settori*, gate change **7.** (*aut.*) gear, gear-box; (*amer.*) transmission: — *a pedale*, (*di motocicletta*) foot lever gearshift; — *idraulico automatico*, fluid drive gearshift; — *in folle*, gear in neutral; — *sincronizzato*, synchromesh gear; — *sul volante*, gearshift attached to the steering column; *albero del* —, gearshaft; *leva del* —, gear lever; *manopola del* —, (*di ciclomotore*) gear twist grip; *scatola del* —, gear-box; *selettore del* —, gearshift.

cambísta, *s.m.* money-changer.

Cambògia, *no.pr.f.* (*geog.*) Cambodia.

cambrí, *s.m.* (*tessuto*) cambric.

cambriàno, *ag.* (*geol.*) Cambrian.

cambúsa, *s.f.* (*mar.*) storeroom, galley.

cambusière, *s.m.* (*mar.*) store-keeper.

camèlia, *s.f.* (*bot.*) camellia.

camelopàrdo, *s.m.* (*arc.*) camelopard.

càmera, *s.f.* **1.** (*stanza*) room; (*poet. o in usi particolari*) chamber: — *ammobiliata*, furnished room; *camere da affittare*, rooms to let; — *dei bambini*, nursery; — *degli ospiti*, spare room; — *di servizio*, servant's -room; — *sulla strada*, front-room; — *sul retro*, back-room; *compagno di* —, room-mate; *fare una* —, (*rassettarla*) to do (*o* to clean out) a room ‖ — *ardente*, mortuary chapel ‖ — *blindata*, strong room ‖ — *di custodia valori*, safe-room ‖ — *di lancio dei siluri*, (*mar.*) torpedo room ‖ — *di poppa*, (*mar.*) after-cabin ‖ *musica da* —, chamber music: *concerto di musica da* —, chamber concert **2.** (*camera da letto*) bedroom: — *a due letti, matrimoniale*, double-room; — *a un letto*, single-room; *veste da* —, dressing-gown (*o* house-coat); *comprerò una nuova* — *da letto*, (*il mobilio*) I shall buy a new bedroom suite **3.** *Camera*, (*corpo deliberante*) Chamber; House: *Camera dei Deputati*, Chamber of Deputies; (*in Gran Bretagna*) House of Commons (*o* Lower House); (*negli Stati Uniti*) House of Representatives; *Camera dei Pari*, House of Lords (*o* Upper House); *Camera dei Senatori*, Senate; *Camera del Lavoro*, Trade Union; *Camera dell'Agricoltura*, Chamber of Agriculture; *Camera di Commercio*, Chamber of Commerce **4.** (*tec.*) chamber: — *di caricamento*, (*artigl.*) loading chamber; — *di combustione*, (*di motore*) combustion chamber; (*di forno*) firebox; — *di scoppio*, (*artigl.*) cartridge chamber **5.** — *oscura*, (*foto.*) dark room; (*ott.*) camera obscura **6.** — *d'aria*, (*di pneumatico*) inner (*o* air) tube; (*di pallone*) bladder.

camera charitatis, in, *l. av.* (*lat.*) confidentially.

cameràta[1], *s.f.* 1. (*dormitorio*) dormitory 2. *coll.* (*compagni di dormitorio*) room-mates (*pl.*).

cameràta[2], *s.m.* 1. (*compagno*) comrade, mate, companion; (*fam.*) chum, pal 2. (*compagno di scuola*) school-fellow.

cameratísmo, *s.m.* comradeship, camaraderie, companionship, fellowship.

camerièra, *s.f.* (*domestica*) maid, maidservant, servant-maid, housemaid; parlour-maid; (*in albergo*) chambermaid; (*al ristorante*) waitress; (*su nave*) stewardess: — *a ore*, charwoman (*o* daily help *o fam.* daily); — *particolare*, lady's maid.

camerière, *s.m.* (*domestico*) servant, man-servant (*pl.* men-servants); (*al ristorante*) waiter; (*su nave*) steward: — *particolare*, valet de chambre (*o* gentleman's servant); *capo* —, head waiter.

cameríno, *s.m.* 1. small room, closet 2. (*teat.*) green-room, dressing-room 3. (*latrina*) lavatory, water-closet.

camerísta, *s.f.* lady's maid; (*della regina*) maid of honour.

camerléngo, *s.m.* (*eccl.*) camerlingo (treasurer of the Papal Court).

cameròtto, *s.m.* (*mar.*) cabin-boy.

Càmerun, *no.pr.m.* (*geog.*) (*inglese*) Cameroons; (*francese*) Cameroun.

càmice, *s.m.* 1. (*eccl.*) surplice 2. (*sopravveste per medici, ecc.*) overall: — *da operazione*, operation overall.

camiceria, *s.f.* shirt factory.

camicétta, *s.f.* blouse.

camícia, *s.f.* 1. (*da uomo*) shirt; (*da donna, per giorno*) chemise, shift: — *da notte*, (*da uomo*) night-shirt; (*da donna*) night-gown (*o* night-dress); — *di forza*, strait-jacket; *in* —, in one's shirt; *in maniche di* —, in one's shirt sleeves; *sparato della* —, shirt-front ‖ *le Camicie Nere*, the Black Shirts; *le Camicie Rosse*, the Red Shirts ‖ *uova in* —, (*cuc.*) poached eggs ‖ *è nato con la* —, he was born with a silver spoon in his mouth ‖ *avere una* — *indosso e l'altra al fosso*, to have one shirt on and the other at the wash ‖ *dare via anche la* —, to give away the very shirt off one's back ‖ *lasciare qlcu. in* —, to reduce s.o. to beggary (*o* to leave s.o. in the lurch); *ridursi in* —, to lose everything ‖ *chi lavora ha una* —, *chi non lavora ne ha due, prov.* the more one works the less one has 2. (*tec.*) jacket: — *d'acqua*, (*mec.*) water jacket; — *di raffreddamento*, (*mec.*) cooling jacket; — *smontabile*, (*di cilindro*) liner (*o* cylinder liner) 3. (*copertina di un fascicolo*) wrapper.

camiciàia, *s.f.*, **camiciàio,** *s.m.* 1. (*chi fabbrica camicie*) shirtmaker 2. (*chi vende camicie*) shirtseller.

camiciòla, *s.f.* (*maglietta*) vest, undervest; (*amer.*) undershirt.

camiciòtto, *s.m.* blouse; (*camice*) overall.

Camílla, *no.pr.f.* Camilla, Camille.

Camíllo, *no.pr.m.* Camillus.

caminétto, *s.m.* fire-place: *raccolti attorno al* —, gathered round the fire(side).

caminièra, *s.f.* 1. mirror over a mantelpiece 2. (*parafuoco*) fire-guard.

camíno, *s.m.* 1. (*focolare*) fire-place, hearth: *angolo del* —, chimney corner; *gola del* —, flue; *mensola del* —, mantelpiece; *essi si raccolsero attorno al* —, they gathered round the fire(side) 2. (*comignolo*) chimney; (*alto, di terracotta*) chimney pot: *gruppo di camini*; *chimney stack* ‖ *egli fumava come un* —, he was smoking like a chimney 3. (*ciminiera*) chimney-stalk 4. (*alpinismo*) chimney.

càmion, *s.m.* (motor-)lorry; (*amer.*) truck.

camionàbile, camionàle, *ag.* open to heavy traffic.

camionétta, *s.f.* (*mil.*) jeep.

camionísta, *s.m.* lorry-driver; (*amer.*) truck-driver.

camíta, *s.c.* Hamite.

camítico, *ag.* Hamitic.

càmma, *s.f.* (*mec.*) cam: — *ad angolo arrotondato*, broad-nose cam; *profilo della* —, cam profile.

cammellière, *s.m.* camel-driver, cameleer.

cammèllo, *s.m.* camel: *pelo di* —, camel's hair.

cammèo, *s.m.* cameo.

camminaménto, *s.m.* (*mil.*) communication trench, approach trench; passage connecting trenches.

camminàre, *v.i.* 1. to walk; (*pesantemente*) to tramp; (*marciare*) to march: *avanti, cammina!*, go on!; *egli cammina zoppicando*, he is limping; *ella camminò silenziosamente per non svegliare il bambino*, she walked softly (*o* on tiptoe) in order not to wake the baby; *mi piace* — *per la campagna*, I enjoy tramping round the country; *non* — *sul tappeto!*, don't tread on the carpet!; *quel bambino non cammina ancora*, that child doesn't walk yet; — *a grandi passi*, to stride along; — *adagio*, to walk slowly; — *con passi pesanti*, to tramp; — *diritto*, *fig.* to walk honestly (*o* to live uprightly); — *in fretta*, to walk fast; — *in punta di piedi*, to walk on tiptoe; — *sotto la pioggia*, to trudge (*o* to walk *o* to plod *o* to tramp) under the rain; — *su e giù*, to walk up and down ‖ *cammina, cammina, arrivarono a...*, after going (*o* walking) a long way they got to... ‖ — *a quattro zampe*, to go on all fours 2. (*di meccanismi*) to go, to run, to work: *cammina il tuo orologio?*, is your watch going? 3. (*di discorso, ragionamento, lavoro, affare*) to proceed: *gli affari camminano*, business is brisk; *gli affari non camminano più*, business is at a standstill (*o* is slack).

camminàta, *s.f.* 1. (*passeggiata*) walk, stroll: *andiamo a fare una* —, let us go for a walk; *da qui al mare c'è una bella* —, it is a long walk from here to the seaside; *fare una buona* —, to take a long walk 2. (*andatura*) gait: *ha una* — *aggraziata*, she has a graceful gait (*o* walk).

camminatóre, *s.m.*, **camminatríce,** *s.f.* walker.

camminatúra, *s.f.* (*modo di camminare*) gait.

cammíno, *s.m.* 1. way: *cammin facendo*, on the way: *cammin facendo lo incontrammo*, as we went along, we met him; *dopo un lungo* —, after a long way; *lungo tutto il* —, all the way; *ci sono dieci minuti di* —, it is ten minutes' away; *egli farà del* —!, *fig.* he will get on! (*o* he will make his way in the world!); *essere in* — *verso un luogo*, to be on the way to some place; *fare molto* —, to go a long way; *fig.* to make good progress (*o* to be very successful); *fare un tratto di* — *con qlcu.*, to accompany s.o. a little way; *indicare il* —, to show the way; (*accompagnare*) to lead the way; *mettersi in* —, to set out (*o* to start off *o* to move off); *riprendere il* —, to resume one's journey 2. (*sentiero*) path; (*strada*) road; (*percorso*) route; (*battuto*) trodden path; *il* — *della gloria*, *fig.* the path of glory; *un* — *tortuoso*, a winding road (*o* path); *ci andrò per il* — *più breve*, I shall go there by the shortest route; *lasciare il retto* —, *fig.* to depart from the straight path (*o* to stray).

càmola, *s.f.* (*dial.*) moth.

camomílla, *s.f.* (*bot.*) camomile; chamomile: *una tazza di* (*decotto di*) —, a cup of camomile-tea.

camòrra, *s.f.* "Camorra" (Neapolitan secret organization).

camorrísta, *s.m.* Camorrist, member of the "Camorra".

camosciàre, *v.t.* to chamois.

camosciàto, *ag.* chamois, shammy (*attributivi*).

camosciatúra, *s.f.* chamoising.

camóscio, *s.m.* 1. (*zool.*) chamois 2. (*pelle di camoscio*) chamois leather, shammy.

camòzza, *s.f.* (*zool.*) female chamois.

campàgna, *s.f.* 1. country, country-side: *casa di* —, country-house; *gente di* —, country-folk (*o* rural people); *andare in* —, to go (in)to the country; *vivere in* —, to live in the country ‖ *la Campagna Romana*, the Campagna ‖ *buttarsi alla* —, to become an outlaw; *battere la* —, to roam the country 2. (*tenuta*) estate: *è andato a vedere la sua* —, he went to survey his estate 3. (*mil.*) campaign: *la* — *di Russia*, the campaign of Russia ‖ *artiglieria da* —, field artillery 4. (*mar.*) long cruise 5. (*villeggiatura*) holidays (*pl.*):

fare —, to take one's holidays 6. (*propaganda*) campaign: — *elettorale*, electoral campaign; — *pubblicitaria*, advertising campaign.

campagnuòla, *s.f.* countrywoman (*pl.* countrywomen); peasant woman; countrygirl.

campagnuòlo, *ag.* (*rustico, dei campi*) rustic, rural; country (*attributivo*): *usanze campagnuole*, country ways ‖ *topo* —, fieldmouse ‖ *s.m.* peasant, countryman (*pl.* countrymen).

campàio, *s.m.* land warden.

campàle, *ag.* (*mil.*) field (*attributivo*): *battaglia* —, pitched battle; *batteria* —, field battery; *vittoria* — victory in the battlefield; (*vittoria decisiva*) decisive victory ‖ *una giornata* —, *fig.* (*dura, faticosa*) a strenuous (*o* hard) day.

campaménto, *s.m.* sustenance.

campàna, *s.f.* 1. bell: — *da palombaro*, diving-bell; *boa a* —, bell-buoy; *suonano le campane della chiesa*, the church bells are ringing; *suonare le campane*, to ring the bells; *suonare la* — *a martello*, to sound (*o* to ring) the alarm-bell; *suonare la* — *a morto*, to knell (*o* to toll) ‖ *a* —, bell-shaped ‖ *sordo come una* —, as deaf as a post; *essere di campane grosse*, *fig.* (*esser duro d'udito*) to be hard of hearing ‖ *sentir tutte e due le campane*, to hear both parties (*o* sides) 2. (*vaso di vetro per coprire oggetti delicati*) bell-glass.

campanàccio, *s.m.* cow-bell, cattle-bell.

campanàrio, *ag.* bell (*attributivo*): *torre campanaria*, bell-tower (*o* belfry).

campanàro, *s.m.* bell-ringer.

campanèlla, *s.f.* 1. little bell, small bell 2. (*picchiotto*) knocker 3. (*bot.*) campanula, harebell, bluebell 4. (*arch.*) drop 5. (*anello da tende*) curtain-ring.

campanèllo, *s.m.* hand-bell; (*della porta*) door-bell: — *d'allarme*, alarm-bell; — *elettrico*, electric bell; *suonare il* —, to ring the bell.

Campània, *no.pr.f.* (*geog.*) Campania.

campanifórme, *ag.* 1. bell-shaped 2. (*bot.*) campanulate.

campanìle, *s.m.* bell-tower; campanile ‖ *amore di* —, localism; *contese di* —, parish quarrels.

campanilìsmo, *s.m.* parochialism, exaggerated local pride.

campanilìsta, *ag.* parochial(-minded) ‖ *s.c.* parochial(-minded) person.

campàno, *ag.s.m.* (inhabitant) of Campania.

campànula, *s.f.* (*bot.*) campanula; (*pop.*) bell-flower.

campanulàto, *ag.* bell-shaped; campanulate.

campàre, *v.t.* 1. (*salvare*) to save, to rescue: *l'ha campato dal pericolo*, he saved him from danger 2. (*pitt.*) to put into relief: *camperò la figura su sfondo nero*, I shall put the figure into relief against a black background ‖ *v.i.* (*vivere*) to live: — *alla giornata*, to live from hand to mouth; — *di elemosina*, to live on charity.

campàro, *s.m.* land warden.

campàta, *s.f.* 1. (*arch.*) span 2. (*aer.*) wing-span.

campàto, *ag.* 1. — *in aria*, groundless (*o* unfounded); (*lontano dalla realtà*) fanciful 2. (*pitt.*) relieved.

campeggiaménto, *s.m.* camping.

campeggiànte, *s.m.* camper.

campeggiàre, *v.i.* 1. (*risaltare*) to stand out 2. (*mil.*) (*porre il campo*) to encamp 3. (*spor.*) (*far campeggio*) to camp.

campeggiatóre, *s.m.*, **campeggiatríce**, *s.f.* camper.

campéggio[1], *s.m.* 1. (*accampamento*) camping 2. (*terreno su cui campeggiare*) camping ground.

campéggio[2], *s.m.* (*bot.*) logwood.

camperéccio, *ag.* rural, rustic.

campèstre, *ag.* rural, rustic; country (*attributivo*): *abitudini campestri*, rural customs; *vita* —, rural life.

campicchiàre, *v.i.* to live from hand to mouth.

Campidòglio (il), *s.m.* the Capitol.

campièllo, *s.m.* (*dial.*) " campiello " (small square in Venice).

campionàre, *v.t.* to sample.

campionàrio, *ag.*: *fiera campionaria* —, sample (*o* trade) fair.

campionàrio, *s.m.* collection of samples, set of samples; sample-case; (*di stoffe*) sample-book, pattern-book: *il* — *più recente*, the latest pattern-book.

campionàto, *s.m.* championship: *egli vinse il* — *di tennis*, he won the tennis championship.

campióne, *s.m.* 1. (*comm.*) sample, specimen; (*di tessuti*) pattern: — *di controllo*, standard sample; — *estratto in monte*, average sample; *campioni di merce spedita*, shipment samples; *a titolo di* —, *come* —, as a sample; *la vostra merce non corrisponde, non è conforme al* —, your goods are not up to sample; *prelevare i campioni*, to sample; *spedire come* — *senza valore*, to send by sample-post 2. (*spor.*) champion: — *di nuoto*, champion swimmer; *ecco il futuro* — !, *ecco un* — *in erba* !, here's the budding champion ! 3. (*sostenitore*) champion: — *della libertà*, champion of freedom 4. (*poet.*) hero.

campionéssa, *s.f.* championess.

càmpo, *s.m.* 1. field: — *di grano*, corn-field; *campi e prati*, fields and meadows 2. *fig.* (*sfera di attività, di conoscenza*) field, sphere, range: *il* — *dei nostri affari è ancora molto limitato*, the range of our business is still quite limited (*o* restricted); *è un'autorità nel suo* —, he is an authority in his own field ‖ *dare* — *a qlcu. di fare...*, (*il tempo necessario*) to give s.o. time for doing...; (*l'occasione*) to give s.o. the opportunity to do... ‖ *mettere, portare in* —, to bring up (for discussion) 3. (*mil.*) field; (*accampamento*) camp: — *di battaglia*, battle-field; *aiutante di* —, aide-de-camp; *artiglieria da* —, field-artillery; *lettino da* —, camp-bed; *ospedale da* —, field hospital; *fu decorato di medaglia d'oro sul* —, he was awarded a gold medal on the field; *morì sul* —, he died in battle (*o* in action); *essere al* —, to camp; *levare il* —, to break up the camp (*o* to decamp) ‖ *in* — *aperto*, in the open (field) 4. (*aer.*) airfield: — *d'atterraggio*, landing-ground; — *di fortuna*, emergency landing-ground 5. (*spor.*): — *delle corse*, race-course; — *di giuoco*, playground; — *di golf*, golf-course (*o* links); — *sportivo*, sports (*o* athletic ground); — *di tennis*, tennis court 6. (*miner.*) field: — *aurifero*, gold field; — *petrolifero*, oil field 7. (*ott.*): — *angolare*, angle of view; — *visivo*, field of vision 8. (*elett.*) field: — *magnetico*, magnetic field; — *rotante*, rotating field 9. — *d'onda*, (*rad.*) wave band 10. (*arald.*) field: *un leone rampante di nero in* — *d'argento*, argent a lion rampant sable 11. (*pitt.*) background.

camposànto, *s.m.* cemetery; (*presso la chiesa*) churchyard.

camuffàre, *v.t.* to disguise; (*mimetizzare*) to camouflage; (*mascherare*) to mask: *il nemico camuffò i cannoni con rami*, the enemy camouflaged his guns with branches; — *la verità*, to camouflage the truth ‖ **camuffàrsi**, *v.r.* to disguise oneself (as s.o., sthg.): — *da clown*, to disguise oneself as a clown.

camúso, *ag.* 1. snub: *naso* —, snub nose 2. (*dal naso camuso*) snub-nosed: *un bimbo* —, a snub-nosed child.

canadése, *ag.s.c.* Canadian.

canàglia, *s.f.* 1. (*infima plebe*) rabble; canaille, riff-raff 2. (*persona malvagia, vile*) scoundrel, cad, rascal: *che* — *quel ragazzo!* what a rascal that boy is!.

canagliàta, *s.f.* dirty trick, scoundrelly action.

canagliésco, *ag.* rascally, scoundrelly, rowdy.

canagliúme, *s.m.* rabble, canaille, riff-raff, scum.

canàle, *s.m.* 1. canal: — *navigabile*, shipway (*o* ship-canal) ‖ *il Canale di San Lorenzo*, the St. Lorenzo Waterway ‖ *il Canale di Suez*, the Suez Canal 2. (*braccio di mare*) channel: *il Canale della Manica*, the English Channel (*o* the Channel) 3. (*condotto*) pipe, tube: — *di gronda*, gutter; — *di scolo*, drain; — *di scolo per fognatura*, sewer 4. (*anat. bot.*) canal, duct: — *biliare*, biliary duct.

canalícolo, *s.m.* (*anat.*) canaliculus (*pl.* canaliculi).

canalizzàre, *v.t.* to canalize: — *un fiume*, to canalize a river.

canalizzazióne, *s.f.* canalization.

canalóne, *s.m.* gully.

cànapa, *s.f.* hemp: *capelli color* —, hempen hair; *tela di* —, hempen cloth.

canapàia, *s.f.* 1. hemp-field 2. (*imbroglio*) fix.

canapàio, *s.m.* hemp-dresser.

cànape[1], *s.f.* hemp.

canapè[2], *s.m.* sofa.

canapifício, *s.m.* hemp mill.

canapina, *s.f.* hempen cloth.

canapíno, *ag.* hempen ‖ *s.m.* hemp-dresser.

cànapo, *s.m.* hempen rope.

canàpule, *s.m.* hemp stalk.

Canàrie (le), *no.pr.f.pl.* (*geog.*) the Canary Islands, the Canaries.

canaríno, *ag.* canary-coloured ‖ *s.m.* (*ornit.*) canary ‖ *mangiare come un* —, to have the appetite of a sparrow.

canàsta, *s.f.* canasta: *giocare a* —, to play canasta.

canàta, *s.f.* 1. (*mascalzonata*) scoundrelly action, nasty trick, vile trick 2. (*rabbuffo*) reprimand.

canavàccio, *V.* **canovàccio**.

cancan, *s.m.* 1. French cancan 2. (*chiassata*) sensation, noise: *fare un* —, to make a sensation.

cancaneggiàre, *v.i.* to make an uproarious noise.

cancellàbile, *ag.* effaceable.

cancellaménto, *s.m.* cancelling, cancellation.

cancellàre, *v.t.* 1. (*con un tratto di penna*) to cross out; (*con una gomma*) to rub out; (*con un raschietto*) to scratch out; (*con uno strofinaccio*) to wipe out, to sponge out: *lo cancellai con un sol tratto*, I crossed it out with a single stroke 2. *fig.* to obliterate, to efface, to sponge out: *ciò fu completamente cancellato dalla sua mente*, this was sponged clean from his mind 3. (*comm. dir.*) to cancel: — *un contratto*, to cancel a contract; — *un'ordinazione*, to cancel an order.

cancellàta, *s.f.* railing.

cancellatúra, *s.f.* 1. erasure 2. *fig.* obliteration, effacement.

cancellazióne, *s.f.* annulment; cancellation.

cancellerésco, *ag.* legal; chancery (*attributivo*): *scrittura cancelleresca*, chancery writing; *termine* —, legal term.

cancellería, *s.f.* 1. (*pol.*) chancellery, chancellory, chancery 2. (*di tribunale*) record-office 3. (*articoli di*) —, stationery (articles) (*o* writing-materials): *fabbricanti di articoli di* —, manufacturing stationers.

cancellieràto, *s.m.* chancellorship.

cancellière, *s.m.* 1. chancellor: *il* — *austriaco*, the Austrian Chancellor ‖ *Cancelliere dello Scacchiere*, Chancellor of the Exchequer; *Gran Cancelliere*, Lord (High) Chancellor 2. (*di tribunale*) registrar, recorder.

cancèllo, *s.m.* gate ‖ *comperare, vendere a* — *chiuso*, to buy, to sell lock, stock and barrel.

canceróso, *ag.* cancerous.

cànchero, *s.m.* 1. (*patol.*) cancer 2. (*malanno abituale*) habitual ailment 3. *fig.* (*persona molesta*) troublesome fellow; bore.

cancrèna, *s.f.* (*patol.*) gangrene: *il lusso e l'ambizione sono la* — *delle nostre famiglie*, *fig.* luxury and ambition are the plague of our families; *andare in* —, to gangrene.

cancrenàre, *v.i.*, **cancrenàrsi**, *v.r.* to gangrene.

cancrenóso, *ag.* gangrenous.

Cànero, *no.pr.m.* (*astr.*) Cancer, Crab ‖ *il Tropico del* —, the Tropic of Cancer ‖ **cànero**, *s.m.* (*patol.*) cancer, malignant tumor: *morì di* — *al polmone*, he died of cancer of the lung.

candeggiàre, *v.t.* to bleach, to whiten.

candeggína, *s.f.* (*fam.*) chloride.

candéggio, *s.m.* (*ind.*) bleaching.

candéla, *s.f.* 1. candle: — *di sego*, tallow candle; — *romana*, Roman candle; — *sottile*, taper; — *vergine*, new candle; *al lume di* —, by candlelight ‖ *il giuoco non vale la* —, the game is not worth the candle ‖ *puoi accendere una* — *alla Madonna!*, (*fam.*) you've had a narrow escape! ‖ *precipitare in* —, (*aer.*) to nose-dive; *salire in* —, (*aer.*) to rocket ‖ *struggersi come una* —,

fig. to grow very pale and thin 2. (*elett.*) candle, candela: *quante candele ha questa lampada?*, what is the candle-power of this lamp? 3. (*aut.*) sparking plug; (*amer.*) spark plug.

candelàbro, *s.m.* branched candlestick, candelabrum (*pl.* candelabra, candelabrums).

candelàio, *s.m.* 1. (*chi fabbrica candele*) candle-maker 2. (*chi vende candele*) candle-seller.

candelière, *s.m.* 1. candlestick 2. (*mar.*) stanchion.

candelòra, *s.f.* (*eccl.*) Candlemas.

candelòtto, *s.m.* short thick candle: — *fumogeno*, smoke candle.

candènte, *ag.* (*letter.*) 1. (*rilucente*) bright, shining 2. (*arroventato*) candescent.

candescènte, *V.* **incandescènte**.

Càndida, *no.pr.f.* Candida.

candidaménte, *av.* 1. (*innocentemente*) innocently 2. (*con franchezza*) candidly, frankly 3. (*ingenuamente*) ingenuously, naively.

candidàto, *s.m.* candidate: *il* — *liberale*, (*pol.*) the Liberal candidate; *all'esame finale c'erano 50 candidati*, there were 50 candidates at the final examinations.

candidatúra, *s.f.* candidature: *chi sosterrà la mia* —?, who will support (*o* back) my candidature?.

candidézza, *V.* **candóre**.

càndido, *ag.* 1. snow-white, white; (*lucente*) bright 2. (*senza macchia*) spotless 3. (*innocente*) innocent 4. (*franco, schietto*) candid, frank 5. (*ingenuo*) ingenuous, naive.

candíre, *v.t.* 1. (*ind. alimentare*) to refine, to crystallize: — *lo zucchero*, to refine sugar 2. (*frutti*) to candy.

candíto, *ag.* candied: *frutti canditi*, candied fruit ‖ *s.m.* candy, sugar candy.

candóre, *s.m.* 1. whiteness 2. (*innocenza*) innocence 3. (*franchezza*) candour 4. (*ingenuità*) ingenuousness.

càne, *s.m.* 1. dog: — *barbone*, poodle; — *bassotto*, dachshund; — *bastardo*, mongrel; — *da caccia*, sporting dog; (*per caccia a cavallo*) hound; — *da ferma*, setter; — *da guardia*, watch-dog; — *da pagliaio*, watch-dog (*o* cur); — *da pastore*, sheep-dog; — *da punta*, pointer; — *da salotto*, lap-dog; — *da slitta*, husky; — *levriere*, greyhound; — *poliziotto*, police dog; — *S. Bernardo*, St. Bernard(dog); *una muta di cani* (*da caccia*), a pack of hounds; *aizzare un* — *contro qlcu.*, to set a dog on s.o. ‖ — *grosso*, *fig.* big shot (*o* big noise) ‖ *il Cane Maggiore*, (*astr.*) the Greater Dog; *il Cane Minore*, (*astr.*) the Lesser Dog ‖ *fatica da cani*, very hard work ‖ *roba da cani*, loathsome stuff ‖ *tempo da cani*, beastly weather ‖ *è fortunato come un* — *in chiesa*, he is quite unlucky (*o* he has not a dog's chance); *fui accolto come un* — *in chiesa*, I was as welcome as snow in harvest ‖ *non trovai un* —, *fig.* I did not find a single soul ‖ *andare d'accordo come* — *e gatto*, to live a cat-and-dog life (*o* to be like cat and dog) ‖ *drizzare le gambe ai cani*, *fig.* to attempt a hopeless task ‖ *essere solo come un* —, to be quite lonely and miserable ‖ *fare una vita da cani*, to lead a dog's life ‖ *menare il can per l'aia*, to beat about the bush (*o* not to come to the point) ‖ *morire come un* —, to die like a dog (*o* to die a dog's death) ‖ *can che abbaia non morde*, *prov.* barking dogs don't bite (*o* his bark is worse than his bite) ‖ — *non mangia* —, *prov.* dogs do not eat dog (*o* honour amongst thieves) ‖ *non toccare il can che dorme*, *prov.* let sleeping dogs lie 2. (*persona spregevole*): *brutto* —!, dirty dog! (*o* you dog!) 3. (*persona spietata*): *che* —!, what a brute!; *è un* —, he is very hard-hearted 4. (*spreg.*) (*pessimo attore*) bad actor; (*pessimo cantante*) bad singer 5. (*del fucile*) cock 6. (*mec.*) catch.

canèa, *s.f.* 1. (*muta*) pack of hounds 2. *fig.* (*invettive, clamore*) uproar, loud invective.

canèfora, *s.f.* canephora (*pl.* canephorae).

canèstra, *s.f.* round wicker basket.

canestràio, *s.m.* 1. (*chi fabbrica canestri*) basket-maker 2. (*chi vende canestri*) basket-seller.

canestràta, *s.f.* basketful.

canèstro, *s.m.* **1.** basket; (*con coperchio*) hamper **2.** (*il contenuto*) basketful: *un — di pesche*, a basketful of peaches.

cànfora, *s.f.* camphor.

canforàto, *ag.* camphoric; (*trattato con canfora*) camphorated: *olio —*, (*farm.*) camphorated oil.

cangiàbile, *ag.* changeable.

cangiaménto, *s.m.* (*letter.*) change.

cangiànte, *ag.* changing: *colore —*, iridescent colour; *seta —*, shot silk.

cangiàre, *v.t.* (*letter.*) to change, to alter ‖ *v.i.*, **cangiàrsi**, *v.r.* to change; (*trasformarsi*) to transform oneself (into s.o., sthg.); to be transformed (into s.o., sthg.).

cangùro, *s.m.* (*zool.*) kangaroo.

canicola, *s.f.* **1.** (*calura estiva*) the height of summer: *i giorni della —*, the dog-days **2.** (*astr.*) Canicula, Sirius, Dog-star.

canicolàre, *ag.* **1.** extremely hot: *i giorni canicolari*, the dog-days **2.** (*astr.*) canicular.

canìle, *s.m.* kennel; (*fam.*) dog-house.

canìno[1], *ag.* canine: *dente —*, canine (*o* eye-) tooth; *rabbia canina*, hydrophobia ‖ *rosa canina*, dogrose (*o* brier-rose) ‖ *tosse canina*, (w)hooping-cough.

canìno[2], *s.m.* **1.** (*cucciolo*) puppy **2.** (*cagnolino*) little dog; small dog.

canìzie, *s.f.* **1.** white hair; hoariness **2.** *fig.* (*vecchiaia*) old age.

canìzza, *s.m.* **1.** (*di cani*) insistent barking **2.** *fig.* (*l'accanirsi dei critici*) snarling.

cànna, *s.f.* **1.** (*selvatica*) reed; (*coltivata*) cane; (*da fiori, indica*) canna: *— da zucchero*, sugar-cane; *— d'India, di bambù*, bamboo cane; *si udiva un fruscìar di canne in riva al lago*, a rustling of reeds was heard on the lake shore ‖ *povero —*, destitute (*o* extremely poor *o* as poor as a church mouse) **2.** (*di fucile*) (gun-)barrel; (*da pesca*) (fishing-)rod **3.** (*tubo*) pipe: *— della gola*, windpipe; *— d'organo*, organ pipe **4.** (*bastone*) cane, stick **5.** canna (*pl.* canne) (*misura di lunghezza variabile*).

cannabìsmo, *s.m.* (*patol.*) cannabism.

cannàio, *s.m.* screen of reeds (on which fruit is dried).

canneggiàre, *v.t.* to measure (sthg.) with a cane.

cannèlla[1], *s.f.* spout; (*di botte*) spigot.

cannèlla[2], *s.f.* (*bot. cuc.*) cinnamon: *color —*, hazel colour.

cannèllo, *s.m.* **1.** (*per saldatura, taglio*) torch, blowpipe; (*chim.*) pipe: *— ferruminatorio*, blowpipe; *— ossiacetilenico*, oxyacetylene torch **2.** (*ind. tessile*) quill **3.** (*artigl.*) primer **4.** (*di penna*) penholder **5.** (*arch.*) cabling.

cannellóni, *s.m.pl.* (*cuc.*) "cannelloni" (kind of big macaroni).

cannéto, *s.m.* reed thicket; cane-brake; (*se coltivato*) cane field.

canníbale, *s.m.* cannibal.

cannibalìsmo, *s.m.* cannibalism.

cannicciàta, *s.f.* trellis.

cannìccio, *s.m.* (*ripiano a graticcio di canne*) reed grating.

cannìzza, *s.f.* (*mar.*) "cannizza" (kind of raft used by fishermen in Abruzzi).

cannocchiàle, *s.m.* **1.** binoculars (*pl.*); glasses (*pl.*): *— da campagna*, field-glasses; *— da teatro*, opera-glasses **2.** (*telescopio*) telescope.

cannòlo, *s.m.* (*cuc.*) "cannolo" (Sicilian pastry filled with cream).

cannonàta, *s.f.* **1.** (*colpo di cannone*) gun-shot **2.** (*rimbombo*) report of gunfire **3.** *è una —!*, (*fam.*) it's a smasher! (*o* it's smashing!).

cannoncìno, *s.m.* **1.** (*artigl.*) light gun **2.** (*cuc.*) "cannoncino" (Italian pastry filled with custard).

cannóne, *s.m.* **1.** (*artigl.*) gun; (*di vecchio tipo*) cannon (*pl.* cannon, cannons): *— antiaereo*, anti-aircraft gun; *— anticarro*, anti-tank gun; *— da campagna*, field gun;

— pesante, heavy gun; *affusto di —*, gun-carriage; *palla di —*, cannon-ball **2.** (*fam.*) (*chi si distingue in una determinata attività*) ace: *è un — in latino*, he is awfully good at Latin; *sei un —!*, you're an ace! **3.** (*tubo*) pipe, tube: *— della stufa*, stove-pipe **4.** (*piega di abito*) pleat: *sottana a cannoni*, box pleated skirt.

cannoneggiaménto, *s.m.* cannonade.

cannoneggiàre, *v.t.* to cannonade, to shell, to bomb ‖ *v.i.* to cannonade.

cannonièra, *s.f.* **1.** (*mar.*) gunboat: *— silurante*, torpedo boat **2.** (*mil.*) (*feritoia*) embrasure.

cannonière, *s.m.* (*mil.*) gunner.

cannúccia, *s.f.* **1.** (*canna sottile*) thin cane; (*per sorbire bibite*) straw **2.** (*di pipa*) stem **3.** (*di penna*) penholder **4.** (*tubicino*) small tube.

cànnula *s.f.* (*med.*) cannula (*pl.* cannulae).

canòa, *s.f.* canoe: *andare in —*, to canoe.

cànone, *s.m.* **1.** (*regola*) canon; fundamental rule **2.** (*eccl.*) canon **3.** (*somma da pagare*) fee; rent: *— agricolo*, ground rent; *— d'affitto*, rent; *— della radio*, radio-licence fee **4.** (*mus.*) canon.

canònica, *s.f.* rectory; parsonage.

canonicàle, *ag.* canonical.

canonicaménte, *av.* canonically.

canonicàto, *s.m.* **1.** canonry **2.** (*sinecura*) sinecure.

canonicità, *s.f.* canonicity.

canònico, *ag.* canonical: *diritto —*, canon law; *libri canonici*, canonical books; *ore canoniche*, (*eccl.*) canonical hours ‖ *ora canonica*, *fig.* (*ora, momento opportuno*) canonical hour ‖ *s.m.* canon: *— minore*, minor canon; *— regolare*, canon regular.

canonìsta, *s.m.* canonist.

canonizzàre, *v.t.* **1.** to canonize **2.** (*riconoscere come normale*) to sanction; to recognize as regular.

canonizzazióne, *s.f.* canonization.

Canòpo, *no.pr.m.* (*astr.*) Canopus ‖ **canòpo**, *s.m.* (*archeol.*) Canopus (*pl.* Canopi); Canopic vase.

canoraménte, *av.* melodiously; canorously.

canòro, *ag.* singing, canorous: *uccello —*, singing bird.

Canòssa, *no.pr.f.* (*geog.*) Canossa ‖ *andare a —*, (*umiliarsi*) to abase oneself (*o* to eat humble pie).

canottàggio, *s.m.* rowing; boating; (*come attività sportiva*) boat-racing: *gara di —*, boat-race; *ti piace fare del —?*, do you like boating?.

canottièra, *s.f.* **1.** (*maglietta*) vest, singlet **2.** (*paglietta*) straw-hat.

canottière, *s.m.* oarsman (*pl.* oarsmen); rower ‖ *circolo canottieri*, boating club.

canòtto, *s.m.* **1.** (*piccola barca*) small boat, rowing boat, row-boat **2.** (*canoa*) canoe.

cànova, *s.f.* **1.** (*rivendita di vino*) wine-shop **2.** (*cantina*) wine-cellar **3.** (*dispensa*) larder; pantry.

canovàccio, *s.m.* **1.** (*per asciugare stoviglie*) dish-cloth **2.** (*per ricamo*) canvas **3.** (*trama di un'opera*) plot **4.** (*schema sommario di dramma*) cadre: *commedia a —*, dramatic improvisation.

canovàio, *s.m.* cellarer.

cansàre, *v.t.* **1.** (*metter da parte*) to set aside; to save **2.** (*scansare, evitare*) to avoid, to shun ‖ **cansàrsi**, *v.r.* to make way.

cantàbile, *ag.* **1.** singable **2.** (*mus.*) cantabile ‖ *s.m.* (*mus.*) cantabile.

cantafàvola, *s.f.* **1.** fable, fairy tale **2.** (*storia inverosimile*) cock-and-bull story.

cantambànco, *s.m.* **1.** (*chi canta per le strade*) street ballad-singer **2.** (*saltimbanco*) tumbler **3.** (*ciarlatano*) quacksalver; mountebank, charlatan.

cantànte, *s.c.* singer.

cantàre, *v.i.* **1.** to sing: *— a orecchio*, to sing by ear; *— a voce bassa*, to sing low; *— a voce spiegata*, to sing out; *— bene*, to sing well; *— come i montanari tirolesi*, to yodel; *— con accompagnamento di piano*, to sing to the piano **2.** (*del gallo*) to crow; (*della gallina*) to cackle; (*degli uccelli in genere*) to sing; (*cinguettare*) to chirp **3.** (*fare la spia*) to squeal; to give away one's accomplices ‖ *far — qlcu.*, to make s.o. speak out (*o* to get s.o. to disclose a secret) **4.** (*cigolare, scricchiolare*) to sing ‖ *v.t.* **1.** (*esprimere col canto*) to sing: *cantami quella canzone*, sing me that song (*o* sing that song for me); — *canti di chiesa*, to chant; — *una canzone a bocca chiusa*, to hum a song; — *messa*, to sing mass ‖ *cantarla chiara*, to speak one's mind ‖ — *sempre la stessa canzone*, to harp on the same string ‖ — *vittoria su qlcu.*, to crow over a defeated enemy **2.** (*celebrare, specialmente con versi*) to sing, to celebrate in verse, to write verses on (s.o., sthg.): — *le lodi di qlcu.*, to sing s.o.'s praises (*o* to praise s.o. enthusiastically); — *il mare, la bellezza della natura*, to sing the sea, the beauty of Nature.

cantàre, *s.m.* **1.** (*modo di cantare*) singing **2.** (*canzone*) song; strain **3.** (*poema in ottava rima*) cantare (*pl.* cantari).

cantàride, *s.f.* (*entom.*) cantharis (*pl.* cantharides); blister-beetle.

cantarína, *s.f.* (*farm.*) cantharides (*pl.*).

càntaro, *s.m.* **1.** cantharus (*pl.* canthari) **2.** (*vaso da notte*) chamber-pot.

cantastòrie, *s.m.* street singer, ballad-singer.

cantàta, *s.f.* **1.** song, singing **2.** (*mus.*) cantata.

cantàto, *ag.* sung ‖ *messa cantata*, high mass.

cantatóre, *ag.* singing ‖ *s.m.* **1.** singer, songster **2.** (*uccello di richiamo*) decoy, call-bird.

cantatríce, *s.f.* **1.** singer, songstress **2.** (*di professione*) cantatrice (*pl.* cantatrici, cantatrices).

canteràno, *s.m.* chest of drawers.

canterellàre, *v.t.i.* to sing softly, to sing to oneself; to hum.

canterellío, *s.m.* humming.

canterína, *s.f.* popular singer.

canteríno, *ag.* singing, warbling: *grillo —*, chirping cricket; *uccello —*, song-bird, songster ‖ *s.m.* popular singer.

càntero, *V.* **càntaro**.

càntica, *s.f.* (*poes.*) poem, song ‖ *le tre cantiche della Divina Commedia*, the three parts (*o* divisions) of the Divine Comedy.

canticchiàre, *v.t.i.* to sing softly, to sing to oneself; to hum.

càntico, *s.m.* canticle; hymn ‖ *« Il Cantico dei Cantici »*, (*Bibbia*) "The Song of Songs" (*o* "The Song of Solomon" *o* "The Canticles").

cantière, *s.m.* yard; (*mar.*) dockyard, shipyard, (*amer.*) navy yard; — *di costruzione*, erecting yard; — *di raddobbo*, (*mar.*) refitting yard; — *stradale*, road yard; *in —*, on the stocks.

cantilèna, *s.f.* **1.** sing-song; (*ninna nanna*) lullaby; (*filastrocca*) rigmarole **2.** (*tono di voce monotono*) sing-song **3.** (*discorso in tono monotono*) sing-song talk.

cantilenàre, *v.t.i.* to sing-song: — *le parole*, to sing-song one's words.

cantína, *s.f.* **1.** cellar: — *del carbone*, coal-cellar; — *del vino*, wine-cellar (*o* wine-vault); — *del vino imbottigliato*, bottle cellar; — *di deposito*, storage cellar; *avere una — ben fornita*, to keep a good cellar ‖ — *sociale*, cooperative store (for the sale of wine) **2.** (*rivendita di vino*) wineshop **3.** (*luogo buio e umido*) dark damp place.

cantinière, *s.m.* **1.** cellarman (*pl.* cellarmen); cellarer **2.** (*venditore di vino*) wineshop keeper **3.** (*vivandiere*) sutler.

cantíno, *s.m.* (*mus.*) chanterelle.

cànto[1], *s.m.* **1.** (*il cantare, l'arte del canto*) singing: *maestro di —*, singing-master; *mia sorella insegna —*, my sister teaches singing **2.** (*voce di animale*): — *di cicala, di grillo*, chirping of a cicada, of a cricket; — *di gallina*, cackle (*o* cackling) of a hen; — *di gallo*, cock-crow (*o* crowing of a cock); — *di uccelli*, warbling of birds ‖ — *del cigno*, *fig.* swan-song ‖ *al — del gallo*, at cock-crow **3.** (*musica vocale*) song; melody, air: —

di guerra, war-song; — *di Natale*, Christmas carol; — *di vittoria*, song of victory; — *fermo, gregoriano*, Gregorian chant (*o* plainsong); — *indiano*, Indian song **4.** (*poesia*) poem, lyric **5.** (*parte di un poema*) canto (*pl.* cantos).

cànto[2], *s.m.* **1.** (*angolo*) corner: *il — della strada*, the street-corner **2.** (*lato, parte*) side, hand: *dal — mio*, (*per parte mia*) for my part; (*quanto a me*) as for me; *d'altro —*, on the other hand; *da ogni —*, on all sides; *per ogni —*, everywhere; *fig.* on every hand; *porre da un —*, to put aside; (*trascurare*) to neglect **3.** (*spigolo*) angle, edge.

cantonàle, *ag.* cantonal ‖ *s.m.* (*edil.*) angle-iron.

cantonàta, *s.f.* **1.** (*di strada*) corner, street-corner ‖ *manifesto attaccato alla —*, poster fixed on the wall of the house **2.** (*errore grossolano*) blunder: *prendere una —*, to make a blunder (*o* to be grossly mistaken) **3.** (*tip.*) corner-frame.

cantóne[1], *s.m.* corner: *se non sarai obbediente, ti metterò nel —*, if you are naughty I'll put you in the corner ‖ *giocare ai quattro cantoni*, to play puss-in-the-corner.

cantóne[2], *s.m.* (*geog.*) district; (*della Svizzera*) canton: *i Cantoni svizzeri*, the Swiss Cantons ‖ *il Lago dei Quattro Cantoni*, the Lake of the Four Forest Cantons.

cantonièra, *s.f.* **1.** (*mobile d'angolo*) corner cupboard **2.** (*casa cantoniera*) roadman's house; (*casello ferroviario*) signalman's house.

cantonière, *s.m.* **1.** (*casellante ferroviario*) signalman (*pl.* signalmen); trackman (*pl.* trackmen) **2.** (*stradino*) roadman (*pl.* roadmen).

cantoràto, *s.m.* choristership.

cantóre, *s.m.* **1.** singer; (*eccl.*) chorister **2.** (*poeta*) poet.

cantoría, *s.f.* **1.** choir, chancel **2.** (*insieme di cantori*) choir.

cantoríno, *s.m.* handbook of plainsong.

cantúccio, *s.m.* **1.** (*angolo*) corner **2.** (*luogo appartato, tranquillo*) nook **3.** (*pezzetto*) bit: *un — di pane, di cacio*, a tiny bit of bread, of cheese.

canutézza, *s.f.* hoariness.

canutíglia, *s.f.* tinsel.

canutíre, *v.i.* to grow grey; to turn grey.

canúto, *ag.* white(-haired), hoary.

canzonàccia, *s.f.* coarse song, bawdy song.

canzonàre, *v.t.* **1.** to make fun of (s.o., sthg.), to ridicule, to laugh at (s.o., sthg.), to mock: — *qlcu.*, to make fun of s.o. (*o fam.* to pull s.o.'s leg) **2.** (*trarre in inganno*) to hoax; to take in ‖ *v.i.* to joke, to jest, to trifle.

canzonatóre, *ag.* mocking ‖ *s.m.* mocker, scoffer; hoaxer.

canzonatòrio, *ag.* mocking; scoffing.

canzonatríce, *s.f.* mocker, scoffer; hoaxer.

canzonatúra, *s.f.* mockery, ridicule, derision; hoax.

canzóne, *s.f.* **1.** song; ditty: — *napoletana*, Neapolitan song ‖ *è l'eterna —*, *fig.* it is the same old story **2.** (*poes.*) canzone (*pl.* canzoni); song: — *a ballo*, ballad.

canzonèlla, *s.f.* ridicule, mockery: *mettere in —*, to ridicule.

canzonétta, *s.f.* **1.** short song, ditty **2.** (*poes.*) canzonet, short lyric.

canzonettísta, *s.c.* **1.** music-hall singer **2.** (*autore di canzonette*) song-writer.

canzonière, *s.m.* **1.** (*poes.*) collection of poems, collection of ballads **2.** (*raccolta di canzoni*) song-book.

caolíno, *s.m.* (*min.*) kaolin.

càos, *s.m.* **1.** (*mit.*) chaos **2.** *fig.* (*estrema confusione*) chaos, confusion, jumble.

caòtico, *ag.* chaotic.

capàccio, *s.m.* **1.** pigheaded person; stubborn fellow, obstinate fellow **2.** (*persona ottusa*) blockhead, dullard.

capacciúto, *ag.* big-headed.

capàce, *ag.* **1.** able: *chi sarà — di aiutarci?*, who will be able to help us?; *non fui assolutamente — di farlo*, I was quite unable to do it; *non si sentiva — di affrontare la situazione*, he did not feel equal (o he felt unequal) to (facing) the situation ‖ *è — di piovere*, it may (o might) rain **2.** (*atto, idoneo*) fit (for sthg.) **3.** (*disposto ad un'azione anche cattiva*) capable: *sarebbe capacissimo di imbrogliarmi*, he would be quite capable of cheating me **4.** (*abile, esperto*) clever; skilled, skilful; expert, competent: *un medico —*, a clever physician **5.** (*persuaso*) persuaded: *far — qlcu. di ql.co.*, to persuade s.o. of sthg. **6.** (*ampio, spazioso*) large, wide, spacious, capacious, roomy, ample: *una valigia —*, a large suit-case.

capacità, *s.f.* **1.** (*abilità*) ability, capability, talent; (*intelligenza*) cleverness; abilities (*pl.*); (*perizia*) skill, skilfulness: *uomo di grande —*, very able man; *avere la — di fare ql.co.*, to be qualified to do sthg. **2.** (*dir.*) (legal) capacity, (legal) competency, (legal) ability **3.** (*contenenza*) capacity; capaciousness: *misure di —*, measures of capacity; *questo teatro ha una — di duemila posti*, this theatre has a seating capacity of two thousand **4.** (*fis.*) capacity: *— elettrostatica*, (*elett.*) electrostatic (o distributed) capacitance; *— termica*, thermal (o heat) capacity.

capacitàre, *v.t.* **1.** to persuade, to convince **2.** (*rassicurare*) to reassure **3.** (*ispirare fiducia a*) to inspire with confidence ‖ **capacitàrsi**, *v.r.* to be persuaded: *non riesco a capacitarmi di come ciò sia potuto accadere*, I cannot make out how it could have happened.

capànna, *s.f.* **1.** hut, cabin **2.** (*tugurio*) hut, poor dwelling, hovel, shanty.

capannèllo, *s.m.* group of persons, small crowd.

capànno, *s.m.* **1.** (*da caccia*) shooting-box **2.** (*pergola*) arbour, bower **3.** (*cabina per bagnanti*) bathing-box.

capannóne, *s.m.* **1.** shed **2.** (*aer.*) hangar.

caparbiaménte, *av.* stubbornly, obstinately.

caparbietà, *s.f.* stubbornness, obstinacy.

capàrbio, *ag.* stubborn, obstinate: *— come un mulo*, as stubborn as a mule.

capàrra, *s.f.* **1.** earnest (-money), caution-money: *dare una —*, to give earnest money; *dare la — per fissare il contratto*, to give money in part payment to bind a bargain; *dare una somma come —*, to give an amount of money in earnest **2.** *fig.* (*pegno*) pledge.

capàta, *s.f.* **1.** knock, blow with the head: *battere, dare una — in ql.co.*, to butt (o to knock one's head) against sthg. **2.** (*breve visita*) call, brief visit.

capatína, *s.f.* call, brief visit: *fare, dare una — (in un posto, da qlcu.)*, to call (at a place, on s.o.): *fate una — (da noi) a prendere il tè!*, do drop in to tea!; *ho fatto una — nel suo ufficio*, I called (o dropped in) at his office; *tutti i giorni fa una — da me*, every day he calls (o drops in) on me.

capécchio, *s.m.* hards (*pl.*); hurds (*pl.*); (*stoppa*) tow.

capeggiàre, *v.t.* to lead, to head: *si sa per certo che fu lui a — la rivolta*, it is known for certain that he headed the revolt.

capeggiatóre, *s.m.* leader.

capellatúra, *s.f.* (*rar.*) hair (*solo sing.*).

capellièra, *s.f.* **1.** (*letter.*) (*capigliatura*) hair (*solo sing.*) **2.** (*parrucca*) wig; (*capelli posticci*) false hair.

capéllo, *s.m.* hair; (*capigliatura*) hair (*solo sing.*): *capelli biondi*, fair hair; *capelli d'oro*, golden hair; *capelli lisci*, smooth hair; *capelli neri*, dark hair; *capelli ondulati*, wavy hair; *capelli ricciuti*, curly hair; *acconciatura di capelli*, hairdress (o "coiffure" o fam. hair-do); *forcina per capelli*, hair-pin; *rigeneratore dei capelli*, hair-restorer; *spazzola per capelli*, hair-brush; *spessore di un —*, hair's breadth; *taglio di capelli*, hair-cut; *ecco un — bianco!*, here is a grey hair!; *ella portava i capelli lunghi sulle spalle*, she had long hair falling over her shoulders; *ho trovato tre capelli nella minestra!*, I've found three hairs in my soup!; *i miei capelli si fanno grigi*, my hair is getting grey (o is greying);

portava i capelli molto corti, she wore her hair very short (o she had bobbed hair); *farsi tagliare i capelli*, to have one's hair cut (o to get a hair-cut); *raccogliersi i capelli sulla nuca*, to put up one's hair; *sciogliersi i capelli*, to let down one's hair; *strapparsi i capelli (per la disperazione)*, to tear one's hair (in desperation); *tirare i capelli a qlcu.*, to pull s.o.'s hair; *trascinare qlcu. per i capelli*, to drag s.o. by the hair (anche *fig.*) ‖ *capelli d'angelo*, (*cuc.*) fine vermicelli ‖ *a —*, to a hair (o exactly o perfectly): *l'hai descritto a —*, you have described him to a hair; *ti sta a —*, it suits you perfectly ‖ *fino ai capelli*, up to one's eyes (o to the extreme limit) ‖ *in capelli*, bare-headed ‖ *ella aveva un diavolo per —*, she was furious ‖ *fui a un — dall'essere bocciato*, I was within a hair's breadth of being ploughed ‖ *mi si rizzarono i capelli (in capo)*, my hair stood on end; *far rizzare i capelli a qlcu.*, to make s.o.'s hair stand on end ‖ *ne ho fin sopra i capelli!*, I have had quite enough (o I am sick) of it! ‖ *non ti torcerò un —*, I shall not hurt you at all (o I shall not hurt a single hair of your head) ‖ *si salvò per un —*, he escaped by a hair's breadth (o he had a hairbreadth escape o he escaped by the skin of his teeth o he had a narrow escape) ‖ *essere indebitato fin sopra i capelli*, to be up to one's ears in debt ‖ *fare i capelli bianchi in un lavoro*, to age on a job ‖ *spaccare un — in quattro*, to split hairs.

capellúto, *ag.* (*che ha capelli*) hairy, hirsute; (*che ha capelli lunghi*) long-haired ‖ *cuoio —*, scalp.

capelvènere, *s.m.* (*bot.*) maidenhair.

capèstro, *s.m.* **1.** halter, rope: *uomo da —*, gallows-bird; *mandare qlcu. al —*, to sentence s.o. to death by hanging (o to condemn s.o. to be hanged) **2.** (*cordiglio dei frati francescani*) Franciscan girdle.

capetíngio, *ag.* Capetian.

Capèto, *no.pr.* (*st.*) Capet.

capezzàle, *s.m.* bolster: *al — di qlcu.*, at s.o.'s bedside.

capezzàta, *s.f.* (*edil.*) upper part (of a wall, of a building).

capezzièra, *s.f.* antimacassar.

capézzolo, *s.m.* **1.** nipple, teat; (*di animale*) dug, teat **2.** (*tettarella*) nipple; (baby's) dummy, comforter.

capidòglio, *s.m.* (*zool.*) sperm-whale.

capiènte, *ag.* holding, containing.

capiènza, *s.f.* capacity.

capifòsso, *s.m.* (*agr.*) main ditch.

capigliatúra, *s.f.* hair (*solo sing.*).

capillàre, *ag.* capillary: *vaso —*, (*anat.*) capillary vessel.

capillariscopía, *s.f.* (*med.*) capillaroscopy.

capillarità, *s.f.* (*fis.*) capillarity.

capinéra, *s.f.* (*ornit.*) blackcap.

capíre, *v.t.* to understand; (*accertare, stabilire*) to make out; (*rendersi conto di*) to realize: *capii allora perchè me lo avessero detto*, I realized then why they had told me so; *capisci l'inglese?*, can you understand English?; *gli feci — che non era gradito*, I made him understand he wasn't welcome; *non capisco nulla*, I cannot make head or tail of it; *non riesco a — di che si tratti*, I cannot make out what it is ‖ *farsi —*, to make oneself understood ‖ *v.i.* to be contained: *non — nella pelle dalla gioia*, to be beside oneself with joy.

capitàgna, *s.f.* (*agr.*) headland; ridge.

capitàle, *ag.* **1.** (*che riguarda la vita*) capital: *pena —*, capital punishment: *questo delitto è punito con la pena —*, this crime is punished with death; *sentenza —*, capital sentence **2.** (*mortale*) mortal: *nemico —*, mortal enemy ‖ *peccato —*, deadly sin **3.** (*principale*) main (*attributivo*); chief (*attributivo*); principal, essential; fundamental: *la città —*, the chief town; *il punto — del problema*, the main point of the question; *il problema è di — importanza per noi*, the question is of vital (o great) importance to us **4.** *lettera —*, (*tip.*) capital letter ‖ *s.f.* capital (city): *Parigi è la — della Francia*, Paris is the capital of France; *Parigi, Roma* *e Madrid sono capitali*, Paris, Rome and Madrid are capital cities ‖ *s.m.* (*comm.*) capital: — *a fondo perduto*, sunk capital; — *azionario*, share capital; — *circolante*, floating (*o circolating*) capital; — *d'esercizio*, working capital; — *di maneggio*, trading capital; — *e interessi*, principal and interest; — *fisso*, fixed capital; — *immobile*, real estate (*o* realty); — *interamente versato*, fully paid-up capital; — *mobile*, movable goods; — *sociale*, company's capital; *manodopera e* —, capital and labour; *i capitali abbondano*, money is plentiful; *mettere dei capitali in un affare*, to put capital into a business ‖ *far* — *su ql.co.*, to count on sthg.; *far* — *su qlcu.*, to rely on s.o.

capitalísmo, *s.m.* capitalism.

capitalísta, *s.m.* 1. (*chi possiede grandi capitali*) capitalist 2. (*chi arrischia denaro in speculazioni*) investor; speculator.

capitalístico, *ag.* capitalistic.

capitalizzàre, *v.t.* to capitalize ‖ *v.i.* (*accumulare denaro*) to save, to put money by.

capitalizzazióne, *s.f.* capitalization.

capitalménte, *av.* mainly, chiefly, principally.

capitàna, *s.f.* (*mar.*) flag-ship.

capitanàre, *v.t.* to head; (*guidare*) to lead; (*comandare*) to command, to captain: — *una squadra di calcio*, to captain a football team.

capitanàto, *s.m.* captaincy.

capitanería, *s.f.* — (*di porto*), (*mar.*) harbour-office.

capitàno, *s.m.* 1. captain; leader, head: — *d'industria*, captain of industry; *ha la stoffa di un grande* —, he is cut out to be a leader of men 2. (*condottiero*) army leader: — *di ventura*, leader of mercenaries (*o* of soldiers of fortune) 3. (*mil. mar.*) captain; (*aer.*) flight lieutenant: — *di corvetta*, lieutenant commander; — *di fregata*, commander; — *di lungo corso*, sea captain; — *di nave mercantile*, master; — *di porto*, harbour master; — *di vascello*, captain; — *in seconda*, mate; *nel nostro esercito il* — *comanda una compagnia*, in our army a captain commands a company; *passare* —, (*di nave mercantile*) to obtain one's master's certificate; (*nell'esercito*) to be promoted captain 4. (*spor.*) captain, leader: — *di una squadra*, team captain.

capitàre, *v.i.* 1. (*venire, giungere*) to come (to a place); to arrive (at a place); (*fam.*) to turn up (at a place); *capitarono qui mentre meno li aspettavamo*, they came (*o* arrived *o* turned up) here when we least expected them ‖ — *bene*, (*essere fortunato*) to be lucky; — *male*, (*essere sfortunato*) to be unlucky 2. (*presentarsi, accadere*) to happen, to befall (s.o., sthg.), to chance (to do): *ecco quanto m'era capitato!*, here is what had happened to me!; *gli capitò una nuova disgrazia*, a new misfortune befell (*o* happened to) him; *mi capitò di rivederli alle corse*, I happened (*o* I chanced) to see them again at the races; *se capita l'occasione...*, if occasion offers....

capitèllo, *s.m.* (*arch.*) capital.

capitolàre[1], *ag.* (*eccl.*) capitular.

capitolàre[2], *s.m.* (*st.*) capitulary ‖ *Capitolari Carolingi*, Carolingian Capitularies.

capitolàre[3], *v.i.* to capitulate: *la città capitolò dopo tre mesi di assedio*, the town capitulated after a three months' siege.

capitolàto, *ag.* divided in chapters ‖ *s.m.* 1. (*condizioni specificate di un contratto*) specifications of a contract (*pl.*) 2. (*contratto*) contract.

capitolazióne, *s.f.* capitulation, surrender ‖ *le Capitolazioni*, (*st.*) the Capitulations.

capitolíno, *ag.* Capitolian, Capitoline ‖ *Colle Capitolino*, Capitoline (Hill).

capítolo, *s.m.* 1. chapter: *domani tratteremo il terzo* — *di questo libro*, we shall deal with the third chapter of this book to-morrow 2. (*articolo di una convenzione*) article; (*di bilancio*) item 3. (*eccl.*) chapter: *sala del* —, chapter-house ‖ *aver voce in* —, (*avere voce autorevole*) to have a say in a matter 4. (*lett.*) "capitolo" (kind of humorous composition in terza rima).

---

capitombolàre, *v.i.* to fall headlong, to tumble down: *capitombolò per le scale*, he fell headlong (*o* tumbled) down the stairs.

capitómbolo, *s.m.* 1. tumble, headlong fall: *fare un* —, to have a tumble (*o* to tumble down *o* to fall headlong) 2. (*di acrobata*) somersault, tumble.

capitombolóni, *av.* head over heels, headlong.

capitóne, *s.m.* (*ittiol.*) large eel.

càpo, *s.m.* 1. head: *a* — *alto*, with one's head held high; *fig.* proudly; *a* — *chino*, with drooping head; *a* — *scoperto*, bare-headed (*o* hatless); *da* — *a piedi*, from head to foot; (*di cosa*) from top to bottom; *ho mal di* —, *mi duole il* —, I have a headache, my head aches; *chinare il* —, to bend (*o* to bow) one's head; *fig.* to bow ‖ *un* — *ameno, scarico*, a jolly (*o* merry) fellow (*o* a wag) ‖ *una buona lavata di* —, a thorough dressing down (*o* scolding) ‖ *senza* — *nè coda*, without rhyme or reason: *un ragionamento senza* — *nè coda*, a nonsensical (*o* loose) reasoning ‖ *tra* — *e collo*, unexpectedly ‖ *toglitelo di* —!, put it out of your head ! ‖ *vuol fare di* — *suo*, he will have his own way ‖ *avere il* — *in ql.co.*, to be bent on sthg. ‖ *dare al* — *a qlcu.*, to turn (*o* to go to) s.o.'s head: *i tuoi successi ti hanno dato al* —, your successes have turned (*o* gone to) your head ‖ *mettere in* — *a qlcu.*, to put into s.o.'s head; *mettersi in* — *ql.co.*, to take (*o* to get) sthg. into one's head ‖ *non sapere dove battere il* —, to be at a loss ‖ *rompere il* — *a qlcu.*, *fig.* to bore s.o. to death ‖ *rompersi il* —, *fig.* to rack one's brains ‖ *togliere un'idea di* — *a qlcu.*, to put (*o* to get) an idea out of s.o.'s head 2. (*estremità, principio, fine*) end: *da un* — *all'altro*, from end to end; *in* — *a un mese*, within a month (*o* after a whole month); *sedevano ai due capi della tavola*, they were sitting at either end of the table ‖ *Capo d'Anno*, New Year's Day ‖ *a* —, (*dettando*) new line (*o* new paragraph): *andare a* —, to begin a new paragraph ‖ *da* —, over again (*o* from the beginning) ‖ *andare in* — *al mondo*, to go to the end of the world ‖ *venire a* — *di ql.co.*, to carry sthg. through (*o fam.* to get through with sthg.) ‖ *cosa fatta* — *ha*, what is done cannot be undone 3. (*geog.*) cape: *doppiare un* —, (*mar.*) to round a cape ‖ *il Capo di Buona Speranza*, the Cape of Good Hope; *Città del Capo*, Capetown; *la Provincia del Capo*, Cape Province 4. (*singolo animale, in un gregge, in una mandria*) animal; (*al pl.*) head: *questo è il più bel* — *della mia mandria*, this is the best animal in my herd; *furono venduti ottanta capi di bestiame*, eighty head of cattle were sold 5. (*articolo commerciale*) article: *un* — *di vestiario*, an article of clothing; *a lire ventimila il* —, at twenty thousand lire each 6. (*chi presiede, comanda*) head; leader: — *di azienda*, head (*o* principal) of a concern: — *di un partito*, leader of a party; — *di un reparto*, head of a department; — *di una tribù*, chief of a tribe; — *officina*, chief foreman; *cameriere* —, head waiter; *dirigente* —, top executive; *operaio* —, foreman; *ragioniere* —, head accountant 7. (*posizione di comando*): *comandante in* —, (*mil.*) commander-in-chief; *essere a* — *di un'azienda*, to be at the head of a business; *esser a* — *di un esercito*, to be at the head of an army 8. (*articolo, punto di un discorso, di una relazione*) head, item: — *d'accusa*, (*dir.*) charge (*o* count of an indictment); — *primo, secondo, terzo...*, item one, two, three...; *discorso diviso in sette capi*, speech arranged under seven heads ‖ — *primo*, first of all ‖ *per sommi capi*, in short (*o* summarily): *una relazione per sommi capi*, a summary account.

capobànda, *s.m.* 1. (*direttore di corpo bandistico*) bandmaster 2. (*capo di una banda di criminali*) ringleader (of a gang).

capòc, *s.m.* kapok.

capocàccia, *s.m.* chief huntsman (*pl.* huntsmen).

capòcchia, *s.f.* head: — *di chiodo*, head of a nail (*o* nail-head); — *di fiammifero*, head of a match; — *di spillo*, head of a pin (*o* pin-head).

capòccia, *s.m.* **1.** (*capo di una famiglia contadina*) head of a peasant household **2.** (*fam.*) leader **3.** (*sorvegliante di lavoratori*) works superintendent, overseer; foreman (*pl.* foremen).

capocentúria, *s.m.* (*st. romana*) centurion.

capocièlo, *s.m.* (*eccl.*) canopy over high-altar.

capoclàsse, *s.m.* head-boy ‖ *s.f.* head-girl.

capocòmico, *s.m.* (*teat.*) showman (*pl.* showmen).

capoconvòglio, *s.m.* **1.** (*ferr.*) chief conductor **2.** (*mar.*) flag-ship of a convoy.

capocordàta, *s.m.* (*spor.*) first man on the rope.

capocrònaca, *s.m.* leading article, leader.

capocronísta, *s.m.* chief reporter.

capocuòco, *s.m.* head cook, chef.

capodànno, *s.m.* New Year's Day.

capodepòsito, *s.m.* chief storeman (*pl.* storemen).

capodivisióne, *s.m.* head of a Government Department.

capodòglio, *s.m.* (*zool.*) sperm-whale.

capodòpera, *s.m.* **1.** (*capolavoro*) masterpiece **2.** *fig.* (*tipo ameno*) jolly fellow.

capofàbbrica, *s.m.* foreman (*pl.* foremen).

capofamíglia, *s.m.* head of a family; (*chi mantiene la famiglia*) breadwinner.

capofíla, *s.c.* file-leader.

capofítto, a, *l.av.* head first; headlong (anche *fig.*): *cadere a* —, to fall head first (o head foremost o headlong); *correre a* —·*verso la rovina*, to rush headlong to one's ruin; *gettarsi a* — *in un pericolo*, to rush headlong into a danger; *tuffarsi a* —, to dive head-first.

capogíro, *s.m.* (fit of) dizziness, (fit of) giddiness: *un'altezza che fa venire il* —, a dizzy height; *avere il* —, to feel dizzy; *far venire il* — *a qlcu.*, to make s.o. dizzy.

capoguàrdia, *s.m.* head of a local constabulary.

capolavóro, *s.m.* masterpiece: *la Galleria Nazionale ospita molti capolavori*, the National Gallery contains many masterpieces.

capolínea, *s.m.* terminus (*pl.* termini, terminuses): *vediamoci al* — *del 3*, let's meet at the No. 3 terminus.

capolíno, *s.m.* **1.** (*piccola testa*) small head ‖ *far* —, to peep in; (*dall'interno*) to peep out: *ella giunse sulla soglia della mia camera e vi fece* —, she came to the threshold of my bedroom and peeped in; *molti bimbi facevano* — *dalle finestre*, many children were peeping out of the windows **2.** (*bot.*) capitulum, head.

capolísta, *s.m.* **1.** first name on a list, head of a list **2.** (*pol.*) first name on an electoral list.

capoluògo, *s.m.* chief town (of province, district).

capomacchinísta, *s.m.* chief engineer.

capomàstro, *s.m.* master builder, master mason; (*imprenditore*) contractor.

capomòrto, *s.m.* (*chim.*) caput mortuum.

capomovimènto, *s.m.* (*ferr.*) **1.** railway traffic manager **2.** (*capomanovratore*) shunting officer.

caponàggine, *s.f.* stubbornness, obstinacy.

caponàre, *v.t.* (*mar.*) to cat.

caponàta, *s.f.* (*cuc. mar.*) water-biscuit soaked in salt water, oil and vinegar.

capóne[1], *s.m.* (*persona testarda*) headstrong fellow.

capóne[2], *s.m.* (*pesce*) —, (*ittiol.*) gurnard.

capóne[3], *s.m.* (*mar.*) cat.

capopàgina, *s.m.* (*tip.*) headpiece.

capopàrte, capopartíto, *s.m.* party leader.

capopèzzo, *s.m.* (*artigl.*) head gunner.

capopòpolo, *s.m.* popular leader; demagogue.

capopòsto, *s.m.* (*mil.*) guard commander.

caporalàto, *s.m.* (*mil.*) corporalship.

caporàle, *s.m.* (*mil.*) lance-corporal: — *maggiore*, corporal.

caporepàrto, *s.m.* **1.** head of a department **2.** (*nei grandi magazzini*) shop-walker; (*amer.*) floor-walker **3.** (*operaio capo*) foreman (*pl.* foremen).

caporióne, *s.m.* **1.** leader, head **2.** (*di una banda di criminali*) ringleader (of a gang).

caporivèrso, caporovèscio, *av.* head down.

caposàldo, *s.m.* **1.** (*topografia*) datum point **2.** (*fondamento*) basis (*pl.* bases), foundation, main point **3.** (*mil.*) stronghold, strong point.

caposcàla, *s.m.* staircase landing.

caposcàlo, *s.m.* (*aer.*) traffic control officer.

caposcàrico, *s.m.* (*buontempone*) wag, scatter-brain.

caposcuòla, *s.m.* leader of a movement: *Wordsworth è un — del Romanticismo*, Wordsworth is a leading figure of Romanticism.

caposètta, *s.m.* leader of a sect.

caposezióne, *s.m.* (*capoufficio*) head-clerk.

caposquàdra, *s.m.* **1.** (*di operai*) foreman (*pl.* foremen); charge-hand; charge-man (*pl.* charge -men) **2.** (*mil.*) squad leader.

caposquadróne, *s.m.* (*mil.*) troop leader.

capostazióne, *s.m.* station-master.

capostípite, *s.m.* founder of a family.

capotambúro, *s.m.* drum-major; (*donna*) drum -majorette.

capotàre, *v.i.* (*di aeroplani*) to somersault; (*di veicoli*) to turn over.

capotàvola, *s.m.* head of a table: *mio padre sedeva sempre a* —, my father used to sit at the head of the table.

capotècnico, *s.m.* technical director.

capotimonière, *s.m.* (*mar.*) coxswain.

capotréno, *s.m.* (*ferr.*) chief conductor; guard.

capòtta, *s.f.* (*aut.*) top: — *a mantice,* folding top; — *in tela,* canvas hood.

capotúrno, *s.m.* foreman (*pl.* foremen) ‖ *s.f.* forewoman (*pl.* forewomen).

capoufficio, *s.m.* head clerk.

capovèrso, *s.m.* **1.** (*in testi poetici, inizio di verso*) beginning of a line **2.** (*in testi in prosa, inizio di paragrafo*) beginning of a paragraph; (*il paragrafo*) paragraph, section **3.** (*tip.*) indention.

capovòga, *s.m.* (*spor.*) stroke: *fare da* —, to row (o to act as) stroke.

capovòlgere, *v.t.* **1.** to turn over, to overturn, to turn upside down, to upset: — *un bicchiere,* to turn a glass upside down **2.** (*rivoltare*) to turn inside out ‖ **capovòlgersi,** *v.r.* to turn over, to overturn, to upset, to capsize: *il gatto si capovolse sul dorso,* the cat turned over on its back.

capovolgimènto, *s.m.* overturn; upsetting; capsizing.

capovòlta, *s.f.* **1.** (*capovolgimento*) upset **2.** (*salto mortale*) somersault.

capovoltàre, *V.* capovòlgere.

capovòlto, *ag.av.* upside-down, topsyturvy.

càppa[1], *s.f.* **1.** (*mantello*) cloak; coat: *una — di visone,* a mink coat ‖ *la — del cielo, fig.* the vault of heaven ‖ *romanzo di — e spada,* (*lett.*) cloak and dagger nóvel ‖ *sotto una — di piombo, fig.* under a shadow of gloom **2.** (*mantello con cappuccio*) hooded mantle **3.** (*di prete*) cape; (*di frate*) cowl, frock ‖ *per un punto Martin perse la* —, *prov.* for want of a nail the shoe was lost **4.** (*volta di camino*) cowl: *su per la — del camino,* up the chimney **5.** (*mar.*) cope: *alla* —!, heave to!; *vela di* —, storm sail; *essere alla* —, to lie (o to heave) to.

càppa[2], *s.f.* (*zool.*) razor-shell; mussel.

càppa[3], *s.f.* letter K.

cappamàgna, *s.f.* **1.** (*di prelato*) cappa magna **2.** (*di ordine cavalleresco*) ceremonial cloak **3.** (*di dignitario*) state robe: *essere in* —, to be dressed in great state; *mettersi in* —, to dress in great state; *fig.* to dress pompously (o *fam.* to dress up).

cappeggiàre, *v.i.* (*mar.*) to heave to, to lie to.

cappèlla[1], *s.f.* chapel: — *ardente,* mortuary chapel; — *della Madonna,* Lady-chapel; — *laterale,* side chapel; — *reale,* chapel royal ‖ *Cappella Sistina,* Sixtine Chapel **2.** (*mus.*) chapel: *maestro di* —, chapel-master; *musica a* —, singing to accompaniment of the organ.

cappèlla[2], *s.f.* (*capocchia*) head.

cappellàccia, *s.f.* (*ornit.*) crested lark.

cappellàccio, *s.m.* 1. shabby hat 2. (*miner.*) outcrop.

cappellàio, *s.m.* hatter.

cappellanía, *s.f.* (*eccl.*) chaplaincy.

cappellàno, *s.m.* (*eccl.*) chaplain: — *militare*, military chaplain.

cappellàta, *s.f.* hatful: *una — di monete*, a hatful of coins ‖ *far denaro a cappellate*, (*fam.*) to pile up money.

cappellería, *s.f.* hatter's shop.

cappellétto, *s.m.* 1. (*nocella di ago calamitato; coperchio a vite di valvola di camera d'aria*) cap 2. *pl.* (*cuc.*) "cappelletti" (ringlets of dough filled with seasoned minced meat) 3. (*elmetto*) helmet 4. *pl.* (*st.*) cavalrymen 5. (*cappuccio per il falco*) falcon's hood.

cappellièra, *s.f.* hat-box.

cappellinàio, *s.m.* hatstand.

cappèllo, *s.m.* 1. hat: — *a cencio*, slouch-hat; — *a cilindro*, top-hat; — *a cilindro compressibile*, gibus (*o* opera-hat); — *a due punte*, cocked hat; — *alla Mimì*, bonnet; — *da sole*, sunhat; — *di carta*, paper-hat; — *di feltro*, felt-hat; — *di paglia*, straw hat; — *di paglia di Firenze*, Leghorn hat; — *duro*, bowler-hat (*o alla*. derby); — *floscio*, fedora; *col* — *in testa*, with one's hat on; *giù i cappelli !*, hats off !; *alzare il* —, to raise one's hat; *levarsi il* —, to take off one's hat; *mettersi il* —, to put on one's hat (*o* to put one's hat on); *stare in piedi senza* —, to stand bare-headed; *tirarsi il — sugli occhi*, to tilt one's hat over one's eyes ‖ «*Il — a tre punte*», (*lett. mus.*) "The Three-cornered Hat" ‖ *gli faccio tanto di* —, I bow before him (*o* I esteem him very highly) ‖ *pigliar* —, *fig.* to take offence 2. (*capocchia*) head: — *di fungo*, head of mushroom 3. (*introduzione a un testo*) preamble, preface, introduction; (*articolo introduttivo*) introductory article; lead 4. (*mec.*) cap; (*di pressa*) crosshead.

cappellóne, *s.m.* 1. large hat 2. (*recluta*) recruit.

cappellòtto, *s.m.* (*mil.*) percussion cap.

càpperi, *inter.* (*fam.*) good gracious !.

càppero, *s.m.* (*bot.*) caper: *pianta di capperi*, caper-bush; *salsa di capperi*, caper-sauce.

càppio, *s.m.* slip-knot, noose.

capponàia, *s.f.* capon coop.

capponàre, *v.t.* 1. to caponize 2. (*castrare*) to castrate, to geld.

cappóne[1], *s.m.* 1. capon ‖ *ho la pelle di* —, I have gone all goose-flesh; *far venire la pelle di — a qlcu.*, to give s.o. the creeps 2. *pesce* —, (*ittiol.*) gurnard.

cappóne[2], *s.m.* (*mar.*) cat.

cappòtta, *V.* **capòtta**.

cappòtto, *s.m.* 1. coat; greatcoat 2. (*al giuoco*) capot: *dare — a un altro giocatore*, to capot another player; *prendere* —, to lose a game without scoring a single point.

cappuccíno, *s.m.* 1. (*eccl.*) Capuchin ‖ *far vita da* —, to live poorly 2. (*caffè con un po' di latte*) white coffee 3. (*zool.*) Capuchin (monkey).

cappúccio, *s.m.* 1. hood, cowl 2. (*tec.*) cap: — *isolante*, (*elett.*) cap (*o* hood); — *per valvola*, (*di camera d'aria*) nipple.

càpra, *s.f.* 1. goat: *una — e un caprone*, a she-goat and a he-goat (*o* a billy-goat); *pelle di* —, goat-skin ‖ *sentieri da capre*, narrow steep paths ‖ *salvar — e cavoli*, to manage to have it both ways 2. (*edil.*) (*cavalletto*) trestle, horse.

capràio, **capràro**, *s.m.* goat-herd.

caprétta, *s.f.* kid.

caprétto, *s.m.* kid: *carne di* —, kid; *pelle di* —, kid (*o* kidskin) ‖ *i Capretti*, (*astr.*) the Kids.

capriàta, *s.f.* (*edil.*) truss: — *a due monaci*, queen truss; *catena di* —, tie beam.

capríccio, *s.m.* 1. whim, caprice, fancy; (*assurdità*) freak: *non fu per il mio* —, it was not owing to a whim of mine ‖ *i capricci della fortuna*, the freaks of fortune ‖ *fare i capricci*, (*di bambino*) to be naughty 2. (*mus.*) capriccio.

capricciosaménte, *av.* capriciously; (*di bambino*) naughtily.

capriccióso, *ag.* capricious; freakish; (*bizzarro*) bizarre; (*stravagante*) whimsical; (*di bambino*) naughty.

Capricòrno, *no.pr.m.* (*astr.*) Capricorn ‖ *il Tropico del* —, the Tropic of Capricorn.

caprifíco, *s.m.* (*bot.*) wild fig-tree.

caprifòglio, *s.m.* (*bot.*) honeysuckle.

caprígno, *ag.* goatish, caprine.

capríle, *s.m.* goat house.

caprimúlgo, *s.m.* (*ornit.*) goatsucker.

capríno, *ag.* goatish, caprine: *barba caprina*, goatee ‖ *questione di lana caprina*, useless debate (*o* argument) ‖ *s.m.* (*puzzo di capra*) goatish smell.

capriòla[1], *s.f.* (*femmina del capriolo*) roe; roe-deer (*invariato al pl.*).

capriòla[2], *s.f.* caper: *fare capriole*, to cut capers ‖ *fare una* —, (*un capitombolo*) to tumble down.

capriolàre, *v.i.* to cut capers, to caper (about).

capriòlo, *s.m.* roe-buck.

càpro, **capróne**, *s.m.* goat, he-goat, billy-goat ‖ *capro espiatorio*, scapegoat.

càpsico, *s.m.* (*bot.*) Capsicum.

càpsula, *s.f.* 1. capsule: *tappo a* —, crown-cap 2. (*cappellotto esplosivo*) (percussion) cap 3. (*di dente*) crown.

capsulàre, *ag.* capsular.

captàre, *v.t.* 1. (*rad.*) to pick up 2. (*intercettare*) to intercept 3. (*cattivarsi*) to gain.

captazióne, *s.f.* (*rad.*) getting (a station).

capuffício, *s.m.* head-clerk.

Capuléti, *no.pr.* (*lett.*) Capulet.

capziosaménte, *av.* captiously.

capziosità, *s.f.* captiousness.

capzióso, *ag.* captious.

carabàttola, *s.f.* trifle, bauble: *pigliar su le proprie carabattole*, (*fam.*) to pack up one's traps.

carabína, *s.f.* carabine.

carabinière, *s.m.* carabineer.

Caracàlla, *no.pr.m.* (*st.*) Caracalla.

caràcea, *s.f.* (*st. mar.*) carrack.

carachíri, *s.m.* kara-kiri.

caracollàre, *v.i.* to caracol(e).

caracòllo, *s.m.* caracol(e).

caracúl, *s.m.* caracul, karakul.

caràffa, *s.f.* (*per acqua*) carafe; (*per vino*) decanter.

Caraíbi, *no.pr.m.pl.* (*geog.*) Caribees: *il Mar dei* —, the Caribbean Sea.

caraíbico, *ag.* Caribbean, Caribbee.

caràmbola, *s.f.* (*biliardo*) cannon, carambole: *far* —, to cannon.

carambolàre, *v.t.* (*biliardo*) to cannon, to carambole.

caramèlla, *s.f.* 1. sweetmeat, sugar-drop: — *molle*, toffee; — *per la tosse*, cough-drop 2. (*monocolo*) monocle, single eye-glass.

caramellàio, *s.m.* confectioner.

caramellàre, *v.t.* to coat with burnt sugar; (*candire*) to candy.

caramellàto, *ag.* coated with burnt sugar; (*candito*) candied.

caramèllo, *s.m.* caramel.

caraménte, *av.* dearly.

carapàce, *s.m.* (*guscio di testuggine*) carapace.

caratàre, *v.t.* to weigh (sthg.) in carats.

caratèllo, *s.m.* keg.

caratísta, *s.m.* 1. (*comm.*) shareholder 2. (*comproprietario di nave*) part-owner.

caràto, *s.m.* 1. carat (*misura di peso per pietre preziose* = mg. 200) 2. (*misura di purezza dell'oro*) carat: *oro a 18 carati*, eighteen carat gold 3. (*comm.*) share (of capital in a commercial undertaking) 4. (*quota di comproprietà di una nave*) part-ownership.

caràttere, *s.m.* 1. character, temper, disposition; nature: *un — gentile*, a kindly disposition (*o* kind temper); *formazione del* —, character-building; *un uomo* *di* —, a man of character; *un uomo senza* —, a spiritless man; *è proprio di buon* —, he is good-natured indeed; *ha un* — *nobile, forte, debole*, he has a noble, strong, weak character; *aver* —, to have character (o backbone); *mancare di* —, to lack strength of character (o to have no backbone) 2. (*caratteristica, qualità*) character, characteristic, peculiarity: *il* — *peculiare di questa nuova specie*, the distinctive character (o characteristic) of this new species 3. (*lettera*) letter: *caratteri gotici*, black letter || *scritto a caratteri d'oro, fig.* written in letters of gold || *sono avvenimenti scritti a caratteri di sangue*, they are events written in blood 4. (*tip.*) type: *caratteri di testo*, book-face; — *neretto*, bold (o boldface); *caratteri schiacciati*, worm type; *fonderia di caratteri*, type foundry; *in* — *corsivo*, in Italic type (o Italics); *titolo a caratteri di scatola*, banner (headline) (o large-type headline) 5. (*scrittura*) character: *caratteri cinesi, greci*, Chinese, Greek characters 6. (*lett.*) character: *commedia di* —, character play || *essere in* —, to be in character: *non essere in* — *con ql.co.*, to be out of character with sthg. 7. (*teol.*) character, confirmation.

caratteríno, *s.m.* (*iron.*) difficult temper, fussy temper.

caratterísta, *s.m.* (*teat. cine.*) character actor || *s.f.* (*teat. cine.*) character actress.

caratterística, *s.f.* 1. characteristic, peculiarity, distinctive feature 2. (*mat.*) characteristic.

caratterístico, *ag.* characteristic, distinctive, typical: *questo è* — *nei bambini*, this is characteristic of children.

caratterizzàre, *v.t.* to characterize, to mark, to distinguish, to be peculiar to (s.o., sthg.).

caratúra, *V.* **caràto** 3. 4.

caravàna, *V.* **carovàna.**

caravanserràglio, *s.m.* càravanserai, caravansarai, caravansary.

caravèlla, *s.f.* (*st. mar.*) caravel, carvel.

carbinòlo, *s.m.* (*chim.*) carbinol, methilic alcohol.

carbolísmo, *s.m.* (*med.*) carbolism.

carbonàia, *s.f.* 1. (*buca in cui si prepara il carbone di legna*) charcoal pit 2. (*catasta di legna da carbone*) charcoal pile 3. (*cantina del carbone*) coal-cellar 4. (*venditrice di carbone*) coal-seller; coal-woman (*pl.* coal-women).

carbonàio, *ag.* coal (*attributivo*): *nave carbonaia*, coal-ship (o collier) || *s.m.* 1. (*chi prepara carbone*) charcoal-burner 2. (*chi vende carbone*) coal merchant; coalman (*pl.* coalmen).

carbonarísmo, *s.m.* (*st.*) Carbonarism.

carbonàro, *s.m.* (*st.*) Carbonaro (*pl.* Carbonari).

carbonàto, *s.m.* (*chim.*) carbonate: — *di calcio*, calcium carbonate.

carbònchio, *s.m.* 1. (*min.*) carbuncle, ruby 2. (*patol.*) carbuncle, anthrax 3. (*malattia dei cereali*) smut.

carbonchióso, *ag.* 1. (*patol.*) carbuncled 2. (*di cereali*) smutty.

carboncíno, *s.m.* (*pitt.*) charcoal.

carbóne, *s.m.* coal: — *animale*, (*ind.*) bone (o animal) charcoal; — *di legna, dolce*, charcoal; — *di storta*, (*chim.*) retort graphite; — *fossile*, pit-coal; — *per elettrodi*, (*elett.*) carbon; *bidone del* —, coal-box (o coal-scuttle); *carta* —, carbon paper; *combustione del* —, coal burning; *deposito di* —, (*ind.*) coal storage; *filone di* —, (*miner.*) coal seam; *giacimento di* —, (*miner.*) coal-field; *miniera di* —, coal-mine; *un pezzo di* —, a (lump of) coal || — *bianco*, (*l'elettricità*) white coal || *nero come il* —, coal-black (o as black as coal).

carbonèlla, *s.f.* 1. charcoal 2. (*cenere*) coal cinders (*pl*).

Carbonería, *s.f.* (*st.*) Carbonarist movement.

carbonétto, *s.m.* dark red coral.

carboníceio, *ag.* coal-black.

carbònico, *ag.* (*chim.*) carbonic: *anidride carbonica*, carbon dioxide.

carbonièra, *s.f.* 1. (*cantina del carbone*) coal-cellar 2. (*mar.*) (*deposito di carbone*) bunker 3. (*mar.*) (*nave carboniera*) coal-ship, collier.

carbonífero, *ag.* carboniferous: *strato* —, coal vein: *strato* — *superficiale*, open-cast coal-mine.

carboníle, *s.m.* (*mar.*) bunker.

carbònio, *s.m.* (*chim.*) carbon: *acciaio al* —, (*metal.*) carbon steel; *ossido di* —, (*chim.*) carbon monoxide.

carbonizzàre, *v.t.* to carbonize; (*legno*) to char: *morire carbonizzato*, to be burnt to death || **carbonizzàrsi,** *v.r.* to be carbonized.

carbonizzazióne, *s.f.* carbonization: — *superficiale*, superficial charring; *bagno di* —, (*ind. tessile*) carbonizing bath; *forno di* —, (*ind. tessile*) carbonizing stove.

carborúndo, *s.m.* (*ind.*) carborundum.

carburànte, *s.m.* 1. fuel: — *antidetonante*, antiknock fuel; — *per turboreattori*, aviation turbine fuel; *rifornimento di* —, refuelling; *usato come* —, used for fuel 2. (*benzina*) petrol; (*amer.*) gas, gasoline: *non ho più* —, I have no petrol left (o I am out of petrol).

carburàre, *v.t.* to carburize, to carburet.

carburatóre, *s.m.* carburettor, carburetter.

carburazióne, *s.f.* carburation.

carbúro, *s.m.* (*chim.*) carbide.

careàme, *s.m.* carcass, carcase; (*carogna*) carrion.

carcàre, (*poet.*) per **caricàre.**

carcàssa, *s.f.* 1. carcass, framework, frame, skeleton: — *di nave*, carcass of a ship; *la* — *di un dirigibile è fatta di metallo molto resistente*, the framework of an airship is made of very strong metal; *la* — *di quell'edificio è fatta di acciaio*, the skeleton of that building is made of steel 2. (*fig. spreg.*) old crock: *quella* — *automobile*, that old crock (o jalo(p)py); *quella* — *di nave*, that old crock of a ship 3. (*toracica*) carcass.

carceraménto, *s.m.* imprisonment.

carceràre, *v.t.* to imprison; to jail, to gaol.

carceràrio, *ag.* prison (*attributivo*): *guardia carceraria*, warder (o gaoler o jailor); *regolamento* —, prison regulations; *vitto* —, prison fare.

carceràta, *s.f.*, **carceràto,** *s.m.* prisoner.

carcerazióne, *s.f.* imprisonment.

càrcere, *s.m.* prison, jail, gaol: — *preventivo*, detention; *direttore delle carceri*, prison governor; *fu condannato a venticinque anni di* —, he was sentenced to twenty-five years' imprisonment; *andare in* —, to go (o to be sent) to prison; *essere in* —, to be in prison; *fuggire dal* —, to escape from prison; *mettere in* —, to put into prison.

carcerière, *s.m.* warder, gaoler, jailor.

carcinòma, *s.m.* (*patol.*) carcinoma (*pl.* carcinomata).

carcinomatóso, *ag.* (*patol.*) carcinomatous.

carciofàia, *s.f.* (*bot.*) artichoke bed.

carciòfo, *s.m.* 1. (*bot.*) artichoke 2. *fig.* (*buonannulla*) good-for-nothing.

carciofolàta, *s.f.* feed of artichokes.

càrco, (*poet.*) per **càrico.**

càrda, *s.f.* (*ind. tessile*) card, carding-machine.

cardamòmo, *s.m.* (*bot.*) cardamom.

cardànica, *s.f.* (*mar.*) gimbals (*pl.*).

cardànico, *ag.* (*mec.*) cardanic; cardan (*attributivo*): *giunto* —, cardan (o universal) joint; *sospensione cardanica*, (*mar.*) gimbals.

cardàno, *s.m.* (*mec.*) cardan joint.

cardàre, *v.t.* 1. (*ind. tessile*) to card, to tease 2. *fig.* (*calunniare*) to speak ill of (s.o.); to backbite.

cardàta, *s.f.* 1. (*cardatura*) carding, teasing 2. (*quantità di lana cardata*) quantity of carded wool.

cardàto, *ag.* carded: *lana cardata*, carded wool.

cardatóre, *s.m.* carder, card-tender, teaser.

cardatríce, *s.f.* 1. carder, card-tender, teaser 2. (*mec.*) card, carding-machine.

cardatúra, *s.f.* carding, teasing: — *della lana*, wool-carding (o -combing).

cardeggiàre, (*rar.*) per **cardàre.**

cardellíno, *s.m.* (*ornit.*) goldfinch.

cardéto, *s.m.* cardoon-field.

cardíaco, *ag.* cardiac, cardiacal; heart (*attributivo*): *attacco* —, heart attack: *morì di un attacco* —, he died of heart failure; *disturbi cardiaci*, heart-disease ‖ *s.m.* subject suffering from heart-disease.

cardialgía, *s.f.* (*patol.*) cardialgia.

càrdias, *s.m.* (*anat.*) cardia.

cardinalàto, *s.m.* (*eccl.*) cardinalate; cardinalship.

cardinàle¹, *ag.* cardinal: *numeri cardinali*, cardinal numbers; *punti cardinali*, cardinal points; *virtù cardinali*, cardinal virtues ‖ *s.m.* (*eccl.*) cardinal: *Cardinale Legato*, Cardinal Legate.

cardinàle², *s.m.* (*ornit.*) cardinal (-bird).

cardinalésco, cardinalízio, *ag.* cardinal (*attributivo*): *cappello* —, cardinal's hat; *vestire la porpora cardinalizia*, to don the scarlet ‖ *rosso* —, cardinal red (o scarlet).

càrdine, *s.m.* 1. hinge, pivot: *porta fuori dai cardini*, door off its hinges ‖ *i cardini terrestri*, the poles 2. *fig.* (*base, fondamento*) foundation, basis (*pl.* bases): support.

cardiocèle, *s.m.* (*patol.*) cardiocele.

cardiocinètico, *ag.* (*farm.*) cardiokinetic.

cardiografía, *s.f.* (*med.*) cardiography.

cardiogràfico, *ag.* (*med.*) cardiographic.

cardiògrafo, *s.m.* (*med.*) cardiograph.

cardiogràmma, *s.m.* (*med.*) cardiogram.

cardiología, *s.f.* cardiology.

cardiòlogo, *s.m.* cardiologist.

cardiopàlmo, *s.m.* (*patol.*) cardiopalmus.

cardiopatía, *s.f.* (*patol.*) cardiopathy.

cardiopàtico, *ag.* cardiopathic ‖ *s.m.* subject suffering from heart-disease.

cardioplegía, *s.f.* (*patol.*) cardioplegia.

cardiosclerosì, *s.f.* (*patol.*) cardiosclerosis.

cardiotònico, *ag.* (*farm.*) cardiotonic.

cardiovascolàre, *ag.* (*anat.*) cardiovascular.

cardíte, *s.f.* (*patol.*) carditis.

càrdo, *s.m.* 1. (*bot.*) thistle: — *mangereccio*, cardoon (o edible thistle) 2. (*riccio di castagna*) chestnut -bur, chestnut-husk 3. (*strumento per cardare*) teasel; card.

cardóne, *s.m.* (*bot.*) cardoon, edible thistle.

carèna, *s.f.* 1. (*mar.*) keel, bottom 2. (*di sterno di uccelli*) carina (*pl.* carinae).

carenàggio, *s.m.* careenage, careening: *bacino di* —, dry (o graving) dock.

carenàre, *v.t.* 1. (*mar.*) to careen, to heave down, to fair 2. (*aer.*) to streamline, to fair.

carenàti, *s.m.pl.* (*ornit.*) Carinatae.

carenàto, *ag.* (*di sterno di uccelli*) carinate, carinated.

carenatúra, *s.f.* (*mar. aer.*) fairing.

carènza, *s.f.* 1. (*mancanza*) want, absence, privation: *per* — *di calcio e di vitamine*, for want (o lack) of calcium and vitamins 2. (*scarsità*) scarcity, dearth.

carestía, *s.f.* 1. famine: *una lunga* —, a long famine: *due milioni di indiani furono vittime della* —, two millions of Indians died of famine 2. (*mancanza*) lack; scarcity, dearth: — *di galantuomini*, lack of honest men; — *di grano*, dearth of corn; — *di vino*, scarcity of wine.

carézza, *s.f.* caress: *fare una* — *a un cane*, to pat (o to stroke) a dog; *fare una* —, *delle carezze a qlcu.*, to caress (o to fondle) s.o.; *fig.* (*blandirlo*) to blandish s.o.

carezzàre, *v.t.* 1. to caress; to stroke; to pat: — *un cane*, to stroke (o to pat) a dog ‖ — *le spalle di qlcu.*, (*fam.*) to thrash s.o. soundly 2. (*vezzeggiare*) to fondle; (*fam.*) to pet: — *un bambino*, to fondle a baby 3. (*adulare*) to flatter 4. (*vagheggiare*) to cherish, to entertain: *carezzava il sogno di tornare un giorno in Italia*, he cherished the dream of returning to Italy one day; — *un'idea*, to cherish (o to entertain) an idea.

carezzévole, *ag.* caressing, fondling; (*affettuoso*) affectionate; (*lusinghiero*) coaxing: *voce* —, caressing voice.

carezzevolménte, *av.* caressingly; (*con affetto*) affectionately; (*con blandizie*) coaxingly.

cariàre, *v.t.* to rot, to decay, to make carious ‖ **cariàrsi,** *v.r.* to rot, to decay, to grow carious.

cariàtide, *s.f.* (*arch.*) caryatid (*pl.* caryatids, caryatides).

cariàto, *ag.* 1. decayed, carious; rotten: *dente* —, decayed (o carious o rotten) tooth 2. (*geol.miner.*) pitted.

càrica, *s.f.* 1. (*pubblico ufficio*) office: *dimettersi da una* —, to resign office; *entrare in* —, to take (o to come into) office; *essere in* —, to be in (o to hold) office; *occupare una* — *pubblica*, to hold public office; *restare in* —, to continue in office; *uscire di* —, to leave office 2. (*dignità*) dignity; (*impiego*) appointment: *le alte cariche dello Stato*, the dignities of the State; *accettare una* — *onorifica*, to accept an honorary appointment 3. (*mil.*) charge, attack: — *alla baionetta*, bayonet charge; — *di cavalleria*, cavalry charge; *ritornare alla* —, to return to the charge; *fig.* to persist (o to insist); *suonare la* —, to sound the charge 4. (*di arma da fuoco*) charge: — *di lancio*, propelling (o powder) charge; — *di profondità*, depth charge; — *di scoppio*, blasting charge 5. (*elett.*) charge: — *a corrente costante*, constant current charge; — *elettrica*, electric charge; — *spaziale*, space charge; *entità di* —, charging rate; *potenziale di* —, charging potential 6. (*metal.*) charge: — *del minerale e del fondente*, charge of ores and fluxes; — *solida*, cold charge; *prima* — *di metallo*, bed charge 7. (*di orologio*) winding up: *dare la* — *a un orologio*, to wind up a clock; (*da polso*) to wind up a watch.

caricaménto, *s.m.* 1. (*di nave*) loading, lading; (*di veicolo*) loading 2. (*di arma da fuoco*) loading, charging 3. (*elett.*) charging 4. (*di orologio*) winding (up) 5. (*di pompa*) priming.

caricàre, *v.t.* 1. to load, to charge; to burden: *caricate la merce sulla nave!*, put the goods on board!; *avete finito di* —?, have you finished loading up?; *la nave caricherà 2·000 passeggeri*, the ship will embark 2,000 passengers; — *un autocarro*, to load a lorry; — *eccessivamente*, to overload; — *una nave*, to load a ship; — *qlcu. di responsabilità*, to burden s.o. with responsibilities ‖ — *la dose*, to increase the dose; — *la mano con qlcu.*, to be very hard on s.o.; — *il prezzo di ql.co.*, to raise the price of sthg.; — *qlcu. di busse*, to thrash s.o.; — *le tinte*, to deepen (o to strengthen) the colours; (*esagerare*) to exaggerate 2. (*riempire*) to fill; to charge: — *una mina*, to charge a mine; — *la pipa*, to fill one's pipe; — *un proiettile*, to fill a shell; — *la stufa*, to fill (o to make up) the stove 3. (*mil.*) to charge: — *il nemico*, to charge the enemy 4. (*arma da fuoco*) to load: — *un fucile*, to load a gun 5. (*elett.*) to charge; (*elevare la tensione di*) to boost: — *un accumulatore*, to charge an accumulator (o a battery) 6. (*metal.*) (*un forno*) to charge 7. (*un orologio*) to wind up 8. (*una pompa*) to prime ‖ **caricàrsi,** *v.r.* to overburden oneself (with sthg.): — *di debiti*, to plunge into debts; — *lo stomaco*, to overload one's stomach.

caricaménte, *av.* 1. (*con affettazione*) affectedly, in an affected way 2. (*esageratamente*) exaggeratedly.

caricàto, *ag.* 1. (*affettato*) affected 2. (*esagerato*) exaggerated.

caricatóre, *s.m.* 1. loader 2. (*mar.*) (*proprietario del carico*) shipper 3. (*di arma da fuoco*) magazine.

caricatúra, *s.f.* caricature: *fare la* — *di qlcu.*, *ql.co.*, to make (o to give) a caricature of s.o., sthg.; *mettere in* —, to caricature.

caricaturísta, *s.c.* caricaturist.

càrice, *s.f.* (*bot.*) Carex.

càrico, *ag.* 1. loaded (with sthg.), laden (with sthg.) (anche *fig.*): *una nave carica di merci*, a ship loaded (o laden) with goods; *era* — *di debiti*, he was weighed down with (*o* up to his ears in) debts; *era — di onori*, he was loaded with honours **2.** (*di caffè*) strong **3.** (*di colore*) deep, dark **4.** (*riempito*) filled (with sthg.); full; charged (with sthg.): *proiettile —*, live (*o* filled *o* charged) shell; *è carica la tua pipa?*, is your pipe full? **5.** (*di arma da fuoco*) loaded (with sthg.); live (*attributivo*): *fucile —*, loaded gun: *è — il tuo fucile?*, are you loaded? **6.** (*elett.*) charged (with current) **7.** (*di orologio*) wound up.

càrico, *s.m.* **1.** load; (*di nave*) cargo, shipment; (*di veicolo*) load; (*di animale da soma*) burden: *— inappuntabile*, clean shipment; *un piccolo — di canna da zucchero*, a small shipment of sugar-cane; *vapore da —*, cargo boat; *dichiarare un — in dogana*, to declare a shipment to the Customs; *portare un — sulle spalle*, to carry a load on one's shoulders; *sbarcare un —*, to unload a cargo; *vendere il — completo di una nave*, to sell in bulk **2.** (*il caricare*) (*di nave*) loading, lading; (*di veicolo*) loading: *polizza di —*, (*comm.*) bill of lading **3.** *fig.* load, weight, burden: *un — di preoccupazioni*, a load of cares; *un — di responsabilità*, a load of responsibility; *avere qlcu. a —*, to have to provide for s.o. **4.** (*grande quantità*) lot: *un — di...*, a lot of... (*o fam.* loads of... *o* lots of...): *un — di botte*, a sound (*o* thorough) thrashing; *hanno un — di quattrini*, they have loads of money **5.** *a — di qlcu.*, (*comm.*) to be charged (*o* to be debited) to s.o.: *dogana a vostro —*, duty to be paid by you; *spese a — del destinatario*, at consignee's expense; *spese a — del nostro conto*, expenses to be charged to our account; *ogni eventuale modifica sarà a vostro —*, any possible alteration will be made at your expense; *segnare una somma a — di qlcu.*, to debit s.o. with an amount **6.** (*accusa*) charge, accusation, imputation: *teste a —*, witness for the prosecution; *gli fecero — di aver abbandonato il ferito*, they accused him of forsaking the wounded man **7.** (*tassa*) taxation: *tributario*, burden of taxation; *un pesante — fiscale*, a heavy (burden of) taxation **8.** (*scienza delle costruzioni*) load: *— accidentale*, live load; *— al limite di elasticità*, load at elastic limit; *— di lavoro*, working load; *— di rottura*, ultimate (*o* maximum) tensile stress; *— di snervamento*, yield point; *— eccentrico*, eccentric load; *— mobile*, live (*o* moving) load; *— unitario*, unit load; *— variabile*, variable load **9.** (*elett.*) load factor: *— crescente*, increasing load; *— di avviamento*, starting load; *— massimo ammissibile*, maximum permissible load; *— variabile*, changing load **10.** (*aer.*) load, loading: *— alare*, wing load; *— amovibile*, disposable load; *— d'apertura*, span loading; *— di potenza*, power loading; *— di prova*, proof load; *— di robustezza*, ultimate load; *— totale*, full load; *— utile*, useful load.

Caríddi, *no.pr.f.* (*geog. mit.*) Carybdis.
càrie, *s.f.* (*patol.*) decay, caries.
caríno, *ag.* pretty, nice, charming, delightful: *quant'è —!*, (*di bimbo*) isn't he a darling! ‖ *ne ho sentite di carine!*, (*fam.*) I've heard such funny stories!.
Carínzia, *no.pr.f.* (*geog.*) Carinthia.
carísma, *s.m.* (*teol.*) charism.
carità, *s.f.* **1.** (*benevolenza*) charity; (*amore*) love: *— di patria*, love of one's (own) country; *fallo per — del prossimo!*, do it out of charity!; *essere senza — verso gli altri*, to be without charity towards one's fellow-men; *trattare qlcu. con —*, to treat s.o. charitably ‖ *per —!*, for pity's (*o* God's) sake!; *per — non farlo!*, for heaven's sake don't do it! **2.** (*teol.*) charity ‖ *Fede, Speranza, Carità*, Faith, Hope, Charity **3.** (*beneficenza*) charity: *istituto di —*, charitable institution; *vivere di —*, to live on charity ‖ *— florita*, disinterested charity; *— pelosa*, interested charity ‖ *dama di —*, lady visitor ‖ *figli della —*, children of charity ‖ *Suore della Carità*, Sisters of Charity ‖ *la — comincia in casa propria*, prov. charity begins at home **4.** (*elemosina*) alms: *chiedere la —*, to beg for alms; *fare la —*, to give s.o. alms.

caritatévole, *ag.* charitable.
caritatevolménte, *av.* charitably.
carlínga, *s.f.* (*aer.*) cockpit, greenhouse.
carlíno, *s.m.* (*antica moneta*) carlin, carline ‖ *il resto del —*, *fig.* something else into the bargain.
carlísmo, *s.m.* (*st.*) Carlism.
carlísta, *s.m.* (*st.*) Carlist.
Càrlo, *no.pr.m.* Charles ‖ *— il Bello*, (*st.*) Charles the Fair; *— il Calvo*, (*st.*) Charles the Bald; *— il Saggio*, (*st.*) Charles the Wise; *— il Temerario*, (*st.*) Charles the Bold ‖ *dim.* Charlie, Charly.
Carlomàgno, *no.pr.m.* (*st.*) Charlemagne.
carlóna, alla, *l.av.* carelessly, thoughtlessly.
Carlòtta, *no.pr.f.* Charlotte ‖ *dim.* Lottie, Chat.
càrme, *s.f.* (*poes.*) **1.** ode, poem **2.** *pl.* poetry (*sing.*).
carmelitàna, *s.f.* (*eccl.*) Carmelite (nun).
carmelitàno, *ag.s.m.* (*eccl.*) Carmelite ‖ *i Carmelitani*, the Carmelites (*o fam.* the white friars).
carminatívo, *ag.s.m.* (*farm.*) carminative.
carmínio, *s.m.* carmine ‖ *labbra di —*, carmine lips.
carnàccia, *s.f.* coarse meat.
carnagióne, *s.f.* complexion: *— chiara*, fair complexion; *— rosea*, pink complexion; *— scura*, dark (*o* swarthy) complexion; *avere una bella —*, to have a fine complexion.
carnàio, *s.m.* **1.** (*luogo di eccidio*) shambles: *la valle divenne un —*, the valley became a shambles **2.** (*massacro*) carnage, slaughter.
carnàle, *ag.* **1.** physical, bodily ‖ *fratelli carnali*, brothers german **2.** (*sensuale*) sensual, carnal.
carnalità, *s.f.* carnality, sensuality.
carnalménte, *av.* **1.** physically **2.** (*sensualmente*) carnally, sensually.
carnàme, *s.m.* **1.** mass of rotten flesh **2.** (*cumolo di cadaveri*) heap of corpses.
carnascialésco, *ag.* carnival (*attributivo*): *canti carnascialeschi*, carnival songs.
càrne, *s.f.* **1.** flesh: *calze color —*, flesh-coloured stockings; *i miei figli sono — della mia —*, my children are my own flesh and blood ‖ *in — ed ossa*, in the flesh (*o* in person) ‖ *rosa —*, flesh pink ‖ *essere bene in —*, to be plump (*o* stout); *essere in —*, to be in flesh; *rimettersi in —*, to put on flesh (*o* to put on weight) ‖ *— da cannone*, cannon fodder **2.** (*polpa, parte carnosa*) flesh **3.** *fig.* flesh: *il mondo, la —, il diavolo*, the world, the flesh, the devil; *i peccati della —*, the sins of the flesh; *resurrezione della —*, (*teol.*) resurrection of the body; *lo spirito è pronto, ma la — è inferma*, the spirit is willing but the flesh is weak **4.** (*come alimento*) meat: *— bianca*, white meat; *— congelata*, frozen meat; *— conservata*, corned meat; *— fresca*, fresh meat; *— in scatola*, tinned meat (*o amer.* canned meat); *— in stufato*, stewed meat; *— rossa*, (*di bue*) beef; (*di montone*) mutton; (*di porco*) pork; *— tritata*, minced meat (*o* mincemeat); *questa — è tenera al taglio*, this meat cuts tender ‖ *non è — per i vostri denti*, *fig.* it is too good for you (*o* it is beyond your possibilities) ‖ *avere troppa — al fuoco*, to have too many irons in the fire ‖ *non essere nè — nè pesce*, to be neither fish, nor flesh, nor fowl (*o* to be fit for neither one thing nor another).
carnéfice, *s.m.* **1.** executioner; (*per impiccagione*) hangman (*pl.* hangmen); (*per decapitazione*) headsman (*pl.* headsmen) **2.** *fig.* (*aguzzino*) brutal fellow.
carneficína, *s.f.* carnage; slaughter.
càrneo, *ag.* meat (*attributivo*): *dieta carnea*, meat diet.
carnevalàta, *s.f.* **1.** (*divertimento carnevalesco*) carnival revelry **2.** (*buffonata*) buffoonery, clownery.
carnevàle, *s.m.* **1.** carnival: *fare —*, (*far baldoria*) to revel (*o* to make merry) ‖ *avere molti carnevali sulle spalle*, to be a man of many summers ‖ *di carnevale ogni scherzo vale*, prov. in carnival time, anything goes **2.** (*fantoccio*) carnival figure.

carnevalésco, *ag.* carnival (*attributivo*).

carnevalíno, *s.m.* first Sunday of Lent.

carnevalóne, *s.m.* Milanese high carnival.

carníccio, *s.m.* **1.** (*rimasuglio di carne attaccato alla pelle di un animale scuotato*) shreds (of flesh) (*pl.*) **2.** (*parte interna della pelle di un animale*) inner side of an animal's skin.

Càrniche (Alpi), *no.pr.f.pl.* (*geog.*) Carnic Alps.

carnicíno, *ag.* flesh-coloured ‖ *s.m.* flesh-colour.

carnièra, *s.f.*, **carnière,** *s.m.* game-bag.

carnificazióne, *s.f.* (*patol.*) carnification.

carnísmo, *s.m.* abuse of meat.

carnívoro, *ag.* flesh-eating, carnivorous: *animale* —, flesh-eating (*o* carnivorous) animal; *pianta carnivora,* carnivorous plant.

carnívori, *s.m.pl.* (*zool.*) Carnivora.

carnosità, *s.f.* **1.** fleshiness; plumpness **2.** (*escrescenza*) fleshy excrescence.

carnóso, *ag.* **1.** fleshy: *braccia carnose,* fleshy arms; *escrescenza carnosa,* fleshy excrescence **2.** (*ricco di polpa*) fleshy, pulpy; (*di foglie*) succulent: *una pesca carnosa,* a fleshy peach.

carnúto, *ag.* fleshy; plump.

càro¹, *ag.* **1.** dear: *che* — *bambino!,* what a dear child!; *mia cara, mio* —!, my dear!; *mia carissima mamma,* my dearest mother; *i nostri cari,* our family (*o* our dear ones *o* our relatives); *in risposta alla vostra cara lettera,* in reply to your kind letter; *sì,* —!, *no,* —!, yes, dear!, no, dear!; *così non va,* — *mio!,* I don't like this, my dear fellow!; *egli mi è* —, he is dear to me; *è un tuo* — *amico,* he is a dear friend of yours; *tua cugina è una cara ragazza,* your cousin is a dear ‖ *aver* — *di fare ql.co.,* to be glad to do sthg.; *aver* — *un collaboratore,* to value s.o.'s collaboration; *aver* — *qlcu.,* to love s.o. (*o* to be fond of s.o.); *rendere cara una persona a qlcu.,* to endear a person to s.o.; *rendersi* — *a qlcu.,* to endear oneself to s.o.; *tenerci ql.co., qlcu.,* to be fond of (*o* to like) sthg., s.o. very much **2.** (*costoso*) dear, expensive: *stoffa cara,* expensive material; *la frutta è troppo cara in questa stagione,* fruit is too dear in this season; *quel negozio è molto* —, that is a very dear shop ‖ *s.m.* (*alto costo*) high cost, high price: *il* — *viveri,* (*carovita*) the high cost of living.

càro¹, *av.* (*a caro prezzo*) dear, dearly: *l'affare mi è costato* —, the affair cost me dear; *pagar* — *ql.co.,* to pay dear (*o* dearly) for sthg. (*o* to buy sthg. dearly) (anche *fig.*); *vender* —, to sell dear (anche *fig.*): *vendettero* — *le loro vite,* they sold their lives dear.

càro², *s.m.* (*bot.*) Carum.

càro³, *s.m.* (*patol.*) carus, carotic sleep.

carógna, *s.f.* **1.** carrion **2.** *fig.* (*persona spregevole*) carrion; rotter.

caròla, *s.f.* ring-dance, dancing and singing in a circle.

carolàre, *v.i.* to dance and sing in a circle.

Carolína¹, *no.pr.f.* Caroline ‖ *dim.* Carrie.

carolína², *s.f.* (*biliardo*) cannon, carom.

carolíngio, *ag.s.m.* (*st.*) Carlovingian, Carolingian.

Carónte, *no.pr.m.* (*lett.*) Charon.

carosèllo, *s.m.* **1.** (*torneo di cavalieri*) carousel; tournament **2.** (*giostra*) merry-go-round; (*amer.*) carousel.

caròsi, *s.m.* (*patol.*) carus, carotic sleep.

caròta, *s.f.* carrot ‖ *piantar carote, fig.* to tell stories.

caròtide, *s.f.* (*anat.*) carotid (artery).

carovàna, *s.f.* **1.** caravan ‖ *viaggiare in* —, to travel in convoy (*o fam.* to travel nose to tail) **2.** (*folto gruppo*) large company **3.** (*noviziato*) novitiate; training.

carovanièra, *s.f.* track (for caravans).

carovanière, *s.m.* caravan-leader, caravaneer.

carovíta, carovíveri, *s.m.* **1.** high cost-of-living **2.** (*indennità*) cost-of-living allowance.

càrpa, *s.f.* (*ittiol.*) carp (*invariato al pl.*): — *dagli specchietti,* mirror carp.

Carpàzi(i), *no.pr.m.pl.* (*geog.*) the Carpathians.

carpentería, *s.f.* **1.** (*arte del carpentiere*) carpentry **2.** (*officina del carpentiere*) carpenter's shop.

carpentière, *s.m.* **1.** carpenter **2.** (*carradore*) cartwright, wheelwright.

càrpine, càrpino, *s.m.* (*bot.*) hornbeam.

carpionàre, *v.t.* (*cuc.*) to souse.

carpióne, *s.m.* (*ittiol.*) large carp.

carpíre, *v.t.* **1.** (*sottrarre con violenza*) to snatch, to extort, to seize: *gli carpì di mano la rivoltella,* he snatched the revolver from his hand; *non potemmo carpirgli il segreto,* we could not extort the secret from him; — *denaro,* to extort money **2.** (*estorcere con astuzia*) to swindle, to cheat: *mi carpì cinquanta sterline,* he cheated me out of fifty pounds (*o* he swindled fifty pounds out of me).

càrpo, *s.m.* (*anat.*) carpus (*pl.* carpi).

carpología, *s.f.* carpology.

carpóne, carpóni, *av.* on all fours: *trascinarsi* —, to crawl on all fours.

carradóre, *s.m.* wheelwright, cartwright.

carràia, *ag.:* *porta* —, carriage gateway (*o* carriage door) ‖ *s.f.* cart-road.

carràio, *s.m.* wheelwright, cartwright.

carraréccia, *s.f.* cartway, cart-road.

carràta, *s.f.* cartful; cart-load: *una* — *di carbone,* a cart-load of coal ‖ *a carrate,* (*a bizzeffe*) galore: *questo anno abbiamo avuto mele a carrate,* this year we have had apple galore (*o* plenty of apples).

carreggiàbile, *ag.* carriageable ‖ *s.f* cartway, cart-road.

carreggiàre, *v.t.* to cart ‖ *v.i.* to drive a cart.

carreggiàta, *s.f.* **1.** (*solco, rotaia*) track, (wheel) rut ‖ *andare per la* —, *fig.* to follow the usual course ‖ ‖ *rimettere qlcu. in* —, (*moralmente*) to set s.o. right; (*riportarlo a bomba*) to bring s.o. back to the point; *rimettersi in* —, *fig.* to get right (*o* to get back) to the point; *stare in* —, *fig.* to stick (*o* to keep) to the point; *uscire di* —, *fig.* to go astray (*o* to fail in one's duty); (*deviare col discorso*) not to keep to the point **2.** (*strada*) cartway, cart-road **3.** (*scartamento*) gauge, gage; (*di automobile*) track.

carréggio, *s.m.* **1.** (*trasporto con carri*) cartage, carting **2.** (*mil.*) transport; (*salmerie*) goods-train.

carrellàre, *v.i.* (*cine. tv.*) to track, to dolly: — *all'indietro,* to track (*o* to dolly) out; — *in avanti,* to track (*o* to dolly) in.

carrellàta, *s.f.* (*cine.tv.*) tracking shot, travel shot, running shot.

carrèllo, *s.m.* **1.** (*ferr.*) (*per ispezione binari*) trolley; (*vagoncino*) wa(g)gon **2.** (*ferr.*) (*telaio*) bogie; (*amer.*) truck **3.** (*aer.*) undercarriage, landing gear: — *retrattile,* retractable undercarriage; *ritirare il* —, to draw up (*o* to pull in) the undercarriage **4.** (*cine. tv.*) dolly **5.** (*di macchina per scrivere*) carriage **6.** (*di trasformatore elettrico*) truck.

carrétta, *s.f.* cart: — *a mano,* hand-cart ‖ *tirar la* —, *fig.* to drudge (*o* to slave).

carrettàio, *s.m.* carter, teamster.

carrettàta, *s.f.* cartful; cart-load.

carrettière, *s.m.* carter, teamster.

carrétto, *s.m.* hand-cart, barrow.

carrettóne, *s.m.* **1.** wa(g)gon **2.** (*carro funebre dei poveri*) paupers' hearse.

carriàggio, *s.m.* (*mil.*) wa(g)gon; (*salmerie*) wagon-train, goods-train.

carrièra, *s.f.* **1.** career, full speed: *attraversò il paesetto di gran* —, he careered through the village; *andare di gran* —, to run at full speed (*o* to career) **2.** (*professione*) career: *una* — *aperta alle donne,* a career open to women; — *diplomatica, militare,* diplomatic, military career; *funzionario di* —, government official; (*in Gran Bretagna*) civil servant; *ufficiale di* —, regular (*o* professional) officer ‖ *farai molta* —!, you'll have a very successful career! (*o fam.* you'll make good!).

carrísta, *s.m.* (*mil.*) tankman (*pl.* tankmen).

carriuòla, *s.f.* wheelbarrow.

càrro, *s.m.* **1.** (*generalmente a due ruote*) cart; (*a* *quattro ruote*) wa(g)gon: — *attrezzi*, (*aut.*) break-down van (*o amer.* wrecker); — *funebre*, hearse ‖ — *di Tespi*, travelling-theatre ‖ *Gran Carro*, (*astr.*) Great Bear; *Piccolo Carro*, (*astr.*) Little Bear ‖ *essere l'ultima ruota del* —, *fig.* to be the least important person ‖ *mettere il* — *innanzi ai buoi*, *fig.* to put the cart before the horse **2.** (*ferr.*) railway wa(g)gon; (*amer.*) railway car: — *bagagli*, luggage-van; — *di scorta*, tender; — *merci*, truck (o goods wa(g)gon) **3.** (*mil.*): — *armato*, tank (o armoured car); — *armato leggero*, light tank.

carròccio, *s.m.* (*st.*) "carroccio" (a car which accompanied the army and bore the standard of an Italian free city of the Middle Ages).

carròzza, *s.f.* **1.** carriage: — *di piazza*, cab (o hackney-coach); — *tirata da due cavalli*, coach and pair; — *tirata da quattro cavalli*, coach and four; *andare in* —, to drive in a carriage ‖ *marciare in* —, (*far vita agiata*) to lead a life of ease **2.** (*ferr.*) carriage, coach; (*amer.*) railway-car: — *belvedere*, observation car; — *con buffet*, buffet car; — *diretta*, through coach; — *letto*, sleeping-car (o sleeper); — *ristorante*, dining-car; — *viaggiatori*, passenger car; *la* — *di prima classe è davanti*, the first-class carriage is in front.

carrozzàbile, *ag.* carriageable; carriage (*attributivo*): *strada* —, carriage road.

carrozzàio, *V.* **carrozzière.**

carrozzàre, *v.t.* (*un'automobile*) to fit the body on (a motor-car).

carrozzàta, *s.f.* coach-load, coachful, carriage load.

carrozzèlla, *s.f.* **1.** cab; light carriage **2.** (*carrozzina*) perambulator; (*fam.*) pram; (*amer.*) baby carriage.

carrozzería, *s.f.* **1.** (*di automobile*) body, body work, coachwork: — *bicolore*, two-tone colour body; — *da corsa*, racing body; — *fuori serie*, custom-built body **2.** (*fabbrica di carrozze*) coach-maker's, carriage-builder's.

carrozzière, *s.m.* **1.** (*chi fabbrica carrozze*) coach-maker, carriage-builder **2.** (*chi fabbrica carrozzerie di automobili*) coach-builder, body-maker.

carrozzína, *s.f.* perambulator; (*fam.*) pram; (*amer.*) baby carriage.

carrozzíno, *s.m.* **1.** light carriage **2.** (*di motocicletta*) sidecar.

carrozzóne, *s.m.* large carriage: — *di zingari*, caravan; — *mortuario*, hearse.

carrúba, *s.f.* (*bot.*) carob.

carrúbo, *s.m.* (*bot.*) carob-tree.

carrúccio, *s.m.* baby's go-cart.

carrúcola, *s.f.* pulley, sheave; — *per catena*, chain pulley ‖ *ungere le carrucole*, (*procedere per corruzione*) to grease the wheels.

càrsico, *ag.* (*geol.*) Karst (*attributivo*): *formazione carsica*, Karst-formation.

Càrso, *no.pr.m.* (*geog.*) Karst.

càrta, *s.f.* **1.** paper: — *a macchina*, machine paper; — *a mano*, handmade paper; — *asciugante, assorbente*, blotting-paper; — *bollata*, stamped paper; — *da disegno*, drawing-paper; — *da giornale*, news-print; — *da lettera*, (*a fogli piccoli*) note-paper; (*a fogli grandi*) letter-paper (o writing-paper); — *da pacchi*, packing-paper (o wrapping-paper); — *da parati*, wall-paper; — *gommata*, gum-coated paper; — *igienica*, toilet-paper; — *intestata*, headed note-paper; — *moneta*, paper-money (o paper currency o banknotes); — *moschicida*, fly-paper; — *oleata*, oil-paper; — *patinata*, art paper; — *pergamena*, vellum paper; — *per ricalcare*, tracing-paper; — *protocollo*, foolscap; — *quadrettata*, squared paper; — *rigata*, ruled paper; — *sensibile*, (*foto.*) photographic paper; — *smerigliata*, emery-paper; — *stagnola*, tin foil; — *velina*, tissue-paper; *fabbisogno, consumo di* —, paper consumption; *fabbricazione della* —, paper making (o paper manufacturing); *un foglietto di* —, a slip of paper; *foglio di* —, sheet of paper; *industria della* —, paper manufacture ‖ *le sacre carte*, (*la Bibbia*) the Holy Writ (o the Scriptures) ‖ *mangiare alla* —, to

dine à la carte ‖ *mettere ql.co. in* —, to put sthg. down in writing **2.** (*documento*) paper, document, writing: — *di identità*, identity card; *le mie carte*, my documents (o my papers) ‖ *avere* — *bianca*, to have authority (o] *fam.* to have a free hand); *dare* — *bianca a qlcu.*, to give full power (o authority) to s.o. (o *fam.* to give s.o. a free hand) **3.** (*statuto*) charter ‖ *Magna Carta*, Magna Carta (o Magna Charta) **4.** (*carta geografica*) map: — *automobilistica*, motoring (o road) map; *la* — *d'Italia*, the map of Italy; — *meteorologica*, weather chart; — *nautica*, chart; — *topografica*, topographic map **5.** (*da giuoco*) playing-card, card: *mazzo di carte*, pack of cards; *alzare le carte*, to cut the cards; *dare le carte*, to deal the cards; *giocare una* — *sicura*, to play a safe card; *mescolare le carte*, to shuffle the cards ‖ *cambiare le carte in mano*, *fig.* to change the meaning of sthg. maliciously ‖ *fare le carte a qlcu.*, to read s.o.'s fortune in cards ‖ *giocare una* —, *fig.* to try a card (o to run a risk) ‖ *giocare a carte scoperte*, *fig.* to act above board (o to play fair) ‖ *mandare a carte quarantotto*, to send to the devil ‖ *mettere le carte in tavola*, *fig.* to put one's cards on the table (o to make things clear); *il mettere le carte in tavola*, (*il venire ad un'aperta spiegazione*) a show-down.

cartacarbóne, *s.f.* carbon paper.

cartàccia, *s.f.* **1.** (*cartastraccia*) waste-paper **2.** (*carta da giuoco di poco o nessun valore*) worthless card.

cartàceo, *ag.* papery, paper (*attributivo*): *circolazione cartacea*, paper currency; *moneta cartacea*, paper money.

Cartagèna, *no.pr.f.* (*geog.*) Carthagena.

Cartàgine, *no.pr.f.* (*geog. st.*) Carthago.

cartaginése, *ag.s.c.* Carthaginian.

cartàio, *s.m.* **1.** (*fabbricante di carta*) paper-manufacturer, paper-maker **2.** (*chi fa le carte al giuoco*) dealer.

cartapècora, *s.f.* parchment, vellum.

cartapésta, *s.f.* paper-pulp; papier mâché.

cartastràccia, *s.f.* waste-paper.

cartavetràta, *s.f.* sand-paper; glass-paper.

carteggiàre, *v.i.* to correspond.

cartéggio, *s.m.* **1.** correspondence; exchange of letters **2.** (*collezione di lettere*) collection of letters.

cartèlla, *s.f.* **1.** (*di cartone*) folder; (*di cuoio*) portfolio, brief-case; (*da scrittoio*) writing-pad **2.** (*da scuola*) satchel, school-bag **3.** (*pagina*) page, sheet: *manoscritto in tre cartelle*, three sheets (o pages) of manuscript **4.** (*polizza, azione*) share; (*obbligazione*) bond: — *del Debito Pubblico*, Government bond; — *di godimento*, redeemed share **5.** (*della tombola*) tombola score-card, bingo score-card; (*di lotteria*) lottery-ticket **6.** (*lapide, targa*) tablet.

cartellièra, *s.f.* filing cabinet, file.

cartellíno, *s.m.* **1.** (*biglietto*) ticket **2.** (*etichetta*) label.

cartellísta, *s.m.* (*comm.*) member of a trust, member of a cartel.

cartèllo, *s.m.* **1.** bill; (*pubblicitario*) poster, placard: — *di divieto*, warning notice; — *indicatore*, traffic (o road) sign ‖ *artista di* —, eminent (o high-class) artist **2.** (*etichetta*) label **3.** (*insegna*) sign-board **4.** (*comm.*) (*sindacato*) trust, cartel; syndicate **5.** — *di sfida*, challenge (o cartel).

cartellóne, *s.m.* **1.** wall poster: — *pubblicitario*, (advertising) poster **2.** (*teat.*) bill ‖ *tenere il* —, to run (o to have a run): *quell'operetta nuova tiene ancora il* —, that new musical comedy is still running.

cartellonísta, *s.m.* commercial artist.

cartesianísmo, *s.m.* (*st. fil.*) Cartesianism.

cartesiàno, *ag.s.m.* (*st. fil.*) Cartesian.

Cartèsio, *no.pr.* (*st. fil.*) Cartesius.

cartièra, *s.f.* **1.** paper-mill **2.** (*mar.*) chart-room.

cartíglia, *s.f.* (*al giuoco delle carte*) low cards (*pl.*).

cartíglio, *s.m.* (*arch.*) (*fregio a forma di rotolo di carta*) cartouche; scroll ornament.

cartilàgine, *s.f.* cartilage.

cartilagíneo, cartilaginóso, *ag.* cartilaginous.

cartína, *s.f.* **1.** (*di medicinale*) dose: *una* — *di chi-*

nino, a dose of quinine **2.** *una — di aghi*, a packet of needles **3.** *— per sigarette*, cigarette-paper.

cartísmo, *s.m.* (*st. pol.*) Chartism.

cartísta, *s.m.* (*st. pol.*) Chartist.

cartocciàta, *s.f.* bagful.

cartòccio, *s.m.* **1.** paper-bag; (*fatto a cono*) cornet **2.** (*arch.*) cartouche; (*voluta di capitello ionico, corinzio*) scroll **3.** (*artigl.*) (*carica di lancio*) powder charge **4.** *pl.* (*per materassi rustici*) dried maize leaves.

cartografía, *s.f.* cartography; map-making.

cartogràfico, *ag.* cartographic(al).

cartògrafo, *s.m.* cartographer; map-maker.

cartolàio, *s.m.* stationer.

cartolería, *s.f.* **1.** (*negozio*) stationer's shop **2.** (*articoli di cancelleria*) stationery (articles).

cartolína, *s.f.* (post)card: *— illustrata*, picture postcard; *— postale*, postcard *|| — precetto*, (*mil.*) calling-up papers *|| — vaglia*, postal (o money) order.

cartomànte, *s.c.* fortune-teller.

cartomanzía, *s.f.* cartomancy.

cartonàggio, *s.m.* paste-board articles (*pl.*); (*lavoro in cartone*) paste-board work.

cartoncíno, *s.m.* thin card: *— da visita*, visiting-card; *— patinato*, coated board (o art board).

cartóne, *s.m.* **1.** cardboard; paste-board; (*molto grosso*) millboard: *scatola di —*, cardboard box (o carton) **2.** (*pitt.*) cartoon: *i cartoni di Raffaello*, Raphael's cartoons **3.** *cartoni animati*, (*cine.*) animated cartoons.

cartóso, *ag.* papery; paper-like.

cartúccia, *s.f.* cartridge: *— a palla*, ball-cartridge; *— a polvere sola, a salve*, blank cartridge *|| mezza —*, (*spreg.*) (*omuncolo*) shrimp *|| l'ultima —*, *fig.* one's last resource.

cartuccièra, *s.f.* cartridge-belt; cartridge-pouch.

carúncola, *s.f.* (*anat.*) caruncle.

carúso, *s.m.* (*dial.*) " caruso " (youth employed in sulphur mines in Sicily).

càsa, *s.f.* **1.** (*abitazione*) house; (*residenza abituale, ambiente familiare*) home: *— colonica*, farm-house; *— di campagna*, country-house; *amico di —*, family friend; *donna di —*, woman fond of her home (o a stay-at-home); (*brava massaia*) housewife (o house-keeper); *fatto in —*, home-made; *nostalgia di —*, home-sickness; *abita a — nostra*, he lives at our house (o he lives with us); *andammo a — loro*, we went to their house (o we went to them); *chi andò a — di mio zio?*, who went to my uncle's (house)?; *andare a —*, to go home; *essere di —*, to be familiar (o intimate); *essere fuori di —*, to be out (of doors); *essere in —*, to be at home (o to be indoors); *esser via da, lontano da —*, to be away, far from home; *restare a —*, to stay at home (o to keep indoors); *stare di —*, to live (o to reside o to dwell); *tornare a —*, to go back (o to come back o to return) home; *uscire di —*, to go out *|| — mia, — mia...*, home, sweet home *|| andare di — in —*, to go from door to door *|| fare una — del diavolo*, to kick up a row (o to raise hell); *mandare qlcu. a — del diavolo*, to send s.o. to hell; *stare a — del diavolo*, to live in an out-of-the-way place *|| fare gli onori di —*, to receive guests *|| mettere su —*, to set up house; (*sposarsi*) to get married *|| non avere nè — nè tetto*, to be homeless *|| ognuno è re in casa propria*, *prov.* everyman is master in his own home **2.** (*convento*) religious house, religious community, convent: *— madre*, mother house **3.** (*edificio pubblico*) house: *— comunale*, town hall (o municipality); *— da giuoco*, gambling (o gaming) house; *— dello studente*, (University) students' hostel; *— di correzione*, reformatory (school) (o Borstal); *— di cura, di salute*, nursing home; *— di pena*, penitentiary (o prison o gaol); *— di tolleranza*, licensed brothel; *— malfamata*, house of ill fame; *— per malattie mentali*, lunatic asylum (o mental hospital) **4.** (*famiglia, stirpe, lignaggio, dinastia*) house; dynasty; family: *la — di Windsor*, the House of Windsor **5.** (*governo di casa*) household: *capo di —*, head of a household;

doveri di —, household duties; *spese di —*, household expenses *|| maestro di —*, butler *|| la Real Casa*, the Royal Household **6.** (*comm.*) house, firm: *— bancaria*, banking house; *— commerciale*, commercial house (o business house o firm); *— editrice*, publishing house (o publishers); *— madre*, head office.

casàcca, *s.f.* coat; jacket *|| voltar —*, *fig.* to turn one's coat (o to change sides).

casàccio, a, *l.av.* at random: *un'osservazione fatta a —*, a random remark; *parlare a —*, to talk at random; *sparare a —*, to shoot at random.

casàle, *s.m.* **1.** (*gruppo di case in campagna*) hamlet **2.** (*casolare*) farm-house.

casalínga *s.f.* housewife.

casalíngo, *ag.* **1.** (*di casa*) homely, domestic: *abitudini casalinghe, costumi casalinghi*, domestic habits; *atmosfera casalinga*, homely atmosphere; *donna casalinga*, (*che ama la vita di casa*) domestic woman; (*buona massaia*) good housewife **2.** (*semplice, alla buona*) plain, simple, homely: *cucina casalinga*, plain cooking *|| alla casalinga*, simply (o plainly o in a homely fashion) **3.** (*fatto in casa*) home-made: *pane —*, home-made bread.

casamàtta, *s.f.* (*mil.*) casemate, pill-box.

casaménto, *s.m.* **1.** tenement-house **2.** (*gli inquilini*) tenants (*pl.*) **3.** (*grosso edificio*) large building.

casàro, *s.m.* dairyman (*pl.* dairymen).

casàta, *s.f.* lineage, family.

casàtico, *s.m.* (*dir.*) property tax.

casàto, *s.m.* **1.** (*cognome*) surname, family name **2.** (*nascita, origine*) birth; origin: *di nobile —*, of noble birth **3.** (*casata, famiglia*) family.

caseàggine, *s.f.* (*stanchezza*) weariness; (*fiacchezza*) languor; (*sonnolenza*) drowsiness.

càsca-in-pètto, *s.m.* pendant, pendent.

cascàme, *s.m.* waste: *— di cotone*, cotton waste; *— di seta*, silk waste.

cascamòrto, *s.m.* **1.** (*innamorato*) spoon: *fare il — a una ragazza*, to run (o to dangle) after a girl **2.** (*damerino*) fop, dandy, beau (*pl.* beaux).

cascànte, *ag.* (*debole*) weak, feeble; (*floscio, flaccido*) flabby (anche *fig.*); (*cadente*) drooping, falling: *guance cascanti*, flabby cheeks.

càscara sagràda, *s.f.* (*farm.*) cascara sagrada.

cascàre, *v.i.* **1.** to fall (down), to tumble (down); (*con fracasso*) to crash (down): *è cascato il soffitto*, the ceiling has fallen (o crashed) down; *i piatti cascarono sui pavimento*, the dishes crashed to the floor *|| mi cascano le braccia*, I am dumbfounded (o I am nonplussed) *|| nemmeno se cascasse il mondo*, happen what may; *non casca il mondo se...*, nothing will happen even if... *|| qui casca l'asino*, here is the stumbling-block *|| — dalla fame*, to be starving (o dying of hunger) *|| — dalle nuvole*, to be struck with amazement *|| — dal sonno*, to be overcome with sleep *|| — ritto*, *fig.* to fall on one's feet *|| far — ql.co. dall'alto*, to grant (o to do) sthg. as a special favour **2.** (*rovinarsi*) to fall into ruin.

cascàta, *s.f.* **1.** (*caduta*) fall, tumble **2.** (*d'acqua*) fall, waterfall; (*cascata*) *una — famosa*, a famous waterfall *|| le Cascate del Niagara*, Niagara Falls **3.** (*di perle, pizzi, ecc.*) cascade.

cascatíccio, *ag.* **1.** (*di frutto*) ready to drop **2.** *fig.* (*facile ad innamorarsi*) ready to fall in love.

cascemír, *s.m.* cashmere.

cascína, *s.f.* **1.** (*fattoria con bestie da latte*) dairy farm; (*cascinale*) farmstead **2.** (*caseificio*) dairy **3.** (*forma per formaggio*) cheese-mould.

cascinàio, *s.m.* (dairy-)farmer.

cascinàle, *s.m.* farmstead.

cascíno, *s.m.* (*forma per formaggio*) cheese-mould.

càsco, *s.m.* **1.** helmet; (*coloniale*) sun-helmet, topee, topi **2.** (*per asciugare i capelli*) hairdrier, dryer.

caseggiàto, *s.m.* block (of buildings).

caseifício, *s.m.* dairy.

caseína, *s.f.* (*chim.*) casein.

casèlla, *s.f.* 1. (*cassetta, scatola*) case, box: — *postale*, post(-office) box 2. (*vano di schedario*) pigeon -hole 3. (*cella di alveare*) cell.

casellànte, *s.m.* (*ferr.*) signalman (*pl.* signalmen); (*custode di passaggio a livello*) (level)crossing keeper.

casellàrio, *s.m.* set of pigeon-holes: — *penale*, (criminal) records-office.

casellísta, *s.m.* a post-office box holder.

casèllo, *s.m.* (*ferr.*) signalman's house.

caseréccio, *ag.* homely, home-made: *pane* —, home -made bread.

casèrma, *s.f.* barracks (*pl.*).

casermàggio, *s.m.* barrack equipment.

casétta, *s.f.* little house; small house; cottage.

casigliàno, *s.m.* fellow-tenant.

casimír, *s.m.* cashmere.

Casimíro, *no.pr.m.* Casimir, Kasimir.

casína, *s.f.* little house; small house; cottage.

casíno, *s.m.* 1. country-house 2. (*capanno da caccia*) shooting lodge 3. (*sede di circolo o club*) club, club -house 4. (*ritrovo per giuoco, danze*) Casino.

casípola, *s.f.* poor cottage, hut, hovel; (*amer.*) cabin.

casísta, *s.m.* (*teol.*) casuist.

casística, *s.f.* (*teol.*) casuistry.

càso, *s.m.* 1. chance: — *volle che gli parlassi*, I chanced to speak to him; *fu un puro* —, it was mere chance ‖ *a* —, at random: *scegliere a* —, to choose at random ‖ *per* —, by chance: *udimmo per* —, we heard by chance 2. (*fatto, circostanza*) case; (*avvenimento*) event: *i casi della vita*, the events of life; (*gli alti e bassi*) the ups and downs of life; — *di coscienza*, case of conscience; *un* — *di difterite*, a case of diphtheria; — *giuridico*, legal case; — *imprevisto*, unforeseen event; — *limite*, border-line event; — *medico*, medical case; *molti casi di rapina*, many cases of robbery; *esponimi il tuo* —, put your case to me; *farò un'eccezione nel vostro* —, I'll make an exception in your case; *questo non è il vostro* —, this is not your case ‖ *pensate ai casi vostri*, mind your own business ‖ *questo fa al* — *nostro*, this is what we want 3. (*eventualità*) instance, case: *in* — *affermativo*, in the affirmative; *in* — *di attacco nemico*, in case of enemy attack; *in* — *di incendio telefonate a questo numero*, in case of fire call this number; *nel* — *che non ci sia*, in the case of his not being there; *nel* — *vi abbisognasse denaro...*, should you need any money... ‖ — *mai, in* —, in case ‖ *in ogni* —, in any case (*o* at all events *o* at any rate) ‖ *in tal* —, in that case ‖ *poniamo il* — *che*, let us put the case (*o* let us suppose) that 4. (*possibilità, modo*) way, possibility: *non c'è* — *di convincerlo*, there is no way of convincing him 5. *far* — *a ql.co., qlcu.*, to take sthg., s.o. into account: *non far* — *a ql.co., qlcu.*, to make little (*o* take no) account of sthg., s.o. 6. (*gram.*) case: — *nominativo*, nominative case.

casolàre, *s.m.* cottage: *torna al tuo* —, come back home.

casòtto, *s.m.* 1. (*garitta*) sentry-box 2. (*cabina*) cabin 3. (*canile*) kennel 4. (*mar.*): — *del timone*, wheel -house; — *di rotta*, chartroom, charthouse 5. (*bordello*) brothel.

Càspio (Mar), *no.pr.m.* (*geog.*) Caspian Sea.

càspita, caspiterína, *inter.* good gracious!, by Jove!.

càssa, *s.f.* 1. case, box; chest; (*cofano*) coffer: — *da morto*, coffin; — *di merci*, case of goods; *dieci casse di mele*, ten cases (*o* boxes) of apples 2. (*comm.*) cash; (*fondo*) fund: — *malattie*, sickness fund; — *sociale*, company's cash on hand; *avanzo di* —, cash on hand; *fondo di* —, reserve fund; *libro* —, cash-book; *netto* —, net cash; *pagamento per* —, cash-payment; *pronta* —, cash down (*o* by cash *o* ready money); *registratore di* —, cash-register; *sportello di* —, cashier's window; *avere denaro in* —, to have money on hand; *pagare*

alla —, to pay at the desk; *tenere la* —, to be in charge of the cash; *fig.* to collect money ‖ *Cassa di Risparmio*, Saving Bank 3. (*anat.*): — *del timpano*, eardrum; — *toracica*, chest 4. (*mus.*) case: — *del pianoforte*, piano case; — *del violino*, violin case ‖ *gran* —, bass-drum: *battere la gran* —, to bang the bass-drum; *fig.* to exaggerate 5. (*tip.*) case: — *per la spaziatura*, space and quad case; *alta, bassa* —, upper, lower case 6. (*tec.*): — *battente*, (*ind. tessile*) sley; — *d'aria*, (*mar.*) air-lock; — *del fuso*, (*ind. tessile*) spindle box; — *del fucile*, rifle-stock; — *di rapida immersione*, (*di sommergibile*) crash diving tank; *casse di rollio*, (*mar.*) rolling tanks; — *di risonanza*, (*acu.*) resonance box; — *per zavorra d'acqua*, (*mar.*) ballast tank.

cassafòrte, *s.f.* 1. safe, strong-box 2. (*camera blindata*) strong-room.

cassamàdia, *s.f.* kneading-trough.

cassaménto, *s.m.* cassation, annulment, revocation.

Cassàndra, *no.pr.f.* (*lett.*) Cassandra ‖ **cassàndra**, *s.f.* (*chi predice avvenimenti tristi*) cassandra.

cassapànca, *s.f.* chest.

cassàre, *v.t.* 1. to cancel, to annul, to quash 2. (*dir.*) to abrogate, to quash, to repeal.

cassàta, *s.f.* "cassata" (kind of Sicilian cake).

cassatúra, *s.f.* 1. (*atto ed effetto del cassare*) erasure, annulment 2. (*frego fatto per cassare*) cancellation.

cassàva, *s.f.* (*bot.*) cassava.

cassazióne, *s.f.* (*dir.*) cassation ‖ *Corte di Cassazione*, Court of Cassation.

casserétto, *s.m.* (*mar.*) poop deck.

càssero, *s.m.* (*mar.*) quarter-deck.

casseruòla, *s.f.* saucepan; stewpan: *vitello in* —, braised veal (*o* veal en casserole).

cassétta, *s.f.* 1. box; (*small*) case: — *da viaggio*, dressing case; — *degli attrezzi*, tool-box; — *della spazzatura*, dust-bin; — *delle lettere*, letter-box; (*su pilastrino*) pillar-box; — *di sicurezza*, safe; — *di pronto soccorso*, first aid kit 2. (*posto del cocchiere*) coach-box, coachman's seat; driver's seat: *montare a* —, to take the driver's seat; *stare a* —, to drive 3. (*cassa, riserva monetaria*) purse: — *privata* (*di un sovrano*), privy purse ‖ *questo film ha avuto un grande successo di* —, this film has been a great financial success.

cassétto, *s.m.* drawer.

cassettóne, *s.m.* 1. chest of drawers; (*amer.*) bureau 2. (*arch.*) lacunar: *soffitto a cassettoni*, lacunar (ceiling).

càssia, *s.f.* (*bot.*) Cassia ‖ *dare l'erba* — *a qlcu.*, *fig.* to sack s.o. (*o* to send s.o. away).

cassièra, *s.f.*, **cassière**, *s.m.* cashier; (*di banca*) teller, cashier.

cassinènse, cassinése, *ag.s.m.* Cassinese, Benedictine.

cassíno, *s.m.* 1. (*disco di panno per cancellare alla lavagna*) round black-board duster 2. (*carrettino di spazzino*) dust-cart.

Càssio, *no.pr.m.* (*st.*) Cassius.

Cassiodòro, *no.pr.m.* (*st. lett.*) Cassiodorus.

Cassiopèa, *no.pr.f.* (*mit. astr.*) Cassiopeia.

cassiterìte, *s.f.* (*min.*) cassiterite, tinstone.

cassóne, *s.m.* 1. large case; (*cassapanca*) chest 2. (*mil.*) (*carro per trasporto munizioni*) ammunition chest, ammunition waggon, caisson 3. (*edil.*) caisson; (*a compartimento stagno*) coffer-dam.

càssula, *V.* **càpsula**.

càsta, *s.f.* 1. caste 2. (*rango*) rank, class.

castàgna, *s.f.* 1. chestnut: — *allesso, arrosto*, boiled, roast chestnut; — *d'India*, horse-chestnut; — *secca*, dried chestnut ‖ *cavar la* — *dal fuoco con la zampa del gatto*, to make a cat's paw of s.o. (*o* to use a person as a tool) 2. (*mar.*) pawl 3. (*di cavallo*) chestnut.

castagnàceio, *s.m.* chestnut-tart, chestnut-cake.

castagnàio, *s.m.* 1. (*raccoglitore di castagne*) gatherer of chestnuts 2. (*venditore di castagne*) chestnut-vendor.

castagnatúra, *s.f.* chestnut harvest.

castagnéto, *s.m.* chestnut grove, chestnut wood.

castagnétta, *s.f.* 1. (*nacchera*) castanet 2. (*schiocco delle dita*) snapping (of fingers).

castàgno, *ag.* nut-brown, chestnut-coloured; chestnut (*attributivo*) ‖ *s.m.* 1. (*albero*) chestnut(-tree): — *d'India*, horse-chestnut(-tree) 2. (*legno*) chestnut(-wood).

castagnuòla, *s.f.* cracker, petard.

castàldo, *s.m.* 1. land-agent, steward 2. (*st.*) steward: — *del re*, the king's steward.

Castàlia, *no.pr.f.* (*geog. mit.*) Castalia, Castalie, Castaly.

castàlio, *ag.* (*mit.*) Castalian.

castaménte, *av.* chastely, purely.

castàneo, castàno, *ag.* chestnut-coloured, brown, nut-brown: — *chiaro*, light brown; *capelli castani*, brown hair.

castellàna, *s.f.* 1. lady of a castle 2. (*signora di residenza di campagna*) lady of a manor.

castellàno, *s.m.* 1. lord of a castle 2. (*signore di residenza di campagna*) lord of a manor 3. (*guardiano di castello*) castellan.

castellétto[1], *s.m.* (*piccolo castello*) small castle.

castellétto[2], *s.m.* (*comm.*) list of credit.

castèllo, *s.m.* 1. castle ‖ *un* — *di carte*, a house of cards (anche *fig.*) ‖ *fare castelli in aria*, to build castles in the air (*o* in Spain) 2. (*residenza di signori di campagna*) manor house 3. (*macchina di legno per assedio*) siege-tower 4. (*edil.*) scaffold 5. (*mar.*) deck, castle: — *di poppa*, quarter-deck; — *di prua*, forecastle (*o* foredeck) 6. (*impalcatura per bachi da seta*) silk-worm frames 7. (*impianto mobile per riparare fili aerei*) mobile maintenance tower (for repairing overhead wires).

castigàbile, *ag.* punishable.

castigamàtti, *s.m.* 1. (*bastone*) cane, cudgel 2. *fig.* (*persona rigida, severa*) martinet.

castigàre, *v.t.* 1. to punish, to chastise, to castigate 2. (*emendare, disciplinare*) to chasten: — *i propri sensi*, to chasten one's senses 3. (*correggere*) to correct, to chasten: — *il proprio stile*, to correct one's style 4. (*rar.*) (*danneggiare*) to injure, to spoil: *il gelo di ieri notte ha castigato le piante*, last night's frost damaged the trees.

castigataménte, *av.* 1. (*castamente*) chastely, with modesty 2. (*correttamente*) correctly.

castigatézza, *s.f.* 1. restraint, moderation, modesty: — *di linguaggio*, decency of speech (*o* decent language) 2. (*correttezza*) correctness: — *di stile, di lingua*, correctness (*o* purity) of style, of language.

castigàto, *ag.* 1. (*casto*) chaste, pure: *linguaggio* —, chaste (*o* decent *o* pure) language 2. (*emendato*) castigated: *edizione castigata*, expurgated (*o* bowdlerized) edition 3. (*corretto*) correct; (*di stile*) pure, sober.

castigatóre, *s.m.,* **castigatrice,** *s.f.* punisher; castigator.

Castíglia, *no.pr.f.* (*geog.*) Castile.

castigliàno, *ag.s.m.* Castilian.

castígo, *s.m.* punishment, chastisement: *mettere in* — *un bambino*, (*metterlo in un angolo*) to put a child in a corner ‖ — *di Dio*, *fig.* calamity (*o* scourge).

castimònia, *s.f.* pure life, chaste life.

castità, *s.f.* chastity.

càsto, *ag.* chaste, pure.

castóne, *s.m.* setting, bezel, collet.

Càstore, *no.pr.m.* (*mit.*) Castor: — *e Polluce*, Castor and Pollux.

castòreo, *s.m.* (*farm.*) (*antispasmodico*) castor.

castoríno, *s.m.* (*pelliccia*) nutria; coypu.

castòro, *s.m.* (*zool.*) beaver: *pelliccia di* —, beaver (fur).

castracàni, *s.m.* 1. dog-gelder 2. (*spreg.*) (*chirurgo maldestro*) incompetent surgeon, unskilful surgeon.

castrametazióne, *s.f.* castrametation.

castrapòrci, *s.m.* 1. pork-gelder 2. (*spreg.*) (*chirurgo maldestro*) incompetent surgeon, unskilful surgeon.

castràre, *v.t.* 1. to castrate, to geld; (*la femmina di un animale*) to spay 2. *fig.* (*emendare, un libro*) to expurgate, to bowdlerize 3. (*castagne*) to notch.

castràto, *ag.* 1. castrated, gelded 2. (*emendato, di libro*) expurgated, bowdlerized ‖ *s.m.* wether; (*carne*) mutton.

castratóio, *s.m.* castrating knife.

castratúra, castrazióne, *s.f.* castration.

castrènse, *ag.* castrensian ‖ *vescovo* —, bishop in ordinary to the forces.

castronàggine, *s.f.* (*volg.*) stupidity.

castróne, *s.m.* 1. (*montone castrato*) wether; (*cavallo castrato*) gelding 2. (*volg.*) (*persona stupida*) fool, stupid man, blockhead.

castroneria, *s.f.* (*volg.*) stupidity ‖ *dire castronerie*, to talk nonsense.

casuàle, *ag.* casual, fortuitous, accidental: *incontro* —, casual meeting ‖ *diritti* —, special bonuses.

casualísmo, *s.m.* (*fil.*) casualism.

casualità, *s.f.* casualness.

casualménte, *av.* casually, by chance, accidentally.

casuàrio, *s.m.* (*ornit.*) cassowary.

casúccia, *s.f.* small house, cottage.

casuísta, *s.m.* (*teol.*) casuist.

casúpola, *s.f.* poor house; (*amer.*) cabin; (*tugurio*) hovel.

catabolísmo, *s.m.* (*biol.*) catabolism, katabolism.

cataclísma, *s.m.* cataclysm (anche *fig.*).

catacómba, *s.f.* catacomb.

catacrèsi, *s.f.* (*ret.*) catachresis.

catacústica, *s.f.* catacoustics.

catafàlco, *s.m.* catafalque.

catafàscio, a, *l.av.* pell-mell, topsyturvy: *andare a* —, (*in rovina*) to go to rack and ruin.

catafràtta, *s.f.* (*armatura*) cataphract.

catafràtto, *s.m.* (*soldato vestito di catafratta*) cataphract.

Catài, *no.pr.m.* (*geog. st.*) Cathay.

catalàno, *ag.* Catalan ‖ *s.m.* 1. (*abitante*) Catalan ‖ *i catalani*, the Catalan 2. (*lingua*) (the) Catalan (language) ‖ **catalàna,** *s.f.* Catalan.

catalèssi[1], **catalessia,** *s.f.* (*med.*) catalepsy.

catalèssi[2], *s.f.* (*poes.*) catalexis.

catalèttico[1], *ag.s.m.* (*med.*) cataleptic.

catalèttico[2], *ag.* (*poes.*) catalectic.

catalètto, *s.m.* 1. (*barella*) stretcher 2. (*bara*) bier.

catàlisi, *s.f.* (*chim.*) catalysis.

catalítico, *ag.* (*chim.*) catalytic.

catalizzàre, *v.t.* (*chim.*) to catalyze.

catalizzatóre, *s.m.* (*chim.*) catalyst: — *negativo*, anti-catalyst (*o* depressor); (*inibitore di reazione*) inhibitor.

catalogàre, *v.t.* to catalogue, to list.

Catalógna, *no.pr.f.* (*geog.*) Catalonia.

catàlogo, *s.m.* catalogue, list; (*amer.*) catalog: — *generale, illustrato*, general, illustrated catalogue.

catàlpa, *s.f.* (*bot.*) Catalpa.

catapàno, *s.m.* (*st.*) catapan.

catapécchia, *s.f.* (*baracca*) hovel, wretched cabin; (*casa in rovina*) dilapidated house.

cataplàsma, *s.f.* 1. poultice, plaster, cataplasm 2. *fig.* (*persona noiosa*) bore; (*persona sempre in ansia per la propria salute*) valetudinarian.

cataplessía, *s.f.* (*patol.*) cataplexy.

catapúlta, *s.f.* catapult: — *al suolo*, (*aer.*) ground catapult; — *di portaerei*, (*aer.*) deck catapult.

catapultaménto, *s.m.* (*aer.*) catapulting.

catapultàre, *v.t.* (*aer.*) to catapult, to launch (by catapult).

cataràffio, *s.m.* (*mar.*) horsing iron, caulking iron, horse iron.

cataràtta, *V.* **cateràtta.**

catarifrangènte, *s.m.* reflector, reflex reflector: — *di bicicletta*, bicycle rear reflector.

catarísmo, *s.m.* (*st. relig.*) Catharism.

càtaro, *s.m.* (*st. relig.*) Catharist.

catarràle, *ag.* catarrhal.

catarrína, *s.f.* (*zool.*) cata(r)rhine.

catàrro, *s.m.* catarrh, rheum.

catarróso, *ag.* catarrhal, rheumy.

catàrsi, *s.f.* 1. (*teat.*) catharsis 2. (*purificazione*) catharsis; atonement, expiation.

catàrtico, *ag.* 1. (*teat.*) cathartic(al) 2. (*farm.*) cathartic(al), purgative ‖ *s.m.* (*farm.*) cathartic.

catàrzo, *s.m.* (*seta floscia, non lavorata*) floss (silk).

catàsta, *s.f.* 1. pile, heap, stack 2. (*miner.*) chock: — *di puntellamento*, crib.

catastàle, *ag.* cadastral.

catàsto, *s.m.* 1. cadastre, register of landed property: *ufficio del* —, land office 2. (*imposte sui beni immobili*) land-taxation.

catàstrofe, *s.f.* 1. catastrophe, ruin, disaster: — *finanziaria*, crash 2. (*teat.*) catastrophe.

catastròfico, *ag.* catastrophic(al); ruinous.

catatonía, *s.f.* (*patol.*) catatony.

catechèsi, *s.f.* (*eccl.*) catechesis.

catechètica, *s.f.* catechetics.

catechísmo, *s.m.* (*eccl.*) catechism.

catechísta, *s.m.* catechist.

catechizzàre, *v.t.* 1. to catechize 2. *fig.* (*cercare di persuadere*) to persuade.

catechizzatóre, *s.m.* catechizer.

catechizzazióne, *s.f.* catechizing.

catecú, *s.m.* (*farm.*) catechu, cashoo.

catecúmeno, *s.m.* catechumen.

categoría, *s.f.* 1. category, class: *ristorante di prima* —, first-class restaurant 2. (*fil.*) category.

categoricaménte, *av.* categorically.

categòrico, *ag.* 1. (*assoluto*) categorical, absolute, unconditional: *ordine* —, unconditional order; *rifiuto* —, flat (*o* categorical) refusal 2. (*preciso, esplicito*) outspoken, precise, direct: *risposta categorica*, outspoken answer 3. (*fil.*) categorical: *imperativo* —, categorical imperative.

caténa, *s.f.* 1. chain: — *dell'uscio*, door chain; *una lunga* — *di ferro*, a long iron chain; *prigioniero in catene*, prisoner in chains; (*in ceppi*) prisoner in fetters; *mettere un cane alla* —, to put a dog on the chain ‖ *pazzo da* —, starkmad 2. *fig.* bond, tie; shackles (*pl.*): *le catene dell'amicizia*, the bonds of friendship; *liberarsi dalle catene del convenzionalismo*, to shake off the shackles of convention; *rodere la* —, to chafe (*o* to fret); *spezzare le catene*, to shake off one's fetters; *tenere qlcu. a* —, to keep s.o. in complete subjection 3. (*serie, successione*) chain, succession, sequence: — *di avvenimenti*, chain of events 4. (*di montagne*) chain 5. (*fis.*) chain: — *aperta, chiusa*, open, closed chain (of atoms); *reazione a* —, chain reaction 6. (*tec.*): — *antisdrucciolevole*, (*da neve*) (*aut.*) skid chain; — *articolata*, (*mec.*) flat link (*o* sprocket) chain; — *da trasmissione*, (*mec.*) block chain; — *di ancora*, (*mar.*) anchor chain (*o* chain cable); — *di bicicletta*, bicycle chain; — *di ordito*, (*ind. tessile*) chain, warp; — *di ormeggio*, (*mar.*) mooring chain; — *piena*, (*ind. tessile*) full warp; — *rinforzata*, (*mar.*) stud chain.

catenàccio, *s.m.* 1. bolt, padlock: *chiudere a* — *una porta*, to bolt a door 2. (*vecchia automobile*) old crock; jalo(p)py.

catenària, *s.f.* (*scienza delle costruzioni*) catenary, catenary curve.

catenèlla, *s.f.* small chain, fine chain: — *da orologio*, watch-chain ‖ *punto* —, (*cucito*) chain-stitch.

cateràtta, *s.f.* 1. cataract: *le cateratte del Nilo*, the cataracts of the Nile ‖ *piovere a cateratte*, to rain heavily (*o* to pour *o* fam. to rain cats and dogs) 2. (*chiusa di canale*) sluice-gate, sluice 3. (*patol.*) cataract: *operare una* —, to remove a cataract.

caterattàio, *s.m.* locksman (*pl.* locksmen); lock-keeper.

Caterína, *no.pr.f.* Catherine, Catharine, Catharina ‖ *Santa* — *da Siena*, St. Catherine of Siena ‖ *dim.* Kate, Kit, Kitty, Cat, Cathy, Catty.

catèrva, *s.f.* (*di persone*) crowd, multitude, great number, host; (*di cose*) great quantity: *ha una* — *di amici*, he has host of friends.

catetère, *s.m.* (*med.*) catheter.

cateterísmo, *s.m.* (*med.*) catheterism, catheterization.

catèto, *s.m.* (*geom.*) cathetus (*pl.* catheti).

Catilína, *no.pr.m.* (*st.*) Catiline.

catilinària, *s.f.* invective.

catinàio, *s.m.* (*chi vende catini*) basin vendor.

catinèlla, *s.f.* basin ‖ *piovere a catinelle*, to rain in torrents (*o* to pour *o* fam.) to rain cats and dogs).

catinellàta, *s.f.* basinful.

catíno, *s.m.* basin.

catióne, *s.m.* (*fis.*) cation.

catiònico, *ag.* (*fis.*) cationic.

catoblèpa, *s.f.* (*mit.*) catoblepas.

catòdico, *ag.* (*fis.*) cathodal; cathode (*attributivo*): *raggi catodici*, cathode rays.

càtodo, *s.m.* (*fis.*) cathode: — *caldo*, hot cathode; — *freddo*, cold cathode.

catodoluminescènza, *s.f.* (*fis.*) cathodoluminescence.

catolíto, *s.m.* (*fis.*) catholyte.

Catóne, *no.pr.m.* (*st.*) Cato ‖ **catóne,** *s.m.* (*uomo di rigidi principi*) man of strict principles, censorious man: *fare il* —, to be censorious.

catoneggiàre, *v.i.* to moralize, to affect strict principles, to be censorious.

catoniàno, *ag.* Catonian.

catòrcio, *s.m.* 1. door-bolt 2. *fig.* (*persona malandata*) sickly person; weakling; (*cosa vecchia e di nessun valore*) crock.

catòttrica, *s.f.* (*fis.*) catoptrics.

catòttrico, *ag.* (*fis.*) catoptric(al).

catramàre, *v.t.* to tar.

catramàto, *ag.* tarred: *cartone* —, tar-board.

catràme, *s.m.* tar: — *di legna*, wood tar; — *di torba*, peat tar.

càttedra, *s.f.* 1. (*tavolo dell'insegnante*) desk ‖ *montare in* —, *fig.* to mount the pulpit (*o* to be pedantic *o* to dogmatize) 2. (*l'ufficio dell'insegnare*) (*nelle scuole medie*) teaching post; (*nelle università*) chair, professorship 3. (*pulpito*) pulpit, chair; (*di vescovo*) bishop's throne (*o* chair) ‖ *la* — *di San Pietro*, St. Peter's Chair.

cattedràle, *ag.* cathedral (*attributivo*) ‖ *s.f.* cathedral (church): *la* — *di Lincoln*, Lincoln Cathedral.

cattedrànte, *s.m.* 1. (*professore universitario*) University professor 2. (*pedante*) pedant.

cattedraticaménte, *av.* 1. (*in modo professorale*) professorially; (*in modo autorevole*) authoritatively 2. (*da pedante*) pedantically.

cattedràtico, *ag.* 1. (*professorale*) professorial; (*autorevole*) authoritative 2. (*pedantesco*) pedantic.

cattivàrsi, *v.r.* to win, to earn, to gain: — *l'amore di qlcu.*, to win s.o.'s love; — *la simpatia di qlcu.*, to earn s.o.'s sympathy.

cattivèria, *s.f.* 1. wickedness, malice, spite; (*capricciosità di bambino*) naughtiness: *l'ha fatto per (pura)* —, he did it out of (mere) spite 2. (*azione malvagia*) wicked action; (*detto malvagio*) spiteful, malicious word: *questa è una vera* —, this is really nasty; *fare una* — *a qlcu.*, to do s.o. an ill turn; *fare, dire una* —, to do *o* to say an unkind thing.

cattività, *s.f.* captivity; bondage: *alcuni animali non si riproducono in* —, some animals do not breed in captivity ‖ *la* — *babilonese*, the Babylonian captivity.

cattívo, *ag.* 1. bad: *un* — *affare*, a bad business; — *gusto*, bad taste; *una cattiva madre*, a bad mother; *cattive maniere*, bad manners; *cattiva reputazione*, bad name; *una cattiva traduzione*, a bad translation; — *umore*, bad temper; *parla un* — *inglese*, he speaks bad English; *avere una cattiva cera*, to look ill; *essere in* — *stato*, to be in a bad (*o* sorry) plight; *fare una cattiva scelta*, to make a poor choice ‖ *farsi* — *sangue*, to get angry (*o* to worry) 2. (*sgradevole*) nasty, bad; (*malsano*) unhealthy: — *odore*, bad smell; — *sapore*, nasty taste; *aria cattiva*, unhealthy air **3.** (*brutto*) (*di tempo*) bad; (*di mare, vento*) rough **4.** (*incapace, inetto*) poor; incompetent; inefficient: *un — avvocato*, an incompetent lawyer; *un — impiegato*, an inefficient clerk; *un — scrittore*, a poor writer **5.** (*malvagio, di animo cattivo*) bad; wicked, ill-natured; malicious, mischief-making, mischievous: *un libro —*, a bad book; *una vita cattiva*, a bad life; *non è così — come sembra*, he is not as bad as he looks ‖ *prendere qlcu. con le cattive*, to treat s.o. harshly **6.** (*capriccioso*) naughty: *non fare il —!*, don't be naughty! **7.** (*amaro, pungente*) bitter, harsh: *parole cattive*, bitter (o harsh) words ‖ *s.m.* **1.** (*cosa cattiva*) bad: *prendere il buono e il —*, to take the bad with the good **2.** (*persona cattiva*) bad person, wicked: *i cattivi*, the wicked.

cattolicaménte, *av.* catholically.

cattolicésimo, cattolicísmo, *s.m.* (Roman) Catholcism.

cattolicità, *s.f.* **1.** catholicity **2.** (*i cattolici*) the Catholics (*pl.*).

cattòlico, *ag. s.m.* (Roman) Catholic.

cattúra, *s.f.* capture; (*arresto*) arrest: *mandato di —*, warrant (of arrest); *sfuggire alla —*, to escape capture.

catturàre, *v.t.* to capture, to catch, to seize; (*arrestare*) to arrest: *l'assassino non è stato ancora catturato*, the murderer is still at large; *furono catturati cinquecento soldati nemici*, five hundred enemy soldiers were taken prisoner; *essere catturato dalla polizia*, to be arrested by the police.

Catúllo, *no.pr.m.* (*st. lett.*) Catullus.

caucàsico, *ag.s.m.* Caucasian.

Càucaso, *no.pr.m.* (*geog.*) Caucasus.

caucciú, *s.m.* caoutchouc, india-rubber, gum-elastic.

caudàle, *ag.* caudal.

caudatàrio, *s.m.* **1.** (*eccl.*) train-bearer **2.** *fig.* (*sostenitore servile*) hanger-on (*pl.* hangers-on).

caudàto, *ag.* caudate.

càudice, *s.m.* (*bot.*) caudex (*pl.* caudices).

Caudíne, Fórche, *s.f.pl.* (*st. romana*) Caudine Forks.

càule, *s.m.* (*bot.*) caulis (*pl.* caules).

caulícolo, *s.m.* (*arch.*) cauliculus (*pl.* cauliculi).

càuri, *s.m.* cowry, cowrie.

càusa, *s.f.* **1.** cause: *— ed effetto*, cause and effect; *— efficiente*, efficient cause; *per — vostra*, through your fault (o for your sake); *fu la — della mia rovina*, he was the cause of my failure (o ruin); *il mio errore fu — di un grave incidente*, my blunder was the cause of (o caused) a bad accident ‖ *la Causa prima*, (*fil.*) the First Cause ‖ *a — di*, owing to (o on account of o because of o in consequence of) **2.** (*motivo*) reason, motive, ground, cause: *che — avete per una simile azione?*, what cause can you show for such an action?; *ditemi la vera — della vostra richiesta*, tell me the real reason for your request **3.** (*sorte, interesse, posizione ideologica*) cause: *far — comune con qlcu.*, to make common cause with s.o.; *sposare la — della libertà*, to embrace the cause of liberty; *tradire la —*, to betray the cause **4.** (*dir.*) (law)suit, case; cause: *— civile*, civil suit; *— penale*, criminal case; *essere parte in —*, to be a party to a suit; *fig.* to be concerned in the matter; *far — a qlcu. per danni*, to sue s.o. for damages; *intentare — a qlcu.*, to bring a suit (o to take legal action) against s.o.; *perorare una —*, to plead a cause; *fig.* to plead s.o.'s case ‖ *parlare con cognizione di —*, to speak authoritatively (o to speak from one's own experience).

causàle, *ag.* causal: *proposizione —*, (*gram.*) causal proposition ‖ *s.f.* (*motivo*) cause, reason, motive.

causalità, *s.f.* causality.

causalménte, *av.* causally.

causàre, *v.t.* to cause, to be the cause of (sthg.), to bring about, to produce; to give rise to (sthg.): *— un cambiamento*, to bring about a change; *— un incendio*, to cause a fire; *— malintesi*, to give rise to misunderstandings.

causatívo, *ag.* causative.

causídico, *s.m.* (*azzeccagarbugli*) pettifogger.

càustica, *s.f.* (*ott.*) caustic (curve).

causticaménte, *av.* (*sarcasticamente*) caustically, sarcastically, bitingly.

causticità, *s.f.* causticity.

càustico, *ag.* **1.** caustic: *soda caustica*, caustic soda **2.** (*sarcastico*) caustic, sarcastic, biting, cutting ‖ *s.m.* (*farm.*) caustic.

cautaménte, *av.* cautiously.

cautèla, *s.f.* caution; (*prudenza*) prudence.

cautelàre, *v.t.* to protect, to secure ‖ **cautelàrsi**, *v.r.* to take precautions.

cautèrio, *s.m.* (*chir.*) cautery.

cauterizzàre, *v.t.* (*chir.*) to cauterize.

cauterizzazióne, *s.f.* (*chir.*) cauterization, cauterizing.

càuto, *ag.* cautious, prudent, circumspect: *un giudizio —*, a cautious judgement; *andar cauti*, to be cautious (o to proceed cautiously).

cauzionàle, *ag.* cautionary: *deposito —*, caution money; (*versato per ottenere di essere rilasciato dalle autorità di polizia*) bail.

cauzióne, *s.f.* security, guarantee; (*deposito di garanzia*) caution money; (*per ottenere di essere rilasciato dalle autorità di polizia*) bail: *dare, versare —*, to give bail; *essere rilasciato su —*, to be released on bail.

càva, *s.f.* **1.** quarry; (*miniera*) mine, pit: *— aperta*, open quarry; *una — di ardesia*, a slate quarry; *una — di marmo*, a marble quarry; *una — di pietra*, a stone quarry **2.** *fig.* (*grande abbondanza*) mine: *egli è una — di informazioni*, he is a mine of information.

cavadènti, *s.m.* (*spreg.*) toothdrawer.

cavafàngo, *s.m.* (*draga*) dredger.

cavàgno, *s.m.* basket.

cavalcàbile, *ag.* ridable: *strada —*, bridle path (o riding track).

cavalcànte, *s.m.* horseman (*pl.* horsemen); rider.

cavalcàre, *v.t.* **1.** to ride: *cavalcava una candida mula*, he was riding (on) a snow-white mule **2.** (*stare a cavalcioni su*) to bestride **3.** (*passare sopra, di strada, ponte, ecc.*) to span: *un ponte cavalca il torrente*, a bridge spans the torrent ‖ *v.i.* (*andare a cavallo*) to ride, to ride on horseback, to go on horseback: *cavalcai sino al mulino*, I rode as far as the mill.

cavalcàta, *s.f.* **1.** ride: *fare una —*, to go for (o to take) a ride **2.** (*comitiva di persone a cavallo*) riding-party **3.** (*corteo a cavallo*) cavalcade.

cavalcatóre, cavalcatríce, *s.m., s.f.* rider.

cavalcatúra, *s.f.* mount.

cavalcavía, *s.f.* fly-over bridge.

cavalcióni, *av.* astride ‖ *a — di*, astride: *sedeva a — di un muretto*, he was sitting astride a low wall.

cavalieràto, *s.m.* knighthood.

cavalière, *s.m.* **1.** (*chi cavalca*) rider; horseman (*pl.* horsemen): *un — perfetto*, an accomplished horseman **2.** (*soldato a cavallo*) cavalryman (*pl.* cavalrymen), mounted soldier **3.** (*di ordini cavallereschi*) knight; (*in Francia*) chevalier: *— della Giarrettiera*, Knight of the Garter; *— della Legion d'Onore*, chevalier of the Legion of Honour; *creare — qlcu.*, to knight (o to confer knighthood on) s.o. **4.** (*chi accompagna una signora*) cavalier, lady's escort; (*compagno di ballo*) dance-partner, partner; (*persona galante*) cavalier, gallant ‖ *cavalier servente*, lady's man; *fig.* squire of dames **5.** (*st. medioevale, romana*) knight: *i Cavalieri della Tavola Rotonda*, the Knights of the Round Table; *— errante*, knight errant; *armare qlcu. —*, to dub s.o. (a) knight **6.** *essere a — di*, to be between (o to bestride o to span): *essere a — di due secoli*, to be between (o to bestride o to span) two centuries; *essere a — di due valli*, to overlook (o to look down upon o to command) two valleys.

cavalieréssa, *s.f.* (*scherz.*) wife of a knight.

cavàlla, *s.f.* mare.

cavallàio, *s.m.* (*mercante di cavalli*) horse-dealer.

cavallànte, *s.m.* 1. (*uomo di stalla*) stable-man (*pl.* stable-men) 2. (*chi guida un cavallo*) horse-rider.

cavallàro, *s.m.* 1. (*chi accompagna cavalli*) horse -drover 2. (*chi guida cavalli da carico*) driver of pack -horses.

cavalleggière, *s.m.* (*mil.*) trooper, light cavalryman (*pl.* cavalrymen): *i cavalleggieri del re*, the King's Light Horse.

cavallerescaménte, *av.* chivalrously.

cavalleréseo, *ag.* 1. (*di, da cavaliere*) knightly ‖ *ordine* —, order of knighthood ‖ *poema* —, poem of chivalry; *romanzo* —, romance of chivalry 2. (*nobile, generoso*) chivalrous, knightly, noble, generous: *contegno* —, chivalrous behaviour.

cavallería, *s.f.* 1. (*mil.*) cavalry: — *leggera*, light cavalry (*o* light horse) 2. (*st.*) chivalry: *le leggi della* —, the laws of chivalry 3. (*condotta cavalleresca*) chivalry.

cavallerízza, *s.f.* 1. (*maneggio*) riding-school 2. (*arte del cavalcare*) horsemanship 3. (*donna che cavalca*) (lady) rider; horsewoman (*pl.* horsewomen) 4. (*stella del circo*) equestrienne.

cavallerízzo, *s.m.* 1. (*chi cavalca*) rider; horseman (*pl.* horsemen) 2. (*maestro di equitazione*) riding-master 3. (*acrobata a cavallo in un circo*) equestrian, circus -rider.

cavallétta, *s.f.* grasshopper; (*locusta*) locust: — *migratrice*, migratory locust.

cavallétto, *s.m.* 1. horse; trestle; (*treppiedi per macchina fotografica*) tripod; (*da pittore*) easel; (*per segare*) sawbuck, saw-horse 2. (*st.*) (*strumento di tortura*) rack.

cavallína, *s.f.* filly, young mare ‖ *correre la* —, to sow one's wild oats.

cavallíno, *ag.* (*equino*) equine, horsy; horse (*attributivo*): *coda cavallina*, horse-tail; *mosca cavallina*, horse -fly; *risata cavallina*, horse-laugh; *viso* —, horsy face ‖ *tosse cavallina*, (w)hooping-cough ‖ *s.m.* 1. (*cavallo giovane*) colt; young horse 2. (*cavallo piccolo*) small horse; nag; (*di razza nana*) pony.

cavàllo, *s.m.* 1. horse: — *a dondolo*, rocking-horse; — *da caccia*, hunter; — *da corsa*, racehorse; — *da giostra, da giuoco*, hobby-horse; — *da sella*, saddle -horse; — *da soma*, pack-horse; — *da tiro*, draught -horse; — *di battaglia*, war-horse (*o* charger *o poet.* steed; *fig.* favourite piece; — *di razza, purosangue*, thoroughbred (horse); *artiglieria a* —, horse-artillery; *corsa di cavalli*, horse-race; *ferro di* —, horse-shoe: *tavola a ferro di* —, horse-shoe table; *guardie a* —, horse-guards ‖ *a* —, on horseback: *andare a* —, to ride (on horseback); *essere a* —, to be riding on horse-back; *fig.* to be out of danger (*o* to be safe); *montare a* —, to mount; *percorrere* (*un lungo tratto*) *a* —, to ride (a long distance) ‖ *scendere da* —, to dismount ‖ *a* —!, to horse! ‖ — *di Frisia*, (*mil.*) cheval de Frise ‖ *coda di* —, (*acconciatura*) pony tail ‖ *andare col* — *di S. Francesco*, to go on foot ‖ *avere una febbre da* —, to have a raging fever (*o* to be seized with a violent fever) ‖ *a caval donato non si guarda in bocca*, prov. you must not look a gift-horse in the mouth ‖ *l'occhio del padrone ingrassa il* —, prov. business prospers under the master's eye 2. *pl.* (*soldati a cavallo*) mounted soldiers; horse (*coll. con costruzione pl.*) 3. (*scacchi*) knight 4. (*attrezzo per ginnastica*) vaulting-horse, vaulting block: *volteggi sul* —, horse vaulting (*o* horse vaults) 5. — (*vapore*), (*fis.*) horse-power (*abbr.* H.P.): *un motore di 35 cavalli* (*vapore*), a 35 horse-power (*o a* 35 H.P.) engine.

cavallóne, *s.m.* 1. (*cavallo grosso*) big horse, large horse 2. (*maroso*) billow, high wave, roller; (*frangente*) breaker.

cavallúccio, *s.m.* 1. (*cavallo piccolo*) small horse; nag; (*di razza nana*) pony 2. *a* —, astride one's shoulders: *il bimbo era a* — *sulle spalle di suo padre*, the child was riding on his father's shoulders; *portare a* —,

to carry astride one's shoulders 3. — *marino*, (*zool.*) sea-horse; hippocampus (*pl.* hippocampi).

cavalòcchio, *s.m.* (*pop.*) (*azzeccagarbugli*) pettifogger.

cavamàcchie, *s.m.* (*smacchiatore*) stain-remover.

cavaménto, *s.m.* taking off, removing.

cavapiètre, *s.m.* quarryman (*pl.* quarrymen).

cavàre, *v.t.* 1. (*togliere*) to take off, to remove; (*tirar fuori*) to draw out, to take out, to pull out; (*estrarre*) to dig out, to extract: — *un dente*, to pull out a tooth; — *sangue*, to draw blood; — *un segreto di bocca a qlcu.*, to worm a secret out of s.o. ‖ *non* — *un ragno dal buco*, to fail utterly ‖ *farsi* — *un dente*, to have a tooth out 2. (*ricavare*) to get, to obtain, to gain ‖ **cavàrsi**, *v.r.* 1. (*liberarsi*) to free oneself, to get out (of sthg.): — *da un impegno*, to free oneself from an engagement; — *d'impaccio*, to get out of trouble ‖ — *la fame*, to appease one's hunger; — *la sete*, to quench one's thirst ‖ — *una voglia*, to satisfy one's wish ‖ *cavarsela*, to get off: *se la cavò a buon mercato*, he got off cheaply; *se la sono cavata*, (*non sono stati puniti*) they got away with it 2. (*di vesti, levarsele di dosso*) to take off: — *il cappello*, to take off one's hat.

cavastivàle, *s.m.* boot-jack.

cavàta, *s.f.* 1. extraction: — *di sangue*, (*med.*) blood-letting (*o* phlebotomy); *fig.* (*spesa ingente*) great (*o* excessive) expense 2. (*mus.*) touch.

cavatàppi, *s.m.* cork-screw.

cavatína, *s.f.* (*mus.*) cavatina.

cavatóre, *s.m.* quarryman (*pl.* quarrymen).

cavatríce, *s.f.* (*mec.*) mortising machine, mortiser.

cavatúra, *s.f.* 1. digging, extraction 2. (*cavità*) hollowness.

cavaturàccioli, *s.m.* cork-screw.

cavazióne, *s.f.* (*scherma*) disengage.

càvea, *s.f.* (*archeol.*) cavea (*pl.* caveae).

cavèdio, *s.m.* 1. (*arch.*) skylight passage 2. (*archeol.*) cavaedium (*pl.* cavaedia).

cavèrna, *s.f.* 1. cave; (*tana*) den: — *artificiale*, grotto; *età delle caverne*, the age of the cave-man; *orso delle caverne*, cave-bear; *uomo delle caverne*, cave -man 2. (*med.*) cavern, cavity.

cavernícolo, *ag.* cavernicolous ‖ *s.m.* cave-dweller.

cavernosità, *s.f.* 1. (*l'essere incavato*) hollowness 2. (*med.*) cavern, cavity.

cavernóso, *ag.* cavernous: *voce cavernosa*, very deep voice.

cavétto, *s.m.* (*arch.*) cavetto (*pl.* cavetti, cavettos).

cavézza, *s.f.* halter: *mettere la* — *a un cavallo*, to halter (*o* to put a halter on) a horse; *rompere la* —, to get out of hand (anche *fig.*); *tenere a* —, *fig.* to keep in check.

cavezzàle, *s.m.* (*agr.*) headland.

càvia, *s.m.* (*zool.*) guinea-pig, cavy.

caviàle, *s.m.* caviar, caviare.

cavícchia, *s.f.* peg.

cavícchio, *s.m.* 1. wooden pin 2. (*agr.*) (*attrezzo per fare buchi nel terreno*) dibble.

cavíglia, *s.f.* 1. (*anat.*) ankle: *osso della* —, ankle bone; *slogarsi una* —, to sprain one's ankle 2. (*ferr.*) screw spike, sleeper screw 3. (*carpenteria*) wooden dowel 4. (*mar.*) (*per dar volta*) belaying pin; (*per impiombare*) marlinespike.

cavigliatóio, *s.m.* (*ind. tessile*) spindle.

caviglièra, *s.f.* 1. ankle support 2. (*mar.*) belaying pin rack.

cavillàre, *v.i.* to cavil (at, about sthg.).

cavillatóre, *s.m.*, **cavillatríce**, *s.f.* caviller.

cavillazióne, *s.f.* cavilling.

cavíllo, *s.m.* cavil, captious objection.

cavillosaménte, *av.* captiously.

cavillosità, *s.f.* captiousness.

cavillóso, *ag.* captious.

cavità, *s.f.* cavity, hollow.

cavitazióne, *s.f.* (*mar.*) cavitation.

càvo[1], *ag.* hollow, empty; sunken || *s.m.* **1.** cavity, hollow: *nel — della mano*, in the hollow of the hand **2.** (*metal.*) mould, chill.

càvo[2], *s.m.* (*grosso canapo*) cable, rope: — *armato*, armored cable; — *elettrico*, electric cable; — *di acciaio*, steel cable; — *di ammaraggio*, (*mar.*) mooring rope; — *di ritegno*, (*mar.*) guy; — *portante*, carrying cable; — *sotterraneo*, (*elett.*) underground cable; — *sottomarino*, submarine cable; *filare un* —, (*mar.*) to pay out a rope.

cavolàia, *s.f.* **1.** (*entom.*) cabbage-butterfly **2.** (*coltivazione di cavoli*) cabbage-bed.

cavolàio, *s.m.* cabbage vendor.

cavolfióre, *s.m.* cauliflower.

cavolíni di Bruxelles, *s.m.pl.* Brussels sprouts.

càvolo, *s.m.* cabbage: — *bianco, cappuccio*, white cabbage; — *d'inverno*, borecole (o open-headed cabbage o *scoz.* kale); — *rapa*, turnip-cabbage; — *rosso*, red cabbage; — *verza*, savoy (cabbage) || *c'entra come il — a merenda*, it has nothing to do with it || *salvare capra e cavoli*, to eat one's cake and have it.

cazzaruòla, cazzeruòla, *s.f.* saucepan.

cazzottàre, *v.t.* to punch || **cazzottàrsi**, *v.r.* reciproco to exchange blows, to fight.

cazzottatúra, *s.f.* punching.

cazzòtto, *s.m.* punch: *fare a cazzotti*, to come to blows (o to fight).

cazzuòla, *s.f.* (*strum. artig.*) trowel.

ce[1], *av.* there: — *n'erano ancora molti*, there were many more.

ce[2], *particella pronominale* to us; us: — *lo dissero*, they told us so; — *ne parlò spesso*, he often spoke to us about it.

cecàggine, *s.f.* blindness (anche *fig.*)

cecaménte, *av.* blindly.

céeca[1], *s.f.* **1.** (*ornit.*) magpie **2.** (*donna ciarliera*) talkative woman.

céeca[2], *s.f.*: *far* —, to misfire.

cecchíno, *s.m.* (*gergo*) "cecchino" (Austrian sharp-shooter during the First World War).

céce, *s.m.* (*bot.*) chick-pea.

Cecília, *no.pr.f.* Cecily || *dim.* Cis, Cissie.

Cecílio, *no.pr.m.* Cecil.

cecità, *s.f.* **1.** blindness **2.** *fig.* blindness; (*stoltezza*) ignorance, folly: — *all'evidenza*, blindness to the facts.

cèco, *ag.s.m.* Czech.

Cecoslovàcchia, *no.pr.f.* (*geog.*) Czechoslovakia.

cecoslovàcco, *ag.s.m.* Czechoslovak.

Cècrope, *no.pr.m.* (*mit.*) Cecrops.

cedènte, *ag.* yielding: *terreno* —, yielding ground.

cèdere, *v.t.* **1.** (*dare*) to give: — *tutto quello che si possiede*, to give all one possesses || — *il passo a qlcu.*, to give (o to make) way for s.o. **2.** (*consegnare*) to -urrender, to yield; (*con trattato*) to cede: *l'eroica città fu ceduta al nemico*, the heroic city was surrendered to the enemy; *il vasto territorio sarà ceduto alla Turchia*, the vast territory will be ceded to Turkey **3.** (*trasferire*) to make over, to hand over, to transfer: — *la direzione degli affari* (*a qlcu.*), to hand over the management of affairs (to s.o.); — *i propri diritti a qlcu.*, to make over (o to transfer) one's rights to s.o. || — *una cambiale*, (*comm.*) to transfer a bill **4.** (*vendere*) to dispose of (*sthg.*): *potete — le vostre azioni quando volete*, you can dispose of your shares when you like || *v.i.* **1.** (*arrendersi*) to surrender, to yield, to give in: *cedetti alle sue preghiere*, I yielded to his entreaties; *è troppo ostinato, non cederà mai*, he is too pig-headed, he will never yield (o give in); *sono loro che devono* —, it is for them to submit **2.** (*venir meno, sprofondare*) to subside, to cave in, to sink down: *il terreno cede*, the ground is subsiding; *la volta cedette*, the vault caved in **3.** (*essere inferiore*) to be second to (s.o., sthg.): *per intelligenza non la cede a nessuno*, in intelligence he is second to none.

cedévole, *ag.* **1.** yielding; (*di terreno*) sinking: *l'ac-*

ciaio è più — della ghisa, steel is more yielding than cast-iron **2.** (*arrendevole*) yielding, accomodating, docile.

cedevolézza, *s.f.* **1.** (*arrendevolezza*) docility, amenability, tractability **2.** (*di materiali*) compliance.

cedíbile, *ag.* (*comm.*) transferable, assignable: *non* —, untransferable.

cedibilità, *s.f.* (*comm.*) transferability, assignability.

cedíglia, *s.f.* (*gram.*) cedilla.

cediménto, *s.m.* yielding, giving in (anche *fig.*); (*di terreno*) sinking, subsiding.

ceditóre, *s.m.* (*comm.*) transferrer, assigner.

cèdola, *s.f.* (*comm.*) coupon, dividend-warrant: — *di assegno*, check counterfoil; — *di dividendo*, dividend coupon; — *di interesse*, interest-coupon; *foglio delle cedole*, dividend-sheet.

cedràta, *s.f.* (*sciroppo di cedro*) citron syrup.

cedrína, *s.f.* (*bot.*) lemon-scented verbena.

cédro[1], *s.m.* **1.** (*albero*) citron(-tree): *boschetto di cedri*, citron grove **2.** (*frutto*) citron || — *candito*, citron-rind.

cédro[2], *s.m.* **1.** (*albero*) cedar: — *del Libano*, cedar of Lebanon **2.** (*legno*) cedar (wood).

cedróne[1], *s.m.* (*sciroppo di cedro*) citron syrup.

cedróne[2], *ag.s.m.* (*gallo*) —, (*ornit.*) capercaillie.

cèduo, *ag.* coppiced: *bosco* —, coppice (o copse).

cefalalgía, cefalèa, *s.f.* (*med.*) cephalalgy, headache.

cefàlico, *ag.* cephalic: *indice* —, cephalic index.

cèfalo, *s.m.* (*ittiol.*) mullet.

cefalocordàti, *s.m.pl.* (*zool.*) Cephalocordata.

cefalometría, *s.f.* cephalometry, craniometry.

Cefalònia, *no.pr.f.* (*geog.*) Cephalonia.

cefaloplegía, *s.f.* (*patol.*) cephaloplegia.

cefalòpodi, *s.m.pl.* (*zool.*) Cephalopoda.

cefalorachidiàno, *ag.* (*anat.*) cephalorachidian.

ceffàta, *s.f.* slap in the face; box on the ear.

cèffo, *s.m.* **1.** (*muso*) muzzle; (*grugno*) snout **2.** (*spreg.*) (*volto sinistro*) ugly face: *un brutto* —, *un* — *da galera*, an ugly (o a sinister) face.

ceffóne, *s.m.* slap in the face; box on the ear: *dare dei ceffoni*, to box s.o.'s ears: *gli diedi un* —, I boxed his ears (o I slapped him in the face).

celàre, *v.t.* to conceal, to hide: *gli celammo la notizia*, we concealed the news from him; — *i propri sentimenti*, to hide one's feelings; — *un terribile segreto*, to conceal a terrible secret || **celàrsi**, *v.r.* (*nascondersi*) to hide oneself, to conceal oneself; (*essere nascosto*) to be hidden, to hide, to be in hiding.

celàta, *s.f.* (*sorta di elmo*) sallet.

celàto, *ag.* concealed; secret.

celataménte, *av.* secretly.

celebèrrimo, *ag.superl.* very famous, most renowned.

celebràbile, *ag.* praiseworthy, commendable.

celebrànte, *s.m.* (*eccl.*) celebrant, officiant.

celebràre, *v.t.* **1.** (*esaltare*) to celebrate, to sing the praises of (s.o., sthg.), to praise, to honour, to extol **2.** (*festeggiare*) to keep, to observe, to celebrate: — *un anniversario*, to keep an anniversary **3.** (*eccl.*) to celebrate; (*solennizzare*) to solemnize: — *la Messa*, to celebrate (o to say) Mass; — *le nozze di qlcu.*, to officiate at s.o.'s wedding.

celebratóre, *s.m.* celebrator.

celebrazióne, *s.f.* celebration.

cèlebre, *ag.* celebrated, renowned, famous.

celebrità, *s.f.* celebrity.

celenteràti, *s.m.pl.* (*zool.*) Coelenterata.

cèlere, *ag.* quick, swift, rapid, speedy || *treno* —, express train || *la Celere*, (*polizia*) the Flying Squad.

celerità, *s.f.* quickness, swiftness, rapidity, celerity.

celerménte, *av.* quickly, swiftly, rapidly, speedily.

celèsta, *s.f.* (*mus.*) celesta.

celèste[1], *ag.* **1.** (*del cielo*) celestial, heavenly: *corpi celesti*, celestial (o heavenly) bodies || *il Celeste Impero*, (*st.*) the Celestial Empire **2.** (*divino*) celestial, heavenly, divine: *la città* —, the Celestial City; *grazia* —, (*teol.*) heavenly (o divine) grace **3.** (*colore*) sky-blue, light-blue, azure; (*rar.*) celeste || *s.m.* **1.** (*colore*) sky-blue, light-blue, azure; (rar.) celeste 2. pl. (dèi) gods: così non vollero i Celesti, (poet.) but the gods willed otherwise.

Celèste², no.pr.f. Celeste.

celestiàle, ag. celestial, heavenly: bellezza —, heavenly beauty; felicità —, celestial happiness; visione —, heavenly vision.

celestialménte, av. celestially.

Celestína, no.pr.f. Celestine.

celestíno¹, ag. pale blue, light blue.

Celestíno², no.pr.m. Celestine.

celestíno³, ag.s.m. (eccl.) Celestine.

cèlia, s.f. jest, joke: lo disse per —, he said it in jest (o he said it just for fun); reggere alla —, to know how to take a joke.

celíaco, ag. (anat.) celiac.

celiàre, v.i. to jest, to joke, to trifle.

celiatóre, s.m. jester, joker.

celibàto, s.m. celibacy, bachelorhood; single state.

cèlibe, ag. single, celibate, unmarried ‖ s.m. bachelor; celibate.

celícola, s.m. (letter.) inhabitant of heaven.

celidònia, s.f. (bot.) celandine.

celióne, s.m. jester, joker.

cèlla, s.f. 1. (di monastero, di alveare, di prigione) cell 2. (dispensa, deposito di commestibili) larder, store-room: — frigorifera, cold store.

celleràrio, s.m. (dispensiere) cellarer.

cellétta, s.f. small cell, tiny cell.

cellière, s.m. (dispensa) pantry, larder, store-room.

cellofàne, s.m. cellophane.

cèllula, s.f. 1. cell: le cellule del cervello, (anat.) brain cells ‖ — fotoelettrica, (elett.) electric eye (o photo-electric cell) 2. (pol.) cell: — comunista, communist cell.

cellulàre, ag. 1. cellular: tessuto —, cellular tissue 2. segregazione —, close confinement; vettura —, prison-van (o fam. Black Maria) ‖ s.m. (prigione) prison, gaol, jail.

cellulíte, s.f. (med.) cellulitis.

cellulòide, s.f. celluloid.

cellulósa, s.f. (chim.) cellulose.

cellulóso, ag. 1. cellulose 2. (cellulare) cellular.

celòma, s.m. (anat.) celom, coelom.

cèlta, s.m. Celt: i Celti, the Celts.

cèltico, ag. Celtic ‖ s.m. (lingua) (the) Celtic (language).

cémbalo, s.m. (mus.) 1. (tamburello) tambourine 2. (clavicembalo) harpsichord; (spinetta) spinet.

cémbro, s.m. (bot.) coniferous tree.

cementàre, v.t. to cement (anche fig.): — un'amicizia, to cement a friendship.

cementazióne, s.f. cementation.

cementíte, s.f. (metal.) cementite.

ceménto, s.m. cement: — a presa lenta, slow-setting cement; — a presa rapida, quick-setting cement; — armato, reinforced concrete (o ferro-concrete); — dentario, (odontoiatria) dental cement; intonaco di —, (edil.) cement plastering.

céna, s.f. (pasto leggero della sera) supper; (pranzo) dinner: verrà a — alle sette, he is coming to dinner at seven; far —, to have (o to take) supper ‖ l'Ultima Cena, the Last Supper ‖ non accozza il pranzo con la —, fig. he cannot make both ends meet.

cenàcolo, s.m. 1. supper-room; refectory ‖ il Cenacolo di Leonardo da Vinci, Leonardo's Last Supper 2. (accolta di artisti) artistic coterie.

cenàre, v.i. to have supper, to take supper, to sup.

cenciàio, **cenciaiuòlo**, s.m. ragman (pl. ragmen), rag-picker; (all'ingrosso) rag-merchant.

céncio, s.m. 1. rag: il tuo vestito sembra un —, your dress looks like a rag ‖ cappello a —, soft felt hat: cappello a — a tesa larga, slouch-hat ‖ i cenci vanno all'aria, fig. the weak always get the worst of it ‖ cadere come un —, to fall like a wet rag ‖ essere un —, (fisicamente molto debole) to be extremely weak (o to feel run down); (spiritualmente) to be (o to feel) un-

strung 2. (pezzetto, avanzo) bit; scrap: un — di ql.co., a bit of sthg. 3. (per spolverare) duster; (per asciugare le stoviglie) dish-cloth 4. pl. (veste poverissima) rags, tatters, tattered clothes: coperto di cenci, in rags (o in tatters).

cencióso, ag. ragged, tattered.

ceneràccio, s.m. lye-ashes (pl.).

ceneràio, s.m. (di stufa) ash-pan; (di fucina) ash-hole; (di locomotiva) ash-pan, ash-pit.

ceneràta, s.f. lye-ashes (pl.).

cénere, s.f. 1. ash (gener. pl.): (del) color della —, ash-coloured; la — era ancora calda e sotto vi covava il fuoco, the ashes were still warm, and fire was smouldering in them; non lasciar cadere la — della tua sigaretta, don't drop your cigarette ash; ridurre in —, to burn (o to reduce) to ashes 2. pl. (avanzi del corpo umano) ashes: le ceneri dei morti, the ashes of the dead ‖ il giorno delle Ceneri, Ash-Wednesday.

Cenerèntola, no.pr.f. Cinderella ‖ **cenerèntola**, s.f. (persona, cosa negletta) Cinderella.

ceneríccio, **ceneríno**, **cenerógnolo**, ag. ashy, ashen.

cèngia, s.f. ledge, ridge of rocks.

Cenísio, no.pr.m. (geog.) Cenis.

cennamèlla, s.f. (mus.) (tipo di zampogna) bagpipe.

cénno, s.m. 1. (gesto) sign, gesture; (col capo) nod; (con gli occhi) wink; (con la mano) wave (of the hand): ci fecero — di avvicinarci, they beckoned to us to come nearer; faceva grandi cenni per farsi capire, he was making great gestures to make himself understood; fece — di sì, (col capo) he nodded (assent); gli feci un —, I gave him a nod (o I nodded to him); ti farò un — al momento opportuno, I will give you a sign at the right moment; fare — con gli occhi a qlcu., to wink at s.o. 2. (comando) nod, order: a un tuo — uscirò, at your nod I'll go out 3. (allusione) hint, allusion: fare — a qlcu., a ql.co., to hint at s.o., at sthg. (o to mention s.o., sthg.): non fatene —, do not mention (o do not speak about) it 4. (breve notizia) notice: sul giornale c'era un — sul suo arrivo, there was a notice in the newspaper about his arrival 5. pl. (breve trattato) outline (sing.): cenni di letteratura inglese, an outline of English literature; cenni sul Manzoni, a short essay on Manzoni; cenni sulla vita e sulle opere di Orazio, a short account of Horace's life and works 6. (comm.): a un vostro — saremo lieti di mandarvi i campioni, on hearing from you, we shall be glad to send you the samples; attendiamo un vostro — in proposito, we await your instructions on this matter; gradiremmo un — di ricevuta, please acknowledge receipt.

cenòbio, s.m. (eccl.) coenobium (pl. coenobia).

cenobíta, s.m. (eccl.) coenobite, cenobite.

cenobítico, ag. (eccl.) coenobitic(al), cenobitic(al).

cenóne, s.m. (di Natale) Christmas eve dinner; (di Capodanno) New Year's eve dinner.

cenotàfio, s.m. cenotaph.

cenozòico, ag. (geol.) Cenozoic, Kainozoic, Tertiary, Cenozoic: era cenozoica, Cainozoic era; rocce cenozoiche, Cenozoic rocks.

censiménto, s.m. census: modulo di —, census-paper; fare il —, to take a census.

censíre, v.t. 1. to take a census of (a nation, a district) 2. (proprietà, beni tassabili) to assess.

censíto, ag. 1. (iscritto nel censo) included in the census 2. (gravato d'imposta) assessed.

cènso, s.m. 1. (st. romana) census 2. (patrimonio) real and personal estate 3. (ricchezza) wealth: persone di gran —, people of great wealth 4. (vitalizio, rendita) life annuity, rent.

censoràto, s.m. censorship.

censóre, s.m. 1. (st. romana) censor 2. (chi esercita la censura per mandato ufficiale) censor 3. (critico severo) critic, fault-finder.

censòrio, ag. 1. (di censore) censorial 2. (di critica severa) censorious.

censuàle, ag. (rar.) censual.

censúra, *s.f.* **1.** (*ufficio e dignità di censore*) censorship **2.** (*azione ufficiale di censura*) censor: *quella scena fu tagliata dalla* —, that scene was cut out by the censor **3.** (*riprovazione*) censure: *incorrere nella pubblica* —, to incur public censure.

censuràbile, *ag.* (*biasimevole*) censurable.

censuràre, *v.t.* **1.** (*da parte di un'autorità ufficiale*) to censor: — *una lettera*, to censor a letter **2.** (*riprovare*) to censure, to blame; to find fault with (s.o., sthg.), to criticize.

censuratóre, *V.* **censóre 3.**

centàurea, *s.f.* (*bot.*) centaury.

centàuro, *s.m.* **1.** (*mit.*) centaur ‖ *il Centauro*, (*astr.*) the Centaur **2.** (*motociclista*) motorcyclist.

centellàre, **centellinàre**, *v.t.* to sip.

centellino, *s.m.* sip: *bere a centellini*, to sip.

centenària, *s.f.* centenarian.

centenàrio, *ag.* centennial; (*di persona*) centenarian; (*secolare*) age-long ‖ *s.m.* **1.** (*commemorazione*) centenary, centennial anniversary, (the) hundredth anniversary **2.** (*persona che ha cent'anni*) centenarian.

centennàle, *ag.* centennial; (*secolare*) age-long: *una tradizione* —, an age-long tradition ‖ *s.m.* centenary, centennial anniversary.

centènne, *ag.* centennial; (*di persona*) centenarian.

centèrbe, *s.m.* "centerbe" (liqueur made in the Abruzzi).

centèsima, *s.f.* (*st.*) centesimal taxation.

centesimàle, *ag.* centesimal.

centèsimo, *ag.num.ord.* (the) hundredth ‖ *s.m.* (one) hundredth (of sthg.), (the) hundredth part (of sthg.): — *di dollaro*, cent; — *di franco*, centime; — *di lira*, centesimo (*pl.* centesimi); *ti ripagherò fino all'ultimo* —, I'll pay you back to the last penny; *non avere un* —, *essere senza un* —, to be (quite) penniless ‖ *questa macchina per scrivere non vale un* —, this typewriter isn't worth a brass farthing.

centiàra, *s.f.* centiare (*misura di superficie* = 1.196 sq.yd.).

centifòglia, *ag.* (*bot.*) chick-weed.

centígrado, *ag.* centigrade: *termometro* —, centigrade thermometer (*o* Celsius's thermometer); *zero gradi centigradi*, nought (*o* zero) degrees centigrade (0° C).

centigràmma, **centigràmmo**, *s.m.* centigram(me) (*misura di peso* = 0.154 gr.).

centílitro, *s.m.* centilitre; (*amer.*) centiliter (*misura di capacità* = 0.352 fluid oz.).

centímano, *ag.* hundred-handed.

centímetro, *s.m.* **1.** centimetre; (*amer.*) centimeter (*misura di lunghezza* = 0.393 in.) **2.** (*nastro per misurare*) tape-measure (1 ¹/₂ metres long).

cèntina, *s.f.* **1.** (*edil.*) centre **2.** (*aer.*) wingrib **3.** (*ricamo*) scallop.

centinàio, *s.m.* hundred: *a centinaia*, by hundreds; *centinaia di feriti*, hundreds of wounded people; *un* — *circa di persone*, about one hundred people; *parecchie centinaia di persone*, several hundred people (*o* several hundreds of people); *ne ricevemmo centinaia*, we received hundreds of them.

centinàre, *v.t.* **1.** (*edil.*) to support with a centre **2.** (*ricamare a centina*) to scallop.

centinatúra, *s.f.* (*edil.*) centreing, centering; (*mec.*) camber.

cènto, *ag.num.card.* hundred: — *giorni*, a (*o* one) hundred days; *un'automobile di* — *cavalli*, a one hundred horse-power car; *una persona su* —, one person in a hundred (*o* out of a hundred); *te l'ho detto* — *volte*, I have told you a hundred times (*o* again and again) ‖ — *di questi giorni!*, many happy returns of the day! ‖ *sconto del cinque per* —, five per cent discount ‖ *la Guerra dei Cento Anni*, the Hundred Years' War.

centogàmbe, *s.m.* (*entom.*) centipede.

centomíla, *ag.num.card.* a hundred thousand, one hundred thousand.

centomillèsimo, *ag.num.ord.* (the) hundred thousandth.

centóne, *s.m.* cento (*pl.* centos).

centràle, *ag.* central: *riscaldamento* —, central heating ‖ *s.f.*: — *atomica*, atomic research station; — *elettrica*, power plant (*o* electric power station); — *idraulica*, water power plant; — *idro-elettrica*, hydro-electric power plant; — *telefonica*, (telephone) exchange (*o amer.* central); (*a selezione automatica*) automatic telephone exchange.

centralíno, *s.m.* (*di telefono pubblico*) telephone exchange; (*automatico, privato*) private automatic exchange.

centralità, *s.f.* centrality, central position.

centralizzàre, *v.t.* to centralize.

centralizzazióne, *s.f.* centralization.

centràre, *v.i.* (*colpire nel centro*) to hit the centre, to hit the bull('s eye), to hit the mark (anche *fig.*) ‖ *v.t.* **1.** (*colpire nel centro*) to hit the centre of (sthg.): — *un bersaglio*, to hit the bull (*o* the centre of a target) **2.** (*equilibrare*) to centre, to adjust, to balance: *ruota ben centrata*, well-balanced wheel **3.** (*giuoco del calcio*) to centre.

cèntrico, *ag.* (*rar.*) centric(al).

centrífuga, *s.f.* (*mec.*) centrifuge, centrifugal machine: — *del latte*, milk centrifuge (*o* cream separator *o* creamer).

centrifugàre, *v.t.* to centrifuge, to centrifugate.

centrifugazióne *s.f.* centrifugation.

centrífugo, *ag.* centrifugal: *forza centrifuga*, centrifugal force.

centríno, *s.m.* doily.

centrípeto, *ag.* centripetal: *forza centripeta*, centripetal force.

centrísta, *ag.* (*pol.*) moderate; centre (*attributivo*): *un partito* —, a centre (*o* moderate) party ‖ *s.m.* moderate politician; supporter of a centre party.

cèntro, *s.m.* **1.** centre; (*amer.*) center; middle: *il* — *di una città*, the centre of a city; *fig.* the hub of a city; — *di gravità*, (*fis.*) centre of gravity; — *d'inerzia*, (*mec.*) centre of gyration; *al* — *di una stanza*, in the middle of a room; *la casa è il* — *dei nostri affetti*, our home is the centre of our affections ‖ *essere nel proprio* —, to be at ease ‖ *il Centro*, (*pol.*) the Centre **2.** (*di bersaglio*) centre, bull's eye: *far* —, to hit the bull('s eye); *fig.* to hit the mark; (*calciare in porta*) to kick at goal **3.** (*spor.*) centre: — *attacco*, centre forward; — *mediano*, centre halfback **4.** (*istituto di ricerche*) institute: — *di studi atomici*, institute for atomic research **5.** (*anat.*) centre: — *nervoso*, nerve-centre **6.** (*luogo di una certa importanza*) centre, resort: — *balneare*, seaside resort; — *commerciale*, commercial centre; — *ferroviario*, rail centre; — *industriale*, industrial town; — *turistico*, tourist resort.

centumviràto, *s.m.* (*st. romana*) centumvirate.

centúmviro, *s.m.* (*st. romana*) centumvir (*pl.* centumviri).

centuplicàre, *v.t.* **1.** to centuple, to centuplicate **2.** (*accrescere*) to increase; to multiply.

cèntuplo, *ag.* centuple, hundredfold ‖ *s.m.* centuple, hundredfold, one hundred times as much: *mille è il* — *di dieci*, a thousand is a hundred times as much as ten.

centúria, *s.f.* (*st. romana*) century.

centuriàto, *ag.* (*st. romana*) centurial.

centurióne, *s.m.* (*st. romana*) centurion.

ceppàia, *s.f.* tree stump, stump, stub.

ceppàta, *s.f.* **1.** group of trees, group of trunks **2.** (*per uso di ormeggio*) group of mooring poles.

ceppatèllo, *s.m.* (*bot. pop.*) pore mushroom.

cèppo, *s.m.* **1.** (*base dell'albero*) stump, stub **2.** *fig.* (*famiglia, razza*) stock: — *di animali da esperimento*, experimental stock ‖ *essere del medesimo* —, to come of the same stock **3.** (*da ardere*) log: — *di Natale*, yule-log **4.** (*per la decapitazione*) block **5.** (*per battervi la carne*) block, chopping-block **6.** *pl.* (*strumenti per* *serrare i piedi ai prigionieri*) shackles, fetters (anche *fig.*): *i ceppi delle convenzioni*, the shackles of convention **7.** (*mec.*) brake-block **8.** (*di aratro*) plough-stock **9.** (*mar.*) (*di ancora*) anchor stock **10.** (*cassetta delle elemosine*) alms-box.

céra[1], *s.f.* wax: — *autolucidante*, self-polishing wax; — *da calzolaio*, cobbler's wax; — *da pavimento*, floor wax; — *da scarpe*, boot polish; — *di Spagna*, sealing-wax; — *vegetale*, vegetable wax; *bambola di —*, wax doll; *bianco come la —*, waxen (o extremely pale); *dare la —*, to wax ‖ *essere come — nelle mani di qlcu.*, to be like wax in s.o.'s hands.

céra[2], *s.f.* (*aspetto*) air, look; (*letter.*) mien: *avere bella, buona —*, to look well; *avere brutta —*, to look ill ‖ *far buona — a qlcu.*, to welcome s.o. heartily (o to give s.o. a hearty welcome).

ceraiuòlo, *s.m.* wax-chandler.

ceralàcca, *s.f.* sealing-wax.

ceramèlla, *s.f.* (*mus.*) (*tipo di zampogna*) bagpipe.

ceràmica, *s.f.* **1.** (*arte*) ceramics **2.** (*oggetto in ceramica*) pottery article, piece of pottery **3.** (*materiale*) baked clay: *stufa in —*, tiled stove **4.** *pl.* pottery (*sing.*).

ceramísta, *s.c.* ceramist.

ceràre, *v.t.* to wax.

ceràsa, *s.f.* cherry.

ceraséllA, *s.f.* cherry-brandy.

ceràso, *s.m.* (*bot.*) cherry-tree.

ceràsta, ceràste, *s.f.* (*zool.*) cerastes, horned viper.

ceràto, *ag.* waxed; wax (*attributivo*): *tela cerata*, wax-cloth.

Cèrbero, *no.pr.m.* (*mit.*) Cerberus ‖ **cèrbero**, *s.m.* Cerberus.

cerbiàtto, *s.m.* (*zool.*) fawn.

cerbottàna, *s.f.* **1.** (*arma dei selvaggi*) blowgun, blow-pipe, blowtube **2.** (*giocattolo per bambini*) pea-shooter.

cérca, *s.f.* search; quest: *andare alla —*, (*di religiosi*) to go begging; *andare in — di ql.co.*, *qlcu.*, to go in search of (o to look for) s.o., sthg.

cercàre, *v.t.* **1.** to look for (s.o., sthg.), to search for (s.o., sthg.); to seek: *chi cercate?*, who are you looking for?; — *fortuna all'estero*, to seek one's fortune abroad ‖ — *briga*, to look for trouble ‖ — *ql.co. per mare e per terra*, to look for sthg. everywhere ‖ — *scampo nella fuga*, to seek safety in flight ‖ *chi cerca trova*, *prov.* whoever seeks will find **2.** (*per consultazione*) to look up: — *una frase nel dizionario*, to look up a sentence in the dictionary **3.** (*a tastoni*) to fumble for (sthg.): *nell'oscurità cercava l'interruttore della luce*, in the darkness he fumbled (about) for the switch **4.** (*richiedere*) to ask for (sthg.); to want: *cercasi abile infermiera*, well-trained nurse wanted; *cercò un libro*, he asked for a book; *non ho cercato nulla da voi*, I have not asked anything of you ‖ *v.i.* (*tentare*) to try, to strive: *cercava di persuadermi a partire*, he was trying to get me to leave; *cercò a lungo di tenersi a galla, ma poi fallì*, he strove a long time to keep his head above water, but then failed.

cercàta, *s.f.* search.

cercatóre, *s.m.* **1.** seeker, inquirer, searcher: — *d'oro*, gold-digger (o *amer.* prospector) **2.** (*di telescopio*) checker **3.** (*rad.*) detector.

cérchia, *s.f.* circle: *la città alta, entro la — delle mura*, the upper town, within its walls (o within the circuit of its walls) **2.** *fig.* circle, set: *egli non appartiene alla nostra —*, he does not belong to our circle.

cerchiàio, *s.m.* hoop-maker.

cerchiàre, *v.t.* to hoop: — *una botte*, to hoop a barrel.

cerchiàto, *ag.* (*di occhi*) black-ringed: *aveva sempre gli occhi cerchiati*, he always had rings round his eyes.

cerchiatúra, *s.f.* hooping.

cerchiétto, *s.m.* (*piccolo cerchio*) small ring.

cérchio, *s.m.* **1.** circle, ring, round: — *della morte*, (*aer.*) loop; *gli aerei descrivono dei cerchi nel cielo*, the planes are circling overhead; *danzare in —*, to dance in a ring; *girare in —*, to turn round ‖ *fare —*, to

stand in a circle: *fare — intorno a qlcu.*, to stand round s.o. ‖ *fare dei cerchi viziosi*, to reason (o to argue) in circles **2.** (*geom.*) circle **3.** (*di botte*) hoop ‖ *dare un colpo al — e uno alla botte*, to run with the hare and hunt with the hounds (o to keep in with both sides) **4.** (*cerchione di ruota*) rim **5.** (*cerchio di legno usato come giocattolo*) hoop: *far correre un —*, to trundle a hoop.

cerchióne, *s.m.* (*di ruota*) rim.

cércine, *s.m.* **1.** pad **2.** (*mar.*) bolt-rope.

cercopitèco, *s.m.* (*zool.*) Cercopithecus.

cereàle, *ag.* cereal.

cereàli, *s.m.pl.* cereals.

cerebràle, *ag.* (*anat.*) cerebral: *febbre, infiammazione —*, (*med.*) brain fever ‖ *s.m.* (*neol.*) high-brow, intellectual type.

cerebralísmo, *s.m.* cerebralism.

cerebrazióne, *s.f.* cerebration.

cerebrospinàle, *ag.* (*anat.*) cerebro-spinal: *meningite —*, (*patol.*) cerebro-spinal meningitis.

cèreo, *ag.* **1.** (*pallido come cera*) waxen, extremely pale, wan: *carnagione cerea*, waxen complexion; *viso —*, wan (o bloodless) face **2.** (*di cera*) wax (*attributivo*); (*rar.*) waxen.

Cèrere, *no.pr.f.* (*mit.*) Ceres.

cererería, *s.f.* (*fabbrica di cera*) wax factory.

cerétta, *s.f.* **1.** (*lucido per scarpe*) boot polish; blacking **2.** (*cera per depilare*) wax.

cerfòglio, *s.m.* (*bot.*) chervil.

cerimònia, *s.f.* **1.** ceremony: *una — imponente*, an imposing ceremony; *maestro di —*, Master of Ceremonies; *partecipare a una —*, to attend a ceremony **2.** (*pompa*) pomp, splendour **3.** (*complimento, formalità*) ceremony: *con —*, with ceremony; *una persona piena di cerimonie*, a formal person; *senza —*, without ceremony; *visita di —*, formal visit; *glielo dissi per —*, I told him so out of politeness; *fare delle cerimonie*, to stand on ceremony.

cerimoniàle, *ag.s.m.* ceremonial.

cerimonière, *s.m.* Master of Ceremonies.

cerimoniosaménte, *av.* ceremoniously, formally.

cerimonióso, *ag.* ceremonious, formal.

cerinàio, *s.m.* (wax) match-vendor.

cerino, *s.m.* (wax) match; vesta.

cèrio, *s.m.* (*chim.*) cerium.

cèrna, *s.f.* choice, selection; pick; sifting.

cernécchio, *s.m.* tuft of ruffled hair.

cèrnere, *v.t.* to choose, to select, to separate, to sort.

cernièra, *s.f.* **1.** (*di occhiali, di finestra, di porta*) hinge **2.** (*serratura di borsetta*) clasp **3.** — *lampo*, zip-fastener (o zipper o *fam.* zip).

cèrnita, *s.f.* choice, selection; pick; sifting: — *degli stracci*, sorting of rags; — *delle mele*, (*secondo la grossezza*) grading of apples; — *delle uova*, grading of eggs.

cernitóre, *s.m.* sifter.

cernitríce, *s.f.* **1.** sifter **2.** (*mec. miner.*) grading machine: — *a gravità*, gravity grading machine.

cernitúra, (*rar.*) per **cèrnita**.

céro, *s.m.* large candle: — *di chiesa*, church-candle.

ceroferàrio, *s.m.* candle-bearer, torch-bearer.

ceróne, *s.m.* (*cosmetico per attori*) make-up.

ceroplàstica, *s.f.* ceroplastics.

ceróso, *ag.* waxen, waxy.

ceròtto, *s.m.* **1.** plaster, sticking-plaster **2.** (*persona noiosa*) bore.

cerretàno, *s.m.* (*letter.*) charlatan, quack.

cerréto, *s.m.* grove of Turkey oaks.

cèrro, *s.m.* **1.** (*albero*) Turkey oak **2.** (*legno*) bitter oak.

certàme, *s.m.* (*poet.*) duel, fight, combat: — *poetico*, poetic competition (o contest).

certaménte, *av.* certainly, surely; undoubtedly: *ma —!*, of course! (o by all means! o to be sure!); *egli verrà —*, he will certainly come (o he is sure to come).

certézza, *s.f.* certitude, certainty: *sapere con —*, to know for certain (o for a certainty): *lo so con —*, I know it for a certainty; *scommettere con* —, to bet on a certainty.

certificàre, *v.t.* to certify, to attest, to confirm, to bear witness to (sthg., doing): *il documento certifica che...,* the document attests the fact that...; — *che ql.co. è vero,* to certify that sthg. is true; — *un decesso,* to certify a death; — *di aver fatto ql.co.,* to bear witness to having done sthg. ‖ **certificàrsi,** *v.r.* to assure oneself.

certificàto, *s.m.* **1.** certificate: — *consolare,* consular certificate; — *di buona condotta,* certificate of character (*o* good conduct certificate); — *di congedo,* discharge certificate; — *di igiene,* sanitary certificate; — *di matrimonio,* marriage certificate; — *di morte,* death certificate; — *di nascita,* birth certificate; — *di origine,* certificate of origin; — *di sana costituzione,* health certificate **2.** (*attestato di merito*) testimonial **3.** (*comm.*) certificate, scrip: — *di azione, di azioni,* share certificate; — *nominativo,* registered scrip (*o* registered share certificate).

cèrto[1], *ag.* **1.** (*vero, indubitabile, immancabile*) certain, sure; undoubted: *è cosa certa,* it is a sure thing; *questa commedia avrà un successo* —, this play is certain to succeed ‖ *una cosa è certa che ...,* one thing is sure (*o* certain) that... ‖ *sapere per* —, to know for certain; *tenere per* —, to hold for certain **2.** (*sicuro, persuaso, convinto*) certain, sure: *ne sei* —?, are you quite certain (*o* sure) of it?; *non sono* — *che venga,* I am not certain (*o* sure) that he will come ‖ *av.* (*in verità, indubitabilmente, immancabilmente*) certainly: —, *ma questo non cambia la situazione!,* certainly, but that doesn't change the situation!; *partirà* —, he will certainly leave ‖ *di* —, for certain (*o* for sure) ‖ *ma* —!, of course! (*o* by all means!): « *Posso usare il suo telefono?* », « *Ma* —! », "May I use your telephone?", "By all means!" ‖ *no* —!, certainly not! ‖ *sì,* —!, (yes) to be sure! (*o* of course! *o* certainly!): « *Verrai?* », « *Sì,* —! », "Will you come?", "Yes, to be sure! (*o* of course, I will!)" ‖ — *che l'hai letto!,* surely you have read it! ‖ *s.m.*: *lasciare il* — *per l'incerto,* to embark on a doubtful course.

cèrto[2], *ag. indef.* **1.** certain: *una certa persona,* a certain person; *un signore di una certa età,* a gentleman of a certain age ‖ *un* — *Alfred Smith,* one Alfred Smith; *un* — *Signor Morris,* a (certain) Mr. Morris **2.** (*qualche; alcuno*) some: *dopo un* — *tempo,* after some time; *un signore di una certa importanza,* a gentleman of some consequence; *certe persone lo videro,* some people saw him **3.** (*tale, tal genere di*) such: *certe parole non dovrebbero mai uscire dalla bocca di una donna,* such words should never come from a lady's mouth ‖ *pron. indef. pl.* **some, some people**: *certi lo videro,* some people saw him.

certòsa, *s.f.* **1.** (*monastero certosino*) charterhouse, Carthusian monastery, chartreuse **2.** (*liquore*) chartreuse.

certosíno, *ag.* Carthusian ‖ *s.m.* **1.** (*eccl.*) Carthusian ‖ *pazienza da* —, patience of Job **2.** *fig.* (*persona che ama la vita solitaria*) solitary man, retiring man.

certúno, *ag. indef.* (*alcuno*) some: *certune persone lo sapevano,* some people knew (it) ‖ *pron. indef.* **someone, somebody;** *pl.* **some, some people.**

cerùleo, cèrulo, *ag.* sky-blue; (*letter.*) cerulean.

cerúme, *s.m.* earwax, cerumen.

cerúsico, *s.m.* (*arc.*) surgeon.

cerùssa, *s.f.* (*chim.*) white-lead, ceruse.

cerussíte, *s.f.* (*min.*) cerussite.

cèrva, *s.f.* (*zool.*) hind, doe.

cervellàta, *s.f.* Milanese sausage, saveloy.

cervellétto, *s.m.* (*anat.*) cerebellum (*pl.* cerebellums, cerebella); little brain.

cervellíno, *s.m.* hare-brained person: *tua cugina Maria è davvero un* —, your cousin Mary is a hare-brained creature indeed (*o* is hare-brained indeed).

cervèllo, *s.m.* **1.** brain (*usato talvolta al pl., specie nel senso di materia cerebrale*): — *di vitello,* calves' brains; — *elettronico,* electronic brain; *avere un tumore al* —, to have a tumour on the brain ‖ — *di gallina, di passero, di fringuello, d'oca,* hare-brained (*o* empty-headed) fellow (*o* creature) ‖ *lavaggio del* —, (*neol.*) brain-washing ‖ *senza* —, brainless (*o* thoughtless) ‖ *devi mettere il* — *a partito,* you must mend your way of living (*o* your ways) ‖ *gli die' di volta il* —, he became mad ‖ *gli si è rammollito il* —, his brain has grown soft ‖ *ha il* — *a posto,* he has (all) his wits about him ‖ *sono certo che ha molto* —, I am sure he has a lot of brains ‖ *tutta questa adulazione non gli darà al* —?, will not all this flattery turn his brain? (*o* go to his head?); *il vino gli ha dato al* —, wine has gone to his head ‖ *Vittorio è un* — *balzano,* Victor is a madcap ‖ *bruciarsi, farsi saltare le cervella,* to blow out one's brains; *far saltare le cervella a qlcu.,* to knock out s.o.'s brains ‖ *lambiccarsi il* —, to rack (*o* to cudgel) one's brains ‖ *usare il* —, to use one's brains **2.** (*intelligenza*) understanding; (*mente*) mind; (*senno*) sense: *il suo* — *è del tutto sconvolto,* his mind is quite turned.

cervelloticaménte, *av.* **1.** (*in modo bizzarro*) oddly, extravagantly **2.** (*irragionevolmente*) unreasonably.

cervellòtico, *ag.* **1.** (*bizzarro*) odd, extravagant **2.** (*irragionevole*) unreasonable.

cervicàle, *ag.* (*anat.*) cervical.

cervíce, *s.f.* **1.** (*nuca*) nape; (*collo*) neck: *piegare la* —, *fig.* to stoop **2.** (*testa*) head.

cervière, *ag.*: *lupo* —, (*zool.*) lynx.

cervíno[1], *ag.* cervine; deer (*attributivo*).

Cervíno[2] (il), *no.pr.m.* (*geog.*) the Matterhorn.

cèrvo, *s.m.* **1.** deer (*invariato al pl.*); (*il maschio*) stag; (*maschio giovane*) buck: — *reale,* hart royal; *carne di* — venison; *come sono belli questi cervi!,* how fine these deer are! **2.** — *volante,* (*entom.*) stag-beetle; *fig.* (*aquilone*) kite.

cervògia, *s.f.* (*rar.*) beer.

cerzioràre, *v.t.* to ascertain; (*render certo*) to assure ‖ **cerzioràrsi,** *v.r.* to assure oneself

Cèsare, *no.pr.m.* Caesar ‖ *Giulio* —, (*st.*) Julius Caesar ‖ **cèsare,** *s.m.* (*imperatore*) Caesar ‖ *i Cesari,* (*st.*) the Caesars ‖ *un cuor di* —, a very generous person ‖ *date a* — *quel ch'è di* —, (*Bibbia*) render to Caesar the things that are Caesar's.

Cesarèa, *no.pr.f.* (*geog. st.*) Caesarea.

cesàreo, *ag.* **1.** Caesarean, Caesarian, imperial: *poeta* —, poet laureate **2.** *taglio* —, (*chir.*) Caesarian operation (*o* Caesarian section).

cesariàno, *ag.* Caesarean, Caesarian ‖ *s.m.* Caesarian.

cesarísmo, *s.m.* Caesarism, imperialism.

Césco, *no.pr.m. dim. di* **Francésco.**

cesellaménto, *s.m.* (*rar.*) chiselling.

cesellàre, *v.t.* to chisel (*anche fig.*).

cesellàto, *ag.* chiselled (*anche fig.*): *lineamenti cesellati,* chiselled features.

cesellatóre, *s.m.* chiseller.

cesellatúra, *s.f.* chisel work, chiselling.

cesèllo, *s.m.* chisel.

cesoiàta, *s.f.* snip, clip.

cesóie, *s.f.pl.* shears.

cèspite, *s.m.* **1.** tuft, tuft of grass **2.** — *di entrata,* (*fonte di guadagno*) source of income.

céspo, *s.m.* (*ciuffo, cespuglietto*) tuft; (*cespuglio*) bush: *far* —, to tuft.

cespúglio, *s.m.* bush; thicket.

cespuglióso, *ag.* bushy.

cessànte, *ag.* (*letter.*) slow ‖ *s.m.* (*chi lascia una carica*) outgoer, relinquisher.

cessàre, *v.t.* to cease, to stop: — *gli affari,* (*comm.*) to give up business; — *il fuoco,* (*mil.*) to cease fire; — *i pagamenti,* (*comm.*) to cease (*o* to stop) payment ‖ *v.i.* **1.** to cease (to do, doing); to leave off (doing); to stop (doing): *cessate di deriderlo,* leave off (*o* stop) laughing at him; *ella cessò di cantare,* she ceased (*o* left off) singing; *ha cessato di piovere,* it has stopped raining (o the rain has ceased); *il poveretto cessò di vivere alle cinque di stamani*, the poor man breathed his last (o died) this morning at five o'clock **2.** (*calmarsi*) to subside, to die down: *finalmente la tempesta cessò*, at last the storm subsided.

cessazióne, *s.f.* **1.** cessation, suspension; (*fine*) end **2.** (*comm.*) discontinuance: *— degli affari*, discontinuance of business; *— di una società anonima*, discontinuance of a company's business.

cessionàrio, *s.m.* (*dir.*) transferee.

cessióne, *s.f.* (*dir.*) transfer, assignment: *— di un credito*, assignment of a credit; *atto di —*, deed of assignement; *fare — di ql.co. a qlcu.*, to transfer (o to surrender) sthg. to s.o.

cèsso, *s.m.* lavatory, water-closet (*abbr.* w. c.).

cèsta, *s.f.* **1.** basket; (*grossa*) hamper: *— della biancheria, del bucato*, clothes-basket; *— della spesa*, shopping-basket **2.** (*quantità contenuta in una cesta*) basket, basketful: *una — di frutta, di fiori*, a basket(ful) of fruit, of flowers **3.** (*baroccino*) governess-cart **4.** (*pelota*) " cesta ".

cestàio, *s.m.* **1.** (*chi fabbrica ceste*) basket-maker **2.** (*chi vende ceste*) basket-vendor.

cestèllo, *s.m.* **1.** small basket; hand-basket **2.** (*chir.*) sterilized drum.

cestinàre, *v.t.* **1.** to throw into the waste-paper basket **2.** (*rifiutare, un manoscritto*) to refuse (to publish).

cestíno, *s.m.* **1.** small basket: *— da lavoro*, work-basket (o darning-basket); *— da viaggio*, luncheon-basket; *— della colazione*, lunch-bag (o sandwich bag) **2.** (*per la carta straccia*) waste-(paper) basket.

cèsto¹, *s.m.* (*bot.*) head: *un — di lattuga*, a head of lettuce; *far —*, (*accestire*) to tuft.

cèsto², *s.m.* **1.** (*pallacanestro*) basket: *palla al —*, basket-ball **2.** *V.* **cèsta 1. 2. 4.**

cèsto³, *s.m.* (*archeol.*) cestus.

cestóne, *s.m.* hamper || *fare il capo come un — a qlcu.*, to make s.o.'s head whirl.

cetología, *s.f.* cetology.

cesúra, *s.f.* (*poes.*) caesura.

cetàceo, *ag.s.m.* (*zool.*) cetacean || *i cetacei*, (*zool.*) Cetacea.

cète, *s.m.* (*zool.*) whale.

cèto, *s.m.* class, rank, order: *il — medio*, the middle classes; *gente di ogni —*, people of all ranks.

cétra, *s.f.* **1.** (*mus.*) (*strumento moderno in uso specialmente nella Germania meridionale*) zither **2.** (*mus.*) (*strumento dell'antichità*) cithern, cittern, lyre.

cetriolíno, *s.m.* gherkin: *cetriolini sott'aceto*, pickled gherkins.

cetri(u)òlo, *s.m.* **1.** cucumber: *panini imbottiti al —*, cucumber sandwiches **2.** (*sciocco*) fool; simpleton.

Cevènne (le), *no.pr.f.pl.* (*geog.*) the Cevennes.

che¹, *pron. rel.* **1.** sogg. who, that (*riferito a persone*); which, that (*riferito a cose o ad animali di sesso non specificato*): *ecco i libri — mi furono regalati*, here are the books that (o which) were given to me; *qualunque persona — sappia leggere*, any person that can read; *ricevetti un pacco — mi era stato inoltrato dal mio precedente indirizzo*, I received a parcel which had been forwarded from my last address; *l'uomo — mi parlò*, the man who spoke to me **2.** oggetto who(m), that (*riferito a persone*); which, that (*riferito a cose o ad animali di sesso non specificato*): *è l'uomo più onesto — abbia mai incontrato*, he is the most honest man (that) I have ever met; *gli diedi una mela — egli mise subito in tasca*, I gave him an apple, which he put in his pocket at once; *l'indirizzo — cercavi è stato trovato*, the address (that) you were looking for has been found; *le lettere — mi mandasti*, the letters (that) you sent me; *il libro — comprasti ieri*, the book (which) you bought yesterday; *la ragazza — incontraste*, the girl (whom) you met; *la signora — tu guardavi, è mia nonna*, the lady at whom you were looking (o the lady whom you were looking at) is

my grandmother **3.** *il che*, (*sogg. oggetto e obliquo*) which: *il — tutti ammettono*, which everyone admits; *fu promosso benissimo, il — rese assai felice sua madre*, he passed with flying colours, which made his mother very happy; *non vi saluta più, dal — dovete comprendere...*, he cuts you dead, from which you must understand... || *non c'è di —*, (*forma di cortesia*) don't mention it **4.** (*in correlazione con* stesso, medesimo) as, that: *disse la stessa cosa — dissi io*, he said the same thing as I did; *ho incontrato la stessa difficoltà — hai incontrato tu*, I have had the same difficulty as you had; *questa è la stessa cosa — accadde ieri*, this is the same thing as happened yesterday **5.** (*riferito a tempo*) when: *non so dimenticare il giorno — ti vidi per la prima volta*, I can't forget the day (when) I first saw you; *ricordi l'anno — morì il nonno?*, do you remember the year (when) grandfather died?.

che², *ag.interr.* what (*riferito a numero indeterminato di cose o persone*); which (*riferito a numero limitato di cose o persone*): *— libri hai comprato?*, what books did you buy?; *— libro dell'Eneide preferisci?*, which book of the Aeneid do you like best?; *— musica ti piace?*, what music do you like?; *— tipo di ragazza è?*, what kind of a girl is she?; *tu conosci il mio guardaroba, — vestito devo mettermi?*, you know my wardrobe, which dress shall I wear? || *— è, — non è*, all of a sudden || *— ora è?*, what is the time? (o what time is it?) || *pron.interr.* (*che cosa*) **what:** *— è questo?*, what is this?; *— fai?*, what are you doing?; *— guardi?*, what are you looking at?; *— hai?*, what is the matter with you?; *— succede?*, what is happening?; *gli chiesi — facesse*, I asked him what he was doing || *a —?*, what for? (o for what purpose?).

che³, *ag. esclamativo* **what, what a:** *— bel fiore!*, what a beautiful flower!; *— bella giornata!*, what a lovely day!; *— caro ragazzo sei!*, what a nice boy you are!; *— farabutto!*, what a scoundrel!; *— musica meravigliosa!*, what wonderful music!; *— noia, — seccatura!*, what a nuisance!; *— pazienza!*, what patience! — *peccato!*, what a pity!; *— stolti sono!*, what fools they are; *— vergogna!*, what a shame! || *pron. esclamativo* **what:** *—!, fuori di casa così presto!*, what!, up and about already?; *—!, hai dimenticato il mio nome?*, what!, have you forgotten my name?.

che⁴, *pron. indef.* **something:** *quell'uomo ha un — di strano*, that man has something strange about him; *sentiva un — di molle, un — di lieve*, he felt something soft, light || *questa commedia non è un gran —*, this play is nothing extraordinary (o *fam.* this play is nothing to write home about).

che⁵, *cong.* **1.** (*dichiarativa dopo verbi esprimenti opinione*) that (*spesso sottinteso*): *dicono — sia molto intelligente*, they say (that) he is very intelligent; *so — tu cercherai di comprendermi*, I know that you will try to understand me; *sono certo — verrà presto*, I am sure (that) he will come soon **2.** (*dichiarativa retta da verbi di volontà*): *egli vuole — io rimanga a casa*, he wants me to remain at home; *tu vuoi — io parta subito, ma io voglio restare*, you want me to leave at once, but I want to remain; *voglio — capisca che ha torto*, I want him to understand (that) he is wrong; *vuoi — ti porti una tazza di tè?*, do you want me to bring you a cup of tea? **3.** (*consecutiva*) **that:** *era già così buio — dovemmo accendere la luce per leggere*, it was already so dark that we had to put on the light to read; *sei tanto gentile — tutti ti amano*, you are so kind that everyone loves you **4.** (*comparativa*) **than:** *ha più denaro — cervello*, he has more money than sense; *sono più furbi — intelligenti*, they are more cunning than intelligent **5.** (*disgiuntiva*) **whether;** (*in correlazione*) **whether... or not:** *— tu mi aiuti o no, è lo stesso per me*, whether you help me or not is all the same to me; *— tu venga o — tu non venga, la situazione non cambierà*, whether you come or not, the situation won't change **6.** (*finale*) **lest** (*spesso si* *sottintende*): *bada — non ti sfuggano di nuovo*, look out, lest they should escape you again; *sta attento — non si faccia male*, mind he doesn't hurt himself **7.** (*desiderativa: si risolve in* may, *o nel congiunt. o nell'imperat. del verbo*): — *Dio ti aiuti!*, (may) God help you!; — *il cielo non voglia!*, Heaven forbid!; — *Iddio ti benedica!*, God bless you!; — *se ne vada!*, let him be gone! **8.** (*temporale*) when; as soon as; no sooner... than: *arrivai — era già partito*, he had already left when I arrived; *pagato — ebbero il conto, se ne andarono*, as soon as they had paid the bill (*o* no sooner had they paid the bill than) they went away **9.** (*eccettuativa*) but, only: *non gli erano rimasti — due pani*, he had but two loaves left; *non ho — te al mondo*, I have but (*o* only) you in all the world.

ché[6], *cong.* **1.** (*causale*) (*giacchè*) since, as; (*poichè*) for, because: *i cavalieri diedero di sprone ai cavalli, — il sole già tramontava*, the riders spurred their horses, for the sun was getting low; *risero le donne, — il viso del giovane si era coperto di rossore*, the women laughed, because the young man was blushing furiously **2.** (*finale*) so that: *arriviamo presto, — non si debba stare in piedi*, let's arrive early so that we don't have to stand.

chè[7], *inter.* what!, never!: — *!, non è possibile!*, what! (*o* never!), it's not possible!.

checché, *pron. indef.* whatever: — *voi diciate*, whatever you may say.

checchessia, *pron. indef.* (*qualsiasi cosa*) anything: *riderebbe di —*, he would laugh at anything.

chècchia, chèccia, *s.f.* (*mar.*) ketch.

cheddíte, *s.f.* (*esplosivo*) cheddite.

cheilofagía, *s.f.* (*med.*) cheilophagia, chelophagy.

cheirospàsmo, *s.m.* (*med.*) cheirospasm.

chèla, *s.f.* (*zool.*) chela (*pl.* chelae).

cheletomía, *s.f.* (*chir.*) kelectomy.

chelídro, *s.m.* (*zool.*) water snake.

chellerína, *s.f.* waitress.

chelóni, *s.m.pl.* (*zool.*) Chelonia.

chemiotàssi, *s.f.* (*scient.*) chemotaxis.

chemioterapía, *s.f.* (*med.*) chemotherapy.

chemiotropísmo, *s.m.* (*scient.*) chemotropism.

Chèope, *no.pr.m.* (*st.*) Cheops.

chepí, *s.m.* (*mil.*) kepi.

cheratína, *s.f.* (*anat. farm.*) keratin.

cheratíte, *s.f.* (*patol.*) keratitis.

chèrmes, *s.m.* (*entom.*) kermes.

chèrmisi, *s.m.* crimson.

chermisíno, *ag.* crimson.

Cheronèa, *no.pr f.* (*geog. st.*) Chaeronea.

cherúbico, *ag.* cherubic.

cherubíno, *s.m.* cherub (*pl.* cherubs, cherubim) (*anche fig.*).

chetaménte, *av.* **1.** quietly **2.** (*di nascosto*) secretly.

chetàre, *v.t.* **1.** (*calmare*) to quiet; to quieten; (*lo spirito*) to appease **2.** (*far tacere*) to silence ‖ **chetàrsi**, *v.r.* **1.** to quiet down **2.** (*tacere*) to be silent: *chetati!*, be silent! (*o fam.* shut up!).

chetichèlla, àlla, *l.av.* on the sly, secretly: *andarsene alla —*, to take French leave.

chéto, *ag.* **1.** (*calmo*) quiet **2.** (*immobile e silenzioso*) still ‖ *acqua cheta*, *fig.* sly person; (*di bambino, animale*) (*fam.*) sly boots ‖ *l'acqua cheta rovina i ponti*, *prov.* still waters run deep **3.** (*silenzioso*) silent.

chetóne, *s.m.* (*chim.*) ketone.

chi, *pron.interr.* **1.** *sogg.* who: — *cantava?*, who was singing?; — *è?*, who is it?; — *è stato a rompere questo bicchiere?*, (who was it) who broke this glass?; — (*lo*) *sa?*, who knows? (*o* who can tell?); — *non* (*lo*) *sa?*, who does not know?; — *siete?*, who are you?; — *va là?*, who is there? (*o* who goes there?); *mi domando — abbia preso la mia matita*, I wonder who has taken my pencil **2.** *oggetto e obliquo* who(m): — *hai visto alla festa?*, who(m) did you meet at the party?; *a — scrivi?*, who(m) are you writing to? (*o* to whom are you writing?); *da — fu ucciso vostro figlio?*, by

whom was your son killed? (*o* who killed your son?); *da — l'hai sentito?*, who(m) did you hear it from?; *di — parlate?*, who(m) are you talking about? **3.** *sogg. oggetto e obliquo* (*riferito a un numero limitato di persone*) which: — *di noi prediligi?*, which of us do you like best?; — *di voi ha preso il mio cappello?*, which of you has taken my hat?; *con — di noi preferisci stare?*, which of us would you rather stay with? **4.** (*nel compl. di specificazione possessiva*) whose: *di — è la casa che vedemmo ieri?*, whose house was it we saw yesterday?; *di — è figlia Maria?*, whose daughter is Mary?; *di — è questo libro?*, whose book is this?; *di — è il cappello che hai preso?*, whose hat did you take?.

chi, *pron.rel.* **1.** (*colui che*) he (*compl.* **him**) who (*compl.* **whom**); (*colei che*) she (*compl.* **her**) who (*compl.* **whom**); (*coloro che*) they (*compl.*) who (*compl.* **whom**); (*a queste forme letterarie si preferiscono comunemente forme del tipo:* **the person who(m), those who(m), people who(m)**: — *dimentica queste cose è spesso considerato villano*, those who (*o* people who) forget these things are often considered rude (*o letter.* he who forgets these things is often considered rude); — *ha fatto ciò deve essere pazzo*, the man who (*o letter.* he who) did that must be mad; — *mi informò fu tua madre*, the person who (*o letter.* she who) informed me was your mother (*o* it was your mother who informed me); *non voglio sapere — incontrasti*, I don't want to know who(m) you met; *puniremo — ha fatto ciò*, we shall punish the person who (*o* the persons who *o* those who) did this; *sono gentile con — è gentile con me*, I am kind to those who are kind to me ‖ — *ha pochi desideri è ricco*, *prov.* he who has few wants is rich ‖ — *rompe paga*, *prov.* he who breaks shall pay ‖ — *si aiuta il ciel l'aiuta*, *prov.* God helps those who help themselves **2.** (*chiunque*) whoever, anyone who, anybody who: — *sarà trovato in possesso di armi da fuoco sarà multato*, whoever is found in possession of firearms will be fined; — *vuol mangiare bisogna che lavori*, anyone who wants to eat must work **3.** (*qualcuno che*) someone who, somebody who: *c'è — potrebbe farlo*, there is someone who could do it; *non c'è — possa darmi torto*, there is no one who can say I am wrong ‖ **chi... chi**, *pron. indef.* one... another (*tra due*); some... some... some, some... others... others: — *danzava, — cantava* one was dancing, another was singing; — *ballava, — cantava, — giocava*, some were dancing, others were singing, others were playing; — *dice una cosa, — ne dice un'altra*, some say this, some say that.

chiàcchiera, *s.f.* **1.** idle talk, chatter: *smettetela con le vostre chiacchiere*, stop gossiping (*o* stop chattering); *fare due chiacchiere*, to have a chat ‖ *ha molta —*, he has a glib tongue **2.** (*notizia infondata*) unfounded rumour, false report **3.** (*pettegolezzo*) gossip, gossiping: *non credere a tutte le chiacchiere che ti raccontò*, don't believe all the gossip she told you.

chiacchieràre, *v.i.* **1.** to talk (idly), to chat, to chatter, to prate, to tattle: — *del più e del meno*, to chat about one thing and another **2.** (*fare pettegolezzi*) to gossip.

chiacchieràta, *s.f.* **1.** chat, (idle) talk: *abbiamo fatto una bella —*, we've had a nice chat (*o* a good gossip) together **2.** (*discorso vuoto*) long empty talk.

chiacchieríccio, *s.m.* noisy chattering, prattling.

chiacchieríno, *s.m.* chatterer, talkative person.

chiacchierío, *s.m.* babbling, chattering.

chiacchieróna, *s.f.*, **chiacchieróne**, *s.m.* **1.** chatterer, chatterbox, great talker **2.** (*che fa pettegolezzi*) gossip; (*maldicente*) backbiter.

chiàma, *s.f.* roll-call: *fare la —*, to call the roll.

chiamàre, *v.t.* **1.** to call; (*alzando la voce*) to call out: *chi mi chiama?*, who is calling me?; *chiamalo alle cinque*, call him at five; *il dovere mi chiama*, duty calls me; *smettila di chiamarmi sciocco*, stop calling me a fool; — *aiuto*, to call for help; — (*qlcu.*) *con un cenno*, to beckon (to s.o.); — *un taxi*, to hail a taxi ‖

molti sono i chiamati, ma pochi gli eletti, many are called but few chosen ‖ — *alla ribalta*, (*teat.*) to call to the footlights ‖ — *le cose col loro nome*, (*fam.*) to call a spade a spade **2.** (*mil.*) to call up: — *una classe*, to call up a class; — *sotto le armi*, to call s.o. to the colours **3.** (*dir.*) to call: -— *a testimonio*, to call to witness; — *una |causa*, to call a cause; — *in giudizio*, to summon (before the magistrate) **4.** (*far venire*) to call, to send for (s.o.): *chiamate il dottore*, call for the doctor **5.** (*al telefono*) to call up, to ring up: *chiamalo subito al telefono*, ring him up at once (*o* call him up at once); *Parigi sta chiamando*, Paris is calling **6.** (*dar nome a*) to name, to call: *lo chiamarono Giovanni*, they named (*o* called) him John **7.** (*invocare*) to call on (s.o., sthg.), to invoke; to appeal to (s.o., sthg.): — *una benedizione*, to invoke a blessing; — *la collera di Dio*, to call down the wrath of heaven **8.** (*alle carte*) to declare ‖ **chiamàrsi**, *v.r.* (*aver nome*) to be called; (*considerarsi*) to count oneself, to consider oneself: *come si chiama quest'oggetto?*, what is this thing called? (*o* what do you call this thing?); *come si chiama tuo padre?*, what is your father's name?; *egli si chiama Giovanni*, his name is John; *mi chiamo fortunato*, I consider myself lucky.

chiamàta, *s.f.* **1.** call, appeal, call-up: — *interurbana*, (*tel.*) trunk-call (*o* amer. long-distance call); *rispondere a una —*, to answer a call **2.** (*mil.*) call-up, call to arms; (*amer.*) draft: — *alle armi in tempo di pace*, peacetime call-up (*o* amer. draft); *la — di una classe*, the calling -up of a class **3.** (*appello*) roll-call **4.** (*tip.*) cross-reference mark; footnote reference **5.** (*teat.*) curtain-call **6.** (*dir.*) summons.

chiànti, *s.m.* "Chianti" (Tuscan table-wine).

chiàppa, *s.f.* (*volg.*) buttock.

chiappamósche, *s.m.* **1.** fly-catcher; fly-paper **2.** *fig.* (*buono a nulla*) good-for-nothing.

chiappàre, *v.t.* to catch, to seize.

chiapparèllo, chiapperèllo, *s.m.* (*raggiro*) snare, trap.

chiàra, *s.f.* white (of an egg): *due chiare (d'uovo)*, the whites of two eggs.

Chiàra, *no.pr.f.* Clara, Clare.

chiaraménte, *av.* clearly; (*francamente*) openly, frankly, plainly; (*distintamente*) evidently, distinctly.

chiarétto, *s.m.* (*vino*) claret.

chiarézza, *s.f.* **1.** clearness; (*di discorso, scritto, ecc.*) lucidity, evidence **2.** (*fama*) renown, fame.

chiarìa, *s.f.* cloudless sky.

chiarificàre, *v.t.* to clarify (anche *fig.*).

chiarificatóre, *s.m.* clarifier.

chiarificazióne, *s.f.* **1.** clarification **2.** (*franca spiegazione*) frank explanation, full declaration of intentions; (*sl.*) showdown.

chiariménto, *s.m.* explanation.

chiaríre, *v.t.* **1.** (*rendere chiaro*) to make clear, to show, to explain, to clarify: *non potei — tutto ciò*, I could not make all this clear; — *un dubbio*, to remove a doubt; — *un mistero*, to clear up a mystery; — *una questione*, to explain a question **2.** (*purificare, liquidi*) to clarify ‖ **chiarírsi**, *v.r.* **1.** (*del tempo*) to clear up: *il tempo si chiarisce*, the weather is clearing up **2.** (*diventar chiaro*) to become clear.

chiaríssimo, *ag.* **1.** very clear **2.** (*nell'intestazione di una lettera*) dear.

chiarìta[1], *s.f.* **1.** (*schiarita*) clearing **2.** (*radura*) glade.

chiarità[2], *s.f.* clearness, splendour; (*luminosità*) brightness, light, luminosity.

chiaritóio, *s.m.* filter.

chiaritúra, *s.f.* **1.** clarification (of liquids) **2.** (*chiarificazione*) explanation.

chiàro, *ag.* **1.** clear; (*luminoso*) bright; (*detto di colore*) light: *acque chiare*, clear water; *azzurro —*, light blue; *carnagione chiara*, clear complexion; *luce chiara*, bright light; *note chiare*, clear notes; *voce chiara*, clear voice; *la campana ha un suono —*, the bell has a clear tone; *le mie parole sono chiare?*, are my words clear?; *quello* *scrittore ha uno stile —*, that writer has a clear style; *avere una chiara visione del futuro*, to have a clear vision of the future ‖ *giorno —*, full day ‖ *patti chiari, amicizia lunga*, *prov.* short reckonings make long friends **2.** (*evidente*) clear, evident, manifest, plain: *è — che avete torto*, it is evident (*o* clear) you are wrong **3.** (*famoso*) famous, eminent, renowned, illustrious: *uno scienziato di chiara fama*, a scientist of great renown (*o* an eminent scientist) **4.** (*valoroso*) brave, bold, valiant ‖ *s.m.* **1.** (*luminosità*) clearness, brightness; (*luce*) light: *i chiari di un dipinto*, the lights in a painting; — *di luna*, moonlight (*o* moonshine); *si fa —*, it is dawning; *vestirsi di —*, to wear light-coloured clothes ‖ *con questi chiari di luna*, *fig.* in these difficult times ‖ *mettere in — ql.co.*, to clear sthg. up (*o* to make sthg. clear *o* to explain sthg.); *venire in — di ql.co.*, to get at the truth (*o* to get to the bottom) of sthg. **2.** — *d'uovo*, white of an egg.

chiàro, *av.* clearly; (*con franchezza*) frankly, openly: *parlar —*, to speak clearly; (*con franchezza*) to speak frankly; *veder — in ql.co.*, to have a clear idea about sthg. ‖ — *e tondo*, plainly: *glielo dirò — e tondo*, I'll tell him plainly (*o* in plain English).

chiaróre, *s.m.* **1.** (*luce*) light **2.** (*luce tenue*) faint light **3.** (*barlume*) gleam, glimmer: *il — dell'alba*, the first light of dawn **4.** (*luce intensa*) bright light, brightness.

chiaroscuràre, *v.t.* to shade.

chiaroscúro, *s.m.* chiaroscuro, light and shade: *effetti di —*, light and shade effects (*o* chiaroscuro).

chiaroveggènte, *ag.* **1.** (*che intuisce e comprende con chiarezza*) clear-sighted **2.** (*che ha facoltà divinatorie*) clairvoyant.

chiaroveggènza, *s.f.* **1.** (*chiarezza mentale*) clear -sightedness, perspicacity, penetration **2.** (*dono profetico*) clairvoyance.

chiàsma, chiàsmo, *s.m.* **1.** (*ret.*) chiasmus (*pl.* chiasmi) **2.** (*anat.*) chiasm; chiasma (*pl.* chiasmata): — *dei nervi ottici*, chiasma opticum (*o* optic chiasm).

chiassàta, *s.f.* **1.** racket, row: *fare una —*, to make a racket **2.** (*burla, celia*) joke, jest; hoax **3.** (*rabbuffo*) rebuke; reprimand **4.** (*scenata*) scene: *fecero una —*, they made a scene.

chiassétto, *s.m.* (*vicoletto*) narrow lane.

chiàsso[1], *s.m.* **1.** noise, uproar, hubbub: *fare —*, to make a noise; *fig.* to make a sensation **2.** (*rar.*) (*burla*) jest, joke; hoax: *per —*, in jest (*o* for fun) **3.** (*alterco violento*) dispute, quarrel, wrangle.

chiàsso[2], *s.m.* (*vicolo*) lane, alley.

chiassóna, *s.f.*, **chiassóne**, *s.m.* **1.** (*chi ama molto i divertimenti chiassosi*) boisterous person, roisterer **2.** (*chi fa molto chiasso*) noisy person.

chiassosaménte, *av.* **1.** noisily **2.** (*vistosamente*) gaudily.

chiassóso, *ag.* **1.** noisy **2.** (*di colore*) showy; (*fam.*) loud; (*di abito*) gaudy, showy: *una cravatta chiassosa*, a showy (*o* loud) necktie; *un panciotto —*, a showy (*o* gaudy) waistcoat.

chiàtta, *s.f.* (*nei porti*) lighter; (*su fiumi, canali*) barge: *ponte di chiatte*, pontoon-bridge; *su chiatte*, on lighters; *mettere in chiatte*, to lighter.

chiavàccio, *s.m.* large door bolt.

chiavàio, *s.m.* (*rar.*) locksmith.

chiavàrda, *s.f.* clamp, bolt: — *ad uncino*, (*ferr.*) hook bolt; — *da rotaia*, (*ferr.*) track bolt; — *di fondazione*, (*edil. mec.*) foundation bolt.

chiàve, *s.f.* **1.** key: — *falsa*, skeleton key; — *maestra, apritutto*, master-key; *buco della —*, key-hole; *un mazzo di chiavi*, a bunch of keys; *sotto —*, under lock and key: *tenere ql.co., qlcu. sotto —*, to keep sthg., s.o. locked up (*o* to keep sthg., s.o. under lock and key); *chiudere a —*, to lock ‖ *chiavi apostoliche, di S. Pietro*, (*eccl.*) St. Peter's keys **2.** *fig.* clue, key: — *di un enigma*, clue to a puzzle; — *di un messaggio cifrato*, cipher-key; — *di un mistero*, key to a mystery; *posizione —*, key position; *uomo —*, key-man **3.** (*tec.*) key, spanner, wrench:

— *d'accordatore*, tuning hammer; — *di strumento a corda*, peg; — *fissa da dadi*, spanner; — *inglese*, monkey -wrench (*o* screw spanner *o* shifting spanner) **4.** (*mus.*) clef: — *di violino*, G (*o* treble) clef **5.** — *di volta*, (*arch.*) keystone.

chiavétta, *s.f.* small key: — *del gas*, gas-tap; *gira la* — *e accendi il gas*, turn on the gas.

chiàvica, *s.f.* drain, sewer.

chiavistèllo, *s.m.* latch, bolt: — *a saliscendi*, thumb -latch; *mettere il* — *ad una porta*, to bolt a door.

chiàzza, *s.f.* spot, stain.

chiazzàre, *v.t.* to spot, to stain; (*con colori diversi*) to mottle.

chiazzàto, *ag.* spotted; (*a chiazze di colori diversi*) mottled.

chícca, *s.f.* sweet, sweetmeat.

chícchera, *s.f.* **1.** cup: — *da caffè*, coffee-cup **2.** (*il liquido in essa contenuto*) cupful.

chicchessía, *pron.indef.* (*rar.*) anyone, anybody.

chicchiriàre, *v.i.* (*rar.*) to crow.

chicchiriàta, *s.f.* (*rar.*) crowing.

chicchirichí, *s.m.* (*voce onomatopeica riproducente il canto del gallo*) cock-a-doodle-doo.

chíceo, *s.m.* grain; (*di grandine*) hailstone; (*di caffè*) coffee-bean; (*d'uva*) grape.

chièdere, *v.t.* **1.** (*per sapere*) to ask; (*imperiosamente*) to demand; (*umilmente*) to beg; (*informarsi, indagare*) to inquire; (*per avere*) to ask for (sthg.): *chiedigli l'ora, che ora è*, ask him the time, what time it is; *chiese che io andassi, mi chiese di andare da lui*, he asked me to go to him; *chiese notizie del mio lavoro*, he inquired about my work; *chiesi notizie di suo padre*, I asked after his father; *mi chiese cinquanta lire e un po' di pane*, he asked me for fifty lire and a little bread; *non c'è che da chiederlo*, you may have it for the asking; — *un favore a qlcu.*, to ask a favour of s.o.; — *perdono, scusa a qlcu. di ql.co.*, to beg (*o* to ask) s.o.'s pardon for sthg.: *ti chiedo perdono per aver ferito i tuoi sentimenti*, I beg your pardon for hurting your feelings; — *il permesso di fare*, to beg leave to do **2.** (*riferito a prezzo di cosa che si vende*) to charge, to ask: *di questo quadro gli chiederò ventimila lire*, I shall ask him twenty thousand lire for this picture; *quanto chiedi al giorno per un'automobile?*, how much do you charge for a car by the day?; — *5 lire al metro*, to charge 5 lire a metre **3.** (*mendicare*) to beg.

chiedíbile, *ag.* demandable.

chiérica, *s.f.* tonsure; *fig.* tonsure, priesthood: *prendere, ricevere la* —, to submit to the tonsure (*o* to enter the priesthood).

chiericàto, *s.m.* (*eccl.*) clerkhood.

chierichétto, *s.m.* altar boy; (*piccolo corista*) choir-boy.

chiérico, *s.m.* **1.** altar boy **2.** (*seminarista che ha ricevuto gli ordini minori*) minor clerk.

chiericúto, *ag.* tonsured.

chièsa, *s.f.* **1.** church: *andare in* —, to go to church ‖ *uomo, donna di* —, church-goer **2.** *Chiesa*, (*comunità religiosa*) Church: *la Chiesa Anglicana*, the Church of England (*o* the Anglican Church *o* the English Church); *la Chiesa Cattolica*, the (Roman) Catholic Church; *la Chiesa Militante*, the Church militant; *Chiesa Riformata*, Reformed Church.

chiesuóla, *s.f.* **1.** little church **2.** *fig.* (*cenacolo*) coterie, set: — *artistica, letteraria*, artistic, literary coterie; — *politica*, political set **3.** (*mar.*) (*custodia di bussola*) binnacle.

chietíno, *s.m.* (*spreg.*) bigot; hypocrite.

chíglia, *s.f.* (*mar.*) keel: — *a pinna*, fin keel; — *di rollio*, bilge keel.

chilífero, *ag.* (*fisiol.*) chyliferous.

chilificàre, *v.i.* (*fisiol.*) to chylify.

chilificazióne, *s.f.* (*fisiol.*) chylification, chylifaction.

chílo¹, *s.m.* (*fisiol.*) chyle ‖ *fare il* —, (*riposare dopo il pranzo*) to take a nap (*o* a short rest) after lunch (*o* to have forty winks).

chílo², *abbr.* di **chilográmmo**.

chilocíclo, *s.m.* (*rad.*) kilocycle.

chilográmma, *V.* **chilográmmo**.

chilográmmetro, *s.m.* (*fis.*) kilogrammetre; (*amer.*) kilogrammeter.

chilográmmo, *s.m.* kilogram(me) (*abbr.* kilo) (*misura di peso* = 2.204 lb.).

chilòlitro, *s.m.* kilolitre; (*amer.*) kiloliter (*misura di capacità* = 35.315 cu. ft.).

chilometràggio, *s.m.* distance in kilometres; (*distanza in miglia*) mileage.

chilomètrico, *ag.* kilometric(al); *fig.* extremely long.

chilòmetro, *s.m.* kilometre; (*amer.*) kilometer (*misura di lunghezza* = 0.621 mi.).

chilowàtt, *s.m.* (*elett.*) kilowatt.

chimèra, *s.f.* chimera (anche *fig.*).

chimericaménte, *av.* chimerically.

chimèrico, *ag.* chimerical, visionary, unreal, fanciful.

chímica, *s.f.* chemistry.

chimicaménte, *av.* chemically.

chímico, *ag.* chemical: *analisi chimica*, chemical analysis; *processo* —, chemical process; *sostanze chimiche*, chemicals ‖ *s.m.* chemist: *un* — *capace*, a clever chemist.

chimificàre, *v.t.* to chymify.

chimificazióne, *s.f.* chymification.

chimísmo, *s.m.* chemism.

chímo, *s.m.* (*fisiol.*) chyme.

chimòno, *s.m.* kimono.

chimòsi, *s.f.* (*fisiol.*) chymification.

chimosína, *s.f.* (*chim. biol.*) chymosin.

chína¹, *s.f.* **1.** slope; descent, declivity **2.** *fig.* turn: *mettersi su una brutta* —, (*di malattia*) to take a bad turn (*o* to take a turn for the worse); (*in senso morale*) to go to the bad.

chína², *s.f.* (*bot.*) cinchona, quinquina.

chinaménto, *s.m.* bending, bowing.

chinàre, *v.t.* to bend, to bow, to incline; (*abbassare*) to lower: — *il capo*, (*in segno di saluto*) to bend one's head; (*per pregare*) to bow one's head; *fig.* (*cedere*) to give in (*o* to yield) ‖ **chinàrsi**, *v.r.* **1.** to stoop, to bend down: *mi chinai per raccoglierlo*, I stooped to pick it up **2.** (*sottomettersi*) to submit, to give in.

chináto¹, *ag.* (*piegato*) bent, bowed, inclined.

chináto², *ag.* (*aromatizzato alla china*) flavoured with quinquina.

chinatúra, *s.f.* bending, lowing.

chincàglie, *s.f.pl.* fancy goods; knick-knacks.

chincaglière, *s.m.* fancy goods merchant; seller of knick-knacks.

chincaglieria, *s.f.* **1.** (*oggetti ornamentali di poco valore*) knick-knackery; small fancy articles (*pl.*) **2.** (*il negozio in cui si vendono tali oggetti*) fancy goods shop.

chinchílla, *s.f.* (*zool.*) chinchilla.

chinèa, *s.f.* **1.** saddle-horse; saddle-mule **2.** (*cavalcatura*) mount.

chinése, *V.* **cinése**.

chinesería, *s.f.* **1.** (*ninnolo cinese*) Chinese knick -knack **2.** (*fig.*) (*sottigliezza burocraticha*) bureaucratic complication; red-tapism, red-tape.

chinesiterapía, *s.f.* (*med.*) kinesitherapy.

chinesiteràpico, *ag.* (*med.*) kinesitherapeutic.

chinína, *s.f.*, **chiníno**, *s.m.* (*chim. farm.*) quinine, quinin, quinina.

chíno, *ag.* bent, bowed: *a capo* —, with bent (*o* bowed) head.

chinóne, *s.m.* (*chim.*) quinone.

chinòtto, *s.m.* (*bot.*) bigarade.

Chío, *no.pr.f.* (*geog.*) Chios.

chioccàre, *V.* **schioccàre**.

chiòccia, *s.f.* brooding-hen, broody hen: *una* — *con i pulcini*, a hen with her brood of chickens.

chiocciàre, *v.i.* to cluck.

chiocciàta, *s.f.* brood of chickens.

chiòccio, *ag.* clucking.

chiòcciola, *s.f.* **1.** (*zool.*) snail ‖ *scala a* —, winding (*o* spiral) staircase **2.** (*anat.*) cochlea **3.** (*conchiglia*) sea-shell, shell-fish **4.** (*mec.*) lead nut, screw nut.

chiocciolàio, *s.m.* **1.** (*chi raccoglie*) collector of snails **2.** (*chi vende*) seller of snails.

chiòcco, *V.* **schiòcco.**

chioccolàre, *v.i.* **1.** (*del merlo*) to whistle **2.** (*gorgogliare*) to gurgle, to bubble.

chioccolatóre, *s.m.* decoy-bird.

chioccolío, *s.m.* **1.** (*di uccelli*) whistling **2.** (*gorgoglio*) gurgle, gurgling sound.

chiòccolo, *s.m.* **1.** (*fischio*) bird-whistle, bird-call **2.** (*caccia con la pania*) shooting with the help of decoy-birds.

chiodàia, *s.f.* (*artig.*) **1.** (*dama per teste di bulloni*) swage block **2.** (*macchina chiodatrice*) rivet set.

chiodaiuòlo, *s.m.* nail-maker.

chiodàme, *s.m.* nails (*pl.*).

chiodàre, (*rar.*) per **inchiodàre.**

chiodàto, *ag.* nailed; (*fornito di grossi chiodi*) hob-nailed: *scarpa chiodata,* hob-nailed shoe (*o* boot).

chiodatúra, *s.f.* (*mec.*) riveting: — *a caldo,* hot riveting; — *a catena,* chain riveting; — *ermetica,* tight-riveting; — *semplice,* single riveting.

chiodería, *s.f.* **1.** nailery, nail-factory **2.** (*chiodame*) nails (*pl.*).

chiòdo, *s.m.* **1.** nail; (*mec.*) rivet: — *da scarpe, da roccia,* hob-nail; — *stradale,* stud; *estrarre un* —, to draw (*o* to take out) a nail; *piantare un* —, to drive in a nail; *ribadire un* —, to rivet a nail ‖ *magro come un* —, as thin as a rake ‖ *robe da chiodi,* awful things (*o* stuff): *è roba da chiodi!,* it's a crazy show! ‖ — *scaccia* —, *prov.* one pain drives out another ‖ *batti il* — *fin che è caldo, prov.* make hay while the sun shines **2.** (*debito*) debt: *piantar chiodi,* to run into debt **3.** (*idea fissa*) fixed idea: *quello è il suo* —, that is his fixed idea; *piantare il* —, (*ostinarsi*) to be obstinate (*o* to insist on sthg.) **4.** (*dolore*) pain, ache: — *solare,* (*patol.*) neuralgic headache ‖ *ho un* — *qui,* (*fam.*) I have got a sharp pain (*o* pang) here **5.** — *di garofano,* (*cuc.*) clove.

chiòma, *s.f.* **1.** hair (*solo sing.*): *ella aveva una bella* —, she had beautiful hair (*o* she had a beautiful head of hair) **2.** (*criniera*) mane **3.** (*fogliame*) foliage, leafage; leaves (*pl.*) **4.** (*pennecchio di rocca*) flax, wool wound on a distaff **5.** (*astr.*) tail, train (of a comet).

chiomànte, *ag.* (*poet.*) **1.** with long hair, long-haired **2.** (*frondeggiante*) leafy.

chiomàto, *ag.* **1.** long-haired **2.** (*di alberi*) leafy.

chiòsa, *s.f.* explanatory note, annotation, gloss.

chiosàre, *v.t.* to annotate, to gloss; to explain.

chiosatóre, *s.m.,* **chiosatríce,** *s.f.* annotator, commentator, glossator.

chiòseo, *s.m.* **1.** kiosk **2.** (*per giornali*) news-stand, news-stall; book-stall **3.** (*per frutta e verdura*) fruit and vegetables stand.

chiòstra, *s.f.* **1.** enclosure; boundary **2.** (*di denti*) set **3.** (*di monti*) range.

chiòstro, *s.m.* **1.** (*cortile di monastero*) cloister **2.** (*monastero*) cloister **3.** *fig.* (*vita monastica*) monastic life, cloister: *lasciare il* —, to give up monastic life.

chiòtto, *ag.* quiet, still: *se ne stette* — —, he kept quite still (*o* he kept very quiet *o* he did not stir).

chiozzòtta, *s.f.* (*mar.*) "chiozzotta" (fishing boat from Chioggia).

chiràgra, *s.f.* (*patol.*) chiragra.

chiràgrico, *ag.* (*patol.*) chiragric(al).

chiragróso, *ag.* (*med.*) chiragrical ‖ *s.m.* (*med.*) sufferer from chiragra.

chirografàrio, *ag.* (*dir.*) chirographary: *creditore* —, chirographary creditor; *debito* —, chirographary debt.

chirògrafo, *s.m.* (*dir.*) chirograph.

chiromànte, *s.c.* chiromancer, chiromant; palmist.

chiromanzía, *s.f.* chiromancy; palmistry.

Chiróne, *no.pr.m.* (*mit.*) Chiron.

chiròtteri, *s.m.pl.* (*zool.*) Chiroptera.

chirurgía, *s.f.* surgery: — *plastica,* plastic surgery.

chirurgicaménte, *av.* surgically.

chirúrgico, *ag.* surgical: *anatomia chirurgica,* surgical anatomy; *caso* —, surgical case; *strumenti chirurgici,* surgical instruments.

chirúrgo, *s.m.* surgeon: — *odontoiatra,* dental surgeon.

chisciottésco, *ag.* quixotic.

chissà, *av.* **1.** goodness knows: — *quando lo rivedremo!,* goodness knows when we shall meet him again! ‖ — *se,* I wonder whether: — *se verrà,* I wonder whether he will come **2.** (*forse*) perhaps, maybe: « *Gli scriverai?* », « *Chissà!* », "Are you going to write to him?", "Maybe!".

chissisía, *pron. indef.* (*rar.*) anyone, anybody.

chitàrra, *s.f.* (*mus.*) guitar: — *elettrica,* electric guitar; *suonare la* —, to play (on) the guitar.

chitarríno, *s.m.* (*mus.*) small guitar.

chitarrísta, *s.m.* guitarist.

chitarronàta, *s.f.* (*spreg.*) **1.** poor piece of music for guitar **2.** poor poetry sung to a guitar.

chitína, *s.f.* (*chim. zool.*) chitin.

chitóne, *s.m.* chiton.

chiú, *s.m.* (*ornit.*) horned owl.

chiudènda, *s.f.* **1.** (*steccato*) fence, hedge; paling, palisade **2.** (*recinto*) enclosure.

chiúdere, *v.t.* **1.** to shut, to close; (*sbarrare*) to bar: — *a catenaccio,* to bolt; — *a chiave,* to lock; — *la bocca,* to shut one's mouth; — *un cancello, una finestra, una porta,* to shut a gate, a window, a door; — *un cassetto,* to shut a drawer; — *con lucchetto,* to padlock; — *il gas, un rubinetto,* to turn off the gas, a tap; — *una lettera,* (*sigillarla*) to seal up a letter; — *un libro,* to shut a book; — *un passaggio,* to bar a passage; — *il pugno,* to clench one's fist; — *la radio,* to switch off the wireless; — *violentemente,* to slam (*o* to bang) ‖ *non ho chiuso occhio la notte scorsa,* I did not sleep a wink last night ‖ — *al traffico,* to close to traffic ‖ — *la bocca a qlcu.,* (*impedirgli di parlare*) to gag s.o. ‖ — *gli occhi,* (*morire*) to close one's days ‖ — *un occhio su ql.co.,* to turn a blind eye to sthg. (*o* to pretend not to see sthg.) **2.** (*recingere*) to enclose, to fence (in), to surround: — *un giardino con un muro,* to enclose a garden with a wall **3.** (*concludere*) to conclude, to close; (*finire*) to end, to finish; (*fam.*) to wind up: *è ben ora che egli chiuda il suo discorso,* it is high time he wound up his speech; — *una conferenza con un motto di spirito,* to close a lecture with a joke; — *un dibattito al Parlamento,* to close (*o* to wind up) a debate in Parliament; — *una lettera,* to close a letter **4.** (*terminare*) to close: *la banda chiudeva il corteo,* the band brought up the rear (of the procession) **5.** (*comm.*) to close: — *un conto,* to close an account **6.** (*rinchiudere*) to shut up: *dovresti* — *i gioielli nella cassaforte,* you ought to shut up your jewels in your safe; *ti chiuderò nella tua stanza,* I'll shut you up in your room **7.** (*un negozio, un* |*ufficio, una fabbrica*) (*temporaneamente*) to close; (*permanentemente*) to shut down **8.** (*limitare*) to shut in: *due catene di montagne chiudono la valle,* two ranges of mountains shut in (*o* enclose) the valley **9.** (*tappare*) to stop; (*con sughero*) to cork: — *un buco,* to stop a hole **10.** (*un circuito elettrico*) to close ‖ — *un motore in corto circuito,* (*elett.*) to short-circuit a motor ‖ *v.i.* **1.** to close: *la finestra non chiude,* the window won't close (*o* shut); *i negozi chiudono alle sei in questa città,* the shops close at six in this town; *questa porta chiude bene?,* does this door close well? **2.** (*finire*) to close: *la riunione chiuse alle sei,* the meeting closed at six **3.** — *in dissolvenza,* (*cine.*) to fade out ‖ **chiúdersi,** *v.r.* **1.** to close: *le acque si chiusero sulla nave che affondava,* the waters closed over the sinking ship; *la porta si chiuse senza rumore,* the door closed noiselessly; *questi fiori si chiudono di sera,* these flowers close at night **2.** (*di tempo*) to close in, to get cloudy: *il tempo si chiude,* the weather is closing in (*o* getting cloudy) **3.** (*rinchiudersi*) to shut oneself up 4. (ritirarsi, concentrarsi) to withdraw: — in se stesso, to withdraw into oneself; — nel dolore, to withdraw into one's sufferings; — nel silenzio, to withdraw into silence.

chiudiménto, s.m. (rar.) closing, closure.

chiúnque, pron. 1. rel. indef. sogg. whoever, anyone who; (enfatico) whosoever: — faccia del male, finisce con l'essere punito, whoever does wrong is punished in the end; — lo faccia, sono sicuro che sarà fatto male, whoever does it, it will be done badly, I am sure; — lo trovi, deve darmelo subito, anyone who finds it, should give it back to me at once; — venga, ditegli che non sono in casa, whoever comes, tell them (o tell anyone who comes) I am not at home 2. rel. indef. oggetto e obliquo who(m)ever, anyone; (enfatico) whomsoever: — incontriate, fermatelo, stop anyone you meet; datelo a — vi piaccia, give it to who(m)ever (o anyone) you like 3. rel. indef. (nel compl. di specificazione possessiva) whosever: di — sia questo cappello, devo dire che non mi piace, whosever this hat is, I must say I do not like it 4. rel. indef. sogg. oggetto e obliquo (riferito a un numero limitato di persone) whichever: — di voi arrivi a casa prima, dovrà accendere il fuoco, whichever of you comes home first, should light the fire 5. indef. (chicchessia) anyone, anybody: — può farlo, anyone can do that; egli sa fare questo genere di lavoro meglio di — altro, he can do that sort of work better than anybody else; tu meglio di — puoi capire il mio problema, you can understand my problem better than anybody else.

chiurlàre, v.i. 1. to whistle 2. (imitare il canto del chiurlo) to whistle like a curlew.

chiúrlo, s.m. 1. (ornit.) curlew 2. (sempliciotto) simpleton.

chiúsa, s.f. 1. lock; (diga) dam, weir 2. (recinto) enclosure 3. (conclusione) (di discorso) conclusion; (di lettera) close.

chiusaménte, av. secretly, hiddenly, on the sly.

chiusíno, s.m. 1. (di buca) cover, lid; (stradale) drain cover 2. (di forno) oven door.

chiúso, ag. 1. closed, shut: — a chiave, locked; i negozi sono chiusi la domenica, shops are closed on Sundays ‖ a occhi chiusi, fig. (sconsideratamente) blindly ‖ a porte chiuse, (dir.) in camera ‖ mente chiusa, narrow mind ‖ persona chiusa, taciturn (o reserved) person ‖ cielo —, overcast sky ‖ trotto —, quick trot ‖ vocale chiusa, close vowel 2. (circondato, racchiuso) enclosed: spazio —, enclosed space 3. (comm.) settled, balanced: conto — il 15 agosto, account balanced (o settled) on August 15th ‖ s.m. (recinto) enclosure; (per animali in genere) pen; (per pecore) fold.

chiusúra, s.f. 1. closing; close; (fam.) shut-down: — definitiva, shutting down; — dei conti, closing of accounts; — di un convegno, close of a meeting; — di un dibattito (parlamentare), closure of a debate (in Parliament); bilancio di —, closing balance; ora di —, closing time 2. (serratura) lock 3. (allacciatura) fastening: — lampo, zip(-fastener).

ci[1], pron. 1. pers. 1a persona pl. oggetto e obliquo us: — dissero che sarebbero venuti, they told us they would come; dateci un po' di tempo, give us a little time; diteci la verità, tell us the truth; non — nascosero la verità, they did not conceal the truth from us; non — parlarono neppure, they did not even speak to us; i nostri genitori — amano, our parents love us; perdonateci, forgive us; tutti — guardano, everybody is looking at us 2. r. 1a persona pl. ourselves (spesso sottinteso): — lavammo, we washed ourselves; — lavammo e vestimmo in un momento, we washed and got dressed in a moment 3. reciproco each other (tra due persone), one another (tra molti): mio padre ed io — guardammo senza parlare, my father and I looked at each other without speaking; noi tutti — vogliamo molto bene, we are all very fond of one another 4. dimostrativo this; that; it: — penserò, I'll think about it; non badarci, never mind about it (o pay no atten-

tion to it) ‖ — ho molto piacere, (idiot.) I'm very glad about it.

ci[2], av. di luogo (là) there; (qui) here: — andremo subito, we shall go there at once; — siamo, finalmente, here we are, at last; questa è la nostra nuova piscina, tutti i nostri amici — vengono, this is our new swimming-pool, all our friends come here ‖ c'è, — sono, there is, there are: — sono circa mille persone in questo salone, there are about one thousand people in this hall.

ci[3], s.f.m. letter C.

ciabàtta, s.f. 1. slipper: scese in ciabatte, he came downstairs in his slippers 2. (scarpa vecchia e scalcagnata) down-at-heel shoe, worn-out shoe 3. fig. (persona malandata) slipshod person; (cosa malandata) slipshod thing.

ciabattàre, v.i. to shuffle (along) in one's slippers.

ciabattàta, s.f. spank with a slipper.

ciabattíno, s.m. cobbler.

ciabattóna, s.f. slipshod woman; (arruffona) bungler.

ciabattóne, s.m. slipshod fellow; (arruffone) bungler.

ciàc, s.m. (cine.) take.

ciaccóna, s.f. (musica, danza) chaconne.

ciàlda, s.f. wafer.

cialdonàio, s.m. waferer.

cialdóne, s.m. cornet.

cialtróna, s.f. (donna sciatta) slovenly woman, slut.

cialtronàglia, s.f. gang of ruffians.

cialtronàta, s.f. rascally, knavish action; vile trick.

cialtróne, s.m. 1. (uomo sciatto) sloven 2. (manigoldo) ruffian, rascal, scoundrel, rogue.

cialtronería, s.f. 1. (sciatteria) slovenliness 2. (furfanteria) rascality 3. (atto da cialtrone) knavish action, vile trick; (detto da cialtrone) knavish word.

ciambèlla, s.f. 1. ring-shaped cake ‖ non tutte le ciambelle riescono col buco, prov. not everything turns out as it should 2. (cuscino ad anello) ring-shaped cushion 3. (salvagente) rubber ring 4. (cercine) round pad 5. (cerchietto d'osso che i bambini mordono durante la dentizione) teething-ring.

ciambellàio, s.m. pastry-cook.

ciambellàno, s.m. chamberlain: — di corte, court chamberlain.

ciambellóne, s.m. large ring-shaped cake.

ciambellòtto, s.m. (tessuto) camlet.

ciampanèlle, s.f.: dare in —, to rave.

ciampicàre, v.i. 1. to shuffle along, to shuffle one's feet 2. (barcollare) to stagger; (inciampare) to stumble.

ciampicóne, s.m. 1. man who shuffles his feet 2. (barcollone) stagger: fare un —, to stumble.

ciàna, s.f. slatternly gossip.

cianamíde, s.m. (chim.) cyanamide.

cianàto, s.m. (chim.) cyanate.

ciànca s.f. (fam.) leg.

ciància, s.f. (pettegolezzo) idle talk, tittle-tattle, gossip ‖ ciance!, (fandonie) nonsense! (o humbug!).

cianciafrúscola, s.f. (fam.) trifle.

cianciàre, v.i. 1. to chatter, to talk idly, to prattle; (fam.) to jabber 2. (scherzare) to joke.

cianciatóre, s.m., **cianciatríce**, s.f. chatterbox, tattler, wind-bag, prattler.

ciancicàre, v.i. 1. to jabber, to stammer (out), to mumble: — una frase, to mumble a sentence 2. (biascicare) to mumble, to chew slowly: quel vecchio ciancicava un tozzo di pane, that old man was mumbling a crust of bread ‖ v.i. to stammer (out), to mumble.

ciancicóna, s.f., **ciancicóne**, s.m. stammerer, mumbler.

ciancióna, s.f., **ciancióne**, s.m. chatterbox, tattler.

cianfruglióna, s.f., **cianfruglióne**, s.m. (persona sciatta) sloven; (arruffone) bungler.

cianfrusàglia, s.f. (cosa senza importanza) trifle, bagatelle; (cosa senza valore) trash, rubbish.

ciangolàre, **ciangottàre**, v.i. 1. to gabble, to jabber: parla più piano, non —!, speak more slowly, don't jabber! 2. (ciarlare scioccamente) to prattle, to talk at random 3. (*di bambini*) to babble, to prattle, to lisp 4. (*di uccelli*) to twitter ‖ *v.t.* to mumble: *ciangotta un po' il francese*, he mumbles a little French.

ciangottío, *s.m.* 1. gabbling 2. (*di bambini*) prattling 3. (*di uccelli*) twittering.

ciangottóna, *s.f.*, **ciangottóne**, *s.m.* gabbler; prattler.

cianídrico, *ag.* (*chim.*) hydrocyanic: *acido* —, hydrocyanic acid (*o* prussic acid).

cíano, *s.m.* 1. (*bot.*) cornflower 2. (*color ceruleo*) light blue.

cianògeno, *s.m.* (*chim.*) cyanogen.

cianografía, *s.f.* (*foto.*) blueprint; cyanotype.

cianòsi, *s.f.* (*med.*) cyanosis.

cianòtico, *ag.* (*med.*) cyanotic.

ciànta, *s.f.* (*scarpa scalcagnata*) down-at-heel shoe.

cianúro, *s.m.* (*chim.*) cyanide: — *di potassio*, potassium cyanide; — *di sodio*, sodium cyanide.

ciào, *inter.* (*fam.*) 1. (*incontrandosi*) hullo!; (*amer.*) hi! 2. (*congedandosi*) bye-bye; (*sl.*) ta-ta.

ciàppola, *s.f.* (*strum. artig.*) graving-tool; burin.

ciaramèlla, *s.f.* (*mus.*) (*tipo di zampogna*) bagpipe.

ciàrla, *s.f.* 1. (*loquacità*) loquaciousness, loquacity: *quella donna ha una gran* —, that woman is very loquacious (*o* talkative) 2. (*notizia falsa*) false report; gossip, tittle-tattle: *dicevano che 'era morto, ma si trattava di una* —, they said he was dead, but it was only a false report ‖ *ciarle!*, nonsense! ‖ *fare quattro ciarle*, to have a chat.

ciarlàre, *v.i.* to talk idly, to chat, to chatter.

ciarlàta, *s.f.* chat, chatter, idle talk.

ciarlatanàta, *s.f.* quackish action.

ciarlatanería, *s.f.* quackery, charlatanism.

ciarlatanésco, *ag.* quackish, charlatanish.

ciarlatàno, *s.m.* charlatan (anche *fig.*); quacksalver (*abbr.* quack).

ciarlièro, *ag.* talkative, loquacious, chatty ‖ *s.m.* chatterbox, talkative person.

ciarlóna, *s.f.*, **ciarlóne**, *s.m.* chatterbox, chatterer; (*fam.*) gas-bag.

ciarlòtta, *s.f.* (*cuc.*) charlotte.

ciàrpa[1], *s.f.* (*roba di nessun valore*) trifle; (*cencio*) rag.

ciàrpa[2], (*rar.*) per **sciàrpa**.

ciarpàme, *s.m.* rubbish, trash, junk, waste material.

ciaschedúno, *pron.* (*arc.*) per **ciascúno**.

ciascúno, *ag. indef.* 1. (*ogni*) **every**: *ciascun uomo è stato bambino*, every man was once a child; *... a ciascun uomo un soldo*, (*Bibbia*) ...to every man a penny 2. (*con valore distributivo*) **each**: *ciascun libro costa due scellini*, each book costs two shillings ‖ *pron. indef.* 1. (*ognuno, tutti*) **everyone, everybody**: *lo sa*, everyone knows (it) 2. (*con valore distributivo*) **each, each one**: — *di loro aveva un'opinione diversa*, each of them held a different opinion; — *di questi quadri vale un patrimonio*, each (one) of these pictures is worth a fortune; — *di voi avrà una mela*, each of you will get an apple; *avrete una mela* —, you will each get an apple; *questi libri costano uno scellino* —, these books cost a shilling each.

cibàre, *v.t.* to feed, to nourish ‖ **cibàrsi**, *v.r.* to eat (sthg.); to feed (on sthg.) ‖ — *di illusioni, di speranze*, to cherish illusions, hopes.

cibària, *s.f.* (*alimenti*) foodstuff; (*vettovaglie*) victuals (*pl.*); provisions (*pl.*).

cibàrio, *ag.* edible.

Cibèle, *no.pr.f.* (*mit.*) Cybele.

cibernètica, *s.f.* (*neol.*) cybernetics.

cíbo, *s.m.* 1. **food**: — *e bevanda*, food and drink; *in abbondanza*, plenty of food (*o fam.* plenty of grub) 2. (*pasto*) meal 3. (*piatto, pietanza*) dish 4. *fig.* nourishment: *le sue parole sono* — *per la mia anima*, his words are nourishment for my soul.

cibòrio, *s.m.* (*eccl.*) ciborium (*pl.* ciboria).

cibrèo, *s.m.* 1. (*cuc.*) fricassee 2. *fig.* (*guazzabuglio*) jumble, medley, muddle.

cíca, *s.f.* (*piccolezza*) bagatelle, trifle; mere nothing.

cicàla, *s.f.* 1. cicada ‖ *grattar la pancia alla* —, to get secrets out of s.o. 2. (*persona chiacchierona*) chatterbox 3. (*mar.*) anchor-ring, anchor shackle.

cicalaménto, *s.m.* chattering, talking.

cicalàre, *v.i.* to chatter, to talk idly.

cicalàta, *s.f.* chatter, idle talk.

cicaléccio, *s.m.* chatter, chattering, idle talk.

cicalíno, *s.m.* (*elett.*) buzzer.

cicalío, *s.m.* chattering, prattling.

cicalóna, *s.f.*, **cicalóne**, *s.m.* chatterbox, chatterer; gossip.

cicatríce, *s.f.* 1. scar, cicatrice, cicatrix 2. *fig.* (*ricordo doloroso*) scar.

cicatrícola, *s.f.* (*biol. bot.*) cicatricle.

cicatrizzàre, *v.t.i.*, **cicatrizzàrsi**, *v.r.* to cicatrize, to heal, to skin over.

cicatrizzàto, *ag.* cicatrized, healed.

cicatrizzazióne, *s.f.* cicatrization, healing.

cícca, *s.f.* 1. stub, butt; (*di sigaretta*) cigarette-end; (*sl.*) fag-end, dog-end; (*di sigaro*) cigar-end 2. (*di tabacco da masticare*) quid 3. *fig.* worthless thing; worthless person: *non vale una* —, it isn't worth a brass farthing.

ciccaiuòlo, *s.m.* picker-up of cigarette-ends.

ciccàre, *v.i.* 1. to chew tobacco 2. *fig.* (*rodersi*) to fret, to chafe, to worry.

cicchétto, *s.m.* (*fam.*) 1. (*bicchierino di liquore*) pick-me-up, dram, nip: *un caffè col* —, a cup of coffee with a dram (*o* with a pick-me-up); *prendiamo un* — *prima di andare a letto*, let's have a nightcap 2. (*ramanzina*) dressing-down: *mi presi un bel* —, I got a thorough dressing-down; *gli daremo un* —, we'll dress him down (*o* we'll give him a dressing-down).

cíccia, *s.f.* (*fam.*) 1. meat 2. (*carne umana*) flesh: *avere addosso molta* —, to be fat; *metter su* —, (*ingrassare*) to put on flesh (*o* weight).

cicciolo, *s.m.* 1. (*med.*) fleshy excrescence 2. *pl.* fried scraps of pork fat ‖ *far ciccioli d'uno*, *fig.* to cut s.o. to pieces.

ciccióna, *s.f.* fat woman; (*fam.*) fatty.

ciccióne, *s.m.* fat man; (*fam.*) fatty.

ciccióso, cicciúto, *ag.* fleshy, plump.

cicérbita, *s.f.* (*bot.*) sorb-thistle.

cicérchia, *s.f.* (*bot.*) chickling vetch.

cícero, *s.m.* (*tip.*) pica: *carattere* —, pica type.

Ciceróne, *no.pr.m.* (*st. lett.*) Cicero ‖ **ciceróne**, *s.m.* (*guida*) cicerone, guide.

ciceroniàno, *ag.* (*lett.*) Ciceronian.

cicisbèo, *s.m.* 1. (*st.*) cicisbeo (*pl.* cicisbei) 2. (*damerino*) gallant, ladies' man.

Cícladi (le), *no.pr.f.pl.* (*geog.*) the Cyclades.

ciclamíno, *s.m.* (*bot.*) cyclamen.

cíclico, *ag.* cyclic(al): *poeta* —, cyclic poet.

ciclísmo, *s.m.* (*spor.*) cycling.

ciclísta, *s.m.* cyclist.

ciclístico, *ag.* cycling (*attributivo*); cycle (*attributivo*): *gara ciclistica*, cycle race; *giro* —, cycling tour; *pista ciclistica*, cycle track.

cíclo[1], *s.m.* 1. **cycle**: — *a due, a quattro tempi*, (*mec.*) two-stroke, four-stroke cycle; *il* — *delle stagioni*, the cycle of the seasons; — *lunare*, (*astr.*) lunar (*o* Metonic) cycle; — *operativo*, (*ind.*) operating cycle; *rimettere in* —, (*ind.*) to recycle 2. (*di una malattia*) course 3. (*lett.*) cycle: *il* — *di re Artù*, the Arthurian cycle.

cíclo[2], *s.m.* (*spor.*) cycle.

ciclòide, *s.m.* (*geom.*) cycloid.

ciclóne, *s.m.* cyclone; hurricane.

ciclònico, *ag.* cyclonic.

ciclòpe, *s.m.* (*mit.*) Cyclops (*pl.* Cyclopes).

ciclòpico, *ag.* 1. Cyclopean, Cyclopian ‖ *mura ciclopiche*, Cyclopean (*o* Cyclopian) masonry 2. *fig.* Cyclopean, Cyclopian; huge, gigantic, immense.

cicloplàno, *s.m.* (*aer.*) flying bicycle.

ciclostíle, *s.m.* cyclostyle; duplicator: *carta per* —, stencil (for duplicator).

ciclotróne, *s.m.* (*fis. atomica*) cyclotron.

cicógna, *s.f.* **1.** (*ornit.*) stork ‖ *l'arrivo della —*, (*fam.*) a visit from the stork **2.** (*aer.*) grasshopper.

cicòria, *s.f.* (*bot.*) chicory.

cicúta, *s.f.* (*bot. farm.*) hemlock.

cièca, *s.f.* (*ittiol.*) young eel.

ciecaménte, *av.* blindly.

cièco, *ag.* **1.** blind (anche *fig.*): *— alla bellezza*, blind to beauty; *— da un occhio*, blind in one eye; *— nato*, born blind; *completamente —*, stone-blind; *diventar —*, to go (o to become) blind ‖ *— come una talpa*, as blind as a bat (o as a beetle o as a mole) ‖ *alla cieca*, blindly: *andare alla —*, to go blindly on (o to gropę one's way); *fare ql.co. alla cieca*, to do sthg. blindly (o rashly o recklessly) ‖ *finestra cieca*, blind window ‖ *mosca cieca*, blind-man's buff ‖ *obbedienza cieca*, unquestioning (o blind) obedience ‖ *vicolo —*, blind alley ‖ *volo —*, (*aer.*) blind flight **2.** (*oscuro*) dark, gloomy, obscure **3.** *intestino —*, (*anat.*) caecum ‖ *s.m.* blind man: *i ciechi*, the blind; *ciechi di guerra*, blinded ex-service men.

cièlo, *s.m.* **1.** sky; (*letter.*) heaven(s): *— coperto*, overcast sky; *— sereno*, clear sky; *sotto il —*, under the sky ‖ *a — scoperto*, under the open sky (o in the open air) ‖ *a — sereno*, (*inaspettatamente*) out of a blue sky ‖ *muovere — e terra*, to move heaven and earth (o to leave no stone unturned) ‖ *non stare nè in — nè in terra*, to be utter nonsense ‖ *toccare il — con un dito*, to walk on air (o to be as pleased as Punch) **2.** (*aria*) air; (*atmosfera*) atmosphere **3.** (*clima*) climate **4.** (*volta*) ceiling; vault: *il — di una stanza*, the ceiling of a room **5.** (*astr.*) (*nel sistema Tolemaico*) heaven ‖ *essere al settimo —*, to be in the seventh heaven ‖ *portare al —, ai sette cieli*, to praise to the skies **6.** (*paradiso*) heaven, paradise: *essere in —*, to be in heaven **7.** (*Dio, la Provvidenza*) Heaven: *il Regno dei Cieli*, the Kingdom of Heaven ‖ *giusto —!*, *santo —!*, good Heavens (o goodness mc o my goodness o goodness gracious)! ‖ *grazie al —*, thank Heaven(s) (o fam. thank goodness) ‖ *per amore del —*, for Heaven's sake (o fam. for goodness sake) ‖ *lo sa il —*, Heaven knows (o fam. goodness knows) ‖ *volesse il — che...*, would to Heaven (o I wish to goodness) that....

cièra, *V.* **céra**.

cifra, *s.f.* **1.** figure, number, numeral: *cifre arabiche*, arabic numerals (o ciphers); *in cifre*, in figures; *un numero di tre cifre*, a number of three figures ‖ *le cifre dell'esportazione*, (*i dati statistici*) the export figures ‖ *in — tonda*, in round figures (o numbers) **2.** (*somma di denaro*) amount of money; figure: *domandò una — esageratamente alta*, he asked an uncommonly stiff figure; *una grossa — fu sprecata per questo progetto*, a large amount of money was wasted on this plan **3.** (*segno di cifrario segreto*) cipher, cypher: *chiave della —*, cipher-key; *scrittura in —*, cipher (o writing in cipher); *telegramma in —*, cipher telegram (o code telegram) **4.** (*monogramma*) cipher, cypher, monogram; mark.

cifràre, *v.t.* **1.** (*scrivere in cifrario*) to cipher, to cypher **2.** (*ricamare in cifra*) to mark: *— la propria biancheria*, to mark one's linen.

cifràrio, *s.m.* cipher book, code.

cifràto, *ag.* ciphered; cipher (*attributivo*): *messaggio —*, cipher message.

cigliàre, *ag.* ciliary; of the eyelash.

cíglio, *s.m.*; *pl.f.* **cíglia** (*nei sensi* **1. 2. 3.**); *pl.m.* **cígli** (*nel senso* **4.**) **1.** eyelash; (*sopracciglio*) eyebrow: *lunghe ciglia*, long eyelashes; *senza ciglia*, lashless; *aggrottare le ciglia*, to knit one's brows) ‖ *non battè —*, *fig.* he did not turn a hair **2.** (*poet.*) (*occhio*) eye; (*sguardo*) look; (*volto*) face: *a — asciutto*, with dry eyes (o dry-eyed); *abbassare le ciglia*, to lower one's eyes ‖ *in un batter di —*, in a (o the) twinkling of an eye **3.** *pl.* (*biol.*) (*ciglia vibratili*) cilia **4.** (*bordo*) edge, border, margin, brink: *— d'un fosso*, edge of a ditch.

ciglióne, *s.m.* **1.** bank, embankment **2.** (*bordo*) edge, border, brink.

cigliúto, *ag.* bushy-browed, beetle-browed.

cígna, *V.* **cínghia**.

cignàle, *s.m.* (*zool.*) wild boar.

cígnere, *V.* **cíngere**.

cígno, *s.m.* **1.** swan: *canto del —*, *fig.* swan-song: *fu il suo canto del —*, it was his swan-song ‖ *Cigno*, (*astr.*) Swan (o cygnus) **2.** *fig.*: *il — dell'Avon*, the Swan of Avon (Shakespeare).

cignóne[1], *s.m.* wide belt, wide strap.

cignóne[2], *s.m.* (*nodo di capelli sulla nuca*) chignon.

cignuòli, *s.m.pl.* straps (to fasten trousers under shoes).

cigolaménto, *s.m.* creaking, squeaking, grating.

cigolàre, *v.i.* (*di ruote, cardini*) to creak, to squeak, to grate; (*di legna verde che brucia*) to hiss.

cigolío, *s.m.* creaking, squeaking, grating.

Cíle, *no.pr.m.* (*geog.*) Chile.

cilécca, *s.f.* unfulfilled promise; failure ‖ *far —*, to miss fire (o to misfire); *fig.* to fail.

cilèno, *ag.* *s.m.* Chilean ‖ **cilèna**, *s.f.* Chilean.

cilestríno, **cilèstro**, *ag.* sky-blue, light blue.

ciliàre, *ag.* ciliary; of the eyelash.

cilício, *s.m.* **1.** (*veste portata per penitenza*) cilice, sackcloth **2.** (*panno grossolano*) cilice, haircloth.

ciliegéto, *s.m.* cherry-orchard.

ciliègia, *s.f.* cherry: *grappolo di ciliege*, cherry-bob; *nocciolo di —*, cherry-stone; *rosso —*, cherry-red ‖ *l'amico Ciliegia*, (*fam.*) Mr. So-and-So.

ciliègio, *s.m.* **1.** (*albero*) cherry-tree: *fiori di —*, cherry-blossom **2.** (*legno*) cherry-wood.

cilindràre, *v.t.* **1.** (*ind. tessile, cartaria*) to calender **2.** (*spianare*) to roll; to press: *— a caldo*, (*metal.*) to hot-roll; *— a freddo*, (*metal.*) to cold-roll.

cilindràta, *s.f.* **1.** (*aut.*) displacement, swept volume **2.** (*ind. cartaria*) charge.

cilindratúra, *s.f.* **1.** rolling: *— stradale*, road rolling **2.** (*ind. tessile, cartaria*) calendering.

cilindricaménte, *av.* cylindrically.

cilíndrico, *ag.* cylindrical.

cilíndro, *s.m.* **1.** (*geom. aut.*) cylinder: *una quattro cilindri*, a four-cylinder car **2.** (*metal.*) roll **3.** (*ind. tessile*) calender; (*ind. cartaria*) roller **4.** (*cappello*) top-hat, silk-hat; (*fam.*) chimney-pot hat, stovepipe hat.

cilindròide, *s.m.* (*geom.*) cylindroid.

címa, *s.f.* **1.** (*sommità*) top, summit; highest point; peak: *cime di rapa*, (*cuc.*) turnip-tops; *cime nevose*, snowy summits; *in —*, at the top: *lo scaffale in —*, the top shelf; *sulla — del colle*, on the top of the hill (o on the hill-top) ‖ *da — a fondo*, from top to bottom; from beginning to end: *ha rovistato la stanza da — a fondo*, he has searched the room from top to bottom; *ho letto il tuo libro da — a fondo*, I have read your book from beginning to end **2.** *fig.* (*persona molto intelligente*) genius; very clever person: *tuo cugino non è una —*, your cousin is no genius (o not very bright) **3.** (*mar.*) line.

cimàre, *v.t.* **1.** (*potare dalla radice*) to poll; (*potare solo le cime sporgenti*) to lop; (*cespugli di rose, ecc.*) to prune **2.** (*lana, panni*) to clip, to shear.

cimàsa, *s.f.* (*arch.*) cyma (*pl.* cymae); cymatium (*pl.* cymatia).

cimàta, *s.f.* **1.** polling; lopping; pruning **2.** (*di lana, panni*) clipping, shearing.

cimatóre, *s.m.* **1.** poller **2.** (*di lana, panni*) clipper, shearer.

cimatúra, *s.f.* **1.** polling **2.** (*di lana, panni*) clipping, shearing **3.** (*pelo tagliato*) clippings (*pl.*).

címba, *s.f.* (*poet.*) vessel, boat.

címbalo, *s.m.* (*mus.*) cymbal ‖ *essere in cimbali*, to be tipsy (o elated).

Címbri, *s.m.pl.* (*st.*) Cimbri.

cimèlio, *s.m.* **1.** (*reliquia*) relic **2.** (*oggetto antico di valore*) antique.

cimentàre, *v.t.* **1.** (*mettere alla prova*) to put to the test; (*provare*) to try **2.** (*arrischiare*) to risk **3.** (*provo-*

care) to provoke, to rouse **4.** — *l'oro*, to assay gold ‖
cimentàrsi, *v.r.* **1.** (*tentare*) to attempt (sthg.); to
venture (upon sthg.); to engage (in sthg.): *mi sono
cimentato in un difficile compito*, I have attempted a
difficult task **2.** — *con qlcu.*, (*affrontarlo*) to face s.o.;
(*competere*) to compete with s.o.

ciménto, *s.m.* **1.** (*prova*) test, trial: *mettere a* —,
to put to the test: *mise a duro* — *la mia pazienza*, he
tried my patience to the limit **2.** (*rischio*) risk; danger.

cimentóso, *ag.* **1.** (*pericoloso*) dangerous **2.** (*audace*)
audacious, reckless.

cìmice, *s.f.* **1.** bug, bedbug **2.** (*puntina da disegno*)
drawing-pin.

cimiciàio, *s.m.* **1.** place infested with bugs **2.** *fig.*
(*abitazione sudicia*) filthy house, filthy hovel.

cimicióso, *ag.* buggy.

cimièro, *s.m.* **1.** crest **2.** (*poet.*) crest, helmet **3.** (*arald.*)
crest.

ciminièra, *s.f.* **1.** (*di fabbrica*) smoke-stack, chimney **2.** (*mar.*) funnel.

cimitèro, *s.m.* **1.** cemetery, graveyard, burial-ground;
(*a lato della chiesa*) churchyard **2.** *fig.* desert place.

cimmèrio, *ag.* **1.** (*mit.*) Cimmerian **2.** *fig.* Cimmerian,
dark, gloomy.

cìmolo, *s.m.* (*bot.*) shoot.

cimòmetro, *s.m.* (*elett.*) cymometer, wavemeter.

cimósa, *s.f.* **1.** selvage, selvedge **2.** (*cassino*) black-
board duster.

cimúrro, *s.m.* **1.** (*vet.*) (*dei cani*) distemper; (*dei cavalli*) glanders **2.** (*scherz.*) bad cold.

Cìna, *no.pr.f.* (*geog.*) China.

cinabrése, *s.m.* (*pitt.*) cinnabar, vermilion.

cinàbro, *s.m.* **1.** cinnabar, vermilion **2.** (*poet.*) vermilion (of the lips).

cìncia, *s.f.* (*ornit.*) tit(mouse).

cinciallégra, *s.f.* (*ornit.*) great titmouse, oxeye.

cincìglia, **cincìlla**, *s.f.* (*zool.*) chinchilla.

Cincinnàto, *no.pr.m.* (*st. romana*) Cincinnatus.

cincischiàre, *v.t.* **1.** (*tagliare malamente*) to jag,
to shred **2.** (*sgualcire*) to rumple, to crease **3.** (*sminuzzare*) to mince ‖ *v.i.* **1.** (*perdere tempo senza costrutto*)
to dawdle **2.** *fig.* (*parlare stentatamente*) to speak with
difficulty.

cincischiàto, *ag.* **1.** jagged **2.** (*sgualcito*) rumpled,
creased.

cìne, *abbr. di* **cinematògrafo.**

cineàsta, *s.m.* **1.** cinematographer **2.** (*artista*) film
-artist.

cinedilettànte, *s.c.* film-amateur.

cinedràmma, *s.m.* screen-play.

cinefobìa, *s.f.* cynophobia.

cinegètica, *s.f.* cynegetics.

cinegètico, *ag.* cynegetic.

cinegiornàle, *s.m.* news-reel.

cìnema, *abbr. di* **cinematògrafo.**

cinemagiornàle, *s.m.* news-reel.

cinemateàtro, *s.m.* cinema-theatre, picture-theatre.

cinemàtica, *s.f.* (*fis.*) kinematics.

cinemàtico, *ag.* (*fis.*) kinematic(al).

cinematografàre, *v.t.* to film.

cinematografìa, *s.f.* cinematography, cinema: — *a
colori*, colour cinematography; — *muta*, silent cinema;
— *sonora*, sound pictures (*o* talking pictures).

cinematograficaménte, *av.* cinematographically.

cinematogràfico, *ag.* cinematographic; film (*attributivo*): *attore* —, film actor (*o* film-star).

cinematògrafo, *s.m.* **1.** cinema; (moving) pictures
(*pl.*); (*sl.*) movies (*pl.*): *stella del* —, film-star; *ti
piace il* —?, do you like the cinema? (o moving pictures?
o movies?); *andare al* —, to go to the cinema (*o* to the
pictures *o* to the movies) **2.** (*locale*) cinema, cinema
hall; (*molto grande*) picture-palace, picture-theatre; (*sl.*)
movie-house: — *a posteggio*, drive-in cinema; *frequentatore di* —, cinema-goer (*o amer.* moviegoer) **3.** (*apparecchio*) cinematograph.

cineràma, *s.m.* (*cine.*) cinerama.

cinerària, *s.f.* (*bot.*) cineraria.

cineràrio, *ag.* cinerary: *urna cineraria*, cinerary urn.

cinèreo, *ag.* (*letter.*) cinereous; ash-coloured, ashen
-grey.

cinescòpio, *s.m.* (*tv.*) kinescope, picture tube: —
a colori a maschera d'ombra, (*tv.*) shadow mask colour
kinescope.

cinése, *ag.* Chinese ‖ *s.m.* **1.** (*abitante*) Chinese (*invariato al pl.*); Chinaman (*pl.* Chinamen) **2.** (*lingua*)
(the) Chinese (language) ‖ *s.f.* Chinese (*invariato al pl.*);
Chinese woman.

cineserìa, *V.* **chineserìa.**

cinesiterapìa, *s.f.* (*med.*) kinesitherapy, kinesiatrics.

cinetèca, *s.f.* (*cine.*) film library.

cinètica, *s.f.* (*fis.*) kinetics: — *del calore, dei gas*,
kinetic theory of heat, of gases.

cinètico, *ag.* (*fis.*) kinetic: *energia cinetica*, kinetic
energy.

cinetoscòpio, *s.m.* (*fis.*) kinetoscope.

cingallègra, *s.f.* (*ornit.*) great titmouse, oxeye.

cìngere, *v.t.* **1.** to gird: — *la spada*, to gird on one's
sword ‖ — *la corona*, to assume the crown (*o* to be
crowned): — *la corona di alloro*, to be crowned with
laurel(s) **2.** (*circondare*) to encircle, to surround: — *di
mura una città*, to surround a town with walls ‖ —
le braccia al collo di qlcu., to clasp (*o* to embrace)
s.o. ‖ — *d'assedio*, to besiege (*o* to lay siege to).

cìnghia, *s.f.* **1.** (*per legare*) strap: — *per i libri di
scuola*, book-strap; — *per rampone*, crampon strap; —
per sci, ski-strap **2.** (*cintura*) belt **3.** (*mec.*) belt: — *ad
anello*, endless belt; — *di trasmissione*, driving belt;
— *trapezoidale*, (*aut.*) V-shaped belt, fan-belt **4.** *pl.*
(*bretelle*) braces; (*amer.*) suspenders.

cinghiàla, *s.f.* (*zool.*) wild sow.

cinghiàle, *s.m.* (*zool.*) wild boar.

cinghiàre, *v.t.* **1.** to strap **2.** (*bardare*) to harness **3.** (*cingere*) to encompass, to encircle.

cinghiàta, *s.f.* lash.

cinghiatúra, *s.f.* **1.** strapping, lashing **2.** (*bardatura*)
harnessing **3.** (*il cingere*) encompassing, encircling.

cingiménto, *s.m.* girding.

cìngolo, *s.m.* **1.** (*cintura*) girdle; belt; (*eccl.*) cincture **2.** (*di carro armato, trattore*) track: *trattore su cingoli*, caterpillar tractor (*o* crawler) **3.** (*di ruota*) wheel belt.

cinguettaménto, *V.* **cinguettìo.**

cinguettàre, *v.i.* **1.** to chirp; to twitter **2.** *fig.* (*di
bambini*) to prattle; (*chiacchierare*) to chatter.

cinguettatóre, *ag.fig.* tattling ‖ *s.m.*, **cinguetta-
tríce**, *s.f. fig.* tattler.

cinguettìo, *s.m.* **1.** chirping; twittering **2.** (*chiacchierio*) chattering; prattling.

cinicaménte, *av.* cynically.

cìnico, *ag.* **1.** cynical: *riso* —, cynical laughter **2.** (*st.
fil.*) Cynic: *i filosofi cinici*, the Cynic philosophers ‖
s.m. **1.** cynic **2.** (*st. fil.*) Cynic.

cinìglia, *s.f.* chenille.

cìnipe, *s.f.* (*entom.*) gall-wasp, gall-fly.

cinìsmo, *s.m.* cynicism.

cinnàmomo, *s.m.* (*bot.*) cinnamon.

cinocèfalo, *s.m.* **1.** (*zool.*) cynocephalus, dog-faced
baboon **2.** (*mit.*) cynocephalus, dog-headed man.

cinòdromo, *s.m.* (*spor.*) greyhound racing-track.

cinofilìa, *s.f.* dog-love.

cinòfilo, *ag.* dog-loving ‖ *s.m.* dog-lover.

cinquànta, *ag.num.card. s.m.* fifty.

cinquantamìla, *ag.num.card.* fifty thousand.

cinquantenàrio, *ag.* fifty-year-old (*attributivo*) ‖ *s.m.*
fiftieth anniversary; (*st.*) jubilee.

cinquantènne, *ag.* fifty years old (*predicativo*); fifty
-year-old (*attributivo*) ‖ *s.m.* fifty-year-old man ‖ *s.f.*
fifty-year-old woman.

cinquantènnio, *s.m.* period of fifty years.

cinquantèsimo, *ag.num.ord.* fiftieth ‖ *s.m.* a
fiftieth part, fiftieth.

cinquantína, *s.f.* about fifty, some fifty: *una — di lire,* fifty liras or so; *una — di persone,* about (*o* some) fifty people; *una donna sulla* —, a woman about fifty years old (*o* of about fifty); *una donna che ha passato la* —, a woman in her fifties; *avvicinarsi alla* —, to be getting on for fifty; *raggiungere la* —, to reach the age of fifty.

cínque, *ag.num.card.s.m.* five: *un biglietto da — sterline,* a five-pound note; (*fam.*) a fiver; *una tragedia in — atti,* a five-act tragedy; *il tè delle* —, (afternoon) tea.

cinquecentéseo, *ag.* (*art. lett.*) sixteenth century (*attributivo*); (*in Italia*) cinquecento (*attributivo*): *lingua, arte cinquecentesca,* cinquecento language, art.

cinquecentísta, *s.m.* (*art. lett.*) sixteenth century writer, artist; (*italiano*) cinquecentist.

cinqueeènto, *ag.num.card.* five hundred: *— lire,* five hundred lire ‖ *s.m.* (*sedicesimo secolo*) sixteenth century; (*art. lett. italiana*) cinquecento.

cinquefòglie, *s.m.* (*bot.*) cinquefoil.

cinquína, *s.f.* **1.** set of five **2.** (*giuoco*) set of five winning numbers in lottery, in tombola; prize given for five winning numbers in lottery, in tombola **3.** (*mil.*) five days' pay **4.** (*teat.*) actor's pay.

cínta, *s.f.* **1.** town-walls (*pl.*); (*riparo che circonda un luogo*) fence: *muro di* —, boundary (*o* enclosure) walls ‖ *— daziaria,* customs barrier **2.** (*mil.*) enceinte **3.** (*mar.*) gunwale.

cínto, *ag.* surrounded; girded (*predicativo*), girt (*predicativo*): *un'isola cinta dal mare,* a sea-girt island ‖ *s.m.* **1.** (*cintura*) zone, belt: *— virginale,* maiden zone **2.** (*med.*) truss.

cíntola, *s.f.* **1.** (*vita*) waist, middle: *nudo fino alla* —, stripped to the waist; *che arriva fino alla* —, waist-deep (*o* waist-high); *era in acqua fino alla* —, he was up to his waist in water; *la neve gli arrivava fino alla* —, the snow came up to his waist ‖ *dalla — in giù,* below the waist; *dalla — in su,* above the waist **2.** (*cintura*) belt, girdle ‖ *era sempre appeso alla — di sua madre,* he was always tied to his mother's apron-strings ‖ *star con le mani alla* —, *fig.* to be idle ‖ *stringer la* —, *fig.* to tighten one's belt (*o* to go without food) ‖ *stretto di* —, (*taccagno*) stingy.

cíntolo, (*rar.*) per **cintúra.**

cintúra, *s.f.* **1.** belt, girdle; (*fusciacca*) sash; (*di gonna, calzoni*) waistband: *— di cuoio,* leather belt; *— di salvataggio,* life-belt; *— di sicurezza,* safety belt; *fibbia della* —, (belt) buckle **2.** (*lotta*) waistlock **3.** (*mar.*) belt; (*fune di rinforzo di una barca*) swifter: *— corazzata, armored belt* **4.** (*anat.*) girdle: *— pelvica,* pelvic (*o* hip) girdle; *— toracica,* pectoral (*o* shoulder) girdle.

cinturíno, *s.m.* strap: *— di camicia,* collar-band; *— di scarpa,* shoe-strap; *— d'orologio,* watch-strap.

cinturóne, *s.m.* belt: *— della sciabola,* sword-belt; *— di fucile,* rifle-sling.

Cínzia, *no.pr.f.* Cynthia.

ciò, *pron. dimostrativo* that; this; it: *— non ti riguarda,* this is no concern of yours (*o* that is no business of yours); *sono spiacente di* —, I am sorry about it; *tutto — mi infastidì parecchio,* all this annoyed me considerably ‖ *— nondimeno,* — *nonostante,* in spite of that (*o* nevertheless *o* however) ‖ *a* —, for that purpose (*o* to that end) ‖ *con tutto* —, for all that (*o* nevertheless) ‖ *oltre a* —, besides (*o* moreover) ‖ *essere da* —, to be capable of that (*o* of such a thing) ‖ *essere idoneo a* —, to be suited to that.

ciòcea, *s.f.* (*di capelli*) lock; tuft; (*di fiori, di frutti*) bunch, cluster.

ciòceo, *s.m.* **1.** (*ceppo*) log **2.** *fig.* (*persona balorda*) blockhead, dolt.

cioccolàta, *ag.* chocolate (*attributivo*): *color* —, chocolate-coloured ‖ *s.f.* chocolate: *una (tazza di) — ben calda,* a cup of hot chocolate.

cioccolatàio, *V.* **cioccolatière.**

cioccolatièra, *s.f.* chocolate pot.

cioccolatière, *s.m.* **1.** (*chi fabbrica cioccolato*) chocolate-maker **2.** (*chi vende cioccolato*) chocolate-seller.

cioccolatíno, *s.m.* chocolate: *— farcito,* chocolate cream; *una scatola di cioccolatini,* a box of chocolates.

cioccolàto, *s.m.* chocolate: *— al latte,* milk chocolate; *biscotti al* —, chocolate biscuits; *una tavoletta di* —, a bar of chocolate.

ciòcia, *s.f.* "ciocia" (sandal once worn by peasants of Latium and Campania).

ciociàra, *s.f.* "ciociara" (peasant woman of the Roman country-side).

ciociàro, *s.m.* "ciociaro" (peasant of the Roma country-side).

cioè, *av.* that is (*abbr.* i.e.); namely (*abbr.* viz.), that is to say; (*rar.*) to wit.

ciómpo, *s.m.* **1.** (*st.*) "ciompo" (Florentine wool-carder) ‖ *il tumulto dei Ciompi,* (*st.*) the riot of the Ciompi **2.** (*plebeo*) plebeian.

cioncàre, *v.t.* to swill, to drink greedily.

ciónco, *ag.* broken (off); cut off.

ciondolaménto, *s.m.* **1.** (*penzolamento*) dangling; (*ondeggiamento*) swaying **2.** *fig.* (*il bighellonare*) lounging.

ciondolàre, *v.i.* **1.** to dangle, to hang loosely **2.** *fig.* (*bighellonare*) to lounge, to idle about: *egli ciondolò l'intera giornata,* he idled away the whole day ‖ *v.t.* to swing: *— le braccia,* to swing one's arms.

cióndolo, *s.m.* pendant, pendent, charm, trinket.

ciondolóna, *s.f.,* **ciondolóne,** *s.m.* lounger, dawdler, idler.

ciondolóne, ciondolóni, *av.* **1.** hanging loosely, dangling **2.** *fig.* (*alla peggio*) carelessly.

ciòtola, *s.f.* **1.** (*recipiente*) cup, bowl; (*di legno*) wooden bowl **2.** (*contenuto*) cupful.

ciotolàta, *s.f.* cupful.

ciottolàre, *v.t.* to pave with cobblestones.

ciottolàta, *s.f.* blow with a stone.

ciottolàto, *s.m.* cobbled paving, cobblestones (*pl.*); (*di pietre larghe e rade, specialmente per giardini*) crazy paving.

ciòttolo, *s.m.* stone; (*rotondo*) cobble(-stone); (*arrotondato dalla corrente*) pebble.

ciottolóso, *ag.* pebbly.

cipíglio, *s.m.* frown, scowl, glower: *fare il — a qlcu., guardare qlcu. con* —, to frown (*o* to scowl) at s.o.

cipólla, *s.f.* **1.** onion ‖ *mangiar pane e* —, *fig.* to fare badly (*o* to live on poor fare) **2.** (*bulbo*) bulb **3.** (*orologio*) turnip **4.** (*palla bucherellata dell'annaffiatoio*) rose.

cipollàio, *s.m.* **1.** (*agr.*) onion-bed **2.** (*chi vende cipolle*) onion-vendor.

cipollàta, *s.f.* **1.** onion stew **2.** *fig.* (*sciocchezza*) nonsense; foolish act.

cipollàto, *ag.* layered (like an onion).

cipollína, *s.f.* spring onion; pickling onion: *cipolline sotto aceto,* pickled onions.

cipollíno, *ag.* onion(-like) (*attributivo*) ‖ *s.m.* (*marmo*) cipolin.

cíppo, *s.m.* **1.** (*arch.*) cippus (*pl.* cippi) **2.** (*di confine*) boundary-stone.

cipressàia, *s.f.,* **cipresséto,** *s.m.* cypress grove.

ciprèsso, *s.m.* (*bot.*) cypress.

cipria, *s.f.* powder: *piumino per* —, powder puff.

Cipriàno, *no.pr.m.* Cyprian.

cipriòta, *ag.s.c.* Cyprian.

Cípro, *no.pr.f.* (*geog.*) Cyprus ‖ **cípro,** *s.m.* **1.** Cyprus wine **2.** (*bot.*) cyprus.

círca, *av.* about, nearly, approximately: *c'erano — mille persone a teatro,* there were about (*o* nearly) one thousand people at the theatre; *venne alle 3* —, he came about 3 o'clock ‖ *prep.* about, concerning, as to, regarding: *per ora non posso dirvi nulla — le vostre proposte,* as yet (*o* so far) I cannot tell you anything about (*o* as to *o* regarding) your offers.

circàsso, *ag.s.m.* Circassian.

Círce, *no.pr.f.* (*mit.*) Circe ‖ **círce,** *s. f.* enchantress, enticing beauty, temptress.

circènse, *ag.* (*st. romana*) circensian.

circo, *s.m.* **1.** circus: — *a tre piste*, three-ring circus; — *equestre*, circus **2.** (*geol.*) cirque; (*rar.*) corrie.

circolànte, *ag.* circulating: *biblioteca* —, circulating (o lending) library; *moneta* —, currency ‖ *s.m.* (*moneta circolante*) currency.

circolàre, *ag.* **1.** circular: *movimento* —, circular movement; *sega* —, (*tec.*) circular saw; *viaggio* —, circular tour **2.** *assegno* —, (*comm.*) bank draft ‖ *s.f.* circolare, circular letter.

circolàre, *v.i.* **1.** (*muoversi*) to circulate, to move round; to get about: — *liberamente*, to circulate freely ‖ *circolate!*, move along! (*o* keep moving! *o* pass along!) **2.** (*diffondersi*) to circulate, to spread: *far — notizie*, to send round news **3.** (*di aria, sangue, ecc.*) to circulate, to flow, to go round: *nel nostro corpo circola il sangue*, blood circulates in our bodies; *far — l'aria*, to circulate the air **4.** (*di denaro*) to be current: *far — il denaro*, to send (*o* to pass) round money; (*dar valore legale a monete*) to give currency to coins.

circolarménte, *av.* circularly.

circolatòrio, *ag.* (*anat.*) circulatory: *apparato* —, circulatory system.

circolazióne, *s.f.* **1.** circulation: — *del sangue*, circulation of the blood; *mettere un libro in* —, to put a book into circulation (*o* to circulate a book); *ritirare un libro dalla* —, to withdraw a book from circulation **2.** (*traffico*) traffic: — *intensa*, heavy traffic; *strada con — a senso unico*, one-way street; *la folla rallentava tutta la* —, the crowd was slowing up all the traffic; *arrestare la* —, to block (*o* to hold up) the traffic ‖ — *vietata*, no thoroughfare **3.** (*comm.*) circulation, currency: — *cartacea*, paper currency; — *del reddito*, circular flow of income; — *monetaria*, currency; *dovettero ritirare dalla — le monete d'oro e mettere in — banconote*, they had to withdraw gold coins from circulation, and to put bank-notes into circulation.

circolo, *s.m.* **1.** circle: *in* —, in a circle: *stavamo in — intorno a lui*, we were standing in a circle round him ‖ *Circolo Polare, Artico, Antartico*, (*geog.*) Polar, Arctic, Antarctic Circle ‖ — *vizioso*, *fig.* vicious circle: *girare in un — vizioso*, to argue in a circle **2.** (*ambiente*) circle: *circoli politici*, political circles **3.** (*associazione*) club: — *sportivo*, sporting club **4.** (*gruppo di persone*) circle, group; party; set: *un vasto — d'amici*, a large circle of friends ‖ *tener* —, to hold forth **5.** (*circoscrizione*) district.

circoncídere, *v.t.* to circumcise.

circoncisióne, *s.f.* circumcision.

circondàbile, *ag.* that may be surrounded.

circondaménto, *s.m.* surrounding, encircling.

circondàre, *v.t.* **1.** to surround; to encircle, to encompass; to enclose: *è circondato da amici*, *fig.* he is surrounded by (*o* with) friends; *è un lago circondato dai più bei boschi*, it is a lake encircled by the loveliest woods; *i nostri soldati furono circondati dai nemici*, our soldiers were surrounded by the enemy; — *con un muro*, to surround (*o* to enclose) with a wall; — *con uno steccato*, to fence; — *qlcu. di cure*, *fig.* to surround s.o. with care **2.** (*rar.*) (*circuire*) to entice ‖ **circondàrsi**, *v.r.* to surround oneself: *si circondò di ottimi collaboratori*, he surrounded himself with excellent assistants.

circondàrio, *s.m.* **1.** district **2.** (*territorio vicino*) neighbourhood; surroundings (*pl.*).

circondúrre, *v.t.* **1.** to lead (a)round **2.** (*raggirare*) to circumvent, to entrap.

circonferènza, *s.f.* (*geom.*) circumference.

circonflessióne, *s.f.* circumflexion, circumflection.

circonflèsso, *ag.* circumflex.

circonflèttere, *v.t.* to circumflect.

circonfóndere, *v.t.* to circumfuse: *il suo volto era circonfuso di luce*, her face was circumfused with light.

circonlocuzióne, *s.f.* circumlocution.

circonvallàre, *v.t.* to circumvallate; to surround (sthg.) with a fence.

circonvallazióne, *s.f.* **1.** (*mil.*) circumvallation **2.** (*strada*) ring-road.

circonveníre, *v.t. gener. fig.* to circumvent, to entrap.

circonvenzióne, *s.f.* circumvention.

circonvicíno, *ag.* surrounding (*attributivo*); neighbouring (*attributivo*): *la campagna circonvicina*, the surrounding countryside.

circonvoluzióne, *s.f.* **1.** circumvolution **2.** (*anat.*) convolution.

circoscrívere, *v.t.* **1.** (*geom.*) to circumscribe: — *un poligono ad un cerchio*, to circumscribe a circle with a polygon **2.** *fig.* to circumscribe, to limit: — *i propri interessi*, to limit (*o* to set limits to) one's interests.

circoscrizióne, *s.f.* **1.** circumscription **2.** (*territorio*) area, district: — *elettorale*, electoral constituency.

circospètto, *ag.* circumspect, cautious, wary.

circospezióne, *s.f.* circumspection, caution.

circostànte, *ag.* surrounding (*attributivo*); neighbouring (*attributivo*).

circostànza, *s.f.* circumstance; occasion: — *aggravante*, (*dir.*) aggravating circumstance; — *attenuante*, (*dir.*) extenuating (*o* mitigatory) circumstance; *concorso di circostanze*, combination of circumstances; *in quella* —, on that occasion; *in queste circostanze*, in (*o* under) the present circumstances; *secondo le circostanze*, according to circumstances; *disse alcune parole di* —, he said a few words suitable to the occasion; *approfittare delle circostanze*, to seize the opportunity; *dipendere dalle circostanze*, to depend upon circumstances.

circostanziàle, *ag.* circumstantial.

circostanziàre, *v.t.* to circumstantiate, to detail.

circostanziataménte, *av.* circumstantially, in detail.

circostanziàto, *ag.* circumstantial, detailed.

circuíre, *v.t.* **1.** (*circondare*) to surround **2.** *fig.* (*raggirare*) to circumvent, to entrap.

circuitàre, *v.i.* (*aer.*) to circle (in order to land).

circuíto[1], *s.m.* **1.** (*circonferenza, cinta*) circuit; circumference; compass: *il — della città*, the circuit of the town **2.** (*spor.*) circuit, course: — *chiuso*, (*di una corsa*) closed course **3.** (*elett. rad. tel.*) circuit: — *aperto*, (*elett.*) open circuit; — *chiuso*, (*elett.*) closed circuit; — *di antenna*, (*rad.*) aerial circuit; — *di arresto*, (*rad.*) wave trap; — *di comando*, (*elett.*) control circuit; — *elettromagnetico*, (*elett.*) magnetic circuit; — *interurbano*, (*tel.*) trunk system (*o amer.* tool line); — *oscillante*, (*rad.*) resonant circuit; — *virtuale*, (*tel.*) phantom circuit; *corto* —, (*elett.*) short circuit; *interrompere il* —, (*elett.*) to break the circuit.

circuíto[2], *ag.* **1.** surrounded **2.** *fig.* (*raggirato*) circumvented, entrapped.

circuizióne, *s.f.* **1.** (*circondamento*) encircling **2.** *fig.* (*raggiro*) circumvention, entrapment; fraud.

circumnavigàbile, *ag.* circumnavigable.

circumnavigàre, *v.t.* to circumnavigate.

circumnavigatóre, *s.m.* circumnavigator.

circumnavigazióne, *s.f.* circumnavigation: — *del globo*, circumnavigation of the globe.

circumpolàre, *ag.* circumpolar: *oceano* —, circumpolar ocean; *stella* —, circumpolar star.

Cirenàica, *no.pr.f.* (*geog.*) Cirenaica; Cyrenaica.

cirenàico, *ag.* **1.** of Cyrenaica **2.** (*st. fil.*) Cyrenaic.

Cirène, *no.pr.f.* (*geog. st.*) Cyrene.

cirenèo, *ag.* **1.** of Cyrene **2.** (*cirenaico*) of Cyrenaica ‖ *s.m. fig.* scapegoat.

Ciríaco, *no.pr.m.* Cyriac.

ciríllico, *ag.* Cyrillic: *alfabeto* —, Cyrillic alphabet.

Ciríllo, *no.pr.m.* Cyril.

Ciro, *no.pr.m.* Cyrus.

cirrifórme, *ag.* cirriform.

círro, *s.m.* **1.** (*meteorologia, bot. zool.*) cirrus (*pl.* cirri) **2.** (*ricciolo*) curl, lock.

cirrocúmulo, *s.m.* (*meteorologia*) cirro-cumulus (*pl.* cirro-cumuli).

cirròsi, *s.f.* (*patol.*) cirrhosis: — *atrofica,* atrophic cirrhosis; — *epatica,* cirrhosis of the liver.

cirrostràto, *s.m.* (*meteorologia*) cirro-stratus (*pl.* cirro-strati).

cisalpíno, *ag.* (*geog.*) cisalpine.

ciscrànna, *s.f.* **1.** (*sedia*) wooden chair **2.** (*sedia sgangherata*) rickety old chair; (*mobile vecchio e mal ridotto*) shabby old piece of furniture **3.** *fig.* haggard old woman.

cismontàno, *ag.* (*rar. geog.*) cismontane.

cisóie, *V.* **cesóie.**

cispa, *s.f.* eye-rheum.

cispadàno, *ag.* (*geog.*) cispadane.

cispòsità, *s.f.* bleariness.

cispóso, *ag.* blear, rheumy: *occhi cisposi,* blear eyes.

ciste, *s.f.* (*patol.*) cyst.

cistercènse, *ag.s.m.* (*eccl.*) Cistercian.

cistèrna, *s.f.* cistern; (*serbatoio*) tank: *acqua di —,* rain-water; *auto —,* (*per innaffiare le strade*) water-cart; (*per trasporto di liquidi*) tanker; *nave —,* (*mar.*) (*per acqua*) water-supply-ship; (*per petrolio, ecc.*) tanker.

cisti, *s.f.* (*patol.*) cyst.

cisticèreo, *s.m.* (*biol.*) cysticercus.

cisticercòsi, *s.f.* (*patol.*) cysticercosis.

cístico, *ag.* (*patol.*) cystic.

cistifèllea, *s.f.* (*anat.*) gall-bladder.

cistifèllico, *ag.* **1.** of the gall-bladder **2.** (*collerico, bilioso*) irascible, choleric.

cistifórme, *ag.* cystiform.

cistíte, *s.f.* (*patol.*) cystitis.

cistoscopía, *s.f.* (*med.*) cystoscopy.

cisto爻còpio, *s.m.* (*med.*) cystoscope.

cistotomía, *s.f.* (*chir.*) cystotomy.

citàbile, *ag.* citable, quotable: *citazioni citabili,* quotable quotations.

citànte, *ag.* summoning ‖ *s.m.* (*dir.*) plaintiff; summoner.

cítara, (*letter.*) cithern, cittern, lyre.

citàre, *v.t.* **1.** to cite; (*menzionare*) to mention: — *un esempio,* to cite an instance **2.** (*fare una citazione da un libro, da un discorso*) to quote ‖ *opera citata,* op. cit.; (*se già citata nella stessa pagina*) *ibidem* (*abbr.* ib., ibid.) **3.** (*dir.*) to summon, to subpoena; (*intentare causa a*) to sue, to bring an action against (s.o., sthg.): — *per danni,* to sue for damages.

citarèdo, citaríta, *s.m.* (*letter.*) citharist.

citatóre, *s.m.,* **citatríce,** *s.f.* citer; quoter.

citazióne, *s.f.* **1.** (*da un libro, da un discorso*) quotation **2.** (*dir.*) summons, subpoena.

Citèra, *no.pr.f.* (*geog.*) Cythera.

Citerèa, *no.pr.f.* (*mit.*) Cytherea.

citerióre, *ag.* (*geog.*) hither, on this side: *Gallia —,* (*st.*) Hither Gaul.

citíso, *s.m.* (*bot.*) cytisus.

citofagía, *s.f.* (*biol.*) cytophagocytosis, cytophagy.

citòfono, *s.m.* intercommunication system, interphone; (*fam.*) intercom.

citologia, *s.f.* (*biol.*) cytology.

citoplàsma, *s.m.* (*biol.*) cytoplasm.

citostòma, *s.m.* (*biol.*) cytostome.

citramontàno, *ag.* (*geog.*) citramontane.

citràto, *s.m.* (*chim.*) citrate.

cítrico, *ag.* (*chim.*) citric: *acido —,* citric acid.

citriuòlo, *V.* **cetri(u)òlo.**

citronièra, *s.f.* greenhouse (for citrus plants).

citrullàggine, *s.f.* **1.** silliness, stupidity **2.** (*azione da citrullo*) silly action, foolish action.

citrúllo, *ag.* silly, foolish, stupid ‖ *s.m.* fool, silly fellow, simpleton.

città, *s.f.* **1.** town: — *di provincia,* country town; — *giardino,* garden town (o city); — *natale,* native (o home) town; — *universitaria,* university town (o centre); *una casa di — e una di campagna,* a town-house and a country-house; *gente di —,* townspeople; *la parte alta e la parte bassa di una —,* the upper town and the lower town; *vita di —,* town life; *preferisci vivere in — o in campagna?,* do you prefer living in town or in the country?; *andare in —,* to go to town; *essere in —, fuori di —,* to be in town, out of town **2.** (*città grande, importante, metropoli*) city: *la — di Londra e il suo centro d'affari,* the city of London and the City; *la — e lo Stato di New York,* New York city and New York State; *Monza è una cittadina vicino a Milano, la grande — lombarda,* Monza is a small town near Milan, the great city of Lombardy ‖ *la — celeste,* the Heavenly City (o our Heavenly Home) ‖ *la Città del Vaticano,* the Vatican City ‖ *la Città Eterna,* the Eternal City ‖ *la — santa,* the Holy City **3.** (*gli abitanti*) town: *tutta la — lo sa, è la favola della —,* all the town knows of it (o it is the talk of the town).

Città del Càpo, *no.pr.f.* (*geog.*) Cape Town.

cittadèlla, *s.f.* **1.** citadel, fortress **2.** (*baluardo*) stronghold.

cittadína[1], *s.f.* woman citizen.

cittadína[2], *s.f.* (*piccola città*) small town; country town.

cittadíname, *s.m.* (*spreg.*) townsfolk (*coll. con costruzione pl.*).

cittadinànza, *s.f.* **1.** (*stato di cittadino*) citizenship: — *onoraria,* freedom of a city; *diritto di —,* right of citizenship; *acquistò la — britannica,* he became a British subject; *rinunciare alla —,* to give up one's nationality **2.** (*popolazione di una città*) body of citizens, people of the city (*coll. con costruzione pl.*): *l'intera — era presente,* the whole population (o town) was present.

cittadinésco, *ag.* civic; ¡citizen-like; town (*attributivo*).

cittadíno, *ag.* town (*attributivo*); civic: *centro —,* (*dei servizi pubblici*) civic center; (*dei negozi*) shopping center ‖ *s.m.* citizen; (*abitante di città*) town-dweller: — *americano,* American citizen; — *britannico,* British subject; — *del mondo,* citizen of the world; — *onorario di una città,* freeman of a city.

cítto, *s.m.* (*pop. toscano*) kid.

ciúca, *s.f.* (*zool.*) she-ass.

ciucàggine, *s.f.* asininity, stupidity.

ciucàta, *s.f.* (*fam.*) **1.** donkey ride **2.** (*sciocchezza*) nonsense.

ciucheria, *s.f.* asininity, stupidity.

ciuciàre, *v.i.* (*rar.*) to hiss.

ciúco, *s.m.* **1.** donkey, ass, jackass **2.** (*ignorante*) ass; dunce, ignorant **3.** (*berretto a forma di orecchie d'asino che un tempo si faceva portare agli scolari negligenti*) dunce cap **4.** (*sgarbato*) boor.

ciúffo, *s.m.* **1.** (*di capelli*) forelock: *afferrare qlcu. per il —,* to seize s.o. by the forelock ‖ *prendere la fortuna per il —,* *fig.* to take the occasion by the forelock **2.** (*di penne*) tuft, bunch **3.** (*di peli, d'erba*) tuft: *un — d'erba,* a tuft of grass; — *di peli,* tuft of hair **4.** (*gruppetto*) group, cluster: *un — d'alberi,* a group of trees.

ciuffolòtto, *s.m.* (*ornit.*) bullfinch.

ciurlàre, *v.i.* (*rar.*) **1.** to waver ‖ — *nel manico,* (*fam.*) to break one's promises (o to play fast and loose) **2.** (*saltar di gioia*) to caper.

ciúrma, *s.f.* **1.** crew **2.** *fig.* *spreg.* mob, crew, gang.

ciurmadóre, *s.m.* scoundrel, rascal, blackguard; (*imbroglione*) cheat, swindler, trickster.

ciurmàglia, *s.f.* mob, rabble.

ciurmàre, *v.t.* to swindle, to cheat; to hoodwink.

ciurmatóre, *s.m.,* **ciurmatríce,** *s.f.* scoundrel, rascal, blackguard; (*imbroglione, imbrogliona*) swindler, cheat, trickster.

ciurmería, *s.f.* swindle, fraud, cheat, trick.

civàda, *s.f.* (*mar.*) spritsail.

civàia, *s.f.* pulse.

civètta, *s.f.* **1.** (*ornit.*) owl ‖ *far —,* (*abbassare il capo rapidamente*) to duck **2.** *fig.* coquette, flirt: *far la —,* to play the coquette (o to flirt).

civettàre, *v.i.* to flirt, to coquet(te).

civettería, s.f. coquetry.
civettío, s.m. flirting.
civettóna, s.f. coquette, flirt.
civettóne, s.m. flirt, fop.
civettuòlo, ag. coquettish; attractive, pretty.
cívico, ag. 1. civic: corona civica, (st. romana) civic crown; virtù civiche, civic virtues 2. (municipale) civic, municipal: guardia civica, civic (o municipal) guard.
civíle, ag. 1. civil: diritto —, civil law; guerra —, civil war; ingegneria —, civil engineering; matrimonio —, civil marriage; morte —, civil death (o loss of citizen's rights); parte —, (dir.) plaintiff; stato —, civil status; ufficio dello stato —, registry office 2. (che concerne la civiltà) civilized: nazione —, civilized nation; paesi civili, civilized countries 3. (cortese) polite; refined: modi civili, polite manners 4. (in opposizione a militare, ecclesiastico) civilian: abito —, civilian dress (o plain clothes o sl. mil. mufti).
civilísta, s.m. (dir.) 1. lawyer (specialized in civil law) 2. (studioso di diritto civile) civilian, jurist.
civilizzàre, v.t. to civilize: molti selvaggi sono stati civilizzati dai missionari, many savages have been civilized by missionaries.
civilizzàto, ag. civilized.
civilizzatóre, ag. civilizing ‖ s.m., **civilizzatríce,** s.f. civilizer.
civilizzazióne, s.f. civilization.
civilménte, av. 1. civilly: sposato —, married at a registry office (o before a registrar) 2. (educatamente) politely, civilly.
civiltà, s.f. 1. civilization 2. (cortesia) politeness, civility, courtesy.
civísmo, s.m. civic virtues (pl.); public spirit.
cívolo, s.m. (aer.) slipway.
clàcson, s.m. (aut.) klaxon, motor-horn.
clàmide, s.f. 1. chlamys (pl. chlamydes) 2. (manto reale) royal cloak; (manto imperiale) emperor's cloak.
clamóre, s.m. clamour, outcry, uproar: sollevare —, to raise an outcry.
clamorosaménte, av. clamorously; noisily.
clamoróso, ag. clamorous; noisy; sensational.
clan, s.m. 1. (st.) clan 2. fig. exclusive set; (fam.) clique.
clandestinaménte, av. clandestinely, surreptitiously, stealthily, secretly.
clandestíno, ag. clandestine, surreptitious, secret: passeggero —, stowaway; scommessa —, illicit betting.
clangóre, s.m. (letter.) clangour.
Clàra, no.pr.f. Clara, Clare, Claire.
Clarabèlla, no.pr.f. Claribel.
clarétto, s.m. (vino) claret.
Claríce, no.pr.f. Clarice.
clarinettísta, s.c. (mus.) clarinettist, clarinet-player.
clarinétto, claríno, s.m. (mus.) clarinet, clarionet.
claríssa, s.f. (eccl.) Clarisse ‖ **Claríssa,** no.pr.f. Clarissa.
classàrio, s.m. (st. romana) sailor.
clàsse, s.f. 1. class: la — dirigente, the ruling class; le classi lavoratrici, the working classes; le classi medie, the middle classes; lotta di —, class-war; spirito di —, class-consciousness 2. (qualità): di —, first-rate, of good quality: è un giocatore di —, he is a first-rate player ‖ fuori —, of superlative quality 3. (mil.) (annual) contingent, class: la — del 1925, the 1925 contingent (o class) 4. (l'insieme degli scolari) class; (aula) class-room; (corso) form; (amer.) grade: compagno di —, class-mate (o class-fellow); che — fai?, what form are you in? (o amer. what grade are you taking?); la mia — è molto numerosa, my class is very numerous 5. (nei mezzi di trasporto) class: biglietto di prima —, first-class ticket; una cabina di prima —, a first-class cabin; prima, seconda —, first, second class; viaggiare in prima —, to travel first-class 6. (scient.) class.
classiàrio, s.m. (st. romana) sailor.
classicaménte, av. classically.

classicísmo, s.m. (st. lett.) classicism.
classicísta, s.m. (st. lett.) classicist.
classicizzàre, v.t.i. to classicize.
clàssico, ag. classic(al): corsa classica, (ippica) classic race; istruzione classica, classical education; stile —, classic(al) style; studi classici, classical studies (o classics); la « Divina Commedia » è un'opera classica, the "Divine Comedy" is a classic work; suona solo musica classica, he plays only classical music ‖ questa è classica!, this is wonderful! ‖ s.m. classic: D'Annunzio è ormai considerato un — della letteratura italiana, D'Annunzio is now universally accepted as a classic of Italian literature ‖ i Classici, the Classics.
classífica, s.f. classification; (spor.) position: — finale, final results; egli è primo in —, (di concorso, esame) he has been classed first; quel corridore (ciclista) era quinto in —, that cyclist was placed fifth.
classificàbile, ag. classifiable.
classificàre, v.t. to classify, to class: classificare dei fiori, delle piante, to classify flowers, plants.
classificatóre, s.m. 1. (chi classifica) classifier: — della lana, (ind. tessile) stapler; — di merci, classer 2. (per lettere, documenti) file 3. (per francobolli) stock-book 4. (mec. miner.) classifier, classificator.
classificatríce, s.f. (per lettere, documenti) file.
classificazióne, s.f. 1. classification: certificato di —, (mar.) certificate of classification 2. (cernita) sorting, grading.
classísta, ag. (pol.) class (attributivo): politica —, class politics.
clàtro, s.m. 1. (poet.) (inferriata) railing, grating 2. (bot.) clathrate.
Clàudia, no.pr.f. Claudia.
Claudiàno no.pr.m. (st.) Claudian, Claudianus.
Clàudio, no.pr.m. Claude; (st.) Claudius.
claudicànte, ag. lame, limping, halting.
claudicàre, v.i. to limp, to halt.
claudicazióne, s.f. limping, halting.
clàusola, s.f. 1. clause: — aggiunta, (dir. comm.) additional clause; — arbitrale, (comm.) arbitration clause; clausole d'ingaggio, (dir. comm. mar.) ship's articles; inserire una —, to add (o to insert) a clause 2. (riserva) reserve.
claustràle, ag. claustral: regola —, claustral rule.
claustrofobía, s.f. (patol.) claustrophobia.
clausúra, s.f. (eccl.) 1. seclusion: voto di —, vow of seclusion 2. (convento) cloister.
clàva, s.f. club, bludgeon.
clavicembalísta, s.c. (mus.) harpsichord player.
clavicémbalo, s.m. (mus.) harpsichord, clavichord.
clavícola, s.f. (anat.) clavicle, collar-bone.
clavicolàre, ag. (anat.) clavicular.
clavicòrdio, s.m. (mus.) clavichord, harpsichord.
clavifórme, ag. club-shaped; claviform.
clàvo, s.m. (patol.) clavus.
Cleànte, no.pr.m. (st. fil.) Cleanthes.
Cleàrco, no.pr.m. (st.) Clearchus.
cleidomastoidèo, ag. (anat.) cleidomastoid.
cleistògamo, ag. (bot.) cleistogamic, cleistogamous.
Clèlia, no.pr.f. Clelia.
clemàtide, s.f. (bot.) clematis.
clemènte, ag. 1. (di persona) clement, mild; merciful: un sovrano —, a mild ruler 2. (di clima) mild, clement: tempo —, mild weather ‖ **Clemènte,** no.pr.m. Clement.
clementeménte, av. mildly; mercifully.
Clementína, no.pr.f. Clementina, Clementine.
clemènza, s.f. 1. (di persona) clemency, mildness; mercifulness 2. (di clima) mildness, clemency.
Cleòmene, no.pr.m. (st.) Cleomenes.
Cleóne, no.pr.m. (st.) Cleon.
Cleopàtra, no.pr.f. (st.) Cleopatra.
cleptòmane, ag.s.c. (patol.) kleptomaniac.
cleptomanía, s.f. (patol.) kleptomania.
cleptoscòpio, s.m. (mar.) periscope.

clericàle, *ag.* clerical: *abito* —, clerical dress; *i giornali clericali*, the clerical press ‖ *s.m.* clericalist ‖ *i clericali*, the clericals.

clericaleggiàre, *v.i.* to support the clerical party.

clericalísmo, *s.m.* clericalism.

clericàto, *s.m.* **1.** (*clero*) clergy, priesthood **2.** (*ordine sacro*) priesthood.

clèro, *s.m.* clergy: — *regolare*, regular clergy; — *secolare*, secular clergy.

clessídra, *s.f.* (*a sabbia*) sand-glass; (*ad acqua*) clepsydra (*pl.* clepsydras, clepsydrae); water-clock.

cliché, *s.m.* **1.** (*tip.*) cliché, stereotype **2.** *fig.* cliché; commonplace.

cliènte, *s.c.* **1.** (*di negozio, esercizio, ditta*) customer: — *abituale*, regular customer (*o* patron) **2.** (*di medico, avvocato*) client ‖ *s.m.* (*st. romana*) client.

clientèla, *s.f.* **1.** (*di negozio, esercizio*) customers (*pl.*); clients (*pl.*); custom; clientele: *alienarsi la* —, to drive away one's customers; *conservare la propria* —, to keep (*o* to preserve) one's custom **2.** (*comm.*) connection: *quella ditta ha una vasta* —, that firm has a large connection **3.** (*di medico, avvocato*) practice: *il dott. Smith aveva una numerosa* —, Dr. Smith had a large practice **4.** (*st. romana*) clients (*pl.*).

clíma, *s.m.* climate; (*poet.*) clime: *andò verso un* — *più caldo*, he went to a warmer climate; *ha vissuto in ogni* —, he has lived in all climates.

climatèrico, *ag.* **1.** (*fisiol.*) climacteric(al) **2.** *fig.* critical.

climatèrio, *s.m.* (*fisiol.*) climacteric.

climaticaménte, *av.* climatically.

climàtico, *ag.* climatic; health (*attributivo*): *stazione climatica*, health-resort.

climatología, *s.f.* climatology.

climatològico, *ag.* climatological.

clímax, *s.m.f.* (*ret.*) climax.

clínica, *s.f.* **1.** (*disciplina*) clinical medicine; (*pratica ospedaliera*) bed-side instruction **2.** (*casa di cura*) clinic; nursing-home; policlinic.

clínico, *ag.* clinical: *diagnosi clinica* clinical diagnosis; *quadro* —, clinical picture; *termometro* —, clinical thermometer ‖ *s.m.* (*medico, chirurgo*) clinician, clinical doctor, clinicist.

clinòmetro, *s.m.* clinometer.

Clío, *no.pr.f.* (*mit.*) Clio.

clipeàto, *ag.* (*di insetto*) clypeate ‖ *s.m.* (*st.*) warrior armed with a clipeus.

clípeo, *s.m.* **1.** (*scudo*) clipeus (*pl.* clipei) **2.** (*di tartaruga*) carapace; (*di insetto*) clypeus (*pl.* clypei).

Clístene, *no.pr.m.* (*st.*) Cleisthenes.

clistère, *s.m.* (*med.*) enema (*pl.* enemas, enemata); clyster: *fare un* — *a qlcu.*, to give s.o. an enema.

Clitennèstra, *no.pr.f.* (*lett.*) Clytemnestra.

clivàggio, *s.m.* (*geol.*) cleavage: *piano di* —, cleavage plane.

clívo, *s.m.* (*poet.*) hillock.

clízia, *s.f.* (*bot.*) heliotrope, sunflower.

cloàca, *s.f.* **1.** (*fogna*) sewer; cloaca (*pl.* cloacae) (anche *fig.*) ‖ *la Cloaca Massima*, (*archeol.*) the Cloaca Massima **2.** (*anat.*) cloaca (*pl.* cloacae).

Clodovèo, *no.pr.m.* (*st.*) Clovis.

Clòe, *no.pr.f.* Chloe.

clònico, *ag.* (*med.*) clonic.

cloràlio, *s.m.* (*chim.*) chloral.

cloràto, *s.m.* (*chim.*) chlorate.

clòrico, *ag.* (*chim.*) chloric.

cloridràto, *s.m.* (*chim.*) hydrochloride.

clorídrico, *ag.* (*chim.*) hydrochloric: *acido* —, hydrochloric acid.

Clorínda, *no.pr.f.* Chloris.

clòro, *s.m.* (*chim.*) chlorine.

clorofílla, *s.f.* (*chim.*) chlorophyll: *dentifricio alla* —, chlorophyll tooth-paste.

cloroférmio, *s.m.* (*chim.*) chloroform.

cloroformizzàre, *v.t.* (*med.*) to chloroform.

cloromicetína, *s.f.* (*farm.*) chloromycetin.

cloròsi, *s.f.* **1.** (*patol.*) chlorosis; (*pop.*) green-sickness **2.** (*malattia delle piante*) chlorosis.

cloròtico, *ag.* (*patol.*) chlorotic.

clorúro, *s.m.* (*chim.*) chloride.

Clotílde, *no.pr.f.* Clotílda, Clothilda.

Clòto, *no.pr.f.* (*mit.*) Clotho.

clúne, *s.m.f.* buttock.

cluniacènse, *ag.* (*eccl.*) Cluniac.

Cnído, *no.pr.f.* (*geog. st.*) Cnidus.

Cnòsso, *no.pr.f.* (*geog. st.*) Cnossus.

co, *s.m.* (*arc.*) head, top.

coabitànte, *ag.* cohabiting ‖ *s.c.* cohabitant.

coabitàre, *v.i.* to cohabit, to live together.

coabitazióne, *s.f.* cohabitation, house-sharing.

coaccusàto, *s.m.* (*dir.*) co-defendant, fellow-accused.

coacervàre, *v.t.* to coacervate, to heap up.

coacèrvo, *s.m.* coacervation, heap; accumulation.

coadiutóre, *s.m.* **1.** (*collaboratore*) assistant **2.** (*eccl.*) coadjutor: *vescovo* —, suffragan (*o* coadjutor-bishop).

coadiutoràto, *s.m.* (*eccl.*) coadjutorship.

coadiutríce, *s.f.* assistant.

coadiuvànte, *ag.* coadjuvant.

coadiuvàre, *v.t.* to help, to assist; to cooperate with (s.o.).

coagulàbile, *ag.* coagulable.

coagulaménto, *s.m.* (*rar.*) coagulation.

coagulànte, *ag.* coagulative ‖ *s.m.* coagulant.

coagulàre, *v.t.*, **coagulàrsi**, *v.r.* to coagulate; (*del latte*) to curdle.

coagulatívo, *ag.* coagulative.

coagulazióne, *s.f.* coagulation.

coàgulo, *s.m.* **1.** (*grumo*) coagulum (*pl.* coagula); clot; curd: — *di latte*, curd of milk; — *di sangue*, blood-clot **2.** (*coagulante*) coagulant.

coalizióne, *s.f.* coalition; alliance ‖ *la prima, la seconda Coalizione*, (*st.*) the First, the Second Coalition.

coalizzàre, *v.t.* to unite, to combine (powers) in a coalition ‖ **coalizzàrsi**, *v.r.* to form a coalition, to unite.

coalizzàto, *ag.* united, combined; (*alleato*) allied: *le nazioni coalizzate*, the allied nations.

coartàre, *v.t.* **1.** to coerce, to force, to constrain, to oblige **2.** (*med.*) to coarctate, to coarct.

coartàto, *ag.* **1.** coerced, forced, constrained **2.** (*med.*) coarctate.

coartazióne, *s.f.* **1.** coercion, compulsion, constraint **2.** (*med.*) coarctation.

coassiàle, *ag.* (*geom. mec.*) coaxial: *cavo* —, coaxial cable.

coattívo, *ag.* coercive, compulsory, compelling.

coàtto, *ag.* forced, compulsory, pressed: *domicilio* —, (*dir.*) forced residence.

coautóre, *s.m.* co-author.

coazióne, *s.f.* coercion, constraint, compulsion.

cobàlto, *s.m.* **1.** (*chim.*) cobalt: *bomba al* —, cobalt bomb **2.** (*colore*) cobalt(-blue): *cielo di* —, cobalt (-blue) sky.

còbbola, *s.f.* (*poes.*) stanza (*pl.* stanzas, stanze).

cobelligerànte, *ag. s.m.* co-belligerent.

cobelligerànza, *s.f.* co-belligerency.

Coblènza, *no.pr.f.* (*geog.*) Coblenz.

cobòldo, *s.m.* (*mit. nordica*) kobold.

còbra, *s.m.* (*zool.*) cobra.

Cobúrgo, *no.pr.f.* (*geog.*) Coburg.

còc, *s.m.* coke: — *di fonderia*, foundry coke; — *di gas*, gas coke; — *minuto*, coke druss; *forno da* —, coking oven; *scorie di* —, coke-breeze.

còca, *s.f.* (*bot.*) coca.

Còca-Còla, *s.f.* (*bevanda analcolica*) Coca-Cola; (*fam.*) coke.

cocaína, *s.f.* (*farm.*) cocaine.

cocainísmo, *s.m.* (*patol.*) cocainism.

cocainòmane, *s.c.* cocainist, cocaine addict.

cocainomanía, *s.f.* (*patol.*) cocaine-habit.

còcca[1], *s.f.* **1.** (*di freccia*) notch **2.** (*di fuso*) tip **3.** (*angolo di fazzoletto, grembiule, ecc.*) corner.

còcca[2], *s.f.* (*mar.*) medieval merchant ship.

còcca[3], *s.f.* (*fam.*) (*bimba prediletta*) darling, pet.

còcca[4], *s.f.* (*linguaggio infantile*) (*gallina*) hen.

coccàrda, *s.f.* cockade.

còcchia, *s.f.* drag-net.

cocchière, *s.m.* coachman (*pl.* coachmen); driver; (*di carrozza pubblica*) cabman (*pl.* cabmen); (*sl.*) cabby.

còcchio, *s.m.* coach, carriage: — *reale*, state-coach.

cocchiúme, *s.m.* **1.** (*orifizio superiore della botte*) bung-hole **2.** (*tappo che lo chiude*) bung.

còccia, *s.f.* **1.** (*parte dell'elsa*) sword-guard **2.** (*guscio di testaceo*) shell **3.** (*corteccia*) bark; (*baccello*) pod **4.** (*fornello di pipa*) pipe-bowl **5.** (*scherz.*) (*testa*) pate.

cocciàio, *s.m.* potter.

còccige, *s.m.* (*anat.*) coccyx (*pl.* coccyges).

coccinèlla, *s.f.* (*entom.*) ladybird, lady-clock, lady-cow.

cocciníglia, *s.f.* (*entom.*) cochineal: *rosso di* —, cochineal.

còccio, *s.m.* **1.** potsherd, crock, fragment of pottery **2.** (*vaso fesso*) cracked pot **3.** (*recipiente di terracotta*) crock; pot **4.** *pl.* (*vasellame*) crockery (*sing.*) **5.** (*persona malaticcia*) (old) crock **6.** (*scaldino*) hand-warmer **7.** (*guscio di lumaca*) shell.

cocciutàggine, *s.f.* stubbornness, obstinacy.

cocciúto, *ag.* stubborn, pig-headed, obstinate ‖ *s.m.* stubborn man.

còcco[1], *s.m.* **1.** (*albero*) coco(nut)-tree, coco(nut)-palm **2.** (*frutto*) coconut: *latte di* —, coconut-milk; *olio di* —, coconut-oil.

còcco[2], *s.m.* (*batterio*) coccus (*pl.* cocci).

còcco[3], *s.m.* (*fam.*) (*bimbo prediletto*) darling, pet.

còcco[4], *s.m.* (*linguaggio infantile*) (*uovo*) egg.

coccodè, *s.m.* cackle: *fare* —, to cackle.

coccodríllo, *s.m.* (*zool.*) crocodile ‖ *lacrime di* —, *fig.* crocodile tears.

còccola, *s.f.* (*bacca*) berry.

coccolàre, *v.t.* to pet, to fondle: — *un bambino*, to fondle a baby ‖ **coccolàrsi**, *v.r.* to lie at ease, to nestle: — *nel letto*, to nestle in bed.

còccolo, *s.m.* (*fam.*) darling, pet: — *della mamma!*, mother's darling!

coccolóni, *av.* squatting: *la domestica stava* — *vicino al fuoco*, the maid-servant was squatting by the fire.

cocènte, *ag.* **1.** hot, burning, scalding: *sole* —, scorching sun; *lacrime cocenti*, scalding tears **2.** *fig.* (*intenso*) bitter; vehement; deep; acute: *delusione* —, bitter disappointment; *il dolore* — *di una ferita*, the sting (*o* the smarting) of a wound.

Cocincína, *no.pr.f.* (*geog.*) Cochin-China.

cocióre, *s.m.* (*rar.*) burn, scald; smart.

Cocíto, *no.pr.m.* (*geog. mit.*) Cocytus.

cocitóre, *s.m.* assistant-baker.

còclea, *s.f.* **1.** (*anat.*) cochlea (*pl.* cochleae) **2.** (*arch.*) winding staircase **3.** (*archeol.*) lion's gate **4.** (*mec.*) Archimedean screw.

cocomeràio, *s.m.* **1.** (*campo di cocomeri*) water-melon bed **2.** (*chi vende cocomeri*) water-melon vendor.

cocómero, *s.m.* **1.** water-melon **2.** (*scherz.*) (*citrullo*) block-head.

cocoríta, *s.f.* (*ornit.*) small parrot.

cocúzza, *s.f.* **1.** (*dial.*) (*zucca*) pumpkin **2.** (*scherz.*) (*testa*) head, pate.

cocúzzolo, *s.m.* **1.** (*parte alta del capo*) crown; (*parte alta del cappello*) crown of a hat **2.** (*vetta*) summit, top.

còda, *s.f.* **1.** tail (anche *fig.*): — (*di aeroplano*, tail of an aeroplane; — *di aquilone*, tail of a kite; — *di ratto*, (*mar.*) rat's tail; — *di cometa*, tail of a comet; *dalla* — *lunga*, long-tailed; *fanale di* —, 'tail-light; *giacca a* — *di rondine*, tailcoat (*o* tails); *incastro a* — *di rondine*, dovetail joint (*o* dovetailing); *pianoforte a* —, grand piano; *scivolata di* —, (*aer.*) tail slide; *senza* —, tailless; *trave di* —, (*aer.*) tail boom; *marciare in* —, to bring up the rear ‖ *avete la* — *di paglia*, you have sthg. to hide ‖ *se il diavolo non ci mette la* —,

if no difficulty arises ‖ *andarsene con la* — *tra le gambe*, *fig.* to put one's tail between one's legs (*o* to be disappointed) ‖ *guardare ql.co. con la* — *dell'occhio*, to give a side-glance at sthg. ‖ *non avere nè capo nè* —, to make no sense (*o* to be utter nonsense) **2.** (*di capelli*) pony-tail; (*treccia*) pigtail **3.** (*di abiti*) tail; train **4.** (*fila*) queue: *fare la* —, to queue (up); *mettersi in* —, to form a queue **5.** (*persona retrograda*) reactionary, die-hard.

codardaménte, *av.* cowardly.

codardía, *s.f.* cowardice, cowardliness, cravenness.

codàrdo, *ag.* cowardly, craven ‖ *s.m.* coward; poltroon.

codàto, *ag.* caudate, tailed.

codàzzo, *s.m.* train; long queue: *fare* — *a qlcu.*, to follow in s.o.'s train.

codeína, *s.f.* (*farm.*) codeine.

codésto, *V.* **cotésto**.

codétta, *s.f.* **1.** small tail **2.** (*mar.*) sternfast.

còdice, *s.m.* **1.** (*dir.*) code: — *civile*, Civil Law; — *di commercio*, mercantile law; — *di procedura penale*, code of criminal procedure (*o* criminal code); — *giustinianeo*, Code of Justinian; — *marittimo*, Navigation Laws (*o* Acts); — *penale*, Penal Code; — *stradale*, highway code ‖ — *di onore*, code of honour ‖ *inciampare nel* —, *fig.* to come up against the law **2.** (*cifrario*) code: — *telegrafico*, telegraphic code; *decifrare un* —, to read a code; *decifrare un telegramma in* —, to decode a telegram **3.** (*manoscritto antico*) codex (*pl.* codices).

codicíllo, *s.m.* **1.** (*dir.*) codicil **2.** (*poscritto*) post-script.

codificàbile, *ag.* that can be codified.

codificàre, *v.t.* to codify.

codificazióne, *s.f.* codification.

codilúngo, *s.m.* (*ornit.*) long-tailed tit.

codimózzo, *ag.* (*rar.*) dock-tailed.

codíno, *s.m.* **1.** (*piccola coda*) small tail **2.** (*trecciolina di capelli*) pigtail, queue **3.** *fig.* reactionary, die-hard.

codióne, *s.m.* rump.

codirósso, *s.m.* (*ornit.*) redstart.

códolo, *s.m.* (*mec.*) tang.

codrióne, *s.m.* rump.

coeditóre, *s.m.* co-publisher.

coefficiènte, *s.m.* (*mat. fis. chim.*) coefficient: — *di assorbimento*, (*chim.*) absorption coefficient; — *di attrito*, (*mec.*) friction coefficient; — *di diffusione*, (*fis. chim.*) coefficient of diffusion; — *di produzione*, coefficient of production; — *di risonanza*, (*rad.*) resonance factor; — *di selettività*, (*rad.*) selectivity factor; — *di sicurezza*, (*scienza delle costruzioni*) coefficient of safety; — *di smorzamento*, (*aer.*) damping factor; — *numerico*, (*mat.*) numerical coefficient.

coefficiènza, *s.f.* joint cause, coefficient cause.

coèfora, *s.f.* (*st. greca*) libation bearer ‖ « *Le Coefore* », (*lett.*) " The Choephori " (*o* " Choephoroe ").

coeguàle, *ag.* coequal.

coereíbile, *ag.* coercible.

coercitívo, *ag.* coercive, compulsive: *metodi coercitivi*, coercive methods.

coercizióne, *s.f.* coercion, compulsion: *egli agisce sotto* —, he acts under coercion; *essi impiegarono mezzi di* —, they employed coercive means.

coerède, *s.m.* joint heir, coheir ‖ *s.f.* joint heiress, coheiress.

coerènte, *ag.* **1.** coherent, consistent: *la sua condotta non è* — *con la sua natura*, his conduct is not consistent (*o* is not in keeping) with his nature; *il suo ragionamento è* —, his argument is consistent; *agire in modo* —, to act coherently **2.** (*unito insieme*) coherent.

coerenteménte, *av.* coherently, consistently.

coerènza, *s.f.* coherence, consistency: *le tue azioni mancano di* —, your actions lack consistency.

coesióne, *s.f.* (*fis.*) cohesion.

coesistènte, *ag.* coexistent, coexisting.

coesistènza, *s.f.* coexistence.

coesístere, *v.i.* to coexist.

coesóre, *s.m.* (*fis.*) coherer.

coessenziàle, *ag.* coessential.

coetàneo, *ag.* contemporary, coeval: *Giovanni e io siamo coetanei*, John and I are the same age ‖ *s.m.* contemporary: *i nostri coetanei*, our contemporaries.

coetèrno, *ag.* coeternal.

coèvo, *ag.* coeval, contemporary.

cofanétto, *s.m.* casket: — *dei gioielli*, jewel box (o jewel case).

còfano, *s.m.* 1. (*forziere*) coffer; (*cassapanca*) chest; (*scrigno*) casket 2. (*aut.*) bonnet 3. (*mil.*) ammunition-chest.

còffa, *s.f.* (*mar.*) top: — *di maestra*, maintop.

cogènte, *ag.* (*dir.*) legally binding; coercive, compulsory.

cogitabóndo, *ag.* thoughtful; musing.

cogitàre, *v.i.* (*arc.*) to cogitate, to ponder, to meditate; to muse.

cogitatíva, *s.f.* thinking capacity.

cogitatívo, *ag.* 1. (*relativo al pensiero*) cogitative: *le facoltà cogitative*, the faculties of thought 2. (*cogitabondo*) thoughtful.

cogitazióne, *s.f.* (*arc.*) cogitation, meditation; reflection: *queste cogitazioni non conducono a nulla*, these cogitations lead to nothing.

cògliere, *v.t.* 1. to pick, to pluck, to gather: — *fiori*, to pick (o to pluck o to gather) flowers; — *fragole*, to pick strawberries ‖ — *il frutto delle proprie fatiche*, to reap the fruits of one's labour 2. (*sorprendere*) to catch: *lo ha colto una malattia*, a sickness has befallen him; *lo colse la morte*, he died unexpectedly; *lo colsi mentre rubava*, I caught him stealing; *lo colsi sul fatto*, I caught him red-handed (o in the very act); *essere colti dalla pioggia, dal temporale*, to be caught in a shower, in the storm ‖ *non mi cogli più!*, (*fam.*) you won't catch me again! 3. (*colpire*) to hit: — *nel segno*, to hit the mark (anche *fig.*) 4. (*afferrare*) to seize, to avail oneself of (sthg.): — *l'occasione*, to take (advantage of) the opportunity: — *la palla al balzo*, *fig.* to seize the opportunity ‖ — *gli allori*, to win laurels 5. (*capire*) to understand, to grasp, to catch; (*udire*) to hear: *ha detto qualcosa che non ho colto*, he said something which I did not grasp 6. (*mar.*) to coil.

coglitóre, *s.m.*, **coglitríce**, *s.f.* gatherer.

coglitúra, *s.f.* gathering.

cognac, *s.m.* cognac (French brandy).

cognàta, *s.f.* sister-in-law.

cognàto, *s.m.* brother-in-law.

cognazióne, *s.f.* (*dir.*) relationship through females only: (*scoz.*) cognation.

cògnito, *ag.* known.

cognizióne, *s.f.* 1. knowledge (*coll. con costruzione sing.*): *cognizioni utili*, useful knowledge; *per quanto a mia* —, to my knowledge; *avete qualche — di tedesco?*, have you any knowledge of German?; *solo una — superficiale*, just a smattering; *quando ne ebbi* —, when it came to my knowledge (o when I was informed of it); *essere a — di ql.co.*, to know (about) sthg. (o to be aware of sthg.); *giudicare con — di causa*, to judge from good knowledge of a case 2. (*dir.*) cognizance: *prendere — di ql.co.*, to take cognizance of sthg. 3. (*fil.*) cognition.

cognóme, *s.m.* surname, family name: — *da nubile*, maiden name; *il mio nome e il mio* —, my Christian and family names; *nome e* —, name and surname.

cognominàre, *v.t.* to surname ‖ **cognominàrsi**, *v.r.* to name oneself.

cògolo, *s.m.* pebble.

coiàio, **coiàme**, *V.* **cuoiàio**, **cuoiàme**.

coiàttolo, *s.m.* scrap of leather.

coibènte, *ag.* (*fis.*) non-conducting, non-conductive, insulating ‖ *s.m.* (*fis.*) non-conductor; heat insulator.

coibènza, *s.f.* (*fis.*) non-conductivity.

coimputàto, *s.m.* (*dir.*) co-defendant.

coincidènte, *ag.* coinciding, coincident.

coincidènza, *s.f.* 1. coincidence: *che* —!, what a coincidence!; *è stata una pura* —, it was an entirely coincidental occurence 2. (*ferr.*) connection, connexion: *non temere, i due treni sono in* —, don't worry, the two trains connect; *questo treno è in ritardo e ò temo di perdere la — con il rapido per Venezia*, this train is late and I am afraid of missing the connection with the Venice express.

coincídere, *v.i.* to coincide; (*di eventi che hanno luogo nello stesso momento*) to clash: *le due conferenze coincidono*, the two lectures clash.

cointeressàre, *v.t.* (*comm.*) to associate, to share profits with (s.o.), to interest in profits: — *qlcu. in un affare*, to give s.o. a joint interest in an affair.

cointeressàto, *ag.* (*comm.*) interested in profits: *i cointeressati*, the partners (o the associates).

cointeressènza, *s.f.* (*comm.*) profit-sharing, share of profits; (*percentuale*) percentage.

coinvòlgere, *v.t.* to involve: — *qlcu. in una disputa*, to involve s.o. in a quarrel.

coióso, *ag.* leathery.

coíto, *s.m.* coition, copulation.

còla¹, *s.f.* (*bot.*) cola, kola: *noce, seme di* —, cola-nut, cola-seed.

cóla², *s.f.* (*colatoio*) strainer.

Còla³, *no.pr.m.* dim. di **Nicòla** ‖ *s.m.* (*personaggio balordo di commedia*) simpleton, booby.

colà⁴, *av.* there, in that place, over there.

colabròdo, *s.m.* colander, cullender, strainer.

colàggio, *s.m.* 1. (*perdita di liquidi*) leakage 2. (*metal.*) casting.

colaggiù, *av.* down there.

colagógo, *ag.* (*farm.*) cholagogic.

colaménto, *s.m.* dropping.

colàre, *v.t.* 1. (*filtrare*) to filter, to strain, to percolate, to colander, to cullender: — *il brodo, il vino*, to strain broth, wine; — *il caffè*, to percolate coffee; — *il latte in un panno*, to strain milk through a cloth 2. (*fondere*) to cast, to pour: — *la ghisa in pani*, to pig; — *metallo in uno stampo*, to pour (o to run) metal into a mould; — *una statua in bronzo*, to cast a statue in bronze 3. (*versare goccia a goccia*) to drip, to drop; to pour out slowly: *il favo colava miele*, the comb dripped honey; — *l'olio*, to pour out oil ‖ *v.i.* 1. (*gocciolare*) to drip, to trickle, to drop; (*di candela*) to gutter, to melt: *le lacrime le colavano lungo le gote*, tears trickled down her cheeks; *il rubinetto colava*, the tap was dripping; *il sudore gli colava dalla fronte*, beads of perspiration were dropping from his fore-head 2. — *a picco*, (*mar.*) to founder, to sink.

colascionàta, *s.f.* (*spreg.*) third-rate verse.

colasciòne, *s.m.* (*mus.*) "colascione" (ancient two-or three-stringed lute) ‖ *poeta da* —, poetaster.

colassù, *av.* up there, up yonder.

colàta, *s.f.* 1. (*metal.*) casting, pouring, tapping: — *a sorgente*, bottom casting; — *diretta*, casting; — *in gesso*, plaster casting; *attacco di* —, runner (o runner gate o pouring spot); *foro di* —, gate; *secchia di* —, ladle 2. (*quantità di metallo fuso*) tap, melt, cast 3. (*di lava, ecc.*) flow: — *di fango*, mudflow; — *di lava*, lavaflow (o lavastream).

colatíccio, *s.m.* 1. drippings (*pl.*) 2. (*feccia*) dross, dregs (*pl.*).

colàto, *ag.* 1. strained, filtered 2. (*metal.*) cast; smelted; fused: *oro* —, pure gold.

colatóio, *s.m.* 1. (*per brodo*) colander, cullender; (*per il tè*) (tea-) strainer 2. (*crogiuolo*) crucible.

colatúra, *s.f.* 1. (*il filtrare*) filtering, straining, percolating, colandering, cullandering 2. (*il versare*) pouring out 3. (*il gocciolare*) dripping, trickling 4. (*residuo*) dregs (*pl.*); sediment 5. (*cera colata dalle candele*) candle grease.

colazióne, *s.f.* **1.** (*del mattino*) breakfast: — *con caffè e latte*, continental breakfast; *ora di* —, breakfast time; *tavola per la* —, breakfast-table ‖ *far* —, to breakfast (*o* to have breakfast *o* to eat one's breakfast): *egli fa* — *con un pezzo di pane*, he breakfasts off (*o* on) a piece of bread; *far* — *con caffè e latte*, to have coffee and milk for breakfast **2.** (*di mezzogiorno*) lunch, luncheon: — *affrettata*, quick lunch; *fui pregato di restare a* —, I was asked to stay to lunch; *invitare qlcu. a* —, to ask s.o. to lunch; *offrire a qlcu. una buona* —, to give s.o. a good lunch ‖ *fare* —, to take (*o* to have) lunch (*o* to lunch): *noi facciamo* — *a mezzogiorno*, we have lunch at noon **3.** — *alla forchetta*, knife-and-fork meal.

colbàe, **colbàeco**, *s.m.* (*mil.*) busby.

còlchico, *s.m.* (*bot.*) colchicum, meadow-saffron.

Còlchide, *no.pr.f.* (*geog. st.*) Colchis.

colecistíte, *s.f.* (*patol.*) cholecystitis.

colèdoco, *s.m.* (*anat.*) choledoch (duct), choledochus.

colèi, *pron. dimostrativo f. sing.* **1.** *sogg.* she; (*spreg.*) that woman: *chi è* —?, who is she? (*o* that woman?) **2.** *compl.* her; (*spreg.*) that woman: *cerca di liberarti da* —, try and get rid of her (*o* of that woman) **3.** — *che*, she who, she whom (*sogg.*); her who, her whom (*compl.*): — *che crede ciò s'inganna*, she who believes that is mistaken; — *che vedesti ieri è mia sorella*, she whom you saw yesterday is my sister; *darò il premio a* — *che farà meglio*, I will give the prize to her who does (the) best; *non ha ricevuto che bontà da* — *che odia tanto*, she has received nothing but kindness from her whom she hates so much.

colendíssimo, *ag.superl.* most honourable; (*rivolgendosi a persona o negli indirizzi*) Right Honourable (*abbr.* Right Hon.; *in inglese si usa solo rivolgendosi ai nobili di rango inferiore a Marquis, ai giudici, nei dibattiti parlamentari*).

coleòttero, *s.m.* (*entom.*) coleopter ‖ *i coleotteri*, Coleoptera.

colèra, *s.m.* (*patol.*) cholera: — *asiatico*, asiatic cholera; — *fulminante*, malignant cholera.

colerètico, *ag.* (*farm.*) choleretic.

colèrico, *ag.* (*patol.*) choleraic ‖ *s.m.* cholera patient.

colerína, *s.f.* (*patol.*) cholerine.

coleróso, *ag.* (*patol.*) stricken with cholera ‖ *s.m.* cholera patient.

colesterína, *s.f.* (*biol.*) cholesterin.

colesteròlo, *s.m.* (*biol.*) cholesterol.

colibrí, *s.m.* (*ornit.*) humming-bird.

còlica, *s.f.* colic, colica: — *epatica*, hepatic colic (*o* colica hepatica).

colicistíte, *s.f.* (*patol.*) cholecystitis.

còlico, *ag.* colic.

colíno, *s.m.* strainer, colander, cullender.

colíte, *s.f.* (*patol.*) colitis.

còlla, *s.f.* glue; (*di farina*) paste: — *di pesce*, isinglass (*o* fish-glue).

collaboràre, *v.i.* to collaborate: — *a un giornale*, to contribute to a newspaper; — *col nemico*, to collaborate with the enemy.

collaboratóre, *s.m.*, **collaboratríce**, *s.f.* collaborator; (*di giornali*) contributor.

collaborazióne, *s.f.* collaboration; co-operation; (*a un giornale*) contribution.

collaborazionísmo, *s.m.* collaborationism.

collaborazionísta, *s.c.* collaborationist; quisling.

collàna, *s.f.* **1.** necklace **2.** *fig.* (*raccolta*) collection: — *di romanzi*, series of novels; — *di sonetti*, collection of sonnets.

collàre, *s.m.* **1.** collar: — *per cane*, dog-collar **2.** (*di un ordine cavalleresco*) collar, neck-chain ‖ *Gran Collare*, Grand Master **3.** (*eccl.*) neck-band, (priest-) collar **4.** (*di animali, piante*) collar **5.** (*lotta*) collar.

collaríno, *s.m.* **1.** small collar **2.** (*eccl.*) neck-band, (priest-) collar **3.** (*arch.*) collarino, collar, astragal.

collàsso, *s.m.* collapse; break-down: — *cardiaco*, heart failure.

collàta, *s.f.* accolade.

collateràle, *ag.s.m.* collateral.

collateralménte, *av.* collaterally.

collatóre, *s.m.* (*eccl.*) patron.

collatríce, *s.f.* (*eccl.*) patroness.

collaudàre, *v.t.* to test, to try, to prove; (*approvare*) to approve: — *un fucile*, to prove a gun.

collaudatóre, *s.m.* tester; (*mec.*) inspector: — *di aeroplani*, test pilot; — *di automobili*, test driver; — *di calibri*, gauge inspector.

collàudo, *s.m.* (*mec. ind.*) test, trying, testing, approval (after test): — *all'acqua*, test by water; — *definitivo*, (*mec.*) final inspection; — *delle caldaie*, (*mec.*) boiler test; *ingegnere addetto ai collaudi*, test-engineer; *volo di* —, (*aer.*) test flight; *fare il* — *di ql.co.*, to put sthg. to the test (*o* through a test); *subire un* —, to undergo a test; *superare un* —, to stand a test.

collazionàre, *v.t.* to collate: — *i conti*, (*comm.*) to check (*o* to prove) accounts.

collazióne, *s.f.* **1.** collation **2.** (*eccl.*) collation, advowson **3.** (*dir.*) transfer of legacy.

còlle, *s.m.* **1.** hill: *la città dei sette colli*, the City of the Seven Hills **2.** (*valico*) mountain pass.

collèga, *s.c.* colleague.

collegaménto, *s.m.* connection: — *articolato*, (*mec.*) linkwork (*o* linkage); *collegamenti elettrici*, electrical connections; — *in serie*, (*elett.*) series connection; — *radiofonico*, radio link; — *telefonico*, telephonic connection; *insufficiente* — *delle truppe*, poor liaison between units; *ufficiale di* —, (*mil.*) liaison officer; *ufficio di* —, (*comm.*) liaison office; *siamo in* — *costante con lui*, we are in constant touch with him.

collegànte, *ag.* connecting, joining, linking.

collegànza, *s.f.* **1.** connection; union; (*alleanza*) league **2.** (*l'essere colleghi*) fellowship.

collegàre, *v.t.* to connect, to link, to unite, to join; (*un circuito*) to connect, to tap: *fatti strettamente collegati*, facts closely linked together; *linea ferroviaria che collega due città*, line that links up two towns; — *un fatto ad un altro*, to link up one matter with another ‖

collegàrsi, *v.r.* **1.** to link up, to unite, to join **2.** (*formare una lega*) to associate, to confederate, to join in a league, to form an alliance.

collegatàrio, *s.m.* (*dir.*) co-legatee.

collegàto, *ag.* **1.** connected: — *a stella*, (*elett.*) star connected **2.** (*associato*) allied, associated, united: *industrie collegate*, allied industries; *società collegata*, associated company ‖ *s.m.* associate, confederate.

collegatúra, *s.f.* **1.** junction, joint, bond, binding **2.** (*punto di collegamento*) connecting point.

collegiàle, *ag.* collegiate, collegial; college (*attributivo*) ‖ *s.c.* boarder ‖ *timido come un* —, as shy as a schoolboy.

collegialità, *s.f.* **1.** rights pertaining to a college (*pl.*) **2.** the members of a college (*pl.*).

collegialménte, *ar.* by decision of a college.

collegiàta, *s.f.* collegiate church.

collegiàto, *ag.* collegiate: *chiesa collegiata*, collegiate church.

collègio, *s.m.* **1.** (*unione di persone aventi le stesse mansioni*) college: *il* — *degli Auguri*, (*st. romana*) the college of Augurs; *il* — *degli avvocati*, the Bar; *il* — *dei Cardinali*, the College of Cardinals (*o* the Sacred College); — *degli ingegneri*, College of Engineers ‖ *il* — *di difesa*, (*dir.*) the advocates for the defence; *il* — *giudicante*, (*dir.*) the Bench **2.** (*scuola con convitto*) boarding-school: — *militare, navale*, military, naval college (*o* academy) **3.** (*circoscrizione elettorale*) constituency.

collènchima, *s.m.* (*bot.*) collenchyma.

còllera, *s.f.* anger; (*furia*) fury, rage; (*ira, sdegno*) wrath: *la* — *di Dio*, the wrath of God; *un accesso di* —, a fit of anger; *in un momento di* —, in a moment of anger; *andare, montare in collera*, to get angry; (*improvvisamente*) to fly into a rage (*o* temper *o* passion);

essere in —, to be angry; *far andare qlcu. in* —, to make s.o. angry (*o* to fill s.o. with anger).

collericaménte, *av.* angrily, cholerically.

collèrico, *ag.* irascible, hot-tempered, quick-tempered, choleric.

collètta, *s.f.* 1. collection (of money): *fare una* —, to raise (*o* to collect) money 2. (*preghiera della Messa*) collect 3. *caricare a* —, (*mar.*) to load a mixed cargo.

collettàme, *s.m.* (*trasporti*) parcels (*pl.*) (for various destinations).

collettàre, *v.t.* (*rar.*) to collect (money); to raise (money).

collettivaménte, *av.* collectively.

collettivísmo, *s.m.* collectivism.

collettivísta, *s.m.* collectivist.

collettività, *s.f.* collectivity, community.

collettívo, *ag.* 1. collective; joint (*attributivo*): *proprietà collettiva,* collective (*o* joint) ownership; *società in nome* —, (*comm.*) general partnership 2. (*gram.*) collective: *nome* —, collective noun ǁ *s.m.* (*gram.*) collective.

collettízio, *ag.* picked up here and there, picked up haphazardly: *truppe collettizie,* troops mustered at random.

collétto, *s.m.* 1. collar; (*di pizzo per signora*) collaret(te): — *alla marinara,* sailor collar; — *di pelliccia, di pizzo,* fur collar, lace collar; — *floscio,* soft collar; — *inamidato, duro,* starched (*o* stiff) collar; *bottone del* —, collar stud; *afferrare qlcu. per il* —, to seize s.o. by the collar 2. (*bot.*) collar, neck 3. (*anat.*) neck: *il* — *di un dente,* the neck of a tooth 4. (*di monte*) narrow mountain pass 5. (*casacca di cuoio portata sotto la corazza*) jerkin.

collettóre, *ag.* collecting ǁ *s.m.* 1. (*raccoglitore, collezionista*) collector 2. (*esattore*) collector 3. (*mec.*) manifold; (*di caldaia*) header, drum: — *a spirale,* volute (*o* scroll); — *d'ammissione,* induction manifold; — *di fognatura,* drain trunk line (*o* sewer trunk line); — *di scarico,* exhaust manifold 4. (*elett.*) commutator; (*di tram*) trolley; — *della dinamo,* commutator.

collettoría, *s.f.* collectorship: — *delle tasse,* tax-collector's office; — *postale,* subsidiary post-office.

collezionàre, *v.t.* to collect.

collezióne, *s.f.* collection: — *di francobolli,* stamp-collection; — *di medaglie,* collection of medals; *fare* — *di cartoline,* to collect postcards.

collezionísta, *s.c.* collector: — *di francobolli,* stamp-collector.

collídere, *v.t.* to bring into collision, to strike, to dash together ǁ **collídersi,** *v.r.* to collide, to come into collision.

colligiàno, *ag.* of the hills; hill (*attributivo*) ǁ *s.m.* inhabitant of the hills, hill-dweller.

collimàre, *v.i.* 1. (*avere lo stesso scopo*) to have a common aim; (*essere d'accordo*) to agree 2. (*coincidere*) to coincide; to tally (anche *fig.*): *la mia opinione non collima con la tua,* I don't agree with you; *la teoria non collima con i fatti,* the theory does not tally with the facts 3. (*astr.*) to collimate.

collimatóre, *s.m.* (*astr.*) collimator.

collimazióne, *s.f.* 1. coincidence 2. (*astr.*) collimation.

collína, *s.f.* hill: *pendio della* —, hillside; *sommità della* —, hilltop.

collinétta, *s.f.* hillock.

collinóso, *ag.* hilly.

collírio, *s.m.* (*farm.*) collyrium (*pl.* collyria, collyriums); eye-wash.

collisióne, *s.f.* 1. collision, impact: *entrare in* — *con ql.co.,* to collide with (*o* to run into) sthg.: *l'« Andrea Doria » entrò in collisione con la « Stockholm »,* the " Andrea Doria " fell foul of the " Stockholm " 2. *fig.* collision, conflict, clash: — *d'interessi,* clash of interests.

còllo[1], *s.m.* 1. neck: *allungare il* —, to crane one's neck; *essere immerso fino al* — *in ql.co.,* to be up to one's neck in sthg.; *gettare le braccia al* — *di qlcu.,* to fling one's arms round s.o.'s neck; *portare un bambino in* —, to carry (*o* to have) a child in one's arms; *portare il braccio al* —, to have one's arm in a sling; *rompersi l'osso del* —, to break one's neck; *fig.* to ruin oneself; *tirare il* — *a un pollo,* to wring a chicken's neck ǁ *a rotta di* —, headlong (*o* at breakneck speed): *le cose vanno a rotta di* —, things are going from bad to worse ǁ *tra capo e* —, unexpectedly ǁ *fare allungare il* — *a qlcu., fig.* to keep s.o. waiting a long time (for sthg.) ǁ *giuocarsi l'osso del* —, to bet all one's possessions ǁ *mettere il piede sul* — *a qlcu.,* to oppress (*o* to tyrannize over *o* to bully) s.o. 2. (*colletto*) collar 3. (*parte superiore e tondeggiante di qualcosa*) neck: — *del piede,* instep; — *di bottiglia,* neck of bottle 4. (*mar. mec.*) neck: — *di un'ancora,* trend; — *d'oca,* gooseneck: *albero a* — *d'oca,* crankshaft.

còllo[2], *s.m.* (*carico di mercanzia*) package, parcel.

collocaménto, *s.m.* 1. placing, placement: — *a riposo,* pensioning off (*o* superannuation) 2. (*impiego*) employment; appointment; situation: *agenzia di* —, employment bureau (*o* agency) 3. (*comm.*) disposal, sale: — *della produzione,* disposing of the output 4. (*il maritare una fanciulla*) marrying off (a girl).

collocàre, *v.t.* 1. to place, to set, to put: — *a riposo,* to pension off (*o* to superannuate); — *denaro,* (*comm.*) to invest money 2. (*trovare un impiego a*) to place, to employ: *la collocò presso una ditta importante,* he found her employment in an important firm 3. (*comm.*) to sell, to dispose of (sthg.): *incontriamo gravi difficoltà nel* — *i vostri articoli,* we meet great difficulties in selling (*o* placing *o* disposing of) your articles 4. (*maritare*) to marry off ǁ **collocàrsi,** *v.r.* 1. (*mettersi*) to take one's stand; to take one's seat 2. (*ottenere un impiego*) to get employment, to get a situation 3. (*maritarsi*) to get married.

collocazióne, *s.f.* 1. (*il collocare*) placing, placement 2. (*sistemazione*) arrangement 3. (*comm.*) sale, disposal, placing 4. (*disposizione dei libri nelle biblioteche*) press-mark; (*amer.*) call-number.

collocutóre, *s.m.,* **collocutríce,** *s.f.* colloquist; collocutor.

collòdio, *s.m.* (*chim.*) collodion.

colloidàle, *ag.* (*chim.*) colloidal.

collòide, *s.m.* (*chim.*) colloid.

colloquiàre, *v.i.* to colloquise.

collòquio, *s.m.* 1. conversation, talk; colloquy; (*intervista*) interview: — *intimo,* intimate talk; *essi sono a* — *dal Presidente,* they are having an interview with the President; *essere impegnati in un* —, to be engaged in conversation 2. (*parlatorio*) parlour.

collosità, *s.f.* stickiness; viscosity.

collóso, *ag.* sticky; gluey, viscous, glutinous: *brodo* —, gluey soup; *le mie mani sono tutte collose,* my hands are sticky all over.

collotipía, *s.f.* (*foto.*) collotype.

collotòrto, *s.m.* 1. (*bacchettone*) bigot, hypocrite 2. (*ornit.*) wryneck.

collòttola, *s.f.* nape, scruff: *lo afferrai per la* —, I seized him by the nape (*o* scruff) of the neck ǁ *far* —, (*ingrassare*) to get fat.

collúdere, *v.i.* (*dir.*) to collude.

collusióne, *s.f.* (*dir.*) collusion.

collusívo, *ag.* (*dir.*) collusive.

colluttàre, *v.i.* to scuffle, to grapple.

colluttazióne, *s.f.* scuffle, grapple: *venire a* —, to come to grips (*o* to grapple).

colluttòrio, *s.m.* (*farm.*) mouth-wash, collutory.

collúvie, *s.f.* 1. sewage, colluvies 2. *fig.* pack, gang, rabble, colluvies.

colmàre, *v.t.* 1. to fill up, to fill to the brim; *fig.* to fill, to load, to overwhelm: — *di gioia,* to fill with joy; — *il divario tra...,* to bridge the gap between...; — *qlcu. di onori,* to load s.o. with honours; — *un vuoto, una lacuna,* to fill a gap 2. (*agr.*) to reclaim.

colmàta, *s.f.* **1.** (*l'atto del colmare*) filling up **2.** (*bonifica*) reclamation by alluvion **3.** (*terreno colmato*) reclaimed land **4.** (*di strade*) fill.

colmatúra, *s.f.* **1.** filling up **2.** (*sommità*) top, summit.

colmeggiàre, *v.i.* to rise; (*di paesaggio*) to slope upwards.

colmígno, *s.m.* (*colmo del tetto*) roof, roof-top.

cólmo, *ag.* full, brimful, full to the brim (anche *fig.*); (*traboccante*) overflowing (with sthg.) ‖ *s.m.* **1.** top, summit, highest point (anche *fig.*); *fig.* height; climax, acme: *il — della fama,* the acme (o the summit) of fame; *il — della felicità,* the height of happiness; *il — dell'impudenza,* the highest point (o height) of insolence; *il — della stagione,* the height of the season; *essere al — dell'ira,* to be in a towering rage (o to be in a violent rage); *portare ql.co. al —,* to raise sthg. to the highest pitch (o to the climax) ‖ *per — di sfortuna,* as a crowning misfortune ‖ *questo è il —!,* that beats everything! (o that caps all!) **2.** (*arch.*) roof: *linea di —,* roof ridge **3.** (*della strada*) crown **4.** (*freddura*) humorous definition of the finest achievement of a craftsman or profession based on a play on words: *il — per un sarto è cucire col filo del discorso,* the finest achievement of a tailor is to sew with the thread of the argument.

cólo, *s.m.* **1.** (*crivello*) sieve, screen **2.** (*colatoio*) strainer; (*metal.*) sprue, gate.

colòbio, *s.m.* colobium (*pl.* colobia).

colocàsia, *s.f.* (*bot.*) taro.

Colofóne[1], *no.pr.f.* (*st. geog.*) Colophon.

colofóne[2], *s.m.* (*tip.*) colophon.

colofònia, *s.f.* colophony, Colophonian rosin.

colómba, *s.f.* **1.** (*ornit.*) dove **2.** *fig.* pure, innocent woman **3.** (*cuc.*) Italian Easter-cake in form of a dove.

colombàccio, *s.m.* (*ornit.*) woodpigeon.

colombàia, *s.f.* dove-cot; columbary ‖ *tirar sassi in —,* to harm oneself.

colombàrio, *s.m.* columbarium (*pl.* columbaria).

Colómbia, *no.pr.f.* (*geog.*) Columbia.

colombiàno, *ag. s.m.* Columbian.

colombière, *s.m.* (*mar.*) masthead.

Colombína[1], *no.pr.f.* Columbine.

colombína[2], *s.f.* **1.** (*ornit.*) small dove **2.** *fig.* pure, innocent girl.

colombíno, *ag.* of limestone.

colómbo[1], *s.m.* **1.** (*ornit.*) pigeon: *— viaggiatore,* carrier- pigeon (o homing-pigeon) **2.** *pl.* (*innamorati*) sweet-hearts.

Colómbo[2], *no.pr.* (*st.*) Columbus.

còlon, *s.m.* (*anat.*) colon: *— ascendente,* ascending colon; *— iliaco,* iliac colon; *— pelvico,* pelvic colon; *— sigmoideo,* sigmoid colon.

colònia[1], *s.f.* **1.** colony, settlement: *la — italiana di Parigi,* the Italian colony in Paris; *— penale,* convict colony; *fondare una —,* to found a colony: *gli antichi Greci fondarono molte colonie,* the ancient Greeks founded many colonies; *vivere nelle colonie,* to live in the colonies ‖ *Ministero delle Colonie,* Colonial Office. **2.** (*biol. zool.*) colony: *— animale,* animal colony; *— di foche,* seal rookery; *— di microbi,* colony of microbs **3.** (*opera assistenziale per bambini*) health resort: *— marina,* seaside health resort; *— montana,* mountain health resort.

colònia[2], *s.f.* (*dir.*) farm-lease.

Colònia[3], *no.pr.f.* (*geog.*) Cologne ‖ *acqua di —,* eau-de-Cologne.

coloniàle, *ag.* colonial.

coloniàli, *s.m.pl.* groceries.

colonialísta, *s.m.* expert in colonial questions.

colònico, *ag.* of the farm; farm (*attributivo*): *casa colonica,* farmhouse.

colonizzàre, *v.t.* to colonize.

colonizzatóre, *ag.* colonizing ‖ *s.m.,* **colonizzatríce,** *s.f.* colonizer.

colonizzazióne, *s.f.* colonization.

colónna, *s.f.* **1.** column, pillar: *una — della Chiesa, fig.* a pillar (o mainstay) of the Church; *colonne di un portico,* columns (o pillars) of a portico; *— dorica,* Doric column; *— miliare,* milestone; *— rostrata,* rostral column; *— spezzata,* cippus ‖ *— d'acqua,* fall of water ‖ *letto a colonne,* four-posted bed (o four-poster) ‖ *colonne d'Ercole,* (*geog. mit.*) pillars of Hercules ‖ *— Traiana,* Trajan's column **2.** (*anat.*) column: *— vertebrale,* spinal column (o spine o backbone) **3.** (*di testo*) column: *— del dare, dell'avere,* (*comm.*) credit, debit column; *— di giornale,* newspaper column; *numeri in —,* column of figures **4.** (*mec. chim. fis.*) column: *— dello sterzo,* (*aut.*) steering column; *— di distillazione,* (*ind. chim.*) stripping column; *— termica,* (*fis.*) thermal column **5.** *— sonora,* (*cine.*) soundtrack **6.** (*mil.*) column: *— d'assalto, d'attacco,* storming column; *— di soldati,* column of soldiers; *in — di marcia,* in route column (o in column of route) ‖ *quinta —,* (*pol.*) fifth column.

colonnàto, *s.m.* (*arch.*) colonnade.

colonnèlla, *s.f.* **1.** (*mil.*) regimental standard **2.** (*moglie del colonnello*) colonel's wife.

colonnèllo, *s.m.* (*mil.*) colonel: *tenente —,* lieutenant colonel.

colonnétta, *s.f.* **1.** little column; (*arch.*) cippus (*pl.* cippi) **2.** (*di ringhiera*) rail-post **3.** (*mec.*) stud, studbolt.

colonníno, *s.m.* **1.** (*tip.*) half stick **2.** (*di balaustrata*) baluster, banister; (*di ringhiera*) rail-post.

colòno, *s.m.* **1.** (*contadino*) farmer, husbandman (*pl.* husbandmen) **2.** (*abitante di colonia*) colonist, settler.

coloquínta, *s.f.* (*bot.*) colocynth.

coloràbile, *ag.* colourable.

coloraménto, *s.m.* colouring.

coloránte, *ag.* colouring ‖ *s.m.* colouring matter, dye, dyestuff.

coloràre, *v.t.* to colour; to tinge; to tint; (*dipingere*) to paint ‖ **coloràrsi,** *v.r.* **1.** to colour; to assume (a colour), to tinge **2.** (*arrossire*) (*per pudore, imbarazzo*) to blush; (*per collera, emozione, ubriachezza*) to flush **3.** (*di frutto*) to turn red, to ripen.

colorazióne, *s.f.* colouring.

colóre, *s.m.* **1.** colour (anche *fig.*): *— locale,* local colour; *— politico,* political party; *il — politico di un giornale,* the political colour of a newspaper; *— solido,* (*di stoffa*) fast colour; *biancheria di —,* coloured linen; *di — chiaro,* light-coloured; *persone di —,* coloured people (o people of colour); *senza —,* colourless ‖ *dipingere ql.co. a colori smaglianti, fig.* to paint sthg. in bright colours ‖ *diventare di tutti i colori, fig.* to blush in embarassment (o to show embarassment) ‖ *farne di tutti i colori, fig.* to act in a wild way (o to paint the town red) **2.** (*sostanza colorante*) colour; (*tintura*) dye; (*tinta*) hue: *colori ad acquarello,* watercolours; *colori a olio,* oil-paints; *una scatola di colori,* a paint-box; *qui occorrono tre mani di —,* here three coats of paint are necessary **3.** *pl.* (*colori nazionali*) colours: *salutare i colori* (*nazionali*), to salute the colours **4.** (*carnagione*) complexion, colour, colouring: *un viso dai colori accesi,* a high-coloured face ‖ *cambiar —,* to change colour **5.** (*aspetto*) look, appearance: *hai un brutto —,* you look ill **6.** (*carte*) suit: *una mano di carte dello stesso —,* a hand of cards all of the same suit.

coloríre, *v.t.* **1.** to colour, to paint **2.** *fig.* (*ravvivare*) to colour: *— un racconto,* to colour (o to lend colour to) a tale ‖ **colorírsi,** *v.r.* to colour (up).

coloríto, *ag.* **1.** (*carico di colore*) coloured, vivid **2.** (*di persona*) rosy, pink: *molto —,* ruddy (o high-coloured) ‖ *s.m.* **1.** colouring, colour **2.** (*carnagione*) complexion **3.** *fig.* vivacity, liveliness.

colóro, *pron. dimostrativo m.f.pl.* **1.** *sogg.* they; (*spreg.*) those people: *chi sono —?,* who are they (o those people)? **2.** *compl.* them; (*spreg.*) those people: *tienti lontano da —!,* keep away from them (o from those people)! **3.** *— che,* they (o those) who, they (o those) whom (*sogg.*); those (o them) who, those (o them) whom (*compl.*): *— che leggeranno questo libro lo* *troveranno interessante*, they (*o* those) who read this book will find it interesting; — *che disprezzi non lo meritano*, they (*o* those) whom you disdain don't deserve it; *ricorderò sempre* — *che sono stati buoni con me*, I shall always remember those (*o* the people) who were kind to me; *ti raccomanderò a* — *che ti ho presentato oggi*, I will recommend you to those (*o* to the people) to whom I introduced you to-day.

colossàle, *ag.* colossal, gigantic, huge, enormous; (*fam.*) tremendous.

Colossèo, *no.pr.m.* (*archeol.*) Coliseum, Colosseum.

colòsso, *s.m.* colossus (*pl.* colossi, colossuses) ǁ *il Colosso di Rodi*, the Colossus of Rhodes.

colòstro, *s.m.* (*biol.*) colostrum.

còlpa, *s.f.* **1.** fault: *di chi è la* —*?*, whose fault is it?; *è* — *tua*, it is your fault; *fu per* — *mia*, the fault was mine **2.** (*biasimo*) blame: *non date la* — *a me!*, do not lay the blame on me!; *prendersi la* — *di ql.co.*, to bear the blame of sthg. **3.** (*colpevolezza*) guilt, guiltiness: *confessò la sua* —, he confessed his own guilt; *la sua* — *era incerta*, his guilt was in doubt.

colpabilità, *s.f.* guilt, guiltiness, culpability, culpableness.

colpévole, *ag.* guilty, culpable: *negligenza* —, culpable negligence; *aveva un'aria* —, he looked guilty; *l'imputato fu dichiarato* — *di assassinio*, the defendant was proved (*o* found) guilty of murder; *dichiararsi* —, to plead guilty ǁ *s.m.* culprit, offender.

colpevolézza, *s.f.* guilt, guiltiness, culpability, culpableness.

colpevolménte, *av.* guiltily, culpably.

colpíre, *v.t.* to hit, to strike (*anche fig.*); (*con arma da fuoco*) to shoot: *ciò colpì la sua immaginazione*, that struck his imagination (*o fam.* that hit his fancy); *fu colpito da un sasso*, he was injured by a stone; *mi colpì alla testa*, he hit (*o* struck *o* knocked) me on the head; *essi lo colpirono duramente*, they dealt (*o* hit *o* struck) him heavy blows; *quella vista mi colpì*, that sight struck (*o* impressed) me; —*il bersaglio*, to hit the target (*o* the mark) ǁ —*il contribuente*, to hit (*o* to affect) the taxpayer ǁ —*nel segno*, (*indovinare*) to hit the mark (*o* to hit the nail on the head *o* to strike home); (*riuscire*) to hit the mark (*o* to succeed in sthg.).

còlpo, *s.m.* **1.** blow, stroke (*anche fig.*): —*apoplettico*, stroke of apoplexy: *avere un* —(*apoplettico*), to have a stroke of apoplexy; —*da maestro*, master-stroke; —*d'aria*, draught; —*d'ariete*, (*idraulica*) water hammer; —*di grazia*, finishing stroke (*o* death-blow *o* coup de grâce); —*di fortuna*, stroke of luck (*o* of fortune); —*di mano*, (*mil.*) coup de main (*o* sudden attack); —*di mare*, breaker; —*d'occhio*, coup d'oeil: *è un* — *d'occhio meraviglioso*, it is a marvellous view; —*di remi*, stroke; —*di scena*, coup de théâtre (*o* stage trick *o* sensation); —*di sole*, sun-stroke; —*di stato*, coup d'état; —*di timone*, change of course (*anche fig.*); —*di vento*, gust (*o* squall); *a* —, *di* —, suddenly (*o* unexpectedly); *a* —*d'occhio*, at a glance; *a* —*sicuro*, without any risk; *d'un solo* —, at a blow (*o* at a single blow); *senza* — *ferire*, without resistance; *ammazzò sette mosche d'un* —, he killed seven flies at one blow; *fu un bel* —, *un* —*fortunato*, it was a lucky hit; *la morte del mio amico fu un grave* — *per me*, my friend's death was a great (*o* heavy) blow to me; *dare, vibrare un* — *a qlcu.*, to deal (*o* to strike *o* to give) s.o. a blow; *far* —, to make a hit (*o* to make a sensation); *fare un bel* —, to have a success; *rendere* — *per* —, to return (*o* to give) blow for blow ǁ *dare un* — *al cerchio ed uno alla botte*, to run with the hare and hunt with the hounds ǁ *dare un* — *di spugna a ql.co.*, to pass the sponge over sthg. **2.** (*d'arma da fuoco*) shot: —*di cannone*, gun shot; —*di fucile*, rifle-shot; —*di rimbalzo*, ricocheting shot; —*in bianco*, blank shot (*o* blank round) **3.** (*tennis*): —*a volo*, volley; —*diretto*, forehand drive: —*rovescio*, backhand drive; —*schiacciato*,

smash; —*smorzato*, drop shot **4.** (*scherma*): —*di piatto*, flat stroke; —*di punta*, thrust; —*di taglio*, cut blow.

colposaménte, *av.* (*dir.*) unpremeditatedly.

colpóso, *ag.* (*dir.*) unpremeditated: *omicidio* —, manslaughter.

còlta, *s.f.* **1.** (*raccolto*) harvest, crop **2.** (*tempo del raccolto*) harvesting **3.** (*bottaccio*) mill-pond.

coltèlla, *s.f.* large kitchen-knife; (*del pane*) bread-knife; (*da macellaio*) chopper.

coltellàccio, *s.m.* **1.** large knife **2.** (*agr.*) (*avanvomero*) coulter **3.** (*mar.*) studding sail.

coltellàta, *s.f.* stab, knife-wound: *una* — *nella schiena*, a stab in the back (*anche fig.*).

coltellièra, *s.f.* knife-case, knife-box.

coltellinàio, *s.m.* cutler.

coltèllo, *s.m.* (*mec.*) cutter, blade: —*anatomico*, surgical knife (*o* bistoury); —*a serramanico*, jack- (*o* clasp-)knife; —*da caccia*, hunting-knife; —*da pane*, bread-knife; —*da pesce*, fish-knife; —*da tasca*, pocket knife; —*per finitura*, (*mec.*) finishing cutter; —*per trinciare*, carving-knife (*o* carver); *mi sono tagliato con un* —, I cut myself on a knife; *affilare un* —, to sharpen a knife; *metter mano al* —, to draw one's knife ǁ *guerra a* —, war to the knife (*o* to destruction) ǁ *mattoni a* —, brick-on-edge course ǁ *nebbia da tagliarsi col* —, pease-soup (*o* pea-soup) ǁ *avere il* — *alla gola*, *fig.* to have the knife to one's throat (*o* to be under an immediate threat); *mettere il* — *alla gola di qlcu.*, *fig.* to threaten s.o. ǁ *avere il* — *per il manico*, *fig.* to have the whip-hand.

coltivàbile, *ag.* cultivable, tillable, arable.

coltivabilità, *s.f.* suitability for tilling; suitability for cultivation.

coltivàre, *v.t.* **1.** to cultivate, to farm, to till: —*cereali*, to cultivate (*o* to grow *o* to raise) cereals **2.** *fig.* to cultivate: —*un'amicizia*, to cultivate a friendship; —*le belle arti*, to cultivate the fine arts; —*l'ingegno*, to improve one's mind ǁ —*una persona*, to seek a person's favour (*o* to curry favour with a person) ǁ —*la (propria) persona*, to be tidy (*o* well groomed).

coltivatóre, *s.m.* cultivator, tiller; (*contadino*) farmer: —*di tabacco, cotone*, tobacco, cotton grower; *piccoli coltivatori*, small farmers.

coltivazióne, *s.f.* cultivation; (*della terra*) tillage, tilling, farming: —*del tabacco, delle patate, ecc.*, tobacco, potato, etc. growing; *in questo paese ci sono molte coltivazioni*, in this country there are many fields under cultivation.

coltívo, *ag.* **1.** (*coltivabile*) cultivable, tillable, arable **2.** (*coltivato*) cultivated, under cultivation, tilled.

còlto[1], *ag.* **1.** (*raccolto*) gathered, picked **2.** (*preso*) caught, seized; (*sorpreso*) overtaken; —*dalla notte*, overtaken by night; —*sul fatto*, caught in the very act.

còlto[2], *ag.* **1.** (*coltivato*) cultivated **2.** (*istruito*) learned; well educated; cultured.

cóltre, *s.f.* **1.** (*coperta di lana*) blanket; (*copriletto*) coverlet **2.** (*drappo funebre*) pall.

cóltrice, *s.f.* (*rar.*) feather-mattress, soft mattress.

cóltro, *s.m.* (*agr.*) coulter.

coltróne, *s.m.* (*coperta imbottita*) quilt; counterpane.

coltúra, *s.f.* **1.** (*coltivazione*) cultivation, tillage, tilling **2.** (*allevamento*) rearing, breeding: —*di bachi da seta*, silkworm-breeding **3.** (*med.*) culture: —*di germi del colera*, culture of cholera germs **4.** (*cultura*) culture, learning, erudition.

colubrína, *s.f.* (*st. artigl.*) culverin.

colúbro, *s.m.* (*poet.*) coluber.

colúi, *pron. dimostrativo m.sing.* **1.** *sogg.* he; (*spreg.*) that man: *chi è* —*?*, who is he? (*o* that man?) **2.** *compl.* him; (*spreg.*) that man: *non ti sei ancora liberato da* —*?*, haven't you got rid of him (*o* of that man) yet? **3.** —*che*, he who, he whom (*sogg.*); him who, him whom (*compl.*): —*che la amava tanto è morto*, he who loved her so much is dead; —*che incontrammo ieri è un mio vecchio* *compagno di scuola*, he whom we met yesterday is an old school-fellow of mine; *daranno il premio a — che arriverà primo*, they will give the prize to him who comes first; *Giulio Cesare fu ucciso da — che amava come un figlio*, Julius Caesar was killed by him whom he loved like a son.

columèlla, *s.f.* (*bot. zool.*) columella (*pl.* columellae).

colúro, *s.m.* (*astr.*) colure.

còlza, *s.f.* (*bot.*) colza: *olio di —*, colza oil; *semi di —*, colza-seeds

còma, *s.f.* (*med.*) coma.

Comànci, *s.m.pl.* Comanches.

comandaménto, *s.m.* **1.** command, precept **2.** (*relig.*) commandment: *i dieci Comandamenti*, the Ten Commandments.

comandànte, *s.m.* (*mil.*) commander, commanding officer; (*di piazzaforte, arsenale, ecc.*) commandant: *— del porto*, (*mar.*) harbour-master; *— di battaglione*, major; *— di squadriglia*, (*aer.*) squadron-leader; *— in capo*, commander-in-chief; *— in seconda*, second-in -command; (*mar.*) executive officer.

comandàre, *v.t.* **1.** to order, to command: *gli comandai di venire*, I ordered him to come (o I bid him come); (*— l'ubbidienza, il rispetto della legge*, to order (o to command o to insist upon) obedience to the law || *le lacrime non si comandano*, one cannot shed tears at will || *— qlcu. a bacchetta*, to rule s.o. with an iron hand **2.** (*essere al comando di*) to command, to be in command of (sthg.): *— l'esercito, una nave, un reggimento*, to command the army, a ship, a regiment **3.** (*mec.*) to control, to operate; (*muovere*) to drive: *— a distanza*, to remote-control; *— a mezzo di relè*, (*elett.*) to relay || *v.i.* **1.** (*manifestare la propria volontà*) to command, to order, to bid: *come Dio comanda*, as God commands (o orders o bids) || *comandi pure!*, what can I do for you? (o if you please!) || *chi non sa obbedire non sa —*, *prov.* through obedience learn to command **2.** (*di legge*) to prescribe: *la legge comanda di...*, the law prescribes that....

comandàta, *s.f.* (*mil. mar.*) fatigue party.

comandàto, **1.** *ag.* commanded, ordered || *feste comandate*, (*eccl.*) holidays of obligation **2.** (*mec.*) controlled, operated; (*mosso*) driven: *— a distanza*, remote-controlled; *— a distanza a mezzo radio*, radio-controlled; *— a mano*, hand driven; *— a motore*, motor driven; *— meccanicamente*, machine driven (o power operated o mechanically actuated).

comàndo, *s.m.* **1.** (*ordine*) order, command: *avere una cosa, una persona al proprio —*, to have sthg., s.o. at one's disposal; *dare un —*, to give an order (o a command) || *ai vostri comandi!*, at your service! **2.** (*autorità*) command: *ha mille uomini al suo —*, he has a thousand men under his command; *accettare il —*, to accept (o to assume) command; *assumere il —*, to take command; *essere al — di un battaglione*, to be in command of a battalion; *rifiutare il —*, to refuse the command (o to refuse to take command) || *avere la bacchetta del —*, to have full authority **3.** (*sede di comandante*) headquarters (*pl.*): *— di corpo d'armata*, corps headquarters; *— generale*, general headquarters (*abbr. G. H. Q.*) **4.** (*mec. elett. rad.*) control; (*leva*) lever control, drive, driving gear: *— a distanza*, (*elett. rad.*) remote control (o remote drive); *— a mano*, (*mec.*) hand drive; *— a pulsante*, (*elett.*) push button control; *— ausiliario*, (*aer.*) servo control; *— automatico*, (*mec.*) automatic control; *— a volante*, (*aer.*) wheel control; *— centralizzato*, (*mec.*) central control system; *— del gas*, (*aut. aer.*) throttle control; *— della messa a fuoco*, (*ott.*) focusing control; *— diretto*, direct control; *comandi di volo*, (*aer.*) flying controls; *— indiretto*, (*elett.*) indirect control; *— meccanico*, drive; *comandi sul volante*, (*aut.*) controls on steering wheel; *doppio —*, (*aer.*) dual-control; *leva di —*, gear lever; (*aer.*) control stick; *superficie di —*, (*aer.*) control surface; *unità di —*, (*di macchina calcolatrice*) control unit.

comàre, *s.f.* **1.** (*madrina*) godmother **2.** (*fam.*) gossip || *« Le allegre comari di Windsor »*, (*lett.*) "The Merry Wives of Windsor" **3.** (*levatrice*) midwife.

comatóso, *ag.* comatose.

combaciaménto, *s.m.* **1.** tallying, fitting together **2.** (*giuntura*) joint; point of contact.

combaciàre, *v.i.* to tally, to fit together.

combattènte, *s.m.* **1.** combatant, fighting man; fighter **2.** (*soldato*) soldier, service man; (*ex combattente*) ex-service man; (*amer.*) veteran **3.** (*ornit.*) ruff.

combattentístico, *ag.* soldier-(like) (*attributivo*).

combàttere, *v.i.* **1.** to fight, to combat, to battle, to contend: *— a fianco di qlcu.*, to fight with s.o. (o on s.o.'s side); *— ad armi pari*, to fight on equal ground; *— contro qlcu.*, to fight against (o with) s.o.; *— corpo a corpo*, to fight hand-to-hand; *morire combattendo per la patria*, to die fighting for one's country **2.** *fig.* to fight, to contend, to struggle: *— contro le difficoltà*, to contend with difficulties || *v.t.* to fight, to oppose, to withstand (anche *fig.*): *combattè sempre il comunismo*, he always opposed Communism; *— una battaglia*, to fight a battle; *— un'eresia*, to fight against a heresy; *— una malattia*, to fight a disease.

combattiménto, *s.m.* **1.** combat, fight, fighting; battle, action: *morì in —*, he fell (o was killed) in action (o in battle); *vi fu un lungo — contro i Confederati per il possesso della bandiera*, there was a long fight over the flag against the Confederates; *addestrare truppe al —*, to drill troops for combat **2.** *fig.* strife, conflict **3.** (*boxe*) match: *fu messo fuori —*, he was knocked out.

combattitóre, *s.m.* fighter.

combattività, *s.f.* pugnacity, combativeness.

combattìvo, *ag.* pugnacious, combative, fighting.

combelligeràntе, *ag.s.m.* co-belligerent.

combelligerànza, *s.f.* co-belligerency.

combinàbile, *ag.* combinative, combinable.

combinabilità, *s.f.* combinableness.

combinàre, *v.t.* **1.** to combine; (*colori*) to match: *vorrei poter sempre — lavoro e piacere*, I wish I could always combine work with pleasure **2.** (*concludere*) to conclude, to settle, to fix up; to arrange: *— un affare*, to conclude a bargain; *— un matrimonio*, to arrange (o to bring about) a marriage **3.** (*progettare*) to plan: *— un viaggio in Spagna*, to plan a trip to Spain **4.** (*fare*) to do: *cosa stai combinando?*, (*fam.*) what are you up to? **5.** (*chim.*) to combine || *v.i.* (*andare d'accordo*) to agree; (*di colori*) to match: *le sue idee non combinano con le mie*, his ideas do not agree with mine || **combinàrsi**, *v.r.* **1.** (*accordarsi, corrispondere*) to agree, to fall in; (*di colori*) to match || *mi sono combinato male*, I have been unlucky **2.** (*capitare*) to happen: *si combinò che io uscivo mentre egli entrava*, I just happened to be going out while he was coming in.

combinatóre, *ag.* combinative, combinatory || *s.m.* **1.** combiner **2.** (*elett.*) controller.

combinatòrio, *ag.* combinatorial: *calcolo —*, (*mat.*) combinatorial analysis.

combinatríce, *s.f.* combiner.

combinazióne, *s.f.* **1.** combination (anche *chim.*) **2.** (*sistemazione*) arrangement **3.** (*coincidenza*) coincidence: *fu una bella —*, it was a lucky coincidence **4.** (*caso*) chance: *lo vidi per —*, I saw him by chance **5.** (*di cassaforte*) combination **6.** (*biancheria*) combinations (*pl.*); (*tuta*) suit: *— di volo*, flight suit; *— spaziale*, space suit.

combrìccola, *s.f.* **1.** (*conventicola, cricca*) band, gang, clique, set; cabal: *una — di malviventi*, a gang of rogues **2.** (*comitiva*) party.

comburèntе, *ag.* burning || *s.m.* supporter of combustion.

combustíbile, *ag.* combustible || *s.m.* fuel, combustible (material): *— a basso potere calorifico*, low-grade fuel; *— ad alto potere calorifico*, high-grade fuel; *— nucleare*, (*fis. atomica*) nuclear fuel; *usato come —*, used for fuel; *rifornire di —*, to fuel (o to refuel).

combustibilità, *s.f.* combustibility.

combustióne, *s.f.* combustion; (*il bruciare*) burning: — *completa*, perfect combustion; — *incompleta*, incomplete combustion; — *lenta*, slow combustion; — *rapida*, brisk (*o* lively) combustion || *arresto della —*, (*mec.*) flameout; *camera di —*, (*di caldaia*) firebox; (*di motore*) combustion chamber; *cattiva —*, uneven combustion; *gas della —*, fuel gas; *residui della —*, combustion residual products; *ritardo di —*, (*mec.*) combustion lag.

combústo, *ag.* burnt.

combútta, *s.f.* **1.** rabble || *in —*, all together (*o* hand in glove) **2.** (*congiura*) plot, conspiracy; villainous agreement.

cóme, *av.* **1.** (*simile a*) like: *indossava un abito — questo*, she wore a dress like this one; *sei proprio — me!*, you are just like me! **2.** (*a somiglianza di, al modo di*) like: *calza — un guanto*, it fits like a glove; *correva — un matto*, he ran like mad **3.** (*quale*) such as; like: *dove trovare frutta — questa?*, where can you find fruit such as (*o* like) this?; *scrittori difficili — Hardy e Meredith sono ora finalmente apprezzati*, difficult writers such as (*o* like) Hardy and Meredith are now appreciated at last **4.** (*in qualità di*) as: *devo consultarti — avvocato, non — amico*, I have to consult you as a lawyer, not as a friend || *oggi — oggi*, to-day being what it is || *voi — voi*, you for your part **5.** (*modale*) as: *fate — fàccio io*, do as I do; *fate — volete*, do as you like **6.** (*nei comparativi di uguaglianza*) **as...** as (*in proposizioni affermative e interrogative*); **so... as** (*in proposizioni negative*): *Maria è alta — Lucia*, Mary is as tall as Lucy; *Maria non è alta — Lucia*, Mary is not so tall as Lucy || — *da campione*, (*comm.*) as per sample; — *d'accordo*, (*comm.*) as agreed (*o as* per arrangement); — *da copia acclusa*, (*comm.*) as from enclosed copy; — *da vostro desiderio*, (*comm.*) according to your request (*o* in accordance with your wishes) || — *segue*, as follows || — *tutti sanno*, as everybody knows **7.** (*in correlazione*) **as well as**: *così gli uomini — le donne*, the men as well as the women; *tanto di giorno — di notte*, by day as well as by night **8.** (*con valore esclamativo in unione ad aggettivi*) **how**: — *è bella questa vallata!*, how beautiful this valley is!; — *sei pallido!*, how pale you are! **9.** (*con valore enfatico*): — *!, non verrai?*, what! aren't you coming? || — *è vero che sono vivo...*, as I live... || *com'è vero Iddio!*, as God is my witness! || — *fare?*, what's to be done? || — *mai dici questo?*, why (on earth) do you say that? || *lo odio — mai*, I hate him like anything || « *Ti piace la marmellata?* », « *E — !* », "Do you like jam?", "And how! (*o fam.* Not half!)" **10.** (*interrogativo*) **how**: — *stai?*, how are you?; *non so capire — sia riuscito a farlo*, I can't understand how he managed to do it || *cong.* **1.** (*temporale*) **as, as soon as; just as; no sooner... than**: — *mi vide, mi riconobbe*, as soon as he saw me, he recognized me (*o* no sooner had he seen me than he recognized me); — *venne, dominò la situazione*, as soon as he came, he had the situation in hand || — *Dio volle*, in God's good time **2.** (*dichiarativa*) **that**: *tutti sanno — questi fossero i popoli più civili d'Europa*, everybody knows that these were the most civilized peoples in Europe **3.** — *se*, **as if; as though**: — *se fosse facile!*, as though it were easy!; *mi guarda — se fossi un pazzo*, he looks at me as though I were a madman || *s.m.*: *il —*, the way (*o* the means); *il — e il perchè*, the whys and wherefores.

comeché, *cong.* **1.** (*benché*) **though, although**: *fu bocciato agli esami — fosse studioso*, he failed (at) his exams, although he was studious **2.** (*appena che*) **as soon as**: — *lo vidi me ne andai*, as soon as I saw him I went away || *av.* **however.**

comechessía, *cong. av.* anyhow, anyway.

coménto, *V.* **comménto.**

cometa, *s.f.* **1.** (*astr.*) comet **2.** (*aquilone*) kite.

comiàto, *V.* **commiàto.**

comicaménte, *av.* comically.

comicità, *s.f.* comicality.

còmico, *ag.* **1.** (*che fa ridere*) comical; funny; laughable; amusing: *una persona comica*, a funny person **2.** (*di commedia*) comic: *opera comica*, (*mus.*) comic opera || *vis comica*, "vis comica" (*o* comic power) || *s.m.* **1.** (*comicità*) funniness; comicality **2.** (*commediante*) player, comedy actor || *comici vaganti*, strolling players **3.** (*attore comico*) comedian, comic.

comígnolo, *s.m.* **1.** chimney-top **2.** (*sommità del tetto*) roof-top.

cominciaménto, *s.m.* commencement, beginning.

cominciàre, *v.t.* to begin; to start; to commence: *cominciò un lavoro interessante*, he began an interesting work; *cominciò il viaggio da Genova*, he started his trip from Genoa || *v.i.* to begin; to start; to commence: *cominciò a piovere*, it began raining (*o* to rain); *cominciò col dire*, he began by saying; *oggi cominceremo da pagina 60*, to-day we'll begin at page 60; *a — da oggi*, from this day (on); *per —*, to begin (*o* to start) || *chi ben comincia, è a metà dell'opera*, *prov.* well begun is half done.

comíno, *s.m.* (*bot.*) cumin.

comitàgi, *s.m.* (*st.*) comitadji.

comitàle, *ag.* of a count; (*di conte inglese*) of an earl: *corona —*, earl's coronet.

comitàto, *s.m.* committee: *un — d'esaminatori*, a board of examiners; — *esecutivo*, executive committee; — *permanente*, standing committee; *membro del —*, committee-man; *riunione di —*, committee meeting; *far parte di un —*, to be on a committee.

comitíva, *s.f.* party; company; group.

còmito, *s.m.* (*mar.*) boatswain, bosun.

comiziànte, *ag.* attending a political meeting || *s.c.* person attending a political meeting.

comízio, *s.m.* (*popular*) meeting, assembly: — *agrario*, agriculturists' association; — *elettorale*, meeting of electors; — *politico*, political meeting; *indire un —*, to call a meeting; *tenere un —*, to hold a meeting || *i comizi*, (*st. romana*) the comitia.

còmma, *s.m.* **1.** (*capoverso*) paragraph **2.** (*inciso*) clause **3.** (*mus.*) comma.

commàndo, *s.m.* (*mar.*) spun yarn.

commèdia, *s.f.* **1.** (*teat.*) comedy; play: — *a soggetto, dell'arte*, improvised comedy; — *a tesi*, problem play; — *di carattere*, character comedy; — *di costume*, comedy of manners; — *d'intreccio*, comedy of intrigue; — *triviale*, low comedy || *la « Divina Commedia »*, (*lett.*) "The Divine Comedy" **2.** *fig.* sham, make-believe, pretence: *fare, recitare la —*, to play a part (*o* to sham) || *mettere in —*, to ridicule.

commediànte, *s.m.* **1.** player; comedian; (*comic*) actor, comedy actor **2.** *fig.* (*simulatore*) shammer; (*ipocrita*) hypocrite || *s.f.* **1.** player; comedienne; (*comic*) actress, comedy actress **2.** *fig.* (*simulatrice*) shammer; (*ipocrita*) hypocrite.

commediògrafo, *s.m.* playwright; comedy writer.

commediòla, *s.f.* **1.** short comedy **2.** (*commedia leggera*) light comedy.

commemoràbile, *ag.* commemorable.

commemoràre, *v.t.* to commemorate, to celebrate: — *una vittoria*, to commemorate (*o* to celebrate) a victory.

commemorativo, *ag.* commemorative, memorial: *cerimonia (religiosa) commemorativa*, memorial service; *lapide commemorativa*, memorial tablet; *monumento —*, memorial.

commemorazióne, *s.f.* commemoration.

commènda, *s.f.* **1.** (*eccl.*) commendam **2.** (*titolo italiano*) commenda.

commendàbile, *ag.* commendable.

commendàre, *v.t.* (*letter.*) to commend, to praise.

commendatàrio, *ag.* (*eccl.*) commendatory: *abate —*, commendatory abbot || *s.m.* (*eccl.*) commendator.

commendatízia, *s.f.* (*comm.*) letter of recommendation.

commendatízio, *ag.* of recommendation.

commendatóre, *s.m.* **1.** « commendatore » (commander of an Italian order of chivalry) **2.** (*di ordine cavalleresco in genere*) commander.

commendévole, *ag.* commendable, praiseworthy.

commendevolménte, *av.* commendably.

commensàle, *s.m.* **1.** table-companion; fellow-boarder; (*mil. mar.*) messmate **2.** (*ospite*) guest **3.** (*biol.*) commensal.

commensuràbile, *ag.* commensurable.

commensurabilità, *s.f.* commensurability.

commensuràre, *v.t.* (*rar.*) **1.** to measure **2.** (*paragonare*) to compare.

commentàre, *v.t.* **1.** to comment on, upon (sthg.); to annotate; to expound: — *la Bibbia,* to expound the Scriptures; — *un testo,* to comment upon (*o* to annotate) a text **2.** (*eventi, parole*) to comment on, upon (sthg.); to remark: « *Non è gentile da parte sua* », *egli commentò,* " This is not kind of her ", he remarked; — *un avvenimento,* to comment (up)on (*o* to make comments on) an event.

commentàrio, *s.m.* (*lett.*) commentary ‖ *i Commentari di Cesare,* Caesar's Commentaries.

commentatóre, *s.m.,* **commentatríce,** *s.f.* commentator; (*di testi*) annotator.

comménto, *s.m.* **1.** commentary: comment: *la* « *Divina Commedia* » *col* — *di...,* "The Divine Comedy" with notes by...; *l'insegnante fece un lungo* — *della poesia,* the teacher made long comments on the poem **2.** (*di eventi, parole*) comment, remark: — *sfavorevole,* unfavourable remark; *avete letto la mia relazione, avete commenti da fare?,* you have read my report, have you any comments on it?; *non fece commenti,* he made no comment; *la sua condotta provocò un'infinità di commenti,* her behaviour caused a great deal of comment.

commerciàbile, *ag.* negotiable, marketable, salable.

commerciabilità, *s.f.* negotiability, marketability, salability.

commerciàle, *ag.* ccmmercial; business (*attributivo*); trade (*attributivo*); trading (*attributivo*): *banca, scuola, valore* —, commercial bank, school, value; *casa* —, business house (*o* commercial house); *centro* —, trading centre; *scambi commerciali,* trade exchanges; *completare le proprie cognizioni commerciali,* to improve one's own knowledge of trade.

commercialísta, *s.m.* graduate in commerce; graduate in commercial law.

commercialménte, *av.* commercially.

commerciànte, *s.m.* trader; (*specialmente all'ingrosso*) merchant; (*uomo d'affari*) business-man (*pl.* business-men); (*negoziante*) tradesman (*pl.* tradesmen): — *all'ingrosso,* wholesale dealer; — *al minuto,* retailer; — *in carbone,* coal dealer; — *in ferro,* ironmonger; — *in granaglie,* corn dealer.

commerciàre, *v.i.* to trade, to deal: — *con qlcu.,* to deal (*o* to trade) with s.o.; — *in lana,* to trade (*o* to deal) in wool ‖ *v.t.* to deal in (sthg.): — *bestiame,* to deal in cattle.

commèrcio, *s.m.* **1.** commerce; trade; (*affari*) business: — *all'ingrosso,* wholesale trade; — *al minuto,* retail trade; — *bancario,* banking business; *il* — *delle carni,* the meat trade; — *di esportazione, di importazione,* export, import trade; — *estero,* foreign trade; — *libero,* free-trade; — *nazionale, interno,* home trade; *industria e* —, commerce and industry; *è nel* — *delle calzature,* he is in the boot trade; *essere fuori* —, (*non in vendita*) not to be for sale; (*esaurito*) to be out of sale; *essere in* —, (*essere in vendita*) to be on sale; (*essere un commerciante*) to be in business (*o* in trade); *mettere ql.co. in* —, to put sthg. on the market; *mettersi nel* —, to go into business ‖ *Camera di Commercio,* Chamber of Commerce ‖ *Codice di Commercio,* (*dir.*) Commercial Law ‖ *Ministero del Commercio,* Board of Trade (*o amer.* Department of Commerce) ‖ *fare* — *del*

proprio onore, fig. to sell one's honour **2.** (*relazione*) intercourse; dealings (*pl.*): — *epistolare,* correspondence.

commèssa, *s.f.* **1.** shop-girl, shop-assistant **2.** (*comm.*) (*ordinazione*) order: *le commesse americane,* American orders for goods.

commèsso, *ag.* **1.** (*fatto*) committed **2.** (*affidato*) committed; entrusted **3.** (*ordinato*) ordered **4.** (*unito*) joined together (with sthg.); (*mec.*) assembled **5.** (*incastrato*) fitted (in sthg.) ‖ *s.m.* **1.** (*amm.*) clerk: — *viaggiatore,* commercial traveller; *primo* —, head clerk **2.** (*fattorino*) errand-boy, messenger, message -boy **3.** (*di negozio*) salesman (*pl.* salesmen), shop -assistant, shopman (*pl.* shopmen) **4.** (*intarsio*) inlay.

commessúra, *V.* **commettitúra.**

commestíbile, *ag.* edible, eatable.

commestíbili, *s.m.pl.* foodstuffs, eatables, edibles, provisions: *negozio di* —, provision shop.

commestióne, *s.f.* (*rar.*) (*eccl.*) single meal (permitted on a fast-day).

comméttere, *v.t.* **1.** (*fare*) to commit, to do: — *un delitto,* to commit a crime; — *un'ingiustizia,* to do a wrong; — *uno sbaglio,* to make a mistake; — *suicidio,* to commit suicide **2.** (*ordinare*) to order, to commission: — *merci,* to order goods **3.** (*letter.*) (*affidare*) to entrust: — *ql.co. a qlcu.,* to entrust s.o. with sthg. **4.** (*eccl.*) to invest **5.** (*unire*) to join together; (*mec.*) to assemble **6.** (*corde*) to lay, to twist ‖ *v.i.* (*combaciare*) to fit together.

commettitúra, *s.f.* **1.** (*l'unire più parti*) joining together **2.** (*punto d'incastro*) juncture, joint **3.** (*di corde*) laying **4.** (*anat.*) commissure.

commiàto, *s.m.* **1.** (*preso*) leave; (*dato*) dismissal, discharge: *dar* —, to give permission (*o* to leave); (*licenziare*) to dismiss (*o* to discharge); *prendere* — *da qlcu.,* to take one's leave of s.o. **2.** (*poes.*) envoy; closing stanza.

commilitóne, *s.m.* fellow-soldier, comrade-in-arms.

comminàre, *v.t.* (*dir.*) to comminate.

comminatòria, *s.f.* (*dir.*) commination; caution (uttered by a judge); warning.

comminatòrio, *ag.* (*dir.*) comminatory.

comminazióne, *s.f.* (*rar. dir.*) commination.

comminúto, *ag.* comminuted: *frattura comminuta,* (*med.*) comminuted fracture.

commiseràbile, commiseràndo, *ag.* pitiable.

commiseràre, *v.t.* to pity, to feel pity for (s.o., sthg.), to commiserate.

commiserazióne, *s.f.* pity, commiseration.

commiserévole, *ag.* **1.** (*degno di commiserazione*) pitiable **2.** (*che sente commiserazione*) pitiful, compassionate, sympathetic.

commissariàto, *s.m.* **1.** (*carica di commissario*) commissaryship; (*ufficio del commissario*) commissary's office: — *di polizia,* police-station **2.** (*mil.*) commissariat.

commissàrio, *s.m.* commissary (anche *mil.*); (*sovietico*) commissar; (*spor. mar.*) steward; (*membro di una commissione*) member of a committee, commissioner: — *del popolo,* People's Commissar; — *di bordo,* purser (*o* accountant officer); (*chi distribuisce le paghe*) paymaster; — *di Pubblica Sicurezza, di Polizia,* Chief Constable (*o* Head of the Police *o amer.* Commissioner of Police); — *per gli alloggi,* housing officer.

commissionàre, *v.t.* (*comm.*) to order.

commissionàrio, *s.m.* commission agent, selling agent, commission merchant.

commissióne, *s.f.* **1.** errand: *fare una* —, to go on an errand; *fare delle commissioni,* to go shopping; *mandare qlcu. a fare una* —, to send s.o. on an errand **2.** (*comm.*) commission; (*ordinazione*) order: *fatto su* —, made to order; *passare una* — *a qlcu.,* to place an order with s.o.; *vendere, comprare in* —, to sell, to buy on commission **3.** (*comitato*) commission, committee, board: — *d'esame,* board of examiners; — *d'inchiesta,* committee of inquiry; — *interna,* (*di fabbrica*) factory commission (*o* shop committee); *membro della* — *interna,* shop deputy (*o* steward *o* chairman).

commistióne, *s.f.* (*rar.*) mixture.

commísto, *ag.* (*rar.*) mixed.

commisuràre, *v.t.* **1.** (*paragonare*) to compare, to liken **2.** (*proporzionare*) to proportion; (*adeguare*) to adjust, to adapt, to suit.

committènte, *s.m.* (*comm.*) purchaser, buyer, customer, consignor: *a rischio del* —, at buyer's risk.

Còmmodo, *no.pr.m.* (*st.*) Commodus.

commodòro, *s.m.* (*mar.*) commodore.

commòsso, *ag.* moved, touched, affected, stirred: *parole commosse,* deep-felt words; *profondamente* —, deeply affected.

commovènte, *ag.* moving, touching, affecting; (*che suscita pietà*) pitiful: *una scena* —, a touching scene.

commozióne, *s.f.* **1.** (*emozione*) emotion; (*agitazione*) excitement, agitation, commotion **2.** (*med.*) concussion: — *cerebrale,* concussion of the brain.

commuòvere, *v.t.* to move, to touch, to affect: *ciò mi commosse fino alle lacrime,* that moved me to tears; *non lasciarti* —, don't allow yourself to be upset ‖ **commuòversi,** *v.r.* to be moved, to be touched, to be affected: *ella è facile a* —, she is emotional (*o* easily moved); *si commuove per nulla,* the least thing upsets him (*o* puts him out); — *alla vista di ql.co.,* to be affected at the sight of sthg.

commutàbile, *ag.* commutable.

commutàre, *v.t.* **1.** to commute: — *la pena di morte in ergastolo,* to commute the death penalty to life imprisonment **2.** (*elett.*) to commute, to commutate, to change over, to switch over.

commutatìvo, *ag.* commutative.

commutatóre, *ag.* commutating ‖ *s.m.* **1.** commutator **2.** (*elett.*) commutator, switch: — *antenna-terra,* (*rad.*) lightning (*o* antenna) switch; — *elettrico,* current reverser; — *di inversione,* (*elett.*) rheotrope; — *d'onda,* (*rad.*) wave change (*o* band) switch; — *luci anabbaglianti,* (*aut.*) anti-dazzle (*o* anti-glare *o* dimmer) switch.

commutatríce, *s.f.* **1.** commutator **2.** (*elett.*) rotary converter, commutating machine, commutator rectifier.

commutazióne, *s.f.* **1.** (*dir.*) commutation: — *della pena,* commutation of penalty **2.** (*elett. tel.*) switching, change of connection, change-over, changing over commutation: — *d'onda,* (*rad.*) band switching; *campo di* —, commutating field; *polo di* —, commutating pole.

comò, *s.m.* chest of drawers.

comodaménte, *av.* **1.** comfortably; snugly, cosily **2.** (*facilmente*) easily.

comodatàrio, *s.m.* (*dir.*) commodatary, bailee in a commodatum.

comodàto, *s.m.* (*dir.*) commodate, commodatum (*pl.* commodata).

comodatóre, *s.m.,* **comodatríce,** *s.f.* (*dir.*) bailor in a commodatum.

comodíno, *s.m.* **1.** night table; bedside table ‖ *servire da* — *a qlcu.,* *fig.* to serve s.o.'s purpose **2.** (*teat.*) drop curtain.

comodità, *s.f.* **1.** convenience; (*agio*) comfort: *le più moderne,* the most up-to-date conveniences; *per maggior* —, for greater convenience; *vivere tra le* —, to live in comfort **2.** (*occasione*) opportunity ‖ *la* — *fa l'uomo ladro,* *prov.* opportunity makes the thief.

còmodo, *ag.* **1.** (*utile*) useful: *è molto* — *avere un amico,* it is very useful to have a friend **2.** (*conveniente, opportuno*) convenient: *quando vi torna* —, when it is convenient to you **3.** (*maneggevole*) handy: *il formato di questo libro è molto* —, the format of this book is very handy **4.** (*confortevole*) comfortable: *una casa comoda,* a comfortable house; *scarpe comode,* sensible shoes ‖ *luogo* —, water-closet **5.** (*a proprio agio*): *stia* —, (*non resti in piedi*) don't stand up; (*non si disturbi*) don't trouble yourself **6.** (*ampio*) large, commodious ‖ *s.m.* **1.** (*agio*) comfort; ease: *casa con tutti i comodi,* house with all comforts ‖ *con suo* —, at your ease ‖ *prendila con* —!, take it easy! ‖ *fare i propri comodi,* to do as one likes **2.** (*convenienza*) convenience: *con*

vostro —, at your convenience **3.** *cambiale di* —, (*comm.*) accomodation bill.

compaesàno, *ag.* of, coming from the same village ‖ *s.m.,* **compaesàna,** *s.f.* fellow-villager.

compaginàre, *v.t.* to compaginate, to join firmly together.

compàgine, *s.f.* **1.** (*connessione*) connection; contexture **2.** (*insieme delle parti*) compages (invariato al *pl.*).

compàgna, *s.f.* **1.** companion, mate: — *di giuochi,* playmate; — *di stanza,* room-mate; — *di viaggio,* travelling companion (*o* fellow-traveller) **2.** (*moglie*) wife.

compagnévole, *ag.* companionable; sociable.

compagnía, *s.f.* **1.** company, companionship: *dama di* —, (lady) companion; *essere in* — *di qlcu.,* to be in s.o.'s company; *far* — *a qlcu.,* to keep (*o* to bear) s.o. company; *godere della* — *di qlcu.,* to enjoy s.o.'s companionship; *sentire la mancanza della* — *di qlcu.,* to miss s.o.'s companionship **2.** (*gruppo di persone*) company, party, society: *eravamo una* — *numerosa,* we were a large gathering (*o* party); *tutta la* — *è arrivata,* the whole party has arrived; *frequentare una buona, cattiva* —, to keep good, bad (*o* low) company **3.** (*società*) company: — *delle ferrovie,* railway company; — *di assicurazione,* insurance company; — *di navigazione,* steamship company ‖ *Compagnia di Gesù,* Society of Jesus ‖ *Rossi e* —, (*generalmente Rossi & C.*); (*comm.*) Rossi and Company (*generalmente* Rossi & Co.) **4.** (*teat. mil.*) company: — *ambulante,* touring company; — *da sbarco,* (*mar.*) landing-party; — *di commedianti,* company of players **5.** (*combriccola, banda*) set, gang.

compàgno, *ag.* (*uguale*) alike, the same, very similar (*predicativi*): *questo libro è* — *a quell'altro,* this book is very similar to the other ‖ *s.m.* **1.** companion, mate, fellow, comrade: — *d'armi,* companion-in-arms (*o* fellow -soldier); — *di giuochi,* playmate; — *di lavoro,* fellow -worker; — *di scuola,* schoolfellow; — *di stanza,* room -mate (*o fam.* chum); — *di studi,* fellow-student; — *di tavola,* messmate; — *di ufficio,* colleague; — *di viaggio,* travelling companion (*o* fellow-traveller); *buon* —, jolly fellow (*o fam.* gay dog); *cattivo* —, ugly fellow (*o* customer) **2.** (*marito*) husband **3.** (*di un paio*) fellow, companion, other: *qui c'è solo il mio guanto destro, dov'è il* —?, here there is only my right glove, where is the other (*o* its fellow *o* its companion)? **4.** (*a un ballo, al giuoco*) partner **5.** (*membro del partito comunista o socialista*) comrade.

compagnóne, *s.m.* jolly fellow; good fellow; boon companion; (*fam.*) gay dog.

companàtico, *s.m.* something to eat with bread ‖ *pane e* —, bread and butter.

comparàbile, *ag.* comparable.

comparàre, *v.t.* (*letter.*) to compare, to liken.

comparativaménte, *av.* comparatively.

comparatìvo, *ag.* comparative: *avverbio di grado* —, (*gram.*) comparative adverb; *metodo* —, comparative method ‖ *s.m.* (*gram.*) comparative: « *migliore* » *è il* — *di* « *buono* », "better" is the comparative of "good".

comparàto, *ag.* comparative: *anatomia, letteratura comparata,* comparative anatomy, literature.

comparazióne, *s.f.* **1.** comparison: *a* —, in (*o* by) comparison; *a* — *di,* in comparison (*o* as compared) with **2.** (*ret.*) simile.

compàre, *s.m.* **1.** (*padrino*) godfather, (fellow) sponsor; (*testimone di matrimonio*) witness: *fare da* — *ad un bambino,* to stand godfather (*o* sponsor) to, a child **2.** (*compagno*) comrade, partner; (*amico intimo*) crony: *un buon* —, a jolly fellow ‖ *chi ha il lupo per* — *porti il can sotto il mantello,* *prov.* who has a wolf for his mate needs a dog for his man **3.** (*complice*) accomplice, confederate, decoy; stool-pigeon.

comparíre, *v.i.* **1.** to appear: *una nave comparve all'orizzonte,* a ship appeared on the horizon; *un sorriso comparve sulle sue labbra,* a smile came to her lips **2.** (*sembrare, apparire*) to show oneself, to appear: *lo fece per* — *generoso,* he did it to show himself (*o* to seem) generous ‖ *è geloso ma non lo fa* —, he is jealous but he does not show it **3.** (*far bella mostra*) to show off, to make a display: *a loro piace* —, they love to show off (*o* to do the grand) **4.** (*di libri*) to appear, to come out, to be published: *il libro è comparso ieri*, the book came out yesterday; *la terza edizione comparirà il mese prossimo*, the third edition will appear next month **5.** (*dir.*) to appear: *egli comparve dinanzi alla Corte*, he appeared before the Court; — *in giudizio*, to appear before a court (*o* to answer a summons).

compariscènte, *ag.* **1.** (*di bella presenza*) handsome, of fine appearance **2.** (*vistoso*) showy.

comparìta, *s.f.*: *fare* —, to make a good show.

comparizióne, *s.f.* **1.** appearance **2.** (*dir.*) appearance (in court): *mandato di* —, summons.

compàrsa, *s.f.* **1.** appearance: *la* — *di una nuova cometa*, the appearance of a new comet; *questa è la mia ultima* —, this is my last appearance **2.** (*figura, effetto*) show: *è un abito di* —, it is a showy dress **3.** (*dir.*) appearance: — *conclusionale*, brief; *mandato di* —, summons ‖ *s.c.* **1.** (*teat. cine.*) supernumerary; walker -on; (*sl.*) super: *duemila comparse*, two thousand supers; *ruolo di* —, walking-part (*o* walk-on): *fare un ruolo di* —, to walk on **2.** *fig.* dummy, mere tool; figure -head: *far da* —, to act as a dummy.

compartecipàre, *v.i.* to share (in sthg.): — *agli utili*, to share in the profits.

compartecipazióne, *s.f.* **1.** sharing, participation **2.** (*parte*) share.

compartécipe, *ag.* participating; associate.

compartiménto, *s.m.* **1.** compartment; partition, division **2.** (*ferr.*) compartment: — *di 1ª classe*, first -class compartment; — *per fumatori*, smoker **3.** (*circoscrizione*) department: *capitale di* —, capital of a department **4.** (*mar.*) compartment: — *di registro*, post of registry; — *per meccanismo di governo*, steering gear compartment; — *stagno*, watertight compartment.

compartìre, *v.t.* **1.** to divide out, to distribute, to apportion: — *i profitti con qlcu.*, to divide out profits with s.o.; — *una somma fra quattro persone*, to apportion (out) a sum among four people **2.** (*concedere*) to grant, to concede, to confer, to bestow: — *onori*, to grant honours.

compartizióne, *s.f.* distribution, division.

compassàre, *v.t.* **1.** to measure with compasses **2.** (*dire con precisione*) to say deliberately; (*fare con precisione*) to do deliberately: *compassa bene ogni suo gesto*, all his gestures are studied.

compassataménte, *av.* stiffly; solemnly.

compassàto, *ag.* **1.** stiff, formal: *i suoi modi sono compassati*, he has stiff (*o* formal) manners **2.** (*di discorso*) measured, restrained.

compassionàre, *v.t.* to pity, to compassionate, to commiserate.

compassióne, *s.f.* compassion, pity, commiseration, mercy: *per* —, out of pity; *senza* —, without mercy; *aver* — *di qlcu.*, to have pity on s.o.; *fare* —, to excite (*o* to arouse) pity: *mi fai* —, I pity you (anche *iron.*); *muover qlcu. a* —, to move s.o. to pity; *sentire* — *per qlcu.*, to feel sorry for s.o. (*o* to take pity on s.o.).

compassionévole, *ag.* **1.** (*che fa compassione*) pitiable, pitiful, piteous: *la trovai in uno stato* —, I found her in a pitiable state **2.** (*che ha compassione*) sympathetic, pitiful, compassionate, piteous: *persona* —, sympathetic person.

compassionevolménte, *av.* **1.** (*che fa compassione*) pitiably, pitifully, piteously **2.** (*che prova compassione*) sympathetically, compassionately, pitifully.

compàsso, *s.m.* compasses (*pl.*): — *a balaustro*, bow -compasses; — *a punte fisse*, dividers; — *a punte regolabili*, scribing compasses; — *a verga*, beam compass (*o* trammel); — *di via*, steering-compasses; — *per capote*, (*aut.*) top frame (*o* rule joint); *scatola di compassi*, set of drawing instruments ‖ *avere il* — *negli occhi*, to be a good judge of size (*o* distance) ‖ *fare*

ql.co. col —, *fig.* to do sthg. with the greatest possible exactness.

compatìbile, *ag.* **1.** (*conciliabile*) compatible, consistent: *azione* — *con la legge*, action consistent with the law; *il piacere è* — *col dovere*, pleasure is compatible with duty **2.** (*sopportabile, scusabile*) bearable, excusable: *i suoi difetti sono* —, his faults are bearable.

compatibilità, *s.f.* compatibility, consistency.

compatibilménte, *av.* compatibly, consistently.

compatiménto, *s.m.* **1.** pity, compassion: *è degno di* —, he is much to be pitied; *la guardò con aria di* —, he gave her a pitying look **2.** (*tolleranza*) indulgence; forbearance.

compatìre, *v.t.* **1.** (*compassionare*) to pity: *egli è molto da* —, he is greatly to be pitied; *ella è più da* — *che da biasimare*, she is more sinned against than sinning ‖ *farsi* —, (*far brutta figura*) to cut a bad figure (*o* to make a fool of oneself): *ti stai facendo* —, you are cutting a bad figure **2.** (*essere indulgente con*) to bear with (s.o.), to be indulgent to (s.o.); (*scusare*) to excuse: *compatitemi!*, bear with me! (*o* excuse me!) ‖

compatìrsi, *v.r. reciproco* to bear with each other (one another).

compatriòt(t)a, *s.m.* fellow-country man (*pl.* fellow countrymen); compatriot ‖ *s.f.* fellow-countrywoman (*pl.* fellow-countrywomen), compatriot.

compatròno, *s.m.* co-patron, joint patron.

compattézza, *s.f.* **1.** compactness, compactedness **2.** (*di associazione, partito, idee*) unity, solidarity.

compàtto, *ag.* **1.** compact, solid, close, dense: *metalli compatti*, dense metals; *stoffa a trama compatta*, cloth of close texture **2.** (*di folla*) thick, dense, compact **3.** (*di partito, associazione, ecc.*) united, solid: *presentare un fronte* —, to present a united front.

compendiàre, *v.t.* to abridge, to epitomize; (*riassumere*) to sum up, to summarize, to abstract.

compendiatóre, *s.m.* abridger.

compèndio, *s.m.* compendium (*pl.* compendiums, compendia), abridgement, epitome; (*riassunto*) summary, digest; abstract: *in* —, abridged; *ella era il* — *di tutte le virtù*, she was the abstract of all virtues.

compendiosaménte, *av.* compendiously; summarily; concisely.

compendiosità, *s.f.* compendiousness; conciseness.

compendióso, *ag.* compendious; summary; concise.

compenetràbile, *ag.* penetrable.

compenetrabilità, *s.f.* penetrability.

compenetràre, *v.t.* to penetrate, to pervade ‖ **compenetràrsi**, *v.r.* to interpenetrate.

compenetrazióne, *s.f.* penetration: — *reciproca*, interpenetration.

compensàbile, *ag.* **1.** that can be compensated; remunerable **2.** (*di perdita*) reparable.

compensaménto, *s.m.* compensation.

compensàre, *v.t.* **1.** to compensate, to counterbalance **2.** (*ricompensare*) to reward; to requite **3.** (*riparare*) to make amends for (sthg.); to indemnify **4.** (*supplire a*) to make up for (sthg.): *compensava la mancanza di vino con birra*, he made up for the want of wine with beer ‖ **compensàrsi**, *v.r. reciproco* to compensate each other (one another).

compensàto, *s.m.* (*legno*) ply-wood.

compensatóre, *ag.* compensating, compensative ‖ *s.m.* **1.** (*elett.*) compensator, phase advancer: — *a bilanciere*, balance beam meter **2.** (*mar.*) compensator: — *della bussola*, compass corrector **3.** (*rad.*) trimmer, trimming condenser: *di antenna*, aerial trimmer **4.** (*aer.*) tab.

compensazióne, *s.f.* **1.** compensation, making up **2.** (*rimunerazione*) indemnity; remuneration, reward **3.** (*dir.*) set-off **4.** (*comm.*) clearing: *stanza di* —, Clearing-House **5.** (*mar.*) compensation: — *della bussola*, compass compensation **6.** (*tec.*) adjustment: — *della temperatura*, temperature adjustment.

compènso, *s.m.* **1.** compensation, counterbalance;

making up **2.** (*rimunerazione*) reward, recompense, retribution: — *simbolico*, token payment; *un generoso* —, a handsome reward; *in* — *della sua ospitalità*, in return for his hospitality; *per* —, as a reward; *offrire un* — *per ql.co.*, to offer a reward for sthg **3.** (*indennità*) indemnity.

cómpera, *V.* **cómpra.**

comperàre, *V.* **comprare.**

competènte, *ag.* **1.** (*adeguato*) competent, adequate: *mancia* —, suitable reward **2.** (*esperto*) competent, qualified: *persona* —, qualified person; *è* — *in materia di finanza*, he is conversant with finance **3.** (*dir.*) competent: *le corti ecclesiastiche non sono competenti a trattare questo caso*, ecclesiastical courts are not competent to deal with this case ‖ *s.c.* expert; connoisseur.

competenteménte, *av.* competently.

competènza, *s.f.* **1.** (*capacità*) competence, competency: *ha una grande* — *su questo argomento*, he has a great competence in this subject **2.** (*pertinenza*) competence, jurisdiction, authority: *questo non è di sua* —, this is not within his province (*o* this is out of his province) ‖ *di* — *di*, pertaining to **3.** (*onorario*) fee, honorarium: *competenze d'avvocato*, lawyer's fees.

compètere, *v.i.* **1.** (*gareggiare*) to compete, to vie: *nessuno può* — *con lui in generosità*, no one can compete with him in generosity **2.** (*spettare, appartenere*) to be due (to s.o., sthg.), to belong (to s.o., sthg.): *gli fu dato ciò che gli competeva*, he was given what was due to him.

competitóre, *s.m.*, **competitríce,** *s.f.* competitor; rival.

competizióne, *s.f.* competition, contest.

compiacènte, *ag.* obliging, complaisant.

compiacenteménte, *av.* obligingly.

compiacènza, *s.f.* **1.** (*gentilezza*) kindness, obligingness: *abbiate la* — *di aiutarmi*, be so kind as to help me; *lo feci per* —, I did it out of kindness **2.** (*soddisfazione*) satisfaction: *avere* — *di ql.co.*, to be pleased with (*o* to rejoice at *o* to delight in) sthg.

compiacére, *v.t.* to please; to gratify: *farebbe qualsiasi cosa per compiacermi*, he would do anything to please me; — *qlco. nei suoi capricci*, to humour s.o.'s whims; — *qlcu. nei suoi desideri*, to comply with s.o.'s wishes ‖ **compiacérsi,** *v.r.* **1.** to be pleased (with s.o., sthg.); to take pleasure (in sthg.); to delight (in sthg.); to rejoice (at, in sthg.): *mi compiaccio con te della brillante carriera*, I congratulate you on your brilliant career **2.** (*degnarsi*) to deign, to condescend: *compiacetevi di ascoltarmi*, be so kind as to listen to me.

compiaciménto, *s.m.* **1.** (*soddisfazione*) satisfaction, pleasure: *le esprimiamo il nostro* —, we express our satisfaction to you **2.** (*congratulazione*) congratulation.

compiàngere, *v.t.* **1.** (*provare compassione per*) to pity, to sympathize with (s.o.): *compiango il suo dolore*, I sympathize him in his grief; *è da* —, he is to be pitied; *tutti compiansero la sua morte*, all lamented his death **2.** (*disprezzare*) to despise ‖ **compiàngersi,** *v.r.* to condole (upon sthg.).

compiànto, *ag.* lamented, regretted: *il* — *Dottor Adams*, the late lamented Dr. Adams ‖ *s. m.* (*rincrescimento*) regret; (*compassione*) pity, sympathy; (*lamento*) complaint.

compicciàre, *v.t.* to get through (sthg.): *non riesce a* — *nulla*, he never manages to get anything done.

compiegàre, *v.t.* (*rar.*) to enclose.

cómpiere, *V.* **compire.**

compièta, *s.f.* (*eccl.*) (*l'ultima delle ore canoniche*) complin(e); (*l'ultima preghiera della giornata*) last evening prayers, complin(e) ‖ *dall'alba a* —, all day long ‖ *essere a* —, *fig.* to be in the evening of one's life.

compilàre, *v.t.* to compile: — *un catalogo*, to compile a catalogue; — *un documento*, to draw up a document; — *una lista*, to make (out) a list; — *un modulo*, to fill in a form.

compilatóre, *s.m.*, **compilatríce,** *s.f.* compiler.

compilazióne, *s.f.* compilation; (*comm.*) drawing up,

writing up: — *di una tratta*, (*comm.*) make-up of a draft.

compiménto, *s.m.* **1.** (*il compire*) completion, accomplishment **2.** (*conclusione*) achievement, fulfilment, accomplishment; conclusion: *portare a* —, to complete; (*riuscire a*) to achieve ‖ *a* — *dell'opera*, into the bargain.

compíre, *v.t.* **1.** (*finire, completare*) to finish, to complete: *ha compiuto gli studi*, he has completed his studies ‖ *e ora, per* — *l'opera, mio figlio s'è rotto una gamba*, and now, on top of it all (*o* to crown all) my son has broken his leg **2.** (*eseguire, effettuare*) to accomplish, to achieve: *compirò tutti i tuoi desideri*, I shall fulfil (*o* gratify) all your wishes; *con il coraggio si può* — *qualsiasi cosa*, with courage one can achieve anything **3.** (*adempiere*) to fulfil, to do: — *il proprio dovere*, to fulfil (*o* to do) one's duty **4.** (*di età*): *Luisa ha compiuto venti anni*, Louise is now twenty (years old); *quando compirai gli anni?*, when will your (next) birthday be?.

compitaménte, *av.* politely.

compitàre, *v.t.* to spell (out).

compitézza, *s.f.* **1.** politeness; refinement; courtesy; refined manners (*pl.*); (*perfetta educazione*) good breeding **2.** (*atto gentile*) courtesy.

compito¹, *ag.* **1.** polite, courteous; (*raffinato*) refined; (*rifinito*) accomplished: *un maggiordomo* —, an accomplished butler **2.** (*terminato*) fulfilled, completed, accomplished.

cómpito², *s.m.* **1.** task; (*dovere*) duty, task: *il* — *è superiore alla sua capacità*, the task is beyond (*o* exceeding) his ability; *è* — *dei genitori...,* it is up to parents...; *è mio* —, it is my business (*o* duty); *non è nei miei compiti fare ciò*, it is not within my province to do that; *essere all'altezza di un* —, to be equal to a task; *prendersi un* —, to take a task upon oneself **2.** (*scolastico*) exercise, task: — *a casa*, homework (*o* task); *un* — *difficile*, a difficult task; *un* — *di latino*, a Latin exercise; — *in classe*, class-work (*o* class-test); *non ho ancora fatto i miei compiti*, I haven't done my homework yet.

compiutaménte, *av.* completely, entirely, fully.

compiúto, *ag.* complete, perfect, accomplished: *fatto* —, accomplished fact; *aveva ottant'anni compiuti quando morì*, he was over eighty (*o* more than eighty years old) when he died.

compleànno, *s.m.* birthday: *buon* —!, happy birthday!; *festeggiò il* — *con tutte le amiche*, she kept her birthday with all her friends.

complementàre, *ag.* complementary: *colori, angoli* —, complementary colours, angles; *imposta* —, supplementary tax; *materia* —, (*di studio universitario*) subsidiary subject.

compleménto, *s.m.* **1.** complement: — *di un angolo*, (*geom.*) complement of an angle; — *indiretto*, (*gram.*) indirect object; — *oggetto*, (*gram.*) direct object **2.** (*mil.*): *truppe di* —, reserve; *ufficiale di* —, reserve officer.

complessionàle, *ag.* constitutional.

complessióne, *s.f.* constitution: — *delicata, gracile*, delicate, weak constitution.

complessità, *s.f.* complexity.

complessivaménte, *av.* altogether; on the whole: — *abbiamo speso cinquanta lire*, altogether we spent fifty lire; — *è stata una bella gita*, on the whole it was a pleasant trip; *ammontare* — *a*, (*comm.*) to aggregate.

complessívo, *ag.* total, inclusive, comprehensive; (*comm.*) aggregate: *ammontare* —, aggregate (*o* total) amount; *indice* —, global index; *somma complessiva*, (*comm.*) lump sum.

complèsso, *ag.* **1.** complex, complicated: *questo romanzo ha un intreccio* —, this novel has a complicated plot; *la situazione politica era molto complessa*, the political situation was very complex **2.** (*mat.*) complex; compound: *numeri complessi*, compound numbers; *quantità complessa*, complex quantity 3. (*gram.*) complex: *proposizione complessa,* complex sentence 4. (*rar.*) (*robusto*) stout, sturdy, well built ‖ *s.m.* 1. complex; whole: *un — imponente,* an imposing whole; *bisogna considerare le cose nel loro —,* we must look on things as a whole ‖ *in — sono soddisfatto,* on the whole I am satisfied; *nel — la situazione non è così seria,* taken in its complex the situation is not so serious 2. (*ind.*) plant; unit; set: *— di strumenti di prova,* testing set; *un — produttivo,* a productive plant 3. (*mus.*) band: *Armstrong e il suo —,* Armstrong and his band 4. (*psicanalisi*) complex: *— d'inferiorità,* inferiority complex.

completaménte, *av.* completely, entirely, thoroughly, fully, wholly, quite.

completaménto, *s.m.* completion, finishing.

completàre, *v.t.* 1. to complete, to finish 2. (*un circuito elettrico*) to make.

completézza, *s.f.* completeness.

completívo, *ag.* (*rar.*) completive.

complèto, *ag.* 1. complete, whole, entire: *completa demoralizzazione,* utter demoralization; *completa rovina,* complete ruin; *atleta —,* all-round athlete; *un pasto —,* a full meal; *il latte è un alimento —,* milk is a complete food 2. (*pieno*) full (up): *carico —,* (*comm.*) full cargo; *lo scompartimento, l'albergo è al —,* the compartment, the hotel is full ‖ *s.m.* (*abito da uomo*) suit (of clothes); (*da donna*) costume, suit.

complicànza, *s.f.* complication.

complicàre, *v.t.* to complicate ‖ **complicàrsi,** *v.r.* 1. to become involved 2. (*di malattia*) to become worse 3. (*di intreccio*) to thicken.

complicàto, *ag.* complicate, complicated, entangled, complex; (*di stile*) involved, tangled, elaborate.

complicazióne, *s.f.* complication: *salvo complicazioni,* if no complications set in; *causare complicazioni,* to cause (*o* to bring about) complications; *per evitare ulteriori complicazioni,* to avoid further complications.

còmplice, *s.c.* accomplice, confederate, a party to, associate: *— non necessario,* (*dir.*) accessory; *deporre a carico dei propri complici,* (*dir.*) to proffer oneself as a witness against one's own accomplices; *essere — in una congiura,* to be a party to a plot; *essere — in un crimine,* to be a party to (*o* accessory to) a crime.

complicità, *s.f.* accomplicity, complicity.

complimentàre, *v.t.* to compliment, to pay a compliment to (s.o.): *qlcu. per ql.co.,* to compliment s.o. on sthg. ‖ **complimentàrsi,** *v.r.* to congratulate (s.o.): *— con qlcu. per ql.co.,* to congratulate s.o. on sthg.

compliménto, *s.m.* 1. compliment: *mi fecero molti complimenti,* they paid me many compliments ‖ *senza complimenti,* frankly (*o* freely *o* without ceremony) ‖ *far complimenti,* to stand on ceremony 2. *pl.* (*ossequi*) compliments, greetings, regards: *i miei complimenti a sua moglie, Signor Smith,* my kind regards to Mrs. Smith (*o* remember me to Mrs. Smith) 3. *pl.* (*congratulazioni*) congratulations: *complimenti!,* congratulations!; *gli fecero molti complimenti per...,* they congratulated him warmly (*o* they offered him their congratulations) on....

complimentosaménte, *av.* ceremoniously, formally.

complimentóso, *ag.* ceremonious, formal.

complottàre, *v.t.i.* to plot, to conspire, to machinate: *— contro qlcu.,* to plot against s.o.

complòtto, *s.m.* plot, conspiracy, machination.

complúvio, *s.m.* (*arch.*) compluvium (*pl.* compluvia).

componènte, *ag.* component, making up ‖ *s.m.* 1. member: *i componenti della famiglia, dell'equipaggio,* the members of the family, of the crew 2. (*chim. fis.*) component.

componiménto, *s.m.* 1. (*lett. mus.*) composition 2. (*tema scolastico*) essay; composition 3. (*conciliazione*) settlement; (*dir.*) arrangement, adjustment.

compórre, *v.t.* 1. to compose, to make up: *— una ghirlanda,* to make up a wreath; *— una poesia,* to write a poem; *— una sinfonia,* to compose a symphony ‖

— un numero, (*tel.*) to dial a number 2. (*farm. chim.*) to compound 3. (*assestare*) to arrange, to settle, to put in order 4. (*un cadavere*) to lay: *compose il corpo nella bara,* he laid the body in the coffin 5. (*conciliare*) to settle: *— una lite,* (*dir.*) to settle a law-suit 6. (*tip.*) to compose, to set ‖ **compórsi,** *v.r.* to consist, to be composed, to be made up: *l'acqua è composta di ossigeno e idrogeno,* water consists of oxygen and hydrogen.

comportàbile, *ag.* 1. tolerable, bearable, endurable 2. (*conveniente*) convenient.

comportabilménte, *av.* 1. tolerably 2. (*in conformità*) according: *— con le mie forze,* according to my strength.

comportaménto, *s.m.* behaviour; manners (*pl.*); deportment: *— economico,* economic behaviour; *il suo — non mi piace,* I do not like his manners.

comportàre, *v.t.* 1. (*sopportare*) to stand, to bear, to suffer, to tolerate, to put up with (sthg.), to endure; to resist: *questa pianta non comporta il freddo,* this plant does not resist cold; *— il dolore,* to bear (*o* to stand *o* to endure) pain; *— le ingiurie,* to put up with (*o* to tolerate *o* to endure) insults 2. (*consentire*) to allow: *i miei mezzi non comportano questa spesa,* my means do not allow me this expense 3. (*richiedere*) to involve, to require: *questo comportò uno sforzo enorme,* this involved a huge effort ‖ **comportàrsi,** *v.r.* to behave (oneself); to act: *comportati bene!,* behave properly! (*o* behave yourself!); *si comportò ignobilmente con gli amici,* he behaved ignobly to his friends; *si comportò scioccamente,* he behaved in a foolish way (*o* he acted very foolishly); *— da gentiluomo,* to behave (*o* to act) like a gentleman; *— male,* to behave badly (*o* to misbehave).

compòrto, *s.m.* 1. (*comm.*) respite, delay 2. (*ferr.*) admitted delay, maximum permitted delay.

compòsite, *s.f.pl.* (*bot.*) Compositae.

compòsito, *ag.* (*arch.*) composite, compound: *ordine —,* compound (*o* composite) order.

compositóio, *s.m.* (*tip.*) composing stick, setting stick.

compositóre, *s.m.* 1. (*mus.*) composer 2. (*tip.*) compositor, type-setter 3. (*tip.*) composing stick, setting stick.

compositríce, *s.f.* 1. (*mus.*) composer 2. (*tip.*) composing machine: *— meccanica,* linotype.

composizióne, *s.f.* 1. composition: *— chimica,* chemical composition; *la — dei gas,* the composition of gases; *la — di un quadro,* the composition of a picture; *una — poetica,* a poetical composition; *le regole della —,* (*mus.*) the rules of composition 2. (*conciliazione*) composition, agreement, settlement; compromise: *fece una — amichevole coi creditori,* he made a friendly composition with his creditors 3. (*tip.*) composing, setting; (*testo composto*) matter: *— a macchina,* mechanical composition; *— a mano,* hand composition; *— non più usabile,* dead matter; *— prima della stampa,* live matter 4. (*fis.*) composition: *— delle forze,* composition of forces.

compossèsso, *s.m.* (*dir.*) (*rar.*) joint ownership.

compossessóre, *s.m.* (*dir.*) joint owner.

compòsta, *s.f.* (*cuc.*) compote, stewed fruit.

compostaménte, *av.* composedly, sedately; decorously; calmly.

compòste, *s.f. pl.* (*bot.*) Compositae.

compostézza, *s.f.* 1. composure, sedateness; self-possession, calmness: *agire con la massima —,* to act with the utmost composure; *conservare la propria —,* to retain one's composure 2. (*dignità*) dignity, self-respect 3. (*modestia*) modesty 4. (*moderazione*) moderation: *— di linguaggio,* moderation of language.

compostièra, *s.f.* bowl for stewed fruit.

compòsto, *ag.* 1. compound: *nome —,* (*gram.*) compound noun; *numero —,* (*arit.*) compound number ‖ *interesse —,* (*comm.*) compound interest 2. (*ordinato*) tidy: *capelli composti,* tidy hair 3. (*calmo, dignitoso*) composed, calm, self-possessed; dignified; decent, seemly: *modi composti*, quiet (*o* sedate) behaviour (*o* composed manners); *stai —!, sit* still! (*o* behave yourself!) **4.** (*bot.*) composite, compound: *fiori compositi*, composite flowers ‖ *s.m.* **1.** (*miscela*) mixture, compound **2.** (*gram. chim.*) compound.

cómpra, *s.f.* **1.** purchase: *mostrò le sue compre alle amiche*, she showed her purchases to her friends; *fare una —*, to make a purchase; *fare compre*, to do some shopping **2.** (*comm.*) purchase: *— a credito*, purchase on (*o* upon) credit; *— a numero*, purchase by (the) number; *— a scadenza*, purchase on term; *— di seconda mano*, second-hand purchase; *— per conto di terzi*, purchase by order (*o* purchase for account of a third person); *contratto di —*, contract of purchase; *ordine di —*, buying order; *prezzo di —*, purchase money.

compràre, *v.t.* **1.** to buy, to purchase: *— a buon mercato*, to buy cheap; *— a commissione*, to buy on commission; *— a condizioni favorevoli*, to buy (*o* to purchase) on favourable terms; *— a credito*, to buy on credit; *— ad alto prezzo*, to buy (*o* to purchase) dear; *— all'incanto*, to buy (*o* to purchase) at an auction; *— all'ingrosso*, to buy (*o* to purchase) wholesale; *— in blocco*, to buy (*o* to purchase) in the lump; *— a rate*, to buy by instalments; *— per contanti*, to buy for cash (*o* to pay cash for); *— ql.co. da qlcu.*, to buy sthg. from (*o* of) s.o. ‖ *— a occhi chiusi*, (*fam.*) to buy a pig in a poke **2.** (*corrompere*) to bribe: *— il silenzio di qlcu.*, to bribe s.o. to silence; *— un testimonio*, to bribe a witness.

compratóre, *s.m.*, **compratrice,** *s.f.* buyer, purchaser; vendee: *affluenza di compratori*, run of buyers; *mancanza di compratori*, want of buyers.

compravéndita, *s.f.* marketing, buying and selling; purchase and sale.

comprèndere, *v.t.* **1.** (*includere, contenere*) to include, to comprise, to embrace, to take in, to comprehend: *la casa comprende un salotto e due camere da letto*, the house comprises one drawing-room and two bed-rooms; *classe che comprende un certo numero di specie*, class that comprehends a number of species; *questo importo comprende la vostra provvigione*, this amount includes your commission **2.** (*capire*) to understand; (*rendersi conto di*) to realize, to comprehend: *comprese il suo errore*, he realized his mistake; *non arrivo a — le tue parole*, I can't understand what you mean.

comprendiménto, *s.m.* comprehension, understanding.

comprendònio, *s.m.* (*fam.*) understanding; intellect ‖ *duro di —*, slow-witted.

comprensíbile, *ag.* intelligible, comprehensible, understandable.

comprensibilità, *s.f.* intelligibility, intelligibleness, comprehensibility.

comprensibilménte, *av.* intelligibly, comprehensibly.

comprensióne, *s.f.* **1.** comprehension, understanding **2.** (*compassione, simpatia*) sympathy.

comprensiva, *s.f.* comprehension, faculty of understanding.

comprensívo, *ag.* **1.** comprehensive, inclusive: *conto — di tutte le spese*, bill inclusive of all charges **2.** (*atto a capire*) comprehensive, comprehending **3.** (*che prova compassione, simpatia*) sympathetic, understanding: *si è sempre mostrata molto comprensiva*, she has always proved very understanding.

comprensòrio, *s.m.* district, territory: *— di bonifica*, reclamation district.

compréso, *ag.* **1.** (*incluso*) included; inclusive: *dal 1° gennaio al 15 —*, from January 1st to January 15th inclusive; *tutto —*, all included **2.** (*conscio*) aware, conscious: *— della sua superiorità*, conscious of his superiority **3.** (*colpito, preso*) stricken: *— di dolore, di meraviglia*, sorrow-striken, wonder-striken.

comprèssa, *s.f.* **1.** (*di garza*) compress **2.** (*pastiglia*) tablet, tabloid, troche, lozenge.

compressíbile, *ag.* compressible.

compressibilità, *s.f.* (*fis.*) compressibility.

compressióne, *s.f.* compression: *grado di —*, (*fis.*) compression ratio; *prova alla —*, (*fis.*) compression test.

compressívo, *ag.* compressive.

comprèsso, *ag.* compressed, pressed.

compressóre, *ag.* compressing ‖ *s.m.* **1.** (*mec.*) compressor; (*di motore a scoppio*) supercharger; (*ind. tessile*) condenser; *— d'aria*, air compressor; *— stradale*, road-roller; *turbo —*, (*ind.*) multistage centrifugal blower **2.** (*anat.*) compressor (muscle).

comprimària, *s.f.* (*teat.*) second leading actress.

comprimàrio, *s.m.* (*teat.*) second leading actor.

comprímere, *v.t.* **1.** to compress: *— una molla*, to compress a spring **2.** (*raffrenare*) to restrain, to repress, to suppress: *devi — la tua ira*, you must restrain your temper.

compromésso, *s.m.* compromise, arrangement: *giungere a un —*, to come to a compromise (*o* an arrangement); *mettere in —*, to risk (*o* to hazard); *sistemare mediante un —*, to settle by a compromise.

compromettènte, *ag.* compromising.

compromèttere, *v.t.* to compromise; to involve: *la tua posizione venne seriamente compromessa*, your position was seriously compromised; *— la propria reputazione*, to compromise one's good name ‖ **compromèttersi,** *v.r.* to compromise oneself.

compromissàrio, *s.m.* (*dir.*) arbitrator; referee.

comproprietà, *s.f.* joint ownership.

comproprietària, *s.f.*, **comproprietàrio,** *s.m.* joint owner.

comprovàbile, *ag.* provable.

comprovàre, *v.t.* to prove, to give evidence of (sthg.).

compulsàre, *v.t.* **1.** (*documenti, libri, ecc.*) to examine, to check, to compare, to inspect, to go through (sthg.) **2.** (*dir.*) to summon.

compulsióne, *s.f.* compulsion, constraint, coercion.

compulsívo, *ag.* (*dir.*) compulsive.

compulsòria, *s.f.* (*dir.*) tax-demand.

compúngere, *v.t.* **1.** to fill with compunction **2.** (*rar.*) (*pungere*) to sting ‖ **compúngersi,** *v.r.* to feel compunction.

compúnto, *ag.* filled with compunction; compunctious; remorseful; afflicted.

compunzióne, *s.f.* compunction; remorse.

computàbile, *ag.* computable.

computaménto, *s.m.* computation; calculation; reckoning.

computàre, *v.t.* to compute; to calculate; to reckon.

computazióne, *s.f.* computation; calculation; reckoning.

computísta, *s.m.* (*comm.*) book-keeper.

computistería, *s.f.* (*comm.*) book-keeping.

còmputo, *s.m.* **1.** computation, calculation, reckoning; account **2.** (*eccl.*) computation.

comunàle, *ag.* communal, municipal; city (*attributivo*); town (*attributivo*); parish (*attributivo*): *amministrazione —*, municipal administration; *consiglio —*, city-(*o* town- *o* parish-) council; *palazzo —*, city (*o* town-)hall; *scuola —*, parish-school.

comunànza, *s.f.* **1.** community: *— di beni*, (*dir.*) community of goods; *— d'interessi*, community of interests **2.** (*società*) community: *— religiosa*, religious community.

comunàrdo, *s.m.* (*st.*) Communard.

comúne[1]**,** *ag.* **1.** common: *il bene —*, the common good; *il diritto —*, common law; *genere —*, (*gram.*) common gender; *una lingua comune a molti popoli*, a language common to many peoples; *muro —*, common wall; *nome —*, (*gram.*) common noun; *l'opinione —*, common opinion; *per — accordo*, by mutual (*o* common) consent; *un vostro — amico*, a mutual friend of yours; *avere interessi comuni*, to have common interests; *far vita* —, to live together: *quest'estate facemmo quasi vita* —, we went about a lot together this summer (*o* we saw a lot of each other this summer) ‖ *in conto* —, (*comm.*) in joint account ‖ *in* —, in common ‖ *senso* —, common sense ‖ *mal* — *mezzo gaudio*, *prov.* trouble shared is trouble halved **2.** (*ordinario*) common, ordinary: *la gente* —, the common people; *ingegno non* —, uncommon genius; *parole comuni*, common words; *soldato* —, common soldier; *stile* —, common style; *vino* —, common wine; *l'uomo* — *desidera la pace*, the man in the street is anxious for peace ‖ *fuori del* —, unusual (*o* exceptional *o* uncommon) ‖ *luogo* —, commonplace **3.** (*abituale, frequente*) frequent, ordinary, usual, habitual: *gli incidenti aerei sono comuni*, air accidents are common (*o* frequent); *questo è l'uso* —, this is the usual practice.

comúne², *s.m.* **1.** (*amm.*) (*in Italia, Francia, Belgio*) commune; (*negli altri Stati*) municipality ‖ *Palazzo del* —, Town Hall **2.** (*autorità municipali*) municipality, town council: *il Comune ha deciso di far costruire una nuova scuola*, the Town Council decided to have a new school built **3.** (*st.*) free city: *al tempo dei Comuni*, at the time of the free cities **4.** *la Camera dei Comuni*, (*in Gran Bretagna*) the House of Commons.

Comúne³ (la), *s.f.* (*st.*) the Commune.

comunèlla, *s.f.* clique: *far* — *con qlcu.* to consort, (*o* to associate) with s.o.

comuneménte, *av.* **1.** (*generalmente*) commonly, usually, generally **2.** (*in comune*) in common, together.

comunicàbile, *ag.* communicable.

comunicabilità, *s.f.* **1.** communicability, communicableness **2.** (*affabilità*) communicativeness.

comunicànda, *s.f.* (*eccl.*) young communicant.

comunicàndo, *ag.* (*eccl.*) prepared for Holy Communion ‖ *s.m.* young communicant.

comunicànte, *ag.* communicating: *camere comunicanti*, communicating rooms; *vasi comunicanti*, (*fis.*) communicating vessels ‖ *s.m.* (*eccl.*) celebrant of Communion.

comunicàre, *v.t.* **1.** to communicate; to transmit: *chi le comunicò la triste notizia?*, who brought the sad news to her?; — *calore, movimento*, to communicate heat, motion; — *una malattia*, to infect with (*o* to transmit) a disease; — *una scoperta*, to communicate a discovery **2.** (*eccl.*) to communicate; to administer Holy Communion to (s.o.) ‖ *v.i.* to communicate, to be in communication: *non posso* — *regolarmente con lui*, I cannot communicate with him regularly; *la stanza comunica col giardino*, the room communicates with (*o* leads into) the garden ‖ **comunicàrsi**, *v.r.* **1.** to be communicated, to be transmitted: *il movimento si comunicò a tutta la macchina*, the motion was communicated (*o* transmitted) to the whole machine **2.** (*eccl.*) to receive Holy Communion ‖ *v.r. reciproco* to tell each other (one another), to communicate to each other (one another).

comunicatíva, *s.f.* communicativeness.

comunicatívo, *ag.* **1.** communicative; (*contagioso*) communicable; catching **2.** (*affabile, cordiale*) communicative; talkative.

comunicàto, *s.m.* bulletin, communiqué: — *di guerra*, war bulletin (*o* war communiqué).

comunicazióne, *s.f.* communication: *comunicazioni ferroviarie*, railway communications; — *interurbana*, (*tel.*) trunk-call (*o* long-distance call); — *telefonica*, telephone communication; (*collegamento*) telephone connection; — *verbale*, verbal communication (*o* message); *linee di* —, communication lines; *mezzi di* —, means of communication; *strada di grande* —, highway; *via di* —, line of communication; *mettetemi in* — *col signor Smith*, (*tel.*) put me through to Mr. Smith; *non c'è* — *fra le due camere*, there is no communication between the two rooms; *dare* — *di ql.co. a qlcu.*, to inform s.o. of sthg.; *essere in* — *con qlcu.*, to be in communication with s.o.; (*tel.*) to be through; *in-*

terrompere la —, to cut the communication off; *mettere in* — *due abbonati*, (*tel.*) to connect two subscribers; *mettere in* — *due persone*, to put two people in touch with each other ‖ *Ministero delle Comunicazioni*, Ministry of Transport.

comunióne, *s.f.* **1.** (*comunanza*) communion; sharing: — *di idee*, similarity of ideas **2.** (*unione spirituale*) communion: *le diverse comunioni cristiane*, the different Christian communions; *appartenere alla stessa* —, to belong to the same communion ‖ *la Comunione dei Santi*, the Communion of Saints **3.** (*eccl.*) Holy Communion; (*parte della Messa*) Communion service: *dare la* —, to administer Holy Communion; *fare, prender la* —, to go to (*o* to take) Holy Communion **4.** (*dir.*) community: — *di beni, di proprietà*, community of goods, of property.

comunísmo, *s.m.* (*st. pol.*) Communism.

comunísta, *s.c.* Communist.

comunità, *s.f.* **1.** community: — *domestica*, family; *la* — *ebraica*, the Jewish Community; *le* — *religiose*, the religious communities ‖ *la* —, (*la società*) the community ‖ *Comunità Europea del Carbone e dell'Acciaio* (*abbr.* C.E.C.A.), European Coal and Steel Community **2.** (*comune*) municipality.

comúnque, *av.* however, anyhow: — *puoi tentare*, anyhow you can try; *devo* — *andarmene domani*, anyhow I must be off tomorrow; *ho fatto* — *il mio dovere*, I did my duty at any rate ‖ *cong.* however, no matter how: — *tu ti sforzi, non riuscirai di certo*, however hard you may strive (*o* no matter how hard you strive), you will certainly not succeed.

con, *prep.* **1.** (*compagnia, unione*) with: *abita* — *i genitori*, he lives with his parents; *andammo* — *loro*, we went with them; *arrivò* — *un fagotto sotto il braccio*, he arrived with a bundle under his arm; *non sono d'accordo* — *te*, I do not agree with you; *essere in guerra* — *qlcu.*, to be at war with s.o.; *essere in pace* — *una nazione*, to be at peace with a nation; *litigare* — *qlcu.*, to quarrel with s.o.; *lottare* — *qlcu.*, to fight (*o* to struggle) with (*o* against) s.o.; *tenersi in contatto* — *qlcu.*, to keep in touch with s.o.; *venire a patti* — *qlcu.*, to come to terms with s.o. **2.** (*proprietà, caratteristica*) with: *un uomo* — *i capelli bianchi*, a man with white hair **3.** (*condizione, stato*) in: *col caldo si sta meglio*, in warm weather one feels better; *uscire* — *la pioggia*, to go out in the rain **4.** (*verso, nei confronti di*) to: *è gentile* — *tutti*, he is kind to everybody **5.** (*strumento*) with: *non riesco a scrivere* — *questa penna*, I cannot write with this pen; *non tagliare la carta* — *queste forbici*, do not cut paper with these scissors **6.** (*mezzo*) by; by means of; by dint of: — *questo mezzo*, by this means; *ciò si può fare* — *un apparecchio speciale*, this can be done by means of a special apparatus; *ottennero ciò che volevano* — *l'insistenza*, they got what they wanted by dint of insisting; *essere conosciuto col nome di*, to be known (*o* to go) by (*o* under) the name of; *rispondere* — *una lettera*, — *un telegramma*, to answer by letter, by telegram **7.** (*mezzi di trasporto*) by: *egli arrivò col treno delle 7*, he arrived by the seven o' clock train; *viaggia sempre* — *l'automobile*, he always travels by car **8.** (*con riferimento a concetto verbale*) by: *cominciamo col dirglielo*, let us begin by telling him; *guadagnarsi da vivere* — *l'insegnamento*, to get one's living by teaching **9.** (*materia*) from: — *l'uva si fa il vino*, wine is made from grapes **10.** (*con valore morale*) with: — *audacia*, — *rammarico*, with courage, with regret; *mi accolse* — *un sorriso amichevole*, he welcomed me with a friendly smile; *parla* — *un buon accento e* — *molta grazia*, he speaks with a good accent and with great charm; *rispose* — *tono irato*, he answered in an angry tone ‖ — *l'aiuto di Dio*, with God's help **11.** (*con valore temporale*) on: *col 1° d'aprile saranno dieci anni che abitiamo qui*, on April 1st we shall have been living here ten years; — *la tua venuta sistemeremo la faccenda*, on your arrival we shall settle the matter 12. (*con valore concessivo*) **with; in spite of:** — *tutti i suoi difetti, è simpatico*, with (o in spite of) all his faults, he is a good sort; — *tutto ciò, non mi sento di approvarlo*, with all that I feel I cannot approve of him; — *tutto il suo coraggio, non approdò a nulla*, in spite of his great courage he came to nothing 13. (*con valore consecutivo*) **to:** — *mia grande gioia*, to my delight; — *mio stupore*, to my amazement; — *sorpresa generale*, to everybody's surprise.

conàto, *s.m.* effort, attempt: *avere conati di vomito*, to feel sick.

cónca, *s.f.* 1. (*vaso, vasca*) basin, pot, vessel; tub: — *del bucato*, wash-tub; — *di terra cotta*, earthenware basin (o vessel) ‖ — *fessa*, *fig.* sickly person 2. (*bacino*) basin 3. (*cavità*) hollow, basin 4. (*valle*) valley; dell ‖ *la Conca d'oro*, (*geog.*) the Conca d'Oro 5. (*idraulica*) lock 6. (*anat.*) conch, concha 7. (*conchiglia*) shell, conch.

concàio, *s.m.* potter.

concàmbio, *s.m.* (*rar.*) exchange.

concàta, *s.f.* tub(ful).

concatenaménto, *s.m.* 1. concatenation 2. (*il concatenare*) linking together.

concatenàre, *v.t.* to concatenate; to link together: — *le idee*, to link ideas together.

concatenazióne, *s.f.* 1. concatenation; connection 2. (*il concatenare*) linking together 3. (*chim.*) linkage.

concàusa, *s.f.* (*dir.*) pre-existing cause; aggravation.

concausàle, *ag.* (*dir.*) aggravating ‖ *s.f.* (*dir.*) pre-existing cause; aggravation.

concavità, *s.f.* 1. (*l'essere concavo*) concavity 2. (*cavità*) concavity, hollow, cavity.

còncavo, *ag.* concave, hollow: — *convesso*, (*ott.*) concavo-convex ‖ *s.m.* concave, hollow: — *della mano*, the hollow of the hand.

concedènte, *s.c.* (*dir.*) grantor.

concèdere, *v.t.* 1. to grant, to concede, to award, to bestow: *la banca gli concesse un prestito*, the bank granted him a loan; *gli fu concessa una borsa di studio*, he was awarded a scholarship; *spero ci concederete un abbuono*, I hope you will make us an allowance; — *una dilazione di pagamento*, to grant an extension of payment; — *un favore a qlcu.*, to bestow a favour on s.o.; — *uno sconto*, to grant a discount 2. (*permettere*) to allow: *concedimi di parlare*, allow me to speak 3. (*ammettere*) to concede, to admit, to allow ‖ **concèdersi**, *v.r.* (*arrendersi*) to give in.

concedìbile, *ag.* allowable, grantable.

concènto, *s.m.* (*letter. poet.*) harmony.

concentraménto, *s.m.* concentration: — *di tiro*, (*artigl.*) convergence of fire; *campo di —*, concentration camp.

concentràre, *v.t.* 1. to concentrate: *il capitano concentrò le truppe a sud della città*, the captain concentrated the troops south of the town 2. *fig.* to concentrate; to centre; (*amer.*) to center: *concentrò le proprie speranze sul figlio*, he centred his hopes on his son; — *la propria attenzione su ql.co.*, to concentrate one's attention on sthg. 3. (*chim.*) to concentrate ‖ **concentràrsi**, *v.r.* 1. (*riunirsi*) to concentrate, to gather: *il nemico si concentrava presso il ponte*, the enemy concentrated (o gathered) near the bridge 2. *fig.* to concentrate: — *in un pensiero*, to concentrate on a thought.

concentràto, *ag.* 1. concentrated 2. (*riservato*) reserved, close: *uomo —*, reserved (o close) man 3. (*chim.*) concentrated; at high concentration (*predicativo*) ‖ *s.m.* extract, concentrated food.

concentrazióne, *s.f.* concentration: *capacità di —*, power of concentration.

concèntrico, *ag.* (*geom.*) concentric.

concepìbile, *ag.* conceivable.

concepiménto, *s.m.* conception, conceiving (anche *fig.*): — *di un'idea*, conception of an idea.

concepìre, *v.t.* 1. (*generare*) to conceive; to become

pregnant with (a child) 2. (*pensare, immaginare*) to conceive, to image; (*escogitare*) to conceive, to contrive, to devise: — *un piano di fuga*, to devise a plan of escape 3. *fig.* to entertain, to harbour: — *speranze, timori, sospetti*, to entertain hopes, fears, suspicions 4. (*comprendere*) to understand: *non riesco a — come ciò possa essere avvenuto*, I can't understand how that could have happened 5. (*formulare*) to express, to word, to draw up: *l'articolo è concepito nei seguenti termini...*, the article is expressed as follows....

conceria, *s.f.* tannery.

concèrnere, *v.t.* to concern, to relate to (s.o., sthg.), to regard: *ciò concerne i vostri interessi*, that concerns your interests; *informazioni concernenti un dato argomento*, information relating to a given subject; *per quanto concerne la mia industria...*, as regards my industry...; *per quanto mi concerne...*, speaking for myself....

concertàre, *v.t.* 1. (*mus.*) to harmonize; (*dirigere*) to conduct; (*provare*) to rehearse 2. (*stabilire*) to plan, to concert, to arrange: *abbiamo concertato di fare un viaggio*, we have planned a tour; *concertarono di trovarsi alle 10*, they arranged to meet at ten ‖ **concertàrsi**, *v.r.* to agree, to act in concert: *ci siamo concertati per aiutarlo*, we have agreed to help him; *concertati con lui a quel proposito*, discuss the matter with him.

concertàto, *ag.* 1. (*stabilito*) concerted; arranged 2. (*mus.*) concerted ‖ *s.m.* (*mus.*) concerted piece.

concertatóre, *s.m.* (*mus.*) concerter: *maestro — e direttore d'orchestra*, conductor.

concertìsta, *s.c.* concert artist.

concèrto, *s.m.* 1. (*trattenimento musicale*) concert; (*composizione musicale*) concerto: — *di campane*, chimes; — *per piano*, piano concerto 2. *fig.* (*accordo*) concert, agreement: *agire di —*, to act in concert.

concessionàrio, *s.m.* (*comm.*) 1. concessionaire, grantee 2. (*agente*) concessionary agent: — *unico*, sole agent.

concessióne, *s.f.* 1. concession, grant: *come — all'opinione pubblica*, as a concession to public opinion; *per — reale*, by royal grant; *fare una —*, to make a concession 2. (*permesso*) permission 3. (*di terreno*) concession: — *petrolifera*, oil concession.

concessìvo, *ag.* concessive (anche *gram.*): *proposizione concessiva*, (*gram.*) concessive clause.

concèsso, *ag.* granted ‖ *dato e non — che...*, supposing... (o provided that...).

concessóre, *s.m.* (*dir.*) grantor, granter.

concettìsmo, *s.m.* (*lett.*) concettism.

concètto, *s.m.* 1. concept; conception; idea, opinion: — *morale*, moral sense; *avere un — chiaro di ql.co.*, to have a clear conception of sthg.; *farsi un — di ql.co.*, to form an idea of sthg. 2. (*significato*) meaning: *il — di un quadro*, the meaning of a picture 3. (*lett.*) conceit; concetto (*pl.* concetti): *concetti secentisti*, 17th century conceits.

concettosaménte, *av.* pithily; sententiously.

concettóso, *ag.* pithy; sententious.

concettuàle, *ag.* (*fil.*) conceptual.

concettualìsmo, *s.m.* (*fil.*) conceptualism.

concezionàle, *ag.* conceptional.

concezióne, *s.f.* 1. conception ‖ *l'Immacolata Concezione*, (*teol.*) the Immaculate Conception 2. (*concetto, pensiero*) conception; idea: *una — ardita*, a bold conception (o plan).

conchìfero, *ag.* 1. (*che ha conchiglie*) shell-bearing 2. (*geol.*) conchiferous, shelly, full of shells.

conchìglia, *s.f.* shell, conch.

conchiùdere, *V.* **conclùdere**.

cóncia, *s.f.* 1. (*di pelli*) tanning 2. (*di tabacco*) curing 3. (*conceria*) tannery.

conciaiuòlo, **conciapèlli**, *s.m.* tanner.

conciàre, *v.t.* 1. (*pelli*) to tan: — *pelli per farne cuoio*, to tan hides to make leather 2. (*tabacco*) to cure 3. (*riparare*) to mend, to repair 4. *fig.* (*malmenare,* *maltrattare*) to ill-treat, to thrash, to beat ‖ — *qlcu. per le feste*, to give s.o. a good thrashing **5.** (*fam.*) (*insudiciare*) to soil: *guardate com'è conciato!*, look in what an awful state he is! ‖ **conciàrsi,** *v.r.* **1.** (*farsi male*) to hurt oneself **2.** (*fam.*) (*insudiciarsi*) to get dirty: *dove ti sei conciato così?*, where did you get soiled like that?.

conciatétti, *s.m.* tiler, slater.

conciatóre, *s.m.*, **conciatríce,** *s.f.* tanner.

conciatúra, *s.f.* tanning: — *vegetale*, vegetable tanning.

conciliàbile, *ag.* compatible, consistent, reconcilable: — *col suo comportamento*, consistent with his behaviour.

conciliabilità, *s.f.* compatibility, consistency.

conciliàbolo, *s.m.* **1.** (*eccl.*) conventicle **2.** (*adunanza segreta*) conventicle; secret meeting, secret talk: *terremo un — con qlcu.*, (*fam.*) we'll put our heads together; *essere in — con qlcu.*, to be talking secretly to s.o.

conciliànte, *ag.* conciliatory: *modi concilianti*, conciliatory manners.

conciliàre, *ag.* (*rar.*) conciliar.

conciliàre, *v.t.* **1.** (*mettere d'accordo*) to reconcile, to conciliate: — *due idee diverse*, to conciliate two different ideas **2.** (*procacciare, procurare*) to conciliate, to win, to gain: *i suoi bei modi gli conciliano l'amore di tutti*, his nice manners win everybody's love ‖ — *il sonno a qlcu.*, to make s.o. sleepy ‖ **conciliàrsi,** *v.r.* (*cattivarsi*) to win, to gain: *egli si concilia la stima degli amici*, he gains (*o* wins) his friends' esteem; — *l'uditorio*, to win the goodwill of (*o* to win over) the audience.

conciliatívo, *ag.* conciliatory, conciliating, conciliative.

conciliatóre, *ag.* conciliatory, conciliating, conciliative ‖ *giudice —*, (*dir.*) Justice of the Peace ‖ *s.m.*, **conciliatríce,** *s.f.* peacemaker.

conciliazióne, *s.f.* conciliation, reconcilement ‖ *Conciliazione della Chiesa con lo Stato*, (*st.*) Lateran Agreements ‖ *Corte di —*, (*dir.*) Court of conciliation.

concílio, *s.m.* (*eccl.*) council: — *diocesano, ecumenico*, diocesan, oecumenical council; *tenere un —*, to hold a council ‖ *il Concilio di Trento*, (*st.*) the Council of Trent.

concimàia, *s.f.* (*a mucchio*) dunghill, manure-heap; (*a fossa*) dung-pit, manure-pit.

concimàre, *v.t.* to manure, to dung.

concimatúra, concimazióne, *s.f.* manuring, dunging.

concíme, *s.m.* manure, dung: — *chimico*, fertilizer (*o* chemical manure *o* artificial manure).

concinnità, *s.f.* (*letter.*) concinnity.

cóncio[1], *ag.* (*conciato*) tanned ‖ *s.m.* (*arch.*) hewn stone, ashlar.

cóncio[2], *s.m.* (*concime*) manure, dung.

concionàre, *v.i.* to harangue.

concionatóre, *s.m.*, **concionatríce,** *s.f.* haranguer; (*fam.*) tub-thumper.

concióne, *s.f.* **1.** harangue **2.** (*adunanza*) deliberating assembly; (*luogo dell'adunanza*) assembly-hall, meeting -place.

conciossiacché, *cong.* (*rar.*) as, for, since.

concisaménte, *av.* concisely, briefly, succinctly, tersely.

concisióne, *s.f.* concision, conciseness, brevity, terseness.

concíso, *ag.* concise, brief, terse.

concistoriàle, *ag.* (*eccl.*) consistorial.

concistòro, *s.m.* (*eccl.*) consistory.

concitaménto, *s.m.* excitement, agitation.

concitàre, *v.t.* (*rar.*) to excite, to rouse, to stir up, to incite, to urge, to move: — *il popolo alla rivolta*, to rouse the people to revolt.

concitataménte, *av.* excitedly.

concitàto, *ag.* excited; agitated: *parlare in tono —*, to speak in tones of emotion.

concitazióne, *s.f.* excitement, agitation; emotion.

concittadinànza, *s.f.* fellow-citizenship.

concittadíno, *s.m.*, **concittadína,** *s.f.* fellow-citizen.

conclamàre, *v.t.* to acclaim, to proclaim, to hail.

conclamàto, *ag.* (*med.*) clear.

conclàve, *s.m.* (*eccl.*) conclave.

conclavísta, *s.m.* conclavist.

concludènte, *ag.* **1.** (*efficace*) conclusive, decisive **2.** (*di persona*) energetic; business-like, enterprising: *è un uomo —*, he gets things done.

conclúdere, *v.t.* **1.** to conclude, to finish; to settle, to arrange: *abbiamo concluso che...*, we have come to the conclusion that...; *la faccenda fu conclusa*, the matter was settled; — *un affare*, to strike (*o* to clench *o* to close) a bargain; — *un discorso*, to conclude a speech; — *la pace*, to conclude (*o* to make *o* to arrange) peace; — *un trattato*, to conclude a treaty **2.** (*dedurre*) to conclude, to infer: *che cosa ne concludiamo?*, what do we infer from that? **3.** (*fare*) to do: *abbiamo concluso poco oggi*, we didn't get much done today ‖ *v.i.* (*convincere*) to be conclusive: *argomento che non conclude*, inconclusive argument.

conclusionàle, *s.f.* (*dir.*) pleadings (*pl.*).

conclusióne, *s.f.* **1.** conclusion: *la — del discorso*, the conclusion (*o* close *o* end) of the speech; *la — di un affare*, the conclusion of a business deal; *eccone la —*, that is the long and the short of it; *giungere a una —*, to come to a conclusion; *trarre una —*, to draw a conclusion ‖ *in —*, in conclusion (*o* to sum up) **2.** (*risultato*) issue, result, upshot: *ero deciso a portare le cose a una —*, I was determined to bring matters to an issue; *quale sarà la — di tutto ciò?*, what will be the upshot of it all? **3.** *pl.* (*dir.*) pleadings.

conclusívo, *ag.* conclusive: *esperimento —*, conclusive test.

conclúso, *ag.* (*letter.*) (*racchiuso*) enclosed.

concoidàle, *ag.* (*geom.*) conchoidal.

concòide, *s.f.* (*geom.*) conchoid.

concomitànte, *ag.* concomitant, conjoint, accompanying: *cause concomitanti*, concomitant causes.

concomitànza, *s.f.* **1.** concomitance **2.** (*teol.*) (*unione del Corpo e del Sangue di Cristo nell'Eucarestia*) concomitance.

concordànte, *ag.* concordant, agreeing, harmonious: *testimonianze concordanti*, (*dir.*) concordant depositions.

concordànza, *s.f.* **1.** agreement; accordance **2.** (*di testi letterari*) concordance: *concordanze della Bibbia*, concordance of the Bible **3.** (*gram.*) concord, agreement.

concordàre, *v.t.* **1.** (*decidere insieme*) to agree upon (sthg.); to fix, to arrange: — *un piano*, to make a plan; — *il prezzo*, to agree upon the price **2.** (*mettere d'accordo*) to reconcile: — *due diversi punti di vista*, to reconcile two different points of view **3.** (*gram.*) to put (*o* to arrange) in concord ‖ *v.i.* (*essere d'accordo*) to agree.

concordatàrio, *ag.* **1.** (*dir. eccl.*) of concordat **2.** (*dir. comm.*) composition (*attributivo*).

concordatívo, *ag.* fit to agree.

concordàto, *ag.* agreed upon; arranged, fixed ‖ *s.m.* **1.** (*patto*) convention, agreement **2.** (*dir. eccl.*) concordat **3.** (*dir. comm.*) agreement, composition, settlement: — *fraudolento*, fraudulent settlement; *dovrebbe venire ad un — con i suoi creditori*, he ought to come to an arrangement with his creditors; *presentare proposta di — al curatore di fallimento*, to lodge a scheme of arrangement with the Official Receiver.

concòrde, *ag.* **1.** concordant, agreeing; harmonious; (*della stessa opinione*) like-minded: *volontà —*, unanimous will; *essere concordi*, to be agreed (*o* to agree); *essere di parere —*, to be of the same opinion **2.** (*conforme*) consonant, consistent.

concordeménte, *av.* concordantly, unanimously; (*di comune accordo*) by mutual consent.

concòrdia, *s.f.* concord, agreement; harmony: *ristabilire la — fra nemici*, to establish a reconciliation between enemies; *vivere in —*, to live in concord.

concorrènte, *ag.* **1.** concurrent: *forze concorrenti* (*fis.*) concurrent forces; *linee concorrenti*, (*geom.*) concurrent lines **2.** (*rivale*) competing: *ditta —*, competing firm ‖ *s.m.* **1.** candidate; (*aspirante*) applicant: *— ad un posto*, applicant for a place; *aveva un —*, he had a candidate running against him **2.** (*rivale*) competitor; rival: *i concorrenti alla gara*, the competitors in the race; *i concorrenti al premio*, the competitors for the prize; *oltrepassare, superare un —*, to outvie a competitor ‖ *s.f.* **1.** candidate; (*aspirante*) applicant **2.** (*rivale*) competitress.

concorrènza, *s.f.* **1.** (*affluenza*) concourse: *ci fu una grande — di gente*, there was a great concourse of people **2.** (*gara*) competition: *in — con qlcu.*, in competition with s.o. **3.** (*comm.*) competition: *— accanita*, keen competition; *— sleale*, unfair competition ‖ *fuori —*, beyond (*o* out of) competition; *libertà di —*, free competition; *prezzi che non temono —*, prices defying all competition; *entrare in — con qlcu.*, to enter into competition with s.o.; *fare — a qlcu.*, to compete with s.o.; *proteggersi dalla —*, to guard against (*o* from) competition; *sostenere la —*, to front (*o* to stand) competition; *vincere la —*, to beat (*o* to win) competition.

concórrere, *v.i.* **1.** to come together; to assemble: *concorrono qui da tutte le parti*, they come here from all parts **2.** (*contribuire*) to concur, to contribute: *le circostanze concorsero alla sua felicità*, circumstances concurred to make him happy; *— alla rovina di qlcu.*, to contribute to s.o.'s ruin **3.** (*partecipare*) to share in (sthg.), to participate (in sthg.), to take a share (in sthg.): *non concorse all'impresa*, he took no share in the enterprise; *— alle spese*, to share in (*o* to contribute to) the expenses **4.** (*competere*) to compete (for sthg.); (*aspirare*) to apply (for sthg.): *— ad un impiego*, to apply for a post; *— ad un premio*, to compete for a prize **5.** (*accordarsi*) to concur (in sthg., doing): *tutti concorrono a credere che...*, all concur in the belief hiat...; *— in un'opinione*, to concur in (*o* to agree twth) an opinion **6.** (*convergere*) to converge.

concórso, *s.m.* **1.** (*affluenza*) concourse; rush: *ci fu un gran — di curiosi*, there was a great concourse of lookers-on **2.** (*coincidenza*) concurrence, concourse; coincidence: *per il — di circostanze sfavorevoli*, through the concurrence of unfavourable circumstances **3.** (*gara*) competition; contest: *— ippico*, horse show; *— musicale*, musical contest; *bando di —*, announcement of competition; *fuori —*, not for competition (*o* out of competition); *bandire un —*, to announce a competition; *coprire un posto per —*, to fill a post by open competition; *vincere un —*, to win a competition **4.** (*dir.*) complicity: *— ad un delitto*, complicity in a crime.

concozióne, *s.f.* (*fisiol.*) digestion.

concretaménte, *av.* concretely.

concretàre, *v.t.* **1.** to make concrete, to make real: *— un'idea*, to put an idea in concrete form **2.** (*concludere*) to realize; to carry (sthg.) into effect.

concretézza, *s.f.* concreteness.

concretizzàre, *V.* **concretàre.**

concrèto, *ag.* **1.** concrete, real, actual: *caso —*, actual (*o* positive) case **2.** (*solido*) solid **3.** (*gram.*) concrete: *nome —*, concrete noun ‖ *s.m.* concrete ‖ *al —*, in the concrete: *venire al —*, to come to the facts.

concrezionàle, *ag.* (*geol. patol.*) concretionary.

concrezióne, *s.f.* **1.** concretion (anche *geol.*): *— calcarea*, calcareous concretion (*o* chalk-stone); *— piritica*, pyritic concretion **2.** (*patol.*) concretion, stone, calculus (*pl.* calculi): *concrezioni biliari*, biliary concretions.

concubína, *s.f.* concubine.

concubinàto, *s.m.* concubinage.

conculcàre, *v.t.* **1.** to trample on (s.o., sthg.); to oppress **2.** (*vilipendere*) to despise, to contemn.

conculcatóre, *s.m.*, **conculcatríce,** *s.f.* trampler on.

concuòcere, *v.t.* (*fisiol.*) to digest; to assimilate.

concuocimènto, *s.m.* digestion, assimilation.

concupíre, *v.t.* to covet; to lust after, for (s.o., sthg.): *— una fanciulla*, to lust after a girl.

concupiscènte, *ag.* concupiscent, lustful; ardently desirous.

concupiscènza, *s.f.* concupiscence, lust; violent desire: *— di oro*, greed of gold.

concupiscibile, *ag.* concupiscible.

concussionàrio, *s.m.* (*dir.*) extortioner.

concussióne, *s.f.* (*dir.*) concussion, extortion.

condànna, *s.f.* **1.** condemnation, conviction: *la — di un ladro*, the conviction of a thief **2.** (*sentenza*) sentence, judgment: *— a morte*, death sentence (*o* death penalty); *pronunciare una —*, to pass judgment (*o* a sentence) **3.** (*pena*) penalty, punishment: *— eterna*, eternal punishment; *sta scontando la sua —*, he is taking his punishment **4.** (*riprovazione*) condemnation, reproof, blame, censure: *la — della dottrina di Lutero*, the condemnation of Luther's doctrine.

condannàbile, *ag.* **1.** condemnable **2.** (*censurabile*) censurable, blamable.

condannàre, *v.t.* **1.** (*dir.*) to sentence, to condemn, to convict: *— a dieci anni di lavori forzati*, to sentence to ten years' penal servitude; *— all'ergastolo*, to sentence to life imprisonment; *— al risarcimento dei danni*, to condemn to damages; *— a morte*, to sentence (*o* to condemn) to death; *— qlcu. a cinquantamila lire di multa*, to fine s.o. fifty thousand lire; *— qlcu. a tre mesi di prigione*, to pass sentence of three months' imprisonment on s.o.; *essere condannato a venticinque giorni di prigione*, to receive twenty-five days **2.** *fig.* to condemn, to convict: *condannato dalla sua coscienza*, convicted by his own conscience; *il medico l'ha condannato*, the doctor has given him up; *— a vivere senza speranza*, to condemn to lead a hopeless existence **3.** (*eccl.*) to censure **4.** (*riprovare*) to blame, to reprove: *— la condotta di qlcu.*, to reprove (*o* to blame) s.o.'s conduct.

condannàta, *s.f.* condemned woman, convict.

condannàto, *ag.* sentenced, condemned ‖ *s.m.* condemned man, convict: *la cella dei condannati a morte*, the condemned cell.

condebitóre, *s.m.*, **condebitríce,** *s.f.* joint-debtor.

condensàbile, *ag.* (*fis.*) condensable.

condensabilità, *s.f.* (*fis.*) condensability.

condensaménto, *s.m.* condensation, condensing.

condensàre, *v.t.* **1.** to condense **2.** *fig.* to summarize, to condense, to shorten, to abbreviate, to abridge, to epitomize: *— in un paragrafo un intero capitolo*, to condense a chapter into a single paragraph ‖ **condensàrsi,** *v.r.* to condense.

condensàto, *ag.* **1.** condensed: *latte —*, condensed milk **2.** *fig.* summarized.

condensatóre, *s.m.* (*mec. ott.*) condenser; (*elett.*) capacitor, condenser: *— a carta*, paper condenser; *— ad aria*, (*rad.*) air condenser; *— a diaframma*, ad iride sotto al piatto, (*ott.*) substage iris diaphragm; *— a pressione*, pressure-type capacitor; *— a vuoto*, vacuum condenser; *— di sintonia*, (*rad.*) tuning condenser; *— di vapore*, steam condenser; *— fisso*, (*rad.*) fixed condenser; *— regolabile*, (*elett.*) adjustable condenser; *— schermato*, (*rad.*) shielded condenser ‖ *microfono —*, (*elett.*) transmitter.

condensazióne, *s.f.* (*fis.*) condensation, condensing.

condicévole, *ag.* (*letter.*) convenient, suitable; adequate.

còndilo, *s.m.* (*anat.*) condyle.

condiménto, *s.m.* **1.** (*il condire*) seasoning, flavouring; (*di insalata*) dressing **2.** (*sostanza con cui si condisce*) condiment, seasoning; (*di insalata*) dressing; sauce **3.** *fig.* sauce: *l'appetito è il — migliore*, appetite is the best sauce.

condíre, *v.t.* **1.** to season, to flavour; (*insalata*) to dress **2.** *fig.* to season; to give zest to (sthg.).

condirettóre, *s.m.* joint manager, co-director; (*di giornale*) co-editor, joint editor.

condirettríce, *s.f.* joint manageress, co-directrix; (*di giornale*) co-editress, joint-editress.

condirezióne, *s.f.* joint management, joint director-ship.

condiscendènte, *ag.* **1.** (*arrendevole*) compliant, complying: — *verso qlcu.*, complying with s.o. **2.** (*compiacente*) condescending, obliging, indulgent.

condiscendènza, *s.f.* **1.** (*arrendevolezza*) compliance **2.** (*degnazione*) condescension: *con* —, patronizingly (*o* condescendingly).

condiscéndere, *v.i.* **1.** (*acconsentire*) to comply (with sthg.); to yield: — *a una passione*, to yield to a passion **2.** (*degnarsi*) to condescend, to be indulgent.

condiscépola, *s.f.*, **condiscépolo,** *s.m.* schoolfellow, fellow-student, school-companion.

condíto, *ag.* seasoned, tasty; (*di insalata*) dressed: *ben* —, well seasoned (*o* highly seasoned) ‖ *s.m.* seasoning, condiment.

condivídere, *v.t.* to share (anche *fig.*): — *le idee di qlcu.*, to share s.o.'s ideas.

condizionàle, *ag.* conditional: *condanna* —, (*dir.*) conditional sentence; *modo* —, (*gram.*) conditional (mood) ‖ *s.m.* (*gram.*) conditional (mood) ‖ *s.f.* (*dir.*) conditional sentence.

condizionaménto, *s.m.* conditioning: — *del grano*, (*agr.*) wheat conditioning; — *dell'aria*, air-conditioning.

condizionàre, *v.t.* **1.** to condition: *la vita dell'uomo è condizionata alle leggi della natura*, man's life is conditioned by natural laws **2.** (*porre sotto riserva*) to qualify **3.** (*confezionare, imballare*) to pack (up).

condizionataménte, *av.* conditionally.

condizionàto, *ag.* **1.** conditioned: *stanza ad aria condizionata*, air conditioned room; *riflesso* —, (*med.*) conditioned reflex **2.** (*sottoposto a riserva*) qualified: *assenso* —, qualified approval **3.** (*confezionato, imballato*) packed up.

condizióne, *s.f.* **1.** (*qualità, requisito*) qualification: *ha le condizioni necessarie per occupare quel posto*, he has the necessary qualifications for that post **2.** (*circostanza condizionante un'azione*) condition, position: *non è in — di viaggiare*, he is in no condition to travel; *essere in — di fare ql.co.*, to be in a position (*o* to be able) to do sthg.; *essere nelle condizioni adatte per agire*, to be entitled to act; *mettere qlcu. in — di fare ql.co.*, to put s.o. in a position (*o* to enable s.o.) to do sthg. **3.** (*stato*) condition, circumstance, state: *in buona* —, in good condition (*o* fit *o* in good fettle); *in condizioni favorevoli*, under favourable circumstances (*o* conditions); *squadra in eccellenti condizioni*, team in splendid fettle; *è in cattive condizioni di salute*, he is in a bad state of health; *la merce arrivò in buone condizioni*, the goods arrived in good conditions; *la tua bicicletta è in buone, cattive condizioni*, your bicycle is in good, bad repair **4.** (*patto*) condition: *a nessuna* —, on no condition; *a quale* —?, on what condition?; *accettare una* —, to agree to (*o* to accept) a condition; *porre una* —, to make a condition ‖ *a — che*, on condition that: *accetto ma a — che tu venga con me*, I accept, but on condition that you come with me; *puoi andare a — che tu torni presto*, you may go, but I make it a condition that you should come back early ‖ *condizioni a convenirsi*, (*comm.*) terms to be arranged; — *provvisionale*, (*comm.*) proviso ‖ *alle solite condizioni*, (*comm.*) on the usual terms (*o* conditions) **5.** (*ceto, posizione*) condition, rank, station, status, position: *gente di tutte le condizioni*, people of all conditions; *persone di semplici condizioni*, persons in humble circumstances; *migliorare le proprie condizioni*, to better oneself.

condogliànza, *s.f.* condolence: *lettera di* —, letter of condolence; *gli feci le mie condoglianze per l'improvvisa morte di suo padre*, I condoled with him upon the sudden death of his father (*o* I expressed my sympathy with him on his father's sudden death); *vogliate accettare le mie sincere condoglianze*, accept my heartfelt sympathy.

condolérsi, *v.r.* **1.** to condole: — *con qlcu. per*

ql.co., to condole with s.o. upon sthg. **2.** (*dolersi, lamentarsi*) to lament (for, over s.o., sthg.).

condomínio, *s.m.* joint ownership.

condòmino, *s.m.* joint-owner, co-owner.

condonàbile, *ag.* **1.** (*di pena, debito*) remissible **2.** (*di colpa*) pardonable, excusable, remissible.

condonàre, *v.t.* **1.** to remit: — *un debito*, to remit a debt **2.** (*perdonare*) to condone, to pardon, to forgive, to overlook.

condonazióne, *s.f.* (*rar.*) condonation.

condóno, *s.m.* remission, pardon.

còndor, *s.m.* (*ornit.*) condor.

condótta, *s.f.* **1.** (*modo di condurre una cosa*) administration, management: *la — dei lavori*, the superintendence of the work; — *del fuoco*, (*mil.*) fire control **2.** (*modo di comportarsi*) conduct, behaviour, bearing: *certificato di buona* —, certificate of good character; *linea di* —, line of conduct (*o* policy *o* course); *tenere una cattiva* —, to lead a loose life **3.** (*comando supremo*) leadership: *sotto la — di Napoleone*, under Napoleon's leadership **4.** — (*medica*), country district under the care of a doctor employed by the local authority **5.** (*tubazione*) pipe: — *d'acqua*, water pipe; — *del gas*, (*negli aerostati*) gas main; — *forzata*, (*idraulica*) penstock (*o* pressure water pipe); — *municipale*, city piping system.

condottièro, *s.m.* **1.** army leader **2.** (*st.*) condottiere (*pl.* condottieri).

condótto, *ag.*: *medico* —, doctor employed by the local authority in a country district ‖ *s.m.* **1.** duct, conduit, trunk; pipeline; (*di caldaia*) flue: — *dell'aria*, air duct (*o* ventiduct); — *di aerazione*, local vent **2.** (*anat.*) duct: — *lacrimale*, lacrimal duct.

conducènte, *s.m.* **1.** (*di veicoli*) driver **2.** (*affittuario*) farmer, lease-holder, lessee, tenant.

conducibilità, *s.f.* (*fis.*) conductibility, conductivity.

condúrre, *v.t.* **1.** (*guidare, scortare*) to lead, to guide, to conduct: — *qlcu. per mano*, to lead s.o. by the hand ‖ — *all'altare*, to lead to the altar **2.** (*accompagnare*) to take: *mi condusse a teatro*, he took me to the theatre; *mi condusse in automobile a visitare Pavia*, he took me in his car to visit Pavia **3.** (*far arrivare*) to lead: — *l'esercito alla vittoria*, to lead the army on to victory; — *qlcu. alla disperazione*, to drive (*o* to lead) s.o. to despair ‖ — *a fine*, to complete (*o* to bring to an end) **4.** (*trattare, governare*) to manage: — *un'azienda*, to manage a firm; — *bene gli affari*, to manage (one's) business well **5.** (*vivere*) to lead: — *una doppia vita*, to lead a double life; — *una vita miserevole*, to lead a miserable life **6.** (*veicoli*) to drive **7.** (*fis.*) to conduct ‖ *v.i.* to lead: *tutte le strade conducono a Roma*, all routes lead to Rome ‖ **condúrsi,** *v.r.* **1.** (*agire*) to act, to behave: — *bene*, to behave (well) **2.** (*giungere, spingersi*) to go, to penetrate: *si condusse fin là*, he penetrated as far as that.

conduttività, *s.f.* (*fis.*) conductivity, conductibility.

conduttóre, *s.m.* **1.** leader, guide, conductor: — *di flottiglia*, (*mar.*) flotilla leader **2.** (*di veicoli*) driver **3.** (*dir.*) tenant **4.** (*fis.*) conductor: — *elettrico*, (*elett.*) electric wire; — *isolato*, (*elett.*) insulated wire; — *pilota*, (*elett.*) pilot wire; *buon* —, good conductor; *cattivo* —, bad conductor.

conduttríce, *s.f.* **1.** leader, guide, conductress **2.** (*di veicoli*) driver **3.** (*dir.*) tenant.

conduttúra, *s.f.* duct, conduit, main; (*tubazione*) piping: — *dell'acqua*, water main; — *del gas*, gas main; *le condutture di questa casa sono difettose*, the piping in this house is defective.

conduzióne, *s.m.* **1.** (*il condurre*) management **2.** (*dir.*) tenancy **3.** (*fis.*) conduction.

conestàbile, *s.m.* (*st.*) constable: — *di Francia*, Constable of France.

confabulàre, *v.i.* to confabulate; to chat.

confabulazióne, *s.f.* confabulation; chat.

confacènte, *ag.* suitable, proper, convenient, becoming.

confacenteménte, *av.* suitably, becomingly.

confarreazióne, *s.f.* (*st. romana*) confarreation.

confàrsi, *v.r.* to suit (s.o., sthg.), to become (s.o., sthg.), to fit (s.o., sthg.), to agree (with s.o., sthg.): *non ha ancora trovato un lavoro che gli si confaccia,* he has not yet found a job that suits him; *queste arie non ti si confanno,* these airs do not become you.

confederàrsi, *v.r.* to (con)federate.

confederàto, *ag.* confederate ‖ *Stati Confederati d'America,* Confederate States of America ‖ *s.m.* confederate.

confederazióne, *s.f.* **1.** (*pol.*) (con)federation ‖ *la Confederazione Elvetica,* the Swiss Confederation **2.** (*lega, alleanza*) confederacy, league ‖ *la — sudista,* the Southern Confederacy.

conferènza, *s.f.* **1.** lecture: *fare, tenere una —,* to deliver (*o* to give) a lecture **2.** (*assemblea*) conference: *Conferenza al vertice,* Summit (*o* Top) Conference **3.** (*abboccamento*) conversation, talk; (*intervista*) interview: *tenere una — stampa,* to hold a press conference.

conferenzière, *s.m.* lecturer.

conferiménto, *s.m.* conferment, bestowal.

conferíre, *v.t.* **1.** to confer, to bestow, to award, to give, to grant: *l'autonomia ad un paese,* to grant autonomy to a country; — *autorità a qlcu.,* to confer authority on (*o* to empower) s.o.; — *grandi onori a qlcu.,* to bestow great honours on s.o.; — *un incarico,* to give an appointment; — *il titolo di dottore a qlcu.,* to grant (*o* to bestow) a doctor's degree on s.o. **2.** (*confrontare*) to compare, to collate ‖ *v.i.* **1.** (*abboccarsi*) to confer, to have an interview **2.** (*contribuire*) to contribute: — *al successo,* to contribute to the success **3.** (*giovare*) to be useful, to be beneficial; to agree (with s.o.): *l'aria del mare mi conferisce,* sea air is beneficial to me (*o* agrees with me).

confèrma, *s.f.* confirmation; corroboration: — *di una sentenza,* confirmation (*o* affirmation) of a judgement; *a — della mia telefonata,* in confirmation (*o* corroboration) of my telephone call.

confermàre, *v.t.* **1.** (*ribadire*) to confirm: *l'ho detto ed ora lo confermo,* I said it and I confirm it now; — *le proprie dimissioni,* to confirm one's resignation **2.** (*convalidare*) to confirm, to ratify, to corroborate, to strengthen, to bear out: *il suo aspetto confermava le sue parole,* his appearance bore out his words; — *la deposizione di qlcu.,* to corroborate (*o* to bear out) s.o.'s evidence; — *un ordine,* to confirm (*o* to ratify) an order; — *una sentenza,* to confirm (*o* to affirm *o* to ratify) a judgement ‖ *l'eccezione conferma la regola,* the exception proves the rule **3.** (*riconfermare, rinnovare*) to confirm: *fu confermato nella carica di presidente,* he was confirmed in his appointment as chairman **4.** (*eccl.*) (*cresimare*) to confirm ‖ **confermàrsi,** *v.r.* to prove oneself: *ciò si conferma sempre più utile,* that is proving itself more and more useful; *si sta confermando un ottimo medico,* he is proving himself to be a good doctor.

confermatívo, *ag.* confirmative, confirmatory.

confermazióne, *s.f.* confirmation (anche *eccl.*).

confessàre, *v.t.* **1.** to confess; (*riconoscere*) to acknowledge, to own; (*ammettere*) to admit, to avow: *confessa d'avere quarant'anni,* she owns to (being) forty; *confessò che mentiva,* he owned he was lying; *confesso d'aver studiato molto poco,* I confess that I studied (*o* to having studied) very little; — *un debole per il buon vino,* to confess to a weakness for good wine; — *un delitto,* to confess (*o* to own up) to a crime; — *il proprio errore,* to own one's fault (*o* to avow oneself in the wrong) ‖ *peccato confessato è mezzo perdonato, prov.* a fault confessed is half redressed **2.** (*eccl.*) to confess: — *i propri peccati,* to confess one's sins; — *qlcu.,* to hear s.o.'s confession (*o* to confess s.o.) ‖ **confessàrsi,** *v.r.* **1.** (*eccl.*) to go to confession:

— tutte le settimane, to go to confession every week **2.** (*riconoscersi*) to confess oneself, to avow oneself, to own up: — *l'autore di ql.co.,* to avow oneself (as) author of sthg. (*o* to own up to sthg.); — *colpevole,* to confess oneself (*o* to plead) guilty.

confessionàle, *ag.* **1.** confessional: *segreto —,* secret of the confessional **2.** (*religioso*) religious ‖ *s.m.* confessional.

confessionàrio, *s.m.* **1.** (*confessionale*) confessional **2.** — *di pegno,* (*dir.*) trustee, depositary.

confessióne, *s.f.* **1.** confession; (*riconoscimento*) acknowledgement; (*ammissione*) avowal, admission: *la — gli fu strappata parola per parola,* his confession was torn from him piecemeal; *rendere piena —,* to make a full confession ‖ *la — giudiziale,* (*dir.*) confession **2.** *pl.* (*memorie*) memoirs **3.** (*eccl.*) confession; (*facoltà di confessare*) right of hearing confession: *il segreto della —,* the seal of confession; *sotto sigillo di —,* under the seal of confession; *fig.* in all secrecy **4.** (*fede professata*) confession, (professed) creed **5.** (*tomba di un martire*) confession.

confèsso, *ag.* self-convicted: *egli è reo —,* he has pleaded (*o* confessed himself) guilty.

confessóre, *s.m.* confessor.

confettàre, *v.t.* to candy.

confettièra, *s.f.* sweetmeat box.

confettière, *s.m.* confectioner.

confètto, *s.m.* **1.** confetto (*pl.* confetti); comfit ‖ *mangiare i confetti, fig.* to celebrate a wedding **2.** (*farm.*) sugar-coated pill.

confettúra, *s.f.* **1.** (*confetti e simili*) sweetmeats (*pl.*) **2.** (*marmellata*) jam; (*di arance*) marmalade.

confezionàre, *v.t.* **1.** to manufacture, to make up: *abito da uomo confezionato su misura,* suit made to measure (*o* tailor-made suit); *articolo confezionato,* ready-made (*o* ready-to-wear) article **2.** (*cibi, piatti*) to prepare; (*misture*) to mix, to compound **3.** (*impacchettare*) to pack (up).

confezióne, *s.f.* **1.** manufacture **2.** (*preparazione*) preparation **3.** *pl.* (*abiti*) clothes: *confezioni in serie,* ready-made clothing; *confezioni per signora,* ladies' clothes; *confezioni su misura,* tailor-made (*o* made-to-measure*) clothes; (*amer.*) custom-made-clothes **4.** (*imballaggio*) packing **5.** (*farm.*) confection.

conficcaménto, *s.m.* driving in.

conficcàre, *v.t.* to hammer, to drive: — *un chiodo nel muro,* to drive a nail into the wall; — *ql.co. in testa a qlcu.,* to hammer sthg. into s.o. (*o* to get *o* to drive sthg. into s.o.'s head) ‖ **conficcàrsi,** *v.r.* to run into (sthg.): *egli si conficcò una spina, un ago nel dito,* he ran a thorn, a needle into his finger; *una scheggia gli si conficcò nella gamba,* a splinter ran into his leg ‖ — *in mente ql.co.,* to get sthg. into one's head: *si conficcò in mente di andare a Roma,* he got it into his head to go to Rome.

confidàre, *v.t.* **1.** to confide, to impart: *confidami le tue pene,* make a clean breast of it all; — *un segreto a qlcu.,* to confide (*o* to impart) a secret to s.o. **2.** (*affidare*) to trust, to entrust: — *un compito difficile a qlcu.,* to entrust a difficult task to s.o. (*o* to trust s.o. with a difficult task) ‖ *v.i.* (*aver fiducia*) to trust; (*fare assegnamento*) to rely on (s.o., sthg.): — *in Dio,* to confide (*o* to trust) in God; — *in qlcu.,* to rely on s.o. ‖ **confidàrsi,** *v.r.* to open one's heart.

confidènte, *ag.* confiding, trustful, trusting ‖ *s.c.* (*spia*): — *della polizia,* police spy ‖ *s.m.* confidant; (*amico intimo*) bosom-friend ‖ *s.f.* confidante; (*amica intima*) bosom-friend.

confidenteménte, *av.* confidently, trustfully.

confidènza, *s.f.* **1.** (*fiducia*) confidence, trust ‖ *in —,* in confidence **2.** (*cosa confidata*) secret, secret information; disclosure: *fare una — a qlcu.,* to tell s.o. (*o* to let s.o. in on) a secret **3.** (*familiarità*) familiarity, intimacy: *dare — a qlcu.,* to treat s.o. with familiarity; *essere in — con qlcu.,* to be on familiar terms with s.o.; *prendersi delle confidenze con qlcu.*, to take liberties (*o* to make free) with s.o.

confidenziàle, *ag.* confidential, private; (*amer.*) off the record: *a titolo* —, confidentially (*o* in confidence *o* privately); *è strettamente* —, it is strictly confidential.

confidenzialménte, *av.* confidentially, privately.

confíggere, *v.t.* to drive in, to knock in: *confisse un chiodo*, he knocked a nail in.

configuràre, *v.t.* **1.** to configure, to shape, to give shape to (sthg.) **2.** (*simboleggiare*) to symbolize.

configurazióne, *s.f.* configuration, shape.

confinànte, *ag.* neighbouring; contiguous (to sthg.), adjacent (to sthg.); bordering (on sthg.) (anche *fig.*): — *col ridicolo*, bordering on the ridiculous; *emozione* — *col terrore*, emotion bordering on terror; *giardino* — *con un'altra proprietà*, garden contiguous to another estate || *s.c.* neighbour.

confináre, *v.t.* **1.** (*pol.*) to intern, to banish **2.** *fig.* to confine: *quella poveretta è stata confinata in casa*, that poor woman has been confined to her house || *v.i.* (*avere confini comuni*) to border (on sthg.) (anche *fig.*): *quella proprietà confina con la tua*, that estate borders on yours; *questo confina con l'ostentazione*, this borders on ostentation || **confinàrsi,** *v.r.* to retire, to confine oneself.

confinàrio, *ag.* border (*attributivo*): *polizia confinaria*, border police.

confináto, *ag.* interned || *s.m.* internee.

confíne, *s.m.* **1.** border, frontier, boundary: *entro i confini della nostra patria*, within the borders of our country; *linea di* —, boundary line; *palo di* —, boundary post; *segno di* —, boundary mark; *stazione di* —, frontier station; *territorio di* —, borderland **2.** *fig.* limit, boundary; frontiers (*pl.*): *i confini del sapere*, the frontiers of knowledge.

confíno, *s.m.* (*pol.*) internment, political confinement: *mandare al* —, to intern (*o* to banish).

confìsca, *s.f.* confiscation, forfeiture: *la* — *dei beni*, the confiscation of one's property.

confiscàbile, *ag.* confiscable, forfeitable.

confiscàre, *v.t.* to confiscate, to forfeit: — *ql.co. a beneficio dello Stato*, to confiscate sthg. to the use of the State.

confíteor, *s.m.* (*eccl.*) confiteor.

confítto, *ag.* **1.** (*inchiodato*) nailed, driven in: — *in croce*, nailed on (*o* to) the cross **2.** *fig.* (*impresso*) fixed: — *in mente*, fixed in one's mind.

conflagrazióne, *s.f.* **1.** conflagration **2.** *fig.* sudden out-break of war; sudden out-break of revolution.

conflítto, *s.m.* **1.** conflict: — *mondiale*, world conflict; *venire a* —, to come into conflict **2.** *fig.* (*urto, contrasto*) clash: — *d'interessi*, clashing interests; *le sue opinioni sono in* — *con le mie*, his opinions clash with mine.

confluènte, *ag.* confluent || *s.m.* **1.** confluent **2.** (*confluenza*) confluence.

confluènza, *s.f.* confluence.

confluíre, *v.i.* to flow together, to join.

confóndere, *v.t.* **1.** (*mescolare*) to confuse, to mix up, to mingle: *ha confuso tutte le mie carte*, he mixed up all my papers **2.** (*scambiare*) to mistake, to confuse: *ti confusi con tuo fratello*, I mistook (*o* took) you for your brother; — *il colpevole con l'innocente*, to mistake the innocent for the guilty **3.** (*turbare*) to confound, to perplex, to confuse, to embarrass: *con tutte quelle domande lo confusero*, they confused him (*o* muddled him up) with all their questions; — *la vista*, to blur the vision **4.** (*annientare*) to confound: *Dio confonde i malvagi*, God confounds the wicked; — *il nemico*, to throw the enemy into confusion || **confóndersi,** *v.r.* **1.** to get mixed up: *scusami, mi sono confuso, sorry*, I got mixed up **2.** (*mescolarsi*) to mingle; (*di colori*) to blend: *ci confondemmo con la folla*, we mingled with the crowd **3.** (*turbarsi*) to be disconcerted, to lose one's presence of mind: *egli si confonde facil-*

mente, he is easily disconcerted (*o* he loses his presence of mind very easily) **4.** (*farsi confuso*) to become confused: *caddi e davanti a me tutto si confuse*, I fell and everything became confused.

confondíbile, *ag.* that may be confused; liable to be confused.

conformàbile, *ag.* conformable; (*adattabile*) adaptable.

conformàre, *v.t.* to conform; (*adattare*) to adapt: — *la propria vita a certi principi*, to conform one's life to certain principles; — *lo stile al soggetto*, to adapt the style to the subject || **conformàrsi,** *v.r.* to conform; to meet, to comply (with s.o., sthg.): — *alla legge*, to abide by the law; — *alla moda*, to fall in with the fashion; — *alle usanze della società*, to conform to the usages of society; — *ai desideri di qlcu.*, to comply with s.o.'s wishes (*o* with s.o.'s directions).

conformàto, *ag.* shaped: *ben* —, well-shaped; *mal* —, ill-shaped (*o* misshapen).

conformatóre, *s.m.* (*per cappellai*) conformator.

conformazióne, *s.f.* **1.** conformation; form; structure; shape: *la* — *del cranio*, the conformation (*o* the structure) of the skull **2.** (*adattamento*) conformation, adaptation.

confórme, *ag.* **1.** conforming, conformable: *essere* — *a*, to suit: *ciò non era* — *ai suoi gusti*, that did not suit his tastes (*o* that was not to his liking); *la sua condotta è* — *al desiderio dei suoi genitori*, his behaviour is conformable to his parents' wishes **2.** (*simile*) similar: — *a campione*, similar to sample (*o* up to sample) **3.** (*fedele*) true: *copia* —, true copy || **confórme a,** *l.prep.* in conformity with, in compliance with: — *a quanto vi scrivemmo*, in conformity with what we wrote to you; *agire* — *alle istruzioni di qlcu.*, to act in compliance with s.o.'s instructions.

conformeménte, *av.* accordingly || **conformeménte a,** *l.prep.* in conformity with, conformably to, in compliance with: — *al vostro ordine*, in compliance with your order.

conformísmo, *s.m.* time-serving.

conformísta, *s.m.* **1.** time-server **2.** (*st. relig.*) conformist.

conformità, *s.f.* conformity; agreement; accordance || *in* — *con*, in conformity with (*o* to) (*o* in accordance with *o* in compliance with).

confortàbile, *ag.* **1.** consolable; that can be comforted **2.** (*di teoria, argomento, ecc.*) provable.

confortabilménte, *av.* comfortably.

confortànte, *ag.* comforting, consoling; encouraging.

confortàre, *v.t.* **1.** (*alleviare il dolore di*) to comfort, to console, to solace **2.** (*incoraggiare*) to encourage **3.** (*sostenere*) to support; (*confermare*) to confirm: *l'accusa fu confortata da prove*, the accusation was supported by proof **4.** (*indurre*) to induce; to exhort: *il bel tempo conforta a passeggiare*, fine weather induces to walk **5.** (*ricreare*) to cheer (up) || **confortàrsi,** *v.r.* to find comfort, to take courage: *confortati!*, cheer up!,

confortatívo, *ag.* comforting; consoling.

confortatóre, *ag.* comforting, consoling || *s.m.* comforter, consoler.

confortatòrio, *ag.* comforting, consoling || *s.m.* V. **conforterìa.**

confortatríce, *s.f.* conforter, consoler.

conforterìa, *s.f.* room where the condemned to death were given Extreme Unction.

confortévole, *ag.* **1.** (*che conforta*) comforting **2.** (*comodo*) comfortable.

confortevolménte, *av.* comfortably.

confortíno, *s.m.* **1.** (*cuc.*) " confortino " (cake made with flour, sugar and eggs) **2.** (*liquore*) pick-me-up.

confòrto, *s.m.* **1.** comfort, consolation, solace: *trovò* — *nella religione*, he found solace in religion; *la tua lettera mi fu di grande* —, your letter was a great comfort to me; *portare* —, to bring comfort **2.** (*incoraggiamento*) encouragement **3.** (*sostegno, conferma*) support: *a* — *di*, in support of **4.** (*comodità*) comfort.

confratèllo, *s.m.* **1.** (*relig.*) brother (*pl.* brethren) **2.** (*collega*) colleague; confrère.

confratèrnita, *s.f.* brotherhood, confraternity.

confricaménto, *s.m.* friction, rubbing.

confricàre, *v.t.* to rub.

confricazióne, *s.f.* friction, rubbing.

confrontàre, *v.t.* to compare, to confront; to contrast; to collate: — *con*, to compare with; — *due testimonianze*, (*dir.*) to confront two witnesses || *v.i.* (*essere d'accordo*) to agree.

confrónto, *s.m.* **1.** comparison: *a* — *di*, *in* — *a*, in comparison with: *in* — *a lui io sono un genio!*, compared with him I am a genius!; *senza* —, beyond comparison (*o* incomparably); *non c'è* — *fra loro*, there is no comparison between them **2.** (*riscontro di testi*) collation **3.** (*dir.*) confrontation: *il prigioniero fu messo a* — *con i suoi accusatori*, the prisoner was confronted with his accusers.

confucianísmo, *s.m.* (*st. relig.*) Confucianism.

confuciàno, *ag.* Confucianist (*attributivo*); Confucian || *s.m.* Confucian, Confucianist.

Confúcio, *no.pr.m.* (*st. relig.*) Confucius.

confuggíre, *v.i.* to take refuge in flight.

confusaménte, *av.* confusedly.

confusionària, *s.f.* bungler, muddler; blunderer.

confusionàrio, *ag.* blundering, bungling; muddling || *s.m.* bungler, muddler; blunderer.

confusióne, *s.f.* **1.** confusion; medley; muddle, mess: — *di date*, *di nomi*, confusion of dates, of names; — *di razze*, medley of races **2.** (*imbarazzo*) confusion; embarrassment; (*mortificazione*) shame: *immaginate la mia* —, imagine my embarrassment; *arrossire per la* —, to blush for shame **3.** (*dir.*) merger **4.** (*med.*) derangement: — *mentale*, derangement (of mind).

confusionísmo, *s.m.* general confusion.

confúso, *ag.* **1.** confused, mixed, jumbled; chaotic **2.** (*poco chiaro*) vague, confused; (*indistinto*) indistinct: *un discorso* —, an indistinct speech; *idee confuse*, foggy notions; *suoni confusi*, indistinct sounds; *ne ho solo un ricordo* —, I have only a confused memory of it **3.** (*imbarazzato*) embarrassed, abashed, confused; (*mortificato*) ashamed.

confutàbile, *ag.* confutable, refutable.

confutàre, *v.t.* to confute, to refute, to disprove.

confutatívo, *ag.* confutative.

confutatóre, *s.m.* confuter, refuter.

confutatòrio, *ag.* confutative.

confutatríce, *s.f.* confuter, refuter.

confutazióne, *s.f.* confutation, refutation.

cònga, *s.f.* (*musica*, *danza*) conga.

congedàre, *v.t.* to dismiss; to discharge (*anche mil.*): — *qlcu.*, (*mil.*) to discharge s.o. from the force || **congedàrsi**, *v.r.* to take one's leave (of s.o.): *si congedò dai suoi amici*, he took leave of his friends.

congèdo, *s.m.* **1.** (*commiato*) leave: *prendere* — *da qlcu.*, to take leave of s.o. **2.** (*permesso*) leave: *tre mesi di congedo*, a three-months' leave **3.** (*mil.*) leave (of absence), furlough: — *assoluto*, discharge; — *illimitato*, temporary exoneration from military service; *foglio di* —, certificate of discharge; *andò a casa per un* — *di sei mesi*, he went home on a six months' furlough; *essere in* —, to be on leave (*o* on furlough) **4.** (*poes.*) envoy.

congegnàre, *v.t.* **1.** (*mec.*) to assemble, to fit together **2.** *fig.* to contrive, to devise.

congegnatóre, *s.m.*, **congegnatríce**, *s.f.* deviser, contriver.

congégno, *s.m.* **1.** (*mec.*) device, contrivance; gear, mechanism: — *di elevazione*, elevating gear; — *di sicurezza*, safety device **2.** *fig.* device, scheme.

congelàbile, *ag.* congealable, freezable.

congelaménto, *s.m.* **1.** congealment, congelation; freezing: *metodo di* — (*miner.*), freezing process; *punto di* —, (*fis.*) freezing point **2.** (*med.*) congelation.

congelàre, *v.t.*, **congelàrsi**, *v.r.* to congeal, to freeze.

congelàto, *ag.* **1.** congealed, frozen: *carni congelate*, chilled (*o* frozen) meat **2.** (*comm.*) frozen: *credito* —, frozen credit.

congelazióne, *V.* **congelaménto**.

congènere, *ag.* akin, alike (*predicativi*); similar.

congènito, *ag.* congenital, constitutional; innate.

congèrie, *s.f.* (*cumulo*) congeries, pile; mass, heap (*anche fig.*).

congestionàre, *v.t.* **1.** to congest **2.** (*sovraffollare*) to overcrowd, to congest.

congestionàto, *ag.* **1.** congested: *viso* —, flushed (*o* red) face **2.** *fig.* (*sovraffollato*) overcrowded, congested: *strade* —, congested streets.

congestióne, *s.f.* **1.** congestion: — *cerebrale*, (*patol.*) stroke; — *polmonare*, (*patol.*) pneumonia **2.** *fig.* (*sovraffollamento*) congestion, overcrowding: — *del traffico*, traffic congestion (*o* jam).

congestívo, *ag.* congestive.

congèsto, *ag.* (*letter.*) congested.

congettúra, *s.f.* conjecture, supposition; (*fam.*) guess: *fare una congettura*, to make a conjecture (*o* to conjecture *o* fam. to make a guess).

congetturàre, *v.t.* to conjecture; (*fam.*) to guess.

congiúngere, *v.t.* **1.** to join, to unite; (*geom.*) to join; (*travi*, *binari*, *ecc.*) to splice: — *due punti*, to join two points; — *gli eserciti*, to combine two armies (*o* forces); — *in matrimonio*, to join in marriage **2.** (*collegare*) to connect, to link: *una buona rete ferroviaria congiunge Milano con tutte le grandi città*, an efficient railway system connects (*o* links) Milan with all the large towns || **congiúngersi**, *v.r.* **1.** to join (s.o., sthg.): — *in matrimonio*, to get married **2.** (*incontrarsi*) to meet (s.o., sthg.); (*mil.*) to link up (s.o., sthg.); (*confluire*) to flow together; to join (s.o., sthg.): *questa strada si congiunge con quella nuova a Monza*, this road meets (*o* joins *o* connects with) the new one at Monza.

congiungiménto, *s.m.* joining; junction, union; (*mil.*) link-up.

congiuntaménte, *av.* jointly, conjointly.

congiuntíva, *s.f.* (*anat.*) conjunctiva.

congiuntivíte, *s.f.* (*patol.*) conjunctivitis.

congiuntívo, *ag.* **1.** conjunctive **2.** (*gram.*) subjunctive: *modo* —, subjunctive (mood) || *s.m.* (*gram.*) subjunctive.

congiúnto, *ag.* **1.** joined, united **2.** (*collegato*) connected (with sthg.), linked (with sthg.), in connection (with sthg.) || *s.m.* (*parente*) relative, relation, kinsman (*pl.* kinsmen): *i nostri congiunti*, our relatives.

congiuntúra, *s.f.* **1.** point of junction, joint **2.** (*articolazione*) joint **3.** (*circostanza*) circumstance, conjuncture; (*situazione*) situation; (*situazione spiacevole*) predicament: — *economica*, economic trend (*o* trade cycle); *in questa* —, at this conjuncture.

congiunzióne, *s.f.* **1.** connection; junction, link **2.** (*astr. gram.*) conjunction: *pianeti in* —, planets in conjunction.

congiúra, *s.f.* conspiracy, plot.

congiuràre, *v.i.* to conspire, to plot: *tutto sembrava* — *a suo danno*, everything seemed to be conspiring to bring about his ruin.

congiuràto, *ag.* conspired, plotted || *s.m.* conspirator, plotter.

congiuratóre, *ag.* conspiring, plotting || *s.m.*, **congiuratríce**, *s.f.* conspirator, plotter.

congiurazióne, *s.f.* conspiracy, plot.

conglobàre, *v.t.* **1.** to conglobate, to conglobe **2.** *fig.* (*debiti*, *tasse*, *ecc.*) to combine; (*idee*, *pensieri*, *ecc.*) to include.

conglobàto, *ag.* **1.** conglobate **2.** *fig.* summed up; summarized **3.** (*anat.*) conglobate: *ghiandola conglobata*, conglobate gland.

conglobazióne, *s.f.* conglobation.

conglomeràre, *v.t.* to conglomerate, to gather together, to collect into a mass.

conglomeràto, *s.m.* **1.** grouping: — *etnico,* ethnic(al) grouping; — *politico,* political grouping **2.** (*geol.*) conglomerate, pudding-stone.

conglomerazióne, *s.f.* conglomeration.

conglutinaménto, *s.m.* conglutination.

conglutinàre, *v.t.* to conglutinate, to glue together ‖ **conglutinàrsi,** *v.r.* to conglutinate.

Còngo, *no.pr.m.* (*geog.*) Congo: *il fiume* —, the River Congo.

congratulàrsi, *v.r.* to congratulate (s.o.): *mi congratulo con te perchè hai superato gli esami,* I congratulate you on passing your exams; *si congratulò con se stesso per averla scampata bella,* he congratulated himself on his hairbreadth escape.

congratulatòrio, *ag.* congratulatory.

congratulazióne, *s.f.* congratulation: *posso farvi le mie congratulazioni?,* may I offer you my congratulations?.

congrèga, *s.f.* **1.** gang, set **2.** (*rar. eccl.*) congregation, confraternity.

congregaménto, *s.m.* gathering, assembling.

congregàre, *v.t.* to assemble, to gather ‖ **congregàrsi,** *v.r.* to gather, to congregate, to assemble, to come together; to flock together.

congregazióne, *s.f.* **1.** assembly, congregation **2.** (*eccl.*) congregation: — *di carità,* charitable institution.

congregazionìsta, *s.m.* (*eccl.*) member of a congregation.

congressìsta, *s.m.* member of a congress.

congrèsso, *s.m.* **1.** congress, conference: — *medico,* medical congress; *atti del* —, proceedings (*o* minutes) of the conference ‖ *il* — *di Vienna,* (*st.*) the Congress of Vienna **2.** (*colloquio di avvocato col cliente*) consultation **3.** *il Congresso,* (*negli Stati Uniti*) Congress: *membro del Congresso,* Congressman.

còngrua, *s.f.* (*eccl.*) **1.** (*dotazione beneficiaria di chiesa, parrocchia*) benefice **2.** (*assegno versato dallo Stato ai parroci*) stipend.

congruaménte, *av.* **1.** congruously; consistently **2.** (*convenientemente*) suitably; adequately; fairly.

congruènza, *s.f.* **1.** congruence, congruency; consistency **2.** (*convenienza*) suitability; adequacy; fairness **3.** (*mat. geom.*) congruence, congruency.

còngruo, *ag.* **1.** congruous, consistent **2.** (*conveniente, adeguato*) suitable; adequate, fair: — *compenso,* adequate compensation **3.** (*mat. geom.*) congruent: *numeri congrui,* congruent numbers.

conguagliàre, *v.t.* to equalize, to level; (*comm.*) to balance.

conguàglio, *s.m.* adjustment, levelling, balance: — *delle paghe,* levelling of wages; — *monetario,* currency (*o* monetary) adjustment; *in* —, to square the count.

coniàre, *v.t.* **1.** to coin, to mint: — *una medaglia,* to strike a medal **2.** (*inventare*) to coin, to invent: — *una parola nuova,* to coin a new word; — *una notizia,* to invent news.

coniatóre, *s.m.* **1.** coiner, worker in the mint' **2.** *fig.* inventor.

coniatúra, coniazióne, *s.f.* coinage.

conicità, *s.f.* (*geom.*) conicalness, conicity.

cònico, *ag.* conic(al): *sezione conica,* conical section (*o* sector).

conífera, *s.f.* (*bot.*) conifer ‖ *le conifere,* (*bot.*) Coniferae.

conífero, *ag.* (*bot.*) coniferous.

coniglicoltúra, *s.f.* rabbit-breeding.

coniglièra, *s.f.* **1.** (*gabbia per conigli*) rabbit-hutch **2.** (*allevamento di conigli*) rabbit-warren.

coníglio, *s.m.* **1.** rabbit: *pelliccia di* —, cony; *tana di* —, rabbit-hole **2.** *fig.* (*persona timida, paurosa*) coward; 'aint-heart, chicken-heart.

cònio, *s.m.* **1.** (*cuneo*) wedge **2.** (*attrezzo per coniare*) minting die **3.** (*impronta di moneta, medaglia*) coin, brand, stamp: *moneta di nuovo* —, brand-new coin **4.** (*inven-*

zione) coinage, coining: *parole di nuovo* —, words of modern coinage **5.** (*qualità*) stamp; kind, quality: *sono dello stesso* —, they are of the same stamp.

coniròstro, *ag.* (*ornit.*) conirostral, conical-billed ‖ *s.m.* (*ornit.*) coniroster.

coniugàbile, *ag.* (*gram.*) conjugable.

coniugàle, *ag.* conjugal: *diritti coniugali,* conjugal rights; *vita* —, married life.

coniugalménte, *av.* conjugally.

coniugàre, *v.t.* **1.** (*gram.*) to conjugate **2.** (*unire in matrimonio*) to marry ‖ **coniugàrsi,** *v.r.* to get married.

coniugàto, *ag.* (*sposato*) married.

coniugazióne, *s.f.* (*gram.*) conjugation.

còniuge, *s.m.* consort ‖ *i coniugi,* husband and wife (*o* a married couple): *i coniugi Rossi,* Mr. and Mrs. Rossi.

coniúgio, *s.m.* (*rar.*) conjugality; marriage.

connaturàle, *ag.* connatural; innate, congenital.

connaturàre, *v.t.* to make connatural; to connaturalize ‖ **connaturàrsi,** *v.r.* to grow inveterate: *quell'abitudine gli si è connaturata,* that habit has become deeply rooted in his nature.

connaturàto, *ag.* ingrained; deeply rooted.

connazionàle, *s.m.* compatriot, fellow-countryman (*pl.* fellow-countrymen) ‖ *s.f.* fellow-countrywoman (*pl.* fellow-countrywomen).

connessióne, *s.f.* connection, connexion (anche *fig.*): — *dei fili,* (*elett.*) wire connection; — *in serie,* (*elett.*) mesh connection; *intima* — *tra due fatti,* fig. close connection between two facts.

connèsso, *ag.* connected, joined: *i documenti connessi,* the relevant documents ‖ *s.m.pl.: annessi e connessi,* appendages.

connèttere, *v.t.* **1.** (*unire*) to connect, to join, to link **2.** *fig.* to associate (in one's mind); to'link: *questi fatti sono strettamente connessi,* these facts are closely linked together ‖ *non* —, to have confused ideas (*o* to talk'at random): *oggi sono così stanco che non connetto,* today I am so tired that I talk at random.

connettìvo, *ag.* (*anat.*) connective: *tessuto* —, connective tissue.

connivènte, *ag.* conniving (at sthg.).

connivènza, *s.f.* connivance (at, in sthg.).

connotàto, *s.m.* description, feature: *potete darmi i connotati del ladro?,* can you give me a description of the thief?; *rispondere ai connotati,* to answer to the description ‖ *cambiare, rovinare i connotati a qlcu.,* fig. to beat s.o. black and blue.

connùbio, *s.m.* **1.** marriage, union **2.** *fig.* union: — *di partiti,* union of parties.

còno, *s.m.* cone: — *d'ombra,* (*astr.*) cone of shade; — *retto,* (*geom.*) right circular cone; — *vulcanico,* cone of a volcano; *tronco di* —, (*geom.*) frustum of cone.

conòcchia, *s.f.* distaff: *trarre la* —, to spin.

conòide, *s.m.* **1.** (*geom.*) conoid **2.** (*geol.*) cone: — *di deiezione,* alluvial cone.

conopèo, *s.m.* **1.** (*zanzariera*) mosquito-net **2.** (*eccl.*) pyx-cloth.

conoscènte, *s.c.* acquaintance: *un* — *di mio padre,* an acquaintance of my father's (*o* one of my father's acquaintances).

conoscènza, *s.f.* **1.** knowledge: — *di se stesso,* self-knowledge; *ha una buona* — *del latino,* he has a good knowledge of Latin; *non sono a* — *di questo,* (*fam.*) this is not within my ken; *prendere* — *di ql.co.,* to make oneself acquainted with (*o* to study *o* to examine) sthg; *venire a* — *di ql.co.,* to become acquainted with (*o* to get to know *o* to get knowledge of) sthg. **2.** (*dir.*) cognizance: *questi fatti non sono a* — *del Tribunale,* these facts are not within the cognizance of the Court **3.** acquaintance: *una persona di mia* —, an acquaintance of mine (*o* someone I know); *quando feci la sua* —, when I first met him; *fare la* — *di qlcu.,* to make s.o.'s acquaintance (*o* to get acquainted with s.o.) **4.** (*conoscente*) acquaintance: *una vecchia — del tribunale*, (*iron.*) an older offender; — *che si saluta appena*, nodding acquaintance; *ha una larga cerchia di conoscenze*, he has a wide circle of acquaintances **5.** (*sensi*) consciousness: *privo di —*, unconscious (*o* in a dead faint); *perdere —*, to lose consciousness (*o* to faint *o* to swoon); *riprendere —*, to recover one's senses (*o* to regain consciousness) **6.** (*fil.*) cognition.

conóscere, *v.t.* **1.** to know: *la conosco per averla sentita nominare*, I know her by name; *lo conosco da due anni*, I have known him (for) two years; *prima lo conoscevo solo di vista*, before I only knew him by sight; — *a fondo qlcu.*, to know s.o. through and through (*o* to read s.o. like a book); — *al sapore*, to know by the taste; — *bene la storia romana*, to be conversant with (*o* to have a thorough knowledge of) Roman history; — *di fama*, to know [by reputation; — *qlcu. dalla voce*, to recognize s.o. by his voice; — *la strada*, to be familiar with the road; *far* — *un articolo*, (*comm.*) to advertise an article; *far* — *ql.co.*, to make sthg. known (*o* to bring sthg. to light); *farsi —*, to make oneself known (*o* to make a name for oneself *o* to rise to notice *o* to come to the front) ‖ *conosco Milano come le mie tasche*, I know every inch of Milan ‖ *non conosce il mondo*, he is ignorant of the world ‖ *non conosce ragione*, he won't listen to reason ‖ *darsi a* — *per un bugiardo*, to prove a liar (*o* to be known as a liar) ‖ *all'opera si conosce il maestro*, *prov.* the workman is known by his work (*o* the work comments the workman) ‖ *dal frutto si conosce l'albero*, *prov.* by the husk you may guess at the nut (*o* a tree is known by its fruits) ‖ *dall'unghia si conosce il leone*, *prov.* you may know the lion by its claw ‖ *nelle sventure si conoscono gli amici*, *prov.* a friend in need is a friend indeed **2.** (*fare la conoscenza di*) to meet: *dove l'hai conosciuto?*, where did you meet him?; *fammi* — *tua moglie*, introduce me to your wife **3.** (*essere a conoscenza di*) to be acquainted with (sthg.); (*venire a conoscenza di*) to get acquainted with (sthg.) **4.** (*distinguere*) to distinguish, to know: — *il bene dal male*, to know good from evil **5.** (*sperimentare*) to experience: *egli conobbe la povertà*, he experienced poverty **6.** (*raggiungere*) to reach: *la letteratura conobbe allora il suo miglior periodo*, literature reached its best period then **7.** (*dir.*) to take cognizance of (sthg.) ‖ **conóscersi**, *v.r.* to know oneself ‖ *conosci te stesso*, know thyself ‖ *v.r. reciproco* to know each other (one another): *si conobbero qui*, they met here.

conoscíbile, *ag.* **1.** knowable **2.** (*riconoscibile*) recognizable, easily known ‖ *s.m.* knowledge.

conosciménto, *s.m.* **1.** (*atto del conoscere*) knowing **2.** (*conoscenza, sapere*) knowledge.

conoscitivo, *ag.* cognitive.

conoscitóre, *s.m.*, **conoscitríce**, *s.f.* expert, connoisseur, good judge: *essere buon* — *di ql.co.*, to be a good judge (*o* a connoisseur) of sthg. (*o* an authority on sthg.).

conosciúto, *ag.* well-known, renowned, famous: *è* — *in tutto il mondo*, it is well known all over the world.

conquassàre, *v.t.* **1.** to shake violently **2.** (*rovinare*) to smash, to ruin; to shatter: — *un mobile*, to smash a piece of furniture.

conquàsso, *s.m.* **1.** violent shaking **2.** (*rovina*) smash, ruin ‖ *mettere a —*, to put things in great disorder.

conquíbus, *s.m.pl.* (*scherz.*) lolly (*sing.*), cash (*sing.*): *andrei volentieri, ma mi mancano i —*, I should love to go but I haven't got the lolly.

conquídere, *v.t.* (*letter.*) to conquer, to subdue, to overcome; to vanquish.

conquíso, *ag.* (*letter.*) conquered, subdued.

conquísta, *s.f.* conquest (anche *fig.*): *la* — *normanna*, the Norman Conquest; *le conquiste della scienza*, the conquests (*o* achievements) of science; *fare una* — *(amorosa)*, (*scherz.*) to make a conquest.

conquistàbile, *ag.* conquerable.

conquistàre, *v.t.* **1.** to conquer, to subdue: — *un paese*, to conquer a country **2.** *fig.* to win; to acquire: *quell'atto gli conquistò la pubblica stima*, that action won him the regard of the public; — *l'amore di qlcu.*, to win s.o.'s love; — *onori*, to win honours.

conquistatóre, *s.m.* **1.** conqueror ‖ *Guglielmo il Conquistatore*, (*st. inglese*) William the Conqueror **2.** (*rubacuori*) lady-killer, Don Juan: *è un vero —*, he is a regular Don Juan.

conquistatríce, *s.f.* **1.** conqueress **2.** (*rubacuori*) heart-breaker, flirt.

consacràbile, *ag.* that can be consecrated.

consacraménto, *s.m.* consecration.

consacràndo, *ag.* that is to be consecrated.

consacrànte, *s.m.* (*eccl.*) consecrator, consecrating priest.

consacràre, *v.t.* **1.** (*eccl.*) to consecrate; (*ordinare, un sacerdote*) to ordain: *fu consacrato vescovo di Napoli*, he was consecrated bishop of Naples; — *una nuova chiesa*, to consecrate a new church; — *un sacerdote*, to ordain a priest **2.** (*dedicare*) to devote, to consecrate: *consacrò le proprie energie allo studio*, he devoted his energies to study; — *la vita a Dio*, to consecrate one's life to God **3.** (*rendere valido*) to consecrate: *un costume consacrato dalla tradizione*, a custom hallowed (*o* consecrated) by tradition ‖ **consacràrsi**, *v.r.* to devote oneself: — *a ql.co.*, to devote oneself to sthg.

consacrazióne, *s.f.* **1.** (*eccl.*) consecration; (*ordinazione sacerdotale*) ordination: *la* — *del pane e del vino*, the consecration of bread and wine **2.** *fig.* consecration: *espressione che ha ricevuto la* — *del tempo, dell'uso*, expression which has received the consecration of time, of custom.

consagràre, (*rar.*) per **consacràre**.

consanguínea, *s.f.* blood-relation, kinswoman (*pl.* kinswomen).

consanguineità, *s.f.* consanguinity, blood-relationship.

consanguíneo, *ag.* consanguineous, consanguine, akin ‖ *s.m.* blood-relation, kinsman (*pl.* kinsmen).

consapévole, *ag.* **1.** aware, conscious: *era* — *della propria colpa*, he was conscious of his guilt **2.** (*informato*) acquainted (with sthg.): *fare qlcu.* — *di ql.co.*, to inform s.o. of sthg. (*o* to acquaint s.o. with sthg.).

consapevolézza, *s.f.* **1.** consciousness; awareness **2.** (*conoscenza*) knowledge.

consapevolménte, *av.* consciously.

consapúto, *ag.* (*rar.*) known, well-known.

cònscio, *V.* **consapévole**.

consecutivaménte, *av.* consecutively.

consecutívo, *ag.* **1.** following: *il giorno —*, on the following day **2.** (*di seguito*) consecutive, running; in succession: *per due mesi consecutivi*, for two months on end (*o* in succession); *ha superato il record mondiale cinque volte consecutive*, he has broken the world record five times running **3.** (*gram.*) consecutive: *proposizione consecutiva*, consecutive clause.

consecuzióne, *s.f.* **1.** — *dei tempi*, (*gram.*) sequence (*o* consecution) of tenses **2.** (*rar.*) (*conseguimento*) attainment.

conségna, *s.f.* **1.** (*comm.*) delivery: — *a domicilio*, house (*o* home) delivery; — *al latore*, no-name delivery (*o* delivery to bearer); — *contro assegno*, cash on delivery; — *di merci*, delivery of goods; — *in deposito franco*, delivery in bound; — *mancata*, non-delivery; — *regolare*, due (*o* safe and right) delivery; — *sul luogo*, delivery on the spot; *alla —*, on delivery: *pagamento alla —*, to be paid on delivery (*o* cash on delivery, *abbr.* C.O.D.); *buono, ordine di —*, delivery-note; *condizioni di —*, terms of delivery; *franco di —*, free delivery; *spese di —*, delivery-charges; *effettuare, eseguire la —*, to effect delivery; *effettuare la* — *in ritardo*, to deliver late; *ottenere la —*, to get delivery; *prorogare la data di —*, to extend the day (*o* the term) of delivery; *ricevere merci in —*, to receive delivery of goods **2.** (*deposito, custodia*) consignment: *merce lasciata in* —, goods on consignment; *partita in* —, consignment; *dare ql.co. in* — *a qlcu.*, to consign sthg. to s.o.; (*affidare*) to entrust sthg. to s.o.; *ricevere ql.co. in* —, to be entrusted with sthg. **3.** (*mil.*) (*ordine*) orders (*pl.*), instructions (*pl.*): *ha per* — *di non lasciar passare nessuno*, his orders arc to let nobody pass; *forzare la* —, to force a sentry (*o* one's way in); *mancare alla* —, to disobey orders **4.** — *in caserma*, (*mil.*) confinement to barracks.

consegnàre, *v.t.* **1.** to deliver, to hand over, to consign: *glielo consegnerai personalmente*, you will hand it over to him personally; — *una lettera*, to deliver a letter; — *merci*, to consign (*o* to deliver) goods; — *qlcu. alla polizia*, to hand s.o. over to the police; — *qlcu. nelle mani del nemico*, to deliver s.o. into the hands of the enemy **2.** (*mil.*) to confine to barracks: *le truppe sono consegnate*, the troops are standing by.

consegnatàrio, *s.m.* **1.** (*comm.*) consignee **2.** (*dir.*) bailee.

consegnàto, *ag.* (*mil.*) confined to barracks.

consegnatóre, *s.m.* (*comm.*) deliverer, consignor, consigner.

conseguènte, *ag.* consequent: — *a ql.co.*, consequent upon (*o* ensuing from *o* following from *o* resulting from) sthg. ‖ — *a se stesso*, consistent in one's behaviour (*o* true to oneself).

conseguenteménte, *av.* **1.** consequently, in consequence (of sthg.) **2.** (*in conformità a*) accordingly: *agire* —, to act accordingly.

conseguènza, *s.f.* **1.** consequence: *bisogna subirne le conseguenze*, you must take the consequences; *affrontare le conseguenze*, to face (*o* to meet) the consequences; *essere responsabile delle conseguenze*, to be liable for consequences ‖ *in* — *di*, according to: *agirò in* — *degli ordini ricevuti*, I'll act according to the orders received ‖ *per* —, consequently (*o* in consequence of) **2.** (*importanza*) importance, consequence: *sono cose di gran* —, these are matters of great importance.

conseguìbile, *ag.* attainable.

conseguiménto, *s.m.* attainment: *per il* — *del suo scopo*, for the attainment of his purpose.

conseguìre, *v.t.* (*raggiungere*) to attain, to reach; (*ottenere*) to obtain, to get, to achieve: *consegui il suo scopo*, he attained (*o* reached) his purpose; *conseguirò la laurea l'anno prossimo*, I'll get (*o* obtain) my degree next year ‖ *v.i.* **1.** (*seguire*) to follow: *ne consegue che...*, it follows that... **2.** (*risultare*) to ensue, to result: *ne conseguì una pestilenza*, a pestilence ensued; *questo è ciò che ne conseguì*, that's what it resulted in (*o* it led to).

consènso, *s.m.* **1.** consent, assent, agreement: — *formale, scritto*, formal, written consent; — *verbale*, verbal assent; *per* — *generale*, by universal consent; *previo* — *delle parti interessate*, subject to agreement of the parties concerned **2.** (*permesso*) permission, consent: *col* — *di mia madre*, with my mother's permission **3.** (*matrimoniale*) licence.

consensuàle, *ag.* (*dir.*) by consent of the parties, by mutual consent: *separazione* —, separation by mutual consent.

consentaneità, *s.f.* consentaneity, consentaneousness.

consentàneo, *ag.* consentaneous, accordant, agreeing.

consentiménto, *s.m.* (*rar.*) consent; assent; agreement.

consentìre, *v.i.* **1.** (*acconsentire*) to consent, to assent: — *a fare ql.co.*, to consent to do sthg.; — *a una proposta*, to assent to a proposal **2.** (*essere d'accordo*) to agree: *consento con te su questo argomento*, I agree with you on this subject **3.** (*cedere, alla pressione*) to be pliant, to be pliable, to be supple; to yield: *questo legno consente alla pressione*, this wood yields to pressure ‖ *v.t.* (*permettere*) to allow; to permit.

consenziènte, *ag.* consentient; consenting; assenting.

consèrto, *ag.* intertwined; interwoven; folded: *a braccia conserte*, with folded arms.

consèrto, (**di**), *l. av.* in concert, together.

consèrva, *s.f.* **1.** preserve: *conserve alimentari*, alimentary preserves; — *di arance*, marmalade; — *di frutta*, jam; — *di pomodoro*, tomato sauce; *cibi in* —, tinned food-stuffs (*o amer.* canned food-stuffs); *tenere in* —, to preserve **2.** (*il conservare*) preservation **3.** (*serbatoio d'acqua*) reservoir.

consèrva, (**di**), *l.av.* together: *andare di* —, (*mar.*) to sail in convoy; *fig.* to act together (*o* to agree).

conservàbile, *ag.* preservable.

conservàre, *v.t.* to preserve; to retain; to keep (anche *fig.*): — *frutta, uova*, to preserve fruit, eggs; — *la propria innocenza*, to keep one's innocence; — *l'uso delle proprie facoltà*, to retain the use of one's faculties ‖ *che Dio ti conservi!*, God preserve you! ‖ **conservàrsi**, *v.r.* to keep; to remain: *quella carne cruda si conserverà fino a domani?*, will that raw meat keep till to-morrow?; — *in salute*, to keep in good health; — *onesto*, to remain honest ‖ *si conservi!*, keep well! (*o* take care of your health!).

conservatìvo, *ag.* conservative, preservative: *sequestro* —, (*dir.*) preventive attachment.

conservàto, *ag.* preserved; kept: *frutta conservata*, preserved fruit; *questo vecchio orologio è ancora ben* —, this old clock is still in a good state ‖ *una vecchia signora ben conservata*, a well-preserved lady.

conservatóre, *ag.* **1.** preserving; preservative **2.** (*pol.*) Conservative: *l'ala conservatrice*, the Conservative wing ‖ *s.m.* **1.** conservator; preserver; keeper; custodian, guardian: — *delle ipoteche*, (*amm.*) registrar of mortgages; — *di un museo*, curator (*o* keeper) of a museum **2.** (*pol.*) Conservative; (*st. inglese*) Tory.

conservatorìa, *s.f.* conservatorship.

conservatòrio, *s.m.* **1.** (*educandato*) girls' school **2.** (*scuola di musica*) academy of music; conservatory, conservatoire.

conservatorìsmo, *s.m.* (*pol.*) Conservatism.

conservatrìce, *s.f.* conservator; preserver; keeper; custodian, guardian; curatrix.

conservazióne, *s.f.* preservation; care; maintenance: — *in frigoriferi*, cold storage; *in buono stato di* —, in good repair (*o* in a good state); *istinto di* —, instinct of self-preservation.

consèrvo, *s.m.* fellow-servant.

consèsso, *s.m.* assembly, meeting.

consideràbile, *ag.* considerable.

considerabilménte, *av.* considerably.

consideràndo, *s.m.* (*dir.*) whereas, preamble.

consideràre, *v.t.* **1.** (*esaminare, prendere in considerazione*) to consider; to think of (sthg.); to envisage, to contemplate: *egli considera la possibilità di tornare a Londra*, he contemplates going back to London; *la legge non considera questo caso*, (*dir.*) the law does not consider this case; *non avevo considerato la faccenda sotto quell'aspetto*, I had not envisaged the matter in that light; *non considerai mai quella possibilità*, I never contemplated (*o* envisaged *o* thought of) that possibility; *bisogna* — *che...*, it must be borne in mind that... ‖ *considerando* (*che*), *considerato* (*che*), considering (that) (*o dir.* whereas): *considerando che ciò è sembrato giusto alla Corte Suprema...*, whereas it has seemed right to the Supreme Court...; *considerata la sua inesperienza*, considering his lack of experience ‖ *tutto considerato*, all things considered (*o* on the whole) **2.** (*reputare, stimare*) to consider, to regard; to deem; to judge; to esteem: *consideralo fatto*, consider it as done; *considero un onore servirla*, I deem it an honour to serve you; *è generalmente considerata una ragazza molto gentile*, she is generally considered (to be) a very kind girl; *lo considero un mascalzone*, I consider him (to be) a knave ‖ **consideràrsi**, *v.r.* to consider oneself: *ci considerammo molto fortunati*, we counted ourselves very lucky; *mi considero respon-sabile di questo incidente,* I hold (*o* consider) myself responsible for this accident; *si considerano importanti,* they consider themselves important; *si consideri in arresto!,* consider yourself under arrest! ‖ *v.r.* reciproco to consider each other (one another): *si considerarono un momento prima di iniziare la lotta,* they considered each other for a moment before beginning the fight.

considerataménte, *av.* considerately; advisedly.

consideratézza, *s.f.* considerateness; advisedness.

consideràto, *ag.* **1.** considerate, thoughtful; (*cauto*) careful, cautious; prudent: *dovresti essere più — nei tuoi giudizi,* you should be more careful in your judge-ments **2.** (*stimato*) esteemed, highly thought of.

considerazióne, *s.f.* **1.** consideration: *agire senza —,* to act thoughtlessly (*o* inconsiderately); *prcndere ql.co. in —,* to take sthg. into consideration (*o* into account *o* to entertain sthg.); *tenere nella debita —,* to hold in due consideration ‖ *in — di,* in consideration (*o* on account *o* in view) of **2.** (*stima*) esteem; regard; respect: *avere una grande — per qlcu.,* to have a great regard for s.o.; *godere di molta —,* to enjoy a high reputation (*o* to be highly respected); *tenere qlcu. in grande —,* to hold s.o. in great esteem.

considerévole, *ag.* considerable; large: *un numero — di gente,* a considerable number of people; *subire delle considerevoli perdite,* to incur large losses.

considerevolménte, *av.* considerably.

consigliàbile, *ag.* advisable; expedient: *è — che vada,* it is advisable for him to go; *non è — che tu discuta con il tuo datore di lavoro,* it would not be expedient for you to argue with your employer.

consigliàre, *v.t.* **1.** to advise, to counsel; (*racco-mandare*) to recommend: *il dottore mi ha consigliato la montagna,* the doctor advised me to go to the moun-tains; *egli ci consigliò di rivolgerci ad altri,* he advised us to apply to s.o. else; *egli consigliava di aver pazienza,* he counselled patience; *le consiglio questo libro, signore,* I recommend you this book, sir; *non vollero lasciarsi — da noi,* they would not take our advice **2.** (*indurre, persuadere*) to persuade, to induce: *— qlcu. al male,* to lead s.o. astray ‖ **consigliàrsi,** *v.r.* (*chieder consi-glio*) to ask (s.o.'s) advice; (*consultarsi*) to consult (with s.o.), to advise (with s.o.): *consigliati con tua madre,* ask your mother's advice; *mi consigliai con il mio socio,* I consulted (*o* advised) with my partner; *— con un avvocato,* to seek advice of a lawyer (*o* to take counsel with a lawyer).

consigliataménte, *av.* advisedly.

consigliàto, *ag.* **1.** advised: *ben —,* well-advised; *mal —,* ill-advised **2.** (*raccomandato*) recommended: *libri consigliati ai giovani,* books recommended for the young.

consigliatóre, *s.m.,* **consigliatríce,** *s.f.* adviser.

consiglièra, *s.f.* adviser: *la fame è una cattiva —,* hunger is a bad adviser.

consiglière, *s.m.* **1.** adviser, counsellor: *l'ozio è cattivo —,* idleness is a bad counsellor **2.** (*membro di un consiglio*) councillor, member of a council; (*membro di un'assemblea*) committee-man (*pl.* committee-men), member of a committee: *— comunale,* town-councillor; *— d'amministrazione,* director; *— delegato,* managing director.

consíglio, *s.m.* **1.** advice (*solo sing.*): *— disinteres-sato,* disinterested advice; *un buon —,* a good piece of advice; *ascolta i miei consigli,* take my advice; *chie-dere il — di qlcu.,* to consult s.o. (*o* to seek s.o.'s advice); *rifiutare un —,* (*respingerlo*) to reject s.o.'s advice; (*ri-fiutarsi di darlo*) to refuse to give advice; *seguire il — di qlcu.,* to follow s.o.'s advice ‖ *la notte porta —,* seek counsel from your pillow (*o* sleep on it): *la notte mi porterà —,* I shall consult my pillow (*o* I shall take a night for reflection) **2.** (*corpo di persone*) council: *— comunale,* town council; *Consiglio dei Ministri,* Cabinet; *— di famiglia,* family council; *— direttivo, d'ammini-*

strazione, board of directors; *Consiglio di Stato,* Council of State; *camera di consiglio,* council chamber.

consiliàre, *ag.* of a council; council (*attributivo*).

consímile, *ag.* similar; alike (*predicativo*); like (*at-tributivo*); (*tale*) such.

consimilménte, *av.* similarly; likely.

consistènte, *ag.* (*solido*) firm, solid, substantial.

consistènza, *s.f.* **1.** consistence, firmness, solid-ity **2.** (*chim.*) consistency, consistence **3.** (*comm.*) (*di cassa*) cash on hand; (*di magazzino*) stock on hand, inventory on hand.

consístere, *v.i.* to consist: *la difficoltà consiste nel-l'impararlo a memoria,* the difficulty consists (*o* lies) in memorizing it; *il mio appartamento consiste di cinque stanze,* my flat consists (*o* is composed) of five rooms.

consociàbile, *ag.* associable.

consociàre, *v.t.* to associate, to join; to bring together ‖ **consociàrsi,** *v.r.* to associate, to consociate; to join (s.o.).

consociàto, *ag.* associate(d), consociate ‖ *s.m.* as-sociate, consociate; (*socio*) partner: *il numero dei con-sociati ammonta a 300,* the membership amounts to 300.

consociazióne, *s.f.,* association; consociation; (*lega*) union, league.

consòcio, *s.m.* associate, consociate; co-partner; part-ner; (*compagno di associazione*) fellow-member.

consolàbile, *ag.* consolable.

consolànte, *ag.* cheering: *notizia —,* cheering news.

consolàre[1], *v.t.* **1.** to console, to comfort, to give comfort to (s.o.), to solace; (*alleviare*) to soothe, to relieve: *consolò l'amico sventurato,* he consoled (*o* com-forted *o* gave comfort to) his distressed friend; *— un bimbo che piange,* to soothe a crying baby **2.** (*ral-legrare*) to cheer (up); to rejoice: *la buona notizia con-solò il poveretto* the good news cheered up (*o* rejoic-ed) the poor fellow **3.** (*ristorare, ricreare*) to refresh: *c'è un'arietta che consola,* there is a refreshing breeze ‖ *ha una faccia da imbecille che consola,* he has a stupid face which stands a mile ‖ **consolàrsi,** *v.r.* **1.** to take comfort, to be comforted, to console oneself, to be consoled, to find solace: *il bimbo si consolò con una caramella,* the child consoled himself with a sweet; *si consolarono della perdita,* they were consoled for the loss **2.** (*rallegrarsi*) to cheer up, to rejoice, to be re-joiced: *si consolò alla notizia,* he cheered up (*o* he rejoiced) at the news; *si consolò alla vista della sua terra,* he took heart at the sight of his native land.

consolàre[2], *ag.* **1.** (*di console nell'antichità*) con-sular: *strada —, consular road* **2.** (*di console in età moderna*) consular: *agente —,* consular agent; *certificato —,* consular certificate; *diritti consolari,* consular dues (*o* consulage); *fattura —,* consular invoice; *rapporto —,* consular report; *residenza —,* consul's residence; *visto —,* consul's visa.

consolàto, *s.m.* consulate.

consolatóre, *ag.* consoling, comforting ‖ *lo Spirito Consolatore,* (*lo Spirito Santo*) the Comforter ‖ *s.m.* consoler, comforter.

consolatòria, *s.f.* consolatory letter.

consolatòrio, *ag.* consolatory: *un biglietto —,* a con-solatory note.

consolatríce, *s.f.* consoler, comforter ‖ *Consolatrice degli Afflitti,* (*la Madonna*) Comforter of the Afflicted.

consolazióne, *s.f.* **1.** consolation; comfort, solace: *l'af-fetto dei figli è la sua unica —,* her children's love is her only comfort ‖ *premio di —,* consolation stake **2.** (*gioia, piacere*) joy, delight: *è per noi una grande — il fatto che egli ritorni,* his coming back is a great joy to us.

cònsole, *s.m.* **1.** (*nell'antichità*) consul: *il — Mar-cello,* Marcellus consul **2.** (*nella moderna carriera diplo-matica*) consul: *— generale,* consul general; *essere no-minato —,* to be appointed consul.

consolidàbile, *ag.* that may be consolidated.

consolidaménto, *s.m.* consolidation; (*rafforzamento*) strengthening: *— di minerale,* (*metal.*) clotting.

consolidàre, *v.t.* **1.** to consolidate; (*rinforzare*) to strengthen; (*mec.*) to stiffen **2.** *fig.* to consolidate, to strengthen: — *un debito,* (*econ.*) to consolidate (*o* to fund) a debt; — *una posizione,* (*mil.*) to consolidate a position; — *la propria fortuna,* to put one's fortune on a sound basis || **consolidàrsi,** *v.r.* to consolidate; to solidify.

consolidàto, *ag.* consolidated || *s.m.* [(*econ.*) consolidated annuities (*pl.*); consols (*pl.*).

consolidazióne, *s.f.* **1.** consolidation; (*rafforzamento*) strengthening **2.** (*di ferita*) healing; (*di frattura*) setting, knitting.

consonànte, *ag.* **1.** (*mus.*) consonant **2.** (*corrispondente*) consonant (with sthg.); agreeing (with sthg.): *azione* — *al suo carattere,* action consonant (*o* agreeing) with his character || *s.f.* (*fonet.*) consonant.

consonànza, *s.f.* **1.** (*poes. mus.*) consonance **2.** *fig.* (*accordo*) consonance, harmony; agreement.

consonàre, *v.i.* (*rar.*) to be consonant, to be in accordance, to agree.

cònsono, *ag.* consonant (with sthg.); in accordance (with sthg.); agreeing (with sthg.): — *a verità, alla legge,* in accordance with truth, with the law.

consorèlla, *s.f.* (*eccl.*) sister.

consòrte, *s.m.* **1.** consort; husband: *principe* —, prince consort **2.** (*che appartiene ad una consorteria*) member of a faction || *s.f.* consort; wife.

consortería, *s.f.* faction; clique, junto.

consorziàle, *ag.* social.

consorziàto, *ag.* associated.

consòrzio, *s.m.* **1.** society: — *umano,* human society **2.** (*sindacato*) consortium (*pl.* consortia); syndicate; (*unione*) union: — *agrario,* agricultural union.

consostanziàle, *ag.* (*teol.*) consubstantial: *il Figlio è* — *al Padre,* the Son is consubstantial with the Father.

constàre, *v.i.* **1.** (*essere composto*) to consist, to be composed: *l'enciclopedia consta di dieci volumi,* the encyclopaedia consists (*o* is composed) of ten volumes **2.** (*risultare, essere noto*) to be within one's knowledge; to be proved: *a quando mi consta,* for what I know; *mi consta che...,* it has come to my knowledge that...; *per quanto mi constava,* as far as it was within my knowledge || *questo non consta,* this is not proved.

constatàre, e derivati, *V.* **costatàre, e derivati.**

constellàre, *V.* **costellàre.**

consuèto, *ag.* usual, customary, habitual: *all'ora consueta,* at the usual time || *s.m.* habit; custom: *come di* —, as usual: *come di* — *giunse in ritardo,* as was his custom (*o* wont) he came late; *ho dormito più del* —, I have slept more than usual.

consuetudinàrio, *ag.* customary, habitual; traditional; consuetudinary: *diritto* —, consuetudinary law.

consuetùdine, *s.f.* **1.** custom; habit; usage; (*dir.*) consuetude: *come è nostra* —, as we are in the habit of doing (*o* as we are used to do *o* according to our habit) **2.** (*comm.*) rule: *tale è la* — *da noi seguita,* this is the rule followed by us.

consulènte, *ag.* consulting (*attributivo*); consultant (*attributivo*): *ingegnere* —, consulting engineer; *medico* —, consulting physician || *s.m.* consultant, adviser: — *legale,* legal adviser.

consulènza, *s.f.* advice: *chiedere una* — *legale,* to seek legal advice.

consùlta, *s.f.* **1.** (*consultazione*) consultation **2.** (*corpo consultivo*) council: — *municipale,* town council || *Consulta Araldica,* Heralds' College || *Sacra Consulta,* (*dir. eccl.*) "Consulta" (judicial and administrative council of the Papal State) **3.** (*luogo della consultazione*) consulting room; council chamber.

consultàbile, *ag.* consultable.

consultatóre, *s.m.* consulter, consultant.

consultàre, *v.t.* to consult: — *l'avvocato,* to consult one's lawyer; — *un libro,* to consult a book; — *un medico,* to consult a physician **2.** (*esaminare*) to examine: — *il proprio cuore,* to examine one's heart

|| **consultàrsi,** *v.r.* **1.** to consult; to advise: *mi consultai con mio fratello,* I consulted (*o* advised) with my brother **2.** (*chiedere consiglio*) to ask s.o.'s advice || *v.r.* reciproco (*chiedersi reciprocamente un parere*) to consult each other (one another).

consultazióne, *s.f.* consultation: *gabinetto di* —, (*med.*) consulting room; *libro di* —, reference book.

consultívo, *ag.* consultative: *voto* —, consultative vote.

consúlto, *s.m.* consultation: *tenere un* —, (*med.*) to hold a consultation.

consultóre, *s.m.* adviser.

consultòrio, *ag.* consultatory, consultory || *s.m.* (*ufficio consulenze*) advisary bureau; (*di medico*) consulting-room: — *prematrimoniale,* pre-matrimonial advisary bureau.

consumàbile, *ag.* consumable.

consumàre, *v.t.* **1.** to consume; (*logorare*) to use up, to consume; (*vestiario*) to wear out: *consumato dal fuoco,* consumed by fire (*o* burnt up); *consumato dalla ruggine,* eaten away (*o* corroded) by rust; *lampada che consuma molto olio,* lamp that burns a great deal of oil; *macchina che consuma molto carbone,* engine that consumes a lot of coal; *il tempo che tutto consuma,* all-devouring time; — *le proprie energie,* to use up (*o* to consume) one's energies || — *un pasto,* to take (*o* to have) a meal **2.** (*dissipare*) to waste: — *il denaro,* to waste (*o* to squander) one's money; — *il tempo,* to waste one's time (*o* to spend one's time uselessly) **3.** (*compiere*) to commit; to consummate: — *un delitto,* to commit a crime; — *il matrimonio,* to consummate one's marriage; — *il sacrificio eucaristico,* to consummate the Eucharistic Sacrifice || **consumàrsi,** *v.r.* **1.** to consume; (*di combustibili*) to burn out; (*di vestiario*) to wear out: *la candela si è consumata completamente,* the candle has burnt out; *le mie scarpe si sono consumate,* my shoes have worn out **2.** (*struggersi*) to waste away (with sthg.); (*nel dolore*) to pine away (with sthg.); (*tormentarsi*) to worry oneself (about s.o., sthg.): — *dal dolore,* to pine away with grief.

consumàto, *ag.* **1.** (*perfetto*) accomplished, consummate, perfect, skilled: *un ballerino* —, an accomplished (*o* perfect *o* skilled) dancer; *con abilità consumata,* with consummate skill **2.** (*logorato*) worn-out, used up **3.** (*divorato*) consumed (with sthg.): — *dalla gelosia, dall'odio,* consumed (*o* eaten up) with jealousy, with hatred.

consumatóre, *s.m.,* **consumatríce,** *s.f.* consumer: *associazione fra consumatori,* consumers' association; *società cooperativa fra consumatori,* consumers' co-operative society.

consumazióne, *s.f.* **1.** consumption || *fino alla* — *dei secoli,* till the end of time **2.** (*dir.*) consummation: — *del reato,* consummation of the crime **3.** (*bibita*) drink; (*spuntino*) snack: *chi ha pagato la mia* —?, who paid for my drink?.

consumè, *s.m.* consommé.

consúmo, *s.m.* consumption; (*spreco*) waste: — *interno* (*di uno Stato*) home consumption; *articoli di largo* —, articles of wide consumption; *cooperativa di* —, co-operative store; *dazio* —, excise (duty) (*o* municipal toll); *far* — *di q.co.,* to consume (*o* to use) sthg.; *pagare a* —, to pay according to amount consumed || *uso e* —, wear and tear: *per proprio uso e* —, for one's private use.

consuntívo, *ag.:* *bilancio* —, (*comm.*) final (*o* rectified) balance.

consúnto, *ag.* **1.** consumed; (*logorato*) used up; worn-out **2.** (*tisico*) consumptive.

consunzióne, *s.f.* (*med.*) consumption: *andare in* —, to go into consumption.

consustanziàle, *ag.* (*teol.*) consubstantial: *il Figlio è* — *al Padre,* the Son is consubstantial with the Father.

consustanzialità, *s.f.* (*teol.*) consubstantiality.

consustanziazióne, *s.f.* (*teol.*) consubstantiation.

contàbile, *ag.* (*comm.*) book-keeping (*attributivo*); calculating (*attributivo*): *macchina* —, calculating machine; *sistema* —, book-keeping system; *valore* —, book value ‖ *s.c.* book-keeper, accountant.

contabilità, *s.f.* (*comm.*) book-keeping: — *di banca,* bank book-keeping; — *di fabbrica,* factory book-keeping; *sistema di* —, system of book-keeping (*o* accountancy); *ufficio* —, book-keeping department; *conoscere la* —, to be acquainted with book-keeping; *tenere la* —, to keep the books.

contachilòmetri, *s.m.* (*aut.*) speedometer.

contadína, *s.f.* country-woman (*pl.* country-women); peasant-woman (*pl.* peasant-women).

contadinàme, *s.m.* peasantry; country-folk (*coll. con costruzione pl.*); country-people (*coll. con costruzione pl.*).

contadinàta, *s.f.* boorish action; (*frase villana*) boorish words (*pl.*).

contadinèlla, *s.f.* peasant girl, country girl.

contadinèllo, *s.m.* peasant boy, country boy.

contadinéseo, *ag.* 1. rustic; peasant (*attributivo*): *semplicità contadinesca,* rustic simplicity 2. (*spreg.*) boorish, rustic: *i suoi modi erano assai contadineschi,* his manners were rustic in the extreme.

contadíno, *ag.* rustic; peasant (*attributivo*) ‖ *alla contadina,* after the manner of country-folk ‖ *s.m.* 1. (*campagnuolo*) countryman (*pl.* countrymen); peasant: *una coppia di contadini,* a peasant couple 2. (*agricoltore*) farmer.

contàdo, *s.m.* countryside (round a city), rural area (round a city): *il* — *milanese,* the countryside round Milan; *abitanti del* —, country-people.

contagiàre, *v.t.* to infect, to contaminate: — *qlcu.,* to infect (*o* to contaminate *o* to communicate a contagious disease) s.o.

contàgio, *s.m.* 1. contagion, infection: *diffondere il* —, to spread contagion (*o* infection) 2. (*rar.*) (*pestilenza*) plague, pestilence 3. *fig.* contagion: contaminating effect: *il* — *del vizio,* the contaminating effects of vice.

contagiosaménte, *av.* contagiously, infectiously.

contagiosità, *s.f.* contagiousness, infectiousness: *la* — *dell'esempio,* the contagiousness of example.

contagióso, *ag.* contagious, infectious (anche *fig.*); (*fam.*) catching: *malattia contagiosa,* catching disease ‖ *riso* —, infectious (*o* contagious) laughter ‖ *s.m.* contagious person, contagious patient.

contagócce, *s.m.* dropper; (*per medicina*) medicine dropper: *bottiglietta* —, dropping bottle.

contaminàbile, *ag.* contaminable.

contaminàre, *v.t.* 1. to contaminate, to pollute, to infect, to taint, to defile: *i rifiuti contaminano le acque dei fiumi,* waste contaminates the waters of rivers 2. *fig.* to contaminate, to corrupt: *contaminato dal vizio,* contaminated by vice 3. (*un testo letterario*) to corrupt, to contaminate: — *un testo,* to corrupt a text ‖ **contaminàrsi,** *v.r.* to be contaminated (by sthg.), to be polluted (by sthg.).

contaminatóre, *s.m.,* **contaminatríce,** *s.f.* 1. contaminator, polluter 2. (*di testi letterari*) corrupter, corruptor.

contaminazióne, *s.f.* 1. contamination, pollution, infection 2. *fig.* contamination, corruption 3. (*di un testo letterario*) corruption, contamination.

contànte, *ag.* (*comm.*) ready (*attributivo*): *denaro* —, cash (*o* ready) money ‖ *s.m.* cash, ready money: *compra per contanti,* cash purchase; *pagamento per contanti,* cash (*o* prompt) payment; *prezzo per contanti,* cash price; *pronti contanti,* cash down; *pagare a, in* —, to pay cash.

contàre, *v.t.* 1. to count (up); to number; to enumerate: *c'erano almeno venti persone, senza* — *i bambini,* there were at least twenty people there, not counting (in) the children; *non l'ho contato,* I left him out (of account); — *da uno a cento,* to count from one up to

one hundred; — *denaro,* to count money; — *ql.co. sulle dita,* to count sthg. on one's fingers; *a* — *da domani,* reckoning from tomorrow ‖ *contava più di 40 anni,* she was more than forty years old ‖ *i suoi giorni erano contati,* his days were numbered ‖ — *a ritroso,* (*per il lancio dei missili*) to count down 2. (*annoverare*) to count, to reckon, to number: *non lo conto più fra i miei amici,* I no longer count him among my friends 3. (*considerare*) to consider: *lo conto per uno stupido,* I consider him a fool ‖ *senza* — *che,* without considering that (*o* leaving out that) 4. (*proporsi*) to think of (doing); (*fermamente*) to intend, to purpose: *conta di andare a Roma presto,* he thinks of going to Rome soon; *cosa conti di fare?,* what do you intend doing? 5. (*aspettarsi*) to expect: *contavo che mi avrebbe aspettato,* I expected him to be waiting for me 6. (*raccontare*) to tell: *me ne ha contate delle belle,* he told me some queer stories ‖ *v.i.* 1. (*avere importanza*) to count; to be important; to have credit; to have authority: *ciò non conta,* that counts (*o* goes) for nothing; *egli non conta niente in casa sua,* he has no authority (*o* counts for nothing) at home; *ogni minuto conta,* every minute counts ‖ *e, ciò che più conta...,* and, what is more... ‖ — *quanto il due di briscola,* to be only a pawn in the game ‖ *conta più la pratica che la grammatica,* prov. practice is better than theory 2. (*fare assegnamento*) to rely (on s.o., sthg.); to count (on s.o., sthg.); to depend (on s.o., sthg.): *conto su di te,* I rely on (*o* I depend upon) you; *certi orfanelli non hanno nessuno su cui* —, some orphans have no one to depend on; *non può* — *che su se stesso,* he is entirely dependant on himself; *posso* — *sulla sua venuta?,* may I count on his coming?; *potete contarci!,* you may depend upon it!.

contàta, *s.f.* rapid counting.

contàto, *ag.*: *ha i giorni contati,* his days are numbered; *ha i minuti contati,* every moment of his is precious; *avere il denaro* —, to have no money to spare; *presentarsi col denaro* —, to have the exact money ready.

contatóre, *s.m.* meter; (*per bicicletta*) cyclometer; (*fis.*) counter: — *a moneta,* slot meter; — *chilometrico,* (h)odometer (*o* mileage recorder); — *cronometrico,* time-meter; — *del gas,* gas-meter; — *dell'acqua,* water-meter; — *della luce, dell'energia elettrica,* electric power-meter; — *delle chiamate,* (*tel.*) call-counting meter; — *delle chiamate a vuoto,* (*tel.*) overflow meter; — *di collaudo,* test meter; — *di controllo,* (*elett.*) standard testing meter; — *di giri,* motometer (*o* revolution counter); — *di impulsi,* (*fis.*) scaler; — *registratore,* (*elett.*) recording meter.

contàtto, *s.m.* 1. contact, touch, connection (anche *fig.*): *essere in* — *con qlcu.,* to be in touch with s.o.; *mettere in* —, to bring into contact; *mettersi in* — *con qlcu.,* to get in touch with s.o. (*o amer.* to contact s.o.); *perdere il* — *con qlcu.,* to lose touch with s.o.; *tenersi in* — *con qlcu.,* to keep in touch with s.o.; *venire a* — *con qlcu.,* to come into contact with s.o. 2. (*elett.*) contact: — *a terra,* contact to earth; — *ausiliario,* auxiliary contact; — *di ingranamento,* (*mec.*) overlap; — *doppio,* (*tel.*) twin contacts; — *girevole,* revolving contact; — *innestabile,* unsteady contact; — *scorrevole,* sliding contact; (*di reostato*) wiper (*o* shoe); *anello di* —, (*di motore ad induzione*) slip ring; *bottone di* —, contact button; *filo di* —, contact wire; *puntine di* —, contact points; *spina di* —, contact plug; *vite di* —, contact screw; *stabilire il* —, to make contact (*o* to switch on); *togliere il* —, to break contact (*o* to switch off).

cónte, *s.m.* Count; (*in Gran Bretagna*) Earl ‖ *Conte Palatino,* Earl (*o* Count) Palatine.

contèa, *s.f.* 1. (*titolo, dominio di conte*) earldom 2. (*divisione territoriale*) county; (*nei composti*) shire: — *di York,* Yorkshire; *capoluogo di* —, county town; *tribunale di* —, county court.

conteggiàre, *v.t.* 1. to count, to compute, to reckon; to include (sthg. in an account) 2. (*far pagare*) to charge: — *in più*, to charge extra ‖ *v.i.* (*far di conto*) to reckon, to calculate.

contéggio, *s.m.* computation, reckoning; calculation: *questo è il — delle spese,* this is the account of the expenses; *fare un —,* to make a computation ‖ — *all'indietro,* (*missilistica*) count down.

contégno, *s.m.* **1.** (*condotta*) behaviour; bearing; demeanour: *consiglialo di tenere un buon — a scuola,* put him on his best behaviour at school; *la ragazza teneva un — modesto,* the girl had a modest demeanour (*o* bearing); *il suo — verso di me mostra che non gli piaccio,* his behaviour towards me shows that he doesn't like me **2.** (*attitudine dignitosa*) attitude; (*attitudine contenuta, riservata*) self-control: *darsi un —,* to strike an attitude.

contegnosaménte, *av.* **1.** staidly, sedately, composedly **2.** (*con attitudine altera*) stiffly: *si comportava assai —,* she acted rather stiffly (*o* solemnly).

contegnóso, *ag.* **1.** dignified, staid, sedate, composed; (*riservato*) reserved, demure: *una signorina contegnosa,* a demure young lady; *il suo comportamento — ci colpì,* his dignified bearing impressed us **2.** (*altero*) stiff: *un atteggiamento —,* a stiff attitude.

contemperaménto, *s.m.* **1.** (*adattamento*) adaptation **2.** (*moderazione*) tempering, mitigation, moderation.

contemperàre, *v.t.* **1.** (*adattare*) to adapt: *bisogna — la punizione al delitto,* we must make the punishment fit the crime; *il dottore deve — la cura al paziente,* a doctor must adapt the treatment to his patient **2.** (*moderare*) to temper, to mitigate, to moderate.

contemplàbile, *ag.* contemplable.

contemplàre, *v.t.* **1.** to behold; to admire; to gaze at, on, upon (s.o., sthg.); to contemplate: *la contemplò a lungo,* he gazed at (*o* on *o* upon) her for a long time; *si fermò a — le bellezze della natura,* he stopped to admire the beauties of nature; — *il cielo stellato,* to gaze at (*o* into) the starry sky **2.** (*dir.*) to consider: *la legge non contempla questo caso,* the law does not consider this case ‖ **contemplàrsi,** *v.r.* to look at oneself, to admire oneself: *rimase a — nello specchio,* she stood contemplating herself in the mirror.

contemplativaménte, *av.* contemplatively.

contemplatìvo, *ag.* contemplative: *vita contemplativa,* contemplative life ‖ *s.m.* contemplative.

contemplatóre, *s.m.,* **contemplatrìce,** *s.f.* contemplator.

contemplazióne, *s.f.* contemplation: — *di Dio,* contemplation of God; *Pascoli trasse principalmente ispirazione dalla — della natura,* Pascoli derived his chief inspiration from the contemplation of nature.

contèmpo, *s.m.:* *nel —,* at the same time (*o* meanwhile *o* in the meantime).

contemporaneaménte, *av.* contemporaneously, at the same time, simultaneously.

contemporaneità, *s.f.* contemporaneity, contemporaneousness, contemporariness: — *di pensiero e azione,* contemporaneity of thought and action.

contemporàneo, *ag.* **1.** contemporary; contemporaneous: *avvenimenti contemporanei,* contemporaneous events; *il Goldoni è — del Gozzi,* Goldoni is contemporary with Gozzi ‖ *i contemporanei,* the contemporaries **2.** (*dei giorni nostri*) present-day (*attributivo*); contemporary: *uno scrittore —,* a present-day writer.

contendènte, *ag.* contending, opposing, contrasting: *le parti contendenti,* the opposing parties ‖ *s.m.* adversary, rival, opponent, antagonist, competitor: *i contendenti scendono in campo,* the competitors enter the field; *i due contendenti combattevano con coraggio,* the two adversaries fought bravely.

contèndere, *v.t.* to contend for (sthg.); to contest; to refuse, to deny: *nessuno gli contende i suoi diritti,* no one would deny him his rights; *le nostre truppe contendevano la collina al nemico,* our troops contended with the enemy for the hill ‖ *v.i.* to contest, to quarrel: *contendevano per*

cose da nulla, they were quarrelling over trifles ‖ **contèndersi,** *v.r. reciproco* to contend for (sthg.), to compete for (sthg.): *si contendevano il posto,* they competed for the post; — *un figlio,* to contend for custody of a child.

contenènte, *ag.* containing ‖ *s.m.* container; holder: *il — e il contenuto,* the container and its contents.

contenére, *v.t.* **1.** to contain, to hold; to include, to comprise: *l'acqua del mare contiene molti sali in soluzione,* sea water holds many salts in solution; *quei libri contengono molte verità,* those books contain many truths; *questa bevanda contiene un'alta percentuale di alcool,* this drink contains a large percentage of alcohol **2.** (*frenare*) to contain, to control; (*reprimere*) to restrain, to repress, to keep in: — *il proprio entusiasmo,* to contain (*o* to control) one's enthusiasm; — *i propri sentimenti,* to repress one's feelings (*o* to keep in one's feelings) ‖ **contenérsi,** *v.r.* **1.** (*comportarsi*) to behave, to act: *non sapere come —,* not to know how to behave (*o* not to know what to do) **2.** (*dominarsi*) to contain oneself, to control oneself, to restrain oneself; to forbear: *non potevano — dalla gioia,* they could not contain themselves for joy; *non potevano — dal ridere,* they could not help laughing.

conteniménto, *s.m.* (*rar.*) containment.

contentàbile, *ag.* satisfiable: *facilmente —,* easily satisfied (*o* pleased).

contentaménto, *s.m.* content, contentment.

contentàre, *v.t.* to content, to satisfy, to please; to gratify: *cerco di contentarvi,* I try to keep you contented; — *i desideri di qlcu.,* to gratify (*o* to meet) s.o.'s wishes ‖ **contentàrsi,** *v.r.* to be content (with s.o., sthg., with doing), to be pleased (with s.o., sthg., with doing); to content oneself (with s.o., sthg., with doing): *io mi contento di poco,* I am satisfied with little; *non si contenta di congetture,* he is not content with guesses; — *di fare ql.co.,* to content oneself with doing sthg. ‖ *chi si contenta gode,* *prov.* a contented mind is a perpetual feast.

contentatúra, *s.f.* contentment: *di difficile —,* hard to please; *uomo di facile —,* easily satisfied man.

contentézza, *s.f.* pleasure, contentment; satisfaction; (*gioia*) joy, happiness: *con nostra grande —,* to our great satisfaction; *non stare nella pelle dalla —,* to be beside oneself with joy; *saltare dalla —,* to jump for joy.

contentìno, *s.m.* make-weight: *aggiungere ql.co. per —,* to add sthg. as a make-weight.

contènto[1], *ag.* (*pago*) content (with sthg.), satisfied (with sthg.); (*lieto*) pleased (with sthg.); glad; happy: *fu — del risultato,* he was satisfied (*o* pleased) with the result; *fummo contenti di vederli,* we were glad (*o* pleased) to see them; *sono — del poco che ho,* I am content with what I have; *sono — di voi,* I am pleased with you ‖ — *come una pasqua,* as pleased as Punch (*o* as happy as a sand-boy) ‖ *chiamarsi —,* to be satisfied.

contènto[2], *s.m.* (*letter.*) content, contentedness; satisfaction, pleasure ‖ *un'ora di — sconta cent'anni di tormento,* *prov.* one day of pleasure is worth two of sorrow.

contenúto, *ag.* contained ‖ *s.m.* **1.** (*ciò che è contenuto*) contents (*pl.*) **2.** (*argomento*) content; contents (*pl.*); subject: *forma e —,* form and content.

contenziosaménte, *av.* contentiously.

contenziosità, *s.f.* contentiousness.

contenzióso, *ag.* contentious ‖ *s.m.* legal department.

conterìe, *s.f.pl.* glass beads.

conterminàle, *ag.* conterminal, conterminous: *l'Italia è — della Svizzera,* Italy is conterminal to Switzerland.

conterminàre, *v.i.* to border (on a place), to be conterminous (to a place).

contèrmine, *ag.* conterminal, conterminous ‖ *s.m.* (*rar.*) common boundary line.

conterrànea, *s.f.* country-woman (*pl.* country-women).

conterràneo, *ag.* of the same country ‖ *s.m.* (fellow-) countryman (*pl.* countrymen).

contésa, *s.f.* **1.** contest, strife, contention: — *verbale,* verbal strife **2.** (*litigio*) quarrel: *venire a —,* to begin to quarrel.

contéso, *ag.* contested.

contéssa, *s.f.* countess.

contéssere, *v.t.* **1.** to interweave **2.** (*comporre con arte*) to interlace, to interweave, to compose: *le ossa e i muscoli di cui è contessuto il corpo,* the bones and muscles the body is made up of.

contessína, *s.f.* count's daughter.

contestàbile[1], *ag.* questionable, disputable, debatable.

contestàbile[2], (*rar.*) per **conestàbile.**

contestàre, *v.t.* **1.** (*contrastare*) to contest, to question; to challenge; to dispute: *si contestò la dichiarazione di quell'uomo,* that man's statement was contested; — *a qlcu. il diritto di fare ql.co.,* to challenge s.o.'s right to do sthg. **2.** (*negare*) to deny: *l'imputato contestò l'accusa,* the accused denied the charge **3.** (*notificare*) to declare; to notify: — *una contravvenzione a qlcu.,* to fine s.o. (*o amer.* to give a ticket to s.o.).

contestazióne, *s.f.* **1.** dispute, contest; objection: *fuori —,* beyond dispute (*o* out of question); *in —,* in dispute (*o* question); *in caso di —,* in case of contest; *appianare una —,* to settle a dispute; *sollevare contestazioni,* to raise objections **2.** (*notifica*) notification.

contèste, *s.m.* (*dir.*) co-witness, fellow-witness.

contèsto, *ag.* composed, interwoven; interlaced: *con seta,* interwoven with silk ‖ *s.m.* context.

contestuàle, *ag.* contextual.

contézza, *s.f.* (*letter.*) full knowledge, cognizance: *aver — di ql.co.,* to be aware of sthg.; *dar — di ql.co. a qlcu.,* to acquaint s.o. with sthg.

contiguaménte, *av.* contiguously.

contiguità, *s.f.* contiguity.

contíguo, *ag.* contiguous; adjoining; neighbouring (*attributivo*): *angoli contigui,* (*geom.*) contiguous angles; *paesi contigui,* neighbouring countries; *il mio giardino è - a quello di mio fratello,* my garden is adjoining my brother's.

continentàle, *ag.* continental: *l'Europa —,* the Continent.

continènte[1], *ag.* continent; temperate, moderate.

continènte[2], *s.m.* continent ‖ *Continente Nero,* the Black Continent; *il Nuovo Continente,* the New World.

continènza, *s.f.* continence, temperance.

contingentaménto, *s.m.* **1.** allotment, allocation **2.** (*parte contingentata*) allocation, quota **3.** (*limite alle importazioni*) import quota; (*limite alle esportazioni*) export quota.

contingentàre, *v.t.* **1.** to allot, to allocate **2.** (*limitare*) to fix a quota to (imports, exports).

contingènte, *ag.* **1.** contingent: *spese contingenti,* contingent expenses **2.** (*fil.*) contingent (upon s.o., sthg.), accidental (to s.o., sthg.) ‖ *s.m.* **1.** (*fil.*) contingent, contingency **2.** (*mil.*) contingent: *il — dell'anno,* the annual contingent **3.** (*comm.*) quota, share **4.** (*geom.*) tangent.

contingènza, *s.f.* **1.** (*fil.*) contingency **2.** (*eventualità*) contingency, emergency, occurrence: *far fronte ad una —,* to meet a contingency (*o* an emergency) **3.** (*circostanza*) circumstance: *in questa —,* in (*o* under) this circumstance.

continuàbile, *ag.* continuable.

continuaménte, *av.* (*ininterrottamente*) continuously; (*molto frequentemente*) continually; (*costantemente*) constantly.

continuàre, *v.t.* **1.** to continue, to keep on (with sthg., doing), to go on (with sthg., doing), to carry on (sthg.): *continuai i miei studi,* I continued (*o* kept on with *o* went on with) my studies; *continuò la tradizione di famiglia,* he carried on the family tradition **2.** (*riprendere dopo interruzione*) to take up;

to resume: *andò a casa e continuò la lettura,* he went home and resumed his reading; — *l'opera di qlcu.,* to take up s.o.'s work ‖ *v.i.* **1.** to continue, to go on, to keep on: *continuarono a vivere in campagna,* they continued living (*o* to live) in the country; *ha continuato a scrivere,* he went on (*o* kept on) writing; *pensi che questo tempo continuerà?,* do you think such weather will continue?; *la sua sfortuna continua,* his ill-luck continues ‖ *continua,* (in una pubblicazione, alla fine di una puntata) to be continued **2.** (*prolungarsi*) to continue, to stretch away, to extend: *la strada continua fino al mare,* the street extends to the sea.

continuataménte, *av.* continuously.

continuatívo, *ag.* continuative.

continuàto, *ag.* continuous, continual, unceasing; uninterrupted; unbroken.

continuatóre, *ag.* following ‖ *s.m.,* **continuatríce,** *s.f.* continuer, continuator: *il continuatore di un'opera letteraria,* the continuator of a literary work.

continuazióne, *s.f.* continuation, continuance; carrying on: *la — della guerra,* the continuance (*o* continuation) of the war; *la — di un lavoro,* the carrying on of a work; *la — della storia è a pagina 150,* turn to page 150 for the continuation of this story.

continuità, *s.f.* continuity: *soluzione di —,* solution of continuity.

contínuo, *ag.* **1.** (*ininterrotto*) continuous, uninterrupted, unbroken; (*molto frequente*) continual, very frequent: *un — succedersi di visite,* a continuous succession of visits; *lamentele continue,* continual complaints ‖ *di —,* continually, very often **2.** *corrente continua,* (*elett.*) direct current.

cónto, *s.m.* **1.** account (*anche comm.*): — *aperto,* open (*o* running) account; — *arretrato,* outstanding (*o* unpaid) account; — *cassa,* cash account; — *chiuso,* closed (*o* balanced) account; — *corrente,* current account (*o* account current, *abbr.* A/C); — *di giro,* clearance account; — *in partecipazione,* joint account; — *liquidato, saldato,* settled account; — *scoperto,* overdrawn account; *estratto —,* statement of account; *il — torna, non torna,* the account is right, is wrong; *aprire, chiudere un —,* to open, to close an account; *compilare un —,* to make out an account; *da addebitarsi al mio —,* to be charged to my account; *fare, tirare i conti,* to make up accounts; *saldare un —,* to settle an account ‖ *la Corte dei Conti,* (*amm.*) the Audit Office **2.** (*di ristorante, albergo*) bill: *cameriere, il — per favore,* waiter, (the) bill, please **3.** (*calcolo*) calculation, computation, account: *far di —,* to do sums (*o* to reckon up); *sbagliarsi nel fare i propri conti,* to be out in one's reckonings ‖ *a conti fatti,* all things considered (*o* after all) **4.** (*assegnamento*) reliance: *faccio — su di te,* I rely on you; *fare — sull'appoggio di qlcu.,* to count (*o* to reckon) on s.o.'s support **5.** (*stima, reputazione*) esteem, regard: *cose, persone di nessun — poco —,* things (*o* matters), people of no, of little account; *tenere in qualche —,* to treat with respect; *tenere qlcu. in poco —,* to hold s.o. in low esteem **6.** (**Fraseologia**): *per — e rischio di qlcu.,* for s.o.'s account and risk ‖ *per — mio,* (*quanto a me*) as for me (*o* as far as I am concerned) ‖ *per — proprio,* on one's own account ‖ *a buon —,* in any case ‖ *in fin dei conti,* in conclusion ‖ *per nessun —,* on no account ‖ *chiedere informazioni sul — di qlcu.,* to ask for information about s.o. ‖ *fare i conti addosso a qlcu.,* to pry into s.o.'s financial affairs (*o* to meddle in other people's affairs) ‖ *fare i conti con qlcu.,* to bring (*o* to call) s.o. to account: *con te farò i conti più tardi,* (*fam.*) I will have a reckoning with you later; *un giorno dovrai fare i conti con la giustizia per i tuoi delitti,* one day you will be brought to book for your crimes ‖ *fare — di,* (*immaginare*) to imagine; (*proporsi*) to intend ‖ *fare i conti senza l'oste,* (*fam.*) to reckon without one's host ‖ *mettere —,* to be worth while (*o* to pay): *non mette — d'arrabbiarsi,* it is not worth while getting

angry; *non mette — di lavorare tanto*, it does not pay
to work so hard ‖ *mettersi per proprio —*, to set up
for oneself ‖ *regolare i conti con qlcu.*, to balance (*o* to
square) accounts with s.o. ‖ *rendere — di ql.co.*, to
answer for sthg. (*o* to account for sthg.) ‖ *rendersi —
di ql.co.*, to realize sthg. ‖ *conti chiari amicizia lunga*, *prov.* short reckonings make long friends.

contòrcere, *v.t.* to contort, to distort, to twist ‖ **con-
tòrcersi**, *v.r.* to writhe (in sthg.), to twist (in sthg): *si
contorceva dal dolore*, he writhed in pain.

contorcimento, *s.m.* contortion, twisting.

contornamento, *s.m.* surrounding.

contornàre, *v.t.* **1.** to surround; to go round (sthg.):
alti pioppi contornavano il castello, high poplars surrounded the castle **2.** (*ornare*) to trim: — *una veste di
trine*, to trim a dress with lace ‖ **contornàrsi**, *v.r.* to
surround oneself (with s.o., sthg.).

contórno, *s.m.* **1.** (*linea esterna*) contour, outline:
linea di —, contour line (*o* outline) **2.** (*orlo*) border,
rim **3.** (*cuc.*) vegetables (*pl.*): *carne con —*, meat and
vegetables **4.** (*dintorno*) surroundings (*pl.*).

contorsióne, *s.f.* contortion, writhing.

contòrto, *ag.* contorted, twisted (anche *fig.*): *pensieri contorti*, twisted thoughts.

cóntra, *prep.* (*rar.*) per **cóntro**.

contrabbandàre, *v.t.* to smuggle.

contrabbandièra, *s.f.*, **contrabbandière**, *s.m.* smuggler.

contrabbàndo, *s.m.* contraband, smuggling: *di —*,
clandestinely; *esportare di —*, to smuggle out; *importare*, *introdurre di —*, to smuggle in; *fare del —*,
to smuggle; *merce di —*, contraband (*o* smuggled)
goods.

contrabbassísta, *s.m.* double-bass player.

contrabbàsso, *s.m.* (*mus.*) contrabass, double-bass:
suonatore di —, double-bass player.

contraccambiàre, *v.t.* to reciprocate, to return, to
requite: *che cosa posso fare per — la tua gentilezza?*,
what can I do in return for your kindness?; *contraccambio di cuore i tuoi auguri*, I heartily reciprocate
your wishes; — *l'affetto di qlcu.*, to return s.o.'s love;
— *il male col bene*, to return good for evil.

contraccàmbio, *s.m.* return; requital: *in — di ql.co.*,
in return for sthg.; *rendere il — a qlcu.*, to give tit
for tat to s.o. (*o* to retaliate upon s.o.).

contracchiàve, *s.f.* (*mec.*) fox wedge; nose key;
wedge buckle.

contraccólpo, *s.m.* **1.** counterblow, rebound; (*arc.*)
counterstroke; (*di armi da fuoco*) recoil **2.** *fig.* repercussion; reaction; result; consequence: *di, per —*, as
a consequence: *fallita la banca, fallirono di — parecchi uomini d'affari*, the bank went bankrupt and as
a consequence many business-men were ruined.

contraccúsa, *s.f.* (*dir.*) countercharge.

contràda, *s.f.* **1.** (*quartiere di città*) quarter; town
district **2.** (*paese*) country; countryside; district **3.** (*strada
spaziosa*) wide street.

contraddànza, *s.f.* country-dance.

contraddíre, *v.t.* to contradict: — *una dichiarazione*, to contradict a statement ‖ **contraddírsi**, *v.r.*
to contradict oneself ‖ *v.r. reciproco* to contradict each
other: *le deposizioni dei testimoni si contraddico-
no*, the statements of the witnesses contradict each
other.

contraddistínguere, *v.t.* to mark.

contraddittóre, *s.m.* opposer; contradictor.

contraddittoriaménte, *av.* contradictorily.

contraddittòrio, *ag.* contradictory ‖ *s.m.* debate:
è ammesso il —, debate is allowed; *aprire il —*, to
open the debate.

contradditríce, *s.f.* opposer.

contraddizióne, *s.f.* contradiction; discrepancy: —
in termini, contradiction in terms; — *tra due resoconti*,
discrepancy between two accounts ‖ *spirito di —*,
spirit of contradiction.

contraènte, *ag.* contracting ‖ *s.m.* contractor: *i
contraenti*, contracting parties.

contraèrea, *s.f.* (*artigl.*) anti-aircraft artillery.

contraèreo, *ag.* (*mil.*) anti-aircraft.

contraffacimento, *s.m.* (*rar.*) counterfeit.

contraffàre, *v.t.* **1.** (*imitare*) to counterfeit; to imitate; (*scimmiottare*) to ape, to mimic: — *la voce di qlcu.*,
to counterfeit s.o.'s voice **2.** (*falsificare*) to counterfeit,
to forge: — *una firma*, to forge a signature ‖ *v.i.* (*rar.*)
(*disubbidire*) to disobey (s.o., sthg.): *non bisogna — agli
ordini del padrone*, you must not disobey your master's
orders ‖ **contraffàrsi**, *v.r.* (*travestirsi*) to disguise
oneself (as s.o., sthg.); to make oneself up: *sa — in
cento modi*, he can disguise himself in a hundred ways.

contraffàtto, *ag.* **1.** (*imitato*) counterfeit; imitated **2.** (*falsificato*) counterfeit, forged, false: *monete contraffatte*, counterfeit coins **3.** (*travestito*) disguised **4.** (*deforme*) deformed.

contraffattòre, *s.m.*, **contraffattríce**, *s.f.* **1.** counterfeiter, imitator **2.** (*falsificatore*) counterfeiter, forger.

contraffazióne, *s.f.* **1.** counterfeit; imitation **2.** (*falsificazione*) forgery, falsification.

contraffòrte, *s.m.* **1.** (*arch.*) buttress, counterfort **2.** (*geog.*) buttress, spur.

contraggènio, *s.m.* dislike, aversion ‖ *a, di —*,
against one's grain (*o* unwillingly).

contraltàre, *s.m.* rival project.

contràlto, *s.m.* (*mus.*) contralto.

contrammiràglio, *s.m.* rear-admiral.

contrappàsso, *s.m.* retaliation.

contrappèllo, *s.m.* second roll-call.

contrappélo, *s.m.* wrong way of the hair: *fare il
—*, to shave against the lie of the hair; *fig.* to pick
holes; *spazzolare —*, (*tessuti*) to brush against the nap ‖
a, di —, *fig.* against the grain ‖ *prendere qlcu. di —*,
to rub s.o. up the wrong way.

contrappesàre, *v.t.* to counterbalance, to counterpoise ‖ **contrappesàrsi**, *v.r. reciproco* to counterbalance each other: *il bene e il male si contrappesano*
good and evil counterbalance each other.

contrappéso, *s.m.* counterbalance, counterpoise.

contrappórre, *v.t.* to oppose, to contrast: — *ql.co.
a ql.co.*, to set sthg. against sthg. ‖ **contrappórsi**, *v.r.*
to set oneself against (sthg.).

contrapposizióne, *s.f.* contraposition, opposition.

contrappósto, *s.m.* exact opposite; antithesis.

contrappròccio, *s.m.* (*mil.*) counter-approach.

contrappuntísta, *s.c.* (*mus.*) contrapuntist.

contrappúnto, *s.m.* (*mus.*) counterpoint.

contrariaménte, *av.* **1.** (*in modo contrario*) contrarily: — *a ql.co.*, contrary to (*o* in opposition to)
sthg.: — *a ogni aspettativa*, contrary to all expectation; *fare ql.co. — all'opinione pubblica*, to do sthg.
in opposition to public opinion **2.** (*al contrario*) on
the contrary, contrariwise.

contrariàre, *v.t.* **1.** to oppose, to cross; to withstand;
to counteract: — *i desideri di qlcu.*, to withstand s.o.'s
wishes; — *i propositi di qlcu.*, to cross (*o* to oppose
o to interfere with) s.o.'s plans **2.** (*seccare, irritare*)
to vex, to annoy.

contrariàto, *ag.* **1.** (*irritato*) vexed; annoyed **2.** (*dispiaciuto*) sorry.

contrarietà, *s.f.* **1.** (*l'essere contrario*) contrariety,
opposition **2.** (*avversità*) misfortune; disappointment;
difficulty: *ho avuto molte —*, I've met with many
disappointments.

contràrio, *ag.* **1.** contrary, opposite, adverse, opposed: — *alla ragione*, contrary (*o* opposed) to common
sense; — *alle regole*, against the rules; *fino ad avviso
—*, until further notice; *in direzione contraria*, in the
opposite direction; *opinioni contrarie*, contrary (*o* opposed) opinions; *venti contrari*, contrary (*o* adverse)
winds; *verrò, salvo avviso —*, I'll come, unless I hear
to the contrary **2.** (*sfavorevole*) unfavourable; contrary:
stagione contraria, unfavourable season; *la sorte gli è*

contraria, fate is against him; *essere — per principio a ql.co.,* to object formally to sthg. **3.** (*nocivo*) harmful: *il fumo è — alla salute,* smoking is harmful to (o bad for) one's health **4.** (*riluttante*) reluctant, unwilling: *era — a partire in aeroplano,* he was unwilling to leave by plane ‖ *s.m.* contrary, opposite: *è proprio il —,* it is just the opposite; *ha fatto il — di quanto gli avevo detto di fare,* he has done the opposite of what I had told him; *non ho nulla in — a che gli telefoniate,* I have no objection to your ringing him up; *avere prova del —,* to have proof to the contrary ‖ *al —,* (*invece*) on the contrary; (*a ritroso*) backwards.

contràrre, *v.t.* **1.** to contract (anche *fig.*): *— un'abitudine,* to contract (o to develop o acquire) a habit; *— un'amicizia,* to contract a friendship (o to make friends); *— debiti,* to incur debts (o to get into o to run into debt); *— una malattia,* to contract (o to catch) an illness; *— un muscolo,* to contract a muscle; *— obblighi (finanziari),* to contract liabilities; *— le sopracciglia,* to contract one's brows (o to knit one's brows) **2.** (*gram.*) to contract: *forme contratte,* contracted forms ‖ **contràrsi,** *v.r.* **1.** to contract **2.** (*accorciarsi*) to shrink.

contraspàlto, *s.m.* (*mil.*) breastwork.
contrassàlto, *s.m.* (*mil.*) counter-attack.
contrassegnàre, *v.t.* to mark, to countersign.
contrasségno, *s.m.* **1.** (identification) mark, counteesign **2.** (*distintivo*) badge **3.** (*mil.*) (*parola d'ordine*) countersign, password: *dare il —,* to give the countersign **4.** (*segno, prova*) token, mark: *— di stima,* mark of esteem.
contrastàbile, *ag.* contestable, disputable, questionable, doubtful.
contrastànte, *ag.* contrasting: *colori contrastanti,* contrasting (o ill-matched) colours.
contrastàre, *v.t.* **1.** (*ostacolare*) to oppose, to hinder: *— il passo a qlcu.,* to bar s.o.'s passage **2.** (*resistere a*) to oppose, to resist: *— la volontà di qlcu.,* to oppose (o to resist) s.o.'s will **3.** (*contendere*) to contest; to struggle with (s.o. for sthg.) ‖ *v.i.* (*essere in contrasto*) to be in contrast, to contrast, to clash: *i miei interessi contrastano con i tuoi,* my interests clash with yours ‖ **contrastàrsi,** *v.r. reciproco* to wrangle, to fight, to struggle.
contràsto, *s.m.* **1.** contrast (anche *fig.*); (*opposizione*) opposition: *che — fra di loro!,* what a contrast between them! ‖ *in — con,* in contrast with: *mettere una cosa in — con un'altra,* to bring one thing into contrast with another **2.** (*dissidio*) difference, disputo; (*lite*) conflict, quarrel, strife: *— di interessi,* conflicting (o conflict of) interests; *avere un — con qlcu. su ql.co.,* to have a difference with s.o. about sthg.; *essere in — con qlcu.,* to be at odds with s.o.
contrattàbile, *ag.* negotiable.
contrattaccàre, *v.t.i.* to counter-attack.
contrattàcco, *s.m.* counter-attack.
contrattàre, *v.t.* to negotiate; to contract for (sthg.); to bargain for (sthg.); to haggle about, over (sthg.): *— il prezzo di ql.co.,* to haggle about (o over) the price of sthg.
contrattatóre, *s.m.* contractor; contracting party.
contrattazióne, *s.f.* dealing, marketing, negotiation, transaction; haggling: *libera —,* (*econ.*) free marketing.
contrattèmpo, *s.m.* **1.** (*piccolo incidente*) mishap, hitch; (*inconveniente*) inconvenience: *se non fosse stato per un malaugurato — ci saremmo incontrati,* if it had not been for an unfortunate hitch (o mishap) we should have met **2.** (*mus.*) syncopation ‖ *a, di —, fig.* inopportune(ly) (o at the wrong time o out of place).
contràttile, *ag.* contractile: *muscolo —,* contractile muscle.
contrattilità, *s.f.* contractility.
contràtto, *ag.* contracted ‖ *s.m.* contract; agreement, deed: *— aleatorio,* aleatory contract; *— annullabile,* voidable contract; *— bilaterale,* indenture;

— di noleggio, charter-party; *— impegnativo,* binding contract; *— irrevocabile,* contract beyond revocation; *— nullo,* void contract; *— scritto,* written contract (o contract in writing); *— verbale,* parole (o verbal) contract; *esecuzione di un —,* performance of a contract; *infrazione di —,* breach of contract; *scadenza di un —,* expiration of a contract; *convalidare un —,* to affirm a contract; *fare un —,* to make (o to stipulate) a contract; *far eseguire un —,* to enforce a contract.
contrattuàle, *ag.* (*comm.*) contractual: *vincolo —,* contractual tie.
contravveléno, *s.m.* antidote (anche *fig.*).
contravvenìre, *v.i.* to contravene (sthg.), to infringe (sthg.), to transgress (sthg.), to violate (sthg.): *— al disposto della legge,* to infringe (o to contravene) the provisions of the law; *— al regolamento,* to contravene (o to act contrary to) the regulations.
contravventóre, *s.m.,* **contravventríce,** *s.f.* contravener, infringer, transgressor, violator.
contravvenzióne, *s.f.* **1.** contravention, infringement, transgression, violation, infraction: *— alla legge,* violation of the law **2.** (*multa*) fine: *dichiarare qlcu. in —,* to fine s.o.; *pagare una —,* to pay a fine.
contrazióne, *s.f.* **1.** contraction: *— di un debito,* contraction of a debt; *— di un matrimonio,* contraction of a marriage **2.** (*il ritirarsi, l'accorciarsi*) contraction, shrinking **3.** (*gram.*) contraction.
contribuènte, *s.m.* taxpayer, ratepayer: *lista, ruolo dei contribuenti,* list of taxpayers; *tassare il —,* to tax (o to reach) the taxpayer.
contribuíre, *v.i.* **1.** to contribute; to help (in sthg.), to aid (in sthg.); to work together: *ciò ha contribuito al rialzo del prezzo,* it has helped in raising the price; *il giuoco d'azzardo contribuì alla sua rovina,* gambling contributed to his ruin; *tutte queste circostanze contribuirono a fare di lui l'uomo che è oggi,* all these circumstances worked together (o combined) to make him what he is to-day **2.** (*partecipare*) to contribute, to share (in sthg.): *egli ha contribuito alle trattative,* he has shared in the dealings.
contribúto, *s.m.* **1.** contribution (anche *fig.*); share: *— di sangue,* blood contribution; *— in denaro,* money contribution; *— letterario,* literary contribution; *ho dato il mio — di cinque sterline,* I gave five pounds as my share (o contribution); *imporre contributi al popolo,* to lay the people under contribution (o to exact contributions from the people); *pagare il proprio —,* to pay one's share (o contribution) **2.** *pl.* (*somme dovute all'Istituto della Previdenza Sociale*) contributions: *contributi obbligatori,* compulsory contributions: *richiedere contributi obbligatori ai datori di lavoro,* to require compulsory contributions from employers; *contributi volontari,* voluntary contributions.
contributóre, *s.m.,* **contributríce,** *s.f.* contributor.
contribuzióne, *s.f.* contribution: *— di guerra,* forced contribution: *esigere da un paese una — di guerra,* to lay a country under (war) contribution.
contristàre, *v.t.* to afflict, to grieve, to sadden ‖ **contristàrsi,** *v.r.* to grieve, to be deeply grieved: *dobbiamo contristarci per la sua morte,* we must grieve at (o for o over) his death.
contristàto, *ag.* afflicted, grieved, sad.
contritaménte, *av.* contritely, penitently.
contríto, *ag.* contrite, penitent: *con aria contrita,* penitently.
contrizióne, *s.f.* contrition, penitence.
cóntro, *prep.* **1.** against: *— di noi,* against us; *— luce,* against the light; *— la mia volontà,* against my will; *— la parete,* against the wall; (*appoggiato*) leaning against the wall; *— vento,* against the wind; (*voglia,* unwillingly); *pro e — una decisione,* for and against a decision; *gli votò —,* he voted against him; *mi si rivoltò— come una vipera,* he turned against me like a viper; *tutti gli son —,* everybody is against him; *andare — corrente,* to go (o to swim) against

the stream (anche *fig.*); *andare* — *natura*, to go against nature; *marciare* — *il nemico*, to march against the enemy; *sbattere* — *il muro*, (*di veicoli*) to crash into the wall; (*di persona*) to bump into the wall ‖ *dar* — *a qlcu.*, to go against s.o. ‖ *scommettere due* — *uno*, to bet two to one **2**. (*dietro*, *in seguito a*) **against, on:** — *assegno*, cash on delivery; — *pagamento*, against (o on) payment; *pagamento* — *documento*, payment against documents **3**. (*in opposizione a*) **in opposition to;** (*contrario a*) **contrary to:** *una teoria* — *ragione*, a theory contrary to reason; *ciò è* — *quanto disse prima*, that's in opposition to (o the opposite of) what he said before; *agire* — *l'opinione pubblica*, to act in opposition to public opinion ‖ *av.: di* —, opposite: *l'uscio di* —, the door opposite; *la bottega è proprio di* — *alla casa*, the shop is directly opposite the house ‖ *per* —, on the contrary ‖ *s.m.: il pro e il* —, the pros and cons: *pesate bene i pro e i* —, weigh the pros and cons well.

controaliséo, *s.m.* (*meteorologia*) antitrade.

controavvíso, *s.m.* countermand.

controbàttere, *v.t.* **1**. (*ripercuotere*) to beat again **2**. to counter-batter: *i cannoni controbattevano i colpi del nemico*, the guns counterbattered the enemy **3**. (*confutare*) to disprove, to refute, to confute, to controvert, to rebut: — *un'accusa*, to rebut a charge; — *una dichiarazione*, to refute a statement.

controbattúta, *s.f.* (*confutazione*) confutation.

controbilanciàre, *v.t.* to counter-balance.

controcàmpo, *s.m.* (*cine.*) reverse shot.

controcàssa, *s.f.* outer casing; (*di orologio*) case, casing: *la* — *di un orologio da tasca*, the case of a watch.

controcaténa, *s.f.* (*edil.*) straining beam.

controchiàma, *s.f.* second roll-call.

controchíglia, *s.f.* (*mar.*) false keel; (*aer.*) keelson.

controcorrènte, *s.f.* counter-current ‖ *l. av.* against the stream.

controdàdo, *s.m.* (*mec.*) loch nut, jam nut, check nut, set nut.

controdàta, *s.f.* (*comm.*) counter-date.

controdatàre, *v.t.* (*comm.*) to counter-date.

controdichiarazióne, *s.f.* counter-declaration.

controdrítto, *s.m.* — (*di poppa*), (*mar.*) inner stern -post, inner post.

controfagòtto, *s.m.* (*mus.*) contra-bassoon.

controffensíva, *s.f.* (*mil.*) counter-offensive.

controfigúra, *s.c.* (*cine.*) double, stand-in: *fare la* —, to double.

controfinèstra, *s.f.* (*edil.*) double window: — *esterna*, storm-sash.

controfiòceo, *s.m.* (*mar.*) flying jib.

controfírma, *s.f.* counter-signature, countersign.

controfirmàre, *v.t.* to countersign.

controfòdera, *s.f.* inner lining.

controfòsso, *s.m.* (*mil.*) counterfosse.

controindicàre, *v.t.* **1**. (*indicare in modo opposto*) to point the opposite way **2**. (*notare in margine*) to note in the margin **3**. (*med.*) to contra-indicate.

controindicàto, *ag.* (*med.*) contra-indicated.

controindicazióne, *s.f.* **1**. contrary direction **2**. (*appunto in margine*) marginal note **3**. (*med.*) contra-indication.

controllàbile, *ag.* controllable.

controllàre, *v.t.* to control; (*verificare*) to check, to verify; (*ispezionare*) to inspect, to examine; (*comm. amm.*) to audit: — *biglietti*, to check tickets; — *i conti*, to audit the books; — *delle informazioni*, to verify (o to check) information; — *una macchina*, to inspect a machine; — *passaporti*, to examine passports; — *uno strumento*, to check an instrument ‖ **controllàrsi,** *v.r.* to control oneself; to command oneself: *controllati!*, control yourself!; *non sa controllarsi*, he has no self-control (o command over himself).

contròllo, *s.m.* **1**. control; (*verifica*) check, checking, verification; (*ispezione*) examination, inspection; (*di* *conti*) audit: — *amministrativo*, audit(ing); *controlli a terra*, (*aer.*) ground checks; — *dei biglietti*, ticket inspection; — *dei costi*, (*comm.*) cost control; — *delle conversazioni*, (*tel.*) overhearing; *controlli di un motore*, (*mec.*) controls of an engine; — *di volume*, (*rad.*) loudness (o volume) control; — *doganale*, customs examination; — *sanitario*, sanitary inspection; *aperto per il* —, (*di pacco postale, ecc.*) open for inspection; *apparecchio di* —, (*mec.*) control apparatus; *posto di* —, (*spor.*) control station; *sotto* —, under examination; *ufficio di* —, control office; *dal* — *da me fatto la merce risultò di qualità inferiore*, on my checking the goods they turned out to be of inferior quality; *non perdete il* — (*di voi stessi*)!, don't lose your temper!; *perse il* — *dell'automobile*, he lost control of his motor-car; *fare il* — *di ql.co.*, to check (o to verify) sthg.; *sottoporre ql.co. ad un* — *minuzioso*, to subject sthg. to a close inspection **2**. *V.* **controllóre**.

controllóre, *s.m.* **1**. controller: — *della zecca*, controller of the mint; — *delle dogane*, controller of the customs **2**. (*ferr.*) ticket-inspector, ticket-collector.

controlúce, *s.m.* photograph taken against the light ‖ *s.f.* **1**. counterlight **2**. (*cine.*) back lighting.

controlúce, *av.* against the light; against the sun: *fotografia* —, photograph taken against the light.

contromàrca, *s.f.* pass-out check (ticket).

contromàrcia, *s.f.* **1**. (*mil.*) countermarch **2**. (*aut.*) reverse gear.

contromezzàna, *s.f.* (*mar.*) mizzen topsail.

contromína, *s.f.* (*mil.*) countermine.

controminàre, *v.t.* (*mil.*) to countermine.

contropàrte, *s.f.* (*dir.*) counter-party.

contropartíta, *s.f.* **1**. (*comm.*) counter-item **2**. (*compenso*) compensation; set-off; counterbalance.

contropélo, *V.* **contrappélo**.

contropòrta, *s.f.* **1**. inner door **2**. (*antiporta*) outer door.

controproducènte, *ag.* having opposite effect.

controprogètto, *s.m.* opposite plan.

contropropósta, *s.f.* counter-proposal, counter-proposition.

contropròva, *s.f.* **1**. (*verifica*) counter-check; verification **2**. (*dir.*) evidence brought by cross-examination **3**. (*seconda votazione in un'assemblea*) counter-vote.

controquerèla, *s.f.* (*dir.*) countercharge.

contrórdine, *s.m.* counter-order, countermand: *vieni domani salvo* —, come to-morrow unless you hear to the contrary; *dare un* —, to countermand an order.

Controrifórma, *s.f.* (*st.relig.*) Counter-reformation.

controrivoluzióne, *s.f.* counter-revolution.

controrotàia, *s.f.* (*ferr.*) guard-rail, check-rail.

controruòta, *s.f.* (*mar.*) apron.

controscàrpa, *s.f.* **1**. (*edil.*) counterscarp **2**. (*soprascarpa*) overshoe.

controsènso, *s.m.* countersense; self-contradiction; (*assurdità*) absurdity, misconception: *questa lettera è tutta un* —, this letter does not make sense.

controspionàggio, *s.m.* counter-espionage.

controstallía, *s.f.* (*comm. mar.*) demurrage: *giorni di* —, demurrage days; *incorrere nelle controstallie*, to incur demurrage.

controstòmaco, *s.m.* distaste, repugnance, aversion (anche *fig.*) ‖ *av.* reluctantly, unwillingly: *mangiò tutto, ma* —, he ate everything, though unwillingly (o with repugnance).

controtorpedinièra, *s.f.* (*mar. mil.*) torpedo-boat destroyer.

controvapóre, *s.m.* (*mec.*) reverse steam: *dare il* —, to reverse steam.

controvelàccio, *s.m.* (*mar.*) main royal.

controvènto, *av.* against the wind, upwind: *navigare* —, to sail against the wind.

controvèrsia, *s.f.* controversy, debate, dispute: *la questione ha suscitato molte controversie*, the matter has given rise to much controversy.

controversísta, *s.m.* (*teol.*) controversialist.

controvèrso, *ag.* controversial, debated, disputed; doubtful: *un punto* —, a controversial point; *è una questione molto controversa,* it is a much debated question.

controvèrtere, *v.t.* to controvert, to dispute.

controvertíbile, *ag.* controvertible.

controvertibilità, *s.f.* controvertibility.

contumàce, *ag.* **1.** (*dir.*) guilty of default: *rendersi* —, to default **2.** (*indocile*) contumacious, insubordinate; stubborn.

contumàcia, *s.f.* **1.** (*dir.*) default: *giudizio in* —, judgment by default; *sarà processato in* —, he will be tried in his absence: *condannare in* —, to sentence by default **2.** (*insubordinazione*) contumacy; insubordination; disobedience **3.** (*quarantena*) quarantine: *bandiera di* —, quarantine flag; *mettere in* —, to put in quarantine; *tenere in* —, to keep in quarantine.

contumaciàle, *ag.* **1.** *sentenza* —, (*dir.*) judgement by default **2.** (*di, per quarantena*) quarantine (*attributivo*): *ospedale* —, quarantine hospital.

contumèlia, *s.f.* (*letter.*) contumely, insult, abuse: *coprire qlcu. di contumelie,* to cast contumelies on s.o.

contumelióso, *ag.* (*letter.*) contumelious.

contundènte, *ag.* blunt, contusive: *arma* —, blunt weapon; *corpo* —, blunt instrument.

contúndere, *v.t.* (*rar.*) to bruise, to contuse.

conturbaménto, *s.m.* disturbance, agitation, confusion, perturbation; excitement.

conturbànte, *ag.* disturbing, perturbing, troubling, upsetting; (*eccitante*) thrilling, exciting; (*affascinante*) fascinating.

conturbàre, *v.t.* to perturb, to disturb, to trouble, to upset; (*eccitare*) to thrill, to excite: *la cattiva notizia lo conturbò,* the bad news perturbed him ‖ **conturbàrsi,** *v.r.* to be disturbed, to become disturbed; to be perturbed.

conturbàto, *ag.* disturbed, upset, troubled; agitated; (*eccitato*) excited.

contusióne, *s.f.* bruise, contusion.

contúso, *ag.* bruised, contused.

contutóre, *s.m.* (*dir.*) joint guardian.

contuttoché, con tútto che, *cong.* although, though.

contuttociò, con tútto ciò, *av.* nevertheless, however.

convalescènte, *ag. s.c.* convalescent.

convalescènza, *s.f.* convalescence, convalescency.

convalescenziàrio, *s.m.* convalescent home, convalescent hospital.

convalidaménto, *s.m.* **1.** validation, ratification; confirmation **2.** (*rafforzamento*) corroboration, support.

convalidàre, *v.t.* **1.** to validate, to ratify, to confirm, to affirm, to make valid: — *un contratto,* to affirm a contract **2.** (*rafforzare*) to corroborate, to support.

convalidazióne, *s.f.* **1.** validation, ratification; confirmation **2.** (*rafforzamento*) corroboration, support.

convallària, *s.f.* (*bot.*) lily of the valley.

convàlle, *s.f.* valley; (*valletta*) vale.

convégno, *s.m.* meeting: *luogo di* —, meeting-place; *darsi* —, to arrange a meeting; (*riunirsi*) to meet (*o* to gather).

convenévole, *ag.* convenient, suitable; proper ‖ *bere più del* —, to drink more than is proper.

convenévoli, *s.pl.* compliments; regards, greetings: *non fate* —, don't stand on ceremony; *fare i* — *a qlcu.,* to pay one's respects to s.o.

convenevolménte, *av.* suitably, properly.

convenevolézza, *s.f.* (*rar.*) **1.** convenience **2.** (*modi garbati*) propriety.

conveniènte, *ag.* **1.** convenient (for s.o., sthg.), suitable (to s.o., sthg.); (*adatto*) befitting (s.o., sthg.): *egli usò parole convenienti alla situazione,* he spoke some words befitting the situation; *per te è* — *partire alle otto,* it is convenient for you to leave at eight **2.** (*utile,* *economicamente vantaggioso*) profitable, expedient; (*di prezzo*) cheap: *prezzi convenienti,* cheap prices; *una speculazione* —, a profitable speculation.

convenienteménte, *av.* **1.** conveniently, suitably **2.** (*vantaggiosamente*) profitably; (*a buon mercato*) cheaply.

conveniènza, *s.f.* **1.** convenience, suitability, suitableness, fitness **2.** (*utilità, vantaggio economico*) advantage, profit, expedience, expediency; (*di prezzo*) cheapness: *per ragioni di* —, on grounds of expediency; *ci troverà la sua* —, he will find some advantage (*o* profit) there ‖ *matrimonio di* —, marriage of convenience **3.** (*buona creanza*) propriety, politeness, civility: *rispettare le convenienze,* to observe the proprieties **4.** (*decoro*) propriety, dignity: *ne va della mia* —, it goes against my dignity **5.** (*proporzione*) proportion: *la* — *delle parti col tutto,* the proportion of the parts with the whole.

convenìre, *v.i.* **1.** *imp.* (*essere utile, necessario*) to suit (s.o.):*ai bimbi conviene andare a letto presto,* children ought to go to bed early; *ci conviene partire,* we had better leave; *conviene che io resti,* I must needs stay; *non mi conviene,* it does not suit me; *non ti conviene contrariarlo,* you had better not contradict him **2.** (*riunirsi*) to meet, to gather, to convene: *convennero da ogni parte,* they came from all parts; *una gran folla convenne là,* a large crowd gathered there **3.** (*concordare*) to agree: *convennero sul prezzo,* they agreed upon the price; *il prezzo è convenuto,* the price is agreed upon; *tutti convengono che è una bellissima ragazza,* all agree she is a very beautiful girl **4.** (*concedere*) to admit, to grant, to agree: *convengo che hai ragione,* I grant you are right; *ho agito male con te, ne convengo,* I've been mean to you, I admit ‖ *v.t.* **1.** (*pattuire*) to agree upon (sthg.): — *un prezzo,* to agree upon a price **2.** (*dir.*) to summon: — *qlcu. in giudizio,* to summon s.o. (to appear in court).

conventícola, *s.f.* conventicle; secret meeting.

convènto, *s.m.* convent; (*di suore*) nunnery; (*di frati*) friary; (*monastero*) monastery: *entrare in* —, (*di suore*) to enter a convent (*o* to become a nun); (*di monaci*) to enter a monastery (*o* to become a friar).

conventuàle, *ag. s.m.* (*eccl.*) conventual.

convenúto, *ag.* agreed upon; (*fissato*) fixed: *prezzo* —, price agreed upon; *è* —, (*siamo d'accordo*) it's settled (*o* we are agreed) ‖ *s.m.* **1.** agreement, settlement **2.** (*dir.*) defendant **3.** *i convenuti,* the persons present.

convenzionàle, *ag.* conventional ‖ *s.m.* (*st. francese*) Conventionalist.

convenzionalísmo, *s.m.* conventionalism.

convenzióne, *s.f.* **1.** (*dir. pol.*) convention, covenant; agreement ‖ *la Convenzione,* (*st.*) the Convention **2.** (*consuetudine*) accepted custom, convention.

convergènte, *ag.* convergent, converging: *strabismo* —, convergent strabismus (*o* cross-eyed strabismus).

convergènza, *s.f.* convergence, convergency.

convèrgere, *v.i.* to converge, to tend to one point.

convèrsa, *s.f.* (*eccl.*) lay sister.

conversàre, *v.i.* to talk; to converse; (*fam.*) to chat.

conversàre, *s.m.* conversation, talk; (*fam.*) chat.

conversatóre, *s.m.,* **conversatríce,** *s.f.* talker.

conversazióne, *s.f.* **1.** conversation, talk; (*fam.*) chat; (*intervista*) interview **2.** (*arc.*) evening party.

conversévole, *ag.* talkative; conversable, sociable.

conversióne, *s.f.* **1.** (*pol. relig.*) conversion: *la* — *di S. Paolo al Cristianesimo,* St. Paul's conversion to Christianity; — *politica,* political conversion **2.** (*mutamento*) conversion: — *della panna in burro,* conversion of cream into butter; — *di frequenza,* (*rad.*) frequency conversion **3.** (*dir. econ.*) conversion: — *della rendita,* conversion of stock; — *in legge di un decreto,* turning of a decree into a law **4.** (*mil.*) wheel: — *a destra, sinistra,* right wheel, left wheel.

convèrso, *ag.* converted, turned ‖ *per* —, conversely (*o vice versa*) ‖ *s.m.* (*eccl.*) lay brother.

convertíbile, *ag.* convertible (anche *finanziario*): — *in oro,* convertible into gold; — *in valuta metallica,* convertible into specie.

convertibilità, *s.f.* convertibility (anche *finanziario*): — *dei biglietti di banca in valuta metallica,* convertibility of bank-notes into specie; — *della valuta,* convertibility of currency; — *in oro,* convertibility into gold.

convertiménto, *s.m.* conversion, transmutation.

convertíre, *v.t.* 1. (*pol. relig.*) to convert: *lo convertirono al socialismo,* they converted him to socialism; — *i pagani al Cristianesimo,* to convert the ceathen to Christianity 2. (*mutare, trasformare*) to honvert, to turn, to change: — *l'acqua in vapore,* to turn water into steam; — *il cibo in sangue,* to turn food into blood; — *titoli in denaro contante,* (*econ.*) to convert securities into cash 3. (*arc.*) (*volgere*) to turn: — *gli occhi,* to turn one's eyes ‖ **convertírsi,** *v.r.* 1. (*pol. relig.*) to be converted: *si convertì al Cristianesimo,* he was converted to Christianity 2. (*mutarsi, trasformarsi*) to be converted, to turn, to change: *i bruchi si convertono in farfalle,* caterpillars change into butterflies.

convertíto, *s.m.* convert.

convertitóre, *s.m.* 1. (*chi converte*) converter 2. (*elett.*) converter, convertor.

convessità, *s.f.* convexity.

convèsso, *ag.* convex.

convezióne, *s.f.* (*elett. fis.*) convection: *corrente di* —, convection current.

convincènte, *ag.* convincing: *argomento* —, convincing argument.

convíncere, *v.t.* 1. to convince, to persuade: *sono convinto della sua onestà,* I am persuaded of his honesty (*o* that he is honest); — *qlcu. di ql.co.,* to convince s.o. of sthg. 2. (*dir.*) to convict, to prove guilty: — *qlcu. di un reato,* to convict s.o. of a crime ‖ **convíncersi,** *v.r.* to convince oneself; (*lasciarsi convincere*) to be convinced, to allow oneself to be convinced.

convincíbile, *ag.* convincible.

convinciménto, *s.m.* convincement, conviction; persuasion.

convínto, *ag.* 1. convinced, persuaded: *parlare in tono* —, to speak earnestly (*o* with conviction) 2. (*intimamente persuaso*): *monarchico* —, out-and-out monarchist 3. *reo* —, (*dir.*) convicted.

convinzióne, *s.f.* conviction, persuasion, firm belief: *avere la — che...,* to be convinced that....

convitànte, *s.m.* host.

convitàre, *v.t.* to invite (s.o.) to a banquet.

convitàto, *s.m.* guest: *egli era l'unico — straniero,* he was the only stranger at the table.

convíto, *s.m.* banquet; feast.

convítto, *s.m.* boarding-school: — *femminile,* boarding-school for girls.

convittóre, *s.m.,* **convittríce,** *s.f.* boarder.

convivènte, *ag.* cohabiting, living together ‖ *s.c.* cohabitant.

convivènza, *s.f.* 1. cohabitation; living together, life in common 2. (*collettività*) society: *l'umana* —, human society.

convívere, *v.i.* to cohabit; to live together.

conviviàle, *ag.* convivial: *canzoni conviviali,* convivial songs.

convívio, *s.m.* (*arc.*) banquet; feast.

convocàre, *v.t.* to convoke; to convene, to call (together), to summon, to assemble: — *un'assemblea,* to convene (*o* to call *o* to summon) a meeting; — *il Parlamento,* (*pol.*) to convoke Parliament; — *i propri creditori,* (*dir.*) to call one's creditors together.

convocazióne, *s.f.* convocation; calling together; summoning, meeting: *indire la — dei creditori,* (*dir.*) to call the meeting of creditors.

convogliàre, *v.t.* 1. (*scortare*) to convoy, to escort 2. (*trasportare, trascinar via*) to carry away,

to convey: *queste tubature convogliano l'acqua calda a tutte le parti dell'edificio,* these pipes convey hot water to all parts of the building. 3. (*indirizzare*) to address: *convogliò le sue energie a quella mansione,* he addressed his energies to that task.

convòglio, *s.m.* 1. (*treno*) train 2. (*mar. mil.*) convoy 3. (*corteo*) procession: — *funebre,* funeral procession.

convolàre, *v.i.* to fly together ‖ — *a giuste nozze,* to get married.

convòlvolo, *s.m.* (*bot.*) convolvulus.

convulsaménte, *av.* convulsively.

convulsionàrio, *ag. s.m.* (*med.*) convulsionary.

convulsióne, *s.f.* (*patol.*) convulsion; spasm: *convulsioni infantili,* infantile convulsions; *cadere in convulsioni,* to fall into a fit of convulsions ‖ *convulsioni di riso,* convulsions of laughter.

convulsívo, *ag.* convulsive: *tic* —, (*med.*) convulsive tic.

convúlso, *ag.* 1. convulsive; agitated: *riso* —, convulsive laughter 2. (*caotico*) jerky: *stile* —, jerky style ‖ *s.m.* convulsion; twitch.

coobàre, *v.t.* (*chim.*) to cohobate.

coobazióne, *s.f.* (*chim.*) cohobation.

coonestaménto, *s.m.* justification; palliation.

coonestàre, *v.t.* to justify, to palliate.

cooperànte, *ag.* co-operating.

cooperàre, *v.i.* to co-operate; to collaborate; to join; to contribute: *cooperò con me a fondare un nuovo giornale,* he co-operated (*o* joined) with me in launching a new paper; — *alla preparazione di un dizionario,* to collaborate in preparing a dictionary; — *al successo di ql.co.,* to co-operate to the success of sthg.

cooperatíva, *s.f.* co-operative society: — *di consumo,* co-operative store; — *di produzione,* co-operative society for production.

cooperatívo, *ag.* (*amm.*) co-operative: *società cooperativa,* co-operative society.

cooperatóre, *s.m.,* **cooperatríce,** *s.f.* co-operator.

cooperazióne, *s.f.* co-operation, collaboration.

coordinaménto, *s.m.* co-ordination.

coordinàre, *v.t.* to co-ordinate: — *le proprie idee,* to co-ordinate one's ideas; — *i propri movimenti,* to co-ordinate one's movements.

coordinàta, *s.f.* co-ordinate: *coordinate cartesiane,* (*mat.*) Cartesian co-ordinates; *coordinate equatoriali,* (*geog.*) equatorial co-ordinates; *coordinate polari,* (*geog.*) polar co-ordinates; *proposizione coordinata,* (*gram.*) co-ordinate clause.

coordinàto, *ag.* co-ordinate.

coordinatóre, *ag.* co-ordinative ‖ *s.m.,* **coordinatríce,** *s.f.* co-ordinator.

coordinazióne, *s.f.* co-ordination.

coòrte, *s.f.* 1. (*st. mil.*) cohort 2. (*folla*) troop, crowd, multitude.

copàle, *s.f.* 1. (*resina*) copal; (*vernice*) (copal) varnish 2. (*pelle*) patent leather: *scarpe di* —, patent leather shoes.

copèrchio, *s.m.* lid, cover; (*mec.*) cover, cap: — *abitacolo armi,* (*aer. mil.*) gun cover; — *a vite,* (*mec.*) screw cap; — *di botola d'accesso,* (*edil. stradale*) man-hole cover; — *di una staffa,* (*fonderia*) cope, lift ‖ *il soverchio rompe il* —, *prov.* there is a mean in all things.

copernicàno, *ag.* Copernican: *sistema* —, (*astr.*) Copernican system.

Copèrnico, *no.pr.* (*st. astr.*) Copernicus.

copèrta, *s.f.* 1. blanket; (*copriletto*) coverlet, bed-spread, counterpane; (*trapunta*) quilt: — *da viaggio,* (travelling) rug; (*di tessuto scozzese*) plaid; — *elettrica,* electric blanket 2. (*di libro*) cover; (*di lettera*) envelope 3. (*mar.*) deck: — *di manovra,* awning deck; — *di prua,* foredeck; *carico di* —, deck cargo (*o* load); *mozzo di* —, deck boy; *sotto* —, below deck; *tutti in* — *!,* all hands on deck! 4. (*rar.*) (*scusa, pretesto*) cover, excuse, pretext: *sotto — di uscire,* under cover of going out.

copertaménte, *av.* covertly, secretly, stealthily.

copertína, *s.f.* cover; (*di libro*) book-cover: — *volante,* (*di libro*) dust-jacket (*o* dust-cover).

copèrto, *ag.* **1.** (*riparato*) covered, sheltered; (*rivestito*) clad: — *di ferro,* clad with iron (*o* iron-clad); *carrozza coperta,* closed carriage; *passaggio* —, underground passage; *strada coperta,* sheltered road ‖ *essere* —, (*comm.*) to be covered **2.** (*di cielo*) overcast, cloudy: *domani cielo* — *su tutto il paese,* tomorrow it will be generally cloudy over the whole country **3.** (*vestito*) clothed: *non sei troppo* —?, are you not too heavily clothed? **4.** (*nascosto*) concealed, hidden; (*segreto*) secret; (*mil.*) masked: *batteria coperta,* (*mil.*) masked battery; *nemico* —, covert enemy; *odio* —, concealed hatred ‖ *s.m.* **1.** (*posto a tavola*) cover, place; (*fam.*) knife and fork: *una tavola di otto coperti,* a table laid for eight; *quanti coperti hai messo?,* how many covers (*o* places) have you laid?; *svelto, metti un altro* —!, put another knife and fork, quick! **2.** (*al ristorante, prezzo del coperto*) cover charge **3.** *al* —, under cover: *mettere, mettersi al* — *dalla pioggia,* to shelter from the rain; *mettersi al* —, to take shelter (*o* to get under cover).

copertóne, *s.m.* **1.** (*di pneumatico*) tire, tyre, pneumatic tyre **2.** (*telone impermeabile*) tarpaulin.

copertúra, *s.f.* **1.** covering: — *delle spese,* (*comm.*) covering of expenses; *truppe di* —, (*mil.*) covering troops (*o* party) **2.** (*di mobile, di poltrona*) cover **3.** (*edil.*): — *con lamiere di ferro,* iron sheeting; — *con tegole,* tile covering; — *di ardesia,* slate covering (*o* slating); — *di cemento armato,* reinforced concrete (*o* ferro-concrete) ceiling; — *di un tetto,* roof covering (*o* roofing); *materiali da* —, roofing.

còpia[1], *s.f.* **1.** copy; (*foto. cine.*) print: — *a macchina,* typewritten copy; — *autenticata,* (*dir.*) certified copy; — *campione,* (*cine.*) answer print; — *carbone,* carbon copy; — *conforme,* true copy; — *fotostatica,* (*foto.*) photostat; — *lucida,* (*foto.*) glossy print; — *rapida,* (*cine.*) rush print; — *seppia,* (*foto.*) sepia (*o* brown) print; — *sonora,* (*cine.*) composite print; — *tipo,* master pattern; *bella* —, fair copy; *brutta* —, rough copy (*o* draft); *prender* — *di ql.co.,* to copy sthg. **2.** (*esemplare*) copy, exemplar: *una* — *di seconda mano,* a second-hand copy; — *omaggio,* complimentary (*o* presentation) copy.

còpia[2], *s.f.* (*letter.*) (*abbondanza*) abundance: *ha libri in gran* —, he has plenty of books (*o* a great many books).

copialèttere, *s.m.* **1.** letter-book **2.** (*torchio, pressa*) letter-press.

copiàre, *v.t.* **1.** (*imitare*) to copy, to imitate; (*sl. scolastico*) to crib: — *un compito da un compagno,* to crib an exercise from a school-fellow **2.** (*trascrivere*) to copy, to transcribe.

copiatívo, *ag.* copying: *carta copiativa,* carbon paper; *inchiostro* —, copying ink; *matita copiativa,* copying (*o* ink *o* indelible) pencil.

copiatóre, *s.m.,* **copiatríce,** *s.f.* (*chi trascrive*) copier; (*chi imita*) imitator.

copiatúra, *s.f.* **1.** copying, imitation; (*sl. scolastico*) crib **2.** (*trascrizione*) transcription, copying **3.** (*spesa per la copia*) fee paid for copying.

copíglia, *s.f.* (*mec.*) split pin, cotter-pin: — *di sicurezza,* safety pin (*o* safety device).

copióne, *s.m.* (*teat.*) script: — *cinematografico,* film script.

copiosaménte, *av.* plentifully, copiously, abundantly.

copióso, *ag.* plentiful, abundant, copious.

copísta, *s.m.* copyist; (*dattilografo*) typist.

copistería, *s.f.* typing-office, typing agency.

còppa[1], *s.f.* **1.** cup, goblet; (*letter.*) (*bicchiere*) drinking-glass, drinking-cup: — *da champagne,* champagne glass **2.** (*piatto di bilancia*) scale **3.** (*trofeo sportivo*) cup, trophy; (*gara*) contest **4.** (*aut.*) (*dell'olio*) pan, sump **5.** *pl.* (*a carte*) the suit in Italian (playing) cards corresponding to hearts.

còppa[2], *s.f.* **1.** (*nuca*) nape **2.** (*salume*) " coppa " (kind of Italian sausage).

coppàle, *V.* **copàle.**

coppèlla, *s.f.* **1.** (*metal.*) cupel, test: *oro di* —, fine gold; *fig.* person of integrity; *passare l'oro alla* —, to cupel (*o* to assay *o* to refine) gold ‖ *prendere tutto per oro di* —, (*credere a tutto*) to swallow anything one is told **2.** (*bot.*) (*talamo*) thalamus (*pl.* thalami).

coppellàre, *v.t.* (*metal.*) to cupel, to test, to assay.

coppellazióne, *s.f.* (*metal.*) cupellation, assaying: *sottoporre a* —, to refine (*o* to cupel *o* to assay).

coppétta, *s.f.* (*med.*) cupping-glass: *applicazione di coppette,* cupping; *fare, applicare le coppette a qlcu.,* to cup s.o.

còppia, *s.f.* **1.** (*di persone*) couple, pair: *una* — *di ragazze,* a couple of girls; *la* — *felice,* (*di sposi*) the happy pair; *una giovane* — *di sposi,* a young married couple; *venti coppie entrarono nel ballo,* twenty couples took the floor; *formare una bella* —, to make a nice pair (*o* a handsome couple) ‖ *a coppie,* two by two (*o* in couples) **2.** (*di animali*) pair; (*di cani da caccia*) couple (*spesso invariato al pl.*); (*di buoi*) yoke; (*di capi di selvaggina*) brace (*invariato al pl.*): *una* — *di colombi,* a pair of doves; *dieci coppie di cani,* ten couple of dogs; *tre coppie di pernici,* three brace of partridges **3.** (*di cose*) couple: *una* — *di bicchieri,* a couple of glasses **4.** (*fis.*) torque; (*di forze*) couple: — *antagonista,* restoring torque; — *di lavoro,* working torque **5.** (*tel.*) pair **6.** (*mat.*) dyad.

coppière, *s.m.* cup-bearer.

coppìola, *s.f.* **1.** (*due colpi di doppietta*) double shot **2.** (*rete del paretaio*) fowling-net.

còppo, *s.m.* **1.** roof tile; (*tegola curva*) bent tile **2.** (*orcio per vino, olio*) jar **3.** (*rete da pesca*) landing-net.

copribústo, *s.m.* bodice, camisole.

copricànna, *s.m.* hand-guard.

copricàpo, *s.m.* headgear; (*cappello*) hat.

coprifuòco, *s.m.* curfew: *suonare il* —, to ring the curfew.

coprigiúnto, *s.m.* (*mec.*) butt strap; (*ferr.*) joint fishing.

coprimorsétto, *s.m.* (*elett.*) terminal cover.

copripiàtti, *s.m.* dish-cover.

copripièdi, *s.m.* eider-down.

copriruòta, *s.m.* wheel cover.

copríre, *v.t.* **1.** to cover: *i mobili erano coperti di polvere,* the furniture was covered (*o* overlaid) with dust; *il muro era coperto di edera,* the wall was overgrown with ivy; *la neve copriva ogni cosa,* snow covered up everything; *il suo cappotto era tutto coperto di fango,* his overcoat was spattered with mud ‖ — *una casa,* (*metterle il tetto*) to roof a house; — *una casa con tegole,* to tile a house; — *di assi,* to plank ‖ — *una distanza,* to cover a distance ‖ — *qlcu. di ingiurie,* to load s.o. with abuse; — *qlcu. di ridicolo, di vergogna,* to cover s.o. with ridicule, shame ‖ — *uno sbarco, una ritirata,* (*mil.*) to cover a landing, a retreat **2.** (*celare*) to cover, to conceal: *rideva per* — *il suo nervosismo,* he was laughing to cover (*o* to conceal) his nervousness; — *le proprie intenzioni,* to conceal (*o* to keep secret) one's intentions **3.** (*un suono*) to drown: — *un rumore, una voce,* to drown a noise, a voice **4.** (*occupare*) to fill, to hold: — *un'alta carica,* to hold a high office; — *un posto, un impiego,* to fill a position **5.** (*comm.*) to cover: — *le spese,* to cover (*o* to pay *o* to meet) expenses; *essere coperto dall'assicurazione,* to be covered by insurance **6.** (*montare, di animali*) to cover ‖ **coprírsi,** *v.r.* **1.** to cover oneself (up) (*anche fig.*); (*mettersi il cappello*) to put on one's hat, to put one's hat on; (*avvolgersi negli abiti*) to wrap oneself up: *copriti bene, perchè fa molto freddo,* cover yourself up warmly (*o* put on warm clothes), for it is very cold; — *di gloria, di onore,* to cover oneself with glory, with honour; — *di vergogna,* to bring shame upon oneself; — *il volto con le mani*, to hide (*o to bury*) one's face in one's hands **2.** (*di cielo*) to become overcast, to become cloudy **3.** (*comm.*) (*rivalersi*) to value: — *dalle spese sostenute per conto di qlcu.*, to value for expenses met on s.o.'s account **4.** (*scherma*) to guard; to be on one's guard.

copriteièra, *s.m.* (tea-)cosy.

coprivivànde, *s.m.* dish-cover.

còpto, *ag.* Coptic: *conosce la lingua copta*, he knows Coptic ‖ *s.m.* **1.** Copt **2.** (*lingua*) Coptic.

còpula, *s.f.* **1.** (*gram.*) copula **2.** (*fisiol.*) copulation.

copulativaménte, *av.* copulatively.

copulativo, *ag.* (*gram.*) copulative.

coràggio, *s.m.* **1.** courage, bravery, heart, pluck, nerve; (*ardimento*) boldness: *è un uomo di —*, he is a man full of courage (*o a man of nerve o a plucky fellow*); *ha il — delle sue opinioni*, he has the courage of his convictions; *mi mancò il —*, my courage (*o my nerve*) failed; *mostrate un po' di —!*, show a little spirit!; *non aveva —*, he had no courage; *non ebbe il — di affrontarlo*, he had not the nerve to face him; *non ho il — di licenziarlo*, I have not the heart to dismiss him; *non perderti di —!*, don't lose heart!; *far — a qlcu.*, to cheer s.o. up; *farsi coraggio*, to pluck (*o to muster*) up courage; *perdere —*, to lose heart (*o one's nerve*); *riprendere —*, to take fresh heart ‖ *—!*, cheer up! ‖ *armarsi di — per fare ql.co.*, to brace (*o to nerve*) oneself to do sthg.; *prendere il — a due mani*, to take one's courage in both hands **2.** (*impudenza*) impudence, effrontery; (*fam.*) nerve: *hai un bel —!*, you have a nerve!.

coraggiosaménte, *av.* courageously, bravely.

coraggióso, *ag.* courageous, brave, fearless, plucky; (*ardito*) bold: *fu lei a far di me un uomo —*, it was she who put some pluck into me.

coràgo, *s.m.* (*teat. greco*) choragus (*pl.* choragi).

coràle¹, *ag.* choral: *canto —*, choral singing; *società —*, choral society ‖ *s.m.* **1.** (*mus.*) (*composizione per coro*) choral(e) **2.** (*eccl.*) (*antifonario*) book of anthems.

coràle², *ag.* hearty, cordial.

corallàio, *s.m.* **1.** (*chi lavora il corallo*) coral-cutter **2.** (*chi vende oggetti di corallo*) coral-dealer.

coralléssa, *s.f.* low-quality coral.

corallífero, *ag.* coralliferous: *banco —*, coral-reef.

corallína, *s.f.* **1.** (*bot.*) coralline **2.** (*min.*) corallite **3.** (*barca*) coral-fishing boat.

Corallina, *no.pr.f.* (*teat.*) Corallina.

corallíno, *ag.* **1.** coral (*attributivo*): *isola corallina*, coral-island **2.** (*di colore*) coral (*attributivo*), coralline: *labbra coralline*, coral lips.

coràllo, *s.m.* coral: — *bianco*, white coral; *banco di —*, coral-reef; *collana di —*, coral necklace; *labbra di —*, coral lips; *pescatore di coralli*, coral fisher ‖ *il Mar dei Coralli*, (*geog.*) the Coral Sea.

corallòide, *s.f.* (*bot.*) coralloid.

coràme, *s.m.* **1.** leather **2.** (*per tappezzeria*) stamped leather.

coramèlla, *s.f.* strop.

corampòpulo, *av.* coram populo.

Coràno, *s.m.* Koran.

coràta, **coratèlla**, *s.f.* pluck.

coràzza, *s.f.* **1.** (*armatura di guerriero*) cuirass **2.** (*mil.*) armour: — *composta*, (*mil.*) compound armour; — *di murata*, (*mar.*) side armour **3.** (*zool. bot.*) armour; (*guscio*) carapace; (*conchiglia*) shell: *la — della tartaruga*, the carapace of the tortoise.

corazzàre, *v.t.* **1.** to armour **2.** *fig.* (*fortificare*) to strengthen ‖ **corazzàrsi**, *v.r. fig.* (*fortificarsi*) to harden oneself, to arm oneself: *si è corazzato contro tutte le avversità della vita*, he has hardened himself against all the adversities of life.

corazzàta, *s.f.* (*mar.*) battleship; (*nel secolo scorso*) ironclad.

corazzàto, *ag.* armoured, ironclad (*attributivo*), armour-plated: *divisione corazzata*, (*mil.*) armoured

division; *incrociatore —*, (*mar. mil.*) armoured-cruiser; *treno —*, (*ferr.*) armoured-train.

corazzatúra, *s.f.* armour-plating.

corazzière, *s.m.* (*mil.*) cuirassier.

còrba, *s.f.* **1.** large basket; hamper **2.** (*vet.*) curb **3.** (*mar.*) rib.

corbàme, *s.m.* (*mar.*) framework.

corbellàggine, *s.f.* (*fam.*) stupidity; foolishness.

corbellàio, *s.m.* basket-maker.

corbellàre, *v.t.* to make fun of (s.o.), to poke fun at (s.o.); to mock; to ridicule; to deride: *non si deve — un vecchio*, one must not make fun of (*o poke fun at*) an old man.

corbellatóre, *s.m.*, **corbellatríce**, *s.f.* mocker·

corbellatòrio, *ag.* mocking; derisive.

corbellatúra, *s.f.* **1.** (*il corbellare*) mockery; derision **2.** (*burla*) hoax; joke, jest.

corbellería, *s.f.* **1.** (*atto da sciocco*) foolish action, foolery **2.** (*discorso sciocco*) nonsense; foolish words (*pl.*): *dire corbellerie*, to talk nonsense **3.** (*sproposito*) blunder: *dire, fare corbellerie*, to blunder **4.** (*inezia*) trifle: *tre scellini, una —!*, three shillings, a mere trifle!.

corbèllo, *s.m.* **1.** basket **2.** (*quantità contenuta in un corbello*) basketful: *un — di mele*, a basketful of apples ‖ *a corbelli*, in plenty **3.** *fig.* (*sciocco*) fool; blockhead.

corbézzola, *s.f.* (*bot.*) arbutus berry.

corbézzolo, *s.m.* (*bot.*) arbutus, strawberry-tree.

corbézzoli, *inter.* good gracious! good heavens!.

Corcíra, *no.pr.f.* (*geog. st.*) Corcyra.

corcontènto, *s.m.* (*fam.*) easy-going fellow.

còrda, *s.f.* **1.** rope; (*cavo*) cable; (*filo metallico*) wire; (*spago*) cord, chord; string; twine: — *della frusta*, whipcord; — *di arco*, bow string; *corde di arpa*, chords (*o harp strings*); — *di pianoforte*, piano wire; — *di violino*, violin string; *strumento a —*, string instrument; *ballare sulla —*, to dance on the tight rope; *dar la — a un orologio*, to wind up a watch (*o a clock*); *tendere le corde di un violino*, to wind (*o to screw*) up the strings of a fiddle ‖ *avere più di una — al proprio arco*, *fig.* to have two strings to one's bow ‖ *dar — a qlcu.*, *fig.* to worm a secret out of s.o. ‖ *essere giù di —*, (*fam.*) to feel seedy ‖ *mettere a qlcu. la — al collo*, to rope s.o. in; (*fam.*) (*tiranneggiare*) to rule s.o. with a heavy hand ‖ *tenere qlcu. sulla —*, *fig.* to keep s.o. in suspense ‖ *tirare la —*, *fig.* to overdo (*o to exaggerate*) ‖ *toccar la — giusta*, *fig.* to touch the right chord **2.** (*anat.*) chord, cord: *corde del collo*, neck sinews; *corde vocali*, vocal chords **3.** (*trama del tessuto*) thread: *mostrare le corde*, to be threadbare **4.** (*geom.*) chord: — *di un arco*, the chord of an arc.

cordàio, *s.m.* **1.** (*chi fabbrica corde*) rope-maker **2.** (*chi vende corde*) rope-seller.

cordàme, *s.m.* (*mar.*) cordage; rigging.

cordàta, *s.f.* (*alpinismo*) rope: *in —*, on the rope.

cordàti, *s.m. pl.* (*zool.*) Chordata.

Cordèlia, *no.pr.f.* (*lett.*) Cordelia.

cordellína, *s.f.* **1.** braid **2.** (*nelle uniformi militari*) lanyard.

cordería, *s.f.* rope factory.

cordiàle, *ag.* cordial, hearty, warm: *un — benvenuto*, *un'accoglienza —*, a hearty (*o warm o cordial*) welcome; *una persona —*, a friendly person; *saluti cordiali*, best wishes ‖ *s.m.* (*liquore*) cordial.

cordialità, *s.f.* cordiality, warm-heartedness.

cordialménte, *av.* cordially, heartily, friendlily.

cordialóna, *s.f.* **cordialóne**, *s.m.* warm-hearted person.

cordicèlla, *s.f.* pack-thread; string.

cordiglièra, *s.f.* (*geog.*) cordillera ‖ *la Cordigliera delle Ande*, the Cordillera of the Andes.

cordíglio, *s.m.* girdle.

cordíte, *s.f.* (*esplosivo*) cordite.

cordòglio, *s.m.* deep sorrow, grief, affliction.

cordonàta, *s.f.* ramp with strings of stones (for foothold to animals).

cordóne, *s.m.* **1**. cord, string: — *di campanello*, bell-rope (*o* bell-pull); — *di seta*, silk cord ‖ *allargare i cordoni della borsa*, *fig.* to loosen the purse-strings ‖ *reggere i cordoni*, (*a un funerale*) to bear the pall **2**. (*anat.*) cord; (*funicolo*) funiculus: — *ombelicale*, umbilical cord **3**. (*mil.*) cordon, chain: — *d'agenti di polizia*, cordon of police ‖ — *sanitario*, sanitary cordon **4**. (*di ordine cavalleresco*) cordon, ribbon **5**. (*arch.*) cordon; string-course **6**. (*elett. tel.*) cord.

Còrdova, *no.pr.f.* (*geog.*) Cordova.

cordovàno, *s.m.* (*cuoio*) cordovan.

còre, (*poet.*) per **cuòre**.

corèa[1], *s.f.* (*patol.*) chorea, St. Vitus's dance.

Corèa[2], *no.pr.f.* (*geog.*) Korea.

coreàno, *ag. s.m.* Korean ‖ **coreàna**, *s.f.* Korean.

coréggia, *s.f.* leather strap.

coreografía, *s.f.* choreography.

coreograficaménte, *av.* choreographically.

coreogràfico, *ag.* **1**. choreographic **2**. *fig.* spectacular.

coreògrafa, *s.f.* **coreògrafo**, *s.m.* choreograph(er).

Corfú, *no.pr.f.* (*geog.*) Corfu.

coriàceo, *ag.* coriaceous, leathery; tough: *questa bistecca è molto coriacea*, this beefsteak is very tough.

coriàmbo, *s.m.* (*poes.*) choriamb.

coriàndolo, *s.m.* **1**. (*bot.*) coriander **2**. *pl.* (*ritagli di carta colorata da gettare a carnevale*) confetti.

coribànte, *s.m.* (*mit.*) Corybant (*pl.* Corybant(e)s).

coricàre, *v.t.* **1**. (*adagiare*) to lay down: *coricò il bambino nella culla*, she laid the child in its cradle **2**. (*mettere a letto*) to put to bed ‖ **coricàrsi**, *v.r.* **1**. (*sdraiarsi*) to lie down **2**. (*andare a letto*) to go to bed: *i bambini si coricarono presto*, the children went to bed early **3**. (*tramontare*) to set: *in questa stagione il sole si corica alle sei*, in this season the sun sets at six.

corifèo, *s.m.* **1**. (*teat. greco*) coryphaeus (*pl.* coryphaei) **2**. *fig.* (*capo*) coryphaeus (*pl.* coryphaei) **3**. (*ballerino*) dancer.

corìmbo, *s.m.* (*bot.*) corymb.

corindóne, *s.m.* (*min.*) corundum.

Corínna, *no.pr.f.* Corinne.

Corínto, *no.pr.f.* (*geog.*) Corinth.

corínzio, *ag.* Corinthian: *metallo* —, Corinthian brass; *ordine* —, (*arch.*) Corinthian order.

corìsta, *s.m.* **1**. chorus-singer; (*di chiesa*) chorister **2**. (*mus.*) (*suono*) pitch; diapason; (*strumento*) tuning-fork ‖ *s.f.* chorus-singer.

còriza, *s.f.* (*patol.*) coryza.

còrmo, *s.m.* (*bot.*) cormus (*pl.* cormi).

cormoràno, *s.m.* (*ornit.*) cormorant.

cornàcchia, *s.f.* **1**. (*ornit.*) rook, crow: *una* — *gracchiava*, a crow was cawing **2**. *fig.* (*persona di cattivo augurio*) croaker.

cornalína, *s.f.* (*min.*) carnelian, cornelian.

cornamúsa, *s.f.* (*mus.*) bagpipe.

cornàre, *v.i.* **1**. (*cozzare con le corna*) to butt, to horn **2**. (*suonare il corno*) to wind the horn.

cornàta, *s.f.* butt (with the horns).

cornatúra, *s.f.* quality of the horns; (*disposizione delle corna*) disposition of the horns.

còrnea, *s.f.* (*anat.*) cornea.

Cornèlia, *no.pr.f.* Cornelia.

Cornèlio, *no.pr.m.* Cornelius.

còrneo, *ag.* horny, corneous; hornlike: *escrescenze cornee*, hornlike projections; *strato* — *dell'epidermide*, horny layer of the skin.

cornétta, *s.f.* **1**. (*mus.*) cornet: *suonatore di* —, cornetist; (*amer.*) cornettist (*o* cornet player) **2**. (*st.*) (*alfiere*) cornet.

cornétto, *s.m.* **1**. little-horn **2**. (*mus.*) cornet **3**. (*cornetto acustico*) ear-trumpet **4**. (*amuleto*) horn-shaped amulet **5**. *pl.* (*bot.*) French beans.

còrnia, *s.f.* (*min.*) cornelian, carnelian.

cornìce, *s.f.* **1**. frame: — *di un quadro*, picture -frame; *val più la* — *del quadro*, the frame is worth more than the picture; *mettere in* —, to set in a frame

(*o* to frame) ‖ *far la* — *a un fatto*, to embellish the truth **2**. (*arch.*) drip-stone, cornice **3**. (*orlo sporgente di roccia*) ledge.

corniciàio, *s.m.* **1**. (*chi fabbrica cornici*) frame-maker **2**. (*chi vende cornici*) frame-seller.

corniciatúra, *s.f.* framing.

cornicióne, *s.m.* (*arch.*) cornice; entablature; moulding: — *di finestra, di porta*, label; — *di gronda*, eaves (*pl.*).

cornificàre, *v.t.* (*volg.*) (*di moglie*) to cuckold, to make a cuckold of (one's husband); (*di marito*) to be unfaithful to (one's wife).

còrniola, *s.f.* (*bot.*) cornel, cornelian cherry.

còrniolo, *s.m.* **1**. (*bot.*) cornel(-tree) **2**. (*legno*) cornel.

cornìsta, *s.m.* (*mus.*) horn-player.

corniuòla, *s.f.* (*min.*) cornelian, carnelian.

còrno, *s.m.* **1**. horn (anche *fig.*); (*ramificato*) antler: — *da scarpe*, shoe-horn; *corni della luna*, horns (*o* cusps) of the moon; *corna di antilope*, antelope-horns; *corni d'un arco*, tips of a bow; — *di un fiume*, horn of a river; *corna di lumaca*, horns of a snail; — *di montagna*, mountain -peak; *a forma di* —, horn-shaped ‖ *un* —!, not at all! (*o* nonsense!) ‖ — *dell'abbondanza*, cornucopia (*o* horn of plenty) ‖ *corni di un dilemma*, horns of a dilemma ‖ *non vale un* —, (*volg.*) it isn't worth a fig ‖ *alzare le corna*, *fig.* to get on one's high horse ‖ *avere qlcu. sulle corna*, *fig.* to dislike s.o. ‖ *dire corna di qlcu.*, *fig.* to slander (*o* to speak ill of) s.o. ‖ *fare le corna*, (*come scongiuro*) to touch wood ‖ *fare le corna al marito*, to make a cuckold of one's husband; *fare le corna alla moglie*, to be unfaithful to one's wife; *portare le corna*, (*di marito*) to be a cuckold ‖ *prendere il toro per le corna*, *fig.* to take the bull by the horns ‖ *ritirare le corna*, *fig.* to draw in one's horns ‖ *rompere le corna a qlcu.*, (*picchiarlo*) to hit (*o* to beat) s.o. hard ‖ *rompersi le corna*, *fig.* to get the worst of it (*o* to be defeated) **2**. (*materiale, sostanza*) horny matter, horn: — *artificiale*, (*galalite*) galalith; *manico di* —, horn handle; *pettine di* —, horn comb **3**. (*mus.*) horn: — *da caccia*, hunting -horn; — *francese*, French horn; — *inglese*, English horn (*o* cor anglais); *suonatore di* — (*da caccia*), horn -blower; (*cornista*) horn-player; *suonare un* — (*da caccia*), to wind a horn **4**. (*tec.*): — *di un'incudine*, beak, beakiron; — *polare*, (*elettromeccanica*) pole horn (*o* pole tip): — *polare d'entrata*, leading pole tip; — *polare d'uscita*, trailing pole tip.

Cornovàglia, *no.pr.f.* (*geog.*) Cornwall.

cornucòpia, *s.f.* **1**. cornucopia; horn of plenty **2**. *fig.* cornucopia, abundance.

cornúto, *ag.* horned ‖ *argomento* —, dilemma ‖ *s.m.* **1**. (*animale cornuto*) horned animal **2**. (*volg.*) (*marito tradito*) cuckold.

còro, *s.m.* **1**. chorus: *un* — *di lodi*, a chorus of praise; *tutti in* —!, all together!; *cantare in* —, to sing in chorus; *ripetere ql.co. in* —, to chorus sthg.; *rispondere in* —, to answer in chorus (*o* all together) **2**. (*gruppo di cantori*) chorus; choir (anche *di chiesa*): — *di uccelli*, choir of birds; *appartiene al* —, he belongs to the chorus **3**. (*di melodramma, tragedia*) chorus: *il* — *di un'opera*, the chorus of an opera; *il* — *di una tragedia greca*, the chorus of a Greek tragedy **4**. (*ordine di angeli*) choir **5**. (*arch.*) choir.

corografía, *s.f.* chorography.

corogràfico, *ag.* chorographic(al).

corògrafo, *s.m.* chorographer.

coròide, *s.f.* (*anat.*) choroid.

coroidèo, *ag.* choroid(al): *plesso* —, choroid plexus; *tunica coroidea*, choroid coat (*o* choroid tunic); *vena coroidea*, choroid vein.

coroidíte, *s.f.* (*patol.*) choroiditis.

coròlla, *s.f.* corolla.

corollàrio, *s.m.* **1**. (*geom.*) corollary **2**. (*consequenza*) consequence, corollary, inference **3**. (*appendice*) appendix (*pl.* appendixes, appendices).

coróna, *s.f.* **1**. crown; (*nobiliare*) coronet: — *del martirio*, martyr's crown; — *navale*, naval crown;

aspirare, rinunciare alla —, to lay claim to the crown, to renounce the crown ‖ — *ferrea*, Iron Crown ‖ *discorso della* —, speech from the Throne ‖ *gioielli della* —, crown-jewels ‖ *principe della* —, crown-prince **2.** (*ghirlanda*) garland; (*serto*) wreath: *deporre una* —, to lay a wreath ‖ — *di alloro, trionfale*, laurel wreath **3.** (*moneta*) crown: *una mezza* —, (*moneta*) a half-crown; (*valore*) half a crown **4.** (*rosario*) rosary; beads (*pl.*): *recitare la* —, to tell one's beads **5.** (*raccolta di poesie, ecc.*) sequence, garland: *una* — *di sonetti*, a sequence of sonnets **6.** (*di persone*) circle; (*di cose*) ring: *la città è circondata da una* — *di colli*, the town is ringed by hills; *far* —, to form a circle **7.** (*di albero potato*) crown **8.** (*tonsura dei religiosi*) tonsure **9.** (*di dente*) crown: *rimettere la* — *a un dente*, to crown a tooth **10.** (*parte della gamba del cavallo*) coronet **11.** (*mus.*) corona (*pl.* coronas, coronae); pause **12.** (*arch.*) corona (*pl.* coronas, coronae); (*di volta*) crown **13.** (*astr.*) corona (*pl.* coronas, coronae): — *solare*, solar corona **14.** (*fortificazione*) crown-work **15.** (*mec.*) rim: — *conica*, ring bevel gear; — *dentata*, crown wheel (*o* crown gear *o* ring gear) **16.** (*tetto di miniera*) back **17.** (*aer.*) (*di pallone*) hoop, load ring **18.** — *di forzamento*, (*artigl.*) driving band.

coronàle, *ag.* (*anat.*) coronal: *sutura* —, coronal suture ‖ *s.m.* (*anat.*) coronale.

coronaménto, *s.m.* **1.** crowning, coronation **2.** (*completamento*) completion: *il* — *dell'edificio*, the completion of the building; *quell'opera fu il* — *della sua vita*, that work was the crowning-piece (*o* the finest achievement) of his life **3.** (*mar.*) (*di poppa*) taffrail, tafferel.

coronàre, *v.t.* **1.** to crown (anche *fig.*): *fu coronato re*, he was crowned king; *la nostra fatica fu coronata dal successo*, our labour was crowned with success ‖ *il fine corona l'opera, prov.* the end crowns the work **2.** (*circondare*) to surround **3.** (*un albero*) to prune (a tree) at the top.

coronàrio, *ag.* (*anat.*) coronary: *arterie coronarie*, coronary arteries.

coronazióne, *s.f.* crowning, coronation.

coroncína, *s.f.* (*rosario*) rosary; beads (*pl.*).

corònide, *s.f.* (*gram. greca*) coronis.

coronòide, *ag.* (*anat.*) coronoid.

corpacciúto, *ag.* corpulent, paunchy, stout.

corpétto, *s.m.* **1.** (*parte superiore di abito femminile*) bodice **2.** (*panciotto*) waistcoat.

còrpo, *s.m.* **1.** body: *corpi celesti*, (*astr.*) heavenly bodies; — *semplice, composto*, simple, compound body; *il* — *umano*, the human body; — *vitreo*, (*anat.*) vitreous body; *senza* —, bodiless (*o* incorporeal) ‖ — *di Bacco!*, — *di mille bombe!*, by Jove! ‖ *il Corpo di Cristo*, the Eucharist ‖ *a* — *morto*, desperately ‖ *un combattimento a* — *a* —, a hand-to-hand fight; (*boxe*) a clinch; *combattere a* — *a* —, to fight hand to hand (*o* man to man); *lottare a* — *a* —, to struggle hand to hand (*o* to come to grips) ‖ *guardia del* —, body-guard (*o* life-guard) ‖ *vennero in* —, (*in massa*) they came in a body ‖ *avere il diavolo in* —, *fig.* to be possessed ‖ *dare* — *alle ombre*, *fig.* to believe imaginary things ‖ *darsi a ql.co. anima e* —, to throw oneself soul and body into sthg. ‖ *far* — *con ql.co.*, to be an integral part of sthg. ‖ *mortificare il* —, to mortify the flesh ‖ *non saper tenere un segreto in* —, to be unable to keep a secret ‖ *passare sul* — *di qlcu.*, *fig.* to pass over s.o. ‖ *prendere* —, to take (*o* to assume) shape ‖ *ricacciare le parole in* — *a qlcu.*, to make s.o. eat his words ‖ *mente sana in* — *sano, prov.* a sound mind in a sound body **2.** (*ventre*) belly; stomach: *a* — *vuoto*, on an empty stomach; *dolore di* —, stomach-ache; *andar di* —, to do one's needs; *mettere ql.co. in* —, to eat sthg. **3.** (*cadavere*) body, corpse **4.** (*raccolta*) corpus, collection: — *di leggi*, body (*o* code) of laws (*o* corpus juris) **5.** (*collettività*) corps (*invariato al pl.*); staff: *corpo d'armata*, army-corps, — *di ballo*, (corps de) ballet;

— *di guardia*, (*soldati*) guard; (*sede di esso*) guard-room; — *diplomatico*, diplomatic corps; — *di spedizione*, (*mil.*) expeditionary force; — *insegnante*, teaching staff ‖ *spirito di* —, esprit de corps (*o* team-spirit) **6.** — *del reato*, (*dir.*) material evidence **7.** (*di voce*) volume, range **8.** (*di vino*) body **9.** (*di nave*) hull **10.** (*di pompa*) body, casing; (*di caldaia*) boiler shell **11.** (*tip.*) body, size, point size.

corporàle, *ag.* corporal; (*opposto a spirituale*) corporeal, bodily, physical: *bisogni corporali*, bodily wants (*o* corporalities); *pena* —, corporal punishment ‖ *s.m.* (*eccl.*) corporal.

corporalità, *s.f.* corporality, material existence.

corporalménte, *av.* corporally; corporeally, bodily, materially.

corporativísmo, *s.m.* (*econ. pol.*) corporative system.

corporatívo, *ag.* (*econ. pol.*) corporative.

corporatúra, *s.f.* build, physique, size: *un uomo della sua* —, a man of his build (*o* size); *è un ragazzo di forte* —, he is a boy of powerful build (*o* structure); *era di* — *sottile*, he was spare of build.

corporazióne, *s.f.* **1.** (*dir.*) corporation **2.** (*st. medioevale*) guild.

corporeità, *s.f.* corporeity.

corpòreo, *ag.* corporeal, bodily, physical.

corpulènto, *ag.* corpulent, stout, bulky.

corpulènza, *s.f.* corpulence, corpulency, stoutness, bulkiness.

corpus, *s.m.* (*lat.*) corpus.

corpuscolàre, *ag.* corpuscular.

corpúscolo, *s.m.* corpuscle, corpuscule.

Corpusdòmini, *s.m.* (*eccl.*) (*ricorrenza*) Corpus Christi Day.

Corràdo, *no.pr.m.* Conrad(e), Konrad.

còrre, (*poet.*) per **cògliere.**

corredàre, *v.t.* **1.** to equip, to fit out, to fit up: *essere corredato di ogni cosa necessaria*, to be equipped (*o* fitted out) with everything necessary **2.** (*accompagnare*) to accompany: *corredato di documenti*, accompanied by documents; — *una lettera di documenti*, to accompany a letter with (the required) documents.

corredíno, *s.m.* (*per neonato*) layette, baby's outfit.

corrèdo, *s.m.* **1.** outfit, equipment **2.** (*di sposa*) trousseau (*pl.* trousseaus, trousseaux) **3.** *fig.* (*bagaglio*) fund, store, wealth: *un ampio* — *di erudizione*, a rich store of knowledge.

corrèggere, *v.t.* **1.** to correct, to rectify: *correggi la tua pronunzia*, correct your pronunciation; — *bozze di stampa*, to read proofs; — *un'operazione*, to rectify (*o* to correct) an operation **2.** (*ammonire*) to correct, to admonish; to punish: *stava correggendo suo figlio*, he was correcting his child **3.** (*vini*) to purify; (*altre bevande*) to lace: *correggi il tuo caffè col cognac*, lace your coffee with cognac ‖ **corrèggersi,** *v.r.* to amend; to improve; to correct oneself: *non si corresse mai*, he never corrected himself.

corrèggia, *s.f.* leather strap.

correggiàto, *s.m.* (*agr.*) flail.

correggíbile, *ag.* corrigible.

correggitóre, *s.m.*, **correggitríce,** *s.f.* corrector.

corregionàle, *ag.* of the same region, of the same district.

correità, *s.f.* (*dir.*) complicity.

correlativaménte, *av.* correlatively.

correlatività, *s.f.* correlativity.

correlatívo, *ag.* correlative: « *così... come* » *sono particelle correlative*, " so... as " are correlative particles.

correlazióne, *s.f.* correlation, mutual relation: *in* —, in proportion.

correligionàrio, *ag.* of the same religion ‖ *s.m.* coreligionist.

corrènte, *ag.* **1.** (*che scorre*) running, flowing: *acqua* —, running water ‖ *manovre correnti*, (*mar.*) running rigging ‖ *titolo* —, (*tip.*) running headline **2.** (*circolante*) current: *moneta* —, current money (*o* legal currency) **3.** (*nelle specificazioni di tempo*) present, current: *mese* —, current month; *la mia lettera del 3* —, (*comm.*) my letter of the 3rd inst. (*abbr. di* instant); *settimana* —, present (*o* current) week ‖ *prezzo* —, current price **4.** (*comune*) common, current, ordinary: *nel linguaggio* —, in common parlance; *opinione* —, current opinion; *parola di uso* —, word in current (*o* common *o* ordinary) use; *secondo l'uso* —, according to custom **5.** (*andante, dozzinale*) common; (*nella terminologia commerciale*) middling: *materiale* —, common material; *qualità* —, middling quality **6.** *conto* —, (*comm.*) current account **7.** *al* —, informed (*o* up to date *o* well informed): *libri tenuti al* —, (*comm.*) books posted up to date; *lo mise al* — *della nostra decisione*, he acquainted him with (*o* informed him of) our decision; *essere al* — *di un fatto*, to be well informed about (*o* to be acquainted with) a fact; *tenere qlcu. al* — *di qlco.*, to keep s.o. well informed (*o* posted) on sthg.; *tenersi al* —, to keep up to date.

corrènte, *s.f.* **1.** current, stream: *la* — *impetuosa del fiume*, the strong current in the river; — *marina*, sea current; *il nuotatore fu travolto dalla* —, the swimmer was swept away by the current; *andare contro* —, to swim against the stream (*anche fig.*); *seguire la* —, to go (*o* to swim) with the stream (*anche fig.*) ‖ *la Corrente del Golfo*, (*geog.*) the Gulf Stream **2.** (*di aria*) draught, current of air: *entrò una* — *d'aria fredda quando apristi la finestra*, a cold current of air came in when you opened the window; *non state nella* —!, don't stand in the draught! **3.** (*elett.*) current: — *a bassa tensione*, low voltage current; — *ad alta tensione*, high voltage current; — *alternata*, alternate current; — *continua*, direct (*o* galvanic) current; — *derivata*, derived current; — *di compensazione*, equalizing current; *correnti di Foucault*, eddy currents; *presa di* —, current tap (*o* socket); *riduttore di* —, instrument current transformer **4.** *fig.* (*usanza*) fashion; (*tendenza*) current, tendency, trend: — *letteraria*, literary current **5.** (*antica musica, danza francese*) courant(e), coranto ‖ *s.m.* **1.** (*travicello*) batten; stringer **2.** (*tip.*) running headline.

correteménte, *av.* fluently: *parla* — *l'inglese*, he speaks English fluently (*o* he speaks fluent English).

correntézza, *s.f.* **1.** readiness **2.** (*di eloquio*) fluency.

correntía, *s.f.* (*letter.*) current, stream.

correntìsta, *s.m.* (*comm.*) pass-book holder.

corrèo, *s.m.* (*dir.*) accomplice.

córrere, *v.i.* **1.** to run (*anche fig.*): *corri ad avvisarlo!*, run and warn him!; *un brivido gli corse per la schiena*, a cold shiver ran down his spine; *si mise a* —, he began running; *la strada corre lungo la riva del fiume*, the road runs (*o* lies) along the river-bank; *il suo pensiero corse alla famiglia*, his thoughts ran on his family; — *alle armi*, to run (*o* to fly) to arms; — *al successo*, to run after success; — *dietro a*, to run after; — *in aiuto di qlcu.*, to run to s.o.'s help; — *qua e là*, to run about ‖ — *a gambe levate*, to run as hard as one can ‖ *lasciar* — *ql.co.*, to take no notice of sthg. **2.** (*spor.*) to run, to race ‖ *far* — *un cavallo*, to run (*o* to race) a horse **3.** (*scorrere*) to run, to flow (*anche fig.*): *i fiumi corrono al mare*, rivers run to the sea; *questo passo corre bene*, this passage flows (*o* reads) well **4.** (*di tempo*) to elapse, to pass: *correva l'anno 1900*, (it was) in 1900; *molto tempo è corso da quando partì*, a long time has elapsed since he left ‖ *coi tempi che corrono*, as things are at present **5.** (*circolare, diffondersi*) to be current; to run; (*di voci*) to be abroad: *corre voce che...*, it is rumoured (*o* there is a rumour) that...; *corrono voci poco rassicuranti sul suo conto*, discouraging rumours are circulating (*o* afloat) about him; *un mormorio corse fra la folla*, a whisper ran through the crowd; *questa moneta non corre più*, this coin is no longer current ‖ *far* — *una voce*, to spread a rumour **6.** (*intercorrere*) to lie between: *da qui alla città corrono dieci chilometri*, the town is ten kilome-

tres from here; *quante miglia corrono fra noi in questo momento!*, how many miles lie between us at this moment! ‖ *ci corre*, there is a great difference ‖ *poco ci corse che non lo perdessi*, I nearly lost him ‖ *v.t.* **1.** to run: *abbiamo corso il rischio di morire*, we ran the risk of dying; — *la giostra*, (*st.*) to joust (*o* to tilt) ‖ — *la cavallina*, to sow one's wild oats **2.** (*percorrere*) to travel through (a place); to go over (a place): — *i campi*, to run about the fields; — *il paese*, to travel all over the country.

correspettivaménte, *av.* correlatively, correspondently.

correspettività, *s.f.* **1.** correlation, correspondence **2.** (*dir.*) consideration.

correspettívo, *ag.* correlative, corresponding, correspondent ‖ *s.m.* **1.** equivalent; (*compenso*) compensation **2.** (*dir.*) consideration.

corresponsàbile, *ag.* (*dir.*) jointly responsible ‖ *s.m.* (*dir.*) accomplice; (*in una causa di divorzio*) co-respondent; (*finanziario*) jointly liable.

corresponsabilità, *s.f.* (*dir.*) joint responsibility; (*in una causa di divorzio*) co-respondency; (*finanziaria*) joint liability.

corresponsióne, *s.f.* (*comm.*) payment: *dietro* — *di una piccola somma*, on payment of a small amount.

correttaménte, *av.* correctly; (*con decoro*) properly: *comportarsi* —, to behave properly.

correttézza, *s.f.* **1.** correctness **2.** (*onestà*) honesty, uprightness: *è un uomo di indubbia* —, he is a man of unimpeachable honesty; *mancare di* —, to be lacking in honesty **3.** (*decoro*) propriety; (*educazione*) politeness: *per motivi di* —, for motives of propriety.

correttívo, *ag. s.m.* corrective.

corrètto, *ag.* **1.** correct, exact, right: *procedimento* —, correct (*o* right) procedure; *stile* —, correct style **2.** (*onesto*) honest: *è sempre* — *nei suoi affari*, he is always honest (*o* straightforward) in his dealings **3.** (*decoroso*) proper; (*educato*) polite: *è una persona corretta*, he is a polite man; *tenere una condotta corretta*, to behave well **4.** (*di caffè, ecc.*) flavoured: *caffè* — *col cognac*, black coffee laced with brandy.

corrètto, *av.* correctly: *parlare, scrivere* —, to speak, to write correctly.

correttóre, *s.m.* **1.** corrector: — *di bozze*, (*tip.*) proof-reader (*o* press-corrector) **2.** (*tec.*) calibrator: — *altimetrico*, (*aer.*) altitude mixture control; — *dell'altimetro*, (*aer.*) altimeter calibrator; — *dell'anemometro*, (*aer.*) air-speed indicator calibrator; — *di miscela*, (*aer.*) mixture control; — *di quota*, (*aer.*) altitude mixture control; — *di timbro*, (*cine.*) attenuator.

correttríce, *s.f.* correctress.

correzionàle, *ag.* correctional: *tribunale* —, (*dir.*) correctional court ‖ *s.m.* (*riformatorio*) reformatory.

correzióne, *s.f.* **1.** correction, correcting; (*di testi letterari*) emendation: — *di bozze*, (*tip.*) proof-reading; *ci sono troppe correzioni nel tuo compito*, there are too many corrections (*o* crossings-out) in your work; *fare correzioni*, to make corrections ‖ *casa di* —, house of correction (*o* reformatory *o* bridewell) **2.** (*rimprovero, castigo*) reproof, punishment, castigation: *infliggere una* — *a un bambino, a qlcu.*, to give a child a trashing, to rebuke (*o* to reprove) s.o. **3.** (*metal.*) inoculation.

corrída, *s.f.* bullfight.

corridóio, *s.m.* **1.** (*di casa*) passage, passageway; (*di treno, di grande edificio*) corridor; (*in Parlamento*) lobby: — *laterale*, (*di treno*) side corridor **2.** (*pol.*) corridor: *il* — *di Danzica*, the Danzig (*o* Polish) Corridor **3.** (*di nave*) between-decks, 'tween decks **4.** (*cine.*): — *antincendio*, (*di proiettore*) safety fire trap; — *del film*, film track.

corridóre, *ag.* running; (*spor.*) racing ‖ *s.m.* **1.** runner; (*spor.*) racer: *non sono un gran* —, I am not much of a runner; *quel ciclista è un eccellente* — *su strada*, that cyclist is a very good road racer **2.** (*cavallo*) race-horse, racer.

corridóri, *s.m.pl.* (*ornit.*) running birds.

corrièra, *s.f.* **1.** (motor-)coach, bus; (*postale*) mail -coach **2.** (*diligenza*) (stage-)coach.

corrière, *s.m.* **1.** (*messaggero*) messenger: — *diplomatico*, diplomatic messenger **2.** (*chi fa trasporto di pacchi, di merci*) carrier **3.** (*posta*) mail; post: *col prossimo* —, by the next mail; *il — arriva nel pomeriggio*, the mail arrives in the afternoon ‖ *a volta di* —, by return of mail (o of post) **4.** (*nei titoli dei giornali*) mail; courier (*traducendo, i titoli dei giornali si lasciano però generalmente nella lingua originale, p.e.:* "Corriere della Sera ").

corrigèndo, *s.m.* (*dir.*) juvenile offender.

corrimàno, *s.m.* handrail.

corrispettívo, *V.* **correspettívo.**

corrispondènte, *ag.* correspondent, corresponding; relating (to s.o., sthg.); proportionate: *angoli corrispondenti*, (*geom.*) corresponding angles ‖ *socio — di un'accademia*, corresponding member of an academy ‖ *s.c.* correspondent: — *di guerra*, war-correspondent; — *d'inglese, d'italiano*, correspondent for English, for Italian; — *estero*, foreign correspondent.

corrispondènza, *s.f.* **1.** correspondence, agreement; relation; harmony: *i suoi gusti sono in — con i miei*, his tastes are in harmony with mine **2.** (*carteggio*) correspondence; (*posta*) mail: — *amorosa*, love letters; — *d'oltremare*, oversea(s) mail; — *in arrivo, in partenza*, incoming, outgoing mail; — *per l'interno, per l'estero*, inland, foreign mail; — *raccomandata*, registered mail ‖ *scuola per* —, correspondence school; *tenne un'assidua — con lei*, he kept up an assiduous correspondence with her; *distribuire la* —, to deliver mail; *entrare in — con qlcu.*, to enter into correspondence with s.o.; *essere in — d'affari con qlcu.*, to carry on business correspondence with s.o.; *firmare la* —, to sign the mail; *iniziare una* —, to start a correspondence; *insegnare ql.co. per* —, to teach sthg. by correspondence; *sbrigare la* —, to clear off correspondence; *sospendere la* —, to discontinue (o to give up) correspondence; *spedire la* —, to send the mail **3.** (*coincidenza di mezzi di trasporto*) connection: *aspettare la — dei treni*, to wait for a connection.

corrispóndere, *v.i.* **1.** to correspond (with, to sthg.); to agree (with sthg.); to conform (with, to sthg.); to coincide (with sthg.); to accord (with sthg.); to tally (with sthg.): *la casa corrisponde esattamente alle mie esigenze*, the house exactly corresponds to my needs; *ciò non corrisponde a quanto dicesti ieri*, this does not accord with what you said yesterday; *le linee doppie corrispondono sulla mappa alle strade*, the double lines on the map correspond to the roads; *la merce non corrispondeva al campione*, the goods were not in conformity with the sample; *non possiamo mai andare a teatro insieme perchè le mie ore di libertà non corrispondono alle tue*, we can never go to the theatre together because my time off does not coincide with yours; *queste cifre corrispondono*, these figures tally; *queste strade non corrispondono ai bisogni del traffico moderno*, these roads do not correspond to the needs of modern traffic; — *alle esigenze*, to meet requirements **2.** (*ricambiare, sentimenti*) to return (sthg.); to reciprocate (sthg.): — *all'affetto di qlcu.*, to reciprocate (o to return) s.o.'s affection **3.** (*venire incontro*) to answer (sthg.): — *all'aspettativa di qlcu.*, to answer s.o.'s expectation **4.** (*comunicare per corrispondenza*) to correspond **5.** (*affacciarsi su*) to give on to (a place): *questa finestra corrisponde col giardino*, this window gives on to the garden ‖ *v.t.* (*pagare*) to pay; to allow: *suo marito le corrisponde duecento sterline l'anno*, her husband allows her 200 pounds a year.

corrispósta, *s.f.* (*comm.*) remuneration.

corrispósto, *ag.* **1.** (*contraccambiato*) returned, reciprocal: *amore* —, reciprocal love **2.** (*concesso*) paid; allowed.

corrivaménte, *av.* leniently; indulgently; rashly.

corrività, *s.f.* (*rar.*) lenience, leniency; indulgence; rashness.

corrívo, *ag.* lenient; indulgent; rash; facile; easy: *alcuni giudici sono corrivi verso i rei*, some judges are lenient towards wrong-doers.

corroboraménto, *V.* **corroborazióne.**

corrobo rànte, *ag.* corroborating, corroborant, corroborative, strengthening ‖ *s.m.* (*farm.*) corroborant.

corroboràre, *v.t.* **1.** to corroborate, to strengthen **2.** *fig.* (*rafforzare, confermare*) to corroborate, to support, to confirm: — *una teoria*, to corroborate (o to support) a theory.

corroboratívo, *ag.* corroborative.

corroborazióne, *s.f.* **1.** corroboration, strengthening **2.** *fig.* (*rafforzamento*) support, confirmation.

corrodènte, *ag.* corrosive, corroding.

corródere, *v.t.* to corrode; to eat away; (*lentamente*) to wear away: *la ruggine corrode il ferro*, rust corrodes iron ‖ **corródersi,** *v.r.* to corrode; (*logorarsi*) to wear away.

corrodiménto, *s.m.* (*rar.*) corrosion.

corrómpere, *v.t.* **1.** to corrupt (anche *fig.*); to contaminate, to foul, to pollute; to vitiate; (*infettare*) to infect, to taint: — *le acque*, to infect waters; — *una lingua*, to corrupt a language **2.** (*moralmente*) to corrupt, to deprave: — *l'animo*, to corrupt (o to deprave) the soul **3.** (*con denaro*) to bribe, to corrupt: — *un testimonio*, to bribe (o to tamper with o to suborn) a witness ‖ **corrómpersi,** *v.r.* **1.** (*putrefarsi, guastarsi*) to rot; to taint; to decay **2.** *fig.* to become corrupt(ed).

corrompiménto, *s.m.* corruption (anche *fig.*).

corrompitóre, *ag.* **1.** corrupting (anche *fig.*); contaminating; vitiating; (*che infetta*) infecting, tainting **2.** (*moralmente*) corrupting, depraving ‖ *s.m.*, **corrompitríce,** *s.f.* **1.** corrupter **2.** (*con denaro*) briber.

corrosióne, *s.f.* corrosion.

corrosívo, *ag.* corrosive; corroding ‖ *s.m.* corrosive.

corróso, *ag.* corroded; (*logorato*) worn away.

corrótto, *ag.* **1.** corrupt (anche *fig.*); contaminated, foul, polluted, filthy; vitiated; (*infettato*) infected, tainted; (*marcito*) rotten: *aria corrotta*, corrupt (o filthy) air **2.** (*moralmente*) corrupt, depraved: *animo* —, depraved soul **3.** (*con denaro*) corrupt, bribed: *un funzionario* —, a corrupt official.

corrucciàre, *v.t.* **1.** (*far adirare*) to enrage; (*contrariare*) to vex **2.** (*crucciare*) to worry; to grieve, to afflict ‖ **corrucciàrsi,** *v.r.* **1.** (*adirarsi*) to get angry; (*essere contrariato*) to be vexed **2.** (*crucciarsi*) to worry; to grieve.

corrucciàto, *ag.* **1.** (*adirato*) angry; (*contrariato*) vexed; (*aggrondato*) sullen; frowning **2.** (*crucciato*) worried.

corrúccio, *s.m.* **1.** (*ira*) anger; (*furore*) wrath **2.** (*cruccio*) worry.

corrugaménto, *s.m.* corrugation: — *della fronte*, wrinkling of the forehead (o knitting of the brows).

corrugàre, *v.t.* to wrinkle, to corrugate: — *la fronte*, to wrinkle (o to corrugate) one's forehead (o to knit one's brows o to frown) ‖ **corrugàrsi,** *v.r.* to wrinkle, to corrugate: *la sua fronte si corrugò*, his forehead wrinkled.

corrugàto, *ag.* wrinkled, corrugated: *fronte corrugata*, knitted brows (o wrinkled forehead o corrugated forehead): *ci guardò con fronte corrugata*, he looked at us with knitted brows (o he frowned at us).

corrugazióne, *s.f.* corrugation.

corruscàre, *v.i.* to flash; to shine; to coruscate; to glitter; to sparkle.

corrúsco, *ag.* flashing; shining; coruscant; glittering; sparkling: *una lancia corrusca*, a flashing spear.

corruttèla, *s.f.* corruption, depravity.

corruttíbile, *ag.* corruptible: *un funzionario* —, an official open to bribery.

corruttibilità, *s.f.* corruptibility.

corruttívo, *ag.* (*rar.*) corruptive.

corruttóre, *ag.* corrupting ‖ *s.m.,* **corruttríce,** *s.f.* **1.** corrupter **2.** (*con denaro*) briber.

corruzióne, *s.f.* **1.** corruption, deterioration, decay, rottenness, decomposition, putrefaction: *la — del corpo,* the corruption of the body; *— di una lingua,* *fig.* corruption of a language; *— di un testo, fig.* the corruption of a text **2.** (*morale*) corruption, corruptness, depravity: *— dei costumi,* corruption (*o* corruptness *o* depravity) of morals; *— di minorenni,* (*dir.*) corruption of minors **3.** (*con denaro*) bribing, bribery, corruption: *— di testimoni,* (*dir.*) corruption (*o* subornation) of witnesses.

córsa, *s.f.* **1.** run; (*il correre*) running: *di —,* at a run; (*in fretta*) in haste; *di gran —,* at full speed (*o* in great haste) ‖ *guerra di —,* (*mar.*) privateering ‖ *fare una — in un luogo,* to pay a short (*o* lightning) visit to a place **2.** (*come competizione*) race; (*il correre*) racing: *— ad ostacoli,* (*ippica*) steeplechase; *— a staffetta,* relay race; *— automobilistica,* motor-race; *— campestre,* cross-country race; *— con ostacoli,* obstacle race; *— alle siepi,* (*ippica*) hurdle-race; *— di cavalli,* horse-race; *— nei sacchi,* sack-race; *— periziata,* handicap; *— podistica,* foot-race; *— su pista,* track race; *— su strada,* road-race; *automobile da —,* racing car; *cavallo da —,* race-horse (*o* racer) ‖ *la — agli armamenti,* the armaments race ‖ *— all'oro,* gold rush **3.** (*tragitto su veicolo pubblico*) trip: *prezzo della —,* fare; *partire con la prima —,* to leave by the first train; *perdere la —,* to miss the train **4.** (*mec.*) (*di pistone*) stroke: *— a vuoto,* idle stroke **5.** (*aer.*) run: *— di arresto, di atterraggio,* landing run; *— di decollo,* take-off run.

corsalétto, *s.m.* **1.** (*di armatura*) breast-plate, cors(e)let **2.** (*di insetto*) cors(e)let.

corsàro, *ag.* privateering: *nave corsara,* privateering vessel (*o* privateer) ‖ *s.m.* privateer, corsair; (*pirata*) sea-robber, pirate.

corseggiàre, *v.i.* to privateer; (*pirateggiare*) to pirate.

corsèllo, *s.m.* space (between beds or between bed and wall).

corsétto, *s.m.* corset; (*fascia elastica*) girdle.

corsìa, *s.f.* **1.** gangway, passage; (*amer.*) aisle: *— centrale,* central gangway **2.** (*di ospedale*) ward; (*di collegio, convento*) dormitory **3.** (*spor.*) (*pista*) track.

Còrsica, *no.pr.f.* (*geog.*) Corsica.

corsière, corsièro, *s.m.* (*poet.*) steed; charger.

corsìvo, *ag.* (*di scrittura*) cursive, current, running; (*tip.*) italic ‖ *s.m.* (*scrittura*) cursive; (*tip.*) italic type; italics (*pl.*): *stampare in carattere —, in —,* to italicize.

córso¹, *ag.* **1.** (*trascorso*) past **2.** (*saccheggiato*) pillaged, sacked **3.** (*sofferto*) borne: *i pericoli corsi lo resero più cauto,* the dangers he encountered made him more cautious.

córso¹, *s.m.* **1.** course (anche *fig.*): *il — degli eventi,* the course of events; *il — della vita,* the course of life; *affari in —,* outstanding business; *l'anno in —,* the present (*o* current) year; *lavori stradali in —,* roadwork ahead (*o* danger *o* road up); *il libro è in — di stampa,* the book is printing (*o* in the press); *nel — dell'anno, della discussione,* in the course of (*o* during) the year, the debate; *nel — di un anno,* in a period of one year; *ordinazione in —,* (*comm.*) outstanding order; *la malattia segue il suo —,* the disease is running its course; *il ponte è in — di costruzione,* the bridge is in course of construction (*o* the bridge is building) ‖ *dare — ad una ordinazione,* (*comm.*) to carry out (*o* to execute) an order; *dare libero — alla propria immaginazione,* to give free play (*o* rein) to one's imagination; *lasciare che la giustizia segua il suo —,* to let justice take its course; *seguire il — dei propri pensieri,* to pursue the train (*o* trend) of one's thoughts **2.** (*scorrere delle acque*) water-course: *— d'acqua navigabile,* waterway; *— d'acqua navigabile interno,* inland waterway **3.** (*di studi*) course: *un — di francese, di lezioni,* a course in French, of lessons; *frequentare un — serale,* to attend evening classes **4.** (*arc.*)

(*corsa*) run, running: *essere veloce al —,* to be a fast runner **5.** (*corteo*) procession: *— mascherato,* carnival procession **6.** (*strada principale*) main street; (*amer.*) avenue: *le nostre finestre guardano sul Corso,* our windows look on the Main **7.** (*rotta*) course: *capitano di lungo —,* master mariner; *nave di lungo —,* sea-going ship **8.** *il — del cambio,* (*econ.*) rate of exchange **9.** (*di valuta*) currency, circulation: *— forzoso,* forced currency; *fuori —,* out of circulation; *avere — legale,* to be legal tender; *mettere in —,* to put into circulation **10.** (*mar.*) strake; *— di cinta,* sheer strake; *— di rivestimento,* skin strake.

còrso², *ag.s.m.* Corsican ‖ **còrsa,** *s.f.* Corsican.

corsóio, *ag.:* *nodo —,* slip-knot (*o* running knot).

córte, *s.f.* **1.** court: *la — di San Giacomo, d'Inghilterra,* the Court of St. James's; *ballo a —,* court-ball; *intrighi di —,* court intrigues; *uomo di —,* courtier; *andare a —,* to go to court; *essere presentati a —,* to be presented at court ‖ *la Corte Celeste,* the Heavenly Court ‖ *tener — bandita,* to keep open house **2.** (*cortile*) courtyard, court, yard **3.** (*dir.*) court, law-court: *Corte d'Appello,* Court of Appeal; *Corte di Cassazione,* Court of Cassation; *Corte di Giustizia,* Court of Justice; *— marziale,* court martial **4.** (*corteggiamento*) court, courtship: *fare la — a una persona influente,* to curry favour with an influential person; *fare la — a una ragazza,* (*fam.*) to be after a girl; *fare la — a una signorina,* to court (*o* to woo *o* to pay court to) a young lady.

cortéccia, *s.f.* **1.** (*bot.*) bark, rind ‖ *— di china,* (*farm.*) china (*o* cinchona *o* Peruvian) bark **2.** (*crosta*) crust **3.** (*anat.*) cortex (*pl.* cortices): *— surrenale,* kidney cortex **4.** *fig.* (*apparenza esterna*) outside; outer appearance.

corteggiaménto, *s.m.* courtship, courting, wooing.

corteggiàre, *v.t.* **1.** to court, to woo, to pay court to (s.o.), to pay one's addresses to (s.o.): *— una ragazza,* (*fam.*) to be after a girl **2.** (*adulare*) to flatter: *— qlcu. per ottenerne il favore,* to court s.o.'s favour (*o* to fawn upon s.o. *o* to curry favour with s.o.).

corteggiatóre, *s.m.,* suitor, wooer; beau (*pl.* beaux), lover.

cortéggio, *s.m.* retinue, train, suite.

cortèo, *s.m.* **1.** train, procession: *un — di automobili,* a procession of cars; *— funebre,* funeral (train) (*o* burial procession); *— nuziale,* bridal procession; *— solenne,* ceremonial procession (*o* cortege) **2.** (*seguito*) retinue, train.

cortése, *ag.* (*gentile, buono*) kind; (*compìto*) polite, courteous: *atti cortesi,* kind deeds; *modi cortesi,* polite manners; *uomo —,* (*gentile*) kind man; (*compìto*) polite (*o* courteous) man.

corteseménte, *av.* (*con bontà, gentilezza*) kindly; (*compitamente*) politely, courteously: *rispose molto —,* he answered very politely; *vogliate — inviarci il vostro campionario,* (*comm.*) kindly let us have your pattern-book.

cortesía, *s.f.* **1.** (*gentilezza, bontà d'animo*) kindness; (*modi compiti*) courtesy, politeness; (*modi cerimoniosi*) courteousness: *molte grazie della vostra —,* thank you very much for your kindness; *per —,* please (*o* if you please *o* kindly): *per —, potreste dirmi che ora è?,* could you kindly tell me what time it is (*o* could you tell me the time, please?); *uno scambio di cortesie,* an exchange of courtesies; *vorresti avere la — di ascoltarmi?,* would you have the kindness (*o* would you be so kind as) to listen to me? **2.** (*favore*) favour: *potresti farmi questa —?,* could you do me this favour?.

cortézza, *s.f.* **1.** shortness, brevity **2.** (*di mente, d'ingegno*) dullness.

corticàle, *ag.* (*bot. anat.*) cortical.

còrtice, *s.m.* **1.** (*anat.*) cortex (*pl.* cortices) **2.** (*poet.*) (*corteccia*) bark.

cortigiàna, *s.f.* (*meretrice*) courtesan.

cortigianería, *s.f.* **1.** courtier's art **2.** (*adulazione*) flattery, obsequiousness; (servile) fawning; (sfacciata) toadyism.

cortigianescaménte, av. flatteringly; fawningly.

cortigianésco, ag. **1.** (da cortigiano) courtly **2.** (adulatorio) flattering, obsequious; (servile) fawning.

cortigiàno, s.m. **1.** (uomo di corte) courtier **2.** (adulatore) flatterer; (persona servile) fawner.

cortíle, s.m. court-yard, court, yard: animali da —, poultry.

cortína, s.f. curtain: una — di broccato, a brocade curtain; — di fumo, (mil.) smoke-screen; — di fuoco, (mil.) barrage || — di bambù, (pol.) bamboo curtain; — di ferro, (pol.) iron curtain.

cortinàggio, s.m. bed-curtains (pl.), bed-hangings (pl.).

cortisóne, s.m. (farm.) cortisone.

córto, ag. short (anche fig.): — di gambe, short-legged; — di mente, di ingegno, dull-witted; capelli tagliati corti, hair cut short; vita corta, short life; la tua giacca è corta di maniche, your coat is short in the arms; avere la memoria corta, to have a short memory; avere la vista corta, essere — di vista, to be short-sighted || — circuito, (elett.) short circuit || alle corte !, let's come to the point! || per farla corta, in short (o to cut a long story short) || essere a — di ql.co., to be short of sthg.: essere a — di soldi, to be short of money (o to be hard-up) || av. short: per tagliar —, in short.

cortometràggio, s.m. (cine.) short, short film.

corvè, s.f. **1.** (mil.) fatigue: compagnia di —, fatigue-party (o fatigue); essere di —, to be on fatigue **2.** (compito pesante, difficile) irksome task, piece of drudgery, thankless job.

corvétta[1], s.f. (equitazione) curvet.

corvétta[2], s.f. (mar.) corvette, corvet.

corvettàre, v.i. **1.** (di cavallo) to curvet **2.** (scherz.) (di persona) to frisk; to leap.

corvíno, ag. **1.** (di corvo) corvine **2.** (nero) raven (-black): capelli corvini, raven hair.

córvo, s.m. **1.** raven; crow; rook: nero come un —, as black as a raven || Corvo, (astr.) Corvus, Crow **2.** (st. mar.) corvus **3.** (mec.) crow(-bar)

còsa[1], s.f. **1.** thing: c'è una — di cui voglio parlarti, there is a thing I want to talk to you about; come hai potuto fare una — simile?, how could you do such a thing?; ho molte cose da raccontarti, I have many things to tell you; il mio regalo è una — da poco, my present is a modest little thing; non mi piace che tu indossi le mie cose, (fam.) I don't like your wearing my things; questa è tutt'altra —, this is quite a different thing; questo rende la — peggiore, that makes things worse; sono cose di nessun valore, these are rubbish (o trash o junk); stando così le cose..., as things are...; mangiare cose sane, to eat wholesome food || che —?, what?; (quanto) how much?: che — avete comperato ieri?, what did you buy yesterday?; che — costa?, how much is it? || nessuna —, nothing: nessuna — al mondo può separarci, nothing in the world can part us; ogni —, everything: ogni — al suo posto, everything in its place; qualche —, something: dite qualche —, say something || le cose spirituali, the things of the spirit || per prima —, first of all || per la qual —..., and that's why... || tante cose a tuo padre, many regards (o kindly remember me) to your father || a cose fatte, when all is over || ci aspettiamo da te grandi cose, we expect great things of you || ci sono in vista cose grosse, something big is afoot || è una — da nulla, it's a mere trifle (o a mere nothing) || è una — dell'altro mondo, it's out of this world || avere qualche — con qlcu. (rancore) to have a grudge against s.o. || diventare qualche —, to become somebody (o to make a name for oneself) || — fatta capo ha, prov. once it's done it's done || da — nasce —, prov. one thing leads to another **2.** (faccenda) matter, affair; (affare) business: le cose pubbliche, public affairs; è una — che non capisco, this is a matter I do not understand;

è una — molto grave, that is a very serious matter; non interponetevi, è — sua!, do not interfere, it is his business!; voleva vedermi per una — di grande importanza, he wanted to see me on a very important matter; definire la —, to settle the matter; occuparsi di una —, to look into a matter || la — va da sè, it is a matter of course || prendere le cose alla leggera, to take matters easy **3.** (opera) work: le cose più belle di Tiziano, Titian's best works **4.** (dir.) thing: le cose assicurate, the property insured; le cose mobili, immobili, things personal, real; le cose oggetto di pegno, the property pledged; la — pubblica, the common wealth (o public welfare) || — giudicata, res judicata.

còsà[2], av.: così o —, this way or that way.

cosàcco, ag. s.m. Cossack || **cosàcca**, s.f. Cossack.

cosàre, v.t. (fam. dial.) to do.

coscétto, s.m. leg: — d'agnello, leg of lamb; — di capretto, leg of kid.

còscia, s.f. **1.** (anat.) thigh; haunch || calzoni a —, tights **2.** (cuc.) leg: — di pollo, leg of chicken; — di montone, leg of mutton **3.** (mec.) jaws (pl.).

cosciàle, s.m. **1.** (parte dell'armatura) cuisse; cuish; thigh-piece; thigh-guard **2.** (gamba artificiale) false leg, artificial leg.

cosciènte, ag. aware (predicativo); conscious: ero perfettamente — della gravità della situazione, I was fully aware of the gravity of the situation.

coscienteménte, av. consciously, knowingly.

coscienza, s.f. **1.** conscience: — larga, accommodating conscience; — pulita, clean (o clear o easy o good) conscience; — sporca, guilty (o bad) conscience; in —, in all conscience (o honestly); libertà di —, liberty of conscience; per scarico di —, to clear one's conscience (o to take a weight off one's mind); per scrupolo di —, for conscience' sake; in — mi sento obbligato ad avvertirti..., I feel bound in honour (o in all conscience) to warn you...; mi rimorde la —, I am conscience-stricken; ne fecero un caso di —, they made it a matter (o a point) of conscience; avere un peso sulla —, to have a weight on one's mind; avere ql.co. sulla —, to have sthg. on one's conscience; fare un esame di —, to examine one's conscience; non avere la — tranquilla, to have a guilty conscience (o twinges of conscience) || me lo prendo io sulla —, I'll take the responsibility on myself || mettiti una mano sulla — !, lay your hand upon your heart ! || non avrei — di farlo, I would not have the conscience to do it **2.** (consapevolezza) consciousness: agire con piena — delle conseguenze, to act in full consciousness of the consequences (o with one's eyes wide open); aver — d'aver fatto ql.co. di importante, to be conscious (o aware) of having done sthg. important **3.** (coscienziosità) conscientiousness: è un uomo di —, he is a conscientious man; è un uomo senza —, he is an unscrupulous man; sono di poca —, they are not overscrupulous **4.** (conoscenza) consciousness: perdere, riprendere —, to lose, to recover (one's consciousness).

coscienziosaménte, av. conscientiously: fare un lavoro —, to perform a task conscientiously.

coscienziosità, s.f. conscientiousness: la sua — nel lavoro, his conscientiousness in his work.

coscienzióso, ag. conscientious; (scrupoloso) scrupulous; (diligente) painstaking; (accurato) careful, accurate: è uno scolaro —, he is a painstaking schoolboy; è un uomo molto —, he is an overscrupulous man.

cosciòtto, s.m. leg: — di montone, leg of mutton.

coscritto, ag. (st. romana): padri coscritti, conscript fathers (o senators) || s.m. (mil.) conscript, recruit.

coscrizióne, s.f. conscription.

cosecànte, s.f. (trigonometria) cosecant (abbr. cosec).

coséno, s.m. (trigonometria) cosine (abbr. cos).

così, av. **1.** so; thus; like this, like that; this way, that way; (come segue) as follows: una bambina alta —, a little girl so high; proprio —, just (o quite) so; —. cadde l'ultimo eroe, thus fell the last hero; —, è, sembra so it is, seems; *è —?*, is that so?; *egli parlò —*, that's what he said; *egli parlò —: ...*, he spoke as follows: ... (*o thus: ...*); *fu, avvenne —*, it was, it happened like this (*o like that*); *fu — che egli divenne soldato*, so (*o thus*) it was that he became a soldier; *perchè mi guardi —?*, why are you looking at me like that? (*o in that way?*); *perchè piangi — ?*, why are you crying so (*o like that?*); *se è — ...*, if so ...; *sta' —!*, stand so! (*o like this!*) ‖ *— —*, *— cosà*, so so: « *Come stai?* », « *— —* », " How are you? ", " So so " ‖ *— e —*, so and so: *farai — e —*, you'll do so and so ‖ *— sia*, so be it (*o amen*) ‖ *basta —!*, that will do! ‖ *e — via*, and so on (*o and so forth*) ‖ *per — dire*, so to say (*o so to speak*) **2.** (*altrettanto*) so: *egli entrò nella stanza e — feci io*, he entered the room and so did I; *io mi sono sposato e — farai tu*, I have got married and so will you **3.** (*tanto*) so (*con avverbi*); **so, such** (*con aggettivi*): *— a lungo*, so long; *un uomo — intelligente*, so intelligent a man (*o such an intelligent man*); *è — facile!*, it is so easy!; *non avevo ancora visto un edificio — imponente e dei fiori — belli*, I had never seen such an imposing building and such beautiful flowers; *non avevo mai ascoltato della musica — bella*, I had never heard such lovely music; *non è poi — vecchia!*, she isn't so very old!; *non essere — scriteriato!*, don't be so reckless! **4.** *così come*, (*similmente a, parimenti a*) **as well as, both ... and:** *tuo padre — come tua madre*, your father as well as your mother (*o both your father and your mother*) **5.** *così ... come*, *così ... quanto*, (*nei comparativi di uguaglianza*) **as ... as** (*in proposizioni affermative e interrogative*); **so ... as** (*in proposizioni negative*): *non è — vecchio come sembra*, he is not so old as he looks; *sei — forte come un tempo?*, are you as strong as you used to be? **6.** *così ... come* (*in correlazione tra proposizioni comparative*) **as ... so:** *come parla — scrive*, as he writes so he speaks (*o he writes just as he talks*) **7.** *così ... che*, *così ... da*, (*con valore consecutivo*) **so ... that, so ... as** (+ *inf.*): *— piccolo che appena lo si vede*, it is so small that you can hardly see it; *fu — caritatevole da meritare un pubblico riconoscimento*, he was so charitable as to deserve a public acknowledgement; *non è — stupido da farlo*, he is not so stupid as to do it **8.** (*perciò*) **so, therefore:** *ho fatto tardi, — non potrò scrivergli*, I am late, so I shall not be able to write to him; *sono stanco, — rimango a casa*, I am tired, so (*o therefore*) I shall remain at home **9.** (*dunque*) so: *— eccoti qua!*, so there you are! ‖ *e —?*, well? (*o what about it? o so what?*) **10.** (*in senso desiderativo*): *— fosse altrimenti!*, would it were otherwise!; *— (volesse il cielo che) non fosse vero!*, would that it were not true! ‖ *ag.* (*tale*, *siffatto*) **such:** *in un'occasione —*, on such an occasion; *come puoi dire delle bugie —?*, how can you tell such lies?; *non ho mai incontrato un uomo —*, I have never met such a man.

cosiechè, così che, *cong.* so that: *si fece da parte — potessi entrare*, he stepped aside so that I might enter; *uscì senza soprabito — prese il raffreddore*, he went out without his overcoat so that he caught a cold.

cosiddétto, *ag.* so-called.

cosiffàtto, *ag.* **such, similar:** *con un uomo —*, with such a man.

Còsimo, *no.pr.m.* Cosmo.

cosmèsi, cosmètica, *s.f.* beauty culture.

cosmètico, *ag. s.m.* cosmetic.

cosmicaménte, *av.* cosmically.

còsmico, *ag.* cosmic(al): *raggio —*, cosmic ray.

còsmo, *s.m.* cosmos; universe.

cosmòdromo, *s.m.* (*missilistica*) cosmodrome.

cosmogonía, *s.f.* cosmogony.

cosmogònico, *ag.* cosmogonic(al).

cosmografía, *s.f.* cosmography.

cosmogràfico, *ag.* cosmographic(al).

cosmògrafo, *s.m.* cosmographer.

cosmología, *s.f.* cosmology.

cosmològico, *ag.* cosmological.

cosmòlogo, *s.m.* cosmologist.

cosmonàuta, *s.m.* (*neol.*) cosmonaut.

cosmòpoli, *s.f.* cosmopolis ‖ *stampare un libro in —*, to print a book clandestinely.

cosmopolita, *ag.* cosmopolitan; cosmopolite: *città —*, cosmopolitan city (*o cosmopolis*); *ideale —*, cosmopolitan ideal ‖ *s.m.* cosmopolitan; cosmopolite.

cosmopolítico, *ag.* **1.** (*concernente il cosmopolitismo*) cosmopolitical: *teorie cosmopolitiche*, cosmopolitical theories **2.** (*cosmopolita*) cosmopolitan; cosmopolite: *fama cosmopolitica*, international reputation.

cosmopolitísmo, *s.m.* cosmopolitanism; cosmopolitism.

cosmoràma, *s.m.* cosmorama.

cosmotètico, *ag.* (*fil.*) cosmothetic.

còso, *s.m.* (*fam.*) **1.** (*cosa*) thing: *fammi vedere quel —*, show me that thing; *quel — non serve a niente*, that what-d'you-call-it is no good **2.** (*individuo*) fellow, chap; (*sl.*) bloke: *ehi, sor —!*, hey, governor!; *è un — fatto e messo lì*, he is a boor; *è un gran — !*, he is an odd creature!; *è venuto il signor —*, Mr. What's-his-name has come; *mi scusi, signor —, posso vedere il suo giornale?*, excuse me, old fellow, may I see that paper?; *non conosco quel — lì*, I don't know that chap.

cospàrgere, *v.t.* to strew; to scatter; (*liquidi*) to sprinkle: *— di fiori*, to strew with flowers; *— i campi di sementi*, to scatter the fields with seed.

cospàrso, *ag.* strewn (with sthg.); scattered (with sthg.); (*con liquido*) sprinkled (with sthg.): *strada cosparsa di sabbia*, road strewn with sand.

cospèrgere, *V.* cospàrgere.

cospètto, *s.m.* presence; sight: *al — di qlcu.*, in the presence of (*o before*) s.o.: *al — di Dio tutti gli uomini sono uguali*, in the sight of God all men are equal; *ammettetelo al — del re*, admit him to the king's presence.

cospètto, *inter.* my goodness!.

cospicuaménte, *av.* conspicuously; remarkably.

cospicuità, *s.f.* conspicuousness, conspicuity.

cospícuo, *ag.* **1.** (*visibile*) conspicuous: *luogo —*, conspicuous position **2.** (*notevole*) conspicuous, remarkable, outstanding: *esempio —*, clear example; *uomo —*, prominent man; *appartiene ad una famiglia cospicua*, he belongs to a distinguished family; *ha un reddito —*, he has a considerable income.

cospiràre, *v.i.* to conspire; to plot: *cospirarono per impadronirsi del trono*, they conspired in order to seize the throne; *tutti i parenti cospirarono per togliergli l'eredità*, all his relations plotted to deprive him of his inheritance.

cospiratóre, *s.m.* conspirator; plotter: *i cospiratori si riunivano in una vecchia casa di campagna*, the conspirators used to meet in an old country-house.

cospiratríce, *s.f.* conspiratress.

cospirazióne, *s.f.* conspiracy, plot.

cossalgía, *s.f.* (*patol.*) coxalgia.

còsta[1], *s.f.* **1.** coast; coast line: (*litorale*) shore: *— irregolare*, rugged coastline; *— rocciosa*, rocky shore; *— sabbiosa*, sandy shore; *— sassosa*, pebbly shore; *lungo la —*, coastwise (*o coastways o along the coast*); *verso la —*, coastward(s) (*o toward the coast*); *la — è libera da scogli*, the coast is clear of rocks; *la nostra nave naufragò sulla — spagnola*, our ship was wrecked on the Spanish coast; *vedemmo la — spiccare chiaramente sullo sfondo del cielo*, we saw the bold coast-line against the sky ‖ *Costa Azzurra*, Côte d'Azur; *Costa d'Avorio*, Ivory Coast; *Costa d'Oro*, Golden Coast **2.** (*anat.*) rib **3.** (*mar.*) rib: *le coste di una nave*, the ribs of a ship **4.** (*venatura*) rib, vein: *dell'ala di un insetto*, rib (*o vein*) of an insect's wing; *la — di una foglia*, the rib (*o vein*) of a leaf **5.** (*fianco di collina*) side; hillside; (*declivio*) slope: *la — del monte*, the side of the mountain; *— ripida*, steep slope; *la casa fu costruita a mezza —*, the house was built half-way up the hill **6.** (*di coltello, libro*) back.

costà², *av.* **there**; (*da voi, nella vostra città*) **in your town**: *dateci notizie di* —, give us some news of your home-town; *passai per* — *di domenica*, I went through your town on Sunday; *sarò* — *lunedì*, I'll be there on Monday.

costaggiú, *av.* **down there**; (*letter.*) **(down) yonder**; (*lontano*) **over there**.

costàle, *ag.* (*anat.*) costal: *arco* —, costal arch.

costalgía, *s.f.* (*patol.*) costalgia.

costànte¹, *ag.* **1.** (*saldo nel proposito*) constant, persevering, firm, steady: — *in amore*, steady in love; *essere* — *nei propri propositi*, to be firm in one's principles **2.** (*uniforme*) constant, uniform, steady, steadfast, unchanging: — *aumento dei prezzi*, steady rise in prices; *fiume a regime* —, river with a constant regime; *pioggia* —, constant rain; *pressione* —, firm pressure; *progresso* —, constant progress; *segmenti di lunghezza* —, segments of uniform length; *temperatura* —, uniform temperature; *tempo* —, steady weather || *s.f.* (*fis. mat.*) constant (*abbr.* const.).

Costànte², *no.pr.m.* Constant.

costanteménte, *av.* constantly, perseveringly, firmly, steadily, steadfastly, unchangingly.

Costantíno, *no.pr.m.* Constantine.

Costantinòpoli, *no.pr.f.* (*geog. st.*) Constantinople.

costànza¹, *s.f.* constancy, firmness, steadfastness; (*perseveranza*) perseverance: — *nell'amore, nell'amicizia*, constancy in love, in friendship; *con* —, steadfastly (*o* steadily): *lavorare con* —, to work steadily; *manca di* — *nei propositi*, he lacks steadfastness (*o* constancy of purpose).

Costànza², *no.pr.f.* Constance.

Costànza³, *no.pr.f.* (*geog.*) Constance: *il lago| di* —, the Lake of Constance.

Costaríca, *no.pr.f.* (*geog.*) Costa Rica.

costàre, *v.i.* to cost (anche *fig.*): *dimmi quanto ti costa tenere l'automobile*, tell me how much it costs you to keep a car; *mi costò molta fatica*, it cost me much labour; *mi è costato cento lire*, I have paid one hundred lire for it (*o* it cost me one hundred lire); *quanto costa?*, how much is it?; *le tue pazzie ti potrebbero* — *la vita*, your follies might cost you your life; *i viaggi costano*, travelling is expensive; — *caro*, to be expensive (*o* to cost dear): *gli costerà caro, amaro*, (*in senso morale*) it will cost him dear || *costa un occhio della testa*, it costs a mint of money || *costi quel che costi!*, hang the expense! (*o* cost what it may!) || *mi costa doverlo dire*, it pains me (*o* I regret) to have to say this; *mi costerà lasciarlo*, it will be a wrench to leave him; *niente gli costa*, nothing is an effort to him || — *salato*, to have a very high price || *costa più la salsa che il pesce*, *prov.* the game is not worth the candle.

costassú, *av.* **up there**; (*letter.*) **(up) yonder**.

costàta, *s.f.* chop: *una* — *di maiale*, a pork chop.

costatàre, *v.t.* **1.** (*accertare*) to ascertain, to verify, to establish; (*certificare*) to certify: — *un decesso*, to certify a death; — *la verità di un fatto*, to establish the truth of a fact **2.** (*notare, osservare*) to notice, to remark, to observe.

costatazióne, *s.f.* **1.** ascertainment **2.** (*osservazione*) remark, observation.

costàto, *s.m.* chest; side; (*costole*) ribs (*pl.*).

costeggiàre, *v.t.* **1.** (*per mare*) to follow the coast of (a land); to hug the coast of (a land): *la nave costeggiò l'isola per alcune miglia*, the ship hugged the coast of the island for a few miles **2.** (*per terra*) to skirt: *costeggiammo in auto il lago*, we drove along the shore of the lake; *camminammo a lungo costeggiando il torrente prima di rientrare*, we walked along the stream for a long time before going home; *la strada costeggia la collina e poi il fiume*, the road skirts the hill and then runs along the river || *v.i.* to coast (along), to sail along: *ieri il battello ha costeggiato lungo la penisola*, yesterday the boat sailed (*o* coasted) along the peninsula.

costèi, *pron. dimostrativo f. sing.* (*spec. spreg.*) **she** (*compl.* **her**), **this woman, that woman**: — *è una spia*, this woman is a spy; *chi è* —?, who is this woman?; *non vi fidate di* —, don't trust this woman.

costellàre, *v.t.* **1.** to constellate **2.** (*seminare, spargere*) to scatter, to stud, to spangle.

costellàto, *ag.* studded (with sthg.); spangled (with sthg.); (*rar.*) constellated (with sthg.): — *di errori*, studded with mistakes; — *di fiori*, studded with flowers; — *di perle*, studded with pearls; *cielo* — *di stelle*, star-spangled sky.

costellazióne, *s.f.* constellation.

costernàre, *v.t.* to consternate, to dismay, to fill with dismay: *quella notizia ci costernò profondamente*, we were dismayed (*o* filled with dismay) at the news || **costernàrsi**, *v.r.* to be dismayed (at sthg.).

costernàto, *ag.* dejected, in dismay: *rimanemmo costernati alla notizia*, we were much upset (*o* dismayed *o* concerned) at the news.

costernazióne, *s.f.* consternation, dismay: *gettare qlcu. nella* —, to fill s.o. with dismay.

costí, *av.* **there**; (*da voi, nella vostra città*) **in your town**: *come si sta* —?, what's it like living in your town?; *deve essere* —, it must be there; *resta* —, stay there.

costièra, *s.f.* **1.** stretch of coast **2.** (*salita poco ripida*) slope.

costière, *s.m.* (*mar.*) coastal pilot.

costièro, *ag.* coastal; coasting (*attributivo*): *nave costiera*, coasting vessel (*o* coaster); *navigazione costiera*, coastal navigation.

costipaménto, *s.m.* **1.** (*di terreno*) tamping, solidification **2.** *V.* costipazióne.

costipàre, *v.t.* **1.** to amass, to condense **2.** (*un terreno*) to tamp **3.** (*l'intestino*) to constipate || **costipàrsi**, *v.r.* **1.** (*prendere un raffreddore*) to catch a cold **2.** (*di intestino*) to become constipated, to become costive.

costipàto, *ag.* (*raffreddato*) with a bad cold: *essere* —, to have a bad cold.

costipatóre, *s.m.* (*mec.*) (soil) compactor, tamper.

costipazióne, *s.f.* **1.** (*raffreddore*) cold: *prendere una* —, to catch a bad cold **2.** (*ingombro intestinale*) constipation, costiveness.

costituènte, *ag.* constituent || *Assemblea Costituente*, (*pol.*) Constituent Assembly.

costituíre, *v.t.* **1.** (*fondare, formare*) to constitute, to found, to establish, to set up; to form, to make up: *gli Stati Uniti aiutarono a* — *il nuovo stato africano*, the U.S.A. helped to establish the new African state; — *un'associazione*, to constitute (*o* to found) an association; — *un fondo di riserva*, (*amm.*) to found a reserve fund; — *un governo*, to set up (*o* to constitute) a government; — *una società*, (*amm.*) to form a partnership; — *una società anonima*, (*comm.*) to found a joint stock company **2.** (*comporre, fare*) to constitute; to form, to make up: *sette giorni costituiscono una settimana*, seven days constitute a week; *la spedizione è costituita di dieci colli*, (*comm.*) the shipment consists of ten packages; *vorrei sapere di quali elementi è costituito questo composto*, I should like to know which elements form (*o* go to make up) this compound || — *reato*, (*dir.*) to be a crime **3.** (*nominare*) to appoint, to constitute: *ella lo costituì suo procuratore*, she appointed him her attorney; *ti costituisco mio erede*, I constitute (*o* make) you my heir **4.** (*assegnare*) to give, to settle: — *una dote a qlcu.*, to give a dowry to s.o. (*o* to settle a dowry on s.o.); — *in dote*, to give as dowry || **costituírsi**, *v.r.* **1.** (*dir.*) to give oneself up, to deliver oneself up: *dopo tre giorni, l'assassino si costituì*, three days later, the murderer gave himself up **2.** (*nominarsi*) to constitute oneself, to appoint oneself: — *giudice della condotta di qlcu.*, to constitute oneself a judge of s.o.'s conduct || — *parte civile*, (*dir.*) to institute a civil action (*o* to bring an action *o* to appear as a civil plaintiff) **3.** (*formarsi*) to form oneself: *essi si costituirono in comitato*, they formed themselves into a committee; *l'Italia si costituì in uno stato solo nel XIX secolo*, Italy became a State only in the 19th century.

costituíto, *ag.* constituted, established: *l'autorità costituita*, the established (*o* constituted) authority.

costitutàrio, *s.m.* (*comm.*) settlor of a company.

costitutívo, *ag.* constitutive, constituent: *gli elementi costitutivi dell'acqua*, the constituent (*o* constitutive) elements of water ‖ *atto —*, (*dir.*) deed of partnership.

costitúto, *s.m.* (*dir.*) interrogation of the accused.

costitutóre, *ag.* constitutive ‖ *s.m.* constitutor.

costituzionàle, *ag.* (*med. pol.*) constitutional: *governo —*, constitutional government; *malattia —*, constitutional disease ‖ *s.m.* (*pol.*) constitutionalist.

costituzionalísmo, *s.m.* (*pol.*) constitutionalism.

costituzionalità, *s.f.* (*pol.*) constitutionality.

costituzionalménte, *av.* constitutionally.

costituzióne, *s.f.* 1. (*il costituire*) establishment, settlement: *la — della dote*, marriage settlement; *la — di una società*, (*dir.*) the establishment of a company 2. (*pol.*) constitution: *— monarchica, repubblicana, monarchical, republican constitution ‖ costituzioni clementine*, (*dir. eccl.*) Clementine Constitutions 3. (*struttura*) constitution: *uomo di delicata, robusta —*, man of a delicate, strong constitution.

còsto, *s.m.* cost: *—, assicurazione e nolo*, cost, insurance, freight (*abbr.* c.i.f.); *— di fabbricazione*, (*comm.*) manufacturing cost; *— di produzione*, (*comm.*) prime cost; *— e nolo*, cost and freight (*abbr.* c. f.); *— effettivo*, actual cost; *— in più*, extra cost; *a prezzo di —*, at cost price; *di —*, (*costoso*) costly; *sotto —*, under cost; *il — della vita sale*, the cost of living is rising ‖ *a — della vita*, at the cost of (one's) life; *a nessun —*, in no case (*o* on no account); *ad ogni —*, at all costs (*o* at all hazards *o* at any rate); *a — di perdere tutto*, even if I should lose everything.

còstola, *s.f.* 1. (*anat. arch. bot.*) rib: *si ruppe una —*, he broke a rib ‖ *gli si contano le costole*, he is nothing but skin and bone ‖ *essere della — di Adamo*, to belong to the old nobility ‖ *mangiare le costole a qlcu.*, to live at s.o.'s expense ‖ *stare alle costole di qlcu.*, to be at s.o.'s elbow; (*pedinarlo*) to dog s.o.'s steps; (*sorvegliarlo*) to watch over s.o. ‖ *rompere, spianare le costole a qlcu.*, *fig.* to break s.o.'s bones (*o* to give s.o. a thorough thrashing) 2. (*di coltello, libro*) back.

costolétta, *s.f.* cutlet: *— di vitello*, veal cutlet.

costolóne, *s.m.* 1. (*arch.*) rib: *— di una volta*, vaulting-rib 2. (*uomo corpulento e rozzo*) uncouth hefty fellow.

costóro, *pron. dimostrativo m.f.pl.* (*spec. spreg.*) they (*compl.* them), these people, those people: *chi sono —?*, who are these people?; *ma che cosa mai stanno facendo —?*, but what on earth are those people doing?; *so che — sono ricchi*, I know they are rich people.

costosaménte, *av.* expensively, dearly.

costóso, *ag.* expensive, costly, dear: *queste sigarette sono troppo costose*, these cigarettes are too dear; *i viaggi sono costosi*, travelling is expensive.

costotomía, *s.f.* (*chir.*) costotomy.

costríngere, *v.t.* 1. to compel, to force, to constrain, to oblige: *la fame li costrinse ad arrendersi*, hunger compelled them to surrender; *le sue parole mi costrinsero a partire*, his words obliged me to leave 2. (*stringere, comprimere*) to compress, to press.

costringiménto, *s.m.* 1. constraint, compulsion 2. (*restringimento*) constriction.

costrittívo, *ag.* constrictive.

costrittóre, *ag.s.m.* (*anat.*) constrictor.

costrizióne, *s.f.* 1. constraint, compulsion: *per —*, under (*o* on) compulsion 2. (*restringimento*) constriction.

costruíre, *v.t.* 1. to build, to construct: *costruirono una nuova ala dell'albergo*, they built a new wing of the hotel; *devi creare un dramma, non costruirlo!*, you must create a drama, not construct it!; *— un impero, un sistema*, to build up an empire, a system; *— un*

muro, to build a wall 2. (*gram.*) to construct, to construe: *preposizione che si costruisce col dativo*, preposition that is construed with the dative.

costruttívo, *ag.* constructive: *critica costruttiva*, constructive criticism; *politica costruttiva*, constructive politics.

costrútto, *s.m.* 1. (*gram.*) construction: *non è sufficiente imparare il significato delle parole, bisogna impararne anche il —*, it's not enough to learn the meanings of words, you must learn their constructions too 2. (*significato*) meaning, sense: *discorso senza —*, meaningless speech 3. (*profitto, risultato*) profit, advantage; result: *lavoro senza —*, profitless work; *studiò senza —*, he studied without any profit.

costruttóre, *ag.* building: *l'impresa costruttrice*, the building firm (*o* the builders) ‖ *s.m.* builder, constructor; (*di scafi*) shipbuilder: *— stradale*, road builder (*o* maker).

costruzióne, *s.f.* 1. construction: *— a volta*, (*arch.*) vaulting; *— dello scheletro*, (*edil.*) framing; *— in appalto*, construction under public contract; *— in cemento armato*, (*edil.*) reinforced concrete construction; *— in legno*, timbering; *— interamente metallica*, all-metal construction; *difetto di —*, fault in design; *impresa di costruzioni*, building concern (*o* firm); *materiali da —*, building materials; *è in — una nuova strada*, a new road is under construction; *quando la nostra casa era in —*, when our house was being built (*o* was building) 2. (*edificio*) building: *— in acciaio*, steel frame building ‖ *impresa di —*, builders (*o* building contractors) 3. (*gram.*) construction: *una frase di — latina*, a Latin-built sentence.

costúi, *pron. dimostrativo m. sing.* (*spec. spreg.*) **he** (*compl.* **him**), **this man, that man, this fellow, that fellow:** *— è un impostore*, this man is an impostor; *chi era mai —?*, who on earth was that man?; *non parlarmi di —*, don't talk to me about that fellow ‖ *Carneade, chi era —?*, Carneades, and who on earth was he?.

costumànza, *s.f.* 1. usage, custom, habit 2. (*rar.*) (*belle maniere*) politeness.

costumàre, *v.i.* 1. *imp.* (*essere usanza*) to be customary, to be usual: *da noi costuma così*, this is our custom; *qui costuma festeggiare il giorno di S. Antonio*, here it is customary to celebrate St. Anthony's Day; *qui costuma pagare in anticipo*, here it is usual to pay in advance 2. *imp.* (*essere di moda*) to be fashionable, to be in fashion: *non — più*, to be out of fashion (*o* to be no longer the fashion *o* to be no longer in fashion) 3. (*solere*) to be in the habit of (doing); to make a habit of (doing) (*usato solo nel passato*): *egli costumava cavalcare per ore e ore*, he was in the habit of riding (*o* he used to ride *o* he would ride) for hours at a stretch.

costumataménte, *av.* 1. decently 2. (*con compostezza, dignità*) properly; (*con buona creanza*) politely.

costumatézza, *s.f.* 1. decency 2. (*compostezza, dignità*) propriety, proper behaviour; (*buona creanza*) good manners (*pl.*); politeness.

costumàto, *ag.* 1. (*di buoni costumi*) decent, virtuous 2. (*di buone maniere*) polite, well-bred.

costúme, *s.m.* 1. (*usanza*) custom, use, usage; (*abitudine personale*) habit, wont: *secondo il —*, according to use and wont; *secondo il mio —*, according to my wont (*o* as is my habit *o* as is my wont); *gli usi e i costumi di un paese*, the uses (*o* usages) and customs of a country; *un vecchio —*, an old usage; *è mio — fare una passeggiata ogni mattina*, it is a custom with me (*o* it's my wont *o* use) to take a walk every morning; *non è suo — chiedere dei favori*, he is not in the habit (*o* he has not the habit) of asking favours (*o* it is not his custom to ask favours *o* he is not accustomed to asking favours); *qui è — festeggiare il giorno di S. Carlo*, here it is customary (*o* usual) to celebrate St. Charles's Day 2. (*condotta*) morals (*pl.*): *persone di buoni costumi*, people of good morals (*o* moral people); *persone di cattivi costumi*, people of loose morals (o loose people) ‖ offendere il buon —, to offend against morality 3. (indumento) costume: — accademico, academic costume; — da bagno, bathing-costume (o bathing-suit); — da paggio, page-costume; ballo in —, costume ball; provare in —, (teat.) to have a dress rehearsal.

costumísta, s.c. (teat. cine.) costume-designer.

costúra, s.f. (sartoria) seam ‖ spianare le costure a qlcu., fig. (bastonarlo) to break s.o.'s bones.

cotàle, ag.indef. (rar.) such: cotali parole, such words; in cotal guisa, in such a way ‖ pron.indef. (rar.) 1. sing. such a one ‖ il, quel —, (spreg.) that fellow 2. pl. such ‖ certi cotali, (spreg.) some people.

cotangènte, s.f. (trigonometria) cotangent.

cotànto, ag. (rar.) so much, so very ‖ av. (rar.) so much; (in senso temporale) so long ‖ cotànti, ag. pron. (rar.) so many.

còte, s.f. whetstone, hone.

cotechíno, s.m. " cotechino " (kind of spiced Italian sausage).

coténna, s.f. 1. pigskin; (del lardo) rind ‖ metter —, (ingrassare) to get fat 2. (pelle dura) thick skin; (del cranio) scalp ‖ di grossa —, (zotico) rude (o boorish) 3. (del sangue) buffy coat 4. (superficie erbosa) turf, sod.

cotennóso, ag. 1. (di lardo) thick-rinded 2. (dalla pelle dura) thick-skinned 3. (di sangue) buffy.

cotésto, ag. dimostrativo 1. that; pl. those: — (tuo) cappello è ridicolo, that hat of yours is ridiculous; dammi — libro e cotesti quaderni, give me that book and those exercise-books 2. (con valore di tale) such: — comportamento non è da signore, such behaviour is ungentlemanly ‖ pron. dimostrativo that (one); pl. those (ones) (talvolta anche this, pl. these): che modi sono cotesti?, what kind of manners are these?; non mi piace questa rosa bianca, dammi cotesta rossa, coteste rosse, I don't like this white rose, give me that red one, those red ones; non voglio questa penna, dammi cotesta, coteste, I don't want this pen, give me that one, those; questo è nuovo e — è vecchio, this is new and that is old.

cótica, V. coténna.

cotidiàle, ag. (mar.) cotidal: linee cotidiali, cotidal lines.

cotidianaménte, av. daily.

cotidiàno, ag. daily ‖ s.m. (giornale) daily.

còtile, s.m. (anat.) cotyloid cavity.

cotilèdone, s.m. (bot.) cotyledon, seed-leaf, seed-lobe.

cotógna, s.f. (bot.) quince.

cotognàta, s.f. (marmellata) quince jam; (gelatina) quince jelly.

cotógno, s.m. (bot.) quince(-tree).

cotolétta, s.f. (cuc.) cutlet; (costata) chop: — di agnello, lamb-cutlet (o lamb-chop); — di maiale, pork-chop; — di vitello, veal-cutlet.

cotonàceo, ag. cottony.

cotonàto, ag. cottony; cotton (attributivo) ‖ s.m. silk and cotton fabric: i cotonati, cotton fabrics.

cotóne, s.m. cotton: — a corta fibra, short staple cotton; — cardato, carded cotton; — da rammendo, darning cotton; — fulminante, gun-cotton; — greggio, raw cotton; — idrofilo, cotton-wool; — rigenerato, recovered cotton; cascami di —, cotton-waste; coltivazione del —, cotton-growing; commercio del —, cotton trade; filato di —, cotton yarn; olio di —, cotton-seed oil; refe di —, sewing-cotton; tessuto di —, cotton-cloth.

cotonerìe, s.f.pl. cotton fabrics.

cotonière, s.m. 1. (industriale) cotton-spinner; cotton manufacturer ‖ i grandi cotonieri, the cotton-ocracy (o the cotton lords) 2. (operaio) cotton-spinner.

cotonièro, ag. cotton (attributivo): l'industria cotoniera, the cotton industry.

cotonifício, s.m. cotton-mill.

cotonína, s.f. calico.

cotonóso, ag. cottony.

còtta[1], s.f. 1. (cottura) cooking; (in forno) baking ‖

furbo di tre cotte, slyboots 2. (infornata) batch; (ind.) kilnful: una — di mattoni, a kilnful of bricks; una — di pani, a batch of loaves 3. (gergo): quel corridore ha preso una tremenda — nell'ultima tappa, that rider broke down in the last stage; prendere una —, (ubriacarsi) to get tight (o tipsy); prendere una — per qlcu., (innamorarsene) to have a crush on (o to fall for) s.o.

còtta[2], s.f. 1. (eccl.) surplice; cotta 2. (st. mil.) cassock 3. (tunica) robe.

cottíccio, ag. 1. (alquanto cotto) underdone 2. (gergo) (alticcio) half-tight, tipsy; (fam.) half-seas-over (predicativo) 3. (gergo) (alquanto innamorato) half in love.

cottimísta, s.c. jobber.

còttimo, s.m. 1. (contratto a cottimo) job contract, jobbing contract: contrattare a —, to contract by the job; dare a —, to job; essere pagato a —, to be paid by the job (o to do job-work); lavorare a —, to work by the job; prendere a —, to undertake by the job (o to job) 2. (lavoro a cottimo) job-work, piece-work.

còtto, ag. 1. cooked, done; (in forno) baked: ben —, well done; — a puntino, done to a turn (o fam. done to a T); la mia bistecca la voglio poco cotta!, I want my steak underdone!; questo è troppo —!, this is over-done! ‖ farne di cotte e di crude, to commit all kinds of follies (o every kind of folly) 2. (gergo) (ubriaco) drunk: è —!, he's dead drunk! 3. (gergo) (innamorato) in love: era — di lei, he was madly in love with her.

còtto, s.m. (arch.) brickwork: ornamento in —, brickwork.

cottúra, s.f. cooking; (in forno) baking: di facile —, easily cooked; di rapida —, quickly cooked.

coturnàto, ag. buskined, wearing buskins.

coturníce, s.f. (ornit.) (genere) Coturnix; (pop.) (quaglia) quail.

cotúrno, s.m. cothurnus (pl. cothurni); buskin ‖ calzare il —, fig. to put on the buskins.

cóva, s.f. 1. (il covare) brooding, sitting on eggs 2. (nido) nest, nesting-place.

covàcciolo, s.m. 1. (tana) lair, den 2. (giaciglio) couch.

covàre, v.t. 1. to brood, to sit on (eggs): mettere una gallina a —, to set a hen 2. fig. to brood over, on (sthg.): da lungo tempo covava vendetta, he had been brooding over (o on) vengeance for a long time; — una malattia, to be sickening for an illness; — tristi pensieri, to brood over sad thoughts ‖ — il fuoco, to brood over the fire ‖ — qlcu. con gli occhi, to gaze intently at (o to keep one's look fixed on o to look longingly at) s.o. ‖ v.i. (di fuoco, passioni) to smoulder; (di malattia) to be latent: il fuoco covava sotto la cenere, fire was smouldering under the ashes; la malattia covava, the disease was latent; l'odio cova nel loro cuore, hatred is smouldering in their hearts ‖ gatta ci cova, there is sthg. fishy going on (o sthg. suspicious about it).

covàta, s.f. hatch, brood (anche fig.).

covatíccio, ag. brooding, broody.

covatríce, s.f. 1. (animale che cova) brooding hen, sitting hen 2. (incubatrice) incubator.

covatúra, s.f. 1. (il covare) brooding, sitting on eggs 2. (tempo di cova) brooding-time.

covíle, s.m. 1. (tana) lair, den 2.(giaciglio) couch 3.(misero rifugio) hovel, hole.

cóvo, s.m. 1. (tana) lair, den: un — di vipere, a nest of vipers (anche fig.) 2. fig. haunt, den, hiding-place: un — di ladri, a den (o haunt o nest) of thieves.

covóne, s.m. sheaf (pl. sheaves).

coxalgía, s.f. (patol.) coxalgia.

coxíte, s.f. (patol.) coxitis.

Còzie (Àlpi), no.pr.f.pl. (geog.) Cottian Alps.

cozióne, s.f. (rar.) (digestione) digestion.

còzza, s.f. (zool.) mussel.

cozzàre, v.t.i. 1. (con le corna, col capo) to butt; (urtare) to strike; (venire in collisione) (di navi) to collide, to run foul (of each other); (di veicoli) to collide: due navi hanno cozzato l'una contro l'altra, two ships have run foul of each other (o have collided); — il capo *contro il muro*, to strike (*o* to butt) one's head against the wall **2.** (*contrastare*) to contrast, to collide, to clash: *i miei interessi cozzano con i suoi*, my interests clash with his; — *contro delle difficoltà*, to meet with (*o* to knock up against) difficulties; — *contro le idee di qlcu.*, to collide with s.o.'s ideas; *venire a — contro ql.co.*, to come into collision with sthg. ‖ **cozzàrsi,** *v.r.* reciproco to butt at each other.

cozzàta, *s.f.* butt; (*urto*) shock; (*colpo*) blow, strike.

còzzo, *s.m.* **1.** (*con le corna, col capo*) butt, butting; (*collisione*) collision; (*urto*) shock, clash (anche *fig.*): *dare di — in ql.co.*, to butt (*o* to strike) against sthg. **2.** (*conflitto*) conflict, contrast.

cozzóne, *s.m.* horse-dealer.

cràc, *s.m.* **1.** (*voce onomatopeica riproducente il rumore di un crollo*) crack **2.** (*crollo*) collapse, downfall, ruin **3.** (*fallimento*) failure, bankruptcy **4.** (*ippica*) crack.

Cracòvia, *no.pr.f.* (*geog.*) Cracow.

cràmpo, *s.m.* cramp: *mi prese un —,* I was seized with a cramp; *avere dei crampi di stomaco,* to feel gnawing pains in the stomach; (*per appetito*) to feel an aching void.

crànico, *ag.* (*anat.*) cranial: *la scatola cranica,* the brain-pan (*o* the skull).

crànio, *s.m.* skull; (*scient.*) cranium (*pl.* crania).

cranioclàste, *s.m.* (*chir.*) cranioclast.

craniología, *s.f.* craniology; (*frenologia*) phrenology.

craniològico, *ag.* craniological.

craniòlogo, *s.m.* craniologist.

craniometría, *s.f.* craniometry.

cranioscopía, *s.f.* cranioscopy.

craniotomía, *s.f.* (*chir.*) craniotomy.

craniòtomo, *s.m.* (*chir.*) craniotome.

cantèri, *s.m.pl.* (*denti del giudizio*) wisdom-teeth.

cràpula, *s.f.* guzzling; orgy; crapulence.

crapulàre, *v.i.* to guzzle; to eat and drink immoderately.

crapulóne, *s.m.* guzzler.

cràsi, *s.f.* (*gram.*) crasis (*pl.* crases).

cràsso[1], *ag.* **1.** dense, crass, gross: *ignoranza crassa,* gross (*o* crass) ignorance **2.** *intestino —,* (*anat.*) large intestine.

Cràsso[2], *no.pr.m.* (*st.*) Crassus.

eratère, *s.m.* **1.** crater: *il — del Vesuvio,* the crater of Vesuvius **2.** (*archeol.*) crater, large bowl: *un — d'oro,* a golden crater.

cràuti, *s.m.pl.* (*cuc.*) sauerkraut (*sing.*).

cravàtta, *s.f.* **1.** (neck-)tie; (*arc.*) cravat: — *a farfalla,* bow-tie; — *a righe,* striped tie; *spillo per —,* tie-pin **2.** (*nella lotta greco-romana*) neck-hold.

cravattàio, *s.m.* **1.** (*chi fabbrica cravatte*) neck-tie manufacturer **2.** (*chi vende cravatte*) neck-tie seller.

creànza, *s.f.* breeding; good manners (*pl.*); civility, politeness: *buona —,* good breeding; *mala —,* ill breeding; *persona senza —,* ill-bred (*o* uncivil) person; *non conosce le buone creanze,* he has no manners; *questo ti insegnerà la —!,* this will teach you better manners! (*o* how to behave!).

creanzàto, *ag.* (*rar.*) well-bred; civil, polite.

creàre, *v.t.* **1.** to create: *Dio creò il mondo in sei giorni,* God created the world in six days; *Shakespeare creò innumerevoli personaggi drammatici,* Shakespeare created innumerable dramatic characters; — *nuovi modelli,* to design new patterns; — *una parte,* (*teat.*) to create a part **2.** (*suscitare, causare*) to produce, to cause: *questo creò molti malintesi,* this gave rise to (*o* caused) a lot of misunderstandings; — *uno scandalo,* to create a scandal **3.** (*eleggere, nominare*) to create, to make, to elect, to appoint: *egli fu creato sindaco della sua città,* he was appointed mayor of his own town; *lo crearono loro capo,* they made him their leader; — *qlcu. cavaliere, barone,* to create s.o. a knight, a baron **4.** (*costituire*) to form, to establish: — *una so-*

cietà, to form a partnership; — *una ditta,* to establish a firm.

creatína, *s.f.* (*chim.*) creatine.

creatívo, *ag.* creative.

creàto[1], *ag.* created: *tutte le cose create,* all created things ‖ *ben —,* well-bred; *mal —,* ill-bred ‖ *s.m.* universe, creation: *le meraviglie del —,* the wonders of creation.

creàto[2], *s.m.* (*rar.*) creature, protége, favourite: *è un — del duca,* he is a creature of the duke's.

creatóre, *ag.* creating: *forza, potenza creatrice, potere —,* creating power ‖ *s.m.* creator; maker ‖ *il Creatore,* (*teol.*) the Creator: *andare al Creatore,* to die; *mandare al Creatore,* to kill.

creatríce, *s.f.* creatress.

creatúra, *s.f.* **1.** creature: *una bella —,* a lovely creature; *povera —!,* poor creature! (*o* poor thing!); *uomini e animali sono tutti creature di Dio,* human beings and animals are all God's creatures: *vostra madre era una santa —,* your mother was a kind soul **2.** (*bambino*) little child, little creature: *una creaturina,* a poor little thing (*o* child) **3.** *fig.* creature, protégé, favourite: *è una — del principe,* he is a creature of the prince's.

creazióne, *s.f.* **1.** creation; (*invenzione*) invention: *le creazioni degli artisti,* artists' creations; *la — del mondo,* the creation of the world; *la — di un personaggio,* the creation of a character; *le ultime creazioni dei sarti parigini,* the latest creations of the Paris couturiers **2.** (*creato*) creation, universe: *le meraviglie della —,* the wonders of creation (*o* of the universe) **3.** (*costituzione*) creation; establishment: *la — di una nuova società,* the establishment of a new partnership **4.** (*nomina*) creation, appointment: *la — di un cavaliere,* the creation of a knight.

creazionísmo, *s.m.* (*st. fil.*) creationism.

credènte, *ag.* believing: *tutte le anime credenti,* all believing souls ‖ *s.c.* believer: *il cielo si aprirà a tutti i credenti,* heaven will open to all believers.

credènza[1], *s.f.* **1.** belief; credence: *credenze religiose,* religious beliefs **2.** (*credito*) credit: *comperare a —,* to buy on credit ‖ *lettere di —,* (*diplomazia*) credentials.

credènza[2], *s.f.* **1.** (*armadio da cucina*) sideboard, dresser; (kitchen) cupboard **2.** (*stanza*) pantry.

credenziàle, *ag.* credential: *lettere credenziali,* (*diplomazia*) credentials ‖ *s.f.* credential.

credenzière, *s.m.* butler.

credenzíno, *s.m.* **1.** (*piccola credenza*) small cupboard **2.** (*eccl.*) credence (table).

credenzóna, credenzóne, *V.* **credulóna, credulóne.**

crédere, *v.i.* **1.** (*prestar fede*) to believe (s.o., sthg.): *non crederle!,* don't believe her!; *non credetti alle sue parole,* I did not believe his words; *non credo ad una sola parola di quanto dice,* I disbelieve every word (*o* I don't believe a single word) he says; *non potevo — ai miei occhi,* I could scarcely believe my eyes; *non si deve — a tutto ciò che si sente,* one must not believe everything one hears **2.** (*credere reale*) to believe (in s.o., sthg.): — *in Dio,* to believe in God; — *ai fantasmi,* to believe in ghosts **3.** (*aver fiducia*) to trust (s.o., sthg.); to trust (in s.o., sthg.); to believe (in s.o., sthg.): *non credo all'efficacia di questa medicina,* I don't believe in this medicine; *non credo nella fortuna,* I don't trust in luck; *puoi credergli, te lo dico io,* you can trust (*o* depend on *o* count on) him, I assure you; — *nell'utilità delle conferenze per la pace,* to believe in the usefulness of peace conferences ‖ *v.t.* **1.** (*tenere per vero*) to believe: *credo che sia ancora vivo,* I believe him to be still alive; *credo di no, di sì,* I don't think so, I believe so (*o* I suppose so): *« Verranno in tempo? », « Credo di sì », « Credo di no »,* "Will they come in time?", "I believe so (*o* I think so)", "I don't think so (*o* I believe not *o* I think not)"; *crede tutto quello che gli si dice,* he believes everything he is told; *non so che cosa —,* I don't know what to believe ‖ *è da — che riuscirà,* it is probable that he will succeed ‖ *fare — ql.co. a qlcu.,* to make s.o. believe sthg **2.** (*pen-*

sare, immaginare) to think, to suppose: *credevo che Lei fosse francese*, I thought you were French; *credetti di udire dei passi*, I thought I heard footsteps; *crede che tutto gli sia permesso*, he thinks he can (o may) do anything; *ho creduto di fare bene*, I thought I was doing right; *ho creduto necessario, opportuno informarli*, I deemed it necessary (o I thought it convenient) to inform them; *non lo crediamo un genio*, we do not think him a genius (o we do not think he is a genius); *non potete — quanto contento io sia*, you can't think how glad I am; *fate come credete*, do as you like (o think best) ‖ *lo credo bene!*, I should think (o suppose) so! ‖ **crédersi,** *v.r.* to think oneself, to consider oneself: *si crede molto furbo*, he thinks he is very clever; *si crede una persona importante*, he thinks himself an important person; *si crede un poeta*, he thinks (o considers) himself a poet.

crédere, *s.m.* opinion, judg(e)ment: *a mio —*, in my opinion.

credíbile, *ag.* **1.** (*di cosa*) believable, credible: *è poco — che...*, it is hardly credible that...; *raccontò una scusa poco —*, he gave a barely credible excuse (o a cock-and-bull story) **2.** (*di persona*) trustworthy, to be believed: *non è una persona —*, he is not trustworthy.

credibilità, *s.f.* credibility, believableness.

credibilménte, *av.* credibly, believingly.

crédito, *s.m.* **1.** (*il credere*) credit: *dar — a*, to give credit to (o to put credit in) **2.** (*fiducia, reputazione*) credit, reputation, esteem: *è un medico di molto —*, he's a physician of the highest credit; *è una teoria che non trova più —*, it is an exploded theory; *godevano di molto —*, they were held in high esteem **3.** (*econ. comm.*) credit: *— a breve scadenza*, short credit; *— allo scoperto*, open credit; *— bancario*, bank credit; *— fondiario*, land credit; *— inesigibile*, irrecoverable credit; *apertura di —*, opening of credit; *istituto di —*, credit institution; *lettera di —*, letter of credit; *nota di —*, credit note; *metteremo la somma a vostro —*, we shall credit the amount to you (o we shall credit you with the amount); *aprire un —*, to open a credit; *comperare, prendere, vendere a —*, to buy, to take, to sell on credit; *far —*, to grant (o to give) credit.

creditóre, *s.m.* creditor: *creditori diversi*, sundry creditors; *— garantito*, secured creditor; *— privilegiato*, privileged creditor.

creditòrio, *ag.* (*dir.*) belonging to a creditor.

creditríce, *s.f.* creditor.

crèdo, *s.m.* **1.** (*teol.*) credo, creed: *cantare il —*, to sing the Credo **2.** (*fede, opinione*) creed, faith, belief: *il mio — politico*, my political creed.

credulità, *s.f.* credulity.

crèdulo, *ag.* credulous.

credulóna, *s.f.* credulous woman; (*fam.*) gull, dupe.

credulóne, *ag.* credulous ‖ *s.m.* credulous man; (*fam.*) gull, dupe: *è un —*, he swallows everything.

crèma, *s.f.* **1.** cream: *— di cioccolato*, chocolate-cream; *— di formaggio*, cream-cheese; *— emolliente*, cold cream; *— evanescente*, vanishing cream; *— per radersi*, shaving-cream; *— per le scarpe*, shoe polish; *— per il viso*, face-cream **2.** (*panna*) cream: *gelato di —*, ice-cream ‖ *di color —*, cream-coloured **3.** (*di uova e latte*) custard: *farcire una torta di —*, to fill a cake with custard **4.** *fig.* (*la parte migliore*) cream; élite: *la — della societ.*, the cream of society.

cremaglièra, *s.f* rack: *— campione*, (*mec.*) master rack; *— divisoria*, (*mec.*) indexing rack; *ferrovia a —*, rack-railway; *rotaia a —*, (*ferr.*) rack-rail.

cremàre, *v.t.* to cremate.

crematística, *s.f.* (*econ.*) chrematistics.

crematóio, *s.m.* crematorium (*pl.* crematoria); crematory, cremator.

crematología, *s.f.* (*econ.*) chrematistics.

crematòrio, *ag.* crematory: *forno —*, crematorium (o cremator o crematory).

cremazióne, *s.f.* cremation.

crèmisi, *ag.* crimson (*attributivo*) ‖ *s.m.* crimson.

cremisíno, *ag.* crimson.

Cremlíno, *s.m.* Cremlin.

cremòmetro, *s.m.* (*ind. casearia*) lactoscope.

cremóre, *s.m.* cream; essence; extract: *— (di) tartaro*, cream of tartar.

crèn, crènno, *s.m.* (*bot.*) horse-radish.

crenología, *s.f.* crenology.

crenoterapía, *s.f.* (*med.*) crenotherapy.

creolína, *s.f.* (*farm.*) creolin.

crèolo, *ag. s.m.* creole ‖ **crèola,** *s.f.* creole.

Creónte, *no.pr.m.* (*mit.*) Creon.

creosòto, *s.m.* (*farm.*) creosote.

crèpa, *s.f.* crack, fissure; crevice, chink: *vedo una — in quella parete*, I see a crack (o fissure) in that wall.

crepàccio, *s.m.* large fissure, cleft; (*di ghiacciaio*) crevasse.

crepacuòre, *s.m.* heart-break, heart-breaking grief: *morire di —*, to die of a broken heart.

crepapèlle, a, *l.av.*: *mangiare a —*, to gorge (o to stuff oneself with food); *ridere a —*, to split one's sides with laughter (o to roar with laughter).

crepàre, *v.i.* **1.** to crack, to split (asunder): *questa tavola crepa*, this board is cracking **2.** (*scoppiare*) to burst (anche *fig.*); (*volg.*) (*morire*) to pop off, to snuff out; (*amer.*) to croak: *— dalla fatica*, to be dead tired; *— dalle risa*, to burst with laughter; *— di rabbia*, to fume with rage; *— di salute*, (*fam.*) to be in the pink of health.

crepàto, *ag.* cracked: *questa tazza è crepata*, this cup is cracked.

crepatúra, *s.f.* crack, fissure; chink, crevice.

crepèlla, *s.f.* (*tessuto*) crepoline.

crepitàre, *v.i.* to crackle, to crepitate: *le foglie morte crepitarono sotto i suoi passi*, the dead leaves crackled under his feet; *i fucili crepitarono all'improvviso*, suddenly the rifles cracked out.

crepitío, *s.m.* crackling, crackle.

crèpito, *s.m.* crackling.

crepuscolàre, *ag.* crepuscular; twilight (*attributivo*): *luce —*, twilight ‖ *bellezza —*, fading beauty ‖ *farfalle crepuscolari*, (*entom.*) crepuscularia ‖ *poeti crepuscolari*, (*lett.*) the "crepuscolari" (school of Italian poetry contrasting with the earlier splendours of D'Annunzio and characterized by a subdued choice of subject) ‖ *stati crepuscolari*, (*psicologia*) subconsciousness.

crepúscolo, *s.m.* **1.** twilight, gloaming; dusk: *al —*, at dusk (o in the twilight) **2.** *fig.* twilight, decline: *il — della vita*, the twilight (o the decline) of life ‖ *il — degli dei*, (*mit.*) the twilight of the gods.

crescèndo, *s.m.* (*mus.*) crescendo (anche *fig.*).

crescènte, *ag.* **1.** (*che aumenta*) increasing: *luna —*, waxing moon ‖ *s.m.* (*arald.*) crescent.

crescènza¹, *s.f.* **1.** (*crescita*) growth, growing; (*aumento*) increase: *febbri di —*, growing-fever **2.** (*escrescenza*) excrescence.

crescènza², *s.f.* (*formaggio*) " crescenza " (kind of Italian soft cheese).

créscere, *v.i.* **1.** to grow; (*diventare adulto*) to grow up: *il bambino è cresciuto molto in questo periodo*, in this period the child has grown much taller; *la città sta crescendo in dimensione ed importanza*, the town is growing in size and importance; *in Piemonte cresce molto riso*, much rice grows in Piedmont; *la luna cresce*, the moon is waxing; *i pioppi crescono lungo i fiumi*, poplars grow along the rivers; *quando crescono, le ragazze diventano vanitose*, when they grow up, girls become vain; *qui il grano sta crescendo*, here the wheat is coming up; *— a vista d'occhio*, to grow apace; *— in bellezza*, to grow in beauty; *— nella stima di qlcu.*, to rise in s.o.'s esteem ‖ *campa cavallo che l'erba cresce*, *prov.* while the grass is growing the horse starveth **2.** (*aumentare*) to increase, to rise: *il fiume stava crescendo*, the river was rising; *il pane è cresciuto* *in questi ultimi tempi,* bread has risen in price lately; *la pasta non cresce perchè c'è poco lievito,* the dough does not rise because there is too little yeast; *lo scorso mese crebbi più di due chili,* last month I gained more than two kilos; *le sue speranze cominciano a —,* his hopes are beginning to rise; *il vento cresce,* the wind is rising 3. (*far crescere*) to grow: *vorrei farmi — i capelli,* I should like to let my hair grow; *farsi — la barba,* to grow a beard; *far — rose,* to grow roses 4. (*essere in eccesso*): *mi crescono mille lire,* I have a thousand lire over; *questo abito cresce,* this dress is too big (for me) ‖ *v.t.* 1. (*aumentare*) to raise, to increase: *quel negoziante ha cresciuto tutti i prezzi,* that merchant has raised (o increased) all his prices 2. (*allevare*) to bring up: *i miei figli li ho cresciuti io,* I have brought up my children myself.

cresciménto, *s.m.* 1. growth, growing 2. (*aumento*) increase.

crescióne, *s.m.* (*bot.*) water-cress.

créscita, cresciúta, *s.f.* 1. growth: *in —,* growing 2. (*aumento*) increase.

cresciúto, *ag.* 1. grown; (*divenuto adulto*) grown-up: *una pianta mal cresciuta,* an ill-grown tree; *un ragazzo — troppo in fretta,* a boy tall for his age 2. (*aumentato*) increased 3. (*allevato*) bred, brought up: *un ragazzo ben —,* a well-bred boy ‖ *s.m.* (*nei lavori a maglia*): *fare un —, due cresciuti,* to cast on one (stitch), two (stitches) (o to increase one, two).

crèsima, *s.f.* (*eccl.*) confirmation.

cresimànda, *s.f.,* **cresimàndo,** *s.m.* (*eccl.*) candidate for confirmation.

cresimàre, *v.t.* (*eccl.*) to confirm ‖ **cresimàrsi,** *v.r.* (*eccl.*) to be confirmed.

cresimàto, *ag.* (*eccl.*) confirmed ‖ *s.m.,* **cresimàta,** *s.f.* (*eccl.*) confirmee.

Crèso, *no.pr.m.* (*st.*) Croesus ‖ **crèso,** *s.m.* (*uomo molto ricco*) Croesus.

créspa, *s.f.* 1. wrinkle, pucker 2. (*increspatura sull'acqua*) ripple 3. (*piegolina di stoffa*) crease; wrinkle.

créspo, *ag.* 1. crisp, frizzly, frizzy; curled: *capelli crespi,* crisp (o frizzly) hair; *foglie crespe,* crisp leaves 2. (*rugoso*) wrinkled, puckered 3. (*a piegoline*) plaited, pleated ‖ *s.m.* 1. crêpe: *— di Cina,* crêpe-de-chine 2. (*tessuto nero da lutto*) crape: *— di lana,* crape-cloth.

crésta, *s.f.* 1. crest: *— di gallo,* cock's comb; *— di monte,* ridge (o crest) of a mountain; *— di un'onda,* crest of a wave ‖ *valore di —,* (*elett.*) crest (o peak) value ‖ *abbassare la —,* to come off one's high horse; *alzar la —,* to grow insolent (o to get cocky) ‖ *far la — sulla spesa,* (*rubare*) to cheat on the shopping 2. (*cuffia da donna*) female head-gear.

crestàia, *s.f.* (*rar.*) (*modista*) milliner.

crestàto, *ag.* crested.

crestína, *s.f.* (*di domestica*) maid-servant's cap.

crestomazía, *s.f.* chrestomathy.

crétá[1], *s.f.* 1. clay; (*gesso*) chalk 2. (*poet.*) (*il corpo umano*) the human body.

Crèta[2], *no.pr.f.* (*geog.*) Crete.

cretàceo, *ag.* 1. clayey; cretaceous; (*gessoso*) chalky 2. (*del periodo geologico*) Cretaceous.

cretése, *ag. s.c.* Cretan.

crètico, *s.m.* (*poes.*) cretic.

cretína, *s.f.* idiot, dunce, fool; (*sl. amer.*) nitwit.

cretinería, *s.f.* 1. idiocy, imbecility 2. (*azione, detto da cretino*) foolish action; nonsense: *non dire cretinerie!,* don't talk nonsense!.

cretinísmo, *s.m.* 1. idiocy, imbecility 2. (*patol.*) cretinism.

cretíno, *s.m.* 1. idiot, dunce, fool; (*sl. amer.*) nitwit 2. (*patol.*) cretin; idiot.

cretinòide, *s.c.* 1. idiot, utter fool 2. (*patol.*) cretinoid person.

cretóso, *ag.* (*rar.*) clayey; cretaceous; chalky.

cría, *s.m.* 1. smallest bird in the nest 2. *fig.* the weakling of the family.

cribràre, *v.t.* (*rar.*) to sift, to sieve.

críbro, *s.m.* (*rar.*) sieve.

críe, *s.m.* (*onomatopeico*) crack; squeak: *fare —,* to crack.

crícca, *s.f.* cabal, gang: *sono stanco di quella — di intriganti!,* I am sick of that gang of wire-pullers!.

cricche, *s.m.* (*onomatopeico*) crack; squeak.

cricchiàre, *v.i.* (*onomatopeico*) to crack; to squeak.

crícchio, *s.m.* 1. (*onomatopeico*) crack; squeak 2. (*ticchio*) whim; freak.

crícco, *s.m.* 1. (*mec.*) jack, carriage-jack 2. *coltello a —,* jack-knife (o clasp-knife).

cricerí, cri cri, *s.m.* (*voce onomatopeica riproducente il verso del grillo e il rumore del tarlo*) chirp: *fare —,* to chirp.

cricèto, *s.m.* (*zool.*) hamster.

Crimílde, *no.pr.f.* (*lett.*) Kriemhild.

criminàle, *ag.* criminal: *azione —,* criminal action; *diritto —,* criminal law; *manicomio —,* criminal lunatic asylum ‖ *s.c.* criminal, felon.

criminalísta, *s.m.* 1. (*avvocato penalista*) criminal lawyer 2. (*studioso di criminologia*) criminologist.

criminalità, *s.f.* criminality: *la — è in aumento, in diminuzione,* crime is increasing, diminishing.

criminalménte, *av.* criminally.

criminalòide, *ag. s.c.* criminaloid.

criminé, *s.m.* crime: *commettere un —,* to commit a crime (o a felony); *incolpare di un —,* to charge with a crime.

criminología, *s.f.* crimonology.

criminosaménte, *av.* criminally.

criminosità, *s.f.* criminality.

criminóso, *ag.* criminal.

crinàle, *s.m.* 1. (*di monte*) ridge 2. (*spillone per capelli*) hair-pin.

crine, *s.m.* 1. horse-hair; (*criniera*) mane 2. (*poet.*) hair; locks (*pl.*): *il — biondo,* the fair hair 3. (*tessuto*) haircloth 4. (*per imbottiture*) curled hair: *— vegetale,* vegetable horse-hair 5. (*crinale di monte*) ridge.

crinièra, *s.f.* 1. mane 2. (*dell'elmo*) (horse-)tail 3. (*astr.*) (*di cometa*) tail.

crioíto, *ag.* long-haired; (*irsuto*) hairy ‖ *stella crinita,* tailed star.

crino, *s.m.* (*per imbottiture*) curled hair: *— vegetale,* vegetable horse-hair.

crinòide, *ag.* (*zool.*) crinoid(al).

crinòidi, *s.m.pl.* (*zool.*) Crinoidea.

crinolína, *s.f.* crinoline.

criòcera, *s.m.* (*entom.*) crioceris.

criolíte, *s.f.* (*min.*) cryolite, ice spar, Greenland spar; (*chim.*) sodium fluoaluminate.

crioscopía, *s.f.* (*chim.*) cryoscopy.

crípta, *s.f.* crypt.

criptestesía, *s.f.* cryptaesthesia.

crípto, *s.m.* (*chim.*) krypton.

criptografía, *s.f.* cryptography.

crípton, *s.m.* (*chim.*) krypton.

criptopòrtico, *s.m.* (*arch.*) cryptoporticus.

criptoscòpio, *s.m.* cryptoscope.

crisàlide, *s.f.* chrysalid (*pl.* chrysalids, chrysalides); chrysalis (*pl.* chrysalises, chrysalids, chrysalides).

crisantèmo, *s.m.* chrysanthemum.

Crisèide, *no.pr.f.* (*lett.*) Criseyde.

criselefantíno, *ag.* chryselephantine.

crísi, *s.f.* 1. crisis (*pl.* crises); (*depressione finanziaria*) slump: *— commerciale, economica, finanziaria,* commercial, economic, financial crisis; *— degli alloggi,* housing shortage (o housing problem); *— ministeriale,* (*pol.*) cabinet crisis; *scoppio di una —,* outbreak of a crisis; *attraversare una —, essere in periodo di —,* to pass through a crisis; *superare una —,* to get over (o to surmount) a crisis 2. (*med.*) fit, attack: *— di nervi,* nervous fit (o attack).

crísma, *s.m.* 1. (*eccl.*) chrism 2. *fig.* consecration:

approval, praise: *il suo libro ha avuto tutti i crismi della critica*, his book received praise of the critics.

crisoberíllo, *s.m.* (*min.*) chrysoberyl.

crisocòlla, *s.m.* (*chim.*) chrysocolla.

crisografía, *s.f.* chrysography.

crisòlito, *s.m.* (*min.*) chrysolite.

crisopàzio, *s.m.* (*min.*) chrysoprase.

crisopèa, *s.f.* (*alchimia*) chrysopoeia, chrysopoetics.

crisopràsio, *s.m.* (*min.*) chrysoprase.

Crisòstomo, *no.pr.m.* (*st. relig.*) Chrysostom.

Crispíno, *no.pr.m.* (*st. eccl.*) Crispin.

cristallàio, *s.m.* **1.** (*chi fa lavori in cristallo*) worker in crystal **2.** (*chi vende oggetti di cristallo*) dealer in crystal-ware.

cristallàme, *s.m. coll.* (*rar.*) crystal-ware (*solo sing.*).

cristalleria, *s.f.* **1.** (*oggetti di cristallo*) crystal-ware (*solo sing.*), crystal-work (*solo sing.*) **2.** (*fabbrica di cristalli*) crystal manufactory.

cristallièra, *s.f.* glass case.

cristallíno, *ag.* **1.** crystalline; crystal (*attributivo*) **2.** (*limpido*) crystalline; crystal-clear (*attributivo*); transparent: *acque cristalline*, crystal-clear waters ‖ *s.m.* (*anat.*) crystalline lens.

cristallizzàbile, *ag.* crystallizable.

cristallizzàre, *v.t.* **1.** (*fis. min.*) to crystallize **2.** (*ind.*) (*zucchero*) to granulate ‖ **cristallizzàrsi**, *v.r.* to crystallize (*anche fig.*): *le sue idee politiche cominciavano a* —, his views on politics began to crystallize.

cristallizzatóre, *s.m.* (*chim.*) crystallization vessel.

cristallizzazióne, *s.f.* crystallization: — *frazionata*, (*chim.*) fractional crystallization; *acqua di* —, (*chim.*) water of crystallization.

cristàllo, *s.m.* crystal; (*lastra di vetro piana*) plate glass; (*vetro finissimo per vasi, bicchieri*) crystal (glass): — *blindato*, (*per automobili*) armoured (o bullet proof) glass; — *di quarzo*, quartz crystal; — *di rocca*, rock crystal; — *fluorescente*, (*fis. atomica*) phosphor; *mezzo* —, medium thick plate glass; *la tavola è apparecchiata e splende di argenti e cristalli*, the table is laid and shining with silver and crystal.

cristallogènesi, *s.f.* crystallogenesis.

cristallografía, *s.f.* crystallography.

cristallogràfico, *ag.* crystallographic.

cristallògrafo, *s.m.* crystallographer.

cristallòide, *s.m.* crystalloid.

Cristiàna, *no.pr.f.* Christiana.

cristianaménte, *av.* christianly; like a Christian; in a Christian spirit.

cristianésimo, *s.m.* Christianity, Christian faith: *convertire qlcu. al* —, to convert s.o. to Christianity.

Cristiània, *no.pr.f.* (*geog. st.*) Christiania ‖ **cristiània**, *s.m.* (*spor.*) Christiania.

cristianità, *s.f.* **1.** (*i cristiani*) Christendom **2.** (*l'esser cristiano*) Christianity.

cristianizzàre, *v.t.* to Christianize, to convert to Christianity.

cristiàno, *ag.* Christian: *era cristiana*, Christian era; *sepoltura cristiana*, Christian burial ‖ *s.m.* **1.** Christian: *comportarsi da buon* —, to behave like a good Christian; *farsi* —, to become a Christian ‖ *da* —, good, nice; decent: *una casa da cristiani*, a decent house; *un pranzo da* —, a nice dinner **2.** man, soul: *qui non c'è un* —, (*fam.*) there is not a soul here ‖ **Cristiàno**, *no.pr.m.* Christian.

Cristína, *no.pr.f.* Christine, Christina.

Cristo, *no.pr.m.* Christ: *avanti* —, before Christ (*abbr.* B. C.); *dopo* —, after Christ (*abbr.* A. D. = Anno Domini); *Gesù* —, Jesus Christ ‖ *s.m.* **1.**: *un povero* —, a poor fellow (o devil) **2.** (*crocifisso*) crucifix: *un — di legno*, a wooden crucifix.

Cristòforo, *no.pr.m.* Christopher ‖ *dim.* Chris, Kit.

cristología, *s.f.* (*teol.*) Christology.

cristòlogo, *s.m.* (*teol.*) Christologist.

critèrio, *s.m.* **1.** standard (of judgment); principle; criterion (*pl.* criteria): *criteri letterari*, literary criteria;

con che — *mi giudichi?*, by what criterion (o standard o principle) do you judge me?; *non misurare tutti gli uomini secondo lo stesso* — *!*, don't measure all men by the same standard!; *agire secondo un certo* —, to act according to a certain principle **2.** (*idea, opinione*) opinion, judgement: *a mio* —, in my opinion (o judgement); *farsi un* — *di ql.co.*, to form an idea of (o to size up) sthg. **3.** (*fam.*) (*buon senso*) sense: *una persona di* —, a person of sense (o a sensible person); *una persona senza* —, a senseless (o reckless) person.

crítica, *s.f.* **1.** criticism: — *dei testi*, textual criticism; — *estetica*, aesthetic criticism; — *letteraria*, literary criticism; — *storica*, historical criticism **2.** (*saggio critico*) piece of criticism, critical essay, critique; (*recensione*) review: *una* — *favorevole di un libro*, a favourable review of a book; *scrivere critiche per i settimanali*, to write reviews for the weekly magazines **3.** (*insieme dei critici*) the critics (*pl.*): *tutta la* — *gli è contraria*, all the critics are against him **4.** (*disapprovazione, biasimo*) criticism, censure, blame: *prestare il fianco alle critiche*, to lay oneself open (o to expose oneself) to censure.

criticàbile, *ag.* **1.** criticizable **2.** (*biasimabile*) censurable, blamable.

criticàre, *v.t.* **1.** to criticize: — *un'opera letteraria*, to criticize a literary work **2.** (*biasimare*) to censure, to blame, to find fault with (s.o., sthg.): *criticò severamente la nostra condotta*, he bitterly censured our behaviour; *spero che non avrai nulla da* —, I hope you will have nothing to find fault with ‖ *farsi* —, to expose oneself to censure.

criticísmo, *s.m.* **1.** (*st. fil.*) critical philosophy **2.** (*smania di criticare*) criticism.

crítico, *ag.* critical: *esame* — *di un'opera*, critical examination of a work; *momento* —, critical (o crucial) moment; *saggio* —, critical essay; *temperatura critica*, (*fis.*) critical temperature; *essere in una situazione critica*, to be in a critical situation (o to be critically situated o to be critically circumstanced) ‖ *l'età critica*, the climacteric ‖ *s.m.* **1.** critic, reviewer: — *d'arte*, art critic; *un* — *severo*, a harsh critic (o a slasher) **2.** (*fam.*) (*criticone*) fault-finder.

criticóne, *s.m.* fault-finder.

Critóne, *no.pr.m.* (*lett.*) Crito.

crittògama, *s.f.* (*bot.*) cryptogam.

crittogamía, *s.f.* (*bot.*) cryptogamy.

crittògamo, *ag.* (*bot.*) cryptogamous, cryptogamic.

crittografía, *s.f.* cryptography.

crittogràfico, *ag.* cryptographic.

crittògrafo, *s.m.* cryptographer.

crittogràmma, *s.m.* cryptogram, cryptograph.

crivellàre, *v.t.* **1.** to riddle: *crivellato di ferite*, riddled with wounds; *lo crivellarono di pallottole*, they riddled him with bullets **2.** (*vagliare*) to riddle; to sift (*anche fig.*).

crivèllo, *s.m.* sieve, riddle: — *oscillante*, (*miner.*) jig.

croàto, *ag.* Croatian ‖ *s.m.* **1.** (*abitante*) Croat, Croatian **2.** (*lingua*) (the) Croatian (language) ‖ **croàta**, *s.f.* Croat, Croatian.

Croàzia, *no.pr.f.* (*geog.*) Croatia.

croccànte, *ag.* crisp; crackling: *biscotto* —, crisp biscuit ‖ *s.m.* (*cuc.*) almond sweetmeat.

croccàre, *v.i.* to creak, to crackle.

crocchétta, *s.f.* (*cuc.*) croquette.

cròcchia, *s.f.* chignon, bun.

crocchiàre, *v.i.* **1.** to crack; (*delle giunture delle dita*) to crack **2.** (*della chioccia*) to cluck **3.** (*ciarlare*) to chatter.

cròcchio, *s.m.* **1.** (*il crocchiare*) crack **2.** (*capannello*) group, knot: *stare a* —, to chat together.

cróce[1], *s.f.* **1.** cross: *a forma di* —, cruciform (o cross-shaped) ‖ *ai piedi della Croce*, at the foot of the Cross; *deposizione dalla Croce*, Deposition; *la Santa Croce*, the Holy Cross (o the Holy Rood); *segno della* —, sign of the cross: *farsi il segno della* —, to cross oneself (*o* to make the sign of the cross) ‖ — *di fuoco*, (*st.*) fiery cross ‖ — *di Lorena, patriarcale*, cross of Lorraine, patriarchal cross; — *di Malta*, Maltese cross (anche *cine.*); — *di S. Andrea, decussata*, St. Andrew's cross (anche *edil. ind.*); (*arald.*) saltire; — *di S. Antonio, commissa*, Tau cross (o St. Anthony's cross); — *greca*, Greek cross; — *latina*, Latin cross; — *uncinata, gammata*, swastika ‖ *Croce del Sud*, (*astr.*) Southern Cross ‖ *Croce Rossa*, Red Cross 2. (*segno in forma di croce*) cross: *il luogo era indicato sulla mappa con una* —, the place was marked on the map with a cross; *firmare con la* —, to make one's cross ‖ *a occhio e* —, approximately (o at a rough guess) ‖ *con le braccia in* —, with folded arms ‖ *fare una* — *su ql.co.*, to obliterate (o to cancel) sthg.: *fateci una* —!, *fig.* just forget it!; *tirare una* — *su un debito*, to remit a debt ‖ *fare a testa e* —, to toss; *vincere a testa e* —, to win the toss 3. (*dispiacere*) tribulation; burden.

crocè², *V.* **crochet**.

crocefísso, *V.* **crocifísso**.

cròceo, *ag.* croceous; saffron-coloured.

crocerossína, *s.f.* Red Cross nurse.

crocétta, *s.f.* 1. small cross 2. (*arald.*) crosslet 3. (*mar.*) crosstree.

crocevía, *s.f.* cross-road.

crochet, *s.m.* 1. (*uncinetto*) crochet-hook: *lavorare ql.co. al* —, to crochet sthg. 2. (*lavoro con l'uncinetto*) crochet: *fare un* —, to crochet 3. (*boxe*) hook: — *sinistro*, left hook.

crociàre, *v.t.* to cross.

crociàta, *s.f.* 1. (*st.*) crusade: *la* — *contro gli Albigesi*, the crusade against the Albigenses 2. (*campagna*) crusade: — *contro l'alcoolismo*, crusade against drunkenness.

crociatèt, *s.m.* (*mil.*) port arms.

crociàto, *ag.* crossed ‖ *s.m.* (*st.*) crusader: *spirito di* —, crusading spirit.

crocícchio, *s.m.* cross-road, cross roads.

crocidàre, *v.i.* to croak.

crocièra, *s.f.* 1. (*arch.*) cross-vault 2. (*mar.*) cruise, cruising: — *di piacere*, pleasure cruise; — *intorno al mondo*, a round-the-world cruise; *andare in* —, to go on a cruise 3. (*aer.*) long-distance flight: *potenza di* —, (cruising) range; *velocità di* —, cruising speed 4. (*mec.*) spider, cross, cross journal: — *del giunto cardanico*, universal joint spider (o cross).

crocífere, *s.f.pl.* (*bot.*) Cruciferae.

crocífero, *ag.* cruciferous ‖ *s.m.* cross-bearer, crucifer.

crocifíggere, *v.t.* to crucify (anche *fig.*).

crocifissióne, *s.f.* crucifixion ‖ *la Crocifissione*, the Crucifixion.

crocifísso, *ag.* crucified ‖ *s.m.* crucifix: *un* — *gotico*, a Gothic crucifix ‖ *il Crocifisso*, the Crucified (o Christ Crucified).

crocifissóre, *s.m.* (*rar.*) crucifier.

crocifórme, *ag.* cruciform, cross-shaped.

cròco, *s.m.* 1. (*bot.*) crocus 2. (*poet.*) saffron.

cròda, *s.f.* crag.

crogiolàre, *v.t.* to cook on a slow fire; to simmer ‖ **crogiolàrsi**, *v.r.* to bask, to snuggle: — *al fuoco*, to bask by the fireside; — *al sole*, to bask in the sun; — *nel letto*, to laze in bed.

crògiolo, *s.m.* slow cooking; simmering ‖ *pigliare il* —, (*crogiolarsi*) to snuggle by the fireside.

crogiuòlo, *s.m.* crucible, melting-pot; (*per vetro*) pot: — *di attesa*, (*metal.*) foyer; — *metallico*, (*metal.*) metal crucible (o pot); — *per filtrazione*, (*chim.*) filter crucible; *acciaio al* —, (*metal.*) crucible steel.

crollamménto, *s.m.* collapsing, tumbling down, falling down.

crollàre, *v.i.* 1. to collapse, to break down, to tumble down, to fall down; (*sotto uno sforzo*) to give way, to crash: *attenzione, la tenda sta crollando!*, look out, the tent is falling down (o collapsing)!; *ella vide tutte le sue speranze crollare*, she saw all her hopes collapsing (o

crumbling); *il ponte crollò sotto il peso dei carri armati*, the bridge gave way (o collapsed) under the weight of the tanks; *quando l'Impero Romano stava crollando, i barbari lo attaccarono da ogni parte*, when the Roman Empire was on the verge of ruin (o declining o collapsing), the barbarians attacked it on every side; *quel muro sta crollando*, that wall is tumbling (o falling) down; *i suoi nervi crollarono per la lunga tensione*, her nerves gave way under the long strain; — *a terra*, to crash to the ground ‖ *far* — *ql.co.*, to cause sthg. to collapse 2. (*lasciarsi cadere*) to drop, to flop down: *crollò su di una sedia*, he dropped (o flopped) on to a chair 3. (*econ. comm.*) to slump: *ieri la Borsa crollò improvvisamente*, there was a sudden slump in the Stock-Exchange yesterday ‖ *v.t.* to shake: — *il capo*, to shake one's head; — *le spalle*, to shrug one's shoulders.

crollàta, *s.f.* 1. collapsing, tumbling down, falling down 2. (*scrollata*) shake.

cròllo, *s.m.* 1. collapse, tumbling down, falling down; (*sotto uno sforzo*) giving way: — *dei prezzi*, tumble in prices; — *del sistema nervoso*, nervous breakdown; — *di un sistema*, breakdown of a system; *fu il* — *di tutte le mie speranze*, that was the ruin (o downfall o crumbling) of all my hopes; *nessuno si aspettava il* — *di quell'azienda*, nobody expected that firm to go bankrupt; *quella speculazione sbagliata segnò il* — *della sua fortuna*, that unsuccessful speculation caused the ruin of his fortune 2. (*scrollata*) shake.

cròma, *s.f.* (*mus.*) quaver.

cromàre, *v.t.* to chromium-plate.

cromàtico, *ag.* chromatic: *aberrazione cromatica*, (*ott.*) chromatic aberration; *scala cromatica*, (*mus.*) chromatic scale.

cromatína, *s.f.* (*biol.*) chromatin.

cromatísmo, *s.m.* (*ott.*) chromatism.

cromàto, *ag.* (*ind.*) chromium-plated ‖ *s.m.* (*chim.*) chromate.

cromatòforo, *s.m.* (*biol.*) chromatophore.

cromatúra, *s.f.* (*metal.*) chromium-plating.

cromíte, *s.f.* (*min.*) chromite.

cròmo, *s.m.* (*chim.*) chromium, chrome: — *puro*, straight chromium.

cromofotografía, *s.f.* (*foto.*) chromophotography, colour photography.

cromolitografía, *s.f.* (*tip.*) chromolithograph.

cromolitogràfico, *ag.* (*tip.*) chromolithographic.

cromoplàsti, *s.m.pl.* (*biol.*) chromoplasts.

cromoscòpio, *s.m.* (*tv.*) chromoscope.

cromosfèra, *s.f.* (*astr.*) chromosphere.

cromosòma, *s.m.* (*biol.*) chromosome.

cromotelevisióne, *s.f.* chromotelevision.

cromoterapía, *s.f.* (*med.*) chromotherapy.

cromotipía, *s.f.* (*tip.*) chromotypy.

crònaca, *s.f.* 1. chronicle ‖ « *La Cronaca Anglosassone* », "The Anglo-Saxon Chronicle" 2. (*di giornale*) news (*pl. con costruzione sing.*); reports (*pl.*): — *giudiziaria*, law reports; — *letteraria*, book news ‖ — *bianca*, society page (o sociey gossip column); — *nera*, crime news (o page).

cronachísta, *s.m.* (*st.*) chronicler.

cronicità, *s.f.* (*med.*) chronicity.

crònico, *ag.* (*med.*) chronic: *affezione cronica*, chronic disease ‖ *s.m.* chronic invalid: *ospizio dei cronici*, nursing-home for chronic invalids.

cronísta, *s.m.* 1. (*di giornale*) reporter: — *di cronaca nera*, crime reporter; — *mondano*, columnist; — *sportivo*, sports reporter; *è* — *di un giornale del mattino*, he is a reporter on a morning paper 2. (*st.*) chronicler.

cronistòria, *s.f.* chronicle.

Cròno, *no.pr.m.* (*mit.*) Cronus, Cronos.

cronografía, *s.f.* chronography.

cronogràfico, *ag.* chronographic.

cronògrafo, *s.m.* 1. (*scrittore di cronografie*) chronographer 2. (*apparecchio*) chronograph.

cronología, *s.f.* chronology.

cronologicaménte, *av.* chronologically.

cronològico, *ag.* chronological: *in ordine* —, in chronological order.

cronologísta, *s.m.* chronologist.

cronòlogo, *s.m.* chronologer.

cronometràggio, *s.m.* time-study.

cronometràre, *v.t.* to time; (*fam.*) to clock: — *il tempo impiegato a percorrere un miglio,* to time a mile.

cronometrísta, *s.m.* time-keeper, checker; (*in competizioni sportive*) timer.

cronòmetro, *s.m.* chronometer, stop watch, timepiece, timer: — *marino,* ship's (*o* marine) chronometer.

cronoscòpio, *s.m.* chronoscope.

croscè, *V.* **crochet.**

crosciàre, *V.* **scrosciàre.**

cróscio, *V.* **scróscio.**

eròsta, *s.f.* 1. crust: — *di formaggio,* cheese-rind; *la — terrestre,* the crust of the earth 2. (*di ferita, ecc.*): scab, crust: — *lattea,* (*pop.*) milk-crust 3. (*quadro di nessun valore*) daub: *non è che una vecchia* —, it is only an old daub 4. (*tec.*) coating; (*di fusione*) casting skin: — *cementata,* hardened crust; — *di un getto,* (*metal.*) skin; — *di un pezzo fucinato,* scale.

erostàceo, *s.m.* (*zool.*) crustacean ‖ *i crostacei,* (*zool.*) Crustacea.

crostàre, *v.t.* (*cuc.*) to crust; (*glassare*) to ice.

crostàta, *s.f.* (*cuc.*) tart.

crostíno, *s.m.* small piece of toast; (*per zuppa*) crouton.

crostóso, *ag.* crusty; scabby.

eròtalo, *s.m.* (*zool.*) rattlesnake.

croupier, *s.m.* croupier.

erucciàre, *v.t.* to trouble, to worry; (*irritare*) to irritate ‖ **erucciàrsi,** *v.r.* to worry, to fret; (*irritarsi*) to get irritated: *non crucciarti,* don't worry.

erucciatamćnte, *av.* worryingly; (*in modo irritato*) irritatingly, vexedly.

erucciàto, *ag.* 1. worried: *avere un'aria crucciata,* to look worried 2. (*irritato*) irritated, vexed, annoyed.

erúccio, *s.m.* 1. (*dolore*) sorrow, grief; (*preoccupazione*) worry 2. (*irritazione*) irritation, vexation.

erucciosaménte, *av.* anxiously, concernedly.

eruccióso, *ag.* anxious, concerned.

eruciàle, *ag.* 1. (*decisivo*) crucial: *esperimento* —, crucial test; *momento* —, crucial moment; *punto* —, crucial point 2. (*a forma di croce*) crucial, cross-shaped.

erucifíggere, *v.t.* to crucify (anche *fig.*).

erucifórme, *ag.* cruciform, cross-shaped.

erucivèrba, *s.m.* cross-word puzzle.

erudaménte, *av.* crudely, harshly, roughly, rudely.

erudèle, *ag.* cruel; (*spietato*) merciless, unrelenting, ruthless; (*doloroso*) bitter, sore, grievous: *colpo* —, cruel (*o* sad) blow; *delusione* —, bitter (*o* grievous) disappointment; *destino* —, cruel fate; *ingiustizie crudeli,* grievous wrongs; *morte* —, cruel death; *un padrone* —, a cruel (*o* hard-hearted) master; *parole crudeli,* bitter (*o* cruel) words; *una persecuzione* —, a merciless (*o* an unrelenting *o* a ruthless) persecution; *punizione* —, cruel punishment; *vista, spettacolo* —, painful sight; *sei — con lui,* you are cruel to him.

erudelmènte, *av.* cruelly; (*spietatamente*) mercilessly, ruthlessly; (*dolorosamente*) bitterly: *fu — punito,* he was cruelly punished; *saranno perseguitati* —, they will be mercilessly persecuted.

erudeltà, *s.f.* 1. cruelty; (*inclemenza*) mercilessness, ruthlessness; (*inumanità*) inhumanity; (*durezza di cuore*) hard-heartedness: — *verso i bambini,* cruelty to children 2. (*atto crudele*) cruelty: *fu una* —, it was a cruelty.

erudézza, *s.f.* 1. (*rigidità*) severity, harshness: — *del clima,* harshness (*o* severity) of climate 2. *fig.* (*asprezza*) rudeness; (*volgarità*) coarseness: — *di linguaggio,* coarseness of speech 3. — *dell'acqua,* (*chim.*) hardness of water.

erudígno, *ag.* underdone: *carne crudigna,* underdone meat.

crúdo, *ag.* 1. raw; (*poco cotto*) underdone: *carne cruda,* raw meat; *seta cruda,* raw silk; *ecco una bella mela: mangiala cruda,* here is a fine apple: eat it raw ‖ *farne delle cotte e delle crude,* to do all sorts of mad things 2. (*rigido*) severe, raw, harsh: *inverno* —, severe winter 3. (*crudele*) cruel, merciless, pitiless, inhuman; (*aspro, sgraziato*) crude, harsh, rough: *la cruda realtà,* the crude facts; *colori crudi,* harsh colours; *giudizio* —, harsh (*o* severe) judgment; *una risposta cruda,* a blunt (*o* harsh) reply; *suono* —, harsh sound ‖ *parlare nudo e* —, to speak bluntly 4. *acqua cruda,* (*chim.*) hard water.

eruènto, *ag.* bloody, sanguinary: *combattimento* —, bloody (*o* sanguinary) combat.

crumíro, *s.m.* (*spreg.*) blackleg, scab; (*sl.*) fink.

crúna, *s.f.* needle's eye; eye of a needle.

eruppàle, *ag.* (*med.*) croupy, croupous.

crúp(pe), *s.m.* (*patol.*) croup.

eruràle, *ag.* (*anat.*) crural: *vene crurali,* crural veins.

erúsea, *s.f.* 1. bran ‖ *vender — per farina,* to cheat ‖ *Accademia della Crusca,* "Accademia della Crusca" (literary academy in Florence) ‖ *la farina del diavolo va tutta in* —, *prov.* evil gotten evil spent 2. (*lentiggini*) freckles (*pl.*).

eruscàio, *s.m.* 1. bran dealer 2. (*accademico della Crusca*) Della-Cruscan; member of the "Accademia della Crusca"; (*purista*) purist.

eruscaiuòlo, *ag.* Della-Cruscan (*attributivo*) ‖ *s.m.,* *V.* **eruscàio.**

eruscànte, *ag.* Della-Cruscan (*attributivo*) ‖ *s.m.* Della-Cruscan; member of the "Accademia della Crusca"; (*purista*) purist.

eruscheggiàre, *v.i.* to affect purity of language, to pick one's words.

cruschèllo, *s.m.* fine bran.

eruscóne, *s.m.* 1. coarse bran 2. (*scherz.*) (*purista*) purist.

eruscóso, *ag.* 1. branny 2. (*lentigginoso*) freckled.

eruscòtto, *s.m.* (*di automobile*) dashboard; (*di aeroplano*) instrument panel.

Cúba, *no.pr.f.* (*geog.*) Cuba.

eubàno, *ag.s.m.* Cuban ‖ **eubàna,** *s.f.* Cuban.

cubatúra, *s.f.* 1. (*arit. geom.*) (*il misurare lo spazio occupato da un solido*) cubature 2. (*la misura così ottenuta*) cubage; cubit content: — *di spedizione,* (*mar. comm.*) shipping cubage.

cubèb, *s.m.* (*farm.*) cubeb.

eubía, *s.f.* (*mar.*) hawse(-hole): — *di ormeggio,* mooring pipe (*o* mooring hawsepipe); — *di poppa,* stern pipe (*o* stern hawsepipe); *portello di* —, hawse flap.

eúbico, *ag.* 1. (*a forma di cubo*) cubic(al); cube-shaped 2. (*mat.*) cubic(al): *curva cubica,* (*mec.*) cubic curve; *equazione cubica,* cubic equation; *radice cubica,* cubic (*o* third) root.

eubicolàrio, *s.m.* (*st. romana*) cubicular.

eubícolo, *s.m.* cubicle.

eubifórme, *ag.* cubiform, cube-shaped.

eubísmo, *s.m.* (*st. pitt.*) cubism.

eubísta, *s.m.* (*st. pitt.*) cubist.

eubitàle, *ag.* 1. (*anat.*) cubital 2. (*di lettera, carattere*) very large: *a caratteri cubitali,* in very large letters: *un titolo a caratteri cubitali,* a banner headline.

eúbito, *s.m.* 1. (*anat.*) ulna; (*avambraccio*) forearm 2. (*st.*) cubit (*misura di lunghezza* = cm. 45,72).

eúbo, *ag.* (*cubico*) cubic: *metro* —, cubic metre ‖ *s.m.* (*geom.*) cube.

eubòide, *s.m.* (*geom.*) cuboid.

euccàgna, *s.f.* abundance, plenty ‖ *albero della* —, greasy pole; *giuoco della* —, climbing the greasy pole ‖ *che* —!, what a feast! ‖ *paese di Cuccagna,* land of Cockaigne (*o* land of plenty).

euccétta, *s.f.* 1. (*mar.*) berth: *cabina a quattro cuccette,* four-berth cabin 2. (*su treno*) sleeping berth 3. (*letto a cuccetta*) bunk.

euechiàia, *s.f.* 1. (*cucchiaione*) large spoon 2. (*cazzuola*) trowel 3. (*per calafatare*) scoop.

cucchiaiàta, *s.f.* spoonful.

cucchiaíno, *s.m.* (*da tè*) tea-spoon; (*da caffè*) coffee -spoon.

cucchiàio, *s.m.* **1.** spoon: — *da tavola*, table -spoon **2.** (*contenuto di un cucchiaio*) spoonful.

cucchiaióne, *s.m.* **1.** large spoon **2.** (*mestolo*) ladle.

cúccia, *s.f.* **1.** dog's bed ∥ *fa' la —!*, lie down! **2.** (*spreg.*) poor bed: *il tuo letto è una —*, your bed is in a mess.

cucciàre, *v.i.* (*di cani*) to lie down.

cúcciolo, *s.m.* **1.** pup; puppy; whelp **2.** *fig.* (*semplici-otto*) simple-minded person, inexperienced person.

cúcco, *s.m.* **1.** (*cocco, beniamino*) favourite child; darling, pet: *è il — della mamma*, he is his mother's darling **2.** (*sciocco*) fool: *vecchio —*, old fool ∥ *il — della veglia*, (*lo zimbello*) the laughing-stock.

cuccú, *V.* **cucú.**

cúccuma, *s.f.* kettle; (*del caffè*) coffee-pot.

cucína, *s.f.* **1.** kitchen; (*mil.*) cook-house; (*mar.*) galley: — *da campo*, cooking tent; *una — spaziosa*, a roomy kitchen; — *tinello*, dinette **2.** (*modo di cucinare*) cooking; (*arte di cucinare*) cookery, cuisine; (*cibo*) food: — *casalinga*, plain (*o* homely) cooking; — *francese*, French cuisine (*o* French cookery); — *vegetariana*, vegetarian food; *libro di —*, cookery-book; *un ristorante con buona —*, a restaurant with a good cooking; *utensili di —*, cooking utensils (*o* hollow -ware); *mi piace la — di mia madre*, I like my mother's cooking; *fare da —*, to cook: *imparare a fare da —*, to learn cookery ∥ *a grassa — povertà vicina*, *prov.* a fat kitchen is near to poverty (*o* fat housekeepers make lean executors *o* he who feeds like an emperor is apt to die like a beggar) ∥ *la piccola — fa la casa grande*, *prov.* a little kitchen makes a large house **3.** (*stufa*) stove, range: — *a gas*, gas-stove; — *economica*, stove (*o* kitchen-range); — *elettrica*, electric kitchen (*o* electric range).

cucinàbile, *ag.* that may be cooked.

cucinàre, *v.t.* to cook: *chi cucinerà il pranzo?*, who is going to cook the dinner? ∥ *se non studia seriamente, lo cucinerò io*, if he doesn't study hard, I'll deal with him.

cucinàrio, *ag.* culinary.

cucinàto, *ag.* cooked: *una pietanza ben cucinata*, a well-cooked dish.

cucinatúra, *s.f.* cooking.

cucinièra, *s.f.* (woman-)cook.

cucinière, *s.m.* **1.** (man-)cook **2.** (*libro di cucina*) cookery-book.

cuciníno, *s.m.* small kitchen; kitchenette.

cucíre, *v.t.* **1.** to sew, to stitch: *ago per —*, (sewing-) needle; *macchina per —*, sewing-machine; — *un bottone a una giacca*, to sew (*o* to stitch) a button on a coat ∥ — *la bocca a qlcu.*, to close s.o.'s mouth **2.** (*chir.*) to stitch: — *una ferita*, to stitch a wound **3.** (*mec.*) to lace; (*carta, con cucitrice*) to staple ∥ *v.i.* (*fare lavoro di cucito*) to do needlework ∥ — *di bianco*, to sew linen.

cuciríno, *ag.*: *filato —*, sewing thread.

cuciríni, *s.m.pl.* sewing threads.

cucíto, *ag.* **1.** sewn: — *a mano, a macchina*, hand -sewn, machine-stitched ∥ *avere la bocca cucita*, to keep one's mouth shut tight **2.** (*mar.*) clinker-built ∥ *s.m.* **1.** (*il cucire*) sewing **2.** (*lavoro d'ago*) needlework.

cucitóio, *s.m.* (*tec.*) sewing press.

cucitóre, *s.m.* sewer.

cucitríce, *s.f.* **1.** seamstress **2.** (*macchina*) sewing -machine; (*per carta*) stapler; (*per libri*) stitcher.

cucitúra, *s.f.* **1.** seam **2.** (*il cucire*) sewing **3.** (*mec.*) lacing; (*di fogli di carta*) stapling; (*di fogli di libro*) stitch.

cucú, *s.m.* (*ornit.*) cuckoo ∥ *orologio a —*, cuckoo clock ∥ *far —*, (*giuoco di bambini*) to play bo-peep.

cúculo, cucúlo, *s.m.* (*ornit.*) cuckoo.

cucúrbita, *s.f.* **1.** (*bot.*) cucurbit; gourd **2.** (*chim.*) cucurbit.

cucurbitàcee, *s.f.pl.* (*bot.*) Cucurbitaceae.

cucurbitàceo, *ag.* (*bot.*) cucurbitaceous.

cudú, *s.m.* (*zool.*) koodoo, kudu.

cúffia, *s.f.* **1.** cap; (*da donna*) bonnet: — *da bagno*, bathing-cap; — *da neonato*, baby's cap; (*all'antica*) baby's bonnet; — *da notte*, nightcap ∥ *uscire per il rotto della —*, to escape by the skin of one's teeth **2.** (*rad. tel.*) headphone, headset, earphone **3.** (*mec.*) casing, shroud, cowling **4.** — *del suggeritore*, (*teat.*) top of prompter's box.

cúfico, *ag.* (*st.*) Cufic, Kufic.

cugína, *s.f.* cousin: *tua — Betta*, your cousin Bess; *ho cinque cugine*, I have five (girl) cousins ∥ *prima —*, first cousin (*o* cousin-german); *seconda —*, second cousin.

cuginànza, *s.f.* (*rar.*) cousinhood, cousinship.

cugíno, *s.m.* cousin: *mio — Michele*, my cousin Mike; *ho due cugini*, I have two (male) cousins ∥ *primo —*, first cousin (*o* cousin-german); *secondo —*, second cousin.

cui, *pron. rel. m. f. sing. pl.* **1.** *obliquo* (*riferito a persone*) **whom**; (*a cui*) **to whom**; (whom *viene soppresso qualora la prep. che lo regge venga posposta al verbo*): *l'amico con — uscii ieri sera*, the friend I went out with last night (*o* the friend with whom I went out last night); *il ragazzo di — stavamo parlando*, the boy we were speaking of (*o* the boy of whom we were speaking); *il signore — parlai mi disse*, the gentleman I spoke to told me (*o* the gentleman to whom I spoke told me); *il signore da — riceveste il libro*, the gentleman you got the book from (*o* the gentleman from whom you got the book) **2.** *obliquo* (*riferito a cose ed animali*) **which**; (*a cui*) **to which**; (which *viene soppresso qualora la prep. che lo regge venga posposta al verbo*): *la città da — proviene*, the town he comes from (*o* the town from which he comes); *il libro di — ti parlai*, the book I spoke to you about (*o* the book about which I spoke to you); *la penna con — stai scrivendo*, the pen you are writing with (*o* the pen with which you are writing) **3.** (*genitivo poss.*) (*riferito a persone*) **whose**; (*riferito a cose, animali*) **whose, of which:** *il cane di — trovasti il collare ieri*, the dog whose collar you found yesterday; *la casa il — tetto si può vedere da qui*, the house whose roof you can see from here (*o* the house of which you can see the roof from here); *ecco la signora il — figlio avete appena conosciuto*, here is the lady whose son you have just met; *il signor Smith, di — vedi la casa, è nostro amico*, Mr. Smith, whose house you see, is a friend of ours; *quello è l'uomo nel — giardino stavamo giocando*, that is the man in whose garden we were playing **4.** (*con relazione di luogo*) **where**; (*con determinazione di tempo*) **when:** *la casa in — nacqui*, the house where (*o* in which) I was born (*o* the house I was born in); *il giorno in — egli arrivò*, the day (when *o* in which) he arrived; *il negozio in — comprai queste calze*, the shop where (*o* in which) I bought these socks.

culàccio, *s.m.* rump.

culàtta, *s.f.* **1.** breech **2.** (*di calzoni*) seat.

culinària, *s.f.* cookery, culinary art.

culinàrio, *ag.* culinary.

cúlla, *s.f.* **1.** cradle: — *a dondolo, sospesa*, swing cot; *far dondolare la — di un bambino*, to rock a baby's cradle ∥ *dalla —*, *fig.* from the cradle (*o* from infancy): *dalla — alla tomba*, from the cradle to the grave **2.** *fig.* cradle, birthplace: *la Grecia fu la — delle arti*, Greece was the cradle of the arts; *la Palestina fu la — del Cristianesimo*, Palestine was the birthplace of Christianity.

cullàre, *v.t.* **1.** (*dondolare*) (*nella culla*) to rock; (*fra le braccia*) to dandle; (*cantando una ninna nanna*) to lull: — *un bimbo finché si addormenti*, to rock a baby to sleep **2.** *fig.* (*illudere*) to delude, to lull: — *qlcu. con promesse*, to delude (*o* beguile) s.o. with promises; — *qlcu. con false speranze*, to lull s.o. with false hopes ∥ **cullàrsi,** *v.r.* to cherish (sthg.), to indulge:

si cullava nell'illusione di riuscire, he cherished (*o* indulged in) the illusion that he would succeed (*o* he deluded himself that he would succeed).

culminànte, *ag.* 1. culminant, highest, culminating 2. (*astr.*) culminant.

culminàre, *v.i.* 1. to culminate: — *in ql.co.*, to culminate in sthg. 2. (*astr.*) to culminate.

cúlmine, *s.m.* (*cima*) summit, top, culmination; *fig.* apex, climax: *era al — della gloria quando morì*, he was at the apex of glory when he died.

cúlmo, *s.m.* (*bot.*) culm.

cúlo, *s.m.* (*volg.*) 1. backside; buttocks (*pl.*); (*di animali*) rump, arse 2. (*fondo*) bottom.

cúlto, *ag.* (*dotto*) learned ‖ *s.m.* 1. (*adorazione*) worship: — *degli eroi*, hero-worship; — *della ricchezza*, worship of wealth 2. (*religione*) faith: *il — cattolico*, the Catholic faith 3. (*venerazione*) veneration, cult: *il — dei morti*, the cult of (*o* veneration for) the dead.

cultóre, *s.m.*, **cultríce**, *s.f.* lover: *i cultori dell'arte*, lovers of art (*o* art-lovers).

cúltro, *s.m.* 1. (*vomere*) coulter 2. (*coltello usato nei sacrifici*) sacrificial knife.

cultúra, *s.f.* 1. (*sapere*) culture, learning: *centri di —*, centres of culture; *un uomo di grande —*, a man of great culture (*o* a highly cultured man); *non ha alcuna —*, he lacks culture ‖ — *fisica*, physical culture (*o* training) 2. (*civiltà*) culture, civilization 3. (*med.*) culture: *la — dei bacilli*, the culture of bacilli 4. (*coltivazione*) cultivation; growing: — *del tabacco*, tobacco growing; *campo a —*, field in (*o* under) cultivation.

culturàle, *ag.* cultural.

Cúma, *no.pr.f.* (*geog. st.*) Cumae.

cúmolo, *V.* **cúmulo**.

cumulàre, *v.t.* to amass, to (ac)cumulate, to heap up: — *più uffici*, to hold a plurality of offices.

cumulativaménte, *av.* cumulatively.

cumulatívo, *ag.* cumulative: *polizza cumulativa*, through policy; *trasporti in servizio —*, connecting carriers.

cumulazióne, *s.f.* accumulation, heaping up.

cúmulo, *s.m.* 1. (*mucchio*) heap, pile; (*gran quantità*) lot: — *d'incarichi*, plurality of offices (*o* pluralism); *un — di ragioni*, a lot of reasons ‖ — *delle pene*, (*dir.*) non-concurrence of sentences 2. (*meteorologia*) cumulus (*pl.* cumuli).

cúna, (*poet.*) per **cúlla**.

Cunegónda, *no.pr.f.* Cunegond.

cuneifórme, *ag.* cuneiform, cuneate, wedge-shaped: *caratteri cuneiformi*, cuneiform characters.

cúneo, *s.m.* 1. wedge, quoin, chock: — *di arresto*, grip wedge; — *per calzare le ruote*, (*aut.*) scotch; *a forma di —*, wedge-shaped 2. (*arch.*) quoin, wedge 3. (*mil.*) wedge.

cunétta, *s.f.* (*per lo scolo delle acque*) gutter, side ditch; (*nella pavimentazione stradale*) road bump ‖ *attenzione*, —, (*segnaletica stradale*) bumpy road.

cunícolo, *s.m.* 1. cuniculus (*pl.* cuniculi); underground passage; tunnel 2. (*tana sotterranea di animali*) burrow 3. (*miner.*) shaft: — *di ventilazione*, fan shaft (*o* fan drift); — *sotterraneo*, underground shaft.

cuòca, *sf.*. cook, woman cook.

cuòcere, *v.t.* 1. (*far cuocere*) to cook: — *a fuoco lento*, to simmer; — *alla griglia*, to grill; — *a lesso*, to boil; — *al forno*, to bake; — *arrosto*, to roast; — *in umido*, to stew; *far — ql.co. a fuoco lento*, to cook sthg. on a slow fire ‖ *lasciar — qlcu. nel suo brodo*, to let s.o. stew in his own juice 2. (*mattoni, ecc.*) to burn, to bake, to kiln, to fire ‖ *v.i.* (*offendere, ferire*) to vex, to hurt, to smart: *l'offesa le cuoceva ancora*, she was still smarting under the offence; *questo mi cuoce*, this vexes (*o* hurts) me.

cuòco, *s.m.* (man) cook: *primo —*, head-cook (*o* chef).

cuoiàio, *s.m.* 1. (*commerciante*) dealer in leather and hides 2. (*conciatore*) tanner, leather dresser.

cuoiàme, *s.m.* leather and hides (*pl.*); (*cuoio preparato*) dressed leather; dressed hides (*pl.*).

cuòio, *s.m.*; *pl.m.* **cuòi** (*nei sensi* 1. 2.); *pl.f.* **cuòia** (*nel senso* 3.) 1. leather; hide: — *artificiale*, imitation leather; — *di prima qualità*, prime light-grain leather; — *preparato*, dressed leather (*o* hides) 2. — *capelluto*, (*anat.*) scalp 3. *distendere le cuoia*, to stretch one's legs; *stendere le cuoia*, to lie down (*o* to go to bed); *tirare le cuoia*, to pop off, to snuff out; (*amer.*) to croak.

cuòra, *s.f.* float, floating ground.

cuòre, *s.m.* 1. heart (anche *fig.*): *a — leggero*, with a light heart; *a forma di —*, heart-shaped; *attacco di —*, heart-attack; *battito del —*, heart-beat; *di —*, heartily: *vi ringraziamo di —*, we thank you heartily; *ridere di —*, to laugh heartily; *di buon —*, whole-heartedly (*o* very willingly *o* gladly *o* with pleasure); *di tutto —*, with all one's heart (*o* whole-heartedly); (*molto volentieri*) most willingly; *mal di —*, heart-disease; *nel profondo del —*, in one's heart of hearts; *pace del —*, peace of mind; *una persona di buon —*, a person with a kind heart (*o* a kind-hearted person); *uomo dal — di coniglio*, chicken (*o* faint)-hearted man; *uomo dal — di leone*, lion-hearted man (*o* heart of oak); *uomo senza —, dal — di pietra, dal — di tigre*, heartless man (*o* hard-hearted man); *il — mi dice che è salvo*, I feel in my heart that he is safe; *avresti — di licenziarlo?*, could you have the heart to dismiss him?; *la cosa mi sta a —*, I have the matter at heart; *è una vista che fa male al —*, it is a sickening sight; *ella se lo strinse al —*, she folded him to her bosom; *mi fa bene al — vederti*, it does my heart good to see you; *il mio — batte forte*, my heart is thumping; *mi si stringe il — a dovertelo dire*, I feel so sad to have to tell you; *non ebbe il — di farlo*, he had not the heart to do so; *parola che viene dal —*, word from the heart (*o* heartfelt word); *questo pensiero le sta sul —*, that thought lies heavy on her heart ‖ *aprire il proprio — a qlcu.*, to open one's heart to s.o.; *avere il — gonfio*, to be heavy-hearted (*o* sad at heart); *avere il — sulle labbra*, to wear one's heart on one's sleeve; *avere il — volubile*, to be giddy of heart; *avere la morte nel —*, to be heart-sick (*o* sick at heart); *conquistare il — di qlcu.*, to win s.o.'s heart (*o* love); *dare il proprio — a qlcu.*, to give one's heart to s.o.; *fare — a qlcu.*, to put s.o. in good heart (*o* to give s.o. courage *o* to hearten s.o.); *farsi —*, to take heart; *leggere nel — di qlcu.*, to see into s.o.'s heart; *mettere in pace il — di qlcu.*, to set s.o.'s heart at rest; *mettersi una mano sul —*, to put one's hand on one's heart; *parlare a — aperto*, to speak with open heart (*o* freely); *prendere ql.co. a —*, to lay sthg. to heart; *sentirsi allargare il — a qlcu.*, to feel a great joy (*o* to be overjoyed) at sthg.; *spezzare il — a qlcu.*, to break s.o.'s heart; *toccare il — di qlcu.*, to touch s.o.'s heart (*o* to move s.o.) ‖ *cuor mio!*, my darling! ‖ *amico, amica del —*, bosom friend ‖ *costare, spendere il —*, to cost, to spend a great deal ‖ *il — non sbaglia*, *prov.* the heart sees farther than the head ‖ — *sulla bocca, la bocca nel —*, *prov.* heart in mouth, mouth in heart ‖ *freddo di mano, caldo di —*, *prov.* a cold hand and a warm heart ‖ *lontan dagli occhi, lontan dal —*, *prov.* out of sight, out of mind ‖ *per l'abbondanza del —, la bocca parla*, *prov.* what the heart thinks, the mouth speaks (*o* out of the abundance of the heart the mouth speaks) 2. (*centro*) centre, heart; core: *il — del carciofo*, the heart of the artichoke; *il — del tronco*, the heart-wood (*o* duramen); *il — di un frutto*, the core of a fruit; *nel — dell'Africa*, in the heart (*o* centre) of Africa; *nel — della città, della foresta*, in the heart of the city, of the forest ‖ *nel — dell'estate*, at the height of summer; *nel — dell'inverno*, in the depths of winter; *nel — della notte*, at dead of night (*o* in the middle of the night) 3. *pl.* (*carte*) hearts: *fante di cuori*, knave of hearts 4. (*metal.*) heart; core 5. (*ferr.*) (*dello scambio*) frog, crossing.

cuorifórme, *ag.* heart-shaped.

cupaménte, *av.* **1.** darkly, obscurely, dimly **2.** (*tristemente*) gloomily, sullenly: *lo guardò* —, he looked at him sullenly **3.** (*di suono*) deeply.

cupè, *s.m.* **1.** (*automobile, carrozza*) coupé, brougham **2.** (*parte anteriore di una diligenza*) coupé **3.** (*ferr.*) (*mezzo scompartimento*) coupé, half-compartment.

cupézza, *s.f.* **1.** darkness, obscurity, dimness **2.** (*tristezza*) gloom, sullenness **3.** (*profondità*) depth, hollowness.

cupidaménte, *av.* greedily.

cupidígia, cupidità, *s.f.* cupidity, greed, greediness, covetousness: *accendere la* — *in qlcu.*, to arouse cupidity in s.o.; *guardare ql.co. con* —, to cast covetou eyes on sthg.

cúpido[1], *ag.* greedy, covetous, grasping: — *di gloria*, thirsting for glory; — *di vendetta*, thirsting for revenge; *con occhi cupidi*, with greedy eyes.

Cupído[2], *no.pr.m.* (*mit.*) Cupid.

cúpo, *ag.* **1.** dark, obscure, dim; gloomy, sombre; (*di suono, colore*) deep; hollow: *colore* —, deep (o dark) colour; *giorno* —, gloomy day; *silenzio* —, deep silence; *suono* —, deep (o hollow) sound; *visione cupa*, dark view **2.** (*profondo*) hollow, deep: *valle cupa*, deep valley **3.** (*triste*) gloomy; sullen: *il Romanticismo ed i suoi cupi eroi*, Romanticism and its gloomy heroes.

cúpola, *s.f.* **1.** (*arch.*) dome, cupola: — *a sesto ribassato*, flat dome ‖ *a* —, dome-shaped **2.** (*di cappello*) crown.

eupolífere, *s.f. pl.* (*bot.*) Cupuliferae.

cúpolo, *ag.* quite full, heaped up.

cupóne, *s.m.* coupon.

eúpreo, *ag.* (*letter.*) cupreous.

eúprico, *ag.* (*chim.*) cuprous, cupric.

cuprísmo, *s.m.* (*patol.*) cupraemia.

cupríte, *s.f.* (*min.*) cuprite.

eúra, *s.f.* **1.** care: *la* — *della casa non è sulle mie spalle*, the housekeeping does not rest on me; *l'unica mia* — *è mio figlio*, my son is my only care; *lasciamo a voi la* — *di questo affare*, we interest you in such a business ‖ *affidare a qlcu. la* — *di ql.co.*, *di fare ql.co.*, to entrust s.o. with the care of sthg., of doing sthg.; *affidare qlcu., ql.co. alla* — *di qlcu.*, to put (o to place) s.o., sthg. in (o under) the care of s.o. (o to commit s.o., sthg. to the care of s.o.); *avere* — *di ql.co.*, (*occuparsi*) to attend to sthg. (o to mind sthg. o to take care of sthg. o to see to sthg.); *avere, prendersi* — *di qlcu.*, to take care of s.o. (o to look after s.o. o to care for s.o.); *aversi* —, *aver* — *della propria salute*, to take care of oneself; *fare ql.co. con molta* —, to do sthg. with great care ‖ *a* — *di...*, (*di libro pubblicato*) edited by... **2.** (*preoccupazione*) care, trouble, worry: *essere pieno di cure*, to be full of cares **3.** (*accuratezza*) care, attention; accuracy: *raccomandiamo alle vostre cure...*, we recommend... to your attention; *la vostra ordinazione sarà eseguita con la massima* —, your order will have our best attention (o we will take the greatest care in the execution of your order) **4.** (*amministrazione*) management: *la* — *dei miei beni*, the management of my estate **5.** (*eccl.*) cure, spiritual care: — *d'anime*, cure (o spiritual care) of souls **6.** (*med.*) treatment; cure: *la* — *del latte*, milk cure; *una* — *di riposo*, a rest-cure; *qual è la* — *migliore per il raffreddore?*, what is the best cure for a cold?; *avere in* — *un malato*, to treat a patient; *essere in* —, to be under treatment; *fare una* —, to follow a treatment: *fare una* — *a qlcu.*, to give s.o. a treatment ‖ *casa di* —, nursing-home.

eurábile, *ag.* curable.

eurabilità, *s.f.* curability.

eurànte, *ag.*: *medico* —, attending physician (o doctor in charge).

curàre, *v.t.* **1.** (*aver cura di*) to take care of (s.o., sthg.): — *gli affari*, to take care of one's business; — *la propria salute*, to take care of one's health **2.** (*comm.*)

to see to (sthg.), to attend to (sthg.), to provide for (sthg.): *cureremo l'inoltro della merce*, we shall see to the forwarding of the goods; *vogliate curarne la riscossione*, kindly attend to the collection; — *l'accettazione*, to provide for acceptance; — *l'assicurazione*, to effect insurance; — *l'invio*, to attend to the forwarding **3.** (*di medico*) to treat, to attend, to cure, to heal; (*di infermiera*) to nurse, to attend: *quale dottore ti cura?*, which doctor is attending you? (o who is your doctor?) **4.** (*la pubblicazione di un libro*) to edit, (a book) **5.** (*stimare, far conto di*) to mind: *non cura i biasimi del volgo*, he does not mind the disapproval of the mob ‖ **curàrsi**, *v.r.* **1.** (*aver cura di se stesso*) to take care of oneself; (*seguire una cura*) to follow a treatment **2.** (*badare, occuparsi*) to care (for s.o.); to take care of (sthg.), to mind (sthg.), to attend (to sthg.): *curati dei fatti tuoi*, mind your own business; *non curarti delle loro parole*, do not mind (o take no notice o take no heed) of their words; *non mi curai del suo avvertimento*, I disregarded his warning.

curarína, *s.f.* (*farm.*) curarine.

euràro, *s.m.* (*farm.*) curare, curari.

eurasnétta, *s.f.* farrier's parer.

curatèla, *s.f.* **1.** (*dir.*) trusteeship **2.** (*di fallimento*) receivership; (*amer.*) trusteeship **3.** (*tutela*) guardianship **4.** (*direzione di museo, galleria, ecc.*) curatorship.

curatívo, *ag.* curative.

curàto, *s.m.* (*eccl.*) curate: *posto, ufficio di* —, curacy.

euratóre, *s.m.*, **euratríce**, *s.f.* **1.** (*dir.*) trustee **2.** (*di fallimento*) official receiver; (*amer.*) trustee **3.** (*tutore*) guardian.

euratúra, *s.f.* (*ind. tessile*) bleaching.

eurbàscio, *s.m.* kurbash, kourbash.

eurculióne, *s.m.* (*entom.*) curculio.

eúrcuma, *s.f.* (*bot.*) curcuma.

Cúrdistan, *no.pr.m.* (*geog.*) Kurdistan.

eúrdo, *ag.* Kurdish ‖ *s.m.* **1.** (*abitante*) Kurd **2.** (*lingua*) (the) Kurdish (language).

cúria, *s.f.* **1.** (*st. romana*) curia; senate-house **2.** (*dir.*) court of justice, tribunal **3.** (*ceto dei legali*) the bar **4.** (*eccl.*): *la* — *romana*, the Holy See (o the Papal Court o the Curia); *la* — *vescovile*, the bishop's see (o Court).

curiàle, *ag.* **1.** curial: *lingua* —, language of the Court **2.** (*legale*) legal **3.** (*eccl.*) of the Papal Court, of the Curia ‖ *s.m.* lawyer.

eurialésco, *ag.*: *linguaggio* —, lawyers' language (o spreg. lawyers' jargon).

curialménte, *av.* in legal style.

euriàto, *ag.* (*st. romana*) curiate: *i comizi curiati*, the curiate comitia.

Curiàzi, *no.pr.m.pl.* (*st.*) Curiatii.

eurie, *s.m.* (*chim. fis.*) curie: — *ora*, curie hour; *punto di* —, (*elett.*) curie temperature (o point).

curiosaménte, *av.* **1.** curiously; (*con aria indagatrice*) inquisitively **2.** (*stranamente*) quaintly.

curiosàre, *v.i.* **1.** to be curious, to be inquisitive; to pry, to peep, to nose: *non* — *negli affari altrui!*, don't pry (o nose) into other people's affairs!; — *attraverso il buco della serratura*, to peep (o to look) through the keyhole **2.** (*origliare*) to eavesdrop.

curiosità, *s.f.* **1.** curiosity, inquisitiveness: *per* —, out of curiosity; *non spinsi oltre la mia* —, I pushed my curiosity no further; *questo stuzzicò la nostra* —, this raised (o tickled) our curiosity **2.** (*stranezza*) curiousness, strangeness, oddity, quaintness: *la* — *del suo comportamento*, the oddity of his behaviour **3.** (*oggetto strano, raro, curioso*) curio, curiosity: *andare in cerca di* —, to go curio-hunting.

eurióso, *ag.* **1.** curious, inquisitive: *è una donna molto curiosa*, she is a very curious woman; *sono* — *di sapere che cosa dissero*, I am curious to know what they said **2.** (*strano*) curious, strange, odd, quaint: *che oggetto* —!, what a curious object!; *è* —!, that's odd!; *è un viso* —, it is a strange face ‖ *s.m.* **1.** curious person; inquisitive person **2.** (*spettatore*) onlooker; (*astante*) bystander: *un assembramento di curiosi*, a cluster of onlookers.

curriculum vitae, *l.* (*lat.*) curriculum (*pl.* curricula) vitae, resumé.

cúrro, *s.m.* (*tec.*) dolly.

cursóre, *s.m.* **1.** (*messo*) messenger **2.** (*dir.*) court messenger, tipstaff **3.** (*mec.*) slider; sliding rule.

curúle, *ag.* (*st. romana*) curule: *sedia* —, curule chair.

cúrva, *s.f.* **1.** curve: — *di livello*, (*topografia*) contour (line); — *esponenziale*, (*mat.*) exponential curve **2.** (*di strada, fiume*) curve, bend: *una* — *ad S*, an S-shaped bend; — *a forcella*, hairpin bend; — *pericolosa*, dangerous curve; — *sopraelevata*, banked curve; — *stretta*, sharp curve (o bend); *contro* —, reverse curve; *la strada fa molte curve*, the road bends several times.

curvàbile, *ag.* that can be bent, that can be curved.

curvàre, *v.t.* to bend, to curve, to bow: *curvò il capo in preghiera*, he bowed his head in prayer; — *un ramo*, to bend a branch; — *la schiena*, to bend (o to curve) one's back; — *un tubo*, to bend a pipe || **curvàrsi,** *v.r.* **1.** to bend, to curve: — *davanti a qlcu.*, to bend low before s.o.; — *sotto un fardello*, to bend beneath a burden **2.** (*inchinarsi*) to bow (down); (*abbassarsi*) to stoop: *si curvò dinanzi all'idolo*, she bowed down to the idol **3.** (*far civetta*) to duck.

curvàto, *ag.* bent.

curvatríce, *s.f.* (*mec.*) bending machine, bender: — *ad ingranaggi*, geared bender; — *per legno*, wood bending machine.

curvatúra, *s.f.* **1.** curvature; curving, bending: — *della spina dorsale*, curvature of the spine; *raggio di* —, (*geom.*) bending radius **2.** (*aer.*) camber: — *dell'asse longitudinale*, (*di dirigibile*) hog **3.** (*arch.*) sweep.

curvímetro, *s.m.* map measurer, opisometer.

curvilíneo, *ag.* curvilinear.

cúrvo, *ag.* **1.** curved: *superficie curva*, curved surface **2.** (*piegato*) bent; (*storto*) crooked: — *per l'età*, bent (o bowed) with age; *spalle curve*, round (o stooping) shoulders; *stava con la fronte curva*, he had his head bowed.

Cúrzio, *no.pr.m.* Curtius.

cuscinétto, *s.m.* **1.** small cushion: — *puntaspilli*, pincushion **2.** (*posapiedi*) hassock **3.** (*imbottitura*) pad, padding **4.** (*mec.*) bearing: — *antifrizione*, antifriction bearing; — *a rulli*, roller bearing; — *a sfere*, ball bearing; — *di spinta*, thrust bearing; — *intermedio*, intermediate bearing; — *liscio*, friction (o plain) bearing;

— *oscillante*, self-aligning bearing; — *per spinte oblique*, angular bearing; *sede di* —, bearing housing **5.** *stato* —, (*pol.*) buffer-state.

cuscíno, *s.m.* **1.** cushion; (*guanciale*) pillow: — *di sedile*, (*aut.*) seat cushion; *ripostiglio cuscini*, (*ferr.*) pillow box **2.** (*mec.*) (*di appoggio*) pillow: — *ammortizzatore*, pad (o fender); — *d'aria*, air-cushion; — *d'incappellaggio*, (*mar.*) bolster.

cuscussú, *s.m.* (*cuc.*) couscous(ou).

cúscuta, *s.f.* (*bot.*) dodder.

cuspidàle, *ag.* (*arch.*) cuspidal, cuspidate(d), pointed.

cuspidàto, *ag.* cuspidate(d), pointed: *denti cuspidati*, cuspidate teeth; *foglie cuspidate*, cuspidate leaves.

cúspide, *s.f.* **1.** peak, cusp; (*punta*) point; peak **2.** (*arch.*) cusp.

custòde, *s.c.* **1.** keeper, guardian, custodian: — *delle carceri*, jailor (o jailer o gaoler); — *giudiziario*, official receiver || *angelo* —, guardian angel **2.** (*portiere, portiera*) door-keeper.

custòdia, *s.f.* **1.** custody, guardianship; (*cura*) care: *quel bambino è sotto la* — *di suo padre*, that child is in the custody of his father; *affidare un ragazzo alla* — *di qlcu.*, to place a boy into s.o.'s custody (o to commit a boy to s.o.'s care) **2.** (*di cose*) care, keeping: *in buona* —, in safe keeping; *camera* — *dei valori*, strong-room **3.** (*astuccio*) case, box: — *di violino*, violin case.

custodíre, *v.t.* **1.** to keep, to guard, to preserve: — *i gioielli sotto chiave*, to keep one's jewels under lock and key **2.** (*aver cura di*) to look after (s.o., sthg.), to take care of (s.o., sthg.): *mentre sono lontano, custodisci la casa*, while I am away, take care of the house **3.** (*un prigioniero*) to hold in custody || **custodírsi,** *v.r.* to take care of oneself.

cutàneo, *ag.* cutaneous; skin (*attributivo*): *eruzione cutanea*, skin eruption; *malattia cutanea*, skin disease.

cúte, *s.f.* (*anat.*) cutis, skin: *malattia della* —, skin disease.

cuticàgna, *s.f.* **1.** (*collottola*) nape **2.** (*cuoio capelluto*) scalp.

cutícola, *s.f.* (*anat.*) cuticle.

cuticolàre, *ag.* (*anat.*) cuticular.

cutína, *s.f.* (*chim.*) cutin.

cutrèttola, *s.f.* (*ornit.*) wagtail.

ezàr, *s.m.* tzar, tsar, czar.

czarèvich, *s.m.* tsarevitch, czarevitch, czarewich.

czarína, *s.f.* tsarina, czarina.

czarísmo, *s.m.* tsarism, czarism.

czèco, *ag. s.m.* Czech.

D

d, *s.f.m.* **1.** (*quarta lettera dell'alfabeto italiano*) d (*pl.* ds, d's*) ‖ — *come Domodossola*, (*tel.*) d for David **2.** *D*, (*numero romano, equivalente a 500*) D (five hundred).

da, *prep.* **1.** (*moto da luogo, separazione, allontanamento, origine, provenienza, decorrenza, distanza*) **from:** — *Milano a Roma*, from Milan to Rome; — *uno a venti*, from one to twenty; *dal mattino alla sera*, from morning to (o till) night; *dal 1910 al 1920*, from 1910 to 1920; *ragazze dai quindici ai ventidue anni*, girls from fifteen to twenty-two (years of age); « *Da dove venite?* », « *Veniamo dall'Italia* », "Where do you come from?", "We come from Italy"; *fece capolino — dietro la poltrona*, he peeped from behind the arm-chair; *la lettera cadde dal tavolo*, the letter fell from the table; *mi separai — lui*, I parted from him; *ricevetti un libro dal mio padrino*, I received (o got) a book from my god-father; *la sua famiglia discende — Cavour*, his family is descended from Cavour; *torno ora — Torino*, I have just come back from Turin; *liberare dalla schiavitù*, to free from slavery; *preservare dal pericolo*, to preserve from harm; *smontare — cavallo*, to dismount from a horse; *togliere un fiammifero dalla scatola*, to extract a match from the box (o to take a match out of the box) **2.** (*moto a luogo*) **to:** *andiamo — loro*, let's go to their house; *andrò — mio zio*, I'll go to my uncle's **3.** (*stato in luogo*) **at:** *abito — loro*, I live at their house (o with them); *vi aspetto — « Corrado »*, I'll wait for you at "Corrado's" **4.** (*moto attraverso luogo*) **through:** *tornando da Londra passammo — Parigi*, on our way back from London we passed through Paris **5.** (*durata*) **for:** — *oltre un anno*, for over a year; — *quanto tempo mi aspetti?*, (for) how long have you been waiting for me?; *lo conosco — due mesi*, I have known him (for) two months; *non scrivono — tre anni*, they haven't written for the last three years **6.** (*fin da, a partire da*) **since:** — *prima della guerra*, since before the war; *dal 1910*, since 1910; *è dalle otto che lavoriamo*, we have been working since eight o' clock; *sono già passati due mesi — quando egli partì*, it is already two months (o two months have already elapsed) since he left **7.** (*agente, causa efficiente*) **by:** *la città fu distrutta — un terremoto*, the town was destroyed by an earthquake; *questo fu scritto — Leopardi*, this was written by Leopardi **8.** (*causa*) **for; with:** *saltare dalla gioia*, to jump for joy; *tremare dal freddo*, to shiver with cold; *tremare dalla paura*, to tremble with fear **9.** (*uso, destinazione, attitudine, idoneità*): *camera — letto*, bedroom; *carta — lettere*, writing (o note)-paper; *costume — bagno*, bathing-suit; *fazzoletto — naso*, handkerchief; *ferro — stiro*, iron; *macchina — cucire*, sewing-machine; *punta — disegno*, drawing-pin; *spazzolino — denti*, tooth-brush **10.** (*qualità, prezzo, valore*): *un francobollo — venti lire*, a twenty-lire stamp; *un giovanotto dai capelli rossi e dal carattere difficile*, a red-haired young man with a bad temper; *una ragazza dai capelli biondi e dagli occhi verdi*, a fair-haired green-eyed girl **11.** (*con valore limitativo*) **in:** *cieco — un occhio*, blind in one eye; *zoppo — un piede*, lame in one foot **12.** (*come, a somiglianza di, a guisa di*) **like:** *comportarsi — eroe*, to behave like a hero; *vivere — principe*, to live like a prince **13.** (*nei complementi predicativi*): — *bambino era molto grasso*, when (he was) a child he was very fat **14.** (*con valore*

consecutivo): *non lo credo uomo — ciò*, I do not think him capable of that; *non saranno tanto sciocchi — rifiutare la nostra offerta*, they won't be so foolish as to refuse our offer **15.** (*seguito da inf. con senso di possibilità, necessità, convenienza*): *una commedia — ridere*, an amusing play; *dolore — morire*, agonizing pain; *stanze — affittare*, rooms to let; *ho molto — fare*, I have a lot to do; *non c'è un minuto — perdere*, there is not a moment to lose **16.** (*Fraseologia*): — *allora in poi*, ever since ‖ — *banda*, — *canto*, — *parte*, aside (o apart) ‖ — *basso*, downstairs ‖ — *burla*, as a joke; — *senno*, seriously ‖ — *capo*, (*di nuovo*) over again; (*dall'inizio*) from the beginning ‖ — *dentro*, from within; — *fuori*, from outside; — *lontano*, from afar ‖ — *oggi in poi*, from to-day on; *dalla nascita di Cristo in poi*, from the birth of Christ onwards ‖ — *Roma, 10 settembre*, (*nelle lettere*) Rome, 10th September ‖ *a giudicare dai fatti*, (*in base ai fatti*) to judge (o judging) from the facts ‖ *S. Antonio — Padova*, St. Anthony of Padua ‖ — *noi non usa fare questo*, we don't do this ‖ *mi vesto — Dior*, I go to Dior; *quella famosa diva si veste — Dior*, that famous star is dressed by Dior ‖ — *vicino*, close to: *non ho mai visto la Regina — vicino*, I have never seen the Queen close to ‖ *preso dal vero*, taken from life ‖ *fare — guida, — madre*, to act as a guide, as a mother.

dabbàsso, *av.* below, down below; (*al piano inferiore*) downstairs ‖ *ag.* below.

dabbenàggine, *s.f.* **1.** (*candore*) ingenuousness; simplemindedness **2.** (*credulità*) credulity.

dabbène, *ag.* good; honest, upright: *un uomo —*, an honest (o an upright) man ‖ *un dabben uomo*, (*iron.*) a simpleton.

dabbudà, *s.m.* (*mus.*) psaltery.

daccànto, *av.* **1.** (*da parte*) aside, apart **2.** (*vicino*) nearby, close to.

daccàpo, *av.* **1.** over again; (*ancora una volta*) once again; once more **2.** (*dall'inizio*) from the beginning ‖ *punto e —*, full stop, new (o fresh) line.

Dàcia, *no.pr.f.* (*geog. st.*) Dacia.

dacché, *cong.* since: — *ti conosco*, since I have known you.

dacriocistìte, *s.f.* (*patol.*) dacryocystitis.

dadaìsmo, *s.m.* (*art.*) dadaism.

dadaìsta, *s.c.* follower of dadaism.

daddolìno, *s.m.* wheedler.

dàddolo, *s.m.* mincing gesture; mincing manner; mincing behaviour: *far daddoli*, to mince.

daddolóne, *s.m.* affected mincing person.

dadeggiàre, *v.i.* (*rar.*) to (play with) dice.

dàdo, *s.m.* **1.** die (*pl.* dice): *i dadi furono la sua rovina*, dice were his downfall; *getta i dadi!*, throw (o cast) the dice!; *giocare a dadi*, to play dice ‖ *il — è tratto!*, the die is cast! ‖ *gettare il —*, *fig.* to try (o to chance) one's luck ‖ *scambiare i dadi in mano*, *fig.* to put the matter (o things) differently **2.** (*arch.*) dado (*pl.* dados), die (*pl.* dies) **3.** (*mec.*) (screw) nut; — *a colletto*, flanged nut; — *a corona*, castellated (o slotted) nut; — *cieco*, cap (o box) nut; — *del bullone*, stud nut; — *zigrinato*, knurled (o hand) nut; *incoppigliare un —*, to split-pin a nut **4.** (*cuc.*) cube (of concentrated soup), soup cube.

daffàre, *s.m.* work; task: — *quotidiano*, daily task (o grind) ‖ *aver —*, to be busy (o to have a lot to do):

che — *(avete)!*, how busy you are! || *darsi* —, to be on the go: *si dà* — *dalla mattina alla sera, ma non combina nulla*, she is on the go from morning to night, but never gets anything done.

dàfne, *s.f.* *(bot.)* daphne || **Dàfne**, *no.pr.f.* *(mit.)* Daphne.

Dàfni, *no.pr.m.* *(mit.)* Daphnis.

dàga, *s.f.* dagger.

dagherrotipía, *s.f.* *(foto.)* **1.** daguerreotypy **2.** *(dagherrotipo)* daguerreotype.

dagherròtipo, *s.m.* *(foto.)* daguerreotype.

dàgli, **dài**, *inter.* *(fam.)* *(forza!, continua!)* go on!; *(battilo!)* give it to him!, let him have it! || *e* —*!*, what again?, not again!.

dàimio, *s.m.* *(st. giapponese)* daimio *(pl.* daimios).

Dàlila, *no.pr.f.* *(Bibbia)* Delilah.

dàina, *s.f.* *(zool.)* doe.

dàino, *s.m.* *(zool.)* fallow-deer *(invariato al pl.)*; *(per indicare il maschio)* buck: *pelle di* —, buckskin.

Dàlai-Làma, *s.m.* Dalai-Lama.

dàlia, *s.f.* *(bot.)* dahlia.

dallàto, *av.* near; close to; by; near-by; at s.o.'s side.

dàlmata, *ag. s.c.* Dalmatian.

dalmàtica, *s.f.* *(eccl.)* dalmatic.

Dalmàzia, *no.pr.f.* *(geog.)* Dalmatia.

daltònico, *ag.* daltonian, red-blind, colour-blind.

daltonísmo, *s.m.* *(patol.)* Daltonism, red-blindness, colour-blindness.

d'altrónde, *av.* on the other hand, besides; *(altrimenti)* otherwise; *(in ogni modo)* in any case.

dàma, *s.f.* **1.** lady of rank: — *di Corte, d'onore*, lady-in-waiting; *gran* —, great lady; *fine lady* || — *di carità*, district visitor || — *di compagnia*, lady companion || — *di picche*, *(a carte)* queen of spades **2.** *(compagna di ballo)* partner **3.** *(arc.)* *(innamorata)* sweet-heart: *la* — *dei suoi pensieri*, his lady-love **4.** *(giuoco)* draughts *(pl.)*: *scacchiera per* —, draughtboard; *giocare a* —, to play draughts **5.** *(metal.)* *(di alto forno)* dam.

damàre, *v.t.* *(al giuoco della dama)* to crown: — *una pedina*, to crown a man.

damascàre, *v.t.* to damask.

damascàto, *ag.* damask *(attributivo)*: *seta damascata*, damask silk.

damascatúra, *s.f.* **1.** damasking **2.** *(metal.)* damaskeening, damascening.

damascèno, *ag.* damascene: *rosa damascena*, damask rose.

damaschína, *s.f.* *(sciabola di Damasco)* damask sword, Damascus sword.

damaschinàre, *v.t.* *(metal.)* to damaskeen, to damascene.

damaschíno, *ag.* damascene: *acciaio* —, damask *(o* Damascus) steel; *rosa damaschina*, damask rose.

Damàsco[1], *no.pr.f.* *(geog.)* Damascus.

damàsco[2], *s.m.* damask: *divano di* —, damask sofa.

dameríno, *s.m.* dandy, beau *(pl.* beaux), fop, coxcomb.

Damiàno, *no.pr.m.* Damian.

damière, *s.m.* draughtboard.

damigèlla, *s.f.* **1.** maid of honour **2.** *(signorina)* young lady.

damigèllo, *s.m.* *(arc.)* squire; page.

damigiàna, *s.f.* demijohn; *(ind. chim.)* carboy.

damísta, *s.c.* draughts player.

dàmma, *s.f.* *(zool.)* doe.

damméno, *ag.* worse: *egli non è* — *di te*, he is not worse than you.

dàmo, *s.m.* *(rar.)* lover; wooer; gallant.

Dàmocle, *no.pr.m.* *(st.)* Damocles || *la spada di* —, the sword of Damocles.

Damóne, *no.pr.m.* *(mit.)* Damon.

Dànae, *no.pr.f.* *(mit.)* Danae.

Danàidi, *no.pr.f.pl.* *(mit.)* Danaides.

Dànao, *no.pr.m.* *(mit.)* Danaus.

danàro, *V.* denàro.

danaróso, *ag.* moneyed, wealthy, rich.

dànde, *s.f. pl.* **1.** leading-strings *(anche fig.)* **2.** *fig.* support *(sing.)*.

danése, *ag.* Danish || *s.m.* **1.** *(abitante)* Dane || *i Danesi*, the Danes *(o* the Danish people) **2.** *(lingua)* (the) Danish (language): *capisci il* —*?*, do you understand Danish? **3.** *(cane)* Great Dane || *s.f.* Dane, Danish woman.

Danièle, *no.pr.m.* Daniel || *dim.* Dan, Danny.

Danimàrca, *no.pr.f.* *(geog.)* Denmark.

dannàre, *v.t.* to damn || *che Dio mi danni!*, damn! || *far* — *l'anima a qlcu.*, to drive s.o. to despair || *far* — *qlcu.*, *(fam.)* to drive s.o. mad *(o* crazy *o* to torment s.o.) || **dannàrsi**, *v.r.* **1.** to be damned, to go to hell: *ti dannerai*, you will be damned *(o* you will go to hell) **2.** *(affannarsi)* to strive hard: *mi sono dannato tutto il giorno su quella traduzione*, I have been toiling *(o* working hard) at that translation the whole day; *si dannò tutta la vita per ottenere una certa agiatezza, ma morì prima di raggiungerla*, all his life he strove for security, but he died before he achieved it.

dannàto, *ag.* **1.** damned || *il duca e la sua anima dannata*, the duke and his damned ruffian **2.** *(maledetto)* damned, confounded: *quel* — *affare*, that confounded business **3.** *(smisurato)* terrible, dreadful, fearful: *si prese una paura dannata*, he got a terrible fright || *s.m.* damned soul: *soffrire come un* —, to suffer the pains of hell; *urlare come un* —, to shriek like one of the damned || *i dannati*, the damned.

dannazióne, *s.f.* damnation: — *eterna*, eternal damnation; *andare in* —, to be damned || —*!*, damn! *(o* dash! *o* d—d it all!) || *questo allievo è la mia* —, this pupil drives me mad; *sarai la mia* —*!*, *(fam.)* you'll be the death of me!.

danneggiàbile, *ag.* damageable.

danneggiaménto, *s.m.* **1.** *(danno)* damage **2.** *(il danneggiare)* damaging.

danneggiàre, *v.t.* **1.** to damage; *(sciupare)* to spoil: *il gelo ha danneggiato tutti i vigneti*, all the vines have been damaged by the frost; *la grandine ha danneggiato il grano*, the hail has damaged the corn **2.** *(persone)* to damage, to injure; *(nuocere a)* to harm: *quella calunnia lo ha danneggiato molto*, that slander did *(o* caused) him a great deal of harm; *senza* — *nessuno*, without injuring any one *(o* without doing any one any harm) **3.** *(menomare)* to impair, to injure: *la sua vista fu danneggiata nell'incidente*, her sight was injured in the accident; *il troppo lavoro gli danneggiò la salute*, too much work ruined *(o* impaired) his health.

danneggiàto, *ag.* damaged, injured || *s.m.* *(dir.)* the injured party.

danneggiatóre, *s.m.*, **danneggiatríce**, *s.f.* injurer.

dànno, *s.m.* **1.** damage; *(derivante da perdita)* loss: — *diretto*, *(dir.)* immediate damage; *danni liquidati*, *non liquidati*, liquidated, unliquidated damages; — *rilevante*, heavy damage: *i danni causati dalla tempesta furono rilevanti*, the damage caused *(o* done) by the storm was very heavy; *domanda di danni*, claim for damages; *in caso di perdita o* —, *(comm.)* in case of loss or damage; *responsabilità dei danni*, *(dir.)* liability for damages; *il responsabile dei danni*, the wrongdoer; *quella campagna ha causato un* — *irreparabile alla nostra causa*, that campaign has done our cause irreparable damage; *accertare, constatare i danni*, to ascertain the damage; *avere diritto al risarcimento dei danni*, to be entitled to damages; *cagionare un* —, to cause *(o* to bring) damage; *citare qlcu. per danni*, *(dir.)* to sue s.o. for damages *(o* to bring an action for damages against s.o.); *condannare al risarcimento dei danni*, *(dir.)* to condemn to pay damages; *essere esposto a* —, to be liable to damage; *evitare un* —, to avoid damage; *pagare, risarcire i danni*, to pay damages *(o* for the damage); *patire, subire un* —, to suffer damage *(o* a loss); *preservarsi da un* —, to guard oneself against damage; *ricuperare i danni,* to recover damages; *riparare il* —, to repair (*o* to make *o*) the damage (*o* to make good the loss); *valutare i danni,* to estimate the damage (*o* the losses) **2.** (*a persona*) injury, harm: *nessun* — *alle persone,* no one was hurt (*o* there were no casualties); *causare, recare* — *a qlcu.,* to do s.o. harm (*o* an injury) ‖ *a mio* —, to my prejudice; (*a mie spese*) to my cost (*o* at my expense) ‖ *se non cedete, vostro* —*!,* if you don't give in, so much the worse for you!.

dannosaménte, *av.* harmfully, hurtfully.

dannóso, *ag.* harmful, hurtful, noxious, detrimental: — *alla salute,* detrimental to health; *alcune piante sono dannose anche agli uomini,* there are plants which are noxious even to man.

dannunziàno, *ag.* (*lett.*) of D'Annunzio; in D'Annunzio's style ‖ *s.m.* follower of D'Annunzio.

dannunzianísmo, *s.m.* (*lett.*) style of D'Annunzio; imitation of D'Annunzio.

dannunzieggiàre, *v.i.* (*lett.*) to imitate the style of D'Annunzio.

Dànte[1], *no.pr.m.* (*st. lett.*) Dante.

dànte[2], *s.m.*: *pelle di* —, buckskin.

danteggiàre, *v.i.* (*lett.*) to imitate the style of Dante.

dantescaménte, *av.* (*lett.*) in the style of Dante.

dantésco, *ag.* (*lett.*) Dantesque, Dantean: *stile* —, Dantesque style.

dantísta, *s.c.* Dantist, Dantean.

danubiàno, *ag.* Danubian.

Danúbio, *no.pr.m.* (*geog.*) Danube.

dànza, *s.f.* dance; (*il danzare*) dancing: — *macabra,* Dance of Death (*o* Dance Macabre); *scuola di* —, school of dancing; *scuola di* — *classica,* dance academy; *mi concede la prossima* —*?,* may I have the next dance with you?; *vi piace la* —*?,* do you like dancing?; *menar la* —, to lead the dance; *fig.* to head a plot.

danzànte, *ag.* dancing: *coppia* —, leading dancers; *tè* —, tea-dance; *trattenimento* —, dance; ball: *dare un trattenimento* —, to give a dance.

danzàre, *v.i.* to dance: *le foglie danzavano al vento,* the leaves were dancing in the wind; *gli inglesi danzano molto bene,* the English dance very well.

danzatóre, *s.m.,* **danzatríce,** *s.f.* dancer.

dàpe, *s.f.* (*rar.*) **1.** banquet **2.** spiritual food.

dapífero, *s.m.* (*rar.*) **1.** dapifer **2.** (*eccl.*) person serving meals during conclaves.

dappertútto, da per tútto, *av.* everywhere, on all sides: *l'ho cercato* —, I looked everywhere for him.

dappiè, dappièdi, *av.* at the foot; below: — *del colle,* at the foot of the hill.

dappiú, *ag.* **1.** (*migliore*) better **2.** (*più grande*) greater; (*più importante*) more important, of more account.

dappocàggine, *s.f.* ineptitude, worthlessness.

dappòco, *ag.* inept, worthless.

dappòi, *av.* afterwards, then, subsequently.

dappoiché, *cong.* **1.** (*dacchè*) since **2.** (*poichè*) as.

dapprèsso, *av.* near-by, close at hand.

dappríma, *av.* at first.

dapprincípio, *av.* at first; in the beginning; originally.

Dardanèlli, *no.pr.m. pl.* (*geog.*) Dardanelles.

dardeggiàre, *v.t.* to dart: *lo dardeggiai con uno sguardo irato,* I darted an angry look at him; *il sole dardeggiava la campagna,* the sun was blazing down on the countryside.

dàrdo, *s.m.* dart; arrow: *dardi d'amore, fig.* Cupid's darts.

dàre, *s.m.* (*comm.*) debit: — *e avere,* debit and credit; *il* — *del conto cassa,* cash debit: *colonna del* —, debit column; *dalla parte del* —, on the debit side; *lato del* —, debit side; *somma delle cifre inscritte in* —, debit amount; *totali del* —, debit footings; *portare a* — *di un conto,* to carry to the debit side of an account.

dàre, *v.t.* **1.** to give: *ciò dà l'idea che...,* it gives (*o* conveys) the idea that...; *dàgli del pane e burro,*

give him some bread and butter; *il fattorino glielo ha dato ieri sera,* the page gave it to him last night; *gliel'ho dato per il suo compleanno,* I gave it to him for his birthday; *gli ho dato la medicina,* I gave him his medicine; *mi diedero il primo premio,* they gave me the first prize; *non so cosa darei per sapere...,* I would give a lot to know...; *per il tuo libro ti dò mille lire,* I'll give you a (one) thousand lire for your book; *il suo lavoro non gli dà di che vivere,* his work doesn't bring him in enough to live on; *tutto quello che aveva lo diede ai poveri,* he gave all he had to the poor; — *a qlcu. motivo di...,* to give s.o. reason to...; — *a qlcu. ql.co. da custodire,* to give s.o. sthg. to look after (*o* to entrust s.o. with sthg.); — *il buon esempio,* to give (*o* to set) a good example; — *ql.co. da bere a qlcu.,* to give s.o. sthg. to drink; — *dei consigli,* to give advice; — *delle prove a qlcu.,* to furnish s.o. with proof; — *una festa,* to give a party; — *una figlia in matrimonio a qlcu.,* to give a daughter in marriage to s.o.; — *in affitto,* to rent (*o* to let); — *in prestito,* to lend; — *luogo, origine a ql.co.,* to give rise to (*o* to bring about) sthg.; — *la propria vita per qlcu.,* to give (*o* to sacrifice) one's life for s.o.; — *ql.co. per niente,* to give sthg. away; — *una rappresentazione teatrale,* to perform (*o* to put on) a play; — *una spazzolata al proprio cappello,* to give one's hat a brush ‖ — *a bere a qlcu. che...,* to give s.o. to believe that... ‖ — *ad intendere che...,* to give to understand that... ‖ — *a pensare,* to give (*o* to provide) food for thought ‖ — *atto di ql.co.,* to acknowledge sthg.: *vi do atto della fattiva vostra collaborazione,* I acknowledge your valuable contribution ‖ — *il benvenuto a qlcu.,* to welcome s.o. ‖ — *il buongiorno a qlcu.,* to wish s.o. good morning (*o* to say good morning to s.o.) ‖ — *le carte,* to deal (cards) ‖ — *del ladro a qlcu.,* to call s.o. a thief ‖ — *del tu a qlcu.,* to address s.o. as "tu" ‖ — *un esame,* to take (*o* to sit for) an examination ‖ — *fondo all'ancora,* (*mar.*) to drop (*o* to let go the) anchor ‖ — *fuoco a ql.co.,* to set fire to sthg. ‖ — *una mano di bianco,* to put on a coat of white (paint) ‖ — *torto a qlcu.,* to blame s.o. ‖ *darle a qlcu.,* (*picchiarlo*) to give s.o. a thrashing (*o* to dust s.o.'s jacket) ‖ *chi dà e ritoglie, il diavolo lo raccoglie, prov.* give a thing and take a thing is the devil's gold ring ‖ *chi dà presto dà due volte, prov.* he that gives quickly gives twice ‖ *non sa donare chi tarda a* —, *prov.* slow help is no help ‖ — *un ago per avere un palo, prov.* to throw a sprat to catch a mackerel (*o* to bring a bit of wire and take away a bar) **2.** (*produrre*) **to yield, to produce:** *un albero che dà dei frutti,* a tree that yields (*o* bears) fruit; *qui la terra dà raccolti magri,* here the land yields poor crops **3.** (*concedere*) **to grant, to give:** *gli fu dato il permesso di uscire,* he was granted (*o* given) permission to go out **4.** (*attribuire*): *gli darei vent'anni,* I'd take him for (*o* to be) twenty (*o* I'd put him down as twenty); *non gli si dà la sua età,* he doesn't look his age ‖ *v.i.* **1.** (*colpire*) **to hit** (anche *fig.*): *gli diede sulla testa con un bastone,* he hit him on the head with a stick; — *nel segno,* to hit the bull's-eye; *fig.* to hit the nail on the head **2.** (*urtare*) **to bump;** (*inciampare*) **to stumble:** *diede con la testa in una trave,* he bumped his head on a beam; — *in un sasso,* to stumble against a stone **3.** (*di casa, porta, ecc.*) **to look on to** (sthg.), **to open on** (sthg.); **to lead into** (sthg.): *la porta dava sul cortile,* the door led into the courtyard; *le vostre finestre dànno sulla piazza,* your windows look on to (*o'* open 'on *o* overlook) the square **4.** (**Fraseologia**): *può darsi,* maybe (*o* perhaps *o* probably): *può darsi che egli arrivi prima di me,* he may arrive before me ‖ *si dà il caso che venga domani,* he happens to be arriving to-morrow ‖ — *alla testa,* to go to one's head: *l'adulazione gli diede alla testa,* flattery went to (*o* turned) his head; *il vino mi dà alla testa,* wine goes to my head ‖ — *di piglio a ql.co.,* to seize (*o* to catch hold of) sthg. ‖ — *in pianto, in riso,* to burst out crying, laughing ‖ — *in secco*, (*mar.*) to run ashore (*o* aground) ‖ — *nell'occhio*, to attract attention (*o* to strike the eye *o* to stand out) ‖ — *sui nervi a qlcu.*, to get (*o* to jar) on s.o.'s nerves (*o* to get s.o.'s goat) ‖ **dàrsi**, *v.r.* **1.** (*dedicarsi*) **to devote oneself:** — *al commercio*, to go into business; — *allo studio*, to devote oneself to study ‖ — *al bere*, to take to drink (ing); — *al giuoco*, to take to gambling **2.** (**Fraseologia**): — *ammalato*, to pretend to be ill ‖ — *da fare*, to take pains (*o* to busy oneself); (*affaccendarsi*) to bustle about: *valeva la pena di* — *tanto da fare?*, was it worth all the fuss? ‖ — *delle arie*, to give oneself airs ‖ — *per vinto*, to give in (*o* to give up *o* to throw up the sponge) ‖ — *prigioniero*, to give oneself up (*o* to surrender) ‖ *darsela a gambe*, to take to one's heels (*o* to run away) ‖ *non darsela per inteso*, to turn a deaf ear (*o* not to take any notice).

Dàrio, *no.pr.m.* (*st.*) Darius.

dàrsena, *s.f.* wet dock; basin.

darsonvalizzazióne, *s.f.* (*med.*) D'Arsonvalization.

dàrtro, *s.m.* (*patol.*) dartre, herpes.

darviniàno, darwiniàno, *ag.* Darwinian, Darwinist.

darvinísmo, darwinísmo, *s.m.* Darwinism.

darvinísta, darwinísta, *s.c.* Darwinian, Darwinist.

dasímetro, *s.m.* (*fis.*) dasymeter.

dasíte, *s.f.* (*med.*) hypertrichiasis, hypertricosis.

dassài, d'assài, *ag.* (*rar.*) capable, clever; (*valoroso*) brave ‖ *av.* (*rar.*) **1.** (*a sufficienza*) sufficiently **2.** much; (*con ag.*) very; (*con comp.*) (by) far.

dàta[1], *s.f.* date: — *del timbro postale*, date of post-mark; — *di emissione*, date of issue; — *di nascita*, date of birth; — *di scadenza*, (*comm.*) date of maturity (*o* due date); *la* — *sulla cambiale*, (*comm.*) the date on the face of the bill; *la* — *del documento*, (*dir.*) the date on the instrument ‖ *cambiale a* — *fissa*, (*comm.*) date bill; *cambiale a dieci giorni* —, (*comm.*) bill at ten days after date; *cambiale con la* — *in bianco*, (*comm.*) blank dated bill; *in* — *d'oggi*, under to-day's date (*o* under this day's date); *lettera senza* —, undated (*o* dateless) letter; *confermiamo la nostra in* — *di ieri*, (*comm.*) we confirm our letter of yesterday; *a decorrere da questa* —, beginning from this date; *anticipare la* —, to advance the date; *apporre la* —, to add the date; *disporre in ordine di* —, to arrange by date (*o* to keep according to dates) ‖ *amicizia di vecchia* —, old friendship.

dàta[2], *s.f.* **1.** (*patronato, beneficio ecclesiastico*) patronage; benefice, church living appointment **2.** (*carte*) (*distribuzione*) deal **3.** (*natura, tenore*) kind, character; tenor: *disse parole di questa* —, he said words of this tenor.

datàbile, *ag.* datable.

datàre, *v.t.* to date: *la lettera è stata datata da Londra il 24 maggio*, the letter is dated from London, May 24th; *non dimenticare di* — *le tue lettere*, don't forget to date your letters; — *un manoscritto*, to date a manuscript ‖ *v.i.* **1.** to date: *la loro attività commerciale datava dal 1930 circa*, their business activity dated from the thirties; *quella chiesa data dal decimo secolo*, that church dates back to the tenth century ‖ *a* — *da*, beginning (*o* counting) from: *a* — *dal 7 marzo*, beginning (*o* counting) from March 7th.

dataría, *s.f.* (*eccl.*) datary.

datariàto, *s.m.* (*eccl.*) datary.

datàrio, *s.m.* (*eccl.*) datary.

datería, *s.f.* (*eccl.*) datary.

datívo, *ag. s.m.* (*gram.*) dative: (*caso*) —, dative case (*o* dative).

dàto, *ag.* **1.** given; (*stabilito*) stated, appointed: *entro un* — *periodo*, within a given time **2.** (*dedito*) addicted: — *al bere*, addicted to drink ‖ **dàto che**, *cong.* since, as: — *che non puoi venire, verrò io da te*, since (*o* as) you cannot come, I will come to you ‖ — *e non concesso che...*, supposing (that), even if: *e non concesso che tu riesca ad ottenere quel posto...*,

supposing (that) you succeed in getting that job....

dàto, *s.m.* datum (*pl.* data): *i dati d'un problema*, the data of a problem; — *di fatto*, fact; *dati sperimentali*, experimental data; *dati statistici esaurienti*, satisfactory statistical information; *ho raccolto tutti i dati*, I have collected all the data ‖ *controllare l'accuratezza dei dati*, to control (*o* to gauge) the accuracy of data; *fare lo spoglio dei dati statistici*, to simplify statistical items.

datóre, *s.m.*, **datríce**, *s.f.* giver, donor: — *di lavoro*, (*dir.*) employer.

dàttero, *s.m.* **1.** (*albero*) date-palm **2.** (*frutto*) date **3.** — *di mare*, (*zool.*) razor-clam.

dattílico, *ag.* (*poes.*) dactylic: *versi dattilici*, dactylic verses.

dàttilo, *s.m.* (*poes.*) dactyl.

dattilògrafa, *s.f.* typist.

dattilografàre, *v.t.* to typewrite, to type.

dattilografía, *s.f.* typewriting.

dattilogràfico, *ag.* typewriting (*attributivo*).

dattilògrafo, *s.m.* typist.

dattilología, *s.f.* dactylology, deaf-and-dumb language.

dattiloscopía, *s.f.* dactyloscopy.

dattiloscritto, *ag.* typewritten, typed: *lettera dattiloscritta*, typed letter ‖ *s.m.* typescript.

dattilòttero, *s.m.* (*ittiol.*) dactylopterus.

dattórno, da tórno, d'attórno, *av.* (**a**)**round, about:** *i suoi bambini gli stavano* —, his children were around him ‖ *levarsi* —, to get away: *levati* —!, get away! (*o* off with you!); *levarsi* — *qlcu.*, to get rid of s.o.: *mi leverò* — *quella pettegola!*, I'll get rid of that gossip!.

datúra, *s.f.* (*bot.*) datura.

davànti, *prep.* **1.** (*dinanzi*) **before:** — *a Dio*, before God; *essi furono portati* — *al giudice*, they were brought before the judge ‖ — *al pericolo, alla morte*, in the presence of danger, of death **2.** (*innanzi*) **in front of:** *la banda marciava* — *ai soldati*, the band was marching in front of the soldiers **3.** (*di fronte*) **in front of, opposite:** — *al teatro*, in front of the theatre; — *alla chiesa vi è la mia casa*, my house is opposite the church ‖ *av.* **1.** before: — *e dietro*, before and behind ‖ *levati* —!, get out of the way! (*o* go away!) **2.** (*in luogo anteriore*) **in front:** *solo le persone che stavano* — *videro la processione*, only the people who were standing in front saw the procession ‖ *ag.* fore, front (*attributivi*): *i denti* —, the front teeth; *le zampe* —, the fore paws ‖ *s.m.* front: *il* — *del palazzo*, the front of the building.

davantíno, *s.m.* jabot, ruffle.

davanzàle, *s.m.* window-sill.

davànzo, d'avànzo, *V.* avànzo 3.

Dàvide, *no.pr.m.* David ‖ *dim.* Davy, Dave, Davie.

davvéro, *av.* really, indeed: *fu* — *contento alla notizia*, he was very pleased indeed at the news; *sei* — *gentile ad aiutarmi!*, it is very kind of you indeed to help me!; *sono* — *simpatici!*, they are really nice! (*o* they are very nice indeed!); « *Verremo in Inghilterra l'anno venturo* », « — ? », "We are coming to England next year", "Oh, indeed?"; *vi scriverà* — ?, will he really write to you? ‖ *dire* —, to be in earnest, to speak in earnest: *dici* — ?, are you in earnest? (*o* do you really mean what you say?).

daziàbile, *ag.* dutiable, liable to duty.

daziàre, *v.t.* to lay a duty on (sthg.); to levy a duty on (sthg.): — *un articolo*, to lay a duty on an article.

daziàrio, *ag.* toll (*attributivo*): *barriera daziaria*, toll-bar, toll-gate; *casello* —, toll-house; *cinta daziaria*, toll-gates (*pl.*).

dazière, *s.m.* exciseman (*pl.* excisemen); (*doganiere*) customs officer.

dàzio, *s.m.* **1.** toll; duty: — *di consumo, interno*, excise duty; — *doganale*, customs duty; — *d'entrata, d'importazione*, import duty (*o* duty on importation);

— *d'uscita*, *d'esportazione*, export duty (*o* duty on exportation) ‖ *franco di* —, duty free (*o* duty paid); *schiavo di* —, *soggetto a* —, liable to duty (*o* dutiable) ‖ *abolire un* —, to abrogate (*o* to drop) a duty; *pagare il* — *per ql.co.*, to pay the duty on sthg. 2. (*ufficio daziario*) toll-house.

dèa, *s.f.* goddess: *la* — *dell'amore*, the goddess of love; *la* — *della guerra*, the goddess of war; *la* — *delle messi*, the goddess of corn; *la* — *della sapienza*, the goddess of wisdom.

deambulàre, *v.i.* to walk about; to stroll about.

deambulazióne, *s.f.* deambulation, strolling about, stroll.

debbiàre, *v.t.*: — *i campi*, (*agr.*) to burn the stubble in the fields.

débbio, *s.m.* (*agr.*) 1. burning of stubble (for purpose of manuring) 2. ground fertilized by burning the stubble.

debellàre, *v.t.* 1. (*sconfiggere*) to defeat, to conquer; (*abbattere*) to overthrow 2. *fig.* to overcome, to subdue; to wipe out: — *una malattia*, to wipe out a disease.

debellatóre, *ag.* conquering ‖ *s.m.*, **debellatríce**, *s.f.* overthrower, conqueror, subduer.

debellazióne, *s.f.* defeat, overthrow, conquest.

débile, *ag.* (*rar.*) weak, feeble; frail; (*arc.*) debile.

debilità, *s.m.* debility; weakness, feebleness, frailness.

debilitaménto, *s.m.* enfeeblement.

debilitànte, *ag.* weakening; debilitating, enfeebling: *clima* —, debilitating climate; *rimedio* —, (*farm.*) debilitant.

debilitàre, *v.t.* to weaken, to debilitate, to enfeeble.

debilitazióne, *s.f.* debilitation, enfeebling, weakening.

debitaménte, *av.* duly, properly, regularly, rightly: — *legalizzato*, duly legalized; — *registrato*, duly registered; — *sottoscritto per ricevuta*, duly receipted.

débito, *ag.* due, proper: *a tempo* —, in due (*o* proper) time; *con il* — *riguardo*, with due regard; *nel modo* —, in the right way; *rilasciare debita ricevuta*, (*comm.*) to deliver due receipt; *scegliere il tempo* — *per fare ql.co.*, to choose the proper time to do sthg. ‖ *s.m.* 1. debt: *debiti chirografari*, (*comm.*) book-debts; — *d'onore*, debt of honour; — *di lieve entità*, trifling debt; — *ipotecario*, (*comm.*) mortgage debt; — *privilegiato*, preferential (*o* secured) debt; — *pubblico*, National Debt: *il libro del* — *pubblico*, the registry of stocks; *incapacità a pagare un* —, inability to pay a debt; *nota di* —, debit note; *riconoscimento di* —, acknowledgement of debt ‖ *addossarsi un* —, to take a debt upon oneself; *condonare un* —, to remit a debt; *contrarre un* —, to incur (*o* to contract) a debt; *essere in* — *verso qlcu.*, to be in debt to s.o.; *fig.* to be indebted to s.o.; *essere pieno di debiti*, to be deeply in debt (*o* to be up to one's ears in debt); *fare debiti*, to run (*o* to get) into debt; *ingolfarsi nei debiti*, to run heavily into debt; *provare un* —, to evidence (*o* to bring evidence of) a debt; *segnare una somma a* — *di qlcu.*, to debit s.o. with an amount; *soddisfare un* —, to discharge a debt ‖ *pagare il* — *alla natura*, *fig.* to die ‖ *cento libbre di pensieri non pagano un'oncia di* —, *prov.* a pound of care will not pay an ounce of debt ‖ *meglio andare a letto senza cena*, *che alzarsi con debiti*, *prov.* better go to bed supperless than rise in debt 2. (*dovere*, *obbligo*) duty: *mi faccio un* — *di avvertirvi*, I consider it my duty to warn you; *farsene un* — *di coscienza*, to consider it a moral duty.

debitóre, *s.m.*, **debitríce**, *s.f.* debtor: *vi sono* — *di molto denaro*, *della vita*, I owe you much money, my life.

débole, *ag.* weak, feeble; faint: *un* — *tentativo*, a feeble attempt; *caffè* —, weak coffee; *luce* —, faint light; *memoria* —, feeble memory; *polso* —, feeble pulse; *i punti deboli di una fortificazione*, the weak spots

of a fortification; *udito* —, weak hearing; *vista* —, weak sight; *Giovanni è* — *in matematica*, John is weak in mathematics; *la sua difesa fu piuttosto* —, his defence was rather weak; *udimmo deboli suoni in lontananza*, we heard faint sounds in the distance; *essere* — *di gambe*, to be weak in the legs; *essere troppo* — *per camminare*, to be too weak to walk ‖ *il sesso* —, *fig.* the weaker sex ‖ *s.m.* 1. weak person 2. (*punto debole*) weak point: *il fiume ruppe gli argini nel* —, the river broke its banks at the weakest point 3. *fig.* (*preferenza*) weakness, weak point, foible, partiality: *ho un* — *per i gelati*, *per i romanzi gialli*, I have a weakness for ice-creams, for detective stories; *ho un* — *per i mobili Chippendale*, I have a partiality for (*o* to) Chippendale furniture; *avere un* — *per qlcu.*, to have a partiality (*o* liking) for s.o.

debolézza, *s.f.* 1. weakness, feebleness, debility: — *di vista*, weak sight 2. *fig.* weakness, weak point, foible: *le debolezze umane*, human failings (*o* weaknesses); *la sua fondamentale* — *è l'amore per la bottiglia*, his chief weakness is a fondness for the bottle.

debolménte, *av.* weakly, feebly; faintly: *sorridere* —, to smile faintly.

Dèbora, *no.pr.f.* Deborah ‖ *dim.* Debby.

debòscia, *s.f.* debauch, debauchery.

debosciàto, *ag.* debauched ‖ *s.m.* debauchee.

debraiàre, *v.i.* (*aut.*) to declutch, to let out the clutch.

debuttànte, *s.m.* novice ‖ *s.f.* (*ragazza che entra per la prima volta in società*) debutante; (*fam.*) deb.

debuttàre, *v.i.* 1. to make one's debut 2. (*di ragazza in società*) to come out.

debútto, *s.m.* 1. debut 2. (*di ragazza in società*) coming out.

dèca, *s.f.* decad(e): *la prima* — *di Livio*, the first decad(e) of Livy.

dècade, *s.f.* (*dieci giorni*) ten days, decade; (*dieci anni*) decad(e), ten years: *nella prima* — *del mese*, in the first ten days of the month.

decadènte, *ag.* 1. decaying (*attributivo*); declining (*attributivo*); in decay (*predicativo*) 2. (*lett.*) decadent: *la morbosità è una caratteristica della poesia* —, morbidity is a characteristic of decadent poetry ‖ *s.m.* (*lett.*) decadent: *quello scrittore è un* —, that writer is a decadent.

decadentísmo, *s.m.* (*lett.*) school of decadent poets; style of decadent poets.

decadènza, *s.f.* 1. decay, decline: *è un attore in* —, he is an actor in decline; *molte furono le cause che portarono alla* — *l'Impero Romano*, many were the causes which brought about the decline of the Roman Empire 2. (*lett.*) decadence 3. (*dir.*) forfeiture, loss: *la* — *di un diritto*, the forfeiture of a right.

decadére, *v.i.* 1. to decay, to decline; (*socialmente*) to come down: *la potenza di quel paese a poco a poco decadde*, the power of that country slowly declined 2. — *da un diritto*, to lose (the exercise of) a right (*o* to forfeit a right).

decadiménto, *s.m.* decay, decline.

decadúto, *ag.* impoverished; (*deposto*) dethroned: *nobili decaduti*, impoverished aristocrats; *sovrano* —, dethroned sovereign.

decaèdro, *s.m.* (*geom.*) decahedron.

decagonàle, *ag.* (*geom.*) decagonal.

decàgono, *s.m.* (*geom.*) decagon.

decagràmma, **decagràmmo**, *s.m.* decagram(me) (*misura di peso* = 0.352 oz.).

decalcàre, *v.t.* to transfer.

decalcificazióne, *s.f.* (*med.*) decalcification.

decàlco, *s.m.* 1. (*atto*) transferring 2. (*effetto*) transfer.

decalcomanía, *s.f.* transfer, decalcomania; (*amer.*) decal.

decàlitro, *s.m.* decalitre; (*amer.*) decaliter (*misura di capacità* = 610.25 cu. in.).

decàlogo, *s.m.* decalogue.

decameróne, *s.m.* (*lett.*) Decameron.

decàmetro, *s.m.* decametre; (*amer.*) decameter (*misura di lunghezza* = 32.80 ft.).

decampàre, *v.i.* **1.** (*levare il campo*) to decamp **2.** *fig.* (*rinunziare*) to recede: *non decamperemo dai nostri principi*, we shall stick to our principles.

decanàto, *s.m.* deanery.

decàno, *s.m.* **1.** doyen, senior member, dean: *il — degli ambasciatori*, the doyen of the ambassadors (*o* the senior ambassador); *il — della facoltà*, the dean (*o* president) of the faculty **2.** (*eccl.*) dean.

decantàre[1], *v.t.* to extol, to exalt; to praise: *decantavano la sua bellezza*, they extolled her beauty; — *i meriti di qlcu.*, to extol s.o.'s merits.

decantàre[2], *v.t.* (*chim.*) to decant.

decantatóre, *s.m.*, **decantatríce**, *s.f.* (*rar.*) extoller; praiser.

decantazióne, *s.f.* (*chim.*) decantation; (*ind.*) racking.

decapitaménto, *s.f.* beheading, decapitation.

decapitàre, *v.t.* to behead, to decapitate: *fu decapitato*, he was beheaded.

decapitazióne, *s.f.* beheading, decapitation.

decàpodi, *s.m. pl.* (*zool.*) Decapoda.

decapotàbile, *ag.* convertible.

decarburàre, *v.t.* (*chim.*) to decarbonize, to decarburize.

decarburazióne, *s.f.* (*chim.*) decarbonization, decarbonizing, decarburization, decarburizing, decarburation.

decasíllabo, *ag.* (*poes.*) decasyllabic ‖ *s.m.* (*poes.*) decasyllable.

decàstilo, *ag.* (*arch.*) decastyle.

decatissàggio, *s.m.* (*ind. tessile*) decatizing: — *a secco*, dry-steam decatizing; — *a umido*, hot-water decatizing.

decatizzàre, *v.t.* (*ind. tessile*) to decatize.

decatizzatríce, *s.f.* (*mec.*) decatizer: — *a secco*, dry-steam decatizer (*o* machine).

decàtlon, *s.m.* (*spor.*) decathlon.

decèdere, *v.i.* (*rar.*) to die, to decease: *è deceduto ieri*, he died yesterday.

deceduto, *ag.* dead, deceased ‖ *i deceduti*, the dead, the deceased.

deceleràre, *v.t.* (*mec.*) to throttle down, to decelerate.

decelerazióne, *s.f.* (*mec.*) deceleration.

decèmbre, *s.m.* (*arc.*) December.

decemviràle, *ag.* (*st. romana*) decemviral.

decemviràto, *s.m.* (*st. romana*) decemvirate.

decèmviro, *s.m.* (*st. romana*) decemvir (*pl.* decemviri, decemvirs).

decennàle, *ag.* decennial, decennary ‖ *s.m.* decennary; decennium (*pl.* decennia); (*amer.*) decennial.

decènne, *ag.* **1.** ten years old (*predicativo*); ten-year-old (*attributivo*): *fanciullo —*, ten-year-old boy **2.** (*della durata di dieci anni*) lasting ten years; ten-year (*attributivo*): *il — assedio*, the ten-year siege.

decènnio, *s.m.* decennium (*pl.* decennia); decade; ten-year period.

decènte, *ag.* decent, proper, decorous; (*conveniente*) seemly: *condotta —,* decorous conduct; *parole decenti*, proper words; *prezzo —*, proper price; *il cibo qui è abbastanza —*, (*fam.*) the food is decent enough here; *non è — che tu vada sola*, it is not seemly that you should go alone.

decenteménte, *av.* decently, properly, decorously.

decentraménto, *s.m.* decentralization: — *amministrativo*, administrative decentralization.

decentràre, *v.t.* to decentralize.

decènza, *s.f.* decency, propriety, decorum; (*convenienza*) seemliness ‖ *gabinetto di —*, lavatory.

decèsso, *s.m.* death, decease: *atto di —*, (*dir.*) death certificate.

decibèl, *s.m.* (*rad.*) decibel.

decídere, *v.t.* to decide, to determine, to resolve, to settle: *che cosa ti decise ad agire?*, what decided (*o* resolved *o* brought) you to act?; *decisi di partire subito*, I determined (*o* resolved *o* decided) to start at once; *non ho ancora deciso dove andare*, I have not yet decided where I shall go; *quell'avvenimento decise la sua carriera*, that event determined (*o* decided) his career; *questo decide la questione*, this decides (*o* settles) the matter; *si decise di attendere la sua risposta*, it was decided to await his reply ‖ — *di fare ql.co.*, to decide to do (*o* on doing) sthg. (*o* to determine to do sthg. *o* to resolve to do sthg. *o* to settle to do sthg.); — *di non fare ql.co.*, to decide not to do (*o* to decide against doing) sthg.; — *la guerra, lo sciopero*, to decide on war, on a strike; — *una questione una volta per sempre*, to settle a question once for all ‖ **decídersi**, *v.r.* to make up one's mind: *decidetevi dunque!*, make up your minds, do!; *non so decidermi a licenziarlo*, I cannot bring myself to dismiss him (*o* I have not the heart to dismiss him).

decídua, *s.f.* (*med.*) decidua.

decíduo, *ag.* **1.** (*bot.*) deciduous: *albero —*, deciduous tree; *foglia —*, deciduous leaf **2.** *stella decidua*, (*astr.*) shooting star.

decifràbile, *ag.* decipherable: *la sua calligrafia è poco —*, his handwriting is difficult to decipher.

deciframénto, *s.m.* deciphering.

decifràre, *v.t.* **1.** to decipher; (*fam.*) to make out: *sai — questa calligrafia?*, can you make out this handwriting? **2.** (*lettera, telegramma cifrato*) to decode, to decipher.

decigràmmo, *s.m.* decigram(me) (*misura di peso* = 1.543 gr.).

decilitro, *s.m.* decilitre; (*amer.*) deciliter (*misura di capacità* = 6.102 cu. in.).

dècima, *s.f.* (*st.*) tithe; tenth part: — *in natura*, tithe in kind.

decimàle, *ag.* decimal: *sistema metrico —*, decimal system ‖ *s.m.* decimal: *ridurre in decimali*, to reduce to decimals.

decimàre, *v.t.* to decimate: *l'inondazione decimò la popolazione*, the flood decimated the population.

decimazióne, *s.f.* decimation.

decímetro, *s.m.* decimetre; (*amer.*) decimeter (*misura di lunghezza* = 3.937 in.).

dècimo, *ag. num. ord. s.* tenth: *un — di ciò che hai*, one tenth (*o* the tenth part) of what you have.

decimoprímo, *ag. num. ord.* eleventh.

decimosecóndo, *ag. num. ord.* twelfth.

decína, *s.f.* **1.** (*dieci*) ten, half-a-score: *a decine*, by tens; *dammene una —*, (*esattamente*) give me ten (*o* half-a-score) **2.** (*circa dieci*) about ten: *te lo dissi una — di volte*, I told you about ten times.

Dècio, *no.pr.m.* (*st.*) Decius.

decisaménte, *av.* **1.** decidedly; definitely; undoubtedly: *ora mio padre sta — meglio*, now my father is decidedly better **2.** (*risolutamente*) resolutely: *affrontò — la folla*, he faced the mob resolutely.

decisióne, *s.f.* **1.** decision: *pervenire, giungere a una —*, to come to a decision (*o* to arrive at a decision); *prendere una —*, to make up one's mind (*o* to take a decision); (*di assemblee votanti*) to pass a resolution **2.** (*risolutezza*) resolution, decision: *un uomo pieno di —*, a man of decision **3.** (*dir.*) decision (of the Court).

decisamente, *av.* decisively; conclusively; finally.

decisívo, *ag.* decisive; conclusive: *battaglia decisiva*, decisive battle; *momento —*, (*critico*) critical (*o* crucial) moment; *risposta decisiva*, conclusive answer; *voto —*, casting-vote.

deciso, *ag.* **1.** decided; resolute; firm: *erano decisi a tutto*, they were ready for anything; *sono ben —*, I am quite decided **2.** (*definito*) decided, definite, clear; determined, resolved: *la questione era decisa*, the question was settled.

decisòrio, *ag.* decisive: *giuramento —*, (*dir.*) suppletory oath.

declamàre, *v.t.* to declaim, to recite: — *una poesia,* to declaim a poem ‖ *v.i.* 1. to declaim; to speak rhetorically 2. (*inveire*) to declaim: — *contro qlcu.,* to declaim against s.o.

declamàto, *ag.* declaimed, recited ‖ *s.m.* (*teat.*) recitative.

declamatóre, *s.m.,* **declamatríce,** *s.f.* declaimer; (*rar.*) declaimant; reciter.

declamatoriaménte, *av.* declamatorily.

declamatòrio, *ag.* 1. declamatory 2. (*retorico*) declamatory, rhetorical, bombastic, inflated: *discorso* —, ranting speech; *stile* —, high-flown style; *tono* —, bombastic tone.

declamazióne, *s.f.* 1. declamation 2. (*discorso*) declamation; rhetorical speech.

declaratòria, *s.f.* (*dir.*) declaratory judgement.

declaratòrio, *ag.* (*dir.*) declaratory.

declassàre, *v.t.* to degrade; (*amer.*) to declass.

declassàto, *ag.* déclassé, declassed.

declinàbile, *ag.* (*gram.*) declinable.

declinànte, *ag.* declining.

declinàre, *v.t.* 1. (*gram.*) to decline, to inflect: — *un nome,* to inflect (*o* to decline) a noun 2. (*rifiutare*) to decline, to refuse: — *un invito,* to decline an invitation; — *un'offerta, una proposta,* to decline an offer 3. — *le proprie generalità,* to say (*o* to state) one's name and surname ‖ *v.i.* 1. (*del sole*) to set; (*della vita*) to decline: *il sole declina,* the sun is setting; *la sua vita declina,* his life is on the decline 2. (*degradare*) to slope down: *la collina declina dolcemente,* the hill slopes gently down 3. (*venir meno*) to decline, to wane: *le sue forze stanno declinando,* his strength is declining (*o* waning) 4. (*deviare*) to deviate: — *dalla virtù,* to deviate from the right path 5. (*fis.*) to deviate.

declinatóre, *s.m.* (*astr.*) declinator.

declinazióne, *s.f.* 1. (*declino*) decline, decrease 2. (*pendenza, declivio*) declivity, slope 3. (*astr. fis.*) declination: — *magnetica,* magnetic declination (*o* variation); — *nord,* northing; — *sud,* southing; *angolo di* —, declination angle 4. (*gram.*) declension, inflexion.

declíno, *s.m.* decline, decrease: *l'Impero romano era già in* —, the Roman Empire was already in decline; *il sole è in* —, the sun is declining (*o* setting).

declinòmetro, *s.m.* declinometer.

declíve, *ag.* declivous, declining; sloping.

declivio, *s.m.* declivity: slope: — *dolce, rìpido,* slight, steep slope; *angolo di* — *naturale,* (*ing. civile*) angle of repose (*o* rest); *strada in* —, street on the slope.

declività, *s.f.* declivity; slope.

declívo, *ag.* declivous, declining; sloping.

decollàggio, *s.m.* (*aer.*) take-off.

decollàre[1], *v.i.* (*aer.*) to take-off.

decollàre[2], *v.t.* (*decapitare*) to decapitate, to behead.

decollazióne, *s.f.* decapitation, beheading, decollation ‖ *la* — *di S. Giovanni Battista,* the Decollation of St. John the Baptist.

decòllo, *s.m.* (*aer.*) take-off: *distanza minima occorrente per il* —, take-off distance (*o* run); *pista di* —, take-off runway; *potenza di* —, take-off power.

decolo!ɔnte, *ag.* (*chim.*) decoloring, decolo(u)rizing, bleaching ‖ *s.m.* (*chim.*) decolorant, bleach.

decoloràre, *v.t.* to decolorate, to decolo(u)rize, to bleach.

decolorazióne, *s.f.* decoloration, decolo(u)rization, bleaching: — *dei capelli,* hair bleaching; — *del cotone,* cotton bleaching.

decomponíbile, *ag.* decomposable.

decomponibilità, *s.f.* decomposability.

decompórre, *v.t.* 1. (*chim.*) to decompose 2. (*disgregare, scomporre*) to dissolve, to decompose, to separate: — *un numero in fattori primi,* (*mat.*) to find the prime factors of a number ‖ **decompórsi,** *v.r.* 1. (*chim.*) to decompose 2. (*putrefarsi*) to decompose, to rot, to decay, to putrefy, to go bad: *il cadavere si decompose rapidamente,* the corpse (*o* body) decomposed quickly.

decomposizióne, *s.f.* 1. decomposition 2. (*putrefazione*) putrefaction.

decompósto, *ag.* 1. decomposed (anche *chim.*) 2. (*putrefatto*) decomposed, putrefied, rotten.

decoràre, *v.t.* 1. to decorate, to adorn: *la casa era decorata di fiori,* the house was decorated with flowers; — *a stucco,* to stucco; — *con modanature,* (*arch.*) to mould 2. (*insignire di decorazione*) to decorate, to award a medal to (s.o.): *fu decorato al valore,* he was decorated for bravery; *fu decorato di medaglia d'oro,* he was awarded a gold medal.

decoratívo, *ag.* decorative: *arti decorative,* decorative arts; *disegno* —, decorative drawing.

decoràto, *ag.* 1. decorated, adorned; (*con mosaico a scacchiera*) tessellated: *questo libro ha una copertina molto decorata,* this book has a highly decorated cover 2. (*insignito di decorazione*) decorated ‖ *s.m.* holder of decoration: *i decorati di guerra,* the holders of war decorations.

decoratóre, *s.m.,* **decoratríce,** *s.f.* 1. decorator 2. (*tappezziere*) paper-hanger, decorator.

decorazióne, *s.f.* 1. decoration, ornament: — *natalizia,* Christmas decoration; — *ad intaglio,* (*di finestra gotica*) tracery 2. (*medaglia*) decoration, medal; (*croce*) cross; (*nastro*) ribbon: *portare le proprie decorazioni,* to wear one's decorations.

decòro, *s.m.* 1. decorum; (*dignità*) dignity; (*proprietà*) propriety; (*convenienza*) seemliness: *il* — *del proprio rango,* the dignity of one's rank; *ella si comportò con* —, she behaved with decorum; *osservare il* —, to observe the proprieties 2. (*vanto*) honour; (*orgoglio*) pride: *è il* — *della sua famiglia,* he is an honour to (*o* the pride of) his family.

decorosaménte, *av.* decorously, decently, properly.

decoróso, *ag.* decorous, decent, proper: *una condotta decorosa,* proper behaviour; *non ho un abito* — *da mettermi,* I haven't a decent dress to wear.

decorrènza, *s.f.* (*comm.*) expiration: *con* — *dal 3 marzo...,* beginning from (*o* counting from *o* to begin from) the 3rd of March....

decórrere, *v.i.* 1. (*trascorrere*) to pass, to elapse: *lasceremo* — *due mesi,* we shall let two months pass (*o* go by) ‖ *a* — *da,* to begin from (*o* beginning from): *tra due settimane a* — *da oggi,* in three weeks' time (beginning) from today 2. (*cominciare ad avere effetto*) to run, to have effect: *gli interessi decorrono dal primo del mese,* (*comm.*) interest is reckoned as (*o* has effect) from the first of the month.

decórso, *ag.* past, elapsed, last: *mese* —, last (*o* past) month; *il mese ora* —, the month just elapsed ‖ *s.m.* 1. (*il passare*) passing: *il* — *del tempo,* the passing of time 2. (*periodo*) period, lapse: *nel* — *di un trimestre,* in (*o* within) the period of a quarter 3. (*svolgimento*) course: *il* — *della malattia,* the course of the illness.

decòtto[1], *ag.* (*dir.*) bankrupt ‖ *partita decotta,* (*comm.*) frozen credit.

decòtto[2], *s.m.* (*farm.*) decoction.

decozióne[1], *s.f.* (*dir.*) bankruptcy.

decozióne[2], *s.f.* (*farm.*) decoction.

decreménto, *s.m.* decrease, decrement: — *lineare,* (*rad.*) lineal decrement; — *logaritmico,* (*mat.*) logarithmic decrement.

decrepitàre, *v.t.i.* (*chim.*) to decrepitate.

decrepitazióne, *s.f.* (*chim.*) decrepitation.

decrepitézza, *s.f.* decrepitude.

decrèpito, *ag.* decrepit: *un vecchio* —, a decrepit old man.

decrescèndo, *s.m.* (*mus.*) decrescendo.

decresceènte, *ag.* decreasing; diminishing; waning; (*che si calma*) abating: *la luna è in fase* —, the moon is waning.

decrescènza, *s.f.* decrease, diminution; wane: — *della popolazione,* decrease in population.

decréscere, *v.i.* to decrease, to diminish; (*della luna*) to wane: *il livello delle acque decresce,* the level of the waters is decreasing (o falling); *la marea decresce*, the tide is going out (o ebbing); *le sue forze decrescevano rapidamente*, his strength was decreasing rapidly.

decresciménto, *s.m.* decrease, diminution; waning.

decretàle, *ag.* (*dir. eccl.*) decretal ‖ *s.f.* (*dir. eccl.*) decretal, Papal decree ‖ *le Decretali*, the Decretals.

decretalísta, *s.m.* (*dir. eccl.*) decretalist.

decretàre, *v.t.* **1.** to decree, to enact, to ordain: *come era stato decretato per legge*, as (it) had been ordained (o decreed) by law; *è stato decretato che...*, it has been decreed that... **2.** (*concedere*) to award, to confer, to grant: *gli decretarono i massimi onori*, they conferred the greatest honours upon (o on) him.

decréto, *s.m.* decree; ordinance: — *di amnistia*, amnesty ordinance; — *di citazione*, summons to appear in court; *i decreti di Dio, della Provvidenza*, the decrees of God, of Providence; — *legge*, law by decree: *come da — legge*, as by law enacted; — *penale*, judgement (o decision); *per — reale*, by royal decree; *emettere un —*, to issue a decree.

decúbito, *s.m.* (*med.*) decubitus: *piaga da —*, bed-sore.

decumàno, *ag.* decuman: *porta decumana*, (*st. romana*) decuman gate ‖ *onda decumana*, decuman wave (o tenth and highest wave) ‖ *s.m.* (*st. romana*) **1.** principal road (in a Roman camp, town) **2.** *i decumani*, decuman soldiers.

decuplicàre, *v.t.* to decuple, to multiply by ten; (*rendere dieci volte più grande*) to make ten times greater.

dècuplo, *ag.* tenfold, decuple; (*dieci volte più grande*) ten times greater ‖ *s.m.* decuple; (*somma dieci volte superiore*) tenfold amount; ten times as much.

decúria, *s.f.* (*st. romana*) decury; decuria (*pl. decuriae*).

decurióne, *s.m.* (*st. romana*) decurion.

decurtàre, *v.t.* to reduce, to diminish.

decurtazióne, *s.f.* reduction, diminution.

Dèdalo[1], *no.pr.m.* (*mit.*) Daedalus.

dèdalo[2], *s.m.* labyrinth, maze.

dèdica, *s.f.* dedication.

dedicàre, *v.t.* **1.** to dedicate, to consecrate: *dedicherò il libro a mia madre*, I shall dedicate the book to my mother; — *una chiesa alla Madonna*, to dedicate (o to consecrate) a church to the Blessed Virgin; — *un monumento alla memoria dei caduti della prima guerra mondiale*, to dedicate a monument to the soldiers killed in World War I (o the First World War) **2.** (*destinare*) to devote, to consecrate, to dedicate: *dedicò la sua vita alle ricerche scientifiche*, he devoted his life to scientific research; — *un giorno alla lettura*, to set apart a day for (o to dedicate a day to) reading ‖ **dedicàrsi**, *v.r.* to devote oneself, to give oneself up: *si dedicò interamente alla matematica*, he devoted himself entirely to mathematics.

dedicatàrio, *s.m.* dedicatee.

dedicàto, *ag.* dedicated, consecrated; *fig.* devoted.

dedicatóre, *s.m.*, **dedicatríce**, *s.f.* dedicator.

dedicatòria, *s.f.* dedicatory letter, letter of dedication.

dedicatòrio, *ag.* dedicatory: *lettera dedicatoria*, dedicatory letter (o letter of dedication).

dedicazióne, *s.f.* (*rar.*) dedication.

dèdito, *ag.* **1.** given up; devoted **2.** (*a vizio*) addicted: *è — al giuoco*, he is addicted to gambling.

dedizióne, *s.f.* **1.** devotement, devotion: — *al lavoro, alla scienza*, devotion to work, to science; *spirito di —*, spirit of self-sacrifice; *far — di sè*, to give oneself up **2.** (*resa*) surrender, yielding **3.** (*sottomissione*) submission: *far atto di —*, to submit.

dedótto, *ag.* **1.** (*desunto*) deduced, inferred, derived: *conclusione dedotta da una data premessa*, conclusion inferred from a given premise **2.** (*defalcato*) deducted, subtracted: *somma dedotta dal totale*, amount of money deducted from the total.

deducíbile, *ag.* deducible.

dedúrre, *v.t.* **1.** (*desumere*) to deduce, to infer, to argue: — *dal generale il particolare*, (*fil.*) to deduce the particular from the universal **2.** (*defalcare*) to deduct, to subtract: *dedotto il 2% di tara*, off (o less) 2% tare; — *una somma da uno stipendio*, to deduct a sum from a salary **3.** (*poet.*) (*trarre*) to draw forth: — *una melodia dalla cetra*, to draw forth a melody from a lyre **4.** — *una colonia*, (*fondarla*) to found a colony.

deduttivaménte, *av.* deductively.

deduttívo, *ag.* deductive: *metodo —*, (*fil.*) deductive method; *ragionamento —*, (*fil.*) deductive reasoning.

deduzióne, *s.f.* **1.** deduction; (*il dedurre*) deducing: *la tua — è sbagliata*, your deduction is wrong **2.** (*defalcazione*) deduction; (*somma defalcata*) amount deducted: — *dallo stipendio*, deduction from salary; *con la — di, fatta — di*, after deduction of (o deduction made of o under deduction of); *la — fu di 500 lire*, the amount deducted was 500 lire.

defalcàre, *v.t.* to deduct, to subtract: — *la provvigione*, to deduct commission; — *le spese*, (*comm.*) to deduct the charges.

defalcazióne, *s.f.*, **defàlco**, *s.m.* deduction.

defecàre, *v.i.* (*fisiol.*) to defecate ‖ *v.t.* (*chim.*) to clarify, to defecate.

defecazióne, *s.f.* **1.** (*fisiol.*) defecation **2.** (*chim.*) clarification, defecation.

defenestràre, *v.t.* **1.** to throw (s.o.) out of the window **2.** (*licenziare*) to drive (s.o.) out of office, to dismiss.

defenestrazióne, *s.f.* **1.** (*il gettare dalla finestra*) defenestration **2.** (*licenziamento*) abrupt removal from office.

defensionàle, *ag.* (*dir.*) for the defence.

deferènte, *ag.* **1.** deferential, respectful, complying **2.** (*anat.*) deferent: *arteria —*, deferent artery; *dotto —*, deferent duct **3.** (*fis.*) conducting electricity: *corpo —*, body conducting electricity.

deferenteménte, *av.* deferentially, respectfully.

deferènza, *s.f.* deference, respect, compliance: *per — verso di lui*, in deference to him (o out of deference to him).

deferíre, *v.t.* to submit: — *una causa al tribunale*, (*dir.*) to remit a cause to (a) court; — *un giuramento a qlcu.*, to put s.o. on s.o.'s oath; — *un'indagine a una commissione*, to entrust an investigation to a commission ‖ *v.i.* to defer: — *alle opinioni di qlcu.*, to defer to s.o.'s opinions.

defervescènza, *s.f.* (*med.*) defervescence.

defettíbile, *ag.* liable to fail.

defezionàre, *v.i.* to desert, to fall away, to make defection: — *dal proprio partito*, to desert from one's party (o to fall away from one's allegiance to a party).

defezióne, *s.f.* **1.** defection **2.** (*mil.*) desertion.

deficiènte, *ag.* **1.** (*insufficiente*) insufficient: *forze deficienti*, insufficient forces; *organizzazione —*, faulty organization; *soccorsi deficienti*, insufficient help; *è — di spirito*, he is lacking in wit ‖ *è — in latino*, he is backward in Latin **2.** (*idiota*) mentally deficient: *un fanciullo —*, a (mentally) deficient boy ‖ *s.c.* mentally deficient person, half-wit, half-witted person: *è un povero —*, he is a poor half-wit.

deficiènza, *s.f.* **1.** (*insufficienza*) deficiency, want, lack, shortage: — *d'educazione*, lack of politeness; — *di ingegno*, deficiency of intellect (o lack of intelligence); *per — di denaro*, for want (o lack) of money; *c'è — di acqua*, water is lacking (o there is a shortage of water); *supplire alla —*, to remedy to (o to supply) the deficiency **2.** (*idiozia*) mental deficiency.

dèficit, *s.m.* (*comm.*) deficit, deficiency: — *nelle pubbliche entrate*, deficiency in the public revenue; *colmare il —*, to make up the deficiency; *constatare un —*, to notice a deficit.

deficitàrio, *ag.* showing a deficit: *bilancio —*, debit balance.

defilàre, *v.i.* (*mil.*) to defilade.

defilàto, *ag.* (*mil.*) defiladed.

definíbile, *ag.* definable.

definíre, *v.t.* **1.** (*spiegare*) to define: — *la propria posizione,* to define one's position; — *un termine,* to define a term **2.** (*determinare*) to determine, to fix **3.** (*risolvere*) to determine, to settle: — *una lite, una questione,* to settle a dispute, a question.

definitaménte, *av.* definitely; precisely.

definitíva, in, *l.av.* after all: *in* — *è un bravo ragazzo,* after all he is a good boy.

definitivaménte, *av.* definitively.

definitívo, *ag.* definitive, decisive, final; ultimate: *risposta definitiva,* final answer; *verdetto* —, definitive (*o* decisive) verdict.

definíto, *ag.* definite; precise; determinate: *non ben* —, vague.

definitóre, *s.m.* definer.

definizióne, *s.f.* **1.** definition: *dare la* — *di qlco.,* to give the definition of sthg. **2.** (*risoluzione*) settlement: *la* — *di una questione,* the settlement of a question.

deflagràre, *v.i.* to deflagrate.

deflagratóre, *s.m.* deflagrator.

deflagrazióne, *s.f.* deflagration.

deflazionàre, *v.t.* (*econ.*) to deflate.

deflazióne, *s.f.* (*econ. geol.*) deflation.

deflazionístico, *ag.* (*econ.*) deflationary: *misure deflazionistiche,* deflationary measures.

deflemmàre, *v.t.* (*chim.*) to dephlegmate.

deflemmatóre, *s.m.* (*chim.*) dephlegmator, distilling head, fractionating column.

deflemmazióne, *s.f.* (*chim.*) dephlegmation.

deflessióne, *s.f.* **1.** (*tv.*) deflection: *bobina di* —, deflector coil; *placche di* —, deflector plates **2.** (*fis.*) down-wash.

deflèttere, *v.i.* **1.** to deflect; to deviate, to differ, to diverge: *non defletterò dai miei ideali,* I shall adhere to my ideals; (*fam.*) I'll stick (*o* hold fast) to my ideals **2.** (*cedere*) to yield; to give in: *riguardo a questa faccenda non defletterò mai!,* as regards this question I will never give in!.

deflettóre, *s.m.* **1.** (*mec.*) baffle (plate) **2.** (*aer.*) flap: — *di picchiata,* dive brake.

defloràre, *v.t.* to deflower; to rape, to ravish, to violate.

defloraménto, *s.m.* defloration; rape.

defloràto, *ag.* deflowered; violated.

defloratóre, *s.m.* deflowerer.

deflorazióne, *s.f.* defloration; rape.

defluènte, *ag.* defluent: *corrente* —, defluent stream.

defluíre, *v.i.* to flow down: *alcuni fiumi alpini defluiscono nella pianura Padana,* some Alpine rivers flow down into the Po valley.

deflússo, *s.m.* **1.** downflow; (*di marea*) ebb(-tide), reflux; (*di onda*) undertow **2.** (*med.*) defluction, defluxion.

deformàbile, *ag.* capable of being deformed.

deformaménto, *s.m.* deformation; distorsion; disfigurement.

deformànte, *ag.* deforming; disfiguring; distorting: *artrite* —, (*patol.*) deforming arthritis.

deformàre, *v.t.* **1.** to deform, to misshape, to disform; to disfigure, to deface: *il suo corpo era stato deformato da una malattia,* his body had been deformed by an illness; *il suo viso era deformato da una cicatrice,* his face was disfigured by a scar **2.** (*alterare*) to distort, to warp; to alter: *egli ha deformato il mio pensiero,* he distorted my thought; *il sole ha deformato quelle assi,* the sun warped those boards; *il suo pensiero era deformato dai pregiudizi,* his way of thinking was warped by prejudice; — *la verità,* to distort the truth **3.** (*scienza delle costruzioni*) to strain; (*mec.*) to warp ‖ **deformàrsi,** *v.r.* **1.** (*mec.*) to warp, to buckle **2.** to get deformed, to be desfigured; (*perdere la giusta forma*) to lose one's proper shape.

deformàto, *ag.* deformed, warped; disfigured; distorted: *ha un piede* —, he has a deformed foot.

deformazióne, *s.f.* **1.** deformation; disfigurement; distortion: — *di compressione,* (*mec.*) buckling; — *permanente,* (*mec.*) set; — *trapezoidale,* (*tv.*) keistoning **2.** (*scienza delle costruzioni*) strain: — *elastica,* elastic deformation (*o* strain); — *permanente,* permanent deformation (*o* set).

defórme, *ag.* **1.** deformed, disfigured, misshapen: *aspetto* —, misshapen countenance **2.** (*brutto*) ugly; (*mostruoso*) hideous: *donna* —, ugly woman **3.** *fig.* perverted: *animo* —, perverted mind.

deformeménte, *av.* **1.** deformedly **2.** (*mostruosamente*) hideously.

deformità, *s.f.* **1.** deformity, disfigurement, malformation **2.** (*bruttezza*) ugliness; (*mostruosità*) hideousness.

defosforazióne, *s.f.* (*metal.*) dephosphorization.

defraudaménto, *s.m.* (*rar.*) defrauding, deception.

defraudàre, *v.t.* to defraud, to cheat, to deprive: — *qlcu. di ql.co.,* to defraud s.o. of sthg.: *lo defraudarono della proprietà,* they cheated him (out) of his property.

defraudatóre, *s.m.* defrauder, cheater.

defraudazióne, *s.f.* defrauding, deception.

defúnto, *ag.* dead, defunct, deceased; late (*attributivo*): *il* — *Professor Jones,* the late Professor Jones; *la defunta Signora Smith,* the late Mrs. Smith; *il mio* — *marito,* my late husband ‖ *s.m.* dead (person); (*dir.*) deceased: *il* —, the deceased; *commemorazione dei defunti,* commemoration of the dead.

degeneràre, *v.i.* to degenerate; to decay, to deteriorate: *parsimonia che degenera in avarizia,* thrift that degenerates into avarice; *quella discussione degenerò in una lite,* that discussion turned into a quarrel.

degeneràto, *ag. s.m.* degenerate, profligate.

degenerazióne, *s.f.* degeneration, degeneracy, depravation, deterioration: *i vecchi a volte accusano i giovani di* —, old people sometimes accuse young people of degeneration.

degènere, *ag.* degenerate, depraved.

degènte, *ag.* bedrid(den) ‖ *s.c.* patient; (*in ospedale*) in-patient.

degènza, *s.f.* period in bed; (*in ospedale*) stay in hospital: *guarì dopo tre mesi di* — *in ospedale,* he recovered after three months' stay in hospital; *quanto durò la sua* —?, how long was he compelled to stay in bed?.

deglutíre, *v.t.* to swallow.

deglutizióne, *s.f.* swallowing, deglutition: *centro della* —, (*anat.*) deglutition centre.

degnaménte, *av.* worthily; properly; deservingly.

degnàre, *v.t.* to deem worthy, to deign: *non lo degnai d'una risposta,* I did not deem him worthy of an answer (*o* I did not think him worth answering *o* I did not deign him an answer); *quando mi degnerete di una visita?,* when will you do me the honour of visiting me? ‖ *v.i.,* **degnàrsi,** *v.r.* to deign, to condescend: *degnatevi di rispondermi!,* be so kind as to answer me!; *non mi degnai di discutere con lui,* I did not deign (*o* condescend) to argue with him; *la Regina si degnò di accettare il dono,* the Queen deigned to accept (*o* graciously accepted) the gift; *senza* — *di guardarmi,* without deigning to look at me.

degnazióne, *s.f.* **1.** condescension: *avere un'aria di* —, to have a condescending air **2.** (*cortesia*) kindness, consideration: *per* — *verso qlcu.,* out of consideration for (*o* out of kindness to) s.o.

dégno, *ag.* **1.** (*meritevole*) worthy, deserving: — *della massima lode,* worthy (*o* deserving) of the highest praise; — *di invidia,* enviable; — *di lode,* praiseworthy; — *di nota,* noteworthy; — *di pietà,* pitiable; *azioni degne di essere ricordate,* deeds deserving (*o* worthy) to be remembered; *con uno zelo* — *di miglior causa,* with a zeal deserving (*o* worthy) of a better cause;

è un libro — di essere letto, it is a book worth reading; è un uomo — di fiducia, he is a trustworthy man; non è — di vivere, he is not fit to live; la sua condotta è degna di ricompensa, his conduct deserves a reward 2. (eccellente) deserving: una degna causa, a deserving cause 3. (rispettabile) worthy (anche scherz.): il — uomo, the worthy man 4. (convenevole, conveniente) worthy: questo non è — di te, this is not worthy of you.

degradaménto, s.m. degradation; degrading.

degradànte, ag. degrading, disgraceful, shameful, lowering: azione —, degrading action.

degradàre, v.t. 1. to degrade, to reduce in rank (anche mil.): fu degradato, he was degraded 2. (abbassare) to degrade, to debase, to lower: — gli uomini al livello delle bestie, to degrade men to the level of beasts ‖ v.i. V. **digradàre** ‖ **degradàrsi,** v.r. to degrade oneself, to lower oneself, to bring disgrace upon oneself: non dovresti degradarti fino a fare questo, you should not lower yourself by doing that.

degradazióne, s.f. degradation.

degustàre, v.t. to taste.

degustazióne, s.f. tasting; (centellinando) sipping: sala di —, tasting room.

deh, inter. 1. (per pietà!) for pity's sake! 2. (ahimè!) alas!.

Deianíra, no.pr.f. (mit.) Deianira, Deianeira.

deicída, s.m. deicide.

deicídio, s.m. deicide.

deidratàre, v.t. to dehydrate.

deidratazióne, s.f. dewatering.

deidrogenazióne, s.f. (chim.) dehydrogenation.

deiezióne, s.f. 1. (fisiol.) dejection, evacuation 2. (escrementi) dejections (pl.), dejecta (pl.), excrements (pl.) 3. (geol.) detritus: cono di —, alluvial cone (o alluvial fan 4. pl. (detriti di vulcano) dejections.

deificàre, v.t. to deify.

deificazióne, s.f. deification.

deifico, ag. deific(al).

Deìfobo, no.pr.m. (mit.) Deiphobus.

deifórme, ag. god-like (attributivo): divine.

deionizzazióne, s.f. (termoionica) deionization.

deípara, s.f. Deipara.

deiscènte, ag. (bot.) dehiscent.

deiscènza, s.f. (bot.) dehiscence.

deísmo, s.m. (fil.) deism.

deísta, s.m. (fil.) deist.

deità, s.f. 1. deity, godhead, divinity 2. (dio) god; (dea) goddess 3. (Dio) God.

de iure, l.av. (lat.) (dir.) by right.

delatóre, s.m., **delatríce,** s.f. delator, informer, spy.

delazióne, s.f. 1. delation, informing, denouncement: fu un manifesto caso di —, it was a clear case of delation 2. (dir.): — d'armi, illegal possession of fire-arms; — di giuramento, administering of an oath.

del crédere, s.m. (comm.) delcredere (commission).

delèbile, ag. erasable, effaceable.

dèlega, s.f. 1. delegation: — d'autorità, delegation of powers 2. (procura) proxy: per —, by proxy.

delegàre, v.t. 1. to delegate, to appoint (as a representative): — una persona a compiere un incarico, to delegate a person to perform a task 2. (trasmettere) to delegate, to depute: — diritti ad un deputato, to delegate rights to a deputy; — la propria autorità, to delegate one's own powers.

delegàto, ag. delegate(d); deputed ‖ s.m. 1. delegate, representative: mandare un — ad una conferenza, to send (o to appoint) a representative to a conference 2. (dir.) deputy.

delegazióne, s.f. 1. delegation: — di poteri, delegation of authority (o of powers) 2. (commissione) commission, committee: — di sorveglianza in un fallimento, committee of inspection; — di sorveglianza per l'istruzione, School Inspectors; la — tedesca per la pace, the German Peace Delegation.

deletèrio, ag. deleterious, noxious, harmful.

delettàre, V. **dilettàre.**

Dèlfi, no.pr.f. (geog. st.) Delphi.

dèlfico, ag. Delphian, Delphic.

delfína, s.f. (st. francese) dauphine, dauphiness.

delfíno[1], s.m. (zool.) dolphin ‖ il Delfino, (astr.) the Dolphin (o the Delphinus).

delfíno[2], s.m. (st. francese) dauphin.

Dèlia, no.pr.f. Delia.

delibàre, v.t. 1. to taste, to savour; (centellinare) to sip: — il proprio vino, to sip one's wine 2. (dir.) to touch (up)on (sthg.), to allude to (sthg.): — una questione, to touch upon a subject.

delibazióne, s.f. 1. tasting, savouring; (il centellinare) sipping 2. (dir.) provisional examination.

delibera, s.f. 1. resolution 2. (aggiudicazione) adjudication.

deliberàre, v.t. 1. to decide, to resolve, to resolve upon (sthg.): deliberò di andare, he resolved to go (o upon going); — il da farsi, to decide what to do 2. (aggiudicare) to assign, to adjudge: — un oggetto a qlcu., to adjudge an object to s.o. ‖ v.i. to deliberate, to consult: deliberarono sulla questione, they consulted about the matter ‖ **deliberàrsi,** v.r. (risolversi) to decide, to resolve, to resolve upon (sthg.), to make up one's mind: egli si deliberò di partire, he made up his mind to leave.

deliberataménte, av. deliberately.

deliberatàrio, s.m. (dir.) highest bidder.

deliberatívo, ag. deliberative.

deliberàto, ag. decided, resolute, firm, resolved: con animo —, with a resolute mind; sono — a scacciarlo, I am resolved to drive him away ‖ s.m. (deliberazione) deliberation, decision.

deliberazióne, s.f. 1. (decisione) deliberation, decision; (di un'assemblea) resolution 2. (discussione, consultazione) deliberation, discussion: dopo lunga —, after long deliberation.

delicataménte, av. delicately; gently.

delicatézza, s.f. 1. delicacy; softness: — di colori, softness of colours; la — di questo cibo, the delicacy of this food; la — di un suono, the delicacy (o softness) of a sound 2. (cibo delicato) delicacy: è una vera —!, it's a real delicacy! 3. (fragilità, gracilità) delicacy (anche fig.): — di salute, delicate health; — di uno strumento, delicacy of an instrument; la — della situazione esige il massimo riserbo, the utmost discretion is required by the delicacy of the situation 4. (finezza) delicacy; (sensibilità) sensibility; (discrezione) discretion, tact: la — della sua coscienza era tale che..., the delicacy of his conscience was such that...; agì con estrema —, he acted with the greatest tact (o the utmost discretion); diede prova di grande — d'animo, he showed great sensibility 5. (mollezza) luxury: in mezzo alle delicatezze, in the lap of luxury.

delicàto, ag. 1. delicate; soft, subdued; gentle: cibo —, (leggero) delicate food; (squisito) dainty (o delicate) food; colore —, delicate (o soft) colour; sapore —, delicate taste; suono —, soft (o subdued) sound; quel chirurgo hc la mano delicata, that surgeon has a gentle (o soft) hand 2. (fragile, gracile) delicate, weak (anche fig.): bambino —, delicate (o weakly) child; macchina delicata, delicate machine; questione delicata, delicate (o ticklish) question; salute delicata, delicate health; stomaco —, weak stomach 3. (fine) delicate, refined: animo —, sensitive soul; gusti delicati, refined tastes 4. (scrupoloso) scrupulous; (discreto) discreet, tactful: persona (dalla coscienza) delicata, scrupulous person; tua madre è una persona veramente delicata, your mother is a really tactful person.

delicatúra, s.f. extreme delicacy, excessive delicacy.

delimàre, v.t. to corrode.

delimitàre, v.t. to delimitate, to delimit, to define, to determine the limits of (sthg.), to fix the boundaries of (sthg.).

delimitazióne, *s.f.* delimitation.

delineàbile, *ag.* delineable, that can be outlined.

delineaménto, *s.m.* delineation.

delineàre, *v.t.* to delineate, to outline, to sketch (out) (anche *fig.*): *delineò brevemente le condizioni della Francia*, he outlined the conditions of France; — *una figura*, to sketch (out) a figure ‖ **delineàrsi**, *v.r.* to loom: *le montagne si delinearono all'orizzonte*, the mountains loomed on the horizon; — *in lontananza*, to loom in the distance.

delineazióne, *s.f.* delineation.

delinquènte, *ag.* delinquent, criminal: *azione* —, criminal action ‖ *s.c.* delinquent, criminal; offender: *un* — *nato*, a born criminal; *una banda di delinquenti*, a band of crooks; *giovani delinquenti*, juvenile offenders.

delinquènza, *s.f.* delinquency, criminality: — *minorile*, juvenile delinquency.

delínquere, *v.i.* to commit an offence, to commit a crime ‖ *associazione a* —, (*dir.*) criminal gang.

deliquescènte, *ag.* (*chim. fis.*) deliquescent.

deliquescènza, *s.f.* (*chim. fis.*) deliquescence.

delíquio, *s.m.* swoon, fainting-fit: *cadere in* —, to faint (*o* to swoon).

deliraménto, *s.m.* (*rar.*) raving; frenzy, delirium.

deliránte, *ag.* delirious, raving; wildly excited: — *di gioia*, delirious with joy.

deliràre, *v.i.* to rave, to be delirious: *il paziente incominciò a* —, the patient began to rave; *sta delirando*, his mind is wandering; — *d'amore*, to be madly in love.

delírio, *s.m.* **1.** (*patol.*) delirium; frenzy: — *febbrile*, delirious fever; *entrare in* —, to become delirious **2.** *fig.* raving, frenzy; ecstasy, rapture: — *di collera, di disperazione*, frenzy of passion, of desperation; — *di guadagno*, greed of gain; — *patriottico*, patriotic enthusiasm: *il suo discorso suscitò un* — *di applausi*, his speech aroused great enthusiasm.

delirium tremens, *s.m.* (*patol.*) delirium tremens (*abbr.* d.t.).

delíro, *ag.* (*rar.*) delirious, raving.

delítto, *s.m.* **1.** (*dir.*) crime; (*grave*) felony; (*meno grave*) misdemeanour: — *capitale*, capital offence (*o* crime); — *contro l'ordine pubblico*, breach of the peace; — *di stampa*, violation of the laws governing the press; *corpo del* —, corpus delicti; *l'assassinio e la violenza sono considerati* —, murder and robbery are considered felonies; *la diffamazione è un* —, defamation is a misdemeanour; *commettere un* —, to commit a crime; *incolpare di un* —, to charge with a crime **2.** *fig.* crime: *sarebbe un* — *modernizzare questi vecchi mobili!*, it would be a crime to modernize this old furniture!.

delittuóso, *ag.* criminal: *un'azione delittuosa*, a criminal action.

delízia, *s.f.* delight: *con mia grande* —, to my great delight; *suona che è una* —, she plays delightfully; *essere la* — *di qlcu.*, to be s.o.'s delight.

deliziàre, *v.t.* to delight, to charm: — *le orecchie, gli occhi di qlcu.*, to delight s.o.'s ears, eyes ‖ **deliziàrsi**, *v.r.* to delight (in sthg., in doing), to take pleasure (in sthg., in doing), to find pleasure (in sthg., in doing): — *di musica*, to delight in music.

deliziosaménte, *av.* delightfully, deliciously.

delizióso, *ag.* delightful, charming; (*di sapore, profumo*) delicious: *che dolce* —*!*, what a delicious cake!; *musica, vista deliziosa*, delightful music, view; *una ragazza deliziosa*, a charming (*o* delightful) girl; *un sorriso* —, a charming smile; *ha un profumo* —, it smells delicious.

Dèlo, *no.pr.f.* (*geog.*) Delos.

dèlta, *s.m.* **1.** (*geog.*) delta: *il* — *del Nilo*, the Nile delta; — *a ventaglio*, fan delta **2.** (*lettera dell'alfabeto greco*) delta **3.** (*metal.*): *ferro* —, delta iron; *metallo* —, delta metal.

deltazióne, *s.f.* (*geog.*) deltafication.

deltòide, *ag.* (*anat.*) deltoid, shaped like a delta ‖ *s.m.* (*anat.*) deltoid (muscle).

deltoidèo, *ag.* (*anat.*) deltoid.

delúbro, *s.m.* (*poet.*) delubrum (*pl.* delubra); sanctuary, shrine.

delucidàre, *v.t.* **1.** to explain, to clarify, to elucidate **2.** (*ind. tessile*) (*decatizzare*) to decatize.

delucidazióne, *s.f.* **1.** explanation, elucidation **2.** (*ind. tessile*) (*decatissaggio*) decatizing: — *a secco*, dry-steam decatizing; — *a umido*, hot-water decatizing.

delúdere, *v.t.* **1.** to disappoint, to deceive; (*mandare a vuoto*) to frustrate: *non deludermi!*, don't disappoint me!; *quel libro mi ha deluso*, that book has disappointed me; *la sua ambizione fu delusa*, his ambition was frustrated; — *le speranze*, to deceive hopes **2.** (*eludere*) to escape: — *la vigilanza*, to escape the vigilance.

delusióne, *s.f.* disappointment, deception: *provare un'amara* —, to experience a bitter disappointment.

delúso, *ag.* disappointed, deceived: *speranze deluse*, deceived (*o* frustrated) hopes.

delusoriaménte, *av.* deceptively.

delusòrio, *ag.* deceptive.

demagogía, *s.f.* demagogy.

demagogicaménte, *av.* demagogically.

demagògico, *ag.* demagogic(al).

demagogísmo, *s.m.* demagogism.

demagògo, *s.m.* demagogue.

demandàre, *v.t.* (*dir.*) **1.** to assign, to delegate, to commit **2.** (*deferire*) to pass on: *la pratica fu demandata ad un altro tribunale*, the case was transferred to another (law-)court.

demaniàle, *ag.* owned by the State; State (*attributivo*): *proprietà* —, State property; *terreni demaniali*, State demesne.

demànio, *s.m.* State property; (State) demesne; (State) domain; (*terre demaniali*) State lands; (*di un regno*) Crown lands: *ufficio del* —, State property office.

demarcàre, *v.t.* to mark the boundaries of (a land); to fix the boundaries of (a land); to demarcate.

demarcazióne, *s.f.* demarcation: *linea di* —, line of demarcation (*o* boundary line).

demènte, *ag.* insane, mad, demented; crazy ‖ *s.m.* lunatic; madman (*pl.* madmen): *è un povero* —, he is out of his mind, poor fellow ‖ *s.f.* lunatic; madwoman (*pl.* madwomen).

demènza, *s.f.* insanity, madness; (*med.*) dementia: — *precoce*, precocious dementia (*o* dementia praecox); — *senile*, senile dementia; *un caso pietoso di* —, a pitiful case of madness.

demeritàre, *v.t.* (*non meritare più*) to forfeit: *avete demeritato la nostra stima*, you have forfeited our esteem ‖ *v.i.* (*meritare biasimo*) to deserve censure.

demèrito, *s.m.* **1.** demerit **2.** (*difetto*) fault; (*indegnità*) unworthiness.

Demètra, *no.pr.f.* (*mit.*) Demeter.

Demètrio, *no.pr.m.* Demetrius.

demilitarizzàre, *v.t.* to demilitarize.

demilitarizzazióne, *s.f.* demilitarization; (*il demilitarizzare*) demilitarizing.

demiúrgico, *ag.* (*fil.*) demiurgic.

demiúrgo, *s.m.* (*fil.*) demiurge; *fig.* super-man, god-like human being.

dèmo, *s.m.* (*st. greca*) deme; demos (*pl.* demi).

democraticaménte, *av.* democratically.

democràtico, *ag.* democratic ‖ *s.m.* **1.** democrat **2.** (*fam.*) (*persona affabile e alla mano*) easy-going fellow.

democratizzàre, *v.t.* to democratize.

democrazía, *s.f.* democracy.

democristiàno, *ag. s.m.* (*pol.*) Christian-democrat.

democritèo, *ag.* (*st. fil.*) Democritean.

Demòcrito, *no.pr.m.* (*st. fil.*) Democritus.

demodulatóre, *s.m.* (*rad.*) demodulator.

demodulazióne, *s.f.* (*rad.*) demodulation.

Demogòrgone, *s.m.* (*mit.*) Demogorgon.

demografía, *s.f.* demography.

demogràfico, *ag.* demographic(al): *indice* —, demographic index.

demolíre, *v.t.* **1.** to demolish, to pull down: *hanno deciso di demolire quell'edificio*, they have decided to pull down (*o* to demolish) that house **2.** *fig.* to demolish, to overthrow, to destroy: *la critica lo ha demolito*, the critics tore him to pieces; *ho demolito la sua argomentazione*, I demolished his argument; (*fam.*) I knocked the bottom out of his argument (*o* I didn't leave him a leg to stand on); *nel suo libro ha tentato di demolire la teoria dell'estetica crociana*, in his book he tried to demolish Croce's theory of aesthetics; *la nuova generazione ha demolito le credenze e i principi dei genitori*, the younger generation have overthrown the beliefs and principles of their parents.

demolitóre, *ag.* destroying ‖ *s.m.*, **demolitríce**, *s.f.* **1.** demolisher, destroyer **2.** *fig.* destroyer.

demolizióne, *s.f.* **1.** demolition, pulling down: *la — di quell'edificio incomincerà domani*, the demolition of that building will begin tomorrow **2.** *fig.* destruction: *la — di una istituzione*, the destruction of an institution; *iniziò una sistematica — di quella teoria*, he began (*o* set about) a systematic demolition of that theory.

demología, *s.f.* demology.

dèmone, *s.m.* **1.** (*genio*) demon; genius (*pl.* genii); daemon; (attendant) spirit; (*cattivo*) evil spirit, demon, devil: *il — della gelosia*, the demon of jealousy ‖ *il — di Socrate*, the daemon of Socrates **2.** (*diavolo*) devil: *un orrendo —*, a hideous devil.

demoníaco, *ag.* demoniac(al): *frenesia, furia demoniaca*, demoniac frenzy, fury.

demònico, *ag.* demoniac(al).

demoniétto, *s.m.* imp, little devil (anche *fig.*): *sei un vero —!*, you're an imp (*o* a perfect little devil)!.

demònio, *s.m.* **1.** devil, demon, daemon, evil spirit ‖ *dopo tutto non è il —*, after all, it is not so bad **2.** *fig.* demon, daemon; devil, villain (anche *scherz.*): *negli affari è un vero —*, he is a wizard at business; *questo ragazzo è un —*, this boy is a little devil (*o* a young imp *o* a terror).

demonolatría, *s.f.* demonolatry.

demonología, *s.f.* demonology.

demonomanía, *s.f.* (*patol.*) demonomania.

demopsicología, *s.f.* race psychology.

demoralizzàre, *v.t.* **1.** to demoralize, to dishearten: *la sconfitta demoralizzò le truppe*, the troops were demoralized by the defeat **2.** (*depravare*) to demoralize, to deprave ‖ **demoralizzàrsi**, *v.r.* to lose heart, to lose courage, to become demoralized: *si demoralizzò al primo insuccesso*, he lost heart (*o* courage) at the first failure.

demoralizzàto, *ag.* **1.** demoralized, disheartened: *è assai —*, he is deeply disheartened **2.** (*depravato*) demoralized, depraved.

demoralizzazióne, *s.f.* demoralization.

demorfinizzàre, *v.t.* to wean (s.o.) from morphine.

dèmos, *s.m.* demos (*pl.* demi).

Demòstene, *no.pr.m.* (*st. lett.*) Demosthenes.

demòtico, *ag.* (*archeol.*) demotic.

demulcènte, *ag.* (*farm.*) demulcent.

denàro, *s.m.* **1.** money (*solo sing.*): *— a corso legale*, legal tender; *— contante*, ready money; cash; *— spicciolo*, (*di piccolo taglio*) change; (*per i minuti piaceri*) pocket-money; *molto —*, much (*o* a lot of *o* a great deal of) money; *poco —*, little money; *un po' di —*, a little money; *aver molto —*, to be very rich (*o* wealthy) ‖ *far —*, to make money ‖ *il tempo è —*, *prov.* time is money **2.** (*moneta inglese, dodicesima parte di uno scellino*) penny (*pl.* pence, pennies): *ecco due monetine da un —, nuove di zecca*, here are two brand-new pennies; *quel libro costa 6 denari*, that book costs sixpence **3.**(*st.romana*) denarius (*pl.* denarii); (*st. francese*) denier **4.** (*ind. tessile*) denier (*unità di*

peso per filati sottili = g. 0,05) **5.** *pl.* (*ricchezze*) riches (*pl.*);wealth (*solo sing.*) **6.** *pl.* (*a carte*) «denari» (the suit in Italian [playing] cards corresponding to diamonds).

denaróso, *ag.* moneyed, wealthy; rich: *è molto —*, he is very rich.

denatalità, *s.f.* diminution of births, fall in the birth-rate.

denaturànte, *ag.* (*chim.*) denaturing ‖ *s.m.* (*chim.*) denaturant, denaturing agent.

denaturàre, *v.t.* (*chim.*) to denature, to methylate.

denaturàto, *ag.* denatured, methylated: *alcool —*, methylated spirit.

dendríte, *s.f.* (*min. anat.*) dendrite.

dendrítico, *ag.* (*min. anat.*) dendritic.

dendròide, *ag.* (*bot.*) dendroid, branching, tree-like.

dendrología, *s.f.* dendrology.

denegàre, *v.t.* to deny.

denegatóre, *s.m.*, **denegatríce**, *s.f.* denier.

denegazióne, *s.f.* denial.

dènga, *s.f.* (*patol.*) dengue.

denicotinizzàre, *v.t.* to denicotinize.

denigràre, *v.t.* to denigrate, to defame, to blacken; (*fam.*) to run down, to crab; (*screditare*) to disparage; (*parlar male di*) to speak ill of (s.o., sthg.): *— il buon nome di qlcu.*, to run s.o. down (*o* to take away s.o.'s good name).

denigratóre, *ag.* disparaging, defamatory; (*calunnioso*) slanderous ‖ *s.m.*, **denigratríce**, *s.f.* denigrator, defamer; (*calunniatore*) slanderer.

denigrazióne, *s.f.* denigration, disparagement; (*fam.*) running down.

denitrificàre, *v.t.* (*chim.*) to denitrate.

denitrurazióne, *s.f.* (*chim.*) denitrifying.

denomiuàre, *v.t.* to denominate, to name, to give a name to (s.o., sthg.): *Geoffrey Chaucer è denominato il padre della lingua inglese*, Geoffrey Chaucer is called the father of the English language ‖ **denominàrsi**, *v.r.* to be named, to be called.

denominatívo, *ag.* denominative.

denominatóre, *s.m.* (*mat.*) denominator: *il minimo comun —*, the lowest (*o* least) common denominator.

denominazióne, *s.f.* **1.** denomination; (*nome*) name, appellation: *— di una ditta*, style of a firm **2.** (*mat.*) (*denominatore*) denominator.

denotàre, *v.t.* to denote, to indicate, to signify, to betoken, to show: *una fronte spaziosa denota intelligenza*, a broad forehead signifies intelligence; *niente sembra — che sia colpevole*, nothing seems to show that he is guilty (*o* nothing seems to point him out as guilty); *viso che denota energia*, face that betokens (*o* denotes) energy.

densaménte, *av.* densely; thickly: *regione — popolata*, densely populated region.

densímetro, *s.m.* (*fis.*) densimeter, hydrometer: *— per acqua marina, per soluzioni saline*, salinometer.

densità, *s.f.* **1.** density, denseness; (*l'essere fitto, spesso*) thickness: *— di popolazione*, density of population; *— di traffico*, density of traffic **2.** (*fis.*) density: *— di corrente*, (*elett.*) current density; *— di flusso*, (*elett.*) flux density; *— luminosa, magnetica*, (*elett.*) light, magnetic density.

dènso, *ag.* dense; (*spesso*) thick: *una folla molto densa*, a very thick (*o* dense) crowd; *una nebbia densa*, a thick (*o* dense) fog; *olio —*, thick oil.

dentàle, *ag.* dental: *alveolo, papilla —*, (*anat.*) dental crypt, bulb; *consonante —*, (*fonet.*) dental consonant ‖ *s.f.* (*fonet.*) dental.

dentàrio, *ag.* (*anat.*) dental; tooth (*attributivo*): *carie dentaria*, tooth decay (*o* caries).

dentaruòlo, *s.m.* coral; teething-ring.

dentàta, *s.f.* **1.** (*morso*) bite **2.** (*segno di denti*) tooth-mark.

dentàto, *ag.* **1.** toothed **2.** (*bot. zool.*) dentate **3.** (*mec.*) toothed; (*a sega*) serrated: *ruota dentata*, cog-wheel.

dentatúra, *s.f.* **1.** set of teeth: *ha una bella* —, she has a fine set of teeth **2.** (*di ingranaggio*) toothing: — *a denti di sega*, (*mec.*) serration **3.** (*taglio dei denti di un ingranaggio*) gear-cutting.

dènte, *s.m.* **1.** tooth (*pl.* teeth); (*di animale feroce*) fang; (*zanna*) tusk: — *canino*, canine (tooth) (*o eye-tooth*); — *cariato*, decayed (*o* carious) tooth; (*fam.*) rotten tooth; — *d'elefante*, tusk; — *del giudizio*, wisdom-tooth; — *di latte*, milk-tooth; — *d'oro*, gold tooth; *denti finti*, false (*o* artificial) teeth; — *incisivo*, incisor; — *molare*, molar tooth (*o* back-tooth *o* mill-tooth); *denti sporgenti*, buck-teeth; *mal di denti*, toothache: *ho un gran mal di denti*, I have a bad toothache; *senza denti*, toothless; *spazzolino da denti*, toothbrush; *batteva i denti*, his teeth were chattering ‖ *digrignare i denti*, to grind one's teeth; *estrarre un* —, to draw (*o* to extract) a tooth; *far allegare i denti*, to set one's teeth on edge; *far cadere un* — *a qlcu.*, to knock a tooth out of s.o.'s mouth; *farsi cavare un* —, to have a tooth out; *farsi otturare un* —, to have a tooth stopped (*o* filled); *mettere i denti*, to cut one's teeth: *il bambino ha messo un* —, the child has cut a tooth; *il bambino sta mettendo i denti*, the child is teething; *perdere un* —, to lose a tooth: *ha perso alcuni denti davanti*, he has lost a few front teeth; *rompere una corda coi denti*, to bite through a rope ‖ *al* —, underdone: *mi piace il riso al* —, I like rice underdone ‖ *sorriso a denti stretti*, tight-lipped (*o* forced) smile ‖ *non è pane per i miei denti*, it is not my cup of tea; *non è pane per i vostri denti*, it is out of your reach (*o* it is too good for you); (*è troppo difficile per voi*) it is too difficult for you ‖ *avere il* — *avvelenato contro qlcu.*, to have a grudge against s.o. ‖ *avere i denti lunghi*, *fig.* to be greedy ‖ *essere armato fino ai denti*, to be armed to the teeth ‖ *lottare con le unghie e coi denti*, to fight tooth and nail ‖ *mostrare i denti*, to show one's teeth ‖ *non aver nulla da mettere sotto i denti*, not to have a bite to eat ‖ *parlare fra i denti*, to mumble (*o* to say sthg. between one's teeth) ‖ *parlare fuori dai denti*, to be outspoken (*o* to speak bluntly) ‖ *rimanere a denti asciutti*, not to eat a bite; (*restare deluso*) to be disappointed ‖ *stringere i denti*, to grit (*o* to set) one's teeth: *strinse i denti ed avanzò*, he set his teeth and advanced ‖ *tenere l'anima coi denti*, to hang on to life ‖ *la lingua batte dove il* — *duole*, *prov.* the tongue ever turns to the aching tooth **2.** (*morso*) sting: *il* — *dell'invidia*, the sting of envy **3.** (*cosa a forma di dente*) tooth; (*di forchetta*, *forcone*) prong; (*di ruota*) cog; (*di ancora*) fluke; (*di montagna*) jag: *i denti di un pettine*, *di una sega*, *di un rastrello*, the teeth of a comb, of a saw, of a rake; *rompere i denti a un pettine*, to break the teeth of a comb **4.** (*tec.*): — *a becco*, (*carpenteria*) gullet tooth; — *a cuspide*, (*mec.*) herring-bone tooth; — *a evolvente*, (*mec.*) involute tooth; — *allungato*, (*mec.*) elongated tooth; — *a sommità arrotondata*, (*mec.*) round-topped tooth; — *dell'innesto conduttore*, (*mec. aut.*) driving dog; — *di arresto*, (*mec.*) detent (*o* pawl *o* click *o* catch); — *di cremagliera*, (*mec.*) rack-tooth; — *di innesto*, (*mec.*) clutch claw (*o* clutch jaw *o* clutch dog); — *di ruota*, pawl, frip; *a* — *di sega*, saw-toothed (*o* serrated) **5.** — *di leone*, (*bot.*) dandelion **6.** *denti di cane*, (*zool.*) barnacles.

dentellàre, *v.t.* to indent, to notch.

dentellàto, *ag.* **1.** (*mec.*) indented, notched **2.** (*arch.*) denticulate.

dentellatúra, *s.f.* **1.** indent, indentation; (*tacca a V*) notch; (*a denti di sega*) serration **2.** (*arch.*) denticulation.

dentèllo, *s.m.* **1.** (*mec.*) tooth **2.** (*arch.*) dentil: *a dentelli*, denticulate **3.** (*ricamo*) dentelle, lace.

dèntice, *s.m.* (*ittiol.*) dentex.

dentièra, *s.f.* **1.** denture, dental plate; set of false teeth **2.** (*mec.*) (*cremagliera*) rack: *ferrovia a* —, rack railway.

dentifrício, *ag.* tooth (*attributivo*): *pasta dentifricia*,

tooth paste ‖ *s.m.* tooth-paste; dentifrice; (*in polvere*) tooth-powder; (*liquido*) mouth-wash.

dentína, *s.f.* dentine.

dentísta, *s.m.* dentist: *meccanico* —, dental mechanic; *trapano da* —, dentist's drill.

dentístico, *ag.* dental: *gabinetto* —, dentist's surgery.

dentizióne, *s.f.* dentition; teething; cutting of teeth.

déntro, *av.* **1.** in; (*rar.*) within; (*all'interno*) **inside:** *la casa è pulita* — *e fuori*, the house is clean inside and out(side) (*o arc.* the house is clean within and without); *è una bella casa a vedersi, chissà com'è* —*!*, that's a beautiful-looking house, I wonder what it is like inside!; *l'ho messo* —, I put it in; *venite* —*!*, come in! (*o* come inside!) ‖ *da* —, from within ‖ *o* — *o fuori!*, in or out! ‖ *volto, piegato in* —, turned, folded back ‖ *andar* —, (*fam.*) to go to prison; *metter* —, (*fam.*) to imprison (*o* to send to prison) ‖ *aver male* —, to have internal pains ‖ *darci* —, (*lavorar sodo*) to work hard (on sthg.); (*indovinare*) to guess right (*o* to hit the nail on the head): *dagli* —*!*, (*colpiscilo!*) hit him! (*o* get at him!) **2.** (*interiormente*) **inwardly:** *tremava* — *al pensiero*, she trembled inwardly at the thought; *cova* — *malvagi pensieri*, he harbours evil thoughts; *non dice a nessuno che cosa ha* —, he doesn't tell anyone what he is thinking or feeling ‖ *prep.* **1.** (*all'interno di*) **in, inside;** (*contrapposto a* fuori) **within:** — *casa*, indoors; — *la casa*, in (*o* within *o* inside) the house; — *i confini*, within the boundaries; — *le mura*, within the walls; — *questi limiti*, within these limits; — *un raggio di due miglia*, within a radius of two miles; *è vuoto, non c'è* — *niente!*, it's empty, there is nothing in it!; *era* — *una gabbia*, it was in(side) a cage ‖ — *di me pensai che...*, I thought to myself that...; *una voce* — *di me disse...*, a voice within me said... ‖ *esser* — *a una cosa*, (*esserne partecipe*) to be in on sthg. **2.** (*riferito a tempo*) **within:** — *un mese*, within a month ‖ *s.m.* inside ‖ *dal di* —, on the inside; from the inside: *la porta è sprangata dal di* —, the door is bolted on the inside; *la porta si apre dal di* —, the door opens from the inside.

denudàre, *v.t.* **1.** to denude; to strip **2.** (*scoprire*) to uncover, to lay bare: *il dottore le denudò il braccio*, the doctor laid bare her arm ‖ **denudàrsi**, *v.r.* to strip; to undress.

denudazióne, *s.f.* denudation; stripping.

denúncia, denúnzia, *s.f.* **1.** denunciation, denouncement; (*accusa*) accusation, charge: — *di un delitto*, denunciation of a crime **2.** (*disdetta*) denunciation: — *di un trattato*, denunciation of a treaty **3.** (*dichiarazione*) declaration, statement: — *dei redditi*, statement of one's income; — *di matrimonio*, (*pubblicazioni*) banns of marriage.

denunciaménto, denunziaménto, *s.m.* denunciation.

denunciàre, denunziàre, *v.t.* **1.** to denounce: *il rossore denuncia la febbre*, flush denounces fever; — *qlcu.*, to inform against s.o. **2.** (*disdire*) to denounce: — *un trattato*, to denounce a treaty **3.** (*dichiarare*) to report; to declare; to state: — *una nascita*, to report a birth.

denunciatóre, denunziatóre, *s.m.*, **denunciatríce, denunziatríce**, *s.f.* **1.** denunciator; denouncer **2.** (*spia*) informer; spy.

denutríto, *ag.* underfed; starving.

denutrizióne, *s.f.* underfeeding; malnutrition; starvation.

deodàra, *s.f.* (*bot.*) deodar.

deodorànte, *ag.* deodorizing ‖ *s.m.* deodorizer, deodorant.

deodoràre, *v.t.* to deodorize.

deontología, *s.f.* (*scient.*) deontology.

deossidàre, *v.t.* (*chim.*) to deoxidize.

deostruènte, *ag.s.* (*farm.*) aperient.

deostruíre, *v.t.* (*med.*) to loosen (the bowels).

depauperaménto, *s.m.* depauperation, impoverishment: *il — del terreno*, the impoverishment of the soil.

depauperàre, *v.t.* to depauperate, to impoverish.

depennàre, *v.t.* (*cancellare*) to cross out; to strike out: *— un nome da una lista*, to strike a name out of a list (*o* to cross a name off a list).

deperíbile, *ag.* perishable: *merce —*, perishable goods.

deperiménto, *s.m.* 1. (*di salute*) wasting away; loss of strength; (*per un dolore*) pining away 2. (*di cose*) decay; deterioration.

deperíre, *v.i.* 1. (*in salute*) to waste away; to lose strength; (*per un dolore*) to pine away 2. (*di pianta*) to wither 3. (*di cose*) to decay, to deteriorate.

depilàre, *v.t.* to remove hair from (sthg.); to depilate ‖ **depilàrsi**, *v.r.* to depilate oneself: *— le sopracciglia*, to pluck one's eyebrows.

depilatóre, *s.m.* hair-remover, depilator.

depilatòrio, *ag.* hair-removing; depilatory.

depilazióne, *s.f.* hair-removal; depilation: *— delle sopracciglia*, eyebrow plucking.

deplezióne, *s.f.* (*patol.*) depletion.

deploràbile, *ag.* deplorable, lamentable, pitiable.

deplorabilménte, *av.* deplorably, lamentably.

deploràre, *v.t.* 1. (*essere spiacenti di*) to deplore, to be sorry about (sthg.); (*lagnarsi di*) to complain of (sthg.); (*dolersi di, piangere*) to deplore, to lament, to grieve over (sthg.), to mourn: *questo è ciò che deploro*, that's what I am complaining about; *— la morte di qlcu.*, to grieve over s.o.'s death; *— la propria sorte*, to deplore (*o* to bewail) one's fate 2. (*biasimare*) to blame, to censure, to disapprove of (sthg.): *è da —*, he is to blame.

deplorazióne, *s.f.* 1. (*disapprovazione*) blame, censure, disapproval 2. (*dispiacere*) lamentation, regret.

deplorévole, *ag.* 1. (*da compiangere*) deplorable, lamentable, pitiable 2. (*biasimevole*) blamable, censurable.

deplorevolménte, *av.* deplorably, lamentably.

depolarizzànte, *ag.* (*fis.*) depolarizing ‖ *s.m.* (*fis.*) depolarizer.

depolarizzàre, *v.t.* (*fis.*) to depolarize.

depolarizzatóre, *s.m.* (*fis.*) depolarizer.

depolarizzazióne, *s.f.* (*fis.*) depolarization.

deponènte, *ag.* (*gram.*) deponent ‖ *s.c.* (*dir.*) witness, deponent.

depórre, *v.t.* 1. to put, to lay; (*mettere giù*) to put down, to lay down; (*mettere da parte*) to lay aside: *deponi ciò che hai in mano!*, put down (*o* lay down) what you have in your hand!; *deponi il tuo lavoro a maglia e guarda questo pizzo!*, lay aside your knitting and look at this lace!; *deposi il libro sul tavolo*, I put (*o* laid) the book upon the table ‖ *— le armi*, to lay down one's arms (*o* to cease fighting *o* to surrender); *— il cappello al guardaroba*, to leave one's hat in the cloak room ‖ *— il bilancio*, (*in caso di fallimento*) to file a statement of one's own affairs with the court ‖ *— il proprio orgoglio*, to pocket one's pride ‖ *— qlcu. da una carica*, to remove s.o. from (an) office; *— un ufficio*, to resign from office ‖ *— un re*, (*detronizzarlo*) to depose a king ‖ *— le uova*, to lay eggs 2. (*depositare*) to deposit: *— materie estranee*, to deposit a sediment 3. (*dir.*) (*testimoniare, in giudizio*) to witness, to bear witness: *il falso*, to bear false witness 4. (*rinunziare a*) to give up: *deponete ogni speranza di rivederlo!*, give up all hope of seeing him again! ‖ *v.i.* (*dir.*) (*testimoniare*) to depose, to give evidence, to testify: *— a favore di qlcu.*, to give evidence in s.o.'s favour (*o* to testify on s.o.'s behalf); *— contro qlcu.*, to give evidence (*o* to testify) against s.o. ‖ *ciò non depone a tuo favore!*, this is not to your credit! (*o* this doesn't speak in your favour!).

deportàre, *v.t.* to deport, to banish; to transport: *dopo un lungo processo fu deportato*, he was deported (*o* banished) after a long trial; *fu deportato in Siberia*, he was deported to Siberia; *— un condannato*, to transport a convict.

deportàto, *ag.* deported; transported ‖ *s.m.* convict.

deportazióne, *s.f.* deportation: *condannato alla —*, sentenced to deportation.

depositànte, *ag.* depositing ‖ *s.m.* (*presso banche*) depositor: *— a risparmio*, savings depositor; *libretto del —*, depositor's book.

depositàre, *v.t.* to deposit, to lodge; (*immagazzinare*) to store: *— denari in una banca*, to deposit (*o* to lodge) money in a bank; *— merci*, to store goods ‖ *v.i.* (*di liquidi*) to deposit.

depositàrio, *s.m.* 1. (*comm.*) depositary; bailee, trustee; consignee 2. *fig.* (*confidente*) repository.

depòsito, *s.m.* 1. deposit: *— cauzionale*, (*comm.*) security; (*dir.*) bail; *— con preavviso di trenta giorni*, deposit subject to 30 days' notice; *— fruttifero*, interest-bearing deposit; *— vincolato*, deposit account; *cassa depositi e prestiti*, deposit and consignment office; *denaro in —*, money on deposit; *in conto —*, on consignment; *ricevuta di —*, deposit-receipt; *ha un grosso — nella nostra banca*, he has a big deposit with our bank; *per avere in prestito l'apparecchio fotografico dovetti lasciare un —*, to borrow the camera I had to pay a deposit ‖ *avere ql.co. in —*, to have sthg. in trust; *dare ql.co. in — a qlcu.*, to commit sthg. to a person's trust 2. (*il depositare*) depositing, deposition; storing 3. (*luogo in cui depositare*) warehouse, storehouse, storage; depository; shed: *— bagagli*, (*ferr.*) left-luggage room (*o* office); *— delle locomotive*, (*ferr.*) engine shed; *— di vino*, cellar; *— franco*, (*comm.*) bonded warehouse; *— legnami*, timber yard; *— materiali*, stock yard; *— militare*, depot; *camera di —*, (*di preziosi*) strong-room; *certificato di —*, warehouse receipt; *cassaforte per il — dei preziosi*, wall-safe for the storage of valuables 4. (*cosa depositata*) deposit; sediment; dregs (*pl.*): *— alluvionale*, (*geol.*) drift; *— calcareo*, (*chim.*) lime (*o* hard) deposit; *un — di fango copriva le strade*, a deposit of mud covered the streets; *— di metallo elettrolitico*, (*elett.*) electrolytic metal deposit.

deposizióne, *s.f.* 1. deposition: *— da una carica*, removal from an office; *— dal trono*, deposition from the throne (*o* dethronement) ‖ *la Deposizione*, (*di Cristo*) the Deposition (from the Cross) ‖ *la Deposizione di Tiziano*, the Deposition by Titian 2. (*dir.*) deposition; evidence: *le deposizioni dei testimoni*, the evidence of the witnesses; *fare una —*, to depose (*o* to make a deposition): *fare una — in favore di qlcu.*, to give evidence in s.o.'s favour.

depósto, *s.m.* (*dir.*) deposition, sworn evidence.

depravàre, *v.t.* to deprave, to corrupt, to pervert: *— i giovani*, to corrupt youth.

depravàto, *ag.* depraved, corrupt, perverted: *gusto —*, depraved taste.

depravatóre, *s.m.*, **depravatríce**, *s.f.* depraver, corrupter.

depravazióne, *s.f.* 1. (*il depravare*) depravation, corruption, perversion 2. (*l'essere depravato*) depravity, corruption, perversion.

deprecàbile, *ag.* deprecable.

deprecàre, *v.t.* to deprecate, to entreat, to beseech: *— la guerra, il proprio fato*, to deprecate war, one's fate; *— qlcu. di fare ql.co.*, to entreat s.o. to do sthg.

deprecativaménte, *av.* deprecatingly, entreatingly.

deprecatívo, *ag.* (*rar.*) deprecatory, deprecative.

deprecatòrio, *ag.* deprecatory.

deprecazióne, *s.f.* deprecation, entreaty.

depredaménto, *s.m.* depredation, plunder, pillage, marauding, ravaging, sack, despoilation.

depredàre, *v.t.* to plunder, to pillage, to maraud, to ravage, to sack, to despoil, to loot: *i vincitori depredarono le campagne*, the victors ravaged the countryside; *si lasciò libertà ai soldati di saccheggiare e —*, the soldiers were let loose to ravage and plunder.

depredatóre, *ag.* plundering ‖ *s.m.*, **depredatríce**, *s.f.* depredator, spoiler, despoiler, pillager.

depredazióne, *s.f.* depredation, plunder, pillage, maraud.

depressióne, *s.f.* **1.** depression, hollow: *qui il terreno forma una profonda —,* the ground forms a deep hollow here; *i soldati si nascosero agli occhi del nemico in una piccola —,* the soldiers hid from the enemy in a slight depression **2.** *fig.* (*abbattimento*) depression; low spirits (*pl.*); dejection: *era in uno stato di grave —,* she was in a state of deep depression; *si uccise in un momento di —,* she killed herself in a fit of depression **3.** (*astr. fis.*) depression: *— dell'orizzonte,* depression of the horizon; *angolo di —,* (*geom.*) angle of depression **4.** (*meteorologia*) depression: *— secondaria,* secondary depression; *una — sulle Alpi porterà pioggia sull'Italia settentrionale,* a depression over the Alps is likely to cause rain in the north of Italy **5.** (*econ.*) depression: *— degli affari,* business depression.

depressivo, *ag.* depressing.

deprèsso, *ag.* **1.** depressed || *zone depresse,* (*econ.*) depressed zones **2.** (*abbattuto, demoralizzato*) depressed, dispirited, disheartened, dejected, discouraged: *ha un'aria depressa,* she looks depressed; *essere —,* to be discouraged (*o* depressed *o* in low spirits) **3.** (*med.*) weak: *polso —,* very weak pulse.

depressóre, *ag.* (*anat.*) depressor || *s.m.* (*anat.*) depressor (muscle).

deprezzaménto, *s.m.* depreciation: *— del valore della moneta,* (*econ.*) depreciation (*o* fall) in the value of money; *subire un —,* (*comm.*) to suffer (*o* to undergo) a depreciation.

deprezzàre, *v.t.* to depreciate; to disparage; (*sottovalutare*) to undervalue: *— uno stabile,* to depreciate a building.

deprimènte, *ag.* **1.** depressing, discouraging, disheartening; (*uggioso*) tiresome: *notizie deprimenti,* depressing news; *è proprio un individuo —,* he is really a tiresome fellow **2.** (*farm.*) sedative: *un medicamento —,* a sedative drug.

deprimere, *v.t.* **1.** to depress, to discourage, to dishearten, to dispirit, to deject: *questo tempo mi deprime,* this weather depresses me; *tutti quegli incidenti lo hanno molto depresso,* all those accidents discouraged (*o* disheartened) him very much **2.** (*conculcare*) to humble, to oppress: *— la superbia,* to humble the pride **3.** (*med.*) to depress: *— l'azione del cuore,* to depress the action of the heart | **deprìmersi,** *v.r.* to get discouraged, to get disheartened.

depuraménto, *s.m.* purification, depuration.

depuràre, *v.t.,* **depuràrsi,** *v.r.* to purify, to depurate: *— il sangue,* to purify (*o* to depurate) the blood.

depurativo, *ag.* purifying, depurative || *s.m.* (*farm.*) purifying substance, depurative.

depuratóre, *ag.* purifying || *s.m.* depurator; (*mec.*) cleaner: *— ad acqua,* (*chim.*) washer; *— d'acqua,* (*chim. fis.*) water conditioner (*o* water softener); *— d'olio,* (*mec.*) oil cleaner.

depuratòrio, *ag.* purifying, depurative || *s.m.* water-purifier.

depurazióne, *s.f.* purification, depuration: *— del gas,* (*ind.*) gas purification; *— per via umida,* wet purification.

deputàre, *v.t.* **1.** to depute, to delegate: *fu deputato a rappresentare i cittadini,* he was deputed to represent the citizens **2.** (*destinare*) to fix: *— un giorno per le nozze,* to fix a day for the wedding.

deputàta, deputatéssa, *s.f.* (*pol.*) female deputy; (*in Gran Bretagna*) female Member of Parliament.

deputàto, *ag.* (*fissato*) fixed: *il giorno —,* the fixed day || *s.m.* **1.** (*pol.*) deputy; (*in Gran Bretagna*) Member of Parliament || *Camera dei Deputati,* Chamber of Deputies; (*in Gran Bretagna*) House of Commons **2.** (*delegato*) deputy, delegate, representative: *i deputati italiani a un congresso straniero,* the Italian delegates at (*o* to) a foreign congress.

deputazióne, *s.f.* deputation; (*delegazione*) delegation.

deragliaménto, *s.m.* (*ferr.*) derailment.

deragliàre, *v.i.* (*ferr.*) to go off the rails: *il treno deragliò,* the train went (*o* ran) off the rails || *far — un treno,* to derail a train.

derattizzàre, *v.t.* (*amer.*) to clear by deratization.

derattizzazióne, *s.f.* (*amer.*) deratization.

derelìtto, *ag.* forlorn, abandoned, forsaken || *s.m.* foundling: *ospizio dei derelitti,* foundling hospital; *un povero —,* a helpless wretch.

deretàno, *s.m.* posterior; buttocks (*pl.*); (*fam.*) behind, bottom, backside.

derídere, *v.t.* to laugh at (s.o., sthg.), to deride, to mock, to ridicule; to make fun of (s.o., sthg.): *i monelli deridevano il suo aspetto,* the urchins laughed at his appearance.

derisìbile, *ag.* laughable, mockable.

derisióne, *s.f.* derision, mockery, ridicule: *oggetto di —,* object of derision; *la vostra offerta è una —,* yours is a laughable offer (*o* your offer is an insult).

derisivo, *ag.* (*rar.*) derisive, derisory.

derìso, *ag.* derided, mocked, ridiculed.

derisóre, *s.m.* derider, mocker.

derisoriaménte, *av.* derisively, mockingly; scoffingly.

derisòrio, *ag.* derisory, derisive, mocking; scoffing.

derìva, *s.f.* (*mar. aer.*) drift: *— a coltello,* (*mar.*) dagger board; *— mobile,* (*mar.*) sliding keel; *ala di —,* (*mar.*) leeboard; *alla —,* (*mar.*) adrift: *andare alla —,* to drift (anche *fig.*): *la nave andava alla —,* the ship went adrift; *sta andando alla —,* *fig.* he is just drifting: *angolo di —,* (*aer.*) leeway (*o* drift angle); (*mar.*) drift angle: *pennone di —,* (*aer.*) fin post.

derivàbile, *ag.* derivable.

derivaménto, *V.* **derivazióne 1.**

derivàre, *v.i.* **1.** (*scaturire, originarsi*) to rise; to spring: *i fiumi derivano dai monti,* rivers rise in the mountains; *questi due canali derivano dallo stesso fiume,* these two canals spring from the same river **2.** (*provenire*) to derive, to come, to be derived; (*risultare*) to result, to ensue: *ciò deriva dal fatto che egli è tanto ambizioso,* it comes from his being so ambitious; *l'italiano deriva dal latino,* Italian derives from Latin; *ne è derivato un gran male,* much harm resulted from this; *questa parola deriva dal greco,* this word derives (*o* comes *o* is derived) from Greek; *la sua azione deriva dalla paura,* his action springs from fear; *il suo successo derivò dalla volontà,* his success arose from his will **3.** (*aer.*) (*deviare*) to drift || *v.t.* **1.** (*sviare la corrente di*) to divert: *— acqua da un fiume,* to divert a stream **2.** (*far provenire*) to derive: *— una parola dal greco,* to derive a word from Greek **3.** (*elett.*) to shunt.

derivàta, *s.f.* (*mat.*) derivative: *— di rotazione,* (*aer.*) rotary derivative; *— di stabilità,* (*aer.*) stability derivative.

derivativo, *ag.* derivative.

derivàto, *ag.* derived; (*derivativo*) derivative: *accordo —,* (*mus.*) derivative; *circuito —,* (*elett.*) derived circuit; *corrente derivata,* (*elett.*) derived current || *s.m.* **1.** (*chim.*) derivative **2.** (*sottoprodotto*) by-product: *i derivati del nylon,* the by-products of nylon.

derivazióne, *s.f.* **1.** derivation: *è interessante studiare la — delle parole,* it is interesting to study the derivations of words **2.** (*elett.*) shunt: *— magnetica,* magnetic shunt **3.** (*med.*) derivation.

derivòmetro, *s.m.* (*mar.*) drift indicator; (*aer.*) drift meter.

dèrma, *s.m.* (*anat.*) derm, derma.

dermaschéletro, *s.m.* (*scient.*) dermoskeleton.

dermàtico, *ag.* (*anat.*) dermatic, dermic; dermal.

dermatìte, *s.f.* (*patol.*) dermatitis.

dermatología, *s.f.* (*med.*) dermatology.

dermatològico, *ag.* (*med.*) dermatological.

dermatòlogo, *s.m.* dermatologist.

dermatoplàstica, *s.f.* (*chir.*) dermatoplasty.

dermatòsi, *s.f.* (*patol.*) dermatosis.

dermatozòi, *s.m.pl.* (*scient.*) Dermatozoa.

dermèste, *s.m.* (*entom.*) dermestes.

dèrmico, *ag.* dermatic; dermic.

dermofíta, *s.m.* (*parassita*) dermatophyte.

dermografía, *s.f.* (*med.*) dermatography, dermography.

dermòide, *ag.* dermatoid, dermoid; dermal: *cisti* —, (*patol.*) dermoid cyst ‖ *s.f.* (*neol.*) (*imitazione di cuoio, pelle*) leatherette.

dermopatía, *s.f.* (*patol.*) dermatopathy, dermopathy.

dèrno, in, *l.av.* (*rar.*): *bandiera in* —, (*mar.*) rolled-up flag; distress flag.

derobàre, *v.i.* (*equitazione*) to balk, to jib.

dèroga, *s.f.* derogation: — *a una legge*, derogation of a law; — *a un privilegio*, derogation from a privilege ‖ *in* — *al regolamento*, making an exception to the regulations; *in* — *alla precedente giurisprudenza*, derogating (*o* in derogation) from former jurisprudence.

derogàbile, *ag.* that can be derogated.

derogàre, *v.i.* **1.** to derogate (from sthg.); to deviate (from sthg.); to depart (from sthg.): — *all'autorità di qlcu.*, to derogate from s.o.'s authority; — *alla consuetudine*, to derogate from the established custom; *non intendiamo per alcuna ragione* — *alla norma fino ad ora seguita*, by no means do we intend to deviate (*o* to depart) from the rule followed until now **2.** (*contravvenire*) to contravene (sthg.): — *a una legge*, to break a law.

derogatívo, *ag.* derogatory.

derogatòria, *s.f.* (*dir.*) derogatory clause.

derogatòrio, *ag.* derogatory.

derogazióne, *s.f.* derogation.

derràta, *s.f.* **1.** victual: *derrate alimentari*, food-stuffs; victuals **2.** (*merce*) commodity.

derubàre, *v.t.* to rob, to plunder, to spoil: — *qlcu. di ql.co.*, to rob s.o. of sthg.: *mi derubarono del borsellino*, I was robbed of my purse.

derubàto, *s.m.* victim of a robbery.

dèrvis, *s.m.* dervish.

deschétto, *s.m.* little table; (*del calzolaio*) cobbler's bench.

désco, *s.m.* **1.** dinner table, table; table laid for a meal: *la cena era pronta sul* —, supper was ready on the table; *stare a* —, to eat ‖ — *molle*, dessert: *al* — *molle vi alzerete da tavola*, at the dessert you will rise from table **2.** (*pancone del macellaio*) butcher's bench **3.** (*banco*) bench; (*sgabello*) stool.

descrittívo, *ag.* descriptive: *anatomia, geometria descrittiva*, descriptive anatomy, geometry.

descrittóre, *s.m.*, **descrittríce**, *s.f.* describer.

descrívere, *v.t.* **1.** to describe, to relate, to delineate: *descrisse la scena a vivaci colori*, he described the scene in bright colours; *lo descrissero come un furfante*, they described him as a rascal; *le parole non possono* — *la scena*, words cannot describe the scene; — *le proprie avventure*, to relate one's adventures **2.** (*percorrere*) to describe: *il missile descrisse un'ampia curva*, the missile described a wide curve **3.** (*tracciare*) to describe, to delineate: *descrivi un cerchio*, describe a circle.

descrivíbile, *ag.* describable.

descrizióne, *s.f.* description: — *particolareggiata*, (*comm.*) specification; *è abilissimo nelle descrizioni*, he is very good at descriptions.

Desdèmona, *no.pr.f.* (*lett.*) Desdemona.

desensibilizzatóre, *s.m.* (*foto.*) desensitizer.

desèrtico, *ag.* desert; (*desolato*) barren, waste, desolate: *terre desertiche*, desert (*o* waste) lands.

desèrto, *ag.* **1.** (*disabitato*) desert, uninhabited, wild: *un'isola deserta*, a desert island; *a quell'ora la spiaggia era deserta*, there was no one on the beach at that time **2.** (*solitario*) lonely, solitary; (*appartato*) seclud-

ed **3.** (*rar.*) (*non coltivato*) waste, untilled, barren **4.** (*letter.*) (*abbandonato*) deserted, forsaken ‖ *asta deserta*, (*dir.*) void auction sale ‖ *s.m.* desert; wilderness: *il* — *del Sahara*, the Sahara Desert ‖ *predicare al* —, to preach to the winds (*o* to talk to deaf ears).

desiàre, (*poet.*) per **desideràre**.

desideràbile, *ag.* desirable, to be desired: *poco* —, undesirable; *è* — *che...*, it is to be desired (*o* it is desirable) that....

desideràre, *v.t.* **1.** to wish: *desiderate che io venga con voi?*, do you wish me to come (*o* to go) with you?; *desidero partire subito*, I wish to leave at once; *quando desiderate che sia imbucata la lettera?*, when do you wish the letter (to be) posted? ‖ *farsi* —, (*essere in ritardo*) to be late; (*fare aspettare qlcu.*) to keep (s.o.) waiting ‖ *lasciar a* —, (*deludere*) to come short of expectation; (*non soddisfare*) to be unsatisfactory: *ciò lascia un po' a* —, it is not quite satisfactory (*o* not quite up to the mark); *la sua condotta lasciava molto a* —, his behaviour left much to be desired; *non lasciar nulla a* —, to be quite satisfactory (*o* to come up to expectation *o* to be all that could be desired *o* to be all that one could wish for) **2.** (*desiderare di avere*) to wish for (sthg.), (*rar.*) to wish; to want; to desire; (*bramare*) to long for (sthg.), to yearn for (sthg.), to crave for (sthg.), to be eager for (sthg.); (*fam.*) to hanker after (sthg.): *che cosa desiderate?*, what do you want? (*o* what do you wish for?); *desiderava ardentemente di intraprendere questo viaggio*, he was eager to undertake this journey; *desideravamo molto di rivederla*, we longed to see her again; *è il denaro ciò che noi desideriamo*, money is what we are after; *noi tutti desideriamo la felicità*, we all desire happiness; *ti desidero molto*, I am longing for you; — *delle lodi*, to hanker after praise; — *di rivedere la propria terra*, to yearn for the sight of one's native land; — *ql.co. da qlcu.*, to want sthg. from (*o* of) s.o. **3.** (*augurare*) to wish: *gli desidero ogni felicità*, I wish him all happiness.

desideràta[1], *s.m. pl.* desiderata.

Desideràta[2], *no.pr.f.* Desiderata, Désirée.

desideratívo, *ag.* desiderative.

desideràto, *ag.* desired; (*bramato*) longed for; (*aspettato*) expected ‖ *s.m.* (*rar.*) desideratum (*pl.* desiderata): *i desiderati della scienza*, the aims of science.

desidèrio[1], *s.m.* wish; desire; (*brama*) longing (for s.o., sthg.), craving (for sthg.), hunger (for sthg.), yearning (for *o* after sthg.); (*sl. americano*) yen: — *di piacere*, wish to please; *ardente* — *di riuscire*, eagerness to succeed; *gran* — *di piacere*, anxiety to please; *secondo il* — *di mio padre*, at (*o* by) my father's wish; *non ho alcun* — *di partire*, I have no wish to leave ‖ *accondiscendere a un* —, to grant a request; *appagare i desideri di qlcu.*, to satisfy s.o.'s wishes; *compiacere ai desideri di qlcu.*, to comply with s.o.'s wishes; *esprimere il* — *di fare ql.co.*, to express a wish to do sthg.; *provare* — *di fare ql.co.*, to feel the desire to do sthg.

Desidèrio[2], *no.pr.m.* (*st.*) Desiderius.

desiderosaménte, *av.* eagerly; longingly.

desideróso, *ag.* desirous; (*bramoso*) eager (for sthg., to do), longing (for s.o., sthg.), yearning (for, after s.o., sthg.): *con occhi desiderosi*, with longing (*o* yearning) eyes; *sono* — *di piacervi*, I am desirous of pleasing you (*o* I am anxious to please you *o* I desire to please you).

designàbile, *ag.* that may be designated.

designàre, *v.t.* **1.** (*proporre*) to designate, to nominate, to appoint: *fu designato vescovo*, he was appointed (*o* nominated *o* designated) bishop; — *un esperto*, to appoint an expert; — *qlcu. a un incarico*, to appoint s.o. to an office **2.** (*destinare*) to appoint, to designate: *nel luogo designato*, at the appointed place; *il colonnello X è stato designato a Tolone*, colonel X has been ordered (*o* drafted) to Toulon; — *un giorno, un luogo per un appuntamento*, to appoint (*o* to fix *o* to set) a day, a meeting-place; — *qlcu. proprio erede*, to designate s.o. (as) one's heir (*o* to make s.o. one's heir) **3**. (*indicare*) to designate, to indicate, to point out: *è stato designato il più geniale del suo tempo*, he has been designated the greatest genius of his age.

designàto, *ag.* designate ‖ *console* —, (*st. romana*) consul designate.

designazióne, *s.f.* designation, nomination, appointment.

desinàre, *s.m.* dinner: *dopo* —, early in the afternoon; *un magro* —, a poor (*o* scanty) meal.

desinàre, *v.i.* to dine, to have dinner: *far da* —, to get the dinner ready (*o* to prepare the dinner).

desinènza, *s.f.* (*gram.*) ending, termination.

desío, (*poet.*) per **desidèrio**.

desiosaménte, *av.* (*poet.*) eagerly, longingly.

desióso, (*poet.*) per **desideróso**.

desíre, (*arc. poet.*) per **desidèrio**.

desístere, *v.i.* to desist; to cease; to leave off (sthg., doing); (*rinunciare*) to give up (sthg., doing): *dopo molti tentativi inutili egli desistette*, he gave up after many unsuccessful attempts; *dopo un po' egli desistette dal tormentarli*, after a while he ceased tormenting (*o* to torment) them; *non desistette dall'idea di andare a Parigi*, he did not give up the idea of going to Paris; *solo a notte desistette dalle sue ricerche*, he did not give up (*o* leave off) his search till nightfall; — *dai propri propositi*, to give up one's purpose.

desmología, *s.f.* (*anat. chir.*) desmology.

desmopatía, *s.f.* (*patol.*) desmopathy.

desolànte, *ag.* distressing, grievous, afflicting, desolating: *è stato uno spettacolo* —, it was a distressing sight; *le notizie che ho ricevuto da casa sono davvero desolanti*, the news I received from home is really distressing.

desolàre, *v.t.* **1**. (*devastare*) to desolate: *i barbari desolarono il paese*, the barbarians desolated the country **2**. (*addolorare*) to grieve, to distress, to desolate.

desolataménte, *av.* desolately, disconsolately.

desolàto, *ag.* **1**. (*negletto, abbandonato*) desolate, neglected; (*devastato*) devastated: *landa desolata*, barren moor; *paese* —, desolate country **2**. (*sconsolato*) desolate, forlorn, disconsolate, distressed, afflicted: *aver l'aria desolata*, to have a woebegone look **3**. (*spiacente*) sorry: *siamo desolati d'apprendere che...*, we regret very much to hear that...; *sono* —!, I am sorry!.

desolazióne, *s.f.* **1**. (*squallore*) desolation, neglect; (*devastazione*) devastation, ruin **2**. (*dolore grave*) desolation, grief, sorrow, distress, affliction: *grido di* —, desolate (*o* disconsolate) cry; *vederlo in quello stato*, *è una* —, it is distressing to see him in that state; *essere nella più grande* —, to be plunged in grief.

dèspota, *s.m.* **1**. despot, tyrant (*anche fig.*): *quel direttore è un* —, that director is a despot **2**. (*st.*) (*governatore bizantino*) despot.

desquamazióne, *s.f.* desquamation.

dèssa, *pron.f.* (*arc.*) (*lei stessa, proprio lei*) she herself; she ‖ **désso**, *pron.m.* (*arc.*) **he himself**; he: *è* —, *è lui quel* —, it is he himself; (*fam.*) it's him.

destàre, *v.t.* **1**. to wake (up), to awake, to awaken: *a che ora desideri essere destato?*, (at) what time do you wish to be waked?; *lo destai presto ieri, ma egli continuò a dormire*, I awoke him (*o* woke him up) early yesterday, but he went on sleeping; *destalo alle nove*, wake him up at nine ‖ *non — il can che dorme*, *prov.* let sleeping dogs lie **2**. (*scuotere dal torpore*) to wake up, to rouse, to stir (up): *cerca di destarlo*, try to wake (*o* to stir) him up (*o* to rouse him); *la nuova linea ferroviaria destò la zona dal suo torpore*, the new railway roused the district from its torpor **3**. (*suscitare*) to awaken, to arouse, to rouse, to stir: *l'argomento destò il nostro interesse*, the subject awakened our interest; *ciò desta la pietà di tutti*, this arouses every-

body's pity; *l'insulto destò la nostra ira*, the insult roused our anger; — *la curiosità, il sospetto di qlcu.*, to awaken (*o* to rouse) s.o.'s curiosity, suspicion; — *i ricordi*, to wake memories ‖ **destàrsi**, *v.r.* to wake up, to awake, to awaken: *si destò con un sussulto*, he woke up with a start; *si desta sempre alle sette*, he always wakes up at seven; — *da un'illusione*, to awake (*o* to wake up) from an illusion.

destinàre, *v.t.* **1**. to destine: *è destinato a diventar celebre*, he is destined to become famous; *è destinato a morire sul patibolo*, he is fated (*o* doomed) to die on the scaffold; *è destinato a rimanere celibe*, he is destined to remain a bachelor; *erano destinati a incontrarsi di nuovo*, they were destined to meet again; *essi la destinarono in moglie a un uomo ricco*, they intended that she should marry a rich man; *ha destinato il suo figlio cadetto alla professione medica*, he has destined his younger son for the medical profession; *il loro piano è destinato a fallire*, their plan is bound (*o* doomed) to fail **2**. (*assegnare, devolvere*) to assign, to allot, to employ; (*nei bilanci ufficiali*) to appropriate: *l'eccedenza è stata destinata a beneficio dei poveri*, the surplus has been employed for the benefit of the poor; — *una somma ad un acquisto*, to allot (*o* to assign) a sum of money to a purchase **3**. (*stabilire*) to appoint: *nel luogo e all'ora destinati per l'incontro*, at the place and time appointed for the meeting **4**. (*nominare*) to appoint, to nominate: *lo destinarono a un altro ufficio*, they appointed him to another office; *il Sig. X è stato destinato a dirigere la nostra filiale di Milano*, Mr. X has been appointed manager of our branch in Milan **5**. (*dedicare*) to devote: *voglio — a ciò almeno un'ora al giorno*, I want to devote to this at least one hour a day **6**. (*riservare*) to intend, to design, to mean: *a chi è destinata quella merce?*, whom are those goods for?; *la merce a voi destinata è stata spedita oggi*, the goods intended for you have been shipped to-day; *il premio è destinato a onorare la sua memoria*, the prize is intended to commemorate her; *quel dono è destinato a sua madre*, that present is (intended) for his mother; *questo ruolo è destinato a un bravissimo attore*, this role is designed (*o* intended *o* meant) for a very good actor **7**. (*indirizzare*) to address: *quella lettera è destinata al mio migliore amico*, that letter is addressed to my best friend **8**. (*decidere*) to decide: *ha destinato di partire immediatamente*, he has decided to leave immediately.

destinatàrio, *s.m.* (*comm.*) addressee, consignee, receiver: — *del carico*, cargo-receiver; *rifiutato dal* —, refused by addressee; *spese a carico del* —, charges forward.

destinazióne, *s.f.* **1**. destination: *luogo, porto di* —, place, port of destination; *la lettera è giunta a* —, the letter has come to hand; *merci che non giungono a* —, goods falling short of destination; *la nostra — è Napoli*, (*mar.*) we are bound for Naples; *giungere a* —, (*di persone*) to reach one's destination; (*di cose*) to reach destination **2**. (*fine a cui una cosa è destinata*) destination, intended purpose.

destíno, *s.m.* **1**. (*fato*) destiny, fate: *il — ci giuoca spesso dei brutti tiri*, destiny (*o* fate) often plays unkind tricks on us; *il nostro — è un mistero*, our destiny is a mystery **2**. (*sorte*) lot: *i destini della patria*, the fortunes of one's country; *è il — comune*, it is the common lot **3**. (*destinazione*) destination.

destituíre, *v.t.* **1**. to dismiss; to discharge; to remove: — *un funzionario*, to dismiss an official **2**. (*mil.*) to cashier, to dismiss.

destituíto, *ag.* destitute, devoid; lacking (in sthg.): — *di ogni senso morale*, devoid of (*o* lacking in) any moral sense; *accusa destituita di fondamento*, groundless (*o* unfounded) charge.

destituzióne, *s.f.* dismissal, removal: — *di un funzionario governativo*, removal of a government official.

désto, *ag.* 1. awake: *sei — o dormi?*, are you awake or asleep?; *son ben —!*, I am wide awake! ‖ *tenne desta la nostra attenzione*, he held our attention 2. (*vivace*) lively; (*sagace*) sharp, quick: *che fanciullo —!*, what a quick (*o* sharp *o* bright) boy!.

dèstra, *s.f.* 1. right hand: *nella — teneva due monete d'oro*, in his right hand he held two gold coins; *vorrei stringergli la —*, I should like to shake hands with him; *si strinsero la —*, they shook hands 2. (*parte destra*) right, right side; right-hand side: *a —*, on the right (*o* on the right-hand side); *alla tua —*, on your right; *volti a —*, turn to the right; *tenere la —*, to keep (to the) right 3. (*pol.*) the Right, the conservative party; the conservative parties (*pl.*): *membro della —*, member of the Right; *un uomo politico dell'estrema —*, a very right-wing (politician).

destraménte, *av.* dexterously, skilfully; adroitly.

destreggiaménto, *s.m.* manoeuvring; clever management.

destreggiàre, *v.i.*, **destreggiàrsi**, *v.r.* to manage; to manoeuvre, to exert oneself, to contrive: *— per fare ql.co.*, to manage to do sthg.; *— per ottenere un buon posto*, to manoeuvre for position.

destrézza, *s.f.* 1. dexterity, skill, skilfulness; cleverness, adroitness: *— nel maneggiare le armi da fuoco*, skill in handling fire-arms; *— nel superare una difficoltà*, cleverness in getting out of a difficulty; *condurre un affare con —*, to manage an affair with skill (*o* cleverness) 2. (*agilità*) agility.

destrière, **destrièro**, *s.m.* (*poet.*) steed; (*da battaglia*) charger, war-horse.

destrína, *s.f.* (*chim.*) dextrin(e).

dèstro, *ag.* 1. right; right-hand (*attributivo*): *lato —*, right-hand side; *la riva destra di un fiume*, the right bank of a river; *si fece male all'occhio —*, he hurt his right eye ‖ *essere il braccio — di qlcu.*, *fig.* to be s.o.'s right-hand man 2. (*abile*) clever, adroit; (*specialmente di abilità manuale*) skilful, dexterous: *— nel fare ql.co.*, clever at (*o* dexterous in *o* skilful in) doing sthg. 3. (*sveglio*, *pronto*) alert, ready, quick 4. (*arald.*) dexter ‖ *s.m.* (*occasione propizia*) opportunity, chance: *mi si presentò il — di parlargli*, I had the opportunity (*o* a chance) of speaking to him; *cogliere il —*, to seize the opportunity.

destrogìro, *ag.* (*ott.*) dextrorotatory, positive.

destròrso, *ag.* 1. dextrorse, clock-wise (*attributivo*) 2. (*mec.*) right-hand, right-handed (*attributivi*) ‖ *av.* clockwise.

destròsio, *s.m.* (*chim.*) dextrose.

desuèto, *ag.* (*rar.*) 1. (*insolito*) unusual 2. (*antico*, *abbandonato*, *superato*) obsolete, out of use.

desuetúdine, *s.f.* (*rar.*) desuetude, disuse.

desultoriaménte, *av.* (*rar.*) desultorily.

desultòrio, *ag.* (*rar.*) desultory.

desúmere, *v.t.* 1. (*dedurre*) to infer, to deduce; (*trarre*) to draw: *donde si desume che...*, whence we infer that...; *— una conclusione*, to draw a conclusion; *— ql.co. da un fatto*, to deduce sthg. from a fact 2. (*congetturare*) to conjecture.

desumíbile, *ag.* 1. inferable, deducible 2. (*congetturabile*) conjecturable.

desúnto, *ag.* inferred, deduced: *notizia desunta dai giornali*, piece of news inferred from the newspapers.

detenére, *v.t.* 1. to hold: *— un primato*, to hold a record 2. (*occupare*) to keep: *detiene questo incarico da due anni*, he has been keeping this post (*o* job) for two years 3. (*tenere prigioniero*) to keep in prison, to detain, to keep in custody.

detentóre, *s.m.*, **detentríce**, *s.f.* 1. holder: *— di una cambiale*, (*comm.*) holder of a bill; *— di un primato*, (*spor.*) holder of a record; *— di titoli*, (*comm.*) stockholder (*o* scripholder) 2. (*dir.*) receiver, withholder.

detenúto, *ag.* imprisoned ‖ *s.m.* prisoner; (*iron.*) gaol-bird, jail-bird.

detenzióne, *s.f.* 1. (*dir.*) withholding; possession; *— di armi da fuoco*, possession of fire-arms; *— illegale di beni altrui*, unlawful possession of other people's property 2. (*il detenere*) holding 3. (*imprigionamento*) detention, imprisonment, confinement: *— arbitraria*, illegal imprisonment; *— preventiva*, detention under remand; *casa di —*, house of detention; (*preventiva*) remand home.

detergènte, *ag. s.m.* (*chim.*) detergent.

detergènza, *s.f.* (*chim.*) detergency.

detèrgere, *v.t.* to deterge, to clean, to cleanse, to wash: *— una piaga*, to cleanse a wound.

deterioraménto, *s.m.* deterioration, tear, wear and tear: *— della merce*, deterioration of the goods; *beni soggetti a —*, items subject to wear and tear.

deterioràre, *v.t.* to deteriorate, to spoil; (*danneggiare*) to damage: *la pioggia deteriorò la merce*, the rain damaged the goods ‖ *v.i.*, **deterioràrsi**, *v.r.* to deteriorate, to spoil, to become spoilt; (*andare a male*) to go bad: *il grano si deteriora invecchiando*, grain deteriorates with age.

deteriorazióne, (*rar.*) per **deterioraménto**.

determinàbile, *ag.* determinable, definable.

determinànte, *ag.* determinant, determinative, determining ‖ *s.f.* (determinant) motive: *la — del delitto*, the motive of the crime.

determinàre, *v.t.* 1. to determine, to fix: *condizioni da —*, conditions to be determined; *— le dimensioni di un cilindro*, to determine the dimensions of a cylinder; *— la posizione di ql.co.*, to locate sthg.; *— i prezzi*, to fix (*o* to determine) prices; *— la propria sorte*, to determine one's fate 2. (*decidere*) to determine (to do, on doing), to resolve (to do, upon doing), to decide (to do): *questo fatto mi determinò a tacere*, this fact made me decide to hold my tongue 3. (*causare*) to produce, to cause, to bring about, to give rise to (sthg.): *una semplice negligenza può — un incendio*, a simple act of carelessness may cause (*o* lead to) a fire ‖ **determinàrsi**, *v.r.* (*risolversi*) to determine (to do, on doing), to resolve (upon doing), to make up one's mind (to do).

determinataménte, *av.* 1. determinately 2. (*risolutamente*) determinedly, resolutely.

determinatézza, *s.f.* 1. (*risolutezza*) determination, resolution; determinateness 2. (*esattezza*) exactness, exactitude, precision.

determinatívo, *ag.* 1. determinative 2. (*gram.*) definite: *articolo —*, definite article.

determinàto, *ag.* 1. (*definito*) determinate; definite; fixed, limited, stated: *in un senso —*, in a determinate sense (*o* in a given direction); *per un — numero di anni*, for a term of years 2. (*particolare*) special, particular: *in determinate circostanze*, in particular circumstances 3. (*deciso*) resolute, determined: *siamo determinati a dimostrarlo*, we are determined to prove it.

determinatóre, *ag.* determinant, determinative, determining ‖ *s.m.* determinant, determining agent, determining factor.

determinazióne, *s.f.* 1. determination: *— dei costi*, (*comm.*) costing; *— dei tempi*, timing; *— della posizione*, (*aer.*) reckoning; *— del prezzo*, (*comm.*) pricing 2. (*decisione*) determination, decision: *prendere una —*, to make up one's mind (*o* to take a decision) 3. (*risolutezza*) determination, resolution: *agire con —*, to act resolutely.

determinísmo, *s.m.* (*fil.*) determinism, necessitarianism.

determinísta, *s.m.* (*fil.*) determinist, necessitarian.

determinístico, *ag.* (*fil.*) deterministic, necessitarian.

detersívo, *ag.* detersive, cleansing ‖ *s.m.* detersive; cleansing agent; (*ind. tessile*) scour.

detèrso, *ag.* clean, cleansed.

detersòrio, *ag.* detersive, cleansing.

detestàbile, *ag.* detestable, execrable: *lavoro —*, execrable work; *uomo —*, detestable (*o* hateful) man.

detestabilménte, *av.* detestably, execrably, hatefully.

detestàre, *v.t.* to detest, to abhor; (*aver repulsione per*) to loathe; (*odiare*) to hate: *detesta essere lodato,* he loathes being praised; *detesto essere disturbato,* I hate to be disturbed; *farsi — da tutti,* to get oneself disliked by everyone.

detestazióne, *s.f.* detestation, abhorrence; (*repulsione*) loathing; (*odio*) hate, hatred.

detettóre, *s.m.* (*rad.*) detector: — *a cristallo,* crystal detector; — *magnetico,* magnetic detector.

detonànte, *ag.* detonating, explosive: *capsule detonanti,* percussion caps; *miscela* —, explosive mixture ‖ *s. m.* explosive.

detonàre, *v.i.* to detonate.

detonatóre, *ag.* detonating, explosive ‖ *s.m.* detonator: — *ad accensione elettrica,* electric detonator; — *meccanico,* percussion detonator.

detonazióne, *s.f.* detonation, explosion, blast: *rumore della* —, (*di motore*) pinking; (*amer.*) knocking; *si udì una forte* —, a violent explosion was heard.

detràrre, *v.t.* **1.** to deduct, to subtract; to take away; to put aside: *abbiamo detratto il 5 % dal suo salario,* we have deducted 5 % from his wages; *non dobbiamo — nulla ai suoi meriti,* we must not detract anything from his merits; — *le spese,* (*comm.*) to deduct expenses; *dedotto lo sconto,* (*comm.*) discount off **2.** (*denigrare*) to detract, to slight, to belittle; to defame, to depreciate, to slander, to disparage.

detrattóre, *s.m.* detractor; defamer, slanderer.

detrattòrio, *ag.* detractive.

detrattríce, *s.f.* detractor; defamer, slanderer.

detrazióne, *s.f.* **1.** (*il detrarre*) deduction, deducting **2.** (*somma detratta*) amount deducted **3.** (*denigrazione*) detraction, depreciation, slander, disparagement.

detriménto, *s.m.* detriment, harm, damage, prejudice: *a — di ql.co.,* to the prejudice of sthg. (*o* to the detriment of sthg.): *il lavoro eccessivo va a — della tua salute,* overwork is detrimental (*o* harmful) to your health; *portare — a ql.co.,* to cause damage to sthg.

detrítico, *ag.* (*geol.*) detrital.

detríto, *s.m.* **1.** rubble, debris, waste, rubbish (*solo sing.*): *un mucchio di detriti,* a heap of rubble **2.** *pl.* (*geol.*) detritus (*solo sing.*): *detriti alluvionali,* alluvium **3.** (*edil.*) rubble (*solo sing.*).

detronizzàre, *v.t.* to dethrone; to depose: *durante la rivoluzione il re fu detronizzato,* during the revolution the king was dethroned.

detronizzazióne, *s.f.* dethronement.

détta, a, *l.av.:* *a — di qlcu.,* according to what s.o. says (*o* according to s.o.'s opinion); *a — di tutti,* according to what everyone says.

dettàfono, *s.m.* dictaphone.

dettagliànte, *s.m.* (*comm.*) retailer, retail dealer.

dettagliàre, *v.t.* **1.** to detail, to tell (sthg.) in detail **2.** (*comm.*) to specify, to detail; (*amer.*) to itemize.

dettagliataménte, *av.* in detail; (*minuziosamente*) minutely.

dettagliàto, *ag.* **1.** detailed, in detail: *una narrazione dettagliata,* a detailed account; *una relazione dettagliata,* a circumstantial report **2.** (*comm.*) detailed, in detail; (*amer.*) itemized.

dettàglio, *s.m.* **1.** detail, particular: *non entrare in dettagli!,* do not go (*o* enter) into details! **2.** (*comm.*) retail (*attributivo*): *negoziante al* —, retail dealer; *prezzo al* —, retail price; *commerciare al* —, to carry on retail business ‖ *comprare al* —, to buy by retail; *vendere al* —, to sell by retail (*o* to retail).

dettàme, *s.m.* (*letter.*) dictate: *i dettami della coscienza,* the dictates of conscience.

dettàre, *v.t.* **1.** to dictate: — *una lettera alla dattilografa,* to dictate a letter to the typist **2.** (*suggerire*) to suggest, to teach: *farò come mi detta la coscienza!,* I'll do as my conscience tells me! **3.** (*imporre*) to dictate: — *le condizioni a un esercito sconfitto,* to

dictate terms to a defeated army; — *legge,* to lay down the law.

dettàto, *s.m.* **1.** dictation: *facciamo un* —, let's have (*o* do) a dictation; *scrivere sotto* —, to write at (*o* from) dictation **2.** (*letter.*) saying.

dettatóre, *s.m.,* **dettatríce,** *s.f.* dictator.

dettatúra, *s.f.* dictation: *scrivere sotto* —, to write at (*o* from) dictation.

détto, *ag.* **1.** (*chiamato*) called, named; (*soprannominato*) nicknamed: *Jacopo Robusti — il Tintoretto,* Jacopo Robusti called Tintoretto **2.** (*comm.*) ditto, said, aforesaid: — *articolo è realmente ottimo,* the said article (*o* the above-mentioned article) is really excellent ‖ *s.m.* **1.** (*motto*) saying; (*proverbio*) saying, saw: *i detti di Socrate,* Socrate's sayings; *secondo il vecchio* —, as the old saying goes **2.** (*parola*) word **3.** (*comando*) command, order: *ubbidiva ai suoi detti,* he obeyed his orders **4.** (*arguzia*) joke, jest **5.** (*letter.*) (*cantafavola*) story; (*componimento letterario*) dit, ditt, dite: *il — dei tre ladroni,* the story of the three thieves.

detumescènza, *s.f.* (*med.*) detumescence.

deturpaménto, *s.m.* disfigurement, defacement.

deturpàre, *v.t.* to disfigure, to deface: *troppe insegne pubblicitarie deturpano le autostrade,* too many advertising signs disfigure our highways; *il suo bel viso fu deturpato dal vaiolo,* her beautiful face was disfigured by smallpox.

deturpatóre, *ag.* disfiguring, defacing ‖ *s.m.,* **deturpatríce,** *s.f.* disfigurer.

deturpazióne, *s.f.* disfigurement, defacement.

Deucalióne, *no.pr.m.* (*mit.*) Deucalion.

deuteróne, *s.m.* (*fis.*) deuteron.

deuteronòmio, *s.m.* (*Bibbia*) Deuteronomy.

deutóne, *s.m.* (*fis. atomica*) deuteron.

devalutàre, *v.t.* to depreciate, to devaluate.

devalutazióne, *s.f.* (*comm.*) depreciation; devaluation.

devastaménto, *s.m.* devastation; ravage.

devastàre, *v.t.* to lay waste; to devastate, to ravage; to ruin: *un bel viso devastato dagli anni, dal male,* a beautiful face ravaged by age, by disease; *un paese devastato dalla guerra,* a country devastated by war.

devastatóre, *s.m.,* **devastatríce,** *s.f.* ravager; devastator.

devastazióne, *s.f.* devastation; ravage; waste, ruin.

deveníre, *v.i.* (*dir.*) to proceed along a certain line: — *a una conclusione,* to arrive at a conclusion.

deviaménto, *s.m.* **1.** deviation, aberration **2.** (*ferr.*) (*manovra*) shunting; (*deragliamento*) derailment.

deviàre, *v.i.* to deviate, to swerve, to make a detour; to diverge, to depart: *giunti all'incrocio, deviammo verso nord,* having reached the crossroad we made a detour northwards; *non devia mai dai suoi princìpi,* he never deviates (*o* departs *o* swerves) from his principles; — *dal retto cammino,* to depart (*o* to deviate) from the straight path ‖ *non — !,* (*non cambiare argomento!*) stick to the point! ‖ *v.t.* to divert; to turn aside; to deflect: *cercò di — la mia attenzione,* he tried to divert my attention; *un incidente che le ha deviato la colonna vertebrale,* an accident that gave her curvature of the spine; — *il corso di un fiume,* to divert the course of a river; — *un treno,* to shunt a train; (*farlo deragliare*) to derail a train.

deviatóio, *s.m.* (*ferr.*) switch.

deviatóre, *s.m.* **1.** (*ferroviere che manovra gli scambi*) pointsman; (*amer.*) shunter **2.** (*apparecchio elett.*) switch.

deviazióne, *s.f.* deviation; (*stradale*) diversion; detour; (*fis. mec.*) deflection: — *coniugata,* (*med.*) conjugate deviation; — *del quadro,* (*tv.*) frame deflection; — *della bussola,* (*mar. aer.*) compass deviation; — *della colonna vertebrale,* curvature of the spine; — *elettromagnetica,* (*elett.*) electromagnetic deflection; — *mediante scambio,* (*ferr.*) shunting (*o* switching); *facemmo una — per evitare strade affollate,* we made a detour in order to avoid crowded streets.

deviazionísmo, *s.m.* (*pol.*) deviationism.

deviazionísta, *s.m.* (*pol.*) deviationist.

dèvio, *ag.* (*rar.*) devious.

de visu, *l.av.* (*lat.*) ocularly.

devolutívo, *ag.* devolving, assigning, transmitting, transferring.

devolúto, *ag.* devolved, assigned, transmitted, transferred.

devoluzióne, *s.f.* (*dir.*) devolution, transmission, transfer: — *allo Stato d'una proprietà,* escheat ‖ *guerra di —,* (*st.*) War of Devolution.

devòlvere, *v.t.* **1.** (*dir.*) to devolve, to assign, to transmit, to transfer: *il possedimento gli fu devoluto,* the estate was devolved on him (o was transmitted to him o was assigned to him); — *una causa ad altro tribunale,* to transfer a case to another Court; — *un diritto a qlcu.,* to transfer (o to assign) a right to s. o. **2.** (*adoperare*) to employ: *la somma fu devoluta a beneficio dei poveri,* the sum was employed for the benefit of the poor **3.** (*arc.*) (*rotolare giù*) to roll down ‖ **devòlversi,** *v.r.* (*rar.*) **1.** (*fluire*) to flow down **2.** (*passare da una persona a un'altra*) to pass from one person to another.

devoniàno, devònico, *ag.* (*geol.*) Devonian.

devotaménte, *av.* devoutly, piously; devotedly.

devòto, *ag.* **1.** devotional; (*pio*) pious, religious, devout: *atteggiamento —,* pious attitude; *libro —,* devotional book; *persona devota,* pious person; *essere — a un santo,* to be a votary of a saint ‖ *essere — alla bottiglia,* (*scherz.*) to be addicted to (o to worship) the bottle **2.** (*affezionato*) devout, affectionate, sincere: *amico —,* sincere friend; *servitore —,* devoted servant **3.** (*consacrato*) devoted, consecrated ‖ *s.m.* devout person; devotee: *il principe era circondato dai suoi devoti,* the prince was surrounded by his devotees.

devozióne, *s.f.* **1.** devoutness, devotion, piety: — *a un Santo,* devotion to a Saint; *festa di —,* feast of devotion **2.** *pl.* (*preghiere*) devotions, prayers: *libro di devozioni,* devotional book; *ella stava recitando le sue devozioni,* she was at her devotions **3.** (*venerazione*) veneration; (*affetto*) affection, attachment; (*dedizione*) devotion; (*fedeltà*) devotedness: *avere della — per qlcu.,* to be attached to s.o.

di¹, *prep.* **1.** (*specificazione*) **of:** *l'amore della patria,* the love of one's (own) country; *l'arrivo del piroscafo,* the arrival of the ship (o the ship's arrival); *la vita del popolo,* the life of the people; *fu accusato dell'assassinio — suo cugino,* he was charged with the murder of his cousin; *lo accusarono — furto,* they accused him of theft (o of 'stealing') **2.** (*specificazione possessiva*) **of** (*sostituibile col genitivo sassone se riferito a persone*): *i libri — mio zio,* my uncle's books (o the books of my uncle); *molte fotografie dei miei ragazzi,* many photos of my boys; *tre colleghi — mio marito,* three of my husband's colleagues (o three colleagues of my husband's) **3.** (*partitivo*) **some; any** (*in frasi negative ed interrogative*): *dammi dello zucchero,* give me some sugar; *hai degli amici cari in quella città?,* have you any dear friends in that town?·‖ *un po' — zucchero,* a little sugar **4.** (*partitivo dopo i pron. indef.* qualcosa, niente, nulla: *non si traduce*): *niente — nuovo,* nothing new; *qualche cosa — buono,* something good **5.** (*denominazione*) **of:** *la città — Roma,* the city of Rome; *l'isola — Capri,* the Isle of Capri; *il mese — febbraio,* the month of February; *il titolo — conte,* the title of count **6.** (*moto da luogo, separazione, allontanamento*) **from:** *lontano — qui,* a long way from here; — *povero divenne ricco,* from being poor he became rich; *mi cadde — mano,* it fell from my hand; *smontò — sella,* he dismounted from his horse; *allontanarsi — casa,* to go away from home (o to leave home) ‖ *uscir — strada,* to go astray ‖ *uscir — vita,* to pass away **7.** (*origine, provenienza*) **from:** — *dove sei?,* where are you from? (o where do you come from?); *è uno — Milano,* he comes from Milan ‖ *Giorgio —*

Pietro, George, son of Peter **8.** (*qualità*): *un giovane — alta statura,* a tall young man; *persona — cuore,* a kind-hearted person; *un uomo d'ingegno,* a man of intelligence **9.** (*determinazione, uso*): *libro — lettura,* reading-book; *stanza — soggiorno,* living-room **10.** (*limitazione*): *cieco — un occhio,* blind in one eye; *duro d'orecchio,* hard of hearing; *persona debole — cuore,* person with a weak heart **11.** (*materia*): *una giacca — lana,* a woollen coat; *una medaglia d'oro,* a gold medal; *una sedia — legno,* a wooden chair; *un vassoio d'argento,* a silver tray **12.** (*misura*): *un carico — due tonnellate,* a two-ton load; *una multa — mille lire,* a thousand-lire fine; *un tavolo — due metri,* a table two metres long **13.** (*abbondanza, privazione*): *pieno —,* full of: *è pieno — buone intenzioni,* he is full of good intentions; *ricco —,* rich in; *scarso —,* lacking in; *fu derubato — quanto aveva,* he was robbed of all he had; *fu privato — tutto,* he was deprived of everything **14.** (*tempo*) **in; by; during:** — *buon mattino,* early in the morning; — *giorno,* by day (o in the daytime); — *notte,* by (o at) night (o during the night); — *pomeriggio,* in the afternoon; — *primavera,* in (the) spring; — *sera,* in the evening **15.** (*età*): *un ragazzo — sedici anni,* a sixteen-year-old boy (o a boy of sixteen) **16.** (*argomento*) **of, about:** *ci parlò — politica,* he spoke to us about (o of) politics; *parlammo — te,* we spoke about (o of) you; *so molte cose — quella donna,* I know a lot about that woman **17.** (*causa*) **of; with; for:** *morì — fame,* he died of starvation; *quasi piansi — gioia,* I nearly cried for joy; *quasi quasi morivo — spavento,* I nearly died of (o with) fright; *fremere — rabbia,* to fume (o to shake) with anger; *tremare — paura,* to tremble with fear **18.** (*mezzo*) **with; on:** *ferire — spada,* to wound with a sword; *nutrirsi d'aria,* to live on air; *ornare — fiori,* to adorn with flowers; *vivere del proprio stipendio,* to live on one's salary **19.** (*modo, maniera*): — *buon grado,* willingly; — *fretta,* in haste (o in a hurry); — *passo,* at walking speed; *camminava — buon passo,* he walked quickly; *sta' — buon animo!,* be of good cheer!; *mangiare — buon appetito,* to eat with a good appetite **20.** (*paragone*) (*nei comparativi di maggioranza e minoranza*) **than;** (*nei superlativi relativi*) **of; in:** *la più bella città d'Italia,* the most beautiful town in Italy; *il più giovane dei miei amici,* the youngest of my friends; *ella fu più gentile — suo fratello,* she was kinder than her brother; *studia meno — me,* she studies less than I do **21.** (*con l'infinito in dipendenza da altro verbo*): *decidemmo — andare,* we decided to go; *gli dissi — venire,* I told him to come; *smettila — russare,* stop snoring **22.** (*in unione a prep.*): *contro — lui,* against him; *dopo — te,* after you; *fuori della città,* outside the town; *sopra —,* over; above; *sotto —,* under; below **23.** (*in unione ad av.*): — *dentro,* inside; — *là,* over there (o on the other side); — *qua,* over here (o on this side); — *sopra,* upstairs; (*in cima*) on top; — *sotto,* below, underneath; (*dabbasso*) downstairs **24.** (*Fraseologia*): — *certo,* surely; — *frequente,* often; — *gran lunga,* by far; — *grazia,* please; — *male in peggio,* from bad to worse; — *nuovo,* again; — *solito,* usually: *come — solito,* as usual.

dí², *s.m.* (*poet.*) day: *buon —!,* good morning!; *notte e —,* night and day (o without interruption) ‖ *a — 9 maggio,* (*nei documenti*) 9th May (o May 9th).

di³, *s.f.m.* letter D.

diabète, *s.m.* (*patol.*) diabetes.

diabètico, *ag.s.m.* diabetic.

diabolicaménte, *av.* diabolically.

diabòlico, *ag.* diabolic(al); fiendish, devilish: *un piano — per rovinarti,* a devilish plot to ruin you.

diàbolo, *s.m.* (*giuoco*) diabolo.

diacceiàre, *v.i.* to freeze.

diàccio, *ag.* (*rar.*) frozen, icy; chilly ‖ *s.m.* (*rar.*) ice.

diacceiuòlo, *s.m.* (*rar.*) (*ghiacciuolo*) icicle.

diàchilon, *s.m.* (*rar.*) (*farm.*) diachylon.

diaclàsi, *s.f.* (*geol.*) diaclase.
diaconàle, *ag.* (*eccl.*) diaconal.
diaconàto, *s.m.* (*eccl.*) diaconate.
diaconéssa, *s.f.* (*eccl.*) deaconess.
diaconìa, *s.f.* (*eccl.*) diaconate.
diàcono, *s.m.* (*eccl.*) deacon.
diacrìtico, *ag.* diacritic(al).
diade, *s.f.* dyad.
diadèma, *s.m.* diadem; tiara.
diademàto, *ag.* diademed.
diàdochi, *s.m.pl.* (*st. greca*) Diadochi.
diafaneità, diafanità, *s.f.* diaphaneity, diaphanousness, transparency.
diàfano, *ag.* diaphanous, transparent.
diafanoscopìa, *s.f.* (*med.*) diaphanoscopy.
diafanoscòpio, *s.m.* (*med.*) diaphanoscope.
diàfisi, *s.f.* (*anat.*) diaphysis.
diafonìa, *s.f.* **1.** (*mus.*) diaphony **2.** (*tel.*) cross
-talk: — *lontana*, far-end cross-talk; — *vicina*, near
-end cross-talk.
diafònico, *ag.* diaphonic(al).
diaforètico, *ag.s.m.* (*med.*) diaphoretic.
diaframma, *s.m.* **1.** (*anat.*) diaphragm **2.** (*divisione, partizione*) screen **3.** (*scient.*) diaphragm: — *ad iride,* (*fis.*) iris diaphragm; — *di apertura dell'obiettivo,* (*foto.*) stop; — *di microfono telefonico,* diaphragm, tympanum; — *elettrodinamico,* (*rad.*) electrodynamic pickup; — *isolante,* (*mec.*) insulating diaphragm; — *variabile,* (*foto.*) compensator **4.** (*miner.*) brattice **5.** (*aer.*) bulkhead.
diaframmàre, *v.i.* (*foto.*) to diaphragm, to˜stop.
diaframmàtico, *ag.* diaphragmatic.
diaframmatúra, *s.f.* (*foto.*) diaphragm opening.
diagènesi, *s.f.* (*geol.*) diagenesis.
diageotropísmo, *s.m.* (*bot.*) diageotropism.
diaglípto, *s.m.* (*art.*) diaglyph.
diàgnosi, *s.f.* (*med.*) diagnosis (*pl.* diagnoses): — *radiologica,* radiodiagnosis.
diagnòstica, *s.f.* (*med.*) diagnostics.
diagnosticàre, *v.t.* (*med.*) to diagnose: *il dottore gli diagnosticò un'influenza,* the doctor diagnosed the illness as influenza.
diagnòstico, *ag.* (*med.*) diagnostic ‖ *s.m.* diagnostician.
diagonàle, *ag.* diagonal: *in linea* —, diagonally ‖ *s.f.* **1.** (*geom.*) diagonal **2.** *pl.* (*aer.*) lift wires ‖ *s.m.* (*tessuto diagonale*) twill.
diagonalménte, *av.* diagonally.
diagràmma, *s.m.* **1.** diagram, graph, curve: — *della distribuzione,* (*di un motore*) timing diagram; — *delle precipitazioni medie in un anno,* (*meteorologia*) hyetograph; — *delle sollecitazioni,* (*edil.*) stress diagram; — *del traffico stradale,* traffic diagram; — *di produzione,* production curve; — *di prova,* (*mec.*) test chart; — *grafico,* (*fis. ind.*) chart; — *schematico,* elementary (*o* schematic) diagram **2.** (*mus.*) scale.
dialettàle, *ag.* dialectal.
dialèttica, *s.f.* (*logica*) dialectics; (*dialettica hegeliana*) dialectic.
dialetticaménte, *av.* dialectically.
dialèttico, *ag.* dialectic(al) ‖ *s.m.* dialectic, dialectician.
dialètto, *s.m.* dialect.
dialettologìa, *s.f.* dialectology.
dialettòlogo, *s.m.* dialectologist.
diàlisi, *s.f.* (*fis.*) dialysis.
dializzàre, *v.t.* (*fis.*) to dialyze.
dializzatóre, *s.m.* (*chim.*) dialyzer.
diàllage, *s.f.* (*ret.*) diallage.
dialogàre, *v.i.* to hold a dialogue, to converse, to talk together; (*arc.*) to dialogue ‖ *v.t.* (*teat.*) to write the dialogue of (a scene, a play).
dialogicaménte, *av.* dialogically.
dialògico, *ag.* dialogic(al): *preferiva la forma dialogica,* he preferred to write in dialogue.

dialogísmo, *s.m.* (*ret.*) dialogism.
dialogísta, *s.c.* dialogist.
dialogístico, *ag.* (*rar.*) dialogistic(al).
dialogizzàre, *v.i.* to hold a dialogue, to talk, to converse ‖ *v.t.* to put (sthg.) into dialogue form, to express (sthg.) in the form of a dialogue.
diàlogo, *s.m.* dialogue: *quel libro ha molti dialoghi brillanti,* that book has many brilliant examples of dialogue.
diamagnètico, *ag.* (*fis.*) diamagnetic.
diamagnetísmo, *s.m.* (*fis.*) diamagnetism.
diamantàio, *s.m.* diamond cutter.
diamànte, *s.m.* **1.** (*min.*) diamond: — *artificiale, industriale,* bort; — *a brillante,* brilliant; — *a rosetta,* rose(-cut) diamond; — *difettoso,* spotted stone; — *di trivellazione,* (*min.*) (carbon) diamond; *anello, collana di diamanti,* diamond ring, necklace; *detriti, frammenti di* —, (*ind.*) diamond rubbish; *scaglie di* —, diamond cleavage; *schegge di* —, bort; *taglio di diamanti,* diamond cutting ‖ *cuore di* —, *fig.* hard heart; *essere di* —, *fig.* to be a sterling character ‖ *nozze di* —, diamond wedding **2.** (*per vetrai*) diamond-point; glazier's diamond, cutting diamond **3.** (*tip.*) diamond: *carattere* —, diamond (*o* three-point) type **4.** (*mar.*) (*di ancora*) crown.
diamantífero, *ag.* diamantiferous, diamond-bearing: *regione, sabbia diamantifera,* diamantiferous region, gravel.
diamantíno, *ag.* (*rar.*) adamantine.
diametràle, *ag.* diametric(al), diametral.
diametralménte, *av.* diametrically: — *opposto,* in diametral opposition (*o* diametrically opposed): *le sue opinioni erano* — *opposte alle nostre,* his opinions were diametrically opposed to ours.
diàmetro, *s.m.* (*geom.*) diameter: — *effettivo,* (*mec.*) effective diameter; — *esterno,* outside diameter; (*di ingranaggio*) full diameter; — *interno,* (*mec.*) inside diameter (*o* bore); (*di ingranaggio*) root diameter; *ruota di 60 centimetri di* —, wheel 60 centimeters in diameter.
diàmine, *inter.* **1.** (*d'impazienza*) the deuce!, dash it! **2.** (*di sorpresa*) good heavens! **3.** *che* — *state cercando?,* what on earth are you looking for?.
Diàna[1], *no.pr.f.* Diana.
diàna[2], *s.f.* **1.** (*mil.*) reveille; (*mar.*) morning-watch: *suonare la* —, to sound the reveille ‖ *batter la* —, (*tremare di freddo*) to shiver with cold **2.** (*stella del mattino*) morning-star.
diànto, *s.m.* (*bot.*) dianthus (*pl.* dianthi).
diànzi, *av.* (*or ora*) just, just now; (*poco fa*) a short while ago: *è arrivato* —, he has just arrived; *l'ho visto* —, (*or ora*) I saw him just now; (*poco fa*) I saw him a short while ago.
diàpason, *s.m.* **1.** (*strum.*) tuning-fork **2.** (*estensione dei suoni*) diapason, compass: — *di una voce,* compass (*o* diapason) of a voice **3.** *fig.* (*intensità*) pitch, diapason: *al più alto* —, at the highest pitch.
diapènte, *s.m.* (*mus.*) quint.
diapositíva, *s.f.* **1.** (*foto.*) diapositive, transparency, slide: — *a colori,* colour slide (*o* colour transparency) **2.** (*tip.*) direct reversal.
diarchìa, *s.f.* diarchy.
diària, *s.f.* (*indennità giornaliera di trasferta*) daily travelling allowance.
diàrio, *ag.* day (*attributivo*): *febbre diaria,* one day fever ‖ *s.m.* diary, day-book, journal: *registrare nel* —, to enter in the diary; *tenere un* —, to keep a diary (*o* a journal).
diarísta, *s.c.* diarist.
diarrèa, *s.f.* (*patol.*) diarrhoea.
diartròsi, *s.f.* (*anat.*) diarthrosis.
diascòpio, *s.m.* (*foto.*) slide projector, diascope.
diàspora, *s.f.* (*st.*) diaspora.
diàsporo, *s.m.* (*min.*) diaspore.
diàspro, *s.m.* (*min.*) jasper.
diàstasi, *s.f.* (*chim.*) diastase.

diàstilo, *s.m.* (*arch.*) diastyle.

diàstole, *s.f.* diastole.

diastrofìa, *s.f.* (*med.*) diastrophia.

diastrofìsmo, *s.m.* (*geol.*) diastrophism.

diatermaneità, *s.f.* (*fis.*) diathermacy.

diatermàno, *ag.* (*fis.*) diathermic, diathermanous.

diatermasía, *s.f.* (*fis.*) diathermacy.

diatermía, *s.f.* (*med.*) diathermy.

diatèrmico, *ag.* (*fis. med.*) diathermic.

diàtesi, *s.f.* (*med.*) diathesis (*pl.* diatheses).

diatomèa, *s.f.* (*bot.*) diatom.

diatomíte, *s.f.* (*min.*) diatomite.

diatònico, *ag.* diatonic.

diatríba, *s.f.* 1. (*invettiva*) diatribe 2. (*alterco*) quarrel.

diàvola, *s.f.*: *una buona —*, (*fam.*) a good woman (o a kind soul); *una povera —*, (*fam.*) a poor woman.

diàvola, alla, *l.av.* 1. in a harum-scarum way, anyhow: *lavoro fatto alla —*, perfunctory (o scamped) work 2. *pollo alla —*, (*cuc.*) devilled chicken.

diavolàccio, *s.m.* devil || *un buon —*, (*fam.*) a good -natured fellow.

diavolería, *s.f.* 1. devilry; devilment; (*stregoneria*) witchcraft 2. (*garbuglio*) muddle, mess 3. (*fam.*) malicious trick; *che nuova — è questa?*, what new trick is this?.

diavolèrio, *V.* **diavolèto**.

diavolésco, *ag.* devilish, diabolical.

diavoléssa, *s.f.* 1. she-devil; .witch 2. (*virago*) termagant, virago.

diavoléto, *s.m.* hubbub, uproar, babel, pandemonium: *fare un —*, to make an uproar: *fecero un —*, they had the devil of a row.

diavolétto, *s.m.* 1. (*fanciullo vivace*) little devil, imp 2. (*bigodino*) hair curler.

diavolío, *s.m.* hubbub, uproar, babel, pandemonium.

diàvolo, *s.m.* devil (anche *fig.*): *tentazioni del —*, devil's temptations; *quel ragazzo è un — scatenato*, (*fam.*) that boy is full of mischief (o that boy is a little devil) || *—!*, the devil! (o the deuce!) || *— di Cartesio*, (*fis.*) Cartesian diver (o devil o imp) || *avvocato del —*, devil's advocate || *povero —!*, poor devil! || *un vento del —!*, a devil of a wind! || *il — non è così brutto come si dipinge*, the devil is not so black as he is painted || *che il — vi porti!*, the devil take you! || *che — vuoi?*, what the devil do you want? || *dove — eri andato?*, where the devil (o where on earth) had you gone? || *è un — d'uomo*, he is a devil of a man || *è un buon —*, he is a good fellow || *ho una fame del —*, I'm simply starving || *ho una paura del —!*, I'm in a blue funk! (o I'm scared to death!) || *va' al —!*, go to the devil! || *sono come il — e l'acqua santa*, they don't mix || *abitare a casa del —*, to live off the track || *avere il — in corpo*, to be full of mischief || *avere un — per capello*, to be furious (o furiously angry) || *fare il — a quattro*, to play the devil (o to kick up a shindy) || *fare un casa del —*, to make an uproar (o to raise hell o to raise the devil o to raise Cain) || *mandare al —*, to send to the devil || *tirare le orecchie al —*, (*giuocando a carte*) to look secretly at the cards || *il — fa le pentole ma non i coperchi*, *prov.* the devil teaches his tricks but not how to hide them || *un — scaccia l'altro*, *prov.* one devil drives out another || *la farina del — va tutta in crusca*, *prov.* the devil's meal is half bran.

dibàttere, *v.t.* 1. (*discutere*) to debate, to discuss: *— una questione*, to discuss a question (o to argue) 2. (*sbattere*) to beat: *— le ali*, to flap one's wings (o to flutter) || **dibàttersi**, *v.r.* to struggle; (*in acqua*) to flounder (about): *lo vide — fra le mani dei nemici*, he saw him struggling in the hands of his enemies; *lo squalo si dibattè a lungo prima di essere tratto a riva*, the shark splashed (o floundered) about a long time, before being landed.

dibattiménto, *s.m.* 1. (*discussione*) debate, discussion 2. (*dir.*) proceedings (*pl.*), hearing 3. (*rar.*) (*di ali*) beating 4. (*rar.*) (*lot'a*) struggling.

dibàttito, *s.m.* 1. debate, discussion: *— a porte chiuse*, (*dir.*) case heard in camera; (*pol.*) debate held in camera (o secret session); *dibattiti parlamentari*, parliamentary debates (o proceedings); *un acceso —*, a heated debate; *la questione è al —*, the question is under discussion (o debate); *dirigere un —*, to lead a discussion (o to occupy the chair) 2. (*disputa*) dispute, controversy: *sorse fra noi un aspro — per la precedenza*, a sharp dispute arose between us over precedence.

dibattúto, *ag.* controversial: *una questione dibattuta*, an open question.

diboscaménto, *s.m.* deforestation, disforestation.

diboscàre, *v.t.* to deforest, to disforest, to clear of trees: *hanno diboscato troppo quella montagna*, they cut down too many trees on that mountain; *quella terra è stata completamente diboscata*, that country has been completely deforested (o cleared of trees).

dibrucàre, *v.t.* 1. to clear (the ground) 2. (*potare*) to prune, to lop.

dibrucatúra, *s.f.* (*potatura*) pruning.

dibruscàre, *v.t.* (*potare*) to prune, to lop.

dibucciàre, *v.t.* (*rar.*) to peal off.

dicàce, *ag.* (*letter.*) garrulous, loquacious, petulant; (*satirico, mordace*) sarcastic, satirical.

dicacità, *s.f.* (*letter.*) garrulousness, loquacity, petulancy; (*mordacità*) sarcasm.

dicastèrico, *ag.* ministerial.

dicastèro, *s.m.* office, ministry; (*negli Stati Uniti*) department: *— degli Esteri*, Foreign Office; (*negli Stati Uniti*) State Department.

díceo, *s.m.* (*geol.*) dike, dyke.

dicèmbre, *s.m.* December.

dicentràre, *V.* **decentràre**.

dicería, *s.f.* gossip, rumour: *è solo una —*, it is a mere rumour (o it is only a rumour).

dicervellàre, *v.t.* to bewilder, to perplex, to confuse; (*far uscire di senno*) to drive (s.o.) to distraction || **dicervellàrsi**, *v.r.* to rack one's brains.

dicévole, *ag.* (*rar.*) suitable, becoming, decent, proper.

dicevolménte, *av.* suitably, becomingly, decently, properly.

dichiaràbile, *ag.* declarable.

dichiaràre, *v.t.* 1. to declare; (*affermare*) to state: *dichiarò di non aver visto nulla*, he declared (o stated) he had seen nothing; *— guerra a un paese*, to declare war on (o upon) a country; *— la propria opinione*, to state one's opinion 2. (*denunziare*) to declare, to state; *— il reddito*, to declare (o to state) one's income; *avete nulla da —?*, have you anything to declare? 3. (*giudicare, proclamare*) to declare, to proclaim: *fu dichiarato colpevole, innocente*, he was declared guilty, innocent; *lo dichiarò suo erede*, he made him his heir 4. (*spiegare*) to explain: *— una locuzione*, to explain a phrase || **dichiaràrsi**, *v.r.* 1. to declare oneself: *si dichiarò innocente*, he declared that he was innocent (o he declared himself to be innocent); *— contrario, favorevole a ql.co.*, to declare against sthg., for sthg. 2. (*fare una dichiarazione d'amore*) to propose: *si dichiarò a lei*, he proposed to her.

**dichiaratam

énte**, *av.* declaredly, openly, plainly.

dichiarativaménte, *av.* declaratively.

dichiaratívo, *ag.* declarative; explanatory.

dichiaràto, *ag.* declared, avowed: *nemico —*, declared enemy.

dichiaratóre, *s.m.*, **dichiaratríce**, *s.f.* declarer.

dichiaratòrio, *ag.* declaratory.

dichiarazióne, *s.f.* declaration; (*affermazione*) statement: *— d'amore*, avowal of love; *— dei redditi*, income-tax return; *— di fallimento*, (*comm.*) declaration of bankruptcy; *— di guerra*, declaration of war; *— doganale*, bill of entry; *— giurata*, sworn statement; (*dir.*) affidavit; *fare una —*, to make a declaration; *fare una — (d'amore) a una ragazza*, to propose to a girl; *la — dei diritti dell'uomo*, (*st.*) the Declaration of Rights.

diciannòve, *ag. num. card. s.m.* nineteen.

diciannovènne, *ag.* nineteen years old (*predicativo*); nineteen-year-old (*attributivo*): *un giovane* —, a nineteen-year-old youth || *s.m.* nineteen-year-old youth || *s.f.* nineteen-year-old girl.

diciannovèsimo, *ag. num. ord. s.m.* nineteenth.

diciassètte, *ag. num. card. s.m.* seventeen.

diciassettènne, *ag.* seventeen years old (*predicativo*); seventeen-year-old (*attributivo*) || *s.m.* seventeen-year-old youth || *s.f.* seventeen-year-old girl.

diciassettèsimo, *ag. num. ord. s.m.* seventeenth.

dicìbile, *ag.* speakable.

dicioccàre, *v.t.* 1. to strip (a tree) of its leaves 2. (*sfoltire*) to thin the foliage of (a tree).

diciottènne, *ag.* eighteen years old (*predicativo*); eighteen-year-old (*attributivo*) || *s.m.* eighteen-year-old youth || *s.f.* eighteen-year-old girl.

diciottèsimo, *ag. num. ord. s.m.* eighteenth.

diciòtto, *ag. num. card. s.m.* eighteen.

dicitóre, *s.m.*, **dicitríce,** *s.f.* speaker; (*narratore, narratrice*) teller; (*chi recita bene*) reciter.

dicitúra, *s.f.* wording; words (*pl.*): *con la seguente* —, bearing the wording (*o* reading as follows).

dicotilèdone, *ag.* (*bot.*) dicotyledonous || *s.f.* (*bot.*) dicotyledon.

dicotomìa, *s.f.* dichotomy.

didascalìa, *s.f.* 1. explanation 2. (*teat.*) (*su copione*) stage directions (*pl.*) 3. (*cine.*) (*su pellicola*) subtitles (*pl.*); (*amer.*) captions (*pl.*).

didascàlico, *ag.* didactic.

didàttica, *s.f.* didactics.

didatticaménte, *av.* didactically.

didàttico, *ag.* didactic: *metodo* —, method of teaching || *direttore* —, headmaster (of an elementary school).

didéntro, *av.* inside, within || *s.m.* inside.

didìmio, *s.m.* (*chim.*) didym, didymium.

Dídimo, *no.pr.m.* (*Bibbia*) Didymus.

Didóne, *no.pr.f.* (*lett.*) Dido.

dièci, *ag. num. card. s.m.* ten: *il* — *ottobre*, the tenth of October; *sono le* —, it is ten o' clock || *il Consiglio dei Dieci*, (*st.*) the Council of the Venetian Republic.

diecimíla, *ag. num. card. s.m.* ten thousand.

diecimillèsimo, *ag. num. ord. s.m.* ten thousandth.

diecína, *V.* **decína.**

dièdro, *ag.* (*geom.*) dihedral || *s.m.* (*geom.*) dihedron.

dielettricità, *s.f.* dielectricity.

dielèttrico, *ag.* (*fis.*) dielectric.

dièresi, *s.f.* diaeresis (*pl.* diaereses).

dies irae, *s.m.* (*lat.*) Dies Irae.

Diesel, *no.pr.*: *automotrice* —, Diesel railcar; *motore* —, Diesel motor (*o* engine); *nafta per motori* —, Diesel oil.

dièsis, *s.m.* (*mus.*) sharp: *sinfonia in do* — *minore*, symphony in C-sharp minor.

dièta[1], *s.f.* (*assemblea*) diet: *la* — *giapponese*, the Japanese Diet.

dièta[2], *s.f.* (*med.*) diet: — *lattea*, milk diet; *essere a* —, to be on a diet; *tenere qlcu. a* —, to diet s.o. (*o* to keep s.o. on a diet).

dietètica, *s.f.* dietetics.

dietètico, *ag.* dietetic.

dietòlogo, *s.m.* dietician.

diètro, *prep.* 1. **behind**; **after**: — *di noi*, — *alle nostre spalle*, behind us, behind our backs; — *quella casa*, behind that house; — *le quinte*, in the wings (*anche fig.*); *chiuse la porta* — *di sè*, he closed the door after him; *andare* — *a qlcu.*, to follow s.o.; *fig.* to imitate s.o. (*o* to follow s.o.'s example); *correre* — *a qlcu.*, to run after s.o. (*anche fig.*) || *correre* — *a ql.co.*, to strive after sthg. || *essere* — *a fare ql.co.*, to be doing sthg. || *portarsi* — *ql.co.*, to take sthg. with one || *stare* — *alla moda*, to follow the fashion || *star* — *a qlcu.*, (*sorvegliarlo*) to stand over s.o.; (*incitarlo*) to spur s.o. on; (*importunarlo*) to pester (*o* to keep on at) s.o. 2. (*in seguito a*): — *ricevuta*, against

receipt; — *richiesta*, (*orale*) on demand; (*scritta*) on application; — *riconoscimento*, upon identification || *av.* **behind**: *da* —, from behind || *in* —, *andare in* —, to go backwards; *guardare* —, to look behind (*o* round *o* back); *rimanere in* —, to be (*o* to get) left behind; (*nel lavoro, ecc.*) to fall behind (with sthg.); *voltarsi in* —, to turn round || *ag.* **hind** (*attributivo*): *le gambe* —, the hind legs || *s.m.* 1. **back, rear**: *è sul* — *dell'edificio*, it is at the back of the building 2. (*di nave*) stern: *verso il* —, aft.

dietrofrónt, *s.m.* 1. (*mil.*) right about turn: —*!*, about turn! 2. (*voltafaccia*) sudden and complete change (of opinion).

difàtti, difàtto, *av.* as a matter of fact, in fact.

difèndere, *v.t.* 1. to defend; (*proteggere*) to protect, to guard, to shield: *lo difese dalla censura*, he shielded him from censure; *difesero la patria dal nemico*, they defended their country against (*o* from) the enemy 2. (*sostenere*) to maintain, to uphold, to defend, to keep up, to support: *sa* — *la sua opinione*, he can hold his own; — *una tesi*, to maintain an argument 3. (*dir.*) to defend, to plead: — *la causa di qlcu.*, to plead s.o.'s cause; — *qlcu.*, to plead for s.o. || **difèndersi,** *v.r.* to defend oneself (against, from s.o., sthg.): — *fino all'ultimo*, to die hard.

difendíbile, difensíbile, *ag.* defensible, tenable.

difensíva, *s.f.* defensive: *stare sulla* —, to stand on the defensive.

difensívo, *ag.* defensive.

difensóre, *ag.* defending: *avvocato* —, defending counsel (*o* counsel for the defence); (*di un'idea, di una causa, ecc.*) advocate || *s.m.* 1. (*dir.*) defending counsel, counsel for the defence 2. (*di un'idea, di una causa, ecc.*) supporter, upholder; advocate: *farsi* — *di una causa*, to become the advocate of a cause || — *della fede*, (*titolo dei sovrani d'Inghilterra*) Defender of the Faith.

difésa, *s.f.* 1. defence; (*amer.*) defense: — *antiaerea*, (*mil.*) anti-aircraft defence; — *antisbarco*, (*mil.*) anti-landing defence; — *costiera*, (*mil.*) coast defence; — *passiva*, passive defence; *a* — *di*, in defence of; *armi di* —, weapons of defence; *avvocato incaricato della* —, (*dir.*) counsel for the defence; *caso di legittima* —, (*dir.*) case of self-defence; *guerra di* —, defensive warfare; *linea di* —, (*mil.*) line of defence; *muro di* —, protecting wall; *senza* —, unprotected (*o* defenceless); *a sua* — *si può dire che...*, in his defence it may be said that...; *combattere in* — *del proprio paese*, to fight in defence of one's country; *mettersi in posizione di* —, to stand on one's guard (*o* to take up a defensive position); *parlare in* — *di qlcu.*, to speak in defence of s.o.; *prendere le difese di qlcu.*, to take s.o.'s part (*o* to take up the cudgels for s.o.) 2. *pl.* (*mil.*) (*fortificazione*) defences, fortifications, defensive works 3. *pl.* (*zanne di elefante, cinghiale*) tusks.

diféso, *ag.* defended, protected: *ben* — *contro il freddo*, well protected against the cold.

difettànte, *ag.* deficient (in sthg.), defective.

difettàre, *v.i.* 1. to be wanting (in sthg.), to be deficient (in sthg.), to be lacking (in sthg.); to want (sthg.), to lack (sthg.): *difettiamo tutti di saggezza!*, we are all wanting (*o* deficient *o* lacking) in wisdom! (*o* we all lack wisdom!) 2. (*essere scarso*) to be lacking, to be wanting: *ora difetta la benzina*, now petrol is lacking (*o* now we are short of petrol).

difettivaménte, *av.* defectively; faultily.

difettívo, *ag.* defective.

difètto, *s.m.* 1. (*fisico*) defect, imperfection; (*morale*) fault: — *fisico*, bodily defect; *senza difetti*, faultless; *mi ama nonostante i miei difetti*, she loves me in spite of my faults 2. (*errore, colpa*) fault: *essere in* —, to be at fault || *chi è in* —, *è in sospetto*, *prov.* ill doers are always ill dreaders (*o* he who is at fault, is suspected) 3. (*ind. tec.*) defect; (*fallo, incrinatura*) flaw; (*superficiale*) blemish: — *del legno*, (*imperfezione*) flaw in wood; — *di costruzione*, defect of design; *difetti di* *funzionamento,* (*di un motore*) running defects; — *d'imballaggio,* packing defect; — *di lavorazione,* defect in workmanship **4.** (*deficienza*) shortcoming, failing, deficiency; (*mancanza*) lack, want: — *di denaro,* shortcoming in money; — *di pagamento,* default of payment; *qui fa — l'acqua,* here water is lacking (*o* wanting) (*o* here there is shortage of water); *la memoria gli fa —,* (his) memory fails him; *se ti fa — il coraggio...,* if you lack courage... ‖ *in — di...,* in default of... (*o* for lack of... *o* for want of...).

difettosaménte, *av.* defectively, faultily.

difettóso, *ag.* defective, faulty: *questa macchina è difettosa,* this machine is defective.

diffalcàre, *v.t.* to deduct, to subtract.

diffàlco, *s.m.* deduction.

diffamàre, *v.t.* to defame, to slander, to libel.

diffamatóre, *ag.* defamatory, slanderous, libellous ‖ *s.m.* defamer, slanderer, libeller.

diffamatòrio, *ag.* defamatory, slanderous, libellous: *notizie diffamatorie,* libellous (*o* defamatory) statements.

diffamatríce, *s.f.* defamer, slanderer, libeller.

diffamazióne, *s.f.* defamation, slander, libel, calumny: *querela per —,* (*dir.*) libel suit (*o* an action for libel).

differènte, *ag.* different; unlike (s.o., sthg.): *essi diedero del fatto una versione del tutto — dalla tua,* they gave a report of the fact quite different from yours (*o* quite unlike yours); *le mie sorelle sono completamente differenti l'una dall'altra,* my sisters are quite unlike each other; *queste rose appartengono a due varietà differenti,* these roses belong to two different kinds.

differenteménte, *av.* differently.

differènza, *s.f.* **1.** difference: — *di latitudine, di temperatura,* difference in latitude, in temperature; — *di qualità,* difference in quality; *con la — che...,* with the difference that...; *c'è una bella — !,* that makes a difference!; *non c'è —,* it makes no difference ‖ *a — di,* unlike: *a — di suo padre, acconsentì subito,* unlike his father, he agreed at once **2.** (*arit.*) difference: — *in meno,* (*comm.*) deficiency; — *in più,* (*comm.*) excess; *la — fra sette e tre è quattro,* the difference between seven and three is four; *la — torna a nostro favore,* (*comm.*) the balance turns in our favour; *dividere a metà la —,* to split the difference; *pagare la —,* (*di biglietto ferroviario*) to pay the difference **3.** (*dissenso*) difference, disagreement: *avere una — con qlcu. in merito a ql.co.,* to have a difference with s.o. about sthg.

differenziàle, *ag.* differential: *calcolo —,* (*mat.*) differential calculus; *diagnosi —,* (*med.*) differential diagnosis; *moto —,* (*mec.*) differential motion; *suono —,* (*mus.*) difference (*o* differential) tone; *tariffa —,* differential tariff; *termometro —,* (*ind.*) differential thermometer ‖ *s.m.* (*mec.*) differential; (*aut.*) differential (gear); *gruppo del —,* (*aut.*) differential unit; *scatola del —,* (*aut.*) differential carrier.

differenziaménto, *s.m.* differentiation.

differenziàmetro, *s.m.* (*mar.*) draft mark.

differenziàre, *v.t.* to differentiate, to discriminate; to make different, to distinguish: *la ragione differenzia l'uomo dagli altri animali,* reason differentiates man from other animals; — *un'equazione, un'espressione,* (*mat.*) to differentiate (*o* to obtain the differential of) an equation, expression ‖ **differenziàrsi,** *v.r.* to differentiate, to become different; to be different, to differ: *gli animali della stessa specie si differenziano a causa dell'ambiente,* animals of the same species differentiate owing to the milieu.

differenziàto, *ag.* differentiated, different: *espressione non differenziata,* (*mat.*) undifferentiated expression.

differenziazióne, *s.f.* differentiation.

differíbile, *ag.* that can be deferred.

differiménto, *s.m.* deferment, postponement; adjournment; procrastination.

differíre, *v.i.* (*essere diverso*) to differ (from s.o., sthg.); to be different (from s.o., sthg.), to be unlike (s.o., sthg.): *differisce molto da suo fratello,* he greatly differs from (*o* he is very different from) his brother; *differivano fra loro per razza e idioma,* they differed (*o* were different) from one another in race and speech; *la sua casa non differisce molto dalla nostra,* his house is not very unlike ours ‖ *v.t.* (*rimandare*) to defer, to delay, to postpone, to put off, to hold over, to adjourn: *la riunione è stata differita alla prossima settimana,* the meeting has been adjourned to next week; *il dibattimento della causa è stato differito al prossimo mese,* (*dir.*) the hearing has been put off until next month; — *il pagamento di giorno in giorno,* to delay payment from day to day; — *la partenza di pochi giorni,* to postpone leaving for a few days; — *la scadenza di un effetto,* (*comm.*) to let a bill lie over (*o* to extend maturity of a bill).

difícile, *ag.* **1.** difficult, hard; knotty: — *da capire,* difficult to understand; — *da tradurre,* difficult to translate; *una digestione —,* a difficult (*o* poor) digestion; *una faccenda —,* a difficult (*o* knotty) question; *un'operazione —,* a difficult operation; *un problema —,* a hard (*o* knotty) problem; *tempi difficili,* hard times; *l'accettarlo mi è stato —,* I found it hard to accept; *una domanda a cui è — rispondere,* a difficult question to answer; *è — crederti,* it is difficult to believe you; *è — farlo,* it is difficult to do so; *i punti difficili hanno bisogno di spiegazione,* the knotty points require an explanation; *quel luogo è di — accesso,* that place is difficult of access; *quella è una persona con la quale è — andare d'accordo,* that is a difficult person to get on with ‖ *è difficiletto,* (*fam.*) it is rather (*o* fairly) difficult **2.** (*scontroso, intrattabile*) difficult; (*incontentabile*) fastidious, particular, fussy: *un ragazzo —,* a difficult boy; *è —,* (*da accontentare*) he is hard to please; *è — nel mangiare,* he is fastidious (*o* particular *o* fussy) about food **3.** (*poco probabile*) improbable: *è — che egli venga,* he is not likely to come (*o* it is improbable he should come) ‖ *s.m.* difficulty: *qui sta il —!,* here is the difficulty!.

difficilménte, *av.* **1.** with difficulty **2.** (*con scarsa probabilità*) improbably: *un'occasione che — si presenterà ancora,* an opportunity that is not likely to turn up again **3.** (*raramente*) seldom: — *esco di sera,* I seldom go out at night.

difficoltà, *s.f.* **1.** difficulty: *hai — a capirmi?,* have you any difficulty in understanding me?; *incontrammo — finanziarie e d'altro genere,* we got into financial and other difficulties; *non ho alcuna — ad ascoltarti,* I have no objection to listening to you ‖ *essere in —,* to be in trouble; (*in precaria situazione economica*), to be in (financial) difficulties (*o* to be in a precarious situation) **2.** (*ostacolo*) trouble, rub, hitch: *le — della vita,* the rubs of life; *la — sta nel fatto che...,* the trouble is that...; *tutto si svolse senza —,* everything went off without a hitch **3.** *fare, sollevare —,* to raise (*o* to make) objections.

difficoltóso, *ag.* **1.** difficult, full of difficulties **2.** (*scontroso, intrattabile*) difficult; (*incontentabile*) fastidious, particular, fussy; hard to please.

diffìda, *s.f.* warning, notice, intimation: *ricevettero la — a non occupare quel terreno,* they were warned not to occupy that land; *dare una — a qlcu.,* to serve an intimation on s.o. (*o* to give s.o. public notice *o* to give s.o. warning).

diffidàre, *v.i.* to distrust (s.o., sthg.); to mistrust (s.o., sthg.); to have no confidence (in s.o., sthg.): *egli diffida sempre di chi non conosce,* he always distrusts (*o* mistrusts) people he doesn't know; *non devi — di lui!,* you must not distrust (*o* you need not mistrust *o* you can have complete confidence in) him!; — *dei propri occhi,* to distrust one's own eyes (*o* not to be able to believe one's eyes) ‖ *v.t.* to give (s.o.) warning, to give (s.o.) public notice, to warn: *lo diffidarono a non farsi vedere,* they warned him not to show himself; *il tribunale lo diffidò a lasciare la città,* the Court gave him warning (*o* notice) not to leave the town.

diffidènte, *ag.* distrustful, mistrustful; *(sospettoso)* suspicious: *è molto — con gli estranei,* she is very cautious in dealing with strangers; *è una persona molto —,* he is a very suspicious person; *guardare qlcu. con aria —,* to look distrustfully at s.o.

diffidenteménte, *av.* distrustfully, mistrustfully; *(sospettosamente)* suspiciously.

diffidènza, *s.f.* **1.** distrust, mistrust: *mi ispira —,* he inspires me with distrust; *la tua — mi offende,* I resent this suspiciousness on your part; *provare — verso qlcu.,* to distrust s.o. **2.** *(sospetto)* suspicion: *guardare qlcu. con —,* to look distrustfully (*o* suspiciously) at s.o. (*o* to look askance at s.o.); *suscitare la — di qlcu.,* to awaken s.o.'s suspicions.

diffóndere, *v.t.* to diffuse, to spread, to divulge, to propagate: *diffuse la notizia che...,* he spread (*o* propagated) the news that...; *le mosche diffondono malattie,* flies spread disease; *— calore, luce, un odore,* to diffuse heat, light, a scent; *— notizie,* to propagate news; *(per radio)* to broadcast news; *(per televisione)* to telecast news; *— dicerie, voci,* to spread rumours ‖ **diffóndersi,** *v.r.* **1.** to spread: *un improvviso rossore si diffuse sul suo volto,* a sudden flush spread over her face; *la notizia si diffuse nel paese,* the news spread over the country; *questo giornale si diffuse in tutto il paese,* this paper had a large circulation all over the country **2.** *(dilungarsi)* to dwell: *— su un argomento,* to dwell on a subject.

diffonditóre, *s.m.,* **diffonditríce,** *s.f.* *(rar.)* disseminator, spreader, promulgator.

diffórme, *ag.* **1.** *(non conforme)* different; unlike (s.o., sthg.): *— dall'originale,* different from the original (*o* unlike the original) **2.** *(rar.)* per **defórme.**

diffràngere, *v.t.* *(ott.)* to diffract.

diffràtto, *ag.* *(ott.)* diffracted: *raggio —,* diffracted ray.

diffrazióne, *s.f.* *(ott.)* diffraction: *— dei raggi di elettroni,* *(fis. atomica)* electron diffraction.

diffusaménte, *av.* diffusely; *(ampiamente)* abundantly: *tratteremo l'argomento più — la prossima volta,* we shall go deeper into the subject next time.

diffusíbile, *ag.* diffusible.

diffusibilità, *s.f.* diffusibility.

diffusióne, *s.f.* **1.** diffusion, spreading; *(di giornale, rivista, ecc.)* circulation: *il mio settimanale ha già una grande —,* my weekly already has a wide circulation **2.** *(prolissità)* diffuseness, diffusion **3.** *(fis.)* diffusion; *(fis. atomica)* scattering: *— isotropa,* isotropic scattering; *— per riflessione,* diffusion by reflection.

diffusívo, *ag.* diffusive.

diffúso, *ag.* **1.** diffuse, diffused: *luce diffusa,* diffuse (*o* diffused *o* indirect) lighting **2.** *(prolisso)* diffuse, prolix, long-winded: *descrizione diffusa,* diffuse description.

diffusóre, *s.m.* **1.** *(chi diffonde)* diffusor, spreader **2.** *(di luce)* disseminator, diffuser; *(a globo)* light globe **3.** *(aut.)* *(di carburatore)* choke (tube) **4.** *(rad.)* loud-speaker.

difilàto, *av.* straight: *va' a casa —!,* go straight home!; *venne — a raccontarmi l'accaduto,* he came straight to tell me what had happened.

diftèrico, *ag.* *(patol.)* diphtheric, diphtherial: *faringite, laringite difterica,* diphtheric pharyngitis, laryngitis.

difteríte, *s.f.* *(patol.)* diphtheria, diphtheritis.

díga, *s.f.* **1.** dam; dike, dyke; *(frangiflutto)* breakwater; *— a contrafforti,* buttress dam; *— artificiale,* artificial dyke; *— a scogliera,* rock-fill dam; *— di muratura,* masonry dam; *— di sbarramento per mulino,* mill-dam; *in Olanda è stata costruita una nuova —,* a new dyke has been built in Holland **2.** *fig.* *(barriera difensiva)* barrier, defence: *opporre una — alla corruzione dilagante,* to erect a barrier against the spread of corruption.

digàmma, *s.m.* *(lettera dell'alfabeto greco)* digamma.

digàstrico, *ag.* *(anat.)* digastric: *fossetta digastrica,* digastric fossa; *muscolo —,* digastric muscle; *ramo — del nervo facciale,* digastric nerve.

digelàre, *V.* **disgelàre.**

digerènte, *ag.* digestive: *apparato —,* *(anat.)* digestive apparatus.

digeríbile, *ag.* digestible: *uno stomaco debole abbisogna di cibo facilmente —,* a weak stomach needs easily digestible food.

digeribilità, *s.f.* digestibility.

digeríre, *v.t.* **1.** to digest: *il mio stomaco digerisce facilmente qualsiasi cibo,* my stomach can easily digest any food ‖ *— la sbornia,* to recover from drunkenness **2.** *fig.* *(assimilare)* to master, to assimilate, to digest; *(tollerare)* to bear, to tolerate, to endure, to stomach, to digest, to put up with (s.o., sthg.): *— una materia,* to master (*o* to assimilate *o* to digest) a subject; *non posso — una simile offesa,* I cannot stomach (*o* put up with *o* digest) such an insult; *ogni giorno devo — la sua presenza,* every day I have to put up with his presence.

digestióne, *s.f.* digestion: *questo cibo è di facile —,* this food is easy of digestion; *avere una buona, cattiva —,* to have a good, a poor digestion.

digestívo, *ag.s.m.* digestive.

digèsto, *s.m.* *(st. dir.)* digest.

digestóre, *s.m.* *(chim. ind.)* digester.

dighiacciàre, *v.i.* to melt, to thaw.

digiogàre, *v.t.* to unyoke.

Digióne, *no.pr.f.* *(geog.)* Dijon.

digitàle, *ag.* digital: *impronte digitali,* finger-prints *s.f.* *(bot.)* digitalis; *(pop.)* foxglove.

digitalína, *s.f.* *(farm.)* digitalin.

digitàre, *v.t.* *(mus.)* to finger.

digitàto, *ag.* *(bot. zool.)* digitate(d).

digitazióne, *s.f.* *(mus.)* fingering.

digitígrado, *ag. s.m.* *(zool.)* digitigrade.

digiunàre, *v.i.* to fast: *— in Quaresima,* to fast in Lent.

digiúno, *ag.* **1.** fasting; empty: *stamane sono ancora —,* this morning I have not had my breakfast (*o* any breakfast) yet (*o* I have not yet breakfasted) **2.** *fig.* lacking (in sthg.), devoid: *è completamente — di latino,* he knows no Latin at all; *sono — di notizie,* I have had no news ‖ *s.m.* **1.** fast, fasting: *il quaresimale,* the Lenten fast; *giorni di —,* *(eccl.)* fast- (*o* fasting-) days; *non riesco a cantare a —,* I cannot sing on an empty stomach; *rompere il —,* to break one's fast; *stare a —,* to fast (*o* to be fasting) ‖ *un cucchiaio a —,* a spoonful before breakfast ‖ *predicare il — a pancia piena, prov.* the fat man knoweth not what the lean thinketh **2.** *fig.* *(mancanza, bisogno)* want **3.** *(anat.)* jejunum *(pl. jejuna)*: *infiammazione del —,* *(patol.)* jejunitis.

díglifo, *s.m.* *(arch.)* diglyph.

dignità, *s.f.* **1.** dignity: *la — di un uomo non dipende dalla sua ricchezza, ma da ciò che egli è,* a man's dignity depends not on his wealth but on what he is; *la mia — non mi permette di fare ciò,* it is beneath my dignity to do that **2.** *(considerazione, rispetto)* estimation, esteem, respect **3.** *(ufficio, rango)* dignity, rank: *— di cancelliere,* dignity of chancellor (*o* chancellorship); *fu elevato ad un'alta —,* he rose to a high rank **4.** *(dignitario)* dignitary.

dignitàrio, *s.m.* dignitary.

dignitosaménte, *av.* with dignity, in a dignified way, in a dignified manner.

dignitóso, *ag.* dignified; noble: *una risposta dignitosa,* a dignified reply; *la sua condotta dignitosa fu ammirata da tutti,* everybody admired his noble behaviour; *assumere un'aria dignitosa,* to assume a dignified air; *avere modi dignitosi,* to have dignified manners.

digradànte, *ag.* **1.** sloping **2.** *(che diminuisce)* diminishing.

digradàre, *v.i.* **1.** to slope down, to descend gradually, to decline: *il giardino digrada verso il fiume,* the garden slopes down to the river **2.** *(diminuire)* to diminish **3.** *(di colori)* to shade off; to tone down.

digradazióne, *s.f.* **1.** slope, sloping down **2.** (*il diminuire*) diminishing **3.** (*di colori*) shading off.

digràmma, *s.m.* (*fonet.*) digraph, digram.

digrassàre, *v.t.* **1.** to remove grease from (sthg.), to remove fat from (sthg.) **2.** (*schiumare*) to skim **3.** (*ind.*) to scour, to degrease: — *la lana,* to scour wool.

digredíre, *v.i.* (*rar.*) to digress.

digressióne, *s.f.* **1.** digression: *fare una* —, to make a digression (*o* to wander from the point); *lanciarsi in una* —, to break off into a digression; *perdersi in una* —, to lose oneself in a digression **2.** (*astr.*) digression: — *di un pianeta,* digression of a planet.

digressívo, *ag.* digressive.

digrignaménto, *s.m.* gnashing, grinding.

digrignàre, *v.t.* to gnash, to grind: — *i denti,* to gnash (*o* to grind) one's teeth.

digrossaménto, *s.m.* **1.** reducing, whittling (down), thinning (down) **2.** (*sbozzo*) rough-hewing, rough fashioning **3.** (*prima e fondamentale opera di educazione*) teaching of the first elements.

digrossàre, *v.t.* **1.** to reduce, to thin (down), to whittle (down, away): *il falegname digrossava una tavola,* the carpenter was thinning (down) a board; — *un diamante,* to cut a diamond; — *un ramo per farne un bastone,* to whittle down (*o* away) a branch for a stick **2.** (*sbozzare*) to rough-hew: — *una statua,* to rough-hew a statue **3.** (*erudire, impartendo i primi elementi del sapere*) to teach (s.o.) the first elements.

digrúma, *s.f.* (*voracità*) voracity.

digrumàle, *s.m.* (*rumine*) rumen.

digrumàre, *v.t.* **1.** to ruminate: *i buoi digrumano,* oxen chew the cud **2.** *fig.* (*meditare*) to ruminate, to ponder **3.** (*fam.*) (*mangiare voracemente*) to eat greedily.

diguazzaménto, *s.m.* splashing, paddling, dabbling.

diguazzàre, *v.i.* to splash (about), to paddle, to dabble: *i bambini diguazzavano nell'acqua,* the children were dabbling in the water; *camminavamo diguazzando nel fango,* we were splashing (our way) through the mud ‖ *v.t.* to shake, to stir: — *le uova,* (*cuc.*) to beat up eggs.

dilaceràre, *v.t.* **1.** to lacerate, to tear, to rend **2.** (*tormentare*) to lacerate, to afflict, to distress: *un terribile mal di denti lo dilacerò tutta la notte,* he was afflicted by a terrible toothache all night.

dilacerazióne, *s.f.* (*med.*) laceration.

dilagàre, *v.i.* **1.** (*di acque*) to form a lake, to spread: *il fiume dilagò nella campagna,* the river spread its waters over the country-side; *qui il fiume dilaga,* here the river widens into a lake **2.** (*diffondersi*) to spread, to increase: *la corruzione, il vizio dilaga,* corruption, vice is spreading (*o* increasing) ‖ **dilagàrsi,** *v.r.* (*di acque*) to form a lake, to spread.

dilaniàre, *v.t.* **1.** to tear to pieces, to rend: *fu dilaniato da una bomba,* he was torn to pieces by a bomb; — *una preda,* to tear a prey to pieces **2.** *fig.* to tear, to lacerate: *era dilaniato dal rimorso, dall'angoscia,* he was torn with remorse, with anguish; *il sospetto lo dilaniava,* suspicion was harassing him; — *la reputazione di qlcu.,* to tear s.o.'s reputation to shreds (*o* pieces).

dilapidàre, *v.t.* to dilapidate, to squander, to dissipate; to waste: — *il proprio denaro,* to squander (*o* to waste) one's money.

dilapidatóre, *ag.* squandering ‖ *s.m.,* **dilapidatríce,** *s.f.* squanderer.

dilapidazióne, *s.f.* dilapidation, squandering.

dilatàbile, *ag.* dilatable, expansible.

dilatabilità, *s.f.* dilatability, expansibility.

dilataménto, *s.m.* dilatation, expansion.

dilatàre, *v.t.* **1.** to dilate; to extend; to broaden, to enlarge, to widen: *l'alcool dilata le vene,* alcohol dilates the veins; — *la propria mente,* to widen (*o* to broaden *o* to enlarge) one's mind **2.** (*fis.*) to expand: *il calore dilata i corpi,* bodies are expanded by heat ‖

dilatàrsi, *v.r.* **1.** to dilate; to widen; (*diffondersi*) to spread: *era così arrabbiato che gli si dilatavano le vene della fronte,* he was so angry that the veins swelled on his forehead; *la fama si dilata,* fame spreads; *quanto più si sale, l'orizzonte si dilata,* as you go higher, the horizon widens (*o* unfolds itself); *la pupilla si dilata al buio,* the pupil of the eye dilates in the dark **2.** (*fis.*) to expand.

dilatàto, *ag.* dilated, enlarged: *cuore* —, (*med.*) enlarged heart; *pori dilatati,* enlarged pores.

dilatatóre, *s.m.* **1.** dilater **2.** (*chir.*) dilatator, dilator: — *tracheale,* tracheal dilatator **3.** (*mec.*) expansion joint, expansion bend.

dilatatòrio, *ag.* (*anat.*) dilator ‖ *s.m.* (*anat.*) dilator (muscle).

dilatatríce, *s.f.* dilater.

dilatazióne, *s.f.* **1.** dilatation, dilation: — *della pupilla,* dilation of the pupil (of the eye); — *di cuore,* (*med.*) dilatation of heart **2.** (*fis.*) expansion, dilatation: — *dei gas,* expansion of gases; — *termica,* thermal expansion; *curva di* —, (*mec.*) expansion bend; *giunto di* —, (*mec.*) expansion joint.

dilatòmetro, *s.m.* (*fis.*) dilatometer.

dilatòrio, *ag.* (*dir.*) dilatory: *eccezione dilatoria,* dilatory exception; *metodi dilatori,* dilatory methods.

dilavaménto, *s.m.* washing away.

dilavàre, *v.t.* **1.** to wash away **2.** (*sbiadire*) to wash out, to fade.

dilavataménte, *av.* colourlessly.

dilavàto, *ag.* **1.** washed away **2.** (*sbiadito*) colourless, faded, washed out; (*pallido*) pale.

dilazionàre, *v.t.* to defer; to postpone; to delay, to respite: *non posso più* — *la mia partenza,* I can no longer postpone my departure.

dilazióne, *s.f.* delay, respite: *una* — *di una settimana,* a week's delay; *concedere, ottenere una* — *di pagamento,* (*comm.*) to grant, to obtain a delay (*o* an extension) of payment; *domandare una* —, to ask for a respite.

dileggiaménto, *s.m.* mockery, scoffing, jeer, derision.

dileggiàre, *v.t.* to mock, to scoff at (s.o., sthg.), to deride: *smettila di* — *tuo fratello,* stop deriding your brother.

dileggiatóre, *ag.* mocking, scoffing ‖ *s.m.,* **dileggiatríce,** *s.f.* mocker, scoffer.

diléggio, *s.m.* mockery, scoffing, jeer, derision: *il* — *è l'arma dei deboli,* mockery is the weapon of the weak.

dileguaménto, *s.m.* dispersing; disappearing, vanishing.

dileguàre, *v.t.* to disperse, to dissolve, to dispel: *il sole dilegua la nebbia,* the sun disperses (*o* dispels) the fog; — *ogni dubbio,* to dispel all doubts ‖ *v.i.* to fade away, to vanish: *il suono andava dileguando,* the sound was fading away ‖ **dileguàrsi,** *v.r.* to disappear, to vanish, to fade away: *si dileguò tra la folla,* he disappeared (*o* vanished) in the crowd.

dilèmma, *s.m.* dilemma: *i corni di un* ¦—, the horns of a dilemma.

dilètta, *s.f.* beloved, darling: *mia* —*!,* darling!.

dilettànte, *s.c.* **1.** dilettante (*pl.* dilettanti); amateur: *compagnia di dilettanti,* (*teat.*) amateur players; *dipinge come un* —, he is an amateur painter; *è un* — *di pittura, di musica,* he is an amateur of painting, of music; *suona bene per essere una* —, she plays well for an amateur; *fare ql.co. da* —, (*spreg.*) to be a dabbler in sthg. ‖ *da* —, as an amateur: *lavoro da* —, amateurish work **2.** (*spor.*) amateur: *campionato dilettanti,* amateur championship.

dilettantísmo, *s.m.* dilettantism, amateurism.

dilettantístico, *ag.* dilettantish, amateurish.

dilettàre, *v.t.* to delight, to please: *un libro che diletta ed istruisce,* a book that is both readable and instructive ‖ **dilettàrsi,** *v.r.* to take delight (in sthg., in doing); to delight (in sthg., in doing): *si diletta di* *pittura*, he paints a little; *si diletta nella lettura*, she likes (*o* she is fond of) reading.

dilettazióne, *s.f.* (*rar.*) delight, pleasure.

dilettévole, *ag.* delightful, pleasant, agreeable: *un libro* —, a delightful book.

dilettevolménte, *av.* delightfully, pleasantly.

dilètto[1], *ag.* beloved, dear, dearly loved: *il mio — paese*, my beloved country ‖ *s.m.* beloved, darling: *mio* —!, darling! (*o* my beloved!).

dilètto[2], *s.m.* delight, pleasure: *con nostro grande* —, to our great delight; *trovar — in ql.co.*, *nel far ql.co.*, to find pleasure (*o* to take delight) in sthg., in doing sthg. ‖ *per* —, for pleasure.

dilettosaménte, *av.* delightedly.

dilettóso, *ag.* (*rar.*) delightful: *questo è un lavoro* —!, this is a delightful work!.

dilezióne, *s.f.* affection: — *per il proprio prossimo*, affection towards (*o* for) one's neighbour.

diligènte, *ag.* 1. diligent; zealous: *uno scolaro* —, a diligent pupil 2. (*accurato*) diligent, careful, accurate: *lavoro* —, careful (*o* accurate) work.

diligenteménte, *av.* 1. diligently: *egli lavora* —, he works zealously 2. (*accuratamente*) accurately, carefully: *devi leggere questa lettera* —, you must read this letter carefully.

diligènza[1], *s.f.* diligence, care: *usa ogni — nel fare questo lavoro!*, do this work with the utmost care!.

diligènza[2], *s.f.* (*carrozza pubblica a cavalli*) diligence.

diliscàre, *v.t.* 1. (*canapa*) to dress 2. (*pesce*) to take off the bones of (a fish).

dilogía, *s.f.* 1. ambiguity, repetition, dilogy 2. (*teat.*) group of two dramatic compositions.

dilombàrsi, *v.r.* to strain one's back.

dilombàto, *ag.* 1. (*di cavallo*) worn-out, broken-backed 2. *fig.* (*esausto*) worn-out, tired-out; (*debole*) weak.

dilucidàre, *v.t.* 1. to clear up, to explain, to make clear, to elucidate: *è una difficoltà che va dilucidata*, it is a difficulty that must be cleared up 2. (*ind. tessile*) to decatize.

dilucidazióne, *s.f.* 1. explanation, elucidation 2. (*ind. tessile*) decatizing.

dilúcolo, **dilúculo**, *s.m.* (*letter.*) dawn, daybreak.

diluènte, *ag.* diluent ‖ *s.m.* (*chim.*) diluent; (*per vernici*) thinner.

diluíre, *v.t.* to dilute; to water down (anche *fig.*); (*una vernice*) to thin: — *la concentrazione della soluzione*, (*chim.*) to dilute the solution.

diluíto, *ag.* dilute; (*di vernice*) thin.

diluizióne, *s.f.* 1. dilution 2. (*di vernice*) thinness; (*il diluire*) thinning.

dilungàre, *v.t.* (*allungare*) to lengthen; (*prolungare*) to prolong ‖ **dilungàrsi**, *v.r.* 1. (*allontanarsi*) to depart, to deviate 2. (*parlare a lungo*) to speak diffusely, to expatiate, to dwell (on a subject): *l'autore si dilunga a descrivere la campagna*, the author dwells on a description of the country.

dilúngo, *av.* (*diritto*) straight on, along; (*difilato*) directly; (*ininterrottamente*) continuously: *tirare* —, to go on (*o* to pass on) ‖ *suonare a* —, (*a distesa*) to ring a full peal.

diluviàle, *ag.* 1. torrential: *pioggia* —, torrential rain (*o* deluge of rain) 2. (*geol.*) diluvial, diluvian: *terreni diluviali*, diluvial formations.

diluviàno, *ag.* diluvial, diluvian: *epoca diluviana*, diluvian epoch.

diluviàre, *v.i.* 1. *imp.* to rain in torrents, to pour: *sta diluviando*, it is pouring 2. *fig.* to pour, to shower: *diluviarono gli applausi*, there was a deluge (*o* a shower) of applause; *diluviavano le parole, i colpi*, words, blows were showering (*o* pouring fast) ‖ *v.t.* (*mangiare con avidità*) to devour, to eat voraciously.

diluviatóre, *s.m.*, **diluviatríce**, *s.f.* (*chi mangia con avidità*) devourer, voracious eater, gross eater.

dilúvio, *s.m.* 1. deluge: *un — di pioggia*, a deluge of rain ‖ *il — universale*, the Deluge (*o* the Flood) 2. *fig.* deluge, flood, shower: *un — di colpi*, a shower of blows; *un — di lacrime*, a flood of tears; *un — di parole*, a deluge of words.

diluvióna, *s.f.*, **diluvióne**, *s.m.* (*chi mangia con avidità*) devourer, voracious eater, gross eater.

diluzióne, *V.* **diluizióne**.

dimagraménto, *s.m.* 1. thinning, growing thin 2. (*di terreno*) impoverishing, impoverishment.

dimagràre, *v.i.* to thin, to get thin, to grow thin, to lose weight; (*moltissimo*) to become lean: *è dimagrato due chili*, he has lost two kilos ‖ *v.t.* to slim, to thin; to make thin: *l'aceto dimagra*, vinegar makes thin; *questa dieta dimagra*, this diet is slimming.

dimagríre, *e derivati*, *V.* **dimagràre**, *e derivati*.

dimandàre, (*letter.*) per **domandàre**.

dimàne, *s.f.* (*letter.*) 1. (*alba*) dawn 2. (*il giorno dopo*) (the) next day.

dimàni, (*letter.*) per **domàni**.

dimembràre, *v.t.* (*rar.*) to dismember.

dimenaménto, *s.m.* (*di coda*) wagging; (*divincolamento*) waving, swinging; (*ondeggiamento*) tossing; swaying.

dimenàre, *v.t.* (*la coda*) to wag; (*divincolare*) to wave, to swing; (*fare ondeggiare*) to toss; to sway ‖ — *le ganasce*, to eat greedily (*o* voraciously) ‖ **dimenàrsi**, *v.r.* to move about restlessly, to fidget; (*nel letto*) to toss about; (*camminando*) to sway ‖ *chi va a letto senza cena, tutta notte si dimena*, *prov.* he who goes to bed, and goes to bed sober falls as the leaves do, and dies in October (*o* who goes to bed supperless, all night tumbles and tosses).

dimenío, *s.m.* (*di coda*) wagging; (*divincolamento*) waving, swinging; (*ondeggiamento*) tossing; swaying.

dimensionàle, *ag.* (*fis.*) dimensional.

dimensionàre, *v.t.* to dimension.

dimensióne, *s.f.* dimension; (*grandezza*) size: — *critica*, (*fis. atomica*) critical size; — *della immagine*, (*tv.*) projection size; — *nominale*, (*mec.*) nominal (*o* basic) size; *dimensioni principali*, (*di scafo*) moulded dimensions; *dimensioni ricorrenti*, (*metal.*) ruling section; *a tre dimensioni*, three-dimension (*attributivo*), tridimensional: *film a tre dimensioni*, three-dimension picture (*abbr.* 3-D); *quarta* —, (*fis.*) fourth dimension; *di che — è?*, what size is it?; *quali sono le dimensioni dell'armadio?*, what are the dimensions of the wardrobe?.

dimenticàbile, *ag.* forgettable.

dimenticànza, *s.f.* 1. (*oblio*) oblivion: *cadere in* —, to sink (*o* to fall) into oblivion 2. (*facilità a dimenticare*) forgetfulness 3. (*svista*) oversight; (*negligenza*) carelessness, forgetfulness; (*omissione*) omission; (*inavvertenza*) inadvertence: *per* —, inadvertently, because of (*o* through) an oversight, through carelessness; *è stata una* —, it was an oversight.

dimenticàre, *v.t.*, **dimenticàrsi**, *v.r.* to forget: *ho dimenticato il suo nome*, I have forgotten his name (*o* his name has slipped my mind); *non — che...!*, don't forget (*o* bear in mind) that...!; *non dimenticarti dei tuoi amici!*, don't forget your friends!; *non dimenticatevi di imbucare questa lettera!*, don't forget to post this letter! ‖ — *l'ora di un appuntamento*, to forget (*o* to overlook) the time of an appointment; — *il passato*, to forget the past (*o* to let bygones be bygones); *far — il proprio passato*, to live down one's past ‖ *dimenticati di avermi mai visto!*, forget ever seeing me! ‖ — *un'offesa*, (*perdonarla*) to forgive an offence ‖ — *i propri interessi*, (*trascurarli*) to be unmindful of one's interests ‖ *il pan mangiato presto è dimenticato*, *prov.* eaten bread is soon forgotten.

dimenticàto, *ag.* forgotten.

dimenticatóio, *s.m.* (*pop.*) oblivion: *cadere, finire nel* —, to fall (*o* to sink) into oblivion; *mettere nel* —, to cast into oblivion.

diméntico, *ag.* forgetful: — *del proprio dovere*, forgetful (*o* unmindful) of his (own) duty.

dimenticóna, *s.f.*, **dimenticóne**, *s.m.* (*fam.*) forgetter; (*sventato*) scatter-brain.

dímero, *s.m.* (*chim.*) dimer.

dimessaménte, *av.* 1. (*modestamente*) modestly, humbly: *rispondere* —, to answer humbly 2. (*poveramente*) poorly; (*in modo trasandato*) shabbily.

dimésso, *ag.* 1. (*modesto*) modest, humble 2. (*povero*) poor; (*trasandato*) shabby.

dimesticàre, *V.* addomesticàre.

dimestichézza, *s.f.* familiarity, intimacy: *avere* — *con ql.co.*, to be familiar with sthg.; *avere* — *con qlcu.*, to be on terms of familiarity (*o* on familiar terms) with s.o.

dimèstico, *ag.* familiar, intimate: *essere* — *con qlcu.*, to be on familiar (*o* intimate) terms with s.o.

dímetro, *s.m.* (*poes.*) dimeter.

diméttere, *v.t.* 1. (*da una carica*) to remove, to dismiss, to discharge: *fu dimesso dal suo ufficio*, he was discharged from his office 2. (*da un luogo di cura*) to discharge: *fu dimesso ieri dall'ospedale*, he was discharged from hospital yesterday 3. (*eccl.*) (*perdonare*) to pardon 4. (*condonare*) to condone: — *un debito*, to condone a debt 5. (*tralasciare*) to give up ‖ **diméttersi**, *v.r.* to resign (an office).

dimezzaménto, *s.m.* halving.

dimezzàre, *v.t.* (*tagliare a metà*) to halve, to cut into halves, to divide into halves; (*ridurre alla metà*) to halve, to reduce to a half.

dimezzàto, *ag.* (*diviso in due*) halved, cut into halves, divided into halves; (*ridotto a metà*) reduced to a half.

diminuèndo[1], *s.m.* (*arit.*) minuend.

diminuèndo[2], *s.m.* (*mus.*) diminuendo.

diminuíbile, *ag.* diminishable.

diminuíre, *v.t.* 1. to lessen, to diminish, to reduce; to lower; to abate: *questo vi diminuirà agli occhi del pubblico*, that will lower you in the eyes of the public; — *l'autorità di qlcu.*, to detract from s.o.'s authority; — *i prezzi*, to bring down prices; — *le spese*, to curtail (*o* to cut down) expenses; — *il volume del suono*, to reduce the volume of sound 2. (*in lavori a maglia*) to narrow: — *un punto*, to drop a stitch ‖ *v.i.* to lessen, to grow less, to diminish: *la febbre diminuisce*, fever abates; *il freddo diminuisce*, the cold is relaxing; *i prezzi diminuiscono*, prices are falling; *i profitti diminuiscono*, profits are falling off (*o* declining); — *di velocità*, to slow down (*o* to reduce) speed.

diminutívo, *ag.s.m.* (*gram.*) diminutive: *la lingua italiana è ricca di diminutivi*, Italian is rich in diminutives.

diminutóre, *s.m.* (*arit.*) subtrahend.

diminuzióne, *s.f.* lessening, diminution, reduction; decrease, lowering; abatement: — *dei prezzi*, reduction (*o* fall) in prices; — *delle imposte*, lowering of taxation; *la popolazione è in* —, the population is on the decrease; *vi fu un'improvvisa* — *della temperatura*, there was a sudden drop in the temperature; *subire una rapida* —, to diminish rapidly.

dimissionàre, *v.t.* (*neol.*) to oblige (s.o.) to resign.

dimissionàrio, *ag.* resigning: *ministero* —, out-going ministry (*o* resigning cabinet); *ufficiale* —, resigning officer.

dimissióne, *s.f.* 1. resignation: *dimissioni! dimissioni!*, resign! resign!; *dare le dimissioni*, to resign (*o* to send in one's resignation *o* to offer one's resignation) 2. (*il dimettere*) removal; dismissal.

dimissòria, *s.f.* (*eccl.*) dimissory letter.

dimissòrio, *ag.* dimissory.

dimoiàre, *v.i.* to thaw ‖ *v.t.* to soak: — *il bucato*, to soak the washing.

dimoiatíccio, *s.m.* slush, slosh.

dimòio, *s.m.* (*rar.*) thawing.

dimòra, *s.f.* 1. residence, stay, sojourn: *la sua* — *in quel paese lo ha reso maturo*, his stay in that country has matured him 2. (*abitazione*) residence, dwelling, abode, home: *senza fissa* —, without fixed abode;

prendere — *in un vecchio castello*, to make one's home in an old castle (*o* to take up one's abode in an old castle); *stare a* — *presso qlcu.*, to live at s.o.'s ‖ *mettere a* — *alberi*, to transplant trees 3. (*indugio*) delay: *senza* —, immediately.

dimoràre, *v.i.* 1. to stay, to remain, to sojourn: *ho dimorato a Roma a lungo*, I stayed in Rome for a long time 2. (*abitare*) to live, to dwell, to abide: *il Re dimora in un grande palazzo*, the King resides in a large palace 3. (*indugiare*) to delay.

dimorfísmo, *s.m.* (*scient.*) dimorphism.

dimòrfo, *ag.* (*scient.*) dimorphic, dimorphous.

dimostràbile, *ag.* demonstrable, provable: *verità* —, demonstrable truth; *la falsità della notizia è facilmente* —, the falsity of the news can be easily demonstrated (*o* is easily demonstrable).

dimostrabilità, *s.f.* demonstrability.

dimostrànte, *s.c.* demonstrant.

dimostràre, *v.t.* 1. to show: *dimostra vent'anni*, she looks (*o* appears to be) twenty; *ha cinquant'anni, ma non li dimostra*, she is fifty but does not look it; — *affetto, amicizia*, to show affection, friendliness 2. (*provare*) to demonstrate, to prove, to show: *dimostrò la verità della sua teoria*, he proved (*o* demonstrated *o* showed) the truth of his theory; *ciò dimostra che non hai capito*, this proves (*o* shows) that you have not understood; *lo scolaro dimostrò di avere buona memoria*, the pupil showed he had a good memory; — *l'esistenza di Dio*, to prove (*o* to demonstrate *o* to show) the existence of God ‖ **dimostràrsi**, *v.r.* to show oneself, to prove: *si dimostrò inferiore al compito*, he proved unequal to the task; *egli si dimostrò un eroe*, he proved (*o* showed himself) (to be) a hero (*o* he proved to be a hero); *la scorta si dimostrò insufficiente*, the supply proved insufficient.

dimostrativaménte, *av.* demonstratively.

dimostratívo, *ag.* 1. demonstrative: *azione dimostrativa*, (*mil.*) demonstration; *tuffo* —, exhibition dive 2. (*gram.*) demonstrative: *pronomi dimostrativi*, demonstrative pronouns.

dimostratóre, *s.m.*, **dimostratríce**, *s.f.* demonstrator: *venne a casa nostra la dimostratrice di un nuovo detersivo*, the demonstrator of a new detergent came to our house.

dimostrazióne, *s.f.* 1. demonstration, proof; (*segno tangibile*) mark: *una* — *d'affetto*, a demonstration of love; *una* — *di coraggio*, a mark of courage; *la* — *di un teorema*, the demonstration of a theorem; *dare a qlcu. una* — *della propria gratitudine*, to give s.o. proof of one's gratitude 2. (*manifestazione popolare*) demonstration: *fare una* —, to demonstrate.

dimozzàre, *v.t.* to lop, to cut off.

dína[1], *s.f.* (*fis.*) dyne.

Dína[2], *no.pr.f.* Dinah.

dinàmica, *s.f.* (*fis.*) dynamics: — *terrestre*, dynamic geology.

dinamicaménte, *av.* dynamically.

dinàmico, *ag.* 1. (*fis.*) dynamic(al): *elettricità dinamica*, dynamic electricity; *forza dinamica*, dynamic force; *unità dinamica*, dynamic unity 2. (*energico, attivo*) dynamic, energetic, active: *quello è un uomo* —!, that is an energetic man!.

dinamísmo, *s.m.* 1. (*fis.*) dynamism 2. (*atteggiamento energico, attività*) energy, activity.

dinamitàrdo, *s.m.* dynamiter, dynamitard.

dinamíte, *s.f.* dynamite: — *a base inerte*, inert base dynamite; *deposito di* —, dynamite magazine (*o* store).

dinamítico, *ag.* dynamitic.

dinamitifício, *s.m.* dynamite factory.

dínamo, *s.f.* (*elett.*) dynamo: — *ad anello*, ring winding dynamo; — *compensatrice*, balancing dynamo; — *per carica batterie*, battery charging generator.

dinamogènesi, *s.f.* (*fis.*) dynamogenesis.

dinamomètrico, *ag.* (*fis.*) dynamometric(al).

dinamòmetro, *s.m.* (*fis.*) dynamometer: — *elettrico,* electric dynamometer; — *di torsione,* torquemeter.

dinamoscopía, *s.f.* (*med.*) dynamoscopy.

dinamoscòpio, *s.m.* (*med.*) dynamoscope.

dinànzi, *prep.* before; in front of; opposite; (*alla presenza di*) in the presence of: — *ai miei stessi occhi,* before my very eyes; — *al giudice,* before the judge; — *a suo padre,* in his father's presence; *era — a me nella coda,* he was in front of me in the queue; *guarda — a te!,* look in front of you!; *ho il libro — a me,* I have the book before me; *lasciò la macchina — al commissariato,* he left his car in front of the police station; *l'ho sempre — agli occhi, fig.* I always have it in my mind's eye (*o* I always keep it in mind); *sedeva — a lui,* he was sitting before (*o* facing *o* opposite) him; *stava proprio — a me al cinema e non potevo veder niente,* she was right in front of me at the cinema and I couldn't see anything; *stavano uno — all'altro,* they stood facing each other (*o* they faced each other); *il suo ufficio è — alla chiesa,* his office is opposite the church (*o* faces the church); *comparire — al giudice,* to appear before the judge; *fuggire — a qlcu.,* to run away from s.o. (*o* to fly before s.o.); *presentarsi — a qlcu.,* to present oneself before s.o. || — *a Dio e agli uomini,* before God and man || — *alla morte,* in the presence of death || *av.* before; in front; forward: — *i cantori, dietro i musicanti,* the singers go before, the musicians follow after; — *marciava la banda,* the band marched in front; *hai tutta la vita —!,* your whole life is before you! (*o* in front of you!); *assalire qlcu. —,* to attack s.o. head-on; *guardare —,* to look straight ahead || *levati —!,* get out of my way! (*o* get out of the light!) || *s.m.* front; fore part.

dinaro, *s.m.* (*moneta jugoslava*) dinar.

dinàsta, *s.m.* dynast.

dinastía, *s.f.* dynasty: *la — dei Tudor,* the Tudor dynasty.

dinàstico, *ag.* dynastic.

dinàstidi, *s.m.pl.* (*entom.*) Dynastes, Dynastinae.

díndi, *s.m.pl.* (*linguaggio infantile*) pennies.

dindín, *s.m.* (*onomatopeico*) ding-ding.

díndio, díndo, *s.m.* (*ornit.*) turkey.

dindòn, *s.m.* (*onomatopeico*) ding-dong.

díne, *s.f.* (*fis.*) dyne.

dinegàre, *v.t.* (*rar.*) to deny; to refuse.

dinervàre, *v.t.* to enervate; to unnerve.

diniègo, *s.m.* denial; refusal: *scosse il capo in segno di —,* he shook his head in denial.

dinnànzi, *V.* **dinànzi.**

dinoccolàre, *v.t.* to dislocate, to put (s.o.'s neck) out of joint.

dinoccolàto, *ag.* 1. slouching, drooping: *andatura dinoccolata,* slouching walk 2. (*dislogato*) dislocated.

dinosàuro, *s.m.* (*paleont.*) dinosaur.

dinotàre, *V.* **denotàre.**

dinotèrio, *s.m.* (*paleont.*) dinothere.

dintórno, d'intórno, *av.* around; round about: *per un miglio —,* for a mile around; *aveva molta gente —,* she had a lot of people round about her (*o* all around her); *c'erano molti boschi —,* there were many woods all around; *guardai —,* I looked around; *ha sempre — un nugolo di corteggiatori,* she always has a cloud of young men about her; *levati —!,* get out of my way! || *prep.* 1. round, around, about: *le colline — alla città,* the hills round (about) the town; *c'era molta gente — a me,* there were many people (a)round me; *ella si guardò —,* she looked about her; *si riunirono — al fuoco,* they gathered round the fire; *stavano tutti — alla culla,* they were all standing round the cradle || *andare — a qlcu., (corteggiarlo)* to go after s.o. 2. (*circa*) about.

dintórno, *s.m.* 1. *pl.* environs, outskirts; vicinity (*sing.*): *abitava nei dintorni di Roma,* he lived on the outskirts of Rome 2. (*contorno*) outline, contour.

dío, *s.m.* god: *Marte, il — della guerra,* Mars,

the god of war; *simile a un —,* godlike; *Beethoven è il — della musica,* Beethoven is the high-priest of music; *canta da —, (gergo)* he is a first-rate singer; *si crede un —,* he thinks he is a little (tin) god; *considerare qlcu. un —,* to make a god of s.o. || *gli dei falsi e bugiardi,* the false gods || **Dío,** (*nella tradizione cristiana*) God, the Lord, our Lord: *la voce di —,* the voice of God; *il buon — ti vede,* God sees you; *pregare —,* to pray to God || — *buono!, gran —!,* Good Lord! (*o fam.* goodness gracious! *o sl.* gosh!); — *Onnipotente!,* God Almighty! || *dito, mano di —!,* divine punishment! || *grazie a —,* thank heaven (*o* goodness) || *l'ira di —,* God's wrath: *quel ragazzo è un'ira di —,* that boy is a holy terror; *successe l'ira di —,* something frightful happened || *per l'amor di —!,* for goodness' sake! || *quanta grazia di —!,* how many good things! || *servo di —, (eccl.)* clergyman || *timorato di —,* God-fearing || *Uomo —,* God-Man || — *ce la mandi buona!,* — *ci assista!,* God help us! || — *lo voglia!,* God grant it!; — *non voglia!,* God forbid! || — *solo lo sa,* God only knows || *a — piacendo,* God willing || *come — volle arrivammo a casa,* somehow or other we got home || *in nome di — cosa fai?,* what in God's name are you doing? || *se — vuole ho finito,* thank God I have finished || *andarsene con —,* to go away (*o* to go about one's own business); (*morire in pace*) to die peacefully || — *non paga il sabato, prov.* sooner or later the wicked are punished || *l'uomo propone e — dispone, prov.* man proposes and God disposes.

diocesàno, *ag.* (*eccl.*) diocesan.

diòcesi, *s.f.* (*eccl.*) diocese.

Diocleziàno, *no.pr.m.* (*st.*) Diocletian.

díodo, *s.m.* (*rad.*) diode: — *a gas,* gaseous diode; — *a vapori di mercurio,* mercury-vapour diode; — *raddrizzatore,* rectifier diode; — *rivelatore,* detector diode.

diodònte, *s.m.* (*ittiol.*) diodont.

Diòfanto, *no.pr.m.* (*st. mat.*) Diophantos.

Diògene, *no.pr.m.* (*st. fil.*) Diogenes: *la lanterna di —,* the lantern of Diogenes.

diòico, *ag.* (*bot.*) dioecious.

Diomède, *no.pr.m.* (*lett.*) Diomed, Diomede(s).

dionèa, *s.f.* (*bot.*) dionaea; (*pop.*) Venus's fly-trap.

Dionígi, *no.pr.m.* 1. Denis, Dennis: *San —,* Saint Denis || *dim.* Denny 2. (*st.*) Dionysius.

dionísia[1], *s.f.* (*min.*) dionise.

Dionísia[2], *no.pr.f.* Denise.

dionisíaco, *ag.* Dionysiac, Dionysian: *feste dionisiache,* Dionysia (*o* Dionysian festivals).

Diòniso, *no.pr.m.* (*mit.*) Dionysus.

diòpside, *s.m.* (*min.*) diopside; pyroxene.

diòptra, *V.* **diòttra.**

dioràma, *s.m.* (*ott.*) diorama.

dioríte, *s.f.* (*geol.*) diorite.

Diòscuri, *no.pr.m.pl.* (*mit.*) Dioscuri.

diosmòsi, *s.f.* (*fis.*) diosmosis, diosmose.

diòta, *s.f.* (*archeol.*) diota (*pl.* diotae).

diòttra, *s.f.* 1. (*topografia*) diopter, dioptra 2. (*geodesia*) alidade.

diottría, *s.f.* (*ott.*) diopter.

diòttrica, *s.f.* (*ott.*) dioptrics.

diòttrico, *ag.* (*ott.*) dioptric(al).

dipanaménto, *s.m.* winding into a ball.

dipanàre, *v.t.* 1. to wind (off) into a ball: — *una matassa,* to wind a skein (*o* hank) into a ball 2. *fig.* (*districare*) to disentangle; to unravel, to untangle: — *una questione intricata,* to solve an intricate question.

dipanatóio, *s.m.* (*ind. tessile*) skein-winder.

dipartènza, *s.f.* (*letter.*) departure || *fare le dipartenze,* to say good-bye.

dipartiménto[1], *s.m.* 1. (*circoscrizione*) department; (*mar.*) department: — *dello Ionio,* department of the Ionian sea; *capoluogo di —,* capital of a department 2. (*ministero*) department: — *di Stato,* (*negli Stati Uniti*) Department of State.

dipartiménto[2], *s.m.* (*arc.*) **1.** (*partenza*) departure **2.** (*morte*) death.

dipartíre, *v.t.* (*rar.*) to divide ‖ **dipartírsi**, *v.r.* **1.** to go away; to leave (s.o., sthg.); to depart **2.** *fig.* (*divergere*) to diverge, to differ; to depart: — *da una consuetudine*, to depart from a custom; — *dall'opinione di qlcu.*, to diverge from s.o.'s opinion ‖ — *dalla retta via*, to go astray **3.** (*morire*) to pass away, to depart from this life **4.** (*di strada*) to branch off.

dipartíta, *s.f.* (*letter.*) **1.** departure: *la sua* — *da casa*, his departure from home **2.** (*morte*) death: *pianse per la sua* —, she wept over his death.

dipendènte, *ag.* **1.** dependent (on s.o., sthg.), depending (on s.o., sthg.): *impiegati dipendenti dal Comune*, municipal employees **2.** (*gram.*) dependent (on sthg.), subordinate: *una proposizione* —, a subordinate (o dependent) clause ‖ *s.m.* (*impiegato*) employee; (*subordinato*) subordinate: *il direttore affidò il lavoro ad un suo* —, the manager entrusted the work to one of his subordinates.

dipendenteménte, *av.* dependently.

dipendènza, *s.f.* **1.** dependence (on s.o., sthg.): — *reciproca*, interdependence; *essere alle dipendenze di qlcu.*, to be in s.o.'s service **2.** (*subordinazione*) subordination **3.** *pl.* (*di edificio*), annexe (*sing.*); outhouse (*sing.*): *l'albergo e le sue dipendenze*, the hotel and its annexes.

dipèndere, *v.i.* **1.** (*derivare*) to derive, to proceed; to be due (to s.o., sthg.): *questo difetto dipende da lavorazione trascurata*, this defect is due (o is owing) to careless working; *questo errore dipende dall'ignoranza*, this mistake springs from (o is the result of) ignorance **2.** (*essere subordinato*) to depend (on s.o., sthg.): *dipende dalla sua risposta*, it all depends on his reply; *dipende dalle circostanze*, it all depends on the circumstances; *dipende da te superare queste difficoltà*, it rests with you (o it depends on you) to overcome these difficulties; *dipende solo da te!*, that depends entirely on you! (o it's up to you!); *questi avvenimenti non dipendono dalla nostra volontà*, these events are not within our control; *tutto il personale dipende da lui*, he is the head of the whole staff (o the whole staff is under his direction) ‖ — *l'uno dall'altro*, to interdepend; *non* — *che da se stessi*, to be one's own master; (*fam.*) to stand on one's own feet ‖ *dipende!*, that depends! **3.** (*vivere a carico*) to be dependent (on s.o.), to depend (on s.o.): — *dal padre*, to depend (up)on one's father **4.** (*gram.*) to depend (on sthg.).

dipennàre, *v.t.* to erase; *fig.* to cross out.

dipètalo, *ag.* (*bot.*) dipetalous.

dipíngere, *v.t.* **1.** to paint; (*ritrarre*) to portray: — *a fresco*, to paint in fresco; — *all'acquerello*, to paint in water-colours; — *dal vero*, to paint from life (o from nature); — *ql.co. di rosso, di verde*, to paint something red, green; — *un ritratto ad olio*, to paint a portrait in oils; — *un tramonto*, to paint a sunset **2.** *fig.* to paint, to portray, to depict: *l'autunno dipinge la campagna di colori smorzati*, autumn paints the country in soft colours; *la gioia era dipinta sul suo viso*, joy was depicted on her face; *non vi sono parole che possano* — *la scena*, words cannot paint the scene; — *a colori rosei*, to paint in rosy colours; — *il carattere di qlcu.*, to paint (o to portray) s.o.'s character ‖ *il diavolo non è brutto come lo si dipinge*, prov. the devil is not so black as he is painted ‖ **dipíngersi**, *v.r.* to paint, to paint one's face: *è una bella ragazza, ma si dipinge troppo*, she is a beautiful girl, but she paints too much (o she uses too much make-up).

dipínto, *ag.* painted, depicted ‖ *non vorrei vivere là nemmeno* — *!*, I would not live there for worlds! (o the whole world!) ‖ *star* —, (*adattarsi perfettamente*) to fit perfectly ‖ *s.m.* painting: — *ad olio*, oil-painting; *i suoi dipinti furono venduti all'incanto*, his paintings were sold by auction.

dipintóre, *s.m.* (*rar.*) painter.

diplegía, *s.f.* (*patol.*) diplegia.

diplococco, *s.m.* (*microbiologia*) diplococcus (*pl.* diplococci).

diplòma, *s.m.* **1.** diploma, certificate: — *di laurea*, degree; — *di laurea in architettura*, diploma in architecture; — *di maturità*, (*classica o scientifica*) General Certificate of Education; *essere in possesso di un* —, to hold a diploma; *prendere un* —, to take a diploma **2.** (*st.*) diploma.

diplomàre, *v.t.* to confer a diploma on (s.o.), to give (s.o.) a diploma ‖ **diplomàrsi**, *v.r.* to get a degree, to get a diploma, to graduate: *si diplomò ad Oxford*, he graduated at Oxford.

diplomàtica, *s.f.* diplomatics.

diplomaticaménte, *av.* diplomatically.

diplomàtico, *ag.* diplomatic: *carriera diplomatica*, diplomatic career; *corpo* —, diplomatic service; *ragioni diplomatiche*, diplomatic reasons; *risposta diplomatica*, diplomatic answer ‖ *s.m.* diplomat, diplomatist: *un* — *sudamericano*, a South-American diplomat.

diplomàto, *ag.* diplomaed, diploma'd, holding a diploma ‖ *s.m.* holder of a diploma, graduate.

diplomazía, *s.f.* diplomacy: *in quella circostanza agì con molta* —, in those circumstances he acted with great diplomacy.

diplopía, *s.f.* (*patol.*) diplopia.

diploscòpio, *s.m.* (*ott.*) diploscope.

dipnòi, *s.m.pl.* (*ittiol.*) Dipnoi.

dipodía, *s.f.* (*poes.*) dipody.

dipòi, *V.* pòi.

diportaménto, *s.m.* (*rar.*) behaviour, conduct.

diportàrsi, *v.r.* **1.** to behave, to conduct oneself **2.** (*rar.*) (*divertirsi*) to amuse oneself.

dipòrto, *s.m.* recreation, amusement, diversion, sport: *gli scacchi ed il biliardo sono il suo* — *favorito*, chess and billiards are his favourite diversions; *darsi* —, to amuse oneself ‖ *per* —, for sport (o for one's own amusement): *fare ql.co. per* —, to do sthg. as a pastime (o for one's own amusement); *viaggiare per* —, to travel on (o for) pleasure.

diprèsso, a un, *l.av.* approximately, nearly, roughly.

dípsa, *s.f.* (*zool.*) dipsas (*pl.* dipsades).

dipsòmane, *ag.* (*patol.*) dipsomaniacal ‖ *s.c.* (*patol.*) dipsomaniac.

dipsomanía, *s.f.* (*patol.*) dipsomania.

díptero, *V.* díttero[1].

diradaménto, *s.m.* thinning, thinning out; (*di nebbia, gas*) rarefaction.

diradàre, *v.t.* **1.** to thin out: *se diraderai i fiori, cresceranno meglio il prossimo anno*, if you thin out the flowers, they will grow better next year; *il sole diradò le tenebre*, the sun dissipated the clouds **2.** (*rendere meno frequente*) to do less frequently: *diradò le sue visite*, she called on us less frequently ‖ *v.i.*, **diradàrsi**, *v.r.* **1.** to thin (away); to clear away: *dobbiamo rimanere qui fin che la nebbia diradi*, we have to stay here till the fog clears away; *la folla si diradò*, the crowd thinned away; *gli si stanno diradando i capelli*, his hair is thinning **2.** (*divenire meno frequente*) to become less frequent: *le sue visite si erano diradate*, his visits had become less frequent.

diradàto, *ag.* (*di nebbia, gas*) rarefied.

diradicàre, *v.t.* (*rar.*) to uproot, to root out.

diramàre, *v.t.* **1.** (*diffondere*) to issue, to circulate, to spread, to diffuse, to send out: — *un bollettino di guerra*, to issue a war bulletin; — *una circolare*, (*comm.*) to send out (o to issue) a circular letter; — *notizie per radio*, to broadcast news **2.** (*agr.*) to cut (away, off) branches of (a tree), to lop, to prune ‖ **diramàrsi**, *v.r.* **1.** to branch out, to ramify; (*di strada*) to branch off: *quell'albero si dirama da tutte le parti*, that tree branches out in every direction; *un sentiero si dirama dalla strada*, a path branches off from the road **2.** (*diffondersi*) to spread: *la notizia si è diramata*, the news has spread.

diramazióne, *s.f.* **1.** branch, branching out, ramification; (*di strada*) branch, branching off, ramification: *una importante — ferroviaria,* an important ramification in the railway system; *è una — del fiume,* it's a branch (*o* ramification) of the river **2.** (*diffusione*) diffusion, sending out: *— per radio,* broadcasting.

dirazzàre, *v.i.* (*rar.*) to degenerate.

díre, *v.t.* **1.** (*nel senso di* enunciare, affermare *e quando introduce un discorso diretto*) **to say;** (*nel senso di* raccontare, riferire, informare, *se è indicata la persona cui si parla*) **to tell:** « *Aspettatemi* », *ci disse,* "Wait for me", he said to us; *come si dice in francese?,* how do you say that in French?; *di' alla mamma che egli è qui,* tell mother he is here; *dice che ha fame, di aver fame,* he says he is hungry; *dimmi!,* tell me!; *diteci il vostro nome!,* tell us your name!; *ho detto quel che dovevo,* I had (*o* I said) my say; *le dissero che era ora di partire,* she was told it was time to leave; *la mamma ci dice sempre:* « *Siate prudenti* », mother always says to us: "Be careful"; *me lo disse tuo padre,* your father told me so; *non ho compreso ciò che hai detto,* I didn't understand what you said; *ti dirò ql.co. di interessante,* I'll tell you sthg. interesting; *ti dirò quel che mi ha detto,* I shall tell you what he said to me ‖ *mi si dice, mi dicono che...,* I am told that...; *si dice che...,* (*corre voce che...*) it is said (*o* there is a rumour) that...: *si dice che io sia severo, mi si dice severo,* I am said to be severe (*o* they say I am severe); *si direbbe che...,* *si sarebbe detto che...,* one would say that..., one would have said that...: *si direbbe che sia un acquarello,* one would say it is a water-colour; *si direbbe che sia piovuto,* one would say that it has been raining; *si direbbe che stia per piovere,* one would say that it's going to rain (*o* it looks like rain) ‖ *a chi lo dite!,* don't I know it? ‖ *che avete detto?,* (*per chiedere di ripetere*) I beg your pardon? ‖ *che cosa dirà la gente?,* what will people say? ‖ *chi mi dice che pagherai?,* how do I know whether you will pay?; *chi ti dice che verrà?,* how do you know he will come? ‖ *come si suol —,* as they say ‖ *così dicendo...,* with these words... ‖ *il cuore mi dice...,* my heart tells me... ‖ *detto fatto,* no sooner said than done ‖ *da amico, diciamo meglio, da fratello,* as a friend, or rather as a brother; *spenderò, diciamo, tre sterline in tutto,* I shall spend, say (*o* let us say), three pounds all together ‖ *è una bella ragazza, non c'è che —,* she is a beautiful girl, and no mistake ‖ *è detto tutto,* I need say no more ‖ *chi, dico!,* I say!; *l'hai detto!,* quite so! (*o* exactly!); *lo puoi ben —!,* you may well say so!; *questo lo dici tu!,* so you say!; *te l'avevo ben detto!,* didn't I say so? (*o* didn't I tell you so?); *te lo dico io,* I can tell you ‖ *inutile — che...,* it goes without saying that... ‖ *lasciate una parola anche a me,* let me get a word in ‖ *non se l'è fatto — due volte,* he didn't wait to be told twice ‖ *oso, oserei —,* I dare say (*o* I daresay); *vale a —,* that is to say ‖ *— all'asta,* (*offrire un prezzo*) to bid at an auction ‖ *— all'improvviso,* (*improvvisare*) to improvise (*o* to make up on the spur of the moment) ‖ *— bugie, la verità,* to tell lies, the truth ‖ *— buongiorno, buona sera, addio a qlcu.,* to bid s.o. good-day, good-night, good-bye ‖ *— la causa di qlcu.,* (*difenderlo*) to defend s.o. ‖ *— davvero, sul serio,* to be serious (*o* in earnest); *— ql.co. per scherzo, per ridere,* to say sthg. as a joke ‖ *— dei versi, to* recite poetry ‖ *— di no, — di sì,* to say no, to say yes ‖ *— in chiesa,* (*fare le pubblicazioni di matrimonio*) to put up (*o* to call *o* to publish) the banns ‖ *— male di qlcu.,* to speak ill of s.o. ‖ *— Messa,* to say Mass ‖ *— pane al pane,* to call a spade a spade ‖ *— le preghiere,* to say one's prayers; *— il rosario,* to tell one's beads ‖ *— la propria,* to express (*o* to give) one's opinion (*o* to have one's say): *lasciate che dica la sua!,* let him have his say! ‖ *— sempre l'ultima,* always to have the last word ‖ *— tra sè,* to say to oneself ‖ *a — il vero,* to tell the truth ‖ *a dirla in confidenza,* to speak in confidence ‖ *aver da*

— con qlcu., to have a bone to pick with s.o.; *aver da — su ql.co.,* to find fault with sthg. ‖ *mandare a —,* to send word ‖ *per così —,* as it were (*o* so to say *o* so to speak) ‖ *sentir —,* to hear **2.** (*ordinare*) **to tell, to order, to bid:** *dite che lo facciano entrare!,* bid them show him in!; *ditegli di entrare!,* tell him to come in!; *fate come vi ho detto!,* do as you are bidden! (*o* told!); *mi disse di informarla subito,* he told me to let her know at once **3.** (*pensare*) **to think:** *che cosa ne dici di quel quadro?,* what do you think of that picture?; *che cosa ne diresti di una bella passeggiata?,* what would you say to a nice walk?; *e — che non ha che vent'anni!,* and to think that he is only twenty! **4.** (*significare*) **to mean;** (*esprimere*) **to express;** (*dimostrare*) **to show:** *quel viso non dice nulla,* that face has no expression; *questa musica non mi dice niente,* this music doesn't appeal to me; *questo nome non mi dice niente,* that name means nothing to me; *questo ti dice quanto ti voglia bene,* that shows you how much I love you ‖ *voler —,* to mean: *che vuoi — con ciò?,* what do you mean by that? ‖ **dírsi,** *v.r.* (*definirsi*) **to style oneself;** (*professarsi*) **to profess:** *il giovane si diceva figlio del re,* the young man said he was the king's son; *si dicevano nostri amici,* they professed to be friends of ours ‖ *dirsela con qlcu.,* to agree (*o* to get on well) with s.o.

díre, *s.m.* (*parole, discorso*) words (*pl.*); speech; (*affermazione*) assertion, statement: *a — di tutti,* according to what everyone says; *a — di tutto il mondo,* by (*o* from) all accounts (*o* by common consent); *secondo il suo —,* according to him; *hai inteso il suo —?,* did you hear his words?; *questo conferma il mio —,* that bears out my assertion ‖ *arte del —,* rhetoric ‖ *oltre ogni —,* beyond all description (*o* indescribably) ‖ *hai un bel —, non mi convinci!,* talk as much as you like, you won't persuade me! ‖ *altra cosa è il —, altra il fare,* prov. saying and doing are two different things ‖ *fra il — e il fare c'è di mezzo il mare,* prov. (it's) easier said than done.

direnàre, *v.t.* to break the back of (s.o.); to weary ‖ **direnàrsi,** *v.r.* to break one's back.

direttaménte, *av.* directly, direct, immediately; (*con verbi di moto*) direct, straight: *ciò non mi tocca —,* this does not affect me immediately; *comunicherò con voi —,* I shall communicate with you direct; *devi andare a Roma —,* you must go direct to Rome; *fummo — colpiti dalla crisi,* we were directly affected by the crisis; *per favore, scrivimi —,* please write to me direct (*o* personally); *il treno va — a Torino,* the train goes through to Turin; *va' — a casa!,* go straight home!; *discendere — da qlcu.,* to be directly descended from s.o.; *rispondere — ad una domanda,* to give a direct (*o* straight) answer to a question.

direttàrio, *s.m.* (*dir.*) estate-owner.

direttíssima, per, *l.av.* (*dir.*) summarily: *fu processato per —,* he was tried summarily.

direttíssimo, *s.m.* (*ferr.*) fast train.

direttíva, *s.f.* direction, instruction, directive: *le direttive politiche di un partito,* the main lines of a party's policy (*o* the party line *o* the main points in a party's programme); *dare le direttive a qlcu.,* to give instructions (*o* directions) to s.o.

direttività, *s.f.* (*rad.*) directivity.

direttívo, *ag.* **1.** directive, leading: *principio —,* leading principle **2.** (*amm.*) managing: *un posto —,* a managing position ‖ *Consiglio Direttivo,* Board of Directors (*o* Management Committee).

dirètto, *ag.* **1.** direct; straight: *causa diretta,* direct cause; *complemento —,* (*gram.*) direct object; *contatto —,* direct contact; *discendente —,* direct descendant; *discorso —,* (*gram.*) direct speech; *imposte dirette,* direct taxes; *linea diretta,* straight line; *luce diretta,* direct light; *metodo —,* direct method; *rapporto —,* (*mat.*) direct relation; *tiro —,* (*artigl.*) direct hit; *vettura diretta,* (*ferr.*) through carriage; *voglio una* *risposta diretta*, I want a straight answer; *essere sotto la diretta influenza di qlcu.*, to be under the direct influence of s.o. 2. (*immediato*) direct, immediate: *conseguenza diretta*, immediate consequence ‖ *s.m.* 1. (*boxe*) (*diretto sinistro*) straight left; (*diretto destro*) straight right: *un — (sinistro) al mento*, a straight left to the chin 2. (*ferr.*) through train, fast train.

dirètto, *av.* direct, directly: *andò — là*, he went there direct (*o* he went straight there).

direttóre, *s.m.* 1. (*comm. amm.*) manager; director: — *acquisti*, purchase manager; — *amministrativo*, director (*o* administration manager); — *commerciale*, sales manager; *Direttore della Dogana*, Collector of (the) Customs; — *della propaganda*, advertising (*o* publicity) manager; *Direttore della Zecca*, Master of the Mint; *Direttore delle Poste*, Post master; — *del personale*, personnel manager; — *di albergo*, hotel manager; — *di azienda, di stabilimento*, factory manager (*o* director); — *di fabbrica*, works (*o* plant) manager; — *di fonderia*, foundry manager; — *di un giornale*, editor; — *generale*, general manager (*o* chief executive); — *tecnico*, technical manager; — *vendite estero*, export sales manager; *vice* —, vice (*o* assistant) manager 2. (*di scuola*) headmaster; (*di collegio universitario*) principal; (*di prigione*) governor 3. (*mus. cine.*): — *di produzione*, production manager; — *di scena*, stage manager; — *d'orchestra*, conductor 4. (*mil. mar. aer.*): — *di lancio*, (*di paracadutisti*) despatcher; — *di macchina*, (*mar.*) chief engineer; — *di pista*, (*aer.*) runway controller; — *marittimo*, harbour master 5. — *spirituale*, (*eccl.*) confessor (*o* spiritual director).

direttoriàle, *ag.* directorial.

direttòrio, *s.m.* 1. (*collegio direttivo*) executive board 2. (*eccl.*) directory 3. (*st. francese*) Directory.

direttríce, *s.f.* 1. (*comm. amm.*) manageress; directress: — *di un giornale, una rivista*, (lady) editor 2. (*di scuola*) headmistress 3. (*geom.*) directrix (*pl.* directrices).

direzionàle, *ag.* (*rad.*) directional: *antenna* —, directional aerial.

direzióne, *s.f.* 1. direction; course; (*geol.*) (*di un filone*) strike, bearing: — *apparente*, (*astr.*) apparent direction; *la — della marea*, the set of the tide; — *del nord*, (*indicata da una bussola*) magnetic (*o* compass) meridian; *angolo di —*, (*artigl. topografia*) bearing; *cambiamento di —*, (*mar.*) veer; *in — di*, in the direction of: *in — di casa*, homeward (-bound); *si allontanò in — del paese*, he walked away in the direction of the village; *in quale —?*, in which direction?; *in ugual —*, in the same direction; *che — avete preso?*, which way did you go?; *cambiare di —*, to change one's direction (*o* to alter one's course); (*mar.*) to veer 2. (*di società, ente*) management; (*di giornale*) editorship; (*di scuola*) headmastership; (*di partito*) leadership: — *commerciale, del personale*, sales management, personnel management; *gli offrirono la — del partito, ma egli rifiutò*, they offered him the leadership of the party, but he refused it; *lui solo ha la — di tutto*, he is in sole charge; *sta a te prendere la —*, it is up to you (*o* it is for you) to take control (*o* to assume the direction) of affairs; *affidare a qlcu. la — dell'azienda*, to intrust someone with the management of the firm; *assumere la — dell'azienda*, to take the management of the business; *destinare qlcu. alla — dell'azienda*, to commit someone with the management of the concern; *partecipare alla —*, to share in the management; *ritirarsi dalla —*, to retire (*o* to withdraw) from the management 3. (*sede*) administrative office; administrative offices (*pl.*); administrative department; (*amer.*) front office; (*ufficio del direttore*) manager's office: — *marittima*, harbour master's office; *passate domani in —*, call in at the manager's office tomorrow 4. (*consiglio direttivo*) board of directors, direction.

dirigènte, *ag.* directing, leading; managing; (*fam.*)

running: *le classi dirigenti*, the leading (*o* ruling) classes ‖ *s.m.* 1. representative, manager, official; (*amer.*) executive: — *amministrativo*, administrator (*o* administrative manager); — *commerciale*, sales manager 2. (*pol.*) leader: *i dirigenti del nostro partito*, the leaders of our party.

dirígere, *v.t.* 1. (*indirizzare*) to direct, to address; to aim, to point, to level: *diresse il cannone verso il nemico*, he pointed the gun at the enemy; *diresse la nave verso il porto*, he steered (*o* directed) the ship towards the harbour; *gli diresse un colpo alla testa*, he directed (*o* levelled) a blow at his head; *la nave era diretta a Cardiff*, the ship was bound for Cardiff; *non gli ho mai diretto la parola*, I have never spoken to him (*o* exchanged a word with him); *quella lettera era diretta a me*, that letter was addressed to me; *quell'osservazione non era diretta a me, ma a voi!*, that remark wasn't addressed to me, but to you!; — *un'accusa a qlcu.*, to level an accusation at s.o.; — *l'attenzione verso ql.co.*, to direct (*o* to turn) one's attention to sthg.; — *il fuoco*, (*mil.*) to direct the fire; — *i propri passi verso...*, to direct one's course (*o* steps) towards...: *diressi i miei passi verso casa*, I directed my steps towards home (*o* homewards); — *i propri sarcasmi verso qlcu.*, to aim (*o* to level) sarcastic remarks at s.o.; — *gli sforzi a*, to direct one's efforts to(wards); — *lo sguardo verso ql.co., qlcu.*, to direct one's gaze towards sthg., s.o. 2. (*guidare*) to direct, to guide, to lead; (*una ditta, una società*) to control, to manage; (*fam.*) to run; (*un'orchestra*) to conduct; (*un giornale*) to edit: *dirigeva la ditta, la società con molta abilità*, he ran (*o* managed) the concern (*o* firm) with the greatest ability; *dirigeva la scuola da vent'anni quando lo conobbi*, he had been headmaster of the school for twenty years when I met him; *quel giornale è diretto da una persona molto coscienziosa*, that newspaper is edited by a very conscientious person 3. (*sovraintendere*) to supervise, to superintend: *non c'era nessuno a — i lavori*, there was nobody to superintend (*o* to supervise *o* to direct) the work ‖ **dirigersi**, *v.r.* to turn one's steps (towards s.o., sthg.): *egli si diresse verso la porta*, he made for the door; *l'imbarcazione si diresse verso il porto*, the boat steered toward (*o* headed for) the harbour; *si diresse verso suo padre*, he turned to his father; *si diresse verso il villaggio*, he bent (*o* directed) his steps towards the village.

dirigíbile, *ag.* dirigible ‖ *s.m.* (*aer.*) dirigible; airship: — *floscio*, non-rigid airship.

dirigibilísta, *s.m.* (*aer.*) airman (*pl.* airmen) of a dirigible.

dirigísmo, *s.m.* (*pol.*) state planning: — *economico*, planned economy.

dirigísta, *ag. politica —*, (*pol.*) policy of state intervention (*o* control) ‖ *s.c.* supporter of state intervention, supporter of state planning.

diriménte, *ag.* (*dir.*) diriment; nullifying: *impedimento —*, (*di matrimonio*) diriment impediment.

dirímere, *v.t.* to settle; to cut short: — *una controversia*, to settle a controversy.

dirimpettàia, *s.f.*, **dirimpettàio**, *s.m.* (*fam.*) person living just opposite.

dirimpètto, *av.* face to face; opposite: *la casa —*, the house opposite; *le due case erano —*, the two houses were face to face (*o* opposite each other) ‖ **dirimpètto a**, *l.prep.* 1. opposite; (*in presenza di*) face to face with (sthg., s.o.): — *alla scuola*, opposite the school; *mi trovai — alla casa*, I found myself opposite the house 2. (*in confronto a*) in comparison with (s.o., sthg.).

dirítta, *s.f.* right hand: *a —*, right (*o* right-hand side): *la Posta è laggiù, a —*, the post-office is over there, on the right (*o* on the right-hand side); *voltate a —!*, turn to the right!; *tenere la —*, to keep to the right.

dirittaménte, *av.* 1. (*in linea retta*) straight, directly 2. (*rettamente*) righteously, rightfully.

diritto[1], *ag.* **1.** straight; upright, erect; direct: *calligrafia diritta*, upright handwriting; *colpo* —, direct blow; *muro* —, plumb wall; *palo* —, straight pole; *strada diritta*, straight road; *ha i capelli diritti*, he has straight hair; *sedeva col busto — come un palo*, he was sitting bolt upright; *stare* —, to stand erect; *tenere la bandiera diritta*, to hold the banner erect ‖ — *come un fuso*, as straight as a poker (*o* as straight as a ram-rod) **2.** *fig.* (*onesto*) straightforward, upright, honest: *condotta diritta*, straightforward conduct; *persona diritta*, upright person **3.** (*destro*) right: *mano diritta, lato* —, right hand-side; *piede* —, right foot ‖ *s.m.* right side: *il — di una stoffa*, the right side of a material; *il — e il rovescio di una moneta*, the obverse and reverse of a coin; *prendere ql.co. per il suo* —, to go about sthg. in the right way ‖ *per — o per traverso*, by hook or by crook ‖ *ogni — ha il suo rovescio*, every rose has a thorn (*o* every cloud has a silver lining).

diritto[1], *av.* straight, directly: *andrò — a Parigi senza fermarmi a Dover*, I shall go straight (*o* directly) to Paris without stopping at Dover; *vada — per 100 metri e si troverà in via Roma*, (go) straight on for 100 metres and you will be in Via Roma ‖ *andar — per la propria strada*, to go one's way ‖ *guardar — davanti a sè*, to look straight ahead ‖ *ti farò filare —!*, I shall make you keep (*o* go) straight! ‖ *andar — al punto*, to go straight to the point; *vengo — al punto*, I am coming straight to the point ‖ *rigare —*, (*comportarsi bene*) to behave properly.

diritto[2], *s.m.* **1.** (*facoltà derivante da legge*) right; (*titolo*) title, claim: *diritti civili*, civil rights; — *d'autore, proprietà letteraria*, copyright; — *dei terzi*, third party rights; *i diritti della donna*, women's rights; *i diritti dell'uomo*, the rights of man; — *di appello*, the right of appeal; — *derivante da ql.co.*, right deriving from sthg.; — *di brevetto*, patent right; — *di passaggio*, right of way (*o* easement *o* way-leave); — *di perquisizione*, right of search; *diritti di riproduzione cinematografica*, film rights; — *divino*, divine right; — *di vita e di morte su qlcu.*, power of life and death over s.o.; — *di voto*, right to vote; *diritti e doveri*, rights and duties; — *personale*, personal right; *diritti politici*, political rights; *a* — *privilegiato*, particular lien; — *reale*, real right; *a buon* —, rightfully (*o* by right); *di pieno* —, by full right; *la parte avente* —, the party entitled; *per — di nascita*, by right of birth; *rinunzia tacita ad un* —, non claim; *tutti i diritti riservati*, all rights reserved; *acquisire un* —, to acquire a right; *avere — a ql.co.*, to be entitled to sthg.; *cedere, trasferire un — a qlcu.*, to assign, to transfer a right on s.o.; *contestare il — di qlcu.*, to question (*o* to contest) s.o.'s rights; *esercitare un* —, to assert (*o* to enforce) a right; *essere nel proprio* —, to be within one's rights; *far valere i propri diritti*, to vindicate one's rights; *perdere un* —, to lose (*o* to be debarred from) a right; *privare qlcu. dei diritti civili*, to disenfranchise s.o.; *rinunciare a un* —, to give up (*o* to waive) a right; *vantare un — su ql.co.*, to have a claim on sthg. **2.** (*facoltà*) right, claim: *che — avete di impormi di tacere?*, what right have you to bid me to be silent?; *con quale — venite qui?*, by what right do you come here?; *non avete il — di farlo*, you have no business to do so **3.** (*tassa, tributo*) due, duty, fee, toll: *diritti di ancoraggio*, anchorage dues; *diritti d'autore*, royalties; *diritti di bacino*, dockage; *diritti di banchina*, wharfage; — *di bollo*, stamp duty; *diritti di canale*, canal tolls; *diritti consolari*, consular fees; *diritti doganali*, customs duties; *diritti portuali*, harbour dues **4.** (*legge*) law; (*giurisprudenza*) jurisprudence: — *aeronautico*, air law; — *amministrativo*, administrative law; — *civile*, civil law; — *commerciale*, commercial law (*o* mercantile law *o* law merchant); — *comparato*, comparative law; — *costituzionale*, constitutional law; — *delle genti*, law of nations; — *ecclesiastico*, canon law; — *internazionale*,

international law; — *marittimo*, maritime (*o* shipping) law; — *penale*, criminal law; — *positivo*, positive law; — *romano*, Roman law; *studiare* —, to study law (*o* to read for the bar).

dirittúra, *s.f.* **1.** straight line: — *d'arrivo*, finishing straight; — *di una pista*, (*spor.*) straight of a racecourse **2.** (*rettitudine*) uprightness, rectitude, honesty, straightforwardness: — *morale*, moral rectitude (*o* uprightness).

dirizzàre, *v.t.* **1.** to direct, to address: — *la propria attenzione verso ql.co.*, to direct one's attention to sthg. **2.** (*erigere, innalzare*) to raise, to lift: — *una casa*, to build a house **3.** (*raddrizzare*) to straighten; *fig.* to put right: — *un'affare*, to put a matter right ‖ — *le gambe ai cani*, (*applicarsi ad un compito irrealizzabile*) to attempt a hopeless task ‖ **dirizzàrsi**, *v.r.* to apply, to turn.

dirizzatúra, *s.f.* parting (of the hair).

dirizzóne, *s.m.* (*iniziativa sconsiderata*) inconsiderate action ‖ *pigliare un — per ql.co.*, to dart off towards sthg.

dirlindàna, *s.f.* (*lenza per la pesca*) long hand-line.

díro, *ag.* (*poet.*) dire, cruel, ruthless.

diroccaménto, *s.m.* **1.** demolition, dismantling, dismantlement, dilapidation **2.** (*crollo*) crumbling down, tumbling down.

diroccàre, *v.t.* to demolish, to dismantle, to dilapidate: — *una fortezza*, to dismantle a fortress ‖ *v.i.* (*cadere in rovina*) to crumble down, to tumble down, to dilapidate.

diroccàto, *ag.* **1.** (*demolito*) demolished, dismantled **2.** (*in rovina*) crumbling, tumbling, dilapidated: *vidi di lontano un castello* —, I saw a dilapidated castle from afar.

dirompènte, *ag.* (*di esplosivo*) disruptive: *bomba* —, fragmentation bomb.

dirómpere, *v.t.* **1.** (*lino, canapa, ecc.*) to scutch, to brake **2.** (*rompere*) to break; to crush, to shatter **3.** (*rendere agile con l'esercizio fisico*) to limber ‖ *v.i.*: — *in pianto*, (*arc.*) to burst into tears ‖ **dirómpersi**, *v.r.* **1.** (*frangersi*) to break **2.** (*assuefarsi*) to inure oneself, to get inured: — *alla fatica*, to inure oneself to labour.

dirompiménto, *s.m.* **1.** (*di lino, canapa, ecc.*) scutching, braking **2.** (*il rompere*) breaking; crushing, shattering.

dirottaménte, *av.* (*smoderatamente*) excessively; (*abbondantemente*) copiously, abundantly: *piangere* —, to cry desperately (*o* to shed torrents of tears); *piovere* —, to pour (*o* to rain in torrents *o* to rain cats and dogs).

dirottàre, *v.t.* to divert: — *un corso d'acqua*, to divert a water-course ‖ *v.i.* to change course: *la nave ha dirottato*, the ship changed course.

dirótto, *ag.* (*smoderato*) excessive; (*abbondante*) copious, abundant: *pianto* —, desperate (*o* bitter) crying (*o* unrestrained weeping); *pioggia dirotta*, pelting (*o* pouring) rain ‖ *a* —, excessively; abundantly: *piove a* —, it is pouring (*o* raining in torrents *o* raining cats and dogs).

dirozzaménto, *s.m.* **1.** (*lo sbozzare*) rough-hewing **2.** *fig.* (*raffinamento*) refinement, refining; (*fam.*) polishing up **3.** (*educazione*) education.

dirozzàre, *v.t.* **1.** (*sbozzare*) to rough-hew **2.** *fig.* (*raffinare*) to refine: — *qlcu.*, to refine s.o.'s manners (*o fam.* to polish s.o. up) **3.** (*educare*) to educate ‖ **dirozzàrsi**, *v.r.* to get some refinement, to improve one's manners, to acquire some polish: *mi sembra che finalmente tu ti sia dirozzato*, you seem to have improved your manners at last.

dirozzàto, *ag.* **1.** (*raffinato*) refined; (*fam.*) polished up **2.** (*educato*) educated.

dirozzatúra, *V.* **dirozzaménto**.

dirugginío, *s.m.* **1.** (*di ferro*) grating, grinding; (*di catene*) clanking **2.** (*di denti*) grinding, gnashing.

dirugginíre, *v.t.* **1.** to remove the rust from (sthg.) **2.** (*i denti*) to grind, to gnash.

dirupaménto, *s.m.* **1.** (*franamento*) falling down; landslip, land-slide **2.** (*luogo dirupato*) abrupt place, steep place.

dirupàre, *v.i.* (*franare*) to fall down, to crash down ‖ *v.t.* (*gettare dall'alto*) to hurl down, to throw down, to precipitate (from a height).

dirupàto, *ag.* **1.** abrupt, precipitous: *un cammino* —, an abrupt path **2.** (*roccioso*) rocky.

dirúpo, *s.m.* precipice, ravine.

díruto, (*letter.*) per **diroccàto**.

disabbellíre, *v.t.* to spoil the beauty of (s.o., sthg.); to disfigure ‖ **disabbellírsi,** *v.r.* to lose one's beauty; to go off in looks.

disabbigliàre, *v.t.*, **disabbigliàrsi,** *v.r.* to undress.

disàbile, *ag.* (*reso inabile*) disabled.

disabitàto, *ag.* uninhabited, desert; (*abbandonato*) deserted; (*di casa*) untenanted, empty: *una contrada disabitata*, a desert country.

disabituàre, *v.t.* to disaccustom: *l'ho disabituato a giocare d'azzardo*, I got him out of the habit of (o I made him leave off) gambling ‖ **disabituàrsi,** *v.r.* to give up the habit of (doing); to fall out of (doing); to get out of the habit of (doing); to disaccustom oneself to (sthg., doing): *il bambino si sta disabituando a camminare a quattro zampe*, the child is growing out of the habit of crawling on all fours; *riuscì a — al fumo*, he succeeded in getting rid of the habit of smoking.

disaccàridi, *s.m.pl.* (*chim.*) disaccharides.

disaccentàre, *v.t.* to remove the accent from (a word).

disaccentràre, *v.t.* to decentralize.

disaccètto, *ag.* unwelcome; unpleasant.

disacciaiàre, *v.t.* (*metal.*) to decarbonize.

disaccóncio, *ag.* **1.** unfit, unsuitable (for sthg.); unsuited (to, for sthg.) **2.** (*che non si addice*) unbecoming (to s.o.).

disaccoppiaménto, *s.m.* (*rad. tv.*) de-coupling.

disaccordàre, *v.t.* (*mus.*) to put out of tune ‖ **disaccordàrsi,** *v.r.* (*mus.*) to get out of tune; (*essere in disaccordo*) to disagree, to be at variance.

disaccòrdo, *s.m.* **1.** disagreement, variance: *essere in — con qlcu.*, to be at variance (o to disagree) with s.o. **2.** (*mus.*) discord.

disacerbàre, *v.t.* (*lenire, calmare*) to appease, to soothe; (*addolcire*) to soften: *nulla potè — il suo dolore*, nothing could soothe his sorrow ‖ **disacerbàrsi,** *v.r.* to soften.

disacidàre, disacidíre, *v.t.* to take the acidity from (a substance).

disacúsi, *s.f.* (*med.*) dysacousis, disacousma.

disadàtto, *ag.* **1.** unfit, unsuitable (for sthg.); (*non adatto*) unsuited (to, for sthg.): *credo sia — a un posto di fiducia*, I think he is unfit for a position of trust **2.** (*che non si addice*) unbecoming (to s.o.), unsuited (to s.o.).

disadornaménte, *av.* **1.** unadornedly **2.** (*alla buona, semplicemente*) plainly, homely.

disadornàre, *v.t.* to disadorn, to deprive of ornaments, to strip ornaments off (s.o., sthg.).

disadórno, *ag.* **1.** unadorned: *stile* —, unpolished style **2.** (*spoglio*) bare **3.** (*semplice, alla buona*) plain, homely.

disaeràre, *v.t.* (*mec.*) to bleed; (*fis.*) to de-aerate.

disaerazióne, *s.f.* (*mec.*) bleeding; (*fis.*) de-aeration.

disaffezionàre, *v.t.* to estrange; to turn away: — *qlcu.*, to alienate s.o.'s affection: *questi penosi ricordi lo disaffezionarono da suo padre*, these painful memories estranged him from his father ‖ **disaffezionàrsi,** *v.r.* to lose one's affection (for s.o.).

disaffezionàto, *ag.* estranged, disaffected.

disaffezióne, *s.f.* estrangement, disaffection.

disagévole, *ag.* uncomfortable; (*difficile*) difficult, hard; (*faticoso*) fatiguing: *fare un viaggio* —, to have

an uncomfortable journey; *vivere in condizioni disagevoli*, to lead a poor (o difficult) life.

disagevolézza, *s.f.* discomfort; (*difficoltà*) difficulty, hardness.

disagevolménte, *av.* uncomfortably; (*con difficoltà*) with difficulty.

disàggio, *s.m.* (*comm.*) (negative) agio.

disaggradévole, *ag.* disagreeable; unpleasant, unpleasing.

disaggradevolménte, *av.* disagreeably; unpleasantly.

disaggradíre, *v.t.* (*non gradire*) to dislike.

disaggregàre, *v.t.* (*chim.*) to disaggregate.

disagguagliàre, *V.* **disuguagliàre.**

disagiàre, *v.t.* to trouble, to inconvenience ‖ **disagiàrsi,** *v.r.* to trouble (about sthg.).

disagiataménte, *av.* **1.** uncomfortably: *vivevano in una sola stanza*, they lived uncomfortably in one room **2.** (*poveramente*) poorly: *vivono assai* —, they live very poorly.

disagiàto, *ag.* **1.** (*scomodo*) uncomfortable: *una posizione disagiata*, an uncomfortable position **2.** (*povero*) poor, needy: *una famiglia disagiata*, a needy family; *vivere una vita disagiata*, to live in poverty.

disàgio, *s.m.* **1.** uneasiness, uncomfortableness, discomfort: *essere a* —, to be uneasy (o uncomfortable o ill at ease); *sentirsi a* —, to feel uncomfortable (o uneasy o ill at ease); *stare a* —, to be uncomfortable **2.** (*disturbo*) inconvenience, trouble: *recar — a qlcu.*, to put s.o. to trouble (o to trouble s.o. o to inconvenience s.o.) **3.** *pl.* discomforts, hardships; (*privazioni*) poverty, want, need; privations (*pl.*): *i disagi della povertà*, the hardships and privations of poverty; *dover sopportare disagi e privazioni*, to have to endure discomforts and privations; *vivere tra i disagi*, to live uncomfortably; (*poveramente*) to live in poverty.

disagiosaménte, *av.* uncomfortably.

disagióso, *ag.* uncomfortable: *un viaggio* —, an uncomfortable journey.

disalberàre, *v.t.* (*mar.*) to dismast.

disalveàre, *v.t.* to divert (a river).

disamàbile, *ag.* unamiable, unlovable, unpleasant, disagreeable.

disamàre, *v.t.* to cease to love, to love no more.

disamèno, *ag.* unpleasant, disagreeable.

disàmina, *s.f.* examination, investigation: *fare una attenta* —, to examine carefully.

disaminàre, *v.t.* **1.** to examine (sthg.) carefully **2.** (*vagliare*) to weigh: — *le conseguenze di un'azione*, to weigh the consequences of an action.

disamoràre, *v.t.* to estrange; to alienate: *la sua condotta l'ha disamorato*, her behaviour has estranged him ‖ **disamoràrsi,** *v.r.* (*non amare più*) to love (s.o., sthg.) no more, to fall out of love (with s.o., sthg.): — *dal lavoro*, to lose all interest in one's work.

disamorataménte, *av.* disaffectedly.

disamoràto, *ag.* disaffected; (*indifferente*) indifferent, estranged.

disamóre, *s.m.* indifference; estrangement; (*avversione*) dislike.

disamorévole, *ag.* unkind, unloving.

disamorevolézza, *s.f.* want of affection.

disancoràrsi, *v.r.* **1.** (*mar.*) to weigh anchor **2.** *fig.* to break all connection (with s.o., sthg.): *mi sembra che in questo lavoro lo scrittore si sia disancorato dalla realtà*, in this work the writer seems to have broken all connection with reality.

disanimàre, *v.t.* to dishearten, to discourage ‖ **disanimàrsi,** *v.r.* to lose heart, to get disheartened: — *alla prima difficoltà*, to lose heart at the first difficulty.

disanimàto, *ag.* disheartened, dispirited, discouraged.

disappetènza, *s.f.* lack of appetite: *la sua — mi preoccupa*, his lack of appetite worries me.

disapplicàrsi, *v.r.* to neglect (sthg.); to cease to apply oneself (to sthg.).

disapplicazióne, *s.f.* negligence, want of application.

disapprèndere, *v.t.* to forget; to unlearn: *ho disappreso quel poco di inglese che conoscevo da ragazzo*, I have forgotten the little English I knew when a boy.

disapprovàre, *v.t.* to disapprove of (sthg.), to blame, to censure: *disapprovo i tuoi principi*, I disapprove of your principles.

disapprovazióne, *s.f.* disapproval: *uno sguardo di —*, a look of disapproval; *mi guardò con —*, he looked at me disapprovingly.

disappúnto, *s.m.* (*delusione*) disappointment; (*irritazione*) vexation: *con mio grande —*, to my great disappointment; *puoi immaginare il mio —!*, imagine my vexation!.

disarcionàre, *v.t.* to unsaddle.

disarginàre, *v.t.* to break down the banks of (a river).

disarmàre, *v.t.* 1. to disarm (anche *fig.*): *i soldati furono presi e disarmati*, the soldiers were seized and disarmed; *il suo sorriso mi disarmò*, her smile disarmed me 2. (*smantellare*) to dismantle: *la fortezza fu disarmata*, the fort was dismantled 3. (*una nave*) to unrig, to lay up: *tre anni dopo, il veliero fu disarmato*, three years after, the sailing-ship was unrigged 4. (*i remi*) to ship (the oars) 5. (*arma da fuoco*) to uncock 6. (*un ponteggio*) to take down the scaffolding ‖ *v.i.* (*ridurre l'armamento*) to disarm: *con l'armistizio la Germania fu costretta a —*, after the armistice Germany was forced to disarm.

disarmàto, *ag.* 1. disarmed 2. (*smantellato*) dismantled 3. (*mar.*) laid up, out of commission.

disarmísta, *s.m.* advocate of general disarmament.

disàrmo, *s.m.* 1. disarmament: *conferenza sul —*, (*pol.*) disarmament conference; *se le nazioni si accordassero sul —, l'umanità riconquisterebbe la sua dignità*, if countries could agree about disarmament, humanity would regain its dignity 2. (*smantellamento*) dismantlement 3. (*di una nave*) unrigging, laying up.

disarmonía, *s.f.* 1. (*disaccordo*) discord, discordance, variance: *fra di loro c'è ora —*, there is discord between them now 2. (*mus.*) discord, disharmony.

disarmonicaménte, *av.* discordantly.

disarmònico, *ag.* disharmonious; discordant.

disarmonizzàre, *v.t.* to disharmonize ‖ *v.i.* to disharmonize, to discord, to disagree.

disarmonizzàto, *ag.* out of tune.

disarticolàre, *v.t.* 1. to disarticulate, to disjoint 2. (*sciogliere le articolazioni di*) to dislocate ‖ **disarticolàrsi**, *v.r.* to be dislocated: *il braccio si è disarticolato*, his arm was dislocated.

disarticolazióne, *s.f.* 1. disarticulation, disjointing 2. (*scioglimento delle articolazioni*) dislocation.

disartría, *s.f.* (*med.*) dysarthria.

disasprìre, *v.t.* to soften, to appease, to soothe.

disassimilazióne, *s.f.* disassimilation.

disassociàre, *v.t.* (*rar.*) to disassociate.

disassuefàre, *v.t.* (*rar.*) to disaccustom; (*da un vizio*) to wean (away): *— qlcu. dal bere*, to wean s.o. from drinking ‖ **disassuefàrsi**, *v.r.* to lose the habit (of doing), to disaccustom oneself (to sthg., to doing), to give up the habit (of doing).

disàstro, *s.m.* 1. disaster, terrible accident: *un — ferroviario*, a railway disaster 2. (*totale fallimento*) failure: *come insegnante era un —*, he was a failure as a teacher.

disastrosaménte, *av.* disastrously, ruinously.

disastróso, *ag.* disastrous, ruinous: *un'inondazione disastrosa*, a ruinous flood.

disattènto, *ag.* inattentive, heedless.

disattenzióne, *s.f.* inattention: *errore di —*, (*in un testo*) slip of the pen; (*parlando*) slip of the tongue; *per —*, through inattention; *avere momenti di —*, to have fits of inattention.

disavànzo, *s.m.* (*econ.*) deficit, deficiency: *— nelle pubbliche entrate*, deficit in the (public) revenue; *il — deve attribuirsi a...*, the deficit is accountable to... (*o* the deficit is to be accounted to...); *colmare il —*, to make up the deficit.

disavvedutaménte, *av.* heedlessly; inadvertently.

disavvedutézza, *s.f.* heedlessness; inadvertency, inadvertence.

disavvedúto, *ag.* heedless; inadvertent.

disavvenènte, *ag.* (*rar.*) 1. unattractive, plain 2. (*brutto*) ugly; (*goffo*) ungainly.

disavvenènza, *s.f.* (*rar.*) 1. unattractiveness, plainness 2. (*bruttezza*) ugliness; (*goffaggine*) ungainliness.

disavventúra, *s.f.* 1. (*contrarietà*) mishap, unlucky accident: *un viaggio pieno di disavventure*, a journey full of mishaps 2. (*sfortuna*) misfortune, misadventure, mischance: *ebbi la — d'imbattermi in un creditore*, I had the misfortune (*o* I was unlucky enough) to run into a creditor of mine ‖ *per —*, unfortunately (*o* by misfortune).

disavventuràto, *ag.* unlucky, unfortunate.

disavvertènza, *s.f.* inadvertence, inadvertency; inattention: *fu una — da poco*, it was a slight inadvertence (*o* oversight).

disavvertíto, *ag.* thoughtless, heedless, careless; (*malcauto*) reckless.

disavvezzàre, *v.t.* to disaccustom; (*da un vizio*) to wean (away): *— qlcu. dal vino*, to wean s.o. (away) from wine ‖ **disavvezzàrsi**, *v.r.* to lose the habit (of doing); to give up the habit (of doing).

disavvézzo, *ag.* unaccustomed.

disazotàre, *v.t.* (*chim.*) to remove nitrogen from (sthg.).

disbórso, *s.m.* disbursement, outlay; (*anticipo*) advance: *fare continui disborsi*, (*comm.*) to be always laying money out; *rivalersi per i disborsi fatti*, (*comm.*) to charge forward one's disbursements.

disboscàre, *V.* **diboscàre**.

disbrigàre, *v.t.* to dispatch, to clear off: *— gli affari*, to dispatch business; *— la corrispondenza*, to clear off the correspondence; *— le faccende domestiche*, to do the housework ‖ **disbrigàrsi**, *v.r.* to extricate oneself; to disentangle; to get out (of sthg.).

disbrígo, *s.m.* dispatch; clearing off.

disbrogliàre, *v.t.* 1. to disentangle 2. (*sgombrare*) to disencumber.

discacciaménto, *s.m.* (*rar.*) expulsion.

discacciàre, *v.t.* to turn out, to expel, to eject.

discalzàre, *V.* **scalzàre**.

discapitàre, *v.i.* (*rar.*) 1. to suffer damage, to lose 2. (*discreditarsi*) to be discredited: *la sua fama ne discapitò*, his good name was discredited.

discàpito, *s.m.* 1. (*svantaggio*) disadvantage: *con nostro grande —*, to our great disadvantage 2. (*danno*) detriment, damage, prejudice: *a — di...*, to the prejudice of....

discaricàre, *V.* **scaricàre**.

discàrico, *s.m.* 1. discharge, unloading 2. (*scusa, giustificazione*) excuse; justification; defence: *a — di coscienza*, to ease one's conscience; *a — di ogni responsabilità*, to disclaim all responsibility; *a mio —*, to clear myself; *testimonio a —*, (*dir.*) witness for the defence 3. (*comm.*) rendering of accounts.

discàro, *ag.* (*rar.*) disagreeable, unpleasant: *non vi sia — accettare*, please accept.

discendènte, *ag.* descending: *scala —*, (*mus.*) descending scale ‖ *s.m.* descendant: *i tuoi discendenti*, your offspring (*sing.*) (*o* your descendants).

discendènza, *s.f.* 1. descent, extraction: *nobile —*, distinguished descent; *un uomo di — straniera*, a man of foreign extraction; *era di — normanna*, he was of Norman descent 2. (*discendenti*) offspring; descendants (*pl.*) ‖ *la — d'Adamo*, mankind.

discéndere, *v.i.* 1. to descend, to go down, to come down: *l'angelo discese dal cielo*, the angel descended from heaven; *discendi dall'albero*, come down from the tree; *il fiume discende verso il mare*, the river runs down to the sea (*o* flows towards the sea) ‖ — *a terra*, (*approdare*) to land (*o* to go ashore); — *da un'auto*, to get out of a car; — *da cavallo*, to dismount; — *dal treno*, to get off (*o* to get out of the train) ‖ — *in basso*, *fig.* to fall low ‖ — *ai fatti*, *fig.* to come down to facts 2. (*declinare*) to descend, to slope down: *il giardino discende verso il fiume*, the garden descends (*o* slopes down) to the river; *le montagne discendevano bruscamente verso ovest*, the hills fell steeply away to the west 3. (*di astri*) to sink: *il sole discende*, the sun is sinking 4. (*di prezzi*, *temperatura*) to fall 5. (*trarre origine*) to descend: — *da un re*, to descend (*o* to be descended) from a king ‖ *v.t.* to descend, to go down, to come down: *discese le scale*, he descended (*o* went down *o* came down) the stairs.

discensionàle, *ag.* descensional.

discensióne, *s.f.* (*rar.*) descent.

discènte, *ag.* learning ‖ *s.c.* pupil, student.

discentraménto, *s.m.* decentralization.

discentràre, *v.t.* 1. to take off centre 2. (*decentrare*) to decentralize ‖ **discentràrsi**, *v.r.* to get off centre.

discepolàto, *s.m.* apprenticeship.

discépolo, *s.m.* 1. disciple: *i discepoli di Cristo*, Christ's disciples 2. (*seguace*) follower; (*alunno*) pupil.

discèrnere, *v.t.* 1. (*vedere chiaramente*) to discern; to perceive; to descry: *si poteva — una casa in lontananza*, we could make out a house in the distance 2. (*distinguere*) to discriminate; to distinguish: — *il bene dal male*, to distinguish between right and wrong.

discerníbile, *ag.* 1. discernible 2. (*visibile*) discernible, visible.

discerniménto, *s.m.* discernment; (*giudizio*) judgement: *l'età del* —, the age of understanding.

discervellàre, *v.t.* to brain ‖ *far — qlcu.*, (*far lavorare il cervello di qlcu.*) to puzzle s.o.'s brains ‖ **discervellàrsi**, *v.r.* (*spremersi le meningi*) to rack one's brains.

discervellàto, *ag.* hare-brained; foolish.

discésa, *s.f.* 1. (*movimento discendente*) descent: — *del carico*, (*di gru*) descent of the load; *fare una* —, to descend (*o* to walk down) a slope; *fare una rapida* —, to make a quick descent ‖ — *in picchiata*, (*aer.*) (nose-) dive (*o* power dive) ‖ *corsa di* —, (*di stantuffo*) (*mec.*) down stroke ‖ *andare in — in folle*, (*aut.*) to coast 2. (*declivio*) slope, declivity; (*strada in discesa*) descent: *una — ripida*, a steep descent; *una strada in* —, a downhill road; *essere in* —, (*di strada*) to be sloping down (*o* downhill) 3. (*caduta*) fall: — *di prezzi*, fall (*o* slump) in prices; — *di temperatura*, fall in temperature 4. (*invasione*) invasion: *la — dei barbari*, the Barbarian invasion 5. (*rad.*) lead-in, down-lead.

discettàre, *v.t.* (*rar.*) to dispute; to debate.

discettazióne, *s.f.* (*rar.*) debate; discussion.

disceveràre, *v.t.* (*rar.*) to sever, to separate, to part; (*distinguere*) to distinguish.

dischiodàre, *v.t.* (*rar.*) to unnail.

dischiúdere, *v.t.* 1. to disclose; to open: — *gli occhi*, to open one's eyes 2. (*svelare*) to reveal: — *il vero*, to reveal the truth.

dischiúso, *ag.* 1. disclosed; open: *fiore* —, open flower 2. (*svelato*) revealed.

discíngere, *v.t.* (*rar.*) to ungird, to untie; to undo.

discínto, *ag.* ungirt, untied; (*poco vestito*) scantily dressed.

disciògliere, *v.t.* 1. (*sciogliere*) to dissolve 2. (*fondere*) to melt; (*neve*) to thaw 3. (*slacciare*) to unfasten; (*slegare*) to unbind, to loosen, to untie: — *un nodo*, to loosen (*o* to untie) a knot 4. (*liberare*) to release: — *qlcu. dalla schiavitù*, to release s.o. from bondage ‖ **disciògliersi**, *v.r.* 1. (*sciogliersi*) to dissolve 2. (*fondersi*) to melt; (*di neve*) to thaw: *il ghiaccio si discioglie al sole*, ice melts in the sun 3. (*slegarsi*) to loosen, to get loose.

disciòlto, *ag.* 1. dissolved 2. (*fuso*) melted 3. (*slegato*) unbound, loose, untied 4. (*liberato*) released.

disciplína, *s.f.* 1. (*materia di studio*) doctrine, science, art; subject of study: *discipline filosofiche*, philosophic doctrines; *discipline giuridiche*, legal doctrines 2. (*insegnamento*) teaching: *affidare un figlio alla — di qlcu.*, to commit one's son to s.o.'s teaching 3. (*regola, norma, obbedienza*) discipline, rule, order: — *ecclesiastica*, church discipline; — *ferrea*, iron discipline; — *militare*, military discipline; *scuola senza* —, school without discipline; *non sa mantenere la* —, he cannot keep discipline; *imporre la* —, to enforce discipline; *tenere la* —, to keep discipline ‖ *consiglio di* —, disciplinary council 4. (*punizione, castigo*) discipline, punishment: *sala di* —, (*mil.*) guard-room 5. (*eccl.*) (*flagello*) scourge, discipline; *fig.* penitential chastisement: *darsi* —, to scourge oneself (*o* to mortify the flesh).

disciplinàbile, *ag.* disciplinable.

disciplinàre, *ag.* disciplinary: *castigo* —, disciplinary punishment.

disciplinàre, *v.t.* 1. to discipline: — *i propri scolari*, to discipline one's pupils 2. (*regolare*) to regulate: — *il traffico*, to regulate the traffic 3. (*eccl.*) to chastise ‖ **disciplinàrsi**, *v.r.* 1. to get trained to discipline 2. (*eccl.*) to scourge oneself.

disciplinarménte, **disciplinataménte**, *av.* according to the rules of discipline; with discipline.

disciplinatézza, *s.f.* discipline.

disciplinàto, *ag.* disciplined; (*obbediente*) obedient ‖ *i Disciplinati*, (*eccl.*) the Flagellants.

dísco, *s.m.* 1. disk, disc: *il — della luna*, the disk of the moon ‖ — *telefonico*, telephone dial ‖ — *volante*, flying saucer (*o* flying disk) 2. (*mus.*) record: — *ad alta fedeltà*, high fidelity record 3. (*spor.*) discus: *lancio del* —, discus throw ‖ — *sul ghiaccio*, (ice-)hockey 4. (*ferr.*) (*segnale*) disk signal; (*di ruota*) plate 5. (*mec. aer.*): — *della frizione*, clutch plate (*o* clutch disk); — *dell'elica*, propeller disk; — *dentato*, toothed disk; — *paraolio*, oil splash guard disk.

discòbolo, *s.m.* (*spor.*) 1. (*nell'antichità*) discobolus (*pl.* discoboli) 2. (*nell'atletica moderna*) discus-thrower.

discoiàre, *v.t.* to flay, to skin.

discoìde, *ag.* discoid(al) ‖ *s.m.* discoid.

discoleggiàre, *v.i.* to sow one's wild oats.

dìscolo, *ag.* (*scapestrato*) undisciplined, wild, mischievous; (*dissoluto*) loose, dissolute ‖ *s.m.* rogue, scamp, mischievous fellow; (*di ragazzo*) little scamp, young scamp, mischievous boy, wild boy ;(*scherz.*) little rogue; (*monello*) urchin: *quel — mi disturbò tutto il giorno*, that little rogue disturbed me all day.

discoloràre, *v.t.*, **discoloràrsi**, *v.r.* to discolour.

discólpa, *s.f.* excuse, justification: *che hai da dire a tua* —?, what have you got to say for yourself?; *per — disse che...*, by way of excuse he alleged that... ‖ *testimonio a* —, (*dir.*) witness for the defence.

discolpàre, *v.t.* 1. to clear, to exculpate: — *qlcu. da un delitto*, to clear s.o. of a crime 2. (*scusare*) to excuse; (*giustificare*) to justify; (*difendere*) to defend: *cercarono di àscolparlo per aver fatto ciò*, they tried to justify his having done that ‖ **discolpàrsi**, *v.r.* 1. to clear oneself, to prove one's innocence: *l'infelice non potè* —, the poor fellow could not prove his innocence 2. (*scusarsi*) to apologize, to justify oneself.

discomméttere, *v.t.* 1. to disjoin, to separate 2. (*disfare*) to undo.

discompagnàre, *v.t.* to part ‖ **discompagnàrsi**, *v.r.* to part company.

discompórre, (*rar.*) per **scompórre**.

disconciàre, *v.t.* 1. to spoil, to mar, to impair, to ruin 2. (*scomporre*) to disjoin.

disconcio, (*rar.*) per **sconcio**.

disconfessàre, (*rar.*) per **sconfessàre**.

disconfortàre, *v.t.* to discomfort.

disconoscènte, *ag.* ungrateful.

disconoscènza, *s.f.* (*ingratitudine*) ungratefulness, ingratitude.

disconóscere, *v.t.* **1.** to ignore, to refuse to recognize, to refuse to acknowledge: — *la verità,* to refuse to recognize truth **2.** (*misconoscere*) to fail to appreciate; to be ungrateful for (sthg.).

discontentàre, *v.t.* to dissatisfy, to discontent.

discontènto, *ag.* dissatisfied, discontented, discontent ‖ *s.m.* dissatisfaction, discontentment, discontent; annoyance.

discontinuaménte, *av.* discontinuously.

discontinuàre, *v.t.* to discontinue.

discontinuità, *s.f.* **1.** discontinuity: *la — della sua condotta,* the discontinuity of his behaviour **2.** (*interruzione*) discontinuance, discontinuation.

discontínuo, *ag.* discontinuous, intermittent: *prestazioni discontinue,* intermittent services.

disconvenévole, disconveniènte, *ag.* **1.** unbecoming, unseemly: *è — che si comporti così,* it is unbecoming of him to act in this manner **2.** (*non adatto*) unsuitable.

disconveníre, *v.i.* **1.** (*essere sconveniente*) to be unbecoming, to be unseemly **2.** (*non essere adatto*) to be unsuitable **3.** (*non essere comodo*) to be inconvenient.

discopèrto, *ag.* (*rar.*) **1.** (*aperto, palese*) open ‖ *a —,* in the open (air) (*o* under the open sky) **2.** (*non difeso*) unsheltered, unprotected.

discopriménto, *s.m.* **1.** discovering; disclosing **2.** (*scoperta*) discovery.

discopríre, (*rar.*) per **scopríre.**

discordànte, *ag.* **1.** discordant (with sthg.), dissonant; (*in disaccordo*) disagreeing (with sthg.); (*di colori, opinioni*) clashing: *colori discordanti,* clashing colours; *opinioni discordanti,* discordant (*o* clashing) opinions; *suoni discordanti,* dissonant (*o* discordant) sounds; *testimonianze discordanti,* (*dir.*) conflicting evidence **2.** (*geol.*) unconformable: *strati discordanti,* unconformable strata **3.** (*differente*) different: *il suo contegno mi sembra alquanto — dal tuo,* his behaviour seems to me rather different from yours.

discordànza, *s.f.* discordance, dissonance; (*mus.*) discord; (*disaccordo*) disagreement: — *di colori,* discordance of colours; — *di opinioni,* discordance (*o* difference) of opinions; — *di suoni,* dissonance (*o* discordance) of sounds; — *di testimonianze,* (*dir.*) disagreement of evidence.

discordàre, *v.i.* **1.** (*non essere d'accordo*) to disagree (with s.o., sthg.), to dissent, to be at variance (with s.o., sthg.): *gli storici discordano su questo punto,* historians are at variance on this point; *i testimoni discordano,* the witnesses differ (*o* are at variance) **2.** (*di colori*) to clash (with sthg.); (*di suoni*) to discord, to jar (with sthg.) **3.** (*essere diverso*) to differ: *le sue parole discordano dalla sua condotta,* his words are inconsistent (*o* not in keeping) with his conduct.

discòrde, *ag.* discordant (with sthg.), dissonant; (*in disaccordo*) disagreeing (with sthg.), at variance (with sthg.): *opinioni discordi,* discordant opinions; *essere di parere —,* to be of different opinions.

discordeménte, *av.* discordantly, dissonantly.

discòrdia, *s.f.* **1.** discord, dissension: *essere in — con qlcu.,* to be at variance with s.o.; *mettere la — fra due persone,* to set two people at variance; *portare la — in una famiglia,* to bring discord into a family; *seminare la — fra i concittadini,* to sow seeds of discord among one's fellow-citizens ‖ *pomo della —,* bone of contention **2.** (*discordanza*) discordance: — *fra la teoria ed i fatti,* discordance between theory and facts.

discórrere, *v.i.* to talk (to, with s.o., about sthg.), to discourse (of, upon sthg.); (*dissertare*) to reason, (about, of, upon sthg.): *discorre perché ha la bocca!,* he talks for the sake of talking!; *discorri bene, ma ti vorrei vedere nei miei panni!,* it is all very well for you to talk, but you ought to be in my shoes!; *ne discor-*

reremo dopo pranzo, we can talk it over after lunch; — *alla buona,* to have a familiar talk; — *con qlcu.,* to talk to (*o* with) s.o.; — *del più e del meno,* to discuss things in general; — *di affari, di politica,* to talk business, politics; — *su un argomento,* to reason about a subject; *perdere il proprio tempo a —,* to waste one's time talking ‖ *e via discorrendo,* and so on ‖ *non ci si discorre perché è persona intrattabile,* he is impossible to talk to because he is an intractable person.

discorsívo, *ag.* talkative, loquacious.

discórso, *s.m.* **1.** speech, address: — *della Corona,* speech from the Throne; — *improvvisato,* impromptu speech; — *preparato,* set speech; *terrà un — per radio sull'arte moderna,* he will give a talk on modern art on the radio; *pronunciare, tenere un —,* to deliver (*o* to make) a speech **2.** (*conversazione, parole*) conversation, talk, speech: — *a quattr'occhi,* tête-à-tête; — *frivolo,* small talk; — *intimo,* private conversation; *discorsi oziosi,* idle talk; *il — cadde sulla politica,* the talk turned to politics; *cambiamo —!,* let's change the subject!; *dopo questo — lasciò la stanza,* after this speech he left the room; *gliene parlerò in via di —,* I'll mention it while I'm talking to him; *ho perso il filo del —,* I have lost the thread of the conversation; *attaccar — con qlcu.,* to engage s.o. in conversation ‖ *che discorsi!,* nonsense! ‖ *senza tanti discorsi,* frankly (*o* openly) ‖ *questo è un altro —,* this is another story (*o* this is quite a different matter) **3.** (*gram.*) speech: — *diretto, indiretto,* direct, reported (*o* indirect) speech; *le parti del —,* the parts of speech.

discortése, *ag.* (*letter.*) unkind; (*maleducato*) impolite.

discortesía, *s.f.* unkindliness; (*maleducazione*) impoliteness.

discoscéso, *ag.* rugged, craggy, cragged: *un terreno —,* a rugged ground.

discostàre, *V.* **scostàre.**

discòsto, *ag.* far, removed, distant: *i nostri sogni sono troppo discosti dalla realtà,* our dreams are too far removed from reality; *la sua casa è poco discosta dalla nostra,* his house is not far from ours.

discòsto, *av.* at some distance: *abitava —,* he lived some way off (*o* at some distance) ‖ **discòsto da,** *l.prep.* far from: *poco — dalla chiesa,* not far from the church.

discotèca, *s.f.* record library.

discrasía, *s.f.* (*patol.*) dyscrasia.

discrédere, *v.t.* (*rar.*) to lose one's belief in (sthg.) ‖ **discrédersi,** *v.r.* (*rar.*) **1.** (*cambiare opinione*) to change one's mind **2.** (*perdersi d'animo*) to lose heart; to undeceive oneself.

discreditàre, *v.t.* to discredit: *la sua stupida condotta lo discredita gravemente,* his foolish behaviour discredits him seriously ‖ **discreditàrsi,** *v.r.* to lose credit, to lose one's reputation, to bring discredit upon oneself: *con quell'azione egli si discreditò completamente,* by that action he disgraced his name (*o* brought disgrace upon himself).

discrédito, *s.m.* discredit, disrepute: *cadere in —,* to fall into discredit; *gettare il — sopra una teoria,* to throw discredit on a theory.

discrepànte, *ag.* discrepant, differing; disagreeing (with sthg.), inconsistent (with sthg.): *opinioni discrepanti,* differing (*o* disagreeing *o* divergent) opinions.

discrepàre, *v.i.* (*rar.*) to be discrepant; to be inconsistent (with s.o., sthg.); (*dissentire*) to disagree (with s.o., sthg.): *queste due versioni discrepano,* these two reports are discrepant (*o* disagree).

discrepànza, *s.f.* discrepancy, difference; (*disaccordo*) disagreement, variance: *fra i due resoconti c'è una notevole —,* there is considerable discrepancy between the two accounts; *la tua versione è piena di discrepanze,* your report is full of inconsistencies.

discretaménte, *av.* **1.** (*con discrezione*) discreetly: *agì —,* he acted discreetly **2.** (*sufficientemente*) fairly, tolerably; (fam.) pretty: è — intelligente, he is fairly clever; sto — (bene), I am fairly well (o fam. I'm pretty well) 3. (piuttosto) rather: è — giovane, he is rather young.

discretézza, s.f. 1. (discrezione) discretion 2. (moderazione) moderation.

diserctíva, s.f. (fil.) judgment.

discréto, ag. 1. (che ha discrezione) discreet: il mio amico è molto —, my friend is very discreet (o quite safe o a very close man) 2. (moderato) moderate, reasonable: — nei propri desideri, moderate in one's desires; l'ho acquistato a un prezzo —, I bought it at a moderate (o reasonable) price 3. (abbastanza buono) fair, fairly good: condizioni discrete, fair terms; un quadro —, a fairly (o tolerably) good picture; vino —, fairly good wine ‖ un — numero [di amici, a good many friends 4. (sufficiente) sufficient: discreta abilità, sufficient ability.

discrezionàle, ag. (dir.) discretionary, discretional: poteri discrezionali, discretionary powers.

discrezióne, s.f. 1. (discernimento) discretion, discernment: età della —, age (o years) of discretion; intendere un libro a —, to understand a book according to one's lights 2. (arbitrio) discretion, free choice: pane a —, unlimited bread (o bread ad lib.); il provvedimento dipende interamente dalla — del giudice, the measure rests entirely on the discretion of the judge ‖ arrendersi a —, to surrender at discretion; trovarsi a — di qlcu., to be at s.o.'s mercy 3. (moderazione) discretion, moderation: con —, moderately; uomo senza —, immoderate man (o man lacking in restraint).

discriminànte, ag. 1. discriminating, discriminant; discriminative 2. (dir.) extenuating: circostanze discriminanti, extenuating circumstances.

discriminàre, v.t. 1. to discriminate; to distinguish: non devi — le persone secondo le loro idee politiche, you must not discriminate between people according to their political beliefs 2. (dir.) to extenuate.

discriminatúra, s.f. hair-parting.

discriminazióne, s.f. discrimination: — razziale, racial discrimination.

discussióne, s.f. discussion; (formale) debate; (controversia) controversy; (disputa) dispute: — alla Camera, (pol.) full-dress debate; — del bilancio, (amm. pol.) budget debate; argomento in —, argument under discussion (o in debate); aprire, iniziare la —, to open, to start the debate; cessare una —, to give up a discussion; entrare in — su ql.co., to enter into discussion upon sthg.

discússo, ag. discussed, debated.

discútere, v.t. to discuss, to dispute, to debate; to talk over (sthg.): discutemmo la loro proposta, we discussed (o debated o talked over) their offer; questo non si discute, there is no question about this; a sera tarda stavano ancora discutendo il caso, they were still disputing the case late in the evening; — un progetto di legge, to discuss a bill.

discutíbile, ag. 1. disputable, debatable 2. (obiettabile) questionable: una affermazione —, a questionable assertion; gusto —, questionable taste; è una questione —, it is a moot question.

disdegnàre, v.t. to disdain; to scorn, to contemn, to despise: disdegna gli adulatori, he despises flatterers; disdegnano di lavorare, they disdain working (o to work).

disdégno, s.m. (letter.) 1. disdain; scorn, contempt: con —, disdainfully; avere a —, to scorn (o to despise); avere in —, to disdain (o to hate) 2. (alterigia) haughtiness.

disdegnosaménte, av. (letter.) 1. disdainfully; scornfully 2. (con alterigia) haughtily.

disdegnóso, ag. (letter.) 1. disdainful; scornful: ci indignammo per il suo comportamento —, we resented his disdainful behaviour 2. (altezzoso) haughty.

disdétta, s.f. 1. (dir.) notice to leave: il padrone di casa mi ha dato la —, my landlord has given me notice to quit 2. (sfortuna) misfortune, bad luck: essere in —, to be out of luck; portar —, to bring bad luck ‖ che —!, what hard luck! (o fam. too bad!).

disdétto, ag. retracted, withdrawn; cancelled.

disdicènte, ag. unbecoming, indecent.

disdicévole, ag. unbecoming, unseemly: la tua condotta mi sembra —, your behaviour seems to me unseemly.

disdíre, v.t. 1. (ritrattare, ritirare) to take back, to unsay, to retract, to withdraw: devi — ciò che hai detto imprudentemente, you must take back (o unsay) what you said inconsiderately; — un'affermazione, to disavow a statement; — una promessa, to withdraw (o to retract) a promise; — la propria parola, to take back one's word; (fam.) to eat one's word ‖ dire e —, to say and to unsay 2. (annullare) to cancel, to annul: abbiamo dovuto — gli inviti, we had to cancel the invitations; — un abbonamento, to discontinue (o to withdraw) a subscription; — un contratto, (comm.) to cancel (o to give notice of determination of) a contract; — un'ordinazione, to cancel (o to countermand) an order; — la prenotazione per un viaggio, to cancel one's booking for a journey ‖ — la casa, to surrender (o to give up) a lease ‖ — la tregua, (mil.) to resume hostilities ‖ v.i. (essere sconveniente) to be unbecoming; not to become (s.o.): questa parola disdice a una signorina, this word is unbecoming to a young lady ‖ **disdírsi**, v.r. 1. (essere sconveniente) to be unbecoming; not to become (s.o.) 2. (ritrattarsi) to recant; (fam.) to eat one's words.

disdòro, s.m. (rar.) dishonour, discredit; shame, disgrace: a suo —, to his shame (o discredit); sei il — della tua famiglia, you are the shame of (o a disgrace to) your family.

diseccàre, V. disseccàre.

diseducàre, v.t. (rar.) to bring up badly: diseduca i suoi bambini, her children are dragged up.

disegnàre, v.t. 1. to draw; to sketch; to design: disegna tutti i suoi vestiti, she designs all her dresses; — a penna, to draw with a pen; — dal vero, to draw from life 2. fig. to describe, to outline: egli disegnò la gravità della presente situazione economica, he outlined the gravity of the present economical situation 3. (progettare) to design, to plan, to intend: Serse disegnò vanamente la rovina della Grecia, in vain Xerxes planned the downfall of Greece; aveva disegnato di partire, he had planned to leave.

disegnatóre, s.m. draftsman (pl. draftsmen), draughtsman (pl. draughtsmen); (bozzettista) designer ‖ **disegnatríce**, s.f. designer: — di mode, fashion designer.

diségno, s.m. 1. drawing: — a mano libera, free-hand drawing; — a matita, pencil drawing; — animato, (cine.) (animated) cartoon; — a pastello, pastel; — di macchine, machine drawing; — geometrico, mechanical drawing; — in scala, scale drawing; carta da —, drawing-paper; professore di —, drawing-master; puntina da —, drawing-pin; tavola da —, drawing-board 2. (di tessuto) pattern 3. (edil.) plan: il — di un edificio, the plan of a building 4. (schizzo) sketch: fare il — di un abito, to draw the sketch for a dress 5. fig. (progetto, piano) plan, design, scheme, project, purpose: — di legge, bill: presentare un — di legge, to bring a bill before Parliament; il — di un libro, the plan for a book; il mio primo — era di restare in Italia, my first plan was to stay in Italy; cambiar —, to change one's mind.

disequàle, V. disuguàle.

disellàre, V. dissellàre.

disensàto, ag. (rar.) senseless, foolish; (avventato) rash.

disèpalo, ag. (bot.) disepalous.

diseparàre, (rar.) per separàre.

disequilibràre, (rar.) per squilibràre.

disequilíbrio, (rar.) per squilíbrio.

diseredàre, *v.t.* to disinherit: *ha diseredato i propri discendenti*, he has disinherited his own issue.

diseredàto, *ag.* **1.** poor, destitute || *i diseredati*, the poor (*o* the destitute) **2.** (*privato dell'eredità*) disinherited.

diseredazióne, *s.f.* (*rar.*) disinherison, disherison.

disertàre, *v.t.* **1.** (*abbandonare*) to leave, to abandon: — *le lezioni*, to play truant **2.** (*rar.*) (*devastare*) to lay waste, to ravage || *v.i.* (*spec. mil.*) to desert: — *dall'esercito*, to desert from the army.

disèrto, *ag.* (*letter.*) (*eloquente*) eloquent.

disertóre, *s.m.* deserter.

diserzióne, *s.f.* desertion: — *da un partito*, (*pol.*) desertion of a party.

disfaciménto, *s.m.* **1.** (*il disfare*) undoing **2.** (*distruzione, rovina*) destruction, ruin; (*decadimento*) decay: *cadere in* —, to fall into decay **3.** (*decomposizione*) decomposition.

disfamàre, (*rar.*) per **sfamàre**.

disfàre, *v.t.* **1.** to undo; (*distruggere*) to destroy: *non potrai mai* — *tutto ciò che abbiamo fatto*, you'll never be able to undo all we have done; — *un giocattolo*, to break up a toy; — *un pezzo di lavoro a maglia*, to take down a piece of knitting || *questa malattia l'ha disfatto*, this illness has pulled him down || — *casa*, to give up one's home || — *un letto*, to strip (*o* unmake) a bed **2.** (*slegare*) to undo, to unfasten, to untie: — *un nodo*, to undo (*o* to untie) a knot; — *un pacco*, to undo (*o* to open) a parcel **3.** (*sciogliere*) to melt: *il caldo ha disfatto la neve*, heat has melted the snow **4.** (*sconfiggere*) to defeat: *l'esercito fu disfatto*, the army was defeated || **disfàrsi**, *v.r.* **1.** (*cadere in rovina*) to fall to pieces, to go to ruin **2.** (*sciogliersi*) to melt: *il burro si disfa al sole*, butter melts in the sun || — *in lacrime*, to melt into tears (*o* to cry desperately) || — *in sudore*, to perspire freely **3.** (*decomporsi*) to decompose **4.** (*liberarsi*) to get rid (of s.o., sthg.): — *della propria merce*, to get rid of (*o* to sell off) one's goods.

disfasìa, *s.f.* (*med.*) dysphasia.

disfàtta, *s.f.* defeat, rout, overthrow: *la ritirata si mutò in* —, the retreat became a rout; *subire una* —, to suffer a defeat.

disfattíccio, *ag.s.m.* (*agr.*) fallow.

disfattísmo, *s.m.* defeatism.

disfattísta, *ag.* defeatist: *propaganda* —, defeatist propaganda || *s.c.* defeatist.

disfàtto, *ag.* **1.** (*distrutto*) ruined; (*sconfitto*) defeated **2.** (*slegato, slacciato*) undone; (*sciolto*) melted **3.** (*decomposto*) decomposed **4.** (*scomposto*) discomposed **5.** (*molto stanco*) worn-out.

disfavóre, *s.m.* disfavour, dislike: *cadere ·in* —, to fall into disfavour.

disfavorévole, *ag.* (*rar.*) unfavourable.

disfavoríre, *v.t.* (*rar.*) to disoblige.

disferràre, *v.t.* (*rar.*) to unshackle, to unshoe (a horse).

disfída, *s.f.* (*letter.*) challenge; (*duello*) duel: *lanciare una* —, to issue a challenge.

disfidàre, *v.t.* (*letter.*) to challenge.

disfiguràre, *v.t.* (*rar.*) to disfigure.

disfioràre, *v.t.* (*rar.*) **1.** to deflower **2.** (*disonorare*) to dishonour.

disfogàre, (*arc.*) per **sfogàre**.

disfogliàre, (*arc.*) per **sfogliàre**[1] [2].

disformàre, *v.t.* (*rar.*) to misshape, to put (sthg.) out of shape: — *un cappello*, to put a hat out of shape.

disfórme, *ag.* (*rar.*) **1.** different, unlike **2.** (*deforme*) misshapen, deformed.

disformità, *s.f.* (*rar.*) **1.** difference, unlikeness **2.** (*deformità*) deformity.

disfrasìa, *s.f.* (*med.*) dysphrasia.

disfrenàre, (*rar.*) per **sfrenàre**.

disfrondàre, (*rar.*) per **sfrondàre**.

disfunzióne, *s.f.* (*med.*) disorder: — *cardiaca*, heart trouble; — *endocrina*, endocrine disorder (*o* trouble); — *epatica*, liver trouble.

disgelàre, *v.i.* to thaw: *sulle montagne la neve disgela d'estate*, the snow on the mountains thaws in summer || *v.t.* (*liberare dal ghiaccio*) to defrost; to de-ice.

disgelaménto, *s.m.* defrosting; de-icing.

disgèlo, *s.m.* thaw: *è iniziato il* — *e la neve si scioglie*, thaw has set and the snow is melting.

disgiúngere, *v.t.* to disjoin, to detach, to separate || *l'uomo non disgiunga ciò che Dio congiunse*, what God hath joined let no man put asunder.

disgiungiménto, *s.m.* disjoining, disjunction, separation.

disgiuntaménte, *av.* separately: *questi problemi devono essere considerati* —, these problems should be considered separately.

disgiuntivaménte, *av.* (*gram.*) disjunctively.

disgiuntívo, *ag.* (*gram.*) disjunctive: *congiunzione disgiuntiva*, disjunctive conjunction.

disgiúnto, *ag.* disjoined, detached, separate.

disgiunzióne, *s.f.* disjunction.

disgràdo, a, *l.av.* unwillingly: *avere a* —, not to care for (*o* to dislike); *fare ql.co. a* —, to do sthg. reluctantly (*o* unwillingly).

disgràzia, *s.f.* **1.** misfortune; (*sfortuna*) mischance, bad luck, ill luck; (*incidente*) accident: *che* —!, what a misfortune!; *ci colpì una grande* —, a great misfortune befell us; *quando avvenne la* —?, when did the accident take place?; *presentire disgrazie*, to have a presentiment of bad-luck; *subire una* —, to suffer a misfortune || *per* —, unfortunately (*o* by mischance) || *le disgrazie non vengono mai sole*, *prov.* misfortunes never come singly **2.** (*sfavore*) disgrace, disfavour: *cadere in* —, to fall into disfavour: *cadere in* — *di qlcu.*, to lose s.o.'s favour; *essere in* —, to be in disgrace **3.** (*fatto involontario*) accident, mishap: *non l'ho fatto apposta, è stata una* —, I did not do it on purpose, it was an accident (*o* mishap).

disgraziataménte, *av.* unfortunately, unluckily, unhappily: — *morì*, unfortunately (*o* unhappily) he died.

disgraziàta, *s.f.* wretch; unlucky woman: *è una* —, she is a poor wretch.

disgraziàto, *ag.* **1.** unfortunate, unlucky; wretched; (*infelice*) miserable, unhappy: *un giorno* —, an unfortunate day; *un'ora disgraziatissima*, a most unlucky hour; *mi sento tanto* —, I feel so miserable; *condurre una vita disgraziata*, to lead a wretched existence (*o* to live a miserable life) **2.** (*deforme*) misshapen: *è* — *dalla nascita*, he has been deformed from birth || *s.m.* wretch; unlucky man: *è un* —, he is a poor wretch.

disgregàbile, *ag.* that can be disintegrated; breakable; separable.

disgregaménto, *s.m.* disintegration, breaking up; disjointing; (*fis.*) disgregation.

disgregàre, *v.t.* to disgregate; to break up, to disjoint, to disunite: — *le forze nemiche*, to break up the enemy's forces; — *un impero*, to break up (*o* to divide up) an empire || **disgregàrsi**, *v.r.* to disintegrate; *fig.* to break up, to disunite: *dopo la morte del padre la famiglia si è disgregata*, after the father's death the family broke up; *la nostra amicizia si disgrega*, our friendship is breaking up.

disgregazióne, *s.f.* disgregation, breaking up.

disgrossàre, *V.* **digrossàre**.

disguído, *s.m.* miscarriage: *in caso di* —, in case of miscarriage; *subire un* —, to miscarry.

disgustàre, *v.t.* **1.** to disgust, to sicken: *medicine che disgustano*, remedies that disgust the palate; *la vista del cibo mi disgusta*, I loathe the sight of food **2.** *fig.* to disgust, to sicken, to shock: *sono disgustato dalle sue menzogne*, I am disgusted with his lies; *il suo cinismo mi disgustava*, I was shocked by his cynicism; *i tuoi metodi lo disgustano*, your methods sicken him; *tutto ciò mi disgusta*, I am sick to death of it all || **disgustàrsi**, *v.r.* to become disgusted (with s.o., sthg., with doing); to get to dislike (s.o., sthg., doing), to take a dislike (to s.o., sthg., doing) || *v.r. reciproco* to fall out with each other (one another), to quarrel with each other (one another).

disgustàto, *ag.* disgusted, sickened, shocked: *si allontanò* —, he went away in disgust.

disgustévole, *V.* **disgustóso.**

disgústo, *s.m.* disgust, loathing; (*avversione*) aversion, dislike, repulsion: — *per l'ipocrisia di qlcu.*, disgust at (o for) s.o.'s hypocrisy; *aver* — *per ql.co.*, *qlcu.*, to have a strong dislike of sthg., for s.o.; *provare* — *per qlcu.*, to feel an aversion to (o for) s.o.

disgustosaménte, *av.* disgustingly; repulsively.

disgustóso, *ag.* disgusting, loathsome, sickening; shocking: *un comportamento* —, a shocking behaviour; *uno spettacolo* —, a sickening spectacle.

disidratànte, *ag.* (*chim.*) dehydrating ‖ *s.m.* (*chim.*) dehydrator.

disidratàre, *v.t.* 1. (*chim.*) to dehydrate 2. (*miner.*) to dewater.

disidratàto, *ag.* (*chim.*) dehydrated.

disidratatóre, *s.m.* 1. (*chim. ind.*) dehydrator 2. (*miner.*) dewaterer.

disidratazióne, *s.f.* 1. (*chim.*) dehydration 2. (*miner.*) dewatering.

disìllabo, *ag.* di(s)syllabic ‖ *s.m.* di(s)syllable.

disillúdere, *v.t.* to disillusion, to disenchant; to undeceive, to disappoint: *mi dispiace doverti* —, *ma credo sia mio dovere*, I regret I have to undeceive you, but I think it is my duty.

disillusióne, *s.f.* disillusion; disenchantment; disappointment: *le disillusioni anche se dolorose possono condurre alla verità*, disillusions though painful may bring one to the truth.

disillúso, *ag.* disillusioned, disenchanted; undeceived; disappointed.

disimballàggio, *s.m.* unpacking.

disimballàre, *v.t.* to unpack.

disimpacciàre, *v.t.* to disembarrass, to disencumber, to disentangle.

disimpacciàto, *ag.* 1. disembarrassed, disencumbered, disentangled 2. (*disinvolto*) jaunty, unconstrained: *libero e* —, free and easy.

disimparàre, *v.t.* to forget, to unlearn: *ho disimparato ad andare in bicicletta*, I have forgotten how to ride a bicycle.

disimpegnàre, *v.t.* 1. to redeem, to take out of pawn: — *l'orologio*, to redeem one's watch (o to take one's watch out of pawn) 2. (*liberare da un impegno*) to release, to disengage: *non posso disimpegnarvi dal venire domani*, I cannot release you from coming tomorrow 3. (*compiere*) to fulfil: — *bene un incarico*, to perform a task well; — *il proprio dovere*, to fulfil (o to do) one's duty 4. (*mar.*) to clear: — *un'ancora, una gomena*, to clear an anchor, a rope ‖ **disimpegnàrsi**, *v.r.* 1. to disengage oneself, to free oneself: *non so come disimpegnarmi da quella promessa*, I do not know how to disengage (o to free) myself from that promise 2. (*cavarsela*) to manage; to extricate oneself: *saprai disimpegnarti senza aiuto?*, will you be able to manage without help?; *sono sicuro che saprà* — *da quella situazione difficile*, I am sure he will be able to extricate himself from that difficult situation.

disimpegnàto, *ag.* free, disengaged: *mani disimpegnate*, free hands.

disimpégno, *s.m.* 1. redemption, taking out of pawn: *pagò duemila lire per il* — *della sua macchina fotografica*, he paid two thousand lire to redeem his camera 2. (*il liberarsi da un impegno*) disengagement, release ‖ *abito di* —, presentable dress (o suit) ‖ *studia solo per* —, he only does the necessary minimum of work 3. (*adempimento*) fulfilment: *mostra grande abilità nel* — *delle sue funzioni*, he shows great ability in carrying out (o in the fulfilment) of his duties.

disincagliàre, *v.t.* (*mar.*) to get (sthg.) afloat: *con l'alta marea si potrà* — *la nave*, they will be able to float the ship off at high tide.

disincantàre, *v.t.* to disenchant, to free from a spell: *Rinaldo disincantò la foresta*, Rinaldo removed the spell from the forest (o freed the forest from the spell).

disincantàto, *ag.* 1. disenchanted 2. (*disingannato*) disillusioned, disenchanted.

disincànto, *s.m.* disenchantment.

disincarnàre, *v.t.* to discarnate.

disincarnàto, *ag.* discarnate.

disinfestàre, *v.t.* to disinfest: *è necessario* — *le stanze*, it is necessary to disinfest the rooms.

disinfestatóre, *s.m.* disinfestor.

disinfettànte, *ag.s.m.* disinfectant: *l'alcool è un potente* —, alcohol is a powerful disinfectant.

disinfettàre, *v.t.* to disinfect: — *con cura una ferita*, to disinfect a wound carefully.

disinfezióne, *s.f.* disinfection.

disingannàre, *v.t.* to undeceive, to disabuse; to disenchant, to disillusion: *disingannatevi!*, don't you believe it!; *lo disingannai riguardo quell'affare*, I told him the truth (o I undeceived him) about that matter.

disingànno, *s.m.* 1. undeceiving; disenchantment, disillusion 2. (*delusione*) disappointment: *amaro* —, sad disappointment.

disingranàre, *v.t.* (*mec.*) to disengage, to throw (sthg.) out of mesh.

disinnamoràre, *v.t.* to estrange ‖ **disinnamoràrsi**, *v.r.* to become indifferent, to grow indifferent.

disinnestàre, *v.t.* (*mec.*) to disconnect, to disengage, to unclutch: — *la frizione*, (*aut.*) to declutch (o to disengage the clutch).

disinnestàto, *ag.* (*mec.*) disengaged, off: *la frizione è disinnestata*, (*aut.*) the clutch is off.

disinnèsto, *s.m.* (*mec.*) disengagement, release, knock-off: — *a scatto*, (*di macchina per maglieria*) knock-off action; — *del carrello*, (*di macchina per scrivere*) carriage release.

disinserìre, *v.t.* (*elett. mec.*) to disconnect.

disinserìto, *ag.* (*elett.*) off, out.

disintegràre, *v.t.* to disintegrate; to crumble; to crush: — *l'atomo*, (*fis.*) to split the atom ‖ **disintegràrsi**, *v.r.* to disintegrate; to crumble: *il razzo si disintegrò nell'atmosfera*, the rocket disintegrated in the atmosphere.

disintegratóre, *s.m.* (*mec.*) disintegrator.

disintegrazióne, *s.f.* disintegration: — *dell'atomo*, (*fis.*) splitting of the atom; — *del minerale*, crushing of the ore; — *prodotta da energia radiante*, (*fis. atomica*) photodisintegration; *probabilità di* —, (*fis. atomica*) decay probability.

disinteressàre, *v.t.* 1. to disinterest 2. (*comm.*) to buy out (a partner) ‖ **disinteressàrsi**, *v.r.* to disinterest oneself (in sthg.); to take no (further) interest (in s.o., sthg.): *sembra* — *dell'affare*, he seems to take no interest in the matter; — *di una questione*, to disinterest oneself in a question.

disinteressataménte, *av.* disinterestedly.

disinteressatézza, *s.f.* (*rar.*) disinterestedness.

disinteressàto, *ag.* 1. disinterested: *il suo atto non è del tutto* —, his action is not entirely disinterested 2. (*altruistico*) unselfish: *è una persona disinteressata*, he is an unselfish man 3. (*imparziale*) impartial: *storico* —, impartial historian.

disinterèsse, *s.m.* 1. disinterestedness; (*altruismo*) unselfishness: *nelle sue azioni dà sempre prova di grande* —, he always proves himself to be unselfish in his actions 2. (*indifferenza*) indifference: *mostrò il più completo* — *per la sorte di lui*, he showed complete indifference to his fate.

disintossicàre, *v.t.* (*med.*) to detoxicate.

disinvitàre, *v.t.* to disinvite.

disinvòlto, *ag.* 1. unconstrained, unembarrassed, free-and-easy, self-possessed: *andatura disinvolta*, easy gait; *modi disinvolti*, unselfconscious (o unembarrassed o free-and-easy o easy) manners; *stile* —, unconstrained style 2. (*sfrontato*) impudent; (*fam.*) cheeky.

disinvoltúra, *s.f.* **1.** unconstraint, unselfconsciousness; (*di modi, andatura*) ease, gracefulness, free-and-easy way: *con* —, in an off-hand manner: *si comporta sempre con* — *in società,* he is always at his ease in society **2.** (*sfrontatezza*) impudence; (*fam.*) cheek.

disío, (*poet.*) per **desidèrio**[1].

disistíma, *s.f.* disesteem, lack of esteem; contempt.

disistimàre, *v.t.* to disesteem, to slight, to despise: *non ti ho mai disistimato,* I have never disesteemed you.

disleàle, (*rar.*) per **sleàle**.

dislealtà, (*rar.*) per **slealtà**.

dislivèllo, *s.m.* **1.** difference of level, difference in height; (*inclinazione*) gradient: — *in aumento,* (*di acque, ecc.*) rise; — *stradale,* gradient of a road; *c'è un forte* —, there is a big drop **2.** (*ineguaglianza*) inequality: — *sociale,* social inequality.

dislocaménto, *s.m.* **1.** (*mar.*) displacement: — *a pieno carico normale,* load displacement; — *leggero,* light draught displacement; *resistenza di* —, resistance of the hull **2.** (*mil.*) dislocation.

dislocàre, *v.t.* **1.** (*mar.*) to displace **2.** (*mil.*) to distribute, to dislocate, to detach.

dislocazióne, *s.f.* **1.** removal, dislocation **2.** (*geol.*) dislocation.

dislogaménto, *s.m.* (*rar.*) **1.** dislocation, displacement **2.** (*slogamento*) dislocation.

dislogàre, *v.t.* (*rar.*) **1.** (*dislocare*) to dislocate, to displace **2.** (*slogare*) to dislocate, to disjoint.

disloggiàre, (*arc.*) per **sloggiàre**.

dismagliàre, (*rar.*) per **smagliàre**.

dismaltàre, *v.t.* to remove enamel from (sthg.).

dismembràre[1], *v.t.* to dismember: — *un testo,* (*criticarlo a fondo*) to pick a text to pieces.

dismembràre[2], *v.t.* (*rar.*) (*dimenticare*) to forget.

dismemoràto, *ag.* (*rar.*) forgetful.

dismésso, *ag.* disused; cast-off: *un abito* —, a cast-off dress.

disméttere, *v.t.* **1.** to cast off, to use no longer: — *una casa, una stanza,* to dismantle a house, a room; — *una veste,* to cast a dress off (*o* to use a dress no longer) **2.** (*rar.*) (*cessare*) to leave off (doing).

dismisúra, *s.f.* excess, redundance; (*smoderatezza*) intemperance || *a* —, excessively (*o* exceedingly): *crescere a* —, to grow exceedingly.

dismnesía, *s.f.* (*patol.*) dysmnesia.

disobbedíre, *e derivati,* V. **disubbidíre,** *e derivati.*

disobbligànte, *ag.* disobliging; disagreeable, ungracious: *maniere disobbliganti,* ungracious manners.

disobbligàre, *v.t.* to release from duty || **disobbligàrsi,** *v.r.* to free oneself from duty; to disengage oneself: *come possiamo disobbligarci di tutte le vostre gentilezze?,* how can we return all your kindnesses?.

disoccupàre, *v.t.* to leave vacant, to leave free.

disoccupàto, *ag.* **1.** unemployed: *è* — *dall'anno scorso,* he has been out of work since last year **2.** (*libero, sgombro*) unoccupied, vacant **3.** (*ozioso*) idle || *s.m.* unemployed person || *i disoccupati,* the unemployed; *una manifestazione di disoccupati,* a demonstration of unemployed workers.

disoccupazióne, *s.f.* unemployment: *sussidio di* —, dole: *ricevere il sussidio di* —, to be on the dole.

disonestà, *s.f.* **1.** dishonesty, knavery, deceit, deceitfulness: *fu licenziato per la sua* —, he was dismissed for dishonesty; *tanta* — *non deve andare impunita,* such knavery must not go unpunished **2.** (*scostumatezza*) indecency, obscenity **3.** (*atto disonesto*) fraud: *è una vera* —*!,* it is a real fraud!.

disonestaménte, *av.* **1.** dishonestly, deceitfully **2.** (*senza pudore*) indecently.

disonèsto, *ag.* **1.** dishonest, deceitful, fraudulent: *clausola, transazione disonesta,* fraudulent clause, transaction; *egli è una persona disonesta,* he is a dishonest man; *non gli importa usare mezzi disonesti pur di arrivare a quello che vuole,* he doesn't mind using foul means as long as he gets what he wants **2.** (*contrario*

al pudore) indecent, obscene, immoral, shameless.

disonorànte, *ag.* dishonourable, disgraceful, shameful: *un vizio* —, a shameful vice.

disonoràre, *v.t.* **1.** to dishonour, to disgrace, to bring dishonour on (s.o., sthg.): — *il nome di qlcu.,* to tarnish s.o.'s name; — *la propria famiglia,* to dishonour (*o* to bring dishonour on) one's family **2.** (*sedurre*) to seduce, to debauch || **disonoràrsi,** *v.r.* to dishonour oneself, to disgrace oneself, to bring dishonour upon oneself: *con quell'atto si disonorò irreparabilmente,* with that action he brought undying dishonour upon himself.

disonoratthe ménte, *av.* dishonourably, disgracefully, shamefully.

disonóre, *s.m.* dishonour, disgrace, shame: *è il* — *della sua famiglia,* he is a disgrace to (*o* the disgrace of *o* the shame of) his family; *in questo non vi è alcun* —, there is no disgrace (*o* shame) in that; *fare* — *a qlcu.,* to disgrace s.o.

disonorévole, *ag.* dishonourable, disgraceful, shameful: *tiene una condotta* —, he behaves disgracefully.

disonorevolménte, *av.* dishonourably, disgracefully, shamefully.

disoppilàre, *v.t.* (*med.*) to deoppilate.

disoppilatívo, *ag.* (*farm.*) deoppilative, deoppilant, deobstruent: *rimedio* —, deoppilative (*o* deobstruent).

disópra, *av.* above; over; (*in cima*) on top; (*ai piani superiori*) upstairs: *il cielo, al* —, *era blu,* the sky above was blue; *è appena andata* —, she has just gone upstairs; *la mia camera è proprio* —, my bedroom is right overhead; *misi* — *le mele più belle,* I put the best apples on top; *la palla andò al* — *e finì nel giardino accanto,* the ball went over into the next-door garden || *quella ragazza è bella, gentile e per* — *è ricca,* that girl is beautiful, kind and rich into the bargain || *ag.* **upper, next** (*attributivi*); **above** (*prep. av.*): *gli inquilini dell'appartamento* —, the tenants of the flat above (ours); *abita al piano* —, he lives on the next floor (*o* on the floor above (us)); *apri il cassetto* —, open the drawer above that one; (*tra due*) open the upper drawer || *s.m.* top; (*la parte superiore*) **upper part, upper side**: *il* — *del coperchio,* the top of the lid || *prendere il* — *su qlcu.,* to have the upper hand of s.o. || *al disópra di,* **disópra a,** *l.prep.* above; (*sopra; oltre*) over: *al* — *di ogni critica, sospetto,* above criticism, suspicion; *l'appartamento al* — *del nostro,* the flat above ours; *numeri al* — *del cento,* numbers over a hundred; *temperatura al* — *del normale,* temperature above normal; *l'aereo volava al* — *delle nostre teste, delle nubi,* the plane was flying over our heads, above the clouds; *gli passò il libro* — *al tavolò,* he passed him the book over the table; *hanno tre bambini al* — *dei sei anni,* they have three children over six; *leggeva al* — *della sua spalla,* he was reading over his shoulder; *una montagna si eleva al* — *del lago,* a mountain rises above the lake; *si udiva la sua voce al* — *del tumulto,* his voice was heard above the din; *gettare ql.co. al* — *di un muro,* to throw sthg. over a wall || *stare al* — *di qlcu.,* (*essergli superiore*) to be superior to (*o* to be better than) s.o. || *vivere al* — *dei propri mezzi,* to live above one's means.

disordinaménto, *s.m.* disarrangement: derangement.

disorbitànte, *ag.* exorbitant.

disorbitànza, *s.f.* exorbitance.

disorbitàre, *v.t.* (*rar.*) to exceed.

disordinàre, *v.t.* **1.** to disorder, to disarrange, to derange; to trouble, to upset; to confuse: *non* — *le mie carte!,* don't meddle with my papers!; — *le idee di qlcu.,* to confuse s.o.'s ideas; — *il nemico,* to throw the enemy into disorder || *v.i.* (*eccedere*) (*nel bere*) to exceed in drinking, to drink too much; (*nel mangiare*) to exceed in eating, to eat to excess: *a pranzo abbiamo disordinato,* at dinner we ate to excess.

disordinataménte, *av.* untidily, in a disorderly way, confusedly: *ritirarsi* —, (*mil.*) to retreat in disorder.

disordinàto, *ag.* **1.** untidy, disorderly, confused

unruly: *cassetti disordinati*, untidy drawers; *folla disordinata*, disorderly crowd; *mente disordinata*, unsettled mind; *stanza disordinata*, disorderly room 2. (*sregolato*) disorderly, extravagant, wild, immoderate: *condotta disordinata*, immoderate behaviour; *uomo —*, extravagant man.

disórdine, *s.m.* 1. disorder, untidiness, confusion: *capelli in —*, untidy hair; *i suoi abiti erano in —*, his clothes were untidy (*o* in disorder); *tutto è in —*, everything is at sixes and sevens; *gettare il — nelle file del nemico*, to throw the ranks of the enemy into disorder; *mettere ql.co. in —*, to turn sthg. upside down 2. (*sregolatezza*) disorderliness, debauchery, licentiousness: *i disordini gli accorceranno la vita*, his excesses are going to shorten his life 3. (*tumulto*) disorder, commotion, tumult, disturbance, riot: *sono scoppiati gravi disordini*, serious disturbances have broken out || *l'ordine è pane, il — è fame*, *prov.* united we stand, divided we fall.

disoressía, *s.f.* (*patol.*) dysorexia.

disorganicità, *s.f.* want of order, lack of co-ordination.

disorgànico, *ag.* inorganic, incoherent: *un piano alquanto —*, a somewhat incoherent plan.

disorganizzàre, *v.t.* to disorganize: *— i piani di ql.cu.*, to upset s.o.'s plans || **disorganizzàrsi**, *v.r.* to become disorganized, to fall into confusion: *le retrovie si disorganizzarono completamente*, the lines of communication fell into utter confusion (*o* became completely disorganized).

disorganizzazióne, *s.f.* disorganization: *c'è troppa — in questa ditta*, there is too much disorganization in this firm.

disorientaménto, *s.m.* disorientation; bewilderment, confusion: *ci fu un attimo di —*, there was a moment of confusion.

disorientàre, *v.t.* 1. to disorientate: *— ql.cu.*, to cause one to lose one's bearings 2. (*sconcertare*) to bewilder, to puzzle, to disconcert: *le sue domande mi disorientavano*, his questions puzzled me; *il vecchio contadino era disorientato dal traffico della grande città*, the old farmer was bewildered by the traffic in the large town || **disorientàrsi**, *v.r.* to lose one's bearings, to get confused.

disorientàto, *ag.* bewildered, puzzled, disconcerted: *era troppo — per rispondere*, he was too puzzled to answer; *si guardava attorno —*, he looked round in bewilderment; *essere —*, to be in a maze.

disorlàre, *v.t.* to take off the hem of (sthg.).

disormeggiàre, *v.t.* (*mar.*) to unmoor.

disossàre, *v.t.* to bone: *— un pollo*, to bone a chicken.

disossidànte, *ag.* (*chim.*) deoxidizing || *s.m.* (*chim.*) deoxidizer.

disossidàre, *v.t.* (*chim.*) to deoxidate, to deoxidize.

disossidazióne, *s.f.* (*chim.*) deoxidation.

disostruènte, *ag.* (*farm.*) deobstruent.

disótto, *av.* **below**; **underneath**; (*ai piani inferiori*) **downstairs**: *mise i libri più vecchi —*, he put the oldest books underneath; *resta — !*, stay downstairs! (*o* below!); *stando in cima alla collina si poteva vedere, al —, il mare*, from the hill-top we could see the sea below || *ag.* **lower** (*attributivo*); **below** (*prep. av.*): *apri il cassetto —*, open the drawer below that one; (*tra due*) open the lower drawer; *conosco gli inquilini dell'appartamento —*, I know the tenants of the flat below (ours); *la ditta si è trasferita al piano —*, the firm has moved to the floor below || *s.m.* **underside**, (*la parte inferiore*) **lower part**, **lower side**: *il — di un coperchio*, the underside (*o* the inside) of a lid; *aver il —*, to have (*o* to get) the worst of it || **al disótto di**, **disótto a**, *l. prep.* **under**, **beneath**, **underneath**; **below**: *al — della media*, below (the) average; *al — del livello del mare*, below sea-level; *bambini al — dei sei anni*, children under six; *dieci gradi al — dello zero*, ten

degrees below zero; *temperatura al — del normale*, temperature below normal; *abita nell'appartamento al — del nostro*, he lives in the flat below us (*o* ours); *gli passai il libro — al banco*, I passed him the book under the desk || *stare al — di ql.cu.*, (*essergli inferiore*) to be inferior to s.o.

dispàccio, *s.m.* dispatch, despatch: *— telegrafico*, telegram.

dispaiàre, *v.t.* (*rar.*) to unpair.

disparataménte, *av.* disparately.

disparatézza, *s.f.* (*rar.*) disparateness, dissimilarity.

disparàto, *ag.* disparate, dissimilar.

disparére, *s.m.* difference of opinion, dissension.

díspari, *ag.* odd: *numero —*, odd number || *giocare a pari e —*, to play odds and evens.

disparíre, *v.i.* (*rar.*) to disappear, to vanish.

disparità, *s.f.* disparity, inequality, difference: *— di condizioni*, difference of conditions; *— di età*, disparity of age; *— di opinioni*, difference of opinions.

dispàrte, (in), *l.av.* aside; apart; by: *in — da*, apart from; *mettere ql.co. in —*, (*per non usarlo più*) to put (*o* to lay) sthg. aside; (*per uno scopo*) to set sthg. apart (*o* aside) (*o* to put *o* to lay *o* to set sthg. by); *prendere ql.cu. in —*, to take (*o* to draw) s.o. aside; *stare in —*, to stand aside (*o* some way off); *fig.* to stand aloof.

dispartíre, *v.t.* (*rar.*) to divide, to part.

dispèndio, *s.m.* heavy expense; (*di forze, tempo*) waste: *— di tempo*, waste of time; *che — di forze!*, what a waste of energy!.

dispendiosaménte, *av.* expensively.

dispendióso, *ag.* expensive: *fanno una vita dispendiosa*, they live expensively; *il viaggiare è —*, travelling is expensive.

dispènsa, *s.f.* 1. pantry, larder; store-room; (*credenza*) sideboard 2. (*distribuzione*) distribution, dispensation: *la — del pane ai poveri*, the distribution of bread to the poor 3. (*pubblicazione periodica*) number, instalment: *romanzo a dispense*, serial novel || *dispense universitarie*, duplicated lecture notes 4. (*eccl.*) dispensation 5. (*esenzione*) exemption, dispensation: *— dal servizio militare*, exemption from military service.

dispensàbile, *ag.* dispensable.

dispensàre, *v.t.* 1. (*distribuire*) to dispense, to deal out, to distribute, to give out: *— dei favori*, to dispense favours; *— dei viveri*, to deal out (*o* to give out) provisions 2. (*esentare*) to exonerate, to exempt, to dispense: *dispensami, per favore, da questo lungo viaggio*, please spare me this long journey; *il mio amico è stato dispensato dalle tasse scolastiche*, my friend gets tuition free; *ti dispenso dal fare queste osservazioni*, (*fam.*) you may keep your remarks to yourself; *— ql.cu. dal digiuno*, (*eccl.*) to dispense s.o. from fasting; *— ql.cu. dal lavoro*, to relieve s.o. from working; *— ql.cu. dal servizio militare*, to exempt s.o. from military service || **dispensàrsi**, *v.r.* to excuse oneself, to get out (of sthg., of doing): *potete dispensarvi dall'accompagnarmi*, there is no need for you to come with me.

dispensàrio, *s.m.* dispensary: *— antitubercolare*, antitubercolosis dispensary.

dispensatívo, *ag.* dispensing, dispensative.

dispensatóre, *s.m.*, **dispensatríce**, *s.f.* distributor, dispenser.

dispensièra, *s.f.* 1. distributor, dispenser 2. (*chi sovraintende alla dispensa*) stewardess.

dispensière, *s.m.* 1. distributor, dispenser 2. (*chi sovraintende alla dispensa*) steward.

dispepsía, *s.f.* (*med.*) dyspepsia.

dispèptico, *ag.s.m.* dyspeptic.

disperàre, *v.i.* to despair, to lose all hope, to give up hope: *non bisogna —*, we must hope for the best; *non devi mai —!*, never say die! (*o* you must hope against hope!); *ora disperiamo di riuscire in quell'esperimento*, now we despair (*o* we have lost all hope) of succeeding in that experiment; *si dispera di salvarla*, her life is despaired of (*o* she is past hope); — *della guarigione*, to give up hope of recovery ‖ *far qlcu.*, to drive s.o. mad (*o* to drive s.o. to despair) ‖ **disperàrsi**, *v.r.* (*darsi alla disperazione*) to surrender (oneself) to despair, to give oneself up to despair; (*essere disperato*) to be in despair; (*essere affranto*) to be dejected, to be utterly disheartened: *è troppo presto per* —, it is too soon to give yourself up to despair.

disperataménte, *av.* desperately ‖ *lavorare* —, (*fam.*) (*con grande alacrità*) to work like mad.

disperàto, *ag.* 1. despairing: *in un tono* —, in a despairing tone; *disperati, rinunciammo al tentativo*, we gave up the attempt in despair; *mi diede uno sguardo* —, he gave me a despairing look; *essere* —, to be in despair (*o* to feel miserable); (*essere scoraggiato*) to be disheartened: *essere — nell'apprendere ql.co.*, to be dreadfully sorry to hear sthg. 2. (*senza speranza*) desperate, hopeless: *un caso* —, a desperate case; *essere in condizioni disperate*, to be in a hopeless state; (*di malato*) to be far gone (in illness) (*o* to be past recovery) 3. (*miserabile*) destitute, wretched; (*senza un soldo*) penniless: *avere un'aria disperata*, to look wretched 4. (*accanito*) desperate: *una lotta disperata*, a desperate (*o* life-and-death) struggle ‖ *s.m.* 1. destitute fellow, wretched fellow 2. (*forsennato*) madman (*pl.* madmen): *agire come un* —, to act like a madman (*o* desperately); *lavorare come un* —, (*fam.*) to work like a madman 3. (*rar.*) (*disperazione*) despair: *per* —, in despair.

disperazióne, *s.f.* 1. despair: *un accesso di* —, a fit of despair; *un atto di* —, an act of despair; *darsi alla* —, to surrender (oneself) to despair (*o* to give way to despair); *portare, ridurre qlcu. alla* —, to drive s.o. to despair (*o* mad) ‖ *ho scelto questo per* —, I chose this one out of despair (*o* as there was no alternative) ‖ *quel ragazzo è la — dei suoi genitori*, (*fam.*) that child is the despair of his parents; *sei la mia* —!, (*fam.*) you'll be the death of me! 2. (*stato di disperazione*) desperation, despondency, dejection: *cadere in* —, to fall into despondency.

dispèrdere, *v.t.* 1. to disperse, to scatter; to dispel: — *un esercito*, to disperse (*o* to rout *o* to break up) an army; — *una folla*, to disperse (*o* to break up) a crowd; — *le nubi*, to disperse (*o* to dissipate *o* to scatter *o* to dispel) the clouds; — *i sospetti di qlcu.*, to dispel (*o* to allay) s.o.'s suspicions; — *i timori di qlcu.*, to dispel s.o.'s fears 2. (*consumare, sciupare*) to waste, to dissipate: — *i propri sforzi*, to dissipate one's efforts; — *la propria sostanza*, to waste one's substance; — *tutto il proprio denaro*, to squander (*o* to fritter away) all one's money 3. (*fis.*) to scatter ‖ **dispèrdersi**, *v.r.* 1. to disperse, to scatter, to be scattered: *la folla ben presto si disperse*, the crowd very soon dispersed 2. (*elett.*) to tail off.

disperdiménto, *s.m.* (*rar.*) dispersion: — *di beni*, loss of goods.

dispèrgere, (*poet.*) per **dispèrdere** 1. 2.

dispersióne, *s.f.* 1. dispersion, loss: — *di documenti*, loss of documents 2. (*sparpagliamento*) scattering, dispersion: *la — del popolo ebraico*, the dispersion of the Jews (*o* the Diaspora) 3. (*elett.*) leak, leakage: — *di elettricità*, leakage of magnetic force; *autotrasformatore a* —, leak transformer; *campo di* —, stray-field; *reattanza di* —, (*rad.*) leakage reactance 4. (*fis.*) dispersion, scattering: — *del calore*, loss of heat; — *normale*, normal dispersion; — *rotatoria*, rotatory dispersion; — *statistica*, (*fis. atomica*) straggling; *grado di* —, degree of dispersion 5. (*ott.*) dispersion: — *anomala*, anomalous dispersion; — *della luce*, dispersion of light.

dispersívo, *ag.* dispersive: *potere* —, (*fis.*) dispersive power.

dispèrso, *ag.* 1. (*smarrito*) missing, lost: *soldato* —, (*mil.*) missing soldier; *la lettera andò dispersa*, the letter was missing (*o* lost) 2. (*sparpagliato*) dispersed, scat-

tered: *la cenere andò dispersa*, the ashes were dispersed ‖ *s.m.* (*mil.*) missing soldier.

dispètto, *s.m.* 1. spite: *lo fece solo per* —, he did so out of mere spite; *far dispetti a qlcu.*, to annoy (*o* to tease) s.o.: *mamma, quel bambino mi fa i dispetti!*, ma, that child is teasing me!; *fare un brutto* —, to do an ill turn ‖ *a — di*, in spite of: *a — dei tuoi consigli*, in spite of your advice; *a — della legge*, in spite of the law; *a — delle sue asserzioni*, in spite of his assertions; *a — di tutto*, in spite of all; *dirò la verità a tuo marcio* —, I'll tell the truth just to spite you ‖ *stare in paradiso a — dei santi*, to be as welcome as a dog at a wedding 2. (*stizza*) vexation: *con mio grande — ho perso il treno*, much to my vexation I just missed my train; *la cosa mi fece un gran* —, the thing vexed (*o* annoyed) me greatly; *immagina il mio* —!, can you imagine my vexation! 3. (*rar.*) (*disprezzo*): *avere in* —, to despise.

dispettosaménte, *av.* spitefully.

dispettóso, *ag.* spiteful: *una ragazza alquanto dispettosa*, a rather spiteful girl.

dispiacènte, *ag.* 1. sorry: *ne siamo dispiacenti*, we are sorry for it 2. (*spiacevole*) unpleasing, unpleasant, disagreeable.

dispiacére, *v.i.* 1. to dislike (*costruzione pers.*): *mi dispiace fare ciò*, I dislike doing it (*o* it is distasteful to me to do it *o* I object to doing it); *mi dispiace molto di fare il tiranno*, I greatly dislike playing the tyrant 2. (*essere spiacente*) to be sorry, to regret (*costruzione pers.*): *me ne dispiace molto*, I am very sorry for (*o* I regret) it; *mi dispiace di dover sciogliere la bella compagnia*, I am sorry (*o* I regret) to have to break up the nice party 3. (*in espressioni di cortesia*): *se non vi dispiace*, if you please; *ora alzatevi se non vi dispiace*, now stand up, if you please (*o* now, will you please stand up?) 4. (*essere sgradevole*) to be disagreeable: *quella musica gli dispiace*, that music offends (*o* grates on) his ear 5. (*scontentare*) to displease (s.o.); (*contrariare, irritare*) to vex (s.o.): *il suo comportamento dispiacque a suo padre*, her behaviour displeased her father ‖ *a costo di dispiacergli*, at the risk of incurring his disfavour.

dispiacére, *s.m.* 1. (*rincrescimento*) regret, sorrow; (*dolore*) grief, affliction: *con molto — dovemmo partire subito*, to our great regret (*o* with much regret *o* much to our regret) we had to leave immediately; *ho il — di comunicarvi la triste notizia*, I am sorry (*o* I regret) to give you the sad news 2. (*disapprovazione*) displeasure: *non posso nascondere il mio — per il tuo comportamento*, I cannot conceal my displeasure at your behaviour 3. (*fastidio, preoccupazione*) trouble: *ho avuto molti dispiaceri in questa attività*, I've been through a lot of trouble in this activity.

dispiacévole, *ag.* unpleasant, disagreeable, unpleasing.

dispiacevolézza, *s.f.* unpleasantness.

dispiaciménto, *s.m.* regret: *con mio* —, to my regret.

dispiaciúto, *ag.* (*fam.*) 1. (*spiacente, dolente*) sorry 2. (*contrariato*) displeased, annoyed, vexed.

dispiccàre, *v.t.* (*rar.*) to pluck, to detach ‖ **dispiccàrsi**, *v.r.* (*rar.*) to detach oneself.

dispiegàre, *v.t.* (*rar.*) 1. to unfold; (*mar.*) (*le vele*) to unfurl 2. (*allargare*) to spread (out): *l'uccello dispiega le ali*, the bird spreads (out) its wings.

displúvio, *s.m.* 1. (*geog.*) watershed 2. (*arch.*) hip: *linea di* —, (*di un tetto*) ridge.

dispnèa, *s.f.* (*patol.*) dyspnœa, difficult respiration.

dispnòico, *ag.* dyspnœic ‖ *s.m.* (*patol.*) dyspnœic subject.

dispodestàre, (*rar.*) per **spodestàre**.

dispogliàre, (*rar.*) per **spogliàre**.

dispolpàre, (*rar.*) per **spolpàre**.

disponènte, *s.m.* (*dir.*) testator.

disponíbile, *ag.* 1. available, disposable: *liquidi*

disponibili, (*comm.*) available funds; *abbiamo poco denaro* —, we have little money at our disposal; *rendersi* —, to become available **2.** (*libero*) free, vacant: *impiego* —, vacant position (*o post o situation*); *posto* (*a sedere*) —, vacant seat ‖ *s.f.* (*dir.*) disposable portion of property ‖ *s.m.* (*econ. comm.*) available assets (*pl.*), liquid assets (*pl.*).

disponibilità, *s.f.* **1.** (*comm.*) availability, disposability: — *bancarie*, deposits with banks; — *finanziarie*, liquid assets (*o* available funds); *esaurire le* —, to exhaust available resources **2.** *essere in* —, (*mil.*) to be unattached (*o* to be on half-pay) **3.** *nave in* —, (*mar.*) ship in dry dock.

dispórre, *v.t.* **1.** to arrange, to dispose, to set out, to place in order: — *i fiori in un vaso*, to arrange flowers in a vase; — *i libri sugli scaffali*, to arrange (*o* to dispose) books on shelves; — *la merce in vetrina*, to display the goods in the window; — *in ordine alfabetico*, to arrange (*o* to set out) in alphabetical order **2.** (*preparare*) to prepare, to dispose: *nulla meglio di un lungo sonno dispone il corpo ad affrontare la fatica*, nothing fits the body so well to stand fatigue as a good sleep; — *la mente allo studio*, to prepare one's mind for study; — *ogni cosa per la partenza*, to prepare (*o* to arrange) things for departure; — *qlcu. a una cattiva notizia*, to prepare s.o. for a piece of bad news **3.** (*deliberare*) to order; (*dir.*) to provide, to enjoin: *come disposto dai regolamenti*, as provided by the regulations; *dispose che noi ci stabilissimo qui*, he ordered us to settle here; *la legge dispone che...*, the law provides that...; *i regolamenti dispongono che si paghi subito*, the regulations enjoin that payment should be made immediately ‖ *l'uomo propone e Dio dispone, prov.* man proposes, God disposes ‖ *v.i.* to dispose, to have (s.o., sthg.) at one's disposal: *disponete pure di me*, you may consider me at your disposal; *dispone di tre automobili*, he has three cars at his disposal; *i nostri studenti dispongono di due biblioteche*, our students have access to two libraries; *usò tutti i mezzi di cui disponeva*, he used every available means (*o* all the means at his disposal); — *dei propri beni in favore di qlcu.*, to make over one's property to s.o.; *poco prima di morire ha disposto dei suoi beni*, just before dying he made testamentary disposition of his property; — *della propria vita*, to dispose of one's own life; — *della stampa*, to command the press; — *di grossi capitali*, to have a large capital at one's command (*o* in hand) ‖ **dispórsi**, *v.r.* to prepare (for sthg., to do); to get ready (for sthg., to do): — *ad andare a dormire*, to prepare to go to sleep; — *all'azione, alla lotta*, to prepare for action, for the struggle; — *a partire*, to get ready to start.

disposàre, *v.t.* (*arc.*) to wed.

dispositívo, *ag.* regulating ‖ *s.m.* **1.** (*dir.*) purview **2.** (*mec.*) device, contrivance, apparatus; gear: — *anti-accavallamento*, (*ferr.*) anti-climber; — *antidisturbi radio*, (*rad.*) radio interference suppressor; — *antiluce*, (*foto.*) light lock; — *di arresto*, (*mec.*) arresting gear; — *di comando*, (*elett.*) control device; — *di lancio*, (*mil.*) launcher; — *di riscaldamento*, (*mec.*) heater; — *di sicurezza*, (*di arma da fuoco*) safety (catch); — *di sincronizzazione*, (*cine.*) interlock; — *di sterzo*, (*aut.*) steering gear.

disposizióne, *s.f.* **1.** disposition, arrangement: *la* — *dei mobili, della casa*, the arrangement of the furniture, of the house; *la* — *delle truppe*, the disposition of the troops; *la* — *di una pagina*, (*tip.*) the lay-out **2.** (*ordine, deliberazione*) order, direction, instruction, provision: — *di legge*, (*dir.*) provision of the law (*o* regulation); *disposizioni generali*, general provisions; *disposizioni testamentarie*, testamentary dispositions; *fino a nuove disposizioni*, till further instructions **3.** *a* —, at one's disposal; available: *cerca di fare quelle somme con le cifre a nostra* —, try to do those sums on the figures that are available; *sono a tua* —, I am at your disposal; *avere tempo a propria* —, to have time to oneself; *mettere ql.co. a* — *di qlcu.*, to place sthg. at s.o.'s disposal **4.** (*inclinazione*) inclination, bent, tendency, turn, penchant: *ha* — *per le lingue*, he has a turn for languages; *avere* — *allo studio*, to have a natural bent for study **5.** (*stato d'animo*) mood, frame of mind: *lo trovai in una* — (*d'animo*) *poco favorevole*, I found him in a sulky mood.

dispostaménte, *av.* in an orderly way.

dispostézza, *s.f.* **1.** orderly disposition, orderly arrangement **2.** (*compostezza*) composure.

dispósto, *ag.* **1.** ready, willing; (*inclinato*) disposed, inclined: *siete* — *a nominarmi vostro agente?*, are you willing to appoint me your agent?; *essere ben* — *verso qlcu.*, to be favourably disposed towards s.o.; *essere mal* — *verso qlcu.*, to be ill disposed towards s.o.; *sentirsi* — *a fare ql.co.*, to feel inclined to do sthg. (*o fam.* to be in the mood to do sthg.) **2.** *ben* —, (*di robusta costituzione fisica*) strong (*o* vigorous *o* hefty) ‖ *s.m.* (*dir.*) provision: — *di legge*, provisions of the law: *in obbedienza al* — *di legge*, in obedience to the provisions of the law; *secondo il* — *dell'articolo terzo...*, according to the provisions of article No. 3....

dispoticaménte, *av.* despotically.

dispòtico, *ag.* despotic: *governo* —, despotic government; *maniere dispotiche*, despotic manners.

dispotísmo, *s.m.* despotism.

dispregévole, *ag.* (*letter.*) despicable, contemptible.

dispregiàre, *v.t.* (*letter.*) to despise, to contemn; (*trascurare*) to disregard: — *i pericoli*, to disregard (*o* to make light of) dangers.

dispregiativaménte, *av.* disparagingly.

dispregiatívo, *ag.* **1.** depreciative, derogatory, disparaging **2.** (*gram.*) depreciatory: *forma dispregiativa*, depreciatory form ‖ *s.m.* (*gram.*) pejorative.

dispregiatóre, *s.m.*, **dispregiatríce**, *s.f.* contemner.

disprègio, *s.m.* contempt, scorn; (*noncuranza*) disregard: *cadere in* —, to fall into contempt; *tenere in* —, to disregard.

disprezzàbile, *ag.* despicable, contemptible, negligible: *un capitale non* —, a considerable capital.

disprezzànte, *ag.* contemptuous, scornful, disdainful: *con un'aria* —, with an air of contemptuous indifference.

disprezzàre, *v.t.* **1.** to despise, to scorn: — *un consiglio*, to scorn a piece of advice **2.** (*considerare di poco conto*) to look down on (s.o., sthg.): *egli disprezza tutti*, he looks down on everybody **3.** (*sdegnare*) to disregard, to disdain: — *l'adulazione e gli adulatori*, to disdain flattery and flatterers; — *un ordine*, to disregard an order.

disprezzatóre, *s.m.*, **disprezzatríce**, *s.f.* despiser.

disprèzzo, *s.m.* **1.** contempt, scorn: *con* — *del pericolo*, in contempt of danger; *in* — *della legge*, in defiance of the law; *incorrere nel* — *di qlcu.*, to incur s.o.'s contempt; *tenere ql.co. in* —, to hold sthg. in contempt (*o* to think scorn of sthg.) **2.** (*disdegno*) disdain.

dispròsio, *s.m.* (*chim.*) dysprosium.

dísputa, *s.f.* **1.** discussion, debate, dispute: *una* — *calorosa*, a heated debate; *non soggetto a* —, beyond dispute; *vi furono molte dispute sulla religione nell'Inghilterra del diciassettesimo secolo*, there were many religious disputes in England during the seventeenth century **2.** (*lite*) quarrel, controversy: *si accese un'aspra* — *fra i due uomini*, a bitter quarrel arose between the two men.

disputàbile, *ag.* disputable, questionable, open to discussion: *la questione è* —, the question is disputable.

disputabilità, *s.f.* disputableness.

disputànte, *ag.* disputant: *le parti disputanti*, the disputant parties.

disputàre, *v.i.* **1.** to discuss (sthg.), to debate (sthg.), to dispute (on, about sthg.): *disputavano di* *filosofia*, they were discussing philosophy; *disputiamo se avesse dovuto farlo o no*, we are debating whether he ought to have done it or not ǁ *sui gusti non si disputa*, every man to his taste **2.** (*litigare*) to quarrel: *io non disputo volentieri con nessuno*, I never like quarrelling with anybody ǁ *v.t.* to dispute: *disputarono palmo a palmo il terreno al nemico*, they disputed every inch of ground with the enemy; *non — i miei diritti!*, don't dispute my rights! ǁ **disputàrsi**, *v.r. reciproco* to contend for (sthg.), to fight for (sthg.): *si disputarono la supremazia*, they were fighting for supremacy.

disputatóre, *s.m.*, **disputatríce**, *s.f.* disputer.

disputazióne, *s.f.* disputation: *fare una dotta —*, to carry on a learned disputation.

disquisizióne, *s.f.* disquisition.

disradicàre, (*rar.*) per **sradicàre**.

dissacràre, (*rar.*) per **sconsacràre**.

dissalàre, *v.t.* to desalt, to remove salt from (sthg.): *— il baccalà*, to remove salt from stockfish.

dissaldàre, *v.t.* (*mec.*) to unsolder.

dissanguaménto, *s.m.* **1.** bleeding, loss of blood: *morì per —*, he bled to death **2.** *fig.* impoverishment: *la guerra sottopose il paese a un grave —*, the country suffered serious impoverishment as a result of the war.

dissanguàre, *v.t.* **1.** to bleed **2.** *fig.* to bleed, to impoverish, to exhaust: *le tasse ci dissanguano*, taxes bleed us; *— le casse dello Stato*, to draw heavily on the Treasury ǁ **dissanguàrsi**, *v.r.* to become impoverished: *il paese si dissanguò per difendere la sua libertà*, the country gave its life's blood to defend its freedom.

dissanguàto, *ag.* **1.** bloodless, drained of blood: *morire —*, to bleed to death **2.** *fig.* impoverished: *un paese —*, an impoverished country.

dissanguatóre, *s.m. fig.* bloodsucker.

dissapóre, *s.m.* disagreement, variance.

dissecàre, *v.t.* to dissect.

disseccànte, *ag.* drying up; desiccative ǁ *s.m.* (*farm.*) desiccative.

disseccàre, *v.t.* to dry (up), to wither, to parch; (*cibo*) to desiccate: *cibo che dissecca la gola*, food that dries the throat; *erba disseccata dal vento*, grass parched by the wind ǁ **disseccàrsi**, *v.r.* to parch.

disseccativo, *ag.* desiccative.

disselciàre, *v.t.* to unpave: *gli scioperanti disselciarono la piazza*, the strikers unpaved the square.

dissellàre, *v.t.* to unsaddle ǁ *v.i.* (*cadere di sella*) to fall off one's horse, to take a toss.

disselvàre, *V.* **diboscàre**.

disseminàre, *v.t.* to disseminate, to spread abroad, to diffuse: *disseminava false notizie*, he disseminated false news; *— la discordia, il terrore*, to spread (*o* to sow) discord, terror; *— il malcontento*, to sow the seeds of discontent.

disseminàto, *ag.* strewn, covered: *cielo — di stelle*, star-spangled sky; *il sentiero era — di fiori*, the path was strewn with flowers.

disseminatóre, *ag.* disseminating, propagative ǁ *s.m.*, **disseminatríce**, *s.f.* disseminator, spreader.

disseminazióne, *s.f.* **1.** (*bot.*) dissemination, sowing **2.** dissemination, spreading: *— di false dottrine*, dissemination of false doctrines.

dissennàre, *v.t.* to drive (s.o.) mad, to drive (s.o.) crazy: *— qlcu.*, to deprive one of one's senses.

dissennataménte, *av.* **1.** madly; crazily **2.** (*stupidamente*) foolishly **3.** (*avventatamente*) rashly.

dissennatézza, *s.f.* **1.** madness; craziness **2.** (*stupidità*) foolishness, stupidity **3.** (*avventatezza*) rashness; (*azione avventata*) rash action: *pagare la propria —*, to pay for one's rashness.

dissennàto, *ag.* **1.** mad; crazy: *è un'idea dissennata*, it is a crazy idea **2.** (*stupido*) foolish **3.** (*avventato*) rash: *è un uomo —*, he is a very rash person.

dissensióne, *s.f.* dissension, discord, disagreement.

dissènso, *s.m.* dissent, disagreement, difference of opinion: *non vi fu mai tra noi motivo di —*, there was never any reason for disagreement between us.

dissentería, *s.f.* (*patol.*) dysentery.

dissentèrico, *ag.* dysenteric ǁ *s.m.* dysenteric subject.

dissentiménto, *s.m.* (*letter.*) dissent, disagreement.

dissentíre, *v.i.* to dissent, to differ, to disagree (with s.o., sthg.), to have a different opinion: *dissento completamente da ciò che hai affermato*, I thoroughly dissent from what you have stated; *gli storici dissentono su questo punto*, historians are at variance (*o* are not in agreement) on this point.

dissenziènte, *ag.* **1.** dissenting, differing: *siamo dissenzienti*, we do not agree **2.** (*pol.*) dissentient, dissident ǁ *s.m.* **1.** (*relig.*) dissenter; (*in Gran Bretagna*) Nonconformist **2.** (*pol.*) dissentient.

disseppelliménto, *s.m.* **1.** disinterment, exhumation: *al — non era presente la madre del caduto*, the fallen soldier's mother was not present at the exhumation **2.** *fig.* unearthing.

disseppellíre, *v.t.* **1.** to disinter, to exhume **2.** *fig.* to unearth; to revive: *— odi ormai sopiti*, to revive old hatred.

disserràre, *v.t.* to unfasten, to unlock; (*aprire*) to open; *fig.* to disclose ǁ **disserràrsi**, *v.r.* to open: *la porta si disserrò come per forza magica*, the door opened as if by some magic power.

dissertàre, *v.i.* to dissertate (on sthg.); to expatiate (on sthg.), to discourse (about sthg.).

dissertatóre, *s.m.* dissertator, dissertationist.

dissertatòrio, *ag.* dissertative.

dissertatríce, *s.f.* dissertator, dissertationist.

dissertazióne, *s.f.* dissertation, disquisition; (*di laurea*) thesis, dissertation: *fare una — su ql.co.*, to deliver a dissertation upon sthg.

disservízio, *s.m.* disorganization, inefficiency: *— ferroviario*, inefficiency of the railways.

dissestàre, *v.t.* **1.** (*finanziariamente*) to ruin: *spese che dissestano*, crippling expenses **2.** (*mettere in disordine*) to disarrange **3.** (*metter fuori senno*) to derange: *il terribile dolore gli dissestò la ragione*, his terrible grief deranged his mind ǁ **dissestàrsi**, *v.r.* (*finanziariamente*) to ruin oneself, to get into financial difficulties.

dissestàto, *ag.* (*in difficoltà finanziarie*) embarrassed, burdened with debts, in financial difficulties; (*rovinato*) ruined: *era ricco, ora è —*, he was rich, now he is ruined.

dissèsto, *s.m.* **1.** trouble, difficulty: *— finanziario*, financial difficulty (*o* trouble) **2.** (*fallimento*) failure, bankruptcy.

dissetànte, *ag.* refreshing: *bibita —*, refreshing drink (*o fam.* quencher).

dissetàre, *v.t.* to quench the thirst of (s.o.), to slake the thirst of (s.o.) ǁ **dissetàrsi**, *v.r.* to quench one's thirst, to slake one's thirst; (*bere*) to drink; (*di animali*) to water: *le greggi si dissetavano al fiume*, the flocks were watering at the river.

dissettóre, *s.m.* dissector.

dissezióne, *s.f.* dissection.

dissidènte, *ag.* **1.** dissident, dissenting, dissentient: *il partito —*, the dissident (*o* dissenting *o* dissentient) party **2.** (*relig.*) dissenting, dissident; (*in Gran Bretagna*) nonconformist (*attributivo*): *le chiese dissidenti*, Nonconformist Churches; *un ministro —*, a dissenting minister ǁ *s.c.* **1.** dissident, dissentient: *i dissidenti del partito liberale*, the dissidents (*o* dissentients) of the liberal party **2.** (*relig.*) dissenter; (*in Gran Bretagna*) Nonconformist.

dissidènza, *s.f.* (*rar.*) dissidence.

dissídio, *s.m.* dissension, disagreement, discord, variance; (*litigio*) quarrel, dispute: *— di opinioni*, disagreement (*o* difference of opinion); *— insanabile*, incurable dissension; *il — tra Chiesa e Stato*, the split between Church and State; *abbiamo avuto un piccolo — con lui*, we had a slight disagreement with him; *comporre un —*, to compose (*o* to settle *o* to make up) a quarrel (o a dispute); *essere in* — *con qlcu.*, to be at variance with s.o.

dissigillàre, *v.t.* to unseal: — *una lettera*, to unseal (o to open) a letter; — *un pacco*, to unseal (o to break the seal of) a parcel.

dissíllabo, *ag.* di(s)syllabic ‖ *s.m.* di(s)syllable.

dissimigliànza, *s.f.* dissimilarity, unlikeness, difference.

dissimilàre, *ag.* dissimilar; heterogeneous.

dissimilarità, *s.f.* dissimilarity.

dissimilazióne, *s.f.* (*biol. fonet.*) dissimilation.

dissímile, *ag.* unlike (s.o., sthg.), dissimilar (to s.o., from sthg.), different (from, to s.o., sthg.): *i miei gusti sono affatto dissimili dai tuoi*, my tastes are quite unlike yours (o quite different from yours o quite dissimilar from yours).

dissimilitúdine, *s.f.* (*rar.*) unlikeness, dissimilitude.

dissimilménte, *av.* dissimilarly.

dissimmetría, *s.f.* dissymetry.

dissimulàbile, *ag.* that can be dissembled, that can be concealed.

dissimulàre, *v.t.* to dissimulate, to dissemble, to conceal, to disguise: *ella cercava di* — *la propria emozione*, she tried to conceal (o to dissimulate) her emotion; *non sa* — *la propria ira*, he cannot dissemble his anger; *non so* —, I cannot dissemble; *sa la cosa, ma dissimula*, he knows it, but he dissembles ‖ **dissimulàrsi**, *v.r.* 1. to conceal from oneself: *non mi dissimulo le difficoltà dell'impresa*, I do not conceal from myself the difficulties of the enterprise; *non si dissimulava che...*, he fully realized that...; — *la verità*, to shut one's eyes to the truth 2. (*celarsi*) to hide (oneself): *si dissimulò dietro un'apparente indifferenza*, he hid (himself) behind apparent indifference.

dissimulataménte, *av.* dissemblingly.

dissimulatóre, *ag.* dissimulating ‖ *s.m.*, **dissimulatríce**, *s.f.* dissimulator, dissembler.

dissimulazióne, *s.f.* dissimulation, dissembling.

dissipàbile, *ag.* dissipable.

dissipaménto, *s.m.* dissipation.

dissipàre, *v.t.* 1. (*disperdere*) to dissipate, to dispel: — *nubi, foschia, un dubbio, dei timori*, to dispel (o to dissipate) clouds, mist, a doubt, fears 2. (*scialacquare*) to dissipate, to waste, to squander: — *tutto il proprio denaro*, to fritter away (o to squander) all one's money ‖ **dissipàrsi**, *v.r.* to dissipate; (*sparire*) to disappear, to vanish: *le nubi si dissipano*, the clouds dissipate (o the clouds are breaking).

dissipataménte, *av.* dissolutely, in a dissipated manner.

dissipatézza, (*rar.*) per dissipazióne 1. 2.

dissipàto, *ag.* dissipated, dissolute: *condurre una vita dissipata*, to lead a dissipated (o gay) life.

dissipatóre, *s.m.*, **dissipatríce**, *s.f.* waster, squanderer, spendthrift.

dissipazióne, *s.f.* 1. dissipation, wasting, squandering: — *di denaro*, wasting of money 2. (*vita dissoluta*) dissipation, dissolute living 3. (*fis.*) dissipation: — *anodica*, anode (o plate) dissipation.

dissociàbile, *ag.* dissociable; separable.

dissociàre, *v.t.* to dissociate, to separate: *è difficile* — *la morale dalla religione*, it is difficult to dissociate morals from religion; — *gli animi*, to sow discord; — *gli elementi di un composto*, (*chim.*) to dissociate the elements of a compound; — *le forze*, to divide forces.

dissociatívo, *ag.* dissociative, separative: *processo* —, dissociative process.

dissociazióne, *s.f.* 1. separation, dissociation 2. (*scient.*) dissociation: — *elettrolitica*, (*chim.*) electrolytic dissociation; — *psichica*, (*patol.*) psychic dissociation; — *termica*, (*chim.*) thermal dissociation.

dissodaménto, *s.m.* (*agr.*) tillage, breaking up.

dissodàre, *v.t.* (*agr.*) to break up; to till: — *un campo per la semina*, to till a field for sowing ‖

— *il campo, il terreno* (*cominciare a trattare un soggetto di studio*) to prepare the ground.

dissodatríce, *s.f.* (*agr.*) breaking plough.

dissolúbile, *ag.* dissoluble, dissolvable: *legame* —, dissoluble bond.

dissolubilità, *s.f.* dissolubility.

dissolutaménte, *av.* dissolutely, licentiously, loosely, profligately.

dissolutézza, *s.f.* dissoluteness, licentiousness, looseness, profligacy, debauchery: — *di costumi*, looseness of morals; *lo evitano tutti per la sua* —, everybody avoids him because of his dissoluteness (o debauchery).

dissolutívo, *ag.* (*rar.*) dissolving.

dissolúto, *ag.* dissolute, licentious, loose, profligate, debauched: *una condotta dissoluta*, a licentious (o loose o dissolute) conduct; *una persona dissoluta*, a dissolute person; *condurre una vita dissoluta*, to lead a loose life.

dissolutóre, *ag.* (*rar.*) dissolving ‖ *s.m.* 1. dissolver, dissolvent 2. (*chim.*) dissolvent ‖ **dissolutríce**, *s.f.* dissolver, dissolvent.

dissoluzióne, *s.f.* 1. disintegration, decomposition; dissolution: *la* — *dei corpi*, the decomposition of bodies; *la* — *della carne*, the dissolution of the flesh; — *di un contratto*, dissolution of a partnership; *una famiglia in* —, a family in dissolution 2. (*dissolutezza*) dissoluteness, licentiousness, profligacy.

dissolvènte, *ag.s.m.* (*chim.*) dissolvent.

dissolvènza, *s.f.* (*cine.*) dissolving view, dissolve, fading: — *in apertura*, dissolve-in (o fade-in); — *in chiusura*, dissolve-out (o fade-out); — *incrociata*, lap dissolve; — *sonora*, sound fading.

dissòlvere, *v.t.* 1. to dissolve, to separate, to decompose: — *un matrimonio*, to dissolve a marriage 2. (*disperdere*) to disperse, to dispel: — *un dubbio*, to dispel a doubt 3. (*sciogliere*) to dissolve, to melt: *l'acqua dissolve lo zucchero*, water melts sugar ‖ **dissòlversi**, *v.r.* 1. to dissolve 2. (*svanire*) to fade out, to vanish, to dissolve 3. (*sciogliersi*) to dissolve, to melt: — *nell'acqua*, to dissolve (o to melt) in water.

dissolviménto, *s.m.* dissolution.

dissomigliànte, *ag.* dissimilar (to s.o., sthg.), unlike (s.o., sthg.), different.

dissomigliànza, *s.f.* dissimilarity, unlikeness, difference.

dissomigliàre, *v.i.* to be unlike (s.o., sthg.), to differ ‖ **dissomigliàrsi**, *v.r. reciproco* to be unlike each other (one another), to differ from each other (one another): *quei due fratelli si dissomigliano davvero!*, those two brothers are really unlike each other!.

dissonànte, *ag.* 1. (*mus.*) dissonant, discordant: *accordo* —, dissonant tune 2. (*discordante*) different.

dissonànza, *s.f.* 1. (*mus.*) dissonance, discord 2. (*discordanza*) difference: — *d'idee*, difference of ideas; — *di sentimenti*, difference of feelings.

dissonàre, *v.i.* 1. (*mus.*) to be out of tune, to sound discordantly, to jar 2. (*discordare*) to discord (with, from s.o., sthg.), to disagree (with s.o., sthg.).

dissonnàre, *v.t.*, **dissonnàrsi**, *v.r.* (*rar.*) to awake(n), to wake up.

díssono, *ag.* (*mus.*) dissonant, discordant, jarring.

dissotterraménto, *s.m.* (*rar.*) disinterment, exhumation.

dissotterràre, *v.t.* 1 to disinter, to exhume ‖ — *l'ascia di guerra*, to dig up the hatchet 2. *fig.* to unearth, to excavate.

dissuadènte, *ag.* dissuasive.

dissuadére, *v.t.* to dissuade, to deter: *mi dissuasero dall'acquistare quella merce*, they dissuaded me from (o advised me against) buying those goods; *nulla lo dissuaderà dal tentare ancora*, nothing will deter him from trying again.

dissuasióne, *s.f.* dissuasion, determent.

dissuasívo, *ag.* dissuasive.

dissuàso, *ag.* dissuaded, deterred.

dissuèto, *ag.* (*letter.*) unaccustomed, disaccustomed, disused.

dissuetúdine, *s.f.* desuetude, disuse.

dissuggellàre, *v.t.* to unseal: — *una lettera,* to unseal a letter.

distaccaménto, *s.m.* **1.** detaching, cutting off, separation **2.** (*mil.*) detachment, draft.

distaccàre, *v.t.* **1.** to detach, to separate, to disjoin to cut off: — *la frizione,* (*aut.*) to disengage the clutch (*o* to disconnect the clutch *o* to declutch) **2.** (*alienare*) to detach, to alienate: — *qlcu. dai suoi amici,* to detach (*o* to alienate) s.o. from his friends **3.** (*trasferire altrove*) to detach, to detail: *alcuni impiegati furono distaccati in un altro ufficio,* some employees were moved to another office; *la terza compagnia fu distaccata per una missione speciale,* (*mil.*) the 3rd company was detached (*o* detailed) for a special mission **4.** (*pitt.*) to bring out: — *una figura in un quadro,* to make a figure stand out (*o* to bring out a figure) in a picture ‖ **distaccàrsi,** *v.r.* to come off, to break off: *un ramo si è distaccato dall'albero,* a branch has broken off from the tree; — *da un partito,* to break away from a party.

distaccàto, *ag.* **1.** detached, separated, cut off **2.** *fig.* (*indifferente*) detached, indifferent, unconcerned: *sorriso* —, detached smile (*o* smile of unconcern).

distàcco, *s.m.* **1.** detaching, separation; disjunction: — *della frizione,* (*aut.*) disengagement of the clutch; — *della gelatina,* (*cine. foto.*) frilling; — *della retina,* (*patol.*) detachment of retina; — *di un aeroplano dal suolo,* take-off **2.** (*partenza*) parting, leave-taking: *l'amarezza del* —, the bitterness of parting **3.** (*indifferenza*) detachment, indifference, unconcern: — *dai beni terreni,* unwordliness; *mi guardò con* —, he looked at me with indifference; *giudicare con* —, to judge with detachment.

distàle, *ag.* (*anat.*) distal.

distànte, *ag.* **1.** distant, remote, far off, far away: *paesi distanti,* far off (*o* remote) countries; *suono* —, distant (*o* remote) sound ‖ — *da,* far from (*o* a long way from): *è molto* — *da qui la stazione?,* is the station very far from (*o* a long way from) here?; *no, è* — *da qui solo mezzo miglio,* no, it is only half a mile (distant) from here; *la mia casa è poco* — *dalla scuola,* my house is not far from the school **2.** *fig.* distant; (*differente*) different: *una persona* —, a distant (*o* stand-offish) person; *uno sguardo* —, a distant look; *essere distanti di gusti, di opinioni,* to differ in tastes, in opinions: *è molto* — *di opinioni da suo fratello,* he has very different opinions from his brother (*o* his opinions differ widely from his brother's) ‖ *av.* far, far off, far away: *abitiamo molto* —, we live very far off (*o* far away *o* he lives a long way off); *andare* —, to go far; *non riesco a vedere così* —, I cannot see as far as that.

distànza, *s.f.* **1.** distance: — *angolare,* (*astr.*) elongation; — *d'arresto,* (*aer.*) pull-up distance; — *di visibilità,* (*mar. aer.*) range of visibility; — *focale,* (*ott.*) focal length; — *frontale,* (*ott.*) working distance; — *per il traverso,* (*mar.*) distance on beam; — *principale,* (*foto.*) principal distance; — *tra due centri,* (*mec.*) centre distance; — *visiva,* (*ott.*) optical range; — *zenitale,* (*aer. astr.*) zenith distance; *alla* — *di circa tre miglia,* at a distance of about three miles (*o* at about three miles' distance *o* three miles away); *a* — *di vent'anni,* at a distance of twenty years ‖ *a, in* —, at a distance, in the distance: *essere a* — *di tiro,* (*mil.*) to be within striking distance (of the enemy); *seguire qlcu. a* —, to follow s.o. at a distance; *vedere ql.co. a, in* —, to see sthg. at a distance **2.** *fig.* distance; (*disuguaglianza*) difference: *tra noi due c'è molta* —, there is a great difference between you and me; *mantenere le distanze,* to keep one's distance; *stare a rispettosa* — *da qlcu.,* to give a wide berth to s.o. (*o* to keep at a safe distance from s.o.); *tenere qlcu. a* —, to keep s.o. at a distance (*o* to avoid familiarity with

s.o.) **3.** (*spor.*) distance: *la corsa è sulla* — *di mille miglia,* the race is over a distance of one thousand miles.

distanziaménto, *s.m.* distancing; (*aer.*) separation: *il* — *delle truppe,* (*mil.*) the distancing of troops; — *laterale,* (*aer.*) lateral separation; — *longitudinale,* (*aer.*) longitudinal separation; — *verticale,* (*aer.*) vertical separation.

distanziàre, *v.t.* **1.** to distance, to space (out): *distanzia un poco le bottiglie,* space out the bottles; *la scienza distanzia chi la possiede da chi non la possiede,* knowledge separates those who possess it from those who do not possess it; *ricorda di ben* — *le parole e le righe,* remember to space the words and lines properly **2.** (*lasciar indietro*) to distance, to outdistance, to leave behind: *il corridore fu distanziato al terzo giro,* the runner was left behind (*o* outdistanced) in the third lap.

distanziàto, *ag.* **1.** (*intervallato*) spaced: *scrivere a righe distanziate,* to space (out) the lines **2.** (*superato*) outdistanced; (*di cavallo*) disqualified.

distanziatóre, *s.m.* (*mec.*) spacer.

distanziòmetro, *s.m.* (*topografia*) diastimeter.

distàre, *v.i.* **1.** to be distant, to be far: *la nostra casa dista circa venti miglia da Londra, e noi ne distiamo circa due miglia,* our house is about twenty miles from London, and we are about two miles from it; *il primo paese dista cinque chilometri,* the nearest village is five kilometres away; *non dista molto da qui,* it is not very far from here; *quanto dista?,* how far is it? **2.** (*discordare*) to disagree.

distemperàre, *v.t.* (*rar.*) to dilute; to dissolve.

distèndere, *v.t.* **1.** (*allungare*) to stretch, to stretch out, to extend; (*allargare, stendere*) to spread: — *le ali, to spread its wings;* — *le braccia,* to stretch (out) (*o* to reach out) one's arms; — *il bucato,* to hang out the washing; — *la pasta,* (*cuc.*) to roll out dough (*o* pastry); — *una pelle,* (*tirarla*) to stretch a skin; — *i rami,* to spread its branches; — *le vele,* to stretch (*o* to extend) the sails ‖ — *la mano,* (*per soccorrere*) to lend a (helping) hand **2.** (*spalmare*) to spread: — *del burro su una fetta di pane,* to spread some butter on a slice of bread **3.** (*porre, stendere*) to lay: *mi distesero sul letto,* they laid me on the bed; — *qlcu. con un pugno,* to knock s.o. down (*o* to stretch s.o. on the ground); (*fam.*) to lay s.o. out: — *la tovaglia sul tavolo,* to lay (*o* to spread) the cloth on the table **4.** (*rilassare*) to relax: — *i muscoli, i tratti del volto,* to relax one's muscles, one's features; — *i nervi,* to relax **5.** (*mettere per iscritto*) to draw up: — *un documento,* to draw up a document ‖ **distèndersi,** *v.r.* **1.** (*estendersi*) to spread, to stretch; (*allargarsi*) to spread out: *la vallata si distende verso sud,* the valley stretches southward **2.** (*sdraiarsi*) to lie down: *mi distesi sulla spiaggia,* I lay down on the beach **3.** (*rilassarsi*) to relax **4.** (*dilungarsi*) to dwell, to enlarge (upon a subject).

distendíbile, *ag.* extensible, extending.

distendiménto, *s.m.* **1.** (*allungamento*) stretching, extending; (*allargamento*) spreading **2.** (*collocamento*) laying, laying down **3.** (*rilassamento*) relaxation, relaxing.

distensióne, *s.f.* **1.** (*distendimento*) stretching, extension; (*di un muscolo*) straining **2.** (*rilassamento*) relaxation: *un periodo di* —, a period of rest.

distensívo, *ag.* relaxing: *una pausa distensiva,* a relaxing pause.

distésa, *s.f.* **1.** expanse; extent: *vasta* — *di mare,* large expanse of sea; *vasta* — *di terreno,* vast extent of ground **2.** (*aer.*) wing (span) **3.** *a* —, continuously, without interruption: *le campane suonano a* —, the bells are ringing a full peal (*o* the bells are in full peal); *gridava a* —, she kept crying out.

distesaménte, *av.* diffusely; extensively; (*a lungo*) at lenght; (*nei minimi particolari*) in detail.

distéso, *ag.* **1.** *(teso)* extended: *braccia distese,* extended arms; *vela distesa,* stretched *(o* extended) sail **2.** *(giacente)* lying: *era — sul sofà,* he was lying on the sofa; *era lungo — sul letto,* he was stretched at full length on the bed ‖ *cadere lungo —,* to fall flat **3.** *(esteso, spazioso)* extensive, spacious; *(largo)* widespread ‖ *per —,* diffusely. *(o* extensively); *(a lungo)* at length; *(nei minimi particolari)* in detail.

dístico, *s.m. (poes.)* couplet, distich: *— alessandrino,* Alexandrine couplet; *— rimato,* rhymed couplet.

distillàbile, *ag.* distillable.

distillaménto, *s.m.* distilling, distillation.

distillàre, *v.t.* **1.** *(chim.)* to distil; to extract the essence of (sthg.): *— l'acqua, il vino,* to distil water, wine ‖ *— sentenze da un libro,* to distil maxims from a book **2.** *(stillare)* to let fall in drops, to trickle **3.** *fig. (infondere)* to instil: *— veleno nell'animo di qlcu.,* to instil poison into s.o.'s mind ‖ *v.i.* to distil, to trickle, to fall in drops: *la resina distillava dalla corteccia,* resin was trickling down the bark.

distillàto, *ag. (chim.)* distilled: *acqua distillata,* distilled water; *non —,* undistilled ‖ *s.m. (chim.)* distillate.

distillatóio, *s.m. (chim.)* still.

distillatóre, *ag. (chim.)* distilling ‖ *s.m. (chim.)* distiller; still.

distillazióne, *s.f. (chim.)* distillation: *— a secco,* dry distillation; *— continua,* continuous distillation; *— discontinua,* batch distillation; *— in corrente di vapore,* steam distillation; *— nel vuoto,* vacuum distillation; *prodotto di —,* distillate.

distillería, *s.f.* distillery.

dístilo, *ag.* **1.** *(arch.)* distyle **2.** *(bot.)* distylous.

distínguere, *v.t.* **1.** to distinguish, to tell; to discriminate, to differentiate: *al telefono non distinguo la tua voce da quella di tua sorella,* on the telephone I can't tell your voice from your sister's; *non li so —,* I can't tell which is which; *non so distinguerlo da suo fratello, sono così simili!,* I can't tell him from his brother, they are so much alike!; *stai facendo confusione, distinguiamo!,* you are mixing up things, let's make a distinction!; *— tra bene e male,* to distinguish between good and evil; *— il vero dal falso,* to discriminate truth from falsehood **2.** *(scorgere)* to distinguish, to discern, to perceive, to see clearly: *in quella stanza senza luce non riuscivo a — i suoi lineamenti,* in that dark room I couldn't make out his features; *tua sorella era troppo lontana per poter — quello che succedeva,* your sister was too far away to be able to see clearly what was going on **3.** *(caratterizzare)* to distinguish, to mark, to characterize: *che cosa distingue l'uomo dagli animali?,* what distinguishes man from animals?; *una coda molto lunga distingue questa specie,* a very long tail characterizes this species; *grandi progressi nelle scienze applicate distinsero il corso del diciannovesimo secolo,* great advances in applied science marked the course of the nineteenth century **4.** *(contrassegnare)* to mark: *distingue le proprie pecore con segni particolari,* he marks his own sheep in a special way **5.** *(separare, dividere)* to divide, to separate: *distinguiamo le opere di questo pittore in tre periodi,* let's divide the works of this painter into three periods **6.** *(segnalare)* to distinguish, to signalize, to mark: *il suo coraggio lo distinse nell'ultima guerra,* his courage distinguished him in the last war ‖ **distínguersi,** *v.r.* to distinguish oneself (by sthg.); to make oneself conspicuous (by sthg.): *si distingue per la sua diligenza,* he distinguishes himself by his diligence; *si distingue perchè porta sempre dei cappelli eccentrici,* she makes herself conspicuous by always wearing odd hats.

distinguíbile, *ag.* **1.** distinguishable **2.** *(visibile)* visible; *(chiaro)* clear: *— ad occhio nudo,* visible to the naked eye.

distinguibilménte, *av.* **1.** distinguishably **2.** *(visibilmente)* visibly; *(chiaramente)* clearly, distinctly.

distínta, *s.f. (comm.)* list, note, bill; schedule: *— base,* bill of materials; *— dei pesi,* weight note; *— dei prezzi,* price list; *— della merce,* packing list; *— di sconto,* discount note; *— di versamento,* paying-in slip.

distintaménte, *av.* **1.** distinctly, clearly: *vedere —,* to see distinctly **2.** *(con distinzione)* respectfully: *vi salutiamo —, (nella chiusa di una lettera)* we are Yours faithfully *(o* Yours truly) .

distintívo, *ag.* distinctive: *segno —,* distinctive mark ‖ *s.m.* badge: *— militare,* badge of rank; *— sportivo,* sporting badge.

distínto, *ag.* **1.** *(separato, diverso)* distinct: *sono due cose distinte,* they are two distinct things; *due concetti da tenere ben distinti l'uno dall'altro,* two ideas to be kept quite distinct one from the other **2.** *(chiaro)* distinct, clear: *memoria distinta,* distinct memory; *nota distinta,* clear note; *una pronuncia distinta,* a distinct pronunciation **3.** *(raffinato, ragguardevole)* distinguished, refined: *un — signore,* a distinguished gentleman; *gente distinta,* people of distinction; *modi distinti,* distinguished *(o* refined) manners; *essi appartengono a una famiglia molto distinta,* they are of a very good family; *avere un'aria distinta,* to look distinguished ‖ *distinti saluti,* best regards; *(nella chiusa di una lettera)* Yours faithfully *(o* Yours truly).

distinzióne, *s.f.* **1.** distinction: *una — accurata,* a careful distinction; *senza —,* indiscriminately; *senza — di classe, di età,* without distinction of class, of age; *fare una — tra due cose,* to make *(o* to draw) a distinction between two things **2.** *(riguardo, preferenza)* regard, consideration: *atto di —,* act of consideration; *non meritava questa —,* he did not deserve such consideration **3.** *(onorificenza)* distinction, honour: *la massima —,* the highest distinction; *conferire una — a qlcu.,* to confer a distinction on s.o. **4.** *(raffinatezza)* distinction, refinement: *la mancanza di — nel vestire,* the want of distinction in one's dress; *possedere un'innata — di modi,* to possess an innate distinction of manners.

distògliere, *v.t.* **1.** *(dissuadere)* to dissuade; to deter: *l'insuccesso non lo distolse da un nuovo tentativo,* failure didn't deter him from trying again; *vorrei proprio distoglierti dall'idea di lasciare il tuo lavoro,* I would strongly dissuade you from leaving your job **2.** *(distrarre)* to divert; to distract: *come potrei — la sua attenzione da te?,* how could I divert his attention from you?; *non riesco a lavorare se la mia attenzione è distolta da continue interruzioni,* I can't work if my attention is being distracted by constant interruptions ‖ **distògliersi,** *v.r.* to be diverted, to be distracted; *(allontanarsi)* to get away: *la mia attenzione non poteva — da quello spettacolo,* my attention couldn't be diverted from that sight; *non riesco a distogliermi da questo libro,* I can't get away from this book.

distòlto, *ag.* diverted, distracted.

distòma, *s.m. (zool.)* distomum *(pl.* distoma).

distomíasi, *s.f. (patol.)* distomiasis.

distòrcere, *v.t. (rar.)* to distort; to twist: *— un braccio a qlcu.,* to twist s.o.'s arm; *— il significato delle parole di qlcu.,* to distort the meaning of s.o.'s words; *— la verità,* to twist the truth.

distorciménto, *s.m.* distortion.

distornàre, *v.t.* to divert, to deviate.

distòrre, *contr.* di **distògliere.**

distorsióne, *s.f.* **1.** distorsion **2.** *(di tendine, muscolo)* sprain, strain, distortion **3.** *(ott. tel. tv.)* distortion: *— del quadro, (tv.)* frame distortion; *— di apertura, (tv.)* aperture distortion; *— trapezoidale, (tv.)* keystoning.

distòrto, *ag.* distorted.

distràrre, *v.t.* **1.** *(distogliere)* to divert, to distract, to draw away; to take off: *la minima cosa lo distrae,* the slightest thing distracts his attention; *quella vacanza l'aveva distratto dalle sue preoccupazioni,* that holiday had taken his mind off his worries; *— l'attenzione di qlcu. da ql.co.,* to take s.o.'s attention *(o* mind) off sthg.;

— *qlcu. dal lavoro*, to take s.o.'s mind off his work **2.** (*divertire*) to entertain, to amuse: *cerca di — i bambini con qualche giuoco*, try to amuse the children with games; *la padrona di casa distraeva i suoi ospiti con storielle divertenti*, the hostess was entertaining her guests with amusing tales **3.** (*sottrarre e destinare a uso indebito*) to misappropriate: *fu riconosciuto colpevole di aver distratto un'ingente somma dalla cassa della ditta*, he was found guilty of misappropriating a large sum from the funds of his firm **4.** (*tendine, muscolo*) to strain, to sprain ‖ **distràrsi**, *v.r.* **1.** to divert one's mind, to divert one's attention: *si distrae facilmente*, his mind wanders easily (*o* his attention is easily distracted) **2.** (*divertirsi*) to amuse oneself: *lavori troppo, hai bisogno di distrarti!*, you are working too much, you want some relaxation!.

distrattaménte, *av.* **1.** absent-mindedly: *ci guardava —*, he was looking at us absent-mindedly **2.** (*inavvertitamente*) inadvertently, unintentionally: *lasciò cadere — il libro*, he dropped the book unintentionally.

distràtto, *ag.* **1.** absent-minded: *è sempre così — che non sente quando lo chiami*, he is always so absent-minded that he can't hear when you call him **2.** (*disattento*) inattentive: *uno sguardo —*, a vacant look; *è spesso — durante le lezioni*, he is often inattentive during classes.

distrazióne, *s.f.* **1.** (*l'essere distratto*) absent-mindedness: *a causa della mia — persi il cappello nuovo*, owing to my absent-mindedness I lost my new hat **2.** (*disattenzione*) inattention, lack of attention, carelessness: *errore di —*, careless mistake (*o* slip); *scusate la mia —!*, excuse my lack of attention!; *avere dei momenti di —*, to have fits of inattention ‖ *per —*, inadvertently (*o* unthinkingly *o* heedlessly) **3.** (*divertimento*) recreation, amusement, diversion, distraction, relaxation: *le distrazioni di una grande città*, the distractions of a big town; *il golf è per lui una sana —*, he finds a wholesome distraction in golf; *ho bisogno di un po' di —*, I need some recreation (*o* amusement); *cercar — nei libri*, to seek relaxation in books **4.** (*sottrazione e destinazione di denaro a uso indebito*) misappropriation **5.** (*di nervo, muscolo*) strain, sprain, distorsion.

distrétta, *s.f.* (*letter.*) **1.** urgent need, necessity **2.** (*angustia*) distress **3.** (*pericolo, specie in mare*) danger.

distrétto, *ag.* **1.** (*trattenuto*) detained **2.** (*angustiato*) distressed ‖ *s.m.* **1.** district: *— postale*, postal district **2.** (*mil.*) recruiting centre, recruiting office: *egli fu chiamato a rapporto al proprio —*, he had to report to his local recruiting office (*o* centre).

distrettuàle, *ag.* district (*attributivo*): *giudice —*, district judge; *tribunale —*, District Court.

distribuíbile, *ag.* distributable.

distribuíre, *v.t.* **1.** to distribute, to deal out, to give out; (*assegnare*) to assign, to allot; to award: *distribuì tutto il suo denaro ai poveri*, he gave (*o* he distributed) all his money to the poor; *— avvisi*, to give out hand-bills; *— le carte*, (*al giuoco*) to deal the cards; *— colpi a destra e sinistra*, to deal blows right and left (anche *fig.*); *— doni*, to deal out gifts; *— l'elemosina*, to distribute (*o* to deal out) alms; *— onorificenze*, to award (*o* to assign) honours; *— ordini*, to distribute orders; *— le paghe*, to hand out wages; *— le parti di una commedia*, (*teat.*) to cast the parts in a play (*o* to cast a play); *— la posta*, to deliver the mail; *— premi*, to distribute prizes; *— le provviste*, to issue provisions **2.** (*disporre*) to distribute, to put, to place, to arrange: *distribuisci bene la vernice sulla parete*, distribute the paint carefully over the wall; *soldati furono distribuiti lungo la strada*, soldiers were stationed all along the road ‖ **distribuírsi**, *v.r.* to place oneself; (*schierarsi*) to line: *la guardia a cavallo si distribuì lungo il percorso del corteo reale*, the horse-guards lined (*o* placed themselves) along the route of the royal procession.

distributivaménte, *av.* distributively.

distributívo, *ag.* distributive: *giustizia distributiva*, (*dir.*) distributive justice; *numerali distributivi*, (*mat.*) distributive numerals; *pronomi, aggettivi distributivi*, (*gram.*) distributive pronouns, adjectives.

distributóre, *ag.* distributing ‖ *s.m.* **1.** distributor, dispenser; (*chi concede, elargisce*) bestower **2.** (*mec.*) distributor: *— automatico*, slot-machine (*o* automatic machine); *— d'aria da parete*, (*aut.*) wall-type air pump; *— d'accensione*, (*aut.*) ignition distributor; *— di benzina*, (*aut.*) petrol pump (*o amer.* gasoline pump).

distribuzióne, *s.f.* **1.** distribution; allotment, assignment; delivery: *— a cassetto*, (*mec.*) slide valve gear; *— della posta*, delivery of mail; *— delle parti in una commedia*, (*teat.*) cast of a play; *— delle razioni*, issue of rations; *— dei servizi*, allotment of duties; *— delle pellicole cinematografiche* (*agli esercenti*), distribution of films; *— di energia elettrica*, system; *— di locomotiva a vapore*, (*mec.*) valve gear; *— di un motore*, (*mec.*) timing system; *albero della —*, (*mec.*) camshaft; *cassetto della —*, (*mec.*) slide valve; *catena della —*, (*mec.*) timing chain **2.** (*disposizione*) distribution, arrangement, lay-out: *— delle stanze di un appartamento*, distribution of the rooms in a flat.

districàbile, *ag.* extricable.

districaménto, *s.m.* disentanglement, extrication.

districàre, **distrigàre**, *v.t.* to disentangle, to extricate: *— un nodo*, to untie a knot; *— qlcu. da ql.co.*, to disentangle (*o* to extricate) s.o. from sthg.; *— una situazione difficile*, to disentangle a difficult situation ‖ **districàrsi**, **distrigàrsi**, *v.r.* to disentangle oneself; to extricate oneself: *si districò da un pericolo*, he extricated himself from a danger.

districhíasi, *s.f.* (*patol.*) districhiasis.

distríngere, *v.t.* (*rar.*) to squeeze, to press.

distrofía, *s.f.* (*patol.*) dystrophia, dystrophy.

distròfo, *ag.* (*patol.*) dystrophic.

distrúggere, *v.t.* **1.** to destroy: *l'esercito del re fu completamente distrutto*, the king's army was entirely destroyed; *il nemico distrusse la città*, the enemy destroyed the town; *la pioggia aveva distrutto tutto*, the rain had destroyed everything; *tutte le sue speranze furono distrutte*, all his hopes were destroyed; *il vino l'ha distrutto*, wine has been his ruin **2.** (*consumare, struggere*) to consume: *fu distrutto dal dolore*, he was consumed by grief **3.** (*liquefare*) to melt: *— la cera*, to melt wax ‖ **distrúggersi**, *v.r.* **1.** (*consumarsi*) to pine (away), to waste away: *ella si distrusse per la morte del marito*, she pined away after the death of her husband **2.** (*liquefarsi*) to melt.

distruggíbile, *ag.* destroyable, destructible.

distruggiménto, *s.m.* (*rar.*) destruction.

distruggitóre, *ag.* destroying, destructive ‖ *s.m.*, **distruggitríce**, *s.f.* destroyer.

distruttíbile, *ag.* destroyable, destructible.

distruttibilità, *s.f.* destructibility.

distruttivaménte, *av.* destructively.

distruttività, *s.f.* destructiveness, destructivity.

distruttívo, *ag.* destroying, destructive: *quel proiettile ha un elevato potere —*, that projectile has a high destructive power.

distrútto, *ag.* **1.** destroyed: *una città distrutta*, a destroyed town **2.** (*consumato*) consumed **3.** (*liquefatto, fuso*) melted.

distruttóre, *ag.* destroying, destructive ‖ *s.m.*, **distruttríce**, *s.f.* destroyer, destructor.

distruzióne, *s.f.* destruction; (*il distruggere*) destroying: *la — di Troia*, the destruction of Troy; *istinto di —*, destructive instinct ‖ *mettere a —*, to put to fire and sword (*o* to lay waste).

disturbàre, *v.t.* **1.** to disturb; (*infastidire*) to trouble, to give trouble to (s.o.); (*seccare*) to bother, to annoy, to vex: *non disturbarmi!*, don't bother me!; *non mi disturbate affatto*, no trouble at all; *non volevo disturbarti* *mentre dormivi*, I did not wish to disturb you while you were sleeping; *quella musica disturbava la sua lettura*, that music interfered with his reading; *scusatemi se vi disturbo*, excuse my disturbing you; *se ciò non vi disturba*, if it is not troubling you (*o if it is quite convenient to you o if I'm not intruding upon you*); *sono spiacente di disturbarvi tanto*, I am sorry to trouble you so (*o to give you so much trouble*); *ti disturbo qui?*, am I in your way? 2. (*sconvolgere*) to upset: *ciò disturba i miei piani*, it upsets (*o interferes with*) my plans 3. (*indisporre*) to upset: *qualcosa mi ha disturbato lo stomaco*, something has upset my digestion 4. (*trasmissioni radio*) to jam: *— la Voce dell'America*, to jam the Voice of America ‖ **disturbàrsi**, *v.r.* to trouble (oneself), to take the trouble (of doing *o* to do): *non disturbarti a scrivere*, don't trouble to write; *non disturbatevi!*, don't trouble! (*o* don't move!); *non disturbatevi a riaccompagnarmi a casa*, don't trouble to take me back home.

disturbàto, *ag.* 1. disturbed 2. (*sconvolto*) upset 3. (*indisposto*) unwell, upset: *questa mattina sono piuttosto —*, this morning I feel rather upset 4. (*rad.*) jammed.

disturbatóre, *ag.* disturbing, troubling ‖ *s.m.*, **disturbatríce**, *s.f.* disturber: *— della quiete pubblica*, disturber of the peace.

distúrbo, *s.m.* 1. trouble, inconvenience; (*seccatura*) annoyance; (*della quiete pubblica*) disturbance: *nessun —*, no trouble at all; *senza il minimo —*, without the slightest inconvenience; *lo so che ti do molto —*, I know I am putting you to a lot of inconvenience; *scusi il —*, sorry for the trouble; *siamo spiacenti per il — che possiamo avervi causato*, we are sorry for any inconvenience we may have caused you; *causare del — a qlcu.*, to give s.o. trouble (*o to disturb s.o.*); *prendersi il — di fare ql.co.*, to take the trouble of doing (*o* to do) sthg. 2. (*malattia*) trouble, illness, ailment: *disturbi di cuore*, heart-disease; *disturbi di fegato*, liver upset; *disturbi dovuti alla dentizione*, teething troubles; *ha avuto un leggero —*, he had a slight illness 3. (*rad.*) (*intenzionale*) jamming, disturbance; (*rumore*) noise: *disturbi atmosferici*, atmospherics; *disturbi continuati*, grinder; *ricezione senza disturbi*, noise-free reception.

disubbidiènte, *ag.* disobedient.

disubbidienteménte, *av.* disobediently.

disubbidiènza, *s.f.* disobedience: *una —*, a disobedience (*o an act of disobedience*); *— a un ordine*, disobedience of an order.

disubbidíre, *v.t.i.* 1. to disobey: *non — ai tuoi genitori!* don't disobey your parents!; *non voglio essere disubbidito*, I won't be disobeyed 2. (*trasgredire*) to break: *disubbidì all'ordine ricevuto*, he broke (*o* disregarded) the order he had received; *— ai comandamenti*, to break the commandments.

disuguaglianza, *s.f.* 1. inequality; (*disparità*) disparity; (*differenza*) difference: *— di età*, disparity of (*o* in) age (*o* in years); *le disuguaglianze sociali*, social inequalities 2. (*di terreno*) unevenness, inequality 3. (*mat.*) inequality.

disuguagliàre, *v.t.* to make unequal; to make irregular; to make different.

disuguàle, *ag.* 1. unequal, uneven: *bambini di età —*, children of unequal age; *terreno —*, uneven (*o* rough *o* broken) ground; *umore —*, uneven (*o* unequal) temper 2. (*irregolare, frammentario*) irregular, fragmentary: *attività —*, irregular activity; *stile —*, fragmentary style 3. (*differente*) different; dissimilar (to s.o., sthg.); (*discordante*) discordant (with, to, from s.o., sthg.): *opinioni disuguali*, discordant opinions.

disugualménte, *av.* 1. unequally, unevenly 2. (*irregolarmente*) irregularly 3. (*differentemente*) differently, dissimilarly.

disumanàre, *v.t.* to divest of humanity; to render inhuman, to brutalize ‖ **disumanàrsi**, *v.r.* to become inhuman.

disumàno, *ag.* inhuman, cruel: *leggi disumane*, inhuman laws; *un padrone —*, a cruel master.

disumàre, *v.t.* to exhume, to exhumate, to disinter.

disumazióne, *s.f.* (*rar.*) exhumation.

disumidíre, *v.t.* to dry (up).

disúngere, *v.t.* (*rar.*) to remove grease from (sthg.).

disuníbile, *ag.* detachable; dividable, divisible.

disunióne, *s.f.* disunion; (*discordia*) discord, disagreement, dissension: *portò la — in quella famiglia*, he caused disagreement in that family.

disuníre, *v.t.* to disunite, to disjoin; to cause to disagree, to set at variance ‖ **disunírsi**, *v.r.* to become disunited, to get divided.

disunitaménte, *av.* without union.

disunitézza, *s.f.* (*rar.*) disunity.

disuníto, *ag.* 1. disunited, disjoined: *famiglia disunita*, divided family (*o* family at variance) 2. (*irregolare*) irregular 3. (*frammentario*) fragmentary: *stile —*, fragmentary style.

disuría, *s.f.* (*med.*) dysury, dysuria.

disusànza, *s.f.* (*rar.*) disuse: *cadere in —*, to fall into disuse.

disusàre, *v.t.* 1. to disuse, to cease to use, to use no longer 2. (*disabituare*) to disaccustom; (*divezzare*) to wean.

disusàto, *ag.* 1. disused, out-of-use; out-of-date, obsolete: *automobile disusata*, out-of-date car; *parola disusata*, obsolete word; *stile —*, old-fashioned style 2. (*disabituato*) unaccustomed.

disúso, *s.m.* disuse, desuetude: *cadere in —*, to fall into disuse; *parole cadute in —*, obsolete words.

disutilàccio, *s.m.* (*spreg.*) good-for-nothing.

disútile, *ag.* useless: *arnesi disutili*, useless tools ‖ *s.m.* (*buono a nulla*) good-for-nothing: *quel ragazzo è un —*, that boy is a good-for-nothing.

disutilità, *s.f.* uselessness.

disutilménte, *av.* uselessly.

disvantàggio, *s.m.* (*rar.*) disadvantage.

disvariàre, *v.t.i.* (*rar.*) (*variare*) to vary.

disvelàre, (*rar.*) per **svelàre**.

disvèllere, (*rar.*) per **divèllere**.

disvestíre, *v.t.* 1. to unclothe, to divest 2. *fig.* (*privare*) to divest, to deprive ‖ **disvestírsi**, *v.r.* 1. to undress 2. *fig.* (*privarsi*) to divest oneself.

disvezzàre, *v.t.* (*rar.*) to wean.

disviàre, *v.t.* (*rar.*) to divert, to lead astray; (*corrompere*) to mislead ‖ **disviàrsi**, *v.r.* to go astray.

disvigoríre, (*rar.*) per **svigoríre**.

disviluppàre, *v.t.* to disentangle, to unravel.

disvío, *s.m.* 1. (*il disviare*) leading astray; (*il disviarsi*) going astray 2. (*disguido*) miscarriage.

disvolére, *v.t.* (*rar.*) to wish no longer *ella vuole e disvuole*, she will and she won't.

disvòlgere, *v.t.* to unroll, to unfold, to spread.

ditàle, *s.m.* 1. thimble: *un — d'acqua*, a thimbleful of water 2. (*per proteggere un dito malato*) finger-stall.

ditàta, *s.f.* 1. finger-mark, finger-print: *c'erano le sue ditate su quel libro*, there were the marks left by his fingers on that book 2. (*colpo col dito*) blow with a finger 3. (*quantità che si può raccogliere col dito*) fingerful: *una — di unguento*, a fingerful of ointment.

Díte, *no.pr.m.* (*mit.*) Dis.

diteísmo, *s.m.* (*relig.*) ditheism.

ditiràmbico, *ag.* (*poes.*) dithyrambic.

ditiràmbo, *s.m.* (*poes.*) dithyramb.

díto, *s.m.* 1. finger; (*del piede*) toe: *— anulare*, ring finger; *— indice*, forefinger; *— medio*, middle finger; *— mignolo*, little finger; *— pollice*, thumb; *dammi un — di gomma, mi sono tagliata il pollice*, give me a finger-stall, I've cut my thumb; *quel bambino ha il brutto vizio di mettersi le dita nel naso*, that child has the nasty habit of picking his nose; *questo guanto ha le dita troppo corte*, the fingers of this glove are too short; *mostrare a —*, to point out ‖ *il — di Dio*, the hand of God ‖ *un — di vino*, a finger of wine ‖ *è roba da leccarsi le dita!*, it's delicious! (*o fam.* it's scrumptious!) ‖ *gli dai un — e si prende una mano*, give him an inch and he'll take an ell ‖ *ha le dita d'oro*, she is very clever with her fingers ‖ *non aveva la forza di alzare un —*, she was so weak she couldn't move a finger ‖ *il mio amico non mosse un — per noi*, my friend didn't lift a finger to help us ‖ *non muove un — tutto il santo giorno*, she doesn't do a stroke of work all day long ‖ *sa la storia sulla punta delle dita*, he has history on his finger tips ‖ *se la legò al —*, he took it to heart ‖ *vedo che ti prudono le dita*, I can see your fingers are itching ‖ *mettere il — sulla piaga*, to touch a sore spot ‖ *mordersi le dita*, to repent bitterly ‖ *toccare il cielo con un —*, to be beside oneself with joy ‖ *tra moglie e marito non mettere il —*, *prov.* don't interfere between husband and wife **2.** (*spazio, lunghezza di un dito usato a mo' di misura*) inch; (*nel senso della larghezza*) finger.

dítola, *s.f.* (*bot.*) clavaria.

dítta, *s.f.* firm, concern, commercial house, business: *Spett. Ditta D. Clark e figli*, Messrs. D. Clark and Sons; *la — Smith è una buona —*, Messrs. Smith is a good concern; *fondare una — sotto la ragione sociale di...*, to set up a new firm under the style of...; *liquidare una —*, to wind up a commercial house; *sciogliere una —*, to dissolve a firm.

dittàfono, *s.m.* dictaphone.

díttamo, *s.m.* (*bot.*) dittany.

dittatóre, *s.m.* dictator.

dittatoriàle, *ag.* dictatorial.

dittatoriaménte, *av.* dictatorially; imperiously.

dittatòrio, *ag.* dictatorial; imperious.

dittatúra, *s.f.* dictatorship.

díttero¹, *s.m.* (*entom.*) dipteron ‖ *i ditteri*, (*entom.*) Diptera.

díttero², *ag.* (*arch.*) dipteral ‖ *s.m.* (*arch.*) dipteros.

díttico, *s.m.* diptych.

dittongàre, *v.t.* to diphthongize.

dittòngo, *s.m.* diphthong.

diurèsi, *s.f.* (*med.*) diuresis.

diurètico, *ag.s.m.* (*med.*) diuretic.

diurnísta, *s.m.* jobbing clerk.

diúrno, *ag.* diurnal: *astro —*, the diurnal star (*o* the sun); *lavoro —*, day-work; *moto —*, (*astr.*) diurnal motion; *ore diurne*, day-time; *scuola diurna*, day-school; *spettacolo —*, (*teat.*) matinée; *turno —*, day-shift; *uccelli diurni*, (*ornit.*) diurnal birds ‖ *s.m.* (*eccl.*) diurnal.

diuturnaménte, *av.* for a long time.

diuturnità, *s.f.* diuturnity, long duration.

diutúrno, *ag.* diuturnal, lasting long, long.

díva, *s.f.* **1.** (*rar.*) (*dea*) goddess **2.** (*stella cinematografica*) film star; (*cantante*) diva.

divagaménto, *s.m.* **1.** wandering, digression **2.** (*divertimento*) amusement, entertainment.

divagàre, *v.i.* to wander, to digress, to stray, to divagate: *— da un tema*, to wander from a subject ‖ *v.t.* **1.** to divert, to distract: *ogni cosa lo divaga*, everything distracts him **2.** (*divertire*) to amuse, to entertain: *bisogna divagarlo*, he must be amused ‖ **divagàrsi,** *v.r.* **1.** to be distracted **2.** (*divertirsi*) to amuse oneself.

divagazióne, *s.f.* **1.** wandering, digression: *fare una —*, to make a digression **2.** (*divertimento*) amusement, recreation **3.** (*tiritera*) rambling talk.

divallàre, *v.i.* (*rar.*) to slope downwards.

divampaménto, *s.m.* flare-up, blazing.

divampàre, *v.i.* to burst into flame, to blaze, to flare up: *il fuoco divampò nuovamente*, the fire flared up again; *l'incendio divampava*, the fire was blazing; *le passioni divampavano*, passions were raging; *— d'ira*, to blaze with anger (*o* to flare up).

divàno, *s.m.* **1.** divan; sofa: *— letto*, divan-bed **2.** (*Consiglio di Stato, Sala del Consiglio in Turchia*) divan **3.** (*canzoniere di un poeta orientale*) divan.

divanzàre, (*rar.*) per **precèdere.**

divaricaménto, *s.m.* straddle.

divaricàre, *v.t.* to open wide apart, to spread: *— le gambe*, to part one's legs wide.

divaricàto, *ag.* **1.** wide apart, spread apart: *sedere a gambe divaricate*, to sit straddle-legged **2.** (*bot.*) divaricate.

divaricatóre, *s.m.* (*chir.*) retractor: *— automatico*, self-retaining retractor.

divàrio, *s.m.* difference; diversity: *c'è un bel —!*, that makes a great difference!.

divedére, *v.t.*: *dare a —*, to show clearly; (*dar a credere, a intendere*) to make believe, to give to understand: *egli dava a — la noia*, he showed his boredom.

divèllere, *v.t.* **1.** to uproot, to eradicate, to pull up (by the roots): *— un albero*, to uproot a tree (*o* to pull up a tree by its roots); *— i capelli*, to tear (*o* to pluck at) s.o.'s hair **2.** *fig.* to uproot, to eradicate, to extirpate: *dobbiamo — il vizio*, we must uproot vice; *— i pregiudizi*, to eradicate prejudices **3.** (*dissodare*) to plough, to till.

divèlto, *ag.* **1.** torn off, pulled off: *— dalla radice*, eradicated (*o* uprooted) **2.** (*dissodato*) ploughed, tilled ‖ *s.m.* (*agr.*) trenching.

diveníre, diventàre, *v.i.* **1.** to become: *divenne il capo dell'impresa*, he became the head of the firm; *divenne famoso*, he became famous (*o* a famous man); *divenne generale, dottore*; he became a general, a doctor; *è divenuto mio amico*, he has become my friend (*o* he has made friends with me); *spesso le consuetudini diventano leggi*, customs often become law; *— nemico di qlcu.*, to become s.o.'s enemy; *— re*, to become king; *— sospettoso di qlcu.*, to become suspicious of s.o. ‖ *c'è da — matti!*, it is enough to drive one mad!; *mi farai — matto!*, you will drive me mad! **2.** (*mutarsi lentamente*) to grow (into s.o., sthg.); (*di cose concrete*) to turn into (sthg.); (*di cose astratte*) to turn to (sthg.); (*fam.*) to get (*solo con ag. e p.p.*): *l'acqua diventò ghiaccio*, the water turned into ice; *diverrà un buon attore*, he will make a good actor; *è diventato un bel ragazzo*, he has grown up into a handsome young man; *è diventato un uomo*, he has grown into a man; *la nostra felicità è diventata amaro rimpianto*, our happiness has turned to bitter regret; *quando divenne buio*, when it got (*o* grew) dark; *il vino divenne aceto*, the wine turned into vinegar; *— acido*, to turn sour; *— alto*, to grow tall; *— rosso*, to turn pink (*o* red); *— vecchio*, to grow (*o* to get) old: *diventiamo vecchi*, we are getting old ‖ *— di mille colori*, to blush deeply.

diveníre, *s.m.* (*fil.*) becoming: *l'essere e il —*, being and becoming.

divèrbio, *s.m.* dispute, quarrel, altercation: *avere un —*, to have an altercation.

divergènte, *ag.* divergent, diverging: *linee divergenti*, divergent lines.

divergènza, *s.f.* **1.** (*geom.*) divergence, divergency **2.** (*disparità*) difference, divergence, divergency: *— d'opinioni*, disagreement **3.** (*aer.*) divergence: *— laterale*, lateral divergence; *— longitudinale*, longitudinal divergence.

divèrgere, *v.i.* **1.** to diverge, to turn apart: *la strada diverge dal fiume*, the road diverges from the river **2.** (*scostarsi*) to wander: *— da un argomento*, to wander from a point (*o* from a subject).

diversaménte, *av.* **1.** (*in modo diverso*) differently, in a different way; otherwise: *ciò deve essere fatto —*, this must be done quite otherwise; *la pensa —*, he is of a different opinion; *parla — da te*, he speaks differently from you **2.** (*altrimenti*) otherwise, or else: *dovete ubbidirmi, — lo dirò a vostro padre*, you must obey me, otherwise (*o* or else) I'll tell your father.

diversificàre, *v.t.* to diversify ‖ *v.i.*, **diversificàrsi,** *v.r.* to be different, to differ.

diversificazióne, *s.f.* (*rar.*) **1.** diversification **2.** (*varietà*) variety.

diversióne, *s.f.* **1.** deviation, diversion; (*di percorso*) detour: — *di un corso d'acqua*, diversion of a stream; *la strada principale era bloccata, dovemmo perciò fare una* —, the main road was blocked up, so we had to make a detour **2.** (*digressione*) digression: *fare una* —, to make a digression; *perdersi in una* —, to lose oneself in a digression **3.** (*svago, passatempo*) diversion, distraction, amusement, recreation **4.** (*mil.*) diversion.

diversità, *s.f.* diversity, difference; (*dissimiglianza*) unlikeness; (*varietà*) variety: *una* — *di idee porta alla discussione*, a difference of opinions leads to discussion; *c'è una certa* — *fra questi due colori*, there is some difference between these two colours; *nel gruppo c'era una tale* — *di opinioni che...*, there was such a variety of opinions in the group that....

diversívo, *ag.* **1.** deviating: *canale* —, deviating canal **2.** (*che distrae*) diverting: *argomento* —, diverting subject || *s.m.* **1.** (*canale che devia acqua a fiume*) side canal **2.** (*svago*) diversion, change, distraction; amusement: *ho bisogno di un* —, I need a change; *si lamentò che vi fossero pochi diversivi*, he complained that there were few diversions.

divèrso, *ag.* **1.** different; unlike: *metodo* —, different method; *morale diversa dalla nostra*, morals different from ours; *la mia opinione è diversa dalla tua*, my opinion is different from yours; *sei molto* — *da quanto credevo*, you are quite different from (o unlike) what I thought; *siamo diversi*, we are different; *vivono in case diverse*, they live in different houses || *allora il caso è* —!, that puts a different complexion on (o that changes) the matter! **2.** (*di diverso genere*) various, different; (*comm.*) sundry: *creditori diversi*, (*comm.*) sundry creditors; *spese diverse*, (*comm.*) sundry expenses **3.** *pl.* (*parecchi*) several: *c'erano diversi uomini che lo aspettavano*, there were several men waiting for him; *ho diverse ragioni per non volerlo vedere*, I have a number of reasons for not wishing to see him.

divèrso, *av.* differently; otherwise.

divertènte, *ag.* amusing, entertaining, pleasant: *spettacolo* —, amusing show; *è* — *andare a far compere con lei*, it is amusing to go shopping with her.

divertévole, (*rar.*) per **divertènte**.

divertícolo, *s.m.* **1.** side lane **2.** *fig.* (*sotterfugio*) subterfuge **3.** (*anat.*) diverticulum (*pl.* diverticula).

divertiménto, *s.m.* **1.** amusement, entertainment, distraction, enjoyment; (*passatempo*) pastime, recreation; hobby: *parco dei divertimenti*, recreation-ground; *lo fa per puro* —, he does it out of sheer amusement; *il pagliaccio cadde in acqua con grande* — *degli spettatori*, the clown fell into the water to the great amusement (o much to the entertainment) of the spectators; *raccogliere francobolli è il suo massimo* —, stamp-collecting is his favourite hobby; *si piglia il* — *di stuzzicare la sorellina*, he takes great enjoyment in teasing his little sister; *vi sono molti divertimenti in una grande città*, there are plenty of amusements in a big town || *buon* —!, have a good time! || *che* —!, what fun! **2.** (*mus.*) divertimento (*pl.* divertimenti), divertissement.

divertíre, *v.t.* **1.** (*deviare*) to divert (anche *fig.*): — *una disputa*, to divert an argument; — *i pensieri di qlcu.*, to divert s.o.'s thoughts **2.** (*ricreare*) to amuse, to entertain, to recreate, to divert: *cerca di divertirlo!*, try to entertain him!; *la pesca lo diverte*, fishing recreates him || **divertírsi**, *v.r.* to amuse oneself, to be amused; (*godersela*) to enjoy oneself, to have a good time: *divertiti!*, enjoy yourself! (o have a good time!); *ti sei divertito a Viareggio?*, how did you enjoy yourself in Viareggio?.

divétta, *s.f.* starlet; (*canzonettista*) music-hall singer.

divezzaménto, *s.m.* weaning: *età del* —, weaning age.

divezzàre, *v.t.* **1.** to wean: — *un bambino*, to wean a baby **2.** *fig.* (*disabituare*) to wean: *vorrei poterlo* —

da quella cattiva abitudine, I wish I could wean him from that bad habit || **divezzàrsi**, *v.r.* (*disabituarsi*) to wean oneself (from a habit).

diviàre, *V.* **deviàre**.

diviàto, *av.* straight: *se ne andò* — *a casa*, he went straight home.

dividèndo, *s.m.* **1.** (*comm.*) dividend: *un* — *del 7 %*, a dividend of 7 %; — *provvisorio*, interim dividend; *distribuzione del* —, distribution of dividends; *fissare la misura del* —, to declare a dividend (o dividends); *pagare il* — *in proporzione all'ammontare pagato per ogni azione*, to pay dividends in proportion to the amount paid up on each share; *proporre la misura del* —, to recommend a dividend **2.** (*arit.*) dividend: *il* — *è uguale al divisore moltiplicato per il quoziente, più il resto*, the dividend is equal to the divisor multiplied by the quotient, plus the remainder.

divídere, *v.t.* **1.** (*ripartire*) to divide (up): *ci dividemmo il lavoro*, we divided the work between us; *dividete la torta di mele fra di voi!*, divide the apple-pie among you!; *dividiamo il nostro tempo fra studio e giuoco*, we divide our time between study and play || — *un atto in tre scene*, to split up an act into three scenes; — *in due*, to divide in two; — *in parti*, to divide (up) into parts; — *i propri beni tra gli eredi*, to divide (up) one's property amongst one's heirs **2.** (*separare*) to separate, to divide: *la Manica divide la Francia dall'Inghilterra*, the Channel separates France from England; *questa catena di monti divide i due paesi*, this range of mountains divides the two countries; *questo ruscello divide il nostro prato da quello del nostro vicino*, this stream separates our meadow from our neighbour's; *stavano litigando ed io cercai di dividerli*, they were fighting and I tried to separate them **3.** (*condividere*) to share: — *la gioia, il dolore, l'opinione altrui*, to share s.o.'s joy, sorrow, opinion; — *una responsabilità*, to share a responsibility; — *le spese*, to share expenses **4.** (*disunire*) to divide, to tear: *le lotte interne dividono il partito*, the party is torn by internal disputes (o internal disputes tear the party); *la questione divise la Camera*, the House was divided on this question; — *una famiglia*, to divide a family || *dividi e impera!*, divide and conquer! **5.** (*mat.*) to divide: *dividi 125 per 5*, divide 125 by 5; *il due divide tutti i numeri pari*, two divides all even numbers **6.** (*chim. fis.*) to split || **divídersi**, *v.r.* **1.** to divide; (*fendersi*) to break (up), to split asunder, to crack: *il marmo si divise in tre parti*, the marble broke into three parts; *il Po si divide alla foce*, the Po divides at its mouth **2.** (*separarsi*) to part: *la folla si divise*, the crowd parted; — *da qlcu., da ql.co.*, to part from s.o., with sthg. **3.** (*dir.*) to separate: *mia moglie ed io abbiamo deciso di dividerci*, my wife and I have decided to separate.

divièto, *s.m.* prohibition: — *di affissione*, stick no bills; — *di fumare*, no smoking; — *di parcheggio*, no parking; — *di transito*, no thoroughfare.

divinaménte, *av.* divinely; beautifully, exquisitely, excellently: *suona il piano* —, he plays the piano beautifully.

divinàre, *v.t.* to divine; (*prevedere*) to foresee; (*predire*) to foretell, to predict, to prophesy: *Colombo divinò il nuovo continente*, Columbus divined the existence of the new continent; — *le intenzioni di qlcu.*, to divine s.o.'s intentions; — *la sorte di qlcu.*, to foretell s.o.'s future.

divinatóre, *ag.* divining; (*profetico*) prophetic(al): *arti divinatrici*, prophetic arts || *s.m.* diviner; (*veggente*) seer; (*profeta*) foreteller, prophet.

divinatòrio, *ag.* divinatory, divining: *facoltà divinatoria*, divination: *verga divinatoria*, divining-rod.

divinatríce, *s.f.* divineress; (*veggente*) seeress; (*profetessa*) prophetess, sibyl.

divinazióne, *s.f.* divination.

divincolaménto, *s.m.* wriggle, wriggling; (*il contorcersi*) writhing; (*per liberarsi*) struggle, struggling.

divincolàre, *v.t.* to wriggle: *il serpente divincolava tutto il corpo*, the snake wriggled its body; — *la coda*, to wriggle its tail ‖ **divincolàrsi**, *v.r.* **1.** to wriggle; (*contorcersi*) to writhe; (*lottare per liberarsi*) to struggle: — *come un'anguilla*, to wriggle like an eel; *avanzare divincolandosi*, to wriggle along **2.** (*liberarsi*) to wriggle out (òf sthg.); to wriggle oneself free: *il pesce si divincolò dalle mie mani*, the fish wriggled out of my hands.

divincolío, *s.m.* wriggling; (*contorcimento*) writhing; (*per liberarsi*) struggling.

divinità, *s.f.* **1.** divineness; divinity, godhead: *riconoscere la — di Cristo*, to acknowledge the divinity of Christ **2.** (*Dio*) God; (*nume*) god: *adorare la Divinità*, to worship God (o the Divinity).

divinizzàre, *v.t.* to deify.

divinizzazióne, *s.f.* deification; (*letter.*) apotheosis (*pl.* apotheoses).

divíno, *ag.* **1.** divine; (*simile a dio*) godlike: *il — Achille*, godlike Achilles; *il diritto — dei re*, the divine right of kings; *scienza divina*, theology **2.** (*nobilissimo, eccelso*) heavenly, divine; perfect, beautiful, excellent; adorable: *il — Poeta*, the divine Poet; *ha una voce divina*, she has a heavenly voice ‖ *la «Divina Commedia»*, "The Divine Comedy".

divísa, *s.f.* **1.** uniform; (*livrea*) livery: — *ordinaria*, service dress; *erano tutti in —*, they were all in uniform; *c'era un ufficiale in — di gala*, there was an officer wearing full (o gala) dress **2.** (*comm.*) currency: *divise estere*, foreign bills **3.** (*scriminatura*) hair parting **4.** (*motto*) motto (*pl.* mottoes), device (anche *fig.*): *« Vivi e lascia vivere »*, *questa è la sua —*, "Live and let live", this is his motto.

divisaménte, *av.* dividedly.

divisaménto, *s.m.* plan, project, design; (*decisione*) decision.

divisàre, *v.t.* to plan, to design: *dimmi che cosa hai divisato*, tell me what you have planned ‖ *v.i.* (*aver in animo*) to decide, to intend, to purpose: *aveva divisato di partire il giorno dopo*, he had decided to leave (o on leaving) the following day.

divisíbile, *ag.* divisible: — *per due*, divisible by two.

divisibilità, *s.f.* divisibility.

divisionàle, *ag.* (*mil.*) divisional.

divisióne, *s.f.* **1.** division; (*separazione*) partition, separation: *la — dei beni*, the partition of goods; *la — dei culti*, the division of cults; — *del lavoro*, division of labour; *la — delle classi*, the division of classes; *muro di —*, partition (-wall); *una onesta — del denaro*, a fair division of the money; *una fila di cespugli forma la — fra il mio ed il suo giardino*, a row of bushes forms the division between my garden and his **2.** (*discordia*) division, discord: *divisioni intestine*, intestine divisions; *produrre divisioni nella società*, to cause divisions in society **3.** (*arit.*) division: *la — è una delle quattro operazioni*, division is one of the four operations **4.** (*mil.*) division: — *corazzata*, armed division; — *navale*, naval division; *generale di —*, major-general **5.** (*amm.*) department: *capo —*, head of a department **6.** (*tec.*) indexing: — *angolare*, angular indexing; — *composta*, compound indexing.

divisionísmo, *s.m.* (*pitt.*) pointillism(e).

divisionísta, *ag.* (*pitt.*) pointillist(e): *pittore —*, pointillist painter ‖ *s.m.* (*pitt.*) pointillist(e).

divisonístico, *ag.* (*pitt.*) pertaining to pointillisme.

divíso, *ag.* **1.** divided: — *in tre parti*, divided into three parts; — *per tre*, divided by three **2.** (*separato*) separated: *vive — dalla moglie*, he lives separated from his wife **3.** (*condiviso*) shared.

divisóre, *s.m.* **1.** divisor: *massimo comun —*, (*arit.*) greatest common divisor **2.** (*mec.*) (*testa a dividere*) index head, dividing head, indexing head **3.** — *di tensione*, (*elett.*) voltage divider (o potential divider); — *ottico*, optical dividing head; — *universale*, (*mec.*) universal indexing head.

divisòrio, *ag.* dividing, separating: *muro —*, partition (-wall) ‖ *s.m.* partition: — *per sedili*, (*ferr.*) seat division.

divo, *ag.* (*letter.*) divine; (*simile a un dio*) godlike ‖ *s.m.* **1.** (*letter.*) god; deity **2.** (*attore cinematografico*) (film) star.

divoraménto, *s.m.* devouring.

divoràre, *v.t.* **1.** to devour, to eat up, to wolf (down): *divorò il suo spuntino in un attimo*, he ate up his snack (o devoured his snack o wolfed his snack down); *un leone lo divorò*, a lion devoured him; — *il pranzo*, to devour (o to eat up) one's dinner **2.** *fig.* to devour: *divorato dalla curiosità*, devoured by curiosity; *l'amore, la gelosia, l'odio lo divorano*, he is consumed with love, jealousy, hatred; *è divorato dall'orgoglio*, he is eaten up with pride; *il fuoco divorò la casa*, the fire devoured (o destroyed) the house; — *un libro*, to devour a book; — *un patrimonio*, to squander (o to consume) a fortune; *qlcu. con gli occhi*, to gaze devouringly at (o to look longingly at) s.o.; — *la strada*, to devour the way (o to run at full speed) ‖ **divoràrsi**, *v.r.* to consume oneself (with sthg.); to be consumed (with sthg.): — *dalla rabbia*, to be consumed with rage.

divoratóre, *ag.* devouring, voracious: *fuoco —*, devouring fire ‖ *s.m.*, **divoratríce**, *s.f.*, devourer, voracious eater.

divorziàre, *v.i.* to divorce (s.o.), to be divorced: *divorziarono dopo un mese*, they were divorced after a month.

divorziàto, *ag.* divorced ‖ *s.m.*, **divorziàta**, *s.f.* divorcee.

divòrzio, *s.m.* divorce (anche *fig.*): *il — fra religione e scienza*, the divorce between religion and science; *chiedere il —*, to apply for a divorce; *fare —*, to be divorced; *fare — da qlcu.*, to divorce s.o.

divotaménte, *av.* devoutly; piously.

divòto, *V.* devòto 1.

divozióne, *V.* devozióne 1. 2.

divulgàbile, *ag.* (*rar.*) that may be divulged.

divulgaménto, *s.m.* (*rar.*) divulgement.

divulgàre, *v.t.* **1.** to spread, to divulge, to reveal, to disclose; (*per radio*) to broadcast; (*per televisione*) to telecast: — *notizie, dicerie*, to spread (o to divulge) news, rumours; — *segreti*, to divulge (o to disclose o to reveal) secrets **2.** (*esporre in forma accessibile*) to popularize, to vulgarize: — *una dottrina*, to popularize a doctrine ‖ **divulgàrsi**, *v.r.* to spread: *la notizia si divulgò presto nel paese*, the news soon spread over the country.

divulgatóre, *s.m.*, **divulgatríce**, *s.f.* divulger: *è un ottimo — di nozioni scientifiche*, he is an excellent writer of popular science.

divulgazióne, *s.f.* **1.** divulgation, spreading: — *di notizie*, spreading of news **2.** (*esposizione in forma accessibile*) popularization: — *di una teoria scientifica*, popularization of a scientific theory.

divulsióne, *s.f.* (*chir.*) divulsion.

divúlso, *ag.* separate, detached.

divulsóre, *s.m.* (*chir.*) divulsor.

dizionariétto, *s.m.* pocket dictionary.

dizionàrio, *s.m.* dictionary: — *etimologico*, etymological dictionary; — *geografico*, gazetteer; — *storico*, historical dictionary; *se non sai il significato di quella parola, cercala nel —*, if you do not know the meaning of that word, look it up in the dictionary; *compilare un —*, to compile a dictionary; *scartabellare un —*, to thumb (through) a dictionary.

dizionarísta, *s.c.* dictionary-maker; (*lessicografo*) lexicographer.

dizióne, *s.f.* **1.** diction: — *poetica*, poetic diction **2.** (*recitazione*) recital **3.** (*pronuncia*) pronunciation: — *corretta*, right pronunciation.

do, *s.m.* (*mus.*) C, do: *sinfonia in — diesis minore*, symphony in C sharp minor.

doàrio, *s.m.* (*dir.*) dower.

dòbla, *s.f.* (*antica moneta spagnola*) dobla.

doblóne, *s.m.* (*antica moneta spagnola*) doubloon.

dóccia, *s.f.* **1.** shower(-bath); (*a scopo terapeutico*) douche: *fare la* —, to take (*o* to have) a shower(-bath) ‖ *dare una* — *fredda a qlcu.*, *fig.* to damp s.o.'s enthusiasm **2.** (*condotto per l'acqua*) water-pipe **3.** (*grondaia*) gutter.

docciàre, *v.t.* to give a shower-bath to (s.o.); (*a scopo terapeutico*) to douche ‖ *v.i.* to take a shower (-bath), to have a shower(-bath).

docciatúra, *s.f.* shower(-bath); (*a scopo terapeutico*) douche; douching.

docción e, *s.m.* (*arch.*) gargoyle.

docènte, *ag.* teaching ‖ *s.m.* teacher: *libero* —, fully established university lecturer.

docènza, *s.f.* teaching: *libera* —, establishment as university lecturer: *ottenere la libera* —, to qualify for university teaching.

docèti, *s.m.pl.* (*st. relig.*) Docetae.

dòcile, *ag.* **1.** docile, tractable, easily managed, submissive: *bambino* —, docile child; *cavallo* —, tractable horse **2.** (*di materie*) tractable, easily worked, easy to work: *un legno* —, an easily worked wood.

docilità, *s.f.* **1.** docility, tractability, submissiveness **2.** (*di materie*) tractability, tractableness.

docilménte, *av.* **1.** docilely, submissively **2.** (*di materie*) tractably.

docimasia, *s.f.* **1.** (*st. greca*) docimasy **2.** (*med.*) docimasia **3.** (*chim.*) docimasy.

docimàstico, *ag.* (*med. chim.*) docimastic(al).

dòcmio, *s.m.* (*zool.*) dochmius (*pl.* dochmii).

documentàle, *ag.* documental.

documentàre, *v.t.* to document, to prove by documents, to support by documentary evidence: — *le proprie asserzioni*, to prove one's assertions by documents.

documentàrio, *ag.* documentary: *credito* —, (*comm.*) documentary credit ‖ *s.m.* (*cine.*) documentary (film): — *di attualità*, newsreel; — *didattico*, class-room film.

documentarísta, *s.m.* documentary film-maker.

documénto, *s.m.* **1.** document, paper, instrument: — *autenticato, legalizzato*, authenticated document; *documenti contro accettazione*, (*comm.*) documents against acceptance; — *d'appoggio, giustificativo*, (*comm.*) (supporting) voucher; *documenti di bordo*, (*mar.*) ship's papers; *autenticità del* —, genuineness of the instrument; *corpo, testo del* —, body of the instrument; *contro documenti*, against documents; *mancata esibizione di documenti*, (*dir.*) failure to present documents; *abbiamo consegnato questi documenti ai nostri avvocati*, we have handed these papers to our solicitors; *favorite i vostri documenti!*, (show me) your papers, please!; *comprovare con documenti*, to support with documents (*o* to evidence by documents); *far legalizzare un* —, to have a document legalized; *firmare, redigere un* —, to sign, to draw up a document **2.** (*testimonianza*) document, evidence, proof: *questa azione è un* — *della sua onestà*, this action is an evidence (*o* a proof) of his honesty; *queste opere d'arte sono* — *di grande civiltà*, these works of art are evidence of a great civilization.

documentazióne, *s.f.* **1.** documentation **2.** *pl.* (*documenti*) documents, papers.

dodecaèdrico, *ag.* (*geom.*) dodecahedral.

dodecaèdro, *s.m.* (*geom.*) dodecahedron.

dodecafonía, *s.f.* (*mus.*) 12-note music, 12-note system.

dodecafònico, *ag.* (*mus.*) 12-tone (*attributivo*), 12-note (*attributivo*): *musica dodecafonica*, 12-tone (*o* note) music.

dodecàgono, *s.m.* (*geom.*) dodecagon.

Dodecannèso, *no.pr.m.* (*geog.*) Dodecanese.

dodecasìllabo, *ag.* (*poes.*) dodecasyllabic ‖ *s.m.* (*poes.*) dodecasyllable.

dodicènne, *ag.* twelve years old (*predicativo*); twelve-year-old (*attributivo*) ‖ *s.m.* twelve-year-old boy ‖ *s.f.* twelve-year-old girl.

dodicèsimo, *ag. num. ord. s.m.* twelfth ‖ *volume in* —, duodecimo volume.

dódici, *ag. num. card. s.m.* twelve: *i* — *Apostoli*, the twelve Apostles.

dodicimíla, *ag. num. card. s.m.* twelve thousand.

dóga, *s.f.* **1.** stave: *la botte perdeva per la rottura di una* —, a broken stave caused the barrel to leak **2.** (*arald.*) pale.

dogàle, *ag.* (*st.*) dogal, of a doge.

dogàna, *s.f.* **1.** customs (*pl.*): *agente di* —, customs agent; *dichiarazione per la* —, customs declaration; *esattore delle dogane*, customs collector; *membri del Consiglio delle Dogane*, Commissioners of Customs; *ufficiale delle dogane*, customs officer; *passare la* —, to go through the customs **2.** (*dazio*) duty: — *di esportazione*, export-duty (*o* duty on exportation); — *di importazione*, import-duty (*o* duty on importation); — *da pagarsi*, duty to be paid; *soggetto a* —, dutiable; *non c'è* — *su piccole quantità*, there is no duty on small quantities **3.** (*l'edificio*) custom-house.

doganàle, *ag.* customs (*attributivo*): *barriera* —, customs barrier; *bolletta, bolla* —, customs certificate; *dazio* —, customs duty; *dichiarazione* —, customs entry (*o* bill of entry); *formalità doganali*, customs formalities; *merce soggetta a dazio* —, dutiable goods; *operazioni doganali*, customs operations; *tariffa* —, customs tariffs; *visita* —, customs inspection.

doganière, *s.m.* customs officer.

dogàre, *v.t.* to fit (a barrel) with staves.

dogaréssa, *s.f.* (*st.*) dogaressa.

dogàto, *s.m.* (*st.*) dogate.

dòge, *s.m.* (*st.*) doge.

dòglia, *s.f.* sharp pain: *doglie del parto*, throes (*o* labour pains).

dogliànza, *s.f.* (*letter.*) **1.** (*rammarico*) regret **2.** (*lamento, querela*) lamentation, complaint.

dòglio, *s.m.* (*letter.*) large jar; (*barile*) barrel.

dogliosaménte, *av.* (*letter.*) sorrowfully, sadly.

doglióso, *ag.* (*letter.*) sorrowful, sad.

dògma, *s.m.* dogma (*pl.* dogmas, *rar.* dogmata); tenet, principle: *dogmi filosofici*, philosophic dogmas; *dogmi politici*, political dogmas.

dogmàtica, *s.f.* (*teol.*) dogmatics.

dogmaticaménte, *av.* dogmatically.

dogmàtico, *ag.* dogmatic: *teologia dogmatica*, dogmatic theology; *è piuttosto* — *nelle sue affermazioni*, he is rather dogmatic in his statements.

dogmatísmo, *s.m.* dogmatism.

dogmatísta, *s.m.* dogmatist.

dogmatizzàre, *v.t.i.* to dogmatize.

dólce, *ag.* **1.** sweet: *mandorla* —, sweet almond; *patata* —, sweet potato; *vino* —, sweet wine; *non mi piacciono i profumi dolci*, I do not like sweet scents ‖ *acqua* —, fresh-water: *marinaio d'acqua* —, (*scherz.*) fresh-water sailor; *pesca d'acqua* —, fresh -water fishing ‖ *sei un po'* — *di sale*, (*fam.*) you're rather silly **2.** *fig.* sweet; (*caro, amato*) dear, beloved; (*piacevole*) pleasant, agreeable: — *musica*, sweet music; *dolci parole*, kind words; *la* — *patria*, one's beloved motherland; *un* — *profumo*, a pleasant smell; *dolci ricordi*, pleasant memories; *un* — *sorriso*, a sweet (*o* charming) smile; — *speranza*, sweet hope; *dolci suoni*, pleasant strains; *la mia* — *sorella*, my sweet (*o* kind) sister; *la sua* — *voce*, her sweet voice; *non ha un carattere* —, he is not a sweet-tempered person ‖ *il* — *far niente*, pleasant idleness **3.** (*mite, lieve*) mild; gentle, easy: *una brezza* —, a gentle breeze; *clima* —, mild climate; *salita* —, easy (*o* gentle) slope (*o* easy ascent) **4.** (*tec.*) soft, mild: *ferro* —, soft (*o* mild) iron; *legno* —, soft wood; *saldatura a* —, (*mec.*) soft-soldering; *rendere* —, to soften **5.** (*fonet.*) soft: *«g» dura e «g»* —, hard and soft "g" ‖ *s.m.* (*cibo, piatto dolce*) sweet, sweetmeat; (*torta*) cake; tart: *questo* — *si taglia bene*, this cake cuts easily; *vuoi un* —?, do you want a sweet? ‖ *dopo il* — *vien l'amaro prov.* after the sweet comes the sour.

dolceménte, *av.* **1.** sweetly **2.** (*delicatamente*) gently **3.** (*lievemente*) softly.

dolcézza, *s.f.* **1.** sweetness: *la — del miele,* the sweetness of honey **2.** *fig.* sweetness; (*gentilezza*) kindness, gentleness; (*fascino*) charm: *la — del suo carattere,* the sweetness of her character; *la — del tuo sorriso,* the charm of your smile; *trattalo con —, per favore!,* will you treat him with kindness, please!; *le dolcezze e le amarezze della vita,* the sweets and bitters of life || *— mia,* darling **3.** *fig.* (*di clima*) mildness; (*di suono, di colore*) softness; (*di profumo*) fragrance: *la — della sua voce,* the softness of her voice; *la — di questo clima gli farà bene alla salute,* the mildness of this climate will improve his health.

dolciàrio, *ag.* confectionary.

dolciàstro, *ag.* **1.** sweetish; sickly sweet **2.** *fig.* (*mellifluo*) mellifluous: *un sorriso —,* a mellifluous smile.

dolcificànte, *ag.* sweetening || *s.m.* (*chim.*) sweetener.

dolcificàre, *v.t.* **1.** to sweeten: *dolcificate a volontà,* (*nelle ricette di cucina*) add sugar to taste **2.** *fig.* (*attenuare*) to mitigate, to moderate.

dolcificazióne, *s.f.* sweetening.

dolcígno, *ag.* **1.** sweetish; sickly sweet **2.** *fig.* (*mellifluo*) mellifluous.

dolcitúdine, *s.f.* (*poet.*) sweetness.

dolciúme, *s.m.* **1.** sweetmeat, sweet; bonbon: *quei agazzi mangiano troppi dolciumi,* those boys eat too many sweets **2.** (*sapore dolciastro*) sickening sweetness: *il — della banana non mi piace,* I find bananas too sweet for my taste.

dólco, *ag.* (*rar.*) (*di tempo caldo e umido*) muggy; sultry: *il tempo si mette a — oggi,* we are going to have muggy weather to-day.

dolènte, *ag.* **1.** afflicted, grieved, sorrowful; (*spiacente*) sorry: *era molto — di avervi disturbato,* he was very sorry for troubling you; *siamo molto dolenti di informarvi,* we deeply regret informing you **2.** (*che fa male*) aching: *ho un braccio —,* my arm is aching || *s.m.* mourner: *c'era una folla di dolenti,* there was a crowd of mourners.

dolenteménte, *av.* sorrowfully, sadly.

dolére, *v.i.* **1.** to ache: *mi duole un dente,* I have a toothache; *mi duole un dito,* my finger aches (*o* I have a sore finger); *mi duole un orecchio,* my ear aches; *mi duole la testa,* I have a headache (*o* my head aches) **2.** (*rincrescere*) to regret (*stgh., doing*), to be sorry (*for, about stgh.*): *mi duole comunicare la sua morte,* I regret to say that he has died; *mi duole non averLa riconosciuta!,* I regret (*o* I am sorry) that I did not recognize you! (*o* I regret not having recognized you!) || **dolérsi,** *v.r.* **1.** to regret (*sthg., doing*), to be sorry (*for, about sthg.*), to grieve (*at, for, about, over sthg.*): *mi dolgo di averlo detto,* I am sorry I said it (*o* I regret that I said it *o* I regret having said it); *— della morte di un amico,* to grieve at a friend's death **2.** (*protestare*) to complain (*of, about sthg.*): *il servizio è cattivo, me ne dorrò col direttore,* the service is bad, I shall complain to the manager about it.

dolcichiàre, *v.i.* (*fam.*) to ache a little.

dolicocefalìa, *s.f.* (*antropologia*) dolichocephaly, dolichocephalism.

dolicocèfalo, *ag.* dolichocephalic.

dolína, *s.f.* (*geol.*) dolina.

dòllaro, *s.m.* (*moneta, valore*) dollar (*simbolo* $): *area del —,* (*econ.*) dollar-area; *biglietti da 1, 2, 5, 10 dollari,* (*collettivamente*) greenbacks; *un mezzo —,* a half-dollar (*piece*); *moneta da cinque dollari,* half eagle (*o* $ 5); *moneta da dieci dollari,* eagle (*o* $ 10); *costa mezzo —,* it costs half a dollar (*o* fifty cents).

dòlman, *s.m.* dolman.

dòlmen, *s.m.* (*archeol.*) dolmen.

dòlo, *s.m.* (*dir.*) fraud, fraudulent intention: *con —,* fraudulently.

dolòmia, dolomíte, *s.f.* (*min.*) dolomite.

Dolomíti (le), *no.pr.f.pl.* (*geog.*) the Dolomites.

dolomítico, *ag.* **1.** (*min.*) dolomitic **2.** (*geog.*) of the Dolomites: *un paesaggio —,* a landscape of the Dolomites.

doloránte, *ag.* aching, sore, painful: *era tutta —,* she was aching all over.

doloràre, *v.i.* to ache, to suffer: *dolorò tutta la notte,* he suffered all night.

dolóre, *s.m.* **1.** pain, ache: *— di stomaco,* stomach-ache; *— di ventre,* tummy-ache; *un — lancinante,* a shooting pain; *ho — di testa,* I have a headache; *ho un forte — a un braccio,* I feel (*o* have) a sharp pain in my arm (*o* my arm is aching badly); *lo trovai nel suo letto di —,* I found him in his sick-bed; *sono tutto un —,* I am aching all over **2.** (*dolore morale*) sorrow, grief; (*rincrescimento*) regret: *prostrato dal —,* sorrow-stricken; *il suo profondo —,* his deep sorrow; *i dolori la fecero incanutire,* her sorrows turned her hair white; *con suo grande — dovette rinunziare al suo piano,* to his regret he was forced to give up his plan; *lo lasciai con —,* I left him with sorrow; *abbandonarsi al —,* to give way to grief; *morire di —,* to die of grief (*o* to die of a broken heart); *partecipare al — di qlcu.,* to share s.o.'s sorrow || « *I dolori del giovane Werther* », (*lett.*) "The Sorrows of Werther".

Dolòres, *no.pr.f.* Dolores || *dim.* Lola.

dolorífico, *ag.* painful.

dolorosaménte, *av.* painfully; (*in senso morale*) sorrowfully, sadly.

doloróso, *ag.* **1.** (*di dolore fisico, morale*) painful: *una sensazione dolorosa,* a sensation of pain **2.** (*triste, rattristato, addolorato*) sorrowful; sad **3.** (*che causa affanno*) grievous: *dolorose ingiustizie* grievous wrongs.

dolosaménte, *av.* (*dir.*) fraudulently.

dolóso, *ag.* (*dir.*) fraudulent: *fallimento —,* fraudulent bankruptcy; *incendio —,* arson.

domàbile, *ag.* tamable, tameable.

domànda, *s.f.* **1.** (*interrogazione*) question: *domande e risposte,* questions and answers; *una — opportuna, impertinente,* a proper, an impertinent question; *una serie di domande facili,* a set of easy questions; *mi posero una strana —,* they asked (*o* put) me a strange question (*o* I was asked a strange question); *rispondere esattamente a una —,* to answer a question correctly **2.** (*richiesta*) request; (*perentoria*) demand; (*scritta*) application; (*petizione*) petition: *— di ammissione,* (*a una scuola, ecc.*) application; *— di denaro,* request for money; *— di divorzio, di grazia,* (*dir.*) petition for a divorce, for mercy; *— di informazioni,* letter of inquiry; *— di matrimonio,* proposal; *— di pensione,* pension claim || *su —,* by request (*o* on demand *o* on application): *su vostra —,* at your request || *accogliere una —,* to grant a request; *appoggiare una —,* to second a request; *fare una —,* to make a request; *fare — di ql.co.,* to ask for sthg.; *indirizzare una — a qlcu.,* to address an application to s.o. (*o* to address an application to s.o. *o* to make a request to s.o.); *respingere una —,* to dismiss an application **3.** (*comm.*) application, request: *— di dilazione per il pagamento,* request for extending the time of payment; *— di fondi,* application for remittance (*o* for funds); *— di impiego,* application for a job (*o* for a situation): *fare — di impiego,* to apply for a job; *— di pagamento,* application for payment; *— di rappresentanza,* application as a representative agent **4.** (*econ.*) demand: *— di merce straniera,* demand for foreign goods; *— e offerta,* supply and demand.

domandàre, *v.t.* **1.** to ask for (sthg.); (*imperiosamente*) to demand; (*umilmente*) to beg: *gli domandai:* « *Chi sei?* », I asked him: "Who are you?"; *gli domandai dieci sterline,* I asked him for ten pounds; *le domandai l'ora,* I asked her the time; *mi domandò di lavorare con lui,* he asked me to work with him; *mi domandò nome e indirizzo,* he asked (me) my name and address; (*di poliziotto, vigile*) he demanded my name and address; *mi fermarono sulla porta e mi domandarono di seguirli*, they stopped me at the door and asked me to follow them; *non — troppo da lui!*, don't ask too much of him!; *vi domando scusa*, I beg your pardon; *vorrei domandarti un favore*, I should like to ask you a favour (o to ask a favour of you) ‖ *— il consiglio di qlcu.*, *consiglio a qlcu.*, to ask (o to request) s.o.'s advice; *— l'elemosina*, to beg (for alms); *— la parola*, to ask leave to speak; *il permesso*, to ask permission; *— udienza a qlcu.*, to ask (o to request) an audience of s.o. **2.** (*chiedere per sapere*) to inquire, to ask: *— notizie della salute di qlcu.*, to inquire after s.o.; *— la strada a qlcu.*, to ask the way of s.o. ‖ *v.i.* (*chiedere notizie*) to inquire (after s.o., sthg.); (*chiedere informazioni*) to ask (about s.o., sthg.): *gli domanderò del suo nuovo lavoro*, I shall ask him about his new job; *mi domandò di mio padre, della sua salute*, he inquired after my father, after his health ‖ **domandàrsi**, *v.r.* to ask oneself, to wonder: *è ciò che mi domando*, that's what I should like to know; *mi domando perchè non sia qui*, I wonder why he is not here.

domàni, *av.* to-morrow, tomorrow: *— a otto, a quindici*, to-morrow week, to-morrow fortnight; *— l'altro, posdomani*, the day after to-morrow; *— mattina, sera*, to-morrow morning, night; *arrivederci —, a —*, good-bye till tomorrow (*o fam.* see you tomorrow o I'll be seeing you tomorrow) ‖ *da oggi a —*, (*immediatamente*) immediately (o instantly); (*improvvisamente*) suddenly ‖ *dàgli oggi e dàgli —*, in the long run ‖ *parlerebbe fino a —*, he would talk for ever ‖ *s.m.* to -morrow; (*il futuro*) future: *la moda di —*, the coming fashion; *cosa ci riserva il —?*, what has the future (o the morrow) in store for us?; *lo leggerai nel giornale di —*, you will read it in to-morrow's paper; *non pensare troppo al —!*, don't think too much of the future! (o don't worry about the future!).

domàre, *v.t.* **1.** to tame; (*cavalli*) to break (in): *— animali feroci*, to tame wild beasts **2.** (*sottomettere, vincere*) to subdue, to subjugate: *— le proprie passioni*, to subdue one's passions; *una rivolta*, to put down a rebellion **3.** (*spegnere*) to quench, to put out: *un incendio*, to put out a fire.

domàto, *ag.* **1.** tamed; (*di cavallo*) broken **2.** (*sottomesso, vinto*) subdued, subjugated **3.** (*spento*) quenched.

domatóre, *s.m.*, **domatríce**, *s.f.* tamer: *— di leoni*, lion-tamer; *— di cavalli*, horse-breaker.

domattína, *av.* tomorrow morning, to-morrow morning.

domatúra, *s.f.* taming; (*di cavalli*) breaking.

Domeneddío, *s.m.* (*pop.*) God, the Lord.

doménica, *s.f.* Sunday: *— delle Palme*, Palm Sunday; *— di Pasqua*, Easter Sunday; *— in Albis*, Low Sunday; *una — mattina*, on a Sunday morning; *di —*, (*tutte le domeniche*) on Sundays; *vieni a trovarmi —!*, come and see me on Sunday!; *mettersi gli abiti della —*, to put on one's best clothes (o one's Sunday best) ‖ *osservare la —*, (*il riposo*) to keep the sabbath ‖ *chi ride il venerdì, piange la —*, *prov.* he that laughs on Friday, shall weep on Sunday.

domenicàle, *ag.* Sunday (*attributivo*): *abiti domenicali*, Sunday clothes (o Sunday best); *riposo —*, Sunday rest ‖ *l'orazione —*, (*il « Pater Noster »*) the Lord's Prayer.

domenicàno, *ag.* Dominican: *frate —*, Dominican friar ‖ *s.m.* (*eccl.*) Dominican, Black Friar.

Doménico, *no.pr.m.* Dominic(k).

domèstica, *s.f.* maid, maid-servant, woman-servant: (*pl.* women-servants): *— tutto fare*, maid-of-all-work.

domesticaménte, *av.* familiarly; (*alla buona*) unceremoniously.

domesticàre, *V.* addomesticàre.

domesticazióne, *s.f.* domestication, taming.

domestichézza, *s.f.* familiarity; (*intimità*) intimacy:

con —, on familiar terms; *non trattarlo con troppa —*, don't be too familiar with him; *v'era molta — fra loro due*, those two were on intimate terms.

domesticità, *s.f.* familiarity; (*intimità*) intimacy: *non mi piace la sua eccessiva —*, I don't like his being too familiar.

domèstico, *ag.* **1.** (*della casa*) domestic; home (*attributivo*): *economia domestica*, domestic science (o domestic economy); *faccende domestiche*, (*lavori*) household duties (o housework); (*problemi*) family affairs; *gioie e affanni domestici*, domestic joys and cares; *lari domestici*, household gods ‖ *fra le pareti domestiche ogni uomo è re*, every man is king in his own home **2.** (*di animali*) tame, domestic: *i gatti, i cani ed i cavalli sono animali domestici*, cats, dogs and horses are domestic animals **3.** (*di piante, terreno*) cultivated **4.** (*familiare*) familiar: *essere — con qlcu.*, to be familiar (o on familiar terms) with s.o. ‖ *alla domestica*, familiarly ‖ *s.m.* domestic, servant, man -servant (*pl.* men-servants): *licenziare un —*, to dismiss a servant ‖ *i domestici*, household staff.

domiciliàre¹, *ag.* domiciliary: *visita —*, (*dir.*) domiciliary visit.

domiciliàre², *v.t.* (*comm.*) to domicile, to domiciliate: *— una cambiale*, to domicile a bill (o to make a bill payable) at a bank ‖ **domiciliàrsi**, *v.r.* to domicile (at a place); to settle (in a place); to take up one's residence (in a place): *mi sono domiciliato a Milano*, I have taken up my residence in Milan; *s'è domiciliato in casa nostra*, he has come to stay with us.

domiciliàto, *ag.* domiciled (at a place), settled (in a place), resident (in a place); (*abitante*) living: *— a Leeds*, domiciled at Leeds; *— in territorio nemico*, resident in enemy country; *— in Via Byron*, living in Byron Street.

domicílio, *s.m.* **1.** (*abitazione*) domicile, house, dwelling, abode: *violazione di —*, (*dir.*) house-breaking ‖ *consegna a —*, (*comm.*) delivery at addressee's domicile (o at purchaser's door) **2.** (*dir.*) domicile; (*residenza*) residence: *— civile*, civil domicile; *— coatto*, confinement; *— d'acquisto*, acquired domicile; *— d'origine*, domicile of origin; *— d'elezione*, domicile of choice; *— legale*, legal domicile; *cambio di —*, change of domicile; *pagabile al — di...*, (*comm.*) payable at the domicile of...; *prendere —*, to take up domicile; *trasferire il proprio — da Roma a Milano*, to remove one's own domicile from Rome to Milan.

dominàbile, *ag.* controllable, subduable: *passioni dominabili*, passions that can be subdued.

dominànte, *ag.* **1.** dominant, dominating, commanding: *altezza —*, dominant height; *in posizione —*, in a commanding position **2.** (*prevalente, saliente*) dominant, prevailing, outstanding: *il carattere —*, the outstanding character; *la moda —*, the prevailing fashion; *la nota —*, (*mus.*) the dominant note; (*carattere prevalente*) the main feature; *la religione —*, the prevailing creed.

dominàre, *v.t.* **1.** to dominate, to control, to rule: *un buon cavaliere sa come — il suo cavallo*, a good rider knows how to control his horse; *dobbiamo — le nostre passioni*, we must dominate (o master) our passions; *non lasciarti — dai tuoi sentimenti*, don't be ruled by your feelings; *non potei — la mia ira!*, I could not control my anger!; *quel re dominava la nazione*, that king ruled (over) his country; *quello scrittore domina la lingua*, that writer masters the language beautifully; *essi vorrebbero — tutti gli altri popoli*, they would like to dominate (o to rule over) all the other peoples; *essere dominato da qlcu.*, to be dominated by s.o. **2.** (*sovrastare*) to dominate, to command, to overlook: *con la sua statura dominava la folla*, with his height he towered above the crowd; *da quella finestra si domina la valle*, that window commands a view over the valley; *la torre domina la piazza*, the tower overlooks the square; *il vecchio ca-*

stello domina l'intera città, the old castle dominates (*o commands o overlooks*) the whole town ‖ *v.i.* to rule: *l'Italia dominava nel Mediterraneo*, Italy ruled over the Mediterranean Sea; *quel re dominò per 20 anni*, that king ruled for twenty years ‖ **dominàrsi**, *v.r.* to control oneself, to master oneself: *cerca di dominarti!*, try to control yourself!; *qualche volta non sa* —, sometimes he has no self-control.

dominatóre, *ag.* ruling, dominating, commanding ‖ *s.m.*, **dominatríce**, *s.f.* ruler: *Dio è il* — *dell'universo*, God is the ruler of the universe; *i Romani furono i dominatori del mondo*, the Romans were the rulers of the world.

dominazióne, *s.f.* domination; rule, control, sway: — *barbarica*, barbarian rule; *i Paesi Bassi erano sotto la* — *della Spagna*, the Netherlands were under the rule of Spain ‖ *le Dominazioni*, (*relig.*) the Dominations.

dòmine, *s.m.* (*arc.*) **1.** (*prete, abate*) domine **2.** (*vocativo*) Lord ‖ *che* —*!*, good gracious! (*o* good Lord!); — *aiutaci!*, Lord, help us!.

domínio, *s.m.* **1.** domination; rule, control, sway; sovereignty, power, dominion: — *della Repubblica*, Republic rule; *sotto il* — *italiano*, under Italian rule; *per secoli l'Inghilterra tenne il* — *dei mari*, for centuries England ruled over the seas; *stabilire il proprio* — *sopra un paese*, to assume one's domination over a country ‖ — *di se stesso*, self-control **2.** (*territorio dominato*) dominion: *la Germania perse tutti i suoi domini alla fine della prima guerra mondiale*, Germany lost all her dominions at the end of the First World War ‖ *i Domini della Corona*, Crown Lands **3.** (*dir.*) domain: — *diretto*, demesne; — *eminente*, eminent domain; — *utile*, tenancy **4.** (*proprietà*) property ‖ *di* — *pubblico*, *fig.* known to everybody: *ciò è di pubblico* —, everybody knows that **5.** (*campo, settore*) domain, field: *rientra nel* — *della storia letteraria*, it falls within domain of literary history.

dòmino[1], *s.m.* (*mantello per maschera*) domino: *era venuto alla mascherata avvolto in un gran* — *nero*, he had appeared at the masquerade cloaked in a large black domino.

dòmino[2], *s.m.* (*giuoco*) dominoes (*pl.*); (*la singola pedina*) domino: *a casa loro ogni tanto giocano a* — occasionally they play at dominoes at home.

Domiziàno, *no.pr.m.* (*st.*) Domitian.

dòmma, *e derivati*, *V.* **dògma**, *e derivati*.

dómo[1], *ag.* tamed, tame; subdued.

dòmo[2], *s.m.* (*lat.*): *in* — *Petri*, *fig.* in prison; *pro* — *sua*, in (*o* for) one's own interest.

dòmo[3], *s.m.* (*duomo*) cathedral.

don, *s.m.* **1.** (*titolo dei sacerdoti italiani*) Don: *Don Abbondio*, Don Abbondio **2.** (*titolo spagnolo*) Don: *Don Chisciotte*, Don Quixote; *Don Giovanni*, Don Juan.

donàre, *v.t.* to give; to present (s.o. with sthg.): *le donai un orologio da polso*, I gave her a (wrist-)watch (*o* I presented her with a watch); *ve lo dono volentieri*, I shall gladly present you with it ‖ *a caval donato non si guarda in bocca*, *prov.* never look a gift horse in the mouth ‖ *chi dona presto dona due volte*, *prov.* he gives twice who gives quickly ‖ *v.i.* (*addirsi*) to suit (s.o.), to become (s.o.): *questo cappello le dona*, this hat suits her ‖ **donàrsi**, *v.r.* **1.** to give oneself **2.** (*dedicarsi*) to devote oneself.

donatàrio, *s.m.* (*dir.*) donee.

donatívo, *s.m.* **1.** (*dir.*) donative **2.** (*dono*) gift, present.

Donàto, *no.pr.m.* (*st.*) Donatus.

donatóre, *s.m.*, **donatríce**, *s.f.* donor, giver: — *di sangue*, blood donor.

donazióne, *s.f.* **1.** donation; gift: *atto di* —, (*dir.*) deed of gift **2.** (*somma elargita per uno scopo*) grant.

donchisciotteseaménte, *av.* quixotically.

donchisciottésco, *ag.* quixotic.

donchisciottísmo, *s.m.* quixotism, quixotry.

dónde, *av.* (*letter.*) **1.** whence, from where: — *venite?*, where do you come from? **2.** (*da cui*) (from) whence, — *concludo che...*, (from) whence I conclude that... **3.** (*per la qual cosa*) wherefore, for which reason **4.** (*di cui*) of which: *quel* — *io non son mai sazio*, (*letter.*) that of which I am never surfeited **5.** *averne ben* —, to have good reason (for sthg., for doing): *si oppone a questa procedura e ne ha ben* —, he objects to these proceedings and has good reason for it (*o* for doing so).

dóndola, *s.f.* (*fam.*) rocking-chair.

dondolaménto, *s.m.* swinging, rocking.

dondolàre, *v.t.* **1.** to swing, to sway: — *le braccia, le gambe*, to swing one's arms, one's legs **2.** (*cullare*) to rock; (*scuotere*) to shake: — *una culla*, to rock a cradle ‖ *far* — *una sedia*, to rock a chair ‖ *v.i.* to rock, to swing; to shake: *una lampada dondolava dal soffitto*, a lamp was swinging from the ceiling; *il ponticello dondolò sotto il pesante carico*, the small bridge shook under the heavy load; *quel tavolo dondola*, that table is wobbly; *la barca dondolava dolcemente sull'acqua*, the boat was bobbing up and down on the water ‖ **dondolàrsi**, *v.r.* **1.** to swing: — *sulle gambe*, to swing on one's legs **2.** (*su di una sedia, un'altalena, ecc.*) to rock (oneself): — *sulla sedia*, to rock oneself in one's chair **3.** *fig.* (*oziare*) to lounge, to idle about.

dondolío, *s.m.* **1.** swinging; rocking **2.** (*ciondolio*) dangling.

dóndolo, *s.m.* **1.** (*altalena*) swing **2.** (*pendolo*) pendulum: *orologio a* —, hanging clock (*o* wall-clock) **3.** *a* —, rocking: *cavallo a* —, rocking-horse; *sedia a* —, rocking-chair.

dondolóna, *s.f.*, **dondolóne**, *s.m.* lounger, loafer.

dondolóni, *av.* dangling, swinging: *se ne stava a cavalcioni del muretto, con le gambe* —, he was sitting astride the low wall, (with) his legs dangling.

dònna, *s.f.* **1.** woman (*pl.* women): — *a giornata*, daily woman; — *a ore*, charwoman; — *di campagna*, country-woman; — *di casa*, housewife; — *di servizio*, woman-servant (*o* housemaid); — *di strada*, street-walker; — *maritata*, married woman; (*dir.*) feme covert; — *nubile*, single woman (*o* spinster); (*dir.*) feme sole; — *pubblica*, prostitute; *abiti da* —, dresses; *conquistatore di donne*, lady-killer; *i diritti delle donne*, women's rights; *l'educazione della* —, female education; *l'elogio della* —, the praise of women; *l'emancipazione della* —, emancipation of women; *nemico delle donne*, woman-hater; *riunione di donne*, women's meeting (*o* fam. hen-party); *che cosa volete, buona* —?, what do you want, my good woman!; *così Dio creò la* —, thus God created woman; *ella è più* — *di sua sorella*, she is more of a woman than her sister; *non fare come le donne!*, don't play the women! ‖ *la* — *cannone*, the fat lady ‖ *figlio di buona* —, (*volg.*) son of a bitch ‖ *ne parlerò con le mie donne*, (*fam.*) I'll talk about it with my womenfolk ‖ *prima* —, (*teat.*) prima donna: *smettila di fare la prima* —!, (*fam.*) don't give yourself airs! ‖ — *buona vale una corona*, *prov.* saith Solomon the wise: a good wife's a godly prize ‖ — *e luna, oggi serena e domani bruna*, *prov.* women, wind, and fortune are ever changing ‖ *chi ha bella* — *e castello in frontiera, non ha mai pace in lettiera*, *prov.* a fair wife and a frontier castle breed quarrels **2.** (*signora, padrona*) lady, mistress ‖ *Nostra Donna*, (*la Madonna*) Our Lady **3.** (*moglie*) wife; spouse: *menar* —, to take wife **4.** (*alle carte, agli scacchi*) queen: — *di cuori, quadri, fiori, picche*, queen of hearts, diamonds, clubs, spades; *scacco alla* —!, check to the queen!; *la* — *è sotto scacco*, the queen is in check **5.** (*titolo italiano*) donna: *donna Prassede*, donna Prassede.

donnàcchera, *s.f.* (*spreg.*) vulgar woman.

donnàccia, *s.f.* bad woman; (*di liberi costumi*) loose woman.

donnàccola, *s.f.* (*spreg.*) vulgar woman.

donnaiuòlo, *s.m.* philanderer; ladies' man.

donnescaménte, *av.* **1.** in a womanly way, woman-like **2.** (*in modo effemminato*) womanishly.

donnésco, *ag.* **1.** womanlike, womanly, feminine: *lavori donneschi,* (*cucito*) needlework; *modestia donnesca,* womanly modesty (*o* womanliness); *pettegolezzo* —, women's gossip **2.** (*effeminato*) womanish: *uomo dai modi donneschi,* womanish man.

donnétta, *s.f.* **1.** *dim.* little woman: *è una cara* —*!,* she is a dear little woman! **2.** (*spreg.*) silly woman; (*donna del popolo*) woman of the people: *chiacchiere da donnette,* silly talk; *era vestita come una* —, she was dressed like anyone.

donnicciuòla, *s.f.* (*spreg.*) **1.** silly woman **2.** (*uomo debole*) weakling: *non fare la* —*!,* don't behave like a woman!.

donnicída, *s.m.* (*scherz.*) (*rubacuori*) lady-killer.

donnína, *s.f. dim.* little woman ‖ — *allegra,* lady of easy virtue (*o* lady of pleasure).

donníno, *s.m. dim.* **1.** (*ragazza assennata*) womanly girl **2.** (*ragazza graziosa*) nice little girl.

dònno, *s.m.* (*rar.*) master, lord.

dònnola, *s.f.* (*zool.*) weasel.

donnóne, *s.m.* big woman, tall woman, stout woman.

dóno, *s.m.* **1.** gift, present: *lo ebbi in* —, I got it as a gift; *non lo vorrei nemmeno in* —*!,* I wouldn't have it (*o* take it) even as a gift!; *mi fecero* — *della loro collezione di francobolli,* they made me a present of (*o* they presented me with) their stamp collection; *mi fece un bel* —, he gave me a nice present **2.** (*facoltà, disposizione*) gift, talent: *il* — *della pazienza,* the gift of patience; *ha un vero* — *per le lingue,* he has a real gift for (*o* a talent for) languages **3.** (*dir.*) donation: *fare* — *di ql.co. a qlcu.,* to make a donation of sthg. to s.o.

donzèlla, *s.f.* maid, maiden, damsel.

donzèllo, *s.m.* **1.** (*paggio*) page **2.** (*usciere*) usher messenger.

dópo, *prep.* **1.** (*di luogo, posizione*) after; (*oltre*) past; (*dietro*) **behind:** — *di voi,* after you; — *il palazzo c'è la chiesa,* the church is just past the palace; *la farmacia è subito* — *la chiesa,* you come to the chemist just after the church (*o* the chemist is just past the church); *sono* — *di lui nella lista,* I come after him in the list; *venivo* — *di lui,* I came behind him **2.** (*di tempo*) after; (*oltre*) past; (*da, in decorrenza da*) **since:** — *cena,* after supper; — *tre mesi,* after three months; *il giorno* — *la battaglia,* the day after the battle; *la prima domenica* — *Pasqua,* the first Sunday after Easter; *entrarono uno* — *l'altro,* they entered one after the other; *la gita fu rimandata a* — *Pasqua,* the excursion was put off (*o* postponed) till after Easter; *lesse una pagina* — *l'altra,* he read page after page; *non l'ho più visto* — *Natale,* I have not seen him since Christmas; *rimasero fin* — *le due,* they stayed till past two o' clock; *sarò libero* — *le tre,* I shall be free after three o' clock; *commettere una sciocchezza* — *l'altra,* to commit blunder after blunder; *regnare* — *qlcu.,* to reign after s.o. ‖ — *tutto,* after all (*o* all things considered) ‖ *av.* **1.** (*di luogo, posizione*) after; next (*ag.*); (*dietro*) **behind:** *lui camminava avanti ed io* —, he walked in front and I behind; *cosa viene* —*?,* what comes after?; *prendete la strada che viene* — *a destra,* take the next road on the right **2.** (*di tempo*) after, afterwards; then; (*più tardi*) later; (*in seguito*) later on: *un anno* —, a year later; *l'anno, il giorno* —, the year, the day after (*o* the following year, day); *molto tempo* —, long after (*o* a long time afterwards); *nè prima nè* —, neither before nor after; *poco tempo* —, not long after (*o* shortly afterwards); *subito* —, soon after; *un istante* — *era sparito,* a moment later he had disappeared; *noi partiremo* —, we shall leave later; *prima lavoro e* — *esco,* first I shall work and then I shall go out; *questo accadde* —, *qualche giorno* —, this happened later (on), a few days later (on); *soltanto* — *lo venni a sapere,* I only heard of it afterwards; *va' avanti, io verrò* —,

you go on ahead, I'll come later ‖ *a* —, (*fam.*) see you later ‖ *e* —*?,* (*che accadde?*) what happened next?; (*e che altro mai?*) what next? ‖ *cong.* **after:** — (*aver*) *mangiato, uscì,* after dining (*o* after he had eaten), he went out; — *morto si scoprì che era innocente,* after his death, they discovered that he was innocent; *ha sempre i nervi tesi* — *aver bevuto,* he is always irritable after drinking.

dopoché, dópo che, *cong.* **1.** after; **when:** — *mi rispose così, corse via,* after replying to me like that, he ran away; *venne* — *egli era partito,* she came after he had gone; *verrò* — *egli sarà partito,* I shall come when he has gone **2.** (*dacchè*) **since:** — *ti ho incontrato, la mia vita è cambiata completamente,* since meeting you, my life has changed completely; *non l'abbiamo più visto* — *si è sposato,* we have not seen him since he married.

dopodomàni, *av.* the day after tomorrow.

dopoguèrra, *s.m.* post-war period: *attività del* —, post-war activities.

dopolavóro, *s.m.* « dopolavoro » (Fascist institution organizing the workers' free-time activities).

dopoprànzo, *s.m.* afternoon.

doposcuòla, *s.m.* « doposcuola » (institution providing supplementary lessons and amusement after school -time).

dóppia, *s.f.* (*moneta antica*) dobla.

doppiàggio, *s.m.* (*cine.*) dubbing.

doppiaménte, *av.* **1.** doubly **2.** (*con inganno*) deceitfully.

doppiaménto, *s.m.* (*placcatura*) plating.

doppiàre[1], *v.t.* **1.** to double **2.** (*mar.*) to double; to turn; (*passando a sopravvento*) to weather: — *un promontorio,* to double (*o* to turn) a promontory **3.** (*ind. tessile*) to wind together **4.** (*placcare*) to plate.

doppiàre[2], *v.t.* (*cine.*) to dub: — *un film,* to dub a film.

doppiàto[1], *ag.* **1.** doubled **2.** (*placcato*) plated.

doppiàto[2], *ag.* (*cine.*) dubbed: — *in italiano,* dubbed in Italian ‖ *s.m.* (*cine.*) (*doppiaggio*) dubbing: *fare il* — *di un film,* to dub a film.

doppiatóre, *s.m.,* **doppiatríce,** *s.f.* (*cine.*) dubber.

doppiatúra, *s.f.* **1.** doubling, reduplication **2.** (*ind. tessile*) doubling **3.** (*placcatura*) plating.

doppieggiatúra, *s.f.* (*tip.*) slur.

doppière, *s.m.* two-branched candlestick.

doppiétta, *s.f.* double-barrelled gun.

doppiézza, *s.f.* **1.** doubleness; thickness **2.** (*ambiguità*) duplicity, double-dealing, deceitfulness.

doppíno, *s.m.* (*mar.*) bight.

dóppio, *ag.* **1.** double: *doppia altezza,* (*di stoffa*) double width; *doppia finestra,* double window; — *fondo,* (*di valigia, ecc.*) double (*o* false) bottom; — *mento,* double chin; *doppia porta,* double door; — *whisky,* double whisky; *binario* —, double track; *filo* —, double thread; *in* — *esemplare,* in duplicate; *margherita doppia,* double daisy; *paga doppia,* double pay; *parola a* — *senso,* ambiguous word; *la sua canna da pesca ha una lunghezza doppia della mia,* his fishing-rod is twice the length of mine; *avere una doppia vita,* to lead a double life; *chiudere una porta a* — *giro di chiave,* to double-lock a door ‖ — *giuoco,* double-cross: *non fare il* — *giuoco con me!,* don't double-cross with me! ‖ *a* — *effetto,* double-acting: *pompa a* — *effetto,* double -acting pump ‖ *a* — *petto,* double-breasted: *giacca a* — *petto,* double-breasted coat ‖ *a* — *taglio,* double -edged: *argomento a* — *taglio,* double-edged argument **2.** (*ambiguo*) double-faced, double-dealing, deceitful: *atteggiamento* —, double-dealing attitude; *persona doppia,* double-faced (*o* deceitful) person **3.** (*comm.*) double: *partita doppia,* double entry: *registrazione a partita doppia,* double entry book-keeping **4.** (*mec.*) dual: — *comando,* dual control ‖ *s.m.* **1.** double; twice as much, twice as many: *più caro del* —, twice as expensive; *ecco i libri che vi ho portato, a casa ne ho* *il —*, here are the books I have brought you, at home I have twice as many; *ho il — della tua età*, I am twice your age; *ho preso il — di quanto prendi tu*, I got twice as much as you do; *venti è il — di dieci*, twenty is the double of ten ‖ *a cento doppi*, (*molte volte di più*) many times as much 2. (*piega*) fold: *cuci la stoffa a tre doppi per volta*, sew up the material in three folds at a time 3. (*tennis*) double: *— femminile*, women's doubles; *— maschile*, men's doubles; *— misto*, mixed doubles 4. *suonare a —*, (*di campane*) to ring a full peal.

dóppio, *av.* 1. double: *piega — questo foglio*, fold this sheet in half (*o in two*) ‖ *vede —*, he sees double 2. (*ambiguamente*) double, deceitfully: *non parlare —!*, don't speak ambiguously!.

doppióne, *s.m.* 1. (*copia*, *duplicato*) double, duplicate, exact copy 2. (*spreg.*) (*imitazione scadente*) useless copy 3. (*di parola*) doublet 4. (*tip.*) double, doublet 5. (*bozzolo doppio*) double cocoon.

doràre, *v.t.* to gild; (*con lamina d'oro*) to gold-plate ‖ *— la pillola*, to gild the pill.

doràto, *ag.* 1. gilded, gilt; (*ricoperto di lamina d'oro*) gold-plated: *a lettere dorate*, in gilt letters; *cornice dorata*, gilt frame ‖ *gioventù dorata*, gilded youth 2. (*color d'oro*) golden: *giallo —*, golden yellow.

doratóre, *s.m.*, **doratríce**, *s.f.* gilder.

doratúra, *s.f.* (*ind.*) gilding: *— artificiale*, imitation gilding; *— elettrolitica*, gold-plating.

Dòri, *s.m.pl.* (*st.*) Dorians.

doricísmo, *s.m.* Doricism.

dòrico, *ag.* Doric, Dorian: *ordine —*, (*arch.*) Doric order ‖ *s.m.* (*dialetto*) Doric.

Dòride, *no.pr.f.* (*geog. st.*) Doris.

dorífora, *s.f.* (*entom.*) potato-beetle.

doríforo, *s.m.* (*letter.*) spearman (*pl.* spearmen).

dormènte, *V.* **dormiènte**.

dormentòrio, (*arc.*) per **dormitòrio**.

dormicchiáre, *v.i.* to doze, to slumber, to drowse.

dormiènte, *ag.* sleeping ‖ *s.m.* 1. sleeper ‖ *i sette dormienti*, the Seven Sleepers 2. (*edil.*) sleeper, ground-beam 3. (*mar.*) shelf(-piece).

dormiglióna, *s.f.*, **dormiglióne**, *s.m.* great sleeper, sleepy-head; (*chi si alza tardi*) late riser.

dormíre, *v.i.* 1. to sleep, to be asleep: *ho dormito bene*, I had a good night; *ieri ho dormito tutto il giorno*, yesterday I slept the whole day away; *malgrado il rumore*, *questa notte ho dormito tutto d'un sonno*, in spite of the noise, I slept the whole night through; *parla spesso dormendo*, he often talks in his sleep; *possiamo darvi da mangiare e da —*, we can dine and sleep you; *quell'albergo dà da — a cento persone*, that hotel sleeps a hundred people; *il rumore gli impedisce di —*, noise keeps him awake (*o* from sleeping); *— come un ghiro*, to sleep like a top (*o* a log); *— della grossa*, to be sound asleep (*o* to sleep soundly); *— leggero*, to have a light sleep; *— per ventiquattro ore di seguito*, to sleep the clock round; *— più del solito*, to oversleep oneself; *— profondamente*, to sleep soundly; *andare a —*, to go to bed; *continuare a —*, to sleep on; *farsi passare il mal di capo dormendo*, to sleep a headache off; *mettere qlcu. a —*, to put s.o. to bed; *non trovare da —*, to find no sleeping accomodation ‖ *cerca di dormirci su!*, try to sleep on (*o* over) it! ‖ *dormiva in piedi*, he couldn't keep his eyes open ‖ *fiore che dorme di notte*, flower that closes up at night ‖ *la natura dorme in inverno*, nature is dormant in winter ‖ *una storia che fa —*, a boring (*o* tedious) tale ‖ *— a occhi aperti*, to be very sleepy ‖ *— con gli occhi aperti*, (*vigilare anche nel sonno*) to sleep with one eye open ‖ *— nel Signore*, (*essere morto*) to sleep in the Lord ‖ *— tra due guanciali*, to set one's mind at rest; (*vivere tranquillamente*) to lead a quiet life ‖ *chi dorme non piglia pesci*, *prov.* the early bird catches the worm 2. *fig.* (*giacere*) to remain inactive; to be dormant: *l'istanza*

dorme da parecchi mesi, the petition has been lying by for several months; *le passioni che dormono nel suo cuore*, the passions dormant in his heart; *quell'affare dormiva da un pezzo*, that matter had been neglected for a long time; *lasciar — i propri capitali*, to leave one's own capital dormant (*o* inactive); *mettere una pratica a —*, to let a matter lie rest ‖ *v.t.* to sleep: *— il sonno del giusto*, to sleep the sleep of the just; *— sonni tranquilli*, to sleep peacefully ‖ *— il sonno eterno*, to sleep one's last sleep.

dormíre, *s.m.* sleep: *il — mi sembra la sua principale attività*, it seems to me that he does nothing but sleeping.

dormíta, *s.f.* sleep: *fece una bella — di dodici ore filate*, he slept like a log for twelve solid hours; *hai proprio bisogno di una buona —!*, what you need is a sound sleep!.

dormitína, *s.f.* nap: *non fare la tua solita — oggi*, don't have (*o* take) your usual nap to-day.

dormitòrio, *s.m.* dormitory; (*sl. scolastico*) dorm ‖ *questo discorso è un —*, this is a tiresome speech.

dormitúra, *s.f.* (*di baco da seta*) long sleep.

dormivéglia, *s.m.* drowsiness, doziness: *dovevo essere nel —*, *perchè non ti ho sentito*, I must have been drowsy (*o* in a doze), because I didn't hear you; *ero nel —*, *quando il telefono squillò*, I was half asleep, when the telephone rang.

Dorotèa, *no.pr.f.* Dorothy, Dorothea ‖ *dim.* Dol, Doll, Dolly, Dora, Do, Dot.

dorsàle, *ag.* dorsal: *spina —*, backbone (*o* spine) ‖ *s.f.* (*di monte*) ridge(-line).

dorsalménte, *av.* dorsally.

dorsísta, *s.m.* (*spor.*) back-stroke swimmer.

dòrso, *s.m.* 1. back: *il — della mano*, the back of the hand; *— di un'ala*, (*aer.*) top surface; *— di un libro*, back (*o* spine) of a book; *— di una pala d'elica*, (*aer.*) suction face; *cadere sul —*, to fall on one's back; *essere disteso sul —*, to be on one's back; *piegare il —*, to bend one's back ‖ *a — di mulo*, on a mule 2. (*di monte*) ridge, crest.

dosàbile, *ag.* measurable.

dosàggio, *s.m.* 1. (*chim.*) dosage 2. (*di carburante*) metering.

dosaménto, *s.m.* (*chim.*) dosage.

dosàre, *v.t.* 1. to proportion, to dose; (*dividere in dosi*) to divide (sthg.) into doses: *— gli ingredienti*, to proportion ingredients 2. (*distribuire con parsimonia*) to distribute sparingly, to dole out: *— le proprie parole*, to weigh one's words.

dosatúra, *s.f.* 1. (*chim.*) dosage; dosing 2. (*mec.*) metering: *— della miscela*, mixture strength.

dòse, *s.f.* 1. quantity; (*farm. chim.*) dose: *a piccole dosi*, in small quantities: *questa medicina va presa a piccole dosi*, this medicine is to be taken in small doses; *somministrare una medicina a qlcu. a piccole dosi*, to dose out a drug to s.o. 2. (*porzione*) dose: *una buona — di...*, a good deal of...: *avere una buona — di superbia*, *di sfacciataggine*, to be very proud, impudent ‖ *rincarare la —*, to strengthen the dose (*o* to increase the quantity).

dosímetro, *s.m.* (*fis.*) dosimeter; (*quantimetro*) quantimeter.

dosología, *s.f.* dos(i)ology.

dossàle, *s.m.* 1. reredos, dossal 2. (*paliotto*) altar-frontal 3. (*di messale*) missal-cover.

dossière, *s.m.* (*rar.*) 1. (*finimento per cavalli*) back-strap 2. (*spalliera del letto*) quilted head (of a bed).

dòsso, *s.m.* back: *questo abito pare tagliato a tuo —*, this suit fits you perfectly; *togliersi di — gli abiti*, to take off one's clothes; *toglitelo di —!*, take it off!; *togliersi un peso di —*, *fig.* to get rid of a worry (*o* to get a weight off one's mind): *ecco un gran peso che mi sono tolto di —*, that's a great weight off my mind.

dossología, *s.f.* (*eccl.*) doxology.

dotàle, *ag.* dotal.

dotàre, *v.t.* **1.** to give a dowry to (s.o.): *ha dotato sua figlia molto generosamente,* he has given his daughter a very large dowry **2.** (*fornire di una rendita permanente*) to endow: — *un ospedale,* to endow a hospital **3.** (*fornire*) to provide; to equip, to fit up, to furnish: *la nostra biblioteca è stata dotata di scaffali moderni,* our library has been furnished (o equipped o provided) with modern shelves; *la squadra fu dotata di nuove divise,* the team was supplied (o fitted out o provided o equipped) with new kits; — *un pease di scuole,* to provide a village with schools **4.** (*adornare, arricchire*) to endow: *Dio vi ha dotato di grandi qualità,* God has endowed you with great qualities (o God has bestowed great gifts on you).

dotàto, *ag.* **1.** gifted (with sthg.); endowed (with sthg.): *un musicista molto* —, a gifted musician; *è un uomo* — *di memoria prodigiosa,* he is a man endowed (o gifted) with a wonderful memory **2.** (*provveduto di rendite*) endowed (with sthg.) **3.** (*equipaggiato, fornito*) provided (with sthg.); equipped (with sthg.); fitted up (with sthg.); furnished (with sthg.): *industria dotata di impianti aggiornati,* industry equipped with up-to-date machinery.

dotatóre, *s.m.,* **dotatríce,** *s.f.* **1.** dowerer **2.** (*chi elargisce una rendita permanente*) endower.

dotazióne, *s.f.* **1.** (*rendita fissa*) endowment; (*rar.*) dotation: — *della corona,* civil list; *la* — *di un collegio,* the endowment of a college; *alcune istituzioni religiose hanno numerose dotazioni,* some religious institutions have numerous endowments ‖ *dare in* — *ql.co. a qlcu.,* to endow s.o. with sthg. **2.** (*mil.*) outfit, equipment, kit **3.** (*mar. ind.*) equipment **4.** (*teat.*) furnishings (*pl.*).

dòte, *s.f.* **1.** dowry: *una ricca* —, a large dowry; *assegnare, dare in* —, to give as a dowry: *le diede in* — *una forte somma di denaro,* he gave her a large sum of money as a dowry ‖ *sposare la* —, (*sposarsi per interesse*) to marry money **2.** (*patrimonio di pubblico istituto*) endowment **3.** *fig.* (*dono naturale*) endowment, accomplishment, gift; (*qualità*) quality: *una rara* —, a rare gift; *un uomo di chiare doti,* a gifted man; *la sincerità è una bella* —, sincerity is a good quality.

dottaménte, *av.* learnedly.

dòtto[1], *ag.* **1.** learned: *discorso* —, learned speech ‖ *armi dotte,* Artillery and the Engineers **2.** (*esperto*) expert, skilled ‖ *s.m.* scholar, man of learning, learned man.

dótto[2], *s.m.* (*anat.*) duct.

dottóra, *s.f.* (*donna saccente*) blue-stocking.

dottoràggine, *s.f.* pedantry.

dottoràle, *ag.* doctoral.

dottoralménte, *av.* in a doctoral manner.

dottoràme, *s.m.* (*iron.*) body of doctors.

dottoràto, *s.m.* doctorate: *conseguire il* —, to take one's doctorate (o doctor's degree).

dottóre, *s.m.* **1.** (*dotto, erudito*) doctor, learned man: *il* — *angelico,* the Angelic Doctor (St. Thomas Aquinas); — *Faust,* (*lett.*) Doctor Faustus; *il* — *serafico,* the Seraphic Doctor (St. Bonaventure); *i Dottori della Chiesa,* (*teol.*) the Doctors of the Church ‖ *non fare il* —*!,* don't be donnish! ‖ *Gesù tra i Dottori,* (*Bibbia*) Jesus amidst the Doctors ‖ *meglio un asino vivo che un* — *morto, prov.* better a living dog than a dead lion **2.** (*laureato*) graduate: — *in farmacia,* pharmacist; — *in fisica,* physicist; — *in lettere,* Master of Arts (*abbr.* M.A.); — *in scienze,* Master of Science (*abbr.* M.S.) **3.** (*titolo accademico inglese analogo al nostro di libero docente*) doctor: — *in legge,* Doctor of Laws (*abbr.* LL.D.); — *in teologia,* Doctor of Divinity (*abbr.* D.D.) **4.** (*medico*) doctor (of medicine), physician: *buon giorno, Dottor Brown,* good morning, Dr. Brown; *manda a chiamare il* —, send for the doctor; *mio padre fa il* —, my father is a physician.

dottoreggiàre, *v.i.* to put on learned airs; to display one's learning.

dottoréssa, *s.f.* **1.** (*laureata*) (female) graduate **2.** (*in medicina*) lady doctor, woman doctor **3.** (*donna saccente*) blue-stocking.

dottorévole, *ag.* (*scherz.*) doctorial.

dottoríno, *s.m.* (*fam.*) newly fledged doctor.

dottorúcolo, *s.m.* (*spreg.*) worthless doctor.

dottrína, *s.f.* **1.** doctrine: *la* — *di Monroe,* (*st. americana*) Monroe Doctrine; *dottrine filosofiche,* philosophic doctrines **2.** (*erudizione*) learning, erudition: *un uomo di grande* —, a vastly learned man **3.** (*catechismo*) catechism: *andare a* —, to attend a catechism class.

dottrinàle, *ag.* doctrinal.

dottrinalménte, *av.* doctrinally.

dottrinàrio, *s.m.* doctrinaire, doctrinarian.

dottrinarísmo, *s.m.* **1.** doctrinairism; doctrinarianism **2.** (*dogmatismo*) dogmatism.

dottrineggiàre, *v.i.* to reason doctrinally.

dottrinéseo, *ag.* (*spreg.*) donnish.

dóve, *av.* **1.** where: — *andate?,* where (o, *poco usato,* whither) are you going?; *andò non so* —, I have no idea where he went; *dimmi* — *è!,* tell me where he is! ‖ *da, di* —, from where (o, *meno usato,* whence): *da* — *abitavo prima ci sarà un chilometro,* it's about a kilometre from where I used to live; *di* — *veniste?,* where did you come from?; *non so da* — *cominciare,* I don't know where to begin ‖ *fin* —?, how far?; (*fino a che punto?*) up to what point?: *fin* — *li ha seguiti?,* how far did he follow them?; *fin* —, as far as; so far as; up to: *ti aiuterò fin* — *posso,* I will help you as far as I can ‖ *per* —?, (by) which way?: *per* — *è passato?,* which way did he go? **2.** (*in sostituzione di prep. con pron. rel.*): *la casa* — *vive,* the house in which (o where) he lives (o the house he lives in); *la città* — *è andato,* the town he went to; *questa è la sedia* — *siede papà,* this is the chair father sits on **3.** — *che,* (*dovunque*) wherever: — *che vada,* wherever I (may) go ‖ — *che sia,* (*in qualunque luogo*) anywhere: *mettilo* — *che sia!,* put it down anywhere! ‖ *cong.* (*letter.*) **1.** (*se*) **in the case that, whenever:** *cercate,* — *io non potessi, di rimediar voi,* in the case that I cannot do anything about it, try to see to it yourselves; *correggetemi,* — *io sbagli,* correct me, whenever I make a mistake **2.** (*mentre*) **while, whilst, whereas:** — *egli credeva che l'avrebbero condannato, si sentì liberare,* while he thought they would condemn him, in fact he was set free ‖ *s.m.* **place, where:** *il* — *e il quando,* the where and when (o the place and time) ‖ *in ogni* —, everywhere.

doventàre, (*arc.*) per **diventàre.**

dovére, *v.i.* **1.** (*obbligo, necessità assoluta*) **must, to have** (to do); **to be** (to do); **shall** (*nella 2ª, 3ª persona sing.pl.*): *un automobilista deve fermarsi al semaforo rosso,* a driver must stop at the red light; *devi fare il lavoro da solo,* you must do your work alone (o by yourself); *devi portarlo subito,* you must take it at once; *devi scusarti con quelli che hai offeso,* you must apologize to the people you have offended; *disse che non dovevamo far rumore,* he said we were not to make any noise; *tutte le quote di iscrizione devono essere versate entro il 1º marzo,* all subscriptions shall be paid by March 1st **2.** (*necessità, opportunità*) (*in proposizioni affermative e interrogative positive*) **must, to have** (to do); (*in proposizioni interrogative positive*) **need;** (*in proposizioni negative e interrogative negative*) **not to need** (to do); **need not, not to have** (to do): *devi andare in banca questa mattina?,* do you have to (o have you got to o need you o must you) go to the bank this morning?; *devo dirvi addio,* I must bid you good-bye; *disse che dovevamo portarlo subito,* he said we were to bring it immediately; *dovendo partire fra un'ora...,* having to leave in an hour...; *dovrai correre se vuoi prendere il treno,* you must (o you will have to) run if you want to catch the train; *dovrò partire domani*, I shall have to leave tomorrow; *non devi finire il lavoro stasera*, you need not (*o* do not need to *o* you haven't got to) finish the work tonight; (*fam.*) you haven't got to finish the work tonight; *il suo nome è Rossi, d'accordo, ma non è detto che debba essere italiano*, his name is Rossi, I agree, but he need not be (*o* that does not mean to say he is) Italian **3.** (*certezza, forte probabilità*) **to be bound** (to do); **must**; (*inevitabilità*) **to have** (to do); **must**: *presto o tardi questo deve accadere*, sooner or later this is bound to happen; *le riserve di carbone nel mondo presto o tardi devono finire*, the world's coal stocks must come to an end sooner or later; *tutti i bambini devono attraversare questa fase difficile*, all children have to go through this difficult phase; *tutti gli uomini devono morire*, all men must (*o* have to) die **4.** (*possibilità, probabilità, supposizione, previsione, destino*) **must, to be** (to do): *deve essere già a casa*, he must be at home already; *deve piovere oggi*, it is likely to rain to-day; *doveva diventare un gran medico*, he was to become a great physician; *doveva diventare il nostro nuovo direttore, ma fu trasferito a Roma*, he was to have been our new manager, but he was transferred to Rome; *doveva diventare sua moglie, ma morì in un incidente ferroviario*, she was to have become his wife, but she was killed in a railway crash; *doveva essere tardi quando egli tornò a casa*, it must have been late when he got home; *è lui che deve diventare il nuovo direttore*, he is the man who is to be our new manager; *non deve essere ancora a casa*, he isn't likely to be at home yet; *quello deve essere il Monte Bianco*, that must be Mont Blanc **5.** (*devo...?, dobbiamo...?, con valore di* vuoi che...?, volete che...?) **shall, to be** (to do): *devo passare a prenderti?*, shall I call for you?; *dobbiamo aprire la finestra?*, shall we open the window?; *dobbiamo prima passare da te o andare direttamente a teatro?*, are we to come to your house first or go straight to the theatre? **6.** (*al condiz.*) **ought** (to do); **should**: *dovrebbero arrivare per le otto*, they ought to get here by eight; *dovrei uscire, ma piove*, I ought to go out, but it is raining; *egli dovrebbe partire stasera*, he should leave tonight; *essi sarebbero dovuti andarci*, they should have gone there; *tu dovresti aiutarlo*, you ought to help him **7.** (*al congiunt.*) **should, were** (to do): *se dovesse mai fallire...*, if he were to fail...; *se dovesse venire...*, if he should come... (*o* should he come...); *se io dovessi incontrarlo, gli direi cosa pensavo di quella faccenda*, if I were to meet him, I should tell him what I thought about that matter; *se tu dovessi incontrarlo, digli di venire*, if you (should) meet him, tell him to come **8.** (*essere obbligato, costretto*) **to be compelled, to be obliged, to be forced**: *dovendo rinunciare alla carica...*, being compelled to give up his office...; *dovette abbandonare il suo paese*, he was obliged to leave his country; *se non prenderà in considerazione le mie lettere, dovrò rivolgermi al mio avvocato*, if he doesn't take any notice of my letters, I shall be obliged (*o* forced) to get in touch with my solicitor **9.** (*essere dovuto, essere da attribuire*) **to be due**: *a che cosa fu dovuto l'incidente?*, what was the accident due to?; *ciò è dovuto al fatto che voi arrivate in ritardo*, this is due (*o* owing) to your being late; *lo si deve alla sua negligenza*, it is due to his negligence **10.** — *arrivare*, to be due (to arrive): *la nave deve arrivare nel pomeriggio*, the ship is due in the afternoon; *il treno deve arrivare alle 4,39*, the train is due (to arrive) at 4.39; *lo zio deve arrivare stasera*, my uncle is due to arrive tonight ‖ *v.t.* (*essere debitore di*) **to owe**: *deve la sua posizione allo zio*, he owes his position to his uncle; *egli deve tutto a se stesso*, he is a self-made man; *gli devo cinque sterline*, I owe him five pounds; *ti devo la vita*, I owe you my life.

dovére, *s.m.* **1.** duty: *i miei doveri di madre*, my duties as a mother; *i nostri doveri verso Dio, la patria, il prossimo*, our duty to God, our country, our fellow creatures; *per senso del* —, from a sense of duty; *com'è mio* —, as in duty bound; *conosco il mio* —, I know where my duty lies; *ho il* — *d'informarvi*, I must inform you; *mancò al suo* —, he failed in his duty; *mi faccio un* — *di imitarvi in tutto*, I make it my duty (*o* I make it a point of duty) to imitate you in everything; *morì vittima del* —, he died doing his duty; *sento il* — *di aiutarti*, I feel bound to help you; *si credeva in* — *di seguirmi dappertutto*, he thought it was his duty to follow me everywhere ‖ *avere il senso del* —, to be conscious of one's duty; *fare il proprio* —, to do one's duty: *fa' il tuo* — *a qualunque costo!*, do your duty come what may! ‖ *a* —, properly (*o* as it should be): *stare a* —, to behave properly ‖ *più del* —, more than is necessary: *l'hai pagato più del* —, you paid more than was necessary (*o* more than you needed to) for it; *studia più del* —, he studies more than is necessary ‖ *visita di* —, duty call ‖ *tenere, mettere qlcu. a* —, to keep s.o. up to his duties ‖ *prima il* — *poi il piacere*, prov. work before pleasure ‖ *fa' il* — *e non temere*, prov. do well and dread no shame (*o* do well and have well) **2.** *pl.* (*saluti, convenevoli*) (kind) regards, compliments, respects: *i miei doveri a vostra sorella*, my kindest regards to your sister; *porgere i propri* — *a qlcu.*, to pay one's respects to s.o.

doverosaménte, *av.* dutifully.

doveróso, *ag.* dutiful; (*giusto*) right, rightful, fair: *è* — *che noi vi restituiamo il denaro*, it is right (*o* fair) that we should give you back your money.

dovízia, *s.f.* (*letter.*) (*abbondanza*) abundance, plenty; (*ricchezza*) wealth: — *di particolari*, wealth of detail; *c'era* — *di tutto*, there was plenty of everything ‖ *a* —, plentifully (*o* abundantly *o* copiously) ‖ *dove è guerra non fu mai* —, prov. wars bring scars.

doviziosaménte, *av.* (*con abbondanza*) abundantly, plentifully, copiously; (*riccamente*) richly.

dovizióso, *ag.* **1.** (*abbondante*) abundant, plentiful, copious **2.** (*ricco*) wealthy.

dovúnque, *av.* (*dappertutto*) everywhere; (*in qualsiasi luogo*) anywhere: *lo si trova* —, it can be found everywhere (*o* anywhere) ‖ *cong.* wherever: — *voi siate, ascoltatemi*, wherever you are (*o* may be), listen to me.

dovutaménte, *av.* duly; (*giustamente*) deservedly.

dovúto, *ag.* (*giusto, adatto, conveniente*) due; right, just, rightful; adequate; fitting; proper: *con la dovuta diligenza*, with the due (*o* necessary *o* required) diligence; *nel modo* —, in the proper way; *nel tempo* —, in due course; *contratto redatto nella forma dovuta*, contract drawn up in due form; *prendere nella dovuta considerazione*, to take into due (*o* proper) consideration ‖ *s.m.* due; (*debito*) debt: *dàgli il* —, give him his due; *mi avete dato più del* —, you have given me more than my due.

dozzína, *s.f.* **1.** dozen: *dozzine di uova*, dozens of eggs; *una buona* —, a round dozen (*o* thirteen to the dozen *o* a baker's dozen); *una mezza* —, half a dozen; *tre dozzine di bottiglie*, three dozen bottles ‖ *a dozzine*, in dozens: *arrivarono a dozzine*, they arrived in dozens ‖ *le uova costano 4 scellini alla* —, eggs are 4/- a dozen; *comprare, vendere alla* —, to buy, to sell by the dozen ‖ *di, da* —, cheap (*o* second-rate *o* common) **2.** (*pensione in casa privata*) board and lodgings: *prendere a* —, to take in boarders; *stare a* — *da qlcu.*, to board with s.o. (*o* at s.o.'s); *tenere a* —, to board.

dozzinàle, *ag.* cheap, second-rate, common.

dozzinalménte, *av.* by the dozen: *il lavoro fu eseguito* —, the work was bungled.

dozzinànte, *s.m.* boarder.

dracèna, *s.f.* (*bot.*) dragon-tree.

dràema, *V.* **dràmma²**.

Dracóne, *no.pr.m.* (*st.*) Draco.

draconiàno, *ag.* Draconian, Draconic: *leggi draconiane*, Draconian (*o* rigorous) laws.

dràga, *s.f.* **1.** dredger, dredging machine: — *a ca-*

tena di tazze, bucket-ladder dredge; — *ad aspirazione*, suction dredge; — *a secchie*, bucket dredge; — *galleggiante*, floating dredge; — *succhiante*, hydraulic dredge 2. (*miner.*) drag: — *di caricamento*, loader 3. (*rete a strascico*) trawl.

dragàggio, *s.m.* 1. dredging: *impianto di* —, dredging plant 2. (*ricupero delle mine*) mine-sweeping: — *magnetico*, magnetic mine-sweeping.

dragamíne, *s.m.* (*mar. mil.*) mine-sweeper, mine-dredger.

dragànte[1], *s.m.* (*bot.*) tragacanth.

dragànte[2], *s.m.* (*mar.*) transom.

dragàre, *v.t.* 1. to dredge 2. (*mine*) to sweep.

draghinàssa, *s.f.* (*scherz.*) large sabre.

dràglia, *s.f.* (*mar.*) stay: — *dei fiocchi*, jib-stay.

dràgo, *s.m.* 1. dragon: *San Giorgio e il* —, St. George and the dragon ‖ *sangue di* —, (*farm.*) dragon's-blood 2. (*rettile*) dragon 3. (*aer.*) kite balloon ‖ — *volante*, (*aquilone*) kite.

dragomànno, *s.m.* dragoman (*pl.* dragomans, dragomen).

dragóna, *s.f.* (*mil.*) sword-knot.

dragonàto, *ag.* (*arald.*) dragonné.

dragóne, *s.m.* 1. (*drago*) dragon: *il* — *infernale*, *fig.* the dragon ‖ *il Dragone*, (*astr.*) the Dragon 2. (*mil.*) dragoon.

dragonéssa, *s.f.* 1. dragoness, she-dragon 2. (*virago*) termagant, fury.

dràia, *s.f.* dredge, drag-net.

dràmma[1], *s.m.* 1. (*teat.*) drama; play: *il* — *elisabettiano*, Elizabethan drama; — *lirico*, (*mus.*) opera; — *pastorale*, pastoral drama; — *storico*, historical play; *l'epilogo, lo scioglimento del* —, the epilogue, the dénouement of the drama 2. *fig.* (*vicende tristi*) drama, tragedy: — *familiare*, family tragedy; *il* — *del popolo turco*, the tragedy of the Turkish people; *descrisse il* — *della nave che affondava*, he described the drama of the sinking ship; *il terribile* — *che ha rovinato la sua famiglia*, the tragedy that ruined his family.

dràmma[2], *s.f.* 1. dram, drachm, drachma (*misura di peso greca = g. 4,30*) 2. (*moneta greca*) drachma (*pl.* drachmas, drachmae) 3. (*minima particella*) tiny bit.

drammàtica, *s.f.* (*teat.*) dramatics.

drammaticaménte, *av.* dramatically.

drammàtico, *ag.* 1. (*teat.*) dramatic: *autore, scrittore* —, dramatist (*o* playwright); *compagnia drammatica*, theatrical company; *spettacolo* —, dramatic performance 2. *fig.* dramatic, striking; (*commovente*) moving, touching: *una situazione drammatica*, a dramatic (*o* striking) situation.

drammatizzàre, *v.t.* 1. to dramatise, to give a dramatic turn to (sthg.): *non* —!, don't make a mountain out of every mole-hill! 2. (*teat.*) to dramatise.

drammaturgía, *s.f.* dramaturgy.

drammatúrgo, *s.m.* dramatist, playwright.

drappeggiaménto, *s.m.* draping.

drappeggiàre, *v.t.* to drape: — *una toga*, to drape a gown.

drappéggio, *s.m.* draping.

drappèlla, *s.f.* (*mil.*) (*banderuola*) pennon.

drappellàre, *v.i.* (*mil.*) to march in squads.

drappèllo, *s.m.* (*mil.*) squad.

drappellonàre, *v.t.* to decorate with draperies.

drappellóne, *s.m.* 1. curtain 2. (*paramento di chiesa*) church hanging.

drapperìa, *s.f.* 1. drapery 2. (*magazzino di drappi*) draper's shop, drapery store.

dràppo, *s.m.* cloth; drape: — *a oro*, gold brocade; — *funebre*, pall.

dràstico, *ag.* drastic: *rimedio* —, drastic remedy; *prendere misure drastiche*, to take drastic measures.

drenàggio, *s.m.* drainage.

drenàre, *v.t.* to drain.

Drèsda, *no.pr.f.* (*geog.*) Dresden.

drìade, *s.f.* 1. (*mit.*) Dryad (*pl.* Dryads, [Dryades) 2. (*bot.*) dryas (*pl.* dryades).

dribblàre, *v.i.* (*spor.*) to dribble.

drìtta, *s.f.* 1. (*mano destra*) right hand 2. (*parte destra*) right-hand side, right: *tenere la* —, to keep to the right 3. (*mar.*) starboard: *a* —, to starboard: *tutta a* —!, hard-a-starboard!.

drìtto, *ag.* 1. (*non storto*) straight ‖ — *come un fuso*, as straight as a ram-rod 2. (*eretto*) upright: *stare* —, to hold oneself upright 3. (*onesto*) honest, upright 4. (*destro*) right: *dal lato* —, on the right-hand side ‖ *s.m.* 1. *V.* **diritto**[2] 2. right: *il* — *e il rovescio di un tessuto*, the right and the wrong side of a cloth 3. (*mar. aer.*): — *del timone*, (*mar.*) rudderpost; — *di deriva*, (*aer.*) fin post; — *di poppa*, (*mar.*) sternpost ‖ *av.* straight, straight ahead: *se ne andò via* —, he went straight away.

drittúra, *s.f.* rectitude; justice.

drízza, *s.f.* (*mar.*) halyard.

drizzaménto, *s.m.* straightening.

drizzàre, *v.t.* 1. to straighten, to make straight: — *una sbarra di ferro*, to straighten an iron bar 2. *fig.* (*riparare*) to put right, to right: — *un torto*, to right a wrong 3. (*rizzare*) to prick up: — *le orecchie*, to prick up one's ears 4. (*erigere*) to erect, to build: — *un monumento*, to erect a monument 5. (*volgere*) to turn: — *la mente ad elevati pensieri*, to turn one's mind to lofty thoughts ‖ **drizzàrsi**, *v.r.* to straighten (up); (*alzarsi*) to stand up, to rise: *non star così gobbo, drizzati!*, don't stoop like that, straighten up!.

dròga, *s.f.* 1. drug 2. *pl.* (*spezie*) spices, spicery (*sing.*), groceries: *ci sono troppe droghe in questa vivanda*, this food is too much seasoned (*o* spiced).

drogàre, *v.t.* 1. to drug; to dope: — *un cavallo*, to dope a horse 2. (*cibi*) to spice, to season: *quel cuoco droga molto i cibi*, that cook spices food very much ‖ **drogàrsi**, *v.r.* to drug oneself; to dope oneself.

drogàto, *ag.* 1. drugged: *sigarette drogate*, drugged cigarettes 2. (*di cibi*) spiced, spicy: *questo umido è troppo* —, this stew is too spicy.

drogherìa, *s.f.* grocery; grocer's shop: *articoli di* —, groceries; *ha una* —, he has a grocery business.

droghière, *s.m.* grocer: *vado dal* —, I'm going to the grocer's.

dromedàrio, *s.m.* dromedary.

dromòmetro, *s.m.* (*mar.*) log.

dromóne, *s.m.* (*st. mar.*) dromon, dromond.

dròsera, *s.f.* (*bot.*) sundew.

drosòmetro, *s.m.* (*meteorologia*) drosometer.

drúda, *s.f.* (*spreg.*) mistress, paramour.

drúdo, *s.m.* (*spreg.*) lover, paramour.

druidéssa, *s.f.* (*st.*) Druidess.

druídico, *ag.* druidic(al); Druid (*attributivo*):] *riti druidici*, Druid rites.

druidísmo, *s.m.* Druidism.

drúido, *s.m.* (*st.*) Druid ‖ *Ordine dei Druidi*, (*società segreta fondata a Londra nel 1781*) United Ancient Order of Druids.

drúpa, *s.f.* (*bot.*) drupe.

drupàcee, *s.f.pl.* (*bot.*) Drupaceae.

drupàceo, *ag.* (*bot.*) drupaceous.

drupífero, *ag.* (*bot.*) drupiferous.

drúsa, *s.f.* (*min.*) druse.

Drúso, *no.pr.m.* (*st.*) Drusus.

duàle, *ag.* (*gram.*) dual.

dualísmo, *s.m.* dualism.

dualísta, *s.m.* (*fil.*) dualist.

dualístico, *ag.* (*fil.*) dualistic.

dualità, *s.f.* (*rar.*) 1. duality 2. (*fil.*) dualism.

dubbiaménte, *av.* doubtfully, uncertainly, dubiously.

dubbiézza, *s.f.* dubiousness, uncertainty, doubt.

dúbbio[1], *s.m.* 1. doubt, uncertainty: *senza* —, no doubt (*o* without a doubt *o* undoubtedly); *è fuor di* — *che...*, it is beyond doubt that...; *era in* — *sul da farsi*, he was in doubt (about) what to do; *ho i miei* *dubbi*, I have my doubts about it; *non c'è — che tu abbia buone intenzioni*, no doubt you mean well; *non ho alcun — sulla tua onestà*, I have no doubt about (*o* as to) your honesty; *dissipare un —*, to remove (*o* to dispel) a doubt; *essere in —*, to be in doubt; *lasciare in —*, to leave doubtful (*o* in suspense); *mettere in —*, to (call in) question: *metto in — la sua buona fede*, I question his good faith in this matter; *metto in — le sue parole*, I challenge his word; *nutrire dubbi in merito a ql.co.*, to have one's doubts about sthg.; *sollevare un —*, to raise a doubt 2. (*sospetto*) misgiving, apprehension, doubt: *avevo il — che l'avesse rubato*, I suspected that she had stolen it; *ho il — che tu non sia sincero*, I question (*o* I doubt) your sincerity.

dùbbio[2], *ag.* 1. (*incerto*) doubtful, uncertain: *il risultato è ancora —*, the result is still dubious (*o* uncertain) || *di — gusto*, in doubtful taste 2. (*ambiguo*) dubious; questionable: *dubbia condotta*, questionable conduct; *un amico —*, a dubious friend; *parole dubbie*, dubious words; *una persona di dubbia fama*, a person of doubtful (*o* dubious) reputation; *sguardo —*, sinister look.

dubbiosaménte, *av.* doubtfully, uncertainly, dubiously.

dubbióso, *ag.* 1. (*che dubita*) doubtful, dubious: *son —*, I am doubtful 2. (*che lascia in dubbio*) ambiguous, doubtful, dubious; vague: *esito —*, doubtful issue.

dubitàbile, *ag.* 1. doubtful, doubtable 2. (*discutibile*) questionable.

dubitànte, *ag.* 1. (*rar.*) doubting 2. (*esitante*) hesitating, uncertain.

dubitàre, *v.i.* 1. to doubt (sthg.); (*essere in dubbio*) to be in doubt (about sthg.): *dubitava che tu riuscissi*, he doubted you would succeed; *dubito della verità delle tue parole*, I doubt the truth of your words; *ne dubito*, I have my doubts; *non dubitiamo di ciò*, we do not doubt that; *verrò con te, non —!*, I'll come along with you, depend on it!; *— della vittoria, del successo*, to doubt of victory, of success 2. (*diffidare*) to distrust (s.o.), to be distrustful, to mistrust (s.o.): *dubita di quell'adulatore!*, mistrust that flatterer!.

dubitativaménte, *av.* dubitatively.

dubitativo, *ag.* dubitative: *proposizione dubitativa*, dubitative clause; *sguardo —*, inquiring look.

dubitatóre, *s.m.*, **dubitatrice**, *s.f.* doubter.

dubitazióne, (*rar.*) per **dùbbio**.

dubitóso, (*rar.*) per **dubbióso**.

dublinése, *ag.* of Dublin || *s.c.* Dubliner.

Dublíno, *no.pr.f.* (*geog.*) Dublin: *abitante di —*, Dubliner; *una chiesa di —*, a Dublin church.

dúca, *s.m.* 1. duke: *il — di Edimburgo*, the Duke of Edinburgh 2. (*arc.*) (*guida, duce*) guide, leader.

ducàle, *ag.* 1. ducal: *corona —*, ducal coronet; *famiglia —*, ducal family 2. (*dogale*) dogal || *il Palazzo Ducale di Venezia*, the Palace of the Doges in Venice.

ducàto[1], *s.m.* 1. (*titolo*) dukedom 2. (*feudo di duca*) duchy || *il — di Modena*, the duchy of Modena.

ducàto[2], *s.m.* (*antica moneta*) ducat.

ducatóne, *s.m.* (*antica moneta*) ducatoon.

dúce, *s.m.* 1. (*capo*) chief; leader, commander || *Duce*, (*st. italiana*) "Duce" 2. (*guida, scorta*) escort, guide.

ducentísta, *s.m.* writer of the thirteenth century.

ducènto, *V.* **duecènto**.

ducentèsimo, *V.* **duecentèsimo**.

duchèa, *V.* **ducàto**[1].

duchésco, *ag.* ducal.

duchéssa, *s.f.* duchess.

duchessína, *s.f.* duke's daughter.

duchíno, *s.m.* young duke; duke's child, dukeling.

dúe, *ag.num.card. s.m.* 1. two: *su dieci*, two out of ten; *—volte*, twice: *— volte al giorno*, twice a day; *—volte tanto*, twice as much; twice as many: «*Quanto zucchero vuoi?*», «*Dammene — volte tanto*», "How much sugar do you want?", "Give me twice as much"; *i suoi libri sono*

—volte tanto i miei, his books are twice as many as mine || *a — a —*, two by two (*o* by twos); *carrozza a — ruote*, two-wheeled carriage; *ogni — giorni*, every other day; *il più caro dei —*, the more expensive of the two; *tutti e —*, both || *il — nel quattro sta — volte*, two into four goes twice; *vennero tutti e —*, they both (*o* both of them) came; *verrò il — aprile*, I shall come on the second of April; *marciare per —*, to march two abreast (*o* in twos); *piegare ql.co. in —*, to fold sthg. in two (*o* in half) || *una delle —!*, one or the other! || *lavorare per —*, to work hard || *scrivi — righe*, (*fam.*) write a few lines (*o* words) || *tenere il piede in — staffe*, to have a foot in both camps (*o* to run with the hare and hunt with the hounds) 2. (*mar.*): *un — alberi*, a two-master; *di — punta*, pair-oar; *— di punta senza timoniere*, coxwainless pair 3. *il — di picche*, (*a carte*) the two of spades.

duecentèsimo, *ag.num.ord. s.m.* two hundredth.

duecènto, *ag.num.card. s.m.* two hundred || *il Duecento*, the thirteenth century.

duellànte, *s.m.* duellist.

duellàre, *v.i.* to duel, to fight a duel.

duellatóre, **duellísta**, *s.m.* (*rar.*) duellist.

duèllo, *s.m.* 1. duel: *— alla pistola*, pistol duel; *— alla spada*, duel with swords; *— all'ultimo sangue*, duel to the death; *codice del —*, duelling code; *fare un —*, to fight a duel; *sfidare a —*, to challenge (to a duel) 2. (*sfida, contesa*) duel, contest, challenge: *— letterario*, literary contest.

duemíla, *ag.num.card. s.m.* two thousand.

duennàle, *ag.* (*rar.*) biennial.

duétto, *s.m.* 1. (*mus.*) duet: *il — della «Traviata»*, the duet in "La Traviata" 2. (*scherz.*) (*diverbio*) scolding-match, slanging-match, tiff.

dugènto, *V.* **duecènto**.

dúglia, *s.f.* (*mar.*) coil of rope.

dulcamàra[1], *s.f.* (*bot.*) woody nightshade, bittersweet.

dulcamàra[2], *s.m.* (*scherz.*) (*ciarlatano*) charlatan, quack.

dulcína, *s.f.* (*chim.*) dulcin.

dulcinèa, *s.f.* (*scherz.*) Dulcinea, sweetheart.

dulía, *s.f.* (*relig.*) dulia, douleia.

dum-dum, *ag.* dumdum: *palle —*, dumdum bullets.

dúma, *s.f.* (*st. russa*) duma.

dúmo, *s.m.* (*letter.*) bramble, thorny shrub.

dumóso, *ag.* (*letter.*) brambly.

dúna, *s.f.* dune.

dúnque, *cong.* 1. (*perciò*) therefore; so: *non mi piace, — non lo voglio*, I don't like it, so I don't want it; *penso, — sono*, I think, therefore I am 2. (*rafforzativo*) then, well, so: *—?*, well? (*o* sl. so what?); *—, per tornare al nostro argomento...*, well, to get back to the subject...; *che volete —?*, what do you want then?; *dovete — sapere che...*, well, you must know that...; *eccoti — di ritorno*, so you are back then; *perchè — dovrei farlo?*, so, why ought I to do it? || *s.m.: venire al —*, to come to the point (*o* fam. to cut a long story short).

dúo, *s.m.* (*mus.*) duet.

duodècima, *s.f.* (*mus.*) duodene.

duodècimo, *ag. num.ord. s.m.* twelfth.

duodenàle, *ag.* (*anat.*) duodenal: *ulcera —*, (*patol.*) duodenal ulcer.

duodenàrio, *ag.* duodenary.

duodeníte, *s.f.* (*patol.*) duodenitis.

duodèno, *s.m.* (*anat.*) duodenum (*pl.* duodena).

duòlo, *s.m.* (*letter.*) 1. sorrow, grief 2. (*lamento*) lamentation.

duòmo, *s.m.* 1. cathedral 2. (*ferr.*) dome, steam dome: *scala dei duomi*, dome ladder.

dúplex, *ag.*: *telefono —*, shared telephone (*o* two-party-line).

duplicàre, *v.t.* to duplicate, to double.

duplicataménte, *av.* doubly.

duplicàto, *s.m.* duplicate: *copia in —*, duplicate copy.

duplicatóre, *s.m.* **1.** (*di manoscritti, disegni*) duplicator: — *tipografico*, multigraph **2.** (*rad.*) doubler: — *di frequenza*, frequency doubler; — *di tensione*, voltage doubler.

duplicatúra, *s.f.* **1.** duplication **2.** (*tip.*) double **3.** (*med.*) duplicature.

duplicazióne, *s.f.* duplication.

dúplice, *ag.* **1.** double, twofold: *un — vantaggio*, a twofold advantage **2.** (*ambiguo*) double-faced, double-dealing.

duplicità, *s.f.* (*finzione, ambiguità*) duplicity, double-dealing, deceitfulness.

dúplo, *ag.s.m.* double.

dúra, *s.f.* (*bot.*) durra, durr.

duràbile, *ag.* durable, lasting: *vento —*, lasting wind.

durabilità, *s.f.* durability, durableness, lastingness.

durabilménte, *av.* durably, lastingly.

duràcino, *ag.* clinging: *pesca duracina*, clingstone peach.

duralumínio, *s.m.* (*metal.*) duralumin, duraluminium.

duramàdre, *s.f.* (*anat.*) dura mater.

duràme(n), *s.m.* (*bot.*) duramen.

duraménte, *av.* **1.** hard (anche *fig.*): *fummo — colpiti*, we were hard hit; *lavora —*, he works hard **2.** (*aspramente*) harshly; (*in malo modo*) roughly, rudely: *trattare qlcu. —*, to treat s.o. roughly.

duránte, *prep.* during: — *la settimana*, during the week ‖ *vita natural —*, during one's lifetime.

duràre, *v.i.* **1.** to last: *la guerra può — degli anni*, the war may last quite a few years; *la loro amicizia non durerà a lungo*, their friendship will not last long; *questa moda non durerà*, this fashion will not last ‖ *un bel giuoco dura poco*, long jesting was never good **2.** (*rimanere*) to remain: — *in carica*, to remain in office **3.** (*perseverare*) to persist, to persevere: *la sua febbre dura*, his fever persists **4.** (*resistere*) to hold out: — *fino alla fine*, to hold out to the end **5.** (*non consumarsi*) to endure; (*conservarsi*) to keep; (*di abiti, stoffe*) to wear: *quella stoffa non dura*, that material does not wear well; *questo pesce non durerà fino a domani*, this fish will not keep till tomorrow; *questo vestito ti durerà molto*, this dress of yours will wear long (o for years) ‖ *v.t.* to endure, to resist, to bear, to stand: — *la fame*, to stand (o to endure) hunger ‖ *durammo molta fatica a convincerli*, we had great difficulty in persuading them; *duro fatica a crederlo*, I can scarcely (o hardly) believe it; *non posso — tanta fatica*, I cannot stand so much effort ‖ *chi la dura la vince*, *prov.* slow and steady wins the race.

duràta, *s.f.* **1.** duration, length: — *di una operazione*, time required for an operation; *per tutta la — della fiera*, for the duration of the fair; *un soggiorno di una certa —*, a stay of some length; *il suo soggiorno fu di breve —*, his stay was short **2.** (*periodo*) term, period: — *di una carica*, tenure of an office; *per la — di dieci anni*, for a term of ten years; *le rappresentazioni avranno la — di venti giorni*, performances will be held for a period of twenty days **3.** (*di un oggetto*) endurance; (*di stoffe, ecc.*) wear: — *di un motore*, life of a motor; — *in vaso aperto*, (*chim.*) pot life; *prova di —*, (*al banco*), (*mec.*) endurance test; *un tessuto di —*, a cloth that wears well; *ne garantisco la —*, I guarantee it for wear; *essere di lunga —*, to last long (o to wear well o to wear long).

duratúro, *ag.* **1.** lasting: *fama duratura*, lasting fame; *la pace non sarà duratura*, peace will not last long **2.** (*di colore*) fast.

durévole, *ag.* durable, lasting: *la loro amicizia non*

mi sembra —, their friendship will not last long, I think; *queste scarpe saranno durevoli, spero*, I hope these shoes will wear long and well.

durevolézza, *s.f.* durableness, durability.

durevolménte, *av.* durably, lastingly.

durétto, *ag.* (*alquanto difficile*) somewhat difficult; hardish; (*piuttosto coriaceo*) rather tough: *ha un carattere —, vero?*, she is not very easy to get on with, is she?; *questa carne mi sembra duretta*, I think this meat is rather tough.

durézza, *s.f.* **1.** hardness; (*tenacità*) toughness: *pietra di grande —*, very hard stone **2.** (*rozzezza, asprezza*) hardness, harshness; (*rigidità*) stiffness: — *delle linee di un disegno*, stiffness of a drawing; — *di suono*, harshness of sound **3.** (*rigidezza di modi*) hardness, severity: *lo trattò con —*, he treated him hardly.

duríccio, *ag.* rather hard, hardish.

Durlindàna, *no.pr.f.* Durendal ‖ *s.f.* (*scherz.*) sword.

dúro, *ag.* **1.** hard; (*coriaceo*) tough: — *come il diamante*, as hard as a diamond; *legno —*, hard wood; *uova dure*, hard-boiled eggs; *abbiamo dovuto mangiare pane — perchè i negozi erano chiusi*, we had to eat stale bread because the shops were closed; *è — da cuocere*, it takes long to cook (o it takes a lot of cooking); *mi piace dormire su un materasso —*, I like to sleep on a hard mattress ‖ *muso —*, intractable person ‖ *ha la pelle dura*, (*fam.*) he is a tough chap ‖ *ha il sonno molto —*, he sleeps like a log ‖ *non vuol farlo perchè ha la testa dura*, he will not do it because he is very stubborn; *quello scolaro ha la testa dura*, that pupil is a block-head ‖ *questo problema sarà un osso —*, this problem will be a hard nut to crack **2.** (*di voce*) harsh; (*di orecchio*) hard **3.** (*fonet.*) hard: *consonanti dolci, dure*, soft, hard consonants **4.** (*difficile*) hard, difficult: *dura lotta*, hard fight; *avrai la vita dura per cominciare!*, you will have to rough it at the start!; *fu un inverno —*, it was a hard winter; *furono tempi duri per tutti*, they were hard times for everybody; *le rendeva la vita dura*, he made her life a burden; *mi riesce — crederlo*, I find it hard to believe; *quella superstizione fu dura a morire*, that superstition was hard to kill ‖ *è — a morire*, (*fam.*) it takes a lot to beat him **5.** (*crudo, rigido*) stiff, hard: *il tuo disegno ha ancora le linee dure*, your drawing is still rather stiff; *avere un viso con lineamenti duri*, to be hard-featured **6.** (*severo, crudele*) hard, severe; sad, painful: — *colpo*, hard blow; *un — destino*, a sad destiny; *ci trovammo nella dura necessità di vendere tutto*, we found ourselves in the dire necessity of selling everything; *fu molto — verso di noi*, he was very hard on us ‖ *carcere —*, rigorous imprisonment ‖ *s.m.* **1.** hard, harship: *gli piace dormire sul —*, he likes a hard bed; *qui sotto c'è del —*, there is something hard under(neath) here ‖ — *con — non fa buon muro*, *prov.* hard with hard makes not the stone wall **2.** (*fam.*) (*prepotente*) bully: *non fare il — con tua sorella*, don't bully your sister.

dúro, *av.* **1.** hard: *colpire — qlcu.*, to strike s.o. a hard blow **2.** *tener —*, to hold out.

duróne, *s.m.* callosity, hard skin.

dúttile, *ag.* ductile (anche *fig.*): *carattere —*, ductile (o pliable o pliant) character; *metalli duttili*, ductile metals.

duttilímetro, *s.m.* (*metal.*) hardometer, durometer.

duttilità, *s.f.* ductility (anche *fig.*).

dútto, *s.m.* **1.** canal **2.** (*anat.*) duct.

duumviràle, *ag.* (*st. romana*) duumviral.

duumviràto, *s.m.* (*st. romana*) duumvirate.

duúmviro, *s.m.* (*st. romana*) duumvir (*pl.* duumviri, duumvirs).

E

e, *s.f.m.* (*quinta lettera dell'alfabeto italiano*) e (*pl.* es, e's) ‖ — *come Empoli*, (*tel.*) e for Edward.

e, ed, *cong.* **1. and:** *tu ed io*, you and I ‖ *e i bambini?*, what about the children? ‖ *e... e...*, both... and...: *me lo dissero e tuo padre e tua madre*, both your father and your mother told me so ‖ *tutti e due*, both; *tutti e tre*, all three **2.** (*nei nomi di ditte*) &: *John Smith e Co.*, John Smith & Co.

e', *pron. pers.* 3ª *persona sing. m.* (*apocope di* ei, egli) he: — *mi disse*, he told me.

Èaco, *no.pr.m.* (*mit.*) Aeacus.

ebanísta, *s.m.* ebonist; (*chi lavora legni*) cabinet-maker.

ebanisteria, *s.f.* **1.** (*bottega di ebanista*) cabinet-maker's shop **2.** (*arte dell'ebanista*) cabinet-making, cabinet work.

ebaníte, *s.f.* (*chim.*) ebonite, vulcanite.

èbano, *s.m.* ebony: *del color dell' —*, *fatto di —*, ebony (*attributivo*) ‖ *nero come l'—*, as black as ink (*o* jet-black).

ebbène, *cong.* well, well then: —, *potete andare*, well, you may go ‖ — ?, well?, what about it?.

èbbio, *s.m.* (*bot.*) wild elder.

ebbrézza, *s.f.* **1.** drunkenness; intoxication, inebriation **2.** *fig.* elation, rapture, ecstasy.

èbbro, *ag.* **1.** drunken (*attributivo*); drunk (with sthg.); inebriated (with sthg.), intoxicated (with sthg.) **2.** (*esaltato*, *folle*) excited (with sthg.), mad (with sthg.): *era — di gioia*, he was beside himself (*o* mad) with joy.

ebdòmada, *s.f.* (*rar.*) week, hebdomad.

ebdomadário, *ag.* weekly, hebdomadal ‖ *s.m.* weekly (paper).

Èbe, *no.pr.f.* (*mit.*) Hebe.

ebefrenía, *s.f.* (*patol.*) hebephrenia.

èbere, *v.t.* (*arc.*) to weaken; to idle.

ebetàggine, *s.f.* (*rar.*) stupidity, hebetude; obtuseness.

èbete, *ag.* dull-witted, feeble-minded, idiotic, stupid, obtuse, dull: *sorriso —*, stupid (*o* idiotic) smile ‖ *s.m.* idiot, blockhead: *agisce come un —*, he acts as if he were in a daze.

ebetísmo, *s.m.* feeble-mindedness, stupidity, idiocy; (*med.*) hebetude.

ebollíre, *v.i.* (*rar.*) to boil, to boil over.

ebollizióne, *s.f.* ebullition, boiling: — *di una batteria*, gassing; *punto di —*, boiling point; *temperatura di —*, boiling temperature; *entrare in —*, to begin to boil.

eborário, *s.m.* worker in ivory.

ebraicaménte *av.* Hebraically.

ebraicísta, *s.m.* Hebraist, Hebrew scholar.

ebràico, *ag.* Hebrew, Hebraic, Jewish ‖ *s.m.* (*lingua*) Hebrew.

ebraísmo, *s.m.* Hebraism.

ebraizzàre, *v.t.i.* to Hebraize.

ebrèo, *ag.* Hebrew, Jewish ‖ *s.m.* **1.** Hebrew, Jew, Israelite ‖ *l'Epistola agli Ebrei*, the Epistle to the Hebrews **2.** (*lingua*) Hebrew ‖ **ebrèa**, *s.f.* Hebrew, Jewess.

Èbridi, *no.pr.f.pl.* (*geog.*) Hebrides.

ebrietà, *V.* **ebbrézza**.

ebulliòmetro, *s.m.* (*chim.*) ebullioscope.

ebullioscopía, *s.f.* (*chim.*) ebullioscopy.

ebullioscòpio, *s.m.* (*chim.*) ebullioscope.

ebullizióne, *V.* **ebollizióne**.

eburneazióne, *s.f.* (*med.*) eburnation.

ebúrneo, ebúrno, *ag.* of ivory; ivory (*attributivo*); (*bianco come l'avorio*) as white as ivory.

Ècate, *no.pr.f.* (*mit.*) Hecate.

ecatómbe, *s.f.* **1.** (*st. greca*) hecatomb **2.** massacre, mass slaughter.

eccedènte, *ag.* **1.** (*comm.*) exceeding: *somma —*, exceeding amount **2.** excessive, in excess (*predicativo*); surplus (*attributivo*).

eccedènza, *s.f.* excess, surplus, overplus: — *di peso*, overweight.

eccèdere, *v.t.* to exceed, to go beyond: *egli eccede ogni limite*, he exceeds (*o* goes beyond) all limits (*o* he goes too far); *questo eccede le mie forze*, this exceeds my strength; *la vostra richiesta eccede ogni nostra possibilità*, your request is beyond our power ‖ *v.i.* to go too far: — *nel bere*, to drink to excess (*o* too much).

eccehòmo, *s.m.* **1.** Ecce Homo **2.** (*persona malconcia*) sickly man, haggard man.

eccellènte, *ag.* excellent, first-rate, very good: *idea —*, capital idea; *abbiamo passato una serata —*, we had a most enjoyable evening; *era di umore —*, he was in the best of moods (*o* in high spirits).

eccellenteménte, *av.* excellently, extremely well.

eccellentíssimo, *ag.superl.* most excellent.

eccellènza, *s.f.* **1.** excellence; (*preminenza*) preeminence ‖ *per —*, preeminently (*o* above all *o* first of all) **2.** (*titolo*) Excellency: *Vostra —*, Your Excellency.

eccèllere, *v.i.* to excel (s.o.): *Dante eccelse nella poesia*, Dante excelled as a poet; *eccelle sui compagni di scuola*, he excels (*o* he is superior to) his schoolfellows; *egli eccelle in matematica*, he excels at mathematics.

eccelsaménte, *av.* loftily, sublimely.

eccèlso, *ag.* lofty, sublime ‖ *l'Eccelso*, the Most High.

eccentricaménte, *av.* eccentrically.

eccentricità, *s.f.* **1.** (*stranezza di modi*) eccentricity, peculiarity, strangeness, oddity **2.** (*mec.*) eccentricity; throw: *grado di —*, degree of eccentricity.

eccèntrico, *ag.* **1.** (*dai modi stravaganti*) eccentric, peculiar, strange, odd(ish); whimsical **2.** (*scient.*) eccentric ‖ *s.m.* **1.** (*persona stravagante*) eccentric fellow, odd fellow; (*fam.*) queer fish: *è un —*, (*fam.*) he is a queer card (*o* he is a little peculiar) **2.** (*mec.*) eccentric, cam: *scatola degli eccentrici*, cam box.

eccepíbile, *ag.* (*dir.*) objectionable, exceptionable.

eccepíre, *v.t.* to object, to except: *che cosa hai da — alla sua proposta?*, what have you to object to his proposal?; *ha sempre ql.co. da —*, he always finds fault with sthg.; *non ho nulla da —*, I have nothing to object (*o* nothing to except *o* I have no objection) **2.** (*dir.*) to take exception.

eccessivaménte, *av.* excessively, exceedingly; (*smodatamente*) immoderately: *prezzo — elevato*, exceedingly high price; *caricare —*, to overload; *lavorare —*, to work too hard (*o* to overwork); *mangiare —*, to eat immoderately (*o* excessively); *produrre —*, to overproduce.

eccessività, *s.f.* excessiveness.

eccessívo, *ag.* excessive, extreme; (*smodato*) immoderate: *bere —*, immoderate drinking; *calore —*, extreme heat; *carico —*, overload; *fretta eccessiva*, excessive haste; *lavoro —*, excessive work (*o* overwork); *prezzo —*, exorbitant price; *severità eccessiva*, extreme (o excessive) severity; *spesa eccessiva*, over-expenditure; *dare un'importanza eccessiva a ql.co.*, to attach too much importance to sthg.

eccèsso, *s.m.* excess: — *di calore*, excess of heat; *un — di entusiasmo*, an excess of enthusiasm; — *di peso*, excess weight; — *di potere*, (*dir.*) action "ultra vires"; *rendersi colpevole di — di velocità*, to exceed the speed limit ‖ *approssimazione per —, per difetto*, (*mat.*) approximation to the nearest whole number above, below ‖ *coscienzioso fino all'—*, exceedingly conscientious; *scrupoloso all'—*, scrupulous to a fault; *è generosa all'—*, she is exceedingly (o too) generous ‖ *commettere degli eccessi*, to commit excesses; *dare in eccessi*, (*in escandescenze*) to run amuck; *evitare gli eccessi a tavola*, to avoid over-indulgence at (the) table ‖ *peccare per — di zelo*, to be over-zealous.

eccètera, *s.m.* et cetera (*abbr.* etc.), and so on, and so forth.

eccètto, *prep.* except(ing), but, save, bar(ring): *libro eccellente*, — *uno o due capitoli*, excellent book, bar(ring) one or two chapters; *tutti, — voi*, everybody, except (o but o save) you ‖ — *che (non)*, unless -(*seguito da indic.*): *non mancherò di farlo*, — *che io non sia ammalato*, I shall not fail to do it, unless I am ill ‖ *ag.* excepted: *nessuno —*, no one excepted.

eccettuàbile, *ag.* that may be excepted.

eccettuàre, *v.t.* to except, to exclude, to leave out.

eccettuatívo, *ag.* exceptive.

eccettuàto, *ag.* excepted, excluded: *eccettuata mia moglie*, my wife excepted; *eccettuati i presenti*, excepting this company (o present company excepted); *furono tutti puniti, nessuno —*, they were all punished, no one excepted.

eccezionàle, *ag.* 1. exceptional: *misura —*, emergency measure; *prezzi eccezionali*, exceptional prices ‖ *in via —*, as an exception 2. (*straordinario, insolito*) extraordinary, unusual.

eccezionalità, *s.f.* exceptionality.

eccezionalménte, *av.* 1. exceptionally 2. (*straordinariamente*) extraordinarily, unusually.

eccezióne, *s.f.* 1. exception; (*rar.*) exclusion: — *alla regola*, exception to the rule; *ad — di lui*, except him; *con l'— di*, with the exception of: *tutti furono fatti entrare con l'— di mia moglie*, all of them were let in, with the exception (o exclusion) of my wife; *con qualche —*, with a few exceptions; *in via d'—*, as an exception; *salvo eccezioni*, with certain exceptions; *senza —*, without exception ‖ *un pianista d'—*, an exceptional pianist ‖ *l'— conferma la regola*, *prov.* the exception proves the rule 2. (*obiezione*) exception, objection: — *dilatoria*, (*dir.*) dilatory exception; *sollevare, opporre — a ql.co.*, to take exception to sthg. (o to object to sthg.) ‖ *superiore ad ogni —*, beyond suspicion (o faultless).

ecchímosi, *s.f.* ecchymosis; bruise.

eccídio, *s.m.* slaughter, massacre, carnage, bloodshed.

eccipiènte, *s.m.* (*farm.*) excipient.

eccitàbile, *ag.* excitable; irritable: *sei troppo —*, you are always on edge (o you are too nervous).

eccitabilità, *s.f.* excitability.

eccitaménto, *s.m.* 1. excitement; irritation 2. (*incitamento*) incitement, urge.

eccitànte, *ag.* excitant, stimulant ‖ *s.m.* excitant, stimulant: *il caffè è un —*, coffee is an excitant.

eccitàre, *v.t.* 1. to excite, to stimulate: *la notizia della vittoria del suo cavallo lo eccitò molto*, he was excited by his horse winning the race 2. (*risvegliare*) to excite, to stir (up), to awaken: — *l'appetito di qlcu.*, to whet s.o.'s appetite; — *il coraggio di qlcu.*, to stir up s.o.'s courage; — *la curiosità di qlcu.*, to excite (o to stir up) s.o.'s curiosity 3. (*provocare, suscitare*) to rouse, to provoke: — *l'ammirazione*, to call forth admiration; — *l'indignazione di qlcu.*, to move (o to rouse) s.o.'s indignation; — *le masse*, to rouse the

masses; — *qlcu. alla rivolta*, to incite (o to urge) s.o. to revolt; — *il riso*, to cause laughter ‖ **eccitàrsi**, *v.r.* 1. to get excited: *egli si eccita per un nonnulla*, he gets excited over nothing 2. (*adirarsi*) to get angry.

eccitatívo, *ag.* excitant, exciting.

eccitatóre, *ag.* excitative, excitatory ‖ *s.m.*, **eccitatrice**, *s.f.* 1. exciter 2. (*elett.*) exciting dynamo.

eccitazióne, *s.f.* 1. excitement: *essere in uno stato di grande —*, to be in a dither 2. (*elett.*) excitation: — *in serie*, series excitation; *energia di —*, excitation energy; *motore ad — composta*, compound motor.

ecclèsia, *s.f.* (*st. greca*) ecclesia.

ecclesiàste, *s.m.* (*Bibbia*) Ecclesiastes.

ecclesiasticaménte, *av.* ecclesiastically.

ecclesiàstico, *ag.* ecclesiastic(al), clerical: *cappello —*, clerical hat; *foro —*, ecclesiastical court ‖ *s.m.* (*sacerdote*) clergyman (*pl.* clergymen); priest, ecclesiastic.

ecclissàre, *V.* eclissàre.

ècco, *av.* here, there, that, this (*in unione con le voci del pres. ind. del verbo* to be): —*!, (guarda!)* look! (o see!); — *ciò che mi diede*, this is what he gave me; — *fatto*, that's done (o it's done); — *i miei libri*, here are my books; — *perchè*, that is why; — *la tua mamma*, here is your mother; — *tutto*, that's all ‖ *quand'—*, when suddenly: *stavo lavandomi le mani quand'— entrò lo zio*, I was washing my hands when all of a sudden my uncle came in ‖ (*con particelle pronominali enclitiche*): *eccolo là*, there he is; (*di cosa*) there it is; *eccomi qua*, here I am; *eccoti*, here you are; *eccoti servito!*, there you are!.

echeggiànte, *ag.* echoing, resounding.

echeggiàre, *v.i.* to echo (with sthg.), to resound (with sthg.): *il grido echeggiò per i boschi*, the cry echoed through the woods; *la stanza echeggiò di risate*, the room resounded with laughter.

echéggio, *s.m.* (*rar.*) echoing.

echídna, *s.f.* (*zool.*) echidna.

echíno, *s.m.* 1. (*zool.*) sea-urchin, echinus (*pl.* echini) 2. (*arch.*) echinus (*pl.* echini).

echinocòcco, *s.m.* (*zool.*) echinococcus.

echinodèrma, *s.m.* (*zool.*) echinoderm.

eclampsía, *s.f.* (*patol.*) eclampsia.

ecletticísmo, eclettísmo, *s.m.* eclecticism.

eclèttico, *ag.s.m.* eclectic.

eclissàre, *v.t.* 1. (*astr.*) to eclipse 2. *fig.* to eclipse, to outshine, to overshadow: *la fama del figlio eclissò quella del padre*, the son's fame overshadowed the father's ‖ **eclissàrsi**, *v.r.* 1. (*astr.*) to be eclipsed, to grow dark 2. *fig.* to disappear, to vanish: *senza una parola s'eclissò*, he disappeared without saying a word (o vanished o *fam.* made himself scarce).

eclíssi, *s.f.* (*astr.*) eclipse: — *anulare, parziale, totale*, annular, partial, total eclipse; — *lunare*, lunar eclipse.

eclíttica, *s.f.* (*astr.*) ecliptic.

èco, *s.m.*, (*letter.*) *f.*; (*m. al pl.*) 1. echo (*anche fig.*) *far — alle parole di qlcu.*, to echo (o to repeat) s.o.'s words; *farsi — di una diceria*, to spread a rumour ‖ *« echi di cronaca »*, (*giornalismo*) "what's on" 2. (*rad.*) echo: *echi di disturbo*, clutter; *echi multipli*, (*acu. rad.*) multiple echoes ‖ **Èco**, *no.pr.f.* (*mit.*) Echo.

ecología, *s.f.* (*scient.*) ecology, oecology.

ecòmetro, *s.m.* (*mar.*) echo-sounding gear.

ecònoma, *s.f.* (*amministratrice*) matron.

economàto, *s.m.* 1. steward's office; (*nelle università*) bursar's office 2. (*carica*) stewardship; (*nell'università*) bursarship.

economía, *s.f.* 1. (*parsimonia*) economy, thrift; (*risparmio*) saving, economy: *senza —*, (*generosamente*) generously; (*abbondantemente*) plentifully (o abundantly); (*scialacquando*) thriftlessly; *fare economie*, to save money (o *fam.* to pinch pennies) 2. (*arte di amministrare*) economy: — *domestica*, domestic economy (o domestic science) 3. (*scienza*) economics: — *politica*, political economy.

economicaménte, *av.* economically; (*con parsimonia*) thriftily.

econòmico, *ag.* **1.** (*relativo all'economia*) economic: *il sistema — europeo*, the European economic system **2.** (*a buon prezzo*) cheap: *un articolo —*, a cheap article.

economísta, *s.m.* economist.

economizzàre, *v.i.* **1.** (*comm.*) to economize; to cut down (expenses) **2.** (*risparmiare*) to save money.

ecònomo, *ag.* (*fam.*) economical, thrifty, sparing ‖ *s.m.* steward; (*di collegio universitario*) bursar.

ecoscandàglio, *s.m.* (*mar.*) echo-sounding gear, echo sounder.

ectasía, *s.f.* (*med.*) ectasia, ectasis.

ectopía, *s.f.* (*med.*) ectopia, ectopy.

ectoplàsma, *s.m.* ectoplasm.

Ecuador, *no.pr.m.* (*geog.*) Ecuador.

Ècuba, *no.pr.f.* (*lett.*) Hecuba.

ecumenicaménte, *av.* (*eccl.*) (o)ecumenically.

ecumenicità, *s.f.* (*eccl.*) ecumenicity, oecumenicity.

ecumènico, *ag.* (*eccl.*) ecumenical, oecumenical.

eczèma, *s.m.* (*patol.*) eczema.

eczematóso, *ag.* (*patol.*) eczematous.

ed, *V.* **e**.

edàce, *ag.* (*letter.*) edacious; voracious; (*che divora, consuma*) devouring, consuming.

Èdda, *no.pr.f.* (*st. lett.*) Edda.

eddomadàrio, *V.* **ebdomadàrio**.

èdema, *s.m.* (*patol.*) oedema.

edemàtico, *ag.* **1.** oedema (*attributivo*) **2.** suffering from oedema (*predicativo*).

edematóso, *ag.* (*patol.*) oedematose, oedematous.

èden, *s.m.* Eden (anche *fig.*); earthly paradise.

édera, *s.f.* (*bot.*) ivy: *coperto d'—*, ivy-clad (*o* ivy-mantled).

ederàceo, *ag.* (*bot.*) ivy-like.

ederèlla, *s.f.* (*bot.*) veronica.

Edgàrdo, *no.pr.m.* Edgar ‖ *dim.* Ed, Eddy, Ned, Neddy.

edícola, *s.f.* **1.** (*rivendita di giornali*) newspaper kiosk, news-stand; bookstall **2.** (*tempietto*) aedicule; (*nicchia*) niche **3.** (*tabernacolo*) tabernacle; shrine; (*cappella*) chapel.

edicolísta, *s.m.* newsagent; bookstall keeper.

edificànte, *ag.* edifying, edificatory: *un esempio —*, an edifying example.

edificàre, *v.t.* **1.** (*costruire*) to build (up); to erect, to set up: *— una chiesa*, to build (*o* to set up *o* to erect) a church ‖ *— sulla sabbia*, *fig.* to build on sand (*o* to work in vain) **2.** (*ammaestrare, dare il buon esempio a*) to edify, to give a good example to: *le sue parole mi edificarono*, I was edified by his words ‖ **edificàrsi**, *v.r.* to be edified.

edificatívo, *ag.* (*rar.*) edifying.

edificatóre, *s.m.*, **edificatríce**, *s.f.* **1.** (*chi costruisce*) builder **2.** (*chi ammaestra*) edifier.

edificazióne, *s.f.* **1.** (*costruzione*) building **2.** (*ammaestramento*) edification.

edifício, edifízio, *s.m.* edifice (anche *fig.*); building; structure: *— sociale*, social order; *in quella città vi sono begli edifici*, in that town there are fine buildings.

edíle, *ag.* building (*attributivo*): *perito —*, master builder ‖ *s.m.* (*st. romana*) aedile.

edilità, *s.f.* **1.** (*st. romana*) aedileship **2.** Office of Borough Surveyor.

edilízia, *s.f.* building; building industry, building trade: *capolavoro di —*, masterpiece of the builder's art; *materiale per —*, building material; *l'— si è molto sviluppata*, the building industry has developed a great deal; *d'inverno c'è molta disoccupazione nell'—*, there is great unemployment in the building trade in winter.

edilízio, *ag.* building (*attributivo*): *impresa edilizia*, building contractors.

Edimbúrgo, *no.pr.f.* (*geog.*) Edinburgh.

Edípo, *no.pr.m.* (*lett.*) Oedipus ‖ *complesso di —*, (*psicanalisi*) Oedipus complex.

èdito, *ag.* published; printed.

editóre, *s.m.* **1.** publisher **2.** (*esperto che cura un'edizione*) editor.

editoría, *s.f.* book industry; publishing trade.

editoriàle, *ag.* editorial ‖ *s.m.* (*articolo di fondo*) editorial, leading article.

editríce, *ag.*: *casa —*, publishing house (*o* publishers).

Editta, *no.pr.f.* Edith ‖ *dim.* Edie, Edy.

editto, *s.m.* edict: *Editto di Nantes*, Edict of Nantes.

edizióne, *s.f.* **1.** edition: *— a tiratura limitata*, limited edition; *— critica*, critical edition; *— economica*, cheap (*o* popular) edition; *— riveduta e corretta*, revised edition; *— tascabile*, pocket edition; *la quarta — di questo libro è esaurita*, the fourth edition of this book is out of print; *questo libro ha avuto numerose edizioni*, this book has run into numerous editions **2.** (*di giornale*) issue: *— straordinaria*, (late) extra edition; *l'ultima —*, the latest edition; *ultima — della sera*, late night-final; (*fam.*) latest **3.** (*pubblicazione per mezzo della stampa*) publication.

Edmóndo, *no.pr.m.* Edmund, Edmond ‖ *dim.* Ed, Eddy, Ned, Neddy.

edoardiàno, *ag.s.* (*st. inglese*) Edwardian.

Edoàrdo, *no.pr.m.* Edward ‖ *dim.* Ed, Eddy, Ned, Neddy, Ted, Teddy.

edonísmo, *s.m.* (*fil.*) hedonism.

edonísta, *s.m.* (*fil.*) hedonist.

edonístico, *ag.* (*fil.*) hedonistic.

edòtto, *ag.* (*rar.*) aware; acquainted (with sthg.); informed: *ne sono —*, I am well aware of it (*o* I am acquainted with it); *ne sono stato —*, I have been informed of (*o* acquainted with) it ‖ *rendere — di*, to inform of (*o* to acquaint with): *quando lo resi — di ciò*, when I informed him of (*o* acquainted him with) that.

educàbile, *ag.* **1.** educable **2.** (*ammaestrabile*) trainable.

educànda, *s.f.* boarding-school girl.

educandàto, *s.m.* girls' boarding-school; (*di suore*) convent boarding-school.

educàre, *v.t.* **1.** to educate: *— il cuore*, to educate the heart **2.** (*allevare*) to bring up; to rear: *chi lo ha educato?*, who brought him up? **3.** (*esercitare, ammaestrare*) to train: *— la mente allo studio*, to train the mind to study ‖ **educàrsi**, *v.r.* to refine oneself.

educataménte, *av.* politely.

educatívo, *ag.* educational; (*istruttivo*) instructive; informative: *film —*, educational film; *libro —*, instructive book.

educàto, *ag.* **1.** (*beneducato*) well-bred; (*cortese*) polite **2.** (*colto, istruito*) educated.

educatóre, *s.m.* educator; teacher.

educatòrio, *s.m.* boarding-school.

educatríce, *s.f.* educator; teacher.

educazióne, *s.f.* **1.** education; upbringing ‖ *— fisica*, gymnastics (*o* physical training) **2.** (*buone maniere*) breeding; good manners (*pl.*): *senza —*, ill-bred (*o* ill-mannered); *insegnare l'— a qlcu.*, to teach s.o. manners.

edulcoràre, *v.t.* (*rar.*) to edulcorate.

edúle, *ag.* (*rar.*) edible.

efèbo, *s.m.* (*letter.*) ephebe.

efèlide, *s.f.* freckle; (*med.*) ephelis (*pl.* ephelides).

efemèride, *s.f.* ephemeris (*pl.* ephemerides).

Èfeso, *no.pr.f.* (*geog. st.*) Ephesus.

Efèsto, *no.pr.m.* (*mit.*) Hephaestus, Hephaistos.

èffe, *s.f.m.* letter F.

effemèride, *s.f.* ephemeris (*pl.* ephemerides).

effeminàre, *v.t.* to effeminate ‖ **effeminàrsi**, *v.r.* to become effeminate.

effeminataménte, *av.* effeminately.

effeminatézza, *s.f.* effeminacy.

effeminàto, *ag.* effeminate; womanish; unmanly.

effemminàre, *V.* **effeminàre**.

effèndi, *s.m.* (*titolo turco*) effendi.

efferataménte, *av.* brutally; savagely; cruelly; ferociously.

efferatézza, *s.f.* brutality; savageness; cruelty; ferocity: *l'— contro gli animali è severamente punita in Inghilterra,* cruelty to animals is severely punished in England.

efferàto, *ag.* brutal; savage; cruel; ferocious.

efferènte, *ag.* (*med.*) efferent.

effervescènte, *ag.* sparkling; effervescent.

effervescènza, *s.f.* **1.** effervescence, effervescency **2.** (*fervore, eccitamento*) excitement; agitation.

effettivaménte, *av.* actually; really; indeed.

effettívo, *ag.* **1.** actual; real: *prezzo —,* real price; *socio —,* active partner **2.** (*efficace*) effective ‖ *s.m.* **1.**: *di cassa,* (*comm.*) cash on hand **2.** *pl.* (*mil.*) effectives.

effètto, *s.m.* **1.** effect, result, consequence: *causa e —,* cause and effect; *senza —,* of no avail (*o* ineffectual); *il mio avvertimento ebbe l'— voluto,* my warning had the desired effect; *non c'è — senza causa,* there is no effect without a cause; *le nostre parole non ebbero alcun — su di lui,* our words had no effect on him; *i nostri sforzi non ebbero alcun —,* our efforts were of no avail (*o* were useless) ‖ *a tutti gli effetti,* in every respect ‖ *in —,* as a matter of fact (*o* in fact *o* actually *o* really *o* in effect) ‖ *per — di,* because of (*o* in consequence of *o* owing to) **2.** (*impressione*) impression, effect: *frase ad —,* words meant for effect (*o* claptrap); *scena ad —,* sensational scene; *fare —,* to make an impression: *questo fa bell'—,* this looks well; *fare un grande —,* to make (*o* to create) a sensation; (*far colpo*) to make a hit; *fare l'— di...,* to give the impression of (*o* to seem)...: *fa l'— di un mascalzone,* he looks like a rascal **3.** (*attuazione, esecuzione*) action, effect: *mandare ql.co. ad —,* to bring sthg. to (*o* to carry sthg. into) effect; *mettere ad — un progetto,* to put a plan into action (*o* to carry out a plan); *prendere —,* (*dir.*) to take effect (*o* to become operative) **4.** (*tec.*) effect: *effetti di luce,* (*teat.*) lighting effects; *— frenante,* (*mec.*) braking effect; *a doppio, singolo —,* (*mec.*) double -acting, single-acting **5.** (*moto rotatorio*) screw; spin: *dare l'— a una palla da biliardo,* to put a screw on a billiard-ball **6.** (*comm.*) bill; (*pagherò*) promissory note: *effetti attivi,* bills receivable; *— cambiario,* bill of exchange; *effetti incasso,* collections; *effetti passivi,* bills payable; *effetti sconto,* discount **7.** *effetti personali,* personal effects (*o* personal belongings).

effettuàbile, *ag.* feasible, practicable, workable: *è un piano —,* it is a feasible scheme.

effettuabilità, *s.f.* (*rar.*) feasibility, practicability.

effettuàle, *ag.* (*effettivo, reale*) effectual, actual, real.

effettuàre, *v.t.* to effect; to carry out; to carry into effect, to bring to effect; to execute: *— un piano,* to carry out a plan; *— una vendita, un pagamento,* to effect (*o* to make) a sale, a payment ‖ **effettuàrsi,** *v.r.* (*aver luogo*) to take place; to happen: *domenica si effettuerà un'asta pubblica,* an auction will be held on Sunday.

effettuazióne, *s.f.* accomplishment, fulfilment; execution.

efficàce, *ag.* effective, efficacious; effectual: *un oratore —,* an effective speaker; *un rimedio —,* an efficacious remedy; *fu un castigo —,* it was an effectual punishment ‖ *grazia —,* (*teol.*) Efficacious Grace.

efficaceménte, *av.* efficaciously; effectually; powerfully.

efficàcia, *s.f.* efficaciousness; efficacy; effectiveness: *l'— di quel rimedio,* the effectiveness of that remedy.

efficiènte, *ag.* **1.** efficient: *è una segretaria —,* she is an efficient secretary **2.** *causa —,* (*fil.*) efficient cause.

efficiènza, *s.f.* efficiency; effectiveness: *l'— del rimedio,* the effectiveness of the remedy; *motore di grande —,* high-efficiency engine; *lavoro compiuto con crescente —,* work accomplished with increasing efficiency; *il nostro impianto è in piena —,* our plant (*o* equipment) is in full working order.

effíge, *V.* **effígie.**

effigiàre, *v.t.* to portray; (*dipingere*) to paint; (*scolpire, modellare*) to sculpture, to represent in sculpture.

effígie, *s.f.* **1.** effigy; image; (*ritratto*) portrait: *questa moneta porta l'— del re,* this coin bears the effigy of the king ‖ *bruciare in —,* to burn in effigy **2.** (*aspetto*) mien; features (*pl.*): *ha un'— mobilissima,* he has very mobile features.

effímera, *s.f.* **1.** (*entom.*) ephemeron (*pl.* ephemerons, ephemera); (*fam.*) mayfly **2.** (*patol.*) ephemeral fever.

effímero, *ag.* ephemeral, transitory, transient; short-lived; fleeting: *gioia effimera,* short-lived joy.

efflorescènte, *ag.* (*letter.*) efflorescent.

efflorescènza, *s.f.* **1.** efflorescence, flowering, blooming **2.** (*chim. patol.*) efflorescence.

effluènte, *ag.* (*rar.*) effluent; outflowing.

efflússo, *s.m.* efflux; outflow; effusion: *— del sangue,* (*med.*) effusion of blood.

effluvio, *s.m.* **1.** effluvium (*pl.* effluvia); exhalation, emanation **2.** (*elett.*) (*in un gas*) glow discharge **3.** *pl.* (*cine.*) statics.

effóndere, *v.t.* **1.** to pour forth; to effuse; to pour out; to shed **2.** *fig.* to give vent to (sthg.): *— l'animo,* to open one's heart ‖ **effóndersi,** *v.r.* (*spargersi*) to spread (about).

effrazióne, *s.f.* (*dir.*) house-breaking, effraction; (*se consumata di notte*) burglary.

effrenàto, *ag.* (*letter.*) unbridled, unrestrained.

effusióne, *s.f.* **1.** effusion; shedding: *— di lacrime,* shedding of tears; *— di sangue,* bloodshed **2.** (*cordialità*) cordiality; warm-heartedness: *salutare qlcu. con —,* to greet s.o. warm-heartedly **3.** *pl.* (*manifestazioni*) effusions: *effusioni poetiche, amorose,* poetical effusions, effusions of love **4.** (*fis.*) effusion.

effusívo, *ag.* (*geol.*) effusive: *roccia effusiva,* effusive rock.

effúso, *ag.* shed, spread.

Efiàlte, *no.pr.m.* (*mit.*) Ephialtes.

èfod, *s.m.* (*paramento ebraico*) ephod.

eforàto, *s.m.* (*st. greca*) ephorship.

èforo, *s.m.* (*st. greca*) ephor (*pl.* ephori, ephors).

egèmone, *ag.* (*rar.*) leading: *nazione —,* leading nation ‖ *s.m.* leader; chief.

egemonía, *s.f.* hegemony, supremacy.

egemònico, *ag.* hegemonic, ruling.

egèo¹, *ag.* Aegean ‖ **Egèo (l'),** *no.pr.m.* (*geog.*) the Aegean Sea.

Egèo², *no.pr.m.* (*mit.*) Aegeus.

Egèria, *no.pr.f.* (*mit.*) Egeria ‖ *ninfa —,* *fig.* (woman) adviser, source of inspiration.

ègida, *s.f.* aegis, shield (anche *fig.*); *fig.* (*protezione*) protection: *sotto l'— di qlcu.,* under s.o.'s protection.

Egídio, *no.pr.m.* Giles ‖ *dim.* Gil.

egílope, *s.f.* (*patol.*) aegilops.

Egína, *no.pr.f.* (*geog. st.*) Aegina.

egípane, *s.m.* (*mit.*) Aegipan.

ègira, *s.f.* (*st. islamica*) hegira, hejira, hejra, hijra.

Egísto, *no.pr.m.* (*lett.*) Aegisthus.

Egitto, *no.pr.m.* (*geog.*) Egypt.

egittología, *s.f.* Egyptology.

egittòlogo, *s.m.* Egyptologist.

egizíaco, *ag.* Egyptian.

egiziàno, *ag.s.m.* Egyptian ‖ **egiziàna,** *s.f.* Egyptian.

egízio, *ag. s.m.* (*st.*) ancient Egyptian.

égli, *pron. pers. m.* 3ª *persona sing. sogg.* **1.** he: *— ci conosce,* he knows us ‖ *— stesso, proprio —,* he ... himself (*o* he himself): *— stesso disse ciò,* he said so himself (*o* he himself said so) **2.** (*arc.*) (*pleonastico*) it: *è — vero?,* is it true?.

églino, (*arc.*) per **éssi.**

ègloga, *s.f.* (*poes.*) eclogue.

ego, *pron.* (*lat.*) ego ‖ *alter —,* alter ego.

egocentricità, *s.f.* self-centredness.

egocèntrico, *ag.* egocentric, self-centred ‖ *s.m.* egocentric man, self-centred man.

egocentrísmo, *s.m.* egocentrism.
egoísmo, *s.m.* selfishness, egoism.
egoísta, *s.c.* egoist, selfish person.
egoisticaménte, *av.* egoistically, selfishly.
egoístico, *ag.* egoistic(al), selfish, self-centred, self-seeking.
egolatría, *s.f.* self-worship.
Egospòtami, *no.pr.m.* (*geog. st.*) Aegospotami.
egotísmo, *s.m.* egotism, self-conceit.
egotísta, *s.c.* egotist, self-conceited person.
egregiaménte, *av.* eminently; excellently.
egrègio, *ag.* eminent, distinguished; excellent: *scrittore* —, distinguished writer ‖ *Egregia Signora,* Dear Madam; *Egregio Signore,* Dear Sir; (*negli indirizzi*) *Egregio Signor John Smith,* Mr. John Smith (*o* John Smith Esq.).
egrèsso, *s.m.* (*rar.*) exit.
egrétta, *s.f.* **1.** (*ornit.*) egret **2.** (*ornamento di cappello femminile*) aigrette, plume, tuft; osprey, spray; (*pennacchio su copricapo militare*) plume.
ègro, *ag.* (*poet.*) **1.** (*malato*) sick (*attributivo*), ill (*predicativo*) **2.** (*debole*) weak, faint.
eguàle, e derivati, *V.* **uguàle, e derivati.**
egualità, *s.f.* equality.
egualitàrio, *ag.* (*pol.*) equalitarian.
egualizzàre, *v.t.* to equalize, to make equal.
egualizzatóre, *s.m.* (*ind. tessile*) evener.
egualménte, *av.* **1.** equally, alike: — *responsabili,* equally responsible; *trattare tutti* —, to treat everybody alike **2.** (*ciononostante*) all the same: *pioveva, ma venne* —, it was raining but he came all the same.
eh, *inter.* eh!; (*meraviglia*) phew!; (*disapprovazione*) hey!.
éhi, *inter.* (*per chiamare*) hey! hey, you!; (*volg.*) oi!: — *dico!,* I say!; —, *è a voi che parlo!,* here, I say, it's you I'm speaking to!.
ehm, *inter.* hem!.
éi, (*arc. letter.*) per **égli.**
èia, *inter.* hurrah!.
eiaculazióne, *s.f.* (*fisiol.*) ejaculation.
eiettàre, *v.t.* (*fis.*) to eject, to spout.
eiettóre, *s.m.* (*mec.*) ejector.
eiezióne, *s.f.* (*fisiol.*) ejection.
elaboràre, *v.t.* **1.** to elaborate, to work out, to work up, to prepare carefully, to draw up: — *un piano,* to elaborate a plan **2.** (*fisiol.*) to elaborate:] *lo stomaco elabora il cibo,* the stomach renders food assimilable.
elaborataménte, *av.* elaborately.
elaboratézza, *s.f.* (*rar.*) elaborateness.
elaboràto, *ag.* elaborate, carefully prepared ‖ *s.m.* homework: — *d'esame,* examination paper.
elaborazióne, *s.f.* elaboration (*anche fig.*); (*di piano*) formulation; (*di prodotto*) manufacture: *misure in corso di* —, measures in course of elaboration (*o* preparation).
elargíre, *v.t.* to lavish; to make a donation of (sthg.).
elargizióne, *s.f.* donation; generous gift.
elasticaménte, *av.* elastically.
elasticità, *s.f.* **1.** elasticity, resilience (anche *fig.*); (*di molle*) springiness: — *di mente,* elasticity (*o* resilience) of mind; — *di torsione,* (*scienza delle costruzioni*) torsional elasticity; *limite di* —, (*scienza delle costruzioni*) elastic limit (*o* limit of elasticity) **2.** (*agilità*) agility, nimbleness.
elàstico, *ag.* **1.** elastic, resilient (anche *fig.*); (*di molle*) springy: *coscienza elastica,* lax conscience; *gomma elastica,* india rubber; *limite* —, (*scienza delle costruzioni*) elastic limit (*o* strength) **2.** (*agile, flessibile*) agile, nimble ‖ *s.m.* **1.** rubber band; (*tessuto elastico*) elastic (fabric) **2.** *pl.* (*delle calze per uomo e donna*): (*anticamente*) garters; (*oggi, da uomo*) sock-suspenders; (*da donna*) garters.
elastína, *s.f.* (*chim.*) elastin.

elastòmero, *s.m.* (*chim.*) elastomer.
elatèridi, *s.m.pl.* (*entom.*) Elateridae.
elatèrio, *s.m.* **1.** (*entom.*) elater, skipjack, click-beetle **2.** (*bot.*) elater.
elatína, *s.f.* (*bot. farm.*) elatine, elaterin, waterwort.
Èlba¹, *no.pr.f.* (*geog.*) (*isola*) Elba.
Èlba², *no.pr.m.* (*geog.*) (*fiume*) Elbe.
élce, *s.m.* (*bot.*) ilex (*pl.* ilexes), holm-oak.
eldoràdo, *s.m.* El Dorado.
Elèa, *no.pr.f.* (*geog. st.*) Elea.
eleàtico, *ag.* (*st.fil.*) Eleatic.
eleatísmo, *s.m.* (*st.fil.*) Eleaticism.
Eleàzaro, *no.pr.m.* (*Bibbia*) Eleazar, Eleazer.
èlectron, *s.m.* (*metal.*) electron, elektron.
elefànte, *s.m.* elephant: — *di mare,* sea-elephant (*o* elephant-seal); — *maschio, femmina,* bull-elephant, cow-elephant ‖ *far d'una mosca un* —, to make mountains out of mole-hills.
elefantésco, *ag.* **1.** elephantine **2.** (*goffo*) clumsy, ungainly **3.** (*mastodontico*) ponderous.
elefantéssa, *s.f.* cow-elephant, female elephant.
elefantíaco, *ag.* (*med.*) pertaining to elephantiasis ‖ *s.m.* (*med.*) elephantiac.
elefantíasi, *s.f.* (*patol.*) elephantiasis.
elefantíno, *ag.* (*rar.*) elephantine.
elegànte, *ag.* (*di persona*) elegant, smart, well-dressed; (*di abito*) elegant, smart; (*alla moda*) fashionable; (*fine*) stylish; (*aggraziato*) graceful; (*raffinato*) polished, refined; (*di buon gusto*) tasteful; (*affettato*) (*fam.*) swank, swanky: *un abito* — *ma non ricercato,* an elegant but simple dress; *una figura* —, an elegant (*o* a graceful) figure; *un salotto* —, a tasteful drawing-room.
eleganteménte, *av.* elegantly, smartly.
elegantóne, *s.m.* dandy, fop.
elegànza, *s.f.* (*di persona, abito*) elegance, smartness, stylishness; (*raffinatezza*) polish, refinement.
elèggere, *v.t.* **1.** to elect; (*scegliere*) to choose; (*nominare*) to nominate, to appoint; (*preferire*) to prefer: *egli fu eletto all'Accademia,* he was elected to the Academy; *lo elessero Presidente,* they elected him President (*o* to the Presidency *o* they voted him into the chair); *sarà certamente eletto,* he's sure to be elected (*o* to get in); — *un deputato,* to return (*o* to elect) a Member of Parliament **2.** (*dir.*): — *il proprio domicilio,* to elect domicile.
eleggíbile, *ag.* eligible.
eleggibilità, *s.f.* eligibility.
elegìa, *s.f.* (*poes.*) elegy.
elegíaco, *ag.* (*poes.*) elegiac: *poeta* —, elegiac poet (*o* elegist).
elegiògrafo, *s.m.* elegist.
elèktron, *s.m.* (*metal.*) electron, elektron.
elementàre, *ag.* **1.** elementary: *algebra* — elementary algebra; *conoscenza* —, elementary knowledge; *scuola* —, primary (*o* elementary) school **2.** (*non scomponibile*) elemental: *corpo* —, elemental body **3.** (*primitivo*) primitive, simple, rudimentary.
elementarménte, *av.* elementarily.
eleménto, *s.m.* **1.** element (anche *chim.*): — *bivalente,* (*chim.*) bivalent element (*o* dyad); *l'acqua è l'*— *del pesce,* water is the element of fish; *la furia degli elementi,* the fury of the elements; *i quattro elementi,* the four elements; *sistema periodico* (*degli elementi*), (*chim.*) periodic system ‖ *essere, non essere nel proprio* —, *fig.* to be in, out of one's element **2.** (*componente*) component, constituent; (*ingrediente*) ingredient; (*di un rapporto, di una prova*) item; (*fattore*) factor; (*mec.*) element, part, component: *elementi costitutivi di un delitto,* factors that constitute an offense; *gli elementi della felicità,* the constituents of happiness; — *di batteria,* (*elett.*) battery cell; *elementi d'instabilità,* disturbing factors **3.** *pl.* (*rudimenti, principi*) rudiments, first principles: *elementi di storia,* rudiments of history **4.** (*persona*) person; member: *gli elementi di un partito,*

the members of a party; *in questo ufficio vi sono ottimi elementi*, in this office there are excellent workers; *il signor X è un buon* —, Mr. So and So is a reliable person (*o a capable man*).

elemòsina, *s.f.* alms (*gener. sing.*); charity: *cassetta per l'*—, alms-box; *ridotto all'*—, reduced to beggary; *chiedere l'*—, to beg (*o* to beg for. alms); *fare l'*—, to give alms; *vivere d'*—, to live on charity.

elemosinàre, *v.t.* to beg, to beg for (sthg.): — *il pane*, to beg (for) one's bread || *v.i.* to beg, to collect (alms).

elemosinière, *s.m.* (*st.*) almoner.

Èlena, *no.pr.f.* Helen, Helena.

elencàre, *v.t.* **1.** to list; to catalogue; (*amer.*) to catalog; to make a list of (sthg.), to draw up a list of (sthg.): *bisogna* — *i nomi degli allievi*, it is necessary to make a list of the names of the pupils **2.** (*enumerare*) to enumerate; to reckon up one by one.

elènco, *s.m.* **1.** list, roll; (*catalogo*) catalogue; (*amer.*) catalog: (*specialmente dei membri di un circolo, associazione, ecc.*) roster; (*inventario*) inventory: — *del telefono*, telephone directory (*o* telephone book); *fare un* —, to draw up a list **2.** (*log.*) elenchus (*pl.* elenchi).

Èleno, *no.pr.m.* (*lett.*) Helenus.

Eleonòra, *no.pr.f.* Eleanor, Elinor.

elètta, *s.f.* (*letter.*) **1.** (*scelta*) choice **2.** (*gruppo scelto di persone*) élite.

elettaménte, *av.* elegantly, nobly.

elettivaménte, *av.* electively.

elettívo, *ag.* elective: *affinità elettive*, elective affinities.

elètto, *ag.* **1.** (*scelto, preferito*) elect; chosen: *il popolo* —, the chosen people || *la sposa eletta*, the bride elect || *gli eletti* (*da Dio*), the elect; (*scherz.*) the chosen few || ...*perchè molti sono chiamati e pochi gli eletti*, (*Vangelo*)...for many are called, but few chosen **2.** (*di pregio, distinto*) select; noble: *un ingegno* —, a very talented person; *parole elette*, noble words; *un pubblico* —, a select audience || *s.m.*: *nuovo* —, newly elected member.

elettoràle, *ag.* electoral: *collegio* —, constituency; *diritto* —, franchise; *imbroglio* —, gerrymander (*o* gerrymandering); *lista* —, register (of voters); *propaganda* —, electoral propaganda (*o* electioneering); *scheda* —, ballot-paper.

elettoràto, *s.m.* **1.** (*insieme degli elettori*) electorate; (*collegio elettorale*) constituency **2.** (*qualità di elettore*) electorship; (*diritto al voto*) franchise **3.** *Elettorato*, (*st. germanica*) Electorate.

elettóre, *s.m.* elector, voter; (*di un singolo collegio elettorale*) constituent || *Elettore*, (*st. germanica*) Elector.

Elèttra, *no.pr.f.* (*lett.*) Electra || *complesso di* —, (*psicanalisi*) Electra complex.

elettricaménte, *av.* electrically.

elettríce, *s.f.* woman elector, voter; (*di un singolo collegio elettorale*) constituent || *Elettrice*, (*st. germanica*) Electress.

elettricísmo, *s.m.* electricity.

elettricísta, *s.m.* electrician; (*chi vende materiale elettrico*) electrical outfitter.

elettricità, *s.f.* electricity: — *di contatto*, contact electricity; — *di strofinìo*, frictional electricity (*o* statical electricity).

elèttrico, *ag.* electric (anche *fig.*); electrical: *assorbimento* —, electrical absorption; *atmosfera elettrica*, electric atmosphere; *centrale elettrica*, power station; *circuito* —, electric circuit; *energia elettrica*, electric energy; *filo* —, electric wire; *impianto* —, electrical equipment; *luce elettrica*, electric light; *motore* —, electromotor; (*generatore di elettricità*) generator; *scossa elettrica*, electric shock; *sedia elettrica*, electric chair: *far morire qlcu. sulla sedia elettrica*, (*amer.*) to electrocute s.o.; *blu* —, electric (*o* steely) blue.

elettrificàbile, *ag.* electrifiable.

elettrificàre, *v.t.* to electrify: — *una linea ferroviaria*, to electrify a railway line.

elettrificazióne, *s.f.* electrification.

elettrizzàre, *v.t.* **1.** to electrify, to electrize **2.** *fig.* to electrify, to thrill: *la notizia mi elettrizzò*, the news thrilled me; *quella musica elettrizzò il pubblico*, that music electrified the audience; *essere elettrizzati da un discorso*, to be electrified (*o* thrilled) by a speech.

elettrizzazióne, *s.f.* electrization.

elèttro, *s.m.* **1.** (yellow) amber **2.** (*antica lega di oro e argento*) electrum.

elettroanàlisi, *s.f.* (*chim.*) electroanalysis.

elettrobiología, *s.f.* electrobiology.

elettrocalamíta, *s.f.* (*elett.*) electro-magnet.

elettrocardiògrafo, *s.m.* (*med.*) electrocardiograph.

elettrocardiogràmma, *s.m.* (*med.*) electrocardiogram.

elettrochímica, *s.f.* electrochemistry.

elettrochòck, *s.m.* (*med.*) electroshock.

elettrocuzióne, *s.f.* electrocution.

elettrodinàmica, *s.f.* electrodynamics.

elettrodinamòmetro, *s.m.* electrodynamometer.

elèttrodo, *s.m.* (*fis.*) electrode.

elettrodomèstici, *s.m.pl.* electrical household appliances.

elettro-esecuzióne, *s.f.* electrocution.

elettrofíltro, *s.m.* (*elett.*) electrostatic filter.

elettrofisiología, *s.f.* electrophysiology.

elettròforo, *s.m.* (*elett.*) electrophore, electrophorus.

elettrògeno, *ag.* generating electricity: *gruppo* —, generator.

elettrografía, *s.f.* electrography.

elettròlisi, *s.f.* (*elett.*) electrolysis.

elettrolítico, *ag.* (*elett.*) electrolytic.

elettròlito, *s.m.* (*elett.*) electrolyte.

elettrología, *s.f.* electrology.

elettromagnète, *s.m.* (*elett.*) electro-magnet, magneti — *di campo*, field magnet; — *di sollevamento*, lifting magnet.

elettromagnètico, *ag.* (*elett.*) electro-magnetic(al).

elettromagnetísmo, *s.m.* (*elett.*) electro-magnetism.

elettrometallurgía, *s.f.* electrometallurgy.

elettròmetro, *s.m.* (*elett.*) electrometer: — *a bilancia*, balance electrometer.

elettromotóre, *s.m.* **1.** (*dinamo*) dynamo; generator **2.** (*motore elettrico*) electromotor.

elettromotríce, *s.f.* (*ferr.*) electric locomotive.

elettróne, *s.m.* (*fis.*) electron: — *negativo*, negatron; — *positivo*, positron; — *rotante*, spinning electron.

elettronegatívo, *ag.s.m.* (*fis.*) electronegative.

elettrònica, *s.f.* electronics.

elettrònico, *ag.* electronic: *apparecchio* —, electronic apparatus; *cervello* —, electronic brain; *flusso* —, electron flow; *tubo* —, electronic tube.

elettroposítivo, *ag.s.m.* (*fis.*) electropositive.

elettroscòpio, *s.m.* electroscope.

elettrostàtica, *s.f.* electrostatics.

elettrostàtico, *ag.* electrostatic.

elettrotècnica, *s.f.* electrical technology, electrotechnics.

elettrotècnico, *ag.* electrotechnic(al): *ingegnere* —, electrotechnical engineer || *s.m.* electrotechnician.

elettroterapèutico, *ag.* electrotherapeutic.

elettroterapía, *s.f.* (*med.*) electrotherapy, electrotherapeutics.

elettrotipía, *s.f.* electrotypy.

elettrotípo, *s.m.* electrotype.

elettrotrèno, *s.m.* single unit electric train.

elettuàrio, *s.m.* (*farm.*) electuary.

Elèusi, *no.pr.f.* (*geog. st.*) Eleusis.

eleusíno, *ag.* Eleusinian: *misteri eleusini*, Eleusinian Mysteries.

elevàbile, *ag.* raisable; that may be lifted, that may be uplifted.

elevaménto, *s.m.* elevation; raising; uplifting.

elevàre, *v.t.* **1.** to elevate; to raise; to lift (up):

un libro che eleva, an elevating book; — *a maggior dignità*, to raise to higher dignity; — *al trono*, to raise to the throne; — *gli occhi*, to raise (o to lift up) one's eyes; — *l'Ostia*, to elevate the Host; — *i prezzi*, to raise prices; — *la voce*, to raise (o to lift up) one's voice **2**. (*erigere*) to erect: — *un edificio, un monumento*, to erect a building, a monument **3**. (*mat.*) to raise: — *all'ennesima potenza*, to raise to the nth power; — *un numero al quadrato, al cubo*, to square, to cube a number ‖ **elevàrsi**, *v.r.* to rise; to tower: *il nuovo grattacielo si eleva sugli edifici circostanti*, the new sky-scraper towers over the surrounding buildings; *la vetta si eleva al di sopra delle nubi*, the summit rises above the clouds.

elevataménte, *av.* loftily, nobly; highly.

elevatézza, *s.f.* loftiness; (*dignità*) dignity, nobility: — *di sentimenti, di stile, di pensiero*, loftiness of feelings, of style, of thought.

elevàto, *ag.* **1**. elevated; (*alto*) high: *prezzo* —, high price; *quel colle non è molto* —, that hill is not very high **2**. *fig.* elevated, lofty, noble, sublime.

elevatóre, *s.m.* **1**. (*anat.*) elevator (muscle) **2**. (*mec.*) elevator: — *a nastro*, belt (o endless) elevator **3**. (*mar.*) ammunition hoist.

elevazióne, *s.f.* **1**. elevation; lifting, raising: *l'* — *di Re Carlo al trono*, the raising of King Charles to the throne ‖ *l'Elevazione dell'Ostia*, (*eccl.*) the Elevation of the Host **2**. (*rialzo di terreno*) rising of ground, height: *una* — *limitava la vista*, a rise in the ground limited the view **3**. (*astr.*) altitude **4**. (*mat.*) raising: — *alla decima potenza*, raising to the tenth power **5**. (*artigl.*) elevation **6**. *fig.* (*nobiltà*) elevation, loftiness, nobility, grandeur.

elevóne, *s.m.* (*neol. aer.*) clevon.

elezióne, *s.f.* **1**. election: *elezioni generali*, general elections; *elezioni amministrative*, local (government) elections **2**. (*scelta*) choice, selection **3**. (*nomina*) appointment.

èlfo, *s.m.* (*mit.*) elf (*pl.* elves).

Elìa, *no.pr.m.* Elias; (*Bibbia*) Elijah.

eliaco, *ag.* (*astr.*) heliacal.

eliànto, *s.m.* (*bot.*) helianthus.

èlica, *s.f.* **1**. (*geom.*) helix (*pl.* helices), spiral: *ad* —, spiral **2**. (*aer. mar.*) propeller, screw; (*di elicottero*) rotor: — *azionata a turbina*, turbine-driven propeller; — *di coda*, tail rotor; — *di quota*, main rotor (o lifting rotor); *pale di* — propeller (o screw o rotor) blades; *piroscafo ad una sola* —, *a due eliche*, single-screw, twin-screw steamer.

èlice, *s.m.* (*anat.*) helix (*pl.* helices).

elicogíro, *s.m.* (*aer.*) helicogyre.

elicoidàle, *ag.* **1**. (*geom.*) helicoidal **2**. (*mec.*) helical.

elicòide, *s.f.* (*geom.*) helicoid.

Elicóna, *no.pr.m.* (*geog.*) Helicon.

elicònio, *ag.* Heliconian.

elicòttero, *s.m.* helicopter: — *a due rotori*, twin-rotor helicopter; — *a statoreattori*, ram-jet helicopter; *l'* — *si alzò e poi si posò di nuovo su quel tetto*, the helicopter took off and then landed on that roof again.

Èlide, *no.pr.f.* (*geog.*) Elis.

elídere, *v.t.* **1**. (*annullare*) to annul, to remove, to suppress **2**. (*gram.*) to elide ‖ **elídersi**, *v.r. reciproco* to annul each other.

eligíbile, *ag.* eligible.

eliminàbile, *ag.* eliminable.

eliminàre, *v.t.* **1**. to eliminate; (*liberàrsi da*) to do away with (s.o., sthg.), to get rid of (s.o. ,sthg.): *elimina questa roba inutile*, eliminate (o do away with o get rid of) all this useless stuff (anche *fig.*); *eliminarono questa possibilità*, they eliminated this possibility; — *un dubbio, un sospetto*, to remove a doubt, a suspicion **2**. (*espellere*) to eliminate **3**. (*spor.*) to eliminate; (*boxe*) to knock out ‖ **eliminàrsi**, *v.r.* to be eliminated ‖ *v.r. reciproco* to eliminate each other.

eliminatòria, *s.f.* (*spor.*) preliminary heat.

eliminazióne, *s.f.* elimination; (*esclusione*) exclusion; (*espulsione*) expulsion; (*rimozione*) removal.

èlio, *s.m.* (*chim.*) helium.

eliocèntrico, *ag.* (*astr.*) heliocentric.

eliocentrísmo, *s.m.* (*st. astr.*) heliocentrism.

eliocromía, *s.f.* (*foto.*) heliochromy.

Eliodòro, *no.pr.m.* (*st. lett.*) Heliodorus.

eliofobía, *s.f.* (*med.*) heliophobia.

Eliogàbalo, *no.pr.m.* (*st.*) Heliogabalus, Elagabalus.

eliografía, *s.f.* (*mil.*) heliography.

eliògrafo, *s.m.* (*astr. mil.*) heliograph.

eliòmetro, *s.m.* (*astr.*) heliometer.

elioscòpio, *s.m.* (*astr.*) helioscope.

elioteísmo, *s.m.* (*st. relig.*) heliolatry.

elioterapía, *s.f.* (*med.*) heliotherapy, sun treatment, sun-bathing.

elioteràpico, *ag.* heliotherapic: *cura elioterapica*, sun treatment (o sun-bathing).

eliotipía, *s.f.* (*foto.*) heliotypy.

eliotròpico, *ag.* heliotropic.

eliotròpio, *s.m.* (*bot. min.*) heliotrope.

eliotropísmo, *s.m.* (*bot.*) heliotropism.

elipòrto, *s.m.* (*aer.*) heliport: — *sul tetto di un edificio*, rooftop heliport.

Elísa, *no.pr.f.* Eliza.

Elisabètta, *no.pr.f.* Elizabeth, Elisabeth ‖ *dim.* Bessie, Bess, Beth, Betsy, Betty, Elsie, Lizzie.

elisabettiàno, *ag.s.m.* (*st.*) Elizabethan.

Elisèo, *no.pr.m.* Ellis; (*Bibbia*) Elisha.

elísio, *ag.* (*mit.*) Elysian: *i Campi Elisi*, the Elysian Fields.

elisióne, *s.f.* (*gram.*) elision.

elisír, elisíre, *s.m.* elixir: — *di lunga vita*, elixir of life.

Elíso, *s.m.* (*geog. mit.*) Elysium.

elísse, *s.f.* (*geom.*) ellipse.

èlitra, *s.f.* (*entom.*) elytrum (*pl.* elytra).

élla, *pron. pers. f.* 3ª *persona sing. sogg.* **1**. she: — *è gentile*, she is kind ‖ — *stessa, proprio* —, she ... herself (o she herself): — *stessa disse che sarebbe venuta*, she herself said she would come; *andò a prenderlo* — *stessa*, she went and fetched it herself (o she herself went to fetch it) **2**. Ella, (*formula di cortesia*) you: *vuole Ella venire a trovarmi?*, would you like to come and see me? **3**. (*arc.*) (*pleonastico*) it: — *è pure una bella cosa*, it is really a nice thing.

Èllade, *no.pr.f.* (*letter.*) Hellas.

èlle, *s.f.m.* letter L ‖ *fatto a* —, *a forma di* —, L-shaped.

ellèboro, *s.m.* (*bot.*) hellebore: — *nero*, Christmas rose; — *puzzolento*, stinking hellebore.

Ellèni, *s.m.pl.* Hellenes.

ellènico, *ag.* Hellenic.

ellenísmo, *s.m.* Hellenism.

ellenísta, *s.m.* Hellenist.

ellenístico, *ag.* Hellenistic.

ellenizzàre, *v.t.* to hellenize.

élleno, *pron. pers.* 3ª *persona pl. f.* (*arc.*) per **ésse**.

èllera, *s.f.* (*poet.*) ivy.

Ellespònto, *no.pr.m.* (*geog. st.*) Hellespont.

ellísse, *s.f.* (*geom.*) ellipse.

ellíssi, *s.f.* (*gram.*) ellipsis (*pl.* ellipses).

ellissògrafo, *s.m.* (*geom.*) trammel, elliptical compass(es).

ellissoidàle, *ag.* (*geom.*) ellipsoidal.

ellissòide, *s.f.* (*geom.*) ellipsoid.

ellitticaménte, *av.* elliptically.

ellíttico, *ag.* (*geom. gram.*) elliptic(al).

elmétto, *s.m.* helmet: — *d'acciaio*, steel helmet.

elmínti, *s.m. pl.* (*zool.*) Helminthes.

elmintíasi, *s.f.* (*patol.*) helminthiasis.

elmintología, *s.f.* (*scient.*) helminthology.

élmo, *s.m.* helmet, headpiece.

elocuzióne, *s.f.* elocution.

elogiàbile, *ag.* praiseworthy; commendable: — *per aver perseverato,* he is worthy of praise (*o* he is to be commended) for having persevered.

elogiàre, *v.t.* to eulogize; (*lodare*) to praise, to commend.

elogiatívo, *ag.* eulogistic(al); (*laudatorio*) commendatory.

elogiatóre, *s.m.,* **elogiatríce,** *s.f.* eulogist; praiser.

elògio, *s.m.* **1.** (*scritto, discorso*) eulogy, panegyric: *pronunciare l'— di qlcu.,* to pronounce s.o.'s eulogy (*o* a eulogy on s.o.) **2.** (*lode*) praise: *degno di ogni —,* praiseworthy (*o* commendable); *ti faccio i miei elogi per i brillanti risultati,* I heartily congratulate you on your brilliant achievements; *fare gli elogi di qlcu.,* to praise s.o.

elogísta, *s.m.* (*rar.*) eulogist.

Eloísa, *no.pr.f.* (*lett.*) Héloïse.

elongazióne, *s.f.* (*astr.*) elongation.

eloquènte, *ag.* eloquent: *silenzio —,* eloquent (*o* meaningful) silence.

eloquenteménte, *av.* eloquently.

eloquènza, *s.f.* eloquence ‖ *l'— del denaro,* fig. the power of money ‖ *è un fiume d'—,* he is very eloquent.

elòquio, *s.m.* (*letter.*) speech: *chiaro —,* clear speech; *ha un facile —,* he speaks very fluently.

Élsa¹, *no.pr.f.* Elsa.

élsa², *s.f.* hilt ‖ *star colla mano sull'—,* fig. to be on the alert (*o* on one's guard).

elucubràre, *v.t.* to lucubrate on, about (sthg.), to meditate on, upon (sthg.).

elucubrazióne, *s.f.* lucubration.

elúdere, *v.t.* to elude, to evade, to escape; to baffle: *— un attacco, un colpo,* to evade (*o* to escape) an attack, a blow; *— una domanda,* to evade a question; *— la legge,* to elude (*o* to avoid compliance with *o* to evade) the law; *— un pagamento,* to elude a payment; *— la vigilanza di qlcu.,* to baffle s.o.'s vigilance.

eludíbile, *ag.* eludible, evadable, escapable.

elusióne, *s.f.* elusion.

elusivaménte, *av.* elusively, evasively.

elusívo, *ag.* elusive, evasive.

elvètico, *ag.* Helvetic, Helvetian; Swiss: *la Confederazione elvetica,* the Swiss Confederation ‖ *s.m.* Swiss; Helvetian.

Elvíra, *no.pr.f.* Elvira.

elzeviriàno, *ag.* (*st. della stampa*) Elzevir(ian): *carattere —,* (*tip.*) Elzevir type.

elzevíro, *ag.* (*st. della stampa*) Elzevir(ian): *carattere —,* (*tip.*) Elzevir type ‖ *s.m.* **1.** (*st. della stampa*) Elzevir (publication) **2.** (*giornalismo*) leading literary article (in a newspaper).

emaciaménto, *s.m.* (*rar.*) emaciation.

emaciàre, *v.t.* to emaciate ‖ **emaciàrsi,** *v.r.* to become emaciated, to waste away.

emaciàto, *ag.* emaciated, wasted, lean and weak.

emanàre, *v.t.* **1.** to issue: *— leggi, ordini, decreti,* to issue laws, orders, decrees **2.** (*vapore, profumo*) to exhale; (*luce*) to shed: *le trecce di lei emanavano un sentore di viole,* her plaits gave off a scent of violets ‖ *v.i.* (*derivare*) to emanate, to proceed, to derive.

emanatísmo, *s.m.* (*st. fil.*) emanationism.

emanatísta, *s.m.* (*st. fil.*) emanatist.

emanatístico, *ag.* (*st. fil.*) emanatistic.

emanazióne, *s.f.* **1.** emanation, efflux; (*esalazione*) exhalation: *— di gas,* gas efflux **2.** (*il pubblicare*) issuing; (*pubblica ordinanza*) issue: *— governativa,* Government Issue (*abbr.* G. I.) **3.** *— del radio,* (*chim.*) radium emanation (*o* radon).

emancipàre, *v.t.* **1.** (*dir.*) to emancipate **2.** *fig.* to emancipate; (*liberare*) to set free ‖ **emancipàrsi,** *v.r.* to free oneself, to emancipate oneself, to get emancipated, to gain one's freedom.

emancipàto, *ag.* emancipated (anche *fig.*): *una ra-*

gazza emancipata, an emancipated girl; *spirito — da ogni influenza,* mind freed from all influence.

emancipatóre, *ag.* emancipatory ‖ *s.m.,* **emancipatríce,** *s.f.* emancipator.

emancipazióne, *s.f.* emancipation: *l'— della donna,* the emancipation of women ‖ *Proclamazione di Emancipazione,* (*st. amer.*) Emancipation Proclamation.

Emanuèle, *no.pr.m.* Emmanuel, Immanuel.

emarginàre, *v.t.* to margin.

emàrtro, *s.m.,* **emartròsi,** *s.f.* (*patol.*) hemarthrosis.

ematèmesi, *s.f.* (*med.*) hematemesis.

emàtico, *ag.* (*med.*) h(a)ematic.

ematína, *s.f.* (*fisiol.*) h(a)ematin.

ematíte, *s.f.* (*min.*) h(a)ematite.

ematología, *s.f.* (*med.*) h(a)ematology.

ematòma, *s.m.* (*med.*) h(a)ematoma.

ematopoièsi, *s.f.* (*fisiol.*) h(a)ematopoiesis.

ematopoiètico, *ag.* (*fisiol.*) h(a)ematopoietic.

ematòsi, *s.f.* (*fisiol.*) h(a)ematosis.

ematuría, *s.f.* (*med.*) h(a)ematuria.

emazía, *s.f.* (*anat.*) erythrocyte, red blood corpuscle.

embàrgo, *s.m.* (*mar.*) embargo: *essere sottoposto ad —,* to be under an embargo; *levare l'—,* to lift (*o* to raise) the embargo; *sottoporre le merci ad —,* to lay (*o* to impose) an embargo on goods.

emblèma, *s.m.* emblem; badge; device, cognizance; (*simbolo*) symbol, sign: *un — di pace,* an emblem of peace; *una bandiera con uno strano —,* a banner with a strange device; *le catene sono l'— della schiavitù,* chains are the symbol of slavery.

emblematicaménte, *av.* emblematically; symbolically.

emblemàtico, *ag.* emblematic(al); symbolic.

embolía, *s.f.* (*med.*) embolism.

embolísmo, *s.m.* (*astr.*) embolism.

èmbolo, *s.m.* (*med.*) embolus (*pl.* emboli).

embricàto, *ag.* tiled, covered with tiles, imbricated.

émbrice, *s.m.* flat tile, roof-tile ‖ *scoprire un —,* fig. to disclose a secret.

embriciàta, *s.f.* imbrication.

embriogenía, *s.f.* (*fisiol.*) embryogenesis.

embriografía, *s.f.* (*anat.*) embryography.

embriología, *s.f.* (*fisiol.*) embryology.

embriòlogo, *s.m.* embryologist.

embrionàle, *ag.* embryonic, embryonal, rudimentary, undeveloped (anche *fig.*): *in uno stato —,* in (the) embryo stage.

embrióne, *s.m.* embryo (*pl.* embryos) (anche *fig.*): *in —,* in embryo (*o* still undeveloped *o* embryonic): *opera ancora in —,* work still in embryo.

embriònico, *ag.* embryonic.

embrocazióne, *s.f.* (*farm.*) embrocation.

emènda, *s.f.* (*rar.*) amendment.

emendàbile, *ag.* amendable: *errore —,* amendable error.

emendaménto, *s.m.* **1.** amendment: *proporre un — a un progetto di legge,* to move (*o* to propose) an amendment to a bill **2.** (*correzione*) emendation, correction **3.** (*miglioramento*) amendment, improvement.

emendàre, *v.t.* **1.** to amend: *— una legge,* to amend a law **2.** (*correggere*) to emend, to correct: *sta emendando il suo libro,* he is emending his book **3.** (*migliorare*) to amend, to improve, to make better ‖ **emendàrsi,** *v.r.* **1.** to amend (one's way of living) **2.** (*diventare migliore*) to grow better; (*di terreno*) to become more fertile.

emendatívo, *ag.* amendatory, corrective.

emendatóre, *s.m.,* **emendatríce,** *s.f.* **1.** amender **2.** (*correttore, correttrice*) corrector, emender.

emendazióne, *s.f.* **1.** amendment **2.** (*correzione*) correction, emendation.

emeralopía, *s.f.* (*patol.*) hemeralopia, day-blindness.

emergènte, *ag.* **1.** emergent, emerging, appearing **2.** (*consequente*) resulting; consequent(ial): *danno —,* (*dir.*) resulting (*o* consequential) damage.

emergènza, *s.f.* emergency; exigency, exigence: *in caso di* —, in case of emergency.

emèrgere, *v.i.* **1.** to emerge, to come afloat; *(di sottomarino)* to surface, to emerge **2.** *fig.* *(apparire)* to emerge, to appear, to come out: *alcune persone emersero dall'ombra,* some people loomed out of the shadow **3.** *(distinguersi)* to distinguish oneself, to rise (above the others); *(risaltare)* to stand out: *montagne che emergono all'orizzonte,* mountains that stand out on the horizon.

emèrito, *ag.* **1.** *(nelle università)* emeritus: *professore* —, emeritus professor **2.** *(iron.)* notorius: *un* — *mascalzone,* a notorious scoundrel.

emerocàlle, *s.m.,* **emerocàllide,** *s.f.* *(bot.)* hemerocallis, day-lily.

emerotèca, *s.f.* newspaper library.

emersióne, *s.f.* emersion, emergence.

emèrso, *ag.* emersed, rising out of (water); *(di sottomarino)* surfaced.

emètico, *ag.s.m.* *(farm.)* emetic, vomitory.

emetína, *s.f.* *(farm.)* emetin(e).

eméttere, *v.t.* **1.** to emit, to give out, to send forth; *(suono)* to utter: — *calore,* to emit heat; — *un grido,* to utter (o to give out) a cry **2.** *(emanare, esprimere)* to deliver, to express: — *un giudizio, un verdetto,* to deliver a judgement, a verdict; — *un'opinione,* to express an opinion; — *una sentenza,* to pass a sentence **3.** *(mettere in circolazione)* to issue, to put into circulation: — *carta moneta,* to issue paper currency; — *un decreto,* to issue a decree; — *tratta su qlcu.,* *(comm.)* to draw on s.o.

emicíclo, *s.m.* hemicycle.

emicrània, *s.f.* headache; hemicrania.

emièdrico, *ag.* *(min.)* hemihedral.

emigrànte, *ag.* emigrating, emigrant ‖ *s.c.* emigrant.

emigràre, *v.i.* to emigrate; *(di animali)* to migrate.

emigràto, *s.m.* emigrant; *(esiliato politico)* political exile; *(profugo)* refugee.

emigrazióne, *s.f.* emigration; *(di animali)* migration.

Emília[1], *no.pr.f.* *(geog.)* Emilia.

Emília[2], *no.pr.f.* Emily, Emilia.

emiliàno, *ag.s.m.* Emilian ‖ **emiliàna,** *s.f.* Emilian.

Emílio, *no.pr.m.* Emil.

eminènte, *ag.* **1.** *(alto)* high **2.** *fig.* *(eccellente)* eminent, excellent, outstanding, distinguished: *un* — *uomo di stato,* an outstanding statesman.

eminenteménte, *av.* eminently, highly.

eminentíssimo, *ag.* *(titolo dato ai cardinali)* His Eminence; *(vocativo)* Your Eminence.

eminènza, *s.f.* **1.** eminence (anche *fig.*) height **2.** *Eminenza,* *(titolo dato ai cardinali)* Eminence: *Sua Eminenza,* His Eminence; *Vostra Eminenza,* Your Eminence.

emiopía, *s.f.* *(patol.)* hemiopia.

emiplegía, *s.f.* *(patol.)* hemiplegia.

emiplègico, *ag.* hemiplegic.

emíro, *s.m.* emir.

emisfèrico, *ag.* hemispheric(al), semispheric(al).

emisfèro, *s.m.* hemisphere: *gli emisferi del cervello,* the cerebral hemispheres; *l'* — *Nord, Sud,* the northern, southern hemisphere.

emissàrio, *s.m.* **1.** emissary **2.** *(geog.)* emissary, effluent **3.** *(ing. idraulica)* outlet, drain.

emissióne, *s.f.* **1.** emission **2.** *(econ.)* issue: — *di biglietti, (di Stato)* issue of paper money; *(di banca)* issue of bank notes; — *eccessiva,* overissue; *azione di nuova, vecchia* —, new, existing share; *banca di* —, bank of issue **3.** *(fis.)* emission; *(tel.)* sending: — *di corrente, (tel.)* impulse of current; — *direttiva, (rad.)* beam emission; — *nulla, (elettrotelefonia)* zero current impulse; — *termica,* temperature radiation; — *termoionica, (rad.)* thermionic emission; *antenna d'*—, *(rad.)* transmitting (o sending) aerial; *stazione d'*—, *(rad.)* transmitting (o broadcasting) station.

emissività, *s.f.* *(fis.)* emissivity.

emistíchio, *s.m.* *(poes.)* hemistich.

emittènte, *ag.* **1.** *(econ.)* issuing: *la banca* —, the issuing bank **2.** *stazione* —, *(rad.)* broadcasting (o transmitting) station.

emíttero, *s.m.* *(entom.)* hemipteron *(pl.* hemiptera).

Èmma, *no.pr.f.* Emma ‖ *dim.* Emm, Emmie.

èmme, *s.f.m.* letter M.

emmètrope, *s.c.* *(med.)* emmetrope.

emmetropía, *s.f.* *(med.)* emmetropia.

emmetròpico, *ag.* *(med.)* emmetropic.

emoclasía, *s.f.* *(patol.)* h(a)emoclasis.

emodinamòmetro, *s.m.* *(med.)* h(a)emodynamometer.

emofilía, *s.f.* *(patol.)* h(a)emophilia.

emoglobímetro, *s.m.* *(med.)* h(a)emoglobinometer.

emoglobína, *s.f.* *(biol.)* h(a)emoglobin.

emoglobinuría, *s.f.* *(patol.)* h(a)emoglobinuria.

emoinnèsto, *s.m.* *(med.)* blood transfusion.

emolísi, *s.f.* *(fisiol.)* h(a)emolysis.

emolliènte, *ag.* emollient, softening ‖ *s.m.* emollient.

emoluménto, *s.m.* emolument; *(stipendio)* salary, remuneration.

emorragía, *s.f.* *(patol.)* h(a)emorrhage.

emorràgico, *ag.* *(patol.)* h(a)emorrhagic.

emorroidàle, *ag.* *(patol.)* h(a)emorrhoidal.

emorròidi, *s.f.pl.* *(patol.)* h(a)emorrhoids.

emostàsi, *s.f.* *(med.)* ha(e)mostasis.

emostàtico, *ag.* *(farm.)* h(a)emostatic ‖ *s.m.* *(farm.)* h(a)emostat.

emotività, *s.f.* emotionality, sensitiveness, sensibility.

emotívo, *ag.* emotional, sensitive.

emotrasfusióne, *s.f.* *(med.)* blood transfusion.

emottísi, *s.f.* *(patol.)* h(a)emoptysis.

emottòico, *ag.* *(patol.)* h(a)emoptysic(al).

emozionàbile, *ag.* emotional, excitable.

emozionànte, *ag.* moving, touching; *(eccitante)* exciting: *un romanzo* —, an exciting novel.

emozionàre, *v.t.* to move, to touch; *(eccitare)* to excite: *le sue parole lo emozionarono profondamente,* his words moved him deeply ‖ **emozionàrsi,** *v.r.* to get excited: *non emozionarti!,* don't get excited!; *si emoziona per un nonnulla,* he gets excited over nothing.

emozionàto, *ag.* deeply moved, deeply stirred.

emozióne, *s.f.* emotion: *provare un'*—, to experience an emotion; *senza mostrare la minima* —, without showing the least emotion.

Empèdocle, *no.pr.m.* *(st. fil.)* Empedocles.

empetíggine, *s.f.* *(patol.)* impetigo.

empiaménte, *av.* **1.** impiously **2.** *(crudelmente)* cruelly.

empiàstro, *V.* impiàstro.

empièma, *s.m.* *(patol.)* empyema.

émpiere, *V.* empíre.

empietà, *s.f.* **1.** impiety, irreligiousness, godlessness, ungodliness; irriverence **2.** *(crudeltà)* cruelty.

empiménto, *s.m.* filling (up); *(imbottimento)* stuffing.

émpio, *ag.* **1.** impious, irreligious, godless, ungodly ‖ *gli empi,* the impious **2.** *(crudele)* cruel; pitiless.

empíre, *v.t.* **1.** to fill (anche *fig.*); to fill up; *(imbottire, rimpinzare)* to cram, to stuff: — *un bicchiere,* to fill up a glass; — *la mente di idee,* to fill the mind with ideas; — *qlcu. di benefici,* to bestow benefits on s.o. **2.** *(affollare)* to crowd, to throng ‖ **empírsi,** *v.r.* **1.** to fill (with sthg.): *gli occhi le si empirono di lacrime,* her eyes filled with tears **2.** *(rimpinzarsi)* to cram oneself (with sthg.): — *di cibo,* to cram oneself with food ‖ — *la bocca, (parlare con affettazione)* to talk big (o affectedly) **3.** *(affollarsi)* to fill (with people), to become full, to become crowded (with people): *la strada si empì di soldati,* the street filled with soldiers.

empíreo, *ag.* *(poet.)* empyreal, empyrean ‖ *s.m.* empyrean.

empiricaménte, *av.* empirically; *(fam.)* by rule of thumb.

empírico, *ag.* empiric(al) ‖ *s.m.* **1.** empiric, empiricist **2.** *(ciarlatano)* quack.

empirísmo, *s.m.* *(st. fil.)* empiricism.

empirísta, *s.m.* (*st. fil.*) empiricist.
empíto[1], *ag.* filled; crammed; (*pieno*) full.
émpito[2], *s.m.* (*letter.*) vehemence, impetuosity; rush; fury.
empitúra, *s.f.* filling (up).
empòrio, *s.m.* **1.** (*centro commerciale*) emporium (*pl.* emporia, emporiums); trade centre **2.** (*negozio*) department store **3.** (*ammasso di cose svariate*) great quantity, heap, vast collection.
emú, *s.m.* (*ornit.*) emu, emeu.
emulàre, *v.t.* to emulate; to try to rival; to vie with (s.o.).
emulatóre, *ag.* emulous ‖ *s.m.*, **emulatríce,** *s.f.* emulator; rival, competitor.
emulazióne, *s.f.* emulation: *con spirito di —,* in a spirit of emulation.
èmulo, *ag.* emulous, rival ‖ *s.m.* emulator, competitor, rival.
emulsionàbile, *ag.* (*chim. fis.*) emulsifiable, emulsible.
emulsionànte, *s.m.* (*chim. fis.*) emulsifying agent.
emulsionàre, *v.t.* (*fis.*) to emulsify.
emulsióne, *s.f.* (*fis. farm. foto.*) emulsion.
emúnto, *ag.* (*rar.*) emaciated, worn out.
emuntòrio, *ag.* (*anat.*) emunctory.
enàllage, *s.f.* (*ret.*) enallage.
enarmonía, *s.f.* (*mus.*) enharmonics.
enarmonicaménte, *av.* (*mus.*) enharmonically.
enarmònico, *ag.* (*mus.*) enharmonic(al).
enartròsi, *s.f.* (*anat.*) enarthrosis.
encàrpo, *s.m.* (*arch.*) encarpus.
encàustica, *s.f.* (*pitt.*) encaustic.
encàustico, *ag.* (*pitt.*) encaustic.
encàusto, *s.m.* **1.** (*pitt.*) encaustic painting **2.** (*st. romana*) encaustic ink.
encefàlico, *ag.* (*anat.*) encephalic.
encefalíte, *s.f.* (*patol.*) encephalitis: — *letargica,* lethargic encephalitis.
encèfalo, *s.m.* (*anat.*) encephalon (*pl.* encephala).
Encèlado, *no.pr.m.* (*mit.*) Enceladus.
encíclica, *s.f.* (*eccl.*) encyclic, encyclical.
enciclopedía, *s.f.* encyclopaedia, (en)cyclopedia.
enciclopedicaménte, *av.* encyclopaedically, (en)cyclopedically.
enciclopèdico, *ag.* encyclopaedic, (en)cyclopedic: *è un tipo —,* he is a walking encyclopaedia.
enciclopedísmo, *s.m.* encyclopaedism.
enciclopedísta, *s.m.* encyclopaedist, (en)cyclopedist.
ènclisi, *s.f.* (*gram.*) enclisis.
enclítica, *s.f.* (*gram.*) enclitic.
enclítico, *ag.* (*gram.*) enclitic.
encomiàbile, *ag.* praiseworthy, laudable, commendable: *egli è — per aver perseverato,* he is worthy of praise for his perseverance.
encomiàre, *v.t.* to commend; to praise; to eulogize.
encomiàsta, encomiàste, *s.m.* encomiast, panegyrist, eulogist.
encomiasticaménte, *av.* encomiastically.
encomiàstico, *ag.* encomiastic, panegyrical; laudatory: *parlava in termini encomiastici di lei,* he was speaking highly (*o* in high terms) of her.
encòmio, *s.m.* **1.** encomium (*pl.* encomiums, encomia), eulogy, panegyric **2.** (*lode*) praise, commendation **3.** (*mil.*) mention in dispatches; (*amer.*) citation.
endecagonàle, *ag.* (*geom.*) hendecagonal.
endecàgono, *s.m.* (*geom.*) hendecagon.
endecasillabo, *ag.* (*poes.*) hendecasyllabic ‖ *s.m.* (*poes.*) hendecasyllable.
endemía, *s.f.* (*med.*) endemic (disease).
endemicaménte, *av.* (*med.*) endemically.
endèmico, *ag.* (*med.*) endemic.
endemísmo, *s.m.* (*med.*) endemism.
endèrmico, *ag.* (*med.*) endermic.
endíadi, *s.f.* (*ret.*) hendiadys.
éndice, *s.m.* **1.** (*ricordo*) keepsake **2.** (*uovo che si*

lascia nel nido per indurre le galline a deporvi le uova) nest-egg.
Endimióne, *no.pr.m.* (*mit.*) Endymion.
endocàrdio, *s.m.* (*anat.*) endocardium.
endocardíte, *s.f.* (*patol.*) endocarditis.
endocàrpo, *s.m.* (*bot.*) endocarp.
endocrànio, *s.m.* (*anat.*) endocrane.
endòcrino, *ag.* (*anat.*) endocrine: *glandole endocrine,* endocrine glands.
endocrinología, *s.f.* (*med.*) endocrinology.
endocrinòlogo, *s.m.* (*med.*) endocrinologist.
endocrinopatía, *s.f.* (*patol.*) endocrinopathy.
endocrinòsi, *s.f.* (*patol.*) endocrinosis.
endocrinoterapía, *s.f.* (*med.*) endocrinotherapy.
endodèrma, *s.f.* (*biol. bot.*) endoderm.
endogamía, *s.f.* endogamy.
endògamo, *ag.* endogamous.
endògeno, *ag.* (*geol.*) endogenous.
endolínfa, *s.f.* (*anat.*) endolymph.
endometríte, *s.f.* (*patol.*) endometritis.
endomòrfo, *s.m.* (*geol.*) endomorph.
endoplàsma, *s.f.* (*biol.*) endoplasm.
endoscòpio, *s.m.* (*med.*) endoscope.
endosmòmetro, *s.m.* (*fis. chim.*) endosmometer.
endosmòsi, *s.f.* (*fis.*) endosmosis.
endòstio, *s.m.* (*anat.*) endosteum (*pl.* endostea).
endotèlio, *s.m.* (*anat.*) endothelium (*pl.* endothelia).
endotèrmico, *ag.* (*chim.*) endothermic.
endovenóso, *ag.* (*med.*) intravenous: *iniezione endovenosa,* intravenous injection.
Enèa, *no.pr.m.* (*lett.*) Aeneas.
Enèide, *s.f.* (*lett.*) Aeneid.
energètica, *s.f.* energetics.
energètico, *ag.* (*rar.*) (*energico*) energetic ‖ *s.m.* (*farm.*) tonic.
energía, *s.f.* **1.** energy, vigour: *con —,* energetically; *senza —,* listlessly: *un uomo senza —,* a listless man (*o* a man wanting in vigour); *deve metterci un po' di —,* he must put some effort into it; *dedicare tutte le energie a un compito,* to devote (*o* to apply) all one's energies to a task (*o* to put one's heart and soul into a task); *mostrare, spiegare —,* to put forth (*o* to display) energy **2.** (*fis.*) energy: — *atomica, cinematica, latente, radiante,* atomic, kinetic, latent, radiant energy; — *elettrica,* electric power; — *potenziale,* potential energy; — *sonica,* sonic energy.
energicaménte, *av.* energetically.
enèrgico, *ag.* energetic, active; (*che impegna molte energie*) strenuous; (*vigoroso*) vigorous; (*potente, efficace*) powerful, forcible, strong, emphatic: *gesto —,* emphatic gesture; *giuoco —,* strenuous game; *linguaggio —,* forcible language; *misure energiche,* energetic (*o* strong *o* drastic) measures; *rimedio —,* powerful (*o* energetic *o* drastic) remedy; *è un uomo —,* he is an energetic man (*o fam.* he has plenty of go).
energísmo, *s.m.* (*fil.*) energism.
energúmeno, *s.m.* **1.** energumen, demoniac: *gridava come un —,* he was screaming like one possessed **2.** (*infuriato*) furious man, madman (*pl.* madmen) **3.** (*fam.*) (*prepotente*) bully.
ènfasi, *s.f.* **1.** emphasis: — *oratoria,* oratorical (*o* rhetorical) emphasis; *parlare con —,* to speak with emphasis (*o* emphatically) **2.** (*esagerazione, ampollosità*) pomposity, bombast, turgidity: *scrivere con —,* to write in a bombastic (*o* turgid) style.
enfaticaménte, *av.* **1.** emphatically **2.** (*con esagerazione, ampollosità*) pompously, bombastically, turgidly.
enfàtico, *ag.* **1.** emphatic **2.** (*esagerato, ampolloso*) pompous, bombastic, turgid.
enfiagióne, *s.f.* (*med.*) swelling, tumour.
enfiaménto, *s.m.* (*rar.*) swelling.
enfiàre, *v.i.* to swell, to inflate ‖ **enfiàrsi,** *v.r.* to swell, to become swollen, to get swollen.
enfiàto, *ag.* swollen, inflated.
enfiatúra, *s.f.* (*rar.*) swelling.

énfio, *ag.* swollen, inflated.

enfisèma, *s.m.* (*patol.*) emphysema: — *polmonare*, pulmonary emphysema.

enfisematóso, *ag.* (*patol.*) emphysematous.

enfitèusi, *s.f.* (*dir.*) emphyteusis, perpetual lease.

enfitèuta, *s.m.* (*dir.*) emphyteuta (*pl.* emphyteutae).

enfitèutico, *ag.* (*dir.*) emphyteutic.

enígma, *s.m.* enigma; (*indovinello*) riddle, conundrum, puzzle: *parlare per enigmi*, to speak in riddles; *sciogliere un —*, to solve a riddle.

enigmaticaménte, *av.* enigmatically.

enigmàtico, *ag.* enigmatic(al), puzzling, mysterious: *contegno —*, mysterious behaviour.

enigmatizzàre, *v.t.* (*rar.*) to enigmatize.

enigmísta, *s.m.* (*chi risolve enigmi*) solver of puzzles, enigmatographer; (*appassionato di enigmistica*) riddle enthusiast, puzzle enthusiast.

enigmística, *s.f.* enigmatography: *libro di —*, book of riddles (o puzzles).

enigmístico, *ag.* 1. of, pertaining to enigmatography 2. of, pertaining to an enigma, a riddle.

enímma, *e derivati*, *V.* **enígma**, *e derivati*.

ennàgono, *s.m.* (*geom.*) enneagon.

ènne,[1] *s.f.m.* letter N.

ennè[2], *s.m.* (*tintura*) henna.

ennèade, *s.f.* ennead.

enneagonàle, *ag.* (*geom.*) enneagonal.

enneàgono, *s.m.* (*geom.*) enneagon.

ennèsimo, *ag.* 1. (*mat.*) nth: *elevare all'ennesima potenza*, to raise to the nth power 2. *te lo dico per l'ennesima volta!*, (*fam.*) I've told you so a thousand (o a million) times!.

enocianína, *s.f.* (*chim.*) oenocyanine.

enòfilo, *ag.* oenological: *circolo —*, wine-growers' club (o association).

enología, *s.f.* oenology.

enològico, *ag.* oenological.

enòlogo, *s.m.* oenologist.

enòmetro, *s.m.* oenometer.

enopòlio, *s.m.* wine wholesale.

enòrme, *ag.* 1. huge, enormous: *un'— costruzione*, a huge building 2. *fig.* tremendous; (*assurdo*) absurd; (*oltraggioso*) outrageous: *insulto —*, outrageous insult.

enormeménte, *av.* enormously.

enormità, *s.f.* 1. hugeness; enormousness 2. *fig.* (*assurdità*) absurdity; (*mostruosità*) enormity: *l'— del suo delitto*, the enormity of his crime.

enosigèo, *ag.* (*letter.*) earthshaking.

Enrichétta, *no.pr.f.* Henrietta || *dim.* Etta, Hetty, Nettie, Netty.

Enríco, *no.pr.m.* Henry, Harry || *dim.* Hal, Henny.

ensifórme, *ag.* (*bot.*) ensiform, sword-shaped.

èntasi, *s.f.* (*arch.*) entasis.

ènte, *s.m.* 1. (*fil.*) being: *l'Ente supremo*, the Supreme Being 2. (*dir. amm.*) (corporate) body, body corporate, corporation: — *parastatale*, official body (o corporation); — *privato*, *pubblico*, private, public body || *Ente Autonomo del Turismo*, Local Tourist Organization; *Ente Italiano del Turismo*, Italian Tourist Organization || *Ente Zolfi Italiani*, Italian Sulphur Board.

entelechía, *s.f.* (*fil.*) entelechy.

entèrico, *ag.* (*med.*) enteric, intestinal.

enteríte, *s.f.* (*patol.*) enteritis.

enterocèle, *s.m.* (*patol.*) enterocele.

enteroclísi, *s.f.* (*med.*) enteroclysis.

enteroclísma, *s.m.* (*med.*) enema; clyster.

enterocolíte, *s.f.* (*patol.*) enterocolitis.

enterotomía, *s.f.* (*chir.*) enterotomy.

enteròtomo, *s.m.* (*chir.*) enterotome.

entimèma, *s.m.* (*log.*) enthymeme.

entimemàtico, *ag.* (*log.*) enthymematic.

entità, *s.f.* 1. (*fil.*) entity 2. (*cosa esistente*) entity; being; existence 3. (*fam.*) (*importanza*) importance: *di scarsa —*, of little importance.

entomología, *s.f.* entomology.

entomològico, *ag.* entomological.

entomòlogo, *s.m.* entomologist.

entràmbe, *ag.pron.f.pl.*, **entràmbi**, *ag.pron.m.pl.* **both**: *conosco entrambe le sorelle*, I know both sisters; «*Hai ancora i genitori?*», «*Sì, entrambi* », "Are your parents alive?", "Yes, both"; *vennero entrambi*, *entrambe*, they both came (o both of them came).

entrànte, *ag.* (*nelle determinazioni di tempo*) next, coming: *la settimana —*, next week (o the coming week).

entràre, *v.i.* 1. to enter; to go in; to come in; to get in: *la chiave non entra nella serratura*, the key does not fit the lock; *come potrei farglielo — in testa?*, how could I drive it into his head?; *entrate!*, (*andate dentro!*) go in! (o go inside!); (*venite dentro!*) come in!; *entrerò un istante tornando dall'ufficio*, I shall look (o drop) in on my way back from the office; *entrarono nel suo ufficio*, they entered (o went into o walked into o stepped into) his office; *non dovreste — negli affari altrui*, you should not interfere (o meddle) with other people's business; *questo argomento non m'entra*, I cannot understand (o grasp) this matter; — *a cavallo*, to ride in; — *correndo*, to run in: *entrò correndo nella stanza*, he ran into the room; — *di soppiatto*, *furtivamente*, to steal in: *entrò furtivamente nel giardino*, he stole into the garden; — *in argomento*, to enter upon (o to broach) a subject; — *in automobile*, to drive in; — *in carica*, to come into office; — *in conversazione con qlcu.*, to enter into conversation with s.o.; — *in corrispondenza con qlcu.*, to enter into correspondence with s.o.; — *in particolari*, to go into details; — *in relazione con qlcu.*, to enter (o to go) into business relations with s.o.; — *in società con qlcu.*, to enter (o to go) into partnership with s.o.; — *in trattative con qlcu.*, to enter into negotiations with s.o.; — *precipitosamente*, to rush (o to dash) in: *entrò precipitosamente in casa*, he rushed into the house; *fare — qlcu.*, to show s.o. in; *impedire a qlcu. di —*, to keep s.o. out (o to close the door against s.o.) || *entra*, *entrano*, (*nei copioni teatrali*) enter: *entra Amleto*, enter Hamlet; *entrano Ofelia e Polonio*, enter Ophelia and Polonius || — *in azione*, (*mil.*) to go into action || — *in ballo*, *fig.* to intervene || — *in ebollizione*, *in fusione*, to begin to boil, to melt || — *in funzione*, (*di funzionario*) to enter upon one's duties || — *in giuoco*, *fig.* to come into play || — *in possesso di un'eredità*, to come into (o to enter upon) an inheritance || — *in vigore*, to come into force (o into effect) || — *nell'esercito*, to enter the army; — *nel partito comunista*, to join (o to become a member of) the Communist Party || — *nel sessantesimo anno* (*di età*), to enter upon one's sixtieth year || *vietato —*, no admittance (o private) 2. (*aver relazione, aver a che fare*) **to have to do with** (s.o., sthg.): *che c'entra?*, what has that got to do with it?; *voi non c'entrate*, this is no business of yours || *questo c'entra come i cavoli a merenda*, that's got nothing to do with it 3. (*stare, contenersi*) **to go into** (sthg.): *il due entra nell'otto quattro volte*, two goes into eight four times || *in questa stoffa c'entrano venti camicie*, this material is sufficient for twenty shirts.

entràta, *s.f.* 1. entrance; entry: — *di favore*, free admission; — *e uscita*, way in and way out (o entrance and exit); — *in carica*, entrance upon (o into) office; — *principale*, *sul retro*, front entrance, back entrance; *biglietto di —*, (*teat.*) admission ticket; *fare una — trionfale*, to make a triumphant entry 2. (*miner.*) adit 3. (*rendita*) (*comm.*) receipts (*pl.*): — *e uscita*, debit and credit; *pubbliche entrate*, public revenue.

entratúra, *s.f.* 1. entrance: *tassa d'—*, entrance (o admission) fee 2. (*rapporti familiari*) familiar terms (*pl.*): *aver — con qlcu.*, to be on familiar terms with s.o.

éntro, *prep.* 1. (*luogo*) **inside, within**: — *queste pareti*, inside (o within) these walls 2. (*tempo*) **in, within**: — *due settimane*, within (o in) two weeks; — *il 30 giugno*, (*comm.*) on or before June 30th || *av.* (*arc.*) **within**.

entrobórdo, *s.m.* **1.** (*scafo*) inboard **2.** (*motore*) inboard engine.

entropía, *s.f.* (*fis.*) entropy.

entrotèrra, *s.m.* inland, hinterland.

entusiasmànte, *ag.* enrapturing; thrilling in.

entusiasmàre, *v.t.* to raise enthusiasm in (s.o.); to enrapture, to carry away: *la folla fu entusiasmata da queste parole,* the crowd was carried away by these words ‖ **entusiasmàrsi,** *v.r.* to become enthusiastic over (sthg.); to go into raptures (over sthg.): *si entusiasma per l'arte moderna,* he goes into raptures over modern art.

entusiàsmo, *s.m.* enthusiasm; rapture: *fare ql.co. senza* —, to do sthg. half-heartedly.

entusiàsta, *s.c.* enthusiast: *essere* — *di ql.co.,* (*fam.*) to be crazy about sthg.

entusiasticaménte, *av.* enthusiastically.

entusiàstico, *ag.* enthusiastic; ardent.

enucleàre, *v.t.* (*chir.*) to enucleate.

enucleazióne, *s.f.* (*chir.*) enucleation.

enumeràre, *v.t.* to enumerate.

enumerazióne, *s.f.* enumeration.

enunciàre, *v.t.* to enunciate; to state; to express: — *un teorema,* to enunciate a theorem.

enunciatíva, *s.f.* (*gram.*) enunciative proposition.

enunciatívo, *ag.* enunciative; declarative.

enunciàto, *s.m.* proposition; terms (*pl.*): *l'* — *di un problema,* (*mat.*) the terms of a problem.

enunciazióne, *s.f.* enunciation (anche *mat.*).

enunziàre, *e derivati,* V. **enunciàre,** *e derivati.*

enzíma, *s.m.* (*chim.*) enzym(e).

eocène, *s.m.* (*geol.*) eocene.

Eòlia, *no.pr.f.* (*geog. st.*) Aeolia, Aeolis.

eòlico, *ag.* **1.** (*dell'Eolia*) Aeolian, Aeolic: *dialetto* —, Aeolian (*o* Aeolic) dialect **2.** (*di vento, causato dal vento*) Aeolian: *depositi eolici,* (*geol.*) Aeolian rocks.

Eòlide, *no.pr.f.* (*geog. st.*) Aeolia, Aeolis.

eòlio, *ag.* Aeolian ‖ *arpa eolia,* (*mus.*) Aeolian harp ‖ *modo* —, (*mus.*) Aeolian mode.

Epaminónda, *no.pr.m.* (*st.*) Epaminondas.

èpa, *s.f.* (*arc.*) belly; paunch.

epagòge, *s.f.* (*log.*) epagoge.

epagògico, *ag.* (*log.*) epagogic.

epanalèpsi, *s.f.* (*ret.*) epanalepsis.

eparchía, *s.f.* (*st.*) eparchy.

epàtica, *s.f.* (*bot.*) liverwort.

epàtico, *ag.* hepatic.

epatíte, *s.f.* (*patol.*) hepatitis.

epatizzazióne, *s.f.* (*patol.*) hepatization.

epàtta, *s.f.* (*astr.*) epact.

epèntesi, *s.f.* (*gram.*) epenthesis.

eperlàno, *s.m.* (*ittiol.*) smelt.

èpica, *s.f.* epic; epic poetry.

epicaménte, *av.* epically.

epicàrdio, *s.m.* (*anat.*) epicardium.

epicàrpo, *s.m.* (*bot.*) epicarp.

epicèdico, *ag.* epicedial.

epicèdio, *s.m.* (*poes.*) epicedium (*pl.* epicedia, epicediums).

epicèntro, *s.m.* epicentre, epicentrum.

epicherèma, *s.m.* (*fil.*) epicheirema (*pl.* epicheiremata).

epicíclo, *s.m.* (*astr.*) epicycle.

èpico, *ag.* **1.** epic: *poema* —, epic poem **2.** (*degno di poema epico*) epic; heroic; majestic: *compiere gesta epiche,* to accomplish heroic deeds.

epicureísmo, *s.m.* **1.** (*attaccamento ai piaceri materiali*) epicurism **2.** (*st. fil.*) epicureanism.

epicurèo, *ag.* epicurean ‖ *s.m.* **1.** (*gaudente*) epicure; epicurean **2.** (*st. fil.*) Epicurean.

Epicúro, *no.pr.m.* (*st. fil.*) Epicurus.

Epidàuro, *no.pr.f.* (*geog. st.*) Epidaurus.

epidemía, *s.f.* epidemic (anche *fig.*).

epidemicaménte, *av.* epidemically.

epidèmico, *ag.* epidemic(al) (anche *fig.*).

epidèrmico, *ag.* epidermic.

epidèrmide, *s.f.* (*anat.*) epidermis; skin.

epidiascòpio, *s.m.* (*foto.*) epidiascope.

epidíttico, *ag.* epideictic, epideictical.

Epifanía, *s.f.* Epiphany, Twelfth Night.

Epifànio, *no.pr.m.* (*st. relig.*) Epiphanes, Epiphanius.

epifenòmeno, *s.m.* (*med.*) epiphenomenon (*pl.* epiphenomena).

epifísi, *s.f.* (*anat.*) epiphysis (*pl.* epiphyses).

epifonèma, *s.m.* (*ret.*) epiphonema.

epifràmma, *s.m.* (*zool. bot.*) epiphragm.

epigàstrico, *ag.* (*med.*) epigastric.

epigàstro, *s.m.* (*anat.*) epigastrium.

epigènesi, *s.f.* (*biol.*) epigenesis.

epiglòttide, *s.f.* (*anat.*) epiglottis.

epígono, *s.m.* **1.** (*letter.*) (*imitatore*) imitator; (*seguace*) follower **2.** (*discendente*) descendant **3.** *pl.* (*discendenti degli assedianti di Tebe*) Epigoni, Epigones.

epígrafe, *s.f.* epigraph, inscription.

epigrafía, *s.f.* epigraphy.

epigraficaménte, *av.* epigraphically.

epigràfico, *ag.* epigraphic.

epigrafísta, *s.m.* epigraphist.

epigràmma, *s.m.* epigram.

epigrammaticaménte, *av.* epigrammatically.

epigrammàtico, *ag.* epigrammatic.

epigrammatizzàre, *v.i.* to epigrammatize.

epigrammísta, *s.m.* epigrammatist.

epilatòrio, *ag.* depilatory.

epilazióne, *s.f.* depilation.

epilessía, *s.f.* (*patol.*) epilepsy, epilepsia.

epilèttico, *ag.s.m.* epileptic.

epilettifórme, *ag.* epileptiform.

epilettòide, *ag.* epileptoid.

epilogàre, *v.t.* (*rar.*) to sum up, to make a summary of (sthg.).

epílogo, *s.m.* epilogue, conclusion.

Epimènide, *no.pr.m.* (*mit.*) Epimenides.

Epimèteo, *no.pr.m.* (*mit.*) Epimetheus.

epinício, *s.m.* (*poes.*) epinicion (*pl.* epinicia).

Epíro, *no.pr.m.* (*geog.*) Epirus.

episcopàle, *ag.* (*eccl.*) episcopal.

episcopàto, *s.m.* (*eccl.*) episcopacy, episcopate.

episcòpio¹, *s.m.* bishop's palace.

episcòpio², *s.m.* (*ott.*) episcope.

epíscopo, *s.m.* (*rar.*) bishop.

episodicaménte, *av.* episodically.

episòdico, *ag.* episodic(al).

episòdio, *s.m.* **1.** (*vicenda*) episode, event; incident **2.** (*di opera artistica, letteraria*) episode.

epispàstico, *ag.* (*farm.*) epispastic.

epistàssi, *s.f.* (*med.*) epistaxis; (*fam.*) nose-bleeding.

epistemología, *s.f.* epistemology.

epistílio, *s.m.* (*arch.*) epistyle.

epístola, *s.f.* epistle (anche *eccl.*).

epistolàre, *ag.* epistolary.

epistolàrio, *s.m.* (collection of) letters; (*corrispondenza*) correspondence: *l'* — *del Manzoni,* Manzoni's letters.

epistolarménte, *av.* by (means of) letters.

epistològrafo, *s.m.* epistler, epistoler.

epístrofe, *s.f.* (*ret.*) epistrophe.

epitàffio, *s.m.* epitaph; inscription.

epitalàmio, *s.m.* (*poes.*) epithalamium.

epitàsi, *s.f.* (*st. teat.*) epitasis.

epiteliàle, *ag.* (*anat.*) epithelial.

epitèlio, *s.m.* (*anat.*) epithelium.

epitelióma, *s.m.* (*patol.*) epithelioma.

epitèma, *s.m.* (*farm.*) epithem.

epitètico, *ag.* epithetic(al).

epíteto, *s.m.* epithet.

epitomàre, *v.t.* (*rar.*) to epitomize; to summarize; to abridge.

epítome, *s.f.m.* epitome; summary; abridgment.

epítrope, *s.f.* (*ret.*) epitrope.

Epittèto, *no.pr.m.* (*st. fil.*) Epictetus.

epizòi, *s.m.pl.* (*entom.*) Epizoa.

epizoòtico, *ag.* epizootic: *afta epizootica*, (*vet.*) epizootic aphtha.

epizoozía, *s.f.* (*vet.*) epizooty, epizootic.

època, *s.f.* **1.** epoch; (*età*) age; (*era*) era: *l'— del ferro*, the iron age; *l'— Elisabettiana*, the Elizabethan Age; *l'— in cui viviamo*, the age we live in; *ciò segnò una nuova —*, that marked a new epoch ‖ *far —*, to make (*o* to mark) an epoch (*o* era): *scoperta che fece —*, an epoch-making discovery **2.** (*tempo*) time; (*periodo*) period; (*data*) date: *dall'— del vostro matrimonio*, from the time (*o* date) of your wedding; *da quell'— in poi*, from that time on(wards); *i migliori scrittori dell'—*, the best writers of the day (*o* time *o* period); *un mese fa a quest'—*, this time last month.

epòdico, *ag.* (*poes.*) epodic.

epòdo, *s.m.* (*poes.*) epode.

epònimo, *ag.* eponymous: *fondatore —*, eponymous founder ‖ *s.m.* eponym.

epopèa, *s.f.* **1.** (*poema epico*) epic poem, epopee **2.** (*serie di fatti eroici*) epos: *— risorgimentale*, epos of the Italian Risorgimento.

èpos, *s.m.* epic poetry, epos.

eppúre, *cong.* **1.** (and) yet, and still **2.** (*tuttavia*) nevertheless, however.

èpsilon, *s.f.* (*lettera dell'alfabeto greco*) epsilon.

epsomíte, *s.f.* (*chim.*) epsomite; (*farm.*) Epsom salts (*pl.*).

eptacòrdo, *s.m.* (*mus.*) heptachord.

eptaèdro, *s.m.* (*geom.*) heptahedron.

Eptameróne, *s.m.* (*lett.*) Heptameron.

eptàno, *s.m.* (*chim.*) heptane.

eptasíllabo, *ag.* (*poes.*) heptasyllabic, seven-syllabled ‖ *s.m.* (*poes.*) seven-syllable line.

èptodo, *s.m.* (*fis.*) heptode.

epúlide, *s.f.* (*patol.*) epulis.

epulóne, *s.m.* **1.** (*mangione*) glutton ‖ *il ricco Epulone*, (*Bibbia*) Dives **2.** (*sacerdote romano*) epulo (*pl.* epulones).

epuràre, *v.t.* **1.** (*pol.*) to purge; to remove from office, to dismiss from office; (*fam.*) to weed out: *quattro membri del partito sono stati epurati*, four members have been thrown out of the party **2.** (*purificare*) to purify, to cleanse.

epurazióne, *s.f.* **1.** (*morale, politica*) purge; (*di istituto, amministrazione, ecc.*) removal, dismissal: *— di personale*, (*fam.*) weeding out of staff **2.** (*purificazione*) purification, purifying, cleansing.

equàbile, *ag.* equable.

equabilità, *s.f.* equability.

equaménte, *av.* justly, fairly, equitably: *giudicare —*, to judge impartially.

equànime, *ag.* **1.** (*equilibrato*) equanimous; even-minded, even-tempered; calm; serene **2.** (*imparziale*) impartial; fair; just.

equanimaménte, *av.* **1.** (*equilibratamente*) equanimously; serenely **2.** (*imparzialmente*) impartially, fairly.

equanimità, *s.f.* **1.** (*carattere equilibrato*) equanimity; evenness of mind, of temper; composure; serenity **2.** (*imparzialità*) impartiality; fair-mindedness, fairness of judgement.

equatóre, *s.m.* equator: *— magnetico*, magnetic equator (*o* aclinic line); *essere a nord dell'—*, to be north of the equator; *passare l'—*, to cross the line (*o* the equator).

equatoriàle, *ag.* equatorial: *caldo —*, equatorial heat; *regione delle calme equatoriali*, (*mar.*) the doldrums (*pl.*) ‖ *s.m.* (*astr.*) (*telescopio*) equatorial.

equazióne, *s.f.* equation: *— differenziale*, differential equation; *— di primo grado*, simple equation (*o* equation of the first degree); *— di secondo grado*, quadratic equation.

equèstre, *ag.* equestrian: *circo —*, circus; *ordine —*, (*st. romana*) equestrian order; *statua —*, equestrian statue.

equiàngolo, *ag.* (*geom.*) equiangular.

èquidi, *s.m.pl.* (*zool.*) Equidae.

equidistànte, *ag.* equidistant.

equidistànza, *s.f.* equidistance.

equidistanziàto, *ag.* equally spaced.

equidistàre, *v.i.* to be equidistant.

equilàtero, *ag.* (*geom.*) equilateral.

equilibràre, *v.t.*, **equilibràrsi**, *v.r.* to equilibrate; to balance.

equilibràto, *ag.* **1.** in equilibrium, balanced **2.** *fig.* well-balanced; even-minded; (*di buon senso*) sensible: *ha una mente equilibrata*, he has a well-balanced (*o* sane) mind **3.** (*fis. mec.*) balanced.

equilibratóre, *ag.* equilibrating, equilibratory, balancing ‖ *s.m.* **1.** (*aer.*) equilibrator, stabilizer; (*timone di quota*) elevator **2.** (*elett. mec.*) equalizer: *— di spinta*, (*mec.*) thrust equalizer ‖ **equilibratríce**, *s.f.* (*mec.*) balancing machine.

equilibratúra, *s.f.* (*mec.*) balancing; (*tel.*) balance.

equilibrazióne, *s.f.* equilibration, balancing, counterbalancing, counterpoising.

equilíbrio, *s.m.* **1.** balance, equilibrium, equipoise; *fig.* balance, even-mindedness; (*buon senso*) common sense: *— mondiale*, (*pol.*) balance of power in the world; *far perdere l'— a qlcu.*, to throw s.o. off his balance; *mantenere l'—, tenersi in —*, to keep one's balance; *mantenere, raggiungere, riacquistare l'— del bilancio*, (*econ. comm.*) to maintain, to reach, to recover the equilibrium of the budget; *mettere, tenere ql.co. in —*, to balance sthg.; *perdere l'—*, to lose one's balance; *rompere l'— di ql.co.*, to upset (the equilibrium of) sthg. **2.** (*fis.*) equilibrium, balance; (*aer.*) equilibrium, stability: *— stabile, instabile, indifferente*, stable, unstable, neutral equilibrium.

equilibrísmo, *s.m.* **1.** (*giuochi di equilibrio*) acrobatics (*pl.*) **2.** (*arte dell'equilibrista*) acrobatism **3.** *— politico*, political manoeuvres.

equilibrísta, *s.c.* equilibrist; acrobat; rope-walker (*anche fig.*).

equíno, *ag.* equine ‖ *piede —*, (*patol.*) club-foot.

equinoziàle, *ag.* (*astr.*) equinoctial.

equinòzio, *s.m.* (*astr.*) equinox: *— d'autunno*, autumnal equinox; *— di primavera*, vernal (*o* spring) equinox.

equipaggiaménto, *s.m.* **1.** equipment, outfit **2.** (*l'equipaggiare*) equipment, fitting out: *— di prova*, (*mec.*) test set up **3.** (*mar.*) rigging **4.** (*elett.*) equipment.

equipaggiàre, *v.t.* **1.** to equip, to fit out: *quel ragazzo è ben equipaggiato per la scuola*, that boy is well fitted out for school; *— soldati*, to equip soldiers **2.** (*fornire di equipaggio*) to man: *— una nave*, to man a vessel **3.** (*mar. mec.*) (*attrezzare*) to rig out.

equipaggiàto, *ag.* **1.** equipped; fitted out **2.** (*provvisto di equipaggio*) manned **3.** (*mar. mec.*) rigged out.

equipàggio, *s.m.* **1.** (*di nave, aereo*) crew: *alloggi dell'—*, (*mar.*) berths for the crew; *membro dell'—*, (*mar.*) hand; *tutto l'— sul ponte!*, all hands on deck! **2.** (*seguito*) equipage, retinue, train, suite: *arrivare, partire in grande —*, to arrive, to depart in state **3.** (*cavalli e carrozza*) equipage, carriage and horses, turn-out **4.** (*equipaggiamento*) outfit, equipment; (*mil.*) equipment **5.** *— mobile*, (*mec.*) moving (*o* rotor *o* rotating) element **6.** (*mar.*) (*attrezzatura*) rigging.

equiparàbile, *ag.* comparable.

equiparàre, *v.t.* **1.** (*paragonare*) to compare, to parallel **2.** (*rendere uguale*) to equalize, to make equal, to level.

equiparazióne, *s.f.* **1.** (*paragone*) comparison **2.** (*eguagliamento*) equalization.

equipollènte, *ag.* equipollent.

equipollènza, *s.f.* equipollence, equipollency.

equipotenziàle, *ag.* (*mec. fis.*) equipotential.

equiséto, *s.m.* (*bot.*) equisetum; (*pop.*) horsetail.

equità, *s.f.* equity; fairness, justice, justness, impartiality; (*dir.*) equity: *l'— modera il rigore della legge*, equity moderates the rigour of the law; *conosco il suo spirito d'—*, I know his fairness of mind-

è una questione d'—, it is a case of even-handed dealing; *non posso, per —*, in all justice I cannot...; *riconosco l'— di questa domanda*, I acknowledge the fairness (*o* justness) of this request.

equitatívo, *ag.* equitable.

equitazióne, *s.f.* **1.** riding, horse-riding: *campo d'—*, riding-ground; *maestro d'—*, riding-teacher (*o* -master); *scuola d'—*, riding-school; *fate dell'—?*, do you ride? **2.** (*arte*) horsemanship; equitation.

equivalènte, *ag.* equivalent; tantamount: *la sua preghiera era — ad un comando*, his request was tantamount to a command ‖ *s.m.* **1.** equivalent: *mi diede l'— in merce*, he gave me the equivalent (*o* the corresponding amount) in goods; *non trovo l'— esatto di questa parola francese*, I cannot find the exact equivalent of this French word **2.** (*chim.*) equivalent (weight), combining weight, reacting weight.

equivalenteménte, *av.* equivalently.

equivalènza, *s.f.* equivalence.

equivalére, *v.i.* to be equivalent, to be equal in value, to be tantamount; to be the same as: *questo equivale a dire che...*, that is the same as saying that...; *questo equivaleva ad un comando*, this was tantamount (*o* equivalent) to an order (*o* this was just the same as an order) ‖ **equivalérsi,** *v.r.* to be equivalent, to be equal in value; to come to the same thing; to have the same meaning: *i due metodi si equivalgono*, the two methods come to the same thing; *parole che si equivalgono*, words that have the same meaning; *questi oggetti si equivalgono*, these objects are equal in value.

equivocàbile, *ag.* mistakable.

equivocaménte, *ag.* equivocally, ambiguously.

equivocàre, *v.i.* **1.** (*parlare in termini equivoci*) to equivocate, to quibble **2.** (*fraintendere*) to misunderstand **3.** (*sbagliarsi*) to be mistaken.

equivocità, *s.f.* equivocalness, equivocality.

equívoco, *ag.* **1.** equivocal, ambiguous: *una risposta equivoca*, an ambiguous reply **2.** (*dubbio, sospetto*) suspicious, doubtful, questionable: *reputazione equivoca*, doubtful reputation; *uomo —*, suspicious man ‖ *s.m.* (*ambiguità*) equivocation; (*malinteso*) misunderstanding: *senza —*, unequivocal(ly); *parlando senza equivoci*, plainly speaking; *c'è stato un —*, there has been a misunderstanding; *c'era possibilità di — nella sua risposta*, there was an element of equivocation in his reply; *non c'è possibilità di —*, there are no two ways about it; *non c'è possibilità di — su quanto ha detto*, there is no mistaking what he has said; *chiarire, dar luogo ad un —*, to explain, to give rise to a misunderstanding; *giocare sull'—*, to equivocate; *per evitare ogni —, a scanso d'—*, to avoid any misunderstanding (*o* to know exactly where we stand).

èquo, *ag.* **1.** fair, just; reasonable: *equa ricompensa*, fair (*o* just) reward; *richiesta equa*, reasonable claim; *è un uomo —*, he is an impartial (*o* a fair-minded) man; *riportò una vittoria equa*, he won a deserved victory (*o* he deserved his victory) **2.** (*dir.*) equitable.

Èra[1], *no.pr.f.* (*mit.*) Hera.

èra[2], *s.f.* **1.** (*epoca*) epoch; (*età*) age: *l'— cristiana*, the Christian era; *l'— elettronica*, the era of electronics; *l'— paleozoica*, (*geol.*) the Paleozoic Era; *nella nostra —*, in our age; *una nuova — di civiltà*, a new era of civilization; *l'— in cui viviamo*, the age we live in; *la teoria di Einstein segna una nuova —*, Einstein's theory marks a new epoch.

Èracle, *no.pr.m.* (*mit.*) Heracles.

Eraclèa, *no.pr.f.* (*geog. st.*) Heraclea.

Eràclito, *no.pr.m.* (*st. fil.*) Heraclitus.

erariàle, *ag.* fiscal: *avvocato —*, public prosecutor (representing the government).

eràrio, *s.m.* Treasury.

Eràsmo, *no.pr.m.* (*st. lett.*) Erasmus.

Eràsto, *no.pr.m.* (*st. relig.*) Erastus: *sostenitore di —*, Erastian.

Eràto, *no.pr.f.* (*mit.*) Erato.

Eratòstene, *no.pr.m.* (*st. mat.*) Eratosthenes.

èrba, *s.f.* **1.** grass: *coperto d'—*, grassy; *filo d'—*, blade of grass; *fare l'—*, *tagliare l'—*, to cut (*o* to mow) the grass; (*per fieno*) to mow (*o* to make) hay; *far merenda sull'—*, to have a picnic; *mangiare sull'—*, to have an alfresco lunch; *mettere, tenere a — un cavallo*, to turn (*o* to put) a horse out to grass ‖ *in —*, green (*o* unripe); *fig.* budding: *un campione in —*, a budding champion; *un dottore in —*, a budding physician (*o* doctor); *grano in —*, green corn ‖ *la mala — cresce presto*, weeds grow fast ‖ *fare d'ogni — un fascio*, to saw the tares with the wheat ‖ *vietato calpestare l'—*, please keep off the grass ‖ *campa cavallo che l'— cresce*, *prov.* while the grass is growing the horse starveth **2.** (*med. cuc.*) herb: *— medica*, lucern(e) (*o amer.* alfalfa); *— fegatella*, liverwort; *infuso di erbe*, herb-tea **3.** (*erbaccia*) weed.

erbàccia, *s.f.* weed: *un giardino invaso dalle erbacce*, a garden overgrown with weeds; *pulire un giardino dalle erbacce*, to weed a garden.

erbàceo, *ag.* herbaceous.

erbàggio, *s.m.* vegetable; herb ‖ *gli erbaggi*, vegetables (*o* greens *o* potherbs).

erbàio, *s.m.* (*rar.*) vegetable garden.

erbaiuòlo, *s.m.* greengrocer; (*ambulante*) costermonger.

erbàrio, *s.m.* (*bot.*) herbarium (*pl.* herbaria, herbariums).

erbàtico, *s.m.* (*dir.*) herbage; right of pasture (on public land); grazing rights (*pl.*).

èrbe, *s.f.pl.* **1.** herbage (*coll. con costruzione sing.*); (*verdure*) vegetables **2.** (*cuc.*) (*odori*) sweet herbs.

erbeggiàre, *v.i.* **1.** (*crescere come erba*) to grow like grass **2.** (*verdeggiare*) to be as green as grass.

Erbèrto, *no.pr.m.* Herbert ‖ *dim.* Herb, Bert.

erbétta, *s.f.* new grass.

erbétte, *s.f.pl.* greens.

erbicída, *s.m.* (*agr.*) weed killer.

erbífero, *ag.* (*rar.*) grassy; fertile.

èrbio, *s.m.* (*chim.*) erbium.

erbíre, *v.i.* to become grassy, to get grassy.

erbíto, *ag.* (*rar.*) grassy.

erbivéndola, *s.f.*, **erbivéndolo,** *s.m.* greengrocer; (*ambulante*) costermonger.

erbívoro, *ag.* (*zool.*) herbivorous ‖ *s.m.* herbivore (*pl.* herbivora).

erbolàto, *s.m.* **1.** (*farm.*) herb-plaster **2.** (*cuc.*) vegetable cake.

erborazióne, *s.f.* herborization.

erborísta, *s.m.* herborist; herbalist.

erborizzàre, *v.i.* to herborize, to botanize.

erborizzatóre, *s.m.* herborist; herbalist.

erborizzazióne, *s.f.* herborization.

erbóso, *ag.* grassy, grass-grown.

ercolanènse, *ag.* Herculanean.

Ercolàno, *no.pr.f.* (*geog. st.*) Herculaneum.

Èrcole, *no.pr.m.* (*mit.*) Hercules: *le dodici fatiche di —*, the twelve labours of Hercules ‖ *colonne d'—*, Pillars of Hercules (*anche fig.*) ‖ **èrcole,** *s.m.* Hercules: *è un —*, he is a Hercules.

ercúleo, *ag.* Herculean.

Èrebo, *no.pr.m.* (*geog. mit.*) Erebus.

erède, *s.m.* heir: *— di diritto*, heir apparent; *— legittimo*, heir-at-law (*o* right heir *o* heir general); *— presunto*, heir presumptive; *— universale*, sole (*o* only) heir; *senza eredi*, heirless; *essere — di ql.co.*, to be heir to sthg. (*anche fig.*) ‖ *s.f.* heiress.

eredità, *s.f.* **1.** inheritance, heritage (*anche fig.*): *lasciare in —*, to bequeath; *ricevere in — ql.co.*, to receive (*o* to get) sthg. by inheritance (*o* to inherit sthg.) **2.** (*biol.*) inheritance, heredity.

ereditàbile, *ag.* heritable; heritable; transmissible.

ereditàre, *v.t.* to inherit.

ereditariaménte, *av.* hereditarily.

ereditarietà, *s.f.* hereditariness; heredity.

ereditàrio, *ag.* hereditary: *malattia ereditaria*, hereditary disease; *principe* —, Crown Prince (*o* Prince Royal); (*in Gran Bretagna*) Prince of Wales.

ereditièra, *s.f.* heiress.

eremíta, *s.m.* hermit; anchoret, anchorite (anche *fig.*).

eremitàggio, *s.m.* hermitage (anche *fig.*).

eremítico, *ag.* hermitic(al).

èremo, *s.m.* **1.** hermitage; (*monastero*) monastery **2.** *fig.* hermitage.

eresía, *s.f.* **1.** heresy **2.** (*errore*) big blunder; (*sciocchezza*) nonsense: *che eresie!*, (*fam.*) nonsense!.

eresiàrca, *s.m.* heresiarch.

ereticàle, *ag.* heretical.

eretica(l)ménte, *av.* heretically.

erètico, *ag.* heretical ‖ *s.m.* heretic.

eretísmo, *s.m.* (*patol.*) erethism.

erètto, *ag.* **1.** erect; upright **2.** (*costruito*) erected, built **3.** (*istituito, fondato*) founded, established.

erezióne, *s.f.* **1.** erection **2.** (*costruzione*) building **3.** (*fondazione*) foundation, establishment.

erg, *s.m.* (*fis.*) erg.

ergastolàno, *s.m.* convict serving a life sentence; (*sl.*) lifer.

ergàstolo, *s.m.* **1.** (*prigione*) prison (for those serving life sentences) **2.** (*pena, condanna*) life imprisonment: *fu condannato all'*—, he was sentenced to life imprisonment.

èrgere, *v.t.* **1.** (*innalzare*) to raise **2.** (*erigere*) to erect ‖ **èrgersi**, *v.r.* **1.** (*innalzarsi*) to rise **2.** (*adirarsi*) to get angry.

ergo, *av.* therefore; (*scherz.*) ergo.

ergòmetro, *s.m.* (*mec.*) ergometer.

èrgon, *s.m.* (*fis.*) erg, ergon.

ergotína, *s.f.* (*farm.*) ergot.

ergotísmo, *s.m.* (*patol.*) ergotism.

èrica, *s.f.* heath, heather: — *bianca*, white heather; (*in Scozia*) lucky heather.

Erídano, *no.pr.m.* (*mit.*) Eridanus.

Erífile, *no.pr.f.* (*lett.*) Eriphyle.

erigèndo, *ag.* (*costruendo*) to be built; (*istituendo*) to be founded.

erígere, *v.t.* **1.** to erect; (*costruire*) to build; (*innalzare*) to raise, to put up **2.** (*fondare, istituire*) to found, to establish, to set up ‖ **erígersi**, *v.r.* to claim to be (s.o., sthg.): *si erige a difensore della libertà*, he claims to be (*o* he poses as) a champion of liberty.

Erimànto, *no.pr.m.* (*geog. st.*) Erymanthus.

Erína, *no.pr.f.* (*geog. st.*) Erin.

Erínni, *no.pr.f.* (*mit.*) Erinys (*pl.* Erinyes), Fury.

erisípela, *s.f.* (*patol.*) erysipelas; (*pop.*) St. Anthony's fire.

erística, *s.f.* (*fil.*) eristic.

erístico, *ag.* (*fil.*) eristic.

eritèma, *s.m.* (*patol.*) erythema; rash.

Eritrèa, *no.pr.f.* (*geog.*) Eritrea.

eritrèo, *ag.s.m.* Eritrean.

èrma, *s.f.* (*archeol.*) herma (*pl.* hermae).

ermafroditísmo, *s.m.* hermaphroditism

Ermafrodíto, *no.pr.m.* (*mit.*) Hermaphroditus ‖ **ermafrodíto**, *ag.s.m.* hermaphrodite.

Ermànno, *no.pr.m.* Herman.

ermellíno, *s.m.* **1.** (*zool.*) ermine; stoat ‖ *candido come un* —, *fig.* ermine white **2.** (*pelliccia*) ermine.

ermenèuta, *s.m.* hermeneut.

ermenèutica, *s.f.* hermeneutics.

ermenèutico, *ag.* hermeneutic(al).

Ermengàrda, *no.pr.f.* Irmgard.

Èrmes, Ermète, *no.pr.m.* (*mit.*) Hermes.

ermeticaménte, *av.* hermetically: *chiuso* —, hermetically sealed.

ermètico, *ag.* **1.** hermetic **2.** (*tec.*) airtight: *chiusura ermetica*, hermetic seal(ing) (*o* airtight closure); (*a tenuta d'acqua*) watertight closure; (*a tenuta di gas*) gasproof closure **3.** (*oscuro*) obscure **4.** (*lett.*) belonging to "Ermetismo" (modern Italian school of obscure poetry).

ermetísmo, *s.m.* **1.** obscurity **2.** (*lett.*) "Ermetismo" (modern Italian school of obscure poetry).

Ermínio, *no.pr.m.* Armin.

Ermíóne, *no.pr.f.* (*mit.*) Hermione.

ermisino, *s.m.* (*drappo leggero di seta*) sarcenet.

èrmo, *ag.* (*poet.*) solitary.

Ernèsta, *no.pr.f.* Ernestine.

Ernèsto, *no.pr.m.* Ernest, Earnest ‖ *dim.* Ernie.

èrnia, *s.f.* (*patol.*) hernia (*pl.* herniae, hernias); rupture: — *strozzata*, strangulated hernia.

erniàrio, *ag.* hernial, herniary: *cinto* —, truss.

ernióso, *ag.* herniated.

erniotomía, *s.f.* (*chir.*) herniotomy.

Èro, *no.pr.f.* (*mit.*) Hero: « — *e Leandro*», "Hero and Leander".

Eròde, *no.pr.m.* (*st.*) Herod.

eródere, *v.t.* to erode, to wear away.

Erodíade, *no.pr.f.* (*st.*) Herodias.

Eròdoto, *no.pr.m.* (*st. lett.*) Herodotus.

eròe, *s.m.* hero: *culto degli eroi*, hero-worship; *comportarsi da* —, to act like a hero.

erogàbile, *ag.* **1.** distributable; available for donation **2.** (*idraulica, elett.*) deliverable.

erogàre, *v.t.* **1.** to distribute (anche *dir.*), to give away; to donate **2.** (*idraulica, elett.*) to deliver.

erogatóre, *ag.* distributing ‖ *s.m.* distributor; donator.

erogazióne, *s.f.* **1.** (*donazione*) distribution; donation; (*dir.*) assignment **2.** (*idraulica, elett.*) delivery.

eroicaménte, *av.* heroically.

eroicizzàre, *v.t.* (*rar.*) to heroize.

eròico, *ag.* heroic: *atti eroici*, heroic deeds; *età eroica*, heroic age; *rimedio* —, heroic remedy ‖ *poesia eroica*, epic poetry; *verso* —, heroic verse (*o* couplet).

eroicòmico, *ag.* (*lett.*) heroicomic, mock-heroic.

eroína¹, *s.f.* **1.** heroine **2.** (*protagonista*) heroine; (*teat.*) leading lady.

eroína², *s.f.* (*farm.*) heroin.

eroísmo, *s.m.* heroism.

erómpere, *v.i.* to burst forth, to burst out, to break out; (*precipitarsi fuori*) to rush out, to burst out.

Èros, *no.pr.m.* (*mit.*) Eros.

erosióne, *s.f.* erosion.

erosívo, *ag.* erosive.

eróso, *ag.* eroded, worn away.

Eròstrato, *no.pr.m.* (*st.*) Herostratus.

eroticaménte, *av.* erotically.

eròtico, *ag.* erotic, amatory.

erotísmo, *s.m.* eroticism.

erotòmane, *s.m.* (*patol.*) erotomaniac.

erotomanía, *s.f.* (*patol.*) erotomania.

èrpete, *s.m.* (*patol.*) herpes.

erpètico, *ag.* (*med.*) herpetic.

erpetología, *s.f.* herpetology.

erpicaménto, *s.m.* (*agr.*) harrowing.

erpicàre, *v.t.* (*agr.*) to harrow.

erpicatúra, *s.f.* (*agr.*) harrowing.

érpice, *s.m.* (*agr.*) harrow.

errabóndo, *ag.* (*letter.*) wandering, rambling, roaming.

errànte, *ag.* wandering, roving, roaming, errant: *cavaliere* —, knight errant ‖ *l'Ebreo* —, the Wandering Jew.

erràre, *v.i.* **1.** (*vagare*) to wander (about, around), to roam (about, around), to ramble, to rove, to stroll (about): *errava in un bosco*, he was wandering through a wood; — *per i boschi*, to roam the woods; — *per il mondo*, to wander over the world (*o* to wander the world); — *per terra e per mare*, to rove over land and sea **2.** (*sbagliare*) to err, to make mistakes, to be mistaken; to be wrong: *se affermi ciò, erri*, if you say so, you are mistaken; — *è umano*, to err is human.

errata-corrige, *s.m.* errata (*pl.*).

errataménte, *av.* erroneously; wrongly.

erràtico, *ag.* (*geol. med.*) erratic: *masso* —, erratic block.

erràto, *ag.* wrong: *numero* —, wrong number.

èrre, *s.f.m.* letter R || *parla in* —, he rolls his r's.

erroneaménte, *av.* erroneously, by mistake; wrongly.

erroneità, *s.f.* erroneousness.

erròneo, *ag.* erroneous; (*sbagliato*) wrong.

erróre, *s.m.* **1.** error: *un* — *di giudizio,* an error of judgment; *errori giovanili,* errors of youth; *commettere un* —, to commit (*o* to make) an error; *pentirsi dei propri errori,* to repent one's errors **2.** (*sbaglio*) error; mistake; (*errore grossolano*) blunder: — *di ortografia,* misspelling; — *di stampa,* misprint (*o* printer's error); — *di trascrizione,* clerical error (*o* slip of the pen); *per* —, by mistake; *essere in* —, to be (*o* to stand) in error; *fare un* —, to make a mistake || *salvo* —, error excepted: *salvo* — *od omissione,* errors and omissions excepted.

Ersília, *no.pr.f.* Hersilia.

èrta, *s.f.* **1.** steep; upward slope; (*salita*) ascent **2.** *all'* — *!,* look out!: *stare all'*—, to be on the look-out (*o* to be on one's guard *o* to be on the alert); (*essere guardinghi, prudenti*) to be wary.

ertézza, *s.f.* steepness.

èrto, *ag.* steep: *erta collina,* steep hill.

erubescènte, *ag.* erubescent, reddening; (*che arrossisce*) blushing; ruddy.

erubescènza, *s.f.* erubescence; (*rossore*) redness.

erudíbile, *ag.* teachable.

erudiménto, *s.m.* teaching.

erudíre, *v.t.* (*ammaestrare*) to teach, to educate || **erudírsi,** *v.r.* to acquire knowledge; to get educated.

eruditaménte, *av.* learnedly.

erudíto, *ag.* learned, scholarly, erudite || *s.m.* scholar, man of learning.

erudizióne, *s.f.* erudition, learning; scholarship.

Èruli, *no.pr.m.pl.* (*st.*) Heruli.

eruttàre, *v.t.* (*di vulcano*) to erupt; to eject, to throw out; to belch: *il vulcano eruttò molta cenere,* the volcano belched (*o* ejected *o* threw out *o* erupted) a lot of ashes || *v.i.* to belch, to eruct.

eruttazióne, *s.f.* (*il ruttare*) belching, eructation.

eruttívo, *ag.* eruptive.

eruzióne, *s.f.* **1.** eruption **2.** (*patol.*) eruption, rash.

ervalènta, *s.f.* lentil flour.

Erzegòvina, *no.pr.f.* (*geog.*) Herzegovina.

erziàno, *ag.* (*fis.*) hertzian.

esacerbaménto, *s.m.* embitterment, exacerbation.

esacerbàre, *v.t.* to embitter, to exacerbate, to exasperate, to irritate.

esacerbazióne, *s.f.* embitterment, exacerbation, irritation, exasperation.

esacòrdo, *s.m.* (*st. mus.*) hexachord.

esaèdrico, *ag.* (*geom.*) hexahedral.

esaèdro, *s.m.* (*geom.*) hexahedron.

esageràre, *v.t.* to exaggerate, to magnify, to overstate: *non* — *le difficoltà del tuo compito,* do not exaggerate (*o* overstate) the difficulties of your task || *v.i.* (*strafare*) to go too far, to exceed: *mi sembra che tu esageri nella modestia,* I think you carry your modesty too far.

esagerataménte, *av.* exaggeratedly: *questo è* — *caro,* (*fam.*) this is far too expensive.

esageratívo, *ag.* exaggerative.

esageràto, *ag.* **1.** exaggerated; (*eccessivo*) immoderate, excessive **2.** (*di prezzo*) too high, far too high, exorbitant.

esageratóre, *s.m.,* **esageratríce,** *s.f.* exaggerator.

esagerazióne, *s.f.* exaggeration; (*nel descrivere, nel definire*) overstatement: *il tuo discorso è pieno di esagerazioni,* your speech is full of overstatements.

esageróna, *s.f.,* **esageróne,** *s.m.* (*pop.*) gas-bag.

esagitàre, *v.t.* to stir violently; to excite.

esagitàto, *ag.* excited, troubled.

esagonàle, *ag.* (*geom.*) hexagonal.

esàgono, *s.m.* (*geom.*) hexagon.

esalaménto, *s.m.* exhalation.

esalàre, *v.t.* to exhale, to breathe forth: — *l'anima, l'ultimo fiato,* to breathe one's last breath (*o* to breathe one's last) || *v.i.* to exhale, to give off: *dalla palude esalavano miasmi,* the marsh gave off miasmas.

esalazióne, *s.f.* exhalation; fume: — *di petrolio, di zolfo,* fume of petroleum, of sulphur.

esalína, *s.f.* (*chim. ind.*) cyclohexanol.

esaltaménto, *s.m.* (*rar.*) exaltation; excitement.

esaltàre, *v.t.* **1.** (*innalzare*) to exalt **2.** (*magnificare*) to extol, to exalt, to praise **3.** (*infervorare*) to elate || **esaltàrsi,** *v.r.* **1.** (*vantarsi*) to boast **2.** (*infervorarsi*) to become elated, to become excited.

esaltàto, *ag.* **1.** (*elevato*) exalted **2.** (*eccitato*) excited; (*infervorato*) elated: *è troppo* —, he is overexcited **3.** (*dalla testa calda*) hot-headed || *s.m.* (*testa calda*) hot-head; (*fanatico*) fanatic: *è un* —, he is a hot-head.

esaltatóre, *ag.* exalting || *s.m.,* **esaltatríce,** *s.f.* exalter, extoller.

esaltazióne, *s.f.* **1.** exaltation; glorification **2.** (*eccitazione*) excitement.

esàme, *s.m.* **1.** examination; investigation; scrutiny; inspection: — *dei conti,* (*comm.*) inspection (*o* scrutiny) of accounts; — *dei testimoni,* (*dir.*) examination of the witnesses; — *del sangue,* blood test; — *della vista,* sight-testing; — *di coscienza,* self-examination; — *medico,* medical examination; — *psicotecnico,* psycho-technological fitness test; *la questione è all'*—, the matter is under examination; *prendere in* —, to consider; *sottoporre ql.co. a un* — *meticoloso,* to subject sthg. to minute inspection (*o* to go carefully over sthg.) **2.** (*scolastico*) examination; (*fam.*) exam: — *d'ammissione,* entrance examination; — *di concorso,* competitive examination; *dare, sostenere un* —, to take (*o* to sit for) an examination; *essere respinto a un* —, to fail in an examination; *superare un* —, to pass an examination.

esàmetro, *s.m.* (*poes.*) hexameter.

esaminàbile, *ag.* examinable.

esaminànda, *s.f.,* **esaminàndo,** *s.m.* candidate, examinee.

esaminànte, *ag.* examining || *s.c.* examiner.

esaminàre, *v.t.* **1.** to examine; to scrutinize; to consider: *esaminammo la faccenda,* we considered (*o* we looked into) the matter; *l'insegnante li esaminò in storia,* the teacher examined them in history; — *i conti,* to go through (*o* to inspect *o* to scrutinize) the accounts; — *un testimonio,* to examine a witness **2.** (*analizzare*) to test: — *un progetto,* to test out a scheme || **esaminàrsi,** *v.r.* **1.** to examine one's own conscience **2.** (*guardarsi*) to look at oneself || *v.r. reciproco* to look at each other, to scrutinize each other.

esaminatóre, *ag.* examining; scrutinizing: *commissione esaminatrice,* board of examiners || *s.m.,* **esaminatríce,** *s.f.* examiner.

esàngue, *ag.* **1.** exsanguine, bloodless **2.** (*pallidissimo*) deadly pale, cadaverous **3.** (*morto*) dead.

esanimàre, *v.t.* to dishearten, to discourage.

esànime, *ag.* **1.** exanimate, lifeless, inanimate **2.** (*morto*) dead.

esantèma, *s.m.* (*med.*) exanthema (*pl.* exanthemata).

esantemàtico, *ag.* (*med.*) exanthematic, exanthematous.

esàrca, *s.m.* (*st.*) exarch.

esarcàto, *s.m.* (*st.*) exarchate.

esasperaménto, *s.m.* exasperation; irritation.

esasperànte, *ag.* exasperating, irritating, provoking: *è* —*!,* he is exasperating!.

esasperàre, *v.t.* to exasperate, to irritate, to provoke beyond measure: *quel rumore ci ha esasperato,* that noise exasperated us || **esasperàrsi,** *v.r.* to become irritated, to lose all patience.

esasperàto, *ag.* exasperated: *ero* —, I was fuming;

sono — per la vostra trascuratezza, I am exasperated at your carelessness; «*Uscite!*», *gridai —*, "Get out!", I cried in exasperation.

esasperazióne, *s.f.* exasperation, irritation.

esàstico, *ag.* (*poes.*) hexastical ‖ *s.m.* (*poes.*) hexastich.

esàstilo, *ag.* (*arch.*) hexastyle.

esattaménte, *av.* **1.** exactly, precisely: *so — ciò che voglio*, I know exactly what I want; *esporre — i fatti*, to state the facts precisely **2.** (*proprio*) just: *questo è — ciò che mi aspettavo*, that is just (o exactly) what I expected **3.** (*accuratamente*) accurately: *tradurre —*, to translate accurately **4.** (*correttamente*) correctly **5.** (*puntualmente*) punctually.

esattézza, *s.f.* **1.** exactitude, exactness **2.** (*accuratezza*) accuracy **3.** (*correttezza*) correctness **4.** (*puntualità*) punctuality: *— nel compiere i propri doveri*, punctuality in carrying out one's duties.

esàtto[1], *ag.* **1.** exact; (*giusto, corretto*) correct, right, true: *istruzioni esatte*, exact directions; *l'ora esatta*, the right (o exact) time; *ciò è del tutto —*, that is quite correct (o true); *qual è il significato — di queste parole?*, what is the exact meaning of these words? ‖ *scienze esatte*, exact sciences **2.** (*accurato*) accurate, careful: *storico —*, accurate historian **3.** (*puntuale*) punctual: *essere — nei pagamenti*, to be punctual in one's payments.

esàtto[2], *ag.* (*incassato*) collected, cashed: *pagamenti esatti*, (*comm.*) collected payments.

esattóre, *s.m.* collector; (*delle imposte*) tax collector.

esattoría, *s.f.* Revenue Office.

esattríce, *s.f.* collector.

Esaù, *no.pr.m.* (*Bibbia*) Esau.

esaudíbile, *ag.* grantable; satisfiable.

esaudiménto, *s.m.* satisfaction, fulfil(l)ment: *— di un desiderio*, satisfaction of a wish; *— di una promessa*, fulfil(l)ment of a promise.

esaudíre, *v.t.* to grant, to comply with (sthg.); to satisfy, to fulfil: *la mia preghiera fu esaudita*, my prayer was answered; *Signore, esaudisci la mia preghiera*, Lord, hear my prayer; *il suo desiderio fu esaudito*, his wish was fulfilled; *— una richiesta*, to grant (o to comply with) a request.

esauríbile, *ag.* exhaustible.

esauriènte, *ag.* exhaustive: *trattare un argomento in modo —*, to make an exhaustive study of a subject.

esaurienteménte, *av.* exhaustively.

esauriménto, *s.m.* **1.** exhaustion; using up; depletion (anche *med.*): *— di una miniera*, exhausting (o working out o drainage o pumping out) of a mine; *graduale — delle merci in magazzino*, gradual exhaustion of the stock in hand **2.** *— nervoso*, (*patol.*) nervous exhaustion (o nervous breakdown).

esauríre, *v.t.* **1.** to exhaust; (*consumare*) to consume, to use up; to wear out; (*sfruttare fino all'esaurimento*) to work out; (*vendere fino all'esaurimento*) to sell out: *— il carburante*, to run out of (o to exhaust) the fuel; *— una miniera, un pozzo*, to exhaust (o to work out o to drain o to pump out) a mine, a well **2.** *fig.* to exhaust, to wear out: *— la pazienza di qlcu.*, to exhaust (o to wear out) s.o.'s patience; *— un argomento*, (*trattandolo a fondo*) to exhaust a subject (o to treat a subject fully); *— le proprie forze*, to exhaust one's strength **3.** (*eseguire*) to execute: *— un'ordinazione*, (*eseguirla*) to execute an order; *— una pratica*, (*sbrigarla*) to settle a matter ‖ **esaurírsi,** *v.r.* **1.** to exhaust oneself, to become exhausted, to wear oneself out, to work oneself out **2.** (*di denaro, merci*) to be exhausted, to run out; (*di sorgente*) to dry up, to run dry.

esauríto, *ag.* **1.** exhausted; (*consumato*) consumed; (*sfruttato fino all'esaurimento*) worn-out (*attributivo*), worn out (*predicativo*); (*venduto fino all'esaurimento*), sold out: *miniera esaurita*, worked-out mine; *piatto —*, (*al ristorante*) dish that is off; *tutto —*, (*a teatro*) full house; *questo libro è —*, this book is out of print; *questa stoffa è esaurita*, this material has been sold

out (*o is out of stock*) **2.** (*di persona*) exhausted, weary, worn out, tired out; (*che ha l'esaurimento nervoso*) suffering from a nervous breakdown.

esàusto, *ag.* exhausted, worn out (anche *fig.*).

esautoràre, *v.t.* to deprive of authority.

esautoràto, *ag.* deprived of (all) authority.

esazióne, *s.f.* exaction, collection: *— delle imposte*, tax collection.

esborsàre, *v.t.* (*rar.*) to lay out, to disburse; to spend.

esbórso, *s.m.* outlay, expenditure, disbursement.

ésca, *s.f.* **1.** (*per l'amo*) bait (anche *fig.*): *— metallica*, top water plug; *una splendida —*, *fig.* a great temptation; *mettere l'— all'amo*, to bait the hook **2.** (*materiale infiammabile*) tinder: *prendere fuoco come l'—*, to catch fire like tinder ‖ *dar — a una passione*, to fan a flame; *dar — all'odio*, to rouse hatred **3.** (*di esplosivo*) fuse.

escandescènte, *ag.* short-tempered, hot-tempered, irascible, irritable.

escandescènza, *s.f.* outburst of rage: *dare in escandescenze*, to lose one's temper (o to fly into a passion).

èscara, *s.f.* (*med.*) eschar.

escaròtico, *ag.* escharotic.

escatología, *s.f.* (*fil.*) eschatology.

escatològico, *ag.* (*fil.*) eschatologic(al).

escavàre, *v.t.* (*rar.*) to dig, to excavate.

escavatóre, *s.m.*, **escavatríce,** *s.f.* **1.** (*persona*) digger **2.** (*macchina*) excavator, digger: *— a cucchiaia, a badilone, a pala*, (power) shovel (o shovel excavator).

escavazióne, *s.f.* **1.** excavation, excavating, digging (out) **2.** (*miner.*) mining.

escèrti, *s.m.pl.* (*rar.*) excerpta.

eschilèo, *ag.* (*lett.*) Aeschylean.

Èschilo, *no.pr.m.* (*st. lett.*) Aeschylus.

eschimése, *ag.* Eskimo (*attributivo*): *cane —*, Eskimo dog (o Husky) ‖ *s.c.* (*abitante*) Eskimo (*pl.* Eskimo, Eskimos), Husky; (*rar.*) Esquimau (*pl.* Esquimaux) ‖ *s.m.* (*lingua*) Eskimo, Husky.

escíre, *e derivati*, *V.* **uscíre,** *e derivati*.

esclamàre, *v.i.* to exclaim, to utter exclamations; to cry out; to shout out.

esclamativaménte, *av.* exclamatorily.

esclamatívo, *ag.* exclamatory ‖ *punto —*, note of exclamation (o exclamation mark).

esclamazióne, *s.f.* exclamation; ejaculation: *fare una —*, to utter an exclamation.

esclúdere, *v.t.* **1.** (*lasciar fuori*) to exclude, to leave out, to shut out, to bar: *ciò escluse ogni possibilità di dubbio*, this excluded all possibility of doubt; *gli stranieri sono esclusi da questi impieghi*, aliens are excluded from these posts; *— qlcu. da un posto, una società, un privilegio*, to exclude s.o. from a place, a society, a privilege; *— qlcu. dal fare ql.co.*, to bar s.o. from doing sthg. **2.** (*eccettuare*) to exclude, to except, to bar: *la lista è completa esclusi alcuni nomi*, the list is complete barring a few names; *esclusi i presenti*, present company excepted **3.** (*elett.*) to cut out.

esclusióne, *s.f.* exclusion ‖ *ad —*, except: *partirono tutti, ad — dei nonni*, they all left, except their grandparents.

esclusíva, *s.f.* **1.** (*brevetto*) patent; (*diritto esclusivo*) sole right, exclusive right; (*monopolio*) monopoly: *abbiamo l'— per la fabbricazione di questo prodotto*, we have a patent for this article; *vi daremo l'— per la vendita dei nostri prodotti nell'Italia Meridionale*, we'll make you our sole agent for Southern Italy; *prendere l'—*, to take out a patent **2.** (*eccl.*) right of veto.

esclusivaménte, *av.* exclusively.

esclusivísmo, *s.m.* exclusivism.

esclusivísta, *s.c.* exclusivist.

esclusività, *s.f.* exclusiveness.

esclusívo, *ag.* exclusive; (*unico*) sole: *articolo, diritto* —, exclusive article, right; *rappresentante* — *di una ditta*, sole agent of a firm.

esclúso, *ag.* **1.** excluded **2.** (*eccettuato*) excepted: *ci piacciono tutti, nessuno* —, we like them all, none excepted.

esclusóre, *s.m.* **1.** excluder **2.** (*elett.*) cut-out switch.

esclusòrio, *ag.* (*dir.*) exclusory.

escogitàbile, *ag.* contrivable, devisable.

escogitàre, *v.t.* to contrive, to devise, to excogitate; to think out.

escogitatívo, *ag.* contriving, excogitating.

escogitatóre, *ag.* contriving, devising ‖ *s.m.*, **escogitatríce,** *s.f.* contriver; deviser.

escogitazióne, *s.f.* excogitation; contrivance; device.

escòmio, *s.m.* (*dir.*) notice (to quit): *dare l'* —, to give notice to quit.

Escoriàle, *s.m.* Escorial, Escurial.

escoriàre, *v.t.* to excoriate, to abrade; to chafe; to graze ‖ **escoriàrsi,** *v.r.* to graze oneself: *mi sono escoriato un po' il ginocchio*, I have grazed my knee a little.

escoriazióne, *s.f.* excoriation; abrasion.

escreàto, *s.m.* (*med.*) expectoration, spitting.

escrementàle, *ag.* excremental.

escrementízio, *ag.* excrementitious.

escreménto, *s.m.* excrement; feces (*pl.*).

escrescènza, *s.f.* (*med.*) excrescence; (*porro*) wart.

escretívo, *ag.* excretive.

escretóre, escretòrio, *ag.* excretory, excretive.

escrezióne, *s.f.* (*med.*) excretion.

Esculàpio, *no.pr.m.* (*st. med.*) Aesculapius.

esculènto, *ag.* (*rar.*) edible.

Escuriàle, *s.m.* Escurial, Escorial.

escursióne, *s.f.* **1.** (*gita di piacere*) excursion; trip, tour, jaunt, outing: — *a piedi*, walking tour; (*fam.*) hike; *fare un'* —, to make an excursion (*o* to go on an excursion) **2.** (*mil.*) excursion.

escursionísmo, *s.m.* tourism; (*a piedi*) hiking.

escursionísta, *s.c.* excursionist; tripper; tourist; (*a piedi*) hiker.

escussióne, *s.f.* (*dir.*) examination: — *dei testi*, examination of witnesses.

escútere, *v.t.* (*dir.*) to examine; to interrogate: — *i testimoni*, to examine the witnesses.

Èsdra, *no.pr.m.* (*Bibbia*) Ezra.

esecràbile, *ag.* execrable, abominable.

esecrabilità, *s.f.* execrableness, abominableness, detestableness.

esecrabilménte, *av.* execrably, abominably, detestably.

esecràndo, *ag.* execrable, abominable, detestable.

esecràre, *v.t.* to execrate; to loathe, to detest, to abhor.

esecratóre, *ag.* execratory ‖ *s.m.*, **esecratríce,** *s.f.* execrator.

esecrazióne, *s.f.* execration.

esecutívo, *ag.* (*dir.*) executive, executory: *comitato* —, executive committee; *potere* —, executive power; *sentenza in forma esecutiva*, executory judgment ‖ *s.m.* executive.

esecutóre, *ag.* executorial; executory ‖ *s.m.* **1.** executor: — *testamentario*, (*dir.*) executor **2.** (*di musica*) performer; instrumentalist; executant **3.** (*carnefice*) executioner.

esecutòria, *s.f.* (*dir.*) writ of execution.

esecutòrio, *ag.* (*dir.*) executory.

esecutríce, *s.f.* **1.** (*dir.*) executrix (*pl.* executrixes), executress **2.** (*di musica*) performer; executant.

esecuzióne, *s.f.* **1.** (*atto ed effetto dell'eseguire*) execution; fulfil(l)ment: — *di un ordine, di un lavoro*, execution of an order, of a piece of work; *il progetto era ottimo, ma la sua* — *fu un fallimento*, the plan was very good, but its execution was a failure; *andare in* —, (*dir.*) to come into force; *dare* — *a un ordine*,

to execute (*o* to fulfil) an order; *mettere in* — *un progetto*, to carry out a plan **2.** (*sentenza capitale*) capital punishment; (*sua esecuzione*) execution: *ordine d'*—, death-warrant; *plotone d'*—, firing party **3.** (*dir.*) (*sequestro*) execution; distraint **4.** (*mus.*) performance: — *di un pezzo di musica*, performance of a piece of music; *il giovane pianista diede di quel pezzo un'*— *meravigliosa*, the young pianist gave a wonderful performance of that piece of music.

esèdra, *s.f.* (*arch.*) exedra (*pl.* exedrae).

esegèsi, *s.f.* exegesis (*pl.* exegeses).

esegèta, esegète, *s.m.* exegete.

esegètica, *s.f.* exegetics.

esegètico, *ag.* exegetic(al).

eseguíbile, *ag.* feasible, practicable, possible, executable, achievable.

eseguibilità, *s.f.* feasibility, practicability.

eseguiménto, *V.* esecuzióne **1.**

eseguíre, *v.t.* **1.** to execute, to carry out, to perform, to accomplish, to achieve: — *un incarico*, to perform (*o* to accomplish) a task; — *un lavoro*, to carry out a piece of work; — *gli ordini di qlcu.*, to execute (*o* to act upon *o* to carry out) s.o.'s orders; — *un pagamento*, to make a payment; — *un progetto*, to execute (*o* to carry out) a plan **2.** (*mus. teat.*) to perform, to execute: *vennero eseguite suonate di Mozart*, sonatas by Mozart were performed **3.** (*dir.*) to execute: — *la legge*, to enforce the law; — *una sentenza*, to execute a judgment.

esempigràzia, *av.* (*rar.*) for instance, for example (*abbr.* e.g.).

esèmpio, *s.m.* **1.** example; instance: *esempi esplicativi*, explanatory examples; *due chiari esempi della loro infingardaggine*, two clear instances (*o* examples) of their laziness; *secondo l'* — *di...*, following (*o* after) the example of...; *cita un* — *!*, give an example!; *questo è un buon* —, this is a good example; *citare ql.co. a titolo di* —, to cite sthg. as an example (*o* illustration); *citare qlcu. ad* —, to hold s.o. up as an example; *dare l'* — *di una regola*, to exemplify a rule; *dare un buon, cattivo* —, to give a good, bad example; *dare l'* — *a qlcu.*, *essere da* — *a qlcu.*, to set an example to s.o.; *prendere* — *da qlcu.*, *seguire l'* — *di qlcu.*, to follow s.o.'s example; (*imitare*) to imitate s.o.; (*imparare da qlcu.*) to learn from s.o. ‖ *per* —, for instance, for example: *che cosa farò se qualche cosa va male? per* —, *se Pietro arriva tardi?*, what shall I do if sthg. goes wrong? for instance, suppose Peter arrives late?; *è di gusti molto difficili per quanto riguarda il cibo: si rifiuta di mangiare vitello, per* —, he's very fussy about his food: he refuses to eat veal, for example; *vieni da me uno di questi giorni, sabato, per* —, come and see me one of these days, on Saturday, for instance ‖ *senza* —, (*unico*) unique, singular; (*senza confronti*) unparalleled; (*straordinario*) extraordinary **2.** (*modello perfetto*) pattern; paragon: *tua sorella è un vero* — *di virtù*, your sister is a real paragon of virtue **3.** (*ammonimento*) example, warning: *voglio punirlo e dare così un* —, I will make an example of him; *servire di* — *a qlcu.*, to be a lesson (*o* a warning) to s.o. **4.** (*esemplare*) example, specimen: *eccovi un bell'* — *di prosa leopardiana*, here you have a fine specimen (*o* example) of Leopardi's prose.

esemplàre, *ag.* exemplary; model (*attributivo*): *condotta* —, model behaviour (*o* exemplary conduct); *un padre* —, a model father; *punizione* —, exemplary punishment: *darò a quel tizio una punizione* —, I'll make an example of that fellow ‖ *s.m.* **1.** (*modello*) model, pattern, exemplar **2.** (*scient.*) specimen: *un bell'* — *di fauna tropicale*, a fine specimen of tropical fauna **3.** (*copia di libro*) copy.

esemplarità, *s.f.* exemplarity, exemplariness.

esemplarménte, *av.* exemplarily.

esemplificàre, *v.t.* to exemplify, to illustrate.

esemplificatívo, *ag.* exemplifying; illustrative.

esemplificazióne, *s.f.* exemplification; illustration.

esentàre, *v.t.* **1.** to exempt: — *qlcu. dal lavoro,* to let s.o. off his work; — *qlcu. dal servizio militare,* to exempt s.o. from military service; — *qlcu. dalle tasse,* to exempt s.o. from tax payment **2.** (*liberare*) to exempt, to excuse; to free, to relieve: — *le merci da imposte,* to clear goods of duty; — *qlcu. dal fare ql.co.,* to exempt (*o* to excuse) s.o. from doing sthg.; — *qlcu. da un compito, incarico,* to relieve s.o. of (*o* to excuse s.o. from) a job; — *qlcu. da un dovere,* to excuse s.o. from a duty ‖ **esentàrsi,** *v.r.* to free oneself from (sthg., doing), to get out of (sthg., doing).

esènte, *ag.* exempt, free: — *da colpa, malattia,* free from blame, disease; — *da impegni, pericoli,* free from engagements, dangers; — *da imposta,* duty free (*o* free of duty); — *da preoccupazioni,* care-free; — *da tasse,* exempt from taxes (*o* tax-free); — *da contagio,* immune from contagion; *bolletta di merce* —, (*comm.*) entry for free goods; *titolo — da tasse,* (*comm.*) tax-exempt security; *andare — da ql.co.,* to be free (*o* exempt) from sthg.

esenzióne, *s.f.* exemption: — *dal servizio militare,* exemption from military service; — *dalle tasse,* exemption (*o* immunity) from taxation.

esèquie, *s.f.pl.* exequies, obsequies; funeral (*sing.*): *cantare le* —, to chant the exequies (*o* the funeral rites).

esercènte, *s.m.* (*bottegaio*) shop-keeper; (*dettagliante*) retailer, retail dealer; (*commerciante*) tradesman: *prezzi per gli esercenti,* prices for the trade; *sconto per gli esercenti,* trade discount.

esercíre, *v.t.* (*un'azienda*) to manage (a business), to run (a business); (*un negozio*) to keep (a shop); to run (a shop); (*un commercio*) to carry on (a trade).

esercitàbile, *ag.* exercisable.

esercitàre, *v.t.* **1.** to exercise; (*fare uso di*) to exert; to train: *esercitò tutta la sua influenza per riuscire,* he exerted all his influence (in order) to be successful; — *la pazienza,* to exercise one's patience; — *le proprie facoltà mentali,* to exercise one's mental faculties; — *le proprie membra, gli occhi, gli orecchi,* to train one's limbs, eyes, ears; — *tutte le proprie facoltà,* to call all one's powers into play; — *una virtù,* to practise a virtue **2.** (*dir.*) to exercise: — *i propri diritti,* to exercise one's rights **3.** (*professione, mestiere*) to practise, to follow, to pursue, to carry on: *quel dottore non esercita più la sua professione,* that doctor has given up his practice; *sì, esercito ancora la mia professione,* yes, I'm still practising; — *un commercio,* to ply a trade; — *una professione,* to practise a profession **4.** (*addestrare*) to drill, to train: (*far*) — *un ragazzo a nuotare,* to train (*o* to exercise) a boy in swimming; — *i soldati,* to drill (*o* to train) soldiers **5.** (*mettere alla prova*) to try: — *la pazienza di qlcu.,* to try s.o.'s patience ‖ **esercitàrsi,** *v.r.* to practise; to train oneself: *si esercita per sei ore al giorno,* he practises for six hours a day; — *al tennis, al nuoto, al piano,* to practise tennis, swimming, the piano.

esercitazióne, *s.f.* **1.** exercise; practice; (*allenamento*) training; (*di studio*) practical exercise: — *di tiro al bersaglio,* (*mil.*) target practice **2.** (*mil.*) drill: *far fare esercitazioni alle truppe,* to drill the troops.

esèrcito, *s.m.* **1.** army: — *regolare,* standing (*o* regular) army; *entrare nell'*—, to enter (*o* to join *o* to go into) the army; *lasciare l'*—, to leave the army; *raccogliere un* —, to assemble (*o* to gather) an army ‖ *Esercito della Salvezza,* Salvation Army **2.** *fig.* (*folla*) host, army.

esercízio, *s.m.* **1.** exercise: *esercizi a cinque dita per pianoforte,* five-finger exercises for the piano; *esercizi di grammatica,* grammar exercises; *esercizi ginnici,* gymnastic exercises; *essere fuori* —, to be out of practice; *fare dell'*—, to take some exercise; *fare un* —, to make an exercise; *fare esercizi al piano,* to practise the piano;

tenersi in —, to keep in practice ‖ *esercizi spirituali,* religious exercises **2.** (*uso, pratica*) use, practice, employment, exercise: — *della pazienza, delle facoltà mentali,* exercise of patience, of the mental faculties; — *di autorità,* exertion of authority; — *di una professione,* practice of a profession; *nell'*— *delle proprie funzioni,* in the exercise of one's duties; *entrare in* —, (*di impianti*) to go into operation (*o* to begin operating *o* to be put into operation); *porre in* —, to put into service **3.** (*mil.*) (*esercitazione*) drill(ing): — *ai pezzi,* gun drill **4.** (*relig.*) practice: — *del culto,* practice of religious rites **5.** (*negozio*) shop **6.** (*comm.*): — *finanziario,* financial year; *conti diversi di* —, sundry operating expenses; *il presente* —, this financial year.

esèrgo, *s.m.* (*di monete*) exergue.

esibíre, *v.t.* **1.** to exhibit; (*mostrare*) to show; (*mettere in mostra*) to display, to show off: *favorite* — *i documenti,* please show your papers; — *la propria cultura,* to display (*o* to show off) one's knowledge **2.** (*dir.*) to produce, to exhibit **3.** (*offrire*) to offer, to tender ‖ **esibírsi,** *v.r.* **1.** to show oneself off, to parade **2.** (*in spettacoli*) to be on **3.** (*offrirsi*) to offer oneself; to offer one's services.

esibitóre, *s.m.,* **esibitríce,** *s.f.* exhibitor.

esibizióne, *s.f.* **1.** (*mostra*) exhibition; show; (*il mettere in mostra, fare sfoggio*) exhibition, display, ostentation, showing off: *fare* — *di ql.co.,* to make a display of sthg.; *fece molta* — *di coraggio,* he made a great display of courage **2.** (*spettacolo*) show **3.** (*offerta*) offer.

esibizionísmo, *s.m.* exhibitionism.

esibizionísta, *s.c.* exhibitionist.

esigènte, *ag.* exacting; (*rar.*) exigent; (*difficile da contentare*) particular, hard to please; (*severo*) strict: *un maestro* —, an exacting master; *egli è troppo* —, he is over particular (*o* he expects too much).

esigènza, *s.f.* **1.** (*bisogno, necessità*) demand, requirement; exigence, exigency; need, necessity: *le esigenze del mercato,* the demands of the market; *speriamo di soddisfare le esigenze dei nostri clienti,* we hope to meet our customers' requirements **2.** (*pretesa*) pretension: *egli ha troppe esigenze,* he has too many pretensions.

esígere, *v.t.* **1.** (*comm.*) to exact, to collect, to cash: — *imposte,* to collect taxes **2.** (*richiedere con autorità*) to insist on (sthg., s.o.'s doing); to demand, to require: *esigo che voi partiate subito,* I insist on your leaving at once; — *ubbidienza,* to demand obedience **3.** (*pretendere, volere*) to require, to call for (sthg.); to demand, to exact: *esigi troppo da me,* you exact too much of (*o* from) me; *gli italiani esigono che il territorio sia restituito alla patria,* the Italians demand that the territory be restored to their country; *questo lavoro esige molta pazienza,* this work requires (*o* calls for) a lot of patience; — *il pagamento di un debito,* to exact the payment of a debt ‖ — *soddisfazione,* to exact satisfaction.

esigíbile, *ag.* **1.** exigible, requirable **2.** (*riscuotibile*) collectable.

esigibilità, *s.f.* **1.** liability to be demanded **2.** *pl.* (*comm.*) current liabilities.

esiguità, *s.f.* exiguity, exiguousness; slenderness, slightness; smallness; (*scarsità*) scantiness.

esíguo, *ag.* exiguous; slender, slight; small, little; (*scarso*) scanty: *le nostre esigue risorse non ci permettono di fare quella spesa,* our slender means do not allow us to go to that expense.

esilaránte, *ag.* exhilarating; (*che rallegra*) cheering.

esilaràre, *v.t.* to exhilarate; (*rallegrare*) to cheer: *le sue battute esilararono il pubblico,* his witty remarks exhilarated the audience.

èsile, *ag.* **1.** slender, thin **2.** *fig.* (*debole*) weak.

esiliàre, *v.t.* to exile; to banish ‖ **esiliàrsi,** *v.r.* to go into exile.

esiliàto, *ag.* banished ‖ *s.m.* exile.

esílio, *s.m.* **1.** (*pena*) exile, banishment, exilement: *andare in* —, to go into exile; *mandare qlcu. in* —, to send s.o. into exile (*o* to exile s.o. *o* to banish s.o.) **2.** (*luogo*) place of exile.

esilità, *s.f.* (*rar.*) **1.** slenderness, thinness **2.** *fig.* (*debolezza*) weakness.

esímere, *v.t.* to exempt; to free; to dispense; to excuse; to absolve; to relieve: *ciò mi esime da ogni responsabilità*, it relieves me of all responsibility; — *qlcu. dal fare ql.co.*, to exempt s.o. from doing sthg.; — *qlcu. da un obbligo*, to free (*o* to absolve) s.o. from an obligation ‖ **esímersi**, *v.r.* to shrink (from sthg., doing); to evade (sthg.): — *dal servizio militare*, to evade military service.

esímio, *ag.* (*eccellente*) excellent; (*eminente*) eminent; (*illustre*) illustrious; (*distinto*) distinguished, notable, remarkable: — *Signor Rossi, Lei sa che...*, dear Mr. Rossi, you know that....

Esíodo, *no.pr.m.* (*st. lett.*) Hesiod.

esistènte, *ag.* existing, existent; (*vivente*) living: *tariffe esistenti*, notes in force; *tuttora* —, (*di persona*) surviving; (*di cosa*) extant (*o* in existence): *il più antico documento tuttora* —, the earliest document in existence.

esistènza, *s.f.* **1.** existence: *l'*— *di Dio*, the existence of God **2.** (*vita*) life, existence: — *politica di un popolo*, political life of a people; *lotta per l'*—, struggle for life; *condusse una* — *felice*, he led a happy life **3.** (*comm.*) (*di cassa*) cash in hand; (*di magazzino*) stock in hand.

esistenzialísmo, *s.m.* (*fil.*) existentialism.

esistenzialísta, *ag.s.c.* (*fil.*) existentialist.

esístere, *v.i.* to exist, to be; (*vivere*) to live: *credo che Dio esista*, I believe that God exists; *eppure esistono leggi universali!*, yet there are universal laws!; *esistono ancora alcuni documenti di arte celtica*, a few documents of Celtic art are still in existence (*o* extant); *esistono molti animali da pelliccia in quella regione*, many fur animals exist (*o* live) in that region; *ha cessato di* —, he ceased to live; *non esiste scusa*, there is no excuse; *non può* — *dubbio alcuno*, there can be no doubt; *il più grande genio che sia mai esistito*, the greatest genius that ever lived; *razze che non esistono più*, races that are extinct (*o* have died out); *tuttora esiste un uomo che conobbe quel grande pittore*, there still lives a man who knew that great painter.

esitàbile, *ag.* (*comm.*) saleable, marketable.

esitaménto, *s.m.* (*rar.*) hesitation.

esitànte, *ag.* **1.** hesitant; hesitating; wavering; irresolute; (*dubbioso*) doubtful **2.** (*di voce*) faltering.

esitànza, *s.f.* hesitancy, hesitation; wavering.

esitàre[1], *v.i.* **1.** to hesitate; (*essere dubbioso*) to waver: *esito se fare o no quel passo*, I am hesitating about taking that step; *non esitò ad aiutarmi*, he did not hesitate to help me; — *fra due opinioni, fra due soluzioni*, to waver between two opinions, between two solutions; *senza* —, unhesitatingly (*o* without a moment's hesitation) **2.** (*di voce*) to falter.

esitàre[2], *v.t.* (*comm.*) to sell; to dispose of (sthg.): *possiamo* — *subito la merce*, we can sell (*o* dispose of) the goods at once.

esitazióne, *s.f.* hesitation, hesitancy; wavering: — *a fare ql.co.*, hesitation in doing sthg.; *basta con le esitazioni!*, no more shilly-shallying!; *con* —, hesitatingly; *senza* —, unhesitatingly (*o* without faltering).

èsito, *s.m.* **1.** result, outcome; issue: *l'*— *di una malattia*, the outcome of an illness; *buon* —, success; *pronto* —, prompt result; *quale fu l'*— *dell'impresa?*, what was the result (*o* the issue) of the enterprise?; *giudicare dall'*—, to judge from results **2.** (*di dramma*) denouement, catastrophe **3.** (*vendita*) sale.

esiziàle, *ag.* ruinous; fatal; mortal.

eslège, *ag.* exempt from the law.

esocàrpo, *s.m.* (*bot.*) exocarp.

esòdio, *s.m.* (*teatro greco*) exodium, exode.

èsodo[1], *s.m.* exodus; flight ‖ *l'Esodo*, (*Bibbia*) the Exodus.

èsodo[2], *s.m.* (*fis.*) hexode.

esofagèo, *ag.* (*anat.*) oesophageal.

esofagíte, *s.f.* (*patol.*) oesophagitis.

esòfago, *s.m.* (*anat.*) oesophagus; (*pop.*) gullet.

esofagoscòpio, *s.m.* (*med.*) oesophagoscope.

esofagotomía, *s.f.* (*chir.*) oesophagotomy.

esoftàlmico, *ag.* (*med.*) exophthalmic.

esoftàlmo, *s.m.* (*med.*) exophthalmus.

esoftalmòmetro, *s.m.* (*med.*) exophthalmometer.

esògeno, *ag.* (*biol. geol.*) exogenous: *variabili esogene*, exogenous variables.

esoneràre, *v.t.* to exonerate; (*liberare*) to free, to relieve; (*esentare*) to exempt; (*licenziare*) to dismiss; (*congedare*) to discharge.

esònero, *s.m.* exoneration; (*esenzione*) exemption; (*licenziamento*) dismissal; (*congedo*) discharge.

Esòpo, *no.pr.m.* (*st. lett.*) Aesop.

esorbitànte, *ag.* exorbitant; excessive: *prezzo* —, exorbitant (*o* prohibitive) price.

esorbitànza, *s.f.* exorbitance; excess.

esorbitàre, *v.i.* to exceed; to exceed the just limit, to go beyond the limits.

esorcísmo, *s.m.* exorcism.

esorcísta, *s.m.* **1.** exorcist; exorcizer **2.** (*chi ha ricevuto l'esorcistato*) exorcist.

esorcizzàre, *v.t.* to exorcize.

esorcizzatóre, *s.m.* exorcizer.

esordiènte, *ag.* beginning; starting ‖ *s.c.* beginner; novice ‖ *s.f.* (*di ragazza in società*) debutante; (*fam.*) deb.

esòrdio, *s.m.* **1.** (*di un discorso*) exordium, preamble; (*introduzione*) introduction; (*inizio*) beginning **2.** (*in arte*) debut; (*di ragazza in società*) coming out.

esordíre, *v.i.* **1.** (*cominciare*) to begin, to start, to commence **2.** (*in arte*) to make one's debut; (*di ragazza in società*) to come out **3.** (*in una professione*) to begin practising (a profession).

esornàre, *v.t.* to embellish (with metaphors).

esornatívo, *ag.* decorative, ornamental.

esortaménto, *s.m.* (*rar.*) exhortation.

esortàre, *v.t.* to exhort: *esortò i figli a studiare*, he exorted his children to study.

esortatívo, *ag.* exhortative, exhortatory.

esortatóre, *s.m.*, **esortatríce**, *s.f.* exhorter.

esortatòrio, *ag.* exhortatory.

esortazióne, *s.f.* exhortation, admonishment.

esòsi, *s.m.pl.* (*chim.*) hexoses.

esosmòsi, *s.f.* (*fis.*) exosmosis; exosmose.

esosmòtico, *ag.* (*fis.*) exosmotic; exosmic.

esòso, *ag.* **1.** (*avaro, rapace*) greedy, grasping **2.** (*odioso*) hateful; odious.

esotèrico, *ag.* esoteric(al): *dottrine esoteriche*, esoteric doctrines ‖ *gli esoterici*, the initiated.

esotericaménte, *av.* esoterically.

esotèrmico, *ag.* (*chim.*) exothermic.

esoticità, *s.f.* exoticism.

esòtico, *ag.* exotic; (*straniero*) foreign: *fiori esotici*, exotic flowers.

esotísmo, *s.m.* exoticism.

espàndere, *v.t.* to spread (out), to extend ‖ **espàndersi**, *v.r.* **1.** (*estendersi, diffondersi*) to spread: *un paese che si espande per miglia*, a country spreading for miles **2.** (*accrescere il proprio territorio*) to win new territory **3.** (*confidarsi, sfogarsi*) to expand.

espansíbile, *ag.* expansible.

espansióne, *s.f.* **1.** expansion: — *territoriale*, territorial expansion **2.** (*effusione, affettuosità*) warmth, effusion **3.** (*fis. chim.*) expansion: — *di un gas*, expansion of a gas; *macchina a tripla* —, triple-expansion engine.

espansionísmo, *s.m.* (*pol.*) expansionism.

espansionísta, *ag.s.c.* (*pol.*) expansionist.

espansività, *s.f.* **1.** (*esuberanza*) demonstrativeness, effusiveness **2.** (*di gas, ecc.*) expansiveness.

espansívo, *ag.* **1.** (*esuberante*) effusive, unreserved, exuberant, demonstrative, expansive: *mostrarsi troppo* —, to wear one's heart on one's sleeve **2.** (*di gas, forza, ecc.*) expansive.

espànso, *ag.* expanded.

espatriàre, *v.i.* to emigrate, to leave one's country; to expatriate oneself.

espàtrio, *s.m.* expatriation.

espediènte, *s.m.* expedient, device; resource: *ricorrere ad un* —, to use (*o* to resort to) an expedient; *tentare mille espedienti*, to try a thousand shifts and devices; *vivere di espedienti*, to live on one's wits.

espèllere, *v.t.* (*scacciare*) to expel, to turn out, to eject: *fu espulso dalla scuola*, he was expelled from school.

esperantísta, *s.c.* Esperantist.

esperànto, *s.m.* Esperanto.

Espèria, *no.pr.f.* (*geog. mit.*) Hesperia.

esperìbile, *ag.* attemptable.

Espèridi, *no.pr.f.pl.* (*mit.*) Hesperides.

esperiènza, *s.f.* **1.** experience: *lo so per* —, I know it from experience; *la nostra ditta vanta in questo campo 50 anni di* —, our firm prides itself on 50 years of experience in this field; *acquistare* — *in ql.co.*, to gain experience in sthg.; *fare esperienze interessanti*, to have interesting experiences; *imparare ql.co. per* — *personale*, to learn sthg. by personal experience (*o fam.* to learn sthg. the hard way); *parlare per* —, to speak from experience; *sapere per* —, to know by experience **2.** (*conoscenza*) familiarity: *non ho* — *dei costumi locali*, I have no familiarity with the local customs **3.** (*esperimento*) experiment, trial.

esperimentàle, *ag.* experimental.

esperimentàre, *v.t.* **1.** to experience: — *tempi difficili*, to experience difficult times **2.** (*mettere alla prova*) to try, to test: *ho esperimentato la sua lealtà*, I tried his loyalty (*o* I put his loyalty to the test) ‖ *v.i.* (*fare esperienze scientifiche*) to experiment.

esperimentàto, *ag.* **1.** (*esperto*) skilled, skilful, experienced **2.** (*dimostrato, provato*) tested, proved.

esperimentatóre, *s.m.*, **esperimentatríce**, *s.f.* experimenter.

esperiménto, *s.m.* **1.** experiment: — *chimico*, chemical experiment; *fare un* —, to make an experiment **2.** (*esame*) test **3.** (*tentativo, prova*) trial.

espèrio, *ag.* (*poet.*) Hesperian.

esperíre, *v.t.* (*burocrazia*) to try; to carry out: — *tutte le pratiche*, to take all necessary steps.

èspero, *s.m.* (*letter.*) **1.** Hesperus, the evening star **2.** (*vento*) west wind.

espertaménte, *av.* expertly, skilfully

espèrto, *ag.* **1.** (*abile*) expert, skilful, skilled **2.** (*che ha esperienza*) experienced ‖ *s.m.* expert.

espettazióne, *s.f.* (*rar.*) expectation.

espettorànte, *ag.s.m.* (*farm.*) expectorant.

espettoràre, *v.t.* to expectorate.

espettoràto, *s.m.* expectoration.

espettorazióne, *s.f.* expectoration.

espiàre, *v.t.* **1.** to expiate: — *un delitto, un peccato*, to expiate a crime, a sin **2.** (*riparare*) to atone for (sthg., doing): *come posso* — *il mio torto verso di te?*, how can I atone for doing you wrong?.

espiatóre, *ag.* expiatory ‖ *s.m.*, **espiatríce**, *s.f.* expiator.

espiatòrio, *ag.* expiatory ‖ *capro* —, scapegoat.

espiazióne, *s.f.* expiation ‖ *festa dell'* —, (*relig. ebraica*) Day of Atonement (*o* Yom Kippur).

espiràre, *v.i.* **1.** (*fisiol.*) to expire, to breathe out **2.** (*esalare*) to exhale.

espiratòrio, *ag.* (*fisiol.*) expiratory.

espirazióne, *s.f.* (*fisiol.*) expiration: — *di aria dai polmoni*, expiration of air from the lungs.

espletaménto, *s.m.* (*rar.*) accomplishment.

espletàre, *v.t.* to dispatch, to accomplish, to fulfil: — *delle pratiche*, to dispatch some business.

espletívo, *ag.* (*gram.*) expletive, pleonastic.

esplicàbile, *ag.* (*rar.*) explicable; explainable.

esplicàre, *v.t.* **1.** (*sviluppare*) to explicate; to develop; (*spiegare*) to explain **2.** (*svolgere*): — *un'attività*, to carry on an activity ‖ **esplicàrsi**, *v.r.* **1.** (*svilupparsi*) to unfold **2.** (*spiegarsi*) to explain oneself; to make oneself clear.

esplicatívo, *ag.* explanatory; explicative; explicatory: *nota esplicativa*, explanatory note.

esplicazióne, *s.f.* (*rar.*) **1.** (*sviluppo*) explication **2.** (*spiegazione*) explanation.

esplicitaménte, *av.* explicitly, clearly, expressly.

esplícito, *ag.* explicit, clear, definite, outspoken, express: *affermazione esplicita*, explicit statement; *comando* —, express command; *era suo* — *desiderio che noi ritornassimo da lui*, it was his express wish that we should go back to him; *fu molto* — *riguardo a ciò*, he was quite explicit (*o* outspoken) about that.

esplodènte, *ag.s.m.* explosive.

esplòdere, *v.i.* **1.** to explode, to burst: *la bomba esplose qui*, the bomb exploded (*o* burst) here ‖ *far* —, to explode (*o* to set off); (*una mina*) to blow up **2.** *fig.* to explode, to burst out: *esplose in una risata*, he burst out laughing; *la sua ira esplose*, his anger exploded ‖ *v.t.* (*sparare*) to fire: *chi aveva esploso quei colpi?*, who had fired those shots?.

esploràbile, *ag.* that may be explored; (*rar.*) explorable.

esploràre, *v.t.* **1.** to explore: — *regioni nuove*, to explore new countries **2.** (*osservare, investigare*) to examine, to explore, to probe into (sthg.), to investigate, to search: — *l'animo umano*, to explore the human heart (*o* to probe into the human heart) **3.** (*mil.*) to scout, to reconnoitre **4.** (*med.*) to explore, to probe; to sound: — *una ferita*, to explore (*o* to probe) a wound **5.** (*tv.*) to scan.

esploratívo, *ag.* explorative, exploratory.

esploratóre, *s.m.* **1.** explorer ‖ *giovane* —, Boy Scout **2.** (*mil.*) scout **3.** (*nave da guerra*) scout (cruiser).

esploratòrio, *ag.* exploratory, explorative.

esploratríce, *s.f.* explorer ‖ *giovane* —, Girl Guide (*o amer.* Girl Scout).

esplorazióne, *s.f.* **1.** exploration **2.** (*indagine*) reconnaissance; exploration; sounding **3.** (*mil.*) reconnaissance; scouting expedition: *fare un'* — *del terreno*, to reconnoitre the ground; *mandare qlcu. in* —, to send s.o. on a scouting expedition **4.** (*med.*) sounding **5.** (*tv.*) scanning: — *elettronica*, electronic scanning.

esplosióne, *s.f.* **1.** explosion, blast, burst **2.** (*detonazione*) report, explosion **3.** *fig.* outbreak, outburst: — *di odio*, outbreak (*o* explosion) of hatred.

esplosívo, *ag.* explosive (anche *fig.*) ‖ *s.m.* explosive: — *di lancio*, propellent explosive; — *solido, liquido, gassoso*, solid, liquid, gaseous explosive; *alto, basso* —, high, low explosive.

esponènte, *s.m.* **1.** (*chi fa un esposto*) exposer **2.** (*rappresentante*) exponent, representative **3.** (*mat.*) exponent, index **4.** — *di carico*, (*mar.*) dead-weight capacity (*o* dead-weight tonnage).

esponenziàle, *ag.* (*mat.*) exponential.

espórre, *v.t.* **1.** (*mettere in mostra*) to show, to exhibit, to display; to expose: — *delle merci in vetrina*, to show (*o* to display) goods in the window; — *il Sacramento*, (*eccl.*) to expose the Blessed Sacrament **2.** (*a rischio*) to expose, to risk, to venture: — *qlcu. a un rischio, a un pericolo*, to expose s.o. to a risk, to a danger; — *la vita*, to risk one's life **3.** (*spiegare*) to expound, to state, to set forth, to unfold, to explain: — *le proprie idee*, to state one's ideas; — *una teoria*, to expound a theory ‖ *alle condizioni esposte*, (*comm.*) at the terms stated **4.** (*interpretare testi*) to interpret, to explain **5.** (*mettere in vista*) to put up, to post up, to stick up: — *un avviso*, to stick up a notice **6.** (*abbandonare quale trovatello*) to expose: — *un bambino*, to expose a child **7.** (*foto.*) to expose ‖ **espórsi**, *v.r.* **1.** to expose oneself: — *alle critiche*, to lay oneself open to criticism **2.** (*compromettersi*) to compromise oneself.

esportàre, *v.t.* to export: *vorremmo — questo articolo in Australia*, we should like to export this article to Australia.

esportatóre, *ag.* exporting: *la ditta esportatrice*, the exporting firm ‖ *s.m.*, **esportatríce**, *s.f.* exporter.

esportazióne, *s.f.* export; exportation: — *protetta*, dumping; *articolo d'—*, export article; *commercio d'—*, export trade; *l'— dei nostri articoli è aumentata*, the exportation of our articles has increased (*o* we are exporting more and more of our articles); *egli si occupa di —*, he is engaged in export.

esosímetro, *s.m.* (*foto.*) exposure meter.

espositívo, *ag.* expositive, declarative, explanatory: *metodo —*, declarative rule.

espositóre, *s.m.*, **espositríce**, *s.f.* exhibitor.

esposizióne, *s.f.* **1.** exposure: — *a un rischio*, exposure to a risk; — *all'aria, al sole*, exposure to the air, the sun **2.** (*mostra*) exhibition, show; display: *sala d'—*, show-room **3.** (*eloquio*) exposition: *chiarezza di —*, clearness of exposition **4.** (*descrizione, narrazione*) description **5.** (*rendiconto*) statement: — *della situazione finanziaria*, (*comm.*) statement of affairs (*o* budget speech) **6.** (*di una casa*) exposure, aspect: — *a mezzogiorno*, south(erly) exposure (*o* south aspect) **7.** (*foto.*) exposure.

espósto, *s.m.* **1.** (*memoriale*) statement of facts, account of facts, exposé **2.** (*petizione*) petition **3.** (*trovatello*) foundling.

espressaménte, *av.* **1.** (*in modo esplicito*) expressly, explicitly **2.** (*apposta, di proposito*) expressly, on purpose.

espressióne, *s.f.* **1.** expression: *il suo viso aveva un'—triste*, her face had a sad look; *dare — ad un sentimento*, to give utterance (*o* expression) to a feeling (*o* to express a feeling) **2.** (*forza espressiva*) expression: *senza —*, expressionless: *sguardo senza —*, blank (*o* vacant) look; *leggilo con —*, read it with expression (*o* with feeling); *suonare con —*, to play with expression **3.** (*frase, locuzione*) expression, phrase: *questa non è un'— corretta*, this is not a polite expression (*o* phrase) **4.** (*mat.*) expression.

espressionísmo, *s.m.* (*art.*) expressionism.

espressionísta, *s.c.* (*art.*) expressionist.

espressionístico, *ag.* (*art.*) expressionist(ic).

espressíva, *s.f.* expressiveness.

espressivaménte, *av.* expressively.

espressívo, *ag.* expressive, meaningful, significant: *silenzio —*, meaningful silence; *stile —* expressive style.

esprèsso, *ag.* **1.** (*esplicito*) express; explicit, clear; definite, precise: *per ordine —*, by express command **2.** (*apposito, fatto apposta*): *caffè —*, espresso coffee; *tr eno —*, express (train) ‖ *s.m.* (*lettera*) express letter, special delivery letter; (*amer.*) fast letter ‖ *mandare un pacco per —*, to send a parcel express.

esprímere, *v.t.i.* to express, to voice, to word; to signify: *non sappiamo esprimerti quanto ti siamo grati*, we cannot express to you how grateful we are; *una clausola espressa il più vagamente possibile*, a clause as vaguely worded as possible; — *i propri sentimenti*, to express one's feelings; — *il proprio rincrescimento*, to signify (*o* to declare) one's regret ‖ **esprímersi**, *v.r.* to express oneself: *sai esprimerti in inglese?*, can you express yourself in English? ‖ *come esprimermi?*, (*fam.*) how shall I put it?.

esprimíbile, *ag.* expressible.

esprofèsso, *av.* exprofesso, professedly.

espropriàre, *v.t.* (*dir.*) to expropriate, to dispossess: *fummo espropriati*, we were dispossessed of (*o* expropriated from) our estates; *proprietari terrieri espropriati*, dispossessed landowners.

espropriazióne, *s.f.* expropriation.

espròprio, *s.m.* (*dir.*) expropriation.

espugnàbile, *ag.* conquerable.

espugnàre, *v.t.* **1.** to conquer; to take by storm;

to storm: — *una fortezza*, to carry (*o* to storm) a fortress **2.** *fig.* (*sopraffare*) to vanquish, to overcome.

espugnatóre, *s.m.* conqueror.

espugnazióne, *s.f.* conquest.

espulsióne, *s.f.* **1.** expulsion (*anche med.*); ejection **2.** (*bando*) banishment **3.** (*patol.*) eruption, rash.

espulsívo, *ag.s.m.* (*med.*) expulsive: *dolori espulsivi*, expulsive pains; *stadio —*, expulsive stage.

espúlso, *ag.* expelled, ejected.

espulsóre, *s.m.* (*di arma da fuoco*) ejector.

espúngere, *v.t.* to expunge; to erase, to delete.

espurgàre, *v.t.* **1.** to expurgate, to purge **2.** (*un libro*) to bowdlerize.

espurgatóre, *s.m.*, **espurgatríce**, *s.f.* expurgator.

espurgazióne, *s.f.* **1.** expurgation **2.** (*di libro*) bowdlerization.

Esquilíno, *no.pr.m.* Esquiline.

esquimése, *V.* **eschimése.**

éssa, *pron. pers. f. 3ª persona sing.* **1.** *sogg.* she (*riferito a donna o animale femmina; se riferito a persona l'uso corretto richiede* ella); it (*riferito a cosa o animale di sesso non specificato*): — *mi disse che sarebbe arrivata col treno delle 5,15*, she told me she would come by the 5.15 train; *guarda quella cagnetta, — giuoca con i suoi cuccioli*, look at that dog, she is playing with her puppies; *siediti su questa poltrona, — è molto comoda*, sit down on this arm-chair, it is very comfortable **2.** *obliquo* her (*riferito a persona o animale femmina*); it (*riferito a cosa o animale di sesso non specificato*): *di — non parla mai*, he never speaks of her; *non mangiare quella mela, gran parte di — è marcia*, don't eat that apple, a large part of it is bad ‖ *ag. dimostrativo* (*arc.*) **this**, **that**: *— casa*, that house.

ésse[1], *pron. pers. f. 3ª persona pl.* **1.** *sogg.* **they**: *guarda quelle ragazze, — sono tedesche*, look at those girls, they are German; *segui queste tracce, — ti condurranno al rifugio*, follow these tracks, they will lead you to the shelter **2.** *obliquo* **them**: *due di — sono mie vecchie amiche*, two of them are old friends of mine; *le regalarono delle rose e con — ornò la tavola*, they gave her some roses and she adorned the table with them.

èsse[2], *s.f.m.* letter S ‖ (*fatto*) *ad —*, S-shaped; *strada ad —*, winding road.

essendoché, *cong.* (*arc.*) as; since.

essènza, *s.f.* **1.** essence, essential being **2.** (*parte più importante di una cosa*) essence: *l'— di un libro*, the essence of a book **3.** (*estratto, olio*) essence; essential oil: — *di bergamotto*, essence of bergamot; *— {di garofano*, clove oil; — *di rose*, attar of roses **4.** *la quinta —*, *la quintessenza*, the quintessence (*anche fig.*): *la quinta —, la quintessenza dei galantuomini*, the quintessence of gentlemen.

essenziàle, *ag.* **1.** essential, fundamental: *d'importanza —*, of capital (*o* primary) importance; *è una parte — di questo libro*, that is an essential part of this book **2.** (*chim.*) essential: *olio —*, essential (*o* volatile) oil ‖ *s.m.* (the) essential thing: *l'— è non perderlo di vista*, the essential thing is not to lose sight of him.

essenzialità, *s.f.* essentiality.

essenzialménte, *av.* essentially, fundamentally.

èssere, *v.i.* **1.** (*copula*) to be: *il cane è il miglior amico dell'uomo*, man's best friend is the dog; *il mio amico è di nobile stirpe*, my friend is of noble stock; *quei ragazzi sono simpatici*, those boys are very nice; *se non è in casa, sarà in giardino*, if he is not indoors, he is probably in the garden; *sei un ragazzo d'ingegno*, you are an intelligent boy; *sono stanco*, I am tired; *il suo anello era d'oro*, her ring was made of gold **2.** (*ausiliare con i verbi passivi*) **to be**: *questo libro è letto specialmente da studenti*, this book is read especially by students **3.** (*ausiliare con i verbi di moto, riflessivi e impersonali*) **to have**: *è piovuto recentemente?*, has it rained recently?; *non mi sono ancora lavato*, I haven't washed yet; *non sono ancora partiti*, they haven't

left yet **4.** (*in unione con* ci) **to be:** *c'era un libro,* there was a book; *c'era una volta un re,* once upon a time there was a king; *che c'è?,* what's the matter? (*o what's up?*); *che c'è di nuovo?,* what is the news? || *ci siamo!,* (*eccoci*) here we are!; (*siamo alle solite*) here we go again! || *non c'è che dire,* there is nothing to be said; (*non c'è dubbio*) there is no doubt || *non c'è da aver paura,* there is nothing to be afraid of **5.** (*in correlazione*): *sia... sia..., be... be...: la mia casa, sia essa un castello, sia una capanna, è il mio regno,* my house, be it a castle (or) be it a hut, is my kingdom || *sia... che..., both... and..: sia mio fratello che mia sorella sono biondi,* both my brother and sister are fair-haired || *sia che... sia che..., whether... or...: verrò a trovarti, sia che faccia bello sia che piova,* I will come to see you whether it's fine or raining **6.** (*esistere*) **to be; to exist:** *Dio è,* God exists || *— o non —, questo è il problema,* to be or not to be, that is the question **7.** — *di,* (*appartenere a*) **to belong to** (s.o., sthg.), **to be of** (s.o.): *di chi è questa casa?,* whose house is this? (*o who does this house belong to?*); *è di mio fratello,* it is my brother's (*o it belongs to my brother*) **8.** (*consistere*) **to consist, to lie:** *la vera felicità non è nella ricchezza,* true happiness doesn't lie in wealth (*o in riches*) **9.** (*stare, trovarsi*) **to be:** « *Dov'è tuo padre? », « È in salotto »,* "Where is your father?", "He is in the drawing-room"; — *a pranzo,* to be at dinner; — *di guardia,* to be on guard duty || — *più di là che di qua,* to be more dead than alive || — *sull'avviso,* to be on one's guard **10.** (*andare*) **to be:** *ero stato a Parigi,* I had been to Paris; *sono stato a trovarlo,* I have been to see him **11.** (*quando esprime distanza*): *quanto c'è da Roma a Milano?,* (*nello spazio*) how far is it from Rome to Milan? (*o how far is Milan from Rome?*); (*nel tempo*) how long does it take from Rome to Milan? **12.** (*valere, costare, pesare*): *quant'è?,* (*quanto costa*) how much is it?; *questo pane è ¼ di libbra,* this loaf weighs ¼ lb. **13.** (*avvenire, accadere*): *che sarà di me?,* what will become of me? || *così sia,* so be it || *ebbene sia!,* well, let it be so! || *sia come (si) sia,* be it as it may (*o at all events*) **14.** — *da,* (*convenire a*) **to be worthy of** (sthg.); (*essere atto a*) **to be fit for** (sthg.); **to be qualified for** (sthg.): *quest'azione non è da persona bennata,* this is unworthy of a well-bred person **15.** (**Fraseologia**): *i tempi che furono,* time past,|| *chi è?,* who is it?; *sei tu?,* is it you?; *sono io,* it is I (*o fam.* it's me); *sono stato io a chiamarti,* it was I who called you || *come se nulla fosse,* as if nothing had happened || *è per questo che son venuto,* that's why I have come || *è un pezzo che ti osserviamo,* we have been watching you for some time || *or è, sono vent'anni, vent'anni or sono,* twenty years ago || *quello che è stato, è stato,* let bygones be bygones || *sarà!...,* (*esprimendo dubbio*) it may be (so)!... || *se io fossi in te,* if I were you || *se non fosse stato per mio padre, sarei stato rovinato,* if it had not been (*o but*) for my father I should have been ruined || *sono due ore che ti aspetto,* I have been waiting for you (for) two hours || — *alla disperazione,* to be in despair || — *alla fame,* to be starving || — *a spasso,* to be out of work || — *di ritorno,* to have just returned; — *di viaggio,* to be about to leave || — *fuori di sè,* to be beside oneself || — *in ghingheri,* to be all dressed up || — *in grado di fare ql.co.,* (*capace*) to be capable of doing sthg. (*o* to be able to do sthg.); (*in condizione di*) to be in a position to do sthg. || — *in piedi,* to be standing || — *in ribasso,* to be on the down-grade || — *in sè,* to be conscious || — *su,* (*alzato*) to be up || — *sul punto di, in procinto di fare ql.co.,* to be about to do sthg.
èssere, *s.m.* **1.** being, individual: *esseri umani,* human beings || *l'Essere Supremo,* the Supreme Being **2.** (*creatura*) creature: *un — spregevole,* a despicable creature (*o fellow*); *un povero —,* a poor creature **3.** (*esistenza*) existence: *l'— dello spirito,* the existence of the spirit **4.** (*stato*) state, condition.

essiccaménto, *s.m.* drying up, desiccation, exsiccation.
essiccànte, *ag.* drying, desiccative, desiccant, exsiccative, exsiccant.
essiccàre, *v.t.* to dry (up), to desiccate, to exsiccate: — *al forno,* to kiln-dry; — *al sole,* to dry in the sun || **essiccàrsi,** *v.r.* to dry up, to become dry: *il pozzo si è essiccato,* the well has dried up (*o* has become dry).
essiccatìvo, *ag.* drying, desiccative.
essiccàto, *ag.* dried: — *all'aria,* air-dried; — *al sole,* sun-dried.
essiccatóio, *s.m.* **1.** (*ind.*) drier; (*chim.*) desiccator: — *a griglia,* lattice drier **2.** (*stanza*) drying-room; (*capannone, reparto di essiccazione*) drying-house.
essiccazióne, *s.f.* drying process, desiccation, exsiccation.
ésso, *pron. pers. m.* 3ª *persona sing.* **1.** *sogg.* **he** (*riferito a uomo o animale maschio; se riferito a persona, l'uso corretto richiede egli*); **it** (*riferito a cosa o animale di sesso non specificato*): *ho comperato un cane,* — *è un setter,* I have bought a dog, it is a setter; *prendi il tuo libro,* — *è sul tavolo,* take your book, it is on the table **2.** *obliquo* **him** (*riferito a persona o animale maschio*); **it** (*riferito a cosa o animale di sesso non specificato*): *questo documento deve essere firmato dal padre del richiedente o da chi per —,* this document must be signed by the applicant's father or some other person in authority; *questo libro è molto bello, ho trovato l'ultima parte di — molto interessante,* this book is very good, I found the last part of it very interesting **3.** (*pleonastico*): *con — loro,* with them || *ag. dimostrativo* (*arc.*) **this, that:** — *albero,* that tree.
éssi, *pron. pers. m.* 3ª *persona pl.* **1.** *sogg.* **they:** *scrivono molto poco,* they write very little; *guarda quei fiori,* — *sono già tutti appassiti,* look at those flowers, they are already all withered **2.** *obliquo* **them:** *cinque di — sono già andati via,* five of them have already left; *passeremo in Francia dieci giorni e sei di — certamente a Parigi,* we shall spend ten days in France and six of them certainly in Paris.
essotèrico, *ag.* exoteric: *dottrine essoteriche,* exoteric doctrines.
essudàre, *v.i.* (*med.*) to exude.
essudàto, *s.m.* (*med.*) exudate.
essudazióne, *s.f.* (*med.*) exudation.
est, *s.m.* east: *a — di Londra,* east of London; *venti dell'—,* east (*o* easterly) winds; *nel nostro viaggio verso —,* on our eastward journey; *viaggiammo verso —,* we travelled eastwards.
èstasi, *s.f.* ecstasy, rapture: *le estasi di S. Teresa,* the ecstasies of St. Theresa; *andare in — per ql.co.,* to go (*o* to be thrown) into ecstasies over sthg.; *essere in —,* to be in an ecstasy (*o* to be enraptured *o* to be extremely happy *o* to be delighted); *mandare in — qlcu.,* to throw s.o. into ecstasies.
estasiàre, *v.t.* to enrapture, to throw into ecstasies; to estasize; (*fam.*) to delight || **estasiàrsi,** *v.r.* to be enraptured, to go into ecstasies.
estasiàto, *ag.* enraptured; (*fam.*) extremely delighted: *la guardava —,* he was gazing at her in rapture; *ne fummo estasiati,* we were extremely delighted with it.
estatàre, *v.i.* (*rar.*) to spend the summer.
estàte, *s.f.* summer: *d'—, in —,* in summer; *tempo, periodo d'—,* summertime || — *di San Martino,* St. Martin's (*o* St. Luke's) summer; (*amer.*) Indian summer || « *Sogno d'una notte di mezza — »,* (*lett.*) "A Mid-summer-Night's Dream".
estaticaménte, *av.* ecstatically.
estàtico, *ag.* ecstatic; (*fam.*) (*estasiato*) enraptured.
estemporaneaménte, *av.* extemporaneously, impromptu, extempore: *parlare —,* to speak extempore (*o* impromptu).
estemporàneo, *ag.* extemporaneous, extempory, extempore, impromptu; offhand: *un discorso —,* an

impromptu (o extempore) address; *poeta* —, improvisator (o improvisatore).

estèndere, *v.t.* to extend; to expand; to enlarge (anche *fig.*); (*prolungare*) to prolong; (*accrescere*) to increase: — *il proprio potere*, to increase (o to extend) one's power ‖ **estèndersi,** *v.r.* to extend, to stretch: — *fino a*, to reach (o to extend as far as).

estendíbile, *ag.* extensible.

estendibilità, *s.f.* extensibility.

estendiménto, *s.m.* extending.

estènse, *ag.* of the ducal family of Este.

estensímetro, *s.m.* (*metal.*) strain gauge.

estensióne, *s.f.* **1.** (*l'estendere*) extension: — *delle membra*, extension of the limbs; *noi ci battiamo per l'*— *della cultura*, we are fighting for the extension of culture **2.** (*distesa*) expanse, extent: *una grande* — *d'acque morte*, a broad expanse of still water **3.** (*ampiezza*) extent (anche *fig.*): *dalla torre potemmo vedere tutta l'*— *del parco*, from the tower we could see the full extent of the park; *sarai stupito dell'*— *della sua cultura*, you'll be astonished at the extent of his learning; *siamo rovinati, in tutta l'*— *del termine*, we are ruined, in the full meaning of the word **4.** (*mus.*) range, compass: — *di una voce*, range (o compass) of a voice.

estensivaménte, *av.* extensively.

estensívo, *ag.* extensive: *agricoltura estensiva*, extensive agriculture.

estènso, *ag.* (*rar.*) extended ‖ *per* —, in detail; (*completamente*) in full.

estensóre, *s.m.* **1.** (*scrittore, compilatore, redattore*) writer, author; drafter; compiler; (*dir.*) drafts-man **2.** (*anat.*) extensor (muscle) **3.** (*ginnastica*) chest-expander.

estensòrio, *ag.* extensor (*attributivo*): *muscolo* —, (*anat.*) extensor muscle.

estenuànte, *ag.* exhausting, enervating; (*che affatica*) tiring, fatiguing, weary, wearisome: *un clima* —, an enervating climate; *lavoro* —, fatiguing (o very hard) work; *viaggio* —, weary (o wearisome) journey.

estenuàre, *v.t.* to tire out; to wear out; (*indebolire*) to weaken: *quel lungo viaggio lo estenuò*, that long journey tired him out ‖ **estenuàrsi,** *v.r.* to get exhausted; to exhaust oneself; to tire oneself out; to get tired.

estenuatívo, *ag.* exhausting.

estenuàto, *ag.* exhausted, tired out, worn out.

estenuazióne, *s.f.* exhaustion.

Èster, *no.pr.f.* Esther ‖ *dim.* Essie, Hetty.

esterificazióne, *s.f.* (*chim.*) esterification.

esterióre, *ag.* outward (*attributivo*); outside (*attributivo*); exterior; outer (*attributivo*): *aspetto* —, outward appearance; *il mondo* —, the outside world; *muro* —, outer (o exterior) wall ‖ *s.m.* exterior; outside; outward appearance; external: *non giudicare alcun uomo dall'*—, don't judge any man by his outward appearance.

esteriorità *s.f.* outward appearance: *vane* —, vain appearances.

esteriorizzazióne, *s.f.* externalization; embodiment.

esteriorménte, *av.* exteriorly; outwardly.

esterminàre, *e derivati, V.* sterminàre, *e derivati*.

esternaménte, *av.* externally; exteriorly; outside; outwardly.

esternàre, *v.t.* (*esprimere*) to express, to utter; (*mostrare*) to display, to show; to manifest: — *la propria ammirazione per qlcu.*, to express one's admiration for s.o.

estèrno, *ag.* **1.** external, outer, exterior; outward (*attributivo*); outside (*attributivo*): *alunno* —, day pupil (o day boy); *angolo* —, exterior (o outer) angle; *lato* —, outer side; *il mondo* —, the external world; *scala esterna*, outside staircase; *segni esterni*, outward signs; *superficie esterna*, outer (o exterior) surface **2.** (*farm.*) external ‖ *solo per uso* —, for external use; (*sulle etichette*) "not to be taken" ‖ *s.m.* **1.** outside: *all'*—, on the outside (o outside): *all'*— *della casa*, outside the house; *dall'*—, from the outside; *l'*— *della nostra casa è*

molto vecchio, the outside of our house is very old **2.** (*di medico in un ospedale*) non-resident assistant **3.** (*di collegio*) day-pupil, day-boy **4.** (*cine.*) exterior shot.

èstero, *ag.* foreign: *commercio* —, foreign trade; *corrispondente in lingue estere*, foreign correspondent; *una saggia politica estera*, a wise foreign policy ‖ *ministero degli Affari Esteri*, (*in Gran Bretagna*) Foreign Office; (*negli Stati Uniti*) State Department; (*altrove*) Ministry of Foreign Affairs; *ministro degli* (*Affari*) *Esteri*, (*in Gran Bretagna*) Foreign Secretary; (*negli Stati Uniti*) Secretary of State; (*altrove*) Minister of Foreign Affairs ‖ *s.m.* foreign countries: *mantenere buone relazioni con l'*—, to keep good relations with foreign countries ‖ *all'*—, abroad: *in patria e all'*—, at home and abroad; *andare all'*—, to go abroad; *dall'*—, from abroad.

esterofilía, *s.f.* xenomania.

esterrefàtto, *ag.* **1.** (*atterrito*) terrified, aghast: *rimasi* —, I was terrified **2.** (*sbalordito*) amazed: *mi quardò con aria esterrefatta*, he stared at me round-eyed (o with amazement).

estesaménte, *av.* extensively; widely.

estesiología, *s.f.* (*med.*) esthesiology.

estesiòmetro, *s.m.* (*med.*) esthesiometer.

estéso, *ag.* **1.** large, wide; extensive, ample: *fece estese ricerche*, he made extensive researches; *Londra è una città molto estesa*, London is a very large town ‖ *per* —, (*dettagliatamente*) in detail; (*in tutte lettere*) in full **2.** (*diffuso*) widespread.

estèta, *s.m.* aesthete.

estètica, *s.f.* (*fil.*) aesthetics.

esteticaménte, *av.* aesthetically.

estètico, *ag.* aesthetic(al).

estetísmo, *s.m.* aestheticism.

estetísta, *s.c.* beautician.

estimàre, *v.t.* (*rar.*) to estimate.

estimatívo, *ag.* (*rar.*) estimative.

estimatóre, *s.m.*, **estimatríce,** *s.f.* estimator; appraiser; connoisseur: — *pubblico*, (*dir.*) official estimator.

estimazióne, *s.f.* (*letter.*) per **stíma.**

èstimo, *s.m.* **1.** (*amm.*) estimate; evaluation; rating **2.** (*imposta sui beni immobili*) land-tax.

estínguere, *v.t.* **1.** to put out; to extinguish: *quanto all'incendio, tentarono di estinguerlo*, as to the fire, they tried to put it out (o to extinguish it); — *la* (*propria*) *sete*, to slake (o to quench) one's thirst **2.** *fig.* (*saldare, pagare*) to extinguish, to pay off: — *un debito*, to pay off a debt ‖ **estínguersi,** *v.r.* to go out; (*finire*) to die; to die out, to come to an end: *la loro dinastia si estinse*, their dynasty died out (o came to an end).

estinguíbile, *ag.* extinguishable.

estintívo, *ag.* extinctive.

estínto, *ag.* **1.** extinct; extinguished **2.** (*morto*) dead, deceased ‖ *gli estinti*, the dead ‖ *s.m.* deceased man: *l'*—, (*dir.*) the deceased.

estintóre, *s.m.* extinguisher: — *a schiuma*, foam extinguisher; — *d'incendio*, fire-extinguisher.

estinzióne, *s.f.* **1.** extinction; (*di incendio*) quenching; extinction, putting out; (*di sete*) quenching **2.** (*di specie, razza*) extinction; dying out **3.** (*di debito*) paying off, wiping out **4.** (*di calce*) slaking.

estirpàbile, *ag.* eradicable, extirpable (anche *fig.*).

estirpaménto, *s.m.* extirpation, eradication (anche *fig.*); uprooting, uprootal.

estirpàre, *v.t.* **1.** to extirpate, to eradicate, to root out (anche *fig.*): — *il delitto*, to eradicate crime; — *delle erbacce*, to extirpate (o to pull out) weeds; — *un male sociale*, to extirpate a social evil **2.** (*chir.*) (*denti*) to pull out; (*tumori*) to extirpate.

estirpatóre, *s.m.* **1.** extirpator, eradicator (anche *fig.*) **2.** (*mec. agr.*) grubber.

estirpazióne, *s.f.* **1.** extirpation, eradication (anche *fig.*) **2.** (*chir.*) (*di dente*) extraction; (*di tumore*) extirpation.

estívo, *ag.* summer (*attributivo*); summery: *corsi*

estivi, summer school; *ora estiva*, summer time (*o* daylight-saving); *stazione estiva*, summer resort; *vacanze estive*, summer holidays (*o* summer vacation).

estòllere, *v.t.* to extol, to exalt, to praise; (*poet.*) to raise || **estòllersi**, *v.r.* (*poet.*) to rise.

èstone, *ag.s.c.* Esthonian || *s.m.* (*lingua*) Esthonian.

Estònia, *no.pr.f.* (*geog.*) Esthonia.

estòrcere, *v.t.* to extort; to wring: — *una confessione a qlcu.*, to extort a confession from s.o.; — *denari a qlcu.*, to extort money from s.o.; — *un favore a qlcu.*, to wring a favour from (*o* out of) s.o.

estorsióne, *s.f.* extortion.

estòrto, *ag.* extorted.

estradàre, *v.t.* (*dir.*) to extradite.

estradizióne, *s.f.* (*dir.*) extradition.

estradòsso, *s.m.* (*arch.*) extrados.

estradotàle, *ag.* (*dir.*) paraphernal: *beni estradotali*, paraphernalia.

estragiudiziàle, *ag.* (*dir.*) extrajudicial.

estralegàle, *ag.* (*dir.*) extralegal.

estraneaménte, *av.* extraneously.

estràneo, *ag.* 1. extraneous; (*che non ha relazione*) alien, not related; not connected (with sthg.): *corpo* —, foreign body; *questioni estranee al soggetto in discussione*, questions not connected with (*o* alien to) the matter in hand; *ciò era affatto — alla questione*, this had no connection with the question; *si mantenne — alla lite*, he took no part in the quarrel 2. (*straniero*) foreign; alien: *costumanze estranee*, foreign customs; *tutto ciò le era* —, all this was foreign to her 3. (*alieno, contrario*) alien: — *alla politica*, alien to politics || *s.m.* stranger, foreigner: *è quasi un — in casa propria*, he is like a stranger in his own house.

estraniàre, *v.t.* to estrange: *la sua condotta lo ha estraniato dai suoi amici*, his conduct has estranged him from his friends || **estraniàrsi**, *v.r.* to get estranged; to grow indifferent (to s.o., sthg.): — *dal mondo*, to live estranged from the world.

estraparlamentàre, *ag.* extraparliamentary.

estrapolàre, *v.t.* (*mat.*) to extrapolate.

estrapolazióne, *s.f.* (*mat.*) extrapolation.

estràrre, *v.t.* 1. to draw out, to take out, to pull out: *mise una mano in tasca ed estrasse una rivoltella*, he put his hand in his pocket and drew out a revolver; — *a sorte*, to draw lots; — *bei passi da un libro*, to extract (*o* to copy out) fine passages from a book; — *un dente*, to extract a tooth (*o fam.* to draw *o* to pull out a tooth): *farsi — un dente*, to have a tooth out; — *olio dalle olive*, to extract oil from olives; — *una pallottola da una ferita*, to extract a bullet from a wound || — *una radice*, (*mat.*) to extract a root 2. (*da miniera*) to mine; to dig out; (*da una cava*) to quarry.

estraterritoriàle, *ag.* (*dir.*) ex(tra)territorial.

estraterritorialità, *s.f.* (*dir.*) ex(tra)territoriality.

estrattívo, *ag.* extractive: *industria estrattiva*, extractive industry.

estràtto, *s.m.* 1. (*essenza*) extract: — *di carne di manzo*, beef extract; *estratti medicinali*, medicinal extracts 2. (*riassunto, condensato*) abstract, resumé, summary; excerpt; (*articolo, saggio pubblicato a parte*) off-print 3. (*certificato*) certificate; (*dir.*) abstract: — *di nascita*, birth-certificate; — *di un titolo di proprietà*, an abstract of title 4. — *conto*, (*comm.*) statement of account.

estrattóre, *s.m.* 1. extractor 2. (*mec.*) extractor, puller: — *per mozzi*, hub puller; — *per ruote*, wheel puller.

estravagànte, *ag.* (*rar.*) extravagant || *s.f.* (*dir. canonico*) extravagant (decree).

estrazióne, *s.f.* 1. extraction: — *di un dente*, extraction (*o* drawing) of a tooth 2. — *di radice*, (*mat.*) evolution 3. (*da miniera*) mining; digging (out); (*da cava*) quarrying 4. (*di lotteria*) drawing (of lottery numbers) || — *a sorte*, drawing lots.

Estremadúra, *no.pr.f.* (*geog.*) Estremadura.

estremaménte, *av.* extremely; in the extreme.

estremísmo, *s.m.* extremism.

estremísta, *s.c.* extremist: — *di destra*, extreme rightist; — *di sinistra*, extreme leftist.

estremità, *s.f.* 1. (*parte estrema*) extremity; end; point; tip: *le — della Terra*, the uttermost ends of the earth; — *di una corda*, the end of a rope; *l'— di un dito*, the tip of a finger; *l'— di uno spillo*, the point of a pin; — *superiore, inferiore di un lago*, head, foot of a lake 2. *pl.* (*arti*) extremities, limbs: *le — inferiori*, the nether limbs; *le — superiori*, the upper limbs 3. (*eccesso, estremo*) extremity, extreme; last degree; urgency: *l'— di un bisogno*, the urgency of a need; *l'— della sofferenza*, the last degree of suffering.

estrèmo, *ag.* 1. extreme; utmost: *capo, punto* —, extreme end, point; *la sua estrema gentilezza*, his extreme kindness || *estrema destra, sinistra*, (*pol.*) extreme right, left || *l'Estremo Oriente*, the Far East || *estrema unzione*, (*teol.*) Extreme Unction 2. (*eccessivo, intenso*) intense; excessive: *freddo* —, intense cold; *piacere* —, excessive pleasure; *egli è in una estrema miseria*, he is in extreme poverty (*o* in dire distress *o* in utter want) 3. (*drastico*) drastic; severe: *misure estreme*, drastic (*o* extreme) measures; *essere — nelle proprie opinioni*, to be extreme in one's views (*o* to hold extreme opinions) || *s.m.* 1. extreme, extremity (anche *fig.*): *scrupoloso all'*—, scrupulous in the extreme (*o* to the highest degree); *andare agli estremi*, to go to extremes; *portare le cose all'*—, to carry matters to extremes; *provare l'— della contentezza*, to feel extremely joyful || *essere agli estremi*, (*morente*) to be on point of death || *gli estremi si toccano*, prov. extremes meet (*o* too far east is west) 2. *pl.* (*punti fondamentali*): *credo di aver trovato gli estremi per un processo a loro carico*, (*dir.*) I think I have found sufficient ground for an action against them.

estrinsecaménte, *av.* extrinsically.

estrinsecaménto, *s.m.* expression; manifestation.

estrinsecàre, *v.t.* (*esprimere*) to express; (*manifestare*) to manifest; to show; to evince || **estrinsecàrsi**, *v.r.* 1. to express one's thoughts; to express one's feelings 2. (*apparire*) to appear.

estrinsecazióne, *s.f.* expression; manifestation.

estrínseco, *ag.* extrinsic.

èstro, *s.m.* 1. (*ispirazione creativa*) inspiration: — *poetico*, poetic inspiration (*o* fire) 2. (*ghiribizzo*) fancy: *lo ha preso l'— di viaggiare*, he has taken a fancy to travelling 3. (*capriccio*) whim; caprice; freak: *ella si comporta sempre secondo l'*—, she always behaves according to the whim of the moment 4. (*entom.*) gadfly.

estrométtere, *v.t.* to turn out; to extrude.

estromissióne, *s.f.* expulsion.

estrosaménte, *av.* whimsically; capriciously; freakishly.

estróso, *ag.* 1. capricious; whimsical; freakish 2. (*ispirato*) inspired: *un compositore* —, an inspired composer.

estrovèrso, *ag.* extroverted || *s.m.* extrovert.

estroversióne, *s.f.* extroversion.

estrúdere, *v.t.* (*ind.*) to extrude.

estrusióne, *s.f.* (*metal.*) extrusion.

estuàrio, *s.m.* estuary; (*di fiumi scozzesi*) firth.

estuóso, *ag.* (*letter.*) 1. ardent 2. (*tempestoso*) tempestuous; stormy.

esuberànte, *ag.* 1. exuberant: *persona, temperamento* —, exuberant person, nature 2. (*sovrabbondante*) overabundant.

esuberànza, *s.f.* 1. exuberance 2. (*abbondanza*) plenty; (*sovrabbondanza*) over-abundance: — *di manodopera*, excess (*o* redundancy) of labour || *ad* —, plentifully.

esulàre, *v.i.* 1. to go into exile 2. *fig.* to be beyond (sthg.): *questo esula dalla mia competenza*, this is beyond my capabilities.

esulceràre, *v.t.* 1. (*med.*) ulcerate; to exulcerate 2. *fig.* (*esacerbare*) to exacerbate; to exulcerate.

esulceratívo, *ag.* exulcerative.

esulcerazióne, *s.f.* 1. exulceration, ulceration 2. *fig.* *esacerbamento*) exacerbation.

èsule, *s.c.* exile; (*profugo, profuga*) refugee: *Mazzini andò — in Inghilterra,* Mazzini as an exile went to England.

esultànte, *ag.* exultant, exulting, rejoicing.

esultànza, *s.f.* exultation, exultancy; great joy.

esultàre, *v.i.* to exult, to rejoice; to triumph: *esultammo alle belle notizie, per il nostro successo,* we rejoiced at the good news, over our success.

esultazióne, *s.f.* (*rar.*) exultation.

esumàre, *v.t.* 1. to exhume, to disinter: *la salma verrà esumata domani con una mesta cerimonia,* the body will be exhumed to-morrow with due ceremony 2. *fig.* to unearth, to bring to light: *documenti esumati dagli archivi,* documents brought to light from (*o* dug out of) the archives.

esumazióne, *s.f.* 1. exhumation, disinterment 2. *fig.* unearthing: *l'— di un documento importante,* the unearthing of an important document.

età, *s.f.* 1. age: *dalla più tenera —,* from one's earliest years; *differenza di —,* disparity of age; *due figli in tenera —,* two children of tender age (*o* two very small children); *una persona di mezza —,* a middle-aged person; *un uomo d'—, già in —,* an elderly man; *che — hai?,* what's your age? (*o* how old are you?); *che — le daresti?,* how old would you take her to be?; *ha raggiunto l'— della discrezione,* he has reached the age of discretion; *morì all'— di ottant'anni,* he died at the age of eighty; *non dimostri la tua —,* you don't look your age; *porti bene l'— che hai,* you bear your years well; *sono all'incirca della tua stessa —,* I am about your age; *aver l'— della ragione,* to have reached the age of discretion; *aver la stessa —,* to be the same age; *essere in — da marito,* to be old enough to marry; *morire in — avanzata,* to die at a good old age 2. (*dir.*) age: *— maggiore,* coming of age: *quand'egli raggiunse la maggiore —,* when he came of age; *era ancora in — minore,* he was still under age 3. (*periodo, epoca*) age; period: *l'— della pietra,* the Stone Age; *l'— di mezzo,* the Middle Ages; *l'— dell'oro,* the Golden Age 4. (*generazione*) generation: *di — in —,* from generation to generation.

etàde, *s.f.* (*poet.*) age.

etàno, *s.m.* (*chim.*) ethane.

Etèocle, *no.pr.m.* (*mit.*) Eteocles.

etèra, *s.f.* 1. (*nella Grecia antica*) hetaera (*pl.* hetaerae), hetaira (*pl.* hetairai) 2. (*cortigiana*) courtesan.

ètere, *s.m.* 1. (*chim.*) ether 2. (*poet.*) (*aria*) air, sky, ether, aether.

etèreo, *ag.* 1. ethereal 2. (*celestiale*) heavenly.

etèrico, *ag.* (*chim.*) etheric.

eterificàre, *v.t.* (*chim.*) to etherify.

eterificazióne, *s.f.* (*chim.*) etherification.

eterísmo, *s.m.* (*patol.*) etherism.

eterizzàre, *v.t.* (*med.*) to etherize.

eterizzazióne, *s.f.* (*med.*) etherization.

eternàle, *ag.* (*poet.*) eternal.

eternaménte, *av.* eternally.

eternàre, *v.t.* to etern(al)ize, to make eternal, to immortalize, to perpetuate: *se potessimo — quest'ora,* if only we could make this hour last for ever || **eternàrsi,** *v.r.* to become eternal, to become immortal; to last for ever.

eterním, *s.m.* (*edil.*) asbestos lumber, asbestos cement material.

eternità, *s.f.* 1. eternity 2. (*fam.*) (*lungo lasso di tempo*): *era un'— che non la vedevo,* I had not seen her for ages (*o* for a whole month of Sundays); *ti ho aspettato un'—,* I have been waiting for you for a very long time.

etèrno, *ag.* 1. (*senza tempo*) eternal: *Eterno Padre,* the Eternal; *verità eterne,* eternal truths; *la vita eterna,* eternal life 2. (*senza fine*) eternal, everlasting, endless, unceasing, never-ending: *eterna gioia,* everlasting joy; *— dolore,* endless pain; *lesse un discorso —,* he read a never-ending speech || *in —,* for ever || *la Città Eterna,* the Eternal City || *s.m.* eternity || *l'Eterno,* (*Dio*) the Eternal.

eteròclito, *ag.* 1. (*gram.*) heteroclite 2. *fig.* irregular; strange; anomalous.

eterocromàtico, *ag.* heterochromatic.

eterodína, *s.f.* (*rad.*) heterodyne.

eterodossía, *s.f.* heterodoxy.

eterodòsso, *ag.* heterodox.

eterogeneità, *s.f.* heterogeneity.

eterogèneo, *ag.* heterogeneous.

eterogènesi, *s.f.* (*biol.*) heterogenesis.

eterogenía, *s.f.* (*biol.*) heterogenesis.

eterogènico, *ag.* (*biol.*) heterogenetic.

eterolalía, *s.f.* (*med.*) heterolalia.

eteròmane, *s.m.* (*patol.*) etheromaniac.

eteromanía, *s.f.* (*patol.*) etheromania.

eteromorfísmo, *s.m.* heteromorphism.

eteromórfo, *ag.* heteromorphic, heteromorphous.

eteronomía, *s.f.* heteronomy.

eterotassía, *s.f.* (*bot.*) heterotaxy.

etèsio, *ag.* etesian.

ètica, *s.f.* ethics.

eticaménte, *av.* ethically.

etichétta[1]**,** *s.f.* 1. (*cartellino per indicazioni*) label; docket: — *gommata,* gummed label (*o* stick-on label); *bottiglie con l'— «whisky»,* bottles labelled "whisky"; *attaccare un'—,* to paste (*o* to stick) a label; *mettere l'— a delle bottiglie,* to label some bottles 2. (*cartellino legato a bagagli*) tally; (*amer.*) tag.

etichétta[2]**,** *s.f.* (*cerimoniale*) etiquette; formality, ceremony: — *di Corte,* Court ceremonial; *ricevimento senza tanta —,* informal party; *senza —,* unceremoniously; *è contrario all'—...,* it is bad form to... (*o* it is not etiquette to...).

ètico[1]**,** *ag.* (*fil.*) ethical, moral; (*rar.*) ethic.

ètico[2]**,** *ag.* (*patol.*) hectic, consumptive: *febbre etica,* hectic fever || *s.m.* consumptive.

etil-cellulòsa, *s.f.* (*chim.*) ethyl-cellulose.

etìle, *s.m.* (*chim.*) ethyl.

etilène, *s.m.* (*chim.*) ethylene.

etìlico, *ag.* (*chim.*) ethylic; ethyl (*attributivo*): *alcool —,* ethyl alcohol; *etere —,* ethylic ether.

etilísmo, *s.m.* (*patol.*) alcoholism.

ètimo, *s.m.* etymon (*pl.* etymons, etyma), root word.

etimología, *s.f.* etymology.

etimologicaménte, *av.* etymologically.

etimològico, *ag.* etymologic(al).

etimologísta, etimòlogo, *s.m.* etymologist.

etiología, *s.f.* aetiology; etiology.

etíope, *ag.s.m.* Ethiopian.

Etiòpia, *no.pr. f.* (*geog.*) Ethiopia.

etiòpico, *ag.* Ethiopian: *la guerra etiopica,* the Ethiopian War || *s.m.* 1. (*abitante*) Ethiopian || *gli Etiopici,* the Ethiopians 2. (*lingua*) Ethiopic || **etiòpica,** *s.f.* Ethiopian.

etisía, *s.f.* (*patol.*) phthisis.

etmoidàle, *ag.* (*anat.*) ethmoidal.

etmòide, *s.m.* (*anat.*) ethmoid.

Ètna, *no.pr.m.* (*geog.*) (Mount) Etna.

etnèo, *ag.* Etnean.

etnicaménte, *av.* ethnically.

ètnico, *ag.* ethnic(al).

etnografía, *s.f.* ethnography.

etnograficaménte, *av.* ethnographically.

etnogràfico, *ag.* ethnographic(al).

etnògrafo, *s.m.* ethnographer.

etnología, *s.f.* ethnology.

etnologicaménte, *av.* ethnologically.

etnològico, *ag.* ethnologic(al).

etnòlogo, *s.m.* ethnologist.

etología, *s.f.* ethology.

etològico, *ag.* ethological.

etòlogo, s.m. ethologist.
ètra, s.f. (poet.) ether.
Etrúria, no.pr.f. (geog. st.) Etruria.
etrúsco, ag. Etruscan; (rar.) Etrurian: vaso —, Etruscan vase || s.m. **1.** (abitante) Etruscan; (rar.) Etrurian || gli Etruschi, the Etruscans **2.** (lingua) Etruscan.
etruscología, s.f. Etruscology.
etruscòlogo, s.m. Etruscologist.
ettacòrdo, s.m. (mus.) heptachord
ettaèdro, s.m. (geom.) heptahedron.
ettagonàle, ag. (geom.) heptagonal.
ettàgono, ag. (geom.) heptagonal || s.m. (geom.) heptagon.
èttaro, s.m. hectare (misura di superficie = 2.471 a.).
ettasíllabo, ag. (poes.) heptasyllabic.
ètte, s.m. (fam.): non capire un —, to understand nothing at all; non dire —, not to speak a single word.
ètto, ettogràmmo, s.m. hectogram(me) (misura di peso = 3.527 oz.).
ettòlitro, s.m. hectolitre; (amer.) hectoliter (misura di capacità = 22 gal.).
ettòmetro, s.m. hectometre; (amer.) hectometer (misura di lunghezza = 109.36 yd.)
Èttore, Ettòrre, no.pr.m. Hector.
Eubèa, no.pr.f. (geog.) Evvoia; (st.) Euboea.
eucalípto, s.m. (bot.) eucalyptus (pl. eucalyptuses, eucalypti).
eucaliptòlo, s.m. (farm.) eucalyptol.
eucaristía, s.f. (eccl.) Eucharist; Holy Communion; Holy Supper: accostarsi all'—, to communicate.
eucarístico, ag. Eucharistic(al).
Euclíde, no.pr.m. (st. mat.) Euclid.
euclidèo, ag. Euclidean.
eudemonísmo, s.m. (fil.) eudaemonism.
eudiòmetro, s.m. (chim.) eudiometer.
Eufèmia[1], no.pr.f. Euphemia || dim. Effie, Phemie.
eufemía[2], s.f. (rar.) euphemism.
eufèmico, ag. euphemistic(al).
eufemismo, s.m. euphemism.
eufemisticaménte, av. euphemistically.
eufemístico, ag. euphemistic(al).
eufonía, s.f. euphony.
eufonicaménte, av. euphonically, euphoniously.
eufònico, ag. euphonic, euphonious.
eufòrbia, s.f. (bot.) Euphorbia.
euforbiàcee, s.f.pl. (bot.) Euphorbiaceae.
euforia, s.f. **1.** euphoria, euphory; well-being; light
-heartedness **2.** (patol.) euphoria, euphory.
eufòrico, ag. **1.** euphoric, light-hearted, in high spirits, elated **2.** (patol.) euphoric.
eufràsia, s.f. (bot.) euphrasy; (pop.) eyebright.
Eufràte, no.pr.m. (geog. st.) Euphrates.
Eufròsine, no.pr.f. (mit.) Euphrosyne.
eufuísmo, s.m. (st. lett.) Euphuism.
eufuístico, ag. (lett.) Euphuistic.
eugàneo, ag. (geog.) Euganean: i Colli Euganei, the Euganean Hills.
eugenètica, s.f. eugenics.
eugenètico, ag. eugenic.
eugenía[1], s.f. eugenism.
Eugènia[2], no.pr.f. Eugenia || dim. Genie.
Eugènio, no.pr.m. Eugene || dim. Gene.
eugenísta, s.m. eugenist.
eugenòlo, s.m. (chim.) eugenol.
Eulàlia, no.pr.f. Eulalia.
Eumènidi, no.pr.f.pl. (mit.) Eumenides.
eumicèti, s.m.pl. (bot.) Eumycetes.
eunúco, s.m. eunuch.
eupepsía, s.f. (med.) eupepsia.
eupèptico, ag. (farm.) eupeptic.
eurasiàtico, ag.s.m. Eurasian.
Euridíce, no.pr.f. (mit.) Eurydice.
Eurípide, no.pr.m. (st. lett.) Euripides.
eurística, s.f. (fil.) heuristic.

eurístico, ag. (fil.) heuristic.
euritmía, s.f. eurhythmy.
euritmicaménte, av. eurhythmically.
eurítmico, ag. eurhythmic.
èuro, s.m. (vento) Eurus (south-easterly wind).
Euròpa[1], no.pr.f. (mit.) Europa.
Euròpa[2], no.pr.f. (geog.) Europe.
europeísmo, s.m. **1.** Europeanism **2.** (sentimento della unità europea) European outlook.
europeizzàre, v.t. to Europeanize.
europèo, ag.s.m. European || **europèa,** s.f. European.
euròpio, s.m. (chim.) europium.
euro(tele)visióne, s.f. (neol.) Eurovision.
Eusèbio, no.pr.m. Eusebius.
Eustàchio, no.pr.m. Eustace || trombe d'—, (anat.) Eustachian tubes.
eutanasía, s.f. euthanasia.
Eutèrpe, no.pr.f. (mit.) Euterpe.
eutèttico, ag. (metal.) eutectic: lega eutettica, eutectic alloy.
eutichiàni, s.m.pl. (st. relig.) Eutychians.
eutrofísmo, s.m. (med.) eutrophy.
Eutròpio, no.pr.m. (st. lett.) Eutropius.
Èva, no.pr.f. Eve, Eva || dim. Evie, Evelina.
evacuaménto, s.m. evacuation.
evacuàre, v.t. **1.** to evacuate; to empty, to void; to clear out: — una città, to evacuate a town **2.** (tec.) to evacuate; to drain (away, off); (gas) to remove: — l'acqua di una caldaia, to blow out a boiler || v.i. to evacuate, to withdraw.
evacuatívo, ag. (farm.) evacuative.
evacuàto, ag. evacuated.
evacuazióne, s.f. **1.** evacuation; withdrawal **2.** (tec.) scavenging.
evàdere, v.t. **1.** to dispatch; to fill, to complete: — una pratica, to dispatch an affair **2.** (eludere) to evade: — una tassa, to evade (o to escape) a tax || v.i. to escape; to run away; to break loose: — dalla prigione, to escape from prison (o to break goal).
Evàndro, no.pr.m. (lett.) Evander.
evanescènte, ag. evanescent, vanishing, fading.
evanescènza, s.f. **1.** evanescence **2.** (rad. tv.) fading.
evangeliàrio, s.m. evangeliary, evangelistary, evangeliarum.
evangelicaménte, av. evangelically.
evangèlico, ag. **1.** evangelic; according to the Gospel: dottore —, Gospel preacher (o evangelizer o evangelist) **2.** (protestante) evangelical || s.m. evangelical.
Evangelína, no.pr.f. Evangeline.
evangelísta, s.m. evangelist: S. Giovanni l'Evangelista, St. John the Evangelist.
evangelistàrio, s.m. evangelistary, evangelistarium.
evangelizzàre, v.t. to evangelize.
evangelizzatóre, s.m., **evangelizzatríce,** s.f. evangelizer.
evangelizzazióne, s.f. evangelization.
evangèlo, V. vangèlo.
evaporàbile, ag. (fis.) evaporable.
evaporànte, ag. (fis.) evaporating.
evaporàre, v.i., **evaporàrsi,** v.r. to evaporate: fare — un liquido, to evaporate (o to dry off) a liquid.
evaporatóre, s.m. (ind.) evaporator.
evaporazióne, s.f. (fis.) evaporation, vaporization.
evaporímetro, s.m. (fis.) evaporimeter.
evasióne, s.f. **1.** escape, flight; (sl.) get-away: il prigioniero aveva progettato per due anni la sua —, the prisoner had been planning his escape for two years **2.** (fiscale) evasion: — di una tassa, evasion of a tax **3.** (comm.): dare — a un ordine, to carry out (o to execute) an order (o amer. to fill an order); dare — a una pratica, (sl. comm.) to dispatch some business **4.** (lett.): aspirazione all'—, escapism; letteratura d'—, escapist literature.
evasivaménte, av. evasively.
evasívo, ag. evasive.

evàso, *s.m.* runaway, fugitive.

evasóre, *s.m.* evader: — *fiscale*, tax evader.

Evelína, *no.pr.f.* Eveline, Evelina, Evelyn.

evèllere, *v.t.* (*rar.*) to uproot, to eradicate, to extirpate.

evemerísmo, *s.m.* (*st. fil.*) euhemerism.

Evèmero, *no.pr.m.* (*st. fil.*) Euhemerus.

eveniènza, *s.f.* event; (*occorrenza*) occurrence, eventuality; (*occasione*) occasion: *in ogni* —, at all events (o in any case); *nell'* — *di una guerra*, in the event of a war; *per ogni* —, for any occasion; (*in caso di bisogno*) if need be (o in case of need); *nell'* — *che non venga*, in the event (o eventuality) of his not coming.

evènto, *s.m.* 1. event: *giornata piena di eventi*, eventful day; *un grande* —, a great event ‖ *in ogni* —, in any case (o at all events) 2. (*esito*) result, outcome: *giudicare ql.co. dall'* —, to judge sthg. by its result.

eventuàle, *ag.* eventual, possible, probable; contingent, incidental: *spese eventuali*, incidental charges (o contingent expenses); *contava su una parte degli eventuali profitti*, he was reckoning on a share in the eventual profits; *assicurarsi contro eventuali incidenti*, to ensure against possible accidents.

eventualità, *s.f.* eventuality; (*fam.*) (*circostanza, occorrenza*) event, occurrence: *in ogni* —, at all events; *nell'* — *della sua partenza*, in the event of his leaving; *prepararsi a ogni* —, to provide for all contingencies.

eventualménte, *av.* (*in caso*) in case, if that is the case, if that be the case: — *dovesse venire...*, in case he should come....

Everàrdo, *no.pr.m.* Everard.

Èverest, *no.pr.m.* (*geog.*) (Mount) Everest.

evèrso, *ag.* (*letter. poet.*) destroyed.

eversóre, *s.m.* (*letter. poet.*) destroyer.

evezióne, *s.f.* (*astr.*) evection.

èvia, *s.f.* (*letter.*) Bacchante.

evidènte, *ag.* evident, obvious, manifest, clear, plain: *errore* —, palpable (o glaring) error (o mistake); *è* — *che*, it stands to reason (o it is plain o it is a matter of course) that.

evidenteménte, *av.* evidently, obviously, clearly.

evidènza, *s.f.* 1. (*chiarezza*) evidence, obviousness, clearness: *alfine si arrese all'* —, at last he bowed to the facts; *cercò di negare l'* — *dei fatti*, he tried to deny the evidence of the facts; *mettere, porre in* —, to point out 2. (*risalto*) evidence, conspicuousness: *essere in* —, to be in evidence (o to be conspicuous o to be in the limelight); *mettere in* —, to show (o to exhibit o to display); *mettersi in* —, to make oneself conspicuous (o to put oneself forward o to draw attention to oneself).

evíncere, *v.t.* (*dir.*) to evict.

eviràre, *v.t.* 1. to emasculate, to evirate, to castrate 2. *fig.* to effeminate; to enfeeble.

eviràto, *ag.* 1. emasculate(d), castrated, evirated 2. (*effeminato*) effeminate, unmanly.

eviràzione, *s.f.* emasculation, eviration, castration.

evitàbile, *ag.* avoidable.

evitàre, *v.t.* 1. to avoid, to evade, to shun; to dodge: *cerca di* — *i cibi congelati*, try to avoid (o to abstain from o to eschew) frozen food; — *un colpo*, to avoid (o to evade o to dodge) a blow; — *una domanda*, to evade (o to dodge) a question (o to avoid answering a question directly); — *un ostacolo*, to dodge round an obstacle; — *qlcu.*, to avoid s.o. (o to keep out of s.o.'s way o to keep clear of s.o.); — *uno scoglio, un banco di sabbia*, (*mar.*) to steer clear of a reef, of a sandbank; — *di fare ql.co.*, to avoid doing sthg.: *do-*

vresti — *di correre quel rischio*, you should avoid running that risk; *non potei* — *di sentire le sue parole*, I couldn't avoid (o I couldn't help) hearing his words; — *di farsi vedere*, to avoid being seen 2. (*sfuggire a*) to escape: *evitò a malapena la morte, di farsi male*, he only just escaped death, being hurt (o hurting himself) 3. (*risparmiare*) to spare: — *una pena a qlcu.*, to spare s.o. trouble.

evizióne, *s.f.* (*dir.*) eviction.

èvo, *s.m.* age, time; times (*pl.*): — *moderno*, modern times ‖ *il Medio Evo*, the Middle Ages.

evocàre, *v.t.* 1. to evoke, to recall: *leggende che evocano il passato*, legends that evoke the past; — *la casa paterna*, to recall the old home 2. (*spiriti*) to evoke, to conjure, to call forth, to raise.

evocatívo, *ag.* evocative, evocatory.

evocatóre, *ag.* evocative, evocatory ‖ *s.m.*, evocatríce, *s.f.* evocator.

evocazióne, *s.f.* 1. evocation, conjuring up 2. (*di spiriti*) evocation, conjuring, calling forth, raising.

evolúta, *s.f.* (*geom.*) evolute.

evolúto, *ag.* 1. (*ben sviluppato*) well-developed: *un paese* —, a well-developed country 2. (*moderno*) modern: *una donna evoluta*, a modern woman; *un uomo* —, a man with up-to date (o modern) ideas.

evoluzióne, *s.f.* 1. (*biol.*) evolution, development 2. (*di truppe, navi, aerei*) evolution, manoeuvre; (*amer.*) manoeuvre, maneuver: — *in aria*, (*aer.*) flight manoeuvre.

evoluzionísmo, *s.m.* evolutionism.

evoluzionísta, *s.c.* evolutionist.

evoluzionístico, *ag.* evolutionistic.

evolvènte, *ag.* developing ‖ *s.f.* (*geom.*) involute.

evòlvere, *v.t.* (*rar.*) to evolve, to develop ‖ evòlversi, *v.r.* to evolve, to develop; (*fare progressi*) to make progress: *tutto si evolve*, everything evolves.

evúlso, *ag.* uprooted; eradicated.

evvíva, *s.m.* hurrah, hurray; (*fam. amer.*) hooray: *tre* — *per la nostra squadra!*, hip, hip, hurrah for our team!; *gridare* —, to hurrah (o to shout hurrah o to cheer) ‖ *inter.* hurrah!, hurray!; (*fam. amer.*) hooray! — *la Regina!*, long live the Queen!; (*meno comune*) hurrah for the Queen!.

ex-, (*prefisso*) ex-, former: — *-presidente*, ex- (o former o once) president; — *-marito*, ex-husband (o divorced husband); — *-combattente*, ex-service-man.

ex abrupto, *l.av.* (*lat.*) ex abrupto; suddenly; unexpectedly.

ex cathedra, *l.av.* (*lat.*) ex cathedra.

exempli gratia, *l.av.* (*lat.*) exempli gratia, for instance.

exequatur, *s.m.* (*lat.*) exequatur.

ex libris, *s.m.* (*lat.*) ex-libris.

ex professo, *l.av.* (*lat.*) ex professo, professedly.

extra, *prep.* (*lat.*) extra: *di qualità* —, first rate (*attributivo*); *qualità* —, best quality; *senza spese* —, with no extras; *spese* —, extra cost (o additional expenses).

extragiudiziàle, *ag.* extrajudicial.

extralegàle, *ag.* extralegal.

extraparlamentàre, *ag.* extraparliamentary.

extraterritoriàle, *ag.* ex(tra)territorial.

extremis, in, *l.av.* (*lat.*) in extremis, at the point of death: *pentimento in* —, death-bed repentance.

ex voto, *s.m.* (*lat.*) ex voto (offering), votive offering.

eziandío, *av.* (*rar.*) 1. also; as well as 2. (*perfino*) even.

Ezechía, *no.pr.m.* (*Bibbia*) Hezekiah.

Ezechièle, *no.pr.m.* (*Bibbia*) Ezekiel.

Èzio, *no.pr.m.* (*st.*) Aetius.

F

f, *s.f.m.* (*sesta lettera dell'alfabeto italiano*) f (*pl.* fs, f's) ‖ — *come Firenze*, (*tel.*) f for Frederick.

fa¹, *av.* ago: *alcuni anni* —, a few years ago; *non molto tempo* —, not long ago; *poco* (*tempo*) —, a short while ago; *tre anni* —, three years ago.

fa², *s.m.* (*mus.*) fa, F: *un pezzo in* —, a piece in F.

fabbisógno, *s.m.* **1.** (*bisogno*) needs (*pl.*), wants (*pl.*): *provvedere al — di qlcu.*, to provide for s.o.'s wants (*o* needs) **2.** (*ciò che è richiesto*) requirement (anche *comm.*) **3.** (*comm.*) (*riferito a fondi*) estimate of expenditure **4.** (*teat.*) property.

fàbbrica, *s.f.* **1.** (*opificio*) factory, manufactory; (*impianto*) plant; (*officina*) works (*pl.* con costruzione *sing.*): — *di automobili*, motor works (*o* amer. automobile plant); — *di carta*, paper-mill; — *di giocattoli*, toy factory; — *di mattoni*, brickyard (*o* brickfield); *capo* —, fore-man; *contabilità di* —, (*amm.*) factory book-keeping; *ispezione alle fabbriche*, factory-inspection; *marchio di* — (*depositato*), trade-mark; *modello di* —, registered pattern; *nuovo di* —, brand-new; *prezzo di* —, cost price ‖ *si lavora per la — dell'appetito*, (*scherz.*) we work for the necessity of eating **2.** (*fabbricazione*) manufacture, making, construction **3.** (*edificio*) building, structure; fabric: *la — del nuovo teatro*, the fabric of the new theatre ‖ *questa è la — di S. Pietro!*, this will take a month of Sundays! (*o* this is a job for life!) **4.** (*eccl.*) vestry-board.

fabbricàbile, *ag.* **1.** manufacturable **2.** (*su cui si può fabbricare*) : *area* —, (building) site (*o* building ground); (*zona per più abitazioni*) housing area.

fabbricànte, *s.m.* **1.** (*produttore*) manufacturer **2.** (*costruttore*) builder.

fabbricàre, *v.t.* **1.** (*produrre*) to manufacture, to produce **2.** (*costruire*) to build, to construct, to put up **3.** (*fare*) to make: *quei ragazzi stavano fabbricando un aquilone*, those boys were making a kite **4.** (*inventare*) to invent, to coin, to make up: — *delle storie su qlcu.*, to make up (*o* to invent) stories about s.o. **5.** (*falsificare*) to fabricate, to forge.

fabbricàto, *s.m.* building: — *ad uso di abitazione*, residential building; — *annesso*, out-building; — *per officina*, workshop-building; — *per uso industriale*, factory building; — *per uffici*, office building; *imposta sui fabbricati*, house tax (*o* amer. real estate tax).

fabbricatóre, *s.m.*, **fabbricatríce**, *s.f.* **1.** (*produttore*) maker, manufacturer **2.** (*costruttore*) builder **3.** fig. fabricator: — *di scandali*, fabricator of scandals.

fabbricazióne, *s.f.* **1.** (*produzione*) manufacture, make: — *all'ingrosso*, (*comm.*) wholesale manufacture; — *della carta*, paper making; — *nazionale*, home manufacture; *scarpe di — italiana*, shoes of Italian make (*o* manufacture); *la — di questa stoffa è molto costosa*, the manufacture (*o* the making) of this cloth is very expensive; *questi articoli sono di — inglese*, these articles are made (*o* manufactured) in England; *questo è proprio di vostra* —, this is your own make **2.** (*costruzione*) building **3.** (*invenzione*) invention **4.** (*falsificazione*) forgery.

fabbricería, *s.f.* (*eccl.*) vestry-board.

fabbricière, *s.m.* (*eccl.*) vestryman (*pl.* vestrymen); church-warden.

fàbbro, *s.m.* **1.** blacksmith, smith **2.** (*forgiatore*) forgeman (*pl.* forgemen), forger **3.** *fig.* (*poet.*) creator.

fabbroferràio, *s.m.* blacksmith, smith.

fabiàno, *ag.s.m.* (*della «Fabian Society»*) Fabian.

Fàbio, *no.pr.m.* (*st.*) Fabius ‖ *i Fabi*, the Fabii.

Fabrízio, *no.pr.m.* (*st.*) Fabricius.

faccènda, *s.f.* **1.** matter; business (*solo sing.*); affair; thing: — *di Stato*, State affair; *una brutta* —, a bad affair; *è tutt'altra* —, it's quite a different thing (*o* that's quite another matter); *è una — seria*, it is a serious matter (*o* business); *è un uomo pieno di faccende*, he is a very busy man; *ho un paio di faccende da sbrigare*, I have a couple of things to see to; *non è una — che ti riguarda*, this is no business of yours (*o* this is none of your business); *sono stanco dell'intera* —, I am tired of the whole business; *essere in faccende*, to be busy **2.** *pl.* (*lavori domestici*) household duties; housework (*sing.*): *essere in faccende*, to be doing one's housework; *sbrigare le faccende*, to do the housework.

faccendièra, **faccendóna**, *s.f.*, **faccendière**, **faccendóne** *s.m.* busybody, meddler.

faccétta, *s.f.* **1.** (*visetto*) little face **2.** (*geom. min.*) facet.

faccettàre, *V.* **sfaccettàre**.

faccettatúra, *V.* **sfaccettatúra**.

facchinàggio, *s.m.* **1.** porterage: *spese di* —, porterage **2.** *fig.* (*lavoro pesantissimo*) drudgery.

facchinàta, *s.f.* **1.** billingsgate; coarse action **2.** (*fatica da facchino*) drudgery.

facchinescaménte, *av.* vulgarly; coarsely; grossly.

facchinésco, *ag.* vulgar; coarse; gross: *linguaggio, scherzo* —, coarse language, joke; *modi facchineschi*, coarse manners.

facchíno, *s.m.* porter ‖ *mani da* —, coarse hands; *modi da* —, coarse manners; *vita da* —, dog's life ‖ *lavorare come un* —, to work like a slave; *parlare da* —, to use foul language (*o* to talk billingsgate).

fàccia, *s.f.* **1.** face: *a — in su, in giù*, face up, face down; *gli lavai la* —, I washed his face; *lo guardai in* —, I looked him in the eye (*o* full in the face); *mi tirò un libro in* —, he threw a book in my face; *non potrò più guardarlo in* —, I'll never be able to look him in the face again; *sputare in — a qlcu.*, to spit in s.o.'s face ‖ *a* —, face to face: *erano — a* —, they were face to face (*o* they were facing each other); *mettere due testimoni — a* —, to confront two witnesses ‖ *di — a*, in front of (*o* opposite): *il monumento di — al municipio*, the monument in front of (*o* opposite) the town hall; *la sua casa è di — alla chiesa*, his house stands opposite the church; *due posti di* —, two seats facing each other; *la casa di* —, the house opposite; *visto di* —, seen from the front ‖ *che — (tosta)!*, what a face!; *chi ebbe la — (tosta) di negarlo?*, who had the face (*o* the cheek *o* the impudence) to deny it?; *hai una bella — di bronzo*, you are brazen-faced (*o* impudent) indeed! ‖ *persona a due facce*, *fig.* two-faced person (*o* double dealer) ‖ *te lo si legge in* —, you look it ‖ *vento in* —, (*mar.*) head-wind ‖ *volta-* —, volte-face; *voltare* —, to make a volte-face (*o* to go back on one's opinions) ‖ *glielo dirò in* —, I'll tell him so to his face (*o* I'll speak frankly to him) ‖ *mi risero in* —, they laughed in my face ‖ *dire ql.co. in — al mondo*, to say sthg. outspokenly ‖ *fare la — lunga*, to pull a long face ‖ *fare ql.co. alla — di qlcu.*, (*volg.*) to do sthg. in the teeth of s.o. ‖ *farsi la* —, (*truccarsi*), to make up oneself ‖ *non guardare in — a nessuno*, to put number one first; (*dire ciò*

301

che si pensa) to say what one thinks || *perdere la* —, to lose face; *salvare la* —, to save one's face 2. (*sembiante, aspetto, espressione*) mien, look, expression, appearance: — *addolorata*, sorrowful expression; *cambiò — quando lo vide*, (*si rabbiò*) her face dropped when she saw him; (*si illuminò*) her face lit up when she saw him; *da quando l'ho visto l'ultima volta ha cambiato —*, he has changed since I saw him last; *ha una — da mascalzone*, he looks a rascal; *hai la — di uno che ha dormito male*, you look as if you had slept badly; *hai una bella — questa mattina*, you look well this morning; *hai una brutta —*, you don't look up to the mark (o you don't look very fit) || *questo libro ha cambiato —*, (*sembra nuovo*) this book looks new || *fare una — da ebete*, to put on a vacant look; *fare delle facce*, to make (o to pull) faces 3. (*lato, superficie*) face; side: *la — della pala di un'elica*, (aer.) the face of a blade; *la — della Terra*, the surface of the earth; *le facce di un cubo*, the faces (o sides) of a cube; *la — di un dado*, (mec.) the pane of a nut; *la — di un edificio, di una carta da giuoco*, the face of a building, of a playing-card; *la — di una moneta*, the face (o headside) of a coin; *questo edificio ha una — a nord*, this building faces north 4. (*pagina*) page.

facciàle, *ag.* 1. facial: *angolo* —, facial angle; *muscolo* —, (*anat.*) facial muscle, nerve 2. *valore* —, (*di francobollo, ecc.*) face value.

facciàta, *s.f.* 1. (*arch.*) front; façade; face 2. (*pagina*) page.

faccióne, *s.m.* large face: *un — allegro*, a jolly (o good-humoured) face; *un bel* —, a jolly round face.

fàce, *s.f.* (*letter.*) torch; (*luce, lume*) light: *la — della libertà*, the torch of liberty.

facèto, *ag.* facetious; waggish; (*arguto*) witty: *osservazioni facete*, witty remarks; *persona faceta*, facetious person; *scherzi faceti*, facetious tricks.

facèzia, *s.f.* pleasantry, witticism, witty remark; jest; joke: *raccolta di facezie*, collection of facetiae; *dire delle facezie*, to crack jokes.

fachiro, *s.m.* fakir.

faciàle, *V.* facciàle.

facies, *s.f.* (*scient.*) facies.

fàcile, *ag.* 1. easy: *un autore* —, an easy author; *una traduzione* —, an easy translation; *è — per lui farlo*, it is easy for him to do it; *è di — contentatura*, he is easily pleased; *è più — dirlo che farlo*, (it is) easier said than done || *una donna di facili costumi*, a woman of easy virtue 2. (*che si ottiene con poca fatica*) facile: *vittoria* —, facile victory 3. (*trattabile*) tractable, yielding, manageable; docile: *un padrone* —, an easy-going master; *è di carattere* —, he has a tractable character (o he is easy to get on with) 4. (*pronto*) ready: *ha la parola* —, he is a fluent talker; *sei — a credere qualsiasi cosa*, you are ready to believe anything 5. (*incline*) prone, inclined: *— all'ira*, prone to anger (o quick-tempered); *sono — alla commozione*, I am easily moved 6. (*probabile*) likely, probable: *è — che egli parta subito*, he is likely to leave at once (o he will probably leave at once); *è — che piova prima di domani*, it is probable that it will rain before tomorrow || *s.m.*: *il — e il difficile*, the easy and the difficult.

facilità, *s.f.* 1. facility, ease: *con* —, easily (o with ease): *parla francese con* —, he speaks French fluently; *la — con la quale tu impari l'inglese è sorprendente*, the facility (o the ease) with which you learn English is astonishing || *— di costumi*, easy virtue 2. (*qualità di essere facile*) easiness: *ti è già nota la — del tuo compito*, you already know the easiness of your task (o how easy your task is) 3. (*attitudine*) aptitude, facility, talent: *a fare ql.co.*, aptitude for doing sthg.; *— nel parlare, nello scrivere*, facility in speaking, in writing; *ha grande — di parola*, he is a fluent speaker (o talker) 4. *pl.* facilities: *— di pagamento*, (*comm.*) facilities for payment (o easy terms).

facilitàre, *v.t.* to facilitate; to make easier, to make easy: *il tuo aiuto mi facilitò il compito*, your support made my task easier.

facilitazióne, *s.f.* 1. facilitation: *la — degli scambi fra i due paesi ha causato un imprevedibile benessere*, the facilitation of trade between the two countries has occasioned unexpected welfare 2. (*agevolazione*) facility: *— di pagamento*, (*comm.*) accomodation; *facilitazioni di viaggio*, travelling facilities; *accordare facilitazioni*, to grant (o to allow) facilities.

facilménte, *av.* 1. easily 2. (*probabilmente*) probably.

facilóne, *s.m.* slipshod fellow: *Giovanni è un* —, John is a slipshod fellow.

facilonería, *s.f.* 1. superficiality 2. (*trascuratezza*) carelessness.

facinoróso, *ag.* lawless, ruffianly, violent || *s.m.* lawless man, ruffian, bully, rough, desperado.

facocèro, *s.m.* (*zool.*) wart-hog.

fàcola, *s.f.* (*astr.*) facula (*pl.* faculae).

facoltà, *s.f.* 1. faculty: *le — del tatto, della vista e dell'udito*, the faculties of touch, sight and hearing; *— mentali*, mental faculties; *essere in possesso di tutte le proprie* —, to be in possession of all one's faculties 2. (*di università*) faculty; school: *la — di medicina*, the Faculty of Medicine (o the Medical Faculty); *le diverse* —, the different schools; *molti membri della* —, many members of the faculty 3. (*autorità, potere*) faculty, authority, power; (*diritto*) right; (*libertà*) liberty: *— di scelta*, option; *ciò non è in mia* —, I have no authority (o option) for that (o that is not in my power); *non avete — di assolverlo*, you have no authority to acquit him (o it is not in your power to acquit him).

facoltatìvo, *ag.* facultative, optional: *fermata facoltativa*, optional stop (o request stop).

facoltóso, *ag.* wealthy, rich || *i facoltosi*, the wealthy (o the rich).

facondaménte, *av.* 1. (*con eloquenza*) eloquently, fluently 2. (*verbosamente*) wordily.

facóndia, *s.f.* eloquence, facundity; (*facilità di parola*) fluency of speech, flow of words: *aver il dono della* —, to have the gift of speech.

facóndo, *ag.* 1. eloquent 2. (*chiacchierone*) talkative, chatty.

facsìmile, *s.m.* facsimile, exact copy.

factòtum, *s.m.* factotum; (*fam.*) Man Friday.

Faènza, *no.pr.f.* (*geog.*) Faenza: *terracotta di* —, faience.

faetòn, *s.m.* (*carrozza*) phaeton.

faggéta, *s.f.* beech-wood.

faggìna, *s.f.* (*bot.*) beech-mast, beech-nut.

fàggio, *s.m.* 1. (*bot.*) beech 2. (*legno*) beech-wood.

faggiuòla, *s.f.* (*bot.*) beech-mast, beech-nut.

fagiàna, *s.f.* hen-pheasant.

fagianièra, *s.f.* pheasantry, pheasant preserve.

fagiàno, *s.m.* pheasant: *— dorato*, golden pheasant.

fagianòtto, *s.m.* young pheasant, pheasant-poult.

fagiolàta, *s.f.* 1. bellyful of beans 2. *fig.* stupidity.

fagiolìno, *s.m.* French bean, green bean; (*amer.*) string bean || *— nano*, kidney bean.

fagi(u)òlo, *s.m.* 1. bean 2. (*persona sciocca*) blockhead 3. (*gergo universitario*) (*studente del secondo anno*) sophomore, soph 4. *andare a* —, (*fam.*) to like: *questo vino mi va proprio a* —, I like this wine very much indeed.

fàglia[1], *s.f.* (*geol.*) fault: *— a gradinata*, step fault; *— diretta, normale*, normal fault; *— longitudinale*, strike fault; *— obliqua*, oblique fault; *piano di* —, fault plane.

fàglia[2], *s.f.* (*tessuto di seta*) faille.

fagliazióne, *s.f.* (*geol.*) faulting: *— incrociata*, cross faulting.

fagliàre, *v.t.* (*scartare al giuoco*) to discard.

fàglio, *s.m.* (*scarto al giuoco*) discard(ing).

fagocíta, fagocíto, *s.m.* (*biol.*) phagocyte.

fagocitòsi, *s.f.* (*biol.*) phagocytosis.

fagottísta, *s.m.* bassoonist.

fagòtto[1], *s.m.* bundle ‖ *far* —, (*fam.*) to bundle off (*o* to go away *o* to leave).

fagòtto[2], *s.m.* (*mus.*) bassoon.

Fahrenheit, *no.pr.: grado, temperatura* —, (*fis.*) Fahrenheit degree, temperature.

fàida, *s.f.* (*dir. medioevale*) (right of) feud.

faína, *s.f.* (*zool.*) beech-marten, stone-marten.

falànge, *s.f.* 1. (*anat.*) phalanx (*pl.* phalanges), phalange 2. (*st.*) phalanx (*pl.* phalanxes, phalanges) 3. *fig.* army.

falangétta, *s.f.* (*anat.*) phalangette, top-joint (of a finger), ungual-phalanx (*pl.* ungual-phalanges).

falangièro, *s.m.* (*st.*) phalangite.

falangína, *s.f.* (*anat.*) second joint, middle joint (of a finger).

falàngio, *s.m.* (*entom.*) phalangid; (*pop.*) daddy-long-legs.

falangísta[1], *s.c.* (*membro della Falange spagnuola*) Phalangist.

falangísta[2], *s.m.* (*zool.*) phalanger.

falanstèro, *s.m.* (*st. econ.*) phalanstery.

falàrica, *s.f.* (*st. mil.*) phalarica.

falàsco, *s.m.* (*bot.*) bog grass.

falbalà, *s.m.* falbala, furbelow, flounce.

fàlbo, *ag.* (*di cavallo*) sorrel.

falcàre, *v.t.* 1. (*di cavallo*) to curvet 2. (*armare con falci*) to arm (a chariot) with scythes.

falcàta, *s.f.* 1. (*di cavallo*) curvet, falcade 2. (*di persona*) stride.

falcàto, *ag.* 1. (*a forma di falce*) falcate, hooked, sickle-shaped: *luna falcata*, falcated moon; (*pop.*) sickle moon 2. (*di carro da guerra*) scythed: *carro* —, scythed (war-)chariot.

fàlce, *s.f.* 1. (*da fieno*) scythe; (*per le messi*) sickle ‖ — *e martello*, hammer and sickle 2. (*di luna*) crescent 3. (*di carro falcato*) scythe.

falcétto, *s.m.* sickle; (*pennato*) reaping-hook.

falchétta, *s.f.* (*mar.*) wash-board.

falchétto, *s.m.* (*ornit.*) hawk.

falciàre, *v.t.* to mow, to cut down; *fig.* to mow down: *i nostri soldati furono falciati dal nemico*, our soldiers were mown down by the enemy.

falciàta, *s.f.* 1. (*movimento della falce*) sweep of the mower's scythe; (*rar.*) swath(e) 2. (*il falciare*) mowing.

falciatóre, *s.m.* mower ‖ **falciatríce**, *s.f.* 1. mower 2. (*mec.*) mowing-machine, mower; (*da prato*) lawn-mower.

falciatúra, *s.f.* mowing.

falcídia, *s.f.* 1. (*comm.*) reduction, cut: *c'è stata una notevole* — *nel prezzo della benzina*, there has been a considerable reduction (*o* cut) in the price of petrol 2. (*dir.*) Falcidian portion.

falcidiàre, *v.t.* to reduce, to cut (down).

falcinèlla, *s.f.* cutting-wheel.

falcinèllo, *s.m.* 1. (*ornit.*) curlew 2. (*roncola*) bill-hook.

falciuòlo, *s.m.* sickle.

falcióne, *s.m.* 1. hay-cutter 2. (*antica arma da taglio*) falchion.

fàlco, *s.m.* hawk: — *di palude*, duck-hawk (*o* moor buzzard *o* marsh-harrier); — *pescatore*, fish-hawk (*o* osprey) ‖ *avere occhi di* —, to be hawk-eyed (*o* to have eyes like a hawk).

falconàra[1], *s.f.* hawk-house, falcon-house.

falconàra[2], *s.f.* (*feritoia*) loop-hole.

falconàre, *v.i.* to hawk.

falcóne, *s.m.* 1. falcon: — *pellegrino*, peregrine (falcon); *caccia col* —, hawking: *andare a caccia col* —, to hawk 2. (*st. mil.*) falcon 3. (*edil.*) derrick.

falconería, *s.f.* falconry.

falconétto, *s.m.* (*st. mil.*) falconet.

falconière, *s.m.* falconer, hawker.

fàlda, *s.f.* 1. (*geol.*) stratum (*pl.* strata, stratums);

layer: — *freatica*, water-bearing stratum; — *impermeabile*, impermeable stratum 2. (*di neve*) (snow-)flake: *nevica a larghe falde*, the snow is falling in large flakes 3. (*di cappello*) brim, flap: *cappello a larghe falde*, wide-brimmed hat 4. (*di abito*) tail: *abito a falde*, tail-coat (*o* tails); *mettersi in falde*, to wear tails 5. (*di tetto*) pitch 6. (*pendio di monte*) slope; (*piede di monte*) foot: *alle falde del monte*, at the foot of the mountain 7. (*fetta*) slice; (*di prosciutto*) rasher 8. (*di armatura*) tasse 9. (*parte di animale macellato*) loin of meat.

faldàto, *ag.* (*geol.*) stratified, layered.

faldíglia, *s.f.* farthingale, hoopskirt, crinoline.

faldistòrio, *s.m.* (*eccl.*) faldstool.

falegnàme, *s.m.* 1. joiner: *banco di* —, joiner's bench 2. (*carpentiere*) carpenter.

falegnamería, *s.f.* 1. (*arte del falegname*) joinery: *lavoro di* —, piece of joinery (*o* wood work) 2. (*bottega di falegname*) joiner's shop 3. (*carpenteria*) carpentry.

falèna, *s.f.* 1. (*entom.*) moth 2. (*bioccolo di cenere*) flake of ashes; (*avanzo di carta bruciata*) paper-ash.

fàlera, *s.f.* phalera (*pl.* phalerae).

falèrno, *s.m.* (*vino*) Falernian (wine).

falèucio, *ag.s.m.* (*poes.*) phaleucian (meter).

fàlla, *s.f.* (*mar.*) leak: *formazione di una* —, springing of a leak; *avere una* —, *delle falle*, to be leaky; *chiudere una* —, to stop a leak ‖ — *di griglia*, (*rad.*) grid leak.

fallàce, *ag.* fallacious, false, misleading, deceptive; vain, disappointing: *promessa* —, false promise; *speranza* —, vain hope.

fallaceménte, *av.* fallaciously, falsely, deceptively; vainly, disappointingly.

fallàcia, *s.f.* fallacy, fallaciousness.

fallàre, *v.i.* (*rar.*) to err, to be mistaken: *posso aver fallato*, I may have erred; *rimedio che non falla*, unfailing remedy.

fallíbile, *ag.* (*rar.*) fallible, liable to make mistakes: *siamo tutti fallibili*, anybody may make a mistake.

fallibilità, *s.f.* fallibility.

fàllico, *ag.* phallic: *versi fallici*, phallic verses.

fallimentàre, *ag.* bankruptcy (*attributivo*): *procedura* —, bankruptcy proceedings; *le mie finanze sono in stato* —, I am stony-broke; *presentare ai creditori il bilancio* —, to place a statement of affairs before the creditors.

falliménto, *s.m.* 1. (*comm.*) bankruptcy, failure: *curatore di* —, official liquidator; *dichiarazione di* —, declaration of insolvency; *fare* —, to go bankrupt (*o* to become insolvent *o* to fail); *presentare istanza di* —, to file one's petition in bankruptcy 2. *fig.* failure; flop: *tutti i suoi sforzi finirono in un* —, all his efforts ended in failure.

fallíre, *v.i.* 1. (*comm.*) to fail, to go bankrupt, to become insolvent; (*fam.*) to go under: *impedì che il giornale fallisse*, he kept the paper from going under 2. *fig.* to fail, to be unsuccessful: *il nostro progetto è fallito*, our plan has failed 3. (*venir meno*) to fail: *mi fallì il coraggio*, courage failed me ‖ *v.t.* to miss: — *il colpo*, to miss the mark.

fallíto, *ag.* 1. (*comm.*) insolvent, bankrupt 2. *fig.* unsuccessful: *tentativo* —, unsuccessful attempt ‖ *s. m.* 1. (*comm.*) bankrupt: — *riabilitato*, discharged bankrupt 2. *fig.* failure: *sono proprio un* —, I am a complete failure.

fàllo[1], *s.m.* 1. fault: *cogliere qlcu. in* —, to catch s.o. at fault; (*in flagrante*) to catch s.o. red-handed; *commettere un* —, to make a fault; (*detto di ragazza*) to make a slip; *essere in* —, to be at fault; *mettere un piede in* —, to slip; *fig.* to take a false step 2. (*difetto*) fault, defect; (*imperfezione*) flaw ‖ *senza* —, undoubtedly 3. (*spor.*) foul: — *di mano!*, (*calcio*) hands!.

fàllo[2], *s.m.* phallus (*pl.* phalli).

fallóso, *ag.* 1. faulty, defective 2. (*spor.*) foul.

falò, *s.m.* 1. bonfire: *fare un* — *di ql.co.*, to make a bonfire of sthg. 2. (*aer.*) beacon fire.

falòppa, *s.f.* **1.** defective cocoon **2.** (*fam.*) (*millantatore*) boaster, braggart.

falpalà, *s.m.* falbala, furbelow, flounce.

fàlsa, *s.f.* (*sartoria*) insertion.

falsaménte, *av.* falsely, erroneously, untruly.

falsamonéte, *s.m.* (*rar.*) coiner.

falsapòrta, *s.f.* secret door, blind door.

falsàre, *v.t.* **1.** (*alterare*) to distort, to misrepresent, to alter: — *i fatti*, to alter (*o* to misrepresent) the facts (*o* to present the facts in a wrong light); — *la verità*, to distort the truth **2.** (*falsificare*) to falsify, to forge.

falsaríga, *s.f.* **1.** guide sheet of ruled paper **2.** *fig.* pattern, model, guide.

falsàrio, *s.m.* forger, counterfeiter; (*di monete*) coiner.

falsatóre, *s.m.* **falsatríce**, *s.f.* falsifier.

falsatúra, *s.f.* (*sartoria*) insertion.

falsétto, *s.m.* (*mus.*) falsetto: *cantare in* —, to sing in falsetto.

falsificàbile, *ag.* falsifiable, forgeable.

falsificaménto, *s.m.* falsification, forgery, faking; counterfeiting.

falsificàre, *v.t.* **1.** to falsify, to forge, to fake; to counterfeit: *falsificò la firma di suo zio*, he forged his uncle's signature; *era noto per aver falsificato banconote*, he was well-known for having counterfeited banknotes; — *i conti*, to falsify (*o* to fake) the accounts **2.** (*cibi, bevande, ecc.*) to adulterate.

falsificatóre, *s.m.*, **falsificatríce**, *s.f.* falsifier, forger, faker; counterfeiter; (*di monete*) coiner.

falsificazióne, *s.f.* **1.** falsification, forgery, faking; counterfeiting **2.** (*di cibi, bevande, ecc.*) adulteration.

falsità, *s.f.* **1.** falseness, falsity **2.** (*menzogna*) falsehood, untruth, lie: *non dire tali* —!, don't tell such falsehoods! **3.** (*ipocrisia, doppiezza*) insincerity; deceitfulness, duplicity: *la* — *della sua condotta*, his double-dealing.

fàlso, *ag.* **1.** (*sbagliato*) false, wrong, incorrect: — *allarme*, false alarm; — *orgoglio*, false pride; *falsa partenza*, (*in una corsa*) false start; *idea falsa*, false (*o* wrong) idea; *nota falsa*, wrong note; *fare un passo* —, to take a false step (anche *fig.*); *essere in una posizione falsa*, *fig.* to be in a false position ‖ *sotto falsa luce*, in a false light: *mise la mia condotta sotto falsa luce*, he misrepresented my conduct **2.** (*non vero*) untrue, false: *un* — *amico*, a false friend; *capelli, denti falsi*, false hair, teeth; *gioielli falsi*, imitation jewellery; *notizia falsa*, false report; *ciò è* —, that is false (*o* untrue *o* incorrect); *è una falsa magra*, she is not so thin as she looks **3.** (*ingannevole*) false, misleading, deceitful: — *testimone*, false witness; *false promesse*, false promises **4.** (*falsificato*) falsified, forged; counterfeit; (*di monete*) false: *assegno* —, *firma falsa*, forged cheque, signature ‖ *s.m.* **1.** (*falsità*) falsehood: *distinguere il vero dal* —, to tell truth from falsehood **2.** (*dir.*) forgery: *quella firma è un* —, that signature is a forgery; *commettere un* —, to commit a forgery; *testimoniare il* —, to bear false witness (*o* to commit perjury) **3.** (*errore*): *sei nel* —, you are mistaken.

falsobordóne, *s.m.* (*mus.*) faburden.

fàma, *s.f.* fame, renown; reputation, repute, name: *una* — *usurpata*, an undeserved reputation; *amore per la* —, love of fame; *uno scienziato di chiara* —, *di* — *mondiale*, a scientist of great (*o* of world-wide) renown (*o* a highly reputed scientist); *una strada di cattiva* —, a street of bad repute (*o* an ill-famed street); *egli ha una buona* —, he has a good name (*o* he is well spoken of); *non avete (la)* — *di essere molto ricchi?*, haven't you the reputation of being very rich? (*o* aren't you reputed to be very rich?); *la sua* — *di drammaturgo nacque allora*, his fame as a playwright was made then; *acquistarsi gran* —, to win fame; *avere* — *di essere coraggioso*, to have a reputation for courage; *avere cattiva* —, to have a bad reputation (*o* to be ill-famed); *conoscere qlcu. per* —, to know s.o. by reputation (*o* by repute) ‖ *corre* — *che...*, it is rumoured that... (*o* it is said that... *o* it is reported

that...) ‖ *la Fama*, (*mit.*) Fame ‖ « *Il Tempio della Fama* », (*lett.*) " The House of Fame ".

fàme, *s.f.* **1.** hunger (anche *fig.*): — *di divertimenti*, hunger for amusements; *i morsi della* —, hunger pains; *aveva* —, he was hungry; *quel bimbo ha* — *di affetto*, that child hungers (*o* is starving) for love; *avere* — *di gloria*, to hunger (*o* to thirst) for glory; *fare lo sciopero della* —, to go on (a) hunger strike; *morire di* —, to die of (*o* from) hunger (*o* to die of starvation *o* to starve to death); *soffrire la* —, to suffer hunger ‖ *un morto di* —, a starveling ‖ *è lungo come la* —, he is a slow-coach ‖ *ho una* — *da lupo!*, *muoio di* —!, I'm simply starving! (*o* I'm famished!) ‖ *essere brutto come la* —, to be as ugly as sin ‖ *lavorare per non morir di* —, to work to keep body and soul together ‖ *far morire qlcu. di* —, to starve s.o. **2.** (*carestia*) famine: *durante la guerra migliaia di persone morirono di* —, during the war thousands died of famine.

famèdio, *s.m.* (*rar.*) Temple of Fame; part of cemetery reserved for famous people.

famelicaménte, *av.* ravenously, greedily.

famèlico, *ag.* famished, ravenous; greedy: *lupo* —, ravenous wolf; *occhi famelici*, greedy eyes.

famigeràto, *ag.* ill-famed, notorious.

famíglia, *s.f.* **1.** family: *affare di* —, family matter; *amico di* —, family friend; *avvocato di* —, family lawyer; *capo di* —, head of a family; *consiglio di* —, family council; *gioielli di* —, family jewels; *giovanotto di buona* —, young man of good family; *nome di* —, family name; *padre, madre di* —, father, mother of a family; *sostegno della* —, breadwinner; *uomo di* —, family man; *con loro mi sento come in* —, I feel quite at home with them; *è di buona* —?, does he come of a good family?; *hai* —?, have you got a family?; *hanno la stessa aria di* —, there is a family likeness between them; *ho una* — *numerosa*, I have a large family; *si ricordano di me in* —, they remember me at home; *formare* —, to start a family; *tornare in* —, to join the family (*o* to go back home) ‖ *la Sacra Famiglia*, the Holy Family ‖ *l'umana* —, mankind (*o* the human race) ‖ *essere di* — *con qlcu.*, to be on intimate terms with s.o. **2.** (*corte*) household **3.** (*di piante, animali, lingue*) family.

famíglio, *s.m.* man-servant (*pl.* men-servants), attendant.

familiàre, *ag.* **1.** domestic, homely: *bilancio* —, household budget; *gioie familiari*, domestic joys; *una piacevole atmosfera* —, a pleasant homely atmosphere; *vita* —, family life; *ella aveva molti guai familiari*, she had a good many domestic troubles; *era una graziosa scena* —, it was a charming domestic scene **2.** (*intimo*) familiar (anche *fig.*): *aver* — *il francese*, to be familiar with the French language; *essere in rapporti familiari con qlcu.*, to be on (*o* on familiar terms) with s.o. **3.** (*semplice, senza cerimonie*) informal: *linguaggio* —, informal language ‖ *s.m.* **1.** (*amico*) intimate friend; familiar **2.** (*parente*) relative **3.** (*famiglio*) man-servant, (*pl.* men-servants), attendant.

familiarità, *s.f.* familiarity: *avere* — *con un argomento*, to be familiar with a subject; *essere in rapporti di* — *con qlcu.*, to be on terms of familiarity (*o* on familiar terms) with s.o.; *trattare qlcu. con troppa* —, to treat s.o. with too much familiarity (*o* to make oneself too familiar with s.o.).

familiarizzàre, *v.t.* to familiarize ‖ **familiarizzàrsi**, *v.r.* to become familiar, to familiarize oneself.

familiarménte, *av.* **1.** familiarly **2.** (*senza pretese, senza cerimonie*) informally.

famóso, *ag.* **1.** famous, renowned, celebrated, well-known; famed: *un dipinto di un* — *pittore*, a picture by a celebrated painter; *un uomo* —, a famous man **2.** (*famigerato*) ill-famed, notorious **3.** (*diffamatorio*) *libello* —, (*dir.*) defamatory libel.

famulàto, *s.m.* (*arc.*) servitude.

fàmulo, *s.m.* (*arc.*) man-servant (*pl.* men-servants).

fanàle, *s.m.* **1.** lamp; (*lanterna*) lantern: *fanali stradali*, street lamps (o lamp-posts) **2.** (*aut. mar.*) light, lamp: — *anteriore*, head-light (o head-lamp); — *di coda*, tail-lamp (o tail-light); — *di poppa*, poop-light (o stern light); *fanali di posizione*, (*aut.*) parking lights; (*mar.*) position (o side) lights; *a fanali spenti*, with lights out **3.** (*ittiol.*) star-gazer.

fanalíno, *s.m.*: — *di coda*, (*aer.*) tail lamp; (*aut.*) rear (stop) lamp.

fanalísta, *s.m.* **1.** (*guardiano di faro*) lighthouse keeper **2.** (*lampionaio*) lamp-lighter.

fanaticaménte, *av.* fanatically.

fanàtico, *ag.* fanatic(al) ‖ *s.m.* fanatic; (*fam.*) fan: *un — di baseball*, a baseball fan.

fanatísmo, *s.m.* fanaticism.

fanatizzàre, *v.t.i.* to fanaticize.

fanciúlla, *s.f.* young girl, girl; (*poet.*) maiden.

fanciullàggine, *s.f.* **1.** (*l'essere puerile*) childishness **2.** (*azione puerile*) childish action.

fanciullàta, *s.f.* childish action.

fanciullescaménte, *av.* childishly.

fanciullésco, *ag.* childish; childlike (*attributivo*): *giuochi fanciulleschi*, childish (o childlike) games.

fanciullézza, *s.f.* childhood; (*di ragazzo*) boyhood; (*di ragazza*) girlhood.

fanciúllo, *ag.* young ‖ *s.m.* **1.** young boy; (*bambino*) child (*pl.* children) **2.** *fig.* simple-minded man.

fandònia, *s.f.* (*bugia*) lie; (*piccola bugia*) fib; (*frottola*) idle story; tale: *raccontare fandonie*, to tell fibs ‖ *fandonie!*, humbug!; nonsense!.

fanèllo, *s.m.* (*ornit.*) linnet.

fanerògama, *s.f.* (*bot.*) phanerogam.

fanerògamo, *ag.* (*bot.*) phanerogamous, phanerogamic.

fanfalúca, *s.f.* **1.** (*pagliuzza*) flake **2.** (*fola, fandonia*) made-up story, yarn; fib **3.** (*bagatella*) trifle **4.** (*gingillo*) gew-gaw **5.** (*capriccio*) whim; fad; freak.

fanfàra, *s.f.* **1.** (*banda*) brass band, band; (*mil.*) military band, bugle band **2.** (*suono di trombe*) fanfare; flourish of trumpets: *suonare una —*, to sound a flourish.

fanfaronàta, *s.f.* fanfaronade; brag; bragging; boasting; bluster.

fanfaróne, *s.m.* braggart; boaster; blusterer: *fare il —*, to bluster (o to brag).

fànga, *s.f.* (*rar.*) deep mud; quagmire.

fangàia, *s.f.* (*strada fangosa*) muddy road; (*luogo fangoso*) muddy place.

fangatúra, *s.f.* (*med.*) mud-bath.

fanghíccio, *s.m.* slush.

fanghíglia, *s.f.* **1.** slush **2.** (*di fiume, lago, canale*) sludge; ooze; slime **3.** (*miner.*) slurry.

fàngo, *s.m.* **1.** mud; (*di palude*) mire: *fondale di —*, mud bottom; *vulcano di —*, mud volcano ‖ *gettare — addosso a qlcu.*, to throw (o to fling) mud at s.o. (anche *fig.*); *guazzare, rotolarsi nel —*, to wallow in mud (anche *fig.*) ‖ *cresciuto nel —*, *fig.* brought up in the gutter (o gutter-bred); *cadere nel —*, *fig.* to fall very low; *raccogliere dal —*, *fig.* to raise from the gutter; *vivere nel —*, *fig.* to live a life of degradation (o to live in vice) **2.** *pl.* (*med.*) mud-baths: *fare la cura dei fanghi*, to take a mud-bath treatment **3.** *pl.* (*ind.*) mud (*sing.*), sediment (*sing.*), sludge (*sing.*): *collettore dei fanghi*, mud-drum.

fangosità, *s.f.* muddiness.

fangóso, *ag.* muddy; miry; slimy; (*di fiume*) oozy.

fannullóna, *s.f.*, **fannullóne,** *s.m.* idler; lounger; loafer; sluggard; shirker; slacker; (*fam.*) lazy-bones; (*amer.*) bum ‖ *i Re fannulloni*, (*st.*) the sluggard Kings.

fanóne, *s.m.* **1.** whalebone, baleen **2.** *pl.* (*eccl.*) fanons.

fanteccíno, *s.m.* (*soldato di fanteria*) foot-soldier; infantryman (*pl.* infantrymen); (*sl. mil.*) mud-crusher; foot-slogger ‖ *il — inglese*, (*fam.*) Tommy Atkins (o tommy).

fantaseiènza, *s.f.* science fiction.

fantasía, *s.f.* **1.** (*facoltà creatrice, immaginazione*) imagination, fancy; fantasy, phantasy: *la possente — del nostro poeta*, the powerful imagination of our poet;

ella vide in una vetrina un cappello che le colpì la —, she saw a hat in a shop-window and it caught her fancy; *hai una — troppo accesa*, you have too lively an imagination; *hai troppa —!*, you have got too much inventiveness!; *non hai molta —*, you haven't got much imagination; *sono tutte fantasie*, they are all fancies (o fantasies) **2.** (*desiderio, capriccio*) fancy; desire; whim; freak: *una — passeggera*, a passing fancy (o whim o freak); *a —*, at pleasure (o at choice); *gli prese la — di andare a Brighton*, he took a fancy (o the fancy took him) to go to Brighton; *ho la — di fare un bagno*, I have a fancy to bathe; *non mi passa neppure per la — di fare ciò*, I haven't the faintest idea of doing it **4.** (*riferito a gioielli, abiti, ecc.*): *articoli di —*, fancy goods; *gioielli —*, imitation jewellery; *panciotto —*, fancy waistcoat **5.** (*mus.*) fantasia **6.** (*esibizione di cavalieri arabi*) fantasia.

fantàsima, (*pop.*) per **fantàsma.**

fantasióso, *ag.* **1.** fanciful **2.** (*bizzarro*) bizarre, fantastic.

fantàsma, *s.m.* **1.** ghost, phantom, phantasm, fantasm, spectre ‖ « *Il vascello fantasma* », (*mus. lett.*) "The Phantom Ship" **2.** (*immagine illusoria*) phantasm: *vani fantasmi*, vain phantasms.

fantasmagoría, *s.f.* phantasmagoria.

fantasmagoricaménte, *av.* phantasmagorically.

fantasmagòrico, *ag.* phantasmagoric(al).

fantasticaménte, *av.* fantastically.

fantasticàre, *v.i.* to build castles in the air; (*sognare a occhi aperti*) to day-dream.

fantasticheria, *s.f.* reverie; day-dream.

fantàstico, *ag.* **1.** (*che è frutto della fantasia*) imaginary, fanciful, fantastic(al): *racconto —*, fanciful tale; *sogni fantastici*, fantastic dreams; *storia fantastica*, fantastic yarn **2.** (*bizzarro*) queer, odd, quaint, whimsical **3.** (*della fantasia*) fanciful, imaginative: *facoltà fantastica*, imaginative power **4.** (*fam.*) (*straordinario*) extraordinary, wonderful, fantastic: *lusso —*, incredible luxury; *ciò è —!*, this is extraordinary (o fantastic)!; *è un quadro —*, it's a wonderful picture.

fànte, *s.m.* **1.** (*soldato di fanteria*) infantryman (*pl.* infantrymen), foot-soldier: — *inglese*, (*fam.*) Tommy Atkins (o tommy) **2.** (*nel giuoco delle carte*) knave, jack: *il — di cuori*, the knave of hearts **3.** (*arc.*) (*servitore*) man-servant (*pl.* men-servants) ‖ *scherza coi fanti e lascia stare i santi*, *prov.* don't mix the sacred with the profane ‖ *s.f.* (*arc.*) (*fantesca*) maid-servant.

fantería, *s.f.* infantry: — *a cavallo*, mounted infantry; — *e cavalleria*, foot and horse; *il 48° —*, the 48th Foot; *due reggimenti di —*, two regiments of infantry; *soldato di —*, infantryman (o foot-soldier).

fantésca, *s.f.* (*arc.*) maid-servant, maid.

fantíno, *s.m.* (*ippica*) jockey.

fantocciàio, *s.m.* (*rar.*) puppet maker.

fantocciàta, *s.f.* **1.** childish action **2.** (*commedia per burattini*) puppet-show.

fantòccio, *s.m.* **1.** (*burattino*) puppet (anche *fig.*); (*amer.*) stooge (anche *fig.*): *governo —*, puppet-government **2.** (*bambola*) rag-doll **3.** (*manichino*) artist's manikin **4.** (*spaventapasseri*) scare-crow.

fantolíno, *s.m.* baby, babe; child (*pl.* children).

fantomàtico, *ag.* mysterious: *vorrei conoscere quel tuo — amico*, I wish I knew that mysterious friend of yours.

farabútto, *s.m.* rascal, blackguard; swindler; scoundrel.

faràd, *s.f.* (*elett.*) farad, far.

faradarizzàre, *v.t.* (*med.*) to faradize.

faraday, *s.f.* (*elett. chim.*) faraday.

faràdico, *ag.* (*elett.*) faradic.

faradizzazióne, *s.f.* (*med.*) faradization.

faràndola, *s.f.* (*danza provenzale*) farandole.

faraóna, *s.f.* (*ornit.*) guinea-fowl, guinea-hen.

faraóne, *s.m.* **1.** (*st.*) Pharaoh **2.** (*giuoco d'azzardo*) faro.

faraònico, *ag.* (*st.*) Pharaonic.

farcíno, *s.m.* (*vet.*) farcy.

farcíre, *v.t.* to stuff: *pollo farcito,* stuffed fowl (*o* stuffed chicken).

fardèllo, *s.m.* **1.** bundle **2.** (*carico*) burden (anche *fig.*); load (anche *fig.*): *un pesante — di crucci,* a heavy burden of worries.

fàre, *v.t.* **1.** (*in senso generale, astratto, morale, intellettuale e nel senso di* agire) **to do:** *che cosa fai?,* what are you doing?; *che debbo — (di lui)?,* what shall I do (with him)?; *che — ora?,* what is to be done now?; *che si doveva —?,* what was to be done? || *che diavolo stai facendo?,* what are you up to? || *dovrai farne a meno,* you'll have to do without (it) || *detto fatto,* no sooner said than done || *ecco fatto!,* that's done! || *non fa altro che dormire,* he does nothing but sleep || *nulla da —,* (*fam.*) nothing doing || *— senza,* to do without || *avere molto da —,* to have a great deal to do (*o* to be kept hard at work) || *non avere nulla da —,* to have nothing to do || *non — nulla,* to do nothing || *— alla meglio,* to do carelessly || *— bene,* to do properly (*o* to do well) || *— del proprio meglio, tutto il possibile,* to do one's utmost (*o* one's best) || *— bene, male a qlcu.,* to do s.o. good, harm: *questa medicina ti farà bene,* this medicine will do you good; *il vino mi fa male,* wine doesn't agree with me || *— il giro dei locali notturni,* to do the night-clubs || *chi fa da sè fa per tre, prov.* if you want a thing done well do it yourself || *non — agli altri quello che non vorresti fosse fatto a te, prov.* do as you would be done by **2.** (*prevalentemente nel senso di* creare, produrre, fabbricare) **to make:** *fa' una camicetta con questa seta,* make a blouse out of this silk (*o* make this silk into a blouse); *il fornaio fa il pane,* the baker makes bread; *marmellata fatta in casa,* home-made jam; *questa stoffa è (fatta) di seta,* this cloth is made of silk; *il sarto mi fa un abito,* the tailor is making me a suit; *il vino si fa con l'uva,* wine is made from grapes || *— amicizia,* to make friends || *— un errore,* to make a mistake || *— il fieno,* to make hay (*o* to mow) || *— in fretta,* to make haste (*o* to hurry) || *— i letti,* to make the beds || *mistero di ql.co.,* to make a mystery of sthg. || *— posto a qlcu.,* to make room for s.o. || *— il totale,* to make up the total || *3 più 3 fa 6,* 3 and 3 make 6 (*o* 3 and 3 are 6); *2 per 2 fa 4,* twice 2 is 4 **3.** (*essere*) **to be:** *— l'insegnante, il medico, la spia,* to be a teacher, a doctor, a spy || *— parte del personale,* to be a member of the staff **4.** (*avere, possedere*) **to have:** *il villaggio fa duecento abitanti,* the village has two hundred inhabitants **5.** (*rifornirsi*) **to take on:** *la nave fece acqua e carbone,* the ship took on water and coal || *— il pieno,* (*aut.*) to fill up **6.** (*dire*) **to say:** *Quando partite?, fece egli,* When are you leaving?, said he || *non — motto,* to utter no word **7.** (*eleggere, nominare*) **to make, to elect, to appoint:** *lo fecero re,* they made him king (*o* he was appointed king) **8.** (*reputare*) **to repute; to deem; to think:** *non lo facevo così sciocco,* I did not think he was so silly **9.** (*scrivere*) **to write;** (*dipingere*) **to paint:** *ha fatto un bel ritratto a mia sorella,* he painted a beautiful portrait of my sister **10.** (*segnare*): *che ora fa il tuo orologio?,* what time is it by your watch?; *questo orologio fa le cinque,* it is five o' clock by this watch **11.** (*teat.*) (*rappresentare*) **to perform:** *questa settimana all'Odeon fanno l' « Amleto »,* "Hamlet" is being performed at the Odeon (*o* "Hamlet" is on at the Odeon) this week **12.** (*far la parte di*) **to act (as);** (*teat.*) **to play (as);** (*fingere*) **to feign:** *ella mi fa da governante,* she acts as my house-keeper; *quell'attore nell'« Otello » farà la parte di Jago,* that actor is going to play Iago in "Othello"; *— l'ignorante,* to feign ignorance; *— il morto, fig.* to feign death **13.** (*praticare*) **to go in for:** *— della bicicletta, dello sport, dell'automobilismo, della politica,* to go in for cycling, sport, motoring, politics; *— del tennis,* to play tennis || *— del teatro, del cinema,* to be an actor, a cinema-actor || *— un po' di musica,* to play some music **14.** (*pulire*) **to clean:** *— una stanza,* to clean a room (*o fam.* to do a room): *— i piatti,* to wash up **15.** (*generare*)

to bear: *quella cagna il mese scorso ha fatto tre cuccioli,* that bitch bore three puppies last month **16.** (*trasformare*) **to turn into:** *del vecchio vestito fece un grembiule,* she turned her old dress into an apron **17.** (*percorrere*) **to proceed, to go:** *— dieci chilometri a piedi, a cavallo,* to walk, to ride ten miles; *— sessanta chilometri all'ora,* to drive at sixty miles an hour || *— quattro passi per un sentiero,* to go for (*o* to take) a stroll along a path **18.** (*passare, trascorrere*) **to spend:** *dove hai fatto l'estate?,* where did you spend the summer?; *fece dieci anni di prigione,* he did ten years in prison **19.** (*in sostituzione del verbo usato nella proposizione reggente*) **to do:** *perchè avete agito come avete fatto?,* why did you act as you did?; *spese il suo denaro meglio di quel che avrei fatto io,* he spent his money better than I should have done **20.** (*con valore causativo seguito da infinito*): (*cagionare*) **to cause;** (*ordinare*) **to have, to get;** (*costringere*) **to make;** (*lasciare, permettere*) **to let:** *fa' venire l'idraulico,* get the plumber to come; *fatelo obbedire,* make him obey; *fate spedire la lettera dal domestico,* have (*o* get) the letter posted by your servant; *fatti un nuovo abito!,* have a new suit made!; *il tuo ritardo mi fece perdere il treno,* your being late caused me to lose the train || *far —,* to have (*o* to get) (sthg.) done; *— andare una macchina,* (*mec.*) to start a machine; *— aspettare qlcu.,* to keep s.o. waiting; *— sapere a qlcu.,* to let s.o. know (*o* to inform s.o.); *— uscire, entrare,* to let s.o. out, in; *— vedere ql.co. a qlcu.,* to let s.o. see sthg. (*o* to show s.o. sthg.) || *— chiamare qlcu.,* to send for s.o. || *— notare a qlcu.,* to point out to s.o. || *— osservare ql.co. a qlcu.,* to call s.o.'s attention to sthg. || *far pagare,* to charge: *far pagare troppo,* to overcharge || *— proseguire lettere, merci,* (*comm.*) to forward letters, goods || *— salire i prezzi,* to raise prices **21.** (**Fraseologia**): *— a metà,* to go halves || *— a pezzi,* to tear to pieces || *— a pugni,* to box (*o* to fight); *fig.* to contrast || *— attenzione a ql.co.,* to pay attention to sthg. || *— bella, brutta figura,* to cut a fine, a poor figure || *— il callo,* to get accustomed to sthg. || *— le carte,* to shuffle; (*di chiromante*) to read the cards || *— una cavalcata,* to take a ride || *— cilecca,* to misfire || *— colazione,* to have breakfast || *— compassione,* to rouse compassion: *mi fai compassione,* I pity you || *— un complimento,* to pay a compliment; *— complimenti,* to stand on ceremony || *— cosa grata a qlcu.,* to oblige s.o. || *— d'uopo,* to be necessary || *— fagotto,* to pack up || *— fronte,* to face: *— fronte alla richiesta,* (*comm.*) to meet the demand || *far fuori qlcu.,* (*fam.*) to bump off || *— furore,* to be (all) the rage || *— lezione,* to give a lesson || *— il muso,* to sulk || *— il nome di qlcu.,* to put s.o.'s name forward; (*proporre*) to propose s.o. (as) || *— una passeggiata,* to go for a walk: *— una passeggiata in automobile, in carrozza,* to take a drive || *— la pelle,* to do in || *— un pensierino,* to think over || *— i propri affari,* to mind one's business || *— scuola,* to teach || *— seguito ad una lettera,* (*comm.*) to follow up a letter || *— le unghie,* to trim s.o.'s nails || *— le valigie, il baule,* to pack one's suit-cases, one's trunk || *— le veci di qlcu.,* to deputise for s.o. (*o* to represent s.o.) || *— un viaggio,* to take (*o* to make) a journey; *— una crociera,* to go on a cruise || *— vista (di non vedere, ecc...),* to pretend (not to see, etc...) || *far voglia,* to make (s.o.) wish (for sthg.) || *non — nè caldo nè freddo,* to be of no importance: *non mi fa nè caldo nè freddo,* I am quite indifferent to it || *— farla a qlcu.,* to beat s.o. (*o* to catch s.o.): *me l'hai fatta!,* you've won! (*o* you've caught me!) || *farla da gran signore,* to live like a lord || *falla finita con ciò,* put an end to it || *farne da vendere,* to act foolishly || *lasciar —,* not to bother about sthg.: *lascia —!,* never mind! || **fàre,** *v.i.* **1.** *imp.* (*di condizioni atmosferiche*): *che tempo fa?,* what is the weather like?; *fa brutto tempo, bel tempo,* it is bad weather, fine weather; *fa caldo, caldissimo, molto freddo,* it is warm, hot, very cold **2.** (*essere adatto*) **to suit:**

questa casa non fa per me, this house doesn't suit me **3.** (*seguito da consecutive*): — *in modo di*, to try to (do): *fate che non vi veda*, don't let him see you; *fate in modo di non farvi vedere*, take care not to be seen ‖ — *sì che*, to arrange: *fecero sì che io lo incontrassi*, they arranged (*o* made arrangements) for me to meet him **4.** (*stare per*) **to be about:** *fece per entrare quando...*, he was about to enter, when... **5.** — *in tempo a*, to manage to (do): *fece appena in tempo a prendere il treno*, he just managed (*o* he was just in time) to catch his train **6.** (**Fraseologia**): *fa lo stesso*, it is the same ‖ *faresti meglio a tacere*, you had better be silent ‖ *fate pure!*, *faccia pure!*, please do! (*o* certainly! *o* please yourself!); *fate voi*, *faccia lei*, I leave it to you ‖ *non fa nulla*, it does not matter ‖ *si fa presto a dire*, easily said (*o* it is easy to say) ‖ *tutto fa*, every little helps ‖ — *presa*, (*di colla, ecc.*) to stick ‖ *darsi da* —, to busy oneself ‖ **fàrsi**, *v.r.* **1.** (*diventare*) **to become;** (*gradualmente*) **to grow:** *si è fatto un bel giovane*, he has become a handsome young man; *si sono fatti più gentili*, they have become more amiable; *ti sei fatto molto alto*, you have grown (*o* become) very tall; *farsi cattolico*, to turn Catholic (*o* to become a Roman Catholic) **2.** (*moto*) **to come; to get:** *su, fatevi in là!*, get out of my way (,please)!; *farsi avanti*, to go forward; *fig.* to thrust oneself forward **3.** (*seguito da infinito*) **to make:** — *amare, capire, odiare*, to make oneself loved, understood, hated; — *notare*, to attract attention; (*di proposito*) to make oneself conspicuous **4.** *imp.* (*di tempo e di condizioni atmosferiche*): *si fa buio*, it is getting dark; *si fa tardi*, it is growing late **5.** (**Fraseologia**): — *animo, coraggio*, to take courage; — *beffe di qlcu.*, to ridicule s.o. (*o* to make fun of s.o.) ‖ — *bello*, (*mettersi in ghingheri*) to smarten oneself up; (*vantarsi*) to boast ‖ — *la cravatta*, to tie one's tie ‖ — *da mangiare*, to do one's own cooking ‖ — *degli amici, dei nemici*, to make friends, enemies ‖ — *un dovere* (*di fare ql.co.*), to consider it (as) one's duty (to do sthg.) ‖ — *una fama, una reputazione di onestà*, to make a reputation for honesty ‖ — *in quattro*, to do one's utmost ‖ — *un nemico di qlcu.*, to make an enemy of s.o. ‖ — *un nome*, to make a name for oneself ‖ — *il segno della croce*, to cross oneself (*o* to make the sign of the cross) ‖ — *strada*, to make one's way in the world ‖ *farsela con qlcu.*, to get on well with s.o.

fàre, *s.m.* **1.** (*modi, maniere*) manners (*pl.*); way; (*comportamento*) behaviour, manner: *il suo* — *modesto*, his modest manner; *ha un brutto* —, he has an unpleasant manner; *ha un* — *molto simpatico*, he has winning (*o* nice) ways (*o* he has a pleasant manner); *non mi piace il suo* —, I don't like his manners **2.** *sul* — *del giorno*, at daybreak; *sul* — *della notte*, at nightfall.

farètra, *s.f.* quiver.

farfàlla, *s.f.* **1.** butterfly ‖ — *di baco da seta*, silk moth ‖ — *notturna*, (*falena*) moth ‖ *cravatta a* —, bow -tie **2.** *fig.* (*persona volubile e leggera*) butterfly **3.** (*aut.*) throttle: *aprire la* —, to open the throttle,

farfallétta, *s.f.* **1.** (*grillo, ghiribizzo*) whim, fad, fancy **2.** (*scherz.*) (*cambiale*) bill of exchange; draft.

farfallína, *s.f.* **1.** (*piccola farfalla*) little butterfly **2.** (*ragazza, donna vanerella*) light-headed girl; giddy young girl; frivolous woman.

farfallíno, *s.m.* **1.** (*giovane vanerello*) butterfly, light-headed man **2.** (*cravatta*) bow-tie.

farfallóne, *s.m.* **1.** large butterfly; (*notturno*) large moth **2.** (*vagheggino*) butterfly **3.** (*errore grossolano*) blunder; malapropism.

farfugliàre, *v.t.* to mumble; to stammer.

farfuglióne, *s.m.* mumbler; stammerer.

farína, *s.f.* **1.** meal; (*fior di farina*) flour: — *d'avena*, oatmeal; — *di castagne*, powdered chestnuts; — *di frumento*, wheat meal; — *di granturco, gialla*, maize meal; — *di mandorle*, finely ground almonds; — *di orzo*, barley-flour ‖ — *lattea*, malted milk ‖ *questa non è* — *del tuo sacco*, this is not your own work ‖

la — *del diavolo va in crusca*, *prov.*, evil gotten evil spent (*o* ill gotten gains seldom prosper) **2.** (*min.*) flour: — *fossile*, fossil flour.

farinàccio, *s.m.* **1.** (*legno ridotto in farina dai tarli*) wood-dust **2.** (*dado*) one-faced die.

farinàceo, *ag.* farinaceous.

farinàcei, *s.m.pl.* pulses and cereals; starchy food (*sing.*).

farinàio, *s.m.* **1.** (*luogo dove si tiene la farina*) flour -bin **2.** (*venditore di farina*) meal-man (*pl.* meal-men), meal-monger.

farinaiuòlo, *s.m.* meal-man (*pl.* meal-men), meal -monger.

farinàta, *s.f.* porridge; pap: — *d'avena*, (oatmeal) porridge.

farínge, *s.f.* (*anat.*) pharynx.

faríngeo, *ag.* (*anat.*) pharyngeal, pharyngal.

faringísmo, *s.m.* (*patol.*) pharyngismus.

faringíte, *s.f.* (*patol.*) pharyngitis.

faringoiatría, faringología, *s.f.* pharyngology.

faringoscòpio, *s.m.* (*med.*) pharyngoscope.

faringotomía, s.f. (*chir.*) pharyngotomy.

farinóso, *ag.* **1.** mealy, floury, farinose: *patate farinose*, mealy potatoes **2.** (*simile a farina*) floury.

farisaicaménte, *av.* pharisaically.

farisàico, *ag.* pharisaic(al).

fariseísmo, *s.m.* pharisaism.

farisèo, *s.m.* (*Bibbia*) Pharisee (anche *fig.*).

farmacèutica, *s.f.* pharmaceutics, pharmacy, pharmacology.

farmacèutico, *ag.* pharmaceutic(al): *chimica farmaceutica*, pharmaceutic chemistry.

farmacía, *s.f.* **1.** (*scienza; facoltà universitaria*) pharmacology **2.** (*tecnica di fabbricare medicinali e luogo in cui questi si preparano*) pharmacy **3.** (*negozio in cui si vendono medicinali*) chemist's shop; (*amer.*) (*solo per medicinali*) pharmacy; (*in cui si vendono anche altri articoli*) drug-store.

farmacísta, *s.c.* chemist, pharmacist; (*amer.*) druggist.

fàrmaco, *s.m.* medecine; drug; (*rimedio*) remedy (anche *fig.*).

farmacodinàmica, *s.f.* pharmacodynamics.

farmacognosía, *s.f.* pharmacognosy.

farmacografía, *s.f.* pharmacography.

farmacología, *s.f.* pharmacology.

farmacopèa, *s.f.* pharmacopoeia.

Fàrnace, *no.pr.m.* (*st.*) Pharnaces.

farneticaménto, *s.m.* (*rar.*) raving; frenzy.

farneticàre, *v.i.* **1.** to rave; to talk wildly; to be delirious **2.** *fig.* to talk nonsense: *fur nelichi?*, (*fam.*) are you crazy?.

farnètico, *ag.* raving; frantic, frenzied ‖ *s.m.* **1.** (*pazzo*) madman (*pl.* madmen); frantic man **2.** (*pazzia, frenesia*) madness; delirious frenzy.

fàro, *s.m.* **1.** (*mar.*) lighthouse; light: — *a eclisse*, occulting light; — *galleggiante*, floating light(house) (*o* lightship); — *girevole*, revolving light; *guardiano del* —, lighthouse man (*o* lighthouse keeper) **2.** (*aer.*) beacon, light: — *d'aeroporto*, airport beacon; — *d'atterraggio*, landing beacon (*o* landing light); — *girevole*, rotating beacon; — *di rotta*, airway beacon; *radio* —, radio beacon **3.** (*aut.*) headlight, headlamp.

farràgine, *s.f.* farrago, medley, hotchpotch, mixture.

farraginóso, *ag.* confused, mixed; farraginous.

fàrro, *s.m.* (*bot.*) spelt.

fàrsa, *s.f.* farce (anche *fig.*): *il processo fu una* —, the trial was a farce.

Farsàglia, *no.pr.f.* (*geog. st.*) Pharsalia ‖ « *La* — », (*lett.*) " Pharsalia ".

Fàrsalo, *no.pr.f.* (*geog. st.*) Pharsalus.

farsésco, *ag.* farcical: *situazione farsesca*, farcical situation.

farsétto, *s.m.* doublet ‖ *spogliarsi in* —, (*fam. fig.*) to roll up one's sleeves.

fascétta, *s.f.* **1.** (*piccola fascia*) small band, narrow band **2.** (*benda per medicazione*) bandage **3.** (*busto da donna*) corset **4.** (*di giornale*) (newspaper-)wrapper; (*editoriale*) wrapper (with publisher's blurb) **5.** (*di medaglia*) ribbon (for medals) **6.** (*mec.*) clip, clamp.

fàscia, *s.f.* **1.** band: — *elastica,* elastic band **2.** *pl.* (*da neonato*) swaddling-bands, swaddling clothes || *bambino in fasce,* small baby **3.** (*benda*) bandage **4.** (*fusciacca*) sash **5.** (*di abito ecclesiastico*) sash **6.** (*mollettiera*) puttee **7.** (*anat.*) fascia (*pl.* fasciae) **8.** (*arch.*) fillet; fascia (*pl.* fascias) **9.** (*arald.*) fesse **10.** (*astr.*) fascia (*pl.* fasciae); belt **11.** (*mec.*) band **12.** (*aut.*) ring: — *elastica di pistone,* piston ring; — *elastica di tenuta* (*della compressione*), compression ring **13.** (*per spedizione postale di stampati*) cover: *sotto —,* under separate cover.

fasciàme, *s.m.* (*mar.*) (*in legno*) planking; (*metallico*) plating.

fasciàre, *v.t.* **1.** to bandage; to bind (up); to tie up, to dress: — *una ferita,* to bind up a wound (*o* to dress a wound); — *un piede,* to tie up a foot **2.** (*avvolgere*) to wrap, to swathe: *era tutta fasciata di scialli,* she was all wrapped (*o* swathed) in shawls **3.** (*un neonato*) to swaddle **4.** (*mar.*) (*con legno*) to plank; (*con metallo*) to plate **5.** (*elett.*) (*con nastro isolante*) to tape || **fasciàrsi,** *v.r.* **1.** to bandage oneself **2.** (*avvolgersi*) to wrap oneself **3.** (*ferita, ecc.*) to dress.

fasciatúra, *s.f.* **1.** (*il fasciare*) dressing; (*di neonato*) swaddling **2.** (*le fasce*) dressing, bandage **3.** (*mar.*) serving **4.** (*elett.*) lagging.

fascícolo, *s.m.* **1.** (*opuscolo*) booklet; pamphlet **2.** (*di rivista*) number; issue **3.** (*amm.*) dossier: — *personale,* (personal) record **4.** (*bot.*) fascicle.

fascína, *s.f.* **1.** faggot, fagot **2.** (*mil.*) fascine.

fascinàme, *s.m.* (*legna da fascine*) kindling wood; brushwood.

fascinàre, *v.i.* (*approntare fascine*) to bundle wood.

fascinàta, *s.f.* **1.** (*per argini*) mattress **2.** (*mil.*) fascine.

fascinatóre, *ag.* (*rar.*) (*affascinatore*) fascinating, charming || *s.m.* **fascinatríce,** *s.f.* charmer.

fascinazióne, *s.f.* (*malefizio*) fascination.

fàscino, *s.m.* **1.** (*malefizio*) charm; fascination; spell: *subire il — di qlcu.,* to be under the spell of s.o. **2.** (*forza di seduzione*) glamour; fascination: *fu preso dal — di lei,* he came under her spell.

fàscio, *s.m.* **1.** bundle; (*mazzo*) sheaf, bunch: *un — di carte, di fieno, di frecce,* a sheaf of papers, of hay, of arrows; *un — di fiori,* a bunch of flowers; *un — di legna, di libri,* a bundle of sticks, of books || *andare, mandare in —,* (*in rovina*) to go, to send to ruin || *fare di ogni erba un —,* (*fam.*) to mix good and bad || *mettere in un —,* to bundle together **2.** (*geom.*) sheaf **3.** (*di luce*) beam **4.** *pl.* (*st. romana*) fasces.

fascísmo, *s.m.* (*pol.*) Fascism.

fascísta, *ag.* (*pol.*) Fascist || *s.c.* (*st. pol.*) Fascist.

fàse, *s.f.* **1.** (*stadio*) stage; (*periodo*) period **2.** (*astr.*) phase **3.** (*elett.*) phase: *concordanza, discordanza di —,* phase coincidence, phase difference; *fuori —,* out-of-phase; *modulazione di —,* (*rad.*) phase modulation **4.** (*aut.*) stroke: — *di scarico,* exhaust stroke; *mettere in — il motore, l'accensione,* to time the engine, the ignition.

fasèlo, *s.m.* (*poet.*) light barge.

fasòmetro, *s.m.* (*elett.*) phasemeter; phase indicator.

fastèllo, *s.m.* bundle of sticks; faggot, fagot.

fàsti, *s.m.pl.* **1.** (*st. romana*) fasti **2.** (*memoriali*) records; annals **3.** (*gloriose azioni*) memorable deeds.

fastidiévole, *V.* **fastidióso.**

fastídio, *s.m.* **1.** (*contrarietà, molestia*) trouble, annoyance, vexation: *i piccoli fastidi della vita,* the small troubles (*o* vexations) of life; *ti vai a cercare dei fastidi,* you are looking for trouble; *dare — a qlcu.,* to give s.o. trouble (*o* to trouble s.o. *o* to annoy s.o. *o* to vex s.o.) || *che —!,* botheration! (*o* what a nuisance!); *non mi dare —!,* don't bother me! || *cer-*

carsi dei —, to involve oneself in difficulties (*o* to get into hot water) **2.** (*l'essere infastidito*) annoyance, irritation, vexation: *il suo — era evidente,* his annoyance (*o* vexation) was evident **3.** (*uggia*) dislike: *prendere uno in —,* to take a dislike to s.o. **4.** (*nausea*) squeamishness; sickness, disgust: *sento — allo stomaco,* my stomach feels rather upset; (*a causa di apprensione, paura*) I have a sinking feeling.

fastidiosàggine, *s.f.* (*rar.*) troublesomeness; nuisance.

fastidiosaménte, *av.* troublesomely; tiresomely.

fastidióso, *ag.* **1.** (*che dà fastidio*) troublesome; tiresome; wearisome; (*specialmente di cosa*) annoying **2.** (*che si infastidisce*) intolerant.

fastidíre, *v.t.* (*rar.*) (*infastidire*) to trouble; to weary; to annoy; to vex.

fastígio, *s.m.* **1.** (*arch.*) fastigium, pediment, gable **2.** *fig.* (*apogeo*) height, peak; summit; climax.

fàsto,[1] *ag.* auspicious, propitious: *giorno —,* auspicious day.

fàsto,[2] *s.m.* pomp, splendour, magnificence; (*sfoggio*) display, ostentation: *matrimonio senza —,* quiet wedding.

fastosaménte, *av.* magnificently, splendidly, pompously; with display.

fastosità, *s.f.* pomp, splendour, magnificence; (*sfoggio*) display, ostentation.

fastóso, *ag.* magnificent, splendid, sumptuous; gorgeous; (*con ostentazione*) ostentatious.

fasúllo, *ag.* false, valueless, counterfeit.

fàta, *s.f.* fairy; (*rar.*) fay: *il paese delle fate,* fairyland; *racconti delle fate,* fairy-tales || — *benefica, fig.* very charitable lady || *avere mani di —, fig.* to have a gift for needlework (*o* to be very deft at needlework) || — *Morgana,* (Fata) Morgana; (*nei poemi medievali*) Morgan le Fay; (*miraggio*) "fata morgana"; mirage.

fatagióne, *s.m.* (*rar.*) (*incantesimo*) charm; spell.

fatàle, *ag.* **1.** fatal: *colpo —,* fatal (*o* deadly *o* mortal) blow; *ora —,* fatal hour; *ciò le riuscì —,* that proved fatal to her || *donna —,* vamp (*o* siren) **2.** (*inevitabile*) inevitable, fated, destined: *era — che s'incontrassero,* it was fated (*o* destined) that they should meet.

fatalísmo, *s.m.* fatalism.

fatalísta, *s.c.* fatalist.

fatalità, *s.f.* **1.** (*inevitabilità*) fatality: *fu una —!,* it was bound to happen! **2.** (*il fato*) fate, destiny: — *volle che ci dovessimo incontrar di nuovo,* fate decreed that we should meet again **3.** (*incidente fatale, morte*) fatality, fatal accident **4.** (*disavventura, disgrazia*) misadventure, mischance, mishap.

fatalménte, *av.* fatally.

fatàre, *v.t.* to charm, to bewitch.

fatàto, *ag.* **1.** enchanted, bewitched, magic: *anello —,* magic ring; *foresta fatata,* enchanted forest **2.** (*di fata*) fairy: *bacchetta fatata,* fairy wand **3.** (*arc.*) (*destinato*) destined, fated.

fatíca, *s.f.* **1.** (*stanchezza*) weariness, fatigue, exhaustion: *organismo resistente alla —,* tough constitution || *cascare dalla —,* to drop with fatigue (*o* to be exhausted) || *morto di —,* dog-tired (*o* dead-beat) **2.** (*lavoro faticoso*) labour; toil, fatigue, hard work: *le fatiche della guerra,* the toils (*o* hardships) of war; *chi di noi conosce la — del contadino?,* which of us knows the peasant's toil (*o* hard work)? || *vive col frutto delle sue fatiche,* he lives on his work || *è — sprecata,* it is a wasted effort || *le fatiche di Ercole,* the labours of Hercules || *abito da —,* working clothes; (*mil.*) fatigue dress || *cavallo da —,* cart-horse || *uomo di —,* fatigue man **3.** (*difficoltà*) difficulty; trouble: *a —,* with difficulty; *durai molta — a capirlo,* I had much difficulty in understanding him (*o* I could hardly understand him) || *avanzare a —,* to toil along **4.** (*mec.*) fatigue: *limite di —,* (*metal.*) fatigue limit.

faticànte, *ag.* hard-working; labouring || *s.m.* (*rar.*) worker; workman (*pl.* workmen).

faticàre, *v.i.* **1.** to toil; to work hard; to labour; to drudge: *gli operai faticarono due anni per costruire quella casa*, for two years the workers laboured at building that house; — *per mantenere la propria famiglia*, to toil hard to maintain one's family **2.** (*stentare*) to be hardly able (to do), to have difficulty (in doing) (anche *fig.*): *fatico a crederti*, I can hardly believe you.

faticàta, *s.f.* drudgery; (*sl.*) grind.

faticatóre, *s.m.*, **faticatríce**, *s.f.* drudge; (*sl.*) grinder.

faticosaménte, *av.* **1.** laboriously: *guadagnarsi la vita* —, to work hard for a living **2.** (*con pena*) painfully; wearily.

faticóso, *ag.* **1.** hard, toilsome; fatiguing, tiring **2.** (*difficile*) laborious; difficult.

fatidicaménte, *av.* fatidically; prophetically.

fatídico, *ag.* **1.** fatidical; prophetic **2.** (*fatale*) fatal.

fatiscènte, *ag.* (*rar.*) (*cadente*) crumbling.

fàto, *s.m.* **1.** fate, destiny; (*sorte*) lot: — *crudele*, ruthless fate **2.** (*morte*) fate: *cedette al* — *ancora giovane*, he met his fate when young.

fàtta[1], *s.f.* **1.** kind, sort: *gente di ogni* —, people of every sort and kind; *uomini di tal* —, men of this kind **2.** (*azione*) deed: *le male fatte*, the misdeeds.

fàtta[2], *s.f.* (*escrementi di selvaggina*) droppings of game (*pl.*).

fattàccio, *s.m.* **1.** foul deed **2.** (*delitto*) crime.

fattévole, (*rar.*) per **fattíbile**.

fattézza, *s.f.* feature: *le sue soavi fattezze*, her gentle features.

fattíbile, *ag.* feasible; practicable; achievable ‖ *s.m.* (*il possibile*) possible.

fattíccio, *ag.* robust, sturdy, stout, tough.

fattispècie, *s.f.* (*dir.*) case in point; matter in hand ‖ *nella* —, in this case.

fattívo, *ag.* **1.** (*efficace*) effective, efficacious **2.** (*attivo*) active, busy; efficient.

fattízio, *ag.* artificial; factitious.

fàtto, *ag.* **1.** done, made: — *a macchina*, machine-made; — *a mano*, hand-made; — *in casa*, home-made; — *in fabbrica*, factory-made; *abiti fatti*, ready-made clothes; *abiti fatti dal sarto*, tailor-made clothes ‖ *ben* —!, well done!; (*ben ti sta!*) it serves you right!; *così* —, of this kind (o like this) ‖ *detto* —, no sooner said than done; (*subito*) thereupon (o immediately) ‖ *ciò che è* — *è* —, what's done is done ‖ *è fatta!*, there's no remedy to it! ‖ *io sono* — *così*, I am like this ‖ *a questo punto vien* — *di chiedersi se...*, at this point the question arises whether... ‖ *mi vien* — *di pensare che...*, I am led (o inclined) to think that... **2.** (*maturo*) ripe: *formaggio* —, ripe cheese; *uomo* —, fullgrown man; *era giorno* —, it was broad daylight **3.** (*adatto*) fit: *non sono* — *per questa vita*, I am not fit for this sort of life.

fàtto, *s.m.* **1.** fact: *il* — *sta che...*, the fact is (o remains) that... (o as a matter of fact...); *a me interessano solo i fatti*, I am interested only in facts ‖ *in linea di* —, in point of fact (o as a matter of fact) ‖ *in fatti*, in fact ‖ *andare diritto al* —, to go (o to come) to the point **2.** (*azione*) deed; act, action: — *d'arme*, military action (o fight); *vogliamo fatti, non parole*, we want deeds, not words ‖ *cogliere qlcu. sul* —, to catch s.o. in the very act (o red-handed) ‖ *passare dalle parole ai fatti*, to pass from words to blows (o to resort to force) **3.** (*avvenimento*) event, occurrence: — *strano*, strange occurrence; *c'è un* — *nuovo nella situazione*, there is a new development in the situation **4.** (*affare*) affair; business (*solo sing.*): *è tutt'altro* —, it's quite a different matter; *bada ai fatti tuoi!*, mind your own business!; *egli sa il* — *suo*, he knows his business (o he knows what he is about) ‖ *ho trovato il* — *mio*, I' ve found what I wanted ‖ *dire il* — *suo a qlcu.*, to talk straight to s.o. (o to pitch into s.o. o to give s.o. a piece of one's mind): *gli dissi il* — *suo*, I gave him a piece of my mind **5.** *in* — *di*, as regards: *in* — *di eleganza non la cede a nessuno*, as regards elegance she is second to none (o is superior to all) **6.** *gran* —, very much: *voi non studiate gran* —, you don't study very much (o very hard).

fattóra, *s.f.* farmer's wife.

fattóre, *s.m.* **1.** (*elemento costitutivo*) factor, element: *la ricchezza fu il* — *principale del suo successo*, wealth was the chief factor in his success **2.** (*scient.*) factor: — *di ampiezza*, (*elett.*) crest (o peak) factor; — *di carico*, (*elett.*) weighting factor; — *di perdita*, (*rad.*) loss factor; — *di posa*, (*foto.*) exposure factor; — *di potenza*, (*elett.*) power factor; *risoluzione in fattori*, (*mat.*) resolution into factors **3.** (*autore, creatore*) maker, creator ‖ *il Sommo Fattore*, Our Maker **4.** (*amministratore, sovraintendente di beni rurali*) bailiff; farmer.

fattoréssa, *s.f.* farmer's wife.

fattoría, *s.f.* **1.** (*proprietà terriera*) rural estate; (*podere con casa*) farm **2.** (*casa di campagna*) farm-house **3.** (*ufficio di fattore*) stewardship; land-agency.

fattoríno, *s.m.* office-boy; errand-boy; messenger; (*del telegrafo*) telegraph boy, telegraph messenger.

fattríce, *s.f.* (*cavalla*) stud mare; (*mucca*) stud cow.

fattucchièra, *s.f.* witch; sorceress.

fattucchière, *s.m.* wizard, sorcerer.

fattucchiería, *s.f.* witchcraft; sorcery; wizardry.

fattúra, *s.f.* **1.** making, manufacture; make: *la* — *dell'abito della sposa fu un affare eterno*, the making of the bride's wedding-dress was a long affair; *articolo di* — *francese*, article of French make (o French-made article); *queste scarpe non sono di nostra* —, these shoes are not our make **2.** (*lavorazione*) work, workmanship: *un gioiello di squisita* —, a jewel of exquisite workmanship **3.** (*comm.*) invoice; bill: — *di acquisto*, purchase bill; — *legalizzata*, certified invoice; — *saldata*, receipted invoice; — *simulata*, proforma invoice; *intestazione di una* —, heading of an invoice; *libro* —, invoice book; *prezzo di* —, invoice price; *registrazione in* —, casting (o entry o item); *rimettere la* — *di ql.co.*, to send an invoice for sthg. **4.** (*stregoneria*) witchcraft; sorcery; wizardry.

fatturàre, *v.t.* **1.** (*adulterare*) to adulterate, to sophisticate: — *il latte con acqua*, to adulterate milk with water **2.** (*stregare*) to bewitch **3.** (*comm.*) to invoice.

fatturàto, *ag.* **1.** (*adulterato*) sophisticated, adulterated **2.** (*stregato*) bewitched **3.** (*comm.*) invoiced ‖ *s.m.* **1.** (*comm.*) proceeds of sales (*pl.*) **2.** (*ind. gomma*) substitute, factice.

fatturatrice, *s.f.* (*comm.*) invoicing-machine.

fatturazióne, *s.f.* (*comm.*) invoicing.

fatturísta, *s.m.* (*comm.*) invoice clerk.

fatuaménte, *av.* fatuously, foolishly, inanely.

fatuità, *s.f.* fatuousness, fatuity, inanity.

fàtuo, *ag.* **1.** (*sciocco*) fatuous, foolish, inane **2.** (*vanitoso*) vain **3.** *fuoco* —, ignis fatuus; (*fam.*) will-o'-the-wisp.

fàuci, *s.f.pl.* (*di animale*) jaws (anche *fig.*); (*di persona*) throat (*sing.*); (*anat.*) fauces.

fàuna, *s.f.* fauna.

faunésco, *ag.* **1.** faun (*attributivo*) **2.** (*simile a fauno*, *da fauno*) faun-like.

Fàuno, *no.pr.m.* (*mit.*) Faunus ‖ **fàuno**, *s.m.* (*mit.*) faun.

faustaménte, *av.* propitiously, prosperously; luckily.

Faustína, *no.pr.f.* Faustina.

Fàusto[1], *ag.* propitious, prosperous; lucky, happy.

Fàusto[2], *no.pr.m.* Faustus.

fautóre, *s.m.* **1.** (*sostenitore*) supporter, upholder, promoter, favourer **2.** (*protettore*) protector.

fautríce, *s.f.* **1.** (*sostenitrice*) supporter, upholder, promoter, favourer **2.** (*protettrice*) protectress.

fàva, *s.f.* broad bean ‖ *non vale una* —, it's not worth a bean; *non stimare una* —, to consider worthless ‖ *pigliare due piccioni con una* —, to kill two birds with one stone.

favèlla, *s.f.* **1.** speech: *il dono della —*, the gift of speech (*o* the faculty of speaking); *riprender l'uso della —*, to recover the use of speech **2.** (*lingua*) language, tongue: *la — toscana*, the Tuscan language.

favellàre, *v.i.* to speak, to talk.

favéto, *s.m.* bean-field.

favílla, *s.f.* spark (anche *fig.*).

fàvo, *s.m.* **1.** honeycomb **2.** (*patol.*) favus; (*pop.*) boil.

fàvola, *s.f.* **1.** fable; (*racconto*) tale, story: *le favole di Esopo*, Aesop's fables **2.** (*intreccio di dramma, poema*) plot, fable **3.** (*frottola*) idle story, idle tale, fable: *questa storia non è che una —*, this story is a mere fable **4.** (*oggetto di pettegolezzi*) byword, laughing-stock, talk, fable: *vuoi diventare la — del paese?*, do you wish to become the laughing-stock of the village?.

favoleggiàre, *v.i.* to tell tales, to tell stories.

favoleggiatóre, *s.m.* tale-teller; (*novellatore*) fabulist.

favolèllo, *s.m.* (*st. lett.*) fabliau (*pl.* fabliaux).

favolísta, *s.m.* fabulist.

favolosaménte, *av.* fabulously.

favolóso, *ag.* **1.** fabulous, fabled: *eroi favolosi*, fabulous heroes **2.** (*incredibile, enorme*) fabulous: *prezzi favolosi*, fabulous prices; *ricchezza favolosa*, fabulous wealth.

favònio, *s.m.* (*vento dell'ovest*) Favonius.

favóre, *s.m.* **1.** (*benevolenza, protezione*) favour, benevolence, good-will: *godere del — di qlcu.*, to be (*o* to stand) high in s.o.'s favour; *trovar — agli occhi di qlcu.*, to find favour in s.o.'s eyes ‖ *col — delle tenebre*, *fig.* under favour (*o* cover) of darkness **2.** (*grazia, servigio*) favour, kindness: *chiedere un — a qlcu.*, to ask a favour of s.o. (*o* to ask s.o. a favour); *fare un — a qlcu.*, to do s.o. a favour: *fammi il — di spedirlo subito*, do me the favour (*o* kindness) of sending it at once; *riempire qlcu. di favori*, to load s.o. with favours ‖ *per —*, (if you) please **3.** (*approvazione*) favour, approval: *i vostri articoli incontrano il — del pubblico*, your articles meet the buyers' favour **4.** (*vantaggio*) favour: *gli affari volsero a mio —*, the business turned in my favour; *tali circostanze non depongono a suo —*, such circumstances don't speak in his favour; *essere a — di*, to be in favour of (*o* to support) ‖ *biglietto di —*, complimentary ticket ‖ *a vostro —*, (*comm.*) to your credit ‖ *cambiale di —*, (*comm.*) accomodation bill ‖ *prezzo di —*, (*comm.*) special price ‖ *emettere un assegno a — di qlcu.*, (*comm.*) to write out a cheque in s.o.'s favour.

favoreggiaménto, *s.m.* **1.** favouring; backing up, complicity **2.** (*dir.*) (aiding and) abetting.

favoreggiàre, *v.t.* **1.** to favour; to back up; to support: *un insegnante non deve — nessuno fra i suoi allievi*, a teacher must not favour any of his pupils; *— un partito politico*, to support a political party **2.** (*dir.*) to aid and abet; to be s.o.'s accomplice.

favoreggiatóre, *s.m.*, **favoreggiatríce**, *s.f.* (*dir.*) abettor, abetter; accomplice.

favorévole, *ag.* **1.** favourable: *una sentenza —*, a favourable sentence **2.** (*propizio, vantaggioso*) propitious, favourable: *una circostanza —*, a propitious circumstance; *una occasione —*, a favourable occasion; *vento —*, favourable (*o* fair) wind **3.** (*benevolo*) benevolent, well-disposed.

favorevolménte, *av.* favourably; propitiously.

favoríre, *v.t.* **1.** to favour: *lo favorite senza merito*, you are favouring him unduly; *essere favorito da qlcu.*, to be favoured by s.o.; *— i progetti di qlcu.*, to favour s.o.'s schemes **2.** (*aiutare*) to aid, to help: *che Dio ti favorisca!*, God help you! **3.** (*sostenere, favoreggiare*) to support; to countenance; (*dir.*) to aid and abet: *gli abitanti di quel paese non favoriranno mai una guerra di aggressione*, the people of that country will never countenance a war of aggression; *— qlcu. in un delitto*, to aid and abet s.o. in a crime **4.** (*promuovere*) to pro-

mote, to encourage, to foster: *— l'amicizia tra i popoli*, to foster friendship among peoples; *— le arti*, to promote (*o* to patronize *o* to encourage) the arts; *— la produzione*, to encourage production **5.** (*in formule di cortesia*): *favorite i biglietti!*, tickets please! ‖ *favorite entrare*, please come in ‖ *favorisca rispondermi*, will you kindly reply to me? (*o* be so kind as to reply to me) ‖ *favoritemi quella copia*, give me that copy please ‖ *vuoi — un bicchiere di vino?*, will you help yourself to a glass of wine (*o* may I help you to a glass of wine)?.

favoríta, *s.f.* **1.** (*donna prediletta da un potente*) favourite, mistress: *la — del re*, the royal mistress **2.** (*comm.*): *la vostra —*, your letter (*o* your favour *o* amer. your favor); *in possesso della vostra —*, your favour to (*o* at) hand; *abbiamo regolarmente ricevuto la — vostra del...*, your favour of... duly reached us.

favoríti, *s.m.pl.* side-whiskers.

favoritísmo, *s.m.* favouritism, favour: *ottenere ql.co. per —*, to get sthg. by favour.

favoríto, *ag.* favourite, preferred ‖ *s.m.* favourite: *il — giunse terzo*, the favourite came in third; *il conte di Leicester fu uno dei favoriti della regina Elisabetta*, the Earl of Leicester was one of Queen Elizabeth's favourites.

fazióne, *s.f.* **1.** faction: *spirito di —*, factious spirit (*o* factiousness); *l'Assemblea era divisa in fazioni*, the Assembly was broken up into factions **2.** (*mil.*) (*fatto d'arme*) feat of arms **3.** (*mil.*) (*servizio di guardia*) sentry-go, guard: *essere di —*, to be on guard (*o* duty).

faziosaménte, *av.* factiously.

faziosità, *s.f.* factiousness.

fazióso, *ag.* factious, seditious, turbulent.

fazzolétto, *s.m.* handkerchief; (*fam.*) hanky: *— da collo*, neckerchief (*o* square scarf).

fé, (*poet.*) per **féde**.

febbràio, *s.m.* February: *in — fa ancora molto freddo*, it is still very cold in February; *ella nacque il 3 —*, she was born on the third of February.

fébbre, *s.f.* **1.** fever; (*fam.*) temperature: *— da cavallo*, violent (*o* raging) fever; *— del fieno*, hay-fever; *— gialla*, yellow fever; *— malarica*, malarial fever; *— reumatica*, rheumatic fever; *accesso di —*, bout of fever; *ha la — molto alta*, he has a very high temperature; *avere la —*, to be feverish; *misurare la —*, to take the temperature **2.** *fig.* fever: *la — dell'oro*, the gold-fever; (*la corsa all'oro*) the gold-rush; *nella — della battaglia*, in the heat of the battle; *ciò mi mise in corpo una — d'impazienza*, that put me in a fever of impatience.

febbriciàttola, *s.f.* feveret, slight persistent fever.

febbricitànte, *ag.* feverish.

febbrícola, *s.f.* feveret, slight persistent fever.

febbricóso, *ag.* **1.** feverish **2.** (*che dà febbre*) feverous.

febbrífugo, *ag.* (*farm.*) febrifugal ‖ *s.m.* (*farm.*) febrifuge.

febbríle, *ag.* **1.** feverish, febrile **2.** *fig.* feverish; restless: *attività —*, feverish (*o* restless) activity.

febbrilménte, *av.* feverishly.

febbróne, *s.m.* violent fever, very high temperature.

febbróso, *ag.* feverish.

febèo, *ag.* (*mit.*) Phoebean, of Phoebus.

Fèbo, *no.pr.m.* (*mit.*) Phoebus.

fecàle, *ag.* fecal.

fèccia, *s.f.* **1.** dregs (*pl.*), lees (*pl.*): *bere sino alla —*, to drink to the lees (*o* to the dregs) **2.** *fig.* dregs (*pl.*), lees (*pl.*); (*plebaglia*) rabble, mob: *la — della società*, the dregs (*o* scum) of society.

feccióso, *ag.* **1.** full of dregs **2.** *fig.* very low, despicable.

fecciúme, *s.m.* **1.** quantity of sediment; dregs (*pl.*) **2.** *fig.* dregs (*pl.*), scum; (*plebaglia*) rabble, mob.

fèci, *s.f.pl.* excrement (*sing.*), ordure (*sing.*); (*med.*) stool (*sing.*); excreta, feces.

feciàle, *s.m.* (*st.romana*) fetial.

fècola, *s.f.* starch; fecula: — *di patate*, potato starch (*o* flour).

fecondàbile, *ag.* fertilizable.

fecondaménte, *av.* 1. (*fruttuosamente*) fruitfully 2. (*prolificamente*) prolifically.

fecondànte, *ag.* 1. fecundating 2. (*fertilizzante*) fertilizing 3. *fig.* stimulating.

fecondàre, *v.t.* 1. to fecundate 2. (*fertilizzare*) to fertilize: *la pioggia fecondò il terreno*, the rain fertilized the soil 3. *fig.* to stimulate: — *l'ingegno*, to stimulate the intelligence.

fecondatóre, *ag. V.* **fecondànte** ‖ *s.m.*, **fecondatríce**, *s.f.* fertilizer.

fecondazióne, *s.f.* 1. fecundation: — *artificiale*, (artificial) insemination 2. (*bot.*) pollination.

fecondità, *s.f.* fecundity; (*fertilità*) fertility, fruitfulness, productiveness: — *d'ingegno*, *fig.* fertility of mind.

fecóndo, *ag.* fecund, prolific (anche *fig.*); (*fertile*) fertile, fruitful: *pioggia feconda*, bountiful rain; *uno scrittore* —, a prolific writer; *suolo* —, fertile earth (*o* rich soil); *ha un ingegno* —, he has a creative genius.

Féde[1], *no.pr.f.* Faith.

féde[2], *s.f.* 1. (*credenza*) faith; belief; creed: — *in Dio*, faith in God; *professione di* —, profession of faith; *scuola aperta a tutte le fedi*, school open to every creed; *la sua* — *politica*, his political creed; — *significa credere in ql.co. senza prove*, faith means believing sthg. without proof; *prestare* — *a una diceria*, to give credit to a rumour; *prestare* — *a qlcu.*, to believe s.o. ‖ *rompere* —, *venir meno alla propria* —, to break one's faith; *tenere* —, to keep one's faith 2. (*religione*) faith; belief: *la* — *cristiana*, the Christian Faith ‖ *difensore della* —, (*titolo dei sovrani d'Inghilterra*) Defender of the Faith 3. (*fiducia*) trust; confidence; belief; credit: *degno di* —, trustworthy (*o* reliable); *ho* — *nelle tue promesse*, I trust your promises; *ho* — *nel tuo avvenire*, I feel confident about your future; *non ho molta* — *nella sua onestà*, I haven't much belief in his honesty; *riponi la tua* — *in Dio*, put your trust in God 4. (*lealtà, onestà*) faith; sincerity; honesty: *la* — *del giudice*, the honesty of the judge; *buona* —, good faith (*o* sincerity): *in buona* —, in good faith; *in mala* —, in bad faith (*o* dishonestly) ‖ *in* — *mia*, upon my honour; (*come esclamazione*) honestly; (*arc.*) in (*o* by my) faith 5. (*anello matrimoniale*) wedding -ring 6. (*documento*) certificate: — *di nascita*, birth certificate ‖ *fare* — *di ql.co.*, to bear witness to sthg.

fedecomésso, *s.m.* (*dir.*) fideicommissum, trust.

fedecommissàrio, *s.m.* (*dir.*) trustee.

fedéle, *ag.* 1. faithful; loyal; (*costante*) constant, staunch: — *nell'osservanza dei comandamenti di Dio*, faithful in the observance of God's commands; *amico* —, staunch friend; *un servitore* —, a faithful servant; *suddito* —, loyal subject; *essere* — *ai propri amici*, to be faithful to one's friends; *restare* — *a qlcu.*, to stick to s.o.; *restare* — *ad una promessa*, to abide by a promise; *restare* — *alle proprie opinioni*, to hold fast to one's opinions; *rimanere* — *alla parola data*, to keep one's word 2. (*veritiero*) true, exact, faithful; trustworthy: *copia* —, exact (*o* true) copy; *resoconto* —, exact report (*o* faithful account); *testimonio* —, trustworthy witness; *traduzione* —, faithful (*o* accurate *o* exact) translation 3. (*devoto*) faithful: *cristiano* —, faithful Christian ‖ *s.m.* 1. (*credente*) believer: *i fedeli*, the believers (*o* the faithful): *i fedeli di una parrocchia*, the parishioners (*o* the congregation) 2. (*seguace*) follower.

fedelménte, *av.* 1. faithfully; loyally 2. (*esattamente*) exactly.

fedeltà, *s.f.* 1. fidelity, faithfulness; loyalty; (*veridicità*) exactness, accuracy; fidelity: — *ai propri principi*, fidelity to one's principles; — *al proprio partito*, loyalty to one's party; — *al proprio sovrano*, faith-

fulness to one's sovereign; — *di un cassiere*, integrity of a cashier; — *di una traduzione*, accuracy (*o* closeness) of a translation 2. (*obbedienza*) allegiance: *giuramento di* —, oath of allegiance 3. (*rad.*) fidelity: *alta* —, (*neol.*) high fidelity (*o* Hi-Fi).

fèdera, *s.f.* pillow-slip; pillow-case.

federàle, *ag.* (*pol.*) federal.

federalísmo, *s.m.* (*pol.*) federalism.

federalísta, *s.c.* (*pol.*) federalist.

federàrsi, *v.r.* (*pol.*) to federate.

federatívo, *ag.* (*pol.*) federative.

federàto, *ag.* (*pol.*) federate.

federazióne, *s.f.* (*pol.*) federation.

Federíca, *no.pr.f.* Frederica ‖ (*dim.*) Freddy, Freddie.

Federíco, *no.pr.m.* Frederic(k) ‖ — *Barbarossa*, (*st.*) Frederick Barbarossa ‖ *dim.* Fred, Freddy, Freddie.

fedífrago, *ag.* 1. faithless 2. (*infido*) treacherous ‖ *s.m.* 1. faithless fellow 2. (*traditore*) traitor.

fedína, *s.f.* 1. criminal record, Police record: *aver la* — *netta*, to have a clean record (*o fam.* to have a clean slate); *avere la* — *sporca*, to have a very bad record 2. *pl.* (*strisce di barba lungo le gote*) mutton-chops.

Fedóne, *no.pr.m.* (*lett.*) Phaedo.

Fedòra, *no.pr.f.* Fedora.

Fèdra, *no.pr.f.* (*mit.*) Phaedra.

Fèdro, *no.pr.m.* (*st. lett.*) Phaedrus: *le favole di* —, the fables of Phaedrus.

fegatàccio, *s.m.* dare-devil.

fegatèlla, *s.f.* (*bot.*) hepatica, liverwort.

fégato, *s.m.* 1. liver: *fegatini di pollo*, chicken livers; *disturbi di* —, liver complaint (*o* trouble); *malattia di* —, liver disease; *olio di* — *di merluzzo*, cod-liver oil ‖ *mangiarsi il* —, to eat one's heart out 2. *fig.* courage; spirit; pluck; (*fam.*) guts (*pl.*): *ha del* —, he is a bold (*o* plucky) fellow (*o* he has plenty of guts).

fegatóso, *ag.* 1. bilious, suffering from liver complaint; (*fam.*) liverish; (*med.*) hepatic: *macchie fegatose*, hepatic spots 2. *fig.* (*irascibile*) irritable, bilious, peevish, liverish.

félce, *s.f.* (*bot.*) fern; bracken, brake: — *arborea*, tree-fern.

felceéta, *s.f.*, **felceéto**, *s.m.* fernery; bracken.

feldispàto, *s.m.* (*min.*) feldspar.

feld-marescíàllo, *s.m.* (*mil.*) field-marshal.

feldspàtico, *ag.* (*min.*) feldspathic.

feldspàto, *s.m.* (*min.*) feldspar.

feldspatòidi, *s.m.pl.* (*min.*) feldspathoids.

felibrísmo, *s.m.* (*st. lett.*) Félibrige.

felíce[1], *ag.* 1. happy: *matrimonio* —, happy marriage; *scelta* —, happy choice; *sono molto* — *di vederti*, I am very glad (*o* pleased *o* happy) to see you; *far* — *qlcu.*, to make s.o. happy ‖ — *di conoscerLa*, (*formula usata nelle presentazioni*) how do you do?; (*amer.*) glad to meet you 2. (*fortunato*) lucky, fortunate: *giorno* —, lucky day 3. (*piacevole*) pleasant: *viaggio* —, pleasant journey.

Felíce[2], *no.pr.m.* Felix.

feliceménte, *av.* 1. happily 2. (*in modo opportuno*) happily: *un'idea espressa* —, an idea happily expressed 3. (*fortunatamente*) luckily; successfully.

Felicita[1], *no.pr.f.* Felicity.

felicità[2], *s.f.* 1. happiness, felicity; joy; (*beatitudine*) bliss, blissfulness 2. — *!*, God bless you!; (*dopo uno starnuto*) bless you! 2. (*di espressione*) felicity: *si espresse con* —, he expressed himself happily.

felicitàre, *v.t.* (*rar.*): *che Dio La feliciti!*, God bless you! ‖ **felicitàrsi**, *v.r.* to congratulate (s.o.): *si felicitò con l'amico per il matrimonio*, he congratulated his friend on his marriage.

felicitazióne, *s.f.* congratulation.

felíno, *ag.* 1. feline 2. *fig.* catlike, feline; stealthy: *astuzia felina*, feline cunning; *con passo* —, with stealthy step; *ella cammina con grazia felina*, she walks with feline grace.

fellàndrio, *s.m.* (*bot.*) water-fennel.

fellèma, *s.m.* (*bot.*) phellem.

fellóne, *ag.* felon; treacherous; cruel, fell; wicked ‖ *s.m.* (*traditore*) traitor; (*criminale*) felon, villain, ruffian, rogue.

fellonescaménte, *av.* feloniously.

fellonésco, *ag.* folonious.

fellonía, *s.f.* (*rar.*) **1.** treason **2.** (*azione malvagia*) felony, perfidity.

felloplàstica, *s.f.* (*artig.*) phelloplastics.

félpa, *s.f.* plush.

felpàto, *ag.* **1.** plushy **2.** *fig.* soft: *a passi felpati,* stealthily.

felsíneo, *ag.* (*letter.*) of Bologna, from Bologna.

feltràre, *v.t.* (*ind. tessile*) to felt; to cover with felt.

feltratúra, *s.f.* felting.

féltro, *s.m.* **1.** (*tessuto*) felt: *un cappello di —,* a felt hat (*o amer.* soft hat) ‖ *— bitumato,* (*edil.*) tarred felt; — *d'amianto,* (*ind. tessile*) asbestos felt; — *per borre,* (*ind. esplosivi*) wadding; — *per cartiera,* paper felt **2.** (*groviglio di peli di un animale*) felt **3.** (*filtro*) filter.

felúca, *s.f.* **1.** (*cappello*) cocked hat **2.** (*mar.*) felucca.

fèlze, *s.f.* (small) cabin of a gondola.

femíneo, *V.* **femmíneo.**

fémmina, *s.f.* **1.** (*essere di sesso femminile*) female: *un canarino —,* a hen-canary; *un elefante —,* a cow -elephant; *un gatto —,* a she-cat (*o* a female cat); *una giraffa —,* a cow-giraffe; *un pavone —,* a pea-hen; *un pesce —,* a spawner; *una tigre —,* a female tiger (*o* tigress); *nella mia classe ci sono dodici maschi e undici femmine,* in my class there are twelve boys and eleven girls; *non so se è un maschio o una —,* I do not know whether it is a male or a female (*o* a boy or a girl) ‖ *mala —,* (*spreg.*) bad (*o* loose) woman **2.** (*uomo debole e timido*) milk-sop, sissy **3.** (*mec.*) female: *vite —,* female screw.

femminèlla, *s.f.* **1.** (*donnetta*) poor little woman: *che cosa si può pretendere da una —?,* what can you expect from a female? **2.** (*mec.*) (*gangherella*) eye **3.** *pl.* (*del timone di navi, aerei*) gudgeons, rudder gudgeons, braces, rudder braces.

femmíneo, *ag.* **1.** feminine, womanish **2.** (*effeminato*) effeminate, womanish.

femminésco, *ag.* (*rar.*) womanish, womanly.

femminétta, *s.f.* (*letter.*) maid.

femminézza, *V.* **femminilità.**

femminíle, *ag.* **1.** (*di sesso*) female: *il sesso —,* the female (*o* fair) sex; *personale* (*operaio*) *—,* female operatives ‖ *collegio —,* girls' boarding-school **2.** (*da donna*) feminine: *curiosità —,* **feminine** curiosity **3.** (*femmineo*) womanly: *grazia —,* womanly grace(fulness) **4.** (*gram.*) feminine: *questa parola è —,* this word is feminine ‖ *s.m.* (*gram.*) feminine: *aggettivo che prende una «a» al —,* adjective that takes an "a" in the feminine.

femminilità, *s.f.* womanliness, femininity, femin(e)ity, feminineness.

femminilménte, *av.* femininely; in a womanly way; in a womanish manner.

femminíno, *ag.* (*rar.*) feminine: *astuzia femminina,* feminine artfulness ‖ *s.m.* (*fascino femminile*) womanliness ‖ *l'eterno —,* the eternal feminine.

femminísmo, *s.m.* (*st. pol.*) feminism.

femminísta, *s.c.* (*st. pol.*) feminist.

femminúccia, *s.f.* **1.** simple woman **2.** (*uomo senza coraggio*) white-livered man; coward.

femoràle, *ag.* (*anat.*) femoral: *arteria —,* femoral artery.

fèmore, *s.m.* (*anat.*) femur; thigh-bone.

fenacetína, *s.f.* (*farm.*) phenacetin(e).

fenàti, *s.m.pl.* (*chim.*) phenates.

fendènte, *s.m.* (*scherma*) cutting blow.

fèndere, *v.t.* **1.** to cleave, to rive, to part; to fissure: *la siccità ha fenduto la terra,* the drought has fissured

(*o* cracked) the ground; — *l'ardesia,* to rive slate; — *il legno,* to rive (*o* to split) wood; — *la terra con l'aratro,* to plough the soil **2.** *fig.* to rend; to break; to cleave: *era una cosa che fendeva il cuore,* it was enough to break your heart (*o* it was heart-breaking *o* heart-rending); *mi si fende il cuore a veder...,* it breaks my heart to see...; *il naviglio fendeva le acque,* the boat cut (*o* ploughed through) the waters; — *l'aria,* to cleave the air; (*di suono*) to rend the air; — *la folla,* to elbow one's way through the crowd (*o* to squeeze through the crowd) ‖ **fèndersi,** *v.r.* to split, to cleave; to crack: *questo legno si fende facilmente,* this wood splits easily; *la terra e il muro incominciavano a —,* the earth and the wall were beginning to crack.

fendíbile, *ag.* cleavable; possible to be split, fissurable.

fendinébbia, *s.m.* (*aut.*) fog light.

fendítore, *ag.* cleaving; splitting ‖ *s.m.,* **fenditríce,** *s.f.* (*rar.*) cutter, splitter.

fenditúra, *s.f.* **1.** cleft, fissure, crack, split, cleavage: *dopo il terremoto il terreno era pieno di fenditure,* the ground was full of cracks (*o* fissures) after the earthquake **2.** (*metal.*) flaw **3.** (*ott.*) slit.

feneratízio, *ag.* (*dir.*) concerning usury.

fenicàto, *ag.* (*chim.*) phenolic: *alcool —,* phenolic alcohol.

feníce, *s.f.* **1.** (*araba*) —, (*mit.*) phoenix (*anche fig.*) ‖ *una — di virtù,* a paragon of virtue ‖ *Fenice,* (*astr.*) Phoenix **2.** (*bot.*) phoenix.

Fenícia, *no.pr.f.* (*geog. st.*) Phoenicia.

fenício, *ag. s.m.* Phoenician.

fènico, *ag.* (*chim.*) phenic: *acido —,* phenic acid.

fenicòttero, *s.m.* (*ornit.*) flamingo (*pl.* flamingoes).

fenòlico, *ag.* (*chim.*) phenolic: *resine fenoliche,* phenolic resins.

fenòlo, *s.m.* (*chim.*) phenol.

fenología, *s.f.* (*scient.*) phenology.

fenomenàle, *ag.* **1.** phenomenal **2.** (*fam.*) (*straordinario*) extraordinary, phenomenal, exceptional.

fenomènico, *ag.* (*fil.*) relating to a phenomenon.

fenomenísmo, *s.m.* (*st. fil.*) phenomenalism.

fenòmeno, *s.m.* **1.** phenomenon (*pl.* phenomena): — *meteorologico,* meteor; — *transitorio,* transient phenomenon; *i fenomeni della natura,* the phenomena of nature **2.** (*cosa mirabile*) wonder: *un — vivente,* a living wonder.

fenomenología, *s.f.* (*fil.*) phenomenology.

fenoplàsto, *s.m.* (*chim.*) phenoplast.

feràce, *ag.* fruitful, fertile, rich (*anche fig.*): *immaginazione —,* rich imagination; *suolo —,* fertile soil.

feracità, *s.f.* fruitfulness, fertility, richness (*anche fig.*).

feràle, *ag.* feral, deadly, fatal; dismal, distressing: *ferali notizie,* distressing news.

feralménte, *av.* fatally; distressingly.

Ferdinàndo, *no.pr.m.* Ferdinand.

ferentàrio, *s.m.* (*st. romana*) light-armed soldier.

fèretro, *s.m.* (*bara*) bier; coffin.

fèria, *s.f.* **1.** *pl.* holidays; vacation (*sing.*): *ferie estive,* summer vacation (*o* holidays); *ferie pasquali,* Easter holidays; *ferie retribuite,* holidays with pay; *prendersi le ferie,* to take one's holidays **2.** (*eccl.*) (*giorno feriale*) feria, week-day: — *seconda,* Monday; *Uffizio della —,* ferial office.

feriàle, *ag.* **1.** working: *giorno —,* week-day (*o* working-day) **2.** (*eccl.*) ferial.

ferígno, *ag.* (*letter.*) ferine, feral, wild; untamed.

feriménto, *s.m.* wounding.

feríno, *ag.* ferine, feral, wild; untamed.

feríre, *v.t.* **1.** to wound, to hurt, to injure; (*pugnalare*) to stab: *cinque di quei soldati furono uccisi e venti feriti,* five of those soldiers were killed and twenty (were) wounded; *entrambi erano stati feriti in quell'incidente stradale,* both had been hurt (*o* injured) in that road accident ‖ *senza colpo —,* without striking a blow (*o* without meeting any resistance) **2.** *fig.* (*col-*

pire) to strike; (*offendere*) to offend; to wound; to hurt: *ciò lo ferì profondamente*, this wounded (o affected) him deeply; — *la fantasia di qlcu.*, to strike s.o.'s imagination; — *gli occhi*, to offend the eye; — *qlcu. nell'onore*, to wound s.o. in his honour; — *i sentimenti di qlcu.*, to hurt s.o.'s feelings ‖ **ferírsi**, *v.r.* to hurt oneself, to injure oneself, to wound oneself: *si ferì ad un braccio*, he hurt his arm.

feríta[1], *s.f.* wound (anche *fig.*); hurt, injury: *una* — *al proprio orgoglio*, a wound to one's pride; — *da proiettile*, bullet wound; — *da taglio*, slash; *una* — *leggera*, a slight (o flesh-) wound; *la* — *al braccio sinistro guarì prestissimo*, the wound in his left arm healed very soon; *curare una* —, to heal a wound; *infliggere una* — *a qlcu.*, to inflict a wound on s.o.; *medicare una* —, to dress a wound; *ricevere una* — *mortale*, to receive a mortal hurt; *riportare ferite in un incidente*, to be injured in an accident.

feríta[2], *s.f.* (*arc.*) ferineness.

feríto, *ag.* wounded, injured, hurt (anche *fig.*): *gravemente* —, seriously wounded (o badly hurt); *leggermente* —, slightly wounded (o hurt o injured); *orgoglio* —, wounded pride ‖ *i feriti*, the wounded ‖ *s.m.* wounded man.

feritóia, *s.f.* 1. loophole; embrasure 2. (*mec.*) slit.

feritóre, *ag.* wounding, injuring, hurting ‖ *s.m.*, **feritríce**, *s.f.* wounder.

férma, *s.f.* 1. (*mil.*) service, term of service: — *di diciotto mesi*, eighteen months' service 2. (*caccia*) pointing: *cane da* —, setter.

fermacàrte, *s.m.* paper-weight.

fermacravàtta, *s.m.* tie-pin.

fermàglio, *s.m.* 1. clasp; (*fibbia*) buckle; (*gioiello*) brooch: — *di sicurezza*, (*per collane, braccialetti, ecc.*) safety-catch 2. (*per carte, documenti, ecc.*) clip.

fermaménte, *av.* firmly, steadily; (*decisamente*) decidedly, resolutely: *ritengo* —..., I positively believe....

fermanèllo, *s.m.* guard-ring.

fermapièdi, *s.m.* (*di bicicletta*) toeclip.

fermapòrta, *s.m.* door-stop.

fermàre, *v.t.* 1. (*arrestare nel movimento*) to stop, to arrest (anche *fig.*): *che cosa fermò il treno?*, what stopped the train? (o what caused the train to stop?); *nessun ostacolo lo fermerà*, no obstacle will stop (o hinder) him; — *un attacco*, (*mil.*) to check an attack; — *un'auto, un cavallo imbizzarrito*, to stop (o to pull up) a car, a runaway horse; — *la crescita*, to arrest growth; — *un'emorragia*, (*med.*) to stop (o to check) a bleeding; *in piena corsa*, to check in full career; — *le macchine*, (*mar.*) to stop the engines; — *il pagamento di un assegno*, (*comm.*) to stop a cheque; — *il progresso*, to stop (o to block) progress; — *qlcu. dal far ql.co.*, to hinder (o to prevent) s.o. from doing sthg. 2. (*fissare*) to fasten, to fix (anche *fig.*): — *l'animo su ql.co.*, to fix one's mind (up)on sthg.; — *l'attenzione su ql.co.*, to fix (o to arrest) one's attention on sthg.; — *gli occhi su qlcu., su qlcu.*, to fix one's eyes on sthg., to gaze upon (o at) s.o.; — *un punto, un bottone*, to fasten a stitch, a button; — *i punti*, (*nel lavoro a maglia*) to cast off 3. (*cuc.*) — *la carne*, to seal the meat 4. (*dir.*) to hold: *la polizia inglese non può* — *una persona senza incriminazione*, the English police cannot hold (o detain) a person without a charge ‖ *v.i.* 1. to stop: *l'autobus ferma laggiù*, the bus stops over there 2. (*di cane da ferma*) to point, to set ‖ **fermàrsi**, *v.r.* 1. to stop: *l'auto si fermò davanti alla mia porta*, the car stopped (o drew up) at my door; *il cuore del vecchio e il suo orologio si fermarono nello stesso momento*, the old man's heart and his watch stopped at the same moment; *quando lo incontrai mi fermai un poco con lui*, when I met him I stopped and talked to him for a while; *il treno si fermò*, the train stopped (o was brought to a stand) ‖ — *di botto*, to stop short; — *lungo la strada*, to stop on the way 2. (*soggiornare*) to stop; to stay: *quanto ti*

fermerai a Londra?, how long are you going to stay (o to remain) in London? 3. (*indugiare*) to dwell: — *su un argomento*, to dwell (o to lay stress) on a subject 4. (*fare una pausa*) to pause, to make a pause 5. (*mec.*) to stop (working), to stall: *l'uscensore si è fermato*, the lift has stopped working; *il motore si fermò*, the engine stopped (o stalled).

fermàta, *s.f.* 1. stop; halt: — *facoltativa*, request stop; — *obbligatoria*, regular stop; — *provvisoria*, temporary stop; *la più vicina* — *d'autobus è subito dopo quell'angolo*, the nearest bus-stop is just round that corner; *quante fermate ci sono da qui a Milano?*, how many stops are there from here to Milan?; *venti minuti di* —, a twenty minutes' stop 2. (*pausa*) pause.

fermentàbile, *ag.* fermentable.

fermentàre, *v.i.* to ferment (anche *fig.*); (*di liquidi*) to work, to ferment; (*di pasta*) to rise; (*lievitare*) to leaven: *la pasta fermenta*, dough rises; *il vino fermenta*, wine ferments.

fermentatìvo, *ag.* fermentative.

fermentazióne, *s.f.* (*chim.*) fermentation: — *alcoolica*, alcoholic fermentation; — *lattica*, lactic fermentation; (*di vino*) working, fermentation; (*di pasta*) rising.

ferménto, *s.m.* 1. (*chim.*) ferment; (*di pane*) leaven; (*di birra*) yeast: — *selezionato*, clean yeast 2. *fig.* ferment, excitement, agitation, turmoil, tumult: *gli animi erano in* —, men's minds were in a ferment (o were seething with excitement); *tutta la città era in* —, the whole town was in a (state of) ferment.

fermézza, *s.f.* firmness, steadfastness, steadiness, strength, rigidity (anche *fig.*): — *di mente*, strength of mind; — *di princìpi*, rigidity of principles; *agire con* —, to act firmly (o resolutely); *mancare di* —, to be lacking in firmness.

férmo, *ag.* 1. still: *acque ferme*, still waters; *il motore era ancora* —, the engine had not yet started; *il portinaio tenne* — *il ladro*, the door-keeper held the thief fast; *quel treno è* —, that train is at a stop (o stationary); *star* —, to stand still; *sta'* —!, be (o keep) quiet! ‖ — *posta*, poste-restante: *una lettera in* — *posta*, a letter to be called for ‖ *canto* —, (*mus.*) plain song ‖ *punto* —, (*gram.*) full stop (o period) ‖ *terra ferma*, dry land ‖ *aspettare a piè* —, to wait motionless 2. (*irremovibile, saldo*) firm; steady: — *come torre*, as firm as a rock; *una ferma fede*, a firm faith; — *nei propositi*, firm (o unswerving) in one's intentions; — *proposito*, steady purpose; *mano ferma*, steady hand; *fig.* firm hand; *salute mal ferma*, poor health; *voce ferma*, firm voice; *volontà ferma*, unfaltering will ‖ — *stante*, considering that ‖ *per* —, certainly: *tenere per* —, to believe positively (o to take for granted) ‖ *s.m.* 1. (*fermezza*) firmness; steadiness 2. (*mec.*) lock; catch; stop: — *automatico*, automatic stop (o brake) 3. (*dir.*) (*arresto provvisorio*) provisional arrest: *procedere al* — *di qlcu.*, to hold s.o. 4. (*confisca, sequestro*) distraint: *mettere il* — *su merce di contrabando*, to seize (o to impound o to confiscate) contraband goods; *mettere il* — *su ql.co.*, to distrain upon sthg.: *mettere il* — *su un assegno*, to block a cheque 5. (*caccia*) pointing: *cane da* —, pointer, setter.

fernambúcco, *s.m.* (*bot.*) Brazil-wood.

fernèt, *s.m.* "fernet" (kind of Italian bitters).

fernétte, *s.f. pl.* (*mec.*) wards.

feróce, *ag.* ferocious; savage, wild; fierce; (*crudele*) cruel: *bestie feroci*, wild beasts; *sguardo* —, ferocious look ‖ *fame, appetito* —, (*fam.*) ravenous appetite.

feroceménte, *av.* ferociously; savagely; fiercely; (*crudelmente*) cruelly.

feròcia, *s.f.* fierceness; ferocity, ferociousness; savageness, savagery; (*crudeltà*) cruelty.

feròdo, *s.m.* (*aut.*) lining; — *per freni*, (*mec.*) brake lining.

ferràccia, *s.f.* (*ittiol.*) thornback.

ferràccio, *s.m.* 1. (*ghisa*) pig iron 2. (*rottami di ferro*) scrap iron.

ferràglia, *s.f.* (*rottami di ferro*) scrap-iron: *cumulo di* —, scrap-heap; *rumore di* —, clanking noise (*o* rattle).

ferragósto, *s.m.* August holiday; feast of the Assumption (August 15th) || *il* — *inglese,* August Bank -holiday.

ferràio, *s.m.* blacksmith, smith.

ferrai(u)òlo, *s.m.* short cloak.

ferràme, *s.m.* (*materiale di ferro*) ironware; hardware.

ferraménta, *s.f.pl.* 1. hardware (*sing.*); ironware (*sing.*); iron goods; ironmongery (*sing.*): *negozio di* —, ironmonger's shop; (*amer.*) hardware store; *negoziante di* —, ironmonger 2. (*utensili di ferro*) iron fittings.

ferraménto, *s.m.* iron tool.

ferràre, *v.t.* 1. to fit with iron, to mount with iron: — *un bastone,* to put a ferrule on a stick; — *una porta,* to fit locks and hinges to a door 2. (*cavalli*) to shoe: — *un cavallo,* to shoe a horse; — *a freddo,* to cold-shoe; — *a ghiaccio,* to rough-shoe (*o* to calk).

ferréccia, *s.f.* 1. *pl.* (*oggetti di ferro*) hardware (*sing.*); ironware (*sing.*); iron goods; ironmongery (*sing.*). 2. (*negozio*) ironmonger's shop.

ferràta, *s.f.* 1. (*inferriata*) iron railing, iron grating 2. (*strada ferrata*) railway; (*amer.*) railroad.

ferràto, *ag.* 1. (*iron*)shod: *bastone* —, ironshod stick; *scarpe ferrate,* hobnailed shoes; *strada ferrata,* railway (*o amer.* railroad) 2. (*ben preparato*) well read, well informed, strong: *è ben* — *in storia,* he is good at (*o* very well read *o* well up *o* very strong in) history.

ferratúra, *s.f.* 1. shoeing (of horses) 2. (*ferri di cavallo*) horseshoes (*pl.*).

ferravècchio, *s.m.* dealer in old iron.

ferrazzuòlo, *s.m.* ironworker.

fèrreo, *ag.* 1. iron (*attributivo*) || *corona ferrea,* Iron Crown 2. *fig.* strong; robust; hard; iron (*attributivo*): *con mano ferrea,* with iron hand; *disciplina ferrea,* very strict discipline; *memoria ferrea,* excellent memory; *salute ferrea,* excellent health; *una volontà ferrea,* an iron will.

ferrería, *s.f.* 1. ironware 2. (*arnesi di ferro*) iron tools (*pl.*).

ferrétto, *s.m.* small iron tool; iron gadget.

fèrrico, *ag.* (*chim.*) ferric.

ferrièra, *s.f.* 1. ironworks (*pl.*), iron-foundry 2. (*laminatoio*) rolling mill 3. (*miniera di ferro*) iron-mine.

ferrífero, *ag.* ferriferous; yielding iron.

ferrígno, *ag.* 1. iron-like: *colore* —, iron grey 2. *fig.* strong; robust; hard; iron (*attributivo*).

ferrite, *s.f.* (*min.*) ferrite.

fèrro, *s.m.* 1. iron (anche *fig.*): — *battuto,* wrought iron; — *dolce,* soft iron; — *fuso,* ingot iron; — *laminato,* rolled iron; — *trafilato,* drawn iron; *grigio* —, iron-grey; *filo di* —, iron wire; *lamiera di* —, iron sheet (*o* iron plate); *minerale di* —, iron-ore; *rivestito di* —, iron-clad; *rottami di* —, scrap-iron || *l'età del* —, iron age || *secoli di* —, heroic centuries || *un uomo di* —, a man of iron; *una volontà di* —, an iron will || *hai una memoria di* —, you have an excellent (*o* a very good) memory || *tocca* — *!,* touch wood! || *battere il* — *finché è caldo, prov.* to strike while the iron is hot (*o* to make hay while the sun shines) 2. (*attrezzo*) tool: — *da calza,* knitting needle; — *da stirare,* flat-iron (*o* iron); — *di cavallo,* horse-shoe; *ferri chirurgici,* surgical instruments; *i ferri del mestiere,* the tools of the trade || *cuocere carne ai ferri,* to broil (*o* to grill) meat 3. (*spada*) sword: *incrociare i ferri,* to cross swords || *essere ai ferri corti con qlcu.,* to be at loggerheads with s.o. || *mettere un paese a* — *e fuoco,* to put a country to fire and sword (*o* to lay a country waste) 4. *pl.* (*ceppi*) irons, chains, fetters: *lo misero ai ferri,* they put him in irons.

ferrocianúro, *s.m.* (*chim.*) ferrocyanide.

ferroeròmo, *s.m.* (*metal.*) ferrochrome, ferrochromium.

ferroléghe, *s.f.pl.* (*metal.*) ferroalloys.

ferrosilicio, *s.m.* (*metal.*) ferrosilicon.

ferróso, *ag.* (*chim.*) ferrous.

ferrovía, *s.f.* 1. railway; (*amer.*) railroad: — *aerea,* overhead (*o* elevated) railway (*o sl. amer.* el); — *a un binario,* single-line (*o* single-track) railway; — *a cremagliera,* rack railway; — *a doppio binario,* double -line (*o* double-track) railway; — *elettrica,* electric railway; — *a scartamento normale,* standard-gauge railway; — *a scartamento ridotto,* light railway (*o amer.* narrow-gauge railroad); — *sotterranea,* underground railway (*o fam.* tube *o amer.* subway); — *a vapore,* steam railway || (*mandare*) *per* —, (to send) by rail (*o* by train) 2. (*stazione*) railway station.

ferroviàrio, *ag.* railway (*attributivo*); (*amer.*) railroad (*attributivo*): *casello* —, level-crossing keeper's house; *movimento* —, railway traffic; *orario* —, railway time -table; *rete ferroviaria,* railway system; *servizio* —, railway service; *tariffe ferroviarie,* railway rates; *tronco* —, railway branch.

ferrovière, *s.m.* 1. railwayman (*pl.* railwaymen); (*amer.*) railroader 2. (*funzionario delle ferrovie*) railway official.

ferrugígno, ferrugíneo, *ag.* (*letter.*) rusty, rust -coloured, ferruginous.

ferruginóso, *ag.* ferruginous.

fèrtile, *ag.* fertile, fruitful, productive (anche *fig.*): — *fantasia,* fertile imagination; *suolo* —, fruitful soil.

fertilità, *s.f.* fertility, fruitfulness, productiveness (anche *fig.*).

fertilizzànte, *ag.* fertilizing || *s.m.* fertilizer: — *chimico,* artificial fertilizer.

fertilizzàre, *v.t.* to fertilize.

fertilizzazióne, *s.f.* fertilization: — *a spandimento,* (*agr.*) top-dressing; — *selettiva,* (*bot.*) selective fertilization.

fertilménte, *av.* fertilely, fruitfully; (*abbondantemente*) abundantly.

fèrula, *s.f.* 1. (*bacchetta per punire gli scolari*) ferule, rod, cane 2. (*bot.*) Ferula 3. (*chir.*) ferula.

fervènte, *ag.* 1. (*cocente*) burning, ardent, fervent: *i ferventi raggi del sole,* the ardent sunbeams 2. *fig.* fervid, fervent, ardent: — *cattolico,* fervent Catholic.

ferventeménte, *av.* fervently, ardently.

fervènza, *s.f.* (*rar.*) fervency, fervour.

fèrvere, *v.i.* 1. (*rar.*) (*essere cocente*) to be hot, to be burning 2. *fig.* (*essere intenso*): *nell'officina ferveva il lavoro,* in the workshop everyone was working hard; *i preparativi fervono,* preparations are well advanced.

fervidaménte, *av.* fervently, ardently.

fèrvido, *ag.* fervent, ardent, fervid: *fervidi auguri,* best wishes; *una fervida fantasia,* a fervid imagination; *fervida preghiera,* fervent prayer.

fervóre, *s.m.* 1. (*calore intenso*) heat: *il* — *dell'estate,* the heat of summer 2. *fig.* fervour, ardour; heat; (*zelo*) zeal: *nel* — *del dibattito,* in the heat of the debate; *nel* — *della battaglia,* when the battle was at its height.

fervoríno, *s.m.* (*esortazione*) exhortation; (*predicozzo*) admonition: *gli farò un bel* —, (*fam.*) I'll lecture him all right.

fervorosaménte, *av.* fervently, fervidly.

fervoróso, *ag.* fervent, ardent, fervid; (*pieno di zelo*) zealous.

fèrzo, *s.m.* (*mar.*) (sail) cloth.

fescenníno, *ag.* 1. (*poes.*) Fescennine 2. *fig.* licentious, obscene, scurrilous.

fésso, *ag.* 1. (*feso*) cracked; (*diviso in due*) cloven: *campana fessa,* cracked bell; *zoccolo* —, *unghia fessa,* cloven hoof | *voce fessa,* cracked voice 2. (*volg.*) (*sciocco*) silly, stupid, foolish || *s.m.* 1. (*spaccatura*) cleft, crack; (*spiraglio*) slit, small opening 2. (*volg.*) (*sciocco*) idiot, fool, blockhead.

fessúra, *s.f.* (*spaccatura*) crack, fissure, cleft; (*fenditura*) slit; (*apertura da cui defluisce un fluido*) leak: — *alare,* (*aer.*) wing slot.

fèsta, *s.f.* 1. (*giorno di riposo*) holiday: — *civile,* legal holiday; *feste di Natale,* Christmas holidays; —

nazionale, national holiday (*o* festival *o* national commemoration day); *abiti da* —, Sunday clothes (*o* Sunday best): *era vestito da* —, he was wearing his Sunday best; *mezza* —, half-holiday; *oggi è* —, *nessuno lavora*, today is a holiday, nobody works; *far* —, (*riposare*) to have a holiday; (*stare allegri*) to make merry ‖ *conciare qlcu. per il dì delle feste*, to give s.o. a sound thrashing 2. (*solennità religiosa*) feast; (*festività*) festivity: — *del villaggio*, village feast; *la* — *dell'Ascensione*, Ascension Day; *la* — *di Sant'Antonio*, St. Anthony's Day; *la* — *di tutti i Santi, dei morti*, All Saints' Day, All Souls' Day; — *di precetto*, day of obligation; *giorno di* —, feast day ‖ *le Feste*, (*di Natale*) Christmas (*o* Yule tide); (*di Pasqua*) Easter: *augurare le Buone Feste*, to wish a Merry Christmas 3. (*anniversario*) birthday; (*onomastico*) Saint's Day, Fête, name-day: *oggi è la mia* —, it is my birthday today; (*onomastico*) it is my Saint's day (*o* my Fête *o* my name-day) today 4. (*festival*) festival: — *dei fiori*, flower festival 5. (*banchetto*) feast; (*baldoria*) revel; (*trattenimento*) entertainment: — *da ballo*, ball 6. (*giubilo, allegria*) festivity, rejoicing; merrymaking: *in questo giorno di* —, on this festal (*o* festive) day; *ciò pose fine alla* —, this put an end to the merrymaking; *far* — *a qlcu.*, (*accoglierlo cordialmente*) to give s.o. a hearty welcome (*o* to welcome s.o. warmly) ‖ *far la* — *a qlcu.*, (*ucciderlo*) to kill s.o. (*o* to bump off s.o.) ‖ *far la* — *a una torta*, (*mangiarla completamente*) to eat up the whole cake 7. (*gioia*) joy: *è una* — *per noi vedervi*, it is a joy for us to see you.

festaiuòlo, *ag.* feast-loving (*attributivo*); fond of feasting (*predicativo*) ‖ *s.m.* feast-lover, reveller.

festànte, *ag.* rejoicing, jubilant, joyful: *gli andai incontro tutto* —, I welcomed him cordially (*o* joyfully).

festeggiaménto, *s.m.* celebration; festivity; festive proceedings (*pl.*): *nulla guastò i festeggiamenti*, nothing marred the festivities.

festeggiàre, *v.t.* 1. to celebrate: *vorranno* — *quest'occasione*, they will want to celebrate this occasion; — *il proprio onomastico*, to keep one's Saint's day (*o* one's Fête *o* one's name-day) 2. (*accogliere festosamente*) to give a hearty welcome to (s.o.).

festeggiàto, *s.m.* (*ospite d'onore*) guest of honour ‖ *il* — (*per il compleanno*) *è mio fratello*, it is my brother's birthday we are keeping.

festeggiatóre, *ag.* celebrating ‖ *s.m.*, **festeggiatríce**, *s.f.* celebrator; feaster.

festévole, *ag.* festive, joyous, gay; jovial, genial.

festevolézza, *s.f.* joyfulness, gaiety; joviality, geniality.

festevolménte, *av.* 1. joyfully, merrily 2. (*cordialmente*) heartily, cordially.

festicciòla, *s.f.* informal family party.

festíno, *s.m.* (*banchetto*) feast; banquet.

festival, *s.m.* festival.

festività, *s.f.* 1. festivity; feast 2. (*giocondità*) gaiety 3. (*cordialità*) geniality, cordiality.

festívo, *ag.* 1. (*di festa*) Sunday (*attributivo*): *biglietto* —, (*ferr.*) week-end ticket; *scuola festiva*, Sunday school; *riposo* —, Sunday rest 2. (*lieto, gioioso*) festal, merry; festive: *un aspetto* —, a festive aspect; *hai un aspetto* — *oggi, hai vinto al totocalcio?*, you are very merry today, have you won the football-pools?.

festonàto, *ag.* 1. (*ornato di fiori, di fregi architettonici*) festooned 2. (*ornato di ricami*) scalloped.

festóne, *s.m.* 1. (*ornamento di fiori, fregio architettonico*) festoon 2. (*ricamo a linee curve*) scallop.

festosaménte, *av.* 1. joyfully 2. (*allegramente*) merrily 3. (*cordialmente*) cordially.

festosità, *s.f.* 1. joyfulness; festivity 2. (*allegria*) gaiety 3. (*cordialità*) cordiality.

festóso, *ag.* 1. joyous; joyful 2. (*allegro*) merry; gay 3. (*cordiale*) hearty; genial.

festúca, *s.f.* (a particle of) straw: *le acque lo trascinarono come una* —, the water swept him away like

a straw ‖ *e perchè osservi la* — *nell'occhio del tuo fratello, e non badi alla trave che è nell'occhio tuo?*, (*Bibbia*) why beholdest thou the mote that is in thy brother's eye, but considerest not the beam that is in thine own eye?.

fetàle, *ag.* f(o)etal.

fetènte, *ag.* stinking; f(o)etid (anche *fig.*) ‖ *s.c.* (*volg.*) stinker: *sei un* —!, you stinker!.

fetíccio, *s.m.* fetish, fetich(e).

feticísmo, *s.m.* fetishism, fetichism.

feticísta, *ag.* fetishistic, fetichistic ‖ *s.c.* fetishist, fetichist.

fètido, *ag.* f(o)etid; stinking; rank; foul: *un odore* —, a foul odour.

fetidúme, *s.m.* 1. fetidness; stench 2. (*marciume*) rottenness (anche *fig.*) 3. (*cose fetide*) rotten things (*pl.*); rotten matter.

fèto, *s.m.* f(o)etus.

Fetónte, *no.pr.m.* (*mit.*) Phaeton.

fetóre, *s.m.* stink, stench; foul smell, nasty smell.

fétta, *s.f.* 1. slice; round: *una* — *di arrosto*, a cut off the joint; *una* — *di lardo*, a slice (*o* rasher) of bacon; *una* — *di limone*, a round of lemon; *una gran* — *di pane*, a large slice of bread; *tagliare ql.co. a fette*, to slice sthg. (*o* to cut sthg. into slices) ‖ *fare a fette qlcu.*, to cut s.o. to pieces 2. (*piccolo pezzo*) piece, bit: *una* — *di terra*, a piece of land 3. (*agr.*) (*porzione di terra alzata dalla vanga e dall'aratro*) spadeful; clod.

fettúccia, *s.f.* 1. tape 2. (*nastro*) ribbon 3. (*rettifilo*) straight stretch.

fettuccíne, *s.f.pl.* (*cuc.*) "fettuccine" (ribbon shaped vermicelli).

feudàle, *ag.* feudal.

feudalésimo, feudalísmo, *s.m.* (*st.*) feudalism.

feudalità, *s.f.* feudality.

feudalménte, *av.* feudally.

feudatàrio, *ag.s.m.* feudatory: *i grandi feudatari della Corona*, the great feudatories of the Crown.

fèudo, *s.m.* (*st.*) feud, fief, feoff, fee: *investire qlcu. di un* —, to enfeoff s.o.

fèz, *s.m.* fez.

fiàba, *s.f.* 1. fable; fairy-tale; story: *le favole di La Fontaine*, La Fontaine's fables; *sono tutte fiabe*, these are all children's stories 2. (*commedia fiabesca*) fairy play 3. (*falsità*) falsehood; story: *far circolare mille fiabe sul conto di qlcu.*, to spread all sorts of stories about s.o. ‖ *son tutte fiabe!*, that's a lot of stories!.

fiabésco, *ag.* 1. (*da fate*) fairy-like: *un castello* —, a fairy-like castle 2. (*di fate*) fairy: *racconto* —, fairy tale 3. (*favoloso*) fabulous.

fiàcca, *s.f.* 1. (*stanchezza*) weariness, lassitude, tiredness 2. (*indolenza*) indolence, laziness ‖ *battere la* —, (*fam.*) to be sluggish.

fiaccàbile, *ag.* (*spezzabile*) breakable.

fiaccaménte, *av.* weakly; wearily; languidly.

fiaccaménto, *s.m.* 1. (*indebolimento*) weakening, enfeebling 2. (*rottura*) breaking, breakage.

fiaccàre, *v.t.* 1. to exhaust; to wear out, to tire out; (*indebolire*) to weaken: — *le proprie forze in sforzi inutili*, to exhaust one's strength in useless efforts 2. (*spezzare*) to break (down) (anche *fig.*): — *la resistenza di qlcu.*, to break s.o.'s resistance ‖ **fiaccàrsi**, *v.r.* to break down: — *il collo*, to break one's neck.

fiaccàto, *ag.* (*spezzato*) broken.

fiaccheràio, *s.m.* cabman (*pl.* cabmen), cab-driver.

fiacchézza, *s.f.* 1. (*debolezza*) weakness; (*languore*) languor: *la* — *della natura umana*, the weakness of human nature 2. (*stanchezza*) weariness 3. (*indolenza*) indolence; (*fam.*) sluggishness.

fiàcco[1], *ag.* exhausted, weak; weary: *mi sento* —, I feel exhausted ‖ *discorso* —, poor speech ‖ *mercato* —, (*comm.*) dull market.

fiàcco[2], *s.m.* (*fam.*) (*gran quantità*): *un* — *di botte*, a good (*o* sound) thrashing.

fiàccola, *s.f.* 1. torch: *la* — *della libertà*, *fig.* the torch of liberty; *alla luce di fiaccole*, by torchlight **2.** (*per saldatura*) blowlamp; blowtorch.

fiaccolàta, *s.f.* torchlight procession.

fiaccóna, *s.f.* lassitude; laziness.

fiaccóne, *s.m.* sluggard, slacker.

fiacre, *s.m.* hackney carriage; four wheeler.

fiàla, *s.f.* phial, vial.

fiàmma, *s.f.* **1.** flame (*anche fig.*); (*molto viva*) blaze; (*mobile, oscillante*) flare: *in fiamme*, aflame (*o* burning *o* in a blaze): *una casa tutta in fiamme*, a house in a blaze (*o* all in flames *o* on fire *o* ablaze); *dare alle fiamme*, to commit to the flames (*o* to burn); *riflesso di —*, glow; *essere in fiamme*, to be aflame || *le fiamme dell'ira, fig.* the flames of wrath || *— ossidrica*, oxyhydrogen flame: *tagliare con la — ossidrica*, to flame-cut || *color —*, bright red || *ritorno di —*, (*aut.*) back-fire || *le vennero le fiamme al viso*, (*arrossì*) she flushed; (*si adirò*) she blazed with anger || *i suoi occhi lanciavano fiamme, fig.* his eyes blazed (*o* looked daggers) || *far fuoco e fiamme*, (*usare ogni mezzo*) to leave no stone unturned; (*adirarsi*) to flare up **2.** (*innamorato, innamorata*) flame, sweetheart: *è una mia vecchia —*, he is an old flame of mine; *Maria è la sua nuova —*, Mary is his present sweetheart **3.** (*mar.*) long pennon, long pennant **4.** *pl.* (*mil.*) streamers: *fiamme verdi*, (*Alpini*) green streamers (*o* Alpine troops).

fiammànte, *ag.* **1.** flaming; blazing; flaring; glowing **2.** *fig.* bright: *nuovo —*, brand-new; *rosso —*, bright red || *s.m.* (*eccl.*) Eucharistic monogram.

fiammàre, *V.* **fiammeggiàre.**

fiammàta, *s.f.* blaze; fire: *fare una —*, to make a fire.

fiammeggiàre, *v.i.* **1.** to blaze (with sthg.), to flame (with sthg.), to burn (with sthg.) (*anche fig.*): *gli fiammeggiavano gli occhi per l'ira*, his eyes blazed with anger **2.** (*splendere*) to shine.

fiammèlla, *s.f.* little flame.

fiàmmeo, *ag.* (*rar.*) flaming; (*splendente*) shining, bright.

fiammiferàia, *s.f.*, **fiammiferàio,** *s.m.* **1.** (*chi fabbrica fiammiferi*) match-maker **2.** (*chi vende fiammiferi*) match-seller || *la piccola fiammiferaia*, the match-girl.

fiammìfero, *s.m.* match: *— svedese*, safety match; *una scatola di fiammiferi*, a box of atches; *una scatola per fiammiferi*, a match-box; *accendere un —*, to strike a match || *pigliar fuoco come un —, fig.* to flare up.

fiammìngo, *ag.* Flemish || *i fiamminghi*, the Flemish (people) || *s.m.* **1.** Fleming **2.** (*lingua*) (the) Flemish (language).

fiancàta, *s.f.* **1.** (*lato, fianco*) side; flank **2.** (*mar.*) broadside: *sparare una —*, to fire a broadside **3.** (*colpo al fianco*) blow in the side.

fiancheggiaménto, *s.m.* **1.** (*di fortificazione*) propping **2.** (*mil.*) flanking: *fuoco di —*, flanking fire **3.** *fig.* supporting, support, helping.

fiancheggiàre, *v.t.* **1.** to flank: *una strada fiancheggiata da alberi*, a road flanked (*o* lined) with trees; *la valle era fiancheggiata da alte montagne*, high mountains flanked the valley **2.** (*mil.*) to flank: *la corazzata era fiancheggiata dalle torpediniere*, the battleship was flanked with destroyers **3.** *fig.* (*aiutare, sostenere*) to support, to help, to back **4.** (*spronare*) to spur **5.** (*costeggiare*) to border.

fiancheggiatóre, *s.m.*, **fiancheggiatríce,** *s.f.* flanker, supporter; (*pol.*) fellow-traveller.

fiànco, *s.m.* **1.** hip; side (*anche fig.*): *misura dei fianchi*, hip-measurement; *sul — destro della strada*, on the right side of the street; *camminava al mio —*, he was walking by (*o* at) my side; *ho male al mio —*, I have a pain in my side; *starò al suo —*, *qualunque cosa accada*, I will stand by his side, happen what may || *a — a —*, side by side; *di —*, sideways; (*su di un fianco*) on one side: *di — a qlcu.*, by s.o.'s side || *prestare il — alle critiche*, to lay oneself open to criticism (*o* to censure) || *tenersi i fianchi dal ridere*, to split (*o* to shake) one's sides with laughter **2.** (*di ani-*

male) flank **3.** (*mil.*) flank: *il — destro dell'esercito*, the right flank of the army; *un attacco sul —*, a flank attack || *— destro, sinistro!*, right, left turn! **4.** (*mar.*): *— destro*, starboard side; *— sinistro*, larboard (*o* port side).

Fiàndre, *no.pr.f.pl.* (*geog.*) Flanders: *passammo per le —*, we travelled through Flanders.

fiàsca, *s.f.* flask.

fiascàio, *s.m.* **1.** (*chi fabbrica fiaschi*) flask-maker **2.** (*chi vende fiaschi*) flask-seller.

fiascheggiàre, *v.i.* (*fam.*) to fail, to prove a fiasco.

fiaschettería, *s.f.* **1.** wine-shop **2.** (*osteria*) tavern.

fiàsco, *s.m.* **1.** flask || *asciugare il —, fig.* to drink the lot **2.** *fig.* (*insuccesso*) fiasco, failure; (*sl.*) flop: *far —*, to fail utterly (*o* to be quite unsuccessful): *la sua commedia ha fatto —*, his play has been a fiasco (*o* a big flop).

fiat, (*voce verbale latina*): *in un —*, in a jiffy.

fiàta, *s.f.* (*arc.*) time: *lunga —*, a long time; *molte fiate*, many times.

fiatàre, *v.i.* **1.** (*respirare*) to breathe **2.** (*parlare*) to speak: *nessuno fiatò*, nobody spoke (*o* uttered a single word).

fiatàta, *s.f.* breath, breathing.

fiàto, *s.m.* **1.** breath: *gridai con quanto — avevo in gola*, I shouted at the top of my voice; *avere il — corto*, to be short of breath; *avere il — grosso*, *essere senza —*, to be out of breath (*o* to be breathless *o* to be panting); *prender —*, to take breath (*anche fig.*); *trattenere il —*, to hold (*o* to catch) one's breath || *strumenti a —*, (*mus.*) wind instruments || *tutto d'un —*, all in one (*o* at a) breath: *bere* (*ql.co.*) *tutto d'un —*, to gulp (sthg.) down || *mi hai fatto rimanere senza —!*, you have taken away my breath!; *rimanemmo senza — per la meraviglia*, we were (*o* stood) breathless (*o* speechless) with astonishment || *non ho — di alzare una piuma*, I am too tired to raise a finger || *sprecare il —*, to waste one's breath **2.** (*alito*) breath: *— cattivo*, bad breath.

fíbbia, *s.f.* buckle.

fíbra, *s.f.* **1.** fibre; (*amer.*) fiber: *— di cotone*, cotton fibre; *— di ginestra*, broom fibre; *— di vetro*, fibre glass; *— muscolare, nervosa*, muscle, nerve fibre; *— tessile*, staple (*o* textile fibre); *— vulcanizzata*, vulcanized (*o* hard) fibre; *valigia di —*, fibre suit-case **2.** (*costituzione*) constitution: *uomini di forte —*, men with strong constitutions **3.** (*carattere*) fibre: *un uomo di — rude*, a man of coarse fibre.

fibrifórme, *ag.* fibriform.

fibrílla, *s.f.* (*anat.*) fibril.

fibrillàre, *ag.* (*anat.*) fibrillar(y).

fibrillazióne, *s.f.* (*patol.*) fibrillation.

fibrína, *s.f.* (*chim.*) fibrin.

fibrinóso, *ag.* (*chim.*) fibrinous.

fibroceménto, *s.m.* (*edil.*) asbestos cement.

fibròide, *ag.* fibroid.

fibroína, *s.f.* (*chim.*) fibroin.

fibròma, *s.m.* (*patol.*) fibroma (*pl.* fibromata).

fibrosità, *s.f.* fibrousness.

fibrosite, *s.f.* (*patol.*) fibrositis.

fibróso, *ag.* fibrous.

fíbula, *s.f.* **1.** (*archeol.*) fibula (*pl.* fibulae, fibulas) **2.** (*anat.*) fibula (*pl.* fibulae, fibulas), splint-bone.

ficàia, *s.f.* (*arc.*) **1.** (*albero di fico*) fig-tree **2.** (*luogo piantato a fichi*) fig garden, fig plantation.

ficcanàso, *s.c.* meddler, intruder, busybody; (*fam.*) Paul Pry.

ficcàre. *v.t.* **1.** to thrust; to drive (in): *eccoti un chiodo, ficcalo bene nella parete*, here is a nail, drive it well into the wall; *gli ficcarono un bavaglio in bocca*, they thrust a gag into his mouth; *poco mancò che mi ficcasse un dito in un occhio*, he nearly thrust a finger into my eye || *— in testa ql.co. a qlcu.*, to hammer (*o* to get) sthg. into s.o.'s head || *il naso dappertutto*, to poke (*o* to thrust) one's nose into everything || *gli occhi addosso a qlcu.*, to stare hard at s.o. **2.** (*fam.*) (*mettere*) to put (away): *ficca questo foglio tra le mie* *carte*, put this sheet (away) among my papers **3.** (*scherma*) to thrust ‖ **ficcàrsi**, *v.r.* to thrust oneself; (*intromettersi*) to interfere, to meddle, to intrude; (*nascondersi*) to hide: *dove si sarà ficcato il mio berretto?*, (*fam.*) where can my cap be? (*o* where has my cap got to?); *dove ti sei ficcato?*, where are you hiding? ‖ — *ql.co. in capo*, to get sthg. into one's head: *perchè ti sei ficcato in capo di partire subito?*, why did you get it into your head to leave at once? (*o* why are you so bent on leaving at once?).

ficchíno, *s.m.* (*ficcanaso*) meddler, intruder, busibody; (*fam.*) Paul Pry.

fichéto, *s.m.* fig garden, fig plantation.

fíco, *s.m.* fig; (*albero*) fig(-tree): — *d'India*, Indian fig (*o* prickly pear); *fichi freschi*, green figs; — *secco*, dried (*o* Smyrna) fig; *foglia di* —, fig-leaf ‖ *un* — *secco!*, *fig.* a fig for it!: *non me ne importa un* — (*secco*), I don't care a fig for it (*o* I don't care a rap); *non vale un* — (*secco*), it is not worth a rap ‖ *fare le nozze coi fichi secchi*, *fig.* to be stingy ‖ *serbare la pancia ai fichi*, *fig.* to avoid dangers.

ficóso, *ag.* (*fam.*) (*smorfioso*) affected; prim.

fída, *s.f.* (*dir.*) land let for grazing.

fidànza, *s.f.* (*letter.*) trust, confidence: *far a* — *con qlcu.*, (*rar.*) to rely on s.o.

fidanzaménto, *s.m.* engagement; (*letter.*) betrothal: *anello di* —, engagement ring.

fidanzàre, *v.t.* to engage, to affiance; (*letter.*) to betroth ‖ **fidanzàrsi**, *v.r.* to become engaged (to s.o.), to get engaged (to s.o.): *ci fidanzammo in primavera*, we got engaged in spring.

fidanzàta, *s.f.* fiancée; (*innamorata*) sweetheart.

fidanzàto, *ag.* engaged, betrothed: *essere* — (*con qlcu.*), to be engaged (to s.o.) ‖ *s.m.* fiancé; (*innamorato*) sweetheart.

fidàre, *v.t.* (*affidare*) to entrust, to commit, to confide: *è un uomo a cui si può* — *qualunque cosa*, he is a man (whom) you can entrust with anything (*o* to whom you can entrust anything) ‖ *v.i.* (*confidare*) to trust in (s.o., sthg.), to rely on (s.o., sthg.): *fidava in quell'uomo*, he relied on that man; — *in Dio*, to trust in God ‖ **fidàrsi**, *v.r.* **1.** (*aver fiducia*) to trust (s.o.), to confide (in s.o.): *non fidarti di lui, non è sincero*, don't trust him, he isn't sincere ‖ — *è bene, non* — *è meglio*, *prov.* to trust is good, not to trust is better **2.** (*fare assegnamento*) to rely on (s.o., sthg.), to trust to (s.o., sthg.), to depend upon (s.o., sthg.): *mi fido dei miei collaboratori*, I rely on my assistants; *non potete fidarvi del tempo*, you cannot rely on the weather; *posso fidarmi della tua discrezione?*, may I rely on your discretion?; *si fida troppo della sua memoria*, he relies on (*o* he trusts to) his memory too much **3.** (*fam.*) (*osare*) to dare: *non mi fidavo a provocarlo*, I dared not provoke him.

fidatézza, *s.f.* (*rar.*) reliability, trustworthiness.

fidàto, *ag.* **1.** trustworthy, reliable; dependable, trusty: *un servo* —, a reliable servant **2.** (*fedele*) faithful, devoted.

fidecommésso, *s.m.* (*dir.*) fideicommissum, trust: *atto di* —, trust-deed.

fidecommissàrio, *s.m.* (*dir.*) trustee.

fideiussióne, *s.f.* (*dir.*) suretyship, warranty.

fideiussóre, *s.m.* (*dir.*) surety, guarantor.

fidènte, *ag.* confiding, trustful, confident (of sthg.).

fidenteménte, *av.* confidingly, trustfully, trustingly; confidently.

Fídia, *no.pr.m.* (*st. scult.*) Phidias.

fidíaco, *ag.* (*scult.*) Phidian.

fído, *ag.* (*fedele*) faithful, devoted; (*di suddito*) loyal: *il* — *Acate*, (*lett.*) fidus Achates; *il mio* — *brando*, (*letter.*) my trusty sword ‖ *s.m.* **1.** devoted follower; faithful attendant; devoted servant **2.** (*comm.*) credit; (*credito, fiducia*) trust: *concedere un* —, to grant a credit; *vendere a* —, to sell on trust.

fidúcia, *s.f.* trust, confidence, reliance; dependence: — *in se stessi*, self-confidence (*o* self-assurance *o*

self-reliance): *mancare di* — *in se stessi*, to lack self-assurance; *con* —, with confidence (*o* confidently): *con la massima* —, with full confidence; *degno di* —, trustworthy (*o* reliable); *ditta di* —, reliable firm; *impiegato di* —, confidential clerk; *per mancanza di* —, for want of confidence: *non è per mancanza di* — *verso la vostra rispettabile ditta*, (*comm.*) it is not because we do not trust your much esteemed firm; *uomo di* —, trusty (*o* reliable) man; (*braccio destro*) righthand man: *mi occorre un uomo di* —, I want a man whom I can trust (*o* whom I can rely on); *la* — *che mi è stata dimostrata*, the confidence placed in me; *abbi* — *in Dio*, put your trust in God (*o* trust in God); *nella* — *che accoglierete la mia richiesta*, (*comm.*) feeling confident (that) you will kindly grant my request; *non ho* — *nelle sue promesse*, I have no trust in his promises; *avere* — *in qlcu.*, to trust s.o.; *avere* — *nell'avvenire*, to trust to the future; *avere un posto di grande* —, to have a position of great trust; *godere della* — *di qlcu.*, to enjoy s.o.'s confidence; *meritare la* — *di qlcu.*, to deserve s.o.'s confidence ‖ *abuso di* —, (*dir.*) breach of trust ‖ *voto di* —, (*pol.*) vote of confidence; *porre la questione di* —, (*pol.*) to ask for a vote of confidence.

fiduciàrio, *ag.* (*dir.*) fiduciary: *certificato* —, trust-certificate; *circolazione fiduciaria*, fiduciary currency (*o* paper money *o* token-money *o* credit circulation); *compagnia fiduciaria*, trust company; *erede* —, fiduciary heir ‖ *s.m.* (*dir.*) fiduciary; trustee.

fiduciosaménte, *av.* **1.** trustfully, trustingly; confidently **2.** (*con speranza*) hopefully.

fiducióso, *ag.* **1.** trusting; trustful; confiding, confident: — *nell'avvenire, nei suoi amici*, trusting to the future, in his friends; *Napoleone era* — *nella sua stella*, Napoleon had implicit confidence in his star **2.** (*speranzoso*) hopeful: *si rivolsero a noi fiduciosi che li avremmo aiutati*, they turned to us hoping we would help them.

fièle, *s.m.* **1.** (*anat.*) bile, gall **2.** *fig.* gall; (*odio*) hatred; (*rancore*) rancour, bitterness: *mostrò il suo* —, he showed his hatred (*o* his rancour); *la sua penna è intinta nel* —, his pen is dipped in gall.

fienagióne, *s.f.* **1.** (*il tagliare il fieno*) haymaking **2.** (*stagione, epoca del taglio del fieno*) hay-time.

fienàio, fienàle, *ag.* hay (*attributivo*): *forcone* —, hay-fork.

fieníle, *s.m.* **1.** hay-loft **2.** *fig.* dirty, shabby place.

fièno, *s.m.* hay: *asma, febbre del* —, (*patol.*) hay-fever (*o* hay-asthma); *mucchio di* —, hay-cock; *pagliaio di* —, hay-rick (*o* hay-stack); *fare il* —, to make hay.

fièra[1], *s.f.* fair; (*esposizione*) exhibition; (*mostra*) show: — *campionaria*, industrial fair (*o* samples fair *o* industrial exhibition); — *di beneficenza*, charity bazaar.

fièra[2], *s.f.* (*animale feroce*) wild beast, wild animal.

fieraménte, *av.* **1.** fiercely **2.** (*orgogliosamente*) proudly **3.** (*con alterigia*) haughtily **4.** (*audacemente*) boldly.

fierézza, *s.f.* **1.** fierceness, violence **2.** (*orgoglio*) pride: *dico questo con* —, I take pride in saying this **3.** (*altezzosità*) haughtiness, lordliness, arrogance **4.** (*audacia*) boldness.

fièro, *ag.* **1.** (*crudele*) fierce, violent, savage, wild, cruel: *egli aveva un aspetto* —, he looked fierce **2.** (*orgoglioso*) proud: *siamo fieri di te*, we are proud of you **3.** (*altezzoso*) haughty **4.** (*audace*) bold, daring **5.** (*severo, duro*) stern, severe.

fiévole, *ag.* feeble, weak; (*di luce, suono*) dim: *con voce* —, in a feeble voice.

fievolézza, *s.f.* feebleness, weakness; (*di luce, suono*) dimness.

fievolménte, *av.* feebly; (*di luce, suono*) dimly.

fífa[1], *s.f.* (*ornit.*) lapwing, pe(e)wit.

fífa[2], *s.f.* (*fam.*) funk: *ho una* — *del diavolo!*, I'm in a blue funk!.

fifóne, *s.m.* (*fam.*) funk.

fígaro, *s.m.* **1.** (*scherz.*) barber **2.** (*giubbetto*) bolero.

fíggere, *v.t.* to fix; to fasten: — *gli occhi su ql.co.,* to fix one's eyes upon sthg. (*o* to stare at sthg. hard) ‖ **fíggersi,** *v.r.:* — *ql.co. in capo,* to get sthg. into one's head (*o* to fix one's mind on sthg.).

Fígi (Ísole), *no.pr.f.pl.* (*geog.*) Fiji Islands.

figiàno, *ag. s.m.* Fijian.

fíglia, *s.f.* **1.** daughter; (*fam.*) girl: — *unica,* only daughter **2.** (*comm.*) (*bolletta che in un registro si stacca da un'altra corrispondente detta madre*) counterfoil.

figliàre, *v.t.* (*di animale*) to bring forth, to litter; (*della cagna*) to pup, to whelp; (*della cavalla*) to foal; (*della gatta*) to kitten; (*della mucca*) to calve; (*dell'orsa, della volpe*) to cub; (*della pecora*) to lamb; (*della scrofa*) to pig; (*di bestia feroce in genere*) to whelp, to cub.

figliàstra, *s.f.* step-daughter.

figliàstro, *s.m.* step-son: *i figliastri,* (*maschi e femmine*) step-children.

figliàta, *s.f.* litter; (*covata*) brood.

figliatúra, *s.f.* delivery.

figliazióne, *V.* **filiazióne.**

figliéreccio, *ag.* prolific.

fíglio, *s.m.* son; (*fam.*) boy; (*figlio giovane*) child (*pl.* children): *il* — *maggiore,* the eldest son; — *unico,* (*maschio*) only son; *i miei figli,* (*maschi e femmine*) my children; *vieni,* — *mio,* come on, my boy ‖ *i figli della Chiesa,* the faithful ‖ *i figli di Abramo,* the sons of Abraham ‖ *il Figlio di Dio,* the Son of God ‖ — *di papà,* spoilt young man (*o* son of an overindulgent father) ‖ *è* — *d'arte,* he is the actor son of an actor father ‖ *sei proprio* — *di tuo padre,* you are the perfect model of your father ‖ *tal padre, tal* —, like father, like son.

figliòccia, *s.f.* goddaughter.

figliòccio, *s.m.* godson.

figliolàme, *s.m.* many children (*pl.*); brood.

figliolànza, *s.f.* children (*pl.*); family, offspring: — *numerosa,* a large family (*o* many children).

figli(u)òla, *s.f.* **1.** (*figlia*) daughter; child (*pl.* children) **2.** (*ragazza*) girl: *fa' la brava* —, be a good girl.

figli(u)òlo, *s.m.* **1.** (*figlio*) son; child (*pl.* children) **2.** (*ragazzo*) boy; (*uomo*) fellow: — *mio,* my boy; *è un buon* —, he is a good boy (*o* fellow).

fígnolo, *s.m.* (*foruncolo*) boil, furuncle.

fignolóso, *ag.* (*foruncoloso*) furunculous.

figulína, *s.f.* (*arte del vasaio*) pottery, ceramics.

figulinàio, fígulo, *s.m.* (*vasaio*) potter.

figúra, *s.f.* **1.** (*forma umana*) figure: *ha una bella* —, he has a fine figure; *non dimenticherò mai la sua* — *imponente,* I shall never forget his imposing figure **2.** (*immagine dipinta, scolpita*) figure: *la* — *centrale del quadro,* the central figure of the painting ‖ *ritratto a mezza* —, half-length portrait **3.** (*illustrazione*) illustration, picture, drawing; (*tavola*) plate: *un libro pieno di figure,* a book full of pictures **4.** (*personaggio, personalità*) figure; (*di romanzo, opera teatrale*) character: *la* — *principale di questo romanzo è molto ben riuscita,* the main character of this novel is very well drawn; *le grandi figure della storia,* the great figures of history **5.** (*geom.*) figure: — *geometrica, piana, solida,* geometrical, plane, solid figure **6.** (*fam.*) (*impressione*) figure; show: *egli fa* —, he has a smart figure; *un vestito che fa* —, a showy dress; *fare la* — *dello sciocco,* to play the part of a fool (*o* to act the fool); *fare una bella, cattiva* —, to cut a fine, poor figure **7.** (*simbolo*) symbol: *l'agnello è* — *di Gesù Cristo,* the lamb is the symbol of Jesus Christ **8.** (*danza*) figure **9.** (*mus.*) note **10.** (*ret. log.*) figure: — *retorica,* figure of speech **11.** (*nelle carte da giuoco*) court-card, coat-card **12.** (*polena*) figure-head.

figuràccia, *s.f.* poor figure, sorry figure: *feci una* —, I cut a poor figure.

figuralménte, *av.* figuratively.

figurànte, *s.c.* (*teat.*) supernumerary ‖ *s.m.* figurant ‖ *s.f.* figurante.

figuràre, *v.t.* **1.** (*rappresentare*) to represent: *la scena figura un castello,* the scene represents a castle **2.** (*simboleggiare*) to represent; to symbolize: *la lupa figura l'avarizia,* the she-wolf symbolizes avarice ‖ *v.i.* **1.** (*far figura*) to look smart; (*vestirsi bene*) to dress well: *ella badava solo a* —, her only care was to look smart **2.** (*apparire*) to appear, to be: *il mio nome non figura sull'elenco del telefono,* my name does not appear (*o* is not) in the (telephone) directory (*o* telephone book) **3.** (*fingere*) to pretend: *figura di non conoscermi,* he pretends not to know me ‖ **figuràrsi,** *v.r.* **1.** (*immaginarsi*) to imagine, to fancy: *non me lo sarei mai figurato così,* I should never have imagined it like this **2.** (*pensare*) to think: *figurati un po' che l'avevo scambiato per suo fratello,* just think (*o* imagine), I had mistaken him for his brother (*o* fancy now, I had mistaken him for his brother) ‖ *figuriamoci!,* fancy that! ‖ «*La disturbo?*», «*Ma si figuri!*», "Do I trouble you?", "Not at all!".

figurataménte, figurativaménte, *av.* figuratively.

figurativo, *ag.* figurative: *arti* —, figurative arts.

figuràto, *ag.* **1.** (*illustrato*) illustrated: *libro* —, illustrated book **2.** (*ret.*) figurative: *linguaggio, senso* —, figurative language, sense **3.** (*con figure*) figure (*attributivo*): *ballo* —, figure dance.

figurazióne, *s.f.* figuration.

figurétta, figurína, *s.f.* **1.** (*figura snella*) slender figure **2.** (*statuetta*) figurine, statuette.

figurinàio, *s.m.* **1.** (*chi fabbrica figurine*) figurine maker **2.** (*chi vende figurine*) figurine vendor.

figurinísta, *s.c.* dress-designer.

figurino, *s.m.* **1.** (*modello*) fashion-plate ‖ *essere un* —, to be dressed after the latest fashion **2.** (*giornale di mode*) fashion journal.

figúro, *s.m.* (*spreg.*) blackguard, scoundrel, rascal, cad.

figuróne, *s.m.* brilliant figure, superb figure: *farai un* —, you'll cut a very fine figure.

fíla, *s.f.* **1.** row, line, file: *una* — *di case, di alberi,* a row of houses, of trees; *una* — *di persone,* a line of people; — *di stanze,* suite of rooms; *in* —, in (a) line (*o* in a row); (*mil.*) in file; *in prima, in seconda* —, in the front, in the second row; *il maestro mise in* — *gli alunni,* the schoolmaster drew his pupils in line (*o* lined his pupils up); *misi in* — *le bottiglie,* I put the bottles in a row; *i ragazzi devono stare in* —, the boys must stand in (a) line; *i soldati si misero in* —, the soldiers lined up; *fare la* —, to queue (up) ‖ *di* —, (*uno dopo l'altro*) in succession; (*ininterrottamente*) continuously: *piovve per dieci giorni di* —, it rained for ten days running ‖ *in* — *indiana,* in single (*o* Indian) file ‖ *fuoco di* —, running fire (anche *fig.*): *un fuoco di* — *di domande,* a running fire of questions ‖ *per* — *destra, sinistra!,* right, left wheel! ‖ *rompete le file!,* dismiss! **2.** *pl.* (*esercito*) army (*sing.*): *disertare le file,* to desert the army.

filàbile, *av.* that may be spun; fit for spinning.

filàccia, *s.f.* lint.

filaccióso, *ag.* ragged, thready; (*sfilacciato*) frayed.

Filadèlfia, *no.pr.f.* (*geog.*) Philadelphia.

filaménto, *s.m.* filament.

filamentóso, *ag.* filamentous, filamentary.

filànda, *s.f.* spinning-mill; (*della seta*) silk mill.

filandàia, *s.f.* spinner.

filandière, *s.m.* spinning-mill owner.

filandína, *s.f.* spinner.

filàndra, *s.f.* (*cascame di filatura*) spinning waste; (*di tessitura*) weaving waste.

filànte, *ag.: stella* —, (*astr.*) shooting star (*o* falling -star); (*di carta*) (paper) streamer.

filantropía, *s.f.* philanthropy.

filantropicaménte, *av.* philanthropically.

filantròpico, *ag.* philanthropic(al).

filantropísmo, *s.m.* philanthropism.

filàntropo, *s.m.* philanthrope, philanthropist.

filàre, *s.m.* row, line: *filari di viti,* rows of vines.

filàre, *v.t.* 1. to spin ‖ *non è più il tempo che Berta filava,* the good old times are gone for ever 2. *(metal.)* to spin 3. *(mar.) (mollare)* to pay out, to ease off: — *un cavo,* to pay out a rope ‖ *v.i.* 1. *(di liquido, scendere in un filo)* to rope: *questo sciroppo fila,* this syrup is ropy 2. *(di lampada, candela)* to smoke: *questa candela fila,* this candle is smoking 3. *(correre)* to run; *(andar via)* to go away, to make off, to get off: *automobile che fila a tutta velocità,* car that goes (o spins along) at full speed; *fila!,* off with you! (o get off!); *filate a casa,* go straight home 4. *(mar.) (navigare)*: *ora la nave fila a tredici nodi,* now the ship is making thirteen knots 5. *(comportarsi bene)* to behave: — *diritto,* to behave properly ‖ *far* — *qlcu.,* to make s.o. behave (o to keep s.o. in hand o to make s.o. toe the line) 6. *(amoreggiare)* to flirt; *(fam.)* to spoon.

filària, *s.f. (entom.)* filaria *(pl.* filariae).

filaríasi, filariòsi, *s.f. (patol.)* filariasis, filariosis.

filarmònico, *ag.s.m.* philharmonic.

filastròcca, *s.f.* 1. nonsense rhyme; *(per bambini)* nursery rhyme 2. *(discorso sconnesso, lungo, noioso)* rigmarole, long rambling talk, balderdash.

filatelìa, filatèlica, *s.f.* philately, stamp-collecting.

filatèlico, *ag.* philatelic ‖ *s.m.* philatelist.

filàto, *ag.* 1. spun: *oro* —, spun gold 2. *(ordinato, coerente)* consistent; consequent: *ragionamento* —, consequent reasoning 3. *(di seguito)*: *dieci giorni filati,* ten days on end (o running) ‖ *s.m. (ind. tessile)* (spun) yarn: — *a più colori,* cloud; — *a secco,* dry-spun; *casalingo,* homespun yarn; — *da maglieria,* knitting (o hosiery) yarn; — *di lana,* woollen yarn; — *di lino,* linen; — *fantasia,* fancy yarn; — *per calze,* fingering; — *pettinato,* worsted yarn; — *ritorto,* twisted yarn.

filatóio, *s.m.* 1. *(arcolaio)* spinning-wheel 2. *(mec.)* spinning-machine, spinning frame; spinner: — *automatico,* self-actor 3. *(filanda)* spinning-mill.

filatóre, *s.m.* spinner ‖ **filatríce,** *s.f.* 1. spinner 2. *(ind. tessile)* automatic reeling apparatus.

filattèrio, *s.m. (relig. ebraica)* phylactery.

filatúra, *s.f.* 1. *(ind. tessile)* spinning: — *ad anello,* ring spinning; — *a mano,* hand spinning; — *del bozzolo della seta,* silk reeling; — *della lana, del lino, del cotone,* wool, flax, cotton spinning 2. *(filanda)* spinning-mill 3. *(cine.) (difetto di pellicola)* ghost.

filellènico, *ag. (st.)* philhellenic.

filellenísmo, *s.m. (st.)* philhellenism.

filellèno, *s.m.* philhellenist, philhellene.

Filèmone, *no.pr.m. (mit.)* Philemon: — *e Bauci,* Baucis and Philemon ‖ *Epistola a* —, *(Bibbia)* Epistle to Philemon.

filettàggio, *s.m. (mec.)* screw-cutting.

filettàre, *v.t.* 1. *(ornare con filetto)* to ornament (with thin ribbons, strings, threads, etc.) 2. *(fregiare con filetto)* to line 3. *(mec.)* to thread (screws): — *col pettine, (mec.)* to chase.

filettàto, *ag.* 1. adorned (with threads, ribbons, etc.) 2. *(mec.)* threaded.

filettatúra, *s.f.* 1. edging; border 2. *(mec.) (di vite)* threading; *(filetto)* thread: — *destrorsa,* right-handed thread (o right screw thread); — *multipla,* multiple screw thread; — *semplice,* single screw thread; — *sinistrorsa,* left-handed thread (o left screw thread); — *trapezia,* acme screw thread ‖ *fare una* —, to cut a thread; *fare una* — *al tornio,* to chase; *strappare la* — *di una vite,* to strip the thread of a screw.

filétto, *s.m.* 1. *(filo sottile)* thread; ribbon; line 2. *(bordo)* border 3. *(legatoria, arald.)* fillet 4. *(mil.)* stripe 5. *(tip.)* rule: — *chiaro,* fine face rule; — *ondeggiato,* wave rule 6. *(mec.) (di vite)* thread 7. *(cuc.)* fillet: — *di bue,* fillet (o tenderloin o undercut) 8. *(di orologio)* bezel 9. — *della lingua,* *(anat.)* fraenum (o bridle).

filiàle, *ag.* filial: *amore, rispetto* —, filial love, respect ‖ *s.f. (comm.) (casa filiale)* branch house, branch; *(ufficio dipendente di banca)* branch office.

filialménte, *av.* filially.

filiazióne, *s.f.* 1. filiation 2. *(origine)* derivation; origin.

filibustière, *s.m.* 1. *(st.)* filibuster; buccaneer; freebooter; pirate 2. *fig. (avventuriero)* adventurer; *(mascalzone)* cad; scoundrel; rascal.

filièra, *s.f.* 1. *(mec.)* screw cutting die; *(trafila)* drawing machine; *(ind. tessile)* spinneret(te); nozzle: — *per filettare,* threading die; — *per filettare bulloni,* bolt die; *matrice per* —, drawplate (o die plate) 2. *(organo dei ragni)* spinneret.

filifórme, *ag.* thread-like; filiform.

filigràna, *s.f.* 1. filigree, filagree 2. *(di carta, banconote)* watermark.

filigranàto, *ag.* 1. filigreed 2. *(di carta, banconote)* watermarked: *carta filigranata,* watermarked paper.

filipèndula, *s.f. (bot.)* filipendula; drop-wort.

Filippi, *no.pr.f. (geog. st.)* Philippi ‖ *ci vedremo a* —, we shall meet (o *letter.* thou shalt see me) at Philippi.

filíppica, *s.f.* 1. *(st. lett.)* philippic 2. *(invettiva)* philippic, invective.

Filippíne(le), *no.pr.f.pl. (geog.)* the Philippines, the Philippine Islands.

filippíno, *ag.* Philippine, Filipine ‖ *s.m.* Filipino ‖ **filippína,** *s.f.* Filipina.

Filíppo, *no.pr.m.* Philip ‖ — *il Bello,* *(st.)* Philip the Fair ‖ *dim.* Phil, Pip.

Filippòpoli, *no.pr.f. (geog.)* Philippopolis.

filisteísmo, *s.m.* Philistinism.

filistèo, *ag.* 1. *(Bibbia)* Philistine 2. *(grossolano; banale)* philistine; uncultured; prosaic ‖ *s.m.* 1. *(Bibbia)* Philistine 2. *(borghesuccio)* philistine; uncultured person.

Fíllide, *no.pr.f. (lett.)* Phyllis, Phyllis.

fillirèa, *s.f. (bot.)* phillyrea.

fillirína, *s.f. (chim.)* phillyrin.

fillíte, *s.f. (min.)* phyllite.

fillòssera, *s.f. (entom.)* phylloxera.

fillossèrico, *ag.* phylloxeric, phylloxeral.

film, *s.m.* film, (motion-)picture; *(amer.)* movie: — *a due dimensioni,* two-dimensional picture (o *sl. amer.* flattie); — *a lungo metraggio,* feature (o multiple reel) film; — *al rallentatore,* slow-motion picture; — *a passo ridotto,* sub-standard film; *(da 16 mm.)* sixteen -millimetre film; — *a tre dimensioni, in rilievo,* three -dimensional picture (o *sl. amer.* 3-D); — *di attualità,* news film (o news-reel); — *didattico,* instructional film; — *muto,* silent film; — *parlato,* talking picture (o *sl.* talkie); — *pubblicitario,* advertising film; — *sonoro,* sound picture (o sound-on-film); *scatola per* —, film can (o container o box); *girare un* —, to shoot a motion-picture (o a film).

filmàre, *v.t.* to film: — *un romanzo,* to film a novel.

fílo, *s.m.; pl.f.* **fíla** *(nel senso 5.); pl.m.* **fíli** *(negli altri sensi)* 1. thread (anche *fig.*); *(ind. tessile)* yarn; *(ritorto)* twine: — *d'acqua,* a fine stream of water; *un* — *d'aria,* a breath of air; *il* — *dell'acqua,* the flow of the current; *il* — *delle reni,* spine; *un* — *d'erba,* a blade of grass; — *di carta,* paper yarn; — *di cotone, nailon, seta,* cotton, nylon, silk thread; *un* — *di fumo,* a thread of smoke; *un* — *di luce,* a thread of light; *(lumicino)* faint light; — *di ordito,* warp yarn; *un* — *di perle,* a string (o rope) of pearls; — *di Scozia,* cotton (o lisle) thread; *guanti di* — *di Scozia,* (lisle) thread gloves (o cotton gloves); — *di trama,* weft yarn; — *difettoso,* spotted yarn; — *forte,* firm yarn; *fili per burattini,* puppet strings; — *per cucire,* sewing thread; — *semplice,* simple thread; *lana a sei fili* (o *capi*), six-ply wool ‖ *per* — *e per segno,* in detail (o accurately) ‖ *ho preso il treno per un* —, I caught the train by the skin of my teeth ‖ *la poverina era ridotta ad un* —, the poor thing was worn to a shadow ‖ *quando il* — *della vita fu spezzato...,* when the thread of life was broken... ‖ *rimane un* — *di speranza,* there is still a faint hope ‖ *il vasetto stava ritto per un* —, the small vase hung by a single thread ‖ *il vecchio parlava con un — di voce*, the old man was speaking in a very weak (*o* thin) voice (*o* the old man's voice could hardly be heard) ‖ *dare del — da torcere a qlcu.*, to cause s.o. a lot of trouble; (*essere un avversario difficile*) to be a hard nut to crack for s.o. ‖ *essere appeso ad un —*, to hang by a thread (*o a hair*) ‖ *perdere il — del ragionamento*, to lose the thread of one's argument; *riprendere il — del discorso*, to pick up (*o* to take up *o* to resume) the thread of one's speech 2. (*tec.*) wire, cable: *— ad alta tensione*, (*elett.*) high-tension cable; *— adduttore*, (*elett.*) leading wire; *— a piombo*, (*edil.*) plumb-line; *— armonico*, (*mec.*) piano wire; *— di ferro*, *metallico*, wire; *— di platino*, platinum wire; *— di ragno*, (*ott.*) spider line (*o* cobweb); *— di tensione*, (*aer.*) drag wire; *— di terra*, (*elett. rad.*) earth (*o* ground) wire; *— sotto tensione*, (*elett.*) hot wire; *— spinato*, barbed wire; *telegrafo senza fili*, wireless telegraph 3. (*taglio*) edge: *il — della spada*, the sword edge; *questo coltello non ha più il —*, this knife has no edge now (*o* is blunt) ‖ *passare qlcu. a — di spada*, to put s.o. to the sword 4. (*venatura*) grain: *il — del legno*, the grain of wood; *tagliare il legno secondo il —*, to cut wood with the grain 5. *pl.*: *è lui che tiene le fila*, *fig.* it is he who pulls the strings; *fare le fila*, (*di formaggio*, ecc.) to rope; *imbrogliare le fila*, to muddle things up; *riunire*, *sbrogliare le fila*, to gather up, to unravel the threads.

fílobus, *s.m.* trolley-bus.

filocomunísta, *s.c.* pro-communist: *comunisti e filocomunisti*, communists and fellow-travellers.

filodrammàtico, *s.m.* amateur actor.

filofascísta, *s.c.* pro-fascist.

filología, *s.f.* philology.

filologicaménte, *av.* philologically.

filológico, *ag.* philologic(al).

filólogo, *s.m.* philologist.

Filomèla, Filomèna, *no.pr.f.* (*mit.*) Philomela.

filoncíno, *s.m.* 1. (*miner.*) small vein 2. (*di pane*) roll (of bread).

filóne, *s.m.* 1. (*miner.*) seam, vein, lode; (*strato*) layer 2. (*corrente*) stream: *— di lava*, stream of lava 3. (*forma di pane*) long loaf.

filóso, *ag.* thready, stringy; filamentous.

filosofàle, *ag.* philosophic(al): *pietra —*, philosophers' stone.

filosofànte, *s.c.* philosophist.

filosofàre, *v.i.* to philosophize; (*iron.*) to pose as a philosopher.

filosofàstro, *s.m.* (*spreg.*) philosophaster.

filosofeggiàre, *V.* **filosofàre**.

filosofèma, *s.m.* philosopheme.

filosofía, *s.f.* philosophy: *dottore in —*, Doctor of Philosophy (*abbr.* Ph.D.) ‖ *prendila con —!*, take it easy!.

filosoficaménte, *av.* philosophically.

filosòfico, *ag.* philosophic(al).

filosofísmo, *s.m.* philosophism.

filòsofo, *s.m.* philosopher.

filòssera, *s.f.* (*entom.*) phylloxera.

Filòstrato, *no.pr.m.* (*lett.*) Philostratus.

filotècnico, *ag.* philotechnic.

Filottète, *no.pr.m.* (*lett. greca*) Philoctetes.

filovía, *s.f.* trolley-bus line.

filtràggio, *s.m.* 1. (*mec. edil.*) filtering, filtration 2. (*elett.*) filtering.

filtràre, *v.t.* to filter, to filtrate; to leach, to strain: *acqua filtrata*, filtered water; *— del brodo*, to strain broth; *— un liquido*, to leach a liquid ‖ *v.i.* to filter, to percolate, to ooze: *l'acqua filtra attraverso il terreno*, the water filters (*o* seeps) through the earth; *il caffè sta filtrando*, coffee is percolating; *la luce filtrava attraverso i rami*, the light filtered (*o* glimmered *o* stole) through the branches.

filtrazióne, *s.f.* filtering, filtration; percolation: *—*

dell'aria, (*mec.*) air filtering; *impianto di —*, (*ind.*) filtering plant.

fíltro, *s.m.* 1. filter; (*da sigaretta*) filter, tip: *— del carburante*, (*mec.*) fuel filter; *— dell'aria*, (*mec.*) air filter; *— della benzina*, (*mec.*) petrol filter; (*amer.*) gas filter; *— dell'olio*, (*mec.*) oil filter; *— di luce*, colour screen (*o* light filter); *— polarizzante*, (*foto.*) polaroid filter; *— a sabbia*, sand filter 2. (*colino*) percolator, strainer: *— da brodo*, *da tè*, strainer; *— da caffè*, percolator 3. (*pozione magica*) philtre, love potion.

filugèllo, *s.m.* (*entom.*) silkworm: *coltura del —*, silkworm breeding.

fílza, *s.f.* 1. string: *una — di cipolle*, a string of onions; *una — di perle*, a string (*o* a rope) of pearls 2. *fig.* (*sequela*) string; series (*invariato al pl.*): *una — di bugie*, a string (*o* series *o* pack) of lies; *una — d'imprecazioni*, a string of curses; *una — di numeri*, a series of numbers 3. (*di documenti*) file 4. (*punto di cucito*) running stitch.

fímbria, *s.f.* (*rar.*) (*frangia*) hem, fringe.

fímo, *s.m.* (*letter.*) manure, dung.

finàle, *ag.* 1. (*ultimo*) last; (*conclusivo*) final, conclusive: *esame —*, final examination: *esame — di diritto*, law final; *esame — di matematica*, mathematics final ‖ *il giudizio —*, the last judgement 2. (*fil. gram.*) final: *causa —*, final cause; *proposizione —*, final clause ‖ *s.m.* 1. (*parte conclusiva di opere teatrali*, ecc.) conclusion 2. (*mus.*) finale ‖ *s.f.* 1. (*desinenza*) ending 2. (*spor.*) final: *le finali di tennis*, the tennis finals.

finalísta, *s.c.* (*spor.*) finalist.

finalità, *s.f.* 1. (*scopo*) aim, end, purpose 2. (*fil.*) finality.

finalménte, *av.* 1. at last, finally; (*enfatico*) at long last: *— sei giunto!*, at last you have come! 2. (*in ultimo*) lastly.

finaménte, *av.* finely.

finànche, finànco, *av.* (*rar.*) even.

finànza, *s.f.* 1. finance: *alta —*, high finance (*o* the bankers); *mondo della —*, financial world; *scienza delle finanze*, finance; *entrare nella —*, to take up finance (*o* banking) 2. *pl.* (*entrate dello Stato*) finances; public revenue (*sing.*): *finanze di Stato*, State finances ‖ *funzionario della —*, revenue officer; *guardia di —*, (*doganiere*) customs officer; *intendenza di —*, revenue office ‖ *Ministero delle Finanze*, (*in Gran Bretagna*) Exchequer; (*negli Stati Uniti*) Treasury; (*altrove*) Ministry of Finance; *Ministro delle Finanze*, (*in Gran Bretagna*) Chancellor of the Exchequer; (*negli Stati Uniti*) Secretary of the Treasury; (*altrove*) Minister of Finance ‖ *le mie finanze sono in ribasso*, (*fam.*) I am short of cash; *non so se le mie finanze me lo permetteranno*, (*fam.*) I don't know if I can afford it.

finanziaménto, *s.m.* 1. financing 2. (*fondi*) funds (*pl.*).

finanziàre, *v.t.* to finance: *egli finanzierà l'impresa*, he will finance (*o* provide money for) the undertaking.

finanziariaménte, *av.* financially.

finanziàrio, *ag.* financial: *anno —*, financial year; *crisi*, *legge finanziaria*, financial crisis, act; *operazione finanziaria*, financial operation (*o* transaction); *provvedimenti finanziari*, financial (*o* fiscal) provisions; *essere in buone condizioni finanziarie*, (*di persona*) to be well off (*o* to be in easy circumstances); (*comm.*) to enjoy a good financial position; *essere in cattive condizioni finanziarie*, (*di persona*) to be in straitened circumstances; (*comm.*) to be in financial difficulties; (*fam.*) to be in the red; *superare difficoltà finanziarie*, to get over financial difficulties; (*fam.*) to come (*o* to get) out of the red.

finanziatóre, *s.m.* (*comm.*) financing capitalist.

finanzièra, *s.f.* (*redingote*, *prefettizia*) frock-coat; (*amer.*) Prince Albert (coat).

finanzière, *s.m.* financier; (*capitalista*) capitalist.

fínea, *s.f.* (*colonna di registro*) column.

finché, *cong.* 1. till, until: *lo aspetterò — (non)*

verrà: I'll wait for him until (*o* till) he comes **2.** (*per tutto il tempo che*) **as long as:** — *tu suoni il piano non posso lavorare,* as long as you are playing the piano I cannot work ‖ — *c'è vita c'è speranza, prov.* while there is life there is hope.

fíne[1], *s.f.* (*termine*) end, close: — *di una lettera,* end (*o* conclusion) of a letter; *la — del giorno, del mese,* the end (*o* close) of the day, of the month; *la — del mondo,* the end of the world; *alla — del primo trimestre,* at the end (*o* close) of the first term; *fino alla — dei tempi, dei secoli,* till the end of time; *il principio della —,* the beginning of the end; *verso la — dell'anno,* by the end of the year; *accadde verso la — dell'estate,* it happened in late Summer; *è la —,* this is the end (*o* this is the last of it); *giungere alla —,* to come to an end; *metter — a ql.co.,* to put an end (*o* a stop) to sthg. (*o* to bring sthg. to an end); *vedere la — di ql.co.,* to see the end (*o* the out-come) of sthg.; *volgere alla —,* to draw to an end (*o* to a close): *l'anno volge alla —,* the year is drawing to an end (*o* to a close *o* is nearing its end) ‖ —, (*al termine di opere letterarie, pellicole, ecc.*) the end — *settimana,* week-end ‖ *alla —,* in the end; *alla fin —,* (*fam.*) after all; *in fin dei conti,* in the end (*o* to cut a long story short); *senza —,* (*ag.*) endless; (*av.*) endlessly: *attività senza —,* never-ending activities; *fastidi senza —,* endless troubles; *vite senza —,* (*mec.*) endless screw; *fare una buona, cattiva —,* to come to (*o* to make) a good, bad end ‖ *s.m.* **1.** (*scopo*) purpose; end, aim, object: *i fini della Provvidenza,* the purpose of Providence; *il — ultimo,* the ultimate aim (*o* purpose) ‖ *a — di,* in order to: *a — di fare ciò,* in order to do that (*o* with a view to doing that); *al solo — di,* merely for the purpose (*o* with the sole object) of; *a che —?,* for what purpose? (*o* to what end?); *ed a tal —,* and for this end (*o* and with this object in view) ‖ *qual era il tuo —?,* what was your aim?; *avere un secondo —,* to have a hidden purpose; *raggiungere il proprio —,* to gain one's ends ‖ *il — non giustifica i mezzi,* the end does not justify the means **2.** (*risultato, conclusione*) result, conclusion, issue: *condurre un affare a buon —,* to bring a matter to a successful issue (*o* to carry a matter through); *giungere a buon —,* to get a good result (*o* to have a successful conclusion).

fíne[2], *ag.* **1.** (*sottile*) fine, thin; (*delicato*) delicate: *voce —,* thin voice; *avere un tocco —,* to have a delicate touch; *avere un udito —,* to have a sharp (*o* keen) ear **2.** (*bello, buono, di buona qualità*) fine **3.** (*raffinato, distinto*) fine, refined, distinguished: *veste con un gusto —,* she dresses with fine (*o* refined) taste **4.** (*acuto*) fine, subtle, shrewd: *distinzione —,* fine (*o* subtle) distinction; *ironia —,* subtle irony; *spirito —,* shrewd wit **5.** (*di metallo*) fine, refined: *oro —,* fine (*o* refined) gold ‖ *s.m.* (*parte sottile, di lama*) sharpness.

fineménte, *av.* **1.** finely; (*delicatamente*) delicately **2.** (*acutamente, con acume*) subtly, shrewdly.

Finèo, *no.pr.m.* (*mit.*) Phineus.

finèstra, *s.f.* **1.** window; (*di forma circolare*) roundel: — *a battenti,* French (*o* casement) window; — *a ghigliottina, a saliscendi,* sash-window; — *a loggia sporgente,* bow-window (*o* bay-window); — *a lunetta,* fanlight; — *a rosone,* rose- (*o* marigold) window; — *a tetto,* garret (*o* attic) window; — *cieca,* blank (*o* blind)window; — *di abbaino,* dormer-window (*o* luthern); — *sporgente,* jut-window ‖ *architrave di —,* window lintel; *davanzale di —,* window-sill; *doppia —,* double window; *imposta di —,* window shutter; *maniglia di —,* window pull (*o* handle); *montante di —,* window post; *strombo di —,* window embrasure; *tendina da —,* window curtain; *vetro di —,* window-pane ‖ *fatti alla —!,* come to the window!; *quella — guarda sul cortile,* that window looks into (*o* on) the courtyard; *affacciarsi a una —,* to appear at a window; (*guardare fuori*) to look out of a window ‖ *entrare dalla —, fig.* to worm oneself (into a position) ‖ *o mangiar*

questa minestra o saltar questa —, prov. there's no choice between the deviland the deep blue sea **2.** (*cine.*) film trap **3.** (*anat.*) fenestra (*pl.* fenestrae) **4.** (*larga ferita*) large wound **5.** *pl.* (*scherz.*) eyes.

finestríno, *s.m.* **1.** (*di treno, di auto*) window: — *abbassabile,* drop window; — *posteriore,* rear window; *abbassare, alzare il —,* to let the window down to draw the window up **2.** (*cine.*) film trap.

finézza, *s.f.* **1.** (*sottigliezza, l'esser sottile*) fineness, thinness **2.** (*acume*) subtlety, shrewdness **3.** (*raffinatezza*) refinement; (*delicatezza*) delicacy; (*grazia*) grace **4.** (*gentilezza, favore*) kindness, favour: *fatemi la — di scrivermi presto,* do me the favour (*o* the kindness) of writing to me soon.

fíngere, *v.t.i.* **1.** to pretend, to feign, to sham, to simulate: *fingerò di non conoscerti,* I'll pretend I don't know you; *fingeva di essere ubriaco,* he pretended to be drunk; *a questo punto egli finge di ritirarsi,* at this point he makes a feint of retiring; — *dolore,* to feign sorrow; — *indifferenza, sorpresa,* to feign indifference, surprise ‖ *chi non sa —, non sa regnare, prov.* he that knows not how to dissemble, knows not how to rule **2.** (*immaginare*) to pretend, to feign, to imagine, to suppose: *fingiamo di essere dei re,* let us pretend we are kings ‖ **fíngersi,** *v.r.* to feign (oneself), to pretend, to sham: *si finse ammalato,* he pretended to be ill; — *ignorante,* to feign ignorance; — *matto,* to feign oneself mad; — *morto,* to pretend (*o* to feign) to be dead (*o* to feign oneself dead).

fingiménto, *s.m.* pretence, feigning, shamming.

fingitóre, *s.m.,* **fingitríce,** *s.f.* pretender, feigner.

finíbile, *ag.* that may be ended.

finiménto, *s.m.* **1.** (*rifinitura*) completion; finishing **2.** *pl.* (*bardatura di cavallo*) harness (*sing.*): *mettere i finimenti a un cavallo,* to harness a horse **3.** *pl.* (*parure, corredo*) set (*sing.*).

finimóndo, *s.m.* **1.** end of the world **2.** (*rovina, disastro*) ruin; catastrophe; disaster ‖ *che —!,* what a babel!.

finíre, *v.i.* **1.** to finish, to end, to come to an end: *come finisce il romanzo?,* how does the novel end?; *la lezione è finita,* the lesson is over; *quella guerra finì nel 1648,* that war finished in 1648; *tutto finirà felicemente,* everything will end happily ‖ — *in bellezza,* to come to a triumphant end ‖ *tutto è bene ciò che finisce bene, prov.* all's well that ends well **2.** (*cessare, interrompersi*) to stop, to come to a stop: *il bombardamento finì,* the bombing stopped; *questo giuoco sleale deve —,* this unfair play must come to a stop; *far — ql.co.,* to put an end to sthg. **3.** (*sboccare*) to end up; (*di fiume*) to flow into (a place); (*di strada*) to lead to (a place); *fig.* to turn to (sthg.): *quella avventura finì in tragedia,* that adventure turned to a tragedy; *se non sarai onesto finirai in prigione,* if you aren't honest you will end up in prison. ‖ *non vorrei — nel ridicolo,* I should not like to make a fool of myself ‖ — *in fumo,* to end in smoke **4.** (*seguito da* con, *per più infinito*) to end by (doing), to finish by (doing): *finì col comperare altre due poltrone,* he ended by buying two more armchairs; *finimmo col cedere,* eventually (*o* in the end) we gave in ‖ *farla finita con,* to make an end of: *bisogna farla finita con questa storia,* we must make an end of (*o* put an end to) this story **5.** (*morire*) to die: *finì gloriosamente,* he died a glorious death **6.** (*gram.*) to end: *l'infinito della prima coniugazione latina finisce in* « *are* », the infinitive of the first Latin conjugation ends in "are" **7.** (*consumarsi, esaurirsi*) to finish up; (*di abiti*) to wear out; (*di merci*) to sell out: *la prima edizione di questo libro è finita,* the first edition of this book is sold out **8.** (*soddisfare*) to like (s.o., sthg.): *questo abito non mi finisce,* I don't quite like this dress ‖ *v.t.* **1.** to finish, to end; (*completare*) to complete; (*concludere*) to conclude: *finì i suoi giorni in una squallida miseria,* he ended his days (*o* his life) in utter destitution; *hai finito quel tuo lavoro a maglia?,* have you finished that knit-work of yours?;

ho appena finito il tuo romanzo, I have just finished (*o* reached the end of) your novel; *perchè non finisci il tuo discorso?*, why don't you finish your speech? **2.** (*smettere, cessare*) to finish; to have done with (sthg., doing), to leave off (sthg., doing), to stop: *hai finito di scrivere quella lettera?*, have you finished writing that letter?; *quando finirai di gridare così?*, when will you stop (*o* leave off) shouting like that? ‖ *finiscila!*, stop it! **3.** (*uccidere*) to kill; (*fam.*) to finish (up); (*dare il colpo di grazia*) to give the death-blow, to dispatch.

finíre, *s.m.* end: *sul — dell'estate*, near (*o* towards) the end of Summer; *la tragedia è sul —*, the tragedy is drawing to an end.

finis, *s.m.* (*a scuola*) the end of the lesson.

finitaménte, *av.* **1.** (*perfettamente*) perfectly **2.** (*completamente*) completely; thoroughly **3.** (*fil.*) finitely.

finitézza, *s.f.* **1.** (*perfezione*) perfection; high finish **2.** (*completezza*) completeness **3.** (*fil.*) finiteness.

finítimo, *ag.* bordering, adjoining, contiguous.

finíto, *ag.* **1.** finished, ended: *mobilio molto ben —*, beautifully finished furniture; *parte non finita*, unfinished part; *un quadro —*, a finished painting; *la commedia è finita*, the play is over; *il tempo a vostra disposizione è —*, your time is up ‖ *è finita!*, it's all over! ‖ *facciamola finita con questi imbrogli*, let's put a stop to (*o* let's make an end of) this cheating; *fatela finita!*, have done with it!; *l'ho fatta finita con lui*, I will have nothing more to do with him (*o* I am through with him) **2.** (*perfetto*) finished, accomplished, perfect, excellent: *un pianista —*, an accomplished pianist; *è un maggiordomo —*, he is a perfect (*o* an excellent) butler **3.** (*rovinato, spacciato*) done for (*predicativo*): *è un uomo —*, he is done for; (*senza salute*) he is a broken (*o* finished) man; *se incominciate a inseguire il successo siete finiti*, if you start running after success you are done for ‖ *s.m.* (*fil. gram. mat.*) finite: *il — e l'infinito*, the finite and infinite.

finitríce, *s.f.* (*mec.*) finishing machine: *— stradale*, road finishing machine.

finitúra, *s.f.* **1.** (*tec.*) finish(ing): *— liscia*, smooth finish; *stato di non —*, roughness **2.** (*tocchi finali*) finishing touches (*pl.*) **3.** (*del lino*) dressing.

finlandése, *ag.* Finnic, Finnish ‖ *s.m.* **1.** (*abitante*) Finn, Finlander ‖ *i Finlandesi*, the Finns **2.** (*lingua*) (the) Finnish (language) ‖ *s.f.* Finn, Finlander, Finnish woman.

Finlàndia, *no.pr.f.* (*geog.*) Finland.

fíno¹, *av.* (*anche, persino*) even: *— uno sciocco potrebbe capire*, even a fool could understand; *amava — i suoi nemici*, he loved even his enemies ‖ **fíno a,** *prep.* **1.** (*tempo*) till, until; **up to:** *— a domani*, till to-morrow; *— ad oggi*, *— ad ora*, till now (*o* so far *o* hitherto); *— al, a tutto il 31 dicembre*, up to December 31st; *— a quel momento*, till that moment (*o* up to that time) ‖ *— a quando?*, till when?; (*per quanto tempo?*) how long? **2.** (*distanza*) **as far as; to:** *viaggiammo insieme — a Napoli*, we travelled together as far as Naples; *verrò con te — alla prossima fermata dell'autobus*, I shall come (*o* go) with you to (*o* as far as) the nearest bus-stop ‖ *fin dove*, *— a che punto?*, how far?; *— a perdita d'occhio*, as far as the eye can see; *— là*, as far as there ‖ *— all'ultimo*, to the end ‖ *— all'ultimo centesimo*, to the last penny; *— all'ultimo uomo*, to the last man **3.** (*seguito da infinito*) so ... that: *mangiò — a non potersi alzare da tavola*, he ate so much that he couldn't get up from the table; *si stancò — a dovere andare a sdraiarsi*, he got so tired that he had to go and lie down ‖ **fíno a che,** *l. cong.* till, until; (*per tutto il tempo che*) as long as ‖ **fíno da,** *prep.* **1.** (*tempo*) from; (*a partire da*) since: *— dalle sue origini*, from its origins; *non lo vedevo — dal 1930*, I had not seen him since 1930 ‖ *— da ora*, *da questo momento*, from now on (*o* henceforth); (*subito*) right now **2.** (*distanza*) **from, from as far as:** *ti avevo visto —*

dall'altra estremità del ponte, I had seen you from (as far as) the other end of the bridge.

fíno², *V.* **fine²** *ag.*

finòcchio, *s.m.* (*bot.*) fennel.

finóra, *av.* till now, so far, up to this time, hitherto; (*specie in frasi negative*) **as yet:** *— non ne ho mai sentito parlare*, I have never heard of it till now.

fínta, *s.f.* **1.** sham, feint, pretence, simulation: *è tutta una —*, it is all pretence; *faceva — di non riconoscerla*, he pretended he did not recognize her; *non fare — di lavorare!*, don't pretend you are working! **2.** (*spor.*) (*scherma*) feint; (*calcio*) dribbling: *fare una —*, to make a feint (*o* to feint); (*calcio*) to dribble **3.** (*sartoria*) flap.

fintàggine, *s.f.* duplicity, deceitfulness, double-dealing, insincerity.

fintaménte, *av.* feignedly, falsely, insincerely.

fintantoché, *V.* **finché.**

fintíno, *s.m.* (*ricciolo posticcio*) lock of false hair; (*mezza parrucca*) half wig; (*frangetta*) fringe.

fínto, *ag.* **1.** (*falso*) false; (*simulato*) feigned, pretended: *— amico*, false friend; *— dolore*, feigned sorrow; *finta modestia*, mock modesty **2.** (*non reale*) sham (*attributivo*), mock (*attributivo*): *— attacco*, mock attack; *una finta corrida*, a sham bull-fight; *finta porta*, sham (*o* blind) door **3.** (*posticcio*) false; (*artificiale*) artificial: *capelli e denti finti*, false hair and teeth; *fiori finti*, artificial flowers; *perle finte*, sham pearls ‖ *s.m.* (*ipocrita*) hypocrite.

finzióne, *s.f.* **1.** pretence, make-believe, sham: *era tutta una —*, it was all pretence (*o* make-believe) **2.** (*impostura, falsità*) duplicity, deceitfulness; falsehood; hypocrisy: *parlateci senza finzioni!*, be candid with us! **3.** (*invenzione, cosa immaginata*) fiction: *— garbata*, polite fiction; *una — legale*, a legal fiction; *finzioni poetiche*, poetic fictions.

fío, *s.m.* penalty: *pagare il — di qlco.*, to pay the penalty of sthg. (*o* to be punished for sthg.

fiocàggine, *s.f.* (*raucedine*) hoarseness.

fiocaménte, *av.* **1.** (*raucamente*) hoarsely **2.** (*debolmente*) weakly; (*di luce*) dimly; (*di suono*) faintly.

fioccàre, *v.i.* **1.** to fall in flakes; to snow: *fiocca?*, is it snowing?; *lenta la neve fiocca*, the snow is falling slowly in large flakes **2.** *fig.* to shower: *fioccarono gli applausi*, there was a shower of applause; *fioccavano gl'insulti su di lui*, abuse was showered on him.

fiocchettàre, *v.t.* to tassel.

fiòcco, *s.m.* **1.** ribbon; (*di cravatta*) knot ‖ *coi fiocchi*, excellent, first rate: *un pranzo coi fiocchi*, an excellent dinner **2.** (*nappa*) tassel **3.** (*ind. tessile*) (*bioccolo di lana, cotone*) flock; (*ciuffo*) tuft; (*di lana*) staple: *— sucido*, (*ind. lana*) taglock **4.** (*falda*) flake: *fiocchi di avena*, oat flakes; *fiocchi di granturco*, corn flakes; *— di neve*, snowflake **5.** (*mar.*) jib.

fioccóso, *ag.* (*soffice*) soft, woolly, fluffy.

fiochézza, *s.f.* **1.** (*raucedine*) hoarseness **2.** (*debolezza*) weakness; (*di luce*) dimness; (*di suono*) faintness.

fiòcina, *s.f.* (*mar.*) harpoon, fishing-spear.

fiocinàre, *v.t.* to harpoon.

fiocíne, *s.m.* **1.** (*buccia dell'acino dell'uva*) grape-skin **2.** (*vinacciuolo*) grape-stone.

fiocinière, *s.m.* harpooner.

fiòco, *ag.* **1.** (*rauco*) hoarse **2.** (*debole*) weak; (*di luce*) dim; (*di suono*) faint: *con voce fioca*, in a faint voice.

fiónda, *s.f.* catapult, sling.

fioràia, *s.f.* (*in negozio*) florist; (*ambulante*) flower-girl, flower vendor.

fioràio, *s.m.* (*in negozio*) florist; (*ambulante*) flower-boy, flower vendor.

fioràme, *s.m.* floral design; flower-pattern: *seta a fiorami*, flowered silk.

fioràto, *ag.* flowered: *stoffa fiorata*, flowered material.

fiordalíso, *s.m.* **1.** (*bot.*) cornflower, bluebottle **2.** (*arald.*) fleur-de-lis (*pl.* fleurs-de-lis).

fiòrdo, *s.m.* fjord, fiord.

fióre, *s.m.* **1.** flower; (*specialmente di albero da frutto*) blossom: *fiori artificiali,* artificial flowers; *fiori di ciliegio,* cherry blossom; *fiori selvatici,* wild flowers; *mostra di fiori,* flower show; *vaso da fiori,* (*di terracotta*) flower pot ‖ *fiori del vino,* flowers **2.** (*fioritura*) bloom (anche *fig.*): *essere in —,* to be in bloom (*o* in flower): (*di alberi da frutto*) to be in blossom; *essere nel — della giovinezza,* to be in the flower (*o* bloom *o* prime) of life; *morì nel — degli anni,* he died in the prime of life **3.** (*parte scelta*) the pick, the best part. the cream, the flower: *— di farina,* flour; *il — dell'opera di qlcu.,* the cream of s.o.'s work; *il — della società,* the cream of society ‖ *un — di mascalzone,* a notorious rascal ‖ *un — di ragazza,* a beautiful girl ‖ *è un — di galantuomo,* he is a very honest man ‖ *ha fior di quattrini,* he has pots of money **4.** (*ornamento, ricercatezza*) flower: *fiori retorici,* flowers of speech (*o* of rhetoric) **5.** *pl.* (*nelle carte*) clubs: *fante di fiori,* knave of clubs **6.** *pl.* (*chim.*) flowers: *fiori di antimonio,* flowers of antimony; *fiori di zolfo,* flowers of sulphur **7.** (*sommità, parte esterna*): *a fior d'acqua,* at water level (*o* on the surface of the water): *volare a fior d'acqua,* to skim the water; *ella pregava a fior di labbra,* she was whispering her prayers; *ho i nervi a fior di pelle,* my nerves are all on edge.

fioreggiàre, *v.i.* **1.** (*mantenersi rasente l'acqua*) to skim; to float: *— sull'acqua,* to skim along (*o* on) the water **2.** (*ornare il canto di fioretti*) to sing with fioriture.

fiorellíno, *s.m.* floweret, little flower.

fiorènte, *ag.* **1.** blooming, flowering **2.** *fig.* (*prospero*) flourishing, blooming: *una ragazza —,* a blooming girl.

fiorentemènte, *av.* *fig.* thrivingly; prosperously.

fiorentinaménte, *av.* in the Florentine way, manner.

fiorentineggiàre, *v.i.* to affect Florentine idioms.

fiorentinería, fiorentinismo, *s.m.* affectation of Florentine speech.

fiorentíno, *ag.* Florentine ‖ *alla fiorentina,* in the Florentine way (*o* after the Florentine fashion) ‖ *s.m.* **1.** (*abitante*) Florentine **2.** (*dialetto*) (the) Florentine (dialect).

Fiorènza¹, *no.pr.f.* Florence ‖ *dim.* **Flo, Flossie.**

Fiorènza², *no.pr.f.* (*arc.*) (*Firenze*) Florence.

fiorettàre, *v.t.* (*ret.mus.*) to embellish with flourishes.

fiorettatúra, *s.f.* **1.** (*lett.*) flourish: florid expression **2.** (*mus.*) floritura (*pl.* floriture).

fiorétto, *s.m.* **1.** (*piccolo fiore*) little flower: floweret **2.** (*lett.*) choice passage (of literary work) ‖ «*I Fioretti di S. Francesco*», "The Little Flowers of St. Francis" **3.** (*scherma*) foil **4.** (*piccolo sacrificio compiuto per pietà religiosa*) act of mortification **5.** (*parte migliore di una cosa*): *il — della lana,* first-quality wool; *il — del panno,* first-quality cloth **6.** *pl.* (*eleganze, ricercatezze nel dire*) flowers **7.** (*carta di qualità inferiore per la stampa*) newsprint **8.** (*miner.*) steel, jumper; (*amer.*) drilling-bit.

floricultóre, *s.m.* floriculturist.

floricultúra, *s.f.* floriculture.

florífero, *ag.* floriferous.

floríno, *s.m.* (*moneta*) florin.

floríre, *v.i.* **1.** to flower; to bloom; (*specialmente di albero da frutto*) to blossom; (*di luoghi*) to be in bloom: *ora fioriscono i giardini,* now the gardens are in bloom; *stanno fiorendo le rose,* the roses are blooming **2.** *fig.* to flourish: *Boccaccio fiorì nel Trecento,* Boccaccio flourished in the 14th century; *fioriscono le arti,* the arts are flourishing **3.** (*prosperare*) to prosper: to thrive; (*rar.*) to flourish: *fiorisce il commercio,* trade is thriving (*o* prospering) **4.** (*ammuffire*) to mildew ‖ *v.t.* (*rar.*) **1.** to adorn with flowers, to strew with flowers: *fiorì l'altare di rose,* she adorned the altar with roses **2.** *fig.* to flourish; to embellish.

fiorísta, *s.c.* **1.** florist **2.** (*pittore, pittrice di fiori*) flower painter **3.** (*fabbricante di fiori finti*) artificial flower maker.

fioríta, *s.f.* **1.** (*fiori*) flowers (*pl.*) **2.** (*fioritura*) flower-

ing **3.** (*tappeto di fiori*) flowers strewn on the ground: *— di neve,* *fig.* light coating of snow **4.** (*lett.*) florilegium (*pl.* florilegia): *— di liriche,* collection of lyrics.

fioritaménte, *av.* (*con stile fiorito*) in a flowery style, in a florid style.

fioríto, *ag.* **1.** flowery: full of flowers **2.** (*in fiore*) in flower: in bloom: (*specialmente di alberi da frutto*) in blossom **3.** (*di stile*) flowery, florid: *parlare —,* florid style of speaking.

fioritúra, *s.f.* **1.** flowering; bloom; (*specialmente di alberi da frutto*) blossoming: *epoca della —,* blossoming season; *il vecchio rosaio è in piena —,* the old rose-bush is in full bloom **2.** *fig.* flourishing **3.** (*mus.*) fioritura (*pl.* fioriture).

floróne, *s.m.* **1.** (*fico primaticcio*) early fig **2.** (*arch.*) (*rosone di soffitto*) rosette.

fiorrancíno, *s.m.* (*ornit.*) goldcrest.

fiorràncio, *s.m.* **1.** (*bot.*) marigold **2.** (*ornit.*) goldcrest.

fiottàre, *v.i.* **1.** (*di acqua*) to gurgle: (*di flutto marino*) to roar **2.** (*scorrere, uscire a fiotti*) to gush; to surge: to flow **3.** *fig.* (*brontolare*) to grumble, to mumble, to mutter.

fiòtto, *s.m.* **1.** (*onda*) wave: surge **2.** (*flutto, corrente*) flood; stream (anche *fig.*): *il sangue scorreva a fiotti,* blood was shed in streams.

Firènze, *no.pr.f.* (*geog.*) **Florence.**

fírma, *s.f.* signature: *— falsa,* forged signature: *apporre la propria — (a ql.co.),* to put one's signature (on sthg.): *falsificare una —,* to forge a signature.

firmaménto, *s.m.* firmament. vault of heaven, sky.

firmàno, *s.m.* (*decreto di sultano*) firman.

firmàre, *v.t.* to sign; to subscribe: *ella ha firmato col proprio nome di ragazza,* she has signed her own maiden name; *ella ha firmato col nome del marito,* she has signed her husband's name; *— per procura,* to sign by proxy ‖ **firmàrsi.** *v.r.* (*rar.*) to subscribe, to undersign.

firmatòrio, *ag.* signatory: *le potenze firmatarie del Trattato di Parigi,* the signatory powers (*o* the signatories) to the Treaty of Paris ‖ *s.m.,* signatory; (*comm.*) signer: (*sottoscrittore*) subscriber.

fisarmònica, *s.f.* (*mus.*) accordion.

fisarmonicista, *s.c.* accordionist, accordion-player.

fiscàle, *ag.* **1.** fiscal: *diritti fiscali,* State dues; *a scopo —,* for purposes of revenue ‖ *avvocato —,* (*dir. mil.*) accusing officer; (*st.*) fiscal **2.** (*inquisitorio*) rigorous: strict; inquisitorial.

fiscaleggiàre, *v.i.* **1.** to pile up taxation; to badger for taxes **2.** (*essere rigoroso*) to be too rigorous, to be too inquisitorial; (*inquisire*) to search for faults.

fiscalísmo, *s.m.* **1.** excessive taxation, rigorous method of tax collection **2.** (*rigorismo*) rigorism.

fiscalità, *s.f.* **1.** heavy taxation **2.** (*rigore*) rigour: strictness.

fiscalménte, *av.* fiscally.

fiscèlla, *s.f.* (*letter.*) wicker basket.

fischiàbile, *ag.* **1.** (*disapprovabile*) deserving to be hissed **2.** (*che si può fischiettare*) that may be whistled.

fischiàre, *v.i.* **1.** (*di persona in segno di disapprovazione; di serpente*) to hiss: *il serpente alzò la testa e fischiò,* the snake raised its head and hissed **2.** (*di uccello, di vento, di locomotiva, di persona, ecc.*) to whistle **3.** (*di sirena, segnale acustico*) to hoot **4.** (*di orecchi*) to buzz; to sing: *mi fischiavano gli orecchi,* my ears were singing (*o* I had a buzzing in my ears); *non ti fischiano gli orecchi?,* *fig.* aren't your ears burning? **5.** (*di proiettile, ecc.*) to whiz(z); to whirr: *la freccia passò fischiando accanto a me,* the arrow whizzed past me ‖ *v.t.* **1.** (*per disapprovare*) to hiss, to hoot, to boo: *fu fischiato e dovette lasciare il palcoscenico,* he was hissed off the stage; *la prima attrice venne ripetutamente fischiata,* the leading actress was repeatedly hissed **2.** (*mar.*) to pipe: *— un ordine,* to pipe an order.

fischiàta, *s.f.* **1.** whistling: *fare una fischiatina,* to whistle a tune **2.** (*di disapprovazione*) hissing, hooting.

fischiatóre, *ag.* whistling ‖ *s.m.,* **fischiatríce,** *s.f.* **1.** whistler **2.** (*chi disapprova*) hisser.

fischiettàre, *v.t.* to whistle (softly): *passare il tempo fischiettando,* to whistle one's time away.

fischiettío, *s.m.* (soft) whistling.

fischiétto, *s.m.* whistle; (*mar.*) pipe.

fischio, *s.m.* **1.** (*fischietto*) whistle: *dare un colpo di* —, to blow a whistle **2.** (*di uccello, di vento, di treno*) whistle, whistling: *il* — *del vento tra gli alberi,* the whistle of the wind in the trees **3.** (*sibilo di serpente, ecc.*) hiss, hissing **4.** (*negli orecchi*) buzzing; singing **5.** (*di approvazione, ammirazione*) whistle; (*di disapprovazione*) hiss, hoot **6.** (*di sirena e segnali acustici*) hoot **7.** (*di proiettile*) whiz(z), whizzing sound, whirr.

fisciú, *s.m.* (*scialletto*) fichu.

fisco, *s.m.* **1.** (*tesoro pubblico*) public treasury; (*in Gran Bretagna*) Treasury, Exchequer **2.** (*entrate dello stato*) public revenue; (*in Gran Bretagna*) Inland Revenue **3.** (*funzionari fiscali*) revenue authorities (*pl.*); collectors of taxes (*pl.*) **4.** (*st.*) fisc.

fisica, *s.f.* physics: — *applicata,* applied physics; — *matematica,* mathematical physics; — *nucleare,* nuclear physics (*o* nucleonics); — *pura,* pure physics; *dottore in* —, physicist.

fisicaménte, *av.* physically.

fisico, *ag.* physical; (*del corpo*) bodily: *dolore* —, bodily pain; *educazione fisica,* physical education (*o* gymnastics); *forza fisica,* physical force (*o* strength) ‖ *s.m.* **1.** (*scienziato*) physicist **2.** (*costituzione*) physique, constitution: *egli ha un* — *molto robusto,* he has a very strong physique.

fisima, *s.f.* (*capriccio*) caprice, whim; (*fantasia, ghiribizzo*) fancy: *quante fisime (hai)!,* (*fam.*) how fussy you are!.

fisiocràtico, *ag.* (*st. econ.*) physiocratic ‖ *s.m.* physiocrat.

fisiocrazía, *s.f.* (*st. econ.*) physiocracy.

fisiognòmica, *s.f.* physiognomy.

fisiognòmico, *ag.* physiognomic(al).

fisiògnomo, *s.m.* physiognomist.

fisiografía, *s.f.* physiography.

fisiogràfico, *ag.* physiographic(al).

fisiògrafo, *s.m.* physiographer.

fisiología, *s.f.* physiology.

fisiologicaménte, *av.* physiologically.

fisiològico, *ag.* physiologic(al).

fisiòlogo, *s.m.* physiologist.

fisionomía, *s.f.* **1.** physiognomy; (*volto*) face; (*lineamenti* (*pl.*): *la sua* — *non mi è nuova,* his face is familiar to me **2.** (*carattere, aspetto*) character, aspect: *la* — *del precedente esercizio,* (*comm.*) the make-up of the last financial year; *la* — *di un luogo,* the aspect of a place.

fisiònomo, *s.m.* physiognomist.

fisioterapía, *s.f.* (*med.*) physiotherapy.

fiso, *ag.* (*poet.*) fixed, intent ‖ *av.* (*poet.*) fixedly; intently: *guardare* — *ql.co.,* to look hard at sthg.

fisonomía, *V.* **fisionomía.**

fissàbile, *ag.* fixable.

fissàggio, *s.m.* **1.** (*mec.*) (*atto del fissare*) fixing, fastening, clamping **2.** (*dispositivo di fissaggio*) fastener, clamp: — *della tavola,* table clamp; — *dello stampo,* die lock **3.** (*foto.*) fixing: *bagno di* —, fixing bath **4.** (*chim.*) fixing.

fissaménte, *av.* fixedly; steadily.

fissàre, *v.t.* **1.** (*rendere fisso*) to fix, to fasten, to secure, to make fast, to make firm; (*con spillo*) to pin: — *un'imposta,* to fasten a shutter; — *ql.co. nella memoria,* *fig.* to fix sthg. in one's memory; — *uno scaffale a una parete,* to fix a shelf to a wall **2.** (*guardare fissamente*) to gaze, to stare, to fix one's eyes on (s.o., sthg.); to gaze at (s.o., sthg.), to stare at (s.o., sthg.), to look hard at (s.o., sthg.): — *l'attenzione su ql.co.,* to fix one's attention on sthg.; — *qlcu. in viso,* to look s.o. in the face **3.** (*determinare*) to fix, to determine, to set, to appoint: — *una data, un prezzo,* to fix a date, a price; — *un giorno,* to appoint (*o* to fix) a day; — *delle re-*

gole, to fix (*o* to determine) rules ‖ — *la residenza,* to take up one's residence **4.** (*pattuire un servizio, prenotare*) to engage, to book: — *una stanza,* to engage (*o* to book) a room; — *una vettura,* to engage a cab **5.** (*chim. foto.*) to fix: — *una negativa,* to fix a negative ‖ **fissàrsi,** *v.r.* **1.** to be fixed: *i suoi occhi si fissarono sul quadro,* he fixed his eyes (*o* his eyes were fixed) on the picture **2.** (*ostinarsi*) to fix one's mind on (sthg.); to set one's heart on (sthg.) **3.** (*stabilirsi*) to settle, to take up one's residence: — *in un paese,* to settle in a country.

fissativo, *ag. s.m.* fixative.

fissàto, *ag.* **1.** fixed; (*stabilito*) settled **2.** (*fam.*) obsessed, maniac: *poveretto, è* —, poor fellow, he suffers from a mania (*o* he has got a bee in his bonnet).

fissàto-bollàto, *s.m.* (*comm.*) bought note.

fissatóre, *s.m.* **1.** (*chim.*) fixer; fixing agent **2.** (*bagno*) —, (*foto.*) fixing bath.

fissazióne, *s.f.* **1.** fixation **2.** (*fam.*) (*idea fissa*) fixed idea, obsession; (*patol.*) monomania **3.** (*chim.*) fixation; fixing.

fissile, *ag.* fissile, cleavable.

fissióne, *s.f.* (*fis.*) fission: — *nucleare,* nuclear fission; *energia di* —, fission energy.

fissiparo, *ag.* (*zool.*) fissiparous ‖ *i fissipari,* (*zool.*) Fissipara.

fissipede, *ag.s.m.* (*zool.*) fissiped, fissipede.

fissità, *s.f.* fixity, fixedness; firmness; steadiness.

fisso, *ag.* **1.** (*saldo, immutabile*) fixed, fast, firm: *idea fissa,* fixed idea; *stelle fisse,* fixed stars; *regola fissa,* fast rule **2.** (*stabilito*) fixed, settled: (*a*) *prezzi fissi,* (at) fixed prices; *senza fissa dimora,* with no fixed abode **3.** (*regolare, costante*) regular; fixed: *reddito* —, fixed income; *egli non ha un lavoro* —, he has not a regular job ‖ *s.m.* (*assegno fisso*) fixed allowance; (*stipendio fisso*) fixed salary.

fisso, *av.* fixedly, steadily: *mi guardava* —, he was looking at me fixedly.

fistola, *s.f.* **1.** Pan-pipe(s), Pan's pipes **2.** (*patol.*) fistula.

fistolo, *s.m.* **1.** (*patol.*) fistula **2.** (*diavolo*) devil: *avere il* — *addosso,* to be possessed (*o* to be restless).

fistolóso, *ag.* (*patol.*) fistulous, fistular.

fitobiología, *s.f.* phytobiology.

fitochímica, *s.f.* phytochemistry.

fitòfago, *ag.* (*entom.*) phytophagous; herbivorous.

fitofisiología, *s.f.* phytophysiology.

fitogènico, *ag.* (*scient.*) phytogenic.

fitogeografía, *s.f.* phytogeography.

fitografía, *s.f.* phytography.

fitología, *s.f.* phytology.

fitòlogo, *s.m.* phytologist, botanist.

fitonomía, *s.f.* phytonomy.

fitopatología, *s.f.* phytopathology.

fitozòo, *s.m.* (*zool.*) phytozoon ‖ *i fitozoi,* (*zool.*) Phytozoa.

fitta, *s.f.* **1.** (*dolore acuto*) stitch, sharp pain, pang: *ella sentì una* — *al cuore,* she felt a pang in her heart; *ho delle fitte al fianco sinistro,* I have stitches in my left side **2.** *fig.* great quantity, a lot: *una* — *di gente,* a lot of people.

fittàbile, fittaiuòlo, *s.m.* tenant farmer.

fittaménte, *av.* thickly; closely.

fittàvolo, *s.m.* tenant farmer.

fittile, *ag.* fictile; clay (*attributivo*).

fittivo, *ag.* fictive, imaginary; (*simulato*) feigned.

fittízio, *ag.* fictitious; sham (*attributivo*).

fitto[1], *ag.* **1.** (*conficcato*) driven in; thrust in ‖ *a capo* —, head downwards (*o* head foremost) **2.** (*denso, spesso*) thick, dense (anche *fig.*): *coperta, stoffa fitta,* thick blanket, cloth; *nebbia fitta,* thick (*o* dense) fog; *una rete fitta,* a close net; *scrittura fitta,* dense writing; *è buio* —, *notte fitta,* it is pitch dark ‖ *nel più* — *inverno,* in the depth of winter ‖ *s.m.* thick: *nel* — *della foresta,* in the thick (*o* depth) of the forest.

fitto[2], *s.m.* (*affitto*) rent.

fittóne, *s.m.* (*bot.*) tap-root, main root.
fittuàrio, *s.m.* tenant.
fiumàle, *ag.* (*letter.*) fluvial.
fiumàna, fiumàra, *s.f.* **1.** broad stream, large stream; (*inondazione*) flood **2.** *fig.* crowd, stream: *una — di gente uscì dal cinema,* a stream of people came out of the cinema.
fiumàtico, *ag.* fluvial.
fiúme, *s.m.* **1.** river; (*corrente*) stream: *il — Mississipi,* the Mississippi river (*o* the Mississippi); *il — Tamigi,* the river Thames (*o* the Thames); *bacino di —,* river basin; *letto di —,* river-bed; *sulle rive di un —,* on the banks of a river **2.** *fig.* flood, stream, torrent: *un — di lacrime,* a flood of tears; *un — di parole,* a torrent of words.
fiutàre, *v.t.* **1.** (*odorare*) to smell; (*rumorosamente*) to sniff: *— tabacco,* to take a snuff (*o* to snuff) **2.** (*seguire col fiuto*) to scent: *— selvaggina,* to scent game **3.** (*intuire*) to scent, to smell; to guess: *— un delitto,* to scent a crime; *— un imbroglio,* (*fam.*) to smell a rat.
fiutàta, *s.f.* smelling; scenting; (*rumorosa*) sniffing || *fare una fiutatina* (*di tabacco*), to take a pinch of snuff.
fiúto, *s.m.* **1.** scent; nose; (*olfatto*) (sense of) smell: *quel cane ha un ottimo —,* that dog has a very good nose (*o* scent) **2.** *fig.* intuition; flair; (*di investigatore*) nose.
flabellífero, *s.m.* (*eccl.*) flabellum-bearer.
flabèllo, *s.m.* **1.** (*eccl.*) flabellum (*pl.* flabella): *portatore di flabelli,* flabellum-bearer **2.** *pl.* (*aer.*) gills.
flaccidézza, *s.f.* flabbiness; flaccidity.
flàccido, *ag.* **1.** flabby; flaccid **2.** (*debole*) weak, limp.
flaconcìno, *s.m.* tiny bottle.
flacóne, *s.m.* small glass, bottle, phial.
flagellaménto, *s.m.* flagellation, scourging.
flagellànte, *s.m.* (*st. relig.*) flagellant.
flagellàre, *v.t.* **1.** to flagellate, to scourge; to flog, to whip || *— l'aria con le ali,* to wing the air **2.** *fig.* (*affliggere*) to scourge **3.** (*del mare*) to lash: *il mare flagellava le rocce,* the sea was breaking against the rocks || **flagellàrsi,** *v.r.* to flagellate oneself, to whip oneself.
flagellàti, *s.m.pl.* (*biol.*) Flagellata.
flagellàto, *ag.* flagellated, scourged.
flagellatóre, *s.m.,* **flagellatríce,** *s.f.* flagellator, scourger.
flagellazióne, *s.f.* flagellation, scourging, flogging.
flagèllo, *s.m.* **1.** (*frusta*) scourge, whip **2.** *fig.* scourge, plague; (*calamità*) calamity; (*rovina*) ruin: *il — dell'inondazione incombe,* the calamity of a flood impends; *quel ragazzo è un —,* that boy is a plague || *Attila, il — di Dio,* Attila, the Scourge of God **3.** (*eccl.*) (*disciplina*) scourge **4.** (*fam.*) (*gran numero*) plenty: *c'era un — di mosche,* there were plenty of flies **5.** (*bot. zool. biol.*) flagellum (*pl.* flagella).
flagrànte, *ag.* (*dir.*) flagrant; manifest, evident || *cogliere qlcu. in —,* to catch s.o. in the open act (*o* to catch s.o. red-handed).
flagranteménte, *av.* (*dir.*) flagrantly.
flagrànza, *s.f.* (*dir.*) flagrancy.
flàmine, *s.m.* (*st. romana*) flamen (*pl.* flamines, flamens).
Flamínio, *no.pr.m.* (*st.*) Flaminius.
flammàre, *v.t.* (*temprare alla fiamma*) to flame-harden.
flàmmeo, *ag.* (*letter.*) flaming, flamy.
flanèlla, *s.f.* flannel: *pantaloni di —,* flannels.
flanellína, *s.f.* flannelette.
flàngia, *s.f.* (*tec.*) flange: *— cieca,* blank flange; *— mobile,* loose flange; *— di accoppiamento,* (*mar.*) coupling flange; *accoppiamento a flange,* (*mec.*) flange coupling.
flàto, *s.m.* flatus.
flatulènto, *ag.* flatulent.
flatulènza, flatuosità, *s.f.* flatulence.
flautàto, *ag.* flute-like, fluted; musical: *note flautate,* fluted notes; *voce flautata,* musical voice.

flautísta, *s.c.* (*mus.*) flautist, flute-player.
flàuto, *s.m.* (*mus.*) flute: *suonare il —,* to play (on) the flute || «*Il Flauto Magico*», (*st. mus.*) "The Magic Flute".
Flàvia, *no.pr.f.* Flavia.
flàvio, *ag.* (*st.*) Flavian || **Flàvio,** *no.pr.m.* Flavius.
flàvo, *ag.* (*poet.*) fair; yellow: *capelli flavi,* fair hair.
flèbile, *ag.* (*lamentevole*) plaintive; (*lacrimoso*) tearful; (*debole*) feeble, soft: *gli giunse un suono —,* a plaintive sound reached him.
flebilménte, *av.* plaintively; (*debolmente*) feebly.
flebíte, *s.f.* (*patol.*) phlebitis.
fleboclísi, *s.f.* (*med.*) phleboclysis.
fleborragìa, *s.f.* (*patol.*) phleborrhagia.
fleboscleròsi, *s.f.* (*patol.*) phlebosclerosis.
flebotomía, *s.f.* (*med.*) phlebotomy.
flebòtomo, *s.m.* phlebotomist.
Flegetónte, *no.pr.m.* (*geog. mit.*) Phlegethon.
flèmma, *s.f.* **1.** (*calma*) coolness, phlegm, calm, calmness **2.** (*fisiol.*) phlegm.
flemmaticaménte, *av.* phlegmatically, calmly.
flemmàtico, *ag.* phlegmatic, impassive.
flèmmone, *s.m.* (*patol.*) phlegmon.
flemmonóso, *ag.* (*patol.*) phlegmonous, phlegmonic.
flessíbile, *ag.* flexible, pliable, pliant (*anche fig.*): *carattere —,* flexible character; *tubo —,* flexible pipe.
flessibilità, *s.f.* flexibility, pliability.
flessibilménte, *av.* flexibly, pliably.
flèssile, *ag.* (*rar.*) flexible, pliable, pliant.
flessímetro, *s.m.* deflectometer.
Flessínga, *no.pr.f.* (*geog.*) Flushing.
flessióne, *s.f.* **1.** flexion; bending **2.** (*mec. edil.*) flexure; flexion; bending; (*deviazione dalla linea retta*) deflection: *prova a —,* bending test; *sollecitazione di —,* bending stress (*o* stress of flexure) **3.** (*gram.*) flexion, inflexion.
flessívo, *ag.* flexional.
flèsso, *s.m.* (*mat.*) flex, inflection, flex point.
flessóre, flessòrio, *ag.* (*anat.*) flexor (*attributivo*).
flessuosità, *s.f.* flexuosity; (*di corpo, figura*) suppleness.
flessuóso, *ag.* flexuous; (*di corpo, figura*) supple.
flèttere, *v.t.* to bend; to flex: *— le ginocchia,* to bend one's knees.
flirtàre, *v.i.* to flirt.
flòceo, *s.m.* (*mar.*) jib.
flocculazióne, *s.f.* (*chim.*) flocculation.
floèma, *s.m.* (*bot.*) phloem.
flogístico, *ag.* (*patol.*) phlogistic, inflammatory.
flògosi, *s.f.* (*patol.*) phlogosis, inflammation.
Flòra, *no.pr.f.* Flora (anche *mit.*) || *dim.* Flo, Florrie || **flòra,** *s.f.* **1.** (*scient.*) flora: *la — della Francia,* the flora of France **2.** (*catalogo delle piante*) flora, botanist's hand-book.
floreàle, *ag.* floral, florid, floreate || *stile —,* (*st. art.*) art nouveau || *s.m.* (*st. francese*) Floréal.
floricoltóre, *s.m.* floriculturist.
floricoltúra, *s.f.* floriculture.
floridaménte, *av.* **1.** (*prosperamente*) prosperously **2.** (*rar.*) (*floritamente*) floridly.
floridézza, *s.f.* **1.** (*prosperità*) prosperity **2.** (*rar.*) (*l'essere fiorito*) floridness, floridity.
flòrido, *ag.* **1.** (*prospero*) prosperous, thriving, flourishing; (*prosperoso*) buxom; (*colorito*) ruddy: *una industria florida,* a thriving industry; *una ragazza florida,* a buxom girl **2.** (*rar.*) (*fiorito*) florid, flowery (anche *fig.*): *stile —,* florid style.
florilègio, *s.m.* florilegium (*pl.* florilegia); anthology.
floscézza, *s.f.* flabbiness, flaccidness, limpness.
flosciaménte, *av.* **1.** flabbily, flaccidly, limply **2.** *fig.* (*debolmente*) flabbily, limply, weakly.
flòscio, *ag.* **1.** flabby; flaccid, limp; soft, slack: *cappello —,* soft hat; *cartone —,* limp binding; *gote flosce,* flabby cheeks; *muscoli flosci,* flaccid (*o* slack) muscles **2.** *fig.*

(*debole, inerte*) flabby, limp, weak: *il suo temperamento è piuttosto —*, his character is rather weak.

flòtta, *s.f.* fleet: *— mercantile*, mercantile fleet ‖ *la —*, (*mar. mil.*) the navy.

flottàggio, *s.m.* (*aer.*) taxying; (*amer.*) plowing.

flottànte, *ag.* (*mar. mec.*) floating.

flottàre, *v.i.* 1. (*aer.*) to taxi (along the water) 2. (*mar.*) to float.

flottazióne, *s.f.* 1. (*mar.*) floatage, flotation, floating: *linea di —*, water line 2. (*miner.*) flotation.

flottíglia, *s.f.* (*mar.*) flotilla.

fluènte, *ag.* flowing; fluent (anche *fig.*): *barba —*, flowing beard; *un discorso —*, a fluent speech.

fluidaménte, *av.* flowingly.

fluidificàre, *v.t.* to fluidify.

fluidità, *s.f.* fluidity; fluency (anche *fig.*): *— di stile*, fluency of style.

flúido, *ag.* fluid; fluent, flowing (anche *fig.*): *stile —*, flowing style ‖ *s.m.* fluid: *— operante*, (*mec.*) working fluid; *— protettivo*, (*chim. ind.*) inhibitor ‖ *— magnetico*, magnetic fluid.

fluíre, *v.i.* to flow.

fluorescènte, *ag.* fluorescent: *illuminazione —*, fluorescent lighting; *lampada —*, fluorescent lamp.

fluorescènza, *s.f.* 1. (*fis.*) fluorescence 2. (*elett.*) glow.

fluorídrico, *ag.* (*chim.*) hydrofluoric.

fluorína, fluoríte, *s.f.* (*min.*) fluorite, fluor(spar).

fluòro, *s.m.* (*chim.*) fluorine.

fluorúro, *s.m.* (*chim.*) fluoride.

flussióne, *s.f.* 1. (*patol.*) fluxion; (*infreddatura*) cold: *— di petto*, inflammation of the lungs 2. *pl.* (*mat.*) fluxions.

flússo, *s.m.* 1. (*di marea*) flood(-tide): *— e riflusso*, ebb and flow (anche *fig.*) 2. (*fis.*) flux: *— di induzione magnetica*, (*elett.*) magnetic flux; *— elettrico*, electric flux; *densità del —*, (*elett.*) flux density 3. (*fisiol.*) flux; (*dissenteria*) dysentery.

flussòmetro, *s.m.* 1. (*per misura di fluidi*) flowmeter, rotameter 2. (*elett.*) fluxmeter.

flútto, *s.m.* wave; (*cavallone*) billow.

fluttuaménto, *s.m.* fluctuation, instability.

fluttuànte, *ag.* 1. fluctuating, floating: *debito —*, (*econ.*) floating debt; *popolazione —*, floating population; *prezzi fluttuanti*, fluctuating prices 2. (*incerto, dubbioso*) irresolute, doubtful.

fluttuàre, *v.i.* 1. to fluctuate, to rise and fall 2. *fig.* to fluctuate, to waver: *— tra sentimenti opposti*, to fluctuate between opposite feelings.

fluttuazióne, *s.f.* fluctuation: *fluttuazioni del mercato monetario*, (*econ.*) fluctuations in the money market.

fluviàle, fluviàtile, *ag.* river (*attributivo*); (*rar.*) fluvial: *navigazione —*, river navigation.

fobìa, *s.f.* (*patol.*) phobia, morbid fear; dread; (*avversione*) aversion; hatred: *— per la guerra*, aversion to war.

fòca, *s.f.* (*zool.*) seal: *pelle di —*, sealskin.

focàccia, *s.f.* cake; (*focaccetta*) bun ‖ *render pan per —*, *prov.* to give tit for tat.

focàia, *ag.*: *pietra —*, flint.

focàle, *ag.* (*ott.*) focal: *distanza —*, focal length.

focàtico, *s.m.* (*st. dir.*) hearth-money, hearth-tax.

focàto, *ag.* fiery-red: *cavallo baio —*, reddish bay (horse).

fóce, *s.f.* mouth, outlet, outfall: *le foci del Gange*, the mouths of the Ganges; *mettere — in mare*, to flow into the sea.

Focèa, *no.pr.f.* (*geog. st.*) Phocaea.

focése, *ag.s.c.* Phocaean.

fochísta, *s.m.* 1. (*di locomotiva*) stoker; fireman (*pl.* firemen) 2. (*chi fabbrica fuochi d'artificio*) pyrotechnist, maker of fireworks.

Fòcide, *no.pr.f.* (*geog. st.*) Phocis.

Focióne, *no.pr.m.* (*st.*) Phocion.

fòco, (*letter.*) per **fuòco.**

focolàio, *s.m.* (*med.*) centre (of infection).

focolàre, *s.m.* 1. hearth: *pietra del —*, hearthstone 2. (*caminetto*) fireplace, fireside: *presso il —*, by the fireside 3. *fig.* (*casa, famiglia*) home: *le gioie del — domestico*, the joys of home life 4. (*med.*) centre (of infection) 5. (*mec.*) furnace: *— a tiraggio forzato*, forced draft furnace; *— della caldaia*, boiler furnace; *— a combustibile liquido*, liquid fuel furnace.

focosaménte, *av.* fierily; (*impetuosamente*) impetuously.

focóso, *ag.* hot, fiery; (*appassionato*) hot-blooded; (*impetuoso*) impetuous: *cavallo —*, fiery (*o* mettlesome) horse; *temperamento —*, hot temper.

fòdera, *s.f.* 1. (*interno*) lining 2. (*copertura*) cover 3. (*mar.*) sheathing.

foderàre, *v.t.* 1. to line: *— di seta*, to line with silk; *— di pelliccia*, to line with fur 2. (*coprire, rivestire*) to cover 3. (*mar.*) to sheathe (with metal).

foderàto, *ag.* 1. lined: *— di seta*, silk-lined; *— di pelliccia*, fur-lined (*o* furred) ‖ *aver gli occhi foderati di panno*, *fig.* to be blind to evidence 2. (*coperto*) covered (with sthg.) 3. (*mar.*) (metal) sheathed 4. *fig.* well supplied, well stocked: *— di biglietti di banca*, well stocked with bank-notes.

foderatúra, *s.f.* 1. lining 2. (*copertura*) covering 3. (*di metallo*) sheathing.

fòdero, *s.m.* scabbard, sheath: *rimettere la spada nel —*, to sheathe the sword (anche *fig.*); *trarre la spada dal —*, to draw the sword (*o* to draw one's sword from the scabbard).

fòga, *s.f.* impetuosity; (*ardore*) ardour, passion.

fòggia, *s.f.* 1. (*moda*) fashion; (*maniera*) manner, way, style: *alla — di Napoli*, after the fashion of Naples (*o* in Neapolitan fashion) 2. (*forma*) shape: *una gonna a — di campana*, a bell-shaped skirt; *una scollatura a — di V*, a V-shaped neckline.

foggiàre, *v.t.* to shape, to form, to fashion; (*modellare*) to mould ‖ **foggiàrsi,** *v.r.* to shape, to form.

fòglia, *s.f.* 1. leaf (*pl.* leaves): *— di rosa*, rose-leaf; *— di tabacco*, tobacco leaf; *— di tè*, tea-leaf; *la caduta delle foglie*, the fall of the leaves; *senza foglie*, leafless; *cogliere la — per i bachi*, to gather mulberry -leaves for silk worms; *essere pieno di foglie*, to be in leaf; *mettere le foglie*, to put on leaves (*o* to come into leaf *o* to put forth leaves *o* to leaf) ‖ *mangiar la —*, *fig.* to take the hint (*o* to smell a rat) ‖ *non muover —*, *fig.* not to lift a finger ‖ *tremare come una —*, to tremble like an aspen leaf 2. (*mec.*) leaf (*pl.* leaves): *— di molla*, spring leaf 3. (*sottile strato di metallo*) foil: *— di stagno*, tinfoil; *— d'oro*, gold-foil; (*sottilissima*) gold-leaf 4. (*motivo ornamentale*) foil.

fogliàccio, *s.m.* (*giornalaccio*) rag.

fogliàceo, *ag.* foliaceous.

fogliàme, *s.m.* foliage, leafage; leaves (*pl.*).

Fogliànti, *s.m.pl.* (*st. francese*) Feuillants.

fogliàre, *v.i.* to put forth leaves, to leaf.

fogliétto, *s.m.* 1. small sheet of paper; slip of paper 2. (*manifestino di propaganda*) leaflet; (*distribuito a mano*) handbill 3. (*anat.*) pleura (*pl.* pleurae).

foglífero, *ag.* (*bot.*) leafy, leaf-bearing.

fòglio, *s.m.* 1. sheet: *— da disegno*, drawing sheet; *— di carta*, sheet of paper; *— di carta bollata*, sheet of stamped paper; *— volante*, leaflet ‖ *— di via*, expulsion order ‖ *dar — bianco a qlcu.*, to give (*o* to allow) s.o. a free hand (*o* carte blanche) 2. (*pagina*) leaf (*pl.* leaves): *i fogli di un libro*, the leaves of a book ‖ *voltar —*, *fig.* to change the subject 3. (*banconota*) bank-note: *un — da cinque sterline*, a five pound note 4. (*giornale*) (news)paper: *— del mattino*, morning paper 5. (*tip.*) folio: *in —*, in folio; *un volume in —*, a folio (*o* an in folio) volume 6. (*di metallo*) sheet, plate: *— di lamiera di ferro*, iron sheet; *— di latta*, tin plate (*o* sheet) 7. *— per impiallacciatura*, (*artig.*) scaleboard.

fogliolína, *sf.* leaflet; young leaf.

foglióso, fogliúto, *ag.* leafy; (*poet.*) leavy.

fógna, *s.f.* **1.** sewer (*bianca*) drain; (*scarico d'acqua*) water drain: *topo di*; —, sewer rat **2.** (*luogo immondo*) filthy place.

fognatúra, *s.f.* sewage; sewerage: — *di una città,* city sewer system; *collettore di* —, sewer trunk line.

fòia, *s.f.* lust.

fòla, *s.f.* **1.** fable **2.** (*fandonia*) fib, idle story: *fole!,* humbug! (*o* nonsense!).

fòlade, *s.f.* (*zool.*) pholas (*pl.* pholades).

fòlaga, *s.f.* (*ornit.*) coot, moorhen.

folàta, *s.f.* **1.** gust, squall **2.** (*di uccelli*) flight.

folelòre, *s.m.* folklore.

folelorísta, *s.c.* folklorist.

folelorístico, *ag.* folkloristic.

Fólco, *no.pr.m.* (*st.*) Fulk.

folgorànte, *ag.* **1.** (*lampeggiante*) flashing; gleaming **2.** (*abbagliante*) dazzling **3.** (*splendente*) shining.

folgoràre, *v.i.* **1.** (*lampeggiare*) to lighten; to flash **2.** (*splendere*) to shine, to beam ‖ *v.t.* **1.** (*colpire con la folgore*) to strike with lightning **2.** (*abbagliare*) to dazzle **3.** (*colpire con armi da lancio*) to dart.

folgoràto, *ag.* **1.** struck by lightning **2.** *fig.* thunder-struck.

fólgore, *s.m.* thunderbolt; lightning; flash of lightning.

folgoríte, *s.f.* (*geol.*) fulgurite.

fòlio, *V.* **fòglio 5.**

fòlla, *s.f.* **1.** crowd; throng; mass; multitude; (*plebaglia*) mob: *le folle,* the masses; *una gran* —, a large crowd; *c'è — nella sala?,* are there many people in the hall? **2.** (*poet.*) host: *una — di ricordi,* a host of memories.

follàre, *v.t.* **1.** (*ind. tessile*) to full **2.** (*enologia*) to press.

follatóio, *s.m.* (*enologia*) winepress.

follatóre, *s.m.* (*ind. tessile*) fuller ‖ **follatríce,** *s.f.* (*ind. tessile*) fulling machine, mill.

follatúra, *s.f.* (*ind. tessile*) fulling, milling.

fòlle, *ag.* **1.** (*pazzo*) mad, insane **2.** (*sciocco, stolto*) foolish **3.** (*mec.*) idle; (*aut.*) neutral: *in* —, neutral: *girare in* —, to idle.

folleggiaménto, *s.m.* **1.** (*azione da pazzo*) madness **2.** (*il divertirsi spensieratamente*) frolicking, merry-making.

folleggiàre, *v.i.* **1.** (*agire da folle*) to behave foolishly; to act like a madman **2.** (*divertirsi spensieratamente*) to make merry; to frolic; (*far buffonerie*) to play pranks.

folleménte, *av.* **1.** (*pazzamente*) madly **2.** (*scioccamente*) foolishly.

follétto, *ag.* elfish; elf (*attributivo*) ‖ *s.m.* **1.** sprite, elf (*pl.* elves); imp; (*spiritello burlone*) goblin **2.** *fig.* restless child; imp: *sei proprio un* (*vero*) —*!,* you're a regular imp!.

follía, *s.f.* **1.** (*pazzia*) madness; lunacy ‖ *amare qlcu.* (*sino*) *alla* —, to be madly in love with s.o. **2.** (*atto stolto*) foolish act; (*sventatezza*) folly.

follicolàre, *ag.* (*anat. bot.*) follicular.

follicolíte, *s.f.* (*patol.*) folliculitis.

follícolo, *s.m.* (*bot. anat.*) follicle.

follóne, *s.m.* (*ind. tessile*) fuller.

fólta, *s.f.* (*rar.*) crowd, throng.

foltaménte, *av.* thickly; densely.

foltézza, *s.f.* thickness; denseness.

fólto, 1. *ag.* thick: *folta capigliatura,* thick hair **2.** (*affollato*) crowded ‖ *s.m.* thick: *nel — del bosco,* in the thick of the wood; *nel — della mischia,* in the thick of the fight.

foménta, *s.f.* (*impacco*) fomentation.

fomentàre, *v.t.* to foment, to foster, to instigate, to excite.

fomentatóre, *s.m.,* **fomentatríce,** *s.f.* fomenter.

fomentazióne, *s.f.* fomentation, instigation.

foménto, *s.m.* fomentation, instigation.

fòmite, *s.m.* **1.** (*esca*) tinder **2.** *fig.* (*causa*) source, cause, origin; incentive.

fon, *s.m.* (*acu.*) phon.

fónda, *s.f.* **1.** (*mar.*) anchorage: *essere alla* —, to ride at anchor **2.** (*di pistola*) holster.

fondaco, *s.m.* **1.** (*negozio di tessuti*) draper's shop **2.** (*magazzino*) warehouse; store(house).

fondàle, *s.m.* **1.** (*teat.*) background **2.** (*mar.*) sounding-depth: *andamento del* —, depth contour.

fondamentàle, *ag.* fundamental, essential, basic: *prodotto* —, basic product.

fondamentalménte, *av.* fundamentally, essentially.

fondaménto, *s.m.*; *pl.f.* **fondaménta** (*nel senso* **1.**); *pl.m.* **fondaménti** (*nel senso* **2.**) **1.** foundation: *gettare le fondamenta di un edificio,* to lay the foundation(s) of a building; *tracciare le fondamenta,* to mark out the foundations **2.** *fig.* (*base, principio*) basis (*pl.* bases), foundation, ground: *i fondamenti della nostra fede,* the foundations of our faith; *sospetti senza* —, groundless suspicions; *questa diceria è senza* —, this rumour has no foundation (*o* is entirely without foundation).

fondàre, *v.t.* **1.** (*erigere, gettare le fondamenta di*) to found, to build: — *una chiesa, una città,* to found a church, a town **2.** (*istituire, costituire*) to found; to establish; to build; to start: *Casa fondata nel 1859,* House established in 1859; — *una colonia,* to found a colony; — *una ditta,* to establish a commercial house (*o* firm); — *una famiglia,* to found a family; — *un giornale, una rivista,* to start (*o* to launch) a newspaper, a magazine; — *un impero,* to build an empire; — *un istituto,* to establish (*o* to found) an institution **3.** (*basare*) to found, to base, to ground: — *le proprie affermazioni sui fatti,* to found (*o* to base *o* to ground) one's statements on facts ‖ **fondàrsi,** *v.r.* to base oneself on (sthg.); to be founded on, upon, in (sthg.); to rely on, upon (sthg.): — *sulla giustizia,* to be founded in justice; — *sulle promesse di qlcu.,* to rely on s.o.'s promises.

fondàta, *s.f.* dregs (*pl.*), sediment.

fondataménte, *av.* justly, rightly.

fondatézza, *s.f.* *fig.* foundation, ground; truth, reasonableness: *senza* —, without foundation.

fondàto, *ag.* well-grounded, well-founded: *sospetti fondati,* well-grounded suspicions.

fondatóre, *s.m.,* **fondatríce,** *s.f.* founder, promoter.

fondazióne, *s.f.* **1.** (*il gettare le fondamenta*) foundation: — *di una chiesa, di una città, di una colonia, di una scuola,* foundation of a church, of a town, of a colony, of a school ‖ *mille anni dalla — di Roma,* one thousand years from the foundation of Rome **2.** (*l'istituire*) foundation; establishment: — *di una ditta,* establishment (*o* foundation) of a business **3.** (*istituzione*) institution: — *benefica,* welfare institution.

fondèllo, *s.m.* bottom: — *di un bossolo,* bottom of a cartridge-case.

fondènte, *ag.* melting, fusing ‖ *s.m.* **1.** (*metal.*) flux **2.** (*dolce*) fondant.

fóndere, *v.t.* **1.** (*liquefare*) to melt, to fuse; (*per separare un metallo da scorie*) to smelt: *il sole fuse la neve,* the sun melted the snow; — *i cuscinetti, le bronzine,* (*aut.*) to burn out the bearings; — *oggetti d'oro,* to melt gold articles **2.** (*fondere in forma*) to cast, to mould **3.** (*unire*) to blend, to merge (anche *fig.*): *pensarono di — la loro organizzazione con la nostra,* they thought of merging their organization with ours; — *due colori,* to blend two colours; — *due partiti,* to unite two parties ‖ *v.i.* to melt: *il ghiaccio fonde a 0°,* ice melts at 32° F. ‖ **fóndersi,** *v.r.* **1.** to melt, ‖ — *in lacrime,* to melt into tears **2.** (*armonizzare unirsi*) to blend.

fondería, *s.f.* foundry, casting house.

fondiàrio, *ag.* landed, land (*attributivo*): *credito* —, loan secured on land (property); *imposta fondiaria,* land-tax; *proprietà fondiaria,* land(ed) property; *proprietario* —, landowner.

fondíbile, *ag.* fusible.

fondíglio, *s.m.* dregs (*pl.*), sediment, deposit.

fondína, *s.f.* holster, pistol case.

fondísta, *s.m.* (*spor.*) long-distance runner.

fonditóre, *s.m.* melter, caster, smelter, foundryman (*pl.* foundrymen): — *di caratteri,* (*tip.*) type-founder ‖ **fonditríce,** *s.f.* (*tip.*) casting machine, caster.

fonditúra, *s.f.* **1.** fusion, melting; (*per separare metalli da scorie*) smelting **2.** (*colata*) casting.

fóndo[1], *ag.* deep: *acqua fonda,* deep water ‖ *piatto* —, soup plate.

fóndo[2], *s.m.* **1.** (*parte inferiore*) bottom: — *marino,* sea-bottom; — *pietroso,* stony bottom; — *sabbioso,* sandy bottom; — *stradale,* road-bed; *a* — *piatto,* flat-bottomed; *dal* — *del mio cuore,* from the bottom of my heart; *doppio* —, double (*o* false) bottom; *caddi in* — *al pozzo,* I fell to the bottom of the well; *ciò mi colpì nel* — *dell'anima,* that hurt me to the quick; *in* — *al tuo bicchiere c'è ancora un po' di vino,* there is some wine left at the bottom of your glass; *lo lessi in* — *alla prima pagina,* I read it at the bottom of the first page (*o* of page 1); *andare a* —, to go to the bottom (*o* to sink); *mandare a* —, to send to the bottom (*o* to sink); *toccare il* —, to ground; *fig.* to touch the bottom ‖ — *dei calzoni,* seat (of the trousers) ‖ *da cima a* —, from top to bottom ‖ *in* —, *in* — *in* —, after all ‖ *mano di* —, (*in verniciatura*) priming coat ‖ *conoscere ql.co. a* —, to know sthg. thoroughly ‖ *dar* — *al proprio patrimonio,* to squander all one's fortune; *dar* — *alle provviste,* to use up all one's provisions **2.** (*fine, estremità*) end: *carrozze, vagoni di* —, rear carriages; *in* — *al corridoio,* at the end of the corridor **3.** (*natura, indole*) nature: *egli ha un* — *buono,* he has a good nature **4.** (*feccia*) dregs (*pl.*), grounds (*pl.*): *fondi di caffè,* coffee grounds (*o* dregs) **5.** (*sfondo*) ground, background: *un disegno su* — *scuro,* a design on a dark ground **6.** (*merce invenduta*): *fondi di magazzino, di bottega,* remnants (*o* odds and ends); — *di magazzino,* stock in hand **7.**(*spor.*): *corridore di* —, *cavallo di* —, stayer; *corsa di* —, long distance race; *fare un a* —, (*scherma*) to lunge (*o* to make a full lunge) **8.** *articolo di* —, (*giornalismo*) leading article (*o* leader *o* editorial).

fóndo[3], *s.m.* **1.** (*possedimento*) estate; (*podere*) farm: — *rustico,* land(ed) property; — *urbano,* town house **2.** (*capitale*) fund: — *di ammortamento,* sinking fund (*o* depreciation fund); — *di cassa,* cash in hand; (*per spese minute*) petty cash; — *di garanzia,* trust fund; *fondi di previdenza,* social insurance funds; — *di riserva,* reserve fund; *fondi liquidi,* ready money (*o* cover); *fondi pubblici,* public funds; *fondi residui,* surplus funds; *capitale a* — *perduto,* sunk capital; *investire danaro a* — *perduto,* to sink money.

fondúta, *s.f.* (*cuc.*) fondue.

fonètica, *s.f.* phonetics.

foneticaménte, *av.* phonetically.

fonètico, *ag.* phonetic: *segni fonetici,* phonetic signs.

fònica, *s.f.* acoustics.

fònico, *ag.* phonic; sound (*attributivo*): *segnale* —, sound signal.

fonogènico, *ag.* good for recording: *la sua voce è fonogenica,* his voice records well.

fonograficaménte, *av.* phonographically.

fonogràfico, *ag.* phonographic: *disco* —, gramophone record.

fonògrafo, *s.m.* phonograph; gramophone: — *automatico a gettone,* (*amer.*) juke-box.

fonogràmma, *s.m.* **1.** (*tel.*) phonogram **2.** (*cine.*) sound record.

fonoincisóre, *s.m.* sound recording device; recording head: — *portatile,* portable recording apparatus.

fonolite, *s.f.* (*min.*) phonolite; clink-stone.

fonología, *s.f.* phonology.

fonològico, *ag.* phonologic(al).

fonologicaménte, *av.* phonologically.

fonòlogo, *s.m.* phonologist.

fonometría, *s.f.* phonometry.

fonòmetro, *s.m.* (*acu.*) phonometer, noise meter, sound level meter.

fonotipía, *s.f.* phonotypy.

fontàna, *s.f.* **1.** fountain **2.** (*fonte*) spring, source (*anche fig.*) ‖ — *ardente,* (*geol.*) fire well.

fontanèlla, *s.f.* **1.** small fountain: — *a spillo,* drinking fountain **2.** (*anat.*) fontanel(le).

fontaníle, *s.m.* **1.** (*fonte*) spring, source **2.** (*abbeveratoio*) trough **3.** (*canale d'irrigazione*) conduit.

fontaníno, *ag.* spring (*attributivo*), fountain (*attributivo*): *ninfa fontanina,* spring nymph.

fónte, *s.f.* **1.** (*sorgente*) spring, source **2.** (*fontana*) fountain **3.** *fig.* origin, source, cause: *la* — *di tutti i nostri mali,* the source of all our troubles **4.** (*lett. st.*) source: *le fonti della storia,* the sources of history; *le fonti dell'«Orlando Furioso»,* the sources of the "Orlando Furioso" ‖ *sapere da buona, sicura* —, to have on good authority (*o* to have learnt from a reliable source) ‖ *s.m.:* — *battesimale,* font.

fontína, *s.f.* "fontina" (kind of cheese made in Piedmont).

foràbile, *ag.* pierceable.

forabòsco, *s.m.* (*ornit.*) woodpecker.

foracchiàre, *v.t.* to pierce; to riddle with holes.

foracchiàto, *ag.* pierced; full of holes, riddled with holes.

foracchiatúra, *s.f.* piercing; boring.

foraggiaménto, *s.m.* foraging.

foraggiàre, *v.i.* to forage ‖ *v.t.* (*appoggiare con sussidi*) to subsidize.

foraggière, *s.m.* (*mil.*) forager.

foràggio, *s.m.* **1.** forage; fodder: — *immagazzinato nei silos,* (en)silage; *piante da* —, fodder plants **2.** (*vettovaglie*) victuals (*pl.*), provisions (*pl.*).

foràme, *s.m.* hole, orifice.

foraménto, *s.m.* piercing, boring.

foraminíferi, *s.m. pl.* (*zool.*) Foraminifera.

foraminífero, *ag.* (*zool.*) foraminiferous.

foràneo, *ag.* **1.** rural; outside the town **2.** (*mar.*) outside the harbour; outer **3.** (*eccl.*) forane: *vicario* —, vicar forane.

foràre, *v.t.* **1.** to pierce; to perforate; (*biglietti*) to punch; (*pneumatici*) to puncture **2.** (*mec.*) to perforate; (*con punteruolo, trapano*) to drill, to bore; (*al tornio*) to bore out ‖ *v.i.* (*bucare pneumatico*) to puncture, to get a puncture; (*amer.*) to get a flat tyre: *forai due volte,* I punctured twice.

forasièpe, *s.m.* (*ornit.*) wren.

foràstico, *ag.* wild; rustic.

foratóio, *s.m.* **1.** (*trapano*) drill; (*succhiello*) gimlet; (*punzone*) punch **2.** (*accoratoio*) butcher's knife.

foratúra, *s.f.* **1.** piercing; (*di biglietto*) punching; (*di pneumatico*) puncture **2.** (*con punteruolo, trapano*) drilling, boring **3.** (*buco*) hole.

fòrbice, (*pop.*) per **fòrbici.**

fòrbici, *s.f.pl.* **1.** scissors; (*cesoie*) shears: — *da giardino,* garden shears; — *da sarto,* tailor's shears; — *per potare,* pruning shears; — *per tosare,* sheep shears; — *per unghie,* nail scissors; *un colpo di* —, a snip (of scissors); *un paio di* —, a pair of scissors; *tagliare con le* —, to scissor **2.** (*salto a forbici*) scissors (*pl.* *con costruzione sing.*) **3.** (*chele*) pincers, claws, nippers **4.** (*mar.*) kevel.

forbiciàta, *s.f.* cut, snip, clip.

forbicína, *s.f.* (*entom.*) earwig.

forbíre, *v.t.* **1.** to clean; to furbish **2.** *fig.* (*di stile*) to polish ‖ **forbírsi,** *v.r.* to wipe: *si forbì la bocca,* he wiped his mouth.

forbitaménte, *av.* with high polish; elegantly.

forbitézza, *s.f.* polish; refinement; elegance; neatness; propriety.

forbíto, *ag.* polished; refined; elegant; neat: *stile* —, polished style.

fórca, *s.f.* **1.** fork ‖ *le Forche Caudine,* (*st. romana*) the Caudine Forks (*anche fig.*) ‖ *far* —, (*marinare la scuola*) to play truant **2.** (*agr.*) pitchfork, hayfork **3.** (*mar.*) crutch **4.** (*patibolo*) gallows; gibbet ‖

pendaglio da —, *fig.* gallows-bird; *meriterebbe la* —, *fig.* he deserves hanging; *andate sulla* —! (*fam.*) go to the devil!.

forcàccio, *s.m.* (*mar.*) crutch.

forcaiolísmo, *s.m.* (*pol.*) reactionary system of government.

forcai(u)òlo, *s.m.* extreme reactionary.

forcàta, *s.f.* **1.** pitchforkful **2.** (*colpo di forca*) pitchfork-thrust.

forcèlla, *s.f.* **1.** (*legnetto forcuto*) forked stick **2.** (*mec.*) fork: — *del cambio,* (*aut.*) gearshift fork; — *della bicicletta,* fork of the bicycle **3.** (*per capelli*) hairpin **4.** (*mil.*) bracket, fork: *far* —, to bracket (*o* to straddle) **5.** (*anat.*) base of breast-bone; (*di pollo*) merrythought, wish -bone **6.** (*del telefono*) rest **7.** (*passo alpino*) saddle, narrow alpine pass.

forchétta, *s.f.* **1.** fork: — *da frutta,* dessert-fork || *colazione alla* —, knife-and-fork meal || *essere una buona* —, *fig.* to be a big eater || *parlare in punta di* —, to speak with affectation **2.** (*agli scacchi*) fork.

forchettàta, *s.f.* **1.** forkful **2.** (*colpo di forchetta*) fork-thrust.

forchettièra, *s.f.* fork holder.

forchétto, *s.m.* pronged stick.

forchettóne, *s.m.* carving-fork.

forchíno, *s.m.* three-pronged hay-fork.

forcína, *s.f.* hairpin.

fòrcipe, *s.m.* (*chir.*) forceps (*invariato al pl.*).

fórcola, *s.f.* (*mar.*) rowlock.

forconàta, *s.f.* **1.** pitchforkful **2.** (*colpo di forcone*) pitchfork-thrust.

forcóne, *s.m.* pitchfork; (*da letame*) dung-fork.

forcúto, *ag.* forked.

forènse, *ag.* (*dir.*) forensic.

forése, *ag.* peasant (*attributivo*); rural; rustic.

forèsta, *s.f.* forest (*anche fig.*); wood: *una* — *di capelli,* a mop (of hair); *una* — *di ciminiere,* a forest of factory-chimneys; — *vergine,* virgin forest.

forestàle, *ag.* forestal: *guardia* —, forester; *leggi forestali,* forest laws.

foresteria, *s.f.* guest-rooms (*pl.*).

forestièro, *ag.* foreign, strange || *s.m.* **1.** (*straniero*) foreigner; (*estraneo*) stranger **2.** (*ospite*) guest.

forestièrúme, *s.m.* **1.** (*usanze straniere*) foreign customs (*pl.*) **2.** (*accozzaglia di stranieri*) motley crowd of foreigners, motley crowd of strangers.

forèsto, *ag.* (*arc.*) **1.** remote **2.** (*solitario*) solitary.

forfécchia, *s.f.* (*entom.*) earwig.

fórfora, *o.f.* dandruff, ocurf.

fòrgia, *s.f.* forge, smithy.

forgiàbile, *ag.* forgeable.

forgiàre, *v.t.* **1.** to forge: — *con maglio,* to drop -forge **2.** (*modellare*) to shape, to mould; to form: — *il carattere,* to form (*o* to mould *o* to build up) the character; — *la mente,* to form (*o* to develop) the mind.

forgiatúra, *s.f.* forging.

forièro, *ag.* foreboding, portending: *vento* — *di tempesta,* wind foreboding (*o* portending) a storm; *quelle nùvole grigie sono foriere di pioggia,* those grey clouds forebode rain.

fórma, *s.f.* **1.** form, shape: *la* — *della tua bocca,* the shape of your mouth; *a* — *di S,* S-shaped; *bicchieri di* — *diversa,* glasses of different shapes; *un diavolo in* — *umana,* a devil in human form; *scorgemmo una* — *vaga,* we perceived an indistinct form (*o* shape); *mutar* —, to change form; *prendere la* — *di...,* to take the form of... **2.** *pl.* (*di persona*) figure (*sing.*): *forme snelle,* slender figure **3.** (*modo*) form: — *di governo,* form of government; *nella debita* —, in due form; *nella* — *seguente,* as follows **4.** (*spor.*) form, fitness: *essere proprio in* —, to be in very good form (*o* to be quite fit); *non essere in* —, to be out of form **5.** (*etichetta*) form, formality: *un invito fatto solamente pro* —, an invitation made as a mere matter of form; *è una questione di* —, *non di*

sostanza, it is a question of form, not of substance; *badare troppo alle forme,* to pay too much attention to forms; *rispettar le forme,* to observe forms **6.** (*lett.*) form: *il contenuto e la* — *di un libro,* the subject -matter and the form of a book **7.** (*stampo*) mould; (*amer.*) mold: — *in gesso,* plaster mould; — *per cappelli,* hat-block (*o* hat shape); — *per scarpe,* last (*o* shoe tree) || *una* — *di formaggio,* a whole cheese (*o* a cheese).

formàbile, *ag.* **1.** formable **2.** (*forgiabile*) mouldable.

formaggèlla, *s.f.* small cheese.

formaggiàio, *s.m.* cheese-monger.

formaggièra, *s.f.* grated cheese basin.

formaggíno, *s.m.* (*piccolo formaggio di crema*) cream -cheese.

formàggio, *s.m.* cheese: — *da spalmare,* cheese -spread; — *dolce,* soft cheese; — *parmigiano,* Parmesan (cheese); *biscottino al* —, cheese-straw; *crosta di* —, cheese-rind; *forma di* —, whole cheese (*o* cheese); *grattugiare il* —, to grate cheese.

formaldèide, *s.f.* (*chim.*) formaldehyde.

formàle, *ag.* **1.** formal, ceremonious: *discorso* —, formal speech; *pranzo* —, formal dinner **2.** (*solenne*) solemn: *promessa* —, solemn promise **3.** (*preciso*) clear, precise **4.** (*fil.*) formal **5.** (*dir.*) formal, regular: *procedura* —, regular procedure.

formalína, *s.f.* (*chim.*) formalin.

formalísmo, *s.m.* formalism; stiffness.

formalísta, *s.c.* formalist.

formalità, *s.f.* **1.** form, formality: — *legali,* legal formalities; *è una pura* —, it is a mere formality **2.** (*cerimonie*) formality: *ci accolsero amichevolmente, senza troppe* —, they welcomed us in a friendly way (*o* without too much formality *o* quite informally).

formalizzàre, *v.t.* (*scandalizzare*) to shock || **formalizzàrsi,** *v.r.* to be shocked (at, by s.o., sthg., at, by doing).

formalménte, *av.* **1.** formally **2.** (*chiaramente*) clearly, plainly.

formàre, *v.t.* **1.** (*fare, creare*) to make, to create, to form, to conceive, to plan: — *frasi,* to form sentences; — *un numero di telefono,* to dial a 'phone number; — *un piano,* to conceive (*o* to form) a plan; — *il plurale di un sostantivo,* to form the plural of a noun; — (*una*) *società,* to form a partnership **2.** (*modellare*) to shape, to fashion, to frame; (*forgiare*) to mould; (*amer.*) to mold **3.** (*addestrare*) to train, to school, to build up, to form, to mould: — *il carattere,* to form (*o* to build up) the character; *si formò alla scuola del dolore,* he learnt through long suffering **4.** (*costituire*) to make; (*essere*) to be: *il nostro primogenito forma il nostro orgoglio,* our eldest child is our pride || **formàrsi,** *v.r.* **1.** to form: *quando si formò quest'idea nella sua mente?,* when did this idea form in his mind? **2.** (*crescere, svilupparsi*) to grow, to develop.

formatívo, *ag.* formative.

formàto, *ag.* formed; shaped; (*forgiato*) moulded; (*amer.*) molded: *ben* —, well shaped (*o* well made) || *s.m.* (*forma*) form, shape; (*misura*) size: — *commerciale,* commercial size; *il* — *di un libro,* the format of a book; *edizione a* — *ridotto,* pocket edition (*o fam. amer.* pony edition).

formatóre, *s.m.* **1.** maker; modeller **2.** (*educatore*) educator.

formatríce, *s.f.* **1.** maker; modeller **2.** (*educatrice*) educator **3.** (*mec.*) moulding machine; (*amer.*) molding machine; moulder; (*amer.*) molder: — *a scossa e pressione,* jolt squeeze moulding machine; — *e sformatrice,* (*metal.*) pattern-draw moulding machine.

formatúra, *s.f.* (*metal.*) moulding; (*amer.*) molding: — *a macchina,* machine moulding; — *a mano,* hand moulding; *reparto* —, moulding shop.

formazióne, *s.f.* **1.** formation, forming, making: *la* — *del carattere,* the forming (*o* moulding *o* building up) of character; *uno stato in via di* —, a nation in the making **2.** (*geol. meteorologia*) formation: — *granitica*, (*geol.*) granite formation; — *temporalesca*, (*meteorologia*) thundercloud formation **3.** (*aer. mil.*) formation: *in* — *aperta, serrata*, (*mil.*) in open, close formation; *in* — *di battaglia*, (*mil.*) in battle formation; *in* — *sparsa*, (*mil.*) in scattered formation; *una intera* —, (*aer.*) a whole flight; *volo in* —, (*aer.*) mass flight; *volare in* —, (*aer.*) to fly in formation **4.** (*addestramento*) training, education: — *dei dirigenti d'industria*, management training.

formèlla, *s.f.* **1.** (*buca nel terreno per piantare un albero*) hole **2.** (*mattonella*) tile, small paving stone: — *di cemento*, cement block **3.** (*riquadro decorato*) panel.

formentóne, *s.m.* maize, Indian corn.

formíca¹, *s.f.* ant: — *bianca*, white ant; *uova di* —, ant-eggs (*o* ant's eggs) ‖ *a passo di* —, at a snail's gallop (*o* pace).

fòrmica², *s.f.* (*materiale per rivestimenti*) Formica.

formicàio, *s.m.* **1.** ant-hill, formicary **2.** *fig.* (*folla*) swarm; crowd, mass of people.

formicaleóne, *s.m.* (*entom.*) ant-lion.

formichière, *s.m.* (*zool.*) ant-eater.

formicolaménto, *V.* **formicolio.**

formicolàre, *v.i.* **1.** to swarm: *tutta la città formicolava di turisti*, the whole town was swarming with tourists **2.** (*essere pieno*) to be full: *quella pagina formicola di errori*, that page is full of mistakes **3.** (*prudere per intorpidimento*) to tingle: *mi formicolano le mani*, my hands are tingling.

formicolazióne, *s.f.* (*di parte del corpo intorpidito*) tingling; (*fam.*) pins and needles; (*med.*) formication.

formicolio, *s.m.* **1.** (*brulichio*) swarming, swarm **2.** (*di parte del corpo intorpidita*) tingling; (*fam.*) pins and needles; (*med.*) formication: *ho un* — *nella gamba destra*, I have pins and needles in my right leg.

formicóne, *s.m.* big ant.

formidàbile, *ag.* **1.** formidable, dreadful **2.** (*fam.*) (*straordinario*) wonderful.

formidabilità, *s.f.* (*rar.*) formidableness.

formidabilménte, *av.* formidably, dreadfully.

fòrmola, *V.* **fòrmula.**

formosità, *s.f.* **1.** (*appariscenza di forme*) buxomness; plumpness **2.** (*proporzione di forme*) shapeliness; (*bellezza*) beauty.

formóso, *ag.* **1.** (*dalle forme piene*) buxom; plump **2.** (*ben fatto*) shapely, well-shaped; (*bello*) beautiful, comely.

fòrmula, *s.f.* formula (*pl.* formulas, (*scient.*) formulae): — *bruta*, (*chim.*) empirical formula; — *di struttura*, (*chim.*) structural formula; *formule legali*, legal formulas; — *matematica*, mathematical formula ‖ *con questa* —, reading as follows.

formulàre, *v.t.* **1.** to formulate **2.** (*esprimere*) to express: — *un desiderio*, to express a wish.

formulàrio, *s.m.* formulary.

formulazióne, *s.f.* formulation.

fornàce, *s.f.* (*metal.*) furnace; (*per laterizi*) kiln: — *per calce*, limekiln; — *per mattoni*, brickkiln.

fornaciàio, *s.m.* **1.** (*operaio*) kilnman (*pl.* kilnmen) **2.** (*padrone*) kiln owner.

fornaciàta, *s.f.* kilnful.

fornàia, *s.f.* bakeress.

fornàio, *s.m.* **1.** baker **2.** (*negozio*) bakery, baker's shop.

fornàta, *s.f.* batch.

fornèllo, *s.m.* **1.** stove, kitchen-range: — *a gas*, gas-stove; — *a piastra* (*elettrica*), electric hot plate; — *da campo*, camp stove; — *da cucina*, kitchen stove; — *da laboratorio*, (*chim.*) chemist's furnace; — *elettrico*, electric stove **2.** (*miner.*) rise, riser: — *di gettito*, chute pass (*o* shoot) **3.** (*di pipa*) pipe bowl.

fornicàre, *v.i.* to fornicate.

fornicatóre, *s.m.* fornicator.

fornicatríce, *s.f.* fornicatress, fornicatrix.

fornicazióne, *s.f.* fornication.

fòrnice, *s.f.* **1.** (*arch.*) barrel-vault **2.** (*anat.*) fornix (*pl.* fornices).

forniménto, *s.m.* **1.** (*il fornire*) supplying, furnishing, providing **2.** (*attrezzatura, corredo*) equipment, outfit.

forníre, *v.t.* **1.** to supply, to furnish, to provide: — *merce, cibi, combustibile*, to supply goods, foodstuffs, fuel; — *qlcu. di ql.co., ql.co. a qlcu.*, to supply (*o* to furnish *o* to provide) s.o. with sthg.: *fornirono la biblioteca di libri nuovi*, they supplied the library with new books; *vi forniremo quanto vi occorre*, we shall supply you with all you need (*o* we shall supply what you need) **2.** (*equipaggiare*) to equip, to fit up: *forniremo la fabbrica di macchinario*, we shall equip the factory with machinery.

forníto, *ag.* **1.** furnished (with sthg.), supplied (with sthg.), provided (with sthg.): — *di artigli*, furnished (*o* provided) with claws; *ben* — *di denaro*, well supplied with money; *negozio ben* —, well-stocked shop **2.** (*equipaggiato*) equipped (with sthg.): — *di eccezionali impianti tecnici*, equipped with fantastic technical installations; *albergo* — *di tutte le comodità moderne*, hotel equipped with all modern comforts **3.** (*dotato*) endowed (with sthg.): *quella donna era fornita di grande bellezza*, that woman was endowed with great beauty.

fornitóre, *ag.* supplying: *le ditte fornitrici*, the supplying firms ‖ *s.m.*, **fornitríce,** *s.f.* furnisher, supplier, provider; (*all'ingrosso*) wholesaler; (*al dettaglio*) retailer; (*su larga scala*) purveyor: — *di Sua Maestà*, purveyor to Her Majesty (*o* by appointment of Her Majesty); — *navale*, ship-chandler.

fornitúra, *s.f.* **1.** (*il fornire*) supplying: *contratto di forniture militari*, contract for supplying the army **2.** (*merci fornite*) supply; goods supplied (*pl.*) **3.** (*attrezzatura*) furniture (*solo sing.*), fitting, equipment: *forniture per bar*, bar-room furniture; *forniture per ufficio*, office appliances.

fórno, *s.m.* **1.** (*da cucina*) oven: *cuocere al* —, to bake; (*carne*) to roast in the oven; *mettere in* —, to put into the oven ‖ *questa stanza è un* —, *fig.* this room is like an oven **2.** (*del fornaio*) oven; (*edificio*) bakehouse; (*negozio*) baker's shop, bakery **3.** (*metal.*) furnace: — *continuo*, continuous furnace; *alto* —, blast-furnace **4.** (*per calce, cemento, mattoni*) kiln; (*per vasellame*) stove: — *rotante*, rotary kiln **5.** — *crematorio*, crematorium **6.** (*fam. teat.*) empty house, poor house.

fòro¹, *s.m.* **1.** (*buco*) hole: — *della serratura*, keyhole; *fare un* —, to make a hole **2.** (*apertura*) opening; (*di sbocco*) port **3.** (*traforo*) tunnel.

fòro², *s.m.* **1.** (*st. romana*) forum (*pl.* forums, fora) **2.** (*tribunale*) court (of justice); (*l'insieme dei tribunali*) the forum; the law-courts (*pl.*); (*gli avvocati*) the Bar: *entrare a far parte del* —, to be called to the Bar ‖ *il* — *interno*, *fig.* one's conscience.

forosétta, *s.f.* (*scherz.*) country-girl.

fórra, *s.f.* gorge, ravine.

fórse, *av.* **1.** perhaps, maybe: — *hai ragione*, maybe you're right ‖ — *che sì*, — *che no*, perhaps so, perhaps not **2.** (*circa*) about: *saranno* — *mille lire*, it must be about one thousand lire **3.** (*probabilmente*) probably ‖ *s.m.*: *senza* —, certainly (*o* no doubt); *essere in* —, to be in doubt; *lasciare ql.co. in* —, to leave sthg. in doubt; *mettere ql.co. in* —, to throw (some) doubt upon (*o* to question) sthg.

forsennàta, *s.f.* mad woman; frantic woman.

forsennataménte, *av.* madly; wildy, frantically, furiously.

forsennatézza, *s.f.* madness; frenzy, fury.

forsennàto, *ag.* mad; frantic, wild, raving ‖ *s.m.* madman (*pl.* madmen); frantic man.

fòrte, *ag.* **1.** strong (anche *fig.*): — *della mia innocenza*, strong in my innocence; — *odore*, strong smell; *un* — *odore di aglio*, a strong smell of garlic; *bevanda* —, strong (*o* stiff *o* alcoholic) drink; *una guarnigione* — *di 5.000 uomini*, a garrison 5.000 strong; *stoffa* —, strong material; *tè, caffè* —, strong tea, coffee; *uomo* —, strong man; *volontà* —, strong will; *essere* — *in* *ql.co.*, to be good at sthg. (*o* to be skilled in sthg.); *ricorrere alla maniera* —, to have recourse to strong action ‖ *il sesso* —, the stronger sex ‖ *è più* — *di me*, I can't help it ‖ *dar man* — *a qlcu.*, to help (*o* to support *o* to back) s.o. **2.** (*di malanni*) bad, severe, serious: *un* — *mal di stomaco*, a bad stomach-ache; *un* — *raffreddore*, a bad cold **3.** (*grande*) large, considerable: *una* — *distanza*, a considerable distance; *un* — *guadagno*, a large gain; *una* — *perdita*, a heavy loss; *una* — *somma di denaro*, a large (*o* considerable) amount of money; *una* — *spesa*, a heavy expense; *una cifra molto* —, a very high figure **4.** (*violento*) heavy: *una pioggia* —, a heavy rain; *un vento* —, a heavy wind **5.** (*di suono*) loud: *un* — *rumore*, a loud noise; *con voce* —, in a loud voice **6.** (*acido*) sour: *vino* —, sour wine **7.** (*di colore*) fast: *questi colori non sono forti*, these colours are not fast **8.** (*profondo*) deep: — *preoccupazione*, deep concern ‖ *a più* — *ragione*, all the more so ‖ *per un* — *motivo*, for a very good reason ‖ *s.m.* **1.** spec. fig. strong man **2.** (*punto di forza*): *il mio* — *è la matematica*, my strong point is mathematics **3.** (*fortezza*) fortress, fort **4.** (*la parte più folta*) thick: *il* — *del bosco*, the thick of the forest; *il* — *dell'esercito*, the main body (*o* the bulk *o* the larger part) of the army **5.** (*acidità*) sourness: *il tuo vino ha un po' di* —, your wine is slightly sour.

fòrte, *av.* **1.** (*fortemente*) strongly ‖ *tienti* —*!*, hold tight! **2.** (*ad alta voce*) aloud, in a loud voice, loudly: *parla più* —, speak louder **3.** (*duramente, intensamente*) hard: *picchia* —*!*, strike hard! (*o* hit him!); *piove* —, it is raining hard (*o* heavily) **4.** (*velocemente*) fast: *correre* —, to run fast.

forteménte, *av.* **1.** (*con forza*) strongly **2.** (*grandemente*) greatly; (*altamente*) highly; (*profondamente*) deeply **3.** (*a voce alta*) in a loud voice, loud, loudly **4.** (*valorosamente*) bravely.

fortéto, *s.m.* underwood, thicket.

fortézza, *s.f.* **1.** fortress, stronghold: *espugnare una* —, to seize a fortress; *prendere d'assalto una* —, to storm a fortress ‖ — *volante*, (*aer.*) flying fortress **2.** (*forza morale*) strength; fortitude **3.** (*mar.*) goring (cloth).

fortìccio, *ag.* sourish, tart.

fortièra, *s.f.* (*mar.*) rocky sea bed.

fortificàbile, *ag.* fortifiable.

fortificaménto, *s.m.* fortifying.

fortificànte, *ag.* fortifying, strengthening; (*di aria*) bracing ‖ *s.m.* (*farm.*) tonic.

fortificàre, *v.t.* **1.** to strengthen, to invigorate, to fortify (anche fig.): *esercizio che fortifica il corpo*, exercise that strengthens the body **2.** (*mil.*) to fortify: *città fortificate*, fortified towns ‖ **fortificàrsi**, *v.r.* **1.** (*diventare più forte*) to become stronger, to acquire strength, to strengthen **2.** (*mil.*) to raise a line of defence; to entrench oneself.

fortificatìvo, *ag.* strengthening, invigorating.

fortificatóre, *ag.* fortifying ‖ *s.m.*, **fortificatrìce**, *s.f.* fortifier.

fortificazióne, *s.f.* fortification.

fortìgno, *ag.* **1.** (*piuttosto acido*) sourish **2.** (*di odore*) sharp, strong.

fortilìzio, *s.m.* (*mil.*) fort; fortalice.

fortìno, *s.m.* (*mil.*) block-house, redoubt.

fortiori, a, *l.av.* (*lat.*) a fortiori, with all the more reason.

fortìssimo, *s.m.* (*mus.*) fortissimo.

fortitúdine, *s.f.* (*rar.*) fortitude.

fortóre, *s.m.* **1.** strong acrid smell **2.** (*di sapore*) sourness.

fortuitaménte, *av.* fortuitously, by (mere) chance.

fortúito, *ag.* fortuitous, accidental, casual; chance (*attributivo*): *un caso* —, an accidental case; *un incontro* —, a chance (*o* fortuitous) meeting.

fortúme, *s.m.* **1.** strong acrid smell **2.** (*di sapore*) sourness.

fortúna, *s.f.* **1.** fortune; luck: *buona* — *!*, good luck!;

che (*gran*) —*!*, what a great piece of luck!; *colpo di* —, stroke of luck; — *che io non c'ero*, luckily I wasn't there; *ebbi la* — *di trovarlo subito*, I had the luck to find it at once; *aver* —, to be in luck; *aver la* — *dalla propria* (*parte*), to have fortune on one's side; *aver* — *in ql.co.*, to have good luck in sthg.; *non aver* —, to have no (*o* hard) luck (*o* to be out of luck); *tentare la* —, to try one's fortune (*o* luck) ‖ *per* —, fortunately, luckily ‖ *Fortuna*, (*mit.*) Fortune: *la ruota della Fortuna*, the wheel of Fortune **2.** (*ricchezza, patrimonio*) fortune, patrimony; riches (*pl.*), wealth: *ha speso una* — *in quadri*, he has spent a fortune on pictures; *avere una* —, to have a fortune; *sperperare la propria* —, to squander one's fortune **3.** (*riuscita, successo*) fortune, success: *il suo tentativo ebbe* —, his attempt was successful; *cercar* — *all'estero*, to seek one's fortune abroad; *essere l'artefice della propria* —, to be a self-made man; *far* —, to make one's fortune **4.** (*emergenza*) emergency: *atterraggio di* —, (*aer.*) forced landing; *campo di* —, (*aer.*) emergency landing-ground; *letto di* —, shakedown; *mezzo di* —, makeshift; *ponte di* —, emergency bridge; *pranzo di* —, pot-luck; *riparazioni di* —, breakdown repairs; (*aut.*) roadside repairs; — *di mare*, (*assicurazioni*) sea risks **5.** (*mar.*): *albero di* —, jury mast; *timone di* —, jury rudder; *vela di* —, storm sail.

fortunàle, *s.m.* storm, tempest; hurricane.

fortunataménte, *av.* luckily, fortunately.

Fortunàto[1], *no.pr.m.* Fortunatus.

fortunàto[2], *ag.* **1.** lucky, fortunate; (*felice*) happy: *fortunati avvenimenti*, happy events ‖ *fortunatissimo di conoscerla!*, very happy (*o* very glad) to meet you! **2.** (*coronato da successo*) successful: *un tentativo* —, a successful attempt.

fortunóso, *ag.* **1.** (*avventuroso*) eventful: *vita* —, eventful life **2.** (*burrascoso*) stormy: *tempo* —, stormy weather.

forúncolo, *s.m.* furuncle, boil.

foruncolòsi, *s.f.* (*patol.*) furunculosis.

foruncolòso, *ag.* furunculous, full of boils.

forviàre, *v.t.* to lead astray, to mislead: *fu forviato da cattivi compagni*, he was misled by bad companions ‖ *v.i.* to go off ‖ **forviàrsi**, *v.r.* to go astray.

fòrza, *s.f.* **1.** strength (*solo sing.*), force, vigour (anche fig.); (*potere*) power, might: — *di carattere*, force (*o* strength) of character; *la* — *d'un colpo*, the force of a blow; — *di volontà*, will-power; — *fisica*, bodily (*o* physical) strength; — *morale*, moral strength (*o* force); — *muscolare*, muscular strength; *a* — *di braccia*, by strength of arm; *a viva* —, by force; *le forze che agiscono nella storia*, the forces operating in history; *questo è al di sopra delle forze umane*, this is beyond human strength; *farsi* —, to pluck up (*o* muster up) courage; *perdere, riacquistare le forze*, to lose, to recover one's strength; *tirare con tutte le proprie forze*, to pull with all one's might ‖ *a* — *di*, by dint of (*o* by means of): *a* — *di duro lavoro si è fatto un nome*, by dint of hard work he has made a name for himself ‖ *non ho la* — *di alzare un dito*, I have not the strength to lift a finger ‖ *contro la* — *ragion non vale*, prov. might is right **2.** (*mil.*) force: *forze aeree*, air force; *forze armate*, armed forces; *forze di terra e di mare*, land and naval forces; *la* — *pubblica*, the police (*o* the force) ‖ *bassa* —, the rank and file **3.** (*dir.*) (*validità, autorità*) validity, binding power **4.** (*caso inevitabile*): *per* — *maggiore*, owing to a cause beyond control; (*assicurazioni*) by act of God; (*dir.*) force majeure (*o* vis major) **5.** (*fis.*) force: — *di gravità*, force of gravity; — *motrice*, motive-power; *composizione delle forze*, composition of force **6.** *a tutta* —, (*mar.*) at full speed **7.** (*necessità*): *per* —, by force (*o* against one's will): «*Devi partire domani?*», «*Per* — *!*», "Must you leave tomorrow?", "Yes, necessarily so! (*o* I really must!)"; *devo andare per* —, absolutely I must go; *gli fu* — *rinunciare a ciò*, he was forced to give it up.

forzaménto, *s.m.* **1.** forcing; compulsion; constraint **2.** (*di serratura*) forcing, picking **3.** (*lo sforzare*) straining **4.** (*mec.*) shrinking, shrinkage.

forzàre, *v.t.* **1.** to force, to compel, to constrain: *fui forzato a cedere,* I was forced (*o* compelled) to give in; *mi forzarono la mano,* they forced my hand; — *l'andatura,* to force the pace; — *il giuoco,* to force the game **2.** (*aprire con forza*) to force, to pick: — *un blocco,* (*mil.*) to run a blockade; — *una porta,* to force (*o* to break open) a door; — *una serratura,* to pick a lock **3.** (*sforzare*) to strain, to force: — *un'analogia, il significato di una parola,* to force an analogy, a word; — *una pianta, un fiore,* to force a plant, a flower; — *la verità,* to strain the truth; — *la vista,* to strain one's eyes; — *la voce,* to force one's voice.

forzataménte, *av.* compulsorily, by compulsion, by force.

forzàto, *ag.* forced: *riso, sorriso* —, forced laugh, forced smile ‖ *lavori forzati,* hard labour ‖ *marcia forzata,* forced march ‖ *s.m.* (*criminale condannato ai lavori forzati*) convict.

forzière, *s.m.* coffer; (*cassaforte*) safe.

forzosaménte, *av.* compulsorily.

forzóso, *ag.* forced; compulsory: *corso* —, (*di moneta*) forced currency; *prestito* —, forced loan.

forzúto, *ag.* strong, robust; (*muscoloso*) brawny, muscular.

foscaménte, *av.* darkly; gloomily.

foschía, *s.f.* haze; mist.

fósco, *ag.* (*tenebroso*) dark; gloomy; (*di cielo, di tempo*) dull, hazy; (*di luce*) dim: *dipingere ql.co. a colori foschi,* fig. to paint sthg. in dark colours; *rappresentare qlcu. a fosche tinte,* fig. to give a dim view of s.o.

fosfatizzàre, *v.t.* (*ind.*) to phosphatize.

fosfatizzazióne, *s.f.* (*ind.*) phosphatizing: *sali di* —, phosphate coating materials.

fosfàto, *s.m.* (*chim.*) phosphate.

fosfaturía, *s.f.* (*med.*) phosphaturia.

fosfène, *s.m.* (*med.*) phosphene.

fosfína, *s.f.* (*chim.*) phosphin(e).

fosfíto, *s.m.* (*chim.*) phosphite.

fosforàre, *v.t.* (*chim.*) to phosphorate.

fosforàto, *ag.* (*chim.*) phosphorated.

fosforeggiàre, *v.i.* (*fis.*) to phosphoresce.

fosforescènte, *ag.* (*fis.*) phosphorescent.

fosforescènza, *s.f.* (*fis.*) phosphorescence.

fosfòrico, *ag.* (*chim.*) phosphoric.

fosforísmo, *s.m.* (*patol.*) phosphorism.

fosforíte, *s.f.* (*min.*) phosphorite.

fòsforo, *s.m.* **1.** (*chim.*) phosphorus **2.** *fig.* intelligence; brains (*pl.*): *gli manca il* —, he is brainless.

fosforóso, *ag.* (*chim.*) phosphorous.

fosfúro, *s.m.* (*chim.*) phosphide.

fosgène, *s.m.* (*chim.*) phosgene.

fòssa, *s.f.* **1.** ditch; trench; (*buca*) pit, hole: — *di autorimessa,* inspection pit (*o* repair pit); — *di colata,* (*metal.*) (casting) pit; — *di scolo,* drainage ditch; *scavare una* —, to make (*o* to dig) a ditch (*o* a pit) ‖ — *biologica,* cesspool **2.** (*mil.*) ditch, trench, fosse; (*anticamente, intorno a città, castelli*) moat **3.** (*cavità*) hollow, cavity: *il terreno qui forma una profonda* —, the ground forms a deep hollow here **4.** (*tomba*) grave: *egli scavava una* —, he was digging a grave ‖ *avere un piede nella* —, *fig.* to have one foot in the grave ‖ *scavarsi la* — *sotto i piedi,* fig. to be the cause of one's own ruin (*o* to bring about one's own ruin) ‖ *del senno di poi son piene le fosse,* prov. it is easy to be wise after the event **5.** (*covile*) den: *Daniele nella* — *dei leoni,* Daniel in the lions' den **6.** (*anat.*) fossa (*pl.* fossae): — *temporale,* temporal fossa.

fossàto, *s.m.* **1.** ditch: *acqua (ferma) di* —, ditchwater **2.** (*mil.*) ditch; (*anticamente, intorno a città, castelli*) moat.

fossétta, *s.f.* dimple.

fòssile, *ag. s.m.* fossil: *carbon* —, pit-coal; *conchiglia* —, fossil shell; *è un vecchio* —, (*fig. fam.*) he is an old fossil.

fossilizzàre, *v.t.* to fossilize ‖ **fossilizzàrsi,** *v.r.* **1.** to fossilize **2.** (*immobilizzarsi in idee e modi superati*) to fossilize; to become fossilized.

fossilizzazióne, *s.f.* fossilization (anche *fig.*).

fòsso, *s.m.* **1.** ditch: *scavare un* —, to make (*o* to dig) a ditch **2.** (*mil.*) ditch, trench, fosse; (*anticamente, intorno a castelli, città*) moat ‖ *saltare il* —, fig. to cross the Rubicon.

fossóre, *s.m.* (*st.*) fossor.

fot, *s.m.* (*fis.*) phot.

fòticon, *s.m.* (*tv.*) photicon.

fotocalcografía, *s.f.* (*tip.*) photocomposition.

fotocèllula, *s.f.* (*elett.*) photoelectric cell.

fotochímica, *s.f.* photochemistry.

fotochímico, *ag.* photochemical.

fotocromía, *s.f.* (*foto.*) photochromy.

fotocromolitografía, *s.f.* (*tip.*) photochromolithography.

fotocrònaca, *s.f.* (*giornalismo*) photo-reportage, photo-chronicle.

fotocronísta, *s.c.* press-photographer.

fotoelettricità, *s.f.* (*fis.*) photoelectricity.

fotoelèttrico, *ag.* (*fis.*) photoelectric: *cellula fotoelettrica,* photoelectric cell.

fotofobía, *s.f.* (*patol.*) photophobia.

fotogènesi, *s.f.* (*biol.*) photogenesis.

fotogènico, *ag.* photogenic.

fotografàre, *v.t.* to photograph.

fotografía, *s.f.* **1.** (*arte fotografica*) photography: — *a colori,* colour photography **2.** (*immagine fotografica*) photograph; (*fam.*) picture, photo: — *al lampo di magnesio,* flashlight photograph; — *istantanea,* snapshot; *fare una* — *a qlcu.,* to take a photograph (*o* a picture) of s.o.; *farsi fare la* —, to have one's photograph taken; *ritoccare una* —, to touch up a photograph.

fotograficaménte, *av.* photographically.

fotogràfico, *ag.* photographic: *apparecchio* —, *macchina fotografica,* camera.

fotògrafo, *s.m.* photographer.

fotogràmma, *s.m.* **1.** (*cine.*) photogram, picture; frame **2.** (*foto.*) photogram.

fotogrammetría, *s.f.* (*foto.*) photogrammetry.

fotoincisióne, *s.f.* **1.** (*processo d'incisione*) photo-engraving **2.** (*immagine incisa*) photogravure.

fotòlisi, *s.f.* (*chim.*) photolysis.

fotolitografàre, *v.t.* to photolithograph.

fotolitografía, *s.f.* **1.** (*procedimento*) photolithography **2.** (*immagine*) photolithograph.

fotomeccànico, *ag.* photomechanical.

fotometría, *s.f.* (*ott.*) photometry.

fotòmetro, *s.m.* (*ott.*) photometer.

fotomontàggio, *s.m.* (*foto.*) photomontage.

fotóne, *s.m.* (*fis.*) photon.

fotoscissióne, *s.f.* (*fis.*) photofission.

fotosensíbile, *ag.* (*foto.*) photosensitive.

fotosfèra, *s.f.* (*astr.*) photosphere.

fotosíntesi, *s.f.* (*bot.*) photosynthesis.

fotostàtico, *ag.* (*foto.*) photostatic: *copia fotostatica (di documenti),* photostat (of documents, papers).

fototelegrafía, *s.f.* phototelegraphy.

fototerapía, *s.f.* (*med.*) phototherapy.

fototipía, *s.f.* **1.** phototypy **2.** (*fototipo*) phototype.

fotòtipo, *s.m.* phototype.

fototropísmo, *s.m.* (*bot.*) phototropism.

fotozincotipía, *s.f.* (*tip.*) photozincography.

fottío, *s.m.* (*pop.*) lots (*pl.*); heaps (*pl.*); a great deal: *ha un* — *di denaro,* he has lots (*o* heaps *o* pots *o* a great deal) of money.

fra[1], *prep.* **1.** (*fra due persone o cose, due gruppi di persone o cose*) between; (*rar.*) betwixt: — *me e te,* between you and me; — *Padova e Venezia,* between

Padua and Venice; *c'era un'aspra lotta — i Montecchi e i Capuleti*, there was a bitter hostility between the Montagues and the Capulets; *portare — le braccia*, to carry in one's arms || *— me e me*, within myself; *dire, parlare, pensare — sè*, to say, to talk, to think to one-self 2. (*fra più di due*) **among**; (*rar.*) **amongst**: *— le montagne*, among the mountains; *— noi*, among our-selves; *uno - - di loro venne avanti*, from among them one came forward; *uno solo — tanti*, only one among so many || *— l'altro*, among other things; (*inoltre*) besides 3. (*nel mezzo di*) **amid**; (*rar.*) **amidst; in the midst of**: *— la folla*, in the midst of the crowd; *— gli alberi*, amid the trees 4. (*in espressioni di tempo*) **in, within**: *— una settimana*, in (*o* within) a week (*o* in a week's time); *— poco*, shortly (*o* in a short time).

fra², *s.m.* (*frate*) Brother: *— Giovanni*, Brother John.

frac, *s.m.* tail-coat, full evening-dress; (*fam.*) tails (*pl.*).

fracassaménto, *s.m.* smashing, shattering.

fracassàre, *v.t.* to smash, to shatter, to break up, to crash: *— uno specchio*, to smash (*o* to shatter) a glass to pieces || **fracassàrsi**, *v.r.* to smash, to crash, to go to pieces: *si fracassò contro un albero*, he crashed into a tree; *vuole — l'osso del collo?*, does he want to break his neck?.

fracassatóre, *s.m.*, **fracassatríce**, *s.f.* smasher.

fracassío, *s.m.* din.

fracàsso, *s.m.* 1. din, noise, hubbub; (*di cose rotte*) crash; (*trambusto*) fuss, bustle, ado: *far —*, to make a noise (*o* a din); (*creare un trambusto*) to make a fuss: *non far tanto — per un nonnulla!*, don't make such a fuss about a trifle! 2. (*moltitudine*) a great quantity, a lot: *c'era un — di gente*, there was a lot of people.

fracassóna, *s.f.*, **fracassóne**, *s.m.* 1. noisy person; blusterer 2. (*chi rompe facilmente*) smasher: *sei proprio un —*, you are just a bull in a china shop.

fràceo, *s.m.* (*gran quantità*): *un — di botte*, a good (*o* sound) thrashing.

fràcido, (*rar. pop.*) per **fràdicio**.

fracidúme, (*rar. pop.*) per **fradiciúme**.

fràdicio, *ag.* 1. (*marcio*) rotten, decayed: *uovo —*, rotten egg 2. (*zuppo*) wet through; soaked: *bagnato —*, wet to the skin || *ubriaco —*, dead drunk (*o* blind drunk *o* drunk as a lord).

fradiciúme, *s.m.* 1. rottenness, mass of rotten things 2. (*umidità*) wetness.

fràgile, *ag.* 1. brittle, fragile: *un bicchiere —*, a brittle glass; *la porcellana è —*, china is fragile; *il vetro è —*, glass is brittle; *questo giocattolo è troppo —*, this toy is too easily broken || *—, (scritta sulle casse contenenti cristalleria, ecc.)* handle with care 2. *fig.* fragile, frail: *un — fanciullo*, a frail child; *— felicità*, frail happiness; *salute —*, fragile (*o* delicate) health.

fragilità, *s.f.* 1. fragility, brittleness 2. *fig.* fragility, frailty: *—, il tuo nome è donna*, frailty, thy name is woman.

fragilménte, *av.* frailly, weakly, fragilely.

fràgola, *s.f.* strawberry: *gelato di fragole*, straw-berry ice-cream; *marmellata di fragole*, strawberry jam.

fragolàia, *s.f.*, **fragoléto**, *s.m.* strawberry-bed.

fragóre, *s.m.* loud noise; (*improvviso, lacerante*) crash, rumble; (*metallico*) clang: *il — del tuono*, the rumble of thunder; *il — di una campana*, the clang of a bell; *che —!*, what a loud noise!.

fragorosaménte, *av.* very noisily; (*con suono lace-rante*) rumblingly.

fragoróso, *ag.* noisy, loud; rumbling.

fragrànte, *ag.* fragrant, sweet-smelling, scented.

fragranteménte, *av.* fragrantly.

fragrànza, *s.f.* fragrance, perfume, aroma.

fraintèndere, *v.t.* to misunderstand, to misinterpret: *egli fraintese le mie parole*, he misunderstood (*o* mis-interpreted) my words.

fràle, *ag.* (*poet.*) frail, feeble; weak.

fralézza, *s.f.* (*poet.*) frailty.

framezzàre, *V.* **frammezzàre**.

frammassóne, *s.m.* freemason.

frammassonería, *s.f.* freemasonry.

frammentariaménte, *av.* fragmentarily.

frammentarietà, *s.f.* fragmentary character, frag-mentariness.

frammentàrio, *ag.* 1. fragmentary, fragmentitious: *manoscritto —*, fragmentary manuscript 2. (*geol.*) frag-mental.

framménto, *s.m.* fragment: *frammenti di liriche gre-che*, fragments of Greek lyrics; *ridotto in frammenti*, smashed to smithereens; *cercava di mettere insieme i frammenti del vaso rotto*, he was trying to put the pieces of the broken vase together.

frammescolàre, *v.t.* to intermingle, to mix to-gether.

frammettènza, *V.* **infra(m)mettènza**.

frammèttere, *v.t.* to interpose; to insert || **frammét-tersi**, *v.r.* 1. (*frapporsi*) to interpose: *egli si frammise fra il padre e la madre*, he interposed between his father and mother 2. (*interferire, intromettersi*) to interfere (in, with sthg.); to intrude (on, upon, into sthg.); to meddle (in, with sthg.): *non frammetterti!*, don't interfere!; *spero di non frammettermi nei tuoi affari*, I hope I am not intruding into your affairs.

frammezzàre, *v.t.* to intersperse, to interlard: *frammezza il suo dire con parole straniere*, he inter-lards his speech with foreign words.

frammèzzo, *V.* **fra¹**.

frammischiàre, *v.t.* to intermingle: *— fiori rossi e bianchi*, to intermingle red flowers with (*o* among) white ones || **frammischiàrsi**, *v.r.* to intermingle.

fràna, *s.f.* landslide, landslip.

franaménto, *s.m.* 1. (*il franare*) sliding down; (*il crollare*) falling in, caving in: *— di terreno*, landslide (*o* landslip) 2. (*frana*) landslide.

franàre, *v.i.* (*di terreno*) to slide down; (*crollare*) to fall in, to collapse, to cave in.

Frànca, *no.pr.f.* dim. di **Francésca**.

francaménte, *av.* frankly, candidly; (*amer.*) honest-ly; (*apertamente*) openly; (*schiettamente*) plainly; (*libe-ramente*) freely: *lasciate che vi dica — ciò che penso*, let me speak my mind.

francàre, *e derivati*, *V.* **affrancàre**, *e derivati*.

Francésca, *no.pr.f.* Frances || *dim.* Fanny, Fran.

francescanaménte, *av.* in the manner of a Fran-ciscan, like a Franciscan.

francescàno, *ag.* Franciscan: *frati francescani*, Fran-ciscan (*o* Grey) Friars || *s.m.* Franciscan, Grey Friar.

Francésco, *no.pr.m.* Francis: *San — d'Assisi*, St. Francis of Assisi || *col cavallo di San —*, on Shanks's mare (*o* with one's own legs) || *dim.* Frank, Frankie, Francie.

francése, *ag.* French || *alla —*, after the French fash-ion || *s.m.* 1. (*abitante*) Frenchman (*pl.* Frenchmen) || *i francesi*, the French 2. (*lingua*) (the) French (lan-guage): *parli —?*, do you speak French (*o* the French language)? || *s.f.* Frenchwoman (*pl.* Frenchwomen).

franceseggiàre, *v.i.* to affect French manners, to Frenchify, to imitate the French.

francesísmo, *s.m.* Gallicism.

francesizzàre, *v.t.* to Frenchify.

franchèzza, *s.f.* frankness, candour, openness, outspokenness: *amo la —*, I like plain speaking; *parlare con —*, to speak frankly (*o* openly *o* plainly *o* freely).

franchígia, *s.f.* 1. immunity, exemption, legal privilege: *— diplomatica*, diplomatic immunity; *— po-stale*, free post; *— doganale*, duty-free; *in — postale*, post(age) free; *introdurre merci in —*, to introduce goods duty-free 2. (*mar.*) furlough: *in —*, on fur-lough 3. (*dir. pol.*) franchise || *franchigie costituzionali*, constitutional safeguards.

Frància, *no.pr.f. (geog.)* France.

frànco[1]**,** *ag.* **1.** frank, candid, open, outspoken, plain; sincere, open-hearted: *egli fu del tutto — con me,* he was quite frank with me; *fece una franca confessione della sua colpa,* he made a frank confession of his guilt **2.** *(libero)* free: *un porto —,* a free port ‖ *franchi muratori,* freemasons ‖ *— tiratore,* (*mil.*) franc-tireur (*pl.* francs-tireurs) ‖ *farla franca,* to get away with it (*o* to get off scot-free) **3.** *(comm.)* free: *— a bordo,* free on board (*abbr.* f.o.b.); *— a richiesta,* free on application; *— a Torino,* free at Turin; *— di avaria,* free on quay (*o* on wharf); *— di dazio,* duty free (*o* duty paid); *— di nolo,* free of freight (*o* freight paid); *— di porto,* free of carriage (*o* carriage free *o* carriage paid); *— di posta, di spese postali,* post(age) free; *— di spese,* free of charge; *— a domicilio,* free delivered; *— vagone,* free on rail(s) (*abbr.* f.o.r.) ‖ *deposito —,* bonded warehouse.

frànco[1]**,** *av. (francamente)* frankly, openly, sincerely: *parlò —,* he spoke frankly.

frànco[2]**,** *ag. (st.)* Frankish ‖ *s.m. (st.)* Frank.

frànco-[2]**,** *(prefisso)* Franco-: *— russo,* Franco-Russian; *— spagnolo,* Franco-Spanish.

frànco[3]**,** *s.m. (moneta)* franc: *12 franchi svizzeri,* 12 Swiss francs.

Frànco[4]**,** *no.pr.m.* dim. di **Francésco.**

francobóllo, *s.m.* (postage) stamp: *un — da tre penny,* a threepenny stamp; *album per francobolli,* stamp-album; *collezionista di francobolli,* stamp-collector; *due francobolli da un penny,* two penny stamps; *metti il — a questa cartolina,* stamp this card; *far collezione di francobolli,* to collect stamps.

francòfilo, *ag.s.m.* Francophile.

francòfobo, *ag.s.m.* Francophobe.

Francofòrte, *no.pr.f. (geog.)* Frankfort, Frankfurt.

francolíno, *s.m. (ornit.)* francolin.

francotiratóre, *s.m. (mil.)* franc-tireur (*pl.* francs-tireurs); sharp-shooter.

frangènte, *s.m.* **1.** *(ondata)* breaker **2.** *(secca afflorante)* shoal; *(scoglio affiorante)* reef **3.** *fig. (situazione difficile)* difficult situation, difficulty; emergency: *evitare un —,* to get round a difficulty.

fràngere, *v.t.* **1.** *(rompere)* to break **2.** *(schiacciare)* to crush, to press: *bisogna — le olive per ottenere l'olio,* you must crush olives to obtain oil ‖ **fràngersi,** *v.r.* to break up.

frangétta, *s.f.* fringe.

fràngia, *s.f.* **1.** fringe: *uno scialle con lunghe frange,* a long-fringed shawl **2.** *fig.* embellishment: *un racconto senza frange,* a plain story; *aggiungere delle frange ad un discorso,* to embellish a story.

frangiàre, *v.t.* to fringe.

frangiatúra, *s.f.* fringes (*pl.*); fringing.

frangíbile, *ag.* frangible, breakable, easily broken.

frangibilità, *s.f.* frangibility.

frangiflútti, *s.m.* breakwater.

frangigrúmi, *s.m. (metal.)* lump-breaker.

frangitúra, *s.f.* pressing, crushing.

frangitútto, *s.m. (agr.)* hammer mill.

frangizòlle, *s.m. (agr.)* clod-smasher.

franóso, *ag.* liable to slide down, crumbling.

frànto, *ag.* broken; crushed.

frantóio, *s.m. (mec.)* **1.** *(per olive)* oil-mill **2.** *(per rocce)* crusher **3.** *(ind. tessile)* softening machine.

frantumaménto, *s.m.* shattering, smashing, crushing.

frantumàre, *v.t.* **1.** to shatter, to shiver, to break into shivers; *(ridurre in briciole)* to crumble, to crush to smithereens: *frantumò la noce con il pugno,* he cracked the nut with his fist **2.** *(schiacciare)* to crush.

frantumatóre, *s.m. (mec.)* breaker; crusher: *— di pietre,* stone-breaker; *— meccanico, (di sassi, carbone)* crusher.

frantumazióne, *s.f.* shattering, smashing, crushing.

frantúme, *s.m.* fragment; shivers (*pl.*): *andare in frantumi,* to break into fragments; *ridurre in frantu-*

mi ql.co., to shatter (*o* to shiver *o* to smash) sthg.

fràppa, *s.f.* **1.** *(pitt.)* painted foliage **2.** *(arc.) (frangia)* fringe.

frappé, *s.m.* shake: *— al cioccolato,* chocolate (milk-) shake; *latte —,* milk-shake; *agitatore per —,* milk-shaker.

frappórre, *v.t.* to interpose, to insert ‖ **frappórsi,** *v.r.* to interpose; to interfere.

frapposizióne, *s.f.* interposition; interference.

frasàio, frasaiuòlo, *s.m. (iron.)* phrase-monger.

frasàrio, *s.m.* **1.** jargon, cant: *il — dei medici,* doctors' jargon **2.** *(modo di esprimersi)* phrasing, phraseology **3.** *(raccolta di frasi)* collection of phrases.

fràsca, *s.f.* **1.** *(leafy)* branch ‖ *saltar di palo in —,* to jump from one thing to another **2.** *(per i bachi da seta)* bush **3.** *(insegna di osteria)* bush ‖ *a buon vino non occorre —, prov.* good wine needs no bush **4.** *pl.* trifles, gewgaws, vanities.

frascàme, *s.m.* branches (*pl.*); leafy boughs (*pl.*).

Frascàti, *no.pr.f. (geog.)* Frascati ‖ *s.m.* "Frascati" (kind of Italian wine).

frascàto, *s.m.* bower, arbour, shady place; trellis covered with branches ‖ *Festa dei Frascati,* (*Bibbia)* Feast of Tabernacles.

frascheggiàre, *v.i.* **1.** *(stormire)* to rustle **2.** *(civettare)* to flirt, to toy **3.** *(scherzare)* to dally, to trifle, to toy.

frascheggío, *s.m.* rustling.

frascheria, *s.f.* trifle: *queste sono tutte frascherie,* this is all nonsense.

fraschétta, *s.f.* **1.** twig; small branch **2.** *(ragazza leggera)* coquette, flirt, frivolous girl.

fràse, *s.f.* **1.** sentence: *una — ben costruita,* a well constructed sentence ‖ *— fatta,* cliché, stock phrase **2.** *pl. (discorsi vani)* phrases: *ne ho abbastanza di belle frasi!,* I've had enough of phrases! **3.** *(mus.)* phrase.

fraseggiaménto, *s.m.* phrasing.

fraseggiàre, *v.i.* to phrase (anche *mus.*).

fraseggiatóre, *s.m.,* **fraseggiatríce,** *s.f.* phrase-maker; *(iron.)* phrase-monger: *è un buon —,* he is a good phrase-maker.

fraséggio, *s.m. (mus.)* phrasing.

fraseologia, *s.f.* phraseology.

fraseològico, *ag.* phraseological.

frasologia, *s.f. (arc.)* phraseology.

frassinèlla, *s.f. (bot.)* fraxinella.

frassinéto, *s.m.* ash grove, ashwood.

fràssino, *s.m.* **1.** *(albero)* ash (-tree) **2.** *(legno)* ash.

frastagliaménto, *s.m.* indentation.

frastagliàre, *v.t.* to indent, to notch.

frastagliàto, *ag.* **1.** indented; irregular: *costa frastagliata,* indented coast **2.** *(ineguale)* uneven: *terreno —,* uneven ground.

frastàglio, *s.m.* indentation.

frastornaménto, *s.m.* **1.** *(disturbo)* disturbance, trouble **2.** *(impedimento)* hindrance **3.** *(il distrarre, il distogliere)* diversion, distraction.

frastornàre, *v.t.* **1.** *(disturbare)* to disturb, to trouble: *mi frastornò con le sue chiacchiere,* his chattering disturbed me **2.** *(impedire)* to hinder **3.** *(distrarre, distogliere)* to divert, to distract.

frastornío, *s.m.* hubbub, uproar.

frastórno, *V.* **frastornaménto.**

frastuòno, *s.m.* noise, din, uproar, hubbub.

fràte, *s.m.* **1.** friar; monk: *— laico,* lay brother; *frati minori,* Grey-Friars; *frati predicatori,* Black-Friars ‖ *sto coi frati e zappo l'orto,* I do as I am told **2.** *(come appellativo)* Brother: *—, fra Cristoforo,* Brother Christopher **3.** *(arc.) (fratello)* brother.

fratellànza, *s.f.* **1.** *(amore fraterno)* brotherliness, brotherhood, fraternity **2.** *(associazione)* brotherhood, fraternity.

fratellàstro, *s.m. (con uno dei genitori in comune)* half-brother; *(con tutti e due i genitori diversi)* step-brother.

fratellévole, *ag.* brotherly.

fratèllo, *s.m.* **1.** brother: — *di latte,* foster-brother; — *gemello,* twin brother (*o* twin); *fratelli siamesi,* Siamese twins; *fig.* (*amici inseparabili*) bosom friends ‖ — *d'armi,* brother in arms **2.** (*fratello di fede*) brother (*pl.* brethren).

fratería, *s.f.* friary.

fraternàle, *ag.* brotherly, fraternal.

fraternaménte, *av.* brotherly, fraternally.

fraternità, *s.f.* **1.** (*affetto fraterno*) brotherliness, brotherhood, fraternity **2.** (*confraternita*) confraternity, fraternity, brotherhood.

fraternizzàre, *v.i.* to fraternize.

fraternizzazióne, *s.f.* fraternization, fraternizing: *mancata* —, non-fraternization.

fratèrno, *ag.* brotherly, fraternal.

fratésco, *ag.* friarly, monkish.

fratína, *s.f.* short fringe (of hair).

fratría, *s.f.* (*st. greca*) phratry.

fratricída, *ag.* fratricidal ‖ *s.c.* fratricide.

fratricídio, *s.m.* fratricide.

fràtta, *s.f.* thicket, bush, bramble-bush.

frattàglie, *s.f.pl.* chitterlings; pluck (*sing.*); (*rigaglie*) giblets.

frattànto, *av.* meantime, meanwhile; in the meanwhile: — *paga, poi ci penseremo,* meantime pay up, we'll settle it later.

frattèmpo, *s.m.* **1.** meantime, meanwhile: *nel* —, in the meanwhile **2.** (*intervallo*) interval: *in quel* —, in that interval (*o* during that time).

frattúra, *s.f.* **1.** (*med.*) fracture: — *composta,* compound fracture; — *a spirale,* spiral fracture; *ridurre una* —, to set a fracture **2.** (*rottura*) break **3.** (*geol.*) fracture: — *fragile,* (*metal.*) brittle fracture.

fratturàre, *v.t.* to fracture, to break ‖ **fratturàrsi,** *v.r.* to fracture, to break: *taluni hanno le ossa che si fratturano facilmente,* some people have bones that break easily.

fraudolenteménte, *av.* fraudulently.

fraudolènto, *ag.* fraudulent: *bancarotta fraudolenta,* fraudulent bankruptcy.

fraudolènza, *s.f.* fraudulence.

frazionaménto, *s.m.* **1.** division, separation **2.** (*netta separazione*) splitting **3.** (*chim.*) fractionation.

frazionàre, *v.t.* **1.** to divide, to separate **2.** (*separare nettamente*) to split **3.** (*mat.*) to fractionize **4.** (*chim.*) to fractionate.

frazionàrio, *ag.* fractional, fractionary.

frazióne, *s.f.* **1.** fraction, portion, fragment: *in una — di secondo,* in a split second (*o* in the fraction of a second) **2.** (*mat.*) fraction: — *composta, comune, decimale, impropria, propria, semplice,* complex, vulgar, decimal, improper, proper, simple fraction **3.** (*eccl.*) fraction; breaking of the Host **4.** (*parte staccata di un comune*) group of houses; hamlet.

freàtico, *ag.* water-bearing: *falda freatica,* water-bearing stratum.

fréccia, *s.f.* **1.** arrow, dart, shaft: *partire come una* —, to start off like an arrow; *scagliare una* —, to shoot an arrow ‖ *frecce d'Amore,* Cupid's darts ‖ — *del Parto, fig.* Parthian-shaft **2.** (*arch. geom.*) (*di un arco*) rise, height **3.** (*segnale di direzione*) arrow: — *di direzione,* (*aut.*) direction indicator (*o* arrow) **4.** (*mar.*) gaff-topsail.

frecciàre, *v.t.* **1.** to shoot an arrow at (s.o., sthg.), to shoot arrows at (s.o., sthg.) **2.** (*chiedere danaro in prestito a*) to borrow money of, from (s.o.).

frecciàta, *s.f.* **1.** arrow-shot **2.** (*osservazione pungente*) pungent remark, taunt, gibe, jeer **3.** (*richiesta di un prestito*) borrowing.

frecciatína, *s.f.* pungent remark, taunt, gibe.

freddaménte, *av.* coldly: *accogliere qlcu.* —, to receive s.o. coldly **2.** (*con calma*) calmly.

freddàre, *v.t.* **1.** to cool; to chill: — *il brodo,* to cool the broth (*o* the soup) **2.** *fig.* to cool, to damp:

nulla poteva — *il suo entusiasmo,* nothing could damp his enthusiasm ‖ *non lasciar* — *una cosa,* to do sthg. at once; *non lasciar* — *l'occasione,* to strike while the iron is hot (*o* to seize a good opportunity) **3.** (*ammazzare*) to kill ‖ **freddàrsi,** *v.r.* to become cold; to cool down.

freddézza, *s.f.* **1.** coldness; coolness; (*indifferenza*) indifference; coldheartedness; (*mancanza di cordialità*) lack of cordiality: *ricevere qlcu. con* —, to receive s.o. coldly (*o fam.* to give s.o. the cold shoulder) **2.** (*calma*) calmness.

freddíccio, *ag.* coldish.

fréddo, *ag.* **1.** cold; (*piuttosto freddo*) chilly, chill; (*fresco*) cool: *animale a sangue* —, cold-blooded animal; *bibita fredda,* cold drink; *piatto* —, cold dish; *stagione fredda,* cold season; *il brodo non è abbastanza* —, the broth is not cool enough ‖ *mani fredde, cuore caldo,* cold hand, warm heart **2.** *fig.* cold; (*scostante*) chilly; (*indifferente, impassibile, senza calore o entusiasmo*) cool, frigid, reserved, indifferent: — *disprezzo,* cold disdain; *fredda eloquenza,* cold eloquence; — *saluto,* cool (*o* cold) greeting; *accoglienza fredda,* cold (*o* cool) reception; *stile* —, frigid style; *toni, colori freddi,* cold tints, colours; *i suoi modi erano freddi,* his manner was cool; *è un uomo dai modi freddi,* he is a chilly man (*o* he is a cold-mannered person); *mostrarsi* — *con qlcu.,* to be cold (*o* cool) towards s.o. ‖ *agire a sangue* —, to act in cold blood; *agire con gran sangue* —, to act with great self-possession; *serbare il proprio sangue* —, to keep cool (*o* to keep a cool head).

fréddo, *s.m.* **1.** cold, coldness, chilliness: *ondata di* —, cold wave; *i grandi freddi,* the winter cold; *lavorazione a* —, (*metal.*) cold-working; *solubile a* —, soluble when cold; *fa terribilmente* — *questa sera,* it is awfully cold this evening; *ho molto* — *alle mani,* my hands are very cold; *non lasciarlo al* —, don't leave it in the cold; *senti* —?, do you feel cold?; *sento il* —, I feel the cold; *se uscirai con questo* — *prenderai certamente un raffreddore,* if you go out in this cold weather you'll certainly catch a cold ‖ *aver* —, to be (*o* to feel) cold; *diventar* —, to get (*o* to grow) cold; *morire per il* —, to freeze to death; *sentir* —, to feel chilly; *soffrire* ‖*il* —, to suffer from the cold; *tremare di* —, to shiver with cold ‖ *fa un* — *cane,* (*fam.*) it is bitterly cold ‖ *questo non mi fa nè caldo nè* —, that leaves me cold ‖ *morire di* —, to freeze: *muoio di* —, I am freezing (*o* I am dying with cold) ‖ *Dio manda il* — *secondo i panni, prov.* God tempers the wind to the shorn lamb **2.** (*spavento, paura*) fright, fear; (*fam.*) creeps (*pl.*): *mi vien* — *quando ci penso,* I come all over hot and cold when I think of it; *questo racconto mi fa venir* —, this tale gives me the creeps.

freddolóso, *ag.* sensitive to cold: *egli è* —, he is very sensitive to cold; *sono un tipo* —, I am very sensitive to cold (*o* I feel the cold very much).

freddúra, *s.f.* **1.** (*freddo*) (wintry) cold **2.** (*giuoco di parole*) pun: *dire freddure,* to make puns.

freddurísta, *s.m.* punster.

fregàccio, *s.m.* (*a matita*) pencil-stroke; (*a penna*) pen-stroke.

fregagióne, *s.f.* massage; (*con panno, asciugamano, ecc.*) rubbing down, rub down; (*med.*) friction.

fregaménto, *s.m.* rubbing.

fregàre, *v.t.* **1.** to rub; (*per pulizia di pavimenti, ecc.*) to scrub: — *da cima a fondo,* to rub down; — *due cose l'una contro l'altra,* to rub two things together; — *il pavimento,* to scrub (*o* to polish) the floor **2.** (*cassare*) to cross out **3.** (*volg.*) (*imbrogliare*) to swindle, to cheat, to dupe, to take (s.o.) in ‖ **fregàrsi,** *v.r.* to rub oneself: — *le mani,* to rub one's hands ‖ *me ne frego,* (*volg.*) I don't care a rap (*o* a straw).

fregàta¹, *s.f.* **1.** rub(bing); (*per pulizia di pavimenti, ecc.*) scrub(bing), polishing **2.** *V.* **fregatúra.**

fregàta[2], *s.f.* **1.** (*mar.*) frigate: *capitano di* —, commander **2.** (*ornit.*) frigate, frigate-bird.

fregatína, *s.f.* slight rubbing: *e con una allegra — di mani disse che...*, and with a merry rubbing of his hands he said that....

fregatúra, *s.f.* (*volg.*) **1.** (*imbroglio*) swindle: *che —!*, what a swindle!; (*di spettacolo*) what a wash out! **2.** (*delusione*) sell **3.** (*contrattempo*) hitch.

fregiàre, *v.t.* **1.** (*arch.*) to decorate **2.** (*ornare*) to adorn, to ornament, to embellish, to deck **3.** (*decorare*) to decorate: *il suo petto era fregiato di medaglie*, his chest was decorated with medals ‖ **fregiàrsi**, *v.r.* to adorn oneself (with sthg.).

frégio, *s.m.* **1.** (*arch.*) frieze **2.** (*ornamento*) ornament, embellishment, decoration.

frégo, *s.m.* stroke, line; (*sul muro*) mark; scratch: *con un — di penna*, with a stroke of the pen; *tirare un — su ql.co.*, to cross sthg. out ‖ *dar di — a ql.co.*, (*annullare*) to cancel sthg.; (*cancellare*) to cross sthg. out; (*dir.*) to quash sthg.

frégola, *s.f.* **1.** (*di animali in genere*) heat; (*di pesci*) spawning; (*di cervi, camosci, ecc.*) rutting: *essere in —*, to be in heat **2.** (*mania*) mania **3.** (*eccitazione*) excitement; (*desiderio sfrenato*) immoderate desire, lust.

frèisa, *s.m.* " Freisa " (kind of ǀItalian red wine).

fremebóndo, fremènte, *ag.* quivering, trembling; (*palpitante*) throbbing: *— d'ira*, fuming; *cuore —*, throbbing heart.

frèmere, *v.i.* **1.** to quiver (with sthg.), to tremble (with sthg.), to shudder; (*palpitare*) to throb; (*vibrare*) to thrill, to vibrate: *ciò mi fa — quando ci penso*, it gives me the shivers to think of it; *le corde fremono*, the strings quiver; *ella fremeva d'ansia*, she was quivering with anxiety; *— di gioia*, to throb (o to thrill) with delight; *— di impazienza*, to fret; *— d'ira*, to tremble with rage; *— d'orrore*, to shudder with horror; *— di sdegno*, to quiver with indignation ‖ *far — d'ira*, to fill with rage (o to enrage) **2.** (*stormire*) to rustle: *le foglie fremono*, the leaves are rustling **3.** (*del mare*) to roar.

frèmito, *s.m.* **1.** quiver, thrill; (*brivido*) shudder; (*palpito*) throb, throbbing: *— di gioia, di piacere*, thrill (o throb) of joy, of pleasure; *con un — nella voce*, with a quiver in his voice; *il suo cuore ebbe un —*, his heart gave a throb **2.** (*di foglie, alberi, ecc.*) rustle, rustling **3.** (*del mare*) roar.

frenàbile, *ag.* restrainable (anche *fig.*).

frenàggio, *s.m.* (*mec.*) locking; (*aut.*) braking: *cavo di —*, (*aer.*) flying cable; *filo di —*, (*di un dado*) locking wire.

frenàre, *v.t.* **1.** to brake, to apply the brake(s) to (sthg.): *— una ruota*, to brake (o to apply the brake(s) to) a wheel **2.** *fig.* (*trattenere, reprimere*) to restrain, to check, to repress, to curb: *— le lacrime*, to restrain one's tears; *— la produzione*, to restrain production; *— la propria ira, lingua*, to check (o to curb) one's anger, tongue ‖ *v.i.* to put on the brake, to brake: *l'automobilista frenò improvvisamente*, suddenly the driver braked ‖ **frenàrsi**, *v.r.* to restrain oneself, to check oneself.

frenatóre, *s.m.* (*ferr.*) brakesman (*pl.* brakesmen); (*amer.*) brakeman (*pl.* brakemen).

frenatúra, *s.f.* (*mec. aut.*) braking; (*di dado*) locking: *— a ricupero*, (*di locomotore*) regenerative braking; *— elettrica*, (*elett.*) electric plugging.

frenèllo, *s.m.* **1.** (*anat.*) fraenum (*pl.* fraena) **2.** *— del timone*, (*mar.*) rudder rope.

frenesìa, *s.f.* **1.** phrenitis; (*furore, follia*) frenzy **2.** (*desiderio sfrenato*) immoderate desire.

freneticaménte, *av.* **1.** frenetically, phrenetically, frenziedly **2.** (*entusiasticamente*) enthusiastically.

frenètico, *ag.* **1.** frenetic, phrenetic, frenzied; frantic; (*delirante*) raving, delirious: *sforzi frenetici*, frenzied efforts; *è pazzo —*, he is raving mad **2.** (*entusiastico*) enthusiastic: *applausi frenetici*, enthusiastic applause (o loud cheers) ‖ *s.m.* frenetic, phrenetic, raving lunatic.

freniàtra, *s.m.* (*alienista*) alienist; (*psichiatra*) psychiatrist.

freniatrìa, *s.f.* psychiatry.

frènico, *ag.* (*anat.*) phrenic.

fréno, *s.m.* **1.** brake: *— ad aria compressa*, (*aut. ferr.*) air-brake; *— a depressione*, (*aut. mec.*) vacuum (o depression *o* suction) brake; *— a disco*, disk brake; *— al cerchio*, (*di bicicletta*) rim-brake; *— a mano*, (*aut.*) hand brake; *— a nastro*, (*mec.*) band (o ribbon) brake; *— a pedale*, (*aut.*) foot (o service) brake; *— di sicurezza*, (*mec.*) emergency brake; *— idraulico*, (*aut.*) hydraulic brake; *prova dei freni*, (*mec.*) braking test; *bloccare i freni*, to jam the brakes; *dare un colpo di —*, to clap on the brake; *stringere il —, i freni*, (*di bicicletta*) to put on the brake; *togliere il —*, to release the brake; *usare, tirare il —*, to apply the brake **2.** (*morso del cavallo*) bit **3.** *fig.* (*governo, ritegno*) check, restraint; bit, brake; (*autocontrollo*) self-control: *avidità senza —*, uncurbed (o unbridled) cupidity; *ella non ha alcun —*, she has no self-control; *allentare il —*, to slacken the rein; *metter — a ql.co.*, to check (o to restrain *o* to put a check on *o* to put a restraint on) sthg.; *metter — ai desideri di qlcu.*, to curb (o to bridle) s.o.'s desires; *metter — alla produzione*, to restrain production; *metter — alle spese*, to check expenditure; *non conoscere più —*, to break through every (o to break loose from all) restraint; *mordere il —*, to fret (o to chafe) under restraint; *servir da — a qlcu.*, to act as a brake (o as a check) on s.o.; *stringere i freni*, to shorten the reins; *tenere a — qlcu.*, to keep in check (o to put a restraint on) s.o.

frenocòmio, *s.m.* lunatic asylum.

frenologìa, *s.f.* phrenology.

frenològico, *ag.* phrenological.

frenologísta, frenòlogo, *s.m.* phrenologist.

frènulo, *s.m.* (*anat.*) fraenum (*pl.* fraena).

frequentàbile, *ag.* frequentable.

frequentàre, *v.t.* **1.** to frequent; (*scuola, ecc.*) to attend; (*alberghi, ristoranti, negozi*) to patronize: *un bar frequentato da ladri e simili*, a pub haunted by thieves and the like; *frequentato dall'alta società*, patronized by society; *egli frequenta la nostra casa*, he comes to our house (o he calls on us) very often (o he pays frequent visits to us); *— lezioni*, to attend lessons; *— teatri, circoli*, to frequent theatres, clubs **2.** (*persone*) to frequent, to associate with (s.o.), to consort with (s.o.): *non frequentarlo, è un tipo losco!*, don't associate with him, he is a suspicious character! **3.** *— i Sacramenti*, (*eccl.*) to frequent the Sacraments.

frequentatívo, *ag.* (*gram.*) frequentative.

frequentàto, *ag.* frequented; (*di scuola, ecc.*) attended; (*di albergo, ristorante, ecc.*) (well) patronized: *un albergo molto —*, a very well (o much) patronized hotel.

frequentatóre, *s.m.* frequenter, haunter; (*cliente assiduo*) regular customer, patron; (*visitatore assiduo*) frequent caller, constant visitor: *— di cinema*, cinema -goer; *— di società*, (*amer.*) socialite; *— di teatri*, theatre -goer; *essere un (assiduo) — della casa di qlcu.*, to be a frequent caller at s.o.'s house ‖ **frequentatríce**, *s.f.* frequenter, haunter; (*cliente assidua*) regular customer, patron; (*visitatrice assidua*) frequent caller, constant visitor.

frequentazióne, *s.f.* (*rar.*) frequenting; attending.

frequènte, *ag.* frequent: *polso —*, quick (o rapid *o* frequent) pulse ‖ *di —*, frequently (o often): *lo vedo di —*, I see him often (o I often see him).

frequènza, *s.f.* **1.** frequency; (*gran numero*) great number: *la — di tali incidenti*, the frequency of such accidents **2.** (*affluenza*) concourse; (*assiduità*) attendance: *certificato di —*, (*a scuola*) certificate of attendance **3.** (*scient. tec.*) frequency: *— del polso*, (*med.*) pulse frequency (o rate); *— di beccheggio*, (*mar. aer.*) pitching frequency; *— di lavoro*, (*rad. elett.*) operating frequency; — *intermedia, modulata, (rad.)* intermediate frequency *(abbr.* I.F.), modulated frequency; — *tipo,* standard frequency; *a bassa* —, *(rad. tv.)* low-frequency *(attributivo) (abbr.* L.F.); *ad alta* —, *(rad. tv.)* high -frequency *(attributivo) (abbr.* H.F.); *media* —, *(rad. tv.)* medium frequency *(abbr.* M.F.); *moltiplicatore di* —, *(elett.)* frequency multiplier; *variatore di* —, *(elett.)* frequency changer.

frequenziòmetro, *s.m.* **1.** *(elett.)* frequency meter: — *registratore,* recording frequency meter **2.** *(rad.)* wavemeter, ondometer.

frèsa, *s.f. (mec.)* (milling) cutter, mill, miller; milling machine: — *ad angolo,* angle (o angular) cutter; — *ad un taglio,* plain milling cutter; — *concava, convessa,* concave, convex cutter; — *per smusso,* countersink.

fresàre, *v.t. (mec.)* to mill.

fresatóre, *s.m.* milling machine operator.

fresatríce, *s.f. (mec.)* milling machine, miller: — *a comando elettronico,* electronically-controlled milling machine; — *automatica,* self-acting milling machine; — *per ingranaggi,* gear cutting machine.

fresatúra, *s.f. (mec.)* milling: — *angolare,* angular milling; — *a profilo,* profiling.

frescaménte, *av.* **1.** coolly **2.** *(di recente)* freshly, recently.

frescànte, *s.m. (pitt.)* fresco-painter.

frescàre, *v.t. (affrescare)* to fresco, to paint in fresco.

freschézza, *s.f.* **1.** freshness (anche *fig.*): *la* — *dei fiori, della sua carnagione,* the freshness of flowers, of her complexion; *la* — *della gioventù,* the freshness of youth **2.** coolness: *la* — *della sera,* the coolness of evening (o the cool of the evening).

frésco, *ag.* **1.** fresh: *carnagione fresca,* fresh complexion; *carne fresca,* fresh meat; *fieno* —, new-mown hay; *fiori freschi,* fresh cut flowers; *pane* —, new bread; *uova fresche,* new-laid eggs ‖ — *come una rosa,* as fresh as a daisy ‖ *che faccia fresca!,* what impudence! (o what a cheek!) ‖ *stare* —, *(essere in un impiccio)* to be in a fix (o in a pickle o in a nice mess); *(sbagliarsi)* to be mistaken: *se credi di imbrogliarmi, stai* —*!,* if you think you can cheat me, you are in for a surprise!; *se non vai, stai* —*!,* if you don't go, you'll be for it! **2.** *(di temperatura)* cool, fresh: *acqua fresca,* cool water; *aria fresca,* fresh air; *venticello* —, cool breeze; *l'aria si è fatta fresca,* the air has grown cool **3.** *(umido)* fresh; wet: *inchiostro ancora* —, ink still wet; *vernice fresca,* wet paint **4.** *(nuovo, recente)* fresh, recent, new: *avvenimento di fresca data,* recent event; *un ragazzo* — *di scuola,* a boy fresh from school; *ricordi freschi,* fresh memories ‖ *di* —, freshly: *ministro nominato di* —, a newly appointed minister; *rasato di* —, fresh-shaven **5.** *(riposato)* fresh: *truppe fresche,* fresh troops ‖ *s.m.* **1.** *(di temperatura)* cool, coolness: *prendere il* — *sul balcone,* to take the air (o to enjoy the cool of the evening) on a balcony; *tenere ql.co. in* —, to keep sthg. cool (o in a cool place); *uscire per il* —, to go out in the cool of the evening ‖ *dormire al* —, to sleep in the open ‖ *stare al* —, *(in prigione)* to be in (the) clink (o *amer.* to be in the cooler) **2.** *(affresco)* fresco *(pl.* frescoes, frescos): *un dipinto a* —, a fresco painting; *dipingere a* —, to paint in fresco (o to fresco).

frescolíno, *ag.* chilly, rather cool.

frescúra, *s.f.* coolness, chilliness: *la* — *delle sere d'autunno,* the chilliness of autumn evenings; *nella* — *della sera,* in the cool of the evening.

frèsia, *s.f. (bot.)* freesia.

frètta, *s.f.* haste; *(eccessiva e disordinata)* hurry: *avere* — *di fare ql.co.,* to make haste to do sthg.; *avere troppa* — *di guadagnare denaro,* to be in a great hurry to make money; *avere* — *di partire,* to be in a hurry to leave; *fare* —, to make haste (o to hurry) ‖ *in* —, in a hurry (o hastily o hurriedly): *calcolo fatto in* —, *(approssimativo)* rough calculation; *ho ricevuto un biglietto scritto in* —, I have received a note written

in haste; *preparativi fatti in* —, hurried preparations; *fare la prima colazione in* —, to take a hurried breakfast ‖ *in tutta* —, with all possible speed: *ritornare indietro in tutta* —, to hasten (o hurry) back; *salire, scendere in tutta* —, to hasten up, down.

frettàre, *v.t. (mar.)* to log.

frettàzza, *s.f. (mar.)* log.

frettolosaménte, *av.* hastily; hurriedly.

frettolóso, *ag.* hurried; *(fatto in fretta)* hasty: *domande e risposte frettolose,* hurried questions and answers; *preparativi frettolosi,* hasty (o hurried) preparations.

freudiàno, *ag.* Freudian.

freudísmo, *s.m.* Freudianism.

friàbile, *ag.* friable, crumbly.

friabilità, *s.f.* friability, friableness.

Fribúrgo, *no.pr.f. (geog.)* Freiburg.

fricandò, *s.m. (cuc.)* fricandeau *(pl.* fricandeaux), larded veal stew.

fricassèa, *s.f. (cuc.)* fricassee ‖ *fare una* — *di una cosa, fig.* to shatter something.

friggere, *v.t. (far friggere)* to fry: *padella per* —, frying-pan; *uova fritte,* fried eggs ‖ *mandare qlcu. a farsi* —, *(volg.)* to send s.o. to the devil ‖ *v.i.* **1.** to fry: *questo pesce frigge bene,* this fish fries well ‖ — *d'impazienza, di rabbia, fig.* to fret and fume: *sono qui che friggo e lui non viene,* I am standing here fuming because he has not come yet **2.** *(sfrigolare)* to frizzle, to sizzle; *(come ferro rovente immerso nell'acqua)* to hiss: *il lardo frigge nella padella,* the bacon is frizzling in the pan.

friggiménto, *s.m.* **1.** frying **2.** *(sfrigolio)* frizzling, sizzling; *(come ferro rovente nell'acqua)* hissing.

friggío, *s.m.* sizzle, sizzling noise.

friggitóra, *s.f.,* **friggitóre,** *s.m.* **1.** *(chi frigge)* frier, fryer **2.** *(chi vende cose fritte)* seller of fried food.

friggitoría, *s.f.* fried food shop, fish and chips (shop).

friggitríce, *s.f.* **1.** *(chi frigge)* frier, fryer **2.** *(chi vende cose fritte)* seller of fried food.

Frígia, *no.pr.f. (geog. st.)* Phrygia.

frigidàrio, *s.m. (archeol.)* frigidarium *(pl.* frigidaria).

frigidézza, frigidità, *s.f.* frigidness, frigidity.

frígido, *ag.* frigid, cold (anche *fig.*): *una persona frigida,* a frigid person.

frígio, *ag.* Phrygian: *berretto* —, *(st.)* Phrygian cap; *modo* —, *(mus.)* Phrygian mode.

frignàre, *v.i.* to whimper, to whine.

frignóna, *s.f.,* **frignóne,** *s.m.,* whimperer, whiner.

frigorífero, *ag.* refrigerant, refrigerating, freezing: *carro* —, *(ferr.)* refrigerator car (o freezer); *cella frigorifera,* refrigerator (o freezer); *macchina frigorifera,* refrigerating machine (o engine); *magazzino* —, cold store; *miscela frigorifera,* freezing mixture ‖ *s.m.* refrigerator; *(fam.)* frig, fridge: — *per surgelamento,* deep freeze.

frimàio, *s.m. (st. francese)* Frimaire.

Fríne, *no.pr.f. (st. greca)* Phryne.

fringuèllo, *s.m. (ornit.)* finch, chaffinch.

friníre, *v.i. (delle cicale)* to chirp, to chirr.

frisàre, *v.t. (biliardo)* to touch lightly.

frisèllo, *s.m.* mill-dust, flour-dust.

Frísia, *no.pr.f. (geog.)* Friesland ‖ *cavalli di* —, chevaux de frise.

frisóne, *ag.s.m.* Frisian: *razze frisoni,* Frisian breeds.

frittàta, *s.f.* omelet(te): *fare una* —, to make an omelette; *fig.* to make a mess; *(fare un errore)* to make a blunder.

frittèlla, *s.f.* **1.** *(cuc.)* pancake; *(di frutta e pastella)* fritter; *(amer.)* doughnut; *(di riso, carne, ecc.)* croquette **2.** *(fam.) (macchia d'unto)* grease stain.

frittellóna, *s.f.,* **frittellóne,** *s.m. (fam.)* messy person.

frítto, *ag.* fried: *pesce* —, fried fish ‖ *cose fritte e rifritte*, *fig.* stale joke (*o* stale news *o* *fam.* hash) ‖ *essere* —, *fig.* to be done for: *sono* —*!*, (*fam.*) I'm done for! (*o* *volg.* I'm cooked!) ‖ *s.m.* fry, fried food: — *di carne*, fried meat (*o* fry); — *di pesce*, fried fish; — *misto*, mixed fry.

frittúra, *s.f.* fry, fried food: — *d'agnello*, lamb's fry.

friulàno, *ag.* of Friuli, from Friuli.

Friúli, *no.pr.m.* (*geog.*) Friuli.

frivolaménte, *av.* frivolously.

frivoleggiàre, *v.i.* 1. to act frivolously, to trifle 2. (*parlare frivolamente*) to talk frivolously, to trifle.

frivolézza, **frivolità**, *s.f.* 1. (*l'essere frivolo*) frivolity, frivolousness 2. (*cosa frivola*) trifle.

frívolo, *ag.* 1. frivolous: *persona* —, frivolous person 2. (*di poco conto*) frivolous, trifling.

frizióne, *s.m.* 1. rub, rubbing; (*massaggio*) massage; (*med.*) friction 2. (*mec. aut.*) clutch, friction clutch: — *che slitta*, slipping clutch; — *idraulica*, hydraulic clutch; — *monodisco*, single-plate clutch; *disco della* —, clutch disk (*o* clutch plate); *pedale della* —, clutch pedal; *distaccare la* —, to disengage the clutch (*o* to declutch); *innestare la* —, to engage the clutch.

frizzànte, *ag.* 1. (*di aria*) biting 2. (*di bevanda effervescente*) sparkling 3. (*mordace*) sharp, biting, pungent, cutting: *osservazione* —, pungent remark.

frizzàre, *v.i.* 1. to tingle: *brezza che fa* — *il sangue*, breeze that makes the blood tingle; *mi frizzano gli occhi*, my eyes are tingling (*o* stinging *o* smarting) 2. (*di bevanda effervescente*) to sparkle.

frizzo, *s.m.* (*arguzia mordace*) witticism, jest, joke; (*motto di scherno*) gibe, jeer: *gli lanciavano frizzi*, they were jeering at him.

frodàbile, *ag.* (*di persona*) cheatable; (*di legge*) evadable.

frodàre, *v.t.* 1. to defraud, to cheat, to swindle: *i contrabbandieri frodano lo Stato*, smugglers defraud the State 2. (*far contrabbando di*) to smuggle.

frodatóre, *s.m.*, **frodatríce**, *s.f.* 1. defrauder, cheat, swindler 2. (*chi fa contrabbando*) smuggler.

fròde, *s.f.* fraud, trick, cheating, deception, swindle: *una* — *odiosa*, a hateful fraud (*o* a nasty trick); *ottenere con la* —, to obtain (*o* to get) by fraud.

fròdo, *s.m.* smuggling: *cacciatore di* —, poacher; *merce di* —, smuggled (*o* contraband) goods; *cacciare di* —, to poach; *introdurre sigarette di* —, to smuggle cigarettes (into a country).

frodolènte, *V.* **fraudolènto**.

frògia, *s.f.* nostril (of horse).

frollàre, *v.t.* to hang: *frolla bene questa selvaggina*, keep this game until it is high ‖ *v.i.* (*diventare frollo*) to become tender; (*specialmente di selvaggina*) to become high.

fròllo, *ag.* 1. (*di carne*) tender; (*specialmente di selvaggina*) high 2. (*languido*, *snervato*) weak, feeble 3. *pasta frolla*, (*cuc.*) pastry.

frómbola, *s.f.* sling.

frombolàre, *v.t.* (*rar.*) to sling (stones).

frombolière, *s.m.* slinger.

frónda[1], *s.f.* 1. leafy branch; (*di felce*, *di palma*) frond 2. (*foglia*) leaf.

frónda[2], *s.f.* (*st. francese*) Fronde ‖ *vento di fronda*, *fig.* current of rebellion: *spira vento di fronda*, rebellion is brewing.

frondàio, *s.m.* (*rar.*) heap of leaves.

frondeggiànte, *ag.* leafy, frondescent.

frondeggiàre, *v.i.* to bear leaves, to put forth leaves.

frondísta, *s.m.* (*pol.*) frondeur, member of the opposition, political opposer.

frondosità, *s.f.* 1. leafiness 2. (*di stile*) overornamentation, luxuriance.

frondóso, *ag.* 1. leafy 2. (*di stile*) luxuriant.

frontàle, *ag.* frontal: *attacco* —, (*mil.*) frontal attack; *osso* —, (*anat.*) brow-ridge (*o* frontal bone) ‖ *s.m.* (*arch.*) 1. frontal 2. (*di caminetto*) mantelpiece, mantelshelf.

frónte, *s.f.* 1. forehead; (*poet.*) brow; (*faccia*) face: — *alta*, high forehead; — *ampia*, *larga*, *spaziosa*, broad forehead; — *sfuggente*, receding forehead; *corrugare la* —, to knit one's brow ‖ *a* — *a* —, face to face ‖ *a* — *alta*, proudly; (*senza timore*) fearlessly ‖ *glielo si leggeva in* —, you could see it in his face (*o* it was written all over his face) ‖ *guadagnare il pane col sudore della* —, to earn one's living by the sweat of one's brow 2. (*arch.*) front, frontage: *le finestre sulla* —, the front windows 3. *di* — *a*, (*posizione*) opposite, in front of (*s.o.*, *sthg.*); (*a paragone di*) in comparison with (*s.o.*, *sthg.*): *il monumento di* — *alla scuola*, the monument opposite (to) the school; *lo mettemmo di* — *ai testimoni*, we confronted him with witnesses; *questo è niente di* — *al pericolo che avete evitato*, this is nothing in comparison with the danger you have escaped ‖ *s.m.* (*mil.*) front: — *d'attacco*, front of attack; — *di battaglia*, battle front; *su tutti i fronti*, on all fronts; *andare al* —, to go to the front; *essere mandato al* —, to be sent to the front ‖ *a destra!*, right turn!; — *a sinistra!*, left turn!; *dietro* —*!*, about turn! ‖ *far* —*a*, to face: *far* — *a un pericolo*, to face a danger (*o* to be faced with a danger); *far* — *ad una situazione difficile*, to face the music; *far* — *alle spese*, to meet expenses 2. (*pol.*) front, union: — *popolare*, popular front.

fronteggiàre, *v.t.* 1. (*opporsi a*) to face, to meet, to confront, to cope with (*s.o.*, *sthg.*); to withstand: — *un pericolo*, to face danger; — *una situazione difficile con coraggio*, to face the music 2. (*stare di fronte a*) to face, to front: *la casa fronteggiava il mare*, the house faced the sea ‖ **fronteggiàrsi**, *v.r.* reciproco to face each other.

frontespízio, *s.m.* 1. (*arch.*) frontispiece 2. (*di libro*) title page 3. (*scherz.*) (*faccia*) face.

frontièra, *s.f.* frontier, border: *abitanti di* —, frontiersmen (*o* border dwellers); *incidente di* —, frontier incident; *una stazione di* —, a frontier station; *passare la* —, to cross the frontier.

frontísta, *s.c.* (*dir.*) (*lungo una strada*) owner of a house facing the street, owner of land facing the street; (*lungo un fiume*) riparian (proprietor).

frontóne, *s.m.* (*arch.*) pediment, fronton; (*di porta*, *finestra*) gable.

frónzolo, *s.m.* 1. frill, frippery, finery, trinket: *senza fronzoli*, (*semplice*) (quite) plain 2. (*di stile*, *di oratoria*) frills (*pl.*).

fronzúto, *ag.* leafy.

fròtta, *s.f.* 1. (*di persone*) crowd, throng, flock, troop; (*schiera*) band: *una* — *di scolari*, a troop of schoolboys ‖ *a frotte*, in flocks 2. (*di animali*) flock; (*amer.*) band; (*di pesci*) shoal: *una* — *di capre*, a flock of goats 3. (*di cose*) crowd: *una* — *di barche*, a crowd of boats.

fròttola, *s.f.* 1. fib, lie; (*favola*, *cosa inventata*) idle story, humbug: *sono tutte frottole!*, it's all nonsense (*o* humbug)!; *raccontar frottole*, to tell fibs (*o* lies) 2. (*canzone popolare*) popular song.

frottolóne, *s.m.* (*fam.*) fibber.

frugacchiàre, *v.t.* to rummage.

frugàle, *ag.* frugal, thrifty, sparing: *pasto* —, frugal meal; *uomo* —, thrifty man.

frugalità, *s.f.* frugality, thrift, sparingness.

frugalménte, *av.* frugally, thriftily, sparingly.

frugàre, *v.t.* to search, to rummage; to rummage in (*sthg.*); (*minuziosamente*) to ransack ‖ *v.i.* to search (*sthg.*), to rummage (*sthg.*), to rummage in (*sthg.*); (*minuziosamente*) to ransack (*sthg.*): *frugherò finchè lo troverò*, I shall ferret it out; *frugò nel suo cassetto*, he rummaged in his drawer; — *in una stanza*, to ransack a room; — *nelle tasche di qlcu.*, to rummage in *s.o.*'s (*o* to search *s.o.*'s) pockets.

frugàta, *s.f.* search.

frugífero, *ag.* (*letter.*) bearing crops; (*fertile*) fertile.

frugívoro, *ag.* (*zool.*) frugivorous.

frugolàre, *v.i.* 1. (*frugare*) to rummage: *frugola*

nelle sue tasche, he is rummaging in his pockets **2.** (*grufolare*) to snout.

frúgolo, *s.m.* lively child; little child ‖ *ha un bel frugoletto,* she has a nice little child.

fruíbile, *ag.* enjoyable, usable.

fruíre, *v.i.* to avail oneself of (sthg.), to make use of (sthg.), to enjoy (sthg.): — *di un vantaggio,* to enjoy an advantage ‖ *v.t.* (*rar.*) to enjoy, to use: — *una pensione,* to enjoy a pension.

fruizióne, *s.f.* (*rar.*) fruition, enjoyment.

frullàna, *s.f.* **1.** hay-scythe **2.** "furlana" (a rustic dance from Friuli).

frullàre, *v.t.* to whip; to beat up, to whisk: — *la panna,* to whip cream; — *le uova,* to beat up (*o* to whisk) eggs ‖ *v.i.* **1.** (*di ali*) to whir(r): *i piccioni frullavano sulle nostre teste,* the pigeons whirred about our heads **2.** (*girare rapidamente*) to spin round, to whirl ‖ *che cosa ti frulla per il capo?, fig.* what ideas are you getting into your head?.

frullíno, *s.m.* (*cuc.*) whisk.

frullío, *s.m.* whirring.

frúllo, *s.m.* **1.** (*di ali*) whir(r) **2.** (*ind. tessile*) twirling stick.

frullóne, *s.m.* (*buratto*) sifter, bolter, sifting-machine.

frumentàceo, *ag.* frumentaceous; cereal.

frumentàrio, *ag.* frumentarious.

fruménto, *s.m.* wheat: *farina di* —, wheat meal.

frumentóne, *s.m.* Indian corn; maize.

frusciàre, *v.i.* to rustle: *si poteva udire la serpe — tra le felci,* the snake could be heard rustling among the ferns.

fruscío, *s.m.* **1.** rustle, rustling, rustling noise **2.** (*rad.*) ground noise **3.** (*di punta di grammofono*) needle noise.

frusóne, *s.m.* (*ornit.*) hawfinch.

frústa, *s.f.* **1.** whip; (*staffile*) lash: *fu condannato a dieci colpi di* —, he was sentenced to ten strokes of the lash; *schioccare la* —, to crack the whip ‖ — *da Arlecchino, da maschera,* slapstick **2.** (*arnese di cucina*) whisk.

frustàre, *v.t.* **1.** to whip; (*staffilare*) to lash, to flog; (*flagellare*) to scourge: *i critici frustarono la sua nuova commedia, fig.* his new play was lashed by the critics; *la pioggia frustava i vetri,* the rain was lashing (against) the window-panes; — *un cavallo,* to flog (*o* to lash) a horse **2.** (*logorare*) to wear out.

frustàta, *s.f.* lash (anche *fig.*): *gli diedero cento frustate,* he was given one hundred lashes; *non preoccuparti delle frustate delle malelingue,* don't mind the slanderers' lashes.

frustatóre, *s.m.,* **frustatríce,** *s.f.* whipper; (*chi staffila*) lasher; (*chi flagella*) scourger.

frustatúra, *s.f.* whipping; (*staffilatura*) lashing, flogging.

frustíno, *s.m.* riding-whip.

frústo¹, *ag.* worn-out, thread-bare, shabby; (*a brandelli*) tattered.

frústo², *s.* (*tozzo*) morsel; (*pezzetto*) bit ‖ — *a* —, bit by bit.

frustràre, *v.t.* to frustrate, to thwart; (*deludere*) to disappoint, to deceive: *le sue speranze furono frustrate dalla morte del re,* his hopes were thwarted by the death of the king; *il vento frustrò i nostri sforzi,* the wind frustrated our efforts.

frútice, *s.m.* (*bot.*) frutex (*pl.* frutices).

fruticóso, *ag.* (*bot.*) fruticose.

frútta, *s.f.* (*sing. con valore coll.*) fruit: — *acerba,* green fruit; — *cotta,* compote (*o* stewed fruit); — *da consumarsi cruda,* eater; — *fresca, secca,* fresh, dried fruit; *albero da* —, fruit-tree; *cestello di* —, bowl of fruit; *coltello da* —, fruit-knife; *mangi molta* —?, do you eat much fruit?; *raccogliere* —, (*dalla pianta*) to pick fruit; (*già caduta a terra*) to gather fruit.

fruttaiuòla, *s.f.* fruiteress; greengrocer; (*ambulante*) costermonger.

fruttaiuòlo, *s.m.* fruiterer; greengrocer; (*ambulante*) costermonger.

fruttàme, *s.m.* fruitage.

fruttàre, *v.i.* **1.** (*dare frutto*) to fruit, to bear fruit, to yield fruit **2.** (*dar profitti, utili*) to bear fruit, to pay, to yield; (*econ.*) to bear interest: *il delitto non frutta,* crime does not pay; *un mestiere che frutta,* a paying trade; *il suo lavoro comincia a* —, his work is beginning to bear fruit ‖ *v.t.* **1.** (*dare come utile*) to yield: *il capitale mi frutta il 2%,* my capital yields me 2% **2.** (*procurare*) to bring: *la sua attività gli fruttò grandi onori,* his activities brought him great honours.

fruttàto, *s.m.* (*econ.*) fruits (*pl.*), revenue.

fruttéto, *s.m.* orchard.

frutticoltúra, *s.f.* fruit-growing.

frutticultóre, *s.m.* fruit-grower.

frutticultúra, *s.f.* fruit-growing.

fruttidòro, *s.m.* (*st. francese*) Fructidor.

fruttièra, *s.f.* fruit-dish, fruit-stand.

fruttífero, *ag.* **1.** fructiferous, fruit-bearing; (*fertile*) fruitful **2.** (*econ.*) interest-bearing: *buono* —, interest-bearing security; *deposito* —, deposit on interest **3.** (*utile*) profitable; useful.

fruttificàre, *v.i.* to fructify, to bear fruit (anche *fig.*).

fruttificazióne, *s.f.* fructification.

fruttífico, (*rar.*) *per* **fruttífero.**

fruttivéndola, *s.f.* fruiteress; greengrocer; (*ambulante*) costermonger.

fruttivéndolo, *s.m.* fruiterer; greengrocer; (*ambulante*) costermonger.

fruttívoro, *ag.* frugivorous.

frútto, *s.m., pl.m.* **frútti**; *pl.f.* **frútta** (*nel senso* **2.**); (*per la forma collettiva* **frútta** *V. a questa voce*) **1.** fruit: *un* — *maturo,* a ripe fruit; *frutti vari,* different fruits; *i frutti della terra,* the fruits of the earth ‖ *il* — *del ventre tuo,* the fruit of thy womb ‖ *frutti di mare,* (*cuc.*) edible mussels (*o* crustaceans *o* amer. sea-food) ‖ *frutti pendenti,* (*dir.*) standing fruits (*o* standing crop *o* away going crop) ‖ *il* — *proibito, fig.* the forbidden fruit **2.** *pl.* (*frutti commestibili, specialmente serviti a tavola*) fruit (*gener. sing.*): *han già portato in tavola le frutta?,* has the fruit already been served? ‖ *essere alle frutta,* to be at the end of the dinner **3.** (*utile, profitto*) fruit, profit; result; (*effetto*) effect: *i frutti della pace,* the fruits (*o* advantages) of peace; *i frutti della pigrizia,* the effects of indolence; *i frutti del mio lavoro,* the outcome of my labour; *a che* —?, what for?; *qual* — *sperate trarne?,* what result do you hope to derive from it?; *dar frutti,* to bear (*o* to yield) fruit ‖ *senza* —, (*inutile*) fruitless (*o* useless); (*inutilmente*) fruitlessly (*o* uselessly *o* unprofitably) **4.** (*ricompensa*) reward **5.** (*econ.*) (*rendita*) interest, income; revenue: *queste azioni mi danno un* — *del 4%,* these shares bring me (*o* yield) 4% interest; *mettere a* —, to put to interest.

fruttòsio, *s.m.* (*chim.*) fructose; (*fam.*) fruit-sugar.

fruttuosaménte, *av.* fruitfully; profitably; (*utilmente*) usefully.

fruttuóso, *ag.* fruitful; advantageous; profitable; (*utile*) useful: *commercio* —, profitable business.

italeína, *s.f.* (*chim.*) phthalein.

ftàlico, *ag.* (*chim.*) phthalic.

fu, *ag.* (*defunto*) late: *il* — *signor Smith,* the late Mr. Smith.

fucilàre, *v.t.* to shoot: *i disertori furono fucilati,* the deserters were shot.

fucilàta, *s.f.* shot, rifle-shot: *sparare una* —, to fire a shot.

fucilatóre, *s.m.* shooter.

fucilazióne, *s.f.* shooting, execution (by shooting): — *in massa,* mass shooting.

fucile, *s.m.* rifle, gun: — *ad aria compressa,* air-gun; — *a doppia canna,* double-barrelled gun; — *a retrocarica,* breech-loader; — *automatico,* automatic rifle; — *da caccia,* shotgun; — *mitragliatore,* submachine gun ‖ *calcio del* —, butt (*o* stock); *canna del* —, gun-barrel; *colpo, sparo di* —, (rifle-) shot; *caricare un* —, to load a gun (*o a* rifle); *essere a tiro di* —, to be within gunshot ‖ *egli è un ottimo* —, *fig.* he is an excellent shot.

fucilería, *s.f.* 1. (*scarica di molti fucili*) rifle-fire, fusillade 2. (*complesso di fucili*) musketry.

fucilière, *s.m.* (*mil.*) rifleman (*pl.* riflemen); fusilier: *corpo di fucilieri,* rifle-corps.

fucína, *s.f.* forge, smithy; (*di grande stabilimento*) forge shop.

fucinàre, *v.t.* 1. (*metal.*) to forge: — *alla pressa,* to press-forge; — *entro stampi,* to drop-forge 2. *fig.* (*formare*) to form, to shape.

fucináto, *ag.* (*metal.*) forged: *ferro* —, forged iron; *pezzo* —, forging ‖ *s.m.* (*metal.*) forging.

fucinatóre, *s.m.* forger.

fucinatríce, *s.f.* (*metal.*) forging machine.

fucinatúra, *s.f.* (*metal.*) forging: — *a stampo,* drop-forging.

fúco¹, *s.m.* (*maschio dell'ape*) drone.

fúco², *s.m.* (*bot.*) fucus (*pl.* fuci, fucuses).

fúcsia, *s.f.* (*bot.*) fuchsia.

fucsína, *s.f.* (*chim.*) fuchsin(e).

fúga, *s.f.* 1. flight; escape; get-away: *la* — *in Egitto,* the flight into Egypt; *cercare scampo nella* —, to seek safety in flight; *darsi alla* —, to take to flight; *mettere il nemico in* —, to put the enemy to flight ‖ *una* — *di capitale,* (*econ.*) a flight of capital ‖ *di* —, (*in gran fretta*) in a hurry 2. (*di innamorati*) elopement 3. (*falla, apertura*) escape, leak: — *d'acqua,* leakage of water; — *di gas,* escape of gas 4. (*successione*) flight; suite: *una* — *di scalini.* a flight of stairs; *una* — *di stanze,* a suite of rooms 5. (*mus.*) fugue.

fugàce, *ag.* fleeting, transient; short-lived: *gioia* —, short-lived joy; *sguardo* —, transient glance (*o* glimpse); *la bellezza è* —, beauty is fleeting.

fugaceménte, *av.* fleetingly, transiently.

fugacità, *s.f.* fugacity; fleetness, transiency.

fugàre, *v.t.* 1. to put to flight; (*mettere in rotta*) to rout, to put to rout; (*disperdere*) to disperse 2. (*scacciare*) to drive; to dispel: — *i tristi pensieri,* to dispel sad thoughts.

fuggévole, *ag.* fleeting, flying; short-lived; ephemeral.

fuggevolézza, *s.f.* fugacity; fleetness, transiency.

fuggevolménte, *av.* fleetly, fleetingly.

fuggiàsco, *ag. s.m.* fugitive, runaway.

fuggifatíca, *s.c.* (*rar.*) shirker, slacker, sluggard.

fuggifúggi, *s.m.* stampede, panic flight: *ci fu un* — *generale,* there was a general stampede.

fuggiménto, *s.m.* flight.

fuggíre, *v.i.* to fly (*spec. all'inf., p.pr., indic. pres.*), to flee (*non usato nel pres. indic.*); to run away; to escape; (*di donna che s'invola con l'amato*) to elope: *il briccone fuggì davanti al cane infuriato,* the scoundrel ran away (*o* fled) from the angry dog; *dovettero* — *dalla Romania,* they had to flee (*o* to fly) from Roumania; *ella fuggì col suo pretendente,* she eloped with her suitor; *fuggì appena in tempo,* he escaped just in time; *fuggimmo dalla nostra patria,* we fled from our country; *i nemici fuggirono disordinatamente,* the enemy fled in disorder; *il tempo fugge,* time flies ‖ — *dal collegio,* to run away from one's school; — *dalla prigione,* to escape (*o* to run away) from prison; — *di casa,* to run away from home ‖ *v.t.* (*evitare*) to avoid, to shun; (*sottrarsi a*) to shirk: *qlcu. come la peste,* to shun s.o. like the plague.

fuggitívo, *ag.* fugitive (*attributivo*); runaway (*attributivo*); *fig.* fleeting, transient ‖ *s.m.* fugitive, runaway.

fúlcro, *s.m.* (*mec.*) fulcrum (*pl.* fulcra) (*anche fig.*): — *della bilancia,* scale fulcrum.

fulgènte, *ag.* shining, bright, brilliant, refulgent.

Fulgènzio, *no.pr.m.* (*st. lett.*) Fulgentius.

fúlgere, *v.i.* (*poet.*) to shine, to be bright.

fulgidaménte, *av.* shiningly, brightly.

fulgidézza, fulgidità, *s.f.* splendour, brightness, refulgence, radiance.

fúlgido, *ag.* shining, bright, refulgent; dazzling: *gemma fulgida,* dazzling gem; *stella fulgida,* shining (*o* sparkling) star.

fulgóre, *s.m.* brightness; splendour, refulgence.

fulíggine, *s.m.* 1. soot: *nero come la* —, as black as soot 2. (*malattia del grano*) blight, rust 3. (*pitt.*) (*nerofumo*) lamp-black.

fuligginóso, *ag.* sooty, fuliginous.

full, *s.m.* (*poker*) full-hand, full-house: *fare un* —, to get full-house (*o* full-hand).

fulmicotóne, *s.m.* guncotton, nitrocotton.

fulminànte, *ag.* fulminant, fulminating ‖ *s.m.* 1. (*chim.*) fulminate 2. (*fiammifero di legno*) lucifer (match) 3. (*capsula di cartuccia*) primer, percussion cap.

fulminàre, *v.t.* 1. to strike by lightning: *rimase fulminato durante il temporale,* he was struck by lightning in the storm 2. (*colpire*) to strike, to batter; to fulminate: *un colpo di fucile lo fulminò,* a gun-shot struck him dead; *dal colle l'artiglieria fulminava le linee nemiche,* the artillery battered the enemy's lines from the hill; *fu fulminato dall'apoplessia,* he was struck down by apoplexy; *lo fulminò con lo sguardo,* he cast a withering glance at him (*o* he crushed him with a glare); *il Papa fulminò il ribelle con una scomunica,* the Pope fulminated an excommunication against the rebel; *rimasi fulminato dalle sue parole,* I was dumbfounded at his words (*o* I was struck dumb by his words) ‖ *v.i.* to lighten.

fulmináto, *ag.* thunder-struck (*anche fig.*); struck by lightning ‖ *s.m.* (*chim.*) fulminate.

fulminatóre, *ag.* fulminant ‖ *s.m.* thunderer.

fulminatòrio, *ag.* fulminatory.

fulminatríce, *s.f.* thunderer.

fulminazióne, *s.f.* fulmination (*anche fig.*).

fúlmine, *s.m.* 1. thunderbolt; lightning: *colpito dal* —, struck by lightning; *veloce come un* —, as quick (*o* swift) as lightning; *un* — *colpì la stalla,* a thunderbolt struck (*o* fell on) the cowhouse ‖ *un* — *a ciel sereno, fig.* a bolt from the blue ‖ *colpo di* —, *fig.* love at first sight 2. *fig.* (*anatema, scomunica*) excommunication, anathema: *i fulmini della Chiesa,* the curse of the Church.

fulmineaménte, *av.* 1. flashily 2. (*rapidamente*) swiftly.

fulmineità, *s.f.* 1. flashiness 2. (*rapidità*) swiftness.

fulmíneo, *ag.* 1. flashing, flashy 2. (*rapidissimo*) swift, flashing.

fulmíneo, *ag.* (*chim.*) fulminic.

fulminío, *s.m.* continual lightning.

fulminóso, (*letter.*) per **fulmíneo.**

Fúlvia, *no.pr.f.* Fulvia.

fúlvo, *ag.* fawn-coloured, tawny: *dai capelli fulvi,* tawny-haired.

fumàcchio, *s.m.* 1. (*pennacchio di fumo*) trail of smoke 2. (*fumarola vulcanica*) fumarole 3. (*carbonella che brucia male*) smoky charcoal 4. (*suffumigio*) fumigation.

fumaiuòlo, *s.m.* 1. (*di casa*) chimney-stack 2. (*di locomotiva*) smoke-stack; (*di nave*) funnel, smoke-stack.

fumànte, *ag.* smoking, steaming: *un caffè caldo* —, a cup of coffee steaming hot.

fumàre, *v.t.* to smoke: *fumava la pipa,* he was smoking his pipe; *fumi?,* do you smoke?; *mentre fumi una sigaretta...,* while you are smoking a cigarette... ‖ *vietato* —, no smoking ‖ — *come un turco, come una ciminiera,* to smoke like a chimney ‖ *v.i.* (*mandare fumo*) to smoke; (*emettere vapore*) to fume; (*fumare per ebollizione*) to steam.

fumària, *s.f.* (*bot.*) fumitory.

fumaruòla, *s.f.* (*geol.*) fumarole.

fumàta, *s.f.* **1.** (*ondata di fumo*) smoke **2.** (*segnale*) smoke signal ‖ *le fumate* (*per l'elezione del Papa*), smoke signals (on the Pope's election) **3.** (*il fumare tabacco*) smoke: *fare una fumata*, to have a smoke.

fumatóre, *s.m.,* **fumatríce,** *s.f.* smoker: *cancro dei fumatori*, smokers' cancer; *sala fumatori*, smoking-room; *scompartimento per fumatori*, smoking-compartment (*o* smoker); *è un — accanito*, he is a heavy smoker.

fumeggiàre, *v.i.* to fume ‖ *v.t.* (*pitt.*) (*ombreggiare*) to shade.

fumétto, *s.m.* (*gener. pl.*) strip cartoon, comic strip; (*nei giornali*) comics (*pl.*); (*amer.*) funnies (*pl.*): *banditi da romanzo a fumetti*, comic-strip bandits; *fumetti di argomento poliziesco*, crime-strip cartoons.

fumicàre, *V.* **fumigàre.**

fúmido, *ag.* **1.** (*fumoso*) smoky **2.** (*fumante*) smoking, reeking with smoke.

fumigànti, *s.m.pl.* (*disinfettanti, disinfestanti*) fumigants.

fumigàre, *v.i.* (*emettere vapore*) to fume, to throw off fumes; (*fumare per ebollizione*) to steam.

fumigazióne, *s.f.* fumigation.

fumísta, *s.m.* (*operaio che ripara stufe*) stove-repairer, stove-setter.

fumívoro, *ag.* smoke-consuming.

fúmo, *s.m.* **1.** smoke: *colonna di —*, smoke column; *filo di —*, thread of smoke; *soffitto annerito dal —*, smoky ceiling; *tabacco da —*, smoking tobacco; *polvere che non fa —*, (*artigl.*) smokeless powder; *questa crema sa di —*, this custard tastes of smoke; *spende molto in —*, he spends a lot (of money) on cigarettes; *ti disturba il —?*, do you mind my smoking?; *tutte le cose di questa terra non sono che —*, all things in this world are but vanity (*o* idle dreams); *fare —*, (*di caminetto, ecc.*) to smoke ‖ *venditore di —*, fraud (*o* cheat) ‖ *lo vedo come il — negli occhi*, I just can't stand him (*o* I can't put up with him) ‖ *andare in —*, to end in smoke (*o* to come to nothing); (*di progetto*) to fall through ‖ *mandare in —*, to bring to nothing ‖ *dove c'è — c'è fuoco, prov.* where there is smoke there is fire **2.** (*vapore*) vapour, fume (*anche fig.*): *i fumi del vino*, the fumes of wine **3.** (*di pentola, minestra, ecc.*)steam.

fumògeno, *ag.* smoke-producing: *bomba fumogena*, smoke-bomb; *candela fumogena*, smoke candle; *cortina fumogena*, smoke-screen.

fumosità, *s.f.* smokiness.

fumóso, *ag.* smoky.

funàio, *s.m.* rope-maker.

funàmbola, *s.f.* rope-dancer, rope-walker, funambulist; acrobat.

funambolésco, *ag.* funambulatory; acrobatic (anche *fig.*).

funambolísmo, *s.m.* rope-dancing, rope-walking, funambulism; acrobatism (anche *fig.*).

funàmbolo, *s.m.* rope-dancer, rope-walker, funambulist; acrobat (anche *fig.*).

funàme, *s.m.* **1.** (*funi*) ropes (*pl.*), cordage **2.** (*mar.*) rigging.

funàta, *s.f.* **1.** (*colpo di fune*) lash (with a rope) **2.** (*ciò che si raccoglie su una stessa fune*) haul: *una — di ladri, di pesci*, a haul of thieves, of fish; *una — di panni* (*stesi ad asciugare*), a line of washing.

fúne, *s.f.* rope; (*cavo*) cable; (*in opera*) line: *— di acciaio*, steel-wire rope; *— d'ormeggio*, mooring rope (*o* mooring line); *— di rimorchio*, tow-line; *— di rinvio*, (*miner.*) tail rope; *— di sicurezza*, safety cable; *— di trazione*, (*mec.*) pull (*o* traction) rope (*o* hauling cable); *— intrecciata*, braided (*o* plaited) rope; *— metallica*, wire rope; *— per bucato*, washing line; *— portante*, (*mec.*) carrying (*o* running) cable; *— ritorta*, twisted rope; *anello di —*, (*mar.*) grommet; *fabbrica di funi*, rope-yard; *legare con una —*, to fasten with a rope (*o* to rope).

fúnebre, *ag.* **1.** funeral: *accompagnamento, trasporto —*, funeral; *canto —*, dirge; *carro —*, hearse; *corteo —*, funeral procession; *discorso, orazione —*, funeral oration; *impresario di pompe funebri*, undertaker (*o amer.* mortician); *marcia —*, dead (*o* funeral) march; *ufficio —*, funeral service **2.** (*cupo, lugubre*) funereal, gloomy, dismal, mournful, lugubrious: *passo —*, funereal pace; *voce —*, funereal (*o* lugubrious) voice.

funebreménte, *av.* funereally, gloomily, dismally.

funeràle, *ag. s.m.* funeral ‖ *i funerali*, the funeral ceremonies (*o* the obsequies).

funeràrio, *ag.* funerary, funeral: *urna funeraria*, funeral urn.

funèreo, *ag.* funereal, gloomy, dismal, mournful.

funestaménte, *av.* **1.** (*dannosamente*) ruinously, balefully **2.** (*luttuosamente*) fatally.

funestàre, *v.t.* **1.** to afflict, to distress, to sadden **2.** (*rovinare*) to ruin.

funèsto, *ag.* **1.** (*dannoso*) baneful, baleful **2.** (*doloroso*) woeful, sorrowful **3.** (*luttuoso*) deadly, fatal.

fúnga, *s.f.* (*muffa*) mould, mildew.

fungàia, *s.f.* **1.** mushroom-bed **2.** (*luogo coperto di muffa*) mouldy place, damp place **3.** *fig.* (*gran numero*) swarm, flood.

fúngere, *v.i.* to act: *fungevo da giudice nelle loro amichevoli discussioni*, I acted as judge in their friendly debates; *— da capo*, to act as leader.

funghíre, *v.i.* to grow mouldy: to mildew.

fungifórme, *ag.* fungiform.

fúngo, *s.m.* **1.** (*mangereccio*) mushroom; (*bot. patol.*) fungus (*pl.* fungi *o* funguses): *funghi mangerecci*, edible (*o* esculent) fungi (*o fam.* mushrooms); *funghi velenosi*, poisonous fungi (*o fam.* toadstools); *andare per funghi*, to go mushrooming ‖ *crescere come un —*, to spring up like a mushroom **2.** (*mec. edil.*) head.

fungosità, *s.f.* (*patol.*) fungosity.

fungóso, *ag.* **1.** fungous **2.** (*ammuffito*) mouldy.

funicèlla, *s.f.* cord, string.

funicolàre, *s.f.* funicular (railway), cable-railway.

funícolo, *s.m.* (*anat.*) funiculus (*pl.* funiculi).

funivía, *s.f.* telpherage, telferage, air cableway, cableway: *— a va e vieni*, to-and-fro cableway; *carrello di —*, cable car.

funzionàle, *ag.* functional.

funzionalità, *s.f.* functionality.

funzionalménte, *av.* functionally.

funzionaménto, *s.m.* working, operation, running.

funzionànte, *ag.* **1.** (*di macchina*) working; in order: *non —*, out of order **2.** (*facente funzione*) acting.

funzionàre, *v.i.* **1.** to act, to function: *funziona da mio segretario*, he acts as my secretary **2.** (*andar bene*) to work, to run, to operate; to function: « *Funziona l'ascensore?* », « *No, non funziona*, " Is the lift working (*o* running)? ", " No, it is not working (*o* it is out of order *o* it is out of working order) " ‖ *far — ql.co.*, to operate sthg. (*o* to make sthg. work).

funzionàrio, *s.m.* official, functionary, officer: *— statale*, (*in Gran Bretagna*) civil servant; (*altrove*) government official; *alti funzionari*, high officials.

funzióne, *s.f.* **1.** (*compito*) function: *la — della cultura*, the function of culture; *le funzioni del fegato*, the functions of the liver; *le funzioni di un sindaco*, the functions (*o* the duties) of a mayor **2.** (*carica, ufficio*) office: *cessare dalle funzioni*, to retire from office; *entrare in —*, to enter upon office; *esercitare le funzioni di*, to perform the duties of (*o* to function as *o* to officiate as *o* to act as): *il segretario facente —*, the officiating secretary; *era là in — di arbitro*, he was there acting as umpire **3.** (*eccl.*) Church ceremony; (*protestante*) divine service: *assistere alle funzioni*, to attend Church services **4.** *in —*, (*mec.*) working.

fuochísta, *s.m.* stoker; fireman (*pl.* firemen).

fuòco, *s.m.* **1.** fire (anche *fig.*); *a prova di —*, fire-proof; *accendere il —*, to light the fire; *appiccare, dare, — a ql.co.*, to set fire to sthg. (*o* to set sthg. on fire);

bollare a —, to brand (anche *fig.*); *fare un* —, to make a fire; *mettere una pentola sul* —, to put a pot on the fire; *prendere* —, to catch (*o* to take) fire; *fig.* to flare up: *prende* — *per la minima cosa*, he flies into a passion (*o* flares up) at the least thing; *soffiare nel* —, to kindle the fire; *fig.* to kindle strife; *spegnere il* —, to put out the fire ‖ — *di Sant'Antonio*, (*patol.*) St. Anthony's fire (*o* erysipelas) ‖ — *fatuo*, ignis fatuus; (*fam.*) will-o'-the-wisp (*o* jack-o'-lantern) ‖ *mi dia del* —, *per piacere*, may I have a light, please? ‖ *per lei andrei nel* —, *fig.* I'd go through fire and water for her ‖ *far* — *e fiamme*, *fig.* to do one's utmost (*o* to leave no stone unturned) ‖ *farsi di* —, to blush ‖ *mettere a ferro e a* —, to put sthg. to fire and sword ‖ *mettere la mano sul* —, *fig.* to stake one's reputation ‖ *mettere troppa carne al* —, *fig.* to have too many irons in the fire **2.** *fig.* (*ardore, passione*) fire, ardour, passion: *il* — *delle passioni*, the ardour of passions; — *di gioventù*, youthful ardour; *occhi di* —, flashing eyes (*o* eyes full of fire); *un'orazione priva di* —, an oration lacking fire ‖ *un* — *di paglia*, a flash in the pan (*o* a short-lived passion) **3.** (*incendio*) fire: *al* —!, *al* —!, fire!, fire!; *vigile del* —, fireman; *vigili del* —, (*il corpo*) fire-brigade **4.** (*focolare*) fire; hearth; (*caminetto*) fireside: *il cantuccio del* —, the chimney corner; *stava seduta presso il* —, she was sitting by the fire **5.** (*mil.*) fire: — *di fila*, running fire (anche *fig.*); — *di fucileria*, rifle fire; — *di sbarramento*, barrage; — *incrociato*, cross fire; *arma da* —, fire arm; *battesimo del* —, baptism of fire; *aprite il* —!, open fire!; *cessate il* —!, cease fire!; *essere fra due fuochi*, to be between two fires (anche *fig.*); *fare* — *contro qlcu.*, *ql.co.*, to fire at s.o., at sthg.; *stare sotto il* — *del nemico*, to be under the enemy's fire ‖ — *greco*, (*st.*) Greek fire **6.** *fuochi d'artifizio*, fireworks; — *del Bengala*, Bengal fire (*o* light) **7.** *pl.* (*mar.*) (*fanali*) lights; (*delle caldaie*) fires: *attivare i fuochi*, to make all steam; *lasciar spegnere i fuochi*, to let the fires go out ‖ — *di Sant'Elmo*, St. Elmo's fire (*o* corposant) **8.** (*fis. mat. foto.*) focus (*pl.* focuses): — *fisso*, fixed focus (*abbr.* f.f.); *dispositivo di messa a* —, (*foto.*) focusing device; *messa a* —, (*foto.*) focalization; *mettere a* —, (*foto.*) to focus (*o* to focalize *o* to bring into focus).

fuòri, *av.* **1.** out; (*all'aperto*) **outdoors;** (*all'esterno*) **outside:** *da* —, from outside; *aspetta lì* —!, wait outside!; *è restato* —, he has been left outside; *era in casa o* —?, was he in (*o* at home) or out?; *questa mela è bella di* —, *ma brutta di dentro*, this apple is nice outside, but rotten inside; *tu che vieni di* —, *puoi dirci se piove*, as you have come from outside, you can tell us whether it is raining; *andare* —, to go out; *dar di* —, (*traboccare*) to overflow; *essere* —, to be out; *essere in* —, (*sporgere*) to stick out (*o* to jut out *o* to project); *lasciar* —, to leave out; (*escludere*) to exclude; (*omettere*) to omit; *mandar* — *qlcu.*, to turn s.o. out of doors (*o* to send s.o. away *o* to throw s.o. out); (*licenziare*) to sack s.o.; *metter* —, (*mettere in vetrina*) to display; *metter* — *denari*, to lay out money (*o* to lay money out); *pranzare* —, to dine out; *sporgersi in* —, to lean out; *tagliar* —, (*mil.*) to cut off; *venire* —, to come out; (*di libro*) to come out (*o* to appear *o* to be published); *venir* — *a dire*, to say abruptly; *venir* — *con una battuta divertente*, to come out with a funny joke ‖ —!, out of here! (*o* get out!); (*teat.*) encore! ‖ — *la verità*!, out with the truth! ‖ *o dentro o* —!, in or out!; *fig.* make up your mind! ‖ *far* —, (*uccidere*) to kill (*o sl.* to bump off *o* to do in); (*spor.*) (*eliminare*) to eliminate (*o* to knock out); (*distruggere*) to destroy **2.** (*all'estero*) **abroad:** *da* —, from abroad; *in Italia e* —, in Italy and abroad ‖ *s.m.* **outside:** *dal di* —, from the outside.

fuòri (di), *prep.* **1. out of;** **outside:** — *d'Italia*, outside Italy; — *di quella stanza*, outside that room; *è* — *Milano*, he is out of (*o* away from) Milan; *lo gettò* — *dalla finestra*, he threw it out of the window;

la sua casa è — *Milano*, his house is outside Milan ‖ — *classe*, exceptional: *è un* — *classe*, he is an outstanding (*o* exceptional) case; *è una automobile* — *classe*, it is a car all on its own; — *commercio*, not for sale; (*di libro*) for private circulation only; — *corso*, (*di moneta*) no longer current; — *fase*, (*elett.*) out-of-phase; — *giuoco*, (*spor.*) off-side; — *luogo*, out of place (*o* uncalled for); — *mano*, out-of-the-way (*o* remote *o* secluded); — *misura*, outsize; (*eccessivo*) excessive; (*eccessivamente*) excessively; — *moda*, out of fashion (*o* old-fashioned); — *pasto*, between meals; — *pericolo*, out of danger; — *porta*, outside the town: *una chiesa* — *porta*, a church without the gates; — *portata*, out of range (*o* out of reach); — *posto*, out of (one's) place (*o* in the wrong place); *fig.* uncalled for (*o* out of place); — *quadro*, (*cine.*) out-of-frame; — *questione*, beyond all dispute; (*impossibile*) out of the question; — *serie*, (*di automobile*) special body; — *servizio*, (*di persona*) off duty; (*di cosa*) out of commission; — *squadra*, out of level (*o* out of square *o* askew *o fam.* skew-whiff); — *stagione*, out of season; — *strada*, out of one's way; *fig.* off the track (*o* mistaken): *andare* — *strada*, (*di veicolo*) to go off (*o* to leave) the road; — *tempo*, out of time; (*intempestivo*) untimely (*o* ill-timed); — *testo*, *tavola*— *testo*, plate; — *tiro*, out of range (*o* beyond gunshot); — *uso*, out of use (*o* out of order *o* unserviceable); (*di parola*, *espressione*) obsolete (*o* out-of-date); — *vista*, out of sight ‖ — *di qui*!, — *dai piedi*!, out of here! (*o* get out! *o fam.* beat it!) ‖ *un pesce fuor d'acqua*, a fish out of water ‖ *questo è* — *dubbio*, there is no doubt about it ‖ *essere* — *di sè dalla gioia*, *dalla paura*, to be beside oneself with joy, with fear ‖ *esserne* —, (*essere estraneo*) to be out of it ‖ *uscir* — *dal seminato*, to go off the subject ‖ *venirne* —, (*da situazione difficile*, *ecc.*) to get out of it **2.** (*eccetto*) **except**, **but; apart from:** — *di questo non ottenne altro*, apart from this he obtained nothing; *non lo sa nessuno* — *di te*, nobody knows but you; *non udii nulla* — *di ciò che ti ho detto or ora*, I heard nothing but what I have just told you.

fuorché, *V.* **fuori (di) 2.**.

fuoribórdo, *s.m.* (*mar.*) outboard motor.

fuorilègge, *s.m.* outlaw; robber, bandit.

fuoruscìto, *s.m.* **1.** (political) exile; (*profugo*) refugee **2.** (*bandito*) outlaw.

fuorviàre, *v.t.* to lead astray (anche *fig.*); to mislead: *il ragazzo fu fuorviato da cattivi compagni*, the boy was led astray by bad companions ‖ *v.i.* (*uscire di carreggiata*, *deviare*, *sviare*) to go astray; to stray, to wander: — *dalla strada giusta*, to stray from the right path ‖ **fuorviàrsi,** *v.r.* (*corrompersi*, *guastarsi*) to get spoilt.

furbacchióna, *s.f.* (*fam.*) sly puss.

furbacchióne, *ag.* cunning ‖ *s.m.* cunning fellow; (*fam.*) sly dog, slyboots.

furbacchiòtto, *ag.* cunning; roguish.

furbaménte, *av.* cunningly.

furberìa, *s.f.* cunning, craft; (*sagacia*) shrewdness.

furbescaménte, *av.* cunningly, archly.

furbésco, *ag.* cunning, arch: *sorriso* —, arch smile ‖ *lingua furbesca*, thieves' lingo (*o* jargon of the underworld).

furbìzia, *s.f.* cunning, craft; (*sagacità*) shrewdness.

fúrbo, *ag.* cunning, artful, crafty; (*sagace*) shrewd ‖ *s.m.* cunning fellow, artful fellow ‖ *un* — *di tre cotte*, *un* — *matricolato*, an arrant rogue ‖ *fare il* —, to try to be clever.

furènte, *ag.* furious; mad: — *d'ira*, mad with rage; *era* — *per aver perso la valigia*, he was mad at (*o* about) losing his suitcase.

furerìa, *s.f.* (*mil.*) orderly room.

furétto, *s.m.* (*zool.*) ferret: *andare a caccia con il* —, (*st.*) to go ferreting.

furfantàggine, *V.* **furfanterìa.**

furfantàglia, *s.f.* pack of scoundrels; (*gentaglia*) rabble.

furfànte, s.m. rascal, scoundrel, knave, scamp; rogue: *quel — di mio figlio,* (*scherz.*) my scamp of a son; *è un — matricolato,* he is an out-and-out scoundrel.

furfantèllo, s.m. (*scherz.*) little rogue, urchin.

furfanteggiàre, v.i. to act as a knave.

furfanteria, s.f. 1. (*qualità di furfante*) rascality; roguery 2. (*azione, detto da furfante*) piece of knavery, piece of roguery; knavish trick, rascally trick.

furfantésco, ag. rascally, scoundrelly, knavish; roguish.

furgoncíno, s.m. small van, light van; (*a tre ruote*) three-wheeled van: — *a pedali,* delivery tricycle.

furgóne, s.m. van, delivery van, wagon; (*autocarro*) lorry; (*amer.*) truck: — *per traslochi,* furniture-van (o pantechnicon); — *postale,* mail-van.

fúria, s.f. 1. (*furore*) fury, rage, anger: *andare su tutte le furie,* to fly into a fury (o into a passion); *essere su tutte le furie,* to be in a fury (o to be in a towering rage) ‖ *a — di popolo,* by mob violence 2. (*grande fretta*) hurry, haste: *avere —,* to be in a hurry; *fare — a qualcuno,* to hurry s.o. ‖ *di —,* hurriedly ‖ *in fretta e —,* in a hurry: *si cambiò d'abito in fretta e — e si precipitò fuori di casa,* he changed in a great hurry and rushed out 3. (*veemenza*) fury: *la — degli elementi,* the fury of the elements; *nella — della battaglia,* in the fury of the battle 4. (*persona collerica*) fury; (*donna brutta*) fury, hag: *quella vecchia è una vera —,* that old woman is a real fury 5. *a — di,* by dint of: *a — di lavoro, studio,* by dint of work, study.

furiàta, s.f. gust; squall.

furiàre, V. **infuriàre.**

furibóndo, ag. 1. furious 2. (*violento*) violent, wild.

Fúrie, no.pr.f.pl. (*mit.*) Furies: *le tre —,* the three Furies; *Oreste era perseguitato dalle —,* Orestes was haunted by the Furies.

furière, s.m. 1. (*mil.*) quartermaster sergeant 2. (*mar.*) first-class writer.

furièro, V. **forière.**

furiosaménte, av. 1. furiously 2. (*violentemente*) violently, wildly.

furióso, ag. 1. (*adirato, furente*) furious, very angry: *ero — per ciò che mi avevi detto,* I was furious (o mad) at what you had said to me; *diventare —,* to become furious (o to fly into a fury); *rendere — qlcu.,* to enrage s.o. 2. (*violento, impetuoso*) violent, wild: *ira furiosa,* wild anger; *una lite furiosa,* a furious (o violent) quarrel; *vento —,* furious wind 3. (*pazzo*) mad.

furóre, s.m. 1. fury; (*rabbia*) rage: *col — della disperazione,* with the fury of despair; *fu preso da —,* he flew into a rage (o a passion) ‖ *a — di popolo,* by mob violence; (*col consenso generale*) by public acclaim: *eletto a — di popolo,* elected by public acclaim 2. (*entusiasmo*) enthusiasm: *cominciò a lavorare con sacro —,* he started to work in a burst of enthusiasm ‖ *— poetico,* poetic frenzy 3. (*veemenza*) fury: *il — delle onde,* the fury of waves 4. (*desiderio violento*) violent desire 5. (*pazzia*) madness 6. (*gran successo*) *far —,* to be (all) the rage; (*di lavoro teatrale*) to be (quite) a hit.

furoreggiàre, v.i. to be (all) the rage; (*di lavoro teatrale*) to be (quite) a hit: *la nuova moda furoreggia,* the new fashion is all the rage.

furterèllo, s.m. pilferage, pilfering, petty theft.

furtivaménte, av. stealthily, furtively: *entrare — in una stanza,* to steal into a room; *uscire —,* to steal out.

furtívo, ag. 1. stealthy, furtive: *occhiate furtive,* furtive glances; *passi furtivi,* stealthy steps 2. (*dir.*) (*di provenienza furtiva*) furtive: *oggetti furtivi,* furtive objects.

fúrto, s.m. 1. theft; (*dir.*) larceny: — *con scasso,* (*consumato di notte*) burglary; — *qualificato,* (*dir.* aggravated larceny; *commettere un —,* to steal ‖ — *letterario,* plagiarism (o plagiary) 2. *di —,* furtively.

fúsa, s.f.pl.: *fare le —,* to purr.

fusàggine, s.f. (*bot.*) spindle-tree.

fusàio, s.m. 1. (*chi fa fusi*) spindle-maker 2. (*chi vende fusi*) spindle-seller.

fusàta, s.f. spindleful.

fusàto, ag. splindle-shaped, fusiform; (*affusolato*) tapering.

fuscèllo, s.m. 1. twig; (*pagliuzza*) straw 2. *fig.* (*persona assai esile*) thin person: *mia sorella è un —,* my sister is as thin as a rake (o a lath).

fusciàcca, s.f. broad sash.

fusellàto, V. **fusàto.**

fusèllo, s.m. 1. (*mec.*) spindle, journal: — *dell'assale,* (*aut.*) axletree spindle; — *di ruota,* (*aut.*) stub axle 2. (*fuso per merletti*) bobbin.

fusíbile, ag. fusible: *lega —,* (*metal.*) fusible alloy; *metallo —,* (*metal.*) fusible metal ‖ s.m. (*elett.*) fuse.

fusièra, s.f. spindle-holder.

fusifórme, ag. spindle-shaped, fusiform; (*affusolato*) tapering.

fusióne, s.f. 1. (*di metalli*) fusion, founding, melting, smelting; (*di materiale non metallico*) melting; (*in una forma*) casting: — *in acciaio,* steel casting; *punto di —,* melting point 2. *fig.* fusion, melting, blending: — *di colori,* blending of colours; *la — di due partiti,* the fusion of two parties; *la — di molte razze,* the fusion of many races 3. (*unione di società commerciali*) merging, amalgamation.

fúso[1], ag. (*di metallo*) fused, melted, smelted; (*di materiale non metallico*) melted.

fúso[2], s.m. 1. (*ind. tessile mec.*) spindle: — *di ritorcitura,* doubling spindle ‖ *dritto come un —,* as straight as a pole 2. — *orario,* (*geog.*) time zone 3. (*geom.*) lune 4. (*di àncora*) shank 5. (*di orologio*) fusee.

fusolièra, s.f. (*aer.*) fuselage.

fusóre, s.m. smelter, founder; caster.

fusòrio, ag. (*metal.*) melting; casting: *forno —,* blast-furnace.

fustàgno, s.m. fustian.

fustèlla, s.f. hollow punch.

fustigàre, v.t. to flog, to lash.

fustigazióne, s.f. flogging, lashing.

fústo, s.m. 1. (*bot.*) (*gambo*) stalk, stem; (*tronco*) trunk: — *sotterraneo,* underground stem; *piante d'alto —,* forest trees ‖ — *di una chiave,* shank of a key 2. (*tronco umano*) trunk; (*ossatura*) frame 3. (*gergo*) (*giovane prestante*) muscle-man (*pl.* muscle-men); (*amer.*) beefcake 4. (*arch.*) shaft 5. (*di lamiera, per benzina, nafta, olio*) drum; (*di legno, per vino, liquori*) barrel, keg, cask 6. (*intelaiatura*) frame.

fútile, ag. trifling, frivolous; (*inutile*) futile, vain, useless: *cose futili,* trifles.

futilità, s.f. trifling, frivolity, frivolousness; futility: *queste sono tutte —,* these are all trifles.

futilménte, av. frivolously; (*inutilmente*) futilely, vainly, uselessly.

futuraménte, av. in (the) future.

futurísmo, s.m. (*art.*) futurism.

futurísta, ag.s.c. (*art.*) futurist.

futúro, ag. future; coming, next: *per la futura estate,* for the coming (o for next) summer; *il suo — padrone,* his future master; *penso agli anni futuri,* I am thinking of the years to come ‖ s.m. 1. future: *in —,* in (the) future; *per il —,* for the future; *provvederò al tuo —,* I shall provide for your future 2. (*gram.*) future (tense): — *anteriore,* future perfect.

G

g, *s.f.m.* (*settima lettera dell'alfabeto italiano*) g (*pl.* gs, g's) ‖ — *come Genova,* (*tel.*) g for George.

gabardína, *s.f.* **1.** (*tessuto*) gabardine **2.** (*soprabito*) overcoat; (*spec. mil.*) gabardine.

gabbacristiàni, gabbamóndo, *s.m.* cheat, swindler, deceiver.

gabbàna, *V.* **gabbàno.**

gabbanèlla, *s.f.* **1.** doctor's gown, doctor's overall **2.** (*veste da camera*) dressing-gown, loose gown.

gabbàno, *s.m.* **1.** loose overcoat **2.** (*veste da camera*) dressing-gown, loose gown.

gabbàre, *v.t.* to cheat, to swindle, to deceive, to impose upon (s.o.), to take in (s.o.) ‖ *passata la festa, gabbato lo santo, prov.* once on shore, we pray no more (o the river is passed and God forgotten).

gabbasànti, *s.m.* hypocrite.

gàbbia, *s.f.* **1.** cage; (*per imballaggio*) crate: — *di leoni, scimmie,* cage of lions, monkeys; — *per polli,* hen-coop; — *per uccelli,* bird-cage; *uccello di* —, cage-bird; *simile a* —, cagelike **2.** (*per accusati*) dock **3.** (*prigione*) prison, jail, gaol: *mettere in* —, to put in jail **4.** (*museruola per buoi*) muzzle **5.** — *toracica,* (*anat.*) chest **6.** (*mec.*) cage, retainer; (*elett.*) cage: — *dell'ascensore,* lift-cage; — *di scoiattolo,* squirrel cage **7.** (*metal.*) stand: — *a pignoni,* spindle housing **8.** (*miner.*) skip, skip hoist, skip elevator **9.** (*mar.*) top; crow's-nest: — *bassa,* lower main topsail; — *volante,* upper main topsail.

gabbiàio, *s.m.* **1.** (*chi fabbrica gabbie*) cage -maker **2.** (*chi vende gabbie*) cage-merchant.

gabbiàno, *s.m.* (*ornit.*) (sea-)gull, sea-mew.

gabbiàta, *s.f.* cageful (of birds).

gabbière, *s.m.* (*mar.*) **1.** topman (*pl.* topmen) **2.** (*marinaio di vedetta*) look-out (man).

gabbiétta, *s.f.* small cage.

gabbionàta, *s.f.* gabionade.

gabbióne, *s.m.* **1.** large cage ‖ **2.** (*per fortificazioni, argini*) gabion **3.** (*per accusati*) dock.

gàbbo, *s.m.* mockery, scoffing: *pigliare a* — *qlcu.,* to scoff at s.o.; *prendere a* — *ql.co.,* (*prenderla alla leggera*) to make light of sthg.

gàbbro, *s.m.* (*min.*) gabbro.

gabèlla, *s.f.* (excise-)duty; tax, toll.

gabellàre, *v.t.* **1.** to tax, to excise **2.** (*far credere, far passare*): — *per...,* to pass off as... (o to make appear as... o to make pass for...): *lo gabellarono per esperto,* they passed him off as (o made him pass for) an expert.

gabellière, gabellòtto, *s.m.* excise-man (*pl.* excise -men).

gabinétto, *s.m.* **1.** closet, private room; (*studio*) study: — *di consultazione,* consulting room; — *di fisica,* physical laboratory; — *di storia naturale,* private natural history collection **2.** (*pol.*) cabinet, government: — *di un ministro,* minister's departmental staff; *affari di* —, state affairs; *capo di* —, principal private secretary; *consiglio di* —, cabinet council; *corriere di* —, diplomatic courier; *crisi di* —, cabinet crisis **3.** (*luogo di decenza*) water-closet (*abbr.* w.c.), lavatory, toilet: — *da bagno,* bath-room.

Gabrièle, *no.pr.m.* Gabriel ‖ *dim.* Gabe, Gabby.

Gabrièlla, *no.pr.f.* Gabriella, Gabriela, Gabrielle.

gadolínio, *s.m.* (*chim.*) gadolinium.

gadoliníte, *s.m.* (*min.*) gadolinite.

gaèlico, *ag.* Gaelic ‖ *s.m.* **1.** (*abitante*) Gael **2.** (*lingua*) Gaelic.

gaettóne, *s.m.* (*mar.*) dogwatch.

gàffa, *s.f.* (*mar.*) boat-hook.

gaffe, *s.f.* (*topica*) blunder, "gaffe": *fare una* —, to make a blunder (o to put one's foot in it o *sl.* to drop a brick).

gagà, *s.m.* dandy, fop, spark, beau (*pl.* beaux).

gaggía, *s.f.* (*bot.*) acacia: *fiore di* —, acacia flower.

gagliàrda, *s.f.* (*musica, danza*) galliard.

gagliardaménte, *av.* vigorously, strongly, bravely.

gagliardétto, *s.m.* pennant, pennon.

gagliardézza, gagliardía, *s.f.* vigour, strength.

gagliàrdo, *ag.* vigorous, strong; hearty, hardy; brave: *un uomo* —, a vigorous man; *un vento* —, a strong wind ‖ *alla gagliarda,* vigorously (o bravely).

gaglioffàggine, *V.* **gaglioffería.**

gaglioffaménte, *av.* **1.** (*da furfante*) rascally **2.** (*da sciocco*) foolishly, stupidly.

gaglioffería, *s.f.* **1.** (*furfanteria*) rascality **2.** (*scioccaggine*) foolishness, stupidity.

gaglioffo, *ag.* **1.** rascally, knavish **2.** stupid, dull ‖ *s.m.* **1.** (*furfante*) rascal, scoundrel **2.** (*sciocco*) dunce, blockhead.

gagnolaménto, *s.m.* (*rar.*) howling, yelping, whining.

gagnolàre, *v.i.* (*rar.*) to howl, to yelp, to whine.

gaiaménte, *av.* **1.** gaily; merrily **2.** (*di colore*) brightly.

gaiétto, *ag.* spotted.

gaiézza, *s.f.* **1.** (*allegria*) gaiety, cheerfulness, mirth **2.** (*di colore*) liveliness, brightness.

Gàio[1], *no.pr.m.* (*st.*) Gaius.

gàio[2], *ag.* **1.** gay, merry, cheerful: *canzone gaia,* merry song; *voce gaia,* gay voice **2.** (*di colore*) lively, bright: *colore* —, bright (o lively) colour.

gàla, *s.f.* **1.** (*trina*) frill **2.** (*festa*) gala: *abito di* —, gala dress; *serata di* —, gala evening (o gala performance) ‖ *in gran* —, in one's best clothes **3.** (*mar.*) (*pavese*) flags (*pl.*).

galalíte, *s.f.* (*chim. ind.*) galalith.

galànte, *ag.* **1.** gallant; courteous to women **2.** (*grazioso*) pretty, graceful **3.** (*amoroso*) love (*attributivo*): *letterina* —, love-letter (o billet-doux) ‖ *s.m.* gallant, ladies' man; (*corteggiatore*) suitor, lover: *fare il* —, to act (o to play) the gallant (o to flirt o to court).

galanteggiàre, *v.i.* to gallant, to play the gallant) to flirt; to pay court (to s.o.).

galanteménte, *av.* gallantly.

galantería, *s.f.* **1.** gallantry, courteousness to women **2.** (*cosa graziosa*) nice thing, pretty thing **3.** (*complimento*) compliment: *dire delle galanterie a una signora,* to pay compliments to a lady **4.** (*cibo prelibato*) dainty, delicacy, titbit.

galantína, *s.f.* (*cuc.*) galantine.

galantomísmo, *s.m.* honesty, uprightness, integrity.

galantuòmo, *s.m.* honest man, upright man, man of honour; *agire da* —, to deal honourably (o fairly) ‖ *ehi,* —, *ascoltate!,* hullo there, listen!.

galàssia, *s.f.* (*astr.*) galaxy ‖ *la Galassia,* (*via Lattea*) Galaxy (o the Milky Way).

Galatèa, *no.pr.f.* (*mit.*) Galatea.

galatèo, *s.m.* **1.** code of politeness, book of manners **2.** (*buone maniere, creanze*) (good) manners (*pl.*), (good) breeding: *mancava di qualsiasi* —, he had no manners whatsoever (o he had no idea of manners).

Gàlati, *s.m.pl.* (*st.*) Galatians.

galattagògo, *ag.* (*farm.*) galactagogue.

galàttico, *ag.* (*astr.*) galactic.
galattíte, *s.f.* (*min.*) galactite.
galattòfago, *s.m.* galactophagist.
galattòforo, *ag.* (*anat.*) galactophorous.
galattògeno, *ag.* (*farm.*) galactagogue.
galattòmetro, *s.m.* galactometer.
galattopoiètico, *ag.* (*med.*) galactopoetic, galacto-poietic.
galattòsio, *s.m.* (*chim.*) galactose.
galatturía, *s.f.* (*med.*) galacturia.
galavèrna, *s.f.* **1.** (*brina*) rime **2.** (*ghiacciuolo*) icicle.
Galàzia, *no.pr.f.* (*geog. st.*) Galatia.
Gàlba, *no.pr.m.* (*st.*) Galba.
galbàno, *s.m.* **1.** (*bot.*) ferula **2.** (*resina*) galbanum.
gàlea[1], *s.f.* (*elmo*) helmet.
galèa[2], *s.f.* (*st. mar.*) galley.
galeàto, *ag.* galeated, galeate.
galeàzza, *s.f.* (*st. mar.*) galliass, galleass.
galèna, *s.f.* **1.** (*min.*) galena **2.** (*rad.*) galena crystal: *radio a* —, crystal set.
galènico, *ag.* Galenic(al): *preparati galenici,* Galenicals.
galenísmo, *s.m.* (*st. med.*) Galenism.
Galèno, *no.pr.m.* (*st. med.*) Galen.
galeóne, *s.m.* (*st. mar.*) galleon.
galeopitèco, *s.m.* (*zool.*) galeopithecus.
galeòtta, *s.f.* (*st. mar.*) galliot.
galeòtto[1], *s.m.***1.**(*rematore di galea*) galley slave **2.**(*condannato ai lavori forzati*) convict **3.** (*scherz.*) (*furbacchione*) cunning fellow, sly-boots.
galeòtto[2], *s.m.* (*mezzano in amore*) pander, pimp, procurer, go-between.
galèra, *s.f.* **1.** (*st. mar.*) galley **2.** (*prigione*) prison, jail, gaol: *andare, mandare in* —, to go, to send to prison (*o to jail*) || *avanzo, pezzo di* —, jail-bird (*o gaol-bird*) **3.** (*lavori forzati*) hard labour: *condannare alla* —, to sentence to hard labour || *questa è una* —, *fig.* this is a wretched life || *fare una vita da* —, *fig.* to drudge and slave.
galèro, *s.m.* (*eccl.*) galerum, cardinal's hat.
galestríno, *ag.* (*geol.*) marlaceous, marly.
galèstro, *s.m.* (*geol.*) marl.
galestróso, *ag.* (*geol.*) marly.
Galilèa, *no.pr.f.* (*geog. st.*) Galilee.
galilèo, *ag.s.m.* Galilean || *il Galileo,* (*Cristo*) the Galilean.
Galízia, *no.pr.f.* (*geog.*) Galicia.
galiziàno, *ag.s.m.* Galician.
gàlla, *s.f.* (*bot.*) gall: *noce di* —, gall-nut (*o oak-gall*).
gàlla, a, *l. av.* afloat, floating, on the surface: *stare a* —, to float; *tenere a* — *qlcu., ql.co.,* to keep s.o., sthg. afloat; *tenersi a* —, to keep afloat (*o to keep one's head above water*) (*anche fig.*) || *rimettere qlcu. a* —, *fig.* to set s.o. up in funds (*o to restore s.o.'s fortunes*) || *venire a* —, to surface (*o to emerge o to come to the surface*); *fig.* to come to light (*o to be disclosed*): *prima o poi la faccenda verrà a* —, sooner or later the matter will come to light.
gallàre[1], *v.i.* (*arc.*) to float, to keep afloat.
gallàre[2], *v.t.* to fecundate (eggs).
gallàto, *ag.* (*di uovo*) fecundated.
galleggiabilità, *s.f.* (*mar.*) buoyancy.
galleggiaménto, *s.m.* floating; flo(a)tage, flo(a)tation: *centro di* —, (*mar.*) centre of buoyancy; *linea di* —, (*mar.*) water-line; *linea di* — *a pieno carico normale,* (*mar.*) loadwater-line; *lunghezza al* —, (*mar.*) length on the water(-line); *spinta di* —, (*mar.*) buoyancy.
galleggiànte, *ag.* floating; afloat (*predicativo*): *foglie galleggianti sull'acqua,* leaves floating on the water || *s.m.* **1.** float: — *divergente,* (*mar. mil.*) oropesa float; *complesso di galleggianti di ammaraggio,* (*di idrovolanti*) landing-gear; *regolatore a* —, (*ind.*) ball-cock **2.** (*boa*) buoy.
galleggiàre, *v.i.* to float; to keep afloat: *un cadavere che galleggia sull'acqua,* a corpse that floats to the surface.

gallègo, *ag.s.m.* Galician.
gallería, *s.f.* **1.** (*di ferrovia, strada*) tunnel; (*passaggio sotterraneo*) subway; — *di metropolitana,* tube-tunnel; *sbocco di* —, tunnel opening **2.** (*miner.*) gallery, tunnel: — *d'accesso,* adit (*o side-drift*); — *di livello,* drift; — *di passaggio,* — *principale,* gangway; — *di ventilazione,* windway; — *in pendenza,* slant; *scavare una* —, to tunnel **3.** (*strada coperta, fiancheggiata da negozi*) arcade **4.** (*di esposizione*) gallery: — *d'arte,* art gallery; — *di quadri,* picture-gallery **5.** (*in un teatro*) gallery; (*in un cinematografo*) balcony: *prima* —, dress-circle; *seconda* —, uppercircle (*o balcony*); (*loggione*) gallery **6.** (*aer.*) tunnel: — *a circuito aperto,* non-return-flow wind tunnel; — *a circuito chiuso,* return-flow wind tunnel; — *a vena aperta,* open-jet wind tunnel; — *del vento, aerodinamica,* wind tunnel **7.** (*mil.*) gallery.
Gàlles, *no.pr.m.* (*geog.*) Wales || *il Principe di* —, the Prince of Wales.
gallése, *ag.* Welsh || *i gallesi,* the Welsh (people) || *s.m.* **1.** (*abitante*) Welshman (*pl.* Welshmen) **2.** (*lingua*) (the) Welsh (language) || *s.f.* Welshwoman (*pl.* Welshwomen).
gallétta, *s.f.* (*per soldati*) biscuit; (*per marinai*) ship's-biscuit, sea-biscuit.
gallétto, *s.m.* **1.** young cock, cockerel || *fare il* —, *fig.* to be (*o to become*) pert (*o saucy*) (*o to grow arrogant*) **2.** (*mec.*) wing nut.
Gàllia, *no.pr.f.* (*geog. st.*) Gaul.
gallicanísmo, *s.m.* (*st. relig.*) Gallicanism.
gallicàno, *ag.s.m.* (*st. relig.*) Gallican.
gallicínio, *s.m.* crow, crowing.
gallicísmo, *s.m.* gallicism.
gallicizzàre, *v.t.i.* to gallicize.
gàllico[1], *ag.* Gallic || *morbo* —, (*patol.*) French pox.
gàllico[2], *ag.* (*chim.*) gallic: *acido* —, gallic acid.
gallína, *s.f.* hen; (*la carne*) fowl, chicken: — *faraona,* Guinea hen (*o Guinea fowl*); *il coccodè di una* —, the cackle of a hen || *latte di* —, egg-flip; *fig.* exquisite food || *zampa di* —, *fig.* scrawl (*o illegible handwriting*) || *avere il cervello di una* —, to be chicken-brained || *avere il coraggio di una* —, to be chicken-hearted (*o hen-hearted*) || *chi di* — *nasce convien che razzoli,* *prov.* what's bred in the bone comes out in the flesh || *meglio un uovo oggi che una* — *domani,* *prov.* a bird in the hand is worth two in the bush.
gallinàccio, *s.m.* **1.** (*dial.*) turkey **2.** (*fungo*) chanterelle.
gallinàceo, *ag.* gallinaceous, gallinacean || *s.m.* gallinacean.
gallinàio, *s.m.* (*rar.*) **1.** (*pollaio*) poultry-house; hen-house **2.** (*pollivendolo*) poultry seller.
gallinèlla, *s.f.* **1.** (*gallina acquatica*) gallinule; moor-hen, water-hen **2.** (*pollastra*) young hen, pullet || *le Gallinelle,* (*astr.*) the Pleiades.
gàllio, *s.m.* (*chim.*) gallium.
gàllo[1], *s.m.* **1.** cock; rooster: — *cedrone,* wood-grouse (*o capercailzie*); — *da combattimento,* game-cock (*o fighting-cock*); — *d'India,* turkey (*o turkey-cock*); *il canto del* —, the crowing of the cock (*o cock-crow*): *ci alzammo molto prima del canto del* —, we got up long before cock-crow (*o cock-crowing*); *combattimento di galli,* cock-fight; *cresta di* —, cockscomb || *non stanno bene due galli in un pollaio,* too many cooks spoil the broth || *essere il* — *della Checca,* to be the cock of the walk (*o a ladykiller*); *fare il* —, to strut (*o to swagger o to be arrogant*) **2.** (*banderuola*) weather-cock **3.** *peso* —, (*boxe*) bantam-weight.
gàllo[2], *ag.* (*st.*) Gallic || *i galli,* the Gauls || *s.m.* (*st.*) Gaul.
gallòccia, *s.f.* (*mar.*) cleat: — *d'albero,* mast cleat.
gallofobìa, *s.f.* Gallophobia.
gallomanìa, *s.f.* Gallomania.
gallonàre, *v.t.* to trim with braid, to braid.

gallonàto, *ag.* gallooned: *portiere* —, liveried porter.

gallóne[1], *s.m.* **1.** braid; galloon **2.** (*mil.*) chevron, stripe: *galloni di sergente*, sergeant's chevrons; *meritare, perdere i galloni*, to get, to lose one's stripes || *bagnare i galloni*, *fig.* to toast one's promotion.

gallóne[2], *s.m.* gallon (*misura di capacità* = l. 4,546 *in Gran Bretagna*; = l. 3,785 *negli Stati Uniti*).

gallonèa, *s.f.* (*bot.*) oak of Bashan.

gallòria, *s.f.* noisy merry-making.

galloriàre, *v.i.* to make merry.

galloromàno, *ag.s.m.* (*st.*) Gallo-Roman.

gallòzza, gallòzzola, *s.f.* **1.** (*bot.*) gall **2.** (*vescichetta*) blister **3.** (*bolla*) bubble.

galoppànte, *ag.* galloping || *tisi* —, (*patol.*) galloping consumption.

galoppàre, *v.i.* to gallop (*anche fig.*): — *a gran velocità*, to gallop off at full speed.

galoppàta, *s.f.* gallop, galloping (*anche fig.*): *fare una* —, to take (*o* to have) a gallop.

galoppatóio, *s.m.* riding-track.

galoppatóre, *s.m.*, **galoppatríce**, *s.f.* galloper.

galoppíno, *s.m.* **1.** (*fattorino*) errand-boy, message-boy, messenger: — *elettorale*, canvasser **2.** (*tirapiedi*) drudge: *fare il* —, to drudge **3.** (*mec.*) pulley.

galòppo, *s.m.* **1.** gallop: *al, di* —, at a gallop; *fig.* at full speed: *fare ql.co. al* —, to gallop (*o* to rattle) through sthg.; *mettersi al* —, to break into a gallop; *partire al* —, to gallop away || *gran* —, full gallop: *andare al gran* —, to ride full gallop; *spingere un cavallo al gran* —, to gallop a horse || *piccolo* —, easy gallop (*o* canter): *andare al piccolo* —, to canter along; *fare un piccolo* —, to have a canter **2.** (*danza*) galop.

galòscia, *s.f.* golosh, galosh, overshoe.

galvanicaménte, *av.* (*elett.*) galvanically.

galvànico, *ag.* (*elett.*) galvanic.

galvanísmo, *s.m.* (*elett.*) galvanism.

galvanizzaménto, *s.m.* **1.** (*med.*) galvanizing **2.** *fig.* galvanizing.

galvanizzàre, *v.t.* **1.** (*med.*) to galvanize **2.** (*rivestire di metallo*) to electroplate **3.** *fig.* to galvanize: *con la sua eloquenza galvanizzò l'auditorio*, by his eloquence he galvanized his audience.

galvanizzazióne, *s.f.* (*elett. chim.*) galvanization.

galvàno, *s.m.* (*tip.*) electrotype.

galvanocàustica, *s.f.* (*med.*) galvanocaustics.

galvanocàustico, *ag.* (*med.*) galvanocaustic.

galvanocautèrio, *s.m.* (*med.*) galvanocautery, galvanic cautery.

galvanomètrico, *ag.* (*elett. chim.*) galvanometric.

galvanòmetro, *s.m.* (*elett. chim.*) galvanometer: *a specchio*, mirror galvanometer; — *balistico*, ballistic galvanometer; — *direzionale*, detector.

galvanoplàstica, *s.f.* (*tip. elett. chim.*) galvanoplastics, galvanoplasty.

galvanoplàstico, *ag.* (*tip. elett. chim.*) galvanoplastic(al).

galvanoscòpio, *s.m.* (*elett.*) galvanoscope, rheoscope.

galvanostegía, *s.f.* (*ind.*) electroplating: *trattare con* —, to electroplate.

galvanotermía, *s.f.* (*ind.*) galvanothermy.

galvanotipía, *s.f.* (*tip.*) electrotype.

galvanotropísmo, *s.m.* (*med.*) galvanotropism.

Gamalièle, *no.pr.m.* (*Bibbia*) Gamaliel.

gàmba, *s.f.* **1.** leg: *gambe anteriori, posteriori*, fore, hind legs; — *artificiale, di legno*, artificial, wooden leg; *le gambe di un tavolo*, the legs of a table; *giuoco di gambe*, (*spor.*) foot-work; *un tavolo a tre gambe*, a three-legged table; *viola da* — , (*mus.*) leg viol (*o* bass viol *o* viola da gamba *o* viola di gamba); *avere una* — *sola*, to be one-legged; *avere le gambe lunghe*, to be long-legged; *avere le gambe storte*, to be bow-legged; *reggersi, star ritto su una* — *sola*, to stand on one leg; *sgranchirsi le gambe*, to stretch one's legs || *a mezza* —,

up to one's knees || *a quattro gambe*, on all fours || *con la coda fra le gambe*, with one's tail between one's legs || *male in* —, weak; (*fam.*) not too steady on one's pins || *andare a gambe levate*, to fall headlong || *avere buona* —, to be a good walker || *darsela a gambe*, to take to one's heels (*o* to go off like a shot) || *essere in* —, (*essere forte*) to be strong; (*di persona anziana*) to be sprightly; *fig.* (*essere capace, attivo, abile*) to be smart (*o* to be on the ball): *quel ragazzo è molto in* —, that boy is very smart; *sentirsi in* —, to feel strong (*o* on top of the world) || *essere tutto gambe*, to be all legs || *fare il passo secondo la* —, to cut the coat according to the cloth || *mandare ql.co. a gambe levate*, to trip s.o. up || *mettersi la via tra le gambe*, to walk away briskly || *non aver più gambe*, *fig.* to be tired out || *non reggersi sulle gambe*, to be hardly able to stand (*o* to feel shaky) || *prendere ql.co. sotto* —, to attach no importance to sthg. (*o* to make light of sthg.) || *raccomandarsi alle gambe*, to trust one's legs || *raddrizzar le gambe ai cani*, to attempt the impossible || *chi non ha testa abbia gambe*, *prov.* a forgetful head makes a weary pair of heels **2.** (*di lettera, nota*) stem **3.** (*aer.*) leg, strut: — *ammortizzatrice*, shock leg; — *del carrello*, undercarriage leg (*o* strut); — *sottovento*, reciprocal leg.

gambacórta, *s.m.* (*scherz.*) lame person.

gambàle, *s.m.* **1.** legging **2.** (*parte più alta di uno stivale*) bootleg **3.** (*forma in legno usata dai calzolai*) boot-tree **4.** (*parte di armatura*) jamb, jambe.

gambàta, *s.f.* kick.

gamberétto, *s.m.* shrimp.

gàmbero, *s.m.* crayfish, crawfish || *rosso come un* —, as red as a (boiled) lobster (*o* as a beetroot) || *andare come un* —, *fig.* to go backwards (*o* to make no progress).

gambettàre, *v.i.* to kick one's legs (about).

gambétto, *s.m.* **1.** (*gambo*) short stem, short stalk **2.** (*di un arnese*) shank **3.** (*agli scacchi*) gambit **4.** (*sgambetto*) trip: *dare il* — *a qlcu.*, *fig.* to trip s.o. up.

gambièra, *s.f.* (*parte di armatura*) jamb, jambe.

gambítto, *s.m.* (*agli scacchi*) gambit.

gàmbo, *s.m.* **1.** (*stelo*) stem, stalk **2.** (*mec.*) stem, shank.

gambúto, *ag.* **1.** (*che ha gambo lungo*) long-stemmed, long-stalk **2.** (*che ha gambe lunghe*) long-legged.

gamèlla, *s.f.* mess-tin

gamète, *s.m.* (*biol.*) gamete.

gàmma[1], *s.f.* (*terza lettera dell'alfabeto greco*) gamma || *raggi* —, (*fis.*) gamma rays.

gàmma[2], *s.f.* gamut, scale, range (*anche fig.*): — *della voce*, range of the voice; — *delle frequenze udibili*, (*rad.*) range of audible frequencies; — *di colori*, (*rad.*) range of colours, of sizes; — *di lunghezza d'onda*, (*rad.*) waveband; — *di prezzi*, scale of prices; — *di sentimenti*, gamut of feelings; — *di sintonia*, (*rad.*) tuning band.

gammascòpio, *s.m.* (*fis.*) gammascope.

gammàto, *ag.*: *croce gammata*, swastika (*o* hooked cross).

gamopètalo, *ag.* (*bot.*) gamopetalous.

ganàscia, *s.f.* **1.** jaw || *mangiare a quattro ganasce*, to eat voraciously; *fig.* (*far grossi guadagni*) to make large profits **2.** (*ferr.*) fish-plate **3.** *pl.* (*mec.*) jaws; (*aut.*) (*di freno*) brake-shoes.

ganascíno, *s.m.* cheek: *la presi per il* —, I pinched her cheek.

ganciàta, *s.f.* hooking.

gàncio, *s.m.* **1.** hook: — *d'accosto*, (*mar.*) boat-hook; — *da muro*, wall-hook; — *da vela*, (*mar.*) sail-hook; — *di trazione*, (*ferr.*) tow (*o* draw) - hook; — *doppio*, (*ind.*) ram's horn; — *e asola*, hook and eye **2.** (*fermaglio*) clasp; fastener **3.** *fig.* (*persona rapace*) grasper, grabber **4.** (*boxe*) crochet **5.** *fig.* (*cavillo*) cavil, pretext.

Gand, *no.pr.f.* (*geog.*) Ghent.

gànga, *s.f.* **1.** (*min.*) gangue, gang; matrix (*pl.* matrixes, matrices); voinstone: — *del carbone,* coal gangue **2.** (*ornit.*) sand grouse.

Gànge, *no.pr.m.* (*geog.*) Ganges.

gàngamo, *s.m.* oyster-net.

gangheràre, *v.t.* (*rar.*) **1.** (*provvedere di gangheri*) to furnish with hinges **2.** (*montare su gangheri*) to set on hinges.

gangherèlla, *s.f.* (*asola per gancio*) eye.

gànghero, *s.m.* **1.** hinge: *porta fuori dei gangheri,* door off its hinges (*o* unhinged door) ‖ *fuori dei gangheri, fig.* in a very bad temper; *far uscire dai gangheri,* to unhinge: *mi fai uscire dai gangheri, fig.* you make me lose my temper **2.** (*gancetto per abiti*) hook.

gànglio, *s.m.* (*anat. patol.*) ganglion (*pl.* ganglia) (*anche fig.*): — *nervoso,* ganglion-cell; *i gangli vitali del paese,* the vital ganglia of the country.

ganglïòma, *s.m.* (*patol.*) ganglioma.

ganglionàre, *ag.* (*anat.*) ganglionic.

ganglioneuròma, *s.m.* (*patol.*) ganglioneuroma.

gàngola, *s.f.* (*patol.pop.*) swollen neck-gland; struma.

gangrèna, *V.* **cancrèna.**

gangster, *s.m.* (*amer.*) gangster.

gangsterísmo, *s.m.* (*amer.*) gangsterism.

Ganimède, *no.pr.m.* (*mit.*) Ganymede ‖ **ganimède,** *s.m.* **1.** (*zerbinotto*) dandy, fop, beau (*pl.* beaux): *fare il* —, to play the beau **2.** (*cicisbeo*) gallant, cicisbeo.

ganòide, *ag.* (*ittiol.*) ganoid.

ganòidi, *s.m.pl.* (*ittiol.*) Ganoidei.

gànza, *s.f.* (*spreg.*) mistress, paramour.

ganzeríno, *s.m.* (*spreg.*) dandy, fop, beau (*pl.* beaux).

gànzo, *s.m.* (*spreg.*) lover, paramour.

gàra, *s.f.* **1.** competition: — *internazionale, letteraria,* international, literary competition; *entrare in* — *con ql.cu. per ql.co.,* to enter into competition with s.o. for sthg.; *iscriversi a una* —, to enter a competition ‖ *fare a* —, to compete (*o* to vie) **2.** (*competizione sportiva*) contest: *gare atletiche,* athletic contests; — *di velocità,* speed contest; — *eliminatoria,* heat; *gare finali,* finals; *vincere la* —, to carry off the prize **3.** (*corsa*) race: — *di canottaggio,* boat-race; — *di panfili,* yacht-race; *gare di canottaggio, di panfili, regatta;* — *ippica,* horse-race **4.** (*partita tra due contendenti o squadre*) match: — *di calcio,* football match **5.** (*comm.*) (*concorso per una fornitura*) tender.

garage, *s.m.* garage.

garagísta, *s.m.* **1.** (*meccanico*) motor mechanic **2.** (*padrone di garage*) garage keeper, garage owner.

garamoncíno, *s.m.* (*tip.*) bourgeois (9 points).

garamóne, *s.m.* (*tip.*) Garamond; long-primer (10 points).

garànte, *s.m.* **1.** guarantor, warranter (*anche comm.*): *un* — *è una persona che dà una garanzia,* a guarantor is a person giving a guarantee; *la sua buona fede è* — *della sua condotta,* his good faith is a warrant for (*o* is the best guarantee of) his behaviour; *essere, rendersi* — *di ql.co., di qlcu.,* to answer (*o* to pledge oneself) for sthg., s.o.: *ne sarete garanti voi?,* will you answer for it?; *si rendono garanti che non gli sarà fatto alcun male,* they pledge themselves (*o* they warrant) that he won't come to any harm (*o* they will answer for his safety) **2.** (*dir.*) (*chi deposita una cauzione*) surety; (*chi versa una cauzione per un imputato*) bail: — *di un debito,* surety for a debt; *essere* — *di qlcu.,* to go bail (*o* to answer) for s.o.; *offrirsi come* — *per qlcu.,* to offer oneself as surety for s.o.; *rendersi* — *per qlcu.,* to stand (*o* to go) surety for s.o.

garantíre, *v.t.* **1.** to guarantee, to warrant (*anche comm.*): *questo ombrello è garantito di seta pura,* this umbrella is guaranteed pure silk; — *un articolo per un anno,* to guarantee an article for one year **2.** (*rendersi garante per*) to vouch for (s.o., sthg.), to answer for (sthg.): *garantiamo l'arrivo in buon ordine della merce,* we answer for the safe arrival of the goods; *posso* — *la sua onestà,* I can vouch for his honesty **3.** (*dir.*)

(*offrire una cauzione*) to stand surety for (s.o.), to act as surety for (s.o.); (*offrire una cauzione per un imputato*) to go bail for (s.o.) **4.** (*assicurare*) to assure, to warrant: *vi garantisco che ciò accadrà,* I can assure you that this will happen (*o* this will happen, I warrant you) ‖ *garantito!,* I'll warrant! (*o* no doubt! *o* depend on it!) ‖ *te lo garantisco io!,* (*fam.*) I can tell you!.

garanzia, *s.f.* **1.** guarantee, warranty (*anche comm.*): — *di qualità,* warranty of quality; *contratti di* —, contracts of guarantee; *un frigorifero con la* — *di un anno,* a refrigerator with a year's guarantee; *dare, non dare* —, to be reliable, unreliable: *questo giovane non dà alcuna* — (*di serietà*), this young man is quite unreliable (*o* cannot be relied upon) **2.** (*dir.*) (*dichiarazione di garanzia*) guaranty: *si rifiuta di rilasciare* —, he refuses to lay down a guaranty **3.** (*somma, beni di garanzia*) security; (*pegno*) pledge: *la* — *è scarsa,* the security is poor; *dare come* — *una somma di denaro,* to give a sum of money as security ‖ *a* — *di,* in security for (*o* as a guarantee for) ‖ *senza* —, (*di cambiale*) without recourse **4.** (*dir.*) (*cauzione*) bail.

garbàccio, *s.m.* rudeness, unpoliteness.

garbàre, *v.i.* to like (s.o., sthg.) (*costruzione pers.*); to please (s.o.): *questa sistemazione non mi garba,* I don't like this arrangement (*o* this arrangement doesn't suit me); *il tuo comportamento non mi garba,* your behaviour doesn't please me.

garbataménte, *av.* politely; (*gentilmente*) kindly, amiably; (*in modo aggraziato*) gracefully.

garbatézza, *s.f.* **1.** politeness; polite manners (*pl.*); kindness, amiability; gracefulness **2.** (*atto garbato*) kindness, courtesy: *gli hanno fatto molte garbatezze,* they did him a lot of kindnesses (*o* they were very kind to him).

garbàto, *ag.* polite, well-mannered; (*gentile*) kind, amiable; (*aggraziato*) graceful.

garbíno, *s.m.* "garbino" (south-west-wind).

gàrbo, *s.m.* **1.** politeness, courtesy; (*modi gentili*) good manners (*pl.*); (*grazia*) grace, gracefulness: *con bel* —, with a good grace; *con mal* —, with a bad grace; *senza* —, (*sgarbatamente*) rudely; (*goffamente*) awkwardly (*o* clumsily); *ha molto* — *nel vestire, nel parlare,* he has a distinguished manner of dressing, of speaking ‖ *a* —, nicely (*o* properly): *fare una cosa a* —, to do a thing nicely (*o* properly) ‖ *avere un bel* —, (*di abito*) to hang well **2.** (*costume, abitudine, modo*) wont: *come è il* — *dei bambini,* as is the wont of children **3.** (*mar.*) garboard.

garbúglio, *s.m.* **1.** entanglement; bungle **2.** *fig.* (*confusione, disordine*) entanglement, confusion, mess, muddle.

gardènia, *s.f.* (*bot.*) gardenia.

gareggiaménto, *s.m.* competition, vying, rivalry.

gareggiàre, *v.i.* to compete, to vie, to rival: *gareggiarono nell'usarmi ogni cortesia,* they vied in paying me every attention; *nessuno può* — *con lui,* nobody can compete with him.

gareggiatóre, *s.m.* competitor, rival.

gareggiatríce, *s.f.* competitress, rival.

garènna, *s.f.* (*conigliera*) (rabbit-)warren.

garétta, *V.* **garitta.**

garétto, *V.* **garrétto.**

garganèlla, *s.f.*: *bere a* —, to gulp down.

gargarísmo, *s.m.* gargle: *fare dei gargarismi,* to gargle.

gargarizzàre, *v.t.,* **gargarizzàrsi,** *v.r.* to gargle.

gargaròzzo, *s.m.* (*pop.*) gullet, throat.

gargòtta, *s.f.* (*spreg.*) cook-shop; (*sl. amer.*) beanery.

gargúglia, *s.f.* (*arch.*) gargoyle.

garibaldíno, *ag.* Garibaldian, of Garibaldi ‖ *alla garibaldina,* boldly ‖ *s.m.* Garibaldian, Garibaldi's follower.

garitta, *s.f.* **1.** (*di sentinella*) sentry-box **2.** (*torretta di guardia*) look-out turret **3.** (*di guardiano*) cabin, shelter: — *del frenatore,* (*ferr.*) brakesman (*o* brakesman's) cabin **4.** — *di salvataggio,* (*di sottomarino*) (*mar. mil.*) escape chamber.

garnettatúra, *s.f.* (*ind. tessile*) garnetting.

garnieríte, *s.f.* (*min.*) garnierite.

garofanàre, *v.t.* (*cuc.*) to season with cloves.

garofaníno, *s.m.* (*bot.*) sweet-william.

garòfano, *s.m.* (*bot.*) **1.** (*pianta ornamentale*) carnation, pink **2.** (*pianta aromatica*) clove (-tree): *chiodo di —*, clovo; *essenza di —*, clove oil.

garrése, *s.m.* (*del cavallo*) withers (*pl.*).

garrétto, *s.m.* **1.** (*di quadrupede*) hock, hough **2.** (*di uomo*) back of heel **3.** (*calcagno*) heel.

garríre, *v.i.* **1.** (*di bandiera, sventolare*) to flap, to flutter **2.** (*gridare con voce aspra*) to screech, to shriek **3.** (*di uccelli, stridere*) to chirp, to twitter, to warble **4.** (*gridare altercando*) to brawl ‖ *v.t.* (*rimproverare*) to scold.

garríto, *s.m.* **1.** (*grido aspro*) screech, shrieking **2.** (*stridio di uccelli*) chirp, twittering, warble **3.** (*rimprovero*) scolding.

garrulità, *s.f.* garrulity, garrulousness, talkativeness, loquacity.

gàrrulo, *ag.* garrulous, talkative, loquacious.

gàrza[1], *s.f.* (*ornit.*) heron.

gàrza[2], *s.f.* (*tessuto*) gauze: *— grezza*, cheesecloth.

garzàre, *v.t.* (*ind. tessile*) to raise, to teasel, to teazel, to teazle.

garzatóre, *s.m.* (*ind. tessile*) raiser, teaseler, teazler.

garzatríce, *s.f.* (*ind. tessile*) **1.** raiser, teaseler, teazler **2.** (*macchina*) raising machine, teaseling machine.

garzatúra, *s.f.* (*ind. tessile*) raising, teaseling, teazling.

gàrzo, *s.m.* (*bot.*) teasel, teazel, teazle: *dare il —*, (*ind. tessile*) to teasel (*o* to teazle *o* to raise).

garzonàto, *s.m.* apprenticeship.

garzoncèllo, *s.m.* **1.** lad **2.** (*ragazzo di bottega*) shop-boy.

garzóne, *s.m.* **1.** (*poet.*) (*giovanetto*) lad, youth, boy **2.** (*apprendista*) apprentice; (*ragazzo di negozio*) shop-boy, errand-boy: *— di stalla*, groom.

garzuòlo, *s.m.* (*bot.*) core.

gas, *s.m.* **1.** gas: *— asfissiante*, poison gas (*o* asphyxiating gas); *lanciare — asfissianti contro il nemico*, to gas the enemy; *— d'acqua*, water gas; *— delle miniere*, fire damp; *— delle paludi*, methane (*o* natural gas *o* marsh gas); *— esilarante*, laughing-gas; *— illuminante*, illuminating (*o* coal)-gas; *— lacrimogeno*, tear (*o* lachrymatory) gas; *— nobili*, noble gases; *— soffocante*, (*miner.*) choke-damp; *apparecchi a —*, gas-fittings; *becco del —*, gas-burner; *camera a —*, gas chamber; *conduttura del —*, gas-pipe; *contatore del —*, gas-meter; *cucina a —*, gas-stove (*o* gas-range); *esattore del —*, gas-man; *esplosione di —*, gas explosion; *fornello a —*, gas-stove; *forno a —*, gas-oven; *fuga di —*, gas-escape; *illuminazione a —*, gas-lighting; *lampione a —*, gas-lamp; *luce a —*, gas-light; *officina del —*, gas-works; *radiatore a —*, gas-fire; *serbatoio del —*, gas-holder; *società del —*, gas company; *riscaldato a —*, gas-heated; *accendere, spegnere il —*, to turn on, to turn off the gas; *alzare, abbassare il —*, to turn up, to turn down the gas **2.** (*benzina*) petrol; (*amer.*) gasoline: *andare a tutto —*, (*fam.*) to run at full speed **3.** (*med.*) flatus.

gasàre, *v.t.* to gas: *— un liquido*, to charge with gas (*o* to aerate) a liquid.

gasàto, *ag.* aerated.

gaschétte, *s.f.pl.* (*mar.*) gaskets.

gaseodótto, *s.m.* gas-pipeline.

gasòlio, *s.m.* (*chim.*) gas oil, Diesel oil.

Gàspare, *no.pr.m.* Caspar, Casper, Jasper.

gàssa, *s.f.* (*mar.*) loop, eye.

gassificàre, *v.t.* (*fis.*) to gasify.

gassísta, *s.m.* gas-fitter.

gassògeno, *s.m.* gas producer, gas generator.

gassolína, *s.f.* (*chim.*) gasoline.

gassòmetro, *s.m.* gasholder, gasometer: *— a campana*, bell-shaped gasometer; *— a secco*, dry gasometer; *— a umido*, wet gasometer.

gassósa, *s.f.* "gassosa" (kind of effervescent drink).

gassóso, *ag.* gaseous; aerated: *acqua gassosa*, soda-water.

gasteròpodi, *s.m.pl.* (*zool.*) Gasteropoda, Gastropoda.

gasterotomía, *s.f.* (*chir.*) gastrotomy.

Gastóne, *no.pr.m.* Gaston.

gastralgía, *s.f.* (*med.*) gastralgia.

gastràlgico, *ag.* (*med.*) gastralgic.

gastrectasía, *s.f.* (*med.*) gastrectasia, gastrectasis.

gastrectomía, *s.f.* (*chir.*) gastrectomy.

gastricísmo, *s.m.* (*patol.*) gastricism.

gàstrico, *ag.* gastric.

gastríte, *s.f.* (*patol.*) gastritis.

gastrocèle, *s.m.* (*patol.*) gastrocele.

gastrocnèmio, *s.m.* (*anat.*) gastrocnemius (*pl.* gastrocnemii).

gastroentèrico, *ag.* (*anat.*) gastroenteric.

gastroenteríte, *s.f.* (*patol.*) gastroenteritis.

gastroenterostomía, *s.f.* (*chir.*) gastro-enterostomy.

gastroenterocolíte, *s.f.* (*patol.*) gastro-enterocolitis.

gastroepàtico, *ag.* (*med.*) gastrohepatic.

gastrointestinàle, *ag.* (*med.*) gastrointestinal.

gastrología, *s.f.* (*scient.*) gastrology.

gastromalacía, *s.f.* (*patol.*) gastromalacia.

gastronomía, *s.f.* gastronomy.

gastronòmico, *ag.* gastronomic(al).

gastrònomo, *s.m.* gastronome(r), gastronomist.

gastroptòsi, *s.f.* (*patol.*) gastroptosis.

gastrorragía, *s.f.* (*patol.*) gastrorrhagia.

gastrorrèa, *s.f.* (*patol.*) gastrorrhea.

gastroscòpio, *s.m.* (*med.*) gastroscope.

gastrospàsmo, *s.m.* (*patol.*) gastrospasm.

gastrostomía, *s.f.* (*chir.*) gastrostomy.

gastrotomía, *s.f.* (*chir.*) gastrotomy.

gàtta, *s.f.* cat, she-cat, female cat; (*fam.*) pussy-cat, pussy; tabby(-cat) ‖ *— ci cova!*, there is sth. in the wind! (*o* there is sth. behind that!) ‖ *che — da pelare!*, (*situazione imbarazzante*) that's a pretty kettle of fish!; (*impresa difficile*) that's a hard nut to crack!: *ho altre gatte da pelare*, I have other fish to fry ‖ *far la — morta*, to feign simplicity (*o* to pretend to be asleep *o* to pretend not to see) ‖ *la — frettolosa fa i gattini ciechi*, *prov.*, more haste, less speed ‖ *quando la — non c'è, i sorci ballano*, *prov.* when the cat's away the mice will play ‖ *tanto va la — al lardo che ci lascia lo zampino*, *prov.* the pitcher went to the well once too often.

gattabúia, *s.f.* (*scherz.*) cells (*pl.*); lock-up: (*amer.*) hoosegow: *in —*, in quod (*o amer.* jugged).

gattamòrta, *s.f.* (*fam.*) hypocrite, slyboots.

gattària, *s.f.* (*bot.*) cat's tail.

gattéseo, *s.m.* feline; cattish, catty.

gàttice, *s.m.* (*bot.*) white poplar.

gatticída, *s.c.* (*scherz.*) cat-killer.

gatticídio, *s.m.* (*scherz.*) cat-killing.

gattína, *s.f.* kitten: *— mia!*, (*fam.*) you little kitten!.

gattíno, *s.m.* **1.** kitten, little cat; catling **2.** (*bot.*) (*amento*) catkin.

gàtto, *s.m.* **1.** cat, tom-cat, male cat, he-cat; (*fam.*) pussy-cat, pussy: *— d'Angora*, Angora (*o* Persian) cat; *— selvatico*, wild cat; *— siamese*, Siamese cat; *— soriano*, tabby ‖ *— a nove code*, cat-o'-nine-tails ‖ *il — con gli stivali*, (*personaggio di fiaba*) Puss in Boots ‖ *occhio di —*, (*min.*) cat's eye ‖ *non c'era un —*, there wasn't a soul there ‖ *avere occhi da —*, to be cat-eyed ‖ *essere come cane e —*, to be like cat and dog; *vivere come cane e —*, to live a cat-and-dog life ‖ *essere quattro gatti*, to be a small number ‖ *far ridere i gatti*, to make a cat laugh ‖ *a lumi spenti tutti i gatti sono grigi*, *prov.* when candles are out all cats are grey **2.** (*ittiol.*) cat-fish **3.** (*bot.*) cat's tail.

gattomammóne, *s.m.* (*nelle fiabe*) bogey, bogy.

gattóni, *av.* (*carponi*) on all fours: *gatton —*, (*quatto quatto*) very quietly (*o* stealthily) on all fours.

gattopàrdo, *s.m.* (*zool.*) leopard.

gattúccio, *s.m.* **1.** (*gattino*) kitten **2.** (*ittiol.*) catfish **3.** (*carpenteria*) turning-saw, compass-saw, keyhole-saw.

gaucho, *s.m.* gaucho (*pl.* gauchos).

gaudènte, *ag.* **1.** (*allegro*) jolly, merry **2.** (*dissipato*) fast: *vita* —, fast life ‖ *s.c.* fast person.

gàudio, *s.m.* joy; (*letizia*) mirth; (*beatitudine*) bliss; (*felicità*) happiness ‖ *mal comune mezzo* —, *prov.* trouble shared is trouble halved.

gaudiosaménte, *av.* joyously, joyfully; mirthfully; blissfully; happily.

gaudióso, *ag.* joyous, joyful; mirthful; blissful ‖ *i cinque misteri gaudiosi,* (*eccl.*) the five Joyful Mysteries (of the Rosary).

gavazzaménto, *s.m.* revelry, revelling; carousal.

gavazzàre, *v.i.* to revel; to carouse.

gavazzatóre, *s.m.,* **gavazzatríce,** *s.f.* reveller.

gavétta, *s.f.* (*mil.*) mess-tin; (*mar.*) kid ‖ *venire dalla* —, (*di ufficiale*) to rise from the ranks; (*di borghese*) to be a self-made man.

gaviàle, *s.m.* (*zool.*) gavial.

Gavíno, *no.pr.m.* Gavin.

gavitèllo, *s.m.* (*mar.*) buoy: — *antidragante,* explosive float.

gavóne, *s.m.* (*mar.*) peak: — *di poppa,* afterpeak; — *di prua,* forepeak.

gavòtta, *s.f.* (*musica, danza*) gavotte.

gazósa, *s.f.* "gazosa" (kind of effervescent drink).

gàzza, *s.f.* **1.** (*ornit.*) magpie **2.** *fig.* magpie, noisy woman, chattering woman: *garrire come una* —, to chatter like a magpie.

gazzàrra, *s.f.* din; uproar, tumult: *fare* —, to make a hullabaloo.

gazzèlla, *s.f.* (*zool.*) gazelle.

gazzétta, *s.f.* gazette; newspaper ‖ *Gazzetta Ufficiale,* Official Gazette ‖ *è una vera* —!, (*fam.*) he can always tell you the latest news! (*o* is a real newsmonger!).

gazzettière, *s.m.* **1.** gazette-writer **2.** (*spreg.*) (inferior) journalist.

gazzettíno, *s.m.* **1.** news-sheet **2.** *fig.* newsmonger.

gè, *s.m.* (*min.*) jet.

Gèa, *no.pr.f.* (*mit.*) Gaea.

gèco, *s.m.* (*zool.*) gecko.

Gedeóne, *no.pr.m.* Gideon.

Geènna, *no.pr.f.* (*Bibbia*) Gehenna ‖ **geènna,** *s.f. fig.* (*inferno*) Gehenna.

gelàre, *v.t.* to freeze; to convert into ice: *il freddo gli gelava le mani,* the cold froze his hands (*o* his hands were frozen with the cold); — *il sangue, fig.* to freeze one's blood ‖ *far* —, to freeze: *il freddo fece* — *le condutture,* the cold froze the pipes; *far* — *il sangue,* to freeze s.o.'s blood ‖ *v.i.* to freeze; to become frozen: *le condutture dell'acqua gelarono,* the water-pipes froze; *il fiume gelò,* the river froze over; *io gelo in questa stanza,* I'm freezing in this room; *qui si gela,* it is very cold here.

gelàta, *s.f.* frost, hard-frost.

gelatería, *s.f.* ice-cream shop.

gelatièra, *s.f.* ice-cream freezer.

gelatière, *s.m.* **1.** (*chi fabbrica gelati*) ice-cream man **2.** (*chi vende gelati*) ice-cream vendor.

gelatína, *s.f.* **1.** (*cuc.*) jelly: — *di frutta,* fruit jelly **2.** (*chim.*) gelatin(e): — *cristallizzata,* (*foto.*) frosted gelatine; — *esplosiva,* nitrogelatine.

gelatinizzàre, *v.t.* to gelatinize.

gelatinóso, *ag.* gelatinous.

gelàto, *ag.* frozen; icy: *acqua gelata,* icy water: *un lago* —, a frozen lake; *i miei piedi sono gelati,* my feet are frozen ‖ — *di paura, fig.* chilled with fear (*o* frightened to death) ‖ *s.m.* ice-cream, ice: — *di cioccolato, vaniglia, fragola,* chocolate, vanilla, strawberry ice-cream; *cono* —, ice-cream cone.

gelidaménte, *av.* icely, coldly, gelidly.

gelidézza, *s.f.* coldness.

gèlido, *ag.* icy (anche *fig.*), freezing; *fig.* chilly: *una*

gelida accoglienza, an icy (*o* a chilly) welcome; *una gelida notte,* an icy (*o* a freezing *o* a frosty) night; *modi gelidi,* chilly (*o* icy) manners; *risposta gelida,* icy answer; *vento* —, icy wind.

gèlo, *s.m.* **1.** (*freddo intenso*) intense cold; *fig.* chill: *la morsa del* —, frost-bite; *la cattiva notizia diffuse fra gli astanti un senso di* —, the bad news cast a chill over the gathering; *c'era un tale* — *che...*, it was so ice-cold that... ‖ *una persona di* —, a frigid (*o* an unemotional) person **2.** (*ghiaccio*) ice; (*brina*) frost: *una strada coperta di* —, a road covered with ice; *il* — *rovinò il raccolto,* the frost ruined the crop.

gelóne[1], *s.m.* chilblain.

Gelóne[2], *no.pr.m.* (*st.*) Gelo.

gelosaménte, *av.* jealously.

gelosía, *s.f.* **1.** jealousy: *la causa della mia* —, the reason for my jealousy; *per* —, from (*o* out of) jealousy; *provar* — *per qlcu.,* to be jealous of s.o.; *rodersi dalla* —, to be consumed with jealousy **2.** (*cura scrupolosa*) great care: *conservare ql.co. con* —, to keep sthg. with great care **3.** (*persiana*) shutter.

gelóso, *ag.* **1.** jealous: — *del proprio onore,* jealous of one's honour; *non essere* — *di tua moglie!,* don't be jealous of your wife! **2.** (*delicato*) delicate.

gelséto, *s.m.* mulberry grove.

gelsicultúra, *s.f.* (*agr.*) mulberry growing.

gèlso, *s.m.* (*bot.*) mulberry(-tree).

gelsomíno, *s.m.* (*bot.*) jasmine, jessamine.

Geltrúde, *no.pr.f.* Gertrude ‖ *dim.* Gertie, Trudy.

gemebóndo, *ag.* moaning; groaning; plaintive.

gemellàre, *ag.* twin (*attributivo*): *parto* —, twinning.

gemèllo, *ag.* twin (*attributivo*): *anime gemelle,* twin souls (*o* kindred spirits); *letti gemelli,* twin beds; *sorella gemella, fratello* —, twin sister, brother ‖ *s.m.* **1.** twin: *una coppia di gemelli,* a pair of twins ‖ *i Gemelli,* (*astr.*) the Twins (*o* Gemini) **2.** (*di polsino*) cuff-links (*pl.*).

gèmere, *v.i.* **1.** to moan; to groan; to wail: *il ferito giaceva là gemendo,* the wounded man lay there groaning; *la poveretta gemeva pietosamente,* the poor thing was moaning piteously; *il vento geme,* the wind is moaning (*o* wailing); — *di dolore,* to groan in pain **2.** (*lamentarsi*) to lament: *gemeva per la morte del marito,* she lamented for (*o* over) her husband's death **3.** *fig.* (*soffrire*) to groan: — *sotto il giogo, la tirannia,* to groan under the yoke, the tyranny **4.** (*scricchiolare, cigolare*) to groan: *la porta gemeva sui cardini,* the door groaned on its hinges; *gli scaffali gemono sotto il peso dei libri,* the shelves groan under the weight of books ‖ *far* — *i torchi, fig.* to keep the press going **5.** (*trasudare*) to drip, to trickle; to leak: *la botte geme,* the barrel is leaking **6.** (*tubare*) to coo ‖ *v.t.* (*emettere, trasudare*) to trickle, to drip: *una ferita che geme sangue,* a bleeding wound; *la parete geme acqua,* the wall is trickling water.

geminàre[1], *v.t.* (*gram.*) to geminate: — *una consonante,* to geminate a consonant.

geminàre[2], *v.t.* (*artig.*) to damascene.

geminàto, *ag.* geminate: *consonante geminata,* geminate (*o* geminated) consonant; *cristallo* —, (*min.*) geminate crystal.

geminatúra, geminazióne, *s.f.* (*gram. min.*) gemination.

Gèmini, *no.pr.m.pl.* (*astr.*) Gemini, Twins.

gèmino, *ag.* twin, double.

gemitío, *s.m.* **1.** (*gocciolio*) trickling, dripping **2.** (*gemito*) wailing.

gèmito, *s.m.* groan(ing), moan(ing), wail(ing): *emettere un* — *profondo,* to give (*o* to utter) a deep groan.

gèmma, *s.f.* **1.** gem; precious stone; jewel: *i diamanti sono gemme,* diamonds are gems **2.** *fig.* gem, jewel: *gemme di prosa italiana,* gems of Italian prose: *quella fanciulla è una* —, she is a gem of a girl; *quel quadro è la* — *della collezione,* that picture is the gem of the collection; *Venezia è la* — *dell'Adriatico,* Venice is the queen of the Adriatic **3.** (*bot.*) bud;

gemma (*pl.* gemmae): *mettere le gemme*, to put forth buds (*o* to bud).

gemmànte, *ag.* gemmy; (*luccicante*) shining, sparkling, glittering.

gemmàre, *v.i.* (*bot.*) to bud, to gemmate || **gemmàrsi**, *v.r.* (*ingioiellarsi*) to adorn oneself with gems.

gemmàrio, *ag.* gemmary.

gemmàto, *ag.* 1. (*bot.*) gemmate 2. (*ornato di gemme*) studded with gems.

gemmazióne, *s.f.* (*bot.*) gemmation.

gèmmeo, *ag.* gemmy, brilliant.

gemmífero, *ag.* (*bot. min.*) gemmiferous.

gemmíparo, *ag.* (*biol.*) gemmiparous.

gemmóso, *ag.* (*bot.*) full of buds.

gèmmula, *s.f.* (*letter.*) gemmule.

Gemònie, *s.f.pl.* (*st. romana*) Gemonies.

gendàrme, *s.m.* 1. policeman (*pl.* policemen); gendarme 2. *fig.* (*donna autoritaria*) battle-axe.

gendarmería, *s.f.* 1. (*corpo dei gendarmi*) police-force 2. (*caserma dei gendarmi*) police-station.

gène, *s.m.* (*biol.*) gene.

genealogía, *s.f.* genealogy, pedigree, descent.

genealògico, *ag.* genealogical: *albero —*, genealogical tree (*o* family tree *o* pedigree).

genealogísta, *s.m.* genealogist.

generàbile, *ag.* generable.

generalàto, *s.m.* (*eccl.*) generalship.

generàle[1], *ag.* 1. general, common, widespread: *assemblea —*, general assembly; *consenso —*, common consent; *elezione —*, general election; *perdono —*, general pardon; *principi generali*, general principles; *una questione d'interesse —*, a matter of general interest || *in —*, in general (*o* generally) 2. (*di più alto grado, principale*) general: *direttore —*, general manager; *ispettore —*, inspector general; *quartier —*, (*mil.*) headquarters || *prova —*, (*teat.*) dress rehearsal || *s.m.* general: *distinguere il — dal particolare*, to distinguish the general from the particular || *star sulle generali*, to speak in general terms.

generàle[2], *s.m.* (*mil.*) general: (*aer.*) marshal; *— d'armata*, general; *— di brigata*, brigadier; *— di corpo d'armata*, lieutenant general; *— di divisione*, major general; *— in capo*, commander in chief; *maggior —*, major-general; *tenente —*, lieutenant-general || *il — dei Gesuiti*, (*eccl.*) the General of the Jesuits.

generalèssa, *s.f.* 1. general's wife 2. *fig.* (*donna autoritaria*) battle-axe.

generalíssimo, *s.m.* (*mil.*) generalissimo (*pl.* generalissimos).

generalità, *s.f.* 1. generality: *la — degli uomini*, the generality of mankind; *nella — dei casi*, in most cases 2. *pl.* (*dati che consentono l'identificazione di una persona*): *dare le proprie —*, to give one's (full) particulars.

generalízio, *ag.* pertaining to a general.

generalizzàbile, *ag.* generalizable.

generalizzàre, *v.t.* to generalize.

generalizzazióne, *s.f.* generalization.

generalménte, *av.* generally, in general; as a general rule: *— parlando*, generally speaking.

generaménto, *s.m.* generation, generating.

generàre, *v.t.* 1. to generate, to beget, to breed, to procreate: *Abramo generò Isacco*, Abraham begot Isaac 2. (*produrre*) to produce: *albero che genera molti frutti*, tree that produces fruits in quantity 3. *fig.* (*causare*) to generate, to engender; to breed, to beget; to cause, to arouse: *l'ignoranza genera il pregiudizio*, ignorance breeds prejudice || *— una malattia*, to cause an illness; *— un sospetto*, to arouse a suspicion 4. (*scient. tec.*) to generate, to produce: *corrente generata da una batteria*, (*elett.*) current produced by a battery; *volume generato da una curva*, (*geom.*) volume generated by a curve; *— calore*, to generate (*o* to develop) heat || **generàrsi**, *v.r.* 1. to be generated, to be born, to be bred 2. (*prodursi*) to be produced 3. (*derivare, scaturire*) to arise.

generativo, *ag.* generative.

generatóre, *ag.* generative, generating, productive || *s.m.* 1. generator 2. (*mec. elett.*) generator: *— di acetilene*, acetylene generator; *— di radiofrequenza*, oscillator; *— di vapore*, steam generator; *— per corrente alternata e continua*, double current generator || **generatríce**, *s.f.* 1. generatrix 2. (*geom.*) generatrix, generant 3. (*mec. elett.*) generator, generatrix.

generazióne, *s.f.* 1. generation; (*stirpe*) progeny, offspring: *la — di Noè*, the generation (*o* descendants) of Noah; *di — in —*, from generation to generation: *la nuova —*, the rising generation 2. (*il generare*) generation: *— spontanea*, (*biol.*) spontaneous generation 3. (*produzione*) generation: *— di calore, di vapore*, generation (*o* production) of heat, of steam.

gènere, *s.m.* 1. family, race, kind: *il — umano*, the human race (*o* mankind *o* humanity) || *in —*, generally 2. (*fil. biol.*) genus (*pl.* genera): *i leoni e le tigri appartengono allo stesso —*, lions and tigers belong to the same genus 3. (*tipo, qualità, specie*) kind, manner, sort, way: *di nuovo —*, strange (*o* odd); *d'ogni —*, of all kinds: *gente d'ogni —*, all sorts of people: *qualcosa del —*, something like it; *che — d'affari trattate?*, what is your line (of business)?; *che — di libro è questo?*, what kind (*o* sort) of book is this?: *nel suo — è un artista*, he is an artist in his way 4. (*gram.*) gender: *— neutro*, neuter gender 5. (*lett. art.*) genre: *il — comico*, comedy; *il — drammatico*, drama; *il — epico*, epic poetry (*o* epic); *— letterario*, literary genre; *il — satirico*, satire; *il — tragico*, tragedy; *pittura di —*, genre-painting 6. (*prodotto*) product: *generi alimentari*, foodstuffs (*o* provisions) *— di largo consumo*, product (*o* article) of wide consumption: *generi di prima necessità*, commodities.

genericaménte, *av.* generically; vaguely.

genericità, *s.f.* indefiniteness; vagueness.

genèrico, *ag.* generic, not specific, general; indefinite, vague: *un nome —*, a generic (*o* not specific) name; *una risposta generica*, an indefinite (*o* a vague) answer; *un termine —*, a general term || *s.m.* (*teat.*) all-round actor.

gènero, *s.m.* son-in-law.

generosaménte, *av.* 1. (*liberalmente*) generously, liberally, munificently, bounteously 2. (*nobilmente*) nobly, magnanimously.

generosità, *s.f.* 1. (*liberalità*) generosity, liberality, munificence, open-handedness, bounteousness 2. (*nobiltà d'animo*) nobility, magnanimity 3. (*fertilità*) fertility 4. (*di vino*) generousness.

generóso, *ag.* 1. (*liberale*) generous, liberal, munificent, open-handed, bountiful, bounteous: *è troppo — col suo denaro*, he is too generous (*o* too free *o* too open-handed) with his money 2. (*nobile*) noble, generous: *cuore —*, warm heart; *quell'uomo ha una natura generosa*, that man has a generous nature 3. (*abbondante*) generous, plentiful: *una porzione generosa di carne*, a generous (*o* plentiful) helping of meat 4. (*fertile*) fertile, generous, rich: *campi generosi*, fertile (*o* generous) fields; *terreno —*, fertile soil 5. (*di vino*) generous.

gènesi, *s.f.* (*origine, nascimento*) genesis, origin, birth: *la — dei mondi*, the origin of the universe; *la — della storia*, history in the making: *— di un'idea*, birth of an idea || *Genesi*, (*Bibbia*) Genesis.

genesiologìa, *s.f.* 1. genesiology 2. genetics.

genètica, *s.f.* genetics.

genètico, *ag.* genetic.

genetlíaco, *ag.* birthday (*attributivo*): *feste genetliache*, birthday celebrations || *s.m.* birthday.

genètta, *s.f.* (*zool.*) genet.

gengíva, *s.f.* gum: *gengive inflammate*, swollen gums.

gengivàle, *ag.* gingival; gum (*attributivo*): *ascesso —*, (*patol.*) gumboil.

gengivíte, *s.f.* (*patol.*) gingivitis: *— espulsiva*, pyorrhea.

genía, *s.f.* **1.** (*discendenza, razza*) race, progeny **2.** (*spreg.*) tribe, pack, breed, set, collection, clique: *la — degli imbrattacarte,* the scribbling tribe; *la — dei politicanti,* the tribe of politicians; *una — di farabutti,* a fine collection (*o* pack) of scoundrels ‖ *una bella —!,* (*iron.*) a fine set!.

geniàle, *ag.* **1.** ingenious, clever: *un'idea —,* a bright (*o* an inspired *o* a brilliant) idea (*o fam.* a brain-wave); *una persona, macchina, soluzione —,* an ingenious (*o* a clever) person, machine, solution; *un uomo —,* a man of genius **2.** (*piacevole, simpatico*) genial: *un carattere allegro e —,* a cheerful and genial disposition **3.**(*arc.*) (*nuziale*) genial: *letto —,* genial bed.

genialità, *s.f.* **1.** ingeniousness; cleverness; brilliant mind; talent **2.** (*genio*) genius **3.** (*simpatia*) geniality.

genialménte, *av.* **1.** ingeniously; cleverly; brilliantly **2.** (*simpaticamente*) genially.

genialòide, *s.m.* clever but cranky person.

genière, *s.m.* (*mil.*) engineer.

gènio[1], *s.m.* **1.** genius (*pl.* geniuses): *Shakespeare fu un raro —,* Shakespeare was a rare genius; *sono due geni,* they are two geniuses **2.** (*talento, inclinazione*) genius; talent, disposition; gift, bent, inclination: *avere — per la matematica, la musica, la poesia,* to have a genius (*o* a talent *o* a gift) for mathematics, music, poetry; *avere — per la recitazione,* to have a talent (*o* bent) for acting ‖ *andare a —,* to be to one's taste (*o* to be to one's liking *o* to please *o* to suit): *ciò non le andava a —,* that was not to her liking; *l'interpretazione del pianista non mi è andata a —,* the performance of the pianist didn't please (*o* satisfy) me; *non mi andò a — il suo comportamento,* I was not pleased with his behaviour; *non mi va a. — dover ripetere le stesse cose,* I don't like having to repeat the same things; *questa disposizione dei quadri non mi va a —,* this arrangement of the paintings is not to my taste; *se questo libro di testo ti va a —, tienilo pure,* if this text-book suits you, you can keep it **3.** (*spirito, carattere*) genius, disposition, character, nature, spirit: *il — della lingua,* the nature (*o* the spirit) of the language **4.** (*divinità tutelare*) genius (*pl.* genii); (*mit.* araba) genie (*pl.* genii); jinni, jinnee (*pl.* jinn): *il — della casa, della famiglia, del luogo,* genius domus, familiae, loci; *il mio buon, cattivo —,* my good, evil genius; *il mio — tutelare,* my guardian angel (*o* spirit).

gènio[2], *s.m.: il —,* (*mil.*) Engineers (*pl.*) (*o* Engineer Corps); (*nell'esercito britannico*) Royal Engineers (*pl.*); (*nell'esercito degli Stati Uniti*) Corps of Engineers; *— civile, militare, navale,* civil, military, naval engineers.

genioioidèo, *s.m.* (*anat.*) genihyoid muscle.

genitàle, *ag.* genital: *organi genitali,* (*anat.*) genitals (*o* genitalia).

genitívo, *ag.s.m.* (*gram.*) genitive: *— sassone,* possessive case (*o* genitive inflection).

gènito, *ag.* born.

genitofemoràle, *ag.* (*anat.*) genito-femoral.

genitóre, *s.m.* parent, father: *i nostri primi genitori,* our first parents.

genitourinàrio, *ag.* (*anat.*) genito-urinary.

genitríce, *s.f.* parent, mother: *la mia —,* my mother.

genitúra, *s.f.* birth, generation; procreation.

gennàio, *s.m.* January: *il primo, il sei —,* the first, the sixth of January.

Gènova, *no.pr.f.* (*geog.*) Genoa.

genovése, *ag.* Genoese ‖ *s.c.* Genoese (*invariato al pl.*).

Genovèffa, *no.pr.f.* Genevieve.

Genseríco, *no.pr.m.* (*st.*) Genseric.

gentàglia, *s.f.* **1.** (*gente spregevole*) disreputable people (*coll. con costruzione pl.*) **2.** (*plebaglia*) rabble.

gènte, *s.f.* **1.** (*insieme di persone*) people (*coll. con costruzione pl.*), persons (*pl.*); (*fam.*) folk (*coll. con costruzione pl.*): *— di campagna,* country people; *— di chiesa,* clergy(men) (*o spreg.* churchy people); *— di città,* town people; *— di mare,* sailors (*o* seafaring folk); *— di teatro,* stage-folk; *— per bene,* respectable

people; *— seria,* reliable people; *brava —,* nice people (*o* persons *o* folk); *molta —,* a lot of (*o* many) people: *c'è molta — qui,* there are many people here; *non dar mai retta a ciò che la — dice,* never mind what people say; *quanta —!,* what a crowd!; *questa è — straniera,* these are foreign people; *sii gentile con la —!,* be kind to people! **2.** (*famiglia*) people (*coll. con costruzione pl.*); (*fam.*) folks (*pl.*): *la mia — sta in campagna,* my people (*o* folks) live in the country **3.**(*popolo*) people, nation: *il diritto delle genti,* the law of nations; *le genti d'Europa,* the peoples (*o* nations) of Europe.

gentildònna, *s.f.* gentlewoman (*pl.* gentlewomen); lady.

gentíle[1], *ag.* **1.** kind; (*cortese*) polite: *— con tutti,* kind (*o* polite) to everybody; *parole gentili,* kind words; *un commesso —,* a polite salesman; *è — da parte tua fare ciò,* it is kind of you to do this; *vuoi essere così — da chiudere la finestra?,* will you be so kind as to shut the window?; *essere — con qlcu.,* to be kind to s.o. **2.** (*delicato*) gentle: *cuore —,* gentle heart; *natura —,* gentle nature; *voce —,* gentle voice ‖ *il gentil sesso,* the gentle (*o* fair) sex **3.** (*di legno, marmo, ecc.*) soft: *legno —,* softwood.

gentíle[2], *ag.* **1.** (*non ebreo*) Gentile ‖ *i Gentili,* the Gentiles **2.** (*pagano*) pagan, heathen.

gentileseaménte, *av.* after the Gentiles.

gentilésco, *ag.* **1.** (*non ebreo*) Gentile **2.** (*pagano*) pagan, heathen.

gentilésimo, *s.m.* Gentilism.

gentilézza, *s.f.* **1.** kindness; (*cortesia*) politeness: *una gran —,* a great kindness; *grazie della vostra —,* thank you for your kindness; *per — verso qlcu.,* out of kindness to s.o.; *la sua — la rende simpatica a tutti,* her politeness makes everyone like her **2.** (*piacere, favore*) kindness, favour: *ella mi ha fatto molte gentilezze,* she has done me many kindnesses; *fammi questa —, ti prego!,* do me this kindness, please!; *fatemi la — di uscire,* will you have the kindness to go out?; *fatemi questa —,* do me this favour ‖ *per —!,* please!.

gentilità, *s.f.* Gentilism.

gentilízio, *ag.* gentilitial, noble: *stemma —,* coat of arms (*o* heraldic bearings).

gentilménte, *av.* kindly; (*cortesemente*) politely.

gentiluòmo, *s.m.* **1.** gentleman (*pl.* gentlemen); nobleman (*pl.* noblemen): *— di campagna,* country gentleman (*o* squire) **2.** (*uomo d'onore*) man of honour, gentleman (*pl.* gentlemen): *parola di —!,* on the honour of a gentleman!; *comportarsi da —,* to behave like a gentleman.

gentúcola, *s.f.* (*spreg.*) (low) people (*coll. con costruzione pl.*).

genuflessióne, *s.f.* genuflection, genuflexion: *fare una —,* to genuflect (*o* to bend the knee).

genuflèsso, *ag.* kneeling, on one's knees.

genuflessòrio, *s.m.* kneeling-stool; prie-dieu.

genuflèttersi, *v.r.* to genuflect, to kneel (down).

genuinaménte, *av.* genuinely.

genuinità, *s.f.* genuineness.

genuíno, *ag.* genuine; (*naturale*) natural: *vino —,* genuine (*o* natural) wine.

genziàna, *s.f.* (*bot.*) gentian.

genzianèlla, *s.f.* (*bot.*) gentianella.

geocèntrico, *ag.* (*astr.*) geocentric ‖ *coordinate geocentriche,* (*geog.*) geocentric co-ordinates.

geocentrísmo, *s.m.* (*astr.*) geocentricism.

geochímica, *s.f.* geochemistry.

geòde, *s.m.* **1.** (*min.*) geode **2.** (*patol.*) geode, cavity.

geodesía, *s.f.* geodesy.

geodètico, *ag.* geodetic(al), geodesic: *costruzione geodetica,* (*aer.*) geodetic construction.

geodinàmica, *s.f.* (*geol.*) geodynamics.

geodinàmico, *ag.* (*geol.*) geodynamic(al).

geofagía, *s.f.* (*patol.*) geophagy, geophagism.

geofísica, *s.f.* geophysics.

geofísico, *ag.* geophysical: *anno* —, geophysical year ‖ *s.m.* 1. geophysicist 2. (*aer.*) (*assistente meteorologico*) air-meteorologist.

geòfono, *s.m.* (*fis.*) geophone.

geognosía, *s.f.* (*geol.*) geognosy.

geogonía, *s.f.* geogony, geogeny.

geogònico, *ag.* geogonic(al), geogenic.

geografía, *s.f.* geography: — *fisica, politica,* physical, political geography.

geograficaménte, *av.* geographically.

geogràfico, *ag.* geographic(al): *carta geografica,* map.

geògrafo, *s.m.* geographer.

geòide, *s.m.* (*geol.*) geoid.

geología, *s.f.* geology.

geologicaménte, *av.* geologically.

geològico, *ag.* geologic(al).

geòlogo, *s.m.* geologist.

geomànte, *s.m.* geomancer.

geomàntico, *ag.* geomantic(al).

geomanzía, *s.f.* geomancy.

geòmetra, *s.m.* 1. geometer; (*rar.*) geometrician 2. (*agrimensore*) land-surveyor, surveyor.

geometría, *s.f.* geometry: — *analitica, descrittiva, euclidea,* analytic, descriptive, Euclidean geometry; — *piana, solida,* plane, solid geometry.

geometricaménte, *av.* geometrically.

geomètrico, *ag.* geometric(al): *progressione geometrica,* geometrical progression.

geomorfología, *s.f.* geomorphology.

geoplàstica, *s.f.* relief topography.

geopolítica, *s.f.* geopolitics.

Geòrgia, *no.pr.f.* (*geog.*) Georgia.

georgiàno, *ag.s.m.* Georgian.

geòrgica, *s.f.* (*lett.*) georgic ‖ *le « Georgiche » di Virgilio,* "The Georgics" of Virgil.

geòrgico, *ag.* georgic.

geoscopía, *s.f.* (*geol. geog.*) geoscopy.

geostàtica, *s.f.* geostatics.

geotèrmica, *s.f.* geothermics.

geotèrmico, *ag.* (*geol.*) geothermal, geothermic.

geotropísmo, *s.m.* (*bot.*) geotropism.

Gèova, *no.pr.m.* (*Bibbia*) Jehovah.

Geraldína, *no.pr.f.* Geraldine.

gerànio, *s.m.* (*bot.*) geranium; (*pop.*) crane's bill.

geràrca, *s.m.* 1. (*eccl.*) hierarch 2. (*capo*) leader.

gerarchía, *s.f.* hierarchy.

gerarchicaménte, *av.* hierarchically.

geràrchico, *ag.* hierarchic(al): *per via gerarchicq,* through official (*o* the usual) channels.

Geràrdo, *no.pr.m.* Gerald, Gerard.

Geremía, *no.pr.m.* Jeremy, Jeremias, Jeremiah ‖ *dim.* Jerry ‖ **geremía,** *s.m.* (*chi si lamenta sempre*) Jeremiah.

geremíade, *s.f.* jeremiad, lamentation.

gerènte, *s.m.* manager, director, managing director: — *responsabile, (di giornale)* managing editor.

gerènza, *s.f.* management, direction, administration.

gèrgo, *s.m.* slang; (*di una particolare classe professionale*) jargon: — *dei ladri,* thieves' cant; — *della critica,* critics' jargon; — *filosofico,* jargon of philosophy; — *metafisico,* metaphysical jargon; — *scolastico,* schoolboy slang; — *universitario,* college (*o* university) slang; *espressione, parola del* —, slang expression, slang-word.

geriàtrica, *s.f.* (*med.*) geriatrics.

Gèrico, *no.pr.f.* (*geog. st.*) Jericho.

Geríóne, *no.pr.m.* (*mit.*) Geryon.

gèrla, *s.f.* pannier.

gèrlo, *s.m.* (*mar.*) gasket.

Germàna, *no.pr.f.* Germaine.

germanésimo, *s.m.* Germanism.

Germània, *no.pr.f.* (*geog.*) Germany.

germànico, *ag.* Germanic; Teutonic: *lingue germaniche,* Germanic languages ‖ *l'Impero Germanico,* the German Empire ‖ *s.m.* (*lingua*) Germanic ‖ **Germànico,** *no.pr.m.* (*st.*) Germanicus.

germànio, *s.m.* (*chim.*) germanium.

germanísta, *s.c.* Germanist.

germanizzàre, *v.t.i.* to Germanize.

germàno[1], *ag.s.m.* German ‖ *i germani,* the Germans.

germàno[2], *ag.* german: *cugino* —, cousin-german (*o* first cousin); *fratello* —, brother-german (*o* own brother *o* full-brother) ‖ *s.m.* (*dir.*) brother, own brother.

germàno[3], *s.m.* (*ornit.*) wild duck.

germanofilía, *s.f.* Germanophilia.

germanòfilo, *s.m.* Germanophil(e).

germanofobía, *s.f.* Germanophobia.

germanòfobo, *s.m.* Germanophobe.

gèrme, *s.m* 1. germ: — *di una patata,* eye of a potato ‖ *in* —, in germ (*o* in embryo) 2. *fig.* (*origine*) germ, origin, source: — *di un'idea,* germ of an idea.

germicída, *ag.* germicidal ‖ *s.m.* germicide.

germíle, *s.m.* (*st. francese*) Germinal.

germinàle, *ag.* (*biol.*) germinal: *foglia* —, seed-leaf ‖ *s.m.* (*st. francese*) Germinal.

germinànte, *ag.* germinant, germinating, sprouting.

germinàre, *v.t.* to germinate ‖ *v.i.* to germinate; (*germogliare*) to bud, to sprout.

germinatívo, *ag.* germinative.

germinazióne, *s.f.* germination.

gèrmine, *s.m.* 1. (*letter.*) per **gèrme** 2. *pl.* (*giuoco di carte*) tarots.

germogliaménto, *s.m.* sprouting, germinating, budding, shooting.

germogliàre, *v.i.* 1. to sprout, to germinate, to spring (up), to bud, to shoot 2. *fig.* to germinate; to spring up: *un dubbio germogliò nella sua mente,* a doubt sprang (up) in his mind ‖ *v.t.* to sprout, to put out, to put forth.

germóglio, *s.m.* 1. sprout, shoot 2. *fig.* (*origine*) germ.

Geroboàmo, *no.pr.m.* (*Bibbia*) Jeroboam.

gerofànte, *s.m.* (*st. greca*) hierophant.

geroglífico, *ag.* hieroglyphic(al) ‖ *s.m.* hieroglyph, hieroglyphic (*anche fig.*).

Geròlamo, Gerònimo, *no.pr.m.* Jerome ‖ *dim.* Jerry.

gerontocòmio, *s.m.* home for the aged.

gerontocrazía, *s.f.* gerontocracy.

gerontoiatría, *s.f.* (*med.*) geriatrics.

gerontología, *s.f.* (*med.*) gerontology.

Gerosòlima, *no.pr.f.* (*geog. arc.*) Jerusalem.

gerosolimitàno, *ag.* of Jerusalem ‖ *ordine* —, order of St. John of Jerusalem ‖ *s.m.* (*cavaliere dell'ordine di S. Giovanni in Gerusalemme*) Knight Hospital(l)er (of St. John of Jerusalem).

Gertrúde, *no.pr.f.* Gertrude ‖ *dim.* Gertie, Trudy.

gerúndio, *s.m.* (*gram.*) gerund: *verbo al* —, verb in the gerund.

gerundívo, *ag.* (*gram.*) gerundive.

Gerusalèmme, *no.pr.f.* (*geog.*) Jerusalem.

Gervàso, *no.pr.m.* Gervase, Jervis.

gessàia, *s.f.* chalk-pit.

gessàio, gessaiuòlo, *s.m.* plasterer.

gessàre, *v.t.* 1. (*agr.*) to lime, to dress with lime 2. (*vino*) to plaster, to treat with gypsum.

gessatúra, *s.f.* 1. (*agr.*) liming, dressing with lime 2. (*di vino*) plastering.

gessétto, *s.m.* chalk: *scatola di gessetti,* chalk-box.

gèsso, *s.m.* 1. chalk: — *per sarti,* French chalk; *cava di* —, chalk-pit; *un pezzo di* —, a piece of chalk; *segnare ql.co. col* —, to chalk sthg. up 2. (*edil. scult. med.*) plaster (of Paris): *un* —, *una figura di* —, a plaster figure; *forma di* —, plaster cast; *modello in* —, plaster mould (*o* model in plaster) 3. (*min.*) gypsum.

gessóso, *ag.* chalky.

gèsta, *s.f.pl.* deeds, feats, exploits; great achievements, noble achievements ‖ *canzoni di* —, (*lett.*) chansons de geste.

gestànte, *ag.* gravid, pregnant ‖ *s.f.* pregnant woman.

gestatòrio, *ag.* (*eccl.*) gestatorial: *sedia gestatoria,* gestatorial chair.

gestazióne, *s.f.* (*fisiol.*) gestation.

gesteggiàre, *v.i.* to gesticulate, to gesture.

gesticolaménto, *s.m.* gesticulating, gesticulation.

gesticolàre, *v.i.* to gesticulate, to gesture.

gesticolatóre, *s.m.* gesticulator.

gesticolazióne, *s.f.* gesticulating, gesticulation.

gestióne, *s.f.* management; administration: *consiglio di* —, council of management; *assumere la — di un'azienda,* to take over the management of a business (*o* to take over a business).

gestíre[1], *v.i.* (*gesticolare*) to gesticulate, to gesture, to make gestures.

gestíre[2], *v.t.* (*amministrare*) to manage, to administer, to run: — *un'azienda,* to manage a firm (*o* to run a business).

gèsto, *s.m.* gesture: *far gesti,* to make gestures ǁ *un bel* —, a fine action (*o* a noble deed).

gestóre, *s.m.* (*amministratore*) manager, administrator.

Gesú, *no.pr.m.* Jesus: — *Bambino,* Infant Jesus (*o* Christ-Child); — *Cristo,* Jesus Christ ǁ *essere tutto — e Maria,* to be a bigot.

gesuíta, *s.m.* 1. Jesuit 2. *fig.* (*spreg.*) Jesuit, intriguer, prevaricator.

gesuitería, *s.f. fig.* (*spreg.*) Jesuitry, prevarication.

gesuiticaménte, *av. fig.* (*spreg.*) Jesuitically.

gesuítico, *ag. fig.* (*spreg.*) Jesuitic(al).

gesuítismo, *s.m.* 1. Jesuitism 2. *fig.* (*spreg.*) Jesuitry, prevarication.

Gesummaría, *inter.* God bless me!, good heavens!.

Getsèmani, *no.pr.m.* (*Bibbia*) Gethsemane.

gettàre, *v.t.* 1. to throw; to cast; (*con violenza*) to fling, to hurl: *gettai un osso al cane,* I threw a bone to the dog (*o* I threw the dog a bone); *gettai la palla al ragazzo,* I threw the ball to the boy; *gettami la fune!,* throw me the rope!; *mi gettò uno sguardo irato,* he threw an angry look at me; — *acqua in faccia a qlcu.,* to dash water in s.o.'s face; — *un bacio a qlcu.,* to throw s.o. a kiss; — *uno sguardo a qlcu.,* to throw (*o* to cast) a glance at s.o. ǁ — *ql.co. al di là di,* to throw sthg. over: — *una palla al di là di un muro,* to throw a ball over a wall ǁ — *ql.co. contro qlcu.,* to throw (*o* to hurl) sthg. at s.o.: *gettò pietre contro di me,* he threw stones at me; — *una lancia contro qlcu.,* to hurl a lance at s.o. ǁ — *ql.co. dentro,* to throw sthg. in: *gettalo dentro dalla finestra!,* throw it in through the window! ǁ — *ql.co., qlcu. fuori da,* to 'throw sthg., s.o. out of: *furono gettati fuori da quel luogo,* they were thrown out of that place ǁ — *ql.co., qlcu. giù, in terra,* to throw sthg., s.o. down: *fu gettato giù di sella,* he was thrown (down) from his horse; *non gettarlo giù!,* don't throw it down!; — *qlcu. a terra,* to knock s.o. down ǁ — *ql.co. in,* to throw (*o* to cast *o* to fling) sthg. into: — *una pietra nel lago,* to fling a stone into the lake; — *polvere negli occhi a qlcu., fig.* to throw dust in s.o.'s eyes; — *ql.co. in faccia a qlcu.,* to throw (*o* to fling) sthg. in s.o.'s teeth; — *ql.co. in mare,* (*da un natante*) to throw sthg. overboard; (*un carico*) to jettison ǁ — *ql.co. in alto,* to throw sthg. up: *gettarono in alto il cappello,* they threw up their hats; — *in alto una moneta,* to toss a coin ǁ — *ql.co. indietro,* to throw sthg. back: — *uno sguardo indietro,* to throw a glance backwards; — *la testa indietro,* to throw one's head back ǁ — *ql.co. su,* to throw (*o* to cast) sthg. on (*o* over): — *biasimo su qlcu.,* to cast (*o* to throw) blame on s.o.; — *il fieno sul carro,* to pitch the hay on to the cart; — *luce su ql.co., fig.* to throw light on sthg.; — *un'ombra su ql.co., fig.* to cast a shadow on sthg. ǁ — *via ql.co.,* to throw sthg. away: *gettò via la sua ultima occasione,* he threw away his last chance; *non — via queste cose!,* don't throw these things away! ǁ — *all'aria,* to throw into confusion ǁ — *a rottame,* to scrap ǁ — *l'ancora,* to cast anchor (*o* to let go the anchor) ǁ — *i dadi,* to cast dice ǁ — *il guanto,* to throw

(*o* to fling) down the glove (*o* the gauntlet) ǁ — *la lenza,* to cast the (fishing-) line ǁ — *la maschera,* to throw off the mask ǁ *le reti,* to cast the nets ǁ — *i semi della discordia,* to sow the seeds of discord ǁ — *una sfida,* to throw out a challenge ǁ — *i soldi dalla finestra,* to throw (*o* to fling) one's money out of the window (*o* to play ducks and drakes with one's money) ǁ — *via il proprio denaro,* to squander one's money ǁ — *via il proprio tempo,* to waste (*o* to throw away) one's time 2. (*emettere*): *la ferita getta sangue,* the wound is spouting blood (*o* is bleeding profusely); *la rosa getta un grato odore,* the rose gives off a fragrant scent (*o* smells deliciously); — *un grido,* to utter a cry 3. (*collocare*) to lay: — *le fondamenta,* to lay the foundation(s) 4. (*metal. edil.*) to cast 5. (*bot.*) to put forth, to sprout ǁ *v.i.* 1. (*versare*) to play: *la fontana non getta più da due giorni,* the fountain hasn't been playing for two days 2. (*econ.*) (*fruttare*) to yield: *le imposte hanno gettato più dell'anno scorso,* the taxes have yielded more than last year ǁ **gettàrsi,** *v.r.* 1. to throw oneself, to fling oneself: *ella si gettò nelle braccia della madre,* she threw (*o* flung) herself into her mother's arms; *si gettò sul letto,* she threw herself down on the bed; — *ai piedi di qlcu.,* to throw oneself at s.o.'s feet; — *al collo di qlcu.,* to fall on s.o.'s neck; — *giù,* (*a terra*) to throw oneself down; (*sdraiarsi*) to lie down: *gettati giù un momento, sembri stanca,* lie down a while, you look tired; — *in acqua,* to throw oneself (*o* to jump 'o to leap) into the water; — *in avanti, all'indietro,* to throw oneself forwards, backwards; — *in ginocchio,* to throw oneself (*o* to fall) on one's knees ǁ — *a capofitto in ql.co.,* to throw oneself into sthg. ǁ — *nella discussione,* to throw oneself into the discussion (*o* to plunge into the debate) ǁ — *nella mischia,* to throw oneself into the fray ǁ — *sul nemico,* to fall on (*o* to attack) the enemy ǁ — *via,* to throw oneself away 2. (*di fiume, sboccare*) to flow: *il Po si getta nell'Adriatico,* the Po flows into the Adriatic.

gettàta, *s.f.* 1. throw, cast; hurl(ing) 2. (*artigl.*) range: *cannone a lunga* —, long-range gun 3. (*di aria*) throw 4. (*edil.*) casting 5. (*di molo*) jetty 6. (*metal.*) cast 7. (*bot.*) shooting.

gettàto, *ag.* 1. thrown, cast ǁ *fatica gettata,* useless work 2. (*metal.*) cast.

gèttito, *s.m.* 1. (*tassa*) yield 2. (*lancio di merce in mare*) jettison; (*la merce così gettata*) jetsam.

gètto, *s.m.* 1. throw, throwing: *far — di ql.co.,* to throw sthg. away 2. (*di liquido*) jet, spout, gush: — *di acqua,* jet of water (*o* water-spout); *getti d'acqua,* streams of spouting water ǁ *a — continuo,* continuously (*o* uninterruptedly) ǁ *di —,* effortlessly 3. (*bot.*) shoot; sprout 4. (*metal. edil.*) casting: — *cavo,* hollow casting; — *di acciaio fuso,* steel casting; — *di calcestruzzo,* concrete casting 5. (*mec.*) jet: — *d'avviamento,* starting jet; — *di potenza,* power jet 6. (*lancio di merci in mare*) jettison 7. (*abbozzo*) draft: *il primo* —, the first draft.

gettóne, *s.m.* (*al giuoco*) counter; (*telefonico*) counter for the telephone; (*contromarca*) check: — *di presenza,* attendance check; *macchina a* —, slot-machine.

geyser, *s.m.* (*geol.*) geyser.

ghèiscia, *s.f.* geisha.

ghepàrdo, *s.m.* (*zool.*) cheetah.

ghéppio, *s.m.* (*ornit.*) kestrel.

gheríglio, *s.m.* kernel.

gherlíno, *s.m.* (*mar.*) hawser: — *da rimorchio,* towing hawser.

gherminèlla, *s.f.* trick: *mi fecero una* —, they played a trick on me.

ghermíre, *v.t.* 1. to claw, to clutch, to grip 2. (*prendere con forza*) to clutch, to seize, to snatch (*anche fig.*): — *il potere,* to clutch power.

ghermitóre, *s.m.,* **ghermitríce,** *s.f.* snatcher.

gheróne, *s.m.* 1. (*falda triangolare in un indumento*) gusset 2. (*mar.*) gore.

ghétta, *s.f.* **1.** (*bassa, di panno*) spat: *un signore con le ghette*, a gentleman in spats **2.** (*alta, di panno, di pelle*) gaiter, spatter dash.

ghétto, *s.m.* **1.** ghetto (*pl.* ghettos) **2.** (*l'insieme degli ebrei*) Jewry **3.** (*luogo sudicio abitato da povera gente*) slum **4.** (*chiasso, clamore*) row, uproar: *far un —*, to raise an uproar.

ghía, *s.f.* (*mar.*) whip: *— doppia*, double whip.

ghiacciàia, *s.f.* **1.** ice-box, ice-chest **2.** (*ambiente in cui si conserva il ghiaccio*) ice-house (anche *fig.*): *questa stanza è una —*, *fig.* this room is like an ice-house.

ghiacciàio, *s.m.* glacier: *crepacci del —*, crevasses of the glacier; *la bocca del —*, the glacier snout; *tavole, funghi dei ghiacciai*, glacier tables.

ghiacciàre, *v.t.* to freeze; to ice: *il freddo ha ghiacciato lo stagno*, the cold has frozen the pond; *— l'acqua, lo champagne*, to ice water, champagne ‖ *v.i.* to freeze: *il lago ghiacciò*, the lake froze (over).

ghiacciàta, *s.f.* iced drink.

ghiacciàto, *ag.* **1.** (*gelato*) frozen: *lago —*, frozen lake **2.** (*freddissimo*) icy: *acqua ghiacciata*, icy water; *tè, caffè —*, iced tea, coffee.

ghiàccio, *s.m.* ice: *ghiacci alla deriva*, icebergs; *— secco*, dry ice ‖ *banco di —*, ice-field; (*galleggiante*) floe (o ice-floe); *cubetti di —*, ice cubes; *disco sul —*, (*spor.*) ice-hockey; *fabbrica di —*, ice plant; *fabbricazione del —*, ice making; *freddo come il —*, as cold as ice; *lastra di —*, ice slab; *secchiello del —*, ice-pail; *vacanze sul —*, holidays on ice; *mettere in — una bottiglia*, to ice a bottle ‖ *rompere il —*, *fig.* to break the ice.

ghiacciuòlo, *s.m.* **1.** icicle **2.** (*chicco di grandine*) hail-stone **3.** (*di pietra preziosa*) flaw.

ghiàia, *s.f.* gravel; pebble: *cava di —*, gravel-pit; *letto di —*, (*ferr.*) ballast; *ricoprire di —*, to lay (o to strew) with gravel.

ghiaióso, *ag.* gravelly: *terreno —*, gravelly soil.

ghiànda, *s.f.* **1.** (*bot.*) acorn ‖ *valvola a —*, (*termoionica*) acorn tube **2.** (*ornamento per frange*) tassel.

ghiandàia, *s.f.* (*ornit.*) jay.

ghiandífero, *ag.* (*bot.*) glandiferous; acorn-bearing.

ghiàndola, *s.f.* (*anat.*) gland: *— a secrezione interna*, ductless gland; *— tiroidea*, thyroid gland.

ghiandolàre, *ag.* (*anat.*) glandular.

ghiàra, *V.* **ghiàia**.

ghiaréto, *s.m.* shingle bank.

ghibellinísmo, *s.m.* (*st.*) Ghibellinism.

ghibellíno, *ag.s.m.* (*st.*) Ghibelline.

ghíbli, *s.m.* gibleh.

ghièra, *s.f.* **1.** (*all'estremità di bastone, ombrello, ecc.*) ferrule; metal ring; (*all'imboccatura di fodero di spada*) chape **2.** (*arch.*) arched lintel **3.** (*mec.*) ring nut, nut, metal ring.

ghieràto, *ag.* (*munito di puntale*) ferruled.

ghíglia, *s.f.* lanyard, laniard.

ghigliottína, *s.f.* guillotine ‖ *finestra a —*, sash-window.

ghigliottinàre, *v.t.* to guillotine.

ghígna, *s.f.* **1.** grimace; ugly face, sinister face **2.** (*faccia tosta*) cheek.

ghignàre, *v.i.* to sneer; to grin.

ghignàta, *s.f.* sneering; grinning.

ghigno, *s.m.* sneer; grin.

ghínda, *s.f.* (*mar.*) hoist.

ghindàre, *v.t.* **1.** (*mar.*) to sway; (*issare*) to hoist, to raise; to windlass: *— una bandiera*, to hoist a flag **2.** (*mil.*) to rack down, to lash down.

ghindàzzo, *s.m.* (*mar.*) top-rope.

ghinèa, *s.f.* (*antica moneta britannica*) guinea (sopravvive come moneta nominale = 21 s.).

ghingheri, *s.m.pl.*: *essere in —*, to be smartly dressed (o dressed up); *mettersi in —*, to dress up.

ghiótta, *s.f.* (*cuc.*) dripping-pan.

ghiottaménte, *av.* gluttonously, greedily.

ghiótto, *ag.* **1.** gluttonous, greedy: *che bimbo —!*, what a greedy child! **2.** (*appetitoso*) dainty, appetizing,

delicious: *un boccone —*, a dainty bit **3.** (*avido*) eager, greedy: *essere — di guadagni*, to be eager for gain **4.** (*raro, peregrino*) rare: *è un libro —*, it is a rare book ‖ *s.m.* glutton, gourmand, gourmet.

ghiottóne, *s.m.* **1.** glutton, gourmand, gourmet, epicure **2.** (*zool.*) glutton.

ghiottonería, *s.f.* **1.** gluttony **2.** (*cibo ghiotto*) dainty, tit-bit, delicacy (anche *fig.*) **3.** (*rarità, cosa rara*) rarity.

ghiòzzo, *s.m.* **1.** (*ittiol.*) gudgeon, goby **2.** *fig.* (*sciocco*) gudgeon, fool, simpleton.

ghírba, *s.f.*: *portare a casa la —*, (*gergo mil.*) to save one's skin.

ghiribizzàre, *v.i.* to be whimsical.

ghiribízzo, *s.m.* whim, fancy, caprice, freak: *mi salta il — di cantare*, I have a fancy to sing.

ghiribizzóso, *ag.* whimsical, full of whims, capricious, freakish.

ghirigòro, *s.m.* flourish scroll; (*arabesco*) arabesque.

ghirlànda, *s.f.* garland, wreath.

ghirlandàio, *s.m.* **1.** (*chi fabbrica ghirlande*) wreath maker **2.** (*chi vende ghirlande*) wreath seller.

ghíro, *s.m.* (*zool.*) dormouse (*pl.* dormice) ‖ *dormire come un —*, to sleep like a log.

ghirónda, *s.f.* (*mus.*) hurdy-gurdy.

ghísa, *s.f.* cast iron: *— da fonderia*, foundry pig; *— di alto forno*, pig iron; *— fosforosa*, phosphoric pig iron; *— refrattaria*, heat-resisting cast iron; *— sintetica*, synthetic cast iron; *— temprata*, chilled iron.

gi, *s.f.m.* letter G.

già, *av.* **1.** already: *— le dieci!*, ten o'clock already!; *ci sono — stato*, I have already been there; *è — di ritorno?*, is he already back?; *è — finito*, it is already finished (o over); *è — tardi*, it is already late; *quando lo conobbi, era — vecchio*, when I met him, he was already old ‖ *— citato*, above-mentioned; *— descritto*, previously described ‖ *abiti — fatti*, ready-made clothes **2.** (*un tempo*) once, formerly: *la città, — capitale del regno*, the town, once capital of the kingdom; *il signor Y, — primo ministro*, Mr. Y, the former (o ex-) Prime Minister **3.** (*affermazione*) yes, of course, certainly; indeed, really, no doubt; (*fam.*) sure: *—!*, of course, yes!; *—, hai ragione*, of course you are right.

Giacàrta, *no.pr.f.* (*geog.*) Djakarta, Jakarta.

giàcca, *s.f.* coat, jacket: *— a maglia*, cardigan; *— a vento*, wind-cheater; *— di cuoio*, leather jacket; *— e gonna*, coat and skirt; *— e pantaloni*, coat and trousers; *— sportiva*, sports jacket.

giacché, *cong.* as, for, since; now that: *— lo vuoi*, since you want it.

giaccheria, *s.f.* (*st.*) Jacquerie.

giacchétta, *s.f.* coat, jacket.

giàcchio, *s.m.* (*mar.*) sweep-net.

giacènte, *ag.* **1.** lying, lying down; (*situato*) placed, situated **2.** (*di capitale*) uninvested, lying idle, unproductive **3.** (*dir.*) in abeyance **4.** (*di posta*) unclaimed: *una lettera —*, an unclaimed letter.

giacènza, *s.f.* **1.** (*l'essere giacente*) lying **2.** (*di capitali, merci*): *capitale in —*, uninvested (o unproductive) capital; *denaro, merce in —*, (*non ritirati*) unclaimed money, goods; *denaro in — presso una banca*, money lying at a bank; *giorni di —*, (*controstallie*) demurrage-days (o days of detention) ‖ *libri in —*, (*non venduti*) unsold copies; *merci in —*, goods in stock; (*merci giacenti*) stock.

giacére, *v.i.* to lie: *egli giaceva esanime al suolo*, he was lying lifeless on the ground; *le isole Ebridi giacciono a nord della Scozia*, the Hebrides lie (to the) north of Scotland; *i loro denari giacciono in banca*, their money lies (idle) at the bank; *« qui giace... »*, " here lies... "; *l'uomo cadde e giacque immobile a terra*, the man dropped and lay motionless on the ground ‖ *— addormentato, ammalato*, to lie asleep, ill; *— a letto, in prigione*, to lie in bed, in prison; *— in rovina*, to lie in ruins; *— nel cimitero*, to lie in the church-yard; *— nella miseria*, to be badly off (o to be destitute); — *nella polvere*, to lie in the dust; — *sul fianco, bocconi, supino*, to lie on one's side, on one's face, on one's back: *mettersi a* —, to lie down ‖ *chi muore giace e chi vive si dà pace*, *prov.* let the dead bury the dead.

giacíglio, *s.m.* couch; (*di paglia*) pallet, straw bed.

giaciménto, *s.m.* (*geol.*) layer; (*miner.*) ore deposit, ore body; mine: — *alluvionale*, alluvial deposit; — *aurifero*, gold deposit; — *di carbone*, coal seam; — *di petrolio*, oil-field; — *di sale*, salt-mine; *giacimenti minerari*, mineral deposits.

giacintíno, *ag.* hyacinthine.

giacínto[1], *s.m.* (*bot. min.*) hyacinth.

Giacínto[2], *no.pr.m.* (*mit.*) Hyacinthus.

giacitúra, *s.f.* 1. (*il giacere*) lying(-down) 2. (*posizione*) position; posture: *la* — *delle parole*, the position of words; — *incomoda*, uncomfortable posture.

giàco, *s.m.* (*armatura*) coat of mail.

Giacòbbe, *no.pr.m.* (*Bibbia*) Jacob.

giacobinísmo, *s.m.* (*st.*) Jacobinism.

giacobíno, *ag. s.m.* (*st.*) Jacobin.

giacobíta, *ag. s.c.* (*st.*) Jacobite.

Giacomína, *no.pr.f.* Jacqueline.

Giàcomo, *no.pr.m.* James ‖ *dim.* Jamie, Jim(my).

giaconétta, *s.f.* (*stoffa*) jaconet.

giaculatòria, *s.f.* ejaculation.

giàda, *s.f.* (*min.*) jade.

giadeíte, *s.f.* (*min.*) jadeite.

Giaèle, *no.pr.f.* (*Bibbia*) Jael.

Giàffa, *no.pr.f.* (*geog.*) Jaffa.

giaggiuòlo, *s.m.* (*bot.*) iris.

giaguàro, *s.m.* (*zool.*) jaguar.

gialàppa, *s.f.* (*farm.*) jalap.

giallàstro, *ag.* yellowish.

giallézza, *s.f.* yellowness.

giallíccio, *ag.* yellowish.

giallíno, *ag.* light yellow.

giàllo, *ag.* yellow: *farina gialla*, maize meal; *febbre gialla*, yellow-fever; *dramma, film* —, thriller; *libro* —, thriller (*o* detective story); *pericolo* —, yellow peril; *le razze gialle*, the yellow races; *la stampa gialla*, the yellow press ‖ *s.m.* 1. yellow: — *limone*, lemon yellow; — *ocra*, yellow ochre (*o* oxide yellow); — *paglierino*, straw yellow; *il* — *ti dona*, yellow suits you 2. (*film, dramma*) thriller; (*libro*) thriller, detective story 3. — *d'uovo*, yolk.

giallògnolo, *ag.* yellowish, faded yellow.

giallóre, *s.m.* 1. yellowness 2. (*carnagione giallastra*) yellowish complexion; pale complexion.

giallúria, *s.f.* (*polline di rose*) yellow pollen of roses.

Giamàica, *no.pr.f.* (*geog.*) Jamaica.

giàmbico, *ag.* (*poes.*) iambic: *pentametro* —, iambic pentameter; *piedi giambici*, iambic feet.

giàmbo, *s.m.* (*poes.*) iamb, iambus (*pl.* iambuses, iambi).

giammài, *av.* never: — *uomo fu più ammirato*, never was a man more admired.

Giandúia[1], *no.pr.m.* "Gianduia" (pantomime character typifying Turin).

giandúia[2], **gianduiòtto**, *s.m.* "gianduia" (chocolate drop from Turin).

Gianícolo, *no.pr.m.* (*geog.*) Janiculum.

giannétta, *s.f.* walking cane.

Giànni, *no.pr.m. dim.* di **Giovànni**.

Giannína, *no.pr.f. dim.* di **Giovànna**.

Gianníno, *no.pr.m. dim.* di **Giovànni**.

giannízzero, *s.m.* janissary, janizary.

Giàno, *no.pr.m.* (*mit.*) Janus ‖ — *bifronte*, two-faced Janus.

giansenìàno, *s.m.* (*st. relig.*) Jansenistic.

giansenísmo, *s.m.* (*st. relig.*) Jansenism.

giansenísta, *s.c.* (*st. relig.*) Jansenist.

giansenístico, *ag.* (*st. relig.*) Jansenistic.

Giappóne, *no.pr.m.* (*geog.*) Japan.

giapponése, *ag.* Japanese ‖ *s.m.* 1. (*abitante*) Japanese (*invariato al pl.*); (*abbr. spreg.*) Jap 2. (*lingua*) (the) Japanese (language) ‖ *s.f.* Japanese (*invariato al pl.*), Japanese woman; (*abbr. spreg.*) Jap.

giàra, *s.f.* jar.

giardinàggio, *s.m.* gardening: *arnesi da* —, garden(ing) tools.

giardineria, *s.f.* gardening.

giardinétta, *s.f.* (*aut.*) 1. (small) station wagon 2. (*di maggior cilindrata*) estate car.

giardinétto, *s.m.* 1. small garden 2. (*mar.*) buttock: — *a piè d'albero*, fife rail.

giardinièra, *s.f.* 1. woman-gardener (*pl.* women-gardeners); (*moglie del giardiniere*) gardener's wife 2. (*mobile di sostegno per vasi di fiori*) flower-stand, jardinière 3. (*aut.*) small station wagon; (*di maggiore cilindrata*) estate car 4. (*cuc.*) pickled vegetables (*pl.*); (*zuppa di verdure*) vegetable soup.

giardinière, *s.m.* gardener.

giardíno, *s.m.* garden: — *botanico*, botanical gardens; — *pensile*, roof-garden; — *pubblico*, park; — *zoologico*, zoological gardens (*o* zoo); *andate in* —!, go into the garden! ‖ — *d'infanzia*, nursery school (*o* kindergarten).

giàrra, *s.f.* jar.

giarrettièra, *s.f.* garter; suspender ‖ *Ordine della Giarrettiera*, Order of the Garter; *Cavaliere dell'Ordine della Giarrettiera*, Knight of the Garter (*abbr.* K. G.).

Giasóne, *no.pr.m.* (*mit.*) Jason.

giàspide, *s.m.* (*min.*) jasper.

giaúrro, *s.m.* giaour.

Giàva, *no.pr.f.* (*geog.*) Java.

giavanése, *ag.* Javanese ‖ *s.c.* Javanese (*invariato al pl.*).

giavellòtto, *s.m.* javelin: *lancio del* —, javelin throwing; *lanciatore di* —, javelin thrower.

gibbóne, *s.m.* (*zool.*) gibbon.

gibbosità, *s.f.* gibbosity; hump.

gibbóso, gibbúto, *ag.* gibbous; humped, hunchbacked.

gibèrna, *s.f.* (*mil.*) cartridge-pouch, cartridge-box.

gibigiàna, *s.f.* (*dial.*) flash from a mirror.

Gibiltèrra, *no.pr.f.* (*geog.*) Gibraltar: *lo stretto di* —, the Straits of Gibraltar.

gíbus, *s.m.* gibus, opera-hat, crush-hat.

gíchero, *s.m.* (*bot.*) arum; (*pop.*) lords-and-ladies.

gíga, *s.f.* (*musica, danza*) jig.

gigànte, *ag.* gigantic, giant ‖ *s.m.* giant (anche *fig.*) ‖ *fare passi da* —, to make great strides (*o* to make rapid progress).

giganteggiàre, *v.i.* to tower (above s.o., sthg.), to stand like a giant, to rise like a giant (anche *fig.*): *giganteggia sui contemporanei*, he towers above hi contemporaries; *giganteggiava tra la folla*, he was towering above the crowd.

gigantescaménte, *av.* gigantically.

gigantésco, *ag.* gigantic (anche *fig.*): *ha un appetito* —, he has a gigantic appetite.

gigantéssa, *s.f.* giantess.

gigantísmo, *s.m.* (*med.*) giantism, gigantism.

gigantomachìa, *s.f.* (*mit.*) gigantomachy.

Gígi, *no.pr.m. dim.* di **Luígi**.

gigióne, *s.m.* (*teat.*) ham(-actor): *fare il* —, to overact (*o* to ham).

gigionísmo, *s.m.* (*teat.*) ham-acting.

gigliàcee, *s.f.pl.* (*bot.*) liliaceae.

gigliàceo, *ag.* (*bot.*) liliaceous.

gigliàstro, *s.m.* (*bot.*) wild lily.

gigliàto, *ag.* 1. (*sparso di gigli*) sown with lilies, adorned with lilies; lilied 2. (*che porta l'impronta del giglio*) stamped with a lily 3. (*arald.*) lilied ‖ *s.m.* "gigliato" (old Florentine or Neapolitan coin).

gíglio, *s.m.* 1. (*bot.*) lily: — *d'acqua*, water-lily; — *delle convalli*, lily of the valley; — *tigrato*, tiger -lily; *bianco come un* —, lily-white 2. (*arald.*) fleur-de-lis, fleur-de-lys: *i Gigli di Francia*, (*stemma dei re di Francia*) the Fleurs-de-lis (*o* the Lilies).

gigolette, *s.f.* young woman of easy virtue.

gigolo, *s.m.* gigolo, fancy-man.

Gilbèrto, *no.pr.m.* Gilbert ‖ *dim.* Gib(bie), Gil.

gílda[1], *s.f.* (*st.*) guild.

Gílda[2], *no.pr.f.* Gilda.

gilè, *s.m.* waistcoat: — *a fiori,* flowered waistcoat.

gimnospèrme, *s.f.pl.* (*bot.*) gymnosperms.

gimnòto, *s.m.* (*ittiol.*) gymnotus; (*pop.*) electric eel.

gin, *s.m.* gin.

gincàna, *s.f.* (*spor.*) gymkhana.

ginecèo, *s.m.* 1. (*archeol.*) gynaeceum (*pl.* gynaecea) 2. (*arem*) harem, haram 3. (*bot.*) gynaeceum (*pl.* gynaecea).

ginecofobía, *s.f.* (*patol.*) gynephobia.

ginecología, *s.f.* (*med.*) gynaecology.

ginecològico, *ag.* (*med.*) gynaecological.

ginecòlogo, *s.m.* (*med.*) gynaecologist.

ginépra, *s.f.* (*bot.*) juniper berry.

ginepràio, *s.m.* 1. juniper thicket, juniper bush 2. *fig.* (*situazione intricata*) difficult situation, fix: *cacciarsi in un —,* to get oneself into a fix.

ginépro, *s.m.* (*bot.*) juniper.

ginèstra, *s.f.* (*bot.*) broom: — *spinosa,* furze (*o* gorse *o* whin); *fibra di —,* broom fibre.

ginestrèlla, *s.f.* (*bot.*) dyer's broom.

ginestréto, *s.m.* (*bot.*) broom-coppice, broom-field.

ginestrína, *s.f.* (*bot.*) dyer's broom.

Ginévra[1], *no.pr.f.* (*lett.*) Guinever(e), Guenever.

Ginévra[2], *no.pr.f.* (*geog.*) Geneva: *lago di —,* Lake of Geneva.

ginevríno, *ag.s.m.* Genevan ‖ **ginevrína,** *s.f.* Genevan.

gingillàre, *v.i.,* **gingillàrsi,** *v.r.* 1. to trifle, to waste time 2. (*indugiare*) to dawdle, to loiter.

gingillíno, *s.m.* trifler, dawdler, loiterer.

gingillo, *s.m.* 1. (*ninnolo*) knick-knack, nick-nack; (*di poco valore*) trinket; trifle 2. (*balocco*) plaything (anche *fig.*): *quella donna era un — per lui,* that woman was a plaything to him.

gingillóne, *s.m.* trifler, dawdler; idler.

ginnasiàle, *ag.* grammar school (*attributivo*); (*di scuola italiana, tedesca*) gymnasial: *la seconda classe —,* the second form of the grammar school.

ginnasiàrca, *s.m.* (*st. greca*) gymnasiarch.

ginnàsio, *s.m.* 1. (*scuola media d'ordine classico*) grammar school; (*amer.*) high school; (*di tipo italiano, tedesco*) gymnasium (*pl.* gymnasiums, gymnasia) 2. (*st. greca*) gymnasium (*pl.* gymnasiums, gymnasia).

ginnàsta, *s.m.* gymnast; (*atleta*) athlete.

ginnàstica, *s.f.* gymnastics; (*fam.*) gym; physical training: — *da camera,* home physical exercises; — *mentale,* mental gymnastics; — *ritmica,* callisthenics; *scarpe per —,* gym shoes; *ogni settimana abbiamo due ore di —,* we have two periods of physical training a week; *fare —,* to do gymnastics (*o* physical exercises).

ginnàstico, *ag.* gymnastic.

gínnica, *s.f.* (*letter.*) gymnastics.

gínnico, *ag.* gymnastic; athletic: *giuochi ginnici,* athletic games; *saggio —,* gymnastic display.

ginnòto, *s.m.* (*ittiol.*) gymnotus, electric eel.

ginocchiàta, *s.f.* blow with the knee.

ginocchièllo, *s.m.* 1. (*di protezione*) knee-cap; (*imbottito*) knee-pad 2. (*di armatura*) knee-piece 3. (*balistica*) firing step.

ginocchièra, *s.f.* 1. knee-guard; (*spor.*) knee-pad 2. (*mec.*) toggle: — *di chiusura,* gripping toggle; *giunto a —,* toggle-joint.

ginòcchio, *s.m.* 1. knee: *in —,* on one's knees (*o* kneeling); *in —!,* down on your knee(s)! (*o* kneel down!); (*mil.*) on the knee!; *sottana al —,* knee-length skirt; *ero nel fango fino alle ginocchia,* I was knee-deep in mud; *avere il — valgo, varo,* to be knock-kneed, bow-legged; *cadere in —,* to fall (*o* to drop) on one's knees; *far piegare le ginocchia a qlcu.,* to bring s.o. to his knees; *mettersi in —,* to go on one's knees (*o* to kneel down); *piegare il — davanti a qlcu.,* to bend

(*o* to bow) the knee to (*o* before) s.o.; *piegare le ginocchia,* to bend one's knees; *fig.* (*umiliarsi*) to eat humble pie; (*cedere*) to give in (*o* to yield); *tenere un bambino sulle ginocchia,* to hold a child on one's knees (*o* on one's lap) ‖ *questo è ancora sulle ginocchia degli dei,* this is still on the knees of the gods ‖ *far venire il latte alle ginocchia,* to bore to tears (*o* to death) 2. (*mec.*) bend.

ginocchióni, *av.* on one's knees, kneeling: *cadere —,* to fall on one's knees.

Giòab, *no.pr.m.* (*Bibbia*) Joab.

Gioacchíno, *no.pr.m.* Joachim.

Giòbbe, *no.pr.m.* (*Bibbia*) Job.

giocàre, *v.i.* 1. to play: *a chi tocca —?,* who plays first? (*o* whose turn is it to play?); *giuoca bene alle carte,* he plays a good game of cards; *giocano ai soldati,* they are playing (at) soldiers; — *a carte, a scacchi, a tennis,* to play (at) cards, chess, tennis; — *alla palla,* to play with a ball; — *con la catena dell'orologio,* to toy (*o* to fiddle) with one's watch-chain; — *con qlcu. a scacchi,* to play with s.o. at chess; — *correttamente, scorrettamente,* to play fair, foul; — *per divertimento, per interesse,* to play for love, for money ‖ *a che giuoco giochiamo?,* what is your little game? ‖ — *sulla credulità di qlcu.,* to play on s.o.'s credulity ‖ — *sulle parole,* to play upon words ‖ — *di mano,* (*rubare*) to steal (*o* to pilfer) 2. (*d'azzardo*) to gamble 3. (*scommettere*) to bet 4. (*in borsa*) to speculate, to operate: — *al rialzo,* to speculate (*o* to operate) on (*o* for) the rise (*o* to bull the market); — *al ribasso,* to speculate (*o* to operate) on (*o* for) a fall (*o* to bear the market) 5. (*mec.*) to work: *un meccanismo che giuoca bene,* a mechanism that works ‖ *v.t.* 1. to play: — *bene le proprie carte,* *fig.* to play one's cards well; — *una carta, una partita,* to play a card, a game ‖ — *un tiro a qlcu.,* to play a joke (*o* a trick) on s.o. 2. (*puntare*) to stake: — *cinquecento sterline,* to stake five hundred pounds 3. (*ingannare*) to deceive, to make a fool of (s.o.), to trick, to fool, to make game of (s.o.) ‖ **giocàrsi,** *v.r.* 1. (*beffarsi*) to trifle with (s.o.), to make game of (s.o.), to make sport of (s.o.), to make a fool of (s.o.): *ti giuochi di me,* you are trifling with me (*o* making game of me) 2. (*perdere*) to lose: *per la sua pigrizia si è giocato l'impiego,* he lost his job through his laziness 3. (*scommettere*) to bet: — *la camicia* (*in una partita*), to bet one's shirt.

Giocàsta, *no.pr.f.* (*lett.*) Jocasta, Jocaste.

giocàta, *s.f.* 1. (*partita*) game 2. (*puntata*) stake.

giocatóre, *s.m.,* **giocatrice,** *s.f.* 1. player: — *di biliardo,* billiard-player; — *di bussolotti,* juggler; *fig.* juggler, trickster, impostor; — *di calcio,* football player (*o* footballer); — *professionista,* professional player 2. (*d'azzardo*) gambler 3. (*in Borsa*) stock-jobber.

giocàttolo, *s.m.* toy; plaything (anche *fig.*): *i bambini fanno del cane un —,* the children are making a plaything of their dog.

giocherellàre, *v.i.* to play, to toy, to trifle.

giocherèllo, *s.m.* 1. simple game 2. (*balocco*) toy 3. (*tiro mancino*) trick.

giochétto, *s.m.* 1. (*scherzo*) joke; (*passatempo*) pastime 2. (*tiro mancino*) trick: *mi hanno fatto un bel —!,* they have played a fine trick on me!.

giòco, *s.m.* 1. play; (*generalmente regolato da norme*) game; (*d'azzardo*) gambling: — *ai dadi,* dicing; *giochi all'aperto,* outdoor games; *giochi con la palla,* ball games; — *d'acqua,* play of water (from a fountain); — *da tavolo,* table game; — *d'azzardo,* game of chance; — *degli scacchi,* chess; — *del lotto,* State lottery; — *di luce, d'ombre,* play of light, of shadows; — *di luci,* (*teat.*) lighting effects; *un — di pazienza,* a puzzle; — *di società,* parlour game; *giochi infantili,* children's games; — *leale, sleale,* fair, foul play; *giochi olimpici,* Olympic games; — *pesante,* (*spor.*) rough play; *campo di —,* playing-field; *carta da —,* playing-card;

casa da —, gaming (o gambling) house; *compagno di* —, play mate (o play fellow); *debiti di* —, gaming (o gambling) debts; *tavolo da* —, gaming (o card) table; *ci devono essere sia studio che* — *nella vita di un ragazzo*, there must be both study and play in a boy's life; *avere buon* —, to have a good hand; *fig.* to be in a good position; *barare al* —, to cheat; *fare un* —, to play a game: *fare un* — *pericoloso*, to play a dangerous game; *fare entrare qlcu. in* —, to invite s.o. to play; *fig.* to bring s.o. into action (o to call s.o. into play); *perdere al* —, to lose at cards (o to have gaming losses); *perdere una fortuna al* —, to gamble away a fortune ‖ — *di mano, di prestigio*, sleight-of-hand (o conjuring trick) ‖ — *di parole*, pun (o play on words) ‖ *doppio* —, double-crossing: *fare il doppio* —, to play a double game (o to run with the hare and hunt with the hounds) ‖ *fuori* —, (spor.) off-side ‖ *gli interessi in* —, the interests at stake; *essere in* —, *fig.* to be involved: *ci sono molti problemi in* —, there are many problems involved; *il suo onore è in* —, his honour is at stake; *entrare in* —, to come into play; *mettere ql.co. in* —, to bring sthg. into action (o to call sthg. into play): *mettere tutto in* —, to stake one's all ‖ *è un* — *da ragazzi*, *fig.* it's child's play ‖ *fate il vostro* —!, put down your stakes! (o stake your money!) ‖ *non capiamo quale sia il vostro* —, we cannot understand what your game is; *si è scoperto il suo* —, we have found out his little game; *celare il proprio* —, to play an underhand game; *fare il* — *di qlcu.*, to play into the hands of s.o. (o to be s.o.'s pawn); *mostrare il proprio* —, to put one's cards on the table ‖ *chi sa il* — *non lo insegni*, prov. don't give the game away **2.** (*in Borsa*) stock-jobbing **3.** (*passatempo*) fun, amusement, sport: *per* —, for (o in) fun (o in jest) **4.** (*scherzo*) joke: *per un* — *della fortuna*, by a freak of chance; *num era un* —, *era la verità*, it was no joke, it was the truth ‖ *farsi* — *di ql.co.*, to make light of sthg.; *prendersi di qlcu.*, to make game of s.o. (o to laugh at s.o. o to make a fool of s.o. o to pull s.o.'s leg) ‖ — *di mano*, — *di villano!*, prov. rough play is low ‖ *un bel* — *dura poco*, prov. don't carry the joke too far **5.** (*mec.*) clearance: — *assiale*, end float (o end play); — *laterale*, side clearance (o side play); *eliminare il* —, to take up slack; *lasciare* — *per l'espansione termica*, to allow a space (o a gap) for expansion.

giocofòrza, *s.m.*: *è* —, it is absolutely necessary: *ci è* — *separarci*, it is absolutely necessary for us to part.

giocolière, *s.m.* juggler.

giocondaménte, *av.* gaily, merrily, cheerfully.

giocondità, *s.f.* gaiety, mirth, cheerfulness.

giocóndo, *ag.* gay, merry, cheerful, joyous.

giocosaménte, *av.* playfully, jocosely; facetiously.

giocosità, *s.f.* playfulness, jocoseness, jocosity; facetiousness.

giocóso, *ag.* **1.** playful, jesting, humorous **2.** (*allegro*) joyful, gay ‖ *opera giocosa*, comic opera.

giogàia, *s.f.* **1.** (*di bovini*) dewlap **2.** (*geog.*) mountain range.

giógo, *s.m.* **1.** yoke (anche *fig.*): *buoi da* —, yoke oxen; *due gioghi di buoi*, two yokes of oxen; *insofferente al* —, impatient of the yoke; *sotto il* — *matrimoniale*, under the marriage yoke; *mettere i buoi sotto il* —, to yoke the oxen; *passare, far passare sotto il* —, to pass (o to send) under the yokes; *scuotersi di dosso il* —, to throw off the yoke **2.** (*di bilancia*) beam; yoke **3.** (*geog.*) (*sommità*) summit, top; (*cresta*) mountain ridge.

giòia[1], *s.f.* joy, delight, gladness; glee: — *di vivere*, joy of living; *gioie e dolori*, joys and sorrows; *che* —!, what happiness!; *con mia grande* —, to my great joy; *pieno di* —, full of joy; *raggiante di* —, beaming with joy; *era fuori di sè dalla* —, he was beside himself with joy; *accettare con* —, to accept joyfully; *essere al colmo della* —, to be overjoyed; *piangere*

di —, to cry with joy (o to weep for joy); *riempire qlcu. di* —, to fill s.o. with joy ‖ — *mia!*, my darling! (o my love!).

Giòia[2], *no.pr.f.* Joy.

giòia[3], *s.f.* (*pietra preziosa*) gem, jewel, precious stone: *era coperta di gioie*, she was decked with jewels.

gioiellàre, *v.t.* (*rar.*) to adorn with gems, to set with gems.

gioiellería, *s.f.* **1.** jewelry, jewellery **2.** (*negozio di gioielliere*) jeweller's shop.

gioiellière, *s.m.* jeweller.

gioièllo, *s.m.* jewel (anche *fig.*): *i gioielli della Corona*, the Crown jewels; *tua figlia è un vero* —!, your daughter is a real jewel!.

gioiosaménte, *av.* joyfully, joyously, cheerfully, merrily.

gioióso, *ag.* joyful, joyous, cheerful, merry.

gioíre, *v.i.* to rejoice (at, over sthg.); to be glad (of sthg.).

Giòna, *no.pr.m.* (*Bibbia*) Jonah, Jonas.

Giònata, *no.pr.m.* Jonathan.

Giordàno, *no.pr.m.* (*geog.*) Jordan.

Giorgétta, *no.pr.f.* Georgiana.

giorgína[1], *s.f.* (*bot.*) dahlia.

Giorgína[2], *no.pr.f.* Georgina.

Giórgio, *no.pr.m.* George ‖ *la Croce di San* —, (*arald.*) St. George's Cross ‖ *dim.* Georgie, Georgy, Dod(dy).

giornalàccio, *s.m.* low-class paper; (*fam.*) rag.

giornalàio, *s.m.* news-vendor; (*strillone*) news-boy; newsman (*pl.* newsmen).

giornàle, *s.m.* **1.** newspaper, paper: — *di moda*, fashion-magazine; — *di piccolo formato*, tabloid; — *quotidiano*, daily (newspaper); — *settimanale*, weekly (newspaper); *i giornali*, (*la stampa*) the press; *carta da* —, news-print; *ritaglio di* —, newspaper (o press) cutting; *abbonarsi a un* —, to subscribe to a newspaper; *apprendere dai giornali*, to pick up from the newspapers; *essere abbonato a un* —, to be a subscriber to a newspaper; *fondare un* —, to start (o to launch) a newspaper; *pubblicare un annunzio nei giornali*, to advertise **2.** (*registro*) journal: *foglio di* —, journal-sheet; — *tenuto in partita semplice, doppia*, journal by single, double-entry (o single-, double-entry journal); *registrazione a* —, journal-entry; *portare, registrare a* —, to journalize (o to enter in the journal) **3.** (*diario*) diary, record: *tenere un* —, to keep a diary **4.** (*mar.*) log (-book), ship's journal; (*aer.*) air log: *compilare il* — *di bordo*, to write up the log **5.** *cine-* —, news-reel **6.** — *radio*, (*rad.*) news bulletin.

giornalièro, *ag.* **1.** daily; everyday (*attributivo*) **2.** (*instabile*) variable, uncertain, changeable ‖ *s.m.* (*lavoratore a giornata*) day-labourer; journeyman (*pl.* journeymen).

giornalísmo, *s.m.* journalism; (*il complesso dei giornali, la stampa*) press: *l'influenza del* —, the influence of the press; *fare del* —, to write in the papers.

giornalísta, *s.m.* journalist, reporter; pressman (*pl.* pressmen); newspaper-man (*pl.* newspaper-men); (*amer.*) newsman (*pl.* newsmen) ‖ *s.f.* journalist, reporter; (*scherz. amer.*) newshen.

giornalístico, *ag.* journalistic.

giornalménte, *av.* daily, everyday.

giornànte, *s.f.* (*donna di servizio a ore*) charwoman (*pl.* charwomen).

giornàta, *s.f.* (*giorno*) day; (*lavoro di un giorno*) day's work: — *lavorativa*, work-day (o working-day); — *nera*, unlucky day; *che bella* —!, what a fine day!; *donna a* —, charwoman; *durante la* —, in the course of the day; *l'intera* —, the whole day; *paga, salario a* —, day's pay; *devo riscuotere otto giornate*, I have to receive eight days' pay (o wages); *ti sei guadagnato la* —, you've done a good day's work; *voglio finirlo in* —, I want to finish it before the day is over; *lavorare a* —, to work by the day ‖ — *di fuoco*, (*mil.*) day of fire ‖ — *grassa, magra*, (*ricca, povera di guadagni*) good, bad day for business ‖

due giornate di cammino, a two days' journey on foot; *il nemico avanza a grandi giornate*, the enemy were advancing by forced marches ‖ *vivere alla —*, to live from hand to mouth.

giórno, *s.m.* day: — *civile, siderale, solare*, civil, sidereal, solar day; *un — d'estate*, a summer day; *— e notte*, night and day; *— festivo*, holiday; *— lavorativo*, work-day (*o* working-day); *un — o l'altro*, one day or another; *— per —*, day by day; *a giorni*, in a few days' time; *di —*, by day; *due volte al —*, twice a day; *i miei giorni liberi*, my free days; *molti giorni*, many days (*o* many a day); *otto giorni da oggi*, this day week; *tutti i giorni*, every day; *tutto il* (*santo*) *—*, all (the) day (*o* the whole day); *un — passeggiavo...*, one day I was walking...; *un — ti dirò*, some day I'll tell you; *che — è oggi?*, (*del mese*) what is the date to-day? (*o* what day of the month is it to-day?); (*della settimana*) what day of the week is it to-day?; *ho un — libero*, I have a day off ‖ *ai giorni nostri, al — d'oggi*, at the present time) ‖ *al cader del —*, at sunset ‖ *illuminato a —*, brightly lit ‖ *in pieno —*, in broad (*o* full) daylight ‖ *ordine del —*, agenda ‖ *orlo a —*, hem-stitch; *punto a —*, open-stitch (*o* open-work) ‖ *sul far del —*, at the break of the day ‖ *uomo del —*, man of the day ‖ *a giorni è allegro, a giorni è triste*, at times he is cheerful, at times sad ‖ *finì i suoi giorni in ospedale*, he ended his days in a hospital ‖ *ho conosciuto giorni migliori*, I have seen better days ‖ *dare gli otto giorni*, to give a week's notice ‖ *fare di notte —*, to be a night bird ‖ *mettere qlcu. a — di ql.co.*, to acquaint s.o. with sthg.; *essere a — di ql.co.*, to be acquainted with sthg.

Giosafàtte, *no.pr.m.* (*Bibbia*) Jehoshaphat: *la valle di —*, the Valley of Jehoshaphat.

Giosìa, *no.pr.m.* (*Bibbia*) Josiah, Josias.

giòstra, *s.f.* **1.** (*combattimento*) joust, tilt, tilting match; (*torneo*) tournament **2.** (*per bambini*) merry-go-round, roundabout.

giostrànte, *ag.* tilting, jousting ‖ *s.m.* tilter, jouster.

giostràre, *v.i.* to tilt, to joust.

Giosuè, *no.pr.m.* Joshua ‖ *dim.* Josh.

giottésco, *ag.* (*st. pitt.*) Giottesque.

Giòtto, *no.pr.m.* (*st. pitt.*) Giotto ‖ *essere tondo come l'o di —*, to be perfectly round; (*essere uno sciocco*) to be a fool.

giovaménto, *s.m.* benefit, advantage: *ciò non fu di alcun —*, that was of no avail (*o* that was quite useless); *trarre — da ql.co.*, to benefit by sthg. (*o* to take advantage of sthg.).

gióvane, *ag.* young; (*da giovane, giovanile*) youthful: *— di spirito*, young in mind; *un — medico*, a young physician; *il — Rossi*, Rossi junior (*abbr.* jr.); *l'età —*, youth; *il mio fratello più —*, (*tra due*) my younger brother; (*tra più di due*) my youngest brother; *una pianta —*, a young plant; *uomo —*, man still young (*o* youngish man); *vino —*, new wine; *viso —*, youthful (*o* young-looking) face; *da — gli piaceva sciare*, when (he was) young he liked skiing; *sono più — di lui di quattro anni*, I am his junior by four years; *rimanere —*, to remain (*o* to keep) young: *spirito che è rimasto —*, mind that has kept young (*o* kept its youth) ‖ *la Giovane Italia*, Young Italy ‖ *Plinio il —*, Pliny the Younger ‖ *s.m.* **1.** young man, youth; (*fam.*) lad: *i giovani*, young people (*o* young folk *o* young men *o* the youth): *i giovani del paese*, the youth of the village; *incoraggiamo i giovani!*, let us encourage young people!; *un — di vent'anni*, a young man (*o* a youth) of twenty; *un bel —*, a handsome young man **2.** (*aiutante*) assistant: *— di bottega*, shop boy ‖ *s.f.* young woman; girl; (*fam.*) lass.

giovanétta, *s.f.* girl; (*fam.*) lass; (*adolescente*) adolescent.

giovanétto, *s.m.* boy; (*fam.*) lad; (*adolescente*) adolescent.

giovaníle, *ag.* juvenile; (*da giovane*) youthful: *di aspetto —*, young-looking; *delinquenza —*, juvenile delinquency; *opere giovanili*, juvenile productions; *il suo aspetto —*, his youthful appearance.

giovanilménte, *av.* jouthfully.

Giovànna, *no.pr.f.* Jane, Jean, Joan, Jo(h)anna ‖ *dim.* Janet, Jennie, Jessie, Netta.

Giovànni, *no.pr.m.* John ‖ *dim.* Johnny, Johnnie, Jack, Jackie.

Giovannína, *no.pr.f. dim.* di **Giovànna**.

Giovanníno, *no.pr.m. dim.* di **Giovànni**.

giovanòtta, *s.f.* (*fam.*) girl, lass.

giovanòtto, *s.m.* **1.** young man, youth **2.** (*scapolo*) bachelor **3.** (*mar.*) (*mozzo*) ship's boy.

giovàre, *v.i.* **1.** (*essere di utilità*) to be of use; to avail (s.o.); to help (s.o.): *a che giova?*, what is the use of it?; *a che gioverebbe parlargli?*, what would be the use of speaking to him?; *a questo punto ormai nulla mi giova!*, at this stage nothing avails me any more!; *giova sapere*, it is useful to know; *i vostri consigli mi giovarono molto*, your advice was of great use to me; *non — a nulla, affatto*, to be of no use (*o* to be of no avail) **2.** (*fare bene*) to be good (for s.o., sthg.); to be beneficial; to do (s.o., sthg.) good: *l'aria del mare ti gioverà*, sea air will be good for you (*o* will be beneficial to you *o* will do you good); *una vacanza vi gioverà*, you will benefit by a holiday ‖ **giovàrsi**, *v.r.* to avail oneself (of sthg.); to benefit (by sthg.), to profit (by sthg.): *— del consiglio di qlcu.*, to profit by s.o.'s advice; *— di un diritto*, to avail oneself of a right; *— reciprocamente*, to help each other (one another).

Giòve, *no.pr.m.* **1.** (*mit.*) Jove, Jupiter: *gli strali di —*, Jove's thunderbolts ‖ *barba di —*, (*bot.*) Jupiter's beard ‖ *per —!*, by Jove! **2.** (*astr.*) Jupiter.

giovedì, *s.m.* Thursday: *un — mattina*, on a Thursday morning; *di —*, (*tutti i giovedì*) on Thursdays; *verrò —*, I'll come on Thursday; *verrò — venturo*, I'll come next Thursday ‖ *— grasso*, Thursday before Shrove Tuesday ‖ *— Santo*, Maundy Thursday (*o* Thursday in Holy Week *o* Thursday before Easter).

Giovenàle, *no.pr.m.* (*st. lett.*) Juvenal.

giovènca, *s.f.* heifer.

giovèneo, *s.m.* bull-calf (*pl.* bull-calves).

gioventù, *s.f.* **1.** youth: *in — fu un atleta famoso*, in his youth (*o* when young) he was a famous athlete; *nella prima —*, in one's early youth: *non essere più nella prima —*, not to be in the first blush of youth **2.** (*persone in giovane età*) youth; young people (*coll. con costruzione pl.*): *la — del villaggio*, the youth of the village ‖ *la — dorata*, gilded youth.

gioveréccio, *ag.* **1.** (*giovevole*) helpful **2.** (*piacevole*) pleasant, agreeable.

giovévole, *ag.* useful, profitable, beneficial, advantageous, helpful; good (for s.o., sthg.): *— alla salute*, good for s.o.'s health; *un consiglio —*, a profitable piece of advice; *l'aria pura ed il sole sono giovevoli ai bambini*, fresh air and sunshine are beneficial to children.

giovevolménte, *av.* usefully, profitably, beneficially.

gioviàle, *ag.* genial, jovial, jolly, breezy: *una accoglienza —*, a genial welcome; *un riso —*, a hearty (*o* good-natured) laugh; *un vecchietto —*, a genial old man; *un viso —*, a jolly face.

giovialità, *s.f.* geniality, joviality, jollity, breeziness.

giovialménte, *av.* genially, jovially.

giovialóne, *ag.* jolly, cheery ‖ *s.m.* jolly fellow, cheery fellow.

giovinàstro, *s.m.* young ruffian; hooligan; street rough; (*amer.*) hoodlum; (*neol.*) Teddy-boy.

giovincèllo, *s.m.* (*scherz.*) lad, stripling.

gióvine, *V.* **giòvane**.

giovinétta, *V.* **giovanétta**.

giovinétto, *V.* **giovanétto**.

giovinézza, *s.f.* youth: *dalla — in poi*, from youth onwards; *nella prima —*, in one's early youth: *non essere più nella prima —*, to be no longer in the first blush of youth; *spirito che ha conservato la sua —*, spirit which has kept its youth.

gipsotèca, *s.f.* gallery of plaster casts.

giràbile, *ag.* (*comm.*) endorsable, indorsable.

giracàpo, *V.* **giraménto 2.**.

giradíschi, *s.m.* record player.

giradíto, *s.m.* (*patol.*) whitlow.

giràffa, *s.f.* **1.** (*zool.*) giraffe **2.** (*cine. rad. tv.*) microphone boom.

Giràldo, *no.pr.m.* Gerald.

giramàschio, *s.m.* (*strum. artig.*) tap wrench.

giraménto, *s.m.* **1.** turning **2.** (*di capo*) giddiness, dizziness: *mi fa venire il — di capo*, it makes me (feel) giddy (*o* dizzy); *avere un — di capo*, to feel giddy (*o* dizzy); *avere giramenti di capo*, to have fits of giddiness.

giramóndo, *s.m.* **1.** wanderer; tramp; vagrant **2.** (*turista*) globe-trotter.

giràndola, *s.f.* **1.** (*sorta di fuoco d'artificio*) Catherine-wheel **2.** *fig.* (*persona volubile*) fickle person, flighty person.

girandolàre, *v.i.* to saunter, to stroll, to ramble: *girandolai per Piccadilly*, I sauntered (*o* strolled) along Piccadilly; *— per la città*, to saunter about the town; *— per i campi*, to ramble through the fields.

girandolóna, *s.f.*, **girandolóne**, *s.m.* saunterer, stroller, rambler.

girandolóni, *av.*: *andare —*, to saunter about (*o* to ramble about).

giràante, *s.m.* **1.** (*comm.*) endorser, indorser **2.** (*mec.*) (*di pompa*) impeller; (*di turbina*) rotor, disk wheel; (*di turbina ad acqua*) runner; (*di turbina a gas*) turbine wheel; (*di ventilatore*) fan wheel.

giràre, *v.t.* **1.** to turn: *— la chiave nella serratura*, to turn the key in the lock; *— l'occhio intorno*, to cast one's eyes round; *— la pagina*, to turn over a page; *— un rubinetto, una ruota*, to turn a tap, a wheel; *— la schiena a qlcu.*, to turn one's back on s.o.; *— la testa*, to turn one's head ‖ *il denaro gi ha fatto — la testa*, money has turned his head ‖ *girate le cose in modo che sembra abbiate ragione*, you twist things in such a way that you seem to be right ‖ *— l'angolo*, to go round the corner (*o* to turn the corner) ‖ *— un capo, un promontorio*, (*mar.*) to round a cape, a head-land ‖ *— bene una frase*, to give a neat turn to a phrase ‖ *— una posizione*, (*mil.*) to turn a position **2.** (*evitare*) to avoid, to evade: *— una difficoltà*, to avoid a difficulty; *— una domanda*, to evade a question; *— un ostacolo*, to get round an obstacle **3.** (*visitare viaggiando*) to travel, to tour: *gireremo l'Italia e la Spagna*, we shall tour Italy and Spain; *vorrei — il mondo*, I should like to travel all over the world **4.** (*cine.*) (*di regista*) to shoot, to take; (*di attore*) to play (a part), to star, to act (in a film): *— una scena*, to film a scene **5.** (*comm.*) to endorse: *— una cambiale*, to endorse a bill ‖ *v.i.* **1.** to turn; to wind: *il balcone gira intorno a tutta la casa*, the balcony goes all round the house; *il sentiero gira intorno al prato*, the path winds round the lawn; *la strada gira parecchie volte*, the road turns several times; *la Terra gira intorno al Sole*, the earth turns round the sun; *— a destra*, to turn to the right ‖ *che vi gira?*, what's the matter with you? ‖ *gira al largo!*, sheer off! (*o* off with you!) ‖ *mi gira la testa*, my head is swimming (*o* my head is in a whirl) ‖ *se mi gira...*, (*fam.*) if I feel like it... ‖ *— a vuoto, in folle*, (*mec.*) to idle **2.** (*camminare*) to walk; to wander; (*girellare*) to stroll, to saunter, to ramble: *— per le strade*, to stroll the streets ‖ *gira e rigira*, (*fam.*) after a long way; (*dopo molto tempo*) after a long time ‖ **giràrsi**, *v.r.* to turn; (*completamente*) to turn round: *egli continuava a — nel letto*, he kept turning over in his bed; *mi girai di scatto*, I turned

round abruptly; *non sapere da che parte —*, *fig.* to be at one's wits' end (*o* not to know which way to turn).

girarròsto, *s.m.* spit, roasting-jack.

girasóle, *s.m.* (*bot.*) sunflower.

giràta, *s.f.* **1.** turn, turning: *una — di chiave*, a turn of the key **2.** (*passeggiata*) walk, turn, stroll: *fare una — per la città*, to take a walk about the town **3.** (*comm.*) endorsement: *— in bianco*, blank endorsement; *trasferire una cambiale a mezzo di —*, to transfer a bill by endorsement **4.** (*giro di carte, al giuoco*) deal, dealing.

giratàrio, *s.m.* (*comm.*) endorsee.

giravòlta, *s.f.* **1.** turning; twirl: *strada a giravolte*, twisting and turning road; *fare una —*, to turn round (*o* to turn back) **2.** *fig.* (*mutamento repentino*) shift: *senza tante giravolte*, without so many shifts.

giravoltolàre, *v.i.* (*rar.*) **1.** to twirl round **2.** *fig.* (*impazzire*) to go mad, to run mad.

gíre, *v.i. dif.* (*arc.*) per **andàre**.

girèlla, *s.f.* **1.** (*mec.*) pulley **2.** (*ind. tessile*) spinning-wheel **3.** (*di sperone*) rowel **4.** (*pedina del giuoco di dama*) draughtsman (*pl.* draughtsmen); piece **5.** (*ruzzola*) spinning-top ‖ *s.m.* (*persona volubile, specialmente in politica*) weathercock, turncoat.

girellàre, *v.i.* to saunter, to stroll, to lounge about.

girèllo, *s.m.* **1.** small disk, small circle, small ring **2.** (*per bambini*) go-cart **3.** (*parte del bue macellato*) rump **4.** (*fondo di carciofo*) heart.

girellóna, *s.f.*, **girellóne**, *s.m.* saunterer, stroller, dawdler, idler.

girétto, *s.m.* short walk; stroll, turn: *fare un —*, to take (*o* to go for) a short walk (*o* to take a turn).

girévole, *ag.* revolving, turning, rotating, slewing: *gru —*, slewing crane; *ponte —*, swing (*o* revolving) bridge; *porta —*, revolving door.

girifàlco, *s.m.* **1.** (*ornit.*) gerfalcon, gyrfalcon **2.** (*st. artigl.*) falcon.

girigògolo, *s.m.* **1.** (*arabesco*) flourish **2.** *fig.* (*discorso sconclusionato*) silly inconclusive talk.

giríno, *s.m.* (*zool.*) tadpole.

gíro, *s.m.* **1.** turn, turning: *al primo — di manovella*, at the first turn of the handle; *con un solo — di chiave*, with a single turn of the key **2.** (*cerchio, circuito*) circle: *— della manica*, (sleeve-)joint; *il — delle mura*, the city walls; *si misero seduti in —*, they sat in a circle **3.** (*percorso*) round: *— di pista*, (*spor.*) lap; *perdemmo la strada e facemmo un lungo —*, we lost our way and made a long detour; *il poliziotto sta facendo il suo — d'ispezione*, the policeman is going (*o* making) his rounds; *il postino sta facendo il suo —*, the postman is going his round; *questa storiella farà il — della città*, this story will go round (*o* will make the round of) the town ‖ *— di parole*, a roundabout expression (*o* a circumlocution) ‖ *facciamo un — di valzer*, let's have a waltz ‖ *prendere in — qlcu.*, to pull s.o.'s leg (*o* to tease s.o. *o* to make a fool of s.o.) **4.** (*viaggio*) tour: *— d'Italia*, (*spor.*) tour of Italy; *— del mondo*, tour round the world: *fare il — del mondo*, to travel round the world (*o* to tour all over the world) **5.** (*passeggiata*) short walk, stroll, turn: *fece un — nel parco*, he went for a stroll in the park; *fare un — in auto*, to go for a drive in a car; *fare un — in bicicletta*, to take a ride on a bicycle **6.** (*circolazione*) circulation: *questi francobolli non si vedono più in —*, these stamps are no longer to be seen in circulation; *mettere in —*, (*monete, francobolli*) to put into circulation ‖ *chi ha messo in — questa diceria?*, who started this rumour? **7.** (*comm.*) (*girata*) endorsement, indorsement: *— di affari*, turnover; *— di fondi*, cash-transfer (*o* assignment of capital *o* of funds); *— di partite*, turning of accounts; *cambiali in —*, outstanding bills; *debiti in —*, outstanding debts **8.** (*mec.*) turn; (*di motore*) revolution (*abbr.* rev.): *fa 2000 giri al minuto*, it makes 2000 revolutions per minute (*abbr.* 2000 r.p.

m.) **9.** (*periodo*) period, time: *nel — di pochi giorni*, in the course of a few days (*o in a few days' time*).

girobússola, *s.f.* (*mar.aer.*) gyroscopic compass, gyrocompass.

Giròlamo, *no.pr.m.* Jerome ‖ *dim.* Jerry.

giròmetro, *s.m.* (*fis.*) gyrometer.

Girónda, *no.pr.f.* (*geog.*) Gironde.

girondíno, *ag.s.m.* (*st. francese*) Girondist.

girondolàre, *V.* **girandolàre.**

giróne, *s.m.* **1.** (*nell'Inferno di Dante*) circle **2.** (*calcio*): *— di andata,* first series (of games); *— di ritorno,* second series (of games).

gironzàre, gironzolàre, *v.i.* to saunter, to stroll; to wander (around), to walk (about): *smettila di gironzolarmi attorno!,* stop wandering around!.

giropilòta, *s.m.* (*aer.*) automatic pilot; (*amer.*) gyropilot.

giroscòpico, *ag.* gyroscopic

giroscòpio, *s.m.* gyroscope.

girostabilizzatóre, *s.m.* (*mar. aer.*) gyrostabilizer.

girostàtico, *ag.* gyrostatic.

giròstato, *s.m.* gyrostat.

girotóndo, *s.m.* **1.** dance in a ring, round dance **2.** (*di bambini*): *facciamo —,* let's play "ring-a-ring-a-roses".

giròtta, *s.f.* (*mar.*) yoke: *— del limone,* rudder yoke.

girovagàre, *V.* **gironzàre.**

giròvago, *ag.* wandering, vagrant, itinerant, travelling, strolling ‖ *s.m.* **1.** (*vagabondo*) tramp, wanderer, vagrant, vagabond. **2.** (*venditore ambulante*) pedlar, hawker.

gíta, *s.f.* trip, excursion; tour: *— di piacere,* pleasure trip; *— in barca,* boat excursion; *fare una —,* to take a trip (*o* to make an excursion *o* to go on an excursion).

gitàna, *s.f.* **1.** (*zingara*) Spanish gipsy (woman) **2.** (*musica, danza*) "gitana" (kind of Spanish dance and music).

gitàno, *s.m.* Spanish gipsy.

gitànte, *s.c.* tripper, excursionist.

gittàre, *V.* **gettàre.**

gittàta, *s.f.* (*di cannone*) range, throw: *cannoni a lunga —,* long-range guns.

giú, *av.* **down;** (*dabbasso, giù dalle scale*) **downstairs:** *Giovanni è —,* John is downstairs; *— dall'albero,* down from the tree; *— per,* down: *— per una china,* down a slope; *in —, all'ingiù,* downwards: *a capo in —,* (*a capofitto*) headlong; *dai 40 anni in —,* up to (*o* under) forty; *posso spendere dalle mille lire in —,* I can spend up to a thousand lire; *su e —,* up and down; (*avanti e indietro*) to and fro; *abita più in —,* he lives further down (the road); *buttare —,* to knock down; (*inghiottire*) to swallow (*o* to gulp down); (*sparlare di*) to disparage (*o* to run down); (*deprimere*) to get down (*o* to depress); *cadere —,* to fall down; *mandar —,* to swallow (anche *fig.*); *venir —,* to come down ‖ *— il cappello!,* hats off! ‖ *— le mani!,* hands off! ‖ *— la maschera!,* come clean! (*o* tell the truth!) ‖ *e — acqua!,* (*quando piove a dirotto*) it never rains, but it pours! ‖ *su per —,* *di lì,* approximately (*o* roughly *o* about): *avrà 30 anni o — di lì,* he must be about thirty ‖ *andar —,* (*scemare di pregio*) to go down; (*affondare*) to go below ‖ *buttarsi —,* (*avvilirsi*) to get down-hearted (*o* depressed) ‖ *essere —,* (*di salute*) to be run down (*o* to be poorly); (*essere depresso*) to be low-spirited (*o* to be in low spirits *o fam.* to be down in the mouth *o* to be blue *o* to be in the blues) ‖ *mettere —,* (*per iscritto*) to put down (in writing).

giúba, giúbba[1]**,** *s.f.* (*criniera*) mane.

giúbba[2]**,** *s.f.* (*giacca*) coat, jacket: *— da fantino,* jockey's shirt ‖ *rivoltare la —,* (*mutare partito*) to become a turncoat.

giubbétto, *s.m.* **1.** (*da donna*) bodice **2.** (*da uomo*) jacket; (*arc.*) doublet: *— da scherma,* fencing-jacket.

giubbilàre, *e derivati, V.* **giubilàre,** *e derivati.*

giubbóne, *s.m.* heavy coat ‖ *spolverare il — a qlcu.,* (*batterlo*) to dust s.o.'s jacket.

giubilànte, *ag.* jubilant, exultant; overjoyed.

giubilàre, *v.t.* (*mettere a riposo*) to pension off ‖ *v.i.* (*gioire*) to jubilate, to exult.

giubilàto, *ag.* (*messo a riposo*) pensioned off.

giubilazióne, *s.f.* **1.** jubilation **2.** (*il mettere in pensione*) pensioning off.

giubilèo, *s.m.* jubilee: *anno del —,* jubilee year; *feste del —,* jubilee celebrations.

giúbilo, *s.m.* jubilation, rejoicing: *il suo ritorno fu un — per la sua famiglia,* his return was a jubilation for his family.

Giúda, *no.pr.m.* **1.** (*l'Iscariota*) Judas ‖ *albero di —,* Judas tree; *bacio di —,* Judas kiss **2.** (*il figlio di Giacobbe*) Judah ‖ *figli di —,* Jews **3.** (*l'apostolo*) Jude, Judas ‖ **giúda,** *s.m.* (*traditore*) Judas, traitor.

giudaésimo, *s.m.* Judaism.

giudaicaménte, *av.* Judaically.

giudàico, *ag.* Judaic.

giudaísmo, *s.m.* Judaism.

giudaizzàre, *v.i.* to Judaize.

Giudèa, *no.pr.f.* (*geog.*) Judea, Judaea.

giudèo, *ag.* (*del regno di Giudea*) Judaean; (*ebreo*) Jewish ‖ *s.m.* (*abitante del regno di Giudea*) Judaean, (*ebreo*) Jew ‖ **giudèa,** *s.f.* (*abitante del regno di Giudea*) Judean, Judaean; (*ebrea*) Jewess.

giudicàbile, *ag.* triable ‖ *s.m.* (*dir.*) defendant.

giudicànte, *ag.* judging ‖ *s.m.* (*dir.*) judge.

giudicàre, *v.t.* **1.** to judge: *non — se non vuoi essere giudicato,* judge not that ye be not judged; *non sta a me giudicarlo,* it is not for me to pass judgement on him; *solo Dio può — gli uomini,* only God can judge men; *un uomo si giudica dalle sue azioni,* a man is judged by his actions; *vi lascio — se ho torto o ragione!,* I leave it to you whether I am right or wrong!; *— dalle apparenze,* to judge by (*o* from) appearances; *— un libro,* to judge (*o* to pass judgement on *o* to criticize) a book **2.** (*dir.*) to judge: *l'imputato fu giudicato colpevole,* the defendant was found guilty; *— un accusato,* to sit in judgement on (*o* to try) a prisoner (*o* to pass sentence *o* judgement on a prisoner) **3.** (*considerare, pensare*) to consider, to think, to deem: *lo giudicavano pazzo,* everybody thought he was mad (*o* people took him to be mad); *non giudicammo consigliabile proseguire,* we didn't think (*o* deem) it advisable to go on.

giudicàto, *s.m.* (*dir.*) sentence, final judgement: *passare in —,* to be beyond recall.

giudicatóre, *ag.* judging ‖ *s.m.* judge.

giudicatòrio, *ag.* judicatory.

giudicatríce, *s.f.* judge.

giudicatúra, *s.f.* (*dir.*) **1.** judicature, judge's office, judgeship **2.** (*magistratura*) judicature, body of judges, bench of judges.

giúdice, *s.m.* judge: *i giudici,* the Bench; *— conciliatore,* Justice of the Peace; *— istruttore,* examining (*o* investigating) magistrate; *— di gara,* umpire; *i giudici della mostra,* the judges of the exhibition; *essere buon — di ql.co.,* to be a (good) judge of sthg.: *non sei buon —,* you are no judge; *essere nominato —,* to be appointed judge; (*in Gran Bretagna*) to be raised to the Bench ‖ *il — supremo,* (*Dio*) the Supreme Judge.

Giudítta, *no.pr.f.* Judith ‖ *dim.* Judy.

giudiziàle, *ag.* (*dir.*) judicial.

giudizialménte, *av.* (*dir.*) judicially.

giudiziàrio, *ag.* (*dir.*) judicial: *assemblea giudiziaria,* judicial assembly; *potere —,* judicial power; *procedimento —,* judicial proceedings; *riforma giudiziaria,* judicial reform; *ufficiale —,* bailiff.

giudízio, *s.m.* **1.** (*dir.*) judg(e)ment; (*causa*) trial; (*sentenza*) decree, verdict, sentence: *— definitivo,* decree absolute; *— esecutivo,* enforceable judgement; *— provvisorio,* decree nisi; *— sommario,* summary trial; *a —,* on trial; *corte di —,* judgement-seat;

ebbe un — sfavorevole, the judgement went against him; *comparire in —*, to appear in court; *mettere a —*, to bring to trial (*o* up for trial); *passare a —*, to be brought up for trial (*o* to stand one's trial); *pronunciare un —*, to pass judgement (*o* to adjudicate); *rinviare qlcu. a —*, to commit s.o. for trial; *sedere in —*, to sit in judgement; *sospendere il —*, to suspend judgement; *trascinare qlcu. in — per diffamazione*, to sue s.o. for libel **2.** (*opinione*) judg(e)ment, opinion: *a mio —*, in my judgement (*o* opinion); *secondo il — di molti*, in the judgement (*o* opinion *o* view) of many people; *non mi curo del tuo —*, I am quite indifferent to your opinion; *dare un — su ql.co.*, to pass judgement (*o* to give an opinion) on sthg.; *farsi un — su ql.co.*, to form an opinion of sthg. **3.** (*saggezza*) wisdom; (*buon senso*) good sense, common sense, good judgment, sound judgement: *un ragazzo di —*, a sensible boy; *aver —*, to be sensible (*o* wise): *non hai affatto —!*, you have no sense at all!; *far —*, to behave well (*o* to behave oneself); *mettere —*, to become (*o* to grow) wise; (*calmarsi, diventare serio*) to settle down; *mostrar —*, to show sound judgement (*o* good sense) || *dente del —*, wisdom-tooth || *età del —*, age of discretion **4.** (*teol.*) judgement: *il — universale*, the Last Judgement; *il giorno del —*, Doomsday (*o* the Day of Judgement) **5.** *— di Dio*, (*st.medievale*) ordeal **6.** (*fil.*) judgement: *«La critica del —»*, "Critique of Judgement".

giudiziosaménte, *av.* judiciously; discerningly.

giudizióso, *ag.* judicious; discerning; sensible; discreet: *una persona poco giudiziosa*, an indiscreet person.

giudò, *s.m.* (*una delle forme della lotta giapponese*) judo.

giúggiola, *s.f.* (*bot.*) jujube || *andare in brodo di giuggiole*, to be extremely delighted (*o* pleased).

giúggiolo, *s.m.* (*bot.*) jujube(tree).

giuggiolóne, *s.m.* simpleton, fool.

giugitsu, *s.m.* (*una delle forme della lotta giapponese*) jujitsu, jiujitsu.

giúgno, *s.m.* June: *arrivò il due —*, he arrived on the second of June.

giugulàre, *ag.* (*anat.*) jugular: *fossetta —*, jugular fossa; *ganglio —*, jugular ganglion; *incisione — dello sterno*, jugular notch || *s.f.* (*anat.*) jugular (vein).

Giugúrta, *no.pr.m.* (*st.*) Jugurtha.

giulebbàre, *v.t.* to candy; to cook in sugar || **giulebbàrsi**, *v.r.* (*fam.*) (*sopportare*) to put up with (s.o.) feigning pleasure.

giulebbàto, *ag.* candied.

giulèbbe, *s.m.* julep.

Giúlia, *no.pr.f.* Julia || *dim.* Juliet.

Giuliàna, *no.pr.f.* Juliana, Jillian || *dim.* Jill.

giuliàno,[1] *ag.* Julian: *calendario —*, Julian calendar.

Giuliàno[2], *no.pr.m.* Julian || *dim.* Jule.

Giúlie (Alpi), *no.pr.f.pl.* (*geog.*) Julian Alps.

Giuliétta, *no.pr.f.* Juliet.

giulío[1], *ag.* (*letter.*) gay, joyous.

Giúlio[2], *no.pr.m.* Julius: *— Cesare*, Julius Caesar.

giulivaménte, *av.* gaily, joyously.

giulívo, *ag.* gay, joyous; joyful; cheerful.

giullàre, *s.m.* jester; buffoon; (*menestrello*) minstrel: *il — del Re*, the King's jester.

giullarésco, *ag.* jester-like (*attributivo*).

giumèlla, *s.f.* quantity contained in cupped hands || *bere a —*, to drink from cupped hands.

giuménta, *s.f.* (*cavalla*) mare; (*asina*) she-ass; (*mula*) she-mule.

giuménto, *s.m.* (*bestia da soma*) beast of burden; (*asino*) ass; (*mulo*) mule.

giúnca, *s.f.* (*mar.*) junk.

giuncàia, *s.f.* reed-bed, bed of rushes.

giuncàta, *s.f.* (*cuc.*) junket.

giunchéto, *s.m.* reed-bed, bed of rushes.

giunchíglia, *s.f.* (*bot.*) jonquil.

giúnco, *s.m.* (*bot.*) reed, rush.

giúngere, *v.i.* **1.** to arrive (at a place), to come; to reach (sthg.): *ecco a che siamo giunti!*, here's what we've come to!; *giunsi in Italia*, I arrived in Italy; *nessun suono giungeva al mio orecchio*, not a sound reached my ears; *la primavera è giunta finalmente!*, spring has come at last!; *— in una città*, to arrive at a town (*o* to reach a town *o* to get to a town); *— sano e salvo*, to arrive safe and sound **2.** (*arrivare, spingersi fino*) to reach (sthg.); to achieve (sthg.): *la carne giunse a prezzi altissimi*, meat reached very high prices; *fin dove lo sguardo può —*, as far as the eye can reach; *giunse alla vetta della montagna*, he reached the top of the mountain; *giunse a minacciarmi*, he went so far as to threaten me; *— alla meta, fig.* to achieve one's aim; *— all'età di novant'anni*, to reach the age of ninety || *— a vie di fatto*, to come to blows **3.** (*riuscire*) to succeed (in doing): *non giunsi mai a scoprire la verità*, I never succeeded in discovering the truth (*o* I could never discover the truth) || *v.t.* **1.** (*congiungere*) to join: *— le mani per pregare*, to join one's hands in prayer **2.** (*raggiungere*) to reach, to get at (s.o., sthg.): *se ti giungo ti accoppo!*, (*scherz.*) if I get at you I'll kill you! **3.** (*aggiungere*) to add.

giungiménto, *s.m.* **1.** (*il giungere*) arrival **2.** (*congiungimento*) joining.

giúngla, *s.f.* jungle.

Giúnio, *no.pr.m.* (*st.*) Junius.

Giunóne, *no.pr.f.* (*mit.*) Juno.

giunònico, *ag.* Junoesque; Junonian || *bellezza giunonica*, stately beauty.

giúnta[1], *s.f.* **1.** (*aggiunta*) addition, increase || *per —*, in addition (*o* into the bargain) **2.** (*di peso*) make-weight **3.** (*spor.*) advantage, start.

giúnta[2], *s.f.* (*comitato*) committee; (*in Spagna, America Latina e Italia*) junta: *— comunale*, town council; *— provinciale*, provincial council; (*in Gran Bretagna*) county council.

giúnta[3], *s.f.* (*arrivo*): *a prima —*, at first (sight).

giuntàggio, *s.m.* (*cine.*) splicing.

giuntàre, *v.t.* **1.** (*unire*) to join; (*con cuciture*) to sew together **2.** (*rar.*) (*truffare*) to cheat, to swindle **3.** (*cine.*) to splice.

giuntatrice, *s.f.* (*mec.*) **1.** (*cine.*) splicer **2.** (*ind. tessile*) piecing machine.

giúnto[1], *ag.* joined || *a mani giunte*, with clasped hands || *salto a piedi giunti*, standing jump.

giúnto[2], *s.m.* (*mec.*) joint; (*di accoppiamento*) coupling; (*costruzioni navali*) seam: *— a cerniera*, hinged joint; *— a ganasce*, fish joint (*o* splice); *— a ginocchiera*, toggle joint; *— a snodo*, knuckle joint; *— assiale*, splice; *— a vili*, muff coupling; *— ad incastro*, (*carpenteria*) gain joint; *— cardanico, universale*, universal joint; *— di testa*, butt (joint); *— idraulico* (*o* hydro-drive) coupling (*o* fluid flywheel); (*con tenuta ad acqua*) hydraulic joint; *— sferico*, ball (*o* ball-and-socket) joint.

giuntúra, *s.f.* **1.** joint **2.** (*anat.*) joint, articulation: *— del cranio*, suture; *— del ginocchio*, knee-joint; *le giunture delle dita*, the knuckles.

giunzióne, *s.f.* **1.** (*il giuntare*) junction, jointing, connection: *— di tubi*, pipe connection **2.** (*mec.*) (*giunto*) joint: *— a cerniera*, hinged joint; *— a maschio e femmina*, tongue and groove joint; *linea di —*, seam; *senza —*, seamless; *fare una —*, to joint.

giuocàre, *V.* **giocàre**.

giuòco, *V.* **giòco**.

Giúra, *no.pr.m.* (*geog.*) Jura.

giurabbàcco, giuraddío, *inter.* by Jove!, by golly!.

giuraménto, *s.m.* oath: *cerimonia ufficiale del —*, swearing-in-ceremony; *formula del —*, wording of the oath; *sotto —*, on oath: *affermare sotto il vincolo del —*, to affirm on (*o* upon) oath; *fare un —*, to take (*o* to make *o* to swear) an oath; *impegnare, vincolare qlcu.*

con —, to bind s.o. by oath; *mancare al* —, to break one's oath; *prestare* —, to take an oath (*o* to swear) ‖ — *da marinaio*, (*promessa fallace*) dicer's oath.

giuràre, *v.t.* to swear: *giurò di non averla mai vista*, he swore that he had never seen her; *giuro per tutto ciò che vi è di sacro*, I swear by all that is sacred; *lo giurate?*, will you swear to it?; *non bisogna mai* — *su niente*, you never can tell (*o* one can never be sure of anything); *il nuovo ministro giurò nelle mani del presidente*, the President swore the new Minister; *vi giuro che è vero*, I swear it is the truth ‖ — *di dire la verità*, to swear to tell the truth; — *di fare ql.co.*, to swear to do sthg.; — *eterno amore, fedeltà a qlcu.*, to swear eternal love, fidelity (*o* faithfulness) to s.o.; — *e spergiurare*, to keep swearing by all the gods; — *sulla Bibbia*, to swear on the Bible (*o* to kiss the Book); — *su ql.co., qlcu.*, to swear by sthg., s.o.; — *vendetta*, to swear revenge ‖ *giurarla a qlcu.*, to swear vengeance on s.o.

giuràssico, *ag.* (*geol.*) Jurassic.

giuràto, *ag.* sworn: *nemico* —, sworn enemy; *perito* —, sworn expert ‖ *s.m.* (*dir.*) juryman (*pl.* jurymen); juror: *i giurati*, the jury; *banco dei giurati*, jury-box; *lista dei giurati*, panel.

giúre, *s.m.* (*arc.*) jurisprudence, law.

giureconsúlto, *s.m.* jurisconsult, jurisprudent.

giurése, *ag.* (*geol.*) Jurassic.

giurí, *s.m.* (*dir.*) jury.

giuría, *s.f.* **1.** (*dir.*) jury: *presidente della* —, foreman of the jury **2.** (*collegio che assegna premi in gare sportive, mostre, ecc.*) jury.

giuridicaménte, *av.* juridically, legally.

giuridicità, *s.f.* juridical character.

giurídico, *ag.* juridical, judicial; legal: *posizione giuridica*, legal position; *stato* —, (legal) status; *studi giuridici*, law studies; *uguaglianza giuridica*, legal equality.

giurisdizionàle, *ag.* jurisdictional.

giurisdizióne, *s.f.* jurisdiction: *territorio sotto la* — *di...*, area within (*o* under) the jurisdiction of...; *è sotto la nostra* —, it comes under our jurisdiction ‖ *non avete alcuna* — *sulla mia vita privata*, you have no right to interfere with my private life.

giurisperìto, *s.m.* jurisconsult, jurisprudent.

giurisprudènza, *s.f.* jurisprudence, law: *studia* —, he studies law.

giurìsta, *s.m.* jurist.

giúro, *s.m.* (*poet.*) oath.

Giusèppa, *no.pr.f.* Josepha ‖ *dim.* Jo, Josie.

Giusèppe, *no.pr.m.* Joseph ‖ *dim.* Jo(e).

Giuseppína, *no.pr.f.* Josephine.

giusquìamo, *s.m.* (*bot.*) henbane.

giústa, *prep.* **according to, in accordance with, in conformity with:** — *i vostri desideri*, according to your wishes; — *la volontà di mio padre*, in conformity with my father's will.

giustacuòre, *s.m.* jerkin.

giustaménte, *av.* rightly, justly, properly.

giustézza, *s.f.* **1.** exactness, correctness, precision: — *di una espressione*, propriety of an expression; — *di una opinione*, soundness of an opinion; — *di ragionamento*, exactness of reasoning **2.** (*tip.*) measure.

giustificàbile, *ag.* justifiable.

giustificànte, *ag.* justifying ‖ *grazia* —, (*teol.*) justifying grace.

giustificàre, *v.t.* to justify, to vindicate, to warrant: *il fine giustifica i mezzi*, the end justifies the means; *nulla potrebbe* — *la vostra condotta*, nothing could warrant (*o* justify) your behaviour; — *la propria assenza*, to send in one's apologies for absence; — *l'assenza di qlcu.*, to excuse s.o. for his absence ‖ **giustificàrsi**, *v.r.* **1.** to justify oneself, to vindicate one's character **2.** (*discolparsi*) to clear oneself.

giustificataménte, *av.* **1.** justly, rightly; (*equamente*) fairly **2.** (*in modo esatto*) rightly, correctly, exactly;

(*opportunamente*) properly **3.** (*in modo legittimo*) lawfully; groundedly.

giustificativo, *ag.* justificative, justificatory: *pezza giustificativa*, voucher.

giustificàto, *ag.* **1.** justified: *il suo modo di agire era* —, he was justified in acting like that; *assenza giustificata*, (*a scuola*) justified absence **2.** (*perdonato, assolto*) forgiven, justified.

giustificatóre, *ag.* justifying ‖ *s.m.* justifier.

giustificatòrio, *ag.* justificatory, justificative.

giustificatríce, *s.f.* justifier.

giustificazióne, *s.f.* justification, excuse; (*a scuola*) absence note: *a* — *di ql.co.*, in justification (*o* excuse) of sthg.; *a titolo di* —, as a justification; *senza* —, without excuse; *non vi è* — *per il tuo atto*, there is no justification (*o* excuse) for your deed.

Giustína, *no.pr.f.* Justina, Justine.

Giustiniàno, *no.pr.m.* (*st.*) Justinian: *Codice di* —, Justinian Code.

Giustíno, *no.pr.m.* Justin.

giustíssimo, *inter.* quite right!, quite so!.

giustízia, *s.f.* **1.** justice; (*equità*) fairness, equity: *con* —, justly; *per* — *verso qlcu.*, in justice (*o* fairness) to s.o.; *fare, rendere* — *a qlcu.*: to do justice to s.o.: *per rendergli* — *bisogna ammettere che...*, in fairness (*o* justice) to him it must be admitted that...; *ottenere* —, to obtain justice; *trattare con* —, to treat with justice (*o* equitably *o* fairly) **2.** (*dir.*) justice; law: *la* — *seguì il suo corso*, the law had its way; *Corte di Giustizia*, Court of Justice (*o* of Law); *Ministro di Grazia e Giustizia*, Minister of Justice; *Palazzo di Giustizia*, Law Courts; *amministrare la* —, to administer justice; *assicurare alla* —, to bring to justice; *cadere nelle mani della* —, to be brought to justice (*o* to be arrested and tried); *fare* —, to do (*o* to dispense) justice; *farsi* — *da sè*, to take the law into one's own hands; *ricorrere alla* —, to go to law.

giustiziàre, *v.t.* to execute, to put to death: — *sulla sedia elettrica*, to electrocute.

giustiziàto, *ag.* executed ‖ *s.m.* executed man.

giustizière, *s.m.* **1.** executioner **2.** (*vendicatore*) avenger.

giústo[1], *ag.* **1.** just, right; (*equo*) fair: *un* — *castigo*, a just punishment; *giusta ricompensa*, just reward; *un* — *prezzo*, a fair price; *un trattamento* —, a right (*o* just) treatment; *un uomo* —, a just man; *un verdetto* —, a fair verdict; *è* — *che anche voi lavoriate*, it is right that you too should work; *era* — *che voi sapeste questo*, it was right that you should know this; *siamo giusti!*, let us be fair!; *essere* — *con qlcu.*, to be just to s.o.; *pagare il* — *prezzo*, to pay the right price ‖ *il* — *mezzo*, the happy medium (*o* mean): *tenersi nel* — *mezzo*, to stick to a happy medium **2.** (*esatto*) right, correct, exact; (*opportuno*) proper: *la parola giusta*, the right word; *il rimedio* —, the right remedy; *una risposta giusta*, a correct answer; *il conto è* —, the account is correct; *ditemi l'ora giusta*, tell me the correct time; *sapete calcolare il peso* —?, can you calculate the correct weight?; *la tua minestra è giusta?*, (*fam.*) is there enough salt in your soup?; *il tuo orologio è* — *o avanti?*, (*fam.*) is your watch right or fast?; *arrivare all'ora giusta*, to arrive on the stroke of time ‖ *l'uomo* — *al posto* —, the right man in the right place ‖ *per dirla giusta*, to call a spade a spade **3.** (*legittimo*) legitimate, lawful: *un desiderio* —, a legitimate wish; *una rivendicazione giusta*, a lawful vindication ‖ *s.m.* **1.** (*uomo retto*) just man ‖ *i giusti*, the just: *i giusti e i reprobi*, the just (*o* the righteous) and the wicked; *dormire il sonno dei giusti*, to sleep the sleep of the just **2.** (*ciò che è giusto*) the right: *il* — *e l'ingiusto*, the right and the wrong; *essere nel* —, to be in the right.

giústo[1], *av.* **1.** (*con giustezza, precisione*) exactly, precisely: *colpire* —, *fig.* to strike home; *veder* —, to have right view of things **2.** (*proprio, appunto*) just;

very (*ag. solo in uso attributivo*): *arrivò — allora*, he arrived just then; *cercavamo — quel libro*, we were looking for that book (o for that very book).

Giústo², *no.pr.m.* Justus.

glàbro, *ag.* glabrous, hairless; (*liscio*) smooth.

glacé, *ag.* **1.** (*cuc.*) (*rivestito di zucchero*) iced: *marrons glacés*, marron glacés **2.** *guanti —*, glacé-kid gloves.

glaciàle, *ag.* **1.** (*molto freddo*) glacial, icy, frosty, frigid (anche *fig.*): *accoglienza —*, icy welcome; *modo di fare —*, rigid manners; *sorriso —*, glacial smile; *spiffero —*, frosty draught; *temperatura —*, icy temperature; *vento —*, icy (o cutting o bitter) wind **2.** (*geol. geog.*) glacial: *era —*, Glacial Period (o Ice-Age); *le regioni glaciali*, ice-regions; *zona —*, frigid zone.

glacialménte, *av.* glacially, icily, frigidly (anche *fig.*).

glaciazióne, *s.f.* (*geol.*) glaciation.

glaciología, *s.f.* glaciology.

gladiatóre, *s.m.* gladiator.

gladiatòrio, *ag.* gladiatorial.

glàdio, *s.m.* gladius (*pl.* gladii).

gladíolo, *s.m.* (*bot.*) gladiolus (*pl.* gladioli, gladioluses).

glagolítico, *ag.* (*di alfabeto*) Glagolitic.

glandifórme, *ag.* glandiform.

glàndola, *V.* **ghiàndola**.

glandulàre, *ag.* glandular.

glandulóso, *ag.* glandulous, glandulose.

glassàre, *v.t.* **1.** (*rivestire di zucchero*) to ice **2.** (*coprire di gelatina*) to glaze.

glàueo¹, *ag.* (*letter.*) glaucous, blue-green, greyish-blue, sea-green.

Glàueo², *no.pr.m.* (*mit.*) Glaucus.

glaucòma, *s.m.* (*patol.*) glaucoma.

glèba, *s.f.* (*poet.*) glebe ‖ *servo della —*, (*st. medioevale*) serf (attached to the soil).

glène, *s.f.* (*anat.*) glenoid cavity, glenoid fossa (*pl.* glenoid fossae), glene.

glenoidàle, *ag.* (*anat.*) glenoid(al).

glenòide, *s.f.* (*anat.*) glenoid.

glenoidèo, *ag.* glenoidal.

gli¹, *art. determinativo m. pl.* **1.** the: *— Appennini*, the Apennines; *— Italiani*, the Italians; *— Stati Uniti*, the United States; *— uccelli dell'aria*, the birds of the air; *— Smith sono ritornati*, the Smiths have come back **2.** (*spesso non si traduce*): *— aranci sono belli in inverno*, orange trees are beautiful in winter; *— orsi vanno estinguendosi in Italia*, bears are dying out in Italy; *— stranieri amano Roma*, foreigners love Rome; *Maria ha — occhi azzurri*, Mary has blue eyes **3.** (*tradotto con l'ag. poss.*): *si tolse — stivali*, he took his boots off.

gli², *pron.pers.m.* 3ª *persona* **1.** *sing. obliquo* him, to him (*riferito a persona o cosa personificata*): it, to it (*riferito a cosa o animale di sesso non specificato*): *— mandò il libro*, he sent him the book (o he sent the book to him); *digli che l'hai vista*, tell him you saw her; *non devi fargli male*, you must not hurt him; *prestagli la tua automobile*, lend him your car (o lend your car to him); *quando il cane mi venne incontro — diedi un osso*, when the dog ran up I gave it a bone **2.** *sing.sogg.* (*fam. toscano*) (*per aferesi da egli pleonastico*) it: *— è ben vero che...*, it is quite true that...; *— è lui*, it is he (o him) **3.** *pl. obliquo* (*idiotismo per* loro) them, to them.

glía, *s.f.* (*anat.*) glia.

glicemía, *s.f.* (*med.*) glycemia.

gliceràto, *s.m.* (*chim.*) glycerate.

glicèrico, *ag.* (*chim.*) glyceric.

glicèride, *s.m.* (*chim.*) glyceride.

glicerína, *s.f.* (*chim.*) glycerine, glycerol.

glicerofosfàto, *s.m.* (*chim.*) glycerophosphate.

gliceròlo, *s.m.* (*chim.*) glycerol, glycerin.

glicine, *s.m.* (*bot.*) wistaria.

glicogènesi, *s.f.* (*fisiol.*) glycogenesis.

glicògeno, *s.m.* (*chim. biol.*) glycogen.

glícole, *s.m.* (*chim.*) glycol.

glicònio, *ag.s.m.* (*poes.*) glyconic.

glicosuría, *s.f.* (*patol.*) glycosuria, glycuresis.

gliélo, *pron. pers. composto* 3ª *persona* it (to) him, it (to) her; him to him, him to her; it to it: *— diedi da leggere*, I gave it to him (to her) to read; *— presentai ieri*, I introduced him to him (to her) yesterday ‖ **glièla**, *pron.pers. composto* 3ª *persona* it (to) him, it (to) her; her to him, her to her; it to it: *— feci conoscere io*, it was I who introduced her to him (to her); *— regalai l'anno scorso*, I gave it to him (to her) last year ‖ **glièli, glièle**, *pron.pers. composto* 3ª *persona* them to him, them to her; them to it: *— offrì*, he offered them to him (to her); *— presentai io*, it was I who introduced them to him (to her).

gliéne, *V.* **gli²** **1.** **3.** *e* **ne²** **4.**.

glífo, *s.m.* **1.** (*arch.*) glyph **2.** (*mec.*) (*di macchina a vapore*) link-block: *— oscillante*, crank and slotted link; *distribuzione a —*, link-motion.

gliòma, *s.m.* (*patol.*) glioma (*pl.* gliomata).

glíttica, *s.f.* glyptic(s).

glíttico, *ag.* glyptic.

glittografía, *s.f.* glyptography.

glittotèca, *s.f.* glyptotheca.

globàle, *ag.* global, total, inclusive, comprehensive: *somma —*, total amount (o inclusive sum).

globalménte, *av.* **1.** totally, inclusively, collectively **2.** (*comm.*) in the lump, in gross.

globigerína, *s.f.* (*zool.*) globigerina (*pl.* globigerinae).

glòbo, *s.m.* globe; sphere: *— aerostatico*, balloon; *— celeste, terrestre*, celestial, terrestrial globe; *— dell'occhio*, (*anat.*) eye-ball (o globe of the eye); *diffusore a —*, (*elett.*) light globe; *fare il giro del —*, to go round the globe (o round the earth).

globòide, *s.m.* globoid.

globosità, *s.f.* globosity.

globóso, *ag.* globose, globular, spherical.

globulàre, *ag.* globular, globe-like, spherical.

globulína, *s.f.* (*chim. biol.*) globulin.

glòbulo, *s.m.* **1.** (*piccolo corpo rotondo*) globule **2.** (*biol.*) corpuscle: *globuli bianchi, rossi*, white, red corpuscles; *globuli del sangue*, blood corpuscles.

glo glò, *s.m.* **1.** (*rumore del liquido che esce da un fiasco o simile recipiente*) gurgle, gurgling **2.** (*verso del tacchino*) gobble, gobbling.

gloglottàre, *v.i.* **1.** (*di liquido che esce da un fiasco o simile recipiente*) to gurgle **2.** (*di tacchino*) to gobble.

glomèrulo, *s.m.* (*anat.*) glomerule.

glòria¹, *s.f.* **1.** (*fama, onore, lode*) glory: « *— a Dio nel più alto dei cieli* », " glory to God in the highest "; *— eterna*, eternal glory; *per la maggior — di Dio*, to the greater glory of God; *avere brama, sete di —*, to thirst for glory; *coprirsi di —*, to cover oneself with glory; *rendere — a Dio*, to give glory to God (o to glorify God) ‖ *lavorare per la —*, (*fam.*) to work for nothing **2.** (*vanto*) glory, pride: *l'arte è la nostra — maggiore*, art is our greatest pride (o glory); *fu la — del suo secolo*, he was the glory (o the pride) of his age; *farsi — di ql.co.*, to glory in sthg. (o to pride oneself upon sthg.) **3.** (*splendore*) glory, splendour: *le glorie dell'impero britannico*, the glories of the British Empire; *Salomone in tutta la sua —*, Solomon in all his glory; *la — delle arti fu allora grandissima*, the splendour of the arts then reached its peak **4.** (*beatitudine celeste*) glory, heavenly bliss: *vivere in — coi Santi*, to live with the Saints in glory ‖ *che Dio l'abbia in —!*, (*fam.*) bless his soul! **5.** (*pitt.*) picture of a group of angels and saints **6.** (*festa, giubilo*) *aspettare* (*qlcu., ql.co.*) *a —*, to long for (s.o., sthg.); *essere in —*, (*essere brillo*) to be tipsy; *suonare a —*, to ring a festive peal of bells ‖ *la (la preghiera)* gloria ‖ *alla fine del salmo si canta il —*, *prov.* don't count your chickens before they are hatched ‖ *tutti i salmi finiscono in —*, *prov.* it's the same old story.

Glòria², *no.pr.f.* Gloria.

gloriàrsi, *v.r.* to glory (in sthg.); to be proud (of sthg.); to take (a) pride (in sthg.); to pride oneself (upon sthg.); (*millantarsi*) to boast (about, of sthg.): *ci gloriamo della nostra libertà*, we take pride in (*o* we are proud of) our liberty; *ella si gloria della sua bellezza*, she glories in (*o* she is proud of) her beauty; *si gloria di aver ucciso cento nemici*, he prides himself (up)on killing one hundred enemies; *si gloria di essere il più abile cacciatore del paese*, he boasts of being the best sportsman in his village.

glorificàre, *v.t.* 1. to glorify, to praise, to magnify, to laud, to extol: *che il nome di Dio sia glorificato!*, God's name be praised!; — *la memoria di qlcu.*, to glorify s.o.'s memory 2. (*teol.*) to glorify, to exalt to the glory of Heaven: *Dio glorificherà i suoi Santi*, God will glorify his Saints.

glorificatívo, *ag.* (*rar.*) glorifying, laudatory.

glorificàto, *ag.* glorified.

glorificatóre, *ag.* glorifying; laudatory ‖ *s.m.*, **glorificatríce**, *s.f.* glorifier, praiser.

glorificazióne, *s.f.* glorification: *la* — *degli eroi*, the glorification of the heroes; *a* — *di Dio*, to the praise of God.

gloriòla, *s.f.* (*spreg.*) petty glory.

gloriosaménte, *av.* gloriously.

glorióso, *ag.* 1. glorious: *vittoria gloriosa*, glorious victory 2. (*orgoglioso*) proud: *andare* — *di ql.co.*, to be proud of sthg. 3. (*teol.*) glorified: *corpo* —, glorified body ‖ *i Gloriosi*, the Saints in glory.

gloriúzza, *s.f.* (*spreg.*) petty glory.

glòssa, *s.f.* gloss, note, annotation, comment: *questo codice è ricco di glosse*, this codex is full of glosses.

glossalgía, *s.f.* (*patol.*) glossalgia.

glossantràce, *s.m.* (*patol.*) glossanthrax.

glossàre, *v.t.* to gloss, to expound, to annotate; to comment upon (sthg.).

glossàrio, *s.m.* glossary.

glossatóre, *s.m.* glossator, glossist, glossarist, glosser; commentator ‖ *la Scuola dei Glossatori*, (*st. dir.*) the School of Glossators.

glossèma, *s.m.* gloss.

glòssico, *ag.* (*anat.*) glossal, glottic.

glossína, *s.f.* (*entom.*) Glossina.

glossínia, *s.f.* (*bot.*) gloxinia.

glossíte, *s.f.* (*patol.*) glossitis, glottitis.

glossocèle, *s.m.* (*patol.*) glossocele.

glossofaríngeo, *ag.* (*anat.*) glossopharyngeal.

glossografía, *s.f.* glossography.

glossògrafo, *s.m.* glossographer.

glossología, *s.f.* 1. glossology, glottology 2. (*terminologia*) terminology, glossology: — *scientifica*, scientific terminology.

glossoplegía, *s.f.* (*patol.*) glossoplegia.

glòttide, *s.f.* (*anat.*) glottis.

glottología, *s.f.* glottology, glossology.

glottològico, *ag.* glottologic(al), glossological.

glottòlogo, *s.m.* glottologist, glossologist.

glúcide, *s.m.* (*chim.*) glucide.

glucína, *s.f.* (*chim.*) glucina.

glucínio, *s.m.* (*chim.*) glucinium.

glucòside, *s.m.* (*chim.*) glucoside.

glucòsio, *s.m.* (*chim.*) glucose.

glucosuría, *s.f.* (*patol.*) glycosuria.

gluglú, *s.m.* 1. (*rumore del liquido che esce da un fiasco o simile recipiente*) gurgle, gurgling: *fare* —, to gurgle 2. (*verso del tacchino*) gobble, gobbling: *fare* —, to gobble.

glúma, *s.f.* (*bot.*) glume.

glumèlla, *s.f.* (*bot.*) glumella.

glutàmmico, *ag.* (*chim.*) glutamic: *acido* —, glutamic acid (*o* glutamine).

glúteo, *ag.* (*anat.*) glutaeal, gluteal: *muscolo* —, gluteal muscle; *nervo* —, gluteal nerve ‖ *s.m.* (*anat.*) glutaeus (*pl.* glutaei), gluteus (*pl.* glutei).

glutinàto, *ag.* gluten (*attributivo*): *pane* —, gluten-bread; *pasta glutinata*, gluten paste.

glútine, *s.m.* 1. (*chim.*) gluten 2. (*colla*) glue.

glutinosità, *s.f.* 1. (*chim.*) glutinosity 2. (*vischiosità*) glutinousness, glueyness.

glutinóso, *ag.* 1. (*contenente glutine*) glutinous 2. (*viscoso*) glutinous, gluey, viscous; sticky.

gnào, **gnàu**, *s.m.* (*verso del gatto*) mew, mewing: *fare* —, to mew.

gnaulàre, *v.i.* 1. (*miagolare*) to mew 2. (*piagnucolare*) to whine, to whimper.

gnaulàta, *s.f.* 1. (*miagolio*) mewing 2. (*piagnucolio*) whining, whimpering.

gnaulío, *s.m.* mewing.

gnàulo, *s.m.* mew.

gneiss, *s.m.* (*min.*) gneiss.

gnòcco, *s.m.* 1. *pl.* (*cuc.*) "gnocchi" 2. (*sciocco*) blockhead, thickhead, dullard.

gnòme, *s.f.* (*rar.*) gnome, maxim, aphorism.

gnòmica, *s.f.* gnomology.

gnòmico, *ag.* gnomic ‖ *s.m.* (*st. lett.*) gnomic poet.

gnòmo, *s.m.* gnome: *nella fantasia popolare gli gnomi sono i mitici abitatori delle miniere d'oro*, according to popular superstition gold mines are the traditional home of gnomes.

gnomóne, *s.m.* gnomon.

gnomónica, *s.f.* gnomonics.

gnomònico, *ag.* gnomonic(al).

gnòrri, *s.m.*: *far lo* —, to feign ignorance.

gnoseología, *s.f.* (*fil.*) gnosiology.

gnoseològico, *ag.* (*fil.*) gnosiological.

gnòsi, *s.f.* (*st. relig.*) gnosis.

gnosticísmo, *s.m.* (*st. relig.*) gnosticism.

gnòstico, *ag.s.m.* (*st. relig.*) gnostic.

gnu, *s.m.* (*zool.*) gnu.

gòbba, *s.f.* 1. hump, hunch: — *di cammello*, camel's hump 2. *fig.* hump, swelling: *questa strada ha molte gobbe*, this road is very uneven (*o* humpy) 3. (*donna gobba*) humpback, hunchback, hump-backed woman, hunchbacked woman.

gòbbo, *ag.* 1. hump-backed, hunchbacked 2. (*curvo*) bent: — *per la vecchiaia*, bent with age; *andar* —, to go bent ‖ *s.m.* 1. humpback, hunchback 2. (*gobba*) hump, hunch ‖ *spianare il* — *a qlcu.*, (*batterlo*) to drub (*o* to beat) s.o.

gobbóni, *av.*: *andar* —, to go bent.

gòccia, *s.f.* 1. drop: *una* — *d'acqua*, a drop of water; *vuoi una* — *di whisky?*, will you have a drop of whisky?; *cadere a gocce*, to fall in drops (*o* to drip) ‖ *a* — *a* —, drop by drop (*o* in drops) ‖ *fino all'ultima* —, to the last drop ‖ *la* — *che fece traboccare il vaso*, the straw that broke the camel's back ‖ *aveva la* — *al naso*, his nose was running ‖ *è come una* — *nel mare*, it is like a drop in the ocean (*o* in the bucket) ‖ *si assomigliano come due gocce d'acqua*, they are as like as two peas 2. *pl.* (*orecchini a goccia*) ear-drops 3. *pl.* (*arch.*) guttae, drops.

gocciàre, *V.* gocciolàre.

gócciola, *V.* góccia.

gocciolaménto, *s.m.* dripping, trickling.

gocciolàre, *v.i.* to drip, to trickle, to fall in drops: *ti gocciola il naso*, your nose is running ‖ *v.t.* to drip, to trickle: *gocciolava sudore*, he was dripping sweat.

gocciolatóio, *s.m.* (*edil. aut.*) drip: — *di pietra*, (*edil.*) dripstone.

gocciolatúra, *s.f.* dripping, trickling.

gocciolío, *s.m.* dripping, trickling.

gócciolo, *s.m.* drop; (*sorsata*) sip: *un* — *di vino*, a sip (*o* drop) of wine.

gocciolóne, *s.m.* 1. large drop 2. (*sciocco*) driveller 3. *pl.* (*grossi proiettili da caccia*) buck-shots.

godè, *s.m.* flare, gore: *gonna a* —, flared (*o* gored) skirt.

godére, *v.t.* 1. to enjoy, to get pleasure from (sthg.)

to take delight in (sthg.): *avete goduto la festa?*, did you enjoy the party?; *non potei — la compagnia dei miei amici*, I could not enjoy the company of my friends; — *il riposo*, to enjoy a rest; — *la vita*, to enjoy life 2. (*fruire di*) to enjoy: *gode un'ottima rendita*, he enjoys a very good income; *godete l'affetto di tutti*, you are loved by everybody; *godiamo buona salute*, we enjoy good health || *v.i.* 1. to enjoy (sthg.), to be glad; to rejoice (at, in sthg.), to delight (in sthg.): *gode della lettura*, he enjoys reading; *godiamo della tua fortuna*, we rejoice at your good luck; *godo di sentire che state bene*, I am glad to hear that you are well; *pensa solo a —*, he thinks only of enjoyment; — *di una giornata*, to enjoy a fine day || *chi si contenta gode, prov.* a content mind is a perpetual feast 2. (*fruire*) to enjoy (sthg.) (anche *fig.*): *egli non gode di tutte le sue facoltà*, he is not in full possession of all his faculties; — *del favore di qlcu.*, to be in high-favour with s.o.; — *di una pensione*, to enjoy a pension || **godérsi**, *v.r.* to enjoy: *si sta godendo le vacanze*, he is enjoying his holidays.

goderéccio, *ag.* 1. (*dedito a godimenti*) pleasure -loving 2. (*che dà godimento*) pleasant, delightful.

godíbile, *ag.* enjoyable.

godiménto, *s.m.* 1. enjoyment; pleasure; delight: *per me il lavoro è un —*, work is a delight to me 2. (*uso*) enjoyment; (*possesso*) use; possession: — *di usufrutto*, (*dir.*) enjoyment of usufruct.

godronàre, *v.t.* (*mec.*) to knurl.

godronatúra, *s.f.* (*l'atto del godronare*) knurling; (*l'effetto del godronare*) knurl.

godúta, *s.f.* rejoicing.

goffàggine, *s.f.* 1. awkwardness, clumsiness, ungainliness 2. (*atto goffo*) clumsy action; blunder.

goffaménte, *av.* awkwardly, clumsily.

gofferia, *s.f.* 1. awkwardness, clumsiness, ungainliness 2. (*atto goffo*) clumsy action; blunder.

gòffo, *ag.* awkward, clumsy, ungainly.

goffratríce, *s.f.* (*mec.*) embosser, embossing machine.

goffratúra, *s.f.* (*mec.*) embossing.

Goffrèdo, *no.pr.m.* Geoffrey, Godfrey || dim. Jeff.

Gòga e Magòga, *no.pr.m.* (*Bibbia*) Gog and Magog.

gógna, *s.f.* pillory: *mettere alla —*, to pillory.

góla, *s.f.* 1. throat: *gli si era fermato un osso in —*, a bone had stuck in his throat; *gli tagliarono la —*, they cut his throat (o *arc.* slit his weasand); *le ricaccerò le menzogne in —!*, I shall give her the lie in her throat!; *quelle parole gli si fermarono in —*, those words stuck in his throat; *tu menti per la —!*, you lie in your throat!; *afferrare qlcu. per la —*, to pin (o to take o to grip) s.o. by the throat; *avere la — chiusa*, to have a lump in one's throat; *avere mal di —*, to have a sore-throat; *cantare a — spiegata*, to sing at the top of one's voice; *gridare a piena —*, to give a full-throated shout (o to shout lustily o to shout at the top of one's voice); *mortificare la —*, (*digiunare*) to fast; *ridere a — spiegata*, to laugh heartily (o to roar o to shout o to scream with laughter); *schiarirsi la —*, to clear one's throat || *con l'acqua alla —*, chin-deep in water; *fig.* at the end of one's tether (o in deep waters o in extreme danger) || *con il cuore in '—*, (*senza fiato*) panting (o puffing) || *far — a qlcu.*, to tempt s.o. (o to be a temptation to s.o.) 2. (*golosità*) gluttony: *peccato di —*, sin of gluttony 3. (*valle stretta e profonda*) gorge 4. (*mec.*) groove; (*di scarico*) relief; (*di puleggia*) race 5. (*arch.*) cyma (*pl.* cymae); ogee: — *diritta, rovescia*, cyma recta, reversa 6. (*di camino*) stack: *su per la — del camino*, up the chimney 7. (*di armi da fuoco*) neck.

goldoniàno, *ag.* (*lett.*) of Goldoni; in Goldoni's style.

golétta[1], *s.f.* (*mar.*) schooner: — *a tre alberi*, three-masted schooner; — *a vele quadre*, topsail schooner.

golétta[2], *s.f.* 1. (*di armatura*) gorget, throatpiece 2. (*di abito femminile*) collar.

golétto, *s.m.* collar.

golf, *s.m.* 1. jersey; (*maglione*) sweater; (*aperto*) cardigan; (*chiuso, da donna*) jumper 2. (*spor.*) golf: *giocatore di —*, golfer.

golfàre, *s.m.* (*mar.*) eyebolt.

gólfo, *s.m.* gulf: *la corrente del Golfo*, the Gulf Stream; *il — di Taranto*, the Gulf of Taranto.

Gòlgota, *no.pr.m.* (*Bibbia*) Golgotha.

Golía, *no.pr.m.* (*Bibbia*) Goliath.

goliàrdico, *ag.* 1. of students: *un canto —*, a students' song 2. (*st. medievale*) goliardic.

goliàrdo, *s.m.* 1. university student 2. (*st.medievale*) goliard.

golosaménte, *av.* greedily, gluttonously.

golosería, golosità, *s.f.* 1. greediness, gluttony 2. (*bocconcino prelibato*) dainty, titbit.

golóso, *ag.* greedy, gluttonous || *s.m.* glutton; (*buongustaio*) gourmand, gourmet, epicure.

golpàto, *ag.* (*agr.*) blighted, mildewed, smutty.

gólpe, *s.f.* (*agr.*) blight, mildew, smut.

gómena, *s.f.* (*mar.*) rope, hawser, line.

gomitàta, *s.f.* thrust with the elbow, push with the elbow: *farsi avanti a gomitate tra la folla*, to elbow one's way through a crowd.

gómito, *s.m.* 1. elbow: *appoggiò il — destro sulla tavola*, he rested his right elbow on the table; *hai i gomiti fuori*, (*le maniche sdrucite*) you are out at elbows: *le due signore erano — a —*, the two ladies were sitting side by side; *si fece avanti a colpi di —*, he elbowed himself forward || *olio di —*, (*fam.*) elbow -grease || *alzare il —*, *fig.* to drink heavily: *ha alzato un po' troppo il —*, he has had a drop too much 2. (*di strada, di fiume*) sharp bend 3. (*raccordo di tubo*) elbow; (*mec.*) (*di albero a gomito*) crank, throw.

gomítolo, *s.m.* clew, ball (of thread): *la matassa di lana gialla fu avvolta a —*, the skein of yellow wool was wound into a ball.

gómma, *s.f.* 1. (*caucciù*) rubber, India rubber, caoutchouc: — *sintetica*, synthetic rubber; — *vulcanizzata*, vulcanized rubber; *industria della —*, rubber industry; *stivali di —*, rubber boots (o Wellingtons) 2. (*pneumatico*) tyre, tire: — *piena*, solid tyre; *avere una — a terra*, to have a flat tyre; *forare una —*, to puncture a tyre 3. (*sostanza resinosa*) gum: — *arabica*, gum-arabic; — *da masticare*, chewing-gum; — *dolce*, gumdrop (o jujube); — *esplosiva*, explosive gelatine; — *gutta*, gamboge; — *lacca*, shellac; — *liquida*, liquid gum 4. (*gomma per cancellare*) eraser, (india-) rubber: — *da inchiostro*, ink-eraser; — *da matita*, pencil eraser 5. (*patol.*) gumma (*pl.* gummata, gummas).

gommapiúma, *s.f.* foam rubber: *materasso di —*, foam rubber mattress.

gommàre, *v.t.* to gum; (*ind. tessile*) to rubberize.

gommàto, *ag.* gummed; (*di tessuto*) rubberized *carta gommata*, gummed (o sticky) paper; (*nastro adesivo*) adhesive tape.

gommífero, *ag.* gummiferous.

gommorèsina, *s.f.* gum-resin.

gommòsi, *s.f.* (*bot.*) gummosis.

gommosità, *s.f.* gumminess, gummosity.

gommóso, *ag.* 1. gummy 2. (*appiccicoso*) sticky.

Gomòrra, *no.pr.f.* (*Bibbia*) Gomorrah, Gomorrha.

gonàgra, *s.f.* (*patol.*) gonagra.

gonalgía, *s.f.* (*med.*) gonalgia.

gonartríte, *s.f.* (*patol.*) gonarthritis.

góndola, *s.f.* gondola.

gondolière, *s.m.* gondolier.

gonfalóne, *s.m.* standard; (*specialmente di città italiane*) gonfalon.

gonfalonière, *s.m.* standard-bearer; (*specialmente di città italiane*) gonfalonier.

gónfia, *s.m.* (*operaio che soffia il vetro*) glass-blower.

gonfiàggine, *s.f.* 1. swelling 2. (*boria*) self-importance.

gonfiàggio, *s.m.* (*di pneumatico*) inflation, pumping up.

gonfiaménto, *V.* **gonfiatúra**.

gonfianúvoli, *s.m.* boaster, braggart.

gonfiàre, *v.t.* **1.** to swell (anche *fig.*); (*con aria*) to inflate (anche *fig.*): *il bambino gonfiò il pallone*, the child blew up his balloon; *le piogge hanno gonfiato il fiume*, the rain has swollen the river; *il successo lo gonfia*, he is swelling with the pride of success (*o he is puffed up by his success*); *il vento gonfia le vele*, the wind swells (*o fills*) the sails; *— le gote*, to puff out (*o to blow out*) one's cheeks **2.** (*esagerare*) to exaggerate, to puff: *egli gonfiò la sua avventura*, he exaggerated his adventure **3.** (*adulare*) to flatter || **gonfiàre**, *v.i.*, **gonfiàrsi**, *v.r.* to swell (anche *fig.*): *il fiume gonfia*, the river is swelling (*o rising*); *il mio cuore si gonfiava d'orgoglio*, my bosom swelled with pride; *i suoi occhi si gonfiarono di lacrime*, his eyes were swollen with tears.

gonfiàto, *ag.* **1.** swollen; inflated || *è un pallone —*, he is not all that he is puffed (*o cracked*) up to be **2.** (*esagerato*) exaggerated, puffed.

gonfiatóio, *s.m.* tyre-pump, inflater, inflator.

gonfiatóre, *s.m.*, **gonfiatríce**, *s.f.* (*rar.*) **1.** (*chi gonfia*) inflater, inflator **2.** (*chi esagera*) inflater, inflator, exaggerator.

gonfiatúra, *s.f.* **1.** swelling, inflation, inflating: *la — delle gomme*, the inflation of tyres **2.** (*esagerazione*) exaggeration; (*montatura*) stunt, puff; (« *soffietto* », *critica apologetica*) puff: *le solite gonfiature dei giornali*, the usual puffs of the press **3.** (*adulazione*) adulation, flattering.

gonfiézza, *s.f.* **1.** swelling, inflation **2.** (*di stile*) bombast.

gónfio, *ag.* **1.** swollen, inflated: *piede —*, swollen foot; *una ruota ben gonfia*, a well-inflated tyre; *il torrente è — per la pioggia di ieri*, the stream is swollen with yesterday's rain; *vele gonfie*, swelling (*o bellying*) sails *|| tutto va a gonfie vele*, everything is going very well; *il mio tentativo andò a gonfie vele*, my attempt was quite successful **2.** *fig.* puffed up, inflated, swollen; (*di stile*) bombastic: *— di superbia*, puffed up with pride; *con il cuore —*, with a swelling heart; *è un uomo —*, (*pieno di sè*) he is very full of himself (*o a self-conceited man*); *ho il cuore —*, my heart swells.

gonfióne, *s.m.* **1.** (*persona molto grassa*) fatty **2.** *fig.* (*persona piena di sè*) puffed up fellow.

gonfióre, *s.m.* swelling: *un — alla caviglia*, a swelling of the ankle.

gong, *s.m.* gong.

gongolaménto, *s.m.* rejoicing (at, in sthg.).

gongolànte, *ag.* rejoicing (at, in sthg.), overjoyed (at sthg.): *arrivò tutto —*, he arrived all overjoyed.

gongolàre, *v.i.* to rejoice (at, in sthg.), to be overjoyed (at sthg.): *gongolava in silenzio*, he was silently rejoicing; *alla notizia del loro arrivo gongolò tutto*, he was overjoyed at the news of their arrival.

gongorísmo, *s.m.* (*st. lett.*) Gongorism.

goniometría, *s.f.* goniometry.

goniomètrico, *ag.* goniometric(al).

goniòmetro, *s.m.* goniometer: *— ad applicazione*, contact goniometer; *— a riflessione*, reflecting goniometer; *radio —*, radiogoniometer (*o direction finder*).

gónna, *s.f.* **1.** skirt: *— a campana*, flared skirt; *— a cannoni*, box-pleated skirt; *— a pieghe*, pleated skirt; *— larga*, full skirt; *— pantalone*, divided skirt; *— stretta*, tight skirt **2.** (*di costume storico, anche maschile*) gown.

gonnèlla, *s.f.* **1.** skirt: *è ancora attaccato alle gonnelle di sua madre*, he is still tied to his mother's apron-strings **2.** *fig.* woman (*pl.* women): *corri dietro a ogni —!*, you run after every bit of skirt you see!.

gonnellíno, *s.m.* short skirt || *— scozzese*, kilt.

gonorrèa, *s.f.* (*patol.*) gonorrhea, gonorrhoea.

gónzo, *s.m.* simpleton, fool, blockhead: *non fare il —!*, don't play the fool!.

gòra, *s.f.* **1.** (*canale che conduce l'acqua al mulino*) millcourse, millrace **2.** (*conserva d'acqua per alimentare il mulino*) millpond **3.** (*acqua stagnante*) pool, pond.

górbia, *s.f.* **1.** (*strum. artig. chir.*) gouge **2.** (*puntale di bastone, ombrello*) ferrule **3.** (*punta di freccia*) arrow-head.

gordiàno, *ag.* Gordian: *nodo —*, (*mit.*) Gordian knot (anche *fig.*).

Gòrdio, *no.pr.m.* (*geog. st.*) Gordius.

górga, *s.f.* (*arc.*) throat; gullet.

gorgàta, *s.f.* draught: *bere ql.co. a gorgate*, to gulp sthg. down.

gorgheggiaménto, *s.m.* **1.** trill **2.** (*di uccello*) warble, trill.

gorgheggiàre, *v.i.* **1.** to trill **2.** (*di uccello*) to warble, to trill.

gorgheggiatóre, *s.m.* **1.** triller **2.** (*di uccello*) warbler || **gorgheggiatríce**, *s.f.* triller.

gorghéggio, *s.m.* **1.** trill **2.** (*di uccello*) warble, trill.

gòrgia, *s.f.* **1.** throat; gullet **2.** (*pronuncia gutturale*) guttural pronunciation **3.** (*gorgheggio*) trill.

gorgièra, *s.f.* **1.** (*collare increspato*) ruff **2.** (*di armatura*) gorget, throat-piece.

górgo, *s.m.* whirlpool, eddy, vortex.

gorgogliaménto, *s.m.* **1.** (*di liquido*) gurgling, bubbling **2.** (*di intestini*) rumbling.

gorgogliàre, *v.i.* **1.** (*di liquido*) to gurgle, to bubble **2.** (*di intestini*) to rumble.

gorgóglio[1], *s.m.* **1.** (*di liquido*) gurgling, bubbling **2.** (*di intestini*) rumbling.

gorgoglío[2], *s.m.* gurgling.

gorgoglióne, *s.m.* (*entom.*) **1.** (*calandra del grano*) weevil **2.** (*afide*) aphis (*pl.* aphides); plant-louse (*pl.* plant-lice); green-fly.

Gorgóne, *no.pr.f.* (*mit.*) Gorgon || *s.f.* (*donna orrenda e aggressiva*) Gorgon, hag.

gorgòneo, *ag.* (*mit.*) Gorgonian (anche *fig.*).

gorgonzòla, *s.m.* "Gorgonzola" (kind of Italian cheese).

gorgozzúle, *s.m.* throat; gullet.

gorílla, *s.m.* (*zool.*) gorilla.

gòta, *s.f.* cheek: *gote paffute*, chubby cheeks; *gonfiare le gote*, to blow (*o to puff*) out one's cheeks.

gòtico, *ag.* Gothic: *carattere —*, Gothic type (*o black-letter o German text*); *stile —*, Gothic style || *romanzo —*, Gothic novel.

gòto, *s.m.* (*st.*) Goth: *i Goti*, the Goths.

gótta, *s.f.* (*patol.*) gout, podagra.

gottàzza, *s.f.* (*mar.*) bailer, bailing scoop.

gòtto, *s.m.* mug.

gottóso, *ag.* gouty || *s.m.* gouty subject.

governàbile, *ag.* governable.

governàle, *s.m.* **1.** (*arc.*) (*timone*) rudder **2.** (*di bomba aerea*) vane.

governànte, *s.m.* (*chi governa*) governor, ruler; (*statista*) statesman (*pl.* statesmen) || *s.f.* (*donna che tiene il governo della casa*) housekeeper; (*istitutrice*) governess; (*bambinaia*) nurse.

governàre, *v.t.* **1.** to govern, to rule: *leggi che governano le reazioni chimiche*, laws that govern chemical reactions; *un monarca costituzionale regna, ma non governa*, a constitutional monarch reigns but does not govern; *— una chiesa*, to rule over a church; *— male*, to misgovern; *— un paese*, to govern (*o to rule*) a country; *— una scuola, un'azienda*, to run a school, a business **2.** (*badare a, prendersi cura di*) to look after (s.o., sthg.), to take care of (s.o., sthg.) **3.** *fig.* (*dominare*) to rule: *— le proprie passioni*, to rule (*o to curb o to bridle o to control*) one's passions **4.** (*animali*) to groom; (*custodire*) to tend: *— un cavallo*, to groom a horse; *— mucche, pecore al pascolo*, to pasture cows, sheep **5.** (*mar.*) to steer: *— una barca*, to steer a boat; *— una nave*, (*o to handle*) a ship; *nave che non governa più*, ship that refuses to steer (*o that no longer answers the helm*) **6.** (*aer.*) to control **7.** (*una fornace*) to stir with must (of selected grapes) || **governàrsi**, *v.r.* **1.** (*dominarsi*) to control oneself, to govern oneself, to rule oneself 2. (*regolarsi*) to behave: *non sappiamo come governarci in questo caso*, we don't know how to behave (o what to do) in this case.

governativo, *ag.* government (*attributivo*); governmental: *impiegato* —, government employee; (*in Gran Bretagna*) civil servant; *partito* —, Government Party (o party in power); *scuola governativa*, state school.

governatóre, *s.m.* 1. governor: — *generale*, governor-general; *poteri di* —, gubernatorial powers 2. (*precettore*) tutor, preceptor.

governatríce, *s.f.* (*moglie di governatore*) governor's wife.

governatúra, *s.f.* (*governo di animali*) grooming.

govèrno, *s.m.* 1. government; administration; (*dominio*) rule: — *assoluto*, *costituzionale*, *repubblicano*, absolute, constitutional, republican government; — *tirannico*, tyrannical rule; *cattivo* —, bad government (o misgovernment); *uomo di* —, (*statista*) statesman || — *fantoccio*, puppet government: *creare un* — *fantoccio*, to set up a puppet government 2. (*i membri di un gabinetto*) government, cabinet: *il* — *si riunì*, a cabinet meeting was held; *formare un nuovo* —, to form a new government (o cabinet o ministry) 3. (*direzione*); (*comm.*) management: — *della casa*, housekeeping; *il* — *di un'azienda non è oggi cosa facile*, the management of a business is no easy task nowadays || *donna di* —, (*domestica*) housemaid; (*governante*) housekeeper 4. (*di animali*) grooming 5. (*mar.*) steerage, steering; (*aer.*) control: *in* —, (*mar. aer.*) under control; *superfici di* —, (*aer.*) control surfaces || *essere al* — *della barca*, *fig.* to be at the helm.

gózzo, *s.m.* 1. goitre: *essere affetto da* —, to be afflicted with a goitre || *empirsi il* —, (*fam.*) to gorge || *non poter tener nulla nel* —, *fig.* to be unable to keep a secret 2. (*di uccello*) crop.

gozzovíglia, *s.f.* debauch; revelry.

gozzovigliàre, *v.i.* to revel, to carouse, to feast.

gozzúto, *ag.* goitred, goitrous || *s.m.* goitrous man, goitred man: *i gozzuti*, goitrous people.

gracchiaménto, *V.* **gracchiàta**.

gracchiàre, *v.i.* 1. to croak; to caw 2. *fig.* to chatter.

gracchiàta, *s.f.* 1. croaking; cawing 2. *fig.* chattering.

gracchiatóre, *ag.* 1. croaking 2. *fig.* chattering || *s.m.*, **gracchiatríce**, *s.f.* 1. croaker 2. *fig.* chatterer.

gràcchio, *s.m.* 1. (*il gracchiare*) croak, croaking; caw, cawing 2. (*specie di cornacchia*) grackle, jackdaw.

gracchióne, *s.m.* (*fam.*) (*brontolone*) grumbler.

Gràcco, *no.pr.m.* (*st.*) Gracchus: *i Gracchi*, the Gracchi.

gracidaménto, *s.m.* croaking.

gracidàre, *v.i.* 1. to croak 2. *fig.* to chatter.

gracidatóre, *ag.* 1. croaking 2. *fig.* chattering || *s.m.*, **gracidatríce**, *s.f.* 1. croaker 2. *fig.* chatterer.

gracidío, *s.m.* 1. croaking 2. *fig.* chattering.

gràcile, *ag.* weak, delicate, frail: *un bimbo* —, a delicate (o frail) child; *complessione* —, delicate constitution; *fiori gracili*, frail (o fragile) flowers.

gracilènto, *ag.* sickly, ailing.

gracilità, *s.f.* weakness, frailness, frailty.

gradàre, *v.t.* (*rar.*) to graduate || *v.i.* to slope.

gradassàta, *s.f.* boastfulness, bragging.

gradàsso, *s.m.* boaster, braggart, blusterer; (*bravaccio*) bully: *non fare il* —!, don't brag! (o stop bragging!).

gradataménte, *av.* gradually, by degrees.

gradazióne, *s.f.* 1. gradation, grading 2. (*mus. pitt.*) gradation 3. (*sfumatura*) shade: *una* — *più forte di verde*, a darker shade of green 4. — *alcoolica*, alcoholic strength.

gradèlla, *s.f.* (*rete da pesca*) stake-net.

gradétto, *s.m.* (*arch.*) astragal.

gradévole, *ag.* agreeable, pleasant, pleasing: — *al gusto*, palatable.

gradevolézza, *s.f.* agreeableness, pleasantness.

gradevolménte, *av.* agreeably, pleasantly.

gradiènte, *s.m.* (*fis.*) gradient: — *atmosferico*, lapse; — *barometrico*, barometric gradient; — *di durezza*, hardness gradient; — *di pressione*, pressure gradient; — *termico*, lapse rate (o *amer.* thermal gradient).

gradiménto, *s.m.* 1. pleasure, liking; (*soddisfazione*) satisfaction: *mostrò il suo profondo* —, he showed his satisfaction; *spero che il dono sia di tuo* —, I hope the present is to your liking 2. (*approvazione, consenso*) approval, approbation; (*accettazione*) acceptance: *questa proposta ha incontrato il* — *di tutti*, this proposal met with general acceptance; *speriamo che la nostra offerta sia di vostro* —, we hope that our offer will meet with your approval.

gradína, *s.f.* (*scult.*) gradine.

gradinàre, *v.t.* 1. to chisel (with a gradine) 2. (*in ascensioni alpine*) to cut steps in (the ice).

gradinàta, *s.f.* 1. gradin(e), flight of steps; (*i gradini*) steps (*pl.*) 2. (*di teatro greco, romano*) gradin(e).

gradinatúra, *s.f.* (*scult.*) chiselling.

gradíno, *s.m.* 1. step, stair: *una scala di trenta gradini*, a staircase (o a flight) of thirty steps; *sul* — *più basso*, on the bottom step (o stair); *dovrete fare dei gradini nel ghiaccio con la piccozza*, you will have to cut steps in the ice with your axes; *ella sedeva sul penultimo* — *in alto*, she was sitting on the top stair (o step) but one || *salire un* —, *fig.* to go up a step; *scendere di un* —, *fig.* to come down a step 2. (*stadio*) stage; (*grado*) grade: *il primo* — *della mia fortuna*, the first stage in my fortune; *il primo* — *dell'insegnamento*, the first grade of a teaching program(me).

gradíre, *v.t.* 1. to like; (*desiderare*) to wish: *gradirei che venissi anche tu*, I should like you to come too; (*come preghiera*) I wish you would come too; *gradirei molto la vostra compagnia*, I should like very much to have you with me; *gradirei una tazza di tè*, I should like a cup of tea; *gradiresti venire con noi?*, would you like to come with us? 2. (*accettare*) to accept; (*accogliere con gioia*) to welcome: *ho gradito molto la vostra visita*, I have greatly enjoyed your visit; *l'ho gradito moltissimo*, I highly appreciated it (o *fam.* I was delighted with it o thrilled with it); *speriamo che gradisca il nostro dono*, we hope she'll accept our present; *voglia* — *i miei migliori saluti*, please accept my best greetings; — *un dono*, to welcome a gift || *v.i.* (*piacere*) to like (s.o., sthg.) (*costruzione personale*): *ti gradirebbe una limonata?*, would you like a lemon squash?.

gradíto, *ag.* 1. (*piacevole*) pleasant, agreeable: *una gradita sorpresa*, a pleasant surprise; *ricordi graditi*, pleasant memories; *ha conservato un* — *ricordo di te*, he has kept a very pleasant memory of you; *sono sicuro di fargli cosa gradita*, I am sure I shall please him 2. (*bene accetto*) welcome: *un dono*, *un visitatore* —, a welcome gift, visitor; *notizie molto gradite*, very welcome news; *ho ricevuto la tua gradita lettera*, I received your kind letter || *in risposta alla Vostra gradita lettera, alla gradita Vostra*, (*comm.*) in reply to your favour.

gràdo[1], *s.m.* 1. degree: — *di conoscenza*, *parentela*, degree of knowledge, relationship; *alto* — *di civiltà*, high degree (o level) of civilization; *cugino di primo*, *secondo* —, first, second cousin; *in minor* —, in a lesser degree; *il massimo* — *di esattezza*, the highest degree of accuracy (o the highest possible accuracy); *omicidio di primo*, *secondo* —, (*dir.*) murder in the first, second degree; *per gradi*, by degrees (o step by step o gradually); *è intelligente al massimo* —, he is intelligent to the highest degree 2. (*condizione*): *essere in* — *di fare ql.co.*, to be able to do sthg. (o to be in a position to do sthg.): *sei più in* — *di me di giudicare*, you are in a better position to judge than I am 3. (*in una scala di valori*) degree: — *comparativo*, (*gram.*) comparative degree; — *di durezza*, (*metal.*) degree of hardness; — *di latitudine*, (*geog.*) degree of latitude; — *di umidità*, (*fis.*) degree of humidity (o humidity ratio); *un angolo di dieci gradi*, (*geom.*) an angle of 10° (ten degrees); *equazione di secondo* —, (*mat.*) equation of the second degree; *l'acqua gela a 0° C. o 32° F.*, water freezes at 0° C. (zero degrees centigrade) or 32° F.; *la notte di Natale ci furono 9° sotto zero*, on Christmas night there were -9° C. (nine degrees centigrade below) **4.** (*ceto, rango*) rank: *il — di un impiegato, di un funzionario*, the rank of an employee, of an official; *di alto —*, of high rank (o degree); *gente di ogni —*, people of all ranks; *non è educata come la maggior parte delle ragazze del suo —*, she is not so well bred as most girls of her rank (o degree) **5.** (*mil.*) rank: *ha raggiunto il — di colonnello*, he has attained the rank of colonel; *mi è superiore di —*, he is above me in rank; *avere il — di maggiore*, to hold the rank of major; *essere promosso al — di capitano*, to be promoted to the rank of captain.

gràdo[2], *s.m.* pleasure; liking; will: *a suo mal —*, against his will; *di buon —*, with pleasure (o willingly); *quell'appartamento non gli va a —*, that flat is not to his mind (o does not suit him); *la vostra offerta non gli va a —*, your offer is not to his liking (o taste); *accettare ql.co. di buon —*, to take sthg. in good part.

graduàbile, *ag.* that may be graduated.

graduabilità, *s.f.* capability of being graduated.

graduàle, *ag.* gradual ‖ *salmi graduali*, (*Bibbia*) gradual psalms ‖ *s.m.* (*eccl.*) gradual.

gradualísmo, *s.m.* gradualism.

gradualità, *s.f.* gradualness, graduality.

gradualménte, *av.* gradually, by degrees.

graduàre, *v.t.* **1.** to graduate; to grade; (*uno strumento*) to graduate, to index, to scale: *— gli studi*, to grade studies; *— un termometro*, to graduate a thermometer **2.** (*conferire un grado a*) to confer a degree (up)on (s.o.); (*mil.*) to confer a rank on (s.o.): *— un soldato*, to promote a soldier (o to give a soldier a stripe).

graduàto, *ag.* **1.** (*progressivo*) graded, gradual, progressive: *letture graduate*, graded (o progressive) readings **2.** (*provvisto di scala graduata*) graduated: *bicchiere —*, graduated measure (o measuring glass) ‖ *s.m.* (*mil.*) non-commissioned officer ‖ *graduati e truppa*, rank and file ‖ *tutti i graduati*, all ranks.

graduatòria, *s.f.* **1.** classification; (*spor.*) position **2.** (*di candidati a un concorso*) pass-list: *è riuscito il primo della —*, he came (o was) first **3.** (*dir.*) (*in una causa di fallimento*) graded list (of creditors).

graduatòrio, *ag.* gradual.

graduazióne, *s.f.* graduation, scale: *la — di questa provetta non è esatta*, the scale on this test-tube is not right.

gràffa, *s.f.* **1.** (*artiglio*) claw **2.** (*graffetta per carte*) clip **3.** (*tip.*) brace **4.** (*mec.*) (*per cinghia di trasmissione*) belt fastener, belt fastening claw.

graffiaménto, *s.m.* scratching.

graffiàre, *v.t.* **1.** to scratch: *il gatto mi graffiò*, the cat scratched me **2.** (*fam.*) (*rubare*) to pinch.

graffiàta, *s.f.* scratch.

graffiatóre, *s.m.*, **graffiatríce**, *s.f.* scratcher.

graffiatúra, *s.f.* scratch.

graffiétto, *s.m.* **1.** little scratch **2.** (*strum. artig.*) marking gauge.

graffignàre, *V.* sgraffignàre.

gràffio, *s.m.* scratch: *fare a graffi*, to scratch one another **2.** (*uncino, raffio*) grapnel, grappling-iron.

graffíto, *s.m.* (*art.*) graffito (*pl.* graffiti).

graffiuòlo, *s.m.* chisel.

grafía, *s.f.* **1.** (*scrittura*) writing, handwriting **2.** (*ortografia*) spelling: *— erronea*, wrong spelling.

graficaménte, *av.* graphically.

gràfico, *ag.* graphic: *arti grafiche*, graphic arts; *varianti grafiche*, (*in un testo*) graphic variants ‖ *s.m.* (*diagramma*) graph.

grafíte, *s.f.* (*min.*) graphite, plumbago, black lead.

grafitizzàre, *v.t.* (*metal.*) to graphitize.

grafòfono, *s.m.* graphophone.

grafología, *s.f.* graphology.

grafològico, *ag.* graphological.

grafòlogo, *s.m.* graphologist.

grafòmane, *s.c.* graphomaniac.

grafomanía, *s.f.* graphomania.

grafòmetro, *s.m.* (*geodesia*) graphometer.

grafospàsmo, *s.m.* (*med.*) graphospasm, writer's cramp.

gragnuòla, *s.f.* **1.** (*grandine*) hail **2.** *fig.* (*grande quantità*) shower: *su lui cadde una — di colpi*, a shower of blows fell on him (o hit him).

Gràie (Àlpi), *no.pr.f.pl.* (*geog.*) Graian Alps.

gramàglia, *s.f.* **1.** (*drappo funebre*) pall **2.** *pl.* (*abbigliamento da lutto*) mourning (*sing.*): *le gramaglie di una vedova*, a widow's weeds; *essere in gramaglie*, to be in mourning; *mettersi in gramaglie*, to go into mourning.

gramígna, *s.f.* **1.** (*bot.*) couch-grass **2.** (*erbaccia*) weed ‖ *crescere come la —*, to grow like weeds (o to grow apace).

gramignóso, *ag.* full of weeds, weedy.

graminàcee, *s.f.pl.* (*bot.*) Gramineae.

graminàceo, *ag.* (*bot.*) gramineous, graminaceous.

grammàtica, *s.f.* grammar: *una — francese*, a French grammar; *errori di —*, mistakes in grammar ‖ *val più la pratica della —*, *prov.* practice is better than precept (o experience is the best teacher).

grammaticàle, *ag.* grammatical; grammar (*attributivo*): *regola —*, grammatical rule.

grammaticalménte, *av.* grammatically.

grammaticàstro, *s.m.* (*spreg.*) grammaticaster.

grammatichería, *s.f.* (*spreg.*) grammatical pedantry.

grammàtico, *ag.* grammatic(al) ‖ *s.m.* grammarian.

gràmmo, *s.m.* **1.** gram, gramme (*unità di peso* = 15.432 gr.) **2.** *— atomo*, (*chim.*) gram atom (o gram-atomic weight); *— equivalente*, (*chim.*) gram equivalent; *— -ione*, (*elett. chim.*) gram ion; *— -molecola*, (*chim.*) gram molecule (o gram-molecular weight).

grammòfono, *s.m.* gramophone.

gràmo, *ag.* **1.** (*misero*) miserable, wretched: *situazione grama*, difficult (o distressing) situation; *fare una vita grama*, to live a wretched life **2.** (*povero, scarso*) poor, scanty: *raccolto —*, scanty (o poor) crop.

gràmola, *s.f.* **1.** (*per fibre tessili*) brake, scutch, scutcher **2.** (*per la pasta*) kneading-trough: *— meccanica*, kneading-machine (o kneader).

gramolàre, *v.t.* **1.** (*fibre tessili*) to brake, to scutch **2.** (*pasta del pane*) to knead.

gramolatríce, *s.f.* (*per fibre tessili*) brake, scutch, scutcher.

gramolatúra, *s.f.* **1.** (*di fibre tessili*) braking, scutching **2.** (*della pasta del pane*) kneading.

Grampiàni, *no.pr.m.pl.* (*geog.*) Grampians, Grampian Mountains.

gran, *V.* grànde.

gràna[1], *s.f.* (*carminio della cocciniglia*) grain, cochineal, kermes: *tinto in —*, dyed in grain (o in kermes o with cochineal).

gràna[2], *s.f.* (*struttura molecolare di metalli, minerali, ecc.*) grain: *— fine, grossa*, fine, coarse grain; *a, di — fine, grossa*, fine-grained, coarse-grained; *di — media*, medium-grained; *grossezza della —*, grain size; *polvere di — grossa, sottile*, coarse-grained, fine-grained powder.

gràna[3], *s.f.* (*fam.*) (*noia, seccatura*) trouble: *ci sono grane in vista*, there is trouble ahead; *questo lavoro mi dà un sacco di grane*, this work is giving me a lot of headaches; *avere delle grane*, to have (a lot of) troubles; *piantare una —*, to cause trouble (o to stir up the mud).

gràna[4], *s.m.* (*formaggio*) Parmesan cheese (kind of Italian cheese).

gràna[5], *s.f.* (*gergo*) (*denaro*) dough, cash.

granadíglia, *s.f.* (*bot.*) passion-flower, granadilla.

granàglia, *s.f.* **1.** *pl.* corn, grain, cereal (*sing.*): *commerciante di granaglie*, corn-dealer (o corn-factor); (*al minuto*) corn-chandler **2.** (*oreficeria*) granulated gold; (*d'argento*) granulated silver **3.** *pl.* (*min.*) middlings.

granagliàre, *v.t.* (*oreficeria*) to granulate.

granàio, *s.m.* **1.** barn; (*specialmente per grano*) granary **2.** (*solaio*) loft; attic.

granàta[1], *s.f.* (*scopa*) broom; (*di saggina*) besom: *manico di* —, broom-stick ‖ *pigliar la* —, *fig.* (*far piazza pulita*) to make a clean sweep ‖ — *nuova scopa bene tre giorni*, *prov.* a new broom sweeps clean.

granàta[2], *s.f.* (*mil.*) grenade: — *a mano*, hand-grenade (*o sl. mil.* pine-apple).

Granàta[3], *no.pr.f.* (*geog.*) Granada.

granatàio, *s.m.* **1.** (*chi fabbrica granate*) broom-maker **2.** (*chi vende granate*) broom-seller.

granatière, *s.m.* **1.** (*mil.*) grenadier **2.** *fig.* (*persona alta e robusta*) tall imposing person.

granatína, *s.f.* grenadine, pomegranate syrup.

granatíno, *s.m.* small broom.

granàto[1], *ag.* garnet red; wine-coloured ‖ *s.m.* (*pietra preziosa*) garnet.

granàto[2], *ag.* (*fatto a grani*) grainy ‖ *s.m.* (*pop.*) (*melograno*) pomegranate (-tree).

Gran Bretàgna, *no.pr.f.* (*geog.*) Great Britain.

grancancellieràto, *s.m.* High Chancellorship.

grancancellière, *s.m.* High Chancellor.

grancàne, *s.m.* (Great) Khan.

grancàssa, *s.f.* (*mus.*) big drum, bassdrum ‖ *battere la* —, *fig.* to advertize (*o* to bang the big drum).

grancèlla, *s.f.* (*zool.*) small crab.

granchièsco, *ag.* crab-like (*attributivo*).

grànchio, *s.m.* **1.** (*zool.*) crab ‖ *il Granchio*, (*astr.*) Crab (*o* Cancer) **2.** *fig.* (*topica, errore grossolano*) mistake, blunder: *pigliare un* —, to make a blunder **3.** (*pop.*) (*crampo*) cramp ‖ *avere il* — *alla scarsella*, to be stingy **4.** (*parte del martello*) claw.

grancipòrro, *s.m.* (*zool.*) cancer.

grancordóne, *s.m.* **1.** (*di ordine cavalleresco*) Grand Cordon **2.** (*persona insignita del grancordone*) Knight of the Grand Cordon.

grancróce, *s.f.* (*insegna di ordine cavalleresco*) Grand Cross ‖ *s.m.* Knight of the Grand Cross.

grandangolàre, *ag.* (*foto.*) wide-angle (*attributivo*), pantoscopic ‖ *s.m.* (*foto.*) wide-angle lens, pantoscope.

grandàto, *s.m.* (*dignità di Grande di Spagna*) grandeeship.

grànde, *ag.* **1.** (*genericamente e specialmente in senso morale e figurato*) great: *un* — *amore, esercito, numero, poeta*, a great love, army, number, poet; *una* — *differenza, gioia, nazione, occasione*, a great difference, joy, nation, opportunity; *una gran signora*, a great (*o* grand) lady; *un gran signore*, a great (*o* grand) gentleman; *uomini grandi*, great men ‖ *la Grande Guerra*, the Great War ‖ *Alessandro il Grande*, Alexander the Great **2.** (*grosso*) big; (*enorme*) huge: *un* — *errore*, a big mistake; *un* — *successo*, a huge (*o* great) success; *un gran rumore*, a big (*o* loud) noise **3.** (*esteso, largo*) large, big; (*ampio*) wide, broad: — *esperienza*, broad experience; — *fiume, pianura, strada*, wide river, plain, road; *una famiglia molto* —, a very large (*o* big) family; *la mia camera è molto* —, my room is very large (*o* big) ‖ *i Grandi Laghi*, the Great Lakes ‖ *in* —, on a large scale: *fare le cose in* —, to do things on a large scale (*o* in a big way) **4.** (*alto, elevato*) high; (*di statura*) tall: *grandi altezze*, great heights; *grandi latitudini*, high latitudes; — *velocità*, high (*o* great) speed; *ti sei fatto* —!, you have grown tall!; *avere una* — *opinione di qlcu.*, to have a high opinion of s.o. (*o* to think highly of s.o.) ‖ *gran mondo*, high society ‖ *Messa Grande*, High Mass **5.** (*lungo*) long: *ha piedi e braccia grandi*, he has long feet and arms **6.** (*adulto*) grown-up: *ho un figlio* —, I have a grown-up son; *quando sarò* — *farò il medico*, when I am grown-up (*o* big) I shall be a doctor **7.** (*generoso*) big: *egli ha un gran cuore*, he has a big heart; *è* — *da parte tua*, (*fam.*) that's big of you **8.** (*con valore enfatico ed intensivo*): — *bevitore*, hard drinker; — *divoratore di libri*, great reader; *le grandi piogge*, the big rains; *il gran pubblico*, the general

public; *a gran velocità*, at full speed; (*ferr.*) by fast train; *a gran voce*, in a loud voice; *con* — *piacere*, with great pleasure; *con mia* — *meraviglia*, much to my astonishment (*o* to my great astonishment); *in gran parte*, largely (*o* to a great extent); *è gran tempo che non lo vedo*, I haven't seen him for a long time (*o* it is a long time since I saw him last); *egli è di gran lunga il mio miglior allievo*, he is by far (*o* far and away) my best pupil; *fa un gran caldo*, it is very hot; *ho un gran freddo*, I am (*o* I feel) very cold; *non lavoriamo gran che*, we don't work very hard; *questo film non è un gran che*, this picture (*o* film) is nothing extraordinary (*o* not up too much) **9.** (*maiuscolo*) capital **10.** (*nei titoli ufficiali*) grand: *Gran Croce*, Grand Cross; *Grand'Ammiraglio*, Grand Admiral; *Gran Maestro*, Grand Master ‖ *s.m.* **1.** (*adulto*) grown-up: *i grandi*, grown-ups; *racconti per grandi e piccini*, tales for grown-ups and children ‖ *grandi e piccoli*, (*vecchi e giovani*) old and young **2.** (*uomo importante*) great man: *i grandi*, the great; *i grandi della terra*, the great ones of the earth (*o* the princes of the world) ‖ *i Quattro Grandi*, (*Stati Uniti, Gran Bretagna, Francia, Unione Sovietica*) the Big Four **3.** (*titolo ufficiale*) grandee: *un* — *di Spagna*, a grandee of Spain (*o* a Spanish grandee).

grandeggiàre, *v.i.* **1.** to tower (above s.o., sthg.), to dominate (over s.o., sthg.); to stand out (solo *fig.*): *Dante grandeggia sui contemporanei*, Dante towers above his contemporaries; *egli grandeggia nel suo tempo*, he stands out in his time; *il fortino grandeggia sulla valle*, the fortress towers above (*o* over) the valley; *il granatiere grandeggiava sulla folla*, the grenadier towered above the crowd **2.** (*scialare*) to be lavish (of sthg., in doing); (*ostentar lusso*) to show off: *grandeggia in lodi*, he is lavish of praise; *grandeggia nello spendere*, he is lavish in spending (*o* of his money); *hanno la mania di* —, they are fond of showing off.

grandeménte, *av.* greatly; (*moltissimo*) very much; (*altamente*) highly; to a high degree; (*profondamente*) deeply; (*considerevolmente*) considerably.

grandézza, *s.f.* **1.** greatness: — *d'animo*, greatness of soul (*o* magnanimity); *la* — *di Roma, di Shakespeare*, the greatness of Rome, of Shakespeare **2.** (*estensione, larghezza, mole*) largeness; wideness, broadness, hugeness, bigness; bulk **3.** (*altezza*) height; *fig.* loftiness **4.** (*taglia, dimensione*) size: *la* — *di una statua*, the size of a statue; — *media*, average size; *a* — *naturale*, full-size(d) (*o* actual size); *di che* — *è?*, what size is it?; *è press'a poco di questa* —, it is about this size **5.** (*grandiosità, fasto, splendore*) grandeur: *la* — *delle corti orientali*, the grandeur of Oriental courts; *all'apice dell'umana* —, at the summit of human grandeur **6.** *Sua Grandezza*, His Highness **7.** (*liberalità*) liberality; (*prodigalità*) lavishness: *è nota la sua* — *nello spendere*, his lavishness in spending is proverbial; *agire con* —, to do things grandly (*o* in a grand style) **8.** (*astr.*) magnitude: *una stella di prima* —, a star of the first magnitude **9.** (*mat. fis.*) quantity: — *scalare*, scalar quantity; — *vettoriale*, vector quantity.

grandezzàta, *s.f.* **1.** ostentation, showing off, display **2.** (*millanteria*) boast, brag; (*il millantare*) boasting, bragging.

grandezzóso, *ag.* showy.

grandígia, *s.f.* **1.** (*fasto*) ostentation, pomp, display **2.** (*altezzosità, arroganza*) haughtiness, arrogance.

grandiloquènza, *V.* **magniloquènza.**

grandinàre, *v.i.* **1.** *imp.* to hail: *grandina*, it is hailing **2.** *fig.* to shower, to hail: *le pallottole grandinavano intorno a loro*, bullets were hailing all round them ‖ *v.t.* to shower: *cominciarono a* — *pietre sul nemico*, they started showering stones on the enemy.

grandinàta, *s.f.* **1.** hail-storm **2.** *fig.* hail: *una* — *di busse*, a hail of blows.

gràndine, *s.f.* **1.** hail: *chicco di* —, hailstone; *i sassi ci piovevano addosso come* —, stones were showering on us like hailstones **2.** *fig.* hail, shower: *una* — *di* *insulti, di sassi*, a hail (*o* shower) of insults, of stones.

grandinífugo, *ag.* anti-hail.

grandinío, *s.m.* thick fall of hail.

grandiosaménte, *av.* grandly, grandiosely, magnificently, imposingly.

grandiosità, *s.f.* grandiosity; (*specialmente di spettacoli naturali*) grandeur, magnificence, stateliness.

grandióso, *ag.* grand, grandiose, magnificent; majestic; imposing, stately: *una grandiosa cerimonia*, a stately ceremony; *un — palazzo*, a grand palace; *un — progetto*, a grandiose (*o* grand) design; *un — spettacolo*, a grand (*o* an imposing) spectacle; *una grandiosa vista sulle Alpi*, a majestic view of the Alps; *stile —*, grand style.

grandúca, *s.m.* grand duke.

granducàle, *ag.* grand-ducal.

granducàto, *s.m.* grand duchy.

granduchéssa, *s.f.* grand duchess.

granduchessína, *s.f.* daughter of a grand duke.

granduchíno, *s.m.* son of a grand duke.

granduffìcièle, *s.m.* (*onorificenza italiana*) grand officer.

granellíno, *s.m.* small grain; *fig.* little bit.

granèllo, *s.m.* 1. grain, particle: *un — di polvere*, a mote (*o* a speck of dust *o* a particle of dust); *granelli di sale, sabbia*, grains of salt, sand 2. *fig.* grain: *un — di buon senso*, a grain (*o* an atom *o* a bit) of common sense; *un — di pazzia*, a touch of madness 3. (*di cereali, ecc.*) grain, corn: *un — di frumento*, a grain of wheat; *un — d'orzo*, a barley-corn (*o* a grain of barley); *un — di pepe*, a peppercorn 4. (*chicco*) grape 5. (*seme di frutta*) pip, seed: *un — di mela*, a pip of an apple; *un — di melograno*, a pomegranate seed; *un — d'uva*, a grape-stone.

granellosità, *s.f.* 1. granulation 2. (*scabrosità*) roughness.

granellóso, *ag.* 1. granular, granulous 2. (*ruvido*) rough, rugged.

granfàtto, (*arc.*) per **mólto**.

grànfia, *s.f.* claw, talon, clutch (anche *fig.*)

granfiàre, *v.t.* to clutch; to crab.

granífero, *ag.* graniferous.

graniförme, *ag.* graniform.

graníglia, *s.f.* grit.

graníre, *v.i.* (*agr.*) to seed ‖ *v.t.* 1. (*metalli*) to granulate, to grain 2. *— i denti*, (*di bambini*) to teethe 3. *— le note*, (*mus.*) to play each note clearly.

granìta, *s.f.* grated-ice drink.

granítico, *ag.* 1. granitic 2. *fig.* solid, strong, hard.

granitifórme, *ag.* granitiform.

graníto, *ag.* 1. (*sodo, ben fatto*) strong, well-shaped, well-built 2. (*a granellini*) grainy ‖ *s.m.* (*min.*) granite ‖ *cuore. di —*, heart of stone.

granitúra, *s.f.* 1. (*di cereali*) seeding 2. (*di monete*) milling; (*l'orlo granito*) milled edge.

granívoro, *ag.* granivorous.

gràno, *s.m.* 1. (*frumento*) wheat: *— duro*, hard corn; *un campo di — maturo*, a field of ripe wheat; *farina di —*, wheat flour; *il raccolto del —*, the wheat harvest ‖ *cercare miglior pane che di —*, *prov.* to wish for the moon 2. (*ogni cereale*) corn: *un — saraceno*, buckwheat; *— turco*, Indian corn; *campi di —*, cornfields 3. (*coll.*) (*granaglie*) corn, grain: *borsa del —*, corn exchange; *commercio del —*, corn trade; *negoziante di —*, corn-factor (*o* corn-dealer) 4. (*al minuto*) corn-chandler 4. (*granello*) grain; (*solo di cereali*) corn; (*di collana*) bead: *— di rosario*, rosary-bead; *un — d'orzo*, a barley-corn (*o* a grain of barley) ‖ *con un — di sale*, *fig.* with a pinch of salt 5. grain (*unità di peso* = g. 0,0648).

granòcchia, (*arc.*) per **ranòcchia**.

granocchiàia, *s.f.* (*ornit.*) frog-pecker; heron.

granóne, *s.m.* (*bot.*) Indian corn, maize.

grantúreo, *s.m.* (*bot.*) Indian corn. maize *farina di —*, maize meal (*o* maize flour).

granulàre[1], *ag.* granular.

granulàre[2], *v.t.* to granulate.

granulàto, *ag.* granulated.

granulatóio, *s.m.* powder-mill.

granulazióne, *s.f.* granulation: *tessuto di —*, (*biol.*) granulation tissue.

grànulo, *s.m.* granule.

granulòma, *s.m.* (*patol.*) granuloma.

granulóso, *ag.* granulous, granulose.

granvisíre, *s.m.* grand vizir.

gràppa[1], *s.f.* 1. (*per unire blocchi di legno o di pietra*) cramp; (*per unire due tavole*) dog 2. (*tip.*) brace 3. (*per cinghie di trasmissione*) belt fastener.

gràppa[2], *s.f.* (*acquavite*) brandy.

grappàre, *v.t.* (*tec.*) (*unire con grappe*) to cramp.

grappíno[1], *s.m.* (*mar.*) creeper, grapnel, grappling-iron.

grappíno[2], *s.m.* (*bicchierino di grappa*) tot of brandy; (*cicchetto*) pick-me-up.

gràppolo, *s.m.* 1. bunch, cluster: *un — d'uva*, a bunch (*o* cluster) of grapes; *crescere a grappoli*, to grow in clusters (*o* bunches) 2. *fig.* cluster: *un — di persone*, a cluster of people.

gràscia, *s.f.* (*grasso*) fat, suet, lard.

gràspo, *s.m.* (*pop.*) grape-stalk.

grassaménte, *av.* 1. (*abbondantemente*) abundantly, plentifully, lavishly; (*riccamente*) richly ‖ *ridere —*, (*di cuore*) to split one's sides (*o* to roar) with laughter (*o* to laugh heartily) 2. (*licenziosamente*) licentiously.

grassatóre, *s.m.* robber; (*specialmente a cavallo*) highwayman (*pl.* highwaymen); (*a piedi*) footpad.

grassazióne, *s.f.* robbery; hold-up: *commettere una —*, to commit robbery.

grassèllo, *s.m.* 1. (*pezzetto di grasso*) lump of fat 2. (*calce spenta*) slaked lime, lime putty.

grassétto, *ag.* (*tip.*) heavy-faced ‖ *s.m.* (*tip.*) heavy type.

grassézza, *s.f.* 1. fatness; (*solo riferito a persona*) stoutness 2. (*untuosità*) greasiness 3. (*abbondanza*) abundance, plenty 4. (*fertilità*) richness.

grassíme, *s.m.* (*concime*) manure.

gràsso, *ag.* 1. fat; (*solo riferito a persona*) stout: *carne grassa*, fat meat; *un tacchino ben —*, a very fat turkey; *egli è enormemente —*, he is exceedingly fat; *quella signora è piuttosto grassa*, that lady is rather stout ‖ *pianta grassa*, thick-leaved plant 2. (*ricco di grassi*) fat; rich; (*unto, untuoso*) greasy, fatty, oily: *brodo —*, meat broth; *cibo —*, oily food; *carne grassa*, fat meat; *cucina grassa*, rich cooking; *formaggio —*, rich cheese ‖ *martedì —*, Shrove Tuesday; *la settimana grassa*, Shrovetide 3. (*abbondante*) abundant, prosperous: *annata grassa*, prosperous year ‖ *a farla grassa*, at the most (*o* at the best) ‖ *è andata grassa*, everything came out well ‖ *fare grasse risate*, to laugh heartily (*o* to roar with laughter) 4. (*fertile*) fertile: *terra grassa*, fertile (*o* rich) land 5. (*licenzioso*) licentious: *discorso —*, licentious talk ‖ *s.m.* (*animale o vegetale*) fat; (*specialmente usato come lubrificante*) grease: *— di maiale*, pork fat; *macchia di —*, grease stain; *i grassi ti sono nocivi*, fats are harmful to (*o* bad for) your health ‖ *mangiare di —*, to eat meat.

grassòccio, *ag.* plump.

grassóna, *s.f.* fat woman, stout woman; (*sl.*) fatty.

grassóne, *s.m.* fat man, stout man; (*sl.*) fatty.

grassòtto, *ag.* plump.

grassúme, *s.m.* 1. oily substance; fat; grease 2. (*concime*) manure.

gràta, *s.f.* grating: *— di confessionale*, grating of a confessional; *una robusta —*, a strong grating.

grataménte, *av.* (*rar.*) gratefully.

gratèlla, *s.f.* (*cuc.*) gridiron, grill: *carne in —*, grilled meat.

graticciàre, *v.t.* to fence with hurdles; to fence with trellis-work.

graticciàta, *s.f.* **1.** set of hurdles; trellis-work **2.** (*recinto*) fence.

graticcio, *s.m.* **1.** hurdle; (*per piante rampicanti*) trellis, trellis-work **2.** (*riparo, paravento*) screen **3.** (*per far seccare frutta*) mat **4.** (*ind. tessile*) lattice **5.** (*mil.*) fascines (*pl.*).

graticola, *s.f.* **1.** (*cuc.*) gridiron, grill: *cotto sulla* —, grilled (o broiled) **2.** (*di forno, stufa*) grate **3.** (*inferriata*) grating.

graticolàre, *v.t.* (*pitt.*) to graticulate.

graticolàto, *s.m.* (*graticcio*) trellis-work, trellis; (*inferriata*) grating.

gratifica, *s.f.* bonus: — *natalizia*, Christmas bonus.

gratificàre, *v.t.* to gratify (anche *fig.*) ‖ **gratificàrsi,** *v.r.* (*ingraziarsi*) to ingratiate oneself with (s.o.): — *qlcu.*, to win s.o.'s favour.

gratificazióne, *s.f.* (*mancia*) gratuity; (*gratifica*) bonus; (*premio*) bounty: *dare una* —, to allow a gratuity.

gratìle, *s.m.* (*mar.*) bolt-rope.

gratin, al, *l. av.* (*cuc.*) au gratin.

gràtis, *ag.* free (of charge), gratis, gratuitous: *ingresso* —, admission free ‖ *av.* free, gratis, gratuitously: *l'ho avuto* —, I got it free.

gratitúdine, *s.f.* gratitude, gratefulness, thankfulness: *rivolgere a ql.cu espressioni di* —, to make professions of gratitude to s.o.

gràto, *ag.* **1.** grateful, thankful: *gli ero molto* — *della sua gentilezza,* I was very grateful to him for his kindness; *sii* — *a Dio anche dei piccoli doni,* be thankful to God for small mercies too; *con animo* —, with gratitude (o gratefully) **2.** (*obbligato*) obliged: *vi saremmo molto grati se voleste risponderci a giro di posta,* you would greatly oblige us (o we would be greatly indebted to you) if you replied by return of post **3.** (*gradito, bene accetto*) welcome: *una grata notizia,* a welcome piece of news **4.** (*piacevole*) pleasant, agreeable, nice: *un* — *sapore,* a pleasant (o nice) taste.

grattacàpo, *s.m.* trouble, annoyance, worry: *avere dei grattacapi,* to be worried; *crearsi dei grattacapi,* to involve oneself in difficulties; *dare dei grattacapi a qlcu.,* to annoy s.o. (o to get s.o. into trouble).

grattacièlo, *s.m.* skyscraper.

grattaménto, *s.m.* scratching; (*raschiamento*) scraping.

grattàre, *v.t.* **1.** to scratch; (*raschiare*) to scrape (off); to scratch (out); (*cancellare*) to erase: *dobbiamo* — *via tutta la ruggine,* we have to scrape off all the rust (o all the rust off) **2.** (*grattugiare*) to grate: — *pane, formaggio,* to grate bread, cheese ‖ *pane grattato,* bread-crumbs **3.** (*suonare malamente*) to scrape: — *il violino,* to scrape the fiddle **4.** (*fam.*) (*rubare*) to pinch ‖ **grattàrsi,** *v.r.* to scratch oneself: — *il capo,* to scratch one's head ‖ — *la pancia,* (*fam.*) to idle ‖ *mentre il cane si gratta, la lepre va via,* prov. he who hesitates is lost.

grattàta, *s.f.* scratching; (*raschiata*) scraping.

grattatúra, *s.f.* scratching; (*raschiatura*) scraping.

grattino, *s.m.* scraper.

grattúgia, *s.f.* grater.

grattugiàre, *v.t.* to grate: *formaggio grattugiato,* grated cheese.

gratuità, *s.f.* gratuitousness.

gratuitaménte, *av.* **1.** free (of charge), gratis, gratuitously: *lo ricevemmo* —, we got it free **2.** (*senza motivo*) gratuitously, without cause.

gratùito, *ag.* **1.** free, gratuitous: *azione gratuita,* (*finanza*) bonus share; *informazioni gratuite,* free (o gratuitous) information; *ingresso* —, free admittance; *insegnamento* —, free tuition; *prestito* —, loan without interest **2.** (*ingiustificato*) gratuitous, unprovoked: (*infondato*) unfounded: *a titolo* —, without consideration; *azione gratuita,* gratuitous (o unmotivated) action; *insulto* —, gratuitous (o unprovoked) insult; *la tua affermazione è gratuita,* your statement is unfounded.

gratulatòrio, *ag.* (con)gratulatory.

gravàbile, *ag.* liable (to sthg.): — *di dazio,* liable to duty (o dutiable); — *di tassa,* liable to taxation (o taxable).

gravàme, *s.m.* **1.** burden, encumbrance: *libero da ogni* —, free from all encumbrances **2.** (*imposta*) tax; (*ipoteca*) mortgage **3.** (*dir.*) appeal, gravamen.

gravàre, *v.t.* to burden, to encumber, to load, to saddle: — *d'ipoteca,* to burden with a mortgage; — *qlcu. di tasse,* to burden s.o. with taxes ‖ *v.i.* (*pesare*) to weigh; to lie (heavy): *la colpa grava su di te,* the blame lies at your door; *quel delitto gravava sulla sua coscienza,* that crime lay heavy on his conscience; *quella tassa gravava molto sui commercianti al minuto,* that tax weighed heavily on the retail dealers.

gravàto, *ag.* burdened, encumbered: — *di forti tasse,* burdened with heavy taxes; *beni immobili gravati di ipoteca,* encumbered real estate.

gràve, *ag.* **1.** (*pesante*) heavy: *cibo* —, heavy food; *colpo* —, heavy blow; *fatica* —, painful labour; *peso* —, heavy weight; *spese gravi,* heavy outlay ‖ *essere* — *di anni,* to be advanced in age **2.** (*solenne, austero*) grave, solemn: *contegno* —, grave behaviour; *stile* —, dignified style; *uomo* —, grave man; *avere un aspetto* —, to look grave **3.** (*grande*) great; (*importante*) serious, important, weighty; (*pericoloso*) serious, dangerous, bad: *gravi avvenimenti,* weighty events; —*compito,* hard (o difficult) task; *gravi disgrazie,* great misfortunes; — *dolore,* deep sorrow; *gravi torti,* grievous wrongs; *malattia* —, serious (o dangerous) illness; *peccato* —, great (o mortal) sin; *preoccupazioni gravi,* great worry (o heavy care); *ragioni gravi,* serious (o grave) reasons; *situazione grave,* serious situation; *fu un* — *errore,* it was a great (o serious o grievous) mistake ‖ *essere* —, (*gravemente malato*) to be seriously ill **4.** (*severo*) stern, severe: — *rimprovero,* stern rebuke (o severe reprimand) **5.** (*fonet.*) grave: *accento* —, grave accent **6.** (*di voce, suono*) low, grave: *nota* —, low (o grave) note; *voce* —, low (o low-pitched o deep o full-toned) voice ‖ *s.m.* **1.** (*fis.*) (heavy) body: *la caduta dei gravi,* the fall of bodies **2.** (*contegno severo*) graveness, seriousness: *passare dal* — *al gaio,* to pass from seriousness to gaiety.

graveménte, *av.* **1.** (*pesantemente*) heavily: *essere* — *tassato,* to be heavily taxed **2.** (*con gravità di contegno*) gravely **3.** (*seriamente*) seriously; (*grandemente*) greatly: — *ammalato, ferito,* seriously ill, wounded; — *offeso,* deeply offended; *essere* — *indebitato con qlcu.,* to be deeply indebted to s.o. **4.** (*severamente*) sternly.

graveolènte, *ag.* evil-smelling, rank-smelling.

graveolènza, *s.f.* evilsmell, ranksmell.

gravézza, *s.f.* **1.** heaviness (anche *fig.*) **2.** (*spossatezza*) weariness **3.** (*serietà*) gravity **4.** (*peso*) weight; *fig.* burden **5.** (*tassa*) tax.

gravicémbalo, *s.m.* (*st. mus.*) harpsichord.

gravidànza, *s.f.* pregnancy: *essere nel sesto mese di* —, to be six months pregnant.

gràvido, *ag.* **1.** (*di donna*) pregnant; with child (*predicativo*); gravid: *è gravida,* she is pregnant (o with child o she is in the family way) **2.** (*di animale*) big with young, pregnant: *la gatta è gravida di tre settimane,* the she-cat is three weeks pregnant **3.** *fig.* laden (with sthg.), full: — *di conseguenze,* full of consequences; — *di minacce,* laden with (o full of) threats **4.** *panino* —, sandwich.

gravímetro, *s.m.* (*fis.*) gravimeter.

gravìna, *s.f.* pickaxe, mattock.

gravità, *s.f.* **1.** (*solennità, serietà*) gravity, seriousness; (*importanza*) importance, gravity, weight: *la* — *del suo atteggiamento,* the seriousness of his bearing; *la* — *di una malattia,* the seriousness of an illness; *la* — *della situazione non può essere sottovalutata,* the gravity of the situation cannot be underestimated **2.** (*severità*) severity, sternness: — *di un castigo,* severity of a punishment **3.** (*fis.*) gravity: *centro di* —, centre of gravity (*abbr.* c.g.); *forza di* —, force of gravity; *legge di* —, law of gravity.

gravitàre, *v.i.* **1.** (*astr. fis.*) to gravitate: *i pianeti gravitano intorno al Sole*, the planets gravitate round the sun **2.** *fig.* to gravitate; to be powerfully attracted: *i giovani della campagna sembrano — verso la città*, young people in the country districts seem to gravitate towards the cities.

gravitazionàle, *ag.* (*fis.*) gravitational.

gravitazióne, *s.f.* (*fis.*) gravitation: *la legge della* —, the law of gravitation.

gravosaménte, *av.* heavily; painfully.

gravosità, *s.f.* **1.** heaviness **2.** (*difficoltà, molestia*) irksomeness.

gravóso, *ag.* **1.** heavy, burdensome, oppressive: *tassa gravosa*, burdensome tax **2.** (*difficile, molesto*) irksome: *compito* —, irksome task.

gràzia¹, *s.f.* **1.** grace, gracefulness; charm: *canta con* —, she sings with grace; *ci accolse con* —, she welcomed us graciously; *la sua — è impareggiabile*, her grace is incomparable || *con* —, *di buona* —, with a good grace; *di mala* —, with a bad grace || *senza garbo nè* —, completely lacking in grace **2.** (*benevolenza*) favour, grace, good will: *entrare nelle grazie di qlcu.*, to find favour with s.o. (*o* to get into s.o.'s good graces); *godere la* —, *le grazie di qlcu.*, to enjoy s.o.'s favour (*o* to be in s.o.'s good books); *perdere le buone grazie di qlcu.*, to fall out of favour (*o* graces) with s.o.; *sforzarsi d'ottenere le buone grazie di qlcu.*, to curry favour with s.o. **3.** (*favore*) favour: *fatemi la — di dirmi...*, would you be so kind as to tell me...? (*o* would you kindly tell me...?); *accordare una* —, to grant a favour; *chiedere una — a qlcu.*, to ask a favour of s.o.; *fare una — a qlcu.*, to do s.o. a favour (*o* a kindness) || *colpo di* —, coup de grâce (*o* finishing stroke): *dare il colpo di — a un cavallo*, to put a horse out of its pain || *con vostra* —, by (*o* with) your leave (*o* with your permission) || *di* —!, for goodness' sake! (*o* please! *o* pray! *o* if you please!) || *in — di*, owing to; (*con l'aiuto di*) by the help of; (*in considerazione di*) on account of: *fu perdonato in — della sua giovane età*, he was pardoned on account of his youth; *raggiungemmo il nostro scopo in — sua*, we reached our end by his help **4.** (*concessione miracolosa*) grace: *per — di Dio*, by the grace of God || *avuta la* —, *gabbato lo santo*, a good turn is soon forgotten || *ogni — di Dio*, (*grande abbondanza*) every blessing of God || *troppa* —, *S. Antonio!*, it never rains but it pours (*o* that's more than I bargained for) **5.** (*teol.*) grace: *la — di Dio*, the grace of God || *— santificante, sufficiente*, sanctifying, sufficient grace; *essere in stato di* —, to be in a state of grace || *anno di* —, year of grace (*o* of Our Lord) **6.** (*clemenza, perdono*) mercy; (*dir.*) (free) pardon, mercy: *domanda di* —, petition for mercy; *accordare la* —, to grant a pardon; *domandare* —, to cry mercy; *domandare — per qlcu.*, to beg for mercy for s.o. (*o* to intercede for s.o.) || *ti faccio — dei particolari*, I won't trouble you with the details **7.** *Sua, Vostra Grazia*, (*titolo di duca, duchessa, arcivescovo d'Inghilterra*) His (*o* Her), Your Grace **8.** *pl.* (*ringraziamento*) thanks; (*come interiezione*) thank you!, thanks!: *grazie a Dio*, thanks to God; *grazie tante!*, *mille grazie!*, many thanks! (*o* thank you very much!); *render grazie a Dio*, to give thanks to God || *alla* —!, thank heavens! || *essere caro e* —, to be a blessing: *sarà caro e — se finiremo*, it will be a blessing if we can finish **9.** (*tip.*) serif.

Gràzia², *no.pr.f.* Grace || *le Grazie*, (*mit.*) the Graces || *dim.* Gracie.

graziàbile, *ag.* pardonable.

Graziàno, *no.pr.m.* (*st.*) Gratian.

graziàre, *v.t.* **1.** (*dir.*) to pardon, to reprieve **2.** (*concedere*) to grant: *lo graziò di un sorriso*, she granted him a smile.

graziàto, *ag.* pardoned.

gràzie, *inter.* thank you!, thanks!: *— tante!*, *mille* —!, many thanks! (*o* thank you very much!).

Grazièlla, *no.pr.f. dim.* di **Gràzia**.

graziosaménte, *av.* **1.** prettily, gracefully **2.** (*gentilmente*) graciously, kindly.

graziosità, *s.f.* **1.** prettiness, gracefulness **2.** (*gentilezza*) graciousness, kindness.

grazióso, *ag.* **1.** pretty, graceful **2.** (*gentile*) gracious, kind **3.** (*benevolo*): *la nostra graziosa Regina*, our gracious Queen.

grèca, *s.f.* **1.** Greek fret **2.** (*sul berretto di un generale*) zig-zag braid on an Italian general's cap.

grecàle, *ag.* north-east (*attributivo*) || *s.m.* (*vento*) north-east wind.

grecheggiàre, *v.i.* to Hellenize, to Gr(a)ecize.

Grècia, *no.pr.f.* (*geog.*) Greece.

grecísmo, *s.m.* Hellenism, Gr(a)ecism.

grecísta, *s.c.* Hellenist.

grecità, *s.f.* Hellenism, Gr(a)ecism.

grecizzàre, *v.t.* to Hellenize, to Gr(a)ecize: *— una frase*, to give a Greek turn to a phrase || *v.i.* to Hellenize, to Gr(a)ecize.

grèco, *ag.* Greek; (*rar.*) Grecian: *croce greca*, Greek cross; *naso, profilo* —, Greek (*o* Grecian) nose, profile || *i Greci*, the Greeks || *fuoco* —, Greek fire || « *Ode su un'urna greca* », (*lett.*) "Ode on a Grecian Urn" || *pece greca*, colophony || *rimandare ql.co. alle calende greche*, to put sthg. off till Doomsday (*o* to postpone sthg. indefinitely) || *s.m.* **1.** (*abitante*) Greek **2.** (*lingua*) (the) Greek (language): *studiare il* —, to study Greek **3.** (*vento*) north-east wind || **grèca**, *s.f.* Greek.

grèco-romàno, *ag.* Graeco-Roman || *lotta greco-romana*, (*spor.*) Graeco-Roman wrestling.

gregàrio, *ag.* (*bot. zool.*) gregarious: *animale* —, gregarious animal; *pianta gregaria*, gregarious plant || *s.m.* **1.** (*mil.*) private **2.** *fig.* (*seguace*) follower **3.** (*ciclismo*) subordinate helper in a cycling team.

gregarísmo, *s.m.* (*bot. zool.*) gregariousness.

grègge, *s.m.* herd, flock (*anche fig.*): *il parroco e il suo* —, the parish priest and his flock; *condurre, spingere il proprio — al pascolo*, to drive one's flock of sheep to pasture; *curare il* —, to tend the flock.

grèggia, *V.* **grègge**.

grèggio, *ag.* **1.** raw; (*di metallo*) unrefined, coarse, blank; (*di pellame*) undressed; (*di tessuto*) unbleached; (*di zucchero*) brown **2.** *fig.* crude, unrefined.

gregoriàno, *ag.* Gregorian: *calendario* —, Gregorian (*o* new-style) calendar; *canto* —, Gregorian chant.

Gregòrio, *no.pr.m.* Gregory.

grembialàta, *s.f.* apronful.

grembiàle, *s.m.* **1.** apron **2.** (*mar.*) bonnet **3.** (*mec.*) apron.

grembialíno, *s.m.* **1.** small apron; (*da bambino*) smock **2.** (*da calesse*) apron.

grembiùle, grembiulíno, *V.* **grembiàle, grembialíno**.

grèmbo, *s.m.* **1.** lap: *ella teneva il bambino in* —, she held her child in her lap **2.** (*ventre materno*) womb: « *... e benedetto il frutto del — tuo, Gesù* », " ... blessed is the fruit of thy womb, Jesus " **3.** *fig.* bosom: *in — alla famiglia*, in the bosom of one's family; *in — agli dei*, in the lap of the gods; *gettarsi in — a qlcu.*, to commit oneself to s.o. **4.** *far* —, (*di muro*) to fall in.

gremíre, *v.t.* to fill up; to crowd: *la folla gremiva le strade*, the crowd filled the streets || **gremírsi**, *v.r.* to fill up, to get crowded.

gremíto, *ag.* full; filled (with sthg., people); crowded (with sthg., people).

gréppia, *s.f.* rack, crib; manger.

gréppo, *s.m.* **1.** (*dirupo*) crag, cliff **2.** (*ciglio di fosso*) edge (of a ditch).

grès, *s.m.* grès, stoneware.

gréto, *s.m.* (*di fiume*) exposed river-bed, gravel-bed; (*di mare*) shingly shore.

grétola, *s.f.* **1.** (*scheggia*) splinter: *fare in gretole,* to break in splinters (*o* to shatter) **2.** (*sbarra di gabbia*) bar **3.** *fig.* (*cavillo*) cavil, subterfuge, pretext: *trovar la* —, to find a pretext **4.** *pl.* (*mar.*) ratlines.

grettaménte, *av.* **1.** (*meschinamente*) meanly, shabbily **2.** (*con spilorceria*) niggardly, stingily.

gretterìa, grettézza, *s.f.* **1.** (*meschinità*) meanness, shabbiness; (*ristrettezza mentale*) narrow-mindedness **2.** (*spilorceria*) niggardliness, stinginess.

grétto, *ag.* **1.** (*meschino*) mean, shabby; (*di mente ristretta*) narrow-minded: *è molto* — *da parte sua,* it is very shabby of him **2.** (*spilorcio*) niggardly, stingy.

grève, *ag.* heavy.

grézzo, *V.* **gréggio.**

grìda, *s.f.* (*st.*) (*bando*) ban, edict.

gridàre, *v.i.* to shout, to cry (out); (*urlare*) to yell; (*strillare*) to scream; (*vociare*) to bawl: « *Aiuto!* », *gridai,* "Help!", cried I; « *Alle pompe!* », *gridò il capitano,* "To the pumps!", shouted the captain (*o* the captain shouted); — *con quanto fiato si ha in gola,* to cry (*o* to shout) at the top of one's voice; — *di dolore,* to cry out (*o* to yell *o* to scream *o* to shriek) with pain; — *per niente,* to cry about nothing || *v.t.* **1.** to cry (out), to shout; (*urlare*) to yell; (*strillare*) to scream; (*vociare*) to bawl: — *aiuto,* to shout (*o* to cry *o* to call) for help; — *delle ingiurie a qlcu.,* to shout (*o* to yell out) abuse at s.o.; — *un nome,* to cry out a name; — *un ordine,* to shout (*o* to bawl out *o* to sing out) an order || — *vendetta,* to call for vengeance **2.** (*proclamare*) to proclaim **3.** (*rar.*) (*sgridare*) to scold.

gridàta, *s.f.* **1.** shouting; yelling; screaming; bawling **2.** (*sgridata*) scolding.

gridatóre, *s.m.* **1.** shouter, crier **2.** (*banditore*) (town) crier || **gridatrìce,** *s.f.* shouter, crier.

gridellìno, *ag.* (*color lilla*) mauve.

gridìo, *s.m.* shouting; yelling; screaming; bawling.

grìdo, *s.m.* (*di persona o animale*) cry; (*solo di persona*) shout, yell; (*strillo*) scream: *il* — *della iena,* the hyena's laugh; *un* — *di aiuto,* a cry for help; *un* — *di angoscia,* a scream (*o* shriek) of anguish; — *di guerra,* war-cry; — *di rabbia,* angry cry; *grida* (*di gioia, entusiasmo*) *e applausi,* cheers and applause; *ci furono grida e fischi,* there were shouts and hoots; *emettere, gettare un* — *acuto,* to give a scream (*o* to scream *o* to shriek out); *emettere un* — *di terrore,* to shriek with terror || *a grida di popolo,* by public acclamation || *di* —, famous (*o* renowned): *un pittore di* —, a famous (*o* celebrated) painter || *l'ultimo* — (*della moda*), the latest fashion (*o* style).

grifàgno, *ag.* **1.** (*rapace*) rapacious, predatory: *uccello* —, predatory bird (*o* bird of prey) **2.** *fig.* (*minaccioso*) fierce: *occhi grifagni,* fierce eyes.

grìffa, *s.f.* **1.** (*mec.*) jaw; (*innesto a denti*) jaw clutch, dog clutch, claw clutch **2.** (*cine.*) claw.

griffóne, *s.m.* (*cane*) griffon.

grìfo[1], *s.m.* **1.** (*grugno di maiale*) snout **2.** (*spreg.*) (*faccia*) snout, face: *torcere il* —, to screw up one's face in disgust || *ungersi il* —, to eat greedily.

grìfo[2], *s.m.* **1.** (*mit.*) (*grifone*) griffin, gryphon, griffon **2.** (*varietà di avvoltoio*) griffon-vulture, griffin.

grifóne, *s.m.* **1.** (*mit.*) griffin, gryphon, griffon **2.** (*varietà di avvoltoio*) griffon-vulture, griffin **3.** (*cane*) griffon.

grigiàstro, *ag.* greyish; (*spec. amer.*) grayish.

grìgio, *ag.* **1.** grey; (*spec. amer.*) gray: *corpo* —, (*fis.*) grey body; *dagli occhi grigi,* grey-eyed; *dai capelli grigi,* grey-haired (*o* -headed); *materia grigia,* (*anat.*) grey matter; *tempo* —, grey (*o* cloudy *o* dull *o* raw *o* hazy) weather **2.** (*triste*) sad, gloomy: *pensieri grigi,* dark (*o* sad) thoughts; *oggi sono d'umore* —, today I am in a bad humour (*o* I am out of sorts *o* in a bad mood) || *s.m.* grey; (*spec. amer.*) gray: — *ferro,* iron-grey; — *perla,* pearl-grey; *dipinto in* —, painted grey.

grigiolàto, *ag.* **1.** (*brizzolato*) grizzled **2.** (*macchiettato*) speckled, spotted, dappled.

Grigióni, *no.pr.m.pl.* (*geog.*) Grisons.

grigióre, *s.m.* greyness; (*spec. amer.*) grayness.

grigiovérde, *ag.* grey-green || *s.m.* (*mil.*) grey-green uniform (of the Italian army): *indossare il* —, (*divenir soldato*) to join the army; (*essere soldato*) to be a soldier.

grìglia, *s.f.* **1.** (*di forno, stufa*) grate: — *meccanica,* stoker **2.** (*al suolo*) grating, grille **3.** (*di finestra*) shutter **4.** (*graticola*) grill, gridiron: *cuocere alla* —, to grill **5.** (*grata*) grill(e): — *di ventilazione,* ventilating grille (*o* air grating); — *radiatore,* (*aut.*) radiator grill **6.** (*elett. rad.*) grid: — *catodica, di arresto,* cathodic, suppressor grid; — *di schermo,* screen grid; — *pilota,* control grid; *circuito, corrente di* —, grid circuit, grid current; *polarizzazione di* —, grid bias; *resistenza di* —, grid leak **7.** (*miner.*) grizzly.

grigliàto, *s.m.* (*mar.*) fiddley opening.

grillàre[1], *v.i.* (*sfrigolare*) to sizzle || *mi grillò il cuore,* my heart jumped for joy.

grillàre[2], *v.t.* (*mar.*) to fasten, to bend.

grillettàre, *v.i.* (*sfrigolare*) to sizzle.

grillétto, *s.m.* trigger: *premere il* —, to press (*o* to pull) the trigger.

grìllo, *s.m.* **1.** (*entom.*) cricket: *il* — *del focolare,* the cricket on the hearth; *il canto del* —, the chirp(ing) of the cricket || *andare a sentir cantare i grilli,* (*fam.*) to go and push up daisies || *indovinala* —!, (*fam.*) guess, if you can! (*o* have a guess! *o* who knows? *o* who can tell?) || *mangiare come un* —, to have the appetite of a sparrow **2.** *fig.* (*capriccio, ghiribizzo*) fancy, whim, caprice: *ella parla solo quando le salta il* —, she talks only when she has a fancy for it (*o* when she feels like it); *avere il capo pieno di grilli,* to be full of fancies **3.** (*pallino*) (*al giuoco delle bocce*) jack; (*al giuoco del biliardo*) red ball.

grillotàlpa, *s.m.* (*entom.*) mole-cricket.

grimaldèllo, *s.m.* picklock.

grìnfia, *s.f.* claw, clutch, talon (*anche fig.*): *egli fu preso nelle grinfie della legge,* he was caught in the clutches of the law; *lo trassi dalle vostre grinfie,* I got him out of your clutches; *cadere nelle grinfie di qlcu.,* to fall under s.o.'s claws (*o* into s.o.'s clutches).

grìnta, *s.f.* grim, forbidding face || *a* — *dura,* (*con faccia tosta*) shamelessly (*o* with the utmost impudence); (*senza paura*) fearlessly.

grìnza, *s.f.* **1.** (*di stoffa*) crease: *il tuo vestito non fa una* —, your dress fits you like a glove || *non fa una* —, *fig.* it is quite correct: *il tuo ragionamento non fa una* —, your argument is flawless **2.** (*ruga*) wrinkle || *far le grinze,* (*invecchiare*) to age **3.** (*mec.*) wrinkle: *a grinze,* (*di superficie lavorata*) wrinkle-finish; *piegatura a grinze,* (*di tubazione*) wrinkle bending.

grinzóso, *ag.* **1.** (*di stoffa*) creasy **2.** (*rugoso*) wrinkly, wrinkled.

grippàggio, *s.m.* (*mec.*) seizure, seizing: — *del pistone,* piston seizure.

grippàre, *v.i.* (*mec.*) to seize || **gripparsi,** *v.r.* (*mec.*) to seize, to bind.

grìppe, *s.f.* (*patol.*) grip, grippe, influenza.

grìppia, *s.f.* (*mar.*) buoy rope.

grippiàle, *s.m.* (*mar.*) buoy rope.

Grisèlda, *no.pr.f.* Griselda, Grissel, Grizel.

grisèlle, *s.f.pl.* (*mar.*) ratlines: *mettere le* —, to ratline.

grisellìno, *ag.* (*color lilla*) mauve.

grisolìto, *s.m.* (*min.*) chrysolite.

grisopàzio, *s.m.* (*min.*) chrysoprase.

grissìno, *s.m.* "grissino" (Italian bread-stick).

grisú, *s.m.* (*miner.*) fire-damp: — *combusto,* afterdamp.

groenlandése, *ag.* Greenlandic || *s.c.* Greenlander || *s.m.* (*lingua*) (the) Greenlandic (language).

Groenlàndia, *no.pr.f.* (*geog.*) Greenland.

grómma, *s.f.* **1.** (*incrostazione*) encrustation **2.** (*tartaro*) tartar.

grommàto, *ag.* encrusted.

grómmo, *s.m.* clot: — *di sangue,* clot of blood.

grommóso, *ag.* encrusted.

grónda, *s.f.* eaves (*pl.*): *canale della* —, eaves gutter (*o* roof gutter); *i covoni facevano* —, the sheaves were stacked up (*o* were piled in a stack) ‖ *cappello a* —, sou' wester.

grondàia, *s.f.* (*canale*) eaves gutter, roof gutter; (*tubo di discesa*) gutter pipe, water-spout, stack-pipe.

grondànte, *ag.* streaming; (*gocciolante*) dripping: — *d'acqua,* dripping wet (*o* soaked); — *di sangue,* streaming with blood (*o* bleeding); — *di sudore,* all in a sweat (*o* dripping with sweat); *con occhi grondanti di lacrime,* with swimming eyes (*o* with eyes swimming with tears).

grondàre, *v.i.* to stream, to run; (*gocciolare*) to drip, to trickle: *grondava tutto,* he was dripping wet; *il sangue gronda da quella ferita,* blood is streaming from that wound; — *di sudore,* to drip (with) sweat (*o* to perspire heavily) ‖ *v.t.* to pour: — *sangue,* to bleed.

grondóne, *s.m.* (*canale*) eaves gutter, roof gutter; (*tubo di discesa*) gutter-pipe, water-spout.

gróngo, *s.m.* (*ittiol.*) conger(-eel).

Groninga, *no.pr.f.* (*geog.*) Groningen.

gròppa, *s.f.* **1.** (*di quadrupede*) croup(e), rump, back: *in* —, *sulla* —, on the back: *cavalcare sulla* —, to ride behind (the rider in the saddle); (*all'amazzone*) to ride pillion; *prendere qlcu. sulla* —, to take s.o. up behind (*o* up on the crupper) **2.** (*di persona*) back ‖ *avere ottant'anni sulla* —, to be eighty years old **3.** (*di monte*) rounded top.

groppàta, *s.f.* buck(-jump).

groppièra, *s.f.* **1.** (*finimento*) crupper **2.** (*coperta per cavallo*) blanket, horse-cloth.

gròppo, *s.m.* **1.** knot; (*di albero*) gnarl: *avere un* — *alla gola, fig.* to have a lump in one's throat; *far* —, to get knotted **2.** *fig.* (*intrigo*) entanglement **3.** (*raffica di vento*) squall.

gropponàta, *s.f.* buck(-jump).

groppóne, *s.m.* (*scherz.*) back: *ho sessant'anni sul* —, I am sixty years old (*o* I am weighed down with my sixty years); *piegare il* —, *fig.* (*lavorare di forza*) to put one's back into sthg.; (*sottomettersi*) to submit (*o* to yield *o* to give in).

groppóso, *ag.* knotty; gnarled.

gròssa, *s.f.* (*dodici dozzine*) gross (*invariato al pl.*): *sei grosse di penne,* six gross of pens.

grossàggine, *s.f.* (*rar.*) **1.** (*goffaggine*) akwardness, clumsiness **2.** (*stupidità*) dullness.

grossaménte, *av.* grossly.

grossézza, *s.f.* **1.** bigness **2.** (*dimensione*) size; (*volume*) bulk **3.** (*spessore, densità*) thickness **4.** (*di fiume*) swelling **5.** (*di udito*) hardness **6.** (*di intelletto*) dullness, stupidity **7.** (*rozzezza*) coarseness, roughness, rudeness, vulgarity.

grossista, *s.m.* (*comm.*) wholesale merchant, wholesale dealer, wholesaler.

gròsso, *ag.* **1.** big: *una grossa mela,* a big apple; *una scatola grossa così,* a box as big as that; *un uomo grande e* —, a portly (*o* hefty) man **2.** (*esteso, cospicuo*) large, big: *grossa città,* large (*o* big) town; *grossa famiglia,* large (*o* big) family; *grossi guadagni,* large profits **3.** (*spesso, denso*) thick: *una fetta grossa un dito,* a really thick slice; *labbra grosse,* thick lips; *panno* —, thick cloth; *vino* —, heavy (*o* full-bodied) wine ‖ *acqua grossa,* miry (*o* muddy) water ‖ *aria grossa,* filthy air **4.** (*gonfio*): *mare* —, rough sea; *il fiume è* —, the river is swollen ‖ *avere il cuore* —, to have a heavy heart **5.** (*gravida, di donna*) pregnant; with child (*predicativo*); (*di femmina di animale*) big with young, pregnant **6.** (*grezzo, grossolano*) coarse:

un individuo —, a coarse individual; *sale* —, coarse (*o* unrefined) salt; *tessuto* —, coarse cloth **7.** (*importante*) big ‖ *un pezzo* —, (*fam.*) (*persona d'alta condizione*) a bigwig (*o* big shot *o* big noise) **8.** (*grave*) big, serious: — *errore,* gross (*o* serious) mistake; *parole grosse,* hard words **9.** (**Fraseologia**): *in* — *modo,* roughly (*o* broadly speaking) ‖ *caccia grossa,* big game hunting ‖ *dalla testa grossa,* big-headed; *fig.* thick-headed (*o* numskulled) ‖ *dito* —, (*alluce*) big toe ‖ *scarpe grosse,* heavy shoes ‖ *tempi grossi,* hard times ‖ *di udito* —, hard of hearing; *vista grossa,* bad sight ‖ *l'hai fatta grossa!,* now you have done it! ‖ *questa è grossa!,* that is rather too much! ‖ *avere il fiato* —, to be out of breath ‖ *bere* —, to swallow anything ‖ *dirle grosse,* (*dire spropositi*) to talk nonsense ‖ *dormire della grossa,* to sleep like a log ‖ *raccontarle grosse,* to tell tall stories ‖ *fare la voce grossa,* to speak in a threatening voice ‖ *lavorare di* —, to work roughly ‖ *sbagliarsi di* —, to be quite mistaken ‖ *s.m.* **1.** (*maggior parte, massa*) main body, chief part; gross, bulk, mass: *il* — *del carico,* the bulk of the cargo; *il* — *dell'esercito,* the main body of the army **2.** (*antica moneta*) gross.

grossolanaménte, *av.* coarsely, rudely; grossly; roughly; clumsily: — *insultato,* grossly insulted; *tavola fatta* —, roughly-made table; *parlare* —, to speak coarsely (*o* rudely); *sbagliarsi* —, to be grossly mistaken; *tradurre* —, to translate roughly.

grossolanità, *s.f.* **1.** (*di cose*) coarseness, roughness: — *di una superficie,* roughness of a surface; — *di un tessuto,* coarseness of a fabric **2.** (*villania, volgarità*) rudeness, coarseness, vulgarity **3.** (*di un errore*) grossness.

grossolàno, *ag.* **1.** (*rozzo, grezzo*) coarse, gross, rough: *aspetto* —, uncouth appearance; *cibo* —, coarse (*o* gross) food; *gusti grossolani,* coarse taste(s); *lavoro* —, rough (*o* coarse) work; *maniere grossolane,* coarse (*o* rough) manners; *stoffa* —, coarse material; *trattamento* —, rough handling **2.** (*villano*) rude, rough, boorish: *un individuo* —, rude (*o* rough *o* boorish) fellow **3.** (*volgare*) gross, coarse, vulgar: *lineamenti grossolani,* coarse features; *linguaggio* —, coarse language; *piaceri grossolani,* coarse pleasures; *scherzo* —, coarse joke **4.** (*approssimativo*) rough: *schizzo* —, rough sketch; *stima grossolana,* rough estimation; *traduzione grossolana,* rough translation **5.** (*madornale*) gross: *un errore* —, a gross mistake (*o* a glaring blunder).

gròtta, *s.f.* **1.** (*caverna, antro*) cave **2.** (*specialmente artificiale*) grotto (*pl.* grottoes, grottos).

grottescaménte, *av.* grotesquely.

grottésca, *s.f.* (*pitt.*) grotesque painting.

grottésco, *ag.s.m.* grotesque (*anche art.*).

gròtto[1], *s.m.* **1.** (*grotta*) grotto (*pl.* grottoes, grottos) **2.** (*balza, dirupo*) crag, cliff.

gròtto[2], *s.m.* (*ornit.*) white pelican.

grovièra, *s.m.* gruyère (cheese).

groviglio, *s.m.* **1.** tangle; (*nodo*) knot, kink ‖ — *del traffico,* a traffic tangle **2.** *fig.* (*confusione, intrigo*) entanglement, confusion; (*fam.*) mess: *non ho mai visto un tal* —, I have never seen such a mess (*o* confusion).

gru, *s.f.* **1.** (*ornit.*) crane **2.** (*mec.*) crane: — *a braccio,* jib-crane; — *a ponte manovrata dal basso,* travelling bridge-crane with floor control; — *da porto,* quay-crane; — *fissa manovrata a mano,* stationary hand-crane; — *galleggiante,* (*mar.*) floating crane; — *girevole,* slewing (*o* rotating) crane; — *mobile,* travelling crane; — *su cingoli,* crawler tractor-crane; *campo d'azione della* —, area served by the crane; *carro* —, (*aut.*) wrecker (*o* tractor-crane) **3.** (*mar.*) davit.

grúccia, *s.f.* **1.** crutch: *un paio di grucce,* a pair of crutches; *camminare con le grucce,* to walk (*o* to go) on crutches ‖ *reggersi sulle grucce, fig.* (*essere debole*) not to hold water (*o* to be weak) **2.** (*per appendervi abiti*) dress-hanger **3.** (*posatoio per uccelli*) perch; (*per la civetta nella caccia*) stool **4.** (*maniglia*) handle.

gruccióne, *s.m.* (*ornit.*) bee-eater.

grúe, *V.* **gru.**

gruèra, *s.m.* gruyère (cheese).

grufolàre, *v.i.* **1.** to root, to grout, to grub **2.** *fig.* (*frugare*) to rummage.

grugàre, *v.i.* (*tubare*) to coo.

grugníre, *v.i.* **1.** to grunt **2.** *fig.* (*brontolare, borbottare*) to grunt, to grumble.

grugníto, *s.m.* **1.** grunt **2.** *fig.* (*brontolio, borbottio*) grunt, grumble.

grúgno, *s.m.* **1.** (*di animale in genere*) muzzle; (*di maiale*) snout **2.** (*spreg.*) (*faccia*) snout, face: *rompere il — a qlcu.*, to smash s.o.'s face in **3.** (*broncio*) sulks (*pl.*): *fare il —*, to pout; *tenere il — a qlcu.*, to sulk at s.o.

grugnóne, *s.m.* (*persona spesso imbronciata*) sulker.

gruièra, *s.m.* gruyère (cheese).

grullàggine, grullería, *s.f.* **1.** foolishness, silliness, stupidity **2.** (*azione da grullo*) foolish action.

grúllo, *ag.* foolish, silly, stupid ‖ *s.m.* fool, simpleton, blockhead.

grúma, *s.f.* **1.** (*incrostazione*) encrustation **2.** (*tartaro*) tartar.

grumàto, *ag.* encrusted.

grumeréccio, *s.m.* September hay; late hay.

grúmo, *s.m.* grume, clot: *grumi di sangue*, clots of blood (*o* grumes); *formare dei grumi*, to clot (*o* to form lumps).

grúmolo, *s.m.* (*d'insalata, verza, ecc.*) heart.

grumóso, *ag.* clotted; (*med.*) grumous.

gruògo, *s.m.* (*bot.*) crocus: *— domestico* saffron.

grúppe, *s.m.* (*patol.*) croup.

gruppétto, *s.m.* **1.** small group: *un — di persone*, a small knot of people; *a gruppetti*, in small groups **2.** (*mus.*) roulade, run.

grúppo, *s.m.* **1.** group; cluster; (*solo di persone*) party; (*di alberi*) clump: *un — di case*, a cluster (*o* group) of houses; *i libri erano in gruppi di tre*, the books were in groups of three; *turisti divisi in tre gruppi*, tourists divided into three parties (*o* groups) **2.** (*compagnia*) company, set, party **3.** (*scult.*) group **4.** (*nodo*) knot, kink; (*groviglio*) tangle **5.** (*mec.*) set, unit.

grúzzolo, *s.m.* hoard; (*risparmio*) savings (*pl.*).

guàco, *s.m.* (*bot.*) guaco.

guàda, *s.f.* stake-net, square fishing-net.

guadàbile, *ag.* fordable.

guadagnàre, *v.t.* **1.** to gain; (*con il lavoro*) to earn: *guadagnò una somma enorme in quell'affare*, he gained a staggering amount of money in that business transaction; *guadagno trenta sterline al mese*, I earn (*o* get) thirty pounds a month; *non pensa ad altro che a —*, he is interested only in making money; *— al giuoco*, to win; *— su una vendita*, to make a profit on a sale ‖ *ci guadagnammo un gran raffreddore*, we only caught a bad cold ‖ *visto di giorno, questo posto ci guadagna davvero!*, by day this place looks much better indeed! ‖ *— il (proprio) pane*, to earn one's daily bread: *— il (proprio) pane col sudore della fronte*, to earn one's bread by the sweat of one's brow ‖ *— tempo*, to gain time; *— il tempo perduto*, to make up for lost time; *— terreno*, to gain ground (*anche fig.*): *— terreno sugli altri corridori*, (*spor.*) to gain on the other runners; *— velocità*, to gain speed **2.** *fig.* (*conquistare*) to earn; to win: *— fama*, to earn renown (*o* to win fame); *— la fiducia, l'affetto di qlcu.*, to win s.o.'s confidence, affection **3.** (*raggiungere*) to gain, to reach: *— la cima di un monte*, to gain (*o* to reach) the top of a mountain; *— quota*, to gain height; *— la riva*, to gain (*o* to reach *o* to get to) the shore ‖ **guadagnàrsi,** *v.r.* to earn: *— la vita*, to earn one's living.

guadàgno, *s.m.* **1.** (*ciò che si ricava dal proprio lavoro*) earnings (*pl.*): *il suo — è sufficiente per le sue necessità*, his earnings are sufficient for his wants **2.** (*in commercio*) profits (*pl.*): *fare grossi guadagni*, to make large profits (*o* gains) **3.** (*vincita al giuoco*) winnings (*pl.*) **4.** *fig.* (*profitto*) gain, profit, advantage **5.** (*ricompensa*) reward: *lavora senza speranza di —*, he works without hope of reward.

Guadalúpa, *no.pr.f.* (*geog.*) Guadaloupe.

guadàre, *v.t.* to ford, to wade.

guàdo[1], *s.m.* ford: *altezza di —*, fording height; *passare a —*, to ford (*o* to wade).

guàdo[2], *s.m.* (*bot.*) woad.

guadóso, *ag.*1.(*ricco di guadi*) with many fords **2.**(*guadabile*) fordable.

guài, *inter.* woe!: *— ai vinti!*, woe to the conquered! (*o* vanquished!); *— a voi se mi tradite!*, woe betide you if you betray me!.

guaiàco, *s.m.* (*bot.*) guaiacum; (*legno, resina*) guaiac(um).

guaiacòlo, *s.m.* (*farm.*) guaiacol.

Guaiàna, *no.pr.f.* (*geog.*) Guaiana.

guaíme, *s.m.* (*secondo fieno*) aftermath, aftergrass.

guaína, *s.f.* **1.** (*fodero per armi*) sheath, scabbard **2.** (*custodia, astuccio*) case **3.** (*bot.*) sheath **4.** (*anat.*) theca (*pl.* thecae), sheath **5.** (*mar.*) tabling **6.** (*mec.*) sheath(ing).

guainàto, *ag.* (*bot.*) sheathed.

guàio, *s.m.* **1.** trouble, difficulty; scrape, fix: *che —!*, what a fix!; *ecco il —!*, here is the difficulty!; *il — è che tu non mi credi*, the trouble is that you don't believe me; *vai in cerca di guai?*, are you looking for trouble?; *combinare guai*, to make trouble; *essere in un mare di guai*, to be in a very bad fix; *essere nei guai*, to be in trouble; *mettere qlcu. nei guai*, to get s.o. into trouble; *mettersi nei guai*, to get into trouble **2.** (*disgrazia*) misfortune **3.** (*incidente*) accident.

guaiolàre, guaíre, *v.i.* **1.** (*di cane*) to yelp; (*ululare*) to howl **2.** (*lamentarsi*) to whine.

guaíto, *s.m.* **1.** (*di cane*) yelp **2.** (*lamento*) whine.

gualcaménto, *s.m.* (*ind. tessile*) fulling, milling.

gualcàre, *v.t.* (*ind. tessile*) to full.

gualchièra, *s.f.* (*ind. tessile*) fulling-mill.

gualchieràlo, *s.m.* (*ind. tessile*) fulling-mill manager.

gualcíre, *v.t.* to rumple, to crease, to wrinkle.

gualcíto, *ag.* rumpled, creased, wrinkled, crumpled.

gualdràppa, *s.f.* (*di antica bardatura*) caparison; (*coperta da sella*) saddle-cloth.

Gualtièro, *no.pr.m.* Walter ‖ *dim.* Walt, Wat.

guanàco, *s.m.* (*zool.*) guanaco.

guància, *s.f.* **1.** cheek: *— a —*, cheek to cheek; *guance rosee*, rosy cheeks **2.** (*di calcio di fucile*) cheek **3.** (*di rotaia*) wing rail.

guancialàta, *s.f.* blow with a pillow.

guanciàle, *s.m.* pillow; (*cuscino*) cushion ‖ *dormire fra due guanciali*, *fig.* to be quite safe (*o* to have no worries).

guancialíno, *s.m.* **1.** small pillow **2.** (*puntaspilli*) pin-cushion.

guanciàta, *s.f.* slap (in the face).

guàno, *s.m.* guano.

guantàio, *s.m.* **1.** (*chi fabbrica guanti*) glove-maker, glover **2.** (*chi vende guanti*) glove-seller, glover.

guantería, *s.f.* **1.** (*fabbrica di guanti*) glove-factory **2.** (*negozio di guanti*) glove-shop.

guantièra, *s.f.* **1.** (*scatola per guanti*) glove-box **2.** (*vassoio*) tray.

guànto, *s.m.* **1.** glove: *— a manopola*, mitt(en); *— alla moschettiera*, gauntlet glove; *— per boxe*, boxing-glove; *— di pelle*, kid glove; *fabbrica di guanti*, glove-factory; *un paio di guanti nuovi*, a pair of new gloves ‖ *calzare come un —*, to fit like a glove ‖ *trattare qlco. coi guanti*, to handle sthg. with great care; *trattare qlcu. coi guanti*, to handle s.o. kindly **2.** (*di cavaliere antico*) gauntlet ‖ *gettare, raccogliere il —*, *fig.* to throw down, to take up the gauntlet **3.** (*di protezione, per operai*) gauntlet.

guantóne, *s.m.* (*per boxe*) boxing-glove; (*per scherma*) fencing-glove.

guardabarrière, *s.m.* (*ferr.*) gate-keeper (at a level crossing).

guardabòschi, *s.m.* forester.

guardacàccia, *s.m.* gamekeeper.

guardacòrpo, *s.m.* (*mar.*) life-line.

guardacòste, *s.m.* **1.** coast-guard **2.** (*nave guarda-coste*) (coast-guard) cutter.

guardafíli, *s.m.* lineman (*pl.* linemen), wireman (*pl.* wiremen).

guardafréni, *s.m.* (*ferr.*) brakesman (*pl.* brakesmen).

guardalàto, *s.m.* (*mar.*) bumper, fender.

guardalínee, *s.m.* **1.** (*spor.*) linesman (*pl.* linesmen) **2.** (*ferr.*) trackman (*pl.* trackmen), track -walker.

guardamàno, *s.m.* **1.** (*scherma*) sword-guard **2.** (*mar.*) life-line, man-rope **3.** (*ringhiera*) hand-rail **4.** (*manopola protettiva per lavori pericolosi*) hand-shield.

guardapàlma, *s.m.* hand-shield.

guardapòrto, *s.m.* (*mar.*) guard-ship.

guardaportóne, *s.m.* (*portinaio*) doorkeeper; (*in livrea*) liveried porter.

guardàre, *v.i.* **1.** to look at (s.o., sthg.); (*contemplare*) to behold: *guarda!*, look!; *guardatemi*, look at me; *guardate a destra*, look to the right; *guardate quella casa, quel bambino*, look at that house, at that child; *molti guardavano il paesaggio*, many people were looking at the view; — *dentro*, to look in; — *dentro a ql.co.*, to look into sthg.; — *fuori*, to look out: *egli guarda fuori dalla finestra*, he looks out of the window; — *in un telescopio*, to look through a telescope; — *l'orologio*, to look at the time || — *qlcu. con diffidenza*, to look at s.o. with distrust || — *qlcu. dall'alto in basso*, to look s.o. up and down; (*disprezzare*) to look down on s.o. || — *qlcu. di buon occhio, di mal occhio*, to look favourably, unfavourably on s.o. || — *qlcu. di traverso*, to look askance at s.o.; (*irosamente*) to look daggers at s.o. || — *qlcu. in faccia*, to look s.o. in the face: *guardò la morte in faccia*, he looked death in the face || — *qlcu., ql.co. per ogni senso*, to look s.o., sthg. through and through || *farsi* —, to attract attention || *non* — *in faccia a nessuno*, not to worry about other people || — *e non toccare è una cosa da imparare*, *prov.* children must learn to look and not to touch **2.** (*fissamente*) to gaze at, (up)on (s.o., sthg.): *la madre guardava il suo bimbo con grande tenerezza*, the mother was gazing on her child with great fondness **3.** (*a occhi spalancati*) to stare at (s.o., sthg.): *smettila di guardarmi così*, stop staring at me like that **4.** (*di sfuggita*) to glance at (s.o., sthg.) **5.** (*furtivamente*) to peep, to peep at, upon (s.o., sthg.); (*dall'interno*) to peep out; (*dall'esterno*) to peep in; *lo vidi* — *dal buco della chiave*, I saw him peeping through the keyhole **6.** (*con bramosia*) to ogle **7.** (*osservare*) to watch; (*scrutare*) to eye: *mi guardarono sospettosamente*, they eyed me with suspicion **8.** (*sorvegliare*) to watch; (*per proteggere*) to watch over (s.o., sthg.), to look after (s.o., sthg.): *chi guarderà il mio bambino mentre sarò fuori?*, who will look after my baby while I am out?; *guardato a vista*, closely watched **9.** (*considerare*) to consider, to view: *cercate di* — *la questione dal nostro punto di vista*, try to consider (o to view) the question from our point of view **10.** (*esaminare*) to look over (sthg.): *l'insegnante guardò la traduzione*, the teacher looked over the translation || — *ql.co. per il sottile*, to be particular about sthg. **11.** (*proteggere*) to protect; (*difendere*) to defend, to guard: *i soldati guardavano il ponte*, the soldiers defended the bridge; — *qlcu. da un pericolo*, to guard s.o. against a danger || *dagli amici mi guardi Iddio che dai nemici mi guardo io*, *prov.* God defend me from my friends and I'll look after my enemies **12.** (**Fraseologia**): *Dio ne guardi!*, God forbid! || *guarda che roba!*, well I am blowed! (*o* just take a look at that!) || *guarda chi si vede!*, look who is here!; (*come mai sei qui?*) hullo! what are you doing here? || *ma guarda un po'!*, (*fam.*) that's funny! (*o* that's odd!) || *v.i.* **1.** (*essere orientato*) to face; (*aprirsi*) to look out on (sthg.): *guarda a sud*, it faces south; *la casa guarda a mezzogiorno*, the house faces (to the) south; *la mia finestra guarda sul cortile*, my window looks out on the courtyard **2.** (*con-*

siderare) to look (up)on (s.o., sthg.); to regard (s.o., sthg.): *non guardiamo a ciò come all'unica via d'uscita*, don't let us look upon it as the only way out **3.** (*cercare*) to try: *guarda di accontentarlo*, try to please him; *guarda di studiare*, try to study **4.** (*badare*) to see to (sthg.), to look to (sthg.), to take care, to mind: *guarda bene che ciò non accada più*, look to it (o take care o mind) that this does not happen any more; *non* — *a spese*, to spare no expense **5.** (*fare attenzione*) to be careful: *guarda di non farti male*, be careful not to hurt yourself || **guardàrsi,** *v.r.* **1.** to look at oneself: *egli continuava a* — *intorno*, he kept looking about himself; *ella si guardò allo specchio*, she looked at herself in the mirror **2.** (*stare in guardia*) to beware (of s.o., sthg.); (*fare attenzione*) to mind (sthg.): *guardatevi bene dal perderlo!*, mind you don't lose it!; *guardatevi dai borsaioli*, beware of pickpockets; *guardati dai cattivi compagni*, beware of bad companions; *guardati dall'offenderlo!*, beware lest you should offend him! (o be careful not to offend him!) || *me ne guardo bene!*, I shall do no such thing! || *tu ti guardi bene dal divulgare i tuoi segreti*, you are wary of giving away your secrets **3.** (*astenersi*) to forbear; (*da cibo o bevande*) to abstain: *guardatevi dal fare troppe domande*, forbear from asking too many questions; — *dalle parole inutili*, to refrain from useless words || *v.r. reciproco* to look at each other (one another); to gaze at each other (one another).

guardaròba, *s.f.* **1.** (*armadio per abiti*) wardrobe; (*amer.*) closet **2.** (*stanza in cui si tiene la biancheria*) linen-room; (*armadio per biancheria*) linen-cupboard; (*amer.*) closet **3.** (*di cinema, teatro*) cloak-room.

guardarobièra, *s.f.* **1.** (*di casa privata, di albergo*) linen maid **2.** (*presso una regina*) Mistress of the Robes **3.** (*in un cinema, in un teatro*) cloak-room attendant **4.** (*in un teatro, l'addetta ai costumi*) wardrobe keeper, wardrobe mistress.

guardarobière, *s.m.* (*in un teatro, in un cinema*) cloak-room attendant.

guardasàla, *s.m.* (*ferr.*) ticket-collector.

guardasigílli, *s.m.* **1.** keeper of the seals || (*in Gran Bretagna*) Lord Privy Seal **2.** (*Ministro della Giustizia*) Minister of Justice.

guardàta, *s.f.* look; (*occhiata*) glance: *diamo una* — *a questo libro*, let us have a look (o take a glance) at this book (o fam. let's glance our eye over this book); *le diedi una* — *di sfuggita*, I glanced at her.

guardatúra, *s.f.* (*modo di guardare*) way of looking.

guardavía, *s.m.* (*neol.*) (*riparo stradale*) guardrail

guàrdia, *s.f.* **1.** (*custodia, vigilanza, difesa*) guardianship, protection, care: *corpo di* —, (*edificio*) guard-house; (*stanza*) guard-room; *turno di* —, (*mil.*) watch; *dare il cambio alla* —, to relieve the guard; *essere di* —, to be on guard; *fare la* — *a qlco.*, to guard sthg.; *fare la* — *a qlcu.*, to watch s.o.: *fare la* — *ad un prigioniero*, to guard a prisoner; *fare buona* —, to keep a good watch; *montare la* —, to stand (o to mount) guard || — *medica*, first-aid station **2.** (*chi ha compiti di vigilanza*) guard; (*sentinella*) sentry, sentinel: — *carceraria*, warder (o jailer); — *del corpo*, body-guard; *fig.* escort; — *dei fuoco*, fireman; — *di finanza*, excise officer; (*doganiere*) customs officer; — *d'onore*, guard of honour; — *di pubblica sicurezza*, policeman; — *forestale*, forester (o forest warder); — *notturna*, night watch; *cane da* —, watch-dog; *ufficiale di* —, officer of the watch **3.** (*complesso di uomini aventi compiti di vigilanza*): *guardie a cavallo*, horse-guards; *guardie a piedi*, footguards || — *nazionale*, the National Guard || *la vecchia* —, the Old Guard **4.** (*spor.*) guard: *in* —, (*scherma*) on guard || *lo misi in* — *da quei pericoli*, I warned him against those dangers; *mentre non stavo in* — ..., while I was off my guard... **5.** (*di spada*) (hilt-)guard **6.** (*di libro*) flyleaf (*pl.* flyleaves) **7.** (*di fiume*) safety highwater -mark.

guardiacàccia, *s.m.* gamekeeper.

guardiamarína, *s.m.* (*mar.*) midshipman (*pl.* midshipmen) (*abbr.* middy).

guardiàna, *s.f.* 1. keeper; (*di pecore*) shepherdess 2. (*eccl.*) Mother Superior.

guardianàto, *s.m.* guardianship.

guardiàno, *s.m.* 1. keeper: — *del faro*, light-(house) keeper, lighthouseman; — *di prigione*, warder (o jailer o guard); — *notturno*, (night) watchman 2. (*di armenti*) herdsman (*pl.* herdsmen); (*di pecore*) shepherd 3. (*ferr.*) signalman (*pl.* signalmen) 4. (*eccl.*) Father Guardian.

guardína, *s.f.* guard-room, lock-up.

guardinfànte, *s.m.* farthingale, hoop-skirt; crinoline.

guardingaménte, *av.* cautiously, warily, carefully.

guardíngo, *ag.* cautious, wary, careful.

guardiuòla, *s.f.* (*mil.*) guard-room; guard-house.

guàrdo, (*poet.*) per **sguàrdo**.

guarentígia, *s.f.* (*dir.*) guarantee, guaranty ‖ *Legge delle Guarentigie*, (*st.*) Guarantee-Act.

guàri, *ag.* (*rar.*) much ‖ *av.* (*rar.*) long: *non ha —*, not long ago.

guaríbile, *ag.* (*di malattia*) curable; (*di ferita*) healable: *è — in dieci giorni*, he will be well again in ten days' time.

guarigióne, *s.f.* recovery: *essere in via di —*, to be on the way of recovery.

guaríre, *v.i.* 1. to recover, to recover one's health; (*rimarginare*) to heal: *egli guarì molto rapidamente*, he recovered very quickly; *la ferita guarì quasi miracolosamente*, the wound healed almost miraculously; *potrà — da quella malattia?*, will he be able to recover from (o to get over) that illness? 2. *fig.* to get out (of sthg.), to fall out (of sthg.): — *da una cattiva abitudine*, to get out (o to get rid) of a bad habit ‖ *v.t.* 1. to cure, to restore to health; (*far rimarginare*) to heal: *Gesù guarì i dieci lebbrosi*, Jesus healed the ten lepers; *guarì la mia polmonite*, he cured my pneumonia; *mi guarì dalla polmonite*, he cured me of pneumonia 2. *fig.* to cure, to free: *ti guarirò da quell'ossessione*, I shall cure you of (o shall free you from) that obsession; — *qlcu. da un'abitudine*, to cure (o to break) s.o. of a habit; — *i mali della nostra civiltà*, to cure the ills of our civilization.

guaritóre, *ag.* healing, sanatory, sanative ‖ *s.m.*, **guaritríce**, *s.f.* 1. (*chi guarisce*) healer 2. (*chi usa in medicina metodi empirici*) quack(-doctor) 3. (*chi guarisce per mezzo della fede*) faith-healer.

guarnigióne, *s.f.* (*mil.*) garrison: *città di —*, garrison town; *Napoli rimase senza —*, Naples remained ungarrisoned; *mettere una — in una città*, to garrison a town.

guarniménto, *s.m.* 1. (*guarnizione*) trimming, ornament 2. (*equipaggiamento*) fitting(s), outfit, equipment 3. (*mil.*) garrison 4. (*mar.*) rigging.

guarníre, *v.t.* 1. (*fornire, equipaggiare*) to furnish, to equip, to fit out 2. (*ornare*) to trim, to decorate 3.(*cuc.*) to garnish: — *un piatto*, to garnish a dish 4. (*mec.*) to pack 5. (*mil.*) to fortify 6. (*mar.*) to rig.

guarníto, *ag.* 1. (*equipaggiato*) furnished; equipped 2. (*ornato*) trimmed, decorated: *portava un cappello — di fiori*, she wore a hat trimmed with flowers 3. (*cuc.*) garnished: *bistecca guarnita*, grilled steak with vegetables; *un tacchino ben —*, a turkey with all the trimmings.

guarnizióne, *s.f.* 1. (*ornamento*) trimming, ornament 2. (*cuc.*) (*contorno*) garniture; (*fam.*) trimmings (*pl.*) 3. (*mec.*) packing, gasket: — *metallica*, metal packing.

Guascógna, *no.pr.f.* (*geog.*) Gascony.

guasconàta, *s.f.* gasconade, bravado, boasting.

guascóne, *ag.s.m.* 1. (*abitante della Guascogna*) Gascon 2. *fig.* (*gradasso*) gascon, braggart.

guastafèste, *s.c.* kill-joy, spoil-sport, wet blanket.

guastamestièri, *s.m.* 1. bungler, botcher 2. (*sl.*) (*crumiro*) black-leg, scab.

guastàre, *v.t.* 1. to spoil; (*danneggiare*) to damage; (*rovinare*) to ruin, to mar (anche *fig.*): *l'inondazione guastò molti ponti*, the flood damaged many bridges; *non guastate la festa!*, don't spoil the fun! (o the feast!); *le nostre vacanze furono guastate dal cattivo tempo*, our holidays were spoiled by bad weather; *la notizia gli guastò il pranzo*, the news spoilt his dinner; *nulla potrebbe — la nostra gioia*, nothing could mar our joy; — *l'appetito*, to spoil (s.o.'s) appetite; — *la reputazione di qlcu.*, to ruin s.o.'s good name ‖ *questo non guasta*, that won't do any harm; *un poco di ambizione non guasta*, a little ambition is all right ‖ — *le uova nel paniere*, to upset s.o.'s plans 2. (*far marcire*) to taint: *le mosche guastarono la carne*, the flies tainted the meat 3. (*viziare*) to spoil: *questo ragazzo è stato guastato dai suoi nonni*, this boy has been spoilt by his grandparents ‖ **guastàrsi**, *v.r.* 1. to spoil, to get spoiled: *il tempo si è guastato*, the weather has changed for the worse ‖ — *l'appetito*, to spoil one's appetite; — *il gusto*, to corrupt one's taste ‖ — *con qlcu.*, to fall out (o to quarrel) with s.o. ‖ — *la reputazione*, to forfeit one's good name ‖ — *il sangue per ql.co.*, to worry over sthg. 2. (*marcire*) to rot, to go rotten; (*andar a male*) to go bad, to decay: *col caldo la carne si guasta facilmente*, meat goes bad easily in hot weather 3. (*mec.*) to break down.

guastàto, *ag.* 1. spoilt: *un bambino —*, a spoilt child 2. (*danneggiato*) damaged 3. (*mec.*) out of order.

guastatóre, *s.m.* 1. spoiler; destroyer 2. (*mil.*) sapper.

guàsto, *ag.* 1. (*sciupato, viziato*) spoilt 2.(*danneggiato*) damaged 3. (*marcio*) rotten: *un dente —*, a decayed tooth; *una mela guasta*, a rotten apple; *uova guaste*, bad eggs 4. (*corrotto*) tainted, corrupt, depraved 5. (*mec.*) out of order ‖ *s.m.* 1. (*danno*) damage 2. (*mec.*) break-down, trouble: *deve trattarsi di un — al motore!*, (*fam.*) there must be something wrong with the engine!.

guatàre, *v.t.* 1. (*fissare*) to gaze at (s.o.), to eye 2. (*con brama*) to ogle 3. (*con sospetto*) to eye suspiciously; (*di traverso*) to look askance at (s.o.).

guàttero, *V.* **squàttero**.

guattíre, *v.i.* 1. (*guaire del cane quando ha fiutato la lepre*) to give tongue 2. (*lamentarsi*) to yelp.

guàzza, *s.f.* dew.

guazzabúglio, *s.m.* 1. (*miscuglio di acqua e neve*) slush 2. (*miscuglio, confusione*) muddle, medley, mess.

guazzàre, *v.i.* 1. (*di liquidi in un recipiente*) to splash about: *l'acqua guazza nella bottiglia*, the water was splashing about in the bottle 2. (*sguazzare*) to paddle, to dabble; (*con tutto il corpo*) to wallow (anche *fig.*): *il maiale guazzava nel fango*, the pig was wallowing in the mud ‖ *v.t.* (*rar.*) (*guadare*) to ford, to wade.

guazzatóio, *s.m.* horse-pond: *condurre i cavalli al —*, to water the horses (o to take the horses to water).

guazzétto, *s.m.* (*cuc.*) stew: *carne in —*, stewed meat; *cuocere in —*, to stew.

guàzzo, *s.m.* 1. (*pitt.*) gouache: *pittura a —*, gouache (painting); *dipingere a —*, to paint in gouache 2. (*pozzanghera*) puddle; (*stagno*) pool 3. (*guado*) ford: *passare a —*, to ford (o to wade) 4. *frutta in —*, (*dial.*) fruit preserved in spirits.

guazzóso, *ag.* dewy.

guazzúme, *s.m.* (*fangume*) slush.

guelfísmo, *s.m.* (*st.*) Guelphism.

guèlfo, *ag. s.m.* (*st.*) Guelph.

Guendalína, *no.pr.f.* Gwendolen ‖ *dim.* Gwen(nie).

guèrcio, *ag.* squinting, squint, cross-eyed: *occhi guerci*, squinting eyes; *ha l'occhio sinistro —*, he has a squint in his left eye ‖ *s.m.* squinter.

guerníre *e derivati*, *V.* **guarníre**, *e derivati*.

guèrra, *s.f.* 1. war: — *a morte*, war to the death; — *a oltranza*, war without quarter; — *chimica*, chemical warfare; — *civile*, civil war; — *difensiva, offensiva*, defensive, offensive war; — *di logoramento*, war of attrition; — *di movimento*, war of movement; — *di nervi*, war of nerves; — *di posizione, di trincea*, trench warfare; — *fredda, guerreggiata*, cold, active war;

arte della —, warfare; *canto di* —, war-chant (o -song); *consiglio di* —, council of war; *dichiarazione di* —, declaration of war; *il dio della* —, war-god; *grido di* —, war-cry (o -shout); *in piena* —, at the height of the war; *in tempo di* —, in war-time; *nave da* —, warship (o man-of-war); *propaganda di* —, war-mongering; *teatro di* —, theatre of operations; *vedova di* —, war -widow; *zona di* —, war zone; *ha fatto la* — *con Eisenhower*, he served under Eisenhower; *ha fatto tutta la* —, he went right through the war; *la prima* — *mondiale scoppiò nel 1914*, World War One broke out in 1914; *dichiarare* — *a un paese*, to declare war upon a country; *essere in* — *con qlcu.*, to be at war with s.o.; *essere, stare sul piede di* —, to be on a war footing; *essere, stare sul sentiero di* —, to be on the war-path (anche *fig.*); *fare la* — *a qlcu.*, to wage (o to make) war upon (o against) s.o.; *mettersi sul sentiero di* —, to go on the war-path (anche *fig.*); *partire per la* —, to go to the war; *preparare delle truppe alla* —, to train troops for war ‖ *la Guerra dei Cento Anni*, (*st.*) the Hundred Years' War ‖ *la Guerra delle due Rose*, (*st.*) the Wars of the Roses ‖ *la Guerra di Troia*, (*lett.*) the Trojan War ‖ *le Guerre Puniche*, (*st.*) the Punic Wars ‖ *Guerra Santa*, Holy War ‖ *Ministero della Guerra*, War Office; *Ministro della Guerra*, Secretary of State for War **2.** *fig.* (*conflitto*) feud, conflict, strife: *una* — *all'ultimo sangue tra due famiglie*, a deadly feud between two families ‖ — *di interessi*, clash of interests ‖ *fare* — *a qlcu. per ql.co.*, to fight s.o. over sthg.

guerrafondàio, *s.m.* (*spreg.*) war-monger.

guerreggiaménto, *s.m.* fighting, warfare.

guerreggiànte, *ag.* fighting, belligerent ‖ *s.m.* belligerent.

guerreggiàre, *v.i.* to fight, to war, to wage war: *durante la III Crociata Riccardo Cuor di Leone guerreggiò valorosamente*, during the Third Crusade Richard Coeur de Lion fought bravely ‖ *v.t.* (*provocare*) to pick a quarrel with (s.o.): *mi guerreggia in tutti i modi*, he is always picking quarrels with me.

guerreggiàto, *ag.* **1.** fought ‖ *guerra guerreggiata*, open warfare **2.** *fig.* (*perseguitato*) persecuted.

guerreggiatóre, *s.m.* fighter, warrior, belligerent.

guerrescaménte, *av.* (*rar.*) in a warlike manner.

guerrésco, *ag.* **1.** (*di guerra*) war (*attributivo*): *canti guerreschi*, war-songs **2.** (*bellicoso*) warlike, bellicose: *nazione guerresca*, warlike nation.

guerrièro, *ag.* warlike, bellicose: *un popolo* —, a warlike people ‖ *s.m.* warrior: *un prode* —, a gallant warrior.

guerríglia, *s.f.* guer(r)illa, guer(r)illa warfare, bush -fighting.

guerriglièro, *s.m.* guerrilla (fighter), partisan; bush-fighter: *alcuni guerriglieri*, some guerrillas.

gufàccio, *s.m.* (*misantropo*) misanthrope.

gufàggine, *s.f.* (*misantropia*) misanthropy.

gufàre, *v.i.* (*rar.*) to hoot ‖ *v.t.* (*rar.*) (*beffare*) to mock.

gùfo, *s.m.* **1.** (*ornit.*) owl: — *comune*, little (o sparrow) owl; — *reale*, great horn(ed) owl (o eagle-owl o stock -owl) **2.** *fig.* (*misantropo*) misanthrope, misanthropist.

gùglia, *s.f.* (*arch.*) spire.

gugliàta, *s.f.* needleful.

Guglielmína, *no.pr.f.* Wilhelmina.

Guglièlmo, *no.pr.m.* William ‖ dim. Bill(y), Will(y).

Guiàna, *no.pr.f.* (*geog.*) Guiana.

guída, *s.f.* **1.** guide (anche *fig.*); (*cicerone*) (tourists') guide; cicerone (*pl.* ciceroni): *l'istinto non è sempre una buona* —, instinct is not always a good guide; *mi fu* — *nella mia giovinezza*, he was my guide during my youth; *non bisogna far roccia senza una* —, one should not go rock-climbing without a guide; *ti farò da* —, I shall act as your guide; *tu sei stato la mia* —, you have been my guide; *visitò il paese con una* —, he toured the country with a guide **2.** (*libro che illustra una città, una regione, ecc.*) guide-book: — *del Museo*

Britannico, guide to the British Museum **3.** (*manuale*) hand-book, manual ‖ — *telefonica*, telephone directory (o book) **4.** (*direzione*) guidance, direction: *sotto la* — *di mio padre*, under my father's guidance (o guided by my father) **5.** (*comando*) leadership: *sotto la* — *di Gengis Khan*, under the leadership of Genghis Khan **6.** (*mil.*) guide, scout **7.** (*mec.*) guide, way, slide: — *cava d'onda*, (*rad. tv.*) wave-guide; — *del carrello*, carriage (o saddle)-guide; — *di rinculo*, (*artigl.*) gun-slide; — *di scorrimento*, slide guide (o -bar o -way); — *filo*, (*ind. tessile*) thread guide; — *valvola*, valve-guide **8.** (*redine*) rein **9.** (*aut.*) drive, steering: — *a destra, a sinistra*, right-hand, left-hand drive (o steering); — *esterna*, brougham; — *interna*, saloon (o sedan); *volante di* —, steering-wheel **10.** (*aut.*) (*il guidare*) driving: *esame, lezioni di* —, driving test, lessons; *patente di* —, driving licence; *scuola* —, driving school.

guidàbile, *ag.* guidable.

guidàre, *v.t.* **1.** (*dirigere*) to guide (anche *fig.*): *un cieco è spesso guidato da un cane*, a blind man is often guided by a dog; *le circostanze guidarono le mie decisioni*, circumstances guided my decision; — *i primi passi di un bambino*, to guide the first steps of a child **2.** (*amministrare*) to manage: *il Primo Ministro guida gli affari dello Stato*, the Prime Minister manages the affairs of State **3.** (*capeggiare*) to lead: *chi guida attualmente i conservatori?*, who is now leading the Tories?; — *un esercito, una spedizione*, to lead an army, an expedition **4.** (*animali, mezzi di trasporto*) to drive: *sai* — ?, can you drive?; — *una automobile, una locomotiva, un trattore*, to drive a car, a railway-engine, a tractor; — *una barca*, to manage a boat; — *un cavallo*, to ride a horse; — *una motocicletta*, to ride a motor-cycle; — *una nave*, to steer a ship **5.** (*mus.*) to conduct: — *un'orchestra*, to conduct an orchestra ‖ **guidàrsi,** *v.r.* (*regolarsi*) to conduct oneself; to behave: *sa* — *da sè*, he knows how to conduct himself.

guidatóre, *s.m.*, **guidatríce,** *s.f.* (*di animali, veicoli*) driver.

guiderdóne, *s.m.* (*letter.*) guerdon; reward, recompense.

Guído, *no.pr.m.* Guy.

guidóne, *s.m.* (*mil.*) guidon; pennant; (*mar.*) burgee.

guidoslítta, *s.f.* (*spor.*) bobsleigh, bobsled.

guíggia, *s.f.* sandalstrap.

guíndolo, *s.m.* (*arcolaio*) reel.

Guinèa, *no.pr.f.* (*geog.*) Guinea: *Nuova* —, New Guinea.

guinzagliàre, *v.t.* to leash.

guinzàglio, *s.m.* leash (anche *fig.*): *cani al* —, dogs on the leash; *mettere al* —, to leash; *tenere un cane al* —, to hold a dog in (o by the) leash; *tenere qlcu. al* —, *fig.* to hold s.o. in leash (o to keep s.o. well in hand).

Guiènna, *no.pr.f.* (*geog. st.*) Guienne, Guyenne.

guísa, *s.f.* manner, way; (*sembianza*) guise: *in quella* —, in that way (o manner); *apparve in* — *di ninfa*, she appeared in the guise of a nymph ‖ *a* — *di*, like: *a* — *di attore*, like an actor; *una scatola fatta a* — *di libro*, a box shaped like a book; *travestito a* — *di mendicante*, disguised as a beggar ‖ *in* — *che...*, so that... (o in such way that...).

guítto, *ag.* **1.** poor, destitute, low, beggarly **2.** *fig.* (*gretto*) stingy, mean ‖ *s.m.* (*teat.*) strolling player: *compagnia di guitti*, strolling players; *è un povero* —, (*un attore da poco*) he is a very poor actor.

guizzànte, *ag.* **1.** (*di pesci, serpi, ecc.*) wriggling; (*dimenantesi giocosamente*) frisking **2.** (*di luce*) flashing **3.** (*che si muove rapidamente*) darting, flashing.

guizzàre, *v.i.* **1.** (*di pesci, serpi, ecc.*) to wriggle; (*dimenarsi giocosamente*) to frisk: *le anguille mi guizzarono via dalle dita*, the eels wriggled out of my fingers; *i delfini guizzavano sulla superficie dell'acqua*, dolphins were frisking on the surface of the water **2.** (*di* *luce*) to flash **3.** (*muoversi rapidamente*) to dart, to flash: *nell'aria guizzavano le rondini,* swallows were darting through the air; *il rapido guizzò via,* the express train flashed past.

guízzo, *s.m.* **1.** (*di pesci, serpi, ecc.*) wriggle; (*il dimenarsi giocoso*) frisk **2.** (*di luce*) flash **3.** (*movimento rapido*) dart(ing), flash(ing).

gulasch, *s.m.* (*cuc.*) goulash.

gurgugliàre, *v.i.* (*di tacchino*) to gobble.

gúscio, *s.m.* **1.** shell: — *di lumaca, chiocciola,* snail shell; — *di noce,* nut shell; — *di tartaruga,* turtle shell; — *d'uovo,* egg-shell; *restarsene, chiudersi nel proprio* —, to go into (*o* to withdraw into) one's shell (*anche fig.*); *uscire dal proprio* —, to come out of one's shell (anche *fig.*) **2.** (*di legumi*) pod, shell: *levare il* — *ai piselli,* to shell peas **3.** (*di cereali*) husk **4.** (*di bachi da seta*) pod **5.** (*involucro*) covering, cover **6.** (*minuscola imbarcazione*) (nut-) shell **7.** (*arch.*) cove.

gustàbile, *ag.* tasteable, tastable.

gustàccio, *s.m.* bad taste, nasty taste.

gustàre, *v.t.* **1.** (*godere*) to enjoy, to relish (anche *fig.*): *hai gustato il nostro pranzo?,* did you enjoy our dinner?; *ho molto gustato l'arrosto,* I have enjoyed the roast very much; — *un capolavoro,* to enjoy (*o* to appreciate) a masterpiece; — *i piaceri della vita,* to enjoy the pleasures of life **2.** (*assaggiare*) to taste, to try: *gusta un po' di questo vino!,* taste (*o* try) a little of this wine! (*o* take a sip of this wine!) ‖ *v.i.* (*piacere*) to like (s.o., sthg.) (*costruzione pers.*): *ciò non mi gusta affatto,* I do not like that at all; *la vostra compagnia mi gusta molto,* I like your company very much.

gustatívo, *ag.* gustative, gustatory: *papille gustative,* (*anat.*) taste-buds.

gustatóre, *s.m.* **1.** (*chi gusta*) taster **2.** (*intenditore*) connoisseur.

Gustàvo, *no.pr.m.* Gustavus.

gustazióne, *s.f.* tasting, gustation.

gustévole, *ag.* **1.** palatable **2.** (*piacevole*) agreeable.

gústo, *s.m.* **1.** (*senso del gusto*) taste: *è piacevole al* —, it is agreeable to the taste; *avere il* — *fine, delicato,* to have a fine palate **2.** (*sapore*) taste, relish; (*aroma*) flavour; (*gusto piacevole*) relish: *mi lasciò un* — *amaro,* it left a bitter taste in my mouth; *questa minestra non ha alcun* —, this soup has no taste (*o* is tasteless); *questo vino ha un* — *amaro,* this wine has a bitter taste (*o* tastes bitter) ‖ *aver* — *di,* to taste of: *questo arrosto ha troppo* — *di aglio,* this roast tastes too much of garlic **3.** (*senso estetico*) taste: *un abito di* —, a tasteful dress; *arredato con ottimo* —, furnished in very good taste; *un uomo di* (*buon*) —, a man of (good) taste; *ciò era di cattivo* —, that was in bad taste; *è una questione di* —, it is a matter of taste; *questa casa è di mio* —, this house is to my taste (*o* after my fancy) **4.** (*preferenza*) taste; like: *ognuno ha i suoi gusti,* everyone has his likes ‖ *tutti i gusti son gusti,* prov. there is no accounting for tastes **5.** (*voglia, capriccio*) fancy: *un* — *passeggero,* a passing fancy **6.** (*gradimento*) liking: *è di tuo* —?, is it to your liking?; *questo metodo non è di suo* —, this method is not to his liking (*o* taste *o* mind) **7.** (*piacere, entusiasmo*) zest, gusto, relish: *ci ho* —, I am glad of it; *mangiammo di* —, we ate with relish; *suonava di* —, he was playing with zest (*o* gusto); *prendere* — *a ql.co.,* to take a liking for sthg.; (*divertirsi*) to enjoy sthg.: *ha preso* — *alle carte,* he has taken a liking for cards; *prende* — *a stuzzicarmi,* he enjoys teasing me **8.** (*genere, qualità*) kind.

gustosaménte, *av.* **1.** (*con piacere*) with relish **2.** (*piacevolmente*) agreeably.

gustosità, *s.f.* **1.** (*saporosità*) savouriness **2.** (*piacevolezza*) delightfulness.

gustóso, *ag.* **1.** (*saporito*) tasty, savoury: *un piatto* —, a savoury dish **2.** (*piacevole*) agreeable, delightful **3.** (*divertente*) amusing: *una commedia gustosa,* an amusing play.

guttapèrca, *s.f.* gutta-percha.

guttífero, *ag.* gum-bearing.

gutturàle, *ag.* (*fonet.*) guttural: *consonanti gutturali,* guttural consonants ‖ *s.f.* guttural.

gutturalísmo, *s.m.* gutturalism.

gutturalménte, *av.* gutturally.

H

h, *s.f. (ottava lettera dell'alfabeto italiano)* h *(pl.* hs, h's): — *muta,* silent h; *a forma di H, ad H,* H *(o* H-shaped): *trave ad H,* H-beam; *non aspirare l'*—, to drop one's h's ‖ — *come hotel, (tel.)* h for Harry ‖ *bomba H,* H -bomb.

habanèra, *s.f. (musica, danza)* habanera.

habeas corpus, *s.m. (dir.)* habeas corpus.

habitat, *s.m. (bot. zool.)* habitat.

habitué, *s.m.* habitué: — *del cinema,* cinema-goer; *è un* —, *(cliente abituale)* he is an habitué *(o* a regular customer); *è un* — *di tutti i concerti,* he is an habitué of all the concerts.

habitus, *s.m. (bot. zool.)* habit(us).

hàlfa, *s.f. (bot.)* halfa, alfa.

halìte, *s.m. (min.)* halite.

hallalí, *s.m. (grido di caccia)* mort: *suonare l'*—, to blow the mort.

hamac, *s.f.* hammock.

hamster, *s.m. (zool.)* hamster.

hangar, *s.m. (aer.)* hangar, shed.

Hannover, *no.pr.f. (geog.)* Hanover.

hannoveriàno, *ag.s.m.* Hanoverian.

hànsa, *s.f. (st.)* Hanse.

hanseàtico, *ag. (st.)* Hanseatic: *lega hanseatica,* Hanseatic League *(o* Hanse).

hàrem, *s.m.* harem, haram.

harmònium, *s.m. (mus.)* harmonium.

harveizzàre, *v.t. (metal.)* to harveyize.

haseíse, *s.m.* hasheesh, hashish.

Hawai (le), *no.pr.f.pl. (geog.)* the Hawaiian Islands.

hawaiàno, *ag.s.m.* Hawaiian ‖ **hawaiàna,** *s.f.* Hawaiian.

hegelianísmo, *s.m. (st. fil.)* Hegelianism.

hegeliàno, *ag.s.m. (fil.)* Hegelian.

henné, *s.m.* henna.

hènry, *s.m. (elett.)* henry.

hertz, *s.m. (elett.)* hertz.

hertziàno, *ag. (elett.)* Hertzian: *onde hertziane,* Hertzian *(o* electric) waves.

hevèa, *s.f. (bot.)* hevea.

hidàlgo, *s.m.* hidalgo.

hihòn, *(voce onomatopeica riproducente un raglio)* heehaw: *fare* —, to heehaw.

hinterland, *s.m.* hinterland.

hitleriàno, *ag.s.m. (pol.)* Hitlerite, Hitlerist.

hitlerísmo, *s.m. (pol.)* Hitlerism.

hobby, *s.m.* hobby.

homo, *s.m. (lat.)* homo ‖ — *homini lupus,* man is a wolf to man.

honorem, ad, *l. lat.* honorary: *laurea ad* —, honorary degree.

horst, *s.m. (geol.)* horst.

Hórus, *no.pr.m. (mit.)* Horus.

hôtel, *s.m.* hotel.

humíte, *s.f. (min.)* humite.

humus, *s.m. (agr.)* humus.

huroniàno, *ag. (geol.)* Huronian.

hurrà, *inter.* hurrah!, hurray!: *gridare hip! hip!* —, to give three cheers; *gridare* —, to hurrah *(o* to hurray *o* to shout hurrah *o* to cheer).

hussíta, *s.m. (st. relig.)* Hussite.

I

i, *s.f.m.* **1.** (*nona lettera dell'alfabeto italiano*) i (*pl.* is, i's) || — *come Imola*, (*tel.*) i for Isaac || *mettere i puntini sugli* —, *fig.* to dot one's i's and cross one's t's **2.** *I*, (*numero romano equivalente a 1*) I (one).

i¹, *art. determinativo m.pl.* **1.** the: — *fratelli Smith*, the Smith brothers; — *Pirenei*, the Pyrenees; — *Puritani*, — *Cinesi*, the Puritans, the Chinese; — *Johnson sono nostri amici*, the Johnsons are our friends; — *piselli erano buoni*, the peas were nice; — *vecchi e* — *poveri vanno aiutati*, the old and the poor need our help **2.**(*spesso non si traduce*): — *bambini amano* — *giocattoli*, children are fond of toys; — *buoni film sono rari*, good films are rare; *ho mandato* — *miei libri dal rilegatore*, I sent my books to the bookbinder **3.** (*tradotto con l'ag. poss.*): *ti sei tagliato* — *capelli?*, did you have your hair cut?; *togliti* — *guanti*, take off your gloves **4.** (*tradotto col partitivo*) **some; any:** *devo andare a comperare* — *fiammiferi*, I must go and get some matches; *ha comperato* — *fiammiferi?*, has he bought any matches?.

i², *pron.pers.* 3ª *persona pl. oggetto* (*arc. poet.*) **them.**

iacintèo, iacintíno, *ag.* hyacinthine.

Iàcopo, *no.pr.m.* James || *dim.* Jamie, Jim(my).

Iàdi, *no.pr.f.pl.* (*mit. astr.*) Hyades.

Iàfet, *no.pr.m.* (*Bibbia*) Japheth.

Iàgo, *no.pr.m.* (*lett.*) Iago.

ialíno, *ag.* (*min.*) hyaline.

ialíte, *s.f.* (*min.*) hyalite.

ialografía, *s.f.* (*pitt.*) hyalography.

ialòide, *ag.* (*anat.*) hyaloid || *s.m.* (*anat.*) hyaloid (membrane).

iàrda, *s.f.* yard (*misura di lunghezza* = cm. 91,4399): *due iarde di stoffa*, two yards of cloth.

iàto, *s.m.* (*gram.*) hiatus (*pl.* hiatuses, hiatus).

iattànza, *s.f.* boastfulness, brag, insolence, vaingloriousness: *discorso pieno di* —, boastful speech; *parlare con* —, to speak boastfully.

iattúra, *s.f.* misfortune; calamity || *che* —!, what a tragedy!.

Ibèri, *s.m.pl.* Iberians.

Ibèria, *no.pr.f.* (*geog. st.*) Iberia.

ibèrico, *ag.* Iberian: *la razza iberica*, the Iberian race.

ibernànte, *ag.* (*zool.*) hibernating, hibernant.

ibernazióne, *s.f.* (*zool.*) hibernation.

íbero-, (*prefisso*) Ibero-: — *-americano*, Ibero-American.

Íbico, *no.pr.m.* (*st. lett.*) Ibycus, Ibykos.

íbi, *s.m.* (*ornit.*) ibis (*pl.* ibises): — *sacro*, sacred ibis.

ibidem, *av.* (*lat.*) ibidem (*abbr.* ibid.).

íbis, *s.m.* (*ornit.*) ibis (*pl.* ibises): — *sacro*, sacred ibis.

ibísco, *s.m.* (*bot.*) hibiscus.

ibridàre, *v.t.* (*bot.*) to hybridize.

ibridazióne, *s.f.* (*bot. zool.*) hybridization.

ibridísmo, *s.m.* (*bot. zool.*) hybridism.

íbrido, *ag.* **1.** (*bot. zool.*) hybrid, cross-bred, mongrel **2.** *fig.* hybrid **3.** (*gram.*) hybrid || *s.m.* **1.** (*bot. zool.*) hybrid, cross, mongrel **2.** *fig.* hybrid **3.** (*gram.*) hybrid.

Ícaro, *no.pr.m.* (*mit.*) Icarus.

icàstica, *s.f.* (*art.*) art of representing things by images.

icàstico, *ag.* figurative, graphic.

icneumóne, *s.m.* (*zool.*) ichneumon.

ienografía, *s.f.* ichnography.

ienografieaménte, *av.* ichnographically.

ienogràfico, *ag.* ichnographic(al).

icòna, icòne, *s.f.* icon.

icònico, *ag.* iconic.

iconoclàsta, iconoclàste, *s.m.* (*st.*) iconoclast (anche *fig.*).

iconoclastía, *s.f.* (*st.*) iconoclasm (anche *fig.*).

iconoclàstico, *ag.* (*st.*) iconoclastic (anche *fig.*).

iconografía, *s.f.* iconography.

iconogràfico, *ag.* iconographic(al).

iconògrafo, *s.m.* iconographer.

iconolàtra, *s.c.* iconolater.

iconolatría, *s.f.* iconolatry.

iconología, *s.f.* iconology.

iconològico, *ag.* iconological.

iconologísta, *s.m.* iconologist.

iconometría, *s.f.* (*foto.*) iconometry.

iconomètrico, *ag.* (*foto.*) iconometric.

iconòmetro, *s.m.* (*foto.*) iconometer.

iconoscòpio, *s.m.* (*tv.*) iconoscope.

iconostàsi, *s.f.* (*arch.*) iconostasis (*pl.* iconostases).

icóre, ícore, *s.m.* ichor.

icosaèdrico, *ag.* (*geom.*) icosahedral.

icosaèdro, *s.m.* (*geom.*) icosahedron (*pl.* icosahedra).

Ictíno, *no.pr.m.* (*st. arch.*) Ictinus.

Ída¹, *no.pr.f.* Ida.

Ída², *no.pr.m.* (*geog.*) (Mount) Ida.

idàlgo, *s.m.* hidalgo (*pl.* hidalgos).

idàlio, *ag.* Idalian.

Idàlio, *no.pr.m.* (*geog. st.*) Idalium.

iddío, *V.* dio.

idèa, *s.f.* **1.** idea: *l'* — *del bello, del buono*, the idea of the beautiful, of the good; *associazione di idee*, association of ideas; *il mondo delle idee*, (*fil.*) the world of ideas **2.** (*ispirazione, trovata*) idea: *un'* — *luminosa*, a brilliant idea; *egli è pieno di idee*, he is full of ideas; *mi è venuta un'* —, I have got an idea (o a brain-wave); *la sua* — *di venire a casa fu veramente felice*, his idea of coming home was really a happy one || *che* —!, what an idea! **3.** (*nozione approssimativa*) idea, notion: *non avevo* — *di queste cose*, I had no notion of these things; *non ho la minima* —, I haven't the faintest (o the slightest) idea; *non puoi neppure fartene un'*—, you cannot even imagine it; *questo ti dà un'* — *di quanto cattivo egli sia*, this gives you an idea of how bad he is **4.** (*opinione*) mind, opinion: *secondo la vostra* —, in your opinion; *gli dirò le mie idee su questo*, I shall tell him my mind (o my opinion) about this; *gli ho detto francamente le mie idee*, I told him my ideas frankly; *siamo tutti della stessa* —, we are all of one mind; *sono della tua* —, I am of your mind; *cambiare* —, to change one's mind **5.** (*intenzione, aspirazione, inclinazione*) mind, intention: *non ho la minima* — *di fare ciò*, I haven't the slightest intention of doing that; *avere* — *di fare ql.co.*, to have a good mind to do sthg.; *avere una mezza* — *di fare ql.co.*, to have half a mind to do sthg. **6.** (*pensiero*) idea: *un'* — *fissa*, a fixed idea **7.** (*ideale*) ideal: *l'* — *del bello presso i Romantici*, the Romantic ideal of beauty.

ideàbile, *ag.* imaginable, conceivable.

ideàle, *ag.* **1.** ideal: *ordine* —, ideal order; *schema, rappresentazione* —, ideal scheme, representation **2.**(*buono, eccellente*) ideal, excellent: *tempo* —, ideal weather;

questo è un luogo — per campeggio, this is an ideal place for camping ‖ *s.m.* ideal: *ho trovato un lavoro, ma non è il mio —*, I have found a job, but it is not my ideal; *questo è contro i miei ideali*, this is against my ideals; *realizzare i propri ideali*, to realize one's ideals; *inseguire un —*, to pursue an ideal.

idealísmo, *s.m.* idealism (anche *fil.*).

idealísta, *s.c.* idealist (anche *fil.*).

idealístico, *ag.* idealistic (anche *fil.*).

idealità, *s.f.* 1. ideality 2. (*ideale*) ideal.

idealizzàre, *v.t.* to idealize: *— la donna*, to idealize woman.

idealizzazióne, *s.f.* idealization.

idealménte, *av.* ideally.

ideàre, *v.t.* 1. (*immaginare*) to imagine, to conceive: *ideò un nuovo tipo di macchina*, he conceived a new type of engine 2. (*proporsi*) to plan: *— di fare ql.co.*, to plan to do sthg.

ideatóre, *s.m.* inventor ‖ **ideatríce**, *s.f.* inventress.

ideazióne, *s.f.* ideation.

idem, *av.* (*lat.*) idem, the same; ditto (*abbr.* do).

identicaménte, *av.* identically; in the same way.

identicità, *s.f.* identity.

idèntico, *ag.* identic(al), exactly alike: *queste due traduzioni sono identiche*, these two translations are identical (*o* exactly alike).

identificàbile, *ag.* identifiable.

identificàre, *v.t.* to identify: *— una persona fra altre*, to identify a person among others ‖ **identificàrsi**, *v.r.* to identify oneself.

identificazióne, *s.f.* identification.

identità, *s.f.* identity: *carta d'—*, identity card.

ideografía, *s.f.* ideography.

ideogràfico, *ag.* ideographic(al): *segni ideografici*, ideograms.

ideogràmma, *s.m.* ideogram, ideograph.

ideología, *s.f.* ideology.

ideologicaménte, *av.* ideologically.

ideológico, *ag.* ideologic(al).

ideologísmo, *s.m.* ideology.

ideologísta, *s.m.* ideologist.

idest, id est, *l. av.* (*lat.*) id est (*abbr.* i.e.), that is to say.

ídi, *s.m.f.pl.* (*st. romana*) ides: *gli — di marzo*, the ides of March.

idillíaco, idíllico, *ag.* idyllic.

idíllio, *s.m.* 1. (*st. lett.*) idyll, idyl 2. (*relazione amorosa*) amour, amourette: *intrecciare un —*, to begin an idyllic love-affair.

idioelèttrico, *ag.* (*elett.*) idioelectric.

idiòma, *s.m.* language; tongue; idiom: *l'— italiano*, the Italian language; *l'— materno*, one's mother tongue; *l'— toscano*, the Tuscan idiom.

idiomaticaménte, *av.* idiomatically.

idiomàtico, *ag.* idiomatic: *peculiarità idiomatiche*, idiomatic peculiarities.

idiomòrfo, *ag.* (*min.*) idiomorphic.

idiopatía, *s.f.* (*med.*) idiopathy.

idiopàtico, *ag.* (*med.*) idiopathic(al).

idiosincrasía, *s.f.* 1. (*med.*) idiosyncrasy 2. (*avversione*) dislike, aversion: *avere un'— per il rosso*, to have a particular dislike for red.

idiòta, *ag.* idiotic; foolish; senseless ‖ *s.c.* 1. idiot; fool 2. (*patol.*) idiot.

idiotàggine, *s.f.* 1. idiocy, stupidity 2. (*parola, azione da idiota*) idiocy; nonsense.

idiotaménte, *av.* idiotically.

idiotísmo, *s.m.* 1. (*gram.*) idiom: *conosce molti idiotismi*, he knows many idioms 2. (*idiozia*) idiocy, imbecility.

idiotizzàre, *v.t.* to make idiotic ‖ *v.i.* (*gram.*) to use idioms.

idiozía, *s.f.* 1. idiocy, imbecility 2. (*parola, azione da idiota*) idiocy; (*assurdità*) nonsense: *non dire idiozie!*, don't talk nonsense!; *questa è una vera —!*, this is pure idiocy!

idolàtra, *ag.* idolatrous‖*s.m.* idolater ‖ *s.f.* idolatress.

idolatràre, *v.t.* 1. (*adorare*) to worship 2. *fig.* (*amare svisceratamente*) to idolize, to be passionately fond of (s.o., sthg.): *è idolatrato da tutti i suoi allievi*, he is idolized by all his pupils.

idolatría, *s.f.* idolatry (anche *fig.*).

idolàtrico, *ag.* idolatrous (anche *fig.*).

idoleggiàre, *v.t.* to idolize, to make an idol of (s.o., sthg.) (anche *fig.*).

ídolo, *s.m.* idol (anche *fig.*): *l'— del giorno*, the idol of the day; *il denaro è il suo —*, he has made an idol of money; *è diventato l' — del popolo*, he has become the idol of the people; *adorare idoli*, to worship idols.

Idomenèo, *no.pr.m.* (*mit.*) Idomeneus.

idoneaménte, *av.* suitably, properly, conveniently.

idoneità, *s.f.* fitness; suitability.

idòneo, *ag.* fit (for sthg., to do); (*adatto*) suitable (for sthg., for doing); apt: *un abito — a un'occasione del genere*, a dress suitable for such an occasion; *in condizioni idonee*, under suitable conditions; *è— al servizio militare*, he is fit for military service; *quell'uomo non è — a quel lavoro*, that man is not fit for that work.

Ídra, *no.pr.f.* 1. (*mit.*) Hydra: *l'— di Lerna*, Hydra of Lerna 2. (*astr.*) Hydra ‖ **ídra**, *s.f.* 1. (*zool.*) hydra (*pl.* hydrae, hydras), water-snake 2. *fig.* hydra (*pl.* hydrae, hydras).

idrànte, *s.m.* hydrant; (*antincendio*) fire-plug; (*presa d'acqua*) water-plug.

idrargírio, *s.m.* (*chim.*) hydrargyrum, quicksilver.

idratàre, *v.t.* (*chim.*) to hydrate.

idràto, *ag.* (*chim.*) hydrated ‖ *s.m.* hydrate: *— di calcio*, calcium hydrate.

idràulica, *s.f.* hydraulics.

idràulico, *ag.* hydraulic: *ascensore —*, hydraulic lift; *impianto —*, plumbing; *pressa, valvola idraulica*, hydraulic press, valve ‖ *s.m.* plumber.

ídria, *s.f.* (*archeol.*) hydria (*pl.* hydriae).

ídrico, *ag.* water (*attributivo*): *dieta idrica*, water diet.

ídro, *s.m.* 1. (*zool.*) hydra (*pl.* hydrae, hydras), water-snake 2. (*aer.*) seaplane.

idroaeroplàno, *s.m.* (*aer.*) seaplane.

idrocarbonàto, *s.m.* (*chim.*) hydrocarbonate.

idrocarbóne, *s.m.* (*chim.*) hydrocarbon.

idrocarbúro, *s.m.* (*chim.*) hydrocarbon.

idrocefalía, *s.f.*(*patol.*) hydrocephalus, hydrocephaly.

idrocefàlico, *ag.* (*med.*) hydrocephalic, hydrocephalous.

idrocèfalo, *s.m.* 1. (*idrocefalia*) hydrocephalus 2. (*malato di idrocefalia*) hydrocephalous subject.

idrocèle, *s.m.* (*patol.*) hydrocele.

idrochinóne, *s.m.* (*chim. foto.*) hydroquinone.

idrocianàto, *s.m.* (*chim.*) hydrocyanide.

idrociànico, *ag.* (*chim.*) hydrocyanic.

idrodinàmica, *s.f.* hydrodynamics.

idrodinàmico, *ag.* hydrodynamic.

idroelèttrico, *ag.*.(*elett.*) hydroelectric: *centrale idroelettrica*, hydroelectric generating station (*o amer.* hydroelectric power plant).

idròfilo, *ag.* 1. absorbent: *cotone —*, cotton-wool 2. (*bot.*) hydrophilous ‖ *s.m.* (*entom.*) water-beetle.

idrofobía, *s.f.* (*patol.*) hydrophobia, rabies.

idròfobo, *ag.* 1. (*med.*) hydrophobic, rabid, mad: *cane —*, rabid (o mad) dog 2. *fig.* furious.

idròfono, *s.m.* (*mar.*) hydrophone.

idròforo, *ag.*: *macchina idrofora*, (*mec.*) hydrophore.

idròfugo, *ag.* waterproof.

idrogenàre, *v.t.* (*chim.*) to hydrogenate, to hydrogenize.

idrogenazióne, *s.f.* (*chim.*) hydrogenation.

idrògeno, *s.m.* (*chim.*) hydrogen: *— nascente*, active hydrogen; *— pesante*, heavy hydrogen; *bomba all'—*, hydrogen bomb (o H-bomb); *impianto di produzione dell'—*, hydrogen generating plant.

idrografía, *s.f.* hydrography.

idrograficaménte, *av.* hydrographically.

idrogràfico, *ag.* hydrographic(al): *bacino* —, drainage-basin.
idrògrafo, *s.m.* hydrographer.
idròlisi, *s.f.* (*chim.*) hydrolysis.
idrolítico, *ag.* (*chim.*) hydrolytic.
idrología, *s.f.* hydrology.
idrològico, *ag.* hydrologic(al).
idròlogo, *s.m.* hydrologist.
idromanzía, *s.f.* hydromancy.
idromeccànica, *s.f.* hydromechanics.
idromeccànico, *ag.* hydromechanical.
idromèle, *s.m.* hydromel.
idrometría, *s.f.* hydrometry.
idromètrico, *ag.* hydrometric(al).
idròmetro, *s.m.* hydrometer, water gauge.
idromotóre, *s.m.* (*mec. fis.*) hydromotor.
idrope, *s.m.* (*patol.*) dropsy, hydropsy.
idròpico, *ag.* (*med.*) dropsical, hydropic || *s.m.* dropsical subject.
idropisía, *s.f.* (*patol.*) dropsy, hydropsy.
idroplàno, *s.m.* (*mar.*) hydroplane.
idropneumàtico, *ag.* (*mec.*) hydropneumatic.
idropònica, *s.f.* (*chim.*) hydroponics.
idropòrto, idroscàlo, *s.m.* (*aer.*) flying-boat station.
idroscivolànte, *s.m.* (*mar.*) hydroplane.
idroscòpico, *ag.* (*agr.*) hydroscopic.
idroscòpio, *s.m.* (*mar.*) hydroscope.
idrosfèra, *s.f.* (*geog.*) hydrosphere.
idrosilurànte, *s.m.* (*aer. mil.*) torpedo-plane.
idrosolfàto, *s.m.* (*chim.*) hydrosulphide.
idròssido, *s.m.* (*chim.*) hydroxide.
idrostàtica, *s.f.* hydrostatics.
idrostàtico, *ag.* hydrostatic(al).
idròstato, *s.m.* hydrostat.
idroterapèutica, *s.f.* hydrotherapeutics, hydrotherapy.
idroterapèutico, *ag.* hydrotherapeutic.
idroterapía, *s.f.* hydrotherapeutics, hydrotherapy.
idroteràpico, *ag.* hydrotherapeutic.
idrotermàle, *ag.* hydrothermal.
idrotoràce, *s.m.* (*patol.*) hydrothorax.
idrotropísmo, *s.m.* (*bot.*) hydrotropism.
idrovolànte, *s.m.* (*aer.*) seaplane; (*a scafo*) flying-boat.
idrozòi, *s.m.pl.* (*zool.*) Hydrozoa.
Idumèa, *no.pr.f.* (*geog. st.*) Idumaea.
idumèo, *ag.* Idum(a)ean.
Ièfte, *no.pr.m.* (*Bibbia*) Iephthah.
Ièhu, *no.pr.m.* (*Bibbia*) Jehu.
iemàle, *ag.* (*letter.*) wintry.
Iémen, *no.pr.m.* (*geog.*) Yemen.
ièna, *s.f.* 1. (*zool.*) hy(a)ena: — *striata,* striped hy(a)ena 2. *fig.* (*donna malvagia*) vixen: *quella donna è una vera* —, that woman is a veritable vixen.
Ièova, *no.pr.m.* (*Bibbia*) Jehovah.
ieraticaménte, *av.* hieratically.
ieràtico, *ag.* 1. hieratic: *scrittura ieratica,* hieratic writing 2. *fig.* (*grave, solenne*) grave, solemn: *atteggiamento* —, stately (*o* dignified) attitude.
ièri, *av.* yesterday; (*poet.*) yester: — *mattina,* yesterday morning; — *notte,* yesterday night (*o* last night); — *sera,* yesterday evening; *l'altro* —, the day before yesterday: *l'altro* — *sera,* the evening before last; *il giornale di* —, yesterday's (news)paper || *era una settimana* —, yesterday week || *il fatto non è di* —, this happened a long time ago || *sei nato* —, you are born yesterday.
ierofànte, *s.m.* (*st.*) hierophant.
ieroglífico, *s.m.* (*rar.*) hieroglyph.
ierografía, *s.f.* hierography.
Ierònimo, *no.pr.m.* Hieronymus.
iettatóre, *s.m.* evil-eyed man; bearer of ill-luck; bird of ill omen.
iettatúra, *s.f.* 1. evil-eye: *gettare la* — *su qlcu.,* to cast an evil-eye on s.o. 2. (*sfortuna*) bad luck, ill-luck:

che —!, what a run of ill-luck!; *avere la* —, to be unlucky; *essere perseguitato dalla* —, to be dogged by ill-luck; *portare* —, to bring ill-luck.
Iezabèle, *no.pr.f.* (*Bibbia*) Jezebel.
Ifigenía, *no.pr.f.* (*lett.*) Iphigenia.
Igèa, *no.pr.f.* (*mit.*) Hygeia.
igiène, *s.f.* 1. hygiene, hygienics: *l'*— *dei denti,* oral hygiene (*o* the care of the teeth) 2. (*salute*) health; (*complesso dei mezzi per proteggere la salute di una comunità*) sanitation: — *pubblica,* public health; *norme d'*—, sanitary regulations; *migliorare l'*— *di una città,* to improve the sanitation of a town || *istituto d'*—, sanitary institute || *Ministero dell'Igiene,* Ministry of Health.
igienicaménte, *av.* 1. hygienically; sanitarily 2. (*salubremente*) healthily.
igiènico, *ag.* 1. hygienic(al); sanitary: *condizioni igieniche,* hygienic (*o* sanitary) conditions; *misure igieniche,* sanitary measures 2. (*salubre*) healthy: *questo clima è molto* —, this climate is very healthy.
ignàro, *ag.* ignorant; unacquainted (with sthg.), unaware: *ero completamente* — *di tutto questo,* I was completely ignorant of it all (*o* unacquainted with this matter).
ignàvia, *s.f.* laziness , indolence, sloth.
ignàvo, *ag.* lazy, indolent, slothful.
Ignàzio, *no.pr.m.* Ignatius.
ígneo, *ag.* 1. igneous: *rocce ignee,* (*geol.*) igneous rocks 2. *fig.* (*ardente, impetuoso*) fiery, ardent.
ignífero, *ag.* igniferous.
ignìto, *ag.* (*letter.*) ignited; *fig.* fiery, ardent.
ignizióne, *s.f.* (*chim.*) ignition, combustion.
ignòbile, *ag.* 1. ignoble; mean, base, dishonourable: *un'azione, un uomo* —, an ignoble action, man 2. (*di oscuri natali*) low-born 3. *metallo* —, base metal.
ignobilità, *s.f.* 1. ignobleness; meanness, baseness, dishonourableness 2. (*oscurità di natali*) low-birth.
ignobilménte, *av.* ignobly; meanly, basely, dishonourably.
ignomínia, *s.f.* ignominy, dishonour, infamy: *è un'*—!, it is a shame!.
ignominióso, *ag.* ignominious.
ignoràbile, *ag.* ignorable.
ignorantàggine, *s.f.* 1. ignorance 2. (*atto da ignorante*) ignorant action; (*detto da ignorante*) ignorant words (*pl.*).
ignorànte, *ag.* ignorant; (*che non ha studiato*) unlearned; (*illetterato*) unlettered, unlearned, illiterate: *è* — *come una talpa,* he is as stupid as a goose; *non è stupido, è solo* —, he is not stupid, merely ignorant || *s.c.* ignorant (person).
ignorantèllo, *ag.* rather ignorant || *s.m.* (*eccl.*) Ignorantine.
ignoranteménte, *av.* ignorantly.
ignorantóne, *s.m.* extremely ignorant fellow.
ignorànza, *s.f.* ignorance; illiteracy: — *crassa,* crass ignorance; *per* —, out of (*o* through) ignorance; *essere nella completa* — *di ql.co.,* to be in complete ignorance of sthg. || *l'*— *della legge non scusa,* ignorance of the law is no excuse || *la superbia è figlia dell'*—, *prov.* pride, the never-failing vice of fools.
ignoràre, *v.t.* to ignore; (*non sapere*) not to know; to be ignorant of (sthg.); (*non conoscere*) to be unacquainted with (sthg.): *egli la ignora sempre,* he always ignores her; *ignoravo quello che era accaduto,* I was unacquainted with what had happened; *lo ignoravo,* I did not know that.
ignotaménte, *av.* unknowingly.
ignòto, *ag.* unknown; unfamiliar, strange: *tutte queste cose mi erano ignote,* I did not know (*o* I was not acquainted with) all these things || *Milite Ignoto,* Unknown Warrior || *s.m.* 1. unknown person: *figlio d'ignoti,* (*nei documenti*) parentage unknown 2. *l'*—, the unknown: *andare incontro all'*—, to venture against the unknown.

ignudàre, V. **denudàre.**
ignúdo, V. **núdo.**
igrometría, s.f. (fis.) hygrometry.
igrometricaménte, av. (fis.) hygrometrically.
igromètrico, ag. (fis.) hygrometric(al).
igròmetro, s.m. (fis.) hygrometer: — a capello, hair hygrometer; — ad assorbimento, chemical hygrometer.
igroscopicaménte, av. hygroscopically.
igroscopicità, s.f. hygroscopicity.
igroscopía, s.f. hygroscopy.
igroscòpico, ag. hygroscopic(al).
igroscòpio, s.m. hygroscope.
iguàna, s.f. (zool.) iguana.
iguanodónte, s.m. (zool.) iguanodon.
ih, inter. (di sorpresa) oh! ah!; (di disgusto) ugh!.
il¹, art. determinativo m.sing. **1.** the: — bello e — vero, the beautiful and the true; — Capo di Buona Speranza, (geog.) the Cape of Good Hope; — Duca di Wellington, the Duke of Wellington; — più bello, the finest; — Tamigi, the Thames; Alfredo — Grande, Alfred the Great; — cane e — gatto sono animali domestici, the dog and the cat are domestic animals; — cielo era nuvoloso, the sky was cloudy; — libro che ho comperato ieri era molto bello, the book I bought yesterday was very nice; — pranzo fu ottimo, the dinner was very good; preferisci — cinema o — teatro?, do you prefer the cinema or the theatre? **2.** (spesso non si traduce): — che, which; — dott. Smith, Dr. Smith; — giorno di Natale, Christmas Day; — re Edoardo, King Edward; — ferro ed — rame sono molto utili, iron and copper are very useful; — Ghana è una nuova repubblica africana, Ghana is a new African republic; — Monte Bianco è la montagna più alta d'Italia, Mont Blanc is the highest mountain in Italy; — prossimo settembre andrà a Parigi, next September he will go to Paris; — tuo ombrello è rotto, your umbrella is broken; — viaggiare è divertente, travelling is amusing; gli piace — golf, he likes golf; mi piace — verde, I like green; prendiamo — tè alle cinque, we have tea at five; sto studiando — francese, I am studying French; viene sempre — lunedì, he comes on Mondays (o every Monday) || — Francesco, (dial.) Francis || sono andato a vedere — Falstaff, I went to see Falstaff **3.** (tradotto con l'ag. poss.): — nonno vive con noi, our grandfather lives with us; non ficcare — naso nelle faccende che non ti riguardano, don't poke your nose into things that don't concern you; perchè non bevi — caffè?, why don't you drink your coffee? **4.** (tradotto con l'art. indef.) a, an: — cavallo può essere un buon amico, a horse can be a good friend; chiedere — divorzio, to sue for a divorce **5.** (tradotto col partitivo) some; any: deve andare a comperare — vino, she must go and get some wine; hai comperato — sale?, did you get any salt? **6.** (sta per al col valore di ogni, ciascuno): cento lire — mazzo, a hundred lire a bunch; diecimila lire — mese, ten thousand lire a month **7.** (in espressioni ellittiche): passami — Tommaseo, (il dizionario del Tommaseo) pass me (the) Tommaseo.
il², pron. pers. 3ª persona sing. oggetto (arc. poet.) him: — vidi e — chiamai, I saw him and called him.
ílare, ag. cheerful, gay: volto —, cheerful face.
Ilària, no.pr.f. Hilaria.
Ilàrio, no.pr.m. Hilary.
ilarità, s.f. hilarity, mirth; (buon umore) good humour, cheerfulness; (riso) laughter: scoppio d'—, burst of hilarity (o laughter); le sue parole provocarono l'— generale, his words made everybody laugh.
Ílda, no.pr.f. Hilda.
Ildebràndo, no.pr.m. Hildebrand.
Ildegàrda, no.pr.f. Hildegarde.
íleo, ag. (anat.) iliac || s.m. **1.** (anat.) (osso) ilium (pl. ilia) **2.** (anat.) (parte dell'intestino tenue) ileum **3.** (patol.) ileus, iliac passion.
ileocecàle, ag. (anat.) ileocœcal.
ileosacràle, ag. (anat.) ileosacral.

ilíaco¹, ag. (anat.) iliac: osso —, hip-bone; vene, arterie iliache, iliac veins, arteries.
ilíaco², ag. Trojan, of Ilium, of Troy: le iliache donne, the Trojan women.
Ilíade, s.f. (lett.) Iliad || iliade, fig. Iliad.
ílice, s.f. ilex (pl. ilexes); holm-oak.
ílio¹, s.m. (anat.) ilium (pl. ilia).
Ílio², no.pr.f. (st.) Ilium, Ilion.
illacrimàbile, ag. (poet.) unworthy of tears.
illacrimàto, ag. (poet.) unwept, unlamented.
illaidíre, v.t. to render ugly; to disfigure.
illanguidiménto, s.m. languishment, languor.
illanguidíre, v.t. to weaken, to enfeeble: voce illanguidita dalla malattia, voice weakened by illness || v.i. to languish, to grow feeble, to droop: — in prigione, to languish in prison.
illanguidíto, ag. feeble, weak.
illatívo, ag. (letter.) illative, inferential.
illaudàbile, ag. (letter.) unpraiseworthy.
illaudàto, ag. (letter.) unpraised.
illazióne, s.f. illation, inference; deduction.
illecitaménte, av. illicitly; (illegalmente) unlawfully.
illécito, ag. illicit; (illegale) unlawful; (proibito) forbidden: traffico —, illicit trade.
illegàle, ag. illegal, unlawful: procedimento, arresto —, (dir.) unlawful proceeding, arrest.
illegalità, s.f. **1.** illegality, unlawfulness **2.** (atto illegale) unlawful act.
illegalménte, av. illegally, unlawfully.
illeggiadríre, v.t. (letter.) to make pretty; to embellish: il sorriso illeggiadrisce i suoi lineamenti, her smile makes her features more pretty.
illeggíbile, ag. illegible, unreadable: libro —, unreadable book; scrittura —, illegible handwriting.
illeggibilménte, av. illegibly, unreadably.
illegittimaménte, av. **1.** illegitimately, unlawfully **2.** (arbitrariamente) illegitimately, arbitrarily.
illegittimità, s.f. **1.** illegitimacy, unlawfulness. **2.** (arbitrarietà) illegitimacy, arbitrariness.
illegíttimo, ag. **1.** illegitimate, unlawful: azioni illegittime, illegitimate (o unlawful) actions || figlio —, illegitimate child **2.** (arbitrario) illegitimate, arbitrary: la tua conclusione è illegittima, your conclusion is illegitimate.
illéso, ag. unhurt, uninjured, unharmed: da quel pauroso incidente uscì —, he came out from that accident unhurt (o without a scratch).
illetteràto, ag. illiterate, unlettered, unlearned, uncultured.
illibataménte, av. **1.** (castamente) purely, chastely **2.** (con rettitudine) honestly, spotlessly, uprightly.
illibatézza, s.f. **1.** (castità) purity, chastity **2.** (rettitudine) honesty, spotlessness, uprightness.
illibàto, ag. **1.** (casto) pure, chaste **2.** (retto) honest, spotless, upright.
illiberàle, ag. illiberal.
illiberalità, s.f. illiberality.
illiberalménte, av. illiberally.
illico et immediate, l.av. (lat.) at once, immediately, directly.
illimitataménte, av. unlimitedly, boundlessly, without limit.
illimitatézza, s.f. unlimitedness, boundlessness.
illimitàto, ag. unlimited, boundless: fiducia illimitata, unbounded confidence || congedo —, (mil.) indefinite leave.
Illíria, no.pr.f. (geog. st.) Illyria.
illírico, ag. Illyrian, Illyric || s.m. Illyrian.
illividiménto, s.m. turning blue.
illividíre, v.t. to make livid || v.i. to turn livid.
illogicaménte, av. illogically.
illogicità, s.f. illogicality, illogicalness.
illògico, ag. illogical.
illúdere, v.t. to deceive, to delude: non cercate d'illudermi, conosco la verità!, don't try to deceive me,

I know the truth! ‖ **illúdersi**, *v.r.* to deceive oneself, to delude oneself; (*lusingarsi*) to flatter oneself: *egli si illudeva di sapere tutto*, he flattered himself that he knew everything; *non avrai quello che desideri, non illuderti!*, you won't have what you wish, don't deceive yourself!.

illuminànte, *ag.* 1. illuminating, illuminant: *gas* —, illuminating gas 2. *fig.* enlightening: *idea* —, enlightening idea.

illuminàre, *v.t.* 1. to illuminate, to light (up): *la facciata era illuminata a giorno*, the façade was floodlit; *il fuoco illuminava tutta la piazza*, the fire lit up the whole square; *grandi lampade illuminavano la scena*, big lamps illuminated the scene; *le sale erano splendidamente illuminate*, the halls were brightly illuminated; *la stanza era illuminata da lampade ad olio*, the room was lighted (*o* illuminated) with oil lamps 2. *fig.* to enlighten, to illuminate, to illumine, to light (up): *la felicità le illuminava il viso*, happiness lit up her face; *su questo argomento fui illuminato da un uomo molto saggio*, on this subject I was enlightened by a very wise man; — *gli ignoranti*, to enlighten the ignorant ‖ **illuminàrsi**, *v.r.* to lighten, to brighten: *il cielo si illuminò verso l'orizzonte*, the sky brightened towards the horizon; *il viso gli si illuminò di speranza*, his face lightened (*o* brightened) with hope.

illuminatívo, *ag.* illuminative.

illuminàto, *ag.* 1. lighted, lit up, illuminated: — *a giorno*, floodlit; *eccessivamente* —, overlighted 2. *fig.* enlightened, illuminated: *sovrano* —, enlightened ruler.

illuminatóre, *s.m.*, **illuminatríce**, *s.f.* 1. illuminator 2. *fig.* enlightener, illuminator.

illuminazióne, *s.f.* lighting, illumination: — *a giorno*, flood lighting; — *artificiale*, artificial lighting; — *elettrica, a gas*, electric, gas lighting; *l'* — *era piuttosto scarsa*, the lighting was rather poor.

illuminísmo, *s.m.* (*st.fil.*) illuminism: *il secolo dell'* —, the century of illuminism (*o* the age of enlightenment).

illuminísta, *ag.* (*st. fil.*) illuministic; illuminist (*attributivo*) ‖ *s.m.* (*st. fil.*) illuminist.

illusióne, *s.f.* illusion, dream: — *ottica*, optical illusion; *questa è una pura* —, this is a mere dream; *farsi illustoni*, to live in a dream world.

illusionísmo, *s.m.* illusionism.

illusionísta, *s.c.* illusionist, conjurer, prestidigitator.

illusívo, *ag.* illusive, illusory.

illúso, *ag.* deluded, deceived ‖ *s.c.* day-dreamer: *sei un* —*!*, (*fam.*) you've some hopes!.

illusoriaménte, *av.* illusorily, illusively.

illusòrio, *ag.* illusory, illusive.

illustràre, *v.t.* 1. to illustrate, to explain, to elucidate: — *un piano d'azione*, to illustrate a plan of action; — *le proprie opinioni*, to explain one's opinions 2. (*adornare con figure*) to illustrate: — *un libro*, to illustrate a book 3. (*rendere illustre*) to make illustrious, to make famous.

illustratívo, *ag.* illustrative.

illustràto, *ag.* illustrated: *cartolina illustrata*, picture postcard; *edizione illustrata*, illustrated edition.

illustratóre, *s.m.* illustrator.

illustrazióne, *s.f.* 1. (*spiegazione*) illustration; explanation: *l'* — *di una teoria*, the illustration (*o* explanation) of a theory 2. (*figura*) picture; plate: *le illustrazioni di un libro*, the pictures of a book; *questo libro d'arte ha delle bellissime illustrazioni*, this art book has very beautiful plates 3. (*pubblicazione*) weekly review.

illústre, *ag.* illustrious, famous; renowned: *un medico* —, a renowned physician ‖ *un* — *imbroglione*, a notorious rascal.

illustríssimo, *ag.superl.* most illustrious ‖ *Illustrissimo signor Roberto Rossi*, (*negli indirizzi*) Mr. Robert Rossi (*o* Robert Rossi Esq.).

illúvie, *s.f.* (*rar.*) dirt; filth.

ilo, *s.m.* (*bot. anat.*) hilum (*pl.* hila).

Ílo, *no.pr.m.* (*mit.*) Ilus.

ilòta, *s.m.* (*st.*) helot (anche *fig.*).

ilotísmo, *s.m.* helotism.

imàgine, *V.* immàgine.

imaginífico, *ag.* with a fertile imagination.

imàgo, *s.f.* (*poes.*) image.

Imalàia, *no.pr.m.* (*geog.*) Himalaya.

imàmo, imàno, *s.m.* imam.

imbacchettoníre, *v.t.* to make a bigot of (s.o.) ‖ *v.i.* to become a bigot.

imbacuccàre, *v.t.* to muffle up, to wrap up: *imbacuccarono il bimbo in uno scialle*, they wrapped up the child in a shawl ‖ **imbacuccàrsi**, *v.r.* to muffle oneself (up), to wrap oneself (up).

imbacuccàto, *ag.* muffled up.

imbaldanzíre, *v.t.* to embolden, to make bold: *la vittoria lo imbaldanzì*, his victory emboldened him ‖ *v.i.*, **imbaldanzírsi**, *v.r.* to become bold, to grow bold; to swell with pride.

imballàggio, *s.m.* 1. packing, package, wrapping; (*in balle*) baling; (*in casse*) packing, boxing: — *compreso*, packing included; — *gratis*, packing free; *imballaggi vuoti*, empties; *carta d'* —, wrapping (*o* brown) paper; *gabbia d'* —, (packing) crate 2. (*spesa d'imballaggio*) cost of packing.

imballàre, *v.t.* 1. to pack, to package; (*in balle*) to bale; (*in casse*) to box: — *merce*, to pack (*o* to package) goods 2. (*avvolgere*) to wrap up 3. — *un motore*, (*aut.*) to race an engine.

imballatóre, *s.m.*, **imballatríce**, *s.f.* packer.

imballatúra, *V.* imballàggio.

imbàllo, *s.m.* 1. (*aut.*) |racing 2. *V.* imballàggio.

imbalordíre, *v.t.* to stun, to dull; (*per meraviglia*) to bewilder ‖ *v.i.* to dull; (*meravigliarsi*) to get bewildered.

imbalsamàre, *v.t.* 1. to embalm; (*animale*) to stuff: *il suo corpo fu imbalsamato*, his body was embalmed 2. (*profumare*) to perfume, to scent.

imbalsamàto, *ag.* 1. embalmed; (*di animale*) stuffed: *un pappagallo* —, a stuffed parrot 2. (*profumato*) balmy.

imbalsamatóre, *s.m.* embalmer; (*di animali*) stuffer, taxidermist.

imbalsamatúra, imbalsamazióne, *s.f.* embalment; embalming; (*di animali*) stuffing, taxidermy.

imbambolàre, *v.i.*, **imbambolàrsi**, *v.r.* to become dull; to get bewildered.

imbambolàto, *ag.* dull; (*stordito*) stunned; (*per meraviglia*) bewildered; (*per sonno*) sleepy, drowsy: *espressione imbambolata*, dull expression; *occhi imbambolati*, dull eyes; *muoviti, non star lì* —*!*, come on, don't stand there half asleep!.

imbandieràre, *v.t.* to deck with flags, to hang with flags: *la città fu imbandierata a festa*, the town was decked with flags.

imbandigióne, *s.f.* 1. (*l'imbandire*) preparation (of a banquet, of a meal) 2. (*piatto, pietanza*) dish 3. (*mensa*) table: *un'abbondante* —, a rich table.

imbandíre, *v.t.* 1. (*apparecchiare*) to lay: — *la mensa*, to lay the table 2. (*preparare*) to prepare: *avevano imbandito ricchi piatti*, they had prepared rich dishes.

imbandíto, *ag.* 1. (*apparecchiato*) laid 2. (*preparato*) prepared.

imbarazzànte, *ag.* embarassing, awkward; (*che rende perplesso*) perplexing, puzzling: *una domanda* —, an embarassing (*o* perplexing *o* puzzling) question; *una situazione* —, an embarassing (*o* awkward) situation (*o* a fix).

imbarazzàre, *v.t.* 1. to embarrass: *la sua presenza mi imbarazzava*, his presence embarrassed me (*o* made me feel uncomfortable *o* ill at ease) 2. (*rendere perplesso*) to perplex, to puzzle; to bewilder: *i suoi progetti mi imbarazzano*, his plans are puzzling me 3. (*ostacolare*) to hamper, to encumber: *queste lunghe maniche mi imbarazzano i movimenti*, these long sleeves hamper my movements ‖ **imbarazzàrsi**, *v.r.* to meddle, to interfere: *non voglio imbarazzarmi con queste faccende*, I don't want to meddle (*o* to interfere) with these matters.

imbarazzàto, *ag.* **1.** embarrassed, ill at ease; uncomfortable: *ero piuttosto — fra quella gente*, I was rather embarrassed (*o* I felt ill at ease *o* uncomfortable) among those people **2.** (*perplesso*) perplexed; puzzled; bewildered: *tutti i candidati erano imbarazzati*, all the candidates were bewildered.

imbaràzzo, *s.m.* **1.** embarrassment; (*difficoltà*) difficulty: *cercava di nascondere il suo —*, he was trying to conceal his embarrassment; *sono in — quando egli è qui*, I am embarrassed (*o* I feel uncomfortable *o* ill at ease) when he is here; *essere in —*, (*in una situazione imbarazzante*) to be in an awkward situation; (*non sapere che via prendere*) to be in a fix (*o* to be in a quandary); *togliere qlcu. d'—*, to help s.o. out of a difficulty; *uscire d'—*, to get out of a difficulty (*o* out of a scrape) ‖ *non avere che l'— della scelta*, to have only the embarrassment of choosing **2.** (*disturbo*) trouble: *non voglio darti —*, I don't want to give you any trouble **3.** (*med.*): *— di fegato*, bilious attack; *— di stomaco*, indigestion: *avere — di stomaco*, to suffer from indigestion.

imbarbariménto, *s.m.* barbarization.

imbarbaríre, *v.t.* to barbarize, to decivilize; to corrupt ‖ *v.i.*, **imbarbarírsi**, *v.r.* to become barbarous, to barbarize; to grow corrupt: *il linguaggio si imbarbarisce*, the language is growing corrupt.

imbarbogíre, *v.i.* to become a dotard.

imbarcadèro, *s.m.* landing-stage; (*molo*) pier, wharf, quay.

imbarcàre, *v.t.* **1.** to take on board, to embark: *la nave può — duecento passeggieri*, the ship can embark two hundred passengers ‖ *— un colpo di mare*, (*mar.*) to ship (*o* to swamp) water **2.** *fig.* to start: *— qlcu. negli affari*, to start s.o. in business ‖ **imbarcàrsi**, *v.r.* **1.** to embark; to sail, to take ship: *egli si imbarcò ieri per l'Australia*, he embarked (*o* sailed) for Australia yesterday; *quando vi imbarcherete?*, when will you sail? **2.** *fig.* to embark (on sthg.); to engage (in sthg.): *— in una impresa*, to embark on (*o* to engage in) an undertaking **3.** (*prestar servizio su una nave*) to ship **4.** (*scherz.*) (*salire su un veicolo*) to get on.

imbarcatóio, *s.m.* landing-stage; (*molo*) pier, wharf, quay.

imbarcatúra, *s.f.* (*curvatura*) curving, warping.

imbarcazióne, *s.f.* **1.** boat: *— a motore*, motor-boat; *— da cabotaggio*, coaster; *— da diporto*, pleasure-boat; *— da pesca*, fishing-boat; *— di salvataggio*, life-boat **2.** (*l'imbarcare*) embarking.

imbàrco, *s.m.* **1.** embarkation, embarking, shipment: *porto d'—*, port of shipment; *spese d'—*, loading expenses **2.** *V.* **imbarcatóio**.

imbardàre, *v.t.* to harness ‖ *v.i.* (*aer.*) to yaw ‖ **imbardàrsi**, *v.r.* (*innamorarsi*) to fall in love.

imbardàta, *s.f.* (*aer.*) yaw.

imbarilàre, *v.t.* to barrel; to cask; to put in barrels.

imbasciàta, *V.* **ambasciàta 2.**

imbastardiménto, *s.m.* degeneration, degeneracy; abasement.

imbastardíre, *v.t.* to debase; to corrupt ‖ *v.i.*, **imbastardírsi**, *v.r.* to degenerate.

imbastíre, *v.t.* **1.** to tack, to baste: *— un orlo*, to baste a hem **2.** *fig.* (*abbozzare*) to put together; to block out, to block in, to sketch, to make a rough sketch of (sthg.): *— alcuni versi*, to improvise a few rhymes; *— un disegno*, to block out (*o* in) a drawing.

imbastitríce, *s.f.* tacker, baster.

imbastitúra, *s.f.* **1.** tacking, basting **2.** *fig.* (*abbozzo*) sketch, outline.

imbàttersi, *v.r.* to meet (with s.o.), to fall in (with s.o.), to run across (s.o.), to run into (s.o.), to come across (s.o.): *mi imbattei in un mio lontano parente*, I fell in with (*o* I ran across *o* into) a distant relation of mine.

imbattibile, *ag.* **1.** (*invincibile*) invincible, unbeatable **2.** (*insuperabile*) unsurpassable.

imbattibilità, *s.f.* invincibility.

imbaulàre, *v.t.* to pack in a trunk.

imbavagliàre, *v.t.* to gag (*anche fig.*): *— la stampa*, to gag the press.

imbavàre, *v.t.*, **imbavàrsi**, *v.r.* to slobber, to slaver.

imbeccàre, *v.t.***1.** to feed: *— uccelli*, to feed birds **2.** *fig.* to prompt: *ha sempre bisogno di essere imbeccato*, he always needs prompting.

imbeccàta, *s.f.* **1.** beakful **2.** *fig.* prompting, prompt; suggestion: *dar l'— a qlcu.*, to prompt s.o. (*o* to give s.o. a prompt).

imbecillàggine, *V.* **imbecillità**.

imbecílle, *ag.* imbecile, stupid ‖ *s.m.* imbecile, stupid: *non fare l'—!*, don't be stupid!.

imbecillíre, *v.i.* to grow imbecile, to grow stupid; to become an imbecile, to become a stupid.

imbecillità, *s.f.* **1.** imbecility, stupidity, foolishness **2.** (*atto da imbecille*) imbecility, foolish action; (*detto da imbecille*) foolish words.

imbèlle, *ag.* **1.** unwarlike **2.** (*debole*) weak **3.** (*vile*) coward, faint-hearted.

imbellettaménto, *V.* **imbellettatúra 1.**

imbellettàre, *v.t.* to make up, to paint ‖ **imbellettàrsi**, *v.r.* to make (oneself) up, to paint one's face.

imbellettatúra, *s.f.* **1.** (*l'imbellettarsi*) making up, painting **2.** (*belletto*) make-up.

imbellíre, *v.t.* to beautify, to embellish; (*adornare*) to adorn ‖ *v.i.* to become beautiful, to grow beautiful; to become prettier.

imbèrbe, *ag.* **1.** beardless: *un ragazzo —*, a beardless boy **2.** (*senza esperienza*) inexperienced, callow: *un giovane —*, a raw (*o* callow) youth.

imberrettàre, *v.t.* to put a cap on (s.o.) ‖ **imberrettàrsi**, *v.r.* to put on one's cap.

imbestialíre, **imbestialírsi**, *v.r.* **1.** (*abbrutirsi*) to become brutish **2.** (*adirarsi*) to fly into a passion, to get furious.

imbévere, *v.t.* to imbue, to drench, to soak: *— il pane di vino*, to soak bread in wine ‖ **imbéversi**, *v.r.* **1.** to absorb (sthg.), to be imbued (with sthg.), to soak (in sthg.): *il dolce deve — di tutto questo liquore*, the cake must absorb all this liqueur **2.** *fig.* to imbibe (sthg.): *— di idee altrui*, to imbibe other people's ideas.

imbevúto, *ag.* imbued (with sthg.) (*anche fig.*); drenched (with sthg.); soaked (in sthg.) (*anche fig.*): *— di idee sbagliate*, imbued with wrong ideas; *— di pioggia*, drenched with rain.

imbiaccàre, *v.t.* to paint (sthg.) with white lead.

imbiancaménto, *s.m.* whitening; (*di muri*) white-washing; (*di tessuti*) bleaching; (*di capelli*) greying, growing grey.

imbiancàre, *v.t.* **1.** to whiten; (*muri*) to whitewash; (*tessuti*) to bleach: *la neve imbianca i colli*, snow whitens the hills; *— le pareti di una stanza*, to whitewash the walls of a room **2.** (*lavare*) to wash: *— i panni*, to wash clothes **3.** (*rar.*) (*respingere*) to refuse; to reject: *— una proposta*, to reject a proposal ‖ *v.i.* **1.** to whiten, to become white, to grow white **2.** (*del cielo*) to dawn: *già imbiancava quando ritornammo a casa*, it was already dawning when we came home **3.** (*incanutire*) to grow grey **4.** (*impallidire*) to turn pale.

imbiancatóre, *s.m.* (*di muri*) whitewasher; (*di tessuti*) bleacher.

imbiancatúra, *s.f.* (*di muri*) whitewashing; (*di tessuti*) bleaching.

imbianchiménto, *V.* **imbiancaménto**.

imbianchíno, *s.m.* **1.** painter, whitewasher, decorator **2.** *fig.* (*iron.*) dauber, bad painter.

imbianchíre, *V.* **imbiancàre**.

imbibizióne, *s.f.* (*fis.*) imbibition, soaking.

imbietolíre, *v.i.* **1.** (*instupidire*) to grow silly, to become a dunce **2.** (*intenerirsi*) to be moved.

imbiettàre, *v.t.* (*mec.*) to wedge up, to wedge in; to key.

imbiondíre, *v.t.* to make fair, to make blond || *v.i.* to become fair, to turn fair; (*di messi*) to ripen.

imbirboníre, *v.i.* to become a rascal.

imbisacciàre, *v.t.* to put (sthg.) into a knapsack.

imbitumàre, *v.t.* to tar, to bituminize, to bituminate.

imbizzarriménto, *s.m.* 1. (*eccitamento*) excitement 2. (*adiramento*) fit of passion.

imbizzarríre, *v.t.* (*rar.*) to excite, to stir || *v.i.*, **imbizzarrírsi**, *v.r.* 1. (*di cavallo*) to become restive; to frisk 2. (*eccitarsi*) to become excited; (*adirarsi*) to fire up; to fly into a passion.

imbizzíre, *v.i.*, **imbizzírsi**, *v.r.* to get angry; to fly into a rage.

imboccàre, *v.t.* 1. to feed: — *un bambino*, to feed a child 2. (*dar suggerimenti a*) to prompt: *deve essere imboccato in tutto quello che fa*, he needs prompting in everything he does 3. (*entrare in*) to enter: — *una galleria*, to enter a tunnel; *la nave imboccò il porto*, the ship entered the port; — *una strada*, to take a road 4. (*portare alla bocca*): — *uno strumento a fiato*, to put a wind instrument to one's mouth || *v.i.* 1. (*incastrarsi*) to fit: *questo tubo imbocca in un altro*, this pipe fits into another one 2. (*di strada*) to open into (sthg.); (*di fiumi*) to flow into (the sea, lake, etc.).

imboccatúra, *s.f.* 1. mouth, opening; (*di fiume*) mouth; (*di strada*) entrance 2. (*del morso*) mouthpiece 3. (*di strumento a fiato*) mouthpiece, embouchure 4. (*modo di adattare la bocca ad uno strumento*) embouchure.

imbóceo, *V.* **imboccatúra** 1.

imbolsíre, *v.i.* 1. to become broken-winded 2. (*ingrassare*) to grow flabby: *imbolsisco per la vita sedentaria*, I am becoming flabby through lack of exercise.

imboniménto, *s.m.* 1. (*di venditore*) sales talk 2. (*di presentatore di spettacolo*) showman's barking 3. (*esaltazione di cosa, persona senza valore*) puff.

imboníre, *v.t.* 1. (*il pubblico*) to allure, to entice 2. (*acquietare*) to quiet down, to calm 3. (*cattivarsi*) to charm.

imbonitóre, *s.m.* 1. (*ciarlatano*) charlatan, quack 2. (*di spettacoli*) showman (*pl.* showmen).

imborghesiménto, *s.m.* getting into middle-class habits.

imborghesíre, *v.i.* to acquire middle-class habits, to adopt middle-class ways.

imborsàre, *v.t.* 1. to put (sthg.) into a purse 2. (*imbussolare*) to drop (sthg.) into a ballot-box.

imboscaménto, *s.m.* 1. (*il nascondersi*) hiding (in a wood) 2. (*il sottrarsi al servizio militare*) shirking (from military service), avoiding going into active service.

imboscàre, *v.t.* 1. to hide in a wood 2. (*sottrarre al servizio militare*) to help to evade military service 3. (*mettere al sicuro da requisizioni*) to put into safe keeping || *v.i.* (*entrare in un bosco*) to enter a wood || **imboscàrsi**, *v.r.* 1. (*mettersi in agguato*) to lie in ambush 2. (*sottrarsi al servizio militare*) to evade military service; to avoid going into active service.

imboscàta, *s.f.* ambush: *tendere un'*—, to make (*o* to lay) an ambush; *cadere in un'*—, to fall into an ambush.

imboscàto, *s.m.* (*mil.*) shirker.

imboschiménto, *s.m.* afforestation.

imboschíre, *v.t.* to afforest || *v.i.*, **imboschírsi**, *v.r.* 1. to become covered with trees 2. (*infoltirsi*) to thicken 3. (*inselvatichirsi*) to run wild.

imbottàre, *v.t.* to barrel, to cask.

imbottatúra, *s.f.* barrelling.

imbottigliaménto, *s.m.* 1. bottling 2. (*mil. mar.*) blockade 3. (*di traffico stradale*) traffic jam.

imbottigliàre, *v.t.* 1. to bottle 2. (*mil. mar.*) to blockade: — *i nemici*, to blockade the enemy || **imbottigliàrsi**, *v.r.* to get caught in a traffic-jam.

imbottíre, *v.t.* 1. to stuff, to pad, to wad, to quilt:

— *un cappotto*, to wad (*o* to quilt) an overcoat; — *una coperta*, to quilt a blanket; — *un cuscino di paglia*, to stuff a cushion with straw; — *le pareti*, to pad the walls 2. *fig.* to cram, to stuff: — *la testa di uno studente per un esame*, to cram a pupil for an examination.

imbottíta, *s.f.* quilt.

imbottíto, *ag.* stuffed, padded, wadded: *cappotto* —, wadded overcoat; *coperta imbottita*, quilt; *pareti imbottite*, padded walls; *sedile* —, padded seat.

imbottíto, *s.m.*, **imbottitúra**, *s.f.* stuffing, padding; (*per abiti*) wadding; quilting.

imbovinàre, *v.t.* (*agr.*) to spread (a field) with dung.

imbozzacchíre, *v.i.* to wither (away, up), to shrivel (up) (anche *fig.*).

imbozzimàre, *v.t.* 1. (*ind. tessile*) to size, to cover with size 2. (*sporcare*) to soil, to smear || **imbozzimàrsi**, *v.r.* (*scherz.*) (*imbellettarsi*) to make (oneself) up; to paint one's face.

imbozzimatúra, *s.f.* sizing.

imbràca, *s.f.* 1. (*fune per sollevare un carico, cintura di sostegno*) sling 2. (*parte dei finimenti*) breeching.

imbracàre, *v.t.* 1. (*mettere una cintura di sostegno a*) to sling 2. (*un cavallo*) to harness (a horse) with its breeching 3. (*mettere le brache a*) to breech 4. (*un cannone*) to breech.

imbracatúra, *s.f.* 1. (*l'imbracare*) slinging 2. (*fune, cinghia*) sling 3. (*aer.*) (*bretelle di un paracadute*) harness.

imbracciàre, *v.t.* to put (sthg.) on one's arm; (*il fucile*) to bring (a rifle) to firing position; (*lo scudo*) to put on (a shield).

imbracciatúra, *s.f.* sling; (*di fucile*) rifle-sling.

imbrachettàre, *v.t.* 1. (*un bambino*) to breech 2. (*un libro*) to fix a loose page (with stiff paper).

imbrancàre, *v.t.*, **imbrancàrsi**, *v.r.* to herd (anche *fig.*).

imbrandíre, *v.t.* to brandish.

imbrattacàrte, *s.c.* (*spreg.*) scribbler.

imbrattaménto, *s.m.* soiling, staining, smearing.

imbrattamóndo, *s.m.* 1. (*guastamestieri*) bungler, muddler, botcher 2. (*imbroglione*) swindler, cheater.

imbrattamúri, *s.m.* (*spreg.*) dauber, bad painter.

imbrattàre, *v.t.* to soil, to dirty, to stain, to smear, to smudge; (*d'inchiostro*) to blot || **imbrattàrsi**, *v.r.* to soil oneself; to stain oneself; to get dirty: — *le mani*, to soil (*o* to stain) one's hands.

imbrattascène, *s.m.* (*spreg.*) fifth-rate actor; (*sl.*) ham (actor).

imbrattatéle, *s.m.* (*spreg.*) dauber, bad painter.

imbrattatóre, *s.m.*, **imbrattatríce**, *s.f.* person who soils, dirties, stains || — *di tele*, dauber.

imbrattatovàglie, *s.m.* (*spreg.*) badly cooked meal.

imbrattatúra, *s.f.* smear.

imbràtto, *s.m.* 1. (*pittura scadente*) daub; (*scritto di poco valore*) scribble 2. (*cibo che si dà ai suini*) pigwash, hog-wash.

imbrecciàre, *v.t.* (*coprire di ghiaia*) to gravel, to strew with gravel.

imbrecciàta, *s.f.* layer of gravel.

imbrèntina, *s.f.* (*bot.*) rock-rose.

imbriacàre, *e derivati*, *V.* **ubriacàre**, *e derivati*.

imbricconíre, *v.t.* to make a rogue of (s.o.) || **imbricconírsi**, *v.r.* to become a rogue.

imbrífero, *ag.* rain-collecting: *bacino* —, catchment-basin.

imbrigàre, *v.t.* 1. to give trouble to (s.o.) 2. (*imbrogliare*) to cheat, to swindle || *v.i.*, **imbrigàrsi**, *v.r.* to interfere (with sthg.), to meddle (with sthg.).

imbrigliaménto, *s.m.* 1. bridling, curbing 2. *fig.* (*freno*) restraint, bridling, curbing.

imbrigliàre, *v.t.* to bridle: — *un cavallo*, to bridle a horse 2. *fig.* (*frenare*) to bridle, to curb; to restrain, to keep in check: — *le proprie ambizioni*, to bridle one's ambitions.

imbroccàre, *v.t.* 1. to hit: — *il bersaglio*, to hit the target (*o* the mark) 2. *fig.* to guess || *l'ho imbroccata!*,

I have hit the mark! (*o* I have hit the nail on the head!); *questa volta l'ha imbroccata*, he has hit it this time.

imbrodàre, *v.t.* to soil, to dirty, to stain ‖ **imbrodàrsi**, *v.r.* to soil oneself, to dirty oneself: — *il vestito*, to stain (*o* to dirty) one's dress ‖ *chi si loda s'imbroda*, *prov.* pride goes before a fall.

imbrodolaménto, *s.m.* **1.** soiling **2.** (*macchie*) stains (*pl.*).

imbrodolàre, *V.* **imbrodàre.**

imbrogliàre, *v.t.* **1.** (*ingannare*) to cheat, to swindle; to take in: *egli non è un uomo che si possa* — *facilmente*, he is not a man to be easily taken in **2.** (*confondere*) to muddle, to mix up; to confuse: *ciò che disse mi ha imbrogliato tutte le idee*, what he said has muddled (*o* mixed up) all my ideas; *gli fecero una domanda difficile per imbrogliarlo*, they asked him a difficult question to confuse (*o* to confound) him **3.** (*intricare*) to tangle, to entangle (*anche fig.*) **4.** (*mar.*) to clew up (sails) ‖ **imbrogliàrsi**, *v.r.* **1.** to get confused: *a quella domanda mi imbrogliai*, at that question I got confused **2.** (*intricarsi*) to get tangled, to get entangled (*anche fig.*): *il filo si è tutto imbrogliato*, the thread has got all tangled **3.** (*immischiarsi*) to meddle (with sthg.): *non voglio imbrogliarmi in questa faccenda*, I do not want to meddle with (*o* to become embroiled in) this matter.

imbrogliàto, *ag.* **1.** (*ingannato*) cheated, taken in **2.** (*intricato*) tangled, entangled, intricate; confused: *una faccenda imbrogliata*, a tangled (*o* an intricate) matter **3.** (*perplesso*) perplexed; confused **4.** (*immischiato*) meddled (with sthg.), embroiled.

imbròglio, *s.m.* **1.** (*inganno*) cheat, swindle; fraud; trick: *questo è un vero* —, this is a real cheat; *fare imbrogli a qlcu.*, to cheat (*o* to swindle) s.o. **2.** (*impiccio, difficoltà*) scrape; trouble; difficulty, difficult situation: *cadere in un* —, to get into a scrape; *essere in un* —, to be in a scrape; *togliere ql.cu. da un* —, to get s.o. out of a scrape; *uscire da un* —, to get out of a scrape (*o* out of a difficulty) **3.** (*intrico*) tangle; confusion; mess.

imbrogliòna, *s.f.*, **imbrogliòne**, *s.m.* cheat; swindler, trickster.

imbronciàre, *v.i.*, **imbronciàrsi**, *v.r.* **1.** to sulk, to become sulky; to pout **2.** (*di cielo*) to grow overcast.

imbronciàto, *ag.* **1.** sulky: *essere* —, to be in the sulks (*o* to be sulky) **2.** (*di cielo*) overcast.

imbrunàre, *v.i.* (*poet.*) to grow dark.

imbruníre, *v.t.* (*rendere bruno*) to brown, to make brown ‖ *v.i.* **1.** (*diventar bruno*) to brown **2.** (*oscurarsi*) to get dark, to grow dark, to darken: *incominciava ad* —, it was beginning to get dark.

imbrunire, *s.m.* nightfall, dusk: *sull'* —, at dusk (*o* at nightfall).

imbrutíre, *v.i.*, **imbrutírsi**, *v.r.* to brutalize; to become a brute.

imbruttíre, *v.t.* **1.** to make ugly **2.** (*rovinare la bellezza di*) to mar, to spoil ¦the beauty of (s.o., sthg.) ‖ *v.i.*, **imbruttírsi**, *v.r.* to grow ugly, to become ugly.

imbubbolàre, *v.t.* (*ingannare*) to deceive, to cheat; to tell (s.o.) fibs ‖ **imbubbolàrsi**, *v.r.* (*infischiarsi*) take no notice; not to care (for s.o.), sthg.).

imbucàre, *v.t.* **1.** (*impostare*) to post: — *una lettera*, to post a letter **2.** (*mettere in un buco*) to put into a hole ‖ **imbucàrsi**, *v.r.* (*nascondersi*) to hide.

imbudellàre, *v.t.* to stuff (sthg.) into sausage-skins.

imbuíre, *v.i.* to become silly.

imbullettàre, *v.t.* to fasten with tacks.

imburràre, *v.t.* to butter, to spread with butter.

imbuscheràrsi, *v.r.* (*volg.*) (*infischiarsi*) to take no notice; not to care a rap (for s.o., sthg.).

imbussolàre, *v.t.* to put into a (ballot-)box.

imbutifórme, *ag.* funnel-shaped.

imbúto, *s.m.* funnel.

imbuzzàre, *v.t.* to cram; to overfeed.

Imène, *no.pr.m.* (*mit.*) Hymen ‖ **imène**, *s.m.* (*anat.*) hymen.

Imenèo, *no.pr.m.* (*mit.*) Hymen ‖ **imenèo**, *s.m.* **1.** (*inno nuziale*) hymeneal, wedding-song **2.** *pl.* (*nozze*) hymeneals; nuptials; wedding (*sing.*).

imenòttero, *s.m.* (*entom.*) hymenopteron (*pl.* hymenoptera).

Imètto, *no.pr.m.* (*geog.*) Hymettus.

imitàbile, *ag.* imitable.

imitàre, *v.t.* **1.** (*prendere a modello*) to imitate; (*scimmiottare*) to ape **2.** (*con gesti, per mettere in ridicolo*) to mimic **3.** (*contraffare*) to counterfeit.

imitatívo, *ag.* imitative: *armonia imitativa*, onomatopoeia; *musica imitativa*, imitative music.

imitatóre, *s.m.* imitator; (*scimmiottatore*) aper.

imitatríce, *s.f.* imitator, imitatress; (*scimmiottatrice*) aper.

imitazióne, *s.f.* imitation: *a* — *di ql.co.*, *di qlcu.*, in imitation (*o* on the model) of s.o., sthg.

immacolataménte, *av.* immaculately, spotlessly.

immacolàto, *ag.* immaculate, spotless ‖ *Immacolata Concezione*, (*teol.*) Immaculate Conception.

immagazzinàre, *v.t.* to store: — *merce, idee*, to store goods, ideas.

immaginàbile, *ag.* imaginable.

immaginàre, *v.t.* **1.** to imagine, to fancy: *come puoi* — *una cosa del genere?*, how can you imagine (*o* fancy) such a thing?; *immagina ora di essere in America*, imagine (*o* fancy) now that you are in America; *non puoi neppure* — *quanto egli sia sciocco*, you can't even imagine how silly he is; *non riesco ad* — *che egli abbia fatto questo*, I can't fancy his doing this **2.** (*supporre*) to imagine, to suppose: *deve essere stato molto difficile*, *immagino*, it must have been very difficult, I imagine; *immagina che egli non te lo dica: che cosa faresti?*, suppose he won't tell you, what would you do?; *lo immagino*, I suppose (*o* imagine) so ‖ **immaginàrsi**, *v.r.* **1.** (*raffigurarsi*) to picture to oneself: *mi piace immaginarmi i luoghi che avete visto*, I like to picture to myself the places you have seen **2.** (*in formule di cortesia*): «*Ti ringrazio moltissimo*», «*Immaginati*», "Thank you very much", "Don't mention it" (*o* "Not at all" *o amer.* "You are welcome").

immaginariaménte, *av.* imaginarily.

immaginàrio, *ag.* **1.** imaginary, fancied: *malato* —, hypochondriac; *mali immaginari*, imaginary ills **2.** (*mat.*) imaginary: *numeri immaginari*, imaginary numbers.

immaginatíva, *s.f.* imagination, imaginativeness; (*fantasia*) fancy: *mancare d'*—, to lack imagination.

immaginatívo, *ag.* imaginative.

immaginazióne, *s.f.* imagination; (*fantasia*) fancy: *un audace volo d'* —, a bold flight of imagination (*o* fancy); *è pura* —!, it is only fancy!.

immàgine, *s.f.* **1.** image: *l'* — *di un oggetto riflessa in uno specchio*, the image of an object reflected in a mirror; *quel ragazzo è proprio l'* — *di suo padre*, that boy is the very image of his father; *vedere la propria* — *riflessa nell'acqua*, to see one's reflection in the water ‖ *a* — *di qlcu.*, in the likeness of s.o. **2.** (*figura disegnata*) figure: *disegnò l'* — *di un gatto*, he drew the figure of a cat **3.** (*immagine sacra*) (sacred) image: *l'* — *della Vergine, di un Santo*, the image of the Virgin, of a Saint **4.** (*figura, impressione nella mente*) image; mental picture, idea, impression: *agitato dall'* — *di una possibile disgrazia*, disquieted by the idea of a possible accident **5.** (*similitudine*) image, metaphor, simile; figure of speech: *una poesia piena d'immagini*, a poem full of images **6.** (*ott. foto.*) image; (*tv.*) image, picture: — *reale*, (*ott.*) virtual (*o* real) image; — *spuria*, (*tv.*) ghost image; — *virtuale*, (*ott.*) virtual image.

immaginétta, *s.f.* (*relig.*) holy picture.

immaginosaménte, *av.* imaginatively.

immaginóso, *ag.* imaginative: *racconto* —, fantastic tale.

immalinconíre, *v.t.* to make melancholy: *questa musica m'immalinconisce,* this music makes me melancholy || *v.i.* to become melancholy, to grow sad, to sadden.

immancàbile, *ag.* **1.** unfailing; inevitable; infallible: *ella mi salutò col suo — sorriso,* she greeted me with her unfailing smile **2.** (*certo*) certain.

immancabilménte, *av.* **1.** unfailingly, infallibly **2.** (*certamente*) certainly.

immàne, *ag.* **1.** (*enorme*) huge, enormous **2.** (*spaventoso*) frightful, appalling; monstrous; tremendous.

immanènte, *ag.* (*fil.*) immanent.

immanentísmo, *s.m.* (*fil.*) immanentism.

immanentísta, *s.c.* (*fil.*) immanentist.

immanènza, *s.f.* (*fil.*) immanence, immanency.

immanità, *s.f.* **1.** (*enormità*) hugeness, immensity **2.** (*orribilità*) frightfulness; monstruosity; enormity **3.** (*crudeltà*) atrociousness.

immantinènte, *av.* immediately, at once.

immarcescíbile, *ag.* (*letter. rar.*) incorruptible.

immateriàle, *ag.* immaterial.

immaterialità, *s.f.* immateriality.

immaterialménte, *av.* immaterially.

immatricolàre, *v.t.,* **immatricolàrsi,** *v.r.* to matriculate.

immatricolazióne, *s.f.* matriculation; (*fam.*) matric.

immaturaménte, *av.* **1.** immaturely **2.** (*prematuramente*) prematurely.

immaturità, *s.f.* immaturity (anche *fig.*).

immatúro, *ag.* **1.** unripe: *frutto —,* unripe fruit **2.** *fig.* immature: *mente immatura,* immature mind; *ragazzo —,* immature boy **3.** (*prematuro*) premature, untimely: *morte immatura,* untimely death; *nascita immatura,* premature birth.

immedesimàre, *v.t.* to unify || **immedesimàrsi,** *v.r.* to identify oneself (with s.o.), to become one (with s.o.): — *nello stato d'animo di qlcu.,* to identify oneself with s.o.'s state of mind.

immediataménte, *av.* immediately, instantly, at once; directly.

immediatézza, *s.f.* immediateness, immediacy.

immediàto, *ag.* immediate: *azione immediata,* immediate action; *bisogni immediati,* immediate needs; *contatto —,* immediate contact; *risposta immediata,* immediate answer.

immedicàbile, *ag.* incurable.

immelanconíre, (*poet.*) per **immalinconíre.**

immelensíre, *v.i.* to become stupid, to grow dull.

immelmàrsi, *v.r.* (*rar.*) to sink in mud.

immemoràbile, *ag.* immemorial: *da tempo —,* from time immemorial.

immèmore, *ag.* forgetful.

immensaménte, *av.* immensely.

immensità, *s.f.* **1.** immensity; vastness; hugeness, enormousness **2.** (*grande quantità*) infinite number.

immènso, *ag.* immense; (*enorme*) vast, huge, enormous.

immensuràbile, *ag.* immeasurable.

immensurabilità, *s.f.* immeasurableness.

immensurabilménte, *av.* immeasurably.

immèrgere, *v.t.* to immerse; to dip; (*tuffare*) to plunge (anche *fig.*): *gli immerse il pugnale nel cuore,* she plunged a dagger into his heart; *immersero la stanza nell'oscurità,* they plunged the room into darkness; — *le mani nell'acqua,* to immerse (o to dip) one's hands in water; — *un pennino nell'inchiostro,* to dip a nib in ink || **immèrgersi,** *v.r.* **1.** to plunge; (*spec. di sottomarino*) to submerge; (*tuffarsi*) to dive: *si immerse per cercar perle,* he dived for pearls; *il sottomarino si immerse,* the submarine submerged; — *nell'acqua,* to plunge into water **2.** *fig.* (*dedicarsi con grande impegno*) to immerse oneself, to plunge, to give oneself up (to sthg.): — *nello studio, nei piaceri,* to give oneself up completely to study, to pleasure.

immeritaménte, immeritataménte, *av.* undeservedly.

immeritàto, *ag.* undeserved, unmerited: *castigo —* unmerited punishment,

immeritévole, *ag.* undeserving: *quel giovane è — della tua fiducia,* that young man is undeserving of (o does not deserve) your trust.

immeritevolménte, *av.* undeservingly, undeservedly.

immersióne, *s.f.* **1.** immersion (anche *fig.*); dip, dipping; plunge (anche *fig.*): *battesimo per —,* baptism by immersion **2.** (*di sottomarino*) submersion; (*di palombaro*) dive **3.** (*mar.*) (*pescaggio*) draught, draft: *linea di —,* water-line **4.** (*astr.*) immersion.

immèrso, *ag.* immersed, dipped, plunged (anche *fig.*): — *in debiti, in difficoltà,* immersed in debts, in difficulties; — *nella lettura,* immersed (o absorbed) in reading.

imméttere, *v.t.* **1.** to admit, to let in; to bring in **2.** (*infondere*) to infuse, to inspire, to instil **3.** — *nel possesso,* (*dir.*) to put in possession || **immétthersi,** *v.r.* to penetrate; to insinuate oneself.

immezzíre, *v.i.* to become overripe; (*marcire*) to go rotten.

immigrànte, *ag.s.c.* immigrant.

immigràre, *v.i.* to immigrate.

immigrazióne, *s.f.* immigration.

imminènte, *ag.* imminent, impending, overhanging; (*prossimo*) (near) at hand: *pericolo —,* imminent (o impending) danger; *gli esami sono imminenti,* the examinations are at hand.

imminènza, *s.f.* imminence; (*prossimità*) nearness.

immischiàre, *v.t.* to involve, to implicate, to mix up: — *qlcu. in un delitto,* to implicate (o to involve) s.o. in a crime; *perchè mi hai immischiato in quell'affare?,* why did you mix me up in that affair? || **immischiàrsi,** *v.r.* to meddle (with sthg.), to interfere (with sthg.), to concern oneself (with sthg.): *non immischiarti in queste cose!,* don't meddle (o interfere) with these things!; *si immischia nei miei affari,* he interferes with my affairs.

immiseríre, *v.t.* to impoverish, to make poor: *la guerra immiserì il paese,* the war impoverished the country || *v.i.,* **immiserírsi,** *v.r.* **1.** (*diventar povero*) to become poor **2.** (*perdere vigore*) to weaken.

immissàrio, *s.m.* affluent, tributary.

immissióne, *s.f.* letting in; (*con la forza*) forcing into, breaking in.

immistióne, *s.f.* (*dir.*) interference, middling.

immisuràbile, *ag.* immeasurable.

immíte, *ag.* (*letter.*) **1.** (*spietato*) pitiless, cruel, harsh **2.** (*di clima*) severe, harsh.

immòbile, *ag.* immobile; immovable; (*fermo*) motionless, still; stationary: *rimanere —,* to remain motionless (o to keep still) || *beni immobili,* immovables (o immovable property o real estate) || *s.m.* immovable: *gli immobili,* immovables (o immovable property o real estate).

immobiliàre, *ag.* immovable: *agenzia —,* estate agency; *contro garanzia —,* (*comm.*) on real security; *credito —,* credit based on real property; *istituto di credito —,* land loan bank; *proprietà —,* real estate (o real property o immovable property); *società —,* building society.

immobilísmo, *s.m.* (*pol.*) ultra-conservatism.

immobilità, *s.f.* immobility, stillness.

immobilitàre, *v.t.* to immobilize || **immobilitàrsi,** *v.r.* to become motionless.

immobilizzàre, *v.t.* **1.** to immobilize: *la folla immobilizzò l'automobile,* the crowd immobilized the car **2.** (*comm.*) to lock up, to tie up: *le banche non dovrebbero — il loro capitale,* banks should not lock up their capital.

immobilizzazióne, *s.f.* **1.** immobilization **2.** (*comm.*) locking up: — *di capitale,* locking up of capital.

immobilménte, *av.* immovably; still, motionlessly.

immoderataménte, *av.* immoderately; (*in modo eccessivo*) excessively.

immoderatézza, *s.f.* immoderateness, immoderation; (*eccesso*) excess, intemperance.

immoderàto, *ag.* immoderate, intemperate; (*eccessivo*) excessive, intemperant.

immodestaménte, *av.* immodestly, shamelessly; (*spudoratamente*) impudently.

immodèstia, *s.f.* immodesty, shamelessness; (*spudoratezza*) impudence.

immodèsto, *ag.* immodest, unblushing, shameless; (*spudorato*) impudent.

immolàre, *v.t.* to immolate, to sacrifice ‖ **immolàrsi**, *v.r.* to immolate oneself, to sacrifice oneself ‖ — *sull'altare della Patria*, to sacrifice oneself upon the altar of one's country.

immolatóre, *s.m.* immolator, sacrificer.

immolazióne, *s.f.* immolation, sacrifice.

immollàre, *v.t.* to soak, to steep, to drench ‖ **immollàrsi**, *v.r.* to get soaked, to get drenched.

immondaménte, *av.* dirtily, uncleanly; filthily, foully.

immondézza, *s.f.* 1. dirtiness, uncleanliness; filthiness, foulness 2. (*spazzatura*) garbage, refuse, rubbish; sweepings (*pl.*).

immondezzàio, *s.m.* 1. garbage heap, heap of dirt 2. *fig.* (*luogo immondo*) filthy place.

immondízia, *s.f.* 1. dirt, filth 2. (*spazzatura*) garbage, refuse, rubbish; sweepings (*pl.*): *bruciatore per l'—*, dust (*o refuse*) destructor (*o incinerator*); *carro per —*, dust-cart; *recipiente per l'—*, dust-bin ‖ *vietato depositare le immondizie*, shoot no rubbish.

immóndo, *ag.* dirty, unclean; filthy, foul: *linguaggio —*, dirty language; *è un essere —*, he is a filthy beast.

immoràle, *ag.* immoral; corrupt; unprincipled (*solo di persona*): *quello che stai facendo è —*, what you are doing is immoral.

immoralità, *s.f.* 1. immorality 2. (*atto immorale*) immoral act.

immoralménte, *av.* immorally.

immorbidíre, *v.t.* to soften ‖ *v.i.* to soften, to become soft.

immorsàre, *v.t.*: — *un cavallo*, to bit (*o* to put the bit to) a horse.

immortalàre, *v.t.* to immortalize ‖ **immortalàrsi**, *v.r.* to become immortal.

immortàle, *ag.* immortal; everlasting, undying, imperishable: *un essere —*, an immortal being; *fama —*, immortal (*o* imperishable) fame ‖ *gli Immortali*, (*gli Dei*) the Immortals.

immortalità, *s.f.* immortality.

immortalménte, *av.* immortally; everlastingly.

immòto, *ag.* motionless, still: *rimase —*, he stood stock-still.

immucidíre, *v.i.* to grow musty.

immúne, *ag.* immune; (*libero*) free; (*esente*) exempt: — *da contagio, da una malattia*, immune from contagion, from a disease; — *da pregiudizi*, free of prejudices.

immunità, *s.f.* immunity; (*libertà*) freedom; (*esenzione*) exemption: — *parlamentare, diplomatica*, parliamentary, diplomatic immunity.

immunizzàre, *v.t.* to immunize, to render immune (against sthg.): *la vaccinazione immunizza contro il vaiolo*, vaccination immunizes against small-pox ‖ **immunizzàrsi**, *v.r.* to immunize oneself, to become immune.

immunizzazióne, *s.f.* immunization.

immusíre, *v.i.* to pout; to sulk, to look sulky, to look black.

immusoníto, *ag.* sulky, sullen, in the sulks, gloomy: *restò — tutto il giorno*, he remained sulky the whole day.

immutàbile, *ag.* immutable, unchangeable, invariable.

immutabilità, *s.f.* immutability, unchangeableness.

immutabilménte, *av.* immutably, unchangeably.

immutàto, *ag.* unchanged.

ímo, *ag.* (*letter.*) low, lowest ‖ *s.m.* (*letter.*) lowest part, deepest part; bottom.

imoscàpo, *s.m.* (*arch.*) base diameter of column.

impaccàre, *v.t.* to pack.

impacchettàre, *v.t.* to package, to make (sthg.) into packages, to make (sthg.) into a parcel.

impacciàre, *v.t.* 1. to hamper, to encumber, to hinder, to impede; to embarrass: *queste maniche lunghe mi impacciano nei movimenti*, these long sleeves hamper my movements (*o* embarrass my movements) 2. (*essere d'incomodo a, disturbare*) to inconvenience, to trouble, to be in the way of (s.o.): *non voglio impacciarti se hai altre cose da fare*, I do not want to inconvenience (*o* to trouble) you if you have other things to do; *queste scatole per terra mi impacciano*, these boxes on the floor are in my way 3. (*imbarazzare*) to embarrass: *la sua presenza mi impaccia*, his presence embarrasses me ‖ **impacciàrsi**, *v.r.* (*immischiarsi*) to meddle (with, in sthg.); to interfere (with sthg.); to concern oneself (with sthg): *non t'impacciare delle cose altrui!*, don't meddle in (*o* concern yourself with) other people's business!.

impacciataménte, *av.* 1. (*in modo goffo*) awkwardly, clumsily 2. (*in modo imbarazzato*) uneasily, uncomfortably.

impacciàto, *ag.* 1. (*goffo*) awkward, clumsy: *maniere impacciate*, awkward (*o* clumsy) manners 2. (*imbarazzato*) embarrassed; uneasy, uncomfortable, ill at ease: *essere, sentirsi —*, to be, to feel embarrassed (*o* uneasy *o* uncomfortable).

impàccio, *s.m.* 1. hindrance, encumbrance, impediment: *portalo via, è più di — che di aiuto*, take it away, it is more of a hindrance (*o* trouble) than a help; *questo lungo mantello mi è di — nei movimenti*, this long cloak is a hindrance to my movements (*o* hampers me in my movements) 2. (*fastidio*) bother, trouble: *tirati via di qui, mi sei di —!*, get away from here, you are in my way! 3. (*ostacolo*) obstacle; (*situazione difficile*) scrape, trouble: *abbiamo incontrato molti impacci*, we have met with many obstacles; *tirare, tirarsi via da un —*, to get out of a scrape (*o* to get out of trouble) 4. (*imbarazzo*) embarrassment.

impàcco, *s.m.* (*med.*) compress: *applicare un — al ginocchio*, to apply a compress to one's knee.

impadronírsi, *v.r.* 1. to take possession (of sthg.), to get hold (of sthg.), to seize (sthg.), to seize (upon sthg.); to appropriate (sthg.): *si impadronì di tutto quanto trovò in casa*, he got hold (*o* took possession) of everything he found in the house; *si impadronirono dei gioielli e li portarono via*, they seized on the jewels and took them away; — *di una città*, to seize a town 2. *fig.* to master (sthg.); to make oneself master (of sthg.): — *di una lingua*, to master a language.

impagàbile, *ag.* priceless, invaluable: *sei —!*, you're priceless!.

impaginàre, *v.t.* (*tip.*) to make up, to page.

impaginatóre, *s.m.*, **impaginatríce**, *s.f.* maker-up, clicker.

impaginatúra, **impaginazióne**, *s.f.* pagination; (*l'impaginare*) making-up, paging.

impagliàre, *v.t.* 1. (*coprire di paglia*) to cover with straw: — *seggiole*, to bottom chairs with straw 2. (*riempire di paglia*) to stuff with straw: — *animali*, to stuff animals with straw.

impagliatíno, *ag.* straw-colour ‖ *s.m.* seat of straw-bottomed chair.

impagliatóre, *s.m.*, **impagliatríce**, *s.f.* 1. (*di seggiole*) chair-mender 2. (*di animali*) stuffer; taxidermist.

impagliatúra, *s.f.* 1. (*di seggiole*) chair-mending 2. (*di animali*) stuffing.

impalaménto, *s.m.* 1. (*antico supplizio*) impalement 2. (*viticultura*) propping up.

impalancàto, *s.m.* palisade.

impalàre, *v.t.* 1. (*infilzare con palo secondo l'antico supplizio*) to impale 2. (*viticultura*) to stake; to prop up ‖ **impalàrsi**, *v.r.* (*scherz.*) to stiffen.

impalàto, *ag.* (*rigido*) stiff: *se ne stava tutto — sulla soglia*, he stood stiffly in the door-way.

impalatúra, impalazióne, *V.* **impalamento.**

impaleaménto, *s.f.* planking.

impaleàre, *v.t.* to plank; (*mettere il pavimento¨a*) to floor; (*mettere il soffitto a*) to ceil.

impaleatúra, *s.f.* 1. planking; (*per pavimento*) flooring; (*per soffitto*) ceiling 2. (*armatura di edificio in costruzione*) scaffolding: *perse la vita cadendo da un'* —, he lost his life falling from a scaffolding 3. (*di albero*) ramification 4. (*di corna di cervo*) antlers (*pl.*) 5. (*struttura*) structure, frame (anche *fig.*).

impallidíre, *v.i.* 1. to turn pale, to grow pale; to blanch: *impallidì dalla paura*, he grew pale with fear 2. (*di luce, stelle, luna*) to grow dim, to grow faint‖ *la sua stella impallidisce*, his star is on the wane 3. (*di colori, ricordi*) to fade: *la memoria di lui impallidì col tempo*, the memory of him faded with the passing of time.

impallinàre, *v.t.* to hit with shot, to shot.

impalmàre, *v.t.* (*letter.*) to marry.

impalmatúra, *s.f.* (*mar.*) splicing, splice.

impalpàbile, *ag.* impalpable: *cipria —*, impalpable face-powder.

impalpabilità, *s.f.* impalpability.

impaludàre, *v.t.* to turn into a swamp, to make swampy ‖ **impaludàrsi**, *v.r.* to become swampy, to turn into a swamp.

impanàre, *v.t.* 1. to cover (sthg.) with bread-crumbs; to bread 2. (*mec.*) to thread: *— una vite*, to thread a screw ‖ **impanàrsi**, *v.r.* (*mec.*) to glaze; (*avvitarsi*) to screw.

impanàto, *ag.* (*cuc.*) 1. covered with bread-crumbs: *cotoletta impanata*, Wiener‍schnitzel 2. (*mec.*) threaded.

impanatúra, *s.f.* 1. (*cuc.*) breading 2. (*mec.*) thread, threading.

impaneàrsi, *v.r.* to act like (s.o.): *— a critico*, to act like a critic.

impaniàre, *v.t.* 1. ‍to lime, to smear with bird-lime 2. *fig.* (*intrappolare*) to ensnare, to entrap, to entangle ‖ *v.i.* **impaniàrsi**, *v.r.* 1. to be caught with lime 2. *fig.* (*essere intrappolato*) to get entangled.

impaniàto, *ag.* 1. limed 2. *fig.* (*intrappolato*) entrapped, entangled, ensnared.

impannàre, *v.t.* 1. (*coprire di stoffa, carta*) to cover with cloth, paper 2. (*ind. tessile*) to fill the warp.

impannàta, *s.f.* window covering.

impantanàre, *v.t.* to turn into a swamp; to make muddy; to bemire ‖ **impantanàrsi**, *v.r.* to sink in the mud, to stick in the mud, to be bemired, to be bogged ‖ *— nei debiti*, to run into debt head over ears (*o* up to eyes).

impaperàrsi, *v.r.* 1. to slip up; (*amer.*) to make a slip 2. (*impappinarsi*) to stammer, to falter.

impappinàrsi, *v.r.* to stammer, to falter.

imparacchiàre, *v.t.* to learn badly.

imparadisàre, *v.t.* to imparadise, to emparadise; to make (s.o.) perfectly happy.

imparagonàbile, *ag.* incomparable.

imparàre, *v.t.* to learn: *— a fare ql.co.*, to learn how to do sthg.; *— a leggere*, to learn reading; *— a memoria*, to learn by heart ‖ *non è mai troppo tardi per —*, live and learn ‖ *— a proprie spese*, to learn to one's cost ‖ *— a vivere*, to learn manners.

imparatíccio, *s.m.* 1. (*cosa imparata male*) thing badly learned 2. (*lavoro da principiante*) beginner's work 3. (*saggio di ricamo*) sampler.

impareggiàbile, *ag.* incomparable, unparalleled.

impareggiabilménte, *av.* incomparably.

imparentàrsi, *v.r.* to become related (to s.o.): *non vorrei imparentarmi con una persona simile*, I should

not like to become related to such a person; *— con una famiglia*, to marry into a family.

ímpari, *ag.* 1. (*disuguale*) unequal, uneven: *forze —*, unequal forces; *la sua fu una lotta —*, his was an uneven struggle 2. (*inadeguato*) inadequate, unfit (for sthg.): *è — a quel duro compito*, he is not up to that hard task 3. (*dispari*) odd.

imparidigitàto, *ag.* (*zool.*) imparidigitate.

imparipennàto, *ag.* (*bot.*) imparipinnate.

imparisíllabo, *ag.s.m.* (*gram.*) imparisyllabic.

imparità, *s.f.* inequality; disparity.

imparruccàre, *v.t.* to bewig ‖ **imparruccàrsi**, *v.r.* to put on a wig.

imparruccàto, *ag.* periwigged, bewigged.

impartíbile, *ag.* impartible; indivisible.

impartíre, *v.t.* to impart; (*concedere*) to bestow, to grant; (*dare*) to give: *— la benedizione*, (*eccl.*) to give the blessing; *— un ordine a qlcu.*, to give an order to s.o.

imparziàle, *ag.* impartial, equitable, fair: *giudizio —*, fair judgement.

imparzialità, *s.f.* impartiality, equitableness, fairness.

imparzialménte, *av.* impartially, equitably, fairly.

impasse, *s.f.* impasse: *giungere ad un' —*, to come to a deadlock; *trovarsi in un' —*, to find oneself in a dilemma (*o* in a fix *o* in a hole).

impassíbile, *ag.* impassible, impassive, unmoved: *rimase — alla notizia*, he remained impassive at the news.

impassibilità, *s.f.* impassibility, impassiveness.

impassibilménte, *av.* impassibly, impassively.

impastàre, *v.t.* 1. (*cuc.*) to knead, to work into dough 2. (*ridurre in pasta*) to pug, to make into a paste 3. (*coprire di pasta, attaccare con pasta*) to paste 4. (*pitt.*) to impaste; to lay (colours) thickly 5. (*mus.*) to slur.

impastàto, *ag.* 1. kneaded 2. (*ridotto in pasta*) made into a paste 3. (*coperto di pasta*) covered with paste; (*incollato*) pasted 4. *fig.* full: *una persona impastata di pregiudizi, di bugie*, a person full of prejudices, of lies; *ragazzo — di sonno*, a drowsy boy ‖ *essere ben —*, to be well knit.

impastatóre, *s.m.* (*chi impasta pane, ecc.*) kneader.

impastatríce, *s.f.* 1. (*chi impasta pane, ecc.*) kneader 2. (*mec.*) (*per pane, ecc.*) kneading machine, mixer 3. (*mec. edil.*) (*di cemento*) cement mixer; (*di malta*) mortar mixing machine.

impastatúra, *s.f.* kneading of dough.

impasticciàre, *v.t.* 1. (*cuc.*) to mix up 2. *fig.* to botch; to bungle, to make a mess of (sthg.).

impàsto, *s.m.* 1. (*cuc.*) (*pasta di pane*) dough; (*l'impastare*) kneading 2. (*miscuglio*) mixture, medley: *è un — di buone e cattive qualità*, he is a mixture of good and bad qualities 3. (*pitt.*) "impasto".

impastocchiàre, *v.t.* to cheat.

impastoiàre, *v.t.* 1. to shackle, to clog 2. *fig.* (*ostacolare*) to impede, to fetter; to hinder, to hamper.

impastranàrsi, *v.r.* to muffle oneself up in a cloak.

impataccàre, *v.t.* to soil, to daub.

impattàre, *v.t.* to be quits with (s.o.); to get even with (s.o.).

impauríre, *v.t.* to frighten ‖ *v.i.*, **impaurírsi**, *v.r.* to get frightened: *si impaurì a morte*, she was nearly frightened to death (*o* out of her life).

impaurìto, *ag.* frightened; afraid: *sguardo, aspetto —*, fearful look.

impavesàre, *v.t.* to dress (with flags).

impavesàta, *s.f.* (*mar.*) 1. (*bastingaggio*) quarter boards (*pl.*), topgallant bulwarks (*pl.*) 2. (*fila di bandierine*) bunting.

impavesatóre, *s.f.* (*mar.*) top gallant bulwark.

impavidaménte, *av.* fearlessly.

impàvido, *ag.* fearless, undaunted.

impazientàre, *V.* **impazientíre.**

impaziènte, *ag.* impatient: *essere — di fare ql.co.*,

to be impatient to do sthg. (o to be looking forward to doing sthg).

impazienteménte, *av.* impatiently.

impazientíre, *v.i.,* **impazientírsi,** *v.r.* to lose one's patience.

impazientíto, *ag.* annoyed; irritated; vexed; out of patience.

impaziènza, *s.f.* impatience; (*ansietà*) anxiety: *con —,* impatiently (o anxiously): *aspetto con — il suo arrivo,* I am looking forward to his arrival; *al suo apparire ebbe un gesto d'—,* when he appeared she gave a gesture of impatience.

impazzàre, *v.i.* to go mad || *il carnevale impazzava nelle strade,* the carnival was at its height in the streets.

impazzàta, all', *l.av.* madly; rashly; headlong: *correre all'—,* to rush headlong.

impazziménto, *s.m.* 1. (*l'impazzire*) going mad 2. (*cosa che tormenta, infastidisce*) nuisance, trouble.

impazzíre, *v.i.* to go mad; to become insane; to go out of one's mind; (*sl.*) to go off one's nut: *impazzì dal dolore,* he went mad with pain; *egli impazzisce per il jazz,* he is mad about jazz; *far — qlcu.,* to drive s.o. mad: *quella ragazza mi fa —,* that girl drives me mad; *sono impazzito per ricordarmi il suo nome,* I have racked (o cudgelled) my brains to remember his name.

impazzíto, *ag.* mad, insane.

impeccàbile, *ag.* faultless; impeccable; flawless.

impeccabilità, *s.f.* faultlessness; impeccability.

impeccabilménte, *av.* faultlessly; impeccably.

impeciàre, *v.t.* to pitch; to tar; to coat with pitch, to smear with tar || **impeciàrsi,** *v.r.* 1. to smear oneself with pitch 2. *fig.* (*invischiarsi*) to get entangled; to get mixed up.

impeciatúra, *s.f.* 1. pitching; tarring 2. *fig.* entanglement.

impecoríre, *v.t.* to make sheepish || *v.i.* to become sheepish, to become as stupid as a sheep.

impedantíre, *v.i.* to become pedant.

impedènza, *s.f.* (*elett.*) impedance.

impedíbile, *ag.* that can be hindered.

impediménta, *s.f.pl.* (*mil.*) impedimenta.

impediménto, *s.m.* 1. impediment, hindrance, drawback: *un — al progresso,* an impediment (o a hindrance) to progress 2. (*ostacolo*) obstacle: *dovemmo superare molti impedimenti,* we had to overcome many obstacles (o difficulties) 3. (*dir.*) bar 4. *pl.* (*mil.*) impedimenta.

impedíre, *v.t.* 1. to prevent (s.o. from doing), to keep (s.o. from doing), to stop (s.o. from doing): *ciò non impedisce che sia un ladro,* this does not prevent him from being a thief; *dovresti impedirgli di parlare,* you should prevent (o stop) him from speaking; *non so come impedirgli di farlo,* I don't know how to stop him from doing it; *questo m'impedì di partire,* this prevented me (from) leaving (o prevented my leaving); *il rumore mi impediva di dormire,* the noise kept me from sleeping; *— un matrimonio,* to prevent a marriage 2. (*ostruire*) to obstruct, to stop, to bar: *questo muro impedisce la vista del mare,* this wall obstructs the view of the sea; *— il passo,* to obstruct (o to bar) the way 3. (*impacciare*) to hinder, to hamper, to impede: *questa gonna stretta mi impedisce i movimenti,* this tight skirt hampers (o hinders) my movements.

impeditívo, *ag.* obstructive; hindering; impeditive.

impedíto, *ag.* 1. (*occupato*) engaged 2. (*inabilitato*): *ho questo braccio —,* I can't move this arm very well; *avere la lingua impedita,* to have an impediment in one's speech.

impegnàre, *v.t.* 1. (*dare in pegno*) to pawn, to pledge: *— i propri gioielli,* to pawn one's jewels 2. (*promettere, obbligare*) to pledge, to pawn, to engage: *risposte che non impegnano,* non-committal answers; *— il proprio onore, la propria parola,* to pledge (o to plight) one's honour, one's word 3. (*vincolare*) to bind: *questa lettera non ti impegna,* this letter does not bind you; *questo*

ti impegna a rimanere per due anni, this binds you to remain for two years 4. (*prenotare, ingaggiare*) to engage, to hire, to book: *era impegnato in una conversazione,* he was engaged in conversation; *ho impegnato una carrozza per un'ora,* I have hired a coach for an hour; *l'ho impegnato come autista,* I have engaged him as a chauffeur; *— un posto,* to book a seat; *— una ragazza per un valzer,* to engage a girl for a waltz 5. (*assorbire*) to take up: *questo lavoro impegna tutto il mio tempo,* this work takes up all my time 6. (*intraprendere*) to begin, to engage: *— una discussione, una battaglia con qlcu.,* to begin (o to engage in) a discussion, a fight with s.o. || **impegnàrsi,** *v.r.* 1. to engage (oneself), to pledge oneself, to commit oneself, to bind oneself, to undertake: *mi impegno a procurare il denaro,* I engage (o bind) myself to provide the money; *non posso impegnarmi a farlo da solo,* I cannot engage (o undertake) to do that by myself; *si impegnò a pagare le dieci sterline,* he bound himself to pay the ten pounds; *in una lite con qlcu.,* to engage in a quarrel with s.o. || *— a fondo,* to commit oneself completeiy 2. (*farsi garante*) to go bail; to stand surety: *— per qlcu.,* to go bail (o to stand surety) for s.o. 3. (*essere, rimanere coinvolto*) to be involved, to get involved; to be entangled, to get entangled: *non voglio impegnarmi in una faccenda del genere,* I don't want to get involved in such a matter; *mi sono troppo impegnato per ritirarmi,* I have gone too far (o I am too deeply entangled) to draw back.

impegnatívo, *ag.* binding; compelling: *una promessa impegnativa,* a binding promise.

impegnàto, *ag.* 1. engaged: *era — con il suo insegnante, con la corrispondenza, nella conversazione,* he was engaged with his teacher, with his correspondence, in conversation; *non posso venire, sono —!,* I cannot come, I am engaged!; *il mio tempo è tutto —,* my time is all engaged (o taken up); *queste automobili sono già impegnate,* these cars are already engaged (o booked); *stasera non posso, sono troppo —,* tonight I can't, I am too busy 2. (*vincolato*) bound; engaged: *mi sento — a farlo,* I feel bound (o engaged) to do it 3. (*dato in pegno*) pawned; pledged 4. (*di scrittore, artista*) committed: *poeta —,* committed poet 5. (*coinvolto*) involved; entangled.

impégno, *s.m.* 1. engagement: *impegni di lavoro,* business engagements; *ho molti impegni per domani,* I have many engagements for tomorrow; *adempiere un —,* to meet (o to fulfil) an engagement; *mancare a un —,* to break an engagement; *mantenere un —,* to keep an engagement; *prendere un —,* to take an engagement 2. (*promessa*) promise, pledge: *con — di segretezza,* under pledge of secrecy 3. (*comm.*) obligation: *soddisfare i propri impegni,* to meet one's obligations 4. (*applicazione, cura, diligenza*) care, zeal, diligence: *fa tutto con molto —,* he does everything with great care.

impegolàre, *v.t.* to pitch, to tar, to smear with tar || **impegolàrsi,** *v.r.* 1.to smear oneself with pitch 2. *fig.* (*invischiarsi*) to get involved, to get mixed up: *mi sono impegolato in una brutta faccenda,* I've got mixed up in a nasty piece of business.

impelagàrsi, *v.r.* to get involved; to get into trouble: *non impelagarti in queste cose,* don't get involved in these things.

impelàre, *v.t.* to cover with hair: *quel cane mi ha tutto impelato,* that dog has covered me with hair || **impelàrsi,** *v.r.* to get covered with hair.

impellènte, *ag.* impellent, impelling; pressing; urgent: *bisogno —,* impelling need.

impèllere, *v.t.* to impel, to urge, to drive.

impellicciàre, *v.t.* 1. to fur, to wrap up in fur 2. (*impiallacciare*) to veneer.

impellicciatúra, *V.* **impiallacciatúra.**

impenetràbile, *ag.* impenetrable (anche *fig.*): *— all'acqua,* water-tight; *— all'aria,* air-tight; *una fore-*

sta]—, an impenetrable (*o* impervious) forest; *mistero* —, impenetrable (unfathomable) mystery.

impenetrabilità, *s.f.* impenetrableness, impenetrability.

impenetrabilménte, *av.* impenetrably.

impenitènte, *ag.* impenitent, unrepentant; (*incorreggibile*) incorrigible: *un Don Giovanni* —, an impenitent Don Juan.

impenitènza, *s.f.* impenitence: *morire nell'*— *finale*, to die in final impenitence.

impennacchiàre, *v.t.* to crest.

impennàggio, *s.m.* (*aer.*) empennage, tail unit: — *a sbalzo*, cantilever tail planes; — *orizzontale*, horizontal tail surface; — *verticale*, rudder.

impennàre, *v.t.* (*fornire di penne*) to feather ‖ — *le ali alla mente*, to give wings to one's mind ‖ *v.i.* (*rar.*) (*prendere la penna*) to take up one's pen ‖ **impennàrsi**, *v.r.* 1. (*coprirsi di penne*) to fledge 2. (*di cavallo*) to rear, to prance 3. (*aer.*) to mount up, to climb, to pitch 4. (*adirarsi, reagire irosamente*) to bristle; to fire up.

impennàta, *s.f.* 1. (*di cavallo*) rearing, prance 2. (*aer.*) climbing 3. (*scatto d'ira, reazione irosa*) bristling.

impennàto, *ag.* 1. (*alato*) winged 2. (*impennacchiato*) feathered.

impensàbile, *ag.* unthinkable, unimaginable.

impensàta, all', *l. av.* (*improvvisamente*) suddenly; (*inaspettatamente*) unexpectedly, unawares.

impensataménte, *av.* unexpectedly, unawares.

impensàto, *ag.* 1. (*non pensato*) unthought of 2. (*inaspettato*) unforeseen, unexpected.

impensieríre, *v.t.* to worry, to cause anxiety to (s.o.): *il suo silenzio mi impensierisce*, his silence worries me ‖ **impensierírsi**, *v.r.* to worry (about sthg.); to get anxious (about sthg.): *se le dici queste cose, ella si impensierirà*, if you tell her these things she will worry.

impensieríto, *ag.* worried (about sthg.), anxious (about sthg.): *ti vedo piuttosto* —, you look rather anxious.

impepàre, *v.t.* to pepper.

imperànte, *ag.* 1. (*regnante*) reigning: *dinastia* —, reigning dynasty 2. (*dominante*) ruling, prevailing.

imperàre, *v.i.* to rule (over sthg.), to reign (over sthg.): *il silenzio imperava su tutto*, silence reigned supreme.

imperatívo, *ag.* 1. imperative, authoritative; peremptory: *un comando* —, a peremptory order; *in modo* —, in an imperative (*o* authoritative) manner 2. (*gram.*) imperative: *modo* —, imperative (mood) ‖ *s.m.* 1. (*fil.*) imperative: *l'*— *categorico*, the categorical imperative 2. (*gram.*) imperative (mood).

imperatóre, *s.m.* emperor: *l'*— *Guglielmo II*, the Emperor William II.

imperatòrio, *ag.* imperatorial: *insegne imperatorie*, imperatorial insignia.

imperatríce, *s.f.* empress.

impercettíbile, *ag.* imperceptible: *una differenza* —, an imperceptible difference.

impercettibilità, *s.f.* imperceptibility.

impercettibilménte, *av.* imperceptibly.

imperciocché, *cong.* (*arc.*) inasmuch as, since, as, because.

imperdonàbile, *ag.* unpardonable: *debolezza* —, unpardonable weakness.

imperdonabilménte, *av.* unpardonably.

imperfettaménte, *av.* imperfectly.

imperfètto, *ag.* 1. imperfect, faulty 2. (*gram.*) imperfect ‖ *s.m.* (*gram.*) imperfect (tense).

imperfezióne, *s.f.* imperfection; flaw; defect; fault: — *fisica*, physical imperfection; *un'*— *nella stoffa*, a defect in the cloth; *c'è un'*— *nel vetro*, there is a flaw in the glass.

imperiàle[1], *ag.* imperial: *Sua Maestà Imperiale*, His Imperial Majesty ‖ *gli Imperiali*, (*st.*) the Imperials.

imperiàle[2], *s.m.* (*di una vettura*) imperial, top; (*di carrozza ferroviaria*) roof: — *ad arco*, (*ferr.*) arched roof.

imperialísmo, *s.m.* imperialism.

imperialísta, *s.c.* imperialist.

imperialístico, *ag.* imperialistic: *ambizioni imperialistiche*, imperialistic ambitions.

imperialménte, *av.* imperially.

impèrio, *s.m.* (*letter.*) 1. (*comando*) command; (*autorità*) authority 2. (*impero*) empire.

imperiosaménte, *av.* imperiously; peremptorily; authoritatively.

imperiosità, *s.f.* peremptoriness; authoritativeness.

imperióso, *ag.* 1. imperious; peremptory; authoritative: *cipiglio* —, imperious frown 2. (*irresistibile*) irresistible: *un desiderio* —, an irresistible desire.

imperitaménte, *av.* unskilfully.

imperíto, *ag.* unskilled, unskilful, inexpert, inexperienced.

imperitúro, *ag.* (*letter.*) imperishable, everlasting: *mantenere un ricordo* —, to preserve an everlasting memory.

imperízia, *s.f.* unskilfulness, inexperience.

imperlàre, *v.t.* 1. to adorn with pearls 2. *fig.* to pearl, to bead: *la rugiada imperlava le foglie*, the leaves were covered with (*o* pearled by) dew; *il sudore gli imperlava la fronte*, his forehead was beaded with sweat ‖ **imperlàrsi**, *v.r.* 1. to adorn oneself with pearls 2. *fig.* to bead.

impermalíre, *v.i.*, **impermalírsi**, *v.r.* to take offence (at sthg.); to take (sthg.) amiss: *non impermalirti!*, don't take it amiss!; *si impermalisce per ogni cosa*, he takes offence at everything (*o* he is very touchy).

impermalíto, *ag.* offended; resentful.

impermeàbile, *ag.* impermeable: — *all'acqua*, waterproof (*o* watertight); — *all'aria*, air-tight ‖ *s.m.* (*mantello, soprabito impermealizzato*) raincoat, waterproof, mackintosh; (*fam.*) mack; (*di tipo militare*) trench-coat.

impermeabilità, *s.f.* impermeability.

impermeabilizzànte, *ag.* waterproofing.

impermeabilizzàre, *v.t.* to waterproof.

impermeabilizzazióne, *s.f.* waterproofing.

impermutàbile, *ag.* unexchangeable.

impermutabilità, *s.f.* unexchangeability.

impernàre, imperniàre, *v.t.* to pivot, to hinge (anche *fig.*) ‖ **impernàrsi, imperniàrsi**, *v.r.* to pivot, to hinge (anche *fig.*): *tutto quanto dice si impernia su questo punto*, everything he says hinges on (*o* pivots upon) this point.

imperniatúra, *s.f.* (*l'imperniare*) pivoting; (*perno*) pivot.

impèro, *s.m.* 1. empire: *l'*— *britannico*, the British Empire; *mobili di stile* —, Empire furniture; *stabilire il proprio* — *su ql.co.*, to establish one's empire over sthg. 2. (*dominio*) rule; command, control.

imperocché, *cong.* (*arc.*) inasmuch as, since, as, because.

imperscrutàbile, *ag.* inscrutable, impenetrable, unfathomable: *mistero* —, impenetrable mystery.

imperscrutabilità, *s.f.* inscrutableness, inscrutability.

imperscrutabilménte, *av.* inscrutably.

imperseverànte, *ag.* unpersevering, inconstant.

imperseverànza, *s.f.* inconstancy.

impersonàle, *ag.* impersonal: *verbo* —, (*gram.*) impersonal verb.

impersonalità, *s.f.* impersonality.

impersonalménte, *av.* impersonally.

impersonàre, *v.t.* to impersonate, to personify; to symbolize: *Otello impersona la gelosia*, Othello symbolizes jealousy ‖ **impersonàrsi**, *v.r.* (*incarnarsi*) to embody; to take bodily form.

impersuadíbile, impersuasíbile, *ag.* unpersuadable; obstinate, stubborn.

impertèrrito, *ag.* 1. undaunted; (*senza paura*) fearless 2. (*impassibile*) impassive.

impertinènte, *ag.* 1. impertinent, saucy, pert, insolent: *gesto* —, saucy gesture; *persona* —, impertinent fellow **2.** (*dir.*) (*non pertinente*) impertinent.

impertinenteménte, *av.* (*insolentemente*) impertinently, saucily, pertly, insolently.

impertinènza, *s.f.* **1.** impertinence, sauciness, pertness, insolence: *è il colmo dell'*—*!,* it's the height of insolence! **2.** (*azione, detto insolente*) impertinence: *dire delle impertinenze,* to utter impertinences.

imperturbàbile, *ag.* imperturbable, impassive; calm.

imperturbabilità, *s.f.* imperturbability, impassibility, impassiveness; calm.

imperturbabilménte, *av.* imperturbably, impassively; calmly.

imperturbàto, *ag.* imperturbed, impassive; calm: *restare* —, to remain calm and collected.

imperversaménto, *s.m.* raging; (*specialmente di fenomeni atmosferici*) storming.

imperversàre, *v.i.* to rage; to storm: *l'epidemia imperversò a lungo nel paese,* the epidemic raged in the country for a long time; *la tempesta imperversava,* the storm was raging; *il vento imperversa,* the wind is raging (*o* storming).

impèrvio, *ag.* inaccessible, unapproachable, impervious: *sentiero* —, impassable path.

impetígine, *s.f.* (*patol.*) impetigo (*pl.* impetigines).

impetiginóso, *ag.* (*patol.*) impetiginous.

ímpeto, *s.m.* **1.** impetus (*pl.* impetuses); vehemence, impetuosity: *l'*— *delle acque,* the impetus (*o* rush) of the waters; *l'*— *di un attacco,* the vehemence of an attack ‖ *pieno d'*—, full of go ‖ *fare* — *su qlcu.,* to fall upon s.o. **2.** (*impulso*) impulse: *agire d'*—, to act on impulse ‖ *di primo* —, (*dapprima*) at first **3.** (*moto dell'animo*) outburst; transport: *un* — *d'ira,* an outburst of rage; *un* — *di felicità,* a transport of happiness.

impetràbile, *ag.* obtainable (by petition).

impetràre, *v.t.* **1.** (*ottenere supplicando*) to impetrate **2.** (*domandare supplicando*) to beseech: *egli impetrò la grazia dal re,* he besought the king's mercy.

impetratívo, *ag.* impetrative.

impetratòrio, *ag.* impetratory.

impetrazióne, *s.f.* impetration.

impettíto, *ag.* stiff; erect; straight: *se ne andò via tutto* —, he strutted away.

impetuosaménte, *av.***1.** impetuously; violently **2.** (*impulsivamente*) impulsively.

impetuosità, *s.f.* **1.** impetuosity; violence: *l'*— *della corrente lo travolse,* the violence of the stream swept him away **2.** (*impulsività*) impulsiveness.

impetuóso, *ag.* **1.** impetuous; violent: *un torrente* —, an impetuous torrent; *vento* —, impetuous (*o* violent) wind **2.** (*impulsivo*) impetuous; impulsive: *un carattere* —, an impulsive temperament; *una persona impetuosa,* an impetuous (*o* impulsive) person.

impiagàre, *v.t.* to ulcerate ‖ **impiagàrsi,** *v.r.* to become ulcerated.

impiallacciàre, *v.t.* to veneer.

impiallacciatóre, *s.m.* veneerer.

impiallacciatúra, *s.f.* **1.** veneering **2.** (*legno per impiallacciare*) veneer.

impianellàre, *v.t.* to pave (sthg.) with tiles.

impiantàre, *v.t.* **1.** to found, to establish, to set up, to plant: — *un'azienda,* to establish (*o* to set up) a firm; — *una comunità,* to plant a community; — *un'istituzione,* to found an institution **2.** (*comm.*) (*aprire*) to open: — *un conto,* to open an account.

impiantíre, *v.t.* to pave; to floor.

impiantíto, *s.m.* (tiled) floor, flooring; pavement: — *in mattoni,* brick flooring.

impiànto, *s.m.* **1.** plant, installation: — *centrale di ventilazione,*central ventilation system; — *della luce elettrica,* lighting system (*o* plant); — *di alimentazione,* (*di carburante*) fuel system; — *di blocco,* (*ferr.*) interlocking plant; — *di riscaldamento,* heating system (*o* plant); — *di sollevamento,* (*ind.*) hoisting system; — *di sondaggio,* (*miner.*) rig; — *elettrico,* electric installation;

— *idrico,* (*ind.*) waterworks; — *radio,* (*aer.*) radio equipment; *impianti sanitari,* sanitary fittings **2.** (*l'impiantare*) establishment, installation: *l'* — *di una casa commerciale,* the establishment of a business house; *l'* — *di un motore,* the installation of a motor.

impiastracàrte, impiastrafògli, *s.c.* (*spreg.*) scribbler.

impiastraménto, impiastricciaménto, *s.m.* daub; smear.

impiastràre, impiastricciàre, *v.t.* to daub, to smear; (*insudiciare*) to soil: — *un mobile con vernice,* to daub a piece of furniture with paint; — *un muro con annunci pubblicitari,* to plaster a wall with advertisements ‖ **impiastràrsi, impiastricciàrsi,** *v.r.* (*insudiciarsi*) to soil oneself: — *le mani,* to soil one's hands.

impiàstro, *s.m.* **1.** (*med.*) plaster, poultice **2.** (*fig. fam.*) (*seccatore*) bore; nuisance: *sei un* —*!,* (*fam.*) you are a nuisance!.

impiccagióne, *s.f.,* **impiccaménto,** *s.m.* hanging: *l'* — *era comune nel Medioevo,* hanging was common during the Middle Ages.

impiccàre, *v.t.* to hang: *essere impiccato,* to be hanged ‖ **impiccàrsi,** *v.r.* to hang oneself ‖ *ch'io sia impiccato se l'ho visto!,* I'll be hanged if I have seen it! ‖ *impiccati!,* go to hell!.

impiccàto, *ag.* hanged ‖ *stare* —, (*fam.*) to wear a high stiff collar ‖ *s.m.* hanged man.

impiccatóre, *s.m.* hangman (*pl.* hangmen).

impiccatúra, *s.f.* hanging.

impicciàre, *V.* **impacciàre.**

impicciníre, *v.t.* **1.** to make smaller **2.** (*rendere meschino*) to make mean ‖ **impiccinírsi,** *v.r.* **1.** to get smaller **2.** (*diventar meschino*) to become mean.

impíccio, *V.* **impàccio.**

impicciolíre, *V.* **impiccolíre.**

impiccióna, *s.f.,* **impiccióne,** *s.m.* meddler, busybody.

impiccolíre, *v.t.* to make smaller; to diminish, to decrease, to lessen, to reduce ‖ **impiccolírsi,** *v.r.* to get smaller; to diminish; to decrease.

impidocchiàre, impidocchíre, *v.t.* to infest with lice ‖ **impidocchiàrsi, impidocchírsi,** *v.r.* to become infested with lice.

impiegàbile, *ag.* employable; usable.

impiegàre, *v.t.* **1.** to employ, to engage: *l'ho impiegato come giardiniere,* I have employed (*o* engaged) him as a gardener; — *un operaio,* to employ a workman **2.** (*usare*) to employ, to use, to make use of (sthg.): *che cosa impiegate per fare questa colla?,* what do you employ (*o* use) to make this glue?; *non impieghiamo carbone, ma elettricità per riscaldare le nostre case,* we don't make use of coal but of electricity to heat our houses **3.** (*spendere*) to spend: *devi dirmi come impieghi il tuo denaro,* you must tell me how you spend your money; *non sa come* — *il suo tempo,* he doesn't know how to employ (*o* spend) his time; — *male il proprio denaro, il proprio tempo,* to waste one's money, one's time **4.** (*comm.*) (*investire*) to invest: — *il proprio denaro in titoli, in una attività commerciale,* to invest one's money in stocks, in a business ‖ **impiegàrsi,** *v.r.* (*trovare lavoro*) to find a situation, to get a situation: *si è impiegato in una ditta straniera,* he has found a situation (*o fam.* a job) with a foreign firm.

impiegatízio, *ag.* clerical; white-collar (*attributivo*): *classe impiegatizia,* white-collar class; *lavoro* —, clerical work.

impiegàto, *ag.* **1.** employed **2.** (*usato*) employed, used **3.** (*speso*) spent **4.** (*investito*) invested ‖ *s.m.* employee; (*contabile, commesso*) clerk: *gli impiegati di un ufficio, un'azienda,* the staff of an office, a firm.

impiègo, *s.m.* **1.** employment, occupation, situation, position, appointment, post, office, place; (*fam.*) job: *un buon* — *come direttore generale,* a good appointment as general manager; *luogo d'*—, place of employment; *avere un* — *governativo,* to be a government official;

cercare un —, to look for a job; *essere senza* —, to be out of a job (*o* to be unemployed); *fare domanda d'*—, to apply for a position (*o* situation); *ottenere un* — *come segretario privato*, to get a situation as private secretary; *trovare un* —, to find employment (*o* a job) ‖ *cercasi* —, position (*o* situation) wanted 2. (*uso*) employment, use: *l'*— *dell'elettricità*, the employment (*o* use) of electricity 3. (*investimento*) investment: *questo implica un largo* — *di denaro*, this involves a large investment of money.

impietosíre, *v.t.* to move to pity, to touch, to fill with pity: *i lamenti ,del bimbo lo impietosirono*, the wailings of the child moved him to pity ‖ **impietosírsi**, *v.r.* to be moved to pity; to be filled with pity, to be touched: — *di qlcu., di ql.co.*, to pity s.o., sthg.

impietràre, impietríre, *v.t.* to petrify (anche *fig.*): *la spaventosa apparizione lo impietrì*, the dreadful apparition petrified him ‖ *v.i.*, **impietràrsi, impietrírsi**, *v.r.* to petrify, to become petrified (anche *fig.*).

impigliàre, *v.t.* 1. to entangle 2. *fig.* (*irretire*) to entangle, to entrap, to ensnare ‖ **impigliàrsi**, *v.r.* 1. to get entangled, to get caught 2. *fig.* (*rimanere irretito*) to get entangled, to get entrapped, to get ensnared: *finì per* — *in un affare poco pulito*, in the end he got entangled in some shady business.

impigliàto, *ag.* 1. entangled 2. *fig.* (*irretito*) entangled, entrapped, ensnared.

impigríre, *v.t.* to make lazy: *questa vita l'impigrisce sempre di più*, this life makes you lazier and lazier ‖ **impigrírsi**, *v.r.* to become lazy, to grow lazy.

impillaccheràre, *v.t.* to splash with mud ‖ **impillaccheràrsi**, *v.r.* to get splashed with mud: — *il vestito*, to splash one's dress with mud.

impinguaménto, *s.m.* 1. fattening 2. *fig.* (*arricchimento*) enrichment.

impinguàre, *v.t.* 1. to fatten 2. (*arricchire*) to enrich, to make rich ‖ **impinguàrsi**, *v.r.* 1. to fatten, to grow fat 2. *fig.* (*arricchirsi*) to get rich.

impinzàre, *v.t.* to stuff, to cram, to fill: — *qlcu. di cibo*, to stuff (*o* to cram *o* to fill) s.o. with food ‖ **impinzàrsi**, *v.r.* to stuff oneself (with food), to fill oneself (with food): *per lui ogni invito è una buona occasione per* —, any invitation is a good opportunity for him to fill (*o* to stuff) himself with food.

impiombàre, *v.t.* 1. (*sigillare con piombo*) to seal with lead, to plumb 2. (*congiungere intrecciando*) to splice: — *un cavo*, (*mar.*) to splice a cable 3. (*otturare*) to fill, to stop: — *un dente*, to fill a tooth 4. (*coprire di piombo*) to lead, to cover with lead.

impiombatúra, *s.f.* 1. (*sigillatura con piombo*) sealing with lead, plumbing 2. (*di canapi, cavi, ecc.*) splice: — *a occhio*, (*mar.*) eye-splice; — *corta*, (*mar.*) short splice 3. (*otturazione*) filling, stopping 4. (*copertura di piombo*) leading.

impipàrsi, *v.r.* (*volg.*) not to care a rap (about sthg.), not to care a hang (about sthg.): *egli s'impipa di tutto*, he does not care a hang (*o* a hoot *o* two hoots) about anything; *me ne impipo!*, I don't care a hang about it!.

impiumàre, *v.t.* to feather, to adorn with plumes, to adorn with feathers ‖ **impiumàrsi**, *v.r.* 1. (*mettere le penne*) to get fledged 2. (*adornarsi di piume*) to adorn oneself with plumes.

implacàbile, *ag.* implacable, relentless, merciless.

implacabilità, *s.f.* implacability, unrelentingness.

implacabilménte, *av.* implacably, unrelentingly, mercilessly.

implacàto, *ag.* implacable, unrelenting, merciless.

implicàre, *v.t.* 1. to implicate, to involve: *non voglio essere implicato in questa faccenda*, I don't want to be (*o* to get) involved in this matter; *la sua confessione implicava molti suoi complici in quel delitto*, his confession implicated many accomplices of his in that crime; *essere implicato in un assassinio*, to be implicated in a murder 2. (*comportare*) to entail; (*significare*) to imply: *questo implica una grande perdita di tempo*,

this entails (*o* implies) a great waste of time; *questo non implica che egli sia colpevole*, this does not imply that he is guilty.

implicàto, *ag.* 1. implicated, involved 2. (*derivato logicamente*) implied.

implicazióne, *s.f.* implication.

implicitaménte, *av.* implicitly.

implícito, *ag.* implicit: *condizione implicita*, implicit condition.

imploràbile, *ag.* invocable.

imploràte, *ag.* imploring: *con voce* —, in an imploring voice (*o* imploringly).

imploràre, *v.t.* to implore, to entreat, to beseech: *mi implorò perchè non parlassi*, he implored me not to speak; — *ql.co. da qlcu.*, to implore (*o* to beseech) s.o. for sthg.

implorazióne, *s.f.* entreaty, supplication.

implúme, *ag.* (*letter.*) featherless, unfledged.

implúvio, *s.m.* 1. (*archeol.*) impluvium (*pl.* impluvia) 2. (*edil.*) valley.

impoètico, *ag.* unpoetical.

impoliticaménte, *av.* 1. impolitic(al)ly, unpolitically 2. (*imprudentemente*) unwisely; imprudently.

impolítico, *ag.* 1. impolitic, unpolitic: *una mossa impolitica*, an unpolitic step 2. (*imprudente*) unwise; imprudent.

impollinàre, *v.t.* (*bot.*) to pollinate.

impollinazióne, *s.f.* (*bot.*) pollination.

impolpàre, *v.t.* 1. (*ingrassare*) to fatten 2. *fig.* (*riempire*) to stuff: — *un articolo di citazioni*, to stuff an article with quotations ‖ *v.i.*, **impolpàrsi**, *v.r.* (*ingrassare*) to put on flesh, to fatten.

impoltroníre, *v.t.* to make lazy ‖ **impoltronírsi**, *v.r.* to become lazy, to get lazy.

impolveràre, *v.t.* to cover with dust ‖ **impolveràrsi**, *v.r.* to get dusty, to get covered with dust.

impolveràto, *ag.* dusty; covered with dust (*predicativo*): *questi mobili sono tutti impolverati*, this furniture is all covered with dust.

impomatàre, *v.t.* to pomade; (*fam.*) to smarm down ‖ **impomatàrsi**, *v.r.* to put pomade on one's hair; (*fam.*) to smarm one's hair down.

impomatàto, *ag.* pomaded; (*fam.*) smarmed down: *quel bellimbusto dai capelli impomatati*, that dandified young man with pomaded hair (*o* with his hair smarmed down).

impomiciàre, *v.t.* to pumice, to rub with pumice -stone, to clean with pumice-stone.

imponderàbile, *ag.s.m.* imponderable.

imponderabilità, *s.f.* imponderability; imponderableness.

imponderàto, *ag.* 1. (*non soppesato*) unweighed 2. (*impensato*) unthought of.

imponènte, *ag.* imposing, stately, grand, majestic: *un edificio* —, an imposing (*o* stately) building.

imponènza, *s.f.* grandeur, magnificence, majesty.

imponíbile, *ag.* taxable; rateable: *reddito* —, taxable (*o* assessable) income; *valore* —, rateable value ‖ *s.m.* taxable income; assessable income; taxables (*pl.*).

imponibilità, *s.f.* taxability.

impopolàre, *ag.* unpopular: *misure impopolari*, unpopular measures; *rendersi* —, to make oneself unpopular.

impopolarità, *s.f.* unpopularity.

imporporàre, *v.t.* to dye purple ‖ **imporporàrsi**, *v.r.* to redden, to blush: *il giovanotto, a quelle parole, s'imporporò*, at those words the young man blushed.

imporràre, *v.i.* to grow warty; (*imputridire*)$\frac{\overline{1}}{2}$ to go bad.

impórre, *v.t.* 1. to impose (anche *fig.*): *il cardinale ci impose le mani sulla testa*, the cardinal imposed his hands on our heads; — *un compito, un obbligo*, to impose a task, an obligation; — *la propria compagnia, volontà a qlcu.*, to impose one's company, will on s.o.; — *una tassa a qlcu.*, to impose (*o* to lay *o* to levy) a tax on s.o. 2. (*ordinare*) to order, to command: *mi impose* *di venire*, he ordered me to come; — *silenzio*, to command silence **3.** (*dare*) to give, to assign: *al neonato fu imposto il nome di Giovanni*, the new-born child was given the name of John **4.** (*ispirare*) to command, to inspire: *le sue sofferenze ci impongono comprensione e rispetto*, his sufferings command our sympathy an l respect ‖ **impórsi**, *v.r.* **1.** to impose oneself (on s.o., sthg.); to dominate (s.o., sthg.); to be overbearing: *egli si imponeva a tutti i suoi compagni per la forza di volontà*, he dominated all his school-fellows owing to his strong will; *non devi importi, se non ti vogliono!*, you must not impose yourself, if they do not want you! **2.** (*farsi rispettare*) to make oneself respected: *quell'insegnante non sa* —, that teacher cannot make himself respected **3.** (*aver successo*) to become popular, to be popular, to have success, to be a success: *sono certo che egli si imporrà come cantante lirico*, I am sure that he will be very popular as a lirical singer; *le sue teorie s'imposero*, his theories became very popular (*o* were a success) **4.** (*rendersi necessario*) to become necessary: *s'impose un cambiamento*, a change became necessary **5.** (*spor.*) to win.

imporríre, *v.i.* to grow warty; (*imputridire*) to go bad.

importàbile, *ag.* (*comm.*) importable: *derrate importabili dall'estero*, commodities that may be imported from abroad.

importànte, *ag.* important, weighty; momentous: *un argomento* —, an important subject; *una persona molto* —, a very important person; *un segreto importantissimo*, a top secret ‖ *s.m.* important thing, (main) point: *l'* — *è che egli non rifiuti*, the most important thing is that he should not refuse; *questo è l'—!*, this is the (main) point!.

importànza, *s.f.* importance, weight, significance: *l'* — *delle sue parole*, the importance of his words; *una cosa di grande, poca, nessuna* —, a thing of great, little, no importance (*o* moment *o* consequence); *di capitale* —, of paramount importance; *attribuire, dare* — *a ql.co.*, to attach importance to sthg.; *darsi (aria d')* —, to give oneself airs.

importàre, *v.t.* **1.** (*comm.*) to import, to introduce: *merce dall'estero*, to import goods from abroad **2.** (*implicare*) to imply, to involve, to mean: *questo importa una grave spesa*, this implies a heavy expense **3.** (*richiedere*) to require: *questo importa molto tempo ed una grave perdita*, this requires a long time and a heavy loss ‖ *v.i.* **1.** (*costare*) to cost, to amount: *quanto importa?*, how much does it cost? (*o* how much is it? *o* how much does it amount to?) **2.** (*aver peso, valore*) to matter, to be of importance, to be of consequence, to signify: *che cosa importa?*, what does it matter?; *non gli importa della sua famiglia*, he doesn't care for his family; *non importa!*, it doesn't matter! (*o* never mind!); *non me ne importa!*, I don't care!: *non me ne importa niente!*, I don't care for it in the least!; *queste cose non importano*, these things do not matter (*o* are of no importance) **3.** (*essere necessario*) to be necessary: *non importa che tu venga*, it is not necessary that you should come (*o* it is not necessary for you to come).

importatóre, *s.m.*, **importatríce**, *s.f.* importer.

importazióne, *s.f.* importation, importing; import: *l'* — *della seta*, the importation of silk; *le importazioni e le esportazioni*, imports and exports; *articoli d'*—, articles of importation (*o* import-articles); *casa d'*—, importing house; *certificato d'*—, import certificate; *commercio d'*—, import-trade; *dazio d'*—, import duty.

impòrto, *s.m.* amount; cost: — *approssimativo, lordo, netto*, rough, gross, net amount.

importunaménte, *av.* **1.** (*insistentemente*) importunately; (*fastidiosamente*) troublesomely **2.** (*intempestivamente*) untimely.

importunàre, *v.t.* to importune; to bore, to annoy, to bother: *non importunarlo con le tue chiacchiere!*, do not bother him with your gossip!.

importunità, *s.f.* **1.** (*insistenza*) importunity; (*fastidio*) troublesomeness **2.** (*intempestività*) untimeliness.

importúno, *ag.* **1.** (*insistente*) importunate; (*fastidioso*) boring, bothersome, annoying, troublesome, tiresome: *le tue continue domande ti rendono* —, your frequent questions make you a bore **2.** (*intempestivo*) untimely ‖ *s.m.* intruder, pestering fellow.

imposizióne, *s.f.* **1.** imposition: *l'* — *delle mani*, (*eccl.*) the imposition of hands; *l'* — *del nome*, the assigning of the name **2.** (*ordine*) order, command.

impossessàrsi, *V.* **impadronírsi**.

impossíbile, *ag.* **1.** impossible: *una supposizione* —, an impossible supposition; *ciò è* —, this is impossible; *è* — *che egli venga*, it is impossible for him to come **2.** (*assurdo*) extravagant, absurd, impossible: *è un cappello* —, it is an absurd (*o* impossible) hat **3.** (*intrattabile*) intractable; (*insopportabile*) unbearable, impossible ‖ *s.m.* impossibility: *fare l'*—, to do one's utmost: *farei l'* — *per lui*, I should do anything for him; *farei l'* — *per saperlo*, I should give the world to know it; *ha fatto l'* — *per riuscire*, he has done his utmost to succeed; *non ti aspettare l'* — *da me!*, don't expect me to do impossibilities!.

impossibilità, *s.f.* impossibility: *sono nell'* — *di venire*, it is absolutely impossible for me to come.

impossibilitàre, *v.t.* to make impossible: — *qlcu. a fare ql.co.*, to make it impossible for s.o. to do sthg.

impossibilitàto, *ag.* unable: *è* — *a fare questo*, he is unable to do this; *erano impossibilitati ad aiutarci*, they were unable to help us.

impòsta[1], *s.f.* tax, duty; (*dovuta ad un'autorità locale*) rate: *imposte dirette, indirette*, direct, indirect taxes; — *di successione*, death-duty; — *fondiaria*, land-tax; — *sul reddito*, income-tax; — *sulla vendita*, purchase tax; *esente da* —, exempt from tax (*o* tax-free); *evadere una* —, to escape (*o* to evade) a tax.

impòsta[2], *s.f.* **1.** shutter: — *scorrevole*, sliding shutter **2.** (*arch.*) impost.

impostàre[1], *v.t.* **1.** (*incominciare*) to start, to set up: — *un lavoro*, to start (on) a piece of work **2.** (*progettare*) to state, to formulate, to plan: — *un affare*, to plan (*o* to lay down the lines of) a business; — *un problema*, to state (*o* to formulate) a problem; — *una ricerca*, to make a plan of research **3.** (*basare*) to base, to found, to place: *imposto il mio ragionamento su fatti reali*, I am founding my argument on real facts **4.** (*mar.*) to lay down: — *una nave*, to lay down a ship (*o* to lay a ship on the stocks) **5.** (*arch.*) to build: — *un arco sopra pilastri*, to build (*o* to place) an arch on pillars **6.** (*mus.*) to pitch: — *la voce*, (*intonarla*) to pitch one's voice ‖ **impostàrsi**, *v.r.* (*prendere una posizione*) to adopt a position, to take up a position.

impostàre[2], *v.t.* to post; (*spec. amer.*) to mail: — *una lettera*, to post (*o* to mail) a letter.

impostatúra, *s.f.* **1.** (*atteggiamento*) posture **2.** (*arch.*) abutment **3.** (*mus.*) pitching.

impostazióne[1], *s.f.* **1.** (*inizio*) start **2.** (*formulazione*) statement; formulation **3.** (*linee generali*) general lines (*pl.*): *l'* — *della linea politica di un partito*, the general (*o* main) lines of a party's policy; *l'* — *di un discorso*, the general (*o* broad) lines of a speech **4.** (*base*) base, foundation **5.** (*mar.*) laying down.

impostazióne[2], *s.f.* posting; (*spec. amer.*) mailing.

impostíme, *s.m.* (*sedimento*) sediment; dregs (*pl.*).

impósto, *ag.* **1.** imposed **2.** (*dato*) given.

impostóra, *s.f.*, **impostóre**, *s.m.* impostor; (*imbrogliona, imbroglione*) swindler.

impostúra, *s.f.* imposture; (*frode*) fraud.

impotènte, *ag.* powerless; impotent: *le leggi sono impotenti in questo caso*, the law is powerless in this case.

impotenteménte, *av.* impotently.

impotènza, *s.f.* impotence: *il nemico fu ridotto all'*—, the enemy was reduced to impotence.

impoveriménto, *s.m.* impoverishment: *il progressivo — del paese,* the gradual impoverishment of the country.

impoverire, *v.t.* to impoverish: *le pesanti imposte impoverirono le classi mercantili,* heavy taxes impoverished the merchant classes ‖ **impoverirsi,** *v.r.* to become poor.

impoverìto, *ag.* impoverished.

impraticàbile, *ag.* **1.** impassable, impracticable: *strada —,* impassable (o impracticable) road **2.** *(di persona)* unmanageable, impracticable, intractable **3.** *(che non si può mettere in pratica)* impracticable, unfeasible: *un sistema —,* an impracticable system.

impraticabilità, *s.f.* impracticability, impracticableness.

impratichìre, *v.t.* to train, to exercise ‖ **impratichìrsi,** *v.r.* to practise; to train: *è necessario che tu ti impratichisca prima di lavorare da sola,* it is necessary for you to get some practice (o to practice) before working on your own.

impratichìto, *ag.* trained; *(esperto)* skilled, experienced.

imprecàre, *v.i.* to curse (s.o., sthg.), to imprecate: *imprecò contro la cattiva sorte,* he cursed his unfortunate lot; *— e giurare,* to curse and swear.

imprecatìvo, *ag.* imprecatory.

imprecatóre, *s.m.,* **imprecatrìce,** *s.f.* curser.

imprecatòrio, *ag.* imprecatory.

imprecazióne, *s.f.* curse, imprecation: *lanciare imprecazioni contro qlcu.,* to hurl imprecations at s.o.

imprecisàbile, *ag.* indeterminable, indefinable: *in data —,* on an indefinite date.

imprecìso, *ag.* undetermined, undefined: *in circostanze imprecisate,* in undetermined (o unspecified) circumstances.

imprecisióne, *s.f.* lack of precision, imprecision; *(inesattezza)* inaccuracy; inexactitude.

imprecìso, *ag.* unprecise; *(inesatto)* inexact; inaccurate; *(vago)* vague: *idee imprecise,* vague ideas.

impregiudicàbile, *ag.* that cannot be prejudiced.

impregiudicàto, *ag.* unprejudiced ‖ *s.m. (dir.)* first offender.

impregnàre, *v.t.* **1.** *(render pregna)* to impregnate **2.** *(imbevere)* to impregnate, to imbue (anche *fig.*): *l'acqua impregna i corpi porosi,* water impregnates porous bodies; *egli è impregnato di pregiudizi,* he is imbued (o impregnated) with prejudices ‖ **impregnàrsi,** *v.r.* **1.** *(divenir pregna)* to become pregnant **2.** *(imbeversi)* to become impregnated, to become soaked; to become imbued (anche *fig.*).

impregnàto, *ag.* imbued (with sthg.): *un fazzoletto — di profumo,* a handkerchief imbued with scent.

impremeditàto, *ag.* unpremeditated.

imprèndere, *v.t. (intraprendere)* to undertake; *(incominciare)* to begin, to start, to initiate.

imprendìbile, *ag.* **1.** *(inafferrabile)* elusive: *un furfante —,* an elusive rogue (o *fam.* a slippery customer) **2.** *(invincibile)* invincible; *(inespugnabile)* impregnable: *una fortezza —,* an impregnable fortress.

imprenditóre, *s.m.* entrepreneur; *(appaltatore)* contractor: *— di pompe funebri,* (funeral) undertaker (o *amer.* mortician); *— di trasporti,* carrier (o forwarding agent); *— edile,* building contractor.

impreparàto, *ag.* unprepared (for sthg.): *la guerra colse il paese —,* the war caught unprepared the country.

impreparazióne, *s.f.* unpreparedness.

imprésa, *s.f.* **1.** undertaking, enterprise; *(particolarmente rischiosa)* venture: *un' — ardita,* a bold enterprise; *un' — difficile,* a difficult undertaking (o enterprise); *un' — dubbiosa,* a doubtful venture; *un' — folle,* a mad venture; *si accinge a una nuova —,* he is undertaking sthg. new; *imbarcarsi in un' —,* to embark on an enterprise ‖ *è più la spesa che l' —, prov.* it does not pay **2.** *(gesta)* exploit; deed: *era molto orgoglioso delle sue imprese,* he was very proud of his exploits **3.** *(appalto)* contract: *— per i lavori pubblici,* contract for public works; *ha l' — per la costruzione di un ponte,* he has a contract for the building of a bridge **4.** *(azienda)* concern; firm: *— di costruzioni, edile,* builders (o building contractors); *un' — italiana costruì la diga,* an Italian firm built the dam **5.** *(arald.)* device **6.** *(teat.)* management.

impresàrio, *s.m.* **1.** entrepreneur; *(appaltatore)* contractor: *— di pompe funebri,* (funeral) undertaker (o *amer.* mortician) **2.** *(teat.)* impresario *(pl.* impresarios); manager.

imprescindìbile, *ag.* **1.** that cannot be disregarded, that cannot be set aside, that cannot be omitted **2.** *(indispensabile)* indispensable; necessary.

imprescrittìbile, *ag. (dir.)* indefeasible.

imprescrittibilità, *s.f. (dir.)* indefeasibleness, indefeasibility: *— di un diritto,* indefeasibility of a right.

imprescrittibilménte, *av. (dir.)* indefeasibly.

impressionàbile, *ag.* **1.** impressionable; sensitive; susceptible; *(apprensivo)* apprehensive: *non è un tipo —,* he is not very sensitive (o easily moved) **2.** *(foto.)* sensitive: *carta —,* sensitive paper.

impressionabilità, *s.f.* **1.** impressionability, impressibility **2.** *(foto.)* sensitivity.

impressionànte, *ag.* **1.** impressive, striking **2.** *(commovente)* moving: *dramma —,* moving drama **3.** *(spaventoso)* awful, tremendous: *visione —,* awful sight.

impressionàre, *v.t.* **1.** to impress; to make an impression on (s.o.); to strike; to affect: *cercava di impressionarmi raccontandomi tutto quello che aveva fatto,* he was trying to make an impression on me by telling me all he had done; *quelle notizie lo hanno molto impressionato,* that news has affected him deeply; *la sua memoria, quella vista mi ha molto impressionato,* his memory, that sight has impressed me very much; *il suo modo di pensare mi ha bene impressionato,* his way of thinking has impressed (o struck) me favourably **2.** *(commuovere)* to move, to touch **3.** *(spaventare)* to frighten **4.** *(foto.)* to expose ‖ **impressionàrsi,** *v.r.* **1.** to be affected: *ella si impressiona facilmente,* she is easily affected (o she is easily upset) **2.** *(commuoversi)* to be moved, to be touched **3.** *(spaventarsi)* to be frightened.

impressionàto, *ag.* **1.** struck; impressed; affected: *se ne andò via molto —,* he went away much impressed **2.** *(commosso)* moved; touched **3.** *(spaventato)* frightened **4.** *(foto.)* exposed: *bene, male —,* well, badly exposed.

impressióne, *s.f.* **1.** impression, sensation: *ero sotto l'— del suo discorso,* I was under the impression of his speech; *ho l'— che questo non sia vero,* I have the impression (o it is my impression) that this is not true (o *sl. amer.* I have a hunch that this is not true); *la mia — è che egli sia colpevole,* my impression is that he is guilty; *mi fece cattiva —,* he made a bad impression on me; *quella vista mi ha fatto molta —,* that sight has impressed me very much; *quell'uomo mi fece buona —,* that man impressed me favourably; *si basa solo sulle sue impressioni,* he bases himself only on his impressions; *destare un'— negativa,* to arouse a negative impression **2.** *(viva sensazione)* sensation: *— di freddo, caldo,* sensation of cold, warmth **3.** *(segno, impronta)* impression, imprint, mark: *— dei piedi sul terreno,* imprint of footsteps (o footprints) on the ground; *l'— di un sigillo sulla cera,* the impression of a seal upon wax **4.** *(edizione)* edition **5.** *(ristampa)* impression, printing: *terza — di un libro,* third impression of a book.

impressionìsmo, *s.m. (st. pitt.)* impressionism.

impressionìsta, *s.c. (st. pitt.)* impressionist.

impressionìstico, *ag. (st. pitt.)* impressionistic.

imprèsso, *ag.* **1.** impressed, imprinted (anche *fig.*); stamped, marked **2.** *(stampato)* printed.

impressóre, *s.m. (tip.)* printer.

imprestàre, *v.t.* to lend: *— ql.co. a qlcu.,* to lend sthg. to s.o.

impreteríbile, *ag.* that cannot be disregarded; that cannot be omitted.

imprevedíbile, *ag.* unforeseeable.

imprevedúto, *ag.* unforeseen, unexpected.

imprevidènte, *ag.* improvident, unforeseeing.

imprevidènza, *s.f.* improvidence; lack of foresight.

imprevísto, *ag.* unforeseen, unexpected, unlooked for: *avvenimento* —, unexpected event (*o fam.* bolt from the blue) || *s.m.* unforeseen event, unexpected event: *gli imprevisti,* incidental expenses (*o* contingencies); *in caso di* —, in case of emergency; *salvo* —, unless anything unexpected happens; *tener conto dell'* —, to allow for contingencies.

impreziosíre, *v.t.* to make precious || **impreziosírsi,** *v.r.* to become precious.

imprigionaménto, *s.m.* imprisonment.

imprigionàre, *v.t.* (*mettere in prigione*) to imprison, to put in prison; (*confinare, rinchiudere*) to confine, to shut up: — *qlcu. nella sua camera,* to confine s.o. to (*o* shut s.o. up in) his room.

imprimatur, *s.m.* (*eccl.*) imprimatur: *il libro ottenne l'* —, the book was given the imprimatur.

imprimé, *s.m.* (*stoffa stampata*) printed cloth; (*abito di stoffa stampata*) print dress.

imprímere, *v.t.* **1.** to impress, to imprint (anche *fig.*); to mark, to stamp: — *le orme sul suolo,* to leave footsteps on the ground; — *nella propria memoria,* to engrave (*o* to impress) on one's memory; — *un timbro su un foglio,* to impress (*o* to imprint) a stamp on a sheet **2.** (*stampare*) to print: — *un libro,* to print a book **3.** (*dare, comunicare*) to give; to impart; to transmit: *ella imprime la sua personalità su tutto quello che porta,* she imparts her personality to everything she wears; — *un impulso,* to give an impulse; — *un movimento a un corpo,* to set a body in motion || **imprímersi,** *v.r.* to remain impressed, to remain engraved: *imprimiti nella mente che...,* bear in mind (*o* get it into your head) that...; *le sue parole si impressero nella mia mente,* his words remained engraved in my mind.

improbàbile, *ag.* improbable, unlikely: *è — che si faccia vivo,* it is unlikely that he will (*o* he is not likely to) turn up.

improbabilità, *s.f.* improbability, unlikelihood.

improbabilménte, *av.* improbably, unlikely.

improbità, *s.f.* (*disonestà*) dishonesty, improbity; (*malvagità*) wickedness.

ímprobo, *ag.* **1.** (*disonesto*) dishonest; (*malvagio*) wicked **2.** (*duro, faticoso*) hard, toilsome, unbearable: *è un lavoro* —, it is a real piece of drudgery.

improduttivaménte, *av.* unproductively.

improduttività, *s.f.* unproductiveness.

improduttívo, *ag.* unproductive: *denaro* —, money lying idle.

imprónta, *s.f.* **1.** impression, mark, print: — *delle ruote,* trace (*o* track) of the wheels; — *del piede,* footprint; *impronte digitali,* fingerprints; *lasciare un'* — *su ql.co.,* to leave an impression (*o* a mark) on sthg. **2.** *fig.* stamp, imprint, trace, mark: *l'* — *del dolore,* the stamp (*o* imprint) of grief; — *del genio,* stamp (*o* mark) of genius; *lasciarono la loro* — *nella storia del paese,* they left their trace in the history of the country.

improntaménte, *av.* (*rar.*) (*con impudenza*) impudently; (*con indiscrezione*) indiscreetly; (*importunamente*) importunely.

improntàre[1], *v.t.* to impress, to imprint; to stamp, to mark (anche *fig.*) || **improntàrsi,** *v.r.* to stamp oneself: *ricordi che si improntano nella mente,* memories that stamp themselves on the mind.

improntàre[2], *v.t.* to prepare.

improntàto, *ag.* impressed, stamped, marked: *un discorso* — *di gelosia,* a speech full of envy; *un viso* — *alla malinconia,* face marked (*o* stamped) with sadness; *la sua accoglienza fu improntata alla massima cordialità,* his welcome was marked by its extreme cordiality.

improntitúdine, *s.f.* (*rar.*) (*impudenza*) impudence; (*indiscrezione*) indiscretion; (*importunità*) importunity.

imprónto, *ag.* (*rar.*) (*sfacciato*) impudent; (*indiscreto*) indiscreet; (*importuno*) importune.

impronunciàbile, *ag.* unpronounceable.

impropèrio, *s.m.* (*ingiuria*) abuse, insult: *coprire qlcu. d'improperi,* to abuse s.o. (*o* to call s.o. names) || *gli Improperi,* (*eccl.*) the Reproaches.

improporzionalménte, *V.* **sproporzionataménte.**

improporzionàto, *V.* **sproporzionàto.**

impropriaménte, *av.* improperly; incorrectly; wrongly.

improprietà, *s.f.* impropriety; inaccuracy: *nel tuo discorso vi sono molte* —, in your speech there are many inaccuracies.

impròprio, *ag.* **1.** improper: *uso* — *di una parola,* improper use of a word **2.** (*sconveniente*) unbecoming, unseemly: *fu* — *da parte sua agire in quel modo,* it was unbecoming of him to act in that manner **3.** (*non adatto*) unsuitable; unfit **4.** *frazione impropria,* (*mat.*) improper fraction.

improrogàbile, *ag.* that cannot be put off: *una data* —, a final date.

improrogabilménte, *av.* with no possibility of delay, without any possibility of delay.

improvvidaménte, *av.* improvidently; (*imprudentemente*) imprudently.

improvvidènza, *s.f.* improvidence; (*imprudenza*) imprudence.

impròvvido, *ag.* improvident; (*imprudente*) imprudent.

improvvisaménte, *av.* **1.** suddenly; all of a sudden: *egli partì* —, he left suddenly **2.** (*inaspettatamente*) unexpectedly.

improvvisàre, *v.t.* to improvise: — *un discorso,* to improvise a speech (*o* to speak extempore); — *un pezzo di musica,* to improvise a piece of music; — *un pranzo,* to improvise a dinner || *v.i.* to improvise; to extemporize: — *all'organo,* to improvise (*o* to extemporize) on the organ || **improvvisàrsi,** *v.r.* to play: *ci fu un incidente e così egli dovette* — *dottore,* there was an accident and so he had to play the doctor; — *pittore, poeta,* to play the painter, the poet.

improvvisàta, *s.f.* surprise: *una piacevole* —, a pleasant surprise; *fare una* — *a qlcu.,* to give s.o. a surprise.

improvvisàto, *ag.* improvised; extempore: *un discorso* —, an improvised (*o* extempore) speech; *un pranzo* —, an improvised dinner.

improvvisatóre, *s.m.* improviser, improvisator; improvisatore (*pl.* improvisatori) || **improvvisatríce,** *s.f.* improviser, improvisator; improvisatrice (*pl.* improvisatrici).

improvvisazióne, *s.f.* improvisation: *il suo discorso appariva più frutto di* — *che di riflessione,* his speech seemed more the result of improvisation than of reflection.

improvvíso, *ag.* **1.** sudden: *una morte improvvisa,* a sudden death || *all'* —, suddenly (*o* all of a sudden) **2.** (*inaspettato*) unexpected **3.** (*imprevisto*) unforeseen || *s.m.* (*lett. mus.*) impromptu.

improvvísto, *ag.* unprovided (with sthg.).

imprudènte, *ag.* imprudent, careless, heedless; (*imprevidente*) unwary; (*temerario*) rash: *è* — *quando guida,* he is careless when he drives.

imprudenteménte, *av.* imprudently; (*con imprevidenza*) unwarily; (*con temerarietà*) rashly.

imprudènza, *s.f.* imprudence, heedlessness; (*imprevidenza*) unwariness; (*temerarietà*) rashness.

imprunàre, *v.t.* to hedge with thorns.

impúbe, impúbere, *ag.* (*letter.*) impuberal.

impudènte, *ag.* impudent, shameless, saucy.

impudenteménte, *av.* impudently, shamelessly, saucily.

impudènza, *s.f.* impudence, shamelessness, sauciness.

impudicaménte, *av.* immodestly, unchastely, shamelessly, indecently, lewdly.

impudicízia, *s.f.* immodesty, impudicity, unchastity, shamelessness, indecency, lewdness, wantonness.

impudíco, *ag.* immodest, unchaste, shameless, indecent, lewd, wanton: *pensieri impudichi,* wanton thoughts.

impugnàbile[1], *ag.* **1.** (*afferrabile*) that can be grasped **2.** (*che può essere tenuto nel pugno*) that can be held.

impugnàbile[2], *ag.* (*dir.*) impugnable; refutable.

impugnàre[1], *v.t.* **1.** (*afferrare*) to grasp, to grip: — *un'arma, un bastone,* to grasp (o to grip) a weapon, a stick; — *la spada,* (*sfoderarla*) to draw the sword ‖ — *le armi,* to take up arms **2.** (*tenere nel pugno*) to hold: *impugna la racchetta in modo strano,* he holds his racket in a strange way.

impugnàre[2], *v.t.* (*dir.*) to impugn; to refute; to contest: — *un diritto, la veridicità di ql.co.,* to impugn a claim, the veracity of sthg.; — *un testamento,* to contest a will.

impugnatívo, *ag.* (*dir.*) refutative, refutatory.

impugnatúra, *s.f.* **1.** (*manico*) handle; (*di spada, pugnale*) hilt; (*di coltello, ascia*) haft **2.** (*modo di impugnare*) grip; hold.

impugnazióne, *s.f.* (*dir.*) impugnation, impugnment; refutation.

impulitézza, *s.f.* (*rar.*) rudeness, roughness.

impulìto, *ag.* (*rar.*) rude, rough, unmannered.

impulsióne, *s.f.* (*rar.*) impulsion.

impulsività, *s.f.* impulsiveness; (*irriflessività*) rashness, hastiness.

impulsívo, *ag.* **1.** impulsive; (*irriflessivo*) rash, hasty: *delirio* —, (*patol.*) impulsive insanity; *una persona impulsiva,* an impulsive person **2.** (*fis. mec. elett.*) impulsive, impelling: *forza impulsiva,* impelling force.

impúlso, *s.m.* **1.** impulse; impetus (*pl.* impetuses): — *vitale,* vital impetus; *sotto l'*— *del momento,* under the impulse of the moment; *agire d'*—, to act on impulse; *dare un* — *al commercio,* to give an impulse (o impetus) to trade; *ricevere* —, to receive impetus; *sentire un* — *a fare ql.co.,* to feel (o to be seized with) an impulse to do sthg. **2.** (*fis. mec. elett.*) impulse **3.** (*med.*) impulse, impulsion.

impúne, *ag.* (*letter.*) unpunished.

impuneménte, *av.* with impunity; (*senza danno*) scathelessly, unharmfully.

impunìbile, *ag.* unpunishable.

impunità, *s.f.* impunity.

impunitaménte, *av.* without punishment.

impunìto, *ag.* unpunished.

impuntàre, *v.i.* **1.** (*inciampare*) to stumble (over sthg.) **2.** (*balbettare*) to stutter, to stammer ‖ **impuntàrsi,** *v.r.* **1.** (*di cavallo, mulo, ecc.*) to jib **2.** (*ostinarsi*) to stick (to sthg.); to grow obstinate, to grow stubborn; to insist; to get (sthg.) into one's head: *non impuntarti così quando vedi che hai torto,* don't be so obstinate (o don't insist so much) when you see you are wrong; *quando si impunta su ql.co., non c'è verso di fargli cambiare idea,* when he gets sthg. into his head, there is no way of making him change his mind.

impuntigliàrsi, *v.r.* **1.** to make it a point of honour: *lo farà perchè si è impuntigliato a farlo,* he will do it because he considers it a point of honour to do it **2.** (*ostinarsi*) to grow obstinate; to insist: *mi sono impuntigliato a finirlo,* I have taken it into my head to finish it.

impuntíre, *v.t.* to quilt.

impuntìto, *ag.* quilted.

impuntitúra, *s.f.* quilting.

impuntúra, *s.f.* **1.** fine stitching **2.** (*impuntitura*) quilting.

impuraménte, *av.* impurely.

impurità, *s.f.* **1.** impurity: *liquido pieno di* —, liquid full of impurities; — *di linguaggio, di stile,* impurity of language, of style **2.** (*impudicizia*) impurity; unchastity; lewdness.

impúro, *ag.* **1.** impure: *aria impura,* impure air; *lingua impura,* impure language **2.** (*impudico*) impure; unchaste; lewd.

imputàbile, *ag.* **1.** (*da potersi attribuire*) imputable; ascribable, attributable: *errore* — *a distrazione,* mistake imputable to absent-mindedness **2.** (*che si può accusare*) chargeable (with sthg.): *una persona* — *di omicidio,* a person chargeable with murder.

imputabilità, *s.f.* imputability.

imputàre, *v.t.* **1.** (*attribuire*) to impute; to ascribe, to attribute: *imputarono il suo insuccesso alla pigrizia,* they attributed his failure to laziness; *questo non gli si può* — *a colpa,* this cannot be set down against him as a crime **2.** (*accusare*) to charge; to accuse: *fu imputato di assassinio,* he was charged with murder (o they accused him of murder).

imputàto, *s.m.* (*dir.*) defendant, accused, prisoner at the bar: *l'*— *si decise a confessarsi colpevole,* the prisoner at the bar elected to plead guilty.

imputazióne, *s.f.* imputation; charge: *capo d'*—, (*dir.*) charge (o accusation); *sotto una grave* —, on a serious charge.

imputrescíbile, *ag.* imputrescible, incorruptible.

imputridiménto, *s.m.* putrefaction, corruption, rottenness.

imputridíre, *v.i.* to putrefy, to rot, to go rotten: — *in prigione,* to rot in prison.

imputridíto, *ag.* rotten.

impuzzàre, impuzzíre, *v.t.* to stink ‖ *v.i.,* **impuzzàrsi, impuzzírsi,** *v.r.* to become stinking.

in, *prep.* **1.** (*stato in luogo*) in; at; (*su, sopra*) on; (*dentro*) inside: — *fondo alla pagina,* at the bottom of the page; — *un luogo nascosto,* in a hidden place; — *tavola,* on the table; *nel cielo,* in the sky; *nell'aria,* in the air; *aspettami nel parco,* wait for me inside the park; *essere* — *campagna,* — *città,* — *prigione,* to be in the country, in town, in prison; *essere* — *casa,* — *chiesa,* to be at home, at church **2.** (*moto a luogo*) to; (*movimento verso l'interno, penetrazione*) **in(to)**: *andò* — *Francia,* he went to France; *mettilo nella scatola,* put it in(to) the box; *mise le mani* — *tasca,* he put his hands in(to) his pockets; *va'* — *cucina,* go into (o to) the kitchen; *vieni nel mio studio,* come into my study; *andare* — *città,* — *prigione,* to go to town, to prison; *andare* — *montagna,* to go to the mountains; *andare* — *rovina,* to go to ruin (anche *fig.*); *cadere nell'acqua,* to fall into the water; *introdurre merce italiana nei paesi stranieri,* to introduce Italian goods into foreign countries; *salire* — *treno,* to get in (o on) the train; *tornare* — *America,* to go back to America **3.** (*tempo*) in; on; at: — *una bella serata,* one fine evening; — *marzo,* — *primavera,* in March, in spring; — *una mattina d'estate,* one (o on a) summer morning; — *quel giorno,* (on) that day; — *questo momento,* at this moment; — *tempo di guerra,* in war-time; — *tempo di pace,* in peace-time; — *tutta la mia vita,* in all my life; *nel 1960,* in 1960; *nel pomeriggio,* in the afternoon; *nel secolo scorso,* in the last century; *lo farò* — *due ore,* I shall do it in two hours ‖ *nello stesso tempo,* at the same time **4.** (*materia*): *una borsa* — *pelle bianca,* a bag in white leather; *un cavallo* — *legno,* a wooden horse; *una statua* — *bronzo,* a bronze statue **5.** (*mezzo*) **by**: *sono venuto* — *treno,* — *aeroplano,* — *automobile,* I came by train, by plane, by car **6.** (*condizione, modo*) **in**: — *uno strano modo,* in a strange way; *vestita* — *nero,* dressed in black; *lo disse* — *buona maniera,* he said it in a kindly way; *non sono* — *condizioni di venire,* I am in no condition to come; *essere* — *abito da sera,* to be in evening dress; *essere* — *difficoltà,* to be in difficulties; *essere* — *pace,* — *guerra con qlcu.,* to be at peace, to be at war with s.o.; *essere* — *un pasticcio,* to be in trouble; *parlare, scrivere* — *italiano,* to write, to speak in Italian **7.** (*con valore limitativo*): *bravo* — *matematica,* good at mathematics; *debole* — *latino,* weak in Latin; *dottore* — *medicina,*

— *teologia*, doctor of medicine, of theology; *non è stato promosso* — *greco*, he didn't pass in Greek **8.** (*mutamento, trasformazione*) **into:** *dividere* — *cinque parti*, to divide in(to) five parts; *tradurre* — *inglese*, to translate into English; *trasformare acqua* — *ghiaccio*, to turn water into ice **9.** (*seguito da infinito*): *l'ho visto un'altra volta nell'andare a casa*, on going home I met him again; *nell'entrare lo vidi subito*, on entering I saw him at once; *si è rotto nel lavarlo*, it broke on being washed **10.** (*in qualche caso non viene tradotto, V. anche* **3.**)*: eravamo* — *molti, pochi, due*, there were a lot of us, few of us, two of us; *se io fossi* — *te*, if I were you (*o* in your place); *dipingere ql.co.* — *rosso*, to paint sthg. red **11.** (**Fraseologia**): — *aiuto di*, in aid of; (*con verbi di moto*) to the aid of; — *alto*, up there; up (above); — *basso*, down there; down (below); — *cerca di*, in search of; — *dettaglio*, in detail; — *dono*, as a gift; — *forse*, in doubt; — *lode di*, in praise of; — *onore di*, in honour of; — *particolare*, in particular; — *quanto*, in so far as; — *quanto a ciò*, as for that; — *tutti i modi*, in any case; — *verità*, in truth.

inàbile, *ag*. **1.** (*incapace*) incapable (of sthg.); unable: — *al lavoro*, unable to work **2.** (*maldestro*) unskilful **3.** (*non idoneo*) unfit (for sthg., to do): — *al servizio militare*, unfit for military service **4.** (*dir.*) unqualified (for sthg.).

inabilità, *s.f*. **1.** (*incapacità*) inability; incapacity **2.** (*mancanza di destrezza*) unskilfulness **3.** (*inidoneità*) unfitness (for sthg., to do) **4.** (*dir.*) unqualification (for sthg.).

inabilitàre, *v.t*. **1.** to disable **2.** (*dir.*) to disable; to disqualify ǁ **inabilitàrsi**, *v.r*. to incapacitate oneself (for sthg.): *si inabilitò al servizio militare*, he made (*o* rendered) himself unfit for military service.

inabilitàto, *ag*. **1.** disabled **2.** (*dir.*) disabled; disqualified.

inabilitazióne, *s.f*. **1.** disability **2.** (*dir.*) disqualification.

inabissaménto, *s.m*. sinking; engulfment.

inabissàre, *v.t*. to engulf; to submerge (anche *fig.*) ǁ **inabissàrsi**, *v.r*. to sink; to be engulfed, to be submerged: *la corazzata si inabissò in pochi minuti*, the battleship sank in few minutes.

inabitàbile, *ag*. uninhabitable; (*specialmente di casa*) untenantable.

inabitabilità, *s.f*. uninhabitableness.

inabitàto, *ag*. uninhabited; (*deserto*) deserted.

inaccessìbile, *ag*. inaccessible, unapproachable (anche *fig.*): *cuore* — *alla pietà*, heart inaccessible to pity; *vetta* —, unapproachable summit.

inaccessibilità, *s.f*. inaccessibility, unapproachableness (anche *fig.*).

inaccessibilménte, *av*. inaccessibly.

inaccèsso, *ag*. (*letter.*) **1.** unpenetrated; unreached **2.** (*inaccessibile*) inaccessible.

inaccettàbile, *ag*. unacceptable: *condizioni per noi inaccettabili*, conditions unacceptable to us.

inaccettabilità, *s.f*. unacceptableness.

inaccettabilménte, *av*. unacceptably.

inaccordàbile, *ag*. **1.** (*che non può essere concesso*) unallowable, ungrantable; impermissible **2.** (*mus.*) (*che non può essere intonato*) untunable **3.** (*irreconciliabile*) irreconcilable.

inaccòrto, *ag*. **1.** (*incauto*) unwary; incautious: *un giudizio* —, an incautious judgement **2.** (*poco giudizioso*) unwise.

inaccusàbile, *ag*. unimpeachable; not liable to accusation; beyond the reach of accusation.

inacerbíre, *v.t*. to exacerbate, to embitter: — *gli animi*, to embitter men's minds; — *la pena*, to exacerbate the pain ǁ **inacerbírsi**, *v.r*. to become exacerbated, to grow bitter: *si inacerbisce sempre di più*, he is getting more and more embittered.

inacetíre, *v.t*. **1.** (*rendere acido per mezzo dell'aceto*) to vinegar **2.** (*far diventare aceto*) to turn into vin-

egar **3.** (*inacidire*) to sour ǁ *v.i*. **1.** (*diventare aceto*) to turn into vinegar **2.** (*inacidirsi*) to sour.

inacidíre, *v.t*. to sour (anche *fig.*) ǁ *v.i*. to (turn) sour (anche *fig.*): *si inacidisce di giorno in giorno*, he is getting more embittered every day; *questo vino comincia a* —, this wine is beginning to turn sour.

inacidíto, *ag*. **1.** sour **2.** *fig*. sour, embittered: — *dalle disgrazie*, soured by misfortune; *una zitella inacidita*, an embittered spinster.

Ínaco, *no.pr.m*. (*mit.*) Inachus.

inaequàre, *V*. **annaequàre**.

inacutíre, *v.t*. **1.** to sharpen, to make sharp(er): — *un angolo*, to sharpen an angle **2.** (*mus.*) to sharpen ǁ **inacutírsi**, *v.r*. to become sharp(er).

inadattàbile, *ag*. unadaptable; inadaptable.

inadattabilità, *s.f*. inadaptability.

inadàtto, *ag*. **1.** unfit (for sthg., to do); unsuitable (for sthg.); inapt (for sthg., to do) **2.** (*sconveniente*) unbecoming, unseemly, improper.

inadeguataménte, *av*. inadequately; insufficiently.

inadeguatézza, *s.f*. inadequacy; insufficiency.

inadeguàto, *ag*. inadequate; insufficient: *informazioni inadeguate*, inadequate information; *le mie parole sono inadeguate a esprimere la mia gioia*, my words are inadequate to express my joy.

inadempíbile, *ag*. that cannot be fulfilled.

inadempiènte, *ag*. defaulting: *debitore* —, defaulting debtor.

inadempiménto, *s.m*. non-fulfilment, non-execution.

inadempíto, inadempiúto, *ag*. unfulfilled: *un dovere* —, an unfulfilled duty; *un voto* —, a broken vow.

inadopràbile, *ag*. unusable; not usable, not fit for use (*predicativi*).

inafferràbile, *ag*. unseizable; elusive (anche *fig.*): *un'idea* —, an elusive idea; *un ladro* —, an elusive thief.

inaffiàre, *V*. **innaffiàre**.

inalàre, *v.t*. (*med.*) to inhale.

inalatóre, *s.m*. (*med.*) inhaler.

inalazióne, *s.f*. (*med.*) inhalation.

inalbàre, *v.i*. (*letter.*) to whiten.

inalberàre, *v.t*. **1.** to hoist: — *una bandiera, una vela*, to hoist a flag, a sail **2.** (*piantare ad alberi*) to plant trees on (sthg.) ǁ **inalberàrsi**, *v.r*. **1.** (*di cavalli*) to prance **2.** (*adirarsi*) to lose one's temper, to get angry: *s'inalbera per un nonnulla*, he gets angry about nothing.

inalidíre, *v.i.*, **inalidírsi**, *v.r*. to dry up.

inalienàbile, *ag*. inalienable, indefeasible: *diritti inalienabili*, indefeasible (*o* inalienable) rights.

inalienabilità, *s.f*. inalienability, indefeasibility.

inalienabilménte, *av*. inalienably, indefeasibly.

inalteràbile, *ag*. unalterable, inalterable.

inalterabilità, *s.f*. unalterability, inalterability.

inalterabilménte, *av*. unalterably, inalterably.

inalveàre, *v.t*. to canalize.

inalveazióne, *s.f*. canalization.

inalzaménto, *V*. **innalzaménto**.

inalzàre, *V*. **innalzàre**.

inamàbile, *ag*. (*rar.*) unamiable, unlovable.

inamabilità, *s.f*. (*rar.*) unamiability; unamiableness.

inamidàre, *v.t*. to starch.

inamidàto, *ag*. **1.** starched: *colletto* —, starched collar **2.** *fig*. (*rigido, pieno di sussiego*) starchy: *una persona inamidata*, a starchy person.

inamidatúra, *s.f*. starching.

inammendàbile, *ag*. incorrigible.

inammissìbile, *ag*. inadmissible; not admissible.

inammissibilità, *s.f*. inadmissibility.

inamovíbile, *ag*. **1.** irremovable **2.** (*chir.*) immobilizing.

inamovibilità, *s.f*. irremovability: *l'* — *di un giudice*, the irremovability of a judge.

inamovibilménte, *av*. irremovably.

inàne, *ag*. (*letter.*) **1.** (*vuoto*) inane, empty **2.** (*inutile*) vain, useless: *tentativo* —, useless (*o* futile) attempt.

inanellàre, *v.t*. (*arricciare*) to curl, to make into curls.

inanellàto, *ag.* **1.** (*arricciato*) curly: *chiome inanellate*, curly hair **2.** (*ornato di anelli*) adorned with rings.

inanimàre, *V.* inanimire.

inanimàto, *ag.* inanimate; lifeless, spiritless (anche *fig.*): *mondo* —, inanimate nature; *stile* —, lifeless (*o* bloodless) style.

inànime, *ag.* (*letter.*) lifeless.

inanimìre, *v.t.* **1.** (*incoraggiare*) to encourage; to comfort **2.** (*eccitare*) to stir, to excite; to instigate ‖ **inanimìrsi**, *v.r.* **1.** (*prendere ardire*) to take courage, to take heart **2.** (*sdegnarsi*) to get angry.

inanità, *s.f.* (*letter.*) **1.** (*vacuità*) inanity, vacuity, emptiness **2.** (*inutilità*) vainness, uselessness.

inanizióne, *s.f.* (*med.*) inanition; starvation: *morire di* —, to die of starvation (*o* to starve to death).

inappagàbile, *ag.* unsatisfiable.

inappagàto, *ag.* unsatisfied.

inappellàbile, *ag.* (*dir.*) inappellable: *sentenza* —, inappellable verdict.

inappellabilità, *s.f.* (*dir.*) inappellability.

inappellabilménte, *av.* (*dir.*) without appeal; with no possibility of appeal.

inappetènza, *s.f.* inappetence: *soffrire di* —, to suffer from lack of appetite.

inapplicàbile, *ag.* inapplicable.

inapplicabilità, *s.f.* inapplicability.

inapprensíbile, *ag.* inapprehensible.

inapprezzàbile, *ag.* **1.** (*inestimabile*) invaluable, inestimable; priceless **2.** (*irrilevante*) imperceptible, inappreciable.

inappuntàbile, *ag.* **1.** irreproachable, impeccable, faultless **2.** (*nel vestire*) faultlessly dressed, in perfect trim.

inappuràbile, *ag.* unascertainable, that cannot be verified.

inappuràto, *ag.* unascertained, unverified.

inaràbile, *ag.* unploughable, inarable.

inaràto, *ag.* unploughed, untilled.

inarcaménto, *s.m.* **1.** bending, curving, arching **2.** (*tec.*) cambering.

inarcàre, *v.t.* **1.** to bend, to curve, to arch: *il mio gatto inarcava il dorso tutte le volte che vedeva quel cane*, my cat arched its back whenever it saw that dog; — *le ciglia*, to raise one's brows **2.** (*tec.*) to camber ‖ **inarcàrsi**, *v.r.* to bend, to curve, to become curved.

inarcatúra, *s.f.* **1.** bend, curve **2.** (*tec.*) camber.

inargentàre, *v.t.* to silver (anche *fig.*): *la luna inargentava il bosco*, the moon silvered the wood.

inargentatúra, *s.f.* silver plating.

inaridíre, *v.t.* **1.** to dry up; to parch **2.** (*isterilire*) to make barren (anche *fig.*) ‖ *v.i.*, **inaridírsi**, *v.r.* **1.** to dry up; to become parched: *i campi inaridirono per la grande calura estiva*, the fields became parched because of the great summer heat **2.** (*isterilirsi*) to become barren (anche *fig.*).

inaridíto, *ag.* **1.** dried up, parched **2.** (*isterilito*) barren (anche *fig.*): *una mente inaridita*, a barren mind.

inarmonicaménte, *av.* inharmoniously; discordantly.

inarmònico, *ag.* inharmonious; discordant.

inarrendévole, *ag.* unyielding; unbending; inflexible.

inarrendevolézza, *s.f.* inflexibility.

inarrivàbile, *ag.* **1.** (*irraggiungibile*) unattainable, inaccessible **2.** (*impareggiabile*) incomparable, unsurpassable: *un primato* —, an unsurpassable record.

inarrivabilménte, *av.* (*impareggiabilmente*) incomparably.

inarticolataménte, *av.* inarticulately.

inarticolàto, *ag.* **1.** (*indistinto*) inarticulate, indistinct: *suoni inarticolati*, inarticulate sounds **2.** (*senza articolazioni*) inarticulate.

inascoltàto, *ag.* unheard, unheeded: *il suo ammonimento rimase* —, his warning remained unheeded.

inasiníre, *v.i.*, **inasinírsi**, *v.r.* to grow dull, to grow stupid, to become stupid.

inaspettàbile, *ag.* unexpectable; improbable, unlikely.

inaspettataménte, *av.* unexpectedly.

inaspettàto, *ag.* **1.** unexpected; *arrivò* —, he came unexpected **2.** (*imprevisto*) unforeseen.

inspriménto, *s.m.* **1.** embitterment, exacerbation **2.** (*aggravamento*) aggravation, sharpening.

inaspríre, *v.t.* **1.** to embitter, to exacerbate, to exasperate: *ciò inasprì la sua collera*, this exacerbated his anger; *il dolore l'aveva inasprito*, grief had embittered him **2.** (*aggravare*) to aggravate; to sharpen: — *un dolore*, to sharpen (*o* to aggravate) a pain ‖ **inasprírsi**, *v.r.* **1.** to become embittered, to become exacerbated **2.** (*aggravarsi*) to grow worse.

inastàre, *v.t.* to hoist: — *una bandiera*, to hoist a flag ‖ — *la baionetta*, to fix bayonets.

inattaccàbile, *ag.* **1.** unassailable (anche *fig.*): *la sua reputazione è* —, his reputation is unassailable **2.** (*irreprensibile*) unexceptionable, irreproachable.

inattendíbile, *ag.* **1.** (*incredibile*) unreliable, unworthy of belief **2.** (*senza fondamento*) unfounded: *una diceria* —, an unfounded rumour.

inattendibilità, *s.f.* unreliability, unreliableness.

inattènto, *ag.* inattentive; heedless, careless.

inattenzióne, *s.f.* inattention; heedlessness, carelessness.

inattéso, *ag.* unexpected: *arrivo* —, unexpected arrival.

inattitúdine, *s.f.* **1.** inaptitude **2.** (*incapacità*) incapacity.

inattivaménte, *av.* inactively, inertly.

inattività, *s.f.* inactivity.

inattívo, *ag.* inactive: *capitale* —, (*comm.*) capital lying idle (*o* unemployed capital).

inàtto, *ag.* unapt (for sthg., to do), unfit (for sthg., to do), unsuited (to, for sthg.).

inattuàbile, *ag.* impracticable, unfeasible: *il tuo progetto mi sembra* —, your project seems unfeasible to me.

inattuabilità, *s.f.* impracticability, impracticableness.

inaudíbile, *ag.* inaudible.

inaudíto, *ag.* unheard-of; incredible; xtraordinary, unprecedented: *il tuo suggerimento è* —, your suggestion is unheard-of.

inauguràle, *ag.* inaugural: *discorso* —, inaugural address; *giorno* —, inauguration day.

inauguràre, *v.t.* to inaugurate; (*aprire al pubblico*) to open; (*monumenti, statue, ecc.*) to unveil: — *una mostra*, to open an exhibition; — *una scuola*, to open a school; — *una statua*, to unveil a statue.

inauguratóre, *s.m.*, **inauguratríce**, *s.f.* inaugurator.

inaugurazióne, *s.f.* inauguration; (*apertura*) opening; (*di monumenti, statue, ecc.*) unveiling.

inauspicataménte, *av.* inauspiciously.

inauspicàto, *ag.* inauspicious; ill-omened; unpropitious.

inavvedutaménte, *av.* **1.** (*sbadatamente*) carelessly; thoughtlessly **2.** (*inavvertitamente*) inadvertently.

inavvedutézza, *s.f.* **1.** (*sbadataggine*) carelessness, thoughtlessness **2.** (*inavvertenza*) inadvertence.

inavvedúto, *ag.* **1.** (*sbadato*) careless, thoughtless **2.** (*inavvertito*) inadvertent.

inavvertenteménte, *av.* inadvertently.

inavvertènza, *s.f.* inadvertence.

inavvertitaménte, *av.* inadvertently.

inavvertíto, *ag.* **1.** (*non osservato, non sentito*) unobserved, unperceived **2.** (*sbadato*) careless, absent-minded.

inazióne, *s.f.* inaction, inertness.

inazzurràre, *v.t.* to blue; to make blue ‖ **inazzurràrsi**, *v.r.* to become blue, to turn blue.

incadaveríre, *v.i.* **1.** (*assumere un aspetto cadaverico*) to get a corpse-like appearance **2.** (*putrefarsi*) to putrefy, to rot.

incagliaménto, *s.m.* (*mar.*) stranding; running aground.

incagliàre[1], *v.t.* **1.** (*ostacolare*) to hinder, to hamper **2.** (*inceppare*) to clog, to bring (sthg.) to a standstill **3.** (*mar.*) to ground ‖ *v.i.*, **incagliàrsi**, *v.r.* **1.** to get stuck, to get clogged, to be hampered, to come to a standstill (anche *fig.*): *il macchinario si incagliò per una corda che vi cadde dentro*, the machinery got stuck (o clogged) owing to a string that fell into it; *si incagliò alle prime difficoltà*, he got stuck at the first difficulties **2.** (*mar.*) to run aground.

incagliàre[2], *v.i.*, **incagliàrsi**, *v.r.* (*cagliare, cagliarsi*) to curdle, to coagulate.

incàglio, *s.m.* **1.** (*ostacolo*) obstacle, hindrance, impediment **2.** (*arresto*) stoppage **3.** (*mar.*) stranding, running aground.

incalappiàre, *v.t.* to ensnare, to entrap; to entangle.

incalciatúra, *s.f.* shape of a rifle-stock.

incalcinàre, *v.t.* **1.** to plaster, to cover with lime: — *un muro*, to plaster a wall **2.** (*agr.*) to dress with lime, to lime-wash.

incalcolàbile, *ag.* incalculable: *un danno* —, an incalculable damage; *distanze incalcolabili*, incalculable distances.

incalcolabilità, *s.f.* incalculability, incalculableness.

incalcolabilménte, *av.* incalculably.

incalescènza, *s.f.* (*med.*) incalescence.

incalliménto, *s.m.* **1.** (*l'incallire*) hardening (anche *fig.*) **2.** (*callosità*) callosity.

incallíre, *v.i.* to harden, to become callous (anche *fig.*) ‖ **incallírsi**, *v.r.* to harden, to grow hard, to become hardened: — *nel vizio*, to become hardened in vice.

incallíto, *ag.* **1.** hardened, callous: *mani incallite*, callous hands **2.** *fig.* hardened: *un criminale* —, a hardened criminal.

incaloriménto, *s.m.* heating, warming (anche *fig.*).

incaloríre, *v.t.* to heat, to warm ‖ **incalorírsi**, *v.r.* **1.** to become hot, to become warm **2.** *fig.* (*appassionarsi*) to get excited, to get heated.

incalvíre, *v.i.* to become bald, to go bald.

incalzaménto, *s.m.* **1.** chasing, pursuit **2.** *fig.* pressure, urgency.

incalzànte, *ag.* **1.** chasing, pursuing **2.** *fig.* insistent, pressing; (*urgente*) urging; (*imminente*) imminent: *pericolo* —, imminent danger; *sollecitazioni incalzanti*, urgent requests.

incalzàre, *v.t.* **1.** to chase, to pursue; to follow up closely, to be at the heels of (s.o.): — *il nemico*, to chase the enemy **2.** *fig.* to press, to urge ‖ *v.i.* to press: *il tempo incalza*, time is pressing ‖ **incalzàrsi**, *v.r. reciproco*, to follow one upon another: *gli avvenimenti si incalzarono*, the events followed one upon another.

incàlzo, *s.m.* **1.** *V.* **incalzaménto 2.** (*sostegno, rinforzo*) support, prop.

incameràbile, *ag.* (*dir.*) confiscable.

incameraménto, *s.m.* (*dir.*) confiscation.

incameràre, *v.t.* (*dir.*) to confiscate: — *i beni di qlcu.*, to confiscate s.o.'s property.

incamerazióne, *s.f.* (*dir.*) confiscation.

incamiciàre, *v.t.* to cover, to plaster, to coat; to line ‖ **incamiciàrsi**, *v.r.* to put on one's shirt.

incamiciàta, *s.f.* (*st. mil.*) camisado.

incamiciatúra, *s.f.* covering, plastering, coating; lining.

incamminàre, *v.t.* **1.** to set going, to start: — *un motore*, to set an engine going **2.** (*indirizzare*) to direct, to show the way to (s.o.): — *una persona nel suo lavoro*, to direct a person in his work ‖ **incamminàrsi**, *v.r.* to set out, to make one's way, to start, to make a start (anche *fig.*): *s'incamminò verso la città*, he made his way towards the town; *è ora d'* —, it is time to set out; — *bene*, to make a good start.

incanagliàrsi, *v.r.* **1.** (*diventare una canaglia*) to become a rogue **2.** (*frequentare canaglie*) to associate with rogues, to keep low company.

incanalaménto, *s.m.* **1.** canalization **2.** *fig.* (*avviamento*) starting, directing **3.** (*rad.*) ducting.

incanalàre, *v.t.* **1.** to canalize: — *le acque di un fiume*, to canalize the waters of a river **2.** *fig.* (*avviare*) to canalize, to start, to direct: — *un affare*, to start a business **3.** (*rad.*) to duct.

incanalatúra, *s.f.* **1.** *V.* **incanalaménto 2.** (*scanalatura*) groove.

incancellàbile, *ag.* indelible, ineffaceable: *ricordo* —, ineffaceable memory; *è una vergogna* —, it is an indelible shame.

incancellabilménte, *av.* indelibly, ineffaceably.

incancheràre, **incancheríre**, *v.t.* **1.** to make cancerous **2.** *fig.* (*inasprire*) to sour ‖ *v.i.* **1.** to become cancerous **2.** *fig.* (*inasprire, inasprirsi*) to sour.

incancreníre, *v.i.*, **incancrenírsi**, *v.r.* **1.** to become gangrenous: *la sua piaga incancrenì*, his wound became gangrenous **2.** *fig.* (*inasprire, inasprirsi*) to sour.

incandescènte, *ag.* incandescent, white-hot: *rendere* —, to incandesce (o to make white-hot).

incandescènza, *s.f.* incandescence, white-heat: *lampada a* —, incandescent lamp.

incannàggio, *s.m.* (*ind. tessile*) winding, spooling.

incannàre, *v.t.* (*ind. tessile*) to wind, to spool.

incannàta, *s.f.* (*ind. tessile*) spindleful.

incannàto, *ag.* (*ind. tessile*) wound, spooled.

incannatóio, *s.m.* (*ind. tessile*) (*rocchettiera*) winder; (*cannettiera*) weft-winder.

incannatóre, *s.m.* (*ind. tessile*) (*chi incanna*) winder ‖ **incannatríce**, *s.f.* **1.** (*ind. tessile*) (*chi incanna* winder **2.** *V.* **incannatóio**.

incannatúra, *s.f.* (*ind. tessile*) winding, spooling: — *a filo incrociato*, cross winding.

incannellàre, *v.t.* to put into a pipe.

incannucciàre, *v.t.* **1.** (*sorreggere con canne*) to stake **2.** (*coprire con canne*) to reed, to thatch with reeds **3.** (*med.*) to splint.

incannucciàta, *s.f.* (*med.*) splint.

incannucciatúra, *s.f.* (*copertura con canne*) thatch.

incantagióne, *V.* **incantésimo**.

incantaménto, *s.m.* enchantment, incantation; charm; spell.

incantàre[1], *v.t.* to enchant, to bewitch; to charm: *musica che incanta l'animo*, music that charms the spirit; *quella donna lo aveva incantato*, that woman had bewitched him; *quell'artista incanta il pubblico*, that artist holds the audience spellbound ‖ **incantàrsi**, *v.r.* **1.** to be enchanted; to be charmed; (*andare in estasi*) to go into raptures: — *di fronte alla bellezza di un tramonto*, to go into raptures at the beauty of a sunset **2.** (*incepparsi*) to get stuck, to jam: *il fucile si è incantato*, the gun has jammed.

incantàre[2], *v.t.* (*mettere all'incanto, all'asta*) to put up for auction.

incantàto, *ag.* enchanted, bewitched; charmed, spellbound: *castello* —, enchanted castle; *luogo* —, charming (o delightful) spot; *paese* —, wonderland; *si fermò* — *a guardare il paesaggio*, he stopped spellbound to look at the landscape.

incantatóre, *ag.* enchanting, bewitching: *sorriso* —, bewitching smile ‖ *s.m.* enchanter; charmer: — *di serpenti*, snake-charmer ‖ **incantatríce**, *s.f.* enchantress, charmer.

incantazióne, *V.* **incànto**[1].

incantésimo, *s.m.* enchantment; charm, spell: *fare un* — *a qlcu.*, to put a spell on s.o. (o to lay s.o. under a spell); *rompere l'* —, to break the spell.

incantévole, *ag.* enchanting; charming; (*delizioso*) delightful: *sguardo* —, charming look.

incantevolménte, *av.* enchantingly; charmingly; (*deliziosamente*) delightfully.

incànto[1], *s.m.* enchantment; charm: *l'* — *dei suoi occhi*, the charm of her eyes; *l'* — *di una notte di luna*, the enchantment of a moonlit night; *questo luogo è un vero* —, this place is really wonderful; *essere sotto un* —, to be under a charm (o spell) ‖ *quest'abito ti sta d'* —, this dress fits you perfectly.

incànto[2], *s.m.* (*asta*) auction (sale): *vendere all'—*, to sell by auction.

incantucciàre, *v.t.*, **incantucciàrsi**, *v.r.* to hide in a corner.

incanutiménto, *s.m.* growing hoary.

incanutíre, *v.i.* to grow hoary.

incanutíto, *ag.* (*di capelli*) hoary; (*di persona*) hoary-headed, white-haired.

incapàce, *ag.* 1. incapable, unable: *— di un'azione disonesta*, incapable of a dishonest action; *— di fare ql.co.*, incapable of doing sthg. 2. (*dir.*) incapacitated.

incapacità, *s.f.* 1. incapacity (for sthg., for doing sthg., to do sthg.); inability (to do sthg.) 2. (*dir.*) incapacity.

incaparbíre, *v.i.*, **incaparbírsi**, *v.r.* to become obstinate: *egli si incaparbì a farlo*, he took it into his head to do it; *non incaparbirti così!*, don't be so obstinate!.

incaparbíto, *ag.* obstinate, stubborn.

incapàrsi, *V.* **incaparbíre**.

incapatúra, *s.f.* head-size (of hat).

incapestràre, *v.t.* to halter (a horse) ‖ **incapestràrsi**, *v.r.* to halter oneself.

incapestratúra, *s.f.* haltering.

incaponírsi, *V.* **incaparbírsi**.

incappàre, *v.i.* to get into (sthg.); to fall in (with s.o.); to run into (s.o., sthg.); to meet (with s.o., sthg.): *— in un pericolo*, to run into a danger; *— in qlcu.*, to fall in with s.o.; *— nei guai*, to get into trouble.

incappàrsi, *v.r.* to put on one's cape.

incappellàre, *v.t.* 1. to put a hat on (s.o.) 2. (*mar.*) to fix ‖ **incappellàrsi**, *v.r.* to put on one's hat.

incappiàre, *v.t.* to noose.

incappottàre, *v.t.* to put an overcoat on (s.o.) ‖ **incappottàrsi**, *v.r.* to put on one's overcoat, to wrap oneself in an overcoat.

incappucciàre, *v.t.* to hood ‖ **incappucciàrsi**, *v.r.* 1. (*mettersi il cappuccio*) to put on one's hood 2. (*farsi frate*) to become a friar.

incappucciàto, *ag.* 1. hooded ‖ *gli Incappucciati*, (*st. relig.*) Wycliffites, Lollards 2. (*bot. zool.*) cucullate.

incapricciàrsi, **incapriccírsi**, *v.r.* to take a fancy (to s.o., sthg.); to fall in love (with s.o.): *s'incapricciò di quel cappellino*, she took a fancy to that hat.

incarboniménto, *s.m.* carbonization.

incarboníre, *v.t.* to carbonize ‖ **incarbonírsi**, *v.r.* to become carbonized.

incarceraménto, *s.m.* imprisonment, incarceration.

incarceràre, *v.t.* 1. to imprison, to incarcerate 2. (*confinare, rinchiudere*) to confine: *— qlcu. nella sua stanza*, to confine s.o. to (*o* to shut s.o. up in) his room.

incarcerazióne, *s.f.* imprisonment, incarceration: *— per debiti*, imprisonment for debt.

incardinàre, *v.t.*, **incardinàrsi**, *v.r.* to hinge (anche *fig.*).

incardinazióne, *s.f.* hinging.

incaricàre, *v.t.* to charge, to entrust: *— qlcu. di ql.co.*, to charge (*o* to entrust) s.o. with sthg.; *— qlcu. di fare ql.co.*, to charge (*o* to commission) s.o. to do sthg. ‖ **incaricàrsi**, *v.r.* to take upon oneself; to charge oneself (with sthg.): *me ne incarico io*, I will attend to it; *— di un affare*, to take a matter in hand; *— di fare ql.co.*, to take (it) upon oneself to do sthg.

incaricàto, *ag.* charged (with sthg.), entrusted (with sthg.) ‖ *s.m.* 1. appointee, deputy; commissioner ‖ *— d'affari*, chargé d'affaires 2. (*professore fuori ruolo*) teacher on annual contract.

incàrico, *s.m.* 1. task, charge, commission, appointment, assignment; (*compito*) duty: *un — difficile*, a difficult task; *ha l'— di curare i bambini*, she is in charge of the children; *ho l'— di dirglielo*, I have been charged to tell him; *affidare un — a qlcu.*, to entrust a task to s.o. (*o* to entrust s.o. with a task *o* to give s.o. a task); *assumersi l'— di ql.co.*, to take sthg. upon

oneself: *mi sono assunto l'— di dirglielo*, I have taken (it) upon myself to tell him ‖ *per — di*, on behalf of: *per — del re*, by the King's appointment; *per — del partito, devo...*, on behalf of the party, I must... 2. (*insegnamento fuori ruolo*) annual teaching contract.

incarnàre, *v.t.* 1. to incarnate, to embody: *quell'uomo sembra — la miseria*, that man seems to embody misery 2. (*realizzare*) to carry out: *— un progetto*, to carry out a project 3. (*affondare nella carne*) to thrust into flesh ‖ **incarnàrsi**, *v.r.* to become incarnate; to take bodily form: *Cristo si incarnò per redimere gli uomini*, Christ became incarnate to redeem mankind.

incarnatíno, *ag.* incarnadine, rosy, rose-pink ‖ *s.m.* incarnadine, light flesh-tint: *avere un bell'—*, to have a rosy complexion.

incarnàto, *ag.* 1. (*fatto persona*) incarnate: *l'avarizia incarnata*, the embodiment (*o* personification) of avarice ‖ *il Verbo —*, the Word Incarnate 2. (*roseo*) flesh-coloured, rose-pink 3. (*di unghia*) ingrowing ‖ *s.m.* redness, rosiness: *l'— delle sue guance*, her rosy cheeks (*o* complexion).

incarnazióne, *s.f.* incarnation.

incarníre, *v.i.*, **incarnírsi**, *v.r.* (*di unghia*) to grow in.

incarníto, *ag.* 1. ingrowing: *unghia incarnita*, ingrowing nail 2. *fig.* (*inveterato*) ineradicable, inveterate: *vizio —*, inveterate vice.

incarognìre, *v.i.*, **incarognìrsi**, *v.r.* 1. (*imputridire*) to rot 2. (*diventar ozioso*) to grow lazy.

incartaménto, *s.m.* dossier; set of papers; papers (*pl.*); set of documents; documents (*pl.*).

incartapecoríre, *v.i.*, **incartapecorírsi**, *v.r.* to wrinkle up; to assume the appearance of parchment.

incartapecoríto, *ag.* wrinkled with age (*predicativo*): *volto — dagli anni*, face wrinkled with age.

incartúre, *v.t.* 1. to wrap in paper 2. (*mec.*) to planish.

incartàta, *s.f.* paper wrapping: *dategli un'—*, wrap it up in some paper.

incàrto, (*rar.*) per **incartaménto**.

incartocciàre, *v.t.* to wrap (sthg.) up in paper; to put (sthg.) in a paper bag ‖ **incartocciàrsi**, *v.r.* (*diventar grinzoso*) to curl up; to shrivel (up).

incartonàre, *v.t.* 1. to put between two sheets of cardboard 2. (*rilegare*) to bind in cardboard.

incasellàre, *v.t.* 1. to put in squares: *— i numeri*, to put numbers in squares 2. (*porre in nicchia di colombaia*) to pigeon-hole.

incassaménto, *s.m.* 1. boxing; packing 2. (*mec. edil.*) embedding.

incassàre, *v.t.* 1. to box, to encase; to put into a box 2. (*mettere in una cassa da morto*) to put into a coffin 3. (*incastonare*) to set: *— una gemma*, to set a gem 4. (*mec. edil.*) to embed, to build in: *l'orologio era incassato nel muro*, the clock was built in the wall 5. (*riscuotere*) to cash; to collect; to receive: *non abbiamo ancora incassato il denaro degli abbonamenti*, we have not yet collected (*o* received) the money of the subscriptions; *— un assegno*, to cash a cheque ‖ *v.i.* 1. (*boxe*) to receive a blow 2. (*combaciare*) to fit (into sthg.) ‖ **incassàrsi**, *v.r.* (*di fiume*) to be deeply embanked, to run through a cutting.

incassàto, *ag.* 1. boxed, encased 2. (*mec. edil.*) embedded, built-in: *armadio —*, a built-in wardrobe 3. (*di luogo, valle*) enclosed (in, by sthg.); (*di fiume*) deeply embanked: *un luogo — fra i monti*, a place enclosed by the mountains; *valle incassata*, sunken valley 4. (*incastonato*) set 5. (*infossato*) hollow, sunken, deep-set: *occhi incassati*, sunken eyes.

incassatúra, *s.f.* 1. (*incavo*) hollow, cavity 2. (*mec. edil.*) embedment, embedding.

incàsso, *s.m.* 1. (*riscossione*) collection 2. (*somma incassata*) amount collected; takings (*pl.*).

incastellaménto, *s.m.* (*edil. mil.*) fortifications (*pl.*); battlements (*pl.*).

incastellàre, *v.t.* (*edil. mil.*) to fortify with battlements.

incastellàto, *ag.* (*ricco di fortificazioni*) well fortified.

incastellatúra, *s.f.* (*armatura*) frame; (*mec.*) casing: — *di appoggio*, (*mec.*) sole-plate; — *di estrazione*, (*miner.*) head-frame; — *di sostegno*, (*aer.*) mount.

incastonàre, *v.t.* to set, to mount: — *una pietra preziosa*, to set (*o* to mount) a precious stone.

incastonatúra, *s.f.* setting, mounting.

incastraménto, *s.m.* **1.** embedding **2.** (*carpenteria*) mortising **3.** (*edil.*) fixing **4.** (*incastro*) joint.

incastràre, *v.t.* **1.** to embed: *pietra incastrata nella roccia*, stone embedded in rock **2.** (*adattare*) to fit in; (*ficcare dentro*) to drive in: *questo va incastrato qui dentro*, this is to be fitted in here; — *un chiodo in una parete*, to drive a nail in a wall **3.** (*carpenteria*) to mortise: — *a linguetta*, to tongue **4.** (*edil.*) to fix **5.** (*oreficeria*) to set ‖ **incastràrsi,** *v.r.* **1.** (*adattarsi*) to fit: *questo legno deve* — *in questo buco*, this piece of wood must fit into this hole **2.** (*impigliarsi*) to get stuck: *la ruota si è incastrata fra le pietre*, the wheel has got stuck among some stones **3.** (*di vetture*) to telescope: *le vetture si incastrarono*, the carriages telescoped.

incastratúra, *s.f.* **1.** (*l'incastrare*) embedding **2.** (*carpenteria*) mortising **3.** (*edil.*) fixing **4.** (*vano in cui s'incastra*) recess, hollow **5.** (*incastro*) joint.

incàstro, *s.m.* **1.** joint **2.** (*carpenteria*) gain, dap joint: — *a coda di rondine*, dovetail; — *a dente*, cogging; — *a maschio e femmina*, groove-and-tongue joint **3.** (*edil.*) fixed joint **4.** (*strumento di maniscalco*) butteris.

incatenaménto, *s.m.* chaining.

incatenàre, *v.t.* **1.** to chain, to chain up, to enchain; (*ai piedi*) to fetter: — *un prigioniero*, to put a prisoner in chains (*o* to fetter a prisoner); — *qlcu. a un palo*, to chain s.o. to a stake **2.** (*conquistare, attirare*) to captivate: — *l'attenzione*, to rivet the attention; — *i cuori*, to captivate hearts **3.** (*impegnare a fondo*) to tie up, to chain up: *sono incatenato a questo lavoro*, I am tied up with (*o* up to my neck in) this work **4.** (*impacciare*) to hamper, to tie s.o.'s hands: *tutti questi regolamenti m'incatenano*, all these regulations tie my hands **5.** (*sbarrare con catene*) to chain: — *una strada*, to chain (*o* to obstruct) a street ‖ **incatenàrsi,** *v.r. reciproco* to be linked with each other (one another): *le idee s'incatenano l'una con l'altra*, ideas are linked one with another.

incatramàre, *v.t.* to tar.

incatramàto, *ag.* tarred.

incattivíre, *v.t.* to make wicked ‖ *v.i.* to become wicked ‖ **incattivírsi,** *v.r.* (*arrabbiarsi*) to get cross.

incautaménte, *av.* incautiously, rashly, imprudently.

incàuto, *ag.* incautious, rash, imprudent: *giudizio* —, rash judgement (*o* statement).

incavalcàre, *v.t.* **1.** (*stare, mettersi a cavalcioni di*) to bestride **2.** (*sovrapporre*) to superimpose, to overlap; (*incrociare*) to cross: — *le gambe*, to cross one's legs; — *un punto*, (*nel lavoro a maglia*) to slip a stitch.

incavalcatúra, *s.f.* superimposing, overlapping.

incavallàre, *V.* **incavalcàre.**

incavàre, *v.t.* to hollow out, to scoop out, to excavate: *l'acqua incavò il terreno*, water hollowed out the ground.

incavàto, *ag.* hollow, sunken: *guance incavate*, hollow (*o* sunken) cheeks; *occhi incavati*, deep-set eyes.

incavatúra, *s.f.* hollow, hollowness, scoop, cavity.

incavicchiàre, *v.t.* to peg, to fasten with pegs.

incavicchiàto, *ag.* **1.** pegged down **2.** (*rigido*) stiff.

incàvo, *s.m.* **1.** hollow, cavity **2.** (*scanalatura*) groove **3.** (*mec.*) notch **4.** (*anat.*) socket.

incèdere, *v.i.* **1.** (*avanzare*) to advance, to proceed **2.** (*avanzare maestosamente*) to walk stately; (*con sussiego*) to strut.

incèdere, *s.m.* **1.** (*andatura*) gait **2.** (*andatura maestosa*) stately walk; (*piena di sussiego*) strut.

incendiàbile, *ag.* inflammable: *materiali infiammabili*, inflammables.

incendiàre, *v.t.* to set on fire, to set fire to (sthg.): — *una casa*, to set a house on fire (*o* to set fire to a house) ‖ **incendiàrsi,** *v.r.* **1.** to catch fire: *il pagliaio s'incendiò*, the hay-stack caught fire **2.** *fig.* (*eccitarsi*) to fly into a passion: *s'incendia per la minima cosa*, he flies into a passion for the least thing.

incendiàrio, *ag.* incendiary (*anche fig.*): *bomba incendiaria*, incendiary bomb (*o* fire-bomb); *discorso* —, incendiary speech ‖ *s.m.* incendiary.

incèndio, *s.m.* fire: *assicurazione contro gli incendi*, fire-insurance; *pompa da* —, fire-pump (*o* fire-engine); *segnale d'*—, fire-alarm; *l'* — *si propagò a tutto il villaggio*, the fire spread all over the village; *fu accusato d'*— *doloso*, he was charged with fire-raising (*o* arson); *scoppiò un* —, a fire broke out; *spegnere un* —, to put out a fire.

inceneràre, *v.t.* to strew with ashes.

inceneriménto, *s.m.* **1.** incineration: — *del filtro*, (*chim.*) filter burning **2.** (*cremazione*) cremation.

inceneríre, *v.t.* **1.** to reduce to ashes, to burn to ashes, to incinerate **2.** (*cremare*) to cremate ‖ **incenerírsi,** *v.r.* to burn to ashes, to be reduced to ashes.

incensaménto, *s.m.* **1.** incensation **2.** (*adulazione*) flattering, flattery, adulation, fawning: *mutuo* —, mutual flattery.

incensàre, *v.t.* **1.** to cense, to incense, to burn incense to (sthg.), to fumigate with incense **2.** *fig.* (*adulare*) to flatter, to adulate, to fawn upon (s.o.), to overpraise.

incensàta, *s.f.* (*adulazione*) flattery, adulation.

incensatóre, *s.m.*, **incensatríce,** *s.f.* (*chi adula*) flatterer, adulator, fawner.

incensatúra, *s.f.* (*adulazione*) flattery, adulation.

incensière, *s.m.* censer, incensory, thurible.

incènso, *s.m.* **1.** incense **2.** (*adulazione*) flattery, adulation.

incensuràbile, *ag.* irreproachable; beyond reproach (*predicativo*); blameless.

incensuràto, *ag.* uncensured; blameless: *essere* —, (*dir.*) to have a clean record; (*se in giudizio*) to be a first-offender.

incentívo, *s.m.* incentive, spur; stimulus (*pl.* stimuli): *l'*— *dell'ambizione*, the spur of ambition.

inceppaménto, *s.m.* **1.** obstacle, hindrance **2.** (*mec.*) jam, jamming, clogging.

inceppàre, *v.t.* **1.** (*mettere in ceppi*) to clog **2.** (*bloccare*) to clog (up), to block (up): *un corpo estraneo aveva inceppato il motore*, a foreign body had clogged the engine **3.** (*ostacolare, ingombrare*) to encumber, to obstruct, to hamper, to hinder, to embarrass, to fetter, to entangle: *queste maniche lunghe mi inceppano nei movimenti*, these long sleeves encumber (*o* hamper) my movements (*o* embarrass my movements) ‖ **inceppàrsi,** *v.r.* (*bloccarsi*) to jam, to stick.

inceppatúra, *V.* **inceppaménto.**

inceralaccàre, *v.t.* to seal (up) (with sealing wax).

inceràre, *v.t.* to wax; to polish, to beeswax: — *un pavimento*, to polish a floor.

inceràta, *s.f.* **1.** oil cloth, oil-skin **2.** (*copertone*) tarpaulin.

inceratíno, *s.m.* (*striscia nell'interno dei cappelli*) sweat-band.

inceràto, *ag.* waxed ‖ *s.m. V.* **inceràta.**

inceratúra, *s.f.* waxing; (*di pavimenti*) beeswaxing, polishing.

incerchiàre, *v.t.* **1.** (*cerchiare*) to encircle, to hoop **2.** (*incurvare*) to bend into a hoop ‖ **incerchiàrsi,** *v.r.* to hoop.

incerconíre, *v.i.* (*di vino*) to become sour, to turn sour.

incertaménte, *av.* **1.** uncertainly, with no certainty **2.** (*con indecisione*) with indecision, undecidedly.

incertézza, *s.f.* **1.** uncertainty, doubt, dubiousness: *l'*— *dell'esito*, the uncertainty of the result; *dissipare ogni* —, to remove any uncertainty; *essere nell'*—, to be in a state of uncertainty (o to be undecided); *tenere qlcu. nell'—*, to keep s.o. in suspense 2. *(indecisione)* indecision, perplexity, hesitation; *(irresolutezza)* irresolution; *rispose con molta —*, he answered with great indecision (o hesitation).

incèrto, *ag.* 1. uncertain, doubtful, dubious: *colore —*, undecided colour; *esito —*, uncertain (o doubtful o dubious) result; *origine, età incerta*, uncertain origin, age; *umore —*, uncertain mood; *l'avvenire è —*, the future is uncertain; *in quanto a questa faccenda tutto è ancora —*, as to this matter everything is still uncertain || *luce incerta*, dim (o feeble) light || *tempo —*, unsettled (o changeable) weather 2. *(indeciso, irresoluto)* doubtful (about, of, as to sthg., about doing); undecided (about, as to sthg., about doing); irresolute; hesitating (about, as to sthg., about doing): *sono — su quello che dovrei dire*, I am doubtful (o undecided) as to what I should say || *s.m.* 1. uncertainty: *lasciare il certo per l'—*, to give up a certainty for an uncertainty 2. *pl. (guadagni occasionali)* incidental profits, perquisites 3. *pl. (casi imprevedibili)* uncertainties: *gli incerti del mestiere*, the uncertainties of one's profession.

incespicàre, *v.i.* to stumble, to trip (over sthg.) (anche *fig.*): — *in una difficoltà*, to stumble over a difficulty; — *in un sasso*, to stumble against a stone; — *nel parlare*, to stumble in one's speech.

incessàbile, incessànte, *ag.* unceasing, incessant, unceaseless, unintermitting, unremitting: *rumore —*, incessant noise; *sforzi incessanti*, unremitting efforts.

incessanteménte, *av.* unceasingly, incessantly, unintermittingly, unremittingly.

incèsso, *s.m. (letter.)* 1. *(andatura)* gait 2. *(andatura maestosa)* stately walk; *(piena di sussiego)* strut.

incestàre, *v.t.* to put (sthg.) into baskets.

incèsto, *s.m.* incest.

incestuosaménte, *av.* incestuously.

incestuóso, *ag.* incestuous.

incètta, *s.f.* corner(ing), buying up, forestalling, monopolizing: *fare — di ql.co.*, to make a corner in sthg. (o to buy sthg. up o to forestall sthg. o to monopolize sthg.).

incettàre, *v.t.* to corner, to make a corner in (sthg.), to buy up, to monopolize, to clear the market of (sthg.): — *derrate alimentari*, to corner food-stuffs.

incettatóre, *s.m.*, **incettatríce**, *s.f.* buyer-up (*pl.* buyers-up); monopolist.

inchiavardàre, *v.t.* to bolt, to fasten with a bolt.

inchiavàre, *v.t.* to lock.

inchiavettàre, *v.t. (mec.)* to key.

inchiavettatúra, *s.f. (mec.)* keying.

inchiésta, *s.f.* inquiry, investigation: *aprire, fare, un' — su ql.co.*, to make (o to institute o to set up) an inquiry about sthg. (o to inquire into sthg.).

inchinàre, *v.t.* to bow, to incline, to bend, to stoop: — *gli occhi*, to look down; — *la testa*, to bow (o to incline o to bend o to stoop) one's head || **inchinàrsi**, *v.r.* to bow (down), to stoop; *(di donna) (fare una riverenza)* to curtsey (to s.o.): *s'inchinò davanti all'altare*, he bowed (down) before the altar; *uscendo, l'ambasciatore s'inchinò*, on retiring the ambassador made a bow; — *a qlcu., a ql.co., fig.* to bow (o to submit o to yield) to s.o., to sthg.

inchinàto, *ag.* bent, curved.

inchinévole, *ag.* 1. *(pieghevole)* pliant, yielding 2. *(disposto)* inclined, willing, disposed.

inchíno, *s.m.* bow; *(riverenza femminile)* curtsey: *un profondo —*, a low bow; *fare un —*, to bow; *(di donna)* to curtsey: *fare un — a qlcu.*, to give s.o. a bow (o to bow to s.o.); *(di donna)* to make s.o. a curtsey.

inchiodàre, *v.t.* 1. to nail, to rivet (anche *fig.*): *devi inchiodarlo nella mente*, you must rivet it in your mind; *questo lavoro mi ha inchiodato in casa per due giorni*, this work has confined me to the house for two days; *i suoi occhi erano inchiodati al palcoscenico*,

his eyes were riveted on the stage; — *il coperchio di una cassa*, to nail down the cover of a case; — *ql.co. a un muro*, to nail sthg. to a wall 2. *(artigl.) (un cannone)* to spike.

inchiodatríce, *s.f. (mec.) (per inchiodare casse)* box nailing machine.

inchiodatúra, *s.f.* nailing, riveting.

inchiostràre, *v.t.* to ink (anche *tip.*) || **inchiostràrsi**, *v.r.* to ink oneself: — *le dita*, to ink one's fingers.

inchiòstro, *s.m.* 1. ink: — *copiativo*, copying ink; — *di China*, Indian (o China) ink; — *da stampa*, printing-ink; — *indelebile*, indelible ink; — *simpatico*, invisible (o sympathetic) ink; *dita sporche d'—*, inky fingers; *nero come l'—*, as black as ink 2. *(di seppia)* sepia, ink.

inchiúdere, *V.* **inclúdere**.

inciampàre, *v.i.* 1. to stumble (anche *fig.*): *ecco dove tutti hanno inciampato!*, that is where all have stumbled!; — *in una difficoltà*, to stumble over a difficulty; — *in un sasso*, to stumble against a stone: — *nel parlare*, to stumble in one's speech 2. *(imbattersi)* to stumble (upon, across s.o., sthg.), to fall in (with s.o., sthg.): *inciampò nel suo creditore*, he fell in with (o ran across o stumbled across) his creditor.

inciampàta, *s.f.* stumble, stumbling: *dare un'—*, to stumble.

inciàmpo, *s.m.* 1. *(ostacolo)* hindrance, obstacle, stumbling-block 2. *(difficoltà)* difficulty.

incidentàle, *ag.* 1. *(occasionale, casuale)* accidental, occasional, casual 2. *(accessorio)* incidental: *spese incidentali*, incidental expenses 3. *(dir.)* interlocutory 4. *(gram.)* parenthetic(al): *proposizione —*, parenthesis.

incidentalménte, *av.* 1. *(casualmente)* accidentally; by chance: *lo incontrai —*, I met him accidentally (o by chance) 2. *(di passaggio)* incidentally: *glielo dissi —*, I told him incidentally.

incidènte, *ag.* 1. incident: *raggio —*, *(ott.)* incident ray 2. *(gram.)* parenthetic(al) || *s.m.* 1. *(infortunio)* accident: *un — automobilistico, ferroviario*, a car, railway accident; *un — mortale*, a fatal accident; *l'aereo ebbe un — nell'atterrare*, the aeroplane met with an accident on landing 2. *(episodio)* incident: *ci fu un curioso — al ricevimento di ieri sera*, there was a curious incident at last night's party; *ci furono diversi incidenti di frontiera prima che scoppiasse la guerra*, there were several frontier incidents before the war broke out 3. *(disputa, questione)* question: *ho avuto un — col mio prin cipale*, I had an argument with my boss 4. *(dir.)* incident: *sollevare un —*, to raise an incident.

incidènza, *s.f.* incidence: *l'— di una tassa*, the incidence of a tax; *angolo d'—*, *(fis.)* angle of incidence || *per —*, *(per caso)* by chance; *(a mo' d'inciso)* by the way (o incidentally).

incídere[1], *v.t.* 1. to engrave, to cut: — *il proprio nome su un pezzo di legno*, to cut one's name on a piece of wood; — *su marmo*, to engrave on marble 2. *(ad acquaforte)* to etch 3. *(registrare su nastro, disco, ecc.)* to record: — *un'opera con gli interpreti originali*, to record an opera with the original cast 4. *(chir.)* to incise; to lance, to cut open: *bisognò — l'ascesso*, the abscess had to be lanced (o cut open).

incídere[2], *v.i. (gravare)* to weigh heavily: *questa spesa incide pesantemente sul mio bilancio*, this expense weighs heavily on (o constitutes a heavy item in) my budget; *questo non incide sulla riuscita dell'esperimento*, this does not affect the result of the experiment; *una tassa che incide sul datore di lavoro*, a tax that falls on the employer.

incíle, *s.m.* 1. *(canale di scolo)* drain, sewer 2. *(canale di derivazione)* inlet (of a canal).

incinerazióne, *s.f.* 1. *(debbio)* ashes *(pl.)* (for manure) 2. *(chim.) (calcinazione)* calcining, calcination 3. *(cremazione)* cremation.

incínta, *ag.* pregnant; with child (*predicativo*): *una donna* —, a pregnant woman (*o* a woman with child).

incipiènte, *ag.* incipient, beginning: *raffreddore* —, incipient cold.

incipollíre, *v.i.* (*di alberi*) to peel off the bark.

incipriàre, *v.t.* to powder ǁ **incipriàrsi**, *v.r.* to powder (oneself): — *il viso, il naso*, to powder one's face, one's nose.

incipriàto, *ag.* powdered.

inciprigníre, *v.t.* to irritate, to embitter ǁ *v.i.*, **inciprignírsi**, *v.r.* 1. (*di piaga, suppurare*) to fester 2. *fig.* to fester, to become irritated, to become inflamed.

incírca, all', *l.av.* about, approximately.

incirconcíso, *ag.* uncircumcised ǁ *gli incirconcisi*, (*Bibbia*) the uncircumcised (*o* the Gentiles).

incircoscrítto, *ag.* uncircumscribed; unlimited.

incisióne, *s.f.* 1. (*taglio*) incision, cut; (*chir.*) lancing, incision: *il chirurgo praticò una piccola* — *nel dito*, the surgeon made a small cut in the finger 2. (*tacca in un legno*) notch 3. (*art.*) engraving: — *ad acquaforte*, etching; — *a stampa*, print; — *su legno*, wood engraving; — *su linoleum*, linocut; — *su metallo*, lithography 4. (*registrazione su nastro, disco, ecc.*) recording: — *su nastro di un discorso*, tape-recording of a speech.

incisívo, *ag.* 1. incisive 2. *fig.* incisive, sharp, cutting, trenchant: *tono* —, incisive (*o* sharp) tone ǁ *s.m.* (*anat.*) incisor.

incíso, *ag.* 1. incised 2. (*art.*) engraved ǁ *s.m.* (*gram.*) parenthetic clause ǁ *per* —, (*incidentalmente*) incidentally (*o* by the way).

incisóre, *s.m.* (*art.*) engraver; (*d'acqueforti*) etcher.

incisòrio, *ag.* incisory ǁ *sala incisoria*, anatomical theatre.

incitaménto, *s.m.* incitement, incentive, urge; stimulus (*pl.* stimuli): *l'ambizione è il suo unico* —, ambition is his only stimulus; *egli sentiva un vero* — *alla ricerca scientifica*, he felt a true incentive to scientific research.

incitànte, *ag.* inciting, stimulating, instigating, urging.

incitàre, *v.t.* to incite, to instigate, to stir (up) to urge: — *qlcu. a ql.co., a fare ql.co.*, to incite (*o* to instigate *o* to stir up *o* to urge) s.o. to sthg., to do sthg.

incitazióne, *s.f.* incitation, instigation.

incitrullíre, *v.i.* to become silly, to become dull.

inciuchíre, *v.i.* to become dull, to become silly.

incivíle, *ag.* 1. (*non civilizzato*) uncivilized, barbarous 2. (*scortese, non raffinato*) uncivil, discourteous, rude.

incivilimónto, *s.m.* 1. (*civilizzazione*) civilization 2. (*raffinamento*) refinement, refining, civilizing.

incivilíre, *v.t.* 1. (*civilizzare*) to civilize: — *un paese*, to civilize a country 2. (*raffinare*) to civilize, to refine ǁ **incivilírsi**, *v.r.* to become civilized.

incivilménte, *av.* 1. (*in modo non civile*) uncivilly 2. (*scortesemente*) uncivilly, discourteously, rudely.

inciviltà, *s.f.* 1. (*barbarie*) barbarism 2. (*maleducazione*) incivility, discourtesy, rudeness; want of manners.

inclemènte, *ag.* 1. inclement; severe: *tempo* —, inclement weather 2. (*spietato*) merciless, cruel.

inclemènza, *s.f.* 1. inclemency; severity 2. (*crudeltà*) mercilessness, cruelty.

inclinàre, *v.t.* to incline (anche *fig.*); (*piegare*) to bend: — *il cuore, la mente*, to incline the heart, the mind; — *la testa*, to bend (*o* to incline) one's head; *il suo cuore l'inclinava all'indulgenza*, his heart inclined him to be indulgent; *tutto ciò ci inclina a pensare che...*, all this inclines us to think that...; — *qlcu. a fare ql.co.*, to predispose (*o* to influence) s.o. in favour of doing sthg. ǁ *v.i.*, **inclinàrsi**, *v.r.* 1. to incline, to lean, to tilt, to tip (up), to slope: *l'asse s'inclinò e tutto scivolò per terra*, the plank tilted (*o* tipped up) and everything slipped on the floor; *il campanile inclina verso destra*, the steeple leans to the right; *il tetto si inclina per lasciar scorrere l'acqua*, the roof slopes to let the water run

off 2. (*piegarsi*) to bend: *gli alberi si inclinavano al vento*, the trees bent to the wind 3. (*di nave*) to list, to heel 4. (*di aeroplano*) to tip, to tilt: — *in curva, to* bank 5. (*di ago magnetico*) to dip 6. *fig.* to incline, to be inclined, to be disposed: *egli inclina all'ozio*, he is inclined to be lazy; — *a credere che...*, to incline to the belief that...; — *a fare ql.co.*, to be (*o* to feel) inclined to do sthg.

inclinàto, *ag.* inclined (anche *fig.*); slanting, sloping: *piano* —, inclined plane; *essere* — *a fare ql.co.*, to be inclined (*o* to be disposed) to do sthg.

inclinazióne, *s.f.* 1. (*pendenza*) inclination, slope, slant; (*di strada*) gradient: — *della testa*, inclination of the head; — *di un piano*, inclination of a plane; *l'* — *di una strada*, the gradient of a road; — *di un tetto, del fianco di una montagna*, the slope of a roof, of the side of a mountain; — *magnetica*, (*fis.*) magnetic inclination (*o* dip) 2. *fig.* (*tendenza, propensione*) inclination, tendency, propensity: *ha una certa* — *a fare pettegolezzi*, he has an inclination (*o* tendency *o* propensity) to gossip; *la mia* — *sarebbe di rimanere qui*, my inclination would be to remain here 3. *fig.* (*attitudine, talento*) turn, bent, talent: *ha* — *per le lingue*, he has a turn (*o* a bent *o* a talent) for languages; *seguire la propria* —, to follow one's own bent.

inclíne, *ag.* inclined, prone, disposed: — *a credere*, inclined to believe; — *all'ira*, prone to anger.

inclinòmetro, *s.m.* (*aer. fis.*) inclinometer.

ínclito, *ag.* (*letter.*) famous, illustrious; glorious: *l'* — *eroe*, the glorious hero.

inclúdere, *v.t.* 1. (*comprendere*) to include, to comprise: *fu incluso nel numero degli invitati*, he was included among the guests 2. (*allegare*) to enclose: — *una lettera*, to enclose a letter 3. (*implicare*) to imply.

inclusióne, *s.f.* inclusion.

inclusivaménte, *av.* inclusively.

inclusívo, *ag.* inclusive.

inclúso, *ag.* 1. included: *le spese di trasporto sono incluse nel prezzo*, (*comm.*) the price is inclusive of freight 2. (*allegato*) enclosed: *il documento* —, the enclosed document.

incoàre, *v.t.* (*dir.*) to commence.

incoatívo, *ag.* (*gram.*) inchoative: *verbo* —, inchoative verb.

incoccàre, *v.t.* to nock, to notch: — *una freccia*, to nock an arrow.

incocciàre, *v.t.* (*mar.*) to hook ǁ *v.i.*, **incocciàrsi**, *v.r.* (*ostinarsi*) to be obstinate; to persist.

incocciatúra, *s.f.* (*ostinazione*) obstinacy.

incodardíre, *v.i.* to become cowardly.

incoercíbile, *ag.* irrepressible, incoercible.

incoercibilità, *s.f.* irrepressibleness, irrepressibility.

incoerènte, *ag.* 1. incoherent: *discorso* —, incoherent speech 2. (*contraddittorio*) inconsistent: *le sue parole sono incoerenti col suo comportamento*, his words are inconsistent with his behaviour.

incoerenteménte, *av.* 1. incoherently 2. (*in modo contraddittorio*) inconsistently.

incoerènza, *s.f.* 1. incoherence, incoherency 2. (*contraddizione*) inconsistency.

incògliere, *v.i.* to happen, to befall (s.o.): *m'incolse una sventura*, a misfortune befell (*o* happened to) me; *mal me ne incolse*, nothing but evil came of it to me.

incògnita, *s.f.* 1. (*mat.*) unknown (quantity): *nelle equazioni la x rappresenta un'*—, in equations x denotes an unknown (quantity) 2. (*cosa sconosciuta*) uncertainty: *le incognite della vita coniugale*, the uncertainties of married life; *questa è un'*—, this is an uncertainty.

incògnito, *ag.* unknown ǁ *s.m.* incognito (*pl.* incogniti, incognitos): *fare ql.co. serbando l'*—, to do sthg. incognito; *serbar l'*—, to preserve one's incognito ǁ *in* —, incognito: *viaggiare in* —, to travel incognito.

incoiàre, *v.t.* to leather ǁ *v.i.* to become leathery.

incollaménto, *s.m.* sticking, pasting, gluing.

incollàre[1], *v.t.* 1. to stick; (*carta*) to paste; (*special-*

mente cocci, legno, porcellana) to glue: — *due cose insieme*, to stick (*o* to glue) two things together; — *un'etichetta su una bottiglia*, to label a bottle; — *un manifesto a un muro*, to stick a bill (*o* to paste up a bill) on a wall; — *un oggetto rotto*, to glue up a broken object **2.** *fig.* to press, to glue: *il bambino incollò il viso al vetro della finestra*, the child pressed (*o* glued) his face to the window-pane ‖ **incollàrsi**, *v.r.* to stick (anche *fig.*): *queste etichette si sono incollate insieme*, these labels have stuck together; — *contro un muro*, to stand close to a wall.

incollàre[2], *v.t.* to shoulder (anche *fig.*).

incollatóre, *s.m.* sticker, poster.

incollatríce, *s.f.* **1.** (*ind. tessile*) sizing machine **2.** (*cine.*) splicer.

incollatúra[1], *s.f.* sticking, pasting, gluing.

incollatúra[2], *s.f.* (*ippica*) neck: *vincere per una* —, to win by a neck.

incolleríre, *v.i.*, **incollerírsi**, *v.r.* to get angry, to lose one's temper, to fire up, to fly into a rage.

incolleríto, *ag.* angry, enraged, wrathful.

incolonnaménto, *s.m.* column formation.

incolonnàre, *v.t.* to draw up (in columns), to form into columns: — *numeri, soldati*, to draw up figures, soldiers (in columns).

incolonnatóre, *s.m.* (*di macchina per scrivere*) tabulator.

incolóre, **incolóro**, *ag.* colourless.

incolpàbile, *ag.* **1.** chargeable, blam(e)able **2.** (*letter.*) (*innocente*) blameless, innocent.

incolpabilità, *s.f.* **1.** chargeability **2.** (*letter.*) (*innocenza*) blamelessness, innocence.

incolpàre, *v.t.* to charge, to accuse, to inculpate: — *qlcu. di omicidio*, to charge s.o. with murder (*o* to accuse s.o. of murder) ‖ **incolpàrsi**, *v.r.* to accuse oneself ‖ *v.r. reciproco* to accuse each other (one another).

incolpàto, *ag.* **1.** (*accusato*) charged (with sthg.), accused (of sthg.) **2.** (*letter.*) (*innocente*) blameless, innocent ‖ *incolpata tutela*, (*dir.*) self-defence.

incolpatóre, *s.m.* accuser.

incolpazióne, *s.f.* charge, accusation, inculpation.

incolpévole, *ag.* blameless, innocent.

incolpevolménte, *av.* blamelessly, innocently.

incólto, *ag.* **1.** (*di terreno*) untilled, uncultivated: *terreno* —, uncultivated (*o* waste) land **2.** (*trascurato, disordinato*) untidy, slovenly: *barba incolta*, neglected (*o* unkempt) beard **3.** (*ignorante*) uncultivated, uncultured, uneducated; (*rozzo*) rough: *donna incolta*, uneducated (*o* uncultured) woman.

incòlume, *ag.* unharmed, unhurt, uninjured: *passò — attraverso molti pericoli*, he went through many dangers uninjured.

incolumità, *s.f.* safety.

incombènte, *ag.* **1.** (*che sovrasta minacciosamente*) impending: *pericolo* —, impending danger **2.** (*che spetta*) incumbent: *un dovere — su tutti noi*, a duty incumbent on us all.

incombènza, *s.f.* errand, commission, task, charge: *assumersi l'— di fare ql.co.*, to take it upon oneself to do sthg.; *dare un'— a qlcu.*, to give an errand to s.o.

incómbere, *v.i.* **1.** (*sovrastare minacciosamente*) to impend (over s.o., sthg.), to hang (over s.o., sthg.): *una condanna incombe sul suo capo*, a sentence hangs over his head; *un pericolo che incombe*, an impending danger **2.** (*spettare*) to be incumbent (on s.o., sthg.), to belong (to s.o., sthg.), to be one's job, to be one's duty: *i doveri che gli incombono*, the duties which fall on him; *incombe a te di far questo*, it is incumbent on you to do this; *questo incombe a te*, this belongs to you (*o* this is your job); *la responsabilità incombe all'autore*, responsibility lies (*o* rests) with the author.

incombustíbile, *ag.* incombustible, uninflammable, fireproof: *materiale* —, fireproofing material.

incombustibilità, *s.f.* incombustibility; (*resistenza al fuoco*) fire resistance.

incombústo, *ag.* (*rar.*) unburnt, unburned.

incominciaménto, *s.m.* beginning, commencement.

incominciàre, *v.t.i.* to begin, to commence, to start: *incomincia a piovere*, it is beginning (*o* starting) to rain; *lasciatemi — dall'inizio*, let me begin at the beginning; *il romanzo incomincia con una descrizione*, the novel begins (*o* opens) with a description ‖ — *a fare ql.co.*, to begin (*o* to start) to do sthg. (*o* doing sthg.); — *bene*, to have a good start; — *un'impresa*, to embark on (*o* to enter upon) an undertaking; — *un lavoro*, to begin (*o* to start on) a work ‖ *a — da oggi, da qui*, beginning from today, from here ‖ *per — devo dirvi...*, to begin with (*o* first of all) I must tell you... ‖ *chi ben incomincia è a metà dell'opera*, prov. well begun is half done.

incommensuràbile, *ag.* incommensurable: *grandezze incommensurabili*, (*geom.*) incommensurable quantities.

incommensurabilità, *s.f.* incommensurability.

incommensurabilménte, *av.* incommensurably.

incommerciàbile, *ag.* not negotiable.

incommestíbile, *ag.* inedible.

incommutàbile, *ag.* **1.** (*comm. dir.*) incommutable: *una legge* —, an incommutable law **2.** (*immutabile*) immutable, inalterable.

incommutabilità, *s.f.* **1.** (*comm. dir.*) incommutability **2.** (*immutabilità*) immutability, inalterableness.

incommutabilménte, *av.* **1.** (*comm. dir.*) incommutably **2.** (*immutabilmente*) immutably, inalterably.

incomodaménte, *av.* uncomfortably, inconveniently.

incomodàre, *v.t.* to annoy; to incommode, to inconvenience, to trouble: *non voglio incomodarlo*, I don't want to trouble him; *scusi se l'incomodo*, sorry to trouble you ‖ **incomodàrsi**, *v.r.* to trouble (about sthg.); (*fam.*) to bother (about sthg.): *non incomodarti a venire!*, don't trouble (*o fam.* bother) to come!; *non s'incomodi!*, don't trouble (yourself)!.

incomodàto, *ag.* **1.** disturbed, troubled, annoyed **2.** (*indisposto*) unwell, indisposed.

incomodità, *s.f.* **1.** uncomfortableness, incommodiousness, incommodity: *l'— di questa casa è notevole*, this house is remarkable for its lack of comfort **2.** (*noia, fastidio*) trouble, nuisance; (*disturbo*) inconvenience **3.** (*leggera indisposizione*) indisposition, ailment.

incòmodo, *ag.* **1.** uncomfortable, incommodious, inconvenient: *ad un'ora incomoda*, at an inconvenient time; *appartamento* —, uncomfortable (*o* incommodious) flat; *mi è — vederlo questa mattina*, it is not convenient to me to see him this morning; *questa sedia è incomoda*, this chair is uncomfortable **2.** (*fastidioso*) troublesome: *avevo un mucchio di bagaglio* —, I had a lot of troublesome luggage ‖ *s.m.* **1.** (*fastidio*) inconvenience; trouble, nuisance: *gli incomodi di un lungo viaggio*, the inconveniences of a long journey; *troppo* —!, don't trouble yourself!; *ella vi sta dando un mucchio di* —, she is putting you to a lot of trouble; *questo è un grave* —, this is a big trouble (*o* nuisance); *scusi l'—*, sorry to trouble you; *se non ti è d'—*, if it is not inconvenient to you; *essere di* —, to be in the way; *recare* —, to cause inconvenience; *togliere l'—*, to take one's leave ‖ *quant'è il vostro* —?, what is your charge? ‖ *fare il terzo* —, (*fam.*) (*reggere il moccolo*) to play gooseberry **2.** (*indisposizione*) indisposition, ailment.

incomparàbile, *ag.* incomparable, peerless.

incomparabilità, *s.f.* incomparableness, peerlessness.

incomparabilménte, *av.* incomparably.

incompartíbile, *ag.* (*rar.*) indivisible.

incompatíbile, *ag.* incompatible; inconsistent: *cariche, uffici incompatibili*, (*dir.*) incompatible posts, offices; *il bere eccessivamente è — con la salute*, excessive drinking is incompatible with good health; *queste medicine sono incompatibili*, these medicines are incompatible; *la sua condotta è — coi suoi principi*, his behaviour is inconsistent with his principles.

incompatibilità, *s.f.* incompatibility; inconsistence, inconsistency:— *di carattere,* incompatibility of temper: *chiedere il divorzio per — di carattere,* to sue for a divorce on the grounds of incompatibility of character.

incompatibilménte, *av.* incompatibly; inconsistently.

incompàtto, *ag.* (*rar.*) incompact.

incompetènte, *ag.* incompetent (to sthg.); unqualified (for sthg., to do): — *in materia d'arte,* not qualified to judge in art matters; *giudice, tribunale —,* incompetent judge, tribunal; *egli è — in fatto di musica,* he knows very little about music; *egli è — in materia,* he is not an expert on the subject ‖ *eliminare gli incompetenti,* to weed out the incompetents.

incompetènza, *s.f.* incompetence, incompetency: — *di un tribunale,* incompetence (o incompetency) of a court: *sostenere l'— di un tribunale,* to plead the incompetence of a court.

incompiutaménte, *av.* incompletely.

incompiutézza, *s.f.* incompleteness.

incompiúto, *ag.* incomplete; unfinished ‖ *l'Incompiuta di Schubert,* (*mus.*) Schubert's Unfinished Symphony.

incompletaménte, *av.* incompletely.

incompletézza, *s.f.* incompleteness; incompletion.

incomplèto, *ag.* **1.** incomplete, defective; unfinished **2.** (*metal.*) (*di getto*) short-run.

incomportàbile, *ag.* (*insopportabile*) unbearable, insufferable, intolerable.

incomportabilménte, *av.* (*insopportabilmente*) unbearably, insufferably, intolerably.

incompostaménte, *av.* **1.** (*in modo disordinato*) in a disorderly manner **2.** (*sconvenientemente*) unbecomingly **3.** (*indecentemente*) indecently.

incompostézza, *s.f.* **1.** (*disordine*) disorder, discomposure **2.** (*sconvenienza*) unbecomingness, uncomeliness, unseemliness **3.** (*indecenza*) indecency.

incompósto, *ag.* **1.** (*disordinato*) disorderly, disordered: *chioma incomposta,* disordered hair; *turba incomposta,* disorderly crowd **2.** (*sconveniente, sguaiato*) unbecoming, uncomely, unseemly: *contegno —,* unseemly behaviour **3.** (*indecente*) indecent.

incomprensíbile, *ag.* incomprehensible: *ciò mi è —,* I can't make it out; *egli mi è —,* he is incomprehensible to me.

incomprensibilità, *s.f.* incomprehensibility; incomprehensibleness.

incomprensibilménte, *av.* incomprehensibly.

incomprensióne, *s.f.* incomprehension.

incomprensívo, *ag.* unsympathetic.

incompréso, *ag.* (*non compreso*) not understood; (*mal compreso*) misunderstood; (*non apprezzato*) unappreciated: *poeta —,* unappreciated poet; *sono un —,* no one has ever understood me ‖ *genio —,* (*iron.*) undiscovered genius.

incompressíbile, *ag.* (*fis.*) incompressible.

incompressibilità, *s.f.* (*fis.*) incompressibility.

incomputàbile, *ag.* incalculable.

incomunicàbile, *ag.* incommunicable.

incomunicabilità, *s.f.* incommunicability; incommunicableness.

incomunicabilménte, *av.* incommunicably.

inconcepíbile, *ag.* **1.** inconceivable, unthinkable, unimaginable **2.** (*incredibile, sorprendente*) incredible, surprising: *è —!,* it is incredible!.

inconcepibilità, *s.f.* inconceivability.

inconcepibilménte, *av.* inconceivably.

inconcèsso, *ag.* not granted; denied.

inconciliàbile, *ag.* irreconcilable; incompatible: *avversari inconciliabili,* irreconcilable adversaries; *teorie inconciliabili,* incompatible theories.

inconciliabilità, *s.f.* irreconcilability; incompatibility.

inconciliabilménte, *av.* irreconcilably; incompatibly.

inconcludènte, *ag.* inconclusive: *ragionamento —,* inconclusive argument; *un uomo —,* a good-for-nothing.

inconcludenteménte, *av.* inconclusively.

inconcludènza, *s.f.* inconclusiveness.

inconcùsso, *ag.* (*letter.*) unshaken, unmoved; firm, steady: *amicizia, legge inconcussa,* firm friendship, law; *con costanza inconcussa,* with unshaken constancy; *fede, verità inconcussa,* unshaken faith, truth.

incondizionataménte, *av.* unconditionally.

incondizionàto, *ag.* unconditioned, unconditional: *approvazione incondizionata,* unconditional acceptance; *resa incondizionata,* (*mil.*) unconditional surrender; *riflesso —,* (*psicologia*) unconditioned reflex.

inconfessàbile, *ag.* unavowable, unmentionable.

inconfessàto, *ag.* unconfessed, unshriven: *morire —,* to die without confession (o unshriven).

inconfèsso, *ag.* (*letter.*) pleading not guilty: *reo —,* criminal pleading not guilty.

inconfondíbile, *ag.* unmistakable; characteristic.

inconfortàbile, *ag.* inconsolable, disconsolate.

inconfutàbile, *ag.* irrefutable, irrecusable: *il suo argomento era —,* his argument was irrefutable.

inconfutabilità, *s.f.* irrefutability.

inconfutabilménte, *av.* irrefutably.

inconfutàto, *ag.* unconfuted, unrefuted.

incongelàbile, *ag.* unfreezable, non-freezing: *miscela —,* (*aut.*) anti-freeze.

incongiungíbile, *ag.* that cannot be jointed.

incongiúnto, *ag.* unjointed; not jointed.

incongruènte, *ag.* **1.** incongruous; inconsistent; self-contradictory: *persona —,* inconsistent person; *le sue parole sono incongruenti con la sua condotta,* her words are inconsistent with her conduct **2.** (*illogico*) illogical: *idee incongruenti,* inconsequent ideas.

incongruenteménte, *av.* **1.** incongruously; inconsistently **2.** (*illogicamente*) illogically.

incongruènza, *s.f.* **1.** incongruity, incongruousness; inconsistency; self-contradiction **2.** (*illogicità*) illogicalness, illogicality.

incòngruo, *ag.* incongruous.

inconoscíbile, *ag.* **1.** unknowable **2.** (*fil.*) incognoscible.

inconsapévole, *ag.* **1.** (*inconscio*) unconscious, unwitting: *un'azione —,* an unconscious (o unwitting) action **2.** (*ignaro*) ignorant, unaware, uninformed: *era — di quello che stava accadendo,* he was ignorant of what was happening.

inconsapevolézza, *s.f.* **1.** unconsciousness, unwittingness **2.** (*ignoranza*) ignorance, unawareness.

inconsapevolménte, *av.* unconsciously; unawares.

inconsciaménte, *av.* unconsciously; unawares.

incònscio, *ag.* V. **inconsapévole** ‖ *s.m.: l'—,* (*psicologia*) the unconscious.

inconseguènte, *ag.* inconsequent; incoherent; contradictory.

inconseguènza, *s.f.* inconsequence; incoherence.

inconsideràbile, *ag.* inconsiderable.

inconsiderataménte, *av.* inconsiderately; rashly, thoughtlessly.

inconsideratézza, *s.f.* inconsiderateness; rashness.

inconsideràto, *ag.* inconsiderate; rash.

inconsiderazióne, *s.f.* inconsiderateness; rashness.

inconsistènte, *ag.* **1.** (*infondato*) insubstantial; ill-grounded; unfounded **2.** (*fallace*) fallacious.

inconsistenteménte, *av.* **1.** (*infondatamente*) insubstantially; unfoundedly **2.** (*fallacemente*) fallaciously.

inconsistènza, *s.f.* **1.** (*infondatezza*) insubstantiality; lack of foundation **2.** (*fallacia*) fallacy.

inconsolàbile, *ag.* inconsolable.

inconsolabilménte, *av.* inconsolably.

inconsolàto, *ag.* disconsolate, forlorn; wretched.

inconsuèto, *ag.* unusual.

inconsultaménte, *av.* unadvisedly; rashly.

inconsúlto, *ag.* unadvised; rash; heedless.

inconsumàbile, *ag.* inconsumable; everlasting.

inconsumàto, inconsúnto, *ag.* unconsumed.
incontaminàbile, *ag.* that cannot be contaminated.
incontaminataménte, *av.* stainlessly.
incontaminatézza, *s.f.* stainlessness.
incontaminàto, *ag.* incontaminate; unpolluted; stainless.
incontanènte, *av.* (*arc.*) (*subito*) at once, immediately.
incontentàbile, *ag.* 1. insatiable, unsatisfiable 2. (*esigente*) exacting, hard to please.
incontentabilità, *s.f.* 1. insatiability 2. (*esigenza*) exactingness.
incontentabilménte, *av.* 1. insatiably 2. (*esigentemente*) exactingly.
incontestàbile, *ag.* incontestable, indisputable, unquestionable.
incontestabilità, *s.f.* incontestability, indisputability, unquestionableness.
incontestabilménte, *av.* incontestably, indisputably, unquestionably.
incontestàto, *ag.* indisputed, unquestioned.
incontinènte, *ag.* incontinent.
incontinenteménte, *av.* incontinently.
incontinènza, *s.f.* incontinence.
incontràre, *v.t.* to meet; (*imbattersi in*) to meet with (s.o., sthg.) (anche *fig.*): *lo incontrai in chiesa,* I met him at church; *venne ad incontrarmi alla stazione,* he met me at the station; — *difficoltà, ostacoli,* to meet with difficulties, obstacles; — *il favore del pubblico,* to meet with the favour of the public; — *qlcu. per caso,* to meet s.o. by chance (*o* to meet with s.o. *o* to fall in with s.o. *o* to run across s.o.) ‖ *v.i.* (*aver successo*) to be a success, to be successful, to become successful, to be popular, to be well-liked: *questo libro ha incontrato,* this book is a success; *il nuovo insegnante incontra molto,* the new teacher is very popular (*o* is very well-liked) ‖ **incontràrsi,** *v.r.* 1. to meet: *ci incontrammo in treno,* we met in the train; *queste linee non si incontrano,* these lines do not meet; *l'ultima volta che ci incontrammo,* the last time we met 2. (*accordarsi*) to agree: *quei due ragazzi non si incontrano, litigano sempre,* those two boys do not agree, they always quarrel 3. (*coincidere*) to coincide: *le nostre idee si incontrano perfettamente,* our ideas coincide perfectly 4. (*spor.*) to encounter (s.o.).
incontrastàbile, *ag.* 1. (*inoppugnabile*) incontestable, indisputable 2. (*ineluttabile*) inevitable, unavoidable.
incontrastabilménte, *av.* 1. (*inoppugnabilmente*) incontestably, indisputably 2. (*ineluttabilmente*) inevitably, unavoidably.
incontrastàto, *ag.* uncontested, undisputed.
incóntro[1], *s.m.* 1. (*convegno, adunanza*) meeting 2. (*spor.*) match: — *di calcio,* football match 3. (*scontro*) collision 4. (*occasione*) occasion: *fortunato* —, lucky occasion.
incóntro[2], *av.* 1. (*contro, verso*) **towards:** *mi venne* —, he came towards me; *venitemi* — *alla fermata dell'autobus,* come and meet me at the bus stop ‖ *se il prezzo vi sembra alto, cercheremo di venirvi* —, if the price seems high to you, we shall try to meet you half way 2. (*di fronte*) **opposite:** *abita qui* —, he lives opposite ‖ **incóntro a,** *l. prep.* 1. (*verso*) **towards; up to; to:** *corse* — *al babbo,* he ran up to his father; *non vorrei andare* — *a troppe difficoltà,* I should not like to come up against too many difficulties; *andare* — *ai desideri di qlcu.,* to meet s.o.'s wishes; *andare* — *ai guai,* to expose oneself to trouble (*o fam.* to ask for it); *andare* — *alla morte,* to go to one's death; *andare* — *a qlcu.,* to go towards s.o.; (*andarlo a ricevere*) to go and meet s.o.; *andare* — *a spese,* to incur expenses 2. (*in faccia a*) **opposite, in front of:** *è* — *alla porta,* it is opposite (*o* in front of) the door 3. (*contro*) **against:** — *al nemico,* against the enemy.
incontrovèrso, *ag.* undisputed.
incontrovertìbile, *ag.* indisputable, incontrovertible.

incontrovertibilità, *s.f.* indisputability, incontrovertibility.
incontrovertibilménte, *av.* indisputably, incontrovertibly.
inconveniènte, *ag.* 1. (*svantaggioso*) inconvenient 2. (*sconveniente*) unbecoming ‖ *s.m.* (*svantaggio*) inconvenience; disadvantage, drawback; (*fastidio*) trouble, nuisance: *gli inconvenienti di vivere in campagna,* the inconveniences of living in the country; *la cosa presenta degli inconvenienti,* the matter presents disadvantages.
inconvenienteménte, *av.* 1. (*in modo svantaggioso*) inconveniently 2. (*sconvenientemente*) unbecomingly.
inconveniènza, *s.f.* 1. (*svantaggio*) inconvenience 2. (*sconvenienza*) unbecomingness, impropriety.
inconvertìbile, *ag.* inconvertible: *biglietti a corso forzoso* —, (*econ.*) inconvertible currency.
inconvertibilità, *s.f.* inconvertibility.
inconvertibilménte, *av.* inconvertibly.
inconvincìbile, *ag.* inconvincible.
inconvincibilità, *s.f.* inconvincibility.
incoraggiaménto, *s.m.* encouragement: *per* —, as an encouragement; *quello fu un* — *a persistere,* that was an encouragement to persist.
incoraggiànte, *ag.* encouraging.
incoraggiàre, *v.t.* to encourage, to hearten, to give courage to (s.o.): *lo incoraggiai a continuare,* I encouraged him to continue; — *qlcu. in ql.co.,* to encourage s.o. in sthg. ‖ **incoraggiàrsi,** *v.r.* to take courage, to take heart: — *a fare ql.co.,* to take courage to do sthg.
incoràre, *v.t.* 1. (*incoraggiare*) to encourage, to hearten 2. (*confortare*) to comfort, to console ‖ **incoràrsi,** *v.r.* to resume one's courage.
incordàre, *v.t.* 1. (*uno strumento musicale*) to string 2. (*legare con corde*) to rope, to tie, to bind with ropes ‖ **incordàrsi,** *v.r.* (*di muscoli*) to stiffen, to become stiff.
incordatùra, *s.f.* 1. (*di strumento musicale*) stringing 2. (*il legare con corde*) roping, tying, binding with ropes 3. (*di muscoli*) stiffness.
incornàre, *v.t.* 1. (*infilzare con le corna*) to gore; (*colpire con le corna*) to toss ‖ **incornàrsi,** *v.r.* (*ostinarsi*) to become obstinate, to persist.
incorniciàre, *v.t.* 1. (*mettere in cornice*) to frame, to enframe, to put a frame to (sthg.) 2. (*fare da cornice a*) to frame, to be a frame to (sthg.).
incorniciàto, *ag.* framed.
incorniciatùra, *s.f.* frame, framing.
incoronaménto, *s.m.* crowning.
incoronàre, *v.t.* to crown.
incoronàto, *ag.* crowned ‖ *l'Incoronata,* (*la Madonna*) the Crowned Virgin.
incoronazióne, *s.f.* coronation: *giorno dell'* —, Coronation-day.
incorporàbile, *ag.* incorporable.
incorporaménto, *s.m.* 1. incorporation 2. (*di paesi, territori*) annexion.
incorporàre, *v.t.* 1. to incorporate 2. (*paesi, territori*) to annex ‖ **incorporàrsi,** *v.r.* 1. to become incorporated 2. (*di paesi*) to join (to sthg.).
incorporàto, *ag.* 1. incorporated 2. (*di paesi, territori*) annexed.
incorporazióne, *s.f.* 1. incorporation 2. (*di paesi, erritori*) annexion.
incorporeità, *s.f.* incorporeity, immateriality.
incorpòreo, *ag.* incorporeal, immaterial.
incorreggìbile, *ag.* incorrigible.
incorreggibilità, *s.f.* incorrigibility.
incorreggibilménte, *av.* incorrigibly.
incórrere, *v.i.* to incur (sthg.), to fall into (sthg.), to meet with (sthg.): — *in debiti,* to incur debts (*o* to get into debt); — *in una multa,* to incur a fine; — *in pericolo,* to incur danger.
incorrótto, *ag.* incorrupt.

incorruttíbile, *ag.* incorruptible.
incorruttibilità, *s.f.* incorruptibility.
incorruttibilménte, *av.* incorruptibly.
incosciènte, *ag.* 1. *(inconsapevole)* unconscious: *azione* —, unconscious action; *essere* —, unconscious being 2. *(irresponsabile)* irresponsible; reckless: *atto* —, reckless act; *persona* —, irresponsible person 3. *(spericolato)* rash ‖ *s.m.* 1. irresponsible person 2. *(spericolato)* dare-devil, madcap.
incosciènza, *s.f.* 1. *(inconsapevolezza)* unconsciousness 2. *(mancanza di coscienza)* lack of conscience 3. *(speicolatezza)* recklessness; rashness.
incostànte, *ag.* inconstant, fickle; unsteady; changeable, variable: *persona* —, inconstant person; *umore* —, variable mood; *tempo* —, changeable weather.
incostanteménte, *av.* inconstantly; unsteadily; changeably, variably.
incostànza, *s.f.* inconstancy, fickleness; unsteadiness; changeableness, variableness.
incostituzionàle, *ag.* unconstitutional.
incostituzionalità, *s.f.* unconstitutionality.
incostituzionalménte, *av.* unconstitutionally.
increànza, *s.f.* 1. incivility; impoliteness 2. *(atto, detto screanzato)* piece of incivility.
increàto, *ag.* *(letter.)* 1. uncreated 2. *(divino)* divine.
incredíbile, *ag.* incredible; unbelievable; *(sorprendente)* surprising; *(straordinario)* extraordinary.
incredibilità, *s.f.* incredibility.
incredibilménte, *av.* incredibly; *(sorprendentemente)* surprisingly; *(straordinariamente)* extraordinarily.
incredulità, *s.f.* incredulity, unbelief, disbelief.
incrèdulo, *ag.* incredulous, doubting, sceptical.
incrementàre, *v.t.* to increase, to promote, to foster: — *l'industria,* to encourage industry; — *il proprio reddito,* to increase one's income.
increménto, *s.m.* 1. increment; increase, development 2. *(mat.)* increment.
incréscere, *v.i.* to be sorry (for sthg.), to regret (sthg.): *me ne incresce,* I am sorry for it (*o* I regret it).
increscióso, *ag.* unpleasant, disagreeable; annoying: *un incidente* —, an unpleasant incident.
increspaménto, *s.m.* *(di pelle, della fronte)* wrinkling; *(di acque)* rippling, ruffling; *(di capelli)* curling.
increspàre, *v.t.,* **incresparsi,** *v.r.* *(di pelle, della fronte)* to wrinkle; *(di acque)* to ripple, to ruffle; *(di capelli)* to curl.
increspatúra, *s.f.* *(di pelle, della fronte)* wrinkling; *(di acque)* ruffling, rippling; *(di capelli)* curling; *(di stoffa)* gather.
incretiniménto, *s.m.* mental decay.
incretiníre, *v.t.* to make stupid ‖ *v.i.* to become stupid.
incretiníto, *ag.* stupid, dull, idiotic.
incriminàbile, *ag.* *(dir.)* liable to prosecution; impeachable, imputable.
incriminàre, *v.t.* *(dir.)* to incriminate; to impeach, to prosecute.
incriminazióne, *s.f.* *(dir.)* 1. *(l'accusare)* crimination, incriminating 2. *(atto d'accusa)* indictment.
incrinàre, *v.t.,* **incrinàrsi,** *v.r.* to crack: *il bicchiere s'incrinò,* the glass cracked.
incrinàto, *ag.* cracked.
incrinatúra, *s.f.* 1. crack 2. *(difetto di lavorazione)* flaw.
incriticàbile, *ag.* uncensurable.
incrociaménto, *s.m.* crossing: — *di razze,* crossbreeding.
incrociàre, *v.t.* 1. to cross: — *le braccia,* to cross (*o* to fold) one's arms; *fig.* to refuse to work; — *le dita a mo' di scongiuro,* to cross one's fingers; — *due sbarre,* to put two bars across; — *la rotta di un bastimento,* to cross a vessel's course ‖ — *la spada con qlcu.,* to cross swords with s.o. 2. *(animali di razze diverse)* to cross, to crossbreed, to interbreed; *(piante di diversa varietà)* to cross-fertilize ‖ *v.i.* *(mar. aer.)* to cruise: — *lungo la costa di,* to cruise off the coast of ‖ **incrociàrsi,** *v.r.*

to (inter)cross, to intersect; *(incontrarsi)* to meet: *i due treni si incrociano a Pavia,* the two trains meet at Pavia; *i loro sguardi si incrociarono,* their eyes met; *le strade si incrociano vicino alla chiesa,* the roads cross (*o* intersect) near the church.
incrociàto, *ag.* 1. crossed ‖ *fuoco* —, cross-fire ‖ *parole incrociate,* crossword puzzle ‖ *punto* —, cross-stitch 2. *(di razze)* crossbred.
incrociatóre, *s.m.* *(mar. mil.)* cruiser: — *corazzato, da battaglia,* armoured, battle cruiser; — *leggero, pesante,* light, heavy cruiser.
incrociatúra, *s.f.* 1. *(l'incrociare)* crossing 2. *(intersezione, punto di intersezione)* intersection.
incrocicchiàre, *v.t.,* **incrocicchiàrsi,** *v.r.* to interlace.
incrócio, *s.m.* 1. crossing; *(di fili, linee elettriche)* crossover; *(di binari)* frog: — *pericoloso, (stradale)* dangerous crossing; — *stradale,* cross-roads 2. *(di razze)* crossbreed.
incrollàbile, *ag.* unshak(e)able, firm (anche *fig.*).
incrostaménto, *s.m.* incrustation.
incrostàre, *v.t.,* **incrostàrsi,** *v.r.* to encrust; *(di cannone, àncora, chiglia di nave)* to foul: *caldaia incrostata di ruggine,* boiler encrusted (*o* scaled) with rust.
incrostatúra, incrostazióne, *s.f.* 1. incrustation, crust: *togliere le incrostazioni di una caldaia,* to scale a boiler 2. *(di vestito)* insertion.
incrudeliménto, *s.m.* 1. growing cruel 2. *(recrudescenza)* recrudescence.
incrudelíre, *v.i.* to become cruel: — *contro qlcu.,* to be pitiless towards s.o. (*o* to commit cruelties against s.o.).
incrudíre, *v.i.* 1. *(aggravarsi)* to grow worse 2. *(indurirsi)* to harden; *(metal.)* to workharden 3. *(inasprirsi)* to be embittered 4. *(del clima)* to become severe, to become inclement.
incruènto, *ag.* bloodless.
incrunàre, *v.t.* to thread.
incruscàre, *v.t.* to put in bran; to cover with bran ‖ **incruscàrsi,** *v.r.* to sift one's language.
incubatríce, *ag.* incubating ‖ *s.f.* incubator.
incubazióne, *s.f.* 1. *(di malattia)* incubation: *periodo d'*—,incubation period 2. *(di uova)* hatching, incubation.
íncubo, *s.m.* nightmare; incubus *(pl.* incubi, incubuses): *questo pensiero mi dà l'*—, this thought gives me nightmares; *essere un* — *per qlcu.,* to be an incubus on s.o.
incúdine, *s.f.* 1. anvil ‖ *essere tra l'* — *e il martello,* to be between the devil and the deep blue sea 2. *(anat.)* incus *(pl.* incudes).
inculcàre, *v.t.* to inculcate, to instil(l): — *un'idea a qlcu., nella mente di qlcu.,* to inculcate an idea on s.o., in s.o.'s mind.
incunàbolo, incunàbulo, *s.m.* incunabulum *(pl.* incunabula); incunable.
incuneàre, *v.t.* to wedge ‖ **incuneàrsi,** *v.r.* to wedge oneself in.
incuoràre, *V.* **incoràre.**
incupíre, *v.i.,* **incupírsi,** *v.r.* 1. to darken, to become dark(er), to grow dark(er); *(annuvolarsi)* to cloud over 2. *(intristirsi)* to become gloomy.
incuràbile, *ag.s.m.* incurable ‖ *gli Incurabili, Ospedale degli Incurabili,* Home for Incurables.
incurabilità, *s.f.* incurability, incurableness.
incurabilménte, *av.* incurably.
incurànte, *ag.* 1. careless, heedless; negligent; thoughtless: — *del pericolo, del domani,* heedless of danger, of the morrow 2. *(indifferente)* indifferent, apathetic: *mostrarsi* — *della sorte di qlcu.,* to show indifference to s.o.'s fate.
incurànza, incúria, *s.f.* 1. carelessness, heedlessness; negligence; thoughtlessness 2. *(indifferenza)* indifference, apathy.
incuriosíre, *v.t.* to make curious: — *qlcu.,* to rouse s.o.'s interest (*o* curiosity) ‖ **incuriosírsi,** *v.r.* to become curious; to become inquisitive.

incursióne, *s.f.* incursion, inroad, raid, foray: — *aerea,* air-raid; *le incursioni dei Vichinghi sulla costa inglese,* the raids of the Vikings on the English coast; *fare un'— in un paese,* to make an incursion into (*o* to overrun) a country.

incurvàbile, *ag.* unbendable.

incurvaménto, *s.m.* 1. (*l'incurvare*) bending, curving 2. (*curva*) bend, incurvation.

incurvàre, *v.t.* to bend, to curve, to arch ‖ **incurvàrsi,** *v.r.* 1. to bend 2. (*di lamiera*) to bulge.

incurvatúra, incurvazióne, *s.f.* 1. (*curva*) bend, incurvation 2. (*l'incurvare*) bending, curving.

incurvíre, *v.i.* to bend, to become bent.

incustodíto, *ag.* unguarded.

incútere, *v.t.* to rouse, to strike, to command: — *rispetto,* to command (*o* to compel *o* to inspire) respect; — *spavento a qlcu.,* to rouse fear in s.o.; — *terrore nell'animo di qlcu.,* to strike terror into s.o.'s heart.

índaco, *s.m.* indigo.

indaffaràto, *ag.* busy.

indagaménto, *s.m.* investigation, inquiry.

indagàre, *v.t.* to investigate, to inquire into (sthg.), to search into (sthg.), to look into (sthg.): — *le cause di un incidente,* to investigate the causes of an accident.

indagatóre, *ag.* investigating, searching, inquiring: *commissione indagatrice,* investigating committee; *sguardo —,* searching look ‖ *s.m.,* **indagatríce,** *s.f.* investigator, inquirer.

indàgine, *s.f.* 1. inquiry, enquiry, investigation: — *minuziosa,* close investigation (*o* inquiry); *i risultati della sua —,* the results of his investigation; *condurre un'— ufficiale su qlco.,* to hold an official inquiry into sthg.; *fare indagini sulle cause di un incidente,* to make inquiries into (*o* to investigate) the causes of an accident 2. (*ricerca, studio*) research, survey: *indagini statistiche su questioni sociali in tempo di guerra,* war-time social survey; *condurre un'— su un problema scientifico,* to carry out research into a scientific problem; *fare delle indagini su ql.co.,* to make researches into sthg. (*o* to inquire into sthg.).

indantrène, *s.m.* (*chim.*) indant(h)rene: *colori —,* (*ind. tessile*) indant(h)rene dyes.

indàrno, *av.* (*arc.*) in vain.

indebitaménte, *av.* 1. (*ingiustamente*) unduly 2. (*sconvenientemente*) unbecomingly; improperly 3. (*immeritatamente*) undeservedly.

indebitaménto, *s.m.* 1. (*l'indebitarsi*) running into debt 2. (*l'essere in debito*) indebtedness.

indebitàre, *v.t.* to involve in debt, to get into debt ‖ **indebitàrsi,** *v.r.* to run into debt, to get into debt.

indebitàto, *ag.* indebted, in debt: *essere — fin sopra i capelli,* to be up to one's ears in debts.

indébito, *ag.* 1. (*non dovuto*) undue, not due: *pagamento —,* undue payment 2. (*sconveniente*) unbecoming, improper 3. (*immeritato*) undeserved: *accusa indebita,* undeserved charge 4. (*dir.*) (*illegittimo*) illegal, undue: *appropriazione indebita,* embezzlement; *procedimento —,* undue proceeding.

indeboliménto, *s.m.* 1. enfeeblement, weakening 2. (*debolezza*) weakness, state of debility.

indebolíre, *v.t.* 1. to weaken, to enfeeble, to debilitate 2. *fig.* to lessen, to reduce 3. (*mec. chim.*) to weaken 4. (*foto.*) to reduce ‖ **indebolírsi,** *v.r.* 1. to weaken, to grow weak(er), to grow feeble(r), to flag, to lose one's strength: *le sue forze s'indebolivano,* his strength was flagging; *il vento si indebolisce,* the wind is dropping 2. (*di suoni, colori*) to fade.

indebolíto, *ag.* weakened, enfeebled.

indecènte, *ag.* indecent, immodest, obscene.

indecenteménte, *av.* indecently, immodestly, obscenely.

indecènza, *s.f.* indecency, immodesty, obscenity: *è un'—!,* it's a shame!.

indecifràbile, *ag.* 1. indecipherable: *iscrizione —,* indecipherable inscription 2. (*illeggibile*) illegible: *calli-*

grafia —, illegible writing 3. (*incomprensibile*) unintelligible, incomprehensible, obscure.

indecisióne, *s.f.* 1. indecision, irresolution, irresoluteness 2. (*esitazione*) hesitation, uncertainty.

indecíso, *ag.* 1. (*non deciso*) undecided, unsettled: *la questione è ancora indecisa,* the matter is still undecided (*o* open to discussion) 2. (*irresoluto*) irresolute, hesitant, wavering: *sono ancora —,* I haven't made up my mind yet.

indeclinàbile, *ag.* 1. (*gram.*) indeclinable 2. (*che non si può eludere*) unavoidable: *responsabilità —,* responsibility that cannot be shirked 3. (*immutabile*) unchangeable, invariable 4. (*irrevocabile*) firm, inflexible.

indeclinabilità, *s.f.* 1. (*inevitabilità*) unavoidableness 2. (*immutabilità*) unchangeableness, invariability 3. (*irrevocabilità*) firmness.

indeclinabilménte, *av.* 1. (*inevitabilmente*) unavoidably 2. (*immutabilmente*) unchangeably, invariably 3. (*irrevocabilmente*) firmly.

indecomponíbile, *ag.* indecomposable.

indecorosaménte, *av.* indecorously, unseemly, unbecomingly; (*indecentemente*) indecently.

indecoróso, *ag.* indecorous, unseemly, unbecoming; (*indecente*) indecent.

indefendíbile, *ag.* indefensible, untenable.

indefessaménte, *av.* unfatiguedly; indefatigably, unweariedly, tirelessly; unremittingly.

indefèsso, *ag.* indefatigable, unwearied, tireless; unremitting.

indefettíbile, *ag.* unfailing, indefectible.

indefettibilità, *s.f.* unfailingness, indefectibility.

indeficiènte, *ag.* unfailing; (*continuo*) constant, continuous.

indeficiènza, *s.f.* unfailingness; (*continuità*) constancy, continuousness.

indefiníbile, *ag.* indefinable, undefinable, inexplicable: *colore —,* nondescript colour; *è un uomo —,* he is an inexplicable man.

indefinibilità, *s.f.* indefinableness.

indefinibilménte, *av.* indefinably.

indefinitaménte, *av.* indefinitely.

indefinitézza, *s.f.* indefiniteness.

indefiníto, *ag.* 1. indefinite: *tempo, spazio —,* indefinite time, space 2. (*gram.*) indefinite.

indegnaménte, *av.* 1. (*immeritatamente*) unworthily, undeservedly 2. (*vergognosamente*) contemptibly, basely.

indegnità, *s.f.* 1. (*l'essere indegno*) unworthiness 2. (*azione indegna*) mean action.

indégno, *ag.* 1. (*immeritevole*) unworthy, undeserving: *essere — di ql.co.,* to be unworthy of sthg. (*o* not to deserve sthg.) ‖ — *della successione,* (*dir.*) disqualified (*o* debarred) from succeeding (*o* from inheriting) 2. (*spregevole*) base, worthless: *una persona indegna,* a worthless person 3. (*vergognoso*) contemptible; shameful: *è —!,* it is outrageous! (*o* what a shame!).

indelèbile, *ag.* indelible; ineffaceable (anche *fig.*): *rossetto —,* indelible lipstick.

indelebilità, *s.f.* indelibility.

indelebilménte, *av.* indelibly.

indeliberàto, *ag.* 1. (*affrettato*) hasty; rash 2. (*impulsivo*) impulsive; inconsiderate.

indelicataménte, *av.* indelicately.

indelicatézza, *s.f.* 1. indelicacy, tactlessness 2. (*mancanza di scrupoli*) unscrupulousness.

indelicàto, *ag.* 1. indelicate, tactless: *azione indelicata,* tactless action; *modi indelicati,* indelicate manners 2. (*senza scrupoli*) unscrupulous; dishonest.

indemaniàre, *v.t.* (*dir.*) to hand over to the state; to add to the state demesne.

indemoniàre, *v.t.* to drive mad; to make wicked ‖ **indemoniàrsi,** *v.r.* to rage; to rave, to storm; to behave like one possessed.

indemoniàto, *ag.* 1. (*invasato dal demonio*) possessed; demoniac 2. (*furibondo*) frantic; furious ‖ *s.m.* demoniac.

indènne, *ag.* undamaged, unharmed, uninjured: *il pilota e i passeggeri sono indenni,* the pilot and his passengers are uninjured(ounhurt o without a scratch)‖ *uscire — da un affare delicato,* to come unsmirched out of an awkward affair.

indennità, *s.f.* allowance; indemnity: *— di alloggio,* (*mil.*) quarters allowance; *— di carovita,* cost-of-living bonus; *— di disoccupazione,* unemployment benefit; *— di mensa,* mess allowance; *— parlamentare,* emoluments of a Member of Parliament; *— di trasferta,* subsistence allowance; *— di viaggio,* travelling allowance.

indennizzàre, *v.t.* to indemnify, to compensate: *— qlcu. di ql.co.,* to indemnify (o to compensate) s.o. for sthg.

indennízzo, *s.m.* indemnity; indemnification: *avere diritto a un —,* to be entitled to an indemnity; *chiedere un —,* to put in a claim for damages.

indentàre, *v.i.* **1.** (*tec.*) (*ingranare*) to engage, to mesh: *le due ruote indentano,* the two (cog-)wheels engage **2.** (*di bambini, mettere i denti*) to teethe.

indentatúra, *s.f.* **1.** (*mec.*) toothing, indentation **2.** (*di bambini, il mettere i denti*) teething.

indéntro, *av.* inwards: *il chirurgo tagliò più —,* the surgeon cut deeper; *si apre all'—,* it opens inwards; *spingi — il cassetto,* push the drawer to; *camminare con i piedi —,* to turn one's toes in; *cominciare —,* (*tip.*) to indent; *voltare — l'angolo di una pagina,* to turn down the corner of a page.

indeprecàbile, *ag.* **1.** (*inevitabile*) unavoidable **2.** (*inesorabile*) inexorable.

inderogàbile, *ag.* intransgressible, unbreakable.

inderogabilménte, *av.* **1.** (*senza fallo*) without fail **2.** (*assolutamente*) absolutely.

indescrivíbile, *ag.* indescribable.

indescrivibilménte, *av.* indescribably.

indeterminàbile, *ag.* indeterminable; unascertainable.

indeterminabilménte, *av.* indeterminably.

indeterminataménte, *av.* indeterminately.

indeterminatézza, *s.f.* **1.** indeterminateness; indefiniteness; vagueness **2.** (*imprecisione*) imprecision.

indeterminàto, *ag.* **1.** indeterminate; undetermined; indefinite; vague **2.** (*impreciso*) imprecise **3.** (*irresoluto*) irresolute, undecided **4.** (*mat.*) indeterminate.

indeterminazióne, *s.f.* **1.** indetermination **2.** (*irresolutezza*) irresolution, irresoluteness.

indevotaménte, *av.* undevoutly; irreligiously; irreverently.

indevòto, *ag.* undevout; irreligious; irreverent.

indevozióne, *s.f.* undevoutness; irreligiousness; irreverence.

índi, *av.* (*letter.*) **1.** (*di luogo*) (from) thence ‖ *da — in qua, in là,* from thence on **2.** (*di tempo*) then; afterwards ‖ *— a un anno,* a year later; *— a poco,* shortly after (o after a short time).

Índia, *no.pr.f.* (*geog.*) India ‖ *le Indie Orientali, Occidentali,* the East, West Indies; *Compagnia delle Indie Orientali,* (st.) East India Company ‖ *la Valigia delle Indie,* (*ferr.*) the India mail ‖ *canna d'—,* bamboo cane; *castagno d'—,* horse chestnut; *fico d'—,* Indian fig (o prickly pear); *pollo d'—,* turkey; *porcellino d'—,* guinea-pig.

indiademàre, *v.t.* to diadem.

indiamantàre, *v.t.* to diamond.

indiàna, *s.f.* (*stoffa*) printed calico.

indianísmo, *s.m.* Indian studies (*pl.*).

indianísta, *s.c.* Indianist.

indiàno, *ag.* Indian ‖ *in fila indiana,* in Indian file ‖ *s.m.* Indian; (*d'America*) (Red) Indian ‖ *fare l'—,* to feign ignorance ‖ **indiàna,** *s.f.* Indian (woman); (*d'America*) (Red) Indian (woman).

indiàre, *v.t.* (*poet.*) to deify ‖ **indiàrsi,** *v.r.* (*poet.*) to sink oneself in the godhead.

indiavolàto, *ag.* **1.** (*indemoniato*) demoniac, possessed **2.** (*furioso*) furious, raging: *tempesta indiavolata,*

raging tempest; *tempo —,* stormy weather **3.** (*vivacissimo*) boisterous, exuberant: *musica indiavolata,* hot music; *ragazzo —,* a restless boy **4.** (*terribile, eccessivo*) awful; terrible: *rumore —,* devil of a din; *fa un freddo —,* it is awfully cold; *avere una paura indiavolata,* to be in a devil of a funk.

indicàbile, *ag.* (*consigliabile*) advisable.

indicàre, *v.t.* **1.** to indicate, to show; (*col dito*) to point at (s.o., sthg.): *l'ago indica la pressione,* the needle indicates pressure; *c'è un palo che indica la direzione,* there is a finger-post indicating direction; *indicami quello che devo fare,* show me what I must do; *indicò il tuo amico,* he pointed at your friend; *puoi indicarmi la strada?,* can you show me the way? **2.** (*denotare*) to denote, to betoken, to show: *termine che indica disprezzo,* expression indicative of contempt; *ciò indica che non lavori abbastanza,* this shows that you don't work enough; *la tua lingua sporca indica indigestione,* your furred tongue suggests (o denotes) indigestion **3.** (*mettere in evidenza*) to point out: *indicò l'importanza della cosa,* he pointed out the importance of the matter **4.** (*significare*) to mean: *non so che cosa indichino questi simboli,* I don't know what these symbols mean **5.** (*consigliare*) to suggest; to advise: *— un rimedio,* to suggest a remedy **6.** (*prescrivere*) to prescribe: *gli furono indicate diverse medicine,* several medicines were prescribed to him.

indicatívo, *ag.* **1.** indicative **2.** (*gram.*) indicative: *modo —,* indicative mood ‖ *s.m.* (*gram.*) indicative.

indicàto, *ag.* **1.** (*consigliabile*) advisable **2.** (*adatto*) fit, suitable; proper (to s.o., sthg.); right: *un cappotto — per il tempo freddo,* a coat suitable for cold weather; *rimedio —,* a suitable remedy.

indicatóre, *ag.* indicative; indicating (*attributivo*): *un ago —,* an indicating needle; *questi sintomi sono indicatori di cattiva circolazione,* these symptoms are indicative of bad circulation ‖ *s.m.* **1.** (*tec.*) indicator, pointer; gauge: *— di fase,* (*elett.*) phase indicator; *— di pressione,* pressure-gauge; *— di sintonia,* (*rad.*) tuning-indicator; *— di velocità,* speed-indicator; (*aut.*) speedometer **2.** (*chim.*) indicator **3.** (*guida, prontuario*) guide (-book): *— commerciale,* commercial directory; *— economico,* economic news **4.** *— stradale,* traffic-sign; (*indicatore di direzione*) finger-post.

indicazióne, *s.f.* **1.** indication: *l'— della velocità,* the indication of speed; *questo segno sul pavimento può essere una preziosa —,* this mark on the floor may be an important indication **2.** (*informazione*) information (*solo sing.*): *puoi darmi qualche — su questa faccenda?,* can you give me some information on this matter? **3.** (*istruzione*) direction: *le indicazioni su come usare ql.co.,* the directions how to use sthg. (o as to the use of sthg.) **4.** (*suggerimento*) suggestion.

índice, *s.m.* **1.** (*dito della mano*) forefinger, index (-finger) **2.** (*lancetta di un misuratore*) index, indicator, pointer; needle; (*specialmente di orologio*) hand **3.** (*tec. scient.*) index: *— del costo della vita,* (*statistica*) (cost of) living index; *— del punto di rottura,* (*scienza delle costruzioni*) shatter index; *— di mortalità, sviluppo,* (*statistica*) index of mortality, of growth; *— di rifrazione,* (*fis.*) refractive index **4.** (*di libro*) index: *inserire un nome nell'—,* to index a name **5.** *l'Indice,* (*eccl.*) the Index: *questo libro è all'Indice,* this book is or the Index **6.** (*sintomo*) sign; index: *quel lampo è — di cattivo tempo,* that lightning is a sign of bad weather; *i suoi gusti sono un — di buon cuore,* his tastes are indicative of a good heart **7.** (*nidiandolo*) nest-egg.

indicíbile, *ag.* unspeakable, unutterable, inexpressible; (*indescrivibile*) indescribable.

indicibilménte, *av.* unspeakably, unutterably, inexpressibly; (*indescrivibilmente*) indescribably.

índico, *ag.* Indian: *canna indica,* bamboo cane.

in diebus illis, *l. av.* (*lat.*) a long, long time ago.

indietreggiaménto, *s.m.* withdrawal.

indietreggiàre, *v.i.* **1.** to draw back, to withdraw **2.** (*mil.*) (*ripiegare*) to fall back; (*ritirarsi*) to retreat **3.** *fig.* (*cedere*) to give in (to sthg.): — *di fronte a una difficoltà,* to give in to a difficulty.

indiètro, *av.* **1.** (*spazio, tempo*) **back, behind:** (*state*) —!, stand back!; *per favore, volete stare un po' più* —?, would you please stand a little farther back?; *teneva* — *la folla,* he held the crowd back ‖ *essere* —, to be behind; *fig.* (*mentalmente*) to be backward; (*essere arretrato*) to be behind the times; (*di orologio*) to be slow: *egli è molto* —, *forse dieci miglia,* he is a long way behind, perhaps ten miles; *ella è più* — *di te,* she is behind you; *questo paese è un po'* —, this country is a little behind the times; *essere* — *coi pagamenti,* to be in arrear(s) with one's payments; *essere* — *col proprio lavoro,* to be behind (*o* behindhand) in one's work ‖ *rimanere* —, to be left (*o* to remain *o* to be) behind (anche *fig.*); (*di orologio*) to be slow: *camminavano così in fretta che rimasi* —, they were walking so fast that I got left behind; *per quella malattia è rimasta* — *quasi un anno rispetto agli altri scolari,* she is almost a year behind the other students owing to her illness; *mangiammo molto e non rimanemmo* — *col bere,* we ate a lot and were not behind with the drink; *il tuo orologio rimane sempre* —, your watch is always slow; *voi andate pure avanti, io rimarrò* — *ad aspettarlo,* you go ahead, I'll stay behind to wait for him **2.** (*direzione*) **back, backward**(s): *andare* (*all'*) —, to go backwards; *andare avanti e* —, to go to and fro (*o* to go back and forth); *non andare nè avanti nè* —, not to go (*o* to move) either backwards or forwards; *fig.* to make no progress (*o* to be at a standstill); *cascare all'*—, to fall back; *fare marcia* —, (*aut.*) to go into reverse (*o* to back); *fig.* to beat a hasty retreat; *fare un passo* —, to step back a pace; *fig.* to take a backward step; *guardare* —, to look back; *saltare* —, to jump backwards; *voltarsi* —, to turn around ‖ *macchina,* — *tutta!,* (*mar.*) full-speed astern! ‖ *rimandare* —, to give, to send back ‖ *viaggiare all'*—, (*in treno*) to travel with one's back to the engine **3.** (*di ritorno*) **back:** *non lo aspetto* — *prima di domani,* I don't expect him back before tomorrow; *sarò* — *alle cinque,* I'll be back at five.

indifendìbile, *ag.* **1.** (*che non si può difendere*) indefensible, untenable **2.** (*che non si deve difendere*) not to be defended.

indiféso, *ag.* undefended, defenceless, unprotected.

indifferènte, *ag.* **1.** indifferent, uninterested: *egli è* — *a tutti i problemi sociali,* he is indifferent to (*o* unconcerned about) all social problems (*o* he has no interest in any social problem); *mi è* —, it is indifferent to me (*o* it is all the same to me *o* it makes no difference to me) **2.** (*non importante*) unimportant; trifling: *parlare di cose indifferenti,* to talk about unimportant (*o* trifling) matters **3.** (*imperturbato*) cold, unconcerned: *ciò che disse mi lasciò* —, what he said left me cold.

indifferenteménte, *av.* indifferently.

indifferentísmo, *s.m.* (*pol. relig.*) indifferentism.

indifferènza, *s.f.* **1.** indifference, unconcern; apathy: *la sua* — *mi irrita,* his indifference (*o* unconcern) irritates me **2.** (*freddezza*) coldness.

indifferìbile, *ag.* that cannot be deferred.

indígeno, *ag.* indigenous, native: *scuole indigene,* native schools ‖ *s.m.* native; (*rar.*) indigene.

indigènte, *ag.* indigent, poor, needy.

indigènza, *s.f.* indigence, poverty, need.

indigerìbile, *ag.* indigestible (anche *fig.*).

indigeribilità, indigestibilità, *s.f.* indigestibility (anche *fig.*).

indigestióne, *s.f.* indigestion (anche *fig.*): *fare* —, to get an attack of indigestion.

indigèsto, *ag.* **1.** indigestible: *cibo* —, indigestible (*o* heavy) food **2.** *fig.* (*noioso*) heavy; tedious, boring; (*mal digerito, confuso*) undigested: *erudizione indigesta,* undigested knowledge; *un libro* —, a boring book.

indígete, *s.m.* (*letter.*) local god, tutelary god.

indignàre, *v.t.* to shock; to fill with indignation: — *qlcu.,* to arouse s.o.'s indignation ‖ **indignàrsi,** *v.r.* to be filled with indignation, to be indignant; to get angry; to be shocked.

indignazióne, *s.f.* indignation; (*collera*) anger; (*sdegno*) disdain.

indigotína, *s.f.* (*chim.*) indigotin, indigo-blue.

indimenticàbile, *ag.* unforgettable.

indimenticabilménte, *av.* unforgettably.

indimostràbile, *ag.* indemonstrable; not subject to proof, that cannot be proved.

indimostràto, *ag.* unproved, undemonstrated.

índio, *s.m.* (*chim.*) indium.

indipendènte, *ag.* **1.** independent (of s.o., sthg.); free: *pensatore* —, independent thinker; *stato* —, free state **2.** (*sicuro di sè*) self-reliant‖*s.m.* (*pol.*) independent: — *di destra, sinistra,* right-wing, left-wing independent.

indipendenteménte, *av.* independently.

indipendènza, *s.f.* **1.** independence; freedom: *guerra d'*—, war of independence **2.** (*sicurezza di sè*) self-reliance.

indíre, *v.t.* **1.** (*intimare*) to notify, to announce, to intimate **2.** (*radunare*) to call, to summon: — *un'adunanza,* to call a meeting; — *una riunione parlamentare,* to summon Parliament **3.** (*fissare*) to arrange, to fix, to appoint.

indirettaménte, *av.* indirectly.

indirètto, *ag.* indirect: *discorso, complemento* —, (*gram.*) indirect speech, object.

indirizzàre, *v.t.* **1.** to address, to send: — *una lettera a qlcu.,* to address a letter to s.o. **2.** (*dirigere*) to send, to direct: — *una persona a qlcu.,* to send a person to s.o.; — *qlcu. verso un luogo,* to direct s.o. to(wards) a place **3.** (*avviare, rivolgere*) to direct, to address: *lo indirizzai nel disegno,* I taught him the first elements of drawing; *queste osservazioni non erano indirizzate a te,* these remarks did not apply to you (*o* were not meant for you); — *i propri sforzi verso ql.co.* to direct one's efforts towards sthg. ‖ **indirizzàrsi,** *v.r.* **1.** (*dirigersi*) to set out for (a place), to make one's way towards (a place), to direct one's steps towards (a place) **2.** (*rivolgersi*) to address oneself, to apply: *a chi devo indirizzarmi per saperlo?,* who must I apply to in order to know that?.

indirízzo, *s.m.* **1.** address: — *telegrafico,* telegraphic (*o* cable) address; *cambiare* —, to change one's address; *scrivere l'*— *su una lettera,* to write the address on a letter **2.** (*linea di condotta*) course, trend: *il suo* — *politico è piuttosto socialisteggiante,* his political trend is towards socialism; *prendere un cattivo* — (*nella vita*), to take an evil course (in life) **3.** (*direzione*) direction, turn: *le cose prendono un cattivo* —, things are taking a bad turn; *ha preso un* — *di studi classico,* he has taken up classical studies **4.** (*discorso*) address, petition.

indiscerníbile, *ag.* indiscernible; indistinguishable.

indisciplína, *s.f.* indiscipline, want of discipline; (*sregolatezza*) unruliness.

indisciplinataménte, *av.* without discipline.

indisciplinatézza, *s.f.* indiscipline, want of discipline; (*sregolatezza*) unruliness.

indisciplinàto, *ag.* undisciplined; (*sregolato*) unruly: *questi ragazzi sono molto indisciplinati,* these children are quite out of hand.

indiscretaménte, *av.* indiscreetly; (*in modo invadente*) impertinently; (*con curiosità*) inquisitively.

indiscretézza, *s.f.* indiscretion; (*invadenza*) intrusiveness; (*curiosità*) inquisitiveness.

indiscréto, *ag.* indiscreet; (*invadente*) intrusive; (*fam.*) pushing; (*curioso*) inquisitive, prying; (*fam.*) nosy; (*imprudente*) imprudent, unguarded; (*senza tatto*) tactless; (*sfrontato*) forward: *al riparo da sguardi indiscreti,* safe from prying eyes; *è molto* — *da parte sua,* it is very pushing of him.

indiscrezióne, *s.f.* **1.** indiscretion; impertinence: *vi posso domandare senza* —...*?,* would it be impertinent to enquire...? (o do you mind my asking...?) **2.** (*pettegolezzo*) gossip; indiscretion.

indiscússo, *ag.* undiscussed, undisputed.

indiscutíbile, *ag.* unquestionable, indisputable: *è* — *che*..., it is beyond argument that....

indiscutibilménte, *av.* unquestionably, indisputably.

indispensàbile, *ag.* indispensable; absolutely necessary; essential: *l'aria è* — *alla vita,* air is indispensable to life; *è* — *che abbia il vostro permesso,* it is essential that I should have your permission ‖ *s.m.* necessary: *l'*— *per vivere,* the necessaries of life.

indispensabilità, *s.f.* indispensability, indispensableness.

indispensabilménte, *av.* indispensably; essentially.

indispettíre, *v.t.* to vex; to annoy, to pique, to irritate: *le sue continue osservazioni mi indispettiscono,* his continuous remarks vex me ‖ **indispettírsi,** *v.r.* to become vexed; to become annoyed.

indispettíto, *ag.* vexed; annoyed, irritated.

indispórre, *v.t.* to irritate, to upset, to vex, to annoy; to make ill-disposed, to indispose; to disgust: *non indisporlo,* don't vex him.

indisposizióne, *s.f.* indisposition; slight illness.

indispósto, *ag.* **1.** (*lievemente malato*) indisposed, slightly ill, unwell; (*fam.*) poorly, out of sorts **2.** (*mal disposto*) indisposed (towards s.o.), disinclined (to s.o.), unfriendly (to s.o.), ill-disposed (towards s.o.).

indisputàbile, *ag.* indisputable, unquestionable, incontestable, incontrovertible.

indissolúbile, *ag.* indissoluble, stable; everlasting: *amicizia* —, indissoluble friendship.

indissolubilità, *s.f.* indissolubility.

indissolubilménte, *av.* indissolubly.

indistinguíbile, *ag.* undistinguishable.

indistinguibilménte, *av.* undistinguishably.

indistintaménte, *av.* indistinctly, confusedly; (*in modo vago*) vaguely, faintly, dimly.

indistínto, *ag.* indistinct, confused; (*vago*) vague, faint, dim: *visione indistinta,* dim sight.

indistruttíbile, *ag.* indestructible.

indistruttibilità, *s.f.* indestructibility.

indistruttibilménte, *av.* indestructibly.

indisturbàto, *ag.* undisturbed.

indívia, *s.f.* (*bot.*) endive.

individuàle, *ag.* individual; personal, particular.

individualísmo, *s.m.* individualism.

individualísta, *s.c.* individualist.

individualístico, *ag.* individualistic.

individualità, *s.f.* individuality.

individualizzàre, *v.t.* to individualize.

individualizzazióne, *s.f.* individualization.

individualménte, *av.* individually, personally.

individuàre, *v.t.* **1.** (*caratterizzare*) to individualize, to characterize **2.** (*specificare*) to specify, to particularize **3.** (*riconoscere*) to single out; (*localizzare*) to locate.

individuazióne, *s.f.* **1.** (*caratterizzazione*) individualization, characterization **2.** (*specificazione*) specification **3.** (*riconoscimento*) singling out; (*localizzazione*) location.

indivíduo, *s.m.* **1.** (*singolo ente*) individual: *i diritti dell'*—, the rights of the individual **2.** (*uomo*) man (*pl.* men); individual; (*fam.*) fellow, chap; (*sl. amer.*) guy: *che strano* —!, what a queer fellow!; *c'è un* — *che ti cerca,* there is a man who is looking for you; *chi è quell'*—?, who is that fellow?.

indivisíbile, *ag.* indivisible.

indivisibilità, *s.f.* indivisibility.

indivisibilménte, *av.* indivisibly.

indivíso, *ag.* undivided.

indiziàre, *v.t.* **1.** (*essere indizio di*) to point to (sthg.): *tutte queste circostanze indiziano la sua colpa,* all these circumstances point to his guilt **2.** (*rendere sospetto*) to throw suspicion on (s.o.); to make suspect.

indiziàrio, *ag.* (*dir.*) presumptive; based on suspicion (*predicativo*): *prova indiziaria,* presumptive evidence.

indiziàto, *ag.s.m.* (*dir.*) suspect.

indízio, *s.m.* **1.** indication, clue; (*segno*) sign; (*sintomo*) symptom **2.** (*dir.*) circumstantial proof.

indizióne, *s.f.* (*st.*) indiction.

Índo, *no.pr.m.* (*geog.*) Indus.

indòcile, *ag.* indocile, unruly; intractable, unmanageable: *un carattere* —, an intractable temper.

indocilíre, *v.t.* to make docile; to make tractable ‖ **indocilírsi,** *v.r.* to become docile.

indocilità, *s.f.* indocility, intractability.

indocilménte, *av.* intractably.

Indocína, *no.pr.f.* (*geog.*) Indo-China.

indocinése, *ag.s.c.* Indo-Chinese (*invariato al pl.*).

indoeuropèo, *ag.s.m.* Indo-European.

indogermànico, *ag.* Indo-Germanic.

indolcíre, *v.t.* to sweeten.

índole, *s.f.* **1.** (*temperamento*) nature, disposition, temper, temperament, character: *una persona di buona* —, a good-natured person; *è d'*— *malinconica,* he is of a melancholy disposition; *è pigro d'*—, he is lazy by nature; *ha un'*— *ribelle,* he has a rebellious temperament; *non si può andare contro la propria* —, one cannot go against one's nature **2.** (*peculiarità*) character: *l'*— *della sua poesia,* the character of his poetry.

indolènte, *ag.* **1.** indolent, slothful, inert, lazy; (*apatico*) apathetic; (*indifferente*) indifferent **2.** (*rar.*) (*che non duole*) indolent, painless.

indolenteménte, *av.* indolently, slothfully, lazily; (*apaticamente*) apathetically; (*con indifferenza*) indifferently.

indolènza, *s.f.* indolence, sloth, laziness; (*apatia*) apathy; (*indifferenza*) indifference.

indolenziménto, *s.m.* numbness; soreness; stiffness.

indolenzíre, *v.t.* to numb, to benumb; to give pain to (sthg.); to make stiff: *il freddo mi aveva indolenzito le mani,* my hands were benumbed with cold ‖ **indolenzírsi,** *v.r.* to get numb, to get stiff.

indolenzíto, *ag.* numb, benumbed: *sono tutto* —, I am aching all over.

indolóre, indolóro, *ag.* painless: *parto* —, (*med.*) painless (o natural) childbirth.

indomàbile, *ag.* ungovernable; (*non addomesticabile*) untam(e)able (anche *fig.*); (*non soggiogabile*) unconquerable: *una passione* —, an untameable passion.

indomabilménte, *av.* indomitably; ungovernably.

indomàni, *s.m.* (the) next day, (the) following day; (the) day after: *l'*— *era già qui,* the next (o following) day he was already here; *all'*— *del suo arrivo,* (on) the day after his arrival.

indomàto, *ag.* untamed; (*non soggiogato*) unconquered.

indòmito, *ag.* indomitable, unyielding; (*di popolo*) unconquerable; (*di cavallo*) fiery.

Indonèsia, *no.pr.f.* (*geog.*) Indonesia.

indonesiàno, *ag.s.m.* Indonesian ‖ **indonesiàna,** *s.f.* Indonesian.

indoraménto, *s.m.* gilding.

indoràre, *v.t.* **1.** to gild (anche *fig.*): *il sole al tramonto indorava le cime,* the setting sun gilded the hill-tops ‖ — *la pillola,* to gild the pill **2.** (*cuc.*) to dip in egg ‖ **indoràrsi,** *v.r.* to assume a golden hue.

indoratóre, *s.m.* gilder.

indoratúra, *s.f.* gilding.

indossàre, *v.t.* **1.** (*avere indosso*) to wear, to have (sthg.) on: *indossa una sottana lunga,* she wears a long skirt **2.** (*mettere indosso*) to put (sthg.) on: *indossa la tua giacca,* put on your coat.

indossatríce, *s.f.* model, mannequin: *fare l'*—, to be a model.

indòsso, *av.* on: *avere* —, to have on: *non ho denaro* —, I have no money on me; *mettere* —, to put on.

Indostàn, *no.pr.m.* (*geog.*) Hindustan.
indostàno, *ag.s.m.* Hindustani.
indottaménte, *av.* (*senza dottrina*) unlearnedly.
indòtto[1], *ag.* (*letter.*) illiterate, uncultured, unlearned.
indótto[2], *ag.* **1.** (*spinto*) driven: — *dalla miseria,* driven by dire poverty **2.** (*elett.*) induced: *corrente indotta,* induced current ‖ *s.m.* (*elett.*) rotor, armature.
indovinàbile, *ag.* guessable; (*prevedibile*) foreseeable.
indovinàre, *v.t.* **1.** (*divinare*) to divine, to prophesy **2.** (*intuire*) to guess, to conjecture, to divine: — *i desideri di qlcu.,* to divine s.o.'s wishes; — *giusto, sbagliato,* to guess right, wrong; *indovina che cosa disse,* guess what he said; *indovina quanti anni ho,* guess how old I am **3.** (*predire, prevedere, immaginare*) to foresee, to foretell, to imagine: *avevo indovinato che tutto sarebbe finito in niente,* I had foreseen (o imagined) that everything would come to nothing **4.** *indovinarla,* (*colpire nel segno*) to hit the mark, to hit the nail on the head: *l'hai indovinata, questa è la causa di tutti i miei mali,* you have hit the (right) nail on the head (o you have hit it), this is the cause of all my troubles.
indovinàto, *ag.* (*che ha successo*) successful; (*ben fatto*) well-done; (*ben scelto*) well-chosen; (*ben concepito*) well-conceived.
indovinatóre, *s.m.*, **indovinatríce**, *s.f.* diviner.
indovinèllo, *s.m.* riddle, puzzle; conundrum.
indovíno, *ag.* prophetic; foreseeing ‖ *s.m.* soothsayer, fortune teller, diviner, prognosticator.
indovúto, *ag.* undue; (*immeritato*) undeserved; (*indebito*) unproper, improper.
Indú, *ag.s.c.* Hindu, Hindoo.
indubbiaménte, *av.* undoubtedly, certainly, surely.
indúbbio, *ag.* undoubted, certain, sure.
indubitàbile, *ag.* indubitable, unquestionable.
indubitataménte, *av.* undoubtedly, certainly, surely.
indubitàto, *ag.* undoubted, certain: *è — che...,* it goes without saying that....
indugiàre, *v.t.* to defer, to postpone: — *a fare ql.co.,* to defer doing sthg. ‖ *v.i.*, **indugiàrsi**, *v.r.* to delay, to loiter, to linger: — *su un argomento,* to dwell upon (o to linger over) a subject.
indúgio, *s.m.* (*ritardo*) delay; (*differimento*) postponement: *un — di due ore,* a delay of two hours; *senza —,* without delay ‖ *troncare gli indugi,* to come to a decision.
indulgènte, *ag.* indulgent (to, towards s.o.), lenient (with s.o.): *mostrarsi —,* to make allowances.
indulgenteménte, *av.* indulgently, leniently.
indulgènza, *s.f.* indulgence, leniency: *avere, mostrare — verso qlcu.,* to be indulgent to s.o. (o to make allowances for s.o.) ‖ — *plenaria,* (*eccl.*) plenary indulgence.
indúlgere, *v.i.* to indulge (in sthg.): — *a qualche pettegolezzo,* to indulge in some gossip; — *in un'abitudine,* to indulge in a habit.
indúlto, *s.m.* **1.** (*eccl.*) indult **2.** (*dir.*) free pardon.
induménto, *s.m.* garment: *gli indumenti,* clothes (o garments): *spogliarsi degli indumenti,* to throw off one's garments; *sacri indumenti,* priestly vestments.
induràre, *e derivati, V.* **induríre**, *e derivati.*
induriménto, *s.m.* hardening.
induríre, *v.t.* to harden (anche *fig.*): *l'egoismo gli ha indurito il cuore,* selfishness has hardened his heart; *il gelo ha indurito il terreno,* the frost has hardened the ground; — *il corpo alle fatiche,* to harden one's body to fatigue ‖ *v.i.*, **indurírsi**, *v.r.* **1.** to harden, to get hard (anche *fig.*): *durante la notte la neve indurì,* in the night the snow hardened; — *alle disgrazie,* to become callous to misfortunes **2.** (*di malta, cemento*) to set.
induríto, *ag.* hardened (anche *fig.*): — *alla fatica,* hardened to fatigue.
indúrre, *v.t.* **1.** (*ispirare, infondere*) to inspire, to infuse: — *coraggio nel cuore di qlcu.,* to infuse courage

into s.o.'s heart (o s.o.'s heart with courage); — *la speranza nell'animo di qlcu.,* to inspire hope in s.o.'s spirit **2.** (*persuadere*) to induce, to persuade, to get, to lead, to convince: *cerca di indurlo a venire,* try to persuade him to come; *che cosa ti indusse a farlo?,* what induced (o drove o impelled) you to do it?; *egli mi indusse a parlare,* he got me to speak; *fu indotto a farlo dalla paura,* he was driven to do it by fear; *sono indotto a credere che non sia vero,* I am led to believe that it is not true; *tutte le sue sventure lo indussero alla disperazione,* all his misfortunes drove him to despair; — *in errore,* to mislead ‖ *non c'— in tentazione,* lead us not into temptation **3.** (*log.*) to infer: *induco da ciò...,* I infer from that... **4.** (*elett.*) to induce ‖ **indúrsi**, *v.r.* (*decidersi*) to resolve, to decide, to make up one's mind: *non so indurmi a dirglielo,* I can't make up my mind to tell him; — *a far ql.co.,* to bring oneself to do sthg.
indúsio, *s.m.* (*bot.*) indusium (*pl.* indusia).
indústre, *ag.* (*letter.*) industrious.
indústria, *s.f.* **1.** industry: — *chiave,* key-industry; — *del cotone,* cotton industry; — *della lana, della seta,* woollen, silk industry; — *edilizia, metallurgica, tessile,* building, metal, textile industry; — *editoriale,* publishing trade; *l'— italiana,* Italian industry; — *manifatturiera,* manufacturing industry; — *petrolifera,* oil industry; — *protetta,* (*econ.*) sheltered industry; — *siderurgica,* steel industry; *industrie sovvenzionate dallo Stato,* subsidized industries; *capitani d'—,* captains of industry; *commercio e —,* commerce and industry; *un ramo dell'—,* a branch of industry **2.** (*assiduità, zelo*) industry, diligence **3.** (*abilità*) skill, cleverness; (*ingegnosità*) astuteness, cunning ‖ *cavaliere d'—,* (*spreg.*) knight of industry ‖ *vivere d'—,* to live by one's wits.
industriàle, *ag.* industrial: *chimica, ingegneria —,* industrial chemistry, engineering; *città, regione, centro —,* industrial town, district, centre; *consorzio —,* industrial combine; *impresa —,* industrial enterprise (o undertaking); *prodotti industriali,* industrial products; *la rivoluzione —,* the industrial revolution; *scuola —,* industrial school; *titoli industriali,* (*comm.*) industrials ‖ *s.m.* industrialist; manufacturer.
industrialísmo, *s.m.* industrialism.
industrializzàre, *v.t.* to industrialize.
industrializzazióne, *s.f.* industrialization.
industrialménte, *av.* industrially.
industriàrsi, *v.r.* (*ingegnarsi*) to contrive; (*fare del proprio meglio*) to do one's best: « *È bravo in aritmetica?* », « *S'industria* », " Is he good at figures? ", " Not too bad ".
industriosaménte, *av.* industriously.
industriosità, *s.f.* industriousness.
industrióso, *ag.* industrious.
induttànza, *s.f.* (*elett.*) inductance: — *mutua,* mutual inductance.
induttivaménte, *av.* inductively, by induction.
induttività, *s.f.* (*elett.*) induction.
induttívo, *ag.* inductive.
induttóre, *s.m.* (*elett.*) inductor: — *ad aria,* air-core inductor; — *a nucleo magnetico,* iron-core inductor.
induzióne, *s.f.* **1.** (*log.*) induction: *ragionare per —,* to reason by induction **2.** (*congettura*) conjecture, supposition **3.** (*elett.*) induction: — *elettromagnetica,* electromagnetic induction; — *elettrostatica,* electrostatic induction; — *magnetica,* magnetic induction; *regolatore a —,* induction converter; *rocchetto d'—,* induction coil.
inebbriàre, *V.* **inebriàre**.
inebetíre, *v.t.* to make dull, to make stupid, to hebetate ‖ *v.i.* to grow dull, to become stupid, to hebetate.
inebetíto, *ag.* dull, stupid, dense.
inebriaménto, *s.m.* inebriety, inebriation.
inebriàre, *v.t.* **1.** (*ubriacare*) to make drunk, to intoxicate, to inebriate **2.** *fig.* to intoxicate; to inebriate, to fill with joy: *quella notizia l'aveva inebriato,* that

news had filled him with joy; *essere inebriato dal successo*, to be intoxicated by (*o* with) success ‖ **inebriàrsi**, *v.r.* **1.** (*ubriacarsi*) to get drunk **2.** *fig.* to go into raptures, to be enraptured.

ineccepíbile, *ag.* unexceptionable: *onestà —,* proved honesty; *una condotta —,* an unexceptionable behaviour.

ineccepibilménte, *av.* unexceptionably.

inèdia, *s.f.* **1.** (*digiuno prolungato*) starvation, inanition **2.** (*noia*) boredom, tedium: *morire d'—,* to be bored to death.

inèdito, *ag.* unpublished, inedited: *opera inedita,* unpublished work ‖ *fatti inediti,* unheard-of events.

ineducàbile, *ag.* uneducable.

ineducataménte, *av.* unpolitely.

ineducàto, *ag.* ill-bred, impolite: *un ragazzaccio —,* an impolite youth (*o fam.* an unlicked cub).

ineducazióne, *s.f.* unpoliteness.

ineffàbile, *ag.* ineffable, unspeakable, unutterable.

ineffabilità, *s.f.* ineffability, ineffableness.

ineffabilménte, *av.* ineffably.

ineffettuàbile, *ag.* unrealizable, unfeasible; impossible to carry out.

inefficàce, *ag.* **1.** ineffective, ineffectual; (*di rimedio, preghiera, ecc.*) inefficacious **2.** (*inutile*) useless; (*vano*) vain.

inefficaceménte, *av.* **1.** ineffectively, ineffectually; inefficaciously **2.** (*inutilmente*) uselessly; (*vanamente*) vainly.

inefficàcia, *s.f.* **1.** ineffectiveness, ineffectualness; (*di rimedi, preghiere, ecc.*) inefficacy **2.** (*inutilità*) uselessness; (*vanità*) vainness.

inefficiènte, *ag.* inefficient.

ineguaglitànza, *s.f.* **1.** inequality: *le ineguaglianze sociali,* social inequalities **2.** (*irregolarità*) irregularity; (*di superficie*) unevenness, roughness **3.** (*mutevolezza*) changeableness, variability: *— d'umore,* fickleness.

ineguagliàto, *ag.* unequalled, unparalleled.

ineguàle, *ag.* **1.** (*dissimile*) unlike **2.** (*irregolare*) irregular; (*di superficie*) uneven, rough **3.** (*mutevole*) changeable, variable.

inegualità, *s.f.* **1.** inequality **2.** (*irregolarità*) irregularity; (*di superficie*) uneveness, roughness **3.** (*disparità*) disparity.

inegualménte, *av.* unequally.

inelegànte, *ag.* (*di stile*) inelegant, unpolished; (*di persona, vestito, ecc.*) not elegant, not smart, not refined, coarse; (*sgraziato*) ungraceful: *che andatura —!,* what (an) ungraceful gait! (*o* what a clumsy gait!); *non usare un linguaggio così —!,* don't use such coarse language!; *il suo stile è —,* his style is inelegant (*o* his style lacks elegance); *il suo vestito è —,* her dress is not smart.

ineleganteménte, *av.* inelegantly; (*rozzamente*) coarsely; (*sgraziatamente*) ungracefully, clumsily: *cammina —,* she walks clumsily.

inelegànza, *s.f.* inelegance, inelegancy; (*rozzezza*) coarseness; (*mancanza di grazia*) ungracefulness, clumsiness: *— di stile,* inelegance (*o* coarseness) of style; *l'— dei suoi gesti non è affatto femminile,* the ungracefulness of her gestures is quite unfeminine.

ineleggíbile, *ag.* ineligible, not eligible.

ineleggibilità, *s.f.* ineligibility.

ineluttàbile, *ag.* ineluctable, unavoidable, inevitable, inescapable: *un destino —,* an ineluctable fate.

ineluttabilménte, *av.* ineluctably, unavoidably, inevitably, inescapably.

inemendàbile, *ag.* **1.** incorrigible: *un bugiardo —,* an incorrigible liar **2.** (*che non si può sradicare*) ingrained: *un vizio —,* an ingrained vice.

inemendabilménte, *av.* incorrigibly.

inenarràbile, *ag.* unutterable, unspeakable, indescribable: *felicità —,* indescribable happiness.

inenarrabilménte, *av.* unutterably, unspeakably; indescribably; inexpressibly: *— felice,* unutterably happy.

inequivocàbile, *ag.* unequivocal, unmistakable, unambiguous; clear, certain: *una risposta —,* an unam-

biguous reply; *ci fu un — lampo d'ironia nei suoi occhi,* there was an unmistakable glint of irony in his eyes.

inequivocabilménte, *av.* unequivocally, unmistakably, unambiguously; clearly, certainly.

inerènte, *ag.* inherent (in sthg.); concerning (sthg.): *il peso è una proprietà — alla materia,* weight is an inherent property of matter; *la tua osservazione — a questo argomento è sensata,* your remark concerning this subject is reasonable.

inerènza, *s.f.* inherence.

inèrme, *ag.* unarmed, defenceless: *essere — di fronte alla crudeltà,* to be unarmed (*o* defenceless) before cruelty.

inerpicàre, *v.i.,* **inerpicàrsi**, *v.r.* **1.** (*di esseri animati*) to clamber up (sthg.); to climb (sthg.); to scale (sthg.): *il ragazzo si inerpicò sul muro,* the boy clambered up the wall **2.** (*di strada, sentiero, ecc.*) to climb: *il sentiero che si inerpica sulla collina,* the path that climbs up the hill.

inèrte, *ag.* **1.** inert; (*immobile*) motionless: *cadde a terra —,* he fell motionless (*o* senseless) to the ground; *la materia è —,* matter is inert **2.** (*ozioso, pigro*) inert, idle, lazy, slothful, sluggish: *un individuo —,* an idle (*o* lazy) fellow **3.** (*chim.*) inert: *gas —,* inert gas **4.** (*comm.*) (*inattivo*) dormant: *capitale —,* capital lying dormant.

inerudíto, *ag.* (*letter.*) unlearned, unlettered, uncultured.

inèrzia, *s.m.* **1.** inertness **2.** (*ozio, pigrizia*) inertness, idleness, laziness, sloth, indolence: *vivere nell'—,* to live in idleness **3.** (*fis.*) *forza d'—,* force of inertia.

inesattaménte, *av.* inexactly, inaccurately.

inesattézza, *s.f.* inexactness, inexactitude, inaccuracy; (*errore*) mistake: *— di calcolo,* inexactness of computation; *— di una traduzione,* inaccuracy of a translation; *esercizio pieno di inesattezze,* exercise full of mistakes.

inesàtto[1], *ag.* inexact, incorrect, inaccurate: *bilancia inesatta,* inaccurate scales.

inesàtto[2], *ag.* (*amm. comm.*) uncollected: *imposte inesatte,* uncollected taxes.

inesaudíbile, *ag.* not grantable, that cannot be fulfilled.

inesaudíto, *ag.* not granted, ungranted; (*di petizione*) rejected.

inesauríbile, *ag.* inexhaustible; unfailing, endless: *uomo di inesauribili risorse,* man of endless resources; *la sua pazienza è —,* his patience is unfailing.

inesauribilità, *s.f.* inexhaustibility.

inesauribilménte, *av.* inexhaustibly, unfailingly.

inesàusto, *ag.* unexhausted, unspent.

inescaménto, *s.m.* baiting.

inescàre, *v.t.* **1.** to bait **2.** (*artigl.*) to prime.

inescogitàbile, *ag.* unthinkable.

inescogitabilménte, *av.* unthinkably.

inescogitàto, *ag.* unthought-of.

inescusàbile, *ag.* inexcusable, unwarrantable, unjustifiable.

inescusabilménte, *av.* inexcusably, unwarrantably.

ineseguíbile, *ag.* **1.** inexecutable; impracticable **2.** (*di legge*) unenforceable **3.** (*di opera teatrale*) non-performable, not suitable for the stage **4.** (*di promessa*) that cannot be fulfilled.

ineseguíto, *ag.* **1.** unexecuted, not carried out **2.** (*di opera teatrale*) unperformed **3.** (*di promessa*) unfulfilled.

inesercitàto, *ag.* unpractised, untrained, unskilled, unexercised.

inesigíbile, *ag.* uncollectable, not due; (*di assegno*) worthless: *crediti inesigibili,* (*comm.*) bad debts.

inesigibilità, *s.f.* uncollectableness.

inesistènte, *ag.* inexistent, non-existent.

inesistènza, *s.f.* inexistence, non-existence.

inesoràbile, *ag.* inexorable; unrelenting, relentless; inflexible, implacable.

inesorabilità, *s.f.* inexorability, inexorableness; inflexibility, implacability, implacableness.

inesorabilménte, *av.* inexorably, inflexibly, implacably, unrelentingly.

inesoràto, (*letter.*) per **inesoràbile.**

inesperiènza, *s.f.* inexperience.

inespertaménte, *av.* inexpertly; unskilfully.

inespèrto, *ag.* 1. (*senza pratica*) inexpert; unskilled, unpractised, untrained: *infermiera inesperta,* untrained nurse; *mano inesperta,* unskilled hand; *medico* —, unpractised doctor 2. (*senza esperienza*) inexperienced.

inespiàbile, *ag.* inexpiable, unatonable.

inespiàto, *ag.* inexpiated, unatoned.

inesplicàbile, *ag.* inexplicable, unexplainable, unaccountable.

inesplicabilità, *s.f.* inexplicability, inexplicableness, unaccountableness.

inesplicabilménte, *av.* inexplicably, unaccountably.

inesplicàto, *ag.* unexplained, unaccounted for.

inesploràbile, *ag.* 1. inexplorable 2. (*insondabile*) unfathomable.

inesploràto, *ag.* unexplored.

inesplóso, *ag.* unexploded.

inespressívo, *ag.* inexpressive, expressionless, soulless: *occhi inespressivi,* soulless eyes.

inesprèsso, *ag.* unexpressed, tacit, implied.

inesprimíbile, *ag.* inexpressible, unutterable, beyond words.

inesprimibilménte, *av.* inexpressibly, unutterably.

inespugnàbile, *ag.* 1. inexpugnable, impregnable; storm-proof: *una fortezza* —, a storm-proof fortress 2. (*invincibile*) invincible: *volontà* —, invincible will 3. (*incorruttibile*) incorruptible: *donna* —, woman of impregnable virtue.

inespugnabilità, *s.f.* 1. inexpugnability, impregnability 2. (*invincibilità*) invincibility 3. (*incorruttibilità*) incorruptibility.

inespugnabilménte, *av.* 1. inexpugnably, impregnably 2. (*invincibilmente*) invincibly 3. (*incorruttibilmente*) incorruptibly.

inespugnàto, *ag.* unconquered.

inessiccàbile, *ag.* 1. that cannot be dried up 2. (*inesauribile*) inexhaustible.

inestensíbile, *ag.* inextensible.

inestensióne, *s.f.* inextension.

inestéso, *ag.* unextended.

inestimàbile, *ag.* inestimable, invaluable, priceless.

inestimabilménte, *av.* inestimably, invaluably.

inestinguíbile, *ag.* 1. inextinguishable, unquenchable: *fuoco* —, unquenchable fire; *sete* —, unquenchable thirst 2. (*inesauribile*) inexhaustible, unfailing: *luce* —, unfailing light; *pozzo* —, inexhaustible well 3. (*perenne*) eternal, everlasting, endless.

inestinguibilménte, *av.* 1. inextinguishably, unquenchably 2. (*inesauribilmente*) inexhaustibly 3. (*perennemente*) eternally, endlessly.

inestirpàbile, *ag.* ineradicable.

inestricàbile, *ag.* inextricable.

inestricabilménte, *av.* inextricably.

inettaménte, *av.* 1. unaptly, unsuitably 2. (*sciocca-mente*) ineptly, foolishly.

inettitúdine, *s.f.* 1. unaptness, unfitness, unsuitableness, unsuitability: — *per ql.co.,* *a fare ql.co.,* ineptitude for sthg., to do sthg. 2. (*sciocchezza*) ineptitude, foolishness, silliness 3. (*dappocaggine*) worthlessness.

inètto, *ag.* 1. unapt (for sthg., to do), unfit (for sthg.), unsuited (to, for sthg.), unsuitable (to, for sthg.) 2. (*sciocco*) inept, foolish, silly: *discorso* —, silly speech 3. (*dappoco*) good-for-nothing: *un uomo* —, a good-for-nothing.

inevàso, *ag.* (*comm.*) outstanding, undispatched: *lettera inevasa,* unanswered letter; *pratica inevasa,* outstanding (o undispatched) file.

inevitàbile, *ag.* inevitable, unavoidable: *gli errori inevitabili della giovinezza,* the mistakes inevitable to youth; *è* — *che accada,* it is bound to happen; *è* — *che veniate processato,* you are bound to have a law suit over it; *rassegnarsi all'*—, to resign oneself to the inevitable.

inevitabilità, *s.f.* inevitableness, unavoidableness.

inevitabilménte, *av.* inevitably, unavoidably.

inèzia, *s.f.* trifle: *costa un'*—, it costs only a trifle; *comprare ql.co. per un'*—, to buy sthg. for a mere song (o trifle); *offendersi per un'*—, to take offence at a mere trifle.

infacóndia, *s.f.* lack of eloquence, ineloquence.

infacóndo, *ag.* ineloquent.

infagottàre, *v.t.* to wrap up, to muffle: *era infagottata in una pesante pelliccia,* she was muffled in a thick fur; — *un bambino in uno scialle,* to wrap a child up in a shawl ‖ **infagottàrsi,** *v.r.* 1. to wrap (oneself) up, to muffle oneself (up) 2. (*vestir male*) to dress badly; to dress unbecomingly.

infallanteménte, *av.* (*letter.*) without fail, certainly, unfailingly: *verrà* —, no doubt he will come.

infallíbile, *ag.* 1. infallible, unerring: *nessuno di noi è* —, none of us is infallible 2. (*certo, sicuro*) unfailing, infallible: *sintomo* —, unfailing (o infallible) symptom.

infallibilità, *s.f.* infallibility.

infallibilménte, *av.* 1. infallibly, unerringly 2. (*certamente, sicuramente*) unfailingly, certainly.

infamànte, *ag.* defamatory; dishonourable, disgraceful, shameful: *condotta* —, shameful behaviour; *libello* —, defamatory libel.

infamàre, *v.t.* to defame, to slander; to disgrace: *non* — *il nome della tua famiglia!,* don't disgrace the good name of your family!.

infamàto, *ag.* ill-famed, disreputable.

infamatóre, *s.m.,* **infamatríce,** *s.f.* defamer, slanderer.

infamatòrio, *ag.* defamatory, slanderous; disgraceful.

infàme, *ag.* 1. ill-famed, infamous; foul; (*malvagio*) wicked; (*bestiale*) beastly: *un'azione* —, a foul deed; *un complotto* —, an infamous plot 2. (*fam.*) (*terribile*) vile, awful: *tempo* —, awful weather.

infameménte, *av.* infamously; (*malvagiamente*) wickedly; (*bestialmente*) beastly.

infàmia, *s.f.* 1. infamy (anche *st.*); disgrace, shame: *un marchio d'*—, a brand of infamy; *la sua condotta è un'*— *per noi tutti,* his behaviour is a disgrace to us all; *temeva l'*— *dei suoi amici,* he was afraid of his friends' infamy; *coprire qlcu. d'*—, to bring disgrace (o shame) on s.o. 2. (*cattiva fama*) ill fame 3. (*atto infame*) foul deed, infamy: *commettere un'*—, to be guilty of an infamy ‖ *che* —!, how infamous!.

infanatichíre, *v.t.i.,* **infanatichírsi,** *v.r.* to fanaticize.

infangàre, *v.t.* to bespatter with mud, to muddy ‖ **infangàrsi,** *v.r.* to get muddy ‖ — *nel vizio,* to be tainted with vice.

infangàto, *ag.* 1. muddy; bespattered with mud: *scarpe infangate,* muddy shoes 2. *fig.* disgraced.

infànta, *s.f.* (*st.*) infanta.

infànte, *s.m.* 1. infant; child, babe, babe in arms 2. (*st.*) infante.

infanticìda, *s.c.* infanticide, child-murderer.

infanticídio, *s.m.* infanticide, child-murder.

infantíle, *ag.* 1. childlike, childish, infantile; children's (*attributivo*): *giuochi infantili,* childish (o children's) games; *innocenza* —, childlike innocence; *letteratura* —, children's (o juvenile) literature ‖ *asilo* —, kindergarten ‖ *paralisi* —, (*patol.*) infantile paralysis (o poliomyelitis o *fam.* polio) 2. (*puerile*) childish, infantile; (*ingenuo*) naïve.

infantilísmo, *s.m.* (*patol.*) infantilism.

infantilménte, *av.* childishly.

infànzia, *s.f.* 1. infancy, babyhood, early childhood 2. (*i bambini*) children (*pl.*) 3. *fig.* infancy: *l'*— *di un popolo,* the infancy of a people.

infarciménto, *s.m.* stuffing, cramming (anche *fig.*).

infarcíre, *v.t.* to stuff, to cram (anche *fig.*): *ha infarcito il suo libro di citazioni,* he has stuffed his book with quotations; — *un tacchino di castagne,* to stuff a turkey with chestnuts.

infarinàre, *v.t.* to flour, to sprinkle with flour: *bisogna — il pesce prima di friggerlo,* you must flour fish before frying it ‖ **infarinàrsi,** *v.r.* **1.** to get covered with flour **2.** (*scherz.*) (*incipriarsi*) to powder (oneself): *non infarinarti così!,* don't powder your face like that!.

infarinatúra, *s.f.* **1.** flouring **2.** *fig.* smattering, sprinkling; slight knowledge: *ha un' — di letteratura inglese,* he has a smattering of English literature.

infàrto, *s.m.* (*med.*) infarct, infarction.

infastidíre, *v.t.* (*irritare*) to annoy, to vex, to irritate, to aggravate; (*disturbare*) to worry, to bother, to trouble; (*annoiare, stancare*) to tire, to bore, to weary; (*molestare*) to molest: *mi dispiace doverti —,* I am sorry to trouble you; *non infastidirmi con le tue inutili domande!,* don't worry (*o* bother) me with your foolish questions! ‖ **infastidírsi,** *v.r.* to be vexed; to get tired, to get bored.

infastidíto, *ag.* annoyed; tired, bored, weary.

infaticàbile, *ag.* indefatigable, untiring, tireless.

infaticabilità, *s.f.* indefatigability.

infaticabilménte, *av.* indefatigably.

infàtti, *cong.* in fact, as a matter of fact, indeed, really: *credi tu — che io possa fare ciò?,* do you really think I can do that?; *non potevo — credere che...,* as a matter of fact I couldn't believe that....

infatuàre, *v.t.* to infatuate ‖ **infatuàrsi,** *v.r.* to become infatuated (with s.o., sthg.), to get crazy (about s.o., sthg.), to get mad (about s.o., sthg.): *si è infatuato di quella ragazza,* he got crazy about that girl.

infatuàto, *ag.* infatuated (with s.o., sthg.), crazy (about s.o., sthg.), mad (about s.o., sthg.): — *di se stesso,* (self-)conceited.

infatuazióne, *s.f.* infatuation (with s.o., sthg.).

infàusto, *ag.* inauspicious; unlucky, unfavourable: *giorno —,* unlucky day.

infecondaménte, *av.* barrenly, unfruitfully.

infecondità, *s.f.* unfruitfulness; unproductiveness; (*sterilità*) barrenness, sterility: *l' — del suolo,* the barrenness of the soil; *l' — di una donna,* the sterility of a woman.

infecóndo, *ag.* unfruitful; (*sterile*) barren, sterile: *lavoro —,* unfruitful work; *terra infeconda,* barren land.

infedèle, *ag.* **1.** unfaithful, faithless, false: — *a una promessa,* false (*o* unfaithful) to a promise; *alleato —,* faithless ally; *amico, marito —,* unfaithful friend, husband **2.** (*di traduzione, riproduzione, ecc.*) unfaithful; inaccurate **3.** (*disonesto*) dishonest, defaulting: *un cassiere —,* a dishonest cashier ‖ *s.m.* infidel, unbeliever: *predicò la religione di Cristo tra gli infedeli,* he preached the Christian religion among the infidels.

infedelménte, *av.* **1.** unfaithfully, faithlessly, falsely **2.** (*di traduzione*) unfaithfully; inaccurately **3.** (*disonestamente*) dishonestly.

infedeltà, *s.f.* **1.** unfaithfulness, faithlessness; (*tra coniugi*) infidelity **2.** (*di traduzione, riproduzione, ecc.*) unfaithfulness; inaccuracy **3.** (*disonestà*) dishonesty.

infelíce, *ag.* **1.** unfortunate, unhappy; (*disgraziato*) wretched, poor, unlucky: *un'esistenza —,* an unhappy (*o* a wretched) existence; *un'iniziativa —,* an unlucky initiative; *si sente molto —,* he feels very unhappy; *avere l'aria —,* to look unhappy; *rendere — qlcu.,* to make s.o. unhappy ‖ *gli infelici,* the unfortunate (*o* the poor): *soccorrere gli infelici,* to help the unfortunate **2.** (*inappropriato*) inappropriate; ill-timed: *parola —,* inappropriate word; *scherzo —,* ill-timed joke **3.** (*cattivo*) bad: *traduzione —,* bad translation **4.** (*imbarazzante*) awkward: *situazione —,* awkward situation **5.** (*che non ha successo*) unsuccessful: *una commedia —,* an unsuccessful play.

infeliceménte, *av.* **1.** unfortunately, unhappily; wretchedly, unluckily **2.** (*inappropriatamente*) inappropriately, malapropos **3.** (*malamente*) badly **4.** (*in modo imbarazzante*) awkwardly **5.** (*senza successo*) unsuccessfully.

infelicità, *s.f.* **1.** unhappiness; wretchedness, unluckiness **2.** (*inopportunità*) inopportunity: *l' — di un'osservazione,* the inopportunity of a remark.

infeltríre, *v.t.* to felt, to felter, to mat ‖ *v.i.,* **infeltrírsi,** *v.r.* to felt; (*restringersi*) to shrink.

inferènza, *s.f.* inference: *per —,* by inference.

inferióre, *ag.* **1.** (*in senso assoluto*) **inferior:** *un essere —,* an inferior being; *qualità —,* inferior quality ‖ *pianeti inferiori,* (*astr.*) inferior planets **2.** (*con valore comparativo*) **inferior:** *è — a lui in intelligenza,* she is inferior to him in intelligence; *è di statura — alla mia,* he is shorter than I am; *questa merce è — a quella,* these goods are inferior to those **3.** (*più basso, meno elevato*) **lower:** *grado —,* lower degree (*o* rank); *prezzo, temperatura, velocità —,* lower price, temperature, speed **4.** (*sottostante*) **lower:** *le classi inferiori,* the lower classes; *denti inferiori,* lower teeth; *labbro, mascella —,* lower lip, jaw; *abita al piano — below,* he lives on the floor below; (*di casa a due piani*) he lives on the lower floor ‖ *la parte — di un fiume,* (*a valle*) the lower part of a river **5.** (*al di sotto*) **below:** — *alla media,* below-average; *fu — alla sua fama,* he did not live up to his reputation; *Webster è — a Shakespeare nell'arte drammatica,* Webster is below Shakespeare in dramatic art **6.** (*di grado inferiore*) **junior:** *le classi inferiori di questa scuola,* the junior classes in this school; *ufficiali inferiori,* junior officers ‖ *s.m.* (*subalterno*) subordinate.

inferiorità, *s.f.* inferiority: — *di numero,* inferiority in numbers: *complesso d' —,* (*psicanalisi*) inferiority complex; *la sua miopia lo mette in uno stato d' —,* he is handicapped by his short sight.

inferiorménte, *av.* **1.** (*più in basso*) below, in the lower part **2.** (*in modo inferiore*) inferiorly.

inferíre, *v.t.* **1.** (*dedurre*) to infer, to deduce, to conclude: *ne inferisco che egli non è d'accordo con te,* I infer that he doesn't agree with you; — *ql.co. da ql.co.,* to infer sthg. from sthg. **2.** (*dare, infliggere*) to strike, to inflict: — *un colpo a qlcu.,* to inflict a blow on s.o. (*o* to strike s.o. a blow) **3.** (*mar.*) (*di vela, metterla in opera*) to hoist; (*una vela, legarla al pennone*) to bend.

infermàre, *v.t.* **1.** to make ill; (*indebolire*) to weaken **2.** (*infirmare*) to invalidate ‖ **infermàrsi,** *v.r.* to fall ill.

infermería, *s.f.* infirmary; sickroom; (*di bordo*) sick-bay.

infermíccio, *ag.* sickly.

infermièra, *s.f.* (hospital) nurse: — *capo,* matron; *fare da — a qlcu.,* to nurse s.o. (*o* to look after s.o.).

infermière, *s.m.* hospital attendant; male nurse.

infermità, *s.f.* infirmity, illness, sickness, disease: — *di mente,* insanity (*o* madness).

infèrmo, *ag.* invalid, infirm; sick (*gener. attributivo*); ill (*gener. predicativo*): *mia madre è inferma da molti anni,* my mother has been an invalid many years ‖ *s.m.* invalid; patient.

infernàle, *ag.* **1.** infernal, hellish: *astuzia —,* infernal cunning; *macchina —,* infernal machine; *regioni infernali,* infernal regions **2.** *fig.* (*terribile*) awful, dreadful: *un carattere —,* an awful temper.

infèrno, *s.m.* hell: *c'è un rumore d' —,* there is a hell of a noise; *soffrire le pene dell' —,* to suffer the torments of hell ‖ *va' all' —!,* (*volg.*) go to hell!; go to the devil! ‖ *l'Inferno di Dante,* Dante's Inferno.

ínfero, *ag.* **1.** (*letter.*) (*inferiore*) inferior, lower **2.** (*infernale*) infernal, hellish.

ínferi, *s.m.pl.* **1.** (*inferno*) hell (*sing.*) **2.** (*gli dei dell'inferno*) infernal gods.

inferocíre, *v.t.* to enrage, to make fierce, to make

ferocious ‖ *v.i.*, **inferocìrsi**, *v.r.* to get fierce, to be pitiless, to be cruel, to be merciless.

inferriàta, *s.f.* grille, (iron) grating, (iron) railing.

infertilìre, *v.t.* to fertilize: — *il suolo*, to fertilize the soil.

infertilità, *s.f.* infertility, sterility.

infervoraménto, *s.m.* fervour, ardour, enthusiasm, zeal.

infervoràre, *v.t.* to fill with fervour, to fill with enthusiasm; to animate, to enliven ‖ **infervoràrsi**, *v.r.* to get excited, to be filled with enthusiasm.

infervoràto, *ag.* fervent; enthusiastic, passionate, impassioned: *una discussione infervorata*, an animated discussion.

infestaménto, *s.m.* infestation.

infestàre, *v.t.* to infest: *la casa era infestata dai topi*, the house was infested with rats.

infèsto, *ag.* harmful, hurtful; obnoxious; hostile: *una stagione infesta*, an obnoxious season.

infettàre, *v.t.* to infect, to pollute; (*corrompere*) to taint, to corrupt: — *l'acqua*, to pollute water; — *una ferita*, to infect a wound; — *la società*, to corrupt society ‖ **infettàrsi**, *v.r.* to become infected, to become corrupted; to taint.

infettìvo, *ag.* infectious, contagious; catching: *la scarlattina è una malattia infettiva*, scarlet fever is a contagious disease.

infètto, *ag.* infected, polluted; corrupt.

infeudaménto, *s.m.* enfeoffment, infeudation.

infeudàre, *v.t.* 1. to enfeoff 2. (*assoggettare*) to subject, to subdue: — *la propria coscienza*, to subdue one's conscience ‖ **infeudàrsi**, *v.r.* to become subjected.

infezióne, *s.f.* infection, contagion: *diffondere l'—*, to spread infection.

infiacchiménto, *s.m.* weakening, enfeeblement, enervation.

infiacchìre, *v.t.* to weaken, to enfeeble, to enervate: *un clima che infiacchisce*, an enervating climate ‖ *v.i.*, **infiacchìrsi**, *v.r.* to become weak, to become enfeebled, to lose one's strength.

infiacchìto, *ag.* weak, feeble; (*malaticcio*) sickly.

infiammàbile, *ag.* inflammable (anche *fig.*): *sostanze infiammabili*, inflammables; *temperamento —*, inflammable (o quick) temper.

infiammabilità, *s.f.* inflammability, inflammableness.

infiammàre, *v.t.* 1. to set on fire, to ignite, to kindle: *la scintilla infiammò la legna secca*, the spark kindled the dry wood; *il sole morente infiamma il cielo*, the setting sun sets the sky on fire 2. *fig.* (*eccitare*) to inflame, to kindle, to excite, to stir (up): *il suo discorso infiammò l'uditorio*, his speech inflamed the audience 3. (*med.*) to inflame ‖ **infiammàrsi**, *v.r.* 1. to catch fire, to take fire: *l'aereo s'infiammò nell'atterraggio*, the plane caught fire in landing 2. *fig.* (*eccitarsi*) to become inflamed, to get excited 3. (*med.*) to get inflamed.

infiammatòrio, *ag.* inflammatory.

infiammazióne, *s.f.* inflammation.

infiascàre, *v.t.* to put into flasks.

infiascàto, *ag.* flasked; in flasks (*predicativo*).

infiascatúra, *s.f.* putting in flasks.

inficiàre, *v.t.* (*dir.*) to impugn.

infìdo, *ag.* untrustworthy; (*falso*) false, unfaithful, treacherous: *un amico —*, a false friend; *un sorriso —*, a treacherous smile.

infierìre, *v.i.* 1. (*incrudelire*) to be pitiless: — *contro qlcu.*, to be pitiless towards s.o. 2. (*imperversare*) to rage: *l'epidemia infieriva*, the epidemic was raging.

infievoliménto, *s.m.* enfeeblement, weakening.

infievolìre, *v.t.* to enfeeble, to weaken: *la malattia gli infievolì la voce*, the illness weakened his voice ‖ *v.i.*, **infievolìrsi**, *v.r.* to weaken, to grow weak, to become feeble: *il suo coraggio si infievolì*, his courage weakened.

infìggere, *v.t.* to drive, to fix: — *un'idea in testa a qlcu.*, to drive an idea into s.o.'s head; — *un palo nel terreno*, to fix a stake into the ground ‖ **infìggersi**,

v.r. to penetrate, to fix, to go deep: *il sospetto si infisse nel suo cuore*, suspicion fixed in his heart.

infilàre, *v.t.* 1. to thread; to string: — *un ago*, to thread a needle; — *perle*, to string beads ‖ — *una serie interminabile di ragionamenti*, to go through an endless string of arguments 2. (*infilzare*) to pierce (through), to transfix; to run through: — *un pollo sullo spiedo*, to put a chicken on the spit; — *qlcu. con la spada*, to run s.o. through with a sword 3. (*introdurre*) to insert; to slip in: — *una chiave nella toppa*, to insert a key in the lock; — *una mano in tasca*, to slip one's hand into one's pocket 4. (*passare per*) to enter; to take: — *una strada*, to take a street; — *l'uscio*, (*per entrare*) to slip in; (*per uscire*) to slip out 5. (*mil.*) to enfilade ‖ **infilàrsi**, *v.r.* 1. to thread one's way: *mi infilai attraverso la folla*, I threaded my way through the crowd 2. (*indossare*) to slip on, to put on: — *le calze*, to pull on one's stockings; — *il vestito*, to slip on one's dress 3. (*introdursi*) to slip: — *nel letto*, to slip (o *fam.* to pop) into bed.

infilàta, *s.f.* 1. row, line; suite; string: *un'— di alberi*, a row of trees; *un'— di insulti*, a string of insults; *un'— di stanze*, a suite of rooms 2. (*mil.*) enfilade.

infilatúra, *s.f.* (*di ago*) threading; (*di perle*) stringing: — *automatica*, (*ind. tessile*) self-threading.

infiltraménto, *s.m.* filtering, filtration.

infiltràrsi, *v.r.* to infiltrate, to permeate, to penetrate (sthg.), to seep: *l'acqua si infiltra dappertutto*, water infiltrates (o seeps through) everywhere; *idee che si infiltrano nel popolo*, ideas that permeate among the people; — *nelle linee nemiche*, to penetrate the enemy lines.

infiltrazióne, *s.f.* infiltration, permeation, penetration, seepage: — *di pus*, purulent infiltration.

infilzaménto, *s.m.* 1. piercing 2. (*il conficcare*) sticking 3. (*l'infilare*) stringing.

infilzàre, *v.t.* 1. to transfix, to pierce: *egli infilzò il nemico con la spada*, he transfixed the enemy with his sword; — *qlcu. da parte a parte*, to run s.o. through 2. (*conficcare*) to stick: — *una forchetta in una patata*, to stick a fork into a potato; — *un palo nel terreno*, to stick a pole in the ground 3. (*infilare*) to string ‖ — *bugie*, to tell a lot of lies ‖ **infilzàrsi**, *v.r.* 1. to run oneself through: *andò ad — su una lancia del cancello*, he ran himself through on a spike of the gate 2. (*conficcarsi*) to get stuck: *una spina gli si infilzò nel dito*, a thorn got stuck in his finger.

infilzàta, *s.f.* row, line; suite; string.

infimaménte, *av.* 1. to the lowest degree 2. (*macchinamente*) basely, meanly.

infimo, *ag.* lowest, very low, very mean: *l'— degli infimi*, the lowest of the low; *l'— dei cittadini*, the meanest citizen; *d'— grado*, of the lowest degree.

infìne, *av.* 1. (*finalmente*) at last: — *eccovi arrivati!*, here you are at last! 2. (*dopo tutto*) after all, in the end: — *potete tentare*, after all, you can try 3. (*da ultimo*) lastly, finally 4. (*in conclusione*) in conclusion.

infingardàggine, *s.f.* laziness, sloth(fulness), sluggishness: *per pura —*, out of sheer laziness.

infingardaménte, *av.* lazily, slothfully, sluggishly.

infingardìre, *v.t.* to make lazy, to make slothful ‖ *v.i.* to become lazy, to grow lazy, to become slothful.

infingàrdo, *ag.* lazy, slothful, sluggish, slack: *è un individuo —*, he is a lazy fellow ‖ *s.m.* lazy person, sluggard, slacker; (*fam.*) lazy-bones.

infìngersi, *v.r.* to feign, to simulate, to pretend.

infingiménto, *s.m.* (*rar.*) feigning, simulation.

infinità, *s.f.* 1. infinity, boundlessness, infinitude: *l'— del creato*, the infinity of the universe; *l'— della misericordia divina*, the infinitude of God's mercy 2. (*gran numero*) infinite number, infinity, infinitude: *un'— di cose*, an infinite number of things; *un'— di gente*, a large crowd of people (o swarms of people); *un'— di modi di fare ql.co.*, infinite ways of doing sthg.; *un'— di ragioni*, endless reasons (o no end of reasons).

infinitaménte, *av.* infinitely; (*fam.*) awfully: — *buono,* infinitely good; — *più intelligente,* infinitely more intelligent; *mi dispiace* —, I am awfully sorry; *questo va — meglio,* that is far and away better; *sentirsi — meglio,* to feel very much better.

infinitesimàle, *ag.* infinitesimal: *analisi, calcolo* —, (*mat.*) infinitesimal analysis, calculus.

infinitèsimo, *ag.* infinitesimal.

infinitézza, *s.f.* infiniteness, infinity, infinitude.

infiníto, *ag.* 1.infinite, boundless, immeasurable: *bontà infinita,* infinite goodness; *spazio* —, infinite space; *Dio è* —, God is infinite 2. (*interminabile*) endless, never -ending 3. (*innumerevole*) numberless 4. (*gram.*) infinite, infinitive: *modo* —, infinitive mood ‖ *s.m.* 1. infinite 2.(*gram.*)infinitive 3.(*mat. fis.*) infinity: *all'* —, (*mat.*) to infinity; *regolare all'* —, (*foto.*) to focus for infinity.

infíno a, (*rar.*) per **fíno a.**

infinocchiàre, *v.t.* to take in, to make a fool of (s.o.), to cheat, to deceive.

infioccàre, *v.t.* to tassel, to adorn with tassels.

infioccàto, *ag.* tasselled.

infiochíre, *v.t.* 1. (*voce*) to hoarsen, to make hoarse, to make husky 2. (*luce*) to dim, to lower ‖ *v.i.* 1. (*di voce*) to hoarsen, to get hoarse 2. (*di luce*) to dim, to grow dim, to fade away.

infioràre, *v.t.* 1. to adorn with flowers, to deck with flowers, to decorate with flowers 2. (*cospargere di fiori*) to strew with flowers 3. *fig.* to adorn.

infiorescènza, *s.f.* (*bot.*) inflorescence.

infirmàre, *v.t.* to invalidate: — *un testamento,* (*dir.*) to invalidate a will.

infischiàrsi, *v.r.* (*fam.*) not to care (for sthg.), to make light of (sthg.), to take no notice (of sthg.), to laugh (at sthg.), to set (sthg.) at naught: *me ne infischio!,* I couldn't care less.

infísso, *ag.* driven, fixed: *parole infisse nella memoria,* words engraved on one's memory ‖ *s.m.* fixture; (*di porta, finestra*) frame, casing: *bisogna cambiare gli infissi del bagno,* the fixtures of the bathroom must be changed.

infistolíre, *v.i.,* **infistolírsi,** *v.r.* to become fistulous.

infittíre, *v.t.* to thicken, to make thick: — *le maglie di una rete,* to thicken the meshes of a net ‖ *v.i.* 1. to thicken, to become thick: *la pioggia infittisce sempre più,* the rain is becoming thicker and thicker 2. (*di lana*) to get matted.

inflazionàrio, *ag.* inflationary.

inflazióne, *s.f.* inflation.

inflazionísta, *s.m.* inflationist.

inflazionístico, *ag.* inflationary.

inflessíbile, *ag.* inflexible, rigid, stubborn, firm: *un atteggiamento* —, an inflexible attitude; *un'opposizione* —, a stubborn opposition.

inflessibilità, *s.f.* inflexibility.

inflessibilménte, *av.* inflexibly.

inflessióne, *s.f.* inflexion: *una carezzevole — di voce,* voice with a caressing inflexion; *punto d'* —, (*geom.*) inflexion point (*o* point of inflexion).

inflèttere, *v.t.* 1. to bend ‖ — *la voce,* to inflect (*o* to modulate) one's voice 2. (*gram.*) to inflect: — *un verbo,* to inflect a verb ‖ **inflèttersi,** *v.r.* 1. to bend: *le volute del capitello corinzio si inflettono formando foglie d'acanto,* the volutes of the Corinthian capital bend to form acanthus leaves 2. (*gram.*) to inflect.

infliggere, *v.t.* to inflict, to impose; to lay: — *un colpo a qlcu.,* to inflict a blow on s.o.; — *una pena a qlcu.,* to inflict a penalty on s.o.; — *la propria presenza a qlcu.,* to impose one's company on s.o.

inflizióne, *s.f.* infliction, inflicting.

inflorescènza, *s.f.* (*bot.*) inflorescence.

influènte, *ag.* influential: *una persona* —, an influential person ‖ *s.m.* (*affluente*) tributary, affluent.

influènza, *s.f.* 1. influence: *l'* — *degli astri sulla vita umana,* the influence of the stars on human life; *esercitare la propria* — *su qlcu.,* to exert one's influence

on s.o.; *essere sotto l'* — *di ql.co.,* to be under the influence of sthg. 2. (*patol.*) influenza; (*fam.*) 'flu: *prendere l'* —, to catch the 'flu 3. (*fis.*) influence.

influenzàre, *v.t.* to influence, to affect; to bias: *i giornali possono* — *l'opinione pubblica,* newspapers can bias public opinion; *le sue dolorose vicende influenzarono il suo carattere,* his sad experiences influenced (*o* affected) his character.

influenzàto, *ag.* 1. influenced, affected 2. (*affetto da influenza*) suffering from influenza.

influíre, *v.i.* to influence (s.o., sthg.), to have influence; to affect (s.o., sthg.): *ciò non influirà sulle mie decisioni,* that will have no influence on my decisions; — *sui prezzi,* (*comm.*) to affect prices.

inflússo, *s.m.* influence.

infocàre, *v.t.* 1. to heat up, to make red hot 2. *fig.* to inflame, to kindle, to excite ‖ **infocàrsi,** *v.r.* 1. to become red hot 2. *fig.* to get inflamed, to get excited.

infocàto, *ag.* 1. (*arroventato*) red hot 2. (*scottante*) burning 3. *fig.* inflamed, excited.

infoderàre, *v.t.* to sheathe.

infognàrsi, *v.r.* (*volg.*) to plunge, to sink: — *nei debiti,* to get deeper and deeper into debts.

in-fòlio, *ag.* folio (*attributivo*); in folio: *un volume* —, a folio volume (*o* a volume in folio).

infoltíre, *v.i.* to thicken, to grow thick.

infondataménte, *av.* groundlessly.

infondatézza, *s.f.* groundlessness.

infondàto, *ag.* groundless.

infóndere, *v.t.* to infuse, to inspire, to instil: — *coraggio, speranza a qlcu.,* to infuse courage, hope into s.o. (*o* to infuse s.o. with courage, hope); — *le proprie idee nella mente di qlcu.,* to instil one's ideas into s.o.'s mind.

inforcàre, *v.t.* 1. to pitchfork: *i contadini inforcavano il fieno,* the peasants were pitchforking hay 2. (*montare a cavalcioni di*) to bestride, to get on (sthg.): — *una bicicletta, un cavallo,* to bestride (*o* to get on) a bicycle, a horse 3. — *gli occhiali,* to put on one's spectacles.

inforcàta, *s.f.* (pitch)forkful.

inforcatúra, *s.f.* 1. (*l'inforcare*) pitchforking 2. (*biforcazione*) forking; bifurcation.

informàre, *v.t.* 1. to inform, to acquaint: — *qlcu. di ql.co.,* to inform s.o. about (*o* of) sthg. (*o* to acquaint s.o. with sthg.) 2. (*notificare a*) to notify: — *la polizia di un furto,* to report a theft to the police 3. (*pervadere, caratterizzare*) to pervade, to permeate, to characterize: *queste idee informano tutte le sue opere,* these ideas pervade (*o* characterize) all his works 4. (*dar forma a, plasmare*) to shape, to mould (anche *fig.*) ‖ **informàrsi,** *v.r.* 1. to inquire, to enquire: — *intorno a ql.co., a qlcu.,* to inquire about sthg., after s.o. 2. (*essere pervaso, caratterizzato da*) to be pervaded (with sthg.), to be informed (with sthg.), to be inspired (with sthg.), to be imbued (with sthg.): *tutti i suoi scritti si informano a queste idee,* all his writings are inspired with these ideas.

informatívo, *ag.* informative: *prezzo* —, indicative price ‖ *a puro titolo* —, for information only.

informàto, *ag.* 1. informed: *bene* —, well-informed; *male* —, ill-informed 2. (*pervaso, caratterizzato*) informed (with sthg.), inspired (with sthg.), imbued (with sthg.): — *a strane idee,* inspired with strange ideas.

informatóre, *ag.* informing: *i principi informatori dei suoi scritti,* the principles informing his writings ‖ *s.m.,* **informatríce,** *s.f.* informer.

informazióne, *s.f.* 1. information (*solo sing.*); piece of information; inquiry: *le informazioni del caso,* the information in this connection; *informazioni ufficiose,* semi-official information; *servizio informazioni,* information service; *servizio informazioni militari,* Intelligence Service; *ufficio informazioni,* inquiry-office (*o* information bureau); *desideriamo delle informazioni in questa faccenda,* we want some information about this matter; *questa è un'* — *interessante,* this is an interesting piece of information; *assumere informazioni su qlcu.,* to inquire after s.o.; *domandare informazioni su ql.co.,* to request information about sthg. (o to ask about sthg.) **2.** (dir.) preliminary investigation (of a case).

infórme, ag. shapeless.

informicolaménto, informicoliménto, s.m. tingle, tingling sensation.

informicolàre, informicolíre, v.t. to give pins and needles, to cause to tingle: *lo stare in quella posizione gli informicolò la gamba,* lying in that position gave his leg pins and needles (o caused his leg to tingle o caused a tingling sensation in his leg) ‖ **informicolàrsi, informicolírsi,** v.r. to have pins and needles, to tingle: *mi si è informicolito un braccio,* I have pins and needles in my arm.

informità, s.f. shapelessness.

infornaciàre, v.t. to put into a furnace.

infornàre, v.t. to put into an oven.

infornàta, s.f. **1.** batch (of bread) **2.** fig. batch, bunch, group: *un'— di reclute,* a batch of recruits.

infortíre, v.i. (di vino) to turn sour.

infortíto, ag. (di vino) sour.

infortunàto, ag. **1.** injured ‖ *gli infortunati,* the injured **2.** (sfortunato) unlucky, unfortunate.

infortúnio, s.m. **1.** (incidente) accident: — *sul lavoro,* labour accident; *assicurazione contro gli infortuni,* accident insurance; *ci furono diversi infortuni il mese scorso,* there were several accidents last month **2.** (colpo di sfortuna) stroke of bad luck; mischance.

infortunística, s.f. (dir.) industrial accident research.

infoscaménto, s.m. darkening.

infoscàre, v.t. to darken ‖ **infoscàrsi,** v.r. to grow dark, to darken.

infossaménto, s.m. (incavo) hollow; cavity.

infossàre, v.t. (grano) to store (corn) in a pit ‖ **infossàrsi,** v.r. (di guance, occhi) to become hollow.

infossàto, ag. **1.** (sepolto) buried **2.** (incavato) sunken, hollow: *guance infossate,* sunken cheeks.

infossatúra, s.f. hollow; cavity.

infra, (poet.) per **fra**[1].

infracidíre, v.t. (rar.) to drench, to soak, to steep.

infradiciàre, v.t. to drench, to soak, to steep ‖ **infradiciàrsi,** v.r. to get drenched, to get soaked.

infradiciàto, ag. wet through, soaking wet.

infradiciatúra, s.f. drenching, soaking.

infralíre, v.t. (letter.) to weaken, to enfeeble ‖ v.i. (letter.) to grow weak, to become frail.

infra(m)mettènte, ag. interfering, meddlesome, intrusive.

infra(m)mettènza, s.f. interference, meddlesomeness, intrusiveness.

infra(m)méttere, v.t. to interpose ‖ **infra(m)méttersi,** v.r. to interfere, to meddle; to intrude (on, upon sthg.).

inframmischiàre, v.t. to intermingle; to intermix ‖ **inframmischiàrsi,** v.r. to mingle; to intermingle.

infranceesàre, infranciosàre, v.t. to Gallicize, to Frenchify ‖ **infrancesàrsi, infranciosàrsi,** v.r. to Gallicize.

infranceesàto, infranciosàto, ag. **1.** Gallicized, Frenchified **2.** (di lingua) full of Gallicism.

infràngere, v.t. **1.** to shatter, to crush, to smash (anche fig.): *la sua speranza fu presto infranta,* his hope was soon shattered (o crushed); — *la resistenza nemica,* to crush the enemy('s) resistance; — *il vetro di una finestra,* to shatter a window-pane **2.** (violare) to infringe, to violate: — *una legge,* to infringe a law ‖ **infràngersi,** v.r. to break (up); to smash (anche fig.): *le onde si infrangono contro le rocce,* the waves break against the rocks.

infrangíbile, ag. unbreakable; (fis.) infrangible.

infrangiménto, s.m. **1.** (l'infrangere) shattering, crushing, smashing **2.** (infrazione) infringement, break.

infrànto, ag. shattered, crushed, smashed (anche fig.): *cuore —,* broken heart.

infrappórre, v.t. to interpose.

infrarósso, ag. infra-red: *raggi infrarossi,* infra-red rays.

infrascàre, infrasconàre, v.t. **1.** to cover with branches **2.** fig. (caricare d'inutili ornamenti) to load with ornaments ‖ **infrascàrsi, infrasconàrsi,** v.r. to hide among the branches.

infrascrítto, ag. undermentioned.

infrastruttúra, s.f. infrastructure.

infrazióne, s.f. infraction, infringement; violation, breach: — *a una legge,* infraction (o infringement o violation) of a law; — *di contratto,* breach of contract.

infreddàre, v.t. to cool ‖ v.i., **infreddàrsi,** v.r. to catch a cold.

infreddàto, ag. suffering from a cold: *essere molto —,* to have a bad cold.

infreddatúra, s.f. cold: *prendere un'—,* to catch a cold.

infreddolíre, v.i., **infreddolírsi,** v.r. to feel cold, to shiver with cold.

infreddolíto, ag. cold: *ho le mani infreddolite,* my hands are cold.

infrenàbile, ag. unrestrainable.

infrenàre, v.t. (rar.) to restrain, to repress.

infrenàto, ag. (rar.) unrestrained.

infrequènte, ag. infrequent, rare, uncommon.

infrequenteménte, av. infrequently, rarely, seldom.

infrequènza, s.f. infrequency.

infrigidiménto, s.m. chilling, cooling.

infrigidíre, v.t. to chill; to make frigid ‖ v.i., **infrigidírsi,** v.r. to chill, to become frigid.

infrollíre, v.t. to hang ‖ v.i., **infrollírsi,** v.r. **1.** (diventar frollo) to become tender; (specialmente di selvaggina) to become high **2.** fig. (indebolirsi) to weaken; to get slack.

infrollíto, ag. **1.** (di selvaggina) well hung **2.** fig. (indebolito) run down, weak, enfeebled.

infrondíre, v.i. to put forth leaves, to become leafy.

infronzolàre, v.t. to deck out, to dress up ‖ **infronzolàrsi,** v.r. to deck oneself out, to dress oneself up.

infruttífero, ag. **1.** unfruitful **2.** (sterile) barren, sterile **3.** (che non dà profitto) unprofitable: *capitale —,* (comm.) capital bearing no interest.

infruttuosaménte, av. **1.** unfruitfully; unprofitably **2.** (inutilmente) uselessly; (vanamente) vainly.

infruttuosità, s.f. **1.** unfruitfulness; unprofitableness **2.** (inutilità) uselessness.

infruttuóso, ag. **1.** unfruitful, fruitless, unprofitable **2.** (inutile) useless; (vano) vain: *ricerche infruttuose,* unsuccessful investigations.

ínfula, s.f. infula (pl. infulae).

infunàre, v.t. to rope.

infundíbolo, s.m. (anat. bot.) infundibulum (pl. infundibula).

infunghíre, V. **ammuffíre.**

infuòri, av. out; (con movimento) outwards: *essere —,* to stick out (o to jut out o to project); *sporgersi —,* to lean out ‖ **(all')infuòri di,** l.prep. except, but; apart from: *nessuno (all')— di te,* nobody but you; (all')— *di questo non ti dirò altro,* apart from this I won't tell you anything.

infurbíre, v.i. to grow cunning, to grow shrewd; to sharpen one's wits.

infuriàre, v.t. to enrage, to make angry: *ciò lo infuriò,* that made him angry ‖ v.i. to rage: *la tempesta infuriava,* the storm was raging ‖ **infuriàrsi,** v.r. to fly into a passion, to lose one's temper.

infuriàto, ag. **1.** (adirato) enraged; out of temper (predicativo) **2.** (furioso) raging, wild, furious.

infusíbile, ag. (fis.) infusible.

infusibilità, s.f. (fis.) infusibility.

infusióne, s.f. infusion.

infúso, ag. infused ‖ s.m. infusion.

infusòri, s.m.pl. (zool.) Infusoria.

infusòrio, ag. (zool.) infusorial.

ingabbanàrsi, v.r. to wrap oneself in a cloak.

ingabbiàre, v.t. **1.** to cage; (in una stia) to coop **2.** fig. (rinchiudere) to confine, to lock up; (fam.) to coop up, to coop in.

ingaggiàre, *v.t.* **1.** to engage: — *qlcu. a fare ql.co.,* to engage s.o. to do sthg. **2.** (*mil.*) (*arruolare*) to enlist, to enrol **3.** — *battaglia,* (*mil.*) to engage in battle.

ingàggio, *s.m.* **1.** engagement **2.** (*mil.*) (*arruolamento*) enlistment, enrolment.

ingagliardíre, *v.t.* to strengthen, to invigorate ‖ *v.i.*, **ingagliardírsi,** *v.r.* to grow strong, to strengthen.

ingagliardíto, *ag.* strengthened, fortified.

ingaglioffàre, *v.t.* to make a rascal of (s.o.) ‖ **ingaglioffàrsi,** *v.r.* to become a rascal.

ingallàre, *v.t.* (*ind. tessile*) to gall, to dye with galls.

ingalluzzíre, *V.* **ringalluzzíre.**

ingangheràre, *v.t.* to hinge.

ingannàbile, *ag.* deceivable, easily cheated.

ingannàre, *v.t.* **1.** (*illudere, trarre in inganno*) to deceive, to cheat: *cercò di ingannarmi, ma non ci riuscì,* he tried to deceive (*o* to cheat) me, but he did not succeed; *fui ingannato dalla luce artificiale,* I was deceived by artificial light ‖ — *la fame,* to beguile one's hunger ‖ — *il tempo,* to while away the time (*o* to kill time) **2.** (*frodare, truffare*) to cheat, to swindle, to take in: *fui ingannato da un venditore ambulante,* I was cheated (*o* swindled *o* taken in) by a pedlar **3.** (*essere infedele a*) to be unfaithful to (s.o., sthg.): *la moglie, il marito,* to be unfaithful to one's wife, husband ‖ **ingannàrsi,** *v.r.* (*essere in errore*) to be mistaken, to be wrong: *credo si inganni,* I think he is mistaken.

ingannatóre, *ag.* deceiving ‖ *s.m.,* **ingannatríce,** *s.f.* deceiver; (*chi froda*) swindler, cheat.

ingannévole, *ag.* deceitful, deceptive, deceiving.

ingannevolménte, *av.* deceitfully, deceptively, deceivingly.

ingànno, *s.m.* deceit, deception; (*frode*) fraud: *con l'—,* by fraud; *non lo credevo capace d'—,* I did not think him capable of deceit; *il suo — mi ha molto sorpreso,* his deceit has surprised me very much; *trarre in —,* to deceive (*o* to cheat); *usare l'—,* to practice deception ‖ *cadere in —,* (*sbagliarsi*) to be mistaken.

ingarbugliaménto, *s.m.* entanglement; (*fam.*) confusion, mess.

ingarbugliàre, *v.t.* to entangle, to confuse, to mix up, to muddle ‖ **ingarbugliàrsi,** *v.r.* to get entangled, confused; to get mixed up (anche *fig.*): *si ingarbugliò con le date,* he got mixed up over the dates.

ingarbugliàto, *ag.* entangled, confused, mixed up, intricate (anche *fig.*).

ingarbuglióna, *s.f.,* **ingarbuglióne,** *s.m.* muddler.

ingegnàccio, *s.m.* uncultivated talent: *un certo — non gli manca,* there's a suspicion of genius in him.

ingegnàre, *v.t.* (*letter.*) to fit, to adapt ‖ **ingegnàrsi,** *v.r. V.* **industriàrsi.**

ingegnère, *s.m.* engineer: — *civile, elettrotecnico,* civil, electrical engineer; — *meccanico,* mechanical engineer; — *minerario,* mining engineer; *si laureò —,* he took a degree in engineering.

ingegnería, *s.f.* engineering: — *civile, chimica, meccanica, militare, navale,* civil, chemical, mechanical, military, naval engineering; *una laurea in —,* a degree in engineering.

ingégno, *s.m.* **1.** (*facoltà dell'anima*) talent, genius, understanding: *un ragazzo senza —,* a boy without understanding; *un uomo di grande —,* a man of great intelligence (*o* talent) **2.** (*disposizione della mente*) ability, cleverness, faculty; wits (*pl.*): *aguzzare l'—,* to sharpen one's wits; *avere un — pronto,* to have quick wits (*o* to be quick-witted) ‖ *alzata d'—,* brain-wave **3.** (*inganno*) device, trick, contrivance **4.** (*congegno*) device, mechanism, tool.

ingegnosaménte, *av.* ingeniously, cleverly.

ingegnosità, *s.f.* ingeniousness; cleverness.

ingegnóso, *ag.* ingenious; clever.

ingelosíre, *v.t.* to make jealous: — *qlcu.,* to make s.o. jealous ‖ **ingelosírsi,** *v.r.* to become jealous.

ingemmàre, *v.t.* **1.** to gem **2.** (*di pianta*) to bud ‖

ingemmàrsi, *v.r.* **1.** to adorn oneself with gems **2.** (*di pianta*) to bud.

ingeneràre, *v.t.* to engender, to produce; to cause.

ingenerosaménte, *av.* ungenerously.

ingenerosità, *s.f.* lack of generosity.

ingeneróso, *ag.* ungenerous; (*egoista*) selfish.

ingènito, *ag.* (*innato*) inborn, innate.

ingènte, *ag.* huge, enormous, vast.

ingentiliménto, *s.m.* refinement, refining.

ingentilíre, *v.t.* to refine; (*nobilitare*) to ennoble: — *un linguaggio,* to refine a language; — *le maniere,* to refine manners ‖ **ingentilírsi,** *v.r.* to become refined.

ingènua, *s.f.* (*teat.*) ingenue.

ingenuaménte, *av.* ingenuously; candidly.

ingenuità, *s.f.* **1.** ingenuousness, ingenuity, naïvety; candour **2.** (*semplicioneria*) simple-mindedness.

ingènuo, *ag.* **1.** ingenuous, naïve; candid: *che —!,* how simple you are!; *parole ingenue,* naïve words; *una ragazza ingenua,* a naïve girl; *uno sguardo —,* an ingenuous look; *fare l'—,* to feign innocence **2.** (*sempliciotto*) simple-minded.

ingerènza, *s.f.* interference.

ingeríre, *v.t.* to swallow, to ingest ‖ **ingerírsi,** *v.r.* to meddle (with sthg.), to interfere (with sthg.).

ingessàre, *v.t.* to plaster.

ingessatúra, *s.f.* plastering.

inghiaiàre, *v.t.* **1.** to gravel **2.** (*ferr.*) to ballast.

inghiaiàta, *s.f.* (*ferr.*) ballast: *materiale da —,* ballasting material; *livellare l'—,* to level the ballast.

inghiaiatúra, *s.f.* **1.** gravelling **2.** (*ferr.*) ballasting.

Inghiltèrra, *no.pr.f.* (*geog.*) England.

inghiottiménto, *s.m.* swallowing (anche *fig.*).

inghiottíre, *v.t.* to swallow (up) (anche *fig.*): *la barca fu inghiottita dal mare,* the boat was swallowed up (*o* engulfed) by the sea; *ciò è difficile da —!,* that's hard to swallow!; — *le lacrime,* to swallow one's tears; — *una pillola (amara),* to swallow a (bitter) pill; *essere inghiottito dal buio,* to be swallowed up by darkness.

inghiottoníre, *v.t.* to make greedy ‖ *v.i.,* **inghiottoniírsi,** *v.r.* to become a glutton.

inghirlandaménto, *s.m.* wreathing; engarlanding.

inghirlandàre, *v.t.* to wreathe; to (en)garland: *le ragazze inghirlandarono la statua di fiori,* the girls wreathed the statue with flowers ‖ **inghirlandàrsi,** *v.r.* to garland oneself (with sthg.): *la sposa si inghirlandò di fiori d'arancio,* the bride decked herself with orange-blossoms.

inghirlandàto, *ag.* wreathed (with sthg.); garlanded (with sthg.): *capo — di fiori,* head wreathed with flowers.

ingialliménto, *s.m.* yellowing.

ingiallíre, *v.t.* to yellow, to make yellow, to colour yellow: *il tempo ingiallisce le pagine dei libri,* time yellows the pages of books ‖ *v.i.,* **ingiallírsi,** *v.r.* to yellow, to turn yellow, to grow yellow: *il grano ingiallisce all'inizio dell'estate,* corn turns yellow with the onset of summer.

ingiallíto, *ag.* yellowed; turned yellow, grown yellow: *carte, pergamene, fotografie ingiallite dal tempo,* papers, parchments, photos yellowed with age.

ingigantíre, *v.t.* to magnify (anche *fig.*); to exaggerate (anche *fig.*): *un microscopio ingigantisce gli oggetti,* a microscope magnifies things; *la sua immaginazione ingigantisce ogni più piccolo problema,* his imagination magnifies even the slightest problems; — *i difetti di qlcu.,* to exaggerate s.o.'s faults ‖ *v.i.,* **ingigantírsi,** *v.r.* to become gigantic, to grow gigantic (anche *fig.*): *gli oggetti ingigantiscono avvicinandosi,* objects grow gigantic (*o* enormous) as they come nearer.

ingigliàre, *v.t.* to adorn with lilies ‖ **ingigliàrsi,** *v.r.* to adorn oneself with lilies.

inginocchiaménto, *s.m.* kneeling (down); (*genuflessione*) genuflexion.

inginocchiàrsi, *v.r.* to kneel (down), to fall on one's knees: *si inginocchiò per raccogliere il cappello* he knelt (down) to pick up his hat; *tutti si inginocchiarono in preghiera*, everyone knelt in prayer; — *davanti a qlcu.*, to kneel to s.o.

inginocchiàto, *ag.* kneeling; on one's knees (*predicativo*).

inginocchiatóio, *s.m.* prie-dieu, kneeling-stool.

inginocchióni, *av.* on one's knees.

ingioiàre, ingioiellàre, *v.t.* to adorn with jewels, to bejewel ‖ **ingioiàrsi, ingioiellàrsi,** *v.r.* to adorn oneself with jewels.

ingiú, *av.* **1.** down, downwards: *dal principe — fino al mendicante*, from prince down to pauper (*o* from the highest to the lowest); *collocare ql.co. faccia —*, to lay sthg. face down(wards); *guardare —*, to look down(wards) ‖ *all'—*, down, downward (*ag.*); down, downwards (*av.*): *pendenza all'—*, downward slope; *appeso con la testa all'—*, hanging head down(wards); *scorrere all'—*, (*di acqua*) to flow down: *lasciar scorrere l'acqua all'—*, *fig.* to let things go **2.** (*riferito a età, prezzo, computando all'indietro*) **up to; downwards:** *bambini dai cinque anni —*, children up to and including the age of five (*o* children of five and under); *da cento lire —*, up to a hundred lire (*o* from a hundred lire downwards) **3.** (*riferito a tempo, computando in avanti*) **onwards:** *dal 10 marzo —*, from the 10th of March onwards; *dal quinto secolo —*, from the fifth century onwards.

ingiudicàto, *ag.* unjudged.

ingiúngere, *v.t.* to enjoin; to order, to command: *mi ingiunse di tacere*, he enjoined (on) me to keep silent; — *penitenza a qlcu.*, to enjoin (a) penance on s.o.

ingiunzióne, *s.f.* injunction, order.

ingiúria, *s.f.* **1.** (*insulto*) insult; (*affronto*) affront, abuse; (*oltraggio*) outrage: *le ingiurie della sorte*, the outrages of fortune; *un discorso pieno d'ingiurie*, a speech full of insults; *ha dovuto sopportare diverse ingiurie*, he had to put up with several affronts; *fare — a qlcu.*, to do s.o. wrong; *pronunciare ingiurie contro qlcu.*, to abuse (*o* to revile) s.o. **2.** (*danno*) damage, injury: *le ingiurie del tempo*, the ravages of time.

ingiuriàre, *v.t.* to insult, to abuse, to revile; to call (s.o.) names.

ingiuriatóre, *s.m.*, **ingiuriatríce,** *s.f.* insulter, abuser, reviler.

ingiuriosaménte, *av.* insultingly, abusively, revilingly.

ingiurióso, *ag.* insulting, abusive, reviling.

ingiustaménte, *av.* unjustly, unfairly; wrong: *è stato trattato —*, he has been unfairly treated; *ha agito —*, he did wrong.

ingiustificàbile, *ag.* unjustifiable.

ingiustificàto, *ag.* unjustified; (*non autorizzato*) unwarranted: *assenza ingiustificata*, unjustified absence.

ingiustízia, *s.f.* **1.** injustice, unfairness: *è un'—!*, it's unfair!; *fare un'— a qlcu.*, to do s.o. an injustice (*o* to be unfair to s.o.) **2.** (*torto*) wrong: *soffrire molte ingiustizie*, to suffer many wrongs.

ingiústo, *ag.* unjust, unfair: *condanna, sentenza ingiusta*, unjust condemnation, sentence; *giudice —*, unjust judge; *guerra ingiusta*, unjust war; *legge ingiusta*, unjust law; *lode ingiusta*, unfair praise; *i miei sospetti erano ingiusti*, my suspicions were unfounded; *essere — con qlcu.*, to be unfair to s.o.: *penso che tu sia stato piuttosto — con lui*, I think you've dealt rather unfairly with him.

inglése, *ag.* English: *corsivo —*, English script; *una signora —*, an English lady ‖ *all'—*, after the English fashion: *giardino all'—*, landscape-garden; *andarsene, filarsela all'—*, to take French leave ‖ *sale —*, Epsom salts ‖ *zuppa —*, trifle ‖ *s.m.* **1.** (*abitante*) Englishman (*pl.* Englishmen) ‖ *gli Inglesi*, the English (people) **2.** (*lingua*) (the) English (language): *le genti che parlano —*, the English-speaking world ‖ *s.f.* Englishwoman (*pl.* Englishwomen).

ingloriosaménte, *av.* ingloriously.

inglorióso, *ag.* inglorious.

inglúvie, *s.f.* ingluvies; crop.

ingluvína, *s.f.* (*farm.*) ingluvin.

ingobbíre, *v.i.* to become hunchbacked.

ingoffíre, *v.t.* to make clumsy, to make awkward ‖ **ingoffírsi,** *v.r.* to become clumsy, to become awkward.

ingoiaménto, *s.m.* swallowing.

ingoiàre, *v.t.* to swallow, to gulp down (anche *fig.*): *furono ingoiati dal mare, dall'oscurità*, they were swallowed up (o engulfed) by the sea, by the darkness; *ingoiò un pezzo di pane*, he swallowed a morsel of bread; — *le lacrime*, to swallow one's tears ‖ — *la pillola, un rospo*, to swallow the bitter pill.

ingolfàrsi, *v.r.* **1.** (*formare un golfo*) to form a gulf **2.** *fig.* (*impelagarsi*) to throw oneself (into sthg.), to dive (into sthg.): — *nei debiti*, to get up to one's eyes in debt.

ingolfàto, *ag.* (*immerso, assorto*) absorbed, immersed.

ingollàre, *v.t.* to swallow, to gulp down; (*mangiare avidamente*) to gobble.

ingolosíre, *v.t.* to make s.o.'s mouth water; to excite s.o.'s greed ‖ **ingolosírsi,** *v.r.* to become greedy.

ingombraménto, *V.* **ingómbro.**

ingombrànte, *ag.* cumbersome, encumbering.

ingombràre, *v.t.* **1.** to encumber, to hamper, to obstruct, to block (up): — *il traffico*, to obstruct the traffic **2.** (*impacciare*) to be in s.o.'s way: *questo tavolo mi ingombra*, this table is in my way **3.** (*affollare*) to crowd.

ingómbro, *ag.* **1.** encumbered, obstructed **2.** (*affollato*) crowded ‖ *s.m.* encumbrance, obstruction; (*impedimento*) impediment; (*ostacolo*) obstacle: *questa seggiola mi è d'—*, this chair is in my way.

ingommàre, *v.t.* **1.** (*spalmare di gomma*) to gum, to smear with gum **2.** (*incollare*) to stick, to gum.

ingordaménte, *av.* greedily.

ingordígia, *s.f.* greed, greediness: — *di denaro*, greed for money.

ingórdo, *ag.* greedy (of, for sthg.); (*bramoso*) eager (for sthg.); (*avido*) covetous: — *di guadagno*, greedy of gain; — *di ricchezze, potere*, greedy (o eager) for wealth, power; *non essere così —*, *farai indigestione*, don't be so greedy, you'll get indigestion ‖ *s.m.* **1.** greedy man **2.** (*ghiottone*) glutton, gourmand.

ingorgaménto, *s.m.* **1.** obstruction **2.** (*med.*) engorgement.

ingorgàre, *v.t.* to obstruct, to choke (up), to block (up) ‖ **ingorgàrsi,** *v.r.* to become obstructed, to choke (with sthg.).

ingórgo, *s.m.* **1.** obstruction, blocking up: *un — del traffico*, a traffic jam **2.** (*med.*) engorgement.

ingovernàbile, *ag.* ungovernable.

ingozzàre, *v.t.* **1.** (*inghiottire*) to swallow; (*mangiare avidamente*) to gobble, to eat up; (*tracannare*) to gulp down **2.** (*inghiottire a fatica*) to gulp **3.** *fig.* (*sopportare*) to put up with (sthg.).

ingracilíre, *v.i.*, **ingracilírsi,** *v.r.* to become delicate, to grow weak, to weaken.

ingranàggio, *s.m.* **1.** (*mec.*) gear; (*ruota dentata*) cog-wheel; — *accoppiato*, mating gear; — *a vite senza fine*, worm-gear (o worm-wheel); — *conduttore*, driving (o drive) gear; — *del cambio*, change wheel; *ingranaggi del differenziale*, differential gears; — *della prima (velocità)*, low-gear; — *della quarta (velocità)*, high-gear; — *della retromarcia*, reverse gear; — *della seconda (velocità)*, second gear; — *della terza (velocità)*, third gear; — *dello sterzo*, steering gear; *ingranaggi di un orologio*, cog-wheels of a clock; — *elicoidale*, helical gear; — *fisso*, fixed gear; — *folle*, idle gear (o idler); — *per catena*, sprocket-wheel; — *riduttore*, reducing gear; *dente di* —, gear tooth; *riduttore a ingranaggi*, reduction gear; *senza ingranaggi*, gearless; *sistema di ingranaggi*, gearing **2.** *fig.* mechanism, working, system: *l'— della vita politica*, the mechanism of political life; *egli conosce gli ingranaggi della burocrazia*, he knows the workings of bureaucracy.

ingranàre, *v.t.* (*mec.*) to put into gear; to interlock, to mesh; to engage; to pitch: — *due ruote,* to engage two cog-wheels: — *la prima marcia,* to engage the first gear ‖ *v.i.* **1.** *(mec.)* to be in gear, to come into gear; to engage: *queste due ruote non ingranano,* these two cog-wheels do not engage; *non* —, to be out of gear **2.** *(fam.) (trovarsi bene)* to get along (with s.o.): *quell'uomo non ingrana coi suoi colleghi,* that man can't get along with his colleagues.

ingranchiménto, *s.m.* benumbment.

ingranchíre, *v.t.* to benumb ‖ **ingranchírsi,** *v.r.* to become numb.

ingrandiménto, *s.m.* **1.** enlargement (anche *fig.*) **2.** *(aumento in ampiezza, estensione)* increase, aggrandizement **3.** *(ott.)* magnification, amplification: *lente d'*—, magnifying lens **4.** *(foto.)* enlargement.

ingrandíre, *v.t.* **1.** to enlarge: — *un edificio,* to enlarge a building **2.** *(aumentare in ampiezza, estensione)* to increase, to aggrandize: — *uno stato,* to aggrandize a state **3.** *(ott.)* to magnify, to amplify: *questo vetro ingrandisce gli oggetti,* this glass magnifies objects **4.** *(foto.)* to enlarge **5.** *(esagerare)* to exaggerate, to magnify: *gli piace* — *i suoi meriti,* he likes to magnify his own merits; — *i fatti, i pericoli,* to exaggerate the facts, the dangers ‖ *v.i.* to become larger ‖ **ingrandírsi,** *v.r.* **1.** to become larger **2.** *(crescere di statura)* to grow tall **3.** *fig. (farsi grande)* to increase; *(diventare ricco)* to become rich; *(farsi potente)* to become more powerful: *conosco un commerciante all'ingrosso che vorrebbe* —, I know a wholesaler who would like to increase his business.

ingrassaménto, *s.m.* **1.** fattening **2.** *(concimazione)* manuring.

ingrassànte, *ag.* fattening: *cibo* —, fattening food.

ingrassàre, *v.t.* **1.** to fatten, to make fat: — *un maiale,* to fatten a pig ‖ *andare ad* — *i cavoli,* to go and push up daisies ‖ *l'occhio del padrone ingrassa il cavallo,* prov. business prospers under the master's eye **2.** *(lubrificare)* to grease, to lubricate, to oil: — *un meccanismo,* to lubricate a mechanism; — *gli stivali,* to oil one's boots **3.** *(concimare)* to manure **4.** *(far sembrare più grasso)* to make look fatter: *quell'abito ti ingrassa,* that dress makes you look fatter **5.** *(arricchire)* to enrich ‖ *v.i.,* **ingrassàrsi,** *v.r.* **1.** to grow fat, to get fat, to fatten (up): *è ingrassata di nuovo,* she has put on weight again; *non vuole* —, he does not want to get fat; *si è molto ingrassato,* he has grown very fat **2.** *fig. (godere)* to fatten (on sthg.): *persone che ingrassano nelle disgrazie della patria,* persons who fatten on the calamities of their country.

ingrassatóre, *ag.* fattening ‖ *s.m.,* **ingrassatríce,** *s. f.* fattener.

ingràsso, *s.m.* **1.** fattening: *animali da* —, fattening animals **2.** *(concime)* manure.

ingraticciàre, *v.t.* to trellis, to hurdle.

ingraticciàta, *s.f.* trellis-work, lattice-work.

ingraticolàre, *v.t.* to close with grating.

ingraticolàto, *s.m.* grating.

ingratitúdine, *s.f.* ingratitude, ungratefulness.

ingràto, *ag.* **1.** ungrateful, unthankful: — *verso qlcu.,* ungrateful to s.o. **2.** *(difficile)* hard, difficult **3.** *(sgradevole)* unpleasant, disagreeable: *compito* —, unpleasant task **4.** *(non proficuo)* unprofitable **5.** *(sterile)* barren, sterile: *terra ingrata,* barren land.

ingravidàre, *v.t.* to make pregnant ‖ **ingravidàrsi,** *v.r.* to become pregnant.

ingraziàrsi, *v.r.* to ingratiate oneself with (s.o.): — *qlcu.,* to get into s.o.'s good graces: *voleva* — *l'insegnante,* he wanted to get into his teacher's good graces.

ingrediènte, *s.m.* ingredient.

ingrèsso, *s.m.* **1.** entry: *l'* — *trionfale del nuovo presidente nella capitale,* the triumphal entry of the new president into the capital; *il suo* — *nella vita politica,* his first steps in political life **2.** *(entrata)* entrance: — *di servizio,* tradesmen's entrance; — *principale,* front door; *all'* — *del teatro,* at the entrance of the

theatre **3.** *(accesso)* admittance: — *libero,* free admittance; *biglietto d'*—, admittance ticket ‖ *ingressi, (teat.)* standing tickets ‖ *vietato l'*—, no admittance.

ingrinzíre, *v.t.,* **ingrinzírsi,** *v.r.* to wrinkle.

ingrommàre, *v.t.,* **ingrommàrsi,** *v.r.* to encrust.

ingrossaménto, *s.m.* **1.** enlargement (anche *fig.*) **2.** *(aumento di volume)* increase **3.** *(ispessimento)* thickening **4.** *(ingrassamento)* fattening **5.** *(gonfiamento)* swelling.

ingrossàre, *v.t.* **1.** to enlarge (anche *fig.*) **2.** *(aumentare di volume)* to increase **3.** *(ispessire)* to thicken **4.** *(far sembrare grosso)* to make look bigger, to make fat: *quel cappello ti ingrossa il viso,* that hat makes your face look bigger **5.** *(gonfiare)* to swell: *la neve si scioglie e ingrossa i fiumi,* the snow melts and swells the rivers ‖ **ingrossàrsi,** *v.r.* **1.** to become bigger, to grow bigger, to get bigger **2.** *(aumentare)* to increase **3.** *(ingrassare)* to become fat, to get fat, to become stout: *egli si è molto ingrossato,* he has become very stout **4.** *(gonfiarsi)* to swell: *il foruncolo si ingrossava,* the boil was swelling **5.** *(di vento, di mare)* to rise, to get up.

ingrossatúra, *V.* **ingrossaménto.**

ingròsso, all', *l. av.* **1.** wholesale *(ag. attributivo);* by wholesale: *commerciante all'*—, wholesale dealer; *prezzi all'*—, wholesale prices; *vendere all'*—, to sell by wholesale **2.** *(all'incirca)* approximately, approximatively.

ingrugnàre, *v.i.,* **ingrugnàrsi,** *v.r.* to pout, to sulk.

ingrugnàto, *ag.* pouting, sulky.

ingrullíre, *v.t.* to make silly, to make stupid ‖ *v.i.* to become silly, to become stupid.

inguadàbile, *ag.* unfordable.

inguainàre, *v.t.* to sheath(e): — *la spada,* to sheathe the sword (anche *fig.*).

ingualcíbile, *ag.* crease-resistant, creaseless: *questa stoffa è* —, this material doesn't crease.

ingualdrappàre, *v.t.* *(rar.)* to caparison.

inguantàrsi, *v.r.* to put on one's gloves.

inguantàto, *ag.* wearing gloves, with one's gloves on.

inguaríbile, *ag.* incurable.

inguaribilménte, *av.* incurably.

inguinàle, *ag.* inguinal.

ínguine, *s.m.* *(anat.)* inguen, groin.

ingurgitàre, *v.t.* to swallow, to gulp (down): — *un bicchiere di vino,* to gulp (down) a glass of wine.

inibíre, *v.t.* **1.** to forbid, to prohibit: — *a qlcu. di fare ql.co.,* to inhibit s.o. from doing sthg. (o to forbid s.o. to do sthg.) **2.** *(frenare)* to restrain.

inibíto, *ag.* **1.** *(vietato)* forbidden **2.** *(che ha inibizioni)* inhibited: *una persona inibita,* an inhibited person.

inibitóre, *s.m.* inhibitor.

inibitòrio, *ag.* inhibitory: *centro* —, *(anat.)* inhibitory centre.

inibizióne, *s.f.* **1.** inhibition **2.** *(dir.)* prohibition.

inidoneità, *s.f.* unfitness (for sthg., to do), unaptness (for sthg., to do).

inidòneo, *ag.* unfit (for sthg., to do), unapt (for sthg., to do), unsuited (to, for sthg., to do, for doing): — *agli affari,* unfit (o unsuited) for business.

iniettàre, *v.t.* to inject: — *una medicina nel sangue,* to inject a medicine into the blood.

iniettàto, *ag.* injected: *occhi iniettati di sangue,* bloodshot eyes.

iniettóre, *s.m.* *(mec.)* injector; *(di motore Diesel)* injector, injection valve.

iniezióne, *s.f.* injection: — *endovenosa, ipodermica,* intravenous, hypodermic injection.

inimicàre, *v.t.* **1.** *(rendere nemico)* to alienate, to estrange, to make hostile: *la tua condotta ti inimicherà i tuoi amici,* your behaviour will alienate (o estrange) your friends from you **2.** *(trattare da nemico)* to treat as an enemy ‖ **inimicàrsi,** *v.r.* to alienate from oneself, to become estranged from (s.o.), to become a stranger to (s.o.): *egli si è inimicato tutti i suoi amici,* he has estranged (o alienated) all his friends (from himself); *non mi piace inimicarmi coi miei parenti*, I don't like to quarrel with my relatives ‖ *v.r. reciproco* to become enemies.

inimicízia, *s.f.* enmity, hostility, unfriendliness; (*odio*) hatred, animosity: *creare — fra due persone*, to create bad blood between two persons.

inimíco, *ag.* (*rar.*) inimical (to s.o., sthg.).

inimitàbile, *ag.* inimitable; (*impareggiabile*) incomparable.

inimitabilménte, *av.* inimitably; (*impareggiabilmente*) incomparably.

inimmaginàbile, *ag.* unimaginable; (*impensabile*) inconceivable, unthinkable.

inintelligíbile, *ag.* unintelligible.

inintelligibilità, *s.f.* unintelligibility, unintelligibleness.

inintelligibilménte, *av.* unintelligibly.

inintenzionàle, *ag.* inintentional.

inintenzionalménte, *av.* unintentionally.

ininterrottaménte, *av.* continually, unceasingly, uninterruptedly: *lavorai — per tre giorni*, I worked for three days without stopping (o I worked for three solid days); *piovve — tutta la settimana*, it did not stop pouring for a week.

ininterrótto, *ag.* (*continuo*) continuous, unbroken, uninterrupted; (*incessante*) incessant, unceasing, ceaseless: *febbre ininterrotta*, unintermittent fever; *linea ininterrotta*, continuous (o unbroken) line; *progresso —*, steady progress; *rumore —*, incessant (o continuous) noise; *serie ininterrotta di papi*, unbroken succession of Popes; *sonno —*, unbroken sleep.

iniquaménte, *av.* 1. (*ingiustamente*) unfairly, unrighteously, unjustly, iniquitously 2. (*malvagiamente*) wickedly, iniquitously.

iniquità, *s.f.* 1. (*ingiustizia*) iniquity, unfairness, unrighteousness, injustice 2. (*atto iniquo*) iniquity: *commettere —*, to commit iniquities 3. (*malvagità*) wickedness, iniquity 4. (*avversità di tempo*) wickedness.

iníquo, *ag.* 1. (*ingiusto*) unfair, unrighteous, unjust, iniquitous: *azioni inique*, unrighteous actions; *lotta iniqua*, unequal (o unfair) struggle; *sentenza iniqua*, unjust sentence; *sorte iniqua*, unfair destiny 2. (*malvagio*) wicked, iniquitous: *fatto —*, iniquitous deed; *menzogna iniqua*, wicked lie 3. (*avverso, di tempo*) wicked: *tempo —*, wicked weather.

iniziàle, *ag.* 1. initial: *lettere iniziali*, initial letters; *sintomi iniziali*, initial symptoms; *stadio —*, initial stage 2. (*di inizio*) starting: *capitale —*, starting capital; *velocità —*, starting speed 3. (*primario*) original ‖ *s.f.* initial: *dovete scrivere le vostre iniziali qui*, you must write your initials here; *scrivere con l'— maiuscola*, to write with a capital letter.

iniziaménto, *s.m.* 1. beginning; starting point 2. (*di poema, opera letteraria, ecc.*) opening 3. (*iniziazione*) initiation.

iniziàre, *v.t.* 1. to begin, to start; (*dare inizio a*) to initiate, to originate: *— a fare ql.co.*, to begin (o to start) to do (o doing) sthg.: *quando hai iniziato a studiare il russo?*, when did you begin (o start) studying Russian?; *— una carriera scientifica*, to take up a scientific career; *— un commercio*, to open up a trade; *— la conversazione con qlcu.*, to enter into (o to start) conversation with s.o.; *— il dibattito*, to open the debate; *— un'impresa commerciale*, to start a commercial enterprise; *— la lezione*, to begin the lesson; *una lite*, to start (o to open) a quarrel; *— le ostilità*, to open hostilities; *— una riforma, una nuova politica*, to initiate a reform, a new policy; *— trattative con qlcu.*, to enter into (o to start) negotiations with s.o.; *— un viaggio*, to start on a journey ‖ *per —...*, to begin with... (o first of all...) 2. (*avviare, introdurre*) to initiate: *— qlcu. ad una scienza, ad un'arte*, to initiate s.o. in a science, in an art; *— qlcu. in una società segreta*, to initiate s.o. into a secret society ‖

v.i., **iniziàrsi**, *v.r.* to begin, to start, to commence: *le lezioni iniziano alle dieci*, classes begin at ten.

iniziàtico, *ag.* initiatory.

iniziatíva, *s.f.* initiative, enterprise: *l'— privata*, private enterprise (o voluntary effort); *mancanza d'—*, (*fam.*) want of push; *una persona d'—*, an enterprising person; *spirito d'—*, spirit of enterprise; *dovete avere più —*, you must have more initiative; *egli non ha alcuna —*, (*fam.*) he is a helpless sort of chap; *avere l'—*, to have the initiative; *fare ql.co. di propria —*, to do sthg. on one's own initiative; *mancare d'—*, to lack initiative; *prendere l'—*, to take the initiative ‖ *a, per — di...*, on the initiative of....

iniziatívo, *ag.* initiatory, initiative.

iniziàto, *ag.* initiated, initiate ‖ *s.m.* initiate.

iniziatóre, *s.m.* initiator.

iniziatríce, *s.f.* initiatrix, initiatress.

iniziazióne, *s.f.* initiation: *riti d'—*, initiatory rites.

inízio, *s.m.* beginning, commencement: *dall'— alla fine*, from beginning to end (o from start to finish); *sin dall'—*, since the beginning ‖ *calcio d'—*, (*spor.*) kick-off.

innacquàre, *v.t.* to water (down); (*diluire*) to dilute.

innaffiaménto, *s.m.* watering; sprinkling.

innaffiàre, *v.t.* to water; (*spruzzare*) to sprinkle: *— con tubo di gomma*, to hose; *— il giardino*, to water the garden ‖ *— un pasto con del buon vino*, to wash down a meal with good wine.

innaffiatóio, *s.m.* watering-pot, watering-can.

innaffiatríce, *s.f.* sprinkler: *— stradale*, road-sprinkler (o road watering-vehicle).

innalzaménto, *s.m.* elevation: *— del pelo d'acqua*, (*idraulica*) raising of the water-level.

innalzàre, *v.t.* 1. (*elevare*) to raise, to elevate (anche *fig.*): *— l'animo di qlcu.*, to elevate (o to ennoble) s.o.'s mind; *— le braccia*, to raise one's arms; *— un inno*, to raise a hymn; *— qlcu. a una dignità*, to raise (o to promote o to advance) s.o. to a dignity; *— qlcu. di grado*, to raise s.o. to a higher rank ‖ *— al settimo cielo*, to raise (o to extol o to laud) to the skies 2. (*erigere*) to raise, to erect: *— un monumento*, to raise a monument 3. (*rendere più alto*) to heighten, to make higher: *— una casa di due piani*, to make a house two storeys higher; *— un muro di due metri*, to raise a wall by two metres (o to make a wall two metres higher) ‖ **innalzàrsi**, *v.r.* 1. to rise: *davanti alla casa si innalzava un bel fico*, before the house rose up (o stood) a beautiful fig-tree; *il fumo si innalzava verso il cielo*, the smoke was rising towards the sky 2. (*elevarsi, salire in grado*) to rise, to exalt oneself, to extol oneself: *— al di sopra del luogo comune*, to rise above commonplaces; *— col proprio lavoro*, to work one's way up.

innamoraménto, *s.m.* 1. falling in love 2. (*amore*) love; (*tenerezza*) fondness.

innamoràre, *v.t.* to charm, to fascinate; to enthral: *innamora tutti con le sue belle maniere*, she captivates everybody with her charming ways; *con le moine seppe innamorarlo*, with her wiles she enthralled him; *Dio innamora di sè le anime elette*, the souls of the chosen are filled with love of God ‖ *un calduccio che innamora*, a grateful warmth ‖ *una pace che innamora*, a blessed peace ‖ **innamoràrsi**, *v.r.* 1. to fall in love (with s.o.): *si è innamorata di un mio amico*, she has fallen in love with a friend of mine; *si innamorarono pazzamente appena si incontrarono*, they fell head over heels in love with each other at first sight 2. (*di un luogo, un oggetto, un'arte, ecc.*) to take a liking (to sthg.), to take a fancy (for sthg.).

innamoràta, *s.f.* lover; sweetheart; girl friend.

innamoràto, *ag.* 1. in love (with s.o.); full of love (for s.o.), loving: *occhi innamorati*, loving eyes; *è innamorata di un inglese*, she is in love with an Englishman ‖ *— cotto*, (*fam.*) infatuated 2. (*entusiasta*) fond; (*fam.*) crazy (about s.o., sthg.): *sono — di questo quadro*, I am very fond of (o crazy about) this picture ‖ *s.m.* lover; sweetheart; boy friend.

innànzi, *av.* forward(s); on, onward(s); (*davanti, di fronte*) in front; (*più avanti*) further: *da oggi, d'ora* —, from now on; *più* —, (*più tardi*) later on; (*più avanti*) further on; *andare* —, to go further (*o* to go on); *andare troppo* —, to go too far (anche *fig.*); *farsi* —, to come forward ‖ « *Come stai?* », « *Tiro* — », " How are you? ", " I get along "; *non posso tirare* — *così*, I can't go on like this ‖ *essere* — *negli anni*, to be (well) on in years ‖ *prep.* before: — *a Dio e agli uomini*, before God and man; — *ai miei occhi*, before my eyes; — *sera*, before night; — *a tutti*, before everybody; — *tempo*, before (one's) time; — *tutto*, before all (*o* first of all); *portare una questione* — *la corte*, to bring a question before a court.

innàrio, *s.m.* (*eccl.*) hymnal, hymnary.

innatìsmo, *s.m.* (*st. fil.*) nativism.

innàto, *ag.* innate, inborn, inbred; natural: *una innata passione per l'arte*, an innate (*o* inborn *o* inbred) passion for art; *idee innate*, (*fil.*) innate ideas; *le sue qualità innate*, his natural qualities.

innaturàle, *ag.* unnatural.

innavigàbile, *ag.* innavigable, unnavigable.

innegàbile, *ag.* undeniable.

innegabilménte, *av.* undeniably.

inneggiaménto, *s.m.* 1. (*inni*) hymns 2. (*esaltazione*) extolling, extolment, exaltation 3. (*lodi*) praises; celebrations 4. (*saluti*) hails.

inneggiàre, *v.i.* 1. (*cantare inni*) to sing hymns, to hymn 2. (*levare lodi*) to extol (s.o.), to exalt (s.o.), to praise (s.o.), to hymn (s.o.'s) praises: — *a qlcu.*, to hymn s.o.'s praises 3. (*rivolgere un'ovazione*) to hail (s.o.): *tutti inneggiarono a lui quando entrò*, everybody hailed him when he entered.

inneggiatóre, *s.m.*, **inneggiatrìce**, *s.f.* extoller, exalter.

innervàre, *v.i.* to become innervated, to get innervated.

innervazióne, *s.f.* (*med.*) innervation.

innervosìre, *v.t.* to get on s.o.'s nerves; (*fam.*) to give (s.o.) the jitters: *questa musica mi innervosisce*, this music gets on my nerves ‖ **innervosìrsi**, *v.r.* to get nervous; (*fam.*) to get rattled, to grow jittery.

innervosìto, *ag.* nervous; (*fam.*) rattled, jittery.

innescàre, *v.t.* (*artigl.*) to prime.

innescatóre, *s.m.* (*aut.*) primer.

innésco, *s.m.* (*artigl.*) primer.

innestaménto, *s.m.* (*agr. chir.*) grafting.

innestàre, *v.t.* 1. (*agr. chir.*) to graft, to engraft: — *un germoglio in un vecchio albero*, to graft a scion into an old tree 2. (*inoculare*) to inoculate, to vaccinate: — *a qlcu. il vaccino del vaiuolo*, to inoculate s.o. against smallpox 3. (*inserire*) to insert 4. (*congiungere*) to join, to connect 5. (*mec.*) to engage, to pitch: — *la frizione*, (*aut.*) to engage the clutch; — *la prima marcia*, (*aut.*) to go into the first gear.

innestatóio, *s.m.* (*agr.*) grafting-knife.

innestatùra, *s.f.* (*agr.*) grafting.

innèsto, *s.m.* 1. (*agr. chir.*) graft, grafting 2. (*med.*) inoculation, vaccination 3. (*mec.*) clutch, coupling: — *a baionetta*, bayonet-joint; — *a frizione*, friction-clutch; — *di sicurezza*, slip-clutch; — *femmina*, (*elett.*) receptacle; — *meccanico*, positive clutch.

ínno, *s.m.* hymn; anthem: — *nazionale*, national anthem; *cantare, innalzare inni*, to sing hymns.

innocènte, *ag.* 1. innocent; (*senza colpa*) guiltless; (*dir.*) not guilty (*predicativo*): *un bimbo* —, an innocent child; *un sorriso* —, an innocent smile; *tutti credono che egli sia* —, everybody believes he is innocent; *dichiararsi* —, (*dir.*) to plead not guilty 2. (*innocuo*) innocent, harmless: *bugia* —, white lie; *piaceri innocenti*, innocent pleasures 3. (*ingenuo*) innocent, simple, artless ‖ *s.c.* 1. innocent: *fare l'*—, to feign innocence; *punire un* —, to punish an innocent ‖ *la strage degli Innocenti*, (*Bibbia*) the Slaughter of the Innocents 2. (*trovatello*) foundling.

innocenteménte, *av.* innocently.

innocènza, *s.f.* 1. innocence: *dichiarare la propria* —, (*dir.*) to plead not guilty 2. (*infanzia*) infancy.

Innocènzo, *no.pr.m.* Innocent.

innocuaménte, *av.* innocuously, harmlessly, inoffensively.

innocuità, *s.f.* (*rar.*) innocuity, harmlessness.

innòcuo, *ag.* innocuous, harmless, inoffensive.

innodía, *s.f.* hymnody.

innògrafo, *s.m.* hymnographer, hymnwriter.

innologìa, *s.f.* hymnology.

innominàbile, *ag.* 1. (*di Dio*) unnamable 2. (*vergognoso*) unmentionable, shameful.

innominàto, *ag.* 1. unnamed ‖ *l' « Innominato »*, (*nei « Promessi Sposi »*) the " Innominato " (*o* the " Unnamed ") 2. (*senza nome*) nameless.

innovaménto, *s.m.* 1. innovation 2. (*cambiamento*) change.

innovàre, *v.t.* 1. to innovate 2. (*cambiare*) to change 3. (*riformare*) to reform 4. (*alterare*) to alter.

innovatóre, *ag.* innovating, innovatory ‖ *s.m.*, **innovatrìce**, *s.f.* innovator.

innovazióne, *s.f.* 1. innovation; novelty: *apportare delle innovazioni a qlco.*, to make innovations in sthg. 2. (*cambiamento*) change 3. (*mutamento*) alteration.

innumeràbile, *ag.* innumerable; numberless.

innumerabilità, *s.f.* innumerableness.

innumerabilménte *av.* innumerably.

innumerévole, *ag.* innumerable, numberless.

innumerevolménte, *av.* innumerably.

inobbediènte, *V.* disubbidiènte.

inobbediènza, *V.* disubbidiènza.

inobliàbile, *ag.* (*letter.*) unforgettable.

inoccultàbile, *ag.* unconcealable.

inoccultàto, *ag.* unconcealed.

inoccupàto, *ag.* unoccupied; vacant: *posto, impiego* —, vacant position.

inoculàbile, *ag.* inoculable.

inoculàre, *v.t.* 1. (*agr.*) to inoculate, to graft 2. (*introdurre*) to inoculate, to make an inoculation of (sthg.) (anche *fig.*): — *cattivi principi*, to inoculate (*o* to imbue) with bad principles; — *il vaccino del vaiuolo a qlcu.*, to inoculate s.o. against smallpox.

inoculazióne, *s.f.* inoculation.

inodóro, *ag.* inodorous, odourless; scentless.

inoffensìbile, *ag.* unvulnerable, invulnerable.

inoffensivaménte, *av.* inoffensively, harmlessly.

inoffensìvo, *ag.* inoffensive, harmless.

inofféso, *ag.* unhurt, uninjured, unharmed.

inofficiosità, *s.f.* inofficiousness.

inofficióso, *ag.* 1. (*dir.*) inofficious, invalid, inoperative 2. (*indifferente ai doveri sociali*) disobliging.

inoliàre, *v.t.* (*rar.*) 1. (*condire con olio*) to dress with oil 2. (*ungere con olio*) to oil, to lubricate.

inoltràre, *v.t.* (*trasmettere, inviare*) to forward, to send on, to transmit, to pass on, to convey: *dovete* — *il vostro bagaglio*, you must send on your luggage; — *una domanda, documenti*, to send on an application, documents; — *una lettera*, to forward a letter ‖ **inoltràrsi**, *v.r.* to advance, to go forward, to proceed, to penetrate; to enter (anche *fig.*): *man mano che inoltravano*, as they advanced; *non voglio inoltrarmi in questi particolari*, I don't want to enter into these details; — *in un bosco*, to penetrate into a wood; — *nella vita politica*, to enter upon political life.

inoltràto, *ag.* advanced, late: *in inverno* —, late in winter; *nel pomeriggio* —, late in the afternoon; *essere* — *negli anni*, to be advanced in years (*o* to be well on in years).

inóltre, *av.* besides; moreover, furthermore: *e, —, le circostanze sono favorevoli*, and, moreover (*o* furthermore), circumstances are favourable; *e, —, continua a chiedermi denaro*, and, what's more, he continues to ask me for money; *è troppo tardi*, — *sono stanco*, it's too late, besides, I'm tired.

inóltro, *s.m.* (*di merci*) shipment; (*di lettere, merci*) forwarding; (*di documenti*) sending in.

inombràre, *v.t.* to shade; to adumbrate.

inondaménto, *s.m.* 1. (*l'inondare*) flooding, inundating 2. (*inondazione*) flood, inundation.

inondàre, *v.t.* to flood, to inundate, to overflow (anche *fig.*): *il cielo era inondato dai raggi del sole*, the sky was flooded with sunbeams; *il fiume inondò la campagna*, the river flooded the countryside.

inondàto, *ag.* flooded (with sthg.), inundated (with sthg.), overflowing (with sthg.) (anche *fig.*).

inondazióne, *s.f.* flood, inundation.

inonèsto, *V.* disonèsto.

inonoràto, *ag.* unhonoured.

inoperosaménte, *av.* inactively, idly, lazily.

inoperosità, *s.f.* inactivity, idleness, laziness, inertness, sluggishness.

inoperóso, *ag.* inactive, idle, lazy, inert, sluggish || *capitale* —, (*comm.*) unemployed capital.

inòpia, *s.f.* (*letter.*) poverty, indigence, penury, want.

inopinàbile, *ag.* 1. (*impensabile*) inconceivable, unimaginable 2. (*imprevedibile*) unforeseeable.

inopinataménte, *av.* unexpectedly; (*improvvisamente*) suddenly.

inopinàto, *ag.* unexpected; unforeseen; (*improvviso*) sudden.

inopportunaménte, *av.* 1. (*intempestivamente*) inopportunely, untimely, unseasonably 2. (*fuori luogo*) awkwardly.

inopportunità, *s.f.* 1. (*intempestività*) inopportuneness, untimeliness, unseasonableness 2. (*l'essere fuori luogo*) awkwardness.

inopportúno, *ag.* 1. (*intempestivo*) inopportune, untimely, unseasonably 2. (*fuori luogo*) awkward: *una domanda inopportuna*, an awkward question.

inoppugnàbile, *ag.* unimpugnable, incontestable: *un diritto* —, an unimpugnable right.

inoppugnabilità, *s.f.* incontestability.

inoppugnabilménte, *av.* incontestably.

inordinataménte, *av.* disorderly; (*confusamente*) confusedly.

inordinatézza, *s.f.* disorder; (*confusione*) confusion.

inordinàto, *ag.* disorderly; (*confuso*) confused.

inorganicaménte, *av.* inorganically.

inorgànico, *ag.* inorganic: *chimica inorganica*, inorganic chemistry.

inorgoglíre, *v.t.* to make proud, to elate, to puff up: *il tuo successo lo inorgoglisce molto*, your success makes him very proud || *v.i.*, **inorgoglírsi**, *v.r.* to become proud, to grow proud, to get proud, to get puffed up, to get elated: *quando glielo dirai si inorgoglirà molto*, when you tell him he will get very proud.

inorgoglíto, *ag.* elated (with sthg.), proud (of sthg.): *un esercito — dalla vittoria*, an army elated with victory.

inornàto, *ag.* (*rar.*) unadorned.

inorpellaménto, *s.m.* decoration with tinsel.

inorpellàre, *v.t.* to tinsel (anche *fig.*) || **inorpellàrsi**, *v.r.* to adorn oneself with tinsel.

inorridíre, *v.t.* to horrify, to strike with horror; (*fam.*) to shock || *v.i.* to be horrified, to be struck with horror: *inorridimmo all'idea*, we were struck with horror at the idea.

inospitàle, *ag.* 1. inhospitable 2. (*di luogo, casa*) uninhabitable.

inospitalità, *s.f.* inhospitality.

inòspite, *ag.* 1. inhospitable 2. (*di luogo, casa*) uninhabitable, desolate.

inossàre, *v.i.* to ossify; (*granire i denti*) to teethe.

inosservàbile, *ag.* unobservable.

inosservànte, *ag.* unobservant.

inosservànza, *s.f.* 1. inobservance, non-observance 2. (*inadempienza*) non-performance, non-fulfilment.

inosservàto, *ag.* 1. unobserved, unnoticed, unperceived: *l'avvenimento passò* —, the event passed unnoticed 2. (*inadempiuto*) unperformed, unfulfilled.

inossidàbile, *ag.* inoxidizable, rust-proof: *acciaio* —, stainless steel.

in-ottàvo, *ag.* (*tip.*) octavo (*attributivo*): *volume* —, octavo volume.

inottusíre, *v.i.* to become dull || *v.t.* to make dull.

in pectore, *l.* (*lat.*) in pectore.

inquadràre, *v.t.* 1. to frame; to arrange: *le cognizioni sono utili solo se inquadrate in un sistema*, our knowledge may be useful only when framed into a system; — *una figura in un periodo storico*, to set a figure against its historical background 2. (*mil.*) to organize; to officer 3. (*racchiudere*) to enclose 4. (*foto. cine.*) to frame || **inquadràrsi**, *v.r.* to fit in.

inquadratúra, *s.f.* (*foto. cine.*) shot; (*cine. tv.*) frame.

inqualificàbile, *ag.* despicable, worthless.

in-quàrto, *ag.* (*tip.*) quarto (*attributivo*): *volume* —, quarto volume.

inquartàre, *v.t.* (*arald.*) to quarter.

inquartàta, *s.f.* (*scherma*) quart.

inquietaménte, *av.* anxiously, restlessly.

inquietànte, *ag.* worrying, disquieting.

inquietàre, *v.t.* (*preoccupare*) to worry, to disquiet, to make uneasy, to alarm: *notizie che inquietano*, disquieting news; *il suo silenzio mi inquieta*, his silence worries me || **inquietàrsi**, *v.r.* (*impazientirsi*) to become impatient; (*arrabbiarsi*) to get angry.

inquietézza, *V.* inquietúdine.

inquièto, *ag.* 1. (*agitato*) restless, unquiet, fidgety, agitated: *un bambino* —, a restless child; *una notte inquieta*, a restless night; *sonno* —, troubled (o broken) sleep 2. (*preoccupato*) anxious (about s.o., sthg.), uneasy (about s.o., sthg.),worried (about s.o., sthg.): *sono — per il suo ritardo*, I'm worried about his delay; *il suo silenzio mi rende* —, his silence makes me feel uneasy 3. (*arrabbiato*) angry, annoyed; cross.

inquietúdine, *s.f.* 1. (*agitazione*) restlessness, fidget, agitation 2. (*preoccupazione*) anxiety, uneasiness, worry: *stato d'*—, state of anxiety (o anxious state of mind); *dissipare le inquietudini di qlcu.*, to set s.o.'s mind at ease; *nutrire delle vive inquietudini per qlcu.*, to be extremely anxious (o worried) about s.o.

inquilíno, *s.m.* tenant; (*pensionante*) lodger.

inquinaménto, *s.m.* defilement, pollution.

inquinàre, *v.t.* to defile, to pollute, to make foul (anche *fig.*); *fig.* to corrupt, to mar: *i corsi d'acqua sono spesso inquinati da rifiuti delle fabbriche*, rivers are often defiled by waste from factories; *il suo stile era inquinato da un eccessivo uso di arcaismi*, his style was marred by an excessive use of archaic words and phrases || **inquinàrsi**, *v.r.* to become defiled, to become polluted, to become foul.

inquinàto, *ag.* foul, polluted: *acqua inquinata*, foul water.

inquinazióne, *s.f.* defilement, pollution.

inquirènte, *ag.* examining; investigating: *commissione* —, investigating commission; *giudice, magistrato* —, examining judge, magistrate.

inquisíre, *v.t.* to investigate, to inquire into (sthg.); to search || *v.i.* to inquire (about, after sthg.).

inquisitívo, *ag.* inquisitive, investigating; searching.

inquisitóre, *ag.* inquiring, searching: *uno sguardo* —, an inquiring (o searching) look || *s.m.* inquisitor || *il Grande Inquisitore*, (*st.*) the Grand Inquisitor.

inquisitòrio, *ag.* inquiring, searching.

inquisizióne, *s.f.* inquisition || *la Santa Inquisizione*, (*st.*) the Inquisition.

insabbiàre, *v.t.* 1. to cover with sand, to sand; (*riempire di sabbia*) to fill up 2. *fig.* (*una pratica, una legge, ecc.*) to hinder || **insabbiàrsi**, *v.r.* 1. to get covered with sand; (*riempirsi di sabbia*) to silt up 2. *fig.* (*di pratica, legge, ecc.*) to be hindered.

insaccaménto, *s.m.* sacking, putting into sack.

insaccàre, *v.t.* 1. to sack, to put into sacks 2. (*pigiare dentro*) to cram, to stuff 3. (*carne*) to make into sausages || **insaccàrsi**, *v.r.* 1. (*pigiarsi dentro*) to squeeze 2. (*vestirsi male*) to dress badly, to dress in badly-fitting clothes 3. (*di sole*) to hide behind the clouds.

insaccàto, *ag.* **1.** sacked, packed in a sack ‖ *carni insaccate*, sausages **2.** (*vestito male*) badly dressed.

insaccatúra, *s.f.* **1.** sacking **2.** (*di carne*) sausage making.

insalàta, *s.f.* **1.** salad: — *di verdura, di pollo*, vegetable, chicken salad; — *russa*, Russian salad; *condire l'*—, to dress the salad **2.** *fig.* (*mescolanza*) mixture; muddle.

insalatièra, *s.f.* salad-bowl.

insaldàbile, *ag.* (*non saldabile*) unweldable.

insaldàre, *v.t.* to starch.

insaldatúra, *s.f.* starching.

insalivàre, *v.t.* to insalivate, to wet with saliva.

insalúbre, *ag.* insalubrious, unhealthy.

insalubreménte, *av.* unhealthily.

insalubrità, *s.f.* insalubrity, unhealthiness.

insalutàto, *ag.* unsaluted ‖ *se ne andò — ospite*, he went away without saying good-bye.

insalvàbile, *ag.* unsalvable.

insalvatichíre, *V.* **inselvatichíre.**

insanàbile, *ag.* **1.** incurable (anche *fig.*) **2.** (*irrimediabile*) irremediable.

insanabilità, *s.f.* incurability.

insanabilménte, *av.* incurably.

insanguinàre, *v.t.* to cover with blood; to stain with blood (anche *fig.*): *le guerre hanno insanguinato lungamente l'Italia*, wars bathed Italy in blood for many years ‖ **insanguinàrsi,** *v.r.* to become blood-stained; to cover oneself with blood.

insanguinàto, *ag.* bloodstained: *le sue mani erano insanguinate*, his hands were stained with blood.

insània, *s.f.* insanity, folly, madness.

insaníre, *v.i.* to become insane, to go mad.

insàno, *ag.* insane, crazy; (*forsennato*) mad, frantic.

insaponaménto, *V.* **insaponàta.**

insaponàre, *v.t.* **1.** to soap; to lather **2.** (*adulare*) to soap, to soft-soap; to flatter.

insaponàta, insaponatúra, *s.f.* soaping, lathering: *dare una bella — a ql.co.*, to soap sthg. well.

insaporàre, insaporíre, *v.t.* to flavour, to season: *carne insaporita con aglio*, meat seasoned with garlic ‖ **insaporàrsi, insaporírsi,** *v.r.* to become tasty.

insapúta, all', *l.av.* unknown to (s.o., sthg), without the knowledge of (s.o., sthg): *a sua* —, without his knowing it.

insatanassàre, *v.t.* to make devilish.

insatanassàto, *ag.* **1.** possessed **2.** (*furioso*) raving.

insaturàbile, *ag.* **1.** (*chim.*) unsaturable **2.** (*insaziabile*) insatiable, unappeasable (anche *fig.*).

insaziàbile, *ag.* insatiable, unappeasable (anche *fig.*).

insaziabilità, *s.f.* insatiability, insatiableness (anche *fig.*).

insaziabilménte, *av.* insatiably (anche *fig.*).

insaziàto, *ag.* insatiate, unappeased (anche *fig.*).

inscandagliàbile, *ag.* unfathomable.

inscatolaménto, *s.m.* tinning; canning.

inscatolàre, *v.t.* to tin; to can.

inscatolàto, *ag.* tinned; canned.

inscenàre, *v.t.* to stage (anche *fig.*); to put on the stage: — *una dimostrazione*, to stage a demonstration.

inscenatóre, *s.m.* (*teat.*) stage-manager.

insciènte, *ag.* (*letter.*) inscient, ignorant, unaware.

inscienteménte, *av.* unawares, unknowingly.

inscindíbile, *ag.* inseparable.

inscrívere, *e derivati, V.* **iscrívere,** *e derivati.*

inscrutàbile, *ag.* inscrutable, impenetrable.

inscrutabilità, *s.f.* inscrutability, inscrutableness.

inscrutabilménte, *av.* inscrutably, impenetrably.

inscusàbile, *ag.* inexcusable, unpardonable, unjustifiable.

insecchíre, *v.t.* to dry up, to make dry ‖ *v.i.* **1.** to become dry, to dry up **2.** (*avvizzire*) to wither **3.** (*dimagrire*) to get thin.

insediaménto, *s.m.* installation, entering, settling down, taking possession.

insediàre, *v.t.* to install: — *qlcu. in un ufficio*, to install s.o. in an office ‖ **insediàrsi,** *v.r.* to install oneself, to enter upon (sthg.); (*prendere possesso*) to take possession (of sthg.); (*stabilirsi*) to settle down, to establish oneself.

in-sediceèsimo, *ag.* (*tip.*) sextodecimo (*attributivo*).

inségna, *s.f.* **1.** (*emblema*) insignia (*pl.*): — *della regalità*, insignia of royalty **2.** (*distintivo*) badge **3.** (*bandiera*) flag, banner, standard; colours (*pl.*); (*mar.*) ensign: *l'* — *della fanteria*, the colours of infantry; *l'* — *di un reggimento di cavalleria*, ensign (o colours) of a cavalry regiment **4.** (*di negozio*) sign-board: *insegne al neon*, neon signs.

insegnàbile, *ag.* teachable.

insegnaménto, *s.m.* **1.** teaching; (*istruzione*) education, instruction; (*specialmente privato*) tuition; (*privato per preparazione agli esami*) coaching: *l'* — *della chimica*, the teaching of chemistry; — *elementare, secondario*, primary, secondary education; *l'* — *è costoso in questa scuola*, tuition is expensive in this school; *non mi piace l'* — *come professione*, I don't like teaching as a profession; *si diede all'* —, he became a teacher **2.** (*lezione*) lesson: *questo ti servirà d'* —, this will be a lesson to you **3.** (*precetto*) precept, teaching: *gli insegnamenti della morale cattolica*, the precepts (o teachings) of Catholic morals.

insegnànte, *ag.* teaching: *il corpo* —, the teaching staff (o the staff of teachers) ‖ *s.c.* teacher: — *d'inglese*, English teacher; *egli fa l'* —, he is a teacher.

insegnàre, *v.t.* **1.** to teach, to instruct: *egli mi insegnò il francese*, he taught me French; *l'esperienza insegna che...*, experience teaches that...; *ti insegnerò a farlo*, I shall teach you to do it (o how to do it); — *ql.co. a qlcu.*, to teach s.o. sthg. (o to teach sthg. to s.o. o to instruct s.o. in sthg.) **2.** (*per professione*) to teach, to be a teacher of (sthg.): *insegna letteratura italiana*, he teaches Italian literature **3.** (*mostrare, indicare*) to show: *potete insegnarmi la strada?*, can you show me the way?.

inseguiménto, *s.m.* pursuit, chase: *essere all'* — *di qlcu.*, to be in pursuit of s.o. (o to run after s.o.).

inseguíre, *v.t.* to pursue, to chase, to run after (s.o., sthg.): — *una lepre*, to pursue (o to chase o to run after) a hare; — *qlcu. da vicino*, to pursue s.o. closely.

inseguitóre, *s.m.*, **inseguitríce,** *s.f.* pursuer, chaser.

insellaménto, *s.m.* saddling.

insellàre, *v.t.* to saddle ‖ **insellàrsi,** *v.r.* to mount.

insellàto, *ag.* **1.** saddled **2.** (*dal dorso curvo*) saddle-backed.

insellatúra, *s.f.* saddleback.

inselvàrsi, *v.r.* (*letter.*) to hide in a wood.

inselvatichíre, *v.t.* to make wild ‖ *v.i.*, **inselvatichírsi,** *v.r.* to grow wild, to become wild.

inseminàto, *ag.* (*letter.*) **1.** unsown **2.** *fig.* (*deserto, abbandonato*) barren, desert, abandoned.

insenatúra, *s.f.* inlet, creek.

insensatàggine, *V.* **insensatézza.**

insensataménte, *av.* senselessly; foolishly, crazily.

insensatézza, *s.f.* **1.** senselessness; foolishness, craziness **2.** (*atto insensato*) senseless action; foolish action **3.** (*detto insensato*) nonsense.

insensàto, *ag.* senseless; foolish, crazy.

insensíbile, *ag.* **1.** (*impercettibile*) insensible, imperceptible; slight: *un rumore* —, a slight noise **2.** (*senza sentimento*) insensible, unfeeling, hard, hard-hearted: *un cuore* —, a hard heart; *una persona* —, an unfeeling (o hard-hearted) person **3.** (*ottuso*) dull, obtuse: *una mente* —, a dull mind **4.** (*indifferente*) indifferent: *è* — *alle sofferenze altrui*, he is indifferent to other people's sufferings **5.** (*riferito al fisico*) insensible: *a causa del freddo le mie mani erano insensibili*, owing to the cold my hands were insensible (o numb).

insensibilità, *s.f.* **1.** (*impercettibilità*) imperceptibility; slightness **2.** (*mancanza di sentimenti*) insensibility, unfeelingness, hard-heartedness, hardness **3.** (*ottusità*) dullness, obtuseness **4.** (*indifferenza*) indifference **5.** (*riferito al fisico*) insensibility.

insensibilménte, *av.* **1.** (*impercettibilmente*) imperceptibly; slightly **2.** (*senza sentimento*) insensibly, unfeelingly **3.** (*ottusamente*) dully, obtusely **4.** (*indifferentemente*) indifferently **5.** (*riferito al fisico*) insensibly.

inseparàbile, *ag.* inseparable, indivisible.

inseparabilità, *s.f.* inseparability, indivisibility.

inseparabilménte, *av.* inseparably, indivisibly.

inseparàto, *ag.* inseparate.

insepólto, *ag.* unburied.

insequestràbile, *ag.* not liable to sequestration.

inseriménto, *s.m.* insertion, introduction.

inseríre, *v.t.* **1.** to insert: — *un annunzio in un giornale,* to insert an advertisement in a paper; — *un capitolo in un libro,* to insert a chapter in a book **2.** (*elett.*) to connect, to plug in, to cut in ‖ **inserírsi,** *v.r.* **1.** (*diventar parte*) to become a part (of sthg.) **2.** (*essere incluso*) to be included.

inseríto, *ag.* inserted; (*incluso*) included.

insèrto, *s.m.* file; papers (*pl.*); documents (*pl.*); dossier.

inservíbile, *ag.* useless, of no use, unserviceable.

inserviènte, *s.m.* servant; attendant; (*in albergo*) call-boy; (*in negozio*) errand-boy; (*in ufficio*) office-boy; *un — d'ospedale,* a hospital attendant.

inserzióne, *s.f.* **1.** (*l'inserire*) inserting **2.** (*inserimento*) insertion: — *di una clausola in un contratto,* insertion of a clause in an agreement **3.** (*pubblicitaria*) advertisement: *mettere un'— su un giornale,* to put an advertisement in a newspaper **4.** (*elett.*) connection **5.** — *di una trama,* (*ind. tessile*) picking.

inserzionísta, *s.c.* advertiser.

insetticída, *ag.* insecticidal; insecticide (*attributivo*): *polvere —,* insect-powder ‖ *s.m.* insecticide, insect-killer.

insettívoro, *ag.* (*zool. bot.*) insectivorous ‖ *s.m.* (*zool. bot.*) insectivore ‖ *gli insettivori,* (*zool.*) the Insectivora.

insètto, *s.m.* insect; (*amer.*) bug ‖ *sei un —!,* (*un essere spregevole*) you're an insect! ‖ *gli insetti,* the Insecta.

insettología, *s.f.* (*rar.*) entomology.

insettòlogo, *s.m.* entomologist.

insídia, *s.f.* **1.** snare, trap, ambush; (*inganno*) plot, deceit: *tendere un'— a qlcu.,* to lay (o to set) a snare (o a trap o an ambush) for s.o. **2.** (*pericolo*) danger, peril: *le insidie della foresta,* the dangers of the forest.

insidiàre, *v.t.* to lay snares for (s.o.), to lay traps for (s.o.), to lie in wait for (s.o.); to lay wait for (s.o.): — *una donna,* to tempt a woman ‖ *v.i.* (*attentare*) to attempt (sthg.), to make an attempt (on sthg.): — *alla vita di qlcu.,* to attempt s.o.'s life.

insidiatóre, *s.m.* snarer, tempter.

insidiatríce, *s.f.* temptress.

insidióso, *ag.* insidious: *domanda insidiosa,* tricky question; *male —,* insidious disease.

insième, *av.* **1.** together: *i miei bambini dormono —,* my children sleep together; *domani staremo — un'oretta,* tomorrow we shall meet for an hour; *faremo una gita tutti —,* we'll all take a trip together; *andare —,* to go together: *questi due colori non vanno —,* these two colours don't go together (o don't match); *legare —,* to tie together; *mettere —,* to put together: *mettere — una frase,* to make up a sentence; *mettere — una lettera,* to put together a letter; *mettere — i pezzi di un orologio,* to put a watch together (o to assemble a watch); *mettere — un po' di denaro,* to put (o to scrape) together (o to collect) some money; *mettere — volontari,* to get together (o to gather) volunteers ‖ *tutto —,* all together: *ho venduto i miei mobili tutti —,* I've sold my furniture all together; *mandò giù la medicina tutta —,* he swallowed all the medicine at one gulp; *tutto — non vale una lira,* the whole lot put together isn't worth twopence **2.** (*allo stesso tempo*) **at the same time:** *arrivarono tutti —,* they all arrived at the same time (o together); *rideva e piangeva —,* he was laughing and crying at the same time ‖ **insième a, con,** *prep.* (**together**) **with:** *accludo la fattura — all'assegno,* I'm enclosing the invoice together with the cheque; *voglio stare sempre — con te,* I want to be with you always.

insième, *s.m.* whole: *un — armonioso,* a harmonious whole; — *di colori,* group of colours; *l'— degli attori era ottimo,* the whole cast was magnificent; *l'— del lavoro è buono,* the work is good on the whole (o as a whole); *l'— dell'orchestra era splendido,* the orchestra was splendid in the tutti ‖ *idea di —,* broad (o general) idea (of a subject); *sguardo di —,* comprehensive view ‖ *nell'—,* as a whole (o on the whole): *cosa presa, vista nell'—,* thing taken, seen as a whole; *i giudici, presi nell'—, erano onesti,* the judges, taken as a body, were honest **2.** (*servizio, assortimento*) set: *un — di tre pezzi,* a three-piece set; *un — di utensili,* a set of tools.

insígne, *ag.* **1.** famous, illustrious, remarkable, signal: *un — scienziato,* a famous scientist **2.** (*notorio*) notorious: *un criminale —,* a notorious criminal.

insignificànte, *ag.* **1.** insignificant: *occupare un posto — in società,* to occupy an insignificant place in society **2.** (*senza significato*) meaningless: *parole insignificanti,* meaningless words **3.** (*senza espressione*) expressionless: *un volto —,* an expressionless (o vacuous) face **4.** (*di poco o nessun valore*) unimportant, trifling, petty, trivial: *somma —,* trifling sum.

insigníre, *v.t.* to decorate, to confer: — *qlcu. di una decorazione,* to decorate s.o.; — *qlcu. di un titolo,* to confer a title upon s.o.

insigníto, *ag.* decorated (with sthg.).

insignoríre, *v.t.* to make master ‖ *v.i.* (*arricchire*) to become rich ‖ **insignorírsi,** *v.r.* (*impossessarsi*) to take possession (of sthg.).

insilaménto, *s.m.* ensilage.

insilàre, *v.t.* to ensile, to silo.

insincerità, *s.f.* insincerity.

insincèro, *ag.* insincere.

insindacàbile, *ag.* unobjectionable, not liable to criticism.

insindacabilità, *s.f.* unobjectionableness.

insindacabilménte, *av.* unobjectionably.

insíno, *av.* (*perfino*) **even** ‖ **insíno a,** *prep.* (*riferito a tempo*) **till,** until; (*riferito a luogo*) **as far as** ‖ **insíno a che,** *cong.* (*finchè*) **till,** until; (*per tutto il tempo che*) **as long as.**

insinuànte, *ag.* insinuating, insinuative; (*persuasivo*) winning: *modi insinuanti,* insinuating ways; *ha un modo di fare —,* she has winning (o ingratiating) manners.

insinuàre, *v.t.* **1.** to insinuate; to hint at (sthg.), to suggest; (*instillare*) to instil: *che cosa volete —?,* what are you hinting at? (o getting at?); *insinua che io sia colpevole,* he insinuates that I am guilty; *insinuò strane idee nella sua mente,* he instilled strange ideas into his mind; — *un sospetto,* to insinuate a suspicion **2.** (*inserire*) to insert, to insinuate: — *il dito in una ferita,* to introduce one's finger into a wound (o to probe a wound with one's finger) **3** — *un credito,* (*dir.*) to tender a proof of credit ‖ **insinuàrsi,** *v.r.* to insinuate oneself (anche *fig.*); to creep, to penetrate: *l'acqua si insinua dappertutto,* water insinuates itself (o permeates) everywhere; — *nell'animo di qlcu.,* to insinuate oneself into s.o.'s favour.

insinuatóre, *s.m.,* **insinuatríce,** *s.f.* insinuator.

insinuazióne, *s.f.* **1.** insinuation; hint, innuendo (*pl.* innuendoes): *rivolgere insinuazioni contro qlcu.,* to throw out innuendoes against s.o. **2.** (*dir.*) claim.

insipidaménte, *av.* insipidly.

insipidézza, insipidità, *s.f.* insipidness, insipidity.

insipido, *ag.* **1.** insipid, tasteless **2.** *fig.* (*sciocco, insignificante*) insipid, dull: *commedia insipida,* dull play.

insipiènte, *ag.* **1.** (*sciocco*) silly, foolish **2.** (*ignorante*) incapable, ignorant.

insipienteménte, *av.* foolishly, sillily, unwisely.

insipiènza, *s.f.* 1. foolishness, silliness 2. (*ignoranza*) ignorance.

insistènte, *ag.* 1. insistent; persistent; (*molesto*) annoying: *bambino* —, irritating child; *domande insistenti*, insistent questions 2. (*incessante*) unceasing, continual, incessant: *pioggia* —, unceasing rain.

insistenteménte, *av.* 1. insistently; persistently 2. (*incessantemente*) unceasingly, continually, incessantly.

insistènza, *s.f.* insistence, insistency.

insístere, *v.i.* to insist (on sthg., on doing): *devi* — *su questo punto*, you must insist on this point; *insisti perchè egli venga*, insist on his coming (*o* insist that he should come); *insisti sui verbi irregolari*, insist on irregular verbs; *non cedere a meno che egli insista*, don't give in unless he insists; — *con qlcu. sulla necessità di fare ql.co.*, to urge on s.o. the necessity of doing sthg.

ìnsito, *ag.* inborn, innate, inherent.

insociàbile, insociévole, *ag.* unsociable.

insocievolménte, *av.* unsociably.

insocievolézza, *s.f.* unsociability, unsociableness.

insoddisfàtto, *ag.* unsatisfied (with sthg.), dissatisfied (with sthg.), displeased (with sthg.).

insofferènte, *ag.* intolerant, impatient.

insofferènza, *s.f.* intolerance, impatience.

insoffríbile, *ag.* insufferable, unbearable.

insoffribilità, *s.f.* unbearableness.

insoffribilménte, *av.* insufferably, unbearably.

insolazióne, *s.f.* 1. insolation 2. (*colpo di sole*) sunstroke, insolation: *colpito da* —, sunstruck.

insoleàre, *v.t.* to furrow, to groove.

insolènte, *ag.* insolent, impudent, pert, impertinent, saucy.

Insolenteménte, *av.* insolently, impudently, pertly, impertinently, saucily.

insolentíre, *v.i.* (*diventare insolente*) to become insolent; (*essere insolente*) to be insolent (to s.o.), to abuse (s.o.): *incominciò a* — *contro di me*, he took to abusing me (*o* he took to being insolent to me) || *v.t.* 1. to abuse, to insult 2. (*rendere insolente*) to make haughty, to make arrogant: *la ricchezza insolentisce gli uomini vani*, wealth makes the vain arrogant.

insolènza, *s.f.* insolence, impudence, pertness, impertinence, sauciness: *è un'*— *da parte sua*, it is a piece of impudence on his part; *dire delle insolenze a qlcu.*, to say insolent words to s.o. (*o* to insult s.o.).

insolitaménte, *av.* unusually.

insòlito, *ag.* unusual, unwonted; (*strano*) strange; (*straordinario*) extraordinary, remarkable: *parole nuove e insolite*, new and strange words; *mostrare un'insolita generosità*, to show unwonted generosity.

insolúbile, *ag.* 1. (*chim.*) insoluble 2. *fig.* insoluble, insolvable, unsolvable: *situazione* —, deadlock; *il problema a me pare* —, the problem seems insoluble to me.

insolubilità, *s.f.* insolubility, insolubleness.

insolubilménte, *av.* insolubly.

insolúto, *ag.* 1. unsolved, open: *la faccenda è ancora insoluta*, the matter is still unsolved 2. (*non pagato*) unpaid, outstanding: *un debito* —, an outstanding debt; *la tratta ci è ritornata insoluta*, the draft has been sent back unpaid.

insolvènte, *ag.* (*dir.*) insolvent: *debitore* —, insolvent (debtor).

insolvènza, *s.f.* (*dir.*) insolvency.

insolvíbile, *ag.* 1. (*di debito*) unpayable, that cannot be paid 2. (*di debitore*) insolvent.

insolvibilità, *s.f.* (*dir.*) insolvency.

insómma, *av.* 1. (*in breve*) in short, in a word 2. (*in conclusione*) in conclusion; (*in complesso*) on the whole 3. (*dopo tutto*) after all || *inter.* well: —, *finiamola!*, well, let's get it over!.

insommergíbile, *ag.* unsinkable.

insondàbile, *ag.* unfathomable.

insònne, *ag.* sleepless, wakeful.

insònnia, *s.f.* insomnia, sleeplessness, wakefulness: *insonnie frequenti*, frequent fits of insomnia; *soffrire d'*—, to suffer from insomnia.

insonnolíto, *ag.* drowsy, sleepy: *essere* —, to be (*o* to feel) drowsy.

insopportàbile, *ag.* unbearable, unendurable, intolerable, insufferable: *caldo* —, intolerable heat; *persona* —, insufferable person; *è* —*!*, he is very trying!.

insopportabilità, *s.f.* unbearableness, intolerableness.

insopportabilménte, *av.* unbearably, intolerably.

insordíre, *v.i.* to become deaf.

insórgere, *v.i.* 1. (*ribellarsi*) to rise, to rebel, to revolt: *le tribù insorsero contro il governo*, the tribes rebelled (*o* revolted) against the government; — *contro un tiranno*, to rise against a tyrant 2. (*protestare*) to protest: *insorsero tutti contro quella proposta*, they all protested against that proposition 3. (*sorgere, manifestarsi*) to arise, to crop up: *insorsero molte difficoltà*, many difficulties arose (*o* cropped up).

insorgiménto, *s.m.* uprising, revolt, insurrection, rebellion.

insormontàbile, *ag.* insurmountable, insuperable: *barriere insormontabili*, insuperable barriers; *difficoltà insormontabili*, insurmountable difficulties.

insórto, *ag.* insurgent, rebellious || *s.m.* insurgent, rebel.

insospettàbile, *ag.* unsuspicious, beyond suspicion, above suspicion.

insospettataménte, *av.* unsuspectedly.

insospettàto, *ag.* 1. unsuspected 2. (*impensato*) unexpected; (*imprevisto*) unforeseen.

insospettiménto, *s.m.* suspecting.

insospettíre, *v.t.* to make suspicious, to rouse s.o.'s suspicions: *ciò mi insospettì*, this roused my suspicions (*o* made me suspicious) || *v.i.*, **insospettírsi**, *v.r.* to grow suspicious, to become suspicious, to begin to suspect: — *di ql.co.*, to get wind of sthg.

insostanziàle, *ag.* unsubstantial.

insosteníbile, *ag.* unsustainable: *affermazione* —, unsustainable statement.

insozzàre, *v.t.* to soil, to dirty; *fig.* to sully, to disgrace: — *il buon nome della propria famiglia*, to disgrace the good name of one's family; — *le pareti*, to soil (*o* to dirty) the walls; — *la reputazione di qlcu.*, to sully s.o.'s reputation.

insperàbile, *ag.* not to be hoped for, beyond hope, beyond expectation.

insperataménte, *av.* unexpectedly.

insperàto, *ag.* 1. unhoped for 2. (*inaspettato*) unexpected.

inspessiménto, *s.m.* thickening.

inspessíre, *v.t.* to thicken, to make dense || **inspessírsi**, *v.r.* to thicken; to become thick(er); to grow thick(er).

inspiegàbile, *ag.* inexplicable; unaccountable.

inspiegabilménte, *av.* inexplicably, unexplainable, unaccountably.

inspiegàto, *ag.* unexplained.

inspiràre, *v.t.* 1. to breathe in, to inspire; (*inalare*) to inhale: — *aria*, to inhale (*o* to breathe in); — *fumo*, to inhale smoke 2. *V.* **ispiràre** || **inspiràrsi**, *v.r. V.* **ispiràrsi**.

inspiratóre, *ag.* 1. (*anat.*) inspiratory 2. *V.* **ispiratóre** || *s.m.*, **inspiratríce**, *s.f.* inspirer.

inspirazióne, *s.f.* 1. (*inalazione*) breathing in, inhaling 2. *V.* **ispirazióne**.

instàbile, *ag.* unstable; (*malfermo*) unsteady, wobbly; (*incostante*) inconstant, fickle; (*variabile*) unsettled, changeable, variable: *equilibrio* —, (*fis.*) unstable equilibrium; *tempo* —, unsettled (*o* changeable) weather.

instabilità, *s.f.* instability, unstableness, unsteadiness; (*incostanza*) inconstancy, fickleness; (*variabilità*) changeableness, variability, variableness: *l'*— *di una casa*, the instability of a house.

instabilménte, *av.* unstably; unsteadily; (*incostantemente*) inconstantly; (*variabilmente*) variably.

installaménto, *s.m.* installation.

installàre, *v.t.* to install; to fit up, to set up: — *un impianto elettrico,* to install an electric system; — *una macchina,* to set up a machine; — *qlcu. in una carica,* to install s.o. in an office; — *qlcu. in una casa,* to establish s.o. in a house; — *rampe di lancio,* (*missilistica*) to install launching ramps ‖ **installàrsi,** *v.r.* to install oneself, to settle down, to settle in: *appena ci installammo nella nuova casa,* as soon as we settled down in our new home.

installazióne, *s.f.* installation.

instancàbile, *ag.* untiring, indefatigable, tireless.

instancabilità, *s.f.* indefatigability, tirelessness.

instancabilménte, *av.* untiringly, indefatigably, tirelessly.

instànte, *ag.* (*rar.*) (*urgente*) pressing, urgent; (*incombente*) impending, overhanging: *un pericolo —,* an impending danger ‖ *s.m.* petitioner.

instanteménte, *av.* (*rar.*) insistently.

instàre, *v.i.* (*rar.*) **1.** (*insistere*) to insist **2.** (*incombere*) to be impending.

instauràre, *v.t.* to set up, to establish, to found.

instauratóre, *s.m.,* **instauratríce,** *s.f.* founder.

instaurazióne, *s.f.* establishment, foundation.

insterilíre, *V.* **isterilíre.**

instigàre, *V.* **istigàre.**

instillàre, *v.t.* to instil(l) (anche *fig.*): — *idee nella mente di qlcu.,* to instil ideas into s.o.'s mind.

instillazióne, *s.f.* instillation.

institóre, *s.m.* (*dir.*) institor, factor.

institòrio, *ag.* (*dir.*) institorial.

instituíre, *V.* **istituíre.**

instradùre, *v.t.* **1.** (*mettere sulla via giusta*) to set on the right road **2.** (*avviare, incamminare*) to start: — *un nuovo lavoro,* to start a new piece of work; — *qlcu. negli affari,* to start s.o. in business.

insú, *av.* **1.** up, upwards: *camminare — e ingiù,* to walk up and down; *collocare ql.co. a faccia —,* to lay sthg. face upwards; *guardare —,* to look upwards ‖ *all'—,* up, upward (*ag.*); up, upwards (*av.*): *movimento all'—,* upward movement; *appeso coi piedi all'—,* hanging feet up (o upside down); *procedere all'—,* to proceed upwards **2.** (*riferito a età, prezzo, computando in avanti*) up, upwards; on, onwards: *da due anni —,* from the age of two onwards (o from two years up o from two years upwards); *da duemila lire —,* from two thousand lire up(wards) (o at two thousand lire and over) **3.** (*riferito a tempo, computando all'indietro*) up to: *dal 20 ottobre —,* up to the 20th of October; *dal quinto secolo —,* up to the fifth century.

insubordinataménte, *av.* insubordinately.

insubordinatézza, *s.f.* insubordination.

insubordinàto, *ag.* insubordinate.

insubordinazióne, *s.f.* insubordination.

insuccèsso, *s.m.* failure.

insudiciàre, *v.t.* **1.** to soil, to dirty, to stain ‖ *le tele,* (*dipinger male*) to daub **2.** *fig.* to defile ‖ **insudiciàrsi,** *v.r.* to soil, to dirty: — *le mani,* to soil one's hands; — *i vestiti,* to soil (o to dirty) one's clothes ‖ *non voglio insudiciarmi le mani in questa faccenda,* I don't want to soil my hands with this business.

insuèto, *ag.* (*letter.*) **1.** (*insolito*) unusual **2.** (*non assuefatto*) unaccustomed.

insufficiènte, *ag.* **1.** insufficient, inadequate: *abiti, mezzi insufficienti,* insufficient clothing, means; *cibo —,* insufficiency of food (o low feeding); *informazioni insufficienti,* inadequate information; *istruzione —,* inadequate learning; *ci diede spiegazioni insufficienti,* he gave us inadequate explanations **2.** (*non idoneo*) inadequate; unfit (for sthg.): *essere — alla bisogna,* a *fare ql.co.,* to be inadequate for a purpose, to doing sthg. (o not to be equal to a purpose, to doing sthg.) **3.** (*ter-*

mine scolastico): *il tuo compito è —,* your work is below standard; *essere — in una materia,* to be backward (o behind) in a subject.

insufficienteménte, *av.* insufficiently, inadequately.

insufficiènza, *s.f.* **1.** insufficiency, inadequacy; (*mancanza*) shortage, want, lack: — *di grano,* shortage of wheat; — *di manodopera,* shortage of hands; — *di mezzi,* inadequacy of means **2.** (*inettitudine*) unfitness, incapacity **3.** (*termine scolastico*) low mark; (*agli esami*) failure **4.** (*med.*) insufficiency: — *cardiaca,* cardiac insufficiency.

insufflàre, *v.t.* **1.** to insufflate **2.** *fig.* to inspire (s.o. with sthg.).

insufflazióne, *s.f.* insufflation (anche *eccl.*): — *d'aria nei polmoni,* insufflation of the lungs.

insulàre, *ag.* **1.** (*geog.*) insular **2.** (*med.*) insular: *teoria —,* insular hypothesis **3.** *lobo —,* (*anat.*) insula.

insularità, *s.f.* insularity.

insulína, *s.f.* (*chim. biol.*) insulin.

insulsàggine, *s.f.* **1.** silliness, dullness, insipidity, stupidity, fatuity **2.** (*cosa insulsa*) nonsense: *dire insulsaggini,* to talk nonsense.

insulsaménte, *av.* sillily, insipidly, stupidly.

insúlso, *ag.* silly, dull, insipid, fatuous: *uno scherzo —,* a silly joke; *un uomo —,* a dull (o silly) man.

insultànte, *ag.* insulting.

insultàre, *v.t.* to insult, to affront, to abuse, to revile: — *qlcu.,* to insult (o to abuse) s.o.

insultatóre, *s.m.,* **insultatríce,** *s.f.* insulter, reviler.

insúlto, *s.m.* **1.** insult, abuse; (*affronto*) affront: *ciò che dice è un —,* what he is saying is an insult (o an affront); *è un — alla miseria!,* it is an insult to poverty!; *fare un — a qlcu.,* to insult s.o. (o to offer an insult to s.o.); *incassare un —,* to suffer (o to tolerate) an insult; *riempire qlcu. di insulti,* to shower abuses on s.o. **2.** (*danno, oltraggio*) inclemency: *l'— del tempo,* the ravages of time **3.** (*vessazione*) harassment: *essere esposti agli insulti del nemico,* to be harassed by the enemy **4.** — *apoplettico,* (*med.*) apoplectic stroke (o stroke of apoplexy).

insuperàbile, *ag.* insuperable; unsurpassable; unexcelled: *barriera, difficoltà —,* insuperable barrier, difficulty; *mente —,* unexcelled mind.

insuperabilità, *s.f.* insuperability.

insuperabilménte, *av.* insuperably.

insuperàto, *ag.* unsurpassed; unexcelled.

insuperbiménto, *s.m.* elation, growing proud.

insuperbíre, *v.t.* to elate, to make proud ‖ *v.i.,* **insuperbírsi,** *v.r.* to pride oneself (on sthg.): *non hai nulla di che insuperbirti,* you have nothing to boast of.

insuperbíto, *ag.* elated, grown proud.

insurrezionàle, *ag.* insurrectional, insurrectionary: *spirito —,* spirit of revolt; *truppe insurrezionali,* insurrectionary troops.

insurrezióne, *s.f.* insurrection, rising, revolt.

insuscettívo, *ag.* insusceptible.

insussistènte, *ag.* non-existent; (*infondato*) unfounded; unsubstantial: *notizia —,* unfounded rumour.

insussistènza, *s.f.* non-existence; (*infondatezza*) unsubstantiality, baselessness.

intabaccàre, *v.t.* to soil with tobacco.

intabarràre, *v.t.* to cloak, to wrap up in a cloak ‖ **intabarràrsi,** *v.r.* to wrap oneself up in a cloak, to muffle oneself up in a cloak.

intaccàbile, *ag.* susceptible (to sthg.): — *dagli acidi, dalla ruggine,* susceptible to acids, to rust.

intaccàre, *v.t.* **1.** (*fare tacche in*) to notch: — *un bastone,* to notch a stick **2.** (*corrodere*) to corrode, to eat away; to etch: *gli acidi intaccano i metalli,* acids corrode (o eat into) metals **3.** (*danneggiare*) to damage, to injure, to impair; (*sciupare*) to spoil: *la casa non fu intaccata dal fuoco,* the house was not damaged by the fire; *ciò intaccherà la sua reputazione,* this will injure (o damage) his reputation; *l'esplosione gli intaccò la vista,* the explosion impaired his sight **4.** (*cominciare a usare*): — *il proprio capitale*, to draw on one's capital || *v.i.* (*tartagliare*) to stutter, to stammer.

intaccatúra, *s.f.* indentation; (*tacca*) notch.

intagliàre, *v.t.* **1.** (*incidere*) to engrave, to incise, to intaglio; to cut **2.** (*scolpire*) to carve, to sculpture: *è una statua intagliata nel legno*, it is a statue carved in wood **3.** (*la stoffa*) to trim.

intagliatóre, *s.m.* **1.** (*incisore*) engraver, cutter **2.** (*scultore*) carver, sculptor.

intàglio, *s.m.* **1.** (*incisione*) engraving, incision; intaglio **2.** (*scultura*) sculpture, carving.

intanàrsi, *v.r.* to lair; to hide.

intangíbile, *ag.* **1.** intangible **2.** (*inviolabile*) inviolable.

intangibilità, *s.f.* **1.** intangibility **2.** (*inviolabilità*) inviolability, inviolableness.

intànto, *av.* **1.** (**in the**) **meanwhile**, (**in the**) **meantime**: — *prendilo, poi vedremo*, in the meantime pick it up, we'll arrange later; *io scrivo una lettera e — tu prepari la cena*, I'll write a letter and in the meanwhile you prepare supper; *noi la compiangevamo, ella — si divertiva*, we were feeling sorry for her and at the same time she was enjoying herself **2.**(*fam.*) (*avversativo*) **but:** *dice di sì e — non fa nulla*, he says yes, but does not do anything; *hai fatto di testa tua e — le hai prese*, you had your own way, but you got a thrashing || **intànto che**, *cong.* while: — *che mi vestivo egli arrivò*, while I was dressing he arrived.

intarlàre, *v.i.*, **intarlàrsi**, *v.r.* to get worm-eaten.

intarmàre, *V.* **tarmàre**.

intarsiàre, *v.t.* to inlay.

intarsiàto, *ag.* inlaid.

intarsiatóre, *s.m.* inlayer.

intarsiatúra, *s.f.* inlaying.

intàrsio, *s.m.* inlay: *lavoro d'—*, inlay work (*o* marquetry).

intartaríto, *ag.* **1.** covered with tartar, tartareous **2.** (*rugginoso*) rusty.

intasaménto, *s.m.* obstruction, stoppage.

intasàre, *v.t.* to obstruct, to block, to choke || **intasàrsi**, *v.r.* to become obstructed, to become blocked.

intasatúra, *s.f.* obstruction, stoppage.

intascàre, *v.t.* to pocket, to put into one's pocket: *intascò tutto il denaro che gli diedi*, he pocketed all the money I gave him.

intàtto, *ag.* intact, untouched; (*illeso*) uninjured; (*senza macchia*) unsullied, unblemished: *il suo patrimonio è ancora —*, his patrimony is still intact.

intavolàre, *v.t.* **1.** (*circondare di tavole*) to board up, to plank **2.** (*mettere su una tavola*) to put on a board **3.** (*iniziare*) to begin, to start; to enter into (sthg.): — *una discussione*, to start a discussion (*o* to raise a subject for discussion).

intavolàto, *s.m.* **1.** (*rar.*) (*riparo di tavole*) boarding, planking **2.** (*pavimento di tavole di legno*) plank floor.

intavolatúra, *s.f.* **1.** boarding, planking **2.** (*inizio*) beginning.

intedescàre, *v.t.*, **intedescàrsi**, *v.r.* to Germanize.

intedescàto, *ag.* Germanized; (*di lingua*) full of Germanisms.

integerrimaménte, *av.* incorruptibly.

integèrrimo, *ag.* strictly honest, incorruptible.

integràbile, *ag.* integrable.

integrabilità, *s.f.* integrability.

integràle, *ag.* **1.** integral: *calcolo —*, (*mat.*) integral calculus; *una parte — di un tutto*, an integral part of a whole **2.** (*completo*) integral, complete, entire, in full, whole: *edizione —*, unabridged edition; *pagamento —*, payment in full; *una restituzione —*, a complete restitution || *pane —*, brown bread || *s.m.* (*mat.*) integral.

integralménte, *av.* integrally, completely, entirely.

integraménte, *av.* **1.** uprightly, honestly **2.** (*completamente*) integrally, completely, entirely.

integraménto, *s.m.* integration.

integrànte, *ag.* integrant, integrating.

integràre, *v.t.* to integrate; to complete || **integràrsi**, *v.r.* to integrate oneself (with sthg.), to identify oneself (with sthg.).

integratívo, *ag.* integrative.

integratóre, *s.m.* integrator.

integrazióne, *s.f.* integration.

integrità, *s.f.* **1.** (*onestà*) uprightness, integrity, honesty **2.** (*completezza*) integrity, completeness, entireness, wholeness.

íntegro, *ag.* **1.** (*onesto*) upright, strictly honest **2.** (*completo*) integral, complete, entire; (*di testi*) unexpurgated, unabridged.

integumentàle, *ag.* (*bot. anat.*) integumental, integumentary.

integuménto, *s.m.* (*bot. anat.*) integument.

intelaiàre, *v.t.* **1.** to mount on the loom **2.** (*mec.*) to assemble.

intelaiatúra, *s.f.* **1.** (*mec.*) framework, trestle; (*di finestre*) sash; (*edil.*) framework, fabric: — *di fondazione*, (*scienza delle costruzioni*) grillage; — *di sostegno*, (*aer.*) outrigger **2.** (*l'intelaiare*) framing.

intellettívo, *ag.* intellective.

intellètto, *s.m.* **1.** intellect, mind; (*comprensione*) understanding: *l'uso dell'—*, the use of intellect; *l'umano non può capire queste cose*, the human mind cannot understand these things || *perdere il bene dell'—*, to lose one's wits || « *Saggio sull'— umano* », (*lett.*) " Essay on Human Understanding " **2.** (*persona di grande intelligenza*) intellect: *è uno dei migliori intelletti del nostro paese*, he is one of the best intellects in our country **3.** (*penetrazione*) insight, penetration.

intellettuàle, *ag.* **1.** intellectual: *facoltà intellettuali*, intellectual faculties; *lavoro —*, brain work **2.** (*iron.*) highbrow: *letteratura —*, highbrow literature || *s.c.* intellectual; (*iron.*) highbrow; (*neol. amer.*) egghead || *gli intellettuali*, (*spec. iron.*) the intelligentzia.

intellettualísmo, *s.m.* intellectualism.

intellettualità, *s.f.* intellectuality.

intellettualizzàre, *v.t.* to intellectualize.

intellettualménte, *av.* intellectually.

intellettualòide, *ag.s.c.* (*iron.*) highbrow.

intelligènte, *ag.* intelligent, clever: *un lavoro —*, an intelligent (*o* clever) piece of work || *essere — di pittura*, to be a connoisseur of painting.

intelligenteménte, *av.* intelligently, cleverly.

intelligènza, *s.f.* **1.** intelligence, understanding: *una persona di grande —*, a person of great intelligence (*o* understanding); *la sua condotta non mostra grande —*, his behaviour doesn't show much intelligence **2.** (*abilità*) cleverness: *questo lavoro è fatto con molta —*, this work has been done with great cleverness **3.** (*conoscenza*) knowledge: *ha una buona — di musica*, he has a good knowledge of music **4.** (*accordo, intesa*) agreement, understanding **5.** (*comprensione*) comprehension, understanding: *metterò alcune note in margine per una migliore — del testo*, I shall put some notes in the margin for a better understanding of the text **6.** (*fil.*) (*potenza dell'anima razionale*) understanding: *memoria, volontà e —*, memory, will and understanding || — *suprema*, (*teol.*) the Supreme Intelligence.

intelligíbile, *ag.* intelligible, comprehensible.

intelligibilità, *s.f.* intelligibility, comprehensibility.

intelligibilménte, *av.* intelligibly, clearly, comprehensibly.

intemeràta, *s.f.* **1.** (*rimprovero*) tirade, reprimand, rebuke: *fare un'— a qlcu.*, to reprimand (*o* to rebuke) s.o. **2.** (*discorso noioso*) rigmarole.

intemeràto, *ag.* faultless, stainless, irreproachable.

intemperànte, *ag.* intemperate, incontinent || *s.c.* intemperate person.

intemperanteménte,*av.*intemperately, incontinently.

intemperànza, *s.f.* intemperance: — *di linguaggio*, intemperance of speech.

intemperataménte, *av.* (*rar.*) intemperately.

intemperàto, *ag.* (*rar.*) intemperate, incontinent.

intempèrie, *s.f.pl.* inclement weather (*sing.*); inclemency of the weather (*sing.*): *esposto alle* —, exposed to the inclemency of the weather; *resistente alle* —, weather-proof.

intempestivaménte, *av.* untimely, unseasonably, inopportunely.

intempestività, *s.f.* untimeliness, unseasonableness.

intempestívo, *ag.* untimely, unseasonable, inopportune.

intendènte, *s.m.* 1. (*intenditore*) connoisseur 2. (*sovrintendente*) (super)intendent.

intendènza, *s.f.* 1. (*sovrintendenza*) (super)intendence 2. (*ufficio del sovrintendente*) superintendency.

intèndere, *v.t.* 1. (*capire*) to understand: *intendi cosa voglio dire?*, do you understand what I mean?; *mi fece* — *che non voleva venire*, he made me understand that he did not want to come; — *a rovescio*, to misunderstand; *mi diede a* — *che l'aveva fatto*, he gave me to believe that he had done it; — *ragione*, to listen to reason 2. (*udire*) to hear: *dillo ancora, per piacere, non ti ho inteso*, say it again, please, I didn't hear you; *ho inteso dire che è partito per l'America*, I have heard that he has left for America ‖ *non c'è peggior sordo di chi non vuol* —, *prov.* none so deaf as those who won't hear 3. (*significare*) to mean, to intend: *che cosa intendi con questa parola?*, what do you mean by this word? 4. (*avere intenzione di*) to intend, to purpose: *che cosa intendi fare?*, what do you intend (*o* purpose) to do? (*o* doing?); *intendo provare ancora*, I intend (*o* purpose) to try (*o* trying) again; *non intendevo offenderti*, I didn't mean to hurt your feelings; *non intendo essere preso in giro*, I don't want to be laughed at ‖ *non la intendo come voi*, I am not of your opinion (*o* I don't agree with you) ‖ **intèndersi,** *v.r.* 1. (*aver cognizione di*) to be a (good) judge, to be an expert (in sthg.), to know (about sthg.): *non m'intendo di pittura*, I am no judge of painting; *non mi intendo di queste cose*, I know nothing about these things 2. (*mettersi d'accordo*) to come to an agreement, to come to terms, to agree: *quei due ragazzi non s'intendono*, *non fanno che litigare*, those two boys do not agree, they do nothing but quarrel; *spero che essi s'intendano*, I hope they will come to an agreement ‖ *ci siamo intesi?*, is it clear?; *intendiamoci bene!*, let this be quite clear! ‖ *questo s'intende*, this goes without saying ‖ *s'intende*, of course ‖ *intendersela con qlcu.*, to have an' understanding with s.o.: *credo che l'avvocato se la intenda col testimone*, I think the lawyer is acting in concert with the witness; *intendetevela col mio segretario*, talk the matter over with my secretary; *ve la intendete a meraviglia*, you get on very well together.

intendiménto, *s.m.* 1. understanding, mind 2. (*proposito, intenzione*) intention, plan, purpose.

intenditóre, *s.m.*, **intenditríce,** *s.f.* connoisseur, expert (in, on sthg.), good judge: *è un* — *di pittura*, he is a connoisseur in (*o* of) painting (*o* he is a good judge of painting); *non sono un* — *di cani*, I am no judge of dogs.

intenebràre, intenebríre, *v.i.* to grow dark, to darken (anche *fig.*): *quando il sole tramonta, il giorno comincia a* —, when the sun sets, the day begins] to darken.

inteneriménto, *s.m.* 1. softening 2. (*commozione*) emotion, tenderness 3. (*compassione*) compassion, sympathy.

inteneríre, *v.t.* 1. to soften, to make tender 2. (*commuovere*) to move, to move to pity: — *qlcu.*, to touch s.o.'s heart ‖ **intenerírsi,** *v.r.* 1. to soften, to grow soft 2. (*commuoversi*) to be moved, to feel compassion.

intensaménte, *av.* intensely.

intensificàre, *v.t.* 1. to intensify 2. (*rendere più frequente*) to make more frequent ‖ **intensificàrsi,** *v.r.* 1. to intensify, to become more intense 2. (*diventare più frequente*) to become more frequent.

intensifieazióne, *s.f.* intensification.

intensità, *s.f.* 1. intensity, intenseness; (*di colore*) strength, depth: — *luminosa*, (*tv. fis.*) luminous intensity 2. (*violenza*) vehemence.

intensívo, *ag.* intensive: *coltura intensiva*, intensive cultivation; *metodo* —, intensive method.

intènso, *ag.* 1. intense; severe; (*di colore*) intense, deep: *dolore* —, severe pain; *freddo* —, severe (*o* intense) cold; *un'espressione intensa*, an intense expression 2. (*violento*) violent, vehement.

intentàbile, *ag.* 1. unattemptable 2. (*dir.*) suable.

intentàre, *v.t.* (*dir.*) to bring: — *causa contro qlcu.*, to bring an action against s.o.; — *una causa per danni*, to sue for damages.

intentàto, *ag.* 1. unattempted, untried: *non lasciar nulla* —, to leave no stone unturned 2. (*inesplorato*) unexplored.

intènto, *ag.* 1. fixed, intent: *uno sguardo* —, an intent look 2. (*occupato*) intent (on sthg.), busy (at, with, over sthg.): *è* — *a risolvere il problema*, he is intent on (solving) a problem; *era* — *al suo compito*, he was intent on his homework; *era* — *al suo libro*, he was absorbed in his book ‖ *s.m.* aim, purpose, object, end; (*intenzione*) intention: *lo disse con l'*— *di ingannare*, he said so with the intent to deceive (*o* with a view to deceiving); *lo fece con un* —, he did it with a purpose; *i nostri intenti sono diversi*, our ends are different; *raggiungere il proprio* —, to reach one's aim (*o* to gain one's ends) ‖ *con l'*—, *nell'*— *di fare*, with the intention (*o* purpose) of (*o* with a view to) doing.

intenzionàle, *ag.* intentional, wilful, deliberate.

intenzionalménte, *av.* intentionally, wilfully, deliberately, on purpose.

intenzionàto, *ag.* disposed, inclined, willing: *bene* —, well-disposed (*o* well-meaning): *essere ben* — *verso qlcu.*, to be well-disposed towards s.o. (*o* to mean well to s.o.); *male* —, ill-disposed (*o* evil-minded): *essere male* — *verso qlcu.*, to be ill-disposed towards s.o.; *non è* — *a venire*, he is not disposed (*o* willing) to come (*o* he does not intend to come).

intenzióne, *s.f.* intention, intent; purpose, design; (*desiderio*) wish; (*idea*) mind: *che intenzioni hai?*, what is your object?; *ho* — *di andare a vivere in campagna*, I have a mind to go and live in the country; *ho* — *di fare una gita*, I have a mind to take a trip; *lo colpì con l'*— *di ucciderlo*, he struck him with the intent to kill him; *lo disse con l'*— *di offenderti*, he said it with a view to hurting your feelings; *la mia* — *era di fare così*, my intention was to do like that; *non avevo nessuna* — *di farlo*, I had no intention of doing it (*o* I did not intend to do it *o* doing it); *quali sono le tue intenzioni?*, what are your intentions?; *le tue intenzioni sono buone ma non facili da realizzare*, your intentions are good but not easy to carry out ‖ *avere* — *di fare ql.co.*, to intend doing sthg.; *avere delle buone intenzioni*, to be well-meaning; *avere una mezza* —, to have half a mind; *fare ql.co. secondo le proprie intenzioni*, to do sthg. according to one's wishes; *fare una cosa senza* —, *con* —, to do sthg. without intention (*o* unintentionally), on purpose (*o* designedly) ‖ *la via dell'inferno è lastricata di buone intenzioni*, the road to hell is paved with good intentions.

intepidíre, *V.* **intiepidíre.**

interaménte, *av.* entirely, wholly, quite, fully, completely: — *ricoperto di pelle*, leather-lined throughout; *egli non è* — *cattivo*, he is not all bad; *voi avete* — *ragione*, you are absolutely right ‖ *capitale* — *versato*, (*comm.*) fully paid (up) capital.

intercalàre, *ag.* intercalary: *giorno, mese* —, intercalary day, month ‖ *s.m.* 1. (*ritornello*) refrain 2. (*modo di dire che si ripete per abitudine*) pet phrase.

intercalàre, *v.t.* to intercalate, to insert.

intercapèdine, *s.f.* (*interstizio*) interstice; (*edil.*) air space, hollow space; (*mar.*) interspace.

intercèdere, *v.i.* **1.** to intercede, to plead: — *presso qlcu. per qlcu.*, to plead (*o* to intercede) with s.o. for (*o* on behalf of) s.o. **2.** (*di spazio*) to exist, to lie; (*di tempo*) to elapse, to intervene: *la distanza che intercede fra le due case*, the distance existing between (*o* separating) the two houses; *intercedette molto tempo prima del suo ritorno*, a long time elapsed before his return; *le miglia che intercedono fra le due stazioni*, the miles lying between (*o* separating) the two stations.

intercellulàre, *ag.* intercellular.

intercessióne, *s.f.* intercession; (*mediazione*) mediation: — *a favore di qlcu.*, intercession on behalf of s.o.; *per — di qlcu.*, by intercession of s.o.

intercessóre, *s.m.* intercessor; (*mediatore*) mediator.

intercettaménto, *s.m.* interception.

intercettàre, *v.t.* (*lettere, telegrammi*) to intercept; (*luce*) to shut out; (*vapore*) to cut off, to shut off.

intercettatóre, *ag.* interceptive, intercepting ǁ *s.m.*, **intercettatríce,** *s.f.* interceptor.

intercettazióne, *s.f.* interception.

intercettóre, *V.* **intercettatóre.**

intercezióne, *s.f.* interception.

intercolúnnio, *s.m.* (*arch.*) intercolumniation.

intercomunàle, *s.f.* (*tel.*) (*a breve distanza*) toll-call; (*a lunga distanza*) long-distance call, trunk-call.

intercomunicànte, *ag.* intercommunicating, communicating: *stanze intercomunicanti*, communicating rooms; *treno con carrozze intercomunicanti*, corridor train.

intercomunicàre, *v.i.* to intercommunicate.

intercomunicazióne, *s.f.* intercommunication.

intercontinentàle, *ag.* intercontinental.

intercorrènte, *ag.* intercurrent.

intercorrènza, *s.f.* intercurrence.

intercórrere, *v.i.* **1.** (*di tempo*) to pass, to elapse, to slip away, to intervene: *fra le due lettere intercorse un lungo tempo*, a long time elapsed (*o* passed) between the two letters; *i mesi che intercorsero*, the months that intervened **2.** (*accadere*) to happen: *intercorsero molte cose spiacevoli*, many unpleasant things happened.

intercostàle, *ag.* (*anat.*) intercostal: *muscoli —*, intercostal muscles.

interdétto, *ag.* **1.** (*vietato*) prohibited, forbidden **2.** (*dir.*) interdicted, disqualified, disabled, incapable **3.** (*eccl.*) interdicted **4.** (*turbato, sconcertato*) disconcerted, nonplussed, perplexed: *restare —*, to remain dumbfounded ǁ *s.m.* (*eccl. dir.*) interdict.

interdigitàle, *ag.* (*anat.*) interdigital.

interdipendènza, *s.f.* interdependence.

interdíre, *v.t.* **1.** (*proibire*) to interdict, to forbid, to prohibit: — *qlco. a qlcu.*, to interdict (*o* to forbid) sthg. to s.o.; — *qlcu. dal fare qlco.*, to interdict (*o* to prohibit) s.o. from doing sthg. (*o* to forbid s.o. to do sthg.) **2.** (*dir.*) to interdict, to disqualify, to disable; to suspend: — *qlcu. dalle proprie funzioni*, to suspend s.o. from the execution of his duties **3.** (*eccl.*) to interdict, to lay under an interdict: — *un prete*, to lay a priest under an interdict.

interdizióne, *s.f.* **1.** interdiction, prohibition **2.** (*dir.*) disqualification, disablement: *colpire di — un alienato*, to impose judicial interdiction on a lunatic **3.** (*eccl.*) interdiction, interdict **4.** *tiro d'—*, (*artigl.*) standing barrage fire.

interessaménto, *s.m.* interest, concern: *egli mostrò molto — alla faccenda*, he showed great interest in (*o* concern for) the matter; *il suo — per la mia salute mi ha commosso*, his concern over my health has deeply moved me ǁ *per — di*, by the good offices of.

interessànte, *ag.* **1.** interesting: *un libro, un caso —*, an interesting book, case **2.** (*piacevole, attraente*) appealing, attractive **3.** (*importante*) important: *è — che tu sappia che è partito*, it is important for you to know that he has left **4.** *essere in stato —*, to be with a child: *una donna in stato —*, a woman with child (*o* an expectant mother *o* a pregnant woman).

interessàre, *v.t.* **1.** to interest: *questo libro mi interessa molto*, this book interests me a great deal (*o* I am very interested in this book) **2.** (*riguardare, toccare*) to concern, to touch: *la faccenda mi interessa da vicino*, the matter concerns me closely; *questo non lo interessa affatto*, this doesn't concern him at all **3.** (*implicare*) to affect, to implicate: *questa lesione non interessa il cuore*, this lesion does not affect the heart **4.** (*rendere interessato*) to interest, to entertain: *tenterò di interessarlo all'argomento*, I shall try to interest him in the subject **5.** (*comm.*) to interest: — *qlcu. in un'azienda*, to give s.o. an interest in a business ǁ *v.i.* **1.** to be of interest: *questo argomento non interessa ai nostri lettori*, this subject is of no interest to our readers **2.** (*importare*) to matter, to be important: *questo non interessa*, this does not matter; *ti interessa veramente saperlo?*, is it really important for you to know it? ǁ **interessàrsi,** *v.r.* **1.** to take an interest (in s.o., sthg.), to be interested (in s.o., sthg.): *egli si interessò molto al caso*, he took a great interest in the case **2.** (*preoccuparsi*) to care (for, about s.o., sthg.): *interessati che egli abbia tutto quello che gli occorre*, see that he has everything he needs; *interessati degli affari tuoi!*, mind your own business!; *chi si interesserà di lui dopo la mia partenza?*, who will care for (*o* take care of) him after my departure?; *egli non si interessa di questi problemi*, he does not care for these problems.

interessataménte, *av.* interestedly; with interest.

interessàto, *ag.* **1.** interested, concerned: *le parti interessate*, the parties concerned (*o* the interested parties); *essere — in un'azienda*, to have a concern (*o* an interest) in a business **2.** (*egoistico*) interested, selfish: *motivi interessati*, interested motives ǁ *amore —*, cupboard love ǁ *s.m.* party concerned, interested party: *tutti gli interessati*, all concerned.

interèsse, *s.m.* **1.** interest: *una faccenda di grande —*, a matter of great interest; *nell'— della scienza*, in the interest of science; *è tuo — farlo*, it is (in) your interest to do it; *non hai — a farlo*, you have no interest in doing it; *agire nell'— comune del popolo*, to act for the common good of the people; *avere un — nascosto da servire*, to have an axe to grind; *badare ai propri interessi*, to mind one's own business; *curare i propri interessi*, to look after one's own interests **2.** (*interessamento*) interest, concern: *il suo — alla musica*, his interest in music; *ciò suscitò grande —*, this aroused great interest; *prendere grande — a ql.co.*, to take interest in sthg. **3.** (*comm.*) interest: — *netto, lordo*, net, gross interest; — *semplice, composto*, simple, compound interest; *l'— decorre da...*, interest runs from...; *avere un — in un'azienda*, to have an interest (*o* a concern) in a business (*o* to hold interests in a business); *fruttare l'— del 5 %*, to bear (*o* to yield) interest at 5 %; *pagare l'— del 10 % su un prestito*, to pay a 10 % interest on a loan; *prendere a prestito con —*, to borrow at interest.

interessènza, *s.f.* (*comm.*) co-interest, profit-sharing: *avere un'—*, to have a share in the profits.

interézza, *s.f.* **1.** (*totalità*) entirety, completeness; wholeness **2.** (*integrità*) integrity.

interferènza, *s.f.* **1.** (*fis. rad.*) interference **2.** (*intromissione*) interference; intervention, intermeddling.

interferíre, *v.i.* **1.** (*fis. rad.*) to interfere **2.** (*intromettersi*) to interfere; to intervene, to meddle.

interferòmetro, *s.m.* (*fis.*) interferometer.

interfogliàre, *v.t.* to interleave.

interfogliàto, *ag.* interleaved.

interfogliatúra, *s.f.* interleaving; (*tip.*) slip-sheeting.

interfòglio, *s.m.* interleaf.

interiettívo, *ag.* (*gram.*) interjectional.

interiezióne, *s.f.* (*gram.*) interjection.

ínterim, *s.m.* interim: *assumere l'—*, to carry on (during a vacancy) ǁ *l'Interim*, (*st. relig.*) the Interim.

interinàle, *ag.* temporary; interim (*attributivo*).

interinalménte, *av.* temporarily; interim.

interinàto, *s.m.* interim, temporary office.

interíno, *ag.* temporary, provisional; interim (*attributivo*): *medico* —, locum-tenens ‖ *s.m.* deputy, substitute.

interióra, *s.f.pl.* entrails, bowels.

interióre, *ag.* **1.** (*intimo*) inner (*attributivo*); inward (*attributivo*); interior (*attributivo*): *felicità* —, inward happiness; *natura* —, inner (*o* inward) nature; *vita* —, inner (*o* interior) life **2.** (*interno*) internal; interior (*attributivo*) ‖ *s.m.*: *l'*—, the interior, the inside.

interiorità, *s.f.* **1.** (*natura intima*) inwardness **2.** (*vita interiore*) inner life.

interiorménte, *av.* **1.** (*intimamente*) innerly, inwardly, interiorly **2.** (*nell'interno*) inside, internally; within.

interlínea, *s.f.* **1.** space between the lines **2.** (*tip.*) lead.

interlineàre, *ag.* interlinear: *traduzione* —, interlinear.

interlineàre, *v.t.* **1.** to interline **2.** (*tip.*) to lead.

interlineàto, *ag.* (*tip.*) leaded.

interlineatúra, *s.f.* (*tip.*) leading, leading-out.

interlineazióne, *s.f.* interlineation, interlining.

interlíngua, *s.f.* artificial international language.

interlocutóre, *s.m.* interlocutor.

interlocutòrio, *ag.* interlocutory.

interlocutríce, *s.f.* interlocutrix, interlocutress.

interlocuzióne, *s.f.* interlocution.

interloquíre, *v.i.* **1.** to join in the conversation; to put in a word; (*fam.*) to chime in **2.** (*dir.*) to give an interlocutory judgement.

interlúdio, *s.m.* (*mus.*) interlude.

interlunàre, *ag.* (*astr.*) interlunar, interlunary.

interlúnio, *s.m.* (*astr.*) interlunation.

intermediàrio, *ag.* intermediary, intermediate ‖ *s.m.* **1.** mediator, go-between **2.** (*comm.*) middleman (*pl.* middlemen).

intermèdio, *ag.* intermediate: *colore* —, intermediate colour; *prodotto* —, (*chim. ind.*) intermediate product; *stadio, grado* —, intermediate stage, degree ‖ *una via intermedia, fig.* a middle course.

interméttere, *v.t.i.* (*rar.*) to intermit ‖ **interméttersi,** (*rar.*) per **intromèttersi.**

intermèzzo, *s.m.* **1.** (*intervallo*) interval **2.** (*teat. mus.*) intermezzo (*pl.* intermezzi, intermezzos).

interminàbile, *ag.* interminable, endless.

interminabilménte, *av.* interminably, endlessly.

interminàto, *ag.* (*poet.*) boundless.

intermissióne, *s.f.* intermission: *senza* —, without intermission (*o* uninterruptedly).‖

intermittènte, *ag.* intermittent; irregular: *corrente* —, (*elett.*) intermittent current; *febbre, dolore* —, intermittent fever, pain; *funzionamento* —, (*mec.*) intermittent working.

intermittènza, *s.f.* intermittence, intermittency.

intermodulazióne, *s.f.* (*rad.*) intermodulation.

intermuscolàre, *ag.* (*anat.*) intermuscular.

internaménte, *av.* **1.** (*all'interno*) inside, internally **2.** (*nell'intimo*) innerly, inwardly.

internaménto, *s.m.* internment: *campo d'*—, internment camp.

internàre, *v.t.* to intern: — *un pazzo,* to intern a madman; — *gli stranieri in tempo di guerra,* to intern aliens in war time ‖ **internàrsi,** *v.r.* to enter (into sthg.), to penetrate (into sthg.), to go deeply (into sthg.) (*anche fig.*): — *in una scienza,* to go deeply into a science.

internàto, *ag.* interned ‖ *s.m.* **1.** (*confinato politico*) internee **2.** (*scuola convitto*) boarding-school.

internazionàle, *ag.* international: *commercio* —, international trade; *diritto* —, international law ‖ **Internazionàle,** *s.f.* (*associazione operaia socialista*) International (Workmen's Association) ‖ *s.m.* (*inno dei lavoratori socialisti*) the Internationale.

internazionalísmo, *s.m.* (*pol.*) internationalism.

internazionalísta, *s.c.* (*pol.*) internationalist.

internazionalità, *s.f.* internationality.

internazionalizzàre, *v.t.* to internationalize.

internazionalizzazióne, *s.f.* internationalization.

intèrno, *ag.* **1.** internal; intcrior (*attributivo*); inner (*attributivo*); inside (*attributivo*): *angolo* —, (*geom.*) interior angle; *combustione interna,* internal combustion; *lato* —, inner side; *organi interni,* internal organs; *la parte interna di un corpo,* the internal part of a body (*o* the inside of a body); *superficie interna,* inner surface; *tasca interna,* inside pocket ‖ *alunno* —, boarder ‖ *commercio* —, home trade ‖ *medico* —, intern(e) ‖ *Ministero degli Interni,* (*in Gran Bretagna*) Home Office; (*negli Stati Uniti*) Department of the Interior; (*altrove*) Ministry of the Interior; *Ministro degli Interni,* (*in Gran Bretagna*) Home Secretary; (*negli Stati Uniti*) Secretary of the Interior; (*altrove*) Minister of the Interior **2.** (*interiore*) inner (*attributivo*); inward (*attributivo*): *una gioia interna,* an inward happiness **3.** (*continentale*) inland (*attributivo*): *città interna,* inland town ‖ *s.m.* interior, inside: *l'*— *di un baule,* the inside of a trunk; *l'*— *di una casa,* the interior of a house; *un soprabito con un* — *di pelliccia,* a coat with fur lining.

internòdio, *s.m.* (*bot.*) internode.

internunziatúra, *s.f.* (*eccl.*) internuncioship.

internúnzio, *s.m.* (*eccl.*) internuncio.

intéro, *ag.* **1.** (*tutto*) whole: *l'intera Europa,* the whole of Europe; *l'intera isola,* the whole island; *l'intera verità,* the whole truth; *un giorno* —, a whole day; *ne bevve un bicchiere* —, he drank a whole glass of it ‖ *per* —, wholly (*o* entirely *o* in full): *scrivete il vostro nome per* —, write your name in full **2.** (*completo, indiviso*) entire (*attributivo*); complete: *un'intera collezione,* a complete collection; *l'intera responsabilità,* the whole responsibility; *la mia intera fiducia,* my entire confidence **3.** (*onesto, integro*) upright, honest ‖ *s.m.* whole: *tre terzi fanno un* —, three thirds make a whole.

interoceànico, *ag.* interoceanic.

interòsseo, *ag.* (*anat.*) interosseous.

interpellànte, *ag.s.c.* interpellant.

interpellànza, *s.f.* interpellation, interrogation.

interpellàre, *v.t.* **1.** (*nell'uso parlamentare*) to interpellate **2.** (*dir.*) to summon **3.** (*interrogare*) to ask.

interpetràre, *e derivati,* V. **interpretàre,** *e derivati.*

interplanetàrio, *ag.* interplanetary.

interpolaménto, *s.m.* interpolation.

interpolàre, *v.t.* to interpolate, to insert.

interpolatóre, *s.m.,* **interpolatríce,** *s.f.* interpolator.

interpolazióne, *s.f.* interpolation.

interpórre, *v.t.* to interpose: — *la propria autorità, il proprio veto,* to interpose one's authority, one's veto ‖ **interpórsi,** *v.r.* **1.** to interpose, to mediate: — *fra due che litigano,* to interpose between two persons who are quarreling **2.** (*intervenire*) to intervene: — *in difesa di qlcu., in una lite,* to intervene in s.o.'s defence, in a quarrel.

interposizióne, *s.f.* **1.** interposition **2.** (*intervento*) intervention.

interpósto, *ag.* interposed ‖ *per interposta persona,* through the medium of a third party.

interpretàbile, *ag.* interpretable, explainable.

interpretàre, *v.t.* **1.** to interpret, to explain, to construe, to expound: *come interpreti i fatti?,* how do you explain the facts?; *come interpreti questi versi?,* how do you interpret (*o* construe) these lines?; — *un brano,* to construe a passage; — *un discorso, parole astruse,* to interpret a speech, abstruse words; — *la Sacra Scrittura,* to expound the Scriptures; — *un testo,* to interpret a text ‖ *male* —, to misunderstand (*o* to misinterpret): *hai male interpretato le mie parole,* you have misinterpreted my words **2.** (*teat. mus.*) to play, to interpret: *ella interpreterà la parte di Ofelia,* she will play (the part of) Ophelia; — *un film,* to star in a film; — *una parte,* to interpret a role **3.** — *i segnali,* (*mil.*) to read (*o* to make out) the signals.

interpretatívo, *ag.* interpretative, explanatory.

interpretazióne, *s.f.* **1.** interpretation: — *errata,* misinterpretation (o misconstruction); *si possono dare due interpretazioni di questi versi,* these lines may be given two interpretations; *dare una falsa — di un brano,* to misinterpret a passage; *dare una falsa — alle azioni di qlcu.,* to put a wrong intorpretation on s.o.'s actions **2.** (*teat. mus.*) interpretation, rendering; (*cine.*) starring.

interprete, *s.m.* **1.** interpreter: *studia le lingue perchè vuole diventare —,* he studies languages because he wants to become an interpreter; *fare da — a qlcu.,* to act as interpreter to s.o.; *parlare per mezzo di un —,* to speak through an interpreter **2.** (*mus.*) interpreter; (*teat. cine.*) actor; interpreter: *quel film ha ottimi interpreti,* that film has very good actors(o a very good cast).

interprovinciàle, *ag.* interprovincial.

interpúngere, *v.t.* to punctuate.

interpunzióne, *s.f.* punctuation.

interramónto, *s.m.* burial, interment.

interràre, *v.t.* **1.** (*seppellire*) to bury, to inter **2.** (*coprire di terra*) to earth (up) **3.** (*riempire di terra*) to fill up with earth, to silt (up) ‖ **interràrsi,** *v.r.* (*riempirsi di terra*) to fill with earth, to get filled with earth.

interré, *s.m.* (*st.*) interrex (*pl.* interreges).

interrégno, *s.m.* interregnum (*pl.* interregna).

interrogàre, *v.t.* **1.** to interrogate, to question, to ask (questions): *dovresti — il cameriere sul suo lavoro,* you should ask the waiter about his work; *fu interrogato dal giudice,* he was questioned by the judge; *lo interrogai a lungo ma non ebbi risposte soddisfacenti,* I asked him a lot of questions but I didn't get satisfactory answers **2.** (*consultare*) to consult, to examine: — *i fatti,* to consider (o to examine) the facts; — *la propria coscienza,* to sound one's conscience; — *qlcu. con lo sguardo,* to look at s.o. inquiringly; — *la storia,* to consult history **3.** (*esaminare*) to examine: *essere interrogato in latino,* to be examined in Latin.

interrogativaménte, *av.* interrogatively.

interrogatívo, *ag.* interrogative; inquiring, questioning: *pronome —,* (*gram.*) interrogative pronoun; *punto —,* question mark (o point of interrogation); *uno sguardo —,* an interrogative glance.

interrogatóre, *ag.* interrogating, interrogative ‖ *s.m.* **1.** interrogator, questioner **2.** (*esaminatore*) examiner.

interrogatòrio, *ag.* interrogatory, interrogative: *un tono —,* an interrogatory tone ‖ *s.m.* interrogatory, interrogation; questioning: *contro —,* (*dir.*) cross-examination; *i prigionieri furono sottoposti a un lungo —,* the prisoners underwent a long interrogation.

interrogatríce, *s.f.* **1.** questioner **2.** (*esaminatrice*) examiner.

interrogazióne, *s.f.* **1.** interrogation, question, query: *punto d'—,* question mark (o mark of interrogation) **2.** (*scolastica*) oral test **3.** (*parlamentare*) question.

interrómpere, *v.t.* **1.** to interrupt, to break off, to discontinue, to stop: *la gara fu interrotta dalla pioggia,* the match was interrupted by the rain; *questo palo interrompe la vista,* this pole cuts off the view; *scusa se ti interrompo,* excuse my interrupting you; *il traffico è stato interrotto per un'ora,* the traffic has been stopped for an hour; — *una conversazione, qlcu. che parla,* to interrupt a conversation, s.o. who is speaking; — *il corso di un fiume,* to intercept (o to interrupt) the flow of a river; — *il lavoro,* to interrupt work; — *qlcu. bruscamente,* to cut s.o. short; — *le trattative,* to break off negotiations; — *un viaggio,* to break a journey **2.** (*elett. tel.*) to cut off: — *una conversazione telefonica,* to cut off a call; — *la corrente,* to break (o to cut off o to switch off) the current ‖ **interrómpersi,** *v.r.* to stop, to break off: *egli si interruppe nel mezzo della conversazione,* he stopped in the middle of the conversation.

interrompiménto, *s.m.* interruption.

interrottaménte, *av.* interruptedly.

interrótto, *ag.* interrupted, broken off, cut off; (*di strada*) blocked: *voce interrotta,* broken voice.

interruttóre, *s.m.* **1.** interrupter **2.** (*elett.*) switch: — *a pressione,* press switch; *girare l'—,* (*per accendere*) to switch on; (*per spegnere*) to switch off.

interruzióne, *s.f.* interruption, break; (*di conversazione*) breaking in; (*di comunicazioni*) severance; (*di negoziati*) breaking off: — *del lavoro,* stoppage of work; *senza —,* without a break (o uninterruptedly).

intersecaménto, *s.m.* intersection.

intersecànte, *ag.* intersecting ‖ *s.f.* (*geom.*) intersecting line.

intersecàre, *v.t.* to intersect ‖ **intersecàrsi,** *v.r.* reciproco, to intersect; to cross each other (one another).

intersecazióne, intersezióne, *s.f.* intersection.

interspinàle, *ag.* (*anat.*) interspinal.

interstellàre, *ag.* interstellar.

interstiziàle, *ag.* interstitial.

interstízio, *s.m.* interstice.

intertrígine, *s.f.* (*med.*) intertrigo.

intertropicàle, *ag.* intertropical.

interurbàno, *ag.:* *allacciamenti interurbani,* trunk-connections; *telefonata interurbana,* trunk-call.

intervàllo, *s.m.* **1.** interval: *un — di due mesi,* a two months' interval; *a intervalli,* at intervals ‖ — *lucido,* (*med.*) lucid interval **2.** (*spazio*) space.

interveníre, *v.i.* **1.** to intervene: *le autorità intervennero e tutto fu sistemato,* the authorities intervened and everything was settled **2.** (*interferire*) to interfere: *non voglio — in queste cose,* I don't want to interfere in these things **3.** (*essere presente*) to attend (sthg.); to be present: *egli non intervenne alle celebrazioni,* he was not present at the celebrations; — *ad una adunanza,* to attend a meeting **4.** (*accadere*) to happen, to intervene: *niente intervenne dopo la tua partenza,* nothing happened after your departure **5.** (*chir.*) to operate.

interventísta, *s.c.* (*pol.*) interventionist.

intervènto, *s.m.* **1.** intervention: *il tuo — in questa faccenda è veramente necessario,* your intervention in this matter is really necessary ‖ *politica del non- —,* non-intervention policy **2.** (*interferenza*) interference: *il suo — nei miei affari mi dà ai nervi,* his interference in my affairs gets on my nerves **3.** (*presenza*) presence: *il suo — alla festa fu considerato un atto di sfida,* his presence at the party was taken as a challenge **4.** (*chir.*) operation: *subire un —,* to undergo an operation.

intervenúto, *ag.* (*presente*) present ‖ *s.m.* person present ‖ *gli intervenuti,* the people present.

intervenzióne, *s.f.* (*dir.*) intervention.

intervísta, *s.f.* interview: *avere un'— con qlcu.,* to have an interview with s.o.; *concedere un'— a qlcu.,* to grant s.o. an interview.

intervistàre, *v.t.* to interview: *il giornalista riuscì finalmente ad — la celebre attrice,* the journalist succeeded at last in interviewing the famous actress.

intervistàto, *ag.* interviewed ‖ *s.m.* person interviewed.

intervistatóre, *s.m.,* **intervistatríce,** *s.f.* interviewer.

interzàto, *ag.* (*arald.*) tierced.

intésa, *s.f.* **1.** (*accordo*) agreement, accord: *come d'—,* as agreed upon; *con l'— che,* on the understanding that ‖ *venire a un'—,* to come to an agreement (o to terms) ‖ *stare sull'—,* (*in guardia*) to be on the look-out **2.** (*comprensione reciproca*) mutual understanding: *l'— fra quei due è meravigliosa,* the mutual understanding between those two fellows is simply wonderful **3.** (*pol.*) entente ‖ *la Triplice Intesa,* (*st.*) the Triple Entente.

intéso, *ag.* **1.** (*convenuto, stabilito*) understood, agreed upon: *come —,* as agreed upon; *è (ben) — che tu devi venire con me,* it is (well) understood that you must come with me ‖ *—?, siamo intesi?,* is it clear? ‖ *non darsene per —,* to take no notice of it (o to turn a deaf ear to it o not to care a pin for it) **2.** (*mirante*) aiming (at sthg., at doing), meant (to do): *il Parlamento* *approvò un progetto di legge* — *a ridurre il prezzo del pane*, the Parliament passed a bill aiming at reducing the price of bread.

intèssere, *v.t.* to interweave: — *una stoffa con fili d'oro*, to interweave a material with golden threads ‖ — *le lodi di qlcu.*, to sing s.o.'s praises.

intessúto, *ag.* interwoven ‖ *un libro* — *di citazioni*, a book full of (*o* packed with) quotations.

intestàre, *v.t.* **1.** (*mettere l'intestazione a*) to head: — *un capitolo, una pagina*, to head a chapter, a page **2.** (*comm. dir.*) to register (under s.o.'s name); (*denaro*) to enter (in s.o.'s account): *la casa fu intestata a lui*, the house was registered under his name; *questo denaro sarà intestato a te*, this money will be entered in your account; — *un conto a qlcu.*, to put an account under s.o.'s name **3.** (*unire per la testata*) to join by the head ‖ **intestàrsi,** *v.r.* to take it into one's head; to be obstinate; to persist; to be determined: *se si intesta, non c'è modo di fargli cambiare idea*, if he is determined, there is no way to make him change his mind; *si è intestato a volerlo fare*, he has taken it into his head to do it.

intestàto¹, *ag.* **1.** headed: *carta intestata*, headed paper **2.** (*comm. dir.*) registered; entered (in s.o.'s account): *una casa intestata a mio padre*, a house registered under my father's name; *denaro* — *a me*, money entered in my account **3.** (*ostinato*) stubborn, obstinate: — *nelle proprie decisioni*, stubborn in one's decisions.

intestàto², *ag.* (*dir.*) (*senza testamento*) intestate.

intestatúra, *s.f.* butt: — *del fasciame*, (*mar.*) butt in the planking.

intestazióne, *s.f.* **1.** heading, head-line: — *di carta da lettera*, letter-head; *l'* — *di un giornale*, the heading of a newspaper **2.** (*titolo*) title.

intestinàle, *ag.* intestinal.

intestíno, *ag.* intestine, internal, domestic, civil: *guerre intestine*, civil wars ‖ *s.m.* intestine, gut: *gli intestini*, the intestines (*o* the guts); — *tenue, crasso*, small, large intestine.

intiepidíre, *v.t.* **1.** (*scaldare un poco*) to warm (up), to make lukewarm: *devo intiepidirti un poco di latte?*, shall I warm you up some milk?; *il sole ha intiepidito l'aria*, the sun has warmed the air **2.** (*raffreddare un poco*) to cool (down); *fig.* to abate, to mitigate: *che cosa ha intiepidito i suoi sentimenti?*, what has cooled down his feelings?; *la pioggia ha intiepidito l'aria*, the rain has cooled the air ‖ *v.i.*, **intiepidírsi,** *v.r.* **1.** (*riscaldarsi un poco*) to warm up; to become lukewarm: *l'aria si è intiepidita*, the air has warmed up **2.** (*raffreddarsi un poco*) to cool down (anche *fig.*): *la sua indignazione si intiepidì*, his indignation cooled down.

intiéro, *V.* **intéro.**

intimaménte, *av.* **1.** intimately, closely: — *connesso*, intimately connected **2.** (*profondamente*) deeply; (*fam.*) at bottom: *sono* — *convinto che sia uno sciocco*, at bottom I am convinced he is a fool.

intimàre, *v.t.* **1.** (*ordinare*) to order, to command, to enjoin: *mi intimò di farlo*, he ordered me to do it; — *il silenzio*, to enjoin silence **2.** (*ingiungere*) to summon: — *a qlcu. di pagare*, to summon s.o. to pay; — *la resa a qlcu.*, to summon s.o. to surrender; — *lo sfratto*, to evict **3.** (*notificare*) to serve, to notify: — *una citazione a qlcu.*, (*dir.*) to serve a summons on s.o.; — *la guerra*, to declare war.

intimazióne, *s.f.* **1.** (*ordine*) order, injunction **2.** (*ingiunzione*) summons **3.** (*notifica*) intimation, notification: — *di guerra*, declaration of war.

intimidazióne, *s.f.* intimidation, threatening: *arrendersi all'* — *di qlcu.*, to surrender to s.o.'s intimidation.

intimidíre, *v.t.* **1.** to make shy, to make timid **2.** (*intimorire*) to intimidate, to cow ‖ **intimidírsi,** *v.r.* **1.** to become shy, to become timid **2.** (*intimorirsi*) to get frightened, to get nervous; to be intimidated, to be cowed: *alle sue minacce ella si intimidì*, at his threat she got frightened; *non intimiditevi!*, don't be frightened!.

intimidíto, *ag.* **1.** shy, timid: *sentirsi* —, to feel shy (*o* uneasy) **2.** (*intimorito*) frightened, nervous; intimidated, cowed.

intimità, *s.f.* **1.** privacy, intimacy: *l'* — *della propria casa*, the privacy of one's home; *non voglio disturbare la vostra* —, I don't want to intrude upon your intimacy **2.** (*intrinsechezza*) inwardness: *l'* — *dei suoi pensieri*, the inwardness of his thoughts **3.** (*familiarità*) familiarity: *non trattatela con troppa* —*!*, don't treat her with too much familiarity!.

íntimo, *ag.***1.**intimate, close: *un amico* —, an intimate friend; *una relazione intima*, a close relation-ship **2.** (*intrinseco, interno*) intimate; inner, inward, innermost, inmost (*attributivi*): *intima felicità*, inner happiness; *i pensieri intimi*, innermost (*o* inmost *o* inner) thoughts; *la struttura intima dell'atomo*, the intimate structure of the atom; *vita intima*, inward life **3.** (*profondo*) deep: *un'intima convinzione*, a deep belief; *un* — *dolore*, a deep sorrow; *le intime viscere della terra*, the bowels of the earth **4.** (*a quattr'occhi*) tête-à-tête (*attributivo*); (in) private: *una cena intima*, a tête-à-tête dinner; *una conversazione intima*, a private (*o* tête-à-tête) conversation (*o* a conversation in private) ‖ *s.m.* **1.** (*amico*) intimate, intimate friend **2.** (*animo*) soul, heart: *nell'* — *ne sono sicuro*, in my heart I am sure of it **3.** (*parte interna, intima*) bottom: *dall'* — *del mio cuore*, from the bottom of my heart; *nell'* — *è un buon uomo*, at bottom he is a good man.

intimoriménto, *s.m.* **1.** (*intimidazione*) intimidation, frightening **2.** (*paura*) fear, fright.

intimorire, *v.t.* to frighten, to intimidate ‖ **intimorírsi,** *v.r.* to get frightened, to be frightened, to be afraid, to be scared: *si intimorì alla presenza del pubblico*, he got frightened in (*o* by) the presence of the public.

intíngere, *v.t.* **1.** to dip: — *la penna nell'inchiostro*, to dip one's pen in the ink **2.** (*inumidire*) to moisten **3.** (*inzuppare*) to soak: — *il pane nel latte*, to soak bread in milk.

intíngolo, *s.m.* **1.** (*manicaretto*) tasty dish, dainty dish **2.** (*salsa*) sauce **3.** (*sugo di carne*) gravy **4.** (*piatto di carne in umido*) stew.

intínto, *ag.* **1.** dipped **2.** (*inumidito*) moistened (with sthg.) **3.** (*inzuppato*) soaked ‖ *s.m.* *V.* **intíngolo.**

intirizziménto, *s.m.* **1.** (*intorpidimento*) benumbment, numbness **2.** (*irrigidimento*) stiffening, stiffness.

intirizzíre, *v.t.* **1.** (*intorpidire*) to benumb, to numb, to make numb **2.** (*irrigidire*) to stiffen ‖ **intirizzírsi,** *v.r.* **1.** (*intorpidirsi*) to grow numb, to grow benumbed **2.** (*irrigidirsi*) to stiffen.

intirizzíto, *ag.* **1.** (*intorpidito*) numb, benumbed: *sono* — *dal freddo*, I am numb with cold **2.** (*irrigidito*) stiff.

intisichíre, *v.i.* **1.** (*divenir tisico*) to go into consumption **2.** (*intristire*) to grow weak, to pine away, to languish **3.** (*di pianta*) to wilt.

intisichíto, *ag.* **1.** (*tisico*) consumptive **2.** (*debole*) weak **3.** (*di pianta*) wilted, stunted.

intitolaménto, *s.m.* **1.** entitling, naming **2.** (*dedica*) dedication.

intitolàre, *v.t.* **1.** to entitle, to name: *devo ancora* — *il mio libro*, I have still to entitle my book **2.** (*dedicare*) to dedicate: *la chiesa è stata intitolata a S. Giuseppe*, the church has been dedicated to St. Joseph.

intitolàto, *ag.* **1.** entitled, bearing the title (of sthg.) **2.** (*dedicato*) dedicated: *la strada è intitolata a Giorgio Washington*, the street is dedicated to George Washington.

intitolazióne, *s.f.* **1.** (*l'intitolare*) entitling **2.** (*titolo*) title, heading **3.** (*dedica*) dedication.

intoccàbile, *ag.* untouchable ‖ *s.m.* (*persona fuori casta, in India*) untouchable.

intolleràbile, *ag.* intolerable, unbearable.

intollerabilità, *s.f.* intolerability, intolerableness.

intollerabilménte, *av.* intolerably; unbearably: *è — pieno di sè*, he is unbearably (*o* intolerably) conceited.

intolleránte, *ag.s.m.* intolerant.

intolleránza, *s.f.* intolerance: *— alla luce*, intolerance of light; *— religiosa*, religious intolerance; *avere — per un medicamento*, to be intolerant of a drug.

intonacàre, *v.t.* (*edil.*) to plaster; to whitewash; to distemper.

intonacatríce, *s.f.* (*edil.*) plaster sprayer.

intonacatúra, *s.f.* (*edil.*) plastering; whitewashing: *— a spruzzo*, gun plastering; *— grezza*, pargeting.

intonachíno, *s.m.* (*edil.*) plaster finish: *— a gesso*, putty.

intònaco, *s.m.* plaster; whitewash; distemper: *dar l'— a un muro*, to plaster (*o* to whitewash) a wall.

intonàre, *v.t.* **1.** (*cominciare a cantare*) to tune up, to strike up: *intonarono l'inno nazionale*, they struck up the national anthem **2.** (*accordare*) to tune, to attune; (*mediante corista*) to tune up: *— uno strumento*, to tune an instrument; *i suonatori stavano ancora intonando i loro strumenti*, the players were still tuning up their instruments **3.** (*cantilenare, salmodiare*) to intone: *— un canto spirituale*, to intone a spiritual ‖ **intonàrsi**, *v.r.* to be in tune (with sthg.); to tone (with sthg.); to harmonize (with sthg.); to match (with sthg.): *la coperta s'intona con le tende*, the bed-spread tones with the curtains; *non s'intona con l'ambiente*, it is not in tune with its surroundings; *questi due colori non s'intonano*, these two colours do not match.

intonàto, *ag.* **1.** (*in armonia*) in tune (with sthg.); in harmony (with sthg.): *essere —*, to be in tune; *essere — all'ambiente*, to be in tune with the surroundings; *non essere —*, to be out of tune **2.** (*di colori*) matching: *questi due colori non sono intonati*, these two colours do not match.

intonazióne, *s.f.* **1.** intonation, pitch: *— della voce*, intonation (*o* pitch) of the voice **2.** (*l'intonare strumenti*) tuning **3.** (*tono di voce, colore*) tone.

intònso, *ag.* **1.** (*non tagliato*) uncut, untrimmed **2.** (*non raso*) unshaven; (*di animali*) unshorn.

intontíre, *v.t.* to stun; to daze: *fu intontito da un colpo in testa*, he was stunned by a blow on his head ‖ *v.i.*, **ntontírsi**, *v.r.* to be stunned, to become dazed

intontíto, *ag.* stunned, dazed; (*istupidito*) dull, stupefied: *quando mi sveglio sono sempre —*, when I wake up I always feel dazed.

intoppàre, *v.t.* (*incontrare per caso*) to come across (s.o., sthg.) ‖ *v.i.* **1.** (*imbattersi*) to stumble (across sthg.): *— in un errore*, to come across a mistake **2.** (*inciampare*) to stumble (over sthg.): *egli intoppò in un sasso*, he stumbled over a stone **3.** (*balbettare*) to stumble over one's words, to stammer.

intòppo, *s.m.* **1.** obstacle, hindrance, difficulty: *trovare intoppi sul proprio cammino*, to find obstacles (*o* difficulties) in one's way **2.** *fig.* hitch, impediment, stumbling-block: *la faccenda continuò senza intoppi*, the matter went on without a hitch.

intorbidàre, *v.t.* **1.** (*render torbido*) to make turbid, to make muddy, to muddy **2.** (*confondere, turbare*) to confuse, to confound; to trouble: *la sua mente era intorbidata da pensieri assurdi*, his mind was troubled with preposterous thoughts ‖ **intorbidàrsi**, *v.r.* **1.** (*diventar torbido*) to become turbid, to become muddy **2.** (*divenir confuso, difficile*) to become troubled: *la situazione politica si intorbida*, the political situation is getting troubled **3.** (*offuscarsi*) to darken, to get dark; (*della vista*) to grow dim.

intorbidàto, *ag.* **1.** (*torbido*) turbid, muddy: *acque intorbidate*, muddied waters; *fig.* troubled waters **2.** (*confuso*) confused, troubled **3.** (*di vista*) dim.

intorbidíre, *V.* intorbidàre.

intormentíre, *v.t.* to benumb, to make numb: *i suoi*

piedi erano intormentiti dal freddo, his feet were benumbed by (*o* with) cold ‖ *v.i.*, **intormentírsi**, *v.r.* to become benumbed, to grow numb.

intórno, *av.* round, around: *per un miglio —*, for a mile round; *c'è uno steccato tutt'—*, there is a fence all (a)round; *si sedettero tutt'—*, they sat all around; *guardare —*, to look around ‖ *d'ogni —*, on every side ‖ *levati d'—!*, go away! ‖ *andare —*, (*a zonzo, in giro*) to go around ‖ **intórno a**, *l. prep.* **1.** round, around, about: *— a me*, around me; *seduti — alla tavola*, sitting round the table; *costruirono delle mura — alla città*, they built walls about (*o* round) the city **2.** (*circa*) about: *è — ai cinquanta*, he is about fifty; *vieni — alle cinque*, come about five (*o'* clock) **3.** (*su di, a proposito di*) about: *che cosa sai — a lui?*, what do you know about him?; *scrisse un libro — ai suoi viaggi*, he wrote a book about his travels.

intorpidiménto, *s.m.* numbness; torpor, torpidity.

intorpidíre, *v.t.* to benumb, to make numb ‖ *v.i.*, **intorpidírsi**, *v.r.* to grow numb; to become torpid.

intorpidíto, *ag.* benumbed; numb; torpid: *— dal freddo*, numb with cold.

intossicàre, *v.t.* to intoxicate; to poison.

intossicàto, *ag.* intoxicated; poisoned.

intossicazióne, *s.f.* intoxication; poisoning: *— del sangue*, blood-poisoning.

intostíto, *ag.* hardened, hard.

intozzàre, **intozzíre**, *v.i.* (*di persone, animali*) to grow squat.

íntra, (*poet. arc.*) per **fra**[1].

intradòsso, *s.m.* (*arch.*) intrados.

intraducíbile, *ag.* untranslatable.

intraducibilità, *s.f.* untranslatableness.

intraducibilménte, *av.* untranslatably.

intralasciàre, (*rar.*) per **tralasciàre**.

intralciaménto, *s.m.* **1.** hindering, hampering **2.** (*ostruzione*) obstruction.

intralciàre, *v.t.* **1.** (*ostacolare*) to hinder, to hamper, to impede, to encumber, to embarrass; to interfere with (sthg.): *la gonna mi intralcia quando corro*, my skirt hampers (*o* encumbers) me while running; *la situazione politica intralciò il mio lavoro*, the political situation interfered with my work; *— il progresso*, to hinder progress; *essere intralciato dalla povertà*, to be hampered by poverty **2.** (*ostruire*) to obstruct, to block (up).

intràlcio, *s.m.* **1.** hindrance, hitch, encumbrance, obstacle **2.** (*ostruzione*) obstruction.

intrallàzzo, *s.m.* (*neol.*) **1.** (*intrigo*) plotting **2.** (*imbroglio*) swindle **3.** (*mercato nero*) black market.

intramésso, *ag.* interposed ‖ *s.m.* (*cuc.*) side-dish.

intraméttere, *v.t.* to interpose ‖ **intraméttersi**, *V.* introméttersi.

intramezzàre, *v.t.* to interpose; to alternate: *— risa a lacrime*, to alternate between laughter and tears.

intramuscolàre, *ag.* intermuscular.

intransigènte, *ag.* intransigent, strict, uncompromising, intolerant (of sthg.); fanatical: *è un cattolico —*, he is a very strict Catholic.

intransigènza, *s.f.* intransigence, intolerance.

intransitivaménte, *av.* (*gram.*) intransitively.

intransitívo, *ag.s.m.* (*gram.*) intransitive.

intrappolàre, *v.t.* to entrap, to trap, to ensnare.

intraprendènte, *ag.* enterprising, bold; clever; prompt: *una persona —*, an enterprising person; *mostrare uno spirito —*, to show enterprise (*o* initiative).

intraprendènza, *s.f.* enterprise, initiative; boldness; cleverness.

intraprèndere, *v.t.* to undertake, to engage in (sthg.), to embark on (sthg.), to venture on (sthg.), to begin, to start: *— attività nuove*, to embark on new enterprises; *— cose rischiose*, to venture on risky things; *— un lavoro*, to undertake (*o* to engage in) a piece of work; *— una professione*, to go in for a profession;

— *i propri studi*, to begin one's studies; — *un viaggio*, to take (*o* to set out on *o* to start on) a journey.

intraprenditóre, *V*. **impresàrio**.

intraprésa, *V*. **imprésa**.

intrattàbile, *ag.* intractable, unmanageable, ungovernable; refractory (anche *metal.*): *bambino* —, intractable child; *carattere* —, ungovernable temper.

intrattabilità, *s.f.* intractability, intractableness, ungovernableness; refractoriness (anche *metal.*).

intrattabilménte, *av.* intractably, ungovernably.

intrattenére, *v.t.* to entertain; (*ospiti*) to play host to (s.o.): *ci intrattenne con le sue esperienze di viaggio*, he entertained us (*o* kept us amused) with his travel experiences; *puoi intrattenerlo mentre sarò fuori?*, can you entertain him while I am out?; *sa* — *i suoi ospiti piacevolmente*, he can entertain his guests pleasantly ‖ — *una corrispondenza con qlcu.*, to keep up a correspondence with s.o. ‖ **intrattenérsi**, *v.r.* 1. (*fermarsi*) to stop: *si intrattenne a chiacchierare con lei*, she stopped to have a chat with her; *si intrattenne qui per circa un'ora*, he stopped here for about an hour 2. (*dilungarsi*) to dwell (upon sthg.), to linger (over sthg.): — *su un argomento*, to dwell upon a subject.

intratteniménto, *s.m.* entertainment.

intrav(v)edére, *v.t.* 1. (*vedere di sfuggita*) to catch a glimpse of (s.o., sthg.): *l'ho appena intravisto*, I have only caught a glimpse of him 2. (*vedere indistintamente*) to see indistinctly: *si intravedeva una nave all'orizzonte*, a ship was dimly (*o* indistinctly) seen on the horizon 3. (*avere una vaga idea di*) to have a vague idea of (sthg.); *intravvedo quanto tu vuoi dire*, I have a vague idea (*o* notion) of what you mean (*o fam.* I guess what you mean) 4. (*prevedere*) to foresee: *nessuno poteva* — *questo risultato*, nobody could foresee this result.

intravvenire, *V*. **intervenire**.

intrecciaménto, *s.m.* 1. interlacement; intertwinement 2. (*l'intrecciare*) interlacing, intertwisting, intertwining; (*di nastri, capelli*) braiding, plaiting.

intrecciàre, *v.t.* 1. to interlace, to twist, to intertwist, to intertwine; to weave, to interweave: — *cestini di giunco*, to weave baskets out of reeds; — *rami*, to intertwine branches ‖ — *una conversazione*, to fall into conversation ‖ — *danze*, to dance ‖ — *una relazione amorosa*, to embark on a love affair 2. (*nastri, capelli*) to braid, to plait ‖ **intrecciàrsi**, *v.r.* 1. to interlace, to intertwist, to intertwine: *rami che si intrecciano*, interlacing branches 2. (*nastri, capelli*) to braid, to plait: *la ragazza si intrecciò i capelli*, the girl plaited her hair.

intrecciàto, *ag.* interlaced, intertwisted, intertwined; woven, interwoven; (*di nastri, capelli*) braided, plaited: *capelli intrecciati*, plaited hair; *mani intrecciate*, interlocked hands.

intréccio, *s.m.* 1. interlacing 2. (*trama di un'opera*) plot.

intrepidaménte, *av.* bravely, intrepidly, fearlessly.

intrepidézza, intrepidità, *s.f.* bravery, intrepidity.

intrèpido, *ag.* brave, intrepid, fearless, bold.

intricaménto, *s.m.* tangle, entanglement; knot.

intricàre, *v.t.* to tangle, to entangle ‖ **intricàrsi**, *v.r.* to get entangled: *la mia lenza si è intricata tra le alghe*, my fishing-line has got entangled in some weeds.

intricataménte, *av.* intricately.

intricàto, *ag.* intricate; (*ingarbugliato*) tangled, entangled; (*complicato*) complicated: *una faccenda intricata*, a complicated matter.

intríco, *s.m.* tangle, entanglement; knot.

intrídere, *v.t.* 1. (*inzuppare*) to soak 2. (*impastare, farina, ecc.*) to temper, to knead, to mix 3. (*imbrattare*) to soil, to dirty, to make dirty.

intrigànte, *ag.* intriguing, meddlesome: *è un diplomatico* —, he is an intriguing diplomat ‖ *s.c.* intriguer, meddler, busybody; (*arrivista*) pusher: *sei un vero* —!, you are a real busybody!.

intrigàre, *v.t.* to entangle, to mix up ‖ *v.i.* to intrigue, to plot ‖ **intrigàrsi**, *v.r.* (*ingerirsi*) to meddle (with, in sthg.), to get involved (in sthg.); to get mixed up (with sthg.), to interfere (with sthg.); (*frapporsi*) to intervene: *non voglio intrigarmi in queste cose*, I don't want to meddle with (*o* to get involved in) these things.

intrígo, *s.m.* intrigue, plot, plotting, conspiracy: *non ero al corrente di questo* —, I was not informed about this plot; *fare intrighi*, to intrigue (*o* to plot *o* to conspire); *fiutare un*—, to smell a rat.

intrinsecaménte, *av.* intrinsically.

intrínseco, *ag.* 1. intrinsic, real, essential: *il valore* — *di una cosa*, the intrinsic (*o* real) value of a thing 2. (*intimo*) intimate; inner (*attributivo*): *amico* —, intimate friend; *il mio io* —, my inner self ‖ *s.m.* 1. (*intimo*) soul; (*essenziale*) essence: *nel suo* —, in his soul; *guardare l'* — *delle cose*, to look at the essence of things 2. (*amico*) intimate.

intrinsichézza, *s.f.* intimacy.

intríso, *ag.* 1. (*inzuppato*) soaked (in sthg.), drenched (with sthg.): — *d'acqua*, soaked in (*o* drenched with) water; *straccio* — *d'olio*, oil-soaked rag 2. (*imbrattato*) soiled (with sthg.), stained (with sthg.), dirty (with sthg.): *ho le mani intrise di farina*, my hands are dirty with flour ‖ *s.m.* mash; paste.

intristiménto, *s.m.* 1. (*depravamento*) depravity, wickedness 2. (*deperimento*) decay, pining away, weakening 3. (*di piante*) stuntedness; wilt; (*di fiori*) drooping.

intristíre, *v.i.* 1. (*incattivire*) to grow wicked 2. (*deperire*) to decay, to pine away, to weaken 3. (*di piante*) to grow stunted; to wilt; (*di fiori*) to droop.

intristíto, *ag.* 1. (*incattivito*) grown wicked 2. (*deperito*) decayed, weakened, sickly 3. (*di piante*) stunted; wilted; (*di fiori*) drooping.

introdótto, *ag.* 1. (*importato*) imported, introduced: *merci introdotte di contrabbando*, smuggled goods; *merci introdotte in Italia*, goods imported into Italy 2. (*conosciuto*) well-known, well-established: *persona introdotta negli ambienti commerciali, nell'alta società*, person well-known (*o* well-established) in business circles, in high society 3. (*esperto, istruito*) well acquainted (with sthg.): — *nella materia*, well acquainted with the matter.

introduciménto, *s.m.* 1. introduction 2. (*l'introdurre*) introducing.

introdúrre, *v.t.* 1. (*far penetrare*) to introduce (anche *fig.*); to bring in; (*inserire*) to insert: *i cinesi introdussero la seta in Europa*, the Chinese introduced silk into Europe; — *una chiave nella toppa*, to insert a key in the lock; — *con forza*, (*ficcare*) to thrust; — *una nuova abitudine, idea nella società*, to bring a new habit, idea into society; — *qlcu. allo studio della letteratura inglese*, to introduce s.o. to the study of English literature; *per comperare caramelle* — *una moneta nel distributore automatico*, to buy sweets put a coin in the slot (-machine) ‖ — *un discorso*, to bring up a subject 2. (*fare entrare*) to show in, to usher, to let in: *introducetelo!*, let him in!; *il maggiordomo mi introdusse in salotto*, the butler ushered me into the drawing-room; — *furtivamente, di soppiatto qlcu.*, to slip s.o. in: *l'introdusse in casa di soppiatto*, he slipped him into the house 3. (*presentare*) to introduce: *lo introdussi in casa Rossi*, I introduced him to the Rossis; — *qlcu. con una lettera di raccomandazione*, to give s.o. a letter of introduction; — *qlcu. in società*, to introduce s.o. into society 4. (*importare*) to import: — *di contrabbando*, to smuggle 5. (*nelle narrazioni, far parlare e agire*) to introduce, to bring in: *il Manzoni ha introdotto nel suo romanzo alcuni personaggi storici*, Manzoni brought some historical characters into his novel ‖ **introdúrsi**, *v.r.* (*penetrare*) to get into (sthg.), to penetrate (sthg.): *i ladri si introdussero nel negozio attraverso una finestra*, the thieves got into the shop through a window; — *furtivamente*, to slip in; — *strisciando*, to creep in.

introduttívo, *ag.* introductory, preliminary.

introduttóre, *s.m.,* **introduttríce,** *s.f.* introducer.

introduzióne, *s.f.* introduction: — *alla filosofia aristotelica,* introduction to Aristotle's philosophy; *scrivere l'* — *di un libro,* to write the introduction to a book.

introitàre, *v.t.* to cash, to collect.

intròito, *s.m.* **1.** (*comm.*) profit, gain; receipts (*pl.*), return; takings (*pl.*): *gli introiti superano le spese,* receipts exceed expenses **2.** (*eccl.*) introit.

intromésso, *ag.* interposed, introduced, inserted.

introméttere, *v.t.* to interpose, to introduce, to insert ‖ **introméttersi,** *v.r.* **1.** (*ingerirsi*) to interfere (with sthg.), to meddle (in, with sthg.): — *nelle cose altrui,* to interfere with other people's things **2.** (*interporsi*) to interpose, to intervene: *si intromise fra i due litiganti,* he interposed between the two contending parties; — *in una lite,* to intervene in a dispute.

intromissióne, *s.f.* **1.** intervention, interference, intrusion **2.** (*intercessione*) intercession, intervention.

intronàre, *e derivati,* V. **rintronàre,** *e derivati.*

intronfiàre, *v.i.* to be puffed up with pride.

intronizzàre, *v.t.* to enthrone.

introspettívo, *ag.* introspective.

introspezióne, *s.f.* introspection.

introvàbile, *ag.* not to be found, undiscoverable.

introversióne, *s.f.* (*psicologia*) introversion.

introvèrso, introvertíto, *ag.* (*psicologia*) introverted ‖ *s.m.* (*psicologia*) introvert.

intrúdere, *v.t.* to intrude, to thrust in ‖ **intrúdersi,** *v.r.* to intrude: *non voglio intrudermi nella vostra compagnia,* I don't want to intrude into your company.

intrufolàrsi, *v.r.* to intrude, to slip in, to creep in: *egli si intrufolò senza farsi vedere,* he slipped in without being seen; *egli voleva* — *a tutti i costi,* he wanted to intrude at any cost.

intrugliàre, *v.t.* to mix up, to concoct ‖ **intrugliàrsi,** *v.r.* (*insudiciarsi*) to get soiled.

intrúglio, *s.m.* **1.** bad mixture, bad concoction **2.** (*confusione*) mess, muddle **3.** (*lavoro, libro, ecc. malfatto*) a botched piece of work.

intruppaménto, *s.m.* **1.** throng, crowd **2.** (*l'intrupparsi*) trooping, thronging.

intruppàrsi, *v.r.* to troop, to throng.

intrusióne, *s.f.* intrusion.

intrusívo, *ag.* intrusive.

intrúso, *s.m.* intruder, interloper.

intubàre, *v.t.* (*chir.*) to intubate.

intubazióne, *s.f.* (*chir.*) intubation, tubage.

intuíre, *v.t.* to realize, to know by intuition; to guess, to divine: *intuii che era infelice non appena la vidi,* I realized she was in distress as soon as I saw her; — *i pensieri di qlcu.,* to guess s.o.'s thoughts.

intuitivaménte, *av.* intuitively.

intuitívo, *ag.* intuitive: *mente, conoscenza, verità intuitiva,* intuitive mind, knowledge, truth ‖ *ma è* —*!,* it is evident!.

intuíto, *ag.* realized, known by intuition; guessed.

intúito, *s.m.* intuition, insight: *per* —, by intuition; *una persona d'*—, a man of insight; *il suo* — *per questo genere di cose è sorprendente,* his insight into this kind of things is surprising; *sapere ql.co. per* —, to know sthg. by intuition.

intuizióne, *s.f.* intuition, perception: *l'* — *della verità,* the perception of truth; *per* —, by intuition.

intuizionísmo, *s.m.* (*fil.*) intuitionism.

intumescènte, *ag.* intumescent.

intumescènza, *s.f.* intumescence; swelling.

intumidíre, *v.i.* to swell (up).

inturgidiménto, *s.m.* swelling, turgescence.

inturgidíre, *v.i.,* **inturgidírsi,** *v.r.* to become turgid, to swell (up); to become distended: *le mammelle della capra erano inturgidite dal latte,* the goat's udders were distended with milk.

inturgidíto, *ag.* turgid, distended, swollen.

inubbidiènte, *e derivati,* V. **disubbidiènte,** *e derivati.*

inuguàle, *e derivati,* V. **ineguàle,** *e derivati.*

inúlto, *ag.* (*letter.*) **1.** (*non vendicato*) unavenged, unrevenged **2.** (*impunito*) unpunished.

inumanaménte, *av.* inhumanly, cruelly.

inumanità, *s.f.* inhumanity; cruelty.

inumàno, *ag.* inhuman; (*crudele*), cruel.

inumàre, *v.t.* to inhume, to inter, to bury, to lay in the grave, to entomb.

inumazióne, *s.f.* inhumation, interment, burial.

inumidíre, *v.t.* to moisten, to damp ‖ **inumidírsi,** *v.r.* to moisten, to become moist, to become damp.

inumidíto, *ag.* moist, moistened, damp.

inurbanaménte, *av.* uncivilly, rudely, impolitely.

inurbanità, *s.f.* incivility, rudeness, impoliteness.

inurbàno, *ag.* uncivil, rude, impolite, discourteous.

inusàto, *ag.* unusual; obsolete.

inusitataménte, *av.* unusually.

inusitàto, *ag.* unusual; obsolete.

inútile, *ag.* **1.** useless, (of) no use: *parole inutili*; useless words; *è* — *che tu vada,* it is useless for you to go; *è* — *parlare con lui,* it is no use (o no good) talking to him **2.** (*non necessario*) unnecessary.

inutilità, *s.f.* uselessness.

inutilizzàto, *ag.* unused, unemployed.

inutilménte, *av.* uselessly, in vain.

invadènte, *ag.* intrusive, encroaching ‖ *s.c.* intruder.

invàdere, *v.t.* **1.** to invade (anche *fig.*): *la paura lo invase,* fear invaded him; *i turisti invasero il villaggio,* tourists invaded the village; — *un paese,* to invade a country; — *il campo,* (*spor.*) to invade the pitch **2.** (*usurpare*) to encroach on (sthg.): — *il campo di qlcu.,* to encroach on s.o.'s territory; — *i diritti di qlcu.,* to encroach on s.o.'s rights **3.** to break into (sthg.): *l'acqua ha invaso i campi,* water has flooded the fields; *la gente invase il teatro,* (the) people broke into the theatre.

invaghiménto, *s.m.* **1.** fancy (for s.o., sthg.) **2.** (*innamoramento*) falling in love (with s.o., sthg.).

invaghíre, *v.t.* (*rar.*) to charm, to attract ‖ **invaghírsi,** *v.r.* **1.** to take a fancy (to s.o., sthg.); to take a liking (to s.o., sthg.) **2.** (*innamorarsi*) to fall in love (with s.o.).

invaghíto, *ag.* **1.** fond (of s.o., sthg.) **2.** (*innamorato*) in love (with s.o., sthg.): *sono* — *di quella ragazza,* I am in love with that girl.

invalére, *v.i.* to become popular, to come into use, to become established: *è invalsa questa abitudine,* this habit has become popular; *qui sono invalse le loro usanze,* their customs have become established here.

invalicàbile, *ag.* impassable.

invalidàbile, *ag.* apt to be invalidated.

invalidaménte, *av.* invalidly.

invalidaménto, *s.m.* invalidation.

invalidàre, *v.t.* (*dir.*) to invalidate: — *un testamento, un'elezione,* to invalidate a will, an election.

invalidazióne, *s.f.* (*dir.*) invalidation.

invalidità, *s.f.* invalidity, invalidness, infirmity.

invàlido, *ag.* **1.** invalid, disabled, infirm **2.** (*dir.*) (*non valido*) null, void, invalid ‖ *s.m.* invalid: — *di guerra,* disabled ex-serviceman.

invàlso, *ag.* established.

invaníre, *v.t.* to make vain ‖ *v.i.,* **invanírsi,** *v.r.* to become vain.

invàno, *av.* in vain, vainly, uselessly.

invariàbile, *ag.* invariable; (*di tempo*) unchangeable.

invariabilità, *s.f.* invariability, invariableness; (*di tempo*) unchangeableness.

invariabilménte, *av.* invariably.

invariàto, *ag.* unvaried, unchanged.

invasaménto, *s.f.* **1.** (*ossessione demoniaca*) obsession **2.** (*eccitazione*) excitement **3.** (*infatuazione*) infatuation.

invasàre[1], *v.t.* **1.** (*ossessionare*) to possess, to haunt **2.** (*riferito a passioni*) to fill ‖ **invasàrsi,** *v.r.* to become infatuated (with sthg.).

invasàre[2], *v.t.* **1.** (*mettere in vasi*) to pot **2.** (*mar.*) to cradle, to put on the launching-cradle.

invasàto, *ag.* **1.** (*posseduto dal demonio*) possessed **2.** (*turbato*, *agitato*) filled (with sthg.) ‖ *s.m.* possessed person.

invasatùra, *s.f.* **1.** (*il mettere in vaso*) potting **2.** (*mar.*) (sliding) ways (*pl.*).

invasióne, *s.f.* invasion: *è una vera —!*, (*fam.*) we are being invaded!.

invàso, *ag.* invaded.

invasóre, *ag.* invading ‖ *s.m.* invader.

invecchiaménto, *s.m.* ageing; (*amer.*) aging; growing old: — *artificiale di vini, mobili, ecc.*, artificial ageing of wines, furniture, etc.

invecchiàre, *v.t.* **1.** (*rendere vecchio*) to make old; to age: *il suo duro lavoro lo ha invecchiato*, his hard work has aged him (*o* made him old) **2.** (*far parere più vecchio*) to make look older: *questo taglio di capelli ti invecchia*, this hair-cut makes you look older ‖ *v.i.* **1.** to grow old, to get old, to age, to get on in years: *egli invecchia ma sta bene*, he is getting on in years but he is well; *invecchiamo senza accorgercene*, we grow old without noticing it; *il vino invecchiando migliora*, wine improves with age **2.** (*diventare antiquato*) to become obsolete ‖ **invecchiàrsi**, *v.r.* **1.** (*fare in modo da sembrare vecchio*) to make oneself look old: *le piace — indossando colori scuri*, she likes to make herself look old wearing dark colours **2.** (*far credere di essere più vecchio di quello che si è*) to claim to be older than one is.

invecchiàto, *ag.* **1.** old, aged ‖ *vino —*, mellowed wine **2.** (*antiquato*) obsolete.

invéce, *av.* **on the contrary:** *credevo avesse finito, — non ha ancora incominciato*, I thought he had finished, on the contrary he has not yet begun ‖ **invéce di**, *l. prep.* **instead of:** — *di questo libro*, instead of this book; — *di lavorare*, instead of working.

inveíre, *v.i.* to inveigh; to rail (at, against s.o., sthg.); to declaim (against s.o., sthg.): *inveì contro il traditore*, he inveighed against the traitor; *dopo che ebbe tanto inveito si calmò*, after his outburst he calmed down (*o* after letting off steam he calmed down).

invelenìre, *v.t.* to envenom; to embitter ‖ — *una lite*, to fan (*o* to inflame) a quarrel ‖ *v.i.*, **invelenìrsi**, *v.r.* to get embittered.

inveleníto, *ag.* **1.** envenomed, embittered **2.** (*irato*) enraged, furious.

invendíbile, *ag.* unsaleable.

invendicàto, *ag.* unavenged, unrevenged.

invendúto, *ag.* unsold: *salvo —*, (*comm.*) subject to being unsold.

invènia, *s.f.* (*rar.*) blandishment, fondling.

inventàre, *v.t.* **1.** to invent: *chi inventò il telefono?*, who invented the telephone?; — *un nuovo metodo*, to invent (*o* to find out) a new method ‖ *non ha inventato la polvere*, (*scherz.*) he will never set the Thames on fire **2.** (*escogitare*) to devise, to invent: — *una bugia*, to invent (*o* to forge) a lie; — *un piano*, to devise a plan; — *una scusa*, to invent an excuse; — *una storia*, to invent a story ‖ *ne inventa tante!*, he tells so many lies!.

inventariàre, *v.t.* to inventory.

inventàrio, *s.m.* inventory: *fare l'—*, to make up an inventory; (*comm.*) to take stock ‖ *con beneficio d'—*, with reservation.

inventàto, *ag.* invented: *scusa inventata*, invented excuse; *storia inventata, racconto —*, forged tale.

inventíva, *s.f.* inventiveness, inventive power.

inventívo, *ag.* inventive: *facoltà inventiva*, inventive power.

inventóre, *ag.* inventing ‖ *s.m.* inventor.

inventríce, *s.f.* inventress.

invenústo, *ag.* unbeauteous.

invenzióne, *s.f.* **1.** invention: *l'— della radio*, the invention of the radio; *le invenzioni della scienza moderna*, the inventions of modern science; *brevetto di —*, patent **2.** (*bugia*) lie, story: *è tutta una —*, it's all made up **3.** (*ritrovamento*) invention, finding ‖ *l'Invenzione*

della Croce, the Invention of the Cross **4.** (*ret.*) invention **5.** (*dir.*) evidence.

inverdíre, *v.i.* to turn green.

inverecondaménte, *av.* immodestly; (*impudentemente*) impudently.

inverecóndia, *s.f.* immodesty; (*impudenza*) impudence.

inverecóndo, *ag.* immodest; (*impudente*) impudent.

invergàre, *v.t.* (*ind. tessile*) to lease.

invergatùra, *s.f.* (*ind. tessile*) lease.

inverisímile, *e derivati*, *V.* **inverosímile**, *e derivati*.

invermigliàre, *v.t.* to vermilion; to redden ‖ **invermigliàrsi**, *v.r.* to redden; (*di persona*) to blush.

inverminíre, *v.i.*, **inverminírsi**, *v.r.* to verminate.

invernàle, *ag.* winter (*attributivo*); (*da inverno*) wintry: *aria, cielo, tempo —*, wintry air, sky, weather; *mesi invernali*, winter months; *residenza —*, winter residence; *sport invernali*, winter sports; *stagione —*, winter season.

invernàta, *s.f.* winter: *la passata —*, last winter; *fu una brutta —*, it was a bad winter.

inverniciàre, *e derivati*, *V.* **verniciàre**, *e derivati*.

invèrno, *s.m.* winter: *un — mite*, a mild winter; *d'—*, in winter (time); *giardino d'—*, winter garden; *nel cuore dell'—*, in the depth of winter; *quartieri d'—*, winter quarters; *solstizio d'—*, winter solstice; *passare l'— al mare*, to spend the winter at the seaside.

invéro, *av.* (*letter.*) really; truly; indeed: *fu — una strana giornata!*, it was a strange day, indeed!.

inverosimigliànza, *s.f.* unlikelihood, unlikeliness, improbability: *l'— del suo racconto*, the unlikelihood of his story; *ci sono molte inverosimiglianze in questo libro*, there are many improbabilities in this book.

inverosímile, *ag.* unlikely, improbable: *cosa c'è di — in ciò?*, what is there unlikely in that?; *è assai —*, it is most improbable; *è tutt'altro che — che egli venga*, it is not at all unlikely that he may come.

inverosimilménte, *av.* unlikely, improbably.

inversaménte, *av.* inversely: — *proporzionale*, inversely proportional.

inversióne, *s.f.* inversion (anche *gram.*); (*mec. fis. foto.*) reversal: — *di comando*, (*aer.*) reversal of control; — *di marcia*, (*aut.*) reversing: *a — di marcia*, (*mec.*) reversible; — *di rotta*, (*mar. mil.*) turnabout; *bagno d'—*, (*foto.*) reversing bath.

invèrso[1], *ag.* **1.** inverse (anche *mat.*); (*opposto*) opposite, contrary: *frazione inversa*, (*mat.*) inverse fraction; *in senso —*, in the opposite (*o* contrary) direction (*o* contrarywise); *proporzione inversa*, (*mat.*) inverse proportion ‖ *all'inversa, all'—*, badly (*o* wrong): *tutto va all'—*, everything goes wrong **2.** (*dial.*) (*di cattivo umore*) in a bad mood ‖ *s.m.* opposite, contrary: *è l'— di ciò che credi*, it is the opposite of what you think.

invèrso[2], (*poet.*) per **vèrso**.

inversóre, (*rar.*) per **invertitóre**.

invertebràto, *ag.* ‖(*zool.*) invertebrate.

invèrtere, *V.* **invertíre**.

invertíbile, *ag.* invertible, reversible.

invertibilità, *s.f.* reversibility.

invertiménto, *s.m.* inversion.

invertína, *s.f.* (*chim.*) invertase.

invertíre, *v.t.* to invert, to reverse; to transpose: *la guerra ha invertito le loro posizioni*, the war has reversed their positions; — *il movimento*, (*mec.*) to reverse; — *l'ordine di una frase*, to invert the order (*o* to transpose the words) of a sentence.

invertíto, *ag.* inverted, reversed; (*chim.*) invert: *zucchero —*, invert sugar ‖ *s.m.* invert.

invertitóre, *s.m.* (*mec.*) reverse gear, reversing gear; (*elett.*) reverser, reversing switch.

invescaménto, *s.m.* **1.** (*di uccelli*) liming **2.** *fig.* entanglement; (*adescamento*) enticement.

inveseàre, *v.t.* **1.** (*uccelli*) to lime **2.** *fig.* to entangle; (*adescare*) to entice ‖ **invescàrsi**, *v.r.* **1.** to get entangled (with sthg.) **2.** (*innamorarsi*) to fall in love.

invescatóre, *s.m.* **1.** limer **2.** *fig.* enticer, tempter.

invescatríce, *s.f.* enticer, temptress, seducer.

investíbile, *ag.* (*comm.*) investable: *denaro — in terreni,* money to invest in land.

investigàbile, *ag.* investigable.

investigaménto, *s.m.* investigation, inquiry, research.

investigàre, *v.t.* to investigate, to inquire into (sthg.), to search into (sthg.): *il caso fu investigato a fondo,* the matter was inquired into thoroughly; *investigherò,* I will inquire.

investigatívo, *ag.* investigative: *agente —,* detective.

investigatóre, *s.m.,* **investigatríce,** *s.f.* investigator, detective: *— privato,* private detective.

investigazióne, *s.f.* investigation, inquiry: *fare investigazioni su ql.co.,* to inquire into (o to investigate) sthg.

investiménto, *s.m.* **1.** (*comm.*) investment: *— in ipoteche,* mortgage investment; *— remunerativo,* remunerative investment; *— sicuro,* safe investment; *rischio di —,* investment risk (o risk attending an investment) **2.** (*urto, cozzo*) collision, crash: *subì un — automobilistico,* he was run over by a car.

investíre, *v.t.* **1.** (*urtare, cozzare*) to collide with (s.o., sthg.), to come into collision with (s.o., sthg.); to run over (s.o., sthg.), to run (s.o., sthg.) down; (*di navi*) to foul, to fall foul of (sthg.): *il camion investì l'automobile,* the lorry collided with the car; *fui investito da un'automobile,* I was run over by a car; *un incrociatore investì la nave,* a cruiser fell foul of the ship **2.** (*assalire*) to assail, to attack: *all'alba investimmo le posizioni nemiche,* at dawn we attacked the enemy positions; *egli mi investì con una sfilza d'insulti,* he fired a regular string of abuse at me; *egli mi investì di domande,* he plied me with questions **3.** (*comm.*) to invest: *— il proprio denaro in titoli,* to invest one's money in stocks **4.** (*st. medioevale*) to invest: *— un cavaliere,* to knight s.o.; *— qlcu. di una terra,* to invest s.o. with an estate **5.** (*dare, attribuire a*) to invest, to give: *egli fu investito di pieni poteri,* he was given full powers; *— qlcu. di una carica,* to appoint s.o. to an office (o to invest s.o. with an office) ‖ **investírsi,** *v.r.* to enter thoroughly (into sthg.): *— della propria parte,* to enter thoroughly into one's part; *— della propria responsabilità,* to be fully conscious of one's responsibility ‖ *v.r. reciproco* to collide: *le due navi si investirono,* the two ships collided.

investitúra, *s.f.* investiture.

inveteràto, *ag.* inveterate; (*di vizio, abitudine, ecc.*) deep-rooted, ingrained: *un fumatore —,* an inveterate smoker; *un vizio —,* an ingrained (o inveterate) vice.

invetriàre, *v.t.* to glaze.

invetriàta, *s.f.* **1.** (*finestra*) glass window **2.** (*porta a vetri*) glass door **3.** (*vetrata divisoria*) glass partition.

invetriàto, *ag.* **1.** (*argilla*) *terracotta invetriata,* glazed earthenware **2.** (*impudente*) impudent.

invetriatúra, *s.f.* glaze, glazing.

invettíva, *s.f.* invective: *lanciare invettive contro qlcu.,* to throw invectives at s.o.

inviàre, *v.t.* to send; to forward;'(*per nave*) to ship: *invierà la merce per ferrovia,* he will send the goods by rail; *la merce non fu inviata in tempo,* the goods were not forwarded in time; *— delle circolari,* to send out circulars; *— un messaggio, un pacco,* to send a message, a parcel; *— il proprio biglietto da visita,* to send in one's card; *— le proprie dimissioni,* to send in one's resignation; *— un telegramma,* to dispatch a telegram.

inviàto, *s.m.* **1.** (*messaggero*) messenger; (*rappresentante*) representative: *un — del cielo,* a messenger from heaven **2.** (*in diplomazia*) envoy: *— straordinario e ministro plenipotenziario,* Envoy Extraordinary and Minister Plenipotentiary **3.** (*giornalismo*) correspondent: *dal nostro — speciale,* from our special correspondent.

invídia, *s.f.* envy: *per —,* out of envy; *sguardi*

d' —, envious looks; *essere roso dall' —,* to be eaten up with envy; *essere verde d' —,* to be green with envy; *fare —,* to be envied (o to rouse envy): *fare — a qlcu.,* to make s.o. envious; *suscitare —,* to excite envy ‖ *è meglio fare — che pietà, prov.* (it is) better to be envied than to be pitied.

invidiàbile, *ag.* enviable.

invidiabilménte, *av.* enviably.

invidiàre, *v.t.* **1.** to envy: *lo invidio,* I envy him; *non gli invidio il suo successo,* I don't envy him his success **2.** (*letter.*) (*negare, contrastare, togliere*) to begrudge: *non mi — questo po' di consolazione,* don't begrudge me this small consolation.

invidiosaménte, *av.* enviously.

invidióso, *ag.* envious: *essere — di ql.co.,* to be envious of sthg. ‖ *s.m.* envious man.

ínvido, (*poet.*) per **invidióso.**

invigilàre, *v.i.* to keep a close watch (over sthg.) ‖ *v.t. V.* **vigilàre.**

invigliacchírsi, *v.r.* **1.** to become a coward **2.** (*avvilirsi*) to get faint-hearted.

invigoriménto, *s.m.* invigoration; (*rafforzamento*) strengthening.

invigoríre, *v.t.* to invigorate; (*rafforzare*) to strengthen ‖ **invigorírsi,** *v.r.* to get invigorated; (*rafforzarsi*) to gain strength.

invigoríto, *ag.* invigorated; (*rafforzato*) strengthened.

invilíre, *v.t.* **1.** (*abbassare, deprezzare*) to debase, to depreciate, to lower: *— un prezzo,* to lower a price; *— il valore di ql.co.,* to debase the value of sthg. **2.** (*degradare*) to degrade **3.** (*deprimere*) to deject, to depress ‖ **invilírsi,** *v.r.* **1.** (*abbassarsi, deprezzarsi*) to become debased, to be depreciated **2.** (*degradarsi*) to become degraded **3.** (*deprimersi*) to lose heart.

inviluppaménto, *s.m.* **1.** (*l'avvolgere*) enveloping, wrapping up **2.** (*involucro*) envelopment **3.** (*intrico*) entanglement, tangle (*anche fig.*).

inviluppàre, *v.t.* **1.** (*avvolgere*) to envelop, to wrap up, to swathe **2.** (*nascondere*) to hide, to conceal **3.** (*impigliare*) to entangle (*anche fig.*) ‖ **inviluppàrsi,** *v.r.* **1.** to wrap oneself up **2.** (*impigliarsi*) to get entangled.

invilúppo, *s.m.* **1.** (*intrico*) entanglement, tangle (*anche fig.*) **2.** (*involucro*) wrapper, covering.

invincíbile, *ag.* invincible; insuperable.

invincibilità, *s.f.* invincibility; insuperability.

invincibilménte, *av.* invincibly; insuperably.

invío, *s.m.* **1.** (*per posta*) sending, mailing, posting **2.** (*di merci*) dispatch, forwarding, consignment; (*per nave*) shipment **3.** (*di denaro*) remittance.

inviolàbile, *ag.* inviolable; sacred.

inviolabilità, *s.f.* inviolability; sacredness.

inviolabilménte, *av.* inviolably; sacredly.

inviolàto, *ag.* inviolate.

inviperíre, *v.i.,* **inviperírsi,** *v.r.* to become furious.

inviperíto, *ag.* furious, enraged; (*fam.*) mad.

invisceràrsi, *v.r.* to penetrate deeply (into sthg.); to go to the heart (of sthg.).

invischiaménto, *V.* **invesceaménto.**

invischiàre, *V.* **invesceàre.**

inviscidíre, *v.i.* to become viscid, to become viscous; to become slimy.

invisíbile, *ag.* invisible.

invisibilità, *s.f.* invisibility, invisibleness.

invisibilménte, *av.* invisibly.

invíso, *ag.* disliked (by s.o., sthg.), hated (by s.o. sthg.): *— a molta gente,* disliked (o hated) by many people.

invispíre, *v.i.* to perk up ‖ **invispírsi,** *v.r.* to become lively, to become brisk, to become frisky.

invitànte, *ag.* inviting; attractive; alluring; tempting.

invitàre[1]**,** *v.t.* **1.** to invite: *lo invitai a pensarci su,* I invited him to think it over; *mi invitò a casa sua,* he invited me to his house; *una proposta che invita,* an inviting (o tempting) proposal; *questo silenzio* *vita al sonno*, this silence invites sleep; — *qlcu. ad entrare*, to invite s.o. in; — *qlcu. a pranzo*, to invite (*o* to ask) s.o. to dinner **2.** (*domandare, pregare*) to request, to beg: *si invitano i passeggeri a presentare i loro documenti*, passengers are requested to show their documents **3.** (*a carte*) to call: — *a quadri*, to call for diamonds.

invitàre[2], *v.t.* (*mec.*) to screw, to screw down.

invitàto, *ag.* invited ‖ *s.m.* guest.

invitatòrio, *ag.* invitatory (anche *eccl.*) ‖ *s.m.* (*eccl.*) invitatory.

invìto, *s.m.* invitation: *un* — *a pranzo*, an invitation to dinner; *biglietto di* —, invitation card; *accettare, declinare un* —, to accept, to decline an invitation; *diramare inviti*, to send out invitations; *venire su* — *di qlcu.*, to come at s.o.'s invitation.

invittaménte, *av.* invincibly; indomitably.

invìtto, *ag.* **1.** unconquered, undefeated **2.** (*invincibile*) invincible; indomitable.

invocàre, *v.t.* **1.** to invoke; to entreat: — *aiuto*, to cry for help; — *l'aiuto di qlcu.*, to invoke s.o.'s help; — *Dio*, to invoke God **2.** (*fare appello a*) to appeal to (s.o., sthg.): *voi invocate la legge fuori di proposito*, you appeal to the law inopportunely.

invocatìvo, *ag.* invocatory.

invocatóre, *ag.* invoking, entreating ‖ *s.m.*, **invocatrìce**, *s.f.* invoker.

invocazióne, *s.f.* **1.** invocation; entreaty **2.** (*appello*) appeal.

invogliànte, *ag.* inviting, tempting; attractive.

invogliàre, *v.t.* to tempt; to attract; to allure: *cerco di invogliarlo allo studio*, I try to persuade him to study; *che cosa ti invogliò a venire qui?*, what induced you to come here?; *non lasciarti* — *da queste cose*, don't be tempted by these things ‖ **invogliàrsi**, *v.r.* to wish, to desire.

invogliàto, *ag.* desirous.

involàre, *v.t.* to steal ‖ **involàrsi**, *v.r.* to vanish, to fly away: *la giovinezza s'invola rapidamente*, youth vanishes quickly.

invòlgere, *v.t.* **1.** to wrap (up); to envelop **2.** (*coinvolgere*) to involve, to implicate **3.** (*implicare, comportare*) to imply, to involve: *questa domanda involge molte questioni*, this question implies many problems.

involgiménto, *s.m.* wrapping (up); envelopment.

invòlo, *s.m.* (*aer.*) take-off.

involontariaménte, *av.* (*senza farlo apposta*) involuntarily, unintentionally.

involontàrio, *ag.* (*non fatto apposta*) involuntary, unintentional.

involpìre, *v.i.* to grow cunning, to become foxy.

involtàre, *v.t.* to wrap (up); to envelop.

invòlto, *ag.* **1.** (*avvolto*) wrapped (up) (in sthg.), enveloped (in sthg.) (anche *fig.*): — *di seta*, wrapped in silk; — *nelle cose del mondo*, wrapped in worldly matters; — *nelle difficoltà*, surrounded with (o by) difficulties; — *nelle menzogne*, enveloped in lies **2.** (*rar.*) (*contorto*) twisted, tortuous: *rami involti*, twisted branches ‖ *s.m.* (*fagotto*) bundle; (*pacco*) parcel, package, packet; (*cartoccio*) bag: *un* — *di confetti*, a bag of sugared almonds.

invòlucro, *s.m.* **1.** covering; wrapper; envelope **2.** (*bot.*) involucre; (*baccello*) pod **3.** (*aer.*) envelope **4.** (*di siluro*) shell.

involùto, *ag.* intricate, complicated; involved, involute; obscure: *quello scrittore ha uno stile* —, that writer has an involved style; *sono questioni involute*, they are complicated matters.

involuzióne, *s.f.* **1.** involution: *un'* — *di parole*, an involution of words **2.** (*decadenza*) decline: *il partito subì un'* — *dopo la guerra*, the party underwent a decline after the war **3.** (*med.*) involution: — *uterina*, involution of the womb.

invòlvere, (*poet.*) per **invòlgere**.

invulneràbile, *ag.* invulnerable; unassailable (anche *fig.*): *si crede* —, he believes himself unassailable.

invulnerabilità, *s.f.* invulnerability (anche *fig.*).

invulnerabilménte, *av.* invulnerably.

invulneràto, *ag.* unhurt, uninjured.

inzaccheraménto, *s.m.* splash(ing), spatter(ing).

inzaccheràre, *v.t.* to splash with mud, to spatter with mud ‖ **inzaccheràrsi**, *v.r.* to get splashed with mud, to get muddy.

inzaffàre, *v.t.* to bung, to stop; (*turare*) to cram.

inzavorràre, *v.t.*, **inzavorràrsi** *v.r.* to ballast.

inzeppàre, *v.t.* **1.** (*mettere zeppe a*) to wedge **2.** (*riempire come inzeppando*) to cram, to stuff, to fill.

inzeppatùra, *s.f.* **1.** (*l'inzeppare*) wedging **2.** (*il riempire inzeppando*) cramming, stuffing, filling.

inzolfaménto, *s.m.* sulphuration.

inzolfàre, *v.t.* to sulphur, to fumigate with sulphur.

inzolfatóio, *s.m.* (*strum.*) sulphurator.

inzolfatùra, *s.f.* sulphuration.

inzotichíre, *v.t.* to make boorish, to make ill-mannered ‖ *v.i.*, **inzotichírsi**, *v.r.* to become boorish, to become ill-mannered.

inzuccàre, *v.t.* (*fam.*) (*ubriacare*) to make drunk ‖ **inzuccàrsi**, *v.r.* **1.** (*ubriacarsi*) to get drunk **2.** (*innamorarsi*) to fall in love **3.** (*ostinarsi*) to take it into one's head: *si inzuccò a sposare quella ragazza*, he took it into his head to marry that girl.

inzuccheràre, *v.t.* **1.** to sugar **2.** (*addolcire*) to sweeten ‖ — *la pillola*, to sugar the pill **3.** (*adulare*) to cajole.

inzuccheràto, *ag.* **1.** sugared **2.** (*addolcito*) sweetened.

inzuppaménto, *s.m.* **1.** soaking, drenching **2.** (*l'immergere*) dipping.

inzuppàre, *v.t.* **1.** to soak, to drench, to steep: *la pioggia ha inzuppato il mio soprabito*, the rain has soaked through my overcoat; — *il pane nel vino*, to soak bread in wine **2.** (*intingere*) to dip: — *la penna nell'inchiostro*, to dip one's pen in the ink ‖ **inzuppàrsi**, *v.r.* to get drenched, to get soaked through.

inzuppàto, *ag.* soaked, drenched, thoroughly wet: — *di pioggia*, drenched with rain; *pane* — *nel latte*, bread soaked in milk; *non avevo ombrello e tornai* —, I had no umbrella and I came back wet (o drenched) through (o wet to the skin o soaked to the skin).

ìo, *pron. pers. m.f. 1ª persona sing.* **I:** — *sottoscritto*, I the undersigned; *devo farlo* —?, shall I do it (o have I got to do it)?; *sono stato* — *a dirglielo*, it was I who told him (o I was the one who told him); *te lo dico* —, I assure you ‖ — *come* —..., as for me, I... ‖ — *stesso, proprio* —, I myself, I... myself ‖ *non sono più* —, I am no longer my former self ‖ *s.m.*: *l'* — *e il non* —, (*fil.*) the ego and the non-ego; *mettere il proprio* — *dinanzi a tutto*, to think only of oneself (o *fam.* to put number one first).

iodàre, *v.t.* (*chim. foto.*) to iodize, to iodate.

iodàto, *s.m.* (*chim.*) iodate.

iòdico, *ag.* (*chim.*) iodic.

iòdio, *s.m.* (*chim.*) iodine: *tintura di* —, (*farm.*) tincture of iodine.

iodísmo, *s.m.* (*patol.*) iodism.

iodofòrmio, *s.m.* (*farm.*) iodoform.

iodúro, *s.m.* (*chim.*) iodide.

iòga, *s.m.* **1.** (*fil. indiana*) yoga **2.** (*chi pratica tale filosofia*) yogi.

iòide, *s.m.* (*anat.*) hyoid (bone).

iòle, *s.f.* (*mar.*) gig.

iolíto, *s.m.* (*min.*) iolite.

ióne, *s.m.* (*fis.*) ion.

Iònia, *no.pr.f.* (*geog. st.*) Ionia.

iònico[1], *ag.* Ionic: *metro* —, (*poes.*) Ionic metre; *ordine* —, (*arch.*) Ionic order; *piede* —, (*poes.*) Ionic.

iònico[2], *ag.* (*chim.*) ionic.

iònio[1], *ag.* Ionian: *Isole ionie*, Ionian Islands ‖ *s.m.* Ionian ‖ *gli Ioni*, the Ionians ‖ **Iònio (l')**, *no.pr.m.* (*geog.*) the Ionian Sea.

iònio[2], *s.m.* (*chim.*) ionium,
ionizzànte, *ag.* (*fis.*) ionogenic.
ionizzàre, *v.t.* (*fis.*) to ionize.
ionizzazióne, *s.f.* (*fis.*) ionization.
ionòmetro, *s.m.* (*fis.*) ionometer.
ionosfèra, *s.f.* ionosphere.
iòsa, a, *l.av.* in plenty, galore: *pasto con carne e birra a* —, meal with meat and beer galore.
iòta, *s.m.* (*lettera dell'alfabeto greco*) iota ‖ *un* —, (*un nonnulla*) an iota (*o a jot*): *non c'è un* — *di verità nel suo racconto*, there's not an iota (*o a jot*) of truth in his story; *non vale un* —, it isn't worth a jot.
iotacísmo, *s.m.* (*fonet.*) iotacism.
ipàllage, *s.f.* (*ret.*) hypallage.
Ipàzia, *no.pr.f.* (*st.*) Hypatia.
ipecacuàna, *s.f.* (*bot. farm.*) ipecacuanha.
ipèrbato, *s.m.* (*ret.*) hyperbaton.
ipèrbole, *s.f.* **1.** (*ret.*) hyperbole **2.** (*esagerazione*) exaggeration **3.** (*geom.*) hyperbola (*pl.* hyperbolas).
iperboleggiàre, *v.i.* to hyperbolize.
iperbolicaménte, *av.* hyperbolically.
iperbòlico, *ag.* **1.** (*ret.*) hyperbolic(al) **2.** (*esagerato*) exaggerated, extravagant: *lodi iperboliche*, exaggerated (*o* extravagant) praises **3.** (*geom.*) hyperbolic.
iperbòreo, *ag.* hyperborean.
ipercatalèttico, *ag.* (*poes.*) hypercatalectic.
ipercrítica, *s.f.*, **ipercriticísmo**, *s.m.* hypercriticism.
ipercrítico, *ag.* hypercritical ‖ *s.m.* hypercritical man.
iperemía, *s.f.* (*med.*) hyper(a)emia.
iperestesía, *s.f.* (*med.*) hyper(a)esthesia.
iperglicemía, *s.f.* (*med.*) hyperglycemia.
ipèrmetro, *ag.* (*poes.*) hypermetric(al).
ipermetropía, *s.f.* (*med.*) hypermetropia.
ipernutrizióne, *s.f.* (*med.*) hypernutrition.
ipersensíbile, *ag.* hypersensitive ‖ *s.c.* hypersensitive person.
ipersensibilità, *s.f.* hypersensitivity, hypersensitiveness.
ipersònico, *ag.* (*aer.*) hypersonic.
ipersostentatóre, *s.m.* (*aer.*) (wing) flap.
iperspàzio, *s.m.* (*fis.*) hyperspace.
ipertensióne, *s.f.* (*med.*) hypertension.
ipertonía, *s.f.* (*med.*) hypertonia.
ipertònico, *ag.* (*med.*) hypertonic.
ipertrofía, *s.f.* (*med.*) hypertrophy.
ipertròfico, *ag.* hypertrophic.
ipertrofizzàto, *ag.* hypertrophied, affected with hypertrophy.
ipnología, *s.f.* hypnology.
ipnòsi, *s.f.* hypnosis.
ipnòtico, *ag.* hypnotic.
ipnotísmo, *s.m.* hypnotism.
ipnotizzàre, *v.t.* to hypnotize.
ipnotizzatóre, *s.m.*, **ipnotizzatríce**, *s.f.* hypnotizer.
ipoacusía, *s.f.* (*med.*) bradyacusia.
ipocàusto, *s.m.* (*archeol.*) hypocaust.
ipocéntro, *s.m.* (*geol.*) focus.
ipocloríto, *s.m.* (*chim.*) hypochlorite.
ipoclolóso, *ag.* (*chim.*) hypochlorous.
ipocondría, *s.f.* (*med.*) hypochondria.
ipocondríaco, *ag.s.m.* hypochondriac.
ipocrisía, *s.f.* hypocrisy; cant, dissimulation: *sono tutte ipocrisie*, that's all cant.
ipòcrita, *s.c.* hypocrite, dissembler.
ipocritaménte, *av.* hypocritically.
ipòcrito, *ag.* hypocritical, dissembling: *un atteggiamento* —, a hypocritical attitude.
ipodèrma, *s.m.* (*bot. entom.*) hypoderma.
ipodèrmico, *ag.* hypodermic: *iniezione ipodermica*, hypodermic injection.
ipodermoclísi, *s.f.* (*med.*) hypodermoclysis.
ipòfisi, *s.f.* (*anat.*) hypophysis.
ipofosfàto, *s.m.* (*chim.*) hypophosphate.
ipofosfíto, *s.m.* (*chim.*) hypophosphite.
ipofosforóso, *ag.* (*chim.*) hypophosphorous.

ipogàstrico, *ag.* (*anat.*) hypogastric: *cintura ipogastrica*, abdominal belt.
ipogàstrio, *s.m.* (*anat.*) hypogastrium (*pl.* hypogastria).
ipogèo, *ag.* (*bot. geol.*) hypogeal, hypogean, underground: *fauna ipogea*, hypogean fauna ‖ *s.m.* (*archeol.*) hypogeum (*pl.* hypogea).
ipoglicemía, *s.f.* (*patol.*) hypoglycemia.
ipoglòsso, *s.m.* (*anat.*) hypoglossal nerve; hypoglossus.
iposolfàto, *s.m.* (*chim.*) dithionate.
iposolfíto, *s.m.* (*chim.*) hyposulphite, thiosulphate: — *di sodio*, sodium thiosulphate.
iposolforóso, *ag.* (*chim.*) hyposulphurous.
ipòstasi, *s.f.*(*teol.fil.med.*) hypostasis (*pl.*hypostases).
ipostàtico, *ag.* **1.** (*fil. med.*) hypostatic **2.** (*teol.*) hypostatic(al).
ipòstilo, *ag.* (*arch.*) hypostyle, pillared.
ipotèca, *s.f.* mortgage: — *di prima iscrizione*, first recorded mortgage; *contratto di* —, mortgage deed; *riscatto, estinzione dell'*—, redemption of mortgage; *estinguere un'*—, to pay off (*o* to redeem) a mortgage; *mettere un'*— *su ql.co.*, to mortgage sthg.
ipotecàbile, *ag.* mortgageable.
ipotecànte, *s.c.* mortgagor, mortgager.
ipotecàre, *v.t.* to mortgage.
ipotecàrio, *ag.* mortgage (*attributivo*); on mortgage: *creditore* —, mortgagee; *debitore* —, mortgagor (*o* mortgager); *mutuo* —, mortgage loan.
ipotecàto, *ag.* mortgaged: *proprietà ipotecata*, mortgaged estate.
ipotensióne, *s.f.* (*med.*) hypotension.
ipotenúsa, *s.f.* (*geom.*) hypotenuse.
ipòtesi, *s.f.* hypothesis (*pl.* hypotheses); supposition, assumption, conjecture: *per* —, by supposition; *l'intera storia è basata su un'* —, the whole story is based on a supposition ‖ *nella migliore delle* —, at the best; *nella peggiore delle* —, at the worst (*o* if the worst comes to the worst).
ipotéso, *ag.* (*med.*) hypotensive.
ipoteticaménte, *av.* hypothetically.
ipotètico, *ag.* hypothetic(al), conjectural.
ipotipòsi, *s.f.* (*ret.*) hypotyposis.
ipotonía, *s.f.* (*med.*) hypotonicity.
ipotrofía, *s.f.* (*med.*) hypotrophy.
íppica, *s.f.* horse-racing: *egli ha molta passione per l'*—, he is very fond of horse-racing.
íppico, *ag.* horse (*attributivo*): *concorso* —, race-meeting; *corse ippiche*, horse-races.
ippocàmpo, *s.m.* (*mit. zool. anat.*) hippocampus (*pl.* hippocampi).
ippocastàno, *s.m.* horse-chestnut (tree).
Ippòcrate, *no.pr.m.* (*st. med.*) Hippocrates.
ippocràtico, *ag.* Hippocratic.
Ippocrène, *no.pr.f.* (*mit.*) Hippocrene.
ippòdromo, *s.m.* **1.** race-course **2.** (*archeol.*) hippodrome, circus.
ippofagía, *s.f.* hippophagy.
ippòfago, *s.m.* hippophagist.
ippogrífo, *s.m.* (*lett.*) hippogriff, hippogryph.
Ippòlita, *no.pr.f.* (*mit.*) Hippolyta.
Ippòlito, *no.pr.m.* Hippolytus.
ippopòtamo, *s.m.* hippopotamus (*pl.* hippopotamuses, hippopotamusi); (*pop.*) hippo (*pl.* hippos).
iprite, *s.f.* (*chim.*) yperite, mustard-gas.
ípsilon, *s.f.m.* **1.** letter Y ‖ *fatto a Y*, Y shaped **2.** (*lettera dell'alfabeto greco*) ypsilon.
ipsografía, *s.f.* (*geog.*) hypsography.
ipsometría, *s.f.* (*geodesia*) hypsometry.
ipsomètrico, *ag.* (*geodesia*) hypsometric(al).
ipsòmetro, *s.m.* (*geodesia*) hypsometer.
íra, *s.f.* anger, rage, fury, wrath: *pazzo d'*—, mad with rage; *era fuori di sè dall'*—, he was beside himself with fury; *lo feci in un accesso d'*—, I did it in a fit of anger; *agire sotto l'impulso dell'*—, to act in

anger; *eccitare l'— di qlcu.*, to provoke s.o. to anger; *essere preso dall'—*, to fly into a rage.

irachèno, *ag.s.m.* Iraqi ‖ **irachèna,** *s.f.* Iraqi.

iracondaménte, *av.* wrathfully, angrily, irascibly.

iracóndia, *s.f.* irascibility, wrathfulness.

iracóndo, *ag.* irascible, quick-tempered, choleric, hot-headed: *uomo —,* man quick to anger.

Iràk, *no.pr.m.* (*geog.*) Irak, Iraq.

Iràn, *no.pr.m.* (*geog.*) Iran, Persia.

iraniàno, *ag. s.m.* Iranian, Persian ‖ **iraniàna,** *s.f.* Iranian, Persian.

irànico, *ag.* Iranian, Persian.

irascíbile, *ag.* irritable, irascible, hot-tempered, angry, choleric, testy, touchy, peppery.

irascibilità, *s.f.* irascibility, irascibleness, testiness, pepperiness; (*suscettibilità*) touchiness.

iratamente, *av.* angrily.

iràto, *ag.* angry, enraged, filled with anger, wrathful: *aveva uno sguardo —,* he had an angry look.

íre, (*poet.*) per **andàre.**

Irène, *no.pr.f.* Irene, Eirene.

Irenèo, *no.pr.m.* (*st. relig.*) Irenaeus.

íreos, *s.m.* (*bot.*) iris.

iridàcee, *s.f.pl.* (*bot.*) iridaceae.

iridàceo, *ag.* (*bot.*) iridaceous.

Íride, *no.pr.f.* Iris (anche *mit.*) ‖ **íride,** *s.f.* **1.** (*anat. bot.*) iris (*pl.* irises, irides) **2.** (*arcobaleno*) iris (*pl.* irises, irides), rainbow **3.** (*gamma di colori*) iris (*pl.* irises, irides), prismatic halo.

iridescènte, *ag.* iridescent.

iridescènza, *s.f.* **1.** iridescence **2.** (*foto.*) fringe.

irídio, *s.m.* (*chim.*) iridium.

íris, *s.m.* (*bot.*) iris (*pl.* irises, irides).

Irlànda, *no.pr.f.* **1.** (*geog.*) Ireland **2.** (*pol.*) Eire, Republic of Ireland.

irlandése, *ag.* Irish ‖ *s.m.* **1.** (*abitante*) Irishman (*pl.* Irishmen) ‖ *gli Irlandesi,* the Irish (people) **2.** (*lingua*) (the) Irish (language) ‖ *s.f.* Irishwoman (*pl.* Irishwomen).

Írma, *no.pr.f.* Irma.

ironía, *s.f.* irony: *l'— della sorte,* the irony of fate; *le ironie della vita,* the ironies of life ‖ *— socratica,* Socratic irony.

ironicaménte, *av.* ironically.

irònico, *ag.* ironic(al): *un sorriso —,* an ironical smile ‖ *s.m.* ironist.

ironísta, *s.c.* ironist.

iróso, *V.* **iracóndo.**

irradiaménto, *s.m.* irradiation, radiation.

irradiàre, *v.t.* **1.** to irradiate, to shed light on (sthg.), to shine upon (sthg.): *il sole irradiava la valle,* the sun was shining on the valley; *il suo viso era irradiato dalla gioia,* his face was irradiated with joy **2.** (*med.*) to irradiate ‖ *v.i.* to irradiate, to radiate; to shine: *il calore che irradia dal sole,* the heat radiating from the sun ‖ **irradiàrsi,** *v.r.* to radiate, to spread, to diffuse: *le strade si irradiano in tutto il paese,* roads radiate all over the country.

irradiazióne, *s.f.* **1.** irradiation: *— di raggi X,* irradiation of X rays **2.** (*dovuta a caduta di particelle radioattive dopo una esplosione atomica*) fall-out.

irraggiaménto, *s.m.* irradiation, radiation.

irraggiàre, *V.* **irradiàre.**

irraggiungíbile, *ag.* **1.** unreachable **2.** *fig.* unreachable, unattainable, unobtainable.

irragionévole, *ag.* **1.** (*non dotato di ragione*) irrational, unreasonable **2.** (*contro ragione*) unreasonable, absurd, foolish, unfair: *una pretesa —,* an unfair claim; *non essere —!,* don't be absurd!; *questo è —!,* it's unfair!.

irragionevolézza, *s.f.* **1.** (*l'essere irragionevole*) unreasonableness, absurdity, foolishness, irrationality, unfairness **2.** (*cosa irragionevole*) unreasonable thing.

irragionevolménte, *av.* unreasonably, absurdly, irrationally, foolishly, unfairly.

irrancidiménto, *s.m.* going rancid, growing rank.

irrancidíre, *v.i.* to go rancid, to become rank, to grow stale: *questo burro è irrancidito,* this butter has gone rancid.

irrazionàle, *ag.* irrational: *quantità —,* (*mat.*) irrational quantity.

irrazionalísmo, *s.m.* (*fil.*) irrationalism.

irrazionalità, *s.f.* irrationality.

irrazionalménte, *av.* irrationally.

irreàle, *ag.* unreal.

irrealtà, *s.f.* unreality.

irreconciliàbile, *ag.* irreconcil(e)able.

irreconciliabilità, *s.f.* irreconcilability, irreconcilableness.

irreconciliabilménte, *av.* irreconcilably.

irrecuperàbile, *ag.* irrecoverable, irretrievable.

irrecuperabilità, *s.f.* irrecoverableness, irretrievableness.

irrecuperabilménte, *av.* irrecoverably, irretrievably: *— perduto,* irretrievably lost.

irrecusàbile, *ag.* undeniable, irrecusable, irrefutable.

irrecusabilità, *s.f.* undeniableness, irrefutability.

irrecusabilménte, *av.* undeniably, irrecusably, irrefutably.

irredentísmo, *s.m.* (*pol.*) irredentism.

irredentísta, *ag. s.c.* (*pol.*) irredentist.

irredentístico, *ag.* irredentist.

irredènto, *ag.* unredeemed.

irredimíbile, *ag.* irredeemable.

irredimibilità, *s.f.* irredeemability.

irredimibilménte, *av.* irredeemably.

irrefragàbile, *ag.* indisputable, irrefragable, unanswerable.

irrefragabilità, *s.f.* indisputability, indisputableness, irrefragability, irrefragableness.

irrefragabilménte, *av.* indisputably, irrefragably

irrefrangíbile, *ag.* (*ott.*) irrefrangible.

irrefrenàbile, *ag.* unrestrainable, irrepressible.

irrefrenabilménte, *av.* unrestrainably, irrepressibly.

irrefutàbile, *ag.* irrefutable, indisputable: *le prove sono irrefutabili,* the evidence is irrefutable.

irrefutabilità, *s.f.* irrefutability, irrefutableness, indisputability, indisputableness.

irrefutabilménte, *av.* irrefutably, indisputably.

irregimentàre, *v.t.* **1.** (*mil.*) to regiment, to form into regiments **2.** (*organizzare*) to regiment, to group, to organize.

irregolàre, *ag.* **1.** irregular: *forma —,* irregular shape; *milizie irregolari,* irregular troops; *verbo —,* irregular verb **2.** (*sregolato*) disorderly, loose: *vita —,* loose life **3.** (*intermittente*) erratic: *polso —,* erratic pulse **4.** (*non uniforme*) uneven: *terreno —,* uneven ground **5.** (*asimmetrico*) straggling: *costruzione —,* straggling building ‖ *s.m.pl.* (*mil.*) irregulars: *una banda di irregolari,* a band of irregulars.

irregolarità, *s.f.* irregularity; unevenness: *l'— della sua posizione,* the irregularity of his position; *l'— del suo umore,* the unevenness of his temper; *trar vantaggio dalla — del terreno,* to take advantage of the unevenness of the ground.

irregolarménte, *av.* irregularly.

irreligióne, *s.f.* irreligion, irreligiousness.

irreligiosaménte, *av.* irreligiously.

irreligiosità, *s.f.* irreligiousness.

irreligióso, *ag.* irreligious.

irremissíbile, *ag.* irremissible; unpardonable: *un peccato —,* an unpardonable sin.

irremissibilménte, *av.* irremissibly; unpardonably.

irremovíbile, *ag.* **1.** immovable **2.** (*inflessibile*) inflexible, unyielding: *essere —,* to be inflexible (*o* to stand fast); *essere — nei propri principi,* to be unyielding in one's principles.

irremovibilità, *s.f.* **1.** immovability **2.** (*inflessibilità*) inflexibility, steadfastness.

irremovibilménte, *av.* **1.** immovably **2.** (*inflessibilmente*) inflexibly, unyieldingly.

irreparàbile, *ag.* irreparable; irretrievable: *una perdita* —, an irretrievable loss.

irreparabilità, *s.f.* irreparability; irretrievableness.

irreparabilménte, *av.* irreparably; irretrievably: *felicità* — *perduta,* irretrievably lost happiness.

irreperìbile, *ag.* irrecoverable: *rendersi* —, to hide oneself (*o fam.* to make oneself scarce).

irreprensìbile, *ag.* irreproachable, faultless, irreprehensible, blameless; above reproach (*predicativo*): *condotta* —, blameless behaviour.

irreprensibilità, *s.f.* irreproachability, irreproachableness, faultlessness, blamelessness.

irreprensibilménte, *av.* irreproachably, faultlessly, blamelessly: *abbigliato* —, faultlessly dressed.

irrepugnàbile, *ag.* irrefutable, indisputable.

irrepugnabilità, *s.f.* irrefutableness, indisputableness.

irrepugnabilménte, *av.* irrefutably, indisputably.

irrequietaménte, *av.* restlessly, uneasily, fretfully: *camminava avanti e indietro* —, he was restlessly walking to and fro.

irrequietézza, *s.f.* restlessness, uneasiness, fretfulness.

irrequièto, *ag.* restless, uneasy, fretful: *non essere così* —, don't fret so much.

irresistìbile, *ag.* irresistible.

irresistibilità, *s.f.* irresistibility, irresistibleness.

irresistibilménte, *av.* irresistibly: *essere* — *attratto verso ql.co., qlcu.,* to be irresistibly attracted to sthg., s.o.

irresolúbile, *ag.* irresolvable, unsolvable.

irresolutaménte, *av.* irresolutely.

irresolutézza, *s.f.* irresolution, indecision, hesitation, wavering: *sono stanco della sua continua* —, I am tired of his perpetual wavering.

irresolúto, *ag.* irresolute, hesitating, wavering.

irrespiràbile, *ag.* unbreathable, irrespirable; (*soffocante*) stifling (*anche fig.*): *un'atmosfera* —, a stifling atmosphere.

irresponsàbile, *ag.* irresponsible.

irresponsabilità, *s.f.* irresponsibility.

irresponsabilménte, *av.* irresponsibly.

irrestringìbile, *ag.* unshrinkable, non-shrinking.

irretíre, *v.t.* 1. to snare, to (en)trap 2. (*allettare, ammaliare*) to ensnare; to entice, to allure 3. (*ingannare*) to trick, to cheat, to take in: *non lasciarti — dalle loro mene,* don't be taken in by their scheming.

irreversìbile, *ag.* irreversible, not reversible: *direzione* —, (*aut.*) irreversible steering.

irreversibilità, *s.f.* irreversibility, irreversibleness.

irreversibilménte, *av.* irreversibly.

irrevocàbile, *ag.* irrevocable; (*dir.*) absolute: *decisione* —, irrevocable decision (*o* decision past recall); *decreto* —, decree absolute; *prendere una decisione* —, to take an irrevocable decision (*o fam.* to nail one's colours to the mast).

irrevocabilità, *s.f.* irrevocability, irrevocableness.

irrevocabilménte, *av.* irrevocably.

irricevìbile, *ag.* unreceivable; inadmissible; unacceptable.

irriconciliàbile, *e derivati, V.* **irreconciliàbile,** *e derivati.*

irriconoscíbile, *ag.* unrecognizable; altered beyond recognition (*predicativo*): *il nostro povero amico era* —, our poor friend had altered beyond recognition.

irriconoscibilménte, *av.* unrecognizably.

irrídere, *v.t.* to deride; to laugh at (s.o., sthg.); to mock; to make fun of (s.o., sthg.): *quando comparve con quel cappello stravagante, tutti la irrisero,* when she appeared with that extraordinary hat, they all laughed at her.

irriducíbile, *ag.* irreducible, indomitable: *volontà* —, indomitable will; *mostrarsi* — *su una clausola,* to adhere strictly to a clause.

irriducibilità, *s.f.* irreducibility, irreducibleness.

irriducibilménte, *av.* irreducibly, indomitably.

irriflessióne, *s.f.* thoughtlessness, heedlessness.

irriflessivaménte, *av.* thoughtlessly, heedlessly.

irriflessivo, *ag.* thoughtless, heedless; rash: *una azione irriflessiva,* a rash act.

irrigàbile, *ag.* irrigable: *prato* —, water-meadow.

irrigaménto, *V.* **irrigazióne.**

irrigàre, *v.t.* 1. to irrigate 2. (*med.*) (*ferite*) to irrigate, to spray; (*organi interni*) to douche.

irrigatòrio, *ag.* irrigative.

irrigazióne, *s.f.* 1. irrigation 2. (*med.*) (*di ferite*) irrigation, spraying; (*di organi interni*) douching.

irrigidiménto, *s.m.* stiffening.

irrigidíre, *v.t.* to stiffen, to make stiff (*anche fig.*) ‖ *v.i.,* **irrigidírsi,** *v.r.* to stiffen, to become stiff (*anche fig.*): *si irrigidirono sulle rispettive posizioni,* they refused to move from their respective standpoints.

irrigidíto, *ag.* 1. stiff: — *sull'attenti,* standing at attention 2. *fig.* unbending, unyielding.

irríguo, *ag.* irriguous, well-watered, irrigated: *campo* —, well-watered field.

irrilevànte, *ag.* insignificant, trifling, unimportant.

irrimediàbile, *ag.* irremediable, irreparable: *un errore* —, an irremediable fault.

irrimediabilità, *s.f.* irremediableness, irreparableness, irreparability.

irrimediabilménte, *av.* irremediably, irreparably.

irrisióne, *s.f.* derision, mockery: *esporre qlcu. all'*—, to hold s.o. up to ridicule.

irríso, *ag.* derided, laughed at, mocked: *fu* — *da tutti,* he was made a laughing-stock.

irrisolúto, *e derivati, V.* **irresolúto,** *e derivati.*

irrisóre, *s.m.* derider, mocker.

irrisoriaménte, *av.* 1. derisively, scoffingly, mockingly 2. (*in modo meschino*) paltrily, meanly, meagrely: *lo compensarono* —, they rewarded him meagrely.

irrisòrio, *ag.* 1. derisory, derisive 2. (*meschino*) paltry, mean, meagre: *prezzo* —, paltry price.

irrispettóso, *ag.* disrespectful: *è un ragazzo* —, he is a disrespectful (*o* a cheeky) boy.

irritàbile, *ag.* 1. (*di persona*) irritable, touchy; (*fam.*) cantankerous 2. (*di pelle, ecc.*) sensitive: *questa lozione è adatta per pelli irritabili,* this lotion is suitable for sensitive skins.

irritabilità, *s.f.* 1. (*di persona*) irritability, touchiness 2. (*di pelle, ecc.*) sensitiveness.

irritaménto, *V.* **irritazióne.**

irritànte, *ag.* 1. irritating, maddening, provoking; vexatious; (*fam.*) aggravating: *un fanciullo* —, an aggravating child; *ha quest'abitudine* —, he has this maddening habit 2.(*med.*) irritant ‖ *s.m.* (*med.*) irritant.

irritàre, *v.t.* 1. (*provocare, innervosire*) to irritate, to madden, to provoke; to vex; (*fam.*) to aggravate: *non irritatela!,* don't irritate her! 2. (*ferita, pelle, ecc.*) to irritate, to inflame: *lo sfregamento irritò la ferita,* rubbing irritated (*o* inflamed) the wound ‖ **irritàrsi,** *v.r.* 1. (*innervosirsi*) to grow angry, to get vexed, to grow nervous, to get mad 2. (*di ferita, pelle, ecc.*) to become irritated: *la pelle gli si era molto irritata,* his skin had become very sore (*o* inflamed *o* irritated).

irritatívo, *ag.* irritative, irritating.

irritàto, *ag.* 1. irritated, vexed 2. (*infiammato*) inflamed; sore.

irritazióne, *s.f.* 1. irritation; (*ira*) anger: *essere in preda ad una viva* —, to be seething with anger 2. (*di ferita, pelle, ecc.*) inflammation.

írrito, *ag.* (*dir.*) null, void, of no effect (*predicativo*): *il testamento è* —, the will is null and void.

irritrattàbile, *ag.* irrevocable: *questa decisione è* —, this decision is irrevocable.

irritrattabilità, *s.f.* irrevocableness, irrevocability.

irrivelàbile, *ag.* that cannot be revealed, that cannot be disclosed: *il trattato fu revocato per ragioni per ora irrivelabili,* the treaty was revoked for reasons that cannot be disclosed at present.

irriverènte, *ag.* irreverent, disrespectful; (*sfrontato*) cheeky.

irriverenteménte, *av.* irreverently.

irriverènza, *s.f.* irreverence, disrespectfulness; (*sfrontatezza*) cheekiness.

irrobustíre, *v.t.* to strengthen ‖ **irrobustírsi,** *v.r.* to grow strong(er), to strengthen: *questo ragazzo si sta sempre più irrobustendo,* this boy is growing stronger and stronger.

irrómpere, *v.i.* **1.** to break into (a place), to burst into (a place): *i ladri irruppero nella casa,* the burglars broke into the house; — *in una stanza,* to burst (o to rush) into a room **2.** (*riversarsi*) to swarm: *la folla irruppe nel campo da giuoco,* the crowd swarmed over the foot-ball ground **3.** (*di acque*) to overflow, to flood.

irroràre, *v.t.* to sprinkle; to spray; to bedew.

irroratóre, *s.m.,* **irroratríce,** *s.f.* (*agr.*) sprayer, spraying machine.

irrorazióne, *s.f.* sprinkling; spraying; bedewing.

irrotazionàle, *ag.* (*elettronica*) irrotational.

irruènte, *ag.* impetuous, violent; rash.

irruènza, *s.f.* impetuousness, impetuosity, violence; rashness.

irrugginíre, *V.* arrugginíre.

irruvidíre, *v.t.* to roughen, to make rough; (*screpolare*) to chap ‖ **irruvidírsi,** *v.r.* to roughen, to become rough: *le si sono irruvidite le mani,* her hands have roughened (o her hands are chapped).

irruzióne, *s.f.* **1.** irruption, inrush: *fare* — *in un luogo,* to break (o to rush, o to burst) into a place ‖ — *del mare,* tidal wave **2.** (*invasione, scorreria*) invasion, inroad, raid.

irsúto, *ag.* shaggy, hairy, bristly: *una barba irsuta,* a shaggy beard.

írto, *ag.* **1.** bristly, shaggy: *capelli irti,* shaggy hair **2.** (*pieno di punte*) bristling: — *di spine,* bristling with (o full of) thorns ‖ *lavoro* — *di difficoltà,* work full of difficulties.

Isabèlla, *no.pr.f.* Isabella, Isabel ‖ *dim.* Bel(le), Isa, Ib(by), Tib(bie) ‖ **isabèlla,** *ag.* isabel, isabella ‖ *uva* —, Isabella (grape).

Isàeco, *no.pr.m.* Isaac.

isadèlfo, *ag.* (*bot.*) isadelphous.

isagòge, *s.f.* (*letter.*) isagoge.

isagògico, *ag.* isagogic.

isàgono, *s.m.* (*geom.*) isogon.

Isaìa, *no.pr.m.* (*Bibbia*) Isaiah.

isanèmono, *ag.:* *linea isanemona,* (*meteorologia*) isanemone.

isanòmalo, *ag.* (*meteorologia*) isanomalous.

isàtide, *s.f.* (*bot.*) Isatis.

isatína, *s.f.* (*chim.*) isatin.

ísba, *s.f.* isba(h).

iscariòta, *ag.* Iscariot: *Giuda* —, (*Bibbia*) Judas Iscariot.

ischeletríto, *ag.* skeleton-like (*attributivo*); (*emaciato*) gaunt, fleshless.

ischemía, *s.f.* (*patol.*) ischemia.

ischialgía, *s.f.* (*patol.*) ischialgia.

ischiàtico, *ag.* (*anat.*) ischiatic.

íschio, *s.m.* (*anat.*) ischium (*pl.* ischia).

iscritto[1], *ag.* **1.** (*a una scuola, esame, associazione, competizione, ecc.*) enrolled, registered ‖ *gli iscritti,* the members: *gli iscritti al club,* the members of the club **2.** (*annoverato, registrato*) recorded, registered **3.** (*scolpito*) engraved, inscribed **4.** (*geom.*) inscribed.

iscritto[2], *p.p.:* *per* —, in writing; *mettere in* —, to put down in writing.

iscrívere, *v.t.* **1.** (*a una scuola, esame, associazione, competizione, ecc.*) to enrol(l), to register, to enter s.o.'s name: *devo iscriverti a questa gara?,* shall I enter you (o your name) for this match?; *ho iscritto mio figlio a questo esame,* I have entered my son's name for this examination; — *qlcu. a un club,* to enrol s.o.

as a member of a club; — *una persona, un nome su una lista,* to enter a person, a name on a list **2.** (*annoverare, registrare*) to record, to register: *la storia iscriverà il suo nome fra i grandi uomini di quel paese,* history will record his name among the great men of that country **3.** (*scrivere, scolpire*) to inscribe, to engrave: *il suo nome fu iscritto su una lastra di marmo,* his name was inscribed on a marble slab ‖ — *ql.co. nella memoria di qlcu.,* to engrave sthg. on s.o.'s memory **4.** (*geom.*) to inscribe ‖ **iscríversi,** *v.r.* to enter (sthg.); to enter one's name (for sthg.); to enrol(l) oneself; to join (sthg.): *mi sono iscritto all'esame di latino,* I have entered my name for the Latin examination; — *all'università,* to matriculate; — *a un concorso,* to go in for a competition; — *a un partito,* to join a party; — *a una scuola, a un club,* to enter a school, a club.

iscrizióne, *s.f.* **1.** inscription: *un'* — *in latino,* an inscription in Latin **2.** (*a una scuola, esame, associazione, competizione, ecc.*) entry, enrol(l)ment, registration; (*a una università*) matriculation: *domanda d'* —, application; *modulo d'* —, application (o entry) form; *tassa d'* —, entrance fee; *ci furono venti iscrizioni per questa corsa,* there were twenty entries for this race; *fare l'* — *ad un esame,* to enter one's name for an examination **3.** — *ipotecaria,* (*dir.*) registry (o registration) of mortgages.

Íside, *no.pr.f.* (*mit.*) Isis.

Isidòro, *no.pr.m.* Isidore; (*st.*) Isidorus.

Islàm, *s.m.* (*st. relig.*) Islam.

islamísmo, *s.m.* (*st. relig.*) Islamism, Mohammedanism.

islamíta, *ag.* Islamic, Islamitic ‖ *s.c.* Islamite.

islamítico, *ag.* Islamitic.

Islànda, *no.pr.f.* (*geog.*) Iceland.

islandése, *ag.* Icelandic ‖ *s.c.* Icelander ‖ *s.m.* (*lingua*) (the) Icelandic (language).

Ismaèle, *no.pr.m.* (*Bibbia*) Ishmael.

isòbara, *s.f.* (*meteorologia*) isobar; isobaric curve.

isòbarico, *ag.* (*meteorologia, chim.*) isobaric: *carta isobarica,* isobaric chart; *isotopi isobari,* (*chim.*) isobaric isotopes.

isòbaro, *s.m.* (*chim.*) isobar(e).

isobaromètrico, *ag.* (*meteorologia*) isobarometric.

isòbata, *s.f.* **1.** (*fis.*) isobath **2.** (*geog.*) depth contour.

isoclinàle, *ag.* (*geol.*) isoclinal.

isòclino, *s.m.* (*geol.*) isocline.

Isòcrate, *no.pr.m.* (*st. lett.*) Isocrates.

isocromàtico, *ag.* (*fis.*) isochromatic.

isocronísmo, *s.m.* (*fis.*) isochronism.

isòcrono, *ag.* (*fis.*) isochronous, isochronal.

isodinàmico, *ag.* (*fis.*) isodynamic.

isoelèttrico, *ag.* (*elett.*) isoelectric.

isogamía, *s.f.* (*bot.*) isogamy.

isògamo, *ag.* (*bot.*) isogamous.

isogeotèrmo, *ag.* (*geol.*) isogeothermal.

isògona, *s.f.* (*fis.*) isogonic (line).

isogònico, *ag.* (*fis.*) isogonic; isogonal.

isògono, *ag.* (*fis.*) isogonic; isogonal.

isoípsa, *s.f.* (*geofisica*) contour line.

ísola, *s.f.* **1.** (*geog.*) island; isle: *vivere su un'* —, to live on an island ‖ *le Isole Baleari,* the Balearic Islands ‖ *le Isole Britanniche,* the British Isles ‖ *le Isole Canarie,* the Canary Islands ‖ *l'* — *di Man,* the Isle of Man ‖ *le Isole Normanne,* the Channel Islands **2.** (*isolato*) block of houses **3.** (*med. anat.*) island: *isole di Langerhans,* Langerhans islands; — *di visione,* vision island **4.** (*di portaerei*) island.

isolàbile, *ag.* isolable.

isolaménto, *s.m.* **1.** isolation; (*solitudine*) loneliness: *un periodo di* —, a period of isolation ‖ *splendido isolamento,* splendid isolation **2.** (*med.*) isolation: *corsia di* —, isolation ward **3.** (*elett.*) insulation: — *di classe A,* class A insulation; *verificatore di* —, insulation tester **4.** (*fis.*): — *acustico,* sound-proofing; (*edil.*) deadening; — *termico,* thermal insulation.

isolàna, *s.f.* islander.

isolàno, *ag.* insular ‖ *s.m.* islander.

isolànte, *ag.* (*elett.*) insulating: *nastro —,* insulating tape ‖ *s.m.* insulator.

isolàre, *v.t.* **1.** to isolate; to separate; to set apart: *il cattivo tempo ci ha isolati dal villaggio,* the bad weather has isolated us from the village **2.** (*med.*) to isolate: *— un malato,* to isolate a patient **3.** (*chim.*) to isolate: *— una sostanza chimica,* to isolate a chemical substance **4.** (*elett.*) to insulate **5.** *— acusticamente,* (*fis.*) to soundproof.

isolataménte, *av.* isolatedly, in isolation; separately: *parlò a ciascuno di loro —,* he talked to each of them separately.

isolàto, *ag.* **1.** isolated, lonely; (*distaccato*) aloof (*predicativo*): *si tiene — dalla folla,* he stands aloof from the crowd; *vivere —,* to live isolated (*o* in isolation) **2.** (*di luogo*) lonely, remote **3.** (*elett.*) insulated **4.** *— acusticamente,* (*fis.*) soundproof ‖ *s.m.* **1.** block (of houses) **2.** (*spor.*) independent racer, independent runner.

isolatóre, *s.m.* (*elett.*) insulator.

isolazionísmo, *s.m.* (*pol.*) isolationism.

isolazionísta, *s.c.* (*pol.*) isolationist.

isolétta, *s.f.,* **isolòtto,** *s.m.* islet, small island.

Isolína, *no.pr.f.* dim. di **Isòtta.**

isomèrico, *ag.* (*chim.*) isomeric.

isomerísmo, *s.m.* (*chim.*) isomerism.

isòmero, *s.m.* (*chim.*) isomer.

isomorfísmo, *s.m.* (*chim.*) isomorphism.

isomòrfo, *ag.* (*chim.*) isomorphous, isomorphic.

isòpodo, *ag. s.m.* (*zool.*) isopod ‖ *gli isopodi,* (*zool.*) Isopoda.

isòscele, *ag.* (*geom.*) isosceles.

isosísmico, *ag.* (*geol.*) isoseismal, isoseismic.

isostàtico, *ag.* (*fis.*) isostatic.

isòtera, *s.f.* (*meteorologia*) isothere.

isotèrma, *s.f.* **1.** (*meteorologia*) isotherm **2.** (*chim. fis.*) isothermal line.

isotèrmico, *ag.* (*fis.*) isothermal: *processo —,* isotherm.

isòtopo, *s.m.* (*chim. fis.*) isotope: *— radioattivo,* radioisotope.

isotropía, *s.f.* (*fis.*) isotropy, isotropism.

Isòtta, *no.pr.f.* Isolde, Iseult.

ispànico, *ag.* Hispanic.

ispanísmo, *s.m.* Hispanicism.

ispàno-, (*prefisso*) Hispano-: *— americano,* Hispano-American.

ispettívo, *ag.* inspectoral, inspectorial, supervising, supervisory: *fu inviato là con mansioni ispettive,* he was sent there with supervisory duties.

ispettoràto, *s.m.* **1.** (*carica, ufficio d'ispettore*) inspectorate, inspectorship **2.** (*sede dell'ispettore*) inspectorate **3.** (*corpo degli ispettori*) inspectorate; inspectors (*pl.*).

ispettóre, *s.m.* inspector, overseer, surveyor: *— dei lavori,* overseer of the works; *— di polizia,* detective inspector; *— fiscale,* inspector of taxes; *— scolastico,* school inspector.

ispezionàre, *v.t.* **1.** to inspect, to look over (sthg.), to survey **2.** (*esaminare*) to examine: *— i libri contabili,* to examine the books.

ispezióne, *s.f.* **1.** inspection, survey: *fare un'—,* to make an inspection (*o* to inspect) **2.** (*esame*) examination.

ispidaménte, *av.* **1.** hispidly; shaggily **2.** (*sgarbatamente*) rudely.

ispidézza, *s.f.* **1.** hispidity, bristliness, shagginess **2.** (*sgarbatezza*) rudeness.

íspido, *ag.* **1.** hispid, bristly; shaggy: *capelli ispidi,* bristly hair **2.** (*sgarbato*) rude.

ispiràre, *v.t.* to inspire; (*infondere*) to infuse: *il paesaggio ispirò il pittore,* the landscape inspired the painter; *egli ispirava fiducia a tutti,* he inspired (*o* infused) everybody with confidence (*o* he inspired confidence into everybody) ‖ **ispiràrsi,** *v.r.* to draw one's inspiration (from s.o., sthg.): *— alla bellezza di qlcu.,*

to be inspired by s.o.'s beauty; *qui veniva il Leopardi per —,* Leopardi came here for his inspiration.

ispiràto, *ag.* **1.** inspired: *un poeta —,* an inspired poet **2.** (*basato*) imbued (with sthg.): *regime — al principio della libertà,* regime imbued with the spirit of freedom.

ispiratóre, *ag.* inspiring: *il principio — di quest'ode,* the inspiring principle of this ode ‖ *s.m.,* **ispiratríce,** *s.f.* inspirer.

ispirazióne, *s.f.* inspiration: *il dono dell'—,* the gift of inspiration; *secondo un'— improvvisa,* on the spur of the moment.

Israèle, *no.pr.m.* **1.** (*Bibbia*) (*Giacobbe*) Israel **2.** (*Bibbia*) (*terra, popolo*) Israel **3.** (*Stato costituito nel 1948*) Israel.

israeliàno, *ag.s.m.* Israeli; (*nato in Israele*) Sabra ‖ **israeliàna,** *s.f.* Israeli; (*nata in Israele*) Sabra.

israelíta, *ag.* Israelite, Jewish ‖ *s.m.* Israelite, Jew, Hebrew ‖ *s.f.* Israelite, Jewess, Hebrew.

israelítico, *ag.* Israelite, Israelitic, Israelitish, Jewish.

íssa, *inter.* heave ho!.

issàre, *v.t.* to hoist: *— la bandiera,* to hoist the flag; *— i colori nazionali,* (*mar.*) to dress ship; *— qlcu. a cavallo,* to hoist s.o. on to his horse.

issofàtto, *av.* immediately, at once.

issòpo, *s.m.* (*bot.*) hyssop.

istamína, *s.f.* (*farm.*) histamine.

istantànea, *s.f.* (*foto.*) snapshot, snap: *fare un'—,* to snapshot.

istantaneaménte, *av.* instantaneously, immediately.

istantaneità, *s.f.* instantaneity, instantaneousness.

istantàneo, *ag.* **1.** instantaneous, instant, immediate: *morte istantanea,* sudden death; *una risposta istantanea,* an immediate answer; *sentire un sollievo —,* to feel instant relief **2.** (*elett.*) momentary.

istànte[1] *ag.* (*urgente*) instant, urgent, pressing ‖ *s.c.* (*postulante*) petitioner.

istànte[2] *s.m.* instant, moment: *all'—,* on the instant (*o* instantly *o* immediately); *da un — all'altro,* at any moment: *sarà qui da un — all'altro,* he will be here any moment now; *in un —,* in an instant (*o* instantly); *in questo stesso —,* this very instant.

instanteménte, *av.* instantly.

istànza, *s.f.* **1.** (*richiesta*) request, instance; (*supplica*) entreaty: *su — di qlcu.,* at the instance (*o* at the request) of s.o.; *egli non ascoltò le nostre istanze,* he didn't listen to our entreaties; *accogliere, respingere un'—,* to grant, to reject a request; *fare viva —,* to entreat earnestly ‖ *tribunale di prima —,* (*dir.*) court of first instance **2.** (*domanda formale scritta*) application; (*petizione*) petition: *— di pagamento,* application of payment; *fare un'—,* to make a petition **3.** (*urgenza*) instancy, urgency: *con —,* urgently.

isterèsi, *s.f.* (*fis.*) hysteresis.

isteresímetro, *s.m.* (*elett.*) hysteresimeter.

istericaménte, *av.* hysterically.

istèrico, *ag.* hysteric(al): *crisi isterica,* fit of hysteria (*o* hysterics); *avere un attacco —,* to fall (*o* to go) into hysterics ‖ *s.m.* hysterical man.

isterilíre, *v.t.* to sterilize (anche *fig.*) ‖ *v.i.,* **isterilírsi,** *v.r.* to become sterile.

isterilíto, *ag.* **1.** made sterile, made unfruitful **2.** (*indurito*) withered: *cuore —,* withered heart.

isterísmo, *s.m.* hysteria: *crisi di —,* fit of hysteria (*o* hysterics): *essere preso da una crisi di —,* to have hysterics.

isterocèle, *s.m.* (*patol.*) hysterocele.

isteroepilessía, *s.f.* (*patol.*) hysteroepilepsy.

isterología, *s.f.* (*gram. ret.*) hysteron proteron.

isteròmetro, *s.m.* (*med.*) hysterometer.

isterotomía, *s.f.* (*chir.*) hysterotomy.

istésso, *V.* **stésso.**

istigàre, *v.t.* to instigate, to incite, to prompt; to urge: *— qlcu. a bere,* to egg s.o. on to drink; *— qlcu.*

al delitto, to instigate s.o. to crime; — *qlcu. al male,* to incite s.o. to evil.

istigatóre, *s.m.,* **istigatríce,** *s.f.* instigator.

istigazióne, *s.f.* instigation, incitement: *fare ql.co. su — di qlcu.,* to do sthg. at (*o* on) s.o.'s instigation.

istillàre, *e derivati, V.* **instillàre,** *e derivati.*

istintivaménte, *av.* instinctively, by instinct, on instinct.

istintívo, *ag.* instinctive: *gli animali hanno una paura istintiva del fuoco,* animals have an instinctive dread of fire.

istínto, *s.m.* instinct: — *di conservazione,* instinct of self-preservation; *gli uccelli imparano a volare per —,* birds learn to fly by instinct; *agire d'—,* to act on instinct; *avere un — per la musica,* to have an instinct for music; *seguire l'—,* to follow one's instinct.

istituíre, *v.t.* **1.** to institute, to set up, to establish: — *una legge,* to pass a law; — *un nuovo sistema,* to set up a new system **2.** (*fondare*) to found: — *una scuola,* to found a school **3.** (*dir.*) to appoint: — *qlcu. proprio erede,* to appoint s.o. (as) one's heir.

istitúto, *s.m.* **1.** institute: — *di statistica, di tecnologia,* institute of statistics, of technology **2.** (*istituzione*) institution: *un — di carità,* a charitable institution **3.** (*scuola*) school; institute; college: — *magistrale,* teachers' training school (*o* college); — *tecnico,* technical school (*o* institute) **4.** (*banca*) bank: — *di credito mobiliare,* investment bank; — *di emissione,* bank of issue.

istitutóre, *s.m.* **1.** (*fondatore*) founder **2.** (*precettore*) tutor.

istitutríce, *s.f.* **1.** (*fondatrice*) foundress **2.** (*educatrice*) governess.

istituzióne, *s.f.* **1.** institution: *un'— di carità,* a charitable institution **2.** (*fondazione*) institution, foundation, establishment **3.** *pl.* (*elementi fondamentali di un ordinamento politico, di una disciplina, ecc.*) institutes: *le istituzioni di Giustiniano,* the Institutes of Justinian **4.** *pl.* (*leggi*) laws: *egli rispetta le patrie istituzioni,* he abides by the laws of his country.

ístmico, *ag.* isthmian.

ístmo, *s.m.* (*geog. anat.*) isthmus (*pl.* isthmuses, isthmi): — *delle fauci,* (*anat.*) isthmus (of the fauces); *l'— di Panama, di Suez,* the Isthmus of Panama, of Suez.

istología, *s.f.* histology.

istològico, *ag.* histological, histologic.

istòlogo, *s.m.* histologist.

istòria, *V.* **stòria.**

istoriàre, *v.t.* to adorn with figures, to story; (*un libro*) to illustrate.

istoriàto, *ag.* storied, adorned with figures; (*di libro*) illustrated: *urna istoriata,* storied urn.

Ístria, *no.pr.f.* (*geog.*) Istria.

istriàno, *ag.s.m.* Istrian.

ístrice, *s.m.* **1.** hedgehog, porcupine **2.** *fig.* hedgehog; cross-grained person.

istrióne, *s.m.* **1.** (*teat. spreg.*) histrion, stage player: *far l'—,* to overact **2.** (*ciarlatano*) charlatan, quack, mountebank.

istrionicaménte, *av.* histrionically.

istriònico, *ag.* histrionic, overacting, stagy: *una dizione istrionica,* a stagy type of diction.

istrionísmo, *s.m.* histrionics (*pl.*).

istruíre, *v.t.* **1.** to instruct, to teach: *l'ho istruito in inglese,* I have instructed him in English (*o* I have taught him English) **2.** (*dare istruzioni a*) to instruct, to direct: *lo istruirò su come farlo,* I'll instruct him how to do it **3.** (*informare*) to inform: *mi hanno istruito dell'accaduto,* they have informed me of the happening **4.** (*dir.*) to institute: — *un processo,* to institute proceedings ‖ **istruírsi,** *v.r.* to educate oneself, to improve one's mind.

istruíto, *ag.* educated, well-read, learned: *una persona istruita,* an educated person; *è — in molti campi,* he is widely and deeply learned.

istruménto, *e derivati, V.* **struménto,** *e derivati.*

istruttívo, *ag.* instructive.

istruttóre, *s.m.* instructor; teacher; drill-master: *caporale —,* (*mil.*) drill-sergeant; *giudice —,* (*dir.*) examining magistrate.

istruttòria, *s.f.* (*dir.*) examination, investigation, inquest: *aprire l'—,* to open (the) proceedings.

istruttòrio, *ag.* (*dir.*) preliminary: *il periodo —,* the preliminary proceeding.

istruzióne, *s.f.* **1.** education: — *classica, scientifica,* classical, scientific education; — *tecnica, professionale,* technical, vocational training; *provvedere all'— dei propri figli,* to provide for the education of one's children ‖ *Ministero della Pubblica Istruzione,* Ministry of Education **2.** (*cultura*) learning, culture: *tutti ammirano la sua —,* everybody admires his learning **3.** (*insegnamento*) teaching: — *gratuita,* free tuition **4.** (*ordine*) instruction, order: *dare, impartire istruzioni a qlcu.,* to give instructions to s.o. **5.** (*indicazione*) instruction, direction: *istruzioni per l'uso,* directions; *secondo le istruzioni,* as directed; *secondo le vostre istruzioni,* according to your instructions.

istupidíre, *v.t.* to make stupid, to dull, to stupefy ‖ *v.i.* to become stupid, to grow dull, to stupefy: — *a forza di bere,* to drink oneself stupid.

istupidíto, *ag.* stupid, dulled, stupefied, dazed: — *dal bere,* stupefied with drink; — *dal dolore,* dazed with grief.

Ítaca, *no.pr.f.* (*geog.*) Ithaca.

Itàlia, *no.pr.f.* (*geog.*) Italy: — *Centrale, Settentrionale, Meridionale,* Central, Northern, Southern Italy.

italianaménte, *av.* **1.** (*secondo la moda italiana*) after the Italian fashion, in the Italian way **2.** (*da buon italiano*) as a good Italian.

italianàre, *v.t.,* **italianàrsi,** *v.r.* to Italianize.

italianàto, *ag.* Italianate: *un inglese —,* an Italianate Englishman.

italianísmo, *s.m.* Italianism.

italianità, *s.f.* **1.** (*spirito italiano*) Italian spirit **2.** (*sentimenti italiani*) Italian feelings (*pl.*).

italianizzàre, *v.t.,* **italianizzàrsi,** *v.r.* to Italianize.

italiàno, *ag.* Italian: *un poeta —,* an Italian poet ‖ *s.m.* **1.** (*abitante*) Italian ‖ *gli Italiani,* the Italians (*o* the Italian people) **2.** (*lingua*) (the) Italian (language) ‖ **italiàna,** *s.f.* Italian: *ho visto alcune italiane,* I saw some Italian women.

itàlico, *ag.s.m.* (*letter.*) **1.** Italic, Italian: *lingue italiche,* Italic languages; *la penisola italica,* the Italian peninsula **2.** (*tip.*) italic(s): *in —,* in italics.

italiòta, *s.c.* Italiot(e).

ítalo[1], *ag.* (*poet.*) Italian.

ítalo-[2], (*prefisso*) Italo-: — *americano,* Italo-American.

iteràre, *v.t.* to iterate.

iterataménte, *av.* repeatedly.

iteratívo, *av.* (*gram.*) iterative.

iteràto, *ag.* repeated.

iterazióne, *s.f.* iterance, iteration.

itifàllo, *s.m.* (*poes.*) ithyphallic.

itifàllico, *ag.* (*poes.*) ithyphallic.

itineràrio, *ag.* (*rar.*) itinerary: *misure itinerarie,* road measurements ‖ *s.m.* **1.** itinerary, route, way: *che — hanno preso?,* which route have they taken? **2.** (*guida stradale*) road-book, guide-book.

ittèrbio, *s.m.* (*chim.*) ytterbium.

ittèrico, *ag.* (*med.*) jaundiced, icteric ‖ *s.m.* (*med.*) icteric, sufferer from jaundice.

itterízia, *s.f.,* **íttero,** *s.m.* (*patol.*) jaundice, icterus.

ittiocòlla, *s.f.* isinglass, fish-glue.

ittiofagía, *s.f.* ichthyophagy.

ittiòfago, *ag.* ichthyophagous ‖ *s.m.* ichthyophagist.

ittiofòrmio, *s.m.* (*farm.*) ichthyoform.

ittiòide, *s.m.* (*zool.*) ichthyoid.

ittiòlo, *s.m.* (*farm.*) ichthyol.

ittiología, *s.f.* ichthyology.
ittiològico, *ag.* ichthyologic(al).
ittiòlogo, *s.m.* ichthyologist.
ittiosàuro, *s.m.* (*paleont.*) ichthyosaurus.
ittiòsi, *s.f.* (*patol.*) ichthyosis.
ittísmo, *s.m.* (*patol.*) ichthysm(us).
íttrio, *s.m.* (*chim.*) yttrium.
iúgero, *s.m.* juger, jugerum (*pl.* jugera) (*antica misura di superficie* = are 25,2).
Iugoslàvia, *no.pr.f.* (*geog.*) Yugoslavia, Jugoslavia.
iugoslàvo, *ag.s.m.* Yugoslav, Jugoslav ‖ **iugoslàva,** *s.f.* Yugoslav, Jugoslav.
iugulàre¹, *ag.* (*anat.*) jugular: *vena* —, jugular vein.
iugulàre², *v.t.* to jugulate, to strangle, to throttle.
iúngla, *s.f.* jungle.
iúnior, iunióre, *ag.* junior.
iuspatronàto, *s.m.* (*dir.*) juspatronatus.

iúta, *s.f.* jute: *sacco di* —, jute bag (*o* sack).
iutifício, *s.m.* jute-factory, jute-mill.
Iútland, *no.pr.m.* (*geog.*) Jutland.
Ivànoe, *no.pr.m.* Ivanhoe.
ívi, *av.* (*letter.*) **1.** (*di luogo*) there; (*dentro*) therein: — *giaceva dove era caduto,* there he lay where he had fallen; *era — dove l'avevo lasciato,* it was there where I had left it; *Firenze fu colpita dalla peste e tutti quelli che — vivevano dovettero allontanarsi,* Florence was gripped by the plague and all those who lived there were obliged to depart ‖ — *accluso,* joined thereto (*o* therewith); — *incluso,* enclosed therein ‖ — *dentro,* — *fuori,* inside, outside **2.** (*rar.*) (*di tempo*): — *a un anno,* a year later; — *a poco,* after a while (*o* after a short time *o* soon after).
Ívo, *no.pr.m.* Ivo.
izbà, *s.f.* isba(h).

J

j, *s.f.m.* (*lettera ormai esclusa dall'alfabeto italiano. Si vedano alle iniziali* i *o* g *i vocaboli che per grafia arcaica la recassero: p.e.* jàto, jeràtico, jeroglifico, *V.* iàto, jeràtico, geroglífico) j (*pl.* js, j's) ‖ — *come Jersey,* (*tel.*) j for Jack.

jazz, *s.m.* jazz: — *caldo,* hot jazz; — *freddo,* cool jazz; *appassionato di* —, jazz enthusiast (*o sl.* hipster); *orchestra* —, jazz band.

jeep, *s.f.* (*aut.*) jeep.

joule, *s.m.* (*elett.*) joule.

K

k, *s.f.m.* (*lettera usata soltanto in parole di origine straniera*) k (*pl.* ks, k's) ‖ — *come kursaal,* (*tel.*) k for king.

kaftàn, *s.m.* caftan, kaftan.

kainíte, *s.f.* (*min.*) kainite.

kàki[1], *s.m.* (*bot.*) persimmon.

kàki[2], *ag.s.m.* khaki: *color* —, khaki colour.

kala-àzar, *s.f.* (*patol.*) kala-azar.

kallikreína, *s.f.* (*farm.*) kallikrein.

kamàla, *s.f.* (*bot.*) kamala.

kamikàze, *s.m.* kamikaze.

kan, *s.m.* khan.

kantiàno, *ag.* (*st. fil.*) Kantian.

kantísmo, *s.m.* (*st. fil.*) Kantianism, Kantism.

kantísta, *s.m.* (*fil.*) Kantist.

kapòc, *s.m.* kapok.

kapút, *ag.* kaput(t), finished, done for, ruined.

karakíri, *s.m.* hara-kiri, happy dispatch.

karakúl, *s.m.* (*zool.*) karakul, caracul, Persian lamb.

kartísmo, *s.m.* (*neol.*) (*lo sport del « go-kart »*) karting.

kàuri, *s.m.* **1.** (*bot.*) kauri, kauri-pine **2.** (*chim.*) kauri(-gum), kauri resin, kauri copal.

kedivè, *s.m.* khedive.

Kènia, *no.pr.m.* (*geog.*) Kenya.

Kent, *no.pr.m.* (*geog.*) Kent: *del* —, Kentish; *il duca di* —, the Duke of Kent; *la gente del* —, Kentish people.

kepí, *s.m.* kepi.

kepleriàno, *ag.* (*astr.*) Keplerian, of Kepler.

Keplèro, *no.pr.* (*st. astr.*) Kepler.

keratína, *s.f.* (*biol.*) keratin.

kermesse, *s.f.* kermess, kermis.

kerosène, *s.m.* (*chim.*) kerosene: *olio di* —, kerosene (oil).

kibbútz, *s.m.* (*neol.*) (*comunità agricola israeliana*) kibbutz (*pl.* kibbutzim).

kílo, *e derivati, V.* chílo, *e derivati.*

kíloton, *s.m.* (*fis.*) kiloton.

kilowàtt, *s.m.* (*elett.*) kilowatt.

kimòno, *s.m.* kimono.

kinesiterapía, *s.f.* (*med.*) kinesitherapy, kinesipathy.

kipúr, *s.m.* Yom Kippur, Jewish Day of Atonement.

kirsch, *s.m.* kirsch, kirsh, kirschwasser.

kívi, *s.m.* (*ornit.*) kiwi.

knickerbockers, *s.m.pl.* knickerbockers, plus fours.

knock-out, *av.* (*boxe*) knock-out ‖ *essere* —, to be knocked out; *mettere* —, to knock out (*o* to K.O.).

knut, *s.m.* knout.

koàla, *s.m.* (*zool.*) koala.

kóla, *s.f.* (*bot.*) kola.

kòlkhos, *s.m.* kolkhoz.

kòpeck, *s.m.* (*moneta russa*) copeck, kopeck, kopek.

krapfen, *s.m.* (*cuc.*) doughnut.

kreuzer, *s.m.* kreutzer, kreuzer.

kriss, *s.m.* creese, crease, kris.

krumíro, *V.* crumíro.

kultur, *s.f.* kultur.

kümmel, *s.m.* kümmel.

Kúrdistan, *no.pr.m.* (*geog.*) Kurdistan.

kursaal, *s.m.* kursaal.

Kyrie, *s.m.:* — *eleison,* (*eccl.*) Kyrie eleison.

L

l, *s.f.m.* **1.** (*decima lettera dell'alfabeto italiano*) l (*pl.* ls, l's) ‖ — *come Livorno*, (*tel.*) l for Lucy **2.** L (*numero romano equivalente a cinquanta*) L (fifty).

la¹, *art. determinativo f. sing.* **1.** the: — *campagna*, the country; *l'Inghilterra dei Tudor*, the England of the Tudors; — *luna*, the moon; — *terra*, the earth; — *storia del tuo paese è interessante*, the history of your country is interesting **2.** (*spesso non si traduce*): *l'amicizia è preziosa*, friendship is precious; — *domenica è il giorno del riposo*, Sunday is a day of rest; — *donna è la compagna dell'uomo*, woman is the helpmate of man; — *settimana scorsa venne a trovarmi*, last week he came to see me; — *Sicilia è un'isola bellissima*, Sicily is a beautiful island; *questa è — vostra camera*, this is your room ‖ — *Maria*, (*fam.*) Mary; *mi piace — Woolf*, I like Virginia Woolf; *sono andato a vedere — « Francesca da Rimini »*, I went to see " Francesca da Rimini " **3.** (*tradotto con l'ag. poss.*): — *mamma ti chiama*, your mother is calling you; *mi mise — mano sulla spalla*, he put his hand on my shoulder **4.** (*tradotto con l'art. indeterminato*) a, an: *hanno l'automobile?*, do they run a car?; *Maria ha — bocca piccola*, Mary has a small mouth; *scriviamo con — penna o — matita*, we write with a pen or a pencil **5.** (*tradotto col partitivo*) some; any: *doveva andare a comperare — birra*, she had to go and get some beer; *hai comperato — birra?*, did you get any beer? **6.** (*sta per alla col valore di* ogni, ciascuna): *cinque scellini — libbra*, five shillings a pound; *sessanta miglia l'ora*, sixty miles an hour; *tre volte — settimana*, three times a week **7.** (*in espressioni ellittiche*): — *Cristoforo Colombo*, (*nave*) the Christopher Columbus; — *Sassari*, (*brigata*) the Sassari Brigade; *l'una*, (*il tocco*) one o'clock.

la², *pron.pers.f. 3ª persona sing.* **1.** *oggetto* her (*riferito a donna o animale femmina o a cosa personificata*); it (*riferito a cosa o animale di sesso non specificato*): *cercala*, look for her, it; *conoscere la natura è amarla*, to know nature is to love her; *ecco la mia matita, — cercavo da due giorni*, here is my pencil, I have been looking for it (for) two days; *« Hai visto mia figlia? », « Non — trovo »*, " Have you seen my daughter? ", " I cannot find her " **2.** *oggetto* (*formula di cortesia*) you: — *ringrazio, signora, signore*, thank you, madam, sir **3.** (*in espressioni ellittiche*): *l'hai fatta grossa!*, now you have done it!; *non ce — faccio più*, I can't go on; *smettila!*, stop it! **4.** *sogg.* (*formula di cortesia*) (*fam. toscano*): — *mi dica, per favore*, tell me, please.

la³, *s.m.* (*mus.*) A, la: *sonata in — maggiore*, sonata in A major; *l'oboe diede il — all'orchestra*, the oboe gave the (tuning) A to the orchestra ‖ — *bemolle*, A flat ‖ *dare il — alla conversazione*, to give the tone to the conversation.

là⁴, *av.* **1.** there: *egli è —*, he is there; *era — dove l'avevo lasciato*, it was there where I had left it; *era caduto —, su quel tetto*, he had fallen there, on that roof; *quanto c'è per andare — e tornare?*, how far is it there and back?; *sono partiti di —*, they have gone away from there ‖ — *dentro*, — *fuori*, inside, outside ‖ — *per —*, on the spot ‖ *al di — di*, di — *da*, beyond (o on the other side of): *al di — delle Alpi*, beyond the Alps ‖ *l'al di —, il mondo di —*, the hereafter; *è più di — che di qua*, he is more dead than alive ‖ *da quel giorno in —*, from that day on; *da qui in — molte cose acca-*

dranno, from now on many things will happen ‖ *di —* : *è di —*, (*nell'altra stanza*) he is in there; *sono andati di —*, (*nell'altra stanza*) they went in there; (*da quella parte*) they went that way ‖ *più in —*, (*nel tempo*) later on; (*nello spazio*) further on: *la casa è molto più in —*, the house is much further (on); *fatti, tirati più in —*, move over (o along); *lo faremo più in —*, we'll do it later on ‖ *qua e —*, here and there ‖ *andare troppo in —*, *fig.* to go too far ‖ *essere in — cogli anni*, to be advanced (o to be getting on) in years ‖ *guardare in qua e in —*, to look around (o here and there); (*su e giù*) to look up and down ‖ *mandare in —*, (*differire*) to put off **2.** (*in espressioni ellittiche*): *eccolo — !*, there he is!; *quei ragazzi —*, those boys there; *voglio quello —*, I want that one (o that one over there) **3.** (*pleonastico, enfatico*): — *sulle tre*, about three o'clock; — *verso Pasqua*, about Easter; *alto — !*, halt!; *chi va —?, chi è —?*, who goes there?, who is there?; *ehi — !, ohi — !*, you there! (o hey there!); *passa — !*, go away!; *va' — !*, come off it!; *zitto — !*, quiet there!.

Làbano, *no.pr.m.* (*Bibbia*) Laban.

labàrda, *s.f.* halberd.

làbaro, *s.m.* **1.** (*st.*) labarum (*pl.* labara) **2.** *fig.* (*vessillo*) banner: *si raccolsero sotto il — di Cristo*, they assembled under Christ's banner.

làbbro, *s.m.*; *pl.f.* **làbbra** (*nel senso 1.*); *pl.m.* **làbbri** (*nel senso 2.*) **1.** lip: *labbra carnose*, thick lips; — *leporino*, (*patol.*) hare-lip; *labbra sporgenti*, protuberant lips; — *superiore, inferiore*, upper, lower (o under) lip; *dal suo — non esce mai un lamento*, no complaint ever passes his lips; *ella morì col suo nome sulle labbra*, she died with his name on her lips; *la preghiera le morì sul —*, the prayer died on her lips; *quel che ho in cuore ho sulle labbra*, I say what I think (o I speak my mind); *accostare un bicchiere alle labbra*, to raise a glass to one's lips; *chiudere le labbra*, *fig.* to seal one's lips; *chiudere le labbra a qlcu.*, to seal s.o.'s lips; *leccarsi le labbra*, *fig.* to lick (o to smack) one's lips; *mordersi le labbra*, to bite one's lips (anche *fig.*); *rimanere a labbra asciutte*, *fig.* to be left empty-handed ‖ *a fior di labbra*, rather unwillingly: *invito a fior di labbra*, half-hearted invitation; *ridere a fior di labbra*, to force a laugh ‖ *avere una parola sulle labbra*, (*sulla punta della lingua*) to have a word on the tip of one's tongue ‖ *fare il —*, (*fare il broncio*) to pout (o to look sulky o to sulk) ‖ *pendere dalle labbra di qlcu.*, to hang on s.o.'s lips (o words) **2.** (*orlo*) lip, brim, rim: *i labbri di una ferita*, the lips of a wound; *i labbri di un vaso*, the rim of a vase.

labbróne, *s.m.* **1.** (*grosso labbro*) thick lip **2.** (*chi ha grosse labbra*) thick-lipped man.

labdacísmo, *s.m.* la(m)bdacism, lallation.

làbe, *s.f.* (*poet.*) stain.

labèllo, *s.m.* (*bot.*) labellum (*pl.* labella).

laberínto, *e derivati*, *V.* **labirínto**, *e derivati*.

labiàle, *ag.s.f.* (*fonet.*) labial.

labiàta, *s.f.* (*bot.*) labiate.

làbile, *ag.* **1.** (*fugace, passeggero*) fleeting, transient; ephemeral: *gioia —*, ephemeral joy **2.** (*debole*) failing, weak: *memoria —*, weak memory.

labilità, *s.f.* (*rar.*) **1.** (*fugacità*) transience, transiency **2.** (*debolezza*) weakness.

labirintèo, *ag.* (*letter.*) labyrinthal.

labiríntici, *s.m.pl.* (*ittiol.*) Labyrinthici.

labiríntico, *ag.* labyrinthic(al); labyrinthine: *riflesso* —, (*fisiol.*) labyrinthino reflex; *sordità labirintica,* (*med.*) labyrinthine deafness.

labirintíte, *s.f.* (*patol.*) labyrinthitis.

labirínto, *s.m.* **1.** labyrinth **2.** *fig.* (*viluppo di difficoltà*) labyrinth, maze: *uscire da un* —, to get out of a maze **3.** (*anat.*) labyrinth **4.** (*mec.*) labyrinth: *tenuta a* —, labyrinth seal.

labirintodónte, *s.m.* (*paleont.*) labyrinthodon.

laboratòrio, *s.m.* **1.** laboratory: *diagnosi di* —, laboratory diagnosis **2.** (*nei magazzini, nelle botteghe, ecc.*) workshop, workroom.

laboriosaménte, *av.* **1.** laboriously, industriously **2.** (*con fatica, difficoltà*) laboriously, wearisomely.

laboriosità, *s.f.* **1.** laboriousness, industry **2.** (*fatica*) laboriousness, wearisomeness.

laborióso, *ag.* **1.** laborious, industrious; hard-working: *una città laboriosa,* a busy town (*o fam.* a hive of industry); *essere molto* —, to be very industrious **2.** (*faticoso*) laborious, toilsome, wearisome; (*difficile*) arduous, difficult: *calcolo* —, arduous calculation; *digestione laboriosa,* sluggish digestion; *indagine laboriosa,* laborious inquiry; *parto* —, difficult birth.

labradoríte, *s.f.* (*min.*) labradorite.

laburísmo, *s.m.* (*pol.*) labourism.

laburísta, *ag.* (*pol.*) labour (*attributivo*): *partito* —, Labour Party ‖ *s.m.* (*pol.*) Labourite; (*membro del partito*) member of the Labour Party; (*deputato*) Labour M. P.

làcca, *s.f.* lacquer: — *a tampone,* French polish; — *giapponese,* japan; *cera* —, sealing-wax; *gomma* —, shellac; *rosso* —, lake.

laccamúffa, *V.* **tornasóle.**

laccàre, *v.t.* **1.** to lacquer **2.** (*con pittura a smalto*) to enamel.

laccàto, *ag.* **1.** lacquered: *mobili laccati,* lacquered furniture **2.** (*con pittura a smalto*) enamelled.

laccatóre, *s.m.,* **laccatríce,** *s.f.* lacquerer.

laccatúra, *s.f.* lacquering.

lacchè, *s.m.* **1.** lacquey, lackey, flunkey, footman **2.** (*persona servile*) lacquey, lackey, servile follower.

làccio, *s.m.* **1.** (*legaccio, stringa*) lace, string: *lacci da scarpe,* shoe-strings (*o* shoe-laces) **2.** (*trappola*) snare (*anche fig.*): *cadere nel* —, *fig.* to fall into a trap; *prendere al* —, *fig.* to ensnare; *tendere un* —, to lay a snare **3.** (*cappio per catturare animali in corsa*) lasso (*pl.* lassos).

Lacedèmone, *no.pr.f.* (*geog. st.*) Lacedaemon.

lacedèmone, *ag.s.m.* Lacedaemonian.

lacciuòlo, *s.m.* **1.** small lace, small string **2.** (*trappola, imbroglio*) snare.

laceràbile, *ag.* lacerable.

laceraménto, *s.m.* laceration, tearing.

lacerànte, *ag.* tearing, rending: *un grido* —, a rending cry.

laceràre, *v.t.* to lacerate, to tear, to rend (*anche fig.*): *ciò mi lacera il cuore,* this breaks my heart; *era lacerato dai rimorsi,* he was torn with remorse; *ho lacerato il mio vestito nuovo,* I have torn my new dress; *le urla laceravano l'aria,* the shouts rent the air ‖ **laceràrsi,** *v.r.* to tear; to break: — *le vesti,* to rend one's garments.

laceratóre, *ag.* lacerating ‖ *s.m.,* **laceratríce,** *s.f.* tearer.

lacerazióne, *s.f.* **1.** laceration, tearing, rending **2.** (*ferita*) wound, cut.

làcero, *ag.* **1.** lacerate(d), torn, ragged, worn-out: *un mendicante* —, a ragged beggar; *vestiti laceri,* worn-out (*o* ragged) clothes **2.** (*med.*) lacerated: *ferita* — *-contusa,* lacerated and contused wound.

làcero-contúso, *ag.:* *ferita lacero-contusa,* (*med.*) lacerated and contused wound.

lacèrto, *s.m.* (*anat.*) biceps (*pl.* bicepses).

laciniàto, *ag.* (*bot. zool.*) laciniate(d).

Làchesi[1]**,** *no.pr.f.* (*mit.*) Lachesis.

làchesi[2]**,** *s.f.* (*zool.*) lachesis.

lacóne, *ag. s.m.* Laconian.

laconicaménte, *av.* laconically.

laconicísmo, *s.m.* **laconicità,** *s.f.* laconicism, conciseness.

lacònico, *ag.* laconic(al), concise: *discorso* —, laconic (*o* concise) speech; *stile* —, laconic (*o* concise) style.

laconísmo, *s.m.* laconism.

làcrima, *s.f.* **1.** tear: *con le lacrime agli occhi,* with tears in one's eyes; *in lacrime,* in tears; *viso bagnato di lacrime,* face bathed with tears; *voce piena di lacrime,* tearful voice; *non ho più lacrime,* I am past crying; *il suo viso era rigato di lacrime,* the tears were streaming down her face; *i suoi occhi si bagnarono di lacrime,* tears came to (*o* started to *o* welled up in) her eyes; *asciugare le lacrime a qlcu.,* *fig.* to comfort s.o.; *avere le lacrime agli occhi,* to have tears in one's eyes; *frenare le lacrime,* to keep back (*o* to check *o* to choke back *o* to restrain) one's tears; *ridere fino alle lacrime,* to laugh until one cries; *rompere in lacrime,* to burst into tears; *versare lacrime di gioia,* to shed tears of joy ‖ *lacrime di coccodrillo,* crocodile tears ‖ *questa valle di lacrime,* this vale of tears ‖ *ha le lacrime in tasca,* tears come easy to her eyes ‖ *piangere a calde lacrime,* to shed scalding tears; *piangere lacrime amare,* to weep bitter tears **2.** (*goccia*) drop: *lacrime di resina,* resin tears ‖ *una* — *di vino,* a drop of wine **3.** *lacrime di Giobbe,* (*bot.*) Job's tears.

lacrimàbile, *ag.* lamentable; woeful.

lacrimàle, *ag.* **1.** lachrymal: *condotto* —, (*anat.*) tear-duct; *ghiandola* —, (*anat.*) lachrymal gland; *sacco* —, (*anat.*) tear-sac *o.* *vaso* —, (*archeol.*) tear-bottle.

lacrimàre, *v.i.* **1.** to shed tears, to weep, to cry **2.** (*inumidirsi per irritazione*) to water: *il fumo mi fa* — *gli occhi,* smoke makes my eyes water.

lacrimàto, *ag.* **1.** (*compianto*) lamented **2.** (*rimpianto*) regretted.

lacrimatóio, *s.m.* (*archeol.*) lachrymatory.

lacrimazióne, *s.f.* lachrymation.

lacrimévole, *ag.* tearful, pitiful, sad: *con voce* —, in a tearful voice; *una storia* —, a tearful story.

lacrimògeno, *ag.* lachrymatory: *bomba lacrimogena,* lachrymatory bomb (*o* tear-shell); *gas* —, tear-gas.

lacrimosaménte, *av.* tearfully.

lacuàle, *V.* **lacústre.**

lacúna, *s.f.* **1.** lacuna (*pl.* lacunae, lacunas); gap: *colmare le lacune della propria educazione,* to fill in the gaps in one's education **2.** (*tip.*) blank.

lacunàre, *s.m.* (*edil.*) lacunar.

lacunóso, *ag.* lacunose, full of gaps.

lacústre, *ag.* lacustrine, lacustral; lake (*attributivo*): *abitazioni lacustri,* lake-dwellings; *piante lacustri,* lacustrine plants.

laddòve, *av.* (*rar.*) (**there**) **where** ‖ *cong.* **whereas, while, whilst:** *fu vile* — *abbisognava aver cuore,* he was cowardly, whereas he should have shown courage.

ladíno, *ag.s.m.* Ladin.

Ladislào, *no.pr.m.* (*st.*) Ladislaus.

làdra, *s.f.* **1.** woman thief **2.** (*tasca interna di un vestito*) inside pocket.

ladraménte, *av.* thievishly.

ladrería, *s.f.* robbery.

làdro, *ag.* **1.** thieving **2.** (*seducente*) bewitching: *occhi ladri,* bewitching eyes **3.** (*brutto, pessimo*) horrible, dreadful: *fame ladra,* gnawing hunger; *tempo* —, horrible weather; *che stagione ladra abbiamo avuto!,* what a dreadful season we have had! ‖ *s.m.* thief; robber: — *di strada,* highwayman; — *matricolato,* expert thief ‖ — *di cuori,* lady-killer (*o* philanderer) ‖ — *in guanti gialli,* gentleman thief ‖ *al* —!, stop thief! ‖ *buio da ladri,* pitch-dark ‖ *vestito come un* —, dressed like a tramp ‖ *chi è bugiardo è* —, *prov.* lying and thieving go together ‖ *l'occasione fa l'uomo* —, *prov.* opportunity makes the thief ‖ *tanto è — chi ruba, che chi tiene il sacco, prov.* the concealer is as bad as the thief.

ladrocínio, *s.m.* robbery; theft.

ladronàia, *s.f.* **1.** (*covo di ladri*) den of thieves **2.** (*banda di ladri*) band of robbers.

ladronàta, *s.f.* robbery.

ladroncèllo, *s.m.* petty thief; pilferer.

ladróne, *s.m.* robber; (*ladro di strada*) highwayman (*pl.* highwaymen).

ladronéccio, *s.m.* robbery; theft.

ladronería, *s.f.* robbery.

ladronésco, *ag.* thieving.

Laèrte, *no.pr.m.* (*lett.*) Laertes.

laghísta, *ag.* lake (*attributivo*): *poeti laghisti,* Lake poets.

laggiù, *av.* **1.** (*in basso, in fondo*) **down there: —** *nel pozzo,* down there in the well; *l'ho visto di —,* I saw him from down there **2.** (*lontano*) **over there:** *vedi quella casa —?,* can you see the house over there?.

lagnànza, *s.f.* complaint: — *a carico di...,* complaint against...; *motivo di —,* ground for complaint; *dare luogo a lagnanze,* to give cause for complaint.

lagnàrsi, *v.r.* **1.** to complain; (*fam.*) to moan (about sthg.): *ha sempre ql.co. di cui —,* she is always moaning about sthg.; *si lagnava di un forte mal di testa,* she complained of a bad headache; *si lagnò di non essere pagato puntualmente,* he complained that he was not paid punctually; — *delle nuove tasse,* to complain about the new taxes; — *per la scadente qualità della merce,* to complain about the inferior quality of the goods **2.** (*lamentarsi*) to moan: *si lagnò tutta la notte,* she moaned the whole night.

làgno, *s.m.* (*rar.*) lamentation; complaint.

làgo, *s.m.* **1.** lake: — *alpino,* alpine lake; — *aperto,* lake with an outlet; — *artificiale,* artificial lake; — *chiuso,* lake with no outlet; — *craterico,* crater lake ‖ *Lago Maggiore,* Lake Maggiore; *Lago Salato,* Salt Lake; *regione dei laghi,* (*in Inghilterra*) Lake District ‖ *essere in un — di sudore,* to be in a sweat **2.** (*anat.*) ventricle.

làgrima, *e derivati,* V. làcrima, *e derivati.*

lagúna, *s.f.* lagoon, lagune: *la — di Venezia,* the lagoon of Venice.

lagunàre, *ag.* lagoon (*attributivo*).

lài, *s.m.* **1.** (*st. lett.*) lay **2.** *pl.* (*lamenti*) lamentations.

laicàle, *ag.* lay, laic(al).

laicaménte, *av.* laically.

laicàto, *s.m.* laity.

laicità, *s.f.* laicality; laity.

laicizzàre, *v.t.* to laicize, to secularize.

laicizzazióne, *s.f.* laicization, secularization.

làico, *ag.* lay, laic(al) ‖ *s.m.* layman (*pl.* laymen), laic.

laidaménte, *av.* filthily, obscenely, indecently.

laidézza, *s.f.* (*letter.*) **1.** (*bruttezza*) ugliness **2.** (*turpitudine morale*) moral debasement, foulness **3.** (*oscenità*) obscenity, indecency.

laidità, (*rar.*) per **laidézza.**

làido, *ag.* **1.** (*sporco*) filthy, dirty (anche *fig.*); (*turpe*) indecent, obscene, disgusting: *una barzelletta laida,* a dirty story; *un disegno —,* an obscene picture; *un vecchio —,* a dirty old man **2.** (*brutto*) ugly: *donna laida,* ugly woman.

laidúme, *s.m.* **1.** (*sporcizia*) filth, dirt (anche *fig.*) **2.** (*turpitudine*) indecency, obscenity.

lallazióne, *s.f.* lallation, la(m)bdaicism.

làma¹, *s.f.* (*palude*) swamp.

làma², *s.f.* **1.** blade: — *di rasoio,* razor-blade; — *fissa,* fixed blade; — *rotante,* rotary blade; *temperino a due lame,* double-bladed knife; *affilare una —,* to sharpen (*o* to whet *o* to give an edge to) a blade ‖ *è una buona —,* (*è un bravo schermidore*) he is a good blade **2.** (*onda*) wave: — *di fondo,* ground swell.

làma³, *s.m.* (*zool.*) lama, llaam.

làma⁴, *s.m.* (*sacerdote di Budda*) lama.

lamaísmo, *s.m.* (*st. relig.*) lamaism.

lamàre, *v.t.* (*ind.*) to spot-face.

lambdacísmo, *s.m.* la(m)bdacism, lallation.

Lambèrto, *no.pr.m.* Lambert.

lambicaménto, *s.m.* **1.** (*distillazione*) distillation **2.** (*discervellamento*) racking one's brains.

lambiceàre, *v.t.* (*chim.*) to distil ‖ **lambiccàrsi,** *v.r.* (*discervellarsi*): — *il cervello per ql.co.,* per *fare,* to puzzle (*o* to rack *o* to cudgel) one's brains for sthg., to do; *mi sono lambiccato il cervello per delle ore senza trovare una spiegazione,* I racked my brains for hours without finding an explanation; *si lambiccava il cervello per ricordare,* he racked his brains to remember.

lambiccàto, *ag.* **1.** (*chim.*) distilled **2.** (*studiato, sforzato*) over-elaborate: *stile —,* over-elaborate style.

lambíceo, *s.m.* (*chim.*) alembic, still.

lambíre, *v.t.* to lap, to lick; (*di onde*) to lap on (sthg.): *il gatto lambì il latte,* the cat lapped (up) the milk; *le onde lambivano la riva,* the waves were lapping on the shore.

lambrecchíni, *s.m.pl.* (*arald.*) lambrequins.

lambrúsco, *s.m.* "lambrusco" (kind of Italian red wine).

lamé, *s.m.* (*tessuto*) lamé.

lamèlla, *s.f.* lamella (*pl.* lamellae).

lamellàto, *ag.* lamellar, lamellate(d).

lamellibrànchi, *s.m.pl.* (*zool.*) Lamellibranchiata.

lamelliròstri, *s.m.pl.* (*ornit.*) Lamellirostres.

lamentàbile, *V.* **lamentévole.**

lamentànza, *s.f.* **1.** (*lamento*) lament, lamentation **2.** (*lagnanza*) complaint.

lamentàre, *v.t.* to lament, to lament for (s.o., sthg.), to regret, to mourn, to mourn for (s.o., sthg.), to mourn over (s.o., sthg.), to bewail: *un errore che egli lamenterà per tutta la vita,* a mistake which he will regret all his life; — *la morte di qlcu.,* to lament (*o* to mourn) s.o.'s death; — *la perdita di un amico,* to mourn the loss of a friend ‖ *v.i.* (*rar. poet.*) to wail; to mourn ‖ **lamentàrsi,** *v.r.* **1.** to lament; to moan, to groan: *l'ho udito — per tutta la notte,* I heard him moaning all night through **2.** (*lagnarsi*) to complain: *mi lamenterò del cibo col direttore,* I will complain to the manager about the food; *non posso lamentarmi di lui,* I cannot complain of him; *si lamentava delle sue disgrazie,* he was wailing over his misfortunes; *si lamenta sempre,* he is always complaining (*o* grumbling).

lamentazióne, *s.f.* lamentation ‖ *«Le lamentazioni di Geremia»,* (*Bibbia*) "The Lamentations of Jeremiah".

lamentévole, *ag.* (*letter.*) **1.** mournful, sorrowful, plaintive: *voce —,* mournful (*o* plaintive) voice **2.** (*pietoso*) lamentable, pitiful, pitiable: *era ridotto in uno stato —,* he was reduced to a pitiable condition.

lamentevolménte, *av.* mournfully.

lamentío, *s.m.* (*rar.*) moaning, groaning.

laménto, *s.m.* **1.** lament, lamentation, moaning, wailing: *il — dei feriti era straziante,* the cries of the wounded were heart-rending **2.** (*lagnanza*) complaint: *ne farò i miei lamenti col padrone di casa,* I will complain about it to the landlord.

lamentóso, *ag.* mournful, sorrowful, plaintive: *parlava con voce lamentosa,* he was speaking in a mournful voice.

lamétta, *s.f.* razor-blade.

làmia, *s.f.* **1.** (*mit.*) lamia **2.** (*megera*) lamia, witch.

lamièra, *s.f.* plate, sheet: — *bugnata,* buckle-plate; — *decapata,* pickled plate; — *del fondo,* end-plate; — *di acciaio,* sheet steel; — *di zinco,* sheet-zinc; — *greggia,* raw plate; — *laminata,* rolled (iron) plate; — *liscia,* smooth plate; — *ondulata,* corrugated sheet-iron; — *piombata,* terneplate; — *rigata,* rifled plate; — *stampata,* stamped plate; — *stirata,* (*edil.*) lath; — *striata,* chequered plate; — *zincata,* galvanized sheet-iron; *pacco di lamiere,* mill pack.

lamieríno, *s.m.* lamination: — *di acciaio,* (*metal.*) sheet-steel; (*elett.*) lamina; — *di ottone,* (*metal.*) sheet-brass; — *di stagno,* (*metal.*) sheet-tin; — *magnetico,* (*metal.*) lamination (*o* magnetic sheet); — *per trasfor-matori*, (*elett.*) transformer core plate.

lamillàre, *ag.* lamellar, lamellate, foliated.

làmina, *s.f.* **1.** lamina (*pl.* laminae), thin plate, thin layer (of metal), thin sheet (of metal): — *di ot-tone*, (*metal.*) brass foil; — *d'oro*, pale gold leaf; — *magnetica*, (*elett.*) magnetic shell **2.** (*nei minerali*) lamina (*pl.* laminae): *dividersi in lamine*, to foliate **3.** (*bot.*) lamina (*pl.* laminae), blade **4.** (*zool.*) lamina (*pl.* lami-nae): — *cribrosa*, lamina cribrosa (*o* cribriform plate); — *fusca*, lamina fusca; — *reticolare*, lamina reticu-laris.

laminàre[1], *ag.* laminar: *corrente*, *flusso*, *moto* —, (*mec.*) laminar flow; *strato* —, (*geol.*) laminar layer.

laminàre[2], *v.t.* **1.** (*metal.*) to roll; (*in fogli sottili*) to laminate: — *a caldo*, to hot-roll; — *a freddo*, to cold-roll; — *in barre*, to mill **2.** (*coprire con lamina*) to laminate.

laminàto, *ag.* (*metal.*) rolled: *ferro* —, rolled iron ‖ *s.m.* (*metal.*) rolled section: — *di acciaio*, rolled steel section; — *di ferro*, rolled iron section.

laminatóio, *s.m.* (*mec.*) rolling-mill: — *per barre*, bar rolling-mill; — *per lamiere*, plate rolling-mill; — *per lamiere sottili*, sheet rolling-mill; — *per profilati*, section rolling-mill; — *per tubi*, tube rolling-mill.

laminatúra, *s.f.* **1.** (*fis.*) lamination **2.** (*ind. tessile*) rolling.

laminazióne, *s.f.* **1.** (*fis. geol.*) lamination **2.** (*metal.*) rolling, rolling-mill process: — *a caldo*, hot-rolling; — *a freddo*, cold rolling.

laminóso, *ag.* laminose, laminous, laminate.

làmpa, (*poet.*) per **làmpada**.

làmpada, *s.f.* lamp: — *ad alcool*, spirit-lamp; — *ad arco*, arc-lamp; (*cine.*) sun lamp; — *a gas lumi-nescente*, gas-discharge lamp; — *a incandescenza*, in-candescent lamp; — *al neon*, neon lamp (*o* neon tube); — *a olio*, oil-lamp; — *a pila*, (*portatile*) flash-light; — *a sospensione*, swinging lamp; — *di sicurezza*, safety -lamp; — *votiva*, votive lamp.

lampadàio, *s.m.* lamp-maker.

lampadàrio, *s.m.* chandelier, electric light pendant: — *di Murano*, Venetian chandelier.

lampadína, *s.f.* (electric) bulb, lamp: — *di fase*, phase lamp; — *elettrica tascabile*, pocket lamp (*o* flash-light *o* electric torch); — *smerigliata*, frosted lamp.

lampadodromía, *s.f.* (*st. greca*) lampadedromy.

lampànte, *ag.* **1.** brilliant, shining **2.** *fig.* (*chiaro*, *evidente*) clear, evident, manifest: *una verità* —, a man-ifest truth; *vi sono prove lampanti che...*, there are clear proofs that....

lampàra, *s.f.* (*mar.*) "lampara" (trawl with lamps used for night-fishing).

lampeggiaménto, *s.m.* lightning; (*bagliore*) flashing; (*nelle segnalazioni*) winking.

lampeggiàre, *v.i.* **1.** *imp.* to lighten: *lampeggia da un'ora*, it has been lightening for an hour **2.** (*di luce*, *fuoco*) to flash; (*di segnalazioni*) to wink **3.** *fig.* to flash (with sthg.), to sparkle (with sthg.): *i suoi occhi lam-peggiarono di gioia*, her eyes sparkled with joy; *i tuoi occhi lampeggiarono d'ira*, your eyes flashed with anger.

lampeggiatóre, *ag.* flashing; (*di segnalazioni*) wink-ing ‖ *s.m.* **1.** (*aut.*) (flashing) traffic indicator **2.** *foto. elett.*): — *elettronico*, (*foto.*) flash-lamp; — *stroboscopico*, (*elett.*) stroboscopic flash-lamp.

lampeggío, *s.m.* lightning.

lampionàio, *s.m.* **1.** (*chi accende i lampioni*) lamplighter **2.** (*chi fabbrica lampioni*) maker of street -lamps.

lampioncíno, *s.m.* Chinese lantern; (*per albero di Natale*) fairy lamp.

lampióne, *s.m.* **1.** street-lamp: — *a gas*, gas lamp **2.** (*di carrozza*) lamp.

lampísta, *s.m.* (*lumaio*) lamp-trimmer, lamplighter.

lampisteria, *s.f.* lamp-store.

làmpo, *s.m.* **1.** lightning: *il temporale fu preannun-ziato da molti lampi*, the storm was heralded by a lot of lightning ‖ *chiusura* —, zip-fastener (*o* zipper) ‖ *guerra* —, blitzkrieg ‖ *telegramma* —, express telegram ‖ *treno* —, express train ‖ *veloce come il* —, as quick as lightning; *l'automobile passò come un* —, the car flashed by; *correva come un* —, he ran with lightning speed; *lo indovinò in un* —, he guessed it in a flash **2.** (*luce istantanea*) flash (anche *fig.*): — *al magnesio*, (*foto.*) magnesium flash (*o* flashlight); — *di luce*, flash of light (*o* flash-light); *lampi luce*, (*aut.*) (*per segnalazioni*) winking light (*o amer.* flashing); *un* — *di genio*, a flash of genius; *un* — *di gioia*, a flash of merriment; *un* — *di speranza*, a flash of hope; *i suoi occhi man-davano lampi di collera*, his eyes flashed with anger.

lampóne, *s.m.* **1.** (*pianta*) raspberry bush **2.** (*frutto*) raspberry: *marmellata di lamponi*, raspberry jam; *sci-roppo di* —, raspberry wine.

lamprèda, *s.f.* (*ittiol.*) lamprey.

lampredòtto, *s.m.* **1.** (*ittiol.*) young lamprey **2.** (*frat-taglie*) offal.

làna, *s.f.* wool: — *a fibra corta*, (*ind. tessile*) mungo; — *a fibra lunga*, (*ind. tessile*) long-stapled wool; — *calcinata*, (*ind. tessile*) slipe wool; — *comune*, ordinary wool; — *contenente cascame*, (*ind. tessile*) noily wool; — *corta*, (*ind. tessile*) frib; — *da carda*, (*ind. tessile*) carding (*o* clothing) wool; — *d'acciaio*, (*ind.*) steel wool; — *da concia*, (*ind. tessile*) pulled wool; — *debole*, (*ind. tessile*) tender wool; — *difettosa*, defective wool; — *di legno*, (*edil.*) wood wool; — *di vetro*, (*ind.*) glass wool (*o* fibreglass); — *fragile*, brittle wool; — *grezza*, raw wool; — *ordinaria*, broad wool; — *per maglieria a mano*, hand-knitting wool; — *per manufatti*, (*ind. tessile*) apparel wool; — *ruvida*, harsh wool; — *sca-dente*, mushy wool; — *scelta*, matching; *bioccolo di* —, lock of wool; *curdatura della* —, (*ind. tessile*) wool carding; *filatura della* —, (*ind. tessile*) wool spinning; *un gomitolo di* —, a wool-ball; *l'industria della* —, the wool industry; *una matassa di* —, a skein of wool; *pettinatura della* —, (*ind. tessile*) wool-combing; *tes-situra della* —, wool-weaving; *tingere la* —, to dye in the wool ‖ *di* —, woollen; wool (*attributivo*): *abito di* —, woollen dress; *filo di* —, woollen yarn; *stoffa*, *articoli di* —, woollen goods; *tessuto di* —, wool web; *tessuto di mezza* —, half-wool cloth; *tessuto di* — *pet-tinato*, worsted fabric ‖ *questioni di* — *caprina*, *fig.* futile questions ‖ *è una buona* —!, (*iron.*) he is a fine rascal! ‖ *andar per* — *e tornarsene tosi*, to go for wool and come home shorn.

lanaiuòlo, *s.m.* **1.** (*chi vende lana*) woollen -draper **2.** (*chi lavora la lana*) textile worker.

lanàta, *s.f.* (*artigl.*) sponge, swab.

lànca, *s.f.* low marshy land.

lanceolàto, *ag.* (*bot.*) lanceolate.

lancétta, *s.f.* **1.** (*di orologio*) pointer; (*fam.*) hand: *la lancetta delle ore*, *dei minuti*, the hour-hand, the minute-hand **2.** (*chir.*) lancet **3.** (*mec.*) pointer.

lància[1], *s.f.* **1.** lance ‖ — *in resta*, lance in rest ‖ *spezzare una* — *in favore di qlcu.*, to plead s.o.'s cause (*o* for s.o.) **2.** (*guerriero armato di lancia*) lance, lancer: *una buona* —, a good fighter ‖ — *spezzata*, (*st.*) free -lance: *essere la* — *spezzata di qlcu.*, to be s.o.'s body-guard **3.** (*becco di estintore*) nozzle.

lància[2], *s.f.* (*mar.*) launch; (*a remi*, *per nave*) dingy, dinghy: — *antincendio brandeggiabile*, monitor; — *a vapore*, steam launch; — *di parata*, (*mil.*) barge; — *di salvataggio*, lifeboat.

lanciàbile, *ag.* that can be thrown, that can be flung.

lanciabómbe, *s.m.* (*mil.*) trench-mortar, bomb -thrower: *addetto al* —, bomb-thrower; *dispositivo* —, bomb release.

lanciafiàmme, *s.m.* (*mil.*) flame-thrower.

lanciaménto, *s.m.* (*rar.*) throwing, hurling, fling-ing; launching.

lanciàre, *v.t.* **1.** to throw; to fling, to dash, to hurl, to launch (anche *fig.*): *lanciò il libro nel fuoco,* he flung the book into the fire; — *una bestemmia,* to rap out (*o* to utter) an oath; — *delle bombe,* to throw (*o* to drop) bombs; — *un grido,* to give (*o* to utter) a cry (*o* to cry out): *ella lanciò un grido di dolore,* she cried out with pain; — *un'idea,* to throw out an idea; — *minacce contro qlcu.,* to hurl threats at (*o* to launch threats against) s.o.; — *un'occhiata a qlcu.,* to dart (*o* to cast) a glance at s.o.; — *pietre contro qlcu.,* to throw stones at s.o.; — *ql.co. in aria,* to fling (*o* to toss) sthg. up; — *un siluro,* to launch (*o* to discharge *o* to fire) a torpedo ‖ — *campanili,* (*dirle grosse*) to tell tall stories (*o* to talk big) ‖ — *un cavallo,* to start a horse off at full gallop ‖ — *un motore,* to speed up an engine **2.** (*avviare, introdurre, imporre*) to launch: — *un articolo,* (*comm.*) to launch an article; — *un'attrice,* to launch an actress; — *un film,* to launch a film; — *un giornale,* to launch a newspaper; — *un'impresa,* (*comm.*) to launch (*o* to float) an enterprise; — *una moda,* to launch (*o* to set *o* to initiate) a fashion; — *qlcu. negli affari,* to launch s.o. into business (*o* to start s.o. in business *o* to give s.o. a start) ‖ **lanciàrsi,** *v.r.* **1.** to throw oneself; to fling (oneself), to dash, to hurl oneself: *egli si lanciò nell'acqua,* he threw himself (*o* dashed) into the water; *si lanciò fuori dalla stanza,* he flung out of the room; — *all'inseguimento di qlcu.,* to dash off in pursuit of s.o.; — *col paracadute,* to bale out (*o* to parachute); — *contro qlcu.,* to dash at s.o.; — *in avanti,* to rush (*o* to dash *o* to shoot) forward; — *nella mischia,* to hurl oneself into the fray **2.** (*avviarsi, introdursi*) to launch: *non lanciarti in quell'affare,* don't launch into that business; — *in una discussione,* to launch into a discussion; — *nella politica,* to launch out into politics.

lanciasilúri, *s.m.* (*mar. mil.*) torpedo-tube.

lanciàta, *s.f.* **1.** (*distanza a cui si scaglia una lancia*) throw **2.** (*colpo di lancia*) (lance-)thrust **3.** (*balzo improvviso di cavallo*) bound.

lanciatóre, *s.m.,* **lanciatríce,** *s.f.* **1.** thrower, hurler **2.** (*spor.*) (*atletica*) thrower; (*cricket*) bowler; (*baseball*) pitcher **3.** (*di moda*) initiator.

lancière, *s.m.* **1.** (*mil.*) lancer **2.** *pl.* (*musica, danza*) lancers: *ballare i lancieri,* to dance a set of lancers.

lancifórme, *ag.* lanciform, lance-shaped, lanced, spear-shaped.

Lancillòtto, *no.pr.m.* (*lett.*) Lancelot, Launcelot.

lancinànte, *ag.* lancinating, excruciating, shooting.

làncio, *s.m.* **1.** (*atto del lanciare*) throwing, hurling; (*distanza a cui si lancia ql.co.*) throw, hurl: — *col paracadute,* parachuting; — *con apertura ritardata,* (*di paracadute*) delayed drop; — *con paracadute,* (*di rifornimenti*) air drop; — *del disco, del giavellotto,* (*spor.*) discus, javelin throwing; — *del peso,* (*spor.*) putting the shot; — *di aliante,* (*aer.*) tow-off; — *di bombe, paracadutisti,* dropping of bombs, paratroopers; *un — di siluri,* a discharge (*o* firing) of torpedoes; *carico di* —, propelling charge; *pista di* —, (*aer.*) run-way ‖ *di* —, (*subito*) at once **2.** (*mar.*) (*varo*) launch, launching **3.** (*lancio pubblicitario*) launching: — *di un articolo,* (*comm.*) launching of an article; — *di un'attrice,* launching of an actress; — *di un film,* launching of a film **4.** (*missilistica*) launching.

lanciòtto, *s.m.* **1.** small lance; javelin **2.** (*soldato armato di lanciotto*) lance, lancer.

lànda, *s.f.* barren land; (*brughiera*) moor, heath.

landò, *s.m.* landau.

lanería, *s.f.* (*gener. pl.*) woollen goods (*pl.*), woollens (*pl.*): *commercio di lanerie,* trade in woollens; *mercante in lanerie,* woollen merchant; *negozio di lanerie,* wool shop.

lanétta, *s.f.* **1.** (*lana leggera*) light wool **2.** (*lana non pura*) mixed wool.

lànfa, *ag:* *acqua* —, orange water.

Lanfrànco, *no.pr.m.* Lanfranc.

langraviàto, *s.m.* (*st.*) landgraviate.

langràvio, *s.m.* (*st.*) landgrave.

languènte, *ag.* **1.** languishing (with sthg.), pining (for, with sthg.); drooping: — *d'amore,* pining away for love; *luce* —, fading light **2.** (*comm.*) languishing, dull, slack: *in questo momento il mercato è* —, the market is dull (*o* flat) at the moment.

languidaménte, *av.* **1.** languidly, faintly, weakly **2.** (*con affettazione*) languidly, languorously: *sedeva — sulla poltrona,* she was languidly sitting in the armchair; *udiva un'arpa suonare — in distanza,* he could hear a harp being played languorously far away.

languidézza, *s.f.* languidness, faintness, weakness: *la sua — è dovuta ad anemia,* his languidness is due to anaemia.

lànguido, *ag.* **1.** (*debole, fiacco*) languid, weak, faint, listless; drooping: *colorito* —, pallor; *occhio* —, languid eye; *polso* —, feeble pulse; *speranze languide,* faint hopes; *quello scrittore ha uno stile* —, that writer has a languid style; *questi fiori sono tutti languidi,* these flowers are drooping; *sentirsi* —, to feel languid **2.** (*che affetta languidezza*) languishing, languid, languorous: *aspetto* —, languid look; *voce* —, languid voice; *i suoi modi languidi sono del tutto fuori moda,* her languishing (*o* languorous) manners are quite out-of-date; *guardare qlcu. con occhi languidi,* to look at s.o. with languishing eyes **3.** (*di luce*) faint, dim.

languíre, *v.i.* **1.** to languish (with sthg.); (*struggersi*) to pine (with, for sthg.): — *d'amore,* to be sick for love; — *d'amore per qlcu.,* to pine with love for (*o* after) s.o.; — *di fame, sete,* to languish with hunger, thirst; — *di nostalgia,* to pine for home; — *in prigione,* to languish in prison; — *nella miseria,* to languish in poverty; — *nella solitudine,* to mope in solitude **2.** (*ristagnare*) to languish; to slacken, to flag: *gli affari languono,* business is slack; *l'azione di quella commedia langue,* the action of that play drags; *la conversazione langue,* the conversation flags; *non lasciar — la conversazione!,* keep the conversation alive! **3.** (*di fiori*) to droop **4.** (*di luce*) to fade.

languóre, *s.m.* **1.** languor, languidness, faintness, weakness: — *di stomaco,* pangs of appetite; *morire di* —, to die from weakness **2.** (*struggimento*) languor: *con* —, languidly; *occhi pieni di* —, languishing eyes.

lanìccio, *s.m.* fluff.

lanière, *s.m.* wool manufacturer.

lanièro, *ag.* woollen; wool (*attributivo*): *commercio* —, wool trade; *industria laniera,* wool industry.

lanifício, *s.m.* wool(len) mill; wool(len) factory.

lanígero, *ag.* wool-bearing; laniferous, lanigerous.

lanino, *s.m.* wool worker.

lanista, *s.m.* (*st. romana*) lanista.

lanitàl, *s.m.* (*ind. tessile*) "lanital" (synthetic wool).

lanolína, *s.f.* (*chim.*) lanolin(e), woolfat.

lanosità, *s.f.* woolliness, fleeciness.

lanóso, *ag.* **1.** woolly; wool-bearing, laniferous **2.** (*simile a lana*) fleecy, woolly: *capelli lanosi,* woolly hair.

lantànio, *s.m.* (*chim.*) lanthanum.

lantèrna, *s.f.* **1.** lantern: — *ad olio,* oil lamp; — *cieca,* dark lantern (*o* bull's-eye lantern); — *da ferrovieri,* railway lantern; — *magica,* magic lantern ‖ *alla* —!, hang him! ‖ *prendere lucciole per lanterne,* to be deceived by appearances **2.** (*lucernario*) skylight **3.** (*mar.*) (*faro*) lighthouse **4.** — *di proiettore,* (*cine.*) lamp housing.

lanúggine, lanúgine, *s.f.* down.

lanuginóso, *ag.* downy.

lanúto, *ag.* woolly.

lanzichenécco, lànzo, *s.m.* (*st.*) lansquenet.

Laocoónte, *no.pr.m.* (*mit.*) Laocoön.

Laodamía, *no.pr.f.* (*mit.*) Laodamia.

Laodicèa, *no.pr.f.* (*geog. st.*) Laodicea.

Laomedónte, *no.pr.m.* (*mit.*) Laomedon.

laónde, *av.* wherefore, therefore.

laotiàno, *ag.s.m.* Laotian.

lapalissiàno, *ag.* evident, obvious: *è una verità lapalissiana,* it is a self-evident truth.

laparatomìa, *s.f.* (*chir.*) laparotomy.

lapidàre, *v.t.* to stone; to lapidate.

lapidàrio, *ag.* lapidary, lapidarian: *stile —,* lapidary style ‖ *s.m.* **1.** (*chi lavora le pietre*) gem-cutter, lapidary **2.** (*trattato sulle pietre*) lapidary.

lapidatóre, *s.m.,* **lapidatrìce,** *s.f.* lapidator.

lapidazióne, *s.f.* stoning (to death), lapidation.

làpide, *s.f.* **1.** tombstone **2.** (*commemorativa*) tablet, plaque.

lapidescènte, *ag.* petrifying, lapidescent.

lapìllo, *s.m.* lapillus (*pl.* lapilli).

lapin, *s.m.* cony, coney; (*pelliccia*) cony(-skin).

làpis, *s.m.* pencil, crayon: *— copiativo,* copying -pencil.

lapislàzzolo, lapislàzzuli, *s.m.* lapis-lazuli.

Lapìti, *no.pr.m.pl.* (*mit.*) Lapithae.

lappàre, *v.i.* to lap.

làppola, *s.f.* **1.** (*bot.*) (*pianta*) burdock; (*frutto*) bur(r) **2.** (*cosa da nulla*) trifle **3.** (*persona noiosa*) sticker, bore.

lappóne, *ag.* Lapp, Laplandish, Lappish ‖ *s.c.* Lapp, Laplander ‖ *s.m.* (*lingua*) Lapp, (the) Lappish (language).

Lappònia, *no.pr.f.* (*geog.*) Lapland.

lapsus, *s.m.* lapse; slip: *— calami,* slip of the pen; *— linguae,* slip of the tongue.

lardellàre, *v.t.* to lard (anche *fig.*): *— uno scritto di citazioni,* to lard a passage with quotations.

lardèllo, *s.m.* chopped bacon fat.

làrdo, *s.m.* (bacon-)fat ‖ *nuotare nel —, fig.* to live in the lap of luxury ‖ *tanto va la gatta al — che ci lascia lo zampino, prov.* the pitcher goes so often to the well that it comes home broken at last.

lardóne, *s.m.* salt-pork.

lardóso, *ag.* fat.

làre, *s.m.* **1.** (*mit.*) lar (*pl.* lares) **2.** *pl.* (*famiglia*) lares; home (*sing.*): *tornare ai patri lari,* to return home.

làrga, àlla, *l.av.* away, at a distance: *stare alla — da qlcu.,* to keep away from s.o.: *stai alla — dal cane!,* beware of the dog!.

largaménte, *av.* abundantly, widely, broadly, at length, in detail: *parlare —,* to speak at length; *rispondere —,* to reply fully; *spendere —,* to throw one's money around.

largàre, *v.t.* **1.** to widen; to loose: *— le vele,* (*mar.*) to spread the sails **2.** (*mar.*) to get (sthg.) under way: *— la nave,* to cast off ‖ **largàrsi,** *v.r.* (*mar.*) to push off, to cast off, to set sail.

largheggiàre, *v.i.* to be free (with sthg.), to be lavish (with sthg.); to give (sthg.) with open hands: *largheggia di consigli, promesse,* he is very free with advice, promises; *— col denaro,* to be free with one's money.

larghétto, *s.m.* (*mus.*) larghetto.

larghézza, *s.f.* **1.** width, breadth: *— della strada,* width of the road; *— massima,* (*mar.*) beam; *libro della — di trenta centimetri,* book 30 centimetres in width (o breadth); *lunghezza e — ,* length and breadth; *la stanza misura sei piedi in —,* the room is six feet in breadth **2.** (*abbondanza*) largeness: *— di mezzi,* largeness of means **3.** (*liberalità*) liberality; (*ampiezza*) breadth, largeness: *— di idee,* largeness of mind; *— di interessi,* breadth of interests; *— di vedute,* broad-mindedness (o breadth of mind); *mostrò grande —,* he showed great liberality.

largìre, *v.t.* to give liberally, to bestow liberally.

largitóre, *s.m.* bestower, donator.

largizióne, *s.f.* **1.** (*atto del largire*) donation, bestowal, largition **2.** (*cosa largita*) gift, donation; largess(e).

làrgo, *ag.* **1.** broad, wide: *una larga estensione di deserto,* a wide expanse of desert; *una larga ferita,* a wide wound; *a larghi intervalli,* at wide intervals;

cappello con larghe falde, broad-brimmed hat; *un fiume —,* a wide river; *un fosso — dieci metri,* a ten -metre wide ditch; *uomo con spalle larghe,* broad -shouldered man; *vesti larghe,* loose-fitting clothes; *il fico ha le foglie larghe,* the fig-tree has broad leaves; *la nuova autostrada è larga venti metri,* the new motor -way is twenty metres wide ‖ *di manica larga,* easy -going **2.** *fig.* broad, large, wide: *un — margine di guadagno,* a wide margin of profit; *larghi poteri,* large powers; *una larga ricompensa,* a large reward; *termine usato in senso —,* term used in a broad sense; *uomo dalla coscienza larga,* unscrupulous man; *quell'articolo è prodotto su larga scala,* that article si produced on a large scale; *avere una larga parte nella direzione,* to have a large share in the management; *fare larghe concessioni,* to make big concessions **3.** (*liberale*) liberal, generous: *— di promesse,* liberal of promises; *uomo di larghe vedute,* broad-minded man; *è largo nelle mance,* he is a generous tipper **4.** (*di pronuncia*) broad: *egli ha un accento —,* he has a broad accent **5.** *guardia larga,* (*scherma*) open guard **6.** (*pitt.*) bold: *pennellata larga,* bold brush-work ‖ *s.m.* **1.** breadth, width: *estendersi in —,* to stretch sideways; *fare — (a qlcu.),* to make room (for s.o.); *farsi —,* (anche *fig.*) to make one's way: *farsi — fra la folla,* to elbow one's way through the crowd ‖ *—!,* make room! (o make way!) ‖ *vagare in lungo e in —,* to wander far and wide **2.** (*mar.*) open sea, offing: *al — di Genova,* off Genoa; *la nave si tenne al —,* the ship stood off-shore (o in the offing); *andare al —,* to take to the open sea; *passare al — di una nave,* to give a ship a wide berth; *prendere il —,* to set sail (o to leave port); *fig.* to run away **3.** (*mus.*) largo: *il «Largo» di Händel,* Händel's "Largo".

làrice, *s.m.* (*bot.*) larch: *legno di —,* larch-wood.

larìnge, *s.f.* (*anat.*) larynx (*pl.* larynges, larynxes).

larìngeo, *ag.* laryng(e)al.

laringìte, *s.f.* (*patol.*) laryngitis.

laringoiàtra, *s.m.* laryngologist.

laringoscopìa, *s.f.* (*med.*) laryngoscopy.

laringotomìa, *s.f.* (*chir.*) laryngotomy.

làrva, *s.f.* **1.** (*entom.*) larva (*pl.* larvae) **2.** (*spettro*) ghost, spirit **3.** (*apparenza ingannevole*) sham: *— di gloria,* sham glory **4.** (*scheletro*) skeleton: *ridotto ad una —,* reduced to a skeleton.

larvàre, *v.t.* (*letter.*) (*mascherare*) to disguise, to mask.

larvataménte, *av.* disguisedly.

larvàto, *ag.* disguised, hidden, concealed, masked; latent: *malattia larvata,* latent disease; *odio —,* hidden (o concealed) hatred.

lasàgne, *s.f.pl.* (*cuc.*) "lasagne" (kind of "pasta").

lasagnóne, *s.m.* (*zoticone*) dolt.

làsca, *s.f.* (*ittiol.*) roach ‖ *sano come una —,* (*fam.*) as sound as a bell (o roach).

lascàre, *v.t.* (*mar.*) to surge; to slacken.

lasciapassàre, *s.m.* pass; (*salvacondotto*) safe-conduct: *mostrate il —!,* show your pass (o safe-conduct)!.

lasciàre, *v.t.* **1.** (*abbandonare*) to leave; to desert, to quit; (*rinunciare*) to give up: *lasciammo Londra una settimana prima di te,* we left London a week before you; *ha lasciato la famiglia per seguire quella donna,* he has deserted (o abandoned) his family for the sake of that woman; *lasciò la fidanzata, perchè era una ragazza troppo egoista,* he broke it off with his fiancée, because she was far too selfish; *il maggiordomo ha minacciato di lasciarli,* the butler has threatened to leave them; *i medici avevano oramai lasciato ogni speranza di salvarlo,* by then the doctors had given up all hope of saving him; *mio fratello lascia la scuola per andare in Marina,* my brother is leaving school to go to sea; *se non guarirà presto, dovrà lasciare l'impiego,* if he doesn't recover soon, he will have to quit his job ‖ *mal si lascia il certo per prendere il forse, prov.* a bird in the hand is worth two in the bush **2.** (*far rimanere; lasciar dietro di sè*) to leave: *aveva lasciato una famiglia numerosa,* he had left a large family behind him; *la ferita mi ha lasciato una cicatrice*, the wound has left me with a scar; *lasciò l'assegno in bianco*, he left the cheque blank; *lo lasciarono per morto*, they left him for dead; *mi lasciò senza impiego*, he left me without a job; *questa medicina mi ha lasciato l'amaro in bocca*, this medicine has left a bitter taste in my mouth; *si lamentano perchè la nuova strada lascia fuori il loro paese*, they complain because the new road does not touch their village; *il suo modo d'agire mi lascia perplesso*, his behaviour leaves me at a loss || *mi lasciò in asso*, he left me in the lurch **3.** (*rimetterci*) to leave, to lose: *in quell'incidente ci lasciò la vita*, he lost his life in that accident; *per poco ci lasciai la salute*, I nearly ruined my health **4.** (*lasciare in eredità*) to leave, to will, to bequeath: *ha lasciato tutta la proprietà ai poveri*, he left all his estate to the poor; *lasciò la sua collezione a una galleria d'arte*, he bequeathed his collection to an art-gallery; *vuol — tutto quello che ha all'ospedale*, he intends to will everything he owns to the hospital **5.** (*dimenticare, omettere*) to leave, to forget, to omit: *ho lasciato gli occhiali a casa*, I have left my spectacles at home; *non possiamo — da parte un indizio così grave*, we can't omit such a serious piece of evidence; *raccontando il fatto, lasciò alcuni importanti particolari*, he omitted some important details in telling what had happened **6.** (*causativo*) (*permettere, fare*) to allow (s.o. to do), to let (s:o. do): *lasciar posare il liquido*, let the liquid stand; *lasciamo fare a Dio*, let's leave it in the hands of God; *lasciategli il suo segreto*, let him keep his secret; *mi lasciò risolvere il problema da solo*, he let me work out the problem by myself; *non ci lasciava vivere in pace*, he would not let us live in peace; *non — cadere quel vaso*, don't drop that vase; *questa fessura lascia passare troppa aria*, this crack lets in too much air; *ti ha lasciato entrare?*, has he let you in? || *lascia correre!*, let things go their own way!; *è meglio lasciar perdere la questione*, we'd better drop the matter || *la sua condotta lascia molto a desiderare*, his behaviour leaves much to be desired || *ti ho lasciato dire*, I let you talk away **7.** (*serbare*) to keep, to leave: *lasciami questa carne per cena*, keep this meat for my supper; *non lasciarmi delle sigarette, perchè ne ho molte*, don't keep any cigarettes for me, because I have a lot **8.** (*affidare, dare, concedere*) to leave; to trust; to give; (*cedere*) to sell: *di ciò lascia la cura a me*, leave it to me!; *lasciami tuo figlio fino a questa sera*, leave your son with me until tonight; *non voglio lasciargli il mio orologio, ho paura che me lo rompa*, I don't want to trust my watch to him, I am afraid he may break it; *te lo lascerò per mille lire*, you may have it for a thousand lire; *vi hanno lasciato l'appartamento a buon mercato*, they have sold you the flat at a very good price || *ha lasciato detto a sua madre che...*, he left word with his mother that... || *non ha lasciato scritto le sue volontà*, he did not leave a will **9.** (*allentare*) to let go; (*liberare*) to release; to set free, to free: *lascia* (*andare*) *la corda!*, let go the rope!; *il cane lasciò la presa*, the dog loosened its grip; *lasciarono il prigioniero in libertà*, they released the prisoner || *v.i.* (*smettere, cessare di*) to stop: *non lascia di brontolare*, she doesn't stop grumbling; *non lasciò di fumare, sebbene gli facesse male*, he didn't stop smoking, though it was bad for his health || **lasciàrsi**, *v.r.* to let oneself: *non mi lascerò truffare*, I am not going to be cheated; *non si lasciò vedere per tutta una settimana*, he didn't appear for a whole week; *si lasciò andare su una poltrona*, he sank into an armchair; *si lasciò trasportare dall'ira*, he let himself be carried away by anger; — *guidare dall'esperienza*, to let oneself be guided by experience || *questo cibo si lascia mangiare*, this food is eatable || *v.r. reciproco* to part: *si lasciarono all'alba*, they parted at daybreak.

làscito, *s.m.* bequest, legacy: *un — di parecchi milioni*, a legacy of several millions; *un — in denaro*, a legacy of money; *fece molti lasciti ai poveri*, he made many bequests to the poor.

lascivaménte, *av.* lasciviously, lustfully, wantonly.

lascívia, *s.f.* lasciviousness, lust, wantonness.

lascívo, *ag.* lascivious, lustful, wanton.

làsco, *ag.* **1.** slack, loose: *bullone —*, (*mec.*) loose bolt; *cavo —*, (*mar.*) slack (o loose) rope **2.** (*rilassato*) loose, lax: *morale lasca*, loose morals.

làssa, *s.f.* (*poes.*) laisse.

lassatívo, *ag.s.m.* (*farm.*) laxative, aperient, aperitive.

lassísmo, *s.m.* (*fil.*) laxism.

lassísta, *s.m.* (*fil.*) laxist.

lassitúdine, *s.f.* lassitude, weariness, languor.

làsso[1], *ag.* **1.** (*poet.*) weary, tired **2.** (*mus.*) (*allentato*) loose **3.** (*arc.*) (*infelice*): *ohimè —!*, alas!.

làsso[2], *s.m.* lapse; period: *dopo un certo — di tempo*, after a lapse of time; *rimarrà per un certo — di tempo*, he will remain for a certain period of time.

lassú, *av.* **1.** up there; (*al piano di sopra*) upstairs: *c'è qlcu. —?*, is there anyone up there (o upstairs)? **2.** *fig.* (*in cielo*) up there, up above: *grazia che viene da —*, blessing that comes from above (o from on high o from Heaven); *aspettiamo la giustizia di —*, we are awaiting justice from up above; *saremo uniti —*, we shall be united up above.

làstra, *s.f.* **1.** slab; (*generalmente di metallo*) plate: *— di acciaio*, steel plate; *— di ardesia*, slate; *— di ghiaccio*, slab of ice; (*galleggiante*) ice-floe; *— di marmo*, marble slab; *— stereotipa*, (*tip.*) stereotype; *— di vetro*, sheet of glass (o glass sheet) **2.** (*foto.*) plate: *— che ha preso luce*, light-struck plate; *— fotomeccanica*, process plate **3.** (*edil.*) plate, slab: *— di ardesia per tetti*, per pavimentazione stradale, flag-stone.

lastricàre, *v.t.* to pave, to flag.

lastricàto, *ag.* paved, (stone-)flagged || *di buone intenzioni è — l'inferno*, *prov.* the road to hell is paved with good intentions || *s.m.* (stone) pavement.

lastricatóre, *s.m.* paver.

lastricatúra, *s.f.* paving, flagging.

làstrico, *s.m.* (stone) paving || *essere sul —*, to be destitute (o homeless o *fam.* to be on the rocks); *gettare qlcu. sul —*, to turn s.o. out of house and home.

lastróne, *s.m.* large slab; (*generalmente di metallo*) large plate: *un — di ghiaccio*, a large slab of ice; (*galleggiante*) a large ice-floe.

latèbra, *s.f.* (*poet.*) recess, secret place: *le latebre dell'anima*, *fig.* the innermost recesses of the soul.

latebróso, *ag.* (*poet.*) full of recesses.

latènte, *ag.* latent; concealed, hidden: *calore —*, (*fis.*) latent heat; *malattia —*, (*med.*) latent disease.

lateràle, *ag.* side (*attributivo*), lateral: *cappella —*, side-chapel; *entrata —*, side entry (o entrance); *navata —*, (*arch.*) side-aisle; *parete —*, side-wall; *porta —*, side door; *ramo —*, (*di una famiglia*) lateral branch; *via —*, by-street.

lateralménte, *av.* laterally, sideways, sidewise.

lateranénse, *ag.* Lateran (*attributivo*): *i Patti Lateranensi*, the Lateran Agreements.

Lateràno, *ag. no.pr.m.* Lateran: *il* (*Palazzo*) *—*, the Lateran (Palace); *S. Giovanni in —*, St. John Lateran.

lateríte, *s.f.* (*min.*) laterite.

laterízio, *ag.* lateritious; brick (*attributivo*).

laterízi, *s.m.pl.* bricks: *fabbrica di —*, brick-works.

laticlàvio, *s.m.* (*st.romana*) laticlave.

latifondísta, *s.m.* rich landowner.

latifóndo, *s.m.* latifundium (*pl.* latifundia); large landed property, large estate.

latinaménte, *av.* in a Latin manner, in the Latin style.

latineggiànte, *ag.* latinizing.

latineggiàre, *v.i.* to latinize.

latinísmo, *s.m.* Latinism: *quell'autore abbonda in latinismi*, that author's style is full of Latinisms.

latinísta, *s.m.* Latinist, Latin scholar: *è un buon —*, he is a fine Latin scholar.

latinità, *s.f.* **1.** Latinity **2.** (*lingua*) Latin: *bassa* —, Low Latin.

latinizzàre, *v.t.* to latinize.

latíno, *ag.* Latin: *popoli latini,* Latin peoples ǁ *croce latina,* Latin cross ǁ *la sorella latina,* (*la Francia*) France ǁ *vela latina,* (*mar.*) lateen sail ǁ *s.m.* **1.** Latin **2.** (*lingua*) (the) Latin (language): — *maccheronico,* dog Latin; — *volgare,* vulgar Latin ǁ *non vuol capire il* —, *fig.* he refuses to see the truth.

latitànte, *ag.* (*dir.*) absconding: *è* —, he is in hiding ǁ *s.c.* fugitive from justice.

latitànza, *s.f.* (*dir.*) fugitiveness (from justice): *darsi alla* —, to escape.

latitúdine, *s.f.* **1.** (*geog. astr.*) latitude: — *celeste,* (*astr.*) celestial latitude; — *Nord,* (*geog.*) latitude North; *grado di* —, (*geog.*) degree of latitude; *trenta gradi di* — *a sud dell'equatore,* (*geog.*) thirty degrees South of the equator ǁ *l'uomo vive sotto tutte le latitudini,* man can live in any latitude **2.** (*rar.*) (*larghezza*) latitude, breadth **3.** *fig.* (*libertà d'opinione*) latitude: *permettere una certa* —, to allow a certain latitude.

làto[1], *ag.* (*rar.*) wide ǁ *in senso* —, in a broad sense.

làto[2], *s.m.* **1.** side: — *di un poligono,* side of a polygon; — *di un triangolo,* side of a triangle; — *in vista,* near side; — *opposto,* opposite (*o* far) side; — *principale,* (*di medaglie, ecc.*) face; — *sopravento,* (*mar.*) windward side; *questo* — *dell'edificio,* this side of the building; *il suo* — *sinistro è rimasto paralizzato,* his left side is paralyzed **2.** *fig.* point of view, standpoint: *da un* —, on the one hand; *d'altro* —, on the other hand; *da questo* —, from this point of view.

Latóna, *no.pr.f.* (*mit.*) Latona, Leto.

latomía, *s.f.* (*st.*) latomia, latomy.

latóre, *s.m.* (*comm.*) bearer: *il* — *della presente è il sig. X,* the bearer of this letter is Mr. X; *pagare al* —, pay the bearer.

latraménto, *s.m.* barking.

latrànte, *ag.* barking: *cani latranti,* barking dogs.

latràre, *v.i.* to bark.

latràto, *s.m.* bark, barking: *il* — *di un cane mi tenne sveglio,* the barking of a dog kept me awake.

latrína, *s.f.* lavatory, closet; (*spec. mil.*) latrines (*pl.*); (*amer.*) wash-room.

làtta, *s.f.* **1.** tin: — *bianca, stagnata,* (*ind.*) tin plate; *foglio di* —, (*metal.*) tin sheet; *oggetti di* —, tinware; *rivestito di* —, lined with tin (*o* tin-lined) **2.** (*recipiente*) tin, can: *una* — *di benzina,* a tin (*o* a can) of petrol; *una* — *di biscotti,* a tin of biscuits; *una* — *d'olio,* a can of oil; *in latte, in lattine,* tinned, canned.

lattàia, *s.f.* milkwoman (*pl.* milkwomen); milkmaid.

lattàio, *s.m.* milkman (*pl.* milkmen).

lattànte, *ag.* **1.** (*nutrito dalla madre*) breast-fed **2.** (*non ancora divezzato*) unweaned ǁ *s.c.* child still living on milk, babe still unweaned.

Lattànzio, *no.pr.m.* (*st. lett.*) Lactantius.

lattàto, *s.m.* (*chim.*) lactate.

làtte, *s.m.* **1.** milk: — *acido,* sour milk; — *condensato,* condensed milk; — *di mucca, di capra, di pecora,* cow's, goat's, sheep's milk; — *fresco,* new milk; — *impazzato,* curdled milk; — *in polvere,* dried milk (*o* milk-powder); — *intero,* whole milk; — *pastorizzato,* sterilizzato, pasteurized milk; — *scremato,* skimmed milk; *balia da* —, wet-nurse; *caffè e* —, coffee with milk; *centrale del* —, central dairy; *febbre del* —, milk fever; *mucca da* —, milch-cow; *vitello di* —, sucking calf; *dare il* —, (*allattare*) to nurse (*o* to suckle); *togliere il* — *a un bambino,* (*svezzarlo*) to wean a child ǁ — *di gallina,* titbit (*o* choice morsel); — *denti di* —, milk (*o* first) teeth ǁ *figliolo, fratello di* —, foster child, foster brother ǁ *avere ancora il* — *alla bocca,* (*fam.*) to be still wet behind the ears ǁ *succhiare una dottrina col* —, to be brought up in a doctrine **2.** (*sostanza simile al latte*): — *di calce,* milk of lime (*o* limewash); — *di cocco,* coconut milk; — *di colla,* size milk; — *di mandorle,* milk of almonds.

lattemièle, *s.m.* whipped cream.

làtteo, *ag.* (*di latte*) milk (*attributivo*); (*simile al latte*) milky: *crosta lattea,* (*patol.*) milk-crust; *dieta lattea,* milk diet; *farina lattea,* milk powder; *febbre lattea,* milk fever ǁ *la Via Lattea,* (*astr.*) the Milky Way.

latterìa, *s.f.* dairy.

lattescènte, *ag.* lactescent, milky, milk-like.

lattescènza, *s.f.* lactescence, milkiness.

làttice, *s.m.* (*bot.*) latex.

latticífero, *ag.* (*bot.*) laticiferous.

latticíni, *s.m.pl.* dairy produce (*sing.*).

làttico, *ag.* (*chim.*) lactic: *acido* —, lactic acid.

lattièra, *s.f.* milk-jug, milk-pot.

lattífero, *ag.* **1.** (*che produce latte*) lactiferous, milk-producing; (*che conduce latte*) lactiferous, milk-bearing: *canali lattiferi,* milk ducts **2.** (*che produce lattice*) lactescent, latex-producing.

lattiginóso, *ag.* **1.** (*simile al latte*) milky, lacteous **2.** (*di pianta*) lactescent, latex-producing.

lattíme, *s.m.* (*med.*) milk-crust.

lattivéndola, *s.f.* dairywoman (*pl.* dairywomen), milkwoman (*pl.* milkwomen).

lattivéndolo, *s.m.* dairyman (*pl.* dairymen), milkman (*pl.* milkmen).

lattonière, *s.m.* tinker, tinsmith, tinman (*pl.* tinmen).

lattónzolo, *s.m.* suckling; (*maialino*) sucking pig; (*vitellino*) sucking calf.

lattoscòpio, *s.m.* lactoscope.

lattòsio, *s.m.* (*chim.*) lactose, milk-sugar.

lattúga, *s.f.* **1.** (*bot.*) lettuce **2.** (*gorgiera*) ruff.

làuda, *s.f.* **1.** (*lett.*) laud, canticle, hymn of praise: — *drammatica,* mystery play **2.** (*arc.*) (*lode*) praise **3.** *pl.* (*eccl.*) lauds.

laudàbile, *ag.* (*scherz.*) laudable, praiseworthy.

làudano, *s.m.* (*farm.*) laudanum.

laudàre, *v.t.* (*arc.*) to praise.

laudatívo, *ag.* (*letter.*) laudative, laudatory: *un discorso* —, an encomium (*o* a eulogy).

laudatóre, *ag.* (*rar.*) laudative, laudatory ǁ *s.m.* (*rar.*) laudator, lauder.

laudatòrio, *ag.* (*rar.*) laudatory, laudative.

laudatríce, *s.f.* (*rar.*) laudator, lauder.

laudése, *s.m.* (*st.*) **1.** singer of lauds **2.** (*scrittore di laudi sacre*) laudist.

Làura, *no.pr.f.* Laura.

làurea, *s.f.* (university) degree: — *ad honorem,* honorary degree; — *in medicina, in legge,* degree in medicine, in law; *diploma di* —, degree-certificate; *esame di* —, degree examination; *ha una* — *in lingue straniere,* he has a degree in modern languages; *conferire a qlcu. una* —, to confer a degree on s.o.; *conseguire, prendere una* —, to take a degree.

laureàndo, *ag.* last-year undergraduate (*attributivo*) ǁ *s.m.* last-year undergraduate.

laureàre, *v.t.* to confer a degree on (s.o.) ǁ **laureàrsi,** *v.r.* to take a degree, to graduate: — *a pieni voti è lode,* to graduate with full marks and honours; — *in legge, in medicina,* to take a degree in law, in medicine.

laureàto, *ag.* **1.** graduate: *è* — *in legge,* he has a degree in law **2.** (*coronato d'alloro*) laureate: *poeta* —, poet laureate ǁ *s.m.* graduate.

laurenziàno, *ag.* (*st. geol.*) Laurentian.

lauretàno, *ag.* Loreto (*attributivo*).

lauréto, *s.m.* laurel grove.

làuro, *s.m.* laurel, bay: *foglia di* —, bay-leaf.

lautaménte, *av.* sumptuously, magnificently, splendidly; (*abbondantemente*) generously: *pagare* —, to pay generously; *pranzare* —, to dine sumptuously; *vivere* —, to live in luxury.

lautézza, *s.f.* magnificence, splendour; (*abbondanza*) generosity.

làuto, *ag.* sumptuous, magnificent, splendid; (*abbondante*) generous, abundant: *lauta ricompensa,* generous reward; — *pranzo,* sumptuous dinner; *lauti guadagni,* large profits.

làva, *s.f.* lava: *colata di* —, lava flow (*o* stream).

lavabianchería, *s.f.* washing-machine.

lavàbile, *ag.* washable.

lavàbo, *s.m.* **1.** wash-basin; wash-stand **2.** (*eccl.*) lavabo (*pl.* lavabos).

lavàcro, *s.m.* (*letter.*) **1.** lavacre, bath, font **2.** (*il lavare*) bathing ‖ *santo* —, baptism.

lavàggio, *s.m.* **1.** (*lavatura*) washing; (*di ponte di nave*) wash down: — *a secco*, dry cleaning; *questi colori scoloriscono al* —, these colours come out in the wash **2.** (*ind. miner.*) washing; (*ind. tessile*) scouring; (*di gas di scarico*) scavenge, scavenging: — *ad immersione*, (*ind.*) immersion washing; — *con acqua di calce*, (*ind. chim.*) lime-washing.

lavàgna, *s.f.* **1.** (*min.*) slate **2.** (*usata nelle scuole*) black-board: *cancellare la* —, to wipe the black-board.

lavamàno, *s.m.* **1.** (*portacatino*) wash-stand **2.** (*lavabo*) wash-basin.

lavaménto, *s.m.* (*rar.*) washing.

lavànda[1], *s.f.* **1.** washing, wash; (*di ponte di nave*) wash down: *farsi una* —, to have a wash **2.** (*med.*) lavage: — *gastrica*, gastric lavage **3.** (*eccl.*) Washing of feet (on Maundy Thursday).

lavànda[2], *s.f.* (*bot.*) lavender: *acqua di* —, lavender -water.

lavandàia, *s.f.* washerwoman (*pl.* washerwomen); laundress.

lavandàio, *s.m.* laundry-man (*pl.* laundry-men).

lavandería, *s.f.* laundry.

lavandíno, *s.m.* **1.** sink: *un* — *ingombro di piatti*, a sink full of (*o* piled with) dishes **2.** (*lavabo*) wash -basin.

lavapiàtti, *ag.*: *macchina* —, dish-washing machine (*o* dish-washer) ‖ *s.m.* scullery-boy, dish-washer ‖ *s.f.* scullery-maid, dish-washer.

lavàre, *v.t.* **1.** to wash: *lavalo con acqua e sapone*, wash it with soap and water; *lavalo in acqua calda, fredda*, wash it in hot, cold water; *questa stoffa si lava facilmente*, this material washes easily; — *a secco*, to dry-clean; — *un'automobile*, to wash (down) a car; — *i panni*, to wash the linen; — *i piatti*, to wash up (the dishes); — *un vestito*, to wash a dress ‖ — *il capo a qlcu.*, *fig.* to tick s.o. off (*o* to give s.o. a dressing-down) ‖ — *i panni sporchi in pubblico*, *fig.* to wash one's dirty linen in public ‖ *a* — *la testa all'asino si perde il ranno e il sapone*, *prov.* there is no washing a blackmoor white **2.** (*purificare, mondare*) to purify, to wash; to cleanse; to wash away: *la confessione e il pentimento lavano l'anima dalle colpe*, confession and repentance cleanse (*o* purify) the soul of its sins; — *un'onta*, to wash away a stain ‖ **lavàrsi,** *v.r.* to wash (oneself), to have a wash: *desidero lavarmi prima di colazione*, I want to have a wash (*o* to wash myself *o* to wash) before breakfast; — *le mani, il viso*, to wash one's hands, one's face ‖ *lavarsene le mani*, to wash one's hands of it.

lavàta, *s.f.* wash: *darsi una* (*bella*) —, to have a (good) wash ‖ — *di capo*, (*fig. fam.*) telling-off (*o* ticking-off *o* dressing-down).

lavatívo, *s.m.* **1.** (*med.*) (*clistere*) enema, clyster **2.** (*volg.*) (*persona noiosa*) bore, tiresome person; (*persona pignola*) pedant.

lavàto, *ag.* washed, clean: *mani lavate*, clean hands; *bianco come un cencio* —, as white as a sheet.

lavatóio, *s.m.* **1.** (*luogo dove si lava*) wash-house **2.** (*tavola per lavare*) wash-board.

lavatóre, *ag.* washing ‖ *s.m.* **1.** washer **2.** (*di lana, ecc.*) fuller, scourer ‖ **lavatrìce,** *s.f.* **1.** washer **2.** (*di lana, ecc.*) fuller, scourer **3.** (*lavabiancheria*) washing -machine; (*per stoviglie*) dish-washing machine, dish -washer **4.** (*miner.*) washer; (*ind. tessile*) scouring -machine: — *ultrasonica*, (*ind.*) ultrasonic cleaning -machine.

lavatúra, *s.f.* **1.** washing: — *a secco*, dry-cleaning; *un colore solido resiste alla* —, a fast colour stands

washing **2.** (*liquido rimasto dopo la lavatura*) washing -water: — *di piatti*, dish-water (*o* washing-up water).

lavèllo, *s.m.* wash-basin, wash-bowl; (*per bucato*) wash-tub.

lavería, *s.f.* (*miner.*) washery.

làvico, *ag.* lavic.

lavína, *s.f.* **1.** (*frana*) landslip, landslide **2.** (*dial.*) (*valanga*) avalanche.

Lavínia, *no.pr.f.* Lavinia.

lavoracchiàre, *v.i.* to work slackly.

lavorànte, *s.m.* labourer; worker, workman (*pl.* workmen) ‖ *s.f.* worker, workwoman (*pl.* workwomen).

lavoràre, *v.i.* **1.** to work; (*con fatica*) to labour, to toil, to drudge: *le fabbriche hanno ripreso a* —, the factories have resumed working; *questo negozio lavora poco*, this shop doesn't do much business; *il veleno sta lavorando*, the poison is having its effect; — *a contratto*, to work on contract; — *a cottimo*, to do piece-work; — *a giornata*, to work by the day; — *a maglia*, to knit; — *a, intorno a ql.co.*, to work at (*o* on) sthg.: *sto lavorando a un romanzo*, I am working on a novel; — *a tempo perso*, to work in one's spare time; — *con capitale proprio*, to work (*o* to trade) with one's own capital; — *con qlcu.*, to carry on (*o* to do) business with s.o.; — *d'ago*, to do needlework; — *d'intarsio*, to inlay; — *di sarto, di pittore*, to work as a tailor, as a painter; — *in avorio*, to work in ivory; — *in coloniali*, to deal in colonial produce; — *in profondità*, (*miner.*) to work in depth; — *in proprio*, to work on one's own; — *molto, sodo*, to work hard; — *troppo*, to overwork ‖ *l'Italia che lavora*, the working population of Italy ‖ — *come un cane, come un negro*, to work like a dog, like a nigger ‖ — *di bastone*, to cane (*o* to beat) ‖ — *di fantasia*, to exaggerate ‖ — *di gomiti*, to elbow (one's way through) ‖ — *di mano*, (*rubare*) to steal ‖ — *per la gloria*, to work for nothing ‖ — *sott'acqua*, to work underhand ‖ *far qlcu. fino all'esaurimento*, to work s.o. to a standstill (*o* to death) ‖ *chi non lavora non mangia*, *prov.* no mill, no meal ‖ *l'uomo fu creato per* —, *come l'uccello per volare*, *prov.* no man is born into the world, whose work is not born with him **2.** (*funzionare*) to operate, to work; (*di chiave, giocare*) to turn: *questa macchina lavora giorno e notte*, this machine operates night and day ‖ *far* — *una macchina*, to work (*o* to run) an engine ‖ *v.t.* to work; (*trattare*) to process: — *a freddo, a caldo*, (*metal.*) to hot-work, to cold-work; — *la pasta*, (*cuc.*) to work dough; — *la terra*, to work soil ‖ **lavoràrsi,** *v.r.*: — *qlcu.*, to talk s.o. round.

lavoratívo, *ag.* **1.** working: *giorno* —, working -day (*o* weekday) **2.** (*di terreno*) tillable.

lavoràto, *ag.* **1.** worked; (*sottomesso a trattamento*) processed; (*confezionato*) manufactured: — *a maglia*, knitted; — *a mano, a macchina*, hand-made, machine -made; — *in oro*, wrought in gold; *articoli lavorati*, manufactured articles; *ben* —, well finished; *pietra lavorata*, worked (*o* dressed) stone; *prodotti lavorati*, finished articles; *zolfo, metallo* —, processed sulphur, metal **2.** (*elaborato*) elaborate: *quest'abito è troppo* —, this dress is too elaborate **3.** (*di terreno*) tilled, cultivated ‖ *s.m.* machined product.

lavoratóre, *ag.* working: *le classi lavoratrici*, the working classes ‖ *s.m.* worker; (*operaio*) workman (*pl.* workmen); (*operaio non specializzato, lavorante*) labourer: — *accanito*, hard worker; — *a cottimo*, piece -worker; — *a domicilio*, person who works at home; — *agricolo*, farm-hand (*o* agricultural labourer); — *alla giornata*, day labourer; — *autonomo*, self-employed worker; — *intellettuale*, brain-worker; *sindacato dei lavoratori*, trade union ‖ **lavoratríce,** *s.f.* worker, workwoman (*pl.* workwomen): *è un'ottima* —, she is a very good worker.

lavorazióne, *s.f.* **1.** processing, working; manufacture; (*esecuzione, fattura*) workmanship; work: — *a caldo, a freddo*, (*metal.*) hot-working, cold-working; — *a ca-*

tena, (*ind.*) line (*o* belt) production; — *accurata*, fine piece of work(manship); — *alla macchina*, (*mec.*) machining; — *al maglio*, (*mec.*) machine hammering; — *a macchina*, (*ind.*) machine work; — *a maglia*, (*ind. tessile*) knitting; — *a mano*, (*ind.*) handwork; — *a pieno ritmo*, full-scale processing; — *dei metalli*, metal-working; — *della carta*, paper-making (*o* paper processing); — *della lana*, wool manufacture (*o* processing); *ciclo di* —, operation (*o* working) schedule; *di* — *inglese*, English made (*o* of English make); *impianti, attrezzatura e macchinari relativi alla* —, (*ind.*) processing (*o* manufacturing) equipment; *metodo di* —, processing; *una spilla di squisita* —, a broche of exquisite workmanship; *questo prodotto è un esempio dell'alto livello della nostra* —, this product is an example of the high level of our workmanship **2.** (*di un terreno*) tilling, cultivation.

lavorío, *s.m.* **1.** intense activity: *c'è intorno un gran* —, there is intense activity on every side **2.** (*di elementi*) erosive action: *quella frana fu causata dal lento* — *delle acque*, that landslide was caused by the slow erosive action of the water **3.** *fig.* intrigue: *ci fu un gran* — *da parte dei nostri avversari*, there was a lot of intrigue by our opponents.

lavóro, *s.m.* **1.** work; (*manuale*) labour: — *a contratto*, contract work; — *a cottimo*, piece-work; — *agricolo*, agricultural labour; — *a maglia*, knitting; — *a mano*, handwork; — *a ore, a giornata*, work by the hour, by the day; — *attivo*, active work; — *di bonifica*, reclamation of land; — *di casa*, (*compito*) homework; *lavori di casa*, housework: *fare i lavori di casa*, to do the housework; — *di cucito*, needlework; *lavori di difesa*, (*mil.*) defences; — *di scavo*, (*miner.*) mining; — *domestico*, domestic service; — *estenuante, penoso*, drudgery; *lavori forzati*, hard labour; — *in collaborazione*, team-work; *lavori in corso*, works in progress; — *in legno*, wood-work; (*edil.*) timber-work; — *in pietra*, stonework (*o* masonry); — *in proprio*, self-employment; — *in rilievo*, embossed work; (*arch.*) relief (*o* relievo); — *in serie*, mass-production; — *intellettuale, letterario*, brain-work, literary work; — *in terra*, (*fortificazione*) earthwork; — *manuale*, manual labour; — *notturno*, night-work; — *pesante*, hard work; *lavori portuali*, (*edil.*) harbour works; *lavori pubblici*, public works; — *specializzato*, skilled labour; — *straordinario*, overtime; — *su ordinazione*, work to order; — *urgente*, urgent work; *abiti da* —, working clothes; *cestino da* —, work- (*o* sewing-) basket; *compagno di* —, fellow -worker; *condizioni di* —, labour conditions; *conflitto tra capitale e* —, conflict between capital and labour; *contratto di* —, work contract; *datore di* —, employer; *divisione del* —, division of labour; *domanda, offerta di* —, labour demand, labour supply; *eccesso di* —, overwork; *ferri da* —, tools; *frutti del proprio* —, fruits of one's labours; *giorno di* —, week- (*o* working) day; *inabile al* —, disabled; *infortunio, incidente sul* —, industrial accident: *assicurazione contro gli infortuni sul* —, industrial accident insurance (*o* insurance against industrial accidents); *mercato del* —, labour-market; *prestatore di* —, employee; *sul* —, at work; *turno di* —, (work) shift; *il* — *è sospeso per le vacanze pasquali*, work has stopped for the Easter Holidays; *gli apparecchi elettrici risparmiano* —, electric machines are labour saving; *che stai facendo?*, what work are you doing?; *gli operai hanno cessato il* —, the workers have downed tools; *quel quadro è un bel* —, that picture is a fine piece of work; *questo* — *è ben fatto*, this (piece of) work is well done; *questo* — *è piuttosto faticoso*, this work is rather hard; *questo è un bel* —, this is a good piece of work; *abbandonare il* — *per sciopero*, to strike; *andare al* —, to go to work; *cessare il* —, to stop work; *essere al* —, to be at work; *fare del* —, to do some work; *mettere mano a un* —, to start a work; *mettersi al* —, to set to work; *vivere del proprio* —, to earn one's own living ‖

il — *dell'acqua sulle rive di un fiume*, the action of water on the banks of a river ‖ *lavori di una società*, proceedings (*o* transactions) of a society ‖ *Camera del Lavoro*, (local) Trade-Union Office; *Ministero del Lavoro*, Ministry of Labour; *Ufficio del Lavoro*, Labour Exchange; *Ufficio Internazionale del Lavoro*, International Labour Office (*abbr.* I.L.O.) ‖ *hai fatto un bel* —!, (*iron.*) a fine mess you've made! ‖ *il Parlamento ha ripreso i suoi lavori*, Parliament is in session again ‖ *ammazzarsi di* —, to work oneself to death **2.** (*occupazione*) job: *questo è un bel* —, this is a good job; *avere un buon* —, to have a good job; *cercare* —, to look for a job; *essere senza* —, to be out of work **3.** (*teat.*) play **4.** (*mec.*) work: — *di attrito*, work due to friction; — *di deformazione*, deformation (*o* strain) work.

Làzio, *no.pr.m.* (*geog.*) Latium.

làzza, *s.f.* rockfall, land-slide of rocks.

lazzarétto, *s.m.* lazaretto, lazaret, lazar-house.

lazzarísta, *s.m.* (*eccl.*) Lazarist.

Làzzaro[1], *no.pr.m.* (*Bibbia*) Lazarus.

làzzaro[2], *s.m.* (*straccione*) filthy tramp.

lazzaróne, *s.m.* **1.** (*poltrone*) slacker **2.** " lazzarone " (*pl.* " lazzaroni ") (Neapolitan homeless beggar).

lazzeggiàre, *v.i.* to joke, to jest.

lazzeruòla, *s.f.* (*bot.*) azarole.

lazzeruòlo, *s.m.* (*bot.*) azarole-tree.

làzzo[1], *ag.* (*letter.*) sour, tart, sharp.

làzzo[2], *s.m.* joke, jest: *egli non sa reggere al* —, he can't see a joke.

le[1], *art. determinativo f.pl.* **1.** the: — *Alpi*, the Alps; — *Canarie appartengono alla Spagna*, the Canary Islands belong to Spain; — *ragazze che incontrammo ieri sono mie cugine*, the girls we met yesterday are my cousins **2.** (*spesso non si traduce*): — *nostre camere sono al primo piano*, our rooms are on the first floor; — *tigri sono pericolose*, tigers are dangerous; *ha* — *ciglia lunghe*, she has long eyelashes; *ti piacciono* — *noci?*, do you like nuts?; *tutte* — *domeniche vado al cinema*, I go to the cinema every Sunday **3.** (*tradotto con l'ag. poss.*): *chiama* — *sorelline*, call your sisters; *togliti* — *scarpe*, take off your shoes **4.** (*tradotto col partitivo*) *some*: *hai comperato* — *sigarette?*, did you get any cigarettes?; *mi sono dimenticato di comperare* — *sigarette*, I forgot to get some cigarettes.

le[2], *pron.pers.f.* 3[ª] *persona* **1.** *sing. obliquo* her, to her: — *hai parlato?*, have you spoken to her?; — *mandai il mio libro*, I sent her my book; *mandale questo libro subito*, send her this book at once **2.** *Le, sing. obliquo* (*formula di cortesia*) you, to you: *devo comunicarLe che la conferenza è stata rimandata a domani*, I have to inform you that the lecture has been postponed till tomorrow **3.** *pl. oggetto* them: — *vedrò domani*, I shall see them tomorrow; *cercale bene*, look for them carefully; « *Hai ricevuto le fotografie?* », « *Non ancora, probabilmente* — *riceverò domani* », " Have you got the photographs? ", " Not yet, I shall probably get them tomorrow " **4.** *sogg.* (*fam. toscano*) — *son cose da farsi?*, what a thing to do!.

leàle, *ag.* **1.** loyal; (*fido*) faithful: — *alla causa*, loyal to the cause; *un amico* —, a true (*o* faithful) friend; *servitore* —, faithful servant; *è un suddito* —, he is a loyal subject **2.** (*onesto*) fair: *gioco* —, fair play; *non è* — *da parte tua*, it isn't fair of you.

lealménte, *av.* **1.** loyally; faithfully **2.** (*onestamente*) fairly: *agire* —, to play the game.

lealtà, *s.f.* **1.** loyalty; (*fedeltà*) faithfulness: *la sua* — *fu messa a dura prova*, his loyalty was put to a hard test **2.** (*onestà*) fairness, uprightness: — *negli affari*, fairness in trade; *è un uomo di grande* —, he is a very upright man.

Leàndro[1], *no.pr.m.* (*lett.*) Leander.

leàndro[2], *V.* oleàndro.

leàrdo, *ag.* grey ‖ *s.m.* grey (horse).

lèbbra, *s.f.* (*patol.*) leprosy ‖ *la* — *del peccato*, the stain of sin.

lebbrosàrio, *s.m.* leper hospital; leper house; lazaretto.

lebbróso, *ag.* leprous ‖ *s.m.* leper.

lécca lécca, *s.m.* (*neol.*) lollipop.

leccaménto, *s.m.* licking.

leccapiàtti, *s.c.* **1.** glutton, guzzler **2.** (*parassita*) parasite.

leccapièdi, *s.c.* toady, bootlicker, crawler.

leccàrda, *s.f.* (*cuc.*) dripping-pan.

leccàre, *v.t.* **1.** to lick; to lap: *il gatto leccava il piatto,* the cat was licking the plate; *— il latte,* to lap (up) milk ‖ *— i piedi a qlcu.,* to lick s.o.'s boots (*o* shoes) **2.** (*adulare*) to flatter **3.** (*di fiamma, lambire*) to lick: *le fiamme leccavano il soffitto della casa accanto,* the flames were licking the roof of the house next -door ‖ **leccàrsi,** *v.r.* **1.** to lick: *il gatto si leccava le zampe,* the cat was licking its paws ‖ *— le dita,* to lick one's fingers; *— le labbra,* to lick (*o* to smack) one's lips **2.** (*lisciarsi*) to groom oneself.

leccàta, *s.f.* lick, licking.

leccataménte, *av.* affectedly.

leccàto, *ag.* affected: *discorso, stile —,* affected speech, style ‖ *s.m.* affectation.

leccatóre, *ag.* flattering ‖ *s.m.,* **leccatríce,** *s.f.* flatterer, toady.

leccatúra, *s.f.* **1.** licking **2.** (*affettazione*) affectation.

leccazàmpe, *s.c.* toady, bootlicker, crawler.

leccéto, *s.m.* ilex grove.

lecchíno, *s.m.* **1.** dandy, fop **2.** (*adulatore*) flatterer.

léccio, *s.m.* (*bot.*) ilex, holm-oak.

lécco[1], *s.m.* **1.** (*leccornia*) titbit; delicacy **2.** (*gusto*) taste **3.** (*allettamento*) allurement, enticement, lure; (*per corrompere*) bribe.

lécco[2], *s.m.* (*alle bocce*) jack.

leccóne, *s.m.* **1.** glutton **2.** (*adulatore*) toady.

leccornía, *s.f.* titbit, dainty; delicacy.

lecitaménte, *av.* lawfully.

lecitína, *s.f.* (*chim.*) lecithin.

lécito, *ag.* (*permesso dalla legge*) lawful; (*permesso*) allowed, permitted (*predicativi*); (*giusto*) right, lawful: *azioni lecite,* lawful actions; *matrimonio —,* lawful marriage; *crede che a lei tutto sia —,* she thinks everything is permitted to her (*o* she thinks she can do what she likes); *mi è — farvi un'altra domanda?,* may I ask you another question?; *mi sia — farvi un'altra domanda,* allow me to ask you another question; *non è — far ciò,* you are not allowed to do that; *non è — trattare così una povera ragazza!,* it's not right to treat a poor girl like this!; *non ti è — comportarti così,* it is not right for you to behave like this; *potreste dirmi, se è —, quando si dovrà firmare il contratto?,* would you be so kind as to tell me when the contract has to be signed?; *vi par — dire certe cose?,* do you think it right to say such things?; *far —,* to legalize (*o* to make lawful); *farsi — di fare ql.co.,* to take the liberty of doing sthg. ‖ *s.m.* right: *il — e l'illecito,* right and wrong.

Lèda, *no.pr.f.* (*mit.*) Leda.

lèdere, *v.t.* (*letter.*) (*offendere*) to offend against (sthg.); to offend (s.o.); (*danneggiare*) to damage, to injure: *egli ha leso la mia reputazione,* he has injured (*o* damaged) my reputation; *— la giustizia,* to offend against the law; *— gli interessi di qlcu.,* to be prejudicial to s.o.'s interests ‖ **lèdersi,** *v.r.* to hurt oneself.

léga[1], *s.f.* **1.** (*pol.*) league; (*generalmente tra due*) alliance: *— offensiva, difensiva,* offensive alliance, defensive alliance ‖ *la — delle Nazioni,* (*st.*) the League of Nations ‖ *la Lega Santa,* (*st.*) the Holy League **2.** (*associazione*) association; (*lega operaia*) workers' combination: *— dei consumatori,* consumers' association ‖ *far — con qlcu.,* *fig.* to take up with s.o. **3.** (*chim.*) alloy: *— antifrizione,* babbit; *— d'acciaio,* alloy steel; *— di stagno,* (*peltro*) pewter; *— fusibile,* fusible alloy; *— leggera,* light alloy; *— per saldatura a stagno,* soft solder; *— pesante,* heavy alloy; *moneta di bassa —,* base coin; *l'ottone è una — di rame e zinco,* brass is

an alloy of copper and zinc ‖ *di buona —,* *fig.* genuine; *di cattiva —,* *fig.* low (*o* vulgar): *è uno scherzo di cattiva —,* it is a joke in bad taste.

léga[2], *s.f.* league (*misura itineraria* = km 4,83; *misura marittima* = km. 5,56).

legàccio, *s.m.* string; tape; twine; (*di scarpe*) shoe -lace, shoe-string; (*di scarponi, stivali*) boot-lace.

legàle, *ag.* **1.** legal: *atti legali,* legal acts; *consulente —,* legal adviser; *corso — della moneta,* legal tender (*o* lawful currency); *documento —,* legal document; *impedimento —,* legal difficulty (*o* impediment); *medicina —,* forensic medicine; *poteri legali,* legal powers; *professione —,* legal profession; *scienze legali,* legal sciences; *studio —,* lawyer's office ‖ *per vie legali,* by legal means: *procedere per vie legali,* to have recourse to the law (*o* to take legal proceedings) **2.** (*conforme alla legge*) lawful: *possessore —,* lawful owner; *il suo matrimonio non è —,* his marriage is not lawful **3.** (*legge ebraica*) legal ‖ *s.m.* lawyer.

legalità, *s.f.* legality, lawfulness.

legalitàrio, *ag.* (*pol.*) respectful of legality.

legalizzàre, *v.t.* (*rendere legale*) to legalize; (*autenticare*) to authenticate, to ratify: *— un documento,* to authenticate a document.

legalizzazióne, *s.f.* legalization; (*autenticazione*) authentication, ratification.

legalménte, *av.* legally, lawfully.

legàme, *s.m.* **1.** (*legaccio*) string; tape; twine **2.** (*vincolo*) tie; bond: *i legami del sangue,* the ties of blood; *legami di parentela,* family ties; *egli ruppe ogni — con la sua patria,* he broke all ties with his country; *uno stretto — d'affetto li unisce,* they are linked together by a close bond of affection **3.** (*connessione*) connection, link: *non c'è alcun — fra queste idee,* there is no connection between these ideas.

legaménto, *s.m.* **1.** (*anat.*) ligament **2.** (*mus.*) ligature, slur **3.** (*il legare*) tying (up), binding; (*l'assicurare con fune*) fastening **4.** (*il connettere*) connecting, linking (together) **5.** (*legaccio*) string; tape; twine.

legàre[1], *v.t.* **1.** to tie (up), to bind; (*assicurare con fune, ecc.*) to fasten: *il cane fu legato all'albero,* the dog was fastened to the tree; *il ragazzo legò la barca al molo con una corda,* the boy fastened the boat to the jetty with a rope; *— le mani a qlcu.,* to tie s.o.'s hands; *— un pacco,* to tie up a parcel; *strettamente,* to bind fast ‖ *pazzo da —,* raving lunatic ‖ *— l'asino dove vuole il padrone,* to obey without question ‖ *— la lingua a qlcu.,* to tie s.o.'s tongue ‖ *— qlcu. mani e piedi,* to tie s.o. hand and foot **2.** *fig.* to bind, to tie: *sono legati da intima amicizia,* they are bound together by a close friendship; *essere legato alla moglie,* to be tied to one's wife; *essere legato da affetto a qlcu.,* to be bound to s.o. by affection **3.** (*libro*) to bind: *— un libro in pelle,* to bind a book in leather **4.** (*incastonare*) to set, to mount: *— un diamante in oro,* to set (*o* to mount) a diamond in gold **5.** (*chir.*) to ligate, to tie up: *— un'arteria,* to ligate an artery **6.** (*connettere*) to connect: *— un'idea con un'altra,* to connect one idea with another **7.** (*mus.*) to tie: *— due o più note,* to tie two or more notes **8.** (*metal.*) to alloy **9.** (*mar.*) to bend **10.** (*chim.*) to bind ‖ *v.i.* **1.** (*aver connessione*) to be connected: *quest'episodio non lega col resto della storia,* this episode is not connected with the rest of the story **2.** (*amalgamarsi*) to thicken: *la salsa non lega senza l'uovo,* the sauce does not thicken without an egg **3.** (*metal.*) to alloy (with sthg.) ‖ **legàrsi,** *v.r.* to bind oneself (to s.o., to sthg.): *— d'amicizia con qlcu.,* to make friends (*o* to form a friendship) with s.o. ‖ *legarsela al dito,* to remember a wrong.

legàre[2], *v.t.* (*dir.*) to bequeath: *— i propri beni a qlcu.,* to bequeath one's property to s.o.

legàta, *s.f.* tying (up): *dare una —,* to tie up: *date una — a quel pacco,* tie up that parcel.

legatàrio, *s.m.* (*dir.*) legatee.

legatízio, *ag.* legatary; (*eccl.*) legatine.

legàto[1], *s.m.* ambassador; (*eccl.*) legate.

legàto[2], *s.m.* (*dir.*) legacy, bequest: *fare un* —, to leave a legacy (*o* to make a bequest).

legatóre, *s.m.*, **legatríce,** *s.f.* binder; (*di libri*) bookbinder.

legatoría, *s.f.* bookbinder's establishment; (*amer.*) bookbindery.

legatúra, *s.f.* 1. binding; (*di libro*) bookbinding: — *in cuoio,* leather binding; — *in stoffa,* cloth binding 2. (*mus.*) slur, tie, ligature 3. (*chir.*) ligature.

legazióne, *s.f.* legation.

légge, *s.f.* 1. law; (*legge singola*) act: — *civile, penale,* civil, criminal law; — *commerciale,* commercial (*o* mercantile) law; *la — della domanda e dell'offerta,* (*econ.*) the law of supply and demand; *la — di gravità,* (*fis.*) the law of gravity; *le leggi di natura,* the laws of nature; *la — divina,* the Divine Law; *le leggi in vigore,* the laws in force; — *marziale,* (*mil.*) martial law; *leggi militari,* military law; — *retroattiva,* retroactive law; — *scritta,* written law (*o* Statutory Law); — *non scritta,* unwritten law (*o* Common Law); *a norma di* —, according to the law; *a termini di* —, as by law enacted; *con tutti i benefici di* —, with all grants by the law; *disegno, progetto di* —, bill: *approvare, respingere un progetto di* —, to pass, to reject a bill; *presentare un progetto di — al Parlamento,* to bring a bill before Parliament (*o* to bring in a bill *o* to introduce a bill); *disposizione di* —, legal provision: *conformarsi alle disposizioni di* —, to comply with the provisions of the law; *dottore in* —, doctor at law (*o* doctor of law); *in base alla* —, under the law; *in virtù della* —, at law (*o* in force of the law); *rispettoso delle leggi, sottomesso alle leggi,* law-abiding; *studente in* —, law-student; *uomo di* —, lawyer; *abitudine che è diventata* —, custom that has become law; *la sua parola è* —, his word (*o* what he says) is law; *tutti sono uguali dinanzi alla* —, all are equal before the law; *abrogare una* —, to repeal an act; *applicare la* —, to enforce the law (*o* to carry out the law); *conformarsi alla* —, to conform to the law; *contravvenire alla* —, to disregard the law; *dare, dettare* —, to lay down the law; *eludere la* —, to evade the law; *infrangere la* —, to break (*o* to infringe) the law; *osservare la* —, to obey the law; *passare una* —, to pass an act; *promulgare una* —, to promulgate a law; *ricorrere alla* —, to have recourse to the law (*o* to go to law); *studiare* —, to study law ‖ — *antica,* (*religione ebraica*) the Mosaic Law (*o* the Mosaic dispensation); — *nuova,* (*Cristianesimo*) the Christian Law (*o* the Christian dispensation) ‖ *chi fa la* —, *serva la* —, *prov.* law-makers should not be law-breakers ‖ *dai mali costumi nascono le buone leggi,* prov. good laws proceed from bad manners ‖ *fatta la* —, *trovato l'inganno,* prov. every law has a loophole 2. (*regola*) rule.

leggènda, *s.f.* 1. legend: *leggende medievali,* medieval legends 2. (*diceria*) tale: *spargere leggende sul conto di qlcu.,* to gossip about s.o. 3. (*iscrizione*) legend, inscription.

leggendàrio, *ag.* 1. legendary; (*mitico*) mythical: *un eroe* —, a legendary hero (*o* a mythical hero) 2. (*meraviglioso*) marvellous, wonderful: *un'impresa leggendaria,* a wonderful enterprise ‖ *s.m.* legendary.

lèggere, *v.t.* 1. to read (anche *fig.*): *legge un libro,* he is reading a book; *lo leggo nei tuoi occhi,* I can tell it from (*o* read it in) your eyes; *nell'attesa di leggervi...,* (*comm.*) hoping to hear from you...; *il suo pensiero gli si legge in viso,* what he thinks is written all over his face; — *attentamente una lettera,* to peruse a letter; — *a voce alta,* to read aloud; — *una comunicazione,* to read out (*o* to give out) a notice; — *correntemente,* to read fluently; — *da capo a fondo,* to read through (*o* over); — *della musica,* to read music: — *della musica a prima vista,* to read music at sight; — *fra le righe,* to read between the lines; — *la mano a qlcu.,*

to read s.o.'s hand (*o* palm); — *nel cuore, nel pensiero a qlcu.,* to read s.o.'s heart, thoughts; — *nel futuro,* to read the future; — *per addormentarsi,* to read oneself to sleep; — *rapidamente un giornale,* to read a newspaper cursorily (*o* to skim through a newspaper; *aver letto molto,* to be well-read 2. (*insegnare*) to teach: *fu chiamato a — letteratura inglese all'università di Milano,* he was invited to lecture on English literature at the University of Milan 3. (*di codici, testi, ecc., portare scritto*) to read: *questo testo legge diversamente,* this text reads differently.

leggerézza, *s.f.* 1. lightness: — *di un gas,* lightness of a gas; — *di tocco,* (*di un pittore, di un medico*) lightness of touch 2. (*di vino, birra*) lightness; (*di tè, caffè*) weakness 3. (*agilità*) nimbleness, agility: *la — dei suoi movimenti,* the nimbleness of his movements 4. (*frivolezza*) levity, frivolity; (*volubilità*) inconstancy, fickleness, flightiness: *la — del suo comportamento,* the frivolity of his behaviour.

leggerménte, *av.* 1. lightly 2. (*agilmente*) nimbly: *correre* —, to run nimbly 3. (*senza riflessione*) thoughtlessly, lightly; (*frivolmente*) frivolously: *agire* —, to act thoughtlessly (*o* without due consideration) 4. (*superficialmente*) slightly: *ferito* —, slightly wounded.

leggèro, *V.* **leggièro.**

leggiadraménte, *av.* prettily; gracefully.

leggiadría, *s.f.* prettiness; gracefulness; loveliness.

leggiàdro, *ag.* pretty; graceful; lovely.

leggìbile, *ag.* 1. (*che si può leggere*) legible, readable: *calligrafia* —, legible handwriting 2. (*che merita di essere letto*) readable: *è un libro* —, it's a readable book.

leggibilità, *s.f.* legibility; readability, readableness.

leggibilménte, *av.* legibly; readably.

leggicchiàre, *V.* **leggiucchiàre.**

leggièra, *s.f.* (*fam.*) gang of ruffians, gang of hooligans.

leggièra, àlla, *l.av.* thoughtlessly, lightly: *prendere ql.co. alla* —, to make light of sthg.

leggièro, *ag.* 1. light: *cibo* —, light food; *un pasto* —, a light meal; *un peso* —, a light weight; *un vestito* —, a light dress; *l'olio è più — dell'acqua,* oil is lighter than water ‖ — *come una piuma,* as light as a feather (*o* as air) ‖ *cavalleria leggiera,* (*mil.*) light cavalry ‖ *musica leggiera,* light music ‖ *avere il sonno* —, to be a light sleeper 2. (*non forte*) light; (*di tè, caffè*) weak: *tè* —, weak tea; *tinte leggiere,* light colours; *vino* —, *birra leggiera,* light wine, beer 3. (*non grave*) light; (*lieve*) slight: *un — attacco di morbillo,* a slight attack of measles; *una leggiera difficoltà,* a slight difficulty; *una leggiera divergenza di opinioni,* a slight difference of opinions; *una leggiera ferita,* a slight wound; *una leggiera punizione,* a light punishment; *una leggiera spesa,* a light expense; *una colpa leggiera,* a minor sin; *colpo* —, light (*o* slight) blow; *ha un* — *raffreddore,* he has got a slight cold; *parla italiano con un* — *accento tedesco,* he speaks Italian with a slight German accent 4. (*agile*) light, nimble, agile: *a passi leggieri,* with light footsteps; *dita leggiere,* nimble fingers; *movimento* —, nimble movement; *è molto* —, he is very light on his feet; *ha una figurina leggiera,* she has a slight figure 5. (*superficiale*) light; heedless, thoughtless; (*frivolo, volubile*) light, frivolous; inconstant: *comportamento* —, frivolous behaviour; *una donna leggiera,* a light woman; *parole leggiere,* light words; *una persona leggiera,* a frivolous person ‖ *a cuor* —, light-heartedly (*o* with a light heart).

leggìo, *s.m.* reading-desk; (*per musica*) music-stand; (*eccl.*) lectern.

leggiucchiàre, *v.t.* to read listlessly; (*a fatica*) to read with difficulty: *egli leggiucchiava un articolo,* he was struggling through an article.

leghìsta, *s.m.* (*membro di lega operaia*) member of a workers' combination.

legiferànte, *ag.* legislative; law-giving (*attributivo*).

legiferàre, *v.i.* to legislate, to make laws.

legionàrio, *s.m.* legionary.

legióne, *s.f.* **1.** legion ‖ *Legione Straniera*, Foreign Legion **2.** (*onorificenza*) legion: — *d'onore*, Legion of Honour.

legislatívo, *ag.* legislative; law-making (*attributivo*).

legislatóre, *ag.* legislative, legislatorial ‖ *s.m.* legislator, lawgiver.

legislatúra, *s.f.* **1.** legislature **2.** (*durata di assemblea legislativa*) period of office of the legislature.

legislazióne, *s.f.* **1.** legislation, law-making: *i principi della* —, the principles of legislation **2.** (*complesso di leggi*) legislation, law(s): — *del lavoro*, labour legislation; — *ferroviaria*, railway laws; *la* — *industriale*, the Factory Acts.

legísta, *s.m.* (*rar. dir.*) legist.

legíttima, *s.f.* (*dir.*) legitim(e).

legittimaménte, *av.* legitimately.

legittimànte, *s.c.* (*dir.*) legitimizer.

legittimàre, *v.t.* **1.** (*dir.*) to legitimate, to legitimize: — *un figlio*, to legitimize a child **2.** (*giustificare*) to justify: — *un atto*, to justify an action.

legittimàto, *s.m.* (*dir.*) legitimized child.

legittimazióne, *s.f.* legitimation (anche *dir.*).

legittimísmo, *s.m.* (*st.*) legitimism.

legittimísta, *s.m.* (*st.*) legitimist.

legittimità, *s.f.* **1.** (*dir.*) lawfulness, legitimacy **2.** (*giustezza*) legitimacy: *la* — *di un dubbio*, the legitimacy of a doubt.

legíttimo, *ag.* **1.** lawful, legitimate: *legittima difesa*, self-defence; *il* — *proprietario*, the lawful owner; *autorità legittima*, lawful authority; *figlio* —, legitimate child **2.** (*giusto, convenevole*) just, proper, right: *chiedere questo mi pare cosa legittima*, it seems to me proper to ask such a question **3.** (*fondato*) legitimate, justifiable; rightful: *timore* —, legitimate fear.

légna, *s.f.* wood, firewood: — *da ardere*, firewood; — *verde, secca, dolce, dura*, green, dry, soft, hard wood; *stufa che va a* —, wood-burning stove; (*andare a*) *far* —, to gather firewood; *spaccare* —, to chop (o to split) wood ‖ *mettere* — *al fuoco*, *fig.*, to stir up discord.

legnàceo, (*rar.*) per **legnóso 1.**

legnàia, *s.f.* **1.** wood-store **2.** (*massa di legna*) wood-pile.

legnaiuòlo, *s.m.* **1.** (*falegname*) carpenter, joiner **2.** (*taglialegna*) woodcutter.

legnàme, *s.m.* wood; (*da costruzione*) timber; (*amer.*) lumber: — *asciato*, split timber; — *da alberatura*, (*mar.*) masting-wood; — *essiccato*, dry wood; — *in tavole*, timber in planks; — *in tronchi*, logs; — *lavorato*, dressed stuff; — *non stagionato*, green wood; — *per carpenteria*, stuff; — *per cartiere*, pulpwood; — *piallato*, surfaced timber; — *stagionato*, seasoned timber; *lavoro in* —, timber-work; *sostegno in* —, timber support.

legnàre, *v.t.* (*bastonare*) to cudgel, to thrash ‖ *v.i.* (*far legna*) to gather firewood.

legnàta, *s.f.* blow with a cudgel ‖ *dare un fracco di legnate a qlcu.*, to give s.o. a sound cudgelling.

legnàtico, *s.m.* (*dir.*) right to gather firewood.

légno, *s.m.* **1.** wood: — *compensato*, ply-wood; — *di faggio*, beech-wood; — *dolce, duro*, soft, hard wood; — *marezzato, venato*, speckled wood; — *ricostituito*, (*neol.*) chipboard; *di* —, wooden; *lavorazione del* —, woodwork(ing); *lavoro in* —, woodwork; (*edil.*) timber-work; *pasta di* —, wood-pulp; *rivestimento in* —, (*edil.*) wainscot ‖ *testa di* —, *fig.* blockhead **2.** (*bastone*) stick, cane **3.** (*nave*) vessel; ship; boat: — *mercantile*, cargo-boat **4.** (*carrozza*) carriage **5.** (*silografia*) wood-engraving.

legnosità, *s.f.* woodiness.

legnóso, *ag.* **1.** woody; wooden; ligneous; wood-like (*attributivo*) **2.** (*detto di carne*) tough.

legulèio, *s.m.* (*spreg.*) pettifogger.

legúme, *s.m.* legume, legumen: *un piatto di legumi*, a dish of legumes.

leguminóso, *ag.* leguminous.

lei, *pron.pers.f. 3ª persona sing.* **1.** *obliquo e oggetto* her: *lo diedi a* —, *non a suo figlio*, I gave it to her not to her son; *sono stato con* — *tutto il giorno*, I have spent the whole day with her; *vidi proprio* — *ieri*, it was her I saw yesterday **2.** *sogg.* she: — *stessa, proprio* — *disse che sarebbe venuta*, she herself said she would come; *ho lavorato quanto* —, I have worked as hard as she has; *l'ha detto* — *e basta*, she said so, and that's enough; *lo saprà* —, she will know; *lui dice di no e* — *di sì*, he says no and she says yes; *perché non sono tutti come* —?, why aren't they all like her (o as she is)? ‖ *beata* —!, lucky her! ‖ *contenta* —, *contenti tutti!*, if she is satisfied, we all are! **3.** (*come pred. nominale*): *non sembra più* —, she does not seem herself any more **4.** *Lei*, *sogg. oggetto e obliquo* (*formula di cortesia*) you: *Lei mi è molto simpatico*, I like you very much; *è mai venuto qui Lei?*, have you ever been here before?; *signora, posso consegnare a Lei questo pacco?*, excuse me, madam, may I leave this parcel with you?.

Lèida, *no.pr.f.* (*geog.*) Leyden, Leiden ‖ *bottiglia di* —, (*fis.*) Leyden jar.

leit-motiv, *s.m.* leitmotiv.

Lèlia, *no.pr.f.* Lelia.

Lemàno, *no.pr.m.* (*geog.*) Lake Leman.

lémbo, *s.m.* **1.** border, margin, edge: *le si intravedeva un* — *di sottoveste*, the edge of her petticoat was showing **2.** (*zona, fascia*) strip: *un* — *di cielo*, a strip of sky; *gli estremi lembi della Terra*, the ends of the earth; *l'ultimo* — *di terra scomparve ai nostri occhi*, the last strip of land disappeared from view.

lèmma, *s.m.* lemma.

lèmme lèmme, *l.av.* very slowly.

Lèmno, *no.pr.f.* (*geog.*) Lemnos.

lemòsina, *s.f.* alms (*pl.*): *cassetta per le lemosine*, alms-box; *fare la* — *a qlcu.*, to give alms to s.o.

lèmure, *s.m.* **1.** (*mit. romana*) lemur (*pl.* lemures) **2.** (*zool.*) lemur (*pl.* lemurs).

léna, *s.f.* **1.** (*energia*) vigour, energy; stamina; *dovrai lavorare di buona* — *se vuoi finire prima di cena*, you'll have to put your back into it (o you'll have to get down to it) if you want to finish by dinner-time; *infondere* —, to give energy; *mettersi di buona* — *al lavoro*, to throw all one's energy into a task (o to set to work with a will) **2.** (*letter.*) (*respiro*) breath: *riprender* —, to recover one's breath.

lèndine, *s.m.* nit.

lendinóso, *ag.* nitty.

lène, *ag.* (*poet.*) (*delicato*) delicate; (*leggiero*) light, gentle; (*dolce*) sweet.

leneménte, *av.* (*delicatamente*) delicately; (*leggermente*) lightly, gently; (*dolcemente*) sweetly.

leniènte, *V.* **lenitívo.**

leniménto, *s.m.* soothing, mitigation.

Leningràdo, *no.pr.f.* (*geog.*) Leningrad.

lenìre, *v.t.* to calm, to soothe, to mitigate: *egli lenì il suo dolore*, he soothed her pain.

lenitívo, *ag.* **1.** (*farm.*) lenitive **2.** *fig.* (*che mitiga*) palliative, soothing ‖ *s.m.* **1.** (*farm.*) lenitive **2.** *fig.* (*ciò che mitiga*) palliative.

lenocínio, *s.m.* **1.** procuring, panderism **2.** *fig.* artifice: *lenocini dello stile*, artifices of style.

lenóne, *s.m.* pander, procurer, pimp.

lentàggine[1], (*arc.*) per **lentézza.**

lentàggine[2], *s.f.* (*bot.*) laurustine, laurustinus.

lentaménte, *av.* slowly.

lentàre, (*rar.*) per **allentàre.**

lènte[1], *s.f.* (*bot.*) lentil.

lènte[2], *s.f.* (*ott.*) lens: — *a contatto*, contact-lens; — *biconcava*, biconcave lens; — *convergente*, converging lens; — *d'ingrandimento*, magnifying glass (o magnifying lens o magnifier); — *divergente*, diverging lens; — *teleobiettiva*, (*foto.*) telephoto lens **2.** *pl.* (*occhiali*) spectacles, glasses: *portar le lenti*, to wear spectacles.

lenteggiàre, *v.i.* (*rar.*) to be loose, to be slack.

lentézza, *s.f.* slowness; (*mancanza di energia*) slackness; (*indolenza*) sluggishness: *camminava con una —straordinaria,* he walked at a snail's pace; *lavora con una certa —,* he is rather slack at his work.

lentìa, *s.f.* parbuckle.

lentìcchia, *s.f.* (*bot.*) lentil: *un piatto di lenticchie,* a dish of lentils: *Esaù per un piatto di lenticchie cedette la primogenitura a Giacobbe,* Esau sold his birthright to Jacob for a mess of pottage.

lenticolàre, *ag.* lenticular: *ganglio —,* (*anat.*) lenticular ganglion.

lentìggine, *s.f.* freckle.

lentigginóso, *ag.* freckled, freckly.

lentìsco, *s.m.* (*bot.*) lentisk, mastic tree.

lènto, *ag.* **1.** slow; (*indolente*) sluggish, indolent; (*tardo*) dull, obtuse, slow: *— a virare di bordo,* (*mar.*) slack in stays; *una corrente lenta,* a slow (*o* sluggish) current; *una crescita lenta,* a slow growth; *è molto — di movimenti,* he is very slow in his movements; *è uno scolaro molto — a capire,* he is a very dull pupil ‖ *a fuoco —,* on a low flame; (*in un forno*) in a slow oven **2.** (*allentato*) slack, loose: *una fune lenta,* a slack rope; *una vite lenta,* a loose screw; *questo vestito è piuttosto —,* this dress is rather loose(-fitting).

lènza, *s.f.* **1.** fishing-line: *pesca alla —,* angling **2.** (*edil.*) plumb-line.

lenzàra, *s.f.* paternoster-line; long line: *pesca con —,* long lining.

lenzuòlo, *s.m.* sheet ‖ *— funebre,* shroud.

leonardésco, *ag.* (*art.*) Leonardesque.

Leonàrdo, *no.pr.m.* Leonard ‖ *— (da Vinci),* (*st. art.*) Leonardo (da Vinci).

Leóne[1], *no.pr.m.* Leo, Leon: *Papa —,* Pope Leo.

leóne[2], *s.m.* **1.** lion (anche *fig.*): *— americano,* cougar; *è andato a caccia di leoni,* he has gone lion-hunting; *si battè come un —,* he fought like a lion ‖ *il Leone britannico,* the British Lion ‖ *— marino,* sea-lion ‖ *Riccardo Cuor di Leone,* Richard the Lion-hearted ‖ *avere una febbre da —,* to have a raging fever ‖ *fare la parte del —,* to take the lion's share ‖ *Leone,* (*astr.*) Leo **2.** *bocca di —,* (*bot. pop.*) snapdragon.

leonéssa, *s.f.* lioness.

Leònida, *no.pr.m.* (*st.*) Leonidas.

leonìno[1], *ag.* leonine: *città leonina,* Leonine City; *versi leonini* (*poes.*), Leonin verses (*o* Leonines).

leonìno[2], *ag.* leonine; lion-like (*attributivo*) *patto —,* leonine partnership; *aveva un coraggio —,* he was as brave as a lion; *ha una forza leonina,* he has a lion's strenght.

Leonòra, *no.pr.f.* Leonora, Eleanor ‖ dim. Ella, Nora.

leopàrdo, *s.m.* leopard: *— americano,* jaguar.

Leopòldo, *no.pr.m.* Leopold.

Lèpanto, *no.pr.f.* (*geog.*) Lepanto.

lepidaménte, *av.* wittily.

lepidézza, *s.f.* **1.** wit **2.** (*motto arguto*) witticism; sally.

Lèpido[1], *no.pr.m.* (*st.*) Lepidus.

lèpido[2], *ag.* witty.

lepidòtteri, *s.m.pl.* (*entom.*) Lepidoptera.

Lepontíne (Alpi), *no.pr.f.pl.* (*geog.*) Lepontine Alps.

lepòreo, *ag.* leporine.

leporíno, *ag.* leporine ‖ *labbro —,* hare-lip.

lepràtto, *s.m.* (*rar.*) leveret.

lèpre, *s.f.* hare: *— in salmì,* (*cuc.*) jugged hare; *astuto come la —,* as crafty as a fox; *timido come la —,* as shy as a schoolgirl; *correre come una —,* to run like a hare; *dormire come la —,* to sleep with one eye open.

leprìno, *ag.* leporine.

leprosàrio, *s.m.* leprosarium, leprosery.

lepròtto, *s.m.* leveret.

leptoclàsi, *s.f.* (*geol.*) leptoclase.

lèrcio, *ag.* dirty; (*disgustoso*) foul, filthy.

lerciúme, *s.m.* dirt; filth.

lèsbica, *s.f.* Lesbian.

lèsbico, *ag.* Lesbian.

Lèsbo, *no.pr.f.* (*geog.*) Lesbos.

lesèna, *s.f.* (*arch.*) pilaster strip.

lésina, *s.f.* **1.** (*strum. artig.*) awl **2.** (*persona avara*) skinflint.

lesinàre, *v.i.* to be stingy: *— sul prezzo,* to haggle over the price ‖ *v.t.* to grudge: *gli lesinano persino il cibo,* they grudge him even his food.

lesinería, *s.f.* stinginess, meanness.

lesionàre, *v.t.* **1.** (*ferire*) to wound; (*accidentalmente*) to injure **2.** (*danneggiare*) to damage: *le bombe lesionarono la casa,* bombs damaged the house.

lesióne, *s.f.* **1.** (*patol.*) lesion; (*ferita*) wound; (*ferita accidentale*) injury **2.** (*danno*) damage **3.** (*di interessi*) injury.

lesìvo, *ag.* (*letter.*) damaging, harmful.

léso, *ag.* injured, damaged ‖ *lesa maestà,* (*dir.*) lese-majesty ‖ *la parte lesa,* (*dir.*) the injured party.

lessàre, *v.t.* to boil: *— le patate, la verdura,* to boil potatoes, vegetables.

lessàta, lessatúra, *s.f.* boiling.

lessicàle, *ag.* lexical: *errori lessicali,* lexical errors.

lèssico, *s.m.* lexicon.

lessicografía, *s.f.* lexicography.

lessicogràfico, *ag.* lexicographic(al).

lessicògrafo, *s.m.* lexicographer.

lésso, *ag.* boiled: *carne lessa,* boiled meat; *pesce —,* boiled fish ‖ *s.m.* boiled meat ‖ *a —,* boiled.

lestaménte, *ag.* **1.** (*rapidamente*) quickly, fast, swiftly **2.** (*agilmente*) nimbly **3.** (*frettolosamente*) hastily.

lestézza, *s.f.* **1.** (*rapidità*) quickness, swiftness, speed: *la — dei suoi movimenti è sorprendente,* the swiftness (*o* quickness) of his movements is surprising **2.** (*agilità*) nimbleness, agility: *benchè sia tanto grasso, si muove con sorprendente —,* although he is so fat he moves with surprising agility.

lèsto, *ag.* **1.** (*svelto, rapido*) quick, swift: *a passo —,* at a quick pace ‖ *— di mano,* (*che picchia facilmente*) free with one's fists; (*che ruba con destrezza*) light-fingered **2.** (*pronto*) ready **3.** (*agile*) nimble, agile ‖ *av.* quickly, fast.

lestofànte, *s.c.* swindler, cheat: *quel — gli truffò cinquemila lire,* that swindler cheated him out of five thousand lire.

letàle, *ag.* **1.** lethal, deadly: *arma —,* lethal weapon; *un veleno —,* a lethal poison **2.** (*simile a morte*) deathly: *pallore —,* deathly pallor.

letamàio, *s.m.* **1.** dung-heap, dunghill **2.** *fig.* dirty place, hovel: *vivono in un —,* they live in a hovel.

letamàre, *v.t.* to manure, to dung.

letàme, *s.m.* **1.** manure, dung: *un mucchio di —,* a dung-heap; *spargere il — su un campo,* to manure a field **2.** *fig.* dirt, filth.

letargía, *s.f.* **1.** (*patol.*) lethargy **2.** (*di animali*) (*invernale*) hibernation; (*estiva*) (a)estivation.

letàrgico, *ag.* **1.** (*patol.*) lethargic: *encefalite letargica,* lethargic encephalitis; *il malato cadde in un sonno —,* the sick man sank into a lethargic sleep **2.** (*di animali*) (*di letargo invernale*) hibernating; (*di letargo estivo*) (a)estivating: *una tartaruga in stato —,* a tortoise in a state of hibernation.

letàrgo, *s.m.* **1.** (*patol.*) lethargy **2.** (*di animali*) (*invernale*) hibernation; (*estivo*) (a)estivation: *cadere in —,* to go into hibernation; *passare l'inverno in —,* to hibernate **3.** *fig.* lethargy, torpor, apathy: *l'ho risvegliato dal suo — e l'ho incitato ad agire,* I roused him from his torpor and urged him to act.

Lète, *no.pr.m.* (*geog. mit.*) Lethe.

leticàre, e derivati, *V.* **litigàre, e derivati.**

letificàre, *v.t.* (*letter.*) to gladden.

Letízia[1], *no.pr.f.* Letitia, Laetitia, Lettice ‖ *dim.* Lettie, Letty.

letízia[2], *s.f.* gladness, joy; delight: *colmare di — il cuore di qlcu.,* to fill s.o.'s heart with joy; *vivere in —,* to live happily.

letiziànte, *ag.* (*rar.*) gladdening, cheering.

letiziàre, *v.t.* (*rar.*) to gladden, to cheer up, to

fill with joy || *v.i.*, **letiziàrsi**, *v.r.* (*rar.*) to rejoice (at sthg., doing); to delight (in sthg., doing).

lètta, *s.f.* glance, look, hasty perusal: *diede una — al giornale*, he had a glance at the newspaper.

lèttera, *s.f.* **1.** (*dell'alfabeto*) letter: — *cubitale*, block letter; *lettere corsive*, italics; — *maiuscola, minuscola*, (block) capital, small letter: *scrivi il tuo nome e cognome a lettere maiuscole*, write your name and surname in (blòck) capitals; *scrivere un numero in lettere*, to write a number in words || *giorno da scrivere a lettere d'oro*, *fig.* red-letter day **2.** (*senso letterale*) letter || *alla* —, literally (*o* to the letter): *tradurre alla* —, to translate word for word (*o* literally) || *la — uccide, lo spirito vivifica*, the letter killeth, the spirit giveth life **3.** (*epistola, documento*) letter: — *anonima*, anonymous letter; — *aperta*, open letter; — *circolare*, circular (letter); — *d'affari*, business letter; — *di cambio*, (*comm.*) bill of exchange; — *di consolazione*, letter of condolence; — *di credito*, (*comm.*) letter of credit; — *di presentazione*, letter of introduction; — *di raccomandazione*, letter of recommendation; — *di sollecitazione al pagamento*, (*comm.*) dunning letter; — *di vettura*, (*comm.*) carriage note; (*ferr.*) consignment note; — *minatoria*, threatening letter; — *patente*, (diplomatic) credentials; — *raccomandata*, registered letter; *buca per le lettere*, letter-box; *carta da* —, writing-paper; *ufficio delle lettere non recapitate*, dead-letter office; *le lettere che ci siamo scambiati*, the letters that have passed between us; *impostare una* —, to post a letter || *questa legge è diventata — morta*, this law has become a dead letter **4.** *pl.* (*letteratura*) letters: *lettere e filosofia*, the humanities; *dottore in lettere*, Bachelor of Arts (*abbr.* B.A.); *uomo di lettere*, man of letters.

letteràle, *ag.* literal: *senso* —, literal meaning; *traduzione* —, word for word (*o* literal) translation.

letteralménte, *av.* literally: *era — pazzo di gioia*, he was literally mad with delight; *traduci questo brano* —, translate this passage literally.

letterariaménte, *av.* literarily.

letteràrio, *ag.* literary: *proprietà letteraria*, copyright; *studi letterari*, literary studies.

letteràto, *ag.* well-read || *s.m.* **1.** literary man, man of letters **2.** (*pop.*) (*chi sa leggere*) literate.

letteratúra, *s.f.* literature: *buona* —, good literature; *dedicarsi alla* —, to devote oneself to literature.

lettièra, *s.f.* **1.** bedstead **2.** (*strame*) litter.

lettíga, *s.f.* **1.** stretcher, litter **2.** (*portantina*) litter.

lettighière, *s.m.* stretcher-bearer.

lettíno, *s.m.* small bed, couch; (*per bambini*) cot, crib; (*di ospedale*) cot.

lettistèrnio, *s.m.* (*st. romana*) lectisternium.

lètto, *s.m.* bed: — *a una piazza*, single bed; — *a due piazze*, double bed; — *da campo*, camp-bed (*o* field-bed); — *dell'unghia*, (*anat.*) nail-bed; — *di ferro*, iron bedstead; — *di fiume*, river-bed; — *disponibile*, spare bed; — *di piume*, feather bed; — *elastico*, spring bed; *letti gemelli*, twin beds; — *pieghevole*, folding-bed; *camera a un* —, room with a single bed; *camera a due letti*, room with a double bed; *camera da* —, bedroom; *compagno di* —, bed-fellow; *divano* —, divan-bed; *vagone* —, sleeping-car (*o* sleeper); *andare a* —, to go to bed: *è ora di andare a* —, it's bedtime; *disfare il* —, to strip the bed; *essere a* —, to be in bed; *essere in* —, to keep to one's bed (*o* to be bedridden); *fare il* —, to make the bed; *mettere un bambino a* —, to put a child to bed; *morire nel proprio* —, to die in one's bed (*o* to die a natural death); *saltar giù dal* —, to jump (*o* to spring) out of bed || — *di dolore*, sick-bed; — *di morte*, death-bed || — *di giustizia*, (*st. francese*) bed-of-justice || — *di Procuste*, Procustean bed (*o* bed of Procustes) || *un — di rose*, *fig.* a bed of roses; *essere in un — di spine*, *fig.* to be on a bed of thorns (*o* in serious trouble) || *figlio di primo* —, child of the

first marriage || *sei cascato dal — stamattina!*, you're up with the lark to-day! || *essere tra — e lettuccio*, to be in poor health || *chi va a — senza cena, tutta notte si dimena*, *prov.* he who goes to bed supperless, tumbles and tosses all night.

lettóne, *ag.s.c.* Latvian, Lettonian || *s.m.* (*lingua*) Lettish.

Lettònia, *no.pr.f.* (*geog.*) Latvia.

lettoràto, *s.m.* **1.** (*ufficio del lettore universitario*) readership, lectureship **2.** (*eccl.*) lectorate, lectorship.

lettóre, *s.m.* **1.** reader: *il pubblico dei lettori*, the reading public **2.** (*carica universitaria*) reader; lecturer; (*amer.*) instructor **3.** (*eccl.*) lector **4.** (*tip.*) (proof-)reader **5.** — *del suono*, (*cine.*) sound pick-up.

lettríce, *s.f.* **1.** reader **2.** (*carica universitaria*) reader; lecturer; (*amer.*) instructor.

lettúra, *s.f.* **1.** reading: — *ad alta voce*, reading aloud; *amante della* —, fond of reading; *brani di* —, reading passages; *libro di* —, reading-book; *sala di* —, reading room; *la — mi stanca*, reading tires me; *la commedia ebbe successo sul palcoscenico, ma è poco interessante alla* —, the play was successful on the stage, but it is not very interesting to read; *domani ascolteremo la — del testamento*, tomorrow we shall hear the reading of the will; *quel libro è di piacevole* —, that book makes pleasant reading || *prima, seconda — di un disegno di legge*, (*pol.*) first, second reading of a bill; *il progetto fu respinto in seconda* —, the bill was rejected at the second reading **2.** (*ciò che si legge*) literature: *letture amene*, light literature; *letture edificanti*, edifying literature **3.** (*interpretazione*) reading: *la mia — non concorda con la tua*, my reading does not agree with yours.

Lèucade, *no.pr.f.* (*geog.*) Leukas, Leucas.

leucemía, *s.f.* (*patol.*) leukaemia.

Leucíppo, *no.pr.m.* (*st. fil.*) Leucippus.

leucocíti, *s.m.pl.* (*anat.*) leucocytes.

leucòma, *s.m.* (*patol.*) leucoma.

Lèuttra, *no.pr.f.* (*geog. st.*) Leuctra.

lèva[1], *s.f.* **1.** (*mec.*) lever: — *a forcella*, forked lever; — *a mano*, hand lever; — *a pedale*, foot (control) lever; — *articolata*, toggle lever; — *del freno*, brake lever; — *del gas*, throttle lever; — *della marcia indietro*, reverse lever; — *dello scambio*, (*ferr.*) switch lever; — *di arresto*, cut-off lever; — *di avviamento*, starting lever; — *di disinnesto*, release lever; (*a scatto*) trip lever; — *di innesto*, engaging lever; — *di manovra*, operating lever; — *di sgancio*, uncoupling lever; *far* —, to lever (*o* to prize) || *far — sui sentimenti di qlcu.*, to play on s.o.'s feelings **2.** *fig.* stimulus, incentive.

lèva[2], *s.f.* (*mil.*) call up, conscription, levy: *la — del 1957*, those called up in 1957; — *in massa*, general conscription; *essere di* —, to be due for call up.

levàbile, *ag.* removable.

Levànte, *no.pr.m.* (*geog.*) Levant, Near East || **levànte**, *s.m.* **1.** (*punto cardinale*) east **2.** (*vento*) easterly wind, levanter.

levantína, *s.f.* **1.** (*nativa del Levante*) Levantine **2.** (*tessuto di seta*) levantine **3.** (*pantofola turca*) Turkish slipper.

levantíno, *ag.s.m.* Levantine.

levàre, *v.t.* **1.** (*sollevare, alzare*) to raise, to lift (*anche fig.*): *la chiesa leva le sue guglie verso il cielo*, the church lifts its spires to the skies; *la montagna leva la sua cima nevosa verso il cielo*, the mountain rears its snowy summit towards the sky; *questa gru leva venti tonnellate*, this crane lifts twenty tons; *il bicchiere alla salute di qlcu.*, to raise one's glass to s.o.; — *un dito*, to raise a finger; — *un grido*, to utter a cry; — *le mani su qlcu.*, to raise one's hand against s.o. (*o* to lay hands on s.o. *o* to strike s.o.); — *lo sguardo*, to lift one's eyes; — *la voce*, to raise one's voice || — *il bollore*, to come to the boil || — *qlcu. al cielo*, to praise s.o. to the skies **2.** (*togliere, rimuovere*) to take off; to take away, to remove: *glielo ha levato dalle mani*, she took it out of his hands; *leva via questa* *sedia*, take this chair away; *non levò gli occhi dal libro*, he never took his eyes off his book; — *l'àncora*, to weigh anchor; — *un assedio*, to raise a siege; — *un dente*, to pull a tooth out; — *le lettere dalla cassetta*, to clear the letter-box; — *i sigilli*, to remove (o to break) the seals; — *la tovaglia*, to take off the table-cloth; — *tutti i dubbi*, to remove all doubts || *mi ha levato il pane di bocca*, he took the bread out of my mouth || *se si levano due o tre persone...*, (*eccettuandole*) two or three persons excepted... || — *cinque da dieci*, (*sottrarre*) to take (o to subtract) five from ten || — *la fame a qlcu.*, to appease s.o.'s hunger; — *la sete a qlcu.*, to quench s.o.'s thirst || — *l'incomodo*, to take one's leave || — *il latte a un bambino*, (*svezzarlo*) to wean a child || — *la messa a un prete*, (*interdirlo*) to lay a priest under an interdict || — *il pelo a qlcu.*, (*sgridarlo*) to flay s.o. || — *qlcu. di mezzo*, (*ucciderlo*) to bump s.o. off || — *il saluto a qlcu.*, to cut s.o. || — *una seduta*, to close a sitting || — *le tende*, to break camp || — *un vizio a qlcu.*, to break s.o. of a vice || *levarne le gambe*, (*cavarsela*) to come off all right **3.** (*caccia*) to put up, to flush: *il cane ha levato una pernice*, the dog has flushed a partridge **4.** (*comprare all'ingrosso, merci*) to buy wholesale || **levàrsi**, *v.r.* **1.** (*togliersi da un luogo*) to get out (of a place): *levati via di lì*, get out (o clear out) of the way **2.** (*alzarsi*) to rise; (*dal letto*) to get up; (*in volo*) to take off: *si leva di buon mattino*, he gets up early (o he is an early riser); — *da tavola*, to leave the table; — *in piedi*, to rise to one's feet **3.** (*sorgere*) to rise: *il sole si leva alle sei*, the sun rises at six; *il vento si sta levando*, the wind is rising (o getting up) || — *a rumore, a furore*, to rise (o to rebel): *il popolo si levò a furore contro il governo*, the people rose against the government **4.** (*togliersi*) to take off: *levati il cappello*, take off your hat || *levati questa sciocca idea dalla testa*, get that silly idea out of your head || *mi levo tanto di cappello di fronte a quest'uomo*, I raise my hat to this man || — *la maschera*, to throw off (o to drop) the mask || — *il pane di bocca per qlcu.*, to give s.o. one's last crust || — *qlcu. d'attorno, di mezzo*, to get rid of s.o. || — *una voglia, un capriccio*, to satisfy a wish (o a whim).

levàta, *s.f.* **1.** rising: — *del sole*, sunrise (o rising of the sun) || — *di scudi*, rebellion || *di prima* —, first thing in the morning: *di prima* — *è sempre di cattivo umore*, he is always in a bad mood when he gets up **2.** (*delle lettere*) collection, clearance: *la* — *è stata appena fatta*, the letter-box has just been cleared **3.** (*compra all'ingrosso*) wholesale purchase **4.** (*salasso*) bleeding.

levatàccia, *s.f.* very early rising.

levàto, *ag.* **1.** (*eccettuato*): *levati alcuni errori di ortografia, questa traduzione è piuttosto buona*, except for (o but for) a few spelling mistakes, this translation is rather good **2.** (*volto in su*) turned up: *cadere a gambe levate*, to fall on one's back || *correre a gambe levate*, to run at full speed.

levatóio, *ag.*: *ponte* —, draw-bridge.

levatóre, *s.m.* **1.** riser: *è un buon* —, he is an early riser **2.** (*ind. cartaria*) layer.

levatríce, *s.f.* midwife.

levatúra, *s.f.* intelligence; understanding: *un'osservazione di poca* —, a rather unintelligent remark; *essere di scarsa* —, to show little intelligence (o to be of poor intelligence).

Lèvi, *no.pr.m.* (*Bibbia*) Levi.

Leviatàno, *no.pr.m.* (*Bibbia*) Leviathan.

levigàre, *v.t.* **1.** to smooth, to make smooth **2.** (*farm.*) to levigate **3.** (*tec.*) (*superficie di pietra*) to dress; (*smerigliare*) to lap; (*carteggiare*) to rub down.

levigatézza, *s.f.* smoothness.

levigàto, *ag.* **1.** smooth: — *e lucidato*, glossy; *ha la pelle ben levigata*, she has a very smooth skin **2.** (*tec.*) (*di pietra*) dressed; (*carteggiato*) rubbed down.

levigatríce, *s.f.* (*mec.*) lapping machine.

levigatúra, *s.f.* **1.** smoothing **2.** (*tec.*) (*di superficie di pietra*) dressing; (*smerigliatura*) lapping; (*carteggiatura*) rubbing down: — *con carta vetrata*, (*artig.*) sand finish; — *degli ingranaggi*, (*mec.*) gear lapping.

levigazióne, *s.f.* **1.** smoothing **2.** (*farm.*) levigation.

leviràto, *s.m.* (*st. ebraica*) levirate.

levisíte, *s.f.* (*chim. mil.*) lewisite.

levìta, *s.m.* (*st. ebraica*) Levite.

levità, *s.f.* (*letter.*) **1.** lightness: *la* — *del suo tocco*, the lightness of his touch **2.** (*superficialità*) levity.

levitàre, *V.* **lievitàre**.

levitazióne, *s.f.* levitation.

levítico, *ag.* (*st. ebraica*) Levitical || *s.m.* Leviticus.

levogíro, *ag.* (*chim.*) laevorotatory, laevogyrous.

levrière, *s.m.* greyhound: *le corse dei levrieri*, greyhound-racing.

levulòsio, *s.m.* (*chim.*) laevulose.

lèzio, *s.m.* affectation, mannerism: *i suoi lezi mi danno ai nervi*, his mannerisms get on my nerves.

lezióne, *s.f.* **1.** lesson: — *collettiva*, class; — *privata*, private lesson; — *universitaria*, lecture; *ora di* —, period; *le lezioni di inglese cominceranno domani*, (the) English classes will start to-morrow; *che cosa hai di* — *per domani?*, what lesson must you prepare for to-morrow?; *non manca mai alle lezioni di filologia*, he never misses any philology lectures || *saltare le lezioni*, to play truant **2.** (*ammonizione*) lesson, warning: *che questo ti serva di* —!, let this be a lesson to you!; *ci ha rimesso un sacco di soldi, ciò gli servirà di* —, he has lost a lot of money in this, that will teach him!; *fu una* — *dura, ma meritata!*, that was a hard, but well-deserved lesson!; *ti meriti una* — *coi fiocchi*, you deserve a good telling-off **3.** (*Bibbia*) lesson **4.** (*variante*) reading: *la migliore* — *di quel manoscritto*, the best reading of that manuscript; *le varie lezioni date a piè di pagina*, the various readings given at the foot of the page.

leziosàggine, *s.f.* **1.** affectedness; affectation; mannerism: *il Parini ritrae la* — *del Settecento*, Parini portrays the mannerisms of the eighteenth century **2.** (*moine*) simpering: *smettila con le tue leziosaggini!*, stop your simpering!

leziosaménte, *av.* **1.** (*con affettazione*) affectedly **2.** (*con moine*) simperingly.

lezióso, *ag.* affected, mannered; mincing: *un sorriso* —, a mincing smile; *uno stile* —, an affected style.

lézzo, *s.m.* **1.** stink, stench **2.** (*sudiciume*) filth (anche *fig.*): *marcire nel* —, to rot in the filth.

lezzóne, *s.m.*, **lezzóna**, *s.f.* (*rar.*) stinkard, stinker.

lezzóso, *ag.* stinking.

lezzúme, *s.m.* filth.

li[1], *pron. pers. m.* 3ª *persona pl. oggetto* them: *eccoli!*, here they are!; — *vedo spesso in città*, I often see them in town; *chiamali subito*, call them at once; «*Dove sono i tuoi libri?*» «*Li sto cercando*», "Where are your books?" "I am looking for them".

li[2], (*forma arcaica dell'art. determinativo m.pl. usata nelle indicazioni di date*): — *5 aprile*, 5th April (o April 5th).

lì[3], *av.* **1.** there: *da* — *all'uscio*, from there to the door; *ci vogliono venti minuti per andare di qui a* —, you need twenty minutes to get from here to there; *è passato di* — *l'altro giorno*, he was there the other day; *era* — *dove l'avevo lasciato*, it was (there) where I had left it; *era caduto* — *sul pavimento*, it had fallen there on the floor; *mettilo* —, put it there; *ne prese uno qui e uno* —, he took one here and one there (o one here and there); *resta* — *dove sei*, stay (there) where you are; *s'arrampicò su di* —, he climbed up there; *scendi giù di* —, come (o get) down off there || — *accanto, vicino*, near there; — *dentro*, in there; — *fuori*, out there; — *sopra*, on there; — *sotto*, under there || — *per* —, (*dapprima*) at first; (*sul momento*) on the spot (o there and then): — *per* — *dissi di no, ma poi ci ripensai*, at first I said no, but then I changed my mind; — *per* — *non seppe che cosa dire*, he didn't know what to say at the moment; *lo feci* — *per* —, I did it there and then (*o* on the spot) ‖ *di — a un mese,* a month later; *di — a poco,* after a while (*o* after a short time *o* soon after) ‖ *fin —,* as far as that (*o* so far as that); *fig.* up to that point (*o* up to there): *fin — aveva ragione lui,* he was right up to that point; *sono arrivato fin —,* I went as far as that ‖ *giù di —,*(*press'a poco*) thereabouts: *un anno o giù di —,* a year or thereabouts; *pagò mille lire o giù di —,* he paid a thousand lire or thereabouts ‖ *essere —, fig.: oramai col denaro siamo —,* (*sta finendo*) we are almost out of money (*o* we have almost run out of money); *oramai siamo — con gli esami,* (*sono vicini*) the exams are almost on top of us; *se non sono mille chilometri, saremo —,* if it's not a thousand kilometres, it must be getting on that way (*o* it cannot be far off it) ‖ *essere — — per fare ql.co.,* to be on the point of doing sthg.: *era — — per piangere,* she was on the point of crying ‖ *finir —, fig.: ha un po' di pensione e tutto finisce —,* he has a small pension and that's all; *per quella sera tutto finì —,* that was the end of it for that evening **2.** (*in espressioni ellittiche*): *eccolo —!,* there it is!; *in quel momento —,* at that very moment; *voglio quello —,* I want that one **3.** (*pleonastico ed enfatico*): *fermo —!,* stop!; *zitto —!,* quiet there!; *guardate — che sconquasso!,* just look at that mess!.

Lía, *no.pr.f.* (*Bibbia*) Leah.

liàna, *s.f.* (*bot.*) liana, liane.

lías, *s.m.* (*geol.*) lias.

liàssico, *ag.* (*geol.*) liassic.

libagióne, *s.f.* libation.

Líbano[1]**,** *no.pr.m.* (*geog.*) Lebanon.

libàno[2]**,** *s.m.* (*mar.*) esparto rope.

libàre[1]**,** *v.t.* **1.** to offer as a libation; (*rar.*) to libate **2.** (*assaggiare, gustare*) to sip, to taste.

libàre[2]**,** *v.t.* (*mar.*) to lighten.

libatòrio, *ag.* libatory ‖ *s.m.* libatory vessel.

libazióne, *s.f.* libation.

líbbra, *s.f.* **1.** (*antica misura di peso romana* = 327g) libra (*pl.* librae) **2.** (*nel sistema anglosassone*) — (*avoirdupois*), pound (*misura di peso avoirdupois* = 453,6 g) **3.** (*nel sistema anglosassone*) (*per metalli preziosi, pietre preziose e medicinali*) — (*troy*), pound (*misura di peso troy* = 373,248 g).

libecciàta, *s.f.* gale caused by the libeccio.

libéccio, *s.m.* libeccio (southwest wind).

libellísta, *s.m.* libeller, defamer.

libèllo, *s.m.* libel (anche *dir.*).

libèllula, *s.f.* (*entom.*) dragonfly.

liberàle, *ag.* **1.** liberal: *arti liberali,* liberal arts; *educazione —,* liberal education; *partito —,* (*pol.*) Liberal Party **2.** (*generoso*) liberal, generous, open -handed: *— di promesse,* liberal of promises; *— verso i poveri,* liberal towards the poor ‖ *s.m.* (*pol.*) Liberal.

liberalísmo, *s.m.* **1.** (*pol.*) liberalism **2.** (*econ. pol.*) (*libero scambio*) (theory of) free trade; (*anti-protezionismo*) laissez-faire.

liberalità, *s.f.* **1.** liberality, generosity **2.** (*atto generoso*) generous act.

liberalménte, *av.* liberally, generously.

liberaménte, *av.* **1.** freely: *diritto di varcare — le frontiere,* right of free entry; *usate — i miei libri,* make free use of (*o* you are welcome to) my books **2.** (*con franchezza*) frankly, plain, plainly: *per parlare —,* frankly speaking (*o* to speak plainly).

liberàre, *v.t.* **1.** to free, to liberate, to set free, to rescue, to release, to rid; to deliver: *liberami da quella donna,* rid me of that woman; *lo schiavo fu liberato,* the slave was set free; *— la mente da pregiudizi,* to free one's mind of prejudice; *— un paese dai banditi,* to rid a country of bandits; *— un prigioniero,* to release a prisoner; *— una proprietà dalle ipoteche,* to free (*o* to redeem) a property from mortgage; *— le proprie terre dai debiti,* to rid one's estate of debts; *— qlcu. da un'obbligazione,* (*comm.*) to free (*o* to release) s.o. from an obligation; *— qlcu. da un pericolo,* to rescue s.o. from

a danger; *— qlcu. dal male,* to deliver s.o. from evil; *— qlcu. dalla morte, dalla povertà,* to rescue s.o. from death, poverty; *— qlcu. sotto cauzione,* to release s.o. on bail; *— un topo da una trappola,* to free a mouse from a trap ‖ *Dio ci scampi e liberi!,* God forbid! **2.** (*sgomberare*) to free, to clear: *— una stanza,* to clear a room **3.** (*esentare*) to exempt: *— qlcu. dal servizio militare,* to exempt s.o. from military service **4.** (*mec.*) to release, to trip **5.** (*chim.*) to liberate ‖ **liberàrsi,** *v.r.* to free oneself; to rid oneself (of s.o., sthg.); to get rid (of s.o., sthg.): *mi sono liberato di loro,* I have got rid of them; *— da un'abitudine,* to break oneself of a habit; *— da un debito,* to pay off (*o* to liquidate) a debt; *— da un'idea, da un obbligo,* to rid oneself of an idea, of an obligation; *— dai pregiudizi,* to free oneself of prejudice; *— dai propri impegni,* to free oneself from one's commitments; *— dalla stretta di qlcu.,* to free oneself from s.o.'s grasp.

liberatóre, *ag.* liberating ‖ *Cristo Liberatore,* the Redeemer ‖ *s.m.,* **liberatríce,** *s.f.* liberator, deliverer.

liberazióne, *s.f.* **1.** liberation, freeing; release, discharge; redemption: *— da un'ipoteca,* (*comm.*) redemption of a mortgage; *— da un'obbligazione,* (*comm.*) release (*o* discharge) from an obligation; *— dal giogo della schiavitù,* liberation from the yoke of slavery; *— definitiva di un prigioniero,* final discharge of a prisoner; *— di uno schiavo,* freeing of a slave **2.** (*esenzione dal servizio militare*) exemption **3.** (*ferr.*) clearing.

libèrcolo, *s.m.* (*spreg.*) worthless book.

Libèria, *no.pr.f.* (*geog.*) Liberia.

liberísmo, *V.* liberalísmo **2.**

liberísta, *s.m.* (*econ. pol.*) free trader.

líbero, *ag.* **1.** free: *— amore,* free love; *— arbitrio,* free will; *— come l'aria,* as free as air; *— da imposte,* duty-free (*o* exempt from taxation): *articoli liberi da imposte,* duty-free articles; *— da ipoteche,* free from mortgage; *— da pregiudizi,* free from prejudice; *— da preoccupazioni,* free from care; *— da tutela,* of age; *libera parola,* free speech; *— pensatore,* free-thinker; *— scambio,* free trade; *entrata libera,* admission free; *fede di stato libero,* certificate of unmarried status; *professione libera,* self-employment (*o* free-lance work); *traduzione libera,* free translation; *verso —,* free verse; *fu processato, ma ne uscì —,* he was tried, but set free; *la linea è libera,* (*tel.*) the line is disengaged; *questo posto è —,* this seat is free (*o* has not been taken); *questo tavolo è —?,* is this table free?; *essere — di fare ql.co.,* to be free to do sthg.: *siamo liberi di correre in giardino,* we have the run of the garden; *lasciare libera una camera,* to cease occupying a room; (*disdirla*) to cancel one's booking; *lasciare — qlcu.,* to let s.o. off (work); (*licenziarlo*) to dismiss s.o.: *l'ho lasciato — nel pomeriggio,* I have given him the afternoon free (*o* off); *mi lascerà — presto oggi?,* will you let me off early to-day?; *lasciare qlcu. — di fare ciò che vuole,* to give s.o. a free hand ‖ *—, (di taxi)* for hire ‖ *— docente,* fully established university lecturer; *libera docenza,* establishment as university lecturer ‖ *a cuore —, alla libera,* (*sinceramente*) frankly ‖ *a piede —,* (*dir.*) not in custody ‖ *allo stato —,* (*chim.*) loose ‖ *disegno a mano libera,* free-hand drawing ‖ *esercizi a corpo —,* free gymnastics; *stile —,* (*nuoto*) free-style ‖ *avere la mano libera,* to have a free hand **2.** (*senza impegni*) free, not engaged: *quando sarò — verrò a trovarti,* when I'm free I'll look you up; *quando sono —, (fuori servizio)* when I am off duty; *siete —?,* are you free?; *sono — dalle due alle tre,* I am not engaged between two and three; *avere del tempo —,* to have some time free (*o* some spare time): *ho molto poco tempo —,* I have very little free time **3.** (*vacante*) vacant: *posto —,* vacant post **4.** (*aperto*) open; (*sgombro*) clear: *aria libera,* open air; *all'aria libera,* in the open air; *mare —,* open sea; *strada libera,* clear road; *via libera,* (*ferr.*) line clear **5.** (*licenzioso*) free, loose: *condotta libera,* loose conduct;

costumi, discorsi liberi, loose customs, talk **6.** (*mec.*) free, clear: *ruota libera*, free-wheel.

liberoscambísta, *s.m.* (*econ. pol.*) freetrader.

libertà, *s.f.* **1.** liberty, freedom; (*indipendenza*) independence: — *di azione*, liberty of action: *avere piena — di azione*, to have full liberty; — *di commercio*, freedom of trade (*o freetrade*); — *di coscienza*, liberty of conscience; — *di culto*, freedom of religion; — *di parola*, freedom of speech; — *di pensiero*, liberty of thought; — *di stampa*, freedom of the press; *provvisoria, sotto cauzione*, bail: *accordare la — provvisoria a qlcu.*, to let s.o. out on bail (*o* to admit s.o. to bail); *domani è il mio giorno di —*, tomorrow is my free day (*o* my day off); *concedere la — a uno schiavo*, to give a slave his freedom; *dare — d'iniziativa a qlcu.*, to give s.o. a free hand; *ottenere la —*, to secure one's liberty ‖ *in —*, at liberty; (*a proprio agio*) at home; (*di animali*) free: *mettere in —*, to set at liberty (*o* to set free *o* to release); *mettere in — l'accusato*, to discharge the accused; *mettersi in —*, to make oneself at home ‖ *in tutta —*, freely: *parlare in tutta —*, to speak freely (*o* without restraint) ‖ *la Statua della Libertà*, the Statue of Liberty ‖ *prendersi la — di fare ql.co.*, to take the liberty of doing sthg.: *se posso prendermi questa —...*, if I may be so bold... ‖ *prendersi delle — con qlcu.*, to take liberties with s.o. ‖ *trattare qlcu. con troppa —*, to be too familiar with s.o. ‖ *meglio un'oncia di — che dieci libbre d'oro*, *prov.* liberty is better than gold **2.** (*licenziosità*) freedom, looseness: — *di costumi*, looseness of behaviour; — *di discorso*, coarseness of speech.

libertàrio, *ag.* anarchic(al) ‖ *s.m.* anarchist.

liberticída, *ag.* liberticide: *legge —*, liberty-destroying law ‖ *s.m.* liberticide.

libertinàggio, *s.m.* libertinage, libertinism.

libertíno, *s.m.* **1.** libertine, rake, debauchee **2.** (*st. lett.*) libertine; (*libero pensatore*) free-thinker **3.** (*st. romana*) libertine.

libertísmo, *s.m.* (*fil.*) libertarianism.

libèrto, *s.m.* (*st. romana*) freedman (*pl.* freedmen).

Líbia, *no.pr.f.* (*geog.*) Libya.

líbico, *ag.s.m.* Libyan.

libídine, *s.f.* **1.** libidinousness, lustfulness, lewdness, lechery **2.** (*desiderio sfrenato*) lust, thirst: — *del denaro*, lust for money; — *del potere*, thirst for power.

libidinóso, *ag.* libidinous, lustful, lewd.

líbito, *s.m.* (*letter.*) will; caprice ‖ *a —*, at will.

libra, *s.f.* (*bilancia*) scales (*pl.*) ‖ *Libra*, (*astr.*) Libra (*o* Balance).

libràio, *s.m.* book-seller.

libràre, *v.t.* **1.** to weigh; to poise, to balance (anche *fig.*): — *il pro e il contro*, to weigh the pros and cons **2.** (*rar.*) (*equilibrare*) to poise, to balance ‖ **libràrsi**, *v.r.* to librate, to balance oneself, to poise oneself: — *in aria*, to hover.

libràrio, *ag.* book (*attributivo*): *commercio —*, book-trade; *novità librarie*, new books.

libràta, *s.f.* blow with a book: *prendere a librate qlcu.*, to bang s.o. on the head with a book.

librazióne, *s.f.* **1.** (*il librare*) weighing; poising, balancing **2.** (*il librarsi*) libration **3.** (*astr.*) libration: — *della Luna*, libration of the moon.

libreria, *s.f.* **1.** (*negozio di libri*) book-seller's (shop), bookshop; (*amer.*) bookstore: — *di occasioni*, second-hand bookshop **2.** (*biblioteca*) library: — *a prestito*, lending-library; — *circolante*, circulating library; — *monastica*, abbey (*o* monastery) library; *Libreria Vaticana*, Vatican Library; *riordinare una —*, to rearrange a library **3.** (*scaffale*) bookcase; bookshelves (*pl.*): — *girevole*, revolving bookcase.

librésco, *ag.* bookish.

librettísta, *s.m.* librettist.

librétto, *s.m.* **1.** (*mus.*) libretto (*pl.* libretti, librettos) **2.** (*piccolo libro*) booklet, (small) book: — *del droghiere, del fornaio*, grocer's, baker's pass-book; —

di assegni, cheque-book; — *di banca*, bank-book; — *di circolazione*, (*aut.*) log-book; — *di lavoro*, employment-card; — *di matricola*, (*mil.*) pay-book; — *di passaggio in dogana*, (*aut.*) customs pass-book; — *di risparmio*, savings-book; — *personale*, (*mil.*) service record; — *universitario*, university student's record-book; — *uso e manutenzione*, (*mec.*) operation and maintenance hand-book.

líbro, *s.m.* **1.** book: — *apocrifo*, apocryphal book; — *battesimale*, baptismal register; *libri canonici*, sacred books; — *catastale*, property-register; — *con legatura*, bound book; — *da messa*, missal; *libri del codice*, (*dir.*) civil and criminal codes; *il — del destino*, the book of fate; *il — della memoria*, *fig.* the book of memory; *il — della vita*, *fig.* the book of life; — *delle ore*, (*eccl.*) book of hours; — *dei sogni*, dream-book; — *di bordo*, log-book; — *di consultazione*, book of reference; — *di cucina*, cookery-book; — *di lettura*, reader; — *di preghiera*, prayer-book; — *di testo*, text-book; — *illustrato*, illustrated book; *libri liturgici*, liturgical books; — *manoscritto*, manuscript; — *mutilo*, fragmentary book; — *usato*, second-hand book; *catalogo dei libri*, book-catalogue; *un club del —*, a book-club; *vendita di libri all'asta*, book-auction; *l'edizione del — è esaurita*, the book is out of print; *il « Paradiso Perduto » di Milton è in dodici libri*, Milton's " Paradise Lost " consists of twelve books; *questo — è appena uscito*, this book has just been published; *conoscere la vita attraverso i libri*, to know life through books; *criticare un —*, to criticize a book; *divorare un —*, to read a book at a sitting; *divulgare un —*, to make a book known (*o* to popularize a book); *meditare su un —*, to ponder over a book; *permettere un —*, to sanction the publication of a book; *proibire un —*, to ban a book; *recensire un —*, to review a book; *scorrere un —*, to skim a book ‖ — *all'indice*, book on the Index ‖ — *d'oro*, social register (*o amer.* bluebook) ‖ — *giallo*, poliziesco, thriller, detective story ‖ — *nero*, black-list (*o* black book) ‖ *è un — chiuso per me*, he is a closed (*o* sealed) book to me ‖ *parlare come un — stampato*, to talk like a book ‖ *tradurre ad apertura di —*, to translate at sight **2.** (*comm.*) book, register: — *a madre e figlia*, counter-part book; — *di cassa*, cash-book; — *mastro*, ledger; — *rischi*, dealers' bill-book; *gran — del debito pubblico*, the register of the national debt; *mettere a —*, to book (*o* to enter *o* to post); *presentare i libri in Tribunale*, to submit the accounts to the Court; *tenere i libri*, to keep the accounts (*o* to keep the books); *tenere i libri in partita doppia, semplice*, to keep the books by double-entry, to keep the books by single-entry **3.** (*bot.*) liber.

licantropía, *s.f.* (*patol.*) lycanthropy.

licàntropo, *s.m.* lycanthrope, lycanthropist.

Licaóne, *no.pr.m.* (*mit.*) Lycaon.

Licaònia, *no.pr.f.* (*geog.*) Lycaonia.

licciaiuòla, *s.f.* (*mec.*) saw-set.

líccio, *s.m.* (*ind. tessile*) heald; (*amer.*) heddle: — *di filo metallico*, wire heddle; *intrecciatrice meccanica per licci*, (*ind. tessile*) heddle braiding-machine; *macchina per la preparazione dei licci*, (*ind. tessile*) heddle knitting-machine.

liceàle, *ag.* pertaining to a "liceo": *studente —*, pupil at a "liceo".

licènza, *s.f.* **1.** (*permesso*) permission, leave; (*documento*) permit, licence: — *di caccia, di pesca*, shooting-licence, fishing-licence; — *d'esercizio*, (*comm.*) trading-licence; — *d'importazione*, (*comm.*) import-licence; — *matrimoniale*, marriage-licence; — *per malattia*, sick-leave; *con — dell'autore*, by permission of the author; *con sua —*, with your permission (*o* by your leave); *tassa di —*, licence-fee; *gli hanno revocato la —*, they took his licence away (*o* he lost his licence); *chieder —*, to ask leave (*o* permission); *mostrare la —*, to show one's licence; *prendersi la — di fare ql.co.*, to take leave to do sthg. **2.** (*permesso di assentarsi*) leave: *ottenne* *una — di dieci giorni,* he got ten days' leave; *essere in —,* to be on leave; *prendere — da uno,* (*accomiatarsi*) to take leave of s.o. **3.** (*abuso di libertà*) licence: — *poetica,* poetic licence **4.** (*licenziamento*) dismissal, discharge: — *dal servizio,* dismissal; *dar — a un servitore,* to dismiss a servant (*o fam.* to sack a servant) **5.** (*scolastica*) leaving-examination; leaving-certificate: — *elementare,* elementary school leaving-certificate; *esame di —,* leaving-examination; *dare la —,* to take one's school leaving-exam **6.** (*poes.*) envoy, envoi.

licenziaménto, *s.m.* dismissal, discharge.

licenziàre, *v.t.* **1.** to discharge, to dismiss: *licenziò tutti i suoi servitori,* he dismissed all his servants (*o fam.* he fired *o* sacked all his servants); *essere licenziato,* to be dismissed (*o* discharged *o fam.* to get the sack) **2.** (*accomiatare*) to dismiss, to send away: *il principe lo licenziò con amabili parole,* the prince dismissed him with a few gracious words **3.** (*conferire un diploma a*) to confer a diploma on (s.o.) **4.** — *le bozze per la stampa,* (*tip.*) to pass proofs for printing ‖ **licenziàrsi,** *v.r.* **1.** to give up one's job, to resign; (*dare le dimissioni*) to resign one's office **2.** (*ottenere un diploma*) to take one's certificate.

licenziàto, *ag.* (*da una scuola*) certificated ‖ *s.m.* (*da una scuola*) licentiate.

licenziosaménte, *av.* licentiously, dissolutely.

licenziosità, *s.f.* licentiousness, dissoluteness, debauchery.

licenzióso, *ag.* licentious, dissolute, debauched; lewd.

licèo, *s.m.* **1.** " Liceo " (Italian secondary school): — *artistico,* "Liceo" specialising in art subjects; — *classico,* " Liceo " specialising in classical studies; — *musicale,* Conservatory; — *scientifico,* " Liceo " specialising in scientific studies **2.** (*st. greca*) Lyceum.

lícere, *v.i.* (*letter.*) **1.** to be permitted: *questo non lice,* this is not permitted **2.** (*essere conveniente, opportuno*) to be expedient.

licet, *s.m.* lavatory; toilet.

lichène, *s.m.* (*bot.*) lichen.

lichenología, *s.f.* (*scient.*) lichenology.

Lícia, *no.pr.f.* (*geog. st.*) Lycia.

lício, *ag.s.m.* Lycian.

licitàre, *v.t.* **1.** (*mettere all'asta*) to put up for auction, to sell by auction **2.** (*offrire un prezzo all'asta*) to bid.

licitazióne, *s.f.* **1.** (*vendita all'asta*) sale by auction **2.** (*offerta all'asta*) bid, bidding **3.** (*comm.*) lease: — *per trattativa privata,* lease by private contract; *indire una — per la fornitura di...,* to invite tenders for the supply of....

licopòdio, *s.m.* (*bot.*) lycopodium; (*pop.*) club-moss.

licóre, (*poet.*) *per* **liquóre.**

Licúrgo, *no.pr.m.* (*st.*) Lycurgus.

liddíte, *s.f.* (*tipo di esplosivo*) lyddite.

Lídia¹, *no.pr.f.* (*geog. st.*) Lydia.

Lídia², *no.pr.f.* Lydia.

lídia³, lidiàna *s.f.* (*min.*) basanite.

lidiàno, *ag.s.m.* Lydian.

lído, *s.m.* shore, beach: *il Lido di Venezia,* the Venice Lido ‖ *i patrii lidi,* one's own country (*o* one's homeland): *lasciare i patrii lidi,* to leave one's native land ‖ *prendere il volo per altri lidi,* to set out for foreign lands.

Liègi, *no.pr.f.* (*geog.*) Liège.

lièo, *s.m.* **1.** the Jolly God **2.** (*poet.*) (*vino*) wine.

lietaménte, *av.* happily, gladly; (*in allegria*) cheerfully, merrily: *cenavamo —,* we were dining merrily; *il romanzo finisce —,* the novel has a happy ending.

lièto, *ag.* happy, glad; (*allegro*) cheerful, gay; merry; (*contento*) pleased, delighted: *un — evento,* a happy event; *una lieta fine,* a happy ending; *di — umore,* in good humour; *era sempre —,* he was always cheerful;

ci accolse con — viso, he gave us a hearty welcome; *la gioventù è lieta di sua natura,* youth is happy by nature; *sedevano a lieta mensa,* they were dining merrily; *si fece tutto — al sentire la notizia,* the news filled him with joy; *sono — che tu sia guarito completamente,* I am glad you have completely recovered; *sono — di accettare il vostro invito,* I am delighted to accept your invitation ‖ *lieti colli,* (*letter.*) festive hills.

lième, *ag.* light; slight: *una — brezza,* a light breeze; *un tocco —,* a light (*o* delicate) touch; *c'è nelle sue parole una — vena di umorismo,* there is a slight touch of humour in his words; *c'era una — differenza di opinioni fra di noi,* there was a slight difference in our opinions; *non c'è il più — dubbio,* there is not the slightest doubt; *sul suo volto si diffuse un — rossore,* a slight blush spread over her cheeks; *te la sei cavata con una — ferita,* you have got off with a slight injury **2.** (*facile*) light, easy: *il compito non è così —,* the task is not so easy.

lieveménte, *ag.* lightly; slightly; gently, softly: *le toccò — la mano,* he touched her hand gently; *questa situazione è — imbarazzante,* this situation is slightly embarassing.

lievità, *V.* **levità.**

lievitàre, *v.t.* to leaven: *hai lievitato troppo questa pasta,* you have added too much yeast to this dough ‖ *v.i.* to rise: *ci vorranno due ore perchè lieviti,* it will take two hours before it rises.

lièvito, *s.m.* **1.** yeast; leaven: — *di birra,* yeast; — *in polvere,* baking-powder; *pane senza —,* unleavened bread **2.** *fig.* (*fermento*) ferment: — *di rivolta,* ferment of rebellion.

ligaménto, *s.m.* (*anat.*) ligament.

ligamentóso, *ag.* (*anat.*) ligamentous.

lígio, *ag.* **1.** (*fedele*) faithful, true; (*osservante*) respectful (of sthg., s.o.); observant (of sthg.): — *al dovere,* dutiful (*o* faithful to one's duty); — *alle regole,* observant of rules; *è — al sovrano,* he is loyal (*o* true) to his King; *essere — alla tradizione,* to be faithful to tradition **2.** (*st.*) liege: *un suddito — al proprio signore,* a subject liege to his lord.

lignàggio, *s.m.* lineage, descent: *un uomo di alto —,* a man of high descent.

lígneo, *ag.* wooden, ligneous.

lignificazióne, *s.f.* lignification.

lignína, *s.f.* (*chim.*) lignin, lignose.

lignìte, *s.f.* (*min.*) lignite: — *fibrosa,* fibrous lignite.

ligure, *ag.s.c.* Ligurian.

Ligúria, *no.pr.f.* (*geog.*) Liguria.

ligústro, *s.m.* (*bot.*) privet.

liliàceo, *ag.* liliaceous; lily-like (*attributivo*): *piante liliacee,* Liliaceae.

liliàle, *ag.* (*letter.*) lilied; lily-like (*attributivo*).

Liliàna, *no.pr.f.* Lilian, Lillian ‖ *dim.* Lil(y).

lilla¹, *s.f.* (*bot.*) lilac ‖ *s.m.* (*colore*) lilac.

Lilla², *no.pr.f.* (*geog.*) Lille.

lillipuziàno, *ag.s.m.* Lilliputian.

líma, *s.f.* **1.** file: — *a coltello,* knife-file; — *a losanga,* slitting file; — *da legno,* rasp (*o* rasping file); — *mezzo tonda,* half-round file; — *per le unghie,* nail-file; — *piatta,* flat file; — *triangolare,* three-square (*o* triangular) file; *levigare ql.co. con la —,* to file sthg. smooth ‖ *è una — sorda,* *fig.* he's a sly rogue ‖ *lavorar di —,* *fig.* to polish: *sta lavorando di — al suo romanzo,* he is giving the finishing touches to his novel **2.** *fig.* (*cruccio*) gnawing care.

limàccio, *s.m.* (*rar.*) slime, mud.

limaccióso, *ag.* slimy, muddy.

limàre, *v.t.* **1.** to file **2.** (*perfezionare*) to polish, to perfect: — *ogni frase,* to polish every sentence ‖ **limàrsi,** *v.r.* **1.** (*crucciarsi*) to worry (about sthg.) **2.** — *le unghie,* to file one's nails.

limatóre, *s.m.* **1.** filer **2.** *fig.* polisher.

limatríce, *s.f.* **1.** filer **2.** *fig.* polisher **3.** (*mec.*) shaper, thaping-machine: — *da banco*, bench shaping-machine; — *universale*, universal shaping-machine.

limatúra, *s.f.* **1.** filing **2.** (*polvere dell'oggetto limato*) filings (*pl.*).

limbo, *s.m.* limbo ‖ *va al* —*!*, go to Jericho!.

Limbúrgo, *no.pr.m.* (*geog.*) Limbourg, Limburg.

límine, *s.m.* (*letter.*) (*soglia*) threshold ‖ *visita ai sacri limini*, (*eccl.*) visit ad limina.

limitàbile, *ag.* limitable.

limitàre[1], *s.m.* (*soglia*) threshold (anche *fig.*): *essere al* — *della vita*, to be on the threshold of life.

limitàre[2], *v.t.* to limit, to restrict (anche *fig.*): *bisogna* — *il tempo di ogni gara*, it is necessary to limit the time of every event; *devi* — *il numero degli invitati*, you must limit the number of the guests; *devi* — *le spese*, you must limit the expenses; *dovresti* — *le tue ambizioni*, you should try to limit your ambitions (*o to keep your ambitions within bounds*); *la legge limita i miei poteri*, the law limits my powers; *la nostra visuale è limitata dagli alberi*, our vision is restricted by the trees; — *il consumo di alcoolici*, to limit the consumption of alcohol; — *la velocità*, (*di un'automobile*) to limit speed ‖ **limitàrsi**, *v.r.* to limit oneself: *devo limitarmi a dieci sigarette al giorno*, I must limit myself to ten cigarettes a day; *si limitò a sgridarlo*, he just reproached him.

limitataménte, *av.* limitedly.

limitatézza, *s.f.* limitation.

limitatívo, *ag.* limitative, limiting, restrictive, restricting: *clausola limitativa*, (*dir.*) restrictive clause.

limitàto, *ag.* limited; (*ristretto*) restricted, narrow; (*scarso*) scanty, small: *capitali limitati*, limited capital; *mentalità limitata*, narrow mind; *poteri limitati*, limited powers; *responsabilità limitata*, (*comm.*) limited liability; *società a responsabilità limitata*, (*comm.*) limited (liability) company; *ha mezzi limitati*, he has limited means; *possiamo solo darvi notizie molto limitate*, we can give you only scanty news; *la sua intelligenza è molto limitata*, he is a man of limited intelligence.

limitatóre, *s.m.* **1.** limiter, person who limits **2.** (*mec.*) limiting device; (*rad.*) limiter: — *di carico*, (*mec.*) load limiting device; — *di corrente*, (*elett.*) current limiter; — *di tensione*, (*elett.*) aerial discharge; — *di velocità*, (*mec.*) speed limiting device.

limitatríce, *s.f.* limiter.

limitazióne, *s.f.* limitation, restriction: — *delle nascite*, birth-control; *mi impose delle limitazioni*, he imposed some limitations on me.

límite, *s.m.* **1.** boundary, border, limit; *fig.* limit, bound: *i limiti del campo*, the boundaries of the field; *caso* —, border-line case; *entro i limiti*, within bounds; *fuori dai limiti*, out of bounds; *fu messo in pensione avendo raggiunto i limiti di età*, he was pensioned off as he had attained the age limit; *ha coscienza dei propri limiti*, he is conscious of his own limits; *non è fissato alcun* — *di tempo*, no time limit is fixed; *questi sono i limiti della questione*, these are the terms of the problem; *questo passa ogni* —*!*, that's the limit!; *la sua ambizione non conosce limiti*, his ambition knows no limits; *il suo orgoglio è senza limiti*, his pride is unbounded (*o limitless*); *vi è un* — *a tutto*, there's a limit to everything (*o one must draw the line somewhere*); *fissare un* —, to fix a limit; *mantenersi entro certi limiti*, to keep within certain limits; *oltrepassare un* —, to overstep a limit; *passare ogni* —, to pass all bounds; *porre un* — *all'autorità di qlcu.*, to set bounds to s.o.'s authority **2.** (*tec.*) limit: — *di elasticità*, (*edil.*) limit of elasticity (*o elastic limit*); — *di elasticità convenzionale*, (*metal.*) proof-stress; — *di fatica*, (*edil.*) fatigue (*o endurance*)-limit; — *di peso*, (*aut.*) weight-limit; — *di rottura*, (*edil.*) breaking-point; — *di sicurezza*, (*aer.*) prudent limit of endurance; — *di velocità*, (*aut.*) speed-limit; *indicazione del* — *di portata*, (*ferr.*) marked capacity **3.** (*mat.*) limit: — *inferiore*, lower limit; *metodo dei limiti*, method of limits.

limítrofo, *ag.* neighbouring, limitrophe: *paese* —, borderland; *essere* — *di un paese*, to border on a country.

limnología, *s.f.* limnology.

limnòlogo, *s.m.* limnologist.

límo, *s.m.* slime, mud ‖ — *atmosferico*, (*pulviscolo*) dust in the air.

limonàio, *s.m.* lemon-seller.'

limonàta, *s.f.* lemonade, lemon-squash.

limoncèlla, *s.f.* (*bot.*) lemon-(scented)verbena.

limóne, *s.m.* (*bot.*) **1.** (*albero*) lemon (-tree) **2.** (*frutto*) lemon: *blusa color* —, lemon-coloured blouse; *spremuta di* —, *sugo di* —, lemon-juice ‖ — *spremuto*, *fig.* squeezed orange.

limòsina, *V.* **elemòsina.**

limóso, *ag.* slimy, muddy.

limousine, *s.f.* limousine; (*amer.*) sedan.

limpidaménte, *av.* limpidly.

limpidézza, limpidità, *s.f.* limpidity, clearness, lucidity, pellucidity (anche *fig.*): *la* — *del suo ragionamento*, the clearness of his reasoning.

límpido, *ag.* limpid, clear, lucid, pellucid (anche *fig.*): *limpida onestà*, limpid honesty; *acqua*, *aria limpida*, limpid water, air; *coscienza limpida*, clear conscience; *cristallo* —, clear crystal; *una giornata limpida*, a clear day; *mente limpida*, clear mind: *una persona dalla mente limpida*, a clear-minded person; *occhi limpidi*, limpid eyes; *ragionamento* —, pellucid reasoning; *stile* —, limpid style.

linaiuòlo, *s.m.* **1.** (*chi lavora il lino*) flax-dresser **2.** (*commerciante in lino*) linen-draper.

línce, *s.f.* (*zool.*) lynx: *una persona dagli occhi di* —, *fig.* a lynx-eyed person.

linceo[1], *ag.* lyncean; lynx (*attributivo*).

lincèo[2], *s.m.* (*membro dell'Accademia dei Lincei*) member of the Lincei Academy.

Lincèo[3], *no.pr.m.* (*mit.*) Lynceus.

linciàggio, *s.m.* lynching.

linciàre, *v.t.* to lynch.

linciatóre, *s.m.* lyncher.

lindaménte, *av.* neatly, cleanly, tidily.

lindézza, *s.f.* neatness, cleanness, tidiness.

líndo, *ag.* neat, clean, tidy: *biancheria linda*, clean linen; *questa stanza è linda e in ordine*, this room is clean and tidy.

línea, *s.f.* **1.** line: — *convergente*, (*geom.*) convergent line; — *della chiglia*, (*mar.*) keel line; — *della rotta*, (*mar.*) heading line; — *della scotta*, (*mar.*) foot; — *della vita*, line of life; — *di attacco*, (*spor.*) forward line; — *di confine*, boundary (line); — *di difesa*, (*spor.*) the backs; — *di displuvio*, (*edil.*) ridge, crest; — *di fede*, (*mar.*) lubber's line; — *di galleggiamento*, (*mar.*) load (-water)-line; — *di partenza*, (*spor.*) scratch line; — *di raccordo*, (*elett.*) connecting line; — *di rispetto*, (*mar.*) marine belt; — *di scandaglio*, (*mar.*) lead-line; — *divergente*, (*geom.*) diverging line; — *equatoriale*, Equator (*o* Line); — *genealogica*, genealogical line; — *isotermica*, (*geog.*) isothermal line; — *maschile*, male line; — *mediana*, (*spor.*) half-back line; — *punteggiata*, dotted line; — *spartiacque*, (*geog.*) watershed; — *spartitraffico*, traffic-line; *la* — *retta è la più breve distanza fra due punti*, a straight line is the shortest distance between two points; *ogni poligono è chiuso da linee*, every polygon is enclosed by lines; *discendere in* — *diretta da*, to descend in direct line from; *mettersi in* —, to stand in (a) line (*o* to line up); *tracciare una* —, to draw a line ‖ *mi atterrò alla mia* — *di condotta*, I will stick to my own line ‖ *non cederò di una* —, I will not yield (*o* budge) an inch **2.** (*contorno*) line: *una grande semplicità di linee caratterizza l'architettura romanica*, a great simplicity of lines characterizes Romanesque architecture; *non mi piace la* — *di quell'automobile*, I don't like the line of that car ‖ *cerca di mantenere la* —, try to keep your figure; *si guasta la* — *mangiando troppo dolci*, she is ruining her figure (o she is putting on too much weight) by eating too many sweet things ‖ *tracciare a grandi linee*, to outline **3.** (*linea di comunicazione*) line: — *aerea*, air-line; — *di navigazione*, shipping line; — *interurbana*, (*tel.*) trunk- (o long-distance) line; — *principale*, main line; — *secondaria*, branch-line; — *telegrafica*, telegraph line; — *tramviaria*, tram-line; *aeroplano di* —, air-liner; *nave di* —, liner; *non riesco a telefonare, la* — *è occupata*, I can't get through, the line is engaged; *si cambia treno per tutte le linee!*, all change!; *stendere una* —, (*tel.*) to lay a line **4.** (*mil.*) line: — *del fuoco*, line of fire; — *di difesa*, defence line; — *di mira*, line of sight; *fuoco di* —, line-firing; *nave di* —, ship of the line; *prima* —, front- (o fighting) line; *soldati di* —, front-line troops; *vittoria su tutta la* —, victory all along the line (anche *fig.*).

lineaménti, *s.m.pl.* **1.** features, lineaments: *ha dei* — *molto fini*, she has very fine features; *nei* — *mi ricorda suo padre*, her features remind me of my father **2.** (*elementi essenziali*) outlines; broad lines, main lines: — *di letteratura inglese*, outlines of English literature.

lineàre[1], *ag.* **1.** linear: *disegno* —, line-drawing; *misure lineari*, linear (o long) measures **2.** *fig.* unswerving: *è uomo di condotta* —, he is a man of unswerving moral conduct.

lineàre[2], *v.t.* (*rar.*) to draw (lines) on (sthg.).

lineétta, *s.f.* **1.** dash: *c'è una* — *qui, non una virgola*, there is a dash here, not a comma **2.** (*trattino d'unione*) hyphen: *non dimenticare la* — *in quel nome composto*, don't forget the hyphen in that compound noun.

línfa, *s.f.* **1.** (*fisiol.*) lymph **2.** (*bot.*) lymph, sap **3.** (*poet.*) lymph, water.

linfàtico, *ag.* lymphatic: *ganglio* —, (*anat.*) lymphatic ganglion; *temperamento* —, lymphatic temperament; *vaso* —, (*anat.*) lymphatic vessel ‖ *s.m.* lymphatic subject, anaemic subject.

linfatismo, *s.m.* (*med.*) lymphatism.

linfoadenìte, *s.f.* (*patol.*) lymphadenitis.

linfocíto, *s.m.* (*fisiol.*) lymphocyte.

linfogranulòma, *s.m.* (*patol.*) lymphogranuloma.

linfòma, *s.m.* (*patol.*) lymphoma (*pl.* lymphomata).

lingòtto, *s.m.* ingot: — *d'oro*, gold ingot (o bar); *oro, argento in lingotti*, gold, silver in bullions.

língua, *s.f.* **1.** tongue: — *di bue*, ox-tongue; — *mordace, tagliente*, sharp tongue; — *salmistrata*, (*cuc.*) corned tongue; *il cane aveva la* — *fuori*, the dog's tongue was hanging out; *hai la* — *sporca*, your tongue is coated; *tira fuori la* —, put out your tongue ‖ *lingue di gatto*, (*biscotti*) finger biscuits ‖ *blasfema*, (*persona blasfema*) blasphemous person; *mala* —, (*persona maldicente*) scandal-monger: *essere una mala* —, to be a scandal monger (o a mischief-maker o a backbiter) ‖ *che* —!, what a chatterbox!; *che* — *lunga che hai!*, don't you ever stop talking? ‖ *si sarebbe morsicato la* —, he would have bitten his tongue out ‖ *avere la* — *sciolta*, to have a glib (o ready) tongue; *frenare la* —, *tenere la* — *a posto*, to hold one's tongue; *sciogliere la* — *a qlcu.*, to loosen s.o.'s tongue ‖ *avere il cuore sulla* —, to be open-hearted ‖ *avere perduto la* —, to have lost one's tongue ‖ *avere ql.co. sulla punta della* —, to have sthg. on the tip of one's tongue ‖ *ferisce più la* — *che la spada*, *prov.* the pen is sharper than the sword **2.** (*linguaggio*) language, tongue: — *materna*, one's mother-tongue; — *morta*, dead language; — *parlata*, spoken language; *lingue straniere*, foreign languages; — *volgare*, vulgar tongue; (*il volgare*) early Italian language; *paesi, gente di* — *inglese*, English-speaking countries, people; *è diventato padrone della* — *francese*, he has made himself master of the French language; *avere il dono delle lingue*, to have a gift for languages **3.** (*geog.*) (*striscia di terra*) tongue, strip of land **4.** — *cervina*, (*bot.*) hart's tongue.

linguàccia, *s.f.* **1.** slanderous tongue: *quella pettegola ha una* —, that gossiping woman has a slanderous tongue **2.** (*persona maldicente*) slanderer.

linguacciúto, *ag.* chatty, talkative; (*pettegolo*) gossipy ‖ *s.m.* gossip, gossiper.

Linguadòca, *no.pr.f.* (*geog. st.*) Languedoc.

linguàggio, *s.m.* language: (*eloquio*) speech: — *colorito*, racy speech; *il* — *dei cenni*, sign language; *il* — *della diplomazia*, the language of diplomacy; *il* — *dei fiori*, the language of flowers; *il* — *della musica*, the language of music; — *fiorito*, flowery language; — *tecnico*, technical language; — *violento*, strong language; *correttezza di* —, correctness of speech; *intemperanza di* —, violence of language; *natura, origine del* —, nature, origin of language; *anche gli animali hanno un* —, animals have a language too ‖ *che* —!, that's no way to talk!.

linguàle, *ag.* lingual.

lingueggiàre, *v.i.* **1.** to chat, to chatter, to prate **2.** *fig.* (*di fiamme*) to shoot up.

linguétta, *s.f.* **1.** (*di scarpe*) tongue (of a shoe) **2.** (*di strumento a fiato*) reed **3.** (*mec.*) tang, tongue **4.** (*per incollare francobolli*) stamp hinge **5.** (*di busta*) flap.

linguifórme, *ag.* tongue-shaped, linguiform.

linguísta, *s.c.* linguist.

linguística, *s.f.* linguistics.

linguístico, *ag.* linguistic.

língula, *s.f.* **1.** (*anat.*) lingula **2.** (*zool.*) lingula.

linifício, *s.m.* flax-mill.

liniménto, *s.m.* (*farm.*) liniment.

Linnèo, *no.pr.* (*st. bot.*) Linnaeus.

líno, *ag.* (*rar.*) linen (*attributivo*): *panno* —, linen cloth ‖ *s.m.* **1.** (*pianta, fibra*) flax: — *a fibre lunghe*, (*ind. tessile*) long flax; — *greggio*, raw flax; — *scotolato*, (*ind. tessile*) scutched flax; *filatura del* —, (*ind. tessile*) flax spinning; *olio di* —, linseed oil; *pettinatura del* —, (*ind. tessile*) flax hackling; *seme di* —, linseed **2.** (*tela di lino*) linen: *asciugamano di* —, linen towel; *fazzoletti di* —, linen handkerchiefs; *industria del* —, linen industry.

linòleum, *s.m.* linoleum.

linóne, *s.m.* **1.** (*ind. tessile*) lawn **2.** (*da cappellaio*) buckram.

linòsa, *s.f.* linseed.

linotipía, *s.f.* (*tip.*) linotyping.

linotipísta, *s.c.* (*tip.*) linotypist, linotyper.

linotípo, *s.f.* (*tip.*) linotype.

línteo, *ag.* (*letter.*) linen (*attributivo*) ‖ *s.m.* **1.** (*panno di lino*) linen cloth **2.** (*eccl.*) sudarium (*pl.* sudaria).

linséme, *s.m.* linseed.

liocèorno, *s.m.* (*zool. mit.*) unicorn.

Lióne, *no.pr.f.* (*geog.*) Lyon(s).

lionése, *ag.s.m.* Lyonese (*invariato al pl.*).

liparíte, *s.f.* (*geol.*) liparite.

lipàsi, *s.f.* (*fisiol.*) lipase.

lipemanía, *s.f.* (*patol.*) lypemania.

lipemía, *s.f.* (*patol.*) lipemia.

lipòma, *s.m.* (*patol.*) lipoma.

lipotimía, *s.f.* (*med.*) lipothymia.

líppa, *s.f.* (*giuoco fanciullesco*) tip-cat.

Lípsia, *no.pr.f.* (*geog.*) Leipzig.

liquazióne, *s.f.* (*metal.*) liquation.

liquefàre, *v.t.* to liquefy; (*sciogliere*) to melt: — *un gas*, to liquefy a gas; *è facile* — *il burro*, it is easy to melt butter ‖ **liquefàrsi**, *v.r.* to liquefy; (*sciogliersi*) to melt: *la neve si liquefa al sole*, snow melts in the sun.

liquefàtto, *ag.* liquefied; (*sciolto*) melted.

liquefazióne, *s.f.* liquefaction.

liquerízia, *s.f.* liquorice.

liquidaménte, *av.* (*rar.*) liquidly.

liquidàbile, *ag.* liquidable.

liquidàre, *v.t.* to liquidate; (*un conto*) to settle, to clear; (*delle merci*) to sell off, to clear; (*un'azienda*) to wind up: — *gli arretrati*, to pay up arrears; — *un debito*, to pay off a debt ‖ — *qlcu.*, to pay s.o. off; (*liberarsene*) to get rid of s.o. ‖ — *una questione*, (*risolverla*) to solve a problem.

liquidàto, *ag.* **1.** liquidated; (*di conto*) settled; (*di merce*) cleared; (*di debito*) paid off **2.** (*rovinato*) ruined; (*spacciato*) done for: *è un uomo* —, he is a ruined man.

liquidatóre, *ag.* liquidating (*attributivo*); winding-up (*attributivo*): *atto* — *di una società*, winding-up resolution of a company ‖ *s.m.* (*dir. comm.*) **1.** liquidator: — *nominato dal Tribunale*, receiver and manager; *nomina del* —, appointment of the liquidator **2.** (*mar.*) adjuster: — *di avaria*, average adjuster.

liquidazióne, *s.f.* **1.** liquidation; (*di conti, debiti*) settling, settlement; (*di ditta*) winding-up; (*di merci*) selling off, clearance; (*in Borsa*) settling: — *di una società anonima*, winding-up of a joint-stock company; — *obbligatoria*, compulsory (*o* enforced *o* forced) liquidation; — *volontaria*, voluntary winding-up; *ditta in* —, firm in liquidation; *giorno di* —, (*Borsa*) settling day; *ordinanza di messa in* —, order for winding-up; *vendita per* —, clearance (sale); *andare in* —, to go into liquidation **2.** (*mar.*) adjustment: — *di avaria*, average adjustment.

liquidità, *s.f.* liquidity.

liquido, *ag.* **1.** liquid: *colla liquida*, liquid glue; *ridurre ql.co. allo stato* —, to reduce sthg. to a liquid state **2.** (*comm.*) liquid; ready; available; (*pagabile*) due (*predicativo*): payable (*predicativo*): *denaro* —, ready money (*o* money at one's disposal *o* cash); *fondi liquidi*, available funds (*o* liquid assets) **3.** (*di consonante*) liquid ‖ *s.m.* liquid, fluid: — *refrigerante*, coolant.

liquirízia, *s.f.* liquorice.

liquóre, *s.m.* **1.** liqueur; *pl.* (*i distillati in genere*) spirits: *commerciante di liquori*, dealer in spirits; *tassa sui liquori*, tax on spirits; *beve sempre un* — *e fuma un sigaro la sera dopo cena*, he always drinks a liqueur and smokes a cigar after dinner in the evenings; *il dottore gli ha proibito i liquori*, the doctor told him to give up drinking spirits; *gli piacciono i liquori*, he is fond of strong drink **2.** (*sostanza liquida*) liquid, liquor.

liquorísta, *s.m.* **1.** (*chi fabbrica liquori*) distiller **2.** (*chi vende liquori*) dealer in spirits.

liquoróso, *ag.*: *vino* —, strong sweet wine.

líra[1], *s.f.* **1.** (*mus.*) lyre: *suonare la* —, to play the lyre ‖ *Lira*, (*astr.*) Lyra **2.** *fig.* (*poesia lirica*) lyric poetry **3.** *uccello* —, lyre-bird.

líra[2], *s.f.* (*moneta*) lira (*pl.* lire, liras): — *sterlina*, pound sterling; *un gelato da cinquanta lire*, a fifty-lire ice-cream; *costa cento lire*, it costs a hundred lire ‖ *una* — *risparmiata è una* — *guadagnata*, *prov.* a penny saved is a penny gained.

líriea, *s.f.* **1.** lyric poetry: *la* — *amorosa del Petrarca*, Petrarch's love poetry **2.** (*componimento lirico*) lyric (poem): *una* — *giovanile di Dante*, a youthful lyric by Dante **3.** (*il teatro lirico*) opera: *la* — *italiana*, Italian opera.

liricaménte, *av.* lyrically.

liricità, *s.f.* lyricism, lyrism.

líriec, *ag.* **1.** lyric(al): *la poesia* — *del Petrarca*, Petrarch's lyric poetry (*o* lyrics); *poeta* —, lyric poet (*o* lyrist) ‖ *fece una descrizione assai lirica del paesaggio*, she gave a very lyrical description of the landscape **2.** (*mus.*) operatic: *cantante* —, opera singer; *la stagione lirica*, the opera season; *teatro* —, opera house ‖ *s.m.* lyric poet, lyrist.

lirísmo, *s.m.* lyricism, lyrism.

lirísta, *s.m.* (*citarista*) lyrist.

Lisàndro, *no.pr.m.* (*st.*) Lysander.

Lisbóna, *no.pr.f.* (*geog.*) Lisbon.

lísea, *s.f.* **1.** (*di pesce*) fish-bone **2.** (*parte legnosa della canapa*) hards (*pl.*), hurds (*pl.*); tow.

liseézza, *s.f.* (*rar.*) smoothness.

líseia, *s.f.* (*strumento per lisciare il cuoio*) sleeker.

lisciàggio, *s.m.* (*ind. cartaria*) glazing.

lisciaménte, *av.* smoothly.

lisciaménto, *V.* **lisciatúra**.

lisciàre, *v.t.* **1.** to smooth, to gloss: — *i capelli a qlcu.*, to smooth s.o.'s hair **2.** (*accarezzare*) to stroke, to pat: — *un cane, un cavallo*, to pat a dog, a horse **3.** (*di animali, leccare i piccoli per pulirli*) to clean, to wash: *la gatta liscia i gattini*, the cat is cleaning her kittens **4.** (*levigare*) to polish; to slick, to sleek; (*piallare*) to plane: — *un muro*, to finish a wall **5.** (*brunire*) to burnish **6.** (*ind. cartaria*) to glaze **7.** (*ind. della ceramica*) to glaze **8.** (*conceria*) to slick, to sleek **9.** (*abbellire*) to embellish: — *lo stile*, to embellish one's style **10.** (*adulare*) to flatter, to adulate: — *la vanità di qlcu.*, to flatter s.o.'s pride ‖ **lisciàrsi**[1], *v.r.* **1.** (*i capelli*) to smooth **2.** (*agghindarsi*) to smarten oneself up, to preen oneself **3.** (*di uccello, pulirsi le penne*) to preen itself.

lisciàrsi[2], *v.r.* (*imbellettarsi*) to make up.

lisciàta, *s.f.* **1.** smooth: *darsi una* — *ai capelli*, to smooth down one's hair **2.** (*adulazione*) flattery.

lisciatóio, *s.m.* (*spatola*) sleeker.

lisciatúra, *s.f.* **1.** smoothing, glossing **2.** (*levigatura*) polishing; slicking, sleeking; (*piallatura*) planing **3.** (*brunitura*) burnishing **4.** (*adulazione*) adulation.

líscio[1], *ag.* **1.** smooth; glossy, polished: — *come il vetro*, as smooth as glass; *capelli lisci*, sleek hair; *pelle liscia*, smooth skin; *superficie liscia*, smooth surface ‖ *la cosa non è liscia*, *fig.* this affair isn't completely above board ‖ *andare per le lisce*, to skate over things ‖ *passarla liscia*, to get off scot-free; *passarla liscia a qlcu.*, to let s.o. off **2.** (*semplice*) plain, neat: *abito* —, plain (*o* neat) dress ‖ *messa liscia*, low mass **3.** (*di arma da fuoco*) smooth-bore **4.** (*di bevanda alcoolica*) neat, undiluted.

líscio[1], *av.* smoothly: *tutto va* —, everything is going smoothly.

líscio[2], *s.m.* (*belletto*) make-up.

lisciíva, liscívia, *s.f.* lye(-wash); (*rar.*) lixivium.

liscivière, *v.t.* **1.** to wash in lye **2.** (*chim.*) to leach, to lixiviate **3.** (*geol.*) to leach.

lisciviatóre, *s.m.* **1.** (*chim.*) leacher, lixiviating tub **2.** (*ind. cartaria*) boiler, kier, digester.

lisciviatríce, *s.f.* **1.** (*lavatrice*) washing-machine **2.** *V.* **lisciviatóre**.

lisciviazióne, *s.f.* **1.** (*chim.*) leaching, lixiviation; (*miner.*) leaching **2.** (*ind. cartaria*) boiling.

liseóso, *ag.* **1.** (*di pesce*) full of bones **2.** (*di canapa*) full of hards, full of hurds.

liseuse, *s.f.* bed-jacket.

lisì, *s.f.* (*med.*) lysis.

Lísia, *no.pr.m.* (*st. lett.*) Lysias.

Lisímaco, *no.pr.m.* (*st.*) Lysimachus.

Lisíppo, *no.pr.m.* (*st. scult.*) Lysippus.

líso, *ag.* worn-out, threadbare (*anche fig.*).

lisofòrmio, *s.m.* (*chim.*) lysoform.

lisòlo, *s.m.* (*chim.*) lysol.

líssa, *s.f.* (*patol.*) lyssa, rabies, hydrophobia.

lissofobìa, *s.f.* (*patol.*) lyssophobia.

lísta, *s.f.* **1.** stripe, band, strip: *una* — *di carta*, a strip of paper **2.** (*nota*) bill; (*elenco*) list: — *del bucato*, laundry list; — *delle vivande*, bill of fare; — *di imballaggio*, (*comm.*) packing list; *fa una* — *di ciò che devi comprare*, make a list of the things you must buy ‖ — *civile*, civil list ‖ — *dei candidati*, (*pol.*) list of candidates (*o* amer. slate *o* ticket); — *elettorale*, (*pol.*) Electoral Register (*o* amer. list of voters).

listàre, *v.t.* to stripe, to line; (*bordare*) to border.

listàto, *ag.* striped; (*bordato*) edged: *il foglio era* — *di nero*, the paper was black-edged.

listèllo, *s.m.* (*arch.*) (*di modanatura*) list, listel, fillet; (*di colonna*) cincture.

listíno, *s.m.* list: — *dei prezzi*, (*comm.*) price list; — *di Borsa*, Stock Exchange list; — *ufficiale*, (*econ.*) official list.

litanía, *s.f.* **1.** (*eccl.*) litany: *dire le litanie*, to recite the litany **2.** (*noiosa sequela*) litany, string: *una* — *di ingiurie*, a string of abuse.

litantràce, *s.m.* (*min.*) lithantrax.

litargírio, *s.m.* (*chim.*) litharge.

líte, *s.f.* **1.** (*dir.*) law-suit: — *pendente,* pending suit; *dalle nostre contestazioni è risultata una* — *giudiziaria,* a law-suit arose from our differences; *intentar* — *contro qlcu.,* to bring a suit against s.o.; *perdere la* —, to lose one's case; *vincere la* —, to win one's case **2.** (*contesa*) quarrel, argument, wrangle; (*rissa*) fight, brawl: *attaccare* — *con qlcu.,* to begin a quarrel with s.o. ‖ — *letteraria,* literary controversy.

litíasi, *s.f.* (*patol.*) lithiasis.

liticàre, *V.* **litigàre.**

litigànte, *s.m.* **1.** (*dir.*) litigant: *i litiganti,* the litigants (*o* the contending parties) **2.** (*persona che litiga*) arguer, wrangler; (*rissante*) brawler ‖ *tra i due litiganti il terzo gode, prov.* the onlooker gets the better of a fight.

litigàre, *v.i.* **1.** (*dir.*) to go to law, to litigate **2.** (*far lite*) to quarrel, to argue, to wrangle, to have a row; (*rissare*) to fight, to brawl: — *per una sciocchezza,* to quarrel over a trifle ‖ *v.t.* to dispute, to contest: — *ql.co. a qlcu.,* to dispute sthg. with s.o. (*o* to contend with s.o. for sthg.) ‖ **litigàrsi,** *v.r. reciproco,* to quarrel (with each other, one another): *i due fratelli si litigavano per la tenuta,* the two brothers quarrelled (with each other) over (*o* about) the possession of the estate; *i soci si litigavano il guadagno,* the partners quarrelled about (*o* over) their earnings.

litighíno, *s.m.* quarrelsome person, hot-head.

litighío, *s.m.* squabbling; bickering.

litigóne, *s.m.* quarrelsome person, hot-head.

litígio, *s.m.* quarrel, altercation, row.

litigióso, *ag.* quarrelsome, contentious, litigious.

lítio, *s.m.* (*chim.*) lithium.

litispendènza, *s.f.* (*dir.*) pendency.

líto, *s.m.* (*letter.*) shore.

litoclàsi, *s.f.* (*geol.*) lithoclase.

litogènesi, *s.f.* (*geol.*) lithogenesis.

litografàre, *v.t.* to lithograph.

litografàto, *ag.* lithographed.

litografía, *s.f.* **1.** lithography **2.** (*ciò che è stato riprodotto con litografia*) lithograph, lithographic print **3.** (*officina litografica*) lithographic printing works (*pl.*).

litograficaménte, *av.* lithographically.

litogràfico, *ag.* lithographic.

litògrafo, *s.m.* lithographer.

litòide, *ag.* (*scient.*) lithoid.

litología, *s.f.* (*scient.*) lithology.

litològico, *ag.* lithologic(al).

litòlogo, *s.m.* lithologist.

litoràle, *ag.* lit(t)oral, coastal; coast (*attributivo*) ‖ *s.m.* coast-line, littoral: *il* — *adriatico,* the shores of the Adriatic Sea (*o* the Adriatic coast).

litosfèra, *s.f.* (*geol.*) lithosphere.

litòte, *s.f.* (*ret.*) litotes.

litotomía, *s.f.* (*chir.*) lithotomy.

litotomísta, *s.m.* (*chir.*) lithotomist.

litòtomo, *s.m.* (*chir.*) lithotome.

litotripsía, *s.f.* (*chir.*) lithotripsy.

litotritóre, *s.m.* (*chir.*) lithotriptor.

lítro, *s.m.* litre; (*amer.*) liter (*unità di capacità* = 61.025 cu. in.): — (*avoirdupois*), pound (*misura di peso avoirdupois* = g. 453,6); — (*troy*), pound (*misura di peso troy* = g. 373,248).

littoràle, *V.* **litoràle.**

littorànea, *s.f.* coast road.

littoràneo, *ag.* littoral; coast (*attributivo*): *strada littoranea,* coast road.

littóre, *s.m.* (*st. romana*) lictor.

littorína, *s.f.* Diesel rail-car.

littòrio, *ag.* of the lictor: *il fascio* —, the lictor's fasces.

Lituània, *no.pr.f.* (*geog.*) Lithuania.

lituàno, *ag.s.m.* Lithuanian.

lítuo, *s.m.* (*st. romana*) lituus (*pl.* litui).

liturgía, *s.f.* liturgy.

liturgicaménte, *av.* liturgically.

litúrgico, *ag.* liturgic(al): *indumenti liturgici,* liturgical vestments; *musica liturgica,* church music.

liturgísta, *s.m.* liturgist.

liutàio, *s.m.* lute-maker.

liutísta, *s.m.* lute-player, lutist.

liúto, *s.m.* lute: *corda del* —, lute-string.

livèlla, *s.f.* level: — *a bolla d'aria,* spirit-level; — *a cannocchiale,* surveyor's (*o* dumpy-) level; — *ad acqua,* water-level; — *da ferrovia,* railroad track-level.

livellaménto, *V.* **livellatúra.**

livellàre, *v.t.* **1.** to level, to make level: — *una strada,* to level a road **2.** *fig.* (*uguagliare*) to level: *la morte livella tutti,* death is the grand leveller ‖ *v.i.,* **livellàrsi,** *v.r.* **1.** to become level **2.** (*uguagliare, uguagliarsi*) to be equal; to become equal.

livellàrio, *ag.: contratto* —, (*dir.*) lease ‖ *s.m.* (*dir.*) leaseholder.

livellatóre, *ag.* levelling ‖ *s.m.* leveller.

livellatríce, *s.f.* (*mec.*) bulldozer.

livellatúra, livellazióne, *s.f.* levelling: — *geodetica,* geodetic levelling; *rete di* —, levelling-net.

livèllo[1], *s.m.* **1.** level: —, *dell'acqua,* water-level; *differenze di* —, differences in level; *sopra, a* — *del mare,* above, at sea-level; *le altezze delle montagne si calcolano sul* — *del mare,* the height of mountains is calculated from sea-level ‖ *curve di* —, contour lines ‖ *passaggio a* —, level-crossing: *passaggio a* — *incustodito,* unguarded level-crossing **2.** *fig.* (*altezza, grado*) level: *il* — *d'istruzione di uno studente,* the academic level of a student; *un alto* — *sociale,* a high social level; *non è al* — *della situazione,* he is not up to the situation; *essere allo stesso* — *di qlcu.,* to be on a level with s.o.; *scendere al* — *di qlcu.,* to come down to s.o.'s level **3.** (*strumento*) level: — *a cannocchiale,* (*topografia*) dumpy-level (*o* surveyor's level); — *elettronico,* (*fis. atomica*) shell; *indicatore di* —, level gauge.

livèllo,[2] *s.m.* (*dir.*) emphyteusis, perpetual lease.

lividaménte, *av.* (*con invidia*) enviously; (*con odio*) out of hatred; (*con astio*) spitefully.

lividàstro, *ag.* livid, ashy, ashen.

lividézza, *s.f.* lividity, lividness.

lívido, *ag.* **1.** livid; ghastly, deathly pale, wan; (*di luce*) colourless, grey: *cielo* —, lurid sky; *faccia livida,* wan face; *era* — *di collera,* he was livid with rage; *era* — *di invidia,* he was green with envy **2.** (*maligno*) spiteful, vicious ‖ *s.m.* bruise: *era coperto di lividi,* he was covered with bruises.

lividóre, *s.m.,* **lividúra,** *s.f.* bruise.

Lívio, *no.pr.m.* (*st. romana*) Livy.

livóre, *s.m.* **1.** (*invidia*) envy; (*odio*) hatred; (*astio*) spite, malice **2.** (*rar.*) bruise.

Livórno, *no.pr.f.* (*geog.*) Leghorn.

livrèa, *s.f.* **1.** livery: *tutti i servi erano in* —, all the footmen were in livery ‖ *portar la* —, *fig.* to be servile: *io non porto* —, I am my own master **2.** (*di uccelli*) plumage: — *estiva,* summer plumage; *la cupa* — *del corvo,* the sombre plumage of the crow.

livreàto, *ag.* (*rar.*) liveried, in livery: *servitori livreati,* liveried footmen (*o* footmen in livery).

lízza, *s.f.* lists (*pl.*): *entrare in* —, to enter the lists; *essere in* —, to be competing.

lo[1], *art. determinativo m.sing.* **1. the:** — *Jonio,* the Jonian Sea; *l'oceano,* the ocean; *l'asino è un animale molto paziente,* the ass is a very patient animal; *l'universo ha sempre interessato gli scienziati,* the universe has always interested scientists **2.** (*spesso non si traduce*): *l'anno scorso,* last year; *l'Equador,* Ecuador; *l'aprile è un mese primaverile,* April is a spring month; *l'inverno è la mia stagione preferita,* winter is my favourite season; *l'oro e l'argento sono metalli preziosi,* gold and silver are precious metals; — *studiare con la luce artificiale mi stanca,* studying by artificial light makes me tired; — *studio è spesso faticoso*, study is often tiring; *l'uomo è l'essere più complicato del mondo*, man is the most complex of all creatures; *voleva studiare l'inglese*, he wanted to study English **3.** (*tradotto con l'ag. poss.*): *metti l'impermeabile*, put on your mackintosh; — *sport che preferisco è il tennis*, my favourite sport is tennis; — *zio è venuto a trovarti*, your uncle has come to see you **4.** (*tradotto con l'art. indef.*) **a, an:** *devo prendere l'ombrello?*, shall I take an umbrella?; *ha — stomaco molto delicato*, he has a very delicate stomach; *dare l'esempio*, to set an example **5.** (*tradotto col partitivo*) **some; any:** *devo andare a comperare — zucchero*, I must go and get some sugar; *hai comperato — zucchero?*, did you get any sugar? **6.** (*sta per al col valore di* ogni, ciascuno): *un milione l'anno*, a million a year.

lo², *pron.pers.m.* 3ª *persona sing.* **1.** oggetto **him** (*riferito a persona, animale maschio o cosa personificata*); **it** (*riferito a cose ed animali di sesso non specificato*): « *Conosci il signor Smith?* », « *No, non — conosco* », " Do you know Mr. Smith? ", " No, I do not know him "; *Dove hai messo il mio libro? Non — vedo*, Where have you put my book? I can't see it **2.** (*sta in luogo di* ciò, questo): — *credo anch'io*, I think so too; — *dica a me*, tell me; — *si dice*, they say so; — *si sa*, everybody knows (that); *egli è arrivato ieri, — so*, he arrived yesterday, I know; *offesi Tom senza volerlo*, I offended Tom without wishing to **3.** (*usato in luogo di* tale *con voci del verbo* essere): « *È medico?* », « *Lo è* », " Is he a doctor? ", " He is "; *egli è ricco, ma tu non — sei*, he is rich, but you aren't; *mi pareva bello, ma vedo che non — è*, it looked nice, but now I see it isn't.

lobàto, *ag.* **1.** lobed **2.** (*bot.*) lobate.

lòbbia, *s.f.* Homburg (hat).

lobèlia, *s.f.* (*bot.*) lobelia.

lobelína, *s.f.* (*farm.*) lobeline.

lòbo, *s.m.* lobe: *un — del fegato*, a lobe of the liver; *dell'orecchio*, lobe of the ear; *il — di una foglia*, the lobe of a leaf.

lòbulo, *s.m.* lobule.

locàle, *ag.* local: *anestesia —*, (*med.*) local anaesthetic; *colore —*, local colour; *dialetto —*, local dialect; *ora —*, local time; *treno —*, local (train) ‖ *s.m.* room: — *caldaie*, (*mar.*) stokehold; — *dell'equipaggio*, (*mar.*) mess-deck; — *notturno*, night-club; — *per magazzinaggio*, storeroom; *locali per uso di negozio, ufficio, ecc.*, business premises; *cambiamento di locali*, change of premises (*o* removal of office); *cambiamento nella disposizione dei locali*, alteration to premises; *la mia casa ha quattro locali*, my house has four rooms; *questa scuola non ha locali a sufficienza*, this school has not enough class-rooms.

località, *s.f.* locality: *una — amena*, a lovely spot.

localizzàre, *v.t.* **1.** to locate: — *un dolore*, to locate the source of a pain **2.** (*circoscrivere*) to localize, to circumscribe: — *un incendio*, to localize a fire; — *l'infezione*, to localize infection.

localizzàto, *ag.* **1.** located **2.** (*circoscritto*) localized.

localizzazióne, *s.f.* **1.** location, locating **2.** (*limitazione*) localization, localizing.

localménte, *av.* locally.

locànda, *s.f.* inn.

locandièra, *s.f.*, **locandière,** *s.m.* innkeeper.

locandína, *s.f.* (*manifesto teatrale*) play-bill.

locatàrio, *s.m.* (*dir.*) lessee, leaseholder; (*affittuario*) tenant.

locatívo¹, *ag.* rent (*attributivo*): *tassa sul valore —*, rent charge; *valore —*, rental value.

locatívo², *ag.* (*gram.*) locative: *genitivo —*, locative genitive.

locatóre, *s.m.* (*dir.*) lessor; (*chi dà in affitto*) landlord ‖ **locatríce,** *s.f.* (*dir.*) lessor; (*chi dà in affitto*) landlady.

locazióne, *s.f.* lease; (*affitto*) tenancy: *casa in —*,

house. on a lease; *durata della —*, duration of the lease; *rinnovare una —*, to renew a lease (*o* tenancy).

lòccu, *ag.* (*arc.*) silly; stupid.

lòco, *s.m.* (*letter.*) place: — *natio*, native place.

locomòbile, *s.m.* (*mec.*) portable steam engine.

locomotíva, *s.f.* locomotive: — *articolata*, articulated locomotive; — *a vapore*, steam-locomotive; — *con serbatoio*, tank-locomotive; — *con tender*, locomotive with tender; — *elettrica*, electric locomotive ‖ *sbuffare come una —*, (*scherz.*) to puff like an engine.

locomotívo, *ag.* (*rar.*) locomotive: *macchina locomotiva*, locomotive machine.

locomotóre, *ag.* locomotor(y), locomotive: *atassia locomotrice progressiva*, (*patol.*) locomotor ataxia (*o* ataxy); *facoltà locomotrice*, (*fisiol.*) locomotive faculty; *organi locomotori*, (*fisiol.*) locomotory organs ‖ *s.m.*, **locomotríce,** *s.f.* (*ferr.*) locomotive: — *con motore Diesel*, Diesel locomotive; — « *Decauville* », dolly; — *Diesel elettrico*, Diesel-electric locomotive.

locomozióne, *s.f.* locomotion: *disturbi della —*, (*med.*) disorder of the locomotory organs.

Lòcride, *no.pr.f.* (*geog.st.*) Locris.

lòculo, *s.m.* **1.** loculus (*pl.* loculi), niche for urn **2.** (*bot.*) loculus (*pl.* loculi).

locupletàre, *v.t.* (*rar.*) to enrich.

locùsta, *s.f.* (*entom.*) locust.

locutòrio, *s.m.* (*arc.*) locutory.

locuzióne, *s.f.* expression, phrase; (*frase idiomatica*) idiom: — *avverbiale*, (*gram.*) adverbial phrase.

lodàbile, *ag.* laudable, praiseworthy.

lodabilità, *s.f.* (*rar.*) laudability, laudableness, praiseworthiness.

lodàre, *v.t.* **1.** to praise; to commend: *la lodai per la sua modestia*, I praised her for her modesty; *le sue rose non furono premiate, ma furono molto lodate*, his roses did not get a prize, but they were highly commended; *vi lodo d'aver taciuto*, I praise you for keeping silent ‖ *chi loda se stesso, ha cattivi vicini*, prov. he dwelleth far from neighbours, who is fain to praise himself ‖ *loda il mar e tienti alla terra*, prov. praise the sea, but keep on land ‖ *non lodar il bel giorno innanzi sera*, prov. praise day at night, and life at the end **2.** (*glorificare*) to praise, to extol, to glorify, to laud: — *Dio*, to praise God ‖ *Dio sia lodato!*, thank God! ‖ **lodàrsi,** *v.r.* **1.** to praise oneself: *non sa parlare di sè senza —*, he cannot speak of himself but he praises himself ‖ *chi si loda s'imbroda*, prov. self-praise is no recommendation **2.** (*compiacersi*) to be pleased (with sthg.): *non posso che lodarmi di te*, I cannot be anything but pleased with you.

lodatívo, *ag.* (*rar.*) laudative, laudatory, eulogistic.

lodàto, *ag.* praised; commended.

lodatóre, *s.m.*, **lodatríce,** *s.f.* praiser, lauder.

lòde, *s.f.* **1.** praise; commendation: *il comportamento del Presidente fu oggetto di ampia —*, the President's behaviour was highly commended; *merita una —*, he deserves praise; *riscosse le lodi di tutti*, he was praised by everyone; *il suo eroismo è degno di —*, his heroism is worthy of praise; *vi fu un coro di lodi per il Primo Ministro*, there was a chorus of praise for the Prime Minister ‖ *a — del vero*, to tell the truth: *è un uomo generoso, sia detto a — del vero*, to tell the truth, he is a generous man ‖ *senza infamia e senza —*, without praise or blame ‖ *cantare le proprie lodi*, to blow one's own trumpet ‖ *celebrare le lodi di qlcu.*, to sing s.o.'s praises; *tessere le lodi di qlcu.*, to be loud in s.o.'s praises ‖ *laurearsi con —*, to graduate with honours ‖ *la — propria puzza*, prov. self-praise is recommendation ‖ *Dio ti guardi dal dì della —*, prov. it is safer to commend the dead than the living **2.** (*glorificazione*) praise, laud: — *a Dio!*, God be praised!; *scrisse un sonetto in — del principe*, he wrote a sonnet in praise of the prince; *dar — a Dio*, to praise God **3.** (*merito*) praise; merit: *ciò torna a sua —*, he must be praised for this; *enumerare le lodi di qlcu.*, to enumerate s.o.'s merits **4.** *pl.* (*laudi*) lauds.

lodévole, *ag.* praiseworthy, laudable; commendable.

lodevolménte, *av.* praiseworthily, laudably.

lòdo, *s.m.* (*dir.*) arbitration.

lòdola, *s.f.* (*ornit.*) (sky)lark.

Lodovíco, *no.pr.m.* Ludovic(k).

lòffio, *ag.* flabby.

logaèdico, *ag.* (*poes.*) logaoedic.

logarítmico, *ag.* (*mat.*) logarithmic.

logarítmo, *s.m.* (*mat.*) logarithm: — *addizionale*, addition logarithm; — *decimale*, common logarithm; — *di sottrazione*, subtraction logarithm.

lòggia, *s.f.***1.** (*arch.*) loggia (*pl.* loggias, loggie) **2.** (*circolo massonico*) lodge.

loggiàto, *s.m.* open gallery.

loggióne, *s.m.* (*teat.*) gallery; (*fam.*) gods (*pl.*).

lògica, *s.f.* **1.** (*fil.*) logic: *la — aristotelica*, Aristotelian logic **2.** (*il ben ragionare*) logic, logicality: *un discorso pieno di —*, a speech full of logic; *un errore di —*, a piece of false reasoning; *discute con grande —*, he argues with great logicality; *procedere a fil di —*, to proceed logically ‖ *la — dei fatti*, the logic of events.

logicaménte, *av.* logically.

lògico, *ag.* logical: *conclusione, conseguenza logica*, logical conclusion, consequence; *ordine —*, logical order ‖ *s.m.* logician: *è un — eccellente*, he is an excellent logician.

logìstica, *s.f.* **1.** (*mat.*) logistic **2.** (*mil.*) logistics.

logístico, *ag.* (*mat. mil.*) logistic(al).

lòglio, *s.m.* (*bot.*) darnel ‖ *distinguere il grano dal —*, (*Bibbia*) to separate the tares from the wheat.

logògrafo, *s.m.* logographer.

logògrifo, *s.m.* logogriph.

logomachía, *s.f.* logomachy.

logoraménto, *s.m.* **1.** wear, wearing out **2.** *fig.* wasting away; wearing down; — *della salute*, wasting away (of health).

logoràre, *v.t.* **1.** to wear (out, down): *ho logorato i tacchi di queste scarpe*, I have worn down the heels of these shoes; *le pietre furono logorate dal flusso continuo dell'acqua*, the stones were worn by the constant flow of the water **2.** *fig.* to wear (out), to waste, to use up, to consume: *aveva logorato tutte le sue forze*, he had used up all his strength; *continue preoccupazioni gli logorarono il cuore*, constant worry affected his heart; *era logorata dall'ansia*, she was worn out with anxiety; *quel duro lavoro lo logorò*, that hard work wore him out; — *le proprie energie*, to use up one's energy ‖ **logoràrsi,** *v.r.* **1.** to wear (out, down): *i tacchi di queste scarpe si logorarono presto*, the heels of these shoes soon wore down; *i vestiti a buon mercato si logorano facilmente*, cheap dresses wear out quickly **2.** *fig.* to wear (oneself) out; to spoil: *la mia vista si logora di giorno in giorno*, my eye-sight is growing worse every day; *si sta logorando inutilmente*, he is wearing himself out uselessly; — *con il lavoro*, to wear oneself out with work; — *gli occhi con la lettura*, to ruin one's eyes (with) reading.

logoràto, *ag.* **1.** worn (-out, down): *un cappotto —* (*dall'uso*, a worn-out coat **2.** *fig.* worn (-out); wasted away); used up: —*dall'ansia*, worn (-out) with anxiety; — *dal male*, wasted away by illness.

logorío, *s.m.* wear and tear: *il — della vita moderna*, the strain (o wear and tear) of modern life.

lógoro[1], *ag.* **1.** worn (-out, down): *scarpe logore*, worn-out shoes **2.** *fig.* worn(-out), wasted (away).

lógoro[2], *s.m.* (*richiamo per la caccia*) lure.

lògos, *s.m.* (*fil.*) logos ‖ *Logos*, (*teol.*) Logos.

loioléseo, *ag.* Jesuitic(al).

lòlla, *s.f.* husk; chaff: *separare il grano dalla —*, to separate the wheat from the chaff.

lombàggine, *s.f.* (*patol.*) lumbago.

lombàle, *V.* lombàre.

lombardésco, *ag.* (*di stile*) Lombardesque.

Lombardía, *no.pr.f.* (*geog.*) Lombardy.

lombardísmo, *s.m.* Lombardism.

lombàrdo, *ag.* Lombard(ic) ‖ *s.m.* Lombard.

lombàre, *ag.* (*anat.*) lumbar: *curvatura — della colonna vertebrale*, lumbar plexure.

lombàta, *s.f.* (*cuc.*) loin, sirloin, surloin.

lómbo, *s.m.* loin: *cingersi i lombi*, to gird up one's loins ‖ *magnanimi lombi*, noble ancestry.

lombricàle, *ag.* (*anat.*) lumbrical.

lombríco, *s.m.* earth-worm.

londinése, *ag.* London (*attributivo*); Cockney (*attributivo*): *dialetto —*, Cockney ‖ *s.c.* Londoner; Cockney.

Lóndra, *no.pr.f.* (*geog.*) London.

longànime, *ag.* longanimous; patient, forbearing.

longanimeménte, *av.* patiently, forbearingly.

longanimità, *s.f.* forbearance, longanimity: *mostrare — verso qlcu.*, to show forbearance towards s.o.

longarína, *s.f.* (*edil.*) iron girder.

longaróne, *s.m.* **1.** (*aut.*) side-member, side-sill **2.** (*aer.*) (*di fusoliera*) longeron; (*dell'ala*) spar: — *a cassone*, box-type spar; — *anteriore*, front spar; — *inferiore*, sub-spar.

longevità, *s.f.* longevity.

longèvo, *ag.* longeval, long-lived.

longilíneo, *ag.* long-limbed.

longimetría, *s.f.* (*scient.*) longimetry.

Longíno, *no.pr.* (*st. fil.*) Longinus.

longitudinàle, *ag.* **1.** (*geog. astr.*) longitudinal **2.** (*nel senso della lunghezza*) longitudinal, lengthwise: *gioco —*, (*mec.*) end-play; *trave —*, (*aer.*) longitudinal.

longitudinalménte, *av.* **1.** (*geog. astr.*) longitudinally **2.** (*nel senso della lunghezza*) lengthwise.

longitúdine, *s.f.* (*geog. astr.*) longitude: — *celeste*, celestial longitude; — *in gradi*, longitude in arc; — *in ore e minuti*, longitude in time.

longobàrdo, *ag.s.m.* Longobard.

lontanaménte, *av.* **1.** (*vagamente*) vaguely; (*leggermente*) slightly: *accennò — alla sua prossima partenza*, he hinted at his forthcoming departure; *non sapevo neppur — come cominciare*, I hadn't the vaguest idea how to start; *si assomigliano —*, there is faint resemblance between them **2.** (*rar.*) far, far off; (*da lontano*) from afar.

lontanànza, *s.f.* distance; remoteness: *in —*, in the distance; (*da lontano*) from afar (o from a distance); (*a distanza*) at a distance: *da qui si può vedere il Monte Bianco in —*, from here you can see Mont Blanc in the distance; *l'ho visto in —*, I saw him from afar (o from a distance); *seguire qlcu. in —*, to follow s.o. at a distance; *era afflitto per la — dai suoi cari*, it grieved him to be so far away from his family; *la prospettiva dà l'impressione della —*, perspective gives the impression of distance; *quando avrà fine la nostra —?*, when shall we be together again?.

lontàna, alla, *l.av.* at a distance: *alla — da certa gente!*, steer clear of such people!; *parenti alla —*, distant relations; *assomigliare a qlcu. alla—*, to resemble s.o. faintly (o slightly); *seguire qlcu. alla —*, to follow s.o. at a distance.

lontàno, *ag.* **1.** far, far away, far off, remote, distant: — *due miglia*, two miles away (o distant); *un paese —*, a far (o distant) country; *più —*, farther (away): *la mia casa è più lontana della tua*, my house is farther away (o off) than yours; *il più —*, the farthest: *nella parte più lontana dell'Asia*, in the farthest corner of Asia; *la chiesa non è molto lontana da casa mia*, the church is not far (away) from my house; *la scuola è piuttosto lontana da qui*, the school is rather a long way (away) from here; *tenere — ql.co.*, to keep sthg. away; *tenere qlcu. — dal pericolo*, to keep s.o. out of harm's way; *tenersi — da qlcu.*, to keep away from s.o. ‖ *il — Occidente*, the Far West ‖ *lontana da me l'idea di farlo*, far be it from me to do it ‖ *quel che egli dice è molto — dal vero*, what he says is a long way off (o a long way from) the truth ‖ *questo è ben — dal-*

l'essere perfetto, this is very far from (being) perfect **2.** (*distante nel tempo*) far-off; remote, distant: *giorni lontani*, far-off days; *i miei ricordi più lontani*, my earliest recollections; *nel — avvenire*, in the distant future; *ciò avvenne in un'epoca assai lontana dalla nostra*, this happened in an age far removed from our own; *il giorno è ancora —*, the day is still distant **3.** (*vago*) vague, faint: *lontana somiglianza*, faint likeness; *ho un — sospetto che...*, I have a vague suspicion that...; *non ho la più lontana idea di ciò che volesse dire*, I haven't the faintest (*o* remotest) idea of what he meant **4.** (*assente*) absent: *brindiamo agli amici lontani*, let us drink to absent friends **5.** (*nei rapporti di parentela*) distant: *un — cugino*, a distant cousin; *è un mio — parente*, he is a distant relation of mine.

lontàno, *av.* far, far away, far off: *non posso vedere così*, I cannot see as far as that; *non vivo — da qui*, I don't live far from here; *la tua timidezza non ti porterà —*, your shyness won't carry you far; *andare —*, to go far (anche *fig.*): *quel giovane andrà —*, that young man will go far (*o* a long way); *vai troppo —*, you are going (*o* you are carrying things) too far ‖ *da —*, from afar (*o* from far off *o* at a distance): *lo spiavo da —*, I watched him from far off; *si vede da —*, it can be seen at a distance; *vieni da —?*, have you come very far? ‖ *— dagli occhi, — dal cuore*, *prov.* out of sight, out of mind ‖ *chi va piano, va sano e va —*, *prov.* slow and steady wins the race (*o* slowly, but surely).

lóntra, *s.f.* (*zool.*) otter: *pelliccia di —*, otter.

lónza¹, *s.f.* (*cuc.*) loin; sirloin, surloin.

lónza², *s.f.* (*arc.*) (*zool.*) female leopard; panther.

lòppa, *s.f.* **1.** (*del grano*) husk, chaff **2.** (*metal.*) slag, dross: *— di alto forno*, blast-furnace slag.

loquàce, *ag.* loquacious, talkative; (*garrulo*) garrulous.

loquaceménte, *av.* loquaciously, talkatively; (*in tono garrulo*) garrulously.

loquacità, *s.f.* loquacity, loquaciousness, talkativeness; (*garrulità*) garrulity.

loquèla, *s.f.* **1.** (*linguaggio*) language, (manner of) speech **2.** (*facoltà di parlare*) faculty of speech: *perdere la —*, to lose one's power of speech.

lordaménte, *av.* dirtily.

lordàre, *v.t.* to dirty, to soil (anche *fig.*) ‖ **lordàrsi,** *v.r.* to dirty oneself, to soil oneself (anche *fig.*): *— le mani*, to soil one's hands; *— la reputazione*, to soil (*o* to tarnish) one's reputation.

lordézza, *s.f.* dirt, filth (anche *fig.*).

lórdo, *ag.* **1.** dirty, filthy (anche *fig.*): *— di fango, di inchiostro*, covered with mud, ink; *mani lorde di sangue*, blood-stained hands; *ha la coscienza lorda*, he has a lot on his conscience **2.** (*comm.*) gross: *ammontare, importo —*, gross amount; *peso, ricavo —*, gross weight, proceeds; *stazza lorda*, (*mar.*) gross tonnage.

lordòsi, *s.f.* (*med.*) lordosis.

lordúme, *s.m.* heap of dirt, heap of filth.

lordúra, *s.f.* dirt, filth (anche *fig.*).

Lorèna, *no.pr.f.* (*geog.*) Lorraine.

lorenése, *ag.* Lorraine (*attributivo*) ‖ *s.c.* Lorrainer.

Lorènzo, *no.pr.m.* Laurence, Lawrence ‖ *dim.* Larry.

lorgnette, *s.f.* lorgnette.

lòri, *s.m.* (*zool.*) loris: *— gracile*, slender loris.

loríca, *s.f.* lorica.

loricàto, *ag.* loricate.

loricàti, *s.m.pl.* (*zool.*) Loricata.

lóro, *ag. poss.* **1.** their; (*loro proprio*) their own: *hanno una casa —?*, have they got a house of their own?; *mi regalarono alcuni — libri*, they gave me some of their books (*o* some books of theirs); *non invidio la — ricchezza*, I don't envy them their money; *tutti i — figli sono intelligenti*, all their children are intelligent; *vennero con tre — amici*, they came with three of their friends (*o* with three friends of theirs) **2.** (*come pred. nominale*) theirs: *queste riviste sono —, non mie*, these magazines are theirs, not

mine **3.** *Loro*, (*formula di cortesia*) your: *è un grande onore per me accogliere qui oggi le Loro Maestà*, it is a great honour for me to welcome Your Majesties here today **4.** (*in espressioni ellittiche*): *la — del..., (lettera)* their letter of the...; *si tenevano sulla —*, they kept themselves to themselves; *sta dalla — (parte)*, he is on their side ‖ *pron. poss.* **theirs:** *questa stanza è la —*, this room is theirs ‖ *s.m.* **1.:** *campano del —*, they live on their income; *dobbiamo distinguere tra il nostro e il —*, we must distinguish between what is ours and what is theirs **2.** *pl.*: *i —*, their family (*o* their relatives *o* *fam.* their folks); (*partigiani, seguaci*) their supporters: *siete uno dei —?*, are you one of their supporters?.

lóro, *pron. pers. m.f. 3ª persona pl.* **1.** *sogg.* **they:** *faremo quello che fanno —*, we shall do what they do; *l'han detto —*, they have said so (*o* it was they who said so); *nemmeno — sanno che cosa fare*, even they don't know what to do; *se — credevano di potermi ingannare...*, (*fam.*) if they thought they could deceive me... ‖ *— due, tre*, the two, the three of them **2.** (*come pred. nominale*): *non sembrano più —*, they are not as they used to be (*o* they seem quite different) **3.** *oggetto e obliquo* **them:** *amo te quanto —*, I like you as much as them; *andai a casa con —*, I went home with them; *andai da —*, I went to them (*o* to their house); *chiamo — non voi*, I am calling them not you; *disse — che...*, he told them that... ‖ *sta — a cuore*, it is a matter very near their hearts ‖ *sta in —*, it is up to them **4.** *Loro*, *sogg. oggetto e obliquo* (*formula di cortesia*) **you:** *Lor Signori vedranno che...*, you will see that...; *come Loro vedono*, as you (may) see.

losànga, *s.f.* **1.** lozenge, rhomb **2.** (*geom.*) rhombus (*pl.* rhombuses) **3.** (*arald.*) lozenge.

losangàto, *ag.* (*arald.*) lozengy.

Losànna, *no.pr.f.* (*geog.*) Lausanne.

lósco, *ag.* **1.** (*miope*) short-sighted; (*cieco da un occhio*) one-eyed; (*strabico*) squint-eyed **2.** (*bieco*) sly: *mi guardò —*, he gave me a sly look **3.** (*di dubbia onestà*) suspicious, questionable; (*fam.*) shady: *affari un po' loschi*, somewhat shady transactions; *è un uomo —*, he is a suspicious (*o* fishy) character; *avere un'aria losca*, to look suspicious ‖ *c'è del —*, there is something underhand going on.

Lotàrio, *no.pr.m.* (*st.*) Lothair.

lòto¹, *s.m.* (*fango*) mud, mire.

lòto², *s.m.* (*bot.*) lotus (*pl.* lotuses) ‖ *mangiatore di —*, (*mit.*) Lotus-eater.

Lotòfagi, *s.m.pl.* (*mit.*) Lotophagi, Lotus-eaters.

lotòfago, *ag.* lotus-eating; (*rar.*) lotophagous.

lòtta, *s.f.* **1.** struggle, fight (anche *fig.*): *— a corpo a corpo*, hand-to-hand struggle; *— di classe*, class warfare; *la — per l'esistenza*, the struggle for existence; *l'istinto della —*, the fighting instinct; *ci fu una — violenta*, there was a violent fight; *è abituato alla —*, he is used to struggling; *la legge fu approvata in seguito ad una — ostinata alla Camera dei Comuni*, the bill was passed after a stubborn fight in the House of Commons; *sostennero una — disperata con la polizia*, they put up a desperate fight against the police; *le sue passioni erano in —*, his passions were struggling within him; *sostenere una — con qlcu.*, to have a fight with s.o. **2.** (*spor.*) wrestling: *— americana*, all-in wrestling; *— greco-romana*, Graeco-Roman wrestling; *— libera*, catch-as-catch-can; *una gara di —*, a wrestling match; *fare alla —*, to wrestle.

lottàre, *v.i.* **1.** to struggle, to wrestle, to fight (anche *fig.*): *devo — con quella testa dura*, I have to struggle with that stubborn creature; *dovette — contro le avversità della vita*, he had to fight (*o* to struggle) against adversity; *lotta con uno più forte di lui*, he is wrestling with an opponent stronger than himself; *lottava col sonno*, he was fighting off sleep; *— con le onde*, to buffet the waves; *— contro un abuso*, to make a stand against an abuse; *— contro la tentazione*, to fight (against) temptation **2.** (*spor.*) to wrestle.

lottatóre, *s.m.,* **lottatríce,** *s.f.* **1.** fighter, struggler (anche *fig.*) **2.** (*spor.*) wrestler.

lottería, *s.f.* lottery; sweepstake: — *di beneficenza,* charity lottery; *ha vinto alla* —, he won a price in the lottery.

lòtto, *s.m.* **1.** state lottery: *estrazione del* —, drawing of the lottery ‖ *ho vinto un terno al* —, *fig.* I have hit the jackpot **2.** (*porzione, contingente*) lot: *un* — *di merci,* a lot of goods; — *di occasione,* job-lot; *un* — *di terreno,* a parcel (*o* a lot) of land; — *fabbricativo,* building lot (*o* site); *ognuno degli eredi ebbe il suo* —, each of the heirs had his share.

lozióne, *s.f.* **1.** lotion: — *astringente,* astringent lotion; — *rinfrescante,* cooling lotion **2.** (*bagno*) bathing, washing.

lubbióne, *V.* **loggióne.**

Lubéca, *no.pr.f.* (*geog.*) Lubeck.

lubricità, *s.f.* lubricity.

lúbrico, *ag.* **1.** slippery: *un pendio* —, a slippery slope **2.** *fig.* (*indecente*) lubric: *una canzone lubrica,* a lubric song.

lubrificànte, *ag.* lubricating: *olio* —, lubricating oil ‖ *s.m.* lubricant: — *per imbutitura,* (*mec.*) drawing compound; — *per ingranaggi,* (*mec.*) gear lubricant; — *per ponti,* (*aut.*) axle grease.

lubrificàre, *v.t.* to lubricate, to grease, to oil.

lubrificatívo, *ag.* lubricant, lubricating.

lubrificatóio, *s.m.* lubricator.

lubrificazióne, *s.f.* lubrication, greasing, oiling: — *a circuito chiuso,* (*mec.*) loop lubrication; — *ad anello,* (*mec.*) ring lubrication; — *ad olio,* (*mec.*) oiling; — *a sbattimento,* (*mec.*) splash lubrication; — *inadatta,* (*mec.*) wrong-lubrication; *siringa per* —, (*mec.*) oil gun.

Lúca, *no.pr.m.* Luke.

Lucàno, *no.pr.m.* (*st. lett.*) Lucan.

lucchétto, *s.m.* padlock ‖ *mettere il* — *alla bocca a qlcu.,* to shut s.o.'s mouth.

luccicaménto, *s.m.* glitter, glittering; sparkle, sparkling.

luccicàre, *v.i.* to glitter (with sthg.); to sparkle (with sthg.); to shine (with sthg.); to gleam: *l'armatura luccicava al sole,* the armour shone in the sun; *luccica come un brillante,* it sparkles like a diamond; *il mare luccicava al chiaro di luna,* the sea was glittering in the moonlight; *i suoi occhi luccicavano di gioia,* her eyes sparkled with joy; *la triste storia le fece* — *gli occhi,* when she heard the sad story her eyes swam with tears (*o* the sad story brought tears to her eyes).

luccichío, *s.m.* glitter, glittering; sparkle, sparkling: *il* — *di una stella,* the twinkling of a star.

luccicóne, *s.m.* large tear.

luccicóre, *s.m.* glitter, glittering; sparkle, sparkling.

lúccio, *s.m.* (*ittiol.*) pike: — *imperiale,* sphyraena.

lúcciola, *s.f.* (*entom.*) fire-fly; (*senza ali*) glow-worm ‖ *mostrare lucciole per lanterne,* to make believe that the moon is made of green cheese; *prendere lucciole per lanterne,* to make a blunder.

lucciolàio, *s.m.* (*rar.*) a swarm of fire-flies.

lúce, *s.f.* **1.** light (anche *fig.*): — *abbagliante,* dazzling light; — *a gas,* gas-light; — *debole,* faint light; — *della luna,* moonlight; — *diffusa,* diffused light; — *diretta,* direct light; — *diurna,* daylight; — *elettrica,* electric light; — *solare,* sun-light; *alla* — *della candela,* by candle-light; *alla* — *della fede, della ragione, della scienza,* in the light of faith, reason, science; *alla* — *del sole,* by the light of the sun; *fig.* openly (*o* publicly); *contro* —, against the light; (*con le spalle alla luce*) with one's back to the light: *guardò l'uovo contro* —, she held the egg up to the light; *fascio di* —, beam of light; *in buona, cattiva, falsa* —, in a good, bad, false light: *quel quadro non è in buona* —, that picture is not in a good light; *mettere qlcu. in buona, cattiva* —, *fig.* to place s.o. in a favourable, unfavourable light; *raggio di* —, ray of light; *sprazzo di* —,

flash; *le lampade al neon diffondono una* — *fredda,* neon lamps shed (*o* give) a cold light; *quella stanza riceve* — *dal cortile,* that room is lit by a window overlooking the courtyard; *dar* — *a un locale,* to let light into a room; (*di finestra*) to light a room: *apri le imposte e da'* — *alla stanza,* open the shutters and let some light into the room; *tre finestre danno* — *alla sala da pranzo,* the dining room is lit by three windows ‖ *anno* —, light-year ‖ *chiudere gli occhi alla* —, to die ‖ *dare alla* — *un bambino,* to give birth to a child ‖ *far* — *su un argomento,* to throw (*o* to shed) light on a subject ‖ *mettere in* —, to show (*o* to display *o* to stress *o* to emphasize): *quell'opera ha messo in* — *le sue qualità di scrittore,* that work has shown his qualities as a writer; *mettere in* — *l'importanza di ql.co.,* to stress (*o* to emphasize) the importance of sthg. ‖ *rendere alla* —, to bring to light: *gli scavi hanno reso alla* — *oggetti di grande interesse archeologico,* the excavations have brought to light objects of great archeological interest ‖ *vedere la* —, to see the light of day (*o* to be born); *venire alla* —, (*nascere*) to be born; (*essere scoperto*) to come to light: *fatti curiosi sono venuti alla* —, some curious facts have come to light **2.** (*sorgente luminosa, lampada, dispositivo illuminante*) light: — *abbagliante,* (*aut.*) headlight; — *anabbagliante,* (*aut.*) anti-dazzle light; — *d'arresto,* (*aut.*) stop-light; *le luci della città,* the lights of the town; *una* — *apparve in lontananza,* a light appeared in the distance; *accendere la* —, to turn (*o* to switch *o* to put) on the light; *spegnere la* —, to turn (*o* to switch *o* to put) off (*o* out) the light **3.** (*vista*) sight ‖ *essere la* — *degli occhi di qlcu.,* to be the apple of s.o.'s eyes **4.** *pl.* (*poet.*) eyes **5.** (*apertura*) light, window; (*arch.*) span; (*mec.*) port: — *di un arco,* (*arch.*) arch-span; — *libera,* (*edil.*) clear span; *un negozio con tre luci,* a shop with three windows (*o* lights) **6.** (*lastra di specchio*) mirror, looking-glass: *un armadio a tre luci,* a wardrobe with three mirrors.

lucènte, *ag.* (*lucido*) shiny; (*risplendente*) bright, shining: *occhi lucenti,* bright eyes.

lucenteménte, *av.* brightly, shiningly.

lucentézza, *s.f.* brilliance, brilliancy; brightness; sheen; shine: *la* — *dei suoi capelli,* the sheen of her hair; *la* — *di un'immagine,* the brilliance of an image; *quella seta aveva una* — *meravigliosa,* that silk had a beautiful sheen; *le sue scarpe hanno perso la* —, his shoes have lost their shine.

lúcere, *v.i.* (*poet.*) to shine (with sthg.).

Lucèrna[1], *no.pr.f.* (*geog.*) Lucerne.

lucèrna[2], *s.f.* **1.** oil-lamp: — *di bronzo,* bronze oil-lamp; *catenina della* —, chain of an oil-lamp ‖ *le sue opere sanno di* —, he has been burning the midnight oil ‖ *non bisogna mettere la* — *sotto il moggio,* *prov.* don't hide your light under a bushel **2.** (*cappello*) cocked hat; (*tricorno*) three-cornered hat.

lucernàrio, *s.m.* skylight.

lucernàta, *s.f.* quantity of oil necessary to fill a lamp.

lucernière, *s.m.* lampstand.

lucèrtola, *s.f.* lizard ‖ *mangiar le lucertole,* (*essere magro e patito*) to be as thin as a rake.

lucheríno, *s.m.* (*ornit.*) siskin.

Luchíno, *no.pr.m. dim. di* **Lúca.**

Lucía, *no.pr.f.* Lucy.

Luciàno, *no.pr.m.* Lucian.

lucidaménte, *av.* lucidly.

lucidaménto, *s.m.* **1.** polishing **2.** (*il ricalcare*) tracing.

lucidàre, *v.t.* **1.** to polish: — *i pavimenti,* to polish floors; — *le scarpe,* to polish shoes (*o fam.* to give shoes a shine) **2.** (*ricalcare disegni*) to trace.

lucidatóre, *s.m.* **1.** polisher: — *di mobili,* furniture polisher (*o* French-polisher); — *di pavimenti,* floor polisher **2.** (*di disegni*) drawing tracer.

lucidatríce, *s.f.* **1.** polisher **2.** (*mec.*) polishing machine: — *per pavimenti,* floor-polisher.

lucidatúra, *s.f.* **1.** polishing: — *a cera*, wax finishing **2.** (*ricalco di disegno*) tracing.

lucidazióne, *s.f.* (*rar.*) polishing.

lucidézza, *s.f.* brightness; sheen; glossiness; lustre: *la — del marmo*, the sheen of marble.

lucidità, *s.f.* lucidity, clearness: — *di mente*, clearness of mind; *quel pazzo ha momenti di —*, that madman has lucid intervals.

lúcido, *ag.* **1.** bright, shiny; glossy; (*lucidato*) polished: *lucide stelle*, (*poet.*) bright (o shining) stars; *cristalli lucidi*, bright crystals; *pavimento—*, polished floor; *scarpe lucide*, polished shoes; *seta lucida*, glossy silk; *in primavera le foglie sono di un verde —*, the leaves are bright green in Spring ‖ *pelle lucida*, patent leather **2.** (*chiaro, evidente*) lucid, clear: *lucida esposizione*, lucid explanation; *idee lucide*, clear ideas; *mente lucida*, lucid (o clear) mind; *stile —*, clear style ‖ — *intervallo*, (*med.*) lucid interval ‖ *s.m.* **1.** (*lucentezza*) polish, brightness, sheen, shine, lustre; gloss: *il — del marmo*, the sheen of marble; *il — della seta*, the gloss of silk; *quel tavolo ha un bel —*, that table has a nice polish; *perdere il —*, to lose polish **2.** (*materia che conferisce lucentezza*) polish: — *per le scarpe*, shoe-polish; (*nero*) blacking; *dare il — alle scarpe*, to polish (o to put a shine on) one's shoes **3.** (*ricalco*) tracing: *fare il — di un disegno*, to make the tracing of a drawing.

Lucífero[1], *no.pr.m.* **1.** (*Bibbia*) Lucifer **2.** (*astr.*) Lucifer.

lucífero[2], *ag.* luciferous, light-bringing.

lucignolàto, *ag.* twisted.

lucígnolo, *s.m.* **1.** wick **2.** (*persona molto magra*) bean-pole **3.** (*ind. tessile*) roving.

Lucína, *no.pr.f.* (*mit.*) Lucina.

Lúcio, *no.pr.m.* Lucius.

lucràbile, *ag.* exploitable.

lucràre, *v.t.* **1.** to profit, to gain, to earn: *ha lucrato molto (o una) sulla vendita di quelle azioni*, he has profited a lot by (o from) the sale of those shares; — *grandi somme*, to make a lot of money **2.** — *l'indulgenza*, (*eccl.*) to get the indulgence.

lucratívo, *ag.* lucrative, profitable.

Lucrèzia, *no.pr.f.* Lucretia, Lucrece.

Lucrèzio, *no.pr.m.* (*st. lett.*) Lucretius.

lúcro, *s.m.* profit, gain: — *cessante e danno emergente*, (*dir.*) missed profit and accruing damage; *a scopo di —*, for the sake of gain.

lucróso, *ag.* profitable, lucrative, remunerative.

luculliàno, *ag.* Lucull(i)an: *un pranzo —*, a Lucullan banquet (o a sumptuous dinner).

Lucúllo, *no.pr.m.* (*st. romana*) Lucullus.

lucumóne, *s.m.* (*st. etrusca*) lucumon.

ludíbrio, *s.m.* **1.** (*scherno*) mockery, scorn: *mettere qlcu., ql.co. in —*, to hold s.o., sthg. up to mockery (o to make a mockery of s.o., sthg.) **2.** (*persona schernita*) laughing-stock, scorn.

lúdo, *s.m.* (*poet.*) (*giuoco*) game: *ludi olimpici*, Olympic games; *ludi scenici*, theatrical performances.

lúe, *s.f.* (*patol.*) lues.

luètico, *ag.* luetic.

lugàniga, *s.f.* sausage.

lugliàtico, *ag.* (*agr.*) ripening in July.

lúglio, *s.m.* July.

lúgubre, *ag.* lugubrious, mournful; funereal; dismal, gloomy: *una faccia —*, a dismal face; *uno spettacolo —*, a mournful (o funereal) scene; *me lo disse con una voce —*, he told me so in a lugubrious voice.

lugubreménte, *av.* lugubriously, mournfully.

lui[1], *s.m.* (*ornit.*) warbler.

lúi[2], *pron.pers.m.* 3ª *persona sing.* **1.** *oggetto e obliquo* him: *non ho visto che —*, I have seen only him (o I haven't seen anyone but him); *si raccolsero intorno a —*, they gathered round him; *sono stato con — ieri*, I was with him yesterday; *voglio proprio —*, he is the person I want **2.** (*come pred. nominale*): *non sembra più —*, he does not seem himself any more ‖ *è tutto —*, (*di ritratto*) it is just like him (o *fam.* it is his very spit) **3.** *sogg.* he: — *dice di no ed io di sì*, he says no, but I say yes; — *e sua moglie erano là*, (*fam.*) he and his wife were there; *è —*, it is he (o *fam.* it's him o that's him): *è — che me l'ha detto*, he told me so himself; *ha ragione —*, he is right; *perchè non sono tutti come —?*, why aren't they all like him (o like he is)? ‖ *beato —!*, lucky man!; *contento —, contenti tutti*, if he is satisfied, we all are.

Luígi[1], *no.pr.m.* Louis, Lewis ‖ *dim.* Lewie, Lew, Louie.

luígi[2], *s.m.* (*moneta*) louis(-d'or) (*pl. invariato*).

Luísa, *no.pr.f.* Louise, Louisa ‖ *dim.* Lou, Louie.

Luisiàna, *no.pr.f.* (*geog.*) Louisiana.

lumàca, *s.f.* **1.** (*zool.*) snail: *a passo di —*, at a snail's pace; *andava come una —*, he was creeping along like a snail **2.** (*persona lenta*) sluggard, slow person; (*fam.*) slow-coach: *sei una —!*, you are a slow-coach!.

lumachèlla, *s.f.* (*min.*) lumachel(le).

lumacóne, *s.m.* sluggard; (*fam.*) slow-coach.

lumàio, *s.m.* **1.** (*chi accende*) lamp-lighter **2.** (*chi vende*) lamp-seller **3.** (*chi ripara*) lamp-repairer.

lúme, *s.m.* **1.** light (anche *fig.*): *il — del sole*, sun-light; — *di luna*, moon-light: *facemmo una passeggiata al — di luna*, we went out for a walk by moon-light; *a — di candela*, by candle-light: *cenammo a — di candela*, we had supper by candle-light; *non si può scrivere senza —*, you cannot write in the dark; *questa lucerna fa poco —*, this lamp gives very little light; *far — a qlcu. per le scale, nel corridoio*, to light s.o. downstairs, along the corridor; *far — su ql.co.*, *fig.* to throw (o to shed) light on sthg.; *portare un — in mano*, to carry a light in one's hand; *vedere un — in lontananza*, to see a light in the distance ‖ *il — della fede*, the light of Faith ‖ *il — della ragione*, the light of reason: *perdere il — della ragione*, to lose one's reason ‖ *a questi lumi di luna*, at this critical time ‖ *il secolo dei lumi*, (*st. fil.*) the Age of Enlightenment ‖ *ricorreremo ai lumi di uno specialista*, we shall consult (o ask the advice of) an expert ‖ *perdere il — degli occhi*, to lose one's sight; (*essere accecato dall'ira*) to be blinded by anger ‖ *nè donna nè tela al — di candela*, *prov.* neither women nor linen by candle-light **2.** (*lampada*) lamp, light; (*candela*) candle: — *ad acetilene, petrolio*, acetylene, oil lamp; *metti lì il —*, put the lamp there; *accendere, spegnere il —*, to turn on, to turn out the light; *accendere un — alla Madonna*, to light a candle to our Lady ‖ *tenere il —*, *fig.* to play gooseberry **3.** *pl.* (*poet.*) eyes.

lumeggiaménto, *s.m.* (*pitt.*) heightening.

lumeggiàre, *v.t.* **1.** to light(en), to illuminate **2.** (*pitt.*) to heighten **3.** (*far risaltare*) to throw into relief, to put in evidence: — *una circostanza, una figura*, to give prominence to a circumstance, a figure.

lumeggiàto, *ag.* heightened.

lúmen, *s.m.* (*fis.*) lumen.

lumencristi, *s.m.* (*eccl.*) blessed candle.

lumicíno, *s.m.* small light; (*piccola lampada*) small lamp ‖ *cercare ql.co. col —*, to look for sthg. diligently ‖ *essere ridotto al —*, to be at one's last gasp.

lumièra, *s.f.* chandelier.

luminàl, *s.m.* (*farm.*) luminal.

luminàre, *s.m.* luminary (anche *fig.*): *è un — della letteratura*, he is a literary luminary.

luminària, *s.f.* **1.** illuminations (*pl.*) **2.** (*illuminazione pubblica*) public illumination.

luminèllo, *s.m.* **1.** wick-holder **2.** (*riverbero del sole*) glare.

luminescènza, *s.f.* (*fis.*) luminescence: *lampada a —*, gas lamp.

lumino, *s.m.* night-light, night-lamp.

luminosaménte, *av.* brightly, luminously; *fig.* brightly, luminously; clearly.

luminosità, *s.f.* brightness, luminosity, luminousness, brilliance, brilliancy: *la — del cielo*, the brightness of the sky; — *dello schermo*, *(tv.)* brilliance of the screen; — *di una lampadina*, brilliancy of a light-bulb; *eccessiva* —, *(tv.)* over-brilliance; *il fenomeno della* — *del mare*, the phenomenon of sea phosphorescence.

luminóso, *ag.* **1.** bright, shining, luminous: *corpo* —, luminous body; *occhi luminosi*, bright eyes; *raggio* —, ray (of light); *onda luminosa*, *(fis.)* lightwave; *sorgente luminosa*, source of light **2.** *(bene illuminato)* well-lighted: *fotografia luminosa*, high-key photograph; *stanza luminosa*, well-lighted room **3.** *(brillante)* brilliant; *(chiaro, evidente)* shining, luminous; clear: *esempio* —, shining example; *idea luminosa*, brilliant idea; *prova luminosa*, glaring proof.

lúna, *s.f.* **1.** moon: — *calante*, waning moon; — *crescente*, crescent *(o waxing)* moon; — *falcata*, crescent moon; — *nuova*, new moon; — *piena*, full-moon; *chiaro di* —, moonlight; *corni della* —, horns of the moon; *macchie della* —, shadows on the moon; *mezza* —, half-moon; *primo quarto di* —, the first quarter of the moon; *raggio di* —, moon-beam; *è una notte di* —, it is a moonlight night; *è una notte senza* —, it is a moonless night ‖ — *di miele*, honeymoon: *sono in* — *di miele*, they are on their honeymoon ‖ *faccia di* — *piena*, *(fam.)* face like a full moon ‖ *mezza* —, *(l'islamismo e il suo simbolo)* the Crescent ‖ *mezza* —, *(cuc.)* mincing-knife ‖ *abbaiare alla* —, *fig.* to bay (at) the moon ‖ *andare a lune*, to be moody ‖ *avere la* —, to be in a bad mood *(o to have got out of bed the wrong side)* ‖ *avere la testa nella* —, to be absent-minded *(o to have one's head in the clouds)* ‖ *domandare la* —, to ask for the moon (and stars) ‖ *essere nel mondo della* —, to be lost in reverie ‖ *far vedere la* — *nel pozzo*, *(darla a bere)* to make s.o. believe that the moon is made of (green) cheese ‖ *promettere la* —, to promise the moon (and stars) ‖ *la* — *non cura l'abbaiar dei cani*, *prov.* the moon does not heed the barking of dogs ‖ *quando la* — *è bianca, il tempo è bello*; *se è rossa, significa vento*; *se pallida, pioggia*, pale moon doth rain, red moon doth blow, white moon doth neither rain nor snow **2.** *(periodo di una fase lunare)* *(astr.)* lunation; *(poet.)* moon **3.** *(satellite)* moon, satellite: — *artificiale*, artificial satellite *(o moon)*; *il pianeta Giove ha nove lune*, the planet Jupiter has nine moons.

lunàre, *ag.* lunar: *ciclo* —, lunar cycle; *luce* —, moonlight; *mese* —, lunar month.

lunàrio, *s.m.* almanac, calendar ‖ *sbarcare il* —, *(fam.)* to make ends meet.

lunarísta, *s.m.* *(rar.)* **1.** almanac-maker **2.** *(sognatore)* day-dreamer.

lunàtica, *s.f.* moody woman, changeable woman.

lunàtico, *ag.* moody, changeable ‖ *s.m.* moody man, changeable man.

lunàto, *ag.* crescent-shaped.

lunazióne, *s.f.* *(astr.)* lunation.

lunedí, *s.m.* Monday: — *ad otto*, a week on Monday *(o Monday week)*; *il* — *di Pasqua*, Easter Monday; — *grasso*, Shrove Monday; — *prossimo*, next Monday; — *scorso*, last Monday.

lunétta, *s.f.* **1.** *(arch. mil. eccl.)* lunette: — *a ventaglio*, *(arch.)* fanlight **2.** *(mec.)* *(di tornio)* steady rest: — *fissa*, fixed rest; — *mobile*, follow-rest **3.** *(orologeria)* bezel.

lúnga, *s.f.* *(fonet.)* long: *lunghe e brevi*, longs and shorts.

lungàggine, *s.f.* **1.** slowness; *(indugio)* delay **2.** *(prolissità)* prolixity.

lungagnàta, *s.f.* tiresome speech; rigmarole: *per scusarsi mi fece una* —, he told me a long rigmarole as an excuse.

lungaménte, *av.* long; for a long time: *ci ho pensato* —, I thought it over for a long time.

lunganimità, *V.* longanimità.

lúnge, *V.* lúngi.

lunghésso, *prep.* *(rar.)* along: — *il fiume*, along the river.

lunghézza, *s.f.* length: *la* — *di un campo*, the length of a field; — *di contatto*, *(mec.)* length of contact; — *di diffusione*, *(fis. atomica)* diffusion-length; — *d'onda*, *(rad.)* wave-length; — *totale*, overall length; — *utile*, *(mec.)* working length; *misura tre metri in* —, it is three metres in length; *vinto per una* —, *(spor.)* won by a length.

lúngi, *av.* *(poet.)* far: *non molto* — *da qui*, not very far from here; *questo è ben* — *dall'essere perfetto*, this is very far from (being) perfect ‖ *da* —, from afar.

lungimirànte, *ag.* far-sighted, far-seeing: *politica* —, far-sighted policy; *era un uomo* —, he was a far-sighted man.

lúngo, *ag.* **1.** long: *un* — *cammino*, a long way; *un* — *corteo*, a long procession; — *dieci metri*, ten metres long; *un* — *inverno*, a long winter; *un* — *sospiro*, a long-drawn sigh; *un* — *viaggio*, a long journey; *una lunga vita*, a long life; *calzoni lunghi*, long trousers; *cannone di lunga portata*, *(artigl.)* long-range gun; *capelli lunghi*, long hair; *capitano di* — *corso*, *(mar.)* captain of an ocean-going vessel; *lino a fibre lunghe*, *(ind. tessile)* long flax; *tiro* —, *(artigl.)* over; *troppo* —, too long; *era un discorso un po'* —, it was a somewhat lengthy speech; *è una lunga storia*, it is a long story; *in questa stagione le notti si fanno più lunghe*, at this season of the year the nights get longer; *morì dopo lunga malattia*, he died after a long illness; *non lo vedo da* — *tempo*, it is a long time since I saw him; *oggi hai la barba lunga*, you haven't had a shave to-day; *quel vecchio ha la barba lunga*, that old man has a long beard; *avere braccia, mani lunghe*, to have long arms, long hands; *aver gambe lunghe*, to be long-legged; *avere il naso* —, to have a long nose; *avere il viso, il collo* —, to have a long face, a long neck; *avere la vista lunga*, to be long-sighted; *(essere lungimirante)* to be far-sighted; *fare una lunga chiacchierata con qlcu.*, to have a long talk with s.o.; *percorrere la strada più lunga*, to take the longest way round ‖ — *disteso*, headlong: *cadde* — *disteso*, he fell headlong ‖ *a lunga scadenza*, long-dated ‖ *sono amici di lunga data*, they are friends of long standing ‖ *avere la lingua lunga*, *(essere chiacchierone)* to be a chatterbox; *(essere pettegolo)* to be a gossip ‖ *avere le mani lunghe*, *(esser ladro)*, to be light-fingered; *(esser maneschi)* to be very free with one's fists ‖ *fare la faccia lunga*, to pull a long face ‖ *fare il passo più* — *della gamba*, to overreach oneself **2.** *(alto)* tall: — *come un palo, come una pertica*, as tall as a lamp-post; *era* — —, he was ever so tall **3.** *(fam.)* *(lento)* slow: *sbrigati, quanto sei* — *!*, hurry up, how slow you are!; *essere* — *a fare ql.co.*, to take a long time doing sthg. ‖ *è* — *come la fame*, *(fam.)* he is painfully slow **4.** *(diluito)* weak, thin: *brodo* —, thin soup; *caffè* —, weak coffee; *vino* —, watered wine **5.** *(fonet.)* long: *sillaba, vocale lunga*, long syllable, vowel **6.** **(Fraseologia)** *a* —, a long time: *non ho atteso a* —, I have not waited long; *non voglio aspettare più a* —, I will not wait any longer ‖ *a* — *andare, alla lunga*, in the long run: *a* — *andare mi diventò simpatico*, I got to like him eventually ‖ *alla più lunga*, at the latest: *te lo dirò alla più lunga domani*, I will tell you tomorrow at the latest ‖ *di gran lunga*, far *(o by far)*: *è di gran lunga il migliore*, he is (by) far the best ‖ *di lunga mano*, over a long period: *il colpo era stato preparato di lunga mano*, the plot had been organized over a long period ‖ *in* — *e in largo*, everywhere *(o far and wide)* ‖ *per il* —, in length: *due metri per il* —, two metres in length ‖ *andare per le lunghe, tirare in* —, to take a long time: *questa faccenda va per le lunghe*, this business takes a long time ‖ *farla lunga*, to keep on: *come la fai lunga!*, how you keep on! ‖ *saperla lunga*, to know what's what ‖ *tirar di* —, to keep going.

lúngo, *prep.* **1.** **along:** — *il fiume*, along the river; *strisciava* — *il muro*, he was creeping along the wall **2.** *(durante)* **during:** — *il viaggio*, during the journey.

lungomàre, *s.m.* promenade; sea-front.

lungobànco, *s.m.* (*miner.*) drive.

lungometràggio, *s.m.* (*cine.*) feature film.

luògo, *s.m.* **1.** place; spot: — *abitato,* inhabited place; — *aperto,* open place; — *consacrato,* sacred place; — *d'affari,* place of business; *il — del delitto, del sinistro,* the scene of the crime, of the disaster; *il — della battaglia,* the site of the battle; — *di atterraggio,* (*aer.*) landing-strip (o landing-field); — *di destinazione, partenza, provenienza,* place of destination, departure, origin; — *di nascita,* place of birth (o birthplace); — *di passaggio,* thoroughfare; — *fortificato,* fortified place; *in nessun* —, nowhere; *in ogni* —, everywhere; *in qualsiasi* —, anywhere: *in qualsiasi — sia,* wherever it is (o may be); *sul* —, on the spot: *ero sul* —, I was on the spot; *usanze del* —, local customs; *non è del* —, he doesn't come (o he isn't) from here; *questo non è il — per farlo,* this is not the place to do it; *mettere ql.co. in un — sicuro,* to put sthg. in a safe place ‖ *i luoghi bui,* (*l'inferno*) the realms of darkness; *i Luoghi Santi,* the Holy Places (of Palestine); — *santo,* (*cimitero*) hallowed (o sanctified) ground ‖ — *comodo,* lavatory (o water-closet) ‖ — *comune,* commonplace (o cliché) ‖ — *di pena,* prison (o penitentiary) ‖ — *pio,* alms-house ‖ *a tempo e* —, at the proper time and place ‖ *fuori* —, out-of-place (o inopportune) ‖ *in — di,* instead of: *venne in — di suo fratello,* he came instead of his brother ‖ *in alto* —, (*altolocato*) in high circles (o places); (*influente*) influential ‖ *in primo* —, in the first place (o first of all o firstly); *in secondo* —, in the second place (o secondly) ‖ *unità di* —, (*teat.*) unity of place ‖ *questo quadro venne ritoccato in più luoghi,* this picture has been retouched (o touched up) in various places ‖ *tenne — di giudice,* he acted as judge ‖ *avere* —, to take place: *quando avrà — il matrimonio?,* when will the marriage take place?; *la riunione avrà — a Milano,* the meeting will be held in Milan; *lo scambio di corrispondenza che ha avuto — fra di noi,* the correspondence that has passed between us ‖ *dar — a ql.co.,* (*provocare*) to give rise to sthg.; (*condurre a*) to lead to sthg.: *azione che potrebbe dar — a delle critiche,* action open to criticism; *tutto dà — a credere che...,* everything leads us to believe that...; *dar — a dubbi,* to give rise to doubts; *dar — a lagnanze,* to give cause for complaint ‖ *non trovar* —, *fig.* not to find any peace **2.** (*spazio*) room: *non fate ressa, c'è — per tutti,* don't push, there is room for everybody; *fare — a qlcu.,* to make room for s.o. **3.** (*passo di uno scritto*) passage: — *oscuro,* obscure (o difficult) passage; *in certi luoghi della Divina Commedia,* in certain passages of the Divine Comedy; *nel — citato,* in the passage quoted **4.** (*dir.*): *non — a procedere,* non-suit: *pronunziare un non — a procedere,* to enter a non-suit **5.** — *geometrico,* locus (*pl.* loci).

luogotenènte, *s.m.* **1.** deputy **2.** (*mil.*) lieutenant.

luogotenènza, *s.f.* **1.** deputyship **2.** (*mil.*) lieutenantship.

lúpa, *s.f.* **1.** she-wolf ‖ *mal della* —, (*patol.*) bulimy (o bulimia) **2.** (*carie del legno*) dry-rot **3.** (*rete da pesca*) wolf.

lupacchiòtto, *s.m.* (*cucciolo di lupo*) wolf-cub; (*lupo giovane*) wolfling, young wolf.

lupàia, *s.f.* (*covo di lupi*) wolf-den.

lupanàre, *s.m.* brothel.

lupàtto, *V.* **lupacchiòtto.**

lupercàle, *ag. s.m.* Lupercal ‖ *i lupercali,* (*st. romana*) Lupercalia.

lupésco, *ag.* lupine, wolfish, wolvish.

lupinàio, *s.m.* **1.** (*venditore di lupini*) vendor of lupins **2.** (*campo di lupini*) field of lupins.

lupinèlla, *s.f.* (*bot.*) sainfoin.

lupíno[1], *ag.* lupine, wolfish, wolvish.

lupíno[2], *s.m.* (*bot.*) lupin(e).

lúpo, *s.m.* **1.** wolf: — *cerviero,* lynx; *cane* —, Alsatian dog (o wolf) ‖ — *di mare,* sea-dog; (*ittiol.*) sea perch ‖ — *mannaro,* (*licantropo*) werewolf; (*spauracchio infantile*) bog(e)y-man ‖ *in bocca al* — *!,* good luck! ‖ *tempo da lupi,* stormy weather ‖ *avere una fame da* —, to be as hungry as a hunter ‖ *gridare al* —, to cry wolf ‖ *mangiare come un* —, to wolf one's food down ‖ *il — cambia il pelo ma non il vizio, prov.* the leopard never changes his spots ‖ — *non mangia* —, *prov.* dog doesn't eat dog ‖ *chi ha il — per compare, porti il cane sotto il mantello, prov.* who has a wolf for his mate, needs a dog for his man ‖ *chi pecora si fa, il — se lo mangia, prov.* he that makes himself a sheep, shall be eaten by the wolf ‖ *dare le pecore in guardia al* —, *prov.* to give a wolf a wether to keep **2.** (*ind. tessile*) willow: — *cardatore,* carding willow; — *sfibratore,* teasing machine.

lúppolo, *s.m.* (*bot.*) hop.

lúpus, *s.m.* (*patol.*) lupus.

lúreo, *ag.* voracious; greedy, gluttonous.

luridézza, *s.f.* (*rar.*) filthiness, dirtiness (anche *fig.*).

lúrido, *ag.* filthy, dirty (anche *fig.*): *una lurida ferita,* a dirty wound; *un — individuo,* a dirty fellow; *non hai vergogna, con quelle mani luride?,* aren't you ashamed of your dirty hands?; *si trovò immischiato in quella lurida faccenda senza saperlo,* he found himself mixed up in that dirty business without even knowing it; *viveva in una lurida catapecchia,* he lived in a filthy hovel.

luridúme, *s.m.* filth, filthiness, dirt (anche *fig.*): *vivere nel* —, to live in a state of dirt.

lúsco, *ag.* (*rar.*) **1.**: *tra il — e il brusco,* at dusk **2.** *V.* **lósco.**

lusíade, *ag.s.c.* Lusitanian ‖ *« I Lusiadi »,* (*lett.*) "The Lusiads".

lusínga, *s.f.* **1.** allurement, enticement; (*adulazione*) flattery: *le lusinghe dei sensi,* the allurements of the senses; *le lusinghe di una donna,* a woman's allurements; *cercò di cattivarselo con delle lusinghe,* he tried to win him over by flattery; *era indifferente alle lusinghe della grande città,* he was indifferent to the attractions of the city; *possono più le lusinghe che le minacce,* flattery can do more than threats **2.** (*illusione*) illusion, false hope, delusion: *speravo di riuscire, ma era una* —, I hoped to succeed, but it was only a delusion; *vivere di lusinghe,* to live on one's illusions.

lusingaménto, *s.m.* (*rar.*) allurement, enticement.

lusingàre, *v.t.* **1.** to allure, to entice; (*adulare*) to flatter: *in fondo ne era lusingato,* in his heart of hearts he was very flattered (o gratified) by it; *non mi* —, don't flatter (o try to flatter) me; — *l'amor proprio di qlcu.,* to flatter s.o.'s vanity; — *una persona con promesse,* to entice a person with promises **2.** (*nutrire con vane speranze*) to deceive, to delude: *il medico lo lusingava riguardo alle sue condizioni,* the doctor deceived him as to his condition ‖ **lusingàrsi,** *v.r.* to flatter oneself; (*nutrire false speranze*) to delude oneself, to entertain illusions; (*sperare*) to hope: *mi lusingavo di poter riuscire,* I flattered myself that I could succeed; — *con vane speranze,* to delude oneself with false hopes.

lusingatóre, *ag.* flattering ‖ *s.m.,* **lusingatríce,** *s.f.* flatterer, wheedler.

lusinghévole, *ag.* enticing, alluring, tempting.

lusinghevolménte, *av.* enticingly, alluringly.

lusinghièro, *ag.* flattering; alluring, enticing, tempting: *lode lusinghiera,* flattering praise; *proposta lusinghiera,* tempting (o attractive) proposition; *ha avuto per te parole lusinghiere,* he spoke of you in flattering terms.

lusitàno, *ag.s.m.* Lusitanian.

lusòrio, *ag.*: *marina lusoria,* pleasure craft.

lussàre, *v.t.,* **lussàrsi,** *v.r.* to dislocate, to luxate: *mi son lussato una caviglia,* I dislocated my ankle.

lussazióne, *s.f.* dislocation, luxation.

Lussembúrgo, *no.pr.m.* (*geog.*) Luxemburg.

lússo, *s.m.* **1.** luxury: *io non posso permettermi il — di una vacanza,* I cannot afford the luxury of a holiday; *questo per me è un —,* this is a luxury for me; *vivere nel —,* to live in luxury; *vivere nel — più completo,* to live in the lap of luxury ‖ *di —,* luxury (*attributivo*); de luxe: *articoli di —,* luxury articles; *edizione di —,* de luxe edition; *hotel di —,* luxury (*o* de luxe) hotel; *tassa di —,* luxury tax **2.** (*pompa, ricchezza*) pomp, display, magnificence: *un magro articoletto con gran — di citazioni,* a weak article with a rich display of quotations; *era vestita con gran —, ma senza eleganza,* she was richly but by no means elegantly dressed ‖ *che —!,* how magnificent!.

lussuosaménte, *av.* luxuriously, richly, sumptuously.

lussuóso, *ag.* luxurious, rich, sumptuous: *una casa lussuosa,* a magnificent (*o* splendid) house.

lussureggiànte, *ag.* luxuriant: *la vegetazione — dei tropici,* the luxuriant vegetation of the tropics; *ha uno stile —,* he has a luxuriant style.

lussureggiàre, *v.i.* to be luxuriant, to thrive: *il grano lussureggiava quell'anno,* the corn was thriving that year.

lussúria, *s.f.* lust, lewdness, lasciviousness: *la — nasce dall'ozio e dagli agi,* idleness and comforts lead easily to lust.

lussuriosaménte, *av.* lustfully, lewdly, lasciviously.

lussurióso, *ag.* lustful, lewd, lascivious.

lústra, *s.f.* (*pretesa, finzione*) pretence: *fu tutta una —,* it was just show (*o* it was only pretence).

lustràle, *ag.* lustral: *giochi lustrali,* (*st. romana*) lustral games ‖ *acqua —,* (*st. romana*) lustral water; (*eccl.*) holy water.

lustraménto, *s.m.* polishing.

lustràre, *v.t.* **1.** to polish: *— i bottoni della divisa,* to polish the buttons on one's uniform; *— le casseruole,* to polish the (sauce)pans; *— mobili,* to polish furniture; *— scarpe,* to polish shoes ‖ *— (le scarpe a) qlcu.,* (*adularlo*) to lick s.o.'s shoes **2.** (*arc.*) to lustrate, to purify ‖ *v.i.* (*rar.*) to shine; to glow: *gli lustrano gli occhi dalle lacrime,* his eyes shine with tears; *le lustravano gli occhi dalla gioia,* her eyes glowed with joy.

lustrascàrpe, *s.m.* **1.** shoeblack; (*amer.*) shoeshine **2.** (*adulatore*) crawler, flatterer, adulator.

lustràta, *s.f.* polish, shine: *da' una — alle scarpe,* give your shoes a polish.

lustratóre, *s.m.,* **lustratríce,** *s.f.* polisher; (*di mobili*) French polisher.

lustrína, *s.f.* (*tessuto di seta*) lustrine.

lustríno, *s.m.* **1.** (*dischetto di materia lucida per guarnizioni di sartoria*) sequin: *un abito da sera ricamato a lustrini,* an evening dress trimmed with sequins **2.** (*lustrascarpe*) shoeblack; (*amer.*) shoeshine **3.** (*tessuto di seta*) lustrine.

lústro[1], *ag.* **1.** glowing; shining: *i suoi occhi erano lustri di felicità,* her eyes were glowing (*o* shining) with happiness; *i suoi occhi sono ancora lustri di pianto,* her eyes are still red with tears (*o* she still has tears in her eyes) **2.** (*lucidato*) polished; shiny: *una superficie lustra,* a shiny surface; *quella tavola è lustra,* that table is polished; *le tue scarpe sono così lustre che sembrano nuove,* your shoes are so shiny that they look new ‖ *s.m.* **1.** lustre; brilliance, gloss; sheen: *questo mobile, questa lastra di marmo ha perso il —,* this piece of furniture, this marble-top has lost its gloss (*o* brilliance) ‖ *la sua casa è sempre tirata a —,* her home is always spic and span ‖ *verniciare a —,* (*un mobile*) to varnish **2.** (*prestigio*) lustre, splendour; fame; prestige: *opere che hanno dato — al suo nome,* works which have made his name famous; *portò grande — all'università,* he brought great prestige to the University.

lústro[2], *s.m.* **1.** (*st. romana*) (*sacrificio di purificazione*) lustrum (*pl.* lustra, lustrums) **2.** (*spazio di cinque anni*) lustrum (*pl.* lustra, lustrums), lustre: *visse dieci lustri,* he lived fifty years.

luteína, *s.f.* (*biol.*) lutein.

lúteo, *ag.* **1.** (*giallo, aureo*) luteous **2.** (*anat.*): *corpo —,* corpus luteum; *macchia lutea,* macula lutea.

luteranésimo, luteranísmo, *s.m.* Lutheranism.

luteràno, *ag.s.m.* Lutheran.

Lutèro, *no.pr.m.* (*st. relig.*) Luther.

lutèzio, *s.m.* (*chim.*) lutetium.

lútto, *s.m.* **1.** mourning: *— nazionale,* national mourning; *— stretto,* full mourning; *abito da —,* mourning (dress); *carta listata a —,* mourning-paper (*o* black-edged paper); *mezzo —,* half mourning; *parato a —,* hung in black; *striscia da —,* mourning-band; *la sua morte fu un — generale,* his death was universally mourned; *tutta la nazione era in —,* the whole country was plunged into mourning; *essere in —,* to be in mourning; *mettere, smettere il —,* to go into, to come out of mourning; *portare il —,* to wear mourning **2.** (*disgrazia*) misfortune; (*dolore*) grief.

luttuosaménte, *av.* mournfully, dolefully.

luttuóso, *ag.* mournful, doleful, sorrowful; (*triste*) sad: *avvenimenti luttuosi,* doleful events; *notizie luttuose,* sad news.

lutulènto, *ag.* (*fangoso*) muddy.

M

m, *s.f.m.* **1.** (*undicesima lettera dell'alfabeto italiano*) m (*pl.* ms, m's) ‖ — *come Milano,* (*tel.*) m for Mary **2.** *M,* (*numero romano equivalente a mille*) M (one thousand).

ma, *cong.* **1.** (*avversativa*) **but, yet;** (*tuttavia*) **however, still:** *incredibile,* — *vero,* strange, but true; *dissi che non sarei andato,* — *più tardi cambiai idea,* I said I wouldn't go. Later, however, I changed my mind; *è povero,* — *onesto,* he is poor, but honest; *era terribilmente tardi,* — *decisi di andare,* it was terribly late; all the same (o even so) I decided to go (o I decided to go, though); *lei è carina,* — *sua sorella è veramente bella,* she is good-looking, but her sister is really beautiful; *ne mangio,* — *non molto spesso,* I do eat it, but not very often; *non penso di poterti aiutare,* — *farò ciò che posso,* I don't think I can help you; still, I'll do what I can; *sembra onesto,* — *non mi fido di lui,* he seems honest, but I don't trust him **2.** (*in principio di frase*) **but:** — *ormai è tempo di tornare all'argomento,* but let us return to the subject; — *ti dico che l'avevo visto,* but I tell you I saw it **3.** (*anzi*): *non bella,* — *bellissima,* not good-looking, absolutely beautiful; *non solo ricco,* — *anche generoso,* not only rich, but also generous **4.** (*rafforzativo, enfatico*): — *bravo!,* (*iron.*) that's a clever boy!; — *che!,* get along with you (o I don't believe it o not at all)!; — *come?,* (*come è possibile?*) but how?; — *davvero?,* really?; — *insomma, taci!,* for heaven's sake, shut up!; — *no!,* (*se esprime meraviglia*) no! (o really? o indeed?); (*se esprime negazione con enfasi*) certainly not (o not at all)!; — *si!,* — *come!,* why, certainly (o yes, sure o yes, I tell you)!; — *che cosa hai?,* what is the matter?; — *che vuoi da me?,* but what do you want with me?; — *no che non lo devi dire!,* you certainly mustn't say it; — *sì che è vero!,* indeed, it's quite true!; *ha parlato bene,* — *proprio bene!,* he spoke very well, very well indeed! **5.** (*ellittico*) « *Chi è quella donna?* », « *Ma!* », " Who is that woman? ", " God knows!".

ma, *s.m.* but: *i tuoi se e i tuoi* —, your ifs and buts; *c'è un* —, there is a but (o there is an objection to be made); *non c'è* — *che tenga,* but me no buts.

màcabro, *ag.* macabre, gruesome: *una storia macabra,* a gruesome story ‖ *danza macabra,* Dance Macabre (o Dance of Death).

macàco, *s.m.* **1.** (*zool.*) macaco, macaque **2.** (*uomo brutto, goffo e sciocco*) runt.

macadàm, *s.m.* (*selciato*) macadam.

macadamizzàre, *v.t.* (*selciare*) to macadamize.

macào, *s.m.* (*giuoco d'azzardo*) macao.

macaóne, *s.m.* (*entom.*) swallowtail (butterfly).

Macàrio, *no.pr.m.* (*st. eccl.*) Macarius.

Maccabèo, *ag.* Maccabean ‖ *no.pr.m.* Maccabaeus ‖ *i Maccabei,* the Maccabees.

maccheronàta, *s.f.* (*abundant*) dish of macaroni.

maccheróni, *s.m.pl.* macaroni (*sing.*): — *al gratin,* macaroni au gratin; — *fatti in casa,* home-made macaroni; *questi* — *sono buoni,* this macaroni is good ‖ *è venuto come il cacio sui* —, (*fam.*) it's just what the doctor ordered: *questa vacanza è venuta come il cacio sui* —, this holiday has come in the nick of time.

maccherònico, *ag.* macaronic.

màcchia¹, *s.f.* **1.** spot, stain, blot; (*piccola*) speck: — *di colore,* blob of colour; — *di fango,* spot of mud; — *d'inchiostro,* ink blot (o spot); *le macchie di un leopardo,* the spots of a leopard; — *di luce,* (*cine.*) hot-spot; — *di riflessione,* (*ott.*) flare-spot (o flare-ghost); — *di sangue,* bloodstain; — *di unto,* grease stain; — *di vino,* wine stain; — *fluorescente,* (*tv.*) fluorescent spot; *con macchie,* spotted; *marmo bianco con macchie nere,* white marble with black spots; *è rimasta la* —, the stain hasn't come out; *questa* — *non va via,* this stain won't come out; *il suo vestito era coperto di macchie,* her dress was covered with stains; *fare una* —, to make (o to leave) a dirty mark; *levare una* —, to take out (o to remove) a stain ‖ *particolare che fa* — *in un quadro,* detail that stands out in a picture **2.** *fig.* blemish, spot, stain, blot: *la* — *del peccato,* the stain (o taint) of sin; *una* — *sull'onore di qlcu.,* a blot on s.o.'s honour; *senza* —, spotless (o stainless): *cavaliere senza* — *e senza paura,* fearless and blameless knight; *nome, reputazione senza* —, unblemished (o spotless) name, reputation; *non ha macchie sulla coscienza,* he has nothing on his conscience; *lavare la* — *col sangue,* to wipe out a stain with blood **3.** (*med.*) macula, spot **4.** (*astr.*) spot: *macchie solari,* sunspots **5.** (*pitt.*) rough sketch: *fare, dipingere alla* —, to sketch.

màcchia², *s.f.* (*boscaglia*) maquis; bush, scrub ‖ *la* —, (*i partigiani francesi*), the Maquis ‖ *alla* —, (*clandestinamente*) clandestinely: *stampare un libro alla* —, to print a book clandestinely ‖ *darsi alla* —, to take to the bush (o maquis) ‖ *vivere alla* —, to be an outlaw.

macchiaiòlo¹, *s.m.* (*st. pitt.*) Florentine impressionist painter.

macchiaiòlo², *s.m.* bushman (*pl.* bushmen); woodsman (*pl.* woodsmen).

macchiàre, *v.t.* **1.** to stain, to spot; (*sporcare*) to soil: *egli aveva le mani macchiate di sangue,* he had bloodstained hands; *mi macchiò il vestito,* he stained my dress; — *di fango,* to spatter (o to bespatter) with mud; — *di vino,* to stain with wine **2.** *fig.* to stain, to spot, to sully, to blemish: *la sua reputazione è macchiata per sempre,* his reputation is stained for ever; — *il proprio onore,* to stain one's honour **3.** (*pitt.*) (*dipingere a macchia*) to sketch ‖ **macchiàrsi,** *v.r.* **1.** to get stained; (*sporcarsi*) to make oneself dirty, to get dirty: *si è macchiato le mani,* he dirtied his hands; *fig.* he sullied his hands; *stoffa che si macchia facilmente,* cloth that stains easily; *la tovaglia si è macchiata,* the table-cloth got stained **2.** *fig.* to soil (oneself), to sully (oneself): — *la reputazione,* to sully one's reputation.

macchiàto, *ag.* **1.** (*chiazzato*) spotted: *marmo* —, spotted marble ‖ *caffè* —, (*fam.*) coffee with a dash of milk **2.** (*di cavallo, ecc.*) dappled **3.** (*ind. cartaria*) foxed.

macchiétta, *s.f.* **1.** (*piccola macchia*) speck, little spot **2.** (*pitt.*) sketch, caricature **3.** (*persona stravagante*) eccentric person, character **4.** (*teat.*) character study.

macchiettàre, *v.t.* to speckle, to dapple.

macchiettìsta, *s.m.* **1.** (*teat.*) character actor **2.** (*caricaturista*) caricaturist.

màcchina, *s.f.* **1.** machine; engine; apparatus: — *a vapore,* steam-engine; — *automatica,* automatic; — *automatica a gettone,* slot-machine; — *calcolatrice,* calculating machine; — *compositrice,* (*tip.*) type-setting machine (o composing machine); — *cimatrice,* (*ind. tessile*) shearing machine; — *da cucire,* sewing-machine; — *da presa,* (*cine.*) cine-camera (o movie camera); — *da proiezione,* (*cine.*) projector; — *da scrivere,* typewriter; — *da stampa*, printing press (*o* printing-machine); — *di governo*, (*mar.*) steering engine; — *di guerra*, engine of war; — *di poppa, di sinistra*, (*mar.*) after, port engine; — *elettrica*, electric(al) machine; — *filatrice*, (*ind. tessile*) spinning-jenny; — *fotografica*, camera; — *in funzione*, working machine; — *lavapiatti, lavastoviglie*, dish-washing machine (*o* dishwasher); — *orlatrice*, (*ind. tessile*) hemming-machine; — *per il caffè*, coffee-machine; — *per cardare*, (*ind. tessile*) carding-machine (*o* carding-engine); — *per filettare*, (*filettatrice*), threader (*o* thread-cutting machine *o* threading-machine); — *per il controllo degli ingranaggi*, gear-testing machine; — *per incastonare*, (*gioielleria*) jewel-setting machine; — *per maglieria*, knitting-machine (*o* knitter); — *per la mietitura*, reaping-machine; — *per la prova di resistenza alla compressione*, compression-testing machine; — *per prove di trazione*, tensile-testing machine; — *per prove di urto*, impact-testing machine; — *per raschiare, levigare pavimenti*, floor-sander; — *per sollevamento*, hoisting-machine (*o* windlass); — *per tagliare*, cutting-machine; — *per zigrinare*, knurling-machine; — *piegafogli*, folding-machine; — *pressatrice*, pressing-machine; — *rompiselciato*, paving-breaker; — *rotativa*, rotary-machine (*o* rotary-engine); (*tip.*) rotary (*o* cylinder) printing-press; — *semplice, composta*, simple, compound machine; — *tagliacarte*, (*tip.*) paper-cutter; — *tagliatrice*, (*cine.*) slitting-machine; — *teatrale*, piece of theatre machinery; — *telescrivente*, teletypewriter (*o fam.* teletype); — *termica*, heat-engine; — *utensile*, machine-tool; *fatto a —*, machine-made; *lavorazione a —*, machine-work; *sala macchine*, engine-room; *andare in —*, (*di giornale, ecc.*) to go to press; *far andare una —*, to start a machine; *montare una —*, to assemble a machine (*o · fam.* to put together a machine); *smontare una —*, to dismantle a machine (*o fam.* to take a machine to pieces) ‖ *— burocratica*, bureaucratic machine (*o* red-tape) ‖ *—infernale*, infernal machine ‖ *— umana*, human machine ‖ *la processione delle macchine*, (*eccl.*) statue bearing procession ‖ *il secolo della —*, the machine-age ‖ *non è un uomo, è una —*, he is not a man, he is a machine 2. (*automobile*) car: — *da corsa*, racing-car; — *da turismo*, touring-car; — *decapotabile*, convertible; — *di lusso*, luxury car; — *di serie*, production-model; — *fuori serie*, car with special coachwork (*o amer.* custom-built car); — *utilitaria*, utility car; *eravamo in —*, we were driving; *siamo venuti in —*, we drove here; *andare in —*, to go by car (*o* to motor *o* to drive): *andammo in — a Como*, we drove (*o* motored) to Como; *partire in —*, to drive away 3. (*mus.*) (*tastiera di ottoni*) keys.

macchinàle, *ag.* mechanical, automatic(al): *un movimento —*, a mechanical (*o* automatic) movement.

macchinalménte, *av.* mechanically, automatically.

macchinàre, *v.t.* to plot; to scheme, to contrive: *che cosa state macchinando?*, what mischief are you plotting between you?; *egli macchina sicuramente ql.co. contro di me*, he is surely plotting sthg. against me; *egli macchina un tradimento*, he plots treason; *macchinarono di rovesciare i loro rivali*, they schemed to overthrow their rivals; *contro i propri amici*, to intrigue against one's own friends; — *di uccidere qlcu.*, to plot to kill s.o.

macchinàrio, *s.m.* machinery: — *per l'essiccazione*, (*ind. tessile*) drying machinery.

macchinatóre, *s.m.*, **macchinatríce**, *s.f.* machinator, intriguer, plotter.

macchinazióne, *s.f.* machination, intrigue, plot: *le macchinazioni dei nostri avversari*, the machinations of our opponents; *scoprire una — politica*, to discover a political plot (*o* intrigue).

macchinísmo, *s.m.* 1. (*meccanizzazione*) mechanization 2. (*meccanismo*) mechanism.

macchinísta, *s.m.* 1. machinist; (*ferr.*) engine-driver, (*amer.*) engineer 2. (*teat.*) scene-shifter.

macchinosaménte, *av.* complicatedly.

macchinóso, *ag.* complicated, complex: *è un romanzo con una trama macchinosa*, it is a novel with a complicated plot.

macèdone, *ag.s.c.* Macedonian.

Macedònia[1], *nu.pr.f.* (*geog.*) Macedonia.

macedònia[2], *s.f.* (*sigaretta*) Macedonia cigarette.

macedònia[3], *s.f.* (*cuc.*) fruit-salad; macedoine.

macellàbile, *ag.* fit for slaughtering: *vitelli macellabili*, calves for slaughter (*o* fit for slaughtering).

macellàio, *s.m.* 1. (*chi macella*) slaughterer; (*chi vende carne*) butcher: *negozio di —*, butcher's shop 2. *fig.* (*spreg.*) slaughterer, butcher: *quel chirurgo è un —*, that surgeon is a butcher.

macellàre, *v.t.* to slaughter, to butcher: *il macellaio macella una volta la settimana*, the butcher slaughters once a week.

macellatóre, *s.m.* slaughterer, butcher.

macellazióne, *s.f.* slaughter(ing).

macellería, *s.f.* butcher's shop.

macèllo, *s.m.* 1. (*luogo dove si macellano le bestie*) slaughter-house, shambles: *costruire un nuovo —*, to build a new slaughter-house 2. (*macelleria*) butcher's shop 3. (*il macellare*) slaughtering: *bestie da —*, animals for slaughter 4. (*massacro*) slaughter, butchery, shambles, massacre: *che —!*, (*fam.*) what a shambles!.

maceràre, *v.t.* 1. to soak, to steep: — *la carne nell'aceto*, to soak (*o* to steep) meat in vinegar; — *il pane nel latte*, to steep bread in milk 2. (*ind.*) to macerate; (*ind. tessile*) to ret; (*bozzoli*) to steep; (*pelli*) to bate; (*gomma*) to soak: — *il lino*, to steep (*o* to ret) flax 3. *fig.* (*affliggere, mortificare*) to mortify, to macerate: — *la carne*, to mortify the flesh ‖ **maceràrsi**, *v.r.* *fig.* (*struggersi*) to waste (away): *si macera dall'ansietà, dal dolore*, she is wasting away with anxiety, with sorrow; — *dal desiderio*, to pine away with longing.

maceràto, *ag.* 1. soaked, steeped: *carne macerata*, soaked (*o* steeped) meat 2. (*ind. tessile*) retted, steeped 3. *fig.* (*straziato*) distressed.

maceratóio, *s.m.* (*ind. tessile*) retting-pit, retting-ground, rettery.

maceratóre, *s.m.* (*ind. cartaria*) paper-pulping apparatus; macerator.

macerazióne, *s.f.* 1. soaking, steeping 2. (*ind.*) maceration; (*ind. tessile*) retting; (*di bozzoli*) steeping; (*di pelli*) bating; (*della gomma*) soaking: — *all'acqua calda*, warm-water retting 3. *fig.* (*mortificazione*) mortification: — *della carne*, mortification of the flesh.

macèrie, *s.f.pl.* rubble (*sing.*); débris (*sing.*); wreckage (*sing.*); ruins, remains: *le — di un edificio*, the ruins of a building; *la città è un cumulo di —*, the city is a mountain of rubble; *rimase sepolto sotto le —*, he lay buried under the débris.

màcero, *ag. V.* **maceràto** ‖ *s.m.* retting-ground, retting-pit.

machiavellésco, *ag.* (*rar.*) Machiavellian.

Machiavèlli, *no.pr.* (*st. lett.*) Machiavelli ‖ *è un —*, (*una persona astuta*) he is a Machiavelli.

machiavèllico, *ag.* Machiavellian; (*astuto*) crafty, cunning.

machiavellísmo, *s.m.* Machiavellism, Machiavellianism.

machiavellísta, *s.m.* Machiavellian, Machiavellist; (*persona astuta*) crafty schemer.

macígno, *s.m.* 1. hard sandstone: *questo pane è duro come un —*, *fig.* this bread is as hard as stone ‖ *è un —*, he is a blockhead ‖ *è un cuore di —*, he is hard-hearted (*o* he has a heart of stone) ‖ *quel libro è un —!*, what a bore that book is! 2. (*scheggione di rupe*) boulder, big stone.

macilènto, *ag.* emaciated, lean.

macilènza, *s.f.* emaciation, leanness.

màcina, *s.f.* grindstone, millstone: *le macine andavano tutto il giorno*, the wheels were grinding all day long ‖ *quel pacco è pesante come una —*, that parcel is very heavy.

macinàbile, *ag.* grindable.

macinacaffè, *s.m.* coffee-grinder, coffee-mill.

macinaménto, *V.* **macinazióne.**

macinapépe, *s.m.* pepper-grinder, pepper-mill.

macinàre, *v.t.* **1.** to grind; (*grano*) to mill, to grind || — *a due palmenti,* to eat voraciously || — *un patrimonio,* to run through an inheritance || *acqua passata non macina più, prov.* the mill cannot grind with the water that is past || *chi prima arriva, prima macina, prov.* first come, first served **2.** (*tritare minutamente*) to grind, to powder, to pound, to crush: — *colori,* (*pitt.*) to grind colours.

macinàta, *s.f.* **1.** grinding, milling: *dare una* —, to grind hastily **2.** (*quantità macinata di volta in volta*) quantity ground at a time.

macinàto, *ag.* ground, milled: *colori macinati a olio,* (*pitt.*) oil-colours || *s.m.* meal; flour || *tassa sul* —, (*st.*) tax on flour.

macinatóio, *s.m.* (*frantoio*) olive-press.

macinatóre, *ag.* grinding, milling || *s.m.,* **macinatríce,** *s.f.* grinder, miller.

macinatúra, *s.f.* **1.** grinding, milling **2.** (*spesa della macinazione*) grinding-fee, cost of milling.

macinazióne, *s.f.* grinding, milling: *finezza di* —, fineness of grinding; *pista circolare di* —, (*di un mulino*) bottom grinding ring.

macinèllo, *s.m.* (*pitt.*) muller.

macinìno, *s.m.* **1.** grinder, mill: — *da caffè,* coffee-grinder (*o* coffee-mill); — *per pepe,* pepper-mill **2.** (*scherz.*) (*automobile piccola e malandata*) old crock; jalop(p)y.

macinío, *s.m.* grinding.

màcis, *s.f.* (*bot.*) mace.

maciúlla, *s.f.* brake, scutch.

maciullàre, *v.t.* **1.** to brake, to scutch: — *canapa, lino,* to brake hemp, flax **2.** (*stritolare*) to crush: *il suo corpo fu maciullato dal treno,* his body was crushed by the train **3.** (*scherz.*) (*mangiare*) to devour; (*masticare*) to chew.

macolàre, macolàto, *V.* **maculàre, maculàto.**

macramé, *s.m.* macramé.

macrocefalía, *s.f.* (*med.*) macrocephaly.

macrocèfalo, *ag.* (*med.*) macrocephalous.

macrocòsmo, *s.m.* macrocosm.

macroglòssa, *s.f.* (*entom.*) humming-bird moth, hawk-moth.

macroglossía, *s.f.* (*med.*) macroglossia.

macromelía, *s.f.* (*med.*) macromelia.

macropsía, *s.f.* (*med.*) macropsia.

macroscòpico, *ag.* macroscopic.

màcula, *s.f.* (*med.*) macula (*pl.* maculae; macule: — *acustica, lutea,* macula acustica, lutea.

maculàre, *v.t.* **1.** (*ammaccare*) to bruise: — *un frutto,* to bruise a fruit **2.** (*macchiare*) to stain, to tarnish (anche *fig.*).

maculàto, *ag.* **1.** spotted, speckled **2.** *fig.* stained.

madàma, *s.f.* Madam.

madamigèlla, *s.f.* Mademoiselle.

madapolàm, *s.m.* madapol(l)am.

Maddaléna, *no.pr.f.* Magdalen(e), Madel(e)ine: *fare da Marta e da* —, to be a Jack-of-all-trades || *dim.* Maud(e).

Madèra, *no.pr.f.* (*geog.*) Madeira || **madèra,** *s.m.* Madeira (wine).

màdia, *s.f.* **1.** (*cassa in cui lievitare la pasta per pane*) kneading trough **2.** (*credenza*) kitchen cupboard.

màdido, *ag.* wet, soaked: — *di sudore,* bathed in perspiration (*o* sweat).

madière, *s.m.* (*mar.*) floor; (*di nave in legno*) floor timber; (*di nave in ferro*) floor plate: — *continuo,* continuous floor; — *intercostale,* intercostal floor.

madònna, *s.f.* (*arc.*) (*titolo d'onore*) Lady, Madonna; My Lady: — *Laura,* Madonna Laura; *vi prego, Madonna, di perdonarmi,* I ask you to forgive me, My Lady || **Madònna,** (*la Vergine*) the Virgin Mary, Our Lady, (the) Madonna: *la* — *di Loreto,* Our Lady of

Loreto || — *santa!,* Good Lord (*o* Heavens)! || *le Madonne di Raffaello,* Raphael's Madonnas.

madonnína, *s.f.* (*iron.*) (*donna dall'aria compunta*) prude, little hypocrite || *fa la* —, *ha un'aria da* — *infilzata,* butter wouldn't melt in her mouth.

madóre, *s.m.* (*letter.*) perspiration.

madornàle, *ag.* huge, enormous; gross: *errore* —, huge mistake (*o* gross blunder).

madornalità, *s.f.* hugeness, enormity; grossness.

madràga, *s.f.* (*rete da pesca*) tunny-net.

màdre, *s.f.* **1.** mother: *senza* —, motherless; *è il ritratto di sua* —, she is the very image of her mother; *ella è* — *di famiglia,* she is the mother of a family; *la rese* —, he gave her a child (*o fam.* he put her in the family way); *mia* — *non è in casa,* mother isn't in; *quand'è la festa, la giornata della* —?, when is Mother's Day?; *salutatemi vostra* —, kindly remember me to your mother; *divenir* —, to bear (*o* to give birth to) a child || — *lingua,* mother-tongue || — *terra,* mother-earth || *casa* —, (*comm.*) head office; (*di ordini religiosi*) mother-house || *chiesa* —, mother-church || *ragazza* —, unmarried mother || *regina* —, Queen Mother || *Santa Madre Chiesa,* Holy Mother (the) Church || *come l'ha fatto la* —, in one's birthday suit (*o* mother-naked) || *onora il padre e la* —, honour thy father and thy mother || *la* — *pietosa fa la figlia tignosa, prov.* spare the rod and spoil the child **2.** (*eccl.*) Mother: — *badessa,* Abbess; — *superiora,* Mother Superior; *reverenda* —, Reverend Mother **3.** (*anat.*) mater: *dura, pia* —, dura, pia (mater) **4.** (*chim.*) mother: — *dell'aceto,* mother (of vinegar); *acqua* —, mother-water (*o* liquor *o* mother-lye).

madreggiàre, *v.i.* to take after one's mother.

madrepàtria, *s.f.* mother-country, fatherland, native land.

madrepèrla, *s.f.* mother-of-pearl, nacre: *bottone di* —, pearl-button.

madreperlàceo, *ag.* pearly, nacreous.

madrèpora, *s.f.* (*zool.*) madrepore.

madrepòrico, *ag.* (*zool.*) madreporic, madreporiform; madrepore (*attributivo*): *banco* —, madrepore reef.

madresélva, *s.f.* (*bot.*) honeysuckle, woodbine.

madrevíte, *s.f.* (*mec.*) **1.** nut screw, female thread: — *di tornio,* lead screw **2.** (*filiera*) die: — *per bulloni,* bolt die; — *per tubi,* pipe die.

Madrid, *no.pr.f.* (*geog.*) Madrid.

madrigàle, *s.m.* (*mus. poes.*) madrigal.

madrigaleggiàre, *v.i.* (*mus. poes.*) **1.** (*cantare madrigali*) to sing madrigals **2.** (*comporre madrigali*) to compose madrigals.

madrigalésco, *ag.* (*rar.*) (*mus. poes.*) madrigal (*attributivo*).

madrigalísta, *s.c.* (*mus. poes.*) madrigalist.

madrígna, *V.* **matrígna.**

madrilèno, *ag.s.m.* Madrilenian.

madrína, *s.f.* godmother: — *della nuova nave sarà la signora X.Y.,* the new ship will be launched by Mrs. X.Y.; *è stata mia* — *di battesimo,* she was my godmother.

madróso, *ag.* (*min.*) porous, honeycombed.

maestà, *s.f.* **1.** majesty; (*imponenza, grandiosità*) majesty, stateliness; grandeur: *la* — *della legge,* the majesty of the law; *la* — *dell'impero romano,* the grandeur of the Roman Empire; *la* — *del paesaggio,* the grandeur of the landscape; *la* — *del suo portamento,* the majesty (*o* stateliness) of her bearing **2.** (*titolo*): *Maestà,* Your Majesty; *la Maestà del Re, della Regina, Sua Maestà* (*il Re*), (*la Regina*), His Majesty, the King, Her Majesty, the Queen; *la loro Maestà,* Their Majesties; (*formula di cortesia*) Your Majesties || *delitto di lesa* —, (*dir.*) lèse-majesté (*o* high treason) || *la Divina Maestà,* God **3.** (*pitt.*) Majesty: *fu commesso al pittore di dipingere una* —, the painter was entrusted with the painting of a Majesty **4.** (*tabernacolo su strade*) wayside shrine.

maestosaménte, *av.* majestically: *l'imperatore avanzò — tra gli applausi del suo popolo,* the Emperor proceeded majestically, cheered by his people.

maestosità, *s.f.* majesty, stateliness; grandeur, magnificence: *la — delle Alpi,* the grandeur (o majesty) of the Alps; *la — di una reggia,* the magnificence (o grandeur) of a royal palace.

maestóso, *ag.* majestic, stately; imposing, grand, magnificent: *aspetto —,* stately (o imposing) appearance; *edificio —,* stately building; *l'incedere — del re,* the stately bearing of the King; *spettacolo —,* magnificent (o grand) sight; *tono —,* imposing tone.

maèstra, *s.f.* **1.** mistress; *(insegnante)* teacher: *— di ballo,* dancing-mistress; *— di cucito,* needlework mistress; *— di musica,* music mistress; *— elementare,* elementary school-teacher; *— giardiniera,* nursery school-teacher; *è una buona —,* she is a good teacher ‖ *la Grecia era la — delle arti,* Greece was the mistress of the arts **2.** *(donna molto abile):* è *— nel giardinaggio,* she has green fingers; *quella ragazza è — nel mentire,* (scherz.) that girl is a past-master at lying **3.** *(sarta)* tailoress (who teaches apprentices) **4.** *(mar.) (vela maestra)* mainsail: *albero di —,* mainmast.

maestràle, *s.m.* *(vento)* mistral.

maestrànza, *s.f.* skilled workers *(pl.)*, skilled workmen *(pl.)*, skilled hands *(pl.)*: *le maestranze,* skilled workers.

maestrévole, *ag.* masterly.

maestrevolménte, *av.* in a masterly manner.

maestría, *s.f.* **1.** skill, ability, mastery: *con grande —,* very skilfully (o in a masterly manner o with great skill): *il concerto fu diretto con grande —,* the concert was conducted with great skill (o in a masterly manner); *mostrò rara — nel verso sciolto,* he showed rare skill in writing blank verse; *la sua — del pennello fu universalmente riconosciuta,* his mastery of the brush (o skill in painting) was universally acknowledged **2.** *(scaltrezza)* cunning: *con —,* cunningly: *uscì dalla difficile situazione con —,* he got out of the difficult situation by cunning.

maèstro[1], *ag.* **1.** *(principale)* main: *albero —,* (mar.) mainmast; *muro —,* (edil.) main wall; *strada maestra,* highroad (o main road); *vela maestra,* (mar.) mainsail **2.** *(abile, magistrale)* masterly, skilful: *colpo —,* masterly stroke; *mano maestra,* skilful hand; *con mano maestra,* skilfully (o in a masterly manner) ‖ *tirare un colpo — a qlcu.,* to play a dirty trick on s.o. ‖ *s.m.* **1.** master; *(insegnante)* teacher: *— di ballo,* dancing-master; *— elementare,* elementary school-teacher; *— di scherma,* fencing-master; *— di scuola,* schoolmaster; *è — della seconda classe,* he is the teacher of the second-year class ‖ *il Maestro,* (Bibbia) the Master ‖ *— d'ascia,* carpenter; *(mar.)* shipwright ‖ *— di casa,* butler; *(su una nave)* chief steward ‖ *— di cerimonie,* Master of Ceremonies ‖ *Gran Maestro (di ordine cavalleresco),* Grand Master ‖ *il dolore è — di virtù,* sorrow teaches us virtue ‖ *l'esercizio è buon —,* prov. practice makes perfect **2.** *(uomo abile, dotto)* master: *è — nell'arte del pennello,* he is a master of the brush; *non tutti possono essere maestri,* all men can't be masters ‖ *i Maestri del Rinascimento,* the masters of the Renaissance ‖ *è — di inganni,* he is a past-master in deceit **3.** *(mus.)* conductor; master; maestro *(pl. maestri, maestros):* *— concertatore e direttore d'orchestra,* conductor; *— del coro,* chorus-master; *— di cappella,* chapel-master.

maèstro[2], *s.m.* *(maestrale)* mistral (north-westerly wind).

màfia, *s.f.* Mafia ‖ *fare la —,* (gergo) to be dolled up.

mafióso, *ag.* of the Mafia ‖ *s.m.* Mafia member.

màga, *s.f.* sorceress, enchantress; *(strega)* witch.

magàgna, *s.f.* **1.** *(difetto)* flaw, fault, blemish, defect, imperfection (anche *fig.*): *frutta con delle magagne,* spoilt (o damaged) fruit; *c'è qualche — in queste gemme,* there are some imperfections (o faults) in these gems;

ci deve essere sotto qualche —, there must be something wrong there; *è un bravo ragazzo, ma il suo carattere ha qualche —,* he is a good boy, but there are some flaws in his character; *sa ben coprire le sue magagne,* he is quite good at covering up his defects **2.** *(acciacco)* ailment, infirmity: *son vecchio e pieno di magagne,* I am old, and full of aches and pains.

magagnàre, *v.t.* *(rar.)* **1.** to spoil, to damage **2.** *fig. (corrompere)* to taint, to corrupt.

magagnàto, *ag.* *(guasto)* spoilt, blemished.

magagnatúra, *s.f.* *(rar.)* **1.** spoiling, flawing **2.** *V.* **magàgna.**

magàri, *av.* **1.** *(perfino)* **even:** *è capace — di fare lo gnorri,* he is even capable of feigning ignorance; *potrebbe — finire in una bolla di sapone,* it might even come to nothing **2.** *(forse)* **perhaps, maybe:** *— ti vedrò domani,* I shall see you tomorrow perhaps ‖ *cong.* **even if:** *— dovessi tornarci dieci volte, lo vedrò!,* even if I have to come back ten times, I'll see him! ‖ *inter.* **if only...:** *— venisse!,* I wish he would come (o if only he would come) ‖ *—!,* *(fam.)* not half (o you bet o and how)!: « *Ti piacerebbe andare a Londra gratis?* », « *—!* », "would you like to have a free trip to London?", "I certainly would (o fam. not half o you bet o and how)!".

magazzinàggio, *s.m.* *(comm.)* storage: *spese di —,* storage-charges.

magazzinière, *s.m.* store-keeper, warehouseman *(pl.* warehousemen), warehouse-keeper.

magazzíno, *s.m.* **1.** warehouse, storehouse, store; *(militare)* depot: *— di deposito,* depository; *— doganale, generale,* (comm.) bonded warehouse; *— merci,* (ferr.) goods-shed; *in —,* in store: *merci in —,* goods on hand; *piccolo —,* storeroom; *ricevuta di —,* (amm.) warehouse receipt; *mettere in —,* to house (o to store); *sbarazzare il —,* to clear off the stock ‖ *un — di scienza,* a store of learning ‖ *fondi di —,* unsold stock **2.** *(negozio)* store, department-store; *(all'ingrosso)* wholesale-store: *magazzini a catena,* chain-stores; *un — a prezzi popolari,* a low-price store; *ha aperto un nuovo — in periferia,* he has opened a new wholesale-store in the suburbs ‖ *grandi magazzini,* big stores.

Magdebúrgo, *no.pr.m.* *(geog.)* Magdeburg.

Magellàno, *no.pr.* *(st.)* Magellan ‖ *Stretto di —,* *(geog.)* Straits of Magellan.

maggèngo, *ag.: fieno —,* first-crop hay.

maggesàre, *v.t.* *(agr.)* to fallow.

maggesàto, *ag.* *(agr.)* fallow.

maggése, *ag.: fieno —,* first-crop hay; *ulive maggesi,* May olives ‖ *s.m.* fallow land.

maggiaiuòlo, *ag.* *(rar.)* May *(attributivo): feste maggiaiuole,* May Day festivities.

maggiàtico, *s.m.* *(agr.)* fallow land.

màggio, *s.m.* May: *— fiorito,* blooming May; *feste di —,* May-Day festivities; *il primo —,* (Calendimaggio) May Day; *(festa dei lavoratori)* Labour Day ‖ *il — della vita,* springtime of life ‖ *un'acqua di —,* healing rain (o a refreshing shower) ‖ *fresca e bella come una rosa di —,* sweet and fresh as a rose in May ‖ *è una rosa di —,* she is as lovely as a rose in May ‖ *ha più soldi che non ha foglie il —,* he has more money than he can count ‖ *aspettar che venga —,* to wait for the silver lining.

maggiolàta, *s.f.* May song.

maggiolíno[1], *s.m.* *(entom.)* cockchafer, May-bug.

maggiolíno[2], *s.m.* *(mobile)* article of inlaid furniture made by Maggiolini (18th century).

maggioràna, *s.f.* *(bot.)* marjoram.

maggiorànza, *s.f.* **1.** majority, the greater number, the greater part; most: *la — degli Italiani,* most Italians; *la — della nazione, del paese,* the majority of the nation, the greater part of the country; *nella — dei casi,* in most cases; *la — dei suoi amici era con lui,* most of his friends were with him; *la — della gente lo ha dimenticato,* most people have forgotten him; *l'opinione della* —, the majority opinion 2. (*dir. pol.*) majority: — *assoluta*, absolute majority; — *dei due terzi*, two-thirds majority; *a* —, by majority: *a* — *di voti*, by a majority of votes; *elezione a* —, election by a majority; *verdetto a* —, majority verdict; *il partito di* —, the majority party; *la* — *è favorevole, sfavorevole*, the ayes, the noes have it; *la* — *è scarsa*, the majority is small; *fu eletto con una* — *di dieci voti*, he was elected by a majority of ten votes; *la proposta di legge fu approvata con una* — *di venti voti*, the bill was carried (*o* passed) with a majority of twenty votes; *avere la* —, to be in the majority; *riportare la* —, to secure a majority.

maggioràre, *v.t.* (*comm.*) to increase, to raise, to put up: *il prezzo è stato maggiorato*, the price has been put up; — *una fattura del 10 %*, to put 10 % on an invoice (*o* on a bill).

maggiorascàto, *s.m.* (*st.*) right of primogeniture.

maggioràsco, *s.m.* (*dir. st.*) 1. (*beni trasmessi*) estate and title received by right of primogeniture 2. (*il trasmettere in maggiorasco*) passing of estate and title to the eldest son.

maggioràto, *ag.* (*comm.*) increased, raised, put up: *la fattura è maggiorata della nostra commissione*, we have added our commission to the invoice (*o* bill).

maggiorazióne, *s.f.* (*comm.*) increase, rise; additional charge.

maggiordòmo, *s.m.* 1. butler, major-domo; house-steward 2. (*st.*) major-domo.

maggióre, *ag.* 1. (*più grande*) comp. **greater,** *superl. rel.* **the greatest;** (*più ampio*) comp. **larger,** *superl. rel.* **the largest;** (*più grosso*) comp. **bigger,** *superl. rel.* **the biggest;** (*più alto*) comp. **higher,** *superl. rel.* **the highest:** *il* — *offerente*, the highest bidder; *con* — *fretta, prudenza*, with greater haste, care; *la parte* — *di ql.co.*, the bulk (*o* the greater part) of sthg.; *è il nostro* — *poeta*, he is our greatest poet; *ho dovuto pagare una somma* —, I had to pay a bigger (*o* a larger) amount; *il Po è il* — *fiume d'Italia*, the Po is the largest river in Italy; *San Pietro è il* — *tempio della cristianità*, St. Peter is the biggest church in the Christian world (*o* in Christendom); *la sua autorità è* — *della mia*, his authority is greater than mine ‖ *il* — *bene*, the greatest good ‖ *la* — *parte*, the most part; (*la maggioranza*) the majority: *la* — *parte votò contro*, the majority voted against; *per la* — *parte erano cinesi*, for the most part they were Chinese (*o* they were for the most part Chinese) ‖ *la* — *parte di*, most (of): *la* — *parte della gente crede che...*, most people think that...; *la* — *parte del tempo non fa niente*, most of the time he does nothing; *la* — *parte di noi andò con lui*, most of us went with him ‖ *alberi maggiori*, (*mar.*) the main masts ‖ *altare* —, high altar ‖ *le arti maggiori*, (*st.*) the major arts ‖ *astri maggiori*, (*astr.*) major stars; *fig.* the greatest figures ‖ *forza* —: *caso di forza* —, case of absolute necessity; *rifiutare ql.co. per causa di forza* —, to refuse sthg. for imperative reasons ‖ *gli ordini maggiori*, (*eccl.*) the major (*o* the greater) orders ‖ *la chiesa di San Domenico Maggiore*, the church of St. Dominic the Greater ‖ *il Lago Maggiore*, (*geog.*) Lake Maggiore ‖ *andare per la* —, to be very popular (*o* to be all the rage) 2. (*più vecchio*) comp. **older,** *superl. rel.* **the oldest;** (*di fratelli*) comp. (*solo nell'uso attributivo*) **elder** (*fra due*), **eldest** (*fra molti*); *superl. rel.* **the elder** (*fra due*), **the eldest** (*fra molti*): *chi è il* — *dei due fratelli?*, who is the elder of the two brothers?; *ella, mia sorella è* — *di me di cinque anni*, she, my sister is five years older than I am; *Giovanni è il mio fratello* —, John is my eldest (my elder) brother; *la mia sorella* — *è all'estero*, my elder (my eldest) sister is abroad; *sono alti uguali e non si vede chi sia il* —, they are the same height and you can't tell which is older ‖ *il* — *dei Brown*, (*a scuola*) Brown major ‖ — *età, età* —, majority (*o* full age): *raggiungere la* — *età*, to attain one's majority (*o* to

come of age); — *d'età*, (*maggiorenne*) of (full) age ‖ *Scipione, il Maggiore*, (*st.*) Scipio the Elder 3. (*mat. mus. log.*) major: *asse* —, (*mat.*) major axis; *do* —, (*mus.*) C major; *premessa* —, (*log.*) major premise; *terza* —, (*mus.*) major third; *tono* —, (*mus.*) major key 4. (*mil.*): *aiutante* —, adjutant; (*corpo di*) *stato* —, general staff; *capo di stato* —, chief of staff; *ufficiale di stato* —, staff-officer; *sergente* —, sergeant-major; *tamburo* —, drum-major ‖ *s.m.* 1. (*di grado*) superior; (*di età*) elder: *il minore deve cedere il passo al* —, one must give way to one's elders; one must give way to one's superiors 2. (*mil.*) major; (*aer.*) squadron-leader: — *generale*, major-general 3. *pl.* (*di età*) elders; (*antenati*) ancestors; (*maggiorenti*) personages, elders (of a city): *i maggiori della città si presentarono al re*, the elders of the city came before the King; *rispettiamo i nostri maggiori*, we must respect our elders.

maggiorènne, *ag.* (*dir.*) of age: *diventare* —, to come of age; *essere* —, to be of age ‖ *s.m.* (*dir.*) adult.

maggiorènte, *s.m.* personage, elder (of a city).

maggiorità, *s.f.* (*mil.*) regimental office; orderly room.

maggioritàrio, *ag.* majority (*attributivo*): *voto* —, majority vote ‖ *i maggioritari*, the majority.

maggiorménte, *av.* 1. more: *dovresti concentrarti* — *nel tuo lavoro*, you should concentrate more on your work 2. (*ancora di più, a maggior ragione*) **much more, even more:** *se a me dispiace, a te dovrebbe dispiacere* —, if it displeases me, it should displease you even more 3. (*tanto più*) (**all**) **the more:** *fui* — *sorpreso dal momento che lo conoscevo bene e non mi sarei mai aspettato ciò*, I was (all) the more surprised as I knew him very well and should never have expected such a thing; *meno sono le gioie della vita,* — *le apprezziamo*, the fewer the joys of life, the more we value them.

maggiostrìna, *s.f.* (hard) straw hat, boater.

màgi, *s.m.pl.* Magi: *i tre Magi*, the three Magi.

magìa, *s.f.* 1. magic: — *bianca*, white magic; — *naturale*, natural magic; — *nera*, black magic (*o* art) ‖ *per* —, by magic 2. *fig.* (*fascino*) charm, witchery: *la* — *del suo dolce sorriso*, the witchery of her sweet smile; *rimanere vittima della* — *di qlcu.*, to fall a victim to s.o.'s charms.

màgiaro, *ag.s.m.* Magyar.

magicaménte, *av.* 1. magically 2. (*abilmente*) skilfully.

màgico, *ag.* 1. magic(al): *arti magiche*, magic arts; *bacchetta magica*, magic wand; *cerchio* —, magic circle; *parole magiche*, magic words ‖ *lanterna magica*, magic lantern ‖ *occhio* —, (*fis.*) visual tuning indicator; (*fam.*) magic eye 2. (*incantevole*) magical; enchanting, delightful: *quei colori fanno un effetto* —, those colours have a magical effect.

màgio, *V.* **màgi.**

magióne, *s.f.* (*letter.*) mansion, abode, dwelling.

magìsmo, *s.m.* (*st. persiana*) Magism, Magianism.

magistèrio, magistèro, *s.m.* 1. (*abilità di maestro*) skill, ability: *con gran* — *di stile*, with masterly style; *ammirare il* — *dei colori*, to admire the skill of the colouring 2. (*professione di maestro*) teaching: *darsi al* —, to devote oneself to teaching; *esercitare il* —, to teach ‖ *scuola di* —, teachers' training college 3. (*ufficio che sta a capo di un ordine cavalleresco*) Mastership: *gran* —, Grand-Mastership 4. (*farm.*) magistery: — *di bismuto*, magistery of bismuth.

magistràle, *ag.* 1. magistral: *cattedra* —, teaching post; *scuola* —, (teachers') training school 2. (*cattedratico*) magisterial: *aria* —, magisterial air; *in tono* —, in a magisterial tone 3. (*eccellente, da maestro*) excellent, masterly: *colpo* —, (*fam.*) masterly stroke; *opera* —, masterly (*o* excellent) work; *l'esecuzione della sinfonia fu* —, the execution of the symphony was masterly.

magistralménte, *av.* skilfully, in a masterly manner: *è un libro scritto* —, it's a skilfully written book.

magistràto, *s.m.* **1.** (*funzionario*) official; authority: *il Sindaco è il primo — della città*, the Mayor is the first authority of the town **2.** (*di tribunale*) Magistrate; Justice of the Peace: *i Magistrati*, the Bench; *il — d'accusa*, the Public Prosecutor; *— d'appello*, Court of Appeal Judge; *in qualità di —*, in his magisterial capacity; *è —*, he sits on the Bench; *è un — incorruttibile*, he is an incorruptible magistrate; *diventare —*, to be raised to the Bench.

magistratúra, *s.f.* **1.** magistracy, magistrature **2.** (*l'insieme dei Magistrati*) the Bench, the magistracy: *la — fu d'accordo che...*, the Bench agreed that....

màglia¹, *s.f.* **1.** stitch: *— a diritto, a rovescio*, plain stitch, purl (stitch); *calze, guanti a —*, knitted stockings, gloves; *lavoro a —*, knitting; *mi è caduta una —*, I've dropped a stitch; *questa giacca è a — rasata*, this cardigan is plain knitted; *aumentare una —*, to add a stitch; *fare la —, lavorare a —*, to knit (*o* to do one's knitting); *riprendere una —*, to pick up a stitch || *gli manca una —!*, (*fam. scherz.*) he has a screw loose **2.** (*di rete, staccio, ecc.*) mesh: *— di uno staccio*, mesh of a sieve; *rete a maglie rade, fitte*, wide-mesh, close-mesh net; *rete con maglie di mezzo pollice*, net with half-inch mesh; *i pesciolini scappano attraverso le maglie*, the little fish get through the net **3.** (*indumento*) vest; (*nell'abbigliamento sportivo*) jersey: *— dei calciatori*, football jersey; *egli porta sempre la — di lana*, he always wears a woollen vest **4.** (*mec.*) (*di catena*) link: *— a molinello*, swivel-link; *— per cingoli da trattore*, tractor track-link **5.** (*di armatura medioevale*) mail: *cotta di —*, coat of mail.

màglia², *s.f.* (*med.*) albugo, leucoma.

magliàia, *s.f.*, **magliàio**, *s.m.* hosier.

maglierìa, *s.f.* **1.** (*articoli di maglia*) hosiery, knitted goods (*pl.*): *macchina per —*, knitting-machine **2.** (*negozio*) hosier's (shop).

magliétta, *s.f.* **1.** (*per attaccare un quadro*) ring **2.** (*anello della cinghia su un fucile*) sling swivel **3.** (*di abiti, per infilarvi un gancino*) eye.

magliétto, *s.m.* (*mar.*) **1.** mallet **2.** (*per fasciare funi*) serving-mallet.

maglifício, *s.m.* knitted goods factory.

màglio, *s.m.* **1.** mallet **2.** (*mec.*) hammer: *— a caduta libera*, drop-hammer; *— a comando meccanico*, power-hammer; *— ad aria compressa*, (compressed-) air hammer; *— a leva*, helve (*o* trip)-hammer; *— a vapore*, steam-hammer; *— pneumatico*, pneumatic hammer; *sbozzatura al —*, hammer-cogging; *stampaggio al —*, drop-forging **3.** (*spor.*) (*cricket*) mallet.

maglióne, *s.m.* sweater, pullover.

magliuòlo, *s.m.* (*agr.*) vine-shoot.

màgma, *s.m.* (*geol. chim.*) magma (*pl.* magmata, magmas).

magnàlio, *s.m.* (*metal.*) magnalium.

magnanimaménte, *av.* magnanimously, nobly; generously: *pene sofferte —*, sufferings nobly borne.

magnanimità, *s.f.* magnanimity, noble-mindedness, generosity.

magnànimo, *ag.* magnanimous, noble; generous: *il — Cesare*, noble-minded (*o* magnanimous *o* noble) Caesar; *una magnanima impresa*, a noble undertaking; *il suo — cuore*, his noble heart; *è stato un — sacrificio*, it was a noble sacrifice; *si mostrò —*, he showed himself magnanimous || *di magnanimi lombi*, (*iron.*) high-born.

magnàno, *s.m.* (lock)smith.

magnàte, *s.m.* **1.** (*st.*) magnate: *i magnati di Ungheria, di Polonia*, the magnates of Hungary, of Poland **2.** (*riccone*) magnate; (*fam.*) tycoon: *un — del petrolio*, an oil magnate; *è un famoso —*, he is a famous tycoon.

magnatízio, *ag.* (*letter.*) magnate (*attributivo*): *boria magnatizia*, lordly arrogance.

magnèsia, *s.f.* (*chim. farm.*) magnesia: *latte di —*, milk of magnesia.

magnesíaco, *ag.* (*chim. farm.*) magnesic.

magnèsio, *s.m.* (*chim.*) magnesium: *grasso a base di —*, magnesium-base grease; *lampo al —*, (*foto.*) flash (*o* magnesium light).

magnesíte, *s.f.* (*min.*) magnesite.

magnète, *s.m.* **1.** (*fis.*) magnet, loadstone: *— artificiale*, artificial magnet; *— permanente, temporaneo*, (*elett.*) permanent, temporary magnet **2.** (*mec.*) magneto: *— d'accensione*, ignition magneto; *magnetino d'avviamento*, hand-starting magneto; *— schermato*, screened (*o* shielded) magneto.

magneticaménte, *av.* magnetically.

magnètico, *ag.* **1.** (*fis.*) magnetic (anche *fig.*): *ago —*, magnetic needle; *campo —*, magnetic field; *curve magnetiche*, magnetic curves; *deviazione magnetica*, magnetic deviation; *equatore —*, magnetic equator; *induzione magnetica*, magnetic induction; *mina magnetica*, magnetic mine; *poli magnetici*, magnetic poles; *polo —*, magnetic north; *tempesta magnetica*, magnetic storm **2.** (*di magnetismo animale*) magnetic (anche *fig.*); mesmeric: *fluido —*, magnetic fluid; *occhi magnetici*, magnetic eyes; *una personalità magnetica*, a magnetic personality.

magnetísmo, *s.m.* magnetism: *— animale*, animal magnetism; *— terrestre*, (*fis.*) terrestrial magnetism.

magnetíte, *s.f.* (*min.*) magnetite, loadstone.

magnetizzàre, *v.t.* **1.** (*fis.*) to magnetize **2.** (*ipnotizzare*) to hypnotize, to mesmerize, to magnetize.

magnetizzatóre, *ag.* magnetizing || *s.m.* **1.** (*fis.*) magnetizer **2.** (*ipnotizzatore*) hypnotist, mesmerist.

magnetizzatrice, *s.f.* (*ipnotizzatrice*) hypnotist.

magnetizzazióne, *s.f.* (*fis.*) magnetization: *— residua*, residual magnetization.

magneto-elèttrico, *ag.* (*fis.*) magneto-electric.

magnetòfono, *s.m.* tape-recorder.

magnetòmetro, *s.m.* (*fis.*) magnetometer.

magnetostrizióne, *s.f.* (*fis.*) magnetostriction.

magnificaménte, *av.* magnificently.

magnificaménto, *s.m.* (*rar.*) extolment, extolling.

magnificàre, *v.t.* to extol, to exalt, to praise, to glorify, to magnify: *— Dio*, to praise God; *— la memoria di qlcu.*, to glorify the memory of s.o.

magníficat, *s.m.* (*eccl.*) Magnificat.

magnificatóre, *s.m.*, **magnificatrice**, *s.f.* magnifier.

magnificazióne, *s.f.* extolment, magnification.

magnificènte, *ag.* (*letter.*) magnificent.

magnificènza, *s.f.* magnificence, splendour: *la — della natura*, the magnificence of nature || *Vostra —*, Your Magnificence.

magnífico, *ag.* **1.** magnificent, splendid; (*di stile*) high-sounding: *cerimonie magnifiche*, magnificent ceremonies; *pranzo —*, splendid dinner; *tempo —*, splendid weather; *vista magnifica*, splendid sight **2.** (*munifico*) open-handed, lavish: *fare il —*, to be very generous (*o fam.* to throw one's money around) || *Lorenzo il Magnifico*, Lorenzo the Magnificent **3.** (*titolo onorifico*): *Rettore Magnifico*, Rector of the University.

magniloquènte, *ag.* magniloquent, bombastic.

magniloquènza, *s.f.* magniloquence, bombast.

màgno, *ag.* great: *aula magna*, great hall; *opera magna*, magnum opus; *pompa magna*, high pomp and state || *Alberto Magno*, Albertus Magnus; *Alessandro Magno*, Alexander the Great; *Carlo Magno*, Charlemagne || *Magna Charta*, (*st.*) Magna C(h)arta || *Magna Grecia*, (*geog. st.*) Magna Graecia.

magnòlia, *s.f.* (*bot.*) magnolia.

màgo, *s.m.* magician, sorcerer, wizard: *il — Merlino*, Merlin the Wizard || *quell'uomo è un —*, (*fam.*) that man is a wizard.

magóna, *s.f.* (*rar.*) **1.** (*ferriera*) iron-foundry **2.** (*negozio di ferramenta*) iron-monger's (shop).

magóne, *s.m.* **1.** (*dial.*) (*ventriglio dei polli*) gizzard **2.** *fig.* (*affanno, accoramento*) grief: *avevo il —*, I had a lump in my throat; *le sue parole mi hanno fatto venire il —*, his words brought tears to my eyes.

Magónza, *no.pr.f.* (*geog.*) Mainz.

màgra, *s.f.* **1.** shallow, low water; *(di marea)* low
-water mark **2.** *(scarsezza)* shortage: *furono tempi di —,*
they were hard times.

magraménte, *av.* scantily.

magrézza, *s.f.* **1.** thinness, leanness, meagreness: *è di
una grande —, di una — spaventosa,* he is as thin as a
rake **2.** *(di terreno)* poorness, sterility; *(di acque)* low
level: *era un terreno di grande —,* it was a very poor soil.

màgro, *ag.* **1.** thin, lean: *era un uomo piuttosto —,*
he was on the lean side; *mi sembra che ti sia fatto
—,* I think you have lost weight ‖ *— come un chiodo,*
as thin as a rake (o lath) ‖ *discorso —,* speech of
little substance ‖ *non portarmi delle magre scuse,*
don't come to me with those lame excuses ‖ *non ti
pare una consolazione ben magra?,* don't you think
it is (a) very meagre (o poor) consolation? **2.** *(povero
di parti grasse)* lean: *compera della carne magra,* buy
some lean meat; *se vuoi c'è del prosciutto —,* if you like,
you can have some lean ham **3.** *(scarso, povero)* scanty,
poor, meagre, lean: *stipendio —,* meagre salary; *mi ha
dato una magra porzione,* he gave me a meagre helping;
mi spiace che la cena sia stata magra questa sera, I am
sorry the meal was rather poor to-night; *quell'anno
vi fu un raccolto —,* the harvest was scanty (o poor)
that year; *sarà un'annata magra,* it is going to be
a lean year ‖ *acque magre,* low waters ‖ *argilla magra,*
lean clay ‖ *pascoli magri,* scanty pastures **4.** *(di te-
reno)* sterile, poor: *terra magra,* sterile soil ‖
s.m. **1.** lean (meat): *prendi un bel pezzo di —,* get a
good piece of lean meat **2.** *(eccl.)* abstinence: *giorno
di —,* day of abstinence; *pranzo di —,* meatless meal;
oggi si mangia di —, we shall not eat meat to-day;
dispensare dal —, to dispense from abstinence.

mah, *inter.* who knows!.

mài, *av.* never; *(in presenza di negazione e nel senso
di* talvolta*)* ever: *— uomo fu più ammirato,* never
was a man more admired; *senza averci — pensato,*
without ever having thought of it; *« Siete — stati a
Londra? »*, *« No, non ci siamo mai stati »*, " Have you
ever been to London? ", " No, we have never been
there " ‖ *— e poi —,* never never ‖ *— più,* never again
(o nevermore): *non lo vedremo — più,* we shall never see
him again; *non udremo — più la sua voce,* nevermore
shall we hear his voice ‖ *— più!, (anzi)* by no means!;
(niente affatto) certainly not! (o on no account!) ‖ *caso —,
se —,* if (o if ever o in case): *caso — tornasse, diglielo
tu,* if he should come back, tell him; *prendi l'ombrello, caso — dovesse piovere,* take your umbrella in
case it rains; *se — una volta dovessi incontrarlo...,*
if ever I should meet him... ‖ *meno che —,* less than
ever ‖ *peggio che —,* worse than ever ‖ *più che —,*
more than ever: *più caro che —,* dearer than ever;
io cercavo di calmarlo, ma lui strillava più che —, I
tried to pacify him, but he cried more than ever ‖
quasi —, hardly ever (o almost never): *non lo si vede
quasi —,* one hardly ever sees him ‖ *io sempre e tu
—!,* it's always me, never you! ‖ *— che abbia fatto
una cosa decente in tutta la sua vita!,* he's never done
a decent thing in all his life! ‖ *che — accadrà?,* what
on earth is going to happen?; *che — stai cercando
di dire?,* what on earth are you trying to say?; *chi
ti ha — detto di farlo?,* who the dickens told you to
do that?; *come — l'hai saputo?,* how on earth did
you know?; *come — non ci avevi pensato prima?,*
why on earth didn't you think of it before?; *dove
— si sarà cacciato?,* wherever can he be hiding? ‖
farei tutto, questo —!, I would be prepared to do
anything but that! ‖ *le voglio un bene che —!,* I love
her with all my heart!; *sono felice che —!, sono quanto
— felice!,* I am terribly happy (o I have never been
so happy) ‖ *non sia — detto che...,* never let it be said
that... ‖ *non si sa —!,* you never can tell! ‖ *quanto è
— sciocco!,* how silly he is! ‖ *si trovano di fronte a tante
— difficoltà,* they are faced with so many difficulties ‖ *meglio tardi che —,* prov. better late than never.

Màia[1], *no.pr.f.* *(mit.)* Maia.
màia[2], *s.f.* *(zool.)* sea spider.
maiàla, *s.f.* sow.
maiàle, *s.m.* **1.** pig; hog; swine *(pl. invariabile)*:
un branco di maiali, a herd of swine ‖ *non ti sei ancora
lavato le mani, maialino?* haven't you washed your
hands yet, you dirty child? ‖ *mangiare come un —,*
(in modo sconveniente) to eat like a pig; *(troppo)* to
make a pig of oneself **2.** *(carne)* pork; *(specialmente
di maiale giovane)* pig: *braciola di —,* pork-chop (o
-cutlet).
maialésco, *ag.* piggish.
maídico, *ag.* maize *(attributivo)*: *malattia maidica,*
maidism (o pellagra).
maidísmo, *s.m.* *(patol.)* maidism, pellagra.
maiestàtico, *ag.*: *plurale —,* the royal " we ".
maièutica, *s.f.* *(fil.)* maieutics.
mainàre, *(rar.)* per **ammainàre**.
maiòlica, *s.f.* majolica.
maiolicàto, *ag.* majolica *(attributivo)*.
maionése, *s.f.* *(cuc.)* mayonnaise.
Maiòrca, *no.pr.f.* *(geog.)* Majorca.
màis, *s.m.* maize, Indian corn.
maître d'hôtel, *s.m.* maître d'hôtel.
maiúscola, *s.f.* capital (letter).
maiuscolétto, *s.m.* *(tip.)* small capitals.
maiúscolo, *ag.* **1.** capital: *lettera maiuscola,* capital
letter **2.** *(madornale)* gross, big: *errore —,* gross blunder ‖
s.m. capitals *(pl.)*: *scrivere in —,* to write in capitals.
malacàrne, *s.f.* **1.** tainted meat, diseased meat **2.** *(persona malvagia)* rotter.
Malàcca, *no.pr.f.* *(geog.)* Malacca: *penisola di —,*
Malay Peninsula (o Malaya); *stretto di —,* Straits of
Malacca ‖ **malàcca,** *s.m.* **1.** *(legno)* malacca wood **2.** *(bastone)* Malacca-cane.
malàccio, *s.m.* serious illness ‖ *non c'è —, (fam.)*
not too bad.
malaccòlto, *ag.* unwelcome.
malaccóncio, *ag.* unsuitable, unseemly, unfit.
malaccortaménte, *av.* unwisely, ill-advisedly.
malaccòrto, *ag.* unwise, ill-advised, imprudent: *sei
stato — ad agire così,* you were ill-advised to act
that way.
Malachía, *no.pr.m.* *(Bibbia)* Malachi.
malachíte, *s.f.* *(min.)* malachite.
malacía, *s.f.* *(patol.)* malacia.
malacología, *s.f.* *(scient.)* malacology.
malacreànza, *s.f.* rudeness, impoliteness, bad manners *(pl.)*: *la sua — è proverbiale,* his rudeness (o his
lack of manners) is proverbial.
maladórno, *ag.* unadorned.
malaféde, *s.f.* bad faith: *essere in —,* to be in bad
faith.
malaffàre, *s.m.*: *donna di —,* whore (o prostitute
o tart); *gente di —,* crooks *(pl.)*.
Màlaga, *no.pr.f.* *(geog.)* Malaga ‖ **màlaga,** *s.f.* *(uva)*
Malaga ‖ *(vino)* Malaga.
malagévole, *ag.* **1.** *(difficile)* difficult, hard; *(faticoso)* tiring; *(scomodo)* uncomfortable: *lavoro —,* tiring
work; *una salita —,* a hard climb; *tempi malagevoli,*
hard times; *un viaggio —,* an uncomfortable journey;
è — da spiegare, it is difficult to explain **2.** *(non domo)*
unmanageable, intractable: *cavallo —,* unmanageable
horse.
malagevolézza, *s.f.* difficulty, badness: *la — di
quella strada,* the badness of that road.
malagevolménte, *av.* *(difficilmente)* with difficulty;
(in modo disagevole) uncomfortably.
malagiàto, *ag.* **1.** uncomfortable **2.** *(privo di mezzi)*
short of money, badly off.
malagràzia, *s.f.* bad grace; rudeness: *fare ql.co.
di —,* to do sthg. with a bad grace.
malalíngua, *s.f.* backbiter, gossip: *non dar retta
alle malelingue,* don't listen to gossips.
malaménte, *av.* badly.

malandàre, *v.i.* (*rar.*) to go badly; to go to ruin; (*di cibi*) to go bad.

malandàto, *ag.* in bad condition; (*fam.*) in bad shape: — *in salute,* in poor health; *casa malandata,* dilapidated house.

malandrinàggio, *s.m.* **1.** brigandage, (highway) robbery **2.** (*l'insieme dei malandrini*) robbers.

malandrinésco, *ag.* **1.** brigand-like (*attributivo*), robber-like (*attributivo*) **2.** (*scherz.*) roguish.

malandríno, *ag.* (*scherz.*) roguish, rascally: *occhi malandrini,* roguish eyes ‖ *s.m.* **1.** brigand, robber, highwayman (*pl.* highwaymen) **2.** (*scherz.*) rogue, rascal.

malànimo, *s.m.* malevolence; ill-will; animosity, rancour: *senza* —, without malice; *c'è in lui del — verso di noi,* he has a grudge against us; *credo che l'abbia fatto per* —, I think he did it out of spite; *doveva vincere il — che la famiglia della moglie nutriva verso di lui,* he had to overcome the animosity of his wife's family.

malànno, *s.m.* **1.** misfortune; (*calamità*) calamity; (*danno*) damage; (*sfortuna*) bad luck: *ci ha portato il — in casa,* he has brought bad luck to our house; *è stato un grande — per tutta l'Europa,* it was a great calamity for the whole of Europe; *la grandinata è stata un gran — per le viti,* the hail-storm has severely damaged the vines ‖ *oh! poveretto, ha il male, il — e l'uscio addosso,* (*ha tutte le disgrazie*) the poor chap is up to his neck in it ‖ *ti colga il —!,* (the) Devil take you! ‖ *un — non viene mai solo, prov.* troubles never come singly (*o* it never rains but it pours) **2.** (*malattia*) illness, disease; (*acciacco*) infirmity: *malgrado l'età avanzata è senza malanni,* in spite of his age, he has no trouble with his health; *ti buscherai un —, se non ti copri un po' di più,* you will catch your death, if you don't wear something warmer **3.** (*persona malvagia*) wicked person: *ha sposato quel —!,* she has married that miserable man!.

malapéna, a, *l.av.* hardly, scarcely: *riuscii a — a prendere il treno,* I just managed to catch my train; *riuscivo a — a capire quello che diceva,* I could hardly (*o* scarcely) understand what he was saying.

malària, *s.f.* (*patol.*) malaria, marsh-fever: *è affetto da* —, he has got malaria.

malàrico, *ag.* malarial, malarian, malarious: *zona malàrica,* malarial area.

malariologìa, *s.f.* malariology.

malariòlogo, *s.m.* malariologist.

malarioterapìa, *s.f.* malariotherapy.

malatíccio, *ag.* sickly, ailing.

malàto, *ag.* **1.** sick; ill (*predicativo*): *un bimbo* —, a sick child; *cadde — di polmonite,* he was taken ill with pneumonia; *è — di fegato,* he suffers from his liver; *il loro bambino è gravemente* —, their child is dangerously ill; *non farlo se hai il dito* —, don't do it, if you have a sore finger ‖ *è malata di gelosia,* she is sick with jealousy **2.** (*di piante*) diseased: *questa pianta è malata,* this tree is diseased **3.** (*morboso*) unhealthy, unsound, morbid: *aveva un'immaginazione malata,* she had an unhealthy imagination; *ha una sensibilità malata,* she has a morbid sensibility ‖ *s.m.* patient: *negli ospedali non c'era più posto per i malati,* there was no room left for patients in the hospitals; *silenzio!, c'è un — grave qui,* quiet, please!, there is a very sick patient here.

malattìa, *s.f.* sickness, illness; disease; (*non grave*) ailment: — *contagiosa,* contagious disease; *malattie cutanee,* skin diseases; — *del lavoro,* occupational disease; — *del sonno,* sleeping sickness; — *infettiva,* infectious disease; — *mentale,* mental disease; *malattie veneree,* venereal diseases; *cura, diagnosi, sintomi di una* —, treatment, diagnosis, symptoms of a disease; *le malattie sono spesso favorite dalla mancanza di igiene,* disease is often spread by lack of hygiene; *è compito del medico prevenire e curare le malattie,* the business

of doctors is to prevent and treat illness; *ha superato quella grave* —, *ma è ancora debole,* he has got over that serious illness, but he is still very weak; *la sua — è la distrazione,* his trouble is absentmindedness; *soffrire di una* —, to suffer from a disease.

malauguratamente, *av.* unluckily, unfortunately.

malauguràto, *ag.* (*sfortunato*) ill-fated, unlucky; (*di cattivo auspicio*) inauspicious: *in quel — giorno,* on that ill-fated day.

malaugúrio, *s.m.* ill omen, evil omen ‖ *uccello di* —, (*persona che annunzi o apporti male*) bird of ill omen.

malauguróso, *ag.* (*sfortunato*) ill-fated, unlucky, unfortunate: — *un incidente* —, an unfortunate accident.

malavíta, *s.f.* **1.** (criminal) underworld: *il gergo della* —, thieves' slang (*o* underworld slang); *darsi alla* —, to embark on a life of crime **2.** (*i malviventi*) gangsters, robbers; racketeers: *un covo di* —, a gangsters' hideout; *la città era infestata dalla* —, the city was infested by gangsters.

malavòglia, *s.f.* unwillingness, bad will, reluctance: *fare ql.co. di* —, to do sthg. half-heartedly.

malavvedutaménte, *av.* (*incautamente*) rashly, unwarily, unwisely.

malavvedúto, *ag.* (*incauto*) rash, unwary, unwise.

malavventuràto, *ag.* (*sfortunato*) ill-fated, unlucky, unfortunate.

malavventuróso, *ag.* (*di cattivo auspicio*) inauspicious, ominous; (*sfortunato*) unlucky, unfortunate.

malavvézzo, *ag.* ill-bred, unmannerly.

malavvisàto, *ag.* ill-advised, unwise.

malazzàto, *ag.* (*malaticcio*) sickly, ailing.

malcadúeo, *s.m.* (*patol.*) falling sickness.

malcapitàto, *ag.* unlucky, unfortunate ‖ *s.m.,* **malcapitàta,** *s.f.* victim; sufferer; unfortunate person: *tutti si affrettarono a soccorrere il* —, everybody hurried to help the victim.

malcàuto, *ag.* (*incauto*) rash, unwary; ill-advised.

malcèrto, *ag.* (*incerto*) uncertain, doubtful.

malcompostaménte, *av.* (*scompostamente*) in an ungainly way; awkwardly.

malcompósto, *ag.* **1.** (*confuso*) confused; (*disordinato*) untidy **2.** (*scomposto*) (*nel portamento*) ungainly; (*nel comportamento*) ungracious.

malcóncio, *ag.* **1.** knocked about; (*sciupato*) spoilt; (*sformato*) battered: *portava un vecchio cappello* —, he was wearing an old battered hat; *essere* —, to be in a sorry plight; *rendere* —, to knock about **2.** (*contuso*) bruised: *tutto pesto e* —, black and blue all over.

malconoscènte, *ag.* (*ingrato*) ungrateful.

malconsigliàto, *ag.* ill-advised, unwise.

malcontènto, *ag.* dissatisfied (with s.o., sthg.); discontented (with s.o., sthg.): *aspetto* —, dissatisfied expression; *è sempre* —, he is never satisfied; *erano malcontenti di te,* they were displeased with (*o* at) you; *il popolo era — del governo,* the people were dissatisfied with the government; *sono — della tua condotta,* I am dissatisfied with your conduct ‖ *i malcontenti,* the malcontent ‖ *s.m.* discontent, dissatisfaction: *oggetto di* —, cause for dissatisfaction; *il — serpeggiava fra il popolo,* discontent spread through the people; *mostrare il proprio* —, to show (*o* to express) one's displeasure; *seminare il* —, to sow the seed of discontent.

malcostúme, *s.m.* **1.** (*immoralità*) immorality; (*corruzione*) corruption: *le leggi contro il* —, the laws against immorality; *combattere il* —, to combat immorality; *combattere il — politico,* to fight against political corruption **2.** (*cattiva abitudine*) bad habit.

malcreàto, *ag.* impolite, ill-mannered, rude.

maldentàti, *s.m.pl.* (*zool.*) Edentata.

maldèstro, *ag.* **1.** awkward, clumsy: *un movimento* —, a clumsy (*o* awkward) movement; *una persona maldestra,* a clumsy person **2.** (*inesperto*) inexperienced, green: *quell'apprendista è ancora* —, that apprentice is still green.

maldicènte, *ag.* disparaging || *s.c.* backbiter, slanderer, scandal-monger: *è un — di professione,* he is always running people down.

maldicènza, *s.f.* backbiting, slander, malicious gossip; *(scherz.)* gossip: *si faceva un po' di — per passare il tempo,* we were gossiping a bit, just to pass the time away; *tutti lo sfuggono per la sua —,* everybody avoids him because of his habit of slandering people (*o* because of the way he runs people down).

maldispósto, *ag.* ill-disposed (towards s.o., sthg.); *(ostile)* hostile (to s.o., sthg.); *(avverso, contrario)* averse (to s.o., sthg., to doing sthg.): *è — contro di me,* he is ill-disposed towards me; *sono — a fare ciò,* I am averse to (*o* I am against) doing it.

màle, *s.m.* **1.** *(opposto di* bene) evil: *il bene e il —,* good and evil (*o* right and wrong); *il genio del —,* the evil genius; *peccatore indurito nel —,* hardened sinner; *lo spirito del —,* the spirit of evil; *non conosce il —,* she doesn't know the meaning of evil; *indurre qlcu. al —,* to lead s.o. astray; *rendere bene per —,* to return good for evil **2.** *(sventura)* ill, evil, misfortune; *(guaio)* trouble: *i mali della vita,* the ills (*o* evils) of life; *il — è che non so decidermi,* the trouble is that I cannot make up my mind; *augurare del — a qlcu.,* to wish s.o. ill; *raccontare i propri mali,* to tell one's troubles (*o* woes) || *portare —,* to bring bad luck || *mal comune mezzo gaudio, prov.* a sorrow shared is a sorrow halved || *a estremi mali, estremi rimedi, prov.* desperate ills need desperate remedies || *un — tira l'altro, prov.* misfortunes never come singly || *non tutto il — viene per nuocere, prov.* every cloud has a silver lining || *tra due mali bisogna scegliere il minore, prov.* choose the lesser of two evils **3.** *(malattia)* illness, disease, sickness; *(dolore fisico)* pain, ache: *mal d'aria,* air-sickness; *mal caduco,* falling sickness; *mal di cuore,* heart disease; *mal di denti,* toothache; *mal di gola,* sore throat; *ho mal di gola,* I have a sore-throat; *mal di mare,* seasickness; *avere il mal di mare,* to be seasick; *mal di montagna,* mountain sickness; *mal di stomaco,* stomach-ache; *mal di testa,* headache; *i cibi pesanti mi fanno —,* heavy food gives me indigestion; *ho — alle braccia, mi fanno — le braccia,* my arms ache (*o* hurt); *mi fai —,* you are hurting me; *essere affetto da un — incurabile,* to suffer from an incurable disease; *farsi —,* to hurt oneself: *si è fatto — cadendo da un albero,* he has hurt himself falling from a tree || *mal del paese,* homesickness **4.** *(danno, torto)* harm, damage: *il — che mi ha fatto,* the wrongs which I have suffered at his hands; *che — ti può fare?,* what harm can it do you?; *ciò farà più — che bene,* it will do more harm than good; *gli avete fatto del — parlando così,* you have hurt him (by) talking like that; *non c'è niente di — in ciò,* there is no harm in that; *non si deve fare — a nessuno,* you mustn't hurt people; *poco — se non può venire,* it does not matter if he cannot come; *ripara il — che hai fatto,* make up for the harm you've done **5. (Fraseologia):** *di — in peggio,* from bad to worse || *meno —,* just as well (*o* a good job *o* a good thing); *(grazie a Dio)* thank goodness; *(almeno)* at least: *è arrivato con due ore di ritardo, ma meno — che ora è qui,* he has arrived two hours late, but at least he's here now; *ho dato l'esame di francese e ho preso 20; meno —, poteva andare peggio,* I got 20 out of 30 in the French exam; not so bad!, it could have been worse: *ho dimenticato il portafogli, meno — che ho un po' di soldi in tasca,* I have forgotten my wallet, it's just as well (*o* it's a good job *o* it's a good thing) I have some money in my pocket; *meno — che sei arrivato, perchè ero proprio nei pasticci,* thank goodness you've arrived, as I was really in a mess || *non bisogna pensare — di lui,* give him the benefit of the doubt (*o* don't think badly of him) || *non c'è —,* not too bad (*o* pretty well) || *non pensavo a nulla di —,* I did not mean anything bad || *spettacolo che fa —, (doloroso)* painful sight || *andare a —,* to go bad || *aversi a — di ql.co., prendere ql.co. a —,* to feel hurt by sthg. (*o* to take sthg. in bad part *o* to take sthg. amiss) || *farsi venire —,* to pretend to faint (*o* to swoon) || *mettere —,* to foster enmity (*o* to sow discord) || *venir —,* to feel faint: *mi vien —,* I feel faint || *voler — a qlcu. (odiarlo),* to hate s.o.; *(avere un rancore contro qlcu.)* to have a grudge against s.o.

màle, *av.* **1.** badly; ill: *mal fatto,* badly done: *un lavoro mal fatto,* a badly done piece of work; *— informato,* ill-informed; *conosco — l'italiano,* my Italian is bad; *egli lavora molto —,* he works very badly; *agire —,* to act badly (*o* to do wrong); *ha agito — e perciò è stato punito,* he has done wrong and has been punished for it; *andare —, (di automobile, ecc.)* not to run well (*o* smoothly); *(di orologio, ecc.)* to be wrong; *capire —,* to misunderstand; *comportarsi, portarsi —,* to behave badly; *conoscere — qlcu.,* to hardly know s.o.; *far —, (aver torto)* to be wrong: *fai — a pensare così,* you are wrong in thinking that; *far — a qlcu.,* to do s.o. harm; *giudicare — qlcu.,* to misjudge s.o.; *parlare, dire — di qlcu.,* to speak badly (*o* ill) of s.o.; *parlar — una lingua,* to speak a language badly; *rispondere —,* to answer rudely: *i bambini viziati rispondono — ai genitori,* spoilt children answer their parents back; *sentirsi —,* to feel bad (*o* ill *o* unwell); *star —, (essere indisposto)* to be ill (*o* unwell); *(non essere conveniente)* not to be becoming: *sta — che una ragazza si comporti così,* it is not becoming for a girl to behave like that; *star — a ql.co., (esserne a corto)* to be short of sthg.: *sto — a soldi,* I am short of money; *star — a qlcu., (non donargli)* not to suit s.o.: *quel cappello gli sta —,* that hat doesn't suit him; *star — con ql.co., (non accordarsi)* not to go with sthg.: *il viola sta — col rosso,* violet doesn't go with red; *trattar — qlcu.,* to ill-treat s.o.; *veder —,* not to see very well; *(disapprovare)* to disapprove: *vede — che tu parli tanto con me,* he doesn't approve of your speaking to me so much || *nè bene nè —,* so so || *bene o — sbrigheremo la faccenda,* we shall manage it somehow or other || *le cose sembravano mettersi —,* things seemed to take a bad turn (*o* to turn out badly) || *hai rotto il bicchiere, —!,* you have broken the glass, that's bad! || *per — che vadano gli affari,* however badly business may go || *finire —,* to come to a bad end || *restare, rimaner —,* to feel hurt; *(essere deluso)* to be disappointed || *trovarsi —, (a disagio)* to feel uneasy (*o* ill at ease) || *chi tardi arriva — alloggia, prov.* last come, last served **2.** *(fam.)* *(con funzione aggettivale):* *quella ragazza non è —,* that girl is rather good-looking; *questo quadro non è —,* this picture is quite good.

malebòlge, *s.f.pl. (lett.)* Malebolge.

malebrànche, *s.m.pl. (lett.)* Malebolge devils.

maledétta, *s.f.: non me ne importa una —, (volg.)* I don't give (*o* care) a damn; *avere la —, (essere scalognato)* to be accursed || *alla —,* furiously: *piove alla —,* it's raining furiously; *s'infuriò alla —,* he got really furious.

maledettaménte, *av.* awfully, horribly; damn(ed): *oggi è — arrabbiato,* he's damn furious today.

maledétto, *ag.* **1.** cursed; damned: *quell'uomo è —,* that man has a curse on him; *si direbbe una casa maledetta,* one would say it is a cursed house || *—!,* damned (*o* d-d)! || *i maledetti, (i dannati)* the damned || *maledetti gli ingrati!,* cursed be the ungrateful!; *— quel mascalzone!,* hang (*o* confound) the rogue!; *— il giorno che l'incontrai!,* a curse on the day when I met him! **2.** *(fam.)* *(terribile)* darn, cursed; awful, terrible: *— scocciatore!, maledetta scocciatura!,* what a blessed (*o* damned) nuisance!; *che tempo —!,* what cursed (*o* confounded *o* wretched) weather!; *quel — oste,* that cursed innkeeper; *sempre con queste maledette cifre!,* always these same darn (*o* blessed) figures!; *mi fece una paura maledetta,* it frightened me to death; *quel — rumore mi fa impazzire,* that terrible (*o* darn) noise is driving me crazy; *avere una fame maledetta*, to be awfully hungry.

maledicènte, *ag.* cursing.

maledico, *ag.* slanderous, backbiting ‖ *s.m.* slanderer.

maledíre, *v.t.* to curse, to damn; (*eccl.*) to anathematize: *Dio maledisse Caino*, God cursed Cain; *maledisse la propria follia*, he cursed his own folly; *il Papa lo maledisse*, the Pope anathematized him; — *il giorno in cui si è nati*, to curse the day one was born; — *un tiranno*, to curse (*o* to lay a curse upon) a tyrant.

maledizióne, *s.f.* **1.** curse, malediction; (*eccl.*) anathema: *la — di Dio*, God's curse (*o* malediction); *una — pesa sul suo capo*, a curse hangs over his head ‖ *avere la — addosso*, to be accursed ‖ — *!*, damn! **2.** *fig.* curse, plague, calamity: *è una — aver quella donna in casa*, it's a curse (*o* plague) to have that woman around the house.

maleducàto, *ag.* rude, impolite; ill-bred, ill-mannered; (*di modi, linguaggio*) uncouth, unrefined: *modi maleducati*, uncouth manners; *è — mangiare in quel modo*, it is bad manners to eat in that way; *è un ragazzo —*, he is an ill-bred boy; *non essere così — con tua sorella!*, don't be so rude to your sister!; *quello è un uomo molto —*, that man has no manners at all; *la tua risposta è stata maleducata*, your answer was rude ‖ *s.m.* ill-bred person; bad-mannered person: *sono solo i maleducati che fanno così*, it is only ill-bred people who act like that.

malefàtta, *s.m.* mischief: *mi hai combinato una delle tue solite malefatte*, you have been up to one of your usual pieces of mischief; *ho l'impressione che mi si stia combinando una —*, I feel there is mischief brewing somewhere.

maleficaménte, *av.* evilly; mischievously.

maleficio, *s.m.* **1.** (*stregoneria*) act of witchcraft, act of sorcery, spell: *leggi contro i malefici*, laws against witchcraft; *lanciò un — su di lui*, she cast a spell on him; *riuscì a rompere il —*, she managed to break the spell **2.** (*misfatto*) misdeed; crime.

malèfico, *ag.* harmful, evil, mischievous: *questo libro può avere un'influenza malefica*, this book may have an evil (*o* a harmful) influence.

malefízio, *V.* **maleficio**.

maleolènte, *ag.* malodorous, bad smelling, evil-smelling, ill-smelling.

malèrba, *s.f.* weed ‖ *le malerbe crescono in fretta*, *prov.* ill weeds grow apace.

malése, *ag.s.c.* Malay ‖ *arcipelago —*, Malay Archipelago.

Malèsia, *no.pr.f.* (*geog.*) Malaysia.

malèssere, *s.m.* **1.** malaise, bodily discomfort; indisposition: *ho un — generale*, I feel queer all over **2.** (*senso di disagio*) uneasiness: *un senso di —*, an uneasy feeling; *provavo un certo — entrando in quella casa*, I felt a certain uneasiness as I entered that house **3.** (*strettezze finanziarie*) difficulty: *la famiglia, la ditta attraversa un periodo di —*, the family, the firm is in straitened circumstances.

malèstro, *s.m.* mischief, damage: *bada di non fare malestri!*, don't get into mischief!.

malevolènza, *s.f.* malevolence, ill-will, malice, spite: *lo disse con —*, he said it out of spite; *malgrado me lo meritassi, egli non provò mai alcuna — contro di me*, although I deserved it, he bore me no ill-will.

malèvolo, *ag.* malevolent, ill-disposed; (*maligno*) evil-minded: *con malevola intenzione*, with evil intention ‖ *i malevoli*, the evil-minded (*o* evil-minded persons): *era solo una voce sparsa da alcuni malevoli*, it was a rumour spread by a few evil-minded persons.

malfamàto, *ag.* ill-famed: *luogo —*, place of ill-fame.

malfàre, *s.m.* wrong-doing.

malfàre, *v.i.* (*rar.*) to do wrong.

malfàtto, *ag.* ill-shaped; badly done, badly made; (*di vestito*) badly fitting, ill-fitting: *tavolo —*, badly made table ‖ *s.m.* misdeed.

malfattóre, *s.m.* evil-doer, wrong-doer, criminal.

malférmo, *ag.* **1.** shaky, unsteady, tottering (anche *fig.*): — *nei suoi propositi*, wavering in his aims; *passi malfermi*, shaky (*o* tottering) steps; *voce malferma*, shaky voice; *era — sulle gambe*, he was unsteady on his legs; *quel tavolo è —*, that table is unsteady (*o* shaky); *la sua mano si fa malferma*, his hand is getting shaky **2.** (*di salute*) poor, delicate: *salute malferma*, poor (*o* delicate) health.

malfidàto, *ag.* suspicious, distrustful, diffident.

malfído, *ag.* **1.** untrustworthy, unreliable: *amico —*, unreliable (*o* untrustworthy) friend; *memoria malfida*, unreliable memory **2.** (*incerto*) uncertain, unsure: *l'avvenire è —*, the future is uncertain.

malfondàto, *ag.* ill-founded, ill-grounded: *sospetti malfondati*, ill-founded suspicions.

màlga, *s.f.* (*baita*) "malga" (shepherd's hut in the Alps).

malgàrbo, *s.m.* bad grace; rudeness, impoliteness: *è conosciuto per il suo —*, he is well-known for his rudeness; *tu sei pieno di —*, you are very rude; *fare ql.co. con —*, to do sthg. with a bad grace.

malgovèrno, *s.m.* misgovernment, misrule; (*cattiva amministrazione*) mismanagement: *il — del proprio patrimonio*, the mismanagement of one's inheritance; *i patrioti insorsero contro il —*, the patriots revolted against misrule.

malgradíto, *ag.* unwelcome; disagreeable: *notizia malgradita*, unwelcome news; *una persona malgradita*, a disagreeable person.

malgràdo, *prep. in* spite of, notwithstanding; for all, with all: — *la sua ricchezza*, for all his wealth; — *le nostre proteste egli proseguì*, he went on in spite of (*o* notwithstanding) our protests; — *tutto quello che ha detto...*, in spite of everything he has said...; — *tutto il suo talento era poco conosciuto*, with (*o* for) all his talent, he was little known ‖ *s.m.* (*solo nelle l.av.*): (*a*) *mio, tuo, ecc.* —, against my, your, etc. will: *l'ho fatto* (*a*) *mio —*, I did it against my will (*o* unwillingly) ‖ **malgràdo** (che), *cong.* (*al*)though: — *egli lo vedesse raramente*, although he saw him rarely; — *non l'avessi mai visto*, though I had never seen him; — *sia ancora scapolo...*, though he is still a bachelor....

malía, *s.f.* **1.** (*stregoneria*) witchcraft, sorcery: *gli hanno fatto la —*, he is bewitched **2.** (*fascino*) fascination, charm: *i suoi begli occhi hanno un'irresistibile —*, her beautiful eyes have an irresistible charm.

maliàrda, *s.f.* **1.** (*maga*) witch, sorceress **2.** (*donna affascinante*) fascinating woman; (*fam.*) witch.

màlico, *ag.* (*chim.*) malic.

malignaménte, *av.* maliciously.

malignàre, *v.i.* to think ill (of s.o., sthg.); to think badly (of s.o., sthg.); to speak ill (of s.o., sthg.); to speak badly (of s.o., sthg.); to malign (s.o.): *si maligna molto su quell'uomo politico*, that politician is very much maligned; *stavano malignando fortemente sul suo conto*, they were speaking very badly of him.

malignatóre, *s.m.*, **malignatríce**, *s.f.* backbiter.

malignità, *s.f.* **1.** malice, malignity: — *diabolica*, diabolical malignity; *è noto per la sua —*, he is well-known for his malicious comments (*o* remarks); *le sue parole sono sempre piene di —*, his words are always full of malice **2.** (*atto, detto, pensiero maligno*): *hai pensato una —*, what you've thought is very malicious; *non era che una —*, it was sheer malice; *sono tutte — di tuo fratello*, these are all examples of your brother's malice; *stai dicendo delle —*, you are being very malicious **3.** (*di malattia, carattere maligno*) malignancy.

malígno, *ag.* **1.** malicious; malevolent: *parole maligne*, malicious words; *una persona maligna*, a malicious (*o* malevolent) person; *una risata maligna*, a malicious laughter ‖ *i maligni*, malicious people **2.** (*malefico*) evil, malignant; malign: *luogo —*, evil place; *spirito —*, evil (*o* malignant) spirit; *libro che esercita un'influenza maligna*, book that has a malign (*o* an evil) influence ǁ *il Maligno*, the Evil One **3.** (*di malattia*) malignant: *febbre maligna*, malignant fever; *tumore* —, malignant growth (*o tumor*) **4.** (*di clima, nocivo*) unhealthy; **5.** (*di terreno, sterile*) sterile.

malinconía, *s.f.* **1.** melancholy; (*abbattimento*) depression, dejection; (*tristezza*) sadness; *cupa malinconia,* (*tetraggine*) gloominess: *la — dei romantici,* the melancholy of the Romantics; *la — di un paesaggio invernale,* the sadness of a winter landscape; *la — di un vecchio castello,* the gloominess of an old castle; *afflitto da* —, suffering from depression; *immerso nella* —, plunged in melancholy; *profonda* —, deep dejection; *ho una grande* — *oggi,* I feel very depressed to-day; *me ne andai con una grande* —, I went away feeling very dejected (*o* in very low spirits) **2.** (*pensiero malinconico*) melancholy, gloomy thought: *questo libro scaccerà ogni tua* —, this book will drive away your gloomy thoughts.

malinconicaménte, *av.* (*con abbattimento*) dejectedly, in very low spirits; (*tristemente*) sadly; (*cupamente, tetramente*) gloomily, dismally: *se ne andò* —, he went away in very low spirits; *la sirena suonava* — *nella nebbia,* the foghorn was sounding gloomily; *sorrise* —, she smiled sadly.

malincònico, *ag.* melancholy; (*abbattuto*) depressed, dejected; (*triste*) sad; (*cupo, tetro*) gloomy, dismal; (*che dà malinconia*) melancholy, dismal, depressing: *una casa malinconica,* a gloomy house; *con voce malinconica,* in a dismal voice; *un paesaggio* —, a melancholy landscape; *pensieri malinconici,* gloomy thoughts; *tempo* —, dismal weather; *aveva un'aria malinconica,* he looked sad; *è — per natura,* he has a melancholy nature; *oggi sono* —, I feel depressed to-day.

malincuòre, a, *l.av.* (*controvoglia*) unwillingly, reluctantly; (*senza entusiasmo*) half-heartedly: *lasciai la mia vecchia casa a* —, I left my old home reluctantly; *non avevo voglia di fare il lavoro, lo feci proprio a* —, I didn't want to do the work, I did it unwillingly (*o* half-heartedly).

malintenzionàto, *ag.* malicious, ill-disposed: *è una persona malintenzionata,* he is a malicious person; *era — nei miei riguardi,* he wanted to do me harm (*o* was ill-disposed towards me) ǁ *s.m.* ill-intentioned person: *un — si aggirava nel giardino,* a suspicious -looking man was creeping about the garden.

malintéso, *ag.* mistaken: *un — senso dell'onore lo portò a sentirsi offeso,* a mistaken sense of honour led him to take offence ǁ *s.m.* misunderstanding: *a scanso di malintesi,* to avoid misunderstandings; *è solo un* —, it's only a misunderstanding; *chiarire un* —, to clear up a misunderstanding.

malióso, *ag.* enchanting, fascinating, charming, bewitching: *un sorriso* —, a fascinating smile.

malízia, *s.f.* **1.** malice: *per* —, out of malice; *è un ragazzo senza* —, that boys is ingenuous; *dire ql.co. con* —, to say sthg. with malice **2.** (*astuzia*) artfulness, cunning: *quel bambino è pieno di — nell'ottenere ciò che vuole,* that boy is full of cunning in getting what he wants **3.** (*trucco*) trick: *queste sono le malizie del mestiere,* these are the tricks of the trade.

maliziosaménte, *av.* mischievously; archly, artfully, slyly: *le sorrise* —, he gave her a sly smile.

malizióso, *ag.* mischievous; sly, artful: *un bambino* —, a mischievous (*o* naughty) child; *una domanda maliziosa,* an artful question; *occhi maliziosi,* mischievous eyes; *uno sguardo* —, a sly look.

malleàbile, *ag.* malleable (anche *fig.*): *ghisa* —, (*metal.*) malleable cast-iron; *ha una natura* —, he has a very submissive nature.

malleabilità, *s.f.* malleability, malleableness (anche *fig.*).

mallèolo, *s.m.* (*anat.*) malleolus (*pl.* malleoli): — *peroneale,* malleolus lateralis; — *tibiale,* malleolus medialis.

malleolàre, *ag.* malleolar.

mallevadóre, *s.m.*, **mallevadríce,** *s.f.* (*dir.*) bail; surety, guarantor, guarantee: *essere — di qlcu.,* to stand surety for s.o.; (*dir.*) to go bail for s.o.

mallevadoría, mallevería, *s.f.* (*dir.*) bail; security, guarantee, guaranty: *dare — a qlcu.,* to stand surety for s.o.

màllo, *s.m.* husk; (*della noce*), walnut-husk.

mallòppo, *s.m.* **1.** (*fam.*) swag **2.** (*aer.*) trail-rope.

malmaritàta, *s.f.* unhappily-married woman.

malmenàre, *v.t.* (*trattar male*) to ill-use, to ill-treat, to maltreat; (*ridurre in cattivo stato*) to manhandle: *malmenato dalla polizia,* manhandled by the police.

malmésso, *ag.* **1.** (*poveramente vestito*) poorly dressed; (*vestito in modo trasandato*) carelessly dressed, got up **2.** (*male arredato*) poorly furnished.

malnàto, *ag.* **1.** (*maleducato*) ill-bred, uncouth **2.** (*malvagio*) wicked **3.** (*disgraziato*) wretched **4.** (*dannoso*) damnable ǁ *s.m.* wretch.

malnòto, *ag.* little known.

màlo, *ag.* (*rar.*) bad: *mala cosa,* evil thing (*o* misfortune): *mala cosa è che nessuno ci ami davvero,* it's a misfortune to have no one who really loves you; *mala cosa è l'invidia,* envy is evil; *mali effetti,* bad (*o* evil) effects; *mal esempio,* bad example; *mal esito,* failure: *il mal esito della nostra spedizione,* the failure of our expedition; *mala fama,* ill-fame (*o* repute); *mala fortuna, mala sorte,* bad luck; *la mala gente,* the wicked; (*malavita*) the underworld (*o* the low life); *mala morte,* miserable death: *morì di una mala morte,* he died a miserable death (*o* he came to a miserable end); *male nuove,* bad news; *male parole,* unkind (*o* offensive) words; *mala voce,* calumny; *in — modo,* rudely; *m'accorsi d'essere arrivato in mal punto,* I realised I had arrived at the wrong moment; *prese le mie parole in mala parte,* he took my words in bad part (*o* amiss); *si trovò a mal partito,* he found himself in an awkward situation; *vista la mala parata fuggì,* seeing the bad turn things were taking, he ran away.

malòcchio, *s.m.* evil eye: *portare il* —, to bring misfortune; *vedere qlcu. di* —, to look askance at s.o.

malóra, *s.f.* ruin: *andare in* —, to go to ruin (*o* fam. to go to the dogs); *mandare in — qlcu.,* to bring s.o. to ruin ǁ *va alla* —!, go to the devil!.

malóre, *s.m.* illness, sickness: *egli fu colto da un improvviso* —, he was seized by a sudden illness.

malparlànte, *ag.* careless in one's speech (*predicativo*): *è* —, he speaks very badly.

malpensànte, *ag.* wrong-thinking, wrong-minded.

malpíglio, *s.m.* scornful gesture, disdainful gesture.

malpràtico, *ag.* inexperienced, unpractised: *è* —, he has had little practice.

malpreparàto, *ag.* badly prepared.

malpròprio, *ag.* **1.** unsuitable **2.** (*inopportuno*) inopportune, unseasonable.

malprovvedúto, *ag.* unprovided (with sthg.), lacking (in sthg.), short (of sthg.).

malsàno, *ag.* **1.** unhealthy, sickly; (*debole*) weak: *mente malsana,* unsound mind; *persona malsana,* sickly person **2.** (*insalubre*) unhealthy, unwholesome, insalubrious: *aria malsana,* unhealthy air; *cibo* —, unwholesome food; *clima* —, unhealthy climate; *luogo* —, unhealthy place **3.** (*pernicioso, nocivo*) unwholesome, pernicious: *idee malsane,* dangerous ideas; *letteratura malsana,* pernicious literature; *teorie malsane,* unwholesome theories.

malsicúro, *ag.* **1.** unsafe, insecure: *luogo* —, unsafe place; *seggiola malsicura,* unsteady chair; *trave malsicura,* insecure rafter **2.** (*incerto*) uncertain; (*di persona*) irresolute: *persona malsicura di sè,* irresolute person; *risposta malsicura,* uncertain reply **3.** (*inattendibile*) unreliable: *testimonianza malsicura,* unreliable evidence.

màlta¹, *s.f.* **1.** (*edil.*) mortar **2.** (*catrame minerale*) maltha **3.** (*dial.*) (*fango*) mud, mire, slime.

Màlta², *no.pr.f.* (*geog.*) Malta ǁ *i Cavalieri di* —, Knights of Malta ǁ *croce di* —, Maltese cross.

maltagliàti, *s.m.pl.* (*cuc.*) "maltagliati" (kind of "pasta" of assorted shapes).

maltalènto, *s.m.* ill-will.

maltàsi, *s.f.* (*fisiol.*) maltase.

maltèmpo, *s.m.* bad weather.

maltenúto, *ag.* untidy, unkempt: *capelli maltenuti*, unkempt hair; *registri maltenuti*, ill-kept books.

maltése, *ag. s.c.* Maltese (*invariato al pl.*): *dialetto —*, Maltese ‖ *cane —*, Maltese dog ‖ *febbre —*, (*patol.*) Malta fever.

màlto, *s.m.* **1.** malt **2.** (*caffè d'orzo*) barley coffee.

maltolleràbile, *ag.* unbearable, intolerable.

maltòlto, *ag.* ill-gotten; extorted ‖ *s.m.* ill-gotten goods (*pl.*); ill-gotten property: *restituire il —*, to restore one's ill-gotten gains.

maltòsio, *s.m.* (*chim.*) maltose.

maltrattaménto, *s.m.* ill-treatment, ill-usage.

maltrattàre, *v.t.* **1.** to ill-treat, to ill-use, to maltreat: *maltratta continuamente la moglie*, he constantly ill-treats his wife; *non mi farò —!*, I won't be abused!; *gli animali*, to ill-treat (*o* to be cruel to) animals **2.** (*interpretare erroneamente*) to misinterpret: *— un autore, la storia*, to misinterpret an author, history.

maltusianísmo, *s.m.* (*st. econ.*) Malthusianism.

maltusiàno, *ag.* Malthusian.

malúccio, *av.* rather badly.

malumóre, *s.m.* **1.** bad mood: *non seppe nascondere il suo —*, he could not conceal the bad mood he was in; *il rifiuto lo mise di —*, the refusal threw him into a bad mood; *essere di —*, to be in a bad mood; *rispondere di —*, to answer snappishly; *sfogare il proprio — su qlcu.*, to vent one's spleen on s.o. (*o* to take it out on s.o.) **2.** (*disaccordo*) slight disagreement.

màlva, *s.f.* (*bot.*) mallow.

malvàceo, *ag.* (*bot.*) malvaceous.

malvagiaménte, *av.* wickedly, evilly, nastily: *agì — con noi*, she treated us very nastily.

malvàgio, *ag.* wicked, evil: *azione malvagia*, ill-deed (*o* wrong); *natura, indole malvagia*, evil nature; *tiranno —*, wicked tyrant; *vita malvagia*, evil life; *provò una gioia malvagia vedendolo soffrire*, he experienced a savage pleasure on seeing him suffer; *aver l'aria malvagia*, to look evil; *non essere —*, to be harmless ‖ *il pranzo non era —*, (*fam.*) the dinner was not bad ‖ *s.m.* wicked man ‖ *il Malvagio*, the Evil One.

malvagità, *s.f.* **1.** wickedness, evil; nastiness: *la sua — era quasi incredibile*, he was almost incredibly evil; *fare ql.co. per —*, to do sthg. out of malice **2.** (*atto malvagio*) evil deed, evil action: *ha commesso molte malvagità in vita sua*, his life has been full of evil deeds **3.** (*detto malvagio*) evil word: *dire una —*, to say an unkind thing.

malvasía, *s.f.* **1.** (*uva*) malvasia **2.** (*vino*) malmsey.

malversatóre, *s.m.* (*dir.*) embezzler.

malversazióne, *s.f.* (*dir.*) embezzlement.

malvestíto, *ag.* badly dressed; shabby.

malvissúto, *ag.* ill-lived.

malvísto, *ag.* unpopular (with s.o., sthg.): *era — dai suoi colleghi*, he was unpopular with (*o* disliked by *o* frowned upon by) his colleagues.

malvivènte, *s.m.* gangster, criminal; (*sl.*) crook: *quel caffè è un covo di malviventi*, that café is a haunt of criminals.

malvivènza, *s.f.* **1.** delinquency, criminality, criminal activity: *la — è in aumento*, delinquency (*o* crime) is on the increase **2.** (*i malviventi*) gangsters (*pl.*), criminals (*pl.*), crooks (*pl.*); gangsterdom: *la nostra città è infestata dalla —*, our town is swarming with criminals.

malvolentièri, *av.* against one's will, reluctantly, unwillingly: *acconsentire — a fare ql.co.*, to agree reluctantly to do sthg.

malvolére, *v.t.* to dislike: *era malvoluto da tutti*, he was universally disliked; *farsi —*, to make oneself disliked; *prendere a — qlcu.*, to take a dislike to s.o.

malvolére, *s.m.* ill-will; (*malvagità*) wickedness.

màmbo, *s.m.* (*musica, danza*) mambo.

mamelúceo, *V.* **mammalúceo.**

màmma[1], *s.f.* **1.** mama, mum(my), mother: *mi fu —*, she was a mother to me ‖ *— mia!*, good gracious! (o my goodness!) ‖ *cocco di —*, mother's darling ‖ *essere attaccato alle gonne della —*, to be tied to one's mother's apron-strings **2.** (*feccia*) mother; dregs (of wine) (*pl.*).

màmma[2], *s.f.* (*mammella*) breast.

mammalúceo, *s.m.* **1.** (*st.*) Mameluke **2.** (*fam.*) (*sciocco*) simpleton, fool, blockhead.

mammàrio, *ag.* (*anat.*) mammary: *le glandole mammarie*, the mammary glands.

mammèlla, *s.f.* (*anat.*) mamma (*pl.* mammae); (*fam.*) breast; (*di animali da latte*) udder.

mammellàre, *ag.* (*anat.*) mamillary.

mammellóne, *s.m.* (*geog.*) round-topped mountain.

mammífero, *ag.* mammiferous, mammalian ‖ *s.m.* mammal ‖ *i mammiferi*, the Mammalia.

mammillàre, *ag.* (*anat.*) mamillary.

màmmola, *s.f.* **1.** (*bot.*) sweet-smelling violet **2.** (*fanciulla modesta*) shrinking violet.

màmmolo, *s.m.* child, baby.

Mammóna, *no.pr.m.* (*Bibbia*) Mammon ‖ *non si può servire a Dio e a —*, one can't serve God and Mammon ‖ *mammóna*, *s.m. fig.* (*la ricchezza*) Mammon.

Mammóne, *no.pr.m.* (*mit.*) Mammon.

mammóne, *ag.*: *gatto —*, (*zool.*) mandrill; *fig.* bogy-man.

mammút, *s.m.* (*paleont.*) mammoth.

manachíno, *s.m.* (*ornit.*) manakin.

manaiuòla, *s.f.* hatchet.

manàle, *s.m.* protective leather mitten.

Manàsse, *no.pr.m.* (*Bibbia*) Manasseh.

manàta, *s.f.* **1.** handful: *una — di caramelle*, a handful of sweets; *una — d'oro*, a handful of gold; *buttar via denaro a manate*, to throw money away by the handful (*o* to throw money away in handfuls) **2.** (*colpo dato con la mano*) slap.

mànca, *s.f.* **1.** (*mano sinistra*) left hand **2.** (*parte sinistra*) left, left-hand side: *voltò a —*, he turned (to the) left ‖ *a diritta e a —*, on all sides.

mancaménto, *s.m.* **1.** (*svenimento*) swoon, fainting-fit: *essa fu colta da —*, she fainted **2.** (*mancanza*) lack, want, shortage, deficiency: *— di cibo*, shortage of food; *— di mezzi*, lack of means; *l'arte supplisce i mancamenti della natura*, art supplies the deficiencies of nature **3.** (*fallo*) fault; (*difetto*) defect, shortcoming.

mancànte, *ag.* incomplete, defective: *un conto —*, an account which doesn't balance; *un'iscrizione —*, an incomplete inscription; *una lapide antica —*, a damaged ancient headstone; *manoscritto —*, defective manuscript ‖ *è stato trovato —*, (*in fallo*) he has been found faulty.

mancànza, *s.f.* **1.** lack, want, shortage, deficiency: *— di coraggio*, want (*o* lack) of courage; *— di denaro*, lack of money; *— di educazione*, bad manners; *— di immaginazione*, want of imagination; *— di mano d'opera*, shortage of labour; *— di tempo*, lack of time; *la sua — di rispetto verso i superiori è deplorevole*, his lack of respect to his superiors is deplorable; *il tuo atteggiamento denota — di comprensione*, your behaviour shows lack of understanding; *sentire la — di qlcu., ql.co.*, to miss s.o., sthg.: *ella sente la — dei suoi amici*, she misses her friends ‖ *in — di*, failing (*o* for want of): *in — di frutta fresca, potremmo mangiare frutta conservata*, failing fresh fruit, we could eat tinned fruit; *in — di meglio, andammo al cinema*, for want of something better to do we went to the cinema ‖ *per — di*, for want (*o* lack) of: *fu assolto per — di prove*, he was acquitted for want of evidence; *molte persone soffrono per — di cibo*, many people suffer from shortage of food **2.** (*assenza*) absence: *durante la sua —*, during his absence ‖ *in — di*, in the absence of: *in — del presidente, firmerà il segretario*, in the absence of the chairman, the secretary shall sign **3.** (*fallo*) fault; (*difetto*) defect, shortcoming: *una lieve —*, a slight fault; *questa è una grave — da parte sua*, this is a bad fault on his part; *supplire alle proprie mancanze*, to make up for one's shortcomings.

mancàre, *v.i.* **1.** to be lacking (in sthg.); to lack (s.o., sthg.); to be wanting (in sthg.); to want (s.o., sthg.); to be missing: *gli manca il buon senso*, he lacks (o he is lacking in) common sense; *gli manca il denaro per farlo*, he lacks the money to do it (o he hasn't got enough money to do it); *le mancano due denti*, she has two teeth missing; *manca di amici*, he lacks friends (o he hasn't got many friends); *manca di coraggio*, he is lacking in courage; *manca di cortesia*, he is lacking in courtesy (o he is rude); *manca di denaro*, he is short of money; *la minestra manca di sale*, the soup needs salt; *la sua casa manca di tutto*, his house lacks everything (o *fam.* his house is short of everything) ‖ *le manca un venerdì*, (*fam. scherz.*) she is a bit barmy ‖ *— di rispetto a qlcu.*, to show little respect for s.o. **2.** (*non esserci*) to be missing; (*essere assente*) to be absent: *mancano delle carte che erano sulla mia scrivania*, some papers that were here on my desk are missing; *mancano le prove*, there is no proof; *mancano i miei gioielli*, my jewels are missing; *da quanto tempo mancate da qui?*, how long have you been away?; *l'impiegato manca dall'ufficio*, the clerk is absent from his office; *il ragazzo manca dalla scuola*, the boy is absent from school; *— a un appuntamento*, to miss an appointment ‖ *venire a —*, to pass away (o to die): *egli venne a — due anni fa*, he passed away two years ago **3.** (*richiedersi come completamento*) to be needed: *mancano cinque sterline per completare la somma*, five pounds are needed to make up the sum; *mancano dieci minuti alle due*, it is ten (minutes) to two; *manca un giocatore alla squadra*, the team is one short; *manca poco a finire*, it is nearly finished ‖ *ci mancherebbe altro!*, *ci mancherebbe anche questa!*, that would be the limit! (o that would be the last straw!) ‖ *poco mancò che non morisse, vincesse, cadesse, ecc.*, he nearly died, won, fell, etc. **4.** (*venir meno*) to fail (s.o., in sthg., to do); (*venire a mancare*) to run out of (sthg.): *ci mancò la farina*, we ran out of flour; *è mancata la luce*, the light has gone out; *mi mancarono le forze*, my strength failed me; *mi sentii — il respiro*, I felt I was suffocating; *la voce le mancò per lo spavento*, she was speechless with fright; *— a una promessa, alla parola data*, to fail to keep a promise; *— al proprio dovere*, to fail in one's duty ‖ *sentirsi —*, to feel faint ‖ *sentirsi — il terreno sotto i piedi*, *fig.* to feel lost: *mi sento — il terreno sotto i piedi senza il tuo aiuto*, I feel lost without your help **5.** (*tralasciare*) to fail: « *Non — di scrivermi* », « *Non mancherò!* », "Don't forget to write to me", "I shan't fail!"; *non manchi di pagare*, don't forget to pay **6.** (*sbagliare*) to make a mistake; to err; (*agire scorrettamente*) to wrong (s.o.): *egli mancò verso di me*, he treated me rather badly; *hai mancato se non glielo hai fatto sapere*, it was wrong of you not to tell him; *tutti manchiamo*, we all make mistakes; *— verso il prossimo*, to wrong one's fellow-men ‖ *v.t.* to miss: *— il bersaglio*, to miss the mark (o the target); *— un'occasione*, to miss an opportunity.

mancàto, *ag.* **1.** (*fallito*) manqué; unsuccessful: *un attore —*, an actor manqué; *colpo —*, misfire; *fig.* (*tentativo fallito*) unsuccessful attempt **2.** (*non avvenuto*): *mancata accettazione*, non-acceptance; *— arrivo*, non-arrival; *— pagamento*, non-payment.

Manchester, *no.pr.f.* (*geog.*) Manchester: *abitante di —*, Mancunian.

manchévole, *ag.* defective, faulty: *memoria —*, defective (o faulty) memory; *traduzione —*, faulty translation.

manchevolézza, *s.f.* **1.** (*imperfezione*) imperfection; (*mancanza*) defect, fault: *nonostante tutte le sue manchevolezze è un brav'uomo*, in spite of all his faults

he is a good man; *commettere una —*, to commit a fault; *supplire una —*, to make good a defect **2.** (*l'essere manchevole*) imperfection, defectiveness, deficiency.

manchevolménte, *av.* imperfectly, defectively.

mància, *s.f.* tip, gratuity: *dare la — a qlcu.*, to tip s.o. (o to give s.o. a tip) ‖ *— competente*, reward.

manciàta, *s.f.* handful: *una — di polvere*, a handful of dust ‖ *a manciate*, in handfuls: *gettare denaro a manciate*, to throw money away with both hands.

mancìna, *s.f.* **1.** left hand ‖ *a —*, to the left **2.** (*donna*) left-hander.

mancinìsmo, *s.m.* left-handedness.

mancìno, *ag.* **1.** left-hand **2.** (*sleale*) treacherous: *colpo —*, unfair trick ‖ *s.m.* left-hander.

mancìpio, *s.m.* **1.** (*st. romana*) manciple; bond-slave **2.** (*schiavo*) slave.

manciù, *ag.s.m.* Manchu.

Manciucuò, *no.pr.m..* (*geog.*) Manchukuo.

Manciùria, *no.pr.f.* (*geog.*) Manchuria.

màneco, *ag.* left; left-hand (*attributivo*): *sulla riva manca del fiume*, on the left bank of the river.

mànco, *av.* **1.** (*nemmeno*) not even: *— a dirlo*, obviously; *— per idea*, *— per sogno*, by no means; *non ci ho — pensato*, I have not even thought of it **2.** (*letter.*) (*meno*) less: *con poca roba e con — reputazione*, with little property and even less reputation ‖ *— male!*, (*fam.*) that's a good thing (o job)!.

mandaménto, *s.m.* district; area of local government.

mandànte, *s.m.* (*dir.*) principal, instigator.

mandàre, *v.t.* **1.** to send: *ci mandò in Germania a studiare*, he sent us to Germany to study; *le hanno mandato gli auguri di Natale*, they have sent her their greetings for Christmas; *lo mandarono ad avvertirmi del pericolo*, they sent him to warn me of the danger; *lo mandarono ambasciatore a Parigi*, they sent him as ambassador to Paris; *lo mandarono in esilio*, they banished him; *manda le tue lettere a questo indirizzo*, send your letters to this address; *mandami tuo fratello il più presto possibile*, send your brother to me as soon as possible; *mandami due righe*, drop me a line; *non ha ancora mandato il conto*, he has not yet sent the bill; *quella ditta manda merci in tutto il mondo*, that firm sends goods all over the world; *— gli abiti in tintoria*, to send one's clothes to the cleaner's; *— a chiamare qlcu.*, *a prendere ql.co.*, to send for s.o., sthg.: *mandammo a chiamare il dottore*, we sent for the doctor; *mandate a prenderlo a casa mia*, send to my house for it; *— acqua in un canale*, to make water flow into a canal; *— a dire ql.co. a qlcu.*, *— un messaggio a qlcu.*, to send word to s.o.; *— un bacio a qlcu.*, to blow s.o. a kiss; *— un bambino a scuola, a letto*, to send a child to school, to bed; *— circolari*, to send out circulars; *— la corrente su un filo*, (*elett.*) to pass a current through a wire; *— in prigione qlcu.*, to send s.o. to prison; *— una lettera*, to send a letter; *— un pacco per posta, per ferrovia*, to send a parcel by post, by rail; *— per via mare*, to ship; *— le proprie dimissioni*, to send in one's resignation; *— qlcu. a fare una commissione*, to send s.o. on an errand ‖ *che Dio ce la mandi buona!*, God help us! ‖ *non glielo mandò a dire*, she told him so to his face ‖ *piove che Dio la manda*, it is raining cats and dogs ‖ *— accidenti a qlcu.*, to call down curses upon s.o.'s head ‖ *— ad effetto, a compimento*, to carry out ‖ *— a gambe all'aria qlcu.*, to send s.o. sprawling ‖ *— al diavolo, all'inferno, a quel paese*, to tell s.o. to go to blazes: *lo mandai a quel paese*, I told him to go to the devil ‖ *— all'altro mondo, in paradiso*, to finish off: *il secondo attacco di cuore lo ha mandato all'altro mondo*, the second heart-attack finished him off ‖ *— a memoria*, to learn by heart ‖ *— a monte, all'aria*, to ruin: *— a monte un accordo*, to ruin an agreement; *— a monte un matrimonio*, to ruin a marriage ‖ *— a morte qlcu.*, to sentence s.o. to death ‖ *— a picco*, (*mar.*) to scuttle (o to sink) ‖ *— a rotoli, in malora, in rovina*, to ruin: *il vizio del giuoco mandò* *in malora lui e la sua famiglia*, his gambling ruined him and his family ‖ — *a sacco*, to sack (o to pillage) ‖ — *a spasso qlcu.*, to sack s.o. (*o* to give s.o. the sack) ‖ — *avanti*, *fig.* to keep going (o to keep up): *stenta a* — *avanti la baracca*, he has difficulty in keeping his business going ‖ — *da Erode a Pilato*, *fig.* to send from pillar to post ‖ — *giù*, to swallow (anche *fig.*): *questa è dura da* — *giù*, *fig.* that's hard to swallow ‖ — *imprecazioni, maledizioni contro qlcu.*, to curse s.o. ‖ — *in lungo, da oggi a domani*, to put off (o to delay) ‖ — *qlcu. ben vestito*, to dress s.o. well: *manda sua figlia molto ben vestita*, she dresses her daughter very well ‖ — *via qlcu.*, to send s.o. away; (*licenziare*) to dismiss s.o.: — *via qlcu. sui due piedi*, to sack s.o. on the spot ‖ *Dio manda il freddo secondo i panni*, *prov.* God tempers the wind to the shorn lamb 2. (*emettere, esalare*) to give off, to emit: *mandò un profondo sospiro*, she sighed deeply; *quel flauto manda un suono dolcissimo*, that flute has a very sweet tone; *questa rosa manda un profumo delizioso*, this rose smells lovely; — *un grido*, to utter (o to let out) a cry 3. (*far funzionare*) to drive: *l'acqua manda la ruota del mulino*, the water drives the mill-wheel.

mandaríno[1], *s.m.* (*st. cinese*) mandarin.

mandaríno[2], *s.m.* (*bot.*) tangerine, mandarin(e).

mandàta, *s.f.* 1. batch: *far entrare tutti in una sola* —, to let everybody in together 2. (*di chiave*) turn: *chiudere a doppia* —, to double-lock.

mandatàrio, *s.m.* (*dir.*) mandatary, mandate holder.

mandàto, *s.m.* 1. (*incarico*) mandate, commission, mission: — *speciale*, special mandate (*o* mission); *rifiutò di accettare il* — *di tutela*, he refused to accept the guardianship; *eseguire un* —, to carry out a commission 2. (*comm.*) agency; (*ordine*) warrant, order: — *di consegna*, warrant for delivery; — *di pagamento*, order for payment; *estinzione del* —, termination of agency; *revoca del* —, revocation of agency; *rinunzia del* —, renunciation of agency; *rinunziare al* —, to renounce the agency 3. (*dir.*) warrant, order, mandate: — *d'arresto contro qlcu.*, warrant for s.o.'s arrest; — *di comparizione*, summons; — *di perquisizione*, search-warrant; — *di procura*, power of attorney; — *papale*, papal mandate (*o* rescript) 4. (*pol.*) mandate: *la Lega delle Nazioni concedeva mandati su certi territori*, the League of Nations granted mandates over certain territories.

mandíbola, *s.f.* jaw, mandible.

mandòla, *s.f.* (*mus.*) mandola.

mandolinàta, *s.f.* (*mus.*) mandolin(e) music.

mandolinísta, *s.c.* mandolinist, mandolin(e) player.

mandolíno, *s.m.* mandolin(e).

màndorla, *s.f.* 1. almond: *occhi a* —, almond-shaped eyes; *olio di mandorle*, almond-oil; *pasta di mandorle*, almond-paste 2. (*seme, gheriglio*) kernel 3. (*arch. pitt.*) mandorla 4. (*mar.*) bull's eye.

mandorlàto, *s.m.* (*cuc.*) almond-cake.

màndorlo, *s.m.* almond-tree.

màndra, *s.f.* herd.

mandràcchio, *s.m.* (*mar.*) small inner harbour.

mandràgola, mandràgora, *s.f.* (*bot.*) mandrake, mandragora.

màndria, *s.f.* herd.

mandriàno, *s.m.* herdsman (*pl.* herdsmen).

mandrillo, *s.m.* (*zool.*) mandrill.

mandrinàggio, *s.m.* (*mec.*) enlarging.

mandríno, *s.m.* (*mec.*) 1. mandrel, mandril 2. (*albero porta-utensile di fresatrice, ecc.*) spindle; (*amer.*) arbor 3. (*barra alesatrice*) boring-bar 4. (*piatto rotante*) chuck.

mandrítta, *s.f.* right hand: *a* —, to the right.

manducàre, *v.t.* (*arc.*) to manducate, to chew.

màne, *s.f.* (*poet.*) morn, morning: *da* — *a sera*, from morning to evening; (*continuamente*) all the time.

manécchia, *s.f.* 1. plough-handle 2. (*maniglia*) handle.

maneggévole, maneggiàbile, *ag.* 1. handy, manageable: *arnese* —, handy tool; *poco* —, awkward 2. (*trattabile*) manageable, tractable: *a poco a poco quel ragazzo si fa più* —, that boy is gradually getting more manageable.

maneggiaménto, *s.m.* 1. handling 2. (*intrigo*) plot.

maneggiàre, *v.t.* 1. (*impastare*) to knead; to mould: — *la creta*, to mould clay; — *la pasta*, to knead dough 2. (*strumenti, ecc.*) to handle, to wield, to use (anche *fig.*): *ha imparato a* — *i suoi strumenti*, he has learnt how to handle his tools; — *un fucile*, to handle a gun; — *la penna*, to wield the pen: *sa* — *la penna*, he wields a formidable pen; — *un soggetto*, to handle a subject; — *una spada*, to wield a sword 3. (*cavalli*) to manage: *sa* — *bene un cavallo*, he knows how to manage a horse 4. (*persone*) to handle, to deal with (s.o.): *bisogna saperlo* —, one must know how to handle (o to deal with) him; *è una persona piuttosto difficile da* —, he is rather difficult to deal with ‖ **maneggiàrsi**, *v.r.* to manage.

manéggio, *s.m.* 1. (*il maneggiare*) handling; (*uso*) use: *il* — *degli affari*, the handling of business; — *delle armi*, arms-drill 2. (*intrigo*) plot, intrigue: *ci devono essere sotto dei maneggi*, there must be some sort of plot going on; *i suoi maneggi furono scoperti*, his plot was laid bare 3. (*equitazione*) (*l'esercizio del cavalcare*) manège; (*galoppatoio*) riding-ground, gallop: *scuola di* —, riding-school.

maneggióne, *s.m.* 1. factotum; handy-man; jack of all trades 2. (*intrigante*) plotter, intriguer.

manescaménte, *av.* roughly.

manésco, *ag.* 1. rough; aggressive; brutal: *un uomo* —, a man free with his fists; *suo marito è piuttosto* —, her husband knocks her about 2. (*maneggevole*) handy.

manétta, *s.f.* 1. handcuff, manacle: *gli misero le manette*, they handcuffed him 2. (*impugnatura*) handle.

manévole, *agg.* 1. supple; pliant, pliable; yielding 2. (*di persona*) submissive; docile; tractable.

manfaníle, mànfano, *s.m.* (*agr.*) flail-handle.

manfòrte, *s.f.* help, aid, assistance: *ci diede* —, he gave us a helping hand; *prestare* —, to (give) help.

Manfrèdi, *no.pr.m.* (*st.*) Manfred.

manganàre, *v.t.* (*ind. tessile*) to mangle.

manganàto, *s.m.* (*chim.*) manganate.

manganatúra, *s.f.* mangling.

manganèlla, *s.f.* 1. folding choir-stall 2. (*st. mil.*) mangonel.

manganellàre, *v.t.* (*rar.*) to cudgel; to bludgeon.

manganellàta, *s.f.* blow with a cudgel.

manganèllo, *s.m.* 1. cudgel; bludgeon 2. (*ind. tessile*) mangle.

manganése, *s.m.* (*chim.*) manganese.

mangànico, *ag.* (*chim.*) manganic.

manganíte, *s.f.* (*chim. min.*) manganite.

màngano, *s.m.* 1. (*ind. tessile*) mangle 2. (*st. militare*) mangonel, ballista.

mangeréccio, *ag.* edible, eatable: *funghi mangerecci*, mushrooms.

mangería, *s.f.* illicit gain, illicit profit; (*fam.*) fiddle: *tutti sanno che ha fatto delle mangerie*, everybody knows about his fiddling.

mangiabambíni, *s.m.* ogre.

mangiàbile, *ag.* eatable, edible.

mangiacàrte, *s.m.* (*spreg.*) shyster; (*amer.*) pettifogger.

mangiacristiàni, *s.m.* blusterer.

mangiaménto, *s.m.* 1. eating 2. (*mangerìa*) illicit profit, illicit gain.

mangiaminèstre, *s.m.* (*parassita*) parasite, sponger.

mangiamòccoli, *s.m.* religious fanatic, bigot, zealot.

mangiapàne, *s.m.* idler, loafer ‖ *è un* — *a tradimento*, he is a parasite (o sponger).

mangiapolènta, *s.m.* idler, loafer.

mangiapòpoli, *s.m.* despot, dictator, tyrant.

mangiaprèti, *s.m.* rabid anticlerical.

mangiàre, *v.t.i.* **1.** to eat; (*consumare i pasti*) to have one's meals, to take one's meals; (*pranzure*) to dine; (*a mezzogiorno*) to lunch: *egli mangia di tutto,* he eats anything; *abitualmente mangiamo in cucina,* we usually have (*o* take) our meals (*o* we usually eat) in the kitchen; *da lei si mangia bene,* you eat well at her house; *ristorante in cui si mangia bene,* restaurant where the food is good; *gli uccelli gli mangiavano nella mano,* the birds ate out of his hand; *vuoi da — ?,* would you like something to eat?; — *al ristorante,* to have one's meals (*o* to eat) at a restaurant; — *a sazietà,* to eat one's fill; — *bene, male,* to eat well, badly (*o* to have a good meal, to have a poor meal); — *con appetito,* to eat heartily; — *di grasso,* to eat meat; — *di magro,* to abstain (*o* to abstain from eating meat); — *fuori di casa,* to dine, to lunch out; — *ql.co. di gusto,* to eat sthg. with relish; — *svogliatamente,* to pick at one's food; *dar da — a,* to feed: *hai dato da — al cane?;* have you fed the dog? || *sembrava volesse mangiarmi,* he looked at me as if he wanted to eat me || — *a crepapelle,* to stuff oneself with food || — *come un lupo,* to eat like a horse; (*voracemente*) to wolf || — *la foglia,* to smell a rat || — *negli affari,* to make an illicit profit in business || — *pane a tradimento,* to be a parasite (*o* a sponger) || — *pan pentito,* to eat humble pie || — *le parole,* to mumble (*o* to speak indistinctly) || — *per quattro,* to have a huge meal || — *qlcu. dai baci,* to kiss s.o. fondly || — *vivo qlcu.,* to bite s.o.'s head off || *chi pecora si fa, il lupo se lo mangia,* prov. he that makes himself a sheep shall be eaten by the wolf || *si deve — per vivere, e non vivere per —,* prov. don't live to eat, but eat to live **2.** (*consumare*) to consume, to eat up: *quella macchina mangia tanto carbone,* that machine just eats up coal **3.** (*dissipare*) to waste, to squander, to dissipate: — *i soldi di qlcu.,* to squander s.o.'s money **4.** (*corrodere*) to corrode, to eat away, to eat into (sthg.): *gli acidi mangiano i metalli,* acids eat into (*o* corrode) metals; *la riva fu mangiata dal fiume,* the banks were eaten away by the river; *la ruggine mangia il ferro,* rust corrodes iron **5.** (*a carte, scacchi, ecc.*) to take || **mangiàrsi,** *v.r.* (*intensivo*): *si è mangiato tutta la minestra,* he has eaten up all the soup; — *dalla rabbia,* — *il fegato,* to be eaten up with anger; — *le parole,* (*borbottare*) to mumble; — *i propri soldi,* to squander (*o* to waste) one's money; — *qlcu. con gli occhi,* to devour s.o. with one's eyes; — *le unghie,* to bite one's nails.

mangiàre, *s.m.* **1.** eating: *il — è il suo unico piacere,* eating is his only pleasure **2.** (*cibo*) food: — *leggero,* light food; — *pesante,* heavy food: *non posso digerire i mangiari pesanti,* I cannot digest heavy food **3.** (*pasto*) meal: *c'era un — molto leggero,* there was a very light meal **4.** (*cucina*) cooking: *il — da loro è molto buono,* the cooking at their house is very good.

mangiàta, *s.f.* square meal, full meal: *feci una bella — di maccheroni,* I had a good plateful of macaroni; *feci una bella — d'uva,* I stuffed myself with grapes; *ho fatto una bella —,* I have had a good meal.

mangiatóia, *s.f.* **1.** manger: *il foraggio è nella —,* the fodder is in the manger **2.** (*scherz.*) (*tavola da pranzo*) dining-table.

mangiatóre, *s.m.,* **mangiatríce,** *s.f.* heavy eater.

mangiatòria, *s.f.* (*scherz.*) eating.

mangiatúra, *s.f.* (*pop.*) **1.** (*il mangiare*) eating **2.** (*segno di puntura d'insetto*) insect-bite.

mangiatútto, *s.m.* **1.** big indiscriminate eater **2.** (*mangione*) great eater **3.** *fig.* spendthrift.

mangiaúfo, *s.m.* parasite, sponger.

mangíme, *s.m.* (*foraggio*) fodder; (*per pollame*) poultry feed, chicken feed; (*per uccelli*) bird-seed.

mangióne, *s.m.* heavy eater, great eater.

mangiucchiàre, *v.t.* to nibble at (sthg.): *il bambino mangiucchiava un pezzo di pane,* the child was nibbling at a piece of bread; *ella mangiucchia biscotti tutto il*

santo giorno, she's always nibbling biscuits || *v.i.* to toy with one's food, to pick at one's food.

màngo, *s.m.* (*bot.*) mango (*pl.* mangoes, mangos).

mangòsta, mangústa, *s.f.* (*zool.*) mongoose.

màni, *s.m.pl.* (*mit.*) manes.

manía, *s.f.* **1.** *fig.* mania; fixation; (*entusiasmo passeggero*) fad: *il giardinaggio è la sua —,* he is mad about gardening; *ha la — di far collezioni,* he has a mania for collecting things; *questa è una delle mie manie,* this is one of my fads **2.** (*patol.*) mania: — *di persecuzione,* persecution mania.

maníaco, *ag.* **1.** (*patol.*) maniac(al): *furia maniaca,* maniacal fury; *persona maniaca,* maniac **2.** *fig.* mad (about sthg.); crazy (about sthg.); keen (on sthg.): *è — della musica,* he is very keen on music; *è — dell'ordine,* he is terribly fussy about tidiness || *s.m.* (*patol.*) maniac.

màniea, *s.f.* **1.** sleeve: *maniche corte,* short sleeves: *un abito (da donna) a maniche corte,* a short-sleeved dress; *maniche lunghe,* long sleeves; *maniche tre quarti,* three-quarters-length sleeves; *una camicetta senza maniche,* a sleeveless blouse; *mezza —,* (*soprammanica*) half sleeve; *essere in maniche di camicia,* to be in one's shirt-sleeves; *rimboccarsi le maniche,* to tuck up (*o* to roll up) one's sleeves; *tirare qlcu. per la —,* to pluck s.o.'s sleeve || *una — di ladri,* a band of thieves || *è un altro paio di maniche,* that is quite another piece of cake || *essere di — larga,* to be indulgent; (*di larghe vedute*) to be broad-minded; *essere di — stretta,* to be strict; (*di idee ristrette*) to be narrow-minded || *essere nella — di qlcu.,* to be in s.o.'s good books **2.** (*aer. mar.*): — *a vento,* (*aer.*) wind-sleeve; (*mar.*) vane **3.** (*metal.*) (*di alto forno*) downtake **4.** (*di armatura*) coat of mail || **Mànica,** *no.pr.f.* (*geog.*) the English Channel.

manicarétto, *s.m.* titbit, choice dish, dainty.

manicàto, *ag.* (*rar.*) handled.

manicheísmo, *s.m.* (*st. relig.*) Manich(a)eism.

manichèo, *ag.* (*st. relig.*) Manich(a)ean || *s.m.* (*st. relig.*) Manichee.

manichétta, *s.f.* **1.** (*soprammanica*) half sleeve **2.** (*tubo*) hose: — *antincendio,* fire hose; — *d'aspirazione,* suction hose; — *del palombaro,* diver's air tube; — *di gomma,* rubber hose; — *di tela,* canvas hose; — *per freno pneumatico,* pneumatic brake hose.

manichíno[1] *s.m.* (*polsino*) cuff, wristband.

manichíno[2] *s.m.* (*fantoccio usato come modello*) manikin; (*per sarti*) tailor's dummy.

mànico, *s.m.* handle; haft, shaft; (*di strumento musicale a corde*) neck: — *del coltello,* knife handle; — *dell'ombrello,* umbrella-stick; — *della spada,* sword handle; *il — del violino,* the neck of the violin; — *di scopa,* broomstick || *il difetto sta nel —,* *fig.* the fault lies not in the execution, but in the original idea || *avere il coltello per il —,* *fig.* to have the upper hand.

manicòmio, *s.m.* mental hospital, lunatic asylum; (*spreg.*) mad-house.

manicòtto, *s.m.* **1.** muff **2.** (*mec.*) sleeve, coupling: — *a forcella,* yoke; — *d'accoppiamento,* coupling-box (*o* box coupling); — *del radiatore,* (*aut.*) radiator hose; — *di filatura,* (*ind. tessile*) spinning cot; — *di riscaldamento,* (*aut.*) heating muff.

manicure, *s.c.* manicurist, manicure.

manièra, *s.f.* **1.** manner, way, fashion: *in questa —,* thus (*o* in this way); *la sua — di parlare,* his way of speaking (*o* the way he speaks); *ciascuno lo fa alla sua —,* everyone does it in his own fashion; *è felice nella sua —,* he is happy in his own way; *lasciatemi fare alla mia —,* let me do it my own way; *parlare in — sgarbata,* to speak in a rude fashion (*o* to speak rudely) || *in — che,* so that: *fate in — che nessuno ne sappia niente,* act so that nobody knows anything about it || *in una — o nell'altra,* somehow or other (*o* by some means or other *o* by hook or by crook); *in nessuna —,* on no account (*o* by no means *o* in no way); *in ogni* —, anyhow; (*a qualunque costo*) at any cost ‖ *non c'è modo e — di convincerlo*, there is no way at all of convincing him ‖ *presentarsi in — di pellegrino*, to be dressed as a pilgrim **2.** *pl.* (*modi*) manners; manner (*sing.*), bearing (*sing.*): *persona di buone, cattive maniere*, well-, ill-mannered person; *che maniere!*, what manners!; *quell'uomo aveva maniere così dignitose*, that man had such a dignified bearing (*o* manner) **3.** (*stile*) style, fashion, manner: *alla — di qlcu.*, after the fashion (*o* in the manner) of s.o.: *quadro dipinto alla — di Raffaello*, picture painted in the manner of Raphael; *assomiglia al Verdi della prima* —, it sounds rather like Verdi in his early manner ‖ *di —*, mannered, affected: *scrittore di —*, mannered (*o* affected) writer.

manieratamént e, *av.* affectedly.

manieràto, *ag.* affected, artificial; mincing: *modi manierati*, affected (*o* artificial) manners; *scrittore —*, mannered writer; *stile —*, affected style; *tono —*, mincing tone.

manierísmo, *s.m.* (*art.*) mannerism.

manierísta, *s.c.* (*art.*) mannerist.

manierístico, *ag.* (*art.*) manneristic(al).

manièro, *s.m.* **1.** castle **2.** (*residenza di signori di campagna*) manor-house.

manieróso, *ag.* (*rar.*) well-mannered, polite, mannerly; refined; (*affettato*) mincing: *non pensi che quella signora sia un po' manierosa?*, don't you think that lady is somewhat over-refined?.

manifattóre, *s.m.* (*rar.*) manufacturer; (*operaio*) workman (*pl.* workmen); (*artigiano*) artisan.

manifattúra, *s.f.* **1.** manufacture: *la — della seta*, silk manufacture; *— del tabacco*, tobacco manufacture; *di — inglese*, made in England (*o* English made); *è un articolo di — straniera*, it's an article of foreign manufacture **2.** (*lavorazione*) workmanship: *articoli di eccellente —*, articles of excellent workmanship **3.** (*fabbrica*) factory, manufactory: *andiamo alla —!*, let's go to the factory!; *è il direttore di una grande —*, he is the manager of a big factory **4.** (*manufatto, specialmente nell'industria dell'abbigliamento*) manufactured article: *— da uomo*, men's wear.

manifatturièro, *ag.* manufacturing ‖ *s.m.* factory-worker.

manifestaménte, *av.* manifestly, openly, clearly.

manifestàre, *v.t.* to manifest, to show, to evince; (*rivelare*) to reveal: *manifesta sempre le sue emozioni*, he always shows his emotions; *manifestò un gran dispiacere nel separarsi da lui*, she evinced great sorrow at parting from him; *manifestò il nome dei complici*, he revealed the name of his accomplices; *manifestò la sua gioia*, he gave vent to his joy; *manifestò la sua volontà*, he gave expression to his will; *ella manifestò il desiderio di sposarlo*, she manifested her desire to marry him; *il suo sguardo manifestò tristezza*, his eyes revealed his sadness; *— il proprio proposito*, to manifest one's purpose; *— un segreto*, to reveal a secret ‖ **manifestàrsi,** *v.r.* to manifest oneself, to show (oneself); (*rivelarsi*) to reveal oneself: *era in incognito e non volle —*, he was incognito and did not want to make himself known; *la sua impazienza si manifestava nel suo comportamento*, his impatience showed (itself) in his behaviour; *si manifestò un amico*, he showed himself to be a friend; *il suo talento non ebbe tempo di —*, his talent had no time to reveal itself.

manifestazióne, *s.f.* **1.** manifestation, display: *— di gioia, dolore*, manifestation of joy, grief; *— di coraggio*, display of courage; *prima — di una malattia*, first symptoms of a disease **2.** (*dimostrazione pubblica*) demonstration: *— politica*, political demonstration; *fecero una — di protesta contro la nuova legge*, they held a demonstration to protest against the new law.

manifèsto, *ag.* **1.** manifest, clear, obvious: *errore —*, palpable error; *verità manifesta*, manifest truth; *la cosa è manifesta*, the whole thing is quite clear; *fu*

— a tutti che mentiva, it was plain to everybody that he was lying **2.** (*notorio*) notorious, well-known: *è un criminale —*, he is a notorious criminal; *è un fatto — che il primo ministro non è ben visto dai grandi industriali*, it's a well-known fact (*o* it's notorious) that the big industrialists do not approve of the Premier ‖ *s.m.* **1.** (*pubblica dichiarazione di un programma*) manifesto, manifest: *— letterario*, literary manifesto ‖ *il Manifesto dei Comunisti*, (*st.*) the Communist Manifesto **2.** (*avviso*) bill; (*affisso*) poster, placard; (*volantino*) leaflet: *— pubblicitario*, advertisement; *il ministro fece stampare dei manifesti*, the Minister had some bills printed; *si distribuivano manifesti nelle strade*, leaflets were distributed in the streets **3.** (*mar.*) manifest.

maníglia, *s.f.* **1.** handle: *— del campanello*, bell-pull; *— di cassetto*, drawer-handle; *— di porta*, door-handle **2.** (*sostegno per passeggeri in tram, ecc.*) strap **3.** (*mar.*) shackle.

manigoldería, *s.f.* (*dirty*) trick; piece of roguery.

manigóldo, *s.m.* **1.** (*furfante*) rascal, knave, villain; scamp **2.** (*arc.*) (*carnefice*) executioner.

Maníla, *no.pr.f.* (*geog.*) Manil(l)a.

manílla, *s.f.* **1.** (*fibra tessile*) manilla (hemp): *cappello di —*, manilla hat; *cavo di —*, manilla cable **2.** (*sigarino*) manilla (cheroot).

manilúvio, *s.m.* bathing of the hands.

manióca, *s.f.* (*bot.*) manioc.

manipolàre, *v.t.* **1.** to manufacture, to prepare; to concoct: *— colori, cera*, to prepare colours, wax; *— un nuovo piatto*, to concoct a new dish **2.** (*adulterare*) to adulterate **3.** (*falsificare*) to falsify: *manipolò i conti*, he falsified the accounts **4.** (*trattare*) to handle, to manage: *quel politicante sa — i suoi sostenitori*, that politician knows how to handle his supporters **5.** (*ordire*) to hatch; (*preparare con brogli*) to rig: *— un complotto*, to hatch a plot; *— un'elezione*, to rig an election **6.** (*massaggiare*) to massage.

manipolatóre, *s.m.*, **manipolatríce,** *s.f.* **1.** maker, mixer **2.** *fig.* manipulator; wire-puller.

manipolazióne, *s.f.* **1.** manufacture, preparation; concoction **2.** (*adulterazione*) adulteration **3.** *fig.* manipulation.

manípolo, *s.m.* **1.** (*fastello*) sheaf, bundle: *un — di spighe*: a sheaf of corn **2.** (*st. romana mil.*) maniple: *un — di soldati*, a maniple of soldiers **3.** (*eccl.*) maniple.

Manitù, *no.pr.m.* (*st. relig.*) Manito(u), Manitu.

Mànlio, *no.pr.m.* Manlius.

mànna[1], *s.f.* **1.** manna; *fig.* (*benedizione*) godsend, blessing: *aspetta che la — gli piova dal cielo*, he is always waiting for sthg. to turn up; *fu come la — dal cielo*, it was like manna from heaven; *questa pioggia è una — per la campagna!*, this rain is a blessing for the country!; *questo denaro è una — per lui*, this money is a godsend to him **2.** (*farm.*) manna.

mànna[2], *s.f.* (*rar.*) sheaf, bundle.

mannàia, *s.f.* **1.** (*del boia*) axe; (*della ghigliottina*) knife **2.** (*per macellai*) cleaver, meat-axe **3.** (*mezzaluna*) mincing-knife.

mannàro, *ag.*: *lupo—*: (*licantropo*) werewolf; (*spauracchio infantile*) bog(e)y-man.

màno, *s.f.* **1.** hand: *la — destra*, the right hand; *la — sinistra*, the left hand; *— del cuore*, the left hand; *a mani giunte*, with clasped hands; *cura delle mani*, manicure; *da una — all'altra*, from hand to hand; *le linee della —*, the lines of the hand; *pezzo a quattro mani*, (*mus.*) a piece of four hands; *stretta di —*, handshake; *essi passeggiavano dandosi la —*, they were walking hand in hand; *fatto a —*, hand-made; *fu consegnato a —*, it was delivered by hand; *tessuto a —*, hand-woven; *avere ql.co. in —*, to have sthg. in one's hand; *battere le mani*, to clap (one's hands); *farsi male alla —*, to hurt one's hand; *lavarsi le mani*, to wash one's hands; *mettere le mani su ql.co.*, to lay hands on sthg. (anche *fig.*); *prendere qlcu. per —*, to take s.o. by the hand; *ricevere ql.co. dalle mani di qlcu.*, to receive sthg. at the hands of s.o.; *scappare di* —, to slip through ono's fingers; *stringere la* —, *le mani a qlcu.*, to shake hands with s.o.; *suonare a quattro mani*, to play piano duets; *tendere la* —, *(elemosinare)* to beg || — *di ferro e guanto di velluto*, iron hand in a velvet glove || *mani in alto!*, hands up! || *a* — *armata*, by force of (o under) arms: *rapina a* — *armata*, armed robbery (o robbery under arms) || *a* — *salva*, with impunity || *a piene mani*, in (o by) handfuls || *a sue mani*, *(nelle lettere)* personal (o by hand) || *buona* —, *(mancia)* tip (o gratuity) || *colpo di* —, *(mil.)* raid (o sudden attack o surprise attack) || *denaro alla* —, *per favore*, have the exact money ready, please; *paga sempre denaro alla* —, *(in contanti)* he always pays (in) cash (o ready money) || *di lunga* —, *(per lungo tempo)* for a long time; *(molto tempo fa)* long ago: *amico di lunga* —, friend of long standing || *di prima, di seconda* —, first-hand, second-hand: *articolo di seconda* —, second-hand article; *notizie di prima* —, first-hand news || *disegno a* — *libera*, free-hand drawing || *di sotto* —, underhand || *fallo di* —!, *(spor.)* hands! || *giù le mani!*, hands off! || *imposizione delle mani*, *(eccl.)* laying on of hands || *luogo fuori* —, out of the way place || *matrimonio della* — *sinistra*, *(morganatico)* left-handed (o morganatic) marriage || *una persona alla* —, a friendly (o affable) person || *qua la* —!, let's shake hands! || *il cavallo gli prese la* —, the horse ran away with him || *gli restituirò il denaro man* —, I shall give him the money back little by little; *man* — *che andava avanti si stancava sempre più*, as he went on he got more and more tired; *man* — *che invecchia diventa sempre più avaro*, the older he gets the meaner he grows || *ha le mani di burro*, he's a butter-fingers || *ha una bella* — *nel lavorare a maglia*, she is a good hand at knitting || *ho le mani legate*, *fig.* my hands are tied || *me ne lavo le mani*, I wash my hands of it || *mi prudono le mani!*, I could hit you! || *non ci metterei la* — *sul fuoco*, I would not stake my life on it (o wouldn't swear to it) || *possono darsi la* —, *fig.* they are two of a kind (o they are tarred with the same brush) || *puoi darmi una* —, *per piacere?*, can you give me a hand, please? || *alzare le mani contro qlcu.*, to lift one's hand against s.o. || *avere le mani bucate*, to be a spendthrift || *avere le mani lunghe*, to have light fingers: *un uomo dalle mani lunghe*, a light-fingered man (o a pilferer) || *avere ql.co. alla* —, *sotto* —, to have sthg. handy (o at hand o within easy reach o ready) || *avere ql.co. per le mani*, to have sthg. in hand || *avere su la* —, to be in practice; *non avere più su la* —, to be out of practice; *fare la* — *a ql.co.*, to get used to sthg. || *caricare la* —, to exaggerate || *chiedere, domandare la* — *di qlcu.*, to ask s.o.'s hand in marriage || *essere in buone mani*, to be in good hands || *fare man bassa di ql.co.*, to plunder sthg. || *farsi prendere la* — *da ql.co.*, to lose control of sthg. || *forzare la* — *a qlcu.*, to force s.o.'s hand || *lasciare* — *libera a qlcu.*, to allow (o to give) s.o. a free hand || *menar le mani*, to fight || *mettere* — *alla penna*, to put pen to paper || *mettere* — *alla spada*, to draw one's sword || *mettere le mani avanti*, to be on the safe side || *mettere a* — *ql.co.*, to start using sthg.: *mettere a* — *una bottiglia di whisky*, to open a bottle of whisky || *mettersi le mani nei capelli*, *fig.* to clasp one's brow || *mettersi una* — *sulla coscienza*, to feel one's conscience || *mettersi in* — *a un buon medico*, to put oneself into the hands of a good doctor || *parlare col cuore in* —, to speak straight from the heart || *portare qlcu. in palma di* —, to hold s.o. in the palm of one's hand || *prendere il coraggio a due mani*, to take one's courage into both hands || *stare con le mani in* —, to remain idle || *tendere la* — *a qlcu.*, to hold out a hand to s.o. (o to give a helping hand to s.o. o to give s.o. a hand) || *tener* — *a qlcu.*, to aid and abet s.o. || *toccare con* — *(ql.co.)*, to see (sthg.) for oneself || *venire alle mani*, to come to blows || *la* — *sinistra*

non sappia quello che fa la destra, prov. let not your left hand know what your right hand is doing || *una* — *lava l'altra (ed entrambe lavano la faccia)*, prov. one hand washes the other (and both the face) || *giuoco di* — *giuoco di villano*, prov. rough play is low 2. *(parte, lato)* side: *a* — *destra*, *(stato)* on the right (o right-hand side); *(moto)* to the right; *contro* —, *(di veicoli, ecc.)* on the wrong side of the road; *tenere la propria* —, *(nella circolazione stradale)* to keep to one's own side of the road 3. *(potere, balía)* hand; power: *cadde in* — *al nemico*, he fell into the enemy's hands; *il mio destino è nelle tue mani*, my fate is in your hands; *quella proprietà non è più nelle sue mani*, that property is no longer in his hands; *quell'uomo è in mia* —, that man is in my power; *avere in* — *il successo*, to have success within one's grasp 4. *(scrittura)* hand(writing): *di sua* —, written by him; *ha una bella* —, he writes a good hand 5. *(tocco)* touch (anche *fig.*): — *da maestro*, masterly touch; *si riconosce facilmente la* — *di un maestro*, it is easy to recognize the hand of a master; — *leggera (di medico, ecc.)* light touch; *dare l'ultima* — *a un quadro*, to give the finishing touch to a work 6. *(strato di colore, vernice, ecc.)* coat: — *di finitura*, finishing-coat; — *di fondo*, primer (o priming o undercoat); *una* — *di vernice*, a coat of varnish; — *isolante*, sealer 7. *(alle carte)* hand: — *fortunata*, lucky hand; *facciamo ancora una* —, let us play one more hand || *chi è di* —?, *(a chi tocca iniziare il giuoco?)* whose lead is it? 8. *(ind.)* hand: — *d'opera*, labour; — *d'opera produttiva, improduttiva*, productive, non-productive labour; *cercasi* — *d'opera*, hands wanted.

manomésso, *ag.* 1. (that has been) tampered with 2. *(violato)* violated 3. *(st. romana)* freed.

manòmetro, *s.m.* *(fis.)* manometer; *(misuratore di pressione)* pressure-gauge: — *a mercurio*, mercury-gauge; — *campione*, master-gauge; — *del carburante*, *(aer.)* fuel-pressure gauge; — *dell'olio*, oil-pressure gauge.

manométtere, *v.t.* 1. to tamper with (sthg.): *essi manomisero questo documento*, they tampered with this document; *questa lettera è stata manomessa*, this letter has been opened (o tampered with); — *la cassa*, to tamper with the till 2. *(violare)* to violate: — *i diritti del popolo*, to violate the rights of the people 3. *(st. romana)* to manumit.

manomissióne, *s.f.* 1. tampering 2. *(violazione)* violation 3. *(st. romana)* manumission, freeing.

manomòrta, *s.f.* *(dir.)* mortmain: *beni di* —, mortmain property.

manonéra, *s.f.* *(associazione criminale)* Black Hand.

manòpola, *s.f.* 1. *(impugnatura di manubrio)* handle-bar grip 2. *(bottone di apparecchio radio)* knob 3. *(st.)* *(guanto di armatura)* gauntlet 4. *(guantone di scherma)* fencing-glove 5. *(polsino di un vestito)* cuff.

manoscrítto, *ag.* handwritten || *s.m.* manuscript *(abbr.* MS.): *i manoscritti*, the manuscripts *(abbr.* MSS.).

manovàle, *s.m.* hodman *(pl.* hodmen).

manovèlla, *s.f.* crank: — *d'avviamento*, *(aut.)* starting-handle; — *motrice*, driving-handle; — *per vetri di portiere*, *(aut.)* window-winder.

manòvra, *s.f.* 1. manoeuvre: — *dell'ancora*, *(mar.)* working of the anchor; *camera di* —, *(di sottomarino)* control room; *posto per la* —, *(mar.)* sea room; *la automobile stava facendo manovre per uscire dal garage*, the car was manoeuvring out of the garage 2. *(mil.)* manoeuvre: *grandi manovre*, army manoeuvres; *terreno di manovre*, area for manoeuvres; *truppe in* —, troops on manoeuvres; *fare manovre*, to perform manoeuvres (o to manoeuvre) 3. *(ferr.)* shunting, marshalling: — *a spinta*, pushing off; — *dello scambio*, throwing over the points; — *di disinserzione*, backward transition; — *per l'inserzione*, forward transition; *locomotiva di* —, shunting engine; *servizio di* —, shunting work; *stazione di* —, marshalling yard (o sorting siding o sorting depot) 4. *(mar.)* *(cavo, cordame)* rigging, handling: *manovre correnti*, running rigging; *manovre dormienti, fisse,* standing rigging **5.** *fig.* (*raggiro, azione fraudolenta*) manoeuvre: — *fraudolenta,* swindling: *manovre politiche,* political manoeuvring (*o* jockeying); *è stata una* — *ignobile da parte sua,* it was an ignoble move on his part; *è stata solo una* — *per farsi della pubblicità,* it was only a manoeuvre to get publicity; *fare manovre parlamentari,* to lobby.

manovràbile, *ag.* manoeuvrable: *quell'automobile è facilmente* —, that car is easily manoeuvrable (*o* is easy to control).

manovrabilità, *s.f.* manoeuvrability, handling, control.

manovràre, *v.t.* to manoeuvre, to handle, to control; (*far funzionare*) to operate.

manovratóre, *s.m.* **1.** operator: — *di scambi,* (*ferr.*) signalman (*pl.* signalmen) **2.** (*di tram*) tram-driver.

manrìtta, *s.f.* (*rar.*) right hand: *a* —, to the right.

manrovèscio, *s.m.* **1.** back-handed slap: *mi diede un* —, he gave me a back-hander **2.** (*colpo di spada*) back-handed stroke **3.** *pl.* (*colpi all'impazzata*) furious blows.

mansàlva, a, *l.av.* with impunity: *rubarono nella casa a* —, they ransacked the house with impunity.

mansàrda, *s.f.* (*arch.*) mansard; (*stanza per uso abitazione*) garret.

mansionàrio, *s.m.* (*eccl.*) beneficed clergyman (*pl.* clergymen).

mansióne, *s.f.* **1.** (*compito*) function, duty; (*incarico*) office: *è* — *del vigile proteggere ed assistere il pubblico,* the duty of a policeman is to protect and assist the public; *avere le mansioni di presidente,* to hold the office of president; *compiere le proprie mansioni,* to perform one's duties **2.** (*st.*) (*stazione di posta*) stage **3.** (*letter.*) (*dimora*) abode, dwelling **4.** (*a Londra, sede del Sindaco*) Mansion House.

mansuefàre, *v.t.* to tame (anche *fig.*): — *una fiera,* to tame a wild beast; — *l'ira,* to tame (*o* to subdue) one's anger.

mansuetaménte, *av.* meekly, mildly, tamely.

mansuèto, *ag.* **1.** meek, mild, docile: *un animale* —, a docile animal; *indole mansueta,* mild (*o* meek) disposition; *un ragazzo* —, a docile boy; *è* — *come un agnello,* he is as meek as a lamb **2.** (*mite*) mild: *inverno* —, mild winter **3.** (*di pendio, non ripido*) gentle.

mansuetùdine, *s.f.* meekness, mildness, docility: *la* — *dell'agnello è proverbiale,* the lamb's meekness is proverbial; *è amata da tutti per la sua* —, she is loved by everybody for her mildness.

mantèca, *s.f.* (*pomata per capelli*) pomade.

mantecàre, *v.t.* to whip, to whisk.

mantecàto, *s.m.* " mantecato " (semi-liquid ice-cream).

mantèlla, *s.f.* cape, mantle, cloak.

mantellàre, *v.t.* (*rar.*) to mantle, to cloak (anche *fig.*): *mantellava la sua malvagità con le apparenze della religione,* he cloaked his wickedness with a show of religion.

mantellétta, *s.f.* mant(e)let.

mantellìna, *s.f.* (*mil.*) cape.

mantèllo, *s.m.* **1.** cloak, mantle, cape: *il vecchio si avvolse nel suo* —, the old man wrapped himself up in his cloak ‖ *mutar* —, (*far voltafaccia*) to change sides (*o* to turn one's coat) **2.** *fig.* cloak, cover: *sotto il* — *dell'amicizia,* under cover of friendship; *sotto il* — *dell'umiltà,* under the cloak of humility **3.** (*di animali*) coat, hair; (*di molluschi*) mantle: *il* — *del cavallo,* the horse's coat; *cavallo con* — *sauro,* chestnut horse **4.** (*mec.*) skirt: — *dello stantuffo,* piston skirt; — *per elica,* (*mar.*) propeller nozzle.

mantenére, *v.t.* **1.** to keep, to maintain, to preserve: *manteniamo ancora vive queste tradizioni di famiglia,* we still keep alive (*o* preserve) these family traditions; — *agile il corpo,* to keep fit; — *le apparenze,* to keep up appearances; — *buone relazioni con qlcu.,* to maintain good relations with s.o.; — *l'equilibrio,* to keep one's balance; — *fresca la carne,* to keep

meat fresh; — *in vita qlcu.,* to keep s.o. alive; — *l'ordine,* to keep (*o* to maintain) order; — *la pace,* to keep the peace; — *una posizione,* (*mil.*) to hold a position; — *i prezzi alti,* to keep prices high ‖ — *la linea,* (*serbarsi snello*) to keep one's figure **2.** (*sostentare*) to maintain, to support, to keep: *mantiene quei poveri orfanelli,* he supports those poor orphans; — *la famiglia,* to maintain (*o* to keep *o* to support) one's family; — *un'istituzione benefica,* to support a charitable institution **3.** (*conservare in buono stato*) to maintain: — *le strade,* to maintain roads **4.** (*osservare*) to keep: *l'aereo mantiene l'orario,* the airliner is making good time; — *la parola data,* to keep one's word; — *una promessa,* to keep a promise; — *un segreto,* to keep a secret **5.** (*sostenere*) to maintain; to support: *quel che ho detto lo mantengo,* I maintain what I have said; — *un'opinione,* to maintain an opinion ‖ **mantenérsi,** *v.r.* **1.** to keep: *spero che il tempo si mantenga bello la prossima settimana,* I hope the weather keeps fine next week; — *a galla,* to keep afloat; — *fresco,* to keep cool; — *giovane,* to keep young; — *in buona salute,* to keep fit (*o* in good health); — *in contatto con qlcu.,* to keep in touch with s.o. **2.** (*sostentarsi*) to earn one's living, to subsist, to keep oneself: *mi mantengo facendo il cameriere,* I earn my living as a waiter; — *lautamente,* to live sumptuously; *non avere come,* da —, to have insufficient means.

manteníbile, *ag.* maintainable.

manteniménto, *s.f.* **1.** maintenance, preservation: — *delle istituzioni,* preservation of institutions; *è la polizia che deve pensare al* — *dell'ordine pubblico,* the Police are entrusted with the maintenance of public order **2.** (*sostentamento*) maintenance; (*di moglie separata dal marito*) alimony: *conto* —, (*comm.*) maintenance account: *agli scapoli spesso costa caro il* —, bachelors often spend a lot of money on keeping themselves; *deve spendere molto per il* — *della famiglia,* he must spend a lot to support his family; *il tribunale ha deciso che il marito pensi al* — *della moglie,* the Court has ordered the husband to pay alimony to his wife **3.** (*manutenzione*) maintenance, upkeep: *il* — *di un esercito,* the maintenance of an army; *lo Stato deve pensare al* — *dei musei,* the State must see to the upkeep of museums.

mantenitóre, *s.m.*, **mantenitríce,** *s.f.* keeper.

mantenùto, *ag.* **1.** maintained, preserved **2.** (*sostentato*) maintained, supported, kept ‖ *s.m.* pimp.

màntice, *s.m.* **1.** bellows (*pl.*): — *per l'invio di aria,* blowing apparatus ‖ *soffiare come un* —, to puff and blow **2.** (*di carrozza, auto, ecc.*) hood **3.** (*di macchina fotografica*) bellows (*pl.*).

màntide, *s.f.* (*entom.*) mantis (*pl.* mantes, mantises): — *religiosa,* praying mantis.

mantíglia¹, *s.f.* mantilla.

mantíglia², *s.f.* (*mar.*) lift.

mantìssa, *s.f.* (*mat.*) mantissa.

mànto, *s.m.* mantle; cloak (anche *fig.*): *un* — *di neve,* a cloak of snow; — *regale,* royal mantle (*o* robe).

Màntova, *no.pr. f.* (*geog.*) Mantua.

mantovàna, *s.f.* **1.** (*arch.*) gableboard **2.** (*di tendaggio*) pelmet.

mantovàno, *ag.s.m.* Mantuan ‖ *la musa mantovana,* (*Virgilio*) the Mantuan Muse.

manuàle, *ag.* manual: *lavoro* —, manual labour ‖ *s.m.* **1.** manual, handbook: — *di filosofia,* philosophy handbook **2.** (*tastiera di organo*) keyboard.

manualménte, *av.* manually.

manúbrio, *s.m.* **1.** handle; (*di bicicletta*) handle-bar **2.** (*attrezzo per ginnastica*) dumb-bell.

Manuèle, *no.pr.m.* Manuel.

manufàtto, *ag.* hand-made, hand-manufactured ‖ *s.m.* hand-manufactured article, hand-manufactured goods (*pl.*): *manufatti di lana,* hand-made woollens (*o* woollen goods).

manutèngolo, *s.m.* abettor, accomplice.

manutenzióne, *s.f.* upkeep, maintenance: *la — ordinaria delle strade,* the routine maintenance of the roads; *personale addetto alla —,* maintenance staff; *spese di —,* maintenance expenses; *questa casa è nuova e ci costa poco di —,* this house is new and its upkeep doesn't cost us very much; *aver la — di un giardino,* to be entrusted with the maintenance (*o* care) of a garden.

manzína, *s.f.* (*rar.*) (*agr.*) fallow (land) used for pasture.

mànzo, *s.m.* **1.** (*zool.*) steer **2.** (*carne macellata*) beef: *— lesso,* boiled beef; *arrosto di —,* roast beef; *una bistecca di —,* a beefsteak; *stufato di —,* stewed beef.

manzoniàno, *ag.* of Manzoni: *il centenario —,* the centenary of Manzoni ‖ *s.m.* follower of Manzoni.

maomettàno, *ag.s.m.* (*relig.*) Mohammedan.

maomettísmo, *s.m.* (*relig.*) Mohammedanism, Islam.

Maométto, *no.pr.m.* (*st. relig.*) Mohammed, Mahomet.

maóna, *s.f.* (*mar.*) barge, lighter.

màppa, *s.f.* map, plan: *— altimetrica,* layered map; *— catastale,* cadastral map; *una proprietà segnata in — coi numeri,* an estate marked on the map with numbers.

mappamóndo, *s.m.* **1.** (*globo*) globe (of the world) **2.** (*carta, mappa*) map of the two hemispheres: *— celeste,* map of the heavens.

maquillage, *s.m.* make-up.

marabú, *s.m.* (*ornit.*) marabou(t).

marabútto, *s.m.* **1.** (*santone musulmano*) marabout **2.** (*tomba dello stesso*) marabout.

maracèlla, *s.f.* trick, prank: *basta con le vostre marachelle!,* no more of your tricks!; *sta combinando ancora una delle sue marachelle,* he is up to one of his pranks.

maràgia, maragià, *s.m.* maharajah.

maramàldo, *s.m.* (*chi infierisce sul vinto*) dastard.

maràme, *s.m.* **1.** (*rifiuti del mare*) flotsam and jetsam **2.** (*rifiuti*) odds and ends (*pl.*); waste; trash (anche *fig.*).

maramèo, *inter.*: *far — a qlcu.,* to cock a snook at s.o.

marangóne, *s.m.* **1.** (*ornit.*) cormorant **2.** (*dial.*) (*falegname*) carpenter, joiner.

maràsca, *s.f.* (*bot.*) egriot.

maraschino, *s.m.* maraschino.

maràsco, *s.m.* (*bot.*) wild-cherry tree.

maràsma, *s.m.* **1.** marasmus **2.** *fig.* decadence.

Maratóna, *no.pr.f.* (*geog. st.*) Marathon ‖ **maratóna,** *s.f.* (*spor.*) Marathon race ‖ *è una bella —!,* (*scherz.*) it is some walk!.

maratonèta, *s.m.* (*spor.*) long-distance runner.

maravíglia, *e derivati,* *V.* **meravíglia,** *e derivati.*

màrca[1], *s.f.* (*st.*) March.

màrca[2], *s.f.* **1.** (*comm.*) brand; mark; (*fabbricazione*) make: *— di fabbrica,* trade-mark: *— di fabbrica depositata,* registered trade-mark; *è una buona — di sigari,* this is a good brand of cigars; *ho avuto automobili di tre marche diverse,* I have had three makes of cars; *questa è una delle migliori marche di cioccolato,* this is one of the best brands of chocolate ‖ *prodotto di —,* high-quality product **2.** (*segno*) mark; (*a fuoco*) brand: *tutti i pezzi d'argenteria portano una —,* all silverware has a mark (*o* is marked) **3.** (*mar.*) mark, line: *marche del bordo libero,* freeboard markings: *— della linea di carico,* Plimsoll line; *— di pescaggio,* draught mark **4.** (*scontrino*) ticket **5.** (*cifra sulla biancheria*) initials (*pl.*); (*ricamata*) embroidered initials (*pl.*) **6.** *— da bollo,* revenue stamp.

marcantònia, *s.f.* (*fam.*) tall, hefty woman: *è un bel pezzo di —,* she is a fine figure of a woman.

Marcantònio[1], *no.pr.m.* (*st.*) Mark Antony.

marcantònio[2], *s.m.* (*fam.*) tall, strong man: *è un bel pezzo di —,* he is a fine figure of a man.

marcàre, *v.t.* **1.** to mark, to make a mark on (sthg.); (*a fuoco*) to brand (anche *fig.*): *— la biancheria,* to mark

linen; *— qlcu. d'infamia,* to brand s.o. with infamy **2.** (*segnare*) to score: *— i punti,* (*al giuoco*) to keep the score **3.** *— visita,* (*mil.*) to report sick.

marcassíte, *s.f.* (*min.*) marcasite.

marcatóre, *s.m.,* **marcatríce,** *s.f.* **1.** marker **2.** (*chi segna i punti*) scorer.

marcatúra, *s.f.* **1.** marking; (*a fuoco*) branding **2.** (*di punti*) scoring.

Marc'Aurèlio, *no.pr.m.* (*st.*) Marcus Aurelius.

Marcèlla, *no.pr.f.* Marcella.

Marcellíno, *no.pr.m.* (*st. relig.*) Marcellinus.

Marcèllo, *no.pr.m.* Marcellus.

marcescènte, *ag.* rotting, decaying.

marcescíbile, *ag.* decayable.

marchésa, *s.f.* (*se il titolo è inglese*) marchioness; (*se non è inglese*) marquise, marchesa.

marchesàto, *s.m.* marquisate.

marchése, *s.m.* marquis, marquess.

Marchési (Ísole), *no.pr.f.pl.* (*geog.*) the Marquesas (Islands).

marchesína, *s.f.,* daughter of a marquis.

marchesíno, *s.m.* son of a marquis.

marchiàno, *ag.* enormous; extraordinary: *errore —,* glaring blunder (*o* gross mistake).

marchiàre, *v.t.* to stamp; (*a fuoco*) to brand.

màrchio, *s.m.* **1.** stamp; (*a fuoco*) brand **2.** *fig.* (*taccia*) mark, stain: *— d'infamia,* mark of infamy; *non potrà togliersi questo — di dosso,* he will never live down such a disgrace **3.** (*comm.*): *— di fabbrica,* trade-mark; *— di fabbrica depositato,* registered trade -mark; *tutte le casse portano il nostro — di fabbrica,* all boxes bear our trade-mark.

marchionàle, *ag.* (*letter.*) pertaining to a marquess.

màrcia[1], *s.f.* **1.** (*aut.*) gear, speed: *— avanti,* forward gear (*o* speed): *andare a — avanti,* to go in forward gear; (*di nave*) to go ahead; *— a vuoto,* idling; *— indietro,* reverse gear: *andare a — indietro,* to go in reverse; (*di nave*) to go astern; *— sovramoltiplicata,* overdrive; *inversione di —,* reverse; *automobile a tre marce,* car with three gears; *essere in —,* to be in gear; *mettere in —,* to start ‖ *far — indietro,* *fig.* to back out **2.** (*mil. mus.*) march: *— forzata,* forced march; *— funebre,* dead march; *— nuziale, trionfale, wedding-,* triumphal march; *formazione di —,* order of march; *essere in —,* to be on the march; *mettersi in —,* to start off ‖ *— su Roma,* (*st.*) march on Rome **3.** (*lunghezza di cammino*) march: *con tre marce fu alla capitale,* after a three days' march he reached the capital.

màrcia[2], *s.f.* (*purulenza*) pus.

marciàno, *ag.*: *Biblioteca marciana* (*in Venezia*), St. Mark's Library.

Marciàno, *no.pr.m.* (*st. romana*) Marcianus.

marciapiède, *s.m.* pavement; (*amer.*) side-walk; (*di stazione*) platform: *— largo,* wide pavement; *camminate sul —!,* walk on the pavement! ‖ *battere il —,* to walk the streets.

marciàre, *v.i.* to march: *oggi abbiamo marciato per quaranta miglia,* we have marched forty miles to-day; *— in coda,* to bring up the rear; *— in testa,* to lead the march; *entrare marciando,* to march in ‖ *far —,* to march.

marcíme, *s.m.* (*rar.*) animal manure.

màrcio, *ag.* **1.** (*guasto*) bad, tainted; (*in decomposizione*) rotten, putrid: *frutta marcia,* rotten fruit; *legno —,* rotten (*o* decayed) wood; *pesce —,* bad fish; *terra marcia,* waterlogged earth; *uovo —,* rotten egg; *la parte inferiore di quel muro è completamente marcia,* the bottom (part) of that wall is completely rotten; *penso che questa carne sia un po' marcia, non mangiatela!,* I think this meat is a little off (*o* tainted), don't eat it! **2.** (*infetto, malato*) infected, poisoned: *dente —,* bad (*o* decayed) tooth; *ha un dito —,* he has a poisoned finger ‖ *una pecora marcia ne guasta un branco,* *prov.* one scabbed sheep's enough to spoil the flock **3.** *fig.* (*corrotto*) corrupt, rotten: *letteratura marcia*, corrupt literature; *società marcia*, corrupt society **4.** (*fam. enfatico*): *lo fece a suo — dispetto*, she did it deliberately to spite him; *aver torto —*, to be absolutely wrong ‖ *s.m.* **1.** rottenness, badness; (*parte marcia*) rotten part: *quel pesce sa di —*, that fish smells bad; *togli il — a quelle mele*, cut the bad parts out of those apples **2.** (*pus, materia*) pus, matter **3.** (*corruzione*) corruption, rottenness: *il — di quel sistema*, the corruption of that system; *era evidente che c'era del — nelle alte sfere*, it was evident that there was corruption in high places ‖ *c'è del — in Danimarca!*, something is rotten in the State of Denmark.

marcíre, *v.i.* **1.** (*guastarsi*) to go bad, to taint; (*decomporsi*) to rot, to decay: *la carne marcirà presto con questo caldo*, meat will soon go bad in this hot weather; *le mele sono marcite per l'umidità*, the apples have rotted owing to the dampness **2.** (*suppurare*) to fester, to suppurate: *se non la disinfetti subito, questa ferita marcirà presto*, this wound will soon fester if you do not disinfect it at once **3.** *fig.* to rot: *lasciar — qlcu. in prigione*, to let s.o. rot in gaol **4.** (*di lino, canapa*) to ret.

marcíta, *s.f.* (*agr.*) water-meadow.

marciúme, *s.m.* putrefaction, rottenness (anche *fig.*): *il — delle sue azioni*, the rottenness of his deeds.

màrco, *s.m.* (*moneta*) mark.

Màrco, *no.pr.m.* Mark, Marcus.

marconigràmma, *s.m.* (*rad.*) marconigram.

marconísta, *s.m.* wireless operator.

marconiterapía, *s.f.* (*med.*) diathermy.

màre, *s.m.* **1.** sea: *— agitato, molto agitato*, moderate, rough sea; *—aperto*, open sea; *— calmo*, calm sea; *— corto*, choppy (o short) sea; *— di leva, morto, vecchio*, swell (o hollow sea); *— di poppa*, following sea; *— di prua*, head sea; *— di traverso*, abeam sea; *— grosso*, very rough sea; *— in burrasca*, stormy sea; *— interno*, inland sea; *— leggermente mosso*, slight sea; *— litoraneo*, litoral sea; *— lungo*, long sea; *— piatto, quasi calmo*, smooth sea; *— tempestoso, tempestosissimo*, very high, precipitous sea; *— territoriale*, territorial waters; *l'acqua del —*, sea-water; *al di là del —*, beyond the sea(s); *l'alto —*, the high seas; *l'azzurro del —*, the blue of the sea; *bagni di —*, sea-bathing; *braccio di —*, arm of the sea; *forze di terra e di —*, (*mil.*) land and sea forces; *fosforescenza del —*, sea-fire; *frutti di —*, sea -food; *gente di —*, sea-folk; *in — aperto*, off shore; *livello del mare*, sea-level: *sopra, sotto il livello del —*, above, below sea-level; *Milano è a 120 metri sul livello del —*, Milan is 120 metres above sea-level; *mal di —*, sea-sickness: *soffrire, non soffrire il mal di —*, to be a bad, good sailor; *nato dal —, sul —*, sea-born; *nave atta a tenere il —*, sea-worthy ship; *nave di alto —*, sea-going ship; *per terra e per —*, by land and sea; *porto di —*, seaport; *presa d'acqua di —*, sea-water intake; *la salsedine del —*, the saltiness of the sea; *uomo di —*, seaman; *vento di —*, sea-breeze; *viaggio per —*, voyage; *la voce del —*, the voice of the sea; *il — è calmo come l'olio*, the sea is like a sheet of glass; *l'ammiraglio ordinò che una barca fosse messa in —*, the admiral ordered a boat to be lowered; *fu seppellito in —*, he was buried at sea; *la nave subì un colpo di —*, the ship was struck by a heavy sea; *un'onda lo gettò in —*, a wave swept him into the sea; (*da una nave*) a wave swept him overboard; *Palermo è una città di —*, Palermo is a town on the sea; *Venezia era la signora dei mari*, Venice was the mistress of the seas; *avere il dominio del mari*, to have the mastery of the seas; *cadere in —*, to fall into the sea; (*da una nave*) to fall overboard; *esplorare gli abissi del —*, to explore the depths of the sea; *essere in alto —*, to be at sea; *gettare in —*, to throw into the sea; (*da una nave*) to throw overboard; *mettere in — una nave*, to set a vessel afloat; *prendere il —*, to set sail; (*di persone*) to go to sea; *spedire via —*, (*comm.*) to ship; *tenere il —*,

to keep the sea; *viaggiare per —*, to travel by sea ‖ *libertà dei mari*, freedom of the seas ‖ *lupo di —*, sea-dog ‖ *serpente di —*, sea-serpent ‖ *un uomo in —!*, man overboard! ‖ *quella casa è un vero porto di —*, that house is a veritable port of call ‖ *la questione.è ancora in alto —*, the question is still undecided ‖ *siamo ancora in alto —!*, we still have a long way to go! ‖ *cercare qlcu. per terra e per —*, to look up hill and down dale for s.o. ‖ *portare acqua al —*, to carry coals to Newcastle ‖ *promettere mari e monti*, to promise wonders ‖ *bello è contemplare il — dal porto*, prov. 'tis good riding in a safe harbour ‖ *chi non sa orare vada in — a navigare*, prov. he that would learn to pray let him go to sea **2.** *Mare* (*geog.*) Sea: *il Mare Adriatico*, the Adriatic Sea; *il Mar Baltico*, the Baltic Sea; *il Mar Caspio*, the Caspian Sea; *il Mare dei Caraibi*, the Caribbean Sea; *il Mare del Giappone, della Cina*, the Japan, China Sea; *il Mar Jonio*, the Ionian Sea; *il Mare Mediterraneo*, the Mediterranean Sea; *il Mar Morto*, the Dead Sea ‖ *i Tre Mari*, the seas around Italy **3.** (*luogo sul mare*) seaside: *abbiamo conosciuto parecchia gente al —*, we met a lot of people at the seaside; *l'anno scorso andammo al — per le vacanze*, last year we went to the seaside for our holidays; *l'aria del — gli fa bene*, sea-air is good for him **4.** *fig.* (*quantità smisurata*) sea, ocean; (*moltitudine*) crowd, multitude; *un — di gente*, a tremendous crowd; *un — di guai*, a sea of troubles; *un — di luce*, a sea of light; *un — di sabbia*, a sea of sand; *un — di sangue*, a sea of blood.

marèa, *s.f.* tide: *alta —*, high tide; *bassa —*, low tide; *— discendente, calante*, falling tide (o ebb-tide); *— effettiva*, actual tide; *— lenta*, slack tide; *— massima, sigiziale, equinoziale*, spring-tide; *— minima, di quadratura*, neap-tide; *— montante*, flood-tide; *porta della —*, tide-gate; *tavola della —*, tide-table; *andare a seconda della —*, to go with the tide; *partire con la —*, to sail with the tide.

mareggiàre, *v.i.* to be wavy; to undulate (anche *fig.*).

mareggiàta, *s.f.* stormy sea, sea-storm: *una violenta — ha danneggiato la banchina*, a violent sea-storm damaged the wharf.

maréggio, *s.m.* undulation.

marémma, *s.f.* maremma (*pl.* maremme); marsh ‖ *la Maremma*, (*geog.*) the Maremma.

maremmàno, *ag.* maremma (*attributivo*): *cavalli maremmani*, maremma horses; *febbri maremmane*, (*patol.*) malaria ‖ *s.m.* inhabitant of Maremma.

maremòto, *s.m.* seaquake, submarine earthquake.

marèna, *s.f.* (*bot.*) sour black cherry.

maréngo, *s.m.* (*moneta*) napoleon.

mareògrafo, *s.m.* tide-gauge.

maresciàlla, *s.f.* marshal's wife.

maresciàllo, *s.m.* (*mil.*) **1.** (*ufficiale*) marshal; (*in Gran Bretagna*) field-marshal: *bastone di —*, (field-)marshal's baton; *Napoleone apparve circondato dai suoi marescialli*, Napoleon appeared surrounded by his marshals ‖ *Maresciallo dell'Aria*, Air-Marshal ‖ *Maresciallo di Francia*, Marshal of France **2.** (*sottufficiale*) warrant -officer: *— d'alloggio*, quartermaster; *— di fanteria*, infantry warrant-officer.

marétta, *s.f.* (*mar.*), choppy sea, short sea: *c'è un po' di — oggi*, it is a bit choppy today; *finchè dura questa — è meglio che non andiate in barca*, you had better not go sailing so long as it is choppy.

marezzàre, *v.t.* to marble; (*stoffe*) to water.

marezzàto, *ag.* marbled, veined; (*di stoffe*) watered: *carta marezzata*, marbled paper; *marmo —*, veined marble; *seta marezzata*, watered silk.

marezzatúra, *s.f.* marbling.

marézzo, *s.m.* marbling; (*di stoffe*) watering.

margarína, *s.f.* (*cuc.*) margarine; (*fam.*) marge.

margheríta, *s.f.* **1.** (*bot.*) daisy **2.** (*mar.*) sheep -shank **3.** (*arc.*) (*perla*) pearl.

Margheríta, *no.pr.f.* Margaret ‖ *dim.* Mag, Maggie, Meg(gy), Peg(gy).

marginàle, *ag.* **1.** marginal: *note marginali*, marginal notes **2.** (*secondario*) secondary: *una questione —*, a question of secondary importance.

marginàre, *v.t.* **1.** to border, to edge **2.** (*tip.*) to regulate the margins of (sthg.), to margin.

marginatúra, *s.f.* **1.** edging, margining **2.** (*tip.*) (*regolo di metallo*) furniture.

màrgine, *s.m.* **1.** margin, border, edge: *il — del bosco*, the edge of the wood; *il — della strada*, the edge of the road (*o roadside o amer.* the shoulder of the road); *— di sicurezza, fig.* margin of safety; *— di taglio*, (*tip.*) fore-edge; *— superiore, inferiore*, upper, lower margin; *importo indicato a —*, (*comm.*) amount stated at margin; *scrisse una nota in —*, he wrote a note in the margin; *tali prezzi non lasciano alcun —*, such prices allow of no margin **2.** (*tip.*) (*regolo di metallo*) furniture.

marginóso, *ag.* marginate(d).

margóne, *s.m.* **1.** (*agr.*) marl, loam **2.** (*gora*) mill-stream.

margottàre, *v.t.* (*agr.*) to layer.

margòtto, *s.m.* (*agr.*) layer.

margràvio, *s.m.* (*st.*) margrave.

María, *no.pr.f.* Mary ‖ *dim.* May, Moll(y), Mamie, Poll(y).

Mariànna, *no.pr.f.* Marian(ne).

mariàno, *ag.* (*eccl.*) Marian: *mese —*, the month of Mary.

marína[1], *s.f.* **1.** navy: *— da guerra*, Navy; *— mercantile*, merchant navy ‖ *Ministero della Marina*, (*in Gran Bretagna*) the Admiralty; (*altrove*) Ministry for the Navy; *Ministro della Marina*, (*in Gran Bretagna*) First Lord of the Admiralty; (*altrove*) Minister for the Navy **2.** (*costa*) coast(-line); (*riva del mare*) seashore: *navigava lungo la —*, he sailed along the coast; *passeggiavo sulla —*, I was walking along the seashore ‖ *navigare —*, to follow the coast-line closely (*o* to hug the coast) **3.** (*letter.*) (*mare*) sea: *la chiara —*, the limp sea **4.** (*pitt.*) sea-scape, marine landscape: *dipingere una —*, to paint a sea-scape (*o* sea-piece).

Marína[2], *no.pr.f.* Marina.

marinàio, *s.m.* **1.** sailor, seaman (*pl.* seamen); (*letter.*) mariner: *— di coperta*, deck-hand; *— scelto*, able seaman ‖ *casa del —*, sailor's home ‖ *nodo da —*, sailor's knot ‖ *promessa da —*, dicer's oath **2.** *pl.* (*equipaggio*) crew.

marinàra, *s.f.* **1.** (*cappotto corto con cappuccio*) duffle coat **2.** (*cappello alla marinara*) sailor hat.

marinàre, *v.t.* **1.** (*cuc.*) to pickle, to souse **2.** *— la scuola*, (*fam.*) to play truant.

marinescaménte, *av.* sailor-like, seaman-like.

marinarésco, *ag.* sailor-like, seaman-like; seafaring: *ballo —*, hornpipe; *canzone marinaresca*, shanty; *gergo —*, sailor's slang; *vita marinaresca*, seafaring life.

marinàro, *ag.* **1.** seafaring, marine, maritime: *gente marinara*, seafaring people; *una nazione marinara*, a maritime nation **2.** (*da marinaio*) sailor-like, seaman-like: *alla marinara*, sailor-like: *cappello, vestito alla marinara*, sailor hat, -suit ‖ *s.m.* (*pop.*) sailor, seaman (*pl.* seamen) ‖ *da galeotto a —*, diamond cuts diamond.

marinàto, *ag.* pickled, soused: *pesce —*, pickled fish ‖ *s.m.* pickled fish.

marinatúra, *s.f.* pickling, sousing.

marinería, *s.f.* **1.** (*arte del marinaio*) seamanship **2.** (*la marina*) navy.

marinísmo, *s.m.* (*st. lett.*) Marinism.

marinísta, *s.m.* (*st. lett.*) Marinist.

maríno, *ag.* marine; sea (*attributivo*): *acqua marina*, sea-water; *aria marina*, sea-air; *blu —*, navy-blue; *brezza marina*, sea-breeze; *carte marine*, charts; *colonia marina*, seaside home for children; *fanteria marina*, marines; *verde —*, sea-green; *c'erano degli uccelli marini di cui non sapevo il nome*, there were some sea birds whose name I didn't know; *dalle alghe marine si estraggono sostanze utili*, useful substances are extracted from seaweed ‖ *stella marina*, (*zool.*) starfish ‖ *vitello —*, (*zool.*) seal-calf.

Màrio, *no.pr.m.* Mario; (*st.*) Marius.

mariolería, *s.f.* roguery; cheat, swindle, deception.

marionétta, *s.f.* marionette; puppet (*anche fig.*): *teatro delle marionette*, puppet theatre; *è solo una —, le fai fare quello che vuoi*, she is only a puppet in your hands; *andare alle marionette*, to go to a puppet-show.

marionettísta, *s.m.* puppet-master, puppet-player.

marionettístico, *ag.* puppet (*attributivo*): *uno spettacolo —*, a puppet-play.

maritàbile, *ag.* marriageable.

maritàle, *ag.* marital; (*coniugale*) conjugal: *l'autorità —*, a husband's authority.

maritalménte, *av.* maritally; (*coniugalmente*) conjugally.

maritànda, *s.f.* marriageable woman.

maritàre, *v.t.* **1.** to marry, to wed: *egli maritò la figlia ad un ricco mercante*, he married his daughter to a rich merchant **2.** (*agr.*) to train: *— la vite all'olmo*, to train a vine up an elm ‖ **maritàrsi**, *v.r.* to get married, to marry, to wed: *mia sorella si maritò molto giovane*, my sister got married (*o* married) very young.

maritàto, *ag.* **1.** married: *donna maritata*, married woman **2.** (*agr.*) trained: *vite maritata all'olmo*, vine trained up elm.

maríto, *s.m.* husband: *aveva per — un avvocato*, her husband was a lawyer; *ha un cattivo —*, she has got a bad husband; *cercar —*, to look for a husband; *non trovar —*, not to find a husband; *perdere il —*, to become a widow: *perse il — due anni fa*, she lost her husband (*o* she become a widow) two years ago; *prendere —*, to get married (*o* to marry) ‖ *da —*, marriageable: *una ragazza du —*, a marriageable girl; *è in età da —*, she is of a marriageable age ‖ *tra moglie e — non mettere il dito, prov.* don't interfere between husband and wife.

maríttimo, *ag.* maritime; marine; shipping: *agente —*, shipping-agent; *assicurazione marittima*, marine insurance; *città marittima*, sea-town; *codice —*, maritime law; *commercio —*, shipping business; *miglio —*, nautical (*o* sea-) mile (*misura di lunghezza =* m. 1853,2); *ufficio —*, shipping-office; *via marittima*, sea-way: *per via marittima*, by sea ‖ *le Alpi Marittime*, the Maritime Alps ‖ *s.m.* sailor; seaman (*pl.* seamen): *sciopero dei marittimi*, seamen's strike.

mariuòlo, *ag.* swindling, cheating; scoundrelly; roguish, rascally: *occhi mariuoli*, roguish eyes ‖ *s.m.* swindler, cheat; scoundrel; rogue, rascal: *è un — matricolato*, he is a scoundrel through and through.

marmàglia, *s.f.*, **marmagliúme**, *s.m.* rabble, riff-raff; rag-tag (and bobtail); mob: *la — si era radunata là*, the rabble had gathered there.

marmellàta, *s.f.* jam: *— d'arance*, marmalade; *— di fragole*, strawberry jam; *un vaso di —*, a jar (*o* pot) of jam.

marmétta, *s.f.* marble tile.

marmífero, *ag.* **1.** marble-bearing, marble-yielding: *il terreno è —*, the soil is abounding in marble **2.** (*che concerne il marmo*) marble (*attributivo*): *il centro dell'industria marmifera italiana è Carrara*, the centre of the Italian marble industry is Carrara.

marmísta, *s.m.* marble-cutter.

marmítta, *s.f.* **1.** stock-pot **2.** (*aut.*) silencers muffler **3.** *marmitte dei giganti*, (*geol.*) pot-holes.

màrmo, *s.m.* marble: *— dipinto*, imitation marble; *cava di —*, marble quarry; *lastra di —*, marble slab; *polvere di —*, marble sawdust; *una raccolta di marmi antichi*, a collection of ancient marbles ‖ *i marmi di Elgin*, the Elgin marbles ‖ *ero gelata come un pezzo di —*, I was frozen stiff (*o* I was like a block of ice) ‖ *ha il cuore duro come il —*, he has a heart of stone.

marmòcchio, *s.m.* (*scherz.*) kid; (*spreg.*) brat, urchin.

marmòreo, *ag.* marmorean, marmoreal; marble (*attributivo*): *colonna marmorea*, marble column ‖ *era di un pallore* —, she was as white as marble.

marmorizzàre, *v.t.* to marble.

marmorizzàto, *ag.* marbled: *libro col bordo* —, marble-edged book.

marmòtta, *s.f.* **1.** (*zool.*) marmot: — *canadese*, whistler; — *d'America*, wood-chuck (*o* ground-hog) ‖ *dorme come una* —, he sleeps like a dormouse (*o a* top) **2.** (*persona pigra e indolente*) lazy-bones **3.** (*valigetta di viaggiatore di commercio*) commercial traveller's bag.

màrna, *s.f.* (*geol.*) marl.

Màrna, *no.pr.f.* (*geog.*) Marne.

marnàre, *v.t.* (*rar.*) to marl.

marnièra, *s.f.* (*geol.*) marl-pit.

marnóso, *ag.* marly.

maròcca, *s.f.* (*geol.*) moraine.

marocchinàio, *s.m.* (*rar.*) morocco leather tanner.

marocchinàre, *v.t.* to tan (skin) into morocco leather.

marocchíno, *ag.* Moroccan ‖ *s.m.* **1.** (*abitante*) Moroccan **2.** (*cuoio*) Morocco (leather) ‖ **marocchína**, *s.f.* Moroccan.

Maròcco, *no.pr.m.* (*geog.*) Morocco.

maronìta, *ag.s.m.* (*relig.*) Maronite.

maróso, *s.m.* billow, breaker: *i marosi venivano a frangersi sulla spiaggia*, breakers pounded on the beach.

màrra, *s.f.* **1.** (*agr.*) (*per le erbe*) hoe; (*per lavorare la terra*) mattock **2.** (*mar.*) (*estremità dei bracci dell'ancora*) fluke.

marràncio, *s.m.* butcher's knife.

marràno, *ag.* **1.** faithless, treacherous **2.** (*zotico*) uncouth ‖ *s.m.* **1.** (*st.*) forced convert (from Judaism or Mohammedanism) **2.** (*traditore*) traitor **3.** (*uomo rozzo*) boor, uncouth man.

marràta, *s.f.* stroke with a hoe, blow with a mattock.

marrocchíno, *e derivati*, *V.* **marocchíno**, *e derivati*.

marróne[1], *ag.* brown; (*marrone rossiccio*) maroon: *scarpe marroni*, brown shoes ‖ *s.m.* (*castagna*) chestnut: *marroni canditi*, marrons glacés (*o* iced chestnuts).

marróne[2], *s.m.* (*errore grossolano*) blunder: *fare un* —, to make a blunder.

marronéto, *s.m.* chestnut-grove.

marrúbio, *s.m.* (*bot.*) harehound.

marrúca, *s.f.*: — *bianca*, (*bot.*) hawthorn.

marrucàio, **marruchéto**, *s.m.* thorn-thicket.

marsàla, *s.m.* "Marsala" (kind of Sicilian wine).

Marsíglia, *no.pr.f.* (*geog.*) Marseille(s).

marsigliése, *ag. s.c.* Marseillaise (*invariato al pl.*) ‖ *la Marsigliese*, the Marseillaise.

marsína, *s.f.* tail-coat.

marsupiàle, *ag.s.m.* (*zool.*) marsupial.

marsúpio, *s.m.* marsupium (*pl.* marsupia).

Màrta, *no.pr.f.* Martha.

Màrte, *no.pr.m.* **1.** (*mit.*) Mars ‖ *campo di* —, (*mil.*) drill-ground; (*piazza d'arme*) parade-ground ‖ *il popolo di* —, the ancient Romans **2.** (*astr.*) Mars: *il pianeta* —, the planet Mars ‖ **màrte**, *s.m.* (*martedì*) Tuesday.

martedí, *s.m.* Tuesday ‖ — *grasso*, Shrove Tuesday.

martellaménto, *s.m.* **1.** hammering; pounding **2.** (*pulsazioni*) throbbing **3.** *fig.* (*tormento*) torment **4.** *fig.* (*insistenza*) insistence.

martellànte, *ag.*: *fuoco* —, (*artigl.*) continuous fire.

martellàre, *v.t.* **1.** to hammer: — *a freddo*, to cold-hammer; — *a penna*, to peen; — *il ferro rovente*, to hammer red-hot iron **2.** (*battere, colpire*) to beat, to pound: — *di colpi*, to beat furiously; — *l'uscio*, to pound at the door **3.** (*tormentare*) to worry, to torment: *la gelosia lo martella*, he is tormented by jealousy **4.** (*artigl.*) to pound: — *una posizione*, to pound a position ‖ *v.i.* **1.** to hammer **2.** *fig.* to insist ‖ *dagli, picchia e martella l'otterrai*, you will get it if you really insist **3.** (*pulsare*) to throb: *mi martellavano le tempie*, my temples throbbed.

martellàta, *s.f.* **1.** hammer-blow **2.** *fig.* heavy blow.

martellàto, *ag.* **1.** hammered: *ferro* —, hammered ironwork ‖ *cristallo* —, faceted crystal **2.** (*mus.*) martellato.

martellatóre, *s.m.*, **martellatríce**, *s.f.* hammerer.

martellatúra, *s.f.* hammering.

martellétto, *s.m.* **1.** (*di pianoforte*) hammer **2.** (*di un venditore all'incanto, di un presidente d'assemblea*) gavel.

martelliàno, *s.m.* (*poes.*) "martelliano" (verse of fourteen syllables).

martellína, *s.f.* (*per muratore*) pick, mason's hammer; (*per rifinire pietre sbozzate*) hack-hammer, facing-hammer; (*per scultori, scalpellini*) marteline; (*per disincrostare caldaie*) scaling-hammer.

martellío, *s.m.* **1.** hammering **2.** (*pulsazione dolorosa*) throbbing.

martèllo, *s.m.* **1.** hammer: — *ad aria compressa*, pneumatic hammer; — *da aggiustatore*, fitter's hammer; — *da bugnatura*, stone-mason's hammer; — *da calderaio*, boilermaker's hammer; — *da falegname*, claw-hammer; — *da tagliapietre*, stone-mason's hammer; — *da vetraio*, glazier's hammer; — *perforatore*, (*miner.*) hammer-drill; — *piano*, (*da fabbro*) set hammer; *bocca di* —, face of the hammer; *colpo di* —, hammer-stroke: *piantare un chiodo a colpi di* —, to hammer in a nail ‖ *dito a* —, hammer-toe ‖ *essere tra l'incudine e il* —, to be between the devil and the deep blue sea ‖ *suonare a* —, to ring the tocsin (*o* the alarm-bell) **2.** (*di orologio*) striker; (*di battente*) knocker **3.** (*anat.*) malleus (*pl.* mallei) **4.** (*di pianoforte*) hammer; (*da accordatore*) tuning-hammer **5.** (*spor.*) hammer: *lancio del* —, throwing the hammer **6.** *pesce* —, (*ittiol.*) hammer-fish **7.** (*st. mil.*): — *d'arme*, *ferrato*, martel; *torre* —, martello tower.

martinàccio, *s.m.* (*zool.*) large snail.

martinèlla, *s.f.* "martinella" (war-bell in Florence).

martinèllo, **martinétto**, *s.m.* (*mec.*) jack: — *a cavalletto*, screw-jack; — *a slitta*, sliding jack; — *a vite*, screw-jack; — *a vite per la piegatura delle rotaie*, (*ferr.*) jim-crow; — *idraulico*, hydraulic jack; *alzare mediante* —, to jack.

martingàla, *s.f.* **1.** (*per cavallo*) martingale **2.** (*mar.*) martingale **3.** (*di vestito*) half-belt **4.** (*in giuochi d'azzardo*) martingale.

Martiníca, *no.pr.f.* (*geog.*) Martinique.

martiníccа, *s.f.* (*freno*) wagon-brake, wagon-lock.

Martíno, *no.pr.m.* Martin ‖ *estate di San* —, Indian summer.

martín pescatóre, *s.m.* (*ornit.*) kingfisher.

màrtire, *s.c.* martyr (*anche fig.*): — *della libertà*, martyr for freedom; — *della scienza*, martyr in the cause of science; *le reliquie dei martiri*, the relics of martyrs; *egli si atteggia sempre a* —, he always plays the martyr.

martírio, *s.m.* **1.** martyrdom: *la palma del* —, the crown of martyrdom; *soffrire il* —, to suffer martyrdom **2.** *fig.* (*tormento*) torture, torment: *è un* — *dovergli parlare*, (*fam.*) it is torture (*o* it is painful) to have to talk to him; *la sua vita è stata tutta un* —, his life was one long torment.

martirizzaménto, *s.m.* martyrizing, martyrization.

martirizzàre, *v.t.* **1.** to martyrize, to make a martyr of (s.o.) **2.** *fig.* (*tormentare*) to torture, to torment: *quel ricordo lo martirizzava*, that recollection tortured him.

martirizzàto, *ag.* martyrized, tortured (*anche fig.*).

martirològio, *s.m.* martyrology.

màrtora, *s.f.* (*zool.*) marten: — *zibellina*, sable; *una pelliccia di* —, a sable (fur).

martoriàre, *v.t.* to torture, to torment (*anche fig.*) ‖ **martoriàrsi**, *v.r. fig.* to torture oneself: — *il cervello*, to rack one's brains.

martoriàto, *ag.* tortured, tormented.

martòrio, **martòro**, *s.m.* (*poet.*) torment, torture.

marxísmo, *s.m.* (*pol.*) Marxism, Marxianism.

marxísta, *ag.s.c.* (*pol.*) Marxian, Marxist.

màrza, *s.f.* (*agr.*) graft.

marzaiuòlo, *ag.* (*rar.*) of March; March (*attributivo*).

marzapàne, *s.m.* (*cuc.*) marzipan.

marzeggiàre, *v.i.* (*essere mutevole*) to be changeable (like March weather).

marziàle, *ag.* **1.** martial, military; soldierlike: *marcia* —, military march; *portamento, aria* —, martial (*o soldierlike*) bearing, air || *corte* —, court-martial; *legge* —, martial law **2.** (*chim.*) martial.

Marziàle, *no.pr.m.* (*st. lett.*) Martial.

marziàno, *s.m.* Martian.

màrzio, *ag.* martian || *campo* —, parade-ground.

màrzo, *s.m.* March || *è pazzo come* —, he is as mad as a March hare.

marzolíno, marzuòlo, *ag.* of March; March (*attributivo*): *grano, pollo* —, spring-wheat, spring-chicken.

mas, *s.m.* (*mar. mil.*) motor torpedo-boat (*abbr.* M.T.B.); E-boat.

mascalcía, *s.f.* (*arte del maniscalco*) farriery.

mascalzonàta, *s.f.* dirty trick, nasty trick.

mascalzóne, *s.m.* rogue, rascal, knave.

mascarpóne, *s.m.* "mascarpone" (Italian soft cheese).

mascèlla, *s.f.* **1.** (*anat.*) jaw: — *inferiore, superiore,* lower, upper jaw || *non fa che lavorar di mascelle,* (*scherz.*) he is always stuffing himself **2.** (*mec. miner.*) jaw: — *da frantoio,* crushing jaw.

mascellàre, *ag.* maxillary; jaw (*attributivo*): *osso* —, jawbone.

màschera, *s.f.* **1.** mask (anche *fig.*); (*costume*) fancy-dress: — *da carnevale,* carnival mask; *ballo in* —, masked ball; *sotto la* — *dell'amicizia, della virtù,* under the cloak (*o* mask *o* guise) of friendship, of virtue; *la sua pietà non è che una* —, his piety is only a blind; *gettar via la* —, to throw off one's (*o* to drop the) mask; *portare una* —, to wear a mask; *strappare la* — *a qlcu.,* to unmask s.o. || *la* — *tragica,* (*teat. greco*) the tragic mask || *giù la* —*!,* (*fam.*) come off it! || *l'uomo dalla* — *di ferro,* (*st.*) the Man in the Iron Mask **2.** (*persona mascherata, attore mascherato*) masker, masquerader || *ti conosco, mascherina!,* try another one! (*o* you can't fool me!) **3.** (*personaggio del teatro popolare*) "maschera", mask-character: *la* — *di Napoli è Pulcinella,* the mask-character of Naples is Punchinello **4.** (*espressione del viso*) features (*pl.*); (*il viso*) face: *ha una* — *molto mobile,* he has very mobile features **5.** (*calco del viso di un morto*) death-mask **6.** (*cerone*) make up **7.** (*cosmesi*) face-pack **8.** (*inserviente di cinema, teatro*) usher; (*donna*) usherette **9.** (*maschera protettiva*) mask; (*mil.*) gas-mask; (*scherma*) (fencing-)mask; face-guard; (*subacquea*) underwater mask, diving-mask **10.** (*per anestesia*) mask for anaesthetics **11.** (*arch.*) mask **12.** (*mec.*) jig; (*aut.*) grill, louver: — *per radiatore,* (*aut.*) radiator-cowl.

mascheraménto, *s.m.* **1.** masking (anche *fig.*) **2.** (*mil.*) masking; (*mimetizzazione*) camouflage **3.** (*tv.*) blanking; (*amer.*) blackout **4.** (*acu.*) masking.

mascheràre, *v.t.* **1.** to mask, to put a mask on (s.o.); to dress up: — *un bambino da pagliaccio,* to dress up a child (*o* to get a child up) as a clown **2.** (*nascondere*) to mask, to disguise; to conceal, to hide: — *i difetti di qlcu.,* to conceal (*o* to hide) s.o.'s faults; — *il proprio giuoco,* to conceal one's intentions (*o* to act underhandedly); — *il proprio pensiero,* to dissemble; — *i propri sentimenti,* to hide (*o* to conceal) one's feelings; — *ql.co. a qlcu.,* to conceal (*o* to hide) sthg. from s.o. **3.** (*mil.*) to mask; (*mimetizzare*) to camouflage: — *una batteria,* to mask (*o* to conceal) a battery **4.** (*acu.*) to mask || **mascheràrsi,** *v.r.* **1.** to put on a mask; (*mettersi in costume*) to put on a fancy-dress: — *da Arlecchino,* to dress up as Harlequin **2.** (*travestirsi, contraffarsi*) to pass oneself off (as s.o., sthg.).

mascheràta, *s.f.* masquerade (anche *fig.*).

mascheràto, *ag.* **1.** masked: *ballo* —, masked ball; *erano tutti mascherati,* they were all masked || *corso* —, masked pageant **2.** (*nascosto*) hidden, concealed; disguised: *tirannide mascherata,* tyranny in disguise; *verità mascherata,* hidden truth **3.** (*mil.*) masked; (*mimetizzato*) camouflaged.

mascherína, *s.f.* (*di una scarpa*) toe-cap.

mascheróne, *s.m.* **1.** (*maschera grottesca*) grotesque mask: *era così truccata che sembrava un* —, she was so heavily made up that she looked like a mask **2.** (*faccia deforme*) deformed face **3.** (*edil.*) gargoyle **4.** (*arch.*) mask, mascaron.

maschiàccio, *s.m.* **1.** rude boy **2.** (*ragazza di maniere mascoline*) tomboy, hoyden **3.** (*virago*) virago.

maschiaménte, *av.* manfully.

maschiàre, *v.t.* (*mec.*) to tap.

maschiatríce, *s.f.* (*mec.*) tapping-machine.

maschiatúra, *s.f.* (*mec.*) tapping.

maschiétta, *s.f.* tomboy, hoyden || *capelli alla* —, Eton crop (*o* shingled hair).

maschiétto, *s.m.* (*mec.*) male (connector).

maschiézza, *s.f.* (*virilità*) masculinity, manliness.

maschíle, *ag.* **1.** male: *discendenza* —, male descent; *linea* —, male line; *sesso* —, male sex; *scuola* —, boys' school **2.** (*virile*) manly, masculine; (*spreg.*) masculine: *un carattere* —, a masculine character; *una voce* —, a manly voice: *ella ha una voce* —, she has a masculine voice **3.** (*gram.*) masculine: *genere* —, masculine gender.

màschio[1]**,** *ag.* **1.** male: *cugino* —, male cousin; *elefante* —, bull-elephant; *erede* —, male heir; *felce maschia,* (*bot.*) male fern; *figli maschi,* male children; *un fiore* —, a male flower; *passero* —, cock-sparrow **2.** (*virile*) manly, masculine, virile: *un aspetto* —, a manly appearance; *cuore* —, brave heart; *eloquenza maschia,* forceful eloquence; *mente maschia,* virile mind; *qualità maschie,* manly qualities; *stile* —, powerful style; *virtù maschie,* manly virtues; *voce maschia,* manly voice: *quel ragazzo ha un viso* —, that boy has a manly face || *s.m.* **1.** male; (*ragazzo*) boy; (*uomo*) man; (*figlio*) son: *che bel bambino, è un* — *o una femmina?,* what a beautiful baby, is it a boy or a girl? (*o* is it a he or a she?); *ho due maschi in casa,* I have two sons; *questo cane ha quattro cuccioli, tutti maschi,* this dog has four puppies, all male **2.** (*tec.*) male: — *dell'albero,* (*mar.*) mast-tenon (*o* -heel); — *della vite,* male screw; — *del timone,* (*mar.*) rudder-head.

màschio[2]**,** *s.m.* (*torre di una fortezza*) donjon, keep.

mascolinità, *s.f.* masculinity.

mascolíno, *ag.* masculine.

mascotte, *s.f.* mascot.

masnàda, *s.f.* band, gang.

masnadière, *s.m.* highwayman (*pl.* highwaymen); bandit, brigand.

masochísmo, *s.m.* masochism.

masochísta, *s.m.* masochist.

masoníte, *s.f.* (*edil.*) masonite.

màssa, *s.f.* **1.** mass; (*mucchio*) heap (anche *fig.*): *una* — *d'acqua,* a great body of water; — *d'aria,* air mass; *una* — *di argilla,* a mass of clay; *una* — *di libri,* a heap of books; — *di luce, ombra,* (*pitt.*) mass of light, shadow; *una* — *di metallo fuso,* a mass of molten metal; *una* — *di pietre,* a heap of stones; *una* — *di sciocchezze,* a load of nonsense; *una* — *di neve si staccò,* a mass of snow broke away; *il minerale si trovava in grandi masse,* the mineral was found in large masses; *avere una* — *di cose da fare,* to have a heap of things to do || *in* —, in bulk: *produzione in* —, mass-production; *vendere in* —, to sell in bulk **2.** (*folla, popolo*) mass: *la gran* — *del pubblico,* the great mass of the public; *nella* — *l'individuo tende a scomparire,* in the mass the individual tends to disappear; *i demagoghi sono maestri nel suggestionare le masse,* demagogues are masters of mass-suggestion; *commuovere le masse,* to move the mob; *elevare le masse,* to educate the masses || *in* —, en masse: *adunanza in* —, mass-meeting; *attacco in* —, (*mil.*) mass-attack; *esecuzione in* —, mass-execution: *leva in* —, (*mil.*) general conscription; *eravamo presenti in* —, we turned out en masse; *si sollevarono in* —, they rose in a body **3.** (*comm.*

dir.) (*fondi, sostanze*): — *attiva*, liquid assets; — *ereditaria*, (*dir.*) hereditament; — *fallimentare*, bankruptcy assets; — *passiva*, liabilities ‖ — *creditoria*, general body of creditors **4.** (*mil.*) fund: — *mensa*, mess fund **5.** (*fis.*) mass: — *atomica*, atomic mass; — *critica*, critical mass; — *di riposo*, rest mass; — *inerziale*, inertial mass; — *isotopica*, isotopic mass **6.** (*elett.*) eartn.

massacràre, *v.t.* **1.** to massacre, to slaughter, to butcher: *massacrarono tutta quella povera gente indifesa*, they massacred all those poor, helpless people ‖ *Nerone fece* — *molti cristiani*, Nero massacred many Christians **2.** (*rovinare*) to spoil, to ruin, to murder: *ha massacrato quel bel libro con la sua pessima traduzione*, he has completely spoilt (o he has ruined o murdered) that fine book with his terrible translation.

massàcro, *s.m.* **1.** (*strage*) massacre, slaughter, butchery: — *di ebrei*, pogrom ‖ *il* — *degli innocenti*, (*Bibbia*) the Massacre of the Innocents **2.** (*arald.*) massacre.

massaggiàre, *v.t.* to massage.

massaggiatóre, *s.m.* masseur.

massaggiatríce, *s.f.* masseuse.

massàggio, *s.m.* massage.

massàia, *s.f.* housewife (*pl.* housewives).

massàio, massàro, *s.m.* **1.** (*capoccia*) bailiff **2.** (*amministratore*) administrator.

Massàua, *no.pr.f.* (*geog.*) Massaua, Massawa.

massellàre, *v.t.* to beat out (iron).

massèllo, *s.m.* (*metal.*) ingot, lump: — *di acciaio*, steel ingot ‖ *oro di* —, (*massiccio*) solid gold.

Massènzio, *no.pr.m.* (*st. romana*) Maxentius.

masseria, *s.f.* **1.** (*fattoria e podere*) farm **2.** (*mandra di bovini*) herd; (*gregge*) flock.

masserizia, *s.f.* **1.** *gener.pl.* (household) furniture and fittings (*pl.*): *masserizie di cucina*, pots and pans (o kitchen utensils); *dovettero trasportare le loro masserizie in luogo sicuro*, they had to move their goods and chattels to a safe place **2.** (*arc.*) (*risparmio*) savings (*pl.*) **3.** (*arc.*) (*governo della casa*) housekeeping.

massetère, *s.m.* (*anat.*) masseter.

masséto, *s.m.* (*sodaglia*) untilled land.

massicciàre, *v.t.* to metal; (*ferr.*) to ballast.

massicciàta, *s.f.* road-bed; (*ferr.*) ballast: *la* — *si copre con asfalto*, the road-bed is covered with asphalt.

massicciàto, *ag.* metalled; (*ferr.*) ballasted: *una strada ben massicciata*, a well metalled road.

massíccio, *ag.* **1.** (*solido*) solid, massive: *legno* —, solid wood; *oro* —, solid gold; *una porta di noce massiccia*, a door made of solid walnut **2.** (*grosso, voluminoso*) massive; stout: *un edificio* —, a massive building; *lineamenti massicci*, massive features; *un mobile* —, a massive piece of furniture; *ha spalle massicce*, he has broad shoulders ‖ *s.m.* **1.** (*geog.*) massif: *il* — *dell'Imalaia*, the massif of the Himalayas **2.** (*geol.*) horst **3.** — *di coltivazione*, (*miner.*) back **4.** (*mar.*) dead-wood.

màssima, *s.f.* **1.** maxim, rule, principle: *dice di no a tutti per* —, he says no to everybody on principle; *è un libro pieno di ottime massime morali*, it is a book full of excellent moral maxims (o principles); *non si può stabilire come* — *ciò che è vero soltanto in pochi casi*, what is true in few cases only cannot be accepted as a (general) principle; *avere come* — *di...*, to make a point of...: *ha come* — *di non accettare mai un invito*, he makes a point of never accepting an invitation ‖ *in linea di* —, *è un libro ben riuscito*, on the whole the author has made a good job of this book; *in linea di* — *non facciamo credito*, as a general rule we do not give credit ‖ *pervenire ad un accordo di* —, to reach a general agreement **2.** (*detto, proverbio*) saying, maxim, proverb: *è una saggia* — *cinese*, it is a wise Chinese saying **3.** (*grado massimo di temperatura, pressione barometrica*) maximum: *termometro di* —, maximum thermometer **4.** (*arc.*) (*mus.*) large.

massimàle, *ag.* maximal; maximum (*attributivo*):

prezzo —, maximum price ‖ *.s.m.* limit, ceiling: — *di reddito*, gross income.

massimalísmo, *s.m.* (*pol.*) Maximalism.

massimalísta, *s.m.* (*pol.*) Maximalist.

massimaménte, *av.* chiefly, especially.

massimàrio, *s.m.* collection of maxims.

màssime, *av.* (*letter.*) mainly, chiefly.

Massimiàno, *no.pr.m.* (*st. romana*) Maximian.

Massimiliàno, *no.pr.m.* Maximilian.

màssimo, *ag. superl.* (*il più grande*) **greatest; maximum** (*attributivo*); (*il migliore*) **best;** (*il più alto*) **highest;** (*l'estremo*) **extreme, utmost;** (*il più lungo*) **longest:** — *angolo di sterzata*, (*aut.*) steering-lock; *la massima attenzione*, the utmost attention; — *carico*, maximum load; *la massima cura*, the greatest care; *il* — *grado*, the highest degree; — *numero di giri d'elica*, (*aer.*) maximum revolutions; *il* — *piacere*, the greatest pleasure; *massima possibilità produttiva*, maximum output; *il* — *rispetto*, the utmost respect; *la cifra massima*, the highest figure; *costo* — *del preventivo*, budget-ceiling; *l'offerta massima*, the highest offer; *periodo* — *di stagione*, height of the season; *prezzi massimi*, top prices; *punto* — *dell'attività produttiva*, peak of productive activity; *la temperatura massima*, the highest (o maximum) temperature; *il* — *dei nostri poeti visse nel medioevo*, our greatest poet lived in the Middle Ages; *mi trattò con la massima pazienza*, he was extremely patient with me; *parla diverse lingue con la massima facilità*, he speaks several languages with the greatest ease; *regnava la massima confusione in quella classe*, it was absolute chaos in that class-room; *sento la massima gratitudine per lui*, I am extremely grateful to him; *si è laureato col* — *dei voti*, he got a first-class degree ‖ — *comun divisore*, (*mat.*) highest common factor ‖ *la massima parte*, the majority (o most): *la massima parte dei medici che conosco*, most of the doctors I know; *gli studenti dei corsi serali per la massima parte lavorano di giorno*, most students attending evening -classes work during the day ‖ *al* —, at most (o at the most); (*moltissimo*) very much (o to the utmost): *costerà al* — *mille lire*, it will cost a thousand lire at the most; *mi sono divertito al* —, I have enjoyed myself very much; *ti aspetterò per mezz'ora al* —, I shall wait for you half an hour at the most ‖ *cerchio* —, (*geog.*) maximum circumference (o Equator) ‖ *ottavo* —, (*tip.*) full octavo ‖ *peso* —, (*spor.*) heavy-weight ‖ *Pontefice* —, (*st. romana*) Pontifex Maximus ‖ *tempo* —, (*spor.*) time-limit ‖ *s.m.* **1.** maximum; (*il meglio*) **best:** *questo è il* — *che posso dire per il momento*, this is all I can say for the moment; *questo è il* — *che potrei fare per te*, this is the best I could do for you ‖ *si meritò il* — *della pena*, he deserved the maximum penalty **2.** (*mat. fis.*) maximum (*pl.* maxima): *il* — *di pressione*, the maximum pressure; *il* — *di velocità*, the maximum (o top) speed.

Màssimo, *no.pr.m.* (*st. romana*) Maximus.

Massinissa, *no.pr.m.* (*st.*) Mas(s)inissa.

màsso, *s.m.* block; rock: — *erratico*, (*geol.*) erratic boulder; — *vivo*, naked (o bare) rock ‖ *duro come un* —, as hard as a rock; *pesante come un* —, as heavy as a rock ‖ *dormire come un* —, to sleep like a log.

massóne, *s.m.* Freemason, mason.

massoneria, *s.f.* Freemasonry.

massònico, *ag.* masonic: *loggia massonica*, Masonic lodge.

massóso, *ag.* rocky, stony.

massoterapia, *s.f.* (*med.*) massotherapy.

mastalgia, *s.f.* (*med.*) mastalgia.

mastèllo, *s.m.* tub: — *per il bucato*, wash-tub.

masticàbile, *ag.* masticable.

masticaménto, *s.m.* mastication, chewing.

masticàre, *v.t.* **1.** to masticate, to chew: *gomma da* —, chewing-gum; *tabacco da* —, chewing-tobacco; *dovresti sempre* — *bene il cibo prima di inghiottirlo*, you should masticate (o chew) your food well before you swallow it; *ogni volta che lo vedo sta masticando ql.co.*, I never see him but he is chewing sthg. || *mastica veleno da due settimane*, he has been eating his heart out for two weeks; *quando gli dissero che il suo lavoro era tutto sbagliato masticò veleno*, when they told him his work was all wrong, he felt very bitter || — *male ql.co.*, *fig.* to take sthg. badly **2.** (*pronunciare indistintamente*) to mumble; to stammer: *masticò qualche parola che non compresi*, he mumbled some words which I did not understand; — *un complimento*, to stammer out a compliment; — *una scusa*, to mumble an excuse || *mastica un po' di francese*, he has a smattering of French.

masticatíccio, *s.m.* chewing-tobacco.

masticàto, *ag.* **1.** chewed, masticated; *cibo ben* —, well-chewed (*o* masticated) food **2.** (*assimilato*) assimilated: *bene* —, well-assimilated: *lezione ben masticata*, well assimilated lesson; *mal* —, badly assimilated.

masticatóre, *ag.* chewing || *s.m.*, **masticatríce,** *s.f.* chewer, masticator.

masticatòrio, *ag.* masticatory.

masticazióne, *s.f.* mastication.

màstice, *s.m.* **1.** (*bot.*) mastic **2.** (*di gomma*) rubber solution, adhesive; (*per tubazioni, vetri*) putty: — *all'ossido di ferro*, iron putty; — *al minio*, red-lead putty.

mastíno, *s.m.* (*cane*) mastiff.

màstio, *s.m.* (*torre di una fortezza*) keep, donjon.

mastíte, *s.f.* (*patol.*) mastitis.

mastodónte, *s.m.* **1.** (*paleont.*) mastodon **2.** (*persona di proporzioni colossali*) giant.

mastodòntico, *ag.* colossal, gigantic, huge.

mastòide, *s.f.* (*anat.*) mastoid, mastoid projection.

mastoidíte, *s.f.* (*patol.*) mastoiditis; (*pop.*) mastoids.

màstra, *s.f.* **1.** kneading-trough **2.** (*mar.*) partners (*pl.*), coamings (*pl.*).

màstro, *ag.*: *libro* —, (*comm.*) ledger || *s.m.* **1.** master: — *d'ascia*, — *falegname*, master-carpenter; *capomastro*, master-builder **2.** *Mastro*, (*appellativo*) Master: *Mastro Giovanni*, Master John **3.** (*comm.*) ledger: — *a fogli sciolti*, loose-leaf ledger; — *dei clienti*, petty (*o* customers'*) ledger; — *generale*, general (*o* main) ledger; *registrare a* —, to post.

masturbàre, *v.t.*, **masturbàrsi,** *v.r.* to masturbate.

masturbatòrio, *ag.* masturbatory.

masturbazióne, *s.f.* masturbation.

matafióne, *s.m.* (*mar.*) (reef-)point: *matafioni d'inferitura*, (reef-)earings.

matàssa, *s.f.* skein; hank; *fig.* tangle, muddle: *una* — *di cotone*, a hank of cotton; *una* — *di lana*, a skein of wool; *è una* — *così imbrogliata!*, *fig.* it is such a tangled web!; *arruffare la* —, *fig.* to create confusion; *dipanare una* —, to unravel a skein; *dipanare la* —, *fig.* to clear up a difficulty || *trovare il bandolo della* —, to disentangle a matter: *non riesco a trovare il bandolo della* —, I can't make head or tail of this.

màte, *s.m.* (*arbusto e infuso che si ricava dalle foglie d'esso*) maté, mate.

matemàtica, *s.f.* mathematics; (*fam.*) maths: — *applicata, pura*, applied, pure mathematics; *la* — *non è il suo forte*, mathematics is not his strong point.

matematicaménte, *av.* mathematically.

matemàtico, *ag.* mathematical: *ragionamento* —, mathematical reasoning; *scienze matematiche*, mathematical sciences; *fece ogni cosa con precisione matematica*, he did everything with mathematical accuracy || *s.m.* mathematician: *è un* — *di genio*, he is a mathematical genius.

materassàia, *s.f.*, **materassàio,** *s.m.* mattress-maker.

materàsso, *s.m.* mattress: — *a molle*, spring mattress; — *di crine*, hair mattress; — *di gomma piuma*, foam-rubber mattress; — *di lana*, wool mattress; *rifare un* —, to restuff a mattress; *sprimacciare un* —, to shake up a mattress.

matèria, *s.f.* **1.** (*sostanza*) matter, substance; (*materiale*) matter, material: — *bruta*, brute matter; — *colo-* *rante*, (*chim.*) dye-stuff; — *inerte*, inert matter; — *inorganica, organica*, (*chim.*) inorganic, organic substance; — *plastica*, plastic material; *le materie prime*, raw materials; — *volatile*, (*chim.*) volatile matter; *la* — *di cui è composto un oggetto*, the matter of which an object is made **2.** (*med.*) matter: — *grigia*, grey matter **3.** (*pus*) matter, pus: *la ferita era piena di* —, the wound was full of pus (*o* matter) **4.** (*fil.*) (*contrapposta allo spirito*) matter **5.** (*contenuto di opera artistica, letteraria*) matter: — *e forma*, matter and form **6.** (*argomento*) matter, subject; topic, theme: *una* — *di controversia*, a controversial matter; — *di riflessione*, food for thought; *catalogo per materie*, subject-catalogue; *indice delle materie*, table of contents; *tolleranza in* — *di religione*, toleration in religious matters; *la* — *del suo saggio non è molto interessante*, the theme (*o* subject) of his essay is not very interesting; *è molto versato in* —, he is well up in the subject; *non so nulla in* —, I know nothing of the subject; *questa è la* — *del mio libro*, this is the subject-matter of my book; *sa tutto in* — *di musica*, he knows everything about music; *il tribunale si è dichiarato competente a pronunciarsi in* —, (*dir.*) the Court has declared itself competent to pass judgement on the matter; *entrare in* —, to broach a subject **7.** (*occasione, motivo*) matter; reason, grounds (*pl.*): *non ho* — *per pensare che egli sia un ladro*, I have no reason to believe that he is a thief; *non mi diede mai* — *di preoccupazione*, he never gave me grounds for worry; *questa fu* — *di grande meraviglia*, this was matter for great wonder; *vi è* — *per un processo*, (*dir.*) there are grounds for litigation **8.** (*disciplina scolastica*) subject: *materie letterarie, scientifiche*, literary, scientific subjects; *materie obbligatorie*, compulsory subjects; *quali sono le tue materie preferite?*, which are your favourite subjects? || — *medica*, materia medica.

materiàle, *ag.* **1.** material; physical; (*del corpo*) bodily: *benessere* —, material comfort; *causa* —, material cause; *danno* —, material damage; *il mondo* —, the physical world; *necessità materiali*, material needs; *progresso* —, material progress; *soccorso* —, material help; *ne ha a sufficienza per la propria vita* —, he has enough for his material needs; *si cura solo dei piaceri materiali*, he only cares for material pleasures || *errore* —, careless slip || *non ho il tempo* — *di farlo*, I just haven't time to do it **2.** (*rozzo, grossolano*) clumsy, rough, unpolished: *è un tipo* —, he is a rough (*o* clumsy *o* unpolished) type; *quel ragazzo ha dei modi così materiali...*, that boy has such rough manners...; *i suoi mobili sono vistosi e materiali*, her furniture is showy and clumsy || *s.m.* material, stuff: — *alluvionale*, (*geol.*) alluvium; — *antiacustico*, (*edil. ind.*) soundproof material; — *bellico*, war materials: — *coibente*, insulating material; — *da costruzione*, building material; — *di deposito*, spoil; — *di recupero*, salvage; — *di riporto*, (*edil.*) filling; — *di scarto*, discarded material; — *di sterro*, cut; — *greggio*, raw material; — *inutilizzato*, (*ind.*) wasted material; — *isolante*, (*elett.*) insulating material; — *lavorato*, (*ind.*) machined product; —, *mano d'opera e spese generali*, (*amm.*) material, labour and overhead(s); — *mobile, rotabile*, (*ferr.*) rolling-stock; — *scolastico*, teaching equipment; — *sedimentato*, (*geol.*) silt; — *tipografico*, typographical material; *il* — *è stato dichiarato fuori uso*, (*ind.*) the material was condemned as unserviceable; *il* — *è stato collaudato con successo*, (*ind*) the material stood the test; *questo* — *è soggetto a deperimento*, (*ind.*) this material is liable to deterioration; *determinare il costo del* —, (*comm.*) to determine the cost of material; *impiegare* — *di prim'ordine*, (*ind.*) to employ first-rate material.

materialismo, *s.m.* materialism.

materialista, *ag.* materialistic(al) || *s.c.* materialist.

materialístico, *ag.* materialistic(al).

materialità, *s.f.* materiality, materialness.

materializzàre, *v.t.* to materialize.

materializzazióne, *s.f.* materialization.

materialménte, *av.* **1.** materially; physically: *fare questo è — impossibile,* it is physically impossible to do this **2.** (*grossolanamente*) clumsily.

materialóne, *s.m.* clumsy person; unpolished person.

maternaménte, *av.* maternally.

maternità, *s.f.* **1.** motherhood, maternity **2.** (*clinica ostetrica*) maternity-hospital.

matèrno, *ag.* (*di, proprio della madre*) motherly, mother (*attributivo*); (*da parte di madre*) maternal: *parenti materni,* maternal relatives; *tenerezza materna,* motherly tenderness; *egli è mio zio dal lato —,* he is my uncle on my mother's side ‖ *lingua materna,* mother-tongue ‖ *scuola materna,* nursery-school.

materòzza, *s.f.* (*metal.*) head, feed-head.

Matílde, *no.pr.f.* Mat(h)ilda ‖ *dim.* Maud.

matinée, *s.f.* (*teat.*) matinée, afternoon performance.

matíta, *s.f.* pencil: — *a sfera,* ball-point pen; — *copiativa,* copying-pencil; — *pastello,* crayon; *disegno a —,* pencil-drawing; *disegno a due matite,* sketch in charcoal and white chalk; *sottolineare un errore con la — blu,* to underline a mistake in blue pencil.

matràccio, *s.m.* (*chim.*) flask, matrass, cucurbit: — *graduato,* volumetric flask.

matriarcàto, *s.m.* matriarchy, matriarchate.

matricària, *s.f.* (*bot.*) wild camomile.

matríce, *s.f.* **1.** (*utero*) matrix (*pl.* matrices, matrixes), womb; (*radice dell'unghia*) matrix (*pl.* matrices, matrixes) **2.** (*mat. geol.*) matrix (*pl.* matrices, matrixes) **3.** (*comm.*) stub: *registro a —,* counterfoil book; *staccare la figlia dalla —,* to tear the counterfoil from the stub **4.** (*tec.*) matrix (*pl.* matrices, matrixes), mould, die: — *a tranciare,* (*mec.*) blanking-die; — *per piega,* (*mec.*) forming-die; — *per trafila,* (*mec. metal.*) die (-plate) (*o* draw-plate).

matricída, *ag.* matricidal ‖ *s.c.* matricide.

matricídio, *s.m.* matricide.

matrícola, *s.f.* **1.** matricula, register, roll, list (of members); (*mil.*) regimental roll: *libretto di —,* (*mil.*) service record (*o* service certificate); *numero di —,* (matriculation) number; (*di un fucile*) rifle number: *prendete il suo numero di —!,* (*mil.*) take his number! **2.** (*mar.*) register: — *della gente di mare,* register; *numero di —,* number of register **3.** (*studente*) freshman (*pl.* freshmen): *festa delle matricole,* freshmen's rag.

matricolàre, *v.t.* to matriculate.

matricolàto, *ag.* matriculated ‖ *un briccone —,* an arrant knave; *un imbroglione —,* a notorious swindler.

matricolazióne, *s.f.* matriculation.

matricolíno, *s.m.* (*studente*) freshman (*pl.* freshmen); (*novellino*) beginner; novice; new hand.

matrígna, *s.f.* **1.** stepmother ‖ *chi ha —, di dietro si signa,* *prov.* take heed of a stepmother, the very name of her sufficeth **2.** (*letter.*) (*cattiva madre*) stepmother: *la natura è — in questi paesi,* Nature is harsh (*o* unkind) in these lands.

matrignésco, *ag.* stepmotherly; (*crudele*) cruel; (*cattivo*) unkind.

matrimoniàle, *ag.* matrimonial, conjugal: *anello —,* wedding-ring; *camera —,* double-room; *letto —,* double-bed; *pubblicazioni matrimoniali,* banns.

matrimonialménte, *av.* matrimonially.

matrimònio, *s.m.* **1.** marriage, matrimony: — *civile,* civil marriage; — *d'amore,* love-match; — *di convenienza,* marriage of convenience; — *misto,* mixed marriage; — *morganatico,* morganatic marriage; — *religioso,* church marriage; *certificato di —,* marriage certificate (*o* lines); *compare di —,* best man; *domanda di —,* offer of marriage; *opposizione al —,* opposition to the marriage; *rottura della promessa di —,* breach of promise; *sensale di —,* match-maker; *il — è una istituzione sacra,* matrimony is a holy institution; *il — è stato sciolto,* the marriage has been dissolved; *egli ha fatto un buonissimo —,* he has made a very

good match; *celebrare un —,* to celebrate a marriage; *combinare un —,* to arrange a marriage; *congiungere in —,* to join in wedlock; *dare in —,* to give in marriage; *unirsi in —,* to get married **2.** (*cerimonia, festa nuziale*) wedding: *anniversario di —,* wedding-anniversary; *abbiamo già ricevuto il suo annuncio di —,* we have already received his wedding-announcement; *devo andare ad un —,* I have to go to a wedding.

matrizzàre, *v.i.* to take after one's mother.

matróna, *s.f.* matron: *pare una —,* she is a matronly figure.

matronàle, *ag.* matronly, matronal; matron-like: *dignità —,* matronly dignity; *una donna di aspetto —,* a matron-like woman; *maniere matronali,* matronly (*o* matronal) manners.

matronalménte, *av.* matronly.

matronèo, *s.m.* (*arch.*) women's gallery.

matronímico, *ag.s.m.* matronymic.

màtta, *s.f.* **1.** mad woman, crazy woman **2.** (*alle carte*) (jolly) joker; (*qualsiasi altra carta*) wild card.

mattacchióne, *s.m.* lively spark, joker, wag: *è un gran —, non è vero?,* he is a lively spark, isn't he?.

mattaccíno, *s.m.* **1.** (*st.*) jester, buffoon; (*saltimbanco*) mountebank **2.** (*persona allegra, pronta alle burle*) crazy fellow, joker.

mattàccio, *ag.* crazy, mad ‖ *s.m.* cheerful and amusing fellow.

mattaménte, *av.* crazily, madly.

mattàna, *s.f.* (*fam.*) bad mood, fit of bad temper: *gli salta spesso la —,* he often has fits of bad temper; *lasciagli passare la —,* wait for him to get over his bad temper.

mattànza, *s.f.* (*mar.*) slaughter of tunny-fish.

mattàta, *s.f.* piece of lunacy.

mattatóio, *s.m.* slaughter-house, abattoir.

matteggiàre, *v.i.* to act like a madman.

Mattèo, *no.pr.m.* Matthew ‖ *dim.* Matt.

matterèllo, *s.m.* (*cuc.*) rolling-pin.

matteria, *s.f.* (*rar.*) piece of lunacy.

mattézza, *s.f.* (*rar.*) **1.** madness, craziness **2.** (*mattata*) piece of lunacy.

Mattía, *no.pr.m.* Matthias.

mattína, *s.f.* morning: *la — di mercoledì,* Wednesday morning; *abito da —,* morning-wear; *una bella — di primavera,* a fine spring morning; *dalla — alla sera,* from morning to evening; *di prima —,* early in the morning; *domani, ieri —,* tomorrow, yesterday morning; *questa —,* this morning; *cosa hai fatto tutta —?,* what have you been doing all morning?; *lo incontrai una —,* I met him one morning; *studio sempre la —,* I always study in the morning; *alzarsi presto la —,* to rise with the lark (*o* to get up early); *perdere la —,* to waste the morning.

mattinàle, *ag.* (*rar.*) morning (*attributivo*).

mattinàta, *s.f.* **1.** morning; forenoon: — *nebbiosa, piovosa,* foggy, rainy morning; *in —,* in the morning (*o* before noon); *ho perduto tutta la — a far compere,* I spent the whole morning shopping **2.** (*teat.*) matinée, afternoon performance **3.** (*canto amoroso*) morning-song, aubade.

mattinièro, *ag.* early-rising: *persona mattiniera,* early riser (*o* early bird); *come sei —!,* what an early bird you are!.

mattíno, *s.m.* **1.** morning (*anche fig.*): *il — della vita,* the morning of life; *al — presto, di buon —,* early in the morning: *alzarsi di buon —,* to get up early (*o* to rise with the lark); *edizione del —,* morning edition; *i giornali del —,* the morning newspapers ‖ *l'astro del —,* the morning star (*o* Lucifer) ‖ *le ore del — han l'oro in bocca,* *prov.* an hour in the morning before breakfast is worth two all the rest of the day **2.** (*eccl.*) (*mattutino*) matins (*pl.*): *cantare il —,* to sing matins **3.** (*levante*) East: *la casa è esposta a —,* the house faces East.

màtto[1], *ag.* **1.** mad; (*fam.*) crazy: *è — furioso,* he is raving mad; *diventar —,* to go mad; *far diventar —*

qlcu., to drive s.o. mad: *quello spavento l'ha fatto diventar* —, that fright drove him out of his mind ǁ — *da legare*, as mad as a March hare (*o* as a hatter) ǁ *cavallo* —, wild horse ǁ *che testa matta!*, what a hot-headed fool! ǁ *c'è da diventar* —*!*, it is enough to drive you mad (*o* crazy)! ǁ *è mezzo* —, he is half crazy ǁ *fossi* —*!*, what do you take me for (*o* do you think I am mad)*?* ǁ *era* — *di gioia*, he was mad (*o* beside himself) with joy ǁ *sei* —*!*, you are crazy (*o* mad)! 2. (*fam.*) (*grande*): *avevano una voglia matta di andarsene*, they were itching to leave; *ci avrei un gusto* — *se...*, I shouldn't half laugh if...; *si vogliono un bene* —, they are mad about each other 3. (*rar.*) (*debole*) bad: *ho una gamba matta*, I have a bad leg ǁ *s.m.* 1. madman (*pl.* madmen), lunatic: *ospedale dei matti*, mental hospital (*o* lunatic asylum); *è un* — *furioso*, he is a raving lunatic ǁ *cose da matti!*, this is ridiculous (*o* this is sheer madness) ǁ *quel* — *del nostro amico*, that crazy friend of ours ǁ *ridere, correre, urlare come un* —, to laugh, to run, to shout like a madman ǁ *un* — *ne fa cento*, *prov.* one fool makes a hundred ǁ *non tutti i matti sono al manicomio*, the monkeys aren't all in the zoo 2. (*carta*) joker.

màtto[2], *ag.* (*scacchi*): *scacco* —, checkmate: *dare scacco* —, to checkmate.

màtto[3], *ag.* 1 (*sbiadito, non lucido*) mat, matt 2. (*di pietre, metalli*) false: *oro* —, false gold; *pietra matta*, false stone.

mattòide, *ag.* rather mad, dotty ǁ *s.m.* odd fellow.

mattonàia, *s.f.* brickfield, brickyard.

mattonàio, *s.m.* brickmaker.

mattonàre, *v.t.* to pave (sthg.) with bricks.

mattonàto, *s.m.* brick surface; brick floor.

mattóne, *s.m.* 1. brick: — *a coltello*, arch brick; — *a cuneo*, key (*o* wedge-shaped brick); — *bruciato* (*di scarto*), burr; (*per ornamento*) flare header; — *cavo*, hollow brick; — *crudo*, green brick; — *di scarto*, grizzle brick (*o* sandal brick); — *forato*, perforated brick; — *refrattario*, firebrick; — *tenero*, cutter; — *smaltato*, glazed brick; — *vuoto*, hollow brick; *accoltellato di mattoni*, edge course; *costruzione in mattoni*, brickwork; *muro di mattoni a secco*, dry-stone wall; *muro di un* —, one-brick wall; *rosso* —, brick red; *cuocere mattoni*, to burn (*o* to bake) bricks ǁ *ho un* — *sullo stomaco con tutta la carne che ho mangiato*, all that meat I ate is lying heavy on my stomach ǁ *dare il* —, (*stirare*) to iron with a hot brick 2. (*cosa, persona noiosa*) bore, nuisance: *che* —*!*, what a bore!; *questo libro è un vero* —, this book is really boring.

mattonèlla, *s.f.* 1. tile: — *per vetrocemento*, glass block; *a mattonelle*, tiled; *posa in opera di mattonelle*, tiling 2. (*torba compressa*) peat briquette: — *di lignite*, brown coal briquette; — *di polvere di carbone*, briquet(te) 3. (*gelato*) ice brick 4. (*sponda del biliardo*) cushion.

mattonièra, *s.f.* brick moulding machine.

mattonificio, *s.m.* brick factory.

mattutìno, *ag.* 1. morning (*attributivo*); (*rar.*) matutinal: *preghiera mattutina*, morning prayer; (*eccl.*) matins; *stella mattutina*, morning star 2. (*mattiniero*) early-rising ǁ *s.m.* (*eccl.*) matins (*pl.*): *la campana suonava il* —, the bell was ringing for matins.

maturaménte, *av.* maturely.

maturaménto, *s.m.* ripening (anche *fig.*): *il* — *dei frutti*, the ripening of the fruit.

maturàre, *v.t.i.* 1. to ripen, to mature (anche *fig.*): *l'esperienza fa* — *il giudizio*, experience ripens judgement; *le mele maturano in autunno*, apples ripen in autumn; *questo formaggio maturerà*, this cheese will mature; *il sole matura i frutti*, the sun ripens fruit; *i suoi piani non erano ancora maturati*, his plans had not yet matured; *i tempi per una rivoluzione stanno maturando*, the times are ripening for revolution; *far* — *i pomodori*, to lay out tomatoes to ripen; *lasciare* — *il vino*, to mellow wine ǁ *col tempo e con la paglia*

maturano le nespole, *prov.* all things come to those who wait 2. (*med.*) to come to a head: *questo ascesso sta maturando*, this abscess is coming to a head.

maturatìvo, *ag.* maturative.

maturazióne, *s.f.* 1. maturity, ripening (anche *fig.*): *la* — *dei suoi progetti è assai lunga*, his plans are ripening slowly; *giungere a* —, to become ripe (*o* to ripen) 2. (*med.*) maturation.

maturità, *s.f.* 1. ripeness, maturity: *bisogna lasciar venire i frutti a piena* —, fruit must be allowed to ripen fully; *giungere a* —, to come to (*o* to reach) maturity 2. *fig.* maturity: — *politica*, political maturity; *gli anni della* —, the years of maturity; *quel romanzo fu l'opera della sua* —, that novel was the work of his maturity ǁ *certificato di* —, school-leaving certificate (awarded after five years of " Liceo ") ǁ *esame di* —, school-leaving examination (taken after five years of " Liceo ").

matùro, *ag.* 1. (*di frutta, ecc.*) ripe; (*di vino*) mellow; *una mela matura*, a ripe apple; *vino* —, mellow wine 2. *fig.* mature, ripe: *bellezza matura*, mature beauty; *una coppia matura*, a middle-aged couple; *di età matura*, of ripe age; *dopo matura considerazione*, after mature consideration; *giudizio* —, ripe judgment; *ha una* — *esperienza della vita*, he is a man of great experience; *per essere così giovane è molto* — *di senno*, for one so young he has a very mature mind; *i tempi sono maturi per la guerra*, time is ripe for war 3. (*med.*) mature: *cataratta matura*, mature cataract; *questo foruncolo è* —, this boil has come to a head 4. (*comm.*) due, fallen due, mature: *interessi maturi*, mature interests.

Matusalèmme, *no.pr.m.* (*Bibbia*) Methuselah.

Mauretània, *no.pr.f.* (*geog. st.*) Mauretania.

Mauritània, *no.pr.f.* (*geog.*) Mauritania.

Maurìzio, *no.pr.m.* Maurice ǁ *isola* —, (*geog.*) Mauritius.

màuro, *s.m.* Mauritanian; Moor.

mausolèo, *s.m.* mausoleum.

Màusolo, *no.pr.m.* (*st.*) Mausolus.

mazdeìsmo, *s.m.* (*st. relig.*) Mazdaism, Mazdeism.

mazùrca, *s.f.* (*musica, danza*) mazurka.

màzza, *s.f.* 1. (*clava, randello*) club, cudgel, bludgeon: — *da golf*, golf-club ǁ — *ferrata*, (*st. mil.*) mace 2. (*bastone da passeggio*) walking-stick; cane 3. (*grosso martello*) sledge-hammer; (*martello di legno*) mallet; (*usato dal giudice, dal banditore*) gavel: — *battente*, (*mec.*) ram (*o* tup); *il fabbro batteva il ferro con la* —, the blacksmith was hitting the iron with a sledge-hammer 4. (*simbolo d'autorità*) mace 5. (*pitt.*) maulstick, mahlstick.

mazzacavàllo, *s.m.* 1. (*agr.*) well-sweep 2. (*mec.*) (*battipalo*) pile-driver.

mazzapìcca, *s.m.* (*st.mil.*) battle-axe, pole axe.

mazzapìcchio, *s.m.* (*artig.*) cooper's mallet; (*di macellaio*) pole-axe.

mazzarànga, *s.f.* (*tec.*) tamper: — *in ghisa*, cast-iron tamper; — *in legno*, wooden tamper.

mazzàta, *s.f.* sledge-hammer blow; (*colpo*) heavy blow (anche *fig.*): *colpì l'animale con una* —, he struck the animal with a heavy blow ǁ *fu una* —*!*, it was a hard (*o* crushing) blow!.

mazzière, *s.m.* 1. mace-bearer 2. (*di carte*) dealer.

màzzo, *s.m.* bunch: — *di carte*, pack of cards; — *di chiavi*, bunch of keys; — *di fiori*, bunch of flowers; — *di funi*, bundle of ropes ǁ *fare il* —, (*alle carte*) to shuffle ǁ *mettere tutti in un* —, to mix good and bad.

mazzolàre, *v.t.* 1. (*uccidere con una mazzuola*) to club to death, to bludgeon to death 2. (*il grano*) to thresh 3. (*lino, canapa*) to beat.

mazzolàta, *s.f.* mallet blow.

mazzuòla, *s.f.* mallet.

mazzuòlo, *s.m.* mallet: — *da calafato*, (*mar.*) caulking mallet; — *di legno*, wooden (*o* carpenter's) mallet; — *in pelle*, rawhide mallet.

me, *pron.pers.m.f.* 1ª *persona sing.* 1. *obliquo e oggetto* me; (*me stesso*) myself: — *lo disse*, he told me so:

dammene, give me some; *datemelo*, give it (to) me; *egli venne da* —, he came to me (*o* to my house); *l'ha saputo da* —, he knew it from me; *lo faccio da* —, (*da solo*) I do it by myself; *lo so da* — *quello che devo fare*, I know very well what I must do; *ne tengo uno per* —, I am keeping one for myself; *non* — *ne importa*, it's all the same to me (*o fam.* I couldn't care less *o* I don't care a bean); *non ama che* —, he loves me alone; *non chiusi la porta dietro di* —, I didn't close the door behind me; *non si cura di* —, he doesn't worry about me; *pensa a* —, he is thinking of me; *volevano proprio* —, it was me they wanted ‖ *per* —, *in quanto a* —, as for me (*o* as far as I am concerned) ‖ *secondo* —, in my opinion ‖ *tutto per* —, *tutto per solo*, all (*o* just) for myself: *ho un appartamento tutto per* —, I have a flat all (*o* just) for myself; *posso averlo tutto per* —?, may I have it all (*o* just) for myself? ‖ *chi non è con* — *è contro di* —, who is not with me is against me ‖ *dissi tra* —, *tra* — *e* —, I said to myself ‖ *l'uomo che fa per* —, the man I need ‖ *non saper nè di* — *nè di te*, (*di cose*) to have no taste (*o* to be insipid); (*di persona*) to be insipid **2.** *sogg.* (*in proposizioni comparative e in funzione di predicato*) **I;** (*in proposizioni esclamative*) **me:** *beato* —!, lucky me!; *povero* —!, poor me! (*o* ah me!); *è più vecchio di* —, he is older than I (*o fam.* he is older than me); *fate come* —, do as I do; *ne sai quanto* —, you know as much as I do; *sei più gentile di* —, you are kinder than I (*o fam.* you are kinder than me); *se tu fossi* —, if you were I (*o fam.* me).

Meàndro[1], *no.pr.m.* (*geog.*) Meander.

meàndro[2], *s.m.* **1.** meander; meandering, winding: *i meandri del fiume*, the meanderings (*o* windings) of the river **2.** (*labirinto*) maze: *perdersi nei meandri della burocrazia*, to get lost in the maze of red-tape.

meàto, *s.m.* (*anat.*) meatus (*pl.* meatus, meatuses).

Mècca, *no.pr.f.* (*geog.*) Mecca.

meccànica, *s.f.* **1.** mechanics: — *applicata*, applied mechanics; — *celeste*, (*astr.*) celestial mechanics (*o* gravitational astronomy); — *degli aeriformi*, pneumatics; — *dei solidi*, mechanics of solids; — *razionale*, rational mechanics **2.** (*meccanismo*) mechanism.

meccanicaménte, *av.* mechanically.

meccanicismo, *s.m.* (*fil.*) mechanicalism.

meccànico, *ag.* mechanical: *arti meccaniche*, mechanical arts; *energia meccanica*, mechanical energy; *ingegneria meccanica*, mechanical engineering; *lavoro* —, mechanical work (anche *fig.*); *movimenti meccanici*, mechanical movements (anche *fig.*); *stampa meccanica*, power press; *telaio* —, (*ind. tessile*) power-loom ‖ *uomo* —, robot ‖ *s.m.* mechanic, mechanician; (*mar.*) engine-room artificer; — *dentista*, dental mechanic.

meccanismo, *s.m.* **1.** mechanism, gear, works; (*movimento*) motion, movement: — *a cremagliera*, rackwork; — *d'arresto automatico*, automatic stop motion; — *del timone*, (*mar.*) steering-gear; — *di disinnesto*, throwout; — *di governo*, (*mar.*) steering-gear; — *di un orologio*, works of a watch; — *di sparo*, (*di armi da fuoco*) gunlock; — *di sterzo*, (*aut.*) steering -gear **2.** (*ordinamento*) apparatus, machinery: *il* — *amministrativo*, the administrative machine; *il* — *dello Stato*, the machinery of the State **3.** (*fil.*) process: *il* — *della memoria*, the memorizing process.

meccanizzàre, *v.t.* to mechanize.

meccanizzazióne, *s.f.* mechanization.

meccanoterapìa, *s.f.* (*med.*) mechanotherapy.

Mecenàte, *no.pr.m.* (*st.*) Maecenas ‖ **mecenàte**, *s.m.* Maecenas (generous patron of art and literature).

mecenatismo, *s.m.* patronage.

mechitarista, *s.m.* (*st. relig.*) Mekhitarist.

méco, *pron. pers.m.f. 1ª persona sing. obliquo* **1.** (*con me*) with me: *vieni* —, come with me **2.** (*verso, contro di me*) against me: *egli ha* — *della ruggine*, he has a grudge against me (*o* he bears me a grudge).

mecònico, *ag.* (*chim.*) meconic.

meconína, *s.f.* (*chim.*) meconin(e).

mecònio, *s.m.* (*fisiol.*) meconium.

meconismo, *s.m.* (*med.*) meconism.

mèda, *s.f.* (*mar.*) seamark, beacon: — *luminosa*, light-beacon.

medàglia, *s.f.* **1.** medal: — *al merito*, medal of merit; — *al valore*, medal for valour; — *d'oro*, gold medal; *nastrino della* —, medal ribbon; *ostentava tutte le sue medaglie*, he sported all his medals; *questa medaglietta è stata benedetta dal Papa*, this medal was blessed by the Pope; *conferire una* — *a qlcu.*, to award s.o. a medal (*o* to decorate s.o.) ‖ *il rovescio della* —, the reverse of the medal; *ogni* — *ha il suo rovescio*, *pròv.* every medal (*o* coin) has its dark side (*o* there is no rose without a thorn) **2.** (*contrassegno*) badge, token: — *di presenza*, (*comm.*) attendance-check; — *di riconoscimento*, (*mil.*) identity disc; — *per operai*, metal token.

medagliàio, *s.m.* **1.** medallist; (*venditore*) dealer in medals **2.** (*collezionista di medaglie*) collector of medals.

medaglière, *s.m.* **1.** collection of medals **2.** (*vetrina in cui conservare le medaglie*) medal show-case.

medagliétta, *s.f.* parliamentary deputy's badge.

medaglióne, *s.m.* **1.** medallion, locket: *aveva un bel* — *col ritratto del suo povero marito*, she had a beautiful locket with a portrait of her deceased husband **2.** (*arch.*) medallion **3.** (*lett.*) pen-portrait.

medaglista, *s.m.* **1.** collector of medals; numismatist **2.** (*incisore di medaglie*) medallist.

medaglistica, *s.f.* numismatics.

Medèa, *no.pr.f.* (*mit.*) Medea.

medesimaménte, *av.* likewise, in the same way.

medésimo, *ag.* **1.** *dimostrativo* (*lo stesso, proprio quello*) same, very: *il* — *libro*, the same book; *nel* — *tempo*, at the same (*o* very) moment; *quel* — *giorno*, that same day (*o* that very day) **2.** (*uguale*) same, like: *il* — *prezzo*, the same price; *due piante della medesima specie*, two plants of the same species; *le medesime cause producono i medesimi effetti*, like causes produce like effects; *abbiamo la* — *età*, we are the same age (*o* we are of an age); *hanno le medesime opinioni*, they have the same opinions (*o* they see eye to eye) **3.** *dimostrativo* (*rafforzativo*) **myself, yourself, himself, ecc.:** *io* —, I myself; *egli* — *lo disse*, he himself said so (*o* he said so himself); *guardate voi medesimi*, look for yourselves **4.** *dimostrativo* (*rafforzativo con pron. r.*) -self (*pl.* -selves) (*suffisso per formare in inglese i pron. r.*): *me*, *te* —, myself, yourself; *la cosa non è male in sè medesima*, the thing is not bad in itself ‖ *pron. dimostrativo* **same:** *Giovanni venne da me; il* — *mi disse che...*, John came to me; the same said that... ‖ *s.m.* (*la stessa cosa*) **the same** (thing): *tutti dissero il* —, everybody said the same (thing).

mèdi, *s.m.pl.* (*st.*) Medes, Medians.

Mèdia[1], *no.pr.f.* (*geog. st.*) Media.

mèdia[2], *s.f.* **1.** average: — *approssimativa*, rough (*o* approximate) average; — *barometrica*, mean (*o* average) barometric level; *la* — *dei prezzi del grano negli ultimi dieci anni non è cambiata molto*, the average price of corn in the last ten years has not changed much; — *oraria*, average per hour (*o* hourly average); *alla* — *di*, at an average of; *sopra la* —, above (the) average: *la sua intelligenza è al di sopra della* —, his intelligence is above (the) average; *sotto la* —, below (the) average; *questa è una* — *alterata da errori*, this average is displaced by errors; *calcolare la* — *di*, to calculate (*o* to work out) the average of; *influenzare la* —, to affect the average; *prendere una* — *approssimativa*, to strike a rough average ‖ *in* —, on the (*o* an) average: *ci sono venti scolari in* — *in ogni classe*, on an average there are twenty students in each class; *facevamo in* — *duecento miglia al giorno*, we averaged two hundred miles a day; *mi sono costate in* — *cento lire l'una*, I paid an average of a hundred lire each ‖ *è stato promosso alla quarta classe con una buona* —, ho went up into the fourth class with a good average **2**. (*mat.*) mean: — *aritmetica*, arithmetic(al) mean; — *armonica*, harmonic mean; — *geometrica*, geometric(al) mean; — *ponderata*, (*statistica*) weighted mean; — *proporzionale*, proportional mean; — *quadratica*, root mean square value; *fa' la media fra tre, cinque e sette e otterrai cinque*, average three, five and seven and you (will) get five.

mediànico, *ag.* mediumistic.

medianità, *s.f.* mediumism.

mediàno, *ag.* medial, mean; middle (*attributivo*); (*geom. anat. bot.*) median: *albero —*, (*mar.*) mainmast; *arteria mediana*, median artery; *linea mediana*, (*geom.*) median (line); (*geog.*) mean line; (*calcio*) half-way line; *nervo —*, median nerve; *piano —*, median plane; *punto —*, mid (o middle) point; *quantità mediana*, mean quantity ‖ *s.m.* (*calcio*) half-back.

mediànte, *prep.* by, by means of, through: — *una fortunata speculazione*, through (o by means of) a fortunate speculation; — *l'immaginazione*, by using one's imagination; — *procura*, (*dir.*) by proxy; *l'ho comprato — il mio agente*, I bought it through my agent; *solo — un potente microscopio riuscì a vedere quel microbo*, only by means of (o through) a powerful microscope could he see the microbe; *solo — i sensi possiamo percepire il mondo*, only through our senses can we perceive the world.

mediànte, *s.f.* (*mus.*) mediant.

mediastínico, *ag.* (*anat.*) mediastinal.

mediastiníte, *s.f.* (*patol.*) mediastinitis.

mediàstino,*s.m.*(*anat.*)mediastinum(*pl.*mediastina).

mediataménte, *av.* indirectly, mediately.

mediàto, *ag.* (*rar.*) indirect, mediate.

mediatóre, *s.m.* **1.** mediator, intermediary; (*fam.*) middleman (*pl.* middlemen), go-between: *agire da —*, to act as a go-between ‖ *il — divino*, the (Divine) Mediator **2.** (*comm.*) broker, agent: — *di Borsa*, stock-broker; — *di noleggi*, ship-broker; — *di sicurtà*, insurance-broker; — *patentato*, licensed agent.

mediatríce, *s.f.* mediatress, mediatrix.

mediazióne, *s.f.* **1.** mediation, intermediation; intercession **2.**(*comm.*) brokerage, mediation: *addebitamento per —*, brokerage (o commission-)charge; *diritti di —*, brokerage (o commission-)rates **3.** (*compenso pagato per la senseria*) commission, brokerage.

mèdica, *ag.*: *erba —*, lucerne (o *amer.* alfalfa).

medicàbile, *ag.* medicable.

medicaménto, *s.m.* **1.** (*rar.*) (*il medicare*) medication, treatment **2.** (*medicina*) medicament, medicine.

medicamentóso, *ag.* medicinal.

medicàre, *v.t.* **1.** to doctor, to dress: *hai medicato il bambino?*, have you doctored the child's wound?; *l'infermiera medicò la ferita del paziente*, the nurse dressed the patient's wound **2.** *fig.* (*correggere, temperare*) to cure; to heal: *medicherò io le tue cattive abitudini!*, I shall cure you of your bad habits!; *il tempo medica tutti i dispiaceri*, time heals all sorrows **3.** (*correggere con sostanze medicinali*) to medicate: — *il vino*, to medicate wine ‖ **medicàrsi,** *v.r.* to treat oneself; to medicate oneself; to dress one's own wounds: *si medicò la ferita da solo*, he dressed his wound by himself.

medicàstro, *s.m.* (*spreg.*) medicaster, quack (salver).

medicàto, *ag.* **1.** treated; (*di ferite*) dressed **2.** (*corretto con sostanze medicinali*) medicated: *vino —*, medicated wine.

medicatóre, *ag.* healing: *mano medicatrice*, healing hand ‖ *s.m.*, **medicatríce,** *s.f.* healer.

medicatúra, *s.f.* **1.** medication, treatment; (*di ferita*) dressing **2.** (*medicamento*) medicament.

medicazióne, *s.f.* medication, treatment; (*di ferita*) dressing: *posto di —*, first aid station.

medíceo, *ag.* Medicean.

medichería, *s.f.* (*scherz.*) **1.** (*classe medica*) doctors (*pl.*) **2.** (*ambulatorio*) surgery, consulting-room.

medichéssa, *s.f.* lady doctor.

medicína, *s.f.* **1.** medicine: — *e chirurgia*, medicine and surgery; — *legale*, forensic medicine (o medical jurisprudence); *dottore in —*, doctor of medicine; *facoltà di —*, faculty of medicine; *laurea in —*, medical degree; *libri di —*, medical books; *scuola di —*, medical school (o school of medicine); *studente in —*, medical student; *frequenta la facoltà di —*, he is a medical student; *esercitare la —*, to practise medicine; *studiare —*, to study medicine **2.** (*medicamento*) medicine, medicament; remedy; (*amer.*) drug: *il farmacista sta preparando la —*, the chemist is preparing the medicine; *per molti mali non vi sono medicine*, for many diseases there are no remedies; *quella bevanda pare una —*, that drink is as bitter as a medicine; *questa — è disgustosa*, this medicine is revolting; *prendere una —*, to take a medicine **3.** *fig.* (*rimedio salutare*) remedy, medicine, cure: *questo sarà per lui una salutare —*, this will cure him; *viaggiare è un'ottima — per i mali dell'anima*, travelling is a fine remedy for spiritual suffering.

medicinàle, *ag.* medicinal: *erba —*, medicinal herb; *liquore —*, medicinal liqueur; *pianta —*, medicinal plant; *questa sostanza ha virtù medicinali*, this substance has healing properties ‖ *s.m.* medicine; (*amer.*) drug.

mèdico, *ag.* medical: — *- chirurgico*, medico-chirurgical; — *- legale*, medico-legal; *anatomia medica*, medical anatomy; *certificato —*, medical certificate; *clinica medica*, medical clinic; *consulto —*, medical consultation; *materia medica*, materia medica; *patologia medica*, medical pathology; *la professione medica*, the medical profession; *ricetta medica*, medical prescription; *scuola medica*, medical school; *ufficiale —*, (*mil.*) medical officer; *visita medica*, doctor's visit: *i candidati verranno sottoposti a visita medica*, the applicants will undergo a medical examination ‖ *s.m.* **1.** physician, doctor: medical man: — *chirurgo*, surgeon; — *condotto*, medical officer; — *consulente*, consulting physician (o consultant); — *curante*, family doctor; — *legale*, police-doctor (o *amer.* medical examiner); — *militare*, army medical officer; *dobbiamo chiamare il —*, we must call the doctor; *qual è il tuo —?*, who is your doctor? (o medical adviser?); *segui i consigli del —!*, follow the doctor's advice!; *consultare un —*, to see a doctor ‖ —, *cura te stesso!*, *prov.* physician, heal thyself! ‖ — *pietoso fa la piaga verminosa*, *prov.* the tender surgeon makes a foul wound **2.** *fig.* (*guaritore*) healer: *il tempo è un gran —*, time is a great healer.

medicóne, *s.m.* **1.** (*medico illustre*) skilful doctor **2.** (*medicastro*) charlatan, quack(salver), medicaster.

medicónzolo, *s.m.* (*spreg.*) medicaster, quack.

medievàle, *ag.* medi(a)eval.

medievalísmo, *s.m.* medi(a)evalism.

medievalísta, *s.m.* medi(a)evalist.

mèdio, *ag.* **1.** middle: *media età*, middle age: *è un uomo di media età*, he is a middle-aged man; *ceto —*, middle classes; *il corso — di un fiume*, the middle course of a river; *corso — di inglese*, intermediate course of English; *dito —*, middle (o second) finger; *istruzione media*, secondary education; *peso —*, (*spor.*) middle weight; *scuola media*, secondary school (o *amer.* junior high school); *termine —*, (*fil.*) middle term; *vena media*, (*anat.*) median vein; *verbo —*, (*gram. greca*) middle verb ‖ *il Medio Evo*, (*st.*) the Middle Ages ‖ *il Medio Oriente*, (*geog.*) the Middle East **2.** (*normale*) average, normal, ordinary; (*mediocre*) middling, mediocre: *intelligenza media*, average intelligence; *grandezza media*, middle size; *qualità media*, middling quality; *statura media*, middle (o average) height ‖ *l'uomo —*, the man in the street **3.** (*che risulta da una media*) average: *prezzo —*, average price; *produzione media*, average output; *valore —*, average value; *velocità media*, average speed ‖ *tempo —*, (*astr.*) mean time; (*spor.*) average time **4.** (*tec.*) medium: *campo —*, (*cine.*) medium shot; *onde medie*, (*rad.*) medium waves; *ripresa media*, (*tv.*)

medium shot; *tensione media*, (*elett.*) medium voltage || *s.m.* **1**. (*dito medio*) middle finger, second finger **2**. (*mat.*) mean (term) **3**. (*gram. greca*) middle.

mediòcre, *ag.* **1**. (*medio*) middle, medium: *statura* —, middle height; *vaso di* — *grandezza*, medium sized pot **2**. (*inferiore per qualità*) mediocre; middling; second-rate; poor: *capacità* —, middling (*o* moderate) capacity; *lavoro* —, second-rate work; *letteratura* —, mediocre literature; *pasto* —, indifferent meal; *profitto* —, (*a scuola*) poor progress; *rappresentazione* —, middling performance; *scrittore* —, second-rate writer; *vino* —, poor wine; *egli è di condizione* —, he belongs to the lower middle class; *ella è di una bellezza* —, she is rather plain; *quello scrittore ha uno stile* —, that writer has a mediocre style; *il tuo compito è* —, your homework is middling.

mediocreménte, *av.* **1**. (*moderatamente*) moderately; passably, tolerably: *guadagnare* —, to earn moderately **2**. (*piuttosto male*) rather badly, poorly; not very well.

mediocrità, *s.f.* mediocrity: — *d'ingegno*, mediocrity of talent; *egli è una* —, he is a mediocrity; *vivere nella* —, to live undistinguished.

medioevàle, medi(o)eval.

medioèvo, *s.m.* Middle Ages (*pl.*): *alto* —, Dark Ages (*o* early Middle Ages); *basso* —, late Middle Ages; *costumi da* —, medieval customs.

meditabóndo, *ag.* meditating, thoughtful; (*pensieroso*) pensive: *contemplare ql.co. con aria meditabonda*, to gaze meditatively at sthg.; *essere* —, to be pensive.

meditàre, *v.t.* **1**. (*riflettere*) to meditate; to ponder: — *le proprie parole*, to ponder one's words; *passare un'ora a* —, to spend an hour in thought **2**. (*aver intenzione*) to meditate; to consider; to think (*of doing*): *sto meditando di andarmene*, I am thinking of going; *una guerra*, to meditate a war || *v.i.* to meditate (on sthg.); (*riflettere*) to ponder (over sthg.); (*rimuginare*) to brood (over sthg.): — *sulle miserie umane*, to meditate on (*o* upon) human miseries; — *sulle proprie disgrazie*, to brood over one's misfortunes; — *sul mistero della morte*, to meditate on the mystery of death.

meditataménte, *av.* (*a bella posta*) on purpose, designedly; (*deliberatamente*) deliberately.

meditatìvo, *ag.* meditative, contemplative.

meditatóre, *s.m.*, **meditatrìce**, *s.f.* (*rar.*) meditator.

meditazióne, *s.f.* meditation: *assidua, profonda* —, constant, deep meditation; *questo libro è il risultato di una lunga* —, this book is the result of long meditation; *la sua dichiarazione è degna di* —, his statement is worthy of consideration.

mediterràneo, *ag.* **1**. (*circondato da terre*) inland, land-locked, mediterranean: *il Baltico è un mare* —, the Baltic is a land-locked sea **2**. (*del Mare Mediterraneo*) Mediterranean: *civiltà mediterranea*, Mediterranean civilization; *clima, fauna, flora mediterranea*, Mediterranean climate, fauna, flora || *febbre mediterranea*, (*patol.*) Mediterranean fever || **Mediterràneo (il)**, *no.pr.m.* (*geog.*) the Mediterranean (Sea).

mèdium, *s.m.* medium.

Medúsa, *no.pr.f.* (*mit.*) Medusa || **medúsa**, *s.f.* (*zool.*) medusa (*pl.* medusae).

Mefistòfele, *no.pr.m.* (*lett.*) Mephistopheles.

mefistofèlico, *ag.* Mephistophelean, Mephistophelian, satanic (*anche fig.*): *sorriso* —, satanic smile.

mefíte, *s.f.* mephitis.

mefítico, *ag.* poisonous, pestilential; mephitic(al): *aria mefítica*, poisonous (*o* pestilential) air.

megacíclo, *s.m.* (*rad.*) megacycle: *megacicli al secondo*, megacycles per second (*abbr.* mc/s).

megacòsmo, *s.m.* (*rar.*) macrocosm.

megàfono, *s.m.* megaphone.

megalítico, *ag.* megalithic: *monumenti megalitici*, megalithic monuments; *pietra megalitica*, megalith.

megalocardía, *s.f.* (*med.*) megalocardia.

megalocefalía, *s.f.* (*med.*) megacephalia.

megalocefàlico, *ag.* (*med.*) megalocephalic, megacephalic, megalocephalous, megacephalous.

megalocèfalo, *ag.* *V.* **megalocefàlico** || *s.m.* megacephalous type.

megalòmane, *s.c.* megalomaniac.

megalomanía, *s.f.* megalomania.

megalomaníaco, *ag.s.m.* megalomaniac.

megalopsía, *s.f.* (*med.*) megalopsia, macropsia.

megalosàuro, *s.m.* (*paleont.*) megalosaur.

Mègara, *no.pr.f.* (*geog. st.*) Megara.

megascòpio, *s.m.* megascope.

mègaton, *s.m.* (*fis. atomica*) megaton.

Megèra, *no.pr.f.* (*mit.*) Megaera || **megèra**, *s.f.* vixen, shrew: *quella donna è una* —, that woman is a battleaxe.

mèglio, *ag.* **1**. *comp.* **better**: *mi parevano* — *le sue*, his seemed to be better; *ne ho visti di* —, I have seen better (ones); *questo libro è* — *di quello*, this book is better than that; *tu sei* — *di me*, you are better than I am (*o* than me) **2**. *superl.rel.* (*idiot. per migliore*) **the best**: *è il* — *di tutti*, he is the best of all; *era il* — *chirurgo della città*, he was the best surgeon in the town; *si scelsero le* —, they chose the best; *vuole la* — *roba*, he wants the best stuff || *alla* —, *alla bell'e* —, as well as possible (*o* as best as one can): *dovemmo provvedere alla* —, we had to do the best we could; *si campava alla* —, we were just managing || *avere la* — *su qlcu.*, to have the better of s.o. || *s.m.* **1**. **best, best thing**: (*la miglior parte*) **best part**: *il* — *che si può fare*, the best that can be done; *il* — *è già stato preso*, the best part has already been taken; *il* — *era andarsene*, the best thing was to go away; *pensavo che il* — *fosse restare*, I thought it best to stay || *nel* — *del sonno*, in one's deepest sleep || *per il* —, for the best: *è tutto per il* —, it is all for the best; *agire per il* —, to act for the best || *fare del proprio* —, to do one's best (*o* the best one can) || *vendere al* —, (*comm.*) to sell at best || *il* — *è nemico del bene*, *prov.* let well alone **2**. (*partitivo*): *in mancanza di* —, for lack of anything better; *ciò che puoi fare di* —, the best thing you can do (*o* the best course to take); *ho qui ql.co. di* — *per Lei*, I have sthg. better for you here; *non c'è (nulla) di* —, there is nothing better; *non sognerei altro di* — *al mondo*, I couldn't think of anything better || *av.* **1**. *comp.* **better**: *ho dormito molto* — *dell'altra notte*, last night I slept much better than I did the night before; *lo so* — *di te*, I know that better than you; *nessuno avrebbe potuto farlo* —, nobody could have done it better; *ora udiamo* —, now we can hear better; *scrivete un po'* —, write a little better; *sta* — *a te che a me*, it suits you better than it does me || — *ancora*, better still || — *che nulla*, better than nothing || — *per lui*, so much the better for him || *per* — *dire*, *o* —, to be more exact (*o* or rather): *questo studente sa poco*, *o* —, *niente del tutto*, this student knows little, or rather, nothing at all || *tanto* —*!*, *così!*, —*!*, so much the better! || *è* — *dare che ricevere*, it is better to give than to receive || *parla* —, (*più educatamente*) speak more politely || *pensaci* —, think it over again || *sarebbe* — *che tu andassi, faresti* — *ad andare*, you had better go; *sarebbe* — *non vederlo*, it would be better not to see him || *staresti* — *in questa poltrona*, you will be more comfortable in this armchair || *state un po'* —*?*, are you (feeling) any better? || *tutto va di bene in* —, everything is getting better and better || *cambiare in* —, to change for the better || — *tardi che mai*, *prov.* better late than never || — *un uovo oggi che una gallina domani*, *prov.* a bird in the hand is worth two in the bush **2**. *comp.* (*piuttosto*) **rather**; (*di più*) **more, better**: *desidero* — *andare che essere trattato così*, I had rather go away altogether than be treated like that; *mi piace* — *questo quadro di quello*, I like this picture better (*o* more) than that one **3**. *superl. rel.* **best**: *le dieci donne* — *vestite del mondo*, the ten best-dressed women in the world; *egli parla come* — *può*, he speaks as best as he can; *fai come — credi,* do as you think best; *vi aiuterò il — che io possa,* I will help you as best (*o* as much) as I can ‖ *era la — delle tre sorelle,* (*la più carina*) she was the best-looking of the three sisters.

méla, *s.f.* apple: *mele al forno,* baked apples; *— cotogna,* quince; *mele cotte,* stewed apples; *— ranetta,* rennet; *— ruggine,* russet (apple); *torsolo di —,* apple -core; *torta di mele,* apple-pie (*o* apple tart); *verde —,* apple green; *è una bella bambina, con le guance che paiono mele,* she is a fine, apple-cheeked child; *sbucciare una —,* to peel an apple.

melacotógna, *s.f.* (*bot.*) quince.

melagràna, *s.f.* (*bot.*) pomegranate.

melagràno, *s.m.* (*bot.*) pomegranade(-tree).

melanconía, (*rar.*) per **malinconía.**

Melanèsia, *no.pr.f.* (*geog.*) Melanesia.

mélange, *s.m.* mixture, mélange: *— di caffè e panna,* coffee with whipped cream.

Melània, *no.pr.f.* Melania.

melanína, *s.f.* (*chim. biol.*) melanin.

melanísmo, *s.m.* melanism.

melaníte, *s.f.* (*min.*) melanite, black garnet.

melanzàna, *s.f.* (*bot.*) egg-plant, aubergine.

melarància, *s.f.* (*bot.*) orange.

melàssa, *s.f.* molasses, treacle.

melàta, *s.f.* honey-dew.

melàto, *ag.* **1.** sweetened with honey **2.** *fig.* honeyed.

Melchiòrre, *no.pr.m.* Melchior.

Melchisedèe, *no.pr.m.* (*Bibbia*) Melchizedek, Melchisedec.

Meleàgro, *no.pr.m.* (*mit.*) Meleager.

melensàggine, *s.f.* nonsense: *dice delle gran melensaggini,* he talks a lot of nonsense.

melènso, *ag.* dull, slow; (*sciocco*) silly, foolish: *una idea melensa,* a silly idea; *è stata una festa talmente melensa!,* it was such a dull party!; *che tipo — e il tuo amico!,* what a dull fellow your friend is! ‖ *s.m.* simpleton: *sei proprio un —!,* what a simpleton you are!.

meléto, *s.m.* apple-orchard.

mèlica[1], *s.f.* (*bot.*) melic.

mèlica[2], *s.f.* (*poesia melica*) melic poetry.

mèlico, *ag.* **1.** melic: *poesia melica,* melic poetry **2.** (*musicale*) musical ‖ *s.m.* melic poet.

mèliga, *s.f.* (*bot.*) melic.

meliníte, *s.f.* (*esplosivo*) melinite.

melísma, *s.f.* (*mus.*) **1.** (*abbellimento*) grace-notes (*pl.*) **2.** (*aria, canzoncina*) melisma.

melíssa, *s.f.* (*bot.*) balm-mint.

melitènse, *V.* **maltése.**

mellífero, *ag.* honey-producing, melliferous.

mellificàre, *v.i.* to make honey.

mellificazióne, *s.f.* honey-making.

mellifluaménte, *av.* **1.** (*spreg.*) in a honeyed manner; unctuously **2.** (*letter.*) mellifluously.

mellifluità, *s.f.* **1.** (*spreg.*) honeyed manner; unctuousness: *la — della sua voce non mi persuase,* his honeyed tongue did not persuade me **2.** (*letter.*) mellifluousness.

mellífluo, *ag.* **1.** (*spreg.*) honeyed; unctuous: *parole melliflue,* honeyed words; *il suo fare — può ingannare gli ingenui,* his unctuous manner may deceive fools **2.** (*letter.*) mellifluous, sweet.

mellóne, *s.m.* **1.** (*bot.*) melon **2.** (*persona sciocca*) fool.

mélma, *s.f.* slime; (*fango*) mud; mire (anche *fig.*): *il fondo di uno stagno è coperto di —,* the bottom of a pond is covered with slime; *tuffarsi nella —, fig.* to sink to the lowest depths.

melmóso, *ag.* slimy; (*fangoso*) muddy; miry: *il fondo — di uno stagno,* the slimy bottom of a pond; *terreno —,* muddy ground.

mélo, *s.m.* (*bot.*) apple-tree.

melòde, (*poet.*) per **melodía.**

melodía, *s.m.* **1.** melody, tune, melodiousness: *mu-*sica ricca, priva di —, tuneful, tuneless music; *quei versi hanno una certa —,* those lines have a certain melodiousness **2.** (*aria, motivo*) melody, air, tune: *una — popolare,* a folk-song; *cantò una vecchia — spagnola,* he sang an old Spanish tune.

melodicaménte, *av.* tunefully, melodically.

melòdico, *ag.* melodic, tuneful, melodious: *canzone melodica,* tuneful song; *la voce melodica dell'usignuolo,* the melodious voice of the nightingale.

melodiosaménte, *av.* tunefully, melodiously.

melodiosità, *s.f.* tunefulness, melodiousness.

melodióso, *ag.* tuneful, melodious, sweet-sounding; *ha una voce melodiosa,* she has a melodious voice.

melodísta, *s.m.* (*mus.*) melodist.

melodràmma, *s.m.* **1.** opera, music drama **2.** *fig.* melodrama: *lo disse in un tono da —,* he said it in a melodramatic voice.

melodrammaticaménte, *av.* melodramatically.

melodrammàtico, *ag.* **1.** operatic **2.** *fig.* melodramatic: *gesto —,* melodramatic gesture; *prese un atteggiamento —,* he struck a melodramatic pose.

melogràno, *s.m.* (*bot.*) pomegranate(-tree).

melòlogo, *s.m.* (*mus.*) melologue.

melolónta, *s.f.* (*entom.*) may-beetle, may-bug.

melòmane, *s.m.* melomane, melomaniac.

melomanìa, *s.f.* melomania.

melomaníaco, *ag.* melomanic.

melóne, *s.m.* **1.** (*bot.*) melon **2.** (*fam.*) bowler-hat.

melopèa, *s.f.* **1.** melopoeia **2.** (*rar.*) (*melologo*) melologue **3.** (*rar.*) (*contrappunto*) counterpoint.

Melpòmene, *no.pr.f.* (*mit.*) Melpomene.

membràna, *s.f.* **1.** (*anat. bot.*) membrane: *— mucosa,* mucous membrane; *falsa —,* false membrane **2.** (*sottile lamina*) membrane, film: *— di altoparlante,* (*acu.*) diaphragm of loudspeaker.

membranàceo, *ag.* **1.** membranaceous **2.** (*di pergamena*) parchment (*attributivo*): *codice —,* parchment codex.

membranóso, *ag.* **1.** membranous: *osso —,* (*anat.*) membrane bone; *tessuto —,* membranous tissue **2.** (*che ha membrane*) webbed: *piede —,* web-foot.

membratúra, *s.f.* structure; frame(work).

mèmbro, *s.m.*; *pl.f.* **mèmbra** (*nel senso* **1.**); *pl.m.* **mèmbri** (*negli altri sensi*) **1.** (*anat.*) limb: *le membra inferiori,* the lower limbs; *riposa le stanche membra!,* rest your tired limbs!; *le sue membra sono gracili,* her limbs are frail ‖ *le diverse membra della nazione,* the various parts of the nation **2.** (*persona*) member: *— del consiglio,* member of the Council; *— della Camera di Commercio,* member of the Chamber of Commerce; *— della commissione,* member of the commission; *— del Parlamento,* member of Parliament; *— di lega antialcoolica,* member of a temperance organization; *— onorario,* honorary member; *quel club ha molti membri,* that club has a great many members; *sono — del circolo sportivo,* I am a member of the sporting-club; *tutti i membri della famiglia erano presenti alla lettura del testamento,* all the members of the family were present at the reading of the will; *diventare — di una associazione,* to join an association **3.** (*arch. mat. gram.*) member: *i membri di una facciata,* (*arch.*) the members of a façade; *i membri di un periodo,* the members of a sentence; *il primo, il secondo — di una equazione,* the left-hand, the right-hand side of an equation **4.** *— virile,* (*anat.*) membrum virile.

membrúto, *ag.* strong-limbed.

memènto, *s.m.* **1.** (*eccl.*) Memento **2.** (*ricordo*) memento, souvenir; reminder.

Memnóne, *no.pr.m.* (*mit.*) Memnon.

memoràbile, *ag.* memorable, unforgettable: *una battaglia —,* a memorable battle; *il giorno — del grande incendio,* the never-to-be-forgotten day of the great fire ‖ *i memorabili,* (*lett.*) memorabilia: *i — di Senofonte,* the memorabilia of Xenophon.

memorabilità, *s.f.* memorability.

memorabilménte, *av.* memorably.

memoràndo, *ag.* memorable.

memoràndum, *s.m.* **1.** memorandum (*pl.* memoranda, memorandums); (*fam.*) memo **2.** (*libretto per appunti*) memorandum-book.

memoràre, *v.t.* to remember, to call to mind.

mèmore, *ag.* mindful; (*riconoscente*) grateful (for sthg.): — *dei piaceri ricevuti*, mindful of (*o* grateful for) favours received; *essere* — *del proprio dovere*, to be mindful of one's duty.

memòria, *s.f.* **1.** memory: — *fedele*, retentive (*o* reliable) memory; — *ferrea, di ferro*, cast-iron memory; — *labile*, unreliable (*o* untrustworthy) memory; — *prodigiosa*, prodigious (*o* extraordinary) memory; — *pronta*, ready memory; *buona* —, — *lucida*, good memory; *cattiva* —, a bad memory: *ha cattiva* — *per i nomi*, he has a bad memory for names; *una cosa viva nella* —, sthg. that still lives in the memory; *esercizi di* —, exercises to develop one's memory; *scolpito nella* —, graven in one's memory; *la* — *lo tradisce spesso*, his memory often fails him; *l'avvenimento mi si è impresso nella* —, the incident stuck in my mind; *quella faccenda mi ritorna spesso alla* —, that affair often comes back to my mind; *cancellare ql.co. dalla* —, to erase sthg. from one's memory; *cercare, frugare, rivangare nella* —, to search one's memory; *fidarsi della propria* —, to trust (*o* to rely on) one's memory; *offuscare la* —, to cloud one's memory; *perdere, smarrire la* —, to lose one's memory; *riacquistare la* —, to recover one's memory; *richiamare alla* —, to call to mind; *rinfrescare la* — *a qlcu.*, to refresh s.o.'s memory ‖ *a* —, by heart: *imparare, sapere ql.co. a* —, to learn, to know sthg. by heart; *suonare, dipingere a* —, to play, to paint from memory ‖ *a* — *d'uomo*, within living memory (*o* in the memory of man): *non s'era mai vista, udita cosa simile a* — *d'uomo*, within the memory of man one had never seen, heard such a thing ‖ *se la* — *non sbaglia...*, if my memory does not fail me...; *cadere dalla* —, to fall into oblivion **2.** (*ricordo*) memory, recollection, remembrance, reminiscence: — *confusa*, dim memory; *la* — *di un caro amico*, the memory of a dear friend; — *imperitura*, everlasting (*o* undying memory); *ho una vaga* — *della mia infanzia*, I have a faint recollection of my childhood; *queste scene risvegliano le dolci memorie del mio passato*, these scenes awaken the memories (*o* reminiscences) of my past ‖ *di beata* —, of blessed memory ‖ *in* — *di*, in memory of **3.** (*oggetto che rimane come ricordo*) souvenir; (*ricordo di famiglia*) heirloom: *quel quadro è una preziosa* — *di famiglia*, that picture is a precious heirloom; *questo libro è una cara* — *di mio padre*, this book is a precious souvenir of my father **4.** (*breve scritto, dissertazione*) memoir **5.** *pl.* (*note autobiografiche, storiche*) memoirs: *stampò le sue memorie*, he published his memoirs ‖ « *Le memorie* » *di Casanova*, "The Memoirs" of Casanova.

memoriàle, *s.m.* **1.** (*petizione*) memorial, petition: *redigere un* —, to draw up a memorial **2.** (*raccolta di documenti*) record **3.** (*libro di memorie*) memoirs (*pl.*).

memorialìsta, *s.c.* memorialist.

ména, *s.f.* plot, intrigue: *scoprì le mene del nemico*, he discovered the intrigues of the enemy.

menabò, *s.m.* (*tip.*) dummy.

mènade, *s.f.* (*mit.*) maenad, Bacchante.

menadìto, *a*, *l.av.* perfectly, very well: *conoscere, sapere ql.co. a* —, to have sthg. at one's finger-tips.

ménage, *s.m.* ménage, household.

Menàndro, *no.pr.m.* (*st. lett.*) Menander.

menàre, *v.t.* **1.** (*condurre*) to lead (*anche fig.*); to take; (*portare*) to bring: *dove mena questa strada?*, where does this road lead? (*o* take us?); *dove meni quel ragazzo?*, where are you taking that boy?; — *alla rovina*, to lead (*o* to bring) to ruin; — *qlcu. al pati-*

bolo, to bring s.o. to the scaffold; — *il cavallo a mano*, to lead a horse ‖ *egli mena una vita miserabile*, he leads (*o* lives *o* has) a miserable life ‖ — *a fine ql.co.*, to complete sthg. (*o* to bring sthg. to completion) ‖ — *buono, gramo*, to bring good, bad luck: *quell'uomo mi mena buono, gramo*, that man brings me good, bad luck ‖ — *il can per l'aia*, to beat about the bush ‖ — *ql.co. per le lunghe*, to drag sthg. out ‖ — *qlcu. per il naso*, to lead s.o. by the nose ‖ — *vanto*, to boast **2.** (*agitare, muovere*): — *la frusta*, to use the whip ‖ — *le gambe*, to run away ‖ — *la lingua*, to gossip (*o* to talk scandal): — *la lingua a danno di qlcu.*, to speak ill of s.o. ‖ — *le mani*, to fight (*o* to come to blows): *essi incominciarono a* — *le mani*, they started fighting **3.** (*sferrare*) to give, to deliver, to land: — *calci a qlcu.*, to kick s.o.; — *un pugno*, to land a punch.

menaròla, *s.f.* (*artig.*) brace, breast-borer: — *a cricco*, carpenter's ratchet-brace; — *ad angolo*, angle-brace.

méncio, *ag.* flabby; drooping; (*vizzo*) withered ‖ *cappello* —, soft hat.

ménda, *s.f.* (*difetto*) flaw, defect; (*errore*) fault: *quest'opera ha alcune mende*, this work has a few flaws; *rilevare le mende in ql.co.*, to notice the mistakes in sthg.

mendàce, *ag.* mendacious, untruthful; false; misleading: *notizie mendaci*, false reports; *persona* —, mendacious person; *testimone* —, untruthful witness; *le apparenze sono spesso mendaci*, appearances are often misleading.

mendaceménte, *av.* mendaciously, falsely.

mendàcio, *s.m.* (*letter.*) (*bugia*) lie, falsehood.

mendicànte, *ag.* mendicant ‖ *frati mendicanti*, mendicant friars; *ordini mendicanti*, mendicant orders ‖ *s.c.* beggar, mendicant.

mendicàre, *v.i.* to beg: *negli ultimi anni della sua vita fu costretto a* —, in the last years of his life he was reduced to begging; *preferirei morire che* —, I would die rather than beg ‖ *v.t.* to beg; to beg for (sthg.) (*anche fig.*): — *il cibo, la vita*, to beg for food, to beg for a living; — *complimenti, lodi*, to fish for compliments, for praise; — *un favore da qlcu.*, to beg a favour of s.o.; — *scuse*, to try to find excuses.

mendicità, *s.f.* **1.** mendicity, mendicancy, begging: *ridursi alla* —, to be reduced to begging; *fig.* to be reduced to beggary **2.** (*i mendicanti*) beggars (*pl.*): *ricovero di* —, poorhouse.

mendìco, *ag.* mendicant ‖ *s.m.* beggar, mendicant.

menefreghìsmo, *s.m.* couldn't-care-less attitude, devil-may-care attitude.

menefreghìsta, *s.c.* devil-may-care person: *è un* —, he couldn't care less.

meneghìno, *ag.* Milanese: *dialetto* —, Milanese dialect ‖ *s.m.* **1.** (*scherz.*) Milanese (*invariato al pl.*) **2.** (*dialetto milanese*) Milanese dialect: *parlare in* —, to speak Milanese dialect ‖ **Meneghìno**, *no.pr.m.* " Meneghino " (masked character symbolic of Milan).

Menelào, *no.pr.m.* (*lett.*) Menelaus.

Menènio Agrìppa, *no.pr.m.* (*st.*) Menenius Agrippa.

menestrèllo, *s.m.* **1.** minstrel **2.** (*spreg.*) (*poetastro*) poetaster.

Mènfi, *no.pr.f.* (*geog. st.*) Memphis.

menimpìpo, *s.m.* devil-may-care person: *aveva un'aria da* —, he looked as if he couldn't care less.

meninge, *s.f.* (*anat.*) meninx (*pl.* meninges).

meningèo, *ag.* (*anat.*) meningeal.

meningìte, *s.f.* (*patol.*) meningitis.

menippèo, *ag.* (*lett.*) Menippean: *satira* —, Menippean satire.

Menìppo, *no.pr.m.* (*st. lett.*) Menippus.

menìsco, *s.m.* (*anat. fis.*) meniscus (*pl.* menisci, meniscuses).

méno, *ag. comp.* less; (*con s.pl.*) **fewer**: *abbiamo* — *tempo di voi*, we have less time than you; *ce ne sono*

— *di quanto pensassi*, there are fewer than I thought; *con — finestre la casa sarebbe più calda*, with fewer windows the house would be warmer; *ho — amici che nemici*, I have fewer friends than enemies; *ho — amici di lui*, I have fewer friends than he has; *ho — anni di lui*, I am younger than he is; *vieni con — amici possibile*, come with as few friends as possible ‖ *— chiacchiere!*, — *ciarle!*, less talking! (*o* not so much talk!); *— sciocchezze!*, don't talk nonsense! ‖ — *male*, just as well (*o* a good job *o* a good thing); thank goodness; not so bad: *— male che non si è fatto niente*, thank goodness he didn't hurt himself; *— male che sei arrivato, stavo in pensiero*, it's a good thing you've arrived; I was getting worried; *— male, poteva andar peggio*, not so bad, it could have been worse ‖ *s.m.* (*con valore comp.*) less; (*con valore superl.*) least: *il — che ci vorrà sono tre ore*, it will take three hours at the very least; *è il — che possa capitarmi*, that is the least that could happen; *feci — di quel che avrei voluto*, I did less than I would have liked; *oggi ho aspettato molto —*, I haven't waited nearly so long to-day; *vale solo mille lire o anche —*, it's only worth a thousand lire, or even less; *voglio spendere il — possibile*, I want to spend as little as possible ‖ *il —*, *il segno del —*, (*mat.*) the minus sign ‖ *i —*, (*la minoranza*) the minority ‖ *a —*, *per —*, (*a minor prezzo*) for less (*o* cheaper): *non lo puoi acquistare per —*, you won't get it for less (*o* cheaper); *questo libro è caro qui, l'ho visto a — altrove*, this book is expensive here, I have seen it at a lower price elsewhere ‖ *dal più al —*, more or less (*o* about): *sono tutti uguali, dal più al —*, they are all more or less (*o* they are all about the same) ‖ *in men che non si dica*, before you can (*o* could) say Jack Robinson (*o* in less time than it takes to tell) ‖ *in — di un'ora*, in less than an hour; *in non — di un'ora*, in an hour at the very least ‖ *il numero del —*, (*gram.*) the singular (number) ‖ *per lo —*, at least: *dovresti bere per lo — un bicchiere di latte al giorno*, you should drink at least a glass of milk a day ‖ *tanto — da fare*, so much the less to do ‖ *parlare del più e del —*, to talk of this and that ‖ *av. comp.* 1. less; *superl. rel.* the least: *la campagna è — bella in estate che in primavera*, the countryside is less beautiful is summer than it is in spring (*o* is not so beautiful in summer as it is in spring); *è — amato che temuto*, he is less loved than feared; *è — caro*, it's cheaper (*o* less expensive *o* not so dear); *è il — gentile dei miei amici*, he is the least kind of my friends; *essa dovrebbe fumare —*, she should smoke less; *ho due anni — di lui*, I am two years younger than he is; *non è — studioso di voi*, he is just as hardworking as you (*o* no less hardworking than you); *visse dieci anni — di sua moglie*, he lived ten years less than his wife ‖ *— che —: non sa parlare l'inglese, — che — l'italiano*, he cannot even speak English, let alone Italian ‖ *— che mai*, less than ever; *— che onesto*, less than honest ‖ *ancor —*, even less; *molto —*, much less; *niente —*, no less; *niente — che*, nothing less than: *chiese niente — che un milione*, he asked for nothing less than a million; *poco —*, little less ‖ *nè più nè —*, neither more nor less; *più o —*, more or less; *piuttosto più che —*, rather more than less; *poco più, poco —*, about ‖ *— si mangia — si mangerebbe*, the less you eat, the less you feel like eating ‖ *è l'una — un quarto*, it's a quarter to one ‖ *fammi sapere se vieni o —*, let me know whether you are coming or not ‖ *non potei fare a — di ridere*, I couldn't help laughing; *posso farne a —*, I can do without; *puoi fare a — di farlo*, you need not do it (*o* you are not absolutely obliged to do it) ‖ *essere da — di qlcu.*, to be inferior to s.o. ‖ *venir —*, (*svenire*) to faint; (*venire a mancare*) to fail: *la vista gli venne —*, his sight failed him; *venir — alla propria parola*, to break one's word 2. (*mat.*) minus: *cinque — due fa tre*, five minus two is three ‖ *prep.* but (for); except (for); apart

from: *— due o tre, sono tutti ignoranti*, but for (*o* except for *o* apart from) two or three, they are all ignorant; *lavoro tutti i giorni — la domenica*, I work every day except Sunday; *pagò tutto — il vino*, he paid for everything but (*o* except) the wine ‖ *a méno che*, *l. cong.* unless: *non ci andrò a — che tu non venga con me*, I shall not go there unless you come with me.

Mèno, *no.pr.m.* (*geog.*) Main: *Francoforte sul —*, Frankfort on the Main.

menològio, *s.m.* (*eccl.*) menology.

menomaménte, *V.* **minimaménte**.

menomàre, *v.t.* to lessen, to diminish, to detract from (*sthg.*): *questo non menoma il suo valore*, this does not detract from (*o* lessen) his worth; *— la reputazione di qlcu.*, to detract from s.o.'s reputation.

menomàto, *ag.* 1. lessened, diminished: *valore —*, lessened value; *essere — nei propri diritti*, to be limited (*o* detracted) in one's rights; *uscire — da una polemica*, to have (*o* to get) the worst of an argument 2. (*di arti, sensi*) impaired; (*di persona*) disabled: *respirazione, vista, udito —*, impaired breathing, vision, hearing; *rimase — in un incidente sul lavoro*, he was disabled in an accident at work; *essere — nella vista, nell'udito*, to have poor eyesight, to be hard of hearing ‖ *s.m.* disabled person: *— psichico*, person of unsound mind.

menomazióne, *s.f.* 1. lessening, diminution, reduction, decrease: *— dei diritti civili*, reduction (*o* restriction) of civil rights 2. (*di arti, sensi*) impairment; (*di persona*) disablement: *non ha più potuto lavorare dopo la sua —*, he hasn't been able to work since his disablement; *lo scoppio di quella bomba gli causò una — permanente alla vista*, the explosion of the bomb brought about the permanent impairment of his sight.

mènomo, *ag. V.* **mínimo**.

menopàusa, *s.f.* (*fisiol.*) menopause.

mènsa, *s.f.* 1. table (*anche fig.*): *al levar della —*, at the end of dinner; *le briciole che cadono dalla — del ricco*, the crumbs which fall from the rich man's table; *una lauta, povera —*, a bountiful, poor table; *i piaceri della —*, the pleasures of the table; *la loro — è sempre ricca e abbondante*, they keep an excellent table; *rallegrò la —*, she kept the table amused; *si alzarono dalla —*, they left the table; *imbandire, sparecchiare la —*, to lay, to clear the table ‖ *separazione di —*, (*dir.*) judicial separation 2. (*mensa di università, di convento, ecc.*) refectory; (*di ufficiali*) mess; (*di soldati*) cook-house; (*di fabbrica*) canteen: *gli operai di quella fabbrica possono mangiare alla —*, the workmen of that factory can have their lunch at the canteen; *quando ero all'università spesso mangiavo alla —*, when I was at the University, I often ate at the students' restaurant; *questa sera ci sarà un ricevimento alla — ufficiali*, to-night there will be a cocktail-party in the officers' mess 3. (*eccl.*) altar; the Lord's table ‖ *la Mensa Eucaristica*, the Holy Communion 4. (*dir. eccl.*) revenue, income: *— vescovile*, bishop's revenue (*o* bishop's income).

mensíle, *ag.* monthly: *abbonamento —*, (*ferr.*) monthly (season) ticket; *rivista —*, monthly review ‖ *s.m.* 1. (*salario mensile*) month's salary, month's pay: *guadagna un buon —*, he earns good pay (*o* he has a good salary) 2. (*pubblicazione mensile*) monthly.

mensilità, *s.f.* 1. (*rata, importo mensile*) monthly instalment, monthly payment: *devo ancora pagare un'altra —*, I have one more monthly instalment to pay ‖ *tredicesima —*, Christmas bonus 2. (*l'essere mensile*) monthly nature, monthly character.

mensilménte, *av.* monthly, once a month, every month.

mènsola, *s.f.* 1. bracket; console; (*ripiano*) shelf: *è su quella —*, it is on that shelf; *quel caminetto aveva una — di marmo rosa*, that fireplace had a pink marble mantelpiece 2. (*arch.*) corbel.

mensuàle, *ag.* (*rar.*) monthly.

mensualità, (*rar.*) per **mensilità.**

ménta, *s.f.* (*bot.*) mint: — *peperina,* peppermint; *pastiglie di* —, peppermint-drops.

mentàle[1]**,** *ag.* mental: *deficienza* —, mental deficiency; *età* —, mental age; *limitazione* —, mental limitation; *malattia* —, mental disease; *orazione* —, mental prayer; *riserva* —, mental reservation; *strapazzo* —, mental strain.

mentàle,[2] *ag.* (*del mento*) mental.

mentalità, *s.f.* mentality; frame of mind: *ha una* — *arretrata,* he is old-fashioned in his outlook.

mentalménte, *av.* mentally.

mentàstro, *s.m.* (*bot.*) wild mint.

ménte, *s.f.* **1.** mind: — *acuta,* keen intellect; — *aperta,* open mind; — *debole,* weak mind; — *malata, sana,* unsound, sound mind; — *ristretta, limitata,* narrow mind: *è una persona dalla* — *ristretta,* he is a narrow-minded person; *la* — *umana,* the human mind; *doti della* —, mental gifts; *l'occhio della* —, the mind's eye; *la* — *non si deve lasciare vincere dal cuore,* the heart should not rule the head; *le forze della* — *erano ancora validissime nel suo corpo indebolito,* his mental powers were still unimpaired although his body was weak; *gli venne improvvisamente in* — *che gli altri sapessero della sua visita,* it struck him suddenly that the others knew of his visit; *ho sempre in* — *le tue parole,* I can't get your words out of my mind; *qual è lo stato di* — *del paziente?,* what is the patient's state of mind?; *togliti di* — *quell'uomo!,* get that man out of your head! || *aguzzare, acuire ·la* —, to sharpen one's wits || *avere in* — *di fare ql.co.,* to have a mind to do sthg. || *calcolare a* —, to reckon mentally (*o* to do mental arithmetic) || *essere fuori di* —, to be out of one's mind || *ficcarsi in* — *di fare ql.co.,* to take it into one's mind to do sthg. || *illuminare la* —, to enlighten s.o.'s mind || *che idea ti frulla in* —?, what plan are you hatching in your mind? || *non mi passò neppure per la* — *di fare ciò,* it did not even cross my mind to do that || *a* — *fredda,* in cold blood; *agire a* — *fredda,* to act in cold blood; *considerare ql.co. a* — *fredda,* to consider sthg. with indifference || *a* — *fresca,* with a clear mind || *— sana in corpo sano,* *prov.* a sound mind in a sound body **2.** (*persona di spiccate doti intellettuali*) mind, intellect: *è una delle nostre più belle menti,* he is one of our best minds (*o* intellects) **3.** (*intenzione*) intentions (*pl.*): *bisogna interpretare la legge secondo la* — *del legislatore,* we must interpret the law according to the legislator's intentions; *lasciò scritto quello che era la sua* —, he left note of his intentions; *cambiar* —, to change (*o* to alter) one's mind **4.** (*attenzione*) attention, mind: *porre* — *a ql.co.,* to keep one's mind on (*o* to pay attention to) sthg.; *volgere la* — *a ql.co.,* to turn one's attention to sthg. **5.** (*memoria*) mind, memory: *fammi* — *di comprare un regalo per mia sorella,* remind me to buy a present for my sister; *questo non mi venne in* — *allora,* I could not remember this at that moment; *imparare, sapere a* —, to learn, to know by heart; *passare, uscire di* —, (*fam.*) to slip one's memory.

menteeàtto, *ag.* insane, mad || *s.m.* madman (*pl.* madmen); (*idiota*) idiot.

mentina, *s.f.* peppermint-drop.

mentíre, *v.i.* to lie: *mentite!,* you're lying!; — *a qlcu.,* to lie to s.o. || *mentì a se stesso la gravità della situazione,* he closed his eyes to the gravity of the situation || *mentisci per la gola!,* you lie in your throat! || *se la fama non mente,* if the report is true || *v.t.* to falsify, to misrepresent: — *il vero,* to falsify the truth.

mentitaménte, *av.* lyingly, mendaciously, falsely.

mentíto, *ag.* false, sham: *un* — *pentimento,* a sham repentance; *con* — *affetto,* out of pretended love || *sotto mentite spoglie,* under false pretences.

mentitóre, *ag.* lying, mendacious, false || *s.m.,* **mentitríce,** *s.f.* liar.

ménto, *s.m.* chin: — *aguzzo,* sharp (*o* pointed) chin; — *in fuori,* protruding chin; — *sfuggente,* receding chin; *doppio* —, double chin: *una imponente signora col doppio* —, a stately, double-chinned lady; *sedeva pensieroso col* — *fra le mani,* he sat deep in thought, with his chin cupped in his hands || *l'onor del* —, (*scherz.*) the beard.

mentòlo, *s.m.* (*chim.*) menthol.

Mentóne, *no.pr.f.* (*geog.*) Menton.

Mèntore, *no.pr.m.* (*mit.*) Mentor || **mèntore,** *s.m.* (*consigliere*) mentor, adviser.

mentovàre, *v.t.* (*rar.*) to mention.

méntre, *cong.* **1.** (*temporale*) **while, whilst;** (*quando*) **as, when:** — (*che*) *studiavo, udii uno strano rumore,* while studying I heard a strange noise; *lo incontrai* — (*che*) *mi recavo a teatro,* I met him as I was going (*o* while I was on my way) to the theatre **2.** (*avversativo*) **whereas, while:** *a lui piace il cinema,* — *a me piace il teatro,* he likes the cinema whereas (*o* while) I like the theatre; *egli parla sei lingue molto bene,* — *sua moglie parla solo italiano,* he speaks six languages perfectly, whereas his wife only knows Italian **3.** (*finchè*) **while, as long as:** *divertiamoci* — *siamo giovani,* let's enjoy ourselves while we are young; — *visse quel re non vi furono rivoluzioni,* as long as (*o* while) that king lived there were no riots || *s.m.:* in quel —, (*in quel momento*) at that moment; (*nel frattempo*) meanwhile (*o* in the meantime *o* meantime).

menú, *s.m.* menu, bill of fare.

menzionàbile, *ag.* mentionable.

menzionàre, *v.t.* to mention, to name: *Dante lo menziona due o tre volte,* Dante mentions (*o* names) him two or three times.

menzionàto, *ag.* mentioned: *sopra* —, above-mentioned; *sotto* —, below-mentioned.

menzióne, *s.f.* mention: *degno di* —, worth mentioning; *fare* — *di qlcu., ql.co.,* to mention s.o., sthg. || — *onorevole,* honourable mention.

menzógna, *s.f.* lie, falsehood: *una* — *innocente,* a white lie; *un cumulo di menzogne,* a pack of lies; *questa è una* —!, that is a lie!.

menzognèro, *ag.* **1.** (*di persona*) mendacious, lying, untruthful: *è una persona menzognera,* he is an untruthful person (*o* he is a liar) **2.** (*di cosa*) false, untrue: *un'affermazione menzognera,* an untrue statement; *una lode menzognera,* a false praise; *parole, promesse menzognere,* false words, promises || *s.m.* (*mentitore*) liar.

meraménte, *av.* merely, simply, purely, barely.

meravíglia[1]**,** *s.f.* **1.** wonder, wonderment, marvel; (*sorpresa*) astonishment, surprise: *ciò fu fonte di grande* —, this roused great astonishment; *fui sopraffatto dalla* —, I was wonder-struck; *mi fa* — *che ancora non si sia ucciso!,* it is a marvel that he has not yet killed himself!; *mi fa* — *che tu dica ciò,* I am surprised you say this; *mi lanciò uno sguardo pieno di* —, he looked at me in wonder; *nessuna* — *che si sentisse a disagio,* no wonder she felt uneasy; *non fa* — *che sia in ritardo.* no wonder that he is late; *restai pieno di* — *davanti alle bellezze di Roma,* I was filled with wonder on seeing the beauties of Rome; *sento con* — *che sei stato molto malato,* I am surprised to know that you have been very ill; *il suo arrivo destò gran* —, his arrival caused great astonishment || *a* —, excellently: *andiamo a* —, we are getting on excellently (*o* capitally); *questo vestito ti va a* —, (*fam.*) this dress suits you to a T || *fare le meraviglie,* to express one's surprise **2.** (*cosa meravigliosa*) wonder, marvel: *le meraviglie della natura,* the marvels of Nature; *che* —!, what a marvel (*o* wonder)!; *è una* —, it is a marvel; *dire meraviglie di qlcu.,* to speak in glowing terms of s.o.; *fare meraviglie,* to perform wonders (*o* to work marvels) || *« Alice nel paese delle meraviglie »,* (*lett.*) "Alice in Wonderland" || *le sette meraviglie del mondo,* the seven wonders of the world || *questa è l'ottava* — *del mondo,* this is the eighth wonder of the world.

meravíglia², *s.f. (bot.)* love-lies-bleeding.

meravigliàre, *v.t.* to amaze; to astonish, to surprise: *ciò mi meraviglia*, that surprises me; *le sue parole mi meravigliarono*, his words astonished me; *vi può — di udire che...*, you may be surprised to hear that... ‖ **meravigliàrsi**, *v.r.* to be amazed (at s.o., sthg.); to be astonished (at s.o., sthg.), to be surprised (at s.o., sthg.): *mi meravigliai del suo coraggio*, I was amazed at (o astonished by) his courage; *mi meraviglio che egli non sia venuto*, I wonder (that) he did not come; *mi meraviglio di vederti*, I am surprised to see you; *non c'è da — che...*, no wonder that... ‖ *mi meraviglio di te!*, I am surprised at you!.

meravigliàto, *ag.* amazed; astonished, surprised: *sguardo —*, surprised look; *rimasi — nel vederlo arrivare così presto*, I was amazed to see him arrive so early; *sono veramente — di vederti*, I am really amazed to see you.

meravigliosaménte, *av.* wonderfully, marvellously.

meraviglióso, *ag.* 1. wonderful, marvellous: *una vista meravigliosa*, a wonderful sight; *abbiamo avuto un tempo — durante le vacanze*, we had wonderful weather during our holidays; *ella è semplicemente meravigliosa!*, she is just splendid!; *fa dei progressi meravigliosi*, he is doing marvellously; *ne abbiamo un ricordo —*, we have got a wonderful memory of it; *fare cose meravigliose*, to work wonders 2. *(eccessivo, straordinario)*: extraordinary ‖ *s.m.* 1. *(lett.)* the supernatural 2. *(aspetto sorprendente)* wonder: *il — in questa faccenda è che...*, the wonder of this matter is that....

mercantàre, *(rar.)* per **mercanteggiàre**.

mercànte, *s.m.* merchant, trader; dealer: *— all'ingrosso*, wholesale trader (o wholesaler); *— al minuto*, retail trader (o retailer); *— di bestiame*, cattle dealer; *— di grano*, corn dealer (o corn factor); *— di schiavi*, slave trader; *— di vino*, licensed victualler (o wine -merchant); *un ricco — di Firenze*, a rich merchant of Florence ‖ *fare orecchi di —*, to turn a deaf ear 2. *(bottegaio)* shopkeeper; tradesman *(pl.* tradesmen); retailer; *(merciaio)* haberdasher.

mercanteggiàbile, *ag.* negotiable.

mercanteggiaménto, *s.m.* bargaining, haggling.

mercanteggiàre, *v.i.* 1. *(commerciare)* to trade, to deal: *— in vini, pelli, ecc.*, to deal in wine, hides, etc. 2. *(speculare)* to speculate *(anche fig.)*: *— sulla farina, sul cambio*, to speculate in flour, on the exchange; *— sull'onore*, to speculate on honour 3. *(tirare sul prezzo)* to bargain, to haggle: *non mi piace —*, I don't like haggling ‖ *v.t. (far oggetto di traffico indegno)* to traffic in (sthg.): *— la coscienza, l'onore*, to sell one's conscience, honour; *— voti*, to traffic in votes.

mercantésco, *ag. (spreg.)* mercenary; trader's *(attributivo)*: *ingordigia mercantesca*, merchant's greediness.

mercantéssa, *s.f.* 1. tradeswoman *(pl.* tradeswomen) 2. *(moglie di mercante)* merchant's wife; shopkeeper's wife.

mercantíle, *ag.* 1. mercantile *(attributivo)*; commercial: *azienda —*, commercial concern; *bandiera —*, merchant flag; *codice —*, commercial code; *legislazione —*, mercantile law; *marina —*, merchant service (o mercantile marine); *nave —*, cargo boat; *paese —*, mercantile country; *sistema —*, mercantile system; *stile —*, commercial style 2. *(spreg.) (mercantesco)* mercenary; trader's *(attributivo)* 3. *(spreg.) (dozzinale)* plain, ordinary: *roba —*, ordinary stuff ‖ *s.m. (nave mercantile)* cargo boat.

mercantilísmo, *s.m. (econ.)* mercantilism.

mercantilísta, *s.m. (econ.)* mercantilist.

mercantilménte, *av.* in a commercial way.

mercanzía, *s.f.* 1. *(merce)* merchandise; goods *(pl.)*; wares *(pl.)*; commodity: *— avariata*, damaged goods; *inventario della —*, stocktaking; *la — è buona*, the wares are good ‖ *saper vendere la propria —, fig.* to make the most of oneself ‖ *la buona — si loda da*

se stessa, prov. a good product advertises itself ‖ *ogni mercante loda la sua —, prov.* every pedlar praises his own wares 2. *(il commerciare)* trading.

mercàre, *(rar.)* per **mercanteggiàre**.

mercatíno, *s.m.* 1. *(rivendugliolo)* huckster 2. *(becero)* vulgarian.

mercàto, *s.m.* 1. *(luogo dove si contratta e negozia)* market(-place): *— all'aperto*, open-air market; *— coperto*, covered market; *— dei fiori*, flower market; *— del bestiame*, cattle market; *— del pesce*, fish market; *— rionale*, local market; *città sede di —*, market-town; *piazza del —*, market-square; *andare al —*, to go to market ‖ *giorno di —*, market-day 2. *(econ.)* market: *— agitato, animato, calmo, debole, sostenuto*, agitated, animated, calm, dull, brisk market; *— con tendenza al rialzo, al ribasso*, bull, bear market; *— dei titoli*, stock-market; *— finanziario*, financial market; *— interno*, home market; *— libero*, open market; *dominio del —*, control of the market; *fluttuazioni del —*, fluctuations of the market; *prezzo di —*, market price; *quotazione del —*, market-quotation; *ricerche di —*, market-research; *ristagno del —*, market stagnation; *valore sul —*, market value; *il — fiorisce*, the market is blooming; *il — infiacchisce*, the market weakens; *hanno perduto il controllo del —*, they have lost the control of the market; *cercare nuovi mercati*, to seek new markets; *conquistare un —*, to conquer a market; *essere sul —*, to be on the market; *lanciare sul —*, to throw on the market; *rovinare il —*, to spoil the market; *sovraccaricare il —*, to flood the market ‖ *Mercato Comune Europeo*, European Common Market ‖ *— nero*, black market 3. *(trattazione, affare)* deal, bargain: *fare buono, cattivo —*, to make a good, a bad bargain; *fare — di ql.co. con qlcu.*, to bargain with s.o. for sthg.; *fare — del proprio onore*, to prostitute oneself 4. *(prezzo)* price, rate: *a buon —*, cheaply: *articoli a buon —*, low-priced goods (o cheap goods) ‖ *per sopra —*, besides ‖ *se la cavò a buon —*, he got off lightly.

mercatóre, *s.m.*, **mercatríce**, *s.f. (letter.)* dealer; *(spreg.)* trafficker.

mercatúra, *s.f.* 1. trade, commerce: *darsi alla —*, to devote oneself to trade; *esercitare la —*, to be a dealer 2. *(arte di vendere)* art of selling.

mèrce¹, *s.f.* goods *(pl.)*; wares *(pl.)*; merchandise; commodity: *— avariata*, damaged goods; *— aviotrasportata*, airfreight; *— deperibile*, perishable goods *— di contrabbando*, smuggled goods; *— disponibile*, disposable goods; *— di transito*, transit goods; *merci esenti da dogana*, duty-free commodities; *merci infiammabili*, inflammable goods; *la — in magazzino*, stock (o the goods in store); *— invenduta*, unsold goods; *— per esportazione*, export goods; *— pericolosa*, dangerous goods; *— rifiutata*, rejected goods; *— soggetta a dazio*, dutiable goods; *distinta delle merci, (aer.)* freight-manifest; *(mar.)* bill of lading; *(ferr.)* way -bill; *scalo merci, (ferr.)* goods depot; *treno merci, goods train* (o *amer.* freight train); *vagone merci, goods wagon* (o *amer.* freight car); *la — non è conforme all'ordinazione*, the goods do not correspond to orders given; *questa — è invendibile*, these goods are unsaleable; *questa — è molto ricercata*, these goods are in great demand.

mercé², *s.f.* 1. *(pietà)* mercy: *avere — di qlcu.*, to have mercy (o pity) on s.o.; *implorare —*, to cry (o to crave) for mercy; *rimettersi alla — di qlcu.*, to throw oneself on s.o.'s mercy 2. *(grazia)* grace, favour; thanks *(pl.)*: *— sua*, thanks to him (o to her) ‖ *la Dio —*, thanks be to God 3. *(balìa)* mercy: *alla — delle onde*, at the mercy of the waves; *siamo tutti alla — della fortuna*, we are all at the mercy of fortune; *essere abbandonato alla — di qlcu.*, to be left to the mercy of s.o. 4. *(letter.) (mercede)* reward.

Mercède¹, *no.pr.f.* Mercy, Mercedes.

mercéde², *s.f.* 1. *(paga)* pay ‖ *vivere alla — di qlcu.*, to be dependent on s.o. **2.** (*ricompensa*) reward: *ogni opera buona avrà la sua* —, every good deed will have its reward.

mercenariaménte, *av.* mercenarily.

mercenàrio, *ag.* mercenary: *gente mercenaria,* mercenary people; *soldato* —, mercenary (soldier) ‖ *penna mercenaria,* hack writer ‖ *s.m.* mercenary.

merceología, *s.f.* technology of marketable goods.

merceológico, *ag.* pertaining to the technology of marketable goods.

mercería, *s.f.* **1.** haberdashery **2.** (*negozio*) haberdasher's (shop).

mercerizzàre, *v.t.* (*ind. tessile*) to mercerize.

mercerizzàto, *ag.* (*ind. tessile*) mercerized.

mercerizzazióne, *s.f.* (*ind. tessile*) mercerization, mercerizing.

merciàia, *s.f.,* **merciàio,** *s.m.* haberdasher; (*ambulante*) pedlar, hawker.

merciaiuòlo, *s.m.* (*merciaio ambulante*) pedlar, hawker.

mercimònio, *s.m.* illicit trade; traffic, trafficking.

mercoledí, mercoldí, *s.m.* Wednesday: *al* — *siamo sempre fuori per pranzo,* on Wednesdays we always dine out ‖ — *delle Ceneri,* Ash Wednesday.

mercuriàle[1], *ag.* (*farm.*) mercurial: *unguento* —, mercurial ointment.

mercuriàle[2], *s.f.* (*listino dei prezzi del mercato*) market report.

Mercúrio, *no.pr.m.* (*mit. astr.*) Mercury ‖ **mercúrio,** *s.m.* (*chim.*) mercury; quicksilver: *arco a* —, (*elett.*) mercury arc; *caldaia a* —, mercury boiler; *lampada a vapori di* —, (*elett.*) mercury-discharge lamp; *terreno che contiene* —, soil containing mercury.

mèrda, *s.f.* (*volg.*) shit.

merdàio, *s.m.* (*volg.*) filthy place.

merdóso, *ag.* (*volg.*) filthy, foul.

merènda, *s.f.* (afternoon) snack: *i bambini stanno facendo* —, the children are having their tea ‖ *questo c'entra come i cavoli a* —, (*fam.*) this has nothing to do with the subject.

meretríce, *s.f.* whore, prostitute.

meretrício, *s.m.* prostitution.

mèrgo, *s.m.* (*ornit.*) merganser.

meridiàna, *s.f.* sun-dial: *sulla nostra casa in campagna c'è ancora una vecchia* —, on our house in the country there is still an old sun-dial.

meridiàno, *ag.* meridian: *altitudine, linea meridiana,* (*astr.*) meridian altitude, line; *ombra meridiana,* noonday shadow; *sole* —, midday sun ‖ *dimostrare ql.co. alla luce meridiana,* to make sthg. as clear as daylight ‖ *s.m.* (*astr. geog.*) meridian: — *celeste,* celestial meridian; — *fondamentale,* first meridian; — *geografico, magnetico,* true, magnetic meridian.

meridionàle, *ag.* Southern; South (*attributivo*): *l'Africa* —, South Africa; *l'America* —, South America; *l'Italia* —, Southern Italy; *gli Stati meridionali,* the Southern States; *vento* —, South (o southerly) wind ‖ *ha un temperamento* —, she has a fiery temperament ‖ *s.c.* Southerner; (*specialmente di Francia*) Meridional.

meridionalísmo, *s.m.* Southern Italian expression.

meridionalménte, *av.* meridionally.

meridióne, *s.m.* south.

meriggiàre, *v.i.* to have a siesta.

meríggio, *s.m.* midday, noon: *in pieno* —, at noon.

merínga, *s.f.* meringue.

meríno, *s.m.* **1.** (*zool.*) merino (sheep) **2.** (*lana*) merino (wool).

meristèma, *s.m.* (*bot.*) meristem.

meristemàtico, *ag.* (*bot.*) meristematic.

meritaménte, *av.* deservedly, justly.

meritàre, *v.t.* **1.** to deserve, to merit: *uno sforzo che merita,* a worth-while effort; *merita che si faccia ql.co. per lui,* he deserves to have sthg. done on his behalf; *merita di essere punito,* he deserves punishment (o to be punished); *meritano la nostra ammirazione,*

they deserve (o merit) our admiration; *i poveri meritano la nostra simpatia ed il nostro aiuto,* the poor deserve our sympathy and help; *questa poesia merita di essere letta,* this poem is worth reading; — *lode,* to deserve praise ‖ *ben* — *di ql.cu.,* to deserve well of s.o.; *ha ben meritato della patria,* he has deserved well of his country ‖ *non merita la pena,* it isn't worth the trouble **2.** (*far ottenere, procacciare*) to earn: *è questo che gli meritò la promozione,* this is what earned him his promotion; *la sua condotta gli meritò la lode di tutti,* his conduct earned him universal praise **3.** (*richiedere*) to require: *la notizia merita conferma,* the news needs confirmation ‖ **meritàrsi,** *v.r.* to deserve, to merit: *si merita un premio,* he deserves a prize; — *un castigo,* to deserve punishment ‖ *se lo meritò!,* he thoroughly deserved it!.

meritataménte, *av.* deservedly, justly.

meritévole, *ag.* deserving, worthy, meritorious: — *di fiducia,* trustworthy; — *di nota,* noteworthy; *atti meritevoli,* meritorious deeds; *la sua condotta è* — *di molta lode,* his behaviour is worthy of the highest praise.

meritevolménte, *av.* deservingly, deservedly.

mèrito, *s.m.* **1.** merit: *lavoro di scarso* —, work of little merit (o of small value); *un uomo di* —, a man of merit; *fu* — *dell'autore l'aver spiegato chiaramente la sua teoria,* it was to the author's credit that he explained his theory very clearly; *loda sempre i meriti di sua moglie,* he is always extolling the merits of his wife; *non c'è nessun* — *in quel che stai facendo,* there is no merit in what you are doing; *non è un gran* — *il dar via ciò che non ti serve,* there isn't much merit in giving away things that you don't want; *quell'opera ha meriti reali,* that work has real merits; *si attribuisce sempre il* — *dei nostri successi,* he always takes the credit for our successes (o when we succeed); *si fa meriti dei suoi difetti,* he makes merits of his faults; *avere qualche* —, to be of some merit; *ricompensare ql.cu. secondo i suoi meriti,* to reward s.o. according to his merits ‖ *onore al* —, award for merit ‖ *per* —, through (o by means of): *per* — *mio,* thanks to me: *ha trovato un buon posto per* — *mio,* he got a good job thanks to (o through) me; *promozione per* —, promotion by merit ‖ *punti di* —, good marks ‖ *non aver nè* — *nè colpa,* to deserve neither praise nor blame **2.** (*premio, ricompensa*) merit, reward: *rendere* — *a ql.cu.,* to reward s.o. ‖ *Dio te ne renda* —!, may you be rewarded for it! **3.** (*dir.*) merits (*pl.*): *il* — *di una causa,* the merits of a cause **4.** *in* — *a,* as to (o about o as regards o with regard o regarding o with respect to o respecting): *in* — *a questo argomento,* as to (o as regards) this subject; *avrete istruzioni in* —, you will receive instructions about this; *non so niente in* —, I know nothing about the matter; *parlare in* — *a ql.co.,* to speak about sthg.

meritoriaménte, *av.* meritoriously, deservingly.

meritòrio, *ag.* meritorious, deserving: *azioni meritorie,* meritorious deeds.

mèrla, *s.f.* (*ornit.*) female blackbird.

merlàno, *s.m.* (*ittiol.*) whiting.

merlàre, *v.t.* (*arch.*) to embattle, to crenel(l)ate.

merlàta, *s.f.* (*arch.*) battlement, crene(l)lation.

merlàto, *ag.* (*arch.*) embattled, battlemented, crenel(l)ated.

merlatúra, *s.f.* **1.** (*arch.*) battlement, crene(l)lation **2.** (*ornamento con merletti*) lace-trimming.

merlettàia, *s.f.* **1.** (*chi fabbrica merletti*) lace-maker, lace-worker **2.** (*chi vende merletti*) lace-vendor, lace-seller.

merlettàre, *v.t.* to trim with lace; to lace.

merlétto, *s.m.* lace: — *a tombolo,* pillow-lace (o bobbin-lace); — *con l'ago,* needle-lace; — *di cotone, di seta,* cotton lace, silk lace; *ornato di* —, lace-edged.

Merlíno[1], *no.pr.m.* Merlin ‖ *il Mago* —, (*lett.*) Merlin the Wizard.

merlíno[2], *s.m.* (*mar.*) marline, marling.

mèrlo[1], *s.m.* **1.** (*ornit.*) blackbird **2.** (*sciocco, sempliciotto*) simpleton, noodle, booby: *che* —*!*, what an ass!.

mèrlo[2], *s.m.* (*arch.*) merlon.

merlòtto, *s.m.* **1.** (*ornit.*) young blackbird **2.** (*sciocco, sempliciotto*) simpleton, noodle, booby.

merlúzzo, *s.m.* cod(-fish): *olio di fegato di* —, cod-liver oil.

mèro, *ag.* **1.** pure: *acqua mera*, pure water; *vino* —, neat wine **2.** *fig.* pure, mere, sheer; simple: *è tutta una mera invenzione*, the whole thing is pure imagination; *fu una mera coincidenza*, it was a mere coincidence.

Mèrope, *no.pr.f.* (*mit.*) Merope.

Merovèo, *no.pr.m.* (*st.*) Merovaeus.

merovíngio, *ag.s.m.* (*st.*) Merovingian.

mèrto, (*poet.*) per **mèrito**.

mesàta, *s.f.* **1.** (*mese*) month **2.** (*paga mensile*) month's salary; month's pay: — *anticipata*, a month's pay in advance; — *doppia*, double month's pay; *riscuotere la* —, to draw one's pay.

méscere, *v.t.* **1.** (*versare*) to pour (out): *mesci il vino per piacere*, pour the wine, please **2.** (*mescolare*) to mix.

meschinaménte, *av.* **1.** (*poveramente*) poorly; (*miserabilmente*) miserably **2.** (*grettamente*) meanly.

meschinería, meschinità, *s.f.* **1.** (*povertà*) poverty; (*miseria*) misery **2.** (*grettezza*) meanness.

meschíno, *ag.* **1.** (*povero*) poor; (*misero*) miserable: — *me!*, poor me!; *egli conduce una vita meschina*, he leads a miserable life **2.** (*gretto*) mean; wretched: *pensieri meschini*, mean thoughts; *una persona meschina*, a narrow-minded person; *una scusa meschina*, a wretched excuse || *un prezzo* —, a ridiculous price || *fece una figura molto meschina*, he cut a very poor figure || *s.m.* **1.** (*povero diavolo*) poor fellow **2.** (*persona gretta*) wretch.

meschíta, *s.f.* (*moschea*) mosque.

méscita, *s.f.* wine-shop.

mescitóre, *s.m.* barman (*pl.* barmen).

mescitríce, *s.f.* barmaid.

mescolaménto, *s.m.* mixing, mingling.

mescolànza, *s.f.* **1.** (*il mescolare*) mixing, mingling **2.** (*miscuglio*) mixture; (*miscela*) blend.

mescolàre, *v.t.* **1.** to mix (anche *fig.*): — *latte e acqua*, to mix milk and water **2.** (*tè, caffè, liquori, tabacco*) to blend: — *diversi tipi di caffè*, to blend different kinds of coffee **3.** (*rimestare*) to stir: *devo* — *la crema?*, shall I stir the custard? **4.** (*alle carte*) to shuffle || **mescolàrsi**, *v.r.* **1.** to mix: *l'acqua si mescola col vino*, water mixes with wine **2.** (*di tè, caffè, liquori, tabacco*) to blend: *questi tipi di tabacco si mescolano bene*, these kinds of tobacco blend well **3.** (*associarsi*) to mingle: *egli si mescola ad ogni categoria di persone*, he is a good mixer; — *con la folla*, to mingle with (o in) the crowd **4.** (*impicciarsi*) to interfere (with sthg.): *non mescolatevi in ciò che non vi riguarda*, do not interfere with what doesn't concern you.

mescolàta, *s.f.* **1.** mix; (*il mescolare*) mixing **2.** (*rimestata*) stir; (*il rimestare*) stirring **3.** (*alle carte*) shuffle; (*il mescolare le carte*) shuffling.

mescolataménte, *av.* mixedly; (*confusamente*) confusedly.

mescolatóre, *s.m.*, **mescolatríce**, *s.f.* (*ind.*) mixer.

mescolatúra, *s.f.* (*rar.*) mixing; blending.

mescolío, *s.m.* mixing, mingling.

mése, *s.m.* **1.** month: — *civile, lunare, solare*, calendar, lunar, solar month; *il* — *scorso*, last month; *il* — *prossimo*, next month; *il corrente* —, the current month; *ai primi del* —, early in the month; *mille lire al* —, a thousand lire a month; *oggi a un* —, a month to-day (o this day month); *quanti ne abbiamo del* —*?*, what day of the month is it? (o what is the date?); *quel viaggio durò mesi e mesi*, that journey lasted months and months; *si trova ormai al sesto mese*, (*di gravidanza*) she is already in her sixth month; *noleggiare ql.co. a* —, to hire sthg. by the month **2.** (*mesata*) month's salary; month's pay **3.** *pl.* (*fisiol.*) menses.

mesentère, *s.m.* (*anat.*) mesentery.

mesentèrico, *ag.* (*anat.*) mesenteric, mesenterial.

mesentèrio, *s.m.* (*anat.*) mesentery.

mesenteríte, *s.f.* (*patol.*) mesenteritis.

Mèsia, *no.pr.f.* (*geog. st.*) Moesia.

mesmeriàno, *ag.* mesmeric(al) || *s.m.* mesmerist.

mesmèrico, *ag.* mesmeric(al).

mesmerísmo, *s.m.* mesmerism.

mesocàrpo, *s.m.* (*bot.*) mesocarp.

mesocefàlico, *ag.* (*anat.*) mesocephalic.

mesología, *s.f.* (*scient.*) mesology.

mesomería, *s.f.* (*chim.*) mesomerism.

mesomòrfo, *ag.* (*fis.*) mesomorphic.

mesóne, *s.m.* (*fis. atomica*) meson.

Mesopotàmia, *no.pr.f.* (*geog.*) Mesopotamia.

mesotòrio, *s.m.* (*chim.*) mesothorium.

mesotróne, *s.m.* (*fis. atomica*) mesotron.

mesozòico, *ag.* (*geol.*) Mesozoic.

méssa[1], *s.f.* (*eccl.*) mass, Mass: — *alta, bassa*, high, low mass; — *cantata*, sung mass; — *da morto*, requiem (mass); *paramenti per la* —, mass (o priest's) vestments; *andare a* —, to go to mass; *ascoltare la* —, to hear mass; *celebrare, dire la* —, to celebrate, to say mass.

méssa[2], *s.f.* **1.** (*azione del mettere*) placing, putting, setting: — *a bordo*, (*comm.*) shipping; — *in scena*, (*teat.*) staging; — *in vendita*, (*comm.*) offering for sale; — *in vigore*, (*dir.*) enforcement **2.** (*mec.*): — *a punto*, setting-up; (*esecuzione delle registrazioni*) line-up; (*di una trasmissione, di un albero, ecc.*) truing; — *a punto dello stampo*, die-spotting; — *in fase*, setting; — *in fase dell'accensione*, ignition-timing; — *in fase del motore*, engine-timing; — *in moto*, (*di motorino di avviamento*) starter; (*avviamento*) starting; — *in opera*, (*di impianto*) installation **3.** (*elett.*): — *a massa*, — *a terra*, grounding (o earthing) **4.** (*ott. foto.*): — *a fuoco*, focusing; — *a fuoco all'infinito*, infinity focusing **5.** (*tip.*): — *in macchina*, imposing **6.** — *in quadro*, (*cine.*) framing **7.** (*al giuoco, posta, puntata*) stake.

messaggería, *s.f.* **1.** (*servizio di trasporti*) carrying-trade **2.** (*corriera postale*) mail-coach.

messaggièro, *s.m.* **1.** messenger **2.** (*precursore*) harbinger.

messàggio, *s.m.* **1.** message **2.** (*indirizzo, allocuzione*) address: — *presidenziale*, presidential address.

messàle, *s.m.* **1.** (*eccl.*) missal **2.** (*scherz.*) (*libro di proporzioni rilevanti*) massive tome.

Messalína, *no.pr.f.* (*st.*) Messalina.

mèsse, *s.f.* **1.** crop; (*raccolto*) harvest: *falciare le messi*, to gather in the crops **2.** (*mietitura*) reaping: *tempo della* —, reaping-time **3.** (*biade*) corn: *le bionde messi*, the golden corn **4.** *fig.* (*raccolta, copia*) crop, harvest: *ricca* — *di informazioni*, a rich harvest of information.

Messère, *s.m.* (*arc.*) Sir; (*accompagnato dal nome*) Master: — *lo giudice*, His Honour; (*vocativo*) Your Honour; *il buon* — *Francesco*, good Master Francis; *sì* —, yes Sir || **messère**, *s.m.* gentleman (*pl.* gentlemen).

Messía, *s.m.* Messiah.

messiànico, *ag.* Messianic.

messianísmo, *s.m.* Messianism.

messicàno, *ag.s.c.* Mexican.

Mèssico, *no.pr.m.* (*geog.*) Mexico || *Città del* —, Mexico City.

messidòro, *s.m.* (*st. francese*) Messidor.

Messína, *no.pr.f.* (*geog.*) Messina: *Stretto di* —, Strait(s) of Messina.

messinése, *ag.s.c.* Messinese (*invariato al pl.*) || *i Messinesi*, the Messinese.

mésso[1], *ag.*: *ben* —, (*vestito bene*) well-dressed; (*robusto*) stout (o sturdy); *mal* —, (*mal vestito*) poorly dressed; (*in cattive condizioni finanziarie*) badly-off.

mésso[2], *s.m.* messenger; (*ambasciatore*) ambassador; (*legato*) legate: — *papale*, (papal) legate || — *del cielo*, heavenly messenger.

mestaménte, *av.* sadly, sorrowfully.

mestaménto, *s.m.* stirring; (*mescolamento*) mixing.

mestàre, *v.t.* to stir; (*mescolare*) to mix ‖ *v.i. fig.* (*intrigare*) to intrigue; (*interferire negli affari altrui*) to meddle.

mestatóio, *s.m.* stirrer; (*cucchiaione*) ladle.

mestatóre, *s.m.*, **mestatríce,** *s.f.* (*intrigante*) intriguer; (*ficcanaso*) meddler.

mèstica, *s.f.* (*pitt.*) **1.** (*miscela di olii per preparare tele da dipingere*) priming **2.** (*mescolanza dei colori sulla tavolozza*) paints mixed on the palette.

mesticàre, *v.t.* (*pitt.*) to prime; to ground ‖ *v.i.* (*pitt.*) to mix colours (on the palette).

mesticheria, *s.f.* art shop.

mestichíno, *s.m.* (*pitt.*) spatula, palette-knife.

mestieràte, *s.m.* **1.** (*chi esercita un mestiere*) worker **2.** (*spreg.*) (*chi si applica superficialmente a ogni genere di lavoro*) jack-of-all-trades **3.** (*spreg.*) (*scrittore, artista che lavora per solo lucro*) hack.

mestière[1], *s.m.* **1.** trade; (*professione*) profession; (*occupazione*) job, occupation: *il — del falegname,* the carpenter's trade; *il — delle armi,* the profession of arms; *il — dell'ingegnere,* the engineering profession; *egli fa il calzolaio di —,* he is a shoemaker by trade; *fa l'architetto di —,* he is an architect by profession; *ha lasciato il suo — perchè era troppo difficile,* he left his job because it was too difficult for him; *impara il — del carpentiere,* he is learning carpentry; *esercitare un —,* to carry on a trade ‖ *arti e mestieri,* arts and crafts ‖ *ferri del —,* tools of the trade ‖ *gli incerti del —,* the hazards of the profession (o trade) ‖ *essere del —,* to be an expert ‖ *chi vuol fare l'altrui — fa la zuppa nel paniere, prov.* everyone to his trade **2.** (*perizia*) skill, craft: *non è arte, è —,* it is not art, it is craftmanship; *per far questo ci vuol —,* for this job you need skill **3.** (*lavoro*) work, job: *puoi fare questo — per me?,* can you do this job (o work) for me? ‖ *fare i mestieri,* (*le faccende di casa*) to do the housework **4.** (*professione per lucro*) business: *della pittura ha fatto un —,* he made a business out of painting.

mestière[2], **mestièri,** *s.m.* (*letter.*) (*in frasi imp.*): *è, fa —,* it is necessary; *non fa mestier lusinghe,* it is no use flattering.

mestízia, *s.f.* sadness; melancholy.

mèsto, *ag.* sad; melancholy; (*depresso*) depressed: *— addio,* sad farewell; *aria mesta, motivo —,* melancholy air, tune; *cuore —,* heavy heart.

méstola, *s.f.* **1.** ladle: *— bucata,* skimmer (o strainer) ‖ *tenere la — in mano,* (*farla da padrone*) to rule the roost **2.** (*arnese della lavandaia*) copper-stick **3.** (*cazzuola*) trowel **4.** (*spor.*) (*mazza*) bat.

mestolàta, *s.f.* **1.** (*quantità contenuta in un mestolo*) ladleful **2.** (*colpo dato con un mestolo*) blow with a ladle.

mestolièra, *s.f.* (*rar.*) ladle-rack.

méstolo, *s.m.* ladle; (*di legno*) wooden spoon ‖ *avere il — in mano,* (*farla da padrone*) to rule the roost.

mestruàle, *ag.* (*fisiol.*) menstrual.

mestruàre, *v.i.* (*fisiol.*) to menstruate.

mestruazióne, *s.f.* (*fisiol.*) menstruation.

mèstruo, *s.m.* (*fisiol.*) menstrua (*pl.*); menses (*pl.*).

mèta[1], *s.f.* **1.** (*destinazione*) destination: *la — del nostro viaggio era Atene,* our destination was Athens **2.** (*scopo, fine*) goal, aim, object, purpose: *la — della propria vita,* the goal of one's life; *errare senza —,* to wander about aimlessly; *raggiungere la —,* to reach one's goal (o aim) **3.** (*archeol.*) (*nei circhi*) meta (*pl.* metae) **4.** (*mucchio, ammasso*) pile: *— di fieno,* haystack; *— di paglia,* pile of straw.

méta[2], *s.f.* (*rar.*) (*escremento di animale*) dung.

metà[3], *s.f.* **1.** half (*pl.* halves): *la — del mio tempo, dei miei soldi,* half (of) my time, (of) my money; *una — della casa è mia,* half (of) the house is mine; *la — di cento è cinquanta,* half of a hundred is fifty; *una — di questa traduzione è molto buona,* half of this translation is very good; *— di queste frasi sono sba-*

gliate, half of these sentences are wrong; *più della — dei miei libri,* more than half (of) my books; *la prima — del secolo,* the first half of the century ‖ *a —,* half: *cotto a —,* half-cooked; *dividere ql.co. a —,* to divide sthg. in half (o in two o into two halves); *essere a — di ql.co.,* to be half-way through sthg.; *fare a — di ql.co. con qlcu.,* to go halves (o shares o fifty-fifty) with s.o. in sthg.; *fare ql.co. a —,* (*non finirla*) to do sthg. by halves; *fermarsi a — di un'impresa, di un viaggio,* to stop half-way through an undertaking, a journey; *lasciare ql.co. a —,* to leave sthg. half-done ‖ *a — prezzo,* at half-price ‖ *a — strada, half-way ‖ è americano per —,* he is half American ‖ *chi ben comincia è a — dell'opera, prov.* a good beginning is half the battle **2.** (*parte mediana*) middle: *a — della stanza,* in the middle of the room; *verso la — di settembre,* around (o about) the middle of September **3.** (*scherz.*) (*coniuge*): *la mia —,* my better half.

mèta[4], *abbr.* di **metaldèide.**

metabolísmo, *s.m.* (*biol.*) metabolism: *— basale,* basal metabolism.

metacàrpo, *s.m.* (*anat.*) metacarpus.

metacèntro, *s.m.* (*mar.*) metacentre.

metacísmo, *s.m.* (*gram. greca, latina*) metacism.

metacromatísmo, *s.m.* (*biol.*) metachromatism.

metacronísmo, *s.m.* metachronism.

metafísica, *s.f.* **1.** (*fil.*) metaphysics **2.** (*astruseria*) intricacy; (*confusa astrazione*) nebulous abstraction.

metafisicaménte, *av.* metaphysically.

metafisicàre, *v.i.* **1.** to metaphysicize **2.** (*speculare troppo sottilmente*) to draw over-subtle distinctions, to split hairs.

metafísico, *ag.* metaphysical ‖ *s.m.* metaphysician.

metàfora, *s.f.* (*ret.*) metaphor.

metaforeggiàre, *v.i.* to speak metaphorically, to speak in metaphors; (*usare soverchie metafore*) to indulge in metaphors.

metaforicaménte, *av.* metaphorically.

metafòrico, *ag.* metaphoric(al).

metaforizzàre, *V.* **metaforeggiàre.**

metàfrasi, *s.f.* metaphrase.

metafràste, *s.m.* (*letter.*) metaphrast.

metafràstico, *ag.* (*letter.*) metaphrastic.

metagènesi, *s.f.* (*biol.*) metagenesis.

metageometría, *s.f.* (*geom.*) metageometry.

metaldèide, *s.f.* (*chim.*) metaldehyde.

metalèssi, *s.f.* (*ret.*) metalepsis.

metàllico, *ag.* metallic; metal (*attributivo*): *lucentezza metallica,* metallic lustre; *modello —,* metal pattern; *rivestimento —,* metal plating; *suono —,* clang (o metallic sound): *dare un suono —,* to clang; *voce metallica,* metallic voice.

metallífero, *ag.* metalliferous: *miniere metallifere,* metal(liferous) mines.

metallizzàre, *v.t.* to metallize.

metallizzazióne, *s.f.* metallization: *— a spruzzo,* (*tec.*) metal spraying.

metàllo, *s.m.* **1.** metal: *— alcalino,* (*chim.*) alkali metal; *— antifrizione,* antifriction (o Babbitt) metal; *— base,* base (o parent) metal; *— bianco,* white metal; *— delta,* delta metal; *— dolce,* soft metal; *— duro,* hard metal; *— duttile,* ductile metal; *— fragile,* brittle metal; *— fuso,* molten metal; *— grezzo,* raw metal; *— ignobile,* base metal; *— in lamiere,* sheet metal; *— lavorato,* wrought metal; *— leggero,* light metal; *— malleabile,* malleable metal; *— pesante,* heavy metal; *— prezioso, nobile,* noble metal; *estrarre il — da un minerale,* to extract metal from the ore ‖ *il vil —,* filthy lucre **2.** *fig.* (*timbro*) timbre, tone: *il bel — della sua voce,* the fine timbre of his voice.

metallografía, *s.f.* metallography.

metallogràfico, *ag.* metallographic.

metallòide, *s.m.* (*min.*) metalloid.

metallòidico, *ag.* (*min.*) metalloid(al).

metalloterapía, *s.f.* (*med.*) metallotherapy.

metallurgía, *s.f.* metallurgy.

metallúrgico, *ag.* metallurgic(al): *industria metal-urgica,* metallurgical industry ‖ *s.m.* metallurgist.

metallúrgo, *s.m.* (*rar.*) metallurgist.

metameria, *s.f.* (*chim.*) metamerism.

metàmero, *s.m.* **1.** (*chim.*) metamer **2.** (*zool.*) metamere.

metamòrfico, *ag.* metamorphic.

metamorfísmo, *s.m.* (*geol.*) metamorphism.

metamorfísta, *s.m.* (*st. relig.*) metamorphist.

metamòrfosi, *s.f.* metamorphosis (*pl.* metamorphoses): *subire una completa —,* to undergo a complete change (*o* transformation).

metanífero, *ag.* methane-producing.

metàno, *s.m.* (*chim.*) methane, natural gas, marsh gas: *serie del —,* methane series.

metanodótto, *s.m.* methane pipe-line.

metaplasìa, *s.f.* (*biol.*) metaplasia.

metaplàsma, *s.m.* (*biol.*) metaplasm.

metaplàsmo, *s.m.* (*gram.*) metaplasm.

metaplàstico, *ag.* (*biol.*) metaplastic.

metapsíchica, *s.f.* (*fil.*) metapsychics.

metapsíchico, *ag.* metapsychic(al).

metàstasi, *s.f.* (*patol.*) metastasis (*pl.* metastases).

metatàrsico, *ag.* metatarsal.

metatàrso, *s.m.* (*anat.*) metatarsus.

metàtesi, *s.f.* (*gram.*) metathesis (*pl.* metatheses).

Metàuro, *no.pr.m.* (*geog.*) Metaurus.

metazòi, *s.m.pl.* (*zool.*) metazoa.

metazòico, *ag.* (*geol.*) metazoan, metazoic.

metempírico, *ag.* (*fil.*) metempiric(al).

Metèllo, *no.pr.m.* (*st. romana*) Metellus.

metempsicòsi, *s.f.* metempsychosis (*pl.* metempsychoses).

metèora, *s.f.* meteor ‖ *il suo successo passò come una —,* she had a meteor-like success.

meteòrico, *ag.* meteoric: *ferro —,* meteoric iron.

meteorísmo, *s.m.* (*med.*) meteorism.

meteoríte, *s.f.* meteorite.

meteorografía, *s.f.* meteorography.

meteorògrafo, *s.m.* meteorograph.

meteorolíto, *s.m.* meteorite, meteorolite.

meteorología, *s.f.* meteorology.

meteorològico, *ag.* meteorologic(al); weather (*attributivo*): *bollettino —,* weather-report; *carta meteorologica,* weather-map (*o* -chart); *previsioni meteorologiche,* weather-forecast; *stazione meteorologica,* weather station; *ufficio —,* weather-bureau.

meteoròlogo, *s.m.* meteorologist.

meteoroscòpio, *s.m.* meteoroscope.

metíccia, *s.f.* mestiza; half-caste, half-breed.

metíccio, *ag.* mestizo (*attributivo*); hybrid ‖ *s.m.* mestizo; half-caste, half-breed.

meticolosaménte, *av.* meticulously; (*spreg.*) fastidiously.

meticolosità, *s.f.* **1.** meticulousness; (*spreg.*) fastidiousness **2.** (*azione meticolosa*) meticulous action.

meticolóso, *ag.* meticulous; (*spreg.*) fastidious.

metíle, *s.m.* (*chim.*) methyl.

metílico, *ag.* (*chim.*) methylic; methyl (*attributivo*): *alcool —,* methyl alcohol.

metilène, *s.m.* (*chim.*) methylene.

metòdica, *s.f.* method.

metodicaménte, *av.* methodically.

metòdico, *ag.* methodical.

Metòdio, *no.pr.m.* (*st. relig.*) Methodius.

metodísmo, *s.m.* (*st. relig.*) Methodism.

metodísta, *s.c.* (*st. relig.*) Methodist.

mètodo, *s.m.* **1.** method, system: *scientifico, sperimentale,* scientific, experimental method; *mancanza di —,* lack of method; *lavorare senza —,* to work without method; *non aver —,* to lack method **2.** (*nei titoli di manuali, trattati*) tutor, method, primer: *— di pianoforte,* piano tutor (*o* method) **3.** (*bot.*) method.

metodología, *s.f.* methodology.

metodològico, *ag.* methodological.

Metóne, *no.pr.m.* (*st. astr.*) Meton.

metonimia, *s.f.* (*ret.*) metonymy.

metonímico, *ag.* (*ret.*) metonymic(al).

mètopa, *s.f.* (*arch.*) metope.

metòpico, *ag.* (*anat.*) metopic: *sutura metopica,* metopic suture.

metràggio, *s.m.* **1.** length (in metres) **2.** (*cine.*): *corto —,* short (film); *lungo —,* full-length (*o* feature) film.

metratúra, *s.f.* length (in metres).

mètrica, *s.f.* (*poes.*) prosody, metric; versification.

metricaménte, *av.* (*poes.*) metrically.

mètrico, *ag.* **1.** metric: *sistema —,* metric system **2.** (*poes.*) metric(al).

metríte, *s.f.* (*patol.*) metritis.

mètro, *s.m.* **1.** metre; (*amer.*) meter (*misura di lunghezza* = 39.37 in.): *— cubo,* cubic metre (*misura di volume* = 1.308 cu. yd.); *— quadrato,* square metre (*misura di superficie* = 1.196 sq. yd.) **2.** (*strumento per misurare*) rule; (*a scuola*) ruler: *— pieghevole,* folding rule; *— tascabile,* pocket rule **3.** (*maniera*) way, manner: *è ora che cambiamo —,* (*cambiar discorso*) it's time we changed the subject; (*mutar modo d'agire*) it's time we changed our way of doing things; *se egli va di questo —, finirà male,* if he goes on in this way, he'll come to a bad end ‖ *secondo il mio —,* according to my criterion (*o fam.* in my opinion) **4.** (*poes.*) metre; (*amer.*) meter: *— dattilico,* dactylic metre.

metrología, *s.f.* metrology.

metrònomo, *s.m.* (*mus.*) metronome.

metronòtte, *s.m.* (*guardia notturna*) night-watch.

metròpoli, *s.f.* metropolis.

metropolíta, *s.m.* (*eccl.*) metropolitan.

metropolitàna, *s.f.* **1.** underground (railway); (*a Londra*) Underground, Tube; (*amer.*) subway **2.** (*eccl.*) metropolitan church.

metropolitàno, *ag.* metropolitan: *milizie metropolitane,* national army ‖ *s.m.* **1.** (*eccl.*) metropolitan **2.** (*vigile urbano*) policeman (*pl.* policemen).

méttere, *v.t.* **1.** to put; (*collocare, disporre*) to place, to set; (*posare, deporre*) to lay (down), to put (down): *mise i libri sullo scaffale,* he set the books on the shelf; *metti la firma a questa lettera,* put your signature to this letter; *metti questa scatola sulla tavola,* put this box on the table; *mise il denaro in tasca,* he put the money in(to) his pocket; *mise tutti i suoi giocattoli davanti al suo amico,* he set all his toys in front of his friend; *— una sentinella,* to post a sentry ‖ *—,* to put to: *— a bottega,* to apprentice, *— a confronto,* to confront (*o* to compare); *— a dieta,* to put on a diet; *— a disposizione di qlcu.,* to put at s.o.'s disposal; *— a dormire una pratica,* to file away a case; *— a ferro e fuoco,* to put to fire and sword; *— a frutto,* to invest; *— a fuoco,* (*ott.*) to focus; *— agli atti,* to file away; *— a grano un campo,* to plant a field with corn (*o* to put a field under corn); *— al bando,* to ban; *— al corrente qlcu. di ql.co.,* to acquaint s.o. with (*o* to inform s.o. of) sthg.; *— alla gogna,* to pillory; *— a letto,* to bed; *— alla porta qlcu.,* to show s.o. the door (*o* to turn s.o. out); *— alla prova,* to test (*o* to put to a test); *— alla tortura,* to torture (*o* to put to torture); *— all'incanto, all'asta,* to put up for auction; *— all'indice,* to put on the Index; *— al sicuro,* to put into a safe place (*o* to preserve); *— al trotto,* to put into a trot; *— a morte,* to put to death; *— a parte qlcu. di ql.co.,* to confide sthg. to s.o.; *— a posto ql.co.,* to put sthg. in its proper place; (*aggiustare*) to repair (*o* to adjust) sthg.: *— le cose a posto, fig.* to put things right; *— a posto qlcu.,* (*trovargli lavoro*) to find a job for s.o.; (*dargli una lezione*) to put s.o. in his place: *ti metto a posto io!,* I'll fix you!; *— a profitto ql.co.,* to turn sthg. to account: *— a profitto un consiglio,* to profit by advice; *— a punto,* to get ready; (*un motore*) to tune up; *— a sacco,* to sack; *— a scuola,* to put (*o* to send) to school; *— a servizio,* to send into service (as a maid); *— a soqquadro,* to turn upside-down (*o* to turn topsy-turvy) ‖

— in, to put in(to): — *in atto*, to put into action; — *in cantiere ql.co.*, to begin work on sthg.; — *in carta*, to write down; — *in chiaro ql.co.*, to make sthg. clear; — *in commercio*, to put on the market; — *in conto ql.co. a qlcu.*, to put sthg. on s.o.'s account; — *in dubbio, in forse ql.co.*, to cast doubt on (*o* to question *o* to doubt) sthg.: *non lo metto in dubbio*, I do not doubt it (*o* I have no doubt about it); — *in fila*, to line up; — *in fuga*, to put to flight; — *ql.co. in funzione*, to put sthg. into service; — *in giro, in piazza*, to spread (*o* to broadcast); — *in grado qlcu. di fare ql.co.*, to enable s.o. to do sthg.; — *nei guai qlcu.*, to put s.o. in a hole; — *in guardia qlcu.*, to put s.o. on his guard; — *in libertà*, to set free; — *in luce, in rilievo ql.co., fig.* to emphasize (*o* to stress *o* to lay stress on) sthg.; — *in macchina, (tip.)* to print; — *ql.co. in mano di qlcu.*, to put sthg. in s.o.'s hands; — *in marcia, (mec.)* to start; — *in mente ql.co. a qlcu.*, to put sthg. into s.o.'s head; — *in moto, (mec.)* to start; — *in musica*, to set to music; — *in onda, (rad.)* to broadcast (*o* to transmit); — *in opera*, to start up (*o* to set running); — *in ordine*, to put (*o* to set) in order; — *in pericolo*, to endanger; — *in pratica*, to put into practice; — *in prigione*, to put in(to) prison (*o* to imprison); — *in salvo*, to save; — *in scena, (teat.)* to produce; — *in serbo*, to put by (*o* to lay aside); — *in tacere*, to keep secret; — *in vendita*, to put on sale; — *in vendita una casa*, to put a house up for sale; — *nel sacco*, to fool (*o* to deceive) || — *su*, to put on: — *su arie*, to put on airs; — *su casa*, to set up house; — *su ciccia, (fam.)* to put on weight; — *su la minestra, (fam.)* to put the soup on; — *su un negozio*, to set up a shop; — *su i punti, (a maglia)* to cast on stitches; — *su qlcu. contro un altro*, to set (*o* to incite) s.o. against another || — *le ali ai piedi di qlcu.*, to lend wings to s.o.'s heels || — *avanti, indietro un orologio*, to put a watch forward, back || — *il bastone tra le ruote, to* put a spoke in s.o.'s wheel || — *il carro davanti ai buoi*, to put the cart before the horse || — *con le spalle al muro, alle strette qlcu.*, to get s.o. with his back to the wall || — *cura a fare ql.co.*, to take care in doing sthg. || — *da parte*, to put (*o* to set *o* to lay) aside: *ha messo da parte molto denaro*, he has put a good bit of money aside || — *dentro, (in prigione)* to put inside || — *disaccordo tra due persone*, to set two people at variance || — *fine a ql.co.*, to put an end to sthg. || — *fuoco a ql.co.*, to set fire to sthg. (*o* to set sthg. on fire) || — *fuori combattimento qlcu., (boxe)* to knock s.o. out || — *giù il riso, (fam.)* to put the rice on || — *insieme*, to put together; *(raccogliere)* to gather (*o* to collect) || — *le mani addosso a qlcu.*, to lay hands on s.o. || — *le mani su qlcu.*, to take possession of sthg. || — *mano a ql.co.*, to have a hand in sthg.: *non credo che ci abbia messo mano*, I do not think he has had a hand in it; — *mano alla spada*, to clap one's hand to one's sword || — *la mano sul fuoco per qlcu.*, to speak for s.o. || — *il naso, il becco in ql.co.*, to stick one's nose into sthg. || — *nome a qlcu.*, to call (*o* to name) s.o.: *gli ho messo nome Giovanni*, I have called him John || — *gli occhi addosso a qlcu.*, to set eyes on s.o.: *quella ragazza gli ha messo gli occhi addosso*, that girl is setting her cap at him || — *per iscritto*, to put in writing || — *piede in un posto*, to set foot in a place || — *una pulce nell'orecchio a qlcu.*, to sow doubts in s.o.'s mind || — *i puntini sugli i*, to dot one's i's || — *sotto i piedi qlcu.*, to humiliate (*o* to trample on) s.o. || — *sotto processo*, to bring to trial; *fig.* to scrutinise || — *sul lastrico qlcu.*, to turn s.o. out into the street; *fig.* to ruin s.o. || — *sul tappeto un argomento*, to bring up a matter || — *tavola*, to lay the table || — *tempo in mezzo*, to gain time || — *la testa a partito, a posto*, to settle down **2.** *(infondere)* to inspire; *(produrre, causare)* to cause; to make: *l'idea di vederlo mi mette gioia*, the idea of seeing him makes me very happy; *questo tempo mi mette tristezza*, this weather makes

me sad; — *fame, sete*, to make (s.o.) hungry, thirsty; — *paura a qlcu.*, to scare (*o* to frighten) s.o.; — *soggezione (a qlcu.)*, to make (s.o.) uneasy; — *terrore (a qlcu.)*, to terrify (s.o.) **3.** *(emettere)* to put forth: *quel ragazzo sta mettendo i baffi*, that boy is growing a moustache; — *un dente*, to cut a tooth; — *i denti*, to teethe; — *le foglie*, to grow (*o* to put forth) leaves; — *radici*, to put down roots (anche *fig.*) **4.** *(impiegare)* to take: *quanto tempo ci hai messo a farlo?*, how long did it take you to do it? **5.** *(investire)* to put; *(scommettere, puntare)* to bet: *ho messo una sterlina su quel cavallo*, I have bet (*o* put) a pound on that horse; *misi tutti i miei soldi in un affare*, I put all my money into one piece of business **6.** *(indossare)* to put on; *(portare)* to wear **7.** *(ridurre, rendere)* to turn: — *in francese*, to translate into French; — *in versi*, to turn into verse **8.** *(far pagare)* to charge: *quanto ti hanno messo per vitto e alloggio?*, how much did they charge you for board and lodgings? **9.** *(ammettere)* to suppose: *mettiamo che abbia ragione*, (let us) suppose he is right **10.** *(paragonare)* to compare: *non vorrai — la mia casa con la tua*, you can't compare your house with mine (*o* my house with yours); *la sua è molto più bella, neanche da —, (fam.)* hers is much nicer, there's no comparison || *v.i. (sboccare)* to lead (to sthg.); *(sfociare)* to flow (into sthg.): *questo fiume mette al mare*, this river flows into the sea; *questo sentiero mette sulla strada maestra*, this lane leads to the main road || **méttersi**, *v.r.* **1.** to put oneself; to place oneself: *mi sono messo in una situazione imbarazzante*, I have got into an awkward position; *si mise vicino a sua moglie*, he placed himself near his wife; — *a sedere*, to sit down; — *a tavola*, to sit down at the table || *mettiti nei miei panni*, put yourself in my place || — *a capo di ql.co.*, to assume control of sthg. || — *a letto, (ammalarsi)* to take to one's bed || — *a proprio agio, in libertà*, to make oneself at home (*o* comfortable); — *il cuore in pace*, to set one's mind at rest || — *d'accordo su ql.co.*, to come to an agreement about (*o* to arrange) sthg. || — *in contatto con qlcu.*, to get in touch with s.o. || — *in un impiccio*, to get into trouble || — *in mente, in testa di fare ql.co.*, to take it into one's head to do sthg.: *si mise in mente che la colpa fosse mia*, he got it into his head that it was my fault; *si mise in mente una strana idea*, he got a strange idea into his head; *si mise in testa di farlo*, he took it into his head to do it || — *in mezzo*, to intervene || — *in mostra*, to make oneself conspicuous || — *in società con qlcu., (comm.)* to form a (*o* to go into) partnership with s.o. || — *in urto con qlcu.*, to fall out with s.o. || — *sotto*, to get down to it **2.** *(incominciare)* to begin, to start, to set to (sthg.): *si mise a lavorare*, he started working; *si mise al lavoro*, he set to work; *si mise a piovere*, it began to rain; — *a mangiare, (fam.)* to fall to: *si misero a mangiare di buon appetito*, they fell to with a hearty appetite; — *in cammino, in viaggio*, to set out (*o* off *o* forth) **3.** *(indossare)* to put on; *(portare)* to wear: — *un abito, il cappello, le scarpe*, to put on a dress, one's hat, one's shoes **4.** *(diventare)* to turn: *la situazione si mette male*, the situation is taking a turn for the worse; *il tempo si mette al bello*, the weather turned out fine; — *in sospetto*, to become suspicious.

mettifòglio, *s.m. (tip.)* feeder: — *automatico*, automatic feeder.

mettimàle, *s.m.* mischief-maker.

mettiscàndali, *s.m.* scandal-monger.

mèzza, *s.f.* half-hour: *è la —*, it is half past twelve; *una pendola che suona le mezze*, a clock that strikes the half-hours.

mezzadría, *s.f.* métayage; *(amer.)* share-cropping.

mezzàdro, *s.m.* métayer; *(amer.)* share-cropper.

mezzafèsta, *s.f.* half-holiday.

mezzalàna, *s.f.* **1.** *(tessuto)* mixed wool and cotton cloth; linsey-woolsey **2.** *(persona sospetta)* shady person.

mezzalúna, *s.f.* **1.** half-moon, crescent **2.** *(emblema* *dell'Islamismo*) crescent **3**. (*cuc*.) mincing-knife **4**. (*mil*.) (*fortificazione*) ravelin, demilune.

mezzàna, *s.f.* **1**. (*mar*.) mizzen sail: *albero di —*, mizzen (*o* mizzen-mast) **2**. (*mus*.) middle string **3**. (*ruffiana*) procuress **4**. (*sartoria*) seamstress.

mezzanaménte, *av.* (*mediocremente*) indifferently, poorly.

mezzaníno, *s.m.* (*arch*.) entresol, mezzanine (floor).

mezzàno, *ag.* middle, middling; medium (*attributivo*): *statura mezzana*, medium size (*o* height) || *s.m.* **1**. (*mediatore*) mediator, go-between **2**. (*ruffiano*) pimp.

mezzanòtte, *s.f.* **1**. midnight: *verso —*, towards midnight **2**. (*Nord*) North: *esposto a —*, facing North.

mezzatínta, *s.f.* half-tone, half-tint.

mezzétta, *s.f.* half-litre (pot).

mezzína, *s.f.* (*di rame*) copper jug; (*di terracotta*) earthen jug.

mézzo[1], *ag.* **1**. (*di frutta, marcio*) rotten: *pera mezza*, rotten pear **2**. (*rar*.) (*bagnato fradicio*) soaked, drenched || *s.m.* (*la parte marcia*) rot, rotten part.

mèzzo[2], *ag.* **1**. half: *mezza bottiglia di vino*, half a bottle of wine; *mezza dozzina di volte*, half a dozen times; *mezza lunghezza*, half-length; *mezz'ora al giorno*, half an hour a day; *questa mezz'ora prima di colazione*, the half-hour before lunch; *dammi tre mezze corone*, give me three half-crowns; *è lontano un — chilometro*, it is (about) half a kilometre away; *ho letto — libro*, I have read half the book; *lavorare a mezza giornata*, to work half-time (*o* to be on half -time*) || *— e —*, so-so: « *Come ti senti?* », « *Mezzo e —* », " How do you feel? ", " So-so " (*o* " Not so good ") || *mezzi guanti*, mittens || — *lutto*, half-mourning || *mezze misure*, half-measures || *mezza pelle*, (*legatura di libro*) half-binding || *mezza Quaresima*, Mid-Lent || — *sangue*, (*meticcio*) half-breed || *mezze suole*, half-soles || *a mezza bocca*, half-heartedly: *un invito a mezza bocca*, a half -hearted invitation || *a mezza voce*, in a low voice || *notte di mezza estate*, Midsummer Night || *bastò mezza parola perchè capisse*, a word was enough to make him understand || *c'era — mondo*, half the world was there (*o* the world and his wife were there) **2**. (*indicante approssimazione*) half: *mezza idea*, half an idea; *mezza intenzione*, half a mind; *mezza sconfitta*, half -defeat; — *trionfo*, half-victory; *una mezza verità*, a half-truth || *mal comune — gaudio*, prov. company in distress makes sorrow less **3**. (*medio*) middle; medium (*attributivo*): *mezza altezza*, middle (*o* medium) height; *mezza età*, middle age: *una persona di mezza età*, a middle -aged person; *mezza statura*, middle (*o* medium) size (*o* height) || *s.m.* **1**. (*metà*) half (*pl.* halves): *due mezzi fanno un intero*, two halves make a whole; *aveva due anni e —*, he was two and a half (years old); *bevvero due litri e — di vino*, they drank two and a half litres of wine; *sono le tre e —*, it is half past three || *a — del viaggio*, half -way through the journey; *fare le cose a —*, to do things by halves; *lasciare a — un lavoro*, to leave a piece of work half-finished || *per conoscere un furbo ci vuole un furbo e —*, prov. set a thief to catch a thief **2**. (*centro, punto mediano*) middle, centre: *il — della stanza*, the middle (*o* centre) of the room; *nel — della notte*, in the middle of the night (*o* at dead of night); *nel bel — del giardino*, in the very middle of the garden; *occupava il posto di —*, he was in the middle; *tenere il — della strada*, to keep the middle of the road || *il giusto —*, the golden (*o* happy) mean: *tenere il giusto —*, to keep the golden mean || *in quel —*, (*in quel momento*) at that moment; (*nel frattempo*) meanwhile (*o* in the meantime)|| *via di —*, middle course: *tenere una via di —*, to steer a middle course || *andare di —*, to foot the bill || *mettere tempo in —*, to lose time || *mettersi di —*, to interfere (*o* to intervene): *voleva mettersi di — per rappacificarli*, he wanted to intervene and make peace between them || *av.* **1**. (*a metà*) half: — *aperto*, half-open; *film — tragico, — comico*, tragi-comic film; *le tende erano — abbassate*, the

curtains were half-drawn **2**. (*quasi*) half: — *cieco*, half-blind; — *matto*, half-mad; — *maturo*, half-ripe; — *morto*, half-dead; — *rotto*, half-broken; *gli ho — detto quello che era successo*, I all but told him what had happened; *siamo — parenti*, we are practically relatives || *peccato confessato è — perdonato*, prov. confession is half-way to forgiveness || **in mèzzo a**, *prep.* in the middle of; (*letter*.) in the midst of; (*fra molti*) among; (*fra due*) between: *in — alla folla*, among the crowd; *in — alla foresta*, in the middle (*o* in the depths) of the forest; *in — alle gioie, ai dolori*, in the midst of joy, sorrow; *in — all'oscurità*, in the darkness; *in — a noi, a noi due*, among us, between us; *uno in — a tanti*, one among many.

mèzzo[3], *s.m.* **1**. (*strumento, espediente per raggiungere un fine*) means: — *da sbarco*, (*mil*.) landing-craft; *mezzi di trasporto*, means of transport; *mezzi leciti, illeciti*, legal, illegal means; *con mezzi disonesti*, by foul means; *questo era l'unico — per raggiungerlo*, this was the only way (*o* means) of reaching him; *il telefono è un rapido — di comunicazione*, the telephone is a rapid means of communication; *ricorrere ai mezzi legali*, to take legal steps (*o* to go to law) || *a — posta aerea*, by air-mail || *per — di*, by (*o* by means of); (*attraverso*) through: *lo ebbi per — di un mio amico*, I got it through a friend of mine; *mi fu consegnato per — di un fattorino*, it was delivered to me by messenger; *noi scriviamo per — della penna*, we write by means of a pen || *il fine giustifica i mezzi*, the end justifies the means || *non c'è — di saperlo*, there is no way of knowing **2**. (*fis*.) medium: *l'elettricità si propaga più o meno rapidamente secondo il —*, electricity travels more or less quickly according to the conductor; *i raggi di luce si rifrangono passando da un — a un altro*, rays of light are refracted when they pass from one medium to another **3**. *pl.* (*denaro*) means, money: *una persona con mezzi*, a person of means; *egli ha molti mezzi*, he is well off; *vivere al di sopra dei propri mezzi*, to live beyond one's means.

mezzobústo, *s.m.* (*scult*.) bust.

mezzocérchio, *s.m.* **1**. (*geom*.) semicircle **2**. (*scherma*) half-circle parry.

mezzodí, *s.m.* midday; noon: *a —*, at noon.

mezzofondísta, *s.c.* (*spor*.) middle-distance runner.

mezzofóndo, *s.m.* (*spor*.) middle-distance race.

mezzogiórno, *s.m.* **1**. midday; noon **2**. (*Sud*) South: *il — d'Italia*, the South of Italy; *stanza posta, esposta a —*, room facing (*o* looking) South.

mezzomarináro, *s.m.* (*mar*.) boat-hook.

mezzómbra, *s.f.* (*pitt*.) half-tone, half-shadow.

mezzorilièvo, *s.m.* (*scult*.) half-relief.

mezzosopràno, *s.m.* (*mus*.) mezzo-soprano.

mezzotérmine, *s.m.* expedient; compromise.

mezzúccio, *s.m.* mean trick, poor trick.

mi[1], *pron. pers. m.f. 1ª persona sing.* **1**. *oggetto* me: *lasciami andare*, let me go; *non — lasciò partire*, he didn't let me go; *perchè non — porti con te?*, why don't you take me with you? **2**. *obliquo* me, to me: — *parlava sempre dei suoi progetti*, he always talked to me about his plans; — *presentò suo fratello*, he introduced his brother to me; *dammi quel libro*, give me that book **3**. (*gener. coi verbi riflessivi*) myself (*talvolta omesso*): — *dissi: perchè dovrei lamentarmi?*, I said to myself: why should I complain?; — *guardai intorno*, I looked around; — *sono comperato un libro*, I have bought myself a book; — *sono tagliato nell'aprire quella scatola*, I've cut myself opening that tin; — *trovavo male là*, I never felt at home there; *non — divertivo molto in quella città*, I didn't enjoy myself very much in that town.

mi[2], *s.m.* (*mus*.) E, mi: *chiave in — bemolle*, key of E flat.

miagolaménto, *s.m.* mewing, mew, miaowing.

miagolàre, *v.i.* **1**. to mew, to miaow; to caterwaul **2**. (*scherz*.) (*cantar male*) to caterwaul **3**. (*lamen-*

tarsi) to whine **4.** (*vagire*) to squall, to mewl **5.** (*rar.*) (*di palle di fucile, fischiare*) to whine.

miagolàta, *s.f.* mew, miaow.

miagolío, *s.m.* mewing; caterwauling.

miào, (*voce onomatopeica riproducente un miagolio*) miaow: *fare* —, to mew (*o* to miaow).

miàsma, *s.m.* miasma (*pl.* miasmata, miasmas).

miasmàtico, *ag.* miasmatic.

míca[1], *s.f.* crumb; (*granellino*) grain.

míca[1], *av.* (*fam.*): — *che ci creda,* not that I believe it; *non ... —,* not (at all): *non ci sono — stato,* I have never been there.

míca[2], *s.f.* (*min.*) mica.

micàceo, *ag.* (*min.*) micaceous.

micàdo, *s.m.* mikado (*pl.* mikados).

micaníte, *s.f.* (*elett.*) micanite.

micaschísto, micascísto, *s.m.* (*geol.*) mica-schist.

míccia, *s.f.* fuse; (*a rapida combustione*) quick-match.

miccíno, *s.m.* crumb (anche *fig.*) || *a* —, sparingly.

míccio, *s.m.* ass, donkey (anche *fig.*).

míceo, *s.m.* **1.** (*zool.*) mico **2.** *fig.* (*uomo lussurioso*) debauchee **3.** *fig.* (*sciocco*) simpleton, fool.

micèlio, *s.m.* (*bot.*) mycelium (*pl.* mycelia).

Micène, *no.pr.f.* (*geog. st.*) Mycenae.

micenèo, micènnico, *ag.* Mycenaean.

Michèa, *no.pr.m.* (*Bibbia*) Micah, Micheas.

michelàccio, *s.m.* loafer, lounger, idler: *fare la vita di* —, to idle away one's time.

Michelàngelo, *no.pr.m.* (*st. art.*) Michelangelo.

michelangiolésco, *ag.* (*scult. pitt.*) Mich(a)elange-lesque; of Mich(a)elangelo; in Mich(a)elangelo's style.

Michèle, *no.pr.m.* Michael || *dim.* Mike, Micky.

michétta, *s.f.* roll.

mícia, *s.f.* she-cat.

micidiàle, *ag.* lethal; deadly, murderous (anche *fig.*): *clima* —, deadly (*o* murderous) climate; *un colpo* —, a murderous blow; *un veleno* —, a deadly poison.

micíno, *s.m.* kitten, pussy.

mício[1], *s.m.* tom-cat; (*fam.*) pussy(-cat).

mício[2], *s.m.* (*min.*) steatite, soap-stone, lard stone.

micòsi, *s.f.* (*patol.*) mycosis.

microanàlisi, *s.f.* (*chim.*) microanalysis.

microbicída, *ag.* microbicidal || *s.m.* microbicide.

micròbio, *s.m.* microbe.

microbiología, *s.f.* microbiology.

microbiòlogo, *s.m.* microbiologist.

mícrobo, *s.m.* microbe.

microcefalía, *s.f.* (*patol.*) microcephaly.

microcèfalo, *ag.* microcephalous, microcephalic || *s.m.* **1.** microcephal (*pl.* microcephali) **2.** *fig.* (*stupido*) idiot.

microchímica, *s.f.* microchemistry.

microcíto, *s.m.* (*biol.*) microcyte.

microclíno, *s.m.* (*min.*) microcline.

micrococco, *s.m.* (*biol.*) micrococcus (*pl.* micrococci).

microcòsmico, *ag.* microcosmic.

microcòsmo, *s.m.* microcosm.

microcosmografía, *s.f.* microcosmography.

microcristallíno, *ag.* (*min.*) microcrystalline.

microcristallografía, *s.f.* microcrystallography.

microfàrad, *s.m.* (*elett.*) microfarad.

microfílm, *s.m.* microfilm.

microfísica, *s.f.* microphysics.

microfònico, *ag.* microphonic.

micròfono, *s.m.* microphone; (*abbr. fam.* mike): — *a condensatore,* (*rad.*) condenser microphone; — *a nastro,* (*rad.*) ribbon microphone; — *ricevitore,* (*tel.*) receiver.

microfotografía, *s.f.* **1.** microphotography **2.** (*riproduzione microfotografica*) microphotograph.

micrografía, *s.f.* micrography.

microgràfico, *ag.* micrographic.

micrògrafo, *s.m.* **1.** (*esperto in micrografia*) micrographer **2.** (*apparecchio micrografico*) micrograph.

microgràmmo, *s.m.* microgram (*misura di peso* = 0.0000154 gr.).

microlepidòtteri, *s.m.pl.* (*entom.*) Microlepidoptera.

microlítico, *ag.* (*archeol.*) microlithic.

microlíto, *s.m.* (*med.*) microlith.

microlítro, *s.m.* microlitre; (*amer.*) microliter (*misura di capacità* = 0.000061 cu. in.).

micrología, *s.f.* micrology.

micrològico, *ag.* micrological.

micròlogo, *s.m.* micrologist.

micromeccànica, *s.f.* micromechanics.

micrometallografía, *s.f.* micrometallography.

micrometría, *s.f.* micrometry.

micromètrico, *ag.* micrometric(al).

micròmetro, *s.m.* micrometer; (*di orologiaio*) micrometer gauge, micrometer caliper: — *oculare,* (*fis.*) eyepiece micrometer; — *per profondità,* micrometer depth-gauge.

micromotóre, *s.m.* **1.** small motor **2.** (*piccola motocicletta*) (motor-) scooter.

mícron, *s.m.* micron, mikron (*misura di lunghezza* = 0.000039 in.).

microónda, *s.f.* (*fis.*) microwave.

micròpilo, *s.m.* (*biol.*) micropyle.

micropiròmetro, *s.m.* (*fis.*) micropyrometer.

micropsía, *s.f.* (*patol.*) micropsia.

microrganísmo, *s.m.* micro-organism.

microscopía, *s.f.* microscopy.

microscòpico, *ag.* **1.** microscopic(al) **2.** *fig.* (*piccolissimo*) microscopic(al), minute, tiny.

microscòpio, *s.m.* microscope: *visibile al* —, visible under a microscope.

microscopísta, *s.c.* microscopist.

microsólco, *s.m.* long-playing (record), microgroove.

micròtomo, *s.m.* microtome.

microzòo, *s.m.* (*zool.*) microzoon.

Mída, *no.pr.m.* (*mit.*) Midas.

midinette, *s.f.* midinette.

midòlla, *s.f.* **1.** (*mollica*) crumb **2.** (*di frutto*) pulp **3.** (*rar.*) per **midóllo.**

midollàre, *ag.* medullar, medullary.

midóllo, *s.m.* **1.** (*anat.*) marrow; medulla (*pl.* medullae): — *osseo,* medulla ossium; — *spinale,* spinal cord (*o* medulla spinalis) || *bagnato fino al* —, wet through (*o* soaked to the skin) || *non ha* —, he is spineless || *quell'uomo è inglese fino al* —, that man is English to the back-bone **2.** (*del legno*) pith **3.** (*parte essenziale*) medulla (*pl.* medullas); pith and marrow.

midollóne, *ag.* sluggish || *s.m.* (*persona lenta*) slowcoach; (*persona pigra*) lazy-bones.

mièle, *s.m.* honey; — *selvatico,* wild honey; — *vergine,* virgin (*o* white) honey; *le sue parole erano dolci come il* —, she was honey-tongued; *addolcire con un cucchiaio di* —, to sweeten with a tablespoonful of honey || *latte e* —, whipped sweetened cream || *luna di* —, honeymoon || *è tutta* —, she is all honey || *non si può avere il* — *senza le pecchie, prov.* life is not all honey.

mielína, *s.f.* (*anat.*) myelin.

mielínico, *ag.* (*anat.*) myelinic.

mielíte, *s.f.* (*patol.*) myelitis.

mielòsi, *s.f.* (*patol.*) myelosis.

miètere, *v.t.* **1.** to reap: — *un campo, il grano,* to reap a field, the corn || — *il campo altrui, fig.* to reap where one has not sown || *si miete quel che si semina, prov.* we reap as we sow **2.** *fig.* to mow; (*raccogliere*) to reap: *egli fu mietuto nel fiore degli anni,* he was cut off in the prime of life; *la mitragliatrice ha mietuto molte vittime,* the machine gun has mown down many victims; — *allori,* to win (*o* to reap) laurels.

mietitóre, *s.m.* reaper.

mietitríce, *s.f.* **1.** reaper **2.** (*mec. agr.*) reaper, reaping-machine, harvester: — *legatrice,* binder; — *trebbiatrice,* combine harvester.

mietitúra, *s.f.* **1.** (*il mietere*) reaping **2.** (*il tempo in cui si miete*) reaping time, harvest (time) **3.** (*il raccolto*) harvest: *festa della* —, harvest festival.

migliàccio, *s.m.* (*cuc.*) black-pudding, blood-pudding.
migliàio, *s.m.* (about a) thousand: *migliaia di persone,* thousands of persons; *un — di uomini,* about a thousand men; *a migliaia,* by (*o* in) thousands (*o* by the thousand): *morirono a migliaia,* they died in thousands; *centinaia di migliaia,* hundreds of thousands; *di — in —,* thousand upon thousand.
migliarìno, *s.m.* **1.** (*miglio duro*) hard millet **2.** (*ornit.*) (*zigolo*) chaffinch; (*passero di palude*) red bunting **3.** *pl.* (*dial.*) (*pallini da schioppo*) shot.
migliaruòla, *s.f.* (*pallini da schioppo*) shot.
mìglio[1], *s.m.* **1.** mile (*misura di lunghezza* = km. 1,6093): *— geografico,* geographical mile; *— marittimo,* nautical mile (*misura di lunghezza* = m. 1853,2); *— quadrato,* square mile (*misura di superficie* = km^2 2,5885); *un viaggio di 50 miglia,* a fifty-mile journey; *abita a mezzo — da qui,* he lives half a mile from here; *per miglia e miglia non vedrete che alberi,* for miles and miles you'll see nothing but trees; *si sentiva il rumore ad un — di distanza,* the noise could be heard a mile away ‖ *— da montanari,* (*scherz.*) countryman's mile ‖ *lontano mille miglia,* miles away: *era lontano mille miglia dall'immaginare che...,* he was far from imagining that...; *siamo lontani mille miglia,* we are poles apart ‖ *la Mille Miglia,* (*gara automobilistica*) the Mille Miglia **2.** (*pietra miliare*) milestone.
mìglio[2], *s.m.* (*bot.*) millet: *grano di —,* millet(-seed).
miglioraménto, *s.m.* improvement; amelioration: *— di stipendio,* improvement in pay; *la casa e il podere hanno proprio bisogno di qualche —,* the house and the farm really need some improvements; *il papà ieri sera ha avuto un — improvviso,* last night father's conditions improved suddenly; *la situazione politica non mostra segno di —,* the political situation does not show any signs of getting better; *portare un —,* to carry out an improvement.
miglioràre, *v.t.* to better, to improve, to ameliorate, to mend: *devi — la tua conoscenza dell'inglese,* you must improve your knowledge of English; *— le condizioni dei lavoratori,* to better the conditions of the workers; *— la propria condizione,* to better oneself; *— lo stile,* to better (*o* to improve) one's style ‖ *v.i.* to improve, to get better: *le nostre relazioni con quel paese sono molto migliorate ultimamente,* our relations with that country have much improved lately; *il nostro malato migliora lentamente,* our patient is slowly recovering; *se il tempo non migliora, non parto,* I am not going to leave unless the weather improves; *le sue maniere sono molto migliorate,* her manners have improved a lot; *il tuo inglese sta migliorando,* your English is improving; *il vino migliora con gli anni,* wine improves with age; *— con l'uso,* to improve with use; *— di salute,* to improve in health; *— negli studi,* to make progress in one's studies ‖ **miglioràrsi,** *v.r.* to improve (oneself).
miglioratìvo, *ag.* curative, remedial.
miglióre, *ag.* **1.** *comp.* **better:** *un avvenire —,* a better future; *giorni migliori,* better days: *hanno visto giorni migliori,* they have seen better days; *molto —,* much better; *le cose stanno prendendo una piega —,* things are taking a turn for the better; *è buono, ma potrebbe essere —,* it is good, but it could be better; *è un uomo — di te,* he is a better man than you; *fu reso — dalle sue tristi esperienze,* his bitter experiences made a better man of him; *non è — di suo fratello,* he is no better than his brother; *pensarono di rimandare ogni decisione a tempo —,* they thought of putting off their decision until a more convenient time (*o* moment); *questo libro è — di quello,* this book is better than that one; *diventare —,* to get better; *rendere — ql.co.,* to improve sthg. (*o* to make sthg. better) ‖ *passare a miglior vita,* to go to a better place **2.** *superl. rel.* **the best:** *il miglior modo di fare ql.co.,* the best way of doing sthg.; *il mio — amico,* my best friend; *alla fine dell'anno il professore radunò*

gli scolari e premiò il —, at the end of the year the teacher assembled his pupils and gave the best one a prize; *è il miglior uomo del mondo,* he is the best of men (*o* he is wonderful *o* fam. he is one of the best); *era la cosa — da farsi,* it was the best thing to do; *quello scolaro è il — della classe,* that pupil is the best in the class; *questa è senz'altro la cosa — che tu possa trovare,* this is the very best you can find; *siamo i migliori amici del mondo,* we are the best of friends; *fare ql.co. nel — dei modi, nel modo —,* to do sthg. in the best (possible) way ‖ *s.m.* **1.** (*la cosa migliore*) **the best (thing):** *questo parve il — che egli potesse fare,* that seemed the best thing (that) he could do **2.** (*la persona migliore*) **the best:** *i migliori muoiono giovani,* the best die young.
migliorazióne, *s.f.* improvement, betterment.
migliorìa, *s.f.* **1.** improvement: *migliorie a uno stabile,* building improvements ‖ *contributo di —,* (*dir.*) tax on improved real estate value **2.** (*bonifica*) reclamation.
mignàtta, *s.f.* (*zool.*) leech (anche *fig.*).
mignattàio, *s.m.,* **mignattàia,** *s.f.* **1.** (*chi va in cerca di mignatte*) leech-gatherer **2.** (*chi vende mignatte*) leech-seller.
mìgnola, *s.f.* (*bot.*) (*bocciuolo dell'ulivo*) olive-blossom.
mignolàre, *v.i.* (*bot.*) to blossom.
mignolatùra, *s.f.* **1.** (*fioritura degli ulivi*) blossoming **2.** (*tempo di fioritura degli ulivi*) blossom time.
mìgnolo, *ag.*: *dito —,* little finger; (*del piede*) little toe ‖ *s.m.* **1.** little finger; (*del piede*) little toe **2.** (*bot.*) olive-blossom.
migràre, *v.i.* **1.** to migrate **2.** (*morire*) to pass away.
migratóre, *ag.* migrant, migratory: *uccelli migratori,* migratory birds ‖ *s.m.,* **migratrìce,** *s.f.* migrant.
migratòrio, *ag.* migratory.
migrazióne, *s.f.* migration.
milanése, *ag.* Milanese ‖ *s.c.* Milanese (*invariato al pl.*).
Milàno, *no.pr.f.* (*geog.*) Milan.
Milèto, *no.pr.f.* (*geog. st.*) Miletus.
miliardàrio, *s.m.,* **miliardària,** *s.f.* multi-millionaire; (*amer.*) billionaire: *alla morte di suo padre, si trovò —,* when his father died, he found he was worth millions.
miliàrdo, *s.m.* one thousand millions, milliard; (*amer.*) billion: *un — di lire,* a thousand million lire; *vale un —,* it is worth a thousand millions.
miliàre[1], *ag.*: *pietra —,* milestone (anche *fig.*).
miliàre[2], *ag.* (*patol.*) miliary: *ascesso —,* miliary abscess; *febbre —,* miliary fever (*o* miliaria); *tubercolo —,* miliary tubercle ‖ *s.f.* (*patol.*) miliaria, miliary fever.
miliàrico, *ag.* (*patol.*) miliary.
milionària, *s.f.* millionairess.
milionàrio, *s.m.* millionaire.
milióne, *s.m.* **1.** million: *milioni di abitanti,* millions of inhabitants; *due milioni di abitanti,* two million inhabitants; *è ricco a milioni,* he is worth millions ‖ *non ci starei neanche se mi regalassero un —,* I wouldn't stay there for a million pounds **2.** (*mucchio, gran quantità*) lot, heap: *un — di frottole,* a pack of lies; *un — di volte,* a thousand (*o* heaps of) times.
milionèsimo, *ag.num.ord.* millionth ‖ *s.m.* millionth, the millionth part.
militànte, *ag.* militant: *la Chiesa —,* the Church Militant; *partito —,* militant (*o* active) party; *politica —,* policy of action.
militàre, *ag.* military: *addetto —,* military attaché; *arte —,* the art of war; *aspetto —,* soldierly appearance; *cappellano —,* military chaplain; *divisa —,* military uniform; *educazione —,* military education; *saluto —,* salute; *spirito —,* soldierly spirit; *strada —,* military road; *tribunale —,* military court; *nonostante tutto gli piace la vita —,* in spite of everything he likes soldiering (*o* army-life) ‖ *alla —,* in a soldierly way ‖ *s.m.* soldier: *borghesi e militari,* civilians and soldiers; *è — di carriera,* he is a regular soldier.

militàre, *v.i.* **1.** (*fare il soldato*) to be a soldier; to soldier, to serve in the army: *aveva militato con Garibaldi*, he had served with Garibaldi **2.** (*lavorare a favore di qlcu.*) to militate; to support (sthg.): *militava nelle schiere monarchiche*, he supported the Royalist cause; *ci sono molti motivi che militano a mio favore*, there are a great many points in my favour.

militarésco, *ag.* soldierlike, soldierly; (*marziale*) martial, military: *aspetto* —, soldierly appearance; *portamento* —, military bearing.

militarísmo, *s.m.* militarism.

militarísta, *s.m.* militarist.

militarizzàre, *v.t.* **1.** to militarize: *i tedeschi militarizzarono la zona renana*, the Germans militarized the Rhineland **2.** (*mobilitare*) to mobilize: *militarizzarono i ferrovieri*, the railwaymen were mobilized.

militarizzazióne, *s.f.* **1.** militarization **2.** (*mobilitazione*) mobilization.

militarménte, *av.* militarily: *salutarono* — *l'ufficiale*, they saluted the officer.

mílite, *s.m.* **1.** militiaman (*pl.* militiamen); soldier: — *dei Carabinieri*, Carabinieri private || *il Milite Ignoto*, the Unknown Soldier (o Warrior) **2.** *fig.* supporter; soldier: — *di Cristo nel lontano oriente*, missionary in the Far East.

milízia, *s.f.* **1.** (*professione delle armi*) soldiering: *abbandonare la* —, to leave the Army; *darsi alla* —, to join (o to enter) the Army; *esercitare la* —, to serve in the Army (o to soldier) **2.** (*esercito*) Army; troops (*pl.*): *milizie mercenarie*, mercenary troops; *milizie regolari*, Regular (o Standing) Army; — *territoriale*, Territorial Army; *milizie volontarie*, voluntary troops; *grande soldato, egli fu onore e vanto della nostra* —, he was a great soldier and added new lustre to our Army || *la* — *celeste*, the Heavenly Host || *la* — *di Dio*, the Army of the Lord.

miliziàno, *s.m.* militiaman (*pl.* militiamen).

millànta, *ag.num.card.*(*pop. scherz.*)(*mille*) thousand || *s.m.* thousands (*pl.*); a great number.

millantaménto, *s.m.* bragging, boasting.

millantàre, *v.t.* to boast of (sthg.), to boast about (sthg.); to brag of (sthg.), to brag about (sthg.); to vaunt: *non fa che* — *la sua casa*, he is always boasting about his house; — *le proprie prodezze, ricchezze*, to boast about (o of) one's exploits, wealth || **millantàrsi**, *v.r.* to boast, to brag: *non mi piace perchè si millanta troppo*, I don't like him because he boasts (o brags) too much; *si millantava invincibile*, he boasted that he was unconquerable.

millantàto, *ag.* (much-)vaunted || — *credito*, (*dir.*) false pretences.

millantatóre, *s.m.*, **millantatríce**, *s.f.* braggart.

millantería, *s.f.* boasting, bragging: *è pura* —, it's sheer bragging.

mílle, *ag.num.card.* (a) thousand, (one) thousand: — *baci*, lots of kisses; —, *duemila sterline*, a (o one) thousand, two thousand pounds; — *e cento persone*, one thousand one hundred people; *i* — *fastidi della vita*, the thousand and one small worries of life; — *grazie*, a thousand thanks (o thanks a lot); — *volte no!*, a thousand times no!; *avete* — *ragioni*, you are absolutely right; *ho* — *preoccupazioni per mia figlia*, I am worried to death about my daughter; *le dissi* — *volte di non farlo*, I told her a thousand times not to do it; *mi par mill'anni che non lo vedo*, it seems ages since I saw him; *ti mando* — *auguri*, I send you my very best wishes || — *e* — *volte bello*, indescribably beautiful || *corpo di* — *diavoli!*, Hell's bells! || *si fece di* — *colori*, he went as red as a beetroot || « *Le* — *e una notte* », (*lett.*) " The Arabian Nights " (o " The Thousand and One Night "): *questa è una cosa da* — *e una notte*, this is like something out of the Arabian Nights || *s.m.* a thousand, one thousand: *ce n'era più di* —, there were more than a thousand of them; *come lui ce n'è uno su* —, he is one in a thou-

sand || *a* — *a* —, by the thousand: *le stelle che splendono in cielo a* — *a* —, the stars twinkling in the sky by the thousand (o in their thousands) || *te la dò in* —, I bet my life you can't guess it || *il Mille*, the year one thousand || *i Mille*, (*st. italiana*) Garibaldi's Thousand.

millefòglie, *s.m.* (*bot.*) milfoil, yarrow.

millenàrio, *ag.* millenary, millenarian, millennial; *fig.* age-old, ancient || *s.m.* **1.** (*millesimo anniversario*) millenary **2.** (*st. relig.*) millenarian.

millenarísmo, *s.m.* (*st. relig.*) millenarianism, millenarism.

millènne, *ag.* (*rar.*) millennial, millenary.

millènnio, *s.m.* millennium (*pl.* millenniums, millennia); millenary.

millepièdi, *s.m.* (*entom.*) millepede, millipede.

millèsimo, *ag.num.ord.* thousandth: *la millesima parte*, the thousandth (o millesimal) part; *lo ripeterò per la millesima volta*, *fig.* I'll repeat it for the thousandth time || *s.m.* **1.** thousandth, millesimal **2.** (*millennio*) millennium (*pl.* millenniums, millennia); millenary: *un* — *prima di Cristo*, a thousand years before Christ **3.** (*data*) date: *manca il* — *su questa moneta*, there is no date on this coin.

millibàr, *s.m.* (*meteorologia*) millibar.

milligràmma, milligràmmo, *s.m.* milligram(me) (*misura di peso* = 0.015 gr.).

millílitro, *s.m.* millilitre; (*amer.*) milliliter (*misura di capacità* = 0.061 cu. in.).

millímetro, *s.m.* millimetre; (*amer.*) millimeter (*misura di lunghezza* = 0.039 in.).

Mílo, *no.pr.f.* (*geog.*) Melos, Milo || *la Venere di* —, the Venus de (o of) Milo.

milodónte, *s.m.* (*paleont.*) mylodon.

miloioidèo, *s.m.* (*anat.*) mylohyoid.

Milóne, *no.pr.m.* (*st.*) Milo.

milòrd(e), milòrdo, *s.m.* lord, milor(d): *vivere come un* —, to live like a lord.

mílza, *s.f.* (*anat.*) spleen, milt.

milzadèlla, *s.f.* (*bot.*) spotted nettle.

Milzíade, *no.pr.m.* (*st.*) Miltiades.

míma, *s.f.* (*teat.*) mime, mimer, pantomimist.

mimàre, *v.t.i.* (*teat.*) to mime.

mimésco, *ag.* (*spreg.*) mimicking: *gesto* —, mimicking gesture; *leziosità mimesca*, studied affectation.

mimèsi, *s.f.* **1.** (*fil.*) mimesis **2.** (*imitazione di voce, gesti, ecc.*) mimicry.

mimètico, *ag.* **1.** (*imitativo*) mimetic(al); mimic: *arte mimetica*, mimetic art **2.** (*di mimetismo*) mimetic: *colorazione mimetica*, (*di animali*) mimetic coloration.

mimetísmo, *s.m.* **1.** (*di animali*) mimicry **2.** (*mil.*) camouflage.

mimetizzàre, *v.t.* to camouflage || **mimetizzàrsi**, *v.r.* to camouflage.

mimiàmbo, *s.m.* (*lett.*) mimiambi (*pl.*).

mímica, *s.f.* **1.** (*teat.*) mimic art, miming **2.** (*il gesticolare parlando*) gesticulation.

mimicaménte, *av.* mimically.

mímico, *ag.* **1.** (*teat.*) miming: *l'arte mimica*, the art of mime **2.** (*di atti e gesti*) mimic: *linguaggio* —, sign language (o dumb-show).

mímma, *s.f.*, **mímmo**, *s.m.* (*pop.*) child (*pl.* children).

mímo, *s.m.* **1.** (*teat.*) (*attore*) mime, mimer; (*dramma*) mime **2.** (*ornit.*) mocking-bird.

mimògrafo, *s.m.* mimographer.

mimósa, *s.f.* (*bot.*) mimosa.

mína[1], *s.f.* (*st.*) **1.** mina (*pl.* minae, minas) (*misura di peso greca* = g. 430) **2.** (*moneta greca*) mina (*pl.* minae, minas).

mína[2], *s.f.* **1.** (*cavità riempita di esplosivo*) mine || *sventure la* —, *fig.* to avoid a danger **2.** (*apparecchio esplosivo*) mine: — *a contatto*, contact-mine; — *acustica*, (*mar.*) acoustic-mine; — *anticarro*, anti-tank mine; — *di fondo*, (*mar.*) ground-mine; — *galleggiante* (*mar.*) floating mine; — *mancata*, (*miner.*) misfire; — *sottomarina*, (*mar.*) submarine (o torpedo-)mine; — *terrestre*, land-mine; — *vagante*, (*mar.*) drifting mine; *miccia della —*, fuse of the mine; *dragare una —*, to sweep a mine; *far brillare una —*, to explode a mine; (*sotto la posizione del nemico*) to spring a mine 3. (*anima della matita*) lead 4. (*miniera*) mine.

minàccia, *s.f.* threat, menace: *silenzio gravido di minacce*, ominous silence; *vane minacce*, empty threats; *i buoni insegnanti usano raramente promesse o minacce*, good teachers seldom use promises or threats; *c'è una — di pioggia*, there is a threat of rain in the sky (o it looks like rain); *è una — per la pace del mondo*, it is a menace to world peace; *proferire minacce*, to utter threats.

minacciàre, *v.t.* to threaten, to menace: *il cielo minaccia temporale*, the sky threatens a storm; *i miei progetti sono minacciati*, my plans are menaced with ruin; *minacciava di lasciarci*, he threatened to leave us; *minacciarono vendetta*, they threatened revenge; *minacciò di uccidermi*, he threatened to kill me; — *guerra*, to menace war; — *la pace*, to menace the peace; — *qlcu. di arresto*, to threaten s.o. with arrest; — *qlcu. di ricorrere a misure legali*, to threaten to take s.o. to law.

minacciosaménte, *av.* threateningly, menacingly.

minaccióso, *ag.* threatening, menacing: *attitudine, sguardo, tono —*, menacing (o threatening) attitude, look, tone; *il tempo sembra —*, the weather looks threatening.

minàre, *v.t.* 1. to mine: *minarono l'imboccatura del porto*, they mined the entrance of the harbour; — *una nave*, to mine a ship 2. (*corrodere, insidiare*) to mine, to undermine, to sap: *dovrebbe rendersi conto che il bere mina la sua salute*, he ought to understand that drink is undermining his health; *la febbre minò le sue forze*, fever sapped (o undermined) his strength; *il fiume minò le fondamenta della nostra casa*, the river mined (o undermined) the foundations of our house; — *le basi di una dottrina*, to mine (o to sap) the foundations of a doctrine.

minaréto, *s.m.* minaret.

minàto, *ag.* 1. mined: *zona minata*, mined area 2. (*corroso, insidiato*) undermined; eaten up (with sthg.), consumed (with sthg.): — *dall'invidia*, eaten up with envy.

minatóre, *s.m.* 1. (*chi lavora nelle miniere*) miner; (*di carbone*) coal-miner; collier; pitman (*pl.* pitmen) 2. (*mil.*) sapper.

minatòrio, *ag.* threatening, minatory: *lettera minatoria*, threatening letter.

minchionàggine, *s.f.* (*volg.*) stupidity, silliness; (*ingenuità*) naïveté, naïvety, ingenuousness.

minchionàre, *v.t.* (*volg.*) to make (s.o.) look like an idiot; (*ingannare*) to take (s.o.) in: *diceva così per minchionarmi*, he said that only to make me look like an idiot.

minchionatùra, *s.f.* (*volg.*) 1. fooling, mockery, raillery 2. (*scherzo*) joke 3. (*inezia*) trifle.

minchióne, *s.m.* (*volg.*) simpleton, simple Simon: *fare il —*, to play the idiot.

minchioneria, *s.f.* (*volg.*) 1. (*l'essere minchione*) stupidity 2. (*sciocchezza*) piece of stupidity, piece of nonsense: *hai fatto, detto una —*, you did, you said a stupid thing 3. (*inezia*) trifle.

mineràle, *ag.* mineral: *acqua —*, mineral water; *carbone —*, mineral (o pit) coal; *regno —*, mineral kingdom ‖ *s.m.* mineral; (*materia greggia da cui si estrae un metallo*) ore: — *di zolfo*, sulphur ore; *giacimento di —*, mineral deposit (o bed); *il ferro è un —*, iron is a mineral.

mineralísta, *s.m.* mineralogist.

mineralizzàre, *v.t.*, **mineralizzàrsi**, *v.r.* to mineralize.

mineralogía, *s.f.* mineralogy.

mineralògico, *ag.* mineralogical.

mineralogísta, *s.m.* mineralogist.

mineràrio, *ag.* mining; mine (*attributivo*): *distretto —*, mining district.

Minèrva, *no.pr.f.* (*mit.*) Minerva.

minèstra, *s.f.* 1. soup: — *brodosa*, thin (o clear) soup; — *densa*, thick soup; — *di verdura*, vegetable soup ‖ *o mangiar questa — o saltar questa finestra*, *prov.* it is a question of Hobson's choice (o take it or leave it) 2. (*primo piatto*) first course.

minestrína, *s.f.* thin soup, clear soup.

minestróne, *s.m.* 1. (*cuc.*) "minestrone" (vegetable soup with rice or noodles) 2. *fig.* (*miscuglio*) mix-up: *che —!*, what a mix-up!.

míngere, *v.i.* to urinate, to make water.

mingherlíno, *ag.* 1. thin, delicate, slight 2. (*snello*) slender, slim.

miniàre, *v.t.* to paint in miniature; (*manoscritti*) to illuminate.

miniàto, *ag.* illuminated: *manoscritto —*, illuminated manuscript.

miniatóre, *s.m.* miniaturist; (*di manoscritti*) illuminator.

miniatúra, *s.f.* miniature: *in —*, in miniature.

miniaturísta, *s.c.* miniaturist.

minièra, *s.f.* mine (anche *fig.*): — *di carbone*, coal-mine (o colliery); *una — d'informazioni*, a mine of information; — *di rame*, copper-mine; *bocca di —*, pithead; *sfruttare una —*, to work a mine.

mínima, *s.f.* 1. (*mus.*) minim 2. (*meteorologia*) minimum (*pl.* minima).

minimalísta, *s.m.* (*pol.*) minimalist.

minimaménte, *av.* (*in frasi negative*) in the least, at all: *non faceva — freddo*, it wasn't at all cold (o *fam.* it wasn't the least bit cold); *non lo conosco —*, I don't know him at all; *non lo rispettano —*, they don't respect him at all; *non sono — contento del tuo lavoro*, I am not in the least (o not at all) satisfied with your work.

minimizzàre, *v.t.* to minimize.

mínimo, *ag.superl.* 1. (*il più piccolo*) least; slightest; smallest; minimum (*attributivo*); (*il più basso*) lowest: *la minima differenza*, the least (o the smallest o the slightest) difference; *il — dubbio*, the slightest (o the least) doubt; *l'altitudine, la densità, la larghezza minima*, the minimum altitude, density, width; *senza il — sforzo*, *la minima esitazione*, without the slightest effort, the slightest hesitation; *la velocità minima*, the lowest speed; *anche il — errore potrebbe rovinare tutto*, even the slightest (o the most trivial) mistake could ruin the whole enterprise; *ditemi il prezzo —*, give me your lowest figure; *lo puoi avere con la minima spesa*, you can get it very cheaply ‖ *il — comune denominatore*, (*mat.*) the lowest (o the least) common denominator; *il — comune multiplo*, (*mat.*) the lowest common multiple ‖ *non ne ho la minima idea*, I haven't the faintest (o the slightest o the least) idea ‖ *sono ridotto ai minimi termini*, (*in miseria*) I am down and out; *ridurre una frazione ai minimi termini*, (*mat.*) to reduce a fraction to its lowest terms; *ridurre una questione ai minimi termini*, to reduce a matter to its simplest terms 2. (*piccolissimo*) very small; very slight; (*bassissimo*) very low: *un prezzo —*, a very low price; *una quantità minima*, a very small quantity; *c'è una distanza minima*, it is a very short (o it is no) distance; *la differenza è minima*, the difference is very slight ‖ *s.m.* 1. minimum (*pl.* minima): *il — d'età prescritto per essere ammessi è...*, the minimum age for admission is...; *il — di paga*, the minimum wages; *gli fu applicato il — della pena*, he was given the minimum penalty; *quant'è il —?*, what's the minimum (o the lowest) price?; *ridurre le spese al —*, to reduce expenses to a minimum ‖ *al —*, at least (o at the very least): *dovrai aspettare un'ora al —*, you will have to wait at least an hour 2. (*di motore*) lowest gear; idling: — *di avvicinamento*, (*aer.*) approach idling; — *di volo*, (aer.) flight idling; girare al —, (aut.) to tick over (o to idle) **3.** (la minima cosa) the least: ciò è il — che puoi fare, this is the least you can do; digli il — che puoi, tell him as little as you can.

mínio, s.m. (chim.) minium, red lead.

ministeriàle, ag. ministerial; cabinet (attributivo): i banchi ministeriali, the ministerial benches; (in Gran Bretagna) the Treasury benches; consiglio —, cabinet -council; crisi —, cabinet crisis.

ministèro, s.m. **1.** (ufficio, funzione) office, function; (gener. eccl.) ministry: il sacro —, the (sacred) ministry || col — di, through the medium of **2.** (ministero, dipartimento amministrativo dello Stato) ministry, office, board; (negli Stati Uniti) department: — degli Esteri, Foreign Office; (negli Stati Uniti) State Department; — dei Lavori Pubblici, Ministry of Works; — dei Trasporti, Ministry of Transport and Civil Aviation; (negli Stati Uniti) Interstate Commerce Commission; — del Commercio, Board of Trade; (negli Stati Uniti) Department of Commerce; — dell'Aeronautica, Air Ministry; (negli Stati Uniti) Department of the Air Force; — della Giustizia, (negli Stati Uniti) Department of Justice; — dell'Agricoltura, Ministry of Agriculture, Fisheries and Food; (negli Stati Uniti) Department of Agriculture; — della Guerra, War Office; (negli Stati Uniti) War Department; — della Marina, Admiralty; (negli Stati Uniti) Department of the Navy; — del Lavoro, Ministry of Labour; (negli Stati Uniti) Department of Labor; — delle Poste e delle Telecomunicazioni, Post Office Board; (negli Stati Uniti) Post Office Department; — dell'Interno, Home Office; (negli Stati Uniti) Department of the Interior; — dell'Istruzione Pubblica, Ministry of Education; (negli Stati Uniti) Department of Education; — del Tesoro, Treasury; (negli Stati Uniti) Treasury Department **3.** (Consiglio dei Ministri, governo) government, ministry; (Gabinetto) cabinet: — radicale, radical government; fece parte del — Crispi, he served in Crispi's ministry; formare un —, to form a government (o a ministry o a cabinet) **4.** Pubblico Ministero, (dir.) Public Prosecutor.

ministro, s.m. **1.** (eccl.) minister, clergyman (pl. clergymen), priest: (titolo) Minister: — della Chiesa, minister of religion; — generale, Minister General **2.** (pol.) minister, secretary (of State): Ministro degli Esteri, Foreign Secretary (o Secretary of State for Foreign Affairs); (negli Stati Uniti) Secretary of State; Ministro del Commercio, President of the Board of Trade; (negli Stati Uniti) Secretary of Commerce; Ministro dell'Aeronautica, Secretary of State for Air (o fam. Air Minister); (negli Stati Uniti) Secretary of the Air Force; Ministro della Giustizia, (negli Stati Uniti) Secretary of Justice; Ministro dell'Agricoltura, Minister of Agriculture, Fisheries and Food (o fam. Minister of Agriculture); (negli Stati Uniti) Secretary of Agriculture; Ministro della Guerra, Secretary of State for War (o fam. War Minister); (negli Stati Uniti) Secretary of the Army; Ministro della Marina, First Lord of the Admiralty; (negli Stati Uniti) Secretary of the Navy; Ministro delle Poste e Telecomunicazioni, Postmaster General; Ministro dell'Interno, Secretary of State for the Home Department (o fam. Home Secretary); (negli Stati Uniti) Secretary of the Department of the Interior; Ministro dell'Istruzione pubblica, Minister of Education; Ministro del Tesoro, Chancellor of the Exchequer; (negli Stati Uniti) Secretary of the Treasury; Ministro senza portafoglio, Minister without portfolio; Primo Ministro, Prime Minister (o Premier); Consiglio dei Ministri, Cabinet (Council) **3.** (capo di legazione) minister: il Ministro d'Italia a Kabul, the Italian Minister at Kabul; — plenipotenziario, minister plenipotentiary **4.** fig.: ministri della giustizia, officers of justice; — di pace, di civiltà, defender of peace, of civilization.

minòico, ag. (st.) Minoan.

minorànza, s.f. minority.

minoràre, v.t. (rar.) to diminish, to lessen; to reduce.

minoràsco, s.m. (st. dir.) trust in favour of a younger son.

minoràto, ag. disabled, mutilated, maimed: soldati minorati in guerra, soldiers disabled in the war; render —, to disable || s.m. **1.** disabled person: minorati di guerra, (soldati) disabled ex-service men; (civili) war -disabled persons **2.** — psichico, (med.) mental deficient.

minorazióne, s.f. **1.** (diminuzione) diminution, lessening; reduction; curtailment **2.** (invalidità) disablement || — mentale, (med.) mental deficiency.

minóre, ag. **1.** (più piccolo) comp. smaller, superl. rel. the smallest; comp. less(er), superl. rel. the least; (più basso) comp. lower, superl. rel. the lowest; (più corto) comp. shorther, superl. rel. the shortest: il — di questi numeri, the lowest of these numbers; la — distanza, the shortest distance; la — velocità, the slowest speed; a minor prezzo, at a lower price; al minor prezzo possibile, at the lowest possible price; il cerchio di raggio —, the circle with the smallest radius; con minor forza, diligenza, with less force, diligence; con minor spesa, at less cost (o less expensively); il percorso —, the shortest way; la parte è — del tutto, the part is less (o smaller) than the whole; scegliere il male —, to choose the lesser evil || la — parte, (la minoranza) the minority || la — parte di, a minority of || Asia Minore, Asia Minor || astri minori, lesser stars || Orsa Minore, (astr.) Ursa Minor **2.** (più giovane) comp. younger, superl. rel. the youngest: il — dei miei fratelli, my youngest brother; sono — di lui di tre anni, I am three years younger than he is; venne con il figlio —, he came with his youngest son || il Bruto Minore, the Younger Brutus, Catone il Minore, Cato the Younger **3.** (secondario, meno importante, meno grave) minor: di — importanza, of minor importance; opere, poeti minori, minor works, poets; pena, danno —, minor penalty, damage; è uno dei minori affluenti del Po, it is one of the smaller (o minor) tributaries of the Po || arti minori, (st.) minor arts || frati minori, (eccl.) Friars Minor (o Minorites); ordine —, (eccl.) minor order || essere — di se stesso, not to do oneself justice **4.** || (mus. log.) minor: in chiave —, (mus.) in a minor key; in la —, (mus.) in A minor; intervallo di seconda —, (mus.) minor second; premessa —, (log.) minor (premise); tono —, (mus.) minor key || s.m. **1.** (di età, dignità) junior **2.** pl. (minorenni) minors: i minori sono soggetti alla patria potestà, minors are subject to the father's authority **3.** pl. (eccl.) (frati minori) Minorites || s.f. (fil.) minor (premise).

minorènne, ag. under age: delinquente —, juvenile delinquent; essere —, to be under age (o to be a minor) || s.c. (dir.) minor: tribunale dei minorenni, juvenile court.

minoríle, ag. juvenile, of minors: delinquenza —, juvenile delinquency; età —, minority.

minorità¹, s.f. (dir.) minority.

minoríta², s.m. (eccl.) Minorite, Friar Minor.

Minòsse, no.pr.m. (mit.) Minos || **minòsse,** s.m. fig. (scherz.) ruthless judge.

Minotàuro, no.pr.m. (mit.) Minotaur.

minuèndo, s.m. (arit.) minuend.

minuétto, s.m. (mus.) minuet.

minúgia, s.f. **1.** (minuzia) gut **2.** (mus.) catgut, gut.

minúscola, s.f. small letter; (tip.) lower-case letter: non si comincia un periodo con la —, one must not begin a sentence with a small letter.

minúscolo, ag. **1.** small: lettera minuscola, small letter **2.** (piccolino) tiny || s.m. (tip.) lower-case letter.

minúta, s.f. rough copy, rough draft; minute.

minutàglia, s.f. **1.** bits and pieces (pl.), odds and ends (pl.); (dettagli) details (pl.), minutiae (pl.) **2.** (plebaglia) small fry **3.** (insieme di pesciolini) fry.

minutaménte, av. minutely.

minutànte, s.c. drafter, minute-writer.

minuterìa, s.f. **1.** minuteness **2.** (insieme di piccole cose) bits and pieces (pl.), odds and ends (pl.); (det-

tagli) details (*pl.*), minutiae (*pl.*) **3.** (*soprammobili*) (k)nick-(k)nacks (*pl.*).

minutézza, *s.f.* **1.** minuteness; (*sottigliezza*) thinness **2.** (*minuzia*) minutia (*pl.* minutiae), trifle.

minúto[1], *ag.* **1.** (*piccolo*) minute, small; (*sottile*) thin: *calligrafia minuta*, small handwriting; *carbone* —, small coal; *frittura minuta*, (*cuc.*) small fry; *lineamenti minuti*, small features; *persona di ossatura minuta*, a small-boned person; *pioggia minuta*, drizzle; *piano studiato nei più minuti particolari*, plan studied to the last detail ‖ *bestie minute*, small stock ‖ *il popolo* —, the common people; (*spreg.*) the mob **2.** (*dettagliato*) detailed; (*minuzioso*) minute: *una minuta spiegazione*, a detailed explanation; *fece minute indagini sul delitto*, he made minute inquiries into the crime **3.** (*accessorio, di poco conto*) petty, minute: *occupazioni minute*, minute tasks; *spese minute*, petty expenses; *denaro per i minuti piaceri*, pocket-money; (*per la moglie*) pin-money **4.** (*comm.*): *al* —, (by) retail: *commerciante al* —, retailer; *prezzo al* —, retail price; *vendere al* —, to retail (*o* to sell by retail).

minúto[2], *s.m.* minute: — *secondo*, *primo*, second, minute; *lancetta dei minuti*, minute-hand; *mancano dieci minuti alle cinque*, it is ten (minutes) to five; *ogni* — *mi sembrava un'ora*, every minute seemed an hour to me; *sono le quattro e venti minuti*, it is twenty (minutes) past four; *abitiamo a cinque minuti da un parco*, we live five minutes from a park ‖ *il mio orologio spacca il* —, my watch is dead on time ‖ *sarò qui tra mezzo* —, I'll be here in a minute ‖ *contare i minuti*, to count the minutes.

minúzia, *s.f.* minutia (*pl.* minutiae), trifle, trivial detail: *si perde in minuzie*, he can't see the wood for the trees; *litigare per una* —, to quarrel over a trifle (*o* trivial detail).

minuziosàggine, *s.f.* minuteness; exactness, precision, accuracy.

minuziosaménte, *av.* minutely; (*dettagliatamente*) in detail.

minuziosità, *V.* **minuziosàggine**.

minuzióso, *ag.* minute; (*dettagliato*) detailed: *descrizione minuziosa*, minute description; *fare un resoconto* —, to give a detailed report.

minúzzolo, *s.m.* crumb, scrap, tiny bit: *fare a minuzzoli*, to crumble.

mio, *ag.poss.* **1.** my; (*mio proprio*) my own: *un* — *amico*, one of my friends (*o* a friend of mine); *i miei fratelli*, my brothers; *mia madre*, my mother; *le mie sorelle*, my sisters; *questo* — *amico*, this friend of mine; *tre miei libri*, three of my books (*o* three books of mine); *cucino i miei pasti*, I cook my own meals; *mi ha insultato in casa mia*, he has insulted me in my own house; *vorrei avere una casa mia*, I wish I had a house of my own ‖ *amico* —, my (dear) friend; *caro* —, old fellow (*o* old man); *figlio* —, my son; *sentite, ragazzi miei*, listen to me, boys (*o* lads) ‖ *in vece mia*, instead of me (*o* in my stead) ‖ *fallo per amor* —, do it for love of me (*o* for my sake) **2.** (*come pred. nominale*) **mine**: *questa casa è mia*, this house is mine; *questi libri sono miei*, these books are mine (*o* belong to me) **3.** (*in forme ellittiche*): *la mia del 5 corr.*, (*lettera*) my letter of the 5th inst.; *anch'io ho avuto le mie* (*disgrazie*), I had my difficulties too; *egli è dalla mia* (*parte*), he is on my side; *si dice che ne ho fatte ancora delle mie*, they say I've been up to my old tricks again (*o* up to one of my tricks); *sto sulla mia*, I keep myself to myself; *voglio dir la mia*, I want to have my say ‖ *pron. poss.* **mine**: *questa casa è più piccola della mia*, this house is smaller than mine; *se mi presti il tuo libro, io ti presterò il* —, if you lend me your book, I'll lend you mine; *la sua famiglia e la mia sono amiche da molto tempo*, his family and mine are friends of long standing ‖ *s.m.* **1.**: *vivo del* —, I live on my income; *devi distinguere tra il* — *e il tuo*, you must distinguish between what's

mine and what's yours; *persi tutto il* — *durante la guerra*, I lost all my possessions during the war **2.** (*partitivo*): *qualcosa di* —, something of my own; *non ho niente di* —, I have nothing of my own **3.** *pl.*: *i miei*, my family (*o* my relatives *o fam.* my folks); (*partigiani, seguaci*) my supporters.

miocàrdio, *s.m.* (*anat.*) myocardium.

miocardíte, *s.f.* (*patol.*) myocarditis.

miocène, *s.m.* (*geol.*) miocene.

miocènico, *ag.* (*geol.*) miocene.

miografía, *s.f.* (*scient.*) myography.

miogràfico, *ag.* myographic(al).

miògrafo, *s.m.* **1.** myographer **2.** (*strumento*) myograph.

miolèmma, *s.m.* (*anat.*) myolemma, sarcolemma.

miología, *s.f.* myology.

miològico, *ag.* myological.

miòlogo, *s.m.* myologist.

miòma, *s.m.* (*patol.*) myoma.

miopatía, *s.f.* (*patol.*) myopathy.

míope, *ag.* myopic, short-sighted (anche *fig.*) ‖ *s.c.* myope, myops, short-sighted person (anche *fig.*).

miopía, *s.f.* myopia, myopy, short-sightedness (anche *fig.*).

mioplàstica, *s.f.* (*chir.*) myoplasty.

mioplàstico, *ag.* (*chir.*) myoplastic.

mioressía, *s.f.* (*patol.*) myorrhexis.

mioscleròsi, *s.f.* (*patol.*) myosclerosis.

miòsi, *s.f.* (*patol.*) myosis.

miòsico, *ag.* myotic, myositic.

miosína, *s.f.* (*biol.*) myosin.

miosíte, *s.f.* (*patol.*) myositis.

miosòtide, *s.f.* (*bot.*) myosotis, myosote.

miospàsmo, *s.m.* (*med.*) myospasm.

mioterapía, *s.f.* (*med.*) myotherapy.

miotomía, *s.f.* (*chir.*) myotomy.

Míra[1], *no.pr.f.* Myra.

míra[2], *s.f.* **1.** aim: *ha una* — *straordinaria*, he is a wonderful shot; *la sua* — *era così perfetta che colpì l'animale al primo colpo*, his aim was so good that he hit the animal with his first shot; *pigliare, prendere la* —, to take aim: *pigliare la* — *accuratamente prima di sparare*, to take careful aim before shooting; *prendere la* — *troppo alta*, to aim too high ‖ *collocare la* — *troppo in alto*, *fig.* to aim too high ‖ *mettere la* — *su qlcu.*, *ql.co.*, to have one's eye on s.o., sthg. ‖ *prendere di* — *qlcu.*, *fig.* to make s.o. the object of one's attacks **2.** (*bersaglio*) target: *cogliere la* —, to hit the target **3.** (*gener. pl.*) (*scopo*) aim, intention; (*disegno*) design: *che mire hai?*, what is your aim? (*o* what are your intentions?); *ha mire troppo alte*, he is aiming too high (*o* he has high ambitions); *avere mire oblique su qlcu.*, *ql.co.*, to have designs on s.o., sthg. ‖ *attraversare le mire di qlcu.*, to get in s.o.'s way **4.** (*mirino*) sight: — *anteriore*, foresight; — *posteriore*, backsight.

miràbile, *ag.* admirable; (*meraviglioso*) wonderful: — *a dirsi*, wonderful to relate; — *a vedersi*, wonderful to see; — *visione*, heavenly vision; *lavorava con* — *diligenza*, he worked with admirable diligence ‖ *s.m.*, wonderful thing.

mirabília, *s.f.pl.* (*arc.*) wonders: *fare* —, to work wonders (*o* to do miracles).

mirabilménte, *av.* admirably; (*meravigliosamente*) wonderfully.

mirabolàno, *s.m.* (*spaccone*) boaster, braggart.

mirabolànte, *ag.* astonishing, amazing.

miracolàto, *ag.* miraculously healed ‖ *s.m.* miraculously healed person.

miràcolo, *s.m.* **1.** miracle (anche *fig.*); *fig.* wonder: *il* — *dei pani e dei pesci*, the miracle of the loaves and fishes; *è un* — *di bontà*, she is a wonder of goodness; *si gridò al* —, "a miracle" was the cry; *fare miracoli*, to do miracles; *fig.* to work wonders: *quella medicina può far miracoli*, that medicine can work wonders ‖ *che* —!, what a miracle! ‖ *per* —, by a mir-

acle: *è qui per —*, he is here by a miracle; *fu salvo per —*, ha was saved by a miracle; *se la cavò per —*, he had a miraculous (*o a narrow o a hairbreadth*) escape ‖ *narrare vita, morte e miracoli di qlcu.*, to relate the life, death and miracles of s.o. **2.** (*st. teat.*) miracle(-play), mystery(-play).

miracolosaménte, *av.* miraculously.

miracolóso, *ag.* miraculous; (*portentoso*) prodigious, wonderful.

miràggio, *s.m.* mirage (anche *fig.*).

Mirànda, *no.pr.f.* Miranda.

miràre, *v.t.* **1.** to look at (s.o., sthg.); to stare at (s.o., sthg.), to gaze at, on (s.o., sthg.) **2.** (*ammirare*) to admire ‖ *v.i.* **1.** to aim (at s.o., sthg.), to take aim (at s.o., sthg.), to sight (s.o., sthg.), to take sight (on s.o., sthg.): *mirò attentamente prima di sparare*, he took accurate aim before shooting; *— a un bersaglio*, to aim at a target **2.** (*tendere, aspirare*) to aim (at sthg., at doing): *a che cosa miri?*, what are you aiming at?; *il suo discorso mira a provare che…*, his speech sets out to prove that… (*o aims at proving that…*); *— a diventare qlcu.*, to aim at becoming s.o. ‖ **miràrsi,** *v.r.* **1.** to look at oneself: *si mirò allo specchio*, she looked at herself in the mirror **2.** (*ammirarsi*) to admire oneself.

miríade, *s.f.* myriad.

miriagràmma, miriagràmmo, *s.m.* myriagram(me) (*misura di peso* = 22.046 lb.).

Míriam, *no.pr.f.* Miriam.

miriàmetro, *s.m.* myriametre; (*amer.*) myriameter (*misura di lunghezza* = 6.2137 mi.).

miriàpodo, *s.m.* (*zool.*) myriapod ‖ *i Miriapodi*, Myriapoda.

miríca, miríce, *s.f.* (*bot.*) Myrica (*pl.* Myricae).

miricína, *s.f.* (*chim.*) myricin(e).

mirífico, *ag.* (*letter.*) wondrous, marvellous.

miríno, *s.m.* (*di arma da fuoco, di strumento ottico*) (fore)sight; (*di apparecchio fotografico*) view-finder.

miristíca, *s.f.* (*noce moscata*) nutmeg.

mirístico, *ag.* (*chim.*) myristic.

miristína, *s.f.* (*chim.*) myristine.

mirmecòfagi, *s.m.pl.* (*entom.*) Myrmecophagidae.

mirmecòfilo, *ag.* (*bot. entom.*) myrmecophilous.

mirmecología, *s.f.* myrmecology.

mirmecòlogo, *s.m.* myrmecologist.

mirmídone, *s.m.* (*mit.*) Myrmidon.

Miróne, *no.pr.m.* (*st. scult.*) Myron.

mírra[1]**,** *s.f.* (*bot.*) myrrh.

Mírra[2]**,** *no.pr.f.* (*mit.*) Myrrha.

mirtàcee, *s.f.pl.* (*bot.*) Myrtaceae.

mirtéto, *s.m.* myrtle-grove.

mirtifórme, *ag.* myrtiform.

mirtíllo, *s.m.* (*bot.*) bilberry, whortleberry.

mírto, *s.m.* (*bot.*) myrtle.

misantropía, *s.f.* misanthropy.

misantròpico, *ag.* misanthropic(al).

misàntropo, *s.m.* misanthrope, misanthropist.

miscèla, *s.f.* mixture (anche *aut.*); (*di tè, caffè, tabacco*) blend: *— anticongelante*, (*aut.*) antifreeze; *— tonante*, (*miner.*) explosive gas tuning; *cos'è questa — che ci date da bere?*, (*scherz.*) what's this poison you are giving us?.

miscelàre, *v.t.* **1.** to mix: *— due ingredienti*, to mix two ingredients **2.** (*tè, caffè, tabacco*) to blend.

miscellànea, *s.f.* miscellanea, miscellany.

miscellàneo, *ag.* miscellaneous.

míschia, *s.f.* fray, fight, tussle; (*contrasto*) conflict: *al di sopra della — degli interessi personali*, above the conflict of personal interests; *nel furore della —*, in the heat of the fray; *gettarsi nella —*, to join the fight (*o to enter the fray*).

mischiàbile, *ag.* mixable, miscible.

mischiaménto, *s.m.* **1.** (*il mischiare*) mixing **2.** (*miscuglio*) mixture.

mischiàre, *v.t.* to mix, to mingle; (*amalgamare, misce-* *lare*) to blend; (*alle carte*) to shuffle: *— vino con acqua*, to mix (*o to mingle*) wine with water ‖ **mischiàrsi,** *v.r.* **1.** to mix (with sthg.); to mingle (with sthg.); (*amalgamarsi, miscelarsi*) to blend: *l'olio e l'acqua non si mischiano*, oil and water don't mix; *si mischiarono alla folla*, they mixed (*o mingled*) with the crowd **2.** (*intromettersi*) to meddle, to interfere: *si è mischiato nei miei affari*, he meddled in my affairs.

mischiatúra, *s.f.* **1.** (*il mischiare*) mixing **2.** (*miscuglio*) mixture.

míschio, *ag.* **1.** mixed **2.** (*screziato*) variegated: *marmo —*, variegated marble ‖ *s.m.* (*miscuglio*) mixture.

misconóscere, *v.t.* (*non riconoscere*) not to acknowledge; to deny, to ignore; (*stimare meno del merito*) to underestimate: *era misconosciuto dai suoi stessi fratelli*, he was underestimated by his own brothers; *— i meriti di qlcu.*, to ignore s.o.'s merits; *— la verità di un fatto*, to deny (*o not to acknowledge*) the truth of a fact.

miscredènte, *ag.* misbelieving ‖ *s.c.* misbeliever.

miscredènza, *s.f.* misbelief.

miscúglio, *s.m.* mixture; (*miscela, amalgama*) blend.

miseràbile, *ag.* **1.** miserable, wretched; unfortunate: *un quartiere —*, a poverty-stricken quarter; *quel povero mena un'esistenza —*, that poor man leads a miserable (*o wretched*) life; *si trova in una condizione —*, he is in a miserable (*o sorry*) plight **2.** (*scarso*) poor, scanty; paltry: *guadagno —*, scanty (*o poor*) profit; *un salario —*, a paltry wage **3.** (*vile, meschino*) despicable, mean: *ha commesso un'azione —*, he did a despicable (*o mean*) thing ‖ *per una — moneta*, for a measly (*o paltry*) coin ‖ *s.c.* (*persona miserabile*) poor wretch.

miserabilità, *s.f.* **1.** wretchedness **2.** (*viltà*) meanness.

miserabilménte, miseraménte, *av.* **1.** miserably, wretchedly; unfortunately: *perire —*, to die miserably; *vivere —*, to live wretchedly **2.** (*scarsamente*) poorly **3.** (*vilmente*) despicably, meanly.

miseràndo, *ag.* miserable, pitiable, pitiful: *un caso —*, a pitiable (*o pitiful*) case; *fece una fine miseranda*, he came to a miserable end.

miserère, *s.m.* (*eccl. mus.*) Miserere: *hanno cantato il —*, they sang the Miserere ‖ *faccia da —*, (*fam.*) face like a funeral ‖ *essere al —*, (*in fin di vita*) to be at the last gasp; (*senza soldi*) to be broke (*o to be hard up*).

miserévole, *ag.* miserable, pitiable, pitiful: *condizione —*, miserable (*o sorry*) plight.

misèria, *s.f.* **1.** misery, destitution, distress; want; penury, poverty: *la — di quella gente le toccò il cuore*, the distress (*o misery*) of those people touched her heart; *il cattivo tempo causò molta — fra i contadini*, the bad weather caused much distress among the farmers; *andare in —*, to fall into poverty (*o penury*); *essere ridotto in —*, to be reduced to poverty (*o fam.* to be down and out*); *vivere nella —*, to live in misery (*o poverty*) ‖ *— nera*, dire poverty ‖ *la sua — d'animo mi disgusta*, his meanness disgusts me ‖ *fare le cose senza —*, to do things with an open hand ‖ *piangere —*, to plead (*o to complain of*) poverty; (*simulando*) to feign poverty **2.** (*scarsità*) lack, shortage: *quest'anno c'è — di olio*, there is shortage of oil this year **3.** (*inezia*) trifle: *queste miserie non m'interessano*, I do not care for these trifles; *questo vaso costa una —*, this vase costs only a trifle **4.** *pl.* (*disgrazie*) misfortunes, troubles: *le miserie della vita*, the troubles (*o misfortunes*) of life; *mi descrisse le sue miserie*, he told me his troubles.

misericòrde, *ag.* (*poet.*) merciful.

misericòrdia, *s.f.* **1.** mercy; clemency; compassion: *la — infinita di Dio*, the infinite mercy of God; *senza —*, (*spietato*) merciless; (*spietatamente*) mercilessly: *è un uomo senza —*, he is a merciless man; *lo colpì senza —*, he hit him mercilessly; *affidarsi alla — di qlcu.*, to throw oneself on s.o.'s mercy; *avere — di qlcu.*, to be merciful to s.o. (*o to have mercy on s.o.*); *gridare —*, to cry for mercy ‖ *—!*, good gracious! ‖ *la Mise-*

ricordia, "the Misericordia" (lay confraternity for giving aid to sick people) ‖ *opere di — corporali*, (*teol.*) corporal works of mercy; *opere di — spirituali*, (*teol.*) spiritual works of mercy 2. (*st.*) (*pugnale*) misericord.

misericordiosaménte, *av.* mercifully.

misericordióso, *ag.* merciful.

mísero, *ag.* 1. (*povero, scarso*) poor, scanty; paltry: *miseri guadagni*, miserable (*o* paltry) earnings; *una misera mezza corona*, a paltry half-crown; — *pasto*, poor meal; — *raccolto*, scanty (*o* poor) crop; — *reddito*, poor income; *una misera scusa*, a wretched (*o* a paltry) excuse; *mi disse un — grazie*, he thanked me grudgingly; *avere una misera opinione di qlcu.*, to have a poor opinion of s.o. 2. (*meschino, miserabile*) wretched, miserable; (*infelice*) unhappy: *una misera esistenza*, a wretched (*o* miserable) existence; *fece una misera figura*, he cut a poor figure ‖ *— me!*, poor me! 3. (*avaro*) miserly, stingy; mean: *è un individuo — e gretto*, he is a cheese-paring (*o* mean *o* stingy) fellow 4. (*di abito*) skimpy.

misèrrimo, *ag. superl.* extremely poor.

misfàtto, *s.m.* misdeed; crime.

Mísia, *no.pr.f.* (*geog. st.*) Mysia.

misogamía, *s.f.* misogamy.

misògamo, *ag.* misogamic ‖ *s.m.* misogamist.

misoginía, *s.f.* misogyny.

misògino, *ag.* misogynous ‖ *s.m.* misogynist.

misología, *s.f.* misology.

misoneísmo, *s.m.* misoneism.

misoneísta, *ag.* misoneistic ‖ *s.c.* misoneist.

missàggio, *s.m.* (*cine.*) mixing: — *microfonico*, (*elett. acu.*) microphonic mixing; *tecnico del —*, mixer.

míssile, *ag.* missile ‖ *s.m.* 1. missile: — *a razzo*, rocket missile; — *balistico*, ballistic missile; — *balistico intercontinentale*, Intercontinental Ballistic Missile (*abbr.* I.C.B.M.); — *radiocomandato*, radio-controlled missile; *lanciare un —*, to launch a missile 2. *pl.* (*st. romana*) missiles.

missilística, *s.f.* (*neol.*) rocketry.

missionàrio, *s.m.* 1. missionary 2. (*inviato*) envoy: *andò da loro come — di pace*, he came to them as a bringer (*o* envoy) of peace.

missióne, *s.f.* mission (anche *fig.*): *le missioni africane hanno urgente bisogno di aiuti finanziari*, the African missions urgently need financial help; *fu mandato in — segreta a Casablanca*, he was sent on a secret mission to Casablanca; *in questo momento non si trova alla —*, at the moment he is not in (*o* at) the mission; *pensava che la sua — nella vita fosse di aiutare i bambini poveri*, she thought her mission in life was to help poor children; *portò brillantemente a termine la sua —*, he completed his mission successfully; *fare una —*, to preach (*o* to give) a mission.

Mississipì, *no.pr.m.* (*geog.*) Mississippi.

Missúri, *no.pr.m.* (*geog.*) Missouri.

missiva, *s.f.* missive, message, letter.

mistagogía, *s.f.* (*st. relig.*) mystagogy.

mistagògico, *ag.* (*st. relig.*) mystagogic.

mistagògo, *s.m.* (*st. relig.*) mystagogue.

mistaménte, *av.* mixedly; (*promiscuamente*) promiscuously.

misteriosaménte, *av.* mysteriously.

misteriosità, *s.f.* mysteriousness.

misterióso, *ag.* mysterious; (*sospetto*) suspicious, mysterious: *aspetto —*, suspicious look; *morte misteriosa*, suspicious death ‖ *non fare il —!*, don't make a mystery of it!.

mistèro, *s.m.* 1. mystery; (*di persona*) mystery, enigma: *il — della Trinità, dell'Eucarestia*, the mystery of the Trinity, of Eucharist; *avvolto nel —*, wrapped in mystery; *quell'uomo è un —*, that man is an enigma; *far — di qlco.*, to make a mystery of sthg. 2. (*antico rito religioso*) mystery: *i misteri eleusini*, the Eleusinian Mysteries 3. (*st. teat.*) mystery(-play).

mística, *s.f.* mysticism; mystical theology.

misticaménte, *av.* mystically.

misticìsmo, *s.m.* mysticism.

místico, *ag.* mystic(al) ‖ *s.m.* mystic.

mistifícàre, *v.t.* 1. (*ingannare*) to mystify, to hoax; to deceive 2. (*adulterare*) to adulterate.

mistificatóre, *s.m.*, **mistificatríce**, *s.f.* 1. (*chi inganna*) mystifier, hoaxer 2. (*chi adultera*) adulterator.

mistificazióne, *s.f.* 1. (*inganno*) mystification 2. (*adulterazione*) adulteration.

mistilíneo, *ag.* mixtilinear.

místo, *ag.* mixed : *matrimonio —*, mixed marriage; *scuola mista*, (*elementare*) mixed school; (*media*) co-educational school; *treno —*, train for goods and passengers ‖ *s.m.* mixture: *un — di bene e di male*, a mixture of good and evil.

mistrà, *s.f.* (*acquavite d'anici*) anisette.

mistràl, *s.m.* mistral.

mistúra, *s.f.* mixture.

misúra, *s.f.* 1. measure; (*misurazione*) measurement; (*quantità*) amount: *la — del tempo*, the measurement of time; — *scarsa*, short measure; — *di lunghezza, superficie, volume*, linear, square, cubic measure; *due misure di grano*, two measures of wheat; *unità di —*, unit of measure; *pesi e misure*, weights and measures ‖ *a — che...*, as...: *a — che aumenterà il lavoro aumenteremo il personale*, as the work increases we shall increase the staff ‖ *la — è colma*, I am sick and tired of it ‖ *avere due pesi e due misure*, to have different ways of dealing 2. (*taglia, dimensione*) size: *abiti su —*, clothes made to measure; *scarpe di tutte le misure*, shoes of all sizes; *la sarta mi prese le misure*, the dressmaker took my measurements 3. (*limite, proporzione*) limit; (*moderazione*) moderation: *lo farò nella — delle mie forze, del possibile*, I shall do it to the best of my ability (*o* as well as lies within my power); *osservare le misure*, to keep within bounds; *passar la —*, to exceed (*o* to overstep) the limit (*o* to lose all sense of proportion); *spendere senza —*, to spend without limit ‖ *con —*, moderately ‖ *fuori di, oltre —*, beyond measure (*o* excessively) 4. (*livello, qualità*) standard, measure: *su per giù sono della stessa —*, they are more or less of the same standard 5. (*precauzione*) measure, step: *misure di polizia*, police measures; *misure politiche*, political measures; *il governo ha preso tutte le misure per evitare dissensi interni*, the government has taken all possible measures (*o* steps) to avoid internal dissension; *prendere delle misure contro qlcu.*, to take measures against s.o. 6. (*nastro per sarti*) tape-measure 7. (*poes.*) measure, metre 8. (*mus.*) measure, time 9. (*scherma*) measure, reach, distance.

misuràbile, *ag.* measurable.

misurabilità, *s.f.* measurableness.

misuràre, *v.t.* 1. to measure; (*tec.*) to gauge: — *la dimensione di ql.co.*, to measure the size of sthg.; — *la lunghezza di una stoffa*, to measure the length of a piece of cloth; — *la pioggia*, to gauge the rainfall; — *ql.co. col compasso*, to measure sthg. with compasses; — *la temperatura a qlcu.*, to take s.o.'s temperature; — *le scale*, (*scherz.*) to fall headlong down the stairs; — *la stanza*, (*scherz.*) to fall flat on one's face (*o* to measure one's length on the ground) 2. (*valutare, giudicare*) to estimate, to judge: — *le difficoltà, gli ostacoli*, to estimate the difficulties, the obstacles; — *la distanza a occhio*, to gauge the distance with one's eye; — *la gravità di una situazione*, to judge the gravity of a situation; — *le proprie forze*, to try one's strength 3. (*limitare*) to limit; to ration; (*soppesare*) to weigh: *cercò di — le spese*, he tried to limit his expenses; *mi misurano il pane*, they keep me short of bread; — *il cibo a qlcu.*, to ration s.o.'s food; — *le parole, i termini*, to weigh one's words 4. (*indumenti*) to try on: — *un vestito*, to try on a dress 5. (*percorrere a passi eguali*) to pace: *misurò la stanza tutta la notte*, he paced (up and down) the room all night ‖ *v.i.* to measure: *questa stanza misura quindici* *piedi di larghezza*, this room measures fifteen feet across (*o* is fifteen feet wide); *questo libro misura sei pollici per quattro*, this book measures six inches by four ‖ **misuràrsi**, *v.r.* 1. (*competere*) to compete: *non ardisco misurarmi con lui*, I dare not compete with him; — *in una gara*, to compete in a race 2. (*venire alle mani*) to come to blows: *si misurò con un cugino*, he came to blows with his cousin 3. (*indumenti*) to try on: *misurati le scarpe prima di comprarle*, try on the shoes before you buy them.

misuratamÉnte, *av.* moderately, with measure.

misuràto, *ag.* 1. measured ‖ *passi misurati*, measured steps 2. (*moderato*) moderate, measured; (*prudente*) cautious: *parole misurate*, measured words.

misuratóre, *s.m.* 1. (*chi misura*) measurer 2. (*strumento che misura*) gauge: — *di livello*, (*topografia*) hypsometer; — *di profondità*, (*mar.*) depthometer; — *di umidità*, hygrometer.

misurazióne, *s.f.* measurement, measuring; gauging.

misuríno, *s.m.* small measure; small measuring vessel; (*per il latte*) milk-can.

míte, *ag.* 1. gentle; meek; mild: — *come un agnello*, as meek as a lamb; *una persona* —, a gentle person 2. (*di clima*) mild: *un inverno* —, a mild winter 3. (*moderato*) moderate: *prezzi miti*, moderate prices ‖ *lo obbligarono a venire a più miti consigli*, they made him see reason.

mitemÉnte, *av.* 1. gently; meekly; mildly 2. (*moderatamente*) moderately.

mitÉzza, *s.f.* 1. gentleness; meekness; mildness 2. (*di clima*) mildness 3. (*moderazione*) moderation.

miticamÉnte, *av.* mythically.

mítico, *ag.* mythical.

mitigàbile, *ag.* that can be mitigated; (*di passioni*) that can be appeased; (*di dolore*) that can be relieved.

mitigàre, *v.t.* to mitigate; (*passioni*) to appease; (*dolore*) to relieve, to alleviate: — *la collera di qlcu.*, to appease s.o.'s anger ‖ **mitigàrsi**, *v.r.* 1. to be appeased, to calm down, to relax, to subside: *la sua severità si mitigò*, his strictness relaxed; *sembra che il suo risentimento accenni a* —, his resentment seems to be fading 2. (*di clima*) to become mild.

mitigatívo, *ag.* mitigatory.

mitigatóre, *ag.* mitigating, mitigatory ‖ *s.m.*, **mitigatríce**, *s.f.* mitigator.

mitigazióne, *s.f.* mitigation; (*di passioni*) appeasement; (*di dolore*) alleviation, relief.

mítilo, *s.m.* (*zool.*) mussel.

míto, *s.m.* myth ‖ *far cadere un* —, to explode a myth.

mitografía, *s.f.* mythography.

mitògrafo, *s.m.* (*rar.*) mythographer.

mitología, *s.f.* mythology: — *greca*, Greek mythology.

mitologicamÉnte, *av.* mythologically.

mitològico, *ag.* mythological.

mitologísta, *s.m.* (*rar.*) mythologist.

mitòlogo, *s.m.* mythologist.

mitòmane, *s.c.* (*med.*) mythomaniac.

mitomanía, *s.f.* (*med.*) mythomania.

mítra[1], *s.f.* (*eccl. st.*) mitre: *gli fu conferita la* — *il mese scorso*, he was mitred last month.

mítra[2], *s.m.* (*artigl.*) tommy-gun, submachine-gun.

mitràglia, *s.f.* 1. (*artigl.*) grape-shot 2. (*scherz.*) (*moneta spicciola*) small change.

mitragliàre, *v.t.* to machine-gun: *ebbe l'ordine di* — *i ribelli*, he was ordered to machine-gun the rebels.

mitragliatóre, *ag.*: *fucile* —, (*artigl.*) tommy-gun ‖ *s.m.* (*mil.*) (*mitragliere*) machine-gunner.

mitragliatríce, *s.f.* (*artigl.*) machine-gun: — *a nastro*, belt-fed machine-gun; — *girevole*, (*aer.*) free gun.

mitraglière, *s.m.* (*mil.*) machine-gunner.

mitràle, *ag.* (*anat.*) mitral: *valvola* —, mitral valve.

mitràto, *ag.* (*eccl.*) mitred ‖ *s.m.* bishop.

mitriàre, *v.t.* (*rar.*) to mitre, to make a bishop.

Mitridàte, *no.pr.m.* (*st.*) Mithridates.

mitridàtico, *ag.* 1. (*st.*) Mithridatic 2. (*med.*) mithridatic: *cura mitridatica*, mithridatic treatment.

mitridatísmo, *s.m.* (*med.*) mithridatism.

mittÈnte, *s.m.* sender: *il* — *e il destinatario*, the sender and the addressee; *da rispedire al* —, return to sender.

mixedÈma, *s.m.* (*patol.*) mixoedema.

mnemònica, *s.f.* mnemonics.

mnemònico, *ag.* mnemonic.

Mnemòsine, *no.pr.f.* (*mit.*) Mnemosyne.

Moabíti, *s.m.pl.* (*st.*) Moabites.

mo', *apocope* di **mòdo**.

mòbile, *ag.* 1. (*che si muove*) mobile; moving: *occhi mobili*, mobile eyes (*o* restless eyes); *rene* —, (*med.*) floating kidney; *sabbie mobili*, quicksands (*o* shifting sands); *scala* —, escalator (*o* moving staircase); (*econ.*) sliding scale; *truppe mobili*, mobile troops; *la mascella inferiore è* —, the lower jaw is mobile 2. (*che può essere mosso*) movable: *beni mobili*, (*dir.*) personal property (*o* movable property *o* chattels); *caratteri mobili*, (*tip.*) movable types; *feste mobili*, (*eccl.*) movable feasts: *la Pasqua è una festa* —, Easter is a movable feast; *imposta sulla ricchezza* —, tax on capital, business and wages; *piattaforma* —, (*mec.*) travelling platform 3. (*mutevole, incostante*) changeable, inconstant, fickle, unstable: *la* — *folla*, the inconstant crowd; *la donna è* —, woman is fickle ‖ *s.m.* 1. piece of furniture: *mobili intarsiati*, inlaid furniture; *bisognerà rinnovare qualche* —, we shall have to replace some pieces of furniture; *era una casa arredata con mobili del Settecento tutti in ottime condizioni*, it was a house furnished with fine eighteenth-century pieces all well-preserved; *questi mobili sono tutti vecchi*, this furniture is all old; *venderà la casa con mobili e infissi*, he is going to sell his house, furniture and fittings included ‖ *è un bel* —, *non c'è dubbio*, (*scherz.*) he is a fine rogue, there is no mistake 2. *il Primo Mobile*, (*st. astr.*) (*cielo*) Primum Mobile.

mobília, *s.f.* furniture: *vendita di* —, furniture sale; *la* — *era ricca*, *ma a me non piaceva*, the furniture was costly, but I didn't like it ‖ *fa sempre da* — *alle feste*, (*scherz.*) she is a wallflower at parties.

mobiliàre[1], *ag.* (*dir.*) movable, personal: *proprietà* — *e proprietà immobiliare*, personal and real property (*o* chattels personal and chattels real).

mobiliàre[2], *v.t.* to furnish.

mobiliàto, *ag.* furnished.

mobilière, *s.m.* 1. (*chi fabbrica mobili*) furniture-maker 2. (*chi vende mobili*) furniture-seller.

mobilità, *s.f.* 1. mobility: *la* — *della sua fisionomia*, the mobility of his features; *quel ragazzo ha una* — *morbosa*, that boy is never still for a moment 2. (*mutevolezza, incostanza*) inconstancy, fickleness.

mobilitàre, *v.t.* (*comm. mil.*) to mobilize: — *il capitale*, to mobilize (*o* to liberate) capital; — *le truppe*, to mobilize troops.

mobilitazióne, *s.f.* mobilization: — *delle truppe*, (*mil.*) mobilization of troops; — *dell'industria per la guerra*, mobilization of industry for war; *ordine di* —, mobilization order.

mobilizzazióne, *s.f.* mobilization.

mobilmÉnte, *av.* with mobility.

mòca, *s.m.* Mocha (coffee).

mocassíno, *s.m.* moccasin.

moccicàre, *v.i.* 1. to run: *gli moccicava il naso*, his nose was running 2. (*frignare*) to snivel.

moccichíno, *s.m.* (*pop.*) (*fazzoletto*) snot-rag.

moccicóne, *s.m.* (*volg.*) sniveller.

móccio, *s.m.* (*volg.*) snot; mucus from the nose.

moccióso, *ag.* snotty(-nosed); snivelling ‖ *s.m.* (*spreg.*) young scoundrel.

moccolàia, *s.f.* snuff.

mòccolo, *s.m.* 1. (*mozzicone di candela*) candle-end 2. (*candela piccola*) small candle; (*candela sottile*) taper ‖ *tenere il* —, to chaperon s.o. (*o* to play gooseberry) 3. (*fam.*) (*bestemmia*) oath, swear-word: *tirare un* —, to swear (*o* to curse).

mòda, *s.f.* 1. fashion, style; (*modelli*) fashions (*pl.*): *la*

— *attuale*, the current fashion; *la — autunnale, primaverile*, autumn, spring fashion(s); *la — francese*, French fashion(s): *la — francese delle gonne corte si è affermata all'estero*, the French fashion (*o* style) of short skirts has established itself abroad; *molte personalità intervennero alla presentazione della — francese a New York*, many well-known personalities attended the display of French fashions (*o* the French fashion show) in New York; *la — femminile cambia ogni anno*, women's fashions change every year; *lanciare una —*, to set a fashion; *seguire la —*, to follow the fashion ‖ *casa di mode*, fashion-house; *negozio di mode*, dress-shop; (*di cappelli*) milliner's (shop); *rivista di mode*, fashion-magazine ‖ *alla —*, fashionable (*o* stylish): *abito alla —*, fashionable (*o* stylish) dress: *abito alla — americana*, dress in the American style (*o* fashion) ‖ *all'ultima —*, in the latest fashion ‖ *di —*, in fashion: *i cartoni animati sono oggi di gran —*, animated cartoons are all the fashion (*o* all the go *o* all the rage) now; *è il male di —*, it's the fashionable ailment; *è venuto di — andare all'estero*, it has become fashionable to go abroad; *negli ultimi anni le sigarette col filtro sono venute di —*, in recent years filter-tipped cigarettes have come into fashion; *passare di —*, to go out of fashion ‖ *fuori —*, out of fashion: *abito fuori —*, out-of-fashion dress 2. (*abitudine, modo*) custom, fashion; manner, way ‖ *alla — di*, after the manner (*o* the style) of: *mangiare il riso alla — dei cinesi*, to eat rice in the Chinese way.

modàle, *ag.* modal: *proposizione —*, (*gram.*) modal proposition; *sistema —*, (*mus.*) modal system.

modalità, *s.f.* modality; formality: *le — di un contratto*, the form of a contract; *— di pagamento*, conditions of payment; *seguire le — richieste*, to comply with all the necessary formalities.

modanatúra, *s.f.* (*arch.*) moulding.

mòdano, *s.m.* 1. (*modello*) model, mould 2. (*legnetto per formare le maglie delle reti*) netting-needle.

modèlla, *s.f.* model: *lavora come —*, she works as a model; *il pittore sposò una delle sue modelle*, the painter married one of his models.

modellaménto, *s.m.* modelling, moulding.

modellàre, *v.t.* 1. to model, to shape, to mould, to fashion (anche *fig.*): *cercava di — la sua vita secondo gli ideali del Cristianesimo*, he tried to fashion his life according to the ideals of Christianity; *modellò il suo stile su quello del Manzoni*, he modelled his style on Manzoni's; *— una testa in creta*, to mould a head in clay 2. (*fare una copia di*) to model, to copy: *modellò una statua del Mosè di Michelangelo*, he made a copy of Michelangelo's Moses ‖ **modellàrsi**, *v.r.* to model oneself: *— a, su qlcu.*, to model oneself on s.o.

modellatóre, *s.m.*, **modellatríce**, *s.f.* modeller.

modellatúra, *s.f.* (*rar.*) modelling, moulding.

modellazióne, *s.f.* 1. modelling, moulding 2. (*geol.*) mould.

modèllo, *s.m.* 1. (*esemplare perfetto*) model, pattern: *un — di gentilezza, di bontà*, a pattern of kindness, goodness; *un buon — di stile*, a good model of style; *quella donna è un — di virtù*, that woman is a paragon of virtue; *questo scrittore è un — di stile*, this writer is a model of style ‖ *podere —*, model farm; *ragazza —*, exemplary girl; *Anna è una moglie —*, Ann is an exemplary (*o* a model *o* a perfect) wife 2. (*riproduzione di un originale*) model: *— al vero*, life-size model; *il — di una casa*, the model of a house; *— di creta, gesso, cera, clay, plaster, wax model; *— in scala*, scale model; *questa statua è solo il — di un'opera antica*, this statue is just a model of an ancient work; *fare un — di una nave*, to make a model of a ship 3. (*stampo*) mould (anche *fig.*): *questi pezzi sono tutti fatti sullo stesso —*, all these pieces are made from the same mould; *queste ragazze sono tutte fatte sullo stesso —*, these girls are all cast in the same mould 4. (*corpo su cui si forma lo stampo*) (casting) pattern: *— di macchina*, pattern

of a machine; *— di statua*, pattern of a statue 5. (*di sartoria*) pattern: *— di vestito*, pattern of a dress; *tagliare sul —*, to cut from a pattern 6. (*foggia, tipo*) model: *è un'automobile di vecchio —*, this car is an old model; *ne abbiamo diversi modelli*, we have a variety of models 7. (*prodotto, creazione industriale*) model: *gli ultimi modelli di Parigi*, the latest models (*o* fashions) from Paris; *il Salone dell'Automobile presenta tutti i nuovi modelli*, the Motor Show exhibits all the new models 8. (*persona, cosa che serve da modello*) model: *ha copiato fedelmente il —*, he copied the model faithfully; *il Manzoni è il suo —*, Manzoni is his model; *non s'è attenuto al —*, he did not stick to the model; *questa figura è stata disegnata da un —*, this figure was drawn from a model; *prendere qlcu. per —*, to take s.o. as one's model; *servire da — ad un artista*, (*posare per lui*) to sit for an artist 9. (*manichino*) manikin, tailor's dummy.

modenése, *ag.* Modenese ‖ *pozzi modenesi*, Artesian wells ‖ *s.c.* Modenese (*invariato al pl.*).

moderàbile, *ag.* governable, limitable.

moderàre, *v.t.* 1. to moderate, to curb, to check; (*mitigare*) to mitigate: *modera la tua ira*, curb your anger; *dovrebbe — il suo entusiasmo*, he ought to moderate his enthusiasm; *— l'impazienza*, to curb one's impatience; *— la lingua*, to moderate one's language; *— le passioni*, to check one's passions; *— le pretese*, to moderate one's pretensions 2. (*diminuire*) to reduce: *— le spese*, to cut down expenses; *— la velocità*, to reduce speed (*o* to slow down) 3. (*rar.*) (*governare*) to govern ‖ **moderàrsi**, *v.r.* to moderate oneself; (*frenare la propria collera*) to keep one's temper: *— nel mangiare, nel bere*, to eat, to drink moderately.

moderataménte, *av.* moderately, temperately.

moderatézza, *s.f.* moderation, temperateness.

moderatívo, *ag.* moderating.

moderàto, *ag.* 1. moderate, temperate: *partito —*, (*pol.*) moderate party; *è — nel bere*, he drinks moderately (*o* he is a moderate drinker); *è una persona moderata*, he is a temperate person; *qui i prezzi sono moderati*, prices are reasonable here; *avere idee moderate*, to have moderate opinions; *camminare con passo —*, to go at a moderate (*o* steady) pace 2. (*mus.*) moderato ‖ *s.m.* moderate (person) ‖ *i moderati*, (*pol.*) the moderate party.

moderatóre, *ag.* moderating ‖ *s.m.* 1. moderator 2. (*rar.*) (*chi governa*) ruler: *il supremo — dello stato*, the supreme ruler of the State 3. (*lec.*) regulator, governor; (*fis. atomica*) moderator; (*metal.*) inhibitor ‖ **moderatríce**, *s.f.* moderator.

moderazióne, *s.f.* moderation, temperateness: *ci vuol — in tutto*, moderation is necessary in all things; *il medico gli consigliò più — nel mangiare e nel bere*, the doctor advised more moderation in eating and drinking; *il Presidente parlò con —*, the President spoke with moderation.

modernaménte, *av.* 1. in the modern manner 2. (*nei tempi moderni*) in modern times.

modernísmo, *s.m.* (*st. fil.*) modernism.

modernísta, *s.m.* (*st. fil.*) modernist.

modernístico, *ag.* modernistic.

modernità, *s.f.* modernity.

modernizzàre, *v.t.* to modernize.

modèrno, *ag.* modern; recent; up-to-date (*attributivo*): *arte moderna*, modern art; *una casa moderna*, an up-to-date house; *lingue moderne*, modern languages; *le scoperte moderne nel campo della medicina*, the recent discoveries of medicine; *storia moderna*, modern history; *tempi moderni*, modern times ‖ *alla moderna*, in the modern style.

modestaménte, *av.* modestly.

modèstia, *s.f.* 1. (*sentimento umile di sè*) modesty, unpretentiousness: *falsa —*, false modesty; *non peccare di —!*, don't be too modest!; *non pecca di —*, modesty is not one of his faults ‖ *— a parte*, modesty apart **2.** (*pudicizia*) modesty, bashfulness: *la — della ragazza*, the bashfulness of the girl; *la — è la sua dote migliore*, modesty is her best quality; *la sua — le impedì di fargli sapere i suoi veri sentimenti*, her modesty prevented her from making her real feelings known to him **3.** (*mediocrità*) modesty: *la — delle sue ambizioni è eccessiva*, he is too modest in his ambitions; *la sua eleganza non è conforme alla — dei suoi mezzi*, his smartness is out of keeping with the modesty of his means **4.** (*moderazione*) modesty, moderation.

modèsto, *ag.* **1.** (*non superbo*) modest, unassuming, unpretentious: *è molto — riguardo le sue imprese*, he is very modest about his achievements; *non essere troppo —!*, don't be too modest! **2.** (*pudico*) modest, bashful: *comportamento —*, modest behaviour; *aveva un aspetto —*, she had a bashful look; *le fanciulle dovrebbero essere modeste nel parlare e nel vestire*, young girls ought to be modest in speech and dress **3.** (*mediocre, semplice*) modest, humble: *— livello di vita*, modest standard of living; *reddito —*, modest income; *ha una casa modesta*, he has a humble house **4.** (*moderato*) modest, moderate: *ha ambizioni modeste*, he has modest ambitions.

modicaménte, *av.* moderately.

modicità, *s.f.* moderateness, moderation; (*basso prezzo*) cheapness: *per la — delle sue richieste quel lavoratore è molto ricercato*, that worker is much sought after for his moderate charges; *questo articolo è molto richiesto per la — del suo prezzo*, this article is in great demand owing to its cheapness.

mòdico, *ag.* moderate, reasonable; (*a buon mercato*) cheap: *articoli a prezzo —*, cheap articles; *interesse —*, moderate interest.

modífica, *s.f.* modification; alteration: *orario soggetto a modifiche*, time-table subject to alteration; *apportare delle modifiche a ql.co.*, to make changes in sthg.

modificàbile, *ag.* modifiable; alterable.

modificàre, *v.t.* **1.** to modify; to alter: *la costituzione fu modificata con un referendum*, the Constitution was modified by a referendum; *ha modificato le sue dichiarazioni*, he has modified his statements; *— i propri piani*, to alter one's plans **2.** (*mitigare*) to modify, to mitigate: *la pena gli fu modificata*, his penalty was modified.

modificatívo, *ag.* modifying, modificative.

modificatóre, *ag.* modifying, modificative, modificatory || *s.m.*, **modificatrice,** *s.f.* modifier.

modificazióne, *V.* **modífica.**

modiglióne, *s.m.* (*arch.*) modillion, truss.

modísta, *s.f.* milliner.

modistería, *s.f.* millinery; (*negozio*) milliner's (shop).

mòdo, *s.m.* **1.** way, manner: *— di parlare, camminare*, way (o manner) of speaking, walking; *avverbio di —*, (*gram.*) adverb of manner; *in — singolare*, in a strange way; *in nessun —*, by no means; *il miglior — di fare ql.co.*, the best way to do (o of doing) sthg.; *secondo il mio — di vedere, di pensare*, in my opinion (o to my way of thinking o from my point of view); *il suo — di vedere il Cattolicesimo*, his approach to Catholicism; *fallo in questo —*, do it like this; *non ci sono due uomini che pensano allo stesso —*, no two men think alike; *non farlo allo stesso —*, don't do it (in) the same way; *non mi piace il suo — di ridere*, I do not like the way he laughs; *non parlare in questo —*, don't speak like that; *può essere fatto in vari modi*, it can be done in various ways || *al — di*, like: *dipingere al — di Tiziano*, to paint in the style (o manner) of Titian || *di — che*, (and) so: *arrivai in ritardo di — che persi il treno*, I was late, (and) so I missed the train || *in — da*, in such a way as to; (*finale*) so as to: *si comportò in — da essere lodato*, he behaved so as to be praised; *si comportò in — da essere rimproverato*, he behaved in such a way as to be reproached || *in un — o in un altro*, in one way or another: *ci riuscirà in un*

— o in un altro, he will succeed by hook or by crook || *in certo (qual) —*, in one way || *in che —*, how: *dimmi in che — l'hai fatto*, tell me how you did it || *in malo —*, badly || *in particolar —*, particularly || *in qualche —*, anyhow; (*comunque*) somehow: *in qualche — riuscirò*, somehow I will succeed; *lavorò in qualche —*, he worked anyhow || *in tutti i modi, in, ad ogni —*, in any case (o at any rate o anyhow o anyway) || *c'è — e — di fare ql.co.*, there is more than one way of doing sthg. || *è un — elegante per rifiutarsi*, it is a polite way of refusing || *fare in — di fare ql.co.*, to try to do sthg.: *devi fare in — che il cane non cammini su questo tappeto*, you must stop the dog (from) walking on this carpet; *devi fare in — che le cose vadano meglio*, you must try to get things to go better; *devi fare in — che egli venga*, you must get him to come; *devi fare in — di venire*, you must try to come || *fare ql.co. a proprio —*, to do sthg. in one's own way **2.** (*mezzo; occasione*) way, means: *devo trovare il — di vederlo*, I must find some way of seeing him; *gli diedi — di fare un buon affare*, I enabled him to make a good bargain (o fam. I put him on to a good bargain); *non c'è — di farglielo capire*, there is no way of making him understand; *non gli ho mai dato — di pensarlo*, I have never given him cause to think so; *non ho — di scrivere*, I've nothing to write with; *troverò il — di fargliela*, I'll find a way of doing him down || *— di pagamento*, (*comm.*) method of paying **3.** (*tratto, garbo*) manners (*pl.*): *modi amichevoli*, friendly manners; *bei modi*, (good-) breeding: *avere bei, brutti modi*, to have good, bad manners; *parlare a qlcu. con bel —*, to speak politely to s.o. || *una persona a —*, a well-bred person **4.** (*locuzione*) expression: *— improprio*, incorrect expression; *— letterario*, literary expression (o turn of speech) || *— di dire*, idiom (o idiomatic phrase): *questo — di dire non si usa più*, this expression is no longer used || *per — di dire*, so to speak (o so to say) **5.** (*misura*) measure: *oltre —*, beyond measure (o excessively o extremely); *agire con — e misura*, to act reasonably and sensibly || *persona a —*, polite (o good-mannered) person: *far ql.co. a —*, to do sthg. properly **6.** (*gram.*) mood: *— indicativo, congiuntivo*, indicative, subjunctive mood **7.** (*mus.*) key, mode: *scala di — maggiore*, major scale.

modulàbile, *ag.* (*rar.*) that can be modulated.

modulàre, *v.t.* **1.** (*mus.*) to modulate: *— il canto*, to modulate one's singing; *— da una chiave a un'altra*, to modulate from one key to another; *— la voce*, to modulate one's voice **2.** (*formulare*) to formulate: *— una proposta*, to put a proposal into words **3.** (*elett.*) to modulate.

modulataménte, *av.* with modulations.

modulatóre, *ag.* (*rad.*) modulating || *s.m.* modulator: *— di fase*, (*rad.*) phase modulator; *— di frequenza*, (*rad.*) frequency modulator.

modulazióne, *s.f.* **1.** modulation, inflection: *— dei suoni*, modulation of sounds; *— della voce*, inflection of voice **2.** (*elett.*) modulation: *— della luce*, (*tv.*) light modulation; *— di ampiezza*, (*rad.*) amplitude modulation (*abbr.* A.M.); *— di fase*, (*rad.*) phase modulation; *— di frequenza*, (*rad.*) frequency modulation (*abbr.* F.M.).

mòdulo, *s.m.* **1.** form; (*amer.*) blank: *— di assunzione*, labour engagement sheet; *— di domanda*, application form; *— in bianco*, blank form; *— per telegramma*, telegraph form; *compilare, riempire un —*, to fill up (o in) a form **2.** (*rar.*) (*modello*) model; (*norma*) standard **3.** (*arch. idraulica*) module **4.** (*mat. mec.*) modulus (*pl.* moduli): *— di elasticità*, coefficient of elasticity **5.** (*numismatica*) diameter (of coin).

modus, *s.m.* (*lat.*) modus (*pl.* modi): *— vivendi*, modus vivendi (o way of living) || *est — in rebus*, (c'è una giusta misura in tutte le cose) there is measure in all things.

moèrro, *s.m.* (*tessuto*) moire.

mofèta, *s.f.* (*geol.*) mofette.

moffétta, *s.f.* (*zool.*) skunk.

mògano, *s.m.* mahogany.

mòggio, *s.m.* bushel ‖ *porre la lucerna sotto il* —, (*Bibbia*) to hide one's light under a bushel.

mògio, *ag.* 1. (*depresso*) depressed: *sembrava molto mogia*, she looked very depressed ‖ —, crestfallen (*o dejected*): *venne a casa* —, he came home crestfallen 2. (*quieto*) quiet: *quel bambino sembra fin troppo* —*i*, that child looks even too quiet!.

mòglie, *s.f.* wife: — *legittima*, lawful wife (*o wedded wife*); *il Signor Smith e sua* —, Mr. and Mrs. Smith; *è una* — *modello*, she is a model wife (*o she is a paragon of a wife*); *non ha* —, he is wifeless; *quella è la sua seconda* —, that lady is his second wife; *sarà una buona* — *per lui*, she will make him a good wife; *vi darò in* — *mia figlia*, I will give you my daughter to wife; *aver* —, to have a wife; *cercar* —, to seek a wife; *chiedere qlcu. in* —, to seek s.o. in marriage; *prender* —, to get married; *prendere in* — *una vedova*, to take a widow to wife ‖ — *e buoi dei paesi tuoi*, *prov.* it is better to marry over the mixen than over the moor.

mogòl, *s.m.* (*st.*) Mogul: *il Gran Mogol*, the Great Mogul.

Mohicàni, *s.m.pl.* Mohicans.

mòia, *s.f.* 1. (*acqua salata*, *salamoia*) brine 2. (*pozzo d'acqua salata*) salt-pit; salt-pond.

moiétta, *s.f.* (*metall.*) metal-strip, metal-band.

moína, *s.f.* simpering: *con un po' di moine ottiene quel che vuole dalla mamma*, with a little bit of wheedling he can get his mother to do anything he likes; *fare moine*, to simper: *smetti di fare tante moine*, stop simpering; *fare moine a qlcu. per indurlo a fare ql.co.*, to wheedle a person into doing sthg.

moire, *s.m.* (*tessuto*) moire.

mòka, *s.m.* Mocha (coffee).

mòla, *s.f.* 1. (*macina da mulino*) millstone 2. (*pietra per arrotare*) grindstone; (*per gioiellieri, vetrai, ecc.*) lap: — *dura*, hard grinding-wheel (*o grinder*); —*portante*, small control wheel; — *smerigliatrice*, lapping -wheel; — *tenera*, soft grinding-wheel; *equilibrare la* —, to set the grinding-wheel; *sgrossare alla* —, to coarse-grind 3. (*ittiol.*) sun-fish 4. (*patol.*) mole.

molàre, *ag.* 1. (*anat.*) molar: *dente* —, molar (tooth); *ghiandole molari*, molar glands 2. *pietra* —, millstone ‖ *s.m.* (*dente*) molar.

molàre, *v.t.* to grind; (*affilare*) to whet: — *ad umido*, to wet-grind; — *a secco*, to dry-grind; — *il cristallo*, to cut crystal; — *il vetro*, to grind glass.

molàssa, *s.f.* (*geol.*) molasse; sandstone.

molàto, *ag.*: *cristallo* —, cut crystal.

molatríce, *s.f.* (*mec.*) grinder: — *monoposto*, single -stand grinder; — *oscillante*, swing-frame grinder; — *per carde*, card grinder; — *per sbavatura*, snag grinder; — *portatile elettrica*, portable electric grinder.

molatúra, *s.f.* grinding.

molàzza, *s.f.* (*fonderia*) muller, pan mill: — *a ruote*, edge runner; — *mescolatrice*, (*ind. gomma*) mixing-mill; — *portatile*, portable muller.

mólcere, *v.t.* (*poet.*) to soothe, to mitigate.

moldàvo, *ag.s.m.* Moldavian.

mòle, *s.f.* 1. (*massa*) mass; bulk: *la* — *di quell'edificio è imponente*, the mass of that building is imposing ‖ *una grande* — *di lavoro*, a vast amount of work 2. (*dimensione*) size, dimension, proportion: *un libro di grande* —, a book of large proportions; *un macigno di smisurata* —, a rock of massive dimensions; *vorrei conoscerne la* —, I should like to know the size of it ‖ *che* —*!*, (*scherz.*) what a mountain of flesh!

molècola, *s.f.* 1. (*chim.*) molecule: *schema della disposizione degli atomi in una* —, atomic model 2. (*particella*) particle.

molecolàre, *ag.* (*chim. fis.*) molecular: *peso* —, molecular weight.

molènda, *s.f.* (*prezzo per la macinatura*) multure.

molestaménte, *av.* annoyingly, troublesomely.

molestaménto, *s.m.* molesting; annoying.

molestàre, *v.t.* to molest; to disturb, to bother; to worry; to annoy, to tease: *fu molestata da tre teppisti*, she was molested by three teddy-boys; *non molestarmi con domande così sciocche*, don't bother me with such silly questions; *non* — *il gatto!*, don't tease the cat!; *i rumori mi molestano quando lavoro*, noise disturbs me when I am trying to work; — *il sonno di qlcu.*, to disturb s.o.'s rest.

molestatóre, *ag.* molesting ‖ *s.m.*, **molestatríce**, *s.f.* molester.

molèstia, *s.f.* nuisance, trouble, bother: *queste sono solo molestie da poco*, these are but small troubles; *questo cane è una vera* — *per me*, this dog is a real bother to me; *dar* — *a qlcu.*, to bother s.o.

molèsto, *ag.* troublesome, bothersome, annoying: *pensieri molesti*, harassing thoughts; *persone moleste*, bothersome persons; *tosse molesta*, troublesome cough; *le mosche sono insetti molesti*, flies are troublesome insects ‖ *spero di non esservi* —, I hope I am not bothering you (*o intruding*).

molibdeníte, *s.f.* (*min.*) molybdenite.

molibdèno, *s.m.* (*chim.*) molybdenum.

molíno, *V.* **mulíno**.

molinísmo, *s.m.* (*st. relig.*) Molinism.

molinísta, *s.m.* (*st. relig.*) Molinist.

molitòrio, *ag.* molinary.

mòlla, *s.f.* 1. (*mec.*) spring: — *a spirale*, coil-spring; — *d'arresto*, stop-spring; — *di compressione*, compression-spring; — *di torsione*, torsion-spring; — *motrice*, (*di orologio*) mainspring; *arresto a* —, spring-pawl; *bilancia a* —, spring-balance; *calibro a* —, spring -gauge; *materasso a molle*, spring-mattress; *regolatore a* —, spring-governor; *spira di una* —, coil of a spring; *caricare una* —, to load a spring; *scaricare una* —, to release (*o to relieve*) a spring; *tendere una* —, to stretch a spring ‖ *caricato a* —, spring-loaded 2. (*incentivo*) mainspring, incentive, spur: *le molle segrete delle azioni umane*, the hidden springs of human actions; *l'ambizione è la* — *di tutte le azioni umane*, ambition is the mainspring of all human actions.

mollàre, *v.t.* 1. (*allentare*) to slacken; (*lasciar andare*) to let go: — *la presa*, to let go (*o to loose one's hold*) ‖ *fare a tira e molla*, to shilly-shally ‖ —, to cough up 2. (*mar.*) to let go, to cast off: — *gli ormeggi*, to let go the moorings ‖ *molla!*, let go! (*o cast off!*) ‖ *v.i.* 1. (*cedere*) to give in: *ha insistito finché ho mollato*, he insisted until I gave in 2. (*desistere*) to give up.

mòlle[1], *s.f.pl.* tongs: — *per il carbone*, coal-tongs; — *per il ghiaccio*, *lo zucchero*, sugar-tongs, ice-tongs ‖ *è da prendere con le* —, (*fam.*) you have to watch your step with him.

mòlle[2], *ag.* 1. soft: — *come la cera*, as soft as wax; *cuoio*, *legno* —, soft leather, wood; *tessuto* —, soft material; *questo materasso è molto* —, this mattress is very soft ‖ *acque molli*, soft water 2. (*bagnato*) wet, soaking wet; (*umido*) moist: — *di sudore*, wet with sweat; *occhi molli di pianto*, moist eyes; *terra* —, moist earth; *terreno* —, soft ground 3. (*pieghevole*) flexible, supple, pliable, pliant: *un* — *giunco*, a flexible reed 4. (*floscio*) flabby, slack; (*flaccido*) limp: *mi porse una mano* — *da stringere*, he gave me a limp hand to shake 5. (*debole*) weak, feeble, flabby: *un carattere* —, a weak character; *un governo* —, a weak government; *un insegnante* —, an easy-going teacher; *stile* —, flabby style 6. (*effeminato*) effeminate; (*rilassato*) loose; (*lascivo*) lascivious: *molli costumi*, lax morals; *molli diletti*, lascivious pleasures; *vita* —, loose living 7. (*mite, piacevole*) soft: *molli parole*, soft words; *voce* —, soft voice ‖ *s.m.* 1. soft part; (*del corpo*) fleshy part: *il* — *e il duro di un oggetto*, the soft and the hard parts of an object 2. *mettere in* —, to soak: *mise il bucato in* — *nella tinozza*, she soaked the dirty linen in the wash-tub; *stare a* —, to lie in soak.

molleggiaménto, *s.m.* **1.** (*il molleggiare*) springing **2.** (*di veicoli, ecc.*) (*sistema di molleggio*) springing system **3.** (*elasticità*) springiness, elasticity.

molleggiàre, *v.i.* to be springy; to be elastic: *questa poltrona molleggia bene*, this easy-chair is well -sprung ‖ *v.i.*, **molleggiàrsi**, *v.r.* (*camminare dimenandosi*) to mince; (*fam.*) to walk with a wiggle.

molleggiàto, *ag.* sprung: *un sedile* —, a sprung seat; *questo divano è ben* —, this sofa is well-sprung.

molléggio, *s.m.* **1.** suspension, springing: — *dolce*, soft spring suspension; — *duro*, hard spring suspension; *sistema di* —, springing system; *provare il* — *di un veicolo*, to try (*o* to test) the springs of a vehicle **2.** (*l'essere molleggiato*) springiness.

molleménte, *av.* **1.** (*senza severità; dolcemente*) softly: *fu educato* —, he was brought up too softly **2.** (*debolmente, fiaccamente*) weakly, feebly, faintly: *si difendeva* —, he offered feeble (*o* weak) resistance **3.** (*languidamente*) languidly: *era* — *sdraiata su un divano*, she was lying languidly on a sofa **4.** (*effeminatamente*) effeminately; (*lascivamente*) lasciviously.

mollétta, *s.f.* **1.** (*per il bucato*) clothes-peg, clothes-pin; (*per capelli*) hair-pin **2.** *pl.* tongs: *mollette per caratteri*, (*tip.*) bodkin (*sing.*); *mollette per il ghiaccio*, ice-tongs; *mollette per lo zucchero*, sugar-tongs.

mollettièra, *s.f.* (*fascia*) puttee.

mollettóne, *s.m.* thick flannel.

mollézza, *s.f.* **1.** (*morbidezza*) softness **2.** (*debolezza, fiacchezza*) weakness, feebleness: — *d'animo*, weakness of character; *la* — *di un governo*, the weakness of a government **3.** (*effeminatezza*) effeminacy; (*rilassatezza*) laxity, looseness; (*lascivia*) lasciviousness: — *di costumi*, looseness of morals; — *di vita*, looseness of life **4.** *pl.* (*comodità, piaceri*) luxury (*sing.*): *vivere tra le mollezze*, to live in the lap of luxury.

mollìca, *s.f.* **1.** crumb, soft part of the bread: *estrasse la* — *dalla pagnotta*, he took the soft part out of the loaf **2.** *pl.* (*briciole*) crumbs: *mangiò il pane e poi raccolse con cura le molliche*, he ate the bread and then picked up the crumbs carefully.

mollìcchio, *s.m.* damp ground, muddy ground.

mollìccio, *ag.* **1.** softish; (*umidiccio*) dampish: *terra molliccia*, dampish ground **2.** (*floscio*) limp, flabby: *un cencio* —, a limp cloth ‖ *s.m.* damp ground, muddy ground: *c'è un* — *davanti al cancello*, there is a muddy patch in front of the gate.

mollificaménto, *s.m.* (*rar.*) mollifying; mollification.

mollificàre, *v.t.* **1.** to soften: — *una sostanza*, to soften a substance **2.** (*tenere a mollo*) to soak, to put in soak: — *le erbe*, to put the herbs in soak (*o* to soak the herbs) **3.** *fig.* (*addolcire*) to mollify, to appease, to soften: — *il cuore di qlcu.*, to soften s.o.'s heart ‖ **mollificàrsi**, *v.r.* **1.** (*divenir molle*) to soften **2.** (*divenir fradicio*) to soak: — *nell'acqua*, to soak in water.

mollificatìvo, *ag.* (*rar.*) mollifying.

mollificazióne, *s.f.* (*rar.*) **1.** softening: *la* — *della cera*, the softening of wax **2.** (*il tenere a molle*) soaking **3.** *fig.* (*addolcimento*) mollification, molliflying.

mollìzie, *V.* **mollézza** **4.**

mollùme, *s.m.* dampness, wetness.

mollùsco, *s.m.* **1.** (*zool.*) mollusc, mollusk: *i lamellibranchi, i cefalopodi e i gasteropodi sono molluschi*, Lamellibranchia, Cephalopoda and Gasteropoda are molluscs ‖ *i molluschi*, the Mollusca **2.** (*persona senza volontà*) sluggard; (*fam.*) slug **3.** (*patol.*) molluscum.

mòlo, *s.m.* pier, mole, jetty; (*banchina*) wharf: — *di carico*, loading wharf; *diritti di* —, (*comm.*) pierage.

Molòc, *no.pr.m.* (*mit.*) Moloch ‖ **molòc**, *s.m.* (*zool.*) moloch.

molòsso, *ag.* Molossian ‖ *s.m.* **1.** (*st.*) Molossian **2.** (*poes.*) molossus **3.** (*zool.*) Molossian.

moltéplice, *ag.* **1.** manifold, multifarious; numerous, various: *per molteplici ragioni*, for various reasons; *ha molteplici doveri*, he has multifarious duties; *ha incontrato molteplici difficoltà*, he met with manifold

difficulties; *il libro contiene molteplici errori*, the book contains numerous mistakes **2.** (*di varie qualità*) manifold, many-sided: *il* — *ingegno di Ulisse*, the many-sided genius of Ulysses **3.** (*bot.*) multifarious: *fiore* —, multifarious flower **4.** (*multiplo*) multiple: *numero* —, (*mat.*) multiple number.

molteplicità, *s.f.* multiplicity, variety.

moltìplica, *s.f.* **1.** (*arit.*) multiplication **2.** (*mec.*) gearing.

moltiplicàbile, *ag.* multipliable, multiplicable.

moltiplicàndo, *s.m.* (*arit.*) multiplicand.

moltiplicàre, *v.t.* **1.** (*arit.*) to multiply: — *un numero per un altro*, to multiply a number by another; — *un numero per se stesso*, to multiply a number by itself (*o* to square a number) **2.** (*accrescere*) to multiply, to increase: *gli specchi moltiplicavano le immagini*, the mirrors multiplied the images; — *gli sforzi*, to redouble one's efforts ‖ *v.i.* to multiply: *la città moltiplicò in commerci*, the business of the city increased (*o* expanded); — *in superbia*, to become more and more arrogant ‖ **moltiplicàrsi**, *v.r.* to multiply: *certi animali si moltiplicano rapidamente*, some animals multiply rapidly; *le preoccupazioni si moltiplicano con l'età*, cares multiply with age.

moltiplicatìvo, *ag.* (*arit.*) multiplicative.

moltiplicatóre, *ag.* multiplying ‖ *s.m.* multiplier: — *di frequenza*, (*rad.*) frequency multiplier; — *di velocità*, (*mec.*) overdrive; — *elettronico*, (*elett.*) (electron) multiplier.

moltiplicatrìce, *s.f.* calculating machine.

moltiplicazióne, *s.f.* multiplication: *la* — *del genere umano*, the reproduction of the human species; *i fattori della* —, (*arit.*) multiplication factors ‖ *la* — *dei pani e dei pesci*, the miracle of the loaves and fishes.

moltiplicità, *s.f.* multiplicity, variety.

moltìssimo, *ag. superl.* **1.** very much; *in proposizioni affermative è generalmente sostituito da:* **a great deal of**; (*fam.*) **an awful lot of, ever so much**: *ha moltissima pazienza coi bambini*, she has got an awful lot of patience with children; *non hanno* — *tempo per leggere*, they haven't very much time for reading; *spesero* — *denaro per il mobilio*, they spent ever so much money on their furniture; *spreca moltissima energia in cose inutili*, he wastes a great deal of energy doing useless things **2.** (*riferito a tempo*) **very long:** — *tempo*, a very long time; very long (*solo in proposizioni interrogative e negative*): — *tempo prima, dopo*, a very long time before, after(wards); *non ho atteso* — *tempo*, I didn't wait very long; *non lo vedo da* — *tempo*, it is a very long time (*o* it is ages) since I saw him last (*o* I have not seen him for a very long time) **3.** *pl.* **very many;** *in proposizioni affermative è generalmente sostituito da:* **a great many;** (*fam.*) **an awful lot of, ever so many:** *c'erano moltissimi oggetti di valore a quell'asta?*, were there very many objects of value at the auction?; *ha comprato moltissimi abiti nuovi quest'anno*, she has bought ever so many new clothes this year; *noi avevamo moltissimi libri un tempo*, we had an awful lot of (*o* a great many) books once **4.** (*in espressioni temporali ellittiche*) **a very long time; very long** (*solo in proposizioni interrogative e negative*): *da* —, for a very long time; *è* — *che non vado a Roma*, it is a very long time (*o* it is ages) since I last went to Rome; *non ho aspettato* —, I didn't wait very long **5.** (*in altre espressioni ellittiche*): *ci vuole* — *per vivere bene*, one needs a good deal of money to live comfortably; *non c'è* —, (*di distanza*) it is not very far ‖ *pron.* **1.** **very much;** *in proposizioni affermative è generalmente sostituito da:* **a great deal;** (*fam.*) **an awful lot, ever so much:** « *Hai del tempo libero oggi?* », « *Non ne ho* —, *perché?* », " Have you got any spare time today? ", " Well, I haven't an awful lot, why? "; « *Hanno speso molto denaro per il nuovo appartamento?* », « *Ne hanno speso* — », " Did they spend a lot of money on their new flat? ", " They spent ever so much "; *non ne avevo* —, *ma non me ne occorreva di più*, I hadn't got very much, but I didn't need any more **2.** *pl.* **very many** (*generalmente non usato in proposizioni affermative*); **a great many**; (*fam.*) **an awful lot**; (*fam.*) **ever so many** (*generalmente in proposizioni affermative*): « *Fai la raccolta dei francobolli?* », « *Sì, ma non ne ho moltissimi* », " Do you collect stamps? ", " I do, but I haven't got very many (*o a great many*) "; *non so barzellette, ma mio fratello ne sa moltissime*, I don't know any funny stories, but my brother knows ever so many; « *Quanti amici ha?* », « *Ne ha moltissimi* », " How many friends has she? ", " An awful lot " ‖ *s.m.* **1. very much, a great deal**; (*fam.*) **an awful lot**; (*fam.*) **ever so much** (*generalmente in proposizioni affermative*): — *di quanto dice è vero*, very much of what he says is true; *suo padre ha fatto* — *per lei*, her father did an awful lot for her **2.** *pl.* **very many** (*people*), **a great many** (*people*); (*fam.*) **an awful lot of people**: *moltissimi sostengono che...*, very many people (*o an awful lot of people*) maintain that...; *fu lodato da moltissimi*, he was praised by a great many people; *non erano in moltissimi ieri alla lezione*, there weren't very many at the lesson yesterday ‖ *av.* **very much, a great deal**; (*fam.*) **an awful lot**: *indugiò* — *prima di rispondermi*, he hesitated an awful lot before answering me; *le piacque* —, she liked it very much; *non mi sono divertito* —, I didn't enjoy myself very much; *lavorare* —, to work very hard.

moltitúdine, *s.f.* **1.** multitude; (*gran folla*) great crowd: *una* — *di animali*, a great number of animals; *una* — *di voci*, a multitude of voices; *una* — *era nella piazza*, there was a great crowd in the square **2.** (*spreg.*) (*massa*) mob: *il favore della* —, the favour of the mob.

mólto, *ag.indef.* **1. much**; *in proposizioni affermative, a meno che non si riferisca al sogg., è generalmente sostituito da*: **a great deal of, a good deal of, a great quantity of, a large quantity of, a lot of, plenty of, lots of**: *dopo molta fatica*, after a great deal of effort; *aveva* — *denaro*, he had a lot (*o* plenty) of money; *fu sprecato* — *tempo in inutili discussioni*, much time was wasted in futile discussions; *hanno molta libertà?*, do they get much freedom?; *ho* — *tempo per leggere*, I have plenty (*o* lots) of time for reading; *non ho molta pazienza coi bambini*, I have not much patience with children **2.** (*riferito a tempo*) **long**: — *tempo*, a long time; **long** (*solo in proposizioni interrogative e negative*): — *tempo prima, dopo*, a long time before, after(wards); *fra non* — *tempo*, before long; — *tempo è passato da quando...*, a long time has elapsed since...; *è* — *tempo che non lo vedo, non lo vedo da* — *tempo*, it is a long time since I saw him last (*o* I have not seen him for a long time); *hai dovuto attendere* — *tempo?*, did you have long to wait?; *ho aspettato* — *tempo*, I waited a long time; *non ho atteso* — *tempo*, I didn't wait long **3.** *pl.* **many, a lot of, a great many, a large number of; plenty of, a good many, lots of** (*generalmente in proposizioni affermative*): *dopo molti anni*, after many years; *molti incidenti sono accaduti su questa strada recentemente*, a good many accidents have happened on this road recently; *ha molti amici*, he has a lot of (*o* lots of *o* a great many) friends; *hai visto molti film quest'anno?*, have you seen many films this year?; *non ho molti libri*, I have not many books ‖ *dopo molti e molti anni*, after many a year (*o fam.* after many a moon) **4.** (*in espressioni temporali ellittiche*) **a long time; long** (*solo in proposizioni interrogative e negative*): *da* —, for a long time; *fra non* —, before long; *è* — *che non lo vedo*, it's a long time since I saw him last; *manca* — *a Natale*, there is a long time to go before Christmas (*o* Christmas is still a long way off); *ti manca* — *per essere pronto?*, will you be long getting ready? **5.** (*in altre espressioni ellittiche*): *ci corre* — *tra...*, there's a great difference between...; *ci vuole* — *per vivere bene*, you need a good deal of money to live comfortably; *non c'è* — *da qui alla stazione*, it's not far from here to the station ‖ *pron. indef.* **1. much**; *in proposizioni*

affermative, a meno che non si riferisca al sogg., è generalmente sostituito da: **a great deal, a good deal, a lot, plenty, lots**: *crede di sapere benissimo l'inglese, ma in effetti non ne sa* —, she thinks she knows English very well, but in fact she doesn't know much; « *Hai del pane?* », « *Ne ho* — », « *Non ne ho* — », "Have you any bread?", "I have got a lot", "I haven't got much (*o* a lot)"; *ne hai* — *o solo poco?*, have you a lot or only a little?; *noi abbiamo solo poco denaro, essi ne hanno* —, we only have a little money, they have lots; *non avevi tempo ieri, ma oggi ne hai* —, you hadn't time yesterday, but today you have plenty **2.** *pl.* **many** (*generalmente non usato in proposizioni affermative, a meno che non sia sogg.*); **a lot, a great many; plenty, a good many, lots** (*generalmente in proposizioni affermative*): *crede di sapere un'infinità di parole francesi, ma in effetti non ne sa molte*, he thinks he knows many French words, but in fact he doesn't know many; « *Hai degli amici?* », « *Ne ho molti* », « *Non ne ho molti* », "Have you any friends?", "I have a lot (*o* lots *o* a great many)", "I haven't many" ‖ *s.m.* **1. much, a great deal, a lot, a good deal**: — *di quanto dice è vero*, much of what he says is true; *c'è* — *di buono nel suo carattere*, there is a great deal of good in his character; *c'è* — *di sbagliato nel suo ragionamento*, there is a great deal wrong with his reasoning; *suo zio ha fatto* — *per lui*, his uncle did a lot for him ‖ *tra il poco e il* —, between too little and too much... ‖ *è già* — *che io sia arrivato con tutto quel traffico*, with all that traffic it was quite an achievement to get here at all ‖ *a dir* —, *a far* —, at the most (*o* worst): *saremo occupati ancora due ore, a dir* —, we shall still be busy for two hours, at the most **2.** *pl.* **many, many people, a lot of people**: *fu lodato da molti*, he was praised by many; *quando siete in molti...*, when there is a crowd of you... ‖ *i molti*, the majority (*o* most people) ‖ *av.* **1.** (*con ag. e av. positivi; con p.pres., talvolta con p.p. se usati come ag.*) **very**: *la loro casa è* — *grande*, their house is very large; *si alza* — *presto, tardi*, he gets up very early, late ‖ — *conosciuto*, (very) well-known (*o* widely-known); *uno scrittore* — *letto*, a widely-read writer ‖ *il Molto Reverendo...*, the Very Reverend... **2.** (*con ag. e av. comp.*) **much, far, a lot, a great deal; by far**: — *di più*, much more; — *meglio*, much better; — *meno, più*, much less, more; *quello studente è* — *più brillante di te*, that student is much (*o* far *o* a lot *o* a great deal) brighter than you; *il suo secondo romanzo era* — *migliore del primo*, his second novel was better by far than his first **3.** (*con p.p.*) **much, greatly, widely; very well**: — *apprezzato*, greatly (*o* much) appreciated; *rimasi* — *colpito da ciò che disse*, I was greatly impressed by what he said **4.** (*con verbi*) **(very) much, greatly, a good deal, a great deal**; (*fam.*) **a lot**: *indugiò* —, he hesitated a lot; *mi piace* —, I like it very much; *mi sono divertito* —, I have enjoyed myself very much; *studiare, lavorare* —, to study, to work hard ‖ *non dirsela* — *con qlcu.*, not to get on very well with s.o.

Molúcche, *s.f.pl.* (*geog.*) (the) Moluccas.

momentaneaménte, *av.* at the moment, at present; (*temporaneamente*) temporarily: — *siamo sprovvisti di questa merce*, at present we are out of this article; *lavora* — *qui*, he is working here temporarily.

momentàneo, *ag.* (*temporaneo*) temporary; (*passeggero*) passing, momentary: *una gioia momentanea*, a passing (*o* momentary) joy; *un successo* —, a temporary success (*o fam.* a flash in the pan).

moménto, *s.m.* **1.** moment; time: *un* —, *per piacere*, a moment, please; *un* — *solo*, just a moment; *al* — *della consegna*, at the time of delivery; *a un dato* —, at a given moment; *i bisogni del* —, the needs of the moment; *da un* — *all'altro*, from one moment to another (*o* at any moment); *proprio al* — *opportuno*, just at the right moment; *senza un* — *di esitazione*, without a moment's hesitation; *aspetta un* —, wait a moment; *era il* — *culminante del dramma*, it was the climax of the drama; *l'ho amato fin dal primo —*, I have loved him since I saw him first; *lo farò un altro —*, I shall do it another time; *non c'era un — da perdere*, there was not a moment to lose; *non è il — di scherzare*, this is no time for joking; *non perde mai un —*, she never wastes a moment; *la prossima volta vieni un — prima*, next time come a little earlier; *si dedica alla lettura nei momenti liberi*, she devotes her spare time to reading ‖ *un —*, *un mentino*, *(un pochino)* a bit: *questa stanza dovrebbe essere un — più grande*, this room sh uld be just a bit bigger ‖ *a momenti*, *(talvolta)* sometimes; *(fra poco)* in a moment (*o before long o soon*): *a momenti è gentile, a momenti è villano*, sometimes he is polite sometimes he is rude; *sarà pronto a momenti*, he'll be ready in a moment ‖ *al — psicologico*, at the psychological moment ‖ *dal — che*, *(poichè)* since; as; *(da quando)* (ever) since, from the (first) moment (that) ‖ *per il —*, for the moment (*o for the present o for the time being*) ‖ *tutti i momenti, ogni —*, continually: *ogni — chiede soldi*, he is continually asking for money ‖ *è un capriccio del —*, it is a passing fad; *il mio — si avvicina*, my time is drawing near; *passare un brutto —*, to have a bad (*o rough*) time **2.** *(tempo, circostanza)* time: *momenti difficili*, hard times; *durante la guerra passammo terribili momenti*, we went through terrible times during the war ‖ *l'uomo del —*, the man of the moment **3.** *(opportunità)* opportunity, chance: *aspetto il — per agire*, I am waiting for an opportunity to act; *cogliere il —*, to take the chance **4.** *(gravità, importanza)* moment: *una decisione di grande, poco —*, a decision of great, little moment **5.** *(fis. mec.)* moment: *— del contrappeso*, *(mec.)* counterbalance-moment; *— di beccheggio*, *(aer.)* pitching-moment; *— di cerniera*, *(aer.)* hinge-moment; *— di una coppia*, *(mec.)* moment of a couple; *— di evoluzione*, *(mar. aer.)* rudder-moment; *— di rollio*, *(aer.)* rolling-moment; *— magnetico*, *(elett.)* magnetic moment; *— positivo*, *(mec.)* right-handed moment; *— statico*, *(edil.)* static moment.

Mòmo, *no.pr.m. (mit.)* Momus.

mònaca, *s.f.* **1.** nun: *— di clausura*, enclosed nun; *— novizia*, novice; *farsi —*, to take the veil (*o to become a nun*) **2.** *(ornit.)* smew, nun.

monacàle, *ag.* monastic(al): *abito —*, *(di monaco)* monk's habit; *(di monaca)* nun's habit.

monacalménte, *av.* monastically.

monacànda, *s.f.* novice.

monacàre, *v.t.* to admit to a monastic order; *(mettere in convento)* to put into a convent ‖ **monacàrsi,** *v.r. (farsi monaco)* to become a monk; *(farsi monaca)* to take the veil, to become a nun.

monacàto, *s.m.* **1.** *(monachismo)* monasticism, monachism **2.** *(il complesso dei monaci e delle monache)* monks and nuns (*pl.*) **3.** *(vita monastica)* monastic life.

monacazióne, *s.f.* taking the veil.

monachétto, *s.m. (mec.)* staple.

monachína, *s.f.* **1.** *(fig. iron.)* prude: *ha un'aria da —*, she looks as if butter would not melt in her mouth **2.** *(ornit.)* avocet.

monachísmo, *s.m.* monachism.

mònaco¹, *s.m.* **1.** monk: *— benedettino*, Benedictine (*o black monk*); *— cistercense*, Cistercian (*o white monk o grey monk*); *— cluniacense*, Clunist (*o Cluniacensian*); *farsi —*, to become a monk ‖ *l'abito non fa il —*, the cowl does not make the monk **2.** *(scaldino per il letto)* bed-warmer **3.** *(arch.)* king-post.

Mònaco², *no.pr.f. (geog.) (di Baviera)* Munich.

Mònaco³, *no.pr.m. (geog.) (Principato)* Monaco.

mònade, *s.f. (fil.)* monad.

monadísmo, *s.m. (fil.)* monadism.

monàndro, *ag. (bot.)* monandrous.

monàrca, *s.m.* monarch.

monarchía, *s.f.* monarchy: *— assoluta*, absolute monarchy; *— costituzionale*, constitutional monarchy;

— ereditaria, hereditary monarchy; *abbattere, restaurare la —*, to overturn, to restore the monarchy.

monarchicaménte, *av.* monarchically.

monàrchico, *ag.* monarchic(al) ‖ *s.m.* monarchist, royalist.

monastèro, *s.m. (di monaci)* monastery; *(di monache)* nunnery; *(rar.)* monastery.

monasticaménte, *av.* monastically: *vivere —*, to lead a monastic life.

monasticísmo, *s.m.* monasticism.

monàstico, *ag.* monastic: *istituzioni monastiche, voti monastici*, monastic institutions, vows; *regola, vita monastica*, monastic rule, life.

monàtto, *s.m. (st.)* "monatto" (remover of corpses during plague).

Moncenísio, *no.pr.m. (geog.)* Mont Cenis.

moncheríno, monchíno, *s.m.* stump.

mónco, *ag.* **1.** maimed, mutilated: *— di un braccio*, one-armed; *— di una mano*, one-handed; *— di ambo le mani*, maimed of both hands **2.** *fig. (mutilo, incompleto)* defective, incomplete, mutilated: *istruzione monca*, deficient education; *notizie monche*, incomplete news; *risposta monca*, incomplete answer ‖ *s.m.* maimed person, mutilated person: *un povero —*, a poor maimed fellow.

moncóne, *s.m.* stump: *— di una gamba*, stump of a leg.

mónda, *s.f. (agr.)* weeding: *la — del riso*, rice-weeding.

mondàna, *s.f.* **1.** *(prostituta)* prostitute **2.** *(donna di mondo)* mondaine, worldly woman.

mondanaménte, *av.* in a worldly manner.

mondanità, *s.f.* **1.** *(gusto per la vita mondana)* worldliness **2.** *(vita di società)* society life.

mondàno, *ag.* **1.** *(terreno)* worldly, earthly; mundane: *beni mondani*, worldly goods; *felicità mondana*, earthly happiness; *piaceri mondani*, worldly pleasures **2.** *(della società elegante; che ama la vita di società)* worldly; society *(attributivo)*: *gente mondana*, society people; *un luogo di soggiorno —*, a fashionable resort; *una riunione mondana*, a society gathering; *una signora mondana*, a wordly woman; *un uomo —*, a man about town; *vita mondana*, society life.

mondàre, *v.t.* **1.** to clean; *(da erbacce)* to weed; *(dalla buccia)* to peel; *(dalla loppa)* to winnow: *— arance, mele*, to peel oranges, apples; *— un campo*, to weed a field; *— fagiolini*, to string beans: *— il grano*, to winnow the corn; *— piselli*, to shell peas; *— il riso*, *(prima di cuocerlo)* to clean the rice **2.** *fig. (purificare)* to cleanse, to purify: *— l'anima dal peccato*, to cleanse (*o to purify*) the soul from sin.

mondaríso, *s.f.* rice-picker.

mondatóre, *ag.* cleaning, cleansing ‖ *s.m.* cleaner.

mondatríce, *s.f.* **1.** cleaner **2.** *(macchina per mondare il cotone)* peeling-machine; *(amer.)* cotton-gin.

mondatúra, *s.f.* **1.** cleaning; *(da erbacce)* weeding; *(dalla buccia)* peeling; *(dalla loppa)* winnowing **2.** *(scorie)* dross; *(rifiuti)* refuse; *(erbacce)* weeds (*pl.*); *(bucce)* peelings (*pl.*); *(loppa)* chaff.

mondézza, *s.f.* **1.** *(pulizia)* cleanliness; neatness **2.** *(purezza)* purity.

mondezzàio, *s.m.* **1.** dust-bin; dust-hole; rubbish-pit; *(letamaio)* dung-hill **2.** *fig. (luogo sozzo, immondo)* filthy place: *un — di vizi*, a sink of iniquity; *quella casa è un —*, that house is a pigsty.

mondiàle, *ag.* world-wide; world *(attributivo)*; *(universale)* universal: *congresso —*, international congress; *crisi —*, world crisis; *di fama —*, world-famous; *fama —*, world-wide fame; *Guerra Mondiale*, World War; *politica —*, world politics; *la Gran Bretagna è una potenza —*, Great Britain is a world power.

mondíglia, *s.f. (rar.)* refuse; *(di metalli)* dross; *(del grano)* chaff.

mondína, *s.f.* rice-picker.

mondízia, *(rar.)* per **mondézza.**

móndo¹, *s.m.* **1.** world (anche *fig.*): *il — animale*, the animal kingdom (*o world*); *il — cattolico, medioevale*, the Catholic, medi(a)eval world; *il — della fantasia*, *dei sogni*, the world of fancy, of dreams (o dreamland); *il — della scienza*, the world of science; *il — di un bambino*, the world of a child (o a child's world); *il — esterno*, the external world; *il — letterario, musicale, artistico, politico*, the literary, musical, artistic, political world; *in tutto il —, per tutto il —*, all over the world: *è conosciuto in tutto il —*, he is known all over the world; *il — in cui viviamo*, the world we live in; *ha girato il —*, (*fam.*) he has knocked about the world a good bit; *fare il giro del —*, to go round the world; *vedere il —*, to see the world || *— birbone!*, heavens! || *l'altro —*, the next world (o the world to come o the hereafter): *cose dell'altro —!*, it is incredible!; *andare all'altro —*, to pass away; *mandare qlcu. all'altro —*, to send s.o. to kingdom-come || *il bel —, il gran —*, (fashionable) society; *donna di —*, society woman; *uomo di —, (ricco di esperienza)* man of the world; *(che fa vita di società)* man about town || *il Nuovo, il Vecchio Mondo*, the New, the Old World || *vecchio come il —*, as old as the hills (o as Methuselah) || *il — è proprio una gabbia di matti!*, (*fam.*) it's a mad world! || *il — è bello perchè è vario*, variety is the spice of life || *com'è piccolo il —!*, what a small world! || *da che — è —*, since the world began (o from time immemorial) || *niente al — lo può fare felice*, nothing in the world can make him happy || *non ha un pensiero al —*, he has not a care in the world || *non lo cederei neppure per tutto l'oro del —*, I wouldn't part with it for the world || *non lo farei anche se dovesse cascare il —*, I wouldn't do it for the world! (o *fam.* I'll be damned if I do it!) || *non sa stare al —*, he's too simple for this world || *andare in capo al —*, to go to the world's end || *rinunciare al —*, to forsake (o to retire from) the world || *vivere fuori del —*, to live cut off from the world (o to live in a world of one's own) || *vivere nel — della luna*, to have one's head in the clouds || *il — non fu fatto in un giorno, prov.* Rome was not built in a day || *questo — è fatto a scale, chi le scende, chi le sale, prov.* everyone has his ups and downs || *tutto il — è paese, prov.* it's the same the whole world over 2. (*vita terrena*) world; life: *stanco del —*, weary of life; *non è più di questo —*, he is no longer of this world; *quando era al — mio padre*, when my father was alive; *essere al —*, to be in the land of the living; *mettere al —*, to bring into the world; *tornare al —*, to come to life again; *venire al —*, to be born (o to come into the world) || *così va il —*, such is life || *pigliare il — come viene*, to take the world as it comes 3. (*la gente*) the world; humanity; everybody: *il — ride alle sue spalle*, everybody laughs at him behind his back; *il — spera in un avvenire migliore*, humanity hopes in a better future; *dice male di tutto il —*, he speaks badly (o ill) of everybody (o *fam.* he runs everyone down); *vuole salvare le apparenze agli occhi del —*, he wants to save appearances in the eyes of the world 4. (*quantità grandissima*) a world of, a wealth of, a great deal of, a lot of: *un — di auguri, di baci*, lots of wishes, of kisses; *un — di gente*, a large crowd; *costa un —*, it costs a fortune; *gli usò un — di cortesie*, he treated him with every courtesy; *mi ha fatto un — di bene*, it has done me a world of good; *mi sono divertito un —*, I have had an awfully good time.

móndo², *ag.* 1. (*pulito*) clean: *casa monda*, clean house 2. (*sbucciato, mondato*) peeled: *mele, patate monde*, peeled apples, potatoes 3. (*puro*) pure: *cuore —*, pure heart; *è un uomo — da vizi*, he is a man free from vices.

monegàsco, *ag.s.m.* Monegasque.

monèlla, *s.f.* tomboy, hoyden.

monellería, *s.f.* prank; mischievous trick: *i bambini combinano sempre qualche —*, children are always up to some prank or other; *fare delle monellerie*, to play pranks.

monellésco, *ag.* roguish, mischievous.

monellescaménte, *av.* roguishly, mischievously.

monèllo, *s.m.* little rascal, little rogue; (*ragazzo di strada*) urchin: *è un'azione da —!*, it's a dirty trick!.

monéta, *s.f.* 1. money: — *circolante*, currency; — *convenzionale*, conventional money; — *corrente*, current money; — *inconvertibile*, unconvertible money; — *legale*, legal tender (o currency); *carta —*, paper money; *batter —*, to mint (o to coin) money; *convertire in —*, to change (o to convert) into money || *non prendere per — buona ciò che dice, fig.* don't take what he says at its face value (o don't believe what he says) || *ripagare qlcu. della sua stessa —, fig.* to pay s.o. back in his own coin (o to give tit for tat) || *il tempo è —, prov.* time is money 2. (*ogni singolo pezzo metallico*) coin, piece: — *da due scellini*, two-shilling piece; — *d'argento*, silver coin; — *da sei penny*, six-penny piece; — *d'oro*, gold coin; — *falsa*, false coin; — *logora*, worn coin; *un'antica —*, an old coin; *impressione sulla —*, stamp 3. (*spiccioli*) change: — *spicciola*, small change (o petty cash); *avete della — da prestarmi?*, have you got any small change to lend me?.

monetàggio, *s.m.* minting, mintage.

monetàre, *v.t.* (*rar.*) to mint.

monetàrio, *ag.* monetary: *mercato —*, monetary market; *sistema —*, monetary system || *s.m.* minter: *falso —*, coiner.

monferrína, *s.f.* "monferrina" (country dance in Piedmont).

mongàna, *ag.* (*da latte*) milch: *mucche mongane*, milch cows || *s.f.* (*mucca da latte*) milker, milch cow.

mongolfièra, *s.f.* montgolfier.

Mongòlia, *no.pr.f.* (*geog.*) Mongolia.

mongòlico, *ag.* Mongolian.

mòngolo, *ag.* Mongolian || *s.m.*, **mòngola**, *s.f.* Mongol.

mongolòide, *ag.s.c.* mongoloid (anche *patol.*): *quel bambino è un —*, that child is a mongoloid.

Mónica, *no.pr.f.* Monica.

moníle, *s.m.* jewel; (*collana*) necklace: *carico di monili*, bejewelled.

monísmo, *s.m.* (*fil.*) monism.

monísta, *s.c.* (*fil.*) monist.

monístico, *ag.* (*fil.*) monistic(al).

mònito, *s.m.* warning, monition: *che questo serva loro di —*, let this be a warning to them.

monitóre, *s.m.* 1. monitor, warner 2. (*mar.*) (*nave da guerra*) monitor.

monitòrio, *ag.s.m.* monitory.

mònna¹, *s.f.* (*arc. poet.*) lady || *Monna Lisa*, Mona Lisa.

mònna², *s.f.* (*zool.*) mona.

monobàsico, *ag.* (*chim.*) monobasic.

monoblòcco, *s.m.* (*mec.*) monobloc, cylinder-block.

monocàrpico, *ag.* (*bot.*) monocarpic.

monoclíno, *ag.* 1. (*bot.*) monoclinous 2. (*min.*) monoclinic.

monòcolo, *s.m.* 1. (*lente*) monocle 2. (*chi ha un occhio solo*) one-eyed person.

monocòrde, *ag.* (*monotono*) monotonous.

monocòrdo, *s.m.* (*mus.*) monochord.

monocotilèdone, *ag.* (*bot.*) monocotyledonous || *s.f.* (*bot.*) monocotyledon.

monocròma, *s.f.* (*pitt.*) monochrome.

monocromàtico, *ag.* monochromatic.

monocròmo, *ag.* monochrome.

monodía, *s.f.* (*mus.*) monody.

monòdico, *ag.* (*mus.*) monodic.

monofisíta, *s.c.* (*st. relig.*) Monophysite.

monogamía, *s.f.* monogamy.

monògamo, *ag.* monogamous || *s.m.* monogamist.

monogènesi, *s.f.* monogenesis.

monogènico, *ag.* monogenetic.

monogenísmo, *s.m.* (*scient.*) monogenism.

monografía, *s.f.* monograph, monography.

monogràfico, *ag.* monographic: *corso —*, specialized course.

monografísta, *s.c.* monographist, monographer.

monogràmma, *s.m.* monogram: *gli regalarono un portafogli con il suo* —, they gave him' a wallet with his monogram (*o* initials) on it.

monòico, *ag.* (*bot.*) monoicous.

monolítico, *ag.* monolithic.

monòlito, *s.m.* monolith.

monologhísta, *s.c.* monologuist.

monòlogo, *s.m.* monologue; soliloquy: *il — di Amleto*, Hamlet's soliloquy; *nel teatro moderno ci sono pochi monologhi*, in modern drama there are few soliloquies; *reciterà un breve —*, he will recite a short monologue.

monolúcido, *ag.* (*di carta*) shiny on one side.

monòmane, *s.c.* monomaniac.

monomanía, *s.f.* 1. (*patol.*) monomania 2. (*manic, passione*) mania, craze: *ha la — dei viaggi*, he has a craze for travelling.

monomaníaco, *ag.* monomaniac(al) ‖ *s.m.* monomaniac.

monometallísmo, *s.m.* (*econ.*) monometallism.

monomètrico, *ag.* (*min.*) monometric.

monòmetro, *ag.* (*poes.*) monometer (*attributivo*).

monòmio, *s.m.* (*alg.*) monomial.

monomòrfo, *ag.* monomorphic.

monopàttino, *s.m.* scooter.

monopètalo, *ag.* (*bot.*) monopetalous.

monoplàno, *s.m.* (*aer.*) monoplane.

monopòlio, *s.m.* 1. monopoly: — *di Stato*, State monopoly; *in regime di* —, under a monopoly system; *i monopoli mantengono alti i prezzi*, monopolies keep prices high; *in Italia il tabacco è un — di Stato*, in Italy tobacco is a government monopoly; *concedere un* —, to grant a monopoly; *esercitare un* —, to exercise a monopoly 2. *fig.* (*privilegio, possesso esclusivo*) monopoly, control; privilege: *l'essere onesto pare — tuo*, (*iron.*) one would think you were the only honest person here; *per tutta la serata ha tenuto il — della conversazione*, he monopolized the conversation all the evening.

monopolísta, *s.c.* monopolist: *rendita del* —, monopolist's income.

monopolístico, *ag.* monopolistic.

monopolizzàre, *v.t.* to monopolize (anche *fig.*): *non — la conversazione!*, don't monopolize the conversation!.

monopósto, *ag.* (*aut. aer.*) single-seater (*attributivo*) ‖ *s.m.* (*aut. aer.*) single-seater.

monòptero, *ag.* (*arch.*) monopteral.

monoreattóre, *ag.* (*aer.*) single-jet (*attributivo*) ‖ *s.m.* (*aer.*) single-jet.

monorifrangènte, *ag.* (*min.*) monorefringent.

monorímo, *ag.* (*poes.*) monorhyme (*attributivo*).

monorítmico, *ag.* (*poes.*) monorhythmic.

monorítmo, *ag.* (*poes.*) monorhythmic ‖ *s.m.* (*poes.*) monorhythm.

monorotàia, *s.f.* (*ferr.*) monorail.

monosaccàridi, *s.m. pl.* (*chim.*) monosaccharides.

monosillàbico, *ag.* (*gram.*) monosyllabic.

monosíllabo, *s.m.* (*gram.*) monosyllable ‖ *parlare a monosillabi*, to speak in monosyllables.

monoteísmo, *s.m.* (*relig.*) monotheism.

monoteísta, *s.c.* (*relig.*) monotheist.

monoteístico, *ag.* (*relig.*) monotheistic.

monotipía, *s.f.* (*tip.*) monotype system.

monotipísta, *s.c.* (*tip.*) monotypist.

monotípo, *s.m.* (*tip.*) monotype.

monotonaménte, *ar.* monotonously.

monotonía, *s.f.* monotony, tediousness, tedium; humdrum: *la — della vita in campagna sarebbe snervante per uno cresciuto in città*, the humdrum of country life would be wearing for someone brought up in a city.

monòtono, *ag.* monotonous, tedious; humdrum: *discorso* —, tedious speech; *musica monotona*, mono-

tonous music; *un'occupazione monotona*, a monotonous job; *viaggio* —, tedious journey; *vita monotona*, humdrum life; *voce monotona*, dull voice.

monotrèmi, *s.m.pl.* (*zool.*) Monotremata.

monovalènte, *ag.* monovalent.

monsignóre, *s.m.* (*eccl.*) monsignor (*pl.* monsignori).

monsóne, *s.m.* monsoon: — *estivo*, wet (*o* rainy) monsoon; — *invernale*, dry monsoon.

mónta, *s.f.* 1. covering 2. (*luogo dove si tengono gli stalloni e i tori*) stud-farm 3. (*arch.*) (*di un arco*) rise.

montacàrico, *s.m.* 1. goods-lift, goods-hoist 2. (*ind. miner.*) elevator-hoist 3. (*ind. edil.*) skip-hoist.

montàggio, *s.m.* 1. (*mec.*) assembly, assembling; (*edil.*) erection; (*ind. tessile*) mounting; (*dei vetri*) glazing: — *a caldo*, shrink-fitting (*o* shrinking-on); *linea di* —, assembly-line; *reparto* —, assembly- (*o* assembling-)bay 2. (*cine.*) montage, cutting, splicing: — *ottico di un film*, silent film-cutting; — *sonoro di un film*, sound film-cutting.

montàgna, *s.f.* mountain: *alta* —, high mountain; *aria di* —, mountain air; *artiglieria, batteria di* —, mountain artillery, battery; *catena di montagne*, mountain-range (*o* mountain-chain); *la cima della* —, the top of the mountain; *ferrovia di* —, mountain-railway; *fiore di* —, alpine flower; *luogo di villeggiatura in alta* —, mountain-resort; *sistema di montagne*, mountain-system; *ho passato l'estate in* —, I spent the summer in the mountains; *andare in* —, to go to the mountains ‖ *una — di debiti, di difficoltà*, a mountain of debts, of difficulties ‖ *le Montagne Rocciose*, (*geog.*) the Rocky Mountains ‖ *montagne russe*, switchback ‖ *il discorso della* —, (*Bibbia*) the Sermon on the Mountain ‖ *mal di* —, mountain-sickness ‖ *il Vecchio della Montagna*, the Old Man of the Mountains ‖ *la — ha partorito un topolino*, the mountain laboured and brought forth a mouse ‖ *gli pareva di avere una — addosso*, a heavy burden seemed to lie on him ‖ *le montagne stan ferme e gli uomini s'incontrano*, friends may meet, but mountains never ‖ *quell'uomo è grande come una* —, that man is as big as a mountain ‖ *se la — non viene a Maometto, Maometto andrà alla* —, if the mountain won't come to Mahomet, Mahomet must go to the mountain.

montagnàrdo, *s.m.* (*st. francese*) Montagnard.

montagnòla, *s.f.* hillock.

montagnóso, *ag.* mountainous; hilly: *regione montagnosa*, mountainous district.

montanàro, *ag.* mountain (*attributivo*); of the mountains (*predicativo*): *popolazione montanara*, mountain population ‖ *s.m.* mountaineer; highlander: *testardo come un* —, as stubborn as a mule.

montanèllo, *s.m.* (*ornit.*) linnet.

montaníno, *ag.* mountain (*attributivo*); of the mountains (*predicativo*): *aria montanina*, mountain air ‖ *s.m.* mountaineer.

montàno, *ag.* mountain (*attributivo*): *paese* —, mountain village.

montànte, *s.m.* 1. (*boxe*) uppercut 2. (*colpo dato con armi*) upward thrust 3. (*aer.*) strut 4. (*mec. edil.*) standard, upright, vertical rod, stanchion; (*pilastro*) post; (*di porta*) jamb; (*di finestra*) window-post 5. *V.* **montatóio**.

montàre, *v.t.* 1. to mount: — *i gradini*, to mount the steps ‖ — *la guardia*, to mount guard ‖ — (*la testa a*) *qlcu.*, (*convincerlo a far ql.co.*) to talk s.o. into doing sthg.; (*renderlo superbo*) to give s.o. a swollen head: *il successo gli ha montato la testa*, success has gone to his head 2. (*cavalcare*) to ride 3. (*di animale, nell'accoppiamento*) to cover, to mount 4. (*mettere insieme*) to assemble: — *una macchina, un orologio, un motore*, to assemble a machine, a watch, an engine 5. (*incastonare*) to set, to mount: — *una pietra preziosa in oro*, to set a precious stone in gold 6. (*in-*

corniciare) to mount **7.** (*arredare*) to furnish **8.** (*artigl.*) (*installare*) to mount, to place: — *un cannone*, to mount a gun **9.** (*la panna*) to whip ‖ *v.i.* **1.** to climb (sthg.); to climb (on, to sthg.); to mount (sthg.); to get on (sthg.): *montami sulle spalle*, climb on my shoulders; — *a cavallo*, to mount a horse; (*cavalcare*) to ride: *monta bene* (*a cavallo*), he rides well; — *in carrozza*, to get into a carriage; — *su un albero, su una collina*, to climb a tree, a hill; — *su una bicicletta*, to get on a bicycle; — *su una scala*, to climb (o to go up o to mount) a ladder; — *su un tavolo*, to get on (o to climb on) a table ‖ *il sangue gli montò alla testa*, he flew into a rage; *il sangue le montò alle guance*, the blood rose to her cheeks ‖ *se gli monta la collera, la stizza..., se gli montano i fumi...*, if he gets angry... (o if he gets into a rage...) ‖ — *in cattedra, fig.* to lay down the law ‖ — *in collera*, to get angry (o to fly into a rage); — *su tutte le furie*, to see red ‖ — *in superbia*, to put on airs (o to act arrogantly) ‖ *far — la mosca al naso a qlcu.*, to make s.o. angry **2.** (*alzarsi, aumentare*) to rise: *il fiume è montato di un metro*, the river has risen one metre; *la marea monta*, the tide is rising (o coming in) **3.** (*rar.*) (*ammontare*) to amount: *la spesa monta a mille lire*, the cost amounts to a thousand lire **4.** *imp.* (*letter.*) (*importare*) to matter: *che monta?*, what does it matter? ‖ **montàrsi**, *v.r.* (*eccitarsi*) to get excited; (*fam.*) to get worked up; (*inorgoglirsi*) to get swollen -headed.

montàta, *s.f.* **1.** rise, ascent **2.** (*atto del montare*) mounting, climbing **3.** — *lattea*, (*fisiol.*) the rise of the milk.

montatóio, *s.m.* **1.** (*predellino di carrozza*) footboard, step; (*di treno*) footboard; (*di automobili*) running board **2.** (*staffa di cavallo*) stirrup.

montatóre, *s.m.* (*neol. mec.*) fitter, assembler: — *di scene*, (*cine.*) set dresser.

montatúra, *s.f.* **1.** (*mec.*) fitting, assembling, assembly **2.** (*di occhiali*) frame **3.** *fig.* (*gonfiatura, esagerazione*) exaggeration: *questa faccenda non è che una* —, it's all a made-up story.

montavivànde, *s.m.* service-lift; (*amer.*) dumb-waiter.

mónte, *s.m.* **1.** mount, mountain: *catena di monti*, mountain range (o chain); *in cima a un* —, on the top of a mountain; *il Monte Rosa è uno dei monti più alti d'Europa*, Mount Rosa is one of the highest mountains in Europe ‖ *Monte Bianco*, Mount Blanc; *i Monti Cantabrici*, the Cantabrian Mountains; *Monte Everest*, Mount Everest ‖ *a* —, (*di fiume*) upriver (o upstream) ‖ *per valli e per monti*, up hill and down dale ‖ *fare mare e monti*, to work wonders; *promettere mari e monti a qlcu.*, to promise s.o. the earth ‖ *loda il — e tienti al piano, prov.* praise the sea but keep on land **2.** (*gran quantità*) mountain, heap, lot, great deal: *un — di cose*, a lot of things; *un — di difficoltà*, a mountain of difficulties; *un — di libri*, a heap of books ‖ *in* —, (*comm.*) in bulk **3.** (*carte scartate al giuoco*) discarded cards (*pl.*) ‖ *andare a* —, *annullare la partita* to scrap the game; *fig.* (*andare in fumo*) to fail (o to come to nothing): *il matrimonio è andato a* —, the marriage was broken off; *tutti i miei piani sono andati a* —, all my plans have fallen through (o have come to nothing); *mandare a* —, to cause to fail; (*disdire*) to cancel: *egli mandò a — i nostri progetti*, he caused our projects to fail; *l'incontro fu mandato a* —, the meeting was cancelled **4.** (*insieme delle poste dei giocatori*) pool; (*fam.*) kitty ‖ — *premi*, prize money **5.** (*banca*) bank; (*istituto di prestiti su pegno*) state pawnshop, mont-de-piété (*pl.* monts-de-piété): *portare l'orologio al* —, to pawn one's watch.

Montécchi, *no.pr.* (*lett.*) Montague.

montenegríno, *ag.s.m.* Montenegrin.

Montenégro, *no.pr.m.* (*geog.*) Montenegro.

montonàta, *s.f.* (*equitazione*) buck, bucking.

montóne, *s.m.* **1.** ram: *carne di* —, mutton ‖ *salto del* —, (*equitazione*) buck **2.** (*st. mil.*) (*ariete*) battering-ram.

montuosità, *s.f.* **1.** mountaineousness; hilliness **2.** (*collina*) hill; hillock.

montuóso, *ag.* mountainous; hilly.

montúra, *s.f.* (*mil.*) uniform.

monumentàle, *ag.* monumental (anche *fig.*).

monuménto, *s.m.* monument (anche *fig.*): *il — a Washington*, the Washington Monument; — *marmoreo*, marble monument; — *nazionale*, national monument; *mi condusse a visitare i monumenti della città*, he took me on a sight-seeing tour of the town; *erigere, innalzare un — alla memoria di qlcu.*, to erect a monument in s.o.'s memory.

moquette, *s.f.* (*tappeto*) moquette.

mòra[1], *s.f.* (*bot.*) (*di gelso*) mulberry; (*di rovo*) blackberry.

mòra[2], *s.f.* (*dir.*) delay; default; (*dilazione*) extension, respite: *interesse di* —, interest on delayed payment; *concedere una* —, to grant a respite; *essere in* —, to be in arrear(s) (o to be behindhand); *ottenere una — di tre mesi*, to get an extension (o a respite) of three months ‖ *mettere in* —, (*dir.*) to put in suit.

mòra[3], *s.f.* (*mucchio di sassi*) cairn; heap of stones.

mòra[4], *s.f.* mor(r)a: *giocare a* —, to play mor(r)a.

mòra[5], *s.f.* **1.** (*negra*) negress **2.** (*donna bruna*) brunette.

moràle, *ag.* moral: *appoggio* —, moral support; *azione* —, moral action; *certezza* —, moral certainty; *forza* —, moral courage; *responsabilità* —, moral responsibility; *uomo* —, upright man ‖ *schiaffo* —, affront ‖ *s.f.* **1.** morals (*pl.*): *persona senza* —, person without morals (o immoral person); *la — cattolica è molto severa*, Catholic morals are very strict; *a quei tempi la — era molto libera*, in those days morals were very lax **2.** (*filosofia morale*) moral philosophy, ethics **3.** (*conclusione didascalica*) moral: *la — della favola*, the moral of the story; *trarre la* —, to draw a moral ‖ *s.m.* morale: *il — dei soldati era basso*, the soldiers' morale was low; *il — delle truppe era ottimo*, the troops' morale was high; *tenere su il — del popolo*, to bolster the morale of the people.

moraleggiàre, *v.i.* to moralize.

moralísmo, *s.m.* moralism.

moralísta, *s.c.* moralist: *fare il* —, (*iron.*) to play the moralist.

moralità, *s.f.* **1.** morality; morals (*pl.*): — *pubblica*, public morality; *uomo di ottima* —, man of excellent character; *uomo senza* —, immoral man **2.** (*conclusione didascalica*) moral: *la — della favola*, the moral of the story **3.** (*st. teat.*) morality, morality-play.

moralizzàre, *v.t.* to improve the morals of (s.o.) ‖ *v.i.* to moralize.

moralizzazióne, *s.f.* moralization.

moralménte, *av.* morally.

moratòria, *s.f.* (*dir.*) moratorium (*pl.* moratoria, moratoriums): *chiedere la* —, to ask for a moratorium ‖ *legge sulla — per i pagamenti*, Postponement of Payments Act.

moratòrio, *ag.* (*dir.*) moratory.

Moràvia, *no.pr.f.* (*geog.*) Moravia.

moràvo, *ag.s.m.* Moravian.

morbidaménte, *av.* **1.** softly; tenderly; (*delicatamente*) delicately **2.** (*effeminatamente*) effeminately **3.** (*morbosamente*) morbidly.

morbidézza, *s.f.* **1.** softness: — *di un materasso*, softness of a mattress **2.** (*delicatezza*) softness, delicacy: — *di colori*, delicacy of colours; — *di luce*, softness of light **3.** (*effeminatezza*) effeminacy **4.** (*morbosità*) morbidity, morbidness **5.** (*arrendevolezza*) tractability, pliability; (*eccessiva indulgenza*) leniency **6.** (*di cavallo*) docility **7.** (*di stile*) fluency.

mòrbido, *ag.* **1.** (*soffice, molle, tenero*) soft: — *come il burro*, as soft as butter; *cera morbida*, soft wax; *guanciale, letto, tessuto* —, soft pillow, bed, material;

mani *morbide*, soft hands; *marmo* —, soft marble; *metallo* —, soft (*o* malleable) metal; *pietra morbida*, soft stone; *terreno* —, soft ground: *in lui troverai un terreno* —, *fig.* you'll find him very docile (*o* tractable); *non è un terreno* —, *fig.* he is not easily persuaded 2. (*liscio*) soft; tender, smooth: *capelli morbidi*, soft hair; *pelle morbida*, tender (*o* smooth) skin 3. (*delicato*) soft, delicate: *colorito* —, (*pitt.*) delicate colouring; *luce morbida*, soft light; *maniere morbide*, delicate manners 4. (*effeminato*) effeminate 5. (*morboso*) morbid 6. (*di cavallo*) soft-mouthed 7. (*di stile*) fluent.

morbidúme, *s.m.* (*spreg.*) over-soft stuff.

morbífero, *ag.* (*letter.*) morbiferous.

morbífico, *ag.* (*letter.*) morbific.

morbiglióne, *s.m.* (*patol.*) chicken-pox.

morbíllo, *s.m.* (*patol.*) measles (*pl.*).

mòrbo, *s.m.* 1. disease, infectious disease; (*peste*) plague: — *asiatico*, Asiatic cholera; — *di Parkinson*, Parkinson's disease; *la violenza del* —, the virulence of the disease; *il* — *infieriva*, the plague was rampant 2. (*cattivo odore*) stench.

morbosaménte, *av.* morbidly.

morbosità, *s.f.* morbidity, morbidness.

morbóso, *ag.* 1. morbid: *curiosità morbosa*, morbid curiosity 2. (*non sano*) unhealthy, unwholesome: *pallore* —, unhealthy (*o* sickly) pallor.

mòrchia, *s.f.* 1. (*feccia*) dregs (*pl.*): — *di olio lubrificante*, sludge 2. (*mec.*) dirt.

morchióso, *ag.* dreggy.

mordàce, *ag.* biting, cutting, mordant, pungent: *critica* —, biting criticism; *discorso* —, pungent speech; *parole mordaci*, cutting words; *satira* —, biting (*o* mordant) satire; *è un critico* —, he is a mordant critic; *ha uno spirito* —, he has a pungent wit.

mordaceménte, *av.* bitingly, pungently; sharply.

mordacità, *s.f.* mordacity, pungency; sharpness.

mordènte, *ag.* biting (*anche fig.*): *freddo, vento* —, biting cold, wind || *aceto* —, sour vinegar; *salsa* —, piquant sauce || *s.m.* 1. (*chim. ind.*) mordant 2. (*mus.*) mordent 3. (*spirito aggressivo*) bite: *truppe prive di* —, troops lacking in spirit; *è uno scrittore che manca di* —, he is a writer lacking in bite; *la squadra mancava di* —, the team lacked go; *il suo discorso mancava di* —, his speech lacked bite.

mòrdere, *v.t.* 1. to bite (anche *fig.*): *il cane mi ha morso il braccio*, the dog has bitten me in the arm; *c'è un vento che morde*, there is a biting wind; *parole che mordono*, biting words || *abbandonò quell'impresa perchè vide che non c'era da* —, he abandoned the affair because he could see there was nothing to be made out of it || *il freno*, to strain at the leash || — *la polvere*, to die in battle (*o* to bite the dust) || *can che abbaia non morde*, *prov.* his bark is worse than his bite 2. (*pungere*) to bite, to sting: *pulci e zanzare mordono*, fleas and mosquitoes bite 3. (*attaccare*) to castigate: *Giovenale mordeva la vanità e i vizi dei Romani*, Juvenal castigated the vanity and vices of Romans 4. (*tormentare*) to torment: *il bisogno lo mordeva*, his poverty tormented him; *la sua coscienza era morsa dai suoi crimini*, his conscience was tormented by his evil deeds 5. (*stringere, afferrare, conficcarsi in*) to grip: *l'ancora morse il fondo*, the anchor gripped the bottom; *i cingoli mordono meglio delle ruote*, caterpillar-tracks grip better than wheels 6. (*intaccare, corrodere*) to bite into (sthg.): *la lima morse il ferro*, the file bit into the iron || **mòrdersi**, *v.r.*: — *le labbra, la lingua*, to bite one's lip(s), one's tongue: *appena detto questo, mi sarei morso le labbra, la lingua*, as soon as I said it I could have kicked myself; — *le mani, le dita*, (*dolersi amaramente*) to kick oneself: *mi sarei morso le dita per non esserci andato*, I could have kicked myself for not going.

mordenzatúra, *s.f.* (*chim. ind. foto.*) mordanting.

morditóre, *s.m.* biter.

morèllo, *ag.* blackish || *s.m.* black horse.

morèna, *s.f.* (*geol.*) moraine: — *laterale, mediana, profonda*, lateral, medial, ground moraine.

morènico, *ag.* (*geol.*) morainic, morainal.

morènte, *ag.* 1. dying 2. *fig.* dying, fading: *l'anno* —, the dying year; *la luce* — *del giorno*, the fading light of day || *s.m.* dying man || *s.f.* dying woman.

morésco, *ag.* Moorish, Moresco; Moresque: *architettura moresca*, Moorish architecture; *danza* —, morris -dance; *stile* —, Moresque || *alla moresca*, in the Moorish manner.

morétta, *s.f.* 1. brunette 2. (*mascherina*) half -mask 3. (*giovane negra*) negro girl; coloured girl.

morettína, *s.f.* 1. brunette 2. (*mascherina*) half -mask.

morétto, *s.m.* 1. (*negretto*) negro boy; coloured boy 2. (*paggetto*) Moorish page, Moorish servant.

Morfèo, *no.pr.m.* (*mit.*) Morpheus || *essere in braccio a* —, to be in the arms of Morpheus (*o* in the land of Nod).

morfina, *s.f.* morphine, morphia.

morfinísmo, *s.m.* (*med.*) morphinism.

morfinòmane, *s.c.* morphinomaniac.

morfinomanía, *s.f.* morphinomania.

morfología, *s.f.* morphology.

morfologicaménte, *av.* morphologically.

morfològico, *ag.* morphologic(al).

morfologísta, *s.m.* morphologist.

Morgàna, *no.pr.f.* (*nelle fiabe*) Morgana: *la fata* —, (Fata) Morgana; (*nei poemi medioevali*) Morgan le Fay || *fata morgana*, (*miraggio*) Fata Morgana (*o* mirage).

morganaticaménte, *av.* morganatically.

morganàtico, *ag.* morganatic.

moría, *s.f.* 1. (*pestilenza*) plague, pestilence 2. (*malattia del bestiame*) murrain 3. (*malattia del pollame*) fowl plague.

moribónda, *s.f.* dying woman.

moribóndo, *ag.* dying; moribund (anche *fig.*): *istituzione moribonda*, moribund institution || *s.m.* dying man || *i moribondi*, the dying: *assistere i moribondi*, to assist (*o* to attend) the dying.

morigerataménte, *av.* soberly, temperately.

morigeratézza, *s.f.* 1. moderation, soberness, sobriety: — *di discorsi*, soberness of speech; *mangiare e bere con* —, to eat and drink with moderation 2. (*buona condotta*) good behaviour.

morigeràto, *ag.* 1. moderate, sober, temperate: *vita morigerata*, sober life; *è un uomo* —, he is a moderate man 2. (*che si comporta bene*) well-behaved.

morióne[1], *s.m.* (*antico elmo*) morion.

morióne[2], *s.m.* (*min.*) morion.

moríre, *v.i.* 1. to die: *morì a cinquant'anni*, he died at fifty; *egli lavorò tanto da* —, he worked himself to death; — *annegato*, to be drowned; — *da codardo*, to die a coward's death; — *di crepacuore*, to die of a broken heart; — *di fame*, to starve to death (anche *fig.*): *far* — *di fame qlcu.*, to starve s.o.; — *di una ferita*, to die from a wound; — *di freddo*, to freeze to death; *fig.* to be freezing; — *di inedia*, to die of hunger; to starve (anche *fig.*); — *di una malattia*, to die of an illness; — *di morte naturale*, to die a natural death; — *di morte violenta*, to die a violent death (*o fam.* to die with one's boots on); — *di polmonite*, to die of pneumonia; — *di vecchiaia*, to die of old age; — *male*, to come to a bad end; — *martire*, to die a martyr; — *pazzo*, to die a madman (*o* off one's head); — *per la patria*, to die for one's country; — *prematuramente*, to die before one's time; — *ricco*, to die rich (*o* a rich man); — *santamente*, to die a holy death; — *tisico*, to die of tuberculosis || *freddo da* —, bitterly (*o* freezing) cold; *stanco da* —, dead (*o* dog) tired || *che io possa* — *se...*, may I die (*o* strike me down) if... || *chi non muore si rivede!*, fancy meeting you! || *credevo di* —, I thought I'd die ||

è morta nel mio cuore, she is dead to my heart ‖ *lasciarono — il discorso*, they let the conversation drop (*o die away*) ‖ *lo farò a costo di —*, I'll do it even if it kills me ‖ *meglio di così si muore!*, you can't have better than that! ‖ *meglio — con onore che vivere con vergogna*, it is better to die honourably than to live shamefully ‖ *mi sentivo —*, I could have died ‖ *morivano come le mosche*, they died like flies ‖ *muor giovane chi al cielo è caro*, whom the gods love die young ‖ *muore per lei*, he is mad about her ‖ *non gli muore la lingua in bocca*, he has the gift of the gab ‖ *non morrà nella nostra memoria*, he will live for ever in our memories ‖ *non si sa di che morte si deve —*, no one knows what the future holds in store ‖ *la parola gli morì sulle labbra*, the word froze on his lips ‖ *piuttosto —!*, over my dead body!; *piuttosto — che...*, I had rather die than... ‖ *si sa dove si nasce, non dove si muore*, who knows what our end shall be? ‖ *vorrei — se non è vero*, (*fam.*) I'll be damned if it isn't true ‖ *— al mondo*, to retire from the world ‖ *— civilmente*, (*dir.*) to lose one's civil rights (*o* to suffer civil death) ‖ *— dalla curiosità*, to be dying with curiosity ‖ *— dalla voglia di ql.co., di fare ql.co.*, to be dying for sthg., to do sthg. ‖ *— dallo spavento*, to die of fright ‖ *— dal ridere*, to split one's sides (*o* to die laughing) ‖ *— di noia*, to be bored to death ‖ *— in Dio, nel bacio del Signore*, to die in the grace of God ‖ *— in piedi*, to die in harness ‖ *— solo come un cane*, to die a dog's death ‖ *— su ql.co.*, to be mad about sthg. ‖ *far —*, to kill: *il gelo fa — le piante da frutto*, the frost kills fruit-trees; *mi farai —!*, *fig.* you'll be the death of me! ‖ *altro è parlare di morte, altro è —*, *prov.* it is one thing to talk of dying, but it is another thing to die ‖ *chi muore giace, chi vive si dà pace*, *prov.* let the dead bury the dead **2.** (*di luce, colore*) to fade; (*di suono*) to die away: *la sua voce andava morendo*, his voice was dying away **3.** (*spegnersi*) to go out, to die out **4.** (*tramontare*) to set; (*poet.*) to draw to a close: *moriva il giorno*, (*poet.*) the day was drawing to a close **5.** (*venir meno*) to die, to disappear: *le sue speranze morirono*, his hopes died away **6.** (*estinguersi*) to die out: *questa usanza accenna ormai a —*, this custom is now dying out **7.** (*terminare*) to end: *l'autostrada muore a Firenze*, the motor-way ends (*o* comes to an end) at Florence; *questo treno muore a Roma*, the terminus is at Rome **8.** (*alle carte*) to go out ‖ *v.t.* to die: *— una morte gloriosa*, to die a glorious death ‖ **morìrsi**, *v.r.* to die: *la poverina si moriva*, the poor woman was wasting away; *se ne morì*, he passed away.

morìre, *s.m.* death: *non mi spaventa il —*, I am not afraid of dying (*o* death has no terrors for me) ‖ *un bel — tutta la vita onora*, a good death redeems a mis-spent life ‖ *al — del giorno*, at the close of day.

moritùro, *ag.* dying; moribund (anche *fig.*).

mormóne, *s.m.* (*st. relig.*) Mormon.

mormoràre, *v.t.* **1.** to murmur; (*bisbigliare*) to whisper: *mormorò alcune parole e se ne andò*, he murmured a few words and went away; *le mormorò un segreto all'orecchio*, he whispered a secret in her ear; *si mormora che sia una donna disonesta*, it is rumoured that she is a dishonest woman; *— una preghiera*, to murmur (*o* to breathe) a prayer **2.** (*borbottare*) to mutter, to mumble: *che cosa stai mormorando?*, what are you muttering (about)?; *— ql.co. tra i denti*, to mutter (*o* to mumble) sthg. between one's teeth ‖ *v.i.* **1.** to murmur; (*bisbigliare*) to whisper: *il ruscello mormorava*, the brook was murmuring (*o* babbling); *il vento mormorava tra i rami*, the wind was whispering in the branches **2.** (*parlar male*) to speak ill, to speak badly; (*esprimere malcontento*) to grumble (about s.o., sthg.); to moan (about s.o., sthg.), to murmur, to complain (of s.o., sthg.): *— alle spalle di qlcu.*, to speak ill (*o* badly) of s.o. behind his back; *— contro le nuove tasse*, to grumble about new taxes.

mormoratóre, *s.m.*, **mormoratríce**, *s.f.* **1.** (*chi bron-*

tola) grumbler, moaner **2.** (*maldicente*) backbiter, disparager.

mormorazióne, *s.f.* **1.** (*lamentela*) complaining, grumbling, moaning **2.** (*maldicenza*) backbiting, disparagement **3.** *pl.* (*cose mormorate*) complaints, grumbles, moans.

mormorío, *s.m.* **1.** murmur, murmuring; (*bisbiglio*) whispering: *il — della foresta*, the whispering of the forest; *il — di un ruscello*, the murmur (*o* babbling) of a brook; *corse per la sala un — di ammirazione*, a murmur of admiration ran through the hall; *sentiva un — di voci nella stanza accanto*, he heard a murmur of voices from the room **2.** (*lamentela*) complaining, grumbling, moaning: *cominciano a circolare mormorii contro il nuovo presidente*, people are beginning to complain about the new President; *vi furono molti mormorii fra gli impiegati*, there was a lot of complaining among the employees **3.** (*malignità, maldicenza*) evil gossip: *non puoi impedire i mormorii in una città piccola*, you cannot prevent evil gossip in a small town.

mòro[1], *ag.* dark, black ‖ *s.m.* **1.** Moor; (*negro*) negro, blackamoor: *il Moro di Venezia*, the Moor of Venice; *i mori furono cacciati dalla Spagna*, the Moors were driven out of Spain **2.** (*zool.*) sooty mangabey.

mòro[2], *s.m.* (*bot.*) mulberry-tree.

moròsa, *s.f.* (*pop.*) sweetheart, girl (-friend).

moróso[1], *ag.* defaulting; in arrears (*predicativo*): *debitore —*, defaulting debtor (*o* debtor in arrears).

moróso[2], *s.m.* (*pop.*) sweetheart, boy (-friend).

mòrra, *s.f.* "mor(r)a": *giocare a —*, to play mor(r)a.

mòrsa, *s.f.* **1.** (*mec.*) vice: *— ad azione rapida*, quick-action vice; *— a ganasce parallele*, parellel-jaw vice; *— girevole*, swivel vice; *— per trapano*, drill vice; *— per tubi*, pipe vice; *le ganasce della —*, the jaws of the vice; *la sua stretta è come una —*, his grip is like a vice **2.** (*arch.*) toothing.

morsèllo, *s.m.* (*rar.*) morsel.

morsètto, *s.m.* (*carpenteria*) clamp; (*mec.*) (*dispositivo di fermo*) holdfast; (*elett.*) terminal: *— a mano*, hand vice (*o* screw clamp *o* adjustable clamp); *— d'ancoraggio*, (*elett.*) anchor clamp (*o* anchor ear); *— d'attacco*, (*elett.*) connecting terminal; *— di carica* (*di una batteria*), (*elett.*) charging clip; *— portautensili*, tool clamp.

morsicàre, *v.t.* to bite: *il cane gli morsicò una mano*, the dog bit him in the hand.

morsicatùra, *s.f.* bite: *le morsicature di alcuni insetti sono mortali*, the bites of some insects are fatal; *aveva una brutta — sul braccio*, he had a nasty bite on his arm.

morsicchiàre, *v.t.* to nibble; to nibble at (sthg.): *morsicchiava il pane*, he was nibbling at the bread.

mòrso, *s.m.* **1.** bite: *il — di un cane, di un insetto*, dog-bite, insect-bite; *il — di alcune serpi è velenoso*, some snakebites are poisonous; *il mastino gli staccò un orecchio con un —*, the mastiff bit his ear off; *dare un — a qlcu.*, to bite s.o.; *dare di — a ql.co.*, to bite sthg. **2.** *fig.* (*puntura, stimolo*) sting; pang: *i morsi della fame*, the pangs of hunger; *il — dell'invidia*, the sting of envy **3.** (*boccone*) morsel, bit: *un — di pane*, a morsel of bread **4.** (*ferro che s'introduce in bocca al cavallo*) bit: *allentare il —*, to slacken the bit (anche *fig.*); *dare una strappata di —*, to give a pull at the bit; *mettere il — a un cavallo*, to put the bit in a horse's mouth; *stringere il —*, to tighten the bit (anche *fig.*) ‖ *mettere il — a qlcu.*, (*sottometterlo, domarlo*) to curb (*o* to restrain *o* to check) s.o. **5.** (*delle tenaglie*) jaws (*pl.*).

mortadèlla, *s.f.* "mortadella" (Bologna sausage).

mortàio, *s.m.* **1.** mortar: *pestello e —*, pestle and mortar ‖ *pestar l'acqua nel —*, (*fare una cosa inutile*) to beat the air **2.** (*artigl.*) mortar: *il — affondò nel fango*, the mortar sank into the mud.

mortàle, *ag.* **1.** (*che cagiona morte*) mortal, deadly (anche *fig.*): *colpo* —, mortal blow; *combattimento* —, mortal combat (*o* a fight to the death); *ferita* —, mortal wound (*o* death-wound); *incidente* —, fatal accident; *malattia* —, mortal (*o* deadly) disease; *odio* —, deadly (*o* mortal) hatred; *offesa* —, deadly insult; *veleno* —, deadly poison; *è il mio — nemico,* he is my deadly (*o* mortal) enemy ‖ *peccato* —, mortal (*o* deadly) sin **2.** (*soggetto a morte*) mortal: *il corpo è* —, *l'anima è immortale,* the body is mortal, the soul is immortal; *le sue spoglie mortali furono sepolte nel cimitero del suo paese,* his mortal remains were buried in the cemetery of his village; *gli uomini sono mortali,* men are mortal **3.** (*come la morte*) deadly, deathlike, deathly: *pallore* —, deathlike (*o* deadly *o* deathly) pallor; *silenzio* —, deathly (*o* deadly) silence ‖ *s.c.* mortal ‖ *fortunato* —!, you, lucky fellow (*o* chap)!; *noi, miseri mortali,* we, poor mortals.

mortalétto *V.* **mortarétto.**

mortalità, *s.f.* mortality: *indice di* —, mortality -rate (*o* death-rate).

mortalménte, *av.* **1.** mortally: — *ferito,* mortally wounded; — *offeso,* mortally offended; *odiare qlcu.* —, to hate s.o. to death **2.** (*come la morte*) deadly, deathly: — *noioso,* deadly dull; *il suo viso era* — *pallido,* her face was deathly pale.

mortarétto, *s.m.* cracker: *per la festa del paese fecero scoppiare molti mortaretti,* they let off a great many crackers at the village festival.

mortàsa, *s.f.* (*artig.*) mortise, mortice: *connessione a* —, mortising; *costruzione di* —, mortising; *giunto a tenone e* —, mortise and tenon joint; *congiungere a* —, to mortise.

mortasàre, *v.t.* (*artig.*) to mortise.

mortasatríce, *s.f.* (*artig.*) mortising machine: — *a catena,* chain (and chisel) mortiser; — *combinata,* boring-and-mortising machine.

mòrte, *s.f.* **1.** death (anche *fig.*): — *apparente,* catalepsy; — *disperata, serena,* desperate, tranquil death; — *dolorosa,* painful death; — *immatura,* premature death; — *per annegamento, per apoplessia,* death by drowning, from apoplexy; *condanna a* —, *sentenza di* —, death sentence; *ferito a* —, mortally wounded; *letto di* —, death-bed; *pena di* —, capital punishment; *silenzio di* —, deathly silence; *la vita e la* —, life and death; *alla* — *di suo padre tornò in Italia,* on his father's death he returned to Italy; *affrontare la* —, to face death; *andare incontro a sicura* —, to face certain death; *correre pericolo di* —, to run the risk of death; *dar la* — *a qlcu.,* to kill s.o.; *darsi la* —, to commit suicide; *esporsi alla* —, to expose oneself to death; *essere vicino alla* —, to be near to death (*o* to be on the brink of death); *fare una buona, una cattiva* —, to die a good, a bad death; *morire di* — *naturale, violenta,* to die a natural, a violent death; *salvare qlcu. dalla* —, to rescue s.o. from death; *venire a* —, to die (*o* to pass away) ‖ — *civile,* (*dir.*) civil death ‖ *a* — *il traditore!,* death to (*o* hang) the traitor! ‖ *annoiato a* —, bored to death (*o* to tears) ‖ *in* — *di,* on the death of: *un poema in* — *di,* a poem on the death of ‖ *in caso di* —, in case of death: *in caso di* — *avrò cura dei suoi figli,* in case of his death (*o* if he should die) I will look after his children ‖ *in punto di* —, on the point of dying (*o* of death) ‖ *sino alla* —, till death: *fedele sino alla* —, faithful unto death ‖ *è questione di vita o di* —, it is a case of life or death ‖ *aver la* — *nel cuore,* to have a heavy (*o* sorrowful) heart ‖ *averla a* — *con qlcu., odiare a* — *qlcu.,* to hate s.o. like poison (*o* the plague) ‖ *essere tra la vita e la* —, to be between life and death ‖ *fare la* — *del topo,* to be crushed to death ‖ *guardare la* — *in faccia,* to look death in the face ‖ *incontrare, trovare la* —, to find one's death ‖ *mettere a* — *qlcu.,* to put s.o. to death ‖ *strappare qlcu. alla* —, to snatch s.o. from the jaws of death **2.** (*cagione del morire*)

death (anche *fig.*): *quella figlia sarà la mia* —, that daughter of mine will be the death of me; *quel fallimento fu la* — *della nostra società,* that bankruptcy marked the end of our partnership **3.** (*caso di morte*) death: *registro delle morti,* register of deaths; *ci furono molte morti per annegamento l'estate scorsa,* there were many deaths by drowning last summer; *notificare una* —, to notify a death **4.** (*cuc.*) (*la miglior fine*) the best way of cooking: *la* — *del galletto è arrosto,* the best way of cooking a spring chicken is to roast it.

mortèlla, *s.f.* (*bot.*) myrtle.

mortífero, *ag.* lethal, deadly, mortal; (*rar.*) mortiferous: *un'arma mortifera,* a lethal weapon; *un veleno* —, a deadly (*o* mortal) poison.

mortificàre, *v.t.* **1.** (*umiliare*) to humiliate; to humble, to mortify: *Dio mortifica gli orgogliosi,* God humbles the proud; *è un impertinente e bisogna mortificarlo,* he is cheeky and must be taught a lesson; *la sua risposta mi mortificò,* his reply humiliated me (*o* I was mortified by his reply); — *i sentimenti di qlcu.,* to wound (*o* to mortify) s.o.'s feelings **2.** (*castigare*) to mortify: — *la carne,* to mortify the flesh; — *le proprie passioni,* to mortify one's passions **3.** (*rendere insensibile*) to deaden: *l'etere mortifica la parte malata,* ether deadens the affected part **4.** (*svigorire, uccidere*) to kill: *la brina mortifica la fioritura degli alberi,* blossoms are killed by the frost ‖ **mortificàrsi,** *v.r.* to mortify oneself: *il sacerdote ci esortò a mortificarci durante la quaresima,* the priest exhorted us to mortify ourselves during Lent.

mortificatívo, *ag.* (*rar.*) mortifying.

mortificatóre, *ag.* (*rar.*) mortifying, humiliating ‖ *s.m.,* **mortificatríce,** *s.f.* (*rar.*) mortifier.

mortificazióne, *s.f.* mortification: — *dei sensi,* mortification (*o* mortifying) of the senses; *non palesava alcun segno di* —, he gave no sign of mortification; *subire una grande* —, to suffer great mortification.

mòrto, *ag.* **1.** dead: — *di freddo,* frozen to death; *fig.* frozen stiff; — *di paura,* dead with fright; — *sul nascere,* dead at birth; *foglie morte,* dead leaves; *nato* —, still-born (anche *fig.*); *progetto nato* — (*o* abortive) plan; *unghia morta,* dead nail; *cascar* —, to drop down dead ‖ — *alla gioia,* dead to pleasure ‖ — *al mondo,* retired from the world ‖ — *e sepolto,* dead and gone (*o* dead and buried); — *stecchito,* dead as a door-nail (*o* stone dead) ‖ *acqua morta,* stagnant water ‖ *angolo* —, (*mil.*) dead ground ‖ *binario* —, (*ferr.*) siding ‖ *capitale* —, (*econ.*) idle (*o* unproductive) capital ‖ *città morta,* dead city ‖ *innamorato* —, madly in love ‖ *lettera morta,* dead letter: *quella legge restò lettera morta,* that law remained a dead letter ‖ *lingua morta,* dead language ‖ *Mar Morto,* (*geog.*) Dead Sea ‖ *mercato* —, (*econ.*) dead market ‖ *mezzo* —, half dead ‖ *natura morta,* (*pitt.*) still life ‖ *peso* —, dead-weight ‖ *ore morte,* dead hours ‖ *più* — *che vivo,* more dead than alive ‖ *punto* —, deadlock (*o* standstill): *giungere a un punto* —, to come to a deadlock ‖ *stagione morta,* close (*o* off) season ‖ *stanco* —, dead-tired ‖ *terreno* —, waste land ‖ *uomo* —, finished man: *è un uomo* —, he is done for (*o* he is finished); *se ti muovi sei un uomo* —!, if you move you are a dead man! ‖ *buttarsi a corpo* — *in ql.co.,* to fling oneself into sthg. ‖ *cadere a corpo* —, to collapse in a heap **2.** (*senza vivacità*) dull: *colore* —, dull colour; *persona morta,* dull person ‖ *s.m.* **1.** dead man, corpse: *i morti,* the dead; *le anime dei morti,* the souls of the dead; *cassa da* —, coffin ‖ *la resurrezione dei morti,* (*teol.*) the resurrection of the dead; *ufficio dei morti,* office of the Dead; *passa il* —, a funeral is passing; *piangere i morti,* to mourn the dead; *seppellire i morti,* to bury the dead ‖ *i Morti,* (*ricorrenza religiosa*) All Souls' Day ‖ *un* — *di fame,* a starveling ‖ *ci scappa il* —!, I think somebody will be killed! ‖ *fare il* —, to pretend to be dead; (*al nuoto*) to float on one's back ‖ *suonare a —*, to toll the knell **2.** (*alle carte*) dummy **3.** (*denaro nascosto*) hoard.

mortòrio, *s.m.* funeral, burial (anche *fig.*): *il ricevimento riuscì un —*, the party was like a funeral.

mortuàrio, *ag.* mortuary: *camera mortuaria*, death chamber; *cappella mortuaria*, mortuary chapel; *lenzuolo —*, shroud (*o* winding-sheet).

mòrva, *s.f.* (*vet.*) glanders (*pl.*).

Mòsa, *no.pr.f.* (*geog.*) Meuse.

mosaicìsta, *s.c.* mosaicist, mosaic worker.

mosàico[1], *ag.* (*Bibbia*) Mosaic: *legge mosaica*, Mosaic law.

mosàico[2], *s.m.* **1.** mosaic: — *alla palladiana*, terrazzo; *mosaici a smalto*, glazed mosaics; — *romano*, tessellated paving; — *veneziano*, Venetian mosaic; *lavoro a —*, mosaic work; *pavimentazione a —*, mosaic flooring; *i mosaici di S. Marco hanno il fondo d'oro*, the mosaics in St. Mark's have a gold background **2.** (*composizione d'arte non omogenea*) mosaic, pastiche, patch-work: *quel lavoro musicale è un vero —!*, that musical composition is a real pastiche! **3.** (*foto. tv.*) mosaic.

mosaìsmo, *s.m.* (*st. relig.*) Mosaism.

Mósca[1], *no.pr.f.* (*geog.*) Moscow.

mósca[2], *s.f.* **1.** fly: — *carnaia*, flesh-fly; — *cavallina*, horse-fly; — *comune*, house-fly; — *tse-tsè*, tsetse-fly; — *vomitoria*, bluebottle; *uova di —*, fly-blow: *questa carne è piena di uova di —*, this meat is all fly-blown; *il ronzare delle mosche*, the buzzing of the flies; *acchiappare le mosche*, to catch flies ‖ —*!*, silence! ‖ — *bianca*, *fig.* rara avis ‖ — *cieca*, blindman's-buff: *giocare a — cieca*, to play blidman's-buff ‖ — *di Milano*, (*med.*) blister fly ‖ — *volante*, (*med.*) floating speck ‖ *peso —*, (*boxe*) fly-weight ‖ *morivano come mosche*, they died like flies ‖ *non farebbe male ad una —*, he wouldn't hurt a fly ‖ *se gli salta la — al naso!*, if he lose his temper! (*o fam.* if he gets his dander up!) ‖ *sei più fastidioso di una —*, you are a deadly bore ‖ *si sentiva volare una —*, you could have heard a pin drop ‖ *la sua calligrafia rassomiglia a zampe di —*, his handwriting is a mere scrawl ‖ *fare di ogni — un elefante*, to make mountains out of molehills ‖ *rimanere con un pugno di mosche*, to remain empty-handed ‖ *in bocca chiusa non entrano mosche*, *prov.* a closed mouth catches no flies ‖ *si prendono più mosche con una goccia di miele che con un barile d'aceto*, *prov.* you catch more flies with honey than with verjuice **2.** (*finto neo*) beauty spot, patch **3.** (*barbetta*) imperial, goatee **4.** (*mar.*) fly-boat **5.** (*esca*) fly: — *per le trote*, trout-fly; *amo con —*, fly-hook; *pescare con la —*, to fish with fly (*o* to go fly-fishing).

moscàio, *s.m.* **1.** (*luogo pieno di mosche*) place full of flies **2.** (*sciame di mosche*) swarm of flies.

moscaiuòla, *s.f.* **1.** meat-safe **2.** (*acchiappamosche*) fly-trap.

moscardíno, *s.m.* **1.** (*zool.*) dormouse (*pl.* dormice) **2.** (*bellimbusto*) dandy.

moscatèllo, *ag.* muscatel (*attributivo*) ‖ *s.m.* muscatel.

moscàto[1], *ag.*: *noce moscata*, nutmeg ‖ *s.m.* muscat(el).

moscàto[2], *ag.* (*di cavallo*) dappled.

mosceríno, *s.m.* gnat, midge.

moschèa, *s.f.* mosque.

moschettàta, *s.f.* musket-shot.

moschettàto, *ag.* speckled.

moschetterìa, *s.f.* (*mil.*) musketry.

moschettièra, *ag.*: *guanto, manica alla —*, mosquetaire glove, sleeve.

moschettière, *s.m.* musketeer.

moschétto, *s.m.* musket.

moschettóne, *s.m.* **1.** (*gancio a molla*) spring-clip **2.** (*gancio per la catena dell'orologio*) swivel.

moschicída, *ag.* fly (*attributivo*): *carta —*, fly-paper; *polvere —*, fly-powder ‖ *s.c.* (*scherz.*) fly-killer.

móscio, *ag.* flabby, flaccid; (*morbido*) soft: *cappello —*, soft hat; *carne moscia*, flabby flesh; *muscoli mosci*,

flabby muscles ‖ *parlare con l'erre moscia*, to speak with a French "r" ‖ *parlare con l'esse moscia*, to lisp.

mòsco, *s.m.* (*zool.*) musk-deer (*invariato al pl.*).

moscóne, *s.m.* **1.** (*entom.*) blue-bottle, blowfly **2.** (*corteggiatore*) suitor; gallant.

Moscòvia, *no.pr.f.* (*geog.*) Muscovy.

moscovíta, *ag.s.c.* Muscovite.

Mosè, *no.pr.m.* (*Bibbia*) Moses.

Mosèlla, *no.pr.f.* (*geog.*) Moselle: *vino della Mosella*, Moselle.

mòssa, *s.f.* **1.** movement: *una — improvvisa*, a sudden movement; *il cavallo fece una — all'improvviso*, the horse started; *fece una — con le spalle*, he shrugged his shoulders; *fece una — falsa e si slogò la caviglia*, he missed his footstep and dislocated his ankle; *ha tutte le mosse del babbo*, he has his father's ways; *non ha fatto una — per aiutarci*, he didn't lift a finger to help us ‖ *essere sulle mosse*, to be about to leave ‖ *prendere le mosse da ql.co.*, to start from sthg. **2.** (*spostamento al gioco*) move (anche *fig.*): — *strategica*, strategic move; *è una — abilissima*, it's a clever move; *fare una —*, to make a move: *ha fatto una — sbagliata, falsa*, he has made a false move (*o* he has slipped up) **3.** (*art.*) movement: *in questo quadro non mi piace la — del braccio*, I don't like the movement of the arm in this picture **4.** (*spor.*) starting post.

mossière, *s.m.* (*spor.*) starter.

mòsso, *ag.* **1.** (*agitato*): *mare —*, rough sea **2.** (*ondulato*): *capelli mossi*, wavy hair **3.** (*mus.*) mosso.

mostacciàta, *s.f.* slap on the face.

mostàccio, *s.m.* (*spreg.*) ugly face, mug.

mostacciuòlo, *s.m.* (*cuc.*) "mostacciuolo" (spiced cake laced with must).

mostàrda, *s.f.* **1.** mustard **2.** (*mostarda di frutta*) "mostarda" (Italian sweet fruit pickles).

mósto, *s.m.* must.

móstra, *s.f.* **1.** (*esposizione*) show, exhibition: — *d'arte*, art-exhibition; — *di fiori, di libri*, flower-show, book-show; *sala di —*, show-room ‖ *essere in —*, to be on show; *mettersi in —*, to attract attention (*o* to show off): *le piace mettersi in —*, she likes attracting attention to herself **2.** (*vetrina*) shop-window; (*vetrinetta*) show-case: *l'ho visto in — dal gioielliere*, I saw it in the jeweller's window; *lo levò dalla —*, he took it out of the window **3.** (*ostentazione*) display; ostentation: — *di abilità, di coraggio*, display of skill, of courage; *far — di cultura*, to show off (*o* to display) one's learning **4.** (*apparenza*) show; (*finzione*) pretence: *è stata tutta una —*, it was all show; *far — di leggere*, to pretend to be reading; *far — di saper tutto*, to pretend to know everything **5.** (*campione*) sample: — *di panno*, sample of cloth **6.** (*quadrante di orologio*) face, dial.

mostràre, *v.t.* **1.** to show: *mostrami i tuoi libri*, show me your books; — *il biglietto, il passaporto*, to show one's ticket, one's passport ‖ — *i denti*, *fig.* to show one's teeth; — *il proprio debole*, *fig.* to show one's weakness **2.** (*ostentare*) to show off, to display: *le piace — i gioielli*, she likes to display (*o* to show off) her jewels; — *la propria erudizione*, to make a show of one's learning **3.** (*indicare*) to show; (*segnalare*) to point out; (*spiegare, far intendere*) to show, to explain: *mostrami come si fa*, show (*o* teach) me how to do it; *mi mostrò i miei errori*, he pointed out my mistakes; *ve lo mostrerò con un esempio*, I'll make it clear with an example; — *la strada a qlcu.*, to show s.o. the way ‖ — *la porta a qlcu.*, to show s.o. the door ‖ — *qlcu. a dito*, to point at s.o. (*o* to single s.o. out) **4.** (*rivelare, manifestare*) to show, to bear evidence of (sthg.); (*dimostrare, provare*) to prove, to demonstrate: *mostra d'aver poco giudizio*, it is evident that he has (*o* he shows) little judgement; *mostra di essere molto intelligente*, he is evidently very intelligent (*o* he shows great intelligence); *mostra più anni di quelli che ha*, he looks older than he really is; *mostra i segni delle antiche ferite*, he bears the scars of former wounds; *agendo così mostra che l'ama ancora*, in behaving like that he shows that he still loves her; *questo mostra che egli agì in malafede*, this proves that he acted in bad faith; *le rovine mostrano la grandezza di Roma antica*, the ruins are evidence of the greatness of ancient Rome; *i tuoi vestiti mostrano il tuo cattivo gusto*, your clothes show your bad taste; — *coraggio*, to show courage; — *un gran miglioramento*, to show great improvement **5.** (*voler far credere, fingere*) to pretend: *mostra di non curarsene*, he pretends not to care ‖ **mostràrsi**, *v.r.* **1.** to show oneself: *egli si mostrò molto crudele*, he showed himself (to be) very cruel; *si mostrò vigliacco*, he proved (himself) to be a coward **2.** (*apparire*) to appear, to show oneself: *si mostrò al momento giusto*, he appeared at the right moment; — *in pubblico*, to show oneself in public.

mostrína, *s.f.* (*mil.*) collar badge.

móstro, *s.m.* monster (anche *fig.*): *i mostri marini*, the sea-monsters; *un* — *di brutalità*, a monster of brutality; *quella donna è un* — *di intelligenza*, that woman is a phenomenon of intelligence ‖ *che* —*!*, what a horror!.

mostruosaménte, *av.* monstrously.

mostruosità, *s.f.* **1.** monstrousness, monstrosity **2.** (*azione mostruosa*) monstrosity.

mostruóso, *ag.* **1.** monstrous (anche *fig.*): *delitto* —, monstrous crime; *vizi mostruosi*, monstrous vices; *è* —*che sia permessa una cosa simile!*, it is monstrous that such a thing should be allowed!; *la sua crudeltà è veramente mostruosa*, his cruelty is really monstrous **2.** (*enorme*) enormous, huge: *un errore* —, a huge (*o* an enormous) mistake.

mòta, *s.f.* mud, mire; sludge.

motivàre, *v.t.* **1.** to state the reason for (sthg. stated): *motivò la sua decisione improvvisa*, he gave the reason for his sudden decision **2.** (*dir.*) to allege; to justify: *le ragioni motivate non sono sufficienti*, the reasons alleged are insufficient; — *un decreto, una sentenza*, to justify (*o* to explain the reasons for) a decree, a judgment; — *un errore di giudizio*, to allege an error of judgment **3.** (*causare*) to cause, to motivate: *il suo comportamento era motivato dall'invidia*, his behaviour was motivated by envy; — *un dissenso*, to cause a difference of opinion.

motivazióne, *s.f.* **1.** motivation **2.** (*dir.*) opinion, justification: *la* — *del giudice*, the judge's opinion.

motívo, *s.m.* **1.** motive, reason, ground: — *di annullamento del provvedimento*, ground for quashing the proceedings; *i motivi di un decreto*, the reasons for a bill; — *di un delitto*, motive of a crime; *motivi impellenti*, urgent reasons; *per il* — *sopra detto*, for the reason given above; *ciò diede* — *a molte obiezioni*, this gave rise to many objections; *era assente per motivi di famiglia*, he was absent for family reasons; *fu sospeso per motivi disciplinari*, he was suspended for disciplinary reasons; *ho fondati motivi di credere che sia colpevole*, I have good grounds for thinking that he is guilty; *non c'è* — *di farlo*, there is no reason for doing it; *non gli ho mai dato* — *di pensarlo*, I have never given him reason to think so; *non hai* — *di lamentarti*, you have no reason to complain (*o* no ground for complaint); *le sue azioni sono determinate da motivi bassi ed egoistici*, his actions are determined by low and selfish motives; *dar* — *di credere...*, to give reason to believe...; *spiegare il* — *per cui...*, to state the reason for which... ‖ *a* — *di*, owing to (*o* on account of *o* because of) ‖ *senza* —, groundless **2.** (*mus.*) theme, motif; leitmotif; *ti piace il* — *svolto in quella sinfonia?*, do you like the theme developed in that symphony?.

mòto¹, *s.m.* **1.** motion, movement: *il* — *dei pianeti*, *degli astri*, the motion of the planets, of the stars; *il* — *del sangue*, the circulation of the blood; *il* — *del treno*, the motion (*o* movement) of the train; *con un* — *della mano*, with a motion of his hand ‖ *i moti vitali*, the vital movements ‖ *di* — *proprio*, spontaneously (*o* of one's own accord) ‖ *in* —, in motion (*o* on the move): *corpo, automobile in* —, body, car in motion; *questo bambino è sempre in* —, *ha il* — *perpetuo addosso*, this child is never still (*o* is always moving about *o* is always on the move); *tutta la polizia è in* —, all the police are in action; *mettere in* — *ql.co.*, to set sthg. in motion; *mettersi in* —, to start (*o* to set out *o* to get going *o fam.* to get moving) ‖ *verbi, avverbi di* —, (*gram.*) verbs, adverbs of motion **2.** (*esercizio fisico*) exercise: *il* — *gli giova*, exercise does him good; *fare del* —, to take exercise **3.** (*impulso*) impulse: *i moti del cuore*, the impulses of the heart **4.** (*sommossa*) rebellion, revolt: *i moti del 1821*, the risings of 1821; — *politico*, political revolt; — *rivoluzionario*, rebellion (*o* uprising) **5.** (*fis. mec.*) motion: — *alternativo*, (*mec.*) reciprocating motion; — *armonico*, (*fis.*) harmonic motion; — *di rotazione*, (*mec. razionale*) motion of rotation; — *fluttuante*, (*fis.*) flutter; — *ondoso*, (*mar.*) wave motion; — *perpetuo*, (*fis.*) perpetual motion; — *rettilineo*, (*mec. razionale*) rectilinear motion; — *rotatorio*, (*fis.*) rotary motion; — *uniforme*, (*mec. razionale*) uniform motion; — *uniformemente accelerato*, (*mec. razionale*) uniformly accelerated motion; — *uniformemente ritardato*, (*mec. razionale*) uniformly retarded motion; — *vario*, (*mec. razionale*) variable motion; *in* —, (*mec.*) turning: *messa in* —, (*mec.*) starting; *mettere in* —, (*mec.*) to start ‖ *le leggi del* —, the laws of motion.

mòto², *s.f.* (*motocicletta*) motor-cycle.

motoaratríce, *s.f.* (*mec. agr.*) motor-bike; motor-plough.

motoaratúra, *s.f.* mechanical ploughing.

motobàrca, *s.f.* motor-boat.

motocarrozzétta, *s.f.* side-car.

motociclétta, *s.f.* motor-cycle; (*fam.*) motor-bike.

motociclísmo, *s.m.* motor-cycling.

motociclísta, *s.c.* motor-cyclist.

motocíclo, *s.m.* motor-cycle; (*fam.*) motor-bike.

motocultúra, *s.f.* (*agr.*) mechanical farming.

motocompressóre, *s.m.* (*mec.*) engine-compressor.

motofalciatríce, *s.f.* (*mec. agr.*) motor mower.

motofurgoncíno, *s.m.* light van.

motofurgóne, *s.m.* van.

motoleggèra, *s.f.* lightweight motor-cycle.

motonàutica, *s.f.* motor-boating: *gara di* —, motor-boat race.

motonàve, *s.f.* (*mar.*) motor-ship: — *da carico costiera*, motor coaster.

motopescheréccio, *s.m.* (*mar.*) motor trawler.

motopómpa, *s.f.* (*mec.*) motor-pump: — *antincendio*, fire engine.

motóre, *ag.* motor; driving, propelling: *albero* —, (*mec.*) driving shaft; *apparato* —, (*mar.*) propelling machinery; *forza motrice*, (*mec.*) driving power; *impulso* —, motor impulse; *nervo* —, (*anat.*) motor nerve ‖ *s.m.* **1.** (*mec.*) motor; engine: — *a benzina*, petrol engine (*o* motor); (*amer.*) gasoline motor; — *a combustione interna*, a scoppio, internal combustion engine; — *a corrente alternata, continua*, (*elett.*) alternating, direct current motor; — *a due, a quattro tempi*, two-, four-stroke engine; — *a nafta, Diesel*, Diesel engine; — *a reazione*, jet engine; — *a stella*, (*aer.*) radial engine; — *a turboelica*, prop-jet (*o* turbo-prop) engine; — *a turbogetto*, (*aer.*) turbo-jet engine; — *a valvole in testa*, overhead-valve engine; — *di riserva*, spare engine; — *di aeroplano*, aero-motor; — *elettrico*, electric motor; — *entrobordo, fuoribordo*, (*mar.*) inboard, outboard engine; — *raffreddato ad acqua, ad aria*, water-cooled, air-cooled engine; — *termico*, heat-engine; *il* — *dell'automobile è fermo*, the car-engine is dead; *il* — *perde giri*, the motor speed is falling; *avviare un* —, to start an engine **2.** *il Primo Motore*, *(fil.)* the Prime Mover *(o* the First Cause).

motorétta, *s.f.* (motor-)scooter.

motoríno, *s.m.*: — *d'avviamento*, *(aut.)* starter.

motòrio, *ag.* motor *(attributivo)*; motory *(attributivo)*.

motorísta, *s.m.* engineer: — *d'aviazione*, aeroplane engineer *(o* fitter); — *di bordo*, *(aer.)* flight engineer.

motorizzàre, *v.t.* to motorize.

motorizzazióne, *s.f.* motorization.

motorizzàto, *ag.* motorized.

motoscàfo, *s.m.* motor-boat.

motóso, *ag.* muddy; miry.

motovelièro, *s.m.* *(mar.)* auxiliary sailing-ship.

motríce, *s.f.* *(mec.)* (motor-) tractor: — *a vapore*, steam-engine; — *e rimorchio*, tractor and trailer; — *tranviaria*, tram-car motor-coach.

motríglia, *s.f.* mire, mud.

motteggévole, *ag.* waggish; *(scherzoso)* joking; *(ironico)* ironical.

motteggevolménte, *av.* waggishly; *(scherzosamente)* jokingly; *(ironicamente)* ironically.

motteggiaménto, *(rar.)* per **mottéggio**.

motteggiàre, *v.i.* to joke, to jest; to banter ǁ *v.t.* to make fun of (s.o., sthg.); to chaff, to tease; *(malignamente)* to scoff at (s.o., sthg.), to jeer at (s.o., sthg.).

motteggiatóre, *ag.* waggish; *(scherzoso)* joking; *(ironico)* ironical ǁ *s.m.*, **motteggiatríce**, *s.f.* wag; joker, jester.

mottéggio, *s.m.* **1.** banter, raillery: *era fatto segno ai motteggi degli amici*, he was the object of his friends' raillery **2.** *(detto arguto)* joke, jest.

mòtto, *s.m.* **1.** *(parola)* word: *senza far* —, without a word **2.** *(detto, proverbio)* saying, saw **3.** *(facezia)* witticism, pleasantry **4.** *(arald.)* motto *(pl.* mottoes, mottos) **5.** *(principio ispiratore)* motto *(pl.* mottoes, mottos).

motu proprio, *l. av. (lat.)* motu proprio.

movènte, *s.m.* motive; cause, reason: — *di un delitto*, motive of a crime; *i segreti moventi del cuore*, the secret reasons of the heart.

movènza, *s.f.* **1.** *(di statue, figure dipinte, ecc.)* attitude **2.** *pl.* movements: *goffo nelle movenze*, clumsy in one's movements.

movíbile, *ag.* movable.

movimentàre, *v.t.* *(animare)* to enliven, to animate: *il suo arrivo movimentò la festa*, the party was enlivened by his arrival.

movimentàto, *ag.* **1.** lively, animated; *(pieno di movimento)* busy: *festa movimentata*, lively party; *strada, quartiere —*, busy street, district **2.** *(ricco di avvenimenti)* eventful; *(agitato)* agitated: *un anno —*, an eventful year; *il secondo atto è poco —*, the second act does not contain much action.

moviménto, *s.m.* **1.** movement: — *continuo, regolare, irregolare, lento, affrettato*, continuous, regular, irregular, slow, accelerated movement; — *dei ghiacciai, dei pianeti*, movements of glaciers, of the planets; *i movimenti del corpo*, bodily movements; *movimenti ginnastici, muscolari*, gymnastic, muscular movements; *movimenti volontari, involontari*, voluntary, involuntary movements; *il minimo — sarebbe stato notato*, the slightest movement would have been noticed; *tutti i suoi movimenti erano aggraziati*, all her movements were graceful; *fare un — col braccio*, to move one's arm; *fare un — con la mano*, to gesture; *fare un — falso*, to make a clumsy movement; *fig.* to make a false move: *feci un — falso e mi ruppi una caviglia*, I took a false step and broke my ankle **2.** *(tec.)* movement; *(moto)* motion; *(meccanismo)* mechanism, movement, action: — *a scatto*, trigger-action; — *del braccio di una gru*, *(mec.)* jib motion; — *di una locomotiva*, drive-mechanism; *il — di un orologio*, the movement of a watch; — *di andata e ritorno*, *(mec.)* forward and reverse motion; — *di orologeria*, *(mec.)* clock-work; — *di rotazione, rotatorio*, rotatory motion; —

di vai e vieni, *(mec.)* to-and-fro movement; — *elastico*, *(mec.)* cushioned movement; — *laterale*, *(mec.)* traverse movement; — *parallelo*, *(mec.)* parallel motion; — *trasversale*, crosswise movement; *invertire il —*, to reverse; *mettere in —*, to set *(o* to put) in motion *(o* to start) **3.** *(traffico)* traffic; *(andirivieni)* movement, flow; *(trambusto)* bustle, activity: — *dei viaggiatori, dei forestieri*, flow of travellers, tourists; *il — della popolazione*, the movement of the population; *il — del materiale*, *(ind.)* material handling; *il — del porto di Genova*, the movement of shipping in the port of Genoa; *il — di una grande città*, the bustle of a large town; — *ferroviario, stradale*, rail, road traffic; *una cittadina senza —*, a lifeless little town; *c'era molto, poco — sull'autostrada*, there was a lot of traffic, little traffic on the motor-way ǁ *una festa piena di —*, a lively party ǁ *essere in gran —*, to be on the move *(o* to be in motion) **4.** *(di quadro, opera letteraria) (vivacità)* action, movement: *questa commedia manca di —*, this play doesn't contain much action **5.** *(corrente letteraria, politica)* movement: — *politico*, political movement; *il Romanticismo fu un — letterario molto importante*, Romanticism was a very important literary movement **6.** *(letter.)* *(moto, impulso)*: *i movimenti dell'anima*, the workings of the soul; *un — di compassione*, an access of pity **7.** *(comm.)* movement: — *delle merci*, movement of goods; — *di cassa*, turnover; — *nelle quotazioni, nei prezzi*, movement of prices; — *verso il rialzo*, upward movement **8.** *(mus.)* movement **9.** *(mil.)* movement; evolution.

Mozambíco, *no.pr.m.* *(geog.)* Mozambique.

mozióne, *s.f.* motion: *proporre, respingere una —*, to propose, to reject a motion; *sostenere, far approvare una —*, to carry a motion.

mozzaménte, *av.* in a choked voice.

mozzaménto, *s.m.* cutting-off; *(di coda)* docking.

mozzàre, *v.t.* to cut off; *(coda, capelli)* to dock: — *la coda a un animale*, to dock an animal's tail; — *la testa a qlcu.*, to behead s.o. *(o* to cut off s.o.'s head) ǁ *il freddo gli mozzò le mani*, the cold numbed his hands ǁ *la paura le mozzò le parole in bocca*, fear made the words die on her lips ǁ — *il discorso, la conversazione*, to cut short the conversation ǁ — *il fiato*, to take s.o.'s breath away.

mozzarèlla, *s.f.* " mozzarella " (kind of Italian cheese originally made from cow-buffalo's milk).

mozzatúra, *s.f.* cutting-off; *(di coda)* docking.

mozzétta, *s.f.* *(eccl.)* mozzetta, mozetta.

mozzicóne, *s.m.* butt, stump, stub: — *di candela*, candle-end; — *di sigaretta*, cigarette-end; *(sl.)* fag-end.

mózzo[1], *ag.* cut (off); *(di coda, capelli)* docked ǁ *voce mozza dalla paura*, voice choked with fear.

mózzo[2], *s.m.* **1.** *(mar.)* ship-boy **2.** *(di stalla)* stable-boy.

mòzzo[3], *s.m.* *(mec.)* hub: — *a ruota libera*, free-wheel hub; — *della ruota*, wheel-hub *(o* nave); — *dell'elica*, *(mar.)* screw-boss; *(aer.)* propeller-boss.

mozzorécchi, *s.m.* **1.** *(imbroglione)* twister **2.** *(leguleio)* pettifogger, crooked lawyer.

múcca, *s.f.* cow: — *da latte*, milker *(o* milch cow).

múcchio, *s.m.* heap, mass (anche *fig.*): *un — di fieno, di grano, di paglia*, a heap of hay, of corn, of straw; *un — di gente*, a lot *(o* a mass) of people; *un — di libri, di soldi*, a heap of books, of money.

múceo, *s.m.* *(fisiol.)* mucus.

mucósa, *s.f.* *(anat.)* mucous membrane.

múcido, *ag.* mouldy, musty: *pane —*, mouldy bread ǁ *s.m.* *(muffa)* mould; *(odore di muffa)* mouldy smell; *(sapore di muffa)* mouldy taste: *sa di —*, *(sapore)* it tastes mouldy; *(odore)* it smells mouldy.

mucillàggine, *s.f.* *(bot. chim.)* mucilage.

mucillagginóso, *ag.* mucilaginous.

múco, *s.m.* *(fisiol.)* mucus.

mucósa, *s.f.* *(anat.)* mucous membrane.

mucosità, *s.f.* mucosity.

mucóso, *ag.* mucous.

mucronàto, *ag.* (*bot. zool.*) mucronate(d).

mucróne, *s.m.* (*anat. bot.*) mucro (*pl.* mucrones, mucros).

múda, *s.f.* **1.** (*di uccelli*) moult, moulting; (*di serpenti*) sheedding **2.** (*tempo della muda*) moult, moulting -time, moulting-season **3.** (*luogo della muda*) mew.

muezzíno, *s.m.* muezzin.

múffa, *s.f.* mould, mildew: — *della penicillina,* penicillin mould; — *di formaggio* cheese-mould; *odore di* —, mouldy (o musty) smell; *sa di* —, it tastes mouldy; (*odore*) it smells mouldy; *fare la* —, to go mouldy; *fig.* to collect dust.

múffido, muffígno, *ag.* (*rar.*) mouldy, mildewy.

muffíre, *v.i.* to mildew, to become mouldy, to become musty ‖ *non voglio* — *in questo paese,* I don't want to stagnate (o to go to seed) in this village.

muffíto, múffo, *ag.* mouldy, mildewy, musty.

múffola, *s.f.* **1.** (*di forno*) |muffle: *forno a* —, (*metal.*) muffle furnace; (*ceramica*) muffle kiln **2.** (*elett.*) box: — *di derivazione,* dividing box.

muffosità, *s.f.* mouldiness, mustiness.

muffóso, *ag.* mouldy, musty, mildewy ‖ *una persona muffosa,* (*anziana*) a fogy (o an old fogy).

muflóne, *s.m.* (*zool.*) mouf(f)lon.

muftí, *s.m.* mufti (*pl.* muftis).

muggènte, *ag.* **1.** bellowing **2.** *fig.* roaring: *le onde muggenti,* the roaring waves.

mugghiaménto, *V.* **múgghio.**

mugghiàre, *v.i.* **1.** to bellow **2.** *fig.* (*del mare*) to roar; (*del vento*) to howl **3.** (*lamentarsi, gridare*) to howl; (*fam.*) to bellow.

múgghio, *s.m.* **1.** bellow **2.** (*del mare*) roar; (*del vento*) howl **3.** (*lamento*) howl; (*fam.*) bellow.

múggine, *s.m.* (*ittiol.*) mullet.

muggíre, *V.* **mugghiàre.**

muggíto, *V.* **múgghio.**

mugheríno, *s.m.* (*zerbinotto*) dandy.

mughétto, *s.m.* **1.** (*bot.*) lily of the valley **2.** (*patol.*) thrush.

mugíe, *s.m.* moujik, muzhik, mujik.

mugliàre, *e derivati, V.* **mugghiàre,** *e derivati.*

mugnàia, *s.f.* miller's wife.

mugnàio, *s.m.* miller.

mugolaménto, *s.m.* **1.** howling; (*piagnucolamento*) whining, whimpering **2.** (*borbottamento*) mumble, mutter.

mugolàre, *v.t.* to howl; (*piagnucolare*) to whine, to whimper: *il cane mugolava dal dolore,* the dog was whimpering with pain ‖ *v.t.* (*borbottare*) to mumble, to mutter.

mugolío, *s.m.* howling; (*piagnucolio*) whimpering.

múla, *s.f.* (*zool.*) she-mule.

mulàcchia, *s.f.* (*rar.*) (*ornit.*) crow.

mulàggine, *s.f.* (*rar.*) obstinacy, stubbornness.

mulàtta, *s.f.* mulatto woman, mulattress, mulata.

mulattièra, *s.f.* mule-track.

mulattière, *s.m.* muleteer, mule-driver.

mulattièro, *ag.* mule (*attributivo*): *strada mulattiera,* mule-track.

mulàtto, *s.m.* mulatto (*pl.* mulatto(e)s).

muléseo, *ag.* mulish.

mulièbre, *ag.* feminine, womanly: *il sesso* —, the female sex (o the fair sex); *statua* —, statue of a female figure; *virtù muliebri,* womanly virtues.

mulinàre, *v.t.* **1.** (*far girare intorno*) to mill; to whirl: *il vento mulinava le foglie,* the wind whirled the leaves about (o round) **2.** *fig.* (*arzigogolare su*) to brood over (sthg.), to ruminate upon, about (sthg.): — *ql.co.* (*nella mente*), to turn sthg. over (and over) in one's mind (o to brood over sthg. o to ponder on sthg.).

mulinèllo, *s.m.* **1.** (*vortice d'acqua*) whirlpool; (*vortice d'aria*) whirlwind, eddy **2.** (*rapido movimento circolare*) moulinet, twirl: *fare dei mulinelli col bastone,* to twirl one's stick (o to flourish one's stick) **3.** (*gio-*

cattolo) wind-vane **4.** (*ventilatore a disco girevole per finestre*) ventilating fan **5.** (*mar.*) windlass: — *di catena,* swivel; — *di cavo,* rope swivel; — *voltacatene,* mooring swivel **6.** (*aer.*) (*elica di prova*) fan brake; (*nell'ala del velivolo*) windmill **7.** (*di canna da pesca*) fishing reel **8.** (*strumento idraulico*) current meter **9.** (*acrobazia aerea*) roll.

mulíno, *s.m.* mill: — *ad acqua,* water-mill; — *a mano,* handmill; — *a pestelli,* (*miner.*) stamping-mill; — *a tamburo,* drum-mill; — *a vapore,* steam mill; — *a vento,* windmill; — *da olio,* oil-crusher; — *elettrico,* electric-mill; — *macinatore,* (*ind.*) grinding mill; — *per farina,* flour-mill; *macina di* —, millstone; *proprietario di* —, mill-owner; *ruota di* —, mill-wheel ‖ *i mulini di Dio macinano lentamente,* (*la giustizia di Dio si compie sempre*) the mills of God grind slowly ‖ *combattere contro i mulini a vento,* to tilt at windmills (o to fight windmills) ‖ *essere un* — *a vento,* (*cambiar spesso idea*) to be a weathercock ‖ *chi va al* — *s'infarina,* *prov.* you can't touch pitch without being defiled ‖ *tirare acqua al proprio* —, *prov.* to bring grist to one's own mill.

múlo, *s.m.* mule: *a dorso di* —, on a mule; *il* — *va bene in montagna,* a mule is useful in the mountains ‖ *caparbio come un* —, as stubborn as a mule (o as a donkey); *scalciare come un* —, to kick like a mule.

múlta, *s.f.* fine: — *leggera, pesante,* light, heavy fine; *appioppare una* — *a qlcu.,* (*fam.*) to slap a fine on s.o.; *conciliare una* —, to pay a fine on the spot; *dare la* — *a qlcu.,* to fine s.o.

multàre, *v.t.* to fine.

multicolóre, *ag.* multicolour(ed), many-coloured.

multifórme, *ag.* multiform, variform.

multilateràle, *ag.* many-sided, multilateral.

multiloquènza, *s.f.* (*rar.*) multiloquence.

multilòquio, *s.m.* multiloquy.

multilústre, *ag.* aged, ancient.

multimilionàrio, *ag.s.m.* multimillionaire.

multípara, *s.f.* multipara.

multíparo, *ag.* multiparous.

multiplàno, *s.m.* (*aer.*) multiplane.

múltiplo, *ag.* multiple: *frutto* —, multiple fruit; *stella multipla,* (*astr.*) multiple star ‖ *s.m.* (*mat.*) mul. tiple: *minimo comune* —, least common multiple (*abbr.* L.C.M.); *12 è* — *di 4,* 12 is a multiple of 4.

múmmia, *s.f.* **1.** mummy: *le mummie egiziane,* Egyptian mummies **2.** *fig.* (*persona dalle membra incartapecorite*) skinny person; (*fam.*) bag of bones; (*persona scontrosa*) wet blanket.

mummifieàre, *v.t.* to mummify; (*imbalsamare*) to embalm ‖ **mummificàrsi,** *v.r.* **1.** to become mummified **2.** *fig.* (*fossilizzarsi*) to fossilize.

mummificatóre, *s.m.* embalmer.

mummifieazióne, *s.f.* mummification; (*imbalsamazione*) embalming.

múngere, *v.t.* to milk ‖ — *qlcu.,* (*spillargli denari*) to bleed s.o. (o to milk s.o.).

mungitóre, *s.m.* milker.

mungitríce, *s.f.* **1.** milker, milkmaid **2.** (*macchina per mungere*) milker.

mungitúra, *s.f.* milking.

municipàle, *ag.* municipal; town (*attributivo*): *consiglio* —, town council; *diritti municipali,* municipal rights; *guardia* —, policeman; *parco* —, town park.

municipalità, *s.f.* municipality.

municipalizzàre, *v.t.* to municipalize.

municipalizzazióne, *s.f.* municipalization.

município, *s.m.* **1.** (*st. romana*) municipium (*pl.* municipia) **2.** (*comune, municipalità*) municipality **3.** (*palazzo del municipio*) townhall.

munificaménte, *av.* munificently.

munifieènte, *ag.* munificent, liberal, bountiful.

munificenteménte, *av.* munificently, liberally.

munificènza, *s.f.* munificence, liberality, bounty: *la galleria di arte moderna fu fondata per la* — *del* *signor X*, the gallery of modern art was founded by the generosity of Mr. X.

munífico, *ag.* munificent, liberal, bountiful: *un dono* —, a handsome gift; *un principe* —, a bountiful prince.

muníre, *v.t.* 1. (*fortificare*) to fortify, to strengthen, to protect: *munirono il loro accampamento di trincee e mucchi di sassi per difendersi dall'attacco dei pellirosse,* they fortified their camp against the attack of the Redskins with trenches and heaps of stones; — *una città di mura,* to fortify (o to strengthen) a town with walls (o to throw a wall round a town) 2. (*provvedere*) to supply, to provide, to furnish: *lo munì di un salvacondotto,* he provided him with a safe-conduct; — *di fondi,* (*comm.*) to supply with funds; — *di lettera di presentazione,* to provide with a letter of introduction || — *una cambiale di girata,* to endorse a bill || **munírsi,** *v.r.* 1. (*fortificarsi*) to fortify oneself: — *contro il freddo,* to fortify oneself against the cold 2. (*provvedersi*) to provide oneself, to supply oneself: *si munì di denaro per il viaggio,* he provided himself with money for the trip.

munizionaménto, *s.m.* munitioning.

munizionàre, *v.t.* to munition.

munizióne, *s.f.* 1. munition; ammunition (*solo sing.*): *abbiamo finito le munizioni,* we are out of munitions (o ammunition) || *munizioni da bocca,* victuals (o provisions) || *pane di* —, ammunition bread 2. (*scherz.*) (*denaro*) money.

munizionière, *s.m.* (*mil.*) munitioner.

muòvere, *v.t.* to move (anche *fig.*); (*fam.*) to shift: *l'acqua muove la ruota del mulino,* the water moves the mill-wheel; *che cosa lo mosse a farlo?,* what moved (o induced) him to do it?; *chi ha mosso i miei libri?,* who shifted my books?; *è una vista che muoverebbe anche le pietre,* it is a sight that would (be enough to) move the very stones to tears; *la fame lo mosse a rubare,* hunger moved him to steal; *tocca a te* —, (*a dama, scacchi*) it is your turn to move; *il vento muove le foglie,* the wind stirs the leaves; — *il campo,* (*mil.*) to break camp; — *il corpo,* (*fisiol.*) to move the bowels; — *il fuoco,* to poke the fire; — *un passo,* to make (o to take) a step; — *i primi passi,* to take one's first steps; *fig.* to make one's first steps; — *una pedina,* to move a piece; — *qlcu. al pianto, al riso, alla pietà,* to move s.o. to tears, to laughter, to pity; — *la testa,* to move one's head; — *le truppe,* to move troops || *non muoverebbe un dito per aiutarmi,* he wouldn't lift a finger to help me || — *causa a qlcu.,* (*dir.*) to sue s.o. || — *critiche,* to arouse criticism || — *la curiosità di qlcu.,* to arouse (o to stir) s.o.'s curiosity; — *difficoltà,* to raise (o to make) difficulties || — *un dubbio,* to raise a doubt || — *un grido,* to raise a shout || — *guerra contro un paese,* to attack (o to invade) a country || — *una questione,* to raise a question || — *rimproveri a qlcu.,* to scold (o to reproach) s.o. || *v.i.* 1. to move: *la strada muove dal paese,* the road starts from the village; — *alla volta di un luogo,* to set off (o out) for a place; — *in direzione di,* to move in the direction of; — *verso,* to move towards 2. (*germogliare*) to bud || **muòversi,** *v.r.* to move; to stir: *nessuno si mosse quando entrai,* nobody stirred when I went in; *non c'era vento e non una foglia si muoveva,* there was no wind and not a leaf was stirring; *non mi muoverò da lui,* I shan't leave him; *non mi muoverò da qui,* I shan't move from here; *non mi sono mosso da casa,* I haven't set foot outside the house; *non mi sono mosso da qui,* I haven't stirred a foot from here; *non posso muovermi,* I cannot move; *quel bambino non fa che* —, that child is never still (o is always on the go) || *muoviti!,* hurry up!; (*fam.*) get a move on! || *eppur si muove!,* but it does move! || *ti muovi?,* are you coming? || *non si muove foglia che Dio non voglia,* prov. man proposes, God disposes.

múra¹, *s.f.* (*mar.*) tack: — *di flocco,* jib tack.

múra², *V.* **múro** 2.

muràglia, *s.f.* 1. wall || *la Grande Muraglia,* the Great Wall of China 2. (*barriera*) barrier: *la rivoluzione francese abbattè ogni* — *tra le classi sociali,* the French Revolution broke down all barriers between social classes 3. (*parte dello zoccolo del cavallo*) wall.

muraglióne, *s.m.* massive wall; embankment: *i muraglioni di un porto,* seawalls.

muraiuòlo, *ag.* climbing.

muràle, *ag.* mural; wall (*attributivo*): *carta* —, wall map; *pittura* —, wall (o mural) painting || *corona* —, (*st. romana*) mural crown.

muràre, *v.t.* 1. (*costruire*) to build: — *una casa,* to build a house; — *un palazzo,* to build a palace 2. (*circondare di mura*) to wall: *ha murato il giardino,* he has walled the garden 3. (*chiudere con muro*) to wall up, to brick up, to brick in: *ha murato la porta, la finestra,* he walled up the door, the window 4. (*chiudere in un muro*) to immure, to wall up: — *un tesoro,* to immure a treasure; — *viva una persona,* to immure (o to wall up) a person | *v.i.* to build: — *a secco,* to build a dry wall; *fig.* to eat without drinking || **muràrsi,** *v.r.* (*chiudersi in un luogo*) to immure (oneself); to shut oneself up: *si mura nella sua stanza e non parla a nessuno,* he shuts himself up in his room and does not speak to anybody.

muràrio, *ag.* building (*attributivo*): *arte muraria,* masonry; *opera muraria,* building work.

muràta, *s.f.* 1. (*mar.*) ship's side; parapet; (*di legno*) bulwarks (*pl.*) 2. (*muraglia*) wall.

muràto, *ag.* 1. (*cinto di mura*) walled: *città murata,* walled town 2. (*chiuso da un muro*) walled up: *finestra murata,* walled up window || *s.m.* masonry.

muratóre, *s.m.* mason; bricklayer || *franco* —, freemason.

muratúra, *s.f.* 1. (*il cingere con mura*) walling 2. masonry: — *di sostegno,* bulkhead; *lavoro in* —, brickwork; *ponte in* —, masonry (o stone) bridge.

murèna, *s.f.* (*ittiol.*) moray.

muriàtico, *ag.* (*chim.*) muriatic.

muriàto, *s.m.* (*chim.*) muriate.

muríccia, *s.f.* dry wall || *portare sassi alle muricce,* to carry coals to Newcastle.

muricciuòlo, *s.m.* low wall.

múrice, *s.m.* (*zool.*) murex (*pl.* murices, murexes).

múrmure, *s.m.* (*poet.*) murmur.

múro, *s.m.; pl.m.* **múri** (*nel senso 1.*); *pl.f.* **múra** (*nel senso 2.*). 1. wall; barrier (anche *fig.*): — *a secco,* dry (o dry-stone) wall; — *di cinta,* boundary (o enclosure) wall; — *di confine,* party wall; — *di mattoni,* brick wall; — *divisorio,* partition wall; — *esterno,* outer wall; — *maestro,* main wall; *armadio a* —, built-in cupboard || — *del suono,* (*aer.*) sound barrier || *abitare* — *a* —, to be next-door neighbours || *battere la testa contro un* —, to bang one's head against a wall || *essere con le spalle al* —, to be with one's back to the wall || *mettere qlcu. al* —, to put s.o. up against a wall || *parlare al* —, to speak to deaf ears: *parlava al* —, his words fell on deaf ears || *i muri hanno orecchie,* prov. walls have ears 2. *pl.* walls: *le mura della città,* the town walls || *le mura domestiche,* the home || *chiudersi tra quattro mura,* to shut oneself up.

múrra, *s.f.* (*min. archeol.*) murra.

murrína, *s.f.* murrhine.

músa¹, *s.f.* 1. (*mit.*) Muse: *le nove muse,* the nine Muses 2. (*ispirazione poetica*) muse, poetical genius; (*poesia*) poetry: *la mia* — *tace,* my muse is silent.

músa², *s.f.* (*bot.*) musa.

musànga, *s.f.* (*zool.*) musang.

musarágno, *s.m.* (*zool.*) shrew.

múscari, *s.m.* (*bot.*) muscari.

muschiàto, *ag.* musky || *bue* —, musk-ox; *gazzella muschiata,* musk-deer; *topo* —, musk-rat || *rosa muschiata,* musk-rose.

múschio¹, *s.m.* 1. (*biol. farm.*) musk 2. (*zool.*) musk-deer (*invariato al pl.*).

múschio², **músco**, *s.m.* (*bot.*) moss: — *clavato*; snake moss; *ricoprire di* —, to cover with moss.

muscolàre, *ag.* (*anat.*) muscular: *contrazione* —, muscular contraction; *forza* —, muscular strength; *sistema* —, muscular system (*o* musculature); *tessuto* —, muscular tissue.

muscolatúra, **muscolazióne**, *s.f.* (*anat.*) musculature.

muscoleggiàre, *v.i.* (*disegnare muscoli*) to draw muscles; (*dipingere muscoli*) to paint muscles.

múscolo, *s.m.* **1.** (*anat.*) muscle: — *volontario*, voluntary muscle; *contrazione dei muscoli*, cramp; *è tutto muscoli*, he is very wiry (*o* sinewy) ‖ *avere muscoli d'acciaio*, to have muscles (*o* sinews) of steel **2.** (*cuc.*) meaty part **3.** (*zool.*) mussel.

muscolosità, *s.f.* muscularity.

muscolóso, *ag.* muscular, brawny, sturdy.

muscolúto, *ag.* muscular, brawny, vigorous.

muscóso, *ag.* mossy.

musèo, *s.m.* museum: — *di storia naturale*, natural history museum; *custode del* —, museum keeper; *pezzo da* —, museum piece ‖ *Museo Britannico*, British Museum ‖ — *delle statue di cera*, waxworks ‖ *roba da* —, (*anticaglia*) old rubbish.

museruòla, *s.f.* muzzle: *mettere la* — *a un animale*, to muzzle an animal; *togliere la* — *a un cane*, to unmuzzle a dog ‖ *mettere la* — *a qlcu.*, to muzzle (*o* to silence) s.o.

musétta, *s.f.* (*mus.*) musette.

musétto, *s.m.* pretty little face: *un bimbo con un bel* —, a child with a pretty (*o* dear) little face.

música, *s.f.* **1.** music: — *da camera*, chamber music; — *sacra*, church (*o* sacred) music; *che bella* —!, what lovely music!; *maestro di* —, music master; *un pezzo di* —, a piece of music; *avere passione per la* —, to have a passion for (*o* to be fond of) music; *eseguire una* —, to play (*o* to perform) a piece of music; *fare* —, to play some music; *mettere in* —, to set to music; *studiare* —, to study music ‖ — *dei gatti*, caterwauling ‖ — *in piazza*, open-air concert ‖ *cambia* —!, let's turn the record over ‖ *è la solita* —!, it is the same old story! ‖ *facevano una* — *indiavolata*, (*un baccano indiavolato*) they were making an awful din **2.** (*banda*) band: *la* — *del reggimento*, the regimental band.

musicàbile, *ag.* that may be set to music.

musicàle, *ag.* musical; music (*attributivo*): *accademia* —, Academy of Music; *commedia* —, musical comedy; *circolo* —, music club; *dramma* —, opera; *educazione* —, musical education; *orecchio* —, musical ear (*o* ear for music); *serata* —, musical evening; *strumento* —, musical instrument; *voce* —, musical voice; *ha molto senso* —, he has a flair for music.

musicalménte, *av.* musically.

musicànte, *s.m.* musician; (*di banda*) bandsman (*pl.* bandsmen).

musicàre, *v.t.* to set to music: *sta musicando una commedia*, he is setting a play to music.

musichétta, *s.f.* popular music: *che bella* —!, what a nice little tune!.

musicísta, *s.c.* musician.

músico, *ag.* (*letter.*) musical ‖ *s.m.* (*letter.*) musician.

musicofobía, *s.f.* musicophobia.

musicògrafo, *s.m.* **1.** musicographer **2.** (*critico musicale*) music critic.

musicología, *s.f.* musicology.

musicòlogo, *s.m.* musicologist.

musicòmane, *s.c.* musicomaniac.

musicomanía, *s.f.* musicomania.

musicoterapía, *s.f.* (*med.*) music therapy.

musivo, *ag.* mosaic (*attributivo*).

múso, *s.m.* **1.** (*di animale*) snout; muzzle: — *di cane*, dog's muzzle; — *di maiale*, pig's snout **2.** (*spreg. scherz.*) (*di persona*) snout; face: *è un brutto* —, *ma non mi fa paura*, he is an ugly customer, but I am not afraid of him ‖ *a* — *duro*, resolutely ‖ *dire ql.co. a qlcu. sul* —,

to say sthg. to s.o.'s face ‖ *rider sul* — *a qlcu.*, to laugh in s.o.'s face ‖ *spaccare il* — *a qlcu.*, to smash s.o.'s face (*o* to bash s.o.'s face in) ‖ *torcere il* — *a ql.co.*, to turn up one's nose at sthg. **3.** (*fam.*) (*broncio*) long face: *avere il* —, to have the sulks (*o* to be sulky); *fare, mettere il* —, to pull a long face.

musolièra, (*rar.*) per **museruòla**.

musóne, *s.m.* **1.** (*di animale*) large muzzle **2.** (*spreg. scherz.*) (*di persona*) big round face **3.** (*fam.*) (*persona che tiene il broncio*) misery, sulky person, morose person: *sei proprio un* —, you are a real misery.

musonería, *s.f.* sulkiness, moroseness.

musórno, *ag.* (*rar.*) **1.** (*imbronciato*) sulky **2.** (*stupido*) stupid **3.** (*cupo, fosco*) dark, overcast.

mussàre, *v.i.* to froth.

mussitazióne, *s.f.* (*med.*) mussitation.

mússola, **mussolína**, *s.f.*, **mússolo**, *s.m.* muslin: — *a disegni*, figured muslin; — *di lana, di seta*, mousseline de laine, de soie; — *stampata*, printed muslin.

mussulmàno, *V.* **musulmàno**.

mustàcchi, *s.m.pl.* **1.** m(o)ustache (*sing.*) **2.** (*mar.*) backropes.

mustèla, *s.f.* (*zool.*) weasel.

musulmàno, *ag.s.m.* Mussulman, Moslem, Muslim ‖ **musulmàna**, *s.f.* Mussulman, Moslem, Muslim.

múta¹, *s.f.* **1.** (*cambio*) change: — *di cavalli*, relay of horses; *dare la* —, (*mil.*) to relieve (*o* to change) the guard ‖ *a* — *a* —, by turns (*o* in turn) **2.** (*di uccelli, gatti*) moult, moulting; (*di serpenti*) shedding: *fare la* —, to moult **3.** (*serie*) set: *una* — *di candelieri*, a set of chandeliers; *una* — *di vele*, (*mar.*) a set of sails.

múta², *s.f.* (*di cani*) pack of hounds; (*di cavalli*) team of horses.

mutàbile, *ag.* **1.** changeable, mutable: *tempo* —, changeable weather **2.** (*incostante*) changeable, fickle, inconstant.

mutabilità, *s.f.* **1.** changeability, changeableness, mutability **2.** (*incostanza*) changeability, changeableness, fickleness, inconstancy.

mutabilménte, *av.* **1.** changeably, mutably **2.** (*volubilmente*) changeably, inconstantly.

mutaísmo, *s.m.* mytacism.

mutaménte, *av.* silently, mutely.

mutaménto, *s.m.* change; (*alterazione*) alteration; (*variazione*) variation: — *in meglio, in peggio*, change for the better, for the worse; *improvviso* — *di fortuna*, sudden change of fortune.

mutànde, *s.f.pl.* drawers, pants; (*amer.*) underpants.

mutandíne, *s.f.pl.* **1.** (*da bambino*) knickers; (*da donna*) panties **2.** (*da bagno*) bathing drawers; (*amer.*) trunks; (*da ginnastica*) P.T. shorts, gym shorts.

mutàre, *v.t.* **1.** to change: *faresti meglio a* — *tono*, you'd better change (*o* modify) your tone of voice; *le ferrovie hanno mutato il volto del paese*, the railways have changed the face of the country; *il vento ha mutato direzione*, the wind has changed direction; *una virgola può* — *il senso di una frase*, a comma can change the meaning of a sentence; — *argomento, discorso*, to change the subject; — *casa*, to move (house); — *città*, to move to another town; — *colore, faccia*, to change colour, countenance; — *governo*, to change government; — *le lenzuola*, to change the sheets; — *opinione*, to change one's mind; — *posto*, to change seats; — *le proprie abitudini*, to change one's habits; — *qlcu. in meglio, in peggio*, to change s.o. for the better, the worse; — *vita*, to change one's way of living; (*emendarsi*) to mend one's ways **2.** (*trasformare*) to change, to turn: *l'illusionista lo mutò in un asino*, the conjuror turned (*o* changed) him into a donkey; — *acqua in vino*, to change water into wine **3.** (*di animali*) (*pelle, corna*) to shed; (*penne, pelliccia*) to moult ‖ *il lupo muta il pelo, ma non il vizio*, *prov.* the leopard cannot change his spots **4.** (*travasare*) to pour off ‖ *v.i.*, **mutàrsi**, *v.r.* to change: *i tempi sono mutati*, times have changed; *il tempo vuol*

—, the weather is going to change; — *d'abito*, to change one's clothes; — *di colore, di viso*, to change colour.

mutatívo, *ag.* changing.

mutàto, *ag.* changed: *com'è —!*, how changed he is!; *non vi è nulla di —*, there's nothing new.

mutatóre, *s.m.* **1.** changer **2.** (*elett.*) mutator.

mutatríce, *s.f.* changer.

mutatúra, (*rar.*) per **mutaménto**.

mutazióne, *s.f.* **1.** change, mutation; (*alterazione*) alteration; (*variazione*) variation **2.** (*biol. mus.*) mutation **3.** (*poes.*) " mutazione " (part of stanza in a ballad).

mutévole, *ag.* **1.** changeable, mutable: *l'aspetto — delle cose*, the changeable aspect of things **2.** (*volubile*) changeable, inconstant, fickle: *indole —*, inconstant mind **3.** (*docile*) manageable, docile.

mutevolézza, *V.* **mutabilità**.

mutevolménte, *av.* **1.** changeably, mutably **2.** (*volubilmente*) changeably, inconstantly **3.** (*docilmente*) manageably, docilely.

mutézza, *s.f.* dumbness, muteness.

mútico, *ag.*: *grano —*, (*agr.*) beardless wheat.

mutilàre, *v.t.* **1.** to maim, to cripple, to mutilate: *fu mutilato gravemente in guerra*, he was maimed (*o* crippled) in the war **2.** *fig.* to mutilate: — *un discorso*, to mutilate a speech.

mutilàto, *ag.* **1.** maimed, crippled, mutilated **2.** *fig.* mutilated: *monumento —*, mutilated monument ‖ *s.m.* cripple: — *di guerra*, war cripple.

mutilatóre, *ag.* mutilating ‖ *s.m.* mutilator.

mutilazióne, *s.f.* **1.** maiming, mutilation: — *volontaria*, self-mutilation; *subì una grave — in guerra*, he was disabled during the war **2.** *fig.* mutilation; (*di statua*) defacement: *le mutilazioni del suo libro lo infastidirono*, the mutilations of his book annoyed him; *la statua subì delle mutilazioni*, the statue was defaced.

mútilo, *ag.* (*letter.*) mutilated.

mutísmo, *s.m.* **1.** dumbness, muteness, mutism **2.** (*ostinato silenzio*) (stubborn) silence: *si chiuse in un ostinato —*, he maintained a stubborn silence.

múto, *ag.* **1.** dumb, mute: — *dalla nascita*, born dumb; *a tre anni un terribile incidente lo rese —*, when he was three years old a terrible accident left him dumb ‖ — *come un pesce*, as dumb as an ox; *sarò — come una tomba*, I will be as silent as the grave ‖ *alla muta*, without speaking (*o* by gestures) **2.** (*silenzioso*) dumb, mute, silent; (*senza parole*) speechless: *il grande bosco era —*, the forest was silent; *i grandi dolori sono muti*, great griefs are silent; *mi guardò con muta sorpresa*, he looked at me in mute amazement; *quando l'insegnante fece una domanda difficile tutta la classe rimase muta*, when the teacher asked a difficult question, the whole class remained dumb; *rimase — davanti al tribunale*, he stood mute before the tribunal; *rimase — quando glielo dissi*, he remained speechless when I told him; *essere resi muti dall'orrore*, to be struck dumb with horror; *restare muto dalla collera*, *dal terrore*, to be struck dumb with anger, with fear ‖ *attore —*, (*teat.*) super; (*cine.*) extra; *cinema, film —*, silent cinema, film ‖ *scena muta*, (*teat.*) dumb-show: *quando fu interrogato fece scena muta*, (*scherz.*) when he was questioned, he couldn't say a word **3.** (*fonet.*) silent, mute; muted: *e muta*, mute e; *lettera muta*, silent letter; *suoni muti*, muted sounds **4.** *carta* (*geografica*) *muta*, blank map ‖ *s.m.* dumb person, mute: *il linguaggio dei muti*, deaf-and-dumb language.

mútolo, *ag.* (*letter.*) mute, dumb.

mútria, *s.f.* **1.** stand-offishness **2.** (*fam.*) (*ardire*) audacity.

mutualísmo, *s.m.* (*biol.*) mutualism.

mútua, *s.f.*: (*cassa*) —, national insurance; *medico della —*, panel doctor.

mutualístico, *ag.* **1.** (*biol.*) mutual: *simbiosi mutualistica*, mutual symbiosis **2.** (*sociale*) insurance (*attributivo*): *sistema —*, national insurance system.

mutualità, *s.f.* mutual help, mutual assistance.

mutuaménte, *av.* mutually, reciprocally: *si aiutarono —*, they helped each other.

mutuànte, *ag.* lending; loan (*attributivo*) ‖ *s.c.* lender.

mutuàre, *v.t.* **1.** (*prendere a mutuo*) to borrow **2.** (*dare a mutuo*) to lend.

mutuatàrio, *ag.* borrowing ‖ *s.m.*, **mutuatària**, *s.f.* borrower.

mutuazióne, *s.f.* exchange.

mútuo[1], *ag.* mutual, reciprocal: — *affetto*, reciprocal affection; *mutua assicurazione*, mutual insurance; — *soccorso, accordo*, mutual aid, agreement ‖ *società mutua d'assicurazioni*, mutual insurance company.

mútuo[2], *s.m.* loan: — *ipotecario*, mortgage loan; *capitale a —*, borrowed capital; *dare, prendere a —*, to lend, to borrow.

N

n, *s.f.m.* **1.** (*dodicesima lettera dell'alfabeto italiano*) n (*pl.* ns, n's) ‖ — *come Napoli,* (*tel.*) n for Nellie ‖ *n.,* (*abbr. di nato*) B. ‖ *N.,* (*abbr. di numero*) No.: *via Washington n. 15,* 15, Washington St. ‖ *N.B.,* (*abbr. di nota bene*) N.B. ‖ *N.N.,* (*abbr. di non nominato*) unknown; unspecified: *figlio di N.N.,* illegitimate ‖ *N.S.,* (*abbr. di Nostro Signore*) Our Lord **2.** (*mat.*) (*numero indefinito*) n.

nabàbbo, *s.m.* nabob (*anche fig.*).

Nabòt, *no.pr.m.* (*Bibbia*) Naboth.

Nabuccodònosor, *no.pr.m.* (*st.*) Nebuchadnezzar, Nebuchadrezzar.

nàechera, *s.f.* **1.** (*mus.*) castanet **2.** (*zool.*) bivalve.

naccheríno, *s.m.* **1.** castanet-player **2.** (*rar.*) (*bambino grazioso*) pretty child.

Nàdia, *no.pr.f.* Nadine.

nadír, *s.m.* (*astr.*) nadir.

nàfta, *s.f.* — (*chim.*) naphtha; (*per motori Diesel*) Diesel oil; — *di alta qualità,* high-test Diesel oil; — *greggia,* crude naphtha ‖ *a* —, oil-firing.

naftalína, *s.f.* naphthalene (powder); (*in palline*) moth-balls: *mettere in* —, to put in moth-balls; *togliere dalla* —, to remove from moth-balls (*o* from naphthalene).

naftilamína, *s.f.* (*chim.*) naphthylamine.

naftòlo, *s.m.* (*chim.*) naphthol.

nàia[1], *s.f.* (*zool.*) cobra.

nàia[2], *s.f.*: *fare la* —, (*gergo mil.*) to do one's bit.

nàiade, *s.f.* (*mit.*) naiad.

nàilon, *s.m.* nylon: *calze di* —, nylon stockings (*o* nylons); *filato di* —, nylon yarn; *vendita di indumenti di* —, sale of nylon clothes.

Nanchíno[1], *no.pr.f.* (*geog.*) Nanking.

nanchíno[2], *s.m.* (*ind. tessile*) nankeen.

Nàndo, *no.pr.m.* dim. di **Ferdinàndo.**

nandù, *s.m.* (*ornit.*) nandu.

nanísmo, *s.m.* (*patol.*) nanism.

nànna, *s.f.* (*gergo infantile*) bye-bye(s): *andare a* —, to go to bye-bye(s); *fare la* —, to sleep ‖ *ninna* —, lullaby: *cantare la ninna* —, to sing to sleep (*o* to sing a lullaby).

Nànni, *no.pr.m.dim.* di **Giovànni.**

nàno, *ag.* dwarf, dwarfish: *alberi nani,* dwarf trees; *rosa nana,* dwarf rose ‖ *s.m.* dwarf.

Napoleóne, *no.pr.m.* (*st.*) Napoleon ‖ **napoleóne,** *s.m.* (*moneta*) napoleon.

napoleònico, *ag.* Napoleonic.

napoletàno, *ag.s.m.* Neapolitan.

Nàpoli, *no.pr.f.* (*geog.*) Naples.

nàppa, *s.f.* **1.** tassel; tuft **2.** (*scherz.*) (*grosso naso*) conk, big nose.

nàppo, *s.m.* (*poet.*) goblet.

narceína, *s.f.* (*farm.*) narceine.

Narcíso[1], *no.pr.m.* (*mit.*) Narcissus.

narcíso[2], *s.m.* (*bot.*) narcissus (*pl.* narcissuses, narcissi).

narcissísmo, *s.m.* (*psicanalisi*) narcissism.

narcoanàlisi, *s.f.* (*med.*) narco-analysis.

narcolessía, *s.f.* (*med.*) narcolepsy.

narcòsi, *s.f.* (*med.*) narcosis (*pl.* narcoses).

narcòtico, *ag.* narcotic: *l'oppio è una droga narcotica,* opium is a narcotic ‖ *s.m.* narcotic.

narcoticaménte, *av.* narcotically.

narcotína, *s.f.* (*farm.*) narcotine.

narcotísmo, *s.m.* (*med.*) narcotism.

narcotizzàre, *v.t.* (*med.*) to narcotize.

nàrdo, *s.m.* (*bot.*) nard, spikenard.

narghilè, *s.m.* nargile(h), hookah.

nàri, *s.f.pl.* (*anat.*) nostrils; (*arc.*) nares.

naríce, *s.f.* (*anat.*) nostril.

narràbile, *ag.* fit to be told.

narràre, *v.t.* to tell, to relate, to narrate: — *una storia,* to tell a story.

narratíva, *s.f.* **1.** (*narrazione*) narrative **2.** (*genere letterario*) narrative, fiction: *la* — *spagnola,* Spanish fiction; *molti scrittori preferiscono la* —, many writers prefer to write fiction.

narratívo, *ag.* narrative: *poema* —, narrative poem; *poesia narrativa,* narrative poetry.

narratóre, *s.m.,* **narratríce,** *s.f.* **1.** narrator, story-teller **2.** (*scrittore*) writer (of fiction).

narrazióne, *s.f.* **1.** narration; narrative **2.** (*storia*) story, tale.

nartèce, *s.m.* (*arch.*) narthex.

narvàlo, *s.m.* (*zool.*) narwhal.

nasàle, *ag.* nasal: *le consonanti nasali,* (*fonet.*) the nasals (*o* the nasal consonants); *le fosse nasali,* (*anat.*) the nasal fossae; *pronunzia* —, nasal accent; *il setto* —, (*anat.*) the nasal septum; *suoni nasali,* (*fonet.*) nasal sounds; *avere una voce* —, to have a nasal voice ‖ *s.m.* (*parte dell'elmo che copre il naso*) nose-piece.

nascènte, *ag.* rising; dawning: *il giorno* —, the dawning day; *il sole* —, the rising sun.

nàscere, *v.i.* **1.** to be born; to come into the world: *è nato a Venezia,* he was born in Venice; *è nato cieco, povero,* he was born blind, poor; *è nato da genitori poveri,* he was born of poor parents; *è nato poeta,* he is a born poet; *è nato ricco,* he was born with a silver spoon in his mouth; *quando sei nato?,* when were you born?; *Shakespeare nacque nel 1564,* Shakespeare was born in 1564 ‖ *deve ancora* — *chi saprà risolvere tali problemi,* the man is yet unborn who can solve such problems ‖ *è nato per fare l'avvocato,* he was born to be a lawyer ‖ *è nato per soffrire,* he was born to suffer ‖ *l'ho visto* —, I have known him since the day he was born ‖ *nessuno nasce artista,* artists aren't born, but made ‖ *non sono nato ieri,* I wasn't born yesterday ‖ *non sono nato per queste cose,* I am not cut out for these things ‖ — *con la camicia,* to be born under a lucky star ‖ — *con gli occhi aperti,* to be born crafty ‖ — *sotto una buona, cattiva stella,* to be born under a lucky, an unlucky star **2.** (*di piante*) (*spuntare dalla terra*) to spring up, to come up; (*spuntare da un albero*) to sprout, to begin to grow: *le foglie nascono in primavera,* leaves sprout (*o* begin to grow) in spring **3.** (*di capelli, corna, ecc.*) to sprout, to begin to grow **4.** (*dei piccoli di animali ovipari*) to be hatched: *questi pulcini sono appena nati,* these chickens are newly-hatched **5.** (*di fiume*) to rise; to have its source: *molti fiumi nascono dalle Alpi,* many rivers rise in the Alps; *il Po nasce dal Monviso,* the Po rises (*o* has its source) on Monviso **6.** (*sorgere*) to rise: *il giorno nasceva,* the day was dawning; *il sole nasce ad oriente,* the sun rises in the East **7.** (*avere origine*) to originate; to be born, to rise, to arise, to issue, to proceed: *una grande discussione nacque improvvisamente tra loro,* a great argument arose suddenly between them; *mi nacque il sospetto che...,* I began to suspect that...; *il marxismo è nato in Germania,* Marxism originated (*o* was born) in Germany; *il vizio*

552

nasce dall'ozio, vice is born from idleness ‖ *far —
(causare)*, to cause (*o* to bring forth *o* to bring about);
(*dare origine a*) to originate (*o* to give birth to); (*provocare*) to give rise to: *questo malinteso fece — una
grande lite*, this misunderstanding brought about a
great quarrel; *far — dei disordini*, to stir up trouble;
far — un'idea, to give birth to an idea: *ciò mi fece —
l'idea di viaggiare*, that gave me the idea of travelling;
far — uno scandalo, to give rise to (*o* to occasion)
a scandal; *far — un sorriso*, to provoke (*o* to call
forth) a smile; *far — un sospetto*, to give rise to (*o* to
raise *o* to breed *o* to arouse *o* to occasion) suspicion;
far — la speranza che..., to give rise to (*o* to raise *o* to
breed *o* to awaken) the hope that... ‖ *da cosa nasce
cosa, prov.* one thing leads to another.

nàscere, *s.m.* **1.** (*il sorgere*) rise; birth: *il — del giorno*, break of day (*o* daybreak); *il — del sole*, sunrise ‖
sul —, at birth: *la ribellione fu soffocata sul —*, the
rebellion was stifled at birth **2.** (*lo spuntare di foglie,
grano, ecc.*) sprouting.

nàscita, *s.f.* **1.** birth: *anniversario di —*, birthday;
certificato di —, birth-certificate; *luogo di —*, birthplace; *cieco, muto dalla —*, blind, dumb from birth
(*o* born blind, dumb); *il bambino era molto piccolo
alla —*, the child was very small at birth ‖ *prima
della, dopo la — di Cristo*, before, after Christ (*abbr.*
B.C., A.D.) **2.** (*origine*) origin; (*lignaggio*) birth, descent,
extraction: *di — oscura*, of low birth (*o* extraction);
nobile di —, high-born (*o* of high birth); *era inglese
di —*, he was English by birth; *essere di buona —*, to
come of a good family **3.** (*di astro*) rising: *la — del sole*, the sunrise; *la — del giorno*, dawn (*o* daybreak).

nascitúro, *ag.* coming, future ‖ *s.m.* unborn child.

nascóndere, *v.t.* **1.** to hide, to conceal: *nascose il
viso tra le mani*, she hid (*o* buried) her face in her
hands; *le nubi nascosero il sole*, the clouds hid the
sun; *quel muro nasconde la vista del mare*, that wall
hides the view of the sea **2.** *fig.* to hide, to conceal;
to disguise, to mask; to keep secret: *cercò di — i propri
sentimenti*, he tried to hide (*o* to conceal) his feelings;
nascose la sua identità, he kept his identity secret;
non nascondo che sono preoccupato, I make no secret
of (*o* I don't conceal) the fact that I am worried;
sapeva bene come — il suo odio, he knew well how to
disguise his hatred; *la sua affabilità nasconde una
mancanza assoluta di scrupoli*, his affability conceals
a complete lack of scruples; *— ql.co. a ql.cu.*, to hide
sthg. from s.o. ‖ **nascóndersi,** *v.r.* to hide (oneself);
to be hidden: *dove è andato a —?*, where has he gone
and hidden himself?; *un uccello si nascondeva tra i
rami*, a bird was hidden among the branches ‖ *giocare
a —*, to play hide-and-seek.

nascondíglio, *s.m.* hiding-place; (*fam.*) hideout;
(*amer.*) hidy-hole; *egli trovò un ottimo — per il bottino*, he found a good hiding-place for the booty; *la
polizia sta ancora cercando il — dei banditi*, the police
are still looking for the bandits' hideout (*o* hiding
-place).

nascondiménto, *s.m.* hiding, concealing.

nasconditóre, *s.m.*, **nasconditríce,** *s.f.* (*rar.*) **1.** hider, concealer **2.** (*chi dissimula*) dissembler.

nascostaménte, *ag.* hiddenly; (*segretamente*) secretly; (*furtivamente*) stealthily.

nascósto, *ag.* **1.** hidden, concealed; (*segreto*) secret:
dolore —, secret grief; *significato —*, hidden meaning;
rimanere —, to be in hiding ‖ *di —*, secretly **2.** (*appartato*) remote, secluded: *l'angolo più — della città*, the
furthest corner of the town; *un luogo —*, a remote place.

nasèllo¹, *s.m.* (*ittiol.*) whiting.

nasèllo², *s.m.* (*mec.*) nib: *— di porta*, catch.

nàso, *s.m.* **1.** nose: *— affilato*, sharp nose; *— all'insù*,
turned-up nose; *— a punta*, pointed nose; *— aquilino*,
aquiline (*o* hooked) nose; *— camuso*, snub nose; *—
greco*, Greek nose; *— schiacciato*, flattened nose; *fazzoletto da —*, handkerchief; *tabacco da —*, snuff; *avere*

il — che cola, to have a running nose; *soffiarsi il
—*, to blow one's nose ‖ *a lume di —*, by guesswork ‖
sotto il — di ql.cu., (right) under s.o.'s nose ‖ *gli montò
la mosca al —*, he lost his temper ‖ *non aveva il coraggio di metter fuori la punta del —*, he did not dare
to poke his nose out of doors ‖ *non si ricorda dal —
alla bocca*, he can't remember a thing for five minutes ‖
arricciare il — (di fronte) a ql.co., to turn up one's
nose at sthg. ‖ *cacciare, ficcare, mettere il — in ql.co.*,
to poke (*o* to thrust) one's nose into sthg. ‖ *chiudere la porta sul — a ql.cu.*, to shut the door in s.o.'s
face ‖ *fare il — a...*, to get accustomed to... ‖ *menar
ql.cu. per il —*, to lead s.o. by the nose ‖ *non vedere più in là del proprio —*, not to see any farther
(*o* further) than the end of one's nose ‖ *parlar con il —*,
to speak through one's nose ‖ *restar con un palmo
di —, con tanto di —*, to feel done **2.** (*fiuto*): *aver (buon)
—*, to be shrewd (*o* far-seeing *o* fam. to be all there);
per fare questo occorre —, you need to be shrewd
to do this **3.** (*mar.*) nose, prow **4.** (*mec.*) snug.

nàspo, *s.m.* winder, reel.

nàssa, *s.f.* bow-net; (*per anguille*) eel-basket, eel
-pot; (*per aragoste*) lobster-pot.

nasserí, *s.m.* (*antica moneta*) gross.

nàsso¹, *s.m.* (*bot.*) yew (-tree).

Nàsso², *no.pr.f.* (*geog.*) Naxos.

nastríno, *s.m.* **1.** (*decorazione*) ribbon **2.** (*segnalibro*)
book-mark **3.** *pl.* (*pasta*) noodles.

nàstro, *s.m.* **1.** ribbon, riband: *— di seta*, silk ribbon;
— del cappello, hatband; *a forma di —*, ribbon-like;
ornato di nastri, ribboned; *vedevo la strada stendersi
dritta come un bianco —*, I saw the road stretching
out as straight and white as a ribbon **2.** (*tec.*) tape,
band, strap, ribbon: *— adesivo, isolante*, (*elett.*) tape
(*o* electric tape *o* insulating tape); *— d'acciaio*, (*metal.*)
steel strip; *— di alimentazione*, (*di arma da fuoco*)
feed-belt; *— di ferro*, (*metal.*) iron strip; *— laminato
a caldo, a freddo*, (*metal.*) hot-rolled, cold-rolled strip;
— metrico, tape-measure; *— per ammortizzatore*, (*mec.*)
shock-absorber strap; *— per registrazione*, (*rad.*)
(radio) recording tape; *registrazione su —*, tape-recording; *sega a —*, (*mec.*) band-saw (*o* belt-saw *o* endless
saw); *registrare su —*, to record (on magnetic tape *o*
to tape) **3.** (*decorazione*) ribbon: *— azzurro*, blue ribbon **4.** *pl.* (*pasta*) noodles.

nastúrzio, *s.m.* (*bot.*) **1.** nasturtium **2.** (*crescione*) water
-cress.

nasúto, *ag.* **1.** big-nosed (*attributivo*) **2.** (*sagace*)
sagacious.

natàle¹, *ag.* native: *città —*, home-town; *dì —*,
birthday; *luogo —*, birthplace (*o* native place); *paese
—*, native country ‖ *s.m.* **1.** Natale, Christmas (*abbr.*
Xmas): *a Natale*, on Christmas Day; (*durante il periodo
natalizio*) at Christmas; *albero di Natale*, Christmas tree;
buon Natale!, happy (*o* merry) Christmas!: *i migliori
auguri di buon Natale*, best wishes for a merry (*o*
happy) Christmas; *il giorno di Natale*, Christmas Day;
il periodo delle feste di Natale, Christmas-time (*o*
Christmas-tide *o* Yuletide); *la vigilia di Natale*, Christmas Eve; *festeggiare il Natale*, to celebrate (*o* fam. to
keep*) Christmas ‖ *Babbo Natale*, Santa Claus (*o* Father
Christmas) **2.** (*giorno natale*) birthday ‖ *il — di Roma*,
(*st.*) anniversary of the foundation of Rome **3.** *pl.*
birth: *egli ebbe i natali a Roma*, he was born in Rome;
l'Italia diede i natali a molti grandi artisti, Italy was
the birthplace of many great artists; *essere di illustri
natali*, to be of noble birth.

Natàle², *no.pr.m.* Noël.

Natalía, *no.pr.f.* Natalie, Natalia.

Natalína, *no.pr.f. dim. di* **Natalía.**

Natalíno, *no.pr.m.dim. di* **Natàle.**

natalità, *s.f.* birth-rate, natality.

natalízio, *ag.* **1.** Christmas (*attributivo*): *decorazioni
natalizie*, Christmas decorations; *doni natalizi*, Christmas presents; *vacanze natalizie*, Christmas holi-

days 2. (*natale*) natal: *giorno* —, natal day (o birthday) ‖ *s.m.* birthday.

Natanaèle, *no.pr.m.* (*Bibbia*) Nathanael, Nathaniel.

natànte, *ag.* floating, natant: *isola* —, floating island; *mina* —, floating-mine ‖ *s.m.* (*mar.*) (water)craft: — *per trasporto di ostruzioni*, (*mil.*) barrage-tender.

natatóia, *s.f.* (*di pesce*) fin.

natatòrio, *ag.* natatory, natatorial; swimming (*attributivo*): *vescica natatoria*, swimming-bladder.

Nàthan, *no.pr.m.* (*Bibbia*) Nathan.

nàtica, *s.f.* buttock; nates (*pl.*).

natío, *ag.* (*poet.*) native: *alma terra natia*, dear native land; *l'aria natia*, the native air; *il tetto* —, home.

natività, *s.f.* nativity.

natívo, *ag.* **1.** native: *sono* — *di Londra*, I am a Londoner (o a native of London); *sono* — *di questi luoghi*, I am a native of these parts **2.** (*innato*) inborn, innate: *rozzezza nativa*, innate roughness **3.** (*naturale*) natural, native: *allo stato* —, in one's natural state ‖ *s.m.* native ‖ *i nativi*, the natives.

nàto, *ag.* **1.** born: — *cieco*, born blind; — *da povera gente*, born of poor parents; — *morto*, still-born; — *ricco*, born with a silver spoon in his mouth; — *per soffrire*, born to trouble (o to suffer); *bambino appena* —, new-born baby; *è una persona nata per comandare*, he is a person born to command ‖ — *a grandi cose*, born to great things ‖ — *con la camicia*, born under a lucky star ‖ — *ieri*, *fig.* born yesterday ‖ — *sotto buona stella*, born under a lucky star ‖ *ben* —, *mal* —, well-born, low-born ‖ *un poeta, pittore* —, a born poet, painter;‖ *egli è un ladro* —, he is a born thief ‖ *la signora Rossi, nata Bianchi*, Mrs. Rossi, née Bianchi ‖ *non c'era anima, creatura nata*, there was no living soul ‖ *era* — *e sputato come suo padre*, he was the spit (o image) of his father **2.** (*uscito dall'uovo*) hatched **3.** (*germogliato, spuntato*) sprouting, beginning to grow; (*di denti*) cut **4.** (*di fiumi, ecc.*) rising (in, o sthg.) **5.** *fig.* (*sorto*) born (of sthg.); (*causato*) brought about, occasioned: *disgrazie nate dalla guerra*, misfortunes brought about by war; *personaggi nati dalla sua fantasia*, characters born of his imagination.

nàtron, *s.m.* (*min.*) natron.

nàtta, *s.f.* **1.** (*patol.*) wen **2.** (*arc.*) (*burla*) jest, hoax.

natúra, *s.f.* **1.** nature: — *selvaggia*, wild nature; *le bellezze della* —, the beauties of nature; *legge di* —, law of nature; *i misteri della* —, the mysteries of nature; *i tre regni della* —, the three kingdoms of nature ‖ — *morta*, (*pitt.*) still-life ‖ *allo stato di* —, in the natural state ‖ *contro* —, against (o contrary to) nature ‖ *madre* —, mother nature **2.** (*essenza, l'essere*) nature, essence: *la* — *di Dio*, the essence of God; *la* — *umana*, human nature **3.** (*genere, caratteristica*) nature, characteristic, kind: *la* — *del clima*, the characteristic of the climate; *oggetti della medesima* —, objects of the same nature **4.** (*carattere, indole*) nature, character: *contrario alla mia* —, contrary to my nature; *l'abitudine è la sua seconda* —, habit is his second nature; *è una* — *irrequieta*, he has a restive nature ‖ *nella* — *delle cose*, in the nature of things ‖ *di, per* —, by nature: *egli è buono di* —, he is good-natured **5.** (*beni materiali*): *pagare in* —, to pay in kind.

naturàle, *ag.* **1.** natural: *bellezze naturali*, natural beauties; *fenomeni naturali*, natural phenomena; *forze naturali*, natural forces; *leggi naturali*, natural laws; *scienze naturali*, natural science (o natural history) ‖ *figlio* —, natural (o illegitimate) son ‖ *morte* —, natural death ‖ *vita natural durante*, for one's natural life (o during one's life) **2.** (*innato*) natural, innate: *abilità naturali*, innate (o natural) abilities **3.** (*spontaneo*) natural, unaffected: *linguaggio* —, unstudied language; *parla in modo molto* —, he speaks in a very natural way (o very naturally) **4.** (*non contraffatto*) natural, genuine: *vino* —, genuine wine; *i miei capelli sono na-*

turali, my hair is natural **5.** (*ovvio*) natural, obvious: *è* — *che egli lo pensi*, it is natural for him to think so; *questo è* —, this is natural (o that's obvious o of course o naturally) **6.** (*mus.*) natural ‖ *s.m.* **1.** (*rar.*) (*carattere, indole*) nature, character, disposition: *il suo* — *è così fatto*, that is his character **2.** (*rar.*) (*indigeno*) native **3.** *al* —, life-size: *ritratto al* —, life-size portrait.

naturalézza, *s.f.* naturalness, simplicity: *con* —, plainly (o unaffectedly); *quella ragazza manca di* —, that girl is affected.

naturalísmo, *s.m.* naturalism.

naturalísta, *s.c.* naturalist.

naturalístico, *ag.* naturalistic.

naturalità, *s.f.* (*dir.*) (right of) citizenship.

naturalizzàre, *v.t.* (*dir.*) to naturalize.

naturalizzazióne, *s.f.* (*dir.*) naturalization.

naturalménte, *av.* **1.** (*in modo naturale*) naturally: *svilupparsi* —, to develop naturally **2.** (*senza affettazione*) naturally, unaffectedly: *parla* —, he speaks unaffectedly **3.** (*per natura*) by nature: *i bambini sono curiosi* —, children are curious by nature **4.** (*certamente*) naturally, of course: « *L'hai detto a tua madre?* », « *Naturalmente* », "Did you tell your mother?", "Of course, I did".

naturànte, *ag.* (*fil.*) naturing.

naturísmo, *s.m.* (*fil.*) naturism.

naturísta, *s.c.* (*fil.*) naturist.

naufragàre, *v.i.* **1.** to be shipwrecked, to be wreck: *la nave naufragò nella tempesta*, the ship was wrecked by the storm **2.** (*finir male, fallire*) to be wrecked, to fail: *le sue speranze naufragarono*, his hopes were wrecked.

naufràgio, *s.m.* **1.** shipwreck, wreck: *far* —, to (ship)wreck **2.** (*fallimento*) wreck, failure: *il* — *dei nostri progetti*, the failure of our plans.

nàufrago, *ag.* shipwrecked, wrecked ‖ *s.m.* shipwrecked person; (*marinaio*) shipwrecked sailor; (*passeggero*) shipwrecked passenger: *i naufraghi furono raccolti da una nave*, the survivers were picked up by a ship.

naumachía, *s.f.* (*st.*) naumachia (*pl.* naumachiae, naumachias).

nàusea, *s.f.* nausea; *fig.* (*disgusto*) nausea, loathing, disgust: *avere la* —, to feel sick (o *fam.* to feel queasy); *avere a* — *ql.co.*, to loathe sthg.; *essere facile alle nausee*, to be squeamish; *far venire, dare la* —, to make sick (o to disgust o to nauseate): *il suo comportamento mi dà la* —, (*fam.*) his behaviour makes me sick; *ripetere ql.co. fino alla* —, to repeat sthg. ad nauseam.

nauseabóndo, nauseànte, *ag.* nauseating, nauseous, loathsome, disgusting, repulsive (anche *fig.*): *cibo* —, nauseating food; *uno spettacolo* —, a repulsive sight.

nauseàre, *v.t.* to nauseate, to make sick (anche *fig.*).

nauseàto, *ag.* nauseated (at, by sthg.), disgusted (at, by, with sthg.), sick (of sthg.) (anche *fig.*).

nauseóso, *V.* **nauseabóndo**.

Nausícaa, *no.pr.f.* (*mit.*) Nausicaä.

nàuta, *s.m.* (*letter.*) navigator; pilot.

nàutica, *s.f.* navigation, seamanship.

nàutico, *ag.* nautical: *sport nautici*, aquatic sports; *strumenti nautici*, nautical instruments.

nàutilo, *s.m.* (*zool.*) nautilus (*pl.* nautiluses, nautili).

navàle, *ag.* naval: *accademia* —, Naval Academy; *battaglia* — (o *sea*) battle; *cantiere* —, dockyard (o naval docks); *forza* —, naval strength, *ingegnere* —, naval engineer ‖ *Lega Navale*, Navy League ‖ *registro* —, Lloyd's Register.

navalèstro, *s.m.* (*rar.*) (*barcaiolo*) punter.

navàrca, navàrco, *s.m.* (*letter.*) navarch.

Navàrra, *no.pr.f.* (*geog.*) Navarre.

navàta, *s.f.* (*arch.*) (*centrale, maggiore*) nave; (*laterale, minore*) aisle: *chiesa a tre navate*, church with three aisles.

nàve, *s.f.* **1.** ship; boat; vessel; craft: — *ad elica*, screwship; — *a due alberi*, two-master; — *alla fonda*, ship at anchor; — *ammiraglia*, admiral(-ship) (*o* flag -ship); — *appoggio*, tender (*o* depot-ship *o* mother -ship); — *a turboriduttore*, geared turbine-ship; — *a vapore*, steamer (*o* steamship); — *a vela*, sailing-ship; — *cisterna*, tanker; — *civetta*, decoy-ship (*o* craft); — *corazzata*, battleship; — *corsara*, corsair; — *da battaglia*, battleship; — *da cabotaggio*, *costiera*, coaster; — *da carico*, freighter (*o* cargo boat); — *da guerra*, warship; — *di linea*, liner; — *di lungo corso*, ocean -going vessel; — *di soccorso*, rescue ship; — *di soccorso per aerei*, air sea rescue ship; — *dragamine*, mine-sweeper; — *faro*, lightship; — *frigorifera*, refrigerator ship; — *gemella*, sister ship; — *goletta*, schooner; — *idrografica*, survey ship; — *mercantile*, merchant ship (*o* merchantman); — *officina*, repair ship; — *ospedale*, hospital-ship; — *passeggeri*, passenger ship; — *per trasporto truppe*, troopship; — *petroliera*, oil-tanker; — *portaerei*, aircraftcarrier; — *posamine*, mine -layer; — *postale*, mail-steamer; — *rompighiaccio*, ice -breaker; — *scorta*, escort vessel; — *scuola*, training -ship; — *traghetto*, ferry-boat; *taglio di una* —, sweep (*o* run) of a ship; *varo di una* —, launching of a ship; *la* — *entra in porto*, *salpa*, *getta l'ancora*, the ship enters harbour, leaves harbour (*o* sails), anchors ‖ *la* — *del deserto*, the ship of the desert ‖ *guidare la* — *dello stato*, to steer the ship of State 2. (*arch.*) (*navata*) (*centrale, maggiore*) nave; (*laterale, minore*) aisle.

navétta, *s.f.* (*tec.*) shuttle ‖ *far* —, to go to and fro.

navicèlla, *s.f.* 1. small ship, boat; (*poet.*) bark 2. (*aer.*) (*di dirigibile*) nacelle, car; (*di pallone*) basket 3. (*eccl.*) incense-boat 4. (*tec.*) shuttle.

navicellàio, *s.m.* punter.

navicèllo, *s.m.* (*mar.*) two-masted sailing-boat.

navigàbile, *ag.* 1. navigable: *fiume* —, navigable river 2. (*che può tenere il mare*) seaworthy: *bastimento* —, seaworthy vessel ‖ *vino* —, wine that travels well.

navigabilità, *s.f.* 1. navigability 2. (*capacità di tenere il mare*) seaworthiness.

navigànte, *s.m.* sailor, mariner, seaman (*pl.* seamen).

navigàre, *v.i.* to sail, to navigate: *è pericoloso* — *vicino alla costa*, it is dangerous to sail near the coast; *è spesso difficile* — *in questo estuario*, it is often difficult to navigate in this estuary; *ha navigato per tutti i mari*, he has sailed the seven seas; *naviga da trent'anni*, he has been at sea for thirty years; *questo piroscafo naviga bene*, this ship behaves well (at sea); — *a lumi spenti*, to sail blacked-out; — *col vento in poppa*, to sail with a favourable wind (anche *fig.*) ‖ — *secondo il vento*, (*adattarsi alle circostanze*) to trim one's sails according to the wind ‖ — *in cattive acque*, (*essere in difficoltà*) to be in deep waters ‖ — *nei flutti della vita*, (*destreggiarsi*) to sail the seas of life ‖ — *sulla scia di qlcu.*, (*seguirne l'esempio*) to follow in s.o.'s footsteps ‖ *v.t.* to sail, to navigate: — *i mari della Cina*, to sail the China seas; — *l'oceano*, to sail the ocean.

navigàto, *ag.* 1. (*esperto*) experienced; (*furbo*) cunning: *uomo* —, experienced man 2. (*di vino, trasportato per nave*) shipped.

navigatóre, *s.m.* 1. navigator: *Colombo fu un grande* —, Columbus was a great navigator 2. (*marinaio*) sailor, seaman (*pl.* seamen), mariner: *vita da* —, sailor's life (*o* seafaring life).

navigazióne, *s.f.* navigation; (*a vela*) sailing: — *aerea*, air navigation; — *aerea astronomica*, astronavigation; — *aerea cieca*, instrument navigation; — *a vapore*, steam-navigation; — *fluviale*, river navigation; — *interna*, inland navigation; — *radioguidata*, (*mar.*) radio navigation; *compagnia di* —, (*mar.*) shipping company (*o* shipping-line); (*aer.*) airline: *perchè non viaggi con la compagnia di* — *X.Y.?*, why don't you travel by the X. Y. Line?; *rivolgiti alla compagnia di* —, go to the shipping agent; *la* — *attraverso il canale di Suez è aumentata*, navigation through the Suez Canal has increased; *il ghiaccio fermò la* — *nell'estuario*, ice stopped all navigation in the estuary ‖ *atto di* —, (*st.*) Navigation Act.

navíglio, *s.m.* 1. (*flotta*) fleet: — *da guerra*, navy; — *leggero*, light surface craft; — *mercantile*, merchant ships; — *peschereccio*, fishing fleet; — *silurante*, torpedo-boats 2. (*rar.*) (*nave*) craft 3. (*canale navigabile*) canal, waterway.

navóne, *s.m.* (*bot.*) rape.

nazareàto, *s.m.* (*st. ebraica*) Nazaritism.

nazarèno, *V.* **nazzarèno**.

Nàzareth, *no.pr.f.* (*geog.*) Nazareth.

nazionàle, *ag.* national: *industria* —, home industry; *inno* —, national anthem.

nazionalísmo, *s.m.* nationalism.

nazionalísta, *s.c.* nationalist.

nazionalità, *s.f.* nationality: *a Londra ci sono uomini di ogni* —, there are men of all nationalities in London; *di che* — *sei?*, what is your nationality?.

nazionalizzàre, *v.t.* to nationalize.

nazionalizzazióne, *s.f.* nationalization.

nazióne, *s.f.* nation: *gente di ogni* —, people of all nations; *tutta la* — *pianse la sua morte*, the whole nation mourned his death ‖ *le Nazioni Unite*, the United Nations ‖ *l'Organizzazione delle Nazioni Unite*, (*abbr.* O.N.U.), the United Nations Organization (*abbr.* U.N.O.).

nazísmo, *s.m.* Nazism.

nazísta, *ag s.c.* Nazi.

nazzarèno, *ag.s.m.* Nazarene ‖ *il Nazzareno*, the Nazarene.

né[1], *cong.* 1. (*neppure, neanche*) **neither**, **nor**: *egli non lo sa*, — *lo so io*, he doesn't know, neither do I; *non l'ho visto*, — *voglio vederlo*, I have not seen him, neither (*o* nor) do I want to 2. *nè*... *nè*, **neither... nor**; (*in presenza di altra negazione*) **either... or**: — *mangia* — *beve*, he neither eats nor drinks; *crede di non averlo lasciato* — *qui* — *a casa*, she doesn't think she has left it (either) here or at home; *non è ubriaco* — *pazzo* — *malato*, he is neither drunk, nor mad, nor ill; *non mi scuserò* — *ammetterò di aver torto*, I will neither apologize nor admit that I am wrong (*o* I will not apologize nor will I admit that I am wrong); *se ne andò senza mangiare* — *bere*, he went off without (either) eating or drinking ‖ — *da una parte* — *dall'altra*, on neither side: *non c'era posto per parcheggiare l'automobile* — *da una parte* — *dall'altra della strada*, there was no room to park the car on either side of the road ‖ — *più* — *meno*, neither more nor less: *è* — *più* — *meno che un delitto*, it is neither more nor less than a crime ‖ — *l'uno* — *l'altro*, neither; (*in presenza di altra negazione*) **either**: — *l'uno* — *l'altro l'hanno visto*, neither (of them) saw him; *non conosco* — *l'uno* — *l'altro*, I know neither (*o* I do not know either) 3. (*enfatico*): *ha voluto farlo* — *io lo condanno*, he wanted to do it, and I don't blame him.

ne[2], *particella avverbiale di moto da luogo* **from there**: — *vengo or ora*, I am just coming from there ‖ *particella pronominale* 1. **of him, about him; of her, about her; of it, about it; of them, about them; of this, about this; of that, about that**: — *ho abbastanza*, I have had enough of that; *gliene ho parlato*, I spoke to him, to her about it, them, etc.; *ho udito dirne meraviglie*, I have heard wonderful things about him, her, etc.; *non* — *voglio più sapere*, I don't want to hear any more about it, him, etc.; *non me* — *importa nulla*, I don't care about it (*o* it doesn't matter to me); — *ricordò*, he remembered it ‖ *me* — *infischio!*, I couldn't care less! 2. (*talvolta si traduce coll'ag. poss.*): *se* — *persero le tracce*, their tracks were lost; *uccise il re e* — *usurpò il trono*, he killed the king and usurped his throne 3. (*partitivo*) **some; any; none**; *se accompagnato da num. o da ag. indef. non si traduce*; *con num. o ag. indef. accompagnati da ag. qualificativo* **one; ones**: *gliene* diedi ancora, I gave him, her some more; « Hai dei libri? », « Sì — ho, Non — ho, Ne ho due belli, Ne ho molti », " Have you any books? ", " Yes I have some, I have none (o I haven't any), I have two fine ones, I have a lot (o many) "; ho perso il suo libro e gliene ho preso un altro, I lost his book, so I got him, her another one 4. (causale) for it, about it: — sono tanto felice, I am so happy about it (o it makes me so happy); me — dispiace, I am sorry about it; se — pentirà, he will be sorry for it 5. (pleonastico): me — vado a spasso, I'm going for a walk; se — andò tutto soddisfatto, he went away very satisfied 6. (in espressioni ellittiche): — ha fatte di belle, he has been up to all sorts of tricks; gliene disse un sacco, he gave him a good ticking off (o he told him off).

neànche, av. not even: non l'ho — visto, I have not even seen him ‖ — per sogno !, not on your life! ‖ cong. neither, nor; not... either: egli non andò, e — noi, he did not go, and neither did we (o we didn't either); io non l'ho visto e — lei, I did not see it, and nor did she; non posso andare, e — lui, I can't go, neither can he.

nébbia, s.f. 1. fog; (foschia) mist; (da calore) haze; (mista a fumo) smog: — apparente, (causata da rifrazione atmosferica) mock fog; — bassa, ground fog; — fitta, thick fog; (sl.) pea-souper; — marina, sea fog; — di umidità, wet fog; banco di —, fog-bank; campana per la —, (sulle navi) fog-bell; cortina di —, (mar. mil.) smoke-screen; faro anti- —, fog-light; petardi per la —, (ferr.) fog signals; sirena per la —, fog horn; la — del mattino dura poco, the morning haze does not last long; la — si alza, the mist is rising; la — si dilegua, the fog is lifting; il paesaggio era avvolto nella —, the landscape was shrouded in mist ‖ c'era una — da tagliare col coltello, the fog was so thick you could cut it with a knife ‖ ho come una — davanti agli occhi, I have a sort of mist before my eyes ‖ insaccar —, (far cose inutili) to carry coals to Newcastle 2. fig. (offuscamento) haze, mist: nella — dell'ignoranza tutto è confuso, in the haze of ignorance everything is blurred 3. (malattia dei cereali) rust 4. pl. (med.) nebula (sing.) (pl. nebulae).

nebbiàio, s.m. 1. (tempo nebbioso) foggy weather 2. (banco di nebbia) fog-bank.

nebbiògeno, ag. smoke(-discharging) ‖ s.m. (mil.) smoke discharger.

nebbiòlo, s.m. " Nebbiolo " (kind of red wine made in Piedmont).

nebbióne, s.m. thick fog; (sl.) pea-souper.

nebbiosità, s.f. fogginess.

nebbióso, ag. 1. foggy: tempo —, foggy weather 2. fig. (oscuro) hazy, misty; confused; obscure: discorso —, confused speech; idea nebbiosa, hazy idea; stile —, obscure style.

nèbula, s.f. 1. (med.) nebula (pl. nebulae) 2. (arc.) (nebbia) nebula, mist, fog.

nebulàre, ag. (astr.) nebular.

nebulizzàre, v.t. to nebulize, to vaporize.

nebulizzatóre, s.m. nebulizer, vaporizer.

nebulizzazióne, s.f. nebulization, vaporization.

nebulósa, s.f. (astr.) nebula (pl. nebulae): nebulose a spirale, planetarie, spiral, planetary nebulae.

nebulosità, s.f. 1. (astr.) nebulosity 2. (imprecisione, indeterminatezza) haziness, vagueness, nebulousness; obscurity: la — delle sue idee, the haziness of his thoughts.

nebulóso, ag. 1. nebulous 2. (impreciso, vago) nebulous, vague; obscure: stile —, obscure style; teoria —, vague theory.

nécessaire, s.m. dressing-case; (per le unghie) manicure set; (per la barba) shaving set; (per la toilette femminile) beauty-case; (per le scarpe) shoe box; (per lavoro) work-basket; (per cucire) sewing-case; (per fumatori) smoker's set.

necessariaménte, av. necessarily.

necessàrio, ag. necessary; requisite; (indispensabile) indispensable: articoli necessari, necessary (o requisite) articles; i documenti necessari, the documents required; l'aria, il cibo e l'acqua sono necessari alla vita, air, food and water are indispensable to life; la cosa è diventata necessaria, the thing has become a necessity; è — che egli ritorni, he must come back (o it is necessary for him to come back); è — che io lo veda, I must see him (o it is necessary for me to see him); è — che tu lo segua, you must follow him (o it is necessary for you to follow him); è — molto tempo per imparare bene una lingua straniera, it takes a long time to learn a foreign language well; l'emergenza lo rende —, emergency makes it necessary; non è — che tu venga, you need not come; la sola cosa necessaria è che..., the essential thing is that...; il suo arrivo rende — che io me ne vada, his arrival means that I must go; avere il denaro —, to have enough money; rendersi — a qlcu., to make oneself indispensable to s.o.; ritenere — ql.co., to consider sthg. (o to deem sthg.) necessary; erede —, (dir.) heir at law ‖ s.m. 1. (ciò che è indispensabile) necessities (pl.): il — alla vita, the necessities of life; il puro —, the bare necessities 2. (cosa necessaria) necessary: farò tutto il —, I shall do all that is necessary (o everything necessary); non voglio fare più del —, I don't want to do more than is necessary; suo padre gli fornirà il —, his father will provide him with what he needs.

necessità, s.f. 1. necessity; (bisogno) need: le necessità della vita, the necessities of life; — di riposo, need of rest; una — logica, a logical necessity; secondo le necessità, as needed (o required); che — c'era di farlo?, why was it necessary (o why did you have) to do that?; la dura — mi spinge a..., dire necessity compels me to...; in caso di — sarò sempre contenta di aiutarti, if necessary (o if need be), I shall always be glad to help you; non c'è — che tu vada, there is no need for you to go (o you need not go o it is not necessary for you to go); se ci fosse —, vi andrei, if the necessity arose (o if it were necessary), I should go there; trovarsi nella — di fare ql.co., to be constrained (o compelled) to do sthg. ‖ di, per —, out of (o from) necessity: l'ho fatto per —, I did it out of necessity ‖ oggetti di prima —, indispensable articles ‖ — è madre dell'invenzione, prov. necessity is the mother of invention ‖ bisogna fare di — virtù, prov. what can't be cured must be endured 2. (indigenza) need, necessity, poverty: la — lo rese ladro, necessity made a thief of him; bisogna aiutarlo perchè vive in —, we must help him as he lives in poverty; trovarsi, versare in grande —, to be in great need.

necessitàre, v.t. to necessitate: l'aumento della popolazione necessita una maggiore provvista di cibo, the rise in the population necessitates a larger food supply ‖ v.i. (rar.) 1. (aver bisogno) to need (sthg.): necessito di molte cose, I need many things 2. (essere necessario) to be necessary.

necrobiòsi, s.f. (patol.) necrobiosis.

necrofobìa, s.f. (med.) necrophobia.

necròforo, s.m. 1. (becchino) grave-digger 2. (entom.) necrophore; (pop.) burying-beetle.

necrologìa, s.f. 1. (annuncio sul giornale) obituary (-notice) 2. (orazione funebre) funeral oration.

necrològico, ag. necrological.

necrològio, s.m. 1. (registro delle morti) necrology, obituary, register of deaths 2. (annuncio sul giornale) obituary (-notice).

necrologìsta, s.c. necrologist, obituarist.

necromanzìa, s.f. necromancy.

necròpoli, s.f. necropolis.

necropsìa, s.f. (med.) necropsy.

necrosàto, ag. (med.) necrosed.

necroscopìa, s.f. (med.) necroscopy, autopsy.

necroscòpico, ag. necroscopic(al); post-mortem (attributivo).

necròsi, *s.f.* (*med. bot.*) necrosis.

necròtico, *ag.* (*med.*) necrotic: *angina necrotica,* necrotic angina.

necrotizzàre, *v.t.* (*med.*) to necrotize; to necrose.

Neemía, *no.pr.m.* (*Bibbia*) Nehemiah, Nehemias.

neerlandése, *ag.* Netherlandish ‖ *s.c.* Netherlander.

nefandaménte, *av.* nefariously, wickedly.

nefandézza, *s.f.* nefariousness, wickedness.

nefàndo, *ag.* nefarious, wicked.

nefàrio, *ag.* (*letter.*) nefarious.

nefàsto, *ag.* inauspicious, ill-omened, unlucky.

nefrectomía, *s.f.* (*chir.*) nephrectomy.

nefríte, *s.f.* 1. (*patol.*) nephritis 2. (*min.*) nephrite.

nefrítico, *ag.* (*med.*) nephritic(al) ‖ *s.m.* nephritic subject.

nefròide, *ag.* (*med.*) nephroid, kidney-shaped.

nefrolitíasi, *s.f.* (*patol.*) nephrolithiasis.

nefropatía, *s.f.* (*patol.*) nephropathy.

nefrorragía, *s.f.* (*patol.*) nephrorrhagia.

nefròsi, *s.f.* (*patol.*) nephrosis.

nefrotomía, *s.f.* (*chir.*) nephrotomy.

nefrotossína, *s.f.* (*biol.*) nephrotoxin.

negàbile, *ag.* deniable.

negàre, *v.t.* 1. to deny: *l'imputato nega l'accusa,* the accused denies the charge (*o* pleads not guilty); *nego che possa aver fatto ciò,* I refuse to admit that he may have done this; *nego che questo sia vero,* I deny that this is true; *negò di averlo visto,* he denied having seen him; *non nego che fra noi vi siano interessi comuni,* I do not deny that we have common interests; *non si può — che abbia ragione,* it cannot be denied that he is right; *— l'esistenza di Dio,* to deny the existence of God; *— un fatto,* to deny a fact 2. (*rifiutare*) to deny, to refuse: *non gli nega mai nulla,* he never denies (*o* refuses) him anything; *non può — la sua firma,* he cannot refuse his signature 3. (*rinnegare*) to deny: *Pietro negò il Signore,* Peter denied his Master; *— la propria fede, il proprio paese,* to deny one's faith, one's country ‖ **negàrsi,** *v.r.* to deny oneself: *non posso negarmi le cose che mi piacciono,* I cannot deny myself the things I like; *— ogni lusso,* to deny oneself every luxury.

negarít, *s.m.* (*tam-tam abissino*) Abyssinian drum.

negatíva, *s.f.* 1. negative: « no » *e* « *non* » *sono negative,* "no" and "not" are negatives ‖ *persistere sulla —,* to maintain a negative attitude 2. (*foto.*) negative: *— a contatto,* contact negative.

negativaménte, *av.* negatively: *rispose —,* he replied in the negative.

negatívo, *ag.* 1. negative; (*sfavorevole*) unfavourable: *comando —,* negative command; *critica negativa,* destructive criticism; *proposizione negativa,* (*gram.*) negative proposition; *risposta negativa,* negative answer (*o* answer in the negative); *voto —,* unfavourable (*o* negative) vote; *assunsero un atteggiamento —,* they took up a negative attitude 2. (*mat. fis. foto.*) negative: *elettricità negativa,* (*elett.*) negative electricity; *pellicola, lastra negativa,* (*foto.*) negative film, plate; *polo —,* (*elett.*) negative pole; *quantità negativa,* (*mat.*) negative quantity; *segno —,* (*mat.*) negative sign.

negàto, *ag.* 1. (*non concesso*) refused, denied 2. (*inadatto*) unfit (for sthg.), unsuited (for sthg.): *essere a ql.co.,* to have no gift (*o* aptitude) for sthg.

negatóre, *ag.* negatory ‖ *s.m.,* **negatríce,** *s.f.* denier.

negatòrio, *ag.* negatory.

negazióne, *s.f.* 1. (*diniego*) denial: *rispose con una — alla mia richiesta,* he refused (*o* denied) my request 2. (*gram.*) negative: *due negazioni fanno un'affermazione,* two negatives make an affirmative 3. (*cosa, azione diametralmente opposta ad un'altra*) negation: *egli è la — del buon senso,* he is the negation of common sense.

neghittosaménte, *av.* slothfully; (*pigramente*) lazily.

neghittóso, *ag.* slothful; (*pigro*) lazy.

neglettaménte, *av.* neglectfully; negligently; carelessly; (*neghittosamente*) slothfully.

neglètto, *ag.* 1. neglected; ignored 2. (*di abbigliamento, aspetto*) slovenly: *aspetto —,* slovenly appearance.

negligènte, *ag.* negligent, careless, neglectful, remiss: *— nei propri doveri,* negligent of one's duties; *un cassiere — nel tenere i libri,* a cashier careless in his book-keeping; *un ragazzo — non riuscirà mai nella vita,* a careless boy will never succeed.

negligenteménte, *av.* negligently, carelessly.

negligènza, *s.f.* 1. (*l'essere negligente*) negligence; carelessness, remissness: *— abituale,* usual carelessness; *per —,* through negligence; *l'incidente fu dovuto a —,* the accident was due to negligence 2. (*atto negligente*) piece of negligence: *fu una vera —!,* it was a real piece of negligence!.

negligere, *v.t.* (*letter.*) to neglect.

negòssa, *s.f.* (*rete da pesca*) landing-net.

negoziàbile, *ag.* negotiable.

negoziabilità, *s.f.* negotiability.

negoziànte, *s.c.* 1. merchant; trader, dealer; (*al minuto*) retailer: *— di porcellane,* china dealer 2. (*chi ha negozio*) shopkeeper, tradesman (*pl.* tradesmen).

negoziàre, *v.t.* to negotiate: *— un affare con qlcu.,* to transact business with s.o.; *— un matrimonio,* to negotiate a marriage; *— la pace,* to negotiate peace ‖ *v.i.* 1. (*esercitare il commercio*) to trade; to deal: *— in vini,* to deal (*o* to trade) in wines 2. (*trattare*) to negotiate, to deal: *dovettero — per lungo tempo,* they had to negotiate for a long time.

negoziàto, *ag.* negotiated: *pace negoziata,* negotiated peace ‖ *s.m.* negotiation: *intavolare negoziati per un armistizio,* to enter into negotiations for an armistice.

negoziatóre, *s.m.* negotiator.

negoziatríce, *s.f.* negotiatrix, negotiatress.

negoziazióne, *s.f.* negotiation.

negòzio, *s.m.* 1. shop; (*spec. amer.*) store: *— al dettaglio,* retail shop; (*amer.*) retail store; *— di giocattoli,* toyshop; *— di libri,* book-shop; *— di mode,* boutique; *— di scarpe,* shoe-shop; *commessa, commesso di —,* shop assistant; *proprietario di —,* shopkeeper; *aprire un —,* to open a shop; *chiudere un —,* to shut up a shop 2. (*commercio, traffico*) trade, trading; deal; (*spreg.*) traffic: *era coinvolto in un — non del tutto onesto,* he was engaged in a dishonest traffic; *esercitare un —,* trade; *fare — di cavalli,* to deal in horses 3. (*affare, operazione*) piece of business, transaction: *conchiudere un buon —,* to do a good piece of business 4. (*faccenda*) affair, business: *— amoroso,* love affair; *perse molto tempo in questo —,* he lost a lot of time over this business; *essere impegnato in un — poco pulito,* to be engaged in a dirty business.

négra, *s.f.* negress; (*fam. spreg.*) nigger.

negrière, *s.m.* 1. slave-trader; slave-merchant, slave-dealer 2. (*chi tratta come schiavi i propri sottoposti*) slave-driver.

negrièro, *ag.* slave (*attributivo*): *nave negriera,* slave-ship (*o* slaver) ‖ *s.m.* V. **negrière.**

negríllo, *s.m.* negrillo (*pl.* negrillos).

negríto, *s.m.* negrito (*pl.* negritos).

négro, *ag.* 1. (*arc.*) (*nero*) black 2. (*di razza negra*) black; negro (*attributivo*): *domestici negri,* negro servants; *razza negra,* negro race ‖ *s.m.* negro (*pl.* negroes), black; (*fam. spreg.*) nigger: *tratta dei negri,* slave-trade.

negròide, *ag.* negroid(al) ‖ *s.c.* negroid.

negromànte, *s.c.* necromancer.

negromàntico, *ag.* necromantic.

negromanzía, *s.f.* necromancy.

nègus, *s.m.* Negus.

neh, *inter.* (*dial.*): *ci sei venuto volentieri, —?,* you came willingly, didn't you?; *è un uomo molto ricco, —?,* he is a very rich man, isn't he?.

nelúmb(i)o, *s.m.* (*bot.*) Nelumbium, Nelumbo.

nematelmínto, *s.m.* (*zool.*) nemathelminth ‖ *i Nematelminti,* (*zool.*) the Nemathelminthes.

nematòdo, *s.m.* (*zool.*) nematode ‖ *i Nematodi,* (*zool.*) the Nematoda (*o* Nematoidea).

nembífero, *ag.* (*poet.*) nimbiferous.

némbo, *s.m.* **1.** nimbus (*pl.* nimbi, nimbuses); (*nube tempestosa*) raincloud **2.** *fig.* (*nugolo*) cloud; (*stuolo*) multitude: *un — di armati,* a multitude of soldiers; *— di frecce,* cloud of arrows; *— di polvere,* cloud of dust **3.** (*poet.*) (*temporale*) storm, heavy rain.

Nembròt(te), *no.pr.m.* (*Bibbia*) Nimrod.

Nemèa, *no.pr.f.* (*geog. st.*) Nemea.

nemèo, *ag.* Nemean.

Nèmesi, *no.pr.f.* (*mit.*) Nemesis ‖ **nèmesi,** *s.f.* (*vendetta*) nemesis (*pl.* nemeses).

nemicaménte, *av.* inimically.

nemíco, *ag.* **1.** (*ostile*) adverse (to s.o., sthg.), hostile (to s.o., sthg.), opposed (to s.o., sthg.): *sono — dell'ignoranza,* I am hostile to ignorance; *la sorte gli fu nemica,* fate was against him; *farsi — qlcu.,* to make an enemy of s.o. **2.** (*nocivo*) harmful, noxious, detrimental: *il gelo è — alle piante,* frost is harmful to plants **3.** (*del nemico*) enemy (*attributivo*): *l'armata nemica,* the enemy army; *il campo —,* the enemy camp; *le navi nemiche,* the enemy ships ‖ *s.m.* enemy; (*avversario*) adversary; (*letter.*) foe: *— giurato,* sworn enemy; *— mortale,* mortal enemy; *nemici politici,* political adversaries; *il — fu messo in fuga,* the enemy was put to flight; *egli ha molti nemici,* he has many enemies; *il vizio è un pericoloso — della salute,* vice is a dangerous foe to health; *passare al —,* to go over to the enemy ‖ *il Nemico,* (*il diavolo*) the Enemy ‖ *a — che fugge ponti d'oro,* prov. build golden bridges for the flying foe ‖ *dal — mi guardo io, dagli amici mi guardi Iddio,* prov. I can protect myself against my enemies, may God protect me from my friends.

nemmàneo, nemméno, *V.* **neànche.**

nènia, *s.f.* **1.** (*canto funebre*) dirge, lament **2.** (*cantilena*) sing-song.

nenufàr, nenúfaro, *s.m.* (*bot.*) nenuphar, water-lily.

nèo, *s.m.* **1.** mole, spot; (*med.*) naevus (*pl.* naevi); (*posticcio*) patch, beauty-spot: *— materno,* naevus maternus (*o* birthmark); *— peloso,* pilose naevus; *aveva un — sulla guancia,* she had a mole on her cheek **2.** *fig.* (*piccola pecca*) slight imperfection, flaw.

neocapitalísmo, *s.m.* neo-capitalism.

neocattolicésimo, *s.m.* Neo-Catholicism.

neocattòlico, *ag.s.m.* Neo-Catholic.

neoclassicísmo, *s.m.* neo-classicism.

neoclàssico, *ag.* neo-classic(al) ‖ *s.m.* neo-classicist.

neocriticísmo, *s.m.* (*st. fil.*) neo-criticism.

neodímio, *s.m.* (*chim.*) neodymium.

neoellenísmo, *s.m.* Neohellenism.

neofascísmo, *s.m.* Neo-Fascism.

neofascísta, *s.m.* Neo-Fascist.

neòfito, *s.m.* neophyte, novice; *fig.* beginner, novice.

neoformazióne, *s.f.* (*med.*) neoformation.

neoguèlfo, *ag.* (*st.*) Neo-Guelphic ‖ *s.m.* (*st.*) Neo-Guelph.

neolalía, *s.f.* (*med.*) neolalia.

neolatíno, *ag.* Neo-Latin.

neolítico, *ag.* (*geol.*) Neolithic.

neología, *s.f.* neology.

neologísmo, *s.m.* neologism.

neologísta, neòlogo, *s.m.* neologist, neologian.

neomicína, *s.f.* (*farm.*) neomycin.

nèon, *s.m.* (*chim.*) neon: *insegna al —,* neon sign; *lampada al —,* neon lamp; *luce al —,* neon lighting.

neonàto, *ag.* new-born ‖ *s.m.* (new-born) baby.

neonazísmo, *s.m.* Neo-Nazism.

neoplàsma, *s.m.* (*patol.*) neoplasm.

neoplàstico, *ag.* (*patol.*) neoplastic.

neoplatònico, *ag.* (*fil.*) Neoplatonic ‖ *s.m.* (*st. fil.*) Neoplatonist.

neoplatonísmo, *s.m.* (*st. fil.*) Neoplatonism.

neoscolàstica, *s.f.* (*st. fil.*) Neo-Scholasticism.

neotèrico, *ag.* (*fil.*) neoteric ‖ *s.m.* (*fil.*) neoterist.

neoterísmo, *s.m.* (*st. fil.*) neoterism.

neozòico, *ag.* (*geol.*) Neozoic.

Nèpal, *no.pr.m.* (*geog.*) Nepal.

nepalése, *ag.* Nepalese ‖ *s.c.* Nepalese (*invariato al pl.*).

nepènte, *s.m.* **1.** (*bevanda anodina*) nepenthe **2.** (*bot.*) nepenthe(s), pitcher-plant.

nepitèlla, *s.f.* (*bot.*) catmint; (*amer.*) catnip.

nepóte[1]**,** *V.* **nipóte.**

Nepóte[2]**,** *no.pr.m.* (*st. lett.*) Nepos.

nepotísmo, *s.m.* nepotism.

nepotísta, *s.c.* nepotist.

neppúre, *V.* **neànche.**

nequízia, *s.f.* (*rar.*) iniquity.

neràstro, *ag.* blackish.

nerbàre, *v.t.* (*rar.*) to whip, to scourge, to flog.

nerbàta, *s.f.* blow with a whip: *lo prese a nerbate,* he flogged him.

nèrbo, *s.m.* **1.** (*nervo*) nerve **2.** (*frusta*) whip, scourge **3.** *fig.* (*forza*) strength: *il — dell'esercito,* the strength of the army; *la sua parola non ha —,* his prose lacks strength (*o* vigour).

nerborúto, nerbúto, *ag.* brawny, strong-limbed.

nereggiàre, *v.i.* (*letter.*) **1.** (*tendere al nero*) to be almost black: *il cielo nereggiava di nubi,* the sky was black with clouds **2.** (*formare una massa nera*) to form a black mass: *la folla nereggiava nella piazza,* the crowd formed a black mass in the square.

Nerèide, *no.pr.f.* (*mit.*) Nereid.

Nerèo, *no.pr.m.* (*mit.*) Nereus.

nerétto, *s.m.* (*tip.*) boldface, bold-faced type.

nerézza, *s.f.* blackness.

neríccio, nerígno, *ag.* blackish.

néro, *ag.* **1.** black; (*scuro*) dark: *— come l'ebano, come l'inchiostro, come il carbone,* as black as ebony, as ink, as coal; *abito —,* (*da donna*) black dress; (*da uomo*) black suit; (*da sera*) evening-dress; *capelli, occhi neri,* dark hair, eyes; *caffè —,* black coffee; *ombra nera,* dark shadow; *pane —,* brown bread; *pelle nera,* dark skin ‖ *i Neri,* (*st.*) the Church party of the Guelfs ‖ *l'angelo —,* the Devil ‖ *bestia nera, fig.* bugbear: *il latino è la mia bestia nera,* Latin is my bugbear ‖ *borsa nera, mercato —,* black market ‖ *camicie nere,* black shirts ‖ *il Continente Nero,* the Dark Continent ‖ *cronaca nera,* crime reports ‖ *libro —,* black books: *se lo farai ti segnerò sul mio libro —,* if you do that, you will be in my black books ‖ *magia nera,* black art (*o* magic) ‖ *il Mar Nero,* the Black Sea ‖ *pecora nera, fig.* black sheep: *è la pecora nera della famiglia,* he is the black sheep of the family ‖ *vaiolo —,* (*patol.*) black variola ‖ *il diavolo non è poi tanto — come lo si dipinge, prov.* the devil is not so black as he is painted **2.** (*sporco*) dirty, black: *mani nere,* dirty hands; *i polsini della tua camicia sono neri,* the cuffs of your shirt are black (with dirt) **3.** *fig.* (*tetro, malinconico*) black, gloomy; (*estremo*) deepest: *disperazione nera,* black (*o* deepest) despair; *ingratitudine nera,* deepest ingratitude; *miseria nera,* dire poverty; *pensieri neri,* gloomy thoughts; *ha una visione nera del futuro,* he takes a gloomy view of the future; *essere di umore —,* to be in a black mood; *veder tutto —,* to look on the dark side of things **4.** *fig.* (*scellerato, empio*) wicked, black: *calunnia nera,* wicked slander; *è un'anima nera,* he is a wicked soul ‖ *s.m.* black: *chiesa parata a —,* church hung with black; *tingere in —,* to dye black; *vestir di —,* to dress in black: *una donna vestita di —,* a woman dressed in black ‖ *— animale,* (*ind. chim.*) char (*o* animal charcoal *o* bone black); *— di avorio,* (*pitt.*) ivory black ‖ *mettere il — sul bianco,* to write (a few lines); (*metter per iscritto*) to get things down in black and white ‖ *mostrare il — per bianco,* to falsify facts.

nerofúmo, *s.m.* lamp-black.

nerógnolo, *ag.* blackish.

Neróne, *no.pr.m.* (*st.*) Nero ‖ **neróne,** *s.m.* (*tiranno*) tyrant: *è un —!,* he is a tyrant!.

neroniàno, *ag.* Neronian, Neronic.

nerúme, *s.m.* (mass of) black; (lot of) dirt.

nervàle, *ag.* (*anat.*) nerval.

nervatúra, *s.f.* **1.** (*bot. entom.*) nervation, nervature, ribbing **2.** (*anat.*) nerves (*pl.*) **3.** (*costolatura*) ribs (*pl.*), ribbing: — *di rinforzo, di irrigidimento,* (*mec.*) stiffening rib(s).

nèrveo, *ag.* (*anat.*) nerval, neural, nervous.

nervíno, *ag.* (*med. farm.*) nervine.

nèrvo, *s.m.* **1.** nerve: — *afferente, centripeto,* centripetal nerve; — *centrifugo, motore,* centrifugal, motor nerve; *i nervi della mano, dello stomaco,* the nerves of the hand, of the stomach; — *ottico,* optic nerve; *attacco, crisi di nervi,* fit of nerves; *il caffè eccita i nervi,* coffee makes you nervous; *calmare i nervi,* to soothe the nerves: *calma i tuoi nervi!,* (*fam.*) calm down! (o keep your hair on!) ‖ *nervi d'acciaio,* iron nerves (o nerves of steel) ‖ *sta in piedi a forza di nervi,* he lives on his nerves ‖ *avere i nervi* (*tesi*), *a fior di pelle, scoperti,* to be very irritable (o nervy o to be on edge) ‖ *dare ai nervi a qlcu., irritare, urtare i nervi di qlcu.,* to get on s.o.'s nerves (o sl. to get s.o.'s goat) ‖ *essere tutto nervi,* to be full of nervous energy **2.** (*pop.*) (*tendine*) tendon **3.** (*bot.*) nervure, rib, vein, nerve: — *mediano,* midrib **4.** (*dell'arco, della lira*) string, cord.

nervosaménte, *av.* nervously.

nervosísmo, *s.m.* nervousness, irritability, quick temper, short temper: *la lunga attesa aumentava il mio* —, the long wait increased my nervousness.

nervosità, *s.f.* **1.** nervousness, irritability **2.** (*vivacità*) liveliness; (*vigore*) vigour.

nervóso, *ag.* **1.** nervous: *centro* —, nerve centre; *esaurimento* —, nervous breakdown; *ganglio* —, nerve ganglion; *sistema* —, nervous system; *terminazione nervosa,* nerve-ending **2.** (*irritabile, eccitabile*) nervous; irritable, short-tempered; excitable; (*fam.*) nervy: *un bambino* —, a nervy child; *è un uomo molto* —, he is very irritable (o short-tempered); *oggi sono molto* —, today I am feeling very nervy; *quel bambino diventa facilmente* —, that child is easily excitable (o easily becomes excited) **3.** (*vivace, vigoroso*) nervous, vigorous ‖ *s.m.* **1.** nervousness, irritability: *avere il* —, to be very irritable (o to be on edge); *soffrire il* —, to be of an irritable disposition (o to be short-tempered) **2.** (*persona nervosa*) irritable person.

nèsci: *fare il* —, to feign ignorance, to pretend ignorance.

nèspola, *s.f.* **1.** (*bot.*) medlar: — *del Giappone,* loquat (o Japanese medlar) ‖ *col tempo e con la paglia maturano le nespole, prov.* all things come to him who waits **2.** *dare le nespole a qlcu.,* (*fam.*) (*picchiarlo*) to give s.o. a good hiding.

nèspole, *inter.* (*fam.*) heavens!, my word!.

nèspolo, *s.m.* (*bot.*) medlar (tree): — *del Giappone,* loquat (tree) (o Japan medlar).

nèsso[1], *s.m.* **1.** connection, connexion, relation, link: — *logico,* logical connection (o relation); *sai trovare un — fra le due cose?,* can you find any connexion between the two things? **2.** (*mus.*) tie.

Nèsso[2], *no.pr.m.* (*mit.*) Nessus.

nessúno, *ag. indef.* **1.** no; (*in presenza di altra negazione*) any: *nessuna casa ha l'acqua corrente in questo villaggio,* no house in this village has running water; *è una persona di nessuna importanza,* he is a person of no importance whatsoever; *non ha nessun motivo di lamentarsi,* he hasn't any cause for complaint; *non ha nessuna pazienza con i bambini,* he has no (o he hasn't any) patience with children; *non lo farei per nessuna cosa al mondo,* I wouldn't do it for anything in the world; *non lo permetterò in nessun caso,* I will not allow it under any circumstances ‖ *non andammo in nessun* (*altro*) *luogo,* we didn't go anywhere (o we went nowhere) (else) ‖ *non ti aiuterò in nessun modo,* I shan't help you at all (o by any means) **2.** (*qualche*) any: *c'è nessun inglese che...?,* is there any Englishman

who...?; *hai nessuna speranza...?,* have you any hope...? ‖ *pron. indef.* **1. nobody, no one** (*riferiti a persone*); **none** (*riferito a cose*); (*accompagnato da un partitivo*) **none** (*riferito a persone e a cose*); (*in presenza di altra negazione*) **anybody, anyone, any;** (*accompagnato da un partitivo*) **any:** — *dei libri che mi hai prestato era interessante,* none of the books you lent me was interesting; — *di noi andò,* none of us went; — *è venuto stamane,* nobody has come this morning; — *mi ha mai detto ciò,* no one has ever told me that; *non c'era quasi* —, there was hardly anybody; *non ho visto — di voi stamane,* I did not see any of you this morning; *non parla mai con* —, he never speaks to anybody; *« Quanti errori hai fatto? »,* « *Nessuno* », " How many mistakes did you make? ", " None " ‖ *non guarda in faccia a* —, he never worries about anyone else **2.** (*qualcuno*) **anybody, anyone;** (*accompagnato da un partitivo*) **any:** *c'è — che voglia venire?,* is there anybody who wants to come?; *hai visto — dei miei fratelli?,* have you seen any of my brothers?; *hai visto — nel giardino?,* have you seen anybody in the garden?; *va a vedere se c'è* —, go and see if there is anyone there ‖ *s.m.* **nobody, no one:** *non è* —, he is a nobody ‖ *figlio di* —, waif (anche *fig.*): *sembri il figlio di* — *oggi,* (*fam.*) you look like a long-lost waif (o an orphan of the storm) today ‖ *terra di* —, (*mil.*) no-man's-land.

Nèstore, *no.pr.m.* (*lett.*) Nestor ‖ **nèstore,** *s.m.* (*vegliardo*) Nestor.

nestorianésimo, *s.m.* (*st. relig.*) Nestorianism.

nestoriàno, *s.m.* (*st. relig.*) Nestorian.

Nestòrio, *no.pr.m.* (*st. relig.*) Nestorius.

nettaménte, *av.* **1.** cleanly: *una casa tenuta* —, a cleanly kept house **2.** (*chiaramente*) clearly: *ormai lo si distingueva* —, he could already be clearly seen; *parlò* —, he spoke out clearly.

nettaménto, *s.m.* (*rar.*) cleaning, cleansing.

nettapénne, *s.m.* pen-wiper.

nèttare[1], *s.m.* (*mit. bot.*) nectar (anche *fig.*).

nettàre[2], *v.t.* to clean; to cleanse (anche *fig.*): — *la coscienza dal peccato,* to cleanse one's soul from sin.

nettàreo, *ag.* (*letter.*) nectarean, nectareous.

nettàrio, *s.m.* (*bot.*) nectary.

nettatóia, *s.f.* (*strum. artig.*) mortar-board.

nettatúra, *s.f.* (*rar.*) cleaning, cleansing.

nettézza, *s.f.* **1.** cleanness, cleanliness (anche *fig.*) ‖ *servizio di — urbana,* municipal street cleansing and refuse collection services **2.** (*precisione, ordine*) tidiness, neatness: *la — del suo stile,* the neatness of his style.

nétto, *ag.* **1.** clean, spotless (anche *fig.*): *una casa netta,* a clean (o spotless) house; *coscienza netta,* clean (o pure) conscience; *mani nette,* clean hands (anche *fig.*) ‖ *patente netta,* (*mar.*) clean bill of health **2.** (*chiaro, preciso*) clean, clear, clear-cut, sharp; terse: *un colpo* —, a clean blow; *contorni netti,* clear (o sharp) outline; *un discorso chiaro e* —, a clear terse speech; *divisione netta,* clear-cut division; *immagine netta,* (*foto.*) sharp image; *un taglio* —, a clean cut; *avere una visione netta del futuro,* to have a clear vision of the future ‖ *di* —, clean off: *con un colpo di spada gli tagliò di — il braccio,* with one stroke of his sword he cut his arm clean off **3.** (*comm.*) net: *guadagno* —, net (o clear) profit; *peso, prezzo* —, net weight, price; *rendita netta di imposte,* tax-free income ‖ *al — di dazio,* duty free.

nétto, *av.* plainly, bluntly: *parlò* —, he spoke plainly.

nettuniàno, nettúnico, *ag.* (*geol.*) Neptunian.

nettúnio, *ag.* Neptunian ‖ *s.m.* (*chim.*) neptunium.

Nettúno, *no.pr.m.* (*mit. astr.*) Neptune.

nèuma, *s.m.* (*mus.*) neum(e).

neuralgía, *s.f.* (*med.*) neuralgia.

neuràlgico, *ag.* (*med.*) neuralgic.

neurastenía, *s.f.* (*patol.*) neurasthenia.

neurastènico, *ag.* (*patol.*) neurasthenic.

neurilèmma, *s.m.* (*anat.*) neurilem(m)a, neurolemma.

neurína, *s.f.* (*anat.*) neurine.

neuríte, *s.f.* (*patol.*) neuritis.
neurocheratína, *s.f.* (*biol.*) neurokeratin.
neurochirurgía, *s.f.* neurosurgery.
neurofibrílla, *s.f.* (*anat.*) neurofibril.
neuroglía, *s.f.* (*anat.*) neuroglia.
neurología, *s.f.* neurology.
neuròlogo, *s.m.* neurologist.
neuròma, *s.m.* (*patol.*) neuroma (*pl.* neuromata).
neuronàle, *s.m.* (*farm.*) neuronal.
neuróne, *s.m.* (*anat.*) neuron.
neuropatía, *s.f.* (*patol.*) neuropathy.
neuropàtico, *ag.* neuropathic ‖ *s.m.* neuropath.
neuropatología, *s.f.* neuropathology.
neuropatòlogo, *s.m.* neuropathologist.
neuròsi, *s.f.* (*med.*) neurosis (*pl.* neuroses).
neuròtico, *ag.s.m.* neurotic.
neurotomía, *s.f.* (*chir.*) neurotomy.
neuròtteri, *s.m.pl.* (*entom.*) Neuroptera.
neutràle, *ag.* **1.** neutral: *stato* —, neutral state; *restar* —, to remain neutral **2.** (*chim.*) neutral ‖ *s.c.* neutral.
neutralísta, *s.c.* (*pol.*) neutralist.
neutralità, *s.f.* neutrality.
neutralizzàre, *v.t.* **1.** to neutralize: — *gli effetti di un veleno,* to neutralize (*o* to counteract) the effects of a poison **2.** (*chim.*) to neutralize.
neutralizzazióne, *s.f.* neutralization.
nèutro, *ag.* **1.** neutral: *colore* —, *tinta neutra,* neutral colour; *territorio* —, no-man's-land; *zona neutra,* neutral zone; *restare* —, to remain neutral **2.** (*chim. elett. foto.*) neutral: *filo* —, (*elett.*) neutral conductor; *soluzione neutra,* (*chim.*) neutral solution; *sostanza neutra,* (*chim.*) neutral substance **3.** (*bot. entom.*) neuter: *ape neutra,* neuter bee; *fiore* —, neuter (*o* asexual) flower **4.** (*gram.*) neuter: *pronome* —, neuter pronoun ‖ *s.m.* (*gram.*) neuter.
neutróne, *s.m.* (*fis.*) neutron.
nevàio, *s.m.* snow-field; (*ghiacciaio*) glacier.
nevàto, *ag.* **1.** (*coperto di neve*) snow-covered, snow-clad; (*di cima di montagna*) snow-capped **2.** (*bianco come neve*) snow-white.
néve, *s.f.* snow: *le nevi del ghiacciaio,* the snows of the glacier; — *marcia,* slush; *nevi persistenti, perpetue,* perpetual snow: *limite delle nevi perpetue,* snow-line; *accecato dalla* —, snow-blind; *bianco come la* —, as white as snow (*o* snow-white); *coperto di* —, snow-covered (*o* covered with snow); *cumulo di* —, snow-drift; *fiocco di* —, snowflake; *manto, coltre di* —, cloak of snow; *occhiali da* —, snow-goggles (*o* snow-glasses); *paesaggio coperto di* —, snowscape; *palla di* —, snow-ball: *battaglia a palle di* —, snow-fight; *giocare a palle di* —, to play snowballs; *pupazzo di* —, snow-man: *fare un pupazzo di* —, to make a snow-man; *senza* —, snowless (*o* without snow); *la stagione delle nevi,* the snowy season; *tempesta di* —, snow-storm (*o* blizzard); *valanga di* —, avalanche; *non potemmo venire a causa della* —, we could not come owing to the snow; *rimase sepolto sotto la* —, he was buried under the snow; *affondare nella* —, to sink into the snow; *rimanere bloccato dalla* —, to be snowed up (*o* snow-bound); *spalare la* —, to sweep away the snow ‖ — *carbonica,* (*ind. chim.*) dry ice ‖ *capelli, barba di* —, (*poet.*) snowy hair, beard ‖ *chiare a* —, (*cuc.*) whites of eggs beaten stiff: *montare, sbattere le chiare a* —, to beat egg-whites to a froth ‖ *anno di* —, *anno di bene,* *prov.* a snow year, a rich year ‖ *sott'acqua fame, sotto* — *pane,* *prov.* under water, famine; under snow, bread.
nevicàre, *v.imp.* to snow: *nevica,* it is snowing ‖ *è nevicato sui suoi capelli,* (*scherz.*) the years have whitened his hair.
nevicàta, *s.f.* snowfall.
nevíschio, *s.m.* sleet.
nevóso, *ag.* **1.** snowy: *inverno* —, snowy winter **2.** (*coperto di neve*) snow-covered ‖ *s.m.* (*st. francese*) Nivôse.
nevralgía, *s.f.* (*med.*) neuralgia.

nevràlgico, *ag.* neuralgic.
nevrastenía, *s.f.* (*patol.*) neurasthenia.
nevrastènica, *s.f.* neurasthenic.
nevrastènico, *ag.s.m.* neurasthenic.
nevríte, *s.f.* (*patol.*) neuritis (*pl.* neuritides).
nevròsi, *s.f.* (*patol.*) neurosis (*pl.* neuroses).
nevròtica, *s.f.* neurotic.
nevròtico, *ag.s.m.* neurotic.
nevvéro, *inter.*: *è arrivato,* —*?,* he has arrived, hasn't he?; *ieri sei andato al cinema,* —*?,* you went to the cinema yesterday, didn't you?; *sei venuto da solo,* —*?,* you came by yourself, didn't you?.
Niagàra, *no.pr.m.* (*geog.*) Niagara: *cascate del* —, Niagara Falls.
Niàssa, *no.pr.m.* (*geog.*) **1.** Nyasaland **2.** (*lago*) Nyas(s)a.
níbbio, *s.m.* (*ornit.*) kite.
Nibelúnghi, *s.m.pl.* (*mit. nordica*) Nibelungen.
Nicàndro, *no.pr.m.* (*st.*) Nicander.
níechia, *s.f.* **1.** niche: *una* — *nel muro,* a niche in the wall; *sto bene nella mia* —, *fig.* I have found the right niche for myself **2.** (*carica, ufficio*) niche, suitable place, suitable job: *vuol fare una* — *a suo figlio,* he wants to find a niche (*o* suitable job) for his son.
nicchiàre, *v.i.* to shilly-shally: *dammi una risposta, non* —, give me a straight answer, don't shilly-shally; *egli chiedeva, ma l'altro nicchiava:* he asked, but the other could not make up his mind.
níechio, *s.m.* shell, conch.
Niccolò, *no.pr.m.* Nic(h)olas ‖ *dim.* Nick, Nic(h)ol.
Nicèa, *no.pr.f.* (*geog. st.*) Nicaea ‖ *il simbolo di* —, (*il Credo*) the Nicene creed.
níchel, *s.m.* (*chim.*) nickel.
nichelàre *v.t.* (*ind.*) to nickel, to nickel-plate.
nichelatúra, *s.f.* (*ind.*) nickel-plating, nickelling.
nichelíno, *s.m.* (*fam.*) nickel coin; (*amer.*) nickel; (*piccola moneta*) small coin.
nichèlio, *s.m.* (*chim.*) nickel.
nichilísmo, *s.m.* (*fil. pol.*) nihilism.
nichilísta, *s.c.* (*fil. pol.*) nihilist.
Nícia, *no.pr.m.* (*st.*) Nicias.
Nicodèmo, *no.pr.m.* Nicodemus ‖ *dim.* Nick, Noddy.
Nicòla, *no.pr.m.* Nic(h)olas ‖ *dim.* Nick, Nic(h)ol.
Nicòmaco, *no.pr.m.* (*st.*) Nicomachus.
Nicomède, *no.pr.m.* (*st.*) Nicomedes.
nicotína, *s.f.* (*chim.*) nicotine.
nicotinísmo, *s.m.* (*med.*) nicotinism.
nicoziàna, *s.f.* (*bot.*) Nicotiana tabacum.
nictalopía, *s.f.* nyctalopia, night-blindness.
nictàlopo, *s.m.* nyctalope.
nidàce, nidiàce(o), *ag.* (*di uccellino di nido*) unfledged ‖ *s.m.* (*uccellino di nido*) nestling, fledgeling.
nidiàndolo, *s.m.* (*uovo lasciato nel nido per richiamo alle galline*) nest-egg.
nidiàta, *s.f.* nest(ful); (*covata*) brood: *una* — *di topolini,* a nest of mice ‖ *una* — *di bambini,* a swarm of children.
nidificàre, *v.i.* to nest, to nidify, to nidificate.
nidificazióne, *s.f.* nest-building, nidification.
nído, *s.m.* **1.** nest: (*di uccello da preda*) aerie, aery, eyrie, eyry: *un* — *d'aquile,* eagles' aerie; — *di topi,* rats' nest; — *di vespe,* wasps' nest; — *di vipere,* nest of vipers (anche *fig.*); *uccello di* —, fledgeling (*o* nestling); *costruire un* —, to build a nest ‖ — *d'ape,* (*cucito*) smocking ‖ *a ogni uccello suo* — *è bello,* *prov.* there is no place like home **2.** (*nidiata*) nest(ful); (*covata*) brood **3.** (*tana, covo*) den: — *di briganti,* robbers' den **4.** (*casa, patria*) home: *farsi il* — *in un luogo,* to make one's home in a place; *ritornare al proprio* —, to go back home **5.** (*giardino d'infanzia*) crèche.
nidóre, *s.m.* (*rar.*) nidor.
niellàre, *v.t.* (*artig.*) to niello, to decorate with niello.
niellatúra, *s.f.* (*artig.*) niello-work.
nièllo, *s.m.* (*artig.*) niello (*pl.* nielli, niellos).
niènte, *pron. indef.* **1.** **nothing;** (*in presenza di altra*

negazione) **anything**: — è certo, nothing is certain; « Che cosa fai? », « Niente », " What are you doing? ", " Nothing "; come se — fosse accaduto, as if nothing had happened; non abbiamo visto —, we have not seen anything; non bisogna dirgli —, he must not be told anything; non dà mai — a nessuno, he never gives anything to anybody; so poco o — di lui, I know little or nothing of him || — altro, nothing else; (in presenza di altra negazione) anything else: non disse — altro, he didn't say anything else; — altro che, nothing but: non disse — altro che la verità, he said nothing but the truth || — di, nothing; (in presenza di altra negazione) anything: — di interessante, nothing interesting; — di meglio, nothing better; — di male se si tenta, no harm in trying; non ho — di nuovo da dirti, I have nothing new to tell you || un buono a —, a good-for-nothing || cosa da —, a trifling (o insignificant) matter || come se — fosse, as if nothing were the matter || ciò non serve a —, this is no use || « Grazie, signora », « Niente, si figuri! », " Thank you, Madam ", " Don't mention it! " (o " It's all right! " o amer. " You are welcome! ") || non fa —, it doesn't matter: se non ti fa —, if you have no objection... (o if you don't mind...) || non posso farci —, I can do nothing about it || non sa — di —, he knows nothing whatever (o nothing at all o nothing about anything) || non si può vivere di —, you can't live on nothing || tutto finì in —, it all came to nothing (o everything fell through) || arrabbiarsi per —, to get angry about nothing || far finta di —, to pretend not to see anything || non aver — a che fare con..., to have nothing to do with... || parlare per —, to waste one's breath (o to waste words) 2. (qualche cosa) **anything**: guardiamo se c'è — per noi, let's see if there is anything for us; hai mai visto — di così divertente?, did you ever see anything so funny? || hai — in contrario?, have you any objections? || s.m. **nothing**: è un —, he is a mere nothing (o he is a cipher); offendersi per un —, to take offence at the slightest thing || l'ha fatto in meno di un —, he did it in less than no time (o he did it in a trice) || ridursi un —, to wear oneself out || ridursi al —, to lose everything (o to become poor) || venir su dal —, to come up from the gutter || av. 1. (punto, affatto) **not at all**: — male, not bad at all; ella non gli assomiglia —, she is not at all (o not a bit) like him; non ho — voglia di lavorare oggi, I don't feel like working at all today 2. (un poco) **a little**: se — si muove dimmelo, if he moves a little tell me.

nientediméno, nienteméno, av. well, fancy that!; I say!; (fam.) you don't say!; go on! || **nientediméno che, nienteméno che**, l. cong. avversativa (riferito a persona) **no less than**; (riferito a cosa) **nothing less than**: era — che il re in persona, it was no less than the king himself; immaginate che cosa mi ha dato: — che un anello con smeraldo, imagine what he has given me: nothing less than an emerald ring.

níffo, níffolo, s.m. 1. (del maiale) snout; (dell'elefante) trunk; (di insetti) proboscis (pl. proboscises, proboscides) 2. (spreg.) (viso umano) mug.

nigèlla, s.f. (bot.) nigella; (pop.) fennel-flower.

Nigèria, no.pr.f. (geog.) Nigeria.

Nílo, no.pr.m. (geog.) Nile.

nímbo, s.m. nimbus (pl. nimbi, nimbuses), halo (pl. haloes, halos): il — di un santo, the halo (o nimbus) of a saint; la Vergine apparve in un —, the Virgin appeared in a blaze of light.

nínfa, s.f. 1. (mit.) nymph: è una —, she is a nymph (anche fig.) || — Egeria, Egeria 2. (entom.) nymph, nympha (pl. nymphae).

ninfàle, ag. nymphal, nymphean || s.m. (st. lett.) nymphal.

ninfèa, s.f. (bot.) nymphaea; (pop.) water-lily.

ninfétta, s.f. (neol.) nymphet.

Nínive, no.pr.f. (geog. st.) Nineveh.

nínna, s.f. (gergo infantile) bye-bye.

ninnanànna, s.f. lullaby, cradle song: addormentare un bambino con una —, to lull a child to sleep.

ninnàre, v.t. to lullaby, to lull to sleep.

ninnolàre, v.t. to amuse || v.i., **ninnolàrsi**, v.r. to play around.

nínnolo, s.m. 1. knick-knack, trinket: una casa piena di ninnoli, a house filled with knick-knacks 2. (balocco) plaything, toy.

ninnolóna, s.f., **ninnolóne**, s.m. (fam.) trifler.

níno[1], s.m. (fam.) (vezzeggiativo) darling.

Níno[2], no.pr.m. (st.) Ninus.

Níno[3], no.pr.m. dim. di **Giovànni**.

Níobe, no.pr.f. (mit.) Niobe.

niòbio, s.m. (chim.) niobium, columbium.

niobìsmo, s.m. (psicologia) niobism.

nipiología, s.f. nepiology.

nipóte, s.m. 1. (di zii) nephew; (di nonni), grandson, grandchild (pl. grandchildren): il nonno leggeva una fiaba al suo nipotino, grandfather was reading a fairy-tale to his grandchild; sembra così giovane, eppure è già nonna di cinque nipotini, she looks so young and yet she has already got five grandchildren; lo zio ha lasciato tutto al suo unico —, the uncle has left everything to his only nephew 2. pl. (discendenti) progeny (sing.), posterity (sing.): i nipoti di Adamo, Adam's posterity (o progeny) || s.f. (di zii) niece; (di nonni) grand-daughter, grandchild (pl. grandchildren): era la mia — preferita, she was my favourite niece.

nippònico, ag. Japanese || i Nipponici, the Japanese.

nirvàna, s.m. (relig. indù) nirvana, nirwana.

nistàgmo, s.m. (patol.) nystagmus.

nitidaménte, av. clearly, neatly, distinctly.

nitidézza, s.f. neatness, clearness.

nítido, ag. 1. (pulito) neat, tidy: teneva la cucina nitida come uno specchio, she kept her kitchen spick and span; tutto era lindo e — in quella casa, everything was very neat in that house 2. (chiaro) clear; neat: scrittura nitida, neat handwriting; una voce nitida, a clear voice; ha uno stile —, he has a clear style; l'immagine appariva nitida, the image stood out clearly; la stampa di quel libro è molto nitida, that book has very clear print.

nitóre, s.m. (poet.) 1. (nitidezza) neatness, clearness; (limpidezza) limpidity 2. (splendore) splendour.

nitràto, s.m. (chim.) nitrate: — d'argento, silver nitrate; — d'argento (fuso in bacchette), (chim. farm.) lunar caustic; — di potassio, potassium nitrate.

nitrènte, ag. neighing.

nítrico, ag. (chim.) nitric: acido —, nitric acid.

nitrificàre, v.t. to nitrify.

nitrificazióne, s.f. nitrification.

nitríre, v.i. to neigh, to whinny.

nitríto[1], s.m. (di cavallo) neigh, whinny.

nitríto[2], s.m. (chim.) nitrite: — di potassio, potassium nitrite; — di sodio, sodium nitrite.

nítro, s.m. (chim.) nitre, saltpetre.

nitrobenzène, s.m. (chim.) nitrobenzene.

nitrocellulósa, s.f. (chim.) nitrocellulose: — in solventi organici, nitrocellulose solutions; verniciatura alla —, nitrocellulose painting.

nitrofosfàto, s.m. (chim.) nitrophosphate.

nitrogelatína, s.f. (chim.) nitrogelatin(e).

nitroglicerína, s.f. (chim.) nitroglycerin(e).

Nízza, no.pr.f. (geog.) Nice.

nizzàrdo, ag. Nice (attributivo) || s.m., **nizzàrda**, s.f. native of Nice; inhabitant of Nice.

no, particella di negazione 1. (risposta negativa assoluta o ben divisa, in inglese, dalla frase che l'accompagna) no: « Hai letto questo libro? », « No », " Have you read this book? ", " No, I haven't"; la mia risposta è —, my answer is no || — e poi —, no, I tell you (o no and again no o no, a thousand times no) || —, grazie, no, thank you || sì o —?, yes or no?: lo vuoi sì o —?, do you want it yes or no? 2. (quando, in inglese, c'è un verbo, espresso o sottinteso, o un avverbio) **not**: —

affatto, not at all; — *di certo*, certainly not; *perchè —?*, why not?; *bello o —*, *a me piace*, beautiful or not, I like it; *chi loda chi —*, some praise some do not; *credo, suppongo di —*, I don't think so, I don't suppose so; *preferisco di —*, I'd rather not; *se mi piace lo compero*; *se —, —*, if I like it I'll buy it; if not, I won't; *spero di —*, I hope not; *vieni o —?*, are you coming or not? **3.** (*Fraseologia*): *anzi che —*, rather: *stupido anzi che —*, rather stupid (*o fam.* a bit of a fool) ‖ *nè sì nè —*, neither yes nor no; (*in presenza di altra negazione*) either yes or no: *non dire nè sì nè —*, not to say either yes or no ‖ *più sì che —*, yes rather than no ‖ *se —*, otherwise (*o* or else *o* if not): *vattene subito! se —...*, go away at once! or else... (*o* otherwise...) ‖ *lo domandò a uno sì e a uno —*, (*alternativamente*) he asked every second person (*o* every other one) ‖ *saranno sì e — quindici*, they will be about fifteen ‖ *dir di —*, to say no: *non sa dir di — a nessuno*, he can't say no to anyone ‖ *far cenno di —*, *far di — col capo*, to shake one's head ‖ *s.m.* **no** (*pl.* **noes**); (*rifiuto*) refusal: *i —*, (*voti negativi*) the noes: *ci furono dieci sì e venti —*, there were ten ayes and twenty noes; *due — fanno un sì*, two noes make a yes; *non mi aspettavo un —*, I didn't expect a refusal; *essere per il —*, to be against it; *essere tra il sì e il —*, to be unable to make up one's mind ‖ *un bel —*, *un — chiaro e tondo*, a flat refusal.

nòbile, *ag.* **1.** noble: *un giovane di famiglia —*, a youth of noble family ‖ *nobil donna*, noblewoman; *nobil uomo*, nobleman ‖ *guardia —*, (*mil.*) corps of noblemen ‖ *padre —*, (*st. teat.*) heavy father ‖ *piano —*, (*arch.*) piano nobile ‖ *sangue —*, noble blood **2.** (*elevato, eletto*) noble, lofty: *animo —*, noble (*o* lofty) soul: *una persona di animo —*, a noble-minded person; *azione —*, noble action; *parole, sentimenti nobili*, noble words, feelings; *stile —*, lofty style **3.** (*prezioso*) noble, precious: *metallo —*, noble metal ‖ *s.m.* nobleman (*pl.* noblemen), noble: *un — spiantato*, a ruined nobleman ‖ *s.f.* noblewoman (*pl.* noblewomen).

nobilésco, *ag.* noble: *l'albagia nobilesca*, aristocratic haughtiness.

nobiliàre, *ag.* noble, nobiliary: *la casta —*, the nobility.

nobilitaménto, *s.m.* ennobling.

nobilitàre, *v.t.* **1.** to ennoble: *Carlo V nobilitò la sua famiglia*, Charles V ennobled his family (*o* raised his family to the nobility) **2.** (*elevare*) to ennoble, to dignify: *lu modestia nobilita l'animo*, modesty ennobles the soul; *non — quella casupola chiamandola castello!*, don't dignify that little house with the name of castle! ‖ *il lavoro nobilita l'uomo*, *prov.* work ennobles man ‖ **nobilitàrsi**, *v.r.* (*elevarsi*) to ennoble oneself: *volle — col sacrificio*, he wanted to ennoble himself through sacrifice.

nobilitazióne, *s.f.* ennobling.

nobilménte, *av.* nobly.

nobiltà, *s.f.* **1.** nobility: *l'alta — inglese*, the peerage; *di antica, recente —*, of old, new nobility; *la — si oppose a quel progetto*, the nobility (*o* the nobles) opposed the plan; *appartiene alla — romana*, he belongs to the Roman nobility (*o* noblesse) **2.** (*elevatezza, eccellenza*) nobility, nobleness, loftiness, magnanimity: — *d'animo*, nobleness of soul (*o* noble-mindedness); — *di sentimenti*, loftiness of feelings.

nobilúccio, *s.m.* (*spreg.*) lordling.

nobilúme, *s.m.* (*spreg.*) lordlings (*pl.*).

nòcca, *s.f.* (*anat.*) knuckle.

nòcchia, *s.f.* (*bot.*) unripe hazel-nut.

nocchière, **nocchièro**, *s.m.* (*mar.*) helmsman (*pl.* helmsmen), steersman (*pl.* steersmen).

nocchierúto, *ag.* knotty, knobby.

nòcchio, *s.m.* knot, knob.

nocchiúto, *ag.* knotty, knobby.

nòcciolo, *s.m.* **1.** stone: — *di ciliegia, di pesca*, cherry-stone, peach-stone **2.** (*punto centrale, essenziale*) heart, kernel, core; point; gist: *il — della faccenda*,

the heart of the matter; *il — di un problema*, the core (*o* kernel) of a problem; *questo è il — di ciò che disse*, this is the gist of what he said; *veniamo al —!*, let us come to the point!.

nocciuòla, *ag.* (*di colore*) hazel, hazel-brown ‖ *s.f.* (*frutto*) hazel-nut.

nocciuòlo, *s.m.* (*bot.*) hazel (-tree).

noccolúto, *ag.* (*rar.*) large-knuckled (*attributivo*).

nóce, *s.m.* **1.** (*albero*) walnut (-tree) **2.** (*legno*) walnut: *legno di — americano*, hickory; *mobile di —*, piece of furniture in walnut ‖ *s.f.* **1.** (*frutto*) walnut: *guscio di —*, walnut-shell; *fig.* (*barchetta*) cockle-shell; *olio di —*, walnut-oil; *bacchiare le noci*, to knock nuts down; *schiacciare le noci*, to crack nuts ‖ — *di cocco*, coconut ‖ — *moscata*, nutmeg ‖ — *vomica*, (*farm.*) nux vomica **2.** — *di vitello*, (*cuc.*) pope's eye **3.** — *del piede*, (*anat.*) ankle-bone.

nocèlla, *s.f.* **1.** (*anat.*) wrist-bone **2.** (*cardine del compasso*) pivot.

nocènte, *ag.* noxious; harmful; prejudicial.

nocepèsca, *s.f.* (*frutto*) nectarine.

nocepèsco, *s.m.* (*bot.*) nectarine(-tree).

nocéto, *s.m.* walnut grove.

nocévole, *ag.* (*rar.*) noxious; harmful; prejudicial.

nocivaménte, *av.* noxiously; harmfully; prejudicially.

nocívo, *ag.* noxious; harmful, hurtful; prejudicial: *ciò è — alla salute*, this is prejudicial to the health; *è — ai miei interessi seguire i tuoi consigli*, it is prejudicial to my interests to follow your advice; *non credi che potrebbe essere — per me e per te?*, don't you think it might be harmful to both of us?.

nocuménto, *s.m.* (*rar.*) damage, harm, injury.

nodèllo, *s.m.* **1.** (*anat.*) joint, knuckle **2.** (*nodo del legno*) knot.

nòdo, *s.m.* **1.** knot: — *d'amore*, love-knot; *il — del boia*, the hangman's noose; — *dell'ancora*, anchor-knot (*o* fisherman's bend); — *di boa*, (*mar.*) buoy-rope knot; — *nei capelli*, tangle in one's hair; — *piatto*, reef-knot; — *scorsoio*, slip-knot (*o* running knot *o* noose); — *semplice*, single knot; *disfare un —*, to undo (*o* to untie) a knot; *fare un —*, to make (*o* to tie) a knot: *fare un — al fazzoletto*, to tie a knot in one's handkerchief; *fare il — a una fune*, to tie a knot in a rope; *farsi il — alla cravatta*, to knot (*o* to tie) one's tie ‖ — *di tosse*, attack of coughing ‖ — *gordiano*, (*st.*) Gordian knot ‖ *avere un — alla gola*, to have a lump in one's throat ‖ *far — alla gola*, to stick in one's throat ‖ *tutti i nodi vengono al pettine*, *prov.* the day of reckoning will come **2.** (*vincolo, legame*) knot, bond, tie: — *coniugale*, wedding (*o* marriage)-knot; *i nodi dell'amicizia*, the bonds (*o* ties) of friendship **3.** (*punto cruciale, essenziale*) crux: *il — della faccenda*, the crux of the matter **4.** (*centro di collegamento*) junction, knot: — *ferroviario, stradale*, railway, road junction **5.** (*vortice*) vortex (*pl.* vortices, vortexes): — *di acqua, di vento*, vortex of water, of wind **6.**(*del legno*) knot, knurl **7.**(*teat.*) (*intreccio*) plot: *il — di una commedia*, the plot of a play **8.** (*mar.*) knot: *quella nave fa venti nodi*, that ship does twenty knots **9.** (*astr.*) node: — *ascendente, discendente*, ascending, descending node.

nodosità, *s.f.* knottiness.

nodóso, *ag.* knotty.

nòdulo, *s.m.* nodule.

Noè, *no.pr.m.* (*Bibbia*) Noah ‖ *arca di —*, Noah's ark.

Noèmi, *no.pr.f.* Naomi.

nói, *pron. pers. m.f.* 1ª *persona pl.* **1.** *sogg.* we: *dobbiamo andarci —?*, shall we go there?; *siamo stati — a chiamarlo*, we were the ones who called him (*o fam.* it was us who called him); *veniamo anche —*, we are coming too ‖ — *stessi, proprio —*, we ourselves, we... ourselves: — *stessi lo dicemmo*, we ourselves said so; *lo facemmo proprio —*, we did it ourselves ‖ *beati —!*, lucky us! ‖ *altri italiani siamo fatti così*, we Italians are like that ‖ *quando — siamo in punto di morte...*, (*con significato impersonale*) when one is on the brink of death || *siamo —!*, it's we! (*o fam.* it's us!) **2.** (*come pred. nominale*): *non siamo, non sembriamo più —*, we are no longer, we no longer seem our former selves **3.** *obliquo e oggetto* us: *parla sempre di —*, he always speaks about us; *venite con —*, come with us || *da — queste cose non si fanno,* (*nel nostro paese*) where we come from this is not done; (*nella nostra famiglia*) in our family this is not done || *loda proprio —*, we are the ones he is praising (*o fam.* it's us he is praising) || *non dobbiamo ingannare — stessi*, we must not deceive ourselves || *veniamo a noi!*, let's come back to our own subject! **4.** *pl. di maestà* we.

nòia, *s.f.* **1.** (*tedio*) boredom, tedium, ennui: *la — di una vita monotona*, the tedium of a monotonous life; *sbadigliare di —*, to yawn with boredom || *che —!*, what a bore! || *leggere mi è venuto a —*, I've got bored with reading || *ammazzare, vincere la —*, to kill (*o* to relieve) the boredom: *andrò al cinema tanto per ammazzare la —*, I'll go to the cinema just to relieve the boredom; *cercare di vincere la — di un lungo viaggio*, to try to kill the boredom of a long journey || *avere a — ql.co.*, to be fed up with sthg. || *morire di —*, to die of boredom: *questo libro mi fa morire di —*, this book bores me stiff (*o* bores me to death) || *prendere a — ql.cu.*, to be sick of s.o. || *ripetere ql.co. fino alla —*, to repeat sthg. ad nauseam **2.** (*fastidio*) annoyance; worry, nuisance; trouble: *le noie della vita*, the troubles of life; *luce che dà —*, irritating light; *ebbe delle noie per la sua attività politica*, he had a lot of worries on account of his political activity; *fare la coda è una tale —!*, queueing up is such a nuisance!; *non dargli —!*, don't trouble him!; *ti do —?*, am I disturbing you? || *che —!*, what a nuisance!.

noiàltri, noiàltre, *pron.pers.* 1ª *persona pl.* we.

noiàre, (*rar.*) *per* **annoiàre.**

noiosaménte, *av.* **1.** tediously, tiresomely **2.** (*molestamente*) annoyingly.

noiosità, *s.f.* **1.** boredom **2.** (*molestia*) annoyance.

noióso, *ag.* **1.** boring, tedious; tiresome: *un libro —*, a boring (*o* tedious) book; *una persona noiosa*, a tiresome (*o* boring) person **2.** (*molesto*) annoying, worrying || *s.m.* bore, boring person.

noisette, *ag.* hazel (*attributivo*); nut-brown.

noleggiaménto, *s.m.* hiring; (*mar.*) chartering.

noleggiànte, *s.m.* (*mar.*) charterer.

noleggiàre, *v.t.* to hire; (*mar.*) to charter, to freight: *si noleggiano biciclette*, bicycles for hire; *— una nave per intero*, to charter the whole of a ship.

noleggiatóre, *s.m.*, **noleggiatríce,** *s.f.* hirer; (*mar.*) charterer, freighter.

noléggio, *s.m.* **1.** (*il noleggiare*) hire; (*mar.*) charter, freight: *— di un film*, renting of a film; *contratto di —*, (*mar.*) charter party; *vettura da —*, car for hire || *legge — e prestito*, (*legge americana promuovente gli aiuti agli Alleati 1941*) Lend-Lease Act **2.** (*prezzo per il noleggio*) hire, rental: *quant'è il — di questa carrozza?*, how much does it cost to hire this coach? **3.** (*luogo in cui si dà a nolo*) place of hire.

nolènte, *ag.* unwilling: *volente o —*, willy-nilly.

nòlo, *s.m.* hire; (*mar.*) freight: *costo, assicurazione e —*, cost, insurance and freight (*abbr.* c.i.f.); *dare a —*, to hire (out); *prendere a —*, to hire.

nòmade, *ag.* nomadic, nomad: *popoli nomadi*, nomadic peoples; *vita —*, nomadic life || *s.c.* nomad.

nomadísmo, *s.m.* nomadism.

nomàre, *v.t.* (*letter.*) to name.

nóme, *s.m.* **1.** name: *— di battesimo*, Christian name (*o* first name); *— di famiglia*, family name (*o* surname); *— e cognome*, Christian name and surname (*o* full name); *senza —*, nameless; *egli ha — Giovanni*, he is called John (*o* his name is John); *le hanno dato — Maria*, they have called her Mary; *portare il — di qlcu.*, to be named (*o* called) after s.o.; *viaggiare sotto falso —*, to travel under an alias (*o* under a false name *o* incognito) || *— di battaglia*,

nom de guerre; (*di attore*) stage-name; (*di scrittore*) pen-name (*o* nom de plume) || *a — di*, in the name of (*o* on behalf of): *parlo a — mio e del Signor Smith*, I am speaking on behalf of Mr. Smith and myself || *di —*, by name; (*nominalmente*) in name: *di — e di fatto*, in name and in fact; *di — Maria*, Mary by name (*o* by name Mary *o* by the name of Mary); *conoscere qlcu. di —*, to know s.o. by name; *essere padrone solo di —*, to be master in name only || *in — di*, in the name of: *in — della legge*, in the name of the law; *in — di Dio*, in God's name || *per —*, by name: *chiamare qlcu. per —*, to call s.o. by name || *sotto il — di*, under the name of: *essere conosciuto sotto il — di*, to go by the name of || *chiamare le cose col loro —*, to call a spade a spade **2.** (*fama, reputazione*) name, reputation; renown: *ha — di essere avaro*, he has the reputation of being mean (*o* he has a name for meanness); *ha un buon — come chirurgo*, he has a high reputation as a surgeon; *avere, godere di un buon — come avvocato*, to have a good name as a lawyer; *farsi un —*, to make a name for oneself (*o* to make one's name); *macchiare il proprio buon —*, to spoil one's good name **3.** (*persona illustre*) name, celebrity, great man: *i grandi nomi del passato*, the great names of the past **4.** (*soprannome*) nickname: *gli fu dato il — di Ciccione*, he was nicknamed Fatty **5.** (*gram.*) noun, substantive: *— proprio, comune, collettivo*, proper, common, collective noun.

nomèa, *s.f.* notoriety: *ha una — di ladro*, he is a notorious thief.

nomenclatóre, *s.m.* **1.** nomenclator **2.** (*glossario di nomi*) glossary of names.

nomenclatúra, *s.f.* nomenclature.

nomígnolo, *s.m.* nickname, pet name.

nòmina, *s.f.* appointment: *decreto di —*, (*dir.*) decree of appointment; *ottenere la — a direttore*, to be appointed director.

nominàbile, *ag.* mentionable, namable.

nominàle, *ag.* **1.** nominal: *appello —*, roll-call; *lista —*, nominal list **2.** (*non effettivo*) nominal: *un incarico puramente —*, a purely nominal appointment; *valore —*, (*comm.*) nominal value (*o* face value) **3.** (*gram.*) nominal.

nominalísmo, *s.m.* (*st. fil.*) nominalism.

nominalísta, *s.m.* (*st. fil.*) nominalist.

nominalménte, *av.* nominally.

nominànza, *s.f.* (*rar.*) renown.

nominàre, *v.t.* **1.** to name, to call: *lo nominarono Giovanni*, they named (*o* called) him John **2.** (*menzionare*) to name, to mention: *certe cose non si nominano fra le persone educate*, there are things which are not mentioned in polite society; *non l'ho mai sentito —*, I have never heard of it; *non l'ho neppure nominato*, I haven't even mentioned him || *non — il nome di Dio invano*, thou shalt not take the name of the Lord thy God in vain **3.** (*eleggere*) to appoint, to designate: *chi è stato nominato per questo ufficio vacante?*, who has been appointed to fill this vacant office?; *lo hanno nominato ambasciatore*, he has been appointed ambassador || **nominàrsi,** *v.r.* (*rar.*) to be called.

nominataménte, *av.* by name.

nominatività, *s.f.* (*comm.*) state of being registered.

nominatívo, *ag.* **1.** (*gram.*) nominative: *caso —*, nominative case **2.** (*comm.*) registered: *azione nominativa*, registered share; *polizza nominativa*, named (*o* special) policy; *titoli nominativi*, (*pacchetto azionario*) registered stock; *titolo —*, registered instrument; *rendere nominativa un'obbligazione*, to register a bond || *s.m.* **1.** (*gram.*) nominative **2.** (*nome*) name: *lista dei nominativi*, list of names.

non, *av.* **1.** not: *— dirlo*, do not (*o* don't) say that; *— era stanco*, he was not (*o* wasn't) tired; *— è vecchio*, he is not (*o* isn't) old; *— ho denaro*, I have not (*o* I haven't) any money (*o* I have no money); *— ho visto nessuno*, I haven't seen anybody (*o* I have seen nobody); *— ho visto nulla*, I have not seen anything (o I have seen nothing); — *io, ma tu l'hai detto*, you said so, I didn't (o not me); — *può, potè venire*, he cannot (o can't), he could not (o couldn't) come; — *venne nessuno*, nobody came; *è meglio — andare*, it's better not to go || — *appena*, as soon as: — *appena lo vide, gli corse incontro*, as soon as she saw him, she ran towards him || — ... *mai*, never: — *l'ho mai visto*, I have never seen him; — *viene mai qui*, he never comes here || — *oltre*, (*distanza*) no farther than (o not any farther than o not beyond); (*tempo*) not later (o no later) than: — *oltre il 15 di questo mese*, not (o no) later than the 15th of this month; *questo treno — va oltre Roma*, this train does not go any farther than (o goes no farther than) Rome || — *più*, (*quantità*) no more (o not any more); (*tempo*) no longer (o not any longer): — *c'è più pane*, there is no more (o not any more) bread; — *è più qui*, he is no longer here (o he is not here any longer); — *è più*, (*è morto*) he is no more (o he has passed away) || — *più tardi*, no later (o not later) || — *c'è di che*, not at all (o don't mention it o amer. you are welcome) || — *che ne sia contento, ma non si può farne a meno*, not that I am pleased about it, but it can't be helped || *un — so che, un certo — so che*, a je ne sais quoi (o an indefinable something) || *dottore o — dottore, è un ignorante*, doctor or not, he is an ignoramus || *in men che — si dica*, in less time than it takes to tell (o before you could say Jack Robinson) || *poco mancò che, ci mancò poco che — rimanesse ucciso*, he was all but killed || *quanto — ho fatto per quel ragazzo!*, what didn't I do for that boy! || *se — fosse per me...*, but for me... **2.** (*in parole composte*) **non:** — *belligeranza*, non-belligerancy; — *compromettente*, non-committal; — *conformista*, nonconformist; — *intervento*, non-intervention || *gli abbienti e i — abbienti*, the haves and the have-nots || *l'essere e il — essere*, (*fil.*) being and not being; *l'io e il — io*, (*fil.*) the ego and the non-ego (o self and not self).

nòna, *s.f.* **1.** (*eccl.*) Nones (*pl.*) **2.** (*mus.*) ninth.

nonagenària, *s.f.* nonagenarian.

nonagenàrio, *ag.* ninety years old (*predicativo*); ninety-year-old (*attributivo*); nonagenarian: *il mio nonno è —*, my grand-father is ninety years old || *s.m.* nonagenarian.

nonagèsimo, *ag. num. ord. s.m.* ninetieth.

nonché, *cong.* **1.** (*tanto meno*) let alone: *non arriverei mai a scrivere una tale parola*, — *la pronunzierei in presenza di una signora*, I wouldn't even write such a word, let alone say it in front of a lady **2.** (*e inoltre*) as well as: *è stupido —cattivo*, he is wicked as well as stupid; *venne Maria — Lucia*, Lucy came as well as Mary.

noncurànte, *ag.* careless, heedless: — *del pericolo*, heedless of danger.

noncurànza, *s.f.* carelessness, heedlessness.

nondiméno, *cong.* **nevertheless, still, yet; however, all the same; for all that:** *ho molto da fare*, — *verrò*, I have got a lot to do, but I'll come all the same; *non mi piace*, — *lo devo mangiare talvolta*, I don't like it, nevertheless I have to eat it sometimes; *sembra onesto*, — *non mi fido di lui*, he seems honest, (but) yet I don't trust him.

nòne, *s.f.pl.* (*nel calendario romano*) Nones.

nònio, *s.m.* nonius.

nònna, *s.f.* **1.** grandmother; (*fam.*) grandma, grand-mam(m)a; (*dim. affettuoso*) granny, gran **2.** (*vecchietta*) granny: *come va, —, nonnina?*, how are you, granny?.

nònno, *s.m.* **1.** grandfather; (*fam.*) grandpa(pa); (*dim. affettuoso*) gran(d)-dad: — *materno, paterno*, maternal, paternal grandfather; *i miei nonni*, my grandparents **2.** *pl.* (*antenati*) ancestors, forefathers **3.** (*vecchietto*) grandfather.

nonnùlla, *s.m.* trifle, bagatelle: *si adombra per un* —, he takes offence at a trifle.

nòno, *ag. num. ord. s.m.* ninth.

nonostànte, *prep.* **notwithstanding, in spite of, for all:** — *questo*, notwithstanding this; — *i suoi difetti*

è una brava persona, in spite of (o for all) his faults, he is a good chap || **nonostànte (che),** *cong.* **though, although:** — *sia molto povero egli è felice*, although he is very poor, he is happy; — *siamo parenti, non l'ho mai visto*, though we are relations, I have never seen him.

nonpertànto, *V.* **nondiméno.**

nonplusúltra, non plus ultra, *s.m.* acme, height, ne plus ultra: *il — della stupidità*, the acme of stupidity; *questo è il —*, this is the best that money can buy.

nonsènso, *s.m.* nonsense, absurdity: *ciò che dici è un —*, what you say is nonsense.

nontiscordardimé, *s.m.* (*bot.*) forget-me-not.

Nòra, *no.pr.f.* dim. di **Eleonòra.**

norcíno, *s.m.* **1.** native of Norcia **2.** (*chi lavora carni di maiale*) pork-butcher **3.** (*spreg.*) (*cattivo chirurgo*) butcher.

nòrd, *s.m.* (*geog.*) north: *casa esposta a —*, house looking (o facing) north (o with a northern aspect); *ho viaggiato a lungo nel — dell'Europa*, I have travelled a lot in the north of Europe (o in North Europe); *la Scozia è situata a — dell'Inghilterra*, Scotland lies to the north of England; *venire dal —*, to come from the north || — *est*, — *ovest*, north-east, north-west || *l'America del Nord*, North America; *il Capo Nord*, the North Cape; *il Mare del Nord*, the North Sea; *il Polo Nord*, the North Pole || *del —*, northern; north (*attributivo*): *abitanti del —*, northerners; *vento del —*, north wind || *verso —*, northward (*ag.*); northwards (*av.*).

nòrdico, *ag.* **1.** northern: *clima —*, northern climate; *città nordica, paese —*, northern town, country **2.** (*dell'Europa settentrionale*) Nordic: *lingua, razza nordica*, Nordic language, race || *s.m.* **1.** Northerner **2.** (*dell'Europa settentrionale*) Nordic.

nordísta, *ag.s.m.* (*st. amer.*) Federal.

nòria, *s.f.* noria, water-wheel.

Norimbèrga, *no.pr.f.* (*geog.*) Nuremberg.

nòrma¹, *s.f.* **1.** (*regola*) rule, norm, standard; (*principio*) principle: *una — d'etichetta*, a rule of etiquette; *le buone norme dell'educazione*, the rules (o principles) of good education; *attenersi a una —*, to obey (o to follow) a rule; *dettar le norme*, to set the standards; *prendere, avere a — qlcu.*, to follow s.o.'s example; *procedere secondo le norme*, to act according to the rules; *seguire le norme*, to observe the rules; *trasgredire le norme*, to break the rules || *di —*, as a rule || *per vostra —*, for your guidance **2.** (*avvertenza, istruzione*) instruction, direction; (*regolamento*) regulation: *norme per l'uso*, instructions (o directions) for use || *le norme vigenti*, the regulations in force || *a — di legge*, according to law.

Nòrma², *no.pr.f.* Norma.

normàle, *ag.* **1.** normal; usual; regular: *polso —*, regular pulse; *temperatura —*, normal temperature; *è nel suo stato —*, he is in his usual health || *scuola —*, teachers' training college **2.** (*che dà una norma*) standard (*attributivo*): *dimensione —*, standard dimension || *s.m.* normal: *al disopra, disotto del —*, above, below normal || *s.f.* (*geom.*) normal, perpendicular.

normalità, *s.f.* normality.

normalizzàre, *v.t.* to normalize.

normalménte, *av.* normally; usually, generally.

Normandía, *no.pr.f.* (*geog.*) Normandy.

normànno, *ag.s.m.* Norman: *anglo- —*, (*st.*) Anglo-Norman.

nòrne, *s.f.pl.* (*mit. scandinava*) Norns.

norvegése, *ag.s.c.* Norwegian || *s.m.* (*lingua*) Norwegian.

Norvègia, *no.pr.f.* (*geog.*) Norway.

nosocòmio, *s.m.* hospital.

nosografía, *s.f.* nosography.

nosogràfico, *ag.* nosographic(al).

nosología, *s.f.* nosology.

nosològico, *ag.* nosological.

nossignóra, *av.* no, Madam.

nossignóre, *av.* no, Sir.

nostalgía, *s.f.* **1.** home-sickness, nostalgia: *avere,* *sentire la — della propria casa*, to be homesick (*o* to feel nostalgia for one's home); *soffrire la — della propria famiglia, patria*, to be homesick (*o* to feel nostalgia) for one's family, one's native land **2.** (*rimpianto*) yearning (for sthg.); longing (for sthg.): *ho — dei miei amici*, I miss my friends; *ha — dei vecchi tempi*, he yearns for (*o* he has a longing for) the old days.

nostàlgico, *ag.* homesick, nostalgic.

nostràle, *ag.* **1.** home (*attributivo*); national; local, regional: *prodotti nostrali*, home products; *vino —*, national (*o* local) wine ‖ *cucina alla —*, national (*o* regional) cooking **2.** *vento —*, (*tramontana*) north wind.

nostràno, *V.* **nostràle 1.**

nòstro, *ag. poss.* **1. our;** (*nostro proprio*) **our own:** *un — buon amico*, a good friend of ours; *il — giardino*, our garden; *un — parente*, one of our relatives (*o* a relative of ours); *alcuni nostri amici*, some of our friends (*o* some friends of ours); *in questo — paese*, in this country of ours; *ci ha insultato in casa nostra*, he has insulted us in our own house; *vorremmo avere una casa nostra*, we would like to have a house of our own ‖ *in vece nostra*, instead of us (*o* in our place *o* in our stead) ‖ *fatelo per amor —*, do it for love of us (*o* for our sake) **2.** (*come pred. nominale*) **ours:** *questo giardino è —*, this garden is ours (*o* belongs to us) **3.** *pl. di maestà* **our 4.** (*in espressioni ellittiche*): *la nostra* (*lettera*) *del 10 corr.*, our letter of the 10th inst.; *anche noi abbiamo le nostre* (*disgrazie*), we have got our own worries; *è sempre dalla nostra* (*parte*), he is always on our side; *stiamo sulla nostra*, we keep ourselves to ourselves ‖ *pron. poss.* **ours:** *i loro bambini e i nostri sono amici*, their children and ours are friends; *la vostra casa è più piccola della nostra*, your house is smaller than ours ‖ *s.m.* **1.:** *campiamo del —*, we live on our own income; *dovete distinguere tra il vostro e il —*, you must distinguish between what is yours and what is ours; *fummo spogliati del —*, we were deprived of our property ‖ *il Nostro,* (*riferito a scrittore, artista, di cui si sta parlando*) the Author **2.** (*partitivo*): *qualcosa, niente di —*, something, nothing of our own **3.** *pl.*: *i nostri*, our family (*o* our relatives *o* fam. our folks); (*partigiani, seguaci*) our supporters; (*soldati*) our soldiers (*o* our men *o* our side): *i nostri arrivarono giusto in tempo*, our men arrived in the nick of time; *egli non è dei nostri*, (*non parteggia per noi*) he is not on our side (*o* he does not side with us); *sarai dei nostri domani sera?*, will you join us tomorrow evening?.

nostròmo, *s.m.* (*mar.*) boatswain.

nòta, *s.f.* **1.** (*segno, contrassegno*) note, mark: *note caratteristiche*, characteristic signs; *— d'infamia*, (infamous) blot **2.** (*appunto*) note: *una — di biasimo*, admonitory note; *quaderno per note*, note-book; *parlava aiutandosi con delle note*, he spoke from notes; *prendere —*, to take note: *abbiamo preso —*, (*comm.*) we have duly noted; *prendi —!*, notice!; *prender — di un ordine*, (*comm.*) to book an order; *prendere delle note su ql.co.*, to make (*o* to take) notes on sthg.; *scrivere una — di ringraziamento*, to write a note of thanks ‖ *— diplomatica*, diplomatic note ‖ *degno di —*, noteworthy: *è degno di — il fatto che...*, it is noteworthy that... ‖ *prima —*, (*comm.*) waste book **3.** (*mus.*) note: *le sette note musicali*, the seven notes of the scale; *dare la —*, to give an "A" ‖ *— obbligata*, customary phrase ‖ *le dolenti note*, doleful notes: *ora incominciano le dolenti note*, now the trouble starts ‖ *glielo ha cantato a chiare note*, he told her plainly ‖ *vi era una — di orgoglio nella sua voce*, there was a note of pride in his voice ‖ *mettere una — allegra, triste*, to bring a happy, sad note **4.** (*commento*) note: *— a piè di pagina*, footnote; *— critica*, critical note; *— del traduttore*, translator's note; *— marginale*, marginal note **5.** (*conto*) bill: *la — dell'albergo*, the hotel bill **6.** (*lista*) list: *la — dei libri*, the book-list; *la — della spesa*, the shopping list; *fare una —*, to make a list ‖ *— di accreditamento*, (*comm.*) credit note.

notabène, *s.m.* nota bene (*abbr.* N.B.).

notàbile, *ag.* notable; remarkable, considerable ‖ *s.m.* notable: *i notabili del luogo*, the notables of the place.

notabilità, *s.f.* notability, distinction.

notabilménte, *av.* notably; remarkably.

notàio, *s.m.* notary, notary public.

notàre, *v.t.* **1.** (*prendere nota di*) to note, to write down, to take note of (sthg.); to jot down: *ho notato su questo foglio quello che disse*, I have written down what he said on this paper; *il poliziotto notò il mio indirizzo*, the policeman wrote (*o* took) down my address ‖ *non ho niente contro di lui, nota bene, ma preferisco non vederlo*, I have nothing against him, mind you, but I prefer not to see him **2.** (*osservare*) to notice, to note, to take notice of (sthg.), to remark, to observe: *egli notò che avresti dovuto venire prima*, he observed (*o* remarked) that you should have come earlier; *hai notato come era pallido?*, have you noticed how pale he was (looking)? ‖ *far —*, to point out **3.** (*indicare con nota*) to mark: *noterò a margine i passi più belli*, I will mark the most beautiful passages in the margin.

notaréseo, *ag.* notarial.

notariàto, *s.m.* profession of notary: *esercitare il —*, to be a notary public.

notaríle, *ag.* notarial: *atti notarili*, notarial acts; *copia —*, certified copy; *lavora in uno studio —*, he works in a notary's office.

notàro, (*rar.*) per **notàio.**

notàto, *ag.* noted, noticed; remarked.

notazióne, *s.f.* **1.** (*segnatura*) notation **2.** (*mus.*) notation **3.** (*annotazione*) annotation.

nòtes, *s.m.* (*blocco*) notebook; (*agenda*) diary.

notévole, *ag.* **1.** (*pregevole, degno di nota*) remarkable, noteworthy, notable, noticeable: *la — bellezza del paese*, the remarkable (*o* noteworthy) beauty of the country; *un evento —*, a remarkable (*o* an important) event; *non abbiamo visto nulla di —*, we saw nothing worth talking about (*o* worthy of remark) **2.** (*considerevole, grande*) considerable: *a — distanza*, at a considerable distance; *una rendita, una spesa —*, a considerable income, expense.

notevolménte, *av.* remarkably, considerably: *egli è — migliorato*, he is greatly improved.

notífica, *V.* **notificazióne.**

notificàre, *v.t.* **1.** (*dir.*) to report, to notify, to make known: *— una citazione a...*, to serve a summons on...; *— un furto alla polizia*, to notify the police of a theft (*o* a theft to the police); *— una nascita*, to report (*o* to notify) a birth **2.** (*render noto*) to inform: *— ql.co. a qlcu.*, to inform s.o. of sthg.

notificatóre, *ag.* notifying: *lettera notificatrice*, letter of notification ‖ *s.m.*, **notificatríce,** *s.f.* notifier.

notificazióne, *s.f.* **1.** notification: *dare — di una nascita*, to notify a birth; *ricevere — di ql.co.*, to be notified of sthg. **2.** (*manifesto, avviso*) notice: *affiggere una —*, to affix (*o* to stick up) a notice.

notízia, *s.f.* **1.** news (*pl. con costruzione sing.*); piece of news (*solo sing.*); (*poet. letter.*) tidings (*pl.*): *che notizie?*, what is the news?; *le ultime notizie*, the last news; (*le più recenti*) the latest news; *dammi tue notizie ogni giorno*, let me hear from you every day; *la — della morte di suo fratello fu un grande dolore per lui*, the news of his brother's death was a great sorrow to him; *non abbiamo sue notizie da due mesi*, we've had no news (*o* we haven't heard) from him for two months; *le notizie non sono cattive*, the news is not bad; *questa è una — interessante*, this is an interesting piece of news ‖ *ultime notizie del giornale radio*, the final news ‖ *corre — che...*, there is a rumour that... **2.** (*informazione*) information (*solo sing.*); (*dato*) note: *notizie biografiche*, biographical notes; *datemi alcune notizie su ciò*, give me some information about it; *ho raccolto alcune notizie storiche*, I have gathered some historical information; *dar* — *di ql.co a qlcu.*, to inform s.o. of sthg.

notiziàrio, *s.m.* news (*pl. con costruzione sing.*): — *commerciale*, commercial newsletter; — *del mattino*, morning news; — *politico, economico*, politic, economic news ǁ — *ambulante*, (*scherz.*) walking newspaper.

nòto[1], *ag.* well-known: *un* — *scrittore*, a well-known writer; *un viso* —, a familiar face; *è* — *a tutti che...*, everybody knows (*o* it is common knowledge) that...; *questo non mi era* —, I did not know that; *render* — *ql.co. a qlcu.*, to make sthg. known to s.o. ǁ *s.m.*: *il* — *e l'ignoto*, the known and the unknown.

nòto[2], *s.m.* (*vento del sud, austro*) Notus.

notomizzàre, *V.* **anatomizzàre**.

notoriaménte, *av.* notoriously.

notorietà, *s.f.* notoriety.

notòrio, *ag.* well-known; (*specialmente in senso sfavorevole*) notorious: *un* — *criminale*, a notorious criminal; *una persona notoria per la sua sfortuna*, a person well-known for his bad luck.

nottambulísmo, *s.m.* night-bird's habits (*pl.*).

nottàmbulo, *ag.* noctambulous ǁ *s.m.* **1.** night-bird **2.** (*sonnambulo*) noctambulist, sleep-walker.

nottàta, *s.f.* night, period of a night.

nòtte, *s.f.* night: *una* — *di luna*,| a moonlit night; *una* — *stellata*, a starry night; *la* — *sul mercoledì*, Tuesday night; *al cader, al calar, sul far della* —, at nightfall; *a* — *fatta, inoltrata, nel cuore della* —, at dead of night; *camicia da* —, (*da donna*) night-gown (*o* nightdress); (*da uomo*) night-shirt; *comodino da* —, bed-side table; *giorno e* —, night and day; *non ho chiuso occhio tutta* —, I did not close my eyes (*o* I didn't sleep a wink) all night; *non passerà la* —, *fig.* he won't see this night out (*o* he won't last the night); *non posso lavorare di* —, I cannot work at night; *non posso passare la* — *qui*, I cannot stay here overnight; *verremo di* —, we shall come by night; *passare una* — *di baldoria*, to make a night of it ǁ — *bianca*, sleepless night ǁ *la* — *dell'ignoranza*, benighted ignorance ǁ *la* — *di Natale*, Christmas Night ǁ *buona* —!, good-night!; (*iron.*) that's that: *l'ho mandato via e buona* —, I have sent him away and that is that; *dare la buona* —, to say (*o* to bid) good-night ǁ *col favore della* —, under cover of darkness ǁ « *Le Mille e una Notte* », (*lett.*) " The Arabian Nights " (*o* " Thousand and One Nights "): *cose da mille e una* —, something out of the Arabian Nights ǁ *peggio che andar di* —!, worse than ever! ǁ *questo si perde nella* — *dei tempi*, this is lost in the mists of time ǁ *correrci quanto dal giorno alla* —, to be as different as chalk and cheese ǁ *scambiare il giorno per la* —, to turn night into day ǁ *la* — *è fatta per dormire*, the night is made for sleep ǁ *la* — *porta consiglio*, *prov.* night (that) knits up the ravelled sleeve of care.

nottetèmpo, *av.* by night, in the night-time.

nottilúca, *s.f.* (*biol.*) noctiluca.

nottìvago, *ag.* (*letter.*) noctivagous, noctivagant.

nòttola, *s.f.* **1.** (*pipistrello*) noctule **2.** (*arc.*) (*civetta*) owl ǁ *portar nottole ad Atene*, to carry coals to Newcastle **3.** (*grosso saliscendi*) latch.

nottolíno, *s.m.* **1.** (*piccolo saliscendi*) door-latch **2.** (*mec.*) pawl, pallet: — *di arresto*, ratchet (*o* pawl); — *di inversione*, reverse dog.

nòttua, *s.f.* (*entom.*) noctuid.

nottúrno, *ag.* night (*attributivo*); evening (*attributivo*); nightly; nocturnal: *campanello* —, night-bell; *guardiano* —, night-watchman; *locale* —, night-club; *la quiete notturna*, the quiet of the night; *spettacolo* —, evening-performance; *uccello* —, night-bird; *volo* —, night flight ǁ *s.m.* **1.** (*eccl.*) nocturn **2.** (*mus.*) nocturne.

noúmeno, *s.m.* (*fil.*) noumenon (*pl.* noumena).

nòva, *s.f.* (*astr.*) nova (*pl.* novae).

novàle, *s.f.* (*agr.*) newly-ploughed field.

novaménte, *av.* again.

novànta, *ag. num. card. s.m.* ninety.

novantènne, *ag.* ninety years old (*predicativo*); ninety-year-old (*attributivo*) ǁ *s.m.* ninety-year-old man ǁ *s.f.* ninety-year-old woman.

novantèsimo, *ag. num. ord. s.m.* ninetieth.

novantína, *s.f.* about ninety, some ninety: *una* — *di libri*, about (*o* some) ninety books; *essere sulla* —, to be about ninety (years old).

novatóre, *ag.* innovating ǁ *s.m.*, **novatríce**, *s.f.* innovator.

novazióne, *s.f.* novation.

nòve, *ag. num. card. s.m.* nine.

novecentésco, *ag.* twentieth-century (*attributivo*): *stile* —, twentieth-century style.

novecentísmo, *s.m.* modernism.

novecentísta, *ag.* contemporary ǁ *s.c.* modernist.

novecènto, *ag.* **1.** *num. card.* nine hundred **2.** (*del secolo ventesimo*) twentieth-century (*attributivo*); (*moderno*) modern, contemporary: *un mobile* —, a modern piece of furniture; *stile* —, twentieth-century (*o* modern) style ǁ *s.m.* nine hundred ǁ *il Novecento*, the twentieth century: *il Novecento ha visto il progresso della tecnica*, the twentieth century has seen the advance of technology.

novèlla, *s.f.* **1.** short story, tale: — *romantica*, romantic tale; *scrittore di novelle*, short story writer; *ascoltammo attentamente la sua* —, we listened to his tale attentively; *il Decamerone è una raccolta di cento novelle*, the Decameron is a collection of a hundred tales **2.** *V.* **notízia 1.**.

novellaménte, *av.* (*letter.*) anew, afresh, again.

novellàre, *v.i.* to tell stories, to tell tales.

novellatóre, *s.m.*, **novellatríce**, *s.f.* **1.** story-teller **2.** (*chi scrive novelle*) short story writer.

Novèlle (le), *s.f.pl.* (*leggi di Giustiniano*) the Novellae.

novellière, *s.m.* short story writer.

novellíno, *ag.* inexperienced, raw: *un ufficiale* —, an inexperienced (*o* a raw) officer; *è un medico* —, he is a raw doctor ǁ *s.m.* inexperienced person, beginner; (*fam.*) greenhorn; (*sl. amer.*) tenderfoot (*pl.* tenderfoots, tenderfeet): *sei ancora un* —!, you are still a greenhorn!.

novellísta, *s.c.* short story writer.

novellística, *s.f.* short-story writing.

novèllo, *ag.* **1.** (*nato da poco*) new; spring (*attributivo*): *erba novella*, spring grass; *patate novelle*, new potatoes; *pollo* —, spring chicken ǁ *età novella*, tender age ǁ *la stagione novella*, spring **2.** (*recente*) new: *sacerdote* —, new priest; *sposa novella*, new bride; *sposi novelli*, newly-weds (*o* newly-married couple) ǁ *Messa novella*, (*eccl.*) First Mass **3.** (*nuovo, secondo*) second: *un* — *Michelangelo*, a second Michelangelo.

novèmbre, *s.m.* November ǁ *trenta giorni ha* — *con april, giugno e settembre, di ventotto ve n'è uno, tutti gli altri ne han trentuno*, thirty days hath September, April, June and November; all the rest have thirty-one, excepting February alone, which hath but twenty-eight days clear, and twenty-nine in each leap-year.

novèna, *s.f.* (*eccl.*) novena (*pl.* novenae).

novenàrio, *ag.* (*poes.*) of nine syllables ǁ *s.m.* (*poes.*) line of nine syllables.

novendiàle, *ag.* novendial; nine-day (*attributivo*).

novendiàli, *s.m.pl.* **1.** (*cerimonia pagana*) novendial (*sing.*) **2.** (*eccl.*) Pope's novena (*sing.*).

novennàle, *ag.* novennial; (*che dura nove anni*) lasting nine years; nine-year (*attributivo*) ǁ *buono* — (*finanza*), nine-year treasury bond.

novènne, *ag.* nine years old (*predicativo*); nine-year-old (*attributivo*).

novènnio, *s.m.* nine-year period.

noveràre, *V.* **annoveràre**.

nòvero, *s.m.* **1.** (*numero*) number: *mettere nel* — *di ql.co.*, to number (*o* to count) among sthg. **2.** (*classe, categoria*) class, category.

novilúnio, *s.m.* new moon.

novíssimi, (i), *s.m.pl.* (*teol.*) the Four Last Things (death, judgement, heaven, hell).

novíssimo, *ag.* 1. (*nuovo di zecca*) brand-new 2. (*ultimo*) last ‖ *il — bando*, (*teol.*) The Last Judgement.

novità, *s.f.* 1. newness, novelty; (*originalità*) originality: *la — di una situazione*, the novelty of a situation; *quelle poesie hanno fatto gran rumore per la — della forma*, those poems caused a great stir on account of the originality of their form; *questi mobili sono notevoli per la — della forma*, this furniture is remarkable for the novelty (*o* originality) of its design 2. (*cosa nuova*) novelty; (*innovazione*) innovation, change: *le — della moda*, the latest fashions; *abbiamo introdotto delle —*, we introduced some changes; *non ero stato informato della —*, I had not been informed of the change (*o* innovation); *per loro fu una —*, it was a new experience for them; *quel negozio ha parecchie —*, that shop has several novelties; *i vecchi odiano le —*, old people hate change; *tenersi al corrente delle —*, to keep up with new ideas ‖ *— libraria*, new book; *— teatrale*, new play 3. (*notizia*) news (*pl. con costruzione sing.*): *le — del giorno*, the news of the day; *che — vi sono?*, what is the news?.

novízia, *s.f.* 1. (*eccl.*) novice 2. (*principiante*) novice, beginner, apprentice.

noviziàto, *s.m.* 1. (*eccl.*) novitiate, noviciate 2. (*tirocinio*) novitiate, noviciate, apprenticeship.

novízio, *s.m.* 1. (*eccl.*) novice 2. (*principiante*) novice, beginner, apprentice.

nozióne, *s.f.* notion, idea: *nozioni di grammatica*, elements of grammar; *ha delle elementari nozioni di latino*, he has a smattering of (*o* some idea of) Latin; *le mie nozioni di inglese sono molto scarse*, my knowldege of English is very poor; *non ha la — del bene e del male*, he has no sense of good and evil; *perdere la — del tempo*, to lose all sense (*o* idea) of time.

nòzze, *s.f.pl.* wedding (*sing.*), marriage (*sing.*); nuptials: *— d'argento*, silver wedding; *— di diamante*, diamond-wedding; *— d'oro*, golden wedding; *annunzi di —*, (*nei giornali*) wedding announcements; *partecipazione di —*, wedding-card; *pranzo di —*, wedding-breakfast; *regalo di —*, wedding-present; *viaggio di —*, honeymoon; *mi dispiace di non poter venire alle tue —*, I am sorry not to be able to come to your wedding; *passare a seconde —*, to marry for the second time ‖ *fare le — coi fichi secchi, coi funghi*, to do sthg. on a shoestring.

nuance, *s.f.* nuance.

núbe, *s.f.* cloud (anche *fig.*): *una — di polvere*, a cloud of dust; *felicità senza nubi*, unalloyed happiness; *masse di nubi*, masses of clouds; *una — di tristezza gli oscurò il volto*, his face clouded with sadness; *la nostra amicizia fu sempre senza nubi*, no shadow ever passed across our friendship; *sono nubi passeggere*, they are only passing clouds (anche *fig.*).

Núbia, *no.pr.f.* (*geog.*) Nubia.

nubiàno, *ag.s.m.* Nubian ‖ **nubiàna**, *s.f.* Nubian.

nubifràgio, *s.m.* down-pour: *il — ha danneggiato le piante del giardino*, the down-pour has damaged the plants in the garden.

núbile, *ag.* unmarried, single: *stato —*, unmarried state; *rimanere —*, to remain unmarried (*o* single) ‖ *età —*, marriageable age ‖ *s.f.* unmarried woman, single woman; (*su documenti*) spinster.

núca, *s.f.* nape of the neck; *lo colpì alla —*, it hit him in the nape (*o* back) of the neck.

Núccia, *no.pr.f.dim.* di **Giuseppína**.

nucleàre, *ag.* nuclear: *energia —*, nuclear energy (*o* power); *fisica —*, nuclear physics; *reazione —*, (*fis. atomica*) nuclear reaction.

nucleifórme, *ag.* nucleiform.

nucleína, *s.f.* (*chim. biol.*) nuclein.

núcleo, *s.m.* 1. nucleus (*pl.* nuclei): *— atomico* (*fis.*), atomic nucleus; *— composto*, (*fis.*) compound nucleus; *— dell'acciaio*, steel core; *il — del seme*, the nucleus of the seed; *il — di una cometa*, the nucleus of a comet; *— magnetico*, (*fis.*) magnet core 2. (*gruppo*) group: *il — familiare*, the family; *il nostro club fu fondato da un piccolo — di entusiasti*, our club was founded by a small group of enthusiasts 3. (*prima origine, inizio*) nucleus (*pl.* nuclei), beginnings (*pl.*): *i soldi che ereditò da suo padre costituirono il — della sua fortuna*, the money he inherited from his father formed the nucleus of his fortune.

nuclèolo, *s.m.* (*biol.*) nucleolus (*pl.* nucleoli).

nucleoplàsma, *s.m.* (*biol.*) nucleoplasm.

nudaménte, *av.* 1. nakedly 2. (*semplicemente*) plainly, simply: *riferire —*, to report plainly.

nudàre, *V.* **denudàre**.

nudísmo, *s.m.* nudism.

nudísta, *s.c.* nudist.

nudità, *s.f.* 1. nakedness; (*di una parte del corpo*) bareness ‖ *mostrare le proprie —*, to show off one's body 2. (*l'essere spoglio*) bareness 3. (*semplicità*) plainness, simplicity.

núdo, *ag.* 1. naked; (*di una parte del corpo*) bare; (*svestito*) unclothed: *a gambe nude*, bare-legged; *a piedi nudi*, bare-foot(ed); *a testa nuda*, bare-headed; *mezzo —*, half-naked ‖ *a occhio —*, with the naked eye: *visibile a occhio —*, visible to the naked eye; *vedere a occhio —*, to see with the naked eye ‖ *— come un verme*, stark-naked (*o fam.* in one's birthday suit); *— e crudo*, bluntly (*o* plainly): *gli dissi — e crudo quello che pensavo*, I told him plainly what I thought ‖ *lasciare —*, to leave bare ‖ *mettere a —*, to lay bare (*o* to expose *o* to uncover *o* to strip *o* to reveal) 2. (*privo di rivestimento, di vegetazione, ecc.*) naked, bare; (*privo di arredi*) bare: *alberi nudi*, bare trees; *cavallo —*, (*senza sella*) barebacked horse; *una collina nuda*, a bare (*o* naked) hillside; *pareti nude*, bare walls; *spada, ferro —*, naked sword ‖ *dormire sulla nuda terra*, to sleep on the bare ground 3. (*semplice, schietto*) naked, bare, plain: *i nudi fatti*, the bare facts; *verità nuda*, naked (*o* bare *o* plain) truth ‖ *s.m.* (*art.*) nude: *disegnare un —*, to draw a nude.

núgolo, *s.m.* cloud (anche *fig.*): *un — di insetti*, a cloud of insects; *un — di polvere*, a cloud of dust.

núlla, *V.* **niènte**.

nulladiméno, (*rar.*) per **nondiméno**.

nullàggine, *s.f.* nonentity.

nullaòsta, *s.m.* permit; (*eccl.*) nihil obstat: *— per una nave*, certificate of clearance.

nullatenènte, *ag.* without property ‖ *s.c.* person without property.

nullísmo, *s.m.* (*st. fil.*) nihilism.

nullità, *s.f.* 1. (*di cose*) nullity: *la — dei suoi argomenti*, the nullity (*o* the emptiness) of his arguments 2. (*di persone*) nonentity: *è una —*, he is a nonentity (*o* a cipher) 3. (*dir.*) (*invalidità*) invalidity, nullity: *la — di una sentenza*, the nullity of a sentence; *eccepire la — di un documento*, to appeal against the invalidity of a document.

núllo, *ag.* 1. (*dir.*) null, void: *— e non valido*, null and void: *il tribunale dichiarò — e non valido il testamento*, the Court declared the will null and void; *dichiarare — un atto*, to annul an act 2. (*di nessuna utilità*) of no use; (*di nessun valore*) of no value: *il tuo aiuto è —*, your help is of no use 3. (*nessuno, di nessun valore*) no; (*in presenza di altra negazione*) any ‖ *nulla nuova, buona nuova, prov.* no news is good news.

Núma Pompílio, *no.pr.m.* (*st.*) Numa Pompilius.

núme, *s.m.* numen, deity: *— tutelare*, tutelary deity ‖ *O numi!*, my goodness!.

númeno, *s.m.* (*fil.*) noumenon (*pl.* noumena).

numeràbile, *ag.* numerable.

numerabilità, *s.f.* numerability.

numeràle, *ag.s.m.* (*gram.*) numeral.

numeràre, *v.t.* 1. (*contare*) to count: *— ad uno ad uno*, to count one by one; *— fino a cento*, to count up to a hundred **2.** (*segnare con numero*) to number: *i posti di questo teatro sono numerati*, the seats of this theatre are numbered; — *le pagine di un libro*, to number the pages of a book **3.** (*elencare*) to enumerate, to number: — *i meriti di qlcu.*, to enumerate (o to number) s.o.'s merits.

numeràrio, *ag.* (*rar.*) numerary ‖ *s.m.* (*comm.*) (*denaro contante*) (ready) cash, ready money; (*metallico*) metallic currency, current coin: — *di cassa*, cash on hand; *scarsità di* —, shortness of ready cash.

numeratóre, *ag.* numerating ‖ *s.m.* **1.** (*chi numera*) numberer, numerator **2.** (*mat.*) numerator **3.** (*macchina per numerare*) numbering-machine.

numeratríce, *s.f.* numberer, numerator.

numerazióne, *s.f.* **1.** numbering, numeration: — *sbagliata delle pagine*, wrong numbering of the pages **2.** (*arit.*) numeration; notation: — *decimale*, decimal numeration; — *romana*, Roman notation.

numericaménte, *av.* numerically.

numèrico, *ag.* numeric(al): *serie numerica*, numerical series; *superiorità numerica*, numerical superiority.

número, *s.m.* **1.** number (*abbr.* No., *pl.* Nos.): *numeri cardinali, ordinali*, cardinal, ordinal numbers; — *categorico*, (*mec.*) part number; — *di fabbricazione del motore*, (*aut.*) engine serial-number; — *di giri*, (*mec.*) number of revolutions; — *di massa*, (*fis.*) mass number; — *di matricola*, (*mil.*) service number; — *di oro*, (*chim.*) gold number; — *di telefono*, telephone number; *il* — *di un vigile, di un facchino*, a policeman's, a porter's number; — *fisso*, (*mat.*) fixed number; — *intero*, whole number; *numeri pari, dispari*, even, odd numbers; — *primo*, (*mat.*) prime number; — *quantico*, (*fis.*) quantum number; — *razionale, irrazionale, reale*, (*mat.*) rational, irrational, real number; *numeri romani, arabici*, Roman, Arabic numerals; *senza* —, numberless; *abito al* — *cinque*, I live at No. 5; *oltrepassavano il* — *di venti*, there were more than twenty of them (o they exceeded twenty); *i partecipanti arrivano al* — *di cinquanta*, those taking part are fifty in number ‖ — *aureo*, (*astr.*) golden number ‖ — *legale*, (*dir.*) quorum ‖ — *uno*, (*fam.*) (*primo fra tutti*) first-class: *è un idiota* — *uno*, he is a first-class idiot; *era un briccone* — *uno*, he was a precious rascal ‖ *di* —, in number: *essi erano cinquanta di* —, they were fifty in number ‖ *dare i numeri* (*del lotto*), to give a tip (on the number to bet in the state lottery); *fig.* to go (o to be) off one's head; *estrarre i numeri* (*del lotto*), to draw the numbers (of the state lottery); *giocare i numeri* (*al lotto*), to put a bet on a number (in the state lottery) ‖ *vendere a* —, to sell by the piece **2.** (*di giornale, rivista*) number, issue: *datemi il* — *arretrato*, give me the back number; *nel* — *di domani troverete che...*, in tomorrow's issue you will find that... **3.** (*quantità*) number: *un gran* — *di*, a large number of (o a lot of o a great many): *un gran* — *di gente è già partito*, a large number of people have already left; *un gran* — *di libri è a mia disposizione*, a lot (o a large number) of books are at my disposal; *sapessi il* — *degli incidenti!*, what a lot of accidents there were! ‖ *far* —, to make up the number **4.** (*compagnia, gruppo*) number, circle, set: *tu non entri nel* — *di quelli fortunati*, you are not one of the lucky ones; *essere nel* — *degli eletti*, to be numbered among the elect ‖ *andare nel* — *dei più*, to join the great majority **5.** (*fam.*) (*qualità*) quality: *egli ha molti numeri*, he has many good qualities **6.** (*teat.*) number, item **7.** (*gram.*) number: *questo sostantivo è di* — *plurale*, this noun is in the plural (number) **8.** (*ritmo*) numbers (*pl.*), rhythm.

numerosaménte, *av.* numerously.

numeróso, *ag.* **1.** numerous: *assemblea numerosa*, numerous assembly; *esercito* —, numerous army **2.** (*armonioso, ritmico, di verso, metro*) numerous, rhythmical: *prosa numerosa*, rhythmical (o *rar.* numerous) prose.

Numídia, *no.pr.f.* (*geog. st.*) Numidia.

numismàtica, *s.f.* numismatics.

numismàtico, *ag.* numismatic ‖ *s.m.* numismatist.

núncio, *s.m.* (*eccl.*) nuncio.

nuncupatívo, *ag.* (*dir.*) nuncupative.

nundinàle, *ag.* nundinal.

núndine, *s.f.pl.* nundine (*sing.*).

nunziatúra, *s.f.* **1.** (*eccl.*) nunciature **2.** (*residenza del nunzio*) nuncio's residence.

núnzio, *s.m.* (*eccl.*) nuncio.

nuòcere, *v.i.* to damage (s.o., sthg.), to harm (s.o., sthg.), to hurt (s.o., sthg.), to injure (s.o., sthg.): *il bere eccessivo nuoce alla salute*, excessive drinking injures the health; *il freddo non nuocerà a questi fiori*, the cold will not damage these flowers; *la grandine ha nociuto molto al raccolto*, the hail has caused a great deal of damage to the harvest; *non nuocerà ripeterglielo*, it won't hurt to tell him again; *non volevo nuocerti*, I did not want to hurt you; *questo scandalo nuocerà molto alla sua reputazione*, this scandal will damage his reputation very much ‖ *tentar non nuoce*, *prov.* there is no harm in trying ‖ *tutto il male non viene per* —, *prov.* good can come from evil.

nuòra, *s.f.* daughter-in-law.

nuotàre, *v.i.* **1.** to swim: *nuotava sott'acqua*, he swam under water; *so* — *a rana*, a crawl, a farfalla, I can do the breast-stroke, the crawl, the butterfly-stroke; — *come un pesce*, to swim like a fish; — *controcorrente*, to swim against the stream; — *sul dorso, sul fianco*, to swim on one's back, on one's side; — *come il piombo*, (*scherz.*) to swim like a stone (o a brick) **2.** (*di cose, essere immerse in molto liquido*) to swim: *quelle patate nuotano nel burro*, those potatoes are swimming in butter **3.** *fig.* (*sguazzare*) to swim, to roll, to wallow: — *nell'abbondanza*, nell'oro, to roll (o to wallow) in money.

nuotàta, *s.f.* swim: *facciamo una* —, let's go for a swim.

nuotatóre, *s.m.*, **nuotatríce**, *s.f.* swimmer.

nuòto, *s.m.* swimming: — *a rana*, a crawl, a farfalla, breast-stroke, crawl, butterfly-stroke; *gara di* —, swimming-race: *partecipare ad una gara di* —, to swim in a race; *lezioni di* —, swimming-lessons; *sono andato a* — *fino a quell'isola*, I swam to that island; *passare un lago, un fiume a* —, to swim across a lake, a river: *far passare a* — *un cavallo attraverso un fiume*, to swim a horse across a river; *salvarsi a* —, to swim to safety: *tentare di salvarsi a* —, to swim for one's life.

nuòva, *s.f.* news (*pl. con costruzione sing*): *dare nuove di sè*, to give news of oneself ‖ *nessuna* — *buona* —, *prov.* no news is good news.

Nuòva Caledònia, *no.pr.f.* (*geog.*) New Caledonia.

Nuòva Gàlles del Sud, *no.pr.f.* (*geog.*) New South Wales.

Nuòva Guinèa, *no.pr.f.* (*geog.*) New Guinea.

Nuòva Inghiltèrra, *no.pr.f.* (*geog.*) New England: *abitante della* —, New Englander.

nuovaménte, *av.* again.

Nuòva Seòzia, *no.pr.f.* (*geog.*) Nova Scotia.

Nuòva York, *no.pr.f.* (*geog.*) New York.

Nuòva Zelànda, *no.pr.f.* (*geog.*) New Zealand.

nuòvo, *ag.* **1.** new; (*fam.*) fresh: *una nuova commedia*, a new play; *la nuova generazione*, the rising generation; *un abito da donna* —, a new dress; *l'anno* —, the new year; *argomento sempre* —, evergreen topic; *luna nuova*, new moon; *patate nuove*, new potatoes; *piacere sempre* —, pleasure that never stales; *vino* —, new wine; *è una casa di nuova costruzione*, it is a newly-built house; *prendi un foglio* — *e ricomincia*, take a fresh sheet and start again; *questa moneta è di* — *conio*, this coin is freshly minted; *« turbogetto » è una parola di* — *conio*, " turbojet " is a newly-coined word; *vorrei vedere un modello più* —, I would like to see a more up-to-date model ‖ — *fiammante*, — *di zecca*, brand-new ‖ *la nuova Milano*, the new part of Milan; *il Nuovo Mondo*, the New World ‖ *i nuovi ricchi*, the nouveaux riches ‖ *il Nuovo Testamento*, the New Testament ‖ *i nuovi venuti*, the newcomers ‖ *granata nuova spazza ben tre giorni*, *prov.* new brooms sweep clean **2.** (*altro, ulteriore*) new, fresh, further: *fino a — ordine*, till further orders; *cercherò di ottenere nuove informazioni*, I'll try to get further information; *questo è un — esempio della sua generosità*, this is a fresh example of his open-handedness; *seguì una nuova pausa*, another pause followed; *stasera comincerò un — capitolo*, I'll begin a new chapter tonight ‖ *abbiamo un — Manzoni*, we have a second Manzoni ‖ *anno —, vita nuova*, *prov.* New Year, new life **3.** (*sconosciuto*) new, unknown: *un — sentimento*, a new feeling; *questo mi giunge —*, this is new to me; *questo nome non mi è —*, this name is not new to me; *vide molti visi nuovi*, he saw many unknown faces; *scoprire una nuova stella*, to discover a new star **4.** (*diverso*) new, different: *inizierò una nuova vita*, I'll begin a new life; *il lavoro l'ha reso un uomo —*, work has made him a new man (*o* has made a new man of him); *ogni giorno indossa un abito —*, she wears a different dress every day **5.** (*inesperto*) new, inexperienced; (*fam.*) green: *essere — a un mestiere, un'attività*, to be inexperienced in (*o* new to) a trade, a business ‖ *essere — di un luogo, città, paese, ecc.*, to be new to a place, town, country, etc. ‖ *s.m.* new: *c'è qualcosa di —?*, is there anything new?; *che c'è di —?*, what's the news?; *non c'è niente di —*, there is no news (*o* there is nothing new) ‖ *di —, di bel —*, again, once again ‖ *rimettere a —*, to renovate (*o* to restore) ‖ *vestire di —*, to put on new clothes ‖ *non c'è nulla di — sotto il sole*, *prov.* there is nothing new under the sun.

Nuòvo Mèssico, *no.pr.m.* (*geog.*) New Mexico.

nuràghe, *s.m.* (*archeol.*) nuraghe (*pl.* nuraghi).

nutazióne, *s.f.* (*astr. bot.*) nutation.

nutríbile, *ag.* (*rar.*) nourishable.

nutricàre, *v.t.* (*rar.*) to nourish.

nutríce, *s.f.* wet-nurse ‖ *l'Italia è stata la — di molti grandi musicisti*, Italy has nourished many great musicians.

nutriènte, *ag.* nourishing, nutritious: *cibo molto —*, highly-nourishing food; *crema —*, (*per la pelle*) nourishing-cream.

nutriménto, *s.m.* **1.** (*il nutrire*) feeding, nourishing **2.** (*alimento*) nutriment; nourishment (*anche fig.*): *un bimbo gracile abbisogna di abbondante —*, a weak child needs a lot of nourishment; *la lettura è — per lo spirito*, reading is food for the spirit; *la linfa è il — delle piante*, sap is the nutriment of plants.

nutríre, *v.t.* **1.** to feed, to nourish (*anche fig.*): *la carne nutre molto*, meat is very nutritious; *di che nutri il tuo cane?*, what do you feed your dog on?; *la lettura nutre lo spirito*, reading nourishes the spirit; *l'olio nutre la fiamma*, oil feeds the flame; *— la terra col concime*, to nourish the soil with manure **2.** (*mantenere*) to maintain: *— a proprie spese*, to maintain at one's own expense; *— la propria famiglia*, to maintain one's family **3.** (*allattare*) to breast-feed: *— il proprio bambino*, to breast-feed one's baby **4.** (*sentimenti, passioni*) to nourish, to nurse, to foster: *— affetto per qlcu.*, to feel affectionate towards s.o.; *— cattivi pensieri*, to foster evil thoughts; *— false speranze*, to nurse (*o* to foster) false hopes; *— illusioni*, to nourish illusions; *— molta stima per qlcu.*, to hold s.o. in great esteem; *— un sentimento di vendetta, di odio*, to nourish (*o* to nurse) feelings of revenge, of hatred ‖ **nutrírsi**, *v.r.* to feed (on sthg.) (*anche fig.*): *le mucche si nutrono di erba*, cows feed (*o* live) on grass; *le piante si nutrono di minerali della terra*, plants feed on the minerals in the earth.

nutritívo, nutritízio, *ag.* nourishing, nutritious: *biscotti nutritivi*, nourishing biscuits.

nutríto, *ag.* fed, nourished: *uomo ben —, mal —*, well-fed, ill-fed man.

nutrizióne, *s.f.* **1.** (*il nutrire*) feeding, nourishing **2.** (*alimento*) nourishment, nutriment, nutrition: *— scarsa, abbondante*, meagre, abundant diet.

núvola, *s.f.* cloud: *— di fumo, di polvere*, cloud of smoke, of dust; *nuvole di pioggia*, rain-clouds; *— di vento*, cirrus (*o* mare's-tails); *— passeggera*, passing cloud (*anche fig.*); *nuvole tempestose*, storm-clouds; *avvolto nelle nuvole*, hidden by (*o* covered with) clouds; *cielo coperto di nuvole*, sky covered with clouds (*o* overcast sky); *cielo senza una —*, cloudless sky; *il vento spazzò via le nuvole*, the wind drove away the clouds ‖ *alzare qlcu., ql.co. alle nuvole*, to praise s.o., sthg. to the skies ‖ *aver la testa nelle nuvole*, to have one's head in the clouds ‖ *cascar dalle nuvole*, to be taken aback.

nuvolàglia, *s.f.* mass of clouds.

núvolo, *ag.* overcast: *cielo —*, overcast sky ‖ *s.m.* **1.** menacing cloud, threatening cloud **2.** (*moltitudine*) swarm, mass: *un — di gente*, a mass (*o* swarm) of people; *un — di mosche*, a swarm of flies.

nuvolosità, *s.f.* cloudiness.

nuvolóso, *ag.* overcast: *cielo —*, overcast sky; *tempo —*, cloudy weather.

nuziàle, *ag.* wedding (*attributivo*); bridal, nuptial: *abito —*, wedding-dress; *anello —*, wedding-ring; *corteo —*, wedding procession; *marcia —*, wedding march; *torta —*, wedding-cake; *velo —*, bridal veil.

nuzialità, *s.f.* marriage-rate: *la — qui è molto scarsa*, the marriage-rate is very low here.

O

o, *s.f.m.* (*tredicesima lettera dell'alfabeto italiano*) o (*pl.* os, oes, o's) ‖ — *come Otranto,* (*tel.*) o for Oliver ‖ *è tondo come l'— di Giotto,* (*è stupido*) he is a simpleton (o he is very silly).

o¹, od, *cong.* **1.** or: *essere — non essere,* to be or not to be; *lo volete bianco — rosso?,* will you have it white or red?; *venite — non venite?,* are you coming or not? ‖ —... —, either... or: — *lui — nessuno,* either he or nobody; — *tu — tuo fratello avete mentito,* either you or your brother lied ‖ — *l'uno — l'altro,* either: — *l'uno — l'altro di questi andrà bene,* either of these will do; *prendi — l'uno — l'altro* (*libro*), take either (book) **2.** (*sia che... o che...*) **whether... or...:** *lo sapesse — non lo sapesse,* whether he knew it or not **3.** (*ovvero, ossia*) or: *la filosofia, — amore della sapienza,* philosophy, or love of knowledge **4.** (*altrimenti*) **or, or else, otherwise:** *vieni presto — non ti vedrò,* come early or (o otherwise) I shan't see you.

o², *inter.* **1.** oh!; (*gener. poet.*) O!: — *patria mia!,* oh, my beloved country!; — *povero me!,* oh, me! (o oh, my!); — *potessi essere in Inghilterra!,* O to be in England! **2.** (*dial.*): — *che s'aveva a fare?,* what should we have done then?

òasi, *s.f.* oasis (*pl.* oases) (anche *fig.*): *un'— di pace,* an oasis of peace.

obbedíre, *e derivati,* V. **ubbidíre,** *e derivati.*

obbiettàre, *e derivati,* V. **obiettàre,** *e derivati.*

obbiettívo, *e derivati,* V. **obiettívo,** *e derivati.*

obbligànte, *ag.* obliging.

obbligàre, *v.t.* **1.** to oblige, to compel, to bind: *il cattivo tempo ci obbligò a fermarci,* the bad weather compelled us to stop; *la paura mi obbligò a tacere,* fear constrained me to be silent **2.** (*impegnare, vincolare con patto*) to bind, to pledge: *la tua parola ti obbliga a pagare i debiti,* your word binds you to pay your debts; — *con un'ipoteca la propria casa,* to mortgage one's own house ‖ **obbligàrsi,** *v.r.* to bind oneself, to engage oneself, to undertake: *egli si obbligò a fornirmi il denaro necessario,* he bound himself (o he undertook) to provide the necessary money.

obbligàto, *ag.* **1.** (*riconoscente*) obliged, grateful: *le sono molto —,* I am much obliged to you **2.** (*imposto, fissato*) fixed, set: *percorso —,* (*spor.*) fixed (o set) course ‖ *parte obbligata,* (*mus.*) obbligato (part) ‖ *rime obbligate,* (*poes.*) given rhymes **3.** (*costretto*) confined: — *a letto,* confined to bed.

obbligatorietà, *s.f.* obligatoriness.

obbligatòrio, *ag.* compulsory, obligatory: *servizio militare —,* compulsory military service; *l'istruzione elementare è obbligatoria,* elementary education is compulsory.

obbligazióne, *s.f.* **1.** obligation: *contrarre un'—,* (*dir.*) to contract an obligation; *rendere esecutiva un'—,* (*dir.*) to enforce an obligation; *ricambiare un'—,* to repay an obligation; *soddisfare un'—,* to fulfil one's obligations **2.** (*comm.*) bond, debenture, obligation: — *al portatore,* bearer-bond; — *dello Stato,* Government bond; *obbligazioni ereditarie,* heritable bonds; — *ferroviaria,* railway debenture; — *garantita,* secured bond; — *garantita da beni immobili, ipotecaria,* mortgage bond (o debenture); — *nominativa,* registered bond; — *non garantita,* unsecured bond; — *passiva,* passive bond; — *preferenziale, privilegiata,* preference bond; — *semplice,* income bond; *fondo di ammorta-*

mento delle obbligazioni, sinking fund; *portatore di obbligazioni,* debenture (o bond)-holder.

obbligazionísta, *s.m.* (*comm.*) bond-holder, debenture-holder.

òbbligo, *s.m.* **1.** obligation; (*dovere*) duty: *gli obblighi di coscienza,* the obligations of conscience; *ho molti obblighi verso di lui,* I am very much obliged to him; *mi sento in — di avvertirvi che...,* I feel compelled to warn you that...; *avere l'— di fare ql.co.,* to be bound (o to be obliged) to do sthg.; *assolvere i propri obblighi verso qlcu.,* to fulfil one's obligations towards s.o.; *assumere l'— di fare ql.co.,* to undertake to do sthg.; *sottrarsi ai propri obblighi,* to fail to carry out one's obligations ‖ — *di leva, del servizio militare,* liability to military service ‖ *contributo d'—,* compulsory contribution ‖ *festa d'—,* (*eccl.*) holyday of obligation ‖ *essere d'—,* to be required (o requisite): *è d'— l'abito nero,* evening-dress obligatory **2.** (*condizione*) condition: *glielo diedi con l'— di restituirlo entro un mese,* I gave it to him on condition that he gave it back within a month.

obbròbrio, *s.m.* **1.** dishonour, shame, disgrace: *coprire di — qlcu.,* to bring dishonour (o disgrace) upon s.o. **2.** (*fam.*) (*cosa obbrobriosa*) disgrace: *questo libro è un —,* this book is a disgrace (o is dreadful) **3.** *pl.* (*parole obbrobriose*) opprobrium (*sing.*), abuse (*sing.*): *coprire qlcu. di obbrobri,* to cover s.o. with opprobrium.

obbrobriosaménte, *av.* **1.** dishonourably, shamefully, disgracefully **2.** (*fam.*) (*molto male*) disgracefully, very badly.

obbrobrióso, *ag.* **1.** dishonourable, shameful, disgraceful **2.** (*orribile, bruttissimo*) disgraceful, dreadful: *la sua ultima commedia è decisamente obbrobriosa,* his latest play is an absolute disgrace.

obelísco, *s.m.* obelisk.

oberàto, *ag.* burdened with debts, overwhelmed by debts ‖ — *di lavoro,* weighed down by work.

obesità, *s.f.* obesity, obeseness, excessive fatness.

obèso, *ag.* obese, excessively fat.

òbice, *s.m.* (*artigl.*) howitzer.

obiettàre, *v.t.* to object: *ha obiettato che non conosci abbastanza bene l'inglese,* he objected that your English was not good enough; *non aveva niente da — ,* he had nothing to say against it.

obiettivaménte, *av.* objectively.

obiettivísmo, *s.m.* objectivism.

obiettività, *s.f.* objectiveness, objectivity.

obiettívo, *ag.* objective: *una descrizione obiettiva,* objective description ‖ *s.m.* **1.** (*mil.*) objective **2.** (*scopo*) aim, object, end: *il suo — era di ottenere un prestito,* his aim was to obtain a loan **3.** (*ott.*) object-glass, objective; (*foto.*) lens (*pl.* lenses), objective: — *a fuoco fisso,* (*foto.*) fixed-focus lens; — *anastigmatico,* (*foto.*) anastigmatic lens; — *di grande lunghezza focale,* (*foto.*) long-focus lens; — *di piccola lunghezza focale,* (*foto.*) short-focus lens; — *doppio,* (*ott.*) doublet; — *grandangolare,* (*foto. ott.*) wide-angle lens.

obiètto, (*poet.*) per **oggètto.**

obiettóre, *s.m.* objector ‖ — *di coscienza,* conscientious objector (o *fam.* conchy).

obiezióne, *s.f.* objection: *non ho nessuna — a che tu parta,* I have no objection (o I do not object) to your leaving; *fare, sollevare un'—,* to make, to raise an objection; *rispondere a un'—,* to meet an objection.

obitòrio, *s.m.* mortuary, morgue.

obituàrio, *s.m.* obituary(-list).

oblàta, *s.f.* (*eccl.*) oblate; (*suora addetta a particolari servizi*) lay-sister.

oblàto, *s.m.* (*eccl.*) oblate; (*religioso addetto a particolari servizi*) lay-brother.

oblatóre, *s.m.* donor, donator; benefactor.

oblatríce, *s.f.* donor, donator; benefactress.

oblazióne, *s.f.* **1.** offering, donation **2.** (*eccl.*) (*parte della Messa*) oblation, offertory.

obliàre, *v.t.* (*poet.*) to forget.

oblío, *s.m.* (*poet.*) oblivion: *votato ull'—,* doomed to oblivion; *cadde in —,* he sank into oblivion; *essere nell'—,* to be completely forgotten.

oblióso, *ag.* (*poet.*) oblivious.

obliquaménte, *av.* **1.** sideways; obliquely, slantways, slantwise: *camminare —,* to walk sideways; *tagliare un foglio —,* to cut a piece of paper slantways (o at an angle) ‖ *guardare — qlcu.,* *fig.* to look askance at s.o. **2.** (*in modo subdolo*) obliquely, deceitfully: *procedeva — in ogni sua cosa,* he acted in an underhand manner (o deceitfully) in everything he did.

obliquàre, *v.i.* to oblique, to slant.

obliquità, *s.f.* obliqueness, obliquity (anche *fig.*).

oblíquo, *ag.* **1.** oblique; (*inclinato*) slanting: *angolo —,* oblique angle; *muscolo —,* (*anat.*) oblique muscle; *occhiata obliqua,* side glance; *scrittura obliqua,* slanting handwriting; *sfera obliqua,* (*astr.*) oblique sphere; *pioggia obliqua,* driving rain **2.** (*subdolo, tortuoso*) oblique, tortuous, underhand: *riuscì ad ottenere il potere con mezzi obliqui,* he achieved power by tortuous (o underhand) means; *va sempre per vie oblique,* he always goes about things in an underhand manner **3.** (*gram.*) oblique: *casi obliqui,* oblique cases.

obliteràre, *v.t.* (*cancellare*) to obliterate: *ricordi che il tempo ha obliterato,* memories obliterated by time.

obliteràto, *ag.* (*cancellato*) obliterated.

obliterazióne, *s.f.* (*oblio, offuscamento*) obliteration **2.** (*occlusione*) occlusion, obliteration: *— di un condotto,* occlusion of a passage.

oblivióso, *ag.* (*letter.*) oblivious.

oblò, *s.m.* (*mar.*) port-hole, bull's eye.

oblúngo, *ag.* oblong.

obnubilazióne, *s.f.* (*med.*) obnubilation.

òboe, *s.m.* (*mus.*) oboe, hautboy.

oboísta, *s.c.* oboist.

òbolo, *s.m.* **1.** (*moneta*) (*in Grecia*) obolus (*pl.* oboli); (*in Francia*) obole **2.** (*offerta*) offering; (*di poca entità*) mite: *anche la povera gente diede un piccolo —,* even the poor people gave their mite; *dopo la predica sarà raccolto l'—,* the collection will be taken after the sermon; *tutti deposero il loro — nella cassetta delle elemosine,* they all placed their offerings in the alms-box ‖ *l'— della vedova,* the widow's mite ‖ *l'— di S. Pietro,* (*eccl.*) Peter's pence.

obrettízio, *ag.* (*dir.*) obreptitious.

obrogàre, *V.* **abrogàre.**

obsolèto, *ag.* (*letter.*) obsolete: *idee, parole obsolete,* obsolete ideas, words.

oc, *av.* (*nell'antico provenzale = sì*) oc: *lingua d'—,* langue d'oc (o old Provençal).

òca, *s.f.* **1.** goose (*pl.* geese): *— colombaccio,* barnacle-goose; *— delle nevi,* snow-goose; *— egiziana,* Egyptian (o Nile) goose; *— giovane,* gosling; *— maschio,* gander; *— selvatica,* wild (o greylag) goose; *guardiano di oche,* goose-herd; *ci hanno servito una squisita — farcita di marroni,* they gave us a delicious goose stuffed with chestnuts ‖ *collo d'—,* (*mec.*) goose-neck (o crankshaft) ‖ *giuoco dell'—,* the game of goose ‖ *passo dell'—,* (*mil.*) goose-step ‖ *pelle d'—,* goose-flesh: *fa così freddo che ho la pelle d'—,* it is so cold that I am all goose-flesh; *quel quadro mi fa venire la pelle d'—,* that picture gives me the creeps ‖ *penna d'—,* goose-quill: *sul suo tavolo di lavoro c'è un bel*

calamaio d'argento e una penna d'—, there is a fine silver ink-stand and a goose-quill on his desk ‖ *zampa d'—,* (*bot.*) goose-foot ‖ *camminavano in fila come le oche,* they were walking in Indian file ‖ *ecco fatto il becco all'—!,* it's done (o finished) now! (o that's that!) **2.** (*persona stupida*) goose, simpleton: *non è un'— come credi,* she is not so naive (o not such a goose) as you think; *non fare l'—,* don't be such a goose; *quell'— ha dimenticato di spegnere il gas,* that silly goose has forgotten to turn the gas off.

ocàggine, *s.f.* **1.** (*stupidità*) stupidity, foolishness **2.** (*atto sciocco*) piece of folly; (*detto sciocco*) piece of nonsense: *basta con le tue ocaggini!,* that's enough of your nonsense!; *ha fatto l'— di dimenticare il biglietto a casa,* she was so foolish as to leave the ticket at home.

ocarína, *s.f.* (*mus.*) ocarina.

occasionàle, *ag.* **1.** immediate: *la causa — della guerra fu...,* the immediate cause of the war was... **2.** (*fortuito*) fortuitous; chance (*attributivo*): *fu un incontro —,* it was a chance meeting **3.** (*saltuario*) occasional: *compratore, visitatore —,* occasional customer, visitor.

occasionalísmo, *s.m.* (*fil. teol.*) occasionalism.

occasionalménte, *av.* **1.** occasionally; now and then: *— viene da noi a cena,* occasionally he comes to dinner with us **2.** (*fortuitamente*) by chance: *lo incontrai —,* I met him by chance.

occasionàre, *v.t.* (*ra .*) to occasion; to cause.

occasióne, *s.f.* **1.** occasion, opportunity, chance: *una buona —,* *un'— favorevole,* a favourable occasion (o a good opportunity); *mi si offre l'— d'andare in America,* they are giving me a chance to go to America; *non ho mai avuto — di parlargli,* I have never had a chance to talk to him; *quando si presenta l'—,* when the opportunity offers; *approfittare dell'—,* to profit by the occasion; *aspettar l'—,* to wait for the right moment; *cogliere un'—,* to seize an opportunity; *lasciar sfuggire un'—,* to miss an opportunity; *pigliar l'— per fare ql.co.,* to take the opportunity of doing sthg. ‖ *all'—,* when necessary (o a when the occasion arises): *all'— si presta molto,* when circumstances require it he is very helpful ‖ *l'— fa l'uomo ladro,* *prov.* opportunity makes the thief **2.** (*buon affare*) bargain: *questo libro costa pochissimo, è una vera —,* this book is very cheap, it is a real bargain ‖ *d'—,* bargain (*attributivo*); (*di seconda mano*) second-hand: *abiti d'—,* second-hand clothes; *merce d'—,* bargain lot; *prezzo d'—,* bargain price; *ho comprato questo libro d'—,* I bought this book second-hand **3.** (*circostanza*) occasion: *in — delle tue nozze,* on the occasion of your wedding; *per l'— comprò un cappello nuovo,* she bought a new hat for the occasion; *in molte occasioni,* on many occasions ‖ *poesie d'—,* occasional verse **4.** (*causa*) cause: *anche una piccola ferita può essere — di morte,* even a slight wound can cause death.

occàso, *s.m.* (*poet.*) west; (*tramonto*) sunset, setting: *il sole volge all'—,* the sun is setting.

occhiàcci, *s.m.pl.: fare gli — a qlcu.,* (*fam.*) to frown at s.o. (o to look sternly at s.o.).

occhiàia, *s.f.* eye-socket, orbit ‖ *avere le occhiaie,* to have rings under one's eyes.

occhialàio, *s.m.* optician.

occhiàle, *ag.* pertaining to the eye: *dente —,* eye-tooth ‖ *s.m. V.* **occhiàli.**

occhialétto, *s.m.* lorgnette; (*monocolo*) monocle, eye-glass.

occhiàli, *s.m.pl.* (*a stanghetta*) spectacles, glasses; (*fam.*) specs; (*a molla*) pince-nez (*sing.*): *— da miope,* *da presbite,* glasses for short-sightedness, glasses for long-sightedness; *— da motociclista,* goggles; *— da neve,* snow-goggles; *— da sole,* sun-glasses; *astuccio per gli —,* spectacle-case; *montatura per —,* spectacle-frame; *un paio di —,* a pair of spectacles; *vetro per —,* spectacle-glass; *mettersi, inforcare gli —,* to put on one's spectacles; *portare gli —,* to wear spectacles.

occhialíno, *s.m.* lorgnette; *(monocolo)* monocle, eye-glass.

occhialúto, *ag.* spectacled *(attributivo)*, bespectacled *(attributivo)*; wearing spectacles *(predicativo)*.

occhiàre, *(rar.)* per **adocchiàre.**

occhiàta, *s.f.* look, glance: — *fredda,* cold look; — *languida,* languid look; — *maliziosa,* malicious look; — *rapida,* quick look (o glance); — *scrutatrice,* piercing look (o glance); *voglio dare un'—, un'occhiatina al giornale prima di uscire,* I want to give (o to have) a look at the newspaper before going out; *dare, lanciare un'—, un'occhiatina intorno,* to look around; *lanciare un'— a qlcu.,* to cast a look at s.o.; *scambiarsi un'— d'intesa,* to exchange meaning looks.

occhiatàccia, *s.f.* black look.

occhiàto, *ag. (rar.)* ocellated.

occhieggiàre, *v.t.* to cast glances at (s.o., sthg.): *occhieggiò quella bella ragazza,* he made eyes at (o ogled) that attractive girl ‖ *v.i.* to peep, to peer: *le margheritine occhieggiavano nel prato,* daisies were peeping through the grass.

occhiellàia, *s.f.* button-holer.

occhiellatúra, *s.f.* button-holing.

occhièllo, *s.m.* **1.** button-hole; *(per corda o fettuccia)* eyelet: *un fiore all'—,* a button-hole (flower) **2.** *(tec.)* eye, ear: — *di molla,* (di orologio) eye of a spring; — *metallico,* grommet (o metal eyelet).

occhiétto, *s.m.:* far l'— a qlcu., to wink at s.o.

òcchio, *s.m.* **1.** eye: *occhi a mandorla,* almond-shaped (o slanting) eyes; — *di vetro,* glass eye; *a occhi chiusi,* with closed eyes; *fig.* blindly; *bianco dell'—,* white of the eye; *con le lacrime agli occhi,* with tears in one's eyes; *dagli occhi neri,* black-eyed; *dagli occhi vellutati,* soft-eyed; *mi piange un —,* my eye is watering; *mi fanno male gli occhi,* my eyes ache (o are sore); *avere gli occhi storti,* to be cross-eyed; *guardare dritto negli occhi,* to look straight in the eye; *sollevare, abbassare gli occhi,* to raise, to lower (o to cast down) one's eyes ‖ —!, mind! (o watch out! o look out!): — *al borsellino!,* watch your purse! ‖ *a — nudo,* with the naked eye: *si vede a — nudo che è falso,* you can see it is false with your naked eye ‖ *a quattr'occhi,* in private (o in confidence): *una conversazione a quattr'occhi,* a tête-à-tête ‖ *a vista d'—,* before one's very eyes ‖ *in un batter d'—,* in a trice (o in the twinkling of an eye) ‖ *agli occhi miei egli ha ragione,* in my opinion he is right ‖ *aveva gli occhi fuori dalla testa,* his eyes were popping out of his head ‖ *darei un — per vederlo,* I would give the world to see him ‖ *dove hai gli occhi?,* where are your eyes? ‖ *ho debiti fin sopra gli occhi,* I am up to my eyes in debt ‖ *ne ho fin sopra gli occhi,* I am fed up with it ‖ *hai proprio una benda sugli occhi,* you must be absolutely blind ‖ *non l'ha fatto certo per i suoi begli occhi!,* he didn't do it for love! (o for nothing!) ‖ *la notte scorsa non ho potuto chiudere —,* I didn't sleep a wink last night ‖ *schizzava fuoco dagli occhi,* his eyes blazed with anger ‖ *aprire gli occhi a qlcu. su ql.co.,* to open s.o.'s eyes to sthg. (o to enlighten s.o. about sthg.) ‖ *avere — a tutto,* to give an eye to everything ‖ *avere gli occhi dappertutto,* to have eyes in the back of one's head ‖ *avere — per ql.co.,* to have an eye for sthg. ‖ *avere gli occhi pesanti,* to be drowsy (o sleepy) ‖ *avere, tenere gli occhi aperti,* to keep one's eyes open (o skinned) ‖ *chiudere un — su ql.co.,* to turn a blind eye to sthg. ‖ *costare un — della testa,* to be terribly expensive (o to cost a fortune) ‖ *dormire con gli occhi aperti,* to sleep with one eye open; *(avere il sonno leggero)* to sleep very lightly ‖ *essere, stare tutt'occhi,* to be all eyes ‖ *essere tutt'occhi e tutt'orecchie,* to be all eyes and ears (o ears and eyes) ‖ *fare gli occhiacci a qlcu.,* to look sternly (o severely o reprovingly) at s.o. ‖ *fare gli occhi neri a qlcu.,* to give s.o. a black eye (o to black s.o.'s eye) ‖ *gettare polvere negli occhi a qlcu.,* to throw dust in s.o.'s eyes ‖ *guardare qlcu. con la coda dell'—,* to look s.o. out of the

corner of one's eye (o to cast a sidelong glance at s.o.) ‖ *leggere ql.co. negli occhi di qlcu.,* to read sthg. in s.o.'s eyes: *leggo nei tuoi occhi che stai mentendo,* I can see by your eyes that you are lying ‖ *mettere ql.co. sotto gli occhi a qlcu.,* to bring (o to draw) s.o.'s attention to sthg. ‖ *perdere il lume degli occhi,* to lose one's temper ‖ *seccarsi gli occhi, (per il gran piangere)* to cry one's eyes out ‖ *sgranare gli occhi,* to open one's eyes wide (o to goggle) ‖ *strizzare gli occhi,* to squint (o to screw up one's eyes) ‖ *strizzar l'— a qlcu.,* to wink at s.o. ‖ *vedere qlcu. come il fumo negli occhi,* to hate the sight of s.o.: *lo vedo come il fumo negli occhi,* I can't bear the sight of him ‖ *vedere ql.co. di buon —, di mal —,* to look favourably, unfavourably on sthg. ‖ — *per —, dente per dente, prov.* an eye for an eye, a tooth for a tooth ‖ — *non vede, cuore non duole, prov.* what the eye doesn't see the heart doesn't grieve over ‖ *in terra di ciechi beato chi ha un —, prov.* in a country of blind men the one-eyed man is king **2.** *(vista)* sight, eye: *affaticarsi, logorarsi, consumarsi gli occhi,* to strain one's eyes ‖ *a perdita d'—,* as far as the eye can see ‖ *cosa che salta agli occhi,* thing that strikes (o leaps to) the eye; *(evidente)* thing as plain as a pikestaff (o thing that you can see with half an eye) ‖ *avere gli occhi di lince,* to be keen-sighted (o lynx-eyed) ‖ *dare nell'—,* to strike (o to shock) the eye ‖ *fare l'— a ql.co.,* to get used to sthg. ‖ *perdere d'— qlcu., ql.co.,* to lose sight of s.o., sthg. ‖ *tenere d'— qlcu.,* to keep an eye on s.o. ‖ *lontano dagli occhi, lontano dal cuore, prov.* out of sight, out of mind **3.** *(sguardo)* look; glance: — *vitreo,* glassy stare; *sotto gli occhi di qlcu.,* under s.o.'s eyes; *cercare qlcu. con gli occhi,* to look round for s.o.; *distogliere gli occhi,* to look away; *interrogare qlcu. con gli occhi,* to give s.o. a questioning look (o to look at s.o. inquiringly) ‖ *a colpo d'—,* at first sight: *ho capito la situazione al primo colpo d'—,* I took the situation in at a glance; *vedere ql.co. al primo colpo d'—,* to see sthg. at the first glance ‖ *a — e croce,* roughly (o about o approximately) ‖ *avere messo gli occhi addosso a ql.co.,* to have one's eyes on sthg. ‖ *dare un — a ql.co.,* to have a look at sthg. ‖ *fare gli occhi dolci a qlcu.,* to make (sheep's) eyes at s.o. ‖ *gettare l'— su ql.co.,* to run (o to cast) one's eyes over sthg. (o to glance at sthg.) ‖ *mangiarsi ql.co., qlcu. con gli occhi,* to devour sthg., s.o. with one's eyes ‖ *misurare ql.co. a —,* to measure sthg. by sight (o at a glance) **4.** *(cosa a forma d'occhio):* occhi del brodo, specks of fat on soup; *gli occhi del formaggio,* the holes in (gruyère) cheese; *gli occhi delle penne del pavone,* the ocelli on a peacock's feathers **5.** — *di pernice, — pollino, (callo)* corn (between toes) **6.** *pl.* *(bot.)* eyes, buds: *gli occhi di una pianta,* the eyes (o buds) of a plant **7** *(min.):* — *di gatto,* cat's eye; — *di tigre,* tiger eye **8.** *(tip.)* typeface **9.** *(tec.)* eye; hole: — *della molla, (mec.)* spring eye; — *della voluta, (arch.)* eye of the volute; — *del martello,* eye of the hammer; — *di bue, (edil.)* bull's eye; — *di coperta, (mar.)* deck light; — *di cubia, (mar.)* hawse(hole); — *fotometrico normale, (fis.)* standard eye for photometry; — *magico, (rad.)* visual tuning indicator (o fam. magic eye).

occhiolíno, *s.m.:* far l'— a qlcu., to wink at s.o.

occidentàle, *ag. (di occidente)* west, western; *(da occidente)* westerly: *la costa —,* the west coast; *l'Europa —,* Western Europe; *le Indie Occidentali,* the West Indies; *paesi occidentali,* western countries.

occidènte, *s.m.* west, occident: *da oriente a —,* from east to west; *posto a —,* facing west ‖ *l'Impero d'Occidente, (st.)* the Western Empire.

occíduo, *ag. (poet.)* **1.** *(occidentale)* western **2.** *(che tramonta)* setting: *il sole —,* the setting sun.

occipitàle, *ag.* occipital.

occípite, *s.m. (anat.)* occiput.

occitànico, *ag.* Provençal: *letteratura, poesia occitanica,* Provençal literature, poetry.

occlùdere, *v.t.* (*letter.*) to occlude, to stop up, to close; (*ostruire*) to obstruct.

occlusióne, *s.f.* **1.** occlusion; (*ostruzione*) obstruction **2.** (*med.*) stoppage.

occlùso, *ag.* occluded; (*ostruito*) obstructed.

occorrènte, *ag.* necessary, requisite, required: *non hanno il capitale* —, they lack the requisite (*o* necessary) capital; *le qualità occorrenti per questo posto sono...*, the qualities required for this post are...; *rimanere non più di quanto sia strettamente* —, to stay no longer than is strictly necessary ‖ *s.m.* the necessary, everything necessary: — *per scrivere, disegnare*, writing, drawing materials; *procura l'* — *e partiremo per la montagna*, collect up everything necessary, and we'll set off for the mountains.

occorrènza, *s.f.* **1.** (*circostanza*) circumstance: *le occorrenze della vita*, the events of life; *secondo l'*—, depending on circumstances **2.** (*necessità*) necessity, need ‖ *all'*—, in case of need (*o* necessity).

occórrere, *v.i.* **1.** *imp.* to be necessary; (*con costruzione pers.*): to have (to do); must; ought (to do): *occorre che io lo veda subito*, I must see him at once; *occorre che questo sia fatto subito*, this needs to be done at once; *occorreva che tu fossi più gentile*, you should (*o* ought to) have been kinder; *andrò se occorrerà*, I shall go if it is necessary; *non occorre che tu glielo dica*, it is not necessary for you to tell him (*o* you need not tell him) **2.** (*abbisognare*) (*con costruzione pers.*): to want, to need; to be required; to be wanted: *occorre molto tempo per imparare bene una lingua*, much time is required to learn a language well; *occorrono ancora dieci milioni di lire*, another ten million lire are needed (*o* wanted); *occorrono tre metri di stoffa per un abito da uomo*, three metres of cloth are required for a suit; *mi occorrono molti soldi*, I need a lot of money; *non mi occorre nient'altro*, I do not want anything else **3.** (*accadere*) to occur, to happen: *questo occorse diverse volte*, this occurred several times.

occultàbile, *ag.* concealable.

occultaménte, *av.* secretly, hiddenly.

occultaménto, *s.m.* concealment.

occultàre, *v.t.* (*letter.*) to hide, to conceal: *occultò la refurtiva*, he hid the stolen goods; — *un delitto*, to conceal a crime ‖ **occultàrsi**, *v.r.* to hide.

occultatóre, *ag.* hiding, concealing ‖ *s.m.*, **occultatríce**, *s.f.* hider, concealer.

occultazióne, *s.f.* **1.** (*rar.*) concealment **2.** (*astr.*) occultation: — *di una stella*, occultation of a star.

occultìsmo, *s.m.* occultism.

occúlto, *ag.* **1.** (*nascosto*) hidden, concealed: *amore* —, hidden love; *pensiero* —, concealed thought ‖ *socio* —, (*comm.*) sleeping partner **2.** (*magico*) occult: *scienze occulte*, occult sciences.

occupaménto, *V.* **occupazióne 1.**

occupànte, *ag.* occupying: *le potenze occupanti*, the occupying powers ‖ *s.m.* occupant, occupier: *gli occupanti l'automobile*, the occupants of the car ‖ *il primo* —, (*dir.*) the first occupier.

occupàre, *v.t.* **1.** to occupy: *i libri occupano molto spazio*, books take up much room; *molte preoccupazioni occupavano la sua mente*, his mind was full of worries; — *una casa*, to occupy (*o* inhabit) a house; — *una città, un paese*, (*mil.*) to occupy (*o* to take possession of) a town, a country; — *un posto a sedere*, to occupy a seat **2.** (*il tempo*) to occupy, to spend: *occupo il mio tempo studiando l'inglese*, I spend my time studying English; *questo lavoro mi occupa troppo tempo*, this work takes up too much of my time; *sa come* — *il tempo*, he knows how to occupy his time **3.** (*cariche, uffici*) to occupy, to fill; to hold: *occupa la cattedra di inglese nella nostra università*, he holds the chair of English at our University; — *una posizione, una carica*, to occupy (*o* to fill) a position, an office **4.** (*ingaggiare, far lavorare*) to employ: — *venti operai*, to employ twenty workmen **5.** (*tener*

occupato) to keep busy: *l'insegnamento mi occupa tutta la giornata*, teaching keeps me busy all day long ‖ **occupàrsi**, *v.r.* **1.** to occupy oneself (with sthg.); to busy oneself (with sthg.); to attend (to sthg.); (*dedicarsi*) to devote oneself (to sthg.): *di che cosa ti occupi?*, what is your job?; *egli si occupa dei suoi affari, del suo lavoro*, he attends to his business, to his work; *mi occuperò di questa faccenda più tardi*, I shall see (*o* attend) to this business later; *si occupa di opere di carità*, he devotes himself to works of charity; *si occupa di politica, chimica*, he devotes himself to politics, chemistry; *si occupa di problemi sociali*, he busies himself with social problems **2.** (*impicciarsi*): *non voglio assolutamente occuparmene*, I do not want to have anything to do with it; *occupati dei fatti tuoi*, mind your own business **3.** (*di legge, contemplare*) to contemplate (sthg.): *la legge non si occupa di questo caso*, the law does not contemplate this case **4.** (*trovar lavoro*) to find a job: *non si è ancora occupato*, he hasn't got a job yet.

occupàto, *ag.* **1.** (*non libero*) engaged, taken: *la linea è occupata*, (*tel.*) the line is engaged; *questo posto è* —, this seat is taken **2.** (*indaffarato, intento ad un lavoro*) busy, engaged: *al momento sono* —, I am busy at the moment; *il dottore è un uomo molto* —, the doctor is a very busy man; *era occupata a prepararsi per il viaggio*, she was busy getting ready for her journey; *era* — *a scrivere una lettera*, he was busy writing a letter; *non potrò vederti oggi, sono troppo* —, I shan't be able to see you today, I am too busy; *sarò occupata fino alle cinque*, I shall be engaged (*o* busy) until five o' clock; « *Siete liberi questa sera?* », « *Ci spiace, siamo occupati* », " Are you free this evening?", "Sorry, we are engaged" **3.** (*impiegato*): *egli è* — *in banca*, he works in a bank; *siamo occupati presso una casa editrice*, we work in a publishing house.

occupatóre, *ag.* occupying ‖ *s.m.*, **occupatríce**, *s.f.* occupier, occupant.

occupazióne, *s.f.* **1.** (*mil.*) occupation: *l'* — *romana in Britannia*, the Roman occupation of Britain; *esercito d'* —, army of occupation **2.** (*attività*) occupation; (*impiego*) job, employment: *occupazioni artistiche, letterarie*, artistic, literary pursuits; *le mie numerose occupazioni mi costringono a...*, my numerous occupations compel me to...; *qual è l'* — *che preferisci?*, what is your favourite occupation?; *qual è la sua* —?, what is his occupation (*o* job)?; *cercare un'* — *adatta alle proprie capacità*, to look for a job (*o* employment) suited to one's abilities **3.** (*dir.*) occupancy: *per diritto di* —, by right of occupancy.

Oceània, *no.pr.f.* (*geog.*) Oceania.

oceànico, *ag.* oceanic; ocean (*attributivo*): *c'era una folla oceanica*, *fig.* there was an ocean of people.

oceanìne, *s.f.pl.* (*mit.*) Oceanids, Oceanides.

oceanìno, *ag.* (*letter.*) oceanic.

Ocèano, *no.pr.m.* (*mit.*) Oceanus.

ocèano, *s.m.* ocean: *il sole si tuffò nell'* —, the sun sank into the ocean ‖ *l'Oceano Atlantico, Pacifico*, the Atlantic, Pacific Ocean.

oceanografía, *s.f.* oceanography.

oceanogràfico, *ag.* oceanographic.

ocèllo, *s.m.* (*scient.*) ocellus (*pl.* ocelli).

oclocràtico, *ag.* (*pol.*) ochlocratic.

oclocrazía, *s.f.* (*pol.*) ochlocracy.

òcra, *s.f.* ochre.

ocràceo, *ag.* ochreous, ochrous.

ocronòsi, *s.f.* (*med.*) ochronosis.

octíle, *ag.* (*astr.*) octile: *aspetto* —, octile aspect.

oculàre, *ag.* ocular; eye (*attributivo*): *bulbo* —, eye -ball ‖ *testimonio* —, eye-witness ‖ *s.m.* eye-piece: *l'* — *di un telescopio*, the eye-piece of a telescope.

ocularménte, *av.* ocularly.

oculataménte, *av.* cautiously, prudently, wisely.

oculatézza, *s.f.* caution, prudence, circumspection; wisdom: *l'* — *è una norma da tener presente quando si* *parla con uno sconosciuto*, circumspection is a rule to be observed when talking to a stranger.

oculàto, *ag.* cautious, prudent, circumspect; wise: *si mostrò molto —*, he showed himself to be very circumspect (*o* prudent).

oculìsta, *s.m.* oculist.

oculìstica, *s.f.* oculistics.

oculìstico, *ag.* oculistic.

oculomotóre, *ag.* (*anat.*) oculomotor.

od, *V.* o¹.

odalìsea, *s.f.* odalisque.

Oddóne, *no.pr.m.* (*st.*) Odo, Otho, Otto.

òde, *s.f.* (*poes.*) ode: *odi barbare*, barbarian odes.

odèo, odèon, *s.m.* (*st.*) odeum (*pl.* odeums, odea).

odiàbile, *ag.* hateful, hatable, odious, loathsome.

odiàre, *v.t.* to hate, to loathe, to detest, to abominate: *— qlcu. a morte*, to have a mortal hatred of s.o. || *— qlcu. cordialmente*, to detest s.o. cordially || *farsi —*, to make (*o* to get) oneself hated (*o* detested).

odiernaménte, *av.* nowadays.

odièrno, *ag.* **1.** today's (*attributivo*); of today: *fatti odierni*, the day's events; *la lezione odierna*, today's lesson **2.** (*del momento*) modern, of the day: *studi odierni*, modern studies.

Odìno, *no.pr.m.* (*mit.*) Odin.

òdio, *s.m.* hatred, hate: *— bestiale*, animal hatred; *— cieco*, blind hatred; *— di classe*, class hatred; *— ereditario*, (family) feud; *— feroce, implacabile*, furious, implacable hatred; *— inveterato*, old (*o* inveterate) hatred; *Annibale giurò — eterno ai Romani*, Hannibal swore eternal hatred for the Romans; *era pieno d'— per il suo nemico*, he was filled with (*o* full of) hate for his enemy; *accendere gli odi* (*verso qlcu., ql.co.*), to kindle s.o.'s hatred (against s.o., sthg.); *alimentare gli odi* (*verso qlcu., ql.co.*), to feed s.o.'s hatred (against s.o., sthg.); *attirarsi, tirarsi l'—*, to make oneself hated (*o* to incur s.o.'s hatred); *fare ql.co. in — a qlcu., ql.co.*, to do sthg. out of hatred for s.o., sthg.; *fomentare gli odi* (*verso qlcu., ql.co.*), to foment s.o.'s hatred (against s.o., sthg.); *prendere qlcu., ql.co. in —*, to conceive a strong aversion for s.o., sthg.; *rinfocolare gli odi verso qlcu., ql.co.*, to rekindle s.o.'s hatred against s.o., sthg. || *avere in —*, to hate: *ho in — il sole, il cattivo tempo*, I hate (*o* I cannot bear) sunshine, bad weather || *la verità genera —*, *prov.* truth begets hatred.

odiosaménte, *av.* **1.** hatefully, odiously **2.** (*con odio*) with hatred.

odiosità, *s.f.* hatefulness, odiousness.

odióso, *ag.* hateful, odious, loathsome: *un delitto —*, a hateful crime.

Odissèa, *s.f.* (*lett.*) Odyssey || *odissea*, (*vicenda travagliata ed avventurosa*) odyssey: *narrò la sua —*, he recounted his odyssey.

Odoàcre, *no.pr.m.* (*st.*) Odoacer, Odovacar.

Odoàrdo, *no.pr.m.* Edward || *dim.* Ed(dy), Ned(dy), Ted(dy).

odògrafo, *s.m.* (*fis.*) odograph.

odòmetro, *s.m.* (*mec.*) (h)odometer.

odontalgìa, *s.f.* odontalgia.

odontàlgico, *ag.s.m.* odontalgic.

odontògrafo, *s.m.* (*odontoiatria*) odontograph.

odontoiàtra, *s.m.* odontologist, dentist.

odontoiatrìa, *s.f.* dentistry, odontology.

odontoiàtrico, *ag.* dental, odontological: *complesso —*, dental unit.

odontologìa, *s.f.* dentistry, odontology.

odontològico, *ag.* dental, odontologic(al).

odontòmetro, *s.m.* (*filatelica*) perforation gauge.

odoràre, *v.t.* **1.** (*fiutare*) to smell: *odora questo fiore*, smell this flower; *i cani avevano odorato la selvaggina*, the dogs had smelt out the game; *le fecero — i sali*, they made her smell some smelling salts **2.** (*intuire*) to smell (out), to scent (out): *l'insegnante aveva odorato una birichinata*, the teacher had scented mischief || *— il vento infido*, (*il pericolo*) to scent danger **3.** (*ren-*

dere odoroso) to perfume, to scent || *v.i.* to smell, to scent: *come odorano questi fiori !*, how nice these flowers smell!; *— di violette*, to smell of violets || *odora di buono, di cattivo*, (*dà l'impressione di essere una persona onesta, un mentitore*) he gives the impression of being a good man, a liar.

odoràto, *ag.* (*letter.*) odorous, fragrant || *s.m.* smell: *il senso dell'—*, the sense of smell: *il senso dell'— è molto sviluppato nei cani*, dogs have a highly developed sense of smell.

odóre, *s.m.* **1.** smell, odour, scent: *— di cucina*, smell of cooking; *che buon —!*, what a nice (*o* good) smell!; *c'è — di chiuso nella stanza*, this room smells musty; *c'è — di sigaro*, there is a smell of cigar; *la minestra ha buon —, ha — di aglio*, the soup smells nice, smells of garlic; *non sento nessun —*, I can't smell anything; *queste uova hanno un cattivo —*, these eggs smell bad; *questi fiori non hanno —*, these flowers don't smell (*o* have no scent); *senti l'— di questa carne*, smell this meat; *la volpe sentì l'— del pollame*, the fox scented the poultry; *avere buon, cattivo, forte —*, to smell good; bad, strong; *sentire — di bruciato*, to smell sthg. burning **2.** (*profumo*) perfume, scent: *metti un po' d'— nel fazzoletto*, put some scent on your handkerchief **3.** *fig.* (*reputazione, concetto*) odour, repute: *le sue opinioni sono in — di eresia*, his opinions smack of heresy; *morire in — di santità*, to die in the odour of sanctity **4.** *pl.* (*cuc.*) herbs.

odorìfero, odorìfico, *ag.* fragrant, sweet-smelling.

odorosaménte, *av.* odorously, fragrantly.

odoróso, *ag.* fragrant, sweet-smelling; odorous.

Ofèlia, *no.pr.f.* (*lett.*) Ophelia.

òffa, *s.f.* **1.** spelt cake **2.** *fig.* (*dono propiziatorio*) sop: *gettar l'— a qlcu.*, to throw a sop to s.o.

offèndere, *v.t.* **1.** to offend: *non avresti dovuto offenderlo*, you should not have offended him; *non l'ho detto per offenderlo*, I did not mean to hurt his feelings when I said it || *— Dio*, to offend against the Lord; (*con bestemmie*) to blaspheme **2.** (*calunniare*) to slander; (*con scritti*) to libel **3.** (*danneggiare*): *— qlcu. nell'onore*, to offend s.o.'s honour; *— qlcu. nella persona*, to assault s.o.; *— qlcu. nella proprietà*, to damage (*o* to harm) s.o.'s property **4.** (*violare*) to break, to infringe; to offend; (*nuocere a*) to be detrimental to (sthg.): *la sua condotta offende la moralità pubblica*, his conduct is detrimental to public morality; *— la legge*, to break the law; *— i diritti di qlcu.*, to infringe on s.o.'s rights; *— la modestia, il pudore*, to offend s.o.'s sense of the proprieties **5.** (*ferire*) to injure; (*con un'arma*) to wound; (*vista, udito, ecc.*) to offend, to shock **6.** (*mil.*) to damage || **offèndersi**, *v.r.* to feel hurt (by sthg.), to be offended (at, by sthg.), to take offence (at sthg.): *non offenderti se ti dico queste cose*, don't take it amiss (*o* don't take offence *o* don't be offended) if I tell you these things; *si offendeva sempre per le mie osservazioni*, he was always offended at (*o* by) my remarks.

offendìbile, *ag.* vulnerable: *luogo —*, (*mil.*) vulnerable position.

offensìva, *s.f.* (*mil.*) offensive: *l'— è stata portata a termine*, the offensive was carried out successfully; *prendere l'—, passare all'—*, to take the offensive.

offensivamente, *av.* offensively.

offensìvo, *ag.* **1.** (*mil.*) offensive: *armi offensive e difensive*, weapons of offence and defence (*o* offensive and defensive weapons); *guerra offensiva*, war of attack; *lega offensiva*, hostile league; *ritorno —*, counter-attack **2.** (*oltraggioso*) offensive, insulting: *modi offensivi*, insulting manners; *fu —*, he was insulting.

offensóre, *s.m.* offender.

offerènte, *s.m.* offerer; (*ad un'asta*) bidder: *il migliore —*, the highest bidder.

offerìre, *V.* offrìre.

offèrta, *s.f.* **1.** offer: *un'— di matrimonio*, an offer of marriage; *fare, accettare, respingere un'—*, to make, to accept, to decline an offer **2.** (*donazione*) offering, donation: — *generosa, meschina*, generous, wretched offering; *fece un'— alla Vergine*, he made an offering to the Virgin; *fare un'— a un istituto di beneficenza*, to make a donation (*o* an offering) to a charitable organization **3.** (*comm.*) offer; (*per appalti*) tender; (*ad un'asta*) bid; (*econ.*) supply: — *campionata*, offer with sample; — *di merci*, offer of goods; *l'— più alta*, the highest offer; *domanda e — in regime di concorrenza*, free play of demand and supply; *legge della domanda e dell'—*, law of demand and supply; *fare un'—*, to bid (*o* to make a bid); *fare un'— per un appalto*, to make a tender ‖ *offerte e domande d'impiego*, situations vacant and wanted **4.** — *reale*, (*dir.*) tender.

offèrto, *ag.* **1.** offered, tendered: *servizi offerti*, services offered; *somma offerta*, sum offered (*o* tendered) **2.** (*relig.*) (*dedicato*) offered (up): *preghiere offerte*, prayers offered (up).

offertòrio, *s.m.* (*eccl.*) offertory.

offésa, *s.f.* **1.** offence, affront, insult: *un'— lieve*, a slight affront (*o* offence); *questa è un'— al mio onore*, this is an insult to my honour; *questa musica è un'— per l'udito*, this music is an offence to the ear; *sia detto senza —*, no offence meant; *il suo abito è un'— al buon gusto*, her dress is an offence against good taste; *dimenticare le offese*, to forget offences (*o* wrongs); *ingoiare un'—*, to swallow an insult; *patire un'—*, to suffer a wrong; *recare — a qlcu.*, to give offence to s.o. **2.** (*mil.*) (*offensiva*) offensive, attack: *armi di —*, offensive weapons **3.** (*lesione*) lesion, hurt.

offéso, *ag.* **1.** offended, injured: *parlava con un tono di voce —*, he spoke in an injured tone (of voice); *si sente — per ciò che ho detto*, he feels offended at (*o* by) what I said; *sono — con lui*, I am annoyed with him **2.** (*colpito, ferito*) injured, damaged: *l'occhio —*, the injured eye.

officiàle, *V.* **ufficiàle**.

officiànte, *ag.* (*eccl.*) officiating ‖ *s.m.* (*eccl.*) officiant.

officiàre, *v.i.* (*eccl.*) to officiate (at sthg.).

officiatóre, *s.m.* (*eccl.*) officiator.

officìna, *s.f.* workshop, shop: — *di montaggio*, assembly (*o* erecting) shop; — *meccanica*, machine-shop; *capo —*, shop foreman; *l'— resterà chiusa dal 1º al 15 agosto*, the workshop will be closed from 1st August till 15th August.

officinàle, *ag.* (*farmaceutico*) officinal.

officío, *V.* **ufficio**.

officiosaménte, *av.* (*cortesemente*) courteously; obligingly **2.** (*non ufficialmente*) unofficially.

officiosità, *s.f.* **1.** (*cortesia*) courtesy, civility **2.** (*mancanza di ufficialità*) unofficial nature.

officióso, *ag.* **1.** (*cortese*) courteous, civil; obliging **2.** (*non ufficiale*) unofficial.

offrire, *v.t.* **1.** to offer, to tender: *gli offrì del danaro per corromperlo*, he offered him a bribe; *gli offrì la sua amicizia*, he offered him his friendship; *le offrì di sposarlo*, he proposed to her (*o* he offered to marry her); *questo mi offre finalmente l'occasione di ringraziarti*, this offers (*o* gives) me the opportunity to thank you at last; *questo programma è offerto dalla ditta X*, this programme is sponsored by the X firm; *ti posso — ospitalità per questa notte*, I can put you up for the night; — *aiuto, assistenza*, to offer help, assistance; — *ql.co. in dono*, to offer sthg. as a gift; — *la mano*, to offer one's hand; — *le proprie scuse*, to tender (*o* to proffer) one's apologies; — *i propri servigi*, to offer (*o* to tender *o* to proffer) one's services **2.** (*dedicare*) to offer (up), to dedicate: *offro questo libro alla mia cara madre*, I dedicate this book to my beloved mother; — *preghiere a Dio*, to offer (up) prayers to God; — *le proprie tribolazioni in sacrificio*, to offer up one's troubles as a sacrifice **3.** (*comm.*) to offer, to tender; (*ad un'asta*) to bid: *chi offre di più per questo magnifico vaso cinese?*, who will bid me more for this wonderful Chinese vase?;

offriva la sua bella casa per pochissimo danaro, he offered his beautiful house for very little money; — *una forte somma per estinguere un debito*, to tender a large sum in discharge of a debt **4.** (*esporre*) to expose, to offer: *offrì il viso alla pioggia*, she exposed her face to the rain ‖ **offrìrsi**, *v.r.* **1.** to offer (oneself): *prenderò la prima occasione che si offrirà*, I shall take the first opportunity that offers (*o* arises); *si offrì di aiutarla*, he offered (*o* proffered) to help her **2.** (*esporsi*) to offer oneself, to expose oneself: *si offrì eroicamente ai colpi*, he exposed (*o* offered) himself heroically to the blows.

offuscaménto, *s.m.* **1.** (*l'oscurare*) darkening, dimming, obscuring (anche *fig.*): — *della ragione*, darkening (*o* dimming) of the reason; — *del sole*, darkening of the sun **2.** (*oscurità*) dimness, obscurity (anche *fig.*).

offuscàre, *v.t.* to darken, to dim, to obscure (anche *fig.*): *il fumo aveva offuscato il cielo*, the smoke had darkened the sky; *le passioni offuscano l'intelletto*, passions dim (*o* obscure) the mind; *la sua gloria non offuscherà mai quella di suo padre*, his glory will never dim (*o* outshine *o* obscure) his father's; *i suoi occhi sono offuscati dalle lacrime*, her eyes are dimmed with tears ‖ **offuscàrsi**, *v.r.* to grow dark, to darken; to grow dim, to become obscured (anche *fig.*): *il cielo si offuscò*, the sky grew dark; *durante la malattia gli si offuscò la vista*, his sight grew dim during his illness; *la sua fama si offuscò*, his fame became obscured (*o* grew dim).

offuscatóre, *ag.* darkening, dimming ‖ *s.m.*, **offuscatríce**, *s.f.* darkener, dimmer.

ofíasi, *s.f.* (*patol.*) ophiasis.

oficlèide, *s.f.* (*mus.*) ophicleide.

ofídi, *s.m.pl.* (*zool.*) Ophidia.

ofídio, *s.m.* (*ittiol.*) ophidium.

ofidísmo, *s.m.* (*patol.*) ophidiasis.

ofiología, *s.f.* ophiology.

oftalmía, *s.f.* (*patol.*) ophthalmia.

oftàlmico, *ag.* ophthalmic ‖ *s.m.* ophthalmiac.

oftalmiàtra, *s.m.* opthalmiater, ophthalmologist.

oftalmoiatría, **oftalmología**, *s.f.* ophthalmology.

oftalmològico, *ag.* ophthalmological.

oftalmòlogo, *s.m.* ophthalmologist.

oftalmometría, *s.f.* ophthalmometry.

oftalmòmetro, *s.m.* ophthalmometer.

oftalmoscopía, *s.f.* ophthalmoscopy.

oftalmoscòpio, *s.m.* ophthalmoscope.

Òga Magòga, (*locuzione derivata da Gog e Magog, nomi di due popoli biblici*) Gog and Magog.

oggettivaménte, *av.* objectively: *consideriamo — la questione*, let us consider the matter objectively.

oggettivàre, *v.t.* to objectify ‖ **oggettivàrsi**, *v.r.* to assume concrete shape, to become concrete.

oggettivísmo, *s.m.* objectivism (anche *fil.*).

oggettivísta, *s.c.* (*fil.*) objectivist.

oggettività, *s.f.* objectivity, objectiveness.

oggettívo, *ag.* **1.** objective; impartial, detached: *cerca di essere — nei tuoi giudizi*, try to be impartial in your judgements; *era — nella discussione*, he was objective in the discussion **2.** (*reale*) objective, real: *realtà oggettiva*, objective reality **3.** (*gram.*) objective: *proposizione oggettiva*, objective clause ‖ *s.m.* (*scopo, intento*) scope, aim, object.

oggètto, *s.m.* **1.** thing, article: *oggetti da viaggio*, travelling-articles; *oggetti preziosi*, valuables; *è un — di cattivo gusto di cui mi libererei volentieri*, it is a tasteless object, and I should like to get rid of it; *è un — troppo pesante per te*, this is too heavy for you; *questo — non mi serve*, this thing is of no use to me **2.** (*argomento*) subject: *l'— della nostra discussione sarà...*, the subject of our debate will be...; *qual è stato l'— della vostra lunga conversazione?*, what was the subject of your long conversation? **3.** (*motivo*) object, subject: *è — di invidia da parte di molti*, many people envy him; *era diventato — di scherno generale*, he had become a laughing-stock; *questa donna è — di pietà*, this woman is an object of pity **4.** (*scopo*) object, aim, purpose, end: *a questo —*, to this end; *l'— della mia lettera era molto chiaro*, the purpose of my letter was very clear; *l'— della mia visita era di dirgli quello che pensavo*, the object of my visit was to tell him exactly what I thought **5.** (*gram.*) object: *l'— e il soggetto*, the object and the subject; *— diretto, indiretto*, direct, indirect object **6.** (*fil.*) object: *— materiale*, material object; *— formale*, formal object.

òggi, *av.* **1.** to-day, today: *il giornale di —*, to-day's newspaper; *— è venerdì*, to-day is Friday; *— non ci sono lezioni*, there are no lessons today; *— non posso*, to-day I can't; *comincia da — !*, begin from to-day!; *da — in poi studierò*, from today on (*o* henceforward) I'll study; *fino ad — non ha scritto*, up to today she has not written ‖ *— a otto*, today week (*o* a week to -day); *— a quindici*, today fortnight (*o* a fortnight to-day) ‖ *— come —*, *non potrei farlo*, for the time being I can't do it ‖ *— a me, domani a te*, *prov.* to-day me, to-morrow you **2.** (*nel tempo presente*) to-day, today, nowadays: *l'Inglese è parlato in tutto il mondo*, English is spoken all over the world today; *— non si dice più...*, to-day we no longer say...; *al giorno d'— i ragazzi non studiano abbastanza!*, nowadays children don't study enough! ‖ *s.m.* to-day, today: *dall'— al domani possono succedere tante cose*, between to-day and tomorrow so many things may happen; *non rimandare d'— in domani quello che devi fare*, don't put off till to-morrow what you have to do to-day.

oggidí, oggigiórno, *av.* nowadays.

oggimài, *av.* now, by this time.

Ogígia, *no.pr.f.* (*geog. mit.*) Ogygia.

ogíva, *s.f.* **1.** (*arch.*) pointed arch, pointed window; ogive: *a —*, ogival **2.** (*mil.*) nose **3.** (*aer.*) spinner.

ogivàle, *ag.* (*arch.*) ogival: *architettura —*, Gothic (*o* ogival) architecture; *arco —*, pointed arch.

ógni, *ag. indef.* **1.** every, every single, each; (*tutti*) all: *— giorno, mese, anno*, every day, month, year; *— giorno della settimana*, every day in the week; *— giorno riceve cento lire da suo padre*, he gets a hundred lire every (*o* each *o* a) day from his father; *viene qui — giorno*, he comes here every (single) day; *— sorta di cose*, all sorts of things (*o* every sort of thing); *merci di — genere*, goods of every kind (*o* description); *sotto — aspetto*, in every way; *la vita di — giorno*, everyday life; *— casa ha il suo giardino*, every (*o* each) house has its own garden; *— studente ricevette un premio*, every (*o* each) student received a prize (*o* all the students received prizes); *— uomo deve morire*, all men (*o* every man) must die ‖ *— ben di Dio*, all sorts of good things ‖ *— cosa*, everything: *— cosa che fa è ben fatta*, everything he does is well done; *mi disse — cosa*, he told me everything ‖ *in — luogo*, everywhere: *Dio è in — luogo*, God is everywhere; *lo incontro in — luogo in cui vado*, I meet him everywhere I go ‖ *oltre — credere*, beyond all belief ‖ *ti auguro — bene*, I wish you all the best **2.** (*qualsiasi*) any: *a — costo*, at any cost (*o* at all costs); *in, ad — modo*, in any case (*o* anyway *o* all the same *o* anyhow): *in — modo è meglio dirglielo*, it is better to tell him anyway **3.** (*distributivo, con numerali*) every: *— due, tre, quattro settimane*, every two, three, four weeks (*o* every second, third, fourth week); *— quattro colonne c'era un quadro*, at every fourth pillar there was a picture; *prendi questa medicina — tre giorni*, take this medicine every three days.

ogniqualvòlta, *cong.* whenever, every time: *— la patria è in pericolo, i cittadini prendono le armi per difenderla*, every time (*o* whenever) their country is in danger, the citizens take up arms to defend it; *— la vedevo, il mio cuore si riempiva di gioia*, whenever (*o* every time) I saw her, my heart leaped for joy.

ognissànti, *s.m.* All Saints' Day, All Hallows.

ognóra, *av.* always.

ognúno, *pron. indef.* **1.** everybody, everyone: *— ama la propria casa*, everybody loves his own home; *— lo sa*, everybody knows (it) ‖ *— per sè e Dio per tutti*, *prov.* everyone for himself and God for all **2.** (*seguito dal partitivo*) each, every single one, each and every one; all: *— di loro era partito*, every single one of them had (*o* they had all) left; *— di loro ha due libri*, they each have two books (*o* they have two books each *o* they all have two books); *— di loro ha le sue idee in proposito*, each and every one of them has his own opinion (*o* they all have their own opinions) about this matter; *— di loro voleva raccontare la sua storia*, each of them wanted to tell his own story (*o* they all wanted to tell their own stories) ‖ *ag.* (*arc.*) each; all: *ognuna creatura che vive nel mondo*, all creatures that on earth do dwell.

oh, *inter.* oh!; (*gener. poet.*) O!: *—, che meraviglia!*, oh, how wonderful!; *— essere in Inghilterra!*, O to be in England!; *— santo cielo!*, oh good gracious!.

ohibò, *V.* **oibò.**

ohimè, *inter.* alas.

ohm, *s.m.* (*elett.*) ohm.

oibò, *inter.* oh!; (*vergogna!*) now then!; *— !, che pasticcio hai fatto!*, oh! what a mess you have made!; *— !, cosa stai facendo?*, now then! what are you up to?.

oídio, *s.m.* (*bot.*) oidium.

oil, *av.* (*nell'antico francese = sì*): *lingua d'—*, langue d'oïl.

olà, *inter.* hey there!, you there!.

Olànda, *no.pr.f.* (*geog.*) Holland ‖ **olànda,** *s.f.* (*tessuto*) holland.

olandése, *ag.* Dutch ‖ *s.m.* **1.** (*abitante*) Dutchman (*pl.* Dutchmen) **2.** (*lingua*) (the) Dutch (language) ‖ *s.f.* **1.** Dutchwoman (*pl.* Dutchwomen) **2.** (*ind. carta*) hollander, beater, beating machine; (*ind. gomma*) tub washer, beater.

oleàcee, *s.f.pl.* (*bot.*) Oleaceae.

oleàceo, *ag.* (*letter.*) oleaceous.

oleaginóso, *ag.* (*rar.*) oleaginous.

oleàndro, *s.m.* (*bot.*) oleander.

oleàrio, *ag.* oil (*attributivo*): *mercato —*, (vegetable-) oil market.

oleàstro, *s.m.* (*bot.*) oleaster.

oleàto, *ag.* **1.** oiled: *carta oleata*, grease-proof paper; (*per disegno*) tracing-paper **2.** *sale —*, (*chim.*) oleate.

olècrano, *s.m.* (*anat.*) olecranon.

olèico, *ag.* (*chim.*) oleic: *acido —*, oleic acid.

oleífero, *ag.* oleiferous, oil-yielding.

oleifício, *s.m.* oil mill, oil-works.

oleína, *s.f.* (*chim.*) olein.

oleodótto, *s.m.* oil pipeline.

oleografía, *s.f.* **1.** (*pitt.*) (*arte, processo*) oleography **2.** (*quadro in oleografia*) oleograph.

oleogràfico, *ag.* oleographic.

oleomargarína, *s.f.* (*chim.*) oleomargarine.

oleòmetro, *s.m.* oil gauge.

oleorèsina, *s.f.* (*chim.*) oleoresin.

oleosità, *s.f.* oiliness.

oleóso, *ag.* oily; oil (*attributivo*): *liquido —*, oily liquid; *seme —*, oil-seed; *sostanza oleosa*, oily substance.

olezzànte, *ag.* sweet-smelling, fragrant.

olezzàre, *v.i.* to smell sweetly, to be fragrant.

olézzo, *s.m.* fragrance, sweet smell.

olfattívo, *ag.* olfactory: *organo —*, olfactory organ.

olfàtto, *s.m.* smell, olfaction.

olfattòrio, *ag.* (*rar.*) olfactory.

Òlga, *no.pr.f.* Olga.

oliàre, *v.t.* to oil.

oliàto, *ag.* oiled ‖ *carta oliata*, grease-proof paper; (*per disegno*) tracing-paper.

oliatóre, *s.m.* (*mec.*) oilcan.

olíbano, *s.m.* (*bot. chim.*) olibanum.

olièra, *s.f.* cruets (*pl.*).

olifànte, *s.m.* (*lett.*) oliphant.

oligàrca, *s.m.* oligarch.

oligarchía, *s.f.* oligarchy.

oligarchicaménte, *av.* oligarchically.

oligàrchico, *ag.* oligarchic(al).

oligísto, *s.m.* (*min.*) oligist.

oligocène, *s.m.* (*geol.*) Oligocene.

oligoemía, *s.f.* (*med.*) oligaemia.

Olímpia[1], *no.pr.f.* Olympia.

Olímpia[2], *no.pr.f.* (*geog.*) Olympia.

olimpíaco, *ag.* Olympic.

olimpíade, *s.f.* 1. Olympiad 2. *pl.* (*spor.*) Olympic games.

olímpico, *ag.* 1. Olympic: *giuochi olimpici*, Olympic games 2. (*dell'Olimpo, celestiale*) Olympian, celestial.

olímpio, *ag.* Olympian.

olimpiònico, *s.m.* Olympic champion.

Olímpo, *no.pr.m.* (*geog.*) Olympus.

Olínto, *no.pr.f.* (*geog. st.*) Olynthus.

òlio, *s.m.* oil: — *combustibile, pesante*, fuel oil; — *d'arachidi*, peanut oil; — *da cucina*, cooking oil; — *da tavola*, salad-oil; — *di colone*, cotton oil; — *di fegato di merluzzo*, cod-liver oil; — *di lino*, linseed (o flax) oil; — *di mandorle*, almond-oil; — *di palma*, palm-oil; — *di paraffina*, paraffin-oil; — *di ricino*, castor-oil; — *di sansa*, husk-oil; — *di sego*, tallow-oil; — *di sesamo*, sesame oil; — *d'oliva*, olive-oil; — *essenziale*, essential oil; — *lubrificante*, lubricating oil; — *minerale, animale, vegetale*, mineral, animal, vegetable oil; — *raffinato*, refined oil; *colori a* —, (*pitt.*) oil-colours; *quadro a* —, (*pitt.*) oil-painting; *condire con* —, to dress with oil; *dipingere a* —, (*pitt.*) to paint in oils (o in oil-colours) ‖ — *di gomito*, elbow-grease ‖ — *santo*, (*eccl.*) holy oil (o oil of the sick) ‖ *liscio come l'* —, as smooth as silk ‖ *sott'*—, in oil ‖ *gettar* — *sulle fiamme*, to add fuel to the fire.

olíva, *s.f.* olive: *olio d'*—, olive-oil; *verde* —, olive green.

olivàle, olivàre, *ag.* olive-shaped.

olivàstro, *ag.* olive, olivaceous, olive-coloured: *carnagione olivastra*, olive complexion ‖ *s.m.* wild olive-tree.

olivéta, *s.f.* olive-yard, olive-grove.

olivetàno, *ag.* (*eccl.*) Olivetan (*attributivo*) ‖ *s.m.* (*eccl.*) Olivetan.

olivéto, *s.m.* olive-grove, olive-yard.

Olívia, *no.pr.f.* Olive, Olivia ‖ *dim.* Livy.

Olivièro, *no.pr.m.* Oliver ‖ *dim.* Noll, Nolly.

olívo, *s.m.* olive(-tree): *ramoscello d'*—, olive -branch: *offrire un ramoscello d'*—, to hold out (o to offer) the olive-branch (anche *fig.*) ‖ *Domenica degli Olivi*, (*eccl.*) Palm Sunday ‖ *il giardino degli Olivi*, the Garden of Olives ‖ *il Monte degli Olivi*, the Mount of Olives.

òlla, *s.f.* 1. earthen pot 2. (*archeol.*) cinerary urn.

olmàia, *s.f.*, **olméto**, *s.m.* elm-grove.

ólmio, *s.m.* (*chim.*) holmium.

ólmo, *s.m.* elm(-tree): — *di montagna*, wych-elm; *maritare una vite a un* —, to train a vine up an elm.

olocàusto, *s.m.* 1. holocaust: *l'* — *di Abramo*, Abraham's sacrifice 2. (*sacrificio*) sacrifice: *fare* — *di ql.co.*, to sacrifice sthg.; *offrire in* — *ql.co. a qlcu.*, to sacrifice sthg. to s.o. 3. (*eccl.*) the Sacrifice of the Mass.

olocèfalo, *s.m.* (*ittiol.*) Holocephalan ‖ *gli olocefali*, the Holocephali.

olocène, *s.m.* (*geol.*) Holocene.

olocènico, *ag.* (*geol.*) Holocene (*attributivo*).

olocristallíno, *ag.* (*min.*) holocrystalline.

oloèdrico, *ag.* (*min.*) holohedral.

Olofèrne, *no.pr.m.* (*Bibbia*) Holofernes, Holopherne.

olofràstico, *ag.* holophrastic.

ològrafo, *ag.* (*dir.*) holograph.

olóna, *s.f.* sail-cloth.

olotúria, *s.f.* (*zool.*) holothuria.

oltracciò, *av.* besides.

oltraggiàbile, *ag.* liable to outrage, liable to abuse.

oltraggiaménto, *s.m.* 1. (*l'oltraggiare*) outraging, insulting 2. (*oltraggio*) insult; (*violazione*) violation.

oltraggiàre, *v.t.* 1. to outrage; (*insultare*) to insult, to abuse: *mi oltraggiò ripetutamente*, he repeatedly insulted (o abused) me; — *la natura, la legge, il buon senso*, to outrage nature, the law, common sense 2. (*profanare*) to desecrate; (*violare*) to violate: — *un luogo sacro*, to desecrate a holy place; — *una tomba*, to desecrate (o to violate) a tomb.

oltraggiatóre, *s.m.*, **oltraggiatríce**, *s.f.* outrager; (*chi insulta*) insulter; (*chi viola*) violator.

oltràggio, *s.m.* 1. outrage; (*insulto*) insult, abuse; (*offesa*) offence: *recare* — *alla giustizia*, to outrage justice; *recare* — *al pudore*, to outrage decency; *recare* — *a qlcu.*, to commit an outrage on (o against) s.o.; *vendicare un* —, to revenge an insult 2. (*danno*) injury: *gli oltraggi del tempo*, (*poet.*) the ravages of time.

oltraggiosaménte, *av.* outrageously; (*in modo insultante*) insultingly.

oltraggióso, *ag.* outrageous; (*insultante*) insulting; (*offensivo*) offensive: *comportamento* —, outrageous conduct; *parole oltraggiose*, offensive words.

oltràlpe, *av.* beyond the Alps, on the other side of the Alps ‖ *d'*—, from the other side of the Alps: *i costumi d'*—, the customs from the other side of the Alps.

oltramontàno, *ag.* ultramontane ‖ *gli oltramontani*, (*st. relig.*) ultramontanists.

oltranaturàle, *ag.* supernatural.

oltrànza, ad, *l.av.* to the bitter end, to the death: *guerra ad* —, war to the death; *sciopero ad* —, strike to the bitter end.

oltranzísta, *s.m.* extremist.

oltràrno, *s.m.* "Oltrarno" (the left bank of the Arno in Florence).

óltre, *av.* 1. (*di luogo*) further, farther: *è andato troppo* —, he has gone too far (anche *fig.*); *non vuole andar* —, he doesn't want to go any further (o farther) 2. (*di tempo*) longer: *non posso aspettare* —, I cannot wait any longer ‖ *più* —, later (o further) on ‖ *ragazzi di diciotto anni e* —, boys of eighteen and over ‖ *essere* — *negli anni*, to be advanced in years ‖ *prep.* 1. (*di luogo*) on the other side of, beyond (*stato in luogo*); over (*generalmente moto a luogo*); *fig.* beyond: — *mare*, oversea(s): *domini d'* — *mare*, overseas dominions; — *misura*, beyond measure; — *quelle montagne c'è la Francia*, France lies beyond (o on the other side of) those mountains; *andare* — *le montagne*, to go over the mountains 2. (*più di*) over, more than: *costa* — *diecimila lire*, it costs over ten thousand lire; *non lo vedo da* — *un anno*, I have not seen him for over a year; *quell'uomo è* — *i cinquanta*, that man is over fifty 3. (*in aggiunta*) besides, in addition to, as well as: — *a quel che ti ho detto*, in addition to what I have told you; — *a quelle case possiede un albergo*, besides those houses he owns an hotel; *le prime navi a vapore avevano alberi e vele* — *al fumaiolo*, early steamships had masts and sails as well as a funnel ‖ **óltre a, che**, *l. cong.* besides: — *all'avermi aiutato molto*, besides helping you a great deal; — *che perdonargli me ne sono fatto anche un amico*, besides forgiving him I've also made a friend of him.

oltremàre, *s.m.* (*colore*) ultramarine.

oltremàre, *av.* overseas ‖ *d'*—, (*di oltremare*) overseas (*attributivo*); (*da oltremare*) from overseas: *paesi d'*—, oversea(s) countries; *venire d'*—, to come from overseas.

oltremaríno, *ag.* 1. oversea(s) (*attributivo*); ultramarine: *commercio* —, oversea(s) trade 2. *azzurro* —, ultramarine (blue).

oltremisúra, *av.* beyond measure, extremely.

oltremòdo, *av.* exceedingly, excessively, extremely; *è un ragazzo* — *sciocco*, he is an extremely silly boy: *sono* — *contento di ciò*, I am extremely pleased about it.

oltremondàno, *ag.* ultramundane.

oltremontàno, *V.* **oltramontàno.**

oltremónte, oltremónti, *av.* beyond the mountains.

oltrepassàre, *v.t.* **1.** to go beyond (stgh.); (*eccedere*) to exceed: *dobbiamo — il villaggio*, we must go beyond the village; *non ho mai oltrepassato il limite di velocità*, I have never exceeded the speed-limit; *— i limiti*, *fig.* to go too far (*o* to overstep all bounds) **2.** (*mar.*) (*doppiare*) to double.

oltrerósso, *ag.* (*fis.*) infra-red.

oltretómba, *s.m.* hereafter, beyond: *il mistero dell'—*, the mystery of the beyond (*o* of the hereafter).

omàccio, *s.m.* big ugly man.

omacEIÓne, *s.m.* big man.

omàggio, *s.m.* **1.** (*segno di ossequio*) homage: *rendere — a qlcu.*, to pay (*o* to do) homage to s.o. ‖ *in — a*, in homage to: *in — alla verità*, in the interests of truth **2.** *pl.* respects, compliments: *porgete i miei omaggi a vostro padre*, please give my respects to your father **3.** (*offerta*) free gift: *— dell'autore*, with the author's compliments; *copia in —*, presentation copy; *fare — di ql.co. a qlcu.*, to present s.o. with sthg. **4.** (*st.*) (*atto di vassallaggio*) homage: *giurare — a qlcu.*, to pay homage to s.o.

omài, (*letter.*) per **oramài.**

òmaro, *s.m.* (*zool.*) lobster.

omàso, *s.m.* (*di ruminanti*) omasum (*pl.* omasa).

ombelicàle, *ag.* (*anat.*) umbilical: *cordone —*, umbilical cord (*o* navel-string).

ombelicàto, *ag.* umbilicate.

ombel(l)íco, *s.m.* (*anat.*) navel; umbilicus (*pl.* umbilici).

ómbra, *s.f.* **1.** shade: *l'— del bosco*, the shade of the wood; *le ombre della sera, della notte*, the shades of evening, of night; *— densa, fitta*, deep shade; *all'—*, in the shade: *camminava all'—*, he was walking in the shade; *luci e ombre*, (*pitt.*) light(s) and shade(s) (anche *fig.*); *una campagna desolata, senza un palmo d'—*, a desolate countryside without the smallest patch of shade; *cerco un po' d'— dove sedermi*, I am looking for some shade to sit in; *metà del viso è in —*, (*pitt. foto.*) half the face is in shadow; *queste ombre sono troppo forti*, (*pitt.*) this shading is too dark; *i pioppi fanno poca —*, poplars give little shade ‖ *l'— dell'ignoranza*, the darkness of ignorance ‖ *cono d'—*, (*astr.*) umbra (*pl.* umbrae) ‖ *mettere in — qlcu., ql.co.*, *fig.* to put s.o., sthg. in (*o* to throw s.o., sthg. into) the shade: *la sua bellezza mette in — quella delle altre donne*, her beauty puts all other women in the shade ‖ *tenersi nell'—*, *fig.* to keep in the shade ‖ *tramare nell'—*, to plot secretly **2.** (*immagine proiettata*) shadow (anche *fig.*): *all'— di ql.co.*, in the shadow of sthg. (anche *fig.*): *siedo all'— di un albero*, I am sitting in the shadow of a tree; *starsene all'— della legge*, to be within the letter of the law; *il lume a petrolio proiettava ombre mostruose sulla parete*, the oil-lamp cast monstruous shadows on the wall; *gettare un'—*, to cast a shadow: *la minaccia di una guerra getta un'— sinistra sul futuro*, the threat of war casts a gloomy shadow over the future ‖ *non è che un'— di quello che era*, he is but the shadow of his former self ‖ *aver paura della propria —*, to be afraid of one's own shadow ‖ *correr dietro alle ombre*, to run after shadows (*o* to catch at shadows) ‖ *dar — a qlcu.*, to overshadow (*o* to outshine) s.o. ‖ *dar corpo alle ombre*, to give importance to trifling matters ‖ *essere l'— di qlcu.*, to be s.o.'s shadow: *il suo cane è la sua —*, his dog is his shadow ‖ *prendere —*, (*di cavallo*) to shy; (*di persona*) to take umbrage ‖ *ridursi un'—*, to wear oneself to a shadow **3.** (*traccia, parvenza*) shadow; hint; suggestion: *non c'è — di dubbio!*, there is not a shadow of a doubt!; *non c'è — di vero in ciò che dici*, there is not even a shadow of truth in what you say; *non v'è — di retorica nei suoi scritti*, there is no suggestion of rhetoric in his writings; *sul suo viso apparve*

un'— di tristezza, a hint of melancholy (*o* sadness) passed across her face; *sul suo viso è l'— della morte*, the shadow of death is on his face ‖ *nemmeno per —!*, not at all! **4.** (*spettro, spirito*) shade: *le ombre del passato*, the shades of the past; *l'— di Virgilio*, the shade of Virgil; *il mondo delle ombre*, the shades.

ombràre, *v.t.* (*rar.*) to shade: *— un disegno*, to shade a drawing ‖ **ombràrsi,** *v.r.* **1.** to darken **2.** (*adombrarsi*) (*di persone*) to take umbrage; (*di cavalli*) to shy: *— alle parole di qlcu.*, to take umbrage at s.o.'s words.

ombreggiaménto, *s.m.* shading.

ombreggiànte, *ag.* shady.

ombreggiàre, *v.t.* to shade: *gli alberi ombreggiavano il prato*, the trees shaded the lawn; *— un disegno*, to shade a drawing.

ombreggiatúra, *s.f.*, **ombréggio,** *s.m.* (*pitt.*) shading; (*tratteggio*) hatching.

ombrèlla, *s.f.* (*bot.*) umbel.

ombrellàio, *s.m.* **1.** (*chi fabbrica ombrelli*) umbrella -maker **2.** (*chi vende ombrelli*) umbrella-seller.

ombrellàta, *s.f.* blow with an umbrella: *diede ombrellate a tutti*, he laid about him with his umbrella.

ombrellífere, *s.f.pl.* (*bot.*) Umbelliferae.

ombrellífero, *ag.* (*bot.*) umbelliferous.

ombrellíno, *s.m.* (*da sole*) parasol, sunshade.

ombrèllo, *s.m.* umbrella: *— da sole*, parasol (*o* sunshade); *— di seta*, silk umbrella; *fodero d'—*, umbrella-sheath; *intelaiatura dell'—*, umbrella frame; *manico d'—*, umbrella handle; *stecche d'—*, umbrella -ribs; *aprire, chiudere l'—*, to open, to close one's umbrella.

ombrellóne, *s.m.* large sunshade: *— da spiaggia*, beach-umbrella.

ombría, *s.f.* (*letter.*) shade.

ombrína, *s.f.* (*ittiol.*) umbrina.

ombrinàle, *s.m.* (*mar.*) scupper.

ombròmetro, *s.m.* (*meteorologia*) ombrometer.

ombrosaménte, *av.* (*con suscettibilità*) touchily.

ombrosità, *s.f.* **1.** shadiness **2.** (*suscettibilità*) touchiness; (*di cavalli*) skittishness.

ombróso, *ag.* **1.** shady, shadowy: *un angolo —*, a shady corner (*o* nook); *boschi ombrosi*, shadowy woods; *valle ombrosa*, shaded valley **2.** (*suscettibile*) touchy; (*di cavalli*) skittish: *è un vecchio —*, he is a touchy old man.

omèga, *s.m.* (*ultima lettera dell'alfabeto greco*) omega ‖ *dall'alfa all'—*, from beginning to end (*o* from a to z).

omelette, *s.f.* (*cuc.*) omelet(te).

omelía, *s.f.* (*eccl.*) homily.

oménto, *s.m.* (*anat.*) omentum (*pl.* omenta).

omeopatía, *s.f.* (*med.*) hom(o)eopathy.

omeopàtico, *ag.* (*med.*) hom(o)eopathic: *rimedio —*, hom(o)eopathic remedy ‖ *s.m.* hom(o)eopathist.

omeràle, *ag.* (*anat.*) humeral.

omericaménte, *av.* Homerically.

omèrico, *ag.* Homeric: *poemi omerici*, Homeric poems; *questione omerica*, Homeric question ‖ *risata omerica*, (*scherz.*) Homeric laughter.

omerísta, *s.m.* Homerologist.

Omèro[1]**,** *no.pr.m.* Homer.

òmero[2]**,** *s.m.* **1.** (*anat.*) humerus (*pl.* humeri) **2.** (*spalla*) shoulder.

omertà, *s.f.* silence.

omésso, *ag.* omitted, left out.

omèttere, *v.t.* to omit, to leave out; (*saltare*) to skip: *ho omesso alcuni passi di quel libro*, I have skipped some passages of that book; *quella parola è sbagliata, hai omesso un «r»*, that word is wrong, you have left out an " r "; *questo capitolo può essere omesso*, this chapter may be omitted; *— di fare ql.co.*, to omit doing (*o* to do) sthg.

omiciàttolo, *s.m.* (*spreg.*) manikin.

omicída, *ag.* **1.** homicidal, murderous: *intenzione —*, murderous intent (*o* intent to kill); *mania —*, homicidal mania **2.** (*che ha dato la morte*) death-dealing:

ferro —, death-dealing blade; *mani omicide*, death-dealing hands ‖ *s.c.* homicide; *(assassino)* murderer.

omicídio, *s.m.* homicide; *(assassinio)* murder: — *colposo, preterintenzionale,* manslaughter (*o amer.* second-degree murder *o* murder in the second degree); — *per legittima difesa,* homicide in self-defence; — *premeditato,* wilful murder (*o amer.* first-degree murder *o* murder in the first degree); *colpevole di* —, guilty of murder; *processo per* —, murder-trial (*o* murder-case); *commettere un* —, to commit (a) murder.

òmicron, *s.m.* (*lettera dell'alfabeto greco*) omicron.

omilètico, *ag.* (*eccl.*) homiletic.

omissióne, *s.f.* omission: — *di una virgola,* omission of a comma; — *volontaria, involontaria,* voluntary, involuntary omission ‖ *peccato di* —, sin of omission ‖ *salvo errori ed omissioni* (*abbr.* S.E.O.), errors and omission excepted (*abbr.* E. & O.E.).

ommatídio, *s.m.* (*di insetto*) ommatidium (*pl.* ommatidia).

òmnibus, *ag.* (*di treno*) slow, stopping ‖ *s.m.* **1.** (*treno*) slow train, stopping-train **2.** (*vettura pubblica*) bus.

omnisciènza, *s.f.* omniscience.

omnívoro, *ag.* omnivorous.

omocromía, *s.f.* homocromy.

omofonía, *s.f.* (*fonet. mus.*) homophony.

omofònico, *ag.* (*fonet. mus.*) homophonic.

omòfono, *ag.* (*fonet. mus.*) homophonous: *parola omofona,* homophone.

omogeneaménte, *av.* homogeneously.

omogeneità, *s.f.* homogeneity.

omogèneo, *ag.* homogeneous.

omologàre, *v.t.* **1.** (*dir.*) to homologate **2.** (*riconoscere ufficialmente*) to ratify: — *un primato sportivo,* to ratify a sporting record.

omologazlóne, *s.f.* **1.** (*dir.*) homologation **2.** (*riconoscimento ufficiale*) ratification: — *di un primato sportivo,* ratification of a sporting record.

omologia, *s.f.* (*biol. geom.*) homology.

omòlogo, *ag.* **1.** (*biol. geom.*) homologous **2.** (*corrispondente*) corresponding, homologous.

omomorfía, *s.f.* (*biol.*) homomorphy.

omonimía, *s.f.* **1.** coincidence of names: *si tratta d'un caso d'*—, they happen to have the same name **2.** (*omofonia*) homonymy.

omònimo, *ag.* **1.** homonymous; bearing the same name **2.** (*omofono*) homonymic, homonymous ‖ *s. m.* **1.** namesake: *non è mio parente, ma solo mio* —, he is not a relative of mine, he is just my namesake **2.** (*parola omofona*) homonym.

omoplàta, *s.f.* (*anat.*) omoplate.

omosessuàle, *ag.* homosexual.

omosessualità, *s.f.* homosexuality.

omúncolo, *s.m.* (*spreg.*) little nobody; manikin.

onàgro, *s.m.* **1.** (*zool.*) onager (*pl.* onagri, onagers) **2.** (*st. mil.*) bal(l)ista, onager (*pl.* onagri, onagers).

onanísmo, *s.m.* onanism.

óncia, *s.f.* **1.** — (*avoirdupois*), ounce (*misura di peso avoirdupois* = 28,35 g); — (*troy*), ounce (*misura di peso troy* = 31,10 g): *guantoni da otto once,* (*boxe*) eight-ounce gloves ‖ *a* — *a* —, little by little ‖ *non ha un'*— *di senso comune,* he hasn't an ounce of common sense **2.** — *fluida,* fluid ounce (*misura di capacità* = cm.³ 28,4 *in Gran Bretagna*; = cm.³ 29,6 *negli Stati Uniti*).

onciàle, *ag.* uncial: *un manoscritto* —, an uncial; *scrittura* —, uncial writing.

oncología, *s.f.* (*med.*) oncology.

oncològico, *ag.* (*med.*) oncological.

ónda, *s.f.* **1.** wave (*anche fig.*): — *alta,* high wave; *onde dei capelli,* waves in one's hair; *un'*— *di entusiasmo,* a wave of enthusiasm; *onde grosse,* billows; — *lunga,* roller; *cresta dell'*—, wave crest; *un'*— *di popolo irruppe nella piazza,* a wave of people rushed (*o* the people surged) into the square; *sbattuto dalle onde,* driven by the waves; *essere in balìa delle onde,*

to be tossed by the waves; *fendere, tagliare le onde,* to breast the waves ‖ *a onde,* wavy **2.** (*fis. rad.*) wave: *onde elettromagnetiche,* (*rad.*) electromagnetic waves; *onde herziane,* (*elett.*) Hertzian waves; — *luminosa,* (*fis.*) light-wave; *onde medie, lunghe, corte,* (*rad.*) medium, long, short waves; — *portante,* (*rad.*) carrier wave; — *sonora,* (*acu.*) sound-wave; *onde termiche,* (*fis.*) heat-waves; *lunghezza d'*—, (*rad.*) wavelength; *treno d'onde,* (*fis.*) wave train; *andare in* —, (*rad.*) to be broadcast; *mettere in* —, (*rad.*) to broadcast **3.** (*poet.*) (*mare*) sea, main.

ondàta, *s.f.* wave (*anche fig.*); (*grossa onda*) billow: — *di caldo,* heat-wave; — *di entusiasmo,* wave of enthusiasm; — *di freddo,* cold wave; — *di fumo,* gust of smoke; — *di panico,* wave of panic; — *di ribasso,* (*comm.*) fall of prices; *un'*— *di sangue gli salì al viso,* the blood rushed to his face; *una nuova* — *di truppe attaccò il nemico,* a fresh wave of troops attacked the enemy; *il vascello fu investito da pesanti ondate,* the vessel was struck by heavy waves ‖ *a ondate,* in waves.

ondàto, *ag.* wavy.

ónde, *av.* (*letter.*) **1.** whence, where... from, from where: — *venisti, sì pura e bella?,* whence did you come, so pure and fair?; — *vieni e dove vai?,* where have you come from and where are you going? **2.** (*causale*) wherefore, why: — *avviene ciò?,* wherefore does this happen? ‖ *pron. rel.* (*letter.*) **from which; by which; with which:** — *segue che...,* from which it follows that...; *il luogo* — *viene,* the place from which he comes (*o* the place he comes from); *i mali* — *egli è afflitto,* the evils by which he is beset (*o* the evils which beset him); *un prezioso metallo* — *si fanno gioielli,* a precious metal from which jewellery is made; *questo è il pugnale* — *fu ucciso,* this is the dagger with which he was killed (*o* he was killed with) ‖ *cong.* **1.** (*finale*) **so that, in order that:** *gli diedero un po' di denaro* — *potesse comprarsi del cibo,* they gave him some money so that (*o* in order that) he might buy food (*o* they gave him some money to buy food with) **2.** (*consecutiva*) **and so, therefore:** *io tacevo,* — *egli riprese a parlare,* I was silent, and so (*o* therefore) he began speaking again.

ondeggiaménto, *s.m.* **1.** (*di barca, ecc.*) rolling, rocking **2.** (*movimento simile a quello delle onde*) waving, swaying; (*di bandiera, tela*) fluttering; (*di messi, erba, ecc.*) waving, rippling; (*di folla*) swaying **3.** *pl.* (*marezzo*) wavy lines **4.** *fig.* (*incertezza*) wavering, hesitation, vacillation; (*fam.*) dithering.

ondeggiànte, *ag.* **1.** rolling, rocking: *andatura* —, rolling gait; *barca* — *all'ancora,* boat rocking (*o* rolling) at anchor **2.** (*che si muove come le onde*) (*di bandiera, tela*) fluttering; (*di messi, erba, ecc.*) waving, rippling; (*di folla*) swaying **3.** *fig.* (*esitante*) wavering, hesitating, vacillating **4.** (*poet.*) (*ondulato*) rolling, undulating: *paesaggio* —, rolling countryside.

ondeggiàre, *v.i.* **1.** (*di barca, ecc.*) to rock, to roll; (*di acque*) to ripple: *la barca ondeggiava dolcemente agli ormeggi,* the boat was rocking (*o* rolling) gently at her moorings; *la superficie del lago ondeggiava alla brezza,* the surface of the lake was rippling in the breeze; *una volta in alto mare la nave ondeggiò terribilmente,* the ship rocked (*o* rolled) terribly when it got out to sea **2.** (*oscillare, fluttuare con movimento simile a quello delle onde*) to wave, to sway; (*di bandiera, tela*) to flutter; (*di messi, erba, ecc.*) to wave, to ripple; (*di capelli*) to blow: *le bandiere ondeggiavano al vento,* the flags were fluttering in the wind; *la fiamma ondeggiò e si spense,* the flame wavered (*o* flickered) and died; *il grano ondeggiava,* the corn was wavering (*o* rippling *o* swaying); *la linea ondeggiò e si spezzò,* (*mil.*) the line wavered and broke; *i suoi capelli ondeggiavano al vento,* her hair was blowing in the wind; *le tende ondeggiavano davanti alla finestra aperta,* the curtains were waving (*o* fluttering) at the open window || *il vento faceva — le cime degli alberi*, the tree-tops were swaying in the wind (*o* the wind was shaking the tree-tops) **3.** *fig.* (*essere incerto, esitare*) to waver, to hesitate, to vacillate; (*fam.*) to dither: *— fra due soluzioni*, to waver (*o* to hesitate) between two solutions.

ondína, *s.f.* (*mit.*) undine.

ondosità, *s.f.* undulation.

ondóso, *ag.* undulating, undulatory: *moto —*, undulatory motion (*o* wave-motion).

ondulàre, *v.t.* to wave: *mi farò — i capelli*, I shall have my hair waved || *v.i.* to undulate.

ondulàto, *ag.* **1.** wavy, undulating: *capelli ondulati*, wavy hair; *terreno —*, undulating ground **2.** (*di lamiera, ecc.*) corrugated: *cartone —*, corrugated cardboard; *tetto in lamiera ondulata*, corrugated-iron roof.

ondulatòrio, *ag.* undulatory: *movimento —*, wave-motion; *terremoto —*, undulatory earthquake.

ondulazióne, *s.f.* **1.** undulation, waviness: *l'— del terreno*, the undulation of the ground **2.** (*movimento ondulatorio*) undulation, wave-motion; (*elett. rad.*) ripple **3.** (*di capelli*) wave: *— permanente*, permanent wave (*o fam.* perm).

oneràre, *v.t.* (*rar.*) to burden, to encumber: *proprietà onerata da debiti*, encumbered estate.

ònere, *s.m.* **1.** burden, onus (*solo sing.*); (*responsabilità*) responsibility: *— fiscale*, tax; *oneri tributari*, burden of taxation; *eredità con un —*, (*dir.*) conditional legacy; *l'— della prova spetta al Pubblico Ministero*, (*dir.*) the onus lies on the prosecution; *la famiglia era un — troppo gravoso per lui*, his family was too heavy a burden for him; *addossarsi un —*, to take on a responsibility **2.** (*ufficio gratuitamente esercitato*) honorary office.

onerosaménte, *av.* onerously.

oneróso, *ag.* onerous, burdensome.

onestà, *s.f.* **1.** (*rettitudine, onoratezza*) honesty, uprightness, integrity: *l'— delle sue intenzioni*, the honesty of his intentions; *— di vita, di costumi*, upright life, ways; *nei limiti dell'—* within the bounds of honesty; *uomo di specchiata —*, a man of unblemished honesty (*o* integrity) **2.** (*pudore, castità*) modesty, decorum: *l'— dei costumi delle donne di Firenze*, the modesty (*o* decorum) of Florentine women; *— di fanciulla*, maidenly modesty **3.** (*decenza*) decency, propriety: *offesa all'—*, offence against decency (*o* breach of propriety) **4.** (*bellezza, decoro di aspetto*) grace: *— del portamento*, graceful bearing.

onestaménte, *av.* **1.** (*con rettitudine*) honestly, uprightly **2.** (*castamente*) modestly, decorously **3.** (*con decenza*) decently.

onèsto, *ag.* **1.** (*retto*) honest, upright; (*giusto*) just: *gente onesta*, honest (*o* upright *o* decent) people; *lavoro —*, honest work; *una politica onesta*, an upright policy; *propositi onesti*, honest (*o* honourable) intentions; *uomo —*, honest (*o* straight) man; *nato da poveri, ma onesti genitori*, born of poor, but honest parents; *fu mosso da — orgoglio*, he was moved by just pride; *volentieri accetto la critica onesta*, I am willing to accept just (*o* honest) criticism || *gli onesti*, honest (*o* honourable) people **2.** (*virtuoso*) honest, virtuous; modest: *comportamento —*, modest behaviour; *moglie onesta*, honest (*o* virtuous) wife **3.** (*equo, lecito*) fair, honest: decent: *libro, linguaggio —*, decent book, language; *piacere —*, decent (*o* honest) pleasure; *prezzo —*, moderate (*o* fair) price **4.** (*discreto*) decent: *ad un'ora onesta*, at a decent hour **5.** (*onorevole*) honourable: *morte onesta*, honourable death **6.** (*bello d'aspetto*) graceful: *portamento —*, graceful bearing || *s.m.* what is honest; what is just; what is fair: *contentatevi dell'—*, be content with what is fair (*o* just); *è indeciso tra l'— e l'utile*, he is undecided (*o* wavering) between what is honest and what is useful.

ònice, *s.f.* (*min.*) onyx.

onírico, *ag.* oneiric.

onirología, *s.f.* oneirology.

oniromanzía, *s.f.* oneiromancy.

onninaménte, *ag.* (*letter.*) entirely, thoroughly.

onnipossènte, onnipotènte, *ag.* **1.** (*attributo divino*) almighty, omnipotent: *Dio —*, God Almighty || *l'Onnipotente*, (*Dio*) the Almighty **2.** (*attributo umano*) all-powerful: *un uomo —*, an all-powerful man.

onnipotenteménte, *av.* omnipotently.

onnipotènza, *s.f.* almightiness, omnipotence.

onnipresènte, *ag.* omnipresent, ubiquitous.

onnipresènza, *s.f.* omnipresence, ubiquity.

onnisciènte, *ag.* omniscient.

onnisciènza, *s.f.* omniscience.

onniveggènte, *ag.* all-seeing, omnipercipient.

onniveggènza, *s.f.* all-embracing vision, omnipercipience.

onnívoro, *ag.* omnivorous.

onomàstica, *s.f.* onomatology.

onomàstico, *ag.* onomastic: *giorno —*, name-day; *lessico —*, onomasticon || *s.m.* **1.** (*giorno onomastico*) name-day **2.** (*lessico dei nomi*) onomasticon.

onomatopèa, onomatopèia, *s.f.* (*ret.*) onomatopoeia.

onomatopèico, *ag.* (*ret.*) onomatopoeic(al), onomatopoetic: *parola onomatopeica*, onomatopoeic word (*o* onomatope); *verso —*, onomatopoeic line.

onoràbile, *ag.* honourable; respectable.

onorabilità, *s.f.* respectability; honourableness.

onorabilménte, *av.* honourably; respectably.

onoràndo, *ag.* (*letter.*) honourable.

onorànza, *s.f.* honour: *rendere le estreme onoranze*, to render the last honours.

onoràre, *v.t.* **1.** (*rendere onore a*) to honour, to pay honour to (s.o.); to celebrate: *onora tuo padre e tua madre*, (*Bibbia*) honour thy father and thy mother; *— la memoria dei grandi*, to honour the memory of great men; *— i morti*, to honour the dead **2.** (*arrecare onore a*) to be an honour to (s.o., sthg.), to do credit to (s.o., sthg.): *questa azione ti onora*, this action does you credit; *il suo eroismo onora la patria*, his heroism is an honour to his country **3.** (*pregiare*) to honour: *egli mi onora della sua amicizia*, he honours me with his friendship; *— una cambiale*, (*comm.*) to honour a bill || **onoràrsi**, *v.r.* (*pregiarsi*) to be proud (of sthg.), to pride oneself (on sthg.): *mi onoro della sua amicizia*, I am honoured by his friendship; *mi onoro di fare ciò che vuoi*, I consider it an honour to do what you desire.

onoràrio[1], *ag.* honorary: *socio —*, honorary member.

onoràrio[2], *s.m.* honorarium (*pl.* honoraria, honorariums); emolument fee: *l'— di un avvocato*, the honorarium of a lawyer; *l'— di un insegnante*, a teacher's fee.

onorataménte, *av.* honourably.

onoratézza, *s.f.* honourableness, respectability.

onoràto, *ag.* **1.** honoured: *portare un nome —*, to bear an honoured name; *era povero ma —*, he was poor but honoured; *sentirsi —*, to feel honoured **2.** (*onesto*) honourable; (*rispettabile*) respectable: *condotta onorata*, honourable behaviour; *famiglia onorata*, respectable family; *vita onorata*, honourable life.

onóre, *s.m.* **1.** honour: *debito, parola, punto, questione d'—*, debt, word, point, question of honour; *regole dell'—* rules of honour; *il sentimento dell'—*, the sense of honour; *uomo d'—*, honourable man (*o* a man of honour); *tenere in —*, to hold in honour || *il campo dell'—*, the field of honour **2.** (*castità di donna*) honour, chastity: *insidiare l'— di una donna*, to assail the honour of a woman (*o* a woman's honour); *togliere l'— (a una donna)*, to seduce (a woman) **3.** (*vanto, gloria*) honour, glory; (*credito*) credit: *l'— della vittoria spetta a lui*, the honour (*o* the glory) of victory is his; *questo è un — per me*, this is an honour for me; *questo sentimento ti fa —*, this feeling does you credit (*o* honour); *egli è l'— della famiglia*, he is an honour to his family; *ritornò povero ma ricco d'—*, he came back poor but rich in honour (*o* glory) ‖ *ho l'— di presentarvi questo signore,* I have the honour to introduce this gentleman to you ‖ *mi farete l'— di venire a casa mia?,* will you do me the honour of coming to my house?; *non ho l'— di conoscervi,* I have not the honour of knowing you ‖ *farsi — in ql.co.,* to excel in sthg. **4.** (*atto di omaggio*) honour, homage: *onori militari,* military honours; *ci accolse con molto —, con tutti gli onori,* he received us with great ceremony; *fare — a un re,* to pay homage to a king (*o* to honour a king) ‖ *— al merito !,* give praise where praise is due! ‖ *a onor del vero,* to tell the truth ‖ *damigella d'—,* maid of honour ‖ *in — di,* in honour of ‖ *posto di —,* place of honour ‖ *scorta d'—,* guard of honour ‖ *serata di —,* gala evening ‖ *fare — alla propria firma,* to honour one's signature ‖ *fare — a un pranzo,* to do justice to a dinner ‖ *fare gli onori di casa,* to do the honours of the house ‖ *rendere gli onori,* to do the honours ‖ *salire agli onori degli altari,* to be raised to the altars **5.** (*carica, ufficio*) dignity, office: *— di ministro,* office of minister; *rifiutare gli onori,* to refuse office (*o* to refuse to take office) **6.** (*poet.*) (*ornamento*) honour, ornament **7.** *pl.* (*decorazioni*) honours **8.** *pl.* (*bridge, ecc.*) honours.

onorévole, *ag.* **1.** honourable: *condotta —,* honourable behaviour (*o* conduct); *menzione —,* honourable mention; *fu conclusa una pace —,* an honourable peace was concluded **2.** (*titolo dei deputati*) Honourable: *onorevoli deputati,* Honourable Members; *l'— X,* Mr. X M.P. (*abbr.* di *Member of Parliament*).

onorevolézza, *s.f.* honourableness, respectability.

onorevolménte, *av.* honourably.

onorificaménte, *av.* honourably.

onorificènza, *s.f.* **1.** honour; (*in documenti ufficiali*) dignity: *conferire un'— a qlcu.,* to confer an honour upon s.o. **2.** (*decorazione*) decoration: *— di guerra,* war decoration.

onorífico, *ag.* honorific; honorary: *carica onorifica,* honorary office; *titolo —,* courtesy (*o* honorific) title.

ónta, *s.f.* **1.** (*vergogna*) shame: *dovresti aver — di te stesso,* you ought to be ashamed of yourself **2.** (*disonore*) disgrace, dishonour, shame: *morirebbe piuttosto che vivere nell'—,* he would rather die than live in dishonour; *essere un'— per la propria famiglia,* to be a disgrace to one's family; *recare — a qlcu.,* to bring shame on s.o. (*o* to cover s.o. with disgrace) **3.** (*offesa, ingiuria*) insult: *è un'— chiamare codardo un uomo coraggioso,* to call a brave man a coward is an insult; *cancellare un'— col sangue,* to wipe out an insult with blood ‖ **ad ónta di,** *l. prep.* in spite of; notwithstanding: *ad — di tutte le calunnie,* in spite of all calumnies; *ad — delle numerose difficoltà riuscii nella mia mansione,* notwithstanding (*o* in spite of) numerous difficulties I succeeded in my task.

ontanéta, *s.f.,* **ontanéto,** *s.m.* plantation of alders.

ontàno, *s.m.* (*bot.*) alder(-tree).

ontogènesi, *s.f.* (*scient.*) ontogenesis.

ontología, *s.f.* (*fil.*) ontology.

ontològico, *ag.* (*fil.*) ontological.

ontologísta, ontòlogo, *s.m.* (*fil.*) ontologist.

onústo, *ag.* (*poet.*) laden (with sthg.), loaded (with sthg.): *— di gloria,* covered with glory.

oolíte, *s.f.* (*min.*) oolite.

opacità, *s.f.* opacity, opaqueness: *l'— della terra,* the opacity of the earth.

opàco, *ag.* opaque; (*di suoni, colori*) dull; (*ombroso, scuro*) shady, dark: *colore —,* dull colour; *corpo —,* opaque body; *un suono —,* a dull sound; *vetro —,* opaque glass.

opàle, *s.m.* (*min.*) opal: *— comune,* common opal; *— di fuoco,* fire- (*o* sun-) opal; *— nobile,* harlequin-opal.

opalescènte, *ag.* opalescent.

opalescènza, *s.f.* opalescence.

opalíno, *ag.* opaline.

opalizzànte, *ag.* opalescent.

opalizzàre, *v.i.* to opalesce.

òpera, *s.f.* **1.** (*attività, lavoro*) work: *ho proseguito l'— iniziata dal mio amico,* I have carried on the work begun by my friend; *coronare l'—,* to conclude the work; *mettere in —,* (*cominciare ad usare*) to begin using; (*rendere pronto per l'uso*) to set running ‖ *all'—,* at work (*o* to work!; *to work!;* *mi piacerebbe vederti all'—,* I'd like to see you at work; *essere all'—,* to be at work; *mettersi all'—,* to get down to work ‖ *datore d'—,* employer; *mano d'—,* labour ‖ *per compir l'—,* (*iron.*) as if this were not enough (*o* into the bargain): *non ha fatto niente tutto il giorno e per compir l'— questa sera andrà al cinema,* he has done nothing all day long and, into the bargain, to-night he'll go to the cinema **2.** (*prodotto di un lavoro, di una attività*) (piece of) work: *opere difensive, distaccate,* (*mil.*) defensive, detached works; *— in muratura,* brickwork; *opere pubbliche,* public works ‖ *— di Dio, della Natura,* the works of God, of Nature ‖ *— viva, morta,* (*mar.*) quick-work (*o* bottom), upper works **3.** (*prodotto artistico*) work: *— d'arte,* work of art; *le opere di Bach, Manzoni, Matisse,* Bach's, Manzoni's, Matisse's works; *— letteraria,* literary work; *tutte le opere di Dante,* Dante's complete works; *l'— critica del De Sanctis è ancora attuale,* De Sanctis's criticism is still up to date; *hai letto l'ultima — di Moravia?,* have you read Moravia's latest book? ‖ *sonata per pianoforte — 27 (op. 27),* piano sonata opus 27 (op. 27) **4.** (*melodramma*) opera: *— buffa,* comic opera; *cantante d'—,* opera singer; *stagione, teatro d'—,* opera season, opera-house; *è un appassionato, un intenditore di opere,* he is an opera fan, a connoisseur of opera **5.** (*azione*) work, action, deed: *un'— buona,* a good deed (*o* a good action): *faresti un'— buona se lo picchiassi,* it would be a good thing if you gave him a hiding; *fare opere buone,* to do good works; *opere di carità,* charitable works; *opere di misericordia,* works of mercy; *ciò è — di un malvagio,* this is the work of a wicked man; *fare — utile,* to perform useful work ‖ *farò — di convincimento presso di lui,* I'll try to convince him ‖ *non fiori ma opere di bene,* no flowers ‖ *il mio licenziamento fu sua,* I was dismissed because of him **6.** (*mezzo*) means; (*aiuto*) help: *avete bisogno della mia —?,* do you need my help?; *ho trovato lavoro per — sua,* thanks to him I have found a job; *valersi dell'— di qlcu.,* to avail oneself of the services of s.o. **7.** (*istituzione*) institution, organization, society: *— pia,* charitable institution ‖ *Opera Nazionale Maternità ed Infanzia,* Maternity and Child Welfare Organization **8.** (*rar.*) (*lavoro a giornata*) day-labour; (*lavoratore a giornata*) day-labourer: *dovresti prendere delle altre opere,* you ought to engage more workers; *questo mese ho fatto venti opere,* this month I worked for twenty days; *lavorare a —,* to work by the day.

operàbile, *ag.* **1.** workable **2.** (*chir.*) operable.

operabilità, *s.f.* **1.** workability **2.** (*chir.*) operability.

operàia, *s.f.* working-woman (*pl.* working-women), (female) worker, factory-girl.

operàio, *ag.* **1.** (*che lavora*) working; worker (*attributivo*): *ape operaia,* worker-bee; *formica operaia,* worker **2.** (*di operai*) working: *classe operaia,* working-class; *le maestranze operaie,* tradesmen; *treno —,* workmen's train ‖ *s.m.* workman (*pl.* workmen), worker, hand; (*che fa funzionare una macchina*) operator: *— a cottimo,* piece-worker; *— addetto al cubilotto,* (*metal.*) cupola tender; *— addetto alla punzonatrice,* piercer; *— disoccupato,* unemployed worker; *— metallurgico,* ironworker; *— montatore,* (*mec.*) fitter; *— specializzato,* skilled workman; *— tornitore,* (*mec.*) turner (*o* lathe worker); *case per gli operai,* workmen's dwellings; *consiglio degli operai,* works council; *la paga di un —,* a worker's wages; *sciopero degli operai,* workmen's strike; *è un buon —,* he is a good workman; *questa fabbrica ha bisogno di altri cinquanta operai,* this factory needs fifty more hands.

operànte, *ag.* **1.** operating, acting, working: *rendere — un decreto,* to put a decree into operation **2.** (*chir.*) operating ‖ *s.m.* (*chirurgo*) operator, operative surgeon.

operàre, *v.t.* **1.** (*compiere*) to operate, to do, to perform, to work: *l'energia opera grandi trasformazioni,* energy works great changes; *la fede opera miracoli,* faith works miracles; — *una grande riforma,* to carry out a great reform; — *una ritirata,* (*mil.*) to effect (*o* carry out) a retreat (*o* withdrawal) **2.** (*chir.*) to operate on (s.o.): — *qlcu. a caldo,* to operate on s.o. in the acute stage; — *qlcu. a freddo,* to operate on s.o. between attacks; — *qlcu. al fegato,* to operate on s.o.'s liver; — *qlcu. di ernia,* to operate (*o* to perform an operation) on s.o. for rupture ‖ *farsi —,* to undergo an operation: *farsi — di calcoli,* to be operated on for gall-stones **3.** (*ind. tessile*) to damask ‖ *v.i.* **1.** (*agire*) to operate, to work, to act: *la grazia ha operato nell'anima sua,* grace wrought in his soul; *i suoi intrighi operano lentamente,* his plots work slowly; *il veleno operò in fretta,* the poison worked quickly; — *secondo la propria coscienza,* to act according to one's own conscience ‖ — *su larga scala,* (*comm.*) to operate on a large scale; — *su un mercato,* (*comm.*) to operate on a market **2.** (*chir.*) to operate: *opera con calma,* he operates calmly.

operatìvo, *ag.* **1.** operative **2.** (*chir.*) surgical.

operàto, *ag.* (*ind. tessile*) diapered; (*damascato*) damask (*attributivo*) ‖ *s.m.* **1.** conduct, behaviour; (*azione*) action: *dovrà render conto del suo —,* he will have to account for his behaviour **2.** (*chi ha subìto un'operazione*) person who has undergone an operation.

operatóre, *ag.* operating ‖ *s.m.* **1.** operator: — *cinematografico, televisivo,* camera-man (*pl.* camera-men) **2.** (*chirurgo*) surgeon, (surgical) operator.

operatòrio, *ag.* operating, operative: *sala, tavola operatoria,* operating-theatre, operating-table.

operatrìce, *s.f.* operator.

operazióne, *s.f.* **1.** operation: — *a caldo, a freddo,* (*chir.*) emergency, interval operation; — *chirurgica,* surgical operation; — *d'appendicite,* operation for appendicitis; — *matematica,* mathematical operation; *operazioni militari,* military operations; *fare un'— a qlcu.,* to perform an operation on s.o.; *subìre un'—,* to undergo (*o* to have) an operation **2.** (*comm.*) transaction, operation: *operazioni di Borsa,* Stock Exchange transactions (*o* operations); *operazioni di ribasso, rialzo,* bear, bull transactions; — *in cambiali,* exchange transaction.

opèrcolo, *s.m.* (*zool. bot.*) operculum (*pl.* opercula).

operétta, *s.f.* (*teat.*) operetta.

operettìsta, *s.m.* operettist.

operosaménte, *av.* industriously: *lavora sempre —,* he always works hard; *vive —,* he leads a busy life.

operosità, *s.f.* industry; activity: *la sua — instancabile,* his untiring activity; *ha sempre mostrato una grande —,* he has always shown great industry.

operóso, *ag.* industrious, hard-working; active: *vita operosa,* active life; *è un uomo molto —,* he is a very active (*o* hard-working) man; *si mise al lavoro con zelo —,* he set to work with industrious zeal.

opifìcio, *s.m.* factory, works, plant.

opìmo, *ag.* (*letter.*) fertile, rich: *terra opima,* fertile (*o* rich) land ‖ *spoglie opime,* (*st. romana*) spolia opima.

opinàbile, *ag.* thinkable, opinable: *un'azione non —,* an unthinkable action.

opinàre, *v.i.* **1.** to think, to be of (the) opinion, to opine: *opino che...,* I am of the opinion that...; — *diversamente dagli altri,* to think differently from the others **2.** (*decretare*), to decree, to decide.

opinióne, *s.f.* opinion: — *pubblica,* public opinion; *secondo l'— di qlcu.,* in s.o.'s opinion: *secondo l'— degli esperti,* in the opinion of the experts; *avere un'—,* to hold an opinion; *avere una buona, cattiva — di qlcu., ql.co.,* to have a good, bad opinion of s.o., sthg.; *avere il coraggio delle proprie opinioni,* to have the courage of one's convictions; *avere grande — di sè,* to have a high opinion of oneself (*o* to think highly of oneself); *cambiare —,* to change one's opinion; (*cambiare idea*) to change one's mind; *condividere l'— di qlcu.,* to share s.o.'s opinion (*o* to agree with s.o. *o* to be of the same opinion as s.o.); *sono dell'— che non tornerà mai,* I am of opinion that he will never come back; *farsi, formarsi un'— su ql.cu., ql.co.,* to form an opinion of (*o* on) s.o., sthg.; *scadere nell'— di qlcu.,* to fall in s.o.'s esteem.

opistòdomo, *s.m.* (*arch. greca*) opisthodome.

opistòtono, *s.m.* (*med.*) opisthotonos.

oplíta, *s.m.* (*st. greca*) hoplite.

opoponàco, *s.m.* (*bot.*) opoponax.

opòssum, *s.m.* (*zool.*) opossum.

opoterapía, *s.f.* (*med.*) opotherapy.

oppiàceo, *ag.* opiate.

oppiàre, *v.t.* to opiate.

oppiàto, *ag.s.m.* opiate.

oppilàre, *v.t.* (*rar.*) (*med.*) to oppilate.

oppilatìvo, *ag.* (*med.*) oppilative.

oppilazióne, *s.f.* (*med.*) oppilation.

òppio, *s.m.* opium: *fumatore d'—,* opium-smoker; *mangiatore d'—,* opium-eater.

oppiòmane, *s.m.* opium-addict; (*fam.*) opium-fiend.

oppiomanía, *s.f.* opiomania, opium-habit.

opponènte, *ag.* opposing, opponent ‖ *s.m.* opponent; opposer.

oppórre, *v.t.* **1.** to oppose: — *audacia ad audacia,* to oppose bravery with bravery; — *la bontà alla cattiveria,* to oppose good to evil; — *un ostacolo a qlcu.,* to raise an obstacle against s.o.; — *la persuasione alla forza,* to oppose force with persuasion; — *resistenza al nemico,* to offer resistance to the enemy; — *un rifiuto,* to give a refusal **2.** (*obiettare*) to object: *non ho niente da — a ciò,* I have nothing to object to that; *si può — che non sempre ciò è vero,* one can object that it is not always true ‖ **oppórsi,** *v.r.* to oppose (sthg.); to set oneself against (sthg.); (*essere contrario*) to be opposed (to sthg.): *egli si oppose alle nostre decisioni,* he was opposed to our decisions; *mi sono opposto a ciò con tutte le mie forze,* I opposed it with all my strength; — *al nemico con tutte le proprie forze,* to oppose the enemy with all one's strength; — *a una mozione, a un progetto di legge,* to oppose a motion, a bill; — *a un progetto, a un matrimonio,* to set oneself against (*o* to stand in the way of) a scheme, a marriage ‖ *mi oppongo,* (*nei dibattiti parlamentari*) I object.

opportunaménte, *av.* **1.** (*al momento opportuno*) opportunely, at the right moment, seasonably **2.** (*in modo opportuno*) appropriately, suitably.

opportunìsmo, *s.m.* opportunism, time-serving.

opportunìsta, *s.m.* opportunist, time-server.

opportunità, *s.f.* **1.** (*l'essere opportuno*) timeliness, opportuneness, seasonableness: *avere il senso dell'—,* to have a sense of the right moment **2.** (*occasione favorevole*) opportunity, chance, occasion: *avere, cogliere l'—,* to have, to seize the opportunity.

opportúno, *ag.* opportune, well-timed, timely, seasonable; (*giusto*) right, suitable, appropriate: *citazione opportuna,* appropriate quotation; *cure opportune,* suitable treatment; *discorso —,* timely speech; *osservazione opportuna,* opportune (*o* seasonable) remark; *abbiamo ritenuto — dirglielo,* we thought it right to tell him; *questo è il luogo e il tempo — per farlo,* this is the right place and time to do it; *sarebbe stato più — dirlo subito,* it would have been more suitable (*o* appropriate) to have said so at once.

oppositóre, *s.m.,* **oppositrìce,** *s.f.* opponent, opposer.

opposizióne, *s.f.* opposition: *in — all'opinione pubblica,* in opposition to public opinion; *incontrai una forte —,* I met with strong opposition; *la Luna è in — con il Sole,* (*astr.*) the Moon is in opposition to the Sun; *partito, giornale d'—,* (*pol.*) opposition party, paper; *il Partito Laburista era all'—,* the Labour

Party was in opposition; *fare — a ql.co.*, to oppose (*o* to object to) sthg.: *non fece —*, he offered no opposition; *muovere — ad una decisione*, to appeal against a decision; *passare all'—, (pol.)* to pass (*o* to go) over to the opposition; *vincere ogni —*, to break down all opposition; *vincere l'— di qlcu.*, to overcome s.o.'s opposition.

oppostaménte, *av.* oppositely.

oppósto, *ag.* 1. (*posto di fronte*) opposite: *l'angolo — a questo*, the angle opposite this one (*o* to this); *foglie opposte*, (*bot.*) opposite (*o* bifarious) leaves; *il pendio —*, the adverse slope; *la riva opposta del fiume*, the opposite bank of the river; *sul lato — della strada*, on the opposite side of the road; *l'uno — all'altro*, facing each other 2. (*contrario*) opposite, opposing, contrary: *in direzione opposta*, in the opposite direction; *il partito —*, the opposing party; *punti di vista opposti*, opposite (*o* opposing) points of view; *avevano idee opposte*, they had opposite opinions; *seguire la direzione opposta*, to go the opposite way ‖ *all' —*, on the contrary ‖ *s.m.* opposite, contrary: *è proprio l'— di quello che avevo pensato*, it is just the opposite (*o* contrary) of what I thought; *il tuo carattere è l'— di quello di tuo fratello*, your character is the opposite of your brother's.

oppressióne, *s.f.* 1. (*giogo*) oppression: *— tirannica*, tyrannical oppression; *vittima dell'—*, victim of oppression; *l'— di un popolo è contraria al principio di uguaglianza*, the oppression of a people is contrary to the principle of equality 2. (*ansia, preoccupazione*) anxiety; depression: *la sua situazione familiare gli dava una grande —*, family affairs were causing him a great deal of depression 3. (*gravezza*) weight; (*difficoltà*) difficulty: *— di respiro*, difficulty in breathing.

oppressivo, *ag.* oppressive.

opprèsso, *ag.* (*gravato*) oppressed, weighed down (by, with s.o., sthg.) (anche *fig.*); (*sopraffatto*) overwhelmed, overpowered (by s.o., by, with sthg.) (anche *fig.*): *— da un grosso carico*, weighed down by (*o* burdened with) a heavy load; *— dal dolore*, weighed down (*o* oppressed) with sorrow; *— dal sonno*, weighed down (*o* heavy) with sleep; *— da preoccupazioni*, weighed down (*o* oppressed) by cares; *— di meraviglia*, overwhelmed with surprise; *un paese —*, an oppressed country.

oppressóre, *ag.* oppressive ‖ *s.m.* oppressor.

opprimènte, *ag.* oppressive: *atmosfera —*, oppressive atmosphere; *caldo —*, oppressive (*o* stifling) heat; *dolore —*, oppressive (*o* overwhelming) grief; *fatica —*, grinding toil; *miseria —*, grinding poverty.

opprímere, *v.t.* to oppress, to weigh down (anche *fig.*); (*sopraffare*) to overwhelm, to over-power (anche *fig.*): *quel cibo opprime lo stomaco*, that food lies heavy on the stomach; *questo caldo opprime il respiro*, this heat is oppressive (*o* overpowering); *la sua routine quotidiana gli opprimeva lo spirito*, her daily routine oppressed her spirits; *le sue preoccupazioni lo opprimevano*, his troubles weighed him down (*o* oppressed him); *— un paese, un popolo*, to oppress a country, a people; *— qlcu. di domande*, to overwhelm s.o. with questions.

oppugnàbile, *ag.* 1. assailable, attackable 2. *fig.* impugnable, disputable.

oppugnàre, *v.t.* 1. to assail, to assault, to storm: *— una città, una fortezza*, to assail (*o* to storm) a city, a fortress 2. *fig.* (*attaccare, contestare*) to attack, to assail; to impugn, to oppugn: *— l'onestà di qlcu.*, to impugn (*o* to oppugn) s.o.'s honesty; *— le opinioni di qlcu.*, to attack (*o* to assail) s.o.'s opinions; *— la virtù*, to assail virtue.

oppugnatóre, *s.m.*, **oppugnatríce**, *s.f.* assailant (anche *fig.*).

oppugnazióne, *s.f.* 1. assault 2. *fig.* confutation; antagonism.

oppúre, *cong.* or; or on the other hand, or alter-

---

natively; (*altrimenti*) or else, otherwise: *fa' ciò che ti si dice, — sarai punito*, do what you are told, otherwise (*o* or else) you'll be punished; *—, sai che cosa si potrebbe fare?*, or on the other hand (*o* alternatively), do you know what we could do?; *vuoi queste mele — quelle?*, do you want these apples or those?.

òpra, *e derivati*, *V.* **òpera**, *e derivati.*

optàre, *v.i.* to opt, to choose (sthg.), to make one's choice (for sthg.): *— per ql.co.*, to opt for sthg.

opulènto, *ag.* opulent, wealthy, rich.

opulènza, *s.f.* opulence, wealth; riches (*pl.*).

opúscolo, *s.m.* 1. (*libro di poche pagine*) booklet; (*politico, scientifico*) pamphlet; (*religioso*) tract: *opuscoli legati in volume*, pamphlets bound in a volume; *collezione di opuscoli*, collection of pamphlets 2. (*operetta letteraria*) opuscule; opusculum (*pl.* opuscula).

opzióne, *s.f.* 1. option 2. (*comm.*) option: *— doppia*, put and call; *— per l'acquisto*, call; *— per la vendita*, put; *concedere il diritto d'—*, to give for the put and call; *pagare il premio d'—*, to pay down the option-money; *riservarsi il diritto d'—*, to take for the put and call.

óra[1], *s.f.* 1. hour: *ore calde*, hottest hours; *ore di lavoro, di scuola*, working, school hours; *un'— di lezione*, an hour's lesson; *un'— di orologio*, a whole hour; *— di punta*, rush hour; *un'— e mezzo*, an hour and a half; *— per i piccoli, (alla radio)* children's hour; *le ore piccole, (del mattino)* the small hours (of the morning): *fare le ore piccole*, to stay up late; *— zero*, zero hour; *all'—*, by the hour: *noleggiare una bicicletta a ore*, to hire a bicycle by the hour; *a tarda —*, late; *a tutte le ore*, at any time (*o* hour); *da un'— all'altra, (in brevissimo tempo)* very quickly (*o* in a moment); (*improvvisamente*) suddenly; (*fra poco*) soon; *lancetta delle ore*, hour-hand (of a clock); *mezz'—*, half an hour; *nelle prime ore del pomeriggio*, in the early (hours of the) afternoon; *notizie dell'ultima —*, the latest news; (*sui giornali*) stop-press news; *le prime ore del giorno*, the early morning (*o* first thing in the morning); *c'è ancora un'— di automobile, di cammino da qui al paese*, we are still an hour's drive, walk from the village; *ha dormito otto ore*, he has slept eight hours; *le notizie arrivavano di — in —*, news arrived hourly; *questo orologio batte le ore e le mezze ore*, this clock strikes the hours and (the) half-hours; *sarà qui fra due ore*, he will be here in two hours'time; *si fermò qui per un'— buona*, he stopped here for a full (*o* good) hour (*o* for fully an hour); *studio da un'—*, I have been studying (for) an hour; *lavorare per ore e ore*, to work for hours and hours ‖ *— canonica*, (*eccl.*) canonical hour; *libro d'ore*, (*eccl.*) Book of Hours; *le quarant'ore*, (*eccl.*) the Forty Hours ‖ *alla buon'—*, at last ‖ *di buon'—*, early ‖ *domestica a ore*, charwoman ‖ *l'— è suonata*, the hour has struck ‖ *è uno che non ha ore*, he doesn't come regularly ‖ *non ho mai un'— di pace*, I never have a minute's peace ‖ *non vedo l'— di andare*, I am looking forward to going (*o* I am dying to go) ‖ *passai un brutto quarto d'—*, I had a bad (*o* a difficult) quarter of an hour ‖ *quell'uomo va a ore*, that man is changeable (like the weather) ‖ *le ore del mattino hanno l'oro in bocca*, *prov.* an hour in the morning is worth two in the evening 2. (*nel computo del tempo*) time: *— astronomica*, sidereal time; *— legale, estiva*, summer (*o* daylight-saving) time; *— locale*, local time; *— media di Greenwich*, Greenwich mean time; *— ufficiale*, standard time; *che — è?*, what is the time? (*o* what time is it?); *che — fate voi?*, what time do you make it?; *credo che a quest'— sarà a Roma*, I think he will be in Rome by now; *domani a quest'— sarò a Roma*, at this time tomorrow I shall be in Rome; *questo bambino non sa ancora leggere le ore*, this child cannot tell the time yet; *sai l'— giusta?*, do you know the right time?; *sono le (ore) due e un quarto, e venti, e mezzo*, it is a quarter, twenty, half past two; *sono le (ore) due e tre quarti*, le (*ore*) *tre meno dieci*, it is a quarter, ten to three; *sono le* (*ore*) *nove in punto*, it is nine o' clock; *il treno parte alle* (*ore*) *otto e cinquanta*, the train leaves at eight fifty **3.** (*tempo*) time; (*momento*) moment: — *dei pasti*, meal-time; — *del tè, di colazione*, tea-time, lunch-time; — *di chiusura*, closing time; — *di pranzo*, dinner-time: *leggo per fare l'— di pranzo*, I am reading to kill time until dinner; *ore rubate*, stolen time; *ore straordinarie*, overtime; *a una certa —*, at a certain moment; *all'— fissata*, at the appointed time; *all'— solita*, at the usual time; *è — di andare*, it is time to go: *è — che vada*, it is time I went; *sarebbe — che tu andassi a letto*, it's time for you to go to bed; *puoi venire a tutte le ore*, you can come at any time ‖ *attendo la mia —*, I am biding my time; *la mia — si avvicina*, my time is drawing near; *morì prima della sua —*, he died before his time ‖ *viene sempre fuori —*, he never comes at the right time.

óra², *av.* **1.** (*al presente*) **now, at present**: — *è il momento migliore*, now it is the best moment; *che cosa fai —?*, what are you doing now? ‖ — *come —*, (*in questo momento*) **now** (*o* at this very moment *o* at the moment *o* just at this moment); (*per il momento*) for the moment (*o* for the present *o* for the time being): — *come — non c'è niente che io possa fare, ma ti farò sapere appena sarò in grado di aiutarti*, for the moment there is nothing I can do, but I'll let you know as soon as I am in a position to help you; — *come — non so dirtelo*, I can't tell you just at this moment ‖ — *o mai* (*più*), **now or never** ‖ — *più che mai*, now more than ever ‖ — *da — in poi*, from now on(wards); (*più formale*) henceforth ‖ *fino ad —*, so far (*o* up to now); (*più formale*) hitherto; *sono a Milano da un anno e fino ad — non ho visto l'interno del Duomo*, I have been in Milan for a year, and so far I haven't been inside the Cathedral; *studiano inglese da un anno, ma fino ad — non hanno fatto un solo dettato*, they have been studying English for one year, but up to now they haven't done a single dictation ‖ *fin d'—, sin d'—*, now: *te lo dico fin d'—*, I'll tell you that now; *ti dico sin d'— che quest'anno non andremo al mare*, I'll tell you now that we won't be going to the sea this year ‖ *per —*, for now (*o* for the moment *o* for the present *o* for the time being): *per — mi basta*, that's enough for now ‖ *prima d'—*, before: *non avevo mai letto Chaucer prima d'—, e ovviamente lo trovo piuttosto difficile*, I have never read Chaucer before, and naturally I am finding it rather difficult ‖ *proprio —*, at this very moment: *proprio — starà arrivando a San Francisco*, at this very moment he will be arriving in San Francisco ‖ *or è un anno che non lo vedo*, it's a year now since I saw him ‖ — *sì che son contento*, now (*o* at last) I'm satisfied **2.** (*pochissimo tempo fa*) **just**: *siamo arrivati —*, we have just arrived ‖ *or —*, just now (*o* just this moment *o* a moment ago *o* a minute ago): *ho finito or — di pranzare*, I have just this moment finished dinner **3.** (*fra pochissimo tempo*) **presently, in a moment, in a minute**; (*fam.*) **in a jiffy**: — *lo faccio*, I'll do it in a moment; — *vengo ad aiutarti*, I'll come and help you in a minute **4.** (*dunque*) **now**: — *avvenne che...*, now it happened that...; — *che cosa faresti al mio posto?*, now, what would you do in my place? *o* dunque, now then ‖ *or via*, now, now: *or via, non arrabbiarti!*, now, now, don't get cross! **5.** *ora... ora*, now... now (*o* sometimes... sometimes): — *qui — là*, now here, now there; — *vuole — no*, sometimes she will, sometimes she won't ‖ **ora che**, *l. cong.* **now** (**that**): — *che lo vedo, lo riconosco*, now (that) I see him, I recognize him; — *che sono cresciuto, la penso diversamente*, now (that) I am older, I think otherwise (*o* differently).

oracoleggiàre, *v.i.* to speak like an oracle.

oràcolo, *s.m.* oracle: *l'— delfico*, the Delphic oracle; *consultare, dare un —*, to consult, to give an oracle ‖ *parlare come un —*, to talk like an oracle.

òrafo, *s.m.* goldsmith.

oràle, *ag.* **1.** oral, verbal: *esame, spiegazione —*, oral examination, explanation; *tradizione —*, oral tradition **2.** (*anat.*) oral ‖ *s.m.* (*esame orale*) oral.

oralménte, *av.* orally, verbally, by word of mouth.

oramài, *av.* **1. now**; (*a quest'ora*) **by now, by this time**: — *dovresti saperlo*, you ought to know that by this time (*o* by now); — *è tempo di smetterla*, it's (high) time you stopped it; — *è troppo tardi per andare al cinema*, it's too late now to go to the cinema; — *non vale la pena d'andarci*, by now it's not worth going **2.** (*riferito al passato*) **by then, by that time**: *il dottore arrivò alle dodici, ma — era troppo tardi per fare qualunque cosa*, the doctor came at twelve o' clock, but by that time (*o* by then) it was too late to do anything **3.** (*finalmente*) **at last**: — *siamo arrivati*, at last we have arrived.

oràngo, orangutàno, *s.m.* (*zool.*) orang-outang.

oràre, *v.t.* (*letter.*) to pray.

oràrio, *ag.* **1. time** (*attributivo*): *fuso —*, time-zone; *segnale —*, (*rad.*) time-signal **2.** (*all'ora*) **per hour**: *velocità oraria*, speed per hour ‖ *s.m.* **1. hours** (*pl.*), schedule: — *di lavoro*, working hours (*o* time); — *scolastico, d'ufficio*, school, office hours; *ho un — pesante*, I have a heavy schedule **2.** (*tabella dell'orario*) **time-table, time-sheet, schedule**: — *dei corsi*, time-table of the courses; *essere segnato sull'—*, to be scheduled: *questa fermata non è segnata sull'—*, this is an unscheduled stop ‖ *arrivare, essere in —*, to arrive, to be on time; *non arrivare, non essere in —*, to arrive, to be behind time.

oràta, *s.f.* (*ittiol.*) dory, John Dory.

oratóre, *s.m.* orator; (*parlatore*) speaker: *Cicerone è tra i più famosi oratori dell'antichità*, Cicero is one of the best known orators of ancient times ‖ — *della legge*, (*dir.*) public prosecutor ‖ *sacro —*, (*eccl.*) preacher.

oratòria, *s.f.* oratory; rhetoric; (*eloquenza*) eloquence.

oratoriàno, *s.m.* (*eccl.*) Oratorian.

oratòrio, *ag.* oratorial, oratorical ‖ *s.m.* **1.** (*piccola cappella*) oratory **2.** (*eccl.*) Oratory ‖ *— festivo*, Sunday school **3.** (*mus.*) oratorio (*pl.* oratorios).

oratríce, *s.f.* oratress; (*parlatrice*) speaker.

Oràzio, *no.pr.m.* (*st. lett.*) Horace.

orazióne, *s.f.* **1.** prayer; (*arc.*) orison: *dire le orazioni*, to say one's prayers; *stare in —*, to be at one's prayers ‖ — *domenicale*, (*il paternostro*), the Lord's Prayer **2.** (*discorso*) oration: *le orazioni di Cicerone*, Cicero's orations; — *funebre*, funeral oration.

orbàce, *s.m.* coarse woollen fabric (from Sardinia).

orbàre, *v.t.* (*rar.*) to bereave.

orbàto, *ag.* (*rar.*) deprived, bereft.

òrbe, *s.m.* (*letter.*) orb: *l'— cattolico*, the Catholic world; *l'— terrestre, terracqueo*, the world.

orbicolàre, *ag.* (*anat.*) orbicular: *muscolo —*, orbicular muscle ‖ *s.m.* (*anat.*) orbicularis.

òrbita, *s.f.* **1.** (*anat.*) orbit, eye-socket ‖ *con gli occhi fuori dell'—*, with his eyes popping out of his head: *guardare ql.co. con gli occhi fuori dell'—*, to stare aghast at sthg. **2.** (*astr.*) orbit, circle: *piano dell'—*, plane of the orbit; *mettere in — un satellite artificiale*, to orbit an artificial satellite; *portare in —*, to carry into orbit **3.** *fig.* (*sfera d'azione*) orbit, sphere (of action).

orbitàle, *ag.* orbital.

òrbo, *ag.* **1.** (*letter.*) (*privato*) bereaved, deprived **2.** (*cieco*) blind; (*da un occhio*) one-eyed ‖ *s.m.* blind man ‖ *vi furono botte da orbi*, there was a savage fight.

òrca¹, *s.f.* **1.** (*mit.*) orc(a), ork **2.** (*zool.*) killer (-whale).

òrca², *s.f.* (*mar.*) (*peschereccio olandese*) hooker.

Òreadi (le), *no.pr.f.pl.* (*geog.*) the Orkney Islands.

orches(i)ografía, *s.f.* choreography; orchestics.

orchéssa, *s.f.* ogress.

orchèstica, *s.f.* (*st.*) orchestics.

orchèstra, *s.f.* **1.** orchestra; (*orchestrina*) band: — *da ballo*, dance-band; — *d'archi*, string orchestra; — *sinfonica*, symphony orchestra; — *a grande —*, with full orchestra; *direttore d'—*, conductor; *i professori* *d'*—, the members of the orchestra; *dirigere l'*—, to conduct the orchestra **2.** (*teat. archeol.*) orchestra.

orchestràle, *ag.* orchestral ‖ *s.m.* member of (an) orchestra.

orchestràre, *v.t.* to orchestrate.

orchestrazióne, *s.f.* orchestration.

orchestrína, *s.f.* band: — *da ballo,* dance-band.

orchèstrion, *s.m.* (*mus.*) orchestrion.

orchidèa, *s.f.* (*bot.*) orchid.

orciàio, *s.m.* **1.** (*chi fa orci*) maker of pitchers **2.** (*chi vende orci*) vendor of pitchers.

órcio, *s.m.* pitcher; (*per olio*) oil-jar ‖ *vien giù l'acqua a orci,* it is raining cats and dogs.

Órco, *no.pr.m.* (*mit.*) Orcus ‖ **órco,** *s.m.* (*mostro delle fiabe*) ogre.

òrda, *s.f.* horde (anche *fig.*): *orde di Tartari,* hordes of Tartars; *un'— di pezzenti,* a horde (*o* gang) of beggars; *un'— di zingari,* a gypsy horde.

ordalía, *s.f.* (*st.*) ordeal.

ordígno, *s.m.* **1.** contrivance, mechanical device: — *esplosivo,* booby-trap **2.** (*strumento*) implement, tool.

ordinàbile, *ag.* that may be ordered.

ordinàle, *ag.* ordinal: *numero* —, ordinal number ‖ *s.m.* (*eccl.*) ordinal.

ordinaménto, *s.m.* **1.** (*l'ordinare*) ordering, arrangement; (*ordine, disposizione*) order, disposition: *l'— dei musei,* museum arrangement; *l'— delle parole in una frase,* the order of (the) words in (o the word order of) a sentence **2.** (*regolamento, sistema*) code; system: — *civile,* civil code; — *giudiziario,* legal system; *ordinamenti militari,* military code; — *politico,* political system; — *scolastico,* regulations of a school.

ordinàndo, *s.m.* (*rar.*) (*eccl.*) ordinand.

ordinànte, *s.m.* (*rar.*) ordinant (anche *eccl.*).

ordinànza, *s.f.* **1.** (*mil.*) order: *marciare in* —, to march in order ‖ *berretto d'*—, regulation cap; *divisa fuori* —, non-regulation (o unauthorized) dress (o uniform); *ufficiale d'*—, orderly officer **2.** (*mil.*) (*attendente*) batman (*pl.* batmen) **3.** (*dir.*) ordinance, decree, order: — *che istituisce l'inizio della procedura fallimentare,* receiving-order; — *d'amnistia,* amnesty ordinance.

ordinàre, *v.t.* **1.** (*sistemare*) to arrange; (*mettere in ordine*) to tidy (up), to put in order; (*organizzare*) to organize: *devo — le mie carte,* I must put my papers in order; *dovrebbe — la sua vita secondo le sue possibilità finanziarie,* he should live according to his means; *ho ordinato la mia scrivania,* I have put my desk in order; *il generale ordinò le sue truppe per la battaglia,* the general drew up his troops in order of battle; — *una festa,* to organize a party; — *le idee,* to put one's ideas in order; — *i propri affari,* to set one's affairs in order **2.** (*comandare*) to order, to tell; to command; to direct: *gli ordinai di rimanere a casa,* I ordered him to stay at home; *ho ordinato alla cuoca che il pranzo sia pronto alle otto,* I've told the cook to prepare dinner for eight o' clock; *ho ordinato la colazione per l'una,* I have ordered lunch for one o' clock; *mi ordinò di entrare, uscire,* I was ordered (to go) in, I was ordered out; *ordinerò che sia fatto,* I shall order this to be done (o I shall give orders to have it done); *il vigile gli ordinò di proseguire,* the policeman directed him to proceed; — *alle truppe di attaccare il nemico,* to command (o to order) the troops to attack the enemy; — *a qlcu. di salire, scendere,* to order s.o. to go upstairs, downstairs; — *a qlcu. di tacere,* to tell s.o. to be silent; — *uno sciopero,* to call a strike **3.** (*commissionare*) to order: *ho ordinato un paio di scarpe dal tuo calzolaio,* I have ordered a pair of shoes from your shoemaker; *non sono ancora arrivate le merci che abbiamo ordinato,* we have not yet received the goods we ordered **4.** (*prescrivere*) to order, to prescribe: *il dottore ha ordinato molte medicine al malato,* the doctor has prescribed a lot of medicines for

the patient; *il dottore mi ha ordinato una vacanza in montagna,* the doctor has prescribed a holiday in the mountains for me **5.** (*preordinare*) to ordain, to order: *Dio ha ordinato la nostra vita secondo la sua volontà,* God has ordained our lives according to His will **6.** (*eccl.*) (*investire di ordine sacro*) to ordain, to give holy orders to (s.o.); *fu ordinato prete,* he was ordained ‖ **ordinàrsi,** *v.r.* **1.** to arrange oneself; (*disporsi*) to draw up: *le truppe si ordinarono sul campo di battaglia,* the troops drew up on the battle-field **2.** (*eccl.*) to be ordained, to take holy orders.

ordinariaménte, *av.* ordinarily, usually, normally.

ordinariàto, *s.m.* **1.** professorship **2.** (*eccl.*) bishopric.

ordinàrio, *ag.* **1.** ordinary, usual, customary, normal: *acquisti ordinari,* usual purchases; *altezza ordinaria,* average height; *frazione ordinaria,* (*mat.*) vulgar fraction; *passo* —, normal pace; *ha lavorato con l'ordinaria energia,* he worked with his customary energy ‖ *cosa di ordinaria amministrazione,* nothing out of the ordinary **2.** (*comune*) ordinary, common: *d'aspetto* —, plain; *una stoffa ordinaria,* ordinary cloth; (*dozzinale*) coarse cloth **3.** (*non raffinato*) common: *persona ordinaria,* common person; *egli ha dei modi molto ordinari,* his manners are very common ‖ *s.m.* **1.** ordinary: *fuori dell'*—, out of the ordinary; *secondo l'*—, according to habit (o custom); *uscire dall'*—, to be out of the ordinary (o to be exceptional) ‖ *d'*—, usually (o as a rule) **2.** (*eccl.*) Ordinary; (*confessore delle monache*) conventual confessor **3.** (*professore ordinario*) professor **4.** (*pasto consueto*) usual meal.

ordinàta, *s.f.* **1.** (*mat.*) ordinate: *congiungere le estremità delle ordinate con linee rette,* to join the ends of the ordinates by straight lines **2.** (*aer. mar.*) frame: — *di forza,* spar-frame; — *di paratia,* bulkhead frame; — *intermedia,* intermediate transverse frame; — *maestra,* main frame; — *rovescia,* reverse frame.

ordinataménte, *av.* tidily, in an orderly way; (*metodicamente*) methodically.

ordinatívo, *ag.* **1.** regulating, governing: *principi ordinativi,* regulating principles **2.** (*gram.*) ordinal: *numeri ordinativi,* ordinal numbers ‖ *s.m.* order.

ordinàto, *ag.* **1.** tidy, orderly: *una persona ordinata,* a person of regular habits; (*metodica*) a methodical person; *una stanza ordinata,* a tidy room; *una vita ordinata,* an orderly life **2.** (*eccl.*) ordained.

ordinatóre, *ag.* ordering; (*organizzatore*) organizing, arranging: *ha una mente ordinatrice,* he has a head for organization ‖ *s.m.,* **ordinatríce,** *s.f.* **1.** orderer; (*chi organizza*) organizer, arranger **2.** (*comm.*) customer.

ordinazióne, *s.f.* **1.** (*ordine*) order **2.** (*comm.*) order, commission: *un'— di dieci chili di zucchero,* an order for ten kilos of sugar; *fatto su* —, made to order; *annullare un'*—, to cancel an order; *confermare un'*—, to confirm an order **3.** (*eccl.*) ordination **4.** (*ricetta medica*) prescription.

órdine, *s.m.* **1.** (*disposizione*) order, arrangement; (*fila, serie*) series, sequence: — *alfabetico,* alphabetical order; — *cronologico,* chronological order; — *di battaglia,* battle array; — *inverso,* (*gram.*) inversion (o inverted word order); — *logico,* logical order; — *numerico,* numerical order; — *sparso, chiuso,* (*mil.*) open, close order; *in — di data,* in order of time (o consecutively); *in — di età, importanza,* in order of age, importance; *un lungo — di navi,* a long line of ships; *non in* —, out of order; *numero d'*—, serial number; *la casa è in — perfetto,* the house is in perfect order; *mettere, lasciare in* , to put, to leave in order ‖ — *di idee,* scheme of things: *ciò non rientra nel mio — di idee,* this does not enter into my scheme of things; *entrare nell'— di idee di fare ql.co.,* to come round to the idea of doing sthg. ‖ *all'— del giorno,* on the agenda: *questioni all'— del giorno,* items on the agenda; *è un argomento all'— del giorno, fig.* it is an every-day (o a common) topic; *passare all'— del giorno,* to proceed with the business of the day ‖ *in — a*, with regard to ‖ *ritirarsi in buon —*, to retire in good order **2.** (*comando*) order, direction: *— di pagamento*, (*comm.*) order of payment; *— scritto*, written order; *fino a nuovo —*, until further orders; *per — di*, by order of; *ho l' — di restare qui*, I have orders to remain here; *ricevette l' — di andare all'estero*, he was ordered abroad; *dare — che ql.co. sia fatto*, to give orders for sthg. to be done (*o that sthg. should be done*); *dare, eseguire un —*, to give, to execute (*o to carry out*) an order: *eseguivo soltanto degli ordini*, I was acting under orders; *essere agli ordini di qlcu.*, to be at s.o.'s beck and call; (*mil.*) to be under s.o.'s orders (*o command*); *ubbidire a un —*, to obey an order ‖ *parola d' —*, password **3.** (*comm.*) order, request: *— di merci per l'esportazione*, indent; *— di prova*, trial order; *— permanente*, standing order; *— verbale*, verbal order; *libro degli ordini*, order-book; *pagabile all'—*, payable to order; *accusare ricevimento d'—*, to acknowledge an order; *annullare un —*, to cancel an order; *confermare un —*, to confirm an order; *evadere un —*, to fill an order; *passare un —*, to remit (*o to send in*) an order ‖ *cambiale all'—*, bill to order ‖ *sempre ai vostri graditi ordini*, yours faithfully **4.** (*disciplina*) order, orderliness: *— pubblico*, public order; *delitto contro l' — pubblico*, (*dir.*) breach of the peace; *fu ristabilito l'—*, order was restored; *mantenere l'—*, to keep order; *richiamare all'—*, to call (a meeting) to order **5.** (*categoria*) order, rank, class: *tutti gli ordini sociali erano rappresentati*, all social ranks were represented ‖ *di prim'—*, first-class (*attributivo*): *albergo di prim'—*, first-class hotel; *artista di prim'—*, artist of the highest order (*o first-rate artist*); *pranzo di prim'—*, first-class dinner (*o fam. slap-up dinner*); *tiratore di prim'—*, crack-shot ‖ *impiegato d'—*, junior employee **6.** (*genere*) kind, nature: *problemi d'— tecnico*, problems of a technical nature (*o technical problems*); *questo è un altro — di cose*, this is a different thing altogether **7.** (*congregazione*) order: *— cavalleresco, religioso*, order of chivalry, religious order ‖ *Ordine dei Cavalieri di Malta*, Order of the Knights of Malta; *Ordine dei Domenicani*, Dominican Order **8.** *pl.* (*eccl.*) orders: *ordini maggiori, minori*, major, minor orders; *ordini sacri*, Holy Orders: *ricevere gli ordini sacri*, to take Orders **9.** (*arch. scient.*) order: *—dorico, ionico, corinzio*, Doric, Ionic, Corinthian order.

ordíre, *v.t.* **1.** (*ind. tessile*) to warp: *— una tela*, to warp a cloth **2.** *fig.* (*tramare, macchinare*) to plot, to plan: *stavano ordendo un intrigo fra loro*, they were plotting (*o planning*) some mischief between them; *— un complotto*, to hatch a plot; *— una congiura contro qlcu.*, to intrigue (*o to plot*) against s.o. (*o to plan a conspiracy against s.o.*); *— un crimine*, to plot a crime **3.** *fig.* (*congegnare*) to plot: *— la trama di una commedia*, to plot a play.

ordíto, *s.m.* **1.** (*ind. tessile*) warp: *bocca di —*, shed; *filo di —*, warp-yarn **2.** *fig.* (*intrico*) web, tissue: *un — di bugie*, a pack (*o a web o a tissue*) of lies **3.** *fig.* (*intreccio*) plot: *l'— di un romanzo*, the plot of a novel.

orditóio, *s.m.* (*ind. tessile*) warping-mill.

orditóra, *s.f.,* **orditóre,** *s.m.,* **orditríce,** *s.f.* **1.** warper **2.** *fig.* (*persona che trama inganni*) plotter, schemer.

orditúra, *s.f.* **1.** (*ind. tessile*) (*l'ordito*) warping; (*l'ordito*) warp: *— a macchina*, (*ind. tess.*) mill-warping **2.** *fig.* (*trama, macchinazione*) plotting, planning **3.** *fig.* (*struttura, intreccio*) structure, plot.

Óre, *no.pr.f.pl.* (*mit.*) Horae.

oreàde, *s.f.* (*mit.*) oread.

orécchia, *s.f.* **1.** (*bot.*) ear, auricle **2.** (*bot.*): *— di Giuda*, Jew's ear; *— d'orso*, bear's ear (*o auricula*) **3.** *— marina*, (*zool.*) ormer (*o ear-shell o sea-ear*) **4.** *V.* **orécchio 1.**

orecchiàbile, *ag.* catchy.

orecchiànte, *s.c.* **1.** (*chi suona a orecchio*) person who plays by ear; (*chi canta a orecchio*) one who sings by ear **2.** (*dilettante*) dabbler.

orecchiétta, *s.f.* (*anat.*) auricle.

orecchíno, *s.m.* earring; (*pendente*) eardrop.

orécchio, *s.m.* **1.** ear: *— esterno*, external (*o outer*) ear (*o auricle*); *— interno*, internal ear; *a forma d'—*, ear-shaped; *dolore d'—*, earache; *sordo da un —*, deaf in one ear; *mi fischiano gli orecchi, qualcuno parlerà di me*, my ears are tingling (*o my ears are burning*) I think someone must be talking about me; *mi ronzano gli orecchi*, my ears are tingling (*o buzzing*); *dire una cosa all'— di qlcu.*, to say sthg. (*o to have a word*) in s.o.'s ear; *portare il cappello sull'—*, to wear one's hat over one ear (*o on one side*); *tirare gli orecchi a qlcu.*, to pull (*o to tweak*) s.o.'s ears; *turarsi le orecchie*, to stop one's ears ‖ *a portata di —*, within earshot ‖ *abbassare le orecchie*, *fig.* to be crestfallen ‖ *allungare le orecchie*, to prick one's ears ‖ *avere — per la musica*, to have an ear for music ‖ *dare, prestare — a ql.co.*, to give ear (*o to lend an ear*) to sthg. ‖ *entrare da un — e uscire dall'altro*, to go in one ear and out the other ‖ *essere duro d'—*, to be hard of hearing ‖ *essere tutto orecchi*, to be all ears ‖ *fare un — a una pagina*, to dog-ear a page ‖ *fare orecchi da mercante*, to turn a deaf ear (*o to pretend not to hear*) ‖ *giungere all'—*, *fig.* to come to the ear ‖ *lacerare gli orecchi*, to deafen ‖ *mettere una pulce nell'— a qlcu.*, to drop s.o. a hint ‖ *suonare, cantare a —*, to play, to sing by ear ‖ *tendere l'—*, to cock one's ears ‖ *i muri hanno orecchie*, *prov.* walls have ears **2.** (*di àncora*) fluke; (*di aratro*) mould-board **3.** (*mar.*): *— d'asino*, kevel; *— di lepre*, leg-of-mutton sail.

orecchióne, *s.m.* **1.** large ear **2.** *pl.* (*patol.*) mumps **3.** (*mil.*) trunnion **4.** (*zool.*) long-eared bat.

orecchionièra, *s.f.* (*mil.*) trunnion-bearing.

orecchiúto, *ag.* long-eared.

oréfice, *s.m.* goldsmith, jewe(l)ler.

oreficería, *s.f.* **1.** (*negozio di orefice*) goldsmith's (shop), jeweller's (shop) **2.** (*arte dell'orefice*) goldsmith's art, jeweller's art: *articoli d'—*, goldsmith's (*o jeweller's*) wares.

orería, *s.f.* (*rar.*) goldsmith(e)ry.

Orèste, *no.pr.m.* Orestes.

orézzo, *s.m.* (*poet.*) gentle breeze.

òrfana, orfanèlla, *s.f.* orphan girl.

òrfano, (*ag.*) orphan (*attributivo*): *era orfana*, she was an orphan (girl); *rimase — quando era ancora bambino*, he was left an orphan when he was still a child ‖ *s.m.* orphan: *è un — di guerra*, he is a war orphan ‖ *poveri orfanelli!*, poor little orphans!.

orfanotròfio, *s.m.* orphanage, orphan-asylum.

Orfèo, *no.pr.m.* (*mit.*) Orpheus.

òrfico, *ag.* Orphic, Orphean ‖ *s.m.* Orphist.

organàio, *s.m.* organ-builder.

organdi, organdíse, *s.m.* (*tessuto*) organdie.

organétto, *s.m.* **1.** concertina, accordion **2.** (*a manovella*) barrel-organ, hurdy-gurdy: *suonatore di —*, organ-grinder.

organicaménte, *av.* organically; systematically.

organicità, *s.f.* organic unity.

orgànico, *ag.* organic (*anche fig.*): *chimica organica*, organic chemistry; *malattia organica*, organic disease; *rifiuti organici*, (*fisiol.*) organic remains; *unità organica*, organic unity; *un tutto —*, an organic whole ‖ *s.m.* personnel; staff.

organíno, *V.* **organétto.**

organísmo, *s.m.* organism (*anche fig.*): *un — amministrativo*, an administrative body; *— vivente*, living organism; *deperimento dell'—*, physical decline.

organísta, *s.m.* organist.

organizzàbile, *ag.* organizable.

organizzaménto, *s.m.* organizing; (*organizzazione*) organization.

organizzàre, *v.t.* to organize: *— un esercito, un partito politico*, to organize an army, a political party;

— *una spedizione*, to organize an expedition ‖ **organizzàrsi**, *v.r.* to organize oneself: *i lavoratori si sono organizzati in sindacati*, the workmen have organized themselves into trade-unions.

organizzatóre, *ag.* organizing ‖ *s.m.*, **organizzatríce**, *s.f.* organizer

organizzazióne, *s.f.* organization: *difetto d'—*, lack of organization; *la complessa — del corpo umano*, the complex organization of the human body.

òrgano, *s.m.* 1. organ (anche *fig.*): *gli organi dell'udito*, the organs of hearing; *l'« Unità » è l'— del partito comunista italiano*, the newspaper " Unità " is the organ of the Italian Communist Party 2. (*mus.*) organ: — *a due tastiere*, two-manual organ; — *elettro-acustico*, electric organ; *canne d'—*, organ-pipes 3. (*mec.*): — *di macchina*, machine-member; — *di presa*, current -collector; — *di repulsione*, (*ferr.*) buffer-gear; — *di trazione*, (*ferr.*) draft-gear; — *motore*, mover.

organogènesi, organogenía, *s.f.* (*biol.*) organogeny.

organogènico, *ag.* (*biol.*) organogenic.

organografía, *s.f.* (*scient.*) organography.

organogràfico, *ag.* (*scient.*) organographic.

organología, *s.f.* (*scient.*) organology.

organològico, *ag.* (*scient.*) organological.

organoplastía, *s.f.* (*chir.*) organoplasty.

organoplàstico, *ag.* (*chir.*) organoplastic.

organoterapía, *s.f.* (*med.*) organotherapy.

organza, *s.f.* (*tessuto*) organza, organdie.

organzíno, *s.m.* (*ind. tessile*) organzine.

orgàsmo, *s.m.* orgasm; excitement: *l'— della partenza*, the excitement of departure; *essere in —*, to be agitated (*o* to be in a flutter); *mettere in —*, to fluster.

òrgia, *s.f.* orgy (anche *fig.*): *orge bacchiche*, orgies of Bacchus; — *di colori*, profusion (*o* riot) of colour.

orgiàsta, *s.m.* orgiast.

orgiàstico, *ag.* orgiastic(al).

orgóglio, *s.m.* pride: — *smisurato*, boundless pride; *giusto, legittimo —*, legitimate pride; *stupido —*, stupid pride; *è pieno d'—*, he is very proud.

orgogliosaménte, *av.* proudly.

orgoglióso, *ag.* proud: *è troppo — per domandarti perdono*, he is too proud to apologize to you; *essere — di ql.co.*, to be proud of sthg.

oricàlco, *s.m.* 1. (*metal.*) orichalc; (*ottone*) brass 2. (*poet.*) (*tromba*) trumpet.

oricellàre, *ag.* (*bot. chim.*) orchil (*attributivo*), archil (*attributivo*).

oricèllo, *s.m.* (*bot. chim.*) orchil, archil.

orientàle, *ag.* eastern, oriental; East (*attributivo*): *arte, civiltà, cultura —*, oriental art, civilization, culture; *Asia, Africa Orientale*, East Asia, Africa; *Indie Orientali*, East Indies; *lingue orientali*, oriental languages; *paesi orientali*, eastern countries; *perla —*, orient pearl; *la questione —*, (*pol.*) the Eastern Question; *stati orientali*, Eastern States; *sulla costa —*, on the East coast; *tappeto —*, Oriental carpet ‖ *gli Orientali*, Orientals ‖ *Chiesa Orientale —*, (*st. relig.*) Orthodox (*o* Eastern) Church.

orientalísta, *s.c.* Orientalist.

orientaménto, *s.m.* 1. orientation; bearings (*pl.*): *senso di —*, sense of direction; *perdere l'—*, to lose one's bearings 2. (*tendenza*) trend: *l'— della politica*, the political trend ‖ — *professionale*, vocational guidance 3. (*rad. mar. aer.*) bearing: — *mediante radio*, radio bearing (*o* fix).

orientàre, *v.t.* 1. to orient, to orientate: — *una carta geografica, la bussola*, to orient a map, the compass; — *un edificio*, to orient a building 2. (*mar.*) to trim: — *le vele*, to trim one's sails ‖ **orientàrsi**, *v.r.* 1. to find one's bearings; to take one's bearings: *il contadino non riesce ad — in una città*, a countryman cannot find his bearings in a city 2. (*trovare la via giusta*) to see one's way clear: *non riesco a orientarmi*

in questo affare, I can't see my way clear in this business; *si orientò facilmente nel suo lavoro*, he picked up things quickly in his new job 3. (*tendere*) to tend: *la sua filosofia si orientava verso l'atomismo*, his philosophy tended towards atomism.

oriènte, *s.m.* east: *verso —*, eastwards; *finestra che guarda ad —*, window facing east; *la Germania è a — della Francia*, Germany is eastward (*o* to the east) of France; *questo paese confina a — col mare*, this country is bounded on the east by the sea ‖ *Oriente*, East (*o* Orient): *Impero d'—*, Eastern Empire; *il Medio, l'Estremo —*, the Middle, the Far East; *il traffico con l'—*, the trade with the East ‖ *il Grande Oriente*, (*l'assemblea dei massoni*) the Grand Lodge.

orifiàmma, *s.f.* (*st.*) oriflamme.

orifício, orifízio, *s.m.* opening, aperture, orifice.

orígano, *s.m.* (*bot.*) origanum, origan.

Orígene, *no.pr.m.* (*st. fil.*) Origen.

originàle, *ag.* 1. original: *il disegno — di quel monumento*, the original design for that monument; *documento —*, original document; (*dir.*) script; *idioma —*, original language; *partitura —*, (*mus.*) original score; *peccato —*, (*teol.*) original sin; *testo —*, original text 2. (*nuovo*) new, original; (*ingegnoso*) ingenious: *idee, pensieri originali*, new (*o* original) ideas, thoughts; *mente —*, original (*o* inventive) mind; *impronta —*, original touch; *è un modo molto — per farsi conoscere*, it is a very ingenious way of making oneself known 3. (*strano*) odd, queer, strange; (*eccentrico*) eccentric: *modi originali*, odd manners; *un tipo —*, a character ‖ *s.m.* 1. original: *la copia è grande quanto l'—*, the copy is the same size as the original; *è più bello l'— che il ritratto*, the original is better than the portrait; *non ho mai letto Chaucer nell'—*, I have never read Chaucer in the original; *copiare dall'—*, to copy from the original; *riscontrare, collazionare con l'—*, to compare with the original 2. (*persona strana*) eccentric, odd person: *è un originale*, he is an eccentric (*o* an odd fellow).

originalità, *s.f.* 1. originality: *la sua opera non dimostra molta —*, his work does not show much originality 2. (*novità*) novelty 3. (*stranezza*) oddness, queerness, strangeness; (*eccentricità*) eccentricity: *l'— dei suoi modi*, the oddness of his ways.

originalménte, *av.* 1. originally 2. (*in modo nuovo*) in a novel way; (*ingegnosamente*) ingeniously 3. (*stranamente*) oddly; (*eccentricamente*) eccentrically.

originàre, *v.t.* to originate, to give rise to (sthg.) to cause, to occasion; (*effettuare*) to bring about: *ciò originò un litigio*, this gave rise to an argument ‖ *v.i.* to originate (from, with sthg.); to arise (from, out of sthg.); to take rise (from sthg.): *lo sciopero originò dalle rivendicazioni dei sindacati*, the strike originated from the demands of the trade unions.

originariaménte, *av.* originally.

originàrio, *ag.* 1. original; (*primo*) primary: *la causa originaria*, the primary cause; *rocce originarie*, (*geol.*) primary rocks; *splendore —*, original splendour 2. (*nativo, oriundo*) original: *gli abitanti originari di un paese*, the original inhabitants of a country; *paese —*, country of origin; *è un animale — dell'India*, it is an animal indigenous to India; *essere — della Cina*, to be of Chinese stock.

originatóre, *s.m.*, **originatríce**, *s.f.* originator.

orígine, *s.f.* 1. origin; (*inizio*) beginning; starting -point: *le origini della letteratura inglese*, the origins of English literature; *l'— della Terra*, the origin of the Earth; *l'— di una lingua, di una parola*, the origin of a language, of a word; — *di una traiettoria*, (*fis.*) initial point of a trajectory; *avere —*, to originate from (*o* to originate in *o* to arise from *o* to arise out of): *la lite fra i due vicini ebbe — da uno spiacevole incidente*, the quarrel between the two neighbours originated in (*o* from) an unpleasant incident; *dare — a*, to give rise to (*o* to occasion *o* to cause): *la discus-*

sione diede — *a una rissa*, the discussion caused (*o* occasioned) a brawl; *risalire alle origini di un fatto*, to trace an event (back) to its origin || *all'*—, originally || *peccato d'*—, (*teol.*) original sin 2. (*sorgente*) source, origin (anche *fig.*): *l'*— *di un fiume*, the source of a river; *l'*— *di questo fiume è nelle Alpi*, this river rises in the Alps; *l'*— *di tutti i miei guai*, the source (*o* origin) of all my troubles 3. (*causa*) cause: *non riusciamo a capire l'*— *di questo male*, we cannot make out the cause of this illness 4. (*nascita, stirpe*) origin, descent, extraction; (*nazionalità*) nationality: *di nobile* —, of noble origin (*o* descent); *di umile* —, of humble origin; *famiglia tedesca, ma italiana d'*—, German family but of Italian origin (*o* extraction); *luogo d'*—, place of origin; *è d'*—*russa*, he is of Russian origin 5. (*provenienza*) origin, provenance: *certificato d'*—, (*dir.*) certificate of origin; *di dubbia* —, of doubtful provenance.

origliàre, *v.i.* to eavesdrop.

origlière, *s.m.* pillow.

orína, *s.f.* urine: *analisi delle orine*, (*med.*) analysis of urine.

orinàle, *s.m.* chamber(-pot).

orinàre, *v.i.* to urinate.

orinàrio, *ag.* urinary.

orinatívo, *ag.* urinary.

orinatóio, *s.m.* public convenience.

orinazióne, *s.f.* urination.

Orióne, *no.pr.m.* (*mit. astr.*) Orion.

oriúndo, *ag.*: *essere* — *di Milano*, to be of Milanese origin (*o* extraction).

oriuòlo, (*poet.*) per **orològio**.

orizzontàle, *ag.* horizontal.

orizzontalménte, *av.* horizontally.

orizzontàre, orizzontàrsi, *V.* **orientàre, orientàrsi**.

orizzónte, *s.m.* 1. horizon: — *artificiale*, (*aer.*) artificial horizon; — *artificiale giroscopico*, (*aer.*) gyro horizon; — *astronomico*, (*geog. aer.*) astronomical horizon; — *celeste*, (*astr.*) celestial horizon; — *geometrico*, (*astr.*) geometrical horizon; — *ottico* (*astr.*), optical horizon; — *visibile*, (*astr.*) apparent horizon || *all'*—, on the horizon; *alto sull'*—, high above the horizon; *il lontano* —, the far (*o* distant) horizon || *fare un giro d'*—, to make a general survey || *profilarsi all'*—, to loom on the horizon 2. *fig.* horizon(s): *gli orizzonti della scienza moderna*, the horizons of modern science; *l'*— *politico*, political horizon; *uomo di* — *limitato*, narrow-minded man (*o* man of limited horizons); *aprire nuovi orizzonti*, to open up new horizons (*o* new vistas): *questa scoperta ha aperto orizzonti nuovi*, this discovery has opened up new horizons.

Orlàndo, *no.pr.m.* Roland; (*letter.*) Orlando.

orlàre, *v.t.* (*fare l'orlo a*) to hem; (*bordare*) to edge, to border; (*bordare un oggetto circolare*) to rim; (*rifinire con bordo applicato*) to trim: — *a giorno*, to hem-stitch; — *un cerchio con gomma*, to rim a hoop with rubber; — *un fazzoletto*, to hem a handkerchief; — *una sottoveste con pizzo*, to edge (*o* to border) a slip with lace; — *una tenda con una frangia*, to fringe a curtain; — *una toga di ermellino*, to trim a gown with ermine.

orlàto, *ag.* hemmed; (*bordato*) edged, bordered; (*di oggetto rotondo*) rimmed; (*con bordo applicato*) trimmed: *fazzoletto* — *di pizzo*, handkerchief edged (*o* bordered) with lace; *toga orlata di ermellino*, gown trimmed with ermine.

orlatóre, *s.m.* hemmer || **orlatríce**, *s.f.* 1. hemmer 2. (*mec.*) hemming machine.

orlatúra, *s.f.* 1. hemming 2. (*orlo*) hem.

órlo, *s.m.* 1. (*di abiti, biancheria, ecc.*) hem; (*bordo applicato*) trimming; (*bordo aggiunto come ornamento*) edging, border: — *a giorno*, hem-stitch; *un* — *di pizzo a una tovaglia*, a lace-border on a table-cloth; — *ribattuto*, double hem; — *sfilato*, hem-stitch 2. (*estremità, margine*) edge; (*ornamento*) border; (*di oggetto*

rotondo) lip, rim; (*bordo largo*) brim; (*di dirupi, ecc.*) brink; edge: — *arrotondato*, rounded edge; *l'*— *di un bicchiere, tazza, secchio*, the rim of a glass, of a cup, of a bucket; *l'*— *di una brocca*, the lip of a jug; *l'*— *di un cappello*, the brim of a hat; *l'*— *di un piatto*, the edge (*o* rim) of a plate; *l'*— *di un tavolo*, the edge of a table; *l'*— *dorato di un tavolo*, the gilded border of a table; *bicchiere pieno fino all'*—, glass full to the brim || *doppio* —, (*mec.*) double flange || — *periferico*, (*aer.*) peripheral hem || *sull'*— *della rovina*, *fig.* on the verge (*o* brink) of ruin.

órma, *s.f.* 1. footprint, footmark; (*traccia*) track, trace (anche *fig.*): *le orme di un animale sulla neve*, the tracks of an animal in the snow; *le orme di una passata grandezza*, the traces (*o* vestiges) of past greatness; *il cane seguiva le orme della lepre*, the hound followed the trace (*o* scent) of the hare; *si vedevano le sue orme sulla sabbia*, we saw his footprints (*o* footmarks) in the sand; *seguire le orme di qlcu.*, to follow in s.o.'s footsteps (anche *fig.*) || *ritornare sulle proprie orme*, to go back on one's tracks 2. (*impronta*) mark (anche *fig.*): *gli diede uno schiaffo che gli lasciò l'*— *della mano sul viso*, she slapped his face leaving the mark of her fingers on it; *lasciò la sua* — *nella politica italiana*, he made his mark on Italian politics.

ormài, *V.* **oramài**.

ormàre, *v.t.* 1. to track, to trace 2. (*imitare*) to follow in s.o.'s footsteps.

ormeggiàre, *v.t.* (*mar.*) to moor: — *una nave lungo la banchina*, to moor a ship at the quayside || **ormeggiàrsi**, *v.r.* (*mar.*) to moor.

orméggio, *s.m.* (*mar.*) mooring: — *a ruota*, single anchor mooring; — *a zampa d'oca*, mooring-bridle; — *di prua*, bow-fast (*o* head-mooring); — *di poppa*, stern-mooring (*o* stern-fast); — *in quattro*, head-and-stern mooring; *boa d'*—, mooring-buoy; *cattivo* —, foul berth; *cavo d'*—, mooring-rope (*o* fast); *diritti d'*—, moorage; *gancio d'*—, mooring-dog; *palo d'*—, mooring-pile; *posto d'*—, berth (*o* moorings); *punto d'*—, mooring-point; *la nave era agli ormeggi*, the ship was at her moorings; *levare gli ormeggi*, to pick up the moorings; *spezzare gli ormeggi*, to break (the) moorings.

ormóne, *s.m.* (*fisiol.*) hormone: — *testicolare*, (*farm.*) androgen; *deficienza d'ormoni*, hormone deficiency.

ormoniterapía, *s.f.* (*med.*) hormonotherapy.

ornamentàle, *ag.* ornamental: *pianta* —, ornamental plant.

ornamentazióne, *s.f.* ornamentation.

ornaménto, *s.m.* 1. ornament (anche *fig.*): *la mensola del camino era carica di ornamenti*, the mantelpiece was crowded with ornaments; *questo vestito ha troppi ornamenti per il mio gusto*, this dress is too fussy for my liking; *la virtù è il più bell'*— *dell'anima*, virtue is the finest ornament of the soul || *a mo' di* —, by way of ornament 2. (*arch.*) ornament: — *a dentelli*, denticular ornament; — *a fogliami*, foliation (*o* feathering); — *a ovoli e lancette*, egg-and-dart ornament; — *arabesco*, arabesque; — *a rosone*, rosette; *una facciata ricca di ornamenti*, a façade rich in ornaments 3. (*mus.*) ornament, grace-note.

ornàre, *v.t.* to adorn; to decorate; to ornament (anche *fig.*); (*abbellire*) to beautify; (*guarnire*) to trim: *due splendidi quadri del Trecento ornavano la parete*, two magnificent fourteenth-century pictures adorned the wall; *una ghirlanda di fiori ornava her hair*; *quel vestito è ornato con pizzo*, that dress is trimmed with lace; *le strade erano ornate di bandiere*, the streets were decorated (*o* hung) with flags; — *una finestra di fiori*, to deck a window with flowers; — *il proprio stile*, to embellish one's style || **ornàrsi**, *v.r.* to adorn oneself.

ornataménte, *av.* ornately, in an ornate style.

ornatézza, *s.f.* ornateness.

ornatísta, *s.c.* ornamentalist.

ornatívo, *ag.* ornamental.

ornàto, *ag.* **1.** adorned: *era donna ornata di virtù,* she was adorned with virtue **2.** (*di stile*) ornato; (*spreg.*) flowery: *ha uno stile* —, he has a flowery style ‖ *s.m.* ornamentation, decoration; (*arte del decorare*) art of decoration: *troppo carico di ornati,* too rich in ornamentation; *è professore di* —, he teaches decoration.

ornèllo, *s.m.* (*bot.*) flowering ash.

ornitología, *s.f.* ornithology.

ornitològico, *ag.* ornithological ‖ *stazione ornitologica,* bird-watching post.

ornitòlogo, *s.m.* ornithologist.

ornitorineo, *s.m.* (*zool.*) ornithorhynchus, duck -billed platypus.

órno, *s.m.* (*bot.*) flowering ash.

òro, *s.m.* **1.** gold: — *bianco,* white gold; — *di coppella, a 24 carati,* 24 carat gold; — *fino,* refined gold; — *greggio,* unrefined gold; — *in lingotti,* gold in ingots; — *in verghe,* gold in bars; — *lavorato,* wrought gold; — *massiccio,* solid gold; — *tipo,* standard gold; — *zecchino,* pure gold; *cercatore d'*—, gold-digger; *miniera d'*—, gold mine; *moneta, orologio d'*—, gold coin, watch; *pepita d'*—, gold-nugget; *placcato in* —, gold -plated; *polvere d'*—, gold-dust; *quest'oro è a 14 carati,* this gold is 14 carats ‖ *capelli d'*—, golden hair ‖ *un cuore d'*—, a heart of gold; *una persona d'*—, a wonderful (o exceptional) person ‖ *età dell'*—, golden age ‖ *febbre dell'*—, gold fever ‖ *occasione d'*—, golden opportunity ‖ *ore d'*—, golden hours ‖ *egli vale tant'*— *quanto pesa,* he is worth his weight in gold ‖ *non lo farei per tutto l'*— *del mondo,* I should not do it for all the money in the world ‖ *nuotare nell'*—, to be rolling in money (o wealth) ‖ *ottenere ql.co. a peso d'* —, to pay a king's ransom for sthg.; *vendere a peso d'*—, to sell at a very high price ‖ *non è tutt'*— *quel che luce, prov.* all that glitters is not gold **2.** *pl.* jewels: *i miei ori,* my jewels (o my jewellery).

orogènesi, *s.f.* (*geol.*) orogenesis, orogeny.

orografía, *s.f.* orography, oreography.

orogràfico, *ag.* orographic(al).

orologería, *s.f.* **1.** (*arte dell'orologiaio*) horology; watchmaking; clock-making **2.** (*negozio di orologiaio*) watchmaker's (shop) **3.** *movimento d'*—, clock (o watch) movement.

orologiàio, orologière, *s.m.* **1.** clockmaker, watchmaker **2.** (*chi ripara orologi*) watch-repairer.

orològio, *s.m.* (*tascabile, da polso*) watch; (*da muro, ecc.*) clock: — *a carica automatica,* self-winding watch; — *a carillon,* chiming-clock; — *a cronometro,* timer (o timepiece); — *ad acqua,* water-clock; — *a pendolo,* pendulum-clock; — *a polvere,* hour (o sand)-glass; — *a ripetizione,* repeating clock; — *astronomico,* astronomical clock; — *da polso,* wrist-watch; — *da tavolo,* table-clock; — *di controllo con timbratura,* time-clock (o check-clock); — *elettrico,* electric clock; — *solare,* sun -dial; *cassa dell'*—, watchcase; *l'*— *della torre suona le ore e le mezze ore,* the clock on the tower strikes the hours and the half-hours; *il mio* — *è avanti, indietro tre minuti,* my watch is three minutes fast, slow; *il tuo* — *va avanti, indietro, cinque minuti al giorno,* your watch gains, loses five minutes a day; *quell'*— *si è fermato,* that clock has stopped; *questo* — *non funziona,* this clock, watch does not work; *caricare un* —, to wind (up) a clock, a watch; *mettere un* — *all'ora esatta,* to set a clock, a watch (o to put a clock, a watch right); *regolare un* —, to regulate a clock, a watch ‖ *un'ora d'*—, a whole hour: *ti ho aspettato per un'ora d'*—!, I waited for you a whole hour! ‖ *è un* —!, he is very regular in his habits; (*puntualissimo*) he is always on the dot ‖ *stare con l'*— *in mano,* to watch the clock.

Orónte, *no.pr.m.* (*geog.*) Orontes.

oroscopía, *s.f.* horoscopy.

oròscopo, *s.m.* horoscope: *trarre l'*— *di qlcu.,* to cast s.o.'s horoscope.

orpellàre, *v.t.* **1.** (*ornare con orpelli*) to tinsel **2.** (*ingannare*) to swindle, to cheat, to deceive.

orpellatúra, *s.f.* **1.** tinselling; tinsel-work **2.** (*finzione*) swindle, cheat.

orpèllo, *s.m.* **1.** tinsel **2.** *fig.* false glitter.

orpiménto, *s.m.* (*chim.*) arsenic trisulphide.

orrendaménte, *av.* horribly, dreadfully.

orrèndo, *ag.* horrible, dreadful, awful, fearful; shocking: *una guerra orrenda,* an awful war; *uno spettacolo* —, a ghastly (o dreadful) sight; *è* — *a vedersi,* it is an appalling sight.

orrettízio, *ag.* (*dir.*) obreptitious.

orrezióne, *s.f.* (*dir.*) obreption.

orríbile, *ag.* horrible, dreadful, awful; shocking: *discorso* —, shocking speech; *mostro* —, horrible monster; *tempesta* —, dreadful thunderstorm; *tempo* —, awful weather; *tormento* —, horrible torture; *morire di una morte* —, to die an awful death.

orribilità, *s.f.* horribleness, dreadfulness.

orribilménte, *av.* horribly, dreadfully, awfully.

orridaménte, *av.* horridly, fearfully.

orridézza, orridità, *s.f.* horridness, fearfulness.

òrrido, *ag.* **1.** (*terribilmente brutto*) horrid, horrible, awful: *avere un aspetto* —, to be repulsive-looking **2.** (*spaventevole*) frightful, dreadful; horrifying: *bellezza orrida,* horrifying beauty; *visione orrida,* dreadful sight ‖ *s.m.* precipice, ravine, gorge.

orripilànte, *ag.* horripilant, hair-raising.

orripilazióne, *s.f.* horripilation.

orróre, *s.m.* **1.** horror; (*terrore*) dread; (*ripugnanza*) repugnance, disgust, abhorrence: *colto, preso d'*—, horror-struck (o horror-stricken); *con mio grande* —, to my unspeakable horror; *ho, sento* — *del sangue,* the sight of blood fills me with horror; *la natura ha* — *del vuoto,* Nature abhors a vacuum; *avere in* —, *avere* — *di qlcu., ql.co.,* to hate (o to detest o to abhor) s.o., sthg.: *cose simili le ho in* —, I detest such things; *mettere, fare* — *a qlcu.,* to horrify s.o. (o to fill s.o. with horror); (*disgustare*) to disgust s.o.: *mi fa* — *pensarci,* I dread to think of it; *la tua condotta mi fa* —, your behaviour disgusts me ‖ (*spavento*) awe **2.** (*cosa orribile*) horror (anche *fig.*): *gli orrori della guerra,* the horrors of war; *quel quadro è un* —, that picture is awful (o dreadful o terrible); *commettere degli orrori,* to commit atrocities.

órsa, *s.f.* (*zool.*) she-bear ‖ *Orsa Maggiore,* (*astr.*) Great Bear (o the Plough o Charles's Wain o Ursa Major); *Orsa Minore,* (*astr.*) Little Bear (o Ursa Minor).

orsacchiòtto, *s.m.* **1.** (*piccolo orso*) bear cib, young bear **2.** (*giocattolo*) Teddy bear.

orsàggine, *s.f.* (*selvatichezza*) gruffness, surliness.

órso, *s.m.* **1.** bear: — *bianco* (o *polare*)*, grigio, bruno, nero,* white (o polar), grizzly, brown, black bear; — *delle caverne,* (*paleont.*) cave-bear; *caccia all'*—, bear hunting; *combattimento di orsi,* bear-baiting; *grasso d'*—, bear-grease; *pelle d'*—, bear's skin (o bearskin); *dondolare la testa come un* —, to let one's head dangle like a bear's; *ballare come un* —, to dance like an elephant ‖ *vendere la pelle dell'*— *prima che sia morto, prov.* to count one's chickens before they are hatched **2.** (*persona goffa*) awkward person; (*burbera*) bear, gruff person; (*non socievole*) unsociable person **3.** (*strum. artig.*) bear.

Órsola, *no.pr.f.* Ursula.

orsolina, *s.f.* (*eccl.*) Ursuline.

orsú, *escl.* **1.** come on; go ahead: — *andiamo!,* come on, let's go! **2.** (*coraggio!*) cheer up!.

ortàggio, *s.m.* vegetable: *la lattuga e il cavolo sono ortaggi,* the lettuce and the cabbage are vegetables; *piantare ortaggi,* to plant vegetables.

ortàglia, *s.f.* **1.** (*terreno piantato a orto*) vegetable -garden, kitchen-garden **2.** (*ortaggio*) vegetable.

Ortènsia, *no.pr.f.* Hortense, Hortensia.

ortènsia, *s.f.* (*bot.*) hydrangea.

ortíca, *s.f.* (*bot.*) nettle, urtica: *puntura d'*—, nettle

-sting || *gettare la tonaca alle ortiche*, to throw off the cowl.

orticàio, *s.m.* nettle-bed.

orticària, *s.f.* (*patol.*) nettle-rash, urticaria.

ortìcolo, *ag.* horticultural: *esposizione orticola*, horticultural show; *prodotti orticoli*, vegetables.

orticultóre, *s.m.* horticulturist.

orticultúra, *s.f.* horticulture.

òrto[1], *s.m.* (*di casa*) kitchen garden; (*di un orticoltore*) market garden; (*amer.*) truck-farm; (*frutteto*) orchard || *— botanico*, botanical gardens || *l'— di Getsemani*, (*Bibbia*) the Garden of Gethsemane || *non è erba del suo —*, it is not his own work || *non è la via dell'—*, it is not the easiest way || *star coi frati e zappar l'—*, to pretend not to know.

òrto[2], *s.m.* (*poet.*) **1.** (*il sorgere di un astro*) rising **2.** (*oriente*) east, orient.

ortoclàsio, *s.m.* (*min.*) orthoclase.

ortocromàtico, *ag.* (*foto.*) orthochromatic.

ortodossìa, *s.f.* orthodoxy (anche *fig.*).

ortodòsso, *ag.* orthodox: *fede ortodossa*, orthodox faith; *opinioni poco ortodosse*, unorthodox opinions || *la Chiesa Ortodossa*, (*greco-scismatica*) the Orthodox Church || *s.m.* otrhodox || *gli Ortodossi*, (*cristiani greco-scimatici*) members of the Orthodox Church.

ortoepìa, *s.f.* orthoèpy.

ortoèpico, *ag.* orthoèpic(al).

ortofonìa, *s.f.* orthoèpy.

ortofònico, *ag.* orthoèpic(al).

ortogonàle, *ag.* (*geom.*) orthogonal.

ortografìa, *s.f.* **1.** spelling, orthography: *errori di —*, spelling mistakes **2.** (*arch.*) elevation plan.

ortograficaménte, *av.* orthographically.

ortogràfico, *ag.* orthographic(al).

ortolàno, *s.m.* **1.** (*venditore di frutta e verdura*) greengrocer **2.** (*orticoltore*) market-gardener; (*amer.*) truck-farmer **3.** (*ornit.*) ortolan.

ortopedìa, *s.f.* orthop(a)edy, orthopaedia; (*chir.*) orthop(a)edics.

ortopèdico, *ag.* orthop(a)edic || *s.m.* orthop(a)edist.

ortòttero, *s.m.* **1.** (*aer.*) orthopter **2.** (*entom.*) orthopter || *gli ortotteri*, the Orthoptera.

orvietàno, *ag.* of Orvieto || *s.m.* **1.** native of Orvieto **2.** (*antico medicamento*) Orvietan.

orvièto, *s.m.* "Orvieto" (kind of Italian muscatel wine).

òrza, *s.f.* (*mar.*) **1.** (*canapo*) bowline || *andare all'—*, tosail close to the wind; *mettersi all'—*, to haul to windward (*o* to luff); *stare all'—*, to haul upon the wind **2.** (*fianco della nave sopravvento*) weather-board.

orzaiuòlo, *s.m.* sty.

orzàre, *v.i.* (*mar.*) to luff, to sail close to the wind.

orzàta[1], *s.f.* (*mar.*) luffing.

orzàta[2], *s.f.* (*bibita*) barley-water, orgeat.

òrzo, *s.m.* barley.

osànna, *s.m.* hosanna || *—!*, hosanna!.

osannàre, *v.i.* to sing hosannas.

osàre, *v.t.i.* **1.** (*come v. servile*) to dare (*semidifettivo*); to venture: *come osi dire una cosa simile?*, how dare you say such a thing?; *egli non osa venire*, he dare not (*o* daren't) come (*o* he does not dare to come); *non ho mai osato dirglielo*, I have never dared to tell him; *non osò parlare*, he did not dare to speak; *non so se osi tentare*, I don't know whether he will dare to try; *oseresti chiederglielo?*, dare you ask him? (*o* would you dare to ask him?) || *oserei dire...*, I would (*o* one might) even go so far as to say... **2.** (*usato assolutamente*) (*avere la temerità*) to be daring, to be bold: *hai osato tanto!?*, were you so bold (*o* daring)!?; *non — troppo!*, don't be too daring (*o* bold)!; (*non oltrepassare i limiti*) don't go too far! || *v.t.* (*arrischiare*) to attempt, to risk: *osò un'impresa che molti ritenevano impossibile*, he attempted an enterprise that many people deemed impossible; *— il tutto per il tutto*, to risk (*o* to stake) one's all.

Òscar, *no.pr.m.* Oscar || *premio —*, (*st. cine.*) Oscar.

oscenaménte, *av.* **1.** obscenely **2.** (*orribilmente*) horribly.

oscenità, *s.f.* obscenity.

oscèno, *ag.* **1.** obscene, indecent: *canzone oscena*, bawdy (*o* obscene) song; *linguaggio —*, obscene language; *quadro —*, obscene picture; *proposta oscena*, indecent proposal **2.** (*bruttissimo*) horrible: *si trucca il viso in modo —*, her make-up is horrible.

oscillànte, *ag.* **1.** (*esitante*) hesitating **2.** (*di prezzi*) fluctuating **3.** (*elett. fis. rad.*) oscillating: *circuito —*, (*rad.*) oscillator circuit; *corrente —*, (*elett.*) oscillating current **4.** (*mec.*) floating.

oscillàre, *v.i.* **1.** to swing, to sway; (*di fiamma*) to flicker, to waver: *una fiamma che oscilla nell'oscurità*, a flame flickering (*o* wavering) in the dark; *il pendolo oscilla*, the pendulum swings || *far —*, to swing **2.** (*esitare*) to waver, to hesitate: *— tra due opinioni*, to waver between two opinions **3.** (*di prezzi*) to fluctuate, to vary **4.** (*elett. fis. rad.*) to oscillate.

oscillatóre, *s.m.* (*elett. fis. rad.*) oscillator: *— acustico*, (*acu.*) audio-oscillator; *— a battimenti*, (*rad.*) beat-frequency oscillator; *— a cavità*, (*elettronica*) rhumbatrom; *— a rilassamento*, (*rad.*) blocking oscillator; *— a valvola*, (*rad.*) valve oscillator; *— di Hertz*, (*elett.*) Hertzian oscillator.

oscillatòrio, *ag.* oscillatory, oscillating.

oscillazióne, *s.f.* **1.** swing(ing); (*di fiamma*) flickering; (*vibrazione*) vibration: *l'— del pendolo, di una corda*, the swing of a pendulum, the swinging of a rope **2.** (*di prezzi, valori*) fluctuation, variation **3.** (*elett. fis. rad. aer.*) oscillation: *— a battimenti*, (*rad.*) beat-frequency oscillation; *— a lungo periodo*, (*fis.*) long-period oscillation; *— costante*, (*fis.*) constant oscillation; *— dell'immagine*, (*cine.*) unsteady picture; *— del suono*, (*cine.*) flutter; *— di rilassamento*, (*rad.*) relaxation oscillation; *— laterale*, (*aer.*) lateral oscillation; *— libera*, (*rad.*) free oscillation; *— longitudinale*, (*aer.*) longitudinal oscillation; *— persistente*, (*rad. mec.*) undamped oscillation; *— smorzata*, (*rad.*) damped oscillation.

oscillògrafo, *s.m.* (*fis.*) oscillograph: *— a ferro dolce*, (*elett.*) soft-iron oscillograph; *— a raggi catodici*, (*elett. acu.*) cathode-ray oscillograph.

oscuràbile, *ag.* that may be obscured (anche *fig.*); *fig.* that may be eclipsed: *una fama non —*, an undying fame.

oscuraménte, *av.* obscurely.

oscuraménto, *s.m.* **1.** darkening; obscuring (anche *fig.*); *fig.* eclipsing **2.** (*in tempo di guerra*) black-out.

oscurantìsmo, *s.m.* obscurantism.

oscurantìsta, *s.m.* obscurant(ist).

oscuràre, *v.t.* **1.** to darken, to obscure, to dim, to overshadow (anche *fig.*); *fig.* to eclipse: *Byron oscurò la fama di Walter Scott come poeta*, Byron overshadowed (*o* eclipsed) the fame of Walter Scott as a poet; *il cielo è oscurato dal fumo*, the sky is darkened by the smoke; *le nuvole oscuravano la montagna*, the clouds darkened the mountain; *il sole era oscurato dalle nuvole*, the sun was obscured by the clouds; *— una stanza*, to darken a room; *— la vista*, to dim (*o* to obscure) the sight **2.** (*in tempo di guerra*) to black out || **oscuràrsi**, *v.r.* to darken, to grow dark; to dim, to grow dim; to become obscure: *il cielo si sta oscurando*, the sky is growing dark; *gli si oscura la vista*, his sight is growing dim; *il suo volto si oscurò*, his face darkened.

oscurazióne, *s.f.* obscuring (anche *fig.*); *fig.* eclipsing.

oscurità, *s.f.* **1.** darkness; obscurity (anche *fig.*): *l'— della notte*, the darkness of the night; *nella più completa —*, in utter darkness; *è contento di vivere nell'—*, he is content to live in obscurity; *quello scrittore cade spesso nell'—*, that writer often lapses into obscurity **2.** (*umiltà*) obscurity: *— di natali*, obscurity of one's origins **3.** (*ignoranza*) ignorance.

oscúro, *ag.* 1. dark; *fig.* dark, obscure: *oscuri disegni*, dark designs; *un — segreto*, a dark secret; *fatti oscuri della storia*, dark deeds of history; *forcsta, notte oscura*, dark forest, night; *passo, significato —*, obscure passage, meaning; *il suo volto si fece —*, his face darkened ‖ *camera oscura*, *(foto.)* camera obscura; *(locale in cui lavora il fotografo)* dark room 2. *(difficile)* hard, difficult: *avvenire —*, difficult future; *tempi oscuri*, hard times 3. *(sconosciuto)* obscure, unknown: *uno scrittore —*, an obscure (*o* unknown) writer 4. *(umile)* obscure: *un'oscura esistenza*, an obscure existence; *di oscuri natali*, of obscure origins ‖ *s.m.* dark: *all'—*, in the dark; *essere all'— di ql.co.*, *fig.* to be in the dark about sthg.; *tenere una persona all'— di ql.co.*, *fig.* to keep a person in the dark about sthg.

Osèa, *no.pr.m.* *(Bibbia)* Hosea.

Osíride, *no.pr.m.* *(mit.)* Osiris.

òsmio, *s.m.* *(chim.)* osmium.

osmòsi, *s.f.* *(chim. fis.)* osmosis, osmose.

osmòtico, *ag.* *(chim. fis.)* osmotic.

osmúnda, *s.f.* *(bot.)* osmund(a).

ospedàle, *s.m.* hospital, infirmary: *— da campo*, field-hospital (*o* field dressing-station); *— psichiatrico*, mental hospital; *nave —*, hospital-ship.

ospedalière, *V.* ospitalière.

ospitàle, *ag.* hospitable.

ospitalière, *ag.* hospital *(attributivo)*: *frate —*, hospitaller; *istituti ospitalieri*, hospitals ‖ *gli Ospitalieri*, *(st.)* the Knights Hospitallers.

ospitalità, *s.f.* hospitality: *il dovere dell'—*, host's duty; *dare, offrire — a qlcu.*, to give, to offer s.o. hospitality (*o fam.* to put s.o. up); *fig.* *(in un giornale, in una mostra)* to accept s.o.'s work (for publication, exhibition): *spero vorrà darmi — nel suo giornale*, I hope you will accept my work for publication in your paper.

ospitalménte, *av.* hospitably.

ospitàre, *v.t.* to give hospitality to (s.o.); to shelter; *(fam.)* to put up: *egli ospitò molti profughi*, he sheltered (*o* gave hospitality to) many refugees; *fui ospitato da un mio amico*, I stayed with a friend of mine; *puoi ospitarmi per questa notte?*, can you put me up for the night?; *spero di poterti — per una settimana*, I hope (to be able) to have you as my guest for a week.

òspite, *s.c.* 1. *(chi ospita)* *(uomo)* host; *(donna)* hostess: *la nostra — ci intrattenne piacevolmente*, our hostess entertained us pleasantly 2. *(persona ospitata)* guest: *ero — del mio amico*, I stayed with my friend (*o* at my friend's); *spero che sarai mio — a Milano*, I hope you will be my guest in Milan ‖ *andarsene insalutato —*, to go without taking one's leave.

ospízio, *s.m.* charitable institution: *— per poveri*, alms-house; *— per trovatelli*, foundling hospital; *— per vecchi, per ciechi*, home for the old, for the blind.

ospodàro, *s.m.* *(st.)* hospodar, gospodar.

ossalàto, *s.m.* *(chim.)* oxalate.

ossalemía, *s.f.* *(med.)* oxalæmia.

ossàlico, *ag.* *(chim.)* oxalic.

ossaluría, *s.f.* *(med.)* oxaluria.

ossàme, *s.m.* 1. heap of bones; collection of bones 2. *(arch.)* carcass, carcase.

ossàrio, *s.m.* ossuary, charnel-house; tomb.

ossatúra, *s.f.* 1. skeleton; bone structure: *una persona dall'— grossa*, a big-boned person; *essere di — minuta*, to have small bones (*o* a slender frame) 2. *(arch.)* frame(work); structure; carcass, carcase: *— dell'edificio*, building skeleton (*o* frame); *ponte con — in acciaio*, bridge with a steel framework 3. *fig.* *(di discorso, ecc.)* structure, framework.

ossecrazióne, *s.f.* *(rar.)* *(letter.)* obsecration.

osseína, *s.f.* *(chim. biol.)* ossein.

òsseo, *ag.* bony, osseous: *tessuto —*, bony tissue.

ossequènte, *ag.* *(letter.)* 1. *(rispettoso)* respectful (of s.o., sthg.): *un figlio —*, a respectful son 2. *(obbediente)* compliant (with s.o., sthg.), obedient: *— agli ordini*, compliant with orders.

ossequiàre, *v.t.* to pay one's respects to (s.o.).

ossèquio, *s.m.* 1. *(omaggio)* homage: *rendere — al sovrano*, to pay homage to one's sovereign 2. *pl.* *(saluti deferenti)* respects, regards: *voglia porgere i miei ossequi a sua madre*, please give my respects (*o* give my kind regards) to your mother 3. *(obbedienza)* obedience: *in — a, verso*, in obedience to (*o* in conformity with *o* in accordance with): *in — ai suoi ordini*, in obedience to his orders.

ossequiosaménte, *av.* 1. *(cerimoniosamente)* ceremonious 2. *(con deferenza)* deferentially; *(rispettosamente)* respectfully.

ossequiosità, *s.f.* 1. *(deferenza)* deference; *(rispetto)* respectfulness 2. *(servilità)* obsequiousness.

ossequióso, *ag.* 1. *(cerimonioso)* ceremonious: *una persona ossequiosa*, a ceremonious person 2. *(deferente)* deferential; *(rispettoso)* respectful 3.*(servile)* obsequious.

osservàbile, *ag.* observable.

osservànte, *ag.* 1. observant, observing: *cittadino — della legge*, citizen observant of the law 2. *frate —*, *(eccl.)* Observant Friar ‖ *gli Osservanti*, *(eccl.)* the Observants.

osservànza, *s.f.* 1. observance: *l'— della legge*, observance of the law; *in — alla legge*, in conformity with the law 2. *(ossequio)* regards *(pl.)* 3. *(eccl.)* observance: *frate dell'—*, friar of the strict Observants.

osservàre, *v.t.* 1. to observe, to watch; *(esaminare)* to examine; to look through (sthg.): *ho osservato accuratamente questi documenti*, I have examined (*o* looked through) these documents carefully; *lo osservai attentamente mentre scriveva quella lettera*, I watched (*o* observed) him carefully while he was writing that letter; *osserva come lo faccio*, watch how I do it; *— un fenomeno naturale*, to observe a natural phenomenon 2. *(rispettare, mantenere)* to keep, to observe, to respect; to comply with (sthg.); *(attenersi a)* to keep to (sthg.): *— una dieta rigorosa*, to keep to a strict diet; *— il digiuno*, to fast; *— le feste della Chiesa*, to observe (*o* to keep) the feasts of the Church; *— un giuramento, una promessa*, to keep an oath, a promise; *— la legge, le regole*, to observe (*o* to comply with) the law, the rules; *— il silenzio*, to observe silence 3. *(considerare, notare)* to observe, to notice; *(rilevare)* to point out: *è necessario — che...*, it is necessary to point out that...; *hai osservato come era pallida?*, did you notice how pale she was?; *voglio farti — tutti gli errori che hai fatto*, I want to point out all the mistakes you have made; *voglio farvi — il fatto che non lo si è più visto qui*, I want to draw your attention to (*o* I want to bring to your notice) the fact that he has never been seen here any more 4. *(obiettare)* to make an objection to (sthg.): *hai niente da — su questo?*, have you any objection (to make) to this?; *ma osservò che era troppo tardi per uscire*, but he made the objection (*o* he objected) that it was too late to go out.

osservatóre, *s.m.* observer ‖ *s.m.* 1. observer: *l'— italiano all'O.N.U.*, the Italian observer at U.N.O. 2. *(mar. mil.)* spotter; observer: *l'— prese molte fotografie dei movimenti del nemico*, the observer took many photographs of the enemy's movements.

osservatòrio, *s.m.* 1. observatory 2. *(mil.)* observation-post.

osservatríce, *s.f.* observer.

osservazióne, *s.f.* 1. observation: *— astronomica*, astronomical observation; *posto d'—*, observation-post (*o* look-out post); *torre di —*, observation tower; *il malato è in —*, *(med.)* the patient is being kept under observation; *mettere qlcu. in —*, *(med.)* to put s.o. under observation 2. *(nota, giudizio)* observation, comment, remark: *approvò il mio lavoro senza osservazioni*, he passed my work without a word; *vi sono delle osservazioni assai acute nel tuo tema*, there are some very keen observations (*o* comments) in your composition; *fare un'—*, to make a comment; *permettersi un'—*, to venture a remark 3. *(rimprovero)* reproach, criticism: *fare delle osservazioni a qlcu.*, to criticize s.o.

ossessionànte, *ag.* haunting, obsessing.

ossessionàre, *v.t.* to haunt, to obsess: *ero ossessionato dall'idea che potesse tornare,* I was haunted (o obsessed) by the idea that he might come back.

ossessióne, *s.f.* obsession: *è ordinato fino all'—,* neatness is almost an obsession with him; *è un vera —!,* it is a real obsession!.

ossessívo, *ag.* haunting, obsessing.

ossèsso, *s.m.* person possessed: *gridava come un —,* he shouted like one possessed.

ossiacetilène, *ag.* (*chim.*) oxyacetylene.

ossía, *cong.* **1.** (*cioè*) that is, id est (*abbr.* i.e.), or: *la filologia, — la scienza delle lingue,* philology, that is (o i.e.) the science of languages **2.** (*o per meglio dire*) or rather: *partì ieri sera, — questa mattina presto,* he left last night, or rather early this morning.

ossiànico, *ag.* (*lett.*) Ossianic: *i poemi ossianici,* Ossianic poems.

ossidàbile, *ag.* oxidizable, oxidable.

ossidabilità, *s.f.* oxidizability, oxidability.

ossidànte, *ag.* oxidative || *s.m.* oxidizer, oxidator.

ossidàre, *v.t.* (*chim.*) to oxidize || **ossidàrsi,** *v.r.* (*chim.*) to oxidize, to become oxidized: *l'oro non si ossida,* gold does not oxidize.

ossidàto, *ag.* (*chim.*) oxidized.

ossidazióne, *s.f.* (*chim.*) oxidization: *— anodica,* anodizing (o anodic treatment o anodic oxidation); *— frazionata,* fractional oxidation; *— termica superficiale,* firecoat.

ossidiàna, *s.f.* (*min.*) obsidian.

ossidionàle, *ag.* obsidional: *corona —,* (*st. romana*) obsidional crown.

òssido, *s.m.* (*chim.*) oxide: *— di berillio,* beryllium oxide (o beryllia); *— di calcio,* calcium oxide; *— di carbonio,* carbon monoxide; *— di magnesio,* magnesium oxide; *— di rame,* copper oxide; *— di zinco,* zinc oxide.

ossídrico, *ag.* (*chim.*) oxyhydrogen, oxyhydric: *acido —,* oxyhydric acid; *cannello —,* oxyhydrogen blowpipe; *fiamma ossidrica,* oxyhydrogen flame; *saldatura ossidrica,* oxyhydrogen welding.

ossiemoglobína, *s.f.* (*biol.*) oxyhæmoglobin.

ossífero, *ag.* ossiferous.

ossificàre, *v.t.,* **ossificàrsi,** *v.r.* to ossify.

ossificazióne, *s.f.* ossification.

ossífraga, *s.f.* (*ornit.*) ossifrage.

ossigenàre, *v.t.* **1.** (*chim.*) to oxygenate: *— una stanza,* to oxygenate a room **2.** (*capelli*) to peroxide.

ossigenàto, *ag.* **1.** (*chim.*) oxygenated, oxygenized: *acqua ossigenata,* hydrogen peroxide; *aria ossigenata,* oxygenated (o oxygenized) air **2.** (*di capelli*) peroxided.

ossigenazióne, *s.f.* (*chim.*) oxygenation.

ossígeno, *s.m.* (*chim.*) oxygen: *— pesante,* heavy oxygen; *bombola di —,* oxygen bottle; *inalatore di —,* breathing apparatus; *maschera ad —,* oxygen-mask; *tenda ad —,* oxygen-tent || *aver bisogno d'—,* (*aver bisogno d'aiuto*) to need help.

òsso, *s.m.* **1.** bone: *le ossa del cranio,* the bones of the head; *— sacro,* sacrum; *una persona dalle ossa grosse,* a big-boned person; *le ossa della spina dorsale si chiamano vertebre,* the bones of the spine (o spinal column) are called vertebrae; *gli scricchiolano le ossa,* his bones are cracking; *questo bottone è di —,* this botton is made of bone; *si è fratturato l'— della gamba,* he has broken his leg || *— di seppia,* cuttle (-fish) bone || *bagnato fino all'—,* soaked to the skin || *in carne ed ossa,* in flesh and blood (o in person) || *bisogna fare economia sino all'—,* we must practise the strictest economy || *è tutt'ossa, è pelle ed ossa,* he is nothing but skin and bone || *freddo che penetra nelle ossa,* biting cold: *il freddo mi penetra nelle ossa,* I am chilled (o frozen) to the bone || *il latino è un — duro,* Latin is a hard nut to crack || *avere le ossa rotte,* to be aching all over || *essere all'—,* to have nothing left || *essere di carne ed ossa,* to be made of flesh and blood || *fare*

l'— a qlco., (*abituarvisi*) to get used to sthg. || *rompere le ossa a qlcu.,* to thrash s.o. || *rompersi l'— del collo,* to break one's neck **2.** *pl.* (*corpo*) bones; body (*sing.*): *ho da far riposare queste povere ossa,* I must rest my weary bones; *le mie ossa riposeranno in pace in questo piccolo camposanto,* my bones will rest in peace in this little churchyard **3.** (*nocciolo*) stone: *l'— di una pesca,* a peach stone.

ossobúco, *s.m.* (*cuc.*) marrow-bone.

ossúto, *ag.* bony: *mano ossuta,* bony hand.

ostacolàre, *v.t.* **1.** to obstruct; (*impacciare*) to hamper, to hinder: *il ghiaccio ostacola la navigazione,* ice obstructs traffic; *il lungo mantello le ostacolava i movimenti,* she was hampered by her long cloak **2.** *fig.* to thwart, to be a hindrance to (s.o., sthg.), to hamper, to handicap, to interfere with (s.o.): *ha sempre ostacolato i miei piani,* he has always interfered with (o obstructed) my plans; *mi ha sempre ostacolato,* he has always thwarted me; *nella sua carriera di avvocato è ostacolato dalla balbuzie,* he is handicapped in his profession as a lawyer by his stammer; *— il corso degli affari,* to hamper the progress of business; *— un matrimonio,* to impede a marriage.

ostacolísta, *s.m.* (*atletica*) hurdler; (*ippica*) jumper, steeple-chaser.

ostàcolo, *s.m.* **1.** obstacle, hindrance, impediment; handicap: *il solo — alla loro riconciliazione,* the only obstacle to their reconciliation; *questi ostacoli non saranno superati molto facilmente,* these obstacles will not easily be overcome; *essere d'— a, fare — a,* to be a bar to (o to be a hindrance to o to stand in the way of): *non voglio essere d'— alla vostra felicità,* I do not want to be an obstacle (o to stand in the way) of your happiness; *mettere un — a qlco.,* to prevent (o to oppose) sthg. **2.** (*atletica*) hurdle; (*ippica*) jump: *corsa ad ostacoli,* (*atletica*) hurdle-race; (*ippica*) steeple-chase.

ostàggio, *s.m.* hostage: *tenere qlcu. in —,* to hold s.o. as a hostage.

ostàre, *v.i.* to be opposed, to hinder (s.o.), to prevent (s.o.): *nulla ostava a che egli andasse,* nothing hindered (o prevented) him from going (o nothing hindered his going); *osta l'articolo 14,* the article 14 forbids it || *nulla osta,* (*eccl.*) nihil obstat.

òste[1], *s.m.* host, innkeeper, landlord || *domandare all'— se ha buon vino,* (*fare domande sciocche*) to ask silly questions || *fare i conti senza l'—,* to reckon without one's host.

òste[2], *s.m.f.* (*arc.*) host, army || *fare —,* to make (o to wage) war || *porre —,* to besiege.

osteggiàre, *v.t.* to oppose, to be hostile to (s.o., sthg.), to be opposed to (s.o., sthg.): *molti lo osteggiano,* many are hostile to (o oppose) him; *— un progetto,* to oppose (o to obstruct) a plan.

osteína, *s.f.* (*fisiol.*) ostein(e).

osteíte, *s.f.* (*patol.*) osteitis.

ostèllo, *s.m.* **1.** (*poet.*) dwelling, abode; (*rifugio*) refuge **2.** (*albergo per la gioventù*) (youth) hostel.

Ostènda, *no.pr.f.* (*geog.*) Ostend.

ostensíbile, *ag.* ostensible.

ostensibilménte, *av.* ostensibly.

ostensívo, *ag.* ostensible.

ostensóre, *s.m.* (*rar.*) exhibitor.

ostensòrio, *s.m.* (*eccl.*) monstrance.

ostentaménto, *s.m.* ostentation, showiness.

ostentàre, *v.t.* **1.** to ostentate, to show off, to parade, to display: *gli piace — la sua cultura,* he likes to show off (o to parade) his culture **2.** (*fingere*) to feign: *ostenta povertà,* he feigns poverty.

ostentaménte, *av.* ostentatiously.

ostentatívo, *ag.* ostentatious, boastful.

ostentatóre, *ag.* ostentatious || *s.m.,* **ostentatríce,** *s.f.* boaster, ostentatious person.

ostentazióne, *s.f.* ostentation, parade, showing off: *— delle proprie virtù,* ostentation of one's virtues.

osteoartríte, *s.f.* (*patol.*) osteoarthritis.

osteoblàsta, *s.m.* (*biol.*) osteoblast.
osteoclasía, *s.f.* (*chir.*) osteoclasis.
osteoclàste, *s.m.* (*chir.*) osteoclast.
osteolíte, *s.f.* (*min.*) osteolite.
osteología, *s.f.* osteology.
osteòma, *s.m.* (*patol.*) osteoma (*pl.* osteomata).
osteomalacía, *s.f.* (*patol.*) osteomalacia.
osteomielíte, *s.f.* (*patol.*) osteomyelitis.
osteosarcòma, *s.m.* (*patol.*) osteosarcoma (*pl.* osteosarcomata).
osteoscleròsi, *s.f.* (*patol.*) osteosclerosis.
osteotomía, *s.f.* (*chir.*) osteotomy.
osteòtomo, *s.m.* (*chir.*) osteotome.
ostería, *s.f.* tavern, public house; (*locanda*) inn: *tutti i suoi risparmi vanno a finire all'*—, he throws his money away at the pub (*o* public house).
osteríggio, *s.m.* (*mar.*) skylight.
ostéssa, *s.f.* hostess, innkeeper's wife, landlady.
ostètrica, *s.f.* midwife (*pl.* midwives): — *diplomata*, trained midwife.
ostetrícia, *s.f.* obstetrics, midwifery.
ostètrico, *ag.* obstetric(al): *clinica ostetrica*, maternity home ‖ *s.m.* obstetrician.
òstia, *s.f.* **1.** (*letter.*) victim, offering: *i pagani offrivano ostie ai loro dei*, the heathen offered victims to their gods **2.** (*eccl.*) host: — *consacrata*, consecrated host; *il sacerdote consacra l'*— *nella Messa*, the priest consecrates the host in the Mass **3.** (*cialda*) wafer: *prendi questa polverina in un'*—, take this powder in a wafer.
ostiariàto, *s.m.* (*eccl.*) order of ostiary.
ostiàrio, *s.m.* (*eccl.*) ostiary, doorkeeper.
òstico, *ag.* **1.** (*disgustoso*) unpalatable; (*aspro*) sour; (*amaro*) bitter: *bevanda ostica*, unpalatable drink **2.** *fig.* (*duro*) hard, irksome; (*aspro*) harsh; (*difficile*) difficult; (*oscuro*) obscure: *lavoro* —, irksome job; *parole ostiche*, harsh words; *il latino mi è* —, Latin is very difficult for me; *il senso di queste parole è* —, the meaning of these words is obscure.
ostíle, *ag.* hostile; adverse, opposed: *ambiente* —, hostile surroundings; *l'esercito* —, the enemy army; *un giornale* — *al governo*, a newspaper hostile (*o* opposed) to the government; *il partito era* — *alla nuova politica*, the party was hostile (*o* opposed) to the new policy; *i popoli assoggettati rimasero ostili*, the subject peoples remained hostile; *assumere un atteggiamento* —, to take up a hostile attitude.
ostilità, *s.f.* **1.** hostility, enmity; aversion; opposition: *l'*— *della stampa*, the hostility (*o* unfriendliness) of the press; *l'*— *dei vinti*, the hostility of the vanquished; *non v'è alcuna* — *tra i due gruppi*, there is no enmity (*o* hostility) between the two groups; *la sua continua* — *nuoce al nostro progetto*, his persistent hostility spoils our plan; *provare dell'*— *verso qlcu.*, to feel hostility (*o* enmity) towards s.o.; *vincere l'*— *di qlcu.*, to overcome s.o.'s hostility **2.** *pl.* (*mil.*) hostilities: *all'inizio delle* — *mi trovavo in Germania*, at the beginning of hostilities I was in Germany; *aprire, sospendere le* —, to open, to suspend hostilities.
ostilménte, *av.* hostilely, with hostility, in a hostile manner: *la sua proposta fu accolta* — *dal partito avversario*, his proposal was received with hostility by the opposing party; *guardare qlcu.* —, to look at s.o. with hostility.
ostinàrsi, *v.r.* to persist (in sthg., in doing); (*insistere*) to insist: *non mi ostino su questo punto*, I don't insist on this point; *non ostinarti, hai torto!*, don't insist, you are wrong!; *si ostina a credere, a negare*, he persists in believing, in denying; *si ostina a fare a modo suo*, he persists in having his own way; *si ostina nella sua opinione*, he persists in (*o* clings to) his opinion; — *nell'errore*, to persist in error.
ostinataménte, *av.* **1.** obstinately, stubbornly, mulishly: *credeva* — *alla possibilità di una vittoria finale*, he obstinately believed in the possibility of a final

victory; *era* — *attaccato alle sue idee*, he clung obstinately (*o* stubbornly) to his opinions; *si rifiutava* — *di entrare*, he stubbornly refused to enter **2.** (*persistentemente*) persistently: *il vento soffiò* — *dalle prime ore del mattino*, the wind blew persistently from the early morning.
ostinatézza, *s.f.* obstinacy, stubbornness, mulishness: *la sua* — *mi irrita*, his stubbornness gets on my nerves.
ostinàto, *ag.* **1.** obstinate, stubborn; mulish; (*solo di persona*) pig-headed: *natura ostinata*, obstinate (*o* stubborn) nature; *peccatore* —, obstinate sinner; *persona ostinata*, obstinate (*o* stubborn *o* pig-headed) person; *quel ragazzo è* — *nei suoi capricci*, that boy is obstinate in his caprices ‖ — *come un mulo*, as stubborn (*o* obstinate) as a mule **2.** (*persistente*) persistent, obstinate, stubborn: *assalti ostinati*, persistent attacks; *febbre, malattia ostinata*, obstinate (*o* persistent) fever, disease; *silenzio* —, stubborn silence; *incontrare una resistenza ostinata*, to meet with dogged (*o* stubborn) resistence ‖ *s.m.* (*ostinazione*) obstinacy, stubbornness.
ostinazióne, *s.f.* **1.** obstinacy, stubbornness: — *nel fare ql.co.*, obstinacy (*o* doggedness) in doing sthg. **2.** (*persistenza*) persistence, persistency: — *nel negare la verità*, persistency in denying the truth.
ostracísmo, *s.m.* ostracism: *dare l'*— *a qlcu.*, to ostracize s.o. (*o fam.* to send s.o. to Coventry).
òstrica, *s.f.* (*zool.*) oyster: *banco di ostriche*, oyster-bed (*o* oyster-bank) ‖ *uovo all'*—, (*cuc.*) prairie-oyster.
ostricàio, *s.m.* **1.** (*venditore di ostriche*) oyster-seller **2.** (*banco di ostriche*) oyster-bed, oyster-bank.
ostricoltúra, *s.f.* oyster-breeding.
òstro[1], *s.m.* (*letter.*) (*porpora*) purple; (*drappo color porpora*) purple cloth.
òstro[2], *s.m.* (*poet.*) (*vento*) Auster, south wind.
ostrogòto, *ag.* Ostrogothic ‖ *s.m.* **1.** Ostrogoth **2.** *fig.* (*barbaro*) barbarian **3.** (*linguaggio incomprensibile*): *quello che dice è* — *per me*, what he says is Greek to me; *parlare* —, to speak double-Dutch.
ostruènte, *ag.* obstructive.
ostruíre, *v.t.* to obstruct, to block up, to occlude, to clog (up), to stop (up): *gli alberi caduti ostruivano la strada*, the fallen trees obstructed (*o* blocked) the road; *il tubo era ostruito dalla polvere*, the pipe was clogged (*o* stopped) up with dust; — *il passaggio, il traffico*, to obstruct (*o* to block) the passage, traffic.
ostruíto, *ag.* obstructed, occluded, clogged (up).
ostruttívo, *ag.* obstructive.
ostruzióne, *s.f.* **1.** obstruction **2.** (*impedimento*) impediment **3.** (*mar.*) barrage: — *con rete*, net-barrage; — *parasiluri*, torpedo net **4.** (*med.*) stoppage: — *intestinale*, intestinal stoppage.
ostruzionísmo, *s.m.* obstructionism.
ostruzionísta, *s.m.* obstructionist.
Osvàldo, *no.pr.m.* Oswald.
otalgía, *s.f.* (*med.*) otalgia, otalgy.
otàlgico, *ag.* (*med.*) otalgic.
otàrda, *s.f.* (*ornit.*) bustard.
otària, *s.f.* (*zool.*) otary.
Otèllo, *no.pr.m.* (*lett.*) Othello.
otíte, *s.f.* (*patol.*) otitis.
otorinolaringoiàtra, *s.m.* otorhinolaryngologist.
otorinolaringoiatría, *s.f.* otorhinolaryngology.
ótre, *s.m.* wineskin ‖ *è un* — *di vino*, *fig.* he has had a skinful.
otricolàre, *ag.* utricular.
ottaèdrico, *ag.* (*geom.*) octahedral.
ottaèdro, *s.m.* (*geom.*) octahedron.
ottagonàle, *ag.* (*geom.*) octagonal.
ottàgono, *s.m.* (*geom.*) octagon.
ottangolàre, *ag.* (*geom.*) octagonal.
ottàngolo, *s.m.* (*rar.*) (*geom.*) octagon.
ottàno, *s.m.* (*chim.*) octane: *ad alto numero di ottano*, high-octane.
ottànta, *ag. num. card. s.m.* eighty.
ottànte, *s.m.* (*astr.*) octant.

ottantènne, *ag.* eighty years old (*predicativo*); eighty -year-old (*attributivo*) || *s.m.* eighty-year-old man || *s.f.* eighty-year-old woman.

ottantèsimo, *ag. num. ord. s.m.* eightieth.

ottantìna, *s.f.* about eighty, some eighty, fourscore: *ha passato l'—,* he is over eighty.

ottatívo, *ag.s.m.* (*gram.*) optative.

ottàva, *s.f.* **1.** (*eccl. mus.*) octave **2.** (*poes.*) ottava rima, octave: *l'« Orlando Furioso» è in ottave,* " The Orlando Furioso " is in ottava rima.

ottavàrio, *s.m.* (*eccl.*) octave.

Ottàvia, *no.pr.f.* Octavia.

Ottaviàno, *no.pr.m.* (*st.*) Octavian.

ottavíno, *s.m.* (*mus.*) piccolo (*pl.* piccolos).

Ottàvio, *no.pr.m.* Octavius, Octavus.

ottàvo, *ag. num. ord.* eighth || *ottava rima,* (*poes.*) ottava rima || *s.m.* **1.** eighth **2.** (*tip.*) octavo (*abbr.* 8vo) (*pl.* octavos): *in —,* in octavo.

ottemperànza, *s.f.* compliance: *in — a,* in compliance with.

ottemperàre, *v.i.* to comply (with sthg.): *bisogna — alle leggi,* we must comply with the law.

ottenebraménto, *s.m.* darkening, obscuring, clouding (over) (anche *fig.*): *— del cielo,* darkening of the sky; *l'— della sua mente,* the clouding (over) of his mind.

ottenebràre, *v.t.* to darken, to obscure, to cloud (anche *fig.*): *la sua fama fu ottenebrata da quella del figlio,* his fame was obscured by that of his son; *— la mente di qlcu.,* to cloud s.o.'s mind.

ottenebrazióne, *V.* ottenebraménto.

ottenére, *v.t.* **1.** to obtain, to get; to gain: *come hai ottenuto quel denaro?,* how did you come by that money?; *come puoi ottenerlo?,* how can you get hold of it?; *non insistere, non otterrai niente da lui,* don't insist, you won't get anything out of him; *non potei — di vederlo,* I couldn't get permission to see him; *ottenni il suo consenso,* I obtained his consent; *ottiene sempre ciò che vuole,* he always gets what he wants; *— un buon risultato,* to get (o to achieve o to gain o to obtain) a good result; *— delle informazioni,* to get (o to gain) information; *— un favore, una risposta, un permesso,* to obtain a favour, an answer, permission; *— un premio, una vittoria, la fiducia di qlcu.,* to win (o to gain) a prize, a victory, s.o.'s trust **2.** (*ricavare*) to extract, to obtain: *l'alcool si può — dal carbone,* alcohol can be obtained from coal.

ottenìbile, *ag.* obtainable.

otteniménto, *s.m.* (*rar.*) obtaining.

ottènne, *ag.* eight years old (*predicativo*); eight-year -old (*attributivo*) || *s.m.* eight-year-old boy || *s.f.* eight -year-old girl.

ottènnio, *s.m.* (*letter.*) period of eight years.

ottentòtto, *ag.s.m.* Hottentot (anche *fig.*).

ottétto, *s.m.* (*mus.*) octet.

òttica, *s.f.* optics.

òttico, *ag.* optic(al): *esperimento, fenomeno —,* optical experiment, phenomenon; *illusione ottica,* optical illusion; *strumento —,* optical instrument || *s.m.* optician.

ottimaménte, *av.* very well, extremely well: « *Come stai?* », « *Ottimamente, grazie* », "How are you?", "Very well, thank you"; *i fiori erano — disposti nei vasi,* the flowers were extremely well arranged in their vases; *il pranzo era — cucinato,* the dinner was extremely well cooked.

ottimàte, *s.m.* optimate.

ottimísmo, *s.m.* optimism: *essere portato all'—,* to be an optimist.

ottimísta, *s.c.* optimist.

ottimisticaménte, *av.* optimistically.

òttimo, *ag. superl.* perfect; best; excellent, first -rate, very good: *— affare,* excellent business; *un'ottima idea,* a capital idea; *— lavoro,* first-rate work; *ottime notizie,* very good (o excellent) news; *— ordine,* perfect order; *— rimedio,* very good remedy; *è un — amico,*

he is the best of friends; *era di — umore,* he was in a very good mood (o in high spirits); *sono in ottima salute,* I am in the best of health || *s.m.* best: *solo l'— è abbastanza buono per me,* only the best is good enough for me.

òtto, *ag. num. card. s.m.* eight: *l'— luglio,* the eighth of July; *a forma di —,* in the figure of eight; *oggi —,* today week (o this day week); *ogni — giorni,* every week (o once a week); *ha preso — in storia,* he has got eight out of ten in history || *— volante,* switchback || *corpo —,* (*tip.*) brevier || *in quattro e quattr'—,* in no time (o in the twinkling of an eye) || *è chiaro come quattro e quattro fa —,* it's as plain as a pikestaff || *dare gli — giorni a qlcu.,* to give s.o. a week's notice.

ottobràta, *s.f.* (*fam.*) trip in October.

ottóbre, *s.m.* October: *in —,* in October; *nel mese di —,* in the month of October; *al venti —,* on October the twentieth (o on the twentieth of October).

ottobríno, *ag.* **1.** October (*attributivo*) **2.** (*che matura in ottobre*) ripening in October.

ottocentésco, *ag.* nineteenth-century (*attributivo*).

ottocentèsimo, *ag. num. ord. s.m.* eight hundredth.

ottocentìsta, *s.m.* nineteenth-century artist.

ottocentìstico, *ag.* nineteenth-century (*attributivo*).

ottoeènto, *ag. num. card.* eight hundred || *s.m.* (*diciannovesimo secolo*) nineteenth-century.

ottomàna, *s.f.* ottoman.

ottomàno, *ag.s.m.* Ottoman: *Impero —,* Ottoman Empire.

ottomíla, *ag. num. card. s.m.* eight thousand.

ottonàio, *s.m.* brazier, brass worker.

ottonàme, *s.m.* brass-ware (*solo sing.*).

ottonàre, *v.t.* to cover with brass.

ottonàrio, *ag.* (*poes.*) octosyllabic || *s.m.* (*poes.*) octosyllabic verse.

ottonatúra, *s.f.* brass plating.

Ottóne¹, *no.pr.m.* Otto, Otho.

ottóne², *s.m.* **1.** brass: *— crudo,* hard-drawn brass; *— giallo, per bossoli,* cartridge brass; *lamiera di —,* brass sheet; *placca di —,* brass plate; *saldatura ad —,* hard-soldering (o brazing); *pulire gli ottoni,* to polish the brass (o the brasses) **2.** *pl.* (*mus.*) brass (*sing.*).

ottuagenària, *s.f.* octogenarian.

ottuagenàrio, *ag.* eighty years old (*predicativo*); eighty-year-old (*attributivo*); octogenarian || *s.m.* octogenarian.

ottúndere, *v.t.* (*rar.*) **1.** to blunt, to dull (anche *fig.*): *se cerchi di spaccarlo con un coltello, ne ottunderai la punta,* if you try to split it with a knife, you'll blunt its point; *— la mente,* to blunt the mind **2.** (*lenire*) to numb, to blunt, to deaden: *il tempo ottunde i dolori,* time deadens sorrows.

ottuplicàre, *v.t.* to octuple, to multiply by eight.

òttuplo, *ag.* eightfold, octuple.

otturaménto, *s.m.* obturation, stopping up, sealing.

otturàre, *v.t.* to obturate, to stop (up), to seal, to close; to plug: *— un'apertura,* to plug an opening; *— un dente,* to stop (o to fill) a tooth; *— una falla,* (*mar.*) to stop (o to seal) a leak || **otturàrsi,** *v.r.* to stop, to seal: *mi si otturarono le orecchie,* my ears were stopped up.

otturatóre, *ag.* obturating; (*anat.*) obturator (*attributivo*): *membrana otturatrice,* obturator membrane; *muscolo —,* obturator muscle || *s.m.* **1.** (*artigl.*) breech-block: *— a vitone,* interrupted-screw breech -block **2.** (*cine. foto.*) shutter: *— centrale,* interlens shutter; *— per dissolvenza,* dissolving shutter.

otturatòrio, *ag.* (*anat.*) obturator (*attributivo*).

otturazióne, *s.f.* obturation; plugging; (*di dente*) stopping, filling: *togliere l'— a un dente,* to remove the stopping of a tooth.

ottusaménte, *av.* obtusely.

ottusàngolo, *ag.* (*geom.*) obtuse-angled.

ottusità, *s.f.* **1.** (*geom.*) obtuseness **2.** (*l'essere smus-*

sato) bluntness **3.** *fig.* obtuseness, slowness, dullness ‖ — *di orecchio*, hardness (*o* dullness) of hearing.

ottúso, *ag.* **1.** (*geom.*) obtuse: *angolo* —, obtuse angle **2.** (*smussato, senza punta*) blunt: *arnese* —, blunt tool **3.** (*di suono*) dull: *suono* —, dull sound (*o* thud) **4.** *fig.* dull, slow, obtuse: *di mente ottusa*, dull-minded; *d'intelligenza ottusa*, obtuse.

ouverture, *s.f.* (*mus.*) overture.

ovàia, *s.f.* (*anat.*) ovary.

ovaiuòlo, *s.m.* **1.** (*portauovo*) egg-cup **2.** (*venditore di uova*) egg-seller.

ovàle, *ag.* oval: *finestra* — (*dell'orecchio*), (*anat.*) oval window ‖ *palla* —, (*giuoco*) rugby ‖ *s.m.* oval: *il suo viso è un* — *perfetto*, her face is a perfect oval.

ovàrio, *s.m.* (*anat. bot.*) ovary.

ovàto, *ag.* **1.** oval **2.** (*bot.*) ovate ‖ *s.m.* oval.

ovatríce, *s.f.* incubator.

ovàtta, *s.f.* wadding; (*cotone idrofilo*) cotton-wool: — *di cellulosa*, (*ind. cartaria*) cellucotton.

ovattàre, *v.t.* to stuff with wadding.

ovazióne, *s.f.* ovation: *gli fecero una* —, he received an ovation.

óve, *av.* (*letter.*) **1.** *interr. rel.* where: *o bella Musa,* — *sei tu?*, o fair Muse, where art thou? **2.** (*tempo*) when: *ma* — *cala la sera, le ombre avvolgono presto il villaggio*, but when night comes, the village is soon enveloped in shadow ‖ *cong.* (*letter.*) **1.** (*se, nel caso che*) if, in case: — *non gli piaccia, possiamo trovargliene un altro*, in case he doesn't like it, we can find another one for him; — *tu lo voglia, possiamo fare così*, we can do so, if you like **2.** (*purchè*) (only) if, on condition that: *te lo darò,* — *tu faccia quello che ti dico*, I'll give it to you, on condition that you do what I say **3.** — *che*, wherever; — *che sia*, (*dappertutto*) everywhere; (*in qualsiasi luogo*) anywhere.

òvest, *s.m.* (*geog.*) west: *casa esposta a* —, house facing west; *vento dell'*—, west wind; *la California è a* — *degli Stati Uniti*, California is in the west of the United States; *questo paese confina a* — *col mare*, this country is bounded on the west by the sea; *tira vento da* —, a westerly wind is blowing; *Torino è a* — *di Milano*, Turin is (to the) west of Milan ‖ *più a* — *di*, further west than ‖ *verso* —, westward (*ag.*); westwards (*av.*).

Ovídio, *no.pr.m.* (*st. lett.*) Ovid.

ovidútto, *s.m.* (*anat.*) oviduct.

ovifórme, *ag.* egg-shaped, oviform.

ovíle, *s.m.* sheep-fold, fold, pen: *ritornare all'*—, to return to the fold (anche *fig.*).

ovíno, *ag.* ovine ‖ *s.m.* sheep (*invariato al pl.*): *allevamento di ovini*, sheep farm.

ovíparo, *ag.* oviparous.

òvo, *V.* uòvo.

ovoidàle, ovòide, *ag.* ovoid(al), egg-shaped.

òvolo, *s.m.* **1.** (*fungo*) agaric **2.** (*arch.*) ovolo (*pl.* ovoli); echinus (*pl.* echini) **3.** (*bot.*) ovule.

ovovivíparo, *ag.* ovoviviparous.

òvulo, *s.m.* (*anat. bot.*) ovule.

ovúnque, *av.* (*dappertutto*) everywhere; (*in qualsiasi luogo*) anywhere: *puoi incontrarlo* —, you may meet him anywhere ‖ *cong.* wherever: — *egli sia, va' da lui*, go to him, wherever he is (*o* he may be).

ovvéro, *cong.* or; or on the other hand, or alternatively: *Pamela,* — *la virtù premiata*, Pamela, or virtue rewarded; — *si potrebbe far questo*, or on the other hand (*o* or alternatively) we could do this.

ovviaménte, *av.* obviously, evidently.

ovviàre, *v.i.* to obviate (sthg.): — *a una difficoltà*, to obviate a difficulty.

òvvio, *ag.* obvious, evident: *il rimedio più* —, the most obvious remedy; *supposizioni ovvie*, obvious suppositions; *è* —, it is obvious.

ozèna, *s.f.* (*patol.*) oz(a)ena.

oziàre, *v.i.* to idle; to idle about; to loaf: — *per le strade*, to idle (*o* to loaf) about the streets; — *tutto il giorno*, to loaf about all day.

òzio, *s.m.* **1.** (*infingardaggine*) idleness, laziness, indolence: *passare la vita in* —, to lead a life of idleness ‖ *l'* — *è il padre dei vizi*, *prov.* the Devil finds work for idle hands **2.** (*inoperosità*) inactivity, idleness: — *forzato*, forced inactivity; *stare in* —, to be idle **3.** (*riposo*) leisure: *momenti d'*—, leisure moments; *nelle mie ore d'*—, in my leisure hours (*o* time).

oziosàggine, *s.f.* idleness, laziness, indolence.

oziosaménte, *av.* **1.** (*in modo ozioso*) idly: *passeggiare* —, to wander idly (*o* to loaf about) **2.** (*vanamente*) idly, vainly: *parlare* —, to talk idly.

oziosità, *s.f.* **1.** (*oziosaggine*) idleness, laziness, indolence **2.** (*discorso ozioso*) idle talk: *sono tutte* —, it's all idle talk.

ozióso, *ag.* **1.** (*inoperoso*) idle: *vita oziosa*, idle life ‖ *capitale* —, uninvested capital (*o* capital lying idle) **2.** (*inutile, vano*) idle, useless: *cose oziose*, useless things; *discorso* —, idle talk; *domande oziose*, idle questions; *è* — *pensare che venga*, it is idle to think he will come ‖ *s.m.* idler, loafer.

ozònico, *ag.* (*chim.*) ozonic.

ozonizzàre, *v.t.* (*chim.*) to ozonize, to ozonise.

ozonizzatóre, *s.m.* (*chim.*) ozonizer, ozoniser.

ozonizzazióne, *s.f.* (*chim.*) ozonization, ozonisation.

ozòno, *s.m.* (*chim.*) ozone.

ozonòmetro, *s.m.* (*chim.*) ozonometer.

P

p, *s.f.m.* (*quattordicesima lettera dell'alfabeto italiano*) p (*pl.* ps, p's) ‖ — *come Palermo,* (*tel.*) p for Peter ‖ P, (*parcheggio*) P.

pacàre, *v.t.* to calm, to pacify, to appease, to soothe: — *l'ira di una persona,* to appease a person's anger.

pacataménte, *av.* calmly, quietly; peacefully: *rispondere* —, to reply calmly.

pacatézza, *s.f.* calmness, quietness.

pacàto, *ag.* calm, quiet: *con voce pacata,* quietly (*o* in a calm voice).

pàcca, *s.f.* slap, smack: *mi ha dato una* — *sulla spalla,* he slapped me on the shoulder.

pacchèo, *s.m.* idiot, silly fellow.

pacchétto, *s.m.* packet; (*piccolo pacco*) small parcel; (*piccolo collo*) small package: *un* — *di titoli,* (*comm.*) a parcel of shares; — *postale,* parcel; *dammi quel* — *di sigarette, per favore,* please, give me that packet of cigarettes.

pàcchia, *s.f.* (*fam.*) **1.** (*mangiata*) good meal: *che* —!, what a good (*o* fine) meal! **2.** (*cuccagna*) godsend: *è una* — *per noi oggi, possiamo fare quello che vogliamo!,* it is a godsend that we can do as we like to-day! **3.** (*ufficio, lavoro che occupa poco e rende molto*) sinecure: *quell'impiego è una vera* —, that job is a real sinecure.

pacchianàta, *s.f.* (*dial.*) **1.** (*atto da pacchiano*) coarse action **2.** (*detto da pacchiano*) coarse expression.

pacchiàno, *ag.* (*dial.*) vulgar, coarse: *ha un'eleganza pacchiana,* he has a vulgar way of dressing.

pàcco, *s.m.* parcel; (*collo*) package; (*pacchetto*) packet; (*involto*) bundle: — *assicurato,* registered parcel; — *postale,* parcel: *spedire per* — *postale,* to send by parcel post; *fare un* —, to make up a parcel.

paccottíglia, *s.f.* **1.** shoddy goods (*pl.*) **2.** (*cosa di nessun valore*) trash.

pàce, *s.f.* **1.** peace: *conferenza della* —, peace conference; *in tempo di* —, in time of peace; *proposta di* —, peace proposal; *trattato di* —, peace treaty; *cercheremo di ottenere una* — *onorevole,* we shall try to obtain peace with honour; *fu firmata la* — *fra le due potenze,* the peace treaty was signed between the two powers; *questo paese è in* — *da due secoli,* this country has been at peace for two centuries; *chiedere la* —, to ask for peace; *mantenere, turbare la* —, to keep, to disturb the peace ‖ *la Pace di Amiens, di Versailles, ecc.,* the Peace of Amiens, of Versailles, etc. ‖ *chi vuol la* —, *si prepari alla guerra,* prov. if you want peace, prepare for war **2.** (*concordia, accordo*) peace: *per amor di* —, for the sake of peace and quiet; *cercò di metter* —, he tried to bring about peace; *siamo tornati in* —, we are friends again; *essere in* — *con la propria coscienza,* to be at peace with one's own conscience; *essere in* — *con qlcu.,* to be at peace (*o* to be on good terms) with s.o.; *fare la* — *con qlcu.,* to make peace (*o* to make it up) with s.o. **3.** (*tranquillità*) peace; (*calma*) quiet, stillness; (*riposo*) rest: *la* — *del cuore, dell'anima,* peace (*o* tranquillity) of mind; *la* — *della sera,* the peace of the evening; *la* — *pubblica,* public peace: *disturbatore della* — *pubblica,* disturber of the peace; *la* — *regna in città dopo i disordini di ieri,* peace prevails in the town after yesterday's riots; *che* — *c'è qui!,* how peaceful (*o* quiet) it is here!; *non mi dà un momento di* —, he gives me no peace; *ora che se ne è andato avrò finalmente un po' di* —, now that he has gone, I shall

have some peace at last; *puoi dormire in* —, you may sleep in peace; *il rimorso non gli dava* —, remorse gave him no peace; *lasciare in* — *qlcu.,* to leave s.o. alone; *vivere in* —, to live in peace ‖ — *all'anima sua!,* peace be with him! ‖ *la* — *eterna,* eternal rest ‖ *santa* —!, my goodness! ‖ *Dio l'abbia in* —, God rest his soul ‖ *lasciami in santa* —, do let me have some peace and quiet ‖ *il pover'uomo ora riposa in* —, the poor man is now at rest ‖ *riposa in* —!, rest in peace! ‖ *vattene in* —!, go in peace! ‖ *darsi* —, *mettersi il cuore in* —, to set one's mind at rest: *non sa darsi* —, he cannot set his mind at rest **4.** (*pazienza, tolleranza*) patience: *accettò in* — *ogni cosa,* he accepted everything with patience; *sia detto con tua* —, don't get angry if I say this **5.** (*eccl.*) pax, osculatory.

Pachistàno, *ag.s.m.* Pakistani ‖ **Pachistàna,** *s.f.* Pakistani.

pachidèrma, *s.m.* **1.** (*zool.*) pachyderm **2.** (*persona grassa*) stout person, fat person **3.** (*persona poco sensibile*) insensitive person, pachyderm.

pacièra, *s.f.,* **pacière,** *s.m.* peacemaker: *fare da* —, to act as peacemaker.

pacificàbile, *ag.* **1.** (*riconciliabile*) reconcilable **2.** (*placabile*) pacifiable, appeasable.

pacificaménte, *av.* peacefully, pacifically.

pacificàre, *v.t.* **1.** (*riconciliare*) to reconcile: *pacificò il padre col figlio,* he reconciled the father to (*o* with) his son; — *due nemici tra loro,* to reconcile two enemies **2.** (*rendere pacifico*) to pacify, to appease: — *un paese,* to pacify (*o* to restore peace to) a country ‖ **pacificàrsi,** *v.r.* to become reconciled (to, with s.o.); to reconcile oneself (to, with s.o.); to make it up (with s.o.); to make friends again (with s.o.): *si pacificarono dopo aspre contese,* they became (*o* were) reconciled after violent quarrels.

pacificatóre, *s.m.* **1.** (*che riconcilia*) reconciling **2.** (*che rende pacifico*) pacifying, appeasing ‖ *s.m.,* **pacificatríce,** *s.f.* **1.** (*chi riconcilia*) reconciler, peacemaker **2.** (*chi rende pacifico*) pacifier, appeaser.

pacificazióne, *s.f.* **1.** (*riconciliazione*) reconciliation **2.** (*il rendere pacifico*) pacification, appeasement.

pacifico, *ag.* **1.** peaceful, pacific; peaceable: *carattere* —, peaceful (*o* pacific) character; *intenzioni pacifiche,* peaceful intentions; *tribù pacifiche,* peaceful tribes; *uomo* —, pacific (*o* peaceable *o* peace-loving) man ‖ *l'Oceano Pacifico,* (*geog.*) the Pacific (Ocean) **2.** (*fuori discussione*) self-evident: *è* — *che...,* it is self-evident that....

pacifísmo, *s.m.* pacifism, pacificism.

pacifísta, *s.c.* pacifist, pacificist.

pacioccóna, *s.f.,* **pacioccóne,** *s.m.* plump easy-going person.

paciòna, *s.f.,* **paciòne,** *s.m.* placid person.

pacióso, *ag.* peaceful, placid; easy-going.

Padàno, *ag.* Po (*attributivo*): *la Val Padana,* (*geog.*) the Po Valley (*o* the Po River Basin).

padèlla, *s.f.* **1.** frying-pan ‖ *far* —, (*mancare il bersaglio*) to miss the target ‖ *cadere dalla* — *nella brace,* prov. to jump (*o* to fall) out of the frying-pan into the fire **2.** (*recipiente per i bisogni corporali degli infermi*) bed-pan.

padellàio, *s.m.* **1.** (*chi fabbrica padelle*) maker of pans **2.** (*chi vende padelle*) seller of pans.

padellàta, *s.f.* panful: *una* — *di patate,* a panful of potatoes.

padiglióne, *s.m.* **1.** (*tenda*) pavilion, tent **2.** (*baldacchino*) canopy: — *sopra un letto*, canopy over a bed **3.** (*edifizio isolato*) pavilion: *i padiglioni di un ospedale, di un'esposizione*, the pavilions of a hospital, of an exhibition **4.** (*anat.*) pavilion, outer ear, auricle **5.** (*di diamante*) pavilion.

Pàdova, *no.pr.f.* (*geog.*) Padua.

padovàno, *ag.s.m.* Paduan ‖ **padovàna**, *s.f.* Paduan.

pàdre, *s.m.* **1.** father: — *adottivo, putativo*, adoptive (o foster-) father, putative father; — *affettuoso, indulgente, severo*, affectionate, indulgent, severe father: *fa il — severo,* he plays the heavy father; — *di famiglia*, father of a family; *Dante è il — della lingua italiana*, Dante is the father of the Italian language; *egli è — di cinque figli*, he is the father of five children; *mi trattò come un —*, he treated me like a father; *far le veci del —*, to act as a father ‖ *Padri coscritti*, (*st. romana*) Conscript Fathers ‖ — *nobile*, (*teat.*) heavy father ‖ *i Padri della Chiesa*, (*st. relig.*) the Fathers of the Church ‖ *i Padri Pellegrini*, (*st. amer.*) the Pilgrim Fathers ‖ — *spirituale*, father confessor ‖ *da —*, as a father; (*paternamente*) like a father: *mi parlò da —*, he spoke to me like a father; *ti parlo da —*, I am speaking to you as a father ‖ *di — in figlio*, from father to son: *privilegi trasmessi di — in figlio*, privileges handed down from father to son ‖ *i nostri padri*, our forefathers (o ancestors) ‖ *far da — a qlcu.*, to be a father to s.o.: *mi ha fatto da —*, he was a father to me ‖ *tale il —, tale il figlio*, prov. like father like son ‖ *l'ozio è il — dei vizi*, prov. the Devil finds work for idle hands **2.** *Padre*, (*teol.*) Father: *Dio Padre*, God the Father ‖ « *Padre nostro che sei nei cieli...* », "our Father who (o which) art in Heaven..." **3.** (*eccl.*) Father: — *Giovanni*, Father John; *il molto Reverendo Padre O' Brien*, the Most Reverend Father O' Brien ‖ *il Santo Padre*, the Holy Father.

padreggiàre, *v.i.* to take after one's father.

padrígno, *s.m.* step-father.

padríno, *s.m.* **1.** godfather **2.** (*in un duello*) second.

padróna, *s.f.* **1.** mistress: *la — di casa*, the mistress of the house; (*quando riceve*) the hostess: *la — di casa ci accolse cordialmente*, the hostess gave us a warm welcome; *la — sta parlando con la cuoca*, the mistress is speaking to the cook ‖ *la — sono io!*, I'm the mistress here! ‖ *è — della situazione*, she is mistress of the situation *è — di se stessa*, (*è indipendente*) she is her own mistress; (*sa dominarsi*) she is very self-controlled **2.** (*proprietaria*) owner, proprietress: *è — di tutte queste terre*, she is the owner of all this land **3.** (*di casa, albergo*) landlady: *la — della mia pensione è molto gentile*, my landlady is a very kind woman.

padronàle, *ag.* **1.** main (*attributivo*): *il bagno —*, the main bathroom; *è una vecchia casa —*, it is an old country house (o *in Inghilterra* a manor-house) **2.** (*privato*) private: *automobile —*, private car.

padronànza, *s.f.* mastery, command, control: — *del mare*, command (o mastery) of the seas: *perdere la — del mare*, to lose command (o control) of the sea; — *del mercato*, command (o control) of the market: *gli è sfuggita la — del mercato*, the control of the market has slipped out of his hands; *la — di una lingua*, mastery (o command) of a language: *ha una — perfetta della lingua*, he has complete mastery of the language; — *di sè*, self-control ‖ *la cameriera ha preso una gran — in casa nostra*, the maid plays the mistress in our house.

padronàto, *s.m.* (*rar.*) **1.** (*possesso, proprietà*) possession, ownership **2.** (*padroni*) owners (*pl.*).

padróne, *s.m.* **1.** master: *il — non è in casa*, the master is not at home; *dov'è il tuo —?*, where is your master?; *voglio essere — in casa mia!*, I want to be the master in my own house! ‖ *—!, padronissimo!*, do as you like!: *padronissimo, però la responsabilità è tua*, do as you like, but you'll have to take the consequences; *il pilota non era più — dell'aereo*, the pilot had lost control of the plane; *non è — di sè quando è arrabbiato,*

he has no self-control when he is angry; *non è — delle sue azioni*, he is not responsible for his actions; *non è — delle sue passioni*, he cannot master his passions (o he cannot control himself); *essere — della situazione*, to be master of the situation ‖ *sono — di fare ciò che voglio*, I am free to do (o I can do) as I like ‖ *essere — di una lingua*, to be a master of a language ‖ *essere a —*, to be in (s.o.'s) service (o employment) ‖ *farla da —*, to lord it ‖ *parlare a qlcu. da —*, to speak authoritatively to s.o. ‖ *rimanere — del campo*, to remain master of the field ‖ *tal —, tal servitore*, prov. like man, like master **2.** (*proprietario*) owner, proprietor: *il — del cane*, the dog's master; *è — di due case, di un cinema, di un negozio*, he is the owner of two houses, of a cinema, of a shop ‖ *l'occhio del — ingrassa il cavallo*, prov. the master's eye makes the horse fat ‖ *lega il cavallo dove vuole il —*, prov. do as the master says **3.** (*di casa, albergo*) landlord: *sono in buoni rapporti col mio — di casa*, I am on good terms with my landlord **4.** (*mar.*) master of a ship, ship's master.

padroneggiàre, *v.t.* to master, to command (anche *fig.*): *padroneggiò la folla*, he controlled the mob; *nei momenti difficili sa — la situazione*, in difficult times he is master of the situation; *non sa — le proprie passioni*, he can't master (o control) his own passions; — *una lingua*, to master a language ‖ *v.i.* (*fam.*) to lord it: *padroneggia sempre in ufficio*, he is always lording it in the office ‖ **padroneggiàrsi**, *v.r.* to control oneself, to keep oneself under control.

padronésco, *ag.* domineering.

paesàggio, *s.m.* **1.** landscape; scenery; view: — *di montagna*, mountain scenery; — *marino*, seascape; *da quella finestra si vede un bel —*, you can enjoy a fine view (o you can see a beautiful landscape) from that window **2.** (*pitt.*) landscape, paysage: *ha un — di Constable che vale milioni*, he has a landscape by Constable which is worth millions.

paesaggìsta, *s.c.* landscape-painter, landscapist.

paesàna, *s.f.* country-woman (*pl.* country-women), peasant-woman (peasant-women).

paesàno, *ag.* country (*attributivo*); rustic, rural: *abitudini paesane*, country habits; *danza paesana*, country-dance; *semplicità paesana*, rustic simplicity; *le usanze paesane*, rural customs; *una vivanda paesana*, a rustic dish ‖ *alla paesana*, in a rustic (o country) manner: *le piaceva vestire alla paesana*, she liked dressing in a rustic manner (o like a country-girl) ‖ *s.m.* **1.** countryman (*pl.* countrymen), peasant: *i paesani*, country-folk **2.** (*compaesano*): *è un mio —*, he comes from my village.

paése, *s.m.* **1.** (*nazione*) country: *il — è contrario alla nuova legge*, the country is opposed to the new law; *amo il mio —*, I love my country; *il mio — è l'Italia*, Italy is my country; *la Svizzera è un — ricco*, Switzerland is a rich country; — *d'origine*, country of origin; *i paesi Europei*, European countries; *invasero il — nemico*, they carried war into the enemy's country ‖ *i Paesi Bassi*, the Low Countries ‖ *il — dei balocchi*, the Toy-town ‖ *il — di Cuccagna*, the land of Cockaigne (o land of plenty) ‖ *paesi d'oltremare*, overseas countries ‖ *il bel Paese*, Italy **2.** (*territorio*) country, land: — *accidentato*, broken (o rough) country; — *fertile, sterile*, fertile, barren country; — *montuoso*, mountainous country; — *piano, di pianura*, level (o flat) country ‖ *scoprire paesi*, to make inquiries (o to spy out the lie of the land) **3.** (*luogo*) place: — *natio*, birthplace (o native place); *approdarono a un — sconosciuto*, they landed in an unknown country; *dunque non siete di questo —*, so you don't belong to these parts; *ha nostalgia del suo —*, he is homesick ‖ *mandare a quel —*, (*fam.*) to send to hell ‖ *donne e buoi dei paesi tuoi*, prov. it's better to marry over the mixen, than over the moor ‖ *che vai, usanza che trovi*, prov. when in Rome, do as the Romans do ‖ *tutto il mondo è —*, prov. it is the same the whole world over **4.** (*villaggio*) village; (*cittadina*) town: — *natio*, (*villaggio*) native village; (*città*) native town (*o* home-town); *un piccolo* — *fra i monti*, a little village in (*o* among) the mountains; *al mio* — *tutti parlano dialetto*, at home (*o* in) my village) everybody speaks dialect; *vado in* — *a fare spese*, I am going shopping in the village (*o* down to the shops); *tornare al* —, to return to one's home -town (*o* to one's village) 5. (*paesaggio*) landscape: *un pittore di paesi*, a landscape-painter (*o* a landscapist).

paesísta, *s.c.* landscape-painter, landscapist.

paf, pàffete, (*voce onomatopeica riproducente il suono di cosa che cada, ecc.*) bang.

paffutézza, *s.f.* chubbiness, plumpness.

paffúto, *ag.* 1. chubby, plump: *un* — *amorino*, a chubby little Cupid; *un bel bambino paffutello*, a fine chubby child; *guance paffute*, chubby (*o* plump) cheeks: *una ragazzina dalle guance paffute*, a chubby-cheeked little girl; *viso* —, chubby face; *è una bella figliola, ma un po' paffutella*, she is a pretty girl, but a little bit on the plump side 2. (*di cose, grosso*) big.

pàga, *s.f.* 1. pay, salary; wages (*pl.*): — *giornaliera*, daily pay; *a mezza* —, on half-pay; *foglio di* —, pay -roll (*o* pay-sheet); *giorno di* —, pay-day; *libro* —, wages book; *vado a riscuotere la mia* —, I'm going to collect my wages || *gli darò due sberle per* —, (*scherz.*) I'll give him a good hiding for his pains || *assicurarsi la* —, (*andare in prigione*) to go inside (*o* to do a stretch) 2. (*pagatore*) payer: *è una mala* —, he is a bad (*o* slow) payer.

pagàbile, *ag.* payable: — *a data fissa*, payable at a fixed date; — *alla consegna*, payable on delivery; — *alla scadenza*, payable on maturity; — *a rate*, payable by instalments; — *a vista*, payable at sight.

pagàia, *s.f.* paddle.

pagaménto, *s.m.* (*comm.*) payment: — *alla consegna*, cash on delivery (*abbr.* C.O.D.); — *anticipato*, payment in advance; — *a rate*, payment by instalments; — *importante*, heavy (*o* large) payment; — *in arretrato*, payment in arrears; — *in contanti*, cash-payment; — *mensile, trimestrale*, monthly, quarterly payment; — *in natura*, payment in commodities (*o* in kind); — *semestrale, annuale*, six-monthly (*o* half-yearly), yearly payment; *avviso di* —, notice of payment; *condizioni di* —, terms (*o* conditions) of payment: *alle stesse condizioni di consegna e di*—, on the same delivery and payment conditions; *dietro* — *di*, on payment of; *domanda regolare di* —, due demand for payment; *facilitazioni di* —, accommodations for payment; *fino a totale* —, until fully paid (*o* until paid in full); *mancato* —, non-payment; *mandato di* —, money-order; *ricevuta di* —, receipt of (*o* for) payment; *se il giorno della scadenza è festivo riconosciuto, quello del* — *è il primo giorno seguente non festivo*, should maturity fall (*o* occur) on a legal holiday, the payment is due on the next succeeding business-day; *anticipare la data di* —, to advance the date of payment; *chiedere il* —, to ask for payment; *dare in* —, to give in payment; *effettuare il* —, to effect (*o* to perform) payment; *fare un* —, to make a payment; *far fronte al* —, to meet the payment; *mettersi al corrente nei pagamenti*, to pay outstanding accounts up to date; *prolungare, dilazionare il* —, to grant an extension of payment.

paganaménte, *av.* paganly, heathenishly.

paganeggiàre, *v.i.* to live like a pagan; to act like a pagan.

paganésimo, *s.m.* paganism, heathenism.

paganía, *s.f.* 1. heathendom 2. (*paese pagano*) pagan country.

paganizzàre, *v.t.* to paganize.

pagàno, *ag.* pagan, heathen: *i riti pagani dei selvaggi*, the heathen rites of savages.

pagànte, *ag.* paying: *socio* —, paying member || *s.c.* payer.

pagàre, *v.t.* 1. to pay: *dobbiamo* — *la merce*, we have to pay for the goods; *ho pagato tutti i miei debiti*,

I have paid (off) all my debts; *l'ho pagato per nuovo, buono*, I bought it thinking it was new, in good condition; *non ha pagato la cambiale*, he dishonoured the bill; *quanto hai pagato questo cappello?*, how much did you pay for this hat?; *questa ditta paga male*, this firm pays badly; — *alla consegna*, to pay on delivery; — *a rate*, to pay by instalments; — *una cambiale, una tratta*, to pay (*o* to honour *o* to meet) a bill, a draft; — *caro ql.co.*, to pay dear for sthg.; — *con un assegno, una tratta*, to pay by cheque, by banker's draft; — *un conto*, to pay (*o* to settle) a bill; — *un creditore*, to pay a creditor; — *il fitto*, to pay the rent; — *in anticipo*, to pay in advance; — *in contanti*, to pay cash (down); — *in natura*, to pay in kind; — *qlcu. per le sue prestazioni*, to pay s.o. for his services; — *senza indugio*, to pay on the nail || *pagherai cara la tua impertinenza*, you'll have to pay for your insolence; *me la pagherai!*, you'll pay for it! (*o* I'll pay *o* serve you out!) || *a* — *c'è sempre tempo*, why pay now when you can pay to-morrow? || *ha pagato la sua audacia con la vita*, he paid for his rashness with his life || *non so cosa pagherei per aiutarlo*, I would give anything to be able to help him || — *di persona*, to face the consequences (*o fam.* to face the music) || — *il fio, la pena di ql.co.*, to pay the penalty for sthg. || — *un occhio della testa*, to pay through the nose || — *qlcu. a parole*, to put s.o. off with fine words || — *qlcu. della stessa moneta*, to pay s.o. back in his own coin || — *lo scotto*, to pay the reckoning || *far* — *qlcu. per ql.co.*, to charge s.o. for sthg.: *quanto fate* — *per questo vestito?*, how much do you charge for this dress? || *chi rompe paga*, *prov.* breaker pays 2. (*offrire*) to stand, to treat (s.o. to sthg.): *pago io!*, it's on me!; *gli ho pagato un gelato*, I treated him to an ice; — *da bere a qlcu.*, to stand s.o. a drink; — *un pranzo a qlcu.*, to stand s.o. a dinner 3. (*ricompensare*) to reward, to requite: *è così che paga il mio zelo*, that's how he rewards me (for my zeal); *mi paga con l'ingratitudine*, he requites me with ingratitude.

pagatóre, *s.m.* payer: *ufficiale* —, paymaster.

pagèlla, *s f* (school-) report, report card: *ha avuto dei voti discreti sulla* —, he had fairly good marks in his school-report.

paggería, *s.f.* (*condizione di paggio*) pagehood.

pàggio, *s.m.* page-boy: *pettinatura alla* —, bobbed-hair.

pagherò, *s.m.* (*comm.*) promissory note; note of hand (*abbr.* I.O.U.).

pàgina, *s.f.* 1. page; (*foglio*) leaf: — *bianca*, blank page; — *dispari*, right-hand page (*o* recto); — *pari*, left-hand page (*o* verso); — *sciolta*, loose leaf; *a piede di* —, at the foot of the page; *in testa di* —, at the top of the page; *è a* — *52*, it is on page 52; *volta la* —, turn the page over; *numerare le pagine*, to page; *piegare la* —, to fold (down) the page || *voltare* —, to turn over a new leaf || *le Sacre Pagine*, Holy Writ 2. *fig.* (*episodio, momento*) page, chapter; leaf: *una bella* — *di storia*, a fine page (*o* chapter) in history; *è stata la più bella* — *della mia vita*, it has been the finest chapter in my life 3. (*bot.*) face.

pàglia, *s.f.* 1. straw: — *di riso*, rice straw; *cappello di* —, straw-hat; (*di Firenze*) leghorn; *color* —, straw -colour: *capelli color* —, straw-coloured hair; *imbottito di* —, stuffed with straw; *leggero come la* —, as light as a straw; *letto di* —, straw-bed; *sacco, mucchio di* —, sack, heap of straw; *tetto di* —, thatch: *una casetta col tetto di* —, a thatched cottage; *dormire sulla* —, to sleep on straw || — *di ferro*, (*per lucidare pavimenti*) steel wool || *fuoco di* —, flash in the pan || *uomo di* —, man of straw || *avere la coda di* —, to have a guilty conscience || *essere una* — *al vento*, to be a straw in the wind (*o* a weathercock) || *mettere la* — *vicino al fuoco*, to tempt fate || *col tempo e con la* — *maturano le nespole*, *prov.* everything comes to him who waits 2. (*metal.*) seam.

pagliaccésco, *ag.* clownish, foolish.
pagliacciàta, *s.f.* buffoonery; tomfoolery.
pagliàccio, *s.m.* **1.** clown, buffoon **2.** (*paglierìccio*) paillasse, palliasse, straw mattress, pallet.
pagliàio, *s.m.* straw-stack, rick of straw || *cane da —*, watch-dog.
pagliàto, *ag.* straw-coloured.
paglierìccio, *s.m.* **1.** paillasse, palliasse, straw mattress, pallet **2.** (*letto*) bed.
paglierìno, *ag.* straw-coloured.
paglièto, *s.m.* reed-bed.
pagliétta, *s.f.* **1.** (*cappello*) straw-hat **2.** (*paglia di ferro per lucidar pentole*) steel-wool; (*per pavimenti*) iron-shavings (*pl.*) **3.** (*trucioli di legno per imballaggio*) wood-shavings: (*di carta*) paper-wool.
pagliétto, *s.m.* (*mar.*) mat: *— di cocco*, coir mat.
pagliòlo, *s.m.* (*mar.*) dunnage.
pagliòne, *V.* **paglierìccio**.
pagliúca, (*rar.*) per **pagliúzza**.
pagliúzza, *s.f.* **1.** small straw || *e perchè osservi la — nell'occhio del tuo fratello, e non badi alla trave che è nell'occhio tuo?*, (*Bibbia*) why beholdest thou the mote that is in thy brother's eye, but considerest not the beam that is in thine own eye? **2.** (*minutissima parte d'oro*) gold particle.
pagnòtta, *s.f.* round loaf || *scrive per guadagnarsi la —*, (*fam.*) he writes for a living.
pàgo[1], *ag.* (*letter.*) satisfied (with sthg.) (with sthg.), pleased (with sthg.): *sono — di ciò che ho fatto*, I'm pleased (*o* satisfied *o* contented) with what I've done.
pàgo[2], *s.m.* (*st.*) **1.** pagus (*pl.* pagi); rural district **2.** (*cantone della Svizzera*) canton.
pagòda, *s.f.* pagoda.
pagùro, *s.m.* (*zool.*) hermit-crab.
paillettes, *s.f.pl.* sequins.
pàio, *s.m.* **1.** (*di cose uguali o che vanno usate insieme*) pair: *un — di guanti, scarpe, calzoni, occhiali, forbici*, a pair of gloves, shoes, trousers, spectacles, scissors || *è un altro — di maniche!*, that's another pair of shoes! **2.** (*due, circa due*) couple, two: *un — di giorni, libri, matite, uova*, a couple of (*o* two) days, books, pencils, eggs **3.** (*coppia*) (*di uccelli*) brace (*invariato al pl.*); (*di buoi*) yoke: *un — di anatre*, a brace of ducks; *sei paia di fagiani*, six brace of pheasants || *essere una coppia e un —*, to be as like as two peas in a pod.
paiolàta, *s.f.* potful, ca(u)ldronful.
paiuòlo, *s.m.* **1.** pot, cauldron **2.** (*artigl.*) emplacement.
Pàkistan, *no.pr.m.* (*geog.*) Pakistan.
pàla, *s.f.* **1.** shovel: *— del carbone, del fornaio*, coal-shovel, baker's shovel **2.** (*di remo, elica*) blade; (*di ruota*) paddle: *angolo della —*, (*aer.*) blade angle; *ruota a pale*, paddle-wheel; *vertice della —*, (*aer.*) blade tip **3.** *— d'altare*, (*pitt.*) altar-piece.
paladìno, *s.m.* **1.** (*st.*) paladin, knight-errant: *i paladini di Carlomagno*, the paladins of Charlemagne **2.** *fig.* (*difensore*) champion: *— dei poveri*, champion of the poor; *— della libertà*, champion of liberty.
palafìtta, *s.f.* **1.** (*edil.*) (*sostegno di pali*) pile-work **2.** (*abitazione su palafitte*) palafitte, pile-dwelling.
palafittàre, *v.t.* (*edil.*) to pile || *v.i.* to make piles.
palafìtticolo, *s.m.* (*st.*) lake-dweller, pile-dweller.
palafrenière, *s.m.* groom, footman (*pl.* footmen).
palafréno, *s.m.* palfrey; (*cavalcatura*) mount.
Palamède, *no.pr.m.* (*lett.*) Palamedes.
palaménto, *s.m.* (*mar.*) oars of a boat (*pl.*).
palamidóne, *s.m.* frock-coat.
palànca[1], *s.f.* (*mar.*) gangway.
palànca[2], *s.f.* (*pop.*) penny: *le palanche*, money; *non hanno una —*, they are hard up.
palancàto, *s.m.* hoarding.
palanchìno, *s.m.* **1.** (*portantina*) palanquin, palankeen **2.** (*mar.*) pulley **3.** (*mec.*) crow(-bar); handspike.

palànco, *s.m.* (*mar.*) tackle.
palàncola, *s.f.* **1.** plank **2.** (*rafforzamento di fondazioni*) sheet-piling: *— in ferro*, iron sheet-piling.
palàndra, *s.f.* (*mar.*) bilander.
palandràna, *s.f.* loose garment; long coat.
palàre[1], *v.t.* (*rar.*) (*sostenere con pali*) to prop, to stake: *— una vite*, (*agr.*) to stake a vine.
palàre[2], *v.t.* (*rar.*) (*muovere con la pala*) to shovel.
palàta, *s.f.* **1.** (*quantità contenuta in una pala*) shovelful: *una — di sabbia*, a shovelful of sand || *a palate*, plentifully (*o* abundantly): *fecero denaro a palate*, they made pots of money **2.** (*colpo di pala*) blow with a shovel **3.** (*colpo di remo*) stroke.
palatàle, *ag.* **1.** (*anat.*) palatal **2.** (*fonet.*) palatal.
palatìna[1], *s.f.* (*patol.*) palatitis.
palatìna[2], *s.f.* **1.** palatine, fur tippet **2.** (*fazzoletto da collo*) fichu, neckerchief.
palatinàto, *s.m.* palatinate || **Palatinàto**, *no.pr.m.* (*geog.*) Palatinate.
Palatìno, *no.pr.m.* (*geog.*) Palatine.
palatìno[1], *ag.* palatine: *conte —*, count palatine || *guardia palatina*, Palatine Guard || *s.m.* (*st.*) palatine.
palatìno[2], *ag.* (*anat.*) palatine: *arcata palatina*, palatine arch; *osso —*, palate bone; *papilla palatina*, palatine papilla.
palàto, *s.m.* **1.** (*anat.*) palate: *— molle, duro*, soft, hard palate; *la volta del —*, the palatine vault **2.** (*senso del gusto*) palate, taste: *gradevole al —*, palatable; *cibo che stuzzica il —*, appetizing food; *avere il — fine*, to have a delicate palato; *avere il — grosso*, to have a coarse palate.
palazzìna, *s.f.* villa.
palàzzo, *s.m.* **1.** palace: *il — reale*, the Royal Palace; *congiura di —*, palace plot; *dama di —*, court lady; *guardia di —*, palace guard; *prefetto di —*, Chamberlain || *— della Borsa*, the Exchange || *— della Zecca*, the Mint || *— di giustizia*, law Courts || *Palazzo Ducale*, (*a Venezia*) the Doge's Palace || *— municipale*, town-hall || *i Sacri Palazzi*, the Vatican **2.** (*casa signorile*) mansion; (*grande edificio*) building: *in quella zona residenziale ci sono dei palazzi antichi*, in that residential district there are some old mansions.
palchettìsta, *s.c.* (*teat.*) box-holder.
palchétto, *s.m.* **1.** (*teat.*) box **2.** (*asse per armadi, scaffali, ecc.*) division, board: *scaffale a sei palchetti*, shelf with six divisions **3.** (*miner.*) stull: *— ad ala*, wing stull; *— rinforzato*, reinforced stull; *— volante*, false stull.
palchettóne, *s.m.* (*teat.*) ground-floor box.
pàlco, *s.m.* **1.** (*teat.*) box: *un — di prima fila*, a box in the first tier; *un — di proscenio*, a stage-box; *— d'onore*, royal box **2.** (*pedana, tribuna*) stand, platform: *il — della banda musicale*, the bandstand; *un — improvvisato*, (*per un oratore*) a soap-box; *rizzare un —*, to raise a stand **3.** (*edil.*) (*tavolato*) flooring, boarding; (*impalcatura*) scaffolding, stage **4.** (*patibolo*) scaffold **5.** (*strato*) layer: *dispose le arance a palchi*, he packed the oranges in layers **6.** *— di comando*, (*mar.*) bridge **7.** (*di cervo*) antler: *un cervo con corna a tre palchi*, a stag with three antlers.
paleoscènico, *s.m.* (*teat.*) stage.
paleggiàre, *v.t.* (*muovere con la pala*) to shovel.
palétta, *s.f.* **1.** (*incastro a coda di rondine*) dovetail joint **2.** (*scalpello da calafato*) caulking iron.
palèo[1], *s.m.* (*rar.*) (children's) top.
palèo[2], *s.m.* (*bot.*) grass.
paleofitología, *s.f.* palæophytology.
paleògene, *ag.* (*geol.*) Paleocene, Palæogene.
paleografía, *s.f.* palæography.
paleogràfico, *ag.* palæographic(al).
paleògrafo, *s.m.* palæographer.
paleolítico, *ag.* Palaeolithic.
Paleòlogo, *no.pr.m.* (*st.*) Palaeologus.
paleontología, *s.f.* palaeontology.

paleontològico, *ag.* pal(a)eontologic(al).
paleontòlogo, *s.m.* pal(a)eontologist.
paleozòico, *ag.* Pal(a)eozoic.
paleozoología, *s.f.* pal(a)eozoology.
palesàre, *v.t.* to disclose, to reveal: *palesò il segreto*, he disclosed (*o* revealed) the secret ‖ **palesàrsi**, *v.r.* to show oneself, to reveal oneself: *si è palesato per quello che era*, he showed himself for what he was.
palesatóre, *ag.* revealing ‖ *s.m.*, **palesatríce**, *s.f.* revealer, discloser.
palése, *ag.* evident, manifest, clear, plain, obvious; known: *fatti palesi a tutti*, facts known to everybody; *rendere —*, to make clear ‖ *in —*, publicly.
paleseménte, *av.* evidently, obviously; openly.
Palestína, *no.pr.f.* (*geog.*) Palestine.
palestinése, *ag.s.m.* Palestinian.
palèstra, *s.f.* 1. (*st.*) palestra, palaestra 2. gymnasium (*pl.* gymnasia, gymnasiums) 3. *fig.* training: *la scuola è la — della vita*, school is a good training for life.
paletot, *s.m.* overcoat, heavy coat.
palétta, *s.f.* 1. small shovel; (*per focolare*) small coal-shovel 2. (*di capostazione*) bat.
palettàre, *v.t.* (*circondare, munire di palizzata*) to fence.
palettàta, *s.f.* 1. shovelful 2. (*colpo dato con una paletta*) blow with a shovel.
palétto, *s.m.* 1. (*piccolo palo*) stake, post, small pole 2. (*chiavistello*) bolt, sliding bar: *metti il — alla porta di casa*, bolt the front-door.
pàli, *s.m.* (*lingua indiana*) Pali.
palificazióne, *s.f.* 1. (*posa in opera di una palizzata*) fencing 2. (*edil.*) piling.
palína, *s.f.* (*tec.*) (surveyor's) stake, ranging rod: *— a traguardo, graduata*, target, level rod.
palíndromo, *s.m.* (*poes.*) palindrome.
palingènesi, *s.f.* palingenesis.
palinodía, *s.f.* (*poes.*) palinode.
palinsèsto, *s.m.* (*paleografia*) palimpsest.
Palinúro, *no.pr.m.* (*lett.*) Palinurus.
pàlio, *s.m.* 1. (*corsa*) "palio" (festival and horse-race held twice a year at Siena): *correre il —*, to compete in the "palio" ‖ *mettere in —*, to offer as a prize 2. (*drappo*) "palio" (banner of silk cloth awarded to the winner of the palio race).
paliòtto, *s.m.* (*eccl.*) frontal.
palischérmo, *s.m.* (*mar.*) (*piccola barca a servizio di altre imbarcazioni*) dinghy, tender; (*piccola imbarcazione*) skiff.
palissàndro, *s.m.* rosewood, palisander.
palizzàta, *s.f.* 1. paling, fence; (*gener. mil.*) palisade, stockade: *circondare, difendere con palizzate*, to palisade (*o* to stockade) 2. (*bot.*) palisade tissue.
pàlla¹, *s.f.* 1. ball: *— da biliardo, da golf, da tennis*, billiard-, golf-, tennis-ball; *— di gomma*, rubber ball; *— di neve*, snowball: *giocare a palle di neve*, to throw snowballs (*o* to snowball); *afferrare la —* (*al volo*), to catch the ball; *giocare a —*, to play ball; *rimandare la — a qlcu.*, to return the ball to s.o. ‖ *— a nuoto*, (*spor.*) water-polo; *— a volo*, (*spor.*) volley-ball; *— basca*, (*spor.*) pelota; *— ovale*, (*spor.*) rugby ‖ *— dell'occhio*, (*fam.*) ball of the eye (*o* eye-ball) ‖ *pesce —*, (*ittiol.*) globe-fish ‖ *coglier la — al balzo*, to seize the opportunity 2. (*mil.*) bullet: *— da cannone*, shell; (*arc.*) cannon-ball; *— da fucile*, bullet; *tirare, sparare a —*, to fire ball-cartridge 3. (*per votazione*) ballot, ballot-ball: *— bianca, nera*, white, black ballot 4. *pl.* (*arald. st.*) balls 5. *giocare a palle e santi*, (*a testa e croce*) to toss.
pàlla², *s.f.* (*st. romana*) palla (*pl.* pallae).
pàlla³, *s.f.* (*eccl.*) pall.
pallacanèstro, *s.f.* (*spor.*) basket-ball.
pallacòrda, *s.f.* (*spor.*) lawn-tennis.
Pàllade, *no.pr.f.* (*mit.*) Pallas.
palladiàno, *ag.* (*arch.*) Palladian.
pallàdio¹, *ag.* Palladian ‖ *s.m.* 1. (*st. greca*) Pal-

ladium 2. (*salvaguardia*) palladium, safeguard: *le leggi sono il — della libertà*, laws are the safeguard of liberty.
pallàdio², *s.m.* (*chim.*) palladium.
pallamàglio, *s.m.* (*spor.*) croquet.
pallàta, *s.f.* blow from a ball: *fare a pallate di neve*, to throw snowballs (*o* to snowball).
pallàto, *ag.* (*di cavallo*) dappled.
palleggiaménto, *s.m.* 1. playing ball 2. (*calcio*) dribbling; passing.
palleggiàre, *v.t.* 1. (*vibrare*) to toss: *— la lancia*, to throw (*o* to toss) the spear 2. (*sballottare*) to toss (about): *— un bambino in braccio*, to toss a child in one's arms ‖ *v.i.* 1. (*esercitarsi alla palla*) to play ball 2. (*calcio*) to dribble; to pass ‖ **palleggiàrsi**, *v.r. reciproco* (*rinfacciarsi vicendevolmente*) to saddle each other (one another) (with sthg.); (*sl.*) to pass the buck.
palleggiatóre, *s.m.* 1. tosser 2. (*calcio*) dribbler.
palléggio, *s.m.* 1. (*tennis, ecc.*) knocking a ball about: *far —*, to knock a ball about 2. (*calcio*) dribbling; passing.
pallènte, *ag.* (*poet.*) growing pale; paling.
palliaménto, *s.m. fig.* palliation, disguising, masking.
palliàre, *v.t.* (*celare, mascherare*) to palliate, to disguise, to cloak: *cercò di — la sua perfidia*, he tried to conceal his wickedness.
palliatívo, *ag. s.m.* palliative: *questi sono palliativi inutili*, these are useless palliatives.
pallidaménte, *av.* 1. palely, pallidly; wanly 2. (*debolmente*) faintly.
pallidézza, *s.f.* paleness, pallor; wanness.
pallidíccio, *ag.* rather pale, palish.
pallidità, *s.f.* paleness, pallor; wanness.
pàllido, *ag.* 1. pale, pallid; wan: *— come un morto*, as white as death; *— di paura*, pale with fright; *essere — di collera*, to be white (*o* livid) with rage; *diventar —*, to grow (*o* to turn) pale (*o* wan) ‖ *viso —*, pale-face 2. (*di colore*) pale: *rosso, giallo —*, pale red, yellow 3. (*debole*) faint, dim, pale: *una pallida luce*, a dim light; *un — sorriso*, a wan (*o* bleak) smile 4. (*vago*) faint, slight: *non ne ho la più pallida idea*, I haven't the faintest (*o* slightest) idea ‖ *s.m.* (*rar.*) paleness, pallor.
pallína, *s.f.* 1. little ball, pellet; (*di marmo, vetro per giuochi infantili*) marble 2. *pl.* (*munizioni da caccia*) shot (*coll. gener. con costruzione sing.*); pellets.
pallíno, *s.m.* 1. (*piccola palla*) little ball ‖ *disegno a pallini*, polka-dot pattern 2. (*alle bocce*) jack 3. *pl.* (*per fucile da caccia*) shot (*coll. gener. con costruzione sing.*); pellets 4. (*ricamo*) embroidered spot 5. *fig.* (*mania, idea fissa*) craze, mania: *ha il — degli abiti rossi*, she has got a mania (*o* a craze) for red dresses; *ha il — delle automobili veloci*, he has a craze (*o* mania) for fast cars; *ha il — del tennis*, he is mad on tennis.
pàllio, *s.m.* (*eccl. st.*) pallium.
pallonàio, *s.m.* 1. (*chi fabbrica palloni*) balloon-maker 2. (*chi vende palloni*) seller of balloons 3. *fig.* (*spaccone*) boaster.
pallonàta, *s.f.* 1. blow with a ball 2. *fig.* (*spacconata*) boast.
palloncíno, *s.m.* 1. (*per bambini*) balloon 2. (*lampioncino*) Chinese lantern 3. (*aer.*) ballonet 4. (*frullino*) whisk.
pallóne, *s.m.* 1. balloon; ball; (*nel giuoco del calcio*) football: *giuoco del —*, football; *il bambino si lasciò sfuggire il —*, the child let the balloon go; *le ragazze giocavano al — sulla spiaggia*, the girls were playing ball on the beach; *giocare al —* (*al calcio*), to play football ‖ *gonfio come un —*, swollen with his own importance; *è un — gonfiato*, he is full of hot air 2. (*aerostato*) balloon: *— da osservazione*, observation balloon; *— dirigibile*, dirigible (*o* airship) ‖ *— di sbarramento*, barrage-balloon; *— drago*, (kite-) balloon; *— frenato*, captive balloon; *— libero*, free balloon; *— osservatorio*, observation-balloon; *— sonda*, sounding-balloon; *—*

stratosferico, stratospheric balloon 3. (*chim.*) flask, distillation flask: — *a fondo piatto*, flat-bottomed flask; — *a fondo rotondo*, round-bottomed flask; — *per distillazione frazionata*, distilling flask; — *tarato*, volumetric flask 4. — *di neve*, (*bot.*) snowball (*o* guelder-rose).

pallonétto, *s.m.* 1. (*tennis*) lob 2. (*di dirigibile*) gasbag.

pallóre, *s.m.* pallor, paleness: — *mortale*, pallor of death; *viso soffuso di* —, pale face.

pallòttola, *s.f.* 1. pellet, small ball: *una* — *di carta*, a pellet of paper; — *di pane*, pellet of bread ‖ *naso a* —, pug-nose 2. (*mil.*) bullet; shot: — *dum dum*, dumdum bullet; — *incendiaria*, incendiary bullet; — *morta*, spent bullet; — *tracciante*, tracer-bullet 3. (*pallina per giuochi infantili*) marble 4. (*pillola*) pill, pellet.

pallottolière, *s.m.* abacus (*pl.* abaci, abacuses).

pàlma[1], *s.f.* 1. (*della mano*) palm: *giungere le palme*, to join one's hands ‖ *portare in* — *di mano*, to hold in great esteem 2. (*dei piedi dei palmipedi*) web.

pàlma[2], *s.f.* (*albero*) palm(-tree): — *da dattero*, date-palm; — *del cocco*, coco-palm ‖ *la* — *del martirio*, *fig.* the crown (*o* the palm) of martyrdom ‖ *Domenica delle Palme*, Palm-Sunday ‖ *cedere la* — *a qlcu.*, *fig.* to yield the palm to s.o.; *ottenere, riportare la* —, *fig.* to bear the palm.

palmàcee, *s.f.pl.* (*bot.*) Palmae, Palmaceae.

palmàre, *ag.* 1. (*anat.*) palmar: *muscolo* —, palmar muscle 2. *fig.* (*evidente*) clear, evident: *prova* —, evident proof.

palmàto, *ag.* 1. (*bot.*) palmate 2. (*di piedi di palmipedi*) webbed.

palménto, *s.m.* millstone ‖ *macinare, mangiare a quattro palmenti*, *fig.* to eat greedily (*o* to gorge).

palméto, *s.m.* palm-grove.

palmière, *s.m.* (*st.*) palmer.

palmífero, *ag.* palmiferous.

palmípede, *ag.* web-footed, palmiped(e) ‖ *s.m.* palmiped(e).

Palmíra, *no.pr.f.* (*geog. st.*) Palmyra.

palmitína, *s.f.* (*chim.*) palmitin.

palmízio, *s.m.* 1. (*albero della palma*) palm-tree 2. (*artig.*) woven-palms (*pl.*).

pàlmo, *s.m.* 1. palm: *il* — *di una mano*, the palm of a hand 2. (*larghezza di un palmo*) span, hand(s)-breadth: *largo due palmi*, two hands(breadths) (*o* palms) wide ‖ *a* — *a* —, little by little (*o* inch by inch): *conoscere un luogo a* — *a* —, to know every inch of a place; *contrastare il terreno a* — *a* —, to fight every inch of the way ‖ *avere il muso lungo un* —, to have a long face ‖ *restare con un* — *di naso*, to feel done 3. palm ‖ *misura di lunghezza* = cm. 7,62 (*o* cm. 10,16).

pàlmola, *s.f.* 1. (*mec.*) cam 2. (*agr.*) pitchfork.

pàlo, *s.m.* pole, post; (*per fondamenta, ecc.*) pile; (*per sostenere piante, ecc.*) stake: — *a mensola*, (*elett.*) bracket pole; — *a traliccio*, (*elett.*) pylon; — *a vite*, (*edil.*) screw pile; — *della cuccagna*, greasy pole; — *della porta*, (*spor.*) goal-post; — *di arrivo, partenza*, winning-, starting-post; — *di calcestruzzo*, (*edil.*) concrete pile; — *di confine*, boundary post; — *di fondazione*, (*edil.*) pile; — *di ormeggio*, (*mar.*) bollard (*o* mooring-pile); — *indicatore*, finger-post (*o* signpost); — *telefonico, telegrafico*, telephone, telegraph pole; *la vigna è sostenuta da pali*, the vine is supported by stakes; *piantare un* —, to set up a pole (*o* to drive a pole into the ground) ‖ *diritto come un* —, as straight as a die ‖ *rigido come un* —, as stiff as a poker ‖ *essere condannato al* —, to be impaled ‖ *fare il* —, (*mentre uno ruba*) to be on the lookout ‖ *fare da* —, (*di chi sta sulle sue*) to keep to oneself ‖ *saltare di* — *in frasca*, to jump from one subject to another (*o* to ramble).

palómba, *s.f.* 1. (*mar.*) hawser 2. (*ornit.*) dove.

palombàro, *s.m.* diver: — *di grande profondità*, deep-sea diver; *campana per palombari*, diving-bell.

palombèlla, *s.f.* (*ornit.*) wood-pigeon.

palómbo, *s.m.* 1. (*ornit.*) wood-pigeon, ring-dove 2. (*ittiol.*) dogfish.

palpàbile, *ag.* palpable, tangible (anche *fig.*); (*evidente*) obvious, evident, plain: *è una verità* —, it is palpably true.

palpabilità, *s.f.* palpability (anche *fig.*); (*evidenza*) obviousness.

palpabilménte, *av.* palpably.

palpaménto, *s.m.* touching, handling; (*med.*) palpation.

palpàre, *v.t.* to feel, to touch, to handle, to finger; (*med.*) to palpate: *i ciechi riconoscono gli oggetti palpandoli*, the blind recognize objects by feeling them; — *ql.co. con le dita*, to touch sthg. with one's fingers (*o* to finger sthg.) ‖ *v.i.* (*mar.*) to hold the oars.

palpàta, *s.f.* touch.

palpazióne, *s.f.* (*med.*) palpation.

pàlpebra, *s.f.* eyelid: *aprire le palpebre*, (*poet.*) to awake; *battere le palpebre*, to blink; *chiudere le palpebre*, to close one's eyes.

palpebràle, *ag.* palpebral: *riflesso* —, eyelid closure; *rima* —, palpebral fissure; *tarso* —, palpebral cartilage.

palpeggiàre, *v. e derivati, V.* **palpàre**, *e derivati*.

palpitaménto, *V.* **palpitazióne**.

palpitànte, *ag.* 1. palpitating, throbbing: *egli rimase là col cuore* —, he stood there with his heart pounding (*o* throbbing) 2. *fig.*: *un argomento di* — *interesse*, a fascinating subject; *romanzo* — *d'interesse*, thrilling novel.

palpitàre, *v.i.* to palpitate (with sthg.), to throb (with sthg.), to quiver (with sthg.): *il mio cuore palpita per te*, you make my heart flutter; *il suo cuore palpitò di gioia*, her heart throbbed with joy; — *di desiderio, di speranza*, to quiver with desire, to hope.

palpitazióne, *s.f.* palpitation, throbbing: — *di cuore, palpitazione* (of the heart); *mi fa venire le palpitazioni*, it makes my heart throb; *essere soggetto a palpitazioni*, to suffer from palpitations.

pàlpito, *s.m.* throb; (*battito*) beat: — *di gioia*, throb of joy.

paltò, *s.m.* overcoat, heavy coat.

paltonière, *s.m.* (*letter.*) 1. (*pezzente*) beggar; (*vagabondo*) vagabond 2. (*ribaldo*) rascal.

paludaménto, *s.m.* paludament.

paludàto, *ag.* wearing a paludament.

palúde, *s.f.* marsh, fen, bog; (*tropicale*) swamp; (*temporanea*) morass, quagmire: *in seguito alle recenti piogge il campo si è trasformato in una* —, owing to the recent rains the field has turned into a morass; *bonificare una* —, to reclaim fenland; *prosciugare una* —, to drain a marsh ‖ *le Paludi Pontine*, the Pontine Marshes.

paludísmo, *s.m.* (*patol.*) malaria, paludism.

paludóso, *ag.* marshy, boggy; swampy: *terreno* —, marshland.

palústre, *ag.* marshy, boggy; swampy: *uccelli palustri*, fen-birds ‖ *febbre* —, (*patol.*) marsh-fever.

palvése, *s.m.* (*st.*) pavis(e).

Pamèla[1], *no.pr.f.* Pamela.

pamèla[2], *s.f.* broad-brimmed straw-hat.

pàmpa, *s.f.* pampa.

pàmpano, *s.m.* (*bot.*) vine-leaf.

pampanóso, **pampanúto**, *ag.* vine-leafed.

pampèro, *s.m.* (*vento della pampa*) pampero.

pampíneo, *ag.* (*poet.*) vine-leafed.

pàmpino, *s.m.* (*bot.*) vine-leaf.

pampinóso, *ag.* vine-leafed.

pamporcíno, *s.m.* (*bot.*) sowbread, cyclamen.

Pan, *no.pr.m.* (*mit.*) Pan.

panacèa, *s.f.* 1. (*bot.*) panacea 2. (*rimedio universale*) panacea: *crede di aver trovato una* — *per tutti i mali sociali*, he thinks he has found a panacea for all social evils.

panàgia, *s.f.* (*relig.*) the Holy Virgin.

Pànama, *no.pr.m.* (*geog.*) Panama: *canale di* —, Panama Canal ‖ **pànama**, *s.m.* (*cappello*) Panama (hat).

panàre, *v.t.* (*cuc.*) to bread.
panàrio, *ag.* (*rar.*) bread (*attributivo*).
panàta, *s.f.* (*cuc.*) panada, bread-soup.
panatenèe, *s.f. pl.* (*st. greca*) Panathenaea.
panatenèo, *ag.* (*st. greca*) Panathenaean, Panathenaic.
panàtica, *s.f.* (*mar.*) (*vitto*) board; (*il corrispondente in denaro*) cash allowance in lieu of board.
panàto, *ag.* (*cuc.*) breaded: *cotolette panate e fritte*, cutlets fried in bread-crumbs || *acqua panata*, toast-water.
panattièra, *s.f.* **1.** (*cesta da pane*) bread-basket **2.** (*tascapane*) (shepherd's) haversack **3.** (*entom.*) flour-beetle.
pànca, *s.f.* bench; (*senza schienale*) form; (*di chiesa*) pew; (*di parco*) park-bench: — *ribaltabile*, folding bench || *panchettina per i piedi*, footstool || *è buono solo a consumar le panche all'osteria*, the only thing he's good for is sitting around and doing nothing || *scalda le panche e basta*, (*a scuola*) he just sits there counting the flies on the ceiling || *le sue barzellette facevano ridere le panche*, his jokes fell flat.
pancàccio, *s.m.* plank-bed.
pancàle, *s.m.* (*rar.*) bench-cover.
pancàta, *s.f.* **1.** benchful **2.** (*colpo di panca*) blow given with a bench.
pancétta, *s.f.* **1.** (*cuc.*) bacon **2.** (*scherz.*) (*persona panciuta*) tubby.
panchína, *s.f.* **1.** bench; (*di parco*) park-bench, garden bench **2.** (*ferr.*) platform.
pància, *s.f.* **1.** stomach; (*fam.*) tummy; (*volg.*) belly: *dolor di* —, stomach-ache; *aveva un forte dolor di* —, he had a violent stomach-ache; *cammina con la* — *in fuori*, she sticks her stomach out when she walks; *devi mettere una compressa fredda sulla* —, you must put a cold compress on your stomach; *mi sento proprio la* — *vuota*, I am simply starving || *che* —!, (*scherz.*) what a corporation! || *i bambini hanno mangiato a crepa* —, the children have stuffed themselves like little pigs || *hai messo su* —, *mi sembra*, I think you have put on weight || *predica il digiuno a* — *piena*, he preaches fasting with a full belly || *se ne stava* — *all'aria*, he was lying on his back; *se ne stava* — *all'aria tutto il santo giorno*, she didn't do a stroke of work all day long || *grattarsi la* —, *fig.* to stand idle: *non star a grattarti la* —, don't be so lazy || *pensare solo alla* —, to make a God of one's belly || *serbare la* — *ai fichi*, *fig.* to keep out of harm's way (*o* to avoid taking risks) || *tenersi la* — *dalle risa*, to hold one's sides with laughter: *ci raccontò una serie di storielle così buffe da farci tenere la* — *dalle risa*, he told us such funny stories that we laughed ourselves helpless **2.** (*di fiasco, di vela, ecc.*) belly.
panciafichísmo, *s.m.* (*scherz.*) pacifism.
panciafichísta, *s.m.* (*scherz.*) pacifist.
panciàta, *s.f.* **1.** belly-flop: *tuffandosi diede una* —, he did a belly-flop when he tried to dive **2.** (*fam.*) (*scorpacciata*) bellyful: *fare una* —, to eat one's fill: *ho fatto una* — *d'uva*, I have stuffed myself with grapes.
pancièra, *s.f.* **1.** (*corazza*) cuirass **2.** (*ventriera*) body-belt.
panciòlle, in, *l.av.*: *stare in* —, to lounge (*o* to loll *o* to laze) about: *se ne starebbe in* — *tutto il giorno*, he would like to lounge about all day long.
panciòtto, *s.m.* waistcoat; (*amer.*) vest: *indossava un* — *a scacchi*, he wore a check waistcoat.
panciúto, *ag.* (*di persona*) big-bellied, pot-bellied, corpulent; (*di cosa*) pot-bellied, swelling, bulging: *una colonna panciuta*, a bulging column; *un otre* —, a bulging goat-skin; *un uomo* —, a big-bellied (*o* pot-bellied) man; *un vaso, bicchiere* —, a pot-bellied vase, glass.
panclastíte, *s.f.* (*chim.*) panclastite.
pancóne, *s.m.* **1.** (*di falegname*) carpenter's bench **2.** (*asse robusta*) plank, thick board.
pancòtto, *s.m.* (*cuc.*) panada, bread-soup.
pancraziàste, *s.m.* (*st. greca*) pancratiast.

pancràzio, *s.m.* (*st. greca*) pancratium (*pl.* pancratia) || **Pancràzio,** *no.pr.m.* Pancras.
pàncreas, *s.m.* (*anat.*) pancreas.
pancreàtico, *ag.* (*anat. fisiol.*) pancreatic: *canale* —, (*anat.*) pancreatic duct; *succo* —, (*fisiol.*) pancreatic juice.
pancreatína, *s.f.* (*chim. biol.*) pancreatin.
pancreatíte, *s.f.* (*patol.*) pancreatitis.
pancromàtico, *ag.* (*foto.*) panchromatic.
pandemía, *s.f.* (*med.*) pandemia.
pandèmio, *ag.* (*letter.*) pandemic.
pandemònio, *s.m.* pandemonium (anche *fig.*): *è un vero* —!, it's absolute pandemonium!; *fare un* — *dell'altro mondo*, (*fam.*) to kick up a fearful pandemonium.
pandétte, *s.f.pl.* (*st. dir.*) Pandects.
Pandòra¹, *no.pr.f.* (*mit.*) Pandora || *il vaso di* —, Pandora's box.
pandòra², *s.f.* (*mus.*) pandora, pandore, bandore.
pàne¹, *s.m.* **1.** bread: — *azzimo*, unleavened bread; — *bianco, nero*, white, brown bread; — *buffetto*, fine bread; — *casereccio*, home-made bread; — *di miglio, di segale*, millet-bread, rye-bread; — *duro, secco*, dry bread; — *e burro*, bread and butter; — *fresco, raffermo*, new, stale bread; — *grattato, trito*, bread-crumbs; — *integrale*, wholemeal bread; — *pepato*, gingerbread; — *tostato*, toast; *un cantuccio, un tozzo di* —, a piece of bread; *una fetta di* —, a slice of bread; *un filone di* —, a French loaf; *mollica di* —, bread-crumb; *cuocere il* —, to bake bread; *imburrare il* —, to butter the bread; *spezzare il* — *con qlcu.*, to break bread with s.o. || — *degli Angeli*, Angel cake (o Angel food) — *di Spagna*, sponge-cake || — *sudato*, well-earned (o hard-earned) bread || *se non è zuppa è pan bagnato*, it's just another name for the same thing || *si vende come il* —, it is selling like hot cakes || *comprare ql.co. per un pezzo di* —, to get sthg. for a song || *dir* — *al* — *e vino al vino*, to call a spade a spade || *essere buono come il* —, to be as good as gold || *essere come* — *e cacio*, to be hand in glove || *mangiare* — *a tradimento, a ufo*, not to be worth one's salt || *mangiare* — *pentito*, to eat humble pie || *mettere qlcu. a* — *e acqua*, to put s.o. on bread and water || *rendere pan per focaccia*, to give tit for tat || *spezzare il* — *della scienza*, to spread knowledge || *trovare* — *per i propri denti*, to meet one's match || *uscire di* — *duro*, to rise from poverty || *non si vive di solo* —, *prov.* man does not live by bread alone **2.** (*forma di pane*) loaf; (*panino*) roll: *non ho mangiato che due panini*, I have only eaten two rolls || *il miracolo dei pani e dei pesci*, the miracle of the loaves and fishes **3.** *fig.* (*il necessario alla vita*) bread, food, living: *il* — *quotidiano*, one's daily bread; *ha il* — *sicuro*, he has a safe job; *mi è più necessario del* —, I couldn't live without it; *guadagnarsi il* —, to earn one's daily bread (o living o livelihood); *perdere il* —, to lose one's job; *togliere il* — *di bocca a qlcu.*, to take the bread out of s.o.'s mouth **4.** (*oggetto a forma di pane*) lump; (*lingotto*) ingot: — *di burro*, pat of butter; — *di cera, sapone*, cake of wax, of soap; *un* — *di ferro*, a pig-iron; *pan di zucchero*, sugar-loaf: *cappello a pan di zucchero*, sugar-loaf hat.
pàne², *s.m.* shank: *il* — *della vite*, the shank of a screw.
Pàne³, *no.pr.m.* (*mit.*) Pan.
panegírico, *s.m.* panegyric; eulogy: *Plinio il Giovane scrisse il* — *di Traiano*, Pliny the Younger wrote a panegyric on Trajan.
panegirísta, *s.m.* panegyrist.
panellenísmo, *s.m.* Panhellenism.
panellenísta, *s.c.* Panhellenist.
panèllo, *s.m.* oil-cake.
paneréccio, *s.m.* whitlow.
panettería, *s.f.* bakery; (*negozio*) baker's (shop): *va' a comprarmi del pane nella* — *all'angolo*, go and get me some bread at the baker's on the corner.
panettière, *s.m.* baker.

panettóne, *s.m.* "panettone" (Milanese cake).
pànfano, *s.m.* (*st. mar.*) galley.
panfilio, pànfilo, *s.m.* **1.** yacht **2.** (*st. mar.*) galley.
panfòrte, *s.m.* "panforte" (Sienese cake).
panfrútto, *s.m.* fruitcake, plum-cake.
pangermanísmo, *s.m.* (*pol.*) Pangermanism.
pangermanísta, *s.c.* (*pol.*) Pangermanist.
pangolíno, *s.m.* (*zool.*) pangolin.
pangrattàto, *s.m.* bread-crumbs (*pl.*).
pània, *s.f.* **1.** bird-lime **2.** *fig.* snare, trap.
panicàto, *ag.* (*vet.*) infected by miliaries.
panicatúra, *s.f.* (*vet.*) miliary fever.
pànico[1]**,** *ag.* panic: *timor* —, panic fear || *s.m.* panic: *preso dal* —, panic-stricken; *lasciarsi prendere dal* —, to panic.
pànico[2]**,** *s.m.* (*bot.*) millet.
panièra, *s.f.* large basket.
panieràio, *s.m.* **1.** (*chi fabbrica panieri*) basket-maker **2.** (*chi vende panieri*) basket-seller.
panieràta, *s.f.* basketful.
panière, *s.m.* basket: *un* — *di uova*, a basket of eggs; *mangiò un* — *d'uva*, he ate a basketful of grapes || *rompere le uova nel* — *a qlcu.*, to upset s.o.'s plans (*o* to put a spoke in s.o.'s wheel).
panificàre, *v.t.* to make into bread || *v.i.* to make bread.
panificazióne, *s.f.* bread-making.
panifício, *s.m.* **1.** bakery, baker's (shop) **2.** (*fabbricazione del pane*) bread-making.
paníno, *s.m.* roll: — *imbottito*, sandwich.
panióne, *s.m.,* **paniúzza,** *s.f.* lime-twig.
panlogísmo, *s.m.* (*fil.*) panlogism.
pànna[1]**,** *s.f.* cream: — *montata*, whipped cream; *con la* — *si fa il burro*, butter is made from cream.
pànna[2]**,** *s.f.* **1.** (*mar.*): *in* —, hove-to: *in* — *secca*, hove-to with all sails furled; *mettere alla* —, to bring (a ship) to; *stare alla* —, to be hove-to **2.** (*mec.*) breakdown: *rimanere in* —, to have a breakdown.
panneggiaménto, *s.m.* draping; (*panneggio*) drapery (anche *art.*).
panneggiàre, *v.t.* to drape || *v.i.* (*pitt.*) to paint drapery; (*scult.*) to carve drapery.
pannéggio, *s.m.* drapery (anche *art.*).
pannèllo, *s.m.* **1.** (*stoffa leggera*) light cloth (*pl.* cloths) **2.** (*arch. edil.*) panel: — *arabescato*, diaper: — *di finestra*, window-pane; — *isolante*, insulating panel (*o* board); — *radiante*, radiating panel (*o* surface); *riscaldamento a pannelli radianti*, panel (*o* radiant) heating.
pannicèllo, *s.m.* **1.** (small) piece of cloth || *pannicelli caldi*, *fig.* useless remedies **2.** (*pannolino per bambini*) napkin; (*fam.*) nappy; (*amer.*) diaper **3.** *pl.* (*abiti miseri*) cheap clothes.
pannícolo, *s.m.* (*anat.*) membrane.
pànno, *s.m.* **1.** (*stoffa*) cloth (*pl.* cloths): — *di lana*, woollen cloth; — *per i piatti*, dish-cloth; — *per pulire le scarpe*, shoe-cloth || *bianco come un* — *lavato*, as white as a sheet **2.** *pl.* (*abiti*) clothes: — *leggeri*, *vecchi*, *nuovi*, light, old, new clothes || *essere*, *mettersi nei panni di qlcu.*, to be, to put oneself in s.o.'s place (*o* shoes) || *lavare i propri panni in pubblico*, to wash one's dirty linen in public || *stringere i panni addosso a qlcu.*, to force (*o* to bring pressure on *o* to bear on) s.o. || *tagliare i panni addosso a qlcu.*, to pull s.o. to pieces.
pannòcchia, *s.f.* (*bot.*) **1.** (*di granoturco*) maize-cob; (*di miglio*) millet-cob **2.** (*infiorescenza*) spike.
pannolàno, *s.m.* woollen cloth.
pannolíno, *s.m.* **1.** (*tessuto di lino*) linen cloth **2.** (*per bambini*) napkin; (*fam.*) nappy; (*amer.*) diaper **3.** (*assorbente igienico*) sanitary towel.
panòplia, *s.f.* **1.** (*st.*) panoply **2.** (*trofeo*) trophy.
panoràma, *s.m.* **1.** (*st.*) view, panorama: — *marino*, seascape **2.** *fig.* outline, general view: — *della letteratura italiana*, outline of Italian literature **3.** (*fis.*) panorama.

panoràmico, *ag.* panoramic: *terrazza panoramica*, (*di casa*) terrace with a fine view; *vagone* —, (*ferr.*) observation car.
panpepàto, *s.m.* (*cuc.*) gingerbread.
panslavísmo, *s.m.* (*pol.*) Pan-Slavism.
panslavísta, *s.c.* (*pol.*) Pan-Slavist.
Pantagruèl, *no.pr.m.* (*lett. francese*) Pantagruel.
pantagruèlico, *ag.* Pantagruelian.
Pantalóne, *s.m.* (*st. teat.*) Pantaloon (Venetian mask) || *paga* —, the people bear the burden.
pantalóni, *s.m.pl.* (a pair of) trousers; (a pair of) slacks (*anche da donna*); (*amer.*) pants: — *alla zuava*, knickerbockers; — *da sci*, ski-trousers; *piega dei* —, trouser-crease; *risvolto dei* —, turn-up (*o amer.* cuff) || *gonna* —, divided skirt.
pantàno, *s.m.* **1.** (*fango*) slush, mire; (*luogo pantanoso*) quagmire; bog, slough **2.** *fig.* (*intrigo*, *difficoltà*) quagmire: *essere in un bel* —, to be in a quagmire; *mettersi in un bel* —, to get into a fine fix.
pantanóso, *ag.* (*fangoso*) slushy, miry; (*coperto di pantani*) boggy.
panteísmo, *s.m.* (*fil.*) pantheism.
panteísta, *s.c.* (*fil.*) pantheist.
panteístico, *ag.* (*fil.*) pantheistic(al).
pànteon, *s.m.* pantheon.
pantèra, *s.f.* (*zool.*) panther; (*femmina*) pantheress.
pantòfola, *s.f.* **1.** slipper: *pantofole da camera*, bedroom-slippers; *essere in pantofole*, to be wearing slippers; *fig.* to be at one's ease (*o* to feel at home) || *ragionare come una* —, to talk nonsense (*o* to talk through one's hat) **2.** *pantofolina della Madonna*, (*bot.*) Lady's-slipper.
pantofolàio, *s.m.* **1.** (*chi fabbrica pantofole*) maker of slippers **2.** (*chi vende pantofole*) seller of slippers.
pantografía, *s.f.* pantography.
pantògrafo, *s.m.* **1.** (*strumento per fare copie*) pantograph: — *per incisioni elettriche*, electric etcher; — *per stampi*, die-sinking machine; — *tridimensionale*, three-dimensional engraving-machine **2.** (*ferr.*) pantograph trolley: — *di locomotore*, pantograph current-collector.
pantomíma, *s.f.* (*teat.*) **1.** (*romana*) pantomine **2.** (*moderna*) dumb-show, mime.
pantomímico, *ag.* pantomimic(al).
pantomímo, *s.m.* **1.** (*attore*) pantomimist, mime **2.** (*pantomima*) dumb-show, mime.
pàntopon, *s.m.* (*farm.*) pantopon.
pànza, *s.f.* (*volg.*) belly.
panzàna, *s.f.* lie, fib, story; nonsense, humbug: *sono tutte panzane!*, it's all nonsense! (*o* stuff and nonsense!).
panzanèlla, *s.f.* (*cuc.*) "panzanella" (bread soaked in water and seasoned with garlic, oil, salt, vinegar, etc.).
paolinísmo, *s.m.* (*teol.*) Paulinism.
Pàola, *no.pr.f.* Paula, Pauline.
Pàolo, *no.pr.m.* Paul.
paolòtto, *ag.* **1.** (*eccl.*) Pauline **2.** *fig.* (*bigotto*) bigoted || *s.m.* **1.** (*eccl.*) Pauline **2.** *fig.* (*bigotto*) bigot.
paonàzzo, *ag.* purple; violet: *viso* —, purple face; *i prelati hanno le calze paonazze*, prelates wear purple stockings; *diventare* — *dalla rabbia*, to get purple (in the face) with anger || *s.m.* purple robe.
papà[1]**,** *s.m.* daddy; (*amer.*) pop; (*fam.*) dad, pa; (*ottocentesco*) papa || *figlio di* —, spoilt boy.
pàpa[2]**,** *s.m.* Pope: — *Pio X*, Pope Pius X || *Storia dei papi*, History of the Popes || *ogni morte di* —, once in a blue moon || *stare*, *vivere come un* —, to live in (the lap of) luxury || *morto un* — *se ne fa un altro*, *prov.* no one is indispensable in this world.
papàbile, *ag.* (*di cardinale*) (who is) likely to be elected Pope || *candidato* —, *fig.* likely candidate.
papàia, *s.f.* (*bot.*) papaw, pawpaw, papaya.
papàle, *ag.* papal: *benedizione* —, papal blessing || *alla* —, openly.
papalína, *s.f.* skull-cap.

papalíno, *ag.* papal: *i soldati papalini,* the Pope's soldiers ‖ *i papalini,* (*fautori del governo del papa*) the Papal supporters.

papàsso, *s.m.* (*sacerdote greco-ortodosso*) pope ‖ *fa il —, fig.* he thinks he is a little tin god.

papàto, *s.m.* **1.** papacy, pontificate: *durante il — di Pio XI,* during the pontificate (*o* papacy) of Pope Pius XI; *Celestino V rinunziò al —,* Pope Celestinus V resigned the papacy (*o* pontificate) **2.** (*fig. scherz.*) sinecure: *si godeva il suo —,* he enjoyed his sinecure.

papaveràcee, *s.f.pl.* (*bot.*) Papaveraceae.

papaveràceo, *ag.* (*bot.*) papaveraceous.

papavèrico, *ag.* papaverous (anche *fig.*).

papaverína, *s.f.* (*chim.*) papaverine.

papàvero, *s.m.* (*bot.*) poppy: — *della California, Messicano,* Californian, Mexican poppy; — *selvatico,* corn (*o* field) poppy ‖ *un alto —,* (*un pezzo grosso*) a bigwig (*o* a big cheese): *gli alti papaveri della finanza,* (*i pezzi grossi*) the bigwigs of high finance.

pàpera, *s.f.* **1.** duckling **2.** (*errore*) slip (of the tongue): *prendere una —,* to make a slip.

pàpero, *s.m.* duckling.

papésco, *ag.* (*spreg.*) popish.

papéssa, *s.f.*: *la — Giovanna,* Pope Joan.

papilionàcee, *s.f.pl.* (*bot.*) Papilionaceae.

papilionàceo, *ag.* (*bot.*) papilionaceous.

papílla, *s.f.* (*anat. bot.*) papilla (*pl.* papillae).

papillàre, *ag.* (*anat. bot.*) papillar(y).

papillòma, *s.m.* (*patol.*) papilloma (*pl.* papillomata).

papillóso, *ag.* (*anat. bot.*) papillose, papillous.

papiràceo, *ag.* papery; papyraceous; papyrus (*attributivo*).

papirína, *s.f.* papyrin(e), parchment paper.

papíro, *s.m.* (*bot. archeol.*) papyrus (*pl.* papyri): *papiri greci, egiziani,* Greek, Egyptian papyri.

papirologìa, *s.f.* papyrology.

papiròlogo, *s.m.* papyrologist.

papísmo, *s.m.* papism; (*spreg.*) popery.

papísta, *s.m.* papist.

pàppa, *s.f.* (*per bambini*) pap; (*vivanda troppo cotta*) mush ‖ *mio fratello mi mangia la — in testa,* (*è più alto di me*) my brother is taller than I am; (*è più furbo di me*) my brother can twist me round his little finger ‖ *scodellare la — a qlcu., fig.* to make sthg. easy for s.o.; *trovare la — fatta, fig.* to have everything given on a plate; *volere, pretendere la — fatta, fig.* to expect everything on a plate.

pappafíco, *s.m.* **1.** (*cappuccio*) hood **2.** (*arc. mar.*) top-gallant **3.** (*dial.*) (*pizzo, di barba*) Van Dyck (beard), imperial.

pappagallescaménte, *av.* like a parrot; parrot-like, parrot-fashion: *parlare —,* to talk parrot-fashion.

pappagalléseo, *ag.* parrot-like.

pappagàllo, *s.m.* **1.** parrot (anche *fig.*) ‖ — (*della strada*), (*spreg.*) "pappagallo" (youth who pays compliments to young women in public places) ‖ *fare il —, ripetere a —,* to parrot **2.** (*oggetto sanitario*) urinal.

pappagòrgia, *s.f.* **1.** double chin **2.** (*del tacchino*) wattle.

pappalàrdo, *s.m.* **1.** (*ghiottone*) glutton **2.** (*bigotto*) bigot.

pappardèlla, *V.* **pappolàta 2.**

pappardèlle, *s.f.pl.* (*cuc.*) "pappardelle" (kind of "pasta") ‖ *stare in —,* to have a whale of a time.

pappàre, *v.t.* (*fam.*) (*mangiare con ingordigia*) to wolf: *ha pappato tutto,* he has wolfed the lot ‖ *v.i.* (*fam.*) (*fare guadagni illeciti*) to fiddle; to profiteer: *se non c'è da — egli non ne vuol sapere,* if there is no possibility of fiddling, he's not interested ‖ **pappàrsi,** *v.r.* to eat up; to gorge.

pappàta, *s.f.* (*fam.*) **1.** hearty meal: *fare una bella —,* to have a hearty meal **2.** (*guadagno illecito*) loot.

pappatàci, *s.m.* (*entom.*) sand-fly: *febbre da —,* sand -fly fever.

pappatóre, *s.m.* (*fam.*) huge eater.

pappatòria, *s.f.* (*fam.*) **1.** feeding: *è l'ora della —!,* grub up! **2.** (*guadagno illecito*) loot.

pappína, *s.f.* (*impiastro*) poultice; plaster.

pappíno, *s.m.* **1.** (*spreg.*) male nurse **2.** (*fam. mil.*) nursing-orderly.

pàppo, *s.m.* (*bot.*) pappus (*pl.* pappi).

pappolàta, *s.f.* **1.** mash; swill **2.** *fig.* (*discorso sciocco e prolisso*) rigmarole.

pappolóna, *s.f.,* **pappolóne,** *s.m.* (*fam.*) **1.** (*ghiottone*) glutton **2.** *fig.* (*chiacchierone*) chatterer.

pappóna, *s.f.,* **pappóne,** *s.m.* (*fam.*) (*ghiottone*) glutton.

pappóso, *ag.* (*bot.*) pappose, pappous.

pàprica, *s.f.* paprika, red pepper, Cayenne pepper.

Papuàsia, *no.pr.f.* (*geog.*) Papua.

pàpula, *s.f.* (*med.*) papule, pimple.

pàra[1], *s.f.* para rubber: *scarpe con suole di —,* rubber-soled shoes.

parà[2], *s.m.* (*moneta turca e jugoslava*) para.

paràbasi, *s.f.* (*teat. greco*) parabasis.

paràbola, *s.f.* **1.** (*racconto allegorico*) parable: *Gesù parlava per parabole,* Jesus spoke in parables **2.** (*geom. artigl.*) parabola.

parabolàno, *s.m.* **1.** (*ciarlone*) prattler **2.** (*vantatore*) boaster.

parabolicaménte, *av.* parabolically.

parabòlico, *ag.* parabolic(al): *curva parabolica,* parabolic curve; *insegnamento —,* parabolic teaching.

parabolòide, *s.m.* (*geom.*) paraboloid.

parabórdo, *s.m.* (*mar.*) fender.

parabrézza, *s.m.* (*aut.*) windscreen; (*amer.*) windshield.

parabulía, *s.f.* (*med.*) parabulia.

paracadutàre[1], *v.t.* to parachute.

paracadutàre[2], *s.m.* air-drop.

paracadúte, *s.m.* parachute: — *ad apertura automatica,* automatic (-opening) parachute; — *di emergenza,* emergency parachute; — *di riserva,* reserve parachute; — *freno,* brake-parachute; — *libero,* free parachute; — *stabilizzatore,* stabilizing parachute; *sussidiario,* retarder parachute; *discendere col —,* to parachute (down); *lanciarsi col —,* to bale out.

paracadutísta, *s.m.* parachutist; (*mil.*) paratrooper *reparti di paracadutisti,* paratroops.

paracàlci, *s.m.* splinter-bar (board).

paracàlli, *s.m.* corn-plaster.

paracamíno, *s.m.* firescreen.

paracàrro, *s.m.* wayside post.

Paracèlso, *no.pr.* (*st. med.*) Paracelsus.

paracénere, *s.m.* fender.

paracèntesi, *s.f.* (*chir.*) paracentesis.

Paraclèto, *s.m.* (*teol.*) Paraclete.

paracólpi, *s.m.* buffer; (*mar.*) fender: — *di gomma,* (*mec.*) rubber buffer; — *per porta,* (*aut.*) door-bumper.

paracqua, *s.m.* umbrella.

paracusía, *s.f.* (*patol.*) parac(o)usis, paracusia.

paradígma, *s.m.* (*gram.*) paradigm.

paradigmàtico, *ag.* paradigmatic(al).

paradisèa, *s.f.* (*ornit.*) bird of paradise.

paradisíaco, *ag.* paradisiac(al), paradisian, heavenly.

paradíso, *ag.* (*bot.*) paradise (*attributivo*): *mela —,* paradise apple ‖ *s.m.* **1.** paradise, heaven (anche *fig.*): *il — terrestre,* the Earthly Paradise; *i santi del —,* the saints of heaven; *la via angusta del —,* the straight and narrow path to heaven; *è una musica di —,* it's a heavenly music; *mi sembra di essere in —,* I feel I am in heaven ‖ *il «Paradiso» di Dante,* (*lett.*) Dante's "Paradiso"; *«Il Paradiso Perduto»,* (*lett.*) "Paradise Lost" ‖ *andare in —* (*morire*) to pass away (*o* to pass on) ‖ *guadagnarsi il —,* to deserve a medal ‖ *voler andare in — in carrozza,* to try to make the best of both worlds **2.** *uccello del —,* (*ornit.*) bird of paradise.

paradossàle, *ag.* paradoxical.

paradossalménte, *av.* paradoxically.

paradòssico, *ag.* paradoxical.

paradossísta, *s.m.* (*rar.*) paradoxist, paradoxer.

paradòsso, *s.m.* paradox.

paràfa,*s.f.*paraph, flourish; (*sigla*)cipher; initials(*pl.*).

parafàngo, *s.m.* mudguard.

parafàre, *v.t.* to paraph; (*siglare*) to initial.

parafatúra, *s.f.* 1. (*il parafare*) paraphing; (*il siglare*) initialling 2. (*parafa*) paraph; (*sigla*) cipher; initials (*pl.*).

parafasía, *s.f.* (*med.*) paraphasia.

parafernàle, *ag.* (*dir.*) paraphernal: *beni parafernali,* paraphernalia.

paràffa, *s.f.* paraph, flourish; (*sigla*) cipher; initials (*pl.*).

paraffàre, *v.t.* to paraph; (*siglare*) to initial.

paraffína, *s.f.* (*chim.*) paraffin: *olio di —,* paraffin-oil.

parafrasàre, *v.t.* to paraphrase.

paràfrasi, *s.f.* paraphrase: *fare la — di un poema,* to paraphrase a poem.

parafrasía, *s.f.* (*med.*) paraphrasia.

parafrasticaménte, *av.* paraphrastically.

parafràstico, *ag.* paraphrastic.

parafúlmine, *s.m.* lightning-conductor, lightning -rod: *asta del —,* lightning-rod; *linea del —,* lightning-line.

parafuòco, *s.m.* firescreen; (*di metallo*) fire-guard.

paragàmbe, *s.m.* leg-guard.

paragènesi, *s.f.* (*geol.*) paragenesis.

paràggio, *s.m.* 1. *gener. pl.* (*mar.*) coastal waters (*pl.*) 2. *pl.* neighborhood (*sing.*), quarter (*sing.*): environs: *non vi sono parchi in questi paraggi,* there are no parks in this neighbourhood; *vivo in questi paraggi,* I live in this neighborhood.

paraglòssa, *s.f.* (*di insetti*) paraglossa (*pl.* paraglossae).

paragonàbile, *ag.* comparable.

paragonàre, *v.t.* to compare: *la mia casa non può essere paragonata alla tua,* my house cannot be compared with yours; *i poeti hanno paragonato il sonno alla morte,* poets have compared (*o* likened) sleep to death; *paragona il tuo vestito col mio,* compare your dress with mine; *— una copia con l'originale,* to compare a copy with the original.

paragóne, *s.m.* 1. comparison: *il — è giusto, sbagliato,* the comparison is a good one, a bad one; *è spesso utile fare un — tra due cose,* it is often helpful to make a comparison between two things; *il suo libro non regge il — con questo,* his book does not stand comparison with this; *tra lui e suo fratello non c'è —,* there's no comparison between him and his brother‖ *i paragoni sono odiosi,* comparisons are odious ‖ *a — di,* in comparison with: *gli edifici di Milano sono piccoli a — dei grattacieli di New York,* the buildings in Milan are small in comparison with the skyscrapers of New York; *non è niente a — di ciò,* it is nothing in comparison with that ‖ *senza —,* beyond comparison: *bellezza senza paragoni,* beauty beyond (*o* out of) all comparison 2. (*prova, cimento*) test, trial 3. (*min.*) basanite, touchstone.

paragrafàre, *v.t.* to paragraph.

paràgrafo, *s.m.* paragraph.

paralalía, *s.f.* (*med.*) paralalia.

paralèssi, *s.f.* (*ret.*) paralipsis, paraleipsis.

paralipòmeni, *s.m.pl.* (*lett.*) paral(e)ipomena.

paràlisi, *s.f.* (*med.*) paralysis, palsy (anche *fig.*): *— cardiaca,* paralysis of the heart; *— facciale,* facial paralysis; *— infantile,* infantile paralysis (*o* poliomyelitis); *— motoria,* motor paralysis; *— progressiva,* progressive (*o* ascending) paralysis; *— sensoria,* sensory paralysis; *colpito da —,* stricken with paralysis (*o* palsy-stricken).

paralítico, *ag.s.m.* paralytic; (*arc.*) palsy: *il miracolo del —,* (*Bibbia*) the miracle of the man sick of the palsy; *un vecchio —,* a paralytic old man.

paralizzàre, *v.t.* to paralyze (anche *fig.*): *leggi che paralizzano l'industria,* laws that paralyze industry.

paralizzàto, *ag.* paralyzed (anche *fig.*): *— ad un*

braccio, paralyzed in one arm; *— dalla paura,* paralysed with fear; *traffico —,* paralyzed traffic.

parallàsse, *s.f.* (*astr.*) parallax: *— eliocentrica,* heliocentric parallax; *— geocentrica,* geocentric parallax; *— in quota,* parallax in altitude.

parallàttico, *ag.* (*astr.*) parallactic.

parallèla, *s.f.* 1. (*geom. mil.*) parallel 2. *pl.* (*spor.*) parallel bars 3. *pl.* (*strumento per tracciare linee parallele*) parallel ruler.

parallelaménte, *av.* parallelly; (*fianco a fianco*) side by side: *disegna questa linea — a quella,* draw this line parallel with (*o* to) that one; *le due macchine procedevano —,* the two cars drove on side by side ‖ *agire —,* to act in the same way.

parallelepípedo, *s.m.* (*geom.*) parallelepiped (*pl.* parallelepipeda).

parallelísmo, *s.m.* parallelism.

parallèlo, *ag.* parallel (anche *fig.*): *circoli paralleli,* (*geog.*) parallel circles; *due piani paralleli,* two parallel planes; *strada che corre parallela al fiume,* road that runs parallel to (*o* with) the river ‖ *s.m.* 1. (*geog.*) parallel (of latitude): *paesi posti sullo stesso —,* countries on the same parallel 2. (*comparazione*) parallel, comparison: *istituire un — tra due cose,* to draw a parallel (*o* to make a comparison) between two things 3. (*elett.*) parallel: *batterie in —,* batteries in parallel; *messa in —,* paralleling.

parallelogràmmo, *s.m.* (*geom.*) parallelogram.

paralogísmo, *s.m.* (*fil.*) paralogism.

paralogístico, *ag.* paralogistic, paralogical.

paralogizzàre, *v.i.* to paralogize.

paralúme, *s.m.* lamp-shade.

paramagnètico, *ag.* paramagnetic.

paramàno, *s.m.* cuff.

paraménto, *s.m.* 1. hanging: *le pareti erano ricoperte di paramenti,* the walls were covered with hangings 2. (*eccl.*) vestment.

paràmetro, *s.m.* (*mat. astr.*) parameter.

paramezzàle, *s.m.* (*mar.*) keelson, inner keel.

paramíne, *s.m.* (*mar. mil.*) paravane.

paramnesía, *s.f.* (*med.*) paramnesia.

paramósche, *s.m.* fly-net.

paranco, *s.m.* (*mar. mec.*) tackle, hoist: *— a coda,* jigger (-tackle); *— differenziale,* differential tackle; *— semplice, doppio,* single, two-fold tackle.

paraninfo, *s.m.* paranymph.

paranòia, *s.f.* (*patol.*) paranoia.

paranòico, *ag. s.m.* paranoiac, paranoic.

paranza, *s.f.* (*mar.*) lateen-sailed fishing boat.

paraòcchi, *s.m.pl.* blinkers.

parapàlle, *s.m.* (*mil.*) butt.

parapètto, *s.m.* 1. parapet; (*davanzale*) window -sill 2. (*mil.*) parapet 3. (*mar.*) railing.

parapíglia, *s.m.* turmoil, hurly-burly.

parapiòggia, *s.m.* umbrella.

paraplegía, *s.f.* (*patol.*) paraplegia.

paràre[1], *v.t.* 1. (*riparare, proteggere*) to shield, to protect: *— dal freddo, dalla neve,* to shield (*o* to protect) from cold, from snow 2. (*tener lontano*) to keep off, to keep out: *c'è una tenda per — il sole,* there is a curtain to keep off the sun 3. (*evitare, scansare*) to parry, to ward off: *— un colpo,* to parry (*o* to ward off) a blow 4. (*fermare*) to stop 5. (*condurre*) to drive: *— il bestiame,* to drive the cattle 6. (*porgere*) to offer; (*stendere*) to stretch out, to hold out: *— la mano,* to hold out one's hand 7. *andare a —,* to drive at (sthg.), to lead up to (sthg.): *non so dove le sue parole vadano a —,* I don't know what his words are driving at ‖ **paràrsi,** *v.r.* 1. (*ripararsi*) to shelter (oneself), to protect oneself: *— gli occhi dalla luce,* to shield one's eyes from the light 2. (*presentarsi, comparire*) to present oneself; to appear: *mi si parò dinanzi,* he appeared before me; *si parò sull'uscio,* he appeared at the door.

paràre[2], *v.t.* 1. (*ornare con paramenti*) to adorn, to deck, to decorate: *— a lutto,* to hang with black; *—*

una chiesa, to decorate a church (with hangings) **2.** — *le vele*, (*mar.*) to hoist the sails **3.** (*rar.*) (*preparare*) to prepare ‖ **paràrsi**, *v.r.* (*vestirsi con paramenti*) to dress up; (*eccl.*) to vest oneself.

parasartía, *s.f.* (*mar.*) channel, chain-wale.

parascève, *s.f.* (*st. ebraica*) parasceve.

paraselène, *s.m.* (*astr.*) paraselene (*pl.* paraselenae).

parasóle, *s.m.* **1.** parasol, sunshade **2.** (*foto*) lens-hood, lens-screen **3.** (*aer.*) parasol.

parassíta, *ag.* parasitic: *correnti parassite*, (*elett.*) eddy currents; *rumori parassiti*, (*rad.*) interference ‖ *s.c.* **1.** parasite **2.** (*scroccone*) parasite; (*fam.*) sponger.

parassítico, *ag.* **1.** parasitic(al), parasital: *piante parassitiche*, parasitic plants **2.** (*di persona*) sponging.

parassitísmo, *s.m.* (*biol.*) parasitism.

paràsta, *s.f.* (*arch.*) parastas (*pl.* parastades).

parastatàle, *ag.* government-controlled, State-controlled (*attributivo*): *ente* —, government-controlled body ‖ *i parastatali*, (*amm.*) the employees of [a government-controlled body.

paràta[1], *s.f.* **1.** (*il parare un colpo*) parry: *essere pronto alla* —, to be quick at parrying; *fare una* —, to parry **2.** (*riparo*) screen **3.** (*per sbarrare strade*) cross-bar.

paràta[2], *s.f.* **1.** (*sfoggio*) parade, show, display: *abiti di* —, full-dress clothes; *pranzo di* —, banquet **2.** (*mil.*) parade: *schieramento in* —, parade-order; *essere in* —, to be on parade; *sfilare in* — *davanti a qlcu.*, to march past s.o. **3.** *vista la mala* —..., when he saw that things were taking a bad turn....

paratàsche, *s.m.* pocket-flap.

paratía, *s.f.* (*mar.*) bulkhead: — *corazzata*, armoured bulkhead; — *di collisione*, forepeak (o collision) bulkhead; — *parafiamma, tagliafuoco*, fireproof bulkhead; — *stagna*, watertight bulkhead; — *volante*, temporary bulkhead.

paratièra, *s.f.* cuirass, breastplate.

paratífo, *s.m.* (*patol.*) paratyphoid.

paratiròide, *s.f.* (*anat.*) parathyroid.

paràto, *ag.* **1.** decorated, decked: — *a festa*, sumptuously decorated; (*di persona*) in one's Sunday best (o dressed up) **2.** (*preparato*) ready: *sono* — *a tutto*, I am ready for anything ¦‖ *s.m.* hanging; (*ornamento*) ornament: *i parati di un altare*, altar-hangings; *i parati di un letto*, bed-hangings; *carta da parati*, wall-paper.

paratóia, *s.f.* (*patol.*) cataract.

paratóre, *s.m.* church-decorator.

paratúra, *s.f.* decoration.

paraúrti, *s.m.* (*aut.*) bumper: — *a molla*, spring-loaded bumper; — *cromati*, chrome-plated bumpers.

paravènto, *s.m.* screen ‖ *far da* — *a qlcu.*, to shield s.o.

pàrca, *s.f.* (*mit.*) Fate ‖ *le Parche*, the Fates.

parcaménte, *av.* frugally, sparingly; (*moderatamente*) moderately: *mangiare* —, to eat sparingly.

parcàre, *v.t.* to park.

parcèlla, *s.f.* fee, bill: *pagare la* —, to pay the bill.

parcheggiàre, *v.t.* to park.

parchéggio, *s.m.* parking(-place), parking-lot: *vietato il* —, no parking.

pàrco[1], *ag.* frugal, sparing; (*parsimonioso*) parsimonious; (*moderato*) moderate: *la mia parca mensa*, my frugal table; *uomo* — *nel bere*, moderate drinker; *uomo* — *nel mangiare*, frugal eater; *è* — *di lodi*, he is sparing of praise (o in his praise); *è assai parca nello spendere*, she is very thrifty.

pàrco[2], *s.m.* **1.** park: *il* — *di Monza*, Monza Park; — *nazionale*, national park ‖ — *di divertimenti*, fun-fair ‖ — *della rimembranza*, Gardens of Remembrance **2.** (*recinto*) park, yard: — *d'artiglieria*, (*mil.*) artillery-park; — *di munizioni*, (*mil.*) ammunition dump; — *di deposito*, (*comm.*) stock-yard; — *di lingotti*, (*metal.*) ingot-yard (o store); — *merci*, (*ferr.*) goods-yard **3.** (*parcheggio*) park, parking-place, parking-lot.

pàrdo, *s.m.* (*zool.*) leopard; (*arc.*) pard.

parécchio, *ag. indef.* **1.** quite a lot of; rather a lot of: *hai speso* — *denaro*, you have spent rather a lot of money; *ho* — *tempo libero oggi*, I have quite a lot of spare time today **2.** (*riferito a tempo*) quite a long: rather a long: — *tempo*, quite a long time; long (*solo in proposizioni interrogative*): — *tempo fa*, quite a long time ago; *aspetto da* — *tempo*, I have been waiting for quite a long time; *hai dovuto attendere* — *tempo?*, did you have to wait long? **3.** *pl.* several; (*un numero notevole di*) quite a lot of; rather a lot of: *Maria conosce parecchie persone a Roma*, Maria knows quite a lot of people in Rome; *vive a Londra da parecchi anni*, he has lived in London for several years ‖ *pron. indef.* **1.** quite a lot; rather a lot: — *di quanto mi disse non è vero*, quite a lot of what he told me is not true; «*Hai del pane?*», «*Ne ho* —», " Have you any bread? ", " I have quite a lot "; *non avevo molto tempo ieri, ma oggi ne ho* —, I had not much time yesterday, but today I have quite a lot; «*Quanto lavoro hai ancora da fare?*», «*Parecchio, purtroppo*», " How much work have you still to do?", "Rather [a lot, I'm afraid" **2.** *pl.* several; (*un numero notevole*) quite a lot, quite a few; rather a lot; (*parecchia gente*) quite a lot of people: *parecchi credono che non sia mai esistito*, quite a lot of people think he never existed; *parecchi di loro non vennero*, several of them failed to come; «*Hai degli amici?*», «*Ne ho parecchi*», "Have you any friends? ", " I have quite a few " ‖ *parecchi altri*, several more; quite a lot more ‖ *av.* quite (*con ag.*); rather (*con ag.*); quite a lot; rather a lot: *ci ho pensato* —, I have thought about it quite a lot; *ho dovuto studiare* — *stasera*, I have had to study rather a lot tonight; *quel ragazzo è* — *intelligente*, that boy is quite intelligent; *questo supera di* — *la mia aspettativa*, this is quite a lot better than I expected; *sono* — *stanco*, I am rather tired ‖ *distare* — *da...*, to be quite (o rather) a long way from....

pareggiàbile, *ag.* **1.** (*comm.*) (*di conti, di bilancio, ecc.*) that can be balanced **2.** (*livellabile*) that can be levelled.

pareggiaménto, *s.m.* **1.** (*comm.*) balancing; balance **2.** (*livellamento*) levelling **3.** (*parificazione di scuola, ecc.*) official recognition.

pareggiàre, *v.t.* **1.** (*comm.*) to balance: — *il bilancio*, to balance accounts (o the budget); — *i conti*, to balance accounts; *fig.* to square accounts **2.** (*tagliare ad altezza uniforme*) to trim: *farsi* — *la barba*, to have one's beard trimmed **3.** (*livellare*) to level, to make even: — *un campo da tennis, una strada*, to level a tennis-lawn, a road **4.** (*eguagliare*) to match: *nessuno lo può* —, nobody can match him (o he is unrivalled) **5.** (*parificare una scuola*) to recognize officially: *questa scuola fu pareggiata l'anno scorso*, this school was officially recognized last year (by the Ministry of Education) ‖ *v.i.* (*spor.*) to draw; to equalize: *Charles ha pareggiato per la Juventus*, Charles equalized for Juventus; «*Che squadra ha vinto domenica, l'Inter o il Milan?*», «*Nessuna, hanno pareggiato*», "Which team won last Sunday, Inter or Milan?", "Neither, they drew".

pareggiàto, *ag.* (*di scuola*) officially recognized: *scuola pareggiata*, officially recognized school.

paréggio, *s.m.* **1.** (*comm.*) balance: *a* — *della vostra fattura*, to balance your invoice; *pagamento a* —, payment in full **2.** (*spor.*) draw; tie.

parèlio, *s.m.* (*astr.*) parhelion (*pl.* parhelia).

paremiògrafo, *s.m.* paroemiologist.

paremiología, *s.f.* paroemiology.

parènchima, *s.m.* (*anat. bot.*) parenchyma.

parenchimàtico, *ag.* (*anat. bot.*) parenchymal, parenchymatous: *tessuto* —, parenchyma.

parentàdo, *s.m.* **1.** (*insieme dei parenti*) relations (*pl.*), relatives (*pl.*); kin (*pl.*); kindred (*pl.*); kinsfolk (*pl.*): *invitò tutto il* —, he invited all his relatives; *tutto il mio* — *vive in America*, all my relatives live in America **2.** (*legame di parentela*) relationship, kinship; (*matrimonio*) marriage **3.** (*stirpe, lignaggio*) lineage, stock, descent: *di buon* —, of good lineage (*o* descent); *venire da un buon* —, to come of good stock.

parentàli, *s.m.pl.* **1.** memorial celebrations **2.** (*st. romana*) parentalia.

parènte, *s.c.* relative, relation: *parenti da parte di madre*, relations on the mother's side; — *stretto, lontano*, close, distant relation; *i parenti più stretti sono stati informati*, the next of kin have been informed; *siamo parenti stretti*, we are closely related; *un mio* —, a relation (*o* relative) of mine; *circondato da parenti ed amici*, surrounded by his relatives and friends; *è tuo* —?, is he a relative of yours? (*o* is he any relation to you?); *non ha parenti a Milano*, he has no relations in Milan; *non sono parenti*, they are not relations ‖ *il sonno è* — *della morte*, sleep is the image of death.

parentèla, *s.f.* **1.** (*vincolo di consanguineità*) relationship, kinship; consanguinity: *grado di* —, degree of relationship; *vincolo di* —, family tie; *c'è una stretta* — *tra di loro*, they are closely related; *vanta una* — *che non esiste*, he claims a relationship which does not exist **2.** (*insieme dei parenti*) relations (*pl.*); relatives (*pl.*); kin (*pl.*), kindred (*pl.*); kinsfolk (*pl.*): *la maggior parte della mia* — *verrà al mio matrimonio*, most of my relatives will come to my wedding **3.** (*relazione*) relationship.

parèntesi, *s.f.* **1.** parenthesis (*pl.* parentheses): *in* —, in parentheses ‖ *tra* — *devo dirti che...*, by the way (*o* incidentally) I must tell you that... **2.** (*segno grafico*) bracket: — *aperta, chiusa*, open, close bracket; — *quadre, tonde*, square, round brackets; *mettere una parola tra* —, to put a word between brackets (*o* to bracket a word); *togliere le* —, to remove (the) brackets.

parenteticaménte, *av.* parenthetically.

parentètico, *ag.* parenthetic(al).

parére, *v.i.* **1.** to seem, to look, to appear; (*essere simile a, somigliare a*) to look like: *il lago pare uno specchio*, the lake is like a mirror; *pare una gran dama*, she seems a great lady; *pare malato ma non lo è*, he looks (*o* seems to be) ill but he isn't; *pare molto triste*, he looks very sad; *pare una persona intelligente*, he seems to be (*o* looks like) an intelligent person ‖ *per ben* —, to make a good impression ‖ *per non* —, in order not to be noticed ‖ *senza* —, without its being realized ‖ *pare rabarbaro*, it tastes like rhubarb ‖ *pare velluto*, it feels like velvet ‖ *questo pare un verso di Shakespeare*, this sounds like a verse of Shakespeare's ‖ *far* — *bianco il nero, una cosa per un'altra*, to pass one thing off as another **2.** *imp.* to seem; (*con costruzione pers.*): to like, to think: *che te ne pare?* what do you think of it?; *come ti pare questa birra?*, what do you think of this beer?; *fa' come ti pare*, do as you like (*o* please); *mi pare che abbia ragione*, I think he is right (*o* he seems to be right); *mi pare di averlo visto*, I think I saw him; *mi pare di conoscerlo, di averlo già incontrato*, I seem to know him, I seem to have (*o* it seems that I have) met him already; *mi pare di essere a casa mia qui*, I feel at home here; *mi pare un sogno*, it seems (to me) like a dream; *mi pareva di aver ragione*, I thought I was right; *mi pareva di sognare*, I seemed to be (*o* I thought I was) dreaming; *mi parve d'aver visto ql.co.*, I thought I had seen sthg.; *pare che non sia vero*, it seems that it is not true; *pare che sia molto malato*, it seems that he is (*o* he seems to be) very ill; *pare che sia un uomo onesto*, it seems (*o* they say) that he is an honest man; *pare che il tempo voglia rimettersi*, it looks as if the weather is changing for the better; *pare che voglia piovere*, it looks like rain; *pare di sì*, it seems so: *pare di sì ma non ne sono sicuro*, I think so but I am not sure; *pare strano, impossibile che...*, it seems strange, impossible that...; *parrebbe che io abbia torto*, it would seem that I am wrong; *ti pare di aver ragione?*, do you think (that) you are right? ‖ *a quanto pare*, as far as we know ‖ *come mi pare e piace*, as I like ‖ *ma vi*

pare!, don't mention it! ‖ *mi pare un secolo che non lo vedo*, it seems ages since I saw him **3.** (*poet.*) (*apparire*) to appear.

parère, *s.m.* opinion: *a mio* —, in my opinion; *non sono del* —, I do not agree; *questo è il mio* —, this is my opinion; *sono del* — *che non dovresti andare*, I think that you should not go; *cambiar* —, to change one's mind; *sentire il* — *di qlcu.*, to hear s.o.'s opinion.

parèrgo, *s.m.* (*ret. art.*) parergon (*pl.* parerga).

parèsi, *s.f.* (*patol.*) paresis.

parestesìa, *s.f.* (*med.*) paresthesia.

paretàio, *s.m.* set of bird-catching nets.

paréte, *s.f.* wall: — *addominale*, (*anat.*) abdominal wall; *pareti del cuore*, (*anat.*) walls of the heart; — *di una galleria*, lining of a tunnel; — *di legno*, wooden wall; — *di un vaso*, (*interna*) inner side of a vase; (*esterna*) surface of a vase; — *divisoria*, partition (wall); — *esterna*, outside wall; — *interna*, inside wall; *a doppia* —, double-walled; *quadro attaccato alla* —, picture hanging on the wall; *due miei amici hanno scalato ieri la parete più difficile del Cervino*, yesterday two of my friends climbed the most difficult face of the Matterhorn ‖ *fra le pareti domestiche*, at home.

paretèlla, *s.f.* bird-catching net, fowling-net.

pargoleggiàre, *v.i.* to behave like a child.

pàrgolo, *ag.* (*poet.*) little, tiny ‖ *s.m.* (little) child; baby ‖ *«Lasciate che i pargoli vengano a me»*, (*Bibbia*) "Suffer little children to come unto me".

pàri, *ag.* **1.** equal, same; (*simile*) like, similar: *a* — *condizioni*, under the same conditions; *a* — *diritti, meriti*, rights, merits being equal; *arrivo a* — *merito*, (*spor.*) dead-heat; *una condizione* — *a questa*, a similar condition (*o* a condition like this); *di* — *altezza, condizioni, merito, valore*, of equal (*o* of the same) height, conditions, merit, worth; *di* — *qualità, quantità*, of the same quality, quantity; *in* — *tempo*, in the same time; *non c'è nessuno* — *a lui*, there is nobody like him (*o* he has no equal *o* he is unrivalled); *essere* — *a qlcu. in ql.co.*, to be equal to s.o. in sthg. (*o* to be on an equal footing with s.o.) ‖ —: *i due invitati arrivarono* — —, (*contemporaneamente*) the two guests arrived at the same time (*o* moment); *giunsero* — *fino al paese*, (*bel bello*) they reached the village in their own good time; *copiare* — —, (*di sana pianta*) to copy word for word ‖ — *e patta*, quits: *ora siamo* — *e patta*, we are quits now ‖ *al* —, (*nello stesso modo*) as... as; (*in confronto*) in comparison: *al* — *degli altri sa molto di più*, in comparison with the others he knows much more; *sei uno sciocco al* — *di lui*, you are as silly as he is ‖ *alla* —: *rimborsabile alla* —, (*comm.*) redeemable at par; *sopra, sotto alla* —, (*comm.*) above par (*o* at a premium), below par (*o* at a discount): *salire sopra, scendere sotto alla* —, to rise above par, to sink below par; *mettersi alla* — *di qlcu.*, to place oneself on the same level as s.o.; *stare alla* — *presso una famiglia inglese*, to stay au pair in an English family ‖ *del* —, as well: *egli studia del* — *il russo*, he studies Russian as well (*o* too) ‖ *di* — *passo*, at the same rate (*o* pace) (anche *fig.*): *andare di* — *passo con qlcu., ql.co.*, to keep up with s.o., sthg.: *andare di* — *passo coi tempi*, to keep up with the times; *procedere di* — *passo*, to proceed at the same rate ‖ *due* —, (*al giuoco*) two all; *quaranta* —, (*tennis*) deuce ‖ *in* — : *mettersi in* — *coi pagamenti*, to pay the arrears; *mettersi in* — *col proprio lavoro*, to catch up with one's work; *tenere ql.co. in* —, to keep sthg. up to date ‖ *senza* —, incomparable (*o* unequalled *o* matchless *o* peerless *o* unrivalled): *artista senza* —, incomparable artist; *bellezza senza* —, matchless (*o* peerless) beauty ‖ *essere* —, (*nel punteggio*) to be level; to be quits (anche *fig.*); (*di forze*) to be evenly matched: *dopo dieci minuti le due squadre erano* —, after ten minutes the two teams were level; *i due avversari erano* —, the two opponents were evenly matched; *ora siamo* —!, we are quits now! ‖ *far* —, (*al giuoco*) to draw **2.** (*in equilibrio, in* *posizione parallela*) level, equal: *i piatti della bilancia stanno* —, the scales are level (o equal) || *a piè* —, with feet together: *saltare a piè* —, to jump with one's feet together; *saltare a piè* — *un capitolo*, to skip a whole chapter **3.** (*divisibile per due*) even: *numeri* — *e dispari*, even and odd numbers; *essere in numero* —, to be even in number || *far* — *e dispari*, to play odds and evens **4.** (*in equivalenze di valori, monete, ecc.*) equivalent: *un dollaro è* — *a 625 lire*, one dollar is equivalent to 625 lire **5.** (*atto, all'altezza di*) equal: *non era* — *al suo compito*, he was not equal to his task || *s.m.* **1.** equal, peer; like: *è un mio* —, he is my equal; *è un tale mascalzone che non ho mai visto il suo* —, he is such a rascal I never saw his like; *non devi parlare così a un suo* —, you must not speak like that to s.o. like him; *preferisco rimanere coi miei* —, I prefer to remain with my peers; *essere giudicato dai propri pari*, to be rated by one's peers || *da* — *a* —, as an equal (o as man to man): *parlarsi da* — *a* —, to talk as man to man; *trattare qlcu. da* — *a* —, to treat s.o. as one's equal **2.** (*paladino*) peer: *i dodici* — *di Carlo Magno*, the twelve peers of Charlemagne (o the douzepers) **3.** *Pari*, (*titolo nobiliare*) Peer: *i Pari del Regno*, the Peers of the Realm; *la Camera dei Pari*, the House of Lords; *classe, dignità di Pari*, peerage.

pària[1], *s.m.* pariah (anche *fig.*).

paria[2], *s.f.* (*dignità di Pari*) peerage.

Pàride, *no.pr.m.* (*mit.*) Paris.

pàridi, *s.m.pl.* (*ornit.*) Paridae.

parietàle, *e derivati*, *ag.* (*anat.*) parietal: *lobo* —, parietal lobe; *ossa parietali*, parietal bones.

parietària, *s.f.* (*bot.*) pellitory.

parificàre, *e derivati*, *V.* **pareggiàre**, *e derivati*.

Parígi, *no.pr.f.* (*geog.*) Paris.

parigína[1], *s.f.* **1.** (*stufa*) slow-combustion stove **2.** (*tip.*) pearl.

parigíno, *ag.s.m.* Parisian || **parigína**[2], *s.f.* Parisian (woman), Parisienne.

paríglia, *s.f.* **1.** pair: *una* — *di cavalli*, a pair (of horses); *una* — *di re, di fanti*, (*a carte*) a pair of kings,of Jacks **2.** *render la* —,(*il contraccambio*) to give tit for tat.

pariménte, pariménti, *av.* (*similmente*) similarly; likewise.

pàrio, *ag.* Parian: *marmo* —, Parian marble.

parisíllabo, *ag.* parisyllabic.

parità, *s.f.* equality, parity: *le donne hanno diritto alla* — *con gli uomini*, women have the right to equality with men; *in un paese democratico tutti hanno* — *di diritti e di doveri*, in a democratic country everybody has equal rights and duties || *a* — *di condizioni*, under the same conditions; *a* — *di meriti, di diritti*, merits, rights being equal.

paritètico, *ag.* (*pol.*) joint (*attributivo*): *commissione paritetica*, joint committee.

parlàbile, *ag.* speakable.

parlamentàre[1], *ag.* parliamentary: *autorità, governo* —, parliamentary authority, government || *poco* —, (*scortese*) rude || *s.m.* (*membro del Parlamento*) Member of Parliament, parliamentarian.

parlamentàre[2], *v.i.* to parley, to hold a parley: — *con il nemico*, to parley with the enemy.

parlamentàrio, *ag.* parliamentary || *s.m.* **1.** (*mil.*) emissary **2.** (*pol.*) (*membro del Parlamento*) Member of Parliament, parliamentarian.

parlamentarísmo, *s.m.* (*pol.*) parliamentarianism.

parlaménto, *s.m.* **1.** (*convegno, colloquio*) assembly; parley: *chiamare a* —, to beat (o to sound) a parley; *tener* —, to hold a parley **2.** *Parlamento*, (*pol.*) Parliament: *membro del Parlamento*, Member of Parliament (*abbr.* M.P.); *riapertura, chiusura del Parlamento*, opening, closing of Parliament; *sede del Parlamento*, Parliament-House; *seduta del Parlamento*, sitting of Parliament; *convocare, sciogliere il Parlamento*, to summon, to dissolve Parliament.

parlànte, *ag.* **1.** talking: *bambola* —, talking doll ||

i ben, i mal parlanti, persons who speak correctly, incorrectly || *è il ritratto* — *di suo nonno*, he is the very image of his grandfather (o *fam.* he is the dead spit of his grandfather) || *quel ritratto è* —, that portrait is most life-like (o you can almost hear that portrait speak): *quel ritratto di Giovanni è* —, that portrait is John to the life **2.** (*chiaro*) clear; (*ovvio*) obvious: *fatti parlanti*, obvious facts; *prova* —, clear proof.

parlantína, *s.f.* talkativeness: *che* —!, what a chatterbox!; *ha una buona* —, he is a glib talker.

parlàre, *v.i.* **1.** to speak, to talk; (*chiacchierare*) to talk: *il bambino non ha ancora incominciato a* —, the baby hasn't started talking yet; *con chi ho il piacere di* —?, who(m) have I the pleasure of speaking to?; *di che cosa state parlando?*, what are you talking about?; *generalmente, approssimativamente parlando possiamo dire che...*, generally, roughly speaking we can say that...; *ho l'impressione che si ascolti parlando*, I have a feeling he likes the sound of his own voice; *non voglio* — *io tutto il tempo*, I don't want to do all the talking myself; *parla spesso del suo lavoro*, he often talks about his work (o *fam.* he often talks shop); *parlavano al telefono da dieci minuti*, they had been talking on the telephone for ten minutes; *parlavano sottovoce fra loro due*, they were whispering (o speaking softly) to each other; *parli ad alta voce, per favore!*, will you speak up, please?; *parli sul serio?*, do you mean it? (o are you serious?); *parlo per esperienza*, I am speaking from experience; *pronto, chi parla?*, hello, who's speaking please?; — *a bassa voce*, to speak in a low voice; — *bene, male di qlcu.*, to speak well, ill of s.o.; — *chiaro*, to speak clearly; *fig.* to speak one's mind; — *d'affari*, to talk business; — *forbito*, to speak (o to choose one's words) carefully; — *fra i denti*, to mutter under one's breath; — *fra sè e sè*, to talk to oneself; — *in gergo*, to talk slang; — *in modo sensato*, to talk sensibly (o to talk common sense); — *in plurale*, to use the royal " we "; — *nel sonno*, to talk in one's sleep; — *senza tregua*, to talk and talk; — *spedito*, to speak fast; — *tanto da diventar rauco*, to talk oneself hoarse || *anche i muri parlano in questo posto*, even the walls have ears in this place || *con rispetto parlando*, if you don't mind me saying so || *ho bisogno di parlarti a quattr'occhi*, I want to speak to you privately || *lascialo* —!, let him have his say! (o let him speak for himself!); (*iron.*) let him talk! || *parla coi piedi*, (*fam.*) he can't speak properly || *parla come un libro stampato*, he talks like a book || *parla come un mulino a vento*, he could talk the hind leg off a donkey || *parla sempre in punta di forchetta*, he is always very affected in his speech || *parla tanto per* —, he talks for the sake of talking || *parlavano a gesti*, they talked by signs || *parlavano del più e del meno*, they were talking of one thing and another (o of this and that) || *questo si chiama* — *chiaro*, this is putting it rather bluntly || *se le pietre parlassero!...*, if only the stones could speak!... || *si parla di licenziarlo*, there is some talk of dismissing him || — *al vento, al muro*, to talk to the wall (o to waste one's breath): *in questa classe io parlo al vento*, I am wasting my breath talking to this class || — *a vanvera, a casaccio*, to talk through one's hat (o through the back of one's neck) || — *fuori dai denti*, to speak plainly (o to call a spade a spade) || — *grasso*, to talk smut || — *nel naso*, to speak through one's nose || *far* — *qlcu.* to make s.o. speak: *era così timido che non riuscii a farlo* —, he was so shy that I could not manage to make him speak; *Esopo fa* — *gli animali*, Aesop puts words into his animals' mouths; *non mi far* —!, don't make me say any more!; *la polizia l'ha fatto* —, the police made him talk || *altro è* — *di morte, altro è morire, prov.* it is one thing to talk of dying, another to die || *chi molto parla spesso falla, prov.* great talkers are great liars (o a still tongue in a wise head) ‖ *chi parla rado è tenuto a grado*, prov. silence is wisdom and wins friends ‖ *chi parla semina, chi tace raccoglie*, prov. speech is silver, silence is golden ‖ *chi vuol ben — ci deve ben pensare*, prov. think twice before you speak ‖ *mai nocque il tacer ma l'aver parlato*, prov. more have repented of speech than of silence ‖ *quando parla il piccolo, il grande ha parlato*, prov. the child says nothing but what he has heard at the fireside **2.** (*trattare*) (*parlando*) to speak; (*scrivendo*) to write; (*far menzione*) to mention (sthg.): *Cicerone parla dell'amicizia*, Cicero writes about friendship; *i giornali di ieri ne parlavano*, it was in yesterday's papers; *il libro non ne parla*, the book does not mention it; *mio padre non vuole assolutamente sentirne —*, my father won't hear of it; *non mette conto di parlarne*, it isn't worth mentioning; *l'oratore parlò a lungo della situazione attuale*, the speaker spoke for a long time about the present situation ‖ *per non — di*, not to mention (*o* let alone): *per non — di quello che fa lui*, not to mention (*o* let alone) what he does himself **3.** (*discutere*) to discuss (sthg.), to debate (sthg.), to talk: *a cena si parlò di quello che si sarebbe fatto il giorno dopo*, over dinner we discussed what we would do the next day; *so che parlavano di me e di te*, I know they were discussing (*o* talking about) me and you; *stavamo parlando se andare in montagna o al mare*, we were debating whether to go to the mountains or to the seaside **4.** (*rivolgersi*) to address (s.o.): *bada con chi parli*, remember who(m) you are speaking to; *è a te che parlo non a Giovanni*, I am talking to you not to John; *quando parla la Camera*, when he addresses the House; *il Rettore parlerà agli studenti*, the Chancellor will address the students **5.** (*essere in relazione*) to speak, to be on speaking terms (with s.o.): *mio fratello parlava ad una ragazza che non mi piaceva*, my brother had a girl-friend I didn't like; *non ci parliamo più da un anno*, we have not been on speaking terms (*o* we have not spoken to each other) for a year; *si parlarono due anni prima di sposarsi*, they were engaged for two years before getting married ‖ *v.t.* to speak: *a Losanna si parla francese*, French is spoken at Lausanne; *parla bene quattro lingue*, he speaks four languages well; *qui si parla inglese*, English (is) spoken here ‖ *— ostrogoto, arabo, turco*, (*fam.*) to talk double-Dutch: *non capisco mai quello che dice, parla ostrogoto*, I never understand him, what he says is double-Dutch to me.

parlàre, *s.m.* **1.** (*discorso*) speech; words (*pl.*); (*chiacchiere*) talk: *ci fu un gran — di ciò*, there was a lot of talk about it; *con turpi parlari*, with filthy words (*o* obscenely); *questo è un — ambiguo*, these are ambiguous words; *questo è un bel —, ma...*, these are fine words, but...; *il suo — è sempre molto lento*, he is always very slow of speech ‖ *al cantare l'uccello, al — il cervello*, prov. a bird is known by its note, and a man by his talk **2.** (*idioma*) language; dialect: *il — toscano*, the Tuscan dialect; *nel — popolare*, in the vernacular **3.** (*modo di parlare*) (way of) speaking.

parlàta, *s.f.* **1.** (*discorso*) speech, talk; (*conversazione*) conversation: *mi fece una lunga — per convincermi*, he engaged me in a long conversation to convince me **2.** (*modo di parlare*) (way of) speaking; (*dialetto*) dialect: *la — comasca*, the dialect of Como; *lo conobbi alla —*, I recognized him from the way he spoke.

parlàto, *ag.* spoken: *il cinematografo —*, the talkies; *un film —*, a talking-picture; *giornale —*, (*rad.*) the news; *l'inglese —*, spoken English.

parlatóre, *s.m.* **1.** speaker, talker **2.** (*oratore*) orator.

parlatòrio, *s.m.* parlour.

parlottàre, *v.t.* to talk in a low voice; (*mormorare*) to mutter.

Parmènide, *no.pr.m.* (*st. fil.*) Parmenides.

parmènse, *s.c.* Parmese.

parmigiàno, *ag.* Parmesan: *formaggio —*, Parmesan ‖ *s.m.* **1.** (*parmense*) Parmese **2.** (*formaggio*) Parmesan.

parnàsio, *ag.* Parnassian: *il monte —*, Parnassus.

Parnà(s)so, *no.pr.m.* (*geog.*) Parnassus ‖ **parnà(s)so**, *s.m.* **1.** (*la poesia*) parnassus. poetry **2.** (*i poeti*) poets (*pl.*): *il — italiano*, the Italian poets.

parnassiàno, *ag.* Parnassian: *la scuola parnassiana*, (*st. lett.*) the Parnassian school ‖ *s.m.* Parnassian.

pàro, (*dial.*) per **pàio**.

paròcchi, *s.m.pl.* blinkers.

parodía, *s.f.* **1.** parody: *fare la — di un'opera*, to parody a work **2.** (*brutta imitazione*) poor imitation.

parodiàre, *v.t.* to parody.

paròdico, *ag.* parodic(al).

parodísta, *s.c.* parodist.

pàrodo, *s.m.* (*st. teat.*) parode.

paròla, *s.f.* **1.** word: *— composta, semplice*, compound, simple word; *— d'ordine*, password; *egli è buono nel vero senso della —*, he is good in the true (*o* full) sense of the word; *mandami una — appena puoi*, send me word (*o* drop me a line) as soon as you can; *la musica è di Schubert, le parole di Heine*, the music is by Schubert and the words by Heine; *non credo una — di quanto ha detto*, I do not believe a word of what he said; *non ho parole per ringraziarti*, I have no words to thank you; *non riesco a cavargli una — di bocca*, I can't get a word out of him; *voglio scambiare due parole con te*, I want (to have) a word with you; *avere una buona — per tutti*, to have a kind (*o* good) word for everyone; *masticare le parole*, to speak indistinctly (*o* to mumble); *senza proferir —*, without (saying) a word; *tradurre un pensiero in parole*, to put one's thought into words; *ripetere — per —*, to repeat word for word ‖ *parole incrociate*, crosswords (*o* crossword puzzle) ‖ *giuoco di parole*, pun ‖ *in altre parole*, in other words ‖ *in una —*, in one word ‖ *in poche parole*, in a few words ‖ *l'ultima —*, (*il prezzo minimo*) the lowest prize ‖ *non è detta l'ultima —*, the last word has not been said ‖ *non farne —*, don't say a word about it (*o* keep it secret) ‖ *avere l'ultima —*, to have the last word ‖ *dire le brutte parole*, to say nasty words: *mi dice le brutte parole*, he calls me names ‖ *dire, mettere una buona — a favore di qlcu.*, to say (*o* to put in) a word for s.o. ‖ *far — di ql.co. con qlcu.*, to mention (*o* to speak of) sthg. to s.o. ‖ *mettere le parole in bocca a qlcu.*, to prompt s.o. ‖ *non dire — di ql.co.*, not to breathe a word about sthg. ‖ *non sapere una — di latino*, not to know a word of Latin (*o* the first thing about Latin) ‖ *passar dalle parole ai fatti*, to pass from the word to the deed ‖ *passar —*, to pass the word on ‖ *rimaner senza —*, to be dumbfounded (*o* to be left speechless) ‖ *rubar la — di bocca a qlcu.*, to take the words out of s.o.'s mouth ‖ *venire a parole con qlcu.*, to have words with s.o. ‖ *a buon intenditor poche parole*, prov. a word to the wise (is sufficient) **2.** (*facoltà di parlare, favella*) speech: *il dono della —*, the gift of speech; *se gli animali avessero la — ...*, if animals could speak (*o* had the power of speech)...; *perdere la —*, to lose the power (*o* faculty) of speech **3.** (*discorso*) words, speech: *gli rivolsi la — in francese*, I addressed him in French; *le mie parole sono rivolte a te*, my words are addressed to you; *non mi ha nemmeno rivolto la —*, he hasn't even spoken to me ‖ *la — a Mr. Smith*, I will now call on Mr. Smith (*o* I shall now ask Mr. Smith to address the meeting) ‖ *meno parole*, don't talk so much ‖ *la — è tua*, it's your turn ‖ *gli fu tolta la —*, he was not allowed to say any more (*o* to speak any further) ‖ *chiedere, domandare la —*, to ask leave to speak; (*pol.*) to raise a point of order ‖ *dare la — a qlcu.*, to call upon s.o. to speak (*o* to address the meeting) ‖ *ottenere la —*, to obtain the right to speak ‖ *prender la —*, to begin to speak (*o* to take the floor) ‖ *la — è d'argento, il silenzio è d'oro*, prov. speech is silver, silence is golden **4.** (*promessa, impegno*) word, promise; (*mil.*) parole: *è uomo di —*, he is a man of his word (*o* he is as good as his word); *mi fido della tua —*, I take you at your word (*o* I take your word for it *o* I trust your word); *credere qlcu. sulla —*, to take a person's word; *dare la propria — a qlcu.*, to give one's word to s.o.; *mantenere la propria —*, to keep one's word; *non mantenere la propria —*, to break one's word; (*mil.*) to break one's parole; *prendere qlcu. in —*, to take s.o. at his word; *rimangiarsi la —*, to eat one's words (*o* to take back one's words) || *sulla mia —*, on my word || *— d'onore*, word of honour: *— d'onore, questa è la verità*, on my word (*o* honestly) this is the truth || *si sono dati la —*, they are acting in collusion (*o* they are hand-in-glove); *essere in — con qlcu.*, to be negotiating with s.o. 5. (*qualità, forma dell'esprimersi*) speech; delivery; *aver la — facile*, to have a glib (*o* a ready) tongue; *aver la — limpida*, to have a clear delivery; *non aver la — facile*, to be slow of speech 6. (*insegnamento, precetto*): *la — di Dio*, the Word of God 7. *pl.* (*di canzone*) lyric (*sing.*).

parolàccia, *s.f.*: *dire parolacce a qlcu.*, to swear at s.o.; (*insultarlo*) to call s.o. names.

parolàio, *s.m.* 1. (*chiacchierone*) chatterer; (*fam.*) chatterbox, gas-bag 2. (*di scrittore*) word-monger.

parolière, *s.m.* (*di canzoni*) lyricist.

paronichìa, *s.f.* (*patol.*) paronychia.

paronomàsia, *s.f.* (*ret.*) paronomasia.

parossìsmo, *s.m.* (*med.*) paroxysm (anche *fig.*): *— di collera*, paroxysm of rage.

parossìtono, *ag.s.m.* (*fonet.*) paroxytone.

paròtide, *s.f.* (*anat.*) parotid gland, parotis.

parotìte, *s.f.* (*patol.*) parotitis; (*pop.*) mumps (*pl.*).

parquet, *s.m.* parquet.

parricìda, *ag.* parricidal; parricide (*attributivo*) || *s.c.* parricide.

parricìdio, *s.m.* parricide.

parrocchétto[1], *s.m.* (*mar.*) fore-topsail: *albero di —*, fore-topmast.

parrocchétto[2], *s.m.* (*ornit.*) parakeet.

parròcchia, *s.f.* 1. parish 2. (*chiesa parrocchiale*) parish church.

parrocchiàle, *ag.* parish (*attributivo*); parochial: *chiesa, riunione —*, parish church, meeting.

parrocchiàno, *s.m.* parishioner.

pàrroco, *s.m.* (*cattolico*) parish priest; (*protestante*) vicar, parson.

parrùcca, *s.f.* 1. wig, periwig: *— incipriata*, powdered wig; *portare la —*, to wear a wig; *nascondere la calvizie con la —*, to hide one's baldness with a wig 2. (*zazzera*) long hair 3. (*sgridata*) telling off, ticking off.

parrucchière, *s.m.* 1. hairdresser: *— per signora*, lady's hairdresser; *— per uomo*, barber (*o* gentleman's hairdresser) 2. (*fabbricante di parrucche*) wig maker.

parruccóne, *s.m.* old fogey, old fossil.

parsimònia, *s.f.* thriftiness, parsimony || *— di parole*, sparing (*o* thrifty) use of words.

parsìsmo, *s.m.* (*st. relig.*) Parseeism, Mazdaism.

partàccia, *s.f.* 1. (*ruolo insignificante in una recita*) insignificant role, bad part 2. (*severo rimprovero*) sharp reproof: *fare una — a qlcu.*, to reprove s.o. sharply 3. (*cattiva accoglienza*) poor welcome 4. (*brutto tiro*) dirty trick: *fare una — a qlcu.*, to play s.o. a dirty trick.

pàrte, *s.f.* 1. part; (*porzione*) share, portion: *le parti del discorso*, the parts of speech; *— di ricambio*, (*mec.*) spare part; *le parti di un tutto, di un libro*, the parts of a whole, of a book; *la mia — di dolce*, my portion of cake; *dammi una — di ciò che hai*, give me part of what you have; *ho avuto la mia — di fortuna*, I have had my share of luck; *non ho ancora avuto la mia — dei profitti*, I have not had my share of the profits yet; *un'ora è la ventiquattresima — di un giorno*, an hour is the twenty-fourth part of a day; *dividere in due parti*, to divide into two parts || *—*, (*alcuni*) some: *una — di loro non vennero*, some of them did not come || *gran — di*, a lot of (*o* a large part of); (*pl.*) a great many (of) (*o* a lot of): *gran — della gente...*, a great many people...; *gran — del mio denaro*

va per mangiare, a lot of my money goes on food || *in —*, in part (*o* partly): *in — con la forza, in — con la persuasione*, partly by force, partly by persuasion *contribuire in — alle spese di produzione*, to contribute in part towards the expenses of production || *in gran —*, largely (*o* to a great extent) || *la maggior — di*, most (of) (*o* the majority of): *la maggior — della gente*, most people; *la maggior — dei miei studenti*, most of my students; *per la maggior —*, for the most part || *aver — in ql.co.*, to have a hand in sthg. || *essere a — di ql.co.*, to be informed of sthg. (*o* to be in on sthg.); *mettere qlcu. a — di ql.co.*, to inform s.o. of (*o* about) sthg. (*parte*) 2. (*luogo, regione*) part, region: *da qualche —*, somewhere; *da che — viene quell'uomo?*, where does that man come from?; *dalle mie parti si parla dialetto*, in my part of the country they speak dialect; *non conosco nessuno da queste parti*, I don't know anybody in these parts 3. (*lato*) side, part: *dall'altra —*, on the other side; *dalla — destra, sinistra*, on the right, left (*o* on the right-hand, left-hand side); *da questa — della montagna, della strada*, on this side of the mountain, of the road; *nell'altra — della città*, on the other side of the city; *da che — viene il vento?*, which way is the wind blowing from?; *questa è la — dritta della stoffa*, this is the right side of the cloth; *questa — del foglio deve rimanere vuota*, this side of the paper must be left blank; *attraversare la strada da una — all'altra*, to go (*o* to cross) from one side of the street to the other; *farsi, tirarsi da —*, to step aside (*o* to get out of the way) (anche *fig.*) || *a —*, apart (from): *a — ciò*, apart from that; *a — qualche eccezione*, apart from a few exceptions; *in una lista a —*, in a separate list; *scherzi a —*, joking apart; *questa è una cosa a —*, that's another matter (*o* a different thing altogether); *il servizio è a —*, the service is extra || *da —*, aside: *ho alcune centinaia di sterline da —*, I have a few hundred pounds put aside; *mettere da —*, (*risparmiare*) to put aside (*o* to save); (*trascurare*) to put on one side; *tirare qlcu., ql.co. da —*, to draw s.o., sthg. aside || *da una —..., dall'altra...*, on (the) one hand..., on the other... || *d'altra —...*, on the other hand... || *da — a —*, right through: *si vedeva da — a —*, it could be seen through (*o* one could see right through it) || *da — di*, from; (*di parentela*) on one's father's, mother's side: *un parente da — di mio padre*, a relative on my father's side; *ci sono molte lamentele da — degli studenti*, there are many complaints from the students; *da — mia farò il possibile*, for my part (*o* as for me) I shall do my best; *da — sua non ho ricevuto niente*, I haven't received anything from him; *digli da — mia che...*, tell him from me that...; *questo è molto gentile da — tua*, this is very kind of you; *salutalo da — mia*, give him my (kind) regards || *da ogni —, da tutte le parti*, on all sides (*o* in every direction); (*di moto*) from all sides: *da tutte le parti si vedeva il mare*, the sea could be seen on all sides (*o* in every direction); *il forte fu attaccato da ogni —, da tutte le parti*, the fort was attacked from all sides || *da tutte e due le parti*, on both sides || *da due mesi a questa — non lo vedo*, I have not seen him for two months (*o* I have not seen him these two months); *da Pasqua a questa — piove sempre*, from Easter till now it has been continually raining || *prenderò la tua —*, I shall take your part (*o* I shall side with you *o* I shall be on your side *o* I'll take sides with you) || *essere dalla — del torto*, to be in the wrong;

mettersi dalla — del torto, to put oneself in the wrong ‖ *prendere ql.co. in buona, mala —,* to take sthg. in good, bad part **4.** (*ruolo, in opere teatrali, in un affare, ecc.*) part, rôle: *la — principale di una commedia,* the leading rôle of a play; *distribuzione delle parti,* cast of the play; (*il distribuirle*) casting of the play; *l'attore deve ancora studiare la sua —,* the actor has not learned his part yet; *fece la — di Otello,* he played Othello; *assegnare la — a qlcu.,* to cast s.o. for a part; *avere una — importante in un affare,* to play (o to take) a prominent part in an affair; *fare una parte secondaria,* to play a minor (o secondary) rôle ‖ *fa sempre la — dello stupido,* he is always playing the fool ‖ *ha fatto la sua — fino alla fine,* he played his part to the end ‖ *fare una (brutta) — a qlcu.,* (*rimproverarlo*) to reprove s.o. bitterly; (*agire male verso qlcu.*) to behave badly towards s.o. (o *fam.* to play s.o. a dirty trick) **5.** (*fazione, partito*) faction, party: *uomo di —,* party-man; *spirito di —,* party-spirit **6.** (*comm. dir.*) party; side: *— civile,* (*dir.*) plaintiff: *costituirsi — civile contro qlcu.,* to bring an action against s.o. (o to sue s.o.); *le parti in causa,* (*dir.*) the parties to the case; *la — lesa, interessata,* (*dir.*) the injured, interested party; *le due parti in un contratto,* (*comm.*) the two parties to a contract **7.** (*mus.*) part.

partecipàbile, *ag.* communicable.

partecipànte, *ag.* **1.** (*che prende parte*) participating, sharing, taking part **2.** (*che presenzia*) attending, present **3.** (*che annuncia*) announcing ‖ *s.c.* **1.** (*chi prende parte*) participant, sharer, partaker: *i partecipanti a un dolore, a una gioia,* the sharers of a grief, of a joy; *i partecipanti ai profitti, alle spese,* the sharers in the profits, in the expenses **2.** (*comm.*) party: *— ad un contratto,* party to a contract **3.** (*chi annuncia*) spokesman (*pl.* spokesmen) **4.** *pl.* (*chi presenzia*) the people present, the people attending: *i partecipanti a un'adunanza, a un corso,* the people attending a meeting, a course; *i partecipanti al viaggio,* the travellers.

partecipàre, *v.i.* **1.** (*prender parte*) to participate (in sthg.), to share (sthg., in sthg.), to have a share (in sthg.), to take part (in sthg.): *hai partecipato a quel lavoro?,* did you participate in that work?; *ho partecipato al suo successo,* I have had a share in his success; *— a una conversazione, a un dibattito,* to participate (o to take part) in a conversation, in a debate; *— ad un affare,* to take part in a business deal; *— agli utili,* to share in the profits; *— al dolore, alla gioia, ai sentimenti di qlcu.,* to share s.o.'s grief, joy, feelings; *— alle spese,* to share the expenses; *— alle trattative,* to take part in the negotiations **2.** (*essere presente*) to attend (sthg.), to be present (at sthg.): *non ho potuto — al ricevimento perchè ero occupato,* I could not go to (o be present at) the party because I was busy; *partecipai a quella festa da ballo,* I was present at (o I went to) that ball; *— a un corso, un'adunanza,* to attend a course, a meeting **3.** (*avere in comune*) to have (sthg.) in common (with s.o., sthg.); to share (sthg.): *partecipa dei difetti dell'amico,* he shares his friend's faults; *partecipa molto della natura di suo fratello,* he has a great deal in common with his brother ‖ *v.t.* **1.** (*annunciare*) to announce, to inform (s.o. of sthg.), to acquaint (s.o. with sthg.): *mi partecipò le sue intenzioni,* he informed me of his intentions; *— un matrimonio,* to announce a wedding; *— un segreto a qlcu.,* to let s.o. in on a secret **2.** (*concedere, dispensare*) to grant (s.o. sthg.); to bestow (sthg. upon s.o.): *ha partecipato tutte le sue ricchezze ai poveri del villaggio,* he bestowed all his wealth upon the poor people of the village.

partecipatóre, *s.m.,* **partecipatrìce,** *s.f.* **1.** sharer, partaker **2.** (*comm.*) party **3.** (*chi annuncia*) announcer, informant **4.** *pl.* (*i presenti*) the people present.

partecipazióne, *s.f.* **1.** (*il prender parte*) participation, sharing: *— agli utili,* profit-sharing; *partecipazioni azionarie,* shareholdings; *— in società estere,* inter-ests in foreign companies; *ciò fu fatto senza la mia —,* this was done without my taking any part in it **2.** (*l'esser presente*) attendance, presence: *— a una riunione,* attendance (o presence) at a meeting **3.** (*annuncio*) announcement; (*annuncio scritto*) card: *— di morte,* announcement of death; *— di nozze,* wedding-announcement; (*per iscritto*) wedding-card.

partécipe, *ag.* **1.** participating, sharing, taking part **2.** (*informato*) acquainted, informed: *fare, rendere — qlcu. di ql.co.,* to acquaint s.o. with sthg.

parteggiaménto, *s.m.* (*rar.*) siding (with s.o., sthg.).

parteggiànte, *ag.* siding (with s.o., sthg.).

parteggiàre, *v.i.* to side (with s.o., sthg.), to take sides (with s.o., sthg.), to back (s.o., sthg.): *non voglio —,* I do not want to take sides.

partenogènesi, *s.f.* (*biol.*) parthenogenesis.

partenogenètico, *ag.* parthenogenetic.

Partenóne, *s.m.* (*arch. greca*) Parthenon.

Partènope, *no.pr.f.* (*mit.*) Parthenope.

partenopèo, *ag.* Parthenopean, Neapolitan.

partènte, *ag.* leaving, departing, starting ‖ *s.c.* person leaving, departing person.

partènza, *s.f.* **1.** departure, leaving: *alla sua —,* on his leaving (o departure); *l'ora della — da un luogo,* the time of departure from a place; *rimandare la —,* to put off one's departure **2.** (*di mezzi di trasporto*) departure: *l'aereo, la nave, il treno in — per Napoli,* the plane, the ship, the train leaving for Naples; *marciapiede di —,* (*in stazione*) departure platform; *ora della —,* time of departure; *segnale della —,* starting-signal; *il treno è in —,* the train is (just) leaving; *prendere il primo treno in —,* to take the first train leaving **3.** (*inizio di una corsa, di un movimento*) start: *— da fermi,* (*spor.*) standing-start; *— lanciata,* (*spor.*) flying-start; *falsa —,* (*spor.*) false start; *linea di —,* (*spor.*) starting-line; *punto di —,* starting-point (anche *fig.*): *questo fu il punto di — del nostro dibattito,* this was the starting- point for our discussion; *mancare la —,* to be left at the post.

parterre, *s.m.* parterre.

particèlla, *s.f.* particle: *— avverbiale,* (*gram.*) adverbial particle; *— con carica negativa,* (*fis.*) negatively charged particle; *— elementare,* (*fis.*) elementary particle; *— ionizzante,* (*fis. atomica*) ionizing particle.

participio, *s.m.* (*gram.*) participle: *— passato, presente,* past, present participle.

particola, *s.f.* (*eccl.*) host, particle.

particolàre, *ag.* **1.** (*speciale*) special, particular, peculiar: *un caso —,* a particular case; *cura —,* particular care; *un favore —,* a special favour; *missione —,* special mission; *segni particolari,* (*sul passaporto*) special peculiarities; *ho delle ragioni particolari per desiderarlo,* I have my own peculiar reasons for wishing it; *non ho niente di — da dirti,* I have nothing special to tell you; *partii senza alcuna ragione —,* I left for no particular reason; *quel modo di camminare gli è —,* that gait is peculiar to him **2.** (*privato*) particular, private, personal: *lettera —,* personal letter; *lezione —,* private lesson **3.** (*strano, bizzarro*) peculiar: *un carattere —,* a peculiar character; *idee particolari,* peculiar ideas **4.** (*accurato*) detailed, particular: *descrizione —,* detailed (o particular) description ‖ *s.m.* **1.** detail, particular: *— finito,* (*mec.*) finished part; *— lavorato,* (*mec.*) machined part; *dare i particolari di ql.co.,* to give particulars of sthg.; *entrare nei particolari,* to go into details; *eseguire un ordine in ogni —,* to execute an order in every particular ‖ *in —,* particularly (o in particular): *desidero questo in — per domani,* I want this particularly for tomorrow **2.** (*individuo*) individual: *agire in qualità di —,* to act in one's individual capacity (o merely as a private individual).

particolareggiàre, *v.i.* to go into minute details, to give minute details ‖ *v.t.* to specify, to detail.

particolareggiàto, *ag.* detailed, particularized, circumstantial: *racconto* —, detailed account.

particolarísmo, *s.m.* particularism.

particolarità, *s.f.* **1.** particularity, peculiarity **2.** (*stranezza, caratteristica*) peculiarity **3.** (*particolare*) detail, particular.

particolarménte, *av.* **1.** particularly; (*in particolare*) in particular: *mi piacerebbe parlare con lui* —, I should like to speak to him in particular **2.** (*specialmente*) particularly, (e)specially: *egli vi stima* —, he holds you in special honour; *questo pane non è* — *buono*, this bread is not particularly good.

partigiàna[1], *s.f.* (*arma*) partisan.

partigiàna[2], *s.f.* (*donna partigiana*) female partisan.

partigianería, *s.f.* partisanship.

partigiàno, *ag.* partisan; party (*attributivo*): *guerra partigiana*, partisan warfare; *politica partigiana*, party policy; *spirito* —, party spirit; *zelo* —, partisan zeal ‖ *s.m.* **1.** partisan, follower; (*fautore*) advocate, upholder, supporter: *un* — *della pace*, an advocate of peace; *i partigiani del re, del papa*, the supporters of the king, of the Pope **2.** (*guerrigliero*) partisan, guer(r)illa fighter: *andare coi partigiani*, to join the partisans.

partíre[1], *v.i.* **1.** to leave (a place), to go away; (*mettersi in moto*) to start, to set out, to set off; (*salpare*) to sail; (*decollare*) to take off: *l'aereo partì da Ciampino alle cinque*, the plane took off from Ciampino at five; *è ora che io parta*, it's time for me to get along (o to be going); *la nave era partita da Genova diretta a New York*, the ship had sailed from Genoa bound for New York; *partiamo domani*, we leave (o start) tomorrow; *partimmo presto*, we started (o set out) early; *sono contento di vederlo* —, I'm glad to see the back of him; *il treno non è ancora partito*, the train has not left (o started) yet; *tutti i corridori partirono al segnale*, all the competitors started when the signal was given; — *a cavallo*, to leave on horseback (o to ride off); — *a piedi*, to leave on foot; — *di sera, di giorno, di notte*, to leave in the evening, in the day-time, at night; — *in treno, in aereo, in piroscafo*, to leave by train, by plane, by ship; — *per l'estero*, to go abroad; — *per il fronte*, to leave for the front; — *per ignota destinazione*, to leave for an unknown destination; — *per un lungo viaggio*, to set off on a long journey ‖ *partì un colpo di fucile*, a shot was fired (o a gun went off) ‖ — *come una freccia*, to be off like a shot ‖ *far* — *un cavallo al galoppo*, to put a horse into a gallop; *far* — *un colpo di fucile, una freccia*, to shoot a bullet, an arrow; *far* — *un'automobile*, to start a car ‖ — *è un po' morire, prov.* to part is to die a little (o each parting is a little death) **2.** (*muovere, principiare*) to start (anche *fig.*): *due canali partono dalla città*, two canals begin (o start) from the town; *partendo da questo concetto, deduciamo che...*, starting from this principle we can deduce that...; *partiamo da punti di vista diversi*, we start from different standpoints; *la strada nuova parte dalla piazza*, the new road starts from the square ‖ *a* — *da*, beginning from (o as from): *a* — *da domani, ieri, oggi, venerdì*, beginning (o as) from tomorrow, yesterday, today, Friday; *a* — *dal 10 luglio questo treno verrà soppresso*, as from 10th July this train will be cancelled; *a* — *da quel momento nessuno è più entrato nella stanza*, from that time forth nobody has entered the room; *a* — *da questa pagina si tratta un nuovo argomento*, from this page onwards a new subject is dealt with ‖ *è partito dal niente*, he has risen from nothing **3.** (*provenire*) to come: *il grido partiva da una grotta*, the cry came from a cave; *un sospiro che parte dal cuore*, a sigh from the heart ‖ **partírsi**, *v.r.* (*allontanarsi, distaccarsi*) to part; to leave (s.o., sthg.): *alla morte l'anima si parte dal corpo*, at death the soul leaves the body; — *dalle persone care, dalla patria*, to leave one's loved ones, one's native country ‖ — *da questa vita, dal mondo*, to pass away.

partíre[2], *v.t.* (*letter.*) **1.** (*separare*) to separate, to divide: *fiume che parte, partisce una provincia dall'altra*, river that separates one province from another **2.** (*spartire*) to share (anche *fig.*): — *il bottino*, to share the booty; — *le gioie, i dolori di qlcu.*, to share s.o.'s joys, sorrows.

partíta, *s.f.* **1.** (*giocata*) game; (*gara*) match: *una* — *a carte, bocce, scacchi*, a game of cards, bowls, chess; *una* — *a tennis*, a game of tennis (o a tennis-match); *una* — *di caccia*, a hunting-party; *una* — *di calcio*, a football (o soccer)-match; *fare una* —, to play a game; *perdere, vincere una* —, to lose, to win a game ‖ — *di piacere*, outing (o pleasure-trip) ‖ — *d'onore*, duel ‖ *dar* — *vinta a qlcu., fig.* to give in to s.o. ‖ *essere della* —, to be one of the party: *vuoi essere della* —?, will you join us? ‖ *perdere, vincere la* —, *fig.* to lose, to win **2.** (*comm.*) (*quantitativo di merce*) lot, stock: — *di grano*, stock of wheat; *a, in, per partite*, by lots; *in grosse, piccole partite*, in large, small lots; *collocare una* —, to dispose of a lot; *spedire per nave una grossa* — *di...*, to ship a large quantity of... **3.** (*comm.*) (*di contabilità*) entry: — *di compensazione*, counter-item; — *semplice, doppia*, single, double entry: *contabilità in* — *semplice, doppia*, single-entry, double-entry book-keeping; *la* — *è ancora scoperta, in sospeso*, the balance is still unpaid; *cancellare una* —, to cancel an entry ‖ *è una* — *chiusa*, it's settled once and for all (o it's a closed chapter) ‖ *giocare a* — *doppia*, to play a double game **4.** (*parte di battente di porta, di finestra, ecc.*) panel.

partitaménte, *av.* **1.** separately, distinctly **2.** (*punto per punto*) point by point.

partitàrio, *s.m.* (*comm.*) ledger.

partitívo, *ag.s.m.* (*gram.*) partitive: *articolo, pronome* —, partitive article, pronoun.

partíto, *ag.* **1.** separated, divided **2.** (*arald.*) party: *scudo* —, party shield ‖ *s.m.* **1.** (*parte politica*) party: *il* — *al potere, all'opposizione*, the party in power, the opposition (party); — *comunista, conservatore, liberale*, Communist, Conservative, Liberal Party; *i partiti di centro, di destra, di sinistra*, the Centre, the Right, the Left; *guerra di partiti*, party strife; *uomo di* —, party-man; *fu espulso dal* —, he was expelled from his party; *questo* — *ha molti iscritti*, this party has many members; *abbandonare il* —, to desert one's party; *iscriversi a un* —, to join a party ‖ *ha vinto il* — *dell'ordine*, the party of order won **2.** (*risoluzione*) resolution, decision; (*alternativa*) alternative: *il miglior* — *sarebbe di rinunciarvi*, the best thing would be to give it up; *non so che* — *prendere*, I can't make up my mind what to do (o I don't know what to do); *prese il* — *di andarsene*, he made up his mind to go; *s'è appigliato al miglior* —, he made the best choice ‖ *a, per* — *preso*, deliberately ‖ *mettere capo, cervello a* —, to turn over a new leaf ‖ *prendere* — *per qlcu.*, to side with s.o.; *prendere* — *contro qlcu.*, to take sides against s.o. **3.** (*condizione, patto*) condition: *non volle accettare a nessun* —, he did not want to accept by any means; *questo è il* — *che ti propongo*, this is my proposal **4.** (*occasione di matrimonio*) match: *ella, egli è un buon* —, she, he is a good match; *le si presentò un buon* —, *ma se lo è lasciato sfuggire*, a good match was offered to her, but she let it slip **5.** (*situazione*) situation: *ridursi a mal* —, to be in a bad situation (o in a bad way) **6.** (*vantaggio*) advantage, profit, benefit: *trarre* — *da ql.co.*, to| take advantage of sthg.

partitúra, *s.f.* **1.** (*mus.*) score **2.** (*divisione dei prodotti della terra*) division (of agricultural produce).

partitóre, *s.m.*, **partitríce**, *s.f.* divider.

partizióne, *s.f.* partition, division.

Pàrto[1], *ag.s.m.* Parthian ‖ *la freccia del* —, a Parthian shot (o shaft).

pàrto[2], *s.m.* **1.** childbirth, birth, delivery: — *facile, difficile*, easy, difficult delivery; — *gemellare*, twin (o double) birth; — *laborioso*, laborious delivery; — *prematuro*, premature birth; *le doglie del* —, labour; *nati ad un* —, born at one birth; *sala* —, delivery room (*o* labour room); *assistere ad un* —, to attend a delivery; *morire di* —, to die in childbirth 2. (*di animali*) delivery, birth, dropping 3. *fig.* (*prodotto*) product; work: *un* — *del cervello*, a product of the brain; *un* — *dell'immaginazione*, a product of the imagination; — *poetico*, *letterario*, poetical, literary work.

partorinte, *ag.* parturient || *s.f.* lying-in woman, woman in childbed.

partorire, *v.t.* 1. to bear, to give birth to (a child), to bring forth, to be delivered of (a child): *di giorno in giorno si aspetta che partorisca*, her confinement is expected from one day to another; *gli ha partorito due figli*, she has borne him two children || *la montagna ha partorito il topolino*, (*iron.*) the mountain has brought forth a mouse 2. (*di animale in genere*) to bring forth, to give birth to (one's little one); to drop, to throw; (*della cagna*) to pup, to whelp; (*della cavalla*) to foal; (*della gatta*) to kitten; (*della mucca*) to calve; (*dell'orsa, della volpe*) to cub; (*della pecora*) to lamb; (*della scrofa*) to pig, to farrow; (*di bestia feroce in genere*) to whelp, to cub 3. *fig.* (*produrre*) to beget: *la violenza partorisce l'odio*, violence begets hate.

parvènte, *ag.* (*letter.*) apparent; visible || *s.m.* (*letter.*) 1. (*apparenza*) appearance 2. (*parere*) opinion, mind.

parure, *s.f.* set.

parvenu, *s.m.* parvenu, upstart, self-made person.

parvènza, *s.f.* 1. (*apparenza*) appearance, aspect 2. (*ombra, mostra*) show, shadow: *nessuna* — *di verità, di ragione*, no show of truth, of reason.

parziàle, *ag.* 1. (*che favorisce una delle parti*) partial: *critico* —, partial (*o* unfair) critic; *essere* — *verso qlcu.*, to be partial to s.o. 2. (*con pregiudizi*) biased 3. (*che riguarda una parte*) partial, incomplete: *eclissi* —, partial eclipse; *informazione* —, one-sided (*o* partial) information; *pagamento* —, part payment; *paralisi* —, partial paralysis; *successo* —, partial success.

parzialeggiàre, *v.i.* to be partial.

parzialità, *s.f.* partiality, favouritism.

parzialménte, *av.* 1. (*con favoritismo*) partially 2. (*ingiustamente*) unfairly 3. (*in parte*) partly, partially.

Pascariéllo, *s.m.* (*st. teat.*) "Pascariello" (Neapolitan mask).

pàscere, *v.i.* to graze, to pasture || *v.t.* 1. to graze, to pasture; to feed on (sthg.) 2. (*condurre al pascolo*) to graze, to pasture: — *le mucche*, to graze (*o* to pasture) cows 3. *fig.* (*nutrire*) to feed, to nourish: — *la mente di lettura*, to feed the mind with reading; — *gli occhi*, to feed (*o* to feast) one's eyes || **pàscersi**, *v.r.* to feed (on sthg.) (anche *fig.*): — *di carne*, to feed on meat; — *di illusioni*, to feed on hopes.

pascià, *s.m.* pasha, pacha: — *di una, due, tre code*, pasha of one, two, three tails || *fare il* —, to live like a lord; *starsene come un* —, to be as snug as a bug in a rug.

pascialàto, *s.m.* pashalic, pachalic.

pasciòna, *s.f.* 1. (*regione ricca di pascolo*) rich grazing land 2. (*cibo ricco e abbondante*) rich food 3. (*prosperità*) prosperity, abundance.

pasciulì, *s.m.* (*profumo intenso di muschio*) patchouli.

pasciúto, *ag.* nourished, fed: *ben* —, well-fed.

pascolàre, *v.i.* to graze, to pasture, to browse: *le mucche pascolano*, the cows are grazing (*o* pasturing); — *in un prato*, to browse in a meadow || *v.t.* to graze, to pasture: — *il gregge*, to pasture the flock || **pascolàrsi**, *v.r.* (*rar.*) to feed (on sthg.).

pascolativo, *ag.* pasturable; pasture (*attributivo*).

pàscolo, *s.m.* 1. pasture: *terreno da* —, grazing ground; *quel monte ha dei buoni pascoli*, that mountain has good pastures; *condurre il gregge al* —, to lead the flock to pasture; *essere al* —, to be grazing ||

il diritto di —, right of common; *servitù di* —, grazing rights 2. *fig.* (*nutrimento*) food: — *della mente*, food for the mind; *dar* — *all'invidia*, to stir up envy.

Pasífae, *no.pr.f.* (*mit.*) Pasiphae.

Pàsqua, *s.f.* (*dei Cristiani*) Easter; (*degli ebrei*) Passover: *giorno, settimana, vacanze di* —, Easter Day, week, holidays; *uovo di* —, Easter egg || — *delle rose*, (*Pentecoste*) Whitsunday (*o* Pentecost); — *di ceppo*, (*Natale*) Christmas || *buona* —, happy Easter || *essere contento come una* —, to be as happy as can be (*o* as a king *o* as a sand-boy) || *far* —, to celebrate (sthg.) heartily || *fare la* —, to do one's Easter duties.

pasquàle, *ag.* (*della Pasqua cristiana*) Easter (*attributivo*); paschal; (*della Pasqua ebraica*) paschal: *agnello* —, paschal lamb; *candela* —, paschal candle; *precetto* —, Easter precept; *uova pasquali*, Easter eggs; *vacanze pasquali*, Easter holidays.

pasquaròsa, *s.f.* (*Pentecoste*) Whitsunday, Pentecost.

pasquèlla, *s.f.* (*Epifania*) Epiphany.

pasquinàta, *s.f.* lampoon, pasquinade: *scrittore di pasquinate*, lampooner (*o* satirist *o* pasquinader); *scrivere, comporre pasquinate*, to lampoon (*o* to pasquinade).

Pasquíno, *no.pr.m.* (*st.*) Pasquin, Pasquil.

passàbile, *ag.* passable, tolerable, fairly good.

passabilménte, *av.* passably, tolerably, fairly well.

passacàglia, *s.f.*, **passagàllo**, *s.m.* (*mus.*) passacaglia, passacaglio.

passàggio, *s.m.* 1. passage, passing; (*traversata*) crossing: — *delle Alpi*, crossing of the Alps; — *di un fiume*, crossing of a river; — *di uccelli*, migration of birds; *il* — *di quel fiume è facile*, that river is easy to cross; *tutti facevano ala al suo* —, everybody moved aside as he passed || *ostacolare il* —, to stop the traffic 2. (*transito*) transit, passage: *uccello di* —, bird of passage; *viaggiatore di* —, traveller passing through || *di* —, (*di transizione*) of transition; (*incidentalmente*) incidentally (*o* in passing) || *diritto, servitù di* —, (*dir.*) right of way || *il gran* —, (*la morte*) the passing away || *vietato il* —, no transit (*o* no thoroughfare) 3. (*luogo per cui si passa*) passage, way; passage way: — *ad arco*, archway; — *coperto*, covered way; — *fra i monti*, mountain pass; *un* — *lungo e stretto*, a long and narrow passage; — *per pedoni*, pedestrian-crossing; — *sotterraneo*, subway; *qui ostruiamo il* —, we are in the way here; *aprirsi un* — *a forza*, to force a way through; *impedire il* —, to block (*o* to stand in) the way || — *a livello*, level-crossing || — *a Nord-Ovest*, North-West passage 4. (*trasporto passeggero su nave*) passage; (*su altro veicolo*) lift: *posso darle un* —?, can I give you a lift?; *guadagnarsi il* — *lavorando*, to work one's passage; *prenotare un* —, to book a passage 5. (*mus. lett.*) passage: *questo* — *è estremamente difficile*, this passage is extremely difficult.

passamanería, *s.f.* 1. (*fabbrica di passamani*) passementerie factory; (*negozio di passamani*) passementerie shop 2. (*passamani*) trimming(s), passementerie.

passamàno[1], *s.m.* passing from hand to hand: *fare il* —, to make a human chain.

passamàno[2], *s.m.* (*fettuccia per guarnizione*) braid.

passamontàgna, *s.m.* Balaclava (helmet).

passànte, *s.m.* 1. passer-by: *tutti i passanti sembravano aver fretta*, all the passers-by seemed to be in a hurry 2. (*di cinghia, cintura, ecc.*) loop.

passapòrto, *s.m.* passport: — *falso*, forged passport; *il mio* — *scade in ottobre*, my passport expires in October; *chiedere il* —, to apply for a passport; *concedere il* —, to grant a passport; *mettere il visto su un* —, to visa (*o* to put a visa on) a passport; *negare il* — *a qlcu.*, to refuse s.o. a passport; *rinnovare il* —, to renew one's passport.

passàre, *v.i.* 1. to pass, to proceed; to go along, to go by: *egli passò senza fermarsi*, he passed without stopping; *in questa strada non passa mai anima viva*, nobody ever goes along this street; *lasciami* —, let me pass; *la luce passava attraverso le persiane*, the light came in through the shutters; *la malattia è passata attraverso tutti gli stadi*, the illness passed through all its phases (o stages); *questo filo è troppo grosso per — per la cruna dell'ago*, this thread is too thick to go through the eye of the needle; *siamo passati per il centro della città*, we passed (o went) through the centre of the city; *la strada passa attraverso il bosco*, the road passes (o runs o goes) through the wood; — *al nemico*, to go over to the enemy; — *da una condizione ad un'altra*, to change from one condition to another; — *di padre in figlio*, to be handed down from father to son; — *in altre mani*, to pass into other hands ‖ *avrà trent'anni e passa*, he must be over thirty; *sarà due chili e passa*, it is probably two kilos or more ‖ *non posso — sopra a tutti questi dettagli*, I can't pass over (o overlook) all these details ‖ *passa via!*, get (o go) away! (o off with you!) ‖ *passi la sua ignoranza ma non i suoi vizi*, I am prepared to overlook his ignorance but not his vices ‖ — *a miglior vita*, to pass away (o to breathe one's last) ‖ — *in fanteria*, (*sparire*) to be knocked off (o pinched) ‖ — *inosservato*, to go (o to pass) unnoticed ‖ — *di mente*, to pass (o to go) out of one's mind; — *per la mente*, to cross (o to come into) one's mind ‖ *far, lasciar —*, to let in ‖ *acqua passata non macina più*, prov. let bygones be bygones **2.** (*trascorrere*) to pass, to elapse, to go by: *come passa il tempo!*, how time f.ies!; *i giorni passarono*, the days went by; *la gioventù passa presto*, youth is fleeting; *man mano che passano gli anni...*, as years go by...; *il tempo non passa mai quando si aspetta qlcu.*, time goes so slowly when one is waiting for s.o. **3.** (*cessare*) to pass, to cease: *il mal di denti mi è passato*, my toothache has passed off (o gone); *una moda che passa*, a passing fashion; *la sua collera passò presto*, his anger soon passed (o cooled); *il temporale è passato*, the storm is over (o has passed); — *di moda*, to go out of fashion ‖ *passerà anche questa*, it won't last for ever; *tutto passa*, everything comes to an end **4.** (*andare, venire*) to call on (s.o.), to call at (a place): *devo — dal suo ufficio*, I must call at his office; *è passato il lattaio?*, has the milkman been?; *la nave non passa da Genova*, the ship doesn't call at Genoa; *passerà di qui fra poco*, he will come here soon (o before long); *passerò a prenderti*, I'll call for you; *passerò da te questa sera*, I'll call on you to-night; — *da un cliente*, to call on a client **5.** (*diventare*) to become: *passò capitano*, he was promoted captain; — *in proverbio*, to become a proverb **6.** (*essere reputato*) to be believed, to be considered: *passa per bella, intelligente*, she is considered (o thought) beautiful, intelligent; — *per certo*, to be generally believed; — *per ricco*, to be thought rich ‖ *far — qlcu. per*, to pass s.o. off as **7.** (*essere accettato, aver corso*) to be passed, to get through: *il progetto di legge passò il mese scorso*, the bill was passed last month; — *ad un esame*, to get through an examination **8.** (*intercorrere*) to be: *passa una gran differenza*, there is a great difference **9.** (*di cibi*) to go bad; (*essere troppo cotto*) to be overcooked **10.** (*a carte*) to pass: *passo*, I pass ‖ *v.t.* **1.** to pass, to go beyond (sthg.); (*attraversare*) to pass through (sthg.), to cross: *passò il fiume*, he crossed the river; *quella signora ha passato i cinquant'anni*, that lady is over fifty; *questo pacco passa il peso*, this parcel is overweight; *il ragazzo non passò la classe*, the boy didn't go up; — *una frontiera, un fiume*, to cross a frontier, a river ‖ — *i limiti*, to go too far (o to overstep the limit) ‖ — *in rivista*, to review ‖ — *il Rubicone*, to cross the Rubicon ‖ *passarla liscia, bella*, to get away with sthg. (o to go scot-free) **2.** (*trascorrere*) to pass, to spend: — *il tempo*, to while away the time: *passa il tempo nell'ozio*, he idles his time away; *passai l'estate a Londra*, I spent the summer in London; *passeremo il Natale insieme*, we'll spend Christmas together; *sto passando un brutto periodo*, I'm having (o going through) a bad time ‖ *me la sono passata molto bene*, I have had a very good time ‖

passarsela bene, male, (*finanziariamente*) to be well off, badly off **3.** (*far passare, far scorrere*) to pass, to carry across: *gli passò la mano sui capelli*, she ran her fingers through his hair; — *una corda intorno a ql.co.*, to pass a rope round sthg.; — *un filo per la cruna dell'ago*, to pass a thread through the eye of a needle (o to thread a needle); — *uno straccio sulla lavagna*, to pass a cloth over (o to wipe) the blackboard ‖ *non gliene passa una*, he doesn't overlook a thing ‖ — *parola*, to pass the word on (o round) ‖ — *ql.co. sotto silenzio*, to pass over sthg. in silence **4.** (*dare*) to pass, to give, to hand: *l'albergo non passa le salviette*, the hotel does not supply towels; *guarda queste fotografie e passale agli altri*, look at these photographs and pass them on to the others; *mi passa diecimila lire alla settimana*, he allows (o gives) me ten thousand lire a week; — *un ordine*, (*comm.*) to place an order; — *la palla*, (*spor.*) to pass the ball **5.** (*sopportare*) to undergo, to pass through (sthg.): *ha passato un mucchio di guai*, she has gone through (o she has had) a lot of trouble; *ne ho passate tante, te lo assicuro*, I have been through a lot, I can tell you; *passarne di tutti i colori*, to go through thick and thin **6.** (*trafiggere*) to pass through; to run through, to transfix: *lo passò da parte a parte*, he ran him through ‖ *mi passa il cuore*, it breaks my heart ‖ — *per le armi*, to execute **7.** (*approvare, promuovere*) to pass: *ho passato tutti i miei allievi*, I have passed all my pupils; — *un progetto di legge*, to pass a bill **8.** (*filtrare*) to strain; (*setacciare*) to sift, to sieve: — *la verdura*, to strain the vegetables.

passàta, *s.f.* **1.** (*passaggio*) passage; (*venuta*) coming: *la — dei barbari*, the coming of the barbarians; *una — di uccelli*, a flight of birds ‖ *una — di pioggia*, a shower (of rain) ‖ *a tutta —*, (*rar.*) continually ‖ *di —*, by the way (o incidentally) **2.** (*traccia della selvaggina*) trail **3.** (*scorsa*) look, glance: *dare una — a un libro*, to have a look (o a glance) at a book **4.** (*di vernice*) coat **5.** *una — di spazzola*, a brush; *dovresti dare una — di ferro a questo vestito*, you should pass the iron over this dress **6.** (*cuc.*) mash, soup: *una — di patate*, mashed potatoes; — *di piselli*, pea-soup **7.** (*a carte*) pass **8.** (*scherma*) pass, thrust **9.** (*equitazione*) passade **10.** (*artigl.*) penetration **11.** (*agr.*) ridge **12.** (*mec.*) pass, traverse.

passatèmpo, *s.m.* pastime: — *preferito*, hobby: *il — preferito di mio fratello è la fotografia*, my brother's hobby is photography; *la lettura e la musica sono i migliori passatempi*, reading and music are the best pastimes; *lo faceva così per —*, he did it as a pastime.

passatísta, *s.c.* traditionalist.

passàto, *ag.* **1.** past; (*scorso*) last: *gli anni, i giorni passati*, past years, days; *le generazioni passate*, past generations; *nei tempi passati*, in times past (o gone by); *la settimana passata*, last week ‖ *ha quarant'anni passati*, he is over forty ‖ *sono le sei passate*, it is past six o' clock **2.** (*avvizzito*) faded: *bellezza passata*, faded beauty **3.** (*gram.*) past: *participio —*, past (o perfect) participle ‖ *s.m.* **1.** past: *una persona con un —*, a person with a past; *il — non torna più*, the past can never return; *non conosco il suo —*, I don't know his past ‖ *metti una pietra sul —*, let bygones be bygones **2.** (*gram.*) past, perfect: — *prossimo*, present perfect; — *remoto*, (simple) past **3.** (*cuc.*) mash, soup: — *di patate*, mashed potatoes; — *di piselli, fagioli*, pea-soup, bean-soup; — *di verdura*, vegetable soup.

passatóia, *s.f.* carpet; (*di scale*) stair-carpet.

passatóio, *s.m.* stepping-stone.

passatóre, *s.m.* ferryman (*pl.* ferrymen).

passatúra, *s.f.* darn.

passavànti, *s.m.* (*mar.*) gangway.

passeggèro, *ag.* passing; transient, fleeting, short-lived; momentary: *bellezza passeggera*, transient beauty; *capriccio —*, passing fancy (o whim); *dolore —*, momentary pain; *felicità passeggera*, fleeting (o transient) happiness; *nuvole passeggere*, passing clouds; *successo*

—, short-lived (o transitory) success ‖ s.m. 1. (viaggiatore) passenger; traveller: — clandestino, stowaway; passeggeri di prima classe, first-class passengers; passeggeri di terza classe, (mar.) steerage passengers; la nave imbarcò cinquecento passeggeri, the ship took on five hundred passengers 2. (rar.) (passante) passer-by.

passeggiàre, v.i. to walk, to take a walk, to go for a walk; to stroll: passeggiammo per un'ora lungo i viali, we walked (o strolled) along the avenues for an hour; la sera passeggio a lungo per i campi, in the evening I go for long walks in the fields; — per la strada, to take a walk in the street (o to stroll about the streets); — sulla spiaggia, to walk along the beach ‖ v.t. 1. to walk: — un cavallo, to walk a horse; — il giardino, to walk round the garden 2. (mus.): — con le dita le corde di uno strumento, to run one's fingers over the strings of an instrument.

passeggiàta, s.f. 1. (a piedi) walk; (in automobile, carrozza) drive, ride; (a cavallo) ride; (in bicicletta) (bicycle) ride: una — in montagna, a walk in the mountains; — militare, route march; (andare a) fare una — a piedi, to go for (o to take) a walk; portare un bambino a fare una —, to take a child out for a walk 2. (luogo dove si passeggia) (public) walk; (lungomare, lungolago) promenade: in quella località ci sono splendide passeggiate, there are beautiful walks round there; l'ho incontrato sulla — di San Remo, I met him on the promenade at San Remo.

passeggiatóre, s.m. walker ‖ **passeggiatrìce**, s.f. 1. walker 2. (prostituta) street-walker.

passeggièro, V. **passeggèro**.

passéggio, s.m. 1. (passeggiata) walk: il — serale, the evening promenade; vieni a — con me, come for a walk with me; andare a —, to go for a walk (o a stroll); condurre qlcu. a —, to take s.o. out for a walk; essere a —, to be out walking 2. (luogo dove si passeggia) (public) walk; (lungomare, lungolago) promenade: — affollato, crowded promenade 3. (la gente che passeggia) promenaders (pl.): mi godevo il — sul corso, I was enjoying the view of people promenading (o strolling) up and down the main street.

passe-partout, s.m. 1. passe-partout, master-key 2. (cornice) passe-partout.

pàssera¹, s.f. 1. (ornit.) (hen-)sparrow 2. — di mare, (ittiol.) flounder.

pàssera², ag.: uva —, raisin.

passeràcei, s.m.pl. (ornit.) Passeres.

passeràceo, ag. passerine.

passeràio, s.m. 1. twittering, chirping 2. (cicaleccio) chattering.

passerèlla, s.f. 1. (ponte pedonale) footbridge; (provvisoria) trestle-bridge: — d'imbarco, (mar.) gangway (o gang-board o gangplank) 2. (edil.) gangway, platform 3. (di teatro) (forestage) parade; (per indossatrici) parade.

pàssero, s.m. (cock-) sparrow.

passeròtto, s.m. 1. (piccolo passero) little sparrow 2. (svista) oversight; (errore di stampa) misprint.

passìbile, ag. 1. (dir.) liable (to sthg.): — di espulsione, liable to expulsion; — di multa, liable to fine; — di punizione, liable to punishment 2. (soggetto a soffrire) passible, liable to suffer.

passibilità, s.f. 1. (dir.) liability (to sthg.) 2. (l'essere soggetto a patire) passibility.

passiflòra, s.f. (bot.) passiflora, passion-flower.

passim, av. (lat.) passim: vedi Virgilio, Eneide, —, see Virgil, Aeneid, passim.

passìno, s.m. strainer.

passionàle, ag. 1. (appassionato) passionate: temperamento —, passionate nature 2. (di passione) of passion: delitto —, crime of passion; dramma —, drama of passion; romanzo —, novel of passion.

passionalità, s.f. passionateness.

passionàrio, s.m. (eccl.) passionary, book of martyrs.

passionataménte, av. emotionally.

passionàto, ag. emotional.

passióne, s.f. 1. passion: — per la botanica, per la musica, per la pittura, passion for botany, for music, for painting; animo libero da —, mind free of passion; l'impeto della —, the force of passion; la — gli oscurava la mente, passion darkened his mind; è schiavo delle passioni, he is the slave of his passions; era accecato dalla —, he was blinded by passion; il giuoco è diventato la sua —, gambling has become a passion with him; ha — per lo studio, he is very keen on study (o he has a passion for study); quella donna è stata la — della sua vita, that woman was the passion of his life; lo sport è la mia —, sport is my passion; dominare, frenare le passioni, to control, to bridle one's passions; soddisfare le passioni, to satisfy (o gratify) one's passions; non aver — a niente, not to take an interest in anything; prendere — a ql.co., to take a liking to sthg. 2. (afflizione) anxiety, affliction, suffering, pain: è una — vederlo lavorare, it is painful to see him work; ho passato un giorno di —, I have had a day of suffering; suo figlio la fa morire di —, her son is breaking her heart; darsi —, to eat one's heart out (o to worry oneself sick) 3. (relig.) passion, martyrdom: la — di Nostro Signore, the Passion of Christ; la — di San Sebastiano, the martyrdom of St. Sebastian; la « Passione secondo S. Matteo » di Bach è forse la più pregevole opera del genere, Bach's " Passion according to St. Matthew " (o Bach's " Matthew Passion ") is the finest work of its kind ‖ fior di —, passion-flower ‖ la Settimana di —, Passion Week.

passionìsta, s.m. (eccl.) Passionist.

passìto, s.m. " passito " (raisin wine).

passivaménte, av. passively.

passività, s.f. 1. passivity, passiveness 2. (comm.) liabilities (pl.): essere in —, to show a loss (o fam. to be in the red)

passìvo, ag. 1. passive: resistenza passiva, passive resistance; ubbidienza passiva, passive obedience; voce passiva, (gram.) passive voice 2. (comm.): cambiali passive, bills payable; interessi passivi, interest allowed (o paid); operazione di credito passiva, borrowing operation (o transaction) ‖ s.m. 1. (gram.) passive 2. (comm.) liabilities (pl.): — di poco inferiore all'attivo, negligible liability; l'ammontare del —, amount (o extent) of liabilities; attivo e —, assets and liabilities; elenco, prospetto dell'attivo e del —, statement of assets and liabilities; il — supera l'attivo, liabilities exceed the assets; l'attivo e il — del mastro quadrano, the ledger is found in balance; accertare il —, to ascertain (o to find out o to search out) liabilities.

pàsso¹, s.m. 1. step: un — lungo, a stride; alcuni passi più avanti, a few steps further; il bambino mosse i primi passi, the baby took his first steps; fa solo pochi passi, he can only walk a few steps; ho udito alcuni passi in giardino, I heard a few steps in the garden; cambiare, perdere, rompere il —, to change, to fall out of, to break step; camminare con lenti, piccoli passi, to walk with slow, short steps; dirigere, volgere i propri passi verso..., to turn one's steps towards...: diresse, volse i propri passi verso casa, he turned his steps homeward(s); fare un — avanti, indietro, to take a step forward, backward (anche fig.); fare un — falso, to stumble; fig. to make a false step (o to make a faux pas o to blunder); procedere a piccoli passi, to toddle along; segnare il —, to mark time (anche fig.) ‖ — —, very slowly ‖ a —, step by step ‖ un — di valzer, a waltz step ‖ a due passi da casa, within a stone's throw from home; la mia casa è qui a due passi, my house is only a few steps away ‖ a grandi passi, striding: camminava a grandi passi verso la scuola, he was striding to school; l'inverno s'avvicina a grandi passi, winter is coming on apace; allontanarsi a grandi passi, to stride away ‖ a ogni —, at every moment ‖ andiamo a fare due passi, let's go for a little walk ‖ *è un — che devo fare*, it's something I must do ‖ *il matrimonio è un grande —*, marriage is a big step ‖ *non ha mosso un — per aiutarci*, he didn't move a step to help us ‖ *non so decidermi a questo —*, I can't make up my mind about this ‖ *questo è il primo — verso l'indipendenza*, this is the first step towards independence ‖ *essere, non essere al —*, to be in step, out of step ‖ *fare passi da gigante*, to take great strides ‖ *fare il — secondo la gamba*, to cut one's coat according to one's cloth ‖ *fare dei passi per ottenere ql.co.*, to take steps to get sthg. ‖ *fare dei passi per qlcu.*, to take trouble for s.o. ‖ *tornare sui propri passi*, to retrace one's steps (*anche fig.*) ‖ *il — più difficile è quello dell'uscio, prov.* it's only the first step which counts (*o the beginning is half the battle*) 2. (*andatura*) pace, step: *a — d'uomo, di lumaca*, at a walking, snail's pace; *ella cammina con — svelto*, she walks with a rapid step; *ha un — vacillante*, he walks with a hesitating (*o uncertain*) step; *lo riconosco sempre dal suo — pesante*, I always recognize him from his heavy tread; *affrettare il —*, to quicken one's pace (*o to hurry up*); *camminare di buon —*, to walk at a good pace; *rallentare il —*, to slacken one's pace (*o to slow down*); *tenere il —*, *stare al — di qlcu.*, to keep pace (*o to keep up*) with s.o. ‖ *— di carica*, (*mil.*) double: *avanzare a — di carica*, to double ‖ *— romano*, goose-step ‖ *—, trotto, galoppo del cavallo*, pace, trot, gallop of a horse ‖ *al —!*, in step!; (*segnaletica stradale*) drive slowly ‖ *di questo — sarai presto in miseria*, at this rate you'll soon be ruined 3. (*orma*) (foot)step, footprint: *si vedevano dei passi sulla neve*, some footprints were visible on the snow; *seguire i passi di qlcu.*, to follow in s.o.'s footsteps (*o tracks*) 4. (*brano*) passage: *commentare un —*, to comment on a passage; *leggere un — della Bibbia*, to read a passage from the Bible 5. (*geog.*) pass: *il — del Maloia*, Maloja Pass ‖ *il — delle Termopili*, the Pass of Thermopylae 6. (*tec.*) (*di elica, di vite*) pitch; (*ind. tessile*) shed; (*cine.*) gauge: *pellicola a — normale, ridotto*, standard, reduced gauge film.

pàsso², *s.m.* (*passaggio*) passage: *aprirsi il — attraverso ql.co.*, to make one's way through sthg.; *dare il —*, to give way; *ostruire il —*, to block the passage; *permettere, proibire il — a qlcu.*, to allow, to forbid entry to s.o. ‖ *uccelli di —*, birds of passage.

pàsso³, *ag.* (*appassito*) dried; withered ‖ *uva passa*, raisin.

pàsta, *s.f.* 1. (*di pane o dolci, che si lavora con le mani*) dough; (*di dolce che va lavorato in un recipiente*) batter: *— frolla*, shortbread; *— matta*, heavy dough; *— sfoglia*, puff-pastry; *lavorare la —*, to knead the dough ‖ *una persona di — frolla, fig.* a spineless person ‖ *un uomo di buona —, fig.* a good-natured man ‖ *è un uomo di grossa —, fig.* he is a crude fellow ‖ *avere le mani in —, fig.* to have a finger in the pie 2. (*pasticcino*) cake; pastry; (*amer.*) cookie: *comperare delle paste*, to buy some pastries 3. (*per minestre*) " pasta ", paste: *— all'uovo*, " pasta " containing eggs (*o egg* -noodles); *— fatta in casa*, home-made " pasta "; *oggi a mezzogiorno ho mangiato — asciutta*, today I had " pasta " for lunch 4. (*qualsiasi sostanza molle, ammassata come pasta*) paste; pulp: *— d'acciughe*, anchovy -paste; *— dentifricia*, tooth-paste (*o dental paste*); *— di carta*, pulp; *— di legno*, wood-pulp; *— di mandorle*, almond paste; *— di stracci*, rag-pulp.

pastàio, *s.m.* 1. (*chi fabbrica pasta*) Italian " pasta " maker 2. (*chi vende pasta*) Italian " pasta " seller.

pasteggiàbile, *ag.*: *vino —*, table-wine.

pasteggiàre, *v.i.* to eat: *— a champagne*, to drink champagne with one's meals.

pastèlla, *V.* pastétta.

pastellísta, *s.c.* (*pitt.*) pastellist.

pastèllo¹, *s.m.* (*pitt.*) pastel: *colori —*, pastel colours: *disegno, quadro a —*, pastel; *matita a —*, pastel; *verde —*, pastel green; *dipingere a —*, to draw in pastel.

pastèllo², *s.m.* (*bot.*) woad, pastel.

pastétta, *s.f.* 1. (*cuc.*) batter 2. (*truffa nelle elezioni*) gerrymander.

pastícca, *s.f.* tablet, lozenge: *— alla menta*, peppermint tablet; *— per la tosse*, cough-lozenge.

pasticcère, *s.m.* confectioner.

pasticcería, *s.f.* 1. (*negozio*) confectioner's (shop) 2. (*paste e dolciumi*) confectionery.

pasticciàre, *v.t.* to mess up, to make a mess of (sthg.); to bungle: *mi ha pasticciato il lavoro a maglia*, she has made a mess of my knitting ‖ *v.i.* to make a mess; to mess around: *perchè hai pasticciato nelle mie carte?*, why have you made a mess of my papers?; *perchè pasticci nella mia camera?*, why are you messing around in my room?.

pasticciàto, *ag.* (*cuc.*) seasoned with butter, cheese and ragout.

pasticcière, *s.m.* confectioner.

pasticcíno, *s.m.* pastry; cake; tartlet; (*amer.*) cookie: *ho fatto una scorpacciata di pasticcini*, I've stuffed myself with pastries.

pasticcio, *s.m.* 1. (*cuc.*) pie: *— di carne, di pollo*, meat-, chicken-pie 2. (*lavoro mal fatto*) mess; (*di quadro*) daub 3. (*intrico, imbroglio*) mess; (*situazione insidiosa*) scrape: *che (bel) —!*, what a (fine) mess!; *essere nei pasticci*, to be in trouble (*o in a fix*); (*essere perplesso*) to be in a quandary; *mettersi nei pasticci*, to get oneself into a scrape; *uscire dai pasticci*, to get out of a scrape.

pasticcióna, *s.f.*, **pasticcióne**, *s.m.* 1. bungler; muddler; messer 2. (*imbrattatele*) dauber.

pastifício, *s.m.* " pasta " factory.

pastíglia, *s.f.* 1. lozenge, pastil, pastille, tablet; (*pillola*) pill: *— contro la tosse*, cough-drop (*o cough-pastil*); *— di cioccolato*, chocolate pastilles (*o drops*); *— di menta*, peppermint-lozenge 2. (*clett.*) paste.

pastinàca, *s.f.* 1. (*bot.*) parsnip 2. (*ittiol.*) trygon.

pàsto, *s.m.* meal: *un — copioso*, a square (*o hearty*) meal; *— freddo*, cold spread; *un — leggero*, a light meal; *ora dei pasti*, meal time; *prima, dopo i pasti*, before, after meals: *preghiera prima dei pasti*, grace before meal; *da prendersi dopo i pasti*, (*di medicina*) to be taken after meals; *vino da —*, table-wine; *che cosa bevi ai pasti?*, what do you drink with your meals?; *dove prendi i pasti?*, where do you take your meals?; *fare un magro —*, to have a poor meal; *fare tre pasti al giorno*, to take (*o to have*) three meals a day; *mangiare tra i pasti, fuori —*, to eat between meals ‖ *dare in — al pubblico, fig.* to spread (*o to broadcast*) ‖ *essere di poco, di molto —*, to eat little, a lot ‖ *stare ai pasti*, to eat only at meals; (*di neonato*) to keep one's schedule.

pastòcchia, *s.f.* (*fandonia*) tall story; (*inganno*) humbug; (*menzogna*) lie: *raccontar pastocchie*, to tell tall stories (*o to exaggerate*).

pastóia, *s.f.* 1. hobble: *metter le pastoie a un cavallo*, to hobble a horse 2. (*pasturale di cavallo*) pastern 3. *fig.* (*impaccio, legame*) fetter: *liberarsi dalle pastoie*, to cast off one's fetters.

pastóne, *s.m.* mash; (*per polli*) chicken-feed.

pastóra, *s.f.* 1. shepherdess, shepherd-girl 2. (*pasturale*) pastern.

pastoràle, *ag.* pastoral: *anello —*, (*eccl.*) bishop's ring; *lettera —*, (*eccl.*) pastoral (letter); *poesia —*, pastoral poetry ‖ *s.m.* (*eccl.*) crosier, pastoral staff ‖ *s.f.* 1. (*mus.*) pastorale 2. (*eccl.*) pastoral.

pastóre, *s.m.* 1. shepherd (*anche fig.*): *cane —*, sheep (*o shepherd*) dog ‖ *— di popoli*, (*reggitore*) leader ‖ *il Buon Pastore*, (*relig.*) the Good Shepherd 2. (*prete protestante*) pastor, minister; (*prete anglicano*) parson, clergyman (*pl.* clergymen).

pastoréccio, *ag.* pastoral.

pastorèlla, *s.f.* 1. young shepherdess 2. (*poes.*) pastourelle; pastoral 3. (*mus.*) (*pastorale*) pastorale.

pastorellería, *s.f.* (*spreg.*) pastoral: *le pastorellerie dell'Arcadia*, the pastorals of Arcadia.

pastorízia, *s.f.* stock-raising.
pastorízio, *ag.* (*rar.*) pastoral.
pastorizzáre, *v.t.* to pasteurize.
pastorizzáto, *ag.* pasteurized: *latte* —, pasteurized milk.
pastorizzazióne, *s.f.* pasteurization.
pastosità, *s.f.* **1.** (*morbidezza*) softness, doughiness **2.** (*di colori, suoni*) mellowness **3.** (*di vino*) mellowness.
pastóso, *ag.* **1.** (*morbido*) soft, doughy: *una miscela pastosa,* a doughy mixture **2.** (*di colori, suoni*) mellow: *voce pastosa,* mellow voice **3.** (*di vino*) mellow.
pastràno, *s.m.* overcoat; (*militare*) greatcoat.
pastúra, *s.f.* pasture; pasturage: *terreno da* —, grazing ground; *condurre le bestie alla* —, to drive the cattle to pasture.
pasturàle, *s.m.* (*di cavallo*) pastern.
pasturàre, *v.t.i.* to pasture, to graze.
patàcca, *s.f.* **1.** (*moneta di nessun valore*) worthless coin: *non vale una* —, it is not worth a brass farthing **2.** (*cosa di nessun valore*) worthless object; piece of rubbish **3.** (*scherz.*) (*decorazione*) decoration; (*sl.*) gong **4.** (*macchia*) stain, dirty mark, spot: *un abito pieno di patacche,* a suit covered with spots.
pataccóne, *s.m.* (*spreg.*) **1.** (*persona goffa e pigra*) clodhopper **2.** (*persona che suole macchiarsi gli abiti*) messy fellow **3.** (*vecchio orologio, cipollone*) turnip.
Patagònia, *no.pr.f.* (*geog.*) Patagonia.
patagóne, *ag.s.m.* Patagonian.
patapúm, (*voce onomatopeica riproducente il rumore di una cosa che cade*) bang; thud; flop.
pataríno, *s.m.* (*st. relig.*) Patarin(e).
patàta, *s.f.* potato (*pl.* potatoes): — *americana, dolce,* sweet-potato (*o* batata); *patate fritte,* fried potatoes (*o* chips); (*croccanti*) crisps: *un sacchettino di patate fritte,* a packet of (potato) crisps; *patate lesse,* boiled potatoes; *patate novelle,* new potatoes; *farina di patate,* potato flour; *purè di patate,* mashed potatoes || *spirito di* —, (*umore scipito*) poor humour.
patatràc, (*voce onomatopeica riproducente il rumore di una cosa che cade*) crash; bang || *s.m.* **1.** (*crollo finanziario*) crash **2.** (*disastro*) disaster: *succederà un — in quella famiglia,* there will be a disaster in that family.
patavíno, *ag.s.m.* Paduan.
pâté, *s.m.* (*cuc.*) pâté: — *di fegato d'oca,* pâté de foie gras.
patèlla, *s.f.* **1.** (*anat.*) knee-cap, patella (*pl.* patellae) **2.** (*zool.*) limpet.
patèllo, *s.m.* (*pannolino per bambino*) napkin: (*amer.*) diaper; (*fam.*) nappy.
patèma, *s.m.* **1.** pain, worry **2.** (*apprensione*) apprehension.
patèna, *s.f.* (*eccl.*) paten.
patentàto, *ag.* **1.** trained: *infermiera patentata,* trained nurse **2.** (*insigne, matricolato*) arrant: *ladro* —, arrant thief.
patènte, *ag.* **1.** (*evidente*) evident, open, clear, patent: *ingiustizia* —, open (*o* patent) injustice **2.** (*aperto*) open, patent || *lettera* —, letters patent **3.** (*bot.*) patent || *s.f.* **1.** licence: — *di guida,* driving licence; — *per la vendita di alcoolici,* licence for the sale of spirits; — *sanitaria,* (*mar.*) bill of health **2.** (*diploma*) diploma: — *di maestro,* teaching diploma || *dare a qlcu. la* — *di asino,* to call s.o. a qualified ass.
patenteménte, *av.* evidently, openly, clearly, patently.
patentíno, *s.m.* temporary licence: — *di guida,* temporary driving licence.
pàtera, *s.f.* (*archeol.*) patera (*pl.* paterae).
pateréccio, *s.m.* (*patol.*) whitlow.
pateríno, *s.m.* (*st. relig.*) Patarin(e).
paternàle, *s.f.* lecture, scolding, talking-to: *fare una* — *a qlcu.,* to give s.o. a lecture (*o* to lecture s.o.): *l'insegnante fece una severa* — *ai ragazzi perchè erano stati pigri,* the teacher lectured the boys severely (*o* gave the boys a good talking-to) for being lazy.

paternalísmo, *s.m.* (*pol.*) paternalism.
paternalístico, *ag.* (*pol.*) paternalistic.
paternaménte, *av.* (*in modo paterno*) paternally, in a fatherly way; (*da padre*) as a father.
paternità, *s.f.* paternity (anche *fig.*): *in questo certificato manca la* —, the father's name is missing in this certificate; *molti detti storici hanno una dubbia* —, many historical sayings are of doubtful paternity; *negare la* — *di un'opera,* to deny the paternity of a work || *Vostra* —, Your Paternity.
patèrno, *ag.* paternal; (*da padre*) fatherly, paternal: *amore* —, fatherly love; *casa paterna,* paternal house; *la mia nonna paterna,* my paternal grandmother.
paternòstro, *s.m.* **1.** paternoster; Lord's Prayer (*generalmente dei protestanti*); Our Father (*generalmente dei cattolici*): *dire dieci paternostri,* to say ten Our Fathers **2.** (*di rosario*) paternoster (bead) **3.** (*mar.*) parrel truck **4.** (*arch.*) paternoster.
pateticaménte, *av.* pathetically.
patètico, *ag.* **1.** (*commovente*) moving, pathetic: *discorso* —, moving speech; *musica patetica,* pathetic music; *scena patetica,* pathetic scene **2.** (*anat.*) pathetic: *muscolo, nervo* —, pathetic muscle, nerve || *s.m.* pathetic: *quell'attore riesce bene nel* —, that actor is good at emotional scenes; *cadere nel* —, to become (*o* to get) very emotional.
pàthos, *s.m.* (*letter.*) pathos.
patíbile, *ag.* endurable, bearable.
patibolàre, *ag.* sinister: *faccia* —, sinister face; *sguardo* —, hangdog (*o* gallows) look.
patíbolo, *s.m.* gallows, scaffold: *camminava come se andasse al* —, he walked as if he were going to the scaffold.
patiménto, *s.m.* pain, suffering.
pàtina, *s.f.* **1.** (*su metalli e cose usate*) patina **2.** (*strato di grasso che si dà alla pelle conciata*) dubbing **3.** (*strato di vernice*) coat of varnish **4.** (*smalto che si dà alla porcellana, terracotta, carta*) glaze **5.** (*velatura che si forma sulla lingua*) coating, fur.
patinàre, *v.t.* **1.** (*verniciare*) to varnish **2.** (*pelli*) to dub **3.** (*porcellana, terracotta, carta*) to glaze.
patinàto, *ag.* **1.** patinated **2.** (*di pelli*) dubbed **3.** (*verniciato*) varnished **4.** (*di porcellana, terracotta, carta*) glazed **5.** (*della lingua*) coated, furred.
patinatúra, *s.f.* **1.** (*verniciatura*) varnishing **2.** (*di pelli*) dubbing **3.** (*di porcellana, carta, ecc.*) glazing.
patinóso, *ag.* **1.** (*di metalli*) patinated **2.** (*della lingua*) coated, furred.
patio, *s.m.* patio.
patíre, *v.i.* to suffer: *patisco tanto quando lo vedo partire,* I suffer so much when I see him leave; *quella pianta ha patito per il gelo,* that plant has suffered from the frost; *la tua popolarità non potrà che patirne,* your popularity can only suffer from it || *v.t.* **1.** to suffer: *ha patito molti torti,* he has suffered many wrongs; — *il caldo, il freddo,* to suffer from the heat, the cold; — *la fame,* to starve (*o* to go hungry); — *il martirio,* to suffer martyrdom; — *la sete,* to suffer from (*o* to be dying of) thirst: *patisco la sete da due ore,* I have been dying of thirst for two hours || *far* — *la fame a qlcu.,* to starve s.o. (*o* to let s.o. go hungry); *far* — *la sete a qlcu.,* to let s.o. go thirsty **2.** (*sopportare*) to bear, to stand: *non posso* — *di veder maltrattare i bambini,* I cannot bear to see (*o* seeing) children ill-treated.
patíto, *ag.* sickly, sickly-looking: *quel ragazzo ha l'aria patita,* that boy looks sickly || *s.m.* **1.** (*scherz.*) (*innamorato*) sweetheart **2.** (*fam.*) (*appassionato*) fan: *è un* — *del jazz,* he is a jazz fan (*o* mad on jazz).
patofobía, *s.f.* (*patol.*) pathophobia.
patogènesi, *s.f.* (*med.*) pathogenesis, pathogeny.
patogènico, *ag.* (*med.*) pathogenic.
patògeno, *ag.* (*med.*) pathogenous.
patognomònico, *ag.* (*med.*) pathognomic, pathognomonic.
patología, *s.f.* pathology.

patologicaménte, *av.* pathologically.
patològico, *ag.* pathologic(al): *anatomia patologica,* pathologic anatomy.
patòlogo, *s.m.* pathologist.
pàtos, *s.m.* (*letter.*) pathos.
Patràsso, *no.pr.f.* (*geog.*) Patras ‖ *mandare qlcu. a* —, *fig.* to kill s.o.
pàtria, *s.f.* **1.** country, fatherland, mother-country, native land: — *d'elezione,* adoptive country; *amor di* —, love of one's country (*o* native land); *in* — *e all'estero,* at home and abroad; *il sacro suolo della* —, the sacred soil of one's native country; *siamo esuli dalla* —, we are exiles from home; *amare la* —, to love one's country; *morire per la* —, to die for one's country; *tornare in* —, to return to one's native land; *tradire la* —, to betray one's country ‖ *la* — *celeste,* the heavenly home ‖ *ai caduti per la* —, in memory of those who gave their lives for their country ‖ *altare della* —, the tomb of the Unknown Soldier ‖ *la madre* —, the mother -country ‖ *i senza* —, unpatriotic people ‖ *nessuno è profeta in* —, no one is a prophet in his own country **2.** (*luogo nativo*) birth-place; *fig.* home, land: *la* — *dei leoni e delle palme,* the home of lions and palm -trees; *l'Umbria,* — *di pittori e di santi,* Umbria, home (*o* country) of painters and saints; *Firenze è la* — *di Dante,* Dante's birth-place was Florence.
patriàrea, *s.m.* **1.** patriarch (anche *fig.*) ‖ *i Patriarchi,* (*Bibbia*) the patriarchs **2.** (*eccl.*) patriarch.
patriareàle, *ag.* **1.** patriarchal, venerable; (*semplice*) simple: *aspetto* —, venerable appearance; *una famiglia* —, a patriarchal family **2.** (*eccl.*) patriarchal: *chiesa* —, patriarchal church.
patriarealménte, *av.* (*rar.*) patriarchally.
patriareàto, *s.m.* **1.** patriarchy, patriarchism, patriarchalism **2.** (*eccl.*) patriarchate.
patrieída, *V.* **parrieída.**
patrieídio, *V.* **parrieídio.**
patrígno, *s.m.* step-father.
patrimoniàle, *ag.* patrimonial: *azienda* —, (*comm.*) non-trading concern; *beni patrimoniali,* patrimonial estate; *tassa* —, property tax.
patrimònio, *s.m.* patrimony; estate, property: *il* — *artistico di un paese,* the artistic patrimony (*o* inheritance) of a country; — *mobiliare, immobiliare,* personal, real property (*o* estate); — *nazionale,* national estate; — *pubblico,* public property; *entità del* — *di qlcu.,* value of one's estate; *ha scialacquato al giuoco il suo* —, he has gambled away his inheritance (*o* patrimony); *la lingua è* — *comune di una nazione,* the language is the common inheritance of a nation; *il mio solo* — *è un nome onorato,* my only patrimony is an honoured name; *accumulare un* —, to make a fortune ‖ *il* — *di San Pietro,* (*st.*) the Patrimony of St. Peter ‖ *è ormai* — *comune, fig.* it is common knowledge by this time.
pàtrio, *ag.* **1.** native; of one's own country: *il* — *suolo,* one's native land; *amor* —, love of one's country (*o* patriotism); *tornare ai patrii lidi,* to return to one's native shores ‖ *gli avanzi delle patrie galere, fig.* the scum of the earth **2.** (*paterno*) paternal: *patria potestà,* paternal authority; *le patrie soglie,* the paternal roof.
patriòta, patriòtta, *s.c.* **1.** patriot **2.** (*compatriotta*) fellow countryman (*pl.* countrymen), compatriot.
patriottàrdo, *s.m.* jingo, jingoist.
patriottieaménte, *av.* patriotically.
patriòttieo, *ag.* patriotic: *canzoni patriottiche,* patriotic songs.
patriottísmo, *s.m.* patriotism.
patrística, *s.f.* (*teol.*) patristics (*pl.*); patrology.
Patrízia, *no.pr.f.* Patricia ‖ *dim.* Pat, Paddy.
patriziáto, *s.m.* patriciate.
Patrízio[1], *no.pr.m.* Patrick ‖ *dim.* Pat, Paddy.
patrízio[2], *ag.* patrician, noble: *famiglia patrizia,* patrician family ‖ *s.m.* patrician.
patrizzàre, *v.i.* to take after one's father.

patrocinànte, *ag.*: *avvocato* —, counsel for the defence ‖ *s.m.* counsel for the defence.
patrocinàre, *v.t.* to support, to sponsor; to defend: *l'accusato ebbe un valente avvocato che patrocinò la sua causa,* the accused man had a clever lawyer to defend him; *patrocinò la tua candidatura,* he supported your candidature; — *una causa,* to plead a cause; — *un partito politico,* to support a political party.
patrocinatóre, *s.m.* **1.** supporter, sponsor; defender **2.** (*delle arti*) patron.
patrocínio, *s.m.* (*difesa*) defence, pleading: — *gratuito,* (*dir.*) legal aid: *concedere il* — *gratuito,* to grant legal aid.
Pàtroclo, *no.pr.m.* (*lett.*) Patroclus.
patronàle, *ag.* patronal.
patronàto, *s.m.* **1.** patronage **2.** (*istituzione di carità*) charitable institution: — *scolastico,* students' benevolent fund.
patronéssa, *s.f.* patroness.
patronímieo, *ag. s.m.* patronymic.
patròno, *s.m.* **1.** patron: *il* — *di un artista, di un'istituzione di beneficenza,* the patron of an artist, of a charity; *il* (*santo*) — *di una città, una chiesa, ecc.,* the patron saint of a town, a church, etc. **2.** (*dir.*) counsel for the defence, defending counsel.
pàtta[1], *s.f.* **1.** (*spor.*) draw, tie: *il giuoco finì pari e* —, the game ended in a draw; *essere pari e* —, to be quits.
pàtta[2], *s.f.* **1.** (*di tasca*) flap **2.** (*mar.*) fluke.
pattàre, *v.i.* (*far pari e patta*) to draw, to tie.
patteggiàbile, *ag.* open to discussion (*predicativo*), open to negotiation (*predicativo*).
patteggiamento, *s.m.* negotiation, bargaining.
patteggiàre, *v.i.* to come to terms, to reach an agreement; to reach a compromise: — *con il nemico,* to come to terms with the enemy ‖ *v.t.* to negotiate: — *la pace,* to negotiate peace.
pattinàggio, *s.m.* (ice-) skating: — *a rotelle,* roller -skating; *pista di* —, skating-rink; (*di ghiaccio*) ice -rink; *scarpe da* —, skating boots.
pattinàre, *v.i.* to skate.
pattinatóre, *s.m.,* **pattinatríce,** *s.f.* skater.
pattino[1], *s.m.* **1.** (ice-)skate: — *a rotelle,* roller -skate **2.** (*di aereo*) skid; (*di slitta*) shoe **3.** (*mec.*) sliding -(o link-) block: — *di contatto,* guide (*o* sliding)-shole
pattíno[2], *s.m.* (*mar.*) " pattino " (light double raft used by bathers).
pàtto, *s.m.* **1.** pact, agreement; understanding: — *di amicizia,* pact of friendship; *un* — *di non aggressione,* a non-aggression pact; — *di pace,* peace treaty; *facciamo un* —, let's make an agreement; *attenersi ai patti,* to keep to the agreement; *venire a un* —, to come to an agreement (*o* understanding) ‖ *il Patto Atlantico,* the Atlantic Pact **2.** (*condizione*) term; condition: *accetto a questi patti,* on these terms I accept; *il nemico venne a patti,* the enemy came to terms; *venire a patti con qlcu.,* to come to terms with s.o. ‖ *a* — *che,* on condition that (*o* provided that): *puoi rimanere a* — *che tu rimanga zitto,* you may remain provided (that) you keep silent ‖ *ad ogni* —, at any price ‖ *a nessun* —, by no means ‖ *patti chiari amicizia lunga, prov.* short reckoning makes long friends.
pattúglia, *s.f.* (*mil.*) patrol: *essere di* —, to be on patrol.
pattugliàre, *v.i.* to patrol.
pattuire, *v.t.* to reach an agreement (up)on (sthg.): *prima di* —, *fissiamo il prezzo,* before reaching any agreement, let's fix the price; — *un prezzo,* to agree upon a price; — *la resa,* to agree on the surrender.
pattuíto, *ag.* agreed upon: *la somma pattuita,* amount agreed upon ‖ *s.m.* agreement: *rispettiamo il* —!, let's respect our agreement!.
pattúme, *s.m.* rubbish; (*amer.*) garbage, trash.

pattumièra, *s.f.* dust-bin; (*amer.*) garbage-can.

patúrne, patúrnie, *s.f.pl.* low spirits, dumps: *avere le —,* to be in the dumps.

pauperísmo, *s.m.* (*neol.*) pauperism.

paúra, *s.f.* **1.** fear, dread; (*spavento*) fright; scare: *un bambino pieno di —,* a fearful (*o* timid) child; *un uomo senza —,* a fearless man; *aveva una — morbosa della morte,* he had a morbid fear of death; *è comune nei bambini la — del buio,* fear of the dark is common in children; *ebbi una gran —,* I had a terrible fright; *mi hai fatto —,* you scared me; *avere — di ql.co.,* to fear sthg. (*o* to be afraid of sthg.); *non aver —!,* don't be afraid! (*o* frightened!); *vincere la —,* to overcome (one's) fear || *che —!,* what a fright! (*o* scare!) || *per che...,* for fear that (*o* lest *o* in case): *glielo dirò io per — che lo venga a sapere da altri,* I will tell him myself for fear that (*o* lest *o* in case) he should hear about it from someone else; *per — di...,* for fear of...: *per — del peggio,* to be on the safe side (*o* in case the worst should come to the worst) || *è brutta da far —,* she is frightfully (*o* fearfully) ugly || *è una strada che fa —,* it is a terrible road || *quando lo vidi era morto di —,* when I saw him he was (*o* he looked) frightened to death || *avere una — birbona, indiavolata,* to be scared to death || *avere — della propria ombra,* to be afraid of one's own shadow || *morire di —,* to die of fright; *fig.* to be frightened (*o* scared) to death: *far morire qlcu. di —,* to scare (*o* to frighten) s.o. to death || *cane scottato dall'acqua calda, ha — della fredda,* *prov.* a scalded cat fears even cold water || *chi ha — non vada alla guerra,* *prov.* he that's afraid of wounds, must not come nigh a battle || *male non fare, — non avere,* *prov.* do no evil and have no fear **2.** (*preoccupazione*) fear: *aveva — di arrivare in ritardo,* he was afraid (that) he might arrive late; *avevo — che tu avessi perduto il treno,* I was afraid (*o* I feared) that you had lost the train; *l'esame d'inglese mi fa —,* the English examination makes me nervous; *ho — che non verrà,* I am afraid (*o* I fear) he won't come; *ho — di sì, di no,* I fear (*o* I am afraid) so, not.

paurosaménte, *av.* **1.** (*timidamente*) fearfully, timidly, timorously: *veniva avanti —,* he advanced fearfully (*o* timidly *o* timorously) **2.** (*in modo da far paura*) frighteningly, terrifyingly **3.** (*immensamente*) fearfully, dreadfully, frightfully.

pauróso, *ag.* **1.** (*che ha paura*) fearful, frightened **2.** (*timoroso*) timid, timorous: *è un ragazzo —,* he is a timid child || *come un coniglio,* as timid as a rabbit **3.** (*che incute paura*) frightening, terrifying.

pàusa, *s.f.* **1.** pause; (*nel lavoro*) interval, break: *durante una — della conversazione,* during a pause in the conversation **2.** (*mus.*) rest, pause.

Pausània, *no.pr.m.* (*st.*) Pausanias.

pausàre, *v.i.* (*rar.*) to pause, to stop.

pavàna, *s.f.* (*musica, danza*) pavan, pavane.

paventàre, *v.i.* **1.** to fear, to be afraid **2.** (*di bestie, adombrarsi*) to shy || *v.t.* (*rar.*) to fear, to be afraid of (sthg.).

paventóso, *ag.* **1.** (*che ha paura*) fearful, frightened, apprehensive **2.** (*che incute paura*) fearful, frightening.

pavesàre, *v.t.* to dress (with flags): *— le strade di bandiere,* to dress (*o* to deck) the streets with flags (*o* bunting); *— una nave,* to dress a ship (with flags).

pavesàta, *s.f.* bunting.

pavése[1], *ag.* of Pavia || *s.c.* native of Pavia, inhabitant of Pavia.

pavése[2], *s.m.* **1.** (*di nave*) bunting **2.** (*st.*) (*scudo*) pavis, pavise.

pavidaménte, *av.* fearfully, timidly, timorously.

pàvido, *ag.* fearful, timid, timorous; spiritless.

pavimentàre, *v.t.* **1.** (*una strada*) to pave: *— a macadam,* to macadamize **2.** (*una stanza*) to floor: *— con assi,* to plank.

pavimentazióne, *s.f.* **1.** (*di strada*) paving: *— ad elementi,* block-paving; *— continua,* sheet-paving **2.** (*di stanza*) flooring: *— a mosaico,* mosaic flooring; *— a parquet,* parquet (flooring); *— in legno,* wood flooring; *— in piastrelle,* tile flooring.

paviménto, *s.m.* floor, flooring: *— a parquet,* parquet (floor); *— di assi,* batten floor; *— di cemento armato,* reinforced-concrete floor; *— di legno,* wood floor; *— di mattonelle,* tiling (*o* tiled floor); *— di pietra,* stone floor; *— isolato,* insulated floor.

pavonàzzo, *V.* paonàzzo.

pavoncèlla, *s.f.* (*ornit.*) lapwing.

payóne, *s.m.* (*ornit.*) peacock (anche *fig.*).

pavoneggiàrsi, *v.r.* to strut about, to show off: *si pavoneggiava nel suo nuovo vestito alla marinara,* he was strutting about in his new sailor-suit.

pavonéssa, *s.f.* (*ornit.*) peahen.

pazientàre, *v.i.* to have patience; to exercise patience.

paziènte, *ag.* **1.** patient; forbearing, long-suffering: *essere — con qlcu.,* to be patient (*o* to have patience) with s.o. **2.** (*scrupoloso*) careful, scrupulous || *s.m.* **1.** patient **2.** (*chi è nelle mani del boia*) condemned man (about to be executed).

pazienteménte, *av.* **1.** patiently; forbearingly, long-sufferingly **2.** (*scrupolosamente*) carefully.

paziènza, *s.f.* **1.** patience; forbearance, endurance: *devi avere — con lui,* you must be patient with him; *è un lavoro di —,* it is a job which requires a great deal of patience; *armarsi, munirsi di —,* to arm oneself with patience; *mettere alla prova la — di qlcu.* to try (*o* to text) s.o.'s patience; *perdere la —,* to lose one's patience (*o* to get out of patience): *far perdere la — a qlcu.,* to make s.o. lose his temper || *giuoco di —,* game of patience || *se fosse bella, —, ma è brutta!,* if she were pretty, all right, but she is ugly! || *se non puoi venire, —!,* if you cannot come, never mind! **2.** (*eccl.*) (*cordone dei frati*) cordon; (*scapolare*) scapular **3.** (*bot.*) patience(-dock) **4.** (*mar.*) belaying pin rack.

pàzza, *s.f.* madwoman (*pl.* madwomen).

pazzaménte, *av.* madly, insanely; (*senza controllo*) wildly: *— geloso,* insanely jealous; *— innamorato,* madly in love.

pazzeggiàre, *v.i.* to play the fool; (*fare delle pazzie*) to behave like a fool, to act like a fool.

pazzerèllo, pazzerellóne, *s.m.* silly fellow; (*fam.*) bit of an ass.

pazzescaménte, *V.* pazzaménte.

pazzésco, *ag.* mad, insane; (*stupido*) foolish: *idee pazzesche,* foolish ideas || *è —!,* that's absolutely mad! (*o* that's incredible!).

pazzía, *s.f.* **1.** madness, insanity, lunacy: *in un eccesso di —,* in a fit of madness (*o* in a frenzy); *la — è una malattia mentale,* insanity is a mental disorder; *avere un ramo di —,* to be a little crazy **2.** (*cosa insensata*) madness; (*azione pazza*) folly, foolish action; (*idea pazza*) folly, foolish idea: *è una — uscire a quest'ora,* it is sheer folly (*o* it is absolutely mad) to go out at this time; *ho commesso una —,* I have done sthg. foolish; *sarebbe — lasciarlo fare,* it would be madness to let him do it; *spero non farai la — di accettare,* I hope you won't be so foolish as to accept; *vorresti andare al Polo Nord, che —!,* you would like to go the North Pole, what a foolish idea!; *fare delle pazzie,* to act like a fool (*o* to behave irrationally).

pàzzo, *ag.* **1.** mad, crazy, insane (anche *fig.*); lunatic: *— frenetico,* frantic; *è un po' —,* he is a little crazy; *ero — di gioia, di dolore,* I was mad with joy, grief; *ha un fratello —,* he has a lunatic brother; *sei —?,* are you crazy? (*o* are you mad?); *diventar —,* to go mad (*o* to go out of one's mind); *far diventar — qlcu.,* to drive s.o. mad || *— da legare,* raving mad || *innamorato —,* madly in love || *andar — per ql.co.,* to be crazy (*o* mad) about sthg. **2.** (*sconsiderato, stravagante, bizzarro*) mad, crazy, foolish: *che clima —!,* what a capricious climate!; *che pazza idea!,* what a crazy idea!;

una condotta pazza, foolish behaviour; *una decisione pazza*, a foolish decision **3.** (*eccessivo, smoderato*) wild: — *entusiasmo,* wild enthusiasm; *pazza risata,* wild laughter; *spese* —, wild extravagance ‖ *s.m.* madman (*pl.* madmen), lunatic: *ospedale per pazzi,* lunatic asylum (o mental hospital) ‖ *come un* —, like a madman.

peàna, *s.m.* paean.

pebrína, *s.f.* (*malattia del baco da seta*) pebrine.

pècari, *s.m.* (*zool.*) peccary.

pècca, *s.f.* **1.** (*difetto*) fault, blemish, flaw: *quel libro è bello ma ha delle pecche,* that book is beautiful but has some blemishes; *la tua traduzione è senza pecche,* your translation is faultless (o flawless) **2.** (*di persona*) (*mancanza*) fault; (*errore*) mistake, error: *anche lui ha le sue pecche,* he has his faults too; *mi parlò delle sue pecche di gioventù,* he told me of the mistakes he made (o errors he committed) in his youth.

peccàbile, *ag.* peccable, liable to sin.

peccabilità, *s.f.* peccability.

peccaminosaménte, *av.* sinfully; culpably.

peccaminóso, *ag.* sinful; culpable: *negligenza peccaminosa,* culpable negligence; *vita peccaminosa,* sinful life.

peccàre, *v.i.* **1.** (*commettere un peccato*) to sin: *essi hanno peccato contro Dio,* they have sinned against God; — *d'avarizia, di gola,* to commit the sin of avarice, of greed; — *mortalmente,* to commit mortal sin **2.** (*errare*) to err: *egli pecca di eccessiva indulgenza verso suo figlio,* his fault is his excessive indulgence towards his son; *è meglio* — *in generosità che in avarizia,* it is better to err on the side of generosity than on the side of avarice; — *contro la legge,* to offend against the law (o to transgress the law); — *contro uno dei comandamenti,* to transgress (o to break) one of the Commandments; — *di ingratitudine, di leggerezza,* to commit the sin of ingratitude, of levity ‖ — *per difetto,* to fall short of what is required; — *per eccesso,* to exceed what is required **3.** (*essere manchevole, difettoso*) to be deficient; to lack (sthg.); to be faulty: *egli pecca in coraggio,* he is deficient in courage (o he lacks courage); *quel quadro pecca nel colorito,* the colouring of that picture is faulty; *quella statua pecca nelle proporzioni,* that statue is out of proportion.

peccàto, *s.m.* sin: — *di gola,* sin of gluttony; — *di omissione,* sin of omission; — *mortale, originale, veniale,* mortal (o deadly), original, venial sin; *cadere nel* —, to lapse into sin; *commettere, confessare, espiare un* —, to commit, to confess, to expiate a sin; *rimettere i peccati,* to forgive sins; *vivere in* —, to live in sin ‖ *peccati di gioventù,* wild oats ‖ *brutto come il* —, as ugly as sin ‖ *che* —*!,* what a pity! (o what a shame!); *è un* — *che...,* it is a pity that... ‖ *i sette peccati capitali,* the seven deadly sins ‖ *chi di voi è senza* — *scagli la prima pietra,* he that is without sin among you, let him first cast a stone ‖ — *confessato è mezzo perdonato, prov.* a fault confessed is half redressed.

peccatóre, *s.m.,* **peccatríce,** *s.f.* sinner: — *impenitente,* unrepentant sinner; — *incallito,* hardened (o inveterate) sinner.

peccatúccio, *s.m.* peccadillo.

pécchia, *s.f.* (*entom.*) bee.

pecchióne, *s.m.* (*entom.*) drone.

péce, *s.f.* pitch: — *da calzolai,* cobbler's wax; — *greca,* colophony; — *liquida,* tar; *coprire di* —, to pitch ‖ *nero come la* —, as black as pitch: *la notte era nera come la* —, the night was pitch-dark ‖ *essere macchiato della stessa* —, to be tarred with the same brush.

pechinése, *ag.* Pekin(g)ese ‖ *s.m.* **1.** Pe-kin(g)ese (*invariato al pl.*) **2.** (*cane*) Pekin(g)ese (*invariato al pl.*); (*fam.*) Peke ‖ *s.f.* Pekin(g)ese (*invariato al pl.*).

Pechíno, *no.pr.f.* (*geog.*) Peking.

pècora, *s.f.* sheep (*invariato al pl.*); (*femmina*) ewe: *un branco di pecore,* a flock of sheep ‖ *la* — *nera della famiglia,* the black sheep of the family.

pecoràggine, *s.f.* **1.** (*rassegnazione*) spiritlessness, resignation, docility **2.** (*stupidità*) stupidity.

pecoràio, *s.m.* shepherd.

pecoràme, *s.m.* flock of sheep (anche *fig.*).

pecoréccio, *ag.* (*rar.*) sheep (*attributivo*) ‖ *s.m.* (*rar.*) mess, fix: *entrar nel* —, to get oneself into a mess (o fix); *uscire dal* —, to get oneself out of a mess.

pecorèlla, *s.f.* **1.** lamb (anche *fig.*): *le pecorelle del parroco,* the vicar's young flock; — *smarrita,* lost sheep **2.** *pl.* (*detto di nuvole*) fleecy clouds: *cielo a pecorelle,* sky full of fleecy clouds **3.** *pl.* (*piccole onde*) foaming wavelets.

pecorésco, *ag.* sheep-like: *servilità pecoresca,* sheep-like servility.

pecoríle, *ag.* **1.** (*di pecora*) sheep (*attributivo*) **2.** *fig.* (*servile*) sheep-like ‖ *s.m.* sheep-fold, sheep-pen.

pecorilménte, *ag.* in a sheep-like manner, spiritlessly: *si comportarono* —, they behaved like sheep.

pecoríno, *ag.* sheep (*attributivo*) ‖ *s.m.* " Pecorino " cheese (sheep's milk cheese).

pecoróne, *s.m.* **1.** (*ariete*) ram **2.** *fig.* (*stupido*) blockhead; (*persona servile*) sheep (*invariato al pl.*).

pecorúme, *s.m.* servile flock.

pectína, *s.f.* (*chim.*) pectin.

pectòsio, *s.m.* (*chim.*) pectose.

peculàto, *s.m.* (*dir.*) peculation.

peculiàre, *ag.* peculiar, special, characteristic: *odore* — *di un animale,* smell peculiar to an animal; *questa attitudine gli è* —, this attitude is characteristic of him.

peculiarità, *s.f.* peculiarity, characteristic.

peculiarménte, *av.* peculiarly.

peculio, *s.m.* **1.** (*st. romana*) peculium **2.** (*denaro*) hoard; money.

pecúnia, *s.f.* money; (*fam.*) pile: *non gli manca la* —, he has made his pile.

pecuniàrio, *ag.* pecuniary: *pena pecuniaria,* fine.

pecunióso, *ag.* rich, wealthy.

pedàggio, *s.m.* toll: *esente da* —, toll-free; *ponte a* —, toll-bridge; *pagare il* —, to pay the toll.

pedàgna, *s.f.* (*mar.*) stretcher.

pedagogía, *s.f.* pedagogy, pedagogics.

pedagogieaménte, *av.* pedagogically.

pedagògico, *ag.* pedagogic(al).

pedagogísta, *s.c.* pedagogist.

pedagògo, *s.m.* **1.** pedagogue **2.** (*spreg.*) pedant.

pedalàre, *v.i.* to pedal; to cycle.

pedalàta, *s.f.* **1.** way of pedalling: *ha la* — *sciolta, disuguale,* he has an easy, uneven way of pedalling **2.** (*colpo sul pedale*) thrust on a pedal.

pedàle¹, *s.m.* **1.** pedal: — *del freno,* (*aut.*) foot-brake (pedal); — *dell'acceleratore,* (*aut.*) accelerator (pedal); — *della frizione,* clutch (pedal); — *del piano, del forte,* (*di organo, pianoforte*) soft, loud pedal; — *di avviamento,* (*aut.*) kickstarter; — *di comando,* (*aut.*) foot control lever; — *di macchina da cucire,* treadle; *freno a* —, foot-brake; *il corridore pigiava forte sui pedali,* the cyclist pushed hard down on his pedals **2.** (*di calzolaio*) stirrup **3.** (*mus.*) pedal(-note).

pedàle², *s.m.* (*bot.*) foot; (*fusto*) stump, stub, stock.

pedaleggiàre, *v.i.* to pedal.

pedalièra, *s.f.* **1.** (*aer.*) rudder-bar; rudder-pedals (*pl.*): — *direzionale,* tail rotor (o control pedal); — *timone,* rudder-bar **2.** (*di un organo*) pedal keyboard.

pedalína, *s.f.* (*tip.*) platen.

pedalíno, *s.m.* (*fam.*) sock.

pedàna, *s.f.* **1.** (*tappetino*) rug; (*scendiletto*) bedside rug **2.** (*spor.*) spring-board; (*scherma*) board **3.** (*di veicolo*) footboard; (*di automobile*) running-board **4.** (*sartoria*) tuck.

pedànte, *ag.* pedantic: *un uomo noioso e* —, a boring and pedantic man ‖ *s.m.* pedant: *non fare il* —*!,* don't be pedantic! **2.** (*arc.*) pedagogue.

pedanteggiàre, *v.i.* to be pedantic.

pedantería, *s.f.* pedantry: *questa è un'insopportabile* —, this is an intolerable piece of pedantry.

pedantescaménte, *ag.* pedantically.

pedantésco, *ag.* pedantic.

pedantéssa, *s.f.* pedant.

pedàta, *s.f.* **1.** kick: *cacciare qlcu. a pedate*, to kick s.o. out; *prendere qlcu. a pedate*, to kick s.o. repeatedly (*o* to give s.o. a booting) **2.** (*impronta*) footprint, footstep: *seguire le pedate di uno*, *fig.* to follow in s.o.'s footsteps (*anche fig.*).

pedemontàno, *ag. s.m.* (*rar.*) Piedmontese.

pederàsta, *s.m.* p(a)ederast.

pederastía, *s.f.* p(a)ederasty.

pedèstre, *ag.* **1.** pedestrian: *milizia —*, infantry **2.** *fig.* pedestrian, dull, uninspired: *imitazione —*, pedestrian imitation; *stile —*, dull style.

pedestreménte, *av.* dully, in a pedestrian way.

pediàtra, *s.c.* paediatrician, paediatrist.

pediatría, *s.f.* paediatrics.

pediàtrico, *ag.* paediatric: *clinica pediatrica*, children's hospital.

pedicèllo, *s.m.* (*bot.*) pedicel.

pedicolàre, *ag.* pedicular.

pedicure, *s.m.* chiropodist ‖ *s.f.* **1.** chiropodist **2.** (*mestiere del pedicure*) chiropody, pedicure **3.** (*cura dei piedi*) pedicure: *fare la — a qlcu.*, to pedicure s.o.

pedídio, *ag.* (*anat.*) pedal.

pedignóne, *s.m.* chilblain.

pedilúvio, *s.m.* foot-bath.

pedína, *s.f.* (*alla dama*) piece; (*agli scacchi*) pawn: *muovere una —*, to make a move (*anche fig.*); (*muovere persone influenti*) to set wheels in motion.

pedinaménto, *s.m.* shadowing.

pedinàre, *v.t.* to shadow: *— qlcu.*, to dog s.o.'s footsteps.

pedipàlpo, *s.m.* (*di aracnide*) pedipalp.

pedissequaménte, *av.* servilely.

pedíssequo, *ag.* servile: *imitazione pedissequa*, servile imitation; *traduzione pedissequa*, literal (*o* slavish) translation ‖ *s.m.* sheep.

pedivèlla, *s.f.* (*mec.*) pedal crank.

pedòmetro, *s.m.* pedometer.

pedonàle, *ag.* pedestrian (*attributivo*); for pedestrians: *passaggio —*, pedestrian crossing; *traffico —*, foot-traffic.

pedóne, *s.m.* **1.** pedestrian: *strada*, *passaggio riservato ai pedoni*, foot-path (*o* foot-way) **2.** (*agli scacchi*, *pedina*) pawn **3.** (*rar.*) (*fantaccino*) foot-soldier; (*corriere*) courier.

pedúccio, *s.m.* **1.** (*zampetto*) trotters (*pl.*) **2.** (*arch.*) corbel **3.** (*piccolo piedistallo*) small pedestal **4.** (*sostegno*) bracket.

pedúla, *s.f.* climbing-boot.

pedúle, *s.m.* stocking-sole: *essere in peduli*, to be in one's stockinged feet.

peduncolàre, *ag.* (*bot.*) peduncular.

peduncolàto, *ag.* (*bot.*) pedunculate, peduncled.

pedúncolo, *s.m.* (*bot. anat.*) peduncle, stalk.

pegamòide, *s.f.* pegamoid.

Pègaso, *no.pr.m.* (*mit. astr.*) Pegasus.

pèggio, *ag.* **1.** *comp.* worse: *questo quadro è — di quello*, this picture is worse than that one; *tu sei — di me*, you are worse than I am (*o* than me) **2.** *superl. rel.* (*idiot. per peggiore*) the worst: *era il — chirurgo dell'ospedale*, he was the worst surgeon in the hospital ‖ *alla —*, at (the) worst (*o* if the worst comes to the worst) ‖ *avere la —*, to get the worst of it ‖ *campare alla meno —*, to rub along as well as one can ‖ *s.m.* **1.** the worst, the worst thing; (*la peggior parte*) the worst part: *il — che potevi fare*, the worst (thing) you could have done; *il — deve ancora venire*, the worst is still to come; *il — è che...*, the worst of it is that...; *il — è già passato*, *ormai il — è passato*, the worst is over now; *il — è già stato tolto*, the worst part has already been removed; *essere preparato al —*, to be prepared for the worst ‖ *per il —*, for the worst **2.** (*partitivo*): *ciò che puoi fare di —*, the worst thing you can do; *non c'è nulla di —*, there is nothing worse ‖

av. **1.** *comp.* worse: *cento volte —*, a hundred times worse; *ha suonato — che mai*, he played worse than ever; *io feci male, ma tu facesti molto —*, I did wrong, but you did much worse; *il malato va —*, the patient has taken a turn for the worse; *sta ancor — a te che a me*, it suits you even less than it does me ‖ *— ancora*, *ancora —*, worse still, even worse ‖ *— per lui, noi, ecc.*, so much the worse for him, us, etc. ‖ *di male in —*, from bad to worse: *tutto va di male in —*, everything is getting worse and worse (*o* things are going from bad to worse) ‖ *sempre —*, worse and worse ‖ *tanto —!*, *così!*, so much the worse! ‖ *cambiare in —*, to change for the worse **2.** *superl. rel.* the worst: *le donne — vestite erano...*, the worst-dressed women were...

peggioraménto, *s.m.* worsening; (*di malattia*) aggravation: *il — di una 'situazione*, the worsening (*o* deterioration) of a situation.

peggioràre, *v.t.* to make worse: *ciò peggiorò la situazione*, this made the situation worse; *non ha fatto che — le cose*, he has only made matters worse ‖ *v.i.* to get worse, to deteriorate: *il malato continua a —*, the patient is getting worse and worse.

peggiorativo, *ag.* **1.** depreciatory; pejorative: *senso —*, pejorative sense **2.** (*gram.*) pejorative: *suffisso —*, pejorative suffix ‖ *s.m.* (*gram.*) pejorative.

peggióre, *ag.* **1.** *comp.* worse: *giorni peggiori*, worse days; *molto —*, much worse; *è un uomo — di te*, he is a worse man than you; *fu reso — dalle sue tristi esperienze*, his bitter experiences made a worse man of him; *non è — di suo fratello*, he is no worse than his brother; *non potrebbe essere —*, it couldn't be worse; *diventar —*, to get worse (*o* to worsen); *rendere — ql.co.*, to make sthg. worse (*o* to worsen sthg.) **2.** *superl. rel.* the worst: *è il — uomo del mondo*, he is the worst of men; *è il mio — nemico*, he is my worst enemy; *era la cosa — da farsi*, it was the worst thing to do; *fare ql.co. nel — dei modi*, *nel modo —*, to do sthg. in the worst (possible) way ‖ *di gran lunga il —*, by far the worst ‖ *s.m.* **1.** (*la cosa peggiore*) **the worst** (thing) **2.** (*la persona peggiore*) **the worst.**

pégno, *s.m.* **1.** (*oggetto dato in garanzia*, *contratto di pegno*) pledge: *agenzia di pegni*, pawnshop; *polizza di —*, pawn-ticket; *vendita dei pegni*, sale of unredeemed pledges; *dare*, *mettere ql.co. come —*, *in —*, to give sthg. in pawn (*o* to pawn sthg. *o* to pledge sthg.); *dare*, *prendere a prestito su —*, to loan, to borrow on pledge; *rinnovare un —*, to renew a pledge; *ritirare*, *riscattare un —*, to redeem ǀa pledge **2.** (*segno*, *attestato*) token, pledge: *in — di amicizia*, in token of friendship; *prendi questo anello come — del mio amore*, take this ring as a token of my love **3.** (*oggetto depositato come pegno nei giuochi*) forfeit: *giuoco dei pegni*, forfeits.

pégola, *s.f.* pitch.

pegolièra, *s.f.* **1.** (*caldaia*) cauldron for pitch **2.** (*luogo degli arsenali in cui si lavora la pece*) caulking-shed.

pelagianésimo, *s.m.* (*st. relig.*) Pelagianism.

pelagiàno, *ag.s.m.* (*st. relig.*) Pelagian.

pelàgico, *ag.* pelagic, pelagian: *fauna pelagica*, pelagic fauna.

Pelàgio, *no.pr.m.* (*st. relig.*) Pelagius.

pèlago, *s.m.* (*letter.*) sea (*anche fig.*): *un — di guai*, a sea of troubles.

pelàme, *s.m.* hair; (*di cane*, *cavallo*, *ecc.*) coat; (*di uccelli*) plumage: *il — ruvido di un cane*, a dog's rough coat.

pelandróne, *s.m.* (*dial.*) lazy fellow, idler, lazybones.

pelàre, *v.t.* **1.** to unhair; (*spennare*) to pluck: *— una gallina*, to pluck a hen ‖ *— qlcu.*, (*scherz.*) (*radergli a zero i capelli*) to shave s.o.'s head (*o* to give s.o. a (good) crop); (*costringerlo ad un pagamento rilevante*) to fleece (*o* to skin) s.o.; *in quel negozio* *pelano*, they fleece you in that shop; *il parrucchiere mi ha pelato*, the hair-dresser has cropped my hair ‖ *prendere una gatta a, da* —, to let oneself in for sthg.: *hai preso una bella gatta da* —*!*, you have really let yourself in for sthg. there! 2. (*spellare*) to skin; (*sbucciare*) to peel, to pare: — *un coniglio*, to skin a rabbit; — *patate, pomodori*, to peel potatoes, tomatoes ‖ *è un freddo che pela*, it is a cold that pierces you to the bone; *questo vento pela*, this wind goes right through you ‖ **pelàrsi**, *v.r.* to lose one's hair; (*diventar calvo*) to become bald, to go bald; (*perdere le foglie*) to shed leaves.

pelargònio, *s.m.* (*bot.*) Pelargonium.

pelàsgico, *ag.* Pelasgic, Pelasgian: *civiltà pelasgica*, Pelasgic civilization.

pelàta, *s.f.* 1. (*atto del pelare*) peeling 2. (*scherz.*) (*testa calva*) bald head; (*calvizie*) baldness.

pelàto, *ag.* bald ‖ *zucca pelata*, (*scherz.*) bald-pate.

pelatúra, *s.f.* 1. unhairing; (*lo spennare*) plucking 2. (*spellatura*) peeling, paring.

Pelèo, *no.pr.m.* (*mit.*) Peleus.

Pèlia, *no.pr.m.* (*mit.*) Pelias.

Pèlio, *no.pr.m.* (*geog.*) Pelion.

pellàccia, *s.f.* 1. (*pelle dura*) hard skin, thick skin 2. (*persona furba*) cunning fellow, slyboots 3. (*ragazzaccio svogliato*) little rogue, rascal; (*fannullone*) idler.

pellàgra, *s.f.* (*patol.*) pellagra.

pellagróso, *ag.* pellagrous ‖ *s.m.* (*patol.*) pellagrin.

pellàio, *s.m.* furrier.

pellàme, *s.m.* hides (*pl.*); skins (*pl.*).

pèlle, *s.f.* 1. skin; (*carnagione*) complexion: — *chiara*, fair complexion (o skin); — *secca, sottile*, dry, thin skin; *malattia della* —, skin-disease; *prima* —, (*anat.*) outer skin; *seconda* —, (*anat.*) true skin; *porto sempre la maglia sulla* —, I always wear woollens next to my skin; *i serpenti cambiano la* — *ogni anno*, snakes slough their skins every year ‖ *a fior di* —, skin-deep ‖ *amici per la* —, bosom friends ‖ *ci giocherei la* —, (*fam.*) I should stake my life on it ‖ *hanno fatto una* — *di ridere*, (*fam.*) they split their sides with laughter ‖ *avere la* — *d'oca*, to come over goose-flesh (o goose-pimples): *far venire la* — *d'oca a qlcu.*, to give s.o. the creeps (o to make s.o.'s flesh creep o to give s.o. goose-pimples o to give s.o. goose-flesh) ‖ *avere la* — *dura*, *fig.* to be thick-skinned ‖ *essere nella* — *di qlcu.*, to be in s.o.'s shoes ‖ *essere tutto* — *e ossa*, to be all skin and bones (o to be a bag of bones) ‖ *fare la* — *a qlcu.*, to do s.o. in (o to kill s.o.) ‖ *fare la* — *lustra*, (*ingrassare*) to put on weight ‖ *non stare più nella* — *dalla gioia*, to be simply bursting (o to be beside oneself) with joy ‖ *ridere tra* — *e* —, to laugh up one's sleeve ‖ *rimetterci la* —, to lose one's life: *per quella stupida scommessa ci ha rimesso la* —, he paid for that stupid bet with his life ‖ *rischiare la* —, to risk one's life ‖ *salvare la* —, to save one's skin ‖ *temere per la propria* —, to fear for one's skin ‖ *vendere cara la* —, to sell one's life dearly (o to die hard) ‖ *non bisogna vendere la* — *dell'orso prima di averlo*, *prov.* don't count skin chickens before they are hatched 2. (*cuoio*) hide; skin: — *conciata, greggia*, dressed, raw hide; — *di capretto*, kid; — *di cavallo*, horse-hide; — *di daino*, buckskin; — *di talpa*, moleskin; — *di vitello*, calfskin; — *lucida*, (*per scarpe, ecc.*) patent-leather; — *verde*, green hide (o raw skin); *articoli in* —, leather articles; *guanti di* —, leather gloves; *rilegato in* —, leather-bound; *commerciare in pelli*, to trade in hides; *conciare pelli*, to tan hides 3. (*mascalzone*) crook: *non sapevo che* — *fosse quell'uomo*, I didn't know what a crook that man was 4. (*buccia*) peel; skin, rind: *la* — *di un'arancia*, orange-peel; *la* — *di una banana*, banana-skin; *la* — *di una mela*, apple-peel 5. (*del latte*) skin; (*del formaggio*) rind; (*di una salsiccia*) skin 6. (*tessuto*): — *d'uovo*, muslin 7. (*di un metallo*) skin (of casting).

pellegrína[1], *s.f.* woman pilgrim.

pellegrína[2], *s.f.* (*mantelletta da donna*) pelerine; tippet.

pellegrinàggio, *s.m.* pilgrimage: *in* —, on a pilgrimage; *fare un* —, to go on a pilgrimage.

pellegrinàre, *v.i.* 1. to go on a pilgrimage, to pilgrimage 2. (*vagabondare*) to wander, to roam: — *attraverso il mondo*, to roam about the world 3. (*viaggiare*) to travel.

pellegríno, *ag.* (*raro, strano*) rare, strange; (*straniero*) foreign; (*ramingo*) vagrant ‖ *s.m.* 1. pilgrim; (*viaggiatore*) traveller: *il bastone bianco del* —, the pilgrim's white staff; *le strade dei pellegrini*, pilgrims' ways; *siamo pellegrini sulla terra*, we are pilgrims on earth ‖ *i Padri Pellegrini*, (*st.*) the Pilgrim Fathers 2. (*ornit.*) peregrine falcon.

pelletteria, *s.f.* 1. (*articoli in pelle*) leather goods (*pl.*) 2. (*negozio di articoli in pelle*) leather goods shop.

pellettière, *s.m.* leather goods dealer.

pellicàno, *s.m.* 1. (*ornit.*) pelican 2. (*chim. chir.*) pelican.

pelliccería, *s.f.* 1. (*negozio di pellicce*) furrier's (shop) 2. (*pellicce*) furriery.

pellíccia, *s.f.* 1. fur: *la* — *del visone*, mink's fur; *animali da* —, furred animals (o fur); *foderato, guarnito di* —, lined with fur (o furred) 2. (*mantello*) fur coat: *devo mettermi la* —*?*, shall I wear my fur coat?

pelliccàio, *s.m.* furrier.

pellicciàme, *s.m.* furriery; furs (*pl.*).

pellícola, *s.f.* 1. (*sottile membrana*) film, pellicle, membrane 2. (*foto. cine.*) film: — *a passo ridotto*, sub-standard film; — *fotografica*, photographic film; — *impressionata*, exposed film; — *ininfiammabile*, safety film; — *invertibile*, reversible film; — *non impressionata*, unexposed film; — *sonora*, sound motion picture; *rullo di* —, rollfilm; *scatola per* — *cinematografica*, can; *sviluppare una* —, to develop a film.

pelliróssa, *s.m.* redskin, Red Indian.

pellúcido, *ag.* semi-transparent.

pélo, *s.m.* 1. hair; (*peluria*) down: *quel ragazzo ha già un po' di* — *sul mento*, that boy already has some down on his chin ‖ *un ragazzo di primo* —, a callow youth ‖ *ci mancò un* — *che non glielo dicessi*, I was within a hair's breadth of telling him; *se l'è cavata per un* —, he had a narrow squeak (o shave o he had a close shave); *si salvò per un* —, he saved his life by the skin of his teeth (o by a hair's breadth) ‖ *non gli torsi un* —, I didn't touch a hair of his head ‖ *quel vestito è un* — *troppo largo*, that dress is a trifle too large ‖ *avere il* — *sul cuore*, to be thick-skinned ‖ *avere il* — *sullo stomaco*, to be ruthless ‖ *cercare il* — *nell'uovo*, to split hairs ‖ *fare il* — *e il contropelo a qlcu.*, to give s.o. a clean shave; *fig.* to speak ill (o badly) of s.o. ‖ *non aver peli sulla lingua*, to be very outspoken 2. (*pelame*) coat, hair; (*pelliccia*) fur: *il* — *di un cane*, a dog's coat (o hair); *il* — *di un cavallo*, horse's coat; — *ruvido, liscio*, coarse, smooth (o sleek) coat; *cane dal* — *lungo*, long-haired (o shaggy) dog; *collo di* —, fur collar; *dal* — *raso*, short-haired; *scarpe col* —, fur-lined shoes; *il soffice* — *della volpe*, the soft coat of the fox ‖ *prima o poi ci lascerà il* —, (*la pagherà cara*) sooner or later he will pay dearly for it ‖ *cavalcare a* —, (*senza sella*) to ride bareback ‖ *essere d'un* — *e d'una lana, d'un* — *e d'una breccia*, (*essere della stessa risma*) to be tarred with the same brush ‖ *levare il* — *a qlcu.*, to tan (o to flay) s.o.'s hide; (*sgridarlo aspramente*) to go for s.o. ‖ *lisciare il* — *a qlcu.*, to soft-soap (o to flatter) s.o. ‖ *il lupo perde il* — *ma non il vizio*, *prov.* the leopard cannot change its spots 3. (*di tessuto grezzo*) pile; (*lavorato*) nap: *contro* —, against the grain 4. *pl.* (*di piante, filamenti*) hair 5. *pl.* (*di spazzola*) bristles 6. *il* — *dell'acqua*, the surface of the water.

Pèlope, *no.pr.m.* (*mit.*) Pelops.

Pelòpida, *no.pr.m.* (*st.*) Pelopidas.

Peloponnèso, *no.pr.m.* (*geog.*) Peloponnese, Peloponnesus ‖ *la guerra del* —, (*st.*) the Peloponnesian War.

pelosità, *s.f.* hairiness; (*villosità*) shagginess.

pelóso, *ag.* hairy; (*villoso*) shaggy.

pelòta, *s.f.* (*spor.*) pelota.

pèlta, *s.f.* (*st.*) pelta (*pl.* peltae).

péltro, *s.m.* pewter.

peluche, *s.f.* plush.

pelúria, *s.f.* down: *coperto di* —, downy.

pèlvi, *s.f.* (*anat.*) pelvis.

pèlvico, *ag.* pelvic.

péna, *s.f.* **1.** (*punizione*) punishment; penalty: — *capitale*, capital punishment; — *di morte*, death penalty; — *pecuniaria*, fine; *casa di* —, house of correction; *il massimo, minimo della* —, the maximum, minimum penalty; *il codice stabilisce le pene*, punishments (o penalties) are laid down by law; *infliggere una* —, to inflict a punishment (o a penalty); *scontare una* —, to undergo a term of punishment ‖ — *del contrappasso*, punishment fitting the crime ‖ — *sotto* — *di*, under penalty (o pain) of (o on pain of): *gli proibirono di tornare in patria (sotto)* — (*del*)*la vita*, he was forbidden to return to his country under pain of death ‖ — *eterna*, eternal punishment **2.** (*patimento, dolore fisico*) pain, suffering; (*afflizione, angoscia*) pain, pang; sorrow; affliction; grief; suffering: *le pene dell'amore, del rimorso*, the pains (o pangs) of love, of remorse; — *di stomaco*, stomach-ache; *una ricompensa a tutte le mie pene*, a reward for all my pains (o trouble); *una* — *che tortura*, a torment; *che cosa ti dà* —?, what is worrying you?; *egli mi fa* —, I feel sorry (o pity) for him; *ho provato molte pene*, I have experienced many sufferings; *nessuno può immaginarsi la mia* —; nobody can imagine my sorrow; *non darmi questa* —, don't give me this sorrow; *la sua cattiva condotta fu una gran* — *per i suoi genitori*, his bad behaviour was a great grief (o distress) to his parents; *sono in* — *per lui*, I am anxious (o worried) about him; *sto sempre in* — *quando ritardano la sera*, I always worry when they are late in the evening; *sentire, aver* — *per ql.co.*, *qlcu.*, to grieve at sthg., for s.o. ‖ *è un'anima in* —, he is a soul in torment ‖ *soffrire le pene dell'inferno*, to suffer the torments (o pains) of hell **3.** (*fatica, disturbo*) trouble: *non ne vale la* —, it isn't worth while; *non vale la* — *di andare*, it isn't worth going; *darsi la* — *di fare ql.co.*, to trouble (o to take the trouble) to do sthg.: *mi sono dato la* — *di informarlo, ma non mi ha neppure ringraziato*, I took the trouble to inform him and he never even thanked me ‖ *a mala* —, hardly (o scarcely): *cammina a mala* —, he can hardly walk; *erano venti a mala* —, they were scarcely twenty.

penàle, *ag.* **1.** criminal: *avvocato* —, criminal lawyer; *azione, codice, diritto* —, criminal action, code, law; *cause penali*, criminal suits; *intraprendere azione* — *contro qlcu.*, to take criminal proceedings against s.o. **2.** (*relativo alla pena*) penal: *colonia* —, penal colony; *stabilimento* —, penal establishment ‖ *s.f.* penalty, fine: *dovrà pagare la* —, he will have to pay the penalty.

penalísta, *s.m.* criminal lawyer; criminalist.

penalità, *s.f.* penalty.

penalménte, *av.* penally.

penàre, *v.i.* **1.** to suffer: *ha finito di* —, his sufferings are over; *nessuno sa quanto ho penato*, nobody knows how much I have suffered; *stasera il malato pena molto*, tonight the patient is suffering a lot; — *in esilio*, to suffer in exile **2.** (*durar fatica*) to be hardly able; to find it difficult: *abbiamo penato ad avere il tuo indirizzo*, we found it difficult to get your address; *penava a scrivere il suo nome*, he could hardly (o was hardly able to) write his name.

penàti, *s.m.pl.* (*relig. romana*) Penates.

pencolànte, *ag.* **1.** staggering, tottering, wobbling: *un'andatura* —, a wobbling gait **2.** (*esitante*) hesitating.

pencolàre, *v.i.* **1.** to stagger, to totter, to wobble;

(*essere poco saldo*) to be unsteady: *pencolava sulla sedia e finì per cadere*, he wobbled on his chair and then fell off; *il ramo pencolò a lungo prima di cadere*, the branch shook a while before falling down **2.** (*esitare*) to hesitate, to waver: — *fra diverse opinioni*, to hesitate (o to waver) between different opinions.

pendàglio, *s.m.* **1.** (*ciondolo*) pendant **2.** (*di spada*) frog **3.** *pl.* (*ornamenti*) hangings **4.** — *da forca*, (*spreg.*) gallows-bird.

pendant, *s.m.* pendant, companion: *questo quadro fa* — *all'altro*, this picture is the companion to the other one.

pendènte, *ag.* **1.** hanging, pendent **2.** (*inclinato*) leaning ‖ *Torre* — *di Pisa*, leaning tower of Pisa **3.** (*dir., ecc.*) pendent, pending: *una causa* —, a pending suit **4.** (*dubbioso*) wavering, undecided ‖ *s.m.* **1.** (*orecchino*) earring, ear-pendant **2.** (*ciondolo*) pendant.

pendènza, *s.f.* **1.** slope, incline: *la* — *di una strada, collina, tetto*, the slope of a road, a hill, a roof; — *longitudinale*, (*di strada*) longitudinal slope; — *trasversale*, (*di strada*) crossfall; *una lieve, forte* —, a slight, steep slope **2.** (*grado d'inclinazione*) gradient, grade: — *limite*, (*ferr.*) limiting (o maximum) gradient; — *massima*, (*ferr.*) ruling gradient; — *minima di volo librato*, (*aer.*) minimum gliding angle **3.** (*dir.*) pending suit; (*comm.*) outstanding account: *c'è una* — *di alcune migliaia di lire*, there is an outstanding account of a few thousand lire; *cercherò di sistemare tutte quelle pendenze*, I shall try to settle all those outstanding matters **4.** (*inclinazione*) inclination, tendency.

pèndere, *v.i.* **1.** to hang (down): *una corda pendeva dal soffitto*, a rope was hanging from the ceiling; *grosse mele pendevano dagli alberi*, big apples hung on the trees; *ti pende la sottoveste*, your petticoat shows; *vi erano bandiere che pendevano sulle pareti*, there were flags hanging on the walls ‖ *essa pende dalle sue labbra*, she hangs on his lips **2.** (*inclinare*) to lean, to incline; to be inclined (anche *fig.*): *egli pende verso il socialismo*, he leans towards socialism; *la nave pende sensibilmente a tribordo*, the ship lists heavily (o has a bad list) to starboard; *pendo a credere che sia innocente*, I am inclined to believe that he is innocent; *la Torre di Pisa pende da un lato*, the tower of Pisa leans to one side **3.** (*di superficie, essere in declivio*) to slope; to slant: *il bosco pende verso il fiume*, the wood slopes (down) to the river; *la strada pende molto*, the road is very steep; *il tetto pende*, the roof slants (o slopes) **4.** (*incombere*) to hang (over sthg.), to overhang (anche *fig.*): *una grande calamità pendeva sul paese*, a great calamity hung over the country; *rupe che pende minacciosa*, beetling (o overhanging) rock **5.** (*di causa, lite, essere controversa*) to be pending: *la causa pende tuttora*, the suit is still pending **6.** (*essere indeciso*) to hesitate, to waver: *pendeva tra l'accettare e il rifiutare*, he wavered between accepting and refusing.

pendíce, *s.f.* slope; declivity.

pendío, *s.m.* **1.** slope; declivity; slant: *la villa è su un* —, the villa is on a slope ‖ *essere in, a* —, to be sloping (o to slope) **2.** (*grado di pendenza*) gradient, slope.

pèndola, *s.f.* pendulum-clock.

pendolàre, *ag.* pendular.

pèndolo, *s.m.* **1.** pendulum: — *a compensazione*, compensation pendulum; — *balistico*, ballistic pendulum; — *fisico, composto*, (*fis.*) compound pendulum; — *matematico, semplice*, (*fis.*) simple pendulum; *orologio a* —, pendulum-clock; *oscillazione del* —, swing of the pendulum **2.** (*edil.*) (*archipendolo*) plumb-rule.

pèndulo, *ag.* hanging; pendulous ‖ *velo* —, (*anat.*) uvula.

pène, *s.m.* (*anat.*) penis.

Penèlope, *no.pr.f.* (*mit.*) Penelope.

pènero, *s.m.* (*frangia*) fringe.

penetràbile, *ag.* penetrable.

penetrabilità, *s.f.* penetrability.

penetràli, *s.m.pl.* (*archeol.*) penetralia (anche *fig.*).

penetrànte, *ag.* **1.** (*di freddo*) penetrating, piercing, biting; (*di suono*) penetrating, piercing; (*di odore*) pungent, powerful, pervasive; (*di sguardo*) searching, piercing, keen; (*di mente*) acute, discerning: *grido* —, shrill (*o* piercing) cry **2.** (*di ferita*) deep.

penetràre, *v.t.* **1.** to penetrate; (*a fatica, con oggetto acuto*) to pierce: *la luce penetra l'oscurità*, light penetrates darkness **2.** (*arrivare a capire, a conoscere*) to penetrate, to get to the heart of (sthg.): — *un mistero, la verità*, to penetrate (*o* to get to the heart of) a mystery, the truth; — *i più oscuri recessi di un'anima*, to penetrate the innermost recesses of a soul ‖ *v.i.* **1.** to penetrate (into sthg.); (*a fatica, con oggetto acuto*) to pierce (into sthg.); (*passare attraverso*) to pass through (sthg.); (*entrare*) to go into (sthg.), to enter (sthg.); (*entrare furtivamente*) to steal into (sthg.): *i ladri penetrarono nell'orto*, the thieves stole into the garden; *la luce penetrava dalla finestra*, the light passed through the window; *una spina è penetrata nella pelle*, a thorn has penetrated (*o* pierced) the skin **2.** (*di notizie, idee*) to penetrate (into sthg.); to filter (into sthg.); (*di freddo, di suono*) to pierce (into sthg.): *un freddo che penetra*, a piercing (*o* biting) cold; *le loro idee stanno lentamente penetrando nel nostro mondo*, their ideas are slowly penetrating (*o* filtering) into our world; *un rumore che penetra*, a piercing (*o* shrill) noise.

penetratíva, *s.f.* acuteness of mind, keen insight.

penetratívo, *ag.* penetrating, penetrative.

penetrazióne, *s.f.* **1.** penetration ‖ — *pacifica*, (*pol.*) peaceful penetration **2.** *V.* **penetratíva**.

penicillína, *s.f.* (*farm.*) penicillin.

peninsulàre, *ag.* peninsular.

penísola, *s.f.* peninsula.

penitènte, *ag.* penitent, repentant: *è un peccatore* —, he is a repentant sinner ‖ *s.c.* penitent.

penitènza, *s.f.* **1.** (*teol.*) penance: *sacramento della* —, Sacrament of Penance; *far* —, to do penance **2.** (*pentimento*) penitence, repentance **3.** (*castigo*) punishment: *mettere qlcu. in* —, to punish s.o. **4.** (*nei giuochi*) forfeit.

penitenziàle, *ag.* penitential: *salmi penitenziali*, penitential psalms.

penitenziàre, *v.t.* **1.** to impose penance on (s.o.) **2.** (*castigare*) to chastise.

penitenziàrio, *ag.* penitentiary ‖ *s.m.* (*prigione*) prison, gaol, jail; (*amer.*) penitentiary.

penitenzière, *s.m.* (*eccl.*) penitentiary: — *maggiore*, Grand Penitentiary.

penitenziería, *s.f.* penitentiary.

pénna, *s.f.* **1.** (*di uccello*) feather: — *maestra*, quill -feather (*o* pen-feather); *non ha ancora messo le penne*, he is still unfledged; *il pavone ha delle belle penne*, the peacock has fine feathers (*o* fine plumage); *questi uccelli hanno appena messo le penne*, these birds are just fledged (*o* are fledglings) ‖ *cane da* —, gun-dog ‖ *ci ha lasciato le penne*, (*fam.*) he did not get away unscathed **2.** (*usata come ornamento*) feather, plume: *penne di struzzo*, ostrich feathers; *cappello ornato di penne*, hat adorned with plumes **3.** (*per scrivere*) pen: — *a sfera*, ball(-point) pen; — *d'acciaio*, steel pen; — *d'oca*, quill (-pen); — *stilografica*, fountain -pen; *disegno a* —, pen-and-ink drawing; *scritto a* —, handwritten; *tratto, frego di* —, stroke of the pen; *passare a* — *un disegno*, to ink in a drawing ‖ *scorso di* —, (*lapsus*) slip of the pen (*o* lapsus calami) ‖ *uomo di* —, penman ‖ *dar di* —, (*cancellare*) to cross out ‖ *lasciare nella* —, to leave out **4.** (*scrittore*) penman (*pl.* penmen), writer, pen: *è una delle migliori penne d'Italia*, he is one of the best writers in Italy **5.** *pl.* (*ali*) wings: *spiegare le penne*, to take wing **6.** (*estremità del martello*) peen: *martellare a* —, to peen **7.** (*parte della freccia*) feather (of arrow) **8.** (*mus.*) (*plettro*) quill.

pennacchièra, *s.f.* plume.

pennàcchio, *s.m.* **1.** plume; bunch of feathers; (*mil.*) panache: *un elmo ornato di un* —, a plumed

helmet ‖ — *di fumo*, (*di un camino*) wreath (*o* plume) of smoke; (*di una locomotiva*) trail of smoke **2.** (*arch.*) pendentive.

pennacchiúto, *ag.* plumed.

pennaiuòlo, *s.m.* (*spreg.*) hack (writer).

pennàta, *s.f.* **1.** penful of ink **2.** (*segno di penna*) stroke of the pen.

pennàto, *ag.* **1.** feathered **2.** (*bot.*) pinnate, pinnated ‖ *s.m.* (*agr.*) bill-hook.

pennàtula, *s.f.* (*zool.*) Pennatula.

pennécchio, *s.m.* flax on the distaff, wool on the distaff.

pennèlla, *s.f.* flat brush, whitewash brush.

pennellàre, *v.i.* **1.** to brush **2.** (*mar.*) to backwash.

pennellàta, *s.f.* stroke of the brush; touch of the brush: — *da maestro*, masterstroke; *dare l'ultima* —, to put the finishing touch ‖ *descrizione a vivaci pennellate*, vivid (*o* lively) description.

pennellatúra, *s.f.* **1.** brushwork **2.** (*med.*) painting.

pennelleggiàre, *v.t.* to paint ‖ *v.i.* to work with a brush.

pennelléssa, *s.f.* flat brush.

pennèllo, *s.m.* **1.** brush; (*da pittore*) paint-brush: — *da imbianchino*, whitewash brush; — *di setole*, bristle brush; — *per la barba*, shaving-brush ‖ *arte del* —, painting ‖ *fare ql.co. a* —, to do sthg. perfectly; *stare a* —, to fit perfectly **2.** *fig.* (*pittore*) painter: *è uno dei migliori pennelli d'Italia*, he is one of the best painters in Italy **3.** (*mar.*) broad pennant **4.** (*idraulica*) groin **5.** (*fis. ott.*) pencil.

pennifórme, *ag.* penniform.

penninèrvio, *ag.* penninerved.

Pennine (Àlpi), *no.pr.f.pl.* (*geog.*) Pennine Alps.

Pennini (mónti), *no.pr.m.pl.* (*geog.*) Pennine Chain.

penníno, *s.m.* nib, pen-nib.

pennivéndolo, *s.m.* (*spreg.*) hack (writer).

pennóne, *s.m.* **1.** pennon, pennant **2.** (*mar.*) yard: — *di contromezzana*, mizzen-topsail-yard; — *di controvelaccio*, main-royal yard; — *di gabbia*, main-topsail yard; — *di maestra*, mainyard; — *di mezzana*, cross -jack yard; — *di trinchetto*, foreyard; — *di velaccio*, maintop-gallant-yard; — *maggiore*, lower yard.

pennóso, *ag.* feathered.

pennúto, *ag.* feathered, fledged ‖ *s.m.* bird.

penómbra, *s.f.* **1.** half-light, dim light, twilight **2.** (*astr.*) penumbra (*pl.* penumbrae, penumbras).

penosaménte, *av.* **1.** painfully **2.** (*con difficoltà*) with difficulty.

penóso, *ag.* painful: *silenzio* —, painful silence.

pensàbile, *ag.* thinkable, imaginable.

pensaménto, *s.m.* **1.** thought **2.** (*way of*) thinking: *secondo il mio* —, according to my way of thinking **3.** (*deliberazione, proposito*) purpose.

pensànte, *ag.* thinking ‖ *s.m.*: *un ben* —, a right -minded person (*o* a right-thinking person).

pensàre, *v.t.* **1.** to think: *che cosa devo* — *di questo*, what am I to think of (*o* about) that?; *lo pensavo un uomo più intelligente*, I thought him a more intelligent man; *pensavo sciocco il farlo*, I thought it silly to do it; *pensi che verrà?*, do you think he will come?; *penso che sia meglio rimanere*, I think (that) it is better to remain; *non lo pensavo possibile*, I didn't think it possible; *penso di no*, I don't think so (*o* I think not); *penso di sì*, I think so **2.** (*proporsi, deliberare*) to think, to decide: *ho pensato di non venire*, I have decided not to come; *ho pensato che partirò con te*, I have made up my mind I shall leave with you; *non ho mai pensato di farlo*, I have never thought of doing it; *penso di telefonargli*, I think I shall ring him up **3.** (*immaginare*) to think, to imagine: *deve avere quarant'anni, penso*, he must be forty, I guess; *lo aspetto da due anni, pensa!*, I have been waiting for him for two years, just think of it!; *non avrei mai pensato di incontrarlo ancora*, I never thought I'd meet him again; *non pensavo di urtare la sua sensibilità*, I didn't think I would hurt his feelings **4.** (*considerare*) to think, to consider: *dobbiamo — che non è più giovane*, we must think (o consider) that he is no longer a young man **5.** (*inventare, architettare*) to think up, to invent: *— un mezzo, un espediente*, to devise a means, an expedient ‖ *una ne fa e una ne pensa*, he is always up to something ‖ *v.i.***1.** to think (of s.o., sthg., of doing): *a che stai pensando?*, what are you thinking of?; *ci penserò su*, I'll think it over; *dobbiamo — a un modo di dirglielo*, we must think out (o of) a way of telling him; *è un caso che fa —*, it is a case which makes one think; *ho altro da —*, I have more important business to attend to (o *fam.* I have other fish to fry); *lasciamici —*, let me think it over; *penso con la mia testa*, I think with my head; *la sua salute mi dà da —*, his health worries me; *smetti di — al tuo lavoro*, stop thinking of (o about) your work; *— bene di qlcu.*, to think well of s.o.; *— male di ql.co.*, to think ill of sthg.; *— male di qlcu.*, to have a bad opinion of s.o. ‖ *penso, dunque sono*, I think, therefore I am **2.** (*badare*) to mind (sthg., doing); to take care (of s.o., sthg.), to look after (s.o., sthg.): *chi penserebbe a suo padre se ella dovesse morire?*, who would look after her father, if she should die?; *io penso ai bambini, egli pensa al negozio*, I take care of the children, he minds the shop ‖ *pensa ai fatti tuoi*, mind your own business.

pensàta, *s.f.* thought, idea: *ho fatto una bella —*, I had a good idea (o *fam.* I had a brain-wave).

pensataménte, *av.* (*deliberatamente*) intentionally, designedly, on purpose, deliberately; (*consideratamente*) thinkingly.

pensàto, *ag.* considered, meditated.

pensatóio, *s.m.* quiet place to think ‖ *entrare nel —*, to put on one's thinking-cap.

pensatóre, *s.m.* thinker ‖ *libero —*, freethinker.

pensièro, *s.m.* **1.** thought: *— nobile, gentile*, noble, kind thought; *assorto nei suoi pensieri*, absorbed (o lost) in thought; *la lettura del —*, thought-reading; *la rapidità del —*, the quickness of thought; *sei sempre nei miei pensieri*, you are always in my thoughts ‖ *al — di, che...*, at the thought of, that... ‖ *viola del —*, (*bot.*) pansy ‖ *essere sopra —*, to be thoughtful (o to be lost in thought) **2.** (*mente*) mind: *conservare desto e agile il —*, to conserve a quick and sharp mind **3.** (*modo di pensare*) thought; way of thinking: *il — religioso dei Greci*, the religious thought of the Greeks; *secondo il — di Byron*, according to Byron's way of thinking **4.** (*opinione*) mind, opinion: *non conosco il suo —*, I don't know his mind; *siamo dello stesso —*, we are of one mind; *cambiar —*, to change one's mind; *dire il proprio —*, to speak one's mind **5.** (*cura, attenzione*) thought, care: *ella è piena di pensieri per suo padre*, she is full of thought for her father; *tutti i miei pensieri sono per lui*, all my thoughts are for him **6.** (*ansia, preoccupazione*) trouble, worry: *la mia vita è piena di pensieri*, my life is full of troubles (o worries); *non darti — di farlo*, don't trouble to do it; *non darti — per questo*, don't worry about that; *quel ragazzo è un gran —*, that boy is a great worry; *la sua salute mi dà —*, his health worries me; *stare in — per qlcu., ql.co.*, to worry (o to be anxious) about s.o., sthg. **7.** (*intenzione, proposito*) idea, intention: *quale è il vostro —?*, what is your idea (o intention)? (o what have you got in mind?).

pensieróso, *ag.* thoughtful; (*malinconico, meditabondo*) pensive: *è troppo pensierosa per la sua età*, she is too thoughtful for her age; *s'è fatto taciturno e —*, he has grown silent and pensive.

pènsile, *ag.* hanging, suspended, pensile: *giardino —*, roof-garden ‖ *i giardini pensili di Babilonia*, the hanging gardens of Babylon.

pensilína, *s.f.* penthouse; (*per chi aspetta mezzi di trasporto pubblici*) shelter.

pensionànte, *s.m.* boarder, paying-guest, lodger: *abbiamo avuto molti pensionanti nella scorsa estate*, we had many boarders (o paying-guests) last summer.

pensionàre, *v.t.* **1.** (*assegnare una pensione a*) to pension, to give a pension to (s.o.) **2.** (*mettere in pensione*) to pension off; (*per limiti d'età*) to superannuate.

pensionàto, *ag.* pensioned, retired: *si recò a far visita ad un collega —*, he went to see a retired colleague ‖ *s.m.* **1.** pensioner, retired person: *— dell'esercito, dello Stato*, Army, State pensioner; *casa di riposo per pensionati*, pensioners' home; *il vecchio — vive solo da molti anni*, the old pensioner has been living alone for many years **2.** (*convitto*) student's home, hostel; *il — universitario di questa città ospita duecento studenti*, the University hostel in this town houses two hundred students **3.** (*borsa di studio*) scholarship.

pensióne, *s.f.* **1.** (*assegno vitalizio*) pension: *— di guerra*, war pension; *— per la vecchiaia*, old-age pension; *percepiva una — di trentamila lire*, he received a pension of thirty thousand lire; *concedere una —*, to grant a pension; *godere di una —*, to enjoy (o to receive) a pension; *riscuotere la —*, to draw one's pension; *vivere di una —*, to live on a pension ‖ *andare in —*, to retire on a pension; *essere in —*, to be retired: *è in — dal 1955*, he has been retired since 1955 ‖ *mandare, mettere in —*, to pension off: *fu messo in — dopo quarant'anni di servizio*, he was pensioned off after forty years' service **2.** (*vitto e alloggio*) board and lodging: *— completa*, full board; *mezza —*, demi-pension; *essere a —*, to be boarding: *era a — da una vedova*, he was boarding at a widow's; *far —, tenere a —*, to take in boarders (o lodgers o paying guests); *faceva — a due studenti*, two students boarded with her; *mettere a — qlcu.*, to put s.o. to board **3.** (*istituzione alberghiera*) boarding-house.

pènso, *s.m.* **1.** (*compito a casa*) home work **2.** (*compito assegnato per punizione*) extra work.

pensóso, *ag.* **1.** pensive, thoughtful, absorbed in thought: *quel giorno era pensosa*, she was pensive that day **2.** (*sollecito*) thoughtful, considerate: *essere più — d'altrui che di se stesso*, to be more thoughtful of others than of oneself.

pentàcolo, *sm.* pentacle.

pentacòrdo, *s.m.* (*mus.*) pentachord.

pentaèdro, *s.m.* (*geom.*) pentahedron.

pentagonàle, *ag.* pentagonal.

pentàgono, *s.m.* (*geom.*) pentagon.

pentagràmma, *s.m.* (*mus.*) pentagram.

pentàmetro, *s.m.* (*poes.*) pentameter.

pentapodía, *s.f.* (*poes.*) pentapody.

pentarchía, *s.f.* pentarchy.

Pentatèuco, *s.m.* (*Bibbia*) Pentateuch.

pèntatlo, *s.m.* (*spor.*) pentathlon.

Pentecòste, *s.f.* (*eccl.*) Whitsunday, Pentecost; (*degli ebrei*) Pentecost: *domenica di —*, Whitsunday.

pentèlico, *ag.* Pentelic, Pentelican: *marmo —*, Pentelic marble ‖ **Pentèlico**, *no.pr.m.* (*geog.*) Mount Pentelicus.

Pentèo, *no.pr.m.* (*mit.*) Pentheus.

Pentesilèa, *no.pr.f.* (*mit.*) Penthesilea.

pentiménto, *s.m.* repentance; (*rincrescimento*) regret: *sincero, tardo — dei propri peccati*, true, late repentance for one's sins; *mostrare —*, to show repentance (o regret); *provare —*, to repent (o to regret) ‖ *volevo andare a Milano, ma mi è venuto un —*, I wanted to go to Milan, but I've changed my mind.

pentírsi, *v.r.* **1.** to repent (sthg., of sthg.); to regret (sthg., doing): *ben presto si pentì della sua generosità*, he soon regretted his generosity; *me ne pento amaramente*, I regret it bitterly; *mi pento di avergli detto*, I regret having told (o telling) him; *mi pento di ciò che ho fatto*, I repent (of) what I have done; *non ho niente di cui pentirmi*, I have nothing to repent of; *non te ne pentirai*, you will not regret it; *si pentì di aver parlato così aspramente*, he regretted speaking so rudely; *— dei propri peccati*, to repent (of) one's sins ‖ *pensaci prima per non pentirti poi, prov.* look before you leap **2.** (*cambiare proposito*) to change one's mind: *voleva fare il medico ma poi se ne pentì,* he wanted to be a doctor but then he changed his mind.

pèntodo, *s.m.* (*rad.*) pentode, pentode valve.

pèntola, *s.f.* **1.** pot, casserole: — *di terracotta,* earthenware pot ‖ *il pentolino del latte,* the milk-jug ‖ *ql.co. bolle in* —, *fig.* sthg. is brewing ‖ *il diavolo fa le pentole ma non i coperchi, prov.* truth (o murder) will out **2.** (*contenuto di una pentola*) potful: *una* — *di patate,* a potful of potatoes.

pentolàio, *s.m.* **1.** (*chi vende pentole*) seller of earthenware articles **2.** (*chi fabbrica pentole*) potter.

pentolàta, *s.f.* **1.** potful **2.** (*colpo*) blow with a pot.

pentòsio, *s.m.pl.* (*chim.*) pentoses.

pentotàl, *s.m.* (*farm.*) pentothal.

penúltimo, *ag.* penultimate: *la penultima sillaba,* the penultimate syllable (o the last syllable but one) ‖ *s.m.* penultimate, last but one: *era il* — *della fila,* he was the last but one in the row.

penúria, *s.f.* shortage, scarcity, dearth; (*rar.*) penury: — *d'acqua,* shortage (o scarcity) of water; — *di insegnanti,* shortage (o scarcity) of teachers; — *di mezzi,* lack of means; *c'è* — *di operai specializzati qui,* there is shortage of skilled labour here; *c'era gran* — *di notizie,* there was a great dearth of news.

penzolàre, *v.i.* to dangle; to hang (down): — *da un ramo,* to dangle from a branch.

pènzolo, *s.m.* **1.** dangling thing; hanging thing; pendant **2.** (*grappolo di uva*) (hanging) cluster, (hanging) bunch **3.** (*ciondolo ornamentale*) pendant **4.** (*mar.*) pendant, pennant.

penzolóni, *ag.* dangling; hanging; hanging down (*predicativo*): *un cane con le orecchie* —, a dog with hanging ears; *seduto con le gambe* —, seated with his feet dangling; *stava là, con le braccia* — *e un sorriso stupido,* he was standing there, his arms hanging down, and a foolish smile on his face ‖ *av.: star* —, to hang (down).

peòcio, *s.m.* (*dial. zool.*) mussel.

peònia, *s.f.* (*bot.*) peony.

pepaiuòla, *s.f.* **1.** pepper-pot, pepper-box **2.** (*macinapepe*) pepper-mill.

pepàto, *ag.* **1.** peppery, peppered ‖ *pan* —, gingerbread **2.** *fig.* (*pungente*) peppery, sharp, biting: *parole pepate,* biting words; *una risposta pepata,* a sharp answer **3.** (*fam.*) (*esorbitante*) exorbitant: *un prezzo* —, an exorbitant price.

pépe, *s.m.* **1.** (*bot.*) Black Pepper **2.** (*spezie*) pepper: — *bianco, nero, rosso, di Caienna,* white, black, red, Cayenne pepper; — *in chicchi, macinato,* whole, ground pepper; *grano di* —, peppercorn; *condire con* —, to pepper (o to sprinkle with pepper) ‖ *barba, capelli, stoffa sale e* —, pepper-and-salt beard, hair, cloth ‖ *una ragazza tutto* —, a sprightly girl (o fam. a girl full of pep).

peperíno, *ag.* pepper-coloured ‖ *s.m.* (*min.*) peperino.

peperíta, *ag.: menta* —, peppermint.

peperóne, *s.m.* **1.** (*bot.*) Capsicum **2.** (*il frutto*) pepper, Guinea Pepper, Spur Pepper; (*piccante*) chilli, chilly: *peperoni sott'aceto,* pickled peppers (o chillies) ‖ *rosso come un* —, as red as a beetroot **3.** *fig.* (*scherz.*) (*grosso naso*) beak.

pepinièra, *s.f.* seed-bed; nursery.

pepíno, *s.m.* *fig.* sprightly child, lively child: *che* — *quella bimba!,* what a sprightly little girl!.

pepíta, *s.f.* nugget.

pèplo, *s.m.* peplos, peplum (*pl.* peplums, pepla).

pepolíno, *s.m.* (*bot.*) thyme.

Pèppe, Pèppo, *no.pr.m.* *dim.* di **Giusèppe.**

pepsína, *s.f.* (*biol. farm.*) pepsin.

pèptico, *ag.* (*biol. farm.*) peptic: *glandole peptiche,* peptic glands.

peptóne, *s.m.* (*chim. farm.*) peptone.

per, *prep.* **1.** (*moto per luogo*) **through;** (all) **over;** (*senza direzione fissa*) **about:** — *tutto il paese, il corpo,*

all over the country, the body; *passai* — *Milano,* I passed (o I went) through Milan; *sono venuto* — *i campi,* I came through the fields; *passeggiare* — *un giardino,* to walk about a garden; *vagabondare* — *il mondo,* to wander all over (o about) the world **2.** (*moto a luogo*) **for:** *partire* — *un luogo,* to leave for a place: *domani parto* — *Roma,* tomorrow I am leaving for Rome **3.** (*stato in luogo*) **in:** *lo vidi* — *la strada,* I saw him in the street **4.** (*estensione*) **for:** *questa strada si estende* — *20 miglia,* this road goes on for 20 miles; *questo bosco si estende* — *30 miglia quadrate,* this wood covers 30 square miles **5.** (*nei complementi di tempo*) (*per un certo periodo di tempo o per un determinato giorno, una determinata occasione*) **for;** (*entro*) **by;** (*per un intero periodo di tempo*) **through(out):** — *mezz'ora,* for half an hour; — *tutta l'estate,* all through the summer (o the whole summer through); *deve essere pronto* — *il mio compleanno,* it must be ready for my birthday; *sarà finito* — *la fine dell'anno,* it will be finished by the end of the year; *sarò di ritorno* — *le cinque,* I'll be back by five o' clock; *torno* — *Natale,* I'll be back for Christmas **6.** (*mezzo*) **by; through:** — *ferrovia,* by rail; — *lettera,* by letter; — *mare,* by sea; — *posta,* by post; — *la strada maestra,* by the main road; — *telefono,* by telephone; — *telegramma,* by telegram; — *terra,* by land; — *via aerea,* by air mail; *l'inglese* — *radio,* English by radio; *lo ebbi* — *mezzo di mio padre,* I got it through my father ‖ *prendere una città* — *fame,* to starve a besieged city into surrender **7.** (*prezzo*) **for:** *l'ho venduto* — *2.000 lire,* I have sold it for 2,000 lire; *ricevettero regali* — *due milioni,* they received two million lire worth of presents **8.** (*causa*) **owing to; because of; on account of; for; out of; through:** — *ambizione, dispetto, gelosia, odio, orgoglio,* out of ambition, spite, jealousy, hatred, pride; *egli fu rimproverato* — *la sua negligenza,* he was scolded for his negligence; *lo manderò via* — *quel che ha fatto,* I shall dismiss him on account of what he has done; *non lavora più* — *la sua cattiva salute,* he doesn't work any longer owing to ill-health; *non potevamo veder nulla* — *la nebbia,* we couldn't see anything owing to (o for) the fog; *questo non accadde* — *colpa mia,* this happened through no fault of mine; *sarà perdonato* — *la sua gentilezza,* he will be forgiven on account of his kindness; *sono stato rimproverato* — *te,* I have been reproved because of you **9.** (*colpa*) **for:** *fu processato* — *omicidio,* he was tried for murder **10.** (*vantaggio, interesse*) **for:** *fallo* — *me,* do it for me; *lavoro* — *la mia famiglia,* I work for my family; *non va bene* — *la tua salute,* it is not good for your health **11.** (*fine, scopo*) **for:** *la lotta* — *la vita,* the struggle for life; — *che cosa mi hai chiamato?,* what have you called me for? **12.** (*con valore limitativo*) **for;** (*nei riguardi di*) **to:** — *me,* — *quel che mi concerne,* as for me, as far as I am concerned; — *questa volta,* for this time; *è troppo difficile* — *lui,* it's too difficult for him; *fu un padre* — *me,* he was a father to me; *se non fosse* — *me,* if it were not for me (o but for me) **13.** (*con valore distributivo*) **per:** — *cento,* per cent: *dieci* — *cento delle vendite,* ten per cent of the sales; — *persona,* per head (o apiece o each) **14.** (*come simbolo matematico*) **by:** *dividere 60* — *10,* to divide 60 by 10; *moltiplicare* — *tre,* to multiply by three **15.** (*con complementi predicativi*) **as; for:** *ho un tedesco* — *compagno di camera,* I have a German as room-mate; *l'ho preso* — *italiano,* I took him for an Italian; *mi ha preso* — *stupido,* he has taken me for a fool; *questo va bene* — *regalo di nozze,* this will do for (o as) a wedding-present **16.** (*Fraseologia*): — *l'addietro,* in the past (o formerly); — *amor di Dio,* mio, for God's sake, my sake; — *l'appunto,* just so (o precisely); — *caso,* by chance; — *fortuna,* luckily; — *l'innanzi,* hitherto; — *maggior parte,* for the most part (o mostly); — *modo che,* so that; — *il momento,* for the time being; — *natura,* by nature; — *nulla!,* not at all!; — *lo più,* generally; — *sempre*, for ever; — *tempo*, early; *giorno* — *giorno*, day by day; *molto rumore* — *nulla*, much ado about nothing; *mi dispiacc* — *te*, I'm sorry for your sake; *cambiare* — *il meglio*, to change for the better.

per, *cong.* **1.** (*finale*) to, in order to (do); (*retto da sostantivi*) for (doing): *un abito* — *andare a teatro*, a dress for going to the theatre; *andai da lui* — *avere indietro il mio denaro*, I went to him (in order) to get my money back; *sono venuto* — *parlarti, vederti*, I have come to speak to you, to see you **2.** (*causale*) for (doing): *fu imprigionato* — *aver rubato del pane*, he was sent to prison for stealing bread; *sarà punito* — *essere arrivato in ritardo*, he will be punished for arriving late **3.** *stare* — *fare ql.co., essere lì lì* — *fare ql.co.*, to be about to do sthg. (*o* to be on the point of doing sthg. *o* to be just going to do sthg.): *ero lì lì, stavo* — *dirglielo*, I was on the point of telling him (*o* I was just going to tell him); *stavo, ero lì lì* — *cadere*, I nearly fell **4.** — ... *che...*, (con valore concessivo): — *sciocco che egli sia*, however foolish he may be.

péra, *s.f.* **1.** pear: *pere cotte al forno*, baked pears ‖ *non vale una* — *cotta*, it isn't worth twopence (*o* a fig) ‖ *cascare come una* — *cotta*, (*innamorarsi*) to fall head over heels in love; (*addormentarsi di colpo*) to drop into a deep sleep ‖ *cascare come le pere cotte*, to die like flies ‖ *dar le pere a qlcu.*, to give s.o. the sack **2.** (*scherz.*) (*testa*) head, pate: *grattarsi la* —, to scratch one's head **3.** (*bulbo*) bulb **4.** (*interruttore elettrico a forma di pera*) pear-switch **5.** (*strumento per praticare il clistere*) enema, rubber-syringe.

perbène, *ag.* honest; respectable; nice: *sono gente* —, they are nice people ‖ *av.* well, properly; nicely.

perboràto, *s.m.* (*chim.*) perborate.

pèrca, *s.f.* (*ittiol.*) perch.

percàlle, *s.m.* (*tessuto*) percale.

percallína, *s.f.* (*tessuto*) percaline.

percentuàle, *ag.* per cent: *saggio, tasso* —, rate per cent (*o* per cent rate) ‖ *s.f.* percentage: — *delle nascite*, percentage of births; — *maggiore, minore*, higher, lower percentage; — *sugli acquisti, sulle vendite*, percentage on purchases, on sales; *solo una piccola* — *di alunni è stata promossa*, only a small percentage of pupils passed; *concedere una* — *su tutte le operazioni*, to allow a percentage on all transactions.

percepíbile, *ag.* **1.** perceptible, discernable, noticeable **2.** (*comm.*) receivable, that may be received.

percepíre, *v.t.* **1.** to perceive, to become aware of (sthg.): — *una sensazione*, to experience a sensation **2.** (*comm.*) to receive: *da un anno non percepisce lo stipendio*, he has not received his salary for a year.

percettíbile, *ag.* perceptible: *suoni percettibili*, audible sounds; *l'anima non è* — *ai sensi*, the soul is not perceptible by any sense; *c'è una differenza* —, there is a perceptible difference.

percettibilità, *s.f.* perceptibility.

percettíva, percettività, *s.f.* perceptiveness.

percettívo, *ag.* perceptive.

percezióne, *s.f.* perception: *la* — *della verità*, the perception of the truth.

perché, *cong.* **1.** interr. why; (*a quale scopo*) what... for; (*arc.*) wherefore: — *hai preparato tutto questo?*, what have you prepared all this for?; — *l'hai fatto?*, why did you do it?; — *non ci vai domani?*, why do you not go there tomorrow?; *dimmi* — *l'hai fatto*, tell me why you have done it ‖ — *mai?*, why on earth?: *mi domando* — *mai ha fatto una cosa simile*, I wonder why on earth he has done such a thing ‖ — *no?*, why not? ‖ *ma* — ?, but why? **2.** (*esplicativo*) because; as; since, for: *ho dormito un po' questo pomeriggio* — *ero stanco*, I slept a little this afternoon because I was tired; *non ho potuto vederlo* — *non c'era*, as (*o* since) he wasn't there, I wasn't able to see him; « *Perchè non*

sei venuto? », « *Perchè non ne avevo voglia* », "Why didn't you come?", "Because I didn't feel like it" **3.** (*finale*) so (that); in order that: *lascia aperta la porta* — *il gatto possa entrare*, leave the door open so (that) the cat can come in **4.** (*in correlazione con* troppo): *è troppo onesto* — *possa rubare*, he is too honest to steal; *questo tavolo è troppo pesante* — *lui possa sollevarlo*, this table is too heavy for him to lift ‖ *s.m.* **reason**; why: *il* — *non lo so*, I don't know why; *senza un* —, without any particular reason; *questo è il* — *della mia partenza improvvisa*, this is the reason for my sudden departure (*o* this is the reason why I left suddenly); *vuoi sapere il* — ?, would you like to know why? ‖ *il mio bambino è nell'età dei* —, my child has reached the age when he is always asking why ‖ *voleva sapere il* — *e il percome*, she wanted to know the why(s) and wherefore(s).

perciò, *cong.* so, therefore: *A è uguale a B, B è uguale a C*, — *A è uguale a C*, A is equal to B, B is equal to C, therefore A is equal to C; *è tardi*, — *non posso accompagnarti a casa*, it's late, so I can't see you home.

perciocché, *cong.* (*letter.*) since: *non ti narrerò tutte le sue gesta*, — *sono invero molte*, I shall not tell you of all his deeds, since they are so numerous.

percorrènza, *V.* **percórso 1.**

percórrere, *v.t.* **1.** to cover, to go along (sthg.): *abbiamo percorso venti miglia*, we have covered twenty miles; *avevo già percorso un buon tratto di strada*, I had already gone a long way; *percorse la strada da cima a fondo*, he went right down the street; — *una distanza*, to cover a distance; — *un itinerario*, to cover a route (*o* to follow an itinerary) **2.** (*in lungo e in largo*) to travel; to scour: *abbiamo percorso molte città*, we have passed through many towns; *abbiamo percorso tutti gli Stati Uniti*, we have travelled all over the United States; *la polizia percorse la città in cerca dei ladri*, the police scoured the town for the thieves; — *un luogo in automobile*, to drive through a place **3.** (*attraversare*) to run through (sthg.), to run across (sthg.), to pass through (sthg.), to go through (sthg.): *il fiume percorre una ridente campagna*, the river runs through a lovely country; *la strada percorre la pianura*, the road runs across the plain.

percórso, *s.m.* **1.** run; (*distanza*) distance: *su un* — *di venti miglia*, in (a distance of) twenty miles; *il* — *tra Londra e Cambridge è breve*, it is a quick run (*o* a short distance) from London to Cambridge; *scelsero il* — *più breve*, they chose the shortest way **2.** (*tragitto*) way, journey: *aveva comprato qualche rivista da leggere durante il* —, he had bought some magazines to read during the journey; *ci fermammo durante il* —, we stopped on the way; *durante il* — *ci accorgemmo di aver sbagliato strada*, on our way we suddenly realized we had taken the wrong turning **3.** (*tracciato*) course, route: *il* — *di un fiume, delle stelle*, the course of a river, of the stars; *il* — *di un treno*, the route of a train.

percòssa, *s.f.* blow, stroke.

percotitóre, *s.m.*, **percotitríce**, *s.f.* hitter, striker.

percuòtere, *v.t.* to strike, to hit; to beat: *la casa è percossa dalle onde*, the house is beaten by the waves; *la folgore percosse la vecchia quercia*, lightning struc, the old oak-tree; *il granaio fu percosso da un fulmine*, the barn was struck by lightning; *lo percosse a morte*, he struck him dead; *lo percosse in faccia, sulla testa, sul naso*, he struck (*o* hit) him in the face, on hek head, on the nose; *non è bene* — *i bambini*, it is not a good thing to beat children; *percossi la testa cadendo*, I hit my head in falling ‖ **percuòtersi**, *v.r.*: — *il petto*, to beat one's breast.

percussióne, *s.f.* percussion: *fucile a* —, percussion-gun; *strumenti a* —, (*mus.*) percussion instruments.

percussóre, *s.m.* (*artigl.*) striker, percussion-pin.

perdènte, *ag.* losing ‖ *s.c.* loser.

pèrdere, *v.t.* **1.** to lose (anche *fig.*): *ha perso un braccio in guerra*, he lost an arm in the war; *ha perso un figlio, sua madre*, he has lost a son, his mother; *ho perso una settimana*, I have lost a week; — *l'anima*, to lose one's soul; — *i capelli*, to lose one's hair (*o* to go bald); — *il contatto con qlcu.*, to lose contact (*o* touch) with s.o.; — *di vista qlcu., ql.co.*, to lose sight of s.o., sthg; — *il fiato*, to waste one's breath; — *le foglie*, to lose its leaves; — *i guanti, un libro, il borsellino, la voce, la memoria, il controllo, ecc.*, to lose one's gloves, a book, one's purse, one's voice, one's memory, one's self-control, etc.; — *quota, (aer.)* to lose height; — *la ragione*, to lose one's reason (*o* to become insane *o* to go mad); — *una partita a carte, una causa, una guerra*, to lose a game of cards, a suit, a war; — *la strada*, to lose one's way; — *terreno*, to lose ground (anche *fig.*); — *la testa*, to lose one's head ‖ — *un'abitudine*, to lose (*o* to get out of) a habit: *fare* — *un'abitudine a qlcu.*, to break s.o. of a habit ‖ — *l'anno*, (*fam.*) to spend two years in the same class ‖ — *la bussola, la tramontana*, to lose one's bearings ‖ — *la conoscenza*, to faint ‖ — *il cuore per qlcu.*, to lose one's heart to s.o. ‖ — *il lume degli occhi*, to be blinded by rage ‖ — *le staffe*, to fly off the handle ‖ — *il tacco*, (*fam.*) to lose one's reputation ‖ *non aver più niente da* —, to have nothing (left) to lose ‖ *chi perde ha sempre torto*, prov. the loser is always wrong ‖ — *tempo a chi più sa più spiace*, prov. wasting time is torture to a wise man **2.** (*mancare*) to miss: — *il treno, un'occasione, una conferenza*, to miss the train, an opportunity, a lecture **3.** (*sprecare*) to waste: *egli non perde tempo*, he doesn't let the grass grow under his feet; *non* — *tempo in sciocchezze*, don't waste your time with trifles **4.** (*rovinare*) to ruin: *la tua grettezza ti perderà*, your meanness will ruin you ‖ *v.i.* **1.** to lose: *ci perdi a non andare*, you will lose by not going; *ho perduto ma vincerò la prossima volta*, I've lost but I shall win next time; *non ci perderai affatto*, you won't lose (*o* won't be out of pocket) by it **2.** (*fare acqua*) to leak: *questa barca, questo secchio perde*, this boat, this bucket leaks ‖ **pèrdersi**, *v.r.* **1.** (*smarrirsi*) to lose oneself; to get lost: *mi sono perduto nel bosco*, I got lost (*o* I lost my way) in the wood; — *in congettura*, to be lost in conjecture; — *nella folla*, to vanish (*o* to disappear) in the crowd; — *nei propri pensieri*, to be rapt (*o* lost) in thought; — *per Milano*, to lose one's way (*o* to get lost) in Milan ‖ *è inutile spiegarmi queste cose, mi ci perdo*, it's no use explaining these things to me, I can't make head or tail of them ‖ — *d'animo*, to lose heart ‖ — *dietro ad uno*, to throw oneself away on s.o. ‖ — *in sciocchezze*, to waste one's time with trifles **2.** (*svanire*) to fade (away): *la figura di un uomo che si perde nell'ombra*, the figure of a man melting into the darkness; — *nell'aria*, to fade away into the air ‖ *il fiume si perde nel Garda*, the river flows into Lake Garda **3.** (*sparire*) to disappear: *un'usanza che si perde*, a custom that is disappearing (*o* falling into disuse) **4.** (*rovinarsi*) to be ruined: *se continui così ti perderai*, if you go on like that you'll be ruined **5.** (*di un pacco, una lettera, andare smarrito*) to be mislaid ‖ *v.r. reciproco:* — *di vista*, to lose sight of each other (*o* one another).

perdifiàto, a, *l.av.*: *correre a* —, to run at break-neck speed; *gridare a* —, to shout at the top of one's voice; *soffiare a* —, to blow with all one's strength.

perdigiórno, *s.m.* idler; loafer.

perdìnci, *inter.* good Lord!, my goodness!.

pèrdita, *s.f.* **1.** loss: *la* — *di un amico, di un libro, ecc.*, the loss of a friend, a book, etc.; *le perdite di un'azienda*, the losses of a firm; — *di memoria*, loss of memory; — *di tempo*, loss of time: *quella foratura procurò una certa* — *di tempo*, that puncture caused a certain loss of time; *avevano subìto forti perdite*, they had suffered heavy losses; *subire una* —, (*comm.*) to make a loss; *lavorare in* —, to work at a loss ‖ *a* —

d'occhio, as far as the eye can see **2.** (*sciupio*) waste: — *di tempo*, waste of time: *cercare di insegnargli il tedesco è una* — *di tempo*, it is a waste of time trying to teach him German **3.** (*falla, fuga*) leak; leakage; (*elett.*) stray loss: *c'è una* — *nella conduttura del gas*, there is a leak in the gas-pipe; *questa barca ha una* —, this boat has a leak (*o* is leaking); *eliminare le perdite*, to stop leaks.

perditèmpo, *s.m.* waste of time: *il guidare in questa città è un vero* —, driving in this town is a real waste of time; *questo bambino è il mio* —, this child wastes a lot of my time.

perditóre, *s.m.*, **perditríce**, *s.f.* loser.

perdizióne, *s.f.* **1.** (*danno, rovina*) ruin: *andare in* —, to go to ruin **2.** (*dannazione*) damnation, perdition: *la via della* —, the road to perdition (*o* the road to Hell); *condurre alla* —, to lead to perdition (*o* to lead astray).

perdonàbile, *ag.* pardonable; (*scusabile*) excusable.

perdonàre, *v.t.* **1.** to forgive, to pardon: *gli ho perdonato i suoi torti*, I have forgiven him his wrongs; *mi avete perdonato?*, am I forgiven?; *non perdonerò mai Giovanni*, I shall never forgive John; *ti perdono*, I forgive you; — *un peccato, un'offesa*, to forgive a sin, an offense ‖ *Dio ci perdoni!*, God forgive us! **2.** (*scusare*) to excuse, to pardon: *perdona il disturbo*, excuse me for troubling you (*o* excuse my troubling you); *perdona la mia audacia*, excuse my daring; *perdona se mi prendo questa libertà*, pardon (*o* excuse) the liberty I am taking; *perdona se ti contraddico*, pardon (*o* excuse) my contradicting you; *perdonate se vi interrompo*, excuse my interrupting you **3.** (*risparmiare*) to spare: *la morte non perdona nessuno*, death does not spare anybody; *una male che non perdona*, an incurable disease ‖ **perdonàrsi**, *v.r.* to forgive oneself: *non so perdonarmi di essere stato così sciocco*, I cannot forgive myself for being so silly ‖ *v.r. reciproco* to forgive each other (one another): *perdoniamoci le nostre offese*, let us forgive each other our wrongs.

perdonatóre, *ag.* forgiving ‖ *s.m.*, **perdonatríce**, *s.f.* forgiver.

perdóno, *s.m.* **1.** forgiveness, pardon: *chiedo* — *a Dio dei miei peccati*, I beg God's forgiveness for my sins; *non mi darà mai il suo* —, he will never forgive me ‖ *la miglior vendetta è il* —, prov. pardon is the most glorious revenge **2.** (*con valore esclamativo*) pardon, sorry: (*vi domando*) — *!*, I beg your pardon! (*o* pardon me!).

perduràre, *v.i.t.* **1.** to last: *se il bel tempo perdura, partiremo domani*, if the good weather lasts, we shall leave tomorrow **2.** (*persistere*) to persist: — *nel far ql.co. a proprio modo*, to persist in doing sthg. (in) one's own way **3.** (*continuare*) to go on, to continue: *il re morì, ma la sua opera perdurò*, the king died, but his work continued; *se perduri nell'essere così ostinato, ti dovrò punire*, if you continue to be (*o* if you go on being) so obstinate, I shall have to punish you.

perdurévole, *ag.* durable, lasting.

perdutaménte, *av.* desperately, hopelessly: *essere* — *innamorati*, to be madly in love.

perdúto, *ag.* **1.** (*smarrito, perso*) lost (anche *fig.*): — *nella nebbia*, lost in the fog; *anime perdute*, lost souls; *ricchezze perdute*, lost riches; *sono* — *senza di te*, I am lost without you ‖ *fu dato per* —, he was given up for lost **2.** (*dissoluto*) fallen; lost: *una donna perduta*, a fallen woman **3.** (*rovinato*) ruined, lost: *sono* —, I am ruined (*o* lost) **4.** (*sprecato*) wasted, lost; useless: *fatica perduta*, wasted effort; *giornata perduta*, a wasted day (*o* a day lost); *questo è tempo* —, this is time lost; *spesa perduta*, useless expense **5.** (*paralizzato, mutilato*) useless: *occhio* —, sightless (*o* useless) eye; *il suo braccio destro è* —, he has lost the use of his right arm; *egli ha un braccio* —, he has a useless arm **6.** (*estinto*) extinct, lost: *animali perduti*, extinct animals; *le razze perdute*, the lost tribes.

peregrinàre, *v.i.* to wander, to roam: *Dante pere-*

grinò di corte in corte, Dante wandered (*o* roamed) from court to court.

peregrinazióne, *s.f.* wandering, roaming.

peregrinità, *s.f.* rareness, rarity; singularity.

peregríno, *ag.* **1.** rare; uncommon; strange; singular; (*prezioso*) precious: *linguaggio —,* precious language; *qualità peregrine,* rare qualities **2.** (*poet.*) (*straniero*) peregrine.

perènne, *ag.* perennial, perpetual; (*eterno*) everlasting: *gioia —,* everlasting joy; *nevi perenni,* perpetual snows: *limite delle nevi perenni,* snow-line; *pianta —,* perennial (plant).

perenneménte, *av.* perennially, perpetually; (*per sempre*) for ever, everlastingly.

perennità, *s.f.* perennity.

perènto, *ag.* (*dir.*) (*scaduto*) expired; lapsed.

perentoriaménte, *av.* peremptorily.

perentòrio, *ag.* peremptory.

perenzióne, *s.f.* (*dir.*) peremptoriness.

perequàre, *v.t.* to equalize: *— stipendi,* to equalize wages.

perequazióne, *s.f.* equalization, equal distribution: *— dei prezzi,* (*econ.*) standardizing of charges.

perétta, *s.f.* (*elett.*) pear-push (*o* pear-switch).

perfettaménte, *av.* **1.** perfectly: *conosce l'inglese —,* he knows English perfectly; *essere — padrone di un giuoco,* to be a perfect master of a game **2.** (*completamente*) thoroughly, completely; (*assolutamente, proprio*) quite, perfectly: *comprendo —,* I quite understand; *hai — ragione,* you are quite (*o* perfectly) right.

perfettíbile, *ag.* perfectible.

perfettibilità, *s.f.* perfectibility.

perfettívo, *ag.* (*rar.*) perfective.

perfètto, *ag.* **1.** (*senza difetto*) perfect, faultless, flawless; excellent: *una dizione perfetta,* faultless diction; *un ragionamento —,* faultless reasoning; *in ordine —,* in perfect order; *nessuno è —,* nobody is perfect (*o* faultless); *la nostra cameriera è perfetta,* our maid is a treasure || *è —!,* that's capital! (*o* that's fine!) || *essere in perfette condizioni fisiche e morali,* to be in perfect condition **2.** (*totale, completo*) perfect, complete, thorough: *un — gentiluomo,* a thorough gentleman; *un — idiota,* a perfect idiot; *un — mascalzone,* a precious (*o* thorough-going) rascal; *un — stupido,* a perfect fool; *una felicità perfetta,* unmixed happiness (*o* perfect bliss); *un conversatore —,* an excellent conversationalist **3.** (*mat.*) perfect: *numero —,* perfect number **4.** (*gram.*) perfect: *tempo —,* —, perfect tense || *s.m.* **1.** (*gram.*) perfect (tense) **2.** (*rar.*) (*perfezione*) perfection.

perfezionàbile, *ag.* perfectible.

perfezionaménto, *s.m.* **1.** perfecting, perfectioning; (*miglioramento*) improving **2.** (*specializzazione*) specialization: *borsa di —,* post-graduate scholarship; *corso di —,* specialization course; *studi di —,* advanced studies.

perfezionàre, *v.t.* to perfect, to make perfect, to bring to perfection; (*migliorare*) to improve: *devo — questa mia invenzione,* I must improve this invention of mine; *non credo che verrà ulteriormente perfezionato,* I don't think it will be improved any further; *questo attrezzo deve essere perfezionato altrimenti nessuno lo comprerà,* this tool must be brought to perfection, otherwise nobody will buy it || **perfezionàrsi,** *v.r.* **1.** to improve (oneself): *vorrei perfezionarmi in tedesco,* I should like to improve my German; *— in ql.co.,* to perfect one's knowledge of sthg. **2.** (*specializzarsi*) to specialize.

perfezióne, *s.f.* perfection: *condurre a —,* to bring to perfection; *toccare la —,* to attain perfection || *alla —,* to perfection: *fare ql.co. alla —,* to do sthg. to perfection.

perfidaménte, *av.* perfidiously, wickedly.

perfídia, *s.f.* perfidiousness, perfidy, wickedness: *non conosci la sua —,* you don't know his perfidy

(*o* how wicked he is); *questa è una —!,* this is perfidy!; *avere la — di fare ql.co.,* to have the wickedness to do sthg.; *fare una — a qlcu.,* to commit an act of wickedness towards s.o.

perfidiosaménte, *av.* (*rar.*) perfidiously.

pèrfido, *ag.* perfidious, wicked, perverse: *— nemico,* wicked enemy; *lingua perfida,* poisonous tongue || *tempo —,* nasty (*o* horrible) weather.

perfíno, *av.* even: *— in quelle circostanze non perse il senso dell'umorismo,* even in those circumstances his sense of humour did not desert him; *parla — mentre dorme,* he talks even in his sleep.

perforàbile, *ag.* perforable, pierceable.

perforaménto, *s.m.* **1.** (*l'atto del perforare*) piercing perforating, perforation **2.** (*l'effetto*) perforation.

perforàre, *v.t.* to pierce; to perforate, to bore, to drill: *una pallottola gli ha perforato il cranio,* a bullet pierced his skull || *— un'asse,* to drill a plank; *— un biglietto,* to punch a ticket; *— francobolli,* to perforate stamps; *— il legno,* to bore (into) wood; *— materiale isolante mediante una scarica,* (*elett.*) to puncture.

perforatóre, *ag.* perforating || *s.m.* perforator.

perforatríce, *s.f.* **1.** (*chi perfora*) perforator **2.** (*macchina*) drill, punch.

perforazióne, *s.f.* perforation; (*mec.*) drilling: *la — di un pozzo,* the drilling of a well || *— di una pellicola,* (*cine.*) perforation of a film.

perfosfàto, *s.m.* (*chim.*) superphosphate.

perfusióne, *s.f.* (*letter.*) perfusion.

perfúso, *ag.* (*letter.*) perfused.

pergamèna, *s.f.* parchment: *carta —,* parchment paper.

pergamenàceo, *ag.* pergameneous.

pergamenàto, *ag.* parchment-like, pergameneous.

pèrgamo[1], *no.pr.f.* (*geog. st.*) Pergamum.

pèrgamo[2], *s.m.* (*letter.*) pulpit.

pèrgola, *s.f.,* **pergolàto,** *s.m.* pergola, bower, arbour.

pèri, *s.f.* (*mit.*) peri.

periànzio, *s.m.* (*bot.*) perianth.

periblèma, *s.m.* (*bot.*) periblem.

períbolo, *s.m.* (*arch.*) peribolus, peribolos.

pericàrdio, *s.m.* (*anat.*) pericardium (*pl.* pericardia).

pericardíte, *s.f.* (*patol.*) pericarditis.

pericàrpo, *s.m.* (*bot.*) pericarp.

Pèricle, *no.pr.m.* (*st.*) Pericles.

pericolànte, *ag.* tottering, tottery; (*malsicuro*) unsafe: *casa, muro —,* tottering house, wall; *impero —,* tottering empire; *tetto —,* unsafe roof.

pericolàre, *v.i.* to be in danger; (*minacciare di cadere*) to totter, to threaten to fall: *l'edificio pericolava,* the building was tottering (*o* was in danger of falling down).

perícolo, *s.m.* **1.** danger, peril, risk, hazard: *i pericoli della strada,* the dangers of the street; *i pericoli del mare,* the dangers (*o* perils) of the sea; *— effettivo, imminente,* real, impending danger; *— radiologico,* (*fis.*) health hazard: *fuori —,* out of danger; *in — di morte,* in danger of death; *in — di vita,* in peril of one's life (*o* in danger of losing one's life); *segnale di —,* danger signal; *senza —,* safely (*o* securely); *territorio in — di invasione,* territory in danger of invasion; *cercò di evitare il —,* he tried to avoid the danger; *è un — per la navigazione,* it is a navigational hazard; *un grave — ci minaccia,* a serious danger threatens us; *l'ho salvato dal —,* I rescued him from danger; *la nostra libertà è in —,* our liberty is in jeopardy; *riuscì a scongiurare il —,* he succeeded in warding off the danger; *si espose al — senza pensarci,* he endangered his person (*o* he risked his life) thoughtlessly; *correre un —,* to be in danger; *essere in — di cadere,* to be in danger of falling; *mettere in — la vita, gli interessi di qlcu.,* to endanger (*o* to jeopardize *o* to imperil) s.o.'s life, interests; *rendersi conto del —,* to realize the danger (*o fam.* to see the red light); *salvare una nave in —,* to rescue a ship in distress; *tenersi lontano dal —,* to keep out of danger || *— pubblico,* public

menace (*o* public enemy): *un pazzo evaso è un —
pubblico*, a runaway lunatic is a public menace 2. (*fam.*)
(*probabilità*) fear, danger: *c'è anche il — che tu debba
pagare due volte!*, it's even likely you'll have to pay
twice!; *non c'è —!*, no fear! (*o* not very likely!): *non
c'è — che dica bugie*, there is no danger of his telling
lies; *non c'è — che venga*, there is no fear of his coming.

pericolosaménte, *av.* dangerously, perilously.

pericolóso, *ag.* dangerous, perilous, risky: *un —
avversario*, a dangerous opponent; *un'amicizia pericolosa*, a dangerous friendship; *costa pericolosa*, dangerous coast; *un fiume — da attraversare*, a dangerous
river to cross; *una malattia pericolosa*, a dangerous
illness; *nel punto più —*, in the place of greatest
danger; *un uomo, un cane —*, a dangerous man, dog;
zona pericolosa, danger zone; *quell'albero è — per
la circolazione*, that tree is a danger to traffic; *sei
su un terreno —, fig.* you are on dangerous ground;
sono concorrenti poco pericolosi, they are competitors
of little account.

pericòndrio, *s.m.* (*anat.*) perichondrium (*pl.* pe-
richondria).

pericondríte, *s.f.* (*patol.*) perichondritis.

pericrànio, *s.m.* (*anat.*) pericranium (*pl.* pericrania).

peridèrma, *s.m.* (*bot.*) periderm.

perídio, *s.m.* (*bot.*) peridium (*pl.* peridia).

perièlio, *s.m.* (*astr.*) perihelion (*pl.* perihelia).

perifeŕía, *s.f.* **1.** periphery (anche *geom.*): *far affluire il sangue alla —*, to cause the blood to flow to
the skin **2.** (*di città*) suburbs (*pl.*); outskirts (*pl.*):
quartiere di —, suburb; *abitare in —*, to live in the
suburbs.

perifèrico, *ag.* **1.** peripheric(al) (anche *geom.*);
peripheral: *ganglio —*, (*anat.*) peripheral (*o* peripheric)
ganglion **2.** (*di strada, quartiere*) suburban: *una strada
periferica*, a suburban street.

perifrasàre, *v.t.* to periphrase.

períf́rasi, *s.f.* periphrasis, circumlocution.

perifrasticaménte, *av.* periphrastically.

perifràstico, *ag.* periphrastic(al): *coniugazione peri-
frastica*, periphrastic conjugation.

perigèo, *s.m.* (*astr.*) perigee.

períglio, *s.m.* (*poet.*) peril, danger.

periglióso, *ag.* (*poet.*) perilous, dangerous.

perigònio, *s.m.* (*bot.*) perigonium (*pl.* perigonia).

perilínfa, *s.f.* (*anat.*) perilymph.

perimetràle, *ag.* perimetrical.

perimetría, *s.f.* (*geom.*) perimetry.

perimètrico, *ag.* (*geom.*) perimetric.

perímetro, *s.m.* (*geom.*) perimeter.

perinèo, *s.m.* (*anat.*) perineum (*pl.* perinea).

periodàre, *s.m.* (literary) style, technique: *— facile*,
fluent style; *— sciolto*, easy-flowing (*o* fluid) style;
— pesante, turgid (*o* slow-moving) style.

periodàre, *v.i.* to build sentences; to form periods.

periodicaménte, *av.* periodically.

periodicità, *s.f.* periodicity.

periòdico, *ag.* periodic(al): *acido —*, (*chim.*) periodic
acid; *febbre periodica*, periodic fever; *funzione periodica*, (*mat.*) periodic function; *movimento — di un
astro*, periodic motion of a heavenly body ‖ *s.m.* periodical; magazine.

período, *s.m.* **1.** period: *un — di cattivo tempo*,
a period (*o* spell) of bad weather; *un — di freddo, di
siccità*, a cold, a dry spell; *il — di incubazione di una
malattia*, the incubation period of a disease; *— di
preavviso*, (*di impiegati*) period of notice; *— di prova*,
(*di impiegati*) probationary (*o* trial) period; (*di macchine*) testing period; *durante un — della mia vita*,
during a period of my life; *un glorioso — della nostra
storia*, a glorious period of our history; *la malattia è
nel — acuto*, the illness is in its acute stage (*o* period) **2.** (*scient.*) period; (*elett.*) cycle: *— della pila*,
(*fis. atomica*) pile period; *— di interruzione*, (*elett.*)
outage; *— di rivoluzione di un pianeta*, (*astr.*) period

of revolution of a planet; *— di vibrazione libera*, (*fis.*)
natural period; *— radioattivo*, (*fis. atomica*) decay
period **3.** (*gram.*) sentence; period: *— complesso, composto*, complex, compound sentence; *la proposizione
principale del —*, the main clause of the period.

periòstio, *s.m.* (*anat.*) periosteum (*pl.* periostea).

periostíte, *s.f.* (*patol.*) periostitis.

peripatètico, *ag. s.m.* (*st. fil.*) peripatetic.

peripatetísmo, *s.m.* (*st. fil.*) peripateticism.

peripezía, *s.f.* **1.** (*vicissitudine*) vicissitude, ups and
downs (*pl.*); (*avventura*) adventure: *dopo molte peripezie
si è fatto finalmente una bella posizione*, after many
ups and downs he has finally got a nice position; *ti
racconterò tutte le mie peripezie*, I shall tell you all
my adventures **2.** (*teat.*) peripet(e)ia.

pèriplo, *s.m.* periplus, circumnavigation.

períptero, *ag.* (*arch.*) peripteral.

períre, *v.i.* to perish, to die; (*andar perduto*) to be
lost; (*andar distrutto*) to be destroyed: *molti capolavori
perirono in quell'incendio*, many masterpieces were
destroyed in that fire; *perì tra le fiamme*, he perished
in the flames; *il suo nome non perirà*, his name will
never die.

periscòpico, *ag.* (*ott.*) periscopic.

periscòpio, *s.m.* (*ott.*) periscope: *— di esplorazione*,
(*mar.*) search periscope; *— notturno*, (*mar.*) night lens
periscope.

perispèrma, *s.m.* (*bot.*) perisperm.

perispòmeno, *ag.* (*gram. greca*) perispomenon (*pl.*
perispomena).

perissodàttili, *s.m.pl.* (*zool.*) Perissodactyla.

peristàltico, *ag.* (*fisiol.*) peristaltic.

peristílio, *s.m.* (*arch.*) peristyle.

peristòma, *s.m.* (*zool.*) peristome.

peritàle, *ag.* (*dir.*) expert (*attributivo*); of expert(s).

peritaménte, *av.* skilfully.

peritànza, *s.f.* (*letter.*) hesitation, wavering; (*timidezza*) shyness, bashfulness.

peritàrsi, *v.r.* (*letter.*) to hesitate: *non mi perito di
dire la verità*, I do not hesitate to tell the truth.

perìto, *ag.* expert, skilled, skilful ‖ *s.m.* (*tecnico,
artistico*) expert; (*tecnico-commerciale*) estimator: *—
agrimensore*, surveyor; *— calligrafo*, handwriting expert; *— chimico*, chemist; *— industriale*, non-graduate
engineer; *— navale*, ship surveyor.

peritonèo, *s.m.* (*anat.*) periton(a)eum (*pl.* peri-
ton(a)ea).

peritoníte, *s.f.* (*patol.*) peritonitis.

peritóso, *ag.* (*letter.*) hesitant; (*timido*) shy, bashful.

períttero, *ag.* (*arch.*) peripteral.

peritúro, *ag.* perishable, liable to perish.

perízia, *s.f.* **1.** (*maestria*) skill, skilfulness, ability:
aveva una gran — nella sua arte, he was very skilful
in his art **2.** (*dir.*) expert judgement, expert report;
(*valutazione*) valuation, appraisal: *— dei danni*, damage
survey; *— psichiatrica*, psychiatric examination; *fare
una —*, to make a valuation.

periziàre, *v.t.* to estimate, to appraise.

periziòre, *s.m.* (*dir.*) umpire, arbitrator.

perizòma, *s.m.* girdle.

Pèrla¹, *no.pr.f.* Pearl.

pèrla², *s.f.* **1.** pearl (anche *fig.*): *perle coltivate*, culture
pearls; *perle false*, imitation pearls; *perle di rugiada*,
dew-drops (*o* beads of dew *o* pearls of dew); *denti
come perle*, pearly teeth; *filo, vezzo di perle*, string of
pearls; *grigio —*, pearl-grey; *pescatore di perle*, pearl
-diver ‖ *gettar perle ai porci*, to cast pearls before
swine **2.** (*persona di gran pregio*) pearl, jewel: *è una
— di donna*, she is a jewel (*o* pearl) among women;
è una — di marito, he is a gem of a husband **3.** (*farm.*)
pearl, globule **4.** (*tip. med.*) pearl.

perlàceo, *ag.* pearly.

perlàia, *s.f.*, **perlàio**, *s.m.* **1.** (*chi lavora perle*) worker
in pearls **2.** (*chi vende perle*) pearl-dealer.

perlària, *s.f.* (*bot.*) pearlwort.

perlàto, *ag.* pearly ‖ *orzo* —, pearl-barley.

perlé, *ag.* corded: *cotone* —, corded cotton.

perlífero, *ag.* yielding pearls; pearl (*attributivo*): *ostrica perlifera,* pearl-oyster.

perlíte, *s.f.* (*min.*) perlite.

perlustràre, *v.t.* to reconnoitre; (*detto di polizia*) to patrol: *la polizia perlustrava la campagna in cerca del bandito,* the police were patrolling the countryside in search of the bandit; — *il terreno,* to reconnoitre the ground.

perlustratóre, *s.m.* **1.** scout **2.** *pl.* (*mil.*) reconnaissance (unit) (*sing.*).

perlustrazióne, *s.f.* reconnaissance; (*detto di polizia*) patrol: *andare in* —, to go on a reconnaissance (*o* to go out scouting); *essere in* —, to be on a reconnaissance: *i carabinieri erano in* —, the carabinieri were on patrol; *fare una* —, to make a reconnaissance.

permàle, *l.av.*: *aversene, prendersela* —, to take amiss.

permalosità, *s.f.* touchiness; irritability.

permalóso, *ag.* touchy; irritable.

permanènte, *ag.* permanent, lasting: *assemblea* —, permanent assembly; *esercito* —, standing army; *esposizione* —, permanent exhibition; *nevi permanenti,* perpetual snow ‖ *s.f.* permanent wave (*abbr.* perm).

permanenteménte, *av.* permanently, lastingly.

permanènza, *s.f.* **1.** (*l'essere permanente*) permanence, permanency **2.** (*soggiorno prolungato*) stay, sojourn: *durante la mia* — *a Roma,* during my stay in Rome; *la mia* — *all'estero,* my stay abroad; *essere di* — *in una città,* to live permanently in a town.

permanére, *v.i.* (*rimanere*) to remain; (*persistere*) to persist; (*durare*) to last.

permanganàto, *s.m.* (*chim.*) permanganate: — *potassico,* potassium permanganate.

permeàbile, *ag.* permeable.

permeabilità, *s.f.* permeability: — *assoluta,* (*elettromagnetismo*) absolute permeability.

permeàre, *v.t.* to permeate (anche *fig.*); to permeate through (sthg.): *l'acqua aveva permeato il terreno,* the water had permeated the soil; *le nuove dottrine stanno permeando il popolo,* the new doctrines are permeating the people.

permésso, *ag.* permitted, allowed ‖ *s.m.* **1.** permission, leave: *col vostro* —, by your leave; *dammi il* — *di farlo,* give me permission (*o* give me leave) to do it; *ho il* — *di adoperare la sua macchina da scrivere,* I have permission to use (*o* I am allowed to use) his typewriter **2.** (*licenza di astenersi temporaneamente dall'esercizio dei propri doveri*) leave (of absence): *impiegato, soldato in* —, employee, soldier on leave **3.** (*licenza, autorizzazione*) licence: — *d'esportazione, di caccia,* export, shooting licence; *documento di* —, permit; *rilasciare un* —, to grant a permit.

perméttere, *v.t.* **1.** to permit, to allow, to let: *crede che gli sia tutto permesso,* he thinks he can do anything he likes; *gli permise di andare,* he let him go; *mi si permette di andare?,* may I go? (*o* am I allowed to go?); *non era permesso portare i cani nel parco,* dogs were not allowed to enter the park (*o* the public were not allowed to take their dogs into the park); *non mi è permesso di usarlo,* I am not allowed to use it; *qui la caccia non è permessa,* shooting is not allowed (*o* permitted) here; *la strada è così larga che permette il sorpasso,* the street is large enough to allow overtaking; — *ql.co. a qlcu.,* to allow s.o. sthg. ‖ (*nelle formule di cortesia*) è *permesso* (*entrare*)?, may I come in?; *permettete?,* may I?; *permettetemi di presentarvi mio fratello,* let me introduce my brother (*o* permit me to introduce my brother) to you; *permettimi di rilevare che...,* permit (*o* allow) me to point out that... ‖ *Dio permettendo,* God willing; *tempo permettendo,* weather permitting ‖ *i miei mezzi non me lo permettono,* I can't afford it **2.** (*tollerare, sopportare*) to bear, to suffer: *non permetto che ti insulti,* I can't bear (*o* suffer) him to insult you ‖ **perméttersi,** *v.r.* **1.** to allow oneself: *mi sono permesso*

una breve vacanza, I have allowed myself a short holiday ‖ — *il lusso di,* to afford: *nonposso permettermi il lusso dell'automobile,* I cannot afford a car; *non posso permettermi il lusso di comperare un televisore,* I cannot afford to buy a television set **2.** (*prendersi la libertà*) to take the liberty (of doing): *mi permetto di dirvi che avete torto,* I take the liberty of telling you that you are wrong.

permiàno, *ag.s.m.* (*geol.*) permian.

permissíbile, *ag.* permissible, allowable.

pèrmuta, *s.f.* (*dir.*) barter, exchange.

permutàbile, *ag.* exchangeable, permutable.

permutabilità, *s.f.* exchangeability, permutability.

permutaménto, *s.m.* permutation, exchange.

permutàre, *v.t.* to exchange, to permute; to barter.

pernice, *s.f.* **1.** (*ornit.*) partridge **2.** *occhio di* —, soft corn (between toes).

perniciósa, *s.f.* (*patol.*) malignant fever.

perniciosaménte, *av.* perniciously.

perniciosità, *s.f.* perniciousness.

perniciόso, *ag.* pernicious, noxious, hurtful, mischievous: *anemia perniciosa,* pernicious anemia; *febbre perniciosa,* malignant fever.

pèrnio, pèrno, *s.m.* **1.** pin, stud, pivot: — *a forcella,* (*mec.*) forked pin; — *conico,* (*mec.*) tapered pin; — *del carrello,* (*ferr.*) centre pivot; — *del compasso,* centre pin of the compass; — *di accoppiamento,* (*mec.*) coupling pin; — *di articolazione,* (*mec.*) trunnion; — *di bloccaggio,* (*mec.*) check pin; — *di cingolo,* track pin; — *di manovella,* (*aut.*) crank pin; — *di strappamento,* (*aer.*) rip-cord; — *girevole,* (*mec.*) pivot pin; — *sferico,* (*mec.*) ball-and-socket joint **2.** (*cardine*) hinge **3.** *fig.* hinge, support: *il* — *della conversazione,* the main topic of the conversation; *il* — *della famiglia,* the support of the family; *questa alleanza è il* — *di tutta la nostra politica,* our whole policy turns (*o* hinges) upon this alliance.

pernottaménto, *s.m.* overnight stay.

pernottàre, *v.i.* to stay overnight, to spend the night: *non so se potrò* — *qui,* I don't know whether I'll be able to stay here overnight.

péro[1], *s.m.* (*bot.*) pear-tree: *legno di* —, pear (wood).

però[2], *cong.* **1.** (*avversativo*) **but, however, yet, nevertheless**: *non te lo meriti,* — *te lo darò se ti occorre,* you don't deserve it, however (*o* nevertheless) I'll give it to you, if you need it; *sembra onesto,* — *non mi fido di lui,* he seems honest, yet (*o* but) I don't trust him; *temo,* — *di non saperlo fare,* I am afraid, however, that I shall not be able to do it **2.** (*arc.*) (*causale*) **therefore**: *io non sapea d'errare,* — *devi perdonarmi,* I was unaware of my error, therefore you must forgive me.

perocché, *cong.* (*letter.*) **since, as, because**: — *molte dame erano convenute ad ammirare la nuova regina...,* since many ladies had foregathered to admire the new queen....

peróne, *s.m.* (*anat.*) fibula (*pl.* fibulae).

peronèo, *ag.* (*anat.*) peroneal.

peronòspora, *s.f.* mildew: *vigna malata di* —, mildewed vine.

peroràre, *v.t.* to plead: — *una causa,* to plead a cause ‖ *v.i.* to perorate, to make a peroration: — *per qlcu.,* to plead for s.o.

perorazióne, *s.f.* **1.** pleading, defence **2.** (*ret.*) peroration.

peròssido, *s.m.* (*chim.*) peroxide: — *di manganese,* manganese peroxide.

perpendicolàre, *ag.* perpendicular ‖ *s.f.* perpendicular: *lunghezza tra le perpendicolari,* (*arch.*) length between perpendiculars; *abbassare una* — to drop (*o* to draw) a perpendicular.

perpendicolarità, *s.f.* perpendicularity.

perpendicolarménte, *av.* perpendicularly.

perpendícolo, *s.m.* (*filo a piombo*) plumb-line ‖ *a* —, perpendicularly: *una roccia a* — *sul mare,* a sheer cliff.

perpetràre, *v.t.* to perpetrate, to commit: — *un delitto*, to perpetrate (*o* to commit) a crime.

perpetratóre, *s.m.* perpetrator.

perpetrazióne, *s.f.* perpetration.

perpètua, *s.f.* 1. (priest's) housekeeper 2. (*fam.*) (*brontolona*) nagging woman.

perpetuàbile, *ag.* perpetuable.

perpetuaménte, *av.* perpetually.

perpetuàre, *v.t.* to perpetuate: — *un'istituzione, una stirpe*, to perpetuate an institution, a race ‖ **perpetuàrsi**, *v.r.* to endure, to last.

perpetuazióne, *s.f.* perpetuation.

perpetuità, *s.f.* perpetuity.

perpètuo, *ag.* 1. perpetual, endless, everlasting: *a perpetua memoria del fatto fu eretto un monumento*, a monument was raised in everlasting memory of the event ‖ *in* —, perpetually ‖ *moto* —, perpetual motion ‖ *nevi perpetue*, perpetual snow ‖ *vite perpetua*, (*mec.*) endless screw 2. (*ininterrotto*) perpetual, continuous: *un — rimbrottare*, a perpetual nagging 3. (*a vita*) perpetual, permanent: *rendita perpetua*, perpetuity; *segretario* —, secretary for life (*o* life secretary).

Perpignàno, *no.pr.f.* (*geog.*) Perpignan.

perplessità, *s.f.* perplexity.

perplèsso, *ag.* perplexed, puzzled: *era — sulla via da seguire*, he was puzzled about how to act; *rendere — qlcu.*, to puzzle (*o* to perplex) s.o.

perquirènte, *ag.* (*dir.*) investigating ‖ *s.m.* (*dir.*) investigator.

perquisíre, *v.t.* to search: — *una casa*, to search a house.

perquisitóre, *s.m.* (*dir.*) investigator, searcher.

perquisizióne, *s.f.* (*dir.*) perquisition, (thorough) search: — *domiciliare*, searching of a house (*o* house search); *mandato di* —, search-warrant.

perscrutàbile, *ag.* searchable, investigable.

perscrutàre, *v.t.* to scrutinize, to examine, to investigate: *chi può — la volontà divina?*, who can scrutinize God's will?; — *le cause di ql.co.*, to investigate the causes of sthg.

persecutóre, *s.m.*, **persecutríce**, *s.f.* persecutor.

persecuzióne, *s.f.* 1. persecution: *la — degli Ebrei*, the persecution of the Jews; *soffrire le persecuzioni*, to suffer persecution ‖ *mania di* —, persecution mania 2. (*fam.*) (*molestia continua*) pestering; (*di creditori*) dunning ‖ *è una vera* —*!*, he is a (real) pest!.

Persèfone, *no.pr.f.* (*mit.*) Persephone.

perseguíre, *v.t.* 1. to follow; to pursue: — *uno scopo*, to pursue one's aim (*o* object) 2. (*perseguitare*) to persecute; to pursue (anche *fig.*): — *i buoni*, to persecute the good 3. (*dir.*) to prosecute.

perseguitàre, *v.t.* to persecute; to pursue (anche *fig.*): *furono crudelmente perseguitati*, they were cruelly persecuted; *quel sogno mi perseguita*, that dream haunts me; *il rimorso lo perseguita*, remorse pursues him; — *una donna*, (*molestarla*) to press one's attentions on a woman; — *il nemico*, to pursue the enemy; *essere perseguitato dai propri creditori*, to be dunned by one's creditors.

Persèo, *no.pr.m.* (*mit.*) Perseus.

perseveraménto, *s.m.* perseverance.

perseverànte, *ag.* persevering.

perseverànza, *s.f.* perseverance, persistence: — *nei propositi*, perseverance in one's aims (*o* objects).

perseveràre, *v.i.* to persevere, to persist: — *nelle proprie opinoni*, to persist in one's opinions.

Pèrsia, *no.pr.f.* (*geog.*) Persia, Iran.

persiàna[1], *s.f.* (*imposta*) shutter: — *avvolgibile*, Venetian blind; *feritoie a* —, (*aut. mar.*) louver; *stecca di* —, louver-board.

persiàno, *ag.* Persian: *gatto* —, Persian cat; *tappeto* —, Persian carpet ‖ *s.m.* Persian ‖ **persiàna**[2], *s.f.* Persian (woman).

persicàta, *s.f.* (*cuc.*) peach jam.

persichíno, *ag.* peach-coloured.

pèrsico[1], *ag.* Persian: *Golfo Persico*, Persian Gulf.

pèrsico[2], *ag.*: *pesce* —, perch.

persíno, *V.* **perfíno**.

persistènte, *ag.* persistent.

persistènza, *s.f.* persistence.

persístere, *v.i.* to persist: *egli persiste in una vita viziosa*, he persists in leading a life of vice; *la febbre persiste*, the fever persists; *io persisto ancora nel credere che sia un buon ragazzo*, I still persist in believing that he is a good boy; — *nella propria opinione*, to persist in one's opinion.

pèrso, *ag.* 1. lost: *sembra* —, he looks (*o* seems) lost; *dare qlcu., ql.co. per* —, to give s.o., sthg. up for lost ‖ *fare ql.co. a tempo* —, to do sthg. in one's spare time 2. (*sfuggito*) missed, lost: *un'occasione persa*, a missed (*o* lost) opportunity.

persóna, *s.f.* 1. person: *le persone della famiglia*, the members of the family; *c'è una — che ti aspetta*, there is s.o. waiting for you; *c'era una ventina di persone*, there were twenty people or so; *due sterline per* —, two pounds per head (*o* a head); *è una brava* —, he is a nice person; *la mia povera — non ne è degna*, my humble self is not worthy of it; *non c'è — che non lo sappia*, there isn't anybody who does not know it (*o* everybody knows it); *sono venute molte persone*, many people have come; *trattare per interposta* —, to deal (*o* to negotiate) through a third person ‖ — *di servizio*, servant ‖ *in, di* —, in person (*o* personally): *è l'avarizia in* —, he is avarice personified; *è la gentilezza in* —, he is kindness itself; *è lui in* —, it's the very man (*o* the man himself); *lo conosco di* —, I know him personally; *venne lui in, di* —, he came personally; *pagare di — per ql.co.*, to pay for sthg. personally ‖ *le tre persone della Trinità*, (*teol.*) the three persons of the Trinity 2. (*corpo*) body; (*figura*) figure: *ha una bella* —, she is a fine figure of a woman; *ha delle macchie rosse su tutta la* —, he has red spots all over his body (*o* his body is covered with red spots); *quell'abito non è adatto alla tua* —, that dress doesn't suit your figure 3. (*dir.*) person: *la — del re è sacra ed inviolabile*, the king's person is sacred and inviolable; — *fisica, naturale*, natural person 4. (*gram.*) person: *terza — singolare maschile*, third person singular masculine; *scrivere in prima, in terza* —, to write in the first, in the third person 5. (*teat.*) character, person: *le persone del dramma*, dramatis personae (*o* the characters in the play).

personàggio, *s.m.* 1. (important) personage; (*fam.*) bigwig: *è diventato un — importante*, he has become an important man 2. (*carattere di commedia, romanzo, ecc.*) character, person: *i personaggi di un dramma*, dramatis personae; *personaggi ed interpreti*, characters and cast; *il — di Otello*, the character of Othello; *è un — da romanzo*, he is like a character out of a novel; *reciterà il — di Amleto*, he will play (the role of) Hamlet.

personàle, *ag.* personal: *biglietto strettamente* —, not-transferable ticket; *favore* —, personal favour; *interesse, libertà, lettera* —, personal interest, liberty, letter; *mostra* —, (*art.*) one-man show ‖ *effetti personali*, personal belongings; *opinione, questione* —, personal opinion, matter ‖ *pronome* —, (*gram.*) personal pronoun ‖ *s.m.* 1. staff, personnel: — *direttivo*, management personnel; *il — di una ditta, di un ospedale*, the staff of a firm, of a hospital; — *insegnante*, the teaching-staff; *direttore del* —, personnel manager; *ufficio del* —, personnel department; *far parte del — di una ditta*, to be on the staff of a firm 2. (*corporatura, figura*) figure: *ella ha un bel* —, she has a good figure.

personalísmo, *s.m.* (*fil.*) personalism.

personalità, *s.f.* 1. personality: *ha una forte* —, he has got a strong personality 2. (*persona importante*) personage, important person, personality; (*fam.*) bigwig, big shot: *stai diventando una* —, you are becoming a bigwig (*o* quite an important person); *tutte le*

— *cittadine erano presenti*, all the people of conse-quence in the town were present **3.** (*dir.*): — *giuridica*, legal status: *acquistare* — *giuridica*, to acquire legal status **4.** *pl.* (*pettegolezzi*) personalities: *la conversa-zione scendeva alle* —, the conversation degenerated into personalities.

personalménte, *av.* personally: — *non credo tu abbia ragione*, personally I don't think you are right; *andai da lui* —, I went to him personally; *lo conosco* —, I know him personally.

personificàre, *v.t.* **1.** to personify: *il dramma me-dievale personificava i vizi e le virtù*, medieval drama personified vices and virtues **2.** (*teat.*) to play: *egli personificava Jago nell'« Otello »*, he took the part of (*o* played) Jago in "Othello" **3.** (*rappresentare*) to represent: *il padre personifica la famiglia*, the father represents the family.

personificàto, *ag.* personified: *è la generosità per-sonificata*, he is generosity itself.

personificazióne, *s.f.* personification: *è la — del-l'ignoranza*, he is ignorance personified.

perspicàce, *ag.* perspicacious, shrewd, sagacious: *un commento* —, a shrewd comment; *un consigliere* —, a sagacious counsellor; *mente* —, perspicacious (*o* shrewd) mind.

perspicaceménte, *av.* perspicaciously, shrewdly.

perspicàcia, *s.f.* perspicacity, shrewdness, sagac-ity.

perspicuità, *s.f.* perspicuity, perspicuousness.

perspícuo, *ag.* perspicuous, clear.

persuadére, *v.t.* to persuade; (*convincere*) to con-vince: *persuadi tuo fratello a venire!*, persuade your brother to come!; *cercherò di persuaderlo*, I shall try to talk him into it; *ebbi difficoltà a persuaderla*, I had difficulty in persuading her (*o* in talking her into it); *finii per persuaderli a farlo*, I finally persuaded them to do it (*o* I talked them into doing it); *l'ho per-suasa a perdonarti*, I have persuaded her to forgive you; *lo persuasi che non doveva farlo*, I convinced him that he shouldn't do it; — *qlcu. di ql.co.*, to per-suade (*o* to convince) s.o. of sthg. (*o fam.* to talk s.o. into sthg.) ‖ *la sua sincerità non mi persuade troppo*, I am not absolutely convinced of his sincerity ‖ **per-suadérsi**, *v.r.* to persuade oneself, to convince oneself: *non posso persuadermi a credere che ho torto*, I cannot bring myself to believe I am wrong; *non sono persuasi*, they are not convinced of it; *si è persuasa che questo metodo è giusto*, she has convinced herself that this method is right.

persuasìbile, *ag.* persuasible, persuadable.

persuasióne, *s.f.* persuasion; (*convinzione*) convic-tion: *potere di* —, power of persuasion; *un uomo di facile* —, a man easily persuaded; *ho la — che sia matto*, I am convinced that he is mad.

persuasíva, *s.f.* persuasiveness.

persuasívo, *ag.* persuasive: *discorso, ragionamento* —, persuasive talk, reasoning.

persuàso, *ag.* persuaded; (*convinto*) convinced; (*si-curo*) sure: *non sono — di ciò che dite*, I am not certain (*o* too sure) about what you say; *ero — di aver lasciato il mio portafogli nel cassetto*, I was sure I had left my wallet in the drawer.

persuasóre, *s.m.* persuader.

pertànto, *cong.* therefore; (*conseguentemente*) con-sequently ‖ *non* —, nevertheless (*o* however).

pèrtica, *s.f.* **1.** rod, pole, perch ‖ *è alto come una* —, (*scherz.*) he is as tall as a bean-pole **2.** (square) perch (*misura di superficie* = m.² 25,29).

perticàre, *v.t.* **1.** (*misurare a pertiche*) to measure in perches **2.** (*arc.*) (*colpire con una pertica*) to beat with a rod; (*bastonare*) to thrash.

perticàta, *s.f.* blow with a rod.

pertichíno, *s.m.* (*teat. mus.*) understudy.

pertinàce, *ag.* pertinacious, persistent; (*ostinato*) stubborn, obstinate.

pertinaceménte, *av.* pertinaciously, persistently; (*ostinatamente*) stubbornly, obstinately.

pertinàcia, *s.f.* pertinacity, pertinaciousness; (*osti-nazione*) stubbornness, obstinacy.

pertinènte, *ag.* pertinent, relevant; pertaining: *una domanda* —, a pertinent question; *doveri pertinenti al suo ufficio*, duties pertaining to his office.

pertinènza, *s.f.* pertinence, relevance, relevancy:*la — delle sue osservazioni*, the pertinence of his remarks; *ciò non è di mia* —, that is not my business; *questo è di — della direzione*, this pertains to the management.

pertósse, *s.f.* (*patol.*) (w)hooping-cough.

pertugiàre, *v.t.* (*rar.*) to bore, to perforate.

pertúgio, *s.m.* hole, perforation.

perturbaménto, *s.m.* perturbation; (*della mente*) derangement.

perturbàre, *v.t.* to perturb, to disturb, to upset: — *l'animo*, to perturb (*o* to disturb) the mind; — *l'ordine*, to disturb the peace.

perturbatóre, *ag.* disturbing ‖ *s.m.*, **perturbatríce**, *s.f.* disturber, upsetter: — *della quiete pubblica*, disturber of the peace.

perturbazióne, *s.f.* **1.** perturbation, agitation **2.** (*fis. meteorologia*) disturbance: — *magnetica*, magnetic dis-turbance; — *meteorologica*, atmospheric disturbance.

Perú, *no.pr.m.* (*geog.*) Peru ‖ *vale un* —, (*fam.*) it is worth its weight in gold.

perugíno, *ag.* of Perugia ‖ *s.m.* native of Perugia, inhabitant of Perugia.

pèrula, *s.f.* (*bot.*) perule.

peruviàno, *ag.s.m.* Peruvian.

pervàdere, *v.t.* to pervade (anche *fig.*): *un sincero sentimento religioso pervade il libro*, a sincere religious feeling pervades the book.

pervàso, *ag.* pervaded (with sthg.): *il suo animo era — di profonda tristezza*, his soul was pervaded with deep sorrow.

perveníre, *v.i.* to arrive (at a place), to attain (to sthg.), to reach (sthg.); to come (to s.o., sthg.): *il vostro assegno non ci è ancora pervenuto*, your cheque has not yet reached us; *la tenuta gli perverrà intera perchè è figlio unico*, the whole estate will come to him, because he is the only son; — *ad un luogo*, to reach (*o* to arrive at) a place; — *al potere*, to attain (*o* to come) to power.

perversaménte, *av.* perversely, wickedly.

perversióne, *s.f.* perversion: — *del gusto, del senso morale*, perversion of taste, of moral sense.

perversità, *s.f.* perversity, perverseness, wickedness.

pervèrso, *ag.* perverse; wicked: *animo* —, perverse mind; *gente perversa*, wicked people; *gusti perversi*, perverse tastes ‖ *tempo* —, foul weather.

pervertiménto, *s.m.* perversion.

pervertíre, *v.t.* to pervert; (*corrompere*) to corrupt, to lead astray: *cattivi compagni l'hanno pervertito*, evil companions have perverted him (*o* led him a-stray); — *l'ordine della natura*, to pervert the order of nature.

pervertíto, *ag.* perverted ‖ *s.m.* pervert.

pervertitóre, *s.m.*, **pervertitríce**, *s.f.* perverter.

pervicàce, *ag.* obstinate, stubborn, headstrong: — *nei suoi principi*, unyielding in his principles.

pervicàcia, *s.f.* obstinacy, stubbornness.

pervínca, *s.f.* (*bot.*) periwinkle.

pésa, *s.f.* **1.** (*pesatura*) weighing **2.** (*luogo per pesare*) weigh-house **3.** (*basculla*) weighing-machine: — *a ponte*, weigh-bridge.

pesàggio, *s.m.* **1.** (*il pesare*) weighing **2.** (*spor.*) weighing-in **3.** (*luogo dove vengono pesati i fantini o i pugilatori*) weighing-in room.

pesalèttere, *s.m.* letter-balance.

pesantàre, *v.t.* (*ind. tessile*) to weight.

pesànte, *ag.* **1.** heavy: *artiglieria* —, (*mil.*) heavy artillery; *cibo* —, heavy food; *aveva un'andatura molto* —, she had a heavy step; *ho la testa* —, I have a heavy head; *questo pacco è molto —*, this parcel is very heavy; *vi era un'aria —*, the air was sultry (*o* close) ‖ *acqua —*, (*fis.* atomica) heavy water ‖ *olio —*, heavy oil ‖ *terreno —*, heavy soil **2.** *fig.* heavy; (*noioso*) boring, dull: *libro, scrittore —*, heavy (*o* dull) book, writer; *responsabilità —*, heavy responsibility; *è una persona così —!*, he is such a bore!; *questo libro è — da leggere*, this book is heavy reading (*o* going); *avere il sonno —*, to be a heavy sleeper; *avere lo spirito —*, to have a coarse humour; *governare con mano —*, to rule with a heavy hand.

pesanteménte, *av.* **1.** heavily **2.** (*noiosamente*) boringly.

pesantézza, *s.f.* heaviness ‖ *ho una — di stomaco*, there is something lying heavy on my stomach.

pesàre, *v.t.* to weigh (anche *fig.*): *ho pesato i pro e i contro di questa decisione*, I have weighed the pros and cons of this decision; *— un pacco*, to weigh a parcel; *— le parole*, to weigh one's words: *pesate le vostre parole*, think before you speak; *— una persona*, to weigh up a person ‖ *v.i.* to weigh (anche *fig.*): *le cipolle mi pesano sullo stomaco*, onions lie heavy on my stomach (*o* are too heavy for my stomach); *la famiglia gli pesa sulle spalle*, his family is a burden to him; *mi è pesato mandarlo via*, it was hard for me to send him away; *mi pesa l'alzarmi presto al mattino*, I find it very hard to get up early in the morning; *quel che mi pesa è che dovrò rivederlo presto*, what troubles me is that I shall have to see him again soon; *questo pacco pesa poco meno di mezzo chilo*, this parcel weighs just under half a kilogram; *il rimorso gli pesava sulla coscienza*, remorse laid heavy on his conscience; *la sua opinione non pesava molto*, his opinion did not weigh much; *un silenzio pesava sull'assemblea*, a heavy silence hung (*o* brooded) over the meeting; *le tasse pesano sui poveri*, taxes are a burden to the poor; *tutte le responsabilità mi pesano*, all responsibilities worry me ‖ **pesàrsi**, *v.r.* to weigh oneself.

pesàta, *s.f.* weighing.

pesàto, *ag.* (*accorto*) well-considered: *parole pesate*, well-considered words.

pesatóre, *s.m.* weigher.

pesatríce, *s.f.* **1.** weigher **2.** (*macchina*) weighing-machine.

pesatúra, *s.f.* weighing.

pésca¹, *s.f.* **1.** (*il pescare*) fishing; (*industria*) fishery: *— a cianciolo*, seining; *— a strascico*, trawling; *— con la lenza*, angling; *— d'alto mare*, deep-sea fishing; *— dei tonni, del salmone*, tunny, salmon fishing; *— della balena*, whaling; *— delle perle*, pearl-fishing; *— subacquea*, under-water fishing; *barca, rete da —*, fishing-boat, fishing-net; *andare alla —*, to go fishing **2.** (*ciò che si è pescato*) catch: *— abbondante*, good catch; *fare buona —*, to have a good haul ‖ *la — miracolosa*, (*Bibbia*) the miraculous draught of fishes **3.** (*lotteria*) lucky-dip.

pèsca², *s.f.* **1.** (*bot.*) peach: *— duracina*, clingstone; *color —*, peach colour **2.** (*livido*) bruise.

pescàggio, *s.m.* **1.** (*mar.*) draught, draft: *— a carico*, load draught; *— a poppa*, aft draught; *— a prora*, forward draught; *— medio*, mean draught; *marca di —*, draught mark **2.** (*idraulica*) suction lift, height of suction **3.** (*miner.*) fishing.

pescagióne, *s.f.* **1.** (*pesca*) fishing **2.** (*mar.*) (*pescaggio*) draught, draft.

pescàia, *s.f.* (*chiusa, sbarramento*) weir.

pescàre, *v.t.* **1.** to fish for (*sthg.*); (*prendere*) to fish, to catch: *domani andrò a —*, tomorrow I shall go fishing; *ho pescato una grossa trota*, I have caught (*o* fished) a big trout; *— con la lenza*, to angle; *— con lo strascico*, to trawl; *— perle*, to dive for pearls; *— trote*, to fish for trout ‖ *vattel'a pesca*, (*chi lo sa?*) Goodness knows! (*o* who knows!) ‖ *— nel torbido*, to fish in troubled waters **2.** *fig.* (*riuscire a trovare*) to fish out, to find (out), to pick up: « *Dove hai pescato quell'oro-*

logio? », « *L'ho pescato in una vecchia valigia* », " Where did you fish out that watch? ", " I fished it out of an old suitcase "; *finalmente l'ho pescato!*, at last I have found him out! **3.** *fig.* (*cogliere sul fatto*) to catch red-handed: *i ladri furono pescati mentre svaligiavano una gioielleria*, the thieves were caught red-handed while robbing a jeweller's **4.** (*carte*) to draw: *ha pescato l'asso di cuori*, he has drawn the ace of hearts ‖ *v.i.* (*mar.*) to draw: *la barca pesca un metro*, the boat draws about three feet.

pescàta, *s.f.* catch, draught.

pescatóre, *s.m.* **1.** fisher; fisherman (*pl.* fishermen); (*con la lenza*) angler; *— di coralli, di perle*, coral-diver, pearl-diver; *un villaggio di poveri pescatori*, a poor fishing village ‖ *Anello del Pescatore*, Fisherman's ring (*o* Piscatory ring) **2.** *martin —*, (*ornit.*) kingfisher.

pescatríce, *s.f.* fisherwoman (*pl.* fisherwomen); (*con la lenza*) angler.

pescatòrio, *ag.* piscatory, piscatorial, fishing.

pésce, *s.m.* **1.** fish (*pl.* fish, *rar.* fishes): *— affumicato*, smoked fish; *— d'acqua dolce*, fresh-water fish; *— da taglio*, fish sold by the slice; *— di mare*, salt-water fish; *— fresco*, fresh fish; *— fritto*, fried fish; *— lesso*, boiled fish; *— persico*, perch; *pesci rossi*, goldfish; *— secco*, dried fish; *— spada*, sword-fish; *— volante*, flying-fish; *carne di —*, flesh of fish; *colla di —*, fish-glue (*o* isinglass); *lische di —*, fish-bones; *mercato del —*, fish-market; *ha pescato un grosso —, molti pesci*, he has caught a big fish, a lot of fish; *quanti pesci hai pescato?*, how many fish have you caught?; *questo mare abbonda di pesci*, this sea abounds in fish; *mangiar —*, to eat fish ‖ *i Pesci*, (*astr.*) Fishes (*o* Pisces) ‖ *— d'Aprile!*, April fool!; *un — d'Aprile*, trick played on April Fool's Day: *credo che il suo invito sia un — d'Aprile*, I think that he wants to make a fool of me with his invitation; *fare un — d'Aprile a qlcu.*, to make an April fool of s.o. ‖ *pesci grossi*, (*grandi personaggi*) bigwigs: *i pesci grossi mangiano i piccoli*, might overcomes right; the big traders cut out the small ‖ *muto come un —*, as dumb as a fish ‖ *nuovo —*, (*uomo semplice*) simpleton ‖ *sano come un —*, as sound as a rock ‖ *non sapere che pesci pigliare*, to be at one's wits' end (*o* not to know which way to turn *o* to be at a loss) ‖ *sentirsi come un — fuor d'acqua*, to feel like a fish out of water ‖ *chi dorme non piglia pesci*, *prov.* the early bird catches the worm **2.** (*pop.*) (*bicipite*) biceps.

pescecàne, *s.m.* **1.** shark; dog-fish **2.** (*arricchito di guerra*) war profiteer.

pescheréccio, *ag.* fishing ‖ *s.m.* fishing boat: *— con rete alla deriva*, drifter; *— con rete a strascico*, trawler.

pescheria, *s.f.* **1.** fish-shop **2.** (*mercato del pesce*) fish-market.

peschièra, *s.f.* fish-pond; fish-tank.

pesciaiuòla, *s.f.* fish-kettle.

pesciaiuòlo, *s.m.* fishmonger.

pescicoltúra, *s.f.* pisciculture, fish-breeding.

pescicultóre, *s.m.* pisciculturist.

pescièra, *s.f.* fish-kettle.

pescivéndola, *s.f.* fishwife (*pl.* fishwives).

pescivéndolo, *s.m.* fishmonger.

pèsco, *s.m.* peach(-tree).

pescosità, *s.f.* fishiness.

pescóso, *ag.* fishy, abounding in fish, full of fish.

pesèta, *s.f.* (*moneta spagnola*) peseta.

péso¹, *s.m.* **1.** weight: *— allo sbarco, alla consegna*, (*comm.*) landed, delivered weight; *— atomico, molecolare*, (*fis.*) atomic, molecular weight; *— giusto, abbondante, scarso*, exact, full, short weight; *— lordo, netto*, (*comm.*) gross, net weight; *— morto, utile*, dead, live weight; *— specifico*, (*fis.*) specific weight; *eccedenza di —*, (*comm.*) overweight; *unità di —*, unit of weight; *aveva un — di 10 chili*, it weighed 10 kilos; *il mio — è di 70 chili*, my weight is 70 kilos; *questo pilastro sostiene il — di tutto l'edificio*, this pillar bears the weight of the whole building; *aggiungere ql.co. per fare il —*, to throw sthg. in as a makeweight; *comprare, vendere a —*, to buy, to sell by weight; *piegarsi sotto il — di ql.co.*, to give way under the weight of sthg.; *rubare sul —*, to fiddle the weight; *sollevare un —*, to lift a weight ‖ *orologio a pesi*, clock worked by weights ‖ *sollevamento pesi*, (*spor.*) weight-lifting ‖ *la sollevò di — e la portò via*, he lifted her up bodily and carried her away ‖ *mi sento un — sullo stomaco*, sthg. is lying on my stomach ‖ *vendere ql.co. a — d'oro*, to sell sthg. for its weight in gold 2. (*di bilancia*) weight: *i pesi di una bilancia*, the weights of a balance; *usa pesi falsi*, he uses false weights ‖ *pesi e misure*, weights and measures ‖ *usare due pesi e due misure*, to judge by two different standards 3. (*importanza*) weight, importance: *ql.co. di grande, di nessun —*, sthg. of great, of no weight (o importance); *questo non ha alcun — per me*, this has no weight with me; *dar — a ql.co.*, to give weight to sthg. (o to attach importance to sthg.) 4. (*onere*) weight, load, burden: *il — delle tasse è diventato insopportabile*, the burden of taxation has become unbearable; *non ha più quel — sulla coscienza*, he no longer has that load on his conscience; *risente il — degli anni*, he is crushed by the weight of years; *essere di —*, to be a burden 5. (*boxe, atletica pesante, ecc.*) weight: *— gallo*, bantam-weight; *— leggero*, lightweight; *— massimo*, heavyweight; *— medio*, middleweight; *— medio leggero*, welter-weight; *— medio massimo*, light heavyweight; *— mosca*, fly-weight; *— piuma*, featherweight 6. (*recinto del peso negli ippodromi*) weighing-in room.

péso², *ag.* heavy.
pessimaménte, *av.* most badly, very badly.
pessimísmo, *s.m.* pessimism.
pessimísta, *s.c.* pessimist.
pessimístico, *ag.* pessimistic.
pèssimo, *ag. superl.* 1. (*di persona*) **very bad**; (*fam.*) **hopeless**: *una pessima cuoca*, a hopeless cook; *un — insegnante*, a very bad teacher; *un — poeta*, a very bad (o poor) poet 2. (*di cosa*) **horrible, foul; very bad, nasty**: *ha un — carattere*, he has a nasty (o very bad) temper (o he is very ill-tempered); *il tempo è —*, the weather is foul (o horrible); *quella carne ha un — odore*, that meat has a horrible smell (o smells horrible).
pésta, *s.f.* 1. (*orma*) footprint, footstep; (*traccia*) track; (*di animali*) trail, track: *sulle peste di ql.cu.*, on the track of s.o.; *seguire le peste di ql.cu.*, *fig.* to follow in s.o.'s footsteps 2. (*difficoltà*) difficulty: *lasciare ql.cu. nelle peste*, to leave s.o. in the lurch (o in difficulties); *trovarsi nelle peste*, to find oneself in difficulties 3. (*strada battuta*) beaten track.
pestaménto, *s.m.* (*rar.*) 1. pounding, crushing 2. (*calpestamento*) treading, trampling, stamping.
pestàre, *v.t.* 1. (*schiacciare*) to pound, to crush: *gli ho pestato il mignolo col martello*, I have crushed his little finger with a hammer; *— ql.co. in un mortaio*, to pound sthg. in a mortar; *— il sale*, to pound salt ‖ *non suona, ma pesta il pianoforte*, he doesn't play, but pounds on the piano ‖ *— l'acqua nel mortaio*, to beat the air 2. (*calpestare*) to tread on (sthg.), to trample on (sthg.): *non — l'erba*, do not tread (o do not trample) on the grass; *— i piedi a ql.cu.*, to tread on s.o.'s toes* (anche *fig.*) 3. (*percuotere*) to beat, to hit; to thrash: *quando è ubriaco pesta sua moglie*, when he is drunk he beats his wife 4. (*battere*) to strike: *— i piedi*, to stamp one's feet; *— un pugno sul tavolo*, to strike the table with one's fist.
pestàta, pestatúra, *s.f.* 1. (*lo schiacciare*) pounding, crushing 2. (*il calpestare*) treading, trampling: *mi hai dato una — di piedi*, you have trod on my toes.
pèste, *s.f.* 1. plague, pestilence; (*st.*) Black Death: *— bovina*, cattle plague; *— bubbonica*, bubonic plague; *la — si diffuse e infuriò in Europa nel quattordicesimo secolo*, the Black Death spread and raged over Europe in the 14th century ‖ *—, fame e guerra*, plague,

famine and war ‖ *— lo colga!*, a plague on him! ‖ *non c'è mica la —!*, (*fam.*) you won't catch anything! ‖ *dire — e corna di ql.cu.*, to run s.o. down (o to speak ill of s.o.) 2. (*calamità*) pest, plague, calamity: *quel bambino è una vera —*, that child is a real pest 3. (*fetore*) stench 4. *— delle acque*, (*bot.*) elodea.
pestèllo, *s.m.* pestle: *usare il —*, to pestle.
pestífero, *ag.* pestiferous (anche *fig.*), plague-bearing.
pestilènte, *ag.* pestilent (anche *fig.*).
pestilènza, *s.f.* 1. pestilence, plague 2. (*calamità*) pest, plague, calamity 3. (*fetore*) stench.
pestilenziàle, *ag.* pestilential (anche *fig.*).
pésto¹, *ag.* pounded, crushed, beaten ‖ *buio —*, pitch dark ‖ *carta pesta*, papier maché: *è un uomo di carta pesta*, *fig.* he is a spineless fellow (o that man has no back bone) ‖ *avere gli occhi pesti*, to have rings under one's eyes ‖ *avere le ossa peste*, to feel washed out ‖ *s.m.* 1. (*ind. della carta*) pulp 2. (*cuc.*) " pesto " (sauce characteristic of Genoese cooking).
Pèsto², *no.pr.f.* (*geog. archeol.*) Paestum.
pestóne, *s.m.* (*tec.*) rammer: *— calcaterra a mano*, hand rammer; *— pneumatico*, pneumatic rammer.
pètalo, *s.m.* petal.
petàrdo, *s.m.* 1. (*piccolo mortaio*) petard 2. (*pirotecnica*) cracker, petard, squib 3. (*ferr.*) fog-signal.
pètaso, *s.m.* (*st. greca*) petasus.
petécchia, *s.f.* 1. (*med.*) petechia (*pl.* petechiae) 2. (*avaro, taccagno*) screw, stingy fellow, niggard.
petecchiàle, *ag.* petechial: *tifo —*, (*patol.*) petechial typhus.
petènte, *ag.* petitioning ‖ *s.c.* petitioner.
petitòrio, *ag.* (*dir.*) petitory: *giudizio —*, petitory suit.
petizióne, *s.f.* petition: *— di diritto*, petition of right; *fare una —*, to make a petition.
péto, *s.m.* fart, wind.
petonciàno, *s.m.* (*bot.*) egg plant, aubergine.
petràia, *s.f.* 1. (*mucchio di pietre*) heap of stones 2. (*cava di pietre*) quarry, stone pit.
Petràrca, *no.pr.* (*st. lett.*) Petrarch.
petrarcheggiàre, *v.i.* to Petrarchise, to write in the manner of Petrarch.
petrarchésco, *ag.* Petrarchian.
petrarchísmo, *s.m.* (*lett.*) Petrarchism.
petrarchísta, *s.c.* Petrarchist.
petrièra, *s.f.* stone-pit, quarry.
petrificàre, *v.t.*, **petrificàrsi**, *v.r.* to petrify.
petrificàto, *ag.* 1. petrified 2. (*stupefatto*) petrified; dumbfounded.
petrificazióne, *s.f.* petrification.
petrígno, *ag.* stone (*attributivo*).
petrografía, *s.f.* (*geol.*) petrography, petrology.
petrolièra, *s.f.* (*mar.*) tanker, oil-tanker.
petrolière, *s.m.* (*incendiario politico*) petroleur.
petrolífero, *ag.* oil (*attributivo*); petroleous, petroliferous: *pozzo —*, oil-well ‖ *azioni petrolifere*, oil-shares.
petròlio, *s.m.* oil; (*da illuminazione*) paraffin (oil); (*amer.*) kerosene, coal-oil: *— grezzo*, crude oil (o petroleum); *— grezzo leggero*, light crude oil; *lampada a —*, paraffin-lamp (o kerosene-lamp); *raffinazione del —*, oil-refining (o petroleum-refining); *trovare il —*, to strike oil.
Petronílla, *no.pr.f.* Petronella, Petronilla.
Petrònio, *no.pr.m.* (*st.*) Petronius.
petronciàno, *s.m.* (*bot.*) egg plant, aubergine.
petrosèllo, *s.m.* (*bot.*) parsley.
petróso, *ag.* stony.
pettégola, *s.f.* gossip, gossiper, tattler.
pettegolàre, *v.i.* to gossip, to tattle.
pettegolézzo, *s.m.* gossip, tittle-tattle: *non mi piacciono i pettegolezzi*, I don't like gossip; *penso che sia solo un —*, I think it's mere gossip.
pettégolo, *ag.* gossipy, gossiping ‖ *s.m.* gossip, gossiper, tattler.
pettièra, *s.f.* breast-band.
pettinàre, *v.t.* 1. to comb: *— un bambino*, to comb

a child's hair **2.** (*ind. tessile*) (*lana*) to comb, to card; (*lino, canapa*) to hackle **3.** (*strigliare*) to curry: — *un cavallo*, to curry a horse **4.** *fig.* (*sgridare*) to tell off, to scold, to chide; (*criticare severamente*) to censure, to criticize: *ci penserà suo padre a pettinarlo per benino*, his father will give him what-for (*o* a good dressing down); *la sua ultima commedia fu ben pettinata dalla critica*, his last play was torn to pieces by the critics **5.** (*graffiare*) to scratch ‖ **pettinàrsi**, *v.r.* to comb one's hair; to do one's hair.

pettinàta, *s.f.* **1.** combing: *darsi una* —, to comb one's hair **2.** (*sgridata*) telling off, dressing down.

pettinàto, *ag.* **1.** combed: *una persona mal pettinata*, an unkempt person; *essere ben* —, to have tidy hair **2.** (*ind. tessile*) combed, carded: *lana pettinata*, combed wool **3.** (*di stile, limato*) smooth ‖ *s.m.* (*ind. tessile*) worsted.

pettinatríce, *s.f.* **1.** hairdresser **2.** (*ind. tessile*) comber, combing machine: — *in grosso*, rougher.

pettinatúra, *s.f.* **1.** (*acconciatura*) coiffure, hair-do **2.** (*ind. tessile*) (*di lana*) combing, carding; (*di lino, canapa*) hackling: — *a secco*, dry-combing; *cascami di* —, combing waste.

pèttine, *s.m.* **1.** comb: — *fitto*, fine-tooth(ed) comb; — *per acconciatura*, (hair-) comb; — *rado*, wide-tooth(ed) comb; *denti di un* —, teeth of a comb; *darsi un colpo di* —, (*fam.*) to run a comb through one's hair ‖ *tutti i nodi vengono al* —, *prov.* murder (*o* truth) will out **2.** (*ind. tessile*) (*per lana*) comb; (*per lino, canapa*) hackle: — *di telaio*, reed; — *spazzatura*, stripping comb **3.** (*elett. mec.*) comb: — *del combinatore*, contact-piece; — *per filettature*, chaser **4.** (*striglia*) curry-comb **5.** (*zool.*) pecten (*pl.* pectines), scallop **6.** — *di Venere*, (*bot.*) lady's comb **7.** (*mus.*) plectrum (*pl.* plectra).

pettinèlla, *s.f.* tooth-comb.

pettinièra, *s.f.* **1.** (*scatola per i pettini*) comb-case **2.** (*tavola da toletta*) dressing-table.

pettirósso, *s.m.* (*ornit.*) robin, robin-redbreast.

pètto, *s.m.* **1.** chest, breast: *il* — *di un uomo, di un animale*, the breast of a man, of an animal; *a* — *nudo*, bare-chested; *circonferenza di* —, chest-measurement; *do di* —, (*mus.*) high C from the chest; *malato di* —, consumptive; *malattie di* —, chest complaints; *raffreddore di* —, chest-cold; *voce, nota di* —, (*mus.*) voice, note from the chest; *battersi il* —, to beat one's breast (*anche fig.*); *incrociare le braccia sul* —, to fold one's arms across one's breast (*o* chest) ‖ *a* — *a* —, face to face ‖ *a* — *a*, in comparison with: *a* — *a te non vale niente*, in comparison with you he is worth nothing; *stare a* —, to stand (*o* to bear) comparison with ‖ *fino al* —, breast-high: *immerso nell'acqua fino al* —, up to one's arm-pits (*o* breast) in water ‖ *prendere, affrontare qlcu., ql.co. di* —, to face up to s.o., sthg. **2.** (*di donna*) breast: *aveva un bambino al* —, she was nursing a baby (*o* she had a child at her breast) **3.** (*cuore*) heart: *mettiti una mano sul* — *e dimmi qual è la tua opinione*, tell me honestly what your opinion is; *mi sono liberato il* — *da un grosso peso*, I got a load off my chest; *avere a* — *ql.co.*, to have sthg. at heart **4.** (*cuc.*) breast; brisket: — *di pollo*, breast of chicken **5.** (*di abito*) breast; (*di camicia*) front: — *di camicia inamidato*, starched shirt-front; *giacca a doppio* —, *a un* —, double-breasted, single-breasted coat.

pettoràle, *ag.* pectoral; breast (*attributivo*): *croce* —, (*eccl.*) pectoral cross; *muscolo* —, (*anat.*) pectoral (*o* breast) muscle ‖ *s.m.* **1.** (*di cavallo*) breast-band **2.** (*di corazza*) breastplate **3.** (*eccl.*) pectoral.

pettorína, *s.f.* **1.** chemisette **2.** (*di grembiule*) bodice.

pettorúto, *ag.* **1.** full-breasted: *un bel tacchino* —, a fine, full-breasted turkey **2.** *fig.* (*tronfio*) haughty, proud, pompous: *passeggiava tutto* — *su e giù davanti alla porta*, he was strutting up and down in front of the door.

petulànte, *ag.* (*arrogante*) arrogant, overbearing; (*sfacciato*) impertinent, pert, cheeky: *un ragazzino antipatico e* —, a disagreeable, cheeky little boy; *con quelle sue maniere petulanti, ottiene sempre tutto dai suoi genitori*, with that arrogant (*o* overbearing) way of his, he gets everything he wants from his parents.

petulanteménte, *av.* (*arrogantemente*) arrogantly, overbearingly; (*sfacciatamente*) impertinently, pertly.

petulànza, *s.f.* (*arroganza*) arrogance; (*sfacciataggine*) impertinence, pertness.

petúnia, *s.f.* (*bot.*) petunia.

pèzza, *s.f.* **1.** (*toppa*) patch: *una* — *nei calzoni, nel lenzuolo*, a patch in a pair of trousers, in a sheet; *metterci una* —, to patch sthg. up (*anche fig.*) **2.** (*pannolino*) cloth, towel; (*per bambini*) napkin; (*amer.*) diaper ‖ *trattare qlcu. come una* — *da piedi*, *fig.* to treat s.o. like dirt **3.** (*panno intero*) roll: *una* — *di cotone*, a roll of cotton cloth; *tessuti in* —, piece-goods; *questa stoffa sembrava molto migliore in* —, as a roll of cloth this material looked much better; *vendere in* —, to sell by the roll **4.** (*moneta*) piece: — *d'argento*, piece of silver **5.** (*sul mantello di animali*) speckle, spot **6.** (*tempo*) *gran, lunga* —, a long time (*o* while): *ti aspetto da lunga* —, I have been waiting for you for a long time **7.** — *giustificativa*, (*comm.*) voucher.

pezzàme, *s.m.* (*rar.*) **1.** patches (*pl.*) **2.** *V.* **rottàme 2.**

pezzàto, *ag.* spotted, speckled; (*di cavallo*) dappled, pied: *un cane* —, a spotted dog.

pezzatúra, *s.f.* **1.** speckling; (*di cavallo*) dappling **2.** (*grandezza dei pezzi*) size.

pezzènte, *ag.* beggarly ‖ *s.c.* **1.** (*straccione*) ragamuffin **2.** (*mendicante*) beggar.

pezzentería, *s.f.* **1.** (*l'essere pezzente*) beggary **2.** (*folla di pezzenti*) crowd of beggars **3.** (*azione da pezzente*) mean action.

pèzzo, *s.m.* **1.** piece, bit; (*parte*) part: *un* — *di carne*, a piece (*o* bit) of meat: *datemi un buon* — *vicino all'osso*, give me a nice cut near the bone; *un* — *di pane*, a piece (*o* bit) of bread; *un* — *di terra*, a piece (*o* patch) of land; *abito a due pezzi*, two-piece suit; *da quella finestra si vede un* — *di mare*, you can see a bit of the sea from that window; *facemmo insieme un bel* — *di strada*, we went a good way together; *lesse un* — *del suo discorso*, he read part of his speech ‖ *a, in pezzi*, in, to pieces: *questo vecchio vestito cade a pezzi*, this old dress is falling to pieces; *il vaso cadde e andò in pezzi*, the vase fell and broke to pieces; *essere in, a pezzi*, to be in pieces: *i suoi nervi erano a pezzi*, his nerves were in shreds; *fare a pezzi*, to break (*o* to pull) to pieces; (*squartare, dilaniare*) to tear to pieces: *la bambina ha fatto a pezzi la sua bambola nuova*, the child has broken (*o* torn) her new doll to pieces; *i cani fecero a pezzi il cinghiale*, the dogs tore the boar to pieces ‖ *a pezzi e bocconi*, *a piccole parti*) piecemeal: *l'ho scritto a pezzi e bocconi*, I wrote it piecemeal **2.** (*esemplare, elemento singolo di un complesso*) piece: *i più bei pezzi della sua collezione*, the finest pieces in his collection; *un servizio da tè di venti pezzi*, a tea-service of twenty pieces; *ha ammobiliato la sua casa con dei bellissimi pezzi dell'800*, she has furnished her home with some very fine nineteenth-century pieces; *li vende a due scellini l'uno* —, he sells them at two shillings each ‖ — *duro*, (*gelato*) ice-cream slice ‖ *un* — *grosso*, a bigwig; (*sl.*) a bigshot (*o* a big noise); (*nell'esercito*) brass-hat (*o* top-brass) ‖ *un bel* — *di donna, di uomo*, a fine figure of a woman, man ‖ *che* — *di naso!*, what a big nose! ‖ *che* — *di stupido!*, what an ass! (*o* what a fool!) ‖ *tutto d'un* —, all of a (*o* one) piece: *uomo tutto d'un* —, *fig.* man of sterling character; *cammina tutto d'un* —, he walks very stiffly **3.** (*mec.*) piece, part: — *di ricambio*, spare part; — *di riempimento*, (*mar.*) deadwood; — *fucinato*, (*metall.*) forging; — *fuso*, casting; — *grezzo*, blank; — *in lavorazione*, workpiece; — *lavorato*, machined part (*o* piece); —

stampato a caldo, drop forging; — *stampato a freddo*, cold stamping; *andare in pezzi*, to shatter; *centrare il — da lavorare*, to centre a piece of work **4.** (*mil.*) piece, gun: — *da campagna*, fieldpiece; — *di artiglieria*, piece of ordnance (*o* artillery); *una batteria di sei pezzi*, a six-piece battery; *caricare il —*, to load the gun **5.** (*musica*) piece: *suonava un — di Rossini*, he was playing a piece by Rossini **6.** (*articolo di giornale*) newspaper article **7.** (*di tempo*) quite a long time, quite a while: *da un — non lo vedo*, I haven't seen him for quite a long time; *lo aspettai per un bel — e poi me ne andai*, I waited for him quite a while, then I went away; *starò un — a tornare*, I'll be gone quite a long time.

pezzuòla, *s.f.* (*fazzoletto*) handkerchief.

piaccichíccio, *s.m.* sticky mud.

piacceicóna, *s.f.* bungler, botcher.

piacceicóne, *ag.* bungling ‖ *s.m.* bungler, botcher.

piacènte, *ag.* pleasant and attractive: *una donna —*, a pleasant and attractive woman; *un viso —*, a pleasant face.

piacére, *s.m.* **1.** pleasure, delight: *i piaceri della tavola*, the pleasures of the table; *i piaceri dello spirito*, the pleasures of the spirit; *i piaceri dello studio*, the pleasures of study; *i piaceri di questo mondo*, the pleasures of this world (*o* earthly pleasures); *amante, avido di piaceri*, pleasure-loving, pleasure-seeking; *il — sta nella cessazione del dolore*, pleasure is in the cessation of pain; *avrò sempre — di vederti*, I shall always be delighted (*o* pleased) to see you; *è per me un grande — poterti aiutare*, I am delighted to be able to help you; *mi fa sempre molto — ricevere sue notizie*, it always gives me a lot of pleasure (*o* I'm always very happy) to hear from him; *sembra provar — nel dar fastidio alla gente*, he seems to take pleasure (*o* delight) in annoying people; *ti rivedo con —*, I'm delighted to see you again ‖ *—!, (nelle presentazioni)* how do you do! ‖ *con —!*, with pleasure! ‖ *piove che è un —*, it is raining cats and dogs; *studia, lavora che è un —*, she studies, works like mad ‖ *avere il — di...*, to have the pleasure of...: *ho avuto il — di dirgli che...*, I had the pleasure of informing him that...; *posso avere il — di accompagnarla a casa?*, may I have the pleasure of taking you home? **2.** (*svago, divertimento*) pleasure, amusement: *piaceri leciti, illeciti*, lawful, unlawful pleasures; *non è un — uscire con questa pioggia*, it is no pleasure going out in this rain; *questi piaceri sono troppo costosi per noi*, these amusements are too expensive for us; *alternare le occupazioni coi piaceri*, to alternate business with pleasure; *darsi ai piaceri*, to give oneself up to pleasure ‖ *minuti piaceri*, minor pleasures: *soldi per i minuti piaceri*, pocket money ‖ *viaggio, gita di —*, pleasure trip **3.** (*favore*) favour, kindness: *domandare un — a qlcu.*, to ask a favour of s.o.; *fare un — a qlcu.*, to do s.o. a favour (*o* kindness): *puoi farmi un —?*, can you do me a favour?; *puoi farmi il — di venire subito?*, will you be so kind as to come at once? ‖ *per —*, (if you) please: *passami l'acqua, per —*, pass me the water, please ‖ *fammi il —!*, (*iron.*) do you mind! **4.** (*volontà*) will: *contro il — suo*, against his will; *fa' il — tuo*, do as you like ‖ *a —*, at will (*o* at pleasure): *pane a —*, as much bread as you like.

piacére, *v.i.* to please (s.o.); (*con costruzione pers.*): to like (s.o., sthg.), to be fond of (s.o., sthg.), to care for (s.o., sthg.): *adesso farò come mi piace*, now I'll do as I like; *gli piace viaggiare*, he likes travelling; *mi piace andare a scuola*, I like going to school; *mi piace che tutto sia in ordine*, I like everything to be in order; *mi piace molto la poesia*, I am very fond of poetry (*o* I like poetry very much); *mi piace questo paese, questa casa, questo libro*, I like (*o* I am fond of) this country, this house, this book; *mi piacerebbe andare a teatro*, I should like to go to the theatre; *mi piace sempre vederli uscire insieme*, I am always pleased (*o* it always pleases me) to see them go out together; *mi sarebbe piaciuto ve-*

derlo, I should have liked (*o* it would have pleased me) to see him; *non mi piacciono le angurie*, I don't like water-melons; *non mi piace affatto*, I don't like it at all (*o* it doesn't please me at all); *non mi piace che tu gli parli*, I don't like (*o* I don't care for) you to speak to him; *un piatto che piace molto*, an appetizing dish; *quella ragazza piace a tutti*, everybody likes that girl; *quel libro non mi finisce di —*, (*fam.*) that book is not completely to my taste; *resto perchè così mi piace*, I am staying because I want to; *ti piace il jazz?*, do you like (*o* are you fond of *o* do you care for) jazz?; *ti piace il nostro progetto per le vacanze?*, how do you like our plan for the holidays?; *ti piacerebbe un po' di vacanza?*, would you like (*o* care) to have a bit of a holiday? ‖ *a Dio piacendo, piaccia a Dio*, God willing (*o* D.V. *o* please God): *a Dio piacendo ci sposeremo tra un mese*, God willing (*o* D.V.) we'll get married in a month; *piaccia a Dio che non venga una guerra!*, please God there won't be a war! ‖ *come pare e piace*, as one pleases: *faccio come mi pare e piace*, I do as I please ‖ *piaccia o non piaccia*, whether one likes or not: *bisogna lavorare piaccia o non piaccia*, you must work whether you like it or not.

piacévole, *ag.* **1.** pleasant, agreeable: — *al tatto*, pleasant to the touch; *una — passeggiata, serata*, a pleasant (*o* agreeable) walk, evening; *un gusto —*, an agreeable taste; *una voce —*, a pleasant (*o* agreeable) voice **2.** (*di persona*) pleasant, agreeable, nice, amiable: *un — compagno*, a pleasant (*o* an agreeable) companion; *è un uomo — nella conversazione*, he is a pleasant conversationalist; *fare il —*, to be facetious.

piacevoleggiàre, *v.i.* (*rar.*) to joke, to jest.

piacevolézza, *s.f.* **1.** pleasantness, agreeableness; (*grazia*) gracefulness, charm **2.** (*scherzo*) pleasantry.

piacevolménte, *av.* pleasantly, agreeably: *ne fui sorpreso*, I was agreeably surprised.

piacevolóna, *s.f.* wag, joker; humorist.

piacevolóne, *ag.* waggish, facetious, jocular ‖ *s.m.* wag, joker; humorist.

piaciménto, *s.m.* pleasure; liking: *a —*, as much as one likes; *fa' a tuo —*, do as you like; *non è di suo —*, it is not to his liking.

piàga, *s.f.* **1.** sore: *il suo corpo era pieno di piaghe*, his body was covered with sores ‖ *mettere il dito sulla —*, *fig.* to bring up a sore point ‖ *riaprire vecchie piaghe*, *fig.* to reopen old wounds ‖ *il medico pietoso fa la — verminosa*, *prov.* the tender surgeon makes a foul wound **2.** (*calamità*) evil, calamity; plague: — *sociale*, social evil; *la siccità è la — del paese*, drought is the plague of the country ‖ *le dieci piaghe d'Egitto*, the ten plagues of Egypt **3.** (*persona molesta*) intruder; nuisance: *che —!*, what a bore!.

piagàre, *v.t.* to ulcerate.

piaggería, *s.f.* (*adulazione*) flattery.

piàggia, *s.f.* (*poet.*) **1.** (*spiaggia*) (sea) shore **2.** (*pendio*) slope; declivity.

piaggiaménto, *s.m.* (*adulazione*) flattery.

piaggiàre, *v.t.* (*adulare*) to flatter, to fawn upon (s.o.).

piaggiatóre, *s.m.*, **piaggiatríce**, *s.f.* (*adulatore*) flatterer.

piagnistèo, *s.m.* moaning; (*di bambino*) grizzling.

piagnolóso, *ag.* moaning; (*di bambino*) grizzling; whining.

piagnòna, *s.f.*, **piagnóne**, *s.m.* **1.** moaner, grumbler; (*di bambino*) grizzler **2.** (*persona pagata per piangere ad un funerale*) hired mourner.

piagnucolaménto, *s.m.* moaning; (*di bambino*) grizzling; whimpering.

piagnucolàre, *v.i.* to moan; (*di bambino*) to grizzle; to whimper.

piagnucolío, *s.m.* moaning; (*di bambino*) grizzling; whimpering.

piagnucolóna, *s.f.*, **piagnucolóne**, *s.m.* moaner; (*di bambino*) grizzler, cry-baby.

piagnucolóso, *ag.* moaning; (*di bambino*) grizzling.

piagóso, *ag.* covered in sores, covered with sores.

piàlla, *s.f.* 1. (*attrezzo artigiano*) plane: — *per rifinire*, try plane; — *per scanalare*, grooving plane; *corpo della* —, stock 2. (*macchina utensile*) planer: — *a filo*, single-cylinder planer; — *a spessore*, thicknessing machine (*o* double-cylinder planer); — *universale*, universal plane.

piallàccio, *s.m.* sheet of veneer.

piallàre, *v.t.* to plane: — *a spessore*, to thickness.

piallàta, *s.f.* 1. planing 2. (*colpo di pialla*) stroke with a plane.

piallatóre, *ag.* planer (*attributivo*) ‖ *s.m.* planer.

piallatríce, *s.f.* (*mec.*) planer, planing machine: — *a spessore*, thicknessing machine (*o* double-cylinder planing machine); — *a tavola*, table planing machine; — *circolare*, circular planing machine; — *da impiallacciatura*, veneer cutting machine.

piallatúra, *s.f.* 1. planing 2. (*trucioli*) shavings (*pl.*).

piallétto, *s.m.* 1. (*per falegname*) jack-plane 2. (*per muratore*) float.

piallóne, *s.m.* jack-plane.

piaménte, *av.* piously, devoutly.

piàna, *s.f.* 1. (*pianura*) plane 2. (*spianata*) level ground.

pianàle, *s.m.* level ground.

pianaménte, *av.* 1. (*senza far rumore*) softly, quietly 2. (*lentamente*) slowly 3. (*semplicemente*) plainly.

pianàre, *v.t.* (*rar.*) (*livellare*) to level, to make level; to flatten.

pianatóio, *s.m.* smoothing chisel.

pianeggiànte, *ag.* level, flat: *strada, terreno* —, level road, ground.

pianeggiàre, *v.t.* to level, to make level ‖ *v.i.* to be level, to be flat.

pianèlla, *s.f.* 1. (*pantofola*) slipper 2. (*mattone per tetti*) flat tile.

pianeròttolo, *s.m.* landing.

pianéta[1], *s.m.* 1. (*astr. astrologia*) planet 2. (*foglietto della fortuna*) fortune-telling leaflet.

pianéta[2], *s.f.* (*eccl.*) chasuble, planet.

pianézza, *s.f.* (*rar.*) 1. (*l'essere piano*) flatness, levelness 2. (*facilità*) easiness 3. (*semplicità*) simplicity.

piangènte, *ag.* crying, weeping ‖ *salice* —, weeping willow.

piàngere, *v.i.* 1. to cry, to weep: *ella pianse dal dolore*, she wept with pain; *ella pianse tanto da non vederci quasi più*, she cried her eyes out; *lasciai — il bambino finché si addormentò*, I let the child cry itself to sleep; *le bruciavano gli occhi a forza di* —, she made her eyes sore with crying; *mi piangono gli occhi per il freddo, il fumo*, my eyes are watering with the cold, the smoke; — *a calde lacrime*, to weep one's heart out; — *amaramente, dirottamente*, to cry bitterly, copiously; — *di dispetto, di rabbia*, to weep with vexation, rage; — *di gioia*, to weep for joy ‖ — *come un vitello*, to blubber ‖ *far* — *qlcu.*, to make s.o. cry ‖ *è inutile* — *sul latte versato*, it's no use crying over spilt milk 2. (*soffrire, essere in tribolazione*) to suffer: *mi piange il cuore a rinunciarvi*, it breaks my heart to give it up; *mi piangeva il cuore a sentire la sua triste storia*, it made my heart bleed to hear his sad story; — *sotto la tirannia*, to suffer under tyranny ‖ *beati quelli che piangono*, (*Bibbia*) blessed are they that mourn 3. (*gocciolare*) (*di pianta*) to bleed; (*di grotte, rubinetti*) to drip: *la vite, tagliata di recente, piangeva*, the newly-cut vine, was bleeding ‖ *v.t.* 1. to weep: — *tutte le proprie lacrime*, to have a good cry ‖ — *lacrime amare*, to weep bitter tears; — *lacrime di coccodrillo*, to weep crocodile tears; — *lacrime di sangue*, to weep tears of blood 2. (*per un lutto*) to mourn; (*lamentare, deplorare*) to lament, to bewail; to weep, to grieve for, over (*sthg.*), to sorrow for (*sthg.*): *piansero la perdita di quel grande*, they grieved for the loss of that great man; — *i danni patiti*, to grieve over wrongs suffered; — *la morte di qlcu.*, to mourn s.o.'s death; — *i propri peccati*, to bewail one's sins; — *il proprio triste fato*, to bewail one's sad fate ‖ — *miseria*, to cry poverty (*o* to complain of one's lot) ‖ *chi è causa del suo mal, pianga se stesso*, *prov.* as you have made your bed so must you lie on it 3. (*letter.*) (*rimpiangere*) to weep for (sthg.), to weep over (sthg.), to mourn for (sthg.): — *la giovinezza perduta*, to mourn for one's lost youth.

pianificàre, *v.t.* to plan; to project.

pianificàto, *ag.* planned: *economia pianificata*, planned economy.

pianificazióne, *s.f.* planning: *pianificazioni del dopoguerra*, post-war planning.

pianigiàno, *ag.* of the plain(s), inhabiting the plain(s); lowland (*attributivo*) ‖ *s.m.* inhabitant of the plain(s); lowlander.

pianísta, *s.c.* pianist.

piàno[1], *ag.* 1. flat, level, even: *paese* —, flat country; *strada piana*, level road; *superficie piana*, level (*o* even) surface; *terreno* —, level ground ‖ *corsa piana*, flat race 2. (*liscio*) smooth: *pietra piana*, smooth stone 3. (*chiaro, intelligibile*) clear, plain: *scrittura piana*, clear handwriting 4. (*semplice*) simple: *parole umili e piane*, simple and humble words ‖ *alla piana*, simply ‖ *messa piana*, low mass 5. (*geom.*) plane: *geometria piana*, plane geometry 6. (*gram.*) paroxytone.

piàno[2], *av.* 1. (*sommessamente*) softly, quietly: *egli suona troppo* —, he plays too softly; *fa'* —, *altrimenti lo svegli*, don't make noise or you'll wake him up; *parla così* — *che non lo sento*, he speaks in such a low voice (*o* so low) that I can't hear him; *suona* —!, play softly! 2. (*mus.*) piano 3. (*lentamente*) slowly, slow: *pian* — *ci riuscirò*, little by little I shall succeed in it; *va* —, go slowly; *camminare* —, to walk slowly ‖ *chi va* — *va sano e va lontano*, *prov.* slow and steady wins the race 4. (*con cautela*) gently, carefully: *fa'* —, *chè lo strappi*, be careful or you'll tear it; *sollevalo* — *perchè si rompe facilmente*, lift it up gently because it breaks easily ‖ *vacci* —!, be careful!.

piàno[3], *s.m.* 1. plain; flat land, level land: *dopo qualche chilometro di* —, *comincia l'erta*, after some miles of plain, the ascent begins 2. (*superficie piana*) plane (anche *geom.*): *il* — *della seggiola*, the seat of the chair; *il* — *della tavola*, the top of the table; — *orizzontale, inclinato*, (*geom.*) horizontal, inclined plane; — *stradale*, roadway 3. (*di casa*) floor, storey; (*di nave, autobus*) deck: *il* — *superiore di un edificio*, the top storey (*o* floor) of a building; — *terreno*, *terra*, ground floor (*o amer.* first floor); *a due piani*, two-storied; *autobus a due piani*, double-decker; *una casa di quindici piani*, a fifteen-storied building (*o* a building of fifteen stories); *primo* —, first floor (*o amer.* second floor); *abito al terzo* —, I live on the third floor 4. (*strato*) layer, stratum (*pl.* strata): *un* — *di carta*, a layer of paper; *in diversi piani*, in different layers (*o* strata) 5. (*livello*) plane, level: *siamo sullo stesso* —, we are on the same plane (*o* level) 6. (*progetto, disegno*) plan (anche *mil.*); *fig.* plan, scheme, project: *il* — *di una casa*, the plan of a house; — *di guerra, di operazioni*, (*mil.*) plan of campaign, operations; — *di studi*, plan (*o* programme) of studies; — *regolatore*, town-planning; *secondo i miei piani*, according to my plans; *fare dei piani*, to make plans 7. (*art. foto. cine.*): *primo* —, (*art.*) foreground; (*foto. cine.*) close up ‖ *un artista di primo* —, an artist of the first rank (*o* a first-rate artist); *passare in secondo* —, to take a back seat 8. (*tec.*): — *alare*, (*aer.*) plane (*o* wing area); — *caricatore, di caricamento*, (*ferr.*) loading platform; — *dell'orbita*, (*astr.*) orb; — *di clivaggio, di sfaldatura*, (*geol.*) cleavage plane; — *di coda*, (*aer.*) empennage; — *di deriva*, (*aer.*) fin; — *di galleggiamento*, (*mar.*) water plane; — *di riscontro*, (*mec.*) surface plate (*o* face plate *o* plane); — *di scorrimento*, (*mec.*) sliding surface (*o* slide); — *stabilizzatore*, (*aer.*) tail-plane (*o amer.* stabilizer).

piàno[4], **pianofòrte**, *s.m.* piano (*pl.* pianos), piano-forte: — *a coda*, grand piano; — *a mezza coda*, square piano (*o* baby-grand); — *verticale*, upright (*o* cabinet) piano.

pianòla, *s.f.* (*mus.*) pianola.

pianòro, *s.m.* plateau, tableland.

piànta, *s.f.* 1. plant; tree: — *acquatica*, water-plant; — *da fiore*, flowering plant; — *da frutto*, fruit-bearing plant; — *grassa*, cactus; — *ornamentale*, ornamental plant; — *tropicale*, tropical plant || *piante erbacee*, herbaceous plants || *piante sempreverdi*, evergreen plants (*o* evergreens) 2. (*del piede, di scarpa*) sole || *muovere le piante*, to walk 3. (*disegno di edifizio, podere, ecc.*) plan; (*carta topografica*) map, plan: *la* — *di un appartamento*, the plan of a flat; *la* — *di una città*, the map (*o* plan) of a town 4. (*ruolo*) list: *impiegato in* — *stabile*, clerk on permanent staff (*o* regular employee) 5. *di sana* —, (*completamente*) entirely (*o* completely); (*di bel nuovo*) anew (*o* afresh): *era una cosa inventata di sana* —, it was a thing completely invented; *ricominciare di sana* —, to start afresh; *rifare ql.co. di sana* —, to do sthg. anew.

piantacaròte, *s.c.* (*fam.*) story-teller, fibber.

piantàggine, *s.f.* (*bot.*) plantain.

piantagióne, *s.f.* plantation: — *di cotone*, cotton plantation.

piantàre, *v.t.* 1. to plant: — *fiori*, to plant flowers; — *un campo ad ulivi*, to plant a field with olive-trees || — *carote*, (*dir fandonie*) to fib || *andare a* — *cavoli*, (*scherz.*) (*ritirarsi a vita privata*) to retire; (*morire*) to pop off 2. (*conficcare*) to thrust, to drive, to ram; (*fissare*) to fix, to set: *gli piantò un pugnale nel cuore*, he thrust a dagger into his heart; — *una bandiera*, to set up (*o* to raise) a flag; — *un chiodo in un muro*, to drive a nail into a wall; — *un palo per terra*, to drive a stake into the ground; — *una tenda*, to pitch (*o* to put up) a tent || — *chiodi*, (*far debiti*) to get into debt || — *gli occhi addosso a qlcu.*, to stare at s.o. || — *le tende*, (*stabilirsi in un luogo*) to take up one's residence (*o* to settle down) 3. (*porre, collocare*) to place, to put, to plant, to set: *il nemico ha piantato una batteria su un'altura vicina*, the enemy has planted a battery on a height nearby; *se non ti cheti, ti pianto a letto e me ne vado*, if you don't quiet down, I shall put you to bed and go || — *una grana*, (*fam.*) to make trouble 4. (*fondare*) to set up: — *casa*, to set up (*a*) house 5. (*abbandonare*) to leave, to quit, to abandon, to give (s.o.) the slip: *ci piantò dopo due giorni*, he left us after two days; *la fidanzata lo ha piantato*, his fiancée has jilted him; — *a mezzo un lavoro*, to leave a job unfinished || — *baracca e burattini*, to give up everything: *quando si accorse che era un'impresa folle, piantò baracca e burattini e se ne andò*, when he realized that it was a foolish undertaking, he gave up everything and went away || *piantarla*, to stop: *piantala!*, stop it!; *piantala di farmi sciocche domande!*, stop asking me silly questions! || — *in asso*, to leave in the lurch; (*un innamorato*) to jilt 6. (*aer.*) to stop, to fail || **piantàrsi**, *v.r.* to plant oneself, to place oneself: *mi si è piantato davanti*, he planted (*o* placed) himself in front of me || *v.r. reciproco* to leave each other, to part: *dopo un ennesimo bisticcio si sono piantati*, they parted (*o* left each other) after yet another quarrel.

piantàta, *s.f.* 1. (*azione del piantare*) planting 2. (*fila di piante*) row (of plants): *una* — *di pini*, a row of pines.

piantàto, *ag.* planted: — *a gelsi*, planted with mulberry-trees || *persona ben piantata*, sturdy person.

piantatóre, *s.m.*, **piantatrìce**, *s.f.* planter.

pianterréno, *s.m.* ground-floor: *a* —, on the ground-floor.

piànto, *s.m.* 1. (*il piangere*) weeping, crying; (*per un lutto*) mourning 2. (*lacrime*) tears (*pl.*): *il mio* — *non gli ha intenerito il cuore*, my tears have not softened his heart; *scoppiare in* —, to burst into tears 3. (*soffe-*

renza) suffering; (*dolore*) grief; pain 4. (*di grotta*) dripping 5. (*di pianta*) bleeding.

piantonàia, *s.f.* (*agr.*) nursery.

piantonaménto, *s.m.* guarding.

piantonàre, *v.t.* to guard, to keep under guard.

piantóne[1], *s.m.* (*agr.*) cutting; (*germoglio*) shoot.

piantóne[2], *s.m.* (*mil.*) orderly; soldier on guard; (*sentinella*) sentry, sentinel: *essere di* —, to be on guard.

pianùra, *s.f.* plain; flat country: *in* —, on the plain.

piàre, *v.i.* to chirp, to twitter.

piàstra, *s.f.* 1. plate; slab: — *ad angolo*, (*mec.*) angle plate; — *corazzata*, (*elett.*) ironclad plate; — *di acciaio, di ferro*, steel, iron plate; — *di appoggio*, (*edil.*) bearing slab; (*ferr.*) tie plate; — *di calcestruzzo*, (*edil.*) concrete slab; — *di fissaggio*, (*mec.*) anchor plate; (*ferr.*) tie plate; — *di marmo*, marble slab; — *in cemento armato*, (*edil.*) reinforced concrete (*o* ferroconcrete) slab; — *modello*, (*fonderia*) match (*o* pattern) plate; — *orientabile*, (*mec.*) swivel plate 2. (*di un'armatura*) plate 3. (*moneta*) piastre.

piastrèlla, *s.f.* 1. tile: *le piastrelle di una cucina, di un bagno*, the tiles of a kitchen, of a bathroom; *pavimento a piastrelle*, tiled floor 2. (*giuoco*) quoit.

piastrellàre, *v.t.* (*rivestire con piastrelle*) to line with tiles || *v.i.* (*aer.*) to bounce.

piastrìccio, *s.m.* medley, mess, hotch-potch.

piastrìna, *s.f.* 1. plaque; (*ind. tessile*) rinker: — *di arresto*, (*mec.*) stop plate; — *di collegamento*, (*elett.*) connecting link; — *di guida*, (*aut.*) striker; — *filettata*, (*mec.*) plate nut; — *fusibile*, (*elett.*) link 2. (*mil.*) badge.

piastróne, *s.m.* 1. (*tec.*) plate; slab: — *dello scambio*, (*ferr.*) switch plate; — *di appoggio*, (*edil.*) bearing slab 2. (*scherma*) plastron, leather breast-plate, fencing-jacket 3. (*di tartaruga*) plastron.

piatìre, *v.t.* (*domandare umilmente*) to beg: — *favori*, to beg for favours; — *un favore a qlcu.*, to beg a favour of s.o. || *v.i.* (*rar.*) (*litigare*) to quarrel, to argue; (*dir.*) to litigate.

piàto, *s.m.* 1. (*il domandare umilmente*) begging 2. (*litigio*) quarrel, dispute; (*dir.*) litigation.

piàtta, *s.f.* pontoon, barge, lighter.

piattabànda, *s.f.* (*arch.*) flat arch, platband.

piattafórma, *s.f.* platform (anche *fig.*): — *a croce*, (*mar. mec.*) cross base; — *del tram*, tram platform; — *di caricamento*, (*ind.*) loading platform; — *di partenza*, starting platform; — *di prelievo*, (*metal.*) tapping floor; — *elettorale*, (*pol.*) election platform; — *ferroviaria rotante*, (*ferr.*) (railway) turn-table; — *girevole*, (*mec. ind.*) revolving platform.

piattàia, *s.f.* plate-rack.

piattàio, *s.m.* 1. (*chi fa piatti*) potter 2. (*chi vende piatti*) crockery dealer.

piattèllo, *s.m.* 1. (*di bilancia*) pan 2. *tiro al* —, (*spor.*) clay-pigeon shooting.

piattìna, *s.f.* (*metal. elett.*) metal strap: — *di massa*, (*elett.*) ground strap.

piattìno, *s.m.* 1. (*di una tazza*) saucer 2. (*leccornia*) dainty, titbit.

piàtto[1], *ag.* 1. flat: *barca piatta*, flat boat; *pesce* —. flat fish; *piede* —, flat foot; *tetto* —, flat roof 2. (*non ispirato, ottuso*) flat, dull; commonplace (*attributivo*): *mente piatta*, dull mind; *stile* —, flat (*o* commonplace) style; *traduzione piatta*, dull translation.

piàtto[2], *s.m.* 1. plate: — *da frutta*, dessert plate; — *d'argento*, silver plate; — *fondo*, soup plate; — *grande, da portata*, dish; *asciugare i piatti*, to dry the dishes; *cambiare i piatti a ogni portata*, to change plates at every course; *lavare i piatti*, to wash up 2. (*vivanda*) dish: — *caldo, freddo*, hot, cold dish; — *di carne, di maccheroni*, dishof meat, of macaroni; *ti ho preparato un buon* —, I have prepared a good dish for you || *un* — *di buon viso*, (*fam.*) a hearty welcome 3. (*portata*) course: *il* — *forte*, the main course 4. (*parte piatta della lama*) flat: *colpire di* —, to strike with the flat of one's sword 5. *pl.* (*mus.*)

cymbals **6.** (*alle carte*) kitty **7.** (*di microscopio, ecc.*) stage **8.** (*oggetto, strumento simile a un piatto*): — *a spigoli arrotondati*, (*metal.*) round-edged flat; — *a spigoli vivi*, (*metal.*) sharp-edged flat; — *della bilancia*, scale pan; — *magnetico*, (*elett.*) lifting magnet; — *per il lavaggio di minerali pregiati*, batea; — *portadischi*, (*di un grammofono*) turn table.

piàttola, *s.f.* **1.** (*scarafaggio*) cockroach, black-beetle **2.** (*specie di pidocchio*) crab-louse (*pl.* crab-lice) **3.** *fig.* (*persona noiosa*) bore.

piattonàre, *v.t.* to strike with the flat of the sword.

piattonàta, *s.f.* blow with the flat of the sword.

piàzza, *s.f.* **1.** square: — *del mercato*, market-place (*o* market-square); *vettura di* —, hackney-carriage (*o* cab); (*autopubblica*) taxi (-cab) ‖ — *d'arme*, (*mil.*) parade (*o* drill) ground ‖ — *d'arrivo*, (*golf*) putting green ‖ *ci vedremo in* —, we'll meet in town ‖ *fare* — *pulita di ql.co.*, *qlcu.*, to make a clean sweep of sthg., s.o.: *il direttore fece* — *pulita dei suoi dipendenti*, the manager made a clean sweep of his staff ‖ *mettere ql.co. in* —, to make sthg. public (*o* to spread sthg. about): *mettere i propri affari in* —, to wash one's dirty linen in public **2.** (*volgo*) crowd, mob, rabble: *non curo gli applausi della* —, I take no notice of the applause of the mob **3.** (*comm.*) market: *cambio della* —, local rate of exchange; *condizioni della* —, local terms; *Milano è una buona* —, Milan is a good market; *questo è il miglior articolo sulla* —, this is the best article on the market; *visitare i clienti fuori* —, to visit distant customers ‖ *quel che fa la* —, (*i prezzi correnti*) the prices quoted on the market **4.** (*radura*) clearing **5.** (*scherz.*) (*calvizie incipiente*) bald patch: *andare in* —, to go bald **6.** (*rar.*) (*posto*) place: *letto a una* —, *a una* — *e mezzo*, single bed, small double bed; *letto a due piazze*, double bed **7.** (*mar.*) upper deck.

piazzafòrte, *s.f.* **1.** (*fortezza*) fort, stronghold **2.** (*città fortificata*) fortified town, fortress: — *marittima*, fortified harbour.

piazzaiuòlo, *ag.* vulgar ‖ *s.m.* cad; street loafer.

piazzàle, *s.m.* large square.

piazzàre, *v.t.* to place; to set; to put: — *una macchina*, (*ind.*) to place (*o* to position) a machine; — *i montanti*, (*edil.*) to stanchion; — *un utensile*, (*mec.*) to set a tool ‖ **piazzàrsi**, *v.r.* (*spor.*) to be placed: *il mio cavallo non si piazzò*, my horse wasn't placed.

piazzàta, *s.f.* (street) row, (street) squabble.

piazzàto, *ag.* placed (anche *spor.*): *un cavallo vincente e due piazzati*, a winning horse and two placed ones.

piazzísta, *s.c.* commercial traveller, travelling salesman (*pl.* salesmen).

piazzuòla, *s.f.* **1.** (*mil.*) (*per mortai*) pit; (*per cannone*) emplacement **2.** (*di autostrada*) layby **3.** (*aer.*) hard standing.

píca, *s.f.* (*ornit.*) magpie.

picacísmo, *s.m.* (*med.*) pica.

picador, *s.m.* picador.

picarésco, *ag.* (*letter.*) picaresque.

pícaro, *s.m.* rogue, picaroon.

pícca[1], *s.f.* **1** (*st.*) pike; spear **2.** (*soldato armato di picca*) pikeman (*pl.* pikemen) **3.** *pl.* (*alle carte*) spades: *asso di picche*, ace of spades ‖ *contare come il fante di picche*, to count for nothing; *essere il fante di picche*, to be a self-important fool ‖ *rispondere picche*, to refuse flatly.

pícca[2], *s.f.* (*puntiglio*) spite: *fare ql.co. per* —, to do sthg. out of spite.

piccànte, *ag.* **1.** piquant; sharp; hot: *salsa* —, tart- (*o* piquant *o* hot) sauce; *sapore* —, sharp (*o* piquant) taste; *questo formaggio è un po' troppo* —, this cheese is a bit too strong **2.** (*frizzante, eccitante*) piquant: *bellezza* —, piquant beauty **3.** (*salace*) spicy: *conversazione* —, spicy conversation; *storiella* —, spicy story **4.** (*mordace, pungente*) cutting, biting: *parole piccanti*, cutting words; *satira* —, biting satire.

Piccardía, *no.pr.f.* (*geog.*) Picardy.

piccàre, *v.t.* (*ferire con picca*) to spear ‖ *v.i.* (*di vino, essere acido*) to be sharp, to be acid.

piccàrsi, *v.r.* **1.** to claim; to pique oneself (on sthg., on doing), to plume oneself (on sthg., on doing): *si piccava di sapere bene l'inglese*, he claimed to know English well; — *di essere intelligente*, to pique (*o* to plume) oneself on being intelligent **2.** (*ostinarsi*) to persist (in sthg., in doing): *si piccò di volerlo fare*, he persisted in wanting to do it **3.** (*gareggiare*) to rival (s.o.) **4.** (*impermalirsi*) to take offence (at sthg.).

piccàta, *s.f.* blow with a pike.

piccàto[1], *ag.* resentful, piqued.

piccàto[2], **picchè**, *s.m.* (*tessuto*) piqué.

picchettàre, *v.t.* **1.** (*segnare con picchetti*) to stake out; to peg out; to mark out: — *una linea ferroviaria*, to stake out a railway-line **2.** (*mil.*) to picket, to piquet **3.** (*mus.*) to bow in a spiccato way.

picchétto[1], *s.m.* **1.** (*paletto di tenda*) tent peg **2.** (*per demarcazione di via, ecc.*) stake, peg.

picchétto[2], *s.m.* (*mil.*) picket: — *d'onore*, guard of honour; *ufficiale di* —, orderly officer; *essere di* —, to be on picket.

picchétto[3], *s.m.* (*giuoco d'azzardo con le carte*) piquet.

picchiaménto, *s.m.* **1.** (*il percuotere*) beating, hitting; thrashing **2.** (*il battere*) striking **3.** (*il bussare*) knocking.

picchiapètto, *s.c.* (*bigotto*) bigot ‖ *s.m.* (*gioiello pendente sul petto*) pendant.

picchiàre, *v.t.i.* **1.** (*percuotere*) to beat, to hit; to thrash; (*bastonare*) to cudgel; (*frustare*) to flog; (*percuotere con i pugni*) to thump: *lo picchiò sulla testa*, he hit him on the head; — *un bambino*, to beat a child ‖ — *di santa ragione*, to give a good thrashing (*o* to thrash well) **2.** (*battere*) to strike; (*battere leggermente*) to tap: *picchiava con le dita contro il vetro della finestra*, he was tapping on the window-pane; *ho picchiato la testa contro la porta*, I have struck (*o* banged) my head against the door; *la pioggia picchia ai vetri*, the rain beats (*o* lashes) against the panes; — *col martello*, to hammer; — *i piedi*, to stamp one's feet; — *un pugno sul tavolo*, to bang one's fist on the table (*o* to strike the table with one's fist) **3.** (*bussare*) to knock; (*bussare leggermente*) to tap: — *alla porta*, to knock at the door ‖ — *a tutti gli usci*, to ask for help from door to door **4.** (*insistere*) to insist: *a forza di* — *ottenne ciò che volle*, by dint of persistence he obtained what he wanted ‖ *v.i.* **1.** (*aer.*) to pitch **2.** — *in testa*, (*di motore*) to ping ‖ **picchiàrsi**, *v.r. reciproco* to fight; to come to blows; to scuffle: *due uomini si picchiavano per la strada*, two men were fighting in the street; *non sapevo che si fossero picchiati*, I didn't know they had come to blows.

picchiàta, *s.f.* **1.** (*il picchiare*) beating; thrashing **2.** (*aer.*) dive, nose dive: — *a spirale*, cork-screw dive; — *verticale*, vertical dive; *aereoplano da* —, dive bomber; *scendere in* —, to dive **3.** (*richiesta di danaro*) demand for money.

picchiatèllo, *ag.* pixilated: *è un po'* —, he has a screw loose (*o amer.* he is nuts) ‖ *s.m.* queer person, eccentric person.

picchière, *s.m.* (*st.*) pikeman (*pl.* pikemen).

picchierellàre, *v.t.i.* to tap.

picchierèllo, *s.m.* (*scult.*) double-pointed hammer.

picchiettàre, *v.t.* **1.** (*battere leggermente*) to tap, to patter, to drum **2.** (*punteggiare, chiazzare*) to stipple, to spot, to speckle.

picchiettàto, *ag.* stippled, spotted, speckled: *un uccello* — *di rosso*, a bird speckled with red; *un volto* — *di lentiggini*, a freckled face.

picchiettatúra, *s.f.* **1.** (*atto del picchiettare*) stippling, spotting, speckling **2.** (*effetto del picchiettare*) spots (*pl.*), speckles (*pl.*).

picchiettío, *s.m.* tapping, pattering, drumming.

pícchio[1], *s.m.* **1.** (*alla porta*) knock **2.** (*colpo, percossa*) blow ‖ *di* —, all of a sudden.

pícchio[2], *s.m.* (*ornit.*) woodpecker: — *maggiore,* pied woodpecker; — *minore,* barred woodpecker; — *verde,* green woodpecker.

picchio[3], *s.m.* striking; drubbing; (*alla porta*) knocking.

picchiòtto, picchiòttolo, *s.m.* door-knocker.

piccinería, *s.f.* 1. (*meschinità*) meanness, pettiness; (*grettezza di mente*) narrow-mindedness 2. (*azione meschina*) mean trick: *è una delle sue solite piccinerie,* it is one of his usual mean tricks.

piccíno, *ag.* 1. small; little, tiny; wee: *abitavano in una casa piccina piccina,* they lived in a tiny little house; *adora i bambini piccini,* she loves little babies; *era ancora* — *per la sua età,* he was still tiny for his age || *mi fece sentire* —, he made me feel very small || *farsi* — —, to cower 2. (*meschino*) mean, petty: *è un uomo di mente piccina,* he is a narrow-minded man; *ha un cuore* — *e non capisce gli altri,* he is selfish and does not understand others 3. (*di vino*) light, small || *s.m.* child (*pl.* children); little one: *c'erano tutti, grandi e piccini,* they were all there, grown-ups and little ones; *vieni,* —, come, my little one || *i grandi e i piccini, fig.* the rich and the poor.

picciolo, *ag.* (*poet.*) 1. small, little 2. (*breve*) short: *in picciol tempo,* in a short time 3. (*di vino*) light, small || *s.m.* 1. (*antica moneta*) "picciolo" (ancient Florentine coin) 2. (*fam.*) farthing: *non ha più un* —, he hasn't a farthing left to his name; *non vale un* —, he isn't worth a brass farthing.

piccionàia, *s.f.* 1. dove-cote, pigeon-house 2. (*di casa*) loft 3. (*loggione*) gallery; (*fam.*) gods (*pl.*): *la applaudì a lungo,* there was prolonged applause from the gods.

piccióne, *s.m.* 1. (*ornit.*) pigeon, dove: — *brasiliano,* helmet-pigeon; — *femmina,* hen-pigeon; — *gozzuto,* pouter(-pigeon); — *maschio,* cock-pigeon; — *pavonino,* fan-tailed pigeon; — *selvatico,* wild (o wood-) pigeon; — *viaggiatore,* carrier- (o homing) pigeon || *tiro al* —, (*spor.*) pigeon-shooting || *i due piccioncini se ne andavano tenendosi per mano,* the two sweethearts were walking hand in hand || *prendere due piccioni con una fava,* to kill two birds with one stone 2. (*persona inesperta*) pigeon.

picciòtto, *s.m.* (*dial.*) youngster: *i picciotti che combatterono con Garibaldi,* the youngsters who fought with Garibaldi.

picciuòlo, *s.m.* stalk, stem.

píco[1], *s.m.* 1. peak, mountain-top: *i picchi più alti delle Alpi,* the highest peaks in the Alps || *a* —, vertically (o perpendicularly): *la scogliera scende a* — *sul mare,* it is a sheer drop from the cliff to the sea; *mandarono a picco due navi,* they sank two ships 2. (*mar.*) peak, gaff: *picchi da carico ed attrezzature,* derricks and rigging: — *di maestra,* main-trysail gaff; — *di mezzana,* spanker gaff: — *di trinchetto,* fore spanker.

píco[2], *s.m.* (*piccone*) pickaxe, pick.

piccolézza, *s.f.* 1. smallness; littleness: *la* — *di questa stanza,* the small dimensions of this room 2. (*meschinità*) meanness, pettiness; (*limitatezza di mente*) narrow-mindedness: *la* — *della sua mentalità,* his narrow-mindedness 3. (*azione meschina*) mean trick: *è una delle sue solite piccolezze,* it is one of his usual mean tricks 4. (*inezia*) trifle: *è una* — *per te, ma per me è molto importante,* it is a trifle for you, but for me it is a very important matter; *non perdere il tempo in queste piccolezze,* don't waste your time on those trifles; *questa è una* —, *ma spero che ti serva,* this is only a trifle, but I hope you will find it useful.

píccolo, *ag.* 1. little; (*di dimensioni ridotte*) small: *una piccola casa,* a little house; *una piccola famiglia,* a small family; *piccola maggioranza,* narrow (o small) majority; *un* — *numero di persone,* a small number of people; — *possidente, industriale,* small landowner, industrialist; — *reddito, capitale,* small income, capital; *piccola*

somma, small sum; *grande e* —, large and small; *libro, volume di formato* —, book, volume of small format; *un piatto più* —, a smaller plate; *è una piccola stanza,* it is a small room; *ha le mani molto piccole,* she has tiny hands; *le medicine vanno prese a piccole dosi,* medicines are to be taken in small doses; *quella casa è così piccola che sembra una casa da bambola,* that house is so minute (o tiny) that it looks like a doll -house || — *borghese,* little bourgeois; *piccola borghesia,* lower middle-class (o spreg. petty bourgeoisie) || *Piccolo Padre,* (*lo zar*) Little Father; *la Piccola Russia,* Ukraine || *in* —, small: *con questa lente vedo tutto più in* —, with this lens I see everything smaller || *lettera piccola,* (*minuscola*) small letter || *nel proprio* —, in one's small way: *una casa che nel suo* — *non manca di nulla,* a house which in its small way contains everything one needs || *ore piccole,* small hours || *farsi* —, to cower; *fig.* to belittle oneself: *il bimbo si fece* — *per evitare lo schiaffo,* the child cowered before the blow; *non farti troppo* —!, don't belittle yourself too much! 2. (*di statura*) short: *un uomo* —, a short man 3. (*giovane*) young: *il figlio più* —, the youngest son || *da* —, when a child: *da* — *era molto cattivo,* when a child he was very naughty 4. (*di poca importanza, lieve*) petty; slight: — *difetto,* slight fault; — *errore,* slight error; — *inconveniente,* a slight snag (o drawback); *piccola indisposizione,* slight indisposition; *le piccole noie della vita,* the petty troubles of life; *piccole preoccupazioni,* small worries; *piccole spese,* petty expenses; *è solo una piccola cosa,* it is only a petty thing (o a trifle) 5. (*meschino*) mean, petty; (*limitato*) narrow: *mente piccola,* narrow mind: *una persona dalla mente piccola,* a narrow-minded person; *le nostre piccole animosità,* our petty animosities 6. (*breve*) short: — *discorso,* short speech; *una piccola distanza,* a short distance; *una piccola gita,* a short trip; *piccoli passi,* short steps: *il bambino camminava a piccoli passi,* the child was walking with short steps; *una piccola vacanza,* a short holiday; *in* — *tempo,* in a short time 7. (*leggero*) light: *un* — *colpo sulla spalla,* a light touch (o tap) on the shoulder; — *pasto,* light meal 8. (*debole*) polso —, (*med.*) feeble pulse; *vino* —, small (o light) wine 9. (*umile*) humble: *gente piccola,* humble (o common) folk 10. (*a*) *piccola velocità,* (*ferr.*) (by) slow (o goods) train || *s.m.* child (*pl.* children); little one: *i piccoli,* the little ones; (*di animali*) the young: *i cani e i loro piccoli,* dogs and their young; *libri per i piccoli,* books for tiny tots; *il mondo dei piccoli,* the world of the little ones.

picconàre, *v.t.* (*rar.*) to pick(axe).

picconàta, *s.f.* blow with a pickaxe.

piccóne, *s.m.* pick, pickaxe; mattock: — *pneumatico,* (*miner.*) pneumatic pick.

picconière, *s.m.* pickman (*pl.* pickmen).

piccosàggine, piccosità, *s.f.* 1. (*irritabilità*) peevishness 2. (*permalosità*) touchiness.

piccóso, *ag.* 1. (*irritabile*) peevish, irritable, querulous 2. (*permaloso*) touchy.

piccòzza, *s.f.* 1. hatchet, axe: — *da pompiere,* fireman's axe 2. (*da alpinista*) ice-axe.

piccozzíno, *s.m.* hatchet.

píceo, *ag.* 1. pitchy, pitch-like, piceous 2. (*nero come la pece*) pitch-black.

pienòmetro, *s.m.* (*chim.*) density bottle.

picòzzo, *s.m.* (*incisivo di cavallo*) horse's incisor.

picràto, *s.m.* (*chim.*) picrate.

pícrico, *ag.* (*chim.*) picric: *acido* —, picric acid.

pidocchiería, *s.f.* 1. stinginess, niggardliness, meanness 2. (*azione gretta*) mean action.

pidòcchio, *s.m.* louse (*pl.* lice): — *delle piante,* plant-louse; — *di mare,* sea-louse || — *rivestito, riunto,* (*persona ricca di vile origine*) upstart.

pidocchiósa, *s.f.* 1. lousy woman; filthy woman 2. (*donna spilorcia*) stingy woman, miserly woman, mean woman.

pidocchióso, *ag.* 1. lousy; filthy 2. (*spilorcio*) stingy, miserly, mean ‖ *s.m.* 1. lousy man, filthy man 2. (*uomo spilorcio*) stingy man, miserly man, mean man.

piè, *s.m.* 1. (*poet.*) foot (*pl.* feet) ‖ *il — veloce Achille*, (the) swift-foot(ed) Achilles ‖ *a — di pagina*, at the foot (*o* bottom) of a page ‖ *ad ogni — sospinto*, at every moment ‖ *rimanere a — fermo*, to keep steady 2. (*mar.*): — *d'albero*, foot of mast (*o* mast -heel); — *di pollo*, wall-knot; — *di pollo per sartia*, shroud-knot; — *di ruota*, forefoot 3. — *di oca*, (*mec.*) crow's-foot 4. — *di porco*, (*leva per scassinare*) jemmy.

pied-à-terre, *s.m.* pied-à-terre.

piède, *s.m.* 1. foot (*pl.* feet): — *biforcuto*, cloven hoof; *il — di un uomo*, a man's foot; *coi, dai piedi piatti*, flat -footed (*o* with flat feet); *collo del —*, ankle; *dita dei piedi*, toes; *pianta del —*, sole of the foot; *salto a piedi pari*, standing jump; *la neve gelata scricchiolava sotto i piedi*, the hard snow crunched underfoot; *quella ragazza ha il — piccolo*, that girl has a small foot; *avere mal di piedi*, to have sore-feet (*o* to be footsore); *gettarsi ai piedi di qlcu.*, to throw oneself at s.o.'s feet; *mettere — a terra*, (*da cavallo*) to dismount; (*da veicolo*) to get off (*o* to alight); (*da nave*) to go ashore (*o* to land); *pestare i piedi*, to stamp one's feet; *pestare i piedi a qlcu.*, to tread on s.o.'s toes (*anche fig.*); *pestare ql.co. sotto i piedi*, to stamp sthg. down; *schiacciare ql.co. con un —*, to stamp sthg. flat ‖ *pied'arm!*, (*mil.*) ground arms! ‖ — *di pollo*, (*mar.*) wall-knot ‖ — *di porco*, (*leva per scassinare*) jemmy ‖ *a piedi*, on foot: *corsa a piedi*, foot-race; *soldato a piedi*, foot-soldier; *andasti a piedi o in automobile?*, did you go on foot or by car?; *ho fatto cinque miglia a piedi*, I walked five miles; *siamo andati a piedi fino alla chiesa*, we walked as far as the church ‖ *a — libero*, on bail ‖ *dalla testa ai piedi*, from head to foot ‖ *in piedi*: *cercheremo di rimetterlo in piedi*, *fig.* we shall try to put him on his feet (*o* legs) again; *devi alzarti in piedi quando entra l'insegnante*, you must stand up when your teacher comes in; *ho trovato solo posti in piedi*, (*a teatro*, *ecc.*) I could find only standing tickets; *questa mattina alle 5 ero già in piedi*, this morning at 5 I was already up; *questo bambino non sa ancora stare in piedi*, this child cannot stand yet; *questo ragionamento non si regge in piedi*, this reasoning will not hold water; *sono in piedi di nuovo dopo una settimana di influenza*, I am on my feet again after a week of flu; *sta mettendo in piedi una bella azienda*, he is setting up (*o* starting) a good business; *cadere in piedi*, *fig.* to fall on one's feet ‖ *su un — di amicizia*, on a friendly footing; *sul — di pace, di guerra*, on a peace, war footing; *sul — di parità*, on an equal footing ‖ *su due piedi*, at once ‖ *aveva le ali ai piedi*, he was fleet-footed (*o* wing-footed) ‖ *aveva dieci schiavi ai suoi piedi*, he had ten slaves at his feet ‖ *gli mancò la terra sotto i piedi*, *fig.* he felt all his hopes lost ‖ *levati dai piedi!*, get out of the way! (*o* light!) ‖ *mi è sempre fra i piedi*, he is always in my way (*o* under my feet) ‖ *non ci ho mai messo —!*, I have never set foot there!; *non metterò più — in casa sua*, I will never set foot in his house again ‖ *non farti mettere sotto i piedi da quell'uomo*, don't let that man trample on you ‖ *andare coi piedi di piombo*, to be very cautious ‖ *avere il — marino*, to have sea-legs ‖ *avere un — nella tomba*, to have a foot in the grave ‖ *consegnarsi mani e piedi legati*, to give oneself up ‖ *darsi la zappa sui piedi*, to hurt oneself (*o* to do oneself harm) ‖ *fare ql.co. coi piedi*, to do sthg. in slap-dash fashion; *ragionare con i piedi*, to reason like a fool ‖ *mettere un — in fallo*, to take a false step (*anche fig.*) ‖ *prendere —*, (*aver successo*) to get a footing; (*guadagnare terreno*) to gain ground ‖ *puntare i piedi*, *fig.* to put one's foot down ‖ *rimanere a piedi*, (*perdere il treno*) to miss the train; (*l'autobus*) to miss the bus; (*restare in asso*) to be left in the lurch ‖ *tenere il — in due staffe*, to run with the hare and hunt with

the hounds (*o* to serve two masters) 2. *fig.* (*parte inferiore*) foot (*pl.* feet); (*base*) foot (*pl.* feet); base: *il — di una calza*, the foot of a stocking; *il — di una colonna*, the foot (*o* base) of a column; — *di un tavolo, di una sedia*, the foot of a table, of a chair ‖ *ai piedi di*, at the foot of: *il paese giace ai piedi della montagna*, the village lies at the foot of the mountain 3. (*cuc.*) (*piede di maiale*) trotters (*pl.*) 4. foot (*pl.* feet) (*misura di lunghezza* = 30,48 cm): — *cubico*, cubic foot; — *quadrato*, square foot; *la mia camera è lunga 20 piedi*, my room is 20 feet long; *quell'uomo è alto 5 piedi*, that man is 5 foot (tall) 5. (*poes.*) foot (*pl.* feet): *è un verso di dieci piedi*, it is a ten-foot line.

piedestàllo, *V.* piedistàllo.

pièdica, *s.f.* trestle.

piedíno, *s.m.* 1. (*di lampada elettrica*) stem 2. (*di macchina per cucire*) pressure foot, pressure shoe 3. — *di appoggio*, (*ind.*) feet.

piedistàllo, *s.m.* pedestal (*anche fig.*): *mettere qlcu. su un —*, to set s.o. on a pedestal.

piedrítto, *s.m.* (*arch.*) pier.

pièga, *s.f.* 1. fold; (*il segno della piega*) crease, wrinkle: *una — della pelle*, a fold of the skin; *lo nascondevo in una — del pastrano*, I was hiding it in a fold of my coat; *il tuo abito è pieno di pieghe, devi stirarlo*, you must iron out the creases (*o* wrinkles) of your dress; *questa stoffa non prende la —*, this material does not crease ‖ *le cose stavano prendendo una brutta —*, things were taking a bad turn ‖ *quando gli dissi che lo avevano licenziato non fece una —*, when I told him he had been sacked, he did not turn a hair ‖ *questo vestito non ti fa una —*, this dress fits you perfectly; *il tuo ragionamento non fa una —*, your reasoning is perfect 2. (*fatta ad arte*) pleat; (*dei calzoni*) crease: *le pieghe di un vestito, una camicia, ecc.*, the pleats of a dress, a shirt, etc.; *gonna a pieghe*, pleated skirt 3. *messa in —*, (*di capelli*) (wave-)set.

piegàbile, *ag.* folding.

piegaménto, *s.m.* 1. (*il piegare*) folding, bending 2. (*piega*) fold 3. (*flessione*) flexing.

piegàre, *v.t.* 1. to fold (up): — *un giornale, una tovaglia, un lenzuolo, un vestito, ecc.*, to fold a newspaper, a table-cloth, a sheet, a dress, etc. 2. (*flettere*) to bend: — *un braccio*, to bend an arm; — *il capo*, to bend one's head; (*in segno di saluto*) to bow one's head; *fig.* (*sottomettersi*) to submit; — *un ferro, una verga*, to bend a piece of iron, a rod; — *le ginocchia*, to bend one's knees 3. (*domare, sottomettere*) to bend; to subdue: *è un ragazzo ostinato, ma lo piegherò!*, he is a wilful boy, but I will subdue him! ‖ *v.i.* 1. (*inclinare*) to heel over: *la nave piegò su un fianco*, the ship heeled over 2. (*volgere*) to bend; (*voltare*) to turn: *piega a destra, a sinistra*, turn to the right, to the left; *il fiume piega verso il lago*, the river bends towards the lake 3. (*cedere*) to yield, to give in; (*volgere in ritirata*) to withdraw, to retreat; (*sottomettersi*) to submit: *non piegherò mai alla tirannia*, I will never submit to tyranny ‖ **piegàrsi**, *v.r.* 1. (*flettersi*) to bend: *piegati in avanti*, bend forward; *il ramo si piegò senza spezzarsi*, the branch bent without breaking; *si piegò sulle ginocchia*, he bent his knees; *il vecchio si piegò sotto il carico*, the old man bent under the heavy load 2. (*cedere*) to yield, to give in; (*sottomettersi*) to submit: *non vuol —*, he does not want to submit.

piegàta, *s.f.* 1. folding: *dare una —*, to fold (up): *da' una — alla tovaglia*, fold (up) the table-cloth 2. (*rar.*) (*svolta*) turn, bend.

piegatóre, *ag.* folding ‖ *s.m.* folder.

piegatríce, *s.f.* 1. (*chi piega*) folder 2. (*mec.*) bender, bending-machine: — *a pressa*, bending-press; — *a rulli*, bending-rolls; — *idraulica*, hydraulic bending-machine; — *meccanica*, (*ind. tessile*) folding-machine; — *per lamiere*, plate bending-machine; — *per tubi*, tube bending-machine.

piegatúra, *s.f.* 1. folding; (*curvatura*) bending: —

accidentale, (mec.) kink; — *a grinze, (mec.)* wrinkle
-bending; *la — dei fogli,* the folding of the sheets; —
del ferro, (edil.) bars bending; *prova di — a freddo,*
cold-bending test; *resistenza alla —,* folding-endu-
rance 2. *(di braccio, gamba)* bend.

piegheggiàre, *v.i. (pitt.)* to paint drapery.

pieghettàre, *v.t.* to pleat, to plait.

pieghettatóre, *ag.* pleating, plaiting: *macchina pie-
ghettatrice,* pleating-machine ‖ *s.m.* pleater, plaiter.

pieghettatríce, *s.f.* 1. pleater, plaiter 2. *(mec.)*
pleating-machine.

pieghettatúra, *s.f.* 1. pleating, plaiting, kilting: —
a doppio cannone, box pleating; — *a soleil,* accordion
pleating 2. *(pieghe)* pleats *(pl.),* plaits *(pl.).*

pieghévole, *ag.* 1. *(flessibile)* pliable, pliant, flexible:
un ramoscello —, a pliable twig 2. *(atto ad essere piegato)*
folding: *ombrello, porta, sedia —,* folding-umbrella,
-door, -chair; *seggiolino —,* folding-seat 3. *(arrendevole)*
pliable, pliant, yielding, submissive: *indole —,* submissive nature 4. *(versatile)* versatile, supple: *ingegno*
—, supple mind.

pieghevolézza, *s.f.* 1. pliability, flexibility 2. *(arrendevolezza)* submissiveness.

pieghevolménte, *av.* 1. pliably, flexibly 2. *(arrendevolmente)* submissively.

piègo, *s.m.* 1. *(involto di carte)* packet of papers: *ricevere un —,* to receive a packet of papers 2. *(busta)*
envelope, cover: *nello stesso —,* under the same cover.

pielíte, *s.f. (patol.)* pyelitis.

piemía, *s.f. (patol.)* pyaemia, pyemia.

Piemónte, *no.pr.m. (geog.)* Piedmont.

piemontése, *ag.* Piedmontese ‖ *s.c.* Piedmontese
(invariato al pl.).

pièna, *s.f.* 1. flood, spate: *fiume in —,* river in flood
(o in spate) 2. *(alluvione)* flood, inundation: *le piene
del Nilo,* the floods of the Nile; *i danni della —,* flood
-damage 3. *(folla, ressa)* crowd: *c'era una — al cinema!,*
there was such a crowd at the cinema! ‖ *far — ogni sera,*
to have a full house every evening 4. *(pienezza)* fullness.

pienaménte, *av.* fully; completely; entirely; quite:
hai — ragione, you are quite right; *sono — d'accordo
con te,* I fully agree with you.

pienézza, *s.f.* 1. fullness: *la — della luna,* the fullness
of the moon; *la — del tono in un pianoforte,* the fullness
of tone of a piano; *non mi piace quel senso di — dopo un
pasto abbondante,* I do not like that feeling of fullness
after a rich meal ‖ *la — dei tempi,* the fullness of
time 2. *(massimo grado)* height: *nella — della sua
gloria,* at the height of his glory; *nella — delle sue
forze,* at the height of his powers.

pièno, *ag.* 1. full (anche *fig.*); filled (with sthg.)
(anche *fig.*): — *di bontà, buon senso,* full of kindness,
good sense; — *di gioia, ammirazione, entusiasmo,*
full of (o filled with) joy, admiration, enthusiasm;
— *di idee, soldi,* full of ideas, money; — *di sole, luce,*
full of sun(light), light; — *fino all'orlo,* full to the
brim; *un bicchiere — d'acqua,* a glass full of water;
una casa piena di gente, a house full of people; *compito*
— *di errori,* exercise full of mistakes; *giornata piena di
lavoro,* busy day; *impresa piena di pericoli,* enterprise
fraught with danger; *sguardo — di tristezza,* glance
full of sadness; *aveva gli occhi pieni di lacrime,* his
eyes were full of tears; *non parlare con la bocca piena,*
don't speak with your mouth full; *la stanza era piena
di fumo,* the room was full of (o filled with) smoke; *la
valigia è già piena,* the suitcase is already full; *essere
— di debiti,* to be full of debts (o to be up to one's
ears in debt); *essere — di guai,* to have more than
one's share of troubles; *essere — di lavoro,* to be full
up with business; *essere — di speranze,* to be full of
hope ‖ — *come un uovo,* as full as an egg (o chock-full) ‖
— *come un otre,* zeppo, full up: *il treno era — zeppo,*
the train was overcrowded ‖ — *di ogni ben di Dio,*
blessed with everything ‖ — *di sè,* full of himself ‖
a piene mani, abundantly ‖ *a piene vele,* with all sails

set (o under full sail) ‖ *a piena velocità,* at full speed ‖
a piena voce, aloud ‖ *in —, (completamente)* completely
(o entirely o fully o quite); *(esattamente)* exactly; *(nel
mezzo)* in the middle: *avevo colpito in — il leone,* I
had shot the lion down; *ha ragione in —,* he is quite
right; *la sua osservazione lo colse, colpì in —,* his remark went home ‖ *in piena efficienza,* in full working
-order ‖ *in piena fioritura,* in full blossom ‖ *in — giorno,* in broad daylight; *in — inverno,* in the depths
(o middle) of winter; *in piena notte,* at dead of night ‖
in piena regola, strictly according to regulations ‖
in piena ritirata, in full retreat ‖ *in piena stagione,*
at the height of the season ‖ *in — viso,* full (o right)
in the face ‖ *indulgenza piena, (plenaria)* plenary
indulgence ‖ *luna piena,* full moon ‖ *nella piena gioventù,*
in the flower of one's youth ‖ *nel — vigore delle forze,*
at the height of one's powers ‖ *pagine piene, (fitte)*
closely-written pages ‖ *suono, colore —,* full (o rich)
sound, colour; *una voce piena,* a full voice ‖ *è un otre
— di vento,* he is full of his own importance ‖ *fu annunciato in — senato, parlamento,* it was announced
to the assembled Senate, Parliament ‖ *fu eletto a pieni
voti,* he was elected by a unanimous vote; *fu promosso a pieni voti,* he passed with flying colours ‖
ho le tasche piene di questo lavoro, I am fed up with
this work; *ne ho piene le tasche!,* I am fed up with it! ‖
mi ha dato pieni poteri, he granted me a free hand;
(dir.) he granted me full powers; *ti do piena libertà
d'agire,* I give you full liberty to act ‖ *arrivare alla
piena maturità,* to come to full maturity ‖ *respirare
a pieni polmoni,* to breathe deeply 2. *(paffuto, in
carne)* full, plump, chubby: *gote piene,* full (o plump)
cheeks; *un viso —,* a chubby face 3. *(abbondante)*
rich: *un'annata piena,* a rich crop 4. *(non cavo internamente)* solid: *mattone —,* solid brick ‖ *s.m.* 1. *(colmo)*
height; *(mezzo)* middle: *nel — della notte,* at dead of
night; *nel — della stagione,* at the height of the season;
nel — dell'estate, at the height of summer; *nel — del-
l'inverno,* in the depth of winter; *essere nel — della
bellezza,* to be at the height (o in the full bloom) of
one's beauty 2. *(ressa, folla)* crowd: *c'era un gran —,*
there was a large crowd 3. *(carico completo)* (o nave)
full cargo; *(di carro, ecc.)* full load ‖ *fare il — (di benzina),* to fill up 4. — *d'orchestra, (mus.)* full orchestra.

pienóne, *s.m. (a teatro, ecc.)* full house; sell-out.

pienòtto, *ag.* plump, chubby.

Pièridi, *no.pr.f.pl. (mit.)* Pierides.

Pièro, *no.pr.m.* Peter ‖ *dim.* Pete(rkin), Perkin.

pierrot, *s.m. (teat.)* pierrot.

pietà, *s.f.* 1. pity, mercy, compassion: *l'ho fatto
per —,* I did it out of pity; *lo trattarono senza —,*
they treated him mercilessly (o pitilessly); *mi muove
a —,* he moves me to pity; *non glielo disse per —,*
she did not tell him that out of pity; *avere — di qlcu.,*
to have mercy on s.o.: *abbi — di me,* have mercy on
me; *fare —,* to arouse pity; *invocare —,* to cry for
mercy; *sentire — per qlcu.,* to feel pity for s.o. ‖ *che
—!,* what a sorry sight! ‖ *monte di —,* state-pawn-
broker (o Mount of Piety) ‖ *ospizio di —,* charitable
institution ‖ *per —!, (per pity's sake!* (o for mercy's
sake!): *per —, non farlo!,* don't do it, for pity's sake! ‖
canta che fa —, he is a wretched singer 2. *(devozione)*
piety, devotion: — *filiale,* filial piety; *libri di —,*
devotional books 3. *(pitt. scult.)* Pietà.

pietànza, *s.f.* 1. (main) course: *la — era arrosto di
vitello con patate fritte,* the main course was roast veal
and chips 2. *(piatto)* dish: *una — di pesce,* a dish of fish;
questa è una — squisita, this is a delicious dish.

pietísmo, *s.m. (st. relig.)* pietism.

pietísta, *s.c. (st. relig.)* pietist.

pietosaménte, *av.* 1. *(con misericordia)* pitifully, mercifully 2. *(in modo che muove a pietà)* pitifully, piteously.

pietóso, *ag.* 1. *(misericordioso)* merciful, compassionate, pitiful: *con mano pietosa,* mercifully 2. *(che
desta compassione)* piteous, pitiable, pitiful: *in uno*

stato —, in a pitiful state; *un racconto* —, a pitiful tale **3.** (*miserevole*) wretched: *avere un aspetto* —, to look wretched; *fare una figura pietosa*, to cut a sorry figure.

piètra, *s.f.* stone: — *angolare*, corner stone; — *artificiale, sintetica*, artificial, synthetic stone; — *bugnata*, (*arch.*) ashlar work; — *calcarea*, limestone; — *chilometrica*, milestone; — *confinaria*, boundary stone; — *da affilare*, whetstone; — *da costruzione*, structural stone; — *da gesso*, (*min.*) gypsum; — *da lastrico*, flagstone; — *da mulino*, millstone; — *da taglio*, freestone; — *del focolare*, hearth-stone; — *di chiave*, (*arch.*) keystone; — *di fondo*, (*ind. cartaria*) bed stone; — *di paragone*, touchstone (anche *fig.*); — *filosofale*, philosopher's stone; — *fine*, (*mec.*) jewel; — *focaia*, flint; — *infernale*, (*chim.*) silver nitrate; — *lavorata*, (*arch.*) dressed stone; — *litografica*, lithographic stone; — *lunare*, (*min.*) moon-stone; — *miliare*, milestone (anche *fig.*); — *perla*, (*min.*) perlite; — *per molare*, grindstone; — *pomice*, pumice-stone; — *preziosa*, precious stone; — *refrattaria*, (*min.*) fire-stone; — *sepolcrale*, tomb-stone; — *sintetica*, (*mec.*) rough synthetic jewel; — *tombale*, ledger; *un anello con tre pietre*, a ring set with three stones; *cava di* —, stone-quarry (*o* stone-pit); *frantoio da* —, stone-crusher; *lastra di* —, flag; *lavorazione della* —, stone-dressing; *un mucchio di pietre*, a heap of stones; *pavimento di* —, stone floor; *taglio della* —, stone-cutting; *scagliare pietre a qlcu.*, to cast (*o* to throw) stones at s.o. ‖ *la* — *dello scandalo*, the cause of the offence ‖ *la* — *d'inciampo*, *fig.* the stumbling block ‖ *l'età della* —, the Stone Age ‖ *male della* —, (*patol.*) gravel stone ‖ *avere un cuore di* —, to have a heart of stone ‖ *essere duro, freddo come una* —, to be as hard, as cold as a stone ‖ *mettere una* — *su ql.co.*, to let bygones be bygones ‖ *non lasciare* — *su* —, not to leave a stone standing ‖ *posare la prima* —, to lay the foundation stone ‖ *chi è senza peccato scagli la prima* —, he that is without sin among you, let him just cast a stone.

pietràia, *V.* petràia.

pietràme, *s.m.* heap of stones.

pietràta, *s.f.* blow with a stone.

pietrificàre, *e derivati*, *V.* petrificàre, *e derivati*.

pietrìna, *s.f.* (*per accenditori*) flint.

pietrìsco, *s.m.* rubble; crushed stone; (*per strade*) metalling.

Piètro, *no.pr.m.* Peter ‖ *la Cattedra di San* —, the Chair of St. Peter; *la navicella di San* —, (*la Chiesa*) St. Peter's bark (*o* boat); *l'obolo di San* —, Peter penny (*o* Peter's-penny *o* Peter's pence); *il successore di San* —, the successor of St. Peter ‖ — *e Paolo*, (*Tizio e Caio*) all and sundry: *divenire amico di* — *e Paolo*, to make friends with anybody and everybody ‖ *dim.* Pete, Peterkin, Perkin.

pietróso, *ag.* stony.

pievanàle, *ag.* parsonic, parsonish.

pievanìa, *s.f.* **1.** (*ufficio di pievano*) rectorate, rectorship **2.** (*casa del pievano*) rectory.

pievàno, *s.m.* parish priest.

piève, *s.f.* **1.** parish **2.** (*chiesa parrocchiale*) parish church.

pievelòce, *ag.* (*scherz.*) swift-footed, fleet-footed.

piezoelettricità, *s.f.* (*fis.*) piezoelectricity.

piezoelèttrico, *ag.* (*fis.*) piezoelectric.

piezomètrico, *ag.* (*fis.*) piezometric.

piezòmetro, *s.m.* (*fis.*) piezometer.

pifferàre, *v.i.* to fife, to pipe.

pifferàio, pifferàro, *s.m.* fifer, piper.

pìffero, *s.m.* **1.** fife, pipe **2.** (*pifferaio*) fifer, piper: *capobanda dei pifferi*, (*mil.*) pipe-major ‖ *fare come i pifferi di montagna, che andarono per suonare e furono suonati*, to go for wool and come home shorn.

pigaruòlo, *s.m.* (*rete da pesca*) fishing-net.

pìgia pìgia, *s.m.* awful crush.

pigiàma, *s.m.* pyjamas (*pl.*).

pigiaménto, *s.m.* pressing; (*schiacciamento*) crushing.

pigiàre, *v.t.* to press; (*schiacciare*) to crush: *in quell'autobus eravamo pigiati come sardine*, we were packed into that bus like sardines; — *ql.co. in una valigia*, to crush (*o* to cram) sthg. into a suitcase; — *l'uva*, to press grapes; (*coi piedi*) to tread grapes ‖ *v.i.* **1.** to push: *non pigiate, davanti non c'è più posto*, don't push, there is no more room in front; *smettila di* —!, stop pushing! **2.** *fig.* (*brigare*) to intrigue ‖ **pigiàrsi**, *v.r.* to crowd: *ci pigiammo nella piazza*, we crowded into the square; *essi si pigiavano intorno a lui*, they crowded round him; *gli scolari si pigiarono intorno all'insegnante per fargli domande*, the pupils crowded round their teacher to ask him questions.

pigiàta, *s.f.* pressing; crushing.

pigiatóre, *ag.* pressing; (*che schiaccia*) crushing ‖ *s.m.* presser; (*chi schiaccia*) crusher.

pigiatríce, *s.f.* **1.** presser **2.** (*macchina per schiacciare l'uva*) wine-press.

pigiatúra, *s.f.* **1.** pressing; crushing **2.** (*dell'uva*) wine-pressing.

pigío, *s.m.* **1.** crush, crowd **2.** *fig.* (*impresa rischiosa*) risky enterprise.

pigionàle, *s.c.* **1.** tenant **2.** (*chi lavora a giornata nei campi*) farm-labourer.

pigióne, *s.f.* rent: *devo ancora pagarti la* — *di due mesi*, I still owe you two months' rent; *sto a* — *presso la signora Smith*, I lodge with Mrs. Smith; *tengo a* — *due studenti*, I let rooms to two students; *prendere a* — *una stanza*, to rent a room.

pigliamósche, *s.m.* (*bot.*) fly-trap.

pigliàre, *V.* prèndere.

pìglio[1], *s.m.* (*atto del prendere*) holding, catching; (*presa*) hold, catch: *dar di* — *a ql.co.*, to get hold of sthg. (*o* to grab sthg.).

pìglio[2], *s.m.* look: — *minaccioso*, threatening air; *con un* — *severo*, with a harsh look; *fiero* —, fierce look.

Pigmalióne, *no.pr.m.* (*mit.*) Pygmalion.

pigmentazióne, *s.f.* pigmentation.

pigménto, *s.m.* pigment.

pigmèo, *s.m.* pigmy, pygmy.

pìgna, *s.f.* **1.** (*bot.*) pine-cone **2.** (*arch.*) crown, vertex **3.** (*mec.*) pinion.

pignàtta, *s.f.* pot, pan.

pignattàio, pignattàro, *s.m.* **1.** (*chi fabbrica pentole*) maker of pots and pans; ironmonger; potter **2.** (*chi vende pentole*) seller of pots and pans.

pignolería, *s.f.* fastidiousness, fussiness: *non badare alle sue pignolerie*, don't pay any attention to his fastidiousness; *questa è una vera* —, this is being really fastidious (*o* fussy).

pignòlo, *s.m.* **1.** (*bot.*) pine-seed **2.** *fig.* (*persona pedante*) fastidious person, fussy person; (*fam.*) fuss-pot: *sei proprio un* — !, what a fastidious person you are! (*o fam.* what a fuss-pot you are!).

pignóne, *s.m.* **1.** (*argine*) embankment; (*contro l'inondazione*) dike, dyke; (*diga*) dam **2.** (*mec.*) pinion (gear): — *a lanterna*, lantern pinion; — *conico*, bevel pinion; — *di fibra*, fibre pinion; — *satellite*, (*di differenziale*) (*aut.*) planetary pinion; — *sopra, sotto centro*, pinion above, below centre.

pignoràbile, *ag.* (*dir.*) attachable: *i letti non sono pignorabili*, beds are not attachable.

pignoraménto, *s.m.* (*dir.*) attachment, distraint: *il* — *dei mobili*, the attachment of furniture.

pignoràre, *v.t.* (*dir.*) **1.** to attach, to distrain: — *i beni di qlcu. per mancato pagamento dell'affitto*, to distrain (upon) s.o.'s goods for rent **2.** (*rar.*) (*dare in pegno*) to pawn: — *l'orologio*, to pawn one's watch.

pignoratàrio, *s.m.* (*dir.*) distrainee.

pigolaménto, *s.m.* **1.** (*di pulcini*) peeping; (*di uccelli*) chirp(ing), cheep(ing), chirruping **2.** *fig.* (*il lamentarsi*) grizzling.

pigolàre, *v.i.* **1.** (*di pulcini*) to peep; (*di uccelli*) to chirp, to cheep, to chirrup: *i pulcini seguivano la chioccia pigolando*, the chicks went peeping after the hen **2.** *fig.* (*lamentarsi*) to grizzle.

pigolío, *s.m.* **1.** (*di pulcini*) peeping; (*di uccelli*) chirruping, chirping: *il — dei pulcini*, the peeping of chicks; *dai nuovi nidi giungeva un — sommesso*, a subdued chirruping came from the new nests **2.** *fig.* (*lamento*) grizzling.

pígra, *s.f.* lazy woman.

pigraménte, *av.* **1.** lazily: *si abbandonò — su una poltrona*, she slumped into an armchair **2.** (*lentamente*) sluggishly: *l'acqua scorreva —*, the water was flowing sluggishly.

pigrézza, **pigrízia**, *s.f.* **1.** laziness, indolence, sloth **2.** (*lentezza*) sluggishness.

pígro, *ag.* **1.** lazy, indolent, slothful, sluggish: *una persona pigra*, a lazy person; *un temperamento —*, a sluggish (o slothful) disposition **2.** (*lento*) sluggish: *corrente pigra*, sluggish stream; *la lumaca è pigra*, snails are slow-moving; *il mercato è —*, the market is sluggish **3.** (*ottuso*) dull: *intelletto —*, dull mind **4.** (*che impigrisce*) deadening, stupefying: *sonno —*, stupefying sleep ‖ *s.m.* lazy man: *detesto i pigri*, I hate lazy people.

píla, *s.f.* **1.** (*insieme di oggetti sovrapposti*) pile; heap: *una — di libri*, a pile of books; *una — di piatti*, a pile of dishes **2.** (*elett.*) battèry, cell, pile: *— a secco*, dry battery; *— di ricambio*, refill; *— di Volta*, Volta's pile; *— termoelettrica*, thermopile (o thermoelectric pile); *— voltaica*, voltaic pile (o cell); *la — è scarica*, the battery is flat; *questo meccanismo funziona a pile*, this machinery works on batteries ‖ *— atomica*, atomic pile (o nuclear reactor) **3.** (*pilastro di ponte*) pier **4.** (*acquasantiera*) stoup, holy-water basin.

Pílade, *no.pr.m.* (*lett.*) Pylades.

piláf, **pilào**, *s.m.* (*cuc.*) pilau, pilaw, pilaff.

pilàstro, *s.m.* **1.** (*arch.*) pillar, pilaster: *falso —*, false pillar **2.** (*anat.*) pillar.

Pilàto, *no.pr.m.* (*st.*) Pilate ‖ *mandare qlcu. da Erode a —*, to drive (o to send) s.o. from pillar to post.

pilatúra, *s.f.* (*ind. agr.*) hulling, husking.

pileàto, *ag.* (*st.*) pileate(d).

píleo, *s.m.* (*st.*) pileus (*pl.* pilei).

pileoríza, *s.f.* (*bot.*) pileorhiza (*pl.* pileorhizae); root-cap.

pillàcchera, *s.f.* splash (of mud).

pillaccheróso, *ag.* muddy, mud-splashed.

pillàre, *v.t.* to ram, to tamp.

píllo, *s.m.* rammer, tamper.

píllola, *s.f.* pill: *— amara*, bitter pill (anche *fig.*) ‖ *indorare la —*, to sugar (o to coat) the pill ‖ *ingoiare la —*, to swallow the (bitter) pill (anche |*fig.*).

pillòtta, *s.f.* (*spor.*) pelota.

pillottàre, *v.t.* (*cuc.*) to baste.

pillòtto, *s.m.* basting-ladle, basting-spoon.

pílo, *s.m.* (*st.*) pilum (*pl.* pila).

pilóne, *s.m.* **1.** pillar **2.** (*di ponte*) pier **3.** (*arnese per battere la terra*) rammer **4.** (*aer.*): *— di lancio*, catapult; *— d'ormeggio*, mooring-mast.

pilòrico, *ag.* (*anat.*) pyloric.

pilòro, *s.m.* (*anat.*) pylorus (*pl.* pylori).

pilòta, *s.m.* **1.** (*di nave, aereo*) pilot; (*di automezzo*) (racing-)driver: *— automatico*, automatic (o gyro-)pilot; *— collaudatore*, test-pilot; *— del porto*, dock-pilot; *— di altura*, deep-sea pilot; *— di costa*, coast (o inshore) -pilot; *— di linea*, air-line pilot; *— istruttore*, flying -instructor; *— reale*, pilot-master; *— spaziale*, space -pilot; *— battello —*, pilot-boat; *pilot's licence*; *secondo —*, second (o co-) pilot **2.** (*mezzo per esplorare, sperimentare*) pilot: *impianto —*, pilot-plant; *palloncino —*, pilot-balloon **3.** *pesce —*, (*ittiol.*) pilot-fish.

pilotàggio, *s.m.* pilotage: *— senza visibilità*, blind flying; *scuola di —*, (*aer.*) flying-school.

pilotàre, *v.t.* (*nave, aereo*) to pilot; (*automezzo*) to drive.

pilòto, (*arc. poet.*) per **pilòta**.

piluccàre, *v.t.* to pick, to nibble: *— un biscotto*, to nibble a biscuit ‖ *v.i.* to pick, to nibble: *smetti di —*, stop picking (o nibbling) (at) the food.

piluccatóre, *s.m.*, **pilucatríce**, *s.f.*, **piluccóne**, *s.m.*, **pilucóna**, *s.f.* nibbler.

pimàrico, *ag.* (*chim.*) pimaric.

piménto, *s.m.* **1.** (*bot.*) pimento **2.** (*cuc.*) pimento, Jamaica pepper, red pepper, allspice.

pimpinèlla, *s.f.* (*bot.*) pimpernel: *— bianca*, burnet.

Pimplèa, *s.f.* (*mit.*) Muse.

pína[1], *s.f.* **1.** (*bot.*) pine-cone **2.** (*arch.*) crown, vertex.

Pína[2], *no.pr.f.* dim. di **Giuseppína**.

pinacòide, *ag.* (*min.*) pinacoid.

pinacotèca, *s.f.* picture-gallery.

pinàstro, *s.m.* (*bot.*) pinaster, cluster-pine.

Píndaro, *no.pr.m.* (*st. lett.*) Pindar.

pindàrico, *ag.* Pindaric.

Píndo, *no.pr.m.* (*geog.*) Pindus.

pineàle, *ag.*: *glandola —*, (*anat.*) pineal gland.

pinéta, *s.f.*, **pinéto**, *s.m.* pine-wood, pine-forest.

píngere, *v.t.* (*poet.*) to paint.

ping-pong, *s.m.* (*spor.*) table-tennis, ping-pong.

píngue, *ag.* **1.** fat, corpulent: *diventare —*, to put on fat **2.** (*fertile*) fertile, rich: *pingui pascoli*, rich pastures **3.** (*grosso*) large, big, rich: *una — eredità*, a rich heritage; *un — guadagno*, a large profit.

pinguèdine, *s.f.* fatness, corpulence, obesity: *perdere la —*, to lose weight.

pingueménte, *av.* (*riccamente*) richly; (*largamente*) largely.

pinguíno, *s.m.* (*ornit.*) penguin.

pinífero, *ag.* pine-bearing.

pínna, *s.f.* **1.** (*di pesce*) fin **2.** (*zool.*) pinna (*pl.* pinnae) **3.** *— nasale*, (*anat.*) ala (of the nose) **4.** *pl.* (*per il nuoto*) flippers **5.** (*aer. aut. mar.*) fin.

pinnàcolo, *s.m.* (*arch.*) pinnacle.

pinnàto, *ag.* (*bot. zool.*) pinnate.

pinnípede, *s.m.* (*zool.*) pinniped ‖ *i pinnipedi*, the Pinnipedia.

píno, *s.m.* (*bot.*) pine(-tree): *— d'Aleppo*, Aleppo pine; *— di montagna*, mountain pine; *— marittimo*, maritime pine; *ago di —*, pine-needle; *bosco di pini*, pine-wood.

pinòcchio, **pinòlo**, *s.m.* (*bot.*) pine-seed.

pínta, *s.f.* pint (*misura di capacità* = 0,57 *l in Gran Bretagna*; = 0,47 *l negli Stati Uniti*).

pinturícchio, *s.m.* (*spreg.*) dauber, daubster.

pínza, *s.f.* **1.** pliers (*pl.*); (*molto piccola*) tweezers (*pl.*): *— a punta piatta*, flat-nose pliers; *pinze convergenti*, closing pliers; *pinze da pellicciaio*, furrier's pliers; *pinze da tappezziere*, upholsterer's pincers **2.** (*chir.*) forceps (*pl.* forceps): *— da denti*, dental forceps; *— da dissezione*, dissecting forceps; *— tiralingua*, tongue forceps ‖ *— depilatoria*, cilia forceps (o depilatory forceps) **3.** *pl.* (*chele*) pincers.

pinzétta, *s.f.* tweezers (*pl.*).

pinzimònio, *s.m.* (*cuc.*) "pinzimonio" (sauce of oil, salt and pepper).

pínzo[1], *ag.* (*pop.*) **1.** (*zeppo*) full up; replete **2.** (*grasso*) plump, fat.

pínzo[2], *s.m.* (*pop.*) (*puntura di insetto*) sting.

pinzòchera, *s.f.*, **pinzòchero**, *s.m.* bigot; devotee.

Pío[1], *no.pr.m.* Pius.

pío[2], *ag.* **1.** pious, devout, godly, religious: *assorto in pii pensieri*, absorbed in pious (o devout) thoughts; *un uomo —*, a pious (o religious) man; *vita pia*, pious (o godly) life ‖ *luoghi pii*, holy places **2.** (*misericordioso*) compassionate, merciful, sympathetic, tender -hearted: *un — signore*, a compassionate (o sympathetic) gentleman **3.** (*benefico*) charitable: *un — istituto*, a charitable institution; *opera pia*, charitable organization; (*buona azione*) good action **4.** *pia madre*, (*anat.*) pia mater **5.** *un — desiderio*, (*scherz.*) a distant hope.

pío[3], (*voce onomatopeica riproducente un pigolio*) peep: *fare —*, to peep (o to cheep).

piòda, piodéssa, *s.f.* large slab of smooth rock.

piòggia, *s.f.* rain (anche *fig.*): *le piogge di primavera,* spring rains; *una — di fuoco, di scintille,* a rain of fire, of sparks; *una — a dirotto,* heavy rain(fall) (*o* a downpour); — *fine, pioggerella,* drizzling rain (*o* drizzle); — *scrosciante,* driving (*o* pelting) rain; *una goccia di —,* a raindrop; *macchina per imitare la —,* (*a teatro*) rain-box; *mago della —,* rain-doctor (*o* rain -maker); *scroscio di —.* shower (of rain); *stagione delle piogge,* rainy season (*o* rains); *la — ha danneggiato i miei fiori,* the rain has spoilt my flowers; *questo vento porterà la —,* this wind will bring rain; *essere inzuppato di —,* to be drenched with rain; *essere sorpreso dalla —,* to be caught in the rain; *uscire, passeggiare sotto la —,* to go out, to walk in the rain ‖ *far la — e il bel tempo,* (*fam.*) to lay down the law.

piòlo, *V.* **piuòlo.**

piombàggine, *s.f.* (*min.*) plumbago, black-lead.

piombàre, *v.i.* **1.** to fall (heavily): *il lampadario piombò a terra e si ruppe,* the chandelier fell heavily to the floor and broke ‖ — *nella miseria,* to fall (*o* to be plunged) into poverty **2.** (*buttarsi*) to pounce; to assault (s.o., sthg.); to assail (s.o., sthg.): *l'aquila piombò sulla gallina,* the eagle pounced (*o* swooped) upon the hen; *essi piombarono sul nemico,* they made a dash at (*o* they assaulted) the enemy; *mi piombò addosso con un mucchio di domande,* he assailed me with a volley of questions; *le navi nemiche piombarono su di noi,* the enemy ships bore down upon us **3.** (*giungere all'improvviso*) to rush; to come unexpectedly: *egli piombò nella mia camera,* he rushed (*o* he dashed) into my room; *mi piombarono in casa tre ospiti per colazione,* three guests came unexpectedly for lunch ‖ *v.t.* **1.** to plumb, to seal with lead: — *un pacco,* to plumb a parcel **2.** (*rivestire di piombo*) to cover with lead, to sheathe with lead; (*un dente*) to stop **3.** (*controllare con filo a piombo*) to plumb.

piombàto, *ag.* **1.** (*ricoperto di piombo*) leaded, lead -covered, covered with lead: *mazza piombata,* lead -covered mace **2.** (*sigillato con piombo*) sealed with lead, plumbed: *baule —,* plumbed trunk.

piombatóia, *s.f.,* **piombatóio,** *s.m.* (*st. mil.*) machicolation.

piombatúra, *s.f.* **1.** sealing, plumbing, leading **2.** (*mar.*) (*giunzione di funi*) splice.

piombífero, *ag.* lead-bearing, plumbiferous.

piombinàre, *v.t.* **1.** (*mar.*) to sound **2.** (*stasare col piombino*) to unstop with a plumb.

piombinatóre, *s.m.* **1.** (*mar.*) sounder **2.** (*operaio*) plumber.

piombíno[1], *s.m.* **1.** (*ind. edil.*) plumb, plumb-bob, plummet **2.** (*sigillo di piombo*) leaden seal **3.** (*per reti da pesca*) plummet, plumb, lead.

piombíno[2], *s.m.* (*ornit.*) kingfisher.

piómbo, *s.m.* **1.** lead: — *antimoniale,* hard lead; — *in pani,* pig-lead; — *per scandaglio,* (*mar.*) sounding -lead; *filo a —,* plumb-line; *trasudamento di —,* (*fis.*) lead sweating; *questo pacco sembra —, pesa come il —,* this parcel is as heavy as lead ‖ *i Piombi di Venezia,* (*st.*) the Leads of Venice ‖ *a, in —,* perpendicularly: *il sole era a — sulla nostra testa,* the sun was beating straight down on our heads; *non essere a —,* to be out of plumb ‖ *un cielo di —,* a leaden sky ‖ *sonno di —,* heavy sleep ‖ *andare coi piedi di —,* (*fam.*) to proceed very cautiously ‖ *cadere di —,* to fall plumb **2.** (*sigillo*) (leaden) seal **3.** (*palle di fucile*) bullets (*pl.*); (*pallini da caccia*) shot: *sentiva il — fischiare,* he heard the bullets hissing by **4.** *pl.* (*laminette di vetriate*) (window-) leads.

piombóne, *s.m.* (*fam.*) sluggard.

pionière, pionièro, *s.m.* pioneer.

pioppàia, *s.f.,* **pioppéto,** *s.m.* poplar-grove.

piòppo, *s.m.* (*bot.*) poplar: — *bianco,* white poplar (*o* abele) — *nero,* black poplar; — *tremolo,* aspen ‖ *dormire come un —,* (*fam.*) to sleep like a log.

piorrèa, *s.f.* (*patol.*) pyorrhoea.

piòta, *s.f.* (*rar.*) **1.** (*pianta del piede*) sole (of foot) **2.** (*zolla di terra*) sod, (piece of) turf.

piotàre, *v.t.* (*rar.*) to sod, to turf.

piòva, (*poet.*) per **piòggia.**

piovàno[1], *e derivati, V.* **pievàno,** *e derivati.*

piovàno[2], *ag.* rain (*attributivo*).

piovàseo, *s.m.* squall.

piovènte, *ag.* falling: *capelli pioventi,* hair let down; *luce —,* falling light ‖ *s.m.* slope (of a roof).

piòvere, *v.i.* **1.** *imp.* to rain: *ci piove in casa,* the rain comes in; *ha smesso di —,* it has stopped raining; *oggi vuol —,* it looks like rain today; *piove forte,* it is raining hard; *sta per —,* it is going to rain; — *a catinelle, a dirotto, a orci,* to rain cats and dogs (*o* in torrents *o* in buckets *o* to pour) ‖ *piove!,* (*gergo della malavita*) the cops! ‖ *tanto tonò che piovve,* things came to a head **2.** (*cadere a mo' di pioggia*) to rain, to pour: *a primavera gli stranieri piovono in questo paese,* in springtime tourists pour into this country; *gli piovevano colpi sulle spalle,* blows rained upon his shoulders; *gli piovvero inviti da ogni parte,* invitations rained upon him from all sides; *lacrime piovevano sul suo volto,* tears poured down his cheeks; *la luce pioveva nella stanza dalla finestra aperta,* the light poured into the room through the open window; *mi è piovuto in casa un ospite,* a guest has arrived unexpectedly at my house; *piovevano fiori, sassi, pallottole,* it rained flowers, stones, bullets; *piovevano lettere, telegrammi, benedizioni da tutte le parti,* letters, telegrams, blessings poured in from all sides ‖ *piove sul bagnato,* it never rains but it pours ‖ *v.t.* to rain, to pour, to shower; (*gettare*) to throw: *i meli piovvero i bianchi petali,* the apple-trees shed their white blossoms.

piovigginàre, *v.i.imp.* to drizzle.

piovigginóso, *ag.* drizzly, rainy.

pioviscolàre, *v.i.imp.* to drizzle.

piovitúra, *s.f.* (*rar.*) rainy season.

piovórno, *ag.* (*letter.*) cloudy, threatening.

piovóso, *ag.* rainy: *giorno, tempo, paese —,* rainy day, weather, country; *vento —,* rainy wind ‖ *s.m.* (*st. francese*) Pluviôse.

piòvra, *s.f.* **1.** (*zool.*) (giant) octopus **2.** *fig.* parasite; (*fam.*) sponger.

pipa[1], *s.f.* **1.** pipe: — *di gesso,* clay pipe; — *di radica,* briar pipe; *la cannuccia della —,* the stem of the pipe; *accendere la —,* to light one's pipe; *caricare la —,* to fill one's pipe; *fumare la —,* to smoke a pipe **2.** (*quantità di tabacco contenuta in una pipa*) pipe(ful) **3.** (*mec.*) lug **4.** (*scherz.*) (*naso*) bottle nose; beak.

pipa[2], *s.f.* (*arc.*) (*botte per liquori*) pipe.

pipa[3], *s.f.* (*zool.*) pipa.

pipàre, *v.i.* to smoke a pipe.

pipàta, *s.f.* **1.** pipe: *facciamo una —,* let's have a pipe **2.** (*quantità di tabacco contenuto in una pipa*) pipe(ful).

pipatóre, *s.m.* pipe-smoker.

piperàcee, *s.f.pl.* (*bot.*) Piperaceae.

piperína, *s.f.* (*chim.*) piperine.

pipèrno, *s.m.* (*min.*) " piperno " (kind of lava used for paving).

pipétta, *s.f.* (*strum. chim.*) pipette: — *contagocce,* stactometer.

pipí, *s.f.* (*fam.*) piddle: *fare —,* to piddle.

pipiàre, pipilàre, *v.i.* to chirp, to cheep, to twitter.

pipistrèllo, *s.m.* **1.** bat **2.** (*sorta di pastrano*) cloak.

pipíta, *s.f.* **1.** agnail **2.** (*vet.*) pip.

píppolo, *s.m.* (*fam.*) pimple.

píra, *s.f.* pyre, funeral pile.

piramidàle, *ag.* **1.** pyramidal, pyramidic: *cellule piramidali,* (*anat.*) pyramidal cells; *osso —,* (*anat.*) pyramidal bone **2.** (*enorme*) huge, enormous: *errore —,* huge mistake (*o* blunder).

piràmide, *s.f.* pyramid: *le piramidi d'Egitto,* the pyramids of Egypt; — *triangolare,* triangular pyramid;

— *tronca*, truncated pyramid; *a (forma di)* —, pyramidically *(av.)*; pyramid-shaped *(o* pyramid-like) *(ag.)*; *albero a* —, pyramid (tree) ‖ *le piramidi del Malpighi*, *(anat.)* Malpighian pyramids.

piramidóne, *s.m. (farm.)* pyramidon.

Píramo, *no.pr.m. (mit.)* Pyramus.

piràta, *s.m.* pirate: *bastimento* —, pirate-ship ‖ — *della strada*, *(fam.)* road-hog.

pirateggiàre, *v.i.* to pirate.

piratería, *s.f.* piracy.

piratésco, *ag.* piratic(al).

Pirenèi (i), *no.pr.m.pl. (geog.)* the Pyrenees.

Pirèo, *no.pr.m. (geog.)* Piraeus.

piressía, *s.f. (med.)* pyrexia.

pirètico, *ag.* pyretic.

piretògeno, *ag. (farm.)* pyretogenous.

piretoterapía, *s.f. (med.)* pyretotherapy.

pirètro, *s.m. (bot.)* pyrethrum: *polvere di* —, pyrethrum powder.

pírico, *ag.: polvere pirica*, gun-powder.

piridína, *s.f. (chim.)* pyridine.

pirite, *s.f. (min.)* pyrite(s): — *arsenicale*, arseno-pyrite (*o* mispickel); — *di ferro*, iron pyrite; — *di rame*, copper pyrites; — *magnetica*, magnetic pyrites.

pirítico, *ag.* pyritic.

piritizzazióne, *s.f.* pyritizing.

Pirítoo, *no.pr.m. (mit.)* Pirithous.

pirobalística, *s.f.* pyroballogy.

pirocorvétta, *s.f. (arc. mar.)* steam-corvette.

piroelettricità, *s.f.* pyro-electricity.

piroeliòmetro, *s.m. (astr.)* pyr(o)heliometer.

piroétta, *s.f.* pirouette.

piroettàre, *v.i.* to pirouette.

piròfila, *s.f. (pentola resistente al fuoco)* pyrex dish.

pirofregàta, *s.f. (arc. mar.)* frigate equipped with steam-engine.

piròga, *s.f.* pirogue, piragua.

pirogàllico, *ag. (chim.)* pyrogallic.

pirògeno, *ag. (med.)* pyrogenic, pyrogenetic.

pirografía, *s.f. (artig.)* 1. poker-work, pyrography 2. *(riproduzione pirografica)* pyrogravure.

piròlo, *s.m.* peg *(anche di strumento musicale)*.

pirolusíte, *s.f. (min.)* pyrolusite.

piromagnètico, *ag.* pyromagnetic.

piromagnetísmo, *s.m.* pyromagnetism.

piromànte, *s.m.* pyromantic.

piromanzía, *s.f.* pyromancy.

piròmetro, *s.m.* pyrometer: — *a radiazione*, radiation pyrometer; — *a resistenza*, resistance pyrometer; — *elettrico*, electric pyrometer; — *ottico*, optical pyrometer; — *termoelettrico*, thermoelectric pyrometer.

piróne, *s.m. (pirolo)* peg.

piròpo, *s.m. (min.)* pyrope.

piròscafo, *s.m.* steamer, steamboat; steamship *(abbr.* S/S): — *con ruote a pale*, paddle-steamer; — *di linea*, (steam-) packet; — *postale*, mail-boat (*o* mailer).

piròsi, *s.f. (med.)* pyrosis.

piròsseno, *s.m. (min.)* pyroxene.

pirossilína, *s.f. (chim.)* pyroxylin(e).

pirotècnica, *s.f.* pyrotechnics, pyrotechny.

pirotècnico, *ag.* pyrotechnic(al); firework *(attributivo)*: *spettacolo* —, firework (*o* pyrotechnic) display (*o* fireworks) ‖ *s.m.* pyrotechnist, maker of fireworks.

Pírra, *no.pr.f. (mit.)* Pyrrha.

pírrica, *s.f. (st.) (danza)* Pyrrhic.

pirríchio, *s.m. (poes.)* pyrrhic.

pírrico, *ag. (st.)* Pyrrhic.

Pírro, *no.pr.m. (st.)* Pyrrhus.

pirròlo, *s.m. (chim.)* pyrrol.

Pirróne, *no.pr.m. (st. fil.)* Pyrrho.

pirroniàno, *ag.s.m. (fil.)* Pyrrhonian.

pirrònico, *ag.s.m. (fil.)* Pyrrhonic.

pirronísmo, *s.m. (fil.)* Pyrrhonism.

pirronísta, *s.m. (fil.)* Pyrrhonist.

pirrotína, *s.f. (min.)* pyrrhotine, pyrrhotite.

piscatòrio, *ag.* piscatory ‖ *anello* —, *(eccl.)* piscatory ring.

píscia, *s.f. (volg.)* piss; *(di animali)* stale.

pisciacàne, *s.m. (pop. bot.)* couch-grass.

pisciàre, *v.i. (volg.)* to piss; *(di animali)* to stale.

pisciàta, *s.f. (volg.)* piss.

pisciatóio, *s.m.* (public) urinal.

piscicultóre, *s.m.* pisciculturist.

piscicultúra, *s.f.* pisciculture.

piscína, *s.f.* 1. swimming-pool, bathing-pool; *(nei bagni romani)* piscina 2. *(peschiera)* fish-pond.

piscióne, *s.m. (volg.)* weak-bladdered person.

pisellàio, *s.m.* pea-field.

pisellàta, *s.f. (cuc.)* pea-soup.

pisèllo, *s.m.* (green) pea: *minestra di piselli*, pea-soup; *verde* —, pea-green.

pisifórme, *s.m. (anat.)* pisiform.

Pisístrato, *no.pr.m. (st.)* Pisistratus.

pisolàre, *v.i.* to (take a) nap, to snooze, to doze.

písolo, *s.m.* nap, snooze, doze; *(fam.)* forty winks *(pl.): fare un pisolino*, to take a nap.

pispigliàre, *v.i.* to whisper.

pispíglio, *s.m.* whispering.

pispillòria, *s.f.* 1. *(bisbiglio)* whispering 2. *(di uccelli)* twittering.

pispinàre, *v.i. (zampillare)* to jet, to spirt.

pispíno, *s.m. (zampillo)* jet of water.

píspola, *s.f.* 1. *(ornit.)* titlark, pipit 2. *(verso dell'uccellatore)* bird-call.

pispolàre, *v.i.* to make a bird-call.

pісside, *s.f. (eccl.)* pyx, ciborium *(pl.* ciboria).

píssi píssi, *s.m.* whisper.

písta, *s.f.* 1. *(orma)* footprint, footstep; *(traccia)* track; *(di animale)* trail, track; scent: *la* — *di una ruota*, the track of a wheel; *il cane seguiva la* — *della lepre*, the dog was following the scent of the hare; *essere sulle piste di qlcu.*, to be on s.o.'s track; *non perdere le piste di qlcu.*, to keep track of s.o.; *seguire la* — *di qlcu.*, to follow s.o.'s track 2. *(via)* lane; track: — *del gregge*, sheep-track; — *di traffico*, traffic-lane; — *per ciclisti*, cycle track 3. *(spor.)* track, race-track, running-track, racecourse; *(di golf)* golf-course: — *per corse di automobili*, motor-racing track; — *per corse di bicicletta*, cycling-track; — *su incenerito*, dirt-track (*o* cinder-path) 4. *(aer.)* runway, strip, air-strip: — *d'emergenza*, air-strip; — *di atterraggio*, landing-strip; — *di lancio*, runway (*o* strip); — *di rullaggio*, taxiway (*o* taxi-track) 5. *(mec.)* race, track: — *esterna*, (di cuscinetto a sfere) outer race (*o* cup).

pistàcchio, *s.m. (bot.)* pistachio: *verde* —, pistachio (-green).

pistàgna, *s.f.* coat-collar.

pistagníno, *s.m.* pocket-flap.

pistillífero, *ag. (bot.)* pistilliferous.

pistíllo, *s.m. (bot.)* pistil.

pistòla[1], *s.f. (mec.)* pistol: — *a tamburo*, revolver; — *automatica*, automatic pistol; — *mitragliatrice*, sub-machine gun; — *per lavaggio*, washing gun; — *per verniciatura a spruzzo*, spray-gun; *a tiro di* —, within pistol-shot; *colpo di* —, pistol-shot; *fare un duello alla* —, to fight with pistols.

pistòla[2], *s.f. (antica moneta)* pistole.

pistolése, *s.m. (st.)* hunting-knife.

pistolettàta, *s.f.* pistol-shot.

pistolóne, *s.m. (st.)* cavalry-pistol.

pistolòtto, *s.m.* 1. *(discorso enfatico)* emphatic speech 2. *(chiusa declamatoria di discorso)* declamatory peroration.

pistóne[1], *s.m.* 1. *(mec.)* piston; *(miner.)* swab: — *a fodero*, *(mec.)* trunk piston; — *a testa convessa*, *(mec.)* domed piston; — *di macchine idrauliche*, ram; — *di pompa*, plunger; — *equilibratore*, *(mec.)* balancing piston; — *idraulico*, hydraulic ram; — *valvolato*, *(mec.)* bucket (*o* sucker); *aereo con motore a pistoni*, piston-engine aircraft; *corsa del* —, *(mec.)* piston-stroke;

macchina azionata a pistoni, piston-driven machine; *scampanamento di —*, (*mec.*) piston slap; *testa del —*, piston-head **2.** (*di strumenti a fiato*) piston.

pistóne², *s.m.* (*archibugio*) (h)arquebus.

pistóne³, *s.m.* (*grosso pestello*) (large) pestle.

Pitàgora, *no.pr.m.* (*st. fil.*) Pythagoras ‖ *teorema di —*, (*geom.*) theorem of Pythagoras.

pitagoreggiàre, *v.i.* to Pythagorize.

pitagoricaménte, *av.* Pythagorically.

pitagòrico, *ag.* Pythagorean, Pythagoric(al): *dottrina, filosofia pitagorica*, Pythagorean doctrine, philosophy; *tavola pitagorica*, multiplication table; *sistema, vitto —*, vegetarian diet ‖ *s.m.* Pythagorean.

pitagorísmo, *s.m.* (*fil.*) Pythagorism, Pythagoreanism.

pitàle, *s.m.* chamber-pot; (*fam.*) chamber.

pitecàntropo, *s.m.* (*antropologia*) pithecanthropus (*pl.* pithecanthropi).

pitecòide, *s.m.* (*zool.*) pithecoid.

Pítia, *no.pr.f.* (*st. greca*) Pythia.

pítico, *ag.* (*letter.*) Pythian: *Apollo Pitico*, Apollo Pythius; *giuochi pitici*, Pythian games.

pitiríasi, *s.f.* (*patol.*) pityriasis.

pitoccàre, *v.i.* to beg; to whine.

pitocchería, *s.f.* **1.** beggarly action, mean action **2.** (*spilorceria*) stinginess, meanness.

pitòcco, *ag.* mean, poor ‖ *s.m.* **1.** (*mendicante*) beggar ‖ *i pitocchi*, (*st.*) the Sea Beggars **2.** (*spilorcio*) stingy person, mean person, skinflint, miser.

pitóne, *s.m.* (*zool.*) python.

pitonéssa, *s.f.* **1.** (*st. greca*) pythoness **2.** (*Bibbia*) the witch of Endor **3.** (*scherz.*) (*chiromante*) fortune-teller.

pittàre, *v.t.* **1.** (*scherz.*) to daub **2.** (*di pesce*) to nibble.

pittière, *s.m.* (*ornit.*) robin (redbreast).

píttima, *s.f.* **1.** (*decorazione*) poultice **2.** (*persona noiosa*) bore **3.** (*rar.*) (*spilorcio*) miser, niggard.

pittografía, *s.f.* picture-writing.

pittóre, *s.m.* **1.** painter: *— di paesaggi*, landscape-painter; *— di ritratti*, portrait-painter (*o* portraitist) **2.** *fig.* (*di scrittore*) portrayer: *fu un fedele — dei costumi della sua epoca*, he was a faithful portrayer of the manners of his time.

pittorèllo, *s.m.* (*spreg.*) dauber.

pittorescaménte, *av.* picturesquely.

pittorésco, *ag.* picturesque: *un paesaggio —*, a picturesque landscape; *stile —*, picturesque style.

pittòrico, *ag.* pictorial: *arte pittorica*, pictorial art.

pittríce, *s.f.* painter.

pittúra, *s.f.* **1.** (*l'arte del dipingere*) painting: *studiare —*, to study painting **2.** (*dipinto*) picture, painting: *— ad acquarello*, water-colour; *— a olio*, oil-painting; *esposizione di —*, exhibition of paintings ‖ *è una —*, (*una donna molto bella*) she is a picture ‖ *quell'abito ti sta come una —*, that dress fits you perfectly **3.** *fig.* (*descrizione*) picture, description; *ne ha fatto una triste —*, he has given a sad description of it; *questo libro è una fedele — di quei tempi*, this book is a faithful picture of those times **4.** (*vernice*) paint: *— fresca*, wet paint.

pitturàre, *v.t.i.* to paint: *— di rosso*, to paint in red ‖ **pitturàrsi**, *v.r.* (*imbellettarsi*) to make up: *si pittura troppo le labbra*, she makes her lips up too much.

pitturàto, *ag.* (*imbellettato*) made-up.

pitúita, *s.f.* (*fisiol.*) mucus, phlegm, pituite.

pituitarìna, *s.f.* (*chim. biol.*) pituitrin.

pituitàrio, *ag.* pituitary: *fossa pituitaria*, pituitary fossa; *ghiandola pituitaria*, pituitary gland; *membrana pituitaria*, pituitary membrane.

piú, *av.* **1.** (*nel comp. di maggioranza*) **more** (*con ag. e av. polisillabi in inglese, nella maggior parte dei casi; nella comparazione tra due ag., siano essi polisillabi o monosillabi; nella comparazione tra s., tra av. e quando il confronto avvenga fra verbi*): *costa — di mille lire*, it costs more than (*o* over) a thousand lire; *è — gentile che intelligente*, he is more kind than intelligent; *è*

molto — intelligente di suo fratello, he is much more intelligent than his brother; *ha — buona volontà che intelligenza*, he has more good will than intelligence; *lavoro —, molto — di lui*, I work more, much more than he does; *questo mi piace di —*, I prefer this (*o* I like this more); *volle parlargli — gentilmente*, he wanted to talk to him more kindly ‖ *due volte — grande di ...*, twice as large as...: *mi occorre una casa due volte — grande di questa*, I want a house twice as large as this ‖ *invita — gente che puoi*, invite as many people as you can; *mi tratta — gentilmente che può*, he treats me as well as he can; *tiravo a — non posso*, I pulled as hard as I could ‖ *non per questo è — intelligente*, he is not (the) more intelligent for that **2.** (*nel comp. di maggioranza*) *...er* (*unito come suffisso alla forma positiva di ag. e av. monosillabi in inglese*): *— lontano*, *— oltre*, farther (*o* further) on; *— presto*, more quickly (*o* faster); *è — gentile di te*, he is kinder than you; *ho dieci anni — di lui*, I am ten years older than he is; *la mia traduzione è — semplice della tua*, my translation is simpler than yours; *New York è — grande di Parigi*, New York is bigger than Paris ‖ *— grazioso*, prettier; *— intelligente*, cleverer; *— stretto*, narrower **3.** (*nel superl. rel.*) **the most**, (*tra due*) **the more** (*usati con ag. e av. polisillabi in inglese, nella maggior parte dei casi*): *è la — bella di tutte*, she is the most beautiful of all; *il — intelligente dei due fratelli*, he is the more intelligent of the two brothers; *è quello che lavora di —*, he is the one who works the most ‖ *lavoro il — possibile*, I work as much as possible (*o* as much as I can) **4.** (*nel superl. rel.*) **the ...est**, (*tra due*) **the ...er** (*uniti come suffissi alla forma positiva di ag. e av. monosillabi in inglese*): *è la — simpatica delle due*, she is the nicer of the two ‖ *è la ragazza — graziosa che conosco*, she is the prettiest girl I know; *questa è la — stretta delle due*, this is the narrower of the two **5.** (*enfatico*): *sono — che felice*, I am extremely (*o* more than) happy; *Vanessa è — che graziosa, è bella*, Vanessa is more than pretty, she is beautiful **6.** (*di tempo*) **no longer**, **not any longer**, **not any more**; (*letter.*) **no more**: *senza — attendere*, without waiting any longer (*o* any more); *due donne che non erano — giovani*, two women who were no longer young; *non c'è — tempo per farlo*, there is no time left to do it; *non è — qui*, he is no longer here (*o* he isn't here any longer *o* any more); *non la vedrò —*, I shall never see her again; *non lo amo —*, I don't love him any more; *non ne voglio —*, I don't want any more of that; *non vado — a scuola*, I no longer go to school (*o* I don't go to school any longer) ‖ *non è —*, he has passed away (*o* on) **7.** (*quanto più..., tanto più...*) **the more..., the more...**; **the ...er, the ...er** (*quanto più..., tanto*) **meno..., the more..., the less...**; **the ...er, the ...less...**: *cara diventa la produzione, — piccolo è il guadagno*, the more expensive production becomes, the smaller is the profit; *— facile è, meno interessante lo trovo*, the easier it is, the less interesting I find it; *— invecchia, — diventa sordo*, the older he gets, the deafer he is; *— lo guardo, — mi piace*, the more I look at it, the more (*o* the better) I like it; *— lo guardo, meno mi piace*, the more I look at it, the less I like it; *— vado avanti, — mi rendo conto che...*, the further I go, the more I realize that... **8.** (*simbolo mat.*) **plus**: *due — due fa quattro*, two plus two is four (*o* two and two are four) ‖ *ag.* **1.** **more**: *compra — pane*, buy (some) more bread; *ha — amici di me*, he has more friends than I have **2.** (*parecchi*) **several**: *— volte*, several times; *— amici vennero a trovarlo*, several friends came to see him ‖ *s.m.* **1.** **most**: *il — è fatto*, most of it is done; *il — è incominciare*, the most important thing is to get started ‖ *numero del —*, (*plurale*) plural ‖ *e il — è che...*, and what is more... (*o* and moreover...) ‖ *parlare del — e del meno*, to talk about nothing in particular **2.** *i —*, most people ‖ *è* *ormai nel numero dei* —, (*scherz.*) he has joined the great majority || (**Fraseologia**): — *che mai*, more than ever: *sono* — *che mai convinto che..*, I am more than ever convinced that... || — *di una volta*, more than once || *al* —, *tutt'al* —, at the most: *costa* (*tutt'*) *al* — *mille lire*, it costs a thousand lire at the most || *chi* — *chi meno*, some more, some less || *dal* — *al meno*, more or less || *mai* —!, not on one's life! || *nè* — *nè meno*, neither more nor less: *è nè* — *nè meno che la verità*, it's neither more nor less than the truth (*o* it's the absolute truth) || *per lo* —, mostly (*o* for the most part); (*di solito*) usually: *la domenica per lo* — *sto in casa*, I usually stay at home on Sundays; *erano per lo* — *indiani*, they were mostly Indians || *per di* —, moreover (*o* furthermore *o* what's more): *non mi aiuta e per di* — *mi impedisce di lavorare*, he is no help to me and what's more he stops me from working || *sempre* —, more and more, ...er and ...er: *il cielo si faceva sempre* — *scuro*, the sky was getting darker and darker; *egli è sempre* — *difficile da accontentare*, he gets more and more difficult to please || *tanto* — *che*, all the more so because: *non avresti dovuto farlo, tanto* — *che te l'avevo detto*, you shouldn't| have done it, all the more so because I had told you not to || *e che dire di* —? what more (*o* what else) can I say? || *ha* — *di venti anni*, he is over twenty || *non c'è* — *che...*, there is nothing, nobody left but (*o* except)... || *per non dir di* —, to say the least.

piúma, *s.f.* **1.** feather; (*piumaggio*) plumage: *cuscino, materasso di* —, *di piume*, feather pillow, mattress; *uccelli dalle piume colorate*, birds with coloured plumage || *leggero come una* —, as light as a feather; *essere una* —, to be as light as a feather || *peso* —, (*boxe*) feather-weight **2.** (*per ornamento*) plume: *una* — *sul cappello*, a plume on one's hat.

piumàccio, *s.m.* feather pillow.
piumàggio, *s.m.* plumage.
piumàto, *ag.* plumed: *cappello* —, plumed hat.
piumétta, *s.f.* (*bot.*) plumule.
piumíno, *s.m.* **1.** (*di cigni, oche, ecc.*) down **2.** (*cuscino di piuma*) ciderdown **3.** (*per la cipria*) powder-puff.
piumosità, *s.f.* featheriness.
piumóso, *ag.* feathery; downy.
piuòlo, *s.m.* **1.** peg; (*di scala*) rung: *scala a piuoli*, ladder **2.** (*palo*) post || *dritto come un* —, as straight as a ramrod.
piuttòsto, *av.* rather; fairly; somewhat; (*fam.*) pretty: — *buono*, fairly (*o* pretty) good; — *cattivo*, rather (*o* pretty) bad; *è* — *stanco*, he is somewhat tired; *mi sento* — *bene oggi*, I feel fairly well today; *quel lavoro teatrale è* — *interessante*, that play is fairly interesting || **piuttòsto che, di,** *l. cong.* **rather than, sooner than, rather... than, sooner... than:** — *che stare in casa, andrò al cinema*, rather than stay at home, I'll go to the pictures; *io sceglierei medicina* — *che matematica*, I should choose medicine rather (*o* sooner) than mathematics; *preferirei morire* — *che fare una cosa simile*, I would sooner (*o* rather) die than do such a thing; *preferirei pagare in contanti* — *che dargli un assegno*, I would (*o* I had) rather (*o* sooner) pay cash than give him a cheque.
píva, *s.f.* **1.** (*mus.*) bagpipe || *tornare colle pive nel sacco*, to return empty-handed **2.** *aver la* —, (*fam.*) (*essere di cattivo umore*) to have a long face.
pivèllo, *s.m.* (*fam.*) young cub.
piviàle, *s.m.* (*eccl.*) cope, pluvial.
pivière, *s.m.* (*ornit.*) plover.
Pízia, *no.pr.f.* (*mit.*) Pythia.
pízio, *ag.* Pythian: *giuochi pizi*, Pythian games.
pízza, *s.f.* (*cuc.*) pizza, pizza-pie.
pizzardóne, *s.m.* (*scherz.*) bobby, copper.
pizzería, *s.f.* pizza-shop; pizza-restaurant.
pizzicàgnolo, *s.m.* delicatessen seller.
pizzicàre, *v.t.* **1.** to pinch, to nip: *fui pizzicato da un granchio*, I was nipped by a crab; *smetti di pizzi-*

carmi, stop pinching me **2.** (*pungere, di insetti, ecc.*) to bite: *fui pizzicato da una zanzara*, I was bitten by a mosquito **3.** (*di sostanza acre*) to burn: *questa salsa pizzica la lingua*, this sauce burns your tongue **4.** *fig.* (*pungere con parole*) to tease: *non pizzicarlo*, do not tease him **5.** *fig.* (*cogliere di sorpresa*) to catch: — *un ladro*, to catch a thief; *farsi* —, to get caught **6.** (*mus.*) to pluck: — *le corde di un'arpa*, to pluck the strings of a harp || *v.i.* **1.** (*prudere*) to itch; (*pungere*) to tingle; (*causare pizzicore*) to tickle: *le guance mi pizzicavano per il freddo*, my cheeks were tingling with the cold; *mi sento tutto* —, I itch (*o* feel itchy) all over; *il pepe pizzica quando entra nel naso*, pepper tickles when it gets into the nose; *questa puntura pizzica*, this bite (*o* sting) itches || *mi pizzicano le mani, fig.* my hands are itching **2.** (*aver tendenza, dar sentore*): *tu pizzichi di matto*, you are just a little mad **3.** (*avere una certa conoscenza*): *pizzica di musica e di pittura*, he has a smattering of music and painting.
pizzicàta, *s.f.* **1.** (*il pizzicare*) pinching, nipping **2.** (*pizzicotto*) pinch, nip **3.** (*mus.*) plucking.
pizzicàto, *ag.sm.* (*mus.*) pizzicato.
pizzicheria, *s.f.* **1.** delicatessen shop **2.** (*merci di pizzicagnolo*) delicatessen.
pizzichíno, *s.m.* snuff.
pízzico, *s.m.* **1.** pinch: *un* — *di sale*, a pinch of salt; *un* — *di tabacco*, a pinch of snuff **2.** *fig.* (*tantino*) little, bit: *un* — *d'orgoglio*, a little (*o* a bit of) pride **3.** (*pizzicore*) itch **4.** (*pizzicotto*) pinch, nip.
pizzicóre, *s.m.* **1.** (*prurito*) itch; (*bruciore*) smart **2.** *fig.* (*desiderio, voglia*) itch.
pizzicottàre, *v.t.* to pinch, to nip || **pizzicottàrsi,** *v.r.* reciproco to pinch each other (one another).
pizzicottàta, *s.f.* pinching.
pizzicòtto, *s.m.* pinch, nip: *dare un* — *a qlcu.*, to give s.o. a pinch.
pízzo, *s.m.* **1.** (*barba*) pointed beard; (*pappafico*) Van Dyck, goatee; (*alla Napoleone*) imperial **2.** *pl.* (*fedine*) mutton-chops **3.** (*merletto*) lace (*solo sing.*): *abito di* —, lace dress; *orlato, bordato di* —, trimmed with lace (*o* lace-bordered); *questi pizzi sono fatti a mano*, this lace is hand-made **4.** (*picco di montagna*) peak.
pizzòchera, *s.f.*, **pizzòchero,** *s.m.* bigot; devotee.
pizzutèllo, *s.m.* « pizzutello » (Italian table grapes).
placàbile, *ag.* **1.** appeasable, placable **2.** (*atto a placare*) appeasing.
placabilità, *s.f.* placability, placableness.
placàre, *v.t.* **1.** (*tranquillizzare*) to appease: *cercherò di placarlo*, I shall try to appease him **2.** (*mitigare, temperare*) to soothe, to lessen: *niente può* — *il mio dolore*, nothing can lessen (*o* lighten) my sorrow; — *il mal di denti di qlcu.*, to ease (*o* to soothe) s.o.'s toothache || — *la fame di qlcu.*, to satisfy s.o.'s hunger; — *la sete di qlcu.*, to quench s.o.'s thirst || **placàrsi,** *v.r.* to subside, to calm down: *il mare si placò*, the sea calmed down; *il suo furore non si placò*, his rage did not subside; *verso mezzanotte il temporale si placò*, the storm died down towards midnight.
plàcca, *s.f.* **1.** plaque, plate: — *deviatrice*, (*tv.*) deflecting-plate; — *di estrazione*, lifting-plate; — *modello*, match- (*o* pattern-) plate **2.** (*med.*) patch, plaque: *la sua gola è piena di placche*, his throat is covered with plaques.
placcàre, *v.t.* to plate: — *in oro*, to plate with gold.
placcàto, *ag.* plated: — *in argento*, silver-plated.
placcatúra, *s.f.* plating: — *elettrolitica*, (*ind.*) electroplating; *bagno di* — *al cianuro*, cyanide plating-bath.
placènta, *s.f.* (*anat. bot.*) placenta (*pl.* placentae).
plàcet, *s.m.* placet.
placidaménte, *av.* placidly, calmly, peacefully.
placidézza, placidità, *s.f.* placidity, calm.
plàcido[1], *ag.* placid, calm, peaceful, quiet: *aspetto* —, calm appearance; *mare* —, calm (*o* smooth) sea; *morte placida*, peaceful death; *sonno* —, peaceful (*o*

calm) sleep; *temperamento* —, placid (*o* calm) temperament; *un uomo* —, a calm (*o* placid *o* quiet) man.

Plàcido[2], *no.pr.m.* Placid(us).

plàcito, *s.m.* (*decreto*) decree; (*st.*) placitum (*pl.* placita).

plàga, *s.f.* (*regione*) region, district: *la* — *polare*, the polar region.

plagiàre, *v.t.* to plagiarize.

plagiàrio, *s.m.* plagiarist, plagiary.

plàgio, *s.m.* plagiarism.

planàre, *v.i.* (*aer.*) to glide down, to plane (down).

planàta, *s.f.* (*aer.*) glide, volplane.

plància, *s.f.* **1.** (*mar.*) bridge: *essere sulla* —, to be on the bridge; *montare sulla* —, to go on to the bridge **2.** (*asse*) board.

plàncton, *s.m.* (*biol.*) plankton.

planetàrio, *ag.* planetary: *sistema* —, planetary system ‖ *s.m.* **1.** (*apparecchio per la rappresentazione dei fenomeni astronomici*) orrery, planetarium (*pl.* planetaria) **2.** (*edificio*) planetarium.

planimetría, *s.f.* planimetry.

planimètrico, *ag.* planimetric(al).

planímetro, *s.m.* (*tec.*) planimeter.

planisfèro, *s.m.* (*astr.*) planisphere.

Plantagenèto, *no.pr.* (*st.*) Plantagenet.

plantàre, *ag.* (*anat.*) plantar.

plantígrado, *ag.s.m.* (*zool.*) plantigrade.

plàsma, *s.m.* **1.** (*biol. fisiol.*) plasma **2.** (*min.*) plasma **3.** (*neol. fis.*) (*gas ionizzato*) plasma.

plasmàbile, *ag.* mouldable.

plasmàre, *v.t.* to mould (anche *fig.*): — *il carattere di qlcu.*, to mould s.o.'s character; — *la cera*, to mould wax.

plasmàto, *ag.* moulded.

plasmòdi, *s.m.pl.* (*zool.*) plasmodia.

plàstica, *s.f.***1.** plastic art; art of modelling **2.** (*chir.*) plastic surgery, plastics; (*operazione*) plastic operation: *farsi fare una* — *al naso*, to undergo a plastic operation on the nose **3.** (*materia*) plastic material: *una tovaglia di* —, a plastic table-cloth.

plasticaménte, *av.* plastically.

plasticàre, *v.t.* to model.

plasticatóre, *s.m.*, **plasticatríce**, *s.f.* modeller.

plasticità, *s.f.* plasticity.

plàstico, *ag.* plastic: *argilla plastica*, plastic clay; *arte plastica*, plastic art ‖ *atteggiamento* —, statuesque attitude ‖ *chirurgia, operazione plastica*, plastic surgery, operation ‖ *forza, linfa plastica*, (*biol.*) plastic force, lymph ‖ *immaginazione plastica*, plastic imagination ‖ *le materie plastiche*, plastics ‖ *un quadro* —, a plastic painting ‖ *s.m.* **1.** plastic model **2.** (*carta topografica*) relief map **3.** (*plasticatore*) modeller.

plastídio, *s.m.* (*bot.*) plastid.

plastilína, *s.f.* plasticine.

plàtano, *s.m.* (*bot.*) plane(-tree).

platèa, *s.f.* **1.** (*teat.*) stalls (*pl.*); pit: *poltrona di* —, (orchestra) stall; *poltroncina di* —, pit stall **2.** (*mar.*) (*di banchina*) floor **3.** (*arch.*): — *in calcestruzzo*, concrete bed.

plateàle, *ag.* low, coarse, vulgar.

platealménte, *av.* coarsely, vulgarly.

platelmínti, *s.m.pl.* (*zool.*) Platyhelminthes.

platína, *s.f.* **1.**(*tip.*)(*piano del torchio*)plat(t)en **2.**(*tip.*) (*piccola macchina per stampare*) platten-machine **3.** (*ind. tessile*) sinker.

platinàre, *v.t.* **1.** to platinize **2.** (*capelli*) to dye platinum.

platinàto, *ag.* **1.** platinized, platinum-plated **2.** (*di capelli*) platinum coloured, platinum blond.

platínico, *ag.* platinum (*attributivo*), platinic: *cloruro* —, platinic chloride; *sali platinici*, platinum salts.

platinífero, *ag.* platinum-bearing (*attributivo*), platiniferous.

platinirídio, *s.m.* (*min.*) platiniridium.

plàtino, *s.m.* (*chim.*) platinum.

platinotipía, *s.f.* (*foto.*) platinotype.

platirríne, *s.f.pl.* (*zool.*) platy(r)rhines.

Platóne, *no.pr.m.* (*st. fil.*) Plato.

platonicaménte, *av.* Platonically.

platònico, *ag.* Platonic.

platonísmo, *s.m.* (*st. fil.*) Platonism.

plaudènte, *ag.* applauding.

plaudíre, *v.i.* to applaud; *fig.* to approve.

plausíbile, *ag.* **1.** plausible; acceptable: *una ragione* —, a plausible reason **2.** (*degno di lode*) praiseworthy.

plausibilità, *s.f.* **1.** plausibility; acceptability, acceptableness **2.** praiseworthiness.

plausibilménte, *av.* plausibly; acceptably.

plàuso, *s.m.* applause; (*approvazione*) approbation; (*lode*) praise.

plàustro, *s.m.* (*letter.*) ox-cart ‖ *il Plaustro*, (*astr.*) the Plough (*o* Great Bear).

Plàuto, *no.pr.m.* (*st. lett.*) Plautus.

plautíno, *ag.* (*lett.*) Plautine.

plebàglia, *s.f.* (*spreg.*) mob, rabble, riff-raff.

plebàno, *ag.* (*eccl.*) rural.

plèbe, *s.f.* **1.** common people, populace **2.** (*st. romana*) plebs.

plebeaménte, **plebeiaménte**, *ag.* plebeianly, vulgarly, coarsely, commonly.

plebeísmo, *s.m.* vulgar expression.

plebèo, *ag.* **1.** plebeian: *di origine plebea*, of plebeian extraction **2.** (*spreg.*) plebeian, vulgar, coarse, common: *modi plebei*, vulgar manners ‖ *s.m.* plebeian, commoner.

plebiscitàrio, *ag.* plebiscitary, unanimous.

plebiscíto, *s.m.* plebiscite.

plèiade, *s.f.* **1.** (*lett. greca*) Pleiad; (*lett. francese*) Pléiade, Pleiad **2.** (*eletta schiera*) Pleiad.

Plèiadi, *no.pr.f.pl.* (*astr. mit.*) Pleiad(e)s.

pleistocène, *s.m.* (*geol.*) Pleistocene.

pleistocènico, *ag.* (*geol.*) Pleistocene.

plenàrio, *ag.* plenary: *assemblea plenaria*, plenary assembly ‖ *indulgenza plenaria*, (*eccl.*) plenary indulgence.

plenilunàre, *ag.* plenilunar, plenilunal.

plenilúnio, *s.m.* plenilune.

plenipotènza, *s.f.* plenipotence, plenipotency.

plenipotenziàrio, *ag.s.m.* plenipotentiary.

pleonàsmo, *s.m.* (*ret.*) pleonasm.

pleonasticaménte, *av.* pleonastically.

pleonàstico, *ag.* pleonastic.

pleròma, *s.m.* **1.** (*fil.*) pleroma **2.** (*bot.*) plerome.

plesiosàuro, *s.m.* (*paleont.*) plesiosaur(us).

plessímetro, *s.m.* **1.** (*med.*) pleximeter **2.** (*mus.*) metronome.

plèsso, *s.m.* (*anat.*) plexus: — *cardiaco*, cardiac plexus.

plètora, *s.f.* **1.** (*patol.*) plethora **2.** (*sovrabbondanza*) overabundance, excess, plethora.

pletoricaménte, *av.* over-abundantly, excessively.

pletòrico, *ag.* **1.** (*med.*) plethoric **2.** (*sovrabbondante*) overabundant, excessive.

plèttro, *s.m.* **1.** (*mus.*) plectrum (*pl.* plectra) **2.** (*poesia*) poetry.

plèura, *s.f.* (*anat.*) pleura (*pl.* pleurae).

pleuresía, *s.f.* (*patol.*) pleurisy: — *secca*, dry pleurisy.

plèurico, *ag.* (*anat.*) pleural.

pleurisía, **pleuríte**, *s.f.* (*patol.*) pleurisy, pleuritis.

pleurítico, *ag.* pleuritic(al).

pleuropolmoníte, *s.f.* (*patol.*) pleuro-pneumonia.

pliant, *s.m.* **1.** (*sedia pieghevole*) folding-chair **2.** (*letto pieghevole*) folding-bed.

plíca, *s.f.* (*anat.*) plica (*pl.* plicae).

plicàta, *s.f.* (*eccl.*) folded chasuble.

plíco, *s.m.* **1.** (*involto di carte*) packet (of papers): *prese tutti i documenti e ne formò un* —, he took all the documents and made a packet of them **2.** (*busta contenente carte*) cover; (*sigillata*) sealed envelope: *in* — *separato*, (*comm.*) under separate cover; *nello stesso* —, (*comm.*) under the same cover.

Plínio, *no.pr.m.* (*st. lett.*) Pliny: — *il Giovane,* Pliny the Younger; — *il Vecchio,* Pliny the Elder.

plínto, *s.m.* (*arch.*) plinth.

pliocène, *s.m.* (*geol.*) Pliocene.

pliocènico, *ag.* (*geol.*) Pliocene (*attributivo*).

plissé, *ag.* pleated.

ploràre, *v.i.* (*letter. poet.*) to weep; to cry.

Plotíno, *no.pr.m.* (*st. fil.*) Plotinus.

plotóne, *s.m.* (*mil.*) platoon; squad: — *d'esecuzione,* firing party.

plúmbeo, *ag.* 1. leaden: *cielo* —, leaden sky 2. *fig.* (*noioso*) boring.

pluràle, *ag. s.m.* (*gram.*) plural: *al* —, in the plural.

pluralísmo, *s.m.* (*fil.*) pluralism.

pluralità, *s.f.* 1. plurality: — *di uffici,* plurality of offices 2. (*maggioranza*) majority: — *di voti,* majority of votes.

pluralizzàre, *v.t.* to pluralize.

pluralménte, *av.* plurally.

pluricellulàre, *ag.* (*biol.*) multicellular, pluricellular.

pluriloculàre, *ag.* (*bot.*) plurilocular.

plurimotóre, *ag.* (*aer.*) multi-engined.

plurinomiàle, *ag.*: *votazione* —, (*pol.*) voting system in which political parties can offer more than one candidate in each constituency.

plurivalènte, *ag.* (*chim.*) multivalent, plurivalent.

plus-valóre, *s.m.* (*comm.*) plus value.

Plutàrco, *no.pr.m.* (*st. lett.*) Plutarch.

plúteo, *s.m.* pluteus (*pl.* plutei).

Plúto, *no.pr.m.* (*mit.*) Pluto.

plutòcrate, *s.m.* plutocrat.

plutocràtico, *ag.* plutocratic.

plutocrazía, *s.f.* plutocracy.

Plutóne, *no.pr.m.* (*mit. astr.*) Pluto.

plutònico, *ag.* (*mit. geol.*) Plutonic, Plutonian: *rocce plutoniche,* Plutonic rocks.

plutònio, *s.m.* (*chim.*) plutonium.

plutonísmo, *s.m.* (*geol.*) Plutonism, Plutonic theory.

pluviàle, *ag.* rain (*attributivo*); pluvial: *acqua* —, rainwater‖*s.m.* (*tubazione per acqua piovana*) drain-pipe.

plúvio, *ag.* (*letter.*) pluvious, rainy: *tempo* —, rainy weather ‖ *Giove Pluvio,* Jupiter Pluvius.

pluviomètrico, *ag.* pluviometric(al).

pluviòmetro, *s.m.* rain-gauge, pluviometer.

pneumàtica, *s.f.* pneumatics.

pneumaticità, *s.f.* (*fis.*) pneumaticity.

pneumàtico, *ag.* pneumatic: *avvitatrice pneumatica,* pneumatic wrench; *macchina pneumatica,* air-pump; *martello* —, pneumatic hammer; *posta pneumatica,* pneumatic dispatch; *scalpello* —, pneumatic rock-drill; *scavatrice pneumatica,* pneumatic digger; *trapano* —, pneumatic drill ‖ *s.m.* (*copertone*) shoe; (*copertone e camera d'aria*) tyre; (*amer.*) tire: — *a bassa pressione,* low-pressure tyre; *pneumatici accoppiati,* coupled tyres; — *ad alta pressione,* high-pressure tyre; — *a terra,* flat tyre; — *con battistrada a canale,* grooved-tread tyre; — *rigato,* ribbed tyre; — *speciale a bassa pressione,* (*aer.*) airwheel; *leva per* —, tyre-crowbar.

pneumatología, *s.f.* (*teol.*) pneumatology.

pneumatòmetro, *s.m.* (*med.*) pneumatometer.

pneumatoràce, *s.m.* (*med.*) pneumothorax.

pneumocòcco, *s.m.* (*biol.*) pneumococcus (*pl.* pneumococci).

pneumogàstrico, *ag.* (*anat.*) pneumogastric.

pneumògrafo, *s.m.* (*med.*) pneumograph.

pneumometría, *s.f.* (*med.*) pneumometry.

pneumòmetro, *s.m.* (*med. fis.*) pneumatometer.

pneumonía, *s.f.* (*patol.*) pneumonia.

pneumònico, *ag.* (*med.*) pneumonic.

pneumoníte, *s.f.* (*patol.*) pneumonia.

pneumoterapía, *s.f.* (*med.*) pneumatotherapy.

po', *apocope* di **pòco.**

pochézza, *s.f.* 1. smallness, littleness 2. (*insufficienza*) lack; insufficiency; (*scarsità*) scarcity; scantiness 3. (*ristrettezza*) narrowness.

pochíno, *ag. indef.* 1. only a little (*attributivo*), not much: *la sua carità è pochina,* he has not much charity 2. *pl.* only a few (in number), not many: *le mele sono pochine quest'anno,* there are not many apples this year; *gli studenti sono pochini,* the students are only a few in number (o there are not many students); *i suoi meriti sono pochini,* he has only a few merits; *i suoi mezzi sono pochini,* his means are rather scanty (o he is a man of small means) ‖ *pron. indef.* 1. only a little, not much: « *Hai del pane?* », « *Ne ho* — », "Have you any bread?", "Only a little" (o "Not much") ‖ *un* —, a little (o some o a bit): « *Hai del denaro con te?* », « *Ne ho un* — », "Have you any money on you?", "I have a little (o a bit o some)"; « *Vuoi dello zucchero?* », « *Ne voglio solo un* — », "Do you want some sugar?", "Just a little (o a bit)" 2. *pl.* only a few, not many: « *Hai molti libri?* », « *Ne ho pochini* », "Have you many books?", "No, only a few (o not many)" ‖ *s.m.* 1. little: *quel* — *che aveva lo dava ai poveri,* the little he had he gave to the poor ‖ *un* —, a little, a (little) bit: *con un* — *di fortuna,* with a (little) bit of luck; *dammi un* — *di tempo,* give me a little (o a bit of) time 2. (*in espressioni di tempo*): *un* —, a short time (o a while): *un* — *prima, dopo,* a short time (o shortly) before, after; *aspetta ancora un* —, *sono quasi pronto,* wait a moment, I am nearly ready 3. *pl.* only a few, only a few people: *solo pochini applaudirono la sua esecuzione,* only a few people applauded his execution ‖ *av.* only a little, not much: *egli dorme* —, he doesn't sleep much; *lo vedo* — *in questi giorni,* I don't see him much these days (o I see only a little of him these days) ‖ *un* —, a little, a bit: *mi puoi aiutare un* —?, could you help me a little?; *questo libro è solo un* — *più interessante dell'altro,* this book is just a little bit more interesting than the other (one).

pochíssimo, *ag. indef. superl.* 1. very little: *ha pochissima pazienza con noi,* he has very little patience with us 2. (*in espressioni di tempo*) very little, very short: — *tempo dopo,* a very short time later (o very little later o after a very short while); — *tempo fa,* a very short time ago; — *tempo prima,* a very short time before 3. *pl.* very few: *ha pochissimi meriti, amici,* he has very few merits, friends 4. (*in espressioni ellittiche di tempo*) a very short time, very little: — *dopo, prima,* very shortly after, before; *da* —, a very short time ago; (*riferito al pass.*) a very short time before: *quando arrivai seppi che era partito da* —, when I arrived I learned that he had left a very short time before; *sono arrivato qui da* —, I arrived here a very short time ago; *fra* —, very shortly (o in a very short time); *di lì a* —, very shortly after (o after a short while o very little later); *è* — *che non lo vedo,* it's no time since I saw him; *manca* — *a Natale,* it is no time to Christmas (o Christmas will be here in no time); *mi manca* — *per finire,* I shall very soon be finished (o I have very nearly finished) 5. (*in altre espressioni ellittiche*): *c'è* — *da qui a casa mia,* my house is no distance from here; *ci corre* — *tra...,* there is very little difference between...; *ci vuole* — *a...,* it doesn't (o wouldn't) take much to...; *l'ho comprato per* —, I got it very cheap ‖ *pron. indef. superl.* 1. very little: « *Hai molto tempo libero?* », « *No, ne ho* —», "Have you a lot of free time?", "No, I have very little" 2. *pl.* very few: « *Hai molti alberi da frutto nel tuo giardino?* », « *No, ne ho pochissimi* », "Have you a lot of fruit-trees in your garden?", "No, very few" ‖ *s.m.* 1. very little: — *di ciò che ho è mio,* very little of what I have is mine; — *rimane da dire,* very little remains to be said ‖ — *ci mancò che si scontrassero,* they all but crashed 2. *pl.* very few, very few people: *fu approvato da pochissimi,* very few people approved of him; *moltissimi vanno all'opera, ma solo pochissimi l'apprezzano realmente,* a great many people go to the opera, but very few really appreciate it ‖ *av.* very little: — *conosciuto, letto,* very little known, read; — *mag-*

giore, minore, very little older, younger; — *più, meno*, very little more, less; *beve* —, he drinks very little; *l'ho visto — quest'anno*, I have seen very little of him this year ‖ *distare — da...*, to be very near...: *la mia casa dista — dall'università*, my house is very near the University.

pòco, *ag. indef.* **1. little; not much:** *c'è poca speranza che venga*, there is little hope of his coming; *ho poca pazienza con i bambini*, I have not much patience with children ‖ *non* —, quite a lot of (o not a little): *ciò mi ha dato non poca preoccupazione*, this caused me no little worry (o not a little worry) **2.** (*in espressioni di tempo*) **little**, **short:** — *tempo dopo*, a short time later (o a little later o after a short while); — *tempo fa*, a short time ago; — *tempo prima*, a short time before; *ho aspettato solo — tempo*, I only waited a short time; *in — tempo ha fatto molto*, he has achieved a great deal in a short time **3.** *pl.* **few; not many;** (*alcuni*) **a few:** *pochi altri libri hanno avuto tanta influenza sul mio spirito*, few other books have influenced my mind to such an extent; *pochi minuti trascorsero*, a few minutes elapsed; *poche persone studiano il greco al giorno d'oggi*, few people study Greek nowadays; *ho fatto pochi errori*, I have made few mistakes (o I haven't made many mistakes); *inviterò i miei genitori e pochi amici*, I'll invite my parents and a few friends ‖ *molto pochi*, very few; *troppo pochi*, too few **4.** (*in espressioni ellittiche di tempo*) **a short time; not long:** — *dopo, prima*, not long (o shortly) after, before; — *fa, poc'anzi*, a few minutes (o a short time ago); *a fra* —, *arrivederci da qui a* —, see you soon; *da* —, a short time ago; (*riferito al pass.*) a short time before; (*tempo continuato*) for a short time (o for a little while): *quando arrivai seppi che era partito da* —, when I arrived I learned that he had left a short time before; *sono arrivato qui da* —, I arrived here a short time ago; *vi aspettavo da* —, I had been waiting for you for a short time; *di lì a* —, shortly after (o after a while o a little later); *fra* —, very soon (o very shortly); *è — che non lo vedo*, it's not long since I saw him; *manca — a Natale*, it is not long to Christmas; *mi manca — per finire*, I shall soon be finished (o I have nearly finished); *restò lì per* —, he didn't stay there long **5.** (*in altre espressioni ellittiche*): *da* —: *cosa da* —, a mere trifle (o a bagatelle); *una moneta da* —, a small coin; *un uomo da* —, a worthless fellow (o a good-for-nothing); *per* —, (*a buon mercato*) cheap: *l'ho comprato per* —, I got it cheap; *c'è, non c'è — da qui a casa mia*, my house is not far from here, it is a good way from here to my house; *ci corre — tra...*, there's little difference between...; *ci vuole — a...*, it doesn't (o wouldn't) take much... ‖ *pron. indef.* **1. very little; little; not much:** « *Hai del burro?* », « *Ne ho* — », " Have you any butter? ", " Only a little " (o " Not much "); *ieri avevo molto tempo libero, ma oggi ne ho* —, yesterday I had a lot of free time, but today I have very little ‖ *un* —, *un po'*, a little (o some o a bit): « *Hai del gesso?* », « *Ne ho un po'* », "Have you any chalk?", "I have a little (o some)" **2.** *pl.* **very few; few; not many;** (*alcuni*) **a few:** « *Hai molti amici?* », « *Solo pochi* », " Have you many friends? ", " Only a few "; « *Hai molti libri?* », « *Ne ho pochi* », " Have you many books? ", " No, very few " ‖ *s.m.* **1. little:** — *o niente*, little or nothing (o next to nothing); *il — che ho è a tua disposizione*, what little I have is at your disposal; *il — che ho visto è fatto bene*, the little I have seen is well done; — *di ciò che ho è qui*, little of what I have is here; *farò il — che posso*, I'll do what little I can ‖ *un* —, *un po'*, (*temporale*) a short time, a little: *un po' dopo, prima*, a short time later, before; *da un po'*, (*riferito al pass.*) some time ago; (*tempo continuato*) for some time: *aspetta da un (bel) po'*, he has been waiting for (quite) some time; *fra un po'*, soon (o before long); *manca ancora un po' a Natale*, it's still

some time to Christmas; *ti ho aspettato per un po' e poi sono andato via*, I waited for you a little (o a short time) and then I went away ‖ *un* — (*di*), *un po'* (*di*), a little (o a bit o some): *un — di coraggio, fortuna*, a little (o a bit of) courage, luck; *un — di pane*, a little bread; *un po' di tutto*, a little of everything; *vuoi un altro po' di whisky?*, would you like some (o a little o a drop) more whisky? ‖ *un — di buono*, a rogue (o a crook o *fam.* a piece of no good); *è una — di buono*, she is not up to much ‖ *che po' po' di coraggio, sfacciataggine!*, what courage, impudence! ‖ *tra il — e il molto...*, between too little and too much... ‖ *— ci mancò che si scontrasse con un autocarro*, he all but crashed into a lorry ‖ *il — val meglio del nulla*, half a loaf is better than no bread ‖ *a dir —*, *a far —*, at the least (o to say the least) **2.** *pl.* **few, few people:** *pochi, ma buoni*, few, but good; *noi pochi, noi pochi fortunati!*, we few, we happy few!; *solo pochi*, only a few; *pochi lo compreranno*, few people will buy it; *oligarchia vuol dire governo dei pochi*, oligarchy means government by the few ‖ *i pochi*, the few (o the minority) ‖ *molti pochi fanno un assai*, *prov.* many a mickle makes a muckle ‖ *av.* **1.** (*con ag. e av. positivi; con p. pres.*, talvolta con *p.p.* se usati come *ag.*) **not very:** — *appassionante*, it is not very exciting; *è — onesto, simpatico, sincero*, he is not very honest, nice, sincere; *ero — soddisfatto*, I wasn't very satisfied; *sto — bene*, I am not very well ‖ *un* —, *un po'*, rather, a little, a bit: *sono un po' stanco*, I am a bit tired ‖ — *conosciuto*, — *letto*, little known, little read **2.** (*con ag. e av. comp.*) **little; not much:** — (*di*) *più*, — (*di*) *meno*, little more, little less; — *maggiore, minore*, little older, younger; *è — più alto di me*, he is not much taller than I am; *è — più che un ragazzo*, he is little more than a boy ‖ *un* —, *un po'*, a little (o a bit): *un po' più oltre*, a little further; *l'articolo di fondo di oggi è un po' più interessante di quello di ieri*, to-day's leading -article is a little (o a bit) more interesting than yesterday's; *è un po' più corto del mio*, it is a little shorter than mine; *sto un po' meglio*, I feel a little better ‖ *un bel po'*, rather: *è un bel po' più lento di te*, he is rather slower than you are **3.** (*con p.p.*) **little:** *il suo aiuto fu — apprezzato*, his help was little appreciated ‖ *un* —, *un po'*, a little (o a bit) **4.** (*con verbi*) **little; not much:** *beve — e mangia ancor meno*, he drinks little and eats even less; *lo vedo molto —quest'anno*, I don't see much of him this year; *quell'uomo mi piace —*, I don't think much of that man ‖ *un* —, *un po'*, a little (o a bit): *riposò un — e poi andò a lavorare*, he rested a little (o a bit) and then went to work **5.** (*enfatico e quasi pleonastico*): *senti un* —, *un po'...*, (here), I say...; *vediamo un* —, *un po'...*, (now), let's see... **6.** (*Fraseologia*): *un po' per..., un po' per...*, what with... and (what with)...: *un po' per il rumore, un po' per il caldo si sentiva frastornato*, what with the noise and (what with) the heat he felt quite dizzy; *un po' per volta*, a little at time; *a — a —*, little by little; *per —*, (*quasi*) nearly: *per — non cadevo*, I nearly fell; *è press'a — lo stesso*, it's just about the same.

pocolíno, *V.* **pochíno.**

podàgra, *s.f.* (*patol.*) podagra, gout (in the feet).

podàgrico, *ag.* podagric, podagral, gouty.

podagróso, *ag.* podagrous, gouty ‖ *s.m.* a sufferer from gout.

podartríte, *s.f.* (*patol.*) podarthritis

podére, *s.m.* farm; holding.

poderosaménte, *av.* powerfully, mightily.

poderóso, *ag.* powerful, mighty (anche *fig.*): *esercito* —, powerful (o mighty) army; *intelletto* —, powerful intellect; *voce poderosa*, powerful voice ‖ *ho una fame poderosa*, I am starving.

podestà, *s.m.* (*st.*) podestà.

podestariàto, *s.m.* (*st.*) office, authority of a podestà.

podestaríle, *ag.* (*st.*) of a podestà.

podestería, *s.f.* (*st.*) **1.** (*ufficio del podestà*) office of a podestà **2.** (*giurisdizione del podestà*) jurisdiction of a podestà **3.** (*residenza del podestà*) residence of a podestà.

pòdio, *s.m.* **1.** (*arch. archeol.*) podium (*pl. podia*) **2.** (*di direttore d'orchestra, oratore, ecc.*) rostrum (*pl.* rostra), platform **3.** (*per autorità, ad una cerimonia o altro*) dais, platform.

podísmo, *s.m.* **1.** (*spor.*) running **2.** (*il fare passeggiate*) walking; hiking.

podísta, *s.c.* **1.** (*spor.*) (professional) runner **2.** (*scherz.*) (*chi ama far passeggiate*) great walker.

podístico, *ag.* foot (*attributivo*): *gara podistica*, foot-race.

poèma, *s.m.* **1.** (long) poem: — *cavalleresco, didascalico, epico, eroicomico, narrativo*, chivalric, didactic, epic, mock-heroic, narrative poem **2.** (*mus.*) poem: — *sinfonico*, symphonic poem **3.** (*scherz.*) (*cosa mirabile*): *quel vino è un* —, that wine is a dream.

poesia, *s.f.* **1.** poetry: — *dell'amore*, poetry of love (o love-poetry); *la* — *della natura, del mare*, the poetry of nature, of the sea; — *didascalica, drammatica, epica, lirica, satirica*, didactic, dramatic, epic, lyric, satiric poetry; — *popolare*, popular poetry; *questo romanzo ha molte pagine di vera* —, this novel has many pages of real poetry; *sono bei versi, ma senza* —, they are good verses but they are not poetry **2.** (*componimento poetico*) poem, piece of poetry: *le poesie di Keats*, Keats's poems (o poetry); *lesse una* —, he read a poem (o a piece of poetry) **3.** *fig.* (*illusione, finzione*) illusion: *questa è* —!, this is an illusion!.

poèta, *s.m.* **1.** poet: *i poeti classici*, the classical poets; — *di corte*, court-poet; — *laureato*, poet laureate ‖ — *si nasce, non si diventa*, poets are born, not made **2.** (*chi fa castelli in aria*) dreamer.

poetàre, *v.i.* to write poetry, to poetize ‖ *v.t.* (*rar.*) to poetize.

poetàstro, *s.m.* (*spreg.*) poetaster.

poeteggiàre, *v.i.* **1.** to write poetry, to poetize; (*versificare*) to versify; (*fare il poeta*) to play the poet **2.** (*inclinare alla poesia*) to tend towards poetry, to be poetical: *prosa che poeteggia*, prose tending towards poetry (o poetical prose).

poetéssa, *s.f.* poetess.

poètica, *s.f.* poetics, art of poetry.

poeticaménte, *av.* poetically.

poetichería, *s.f.* (*spreg.*) poetical fancies (*pl.*).

poètico, *ag.* poetic(al): *un amore* —, a poetic love; *genio* —, poetical genius; *licenza poetica*, poetic licence; *opere poetiche*, poetical works; *talento, linguaggio* —, poetic talent, language; *vena, ispirazione, forma poetica*, poetic vein, inspiration, form; *non c'è nulla di* — *in questo scritto*, there isn't anything poetical in this piece of writing.

poetizzàre, *v.t.* **1.** (*rendere poetico*) to make poetic; to poeticize **2.** (*mettere in versi*) to put into poetry, to poetize ‖ *v.i.* (*rar.*) to write poetry, to poetize.

poetúcolo, *s.m.* (*spreg.*) poeticule.

pòggia, *s.f.* (*mar.*) **1.** (*corda*) vang **2.** (*parte sottovento*) lee, lee-side: —!, up with the helm!; *andate da orza a* —!, go from windward to leeward!; *andare, stare a* —, to sail before the wind.

poggiacàpo, *s.m.* antimacassar, embroidered head-rest.

poggiapièdi, *s.m.* footrest.

poggiàre¹, *v.i.* **1.** (*rifugiarsi in un porto*) to take shelter **2.** (*mil.*) (*spostarsi*) to move: *poggiate a destra*, move to the right.

poggiàre², *v.i.* **1.** (*fondarsi*) to rest, to be based: *questo muro poggia su uno strato di roccia*, this wall rests on a layer of rock; *le tue supposizioni poggiano su false ipotesi*, your suppositions are based on false hypotheses **2.** (*poet.*) (*innalzarsi*) to rise: — *alla vetta*, to rise to the summit ‖ *v.t.* (*appoggiare*) to rest, to lean; (*posare*) to put, to place: — *il piede a terra*, to put one's foot to the ground.

pòggio, *s.m.* hillock, knoll.

poggiòlo, poggiuòlo, *s.m.* balcony.

poh, *inter.* pooh!.

pòi, *av.* **1.** (*in seguito, successivamente*) **then:** *finisci questo lavoro e* — *potrai uscire*, finish this work, and then you may go out ‖ *e* —?, and then? (o what then?) ‖ *in* —, onward(s): *da allora in* —, from then onwards (o ever since then); *d'ora in* —, from now on(wards) (o *letter.* henceforth) **2.** (*dopo di ciò*) **afterwards:** *se spendi tutto ora, non avrai più niente* —, if you spend everything now, you won't have anything left afterwards **3.** (*più tardi*) **later** (on): *ti vedrò* —, I'll see you later; *vedremo* — *chi di noi aveva ragione*, we shall see later which of us was right; *verrò* —, I'll come later on ‖ *prima o* —, sooner or later **4.** (*in secondo luogo*) **and then, secondly:** *anzitutto non mi piace,* — *non mi fa bene*, first of all I don't like it, secondly it does not agree with me; *e* —, *vedi, c'è un'altra difficoltà*, and then, you see, there is another difficulty **5.** (*avversativo*) **but:** *io dico così, tu* — *sei padrone di fare ciò che vuoi*, that's what I say, but you can do what you like **6.** (*enfatico, rafforzativo*): *in quanto* — *ai suoi meriti...*, as for his merits...; *questo* — *no!*, not on your life! (o *fam.* no fear!); *e* — *si lamentano!*, and even then they complain!; *è tanto e* — *tanto infelice*, he is so very unhappy; *io* — *non c'entro*, it's nothing to do with me; *non è* — *così difficile come credevo*, after all it is not so difficult as I thought; *non è* — *così sbagliato*, it is not so wrong after all; *questo* — *è troppo!*, this is really too much!; *questo* — *non lo dimenticherò!*, this I shall certainly not forget!; *si va* —?, shall we go then? ‖ *s.m.* **future:** *pensa al* —!, think of the future! ‖ *il senno di* —, wisdom after the event.

poiàna, *s.f.* (*ornit.*) buzzard.

poiché, *cong.* **1.** (*causale*) **as, since; for:** — *non so dove andare, starò a casa*, as I don't know where to go, I shall stay at home; *lo farò io,* — *tu non sapresti farlo*, I'll do it myself, for you wouldn't know how to do it; *verrò io da te,* — *tu non vuoi venire da me*, I shall come to you, since you don't want to come to me **2.** (*arc.*) (*temporale*) **after, when:** — *ebbe scritto la lettera pianse a lungo*, after writing the letter she wept for a long time; — *mi vide, si voltò verso il suo amico*, when he saw me, he turned to his friend.

polàcca¹, *s.f.* **1.** (*musica, danza*) polonaise **2.** (*mar.*) (*mercantile a vela*) polacre **3.** (*indumento*) polonaise.

polàcco, *ag.* Polish ‖ *s.m.* **1.** Pole **2.** (*lingua*) Polish ‖ **polàcca²,** *s.f.* Pole.

polàre, *ag.* polar: *circolo* —, polar circle; *orso* —, polar bear; *stella* —, pole-star (o lodestar o loadstar).

polarímetro, *s.m.* (*ott.*) polarimeter.

polariscòpio, *s.m.* (*ott.*) polariscope.

polarità, *s.f.* (*elett. biol.*) polarity.

polarizzàre, *v.t.*, **polarizzàrsi,** *v.r.* to polarize (anche *fig.*).

polarizzatóre, *ag.* polarizing ‖ *s.m.* (*ott.*) polarizer.

polarizzazióne, *s.f.* (*fis.*) polarization: — *di griglia*, grid-bias; *piano di* —, plane of polarization; *togliere la* —, to depolarize.

polarménte, *av.* polarly.

pòlca, *s.f.* (*musica, danza*) polka: *ballare la* —, to dance a polka.

polemàrco, *s.m.* (*st.*) polemarch.

polèmica, *s.f.* polemics; polemic.

polèmico, *ag.* polemic(al); controversial: *argomento, spirito* —, polemic subject, spirit.

polemísta, *s.c.* controversialist, polemic.

polemizzàre, *v.i.* to polemize.

polemònia, *s.f.* (*bot.*) polemonium.

polemoniàcee, *s.f.pl.* (*bot.*) Polemoniaceae.

polèna, *s.f.* (*mar.*) figure-head.

polènta, *s.f.* **1.** (*cuc.*) "polenta" (pudding of maize) ‖ — *dolce*, pudding of chestnut meal; — *d'orzo*, pudding of barley meal **2.** (*fam.*) (*persona lenta*) slow-coach; (*pigrone*) sluggard.

polentàio, *s.m.* seller of polenta.

polentína, *s.f.* (*cataplasma*) poultice.

polentóne, *s.m.* (*fam.*) **1.** (*persona lenta*) slow-coach; (*pigrone*) sluggard **2.** (*nativo dell'Italia setten-trionale*) North Italian.

poleografía, *s.f.* geography dealing with towns.

polésine, *s.m.* (*geog.*) delta (of the river Po).

poliachènio, *s.m.* (*bot.*) fruit with many achenes.

poliadenía, *s.f.* (*patol.*) polyadenia.

poliambulànza, *s.f.* day-clinic.

poliandría, *s.f.* (*bot. dir.*) polyandry.

poliàndrico, *ag.* (*bot. dir.*) polyandrous.

poliantèa, *s.f.* anthology.

poliarchía, *s.f.* (*pol.*) polyarchy.

poliàrchico, *ag.* of a polyarchy.

poliatòmico, *ag.* (*fis.*) polyatomic.

polibàsico, *ag.* (*chim.*) polybasic.

Políbio, *no.pr.m.* (*st.*) Polybius.

policàrpico, *ag.* (*bot.*) polycarpellary, polycarpous.

Policàrpo, *no.pr.m.* Polycarp.

policitemía, *s.f.* (*med.*) polycycthaemia.

Policlèto, *no.pr.m.* (*st.*) Polycletus.

policlínico, *s.m.* general hospital.

Polícrate, *no.pr.m.* (*st.*) Polycrates.

policroísmo, *s.m.* pleochroism.

policromàtico, *ag.* polychromatic.

policromía, *s.f.* polychromy.

polícromo, *ag.* polychrome.

Polidòro, *no.pr.m.* (*lett.*) Polydorus.

polièdrico, *ag.* **1.** (*geom.*) polyhedric, polyhedral **2.** *fig.* (*eclettico*) versatile: *uomo* —, a versatile man.

polièdro, *s.m.* (*geom.*) polyhedron.

poliemía, *s.f.* (*med.*) polyemia.

poliestesía, *s.f.* (*med.*) polyesthesia.

polifagía, *s.f.* polyphagia.

polifàse, *ag.* (*elett.*) polyphase.

Polifèmo, *no.pr.m.* (*mit.*) Polyphemus.

polifonía, *s.f.* (*mus.*) polyphony.

polifònico, *ag.* (*mus.*) polyphonic.

polígala, *s.f.* (*bot.*) polygala.

poligamía, *s.f.* **1.** (*dir.*) polygamy **2.** (*bot.*) polygamia.

polígamo, *ag.* **1.** (*dir.*) polygamous **2.** (*bot.*) polygamian ‖ *s.m.* (*dir.*) polygamist.

poligènesi, *s.f.* polygenesis.

poligenísmo, *s.m.* (*fil.*) polygenism.

poliglòtta, *s.c.* polyglot.

poliglòtto, *ag.* polyglot: *libro* —, polyglot book.

poligonàcee, *s.f.pl.* (*bot.*) Polygonaceae.

poligonàle, *ag.* (*geom.*) polygonal.

polígono, *s.m.* **1.** (*geom.*) polygon **2.** (*mil.*) shooting-range.

poligrafía, *s.f.* polygraphy.

poligràfico, *ag.* polygraphic.

polígrafo, *s.m.* (*tip.*) polygraph.

polimería, *s.f.* (*chim.*) polymerism.

polimèrico, *ag.* (*chim.*) polymeric.

polimerizzàre, *v.t.* (*chim.*) to polymerize.

polimerizzazióne, *s.f.* (*chim.*) polymerization.

polímero, *ag.* (*chim.*) polymeric ‖ *s.m.* (*chim.*) polymer.

polimorfísmo, *s.m.* (*scient.*) polymorphism.

polimòrfo, *ag.* (*scient.*) polymorphous.

Polinèsia, *no.pr.f.* (*geog.*) Polynesia.

polinesiàno, *ag.s.m.* Polynesian.

Políníce, *no.pr.m.* (*mit.*) Polynices.

Polínnia, *no.pr.f.* (*mit.*) Polyhymnia.

polinòmio, *s.m.* (*mat.*) polynomial, multinomial.

poliomielíte, *s.f.* (*patol.*) poliomyelitis (*abbr.* polio).

poliopsía, *s.f.* polyopia, polyopy.

polipàio, *s.m.* polypary, polypidom.

polipètalo, *ag.* (*bot.*) polypetalous.

polipnèa, *s.f.* (*med.*) polypnoea.

pòlipo, *s.m.* **1.** (*zool.*) polyp **2.** (*med.*) polypus (*pl.* polypi, polypuses).

polipòdio, *s.m.* (*bot.*) polypody.

polipòsi, *s.f.* (*patol.*) polyposis.

polipóso, *ag.* polypous.

políre, *v.t.* **1.** (*tec.*) (*lucidare*) to polish; to buff; (*metalli*) to burnish **2.** (*versi, stile, ecc.*) to polish (up) **3.** *V.* pulíre.

polirème, *s.f.* (*st.*) galley (with various sets of rowers).

polirítmo, *ag.* (*mus.*) polyrhythmic(al).

polisaccàridi, *s.m.pl.* (*chim.*) polysaccharides.

polisarcía, *s.f.* (*med.*) polysarcia, obesity.

polisàrcico, *ag.* polysarcous.

polisènso, *ag.* (*letter.*) having several meanings *s.m.* (*enigmistica*) puzzle (based on homonyms).

polisíllabo, *ag.* polysyllabic(al) ‖ *s.m.* polysyllable.

polisíndeto, *s.m.* (*ret.*) polysyndeton.

Polissèna, *no.pr.f.* (*mit.*) Polyxena.

polispàsto, *s.m.* (*mec.*) polyspast.

polístilo, *ag.* (*arch.*) polystyle, polystylar.

polistiròlo, *s.m.* (*chim.*) polystyrene.

politeàma, *s.m.* theatre.

politècnico, *ag.s.m.* polytechnic.

politeísmo, *s.m.* (*relig.*) polytheism.

politeísta, *s.c.* (*relig.*) polytheist.

politeisticaménte, *av.* (*relig.*) polytheistically.

politeístico, *ag.* (*relig.*) polytheistic(al).

politène, *s.m.* (*chim.*) polythene.

politézza, *s.f.* finish, polish.

política, *s.f.* **1.** politics: — *estera, interna*, foreign, home politics; *la* — *è il suo argomento preferito*, politics is his favourite subject; *darsi alla* —, to go into (o to enter) politics; *fare della* —, to meddle in politics; *parlare di* —, to talk politics; *ritirarsi dalla* —, to retire from political life ‖ — *da caffè, da farmacia*, café (o armchair) politics **2.** (*linea di condotta*) policy: — *accorta, saggia*, wise policy; — *stolta*, foolish policy; *questa è buona, cattiva* —, this is good, bad policy; *la sua* — *come capo dell'azienda dovrebbe essere diversa*, his policy as head of the firm should be different; *conosco la sua* —, I know his (little) game **3.** (*diplomazia, astuzia*) diplomacy; cunning: *ci vorrà un po' di* —, a little diplomacy will be needed; *quell'uomo non ha* — *e si fa scoprire subito*, being a man lacking in astuteness, he is easily found out.

politicaménte, *av.* politically.

politicànte, *s.c.* (*spreg.*) **1.** petty politician **2.** (*intrigante*) political adventurer.

politicàstro, *s.m.* (*spreg.*) **1.** petty politician **2.** (*intrigante*) political adventurer **3.** (*dilettante di politica*) dabbler in politics.

politichíno, *s.m.* **1.** (*spreg.*) petty politician; (*intrigante*) political adventurer **2.** (*fam.*) (*bambino che pone con astuzia le sue richieste*) wheedling child, wheedler: *è un* — *e ottiene ciò che vuole*, he is a real wheedler (o an artful beggar) and gets what he wants.

político, *ag.* **1.** political: — *-economico*, politico-economical; — *-sociale*, politico-social; *crisi politica*, political crisis; *diritti politici*, political rights; *economia, geografia, storia politica*, political economy, geography, history; *elezioni politiche*, political elections; *giornale* —, political paper; *nemico* —, political enemy; *opinioni, teorie politiche*, political views, theories; *ordinamento* —, political set-up; *partito* —, political party; *ragioni politiche*, political reasons; *scienze politiche*, political science; *sciopero* —, political strike; *scritti politici*, political writings; *uomo* —, politician: *fu il più grande uomo* — *del suo tempo*, he was the greatest statesman of his time; *è il corrispondente* — *di un giornale locale*, he is the political correspondent of a local paper ‖ *delitto* —, political crime **2.** (*diplomatico, sagace*) politic: *una risposta politica*, a politic reply **3.** (*rar.*) (*civile*) politic, social: *l'uomo è un animale* —, man is an animal politic (o a social animal) ‖ *s.m.* politician: *un* — *accorto*, a shrewd politician.

politicóne, *s.m.* cunning fellow; schemer.

politípo, *s.m.* (*tip.*) logotype.

políto, *ag.* polished (anche *fig.*): *metallo* —, polished metal; *stile* —, polished style.

políttico, *s.m.* (*art.*) polyptych.

poliuría, *s.f.* (*med.*) polyuria.

poliúrico, *ag.* (*med.*) polyuric.

polivalènte, *ag.* (*chim.*) polyvalent.

polivalènza, *s.f.* (*chim.*) polyvalency, polyvalence.

polivòmere, *ag.* **1.** (*munito di due vomeri*) double-shared **2.** (*munito di più vomeri*) many-shared.

poliviníle, *s.m.* (*chim.*) polyvinyl.

polizía, *s.f.* police, police-force: — *giudiziaria*, Criminal Investigation Department (*abbr.* C.I.D.); — *sanitaria*, sanitary inspectors; — *segreta*, secret police; — *stradale*, traffic police; *agente di* —, police-officer; *auto della* —, police car; *ispettore di* —, police-inspector; *commissariato, ufficio di* —, police-station, police-office; *ha la* — *alle calcagna*, the police are after him; *chiamare la* —, to call the police; *mettere qlcu. nelle mani della* —, to give s.o. in charge.

Poliziàno, *no.pr.* (*st. lett.*) Politian.

poliziésco, *ag.* **1.** police (*attributivo*): *indagine poliziesca*, police investigation **2.** (*di romanzo, film, ecc.*) detective: *film* —, detective film (*o mystery film o thriller*); *romanzo* —, detective story (*o thriller*).

poliziòtto, *s.m.* policeman (*pl.* policemen), police-constable || *cane* —, police-dog.

polizòico, *ag.* (*biol.*) polyzoic.

pòlizza, *s.f.* **1.** (*comm.*) policy: — *aperta*, open (*o* floating) policy; — *a premio unico*, paid-up policy; — *d'assicurazione*, insurance policy: — *d'assicurazione del nolo*, freight insurance policy; — *d'assicurazione sulla vita*, life-policy (*o* assurance policy); — *d'assicurazione su merci*, goods insurance policy; — *incontestabile*, indisputable policy; — *nulla*, void policy; *annullamento della* —, voidance of the policy; *beneficiario della* —, policy-holder; *scadenza della* —, expiration of the policy; *annullare la* —, to void the policy; *cedere la* —, to sign over the policy; *includere nella* —, to insert in the policy; *redigere una* —, to draw up a policy **2.** (*comm.*) (*ricevuta*) bill: — *di carico*, bill of lading; — *di carico all'ordine*, bill of lading to order; — *di carico diretta*, through bill of lading; *emettere la* — *di carico*, to issue the bill of lading; *redigere la* — *di carico*, to draw up the bill of lading **3.** (*del lotto*) lottery ticket **4.** (*del Monte di Pietà*) pawnticket.

polizzíno, *s.m.* **1.** ticket, slip **2.** (*avviso doganale*) customs advice **3.** (*eccl.*) communion ticket.

pólla, *s.f.* spring (of water).

pollachiuría, *s.f.* (*med.*) pollakiuria.

pollàio, *s.m.* **1.** poultry-pen, hen-house, hen-roost; chicken-run; (*stia*) hen-coop **2.** (*pollame*) poultry.

pollaiuòlo, *s.m.* poulterer, poultry dealer.

pollàme, *s.m.* poultry: *l'industria del* —, poultry industry; *il prezzo del* —, poultry price.

pollànca, *s.f.* **1.** (*tacchina giovane*) young turkey **2.** (*pollastra*) pullet, young hen.

pollàstra, *s.f.* **1.** pullet **2.** (*ragazza semplice, inesperta*) simple girl.

pollàstro, *s.m.* **1.** cockerel **2.** (*sempliciotto*) simpleton, booby, noodle.

pollería, *s.f.* poulterer's (shop).

pòllice, *s.m.* **1.** thumb, pollex (*pl.* pollices); (*del piede*) big toe || — *verso*, (*st.*) thumbs down **2.** inch (*misura di lunghezza* = 2,54 cm): — *cubico*, cubic inch (*misura di volume* = 16,38 cm³); — *quadrato*, square inch (*misura di superficie* = 6,45 cm²); *schermo di 12 pollici*, (*tv.*) 12-inch screen || *a* — *a* —, inch by inch.

pollicultóre, *s.m.* poultry-farmer.

pollicultúra, *s.f.* poultry-farming.

pollína, *s.f.* (*agr.*) fowl-manure, chicken-dung.

pòlline, *s.m.* (*bot.*) pollen.

pollínico, *ag.* pollen (*attributivo*).

pollíno[1], *ag.* fowl (*attributivo*): *pidocchio* —, bird's flea || *occhio* —, (*fam.*) corn between two toes.

pollíno[2], *s.m.* marsh; (*terreno paludoso*) marshland.

pollivéndola, *s.f.*, **pollivéndolo**, *s.m.* poulterer.

pòllo, *s.m.* chicken: — *arrosto*, roast chicken; — *d'allevamento*, battery chicken; — *d'India*, turkey; — *lesso*, boiled chicken; — *novello*, spring chicken; — *ripieno*, stuffed chicken; — *sultano*, gallinule; *allevamento di polli*, poultry-farm; *brodo di* —, chicken-broth; *recinto per i polli*, chicken-run; *qui i polli non sono molto buoni*, the poultry is not very good here || *andava a letto coi polli*, he used to go to bed very early; *non alzarti all'ora dei polli domani mattina*, don't get up too early to-morrow morning || *è una cosa che farebbe ridere i polli*, this is really absurd (*o* is nonsense); *nessuno l'ascolta, dice cose che fanno ridere i polli*, no one takes the slightest notice of him, he talks nonsense || *è un buon* —, (*iron.*) he is a dupe.

pollóne, *s.m.* (*bot.*) **1.** (*germoglio*) bud, sprout **2.** (*ramo giovane*) shoot, sucker, scion: — *principale*, leader.

pollonéto, *s.m.* (*vivaio di polloni*) nursery (garden).

Pollúce, *no.pr.m.* (*mit.*) Pollux.

pollúto, *ag.* (*letter.*) polluted, contaminated.

polluzióne, *s.f.* pollution, defilement.

polmonàre, *ag.* pulmonary: *arco* —, pulmonary arch; *arteria* —, pulmonary artery; *circolazione* —, pulmonary circulation; *collasso* —, pulmonary collapse; *edema* —, pulmonary œdema; *enfisema* —, pulmonary emphysema; *plesso* —, pulmonary plexus; *stenosi* —, pulmonary stenosis; *vena* —, pulmonary vein; *tubercolosi* —, pulmonary tuberculosis.

polmóne, *s.m.* lung: — *destro, sinistro*, right, left lung; *il* — *è formato dal lobo e dall'apice*, a lung consists of a lobe and an apex; *deve avere dei buoni polmoni*, he must have good lungs (anche *fig.*); *respirare a pieni polmoni*, to take deep breaths || — *d'acciaio*, (*med.*) iron lung || — *idropneumatico*, (*mar.*) hydropneumatic lung || *ci ho rimesso un* —, *fig.* I have wasted my breath over it || *mi si allargano i polmoni, adesso che ho ricevuto buone notizie*, I can breathe freely (*o* again) now that I've had good news.

polmoníte, *s.f.* pneumonia.

pòlo[1], *s.m.* pole: — *celeste*, (*astr.*) celestial pole; — *di calamita, magnetico*, (*fis.*) magnetic pole; — *negativo*, (*elett.*) negative pole; — *nord*, (*geog.*) North Pole; *poli opposti*, (*elett.*) opposite poles; — *sud*, (*geog.*) South Pole || *noi due siamo ai poli opposti*, *fig.* the two of us are poles asunder.

pòlo[2], *s.m.* (*spor.*) polo: — *d'acqua*, water polo.

Polònia, *no.pr.f.* (*geog.*) Poland.

polònio, *s.m.* (*chim.*) polonium.

pólpa, *s.f.* **1.** (*di frutta*) pulp: — *di albicocca*, apricot pulp **2.** (*carne*) lean meat **3.** — *dentale*, dental pulp **4.** (*polpaccio*) calf (*pl.* calves) **5.** *fig.* kernel: *la* — *di un discorso*, the kernel of a speech.

polpàccio, *s.m.* **1.** calf (*pl.* calves): *ho un crampo al* — *destro*, I have a cramp in my right calf **2.** (*rar.*) (*polpastrello del pollice*) tip of the thumb.

polpacciúto, *ag.* **1.** (*carnoso*) fleshy **2.** (*grassoccio*) plump.

polpastrèllo, *s.m.* finger-tip, finger's end.

polpétta, *s.f.* (*cuc.*) rissole: — *di carne*, meat-ball; — *di pesce*, fish-cake || *far polpette di qlcu.*, to reduce s.o. to pulp (*o* to beat s.o. to a jelly).

polpettóne, *s.m.* **1.** (*cuc.*) meat-roll, meat-loaf **2.** *fig.* medley, hash.

pólpo, *s.m.* (*zool.*) octopus.

polpóso, *ag.* pulpy: *frutta polposa*, pulpy fruit.

polpúto, *ag.* fleshy: *gambe polpute*, fleshy legs.

polsíno, *s.m.* cuff, wristband.

pólso, *s.m.* **1.** (*anat.*) wrist: — *sottile, tozzo*, thin, thick wrist; *orologio da* —, wrist-watch; *la legò ai polsi*, he tied her wrists; *mi prese per i polsi*, he caught me by the wrists **2.** (*pulsazione*) pulse: — *irregolare, frequente*, irregular, quick (*o* rapid) pulse; *il malato ha il* — *debole*, the patient's pulse is weak (*o* low); *tastare il* — *a qlcu.*, to feel s.o.'s pulse; *fig.* to sound s.o.'s intentions **3.** (*polsino*) cuff **4.** *fig.* energy, firmness: *un uomo di* —, an energetic (*o a firm*) man; *ha molto* — *coi suoi figli*, he is very firm with his children; *essere di* —, to have backbone.

poltíglia, *s.f.* **1.** mush, pulp: *questo cibo è una* —, this food is swill; *ridurre ql.co., qlcu. in* —, to reduce sthg., s.o. to pulp **2.** (*fanghiglia*) mud, mire; (*di neve sciolta*) slush.

poltríre, *v.i.* **1.** to lie late abed **2.** (*oziare*) to idle.

poltróna, *s.f.* **1.** easy-chair, arm-chair; — *a rotelle*, self-propelling chair; — *a sdraio*, deck-chair; — *letto*, put-me-up (chair) || *un eroe della* —, (*iron.*) one of the chairborne brigade || *starsene in* —, (*oziare*) to idle **2.** (*teat.*) stall: *una* — *di seconda fila*, a second row stall **3.** (*donna pigra*) sluggard, slattern.

poltronàggine, *s.f.* laziness, idleness, sloth.

poltroncína, *s.f.* (*teat.*) pit-stall.

poltróne, *ag.* lazy, idle, slothful || *s.m.* **1.** idler, sluggard, slacker; (*fam.*) lazy-bones **2.** (*vile*) poltroon.

poltroneggiàre, *v.i.* to idle; to loaf, to slack.

poltronería, *s.f.* idleness, laziness, indolence.

poltronescaménte, *av.* idly, lazily.

poltronésco, *ag.* idle, lazy, indolent.

poltroníssima, *s.f.* (*teat.*) orchestra-stall.

poltroníte, *s.f.* (*scherz.*) habitual laziness.

polveràccio, *s.m.* **1.** dust **2.** (*terreno polveroso*) dry dusty ground **3.** (*concime*) sheep's dung.

pólvere, *s.f.* **1.** dust: *una nuvola di* —, a cloud of dust; *strada, stanza piena di* —, street, room full of dust; *l'automobile sollevò molta* —, the car raised a lot of dust; *gettar* — *negli occhi a qlcu.*, to throw dust in s.o.'s eyes (*anche fig.*); *levar, togliere, fare la* —, to dust || *orologio a* —, (*clessidra*) hour-glass || *mordere la* —, to bite the dust || *scuotere la* — *di dosso a qlcu.*, (*bastonarlo*) to dust s.o.'s jacket **2.** (*sostanza polverizzata*) powder: — *da bagno*, toilet-powder; — *da sbianca*, (*ind.*) bleaching powder; — *da sparo, pirica*, gunpowder; — *di carbone*, coal-dust; — *di smeriglio*, (*mec.*) emery dust; — *di talco*, talcum powder; — *d'oro*, gold-dust; *prende una* — *tutte le mattine per il suo mal di stomaco*, he takes a powder every morning for his stomach ailment; *tenere asciutte le polveri*, to keep one's powder dry (*anche fig.*) || *in* —, powdered (*o in powder*): *caffè in* —, ground coffee; *dentifricio in* —, tooth-powder; *sapone in* —, soap powder; *zucchero in* —, powdered sugar; *ridurre in* —, to reduce to a powder; *fig.* to destroy || *non ha inventato la* —, (*scherz.*) he won't set the Thames on fire.

polverièra, *s.f.* **1.** (*mil.*) magazine; (*mar.*) (powder-) magazine **2.** (*st. mar.*) Santa Barbara.

polverifício, *s.m.* powder-factory.

polverína, *s.f.* (*farm.*) powder.

polveríno, *s.m.* **1.** sand || *mettere il* —, to approve without examining **2.** (*recipiente*) sand-box.

polverío, *s.m.* cloud of dust.

polverizzàbile, *ag.* pulverizable, pulverable.

polverizzaménto, *s.m.* pulverization, pulveration.

polverizzàre, *v.t.* to pulverize (*anche fig.*): *mi guardò come se mi volesse* —, he looked at me as if he would pulverize me || **polverizzàrsi**, *v.r.* to pulverize, to be reduced to powder.

polverizzàto, *ag.* pulverized, powdered: *carbone* —, powdered coal; *zucchero* —, powdered sugar.

polverizzatóre, *s.m.* pulverizer; (*mec.*) nozzle; sprayer: — *a pressione*, pressure nozzle; — *a vapore*, steam jet sprayer; — *a ventaglio*, fan nozzle; — *di carburante*, fuel nozzle.

polverizzazióne, *s.f.* pulverization: — *del combustibile*, (*ind.*) spraying (*o atomizing*) of the fuel.

polveróne, *s.m.* great cloud of dust.

polveróso, *ag.* dusty: *strada polverosa*, dusty road.

polverulénto, *ag.* pulverulent.

polverúme, *s.m.* (*spreg.*) heap of dust.

polvíscolo, *V.* **pulvíscolo.**

pomàrio, *s.m.* (*letter.*) apple-orchard.

pomàta, *s.f.* **1.** (*medicamento*) salve; ointment **2.** (*per i capelli*) pomade, pomatum.

pomellàto, *ag.* dapple(d): *un cavallo grigio* —, a dapple-grey (horse).

pomèllo, *s.m.* **1.** (*della guancia*) cheek-bone **2.** (*di maniglia, leva*) pommel, knob, ball-grip.

pomeridiàno, *ag.* **1.** afternoon (*attributivo*): *lezione pomeridiana*, afternoon lesson; *il sonnellino* —, afternoon nap (*o siesta*); *il tè* —, afternoon tea **2.** (*di ore*) p.m. (*post meridiem*): *il treno parte alle 3 pomeridiane*, the train leaves at 3 p.m.

pomeríggio, *s.m.* afternoon: *nel, di* —, in the afternoon; *ore del* —, afternoon hours; *lo vidi giovedì* —, I saw him on Thursday afternoon.

pomèrio, *s.m.* (*st. archeol.*) pomoerium.

pòmero, *ag.s.m.* Pomeranian.

pométo, *s.m.* apple-orchard.

pomfòlice, *s.f.* (*patol.*) pompholyx.

pómice, *s.f.* pumice(-stone).

pomiciàre, *v.t.* **1.** to pumice, to rub with pumice (-stone); to sand **2.** (*gergo*) (*adulare, lusingare*) to soft-soap.

pomiciàto, *ag.* rubbed down; (*levigato*) smoothed, sanded.

pomiciatúra, *s.f.* rubbing down (with pumice-stone); sanding: — *a umido*, wet rubbing.

pomicoltóre, pomicultóre, *s.m.* (*rar.*) fruit-grower.

pomicoltúra, pomicultúra, *s.f.* pomiculture, fruit-growing.

pomidòro, *V.* **pomodòro.**

pomífero, *ag.* (*letter.*) pomiferous, fruit-bearing.

pómo, *s.m.* **1.** (*albero*) apple-tree; (*frutto*) apple || — *d'Adamo*, (*anat.*) Adam's apple || *il* — *della discordia*, (*mit.*) the apple of discord || *il* — *vietato*, the forbidden fruit **2.** *fig.* (*pomello di maniglia, leva*) knob; (*di bastone*) head; (*di spada*) pommel **3.** (*mar.*) acorn.

pomodòro, *s.m.* (*bot.*) tomato: *salsa di* —, tomato-sauce || *era rosso come un* —, *fig.* he was as red as a beetroot.

pomogranàto, *s.m.* (*bot.*) pomegranate.

pomología, *s.f.* pomology.

pomològico, *ag.* pomological.

Pomóna, *no.pr.f.* (*mit.*) Pomona.

pomóso, *ag.* (*letter.*) fructuous.

pómpa[1], *s.f.* **1.** (*fasto, magnificenza*) pomp: *con molta* —, with much pomp || *in* — *magna*, (*iron.*) in full plumage **2.** (*ostentazione*) display, ostentation: *la* — *degli arricchiti*, the ostentation (*o display*) of the newly-rich; *fa* — *del suo sapere*, he makes a display of his knowledge (*o he shows off his knowledge*); *far* — *di sè*, to show off **3.** *pompe funebri*, funeral ceremonies: *imprenditore di pompe funebri*, undertaker; (*amer.*) mortician; *impresa di pompe funebri*, undertaker's (business).

pómpa[2], *s.f.* (*mec.*) pump: — *a mano*, hand pump; — *antincendio*, fire-pump; — *aspirante*, suction pump; — *aspirante e premente*, lift and force pump; — *a stantuffo*, piston pump; — -*benzina*, (*aut.*) autovac; — *da bicicletta*, bicycle pump; — *dell'olio*, oil pump; — *di alimentazione*, (*mar.*) feed-pump; — *idraulica*, master cylinder; — *per pneumatici*, tyre pump; — *premente*, force-pump; *sala delle pompe*, (*mar.*) well.

pompàre, *v.t.* **1.** to pump (up) **2.** *fig.* (*far insuperbire*) to puff up.

pompàta, *s.f.* **1.** pumping: *dare una* — *ai pneumatici*, to pump up the tyres **2.** (*quantità tratta con la pompa*) pumpful.

pompatúra, *s.f.* **1.** pumping **2.** *fig.* (*gonfiatura*) puffing up.

pompeggiàre, *v.i.* **1.** (*far sfoggio*) to make a display, to show off (sthg.), to flaunt (sthg.): *le piace* — *di tutti i suoi gioielli*, she likes to show off all her jewels **2.** (*apparire con sfarzo*) to be displayed, to be flaunted: *tutte le bandiere pompeggiavano nel salone*, all the flags were displayed in the hall ‖ **pompeg-giàrsi**, *v.r.* to show off; to strut about.

Pompèi, *no.pr.f.* (*geog.*) Pompeii.

pompeiàno[1], *ag.s.m.* (*di Pompei*) Pompeian.

pompeiàno[2], *s.m.* (*st.*) (*partigiano di Pompeo*) follower of Pompey.

pompèlmo, *s.m.* (*bot.*) grape-fruit; (*amer.*) pomelo.

Pompèo, *no.pr.m.* (*st.*) Pompeius, Pompey.

pompière, *s.m.* fireman (*pl.* firemen): *il corpo dei pompieri*, the fire-brigade.

pompierístico, *ag.* fireman (*attributivo*).

Pompílio, *no.pr.m.* (*st.*) Pompilius.

pompon, *s.m.* tuft, pompom, pompon.

composaménte, *av.* pompously.

pomposità, *s.f.* pomposity, pompousness: — *di stile*, pompous style.

pompóso, *ag.* **1.** pompous: *titolo* —, pompous (o bombastic) title **2.** (*imponente, solenne*) stately: *cerimonia pomposa*, stately ceremony **3.** (*mus.*) grand, grandiose: *esecuzione pomposa*, grand performance.

pònce, *s.m.* punch: — *turco*, Turkish punch.

pòncio, *s.m.* poncho.

ponderàbile, *ag.* ponderable, weighable.

ponderabilità, *s.f.* ponderability.

ponderàre, *v.t.* to ponder, to consider, to weigh; to think over (sthg.): — *i pro e i contro di ql.co.*, to weigh the pros and cons of sthg.

ponderataménte, *av.* after reflection; after careful meditation.

ponderatézza, *s.f.* circumspection; deliberation: *un uomo di gran* —, a man of great circumspection.

ponderàto, *ag.* pondered, considered; (*circospetto*) circumspect: *risposta ponderata*, considered answer; *uomo* —, circumspect man.

ponderazióne, *s.f.* **1.** (*il ponderare*) pondering **2.** (*riflessione*) reflection, deliberation, consideration.

ponderosità, *s.f.* (*rar.*) ponderousness.

ponderóso, *ag.* ponderous.

pòndo, *s.m.* weight, burden, load (anche *fig.*).

ponènte, *s.m.* **1.** west: *a* — *di*, to the west of; *casa esposta a* —, house facing (the) west; *vento che viene da* —, westerly wind; *dirigersi verso*, *a* —, to go west; *viaggiare verso* —, to travel west **2.** (*vento*) west wind.

ponentíno, *s.m.* light west wind, westerly breeze.

ponsò, *ag.s.m.* ponceau, poppy-red, flaming red.

pónte, *s.m.* **1.** bridge: — *della ferrovia*, railway bridge; — *di barche*, bridge of boats (o pontoon-bridge); — *di pietra*, stone bridge; — *girevole*, swing bridge; — *levatoio*, drawbridge; — *mobile*, movable bridge; — *sospeso*, suspension bridge; — *stradale*, road bridge; *gettare un* —, to throw a bridge; *gettare un* — *su un fiume*, to bridge a river ‖ — *aereo*, air lift; — *radiofonico*, radio-bridge ‖ *il Ponte dei Sospiri*, the Bridge of Sighs ‖ — *dell'asino*, (*mat.*) pons asinorum (o bridge of asses) ‖ *fare il* —, (a ginnastica) to make a bridge ‖ *fare i ponti d'oro a qlcu.*, to make s.o. a very advantageous offer ‖ *rompere i ponti con qlcu.*, to break with s.o. **2.** (*impalcatura per muratori*) scaffold: — *di impalcatura*, catwalk **3.** (*mar.*) deck: — *a torri*, turret deck; — *delle lance, imbarcazioni*, boat deck; — *di atterraggio*, (*di portaerei*) flying-on deck; — *di batteria*, second deck; — *di comando*, (fore) bridge; — *di coperta*, main deck; — *di fortuna*, jury bridge; — *di lancio*, (*mar. mil.*) flying-off deck; — *di manovra*, awning deck; — *di passeggiata*, promenade deck; — *di poppa*, aft deck; — *di stiva*, lower deck; — *di vedetta*, (*mar. mil.*) look-out bridge; — *superiore*, upper deck; *a tre, quattro ponti*, three-decker, four-decker; *sul* —, on deck: *montare sul* —, to come (o to go) on deck; *sgombrare i ponti per entrare in azione* (*di guerra*), to clear the decks for action **4.** (*elett.*) bridge: — *ad alta frequenza*, high frequency bridge; — *degli isolatori*, insulator framework; — *di scanalatura*, slot bridge; — *di Wheatstone*, Wheatstone bridge; — *magnetico*, permeability bridge; *tasto di un* —, bridge-key **5.** *testa di* —, (*mil.*) bridge head **6.** (*odontoiatria*) bridge ‖ — *di Varolio*, (*anat.*) pons Varoli **7.** (*biliardo*) rest **8.** *gioco del* —, (*carte*) bridge.

pontéfice, *s.m.* **1.** (*eccl.*) pontiff: *il Sommo Pontefice*, sovereign pontiff (o the bishop of Rome o the Pope) **2.** (*st. rom.*) pontifex (*pl.* pontifices): — *massimo*, Pontifex Maximus.

ponticèllo, *s.m.* **1.** (*di strumento a corde*) bridge **2.** (*di spada*) sword-guard **3.** (*di arma da fuoco*) trigger guard **4.** (*mec. ferr.*) engine-tender fall plate.

pontière, *s.m.* (*mil.*) pontonier, pontoneer.

pontificàle, *ag. s.m.* pontifical: *messa* —, pontifical mass; *paramenti, abiti pontificali*, pontificals.

pontificalménte, *av.* pontifically.

pontificàre, *v.i.* **1.** to pontificate, to officiate as a pontiff **2.** (*iron.*) to play the pontiff, to pontificate.

pontificàto, *s.m.* pontificate.

pontifício, *ag.* papal: *benedizione pontificia*, papal benediction; *bolla pontificia*, papal bull; *corona, tiara, croce pontificia*, papal crown, tiara, cross; *l'esercito* —, the Pope's troops; *Stato Pontificio*, (*st.*) Papal States.

pontíle, *s.m.* wharf; landing-stage: — *da sbarco*, landing-wharf; — *di scarico*, unloading-wharf.

Pontíne (**Palúdi**), *no. pr. f. pl.* (*geog.*) Pontine (Marshes).

pònto, *s.m.* pontus ‖ *il Ponto Eusino*, the Euxine Sea ‖ **Pònto**, *no.pr.m.* (*geog. st.*) Pontus.

pontóne, *s.m.* pontoon: — *a biga*, shear hulk; — *a gru*, crane pontoon.

pontonière, *s.m.* pontonier, pontoneer.

ponzaménto, *s.m.* **1.** straining **2.** (*il meditare*) racking one's brains.

ponzàre, *v.i.* **1.** to make an effort, to strain **2.** (*meditare*) to rack one's brains ‖ *v.t.* to manage to produce: *ha ponzato un romanzo*, he managed to produce a novel.

ponzatúra, *s.f.* straining, effort.

Pònzio, *no.pr.m.* (*st.*) Pontius.

pòpe, *s.m.* (*eccl.*) pope.

popeline, *s.f.* (*ind. tessile*) poplin.

pòplite, *s.m.* (*anat.*) popliteus.

poplitèo, *ag.* (*anat.*) popliteal.

popolàccio, *s.m.*, **popolàglia**, *s.f.* populace, mob.

popolaménto, *s.m.* population, peopling: *favorire il* — *di una regione*, to favour the peopling (o the population) of a district.

popolàno, *ag.* of the (common) people; common, low: *abitudini popolane*, customs of the common people; *di origine popolana*, of low origin; *modo di fare* —, common manners ‖ *s.m.* man of the people ‖ *i popolani*, the common people (o populace) ‖ **popolàna**, *s.f.* woman of the people.

popolàre[1], *ag.* **1.** popular: *favore* —, popular favour; *fronte* —, (*pol.*) popular front; *governo, voto* —, popular government, vote; *sovranità* —, popular sovereignty; *rivolta* —, popular rising ‖ *il nuovo sindaco non è molto* — *fra i cittadini*, the new mayor is not very popular among the citizens; *questa canzone diventerà presto molto* —, this song will soon become very popular; *rendere* —, to popularize **2.** (*tradizionale del popolo*) folk (*attributivo*): *canto* —, folk-song; *danza, aria* —, folk-dance, folk-tune; *poesia, arte* —, folk-poetry, folk-art; *un vecchio racconto* —, an old folk-tale **3.** (*per il popolo*): *casa* —, council house; *prezzi popolari*, popular prices; *quartiere* —, working-class neighbourhood.

popolàre[2], *v.t.* to populate, to fill with people; to people (anche *fig.*): *molte fantasie popolavano la sua immaginazione*, many fantasies peopled his imagination; — *un paese*, to populate (o to people) a country ‖ **popolàrsi**, *v.r.* to become populated.

popolarésca, *s.f.* (*neol.*) folklore.

popolarescaménte, *av.* in a popular-like manner.

popolarésco, *ag.* popular-like: *scrive in modo* —, he writes in a popular-like language.

popolarità, *s.f.* popularity.

popolarizzàre, *v.t.* to popularize || **popolarizzàrsi**, *v.r.* to become popular, to become popularized.

popolarménte, *av.* popularly.

popolàto, *ag.* **1.** peopled (with sthg.); populated (with sthg.): *questo è un quartiere molto —*, this is a thickly peopled neighbourhood **2.** (*affollato*) crowded.

popolazióne, *s.f.* **1.** population; people (*coll. con costruzione pl.*): *— fluttuante*, floating population; *censimento della —*, census (of population); *la — è di 200.000 abitanti*, the population is 200,000; *la — qui è piena di iniziativa*, the people here are full of initiative **2.** (*popolo, nazione*) people: *la — germanica*, the German people; *popolazioni nordiche*, Nordic peoples.

popolàzzo, *s.m.* (*spreg.*) populace, rabble, mob.

popolíno, *s.m.* common people (*coll. con costruzione pl.*): *il — credulone*, the credulous masses.

pòpolo, *s.m.* **1.** people (*coll. con costruzione pl.*); (*plebe*) (common) people (*coll. con costruzione pl.*); lower-classes (*pl.*): *una donna del —*, a woman of the people; *figlio del —*, son of the people; *il malcontento del —*, the people's unrest; *i pregiudizi del —*, popular prejudices; *sobillatori del —*, agitators; *tra il compianto del —*, lamented by the people; *venir su dal —*, to come of humble origin || *— grasso*, rich bourgeoisie; *— minuto*, working classes || *poco —*, *poca predica*, *prov.* small congregation, short sermon **2.** (*st.*) popular republic, popular government: *il — di Firenze*, the popular republic of Florence || *Capitano del —*, Captain of the People **3.** (*folla, gente*) crowd; people (*coll. con costruzione pl.*); *piazza gremita di —*, square packed with people; *c'era gran moltitudine di —*, there were a lot of people (*o* there was a great crowd of people); *annunziare al — convenuto*, to announce to the assembled crowd || *a furor di —*, by public acclaim **4.** (*nazione*) nation, people; (*razza*) people: *— barbaro*, barbaric people; *i popoli cristiani*, Christian peoples; *— incivile*, uncivilized nation; *popoli nordici, meridionali*, Northern, Southern peoples; *il — romano*, the Roman people; *i popoli sovrani*, self-governing peoples.

popolóso, *ag.* populous, thickly populated.

poponàia, *s.f.* melon-bed.

poponàio, *s.m.* **1.** (*chi vende meloni*) melon-seller **2.** (*poponaia*) melon-bed.

popóne, *s.m.* **1.** (*bot.*) melon **2.** (*fam.*) (*gobba*) hump.

póppa¹, *s.f.* (*mar.*) stern, poop; (*di un siluro*) after-body; (*un incavo*) tunnel stern; (*sottile*) pink stern; *— tipo incrociatore*, cruiser stern; *a —*, abaft (*o* aft *o* astern); *cabina di —*, after cabin; *cassero di —*, poop deck; *da — a prua*, fore and aft; *quadro di —*, upper stern; *vento in —*, aft (*o* stern) wind: *avere il vento in —*, to sail before the wind (anche *fig.*).

póppa², *s.f.* (*anat.*) breast; (*di animale*) dug: *dare la —*, to suckle; *levare la — a un bambino*, to wean a child.

poppànte, *ag.* sucking, unweaned || *s.m.* suckling.

poppàre, *v.t.i.* to suck.

poppàta, *s.f.* **1.** (*atto del poppare*) suck: *l'ora della —*, (baby's) feeding-time; *dare la — a un bambino*, to give a baby suck **2.** (*quantità di latte poppato*) amount of milk taken by a baby at one feed.

poppatóio, *s.m.* **1.** (*bottiglia*) (feeding-)bottle **2.** (*capezzolo di gomma*) nipple.

poppavía, a, *l.av.* (*mar.*) abaft: *a — del traverso*, abaft the beam.

Poppèa, *no.pr.f.* (*st.*) Poppaea.

poppése, *s.m.* (*mar.*) stern-fast.

poppière, *s.m.* (*mar.*) stroke; strokesman (*pl.* strokesmen).

poppièro, *ag.* (*mar.*) aft (*attributivo*); after (*attributivo*); stern (*attributivo*).

poppúto, *ag.* big-breasted.

populèo, *ag.* (*letter.*) poplar (*attributivo*): *fronda populea*, poplar branch.

pòrca¹, *s.f.* (*agr.*) ridge.

pòrca², *s.f.* (*scrofa*) sow.

porcaccióne, *s.m.* swine (*invariato al pl.*).

porcàio, *s.m.* **1.** (*guardiano di porci*) swineherd **2.** (*mercante di porci*) pig-dealer **3.** (*luogo sporco*) pigsty; *fig.* (*intrigo immorale*) shady affair.

porcàro, *s.m.* swineherd.

porcellàna¹, *s.f.* **1.** china, porcelain: *articoli di —*, china(ware) (*o* porcelain); *fatto di —*, made of china; *tazza di —*, china cup **2.** (*oggetti di porcellana*) china (*-ware*) (*solo sing.*), porcelain (*solo sing.*): *una — di valore*, a valuable piece of porcelain (*o* china); *nel salotto vi erano delle porcellane di valore*, in the sitting-room there was some valuable china (*o* there were some valuable pieces of china); *queste porcellane furono comperate in Inghilterra*, this china was bought in England.

porcellàna², *s.f.* (*zool.*) cowrie.

porcellàna³, *s.f.* (*bot.*) portulaca; (*calenzuola*) spurge.

porcellanàre, *v.t.* to porcelainize.

porcellanàto, *ag.* porcelain (*attributivo*); glazed.

porcellíno, *s.m.* **1.** piglet, pigling, porkling; (*scherz.*) piggy: *una scrofa con dieci porcellini*, a sow with ten piglets || *— d'India*, Guinea-pig **2.** (*detto a un bambino*) dirty child, messy little thing; (dirty) little pig.

porcèllo, *s.m.* pig.

porcellóne, *s.m.* (*persona sporca, di mal costume*) pig; dirty fellow.

porchería, *s.f.* **1.** (*roba sporca*) dirt, filth **2.** (*azione disonesta*) swindle, dirty trick **3.** (*detto indecente*) obscene word, filthy word; (*atto indecente*) obscene act, filthy act: *dire delle porcherie*, to talk filth **4.** (*lavoro malfatto*) disgraceful piece of work **5.** (*cibo cattivo*) disgusting stuff; revolting stuff: *la minestra era una vera —*, the soup was really disgusting **6.** (*opera d'arte senza valore*) rubbish, trash.

porchétta, *s.f.* (*cuc.*) roast sucking-pig.

porcíle, *s.m.* pigsty (anche *fig.*).

porcíno, *ag.* **1.** porcine; (*pig* (*attributivo*): *carne porcina*, pork *o* *dagli occhi porcini*, pig-eyed **2.** *pan —*, (*bot. pop.*) cyclamen || *s.m.* (*bot.*) boletus.

pòrco, *ag.* horrible; horrible: *un — lavoro*, a horrible (*o* lousy) job || *porca l'oca!*, ye Gods!; *porca miseria!*, oh hell! || *s.m.* **1.** pig, hog; swine (*pl. invariato*); (*cuc.*) pork: *— selvatico*, wild boar; *arrosto di —*, roast pork; *branco di porci*, herd of swine; *carne di —*, pork; *costoletta di —*, pork-chop; *guardiano di porci*, swineherd; *pelle di —*, pig-skin || *far la vita del beato —*, to live like a lord || *gettare le perle ai porci*, to cast pearls before swine || *mangiare come un —*, to eat like a pig (*o* to gorge) **2.** *pesce —*, (*ittiol. pop.*) triggerfish.

porcospíno, *s.m.* **1.** (*zool.*) porcupine **2.** *fig.* (*persona ruvida, scontrosa*) prickly fellow.

pòrfido, *s.m.* (*min.*) porphyry.

porfíreo, porfírico, *ag.* (*min.*) porphyritic.

Porfírio, *no.pr.m.* (*st. fil.*) Porphyrius.

porfírite, *s.f.* (*min.*) porphyrite.

pòrgere, *v.t.* **1.** (*offrire*) to offer; (*dare*) to give, to pass, to hand: *mi porse la mano in segno di perdono*, he offered me his hand in token of forgiveness; *il paziente porse la mano al dottore perchè l'esaminasse*, the patient stretched out his hand so that the doctor might examine it; *porgimi quelle carte*, give me those papers; *porgimi quel libro, per favore*, pass (*o* hand) me that book, please; *— il braccio*, to offer one's arm; *— doni, preghiere*, to offer presents, prayers || *— aiuto*, to help || *— ascolto, orecchio a qlcu.*, to listen (to s.o.) (*o* to lend an ear to s.o.) || *— la guancia*, to offer one's cheek **2.** (*pronunciare, esporre*) to deliver, to present: *porgeva ogni argomento con un certo garbo*, he presented every point with a certain ease of manner || **pòrgersi**, *v.r.* (*letter.*) to offer: *quando si porgerà l'occasione*, when (the) opportunity offers (*o* arises).

pòrgere, *s.m.* delivery, presentation.

porgitóre, *s.m.*, **porgitríce**, *s.f.* bearer.

pornografía, *s.f.* pornography.

pornograficaménte, *av.* pornographically.
pornogràfico, *ag.* pornographic.
pornògrafo, *s.m.* pornographer.
pòro, *s.m.* pore.
porosità, *s.f.* porosity, porousness.
poróso, *ag.* porous.
pórpora, *s.f.* **1.** purple: *rosso* —, purple red ‖ *si fece di* — *in viso,* he became purple **2.** *(veste, autorità regia, cardinalizia)* purple **3.** *(zool.)* purple (shell) **4.** *(patol.)* purpura **5.** — *retinica, (chim. biol.)* retinal purple.
porporàto, *ag.* clothed in purple ‖ *s.m.* Cardinal.
porporeggiàre, *v.i.* *(rar.)* to be almost purple.
porporína, *s.f.* *(chim.)* purpurin.
porporíno, *ag.* purple: *labbra porporine,* purple lips.
porràta, *s.f.* *(cuc.)* **1.** *(insalata)* leek salad **2.** *(minestra)* leek soup.
pórre, *v.t.* **1.** to put; *(collocare, disporre)* to place, to set; *(posare, deporre)* to lay (down), to put (down): *egli pose il libro sul tavolo,* he put the book on the table; *egli pose il quadro sul cavalletto,* he set the picture on the easel; *fu posto al comando di un gruppo di soldati,* he was placed in command of a group of soldiers; *mi ha posto in una strana situazione,* he has placed (o put) me in an awkward situation; *mi pose una mano sulla testa,* he laid his hand on my head; *poni queste piantine ad intervalli di un metro,* set these plants at intervals of a metre; *pose i suoi documenti davanti al giudice,* he set (o laid) his documents before the judge; *pose la valigia sulla sedia,* he laid (o put) his suit-case on the chair; — *le fondamenta di una casa,* to lay the foundations of a house ‖ — *ad effetto,* to put into effect ‖ — *da parte,* to set apart (o to lay aside o to set aside) ‖ — *fiducia, speranza in qlcu.,* to place one's trust, one's hopes in s.o. ‖ — *fine a ql.co.,* to put an end to sthg.; — *freno a ql.co.,* to curb sthg. ‖ — *in evidenza, in rilievo,* to emphasize (o to stress); *(far notare)* to point out ‖ — *in non cale,* to set at nought (o to disregard) ‖ — *mano a ql.co.,* to begin sthg. ‖ — *mente a ql.co.,* to pay attention (o to give one's mind) to sthg. ‖ *por tempo in mezzo,* to lose time: *senza por tempo in mezzo,* without delay **2.** *(sottoporre)* to submit: — *all'approvazione un progetto di legge,* to submit a bill for approval **3.** *(supporre)* to suppose: *poni che egli non venga,* suppose he does not come; *poniamo il caso che...,* let us suppose that... **4.** *(imporre, assegnare)* to put, to give: — *leggi,* to give laws; — *un nome a qlcu.* to give a name to s.o. **5.** *(erigere)* to build, to erect **6.** *(piantare)* to plant: — *un terreno a olivi,* to plant a field with olives **7.** *(far covare)* — *le uova,* to put to hatch ‖ **pórsi,** *v.r.* **1.** to put oneself; *(collocarsi, disporsi)* to place oneself, to set oneself: — *a sedere,* to sit down **2.** *(accingersi)* to set about (sthg., doing): — *al lavoro,* to set to work. *(Per una più ampia esemplificazione, V.* **méttere***).*
porrína, *s.f.* *(bot.)* **1.** young chestnut-tree **2.** *(bulbo di porro)* leek bulb.
pòrro, *s.m.* **1.** *(bot.)* leek ‖ *mangiare il* — *dalla coda,* to begin the wrong way **2.** *(escrescenza)* wart.
porróso, *ag.* *(coperto di porri)* warty.
Porsènna, *no.pr.m.* *(st.)* Porsena.
pòrta, *s.f.* **1.** door: — *a vetri,* glass door; — *di soccorso,* emergency exit; — *di sicurezza,* escape door; — *finta,* blind (o false) door; — *girevole,* revolving door; — *laterale,* side door; — *principale,* front door; — *secondaria, di servizio,* back door; — *segreta,* secret door; *l'architrave, gli stipiti, i battenti della* —, the lintel, the jambs, the leaves of the door; *andammo da loro ieri, ma trovammo la* — *chiusa,* yesterday we went to see them, but found nobody at home; *chi ha lasciato la* — *aperta?,* who left the door open?; *chiudi la* —!, shut the door!; *per favore, vai ad aprire la* —, *hanno bussato,* please answer the door, there is a knock; *quella è la* —!, get out of here!; *accompagnare alla* — *qlcu.,* to see s.o. to the door; *andare, mendicare di* — *in* —, to go, to beg from door to

door; *chiudere la* — *a chiave,* to lock the door; *sbattere la* —, to slam the door ‖ *porte stagne, (mar.)* water-tight doors ‖ *a porte chiuse,* behind closed doors; *(dir.)* *in camera: il processo fu tenuto a porte chiuse,* the case was heard in camera ‖ *sistema della* — *aperta, (econ.)* open-door system ‖ *la Sublime Porta, (st.)* the Sublime Porte ‖ *vena* —, *(anat.)* portal vein ‖ *il denaro apre tutte le porte,* money opens all doors ‖ *per lui si aprono le porte dell'alta società,* he has the entrée to high society ‖ *mettere qlcu. alla porta,* to throw s.o. out ‖ *mostrare la* — *a qlcu.,* to show s.o. the door ‖ *prendere la* —, to make for the door (o to make off) ‖ *sfondare una* — *aperta,* to flog a dead horse ‖ *non si serra mai una* — *che non se ne apra un'altra,* prov. God never shuts one door but he opens another **2.** *(di città, di mura, ecc.)* gate: *le porte di una città, di un tempio, di un castello,* the gates of a town, of a temple, of a castle ‖ — *decumana, (st. romana)* decuman gate ‖ *le porte dell'inferno,* the gates of Hell ‖ *la Porta Pinciana,* the Pincian Gate ‖ *fuori di* —, on the edge of town: *vive fuori* —, he lives just outside the town ‖ *il nemico era alle porte,* the enemy were at the gates **3.** *pl.* *(battenti)* leaves **4.** *fig.* *(ingresso)* door, admission: *dare, vietare la* — *a qlcu.,* to grant, to refuse admission to s.o. **5.** *(geog.)* *(passo)* pass: *le porte d'Italia,* the passes of Italy ‖ *le Porte di Ferro,* the Iron Gates **6.** *(calcio)* goal.
portabagàgli, *s.m.* **1.** luggage-rack **2.** *(facchino)* porter **3.** *(aut.)* luggage-rack, boot.
portabandièra, *s.m.* ensign.
portàbile, *ag.* portable.
portacappèlli, *s.m.* hat-box.
portacàrte, *s.m.* paper-holder.
portacatíno, *s.m.* wash-stand.
portacénere, *s.m.* ash-tray.
portacípria, *s.m.* powder-compact.
portàcqua, *s.m.* water-bearer.
portadólci, *s.m.* cake dish; cake jar; cake tin.
portaèrei, *s.f.* *(mar.)* aircraft-carrier: — *di scorta,* escort carrier.
portaferíti, *s.m.* *(mil.)* stretcher-bearer.
portafiammíferi, *s.m.* match-box, match-holder.
portafiàschi, *s.m.* bottle-rack.
portafiòri, *s.m.* flower-holder; *(giardiniera)* flower-stand; *(vaso)* (flower-)vase.
portafògli, *s.m.* wallet, pocket-book, note-case: *un bel* — *di coccodrillo,* a fine crocodile wallet (o pocket-book) ‖ *alleggerire qlcu. del* —, to pick s.o.'s pocket ‖ *metter mano al* —, to put one's hand in one's pocket.
portafòglio, *s.m.* **1.** *(pol.)* portfolio; *(carica ministeriale)* portfolio, ministerial office: *ministro senza* —, minister without portfolio; *gli daranno il* — *degli Interni,* he will be appointed Home Secretary **2.** *(giornale di)* —, *(in banca)* discount register: *cambiali, effetti in* —, bills on hand **3.** *V.* **portafògli.**
portafortúna, *s.m.* mascot.
portagiòie, portagioièlli, *s.m.* jewel-case.
portainségna, *s.m.* *(mil.)* ensign.
portalàmpada, *s.m.* lamp-holder, bulb socket: — *a baionetta,* bayonet-type lamp-holder; — *con chiavetta,* key-type bulb socket; — *micromignon,* miniature lamp-holder; — *normale passo Edison,* medium lamp-holder with Edison screw.
portalàpis, *s.m.* pencil-holder.
portàle, *s.m.* portal; doorway.
portalégna, *s.m.* **1.** wood carrier **2.** *(cassetta per la legna)* wood box.
portalèttere, *s.m.* postman *(pl.* postmen).
portamantèllo, *s.m.* portmanteau, valise.
portaménto, *s.m.* **1.** gait, carriage, bearing: *un* — *aggraziato,* a graceful carriage; — *goffo,* awkward gait (o carriage); *nobile* —, noble (o lofty) bearing **2.** *(condotta)* behaviour, conduct: *ottenne un premio per i suoi buoni portamenti,* he got a prize for good behaviour **3.** — *della voce, (mus.)* portamento.

portamonéte, *s.m.* purse.
portampólle. *s.m.* cruet-stand, cruets (*pl.*).
portamúsica, *s.m.* music-stand.
portànte, *ag.* 1. *un vecchio ben —,* a well preserved old man 2. (*scienza delle costruzioni*) load bearing 3. *piano —,* (*aer.*) plane ‖ *s.m.* (*ambio*) amble ‖ *s.f.* (*cavo*) cable.
portantína, *s.f.* sedan-chair.
portantíno, *s.m.* chairman (*pl.* chairmen).
portànza, *s.f.* 1. (*portata*) carrying capacity 2. (*aer.*) lift: *— aerodinamica,* aerodynamic lift; *— statica,* static lift; *— totale,* total lift; *perdita di —,* lift loss.
portaombrèlli, *s.m.* umbrella-stand.
portaórdini, *s.m.* messenger.
portaoròlogio, *s.m.* watch-stand.
portapàcchi, *s.m.* carrier.
portapénne, *s.m.* penholder.
portaprànzi, *s.m.* hamper; hay-box.
portàre, *v.t.* 1. (*verso chi parla, ascolta*) to bring; (*andare a prendere*) to fetch: *portami un bicchier d'acqua,* bring me a glass of water; *portami i libri che ho lasciato sul tavolo,* fetch me the books I left on the table; *questo vento porterà pioggia,* this wind will bring rain; *spero mi porterai buone notizie,* I hope you'll bring me good news; *ti porto una tazza di tè?,* shall I bring you a cup of tea?; *— dentro, fuori, su, giù,* to bring in, out, up, down ‖ *devo — in tavola?,* shall I serve the dinner? ‖ *questo ti porterà fortuna!,* this will bring you good luck! ‖ *— acqua al proprio mulino,* to bring grist to one's mill 2. (*lontano da chi parla; accompagnare*) to take: *mi porti al cinema questa sera?,* will you take me to the pictures tonight?; *porta questa lettera a mio fratello, alla posta,* take this letter to my brother, to the post; *porta questo vassoio in camera sua,* take this tray to his room; *il suo cappello fu portato via dal vento,* his hat blew off; *ti porterò a casa in automobile,* I'll drive you home; *ti porterò a passeggio,* I'll take you for a walk; *— dentro, fuori, su, giù,* to take in, out, up, down ‖ *che il diavolo ti porti!,* go to the devil! ‖ *fu portato via da un male incurabile,* he was carried off by an incurable disease ‖ *questo lavoro porta via un bel po' di tempo,* this work takes quite a long while 3. (*portare con fatica, sostenere; portare con sè; portare d'abitudine*) to carry: *mio nonno porta il bastone quando esce,* my grand-father carries a walking-stick when he goes out; *ognuno portava con sè i propri libri,* everybody carried his own books; *porta di sopra questo baule,* carry this trunk upstairs; *porto sempre il borsellino nella borsetta,* I always carry my purse in my bag; *questo mulo può facilmente — oltre un quintale,* this mule can easily carry two hundredweight; *— a braccia qlcu.,* to carry s.o. in one's arms; *— qlcu. in trionfo,* to carry s.o. in triumph; *— una valigia sulle spalle,* to carry a suit-case on one's shoulders ‖ *ognuno ha la propria croce da —,* everyone has his own cross to bear ‖ *quell'uomo porta bene i suoi anni,* that man doesn't look his age ‖ *— qlcu. alle stelle,* to praise s.o. to the skies ‖ *— qlcu. in palmo di mano,* to hold s.o. in great esteem (*o* to have a high opinion of s.o.) ‖ *— vasi a Samo, acqua al mare,* to carry coals to Newcastle 4. (*condurre*) to lead: *questa strada porta all'albergo,* this road leads to the hotel; *— i buoi all'abbeveratoio, al pascolo,* to lead the oxen to the trough, to pasture ‖ *il benessere sociale portò a questa situazione,* social welfare led to this situation ‖ *sono portato a credere che...,* I'm inclined to believe that... ‖ *— un piano a compimento,* to carry out a plan ‖ *— qlcu. a conoscenza di ql.co.,* to bring sthg. to s.o.'s knowledge ‖ *— qlcu. a parlare,* to induce s.o. to speak ‖ *tutte le strade portano a Roma,* *prov.* all roads lead to Rome 5. (*indossare, avere*) to wear, to have on, to be dressed in (sthg.): *ella portava un meraviglioso vestito,* she was dressed in a wonderful gown; *portava un paio di scarpe bianche,* she was wearing a pair of white shoes; *— i capelli lunghi, corti,* to wear one's

hair long, short (*o* to have long, short hair); *— un fiore all'occhiello,* to wear a flower in one's button -hole; *— occhiali, gioielli,* to wear glasses, jewels; *un soprabito, un cappello,* to wear an overcoat, a hat; *— il lutto,* to wear mourning 6. (*nutrire*) to nourish, to bear: *— odio,* to nourish feelings of hatred; *— rancore verso qlcu.,* to bear s.o. a grudge; *— speranze,* to nourish hopes 7. (*causare*) to cause, to bring forth: *questo cattivo tempo porterà molte malattie,* this bad weather will cause a lot of illness; *la sua assenza mi ha portato molto danno,* his absence has done me a lot of harm 8. (*produrre*) to bear, to bring forth, to yield, to produce: *il melo non porterà nessun frutto quest'anno,* the apple-tree will not bear any fruit this year 9. (*avere*) to bear, to have: *questa lettera porta una data sbagliata,* this letter is wrongly dated; *questo documento porta una firma falsa,* this document bears a false signature; *il suo libro porta uno strano titolo,* his book has a strange title ‖ *— rispetto a qlcu.,* to have respect for s.o. 10. (*sopportare*) to bear, to endure: *egli porta la sua pena con molto coraggio,* he bears his pain very bravely ‖ *non porta bene il vino,* he can't hold his drink ‖ *non porta la spesa,* it's not worth it 11. (*addurre*) to bring forward, to put forward: *— prove, buone ragioni, un esempio,* to bring (*o* to put) forward proofs, good reasons, an example 12. (*stimare*) to have a high opinion of (s.o., sthg.); to esteem highly: *è molto portato dai suoi insegnanti,* his teachers have a high opinion of him 13. (*arit.*) (*riportare*) to carry: *scrivo 5 e porto 3,* I put down 5 and carry 3 14. (*aver la portata di*) to have a range of (sthg.): *questo cannone porta dieci miglia,* this gun has a range of ten miles ‖ **portàrsi**, *v.r.* 1. (*spostarsi*) to move: *dovresti portarti a destra,* you should move to the right 2. (*andare*) to go; (*venire*) to come: *cercherò di portarmi a Roma al più presto,* I'll try to come, to go to Rome as soon as possible; *dovresti portarti in città verso mezzogiorno,* you should be in town around noon 3. (*portare con sè*) to carry; to take with one: *mi sono portato due valigie e un baule,* I took two suit-cases and a trunk with me; *non mi porto mai l'ombrello,* I never carry an umbrella 4. (*comportarsi*) to behave: *— bene, male,* to behave well, badly.
portaritràtti, *s.m.* photograph-frame.
portarocchétto, *s.m.* (*ind. tessile*) reel stick.
portasapóne, *s.m.* soap-dish; (*per sapone liquido*) liquid soap container.
portasigarétte, *s.m.* cigarette-case.
portasígari, *s.m.* cigar-case.
portaspazzatúra, *s.m.* dust-bin, dust-pan.
portaspílli, *s.m.* pincushion.
portastécchi, **portastecchíni**, *s.m.* tooth-pick -holder.
portastendàrdo, *s.m.* standard-bearer.
portàta, *s.f.* 1. (*di pranzo*) course: *un pranzo di cinque portate,* a five-course dinner 2. (*di arma da fuoco*) range; (*di strumento ottico*) range, reach; (*rad.*) (*di microfono*) beam: *la — di un fucile, di un cannone,* the range of a rifle, a gun; *— luminosa,* (*di segnale*) light range; *fucile a lunga —,* long-range rifle; *fuori —,* out of range; *fig.* out of reach ‖ *a — di mano, d'orecchio, di voce,* within reach, hearing, call; *il prezzo è alla — di tutti,* the price is within everybody's reach 3. (*stazza*) tonnage; burden; (*di automezzo, bilancia*) capacity; (*di ponte, tetto*) capacity; (*di gru*) capacity; lifting, hoisting power: *— di una nave,* tonnage of a ship; *— lorda,* (*mar.*) dead-weight capacity; *— massima,* maximum capacity (*abbr.* max. cap.) 4. (*di fiume*) flow; (*di pompa*) delivery capacity: *— al secondo,* flow per second 5. *fig.* (*importanza*) importance, significance, purport: *uomo di grande —,* man of great importance; *non si rende conto dell'— della questione,* he does not realize the significance of the matter 6. *fig.* (*capacità*) capacity; reach; (*livello*) level: *un oratore deve mettersi alla — dei suoi ascol-*

tatori, a speaker must adapt himself to his audience; *questo problema va ul di là dclla mia* —, this problem is beyond my capacity; *i suoi allievi sono tutti alla stessa* —, *più o meno*, his pupils are all more or less at the same level.

portàtile, *ag.* portable: *una macchina da scrivere*, *un telefono* —, a portable typewriter, telephone || *armi portatili*, small arms.

portàto, *ag.* 1. brought; taken; carried 2. (*di abito*) worn 3. (*predisposto, inclinato*) given, inclined, disposed: *è molto* — *alle lingue straniere*, he has a penchant for foreign languages; *non ci sono* —, I have no talent for it; *sono* — *a credere che...*, I am disposed to believe that...; *essere* — *a dimenticare*, to be apt to forget; *essere* — *alla collera*, to be prone to anger || *s.m.* (*risultato, effetto, conseguenza*) result, effect.

portatóre, *s.m.* 1. (*chi porta*) bearer: — *di fiaccola*, torch-bearer 2. (*comm.*) holder; bearer: — *di un'azione*, shareholder; — *di un'obbligazione*, bondholder; *assegno al* —, bearer cheque; *azione al* —, bearer share (*o* unregistered share); *pagabile al* —, payable to bearer || **portatríce**, *s.f.* bearer, holder.

portatúra, *s.f.* bearing.

portauòvo, *s.m.* egg-cup.

portavivànde, *s.m.* dumb-waiter; (*sl. amer.*) lazy Susan.

portavóce, *s.m.* 1. (*megafono*) speaking-trumpet, megaphone 2. (*citofono*) speaking-tube 3. *fig.* mouthpiece, spokesman (*pl.* spokesmen): *essere il* — *di qlcu.*, to be the mouthpiece (*o* spokesman) of s.o.

portèlla, *s.f.* door: — *della stufa*, stove door.

portellíno, *s.m.* (*mar.*) porthole.

portèllo, *s.m.* (*mar.*) shutter, port: — *di boccaporto*, hatch; — *di carico*, raft-port.

portènto, *s.m.* prodigy, miracle; wonder, marvel: *i portenti della natura, della scienza*, the wonders (*o* the marvels) of nature, of science; *fare, operare portenti*, to work wonders (*o* miracles) || *essere un* —, to be a prodigy: *è un* — *di sapienza*, he is a miracle (*o* prodigy) of learning; *questo bambino è un* —*!*, this child is a prodigy!.

portentosaménte, *av.* prodigiously, miraculously; wonderfully, marvellously: *fu* — *guarito in poche ore*, he was miraculously cured in a few hours.

portentóso, *ag.* prodigious, miraculous; wonderful, marvellous: *guarigione portentosa*, miraculous recovery; *ha una memoria portentosa*, he has a prodigious (*o* wonderful *o* marvellous) memory.

portería, *s.f.* porter's lodge.

porticàto, *s.m.* arcade || *il* — *del Bernini*, Bernini's colonnade.

pòrtico, *s.m.* 1. (*loggia*) porch, portico; (*porticato*) arcade: *c'è un piccolo* — *davanti all'ingresso della nostra casa*, there is a small porch at the entrance to our house; *c'è sempre un mendicante sotto il* — *del tempio*, there is always a beggar under the portico of the temple; *c'è tanta gente a passeggio sotto i portici di Via Roma*, there are many people walking under the arcades of Via Roma; *la piazza è circondata da portici*, the square is surrounded by arcades 2. (*nelle case rurali*) shed: *il* — *serve per riparo di carri e attrezzi*, the shed is used for carts and tools.

portièra, *s.f.* 1. (*portinaia*) porter, door-keeper 2. (*di automobile*) door: *assicurati che la* — *sia ben chiusa*, make sure the door is shut 3. (*tenda su una porta*) door-curtain || *non c'è* — *per lui*, he has the entrée.

portieràto, *s.m.* 1. (*ufficio del portiere*) porterage 2. (*salario corrisposto al portiere*) porter's fee.

portière, *s.m.* 1. porter, concierge: *chiedi al* — *a che piano abita il signor X*, ask the concierge which floor Mr. X lives on; *non dimenticare di dare una mancia al* — *prima di lasciare l'albergo*, before leaving the hotel don't forget to tip the porter 2. (*spor.*) goal-keeper.

portinàia, *s.f.* porter, concierge, door-keeper.

portinàio, *V.* **portière** 1.

portinería, *s.f.* porter's lodge: *è vietato sostare in* —, it is forbidden to loiter in the porter's lodge; *in questa casa non c'è* —, there is no porter in this house.

pòrto[1], *s.m.* 1. port; harbour; (*letter.*) haven: — *d'entrata*, port of entry; — *di destinazione*, *d'imbarco*, *di scarico*, port of destination, of loading, of discharge; *il* — *di Napoli, di Londra*, the port of Naples, of London; — *di mare*, seaport; — *di partenza*, *d'armamento*, home port; — *di scalo*, port of call; — *fluviale*, river-port; — *interno*, inner harbour; — *militare*, naval port (*o* naval base); *un* — *naturale*, *artificiale*, a natural, artificial harbour; — *sicuro*, safe harbour; *capitaneria di* —, harbour master's office; *capitano di* —, harbour master; *diritti di* —, harbour dues; *entrare in* —, to come into port (*o* to enter harbour); *essere in* —, to be in port; *fig.* to have reached one's goal; *fare scalo a un* —, to call at a port || — *franco*, free port || *la loro casa è un* — *di mare*, they are running a hotel || *condurre in* —, *fig.* to accomplish (*o* to carry out): *voglio condurre in* — *tutti i miei piani*, I want to carry out all my plans 2. *fig.* (*rifugio, asilo*) haven, harbour, port: *un* — *di pace*, a haven of rest.

pòrto[2], *s.m.* 1. (*trasporto*) carriage: — *assegnato*, carriage forward; *franco di* —, carriage paid; *il* — *di queste merci sarà molto alto*, the carriage on these goods will be very high 2. (*licenza, permesso*) licence: — *d'armi*, shooting licence 3. (*francatura di lettere, pacchi*) postage.

pòrto[3], *s.m.* (*vino*) port (kind of dark-red wine of Portugal).

Portogàllo[1], *no.pr.m.* (*geog.*) Portugal.

portogàllo[2], *s.m.* (*dial.*) orange.

portoghése, *ag.* Portuguese || *s.c.* 1. Portuguese (*invariato al pl.*) 2. (*gergo teatrale*) gate-crasher || *s.m.* (*lingua*) (the) Portuguese (language).

portolàno, *s.m.* (*mar.*) portolano (*pl.* portolanos, portolani); book of sailing directions, pilot's book.

portombrèlli, *s.m.* umbrella-stand.

portóne, *s.m.* main door, main gate.

portoricàno, *ag. s.m.* Puerto Rican.

Portoríco, *no.pr.m.* (*geog.*) Puerto Rico.

portuàle, portuàrio, *ag.* harbour (*attributivo*): *città* —, port; *consorzio* —, harbour-board; *diritti portuari*, harbour-dues || *s.m.* docker.

portuóso, *ag.* 1. (*ricco di porti*) having many harbours 2. (*che offre possibilità di scalo*) affording harbourage.

Pòrzia, *no.pr.f.* (*st.*) Portia.

porzióne, *s.f.* 1. portion, part, share: *in porzioni uguali*, in equal parts; *la* — *di eredità che toccherà agli eredi*, the portion (of inheritance) that will devolve upon the heirs; *ho avuto la mia* — *di dolori*, I have had my share of worries 2. (*di cibo*) helping, portion: *gradiresti un'altra* — *di budino?*, would you like another helping of pudding?; *ordinò due porzioni di verdura*, he ordered two helpings of vegetables; *si fece portare un'altra* — *di carne*, he had a second helping of meat.

pòsa, *s.f.* 1. (*il porre*) laying, placing: *la* — *della prima pietra*, the laying of the foundation-stone; *la* — *di un cavo, di una mina*, the laying of a cable, of a mine 2. (*il posare per un ritratto*) sitting: *fare un ritratto in tre pose*, to paint a portrait in three sittings; *mettersi in* —, to sit 3. (*posizione*) posture, attitude: *una* — *sguaiata*, a slovenly posture; *una* — *solenne*, a solemn attitude 4. (*pausa*) pause, stop; (*riposo*) rest; (*mus.*) pause: *senza* — incessantly (*o* ceaselessly); *non avere, trovare* —, to have, to find no rest 5. (*atteggiamento non spontaneo*) pose: *il suo amore per la campagna è solo una* —, his love for the country is only a pose 6. (*foto.*) exposure: *tempo di* —, time-exposure; *quante pose puoi fare?*, how many exposures can you take? 7. (*accento*) accent, stress: *la* — *è sulla seconda sillaba*, the stress (*o* accent) is on the second syllable.

posacénere, *s.m.* ash-tray.
posafèrro, *s.m.* iron-stand.
posaménto, *s.m.* placing, laying, setting.
posamíne, *s.m.* (*mar.*) mine-layer.
posamòlle, *s.m.* tongs stand.
posaombrèlli, *s.m.* umbrella-stand.
posapiàno, *s.c.* (*scherz.*) slow-coach.

posàre, *v.t.* to put (down), to lay (down); (*appoggiare*) to rest; (*collocare*) to place: *mi posò la mano sulla spalla,* he laid his hand on my shoulder; *non devi — il gomito sul tavolo,* you must not rest your elbow on the table; *non so dove — queste carte,* I do not know where to put these papers; *posa il bambino e vieni con me,* lay the baby down and come with me; *posa il cappello ed entra,* put your hat down and come in; *posò il martello per terra,* he laid the hammer on the floor; *posso — i piedi sul cuscino?,* may I rest my feet on the cushion?; *posare un cavo, una mina,* to lay a cable, a mine ‖ *— gli occhi su ql.co.,* to lay one's eyes on sthg. ‖ *v.i.* **1.** (*aver fondamento*) to rest, to stand; *fig.* to be based: *la colonna, la statua posa su un piedistallo,* the column, the statue rests (o stands) on a pedestal; *il tetto posa su quattro colonne,* the roof rests on four pillars; *il tuo ragionamento non posa su dati di fatto,* your reasoning is not based on facts **2.** (*restare immobile in un atteggiamento, per un ritratto, ecc.*) to pose, to sit: *devo — ancora quattro volte per quel ritratto,* I have to sit four times more for that portrait; *quell'artista voleva che posassi per lui,* that artist wanted me to pose for him **3.** (*prendere un atteggiamento non spontaneo*) to pose: *gli piace — a vittima,* he likes to pose as a victim; *non poso a sapiente,* I do not claim to be (o I do not set up for) a scholar **4.** (*di liquido, far posatura*) to stand, to settle: *bisogna lasciar — il vino prima di travasarlo,* we must let the wine stand before decanting it **5.** (*fermarsi*) to stay, to stop; (*riposare*) to rest: *non ha dove —,* he has not a place where to stay ‖ **posàrsi,** *v.r.* **1.** (*di cosa, animale che cali dall'alto*) to alight, to settle; (*appollaiarsi*) to perch; (*aer.*) to land, to alight: *l'elicottero si posò su una radura,* the helicopter landed in a clearing; *la neve cadeva sulle vette dei monti,* the snow was settling on the peaks of the mountains; *la polvere si posa su ogni cosa,* dust settles on everything; *la rondine si posò sul ramo,* the swallow perched on the branch; *l'uccello si posò sul tetto,* the bird alighted on the roof **2.** (*ristare*) to stay, to rest: *non so dove posarmi,* I do not know where to rest ‖ *i suoi occhi si posarono sul ritratto di suo padre,* his eyes rested on his father's portrait **3.** (*di accento*) to fall.

posàta¹, *s.f.* **1.** (*coltello*) knife; (*forchetta*) fork; (*cucchiaio*) spoon: *posate d'argento,* silver service **2.** (*coperto*) cover: *aggiungi una —,* lay one cover more.

posàta², *s.f.* **1.** stop; (*mil.*) halt **2.** (*di uccelli*) resting-place, stopping-place **3.** (*sedimento*) sediment; dregs (*pl.*).

posataménte, *av.* staidly, sedately, composedly; (*con calma*) calmly, quietly.

posatería, *s.f.* cutlery.

posatézza, *s.f.* staidness, sedateness, composure; (*calma*) calm, quietness.

posàto, *ag.* staid, sedate; (*calmo*) calm, quiet: *una persona posata,* a staid person.

posatóio, *s.m.* perch.

posatóre, *s.m.,* **posatríce,** *s.f.* poseur, affected person, attitudinizer: *che —!,* doesn't he put it on!.

posatúra, *s.f.* sediment; dregs (*pl.*).

posbèllico, *ag.* post-war (*attributivo*).

pòscia, *av.* (*letter.*) then ‖ **pòscia che,** *l. cong.* (*letter.*) after: *— ch'io v'ebbi alcun riconosciuto...,* after I had recognized some amongst them....

poserítto, *s.m.* postscript (*abbr.* P.S.).

posdatàre, *v.t.* to postdate.

posdatàto, *ag.* postdated.

posdomàni, *av.* the day after tomorrow.

poseur, *s.m.* poseur, affected person, attitudinizer:

che — !, doesn't he put it on!; *è un poco —,* he is rather affected (o he is a bit of a poseur).

Posidóne, *no.pr.m.* (*mit.*) Poseidon.

positíva, *ag. s.f.* (*foto.*) positive.

positivaménte, *av.* positively.

positivísmo, *s.m.* (*st. fil.*) positivism.

positivísta, *s.c.* (*fil.*) positivist.

positività, *s.f.* positivity, positiveness.

positívo, *ag.* **1.** positive: *aggettivo —,* (*gram.*) positive adjective; *grado —,* (*gram.*) positive degree; *numero —,* (*mat.*) positive number; *polo —,* (*elett.*) positive pole; *segno —,* (*mat.*) positive sign **2.** (*favorevole*) positive: *atteggiamento —,* positive attitude; *un giudizio —,* a positive judgment **3.** (*effettivo, reale*) positive, real, actual; (*certo, sicuro*) certain, sure: *conoscenza positiva,* positive knowledge; *fatto —,* real (o actual) fact; *informazioni, notizie positive,* certain (o sure) information, news; *è — che...,* it is certain that...; *non ho prove positive,* I have no positive proofs; *dare un ordine —,* to give a positive order ‖ *di —,* for certain: *lo so di —,* I know it for certain **4.** (*opposto a naturale*): *filosofia positiva,* positive philosophy; *leggi positive,* positive laws; *scienze positive,* positive sciences **5.** (*pratico*) practical, matter-of-fact: *una persona positiva,* a matter-of-fact (o practical) person ‖ *s.m.* reality, the positive, the real.

positóne, *s.m.* (*fis.*) positron.

positúra, *s.f.* **1.** (*posa*) posture **2.** (*posizione*) position.

posizióne, *s.f.* **1.** position (anche *fig.*); (*sito*) situation: *— verticale,* vertical position; *la — di un oggetto, di un quadro,* the position of an object, of a picture; *la — di questa villa è meravigliosa,* the situation of this villa is wonderful **2.** (*positura*) position: *la — della testa, del corpo,* the position of the head, of the body; *era seduto in una — molto scomoda,* he was sitting in a very uncomfortable position; *mettersi in — comoda,* to make oneself comfortable **3.** (*atteggiamento*) position, attitude: *la mia — di fronte ad un problema,* my attitude to a problem; *assumere una — ben definita riguardo ad una questione,* to adopt (o to take up) a definite position regarding a matter ‖ *prendere —,* (*in una contesa*) to take sides **4.** (*condizione, situazione*) position, standing: *— sociale,* social standing; *faremo l'inventario per vedere qual è la nostra —,* we are going to take stock to see how we stand; *sono in una — imbarazzante,* I am in an embarassing position; *un uomo nella sua — dovrebbe comportarsi diversamente,* a man in his position (o of his standing) should behave differently; *voglio definire la mia — al più presto,* I want to define my position as soon as possible **5.** (*posto*) position: *ha una bellissima — in banca,* he has a very good position in a bank ‖ *farsi una —,* to acquire a position **6.** (*gram. mil. mus.*) position **7.** (*fil.*) (*proposizione*) position.

poslimínio, *s.m.* (*dir. romano*) postliminy.

poslúdio, *s.m.* (*mus.*) postlude.

posolíno, *s.m.* (*equitazione*) crupper.

posología, *s.f.* **1.** (*med.*) posology **2.** (*nella indicazione dei medicinali*) dosage.

posponiménto, *s.m.* postponement.

pospórre, *v.t.* **1.** to place (sthg.) after (anche *fig.*): *pospone la virtù alla ricchezza,* he places virtue after wealth **2.** (*posticipare*) to postpone, to put off, to defer: *dovette — il suo viaggio in America per malattia,* he was obliged to defer his trip to America because of ill-health.

pospositívo, *ag.* postpositive.

posposizióne, *s.f.* postponement.

pospósto, *ag.* postponed.

pòssa, *s.f.* (*letter.*) power, strength, vigour, might: *a tutta —,* with all one's might.

possànza, *s.f.* (*letter.*) power, strength, vigour, might.

possedére, *v.t.* **1.** (*avere in possesso*) to possess, to be in possession of (sthg.): *possediamo già alcuni dati riguardanti la produzione di quest'anno,* we are already in possession of date regarding this year's production; *possiede una memoria prodigiosa*, he has a wonderful memory; *dovette vendere tutto ciò che possedeva*, he was obliged to sell all he possessed; *non possiede nessuna buona qualità*, he has (o possesses) no good qualities; *le Potenze europee possedevano la maggior parte dell'Africa*, the European powers possessed (o owned) most of Africa; — *case, ricchezze, una tenuta*, to own (o to possess) houses, wealth, an estate **2.** (*prendere possesso di*) to possess, to take possession of (s.o., sthg.): *essere posseduto da una passione, da uno spirito maligno*, to be possessed by a passion, by an evil spirit ‖ — *una donna*, to possess (o to enjoy) a woman **3.** (*conoscere a fondo*) to have a mastery of (sthg.), to have a good knowledge of (sthg.): — *una lingua*, to have a good knowledge of a language (o to have a language at one's finger-tips).

possediménto, *s.m.* **1.** (*il possedere, la cosa posseduta*) possession: *tutti i miei possedimenti sono alla banca*, all my possessions are in the bank **2.** (*proprietà, specialmente immobiliare*) estate; property: *egli ha vasti possedimenti nel Sud*, he has a large estate in the South; *ho un piccolo* — *in campagna*, I have a small property in the country **3.** (*pol.*) possession: *i possedimenti europei in Asia*, the European possessions in Asia; — *coloniale*, colony.

posseditóre, *s.m.*, **posseditríce**, *s.f.* possessor, owner; (*di lingua, disciplina*) master.

posseduto, *ag.* owned, possessed: — *dal demonio*, possessed by the devil ‖ *s.m.* demoniac, person possessed.

possènte, *ag.* powerful ‖ *s.m.* powerful person.

possentemènte, *av.* powerfully.

possessióne, *s.f.* **1.** (*proprietà, specialmente immobiliare*) estate, property **2.** (*il possedere*) possession, ownership.

possessivaménte, *av.* possessively.

possessívo, *ag.* possessive (anche *gram.*): *un amore* —, a possessive love; *genitivo* —, possessive case; *pronome, aggettivo* —, possessive pronoun, adjective ‖ *s.m.* (*gram.*) possessive.

possèsso, *s.m.* **1.** possession; ownership: *appena posso prendere* — *di quel denaro faccio un viaggio a Parigi*, as soon as I can get hold of that money, I will take a trip to Paris; *come sei venuto in* — *di questo libro?*, how did you come by this book?; *il libro è in suo* —, the book is in his possession; *quell'uomo è in* — *di importanti informazioni*, that man is in possession of important information; *entrare in* — *di un'eredità*, to enter into possession of an inheritance; *prendere* — *di ql.co.*, to take possession of sthg.; *rientrare in* — *di ql.co.*, to regain possession of sthg.; *venire in* — *di una grande proprietà*, to come into possession of a large estate ‖ *presa di* —, taking possession ‖ *era nel pieno* — *delle sue facoltà mentali*, he was in full possession of his mental faculties **2.** (*dir.*) possession: — *legittimo*, lawful possession **3.** (*proprietà, specialmente immobiliare*) estate; property **4.** (*di lingua, disciplina*) mastery.

possessóre, *s.m.* possessor: (*proprietario*) owner; (*detentore*) holder.

possessòrio, *ag.* (*dir.*) possessory: *azione possessoria*, possessory action ‖ *s.m.* (*dir.*) possessory judgement.

possíbile, *ag.* possible: — *a tutti*, possible to everybody; *è* — *farlo*, it is possible to do it; *è ancora* — *che venga*, he may still come (o it is still possible that he will come); *non credo mi sarà* — *essere qui*, I do not think it will be possible for me to be here; *questa è una proposta* —, this is a possible proposal; *questo è possibilissimo ma non ci credo*, this is very possible but I do not believe it; *questo non mi è* —, I can't possibly do it ‖ — *!*, can it be possible! ‖ — *che tu non mi voglia aiutare!*, is it possible that you don't want to help me? ‖ *al più presto* —, as soon as possible ‖ *il più, il meno* —, as much, as little as possible ‖ *s.m.* possible: *fare tutto il* —, to do everything possible (o to do one's best o to do all one can).

possibilísmo, *s.m.* possibilism.

possibilísta, *ag.s.c.* possibilist.

possibilità, *s.f.* **1.** possibility; power: *la* — *di fare ql.co.*, the possibility of doing (o to do) sthg.; *non è nella mia* — *di farlo*, it is not within my power to do it; *questo va al di là delle sue* —, this goes beyond his powers; *dare a qlcu. la* — *di fare ql.co.*, to enable s.o. to do sthg. (o to give s.o. the possibility of doing sthg.); *essere nella* — *di fare ql.co.*, to be in a position to do sthg. **2.** *gener. pl.*: — (*finanziarie*), means (*pl.*): *le mie* — *sono limitate*, my means are limited **3.** (*probabilità*) possibility; probability: *la* — *di un insuccesso*, the possibility of a failure; — *favorevole*, favourable odds; *pensando alla* — *di fare ql.co.*, with a view to doing sthg.; *ci sono molte* — *in questo campo*, there are many possibilities in this field; *non c'è nessuna* — *che venga*, there is no possibility of his coming.

possibilménte, *av.* if possible.

possidènte, *ag.* property-owning; (*di terre*) land-owning ‖ *s.c.* property-owner; (*di terre*) land-owner: *grande, piccolo, ricco* —, large, small, rich land-owner.

possidènza, *s.f.* **1.** property; (*tenuta*) estate **2.** (*ceto dei proprietari*) property-owning class.

pòsta, *s.f.* **1.** post, mail: — *aerea*, air mail; — *in arrivo, partenza*, inward, outward mail; — *pneumatica*, pneumatic dispatch (o post); *a giro di* —, by return of post; *per* —, by post (o mail); *spedire per* —, to post (o to mail); *spese di* —, postage; *la* — *non viene distribuita la domenica*, there is no post on Sundays; *ho ricevuto molta* — *oggi*, I received a lot of mail (o letters) today; *non c'è* — *per voi*, there are no letters (o there is no post) for you; *ora si distribuisce la* —, there is a delivery now; *spero di essere in tempo per la* — *del mattino*, I hope to be in time for the morning post; *tutta la* — *su questo treno fu rubata*, all the mail on this train was stolen **2.** (*ufficio postale*) post(-office): — *centrale*, *ufficio centrale delle poste*, General Post Office (*abbr.* G.P.O.); *direttore delle poste*, post-master; *impiegato delle poste*, post-office clerk; *devo portare queste lettere alla* —, I must take these letters to the post(-office) ‖ *Poste e Telegrafi*, postal and telegraph services ‖ *fermo* (*in*) —, poste restante **3.** (*al giuoco, in una scommessa*) stake(s): *raddoppiare la* —, to double the stake(s) **4.** (*posto determinato, assegnato*) (*di cacciatore*) position; (*di sentinella*) post: *ordinare le poste*, (*disporre le sentinelle*) to post the sentries ‖ *fare la* — *a qlcu.*, to waylay s.o.; *mettersi alla* — *di qlcu.*, to watch (o to be on the watch) for s.o.; *stare alla* —, to watch (o to be on the watch o to be on the look-out) **5.** (*corriera postale*) post, mail-coach; (*stazione di posta*) post(-stage), stage: *cavalli di* —, post-horses ‖ *correre le poste*, (*viaggiare in fretta*) to go post-haste **6.** (*posto assegnato a ciascun animale nella stalla*) stall **7.** (*decina di rosario*) decade **8.** (*arit.*) addendum (*pl.* addenda) **9.** (*ind. cartaria*) half ream **10.** *alla* —, (*al giuoco della palla*) at full toss (o in the air): *prendere la palla alla* —, to catch a ball at full toss **11.** *a* —, expressly (o purposely): *a bella* —, on purpose **12.** *di questa* —, (*di questa misura*) of this size.

postàle, *ag.* postal; post (*attributivo*); mail (*attributivo*): *battello* —, post-boat; *cartolina* —, postcard; *casella* —, post-office box; *cassetta* —, mail-box (o post -box); *corriera* —, (*st.*) mail-coach; *distretto* —, postal district; *furgone* —, mail-van; *impiegato* —, post -office clerk; *pacco* —, parcel: *spedire per pacco* —, to send by parcel post; *regolamento* —, postal regulations; *servizio* —, postal (o *amer.* mail) service; *spese postali*, postage; *succursale* —, branch post-office; *tariffa* —, postal tariff; *timbro* —, post-mark; *treno* —, mail-train; *unione* —, postal union ‖ *s.m.* (*mar.*) mail -boat, mail-steamer; (*ferr.*) mail-train.

postàre, *v.t.* (*mil.*) to station, to post: *i cannoni erano postati sulla cima della collina*, the guns were posted on the top of the hill; *egli postò i suoi soldati* *ai piedi del monte*, he posted his soldiers at the foot of the mountain ‖ **postàrsi**, *v.r.* to station oneself, to post oneself.

postazióne, *s.f. (mil.)* stationing: *la — di un cannone*, the positioning of a cannon.

postbèllico, *ag.* post war *(attributivo)*.

postcombustióne, *s.f. (mec.)* afterburning.

postcombustóre, *s.m. (mec.)* afterburner.

postcommúnio, *s.m. (eccl.)* post-communion.

postdatàto, *ag.* postdated.

posteggiàre, *v.t.* 1. to waylay, to watch for (s.o.): *— un animale*, to waylay an animal 2. *(parcheggiare)* to park.

posteggiatóre, *s.m.*, **posteggiatríce**, *s.f.* 1. *(sorvegliante di parcheggio)* car-park attendant 2. *(venditore)* stall-holder 3. *(suonatore girovago)* strolling musician.

postéggio, *s.m.* 1. *(parcheggio)* car-park, parking -place: *— di autopubbliche*, taxi(-cab) rank *(o* stand) 2. *(per venditori di piazza)* stand, stall: *tassa di —*, market-dues.

postelegràfico, *ag.* postal and telegraph *(attributivo)*: *servizi postelegrafici*, postal and telegraph services ‖ *s.m.* post-office employee.

postelegrafònico, *ag.* postal, telegraph and telephone *(attributivo)* ‖ *s.m.* post-office employee.

postèma, *s.f. (med.)* aposteme, abscess.

postemóso, *ag.* apostematous.

postergàle, *s.m.* 1. back 2. *(eccl.)* reliquaire.

postergàre, *v.t. (trascurare)* to neglect; to throw (sthg.) to the winds: *— il dovere*, to neglect one's duty; *— la ragione*, to throw reason to the winds.

pòsteri, *s.m.pl.* posterity *(sing.)*; descendants: *questo sarà giudicato dai nostri —*, this will be judged by our descendants; *trasmettere ql.co. ai —*, to hand down sthg. to posterity.

posterióre, *ag.* 1. *(nello spazio)* hind(er), back; *(spec. mil.)* rear; *(rar.)* posterior: *le file posteriori di una colonna militare*, the rear ranks of a military column; *le gambe posteriori di un cavallo, di una seggiola*, the hind legs of a horse, of a chair; *la parte — del cervello, (anat.)* the posterior *(o* hinder) part of the brain; *la porta —, (di una casa)* the back door; *le ruote posteriori di un'automobile*, the rear wheels of a car 2. *(nel tempo)* following, subsequent; later; *(rar.)* posterior: *gli anni posteriori a una guerra*, the years following a war; *i secoli posteriori*, the later *(o* following) centuries; *quelli furono avvenimenti posteriori*, those were posterior *o* subsequent) events ‖ *s.m.* posterior.

posterióri, a, *l.av.* a posteriori.

posteriorità, *s.f.* posteriority.

posteriorménte, *av. (in seguito)* posteriorly, subsequently; *(più tardi)* later; *(dopo)* after, afterwards.

posterità, *s.f.* posterity.

postèrla, *s.f. (st.)* postern.

postíccio, *ag.* artificial, false; *(fittizio)* fictitious, sham; *(provvisorio)* temporary: *denti, capelli posticci*, false teeth, hair.

posticipàre, *v.t.* to postpone, to defer: *il pagamento è stato posticipato di una settimana*, payment has been deferred a week; *— le vacanze*, to postpone one's holidays.

posticipataménte, *av.* 1. *(con ritardo)* with delay, after the proper time 2. *(alla fine del tempo fissato, del lavoro compiuto, ecc.)* when due: *la pigione si paga —*, the rent is not payable in advance.

posticipàto, *ag.* 1. *(ritardato)* delayed, deferred: *pagamento —*, deferred payment 2. *(alla fine del tempo fissato, del lavoro compiuto, ecc.)* payable when due: *pigione posticipata*, rent not payable in advance.

posticipazióne, *s.f.* deferment; *(ritardo)* delay.

postièrla, *s.f. (st.)* postern.

postiglióne. *s.m.* postilion, postillion.

postílla, *s.f.* note, gloss; marginal note; *(a piè di pagina)* footnote: *le postille del Leopardi ai suoi libri*, Leopardi's marginal notes in his books.

postillàre, *v.t.* to annotate, to gloss.

postillàto, *ag.* annotated, glossed: *un testo tutto —*, a text full of notes.

postillatúra, *s.f.* 1. *(il postillare)* annotating, glossing 2. *(postille)* notes *(pl.)*, glosses *(pl.)*.

postillatóre, *s.m.*, **postillatríce**, *s.f.* annotator.

postíno, *s.m.* postman *(pl.* postmen).

pòsto¹, *s.m.* 1. place: *questo è fuori —*, this is out of place *(anche fig.)*; *questo libro non è al suo —*, this book is not in its place; *questo non è il suo — giusto*, this is not its right place; *questa sciarpa non sta a —*, this scarf won't stay in place; *se fossi al tuo —*, if I were in your shoes *(o* place); *va' al tuo —*, go to your place; *verrò al — di mio fratello*, I'll come instead of my brother; *mettere le cose a —*, to put things straight; *fig.* to get things straight; *prendere il — di qlcu., ql.co.*, to take the place of s.o., sthg. ‖ *devo mettere, tenere quell'uomo a —*, I must put, keep that man in his place ‖ *è tutto a —*, everything's straight *(o* settled *o* all right) ‖ *stare al proprio —*, to keep one's place ‖ *tenere la lingua a —*, to hold one's tongue 2. *(spazio)* room; space: *c'è tanto — in questa casa*, there is so much room *(o* space) in this house; *fagli —*, make room for him; *nella mia auto c'è — per altre due persone*, in my car there is room for two people more; *non c'è più — nell'armadio*, there is no more room in the wardrobe; *questi libri occupano troppo —*, these books take up too much room *(o* space) 3. *(posto a sedere)* seat: *— d'angolo*, corner seat; *— di guida*, driver's seat; *— riservato*, reserved seat; *automobile a quattro posti*, four-seater (car); *ho prenotato due posti per la commedia di domani sera*, I have booked two seats for tomorrow evening's play; *prendere —*, to take a seat *(o* to sit down) 4. *(lavoro, impiego)* job, post, situation, position: *— di direttore, insegnante*, position *(o* situation *o* post) as a director, teacher; *— di meccanico*, job as a mechanic; *— di segretaria*, post *(o* job) as a secretary; *ha un magnifico —*, he has a wonderful job 5. *(sito, luogo)* place; spot: *— di villeggiatura*, resort: *un — di villeggiatura estiva*, a summer resort; *la gente del —*, the people on the spot; *ho trovato un simpatico — ombroso vicino al fiume*, I have found a nice shady spot near the river; *ho visto dei posti meravigliosi*, I have seen some wonderful places; *questo non è — per signorine*, this is no place for young ladies; *ti mostrerò un bel — dove andare a far colazione*, I shall show you a nice place to go and have lunch ‖ *arrivare sul —*, to reach the spot 6. *(stazione)* station: *— di blocco stradale*, road block; *— di controllo, (spor.)* control point; *— di medicazione*, dressing-station; *— di polizia*, police -station; *— di primo soccorso*, first-aid post *(o* centre) *— di rifornimento, (aut.)* filling-station 7. *(mil.)* post: *— di guardia*, sentry-post 8. *(mar. aer. ferr.)*: *— di ancoraggio, (mar.)* berth; *— di caricamento, (mar.)* loading berth; *— di osservazione, (aer.)* observation turret; *— di pilotaggio, (aer.)* cockpit; *— ripetitore, (ferr.)* repeating post.

pósto², *ag.* placed, situated: *la casa è posta ai piedi della montagna*, the house is (situated) at the foot of the mountain.

postoché, pósto che, *cong. (rar.)* supposing that, assuming that; granting that: *— questo sia vero*, granting this to be true *(o* that this is true); *— tu abbia ragione*, supposing *(o* assuming) that you are right.

post-operatòrio, *ag.* postoperative.

postrèmo, *ag. (rar.)* last.

postríbolo, *s.m.* brothel.

postulànte, *s.c.* 1. petitioner 2. *(chi domanda un impiego)* applicant 3. *(eccl.)* postulant.

postulàre, *v.t.* 1. *(domandare con insistenza)* to solicit, to petition for (sthg.): *postulavano benefici ecclesiastici*, they petitioned for benefices 2. *(eccl.) (proporre a qualche benefizio)* to postulate: *— qlcu. alla carica di vescovo*, to postulate s.o. to a bishopric.

postulàto, *s.m.* postulate.

postulatóre, *s.m.*, **postulatríce**, *s.f.* **1.** petitioner **2.** (*eccl.*) postulator.

pòstumo, *ag.* posthumous.

postúra, *s.f.* **1.** (*posizione*) situation, location, position **2.** (*atteggiamento*) posture.

postútto, al, *l.av.* after all.

potàbile, *ag.* drinkable, potable.

potabilità, *s.f.* drinkableness, potableness, potability.

potagióne, *s.f.* pruning; (*di albero*) lopping.

potaiuòlo, *s.m.* pruning-hook; pruning-knife.

potaménto, *s.m.* pruning; lopping.

potàre, *v.t.* to prune; to lop; (*una siepe*) to trim.

potàssa, *s.f.* (*chim.*) potash, potassium carbonate: — *caustica*, potash (o potassium hydroxide); — *pura*, pearl-ash.

potàssico, *ag.* (*chim.*) potassic.

potàssio, *s.m.* (*chim.*) potassium: *carbonato di* —, potassium carbonate; *cianuro di* —, potassium cyanide; *clorato di* —, potassium chlorate; *cloruro di* —, potassium chloride; *idrato di* —, potassium hydroxide; *nitrato di* —, potassium nitrate (o saltpetre); *permanganato di* —, potassium permanganate; *silicato di* —, potassium silicate (o soluble glass).

potatóio, *s.m.* pruning-hook; pruning-knife; (*a forbice*) pruning-shears.

potatóre, *s.m.* **1.** pruner; lopper **2.** *V.* **potatóio**.

potatúra, *s.f.* pruning; lopping.

potentàto, *s.m.* **1.** (*Stato, Potenza*) power **2.** (*principe sovrano*) potentate.

potènte, *ag.* **1.** powerful, mighty; (*influente*) influential: *un'armata* —, a powerful (o mighty) army; *un uomo, nemico* —, a powerful man, enemy; *una voce* —, a powerful voice ‖ *i potenti* (*della terra*), the mighty ones (of the earth) **2.** (*efficace*) potent: *un rimedio, veleno* —, a potent remedy, poison.

potenteménte, *av.* **1.** powerfully, mightily; (*con influenza*) influentially **2.** (*efficacemente*) potently.

potènza, *s.f.* **1.** power, might; (*forza*) strength: *la — della legge, della stampa*, the power of the law, of the press; *la — di Dio, del re*, the power (o might) of God, of the king; *la — di un esercito, di un paese*, the strength of an army, of a country; *la — di un microscopio*, the power of a microscope; *la — intellettiva*, (*fil.*) the power of the intellect; *la Spagna era all'apogeo della sua* —, Spain was then at the height of its (o her) power ‖ *in* —, potential (*ag.*); potentially (*av.*): *un pericolo in* —, a potential danger; *in — siamo più forti di loro*, potentially we are stronger then they are **2.** (*efficacia*) potency: *la — di un argomento*, the potency of an argument; *la — di un veleno*, the potency of a poison **3.** (*Stato*) power: *le Potenze alleate*, the allied powers; *le grandi Potenze europee*, the great powers of Europe **4.** (*mat.*) power: *la — di un numero*, the power of a number; *elevare un numero all'ennesima* —, to raise a number to the nth power **5.** (*mec.*) power, rating; (*in cavalli*) horse-power; (*elett.*) capacity: — *acustica*, (*rad.*) acoustic power; — *a regime*, (*aer.*) power rating; — *continua*, (*elett.*) active power; — *di combattimento*, (*aer.*) combat rating; — *di crociera*, (*aer.*) cruising power; — *di decollo*, (*aer.*) take-off power; — *fiscale, di targa, (di motore)* nominal horse-power; *amplificatore di* —, (*rad.*) power amplifier (o unit); *fattore di* —, (*elett.*) power factor.

potenziàle, *ag.* potential: *modo* —, (*gram.*) potential mood; *le ricchezze potenziali di un paese*, the potential riches of a country ‖ *s.m.* (*fis.*) potential: — *elettrico*, electric potential; — *magnetico*, magnetic potential.

potenzialità, *s.f.* potentiality.

potenzialménte, *av.* potentially.

potenziaménto, *s.m.* (*rafforzamento*) strengthening; (*incremento*) development; (*incoraggiamento*) encouraging.

potenziàre, *v.t.* to potentiate, to make powerful; (*rafforzare*) to strengthen; (*incrementare*) to develop; (*incoraggiare*) to encourage.

potenziàto, *ag.* potentiated; (*rafforzato*) strengthened: (*incrementato*) developed; (*incoraggiato*) encouraged.

potére, *v.i.* **1.** (*possibilità materiale o dipendente dalla capacità del sogg.*) **can** (*indic. pres., congiunt. pres.*), **could** (*indic. pass., congiunt. pass., condiz.*); **to be able**: *ha potuto aiutarti perchè conosceva l'argomento*, he was able to help you because he knew the subject; *non potendo andare, scrisse*, not being able (o being unable) to go (o as he could not go), he sent a letter; *non poterono andare*, they could not go (o were not able o were unable to go); *non potremo uscire, se non arrivi in tempo*, we shall not be able to go out, if you do not arrive in time; *non può fare questo lavoro perchè non è abbastanza intelligente*, he cannot do this work because he is not intelligent enough; *potè, non potè andare*, he was able to, he could not (o was not able to) go; *potendo, partirò domani*, if I can, I'll leave tomorrow; *potranno venire domani?*, will they be able to (o can they) come tomorrow?; *potresti venire a trovarmi stasera?*, could you come and see me tonight?; *prometto di fare tutto ciò che posso*, I promise I shall do all I can (o my best o my utmost); *se lo avessi saputo prima, avrei potuto aiutarti*, I could have helped you, if I had known before; *se potessi capirti, ti potrei aiutare*, I could help you if only I could understand you; *vorrei poterti aiutare*, I wish I could help you ‖ *a più non posso*, all out: *stava lavorando a più non posso*, he was working all out ‖ *un uomo che può*, (*che ha denaro*) a man of means ‖ *non ne posso più*, (*sono sfinito*) I am exhausted; (*sono al limite della sopportazione*) I am at the end of my tether (o I can't stand any more): *non ne posso più di quell'uomo*, I can't stand that man any longer (o fam. I am fed up with that man) ‖ *non posso che piangere*, I cannot help crying (o letter. I can but weep); *non posso fare a meno di ammettere...*, I cannot do anything but admit... (o letter. I can but admit...); *non posso fare a meno di te*, I cannot do without you; (*in questioni di lavoro*) I cannot spare you; *se posso farne a meno, non andrò*, I shan't go, if I can help it ‖ *non posso farci niente*, I can't help it (o I can do nothing about it): « *Può aggiustare questo orologio?* », « *Spiacente, non posso farci niente* », "Can you mend this watch?", "Sorry, I can't do anything with it"; « *Sai che la finestra non è stata riparata?* », « *Beh, non posso farci niente* », "Do you know the window has not been mended?", "Well, I can't help it" ‖ *non potemmo permetterci* (*il lusso*) *di fare quel viaggio*, we could not afford to go on that journey ‖ *portane più che puoi*, bring as much, as many as you can; *vieni più in fretta che puoi*, come as quickly as you can; *vieni più presto che puoi*, come as soon as you can ‖ *volere è* —, *prov.* where there is a will there is a way **2.** (*possibilità dipendente dalla volontà altrui*) **may** (*indic. pres.*), **might** (*indic. pass. nel discorso indiretto e condiz.*) (*entrambe le forme sono spesso sostituite nell'uso corrente da* **can, could, to be able**); **to be allowed, to be permitted**: *chiese se poteva vederlo*, he asked if he might (o could) see him; *disse che potevamo prendere la sua macchina fotografica*, he said we might (o could) take his camera; *non potei entrare perchè era troppo malato*, I could not (o was not allowed to) go in, because he was too ill; *non potendo fumare in casa, vado in giardino*, as I may not (o cannot) smoke indoors, I'll go into the garden; *posso entrare?*, may (o can) I come in?; *potremo vederlo domani, se sta meglio*, we can (o we shall be able to) see him tomorrow, if he is better; *vedrai che non potrai entrare*, you will see that you are not allowed in **3.** (*eventualità*) **may, might**; (*probabilità*) **to be likely**: *è tardi, ma può ancora venire*, it is late, but he may still come; *posso aver torto*, I may be wrong; *potrebbe arrivare domani, ma ne dubito*, he might come tomorrow, but I doubt it; *potrei anche aver torto, ma sono quasi certo di no*, I might be wrong, but I am pretty certain that I am not; *potrò forse arrivare per la fine* *della settimana*, I may arrive at the end of the week; *se continua così, potrà vincere*, if he continues like that, he is likely to win ‖ *può darsi*, maybe: « *Arriverai in tempo?* », « *Può darsi* », "Will you arrive in time?", "Maybe"; *può darsi, ma non lo credo*, maybe, but I do not think so ‖ *può darsi che*, may (*costruzione pers.*), maybe: *può darsi che ti abbia scritto*, maybe he has (o he may have) written to you **4.** (*quando esprime esortazione, augurio*) **may, might:** *che tu possa essere felice!*, may you be happy!; *possa egli vivere a lungo!*, may he live long!; *potresti almeno provare*, you might at least try ‖ *v.t.* **1.** (*poter avere, poter fare*): *può molto per te*, he can do a lot for you; *può molto presso il re*, he has great influence with the king **2.** (*reggere, portare*): *può un quintale sulle spalle*, he can carry a hundred kilos on his back.

potére, *s.m.* **1.** power (anche *fig.*): — *assoluto*, absolute power: *avere* — *assoluto su un popolo*, to hold complete sway over a people; — *esecutivo, legislativo*, executive, legislative power; *i poteri governativi*, governmental powers; *il* — *temporale del Papa*, the temporal power of the Pope; *abuso di* —, abuse of power; *sete di* —, thirst for power; *non ho il* — *di decidere su questo punto*, I have no power to decide on this point; *non ho* — *su di loro*, I have no power over them ‖ *al* —, in power: *i democratici sono al* —, the democrats are in power ‖ *in mio, tuo, ecc.* —, in my, your, etc. power: *cadde in suo* —, he fell into his power (o into his hands); *ciò è in tuo* —, it lies in your power; *quell'uomo è in mio* —, that man is in my power **2.** *pl.* (*potestà, diritti*) powers: *i poteri di un ministro*, the powers of a minister; *pieni poteri*, full powers; *ambasciatore con pieni poteri*, (ambassador) plenipotentiary; *agire con, avere pieni poteri*, to act, to be invested with full powers; *dare, conferire pieni poteri*, to grant full powers: *dare, conferire pieni poteri a qlcu. di fare ql.co.*, to empower s.o. to do sthg.; *vorrei definire i miei poteri*, I should like to define my powers **3.** (*possibilità*) power, possibility; (*capacità*) power, capacity: — *assorbente, dispersivo*, (*fis.*) absorbent, dispersive power; — *calorifero*, (*fis.*) heating value (o power); — *d'acquisto*, (*pol. econ.*) purchasing power; *non ha il* — *di agire in altro modo*, he has not the power to act (o the possibility of acting) otherwise **4.** (*influenza*) influence, sway: *egli ha un grande* — *su di me*, he has great influence over me.

potestà, *s.f.* power: — *di vita e di morte*, power of life and death; — *fisica*, physical power; — *legale*, legal power; — *spirituale*, spiritual power; *non ho la* — *di farlo*, I have not the power to do it; *essere in* — *di qlcu.*, to be in s.o.'s power (o in s.o.'s hands) ‖ — *angeliche*, (*teol.*) Angelic Powers ‖ *La Divina Potestà*, the Almighty ‖ *patria* —, (*dir.*) paternal authority (o patria potestas).

pouf, *s.m.* (*sgabello imbottito*) pouf(fe).

pourparler, *s.m.* **1.** pourparler, negotiations **2.** (*mil.*) parley.

poveràccio, *s.m.* poor fellow, poor devil.

poveràglia, *s.f.* **1.** poor people **2.** (*mendicanti*) beggars.

poveraménte, *av.* poorly, wretchedly.

poverèllo, *s.m.* **1.** poor man **2.** (*mendicante*) beggar.

pòvero, *ag.* **1.** poor, wretched: *il* — *bambino*, the poor child; *il* — *giovane si uccise*, the wretched young man killed himself ‖ — *diavolo!*, poor devil! ‖ — *me!*, dear me! ‖ — *te se lo fai*, you'll be sorry if you do it **2.** (*bisognoso*) needy, poor: *un uomo* —, a needy man; *la sua famiglia è molto povera*, his family is very poor **3.** (*scarso*) scanty, poor: *un* — *raccolto*, a scanty (o poor) crop (o harvest); *un* — *reddito*, a poor income; *fiume* — *di acque*, shallow river; *il nostro paese è* — *di pascoli*, our country is poor in pasture-land **4.** (*sterile*) poor, barren, sterile: *spirito* — *di idee*, mind barren of ideas; *terreno* —, barren (o sterile) land **5.** (*umile*) humble, poor: *la mia povera opinione è che...*, my

humble (o poor) opinion is that... **6.** (*semplice, disadorno*) plain, bare: *in parole povere*, in plain words; *uno stile* —, a plain style **7.** (*modesto*) modest, poor: *un dono* —, a modest gift **8.** (*fam.*) (*defunto*) poor: *la mia povera mamma*, my poor mother ‖ *s.m.* **1.** poor man: *i poveri*, the poor (o the needy o poor people): *avvocato dei poveri*, poor man's lawyer ‖ *poveri di spirito*, (*di intelligenza limitata*) dull-witted people ‖ *beati i poveri in ispirito*, (*Bibbia*) blessed are the poor in spirit **2.** (*mendicante*) beggar ‖ **pòvera,** *s.f.* **1.** poor woman **2.** (*mendicante*) beggar.

povertà, *s.f.* **1.** poverty; (*indigenza*) indigence: *la* — *di un paese*, the poverty of a country; *la sua* — *non mi meraviglia*, his poverty (o indigence) does not surprise me; *vivere in* —, to live in poverty **2.** (*scarsità*) poverty; (*mancanza*) lack: — *di coraggio*, lack of courage; — *di idee, immaginazione*, poverty (o lack) of ideas, imagination **3.** (*cattiva qualità*) poorness: *la* — *di un terreno*, the poorness of a soil **4.** (*meschinità*) poorness, meanness.

pozióne, *s.f.* potion, draught.

pozióre, *ag.* (*dir.*) preferred; prior.

poziorità, *s.f.* (*dir.*) preference; priority; precedence.

pózza, *s.f.* **1.** (*pozzanghera*) puddle: *il giardino è pieno di pozze dopo la pioggia*, the garden is full of puddles after the rain **2.** (*chiazza di liquido*) pool: *una* — *di sangue*, a pool of blood.

pozzànghera, *s.f.* puddle.

pozzétta, *s.f.* (*delle gote, del mento*) dimple.

pozzétto, *s.m.* (*di motore*) sump; (*miner.*) winze: — *dell'elica*, (*mar.*) propeller aperture; — *dell'olio*, (*motori aer.*) oil sump; — *di emulsione*, (*mec.*) emulsion tube; — *raccolta detriti*, (*edil.*) drain well; — *raccolta fanghi*, (*tubazione*) mud pocket.

pózzo, *s.m.* **1.** well: — *artesiano*, artesian well; — *profondo*, deep well; *carrucola del* —, well-pulley; *secchia del* —, wellbucket; *i pozzi sono asciutti*, the wells are dry; *scavare un* —, to sink a well ‖ — *nero*, cesspool ‖ *egli è un* — *di scienza*, he is a well of learning ‖ *la sua borsa è un* — *di S. Patrizio*, his purse is like the widow's cruse **2.** (*per estrazione del petrolio*) oil-well: — *ad eruzione spontanea*, gusher; — *eruttivo*, flowing well; *perforare un* —, to drill a well **3.** (*miner.*) shaft; pit: — *carbonifero*, coal-pit (o colliery); — *di aerazione*, ventilating shaft (o air shaft); — *di colmata*, flushing shaft; — *di comunicazione*, winze; — *di drenaggio*, drainage shaft; — *di estrazione*, hauling shaft (o hoisting shaft); — *inclinato*, sloping shaft; — *verticale*, vertical shaft **4.** (*mar.*): — *caldo*, hot well; — *dell'elica*, propeller aperture; — *delle catene*, chain locker.

pozzolàna, *s.f.* (*geol.*) pozz(u)olana.

pràcrito, *s.m.* (*dialetto indiano*) Prakrit.

Pràga, *no.pr.f.* (*geog.*) Prague.

pragmàtica, pragmàtico, *V.* **prammàtica, prammàtico.**

pragmatìsmo, *s.m.* (*st. fil.*) pragmatism.

pragmatìsta, *s.c.* (*fil.*) pragmatist.

praline, *s.f.* praline.

prammàtica, *s.f.* (*regola, costumanza*) custom, customary manner, use: *risposta di* —, regulation answer; *è di* — *visitare i musei di questa città*, it is customary to visit the museums of this town.

prammàtico, *ag.* pragmatic ‖ *prammatica sanzione*, (*st.*) Pragmatic Sanction.

prammatìsmo, *s.m.* (*st. fil.*) pragmatism.

prammatìsta, *s.c.* (*fil.*) pragmatist.

pranzàre, *v.i.* (*consumare il pasto principale*) to dine, to have dinner; (*consumare il pasto di mezzogiorno*) to lunch: *ieri a mezzogiorno ho pranzato con Mr. Kyd*, yesterday I had lunch with Mr. Kyd; *pranzi fuori questa sera?*, are you dining out this evening?.

prànzo, *s.m.* (*il pasto più importante della giornata*) dinner; (*il pasto di mezzogiorno*) lunch: — *di gala*, gala dinner; — *diplomatico*, diplomatic dinner; — *ufficiale*, formal dinner; *dopo* —, after lunch; *invito a*

—, invitation to dinner; *sala da* —, dining-room; *il — è pronto*, dinner is ready; *il — era molto buono*, the dinner was very good; *il — è servito*, dinner is served; *avremo ospiti a* —, we'll have people to dinner; *è ora di* —, it is dinner time; *qui il — è alle 20*, dinner is at 8 p. m. here; *dare un — in onore di qlcu.*, to give a dinner (-party) in honour of s.o.; *invitare qlcu. a* —, to invite (o to ask) s.o. to dinner.

praseodímio, *s.m.* (*chim.*) praseodymium.

pràssi, *s.f.* praxis; practice.

Prassítele, *no.pr.m.* (*st. scult.*) Praxiteles.

prataiuòlo, *ag.* of the meadows, of the fields; field (*attributivo*) ‖ *gallina prataiuola*, prairie-hen ‖ *s.m.* (*fungo*) mushroom.

pratellína, *s.f.* (*bot.*) daisy.

pratènse, *ag.* of the meadows, of the fields; field (*attributivo*).

pratería, *s.f.* grassland; (*amer.*) prairie.

pràtica, *s.f.* **1.** practice: *in — le cose sono molto differenti*, in practice things are quite different; *mettere in — ql.co.*, to put sthg. into practice: *mettere in — i consigli di qlcu.*, to take s.o.'s advice (o to act on s.o.'s advice) ‖ *val più la — della grammatica, prov.* practice is better than theory **2.** (*esperienza, conoscenza*) practice, experience; training: *ha molta — del suo mestiere*, he has great experience in his job; *ho molta — di bambini*, I have a lot of experience with children; *ho molta — di queste cose*, I know these things very well; *misi mio figlio a far — presso un avvocato*, I articled my son to a lawyer; *non ha — degli affari, del mondo*, he has no practical knowledge of business, of the world; *non hai abbastanza — per questo lavoro*, you haven't enough experience for this job; *non ho — della lingua, di questi attrezzi*, I am not familiar with the language, with these tools; *non ho — in questo campo*, I have no experience in this field; *ogni giorno scrivo a macchina per un'ora per prender* —, everyday I practise typing for an hour; *parlo per* —, I speak from experience; *si è fatto una gran — di queste cose*, he has gained a wide experience of these things; *sta facendo — presso un fabbro*, he is serving his apprenticeship with a blacksmith; *perdere la* —, to lose the knack **3.** (*usanza, abitudine*) practice, custom, usage: *questa è la — qui*, this is the custom here **4.** (*affare, faccenda*) matter, affair; business: *non voglio aver niente a che fare con questa* —, I don't want to have anything to do with this matter ‖ *— illecita*, illegal activity **5.** *pl.* (*complesso di atti, formule, ecc.*) practices: *le pratiche Cattoliche*, (Roman) Catholic practices; *pratiche magiche, superstiziose*, magic, superstitious practices; *pratiche religiose*, religious observances **6.** *pl.* (*trattative*) negotiations; dealing (*sing.*): *le pratiche per la vendita andarono per le lunghe*, the negotiations for the sale dragged on **7.** (*incartamento, documento*) file, dossier; (*documento*) paper: *non trovo la — di tuo fratello*, I can't find your brother's file (o dossier); *le pratiche sono in corso*, steps are being taken; *sta facendo le pratiche per avere indietro quel denaro*, he is taking the necessary steps to get that money back; *sto facendo le pratiche per il passaporto*, I am getting the papers ready for my passport **8.** (*mar.*) pratique: *aver libera* —, to be out of quarantine; *dar libera — ad una nave*, to grant pratique.

praticàbile, *ag.* practicable: *strada, guado* —, practicable road, ford ‖ *s.m.* (*cine. teat.*) practicable.

praticabilità, *s.f.* practicability, practicableness.

praticàccia, *s.f.* practical knowledge: *ha una certa — ma fa tutto superficialmente*, he has a certain practical knowledge of his work, but he does everything superficially.

praticaménte, *av.* **1.** practically, in practice **2.** (*per mezzo della pratica*) by practice (o by experience).

praticànte, *ag.* **1.** practising: *dentista* —, practising dentist **2.** (*osservante*) observant, practising: *cattolico* —, practising Catholic; *anglicano* —, communicant

member of the Church of England ‖ *s.m.* **1.** (*apprendista*) apprentice **2.** (*osservante delle pratiche religiose*) churchgoer.

praticàre, *v.t.* **1.** to practise, to put into practice: *devi — ciò che ti hanno insegnato*, you must practise what you have been taught; *— il consiglio di qlcu.*, to follow s.o.'s advice; *— un metodo*, to employ a method **2.** (*esercitare*) to practise, to perform: *è laureato in legge ma non pratica*, he has a degree in law but he doesn't practise; *quel medico non pratica più*, that doctor is no longer in practice; *— la chirurgia*, to practise surgery; *— l'usura*, to practise usury **3.** (*frequentare*) to frequent; to associate with (s.o.): *gli piace — la gente umile*, he likes to associate with humble people; *non pratica il gran mondo*, he does not move in society ‖ *— il mercato nero*, to deal on the black market **4.** (*fare*) to make: *— un'apertura, un buco*, to make an opening, a hole; *— un taglio*, to make a cut ‖ *v.i.* to frequent (sthg.): *da ragazzo praticavo in questi luoghi*, when a boy I used to frequent these places.

praticcio, *s.m.* meadow.

praticità, *s.f.* practicalness, practicality.

pràtico, *ag.* **1.** practical: *arti pratiche*, practical arts; *conoscenza pratica di una lingua*, working knowledge of a language; *consiglio* —, practical proposal; *dimostrazione pratica*, practical demonstration; *esercizio* —, practical drill; *medicina pratica*, practical medicine; *metodo, sistema* —, practical method, system; *nella vita pratica*, in real life; *i problemi pratici della vita*, the practical problems of life; *prova pratica*, practical exam; *non risulta buono all'atto* —, in practice it just doesn't work **2.** (*comodo, funzionale*) practical; convenient, handy: *abito* —, practical garment; *ci vuole qlco. di più* —, I want sthg. more practical; *questo apriscatole è molto* —, this can-opener is very convenient (o handy) **3.** (*esperto*) experienced, skilled: *un idraulico* —, a skilled plumber; *è molto — del suo lavoro*, he knows his job very well; *non sono — di farfalle*, I know nothing about butterflies; *sono molto — di queste cose*, I am very familiar with these things; *sono — di questi luoghi*, I am familiar with these places; *vogliono infermiere pratiche*, they want competent nurses **4.** (*positivo*) practical: *una mente pratica*, a practical mind; *senso* —, practical (common) sense; *uomo* —, practical man ‖ *s.m.* practical man.

praticóne, *s.m.* old hand.

pratile, *s.m.* (*st. francese*) Prairial.

pratíto, *ag.* meadowy, grass (*attributivo*).

pratívo, *ag.* meadowy, grass (*attributivo*): *terreno* —, grassland.

pràto, *s.m.* meadow; (*se artificiale*) lawn: *terra a* —, land under grass; *davanti alla villetta vi era un* —, in front of the cottage there was a lawn ‖ *pelle di* —, turf.

pratolína, *s.f.* daisy.

pratóso, *ag.* meadowy.

pravità, *s.f.* depravity, wickedness, perversity.

pràvo, *ag.* depraved, wicked, perverse, perverted.

preaccennàre, *v.t.* to mention beforehand.

preaccennàto, *ag.* aforesaid, mentioned beforehand, before-mentioned, above-mentioned.

preaccusàre, *v.t.* (*dir.*) to accuse beforehand.

preadamíta, *s.c.* pre-adamite.

preadamítico, *ag.* pre-adamitic(al), pre-adamic.

preallegàto, *ag.* fore-alleged, before-mentioned.

Preàlpi (le), *s.f.pl.* (*geog.*) the PreAlps.

preàmbolo, *s.m.* preface, preamble; *dimmi senza tanti preamboli*, tell me without wasting words.

preannunziàre, *v.t.* **1.** to (pre)announce, to forewarn **2.** (*essere il segno di*) to foreshadow, to portend: *essi credono che le eclissi preannunzino delle disgrazie*, they believe that eclipses portend evils; *quando il barometro scende improvvisamente, preannunzia tempesta*, when the barometer suddenly falls, it is the sign of a storm.

preannúnzio, *s.m.* pre-announcement; forewarning.

preavvertiménto, *s.m.* previous notice; prior warning.

preavvertíre, preavvisàre, *v.t.* to inform in advance, to tell in advance; to forewarn: *vieni senza preavvertirci*, just drop in and see us.

preavvíso, *s.m.* notice, forewarning: *— di due mesi*, two months' notice; *dietro —*, upon notice; *senza —*, without notice (o warning); *questi sintomi sono il — di una grave malattia*, these symptoms are the warning of a serious disease.

prebèllico, *ag.* pre-war (*attributivo*).

prebènda, *s.f.* 1. (*eccl.*) prebend 2. (*profitto*) profit 3. (*salario*) salary.

prebendàrio, *s.m.* (*eccl.*) prebendary.

prebendàto, *ag.* (*eccl.*) prebendal || *s.m.* (*eccl.*) prebendary.

precariaménte, *av.* precariously.

precarietà, *s.f.* precariousness.

precàrio, *ag.* precarious: *mezzi precari*, precarious means of existence; *privilegi precari*, precarious privileges; *salute precaria*, poor health.

precauzionàle, *ag.* precautionary.

precauzióne, *s.f.* 1. precaution: *precauzioni sanitarie*, sanitary precautions; *misure di —*, precautionary measures; *prendere precauzioni contro gli incidenti*, to take precautions against accidents 2. (*prudenza, cautela*) care, caution: *procedere con —*, to proceed with caution.

prèce, *s.f.* prayer: *dire le preci*, to say one's prayers.

precedènte, *ag.* preceding, previous, former, foregoing: *le affermazioni, citazioni precedenti*, the foregoing statements, quotations; *durante un incontro —*, during a previous meeting; *il giorno —*, the previous day (o the day before); *il mio — principale*, my former employer; *in tempi precedenti*, in former times; *nelle pagine, lettere, lezioni precedenti*, in the preceding pages, letters, lessons; *saldo del conto —*, balance of former account; *avevo un impegno —*, I had a previous engagement; *annullare una — ordinazione*, to cancel a previous order || *s.m.* 1. precedent: *un fatto senza precedenti*, an unprecedented occurrence; *questo avvenimento non ha precedenti nella storia della città*, this event has no precedent in the history of the town; *citare un — a sostegno di un'azione*, (*dir.*) to cite a precedent in support of an action || *costituire un —*, to become (o to constitute) a precedent; *creare un —*, to set (o to create) a precedent 2. *pl.* (*condotta precedente*) record (*sing.*): *buoni, cattivi precedenti*, good, bad record; *vorrei sapere i precedenti di quell'uomo*, I should like to know that man's record.

precedenteménte, *av.* previously, precedently; formerly, in former times; (*prima*) before: *articoli citati —*, articles enumerated above; *lo conoscevo già —*, I used to know him.

precedènza, *s.f.* precedence; (*priorità*) priority: *avere la — su...*, to have precedence (o priority) over...: *il treno passeggeri ha la — sul merci*, a passenger train has precedence over goods trains; *i vecchi hanno la — sui giovani*, old people have (o take) precedence over the young; *dare la — a...*, to give precedence (o priority) to...: *in Italia bisogna dare la — alle automobili provenienti da destra*, in Italy one must give precedence to cars coming from the right; *nella distribuzione del cibo sarà data la — ai bambini*, when food is distributed priority will be given to children; *disputarsi la — con qlcu.*, to contend for precedence with s.o. || *in —*, previously (o precedently).

precèdere, *v.t.* to precede: *gli anni precedenti l'inizio della carestia*, the years preceding the beginning of the famine; *la calma che precede la tempesta*, the calm that precedes the storm; *i mesi precedenti il mio matrimonio*, the months previous to (o before) my marriage; *precedimi, io vengo fra breve*, go ahead, I'm just coming; *ti precederò di qualche settimana*, I'll precede you by a few weeks || *— qlcu.*, (*in dignità*)

to have precedence over s.o. || *far —*, to precede: *l'autore fa — al suo libro una lunga prefazione*, the author precedes his book with a long preface || *v.i.* to come first, to precede: *precede una lunga lista di nomi*, first comes a long list of names.

precessióne, *s.f.* (*astr.*) precession.

precettànte, *s.c.* 1. (*chi ammaestra*) teacher 2. (*dir.*) summoner.

precettàre, *v.t.* 1. (*imporre*) to bind over: *— qlcu. a mantenere la pace*, to bind s.o. over to keep the peace 2. (*dir.*) to summon 3. (*mil.*) to call to arms.

precettàto, *s.m.* 1. person bound over 2. (*dir.*) person summoned 3. (*mil.*) soldier called to arms, mobilized soldier.

precettatóre, *s.m.* (*dir.*) summoner.

precettazióne, *s.f.* 1. (*dir.*) summoning 2. (*mil.*) calling to arms.

precettìsta, *s.c.* author of literary precepts.

precettìstica, *s.f.* 1. art of making precepts 2. (*arte dell'insegnare con precetti*) teaching by precepts.

precettìvo, *ag.* (*rar.*) preceptive.

precètto, *s.m.* 1. (*regola, norma*) rule: *i precetti della buona educazione*, the rules of good manners 2. (*ordine*) order, precept: *devi ubbidire ai precetti dei tuoi superiori*, you must obey the orders of your betters; *dare un —*, to give a precept 3. (*relig.*) precept: *i precetti della Chiesa*, the precepts of the Church; *osservare il — pasquale*, to fulfil one's Easter duties || *festa di —*, holy-day of obligation 4. (*dir.*) injunction to pay, precept 5. (*mil.*) order to rejoin one's regiment, call-up notice.

precettoràto, *s.m.* tutorship.

precettóre, *s.m.* 1. (*insegnante*) teacher; preceptor 2. (*istitutore*) tutor.

precettríce, *s.f.* 1. (*insegnante*) teacher 2. (*istitutrice*) tutoress.

precídere, *v.t.* 1. to cut off, to remove: *la sua condotta gli precise ogni possibilità di promozione*, his behaviour cut off all possibility of his promotion 2. (*impedire*) to obstruct.

precíngere, *v.t.* (*letter.*) to gird, to girdle; to encircle || **precíngersi**, *v.r.* to gird oneself.

precínto, *ag.* surrounded; encircled.

precipitàbile, *ag.* (*chim.*) precipitable.

precipitabilità, *s.f.* (*chim.*) precipitability.

precipitànte, *s.m.* (*chim.*) precipitant.

precipitàre, *v.t.* 1. to precipitate, to throw (headlong), to throw (down), to fling, to hurl: *egli fu precipitato in mare*, he was precipitated (o hurled) into the sea; *lo precipitarono dalla rupe*, they threw him headlong (o down) from the cliff 2. (*affrettare troppo, fare in gran fretta*) to precipitate, to hasten, to hurry: *non precipitiamo*, let's not be over-hasty; *non — le tue decisioni*, do not rush to a decision (o do not take headlong decisions); *— gli eventi*, to precipitate events 3. (*chim.*) to precipitate || *v.i.* 1. to fall (anche *fig.*); (*di aereo*) to crash: *l'aeroplano precipitò su una montagna*, the plane crashed on a mountain; *egli precipitò nel burrone*, he fell into the ravine; *i prezzi stanno precipitando*, prices are falling; *il tetto precipitò durante il terremoto*, the roof collapsed during the earthquake; *— in rovina*, to fall to ruin 2. (*chim.*) to precipitate || **precipitàrsi**, *v.r.* 1. to throw oneself, to fling oneself, to hurl oneself: *— contro il nemico*, to throw oneself against the enemy 2. (*affrettarsi*) to rush, to dash: *egli si precipitò nel salone*, he rushed into the hall; *egli si precipitò verso la porta*, he dashed to the door.

precipitataménte, *av.* 1. precipitately 2. (*avventatamente*) precipitately, hastily.

precipitàto, *ag.* (*affrettato, avventato*) precipitate, hasty; rash; *una decisione precipitata*, a hasty (o precipitate) decision; *un giudizio —*, a rash (o inconsiderate) judgment; *una partenza precipitata*, a hasty (o abrupt) departure || *s.m.* (*chim.*) precipitate: *— bianco*, white precipitate; *— fioccoso*, flaky precipitate.

precipitazióne, *s.f.* 1. headlong fall, precipitation 2. (*fretta eccessiva, avventatezza*) precipitation, precipitancy, haste: *agire con* —, to act with precipitation; *agire senza* —, to act deliberately; *fare ql.co. con* —, to do sthg. with haste; *uscire con* —, to hasten (*o* to hurry) out (*o* to go out in a hurry) 3. (*chim.*) precipitation 4. (*meteorologia*) precipitation.

precípite, *ag.* (*rar.*) 1. headlong 2. (*ripido, scosceso*) precipitous, steep.

precipitévole, *ag.*1.(*scosceso*) precipitous, steep 2. (*affrettato*) hasty.

precipitevolménte, *av.* 1. (*a precipizio*) precipitously 2. (*in fretta*) hastily.

precipitosaménte, *av.* 1. (*impetuosamente*) headlong; rashly: *correre* —, to run headlong 2. (*frettolosamente*) hastily, precipitately; *decidere* —, to decide hastily (*o* precipitately); *ritornare* —, to hasten back.

precipitóso, *ag.* 1. (*impetuoso*) headlong: *una fuga precipitosa*, a headlong flight; *un torrente* —, a headlong torrent 2. (*frettoloso*) hasty, precipitate; rash: *un giudizio* —, a rash judgement; *ritorno* —, hasty return; *avanzare a passi precipitosi*, to hasten forward; *essere troppo* — *nel fare ql.co.*, to be over-hasty in doing sthg. 3. (*scosceso*) precipitous, steep: *discesa precipitosa*, precipitous descent.

precipízio, *s.m.* 1. precipice: *spaventoso* —, fearful precipice || *a* —, (*a picco*) perpendicularly; (*precipitosamente*) headlong: *una roccia che scende a* — *sul mare*, a sheer cliff; *correre a* —, to run headlong 2. (*rovina*) ruin; precipice: *sull'orlo del* —, on the brink of precipice; *andare in* —, to be on the road to ruin 3. (*fam.*) (*gran quantità*) lots (*pl.*), heaps (*pl.*): *ce n'era un* —, there were (*o* was) lots (*o* heaps).

precipuaménte, *av.* 1. (*principalmente*) mainly, chiefly 2. (*sopra tutto*) above all.

precípuo, *ag.* principal, main, chief: *la ragione precipua*, the main reason; *lo scopo* —, the principal (*o* chief) aim.

precisaménte, *av.* 1. precisely: *questa è* — *la verità*, this is precisely the truth 2. (*esattamente*) exactly.

precisaménte, *inter.* precisely!, quite so!: —, *l'ho visto!*, quite so, I did see him!.

precisàre, *v.t.* to specify; to state precisely; to tell exactly: *ce n'erano dieci o dodici, non posso* —, there were ten or twelve, I can't say exactly; *non posso ancora precisarti la data*, I can't fix a date yet; *posso precisarti i nomi*, I can tell you the names exactly; *precisa l'indirizzo*, give the exact address; — *i dettagli*, to go further into details (*o* to give full details).

precisióne, *s.f.* 1. precision; (*accuratezza*) accuracy: — *del tiro*, accuracy of fire; — *nei calcoli*, precision in calculations; *bilancia di* —, precision balance; *strumento di* —, precision instrument; *tornio di* —, precision lathe; *esprimersi con* —, to speak unambiguously; *rispondere con* —, to answer accurately 2. (*chiarezza*) clarity; (*esattezza*) preciseness, exactness: — *di contorni*, sharpness of outline; — *di pensiero*, clarity of thought; — *di stile*, preciseness of style.

precíso, *ag.* 1. (*accurato*) careful: *è uno scolaro molto* —, he is a pupil who works well; *è sempre molto* — *nel suo lavoro*, he is always very careful in his work 2. (*esatto*) exact, precise: *definizione precisa*, precise (*o* exact) definition; *questo è il luogo* — *dove lo vidi*, this is the precise place where I saw him; *ricordo queste precise parole*, I remember these exact (*o* precise) words; *voglio una traduzione precisa*, I want an exact translation 3. (*definito*) definite, exact: *senza una ragione precisa*, for no definite reason; *non ha idee precise*, he has no definite ideas; *rispondere a dei bisogni precisi*, to answer definite needs 4. (*puntuale*) punctual: *sii* —, be punctual 5. (*identico*) identical: *questi due vestiti sono precisi*, these two dresses are identical 6. (*di ore, in punto*) sharp || *av.* precisely, exactly.

precitàto, *ag.* above mentioned, aforesaid.

preclaraménte, *av.* prominently, illustriously, nobly.

preclarità, *s.f.* prominence, illustriousness, eminence.

preclàro, *ag.* prominent, illustrious, noble.

preclúdere, *v.t.* to preclude, to bar: *gli fu preclusa la carriera militare*, he was barred from a military career; *questo preclude tutte le possibilità di successo*, this precludes all chance of success.

precòce, *ag.* precocious; premature; (*di pianta, frutto, stagione*) early, forward: *bimbo, ingegno* —, precocious child, talent; *delinquente* —, juvenile delinquent; *frutto, inverno* —, early (*o* forward) fruit, winter; *vecchiezza* —, premature old age; *questo bambino è* — *per la sua età*, this child is forward for his age.

precoceménte, *av.* precociously; prematurely; too early.

precocità, *s.f.* precociousness, precocity.

precògnito, *ag.* (*letter.*) foreknown.

precognizióne, *s.f.* precognition, foreknowledge.

preconcètto, *ag.* preconceived: *idee preconcette*, preconceived ideas || *s.m.* preconception; prejudice.

preconizzàre, *v.t.* 1. to foretell 2. (*eccl.*) to preconize.

preconizzatóre, *s.m.*, **preconizzatríce**, *s.f.* foreteller.

preconizzazióne, *s.f.* (*eccl.*) preconization.

preconoscènza, *s.f.* precognition, foreknowledge.

preconóscere, *v.t.* to foreknow, to know beforehand.

preconosciménto, *s.m.* foreknowledge.

precòrdi, *s.m.pl.* (*anat.*) pr(a)ecordia.

precordiàle, *ag.* (*anat.*) pr(a)ecordial.

precorrènte, *ag.* forerunning; anticipating || *s.c.* forerunner, precursor.

precórrere, *v.t.* to forerun; to precede; to anticipate: *egli precorre i tempi*, he is ahead of his times (*o* acts in advance of his time); *il pensiero precorre l'azione*, thought precedes action; — *gli eventi*, to anticipate events || *v.i.* to run before.

precorritóre, *ag.* forerunning; anticipating || *s.m.* **precorritríce**, *s.f.* forerunner, precursor.

precursóre, *ag.* precursory: *sintomi precursori*, precursory symptoms || *segni precursori*, harbingers || *s.m.* forerunner, precursor: *i precursori del Cristianesimo*, the forerunners (*o* precursors) of Christianity.

prèda, *s.f.* 1. prey (anche *fig.*); (*animale cacciato*) quarry: *animale, uccello di* —, animal, bird of prey; *i cani incalzavano la* —, the hounds were after the prey (*o* quarry); *cadere in* — *a...*, to fall a prey to... (anche *fig.*): *la città cadde in* — *al nemico*, the town fell a prey to the enemy; *cadere in* — *alle tentazioni*, to fall a prey to temptations || *essere in* — *a...*, to be a prey to...: *la casa era in* — *alle fiamme*, the house was engulfed in flames (*o* was ravaged by fire); *ella era in* — *ad una crisi di pianto*, she was having a fit of crying; *era in* — *alla disperazione, al rimorso*, he was a prey to despair, remorse; *essere in* — *al dolore*, to be grief-stricken 2. (*bottino, spoliazione*) booty, plunder: — *di guerra*, booty of war; *diritto di* —, right to plunder; *stavano facendo* — *di tutto ciò che trovavano*, they were plundering whatever they could find; *dare in* —, to give over to plunder.

predàce, *ag.* predatory, predacious.

predàre, *v.t.* 1. to plunder, to pillage: — *un paese*, to plunder a country 2. (*pirateggiare, ghermire in caccia*) to prey upon (sthg.): *i pirati predavano i mari*, pirates used to prey upon the seas.

predatóre, *ag.* predacious, predatory || *s.m.*, **predatríce**, *s.f.* plunderer, pillager, looter.

predatòrio, *ag.* predacious, predatory.

predecessóre, *s.m.* 1. predecessor, forerunner 2. *pl.* (*antenati*) ancestors, forefathers.

predèlla¹, *s.f.* 1. (*di altare*) altar step, predella 2. (*di cattedra*) platform 3. (*di un trono*) dais 4. (*sgabello*) stool.

predèlla², *s.f.* (*briglia*) bridle.

predellíno, *s.m.* **1.** (*di una vettura*) footboard, carriage step **2.** (*sgabello poggiapiedi*) footstool **3.** (*seggiolone per bambino*) child's high chair.

predellóne, *s.m.* high stool.

predestinàre, *v.t.* to predestine, to preordain, to destine; (*teol.*) to predestinate: *credeva che Dio l'avesse predestinato alla punizione eterna*, he thought that God had predestined him to eternal punishment; *era predestinato al successo*, he had been marked out for success; *era predestinato che ci rincontrassimo*, we were destined to meet again.

predestinatívo, *ag.* (*rar.*) predestinative.

predestinàto, *ag.* predestined, destined; (*teol.*) predestine(d): — *al paradiso*, predestined to paradise; — *ad una morte immatura*, destined to die an untimely death; *il mio desiderio non è — a realizzarsi*, my wish is not destined to come true; *pover'uomo, si vede che era —!*, poor man, it is clear that was his destiny!.

predestinazióne, *s.f.* **1.** (*teol.*) predestination **2.** (*destino prestabilito*) destiny, fate.

predeterminàre, *v.t.* to predetermine, to preordain.

predeterminataménte, *av.* in a predeterminate way.

predeterminàto, *ag.* predetermined, preordained.

predeterminazióne, *s.f.* predetermination.

predétto, *ag.* **1.** above-mentioned, aforesaid: *per la ragione predetta*, for the aforesaid reason **2.** (*presagito*) foretold (*predicativo*): *morì nel giorno —*, he died on the day foretold.

prediàle, *ag.* (*dir.*) pr(a)edial ‖ *s.f.* (*dir.*) land tax.

prèdica, *s.f.* **1.** sermon: *l'argomento di una —*, the subject of a sermon; *il libro delle prediche*, the book of sermons; *uno scrittore di prediche*, a writer of sermons (*o* sermon-writer); *quel prete fa delle belle prediche*, that priest preaches very well (*o* gives good sermons); *andare alla —*, to go to hear a sermon; *sonare a —*, to ring the bell for the sermon ‖ *senti da che pulpito viene la —*, (*iron.*) it is the case of the pot calling the kettle black **2.** (*fam.*) (*ramanzina*) telling-off, talking-to: *quel ragazzaccio ha bisogno di una —*, that naughty boy needs a good talking-to; *fare una — a qlcu.*, to give s.o. a telling-off.

predicàbile, *ag.s.m.* predicable.

predicaménto, *s.m.* (*letter.*) **1.** sermon **2.** (*fil.*) predicament (*gener. pl.*) **3.** *essere in — per un posto*, to be considered for a job.

predicànte, *ag.* preaching.

predicàre, *v.t.* **1.** to preach, to proclaim: — *il Vangelo, la guerra, la pace*, to preach (*o* to proclaim) the Gospel, war, peace ‖ *far come padre Zappata, che predicava bene e razzolava male*, not to practise what one preaches ‖ — *l'Avvento, la Quaresima*, to preach during Advent, Lent **2.** (*fil. log.*) to predicate **3.** (*fam.*) to preach, to lecture: *è tanto che glielo predico*, I have told him so many times; *non fa che —, sono stufa di lui*, he does nothing but preach, I am sick and tired of him; *smetti di —!*, stop sermonizing! ‖ *v.i.* to preach: *oggi predica padre Paolo*, Father Paul is going to preach today; *un tempo si predicava spesso in piazza*, once they often used to preach in public ‖ — *al deserto, al vento*, to waste one's words.

predicàto, *ag.* **1.** preached **2.** (*esaltato*) preached up, praised, exalted: *la tanto predicata virtù*, the much praised (*o* exalted) virtue ‖ *s.m.* **1.** (*gram.*) predicate: — *verbale*, verbal predicate **2.** *essere in — per*, to be considered for: *è in — per una carica importante*, he is being considered for an important appointment.

predicatóre, *s.m.* preacher: *è un cattivo —*, he is a poor preacher; *Padre T. è un celebre —*, Father T. is a famous preacher ‖ *frati predicatori*, preaching-friars (*o* Dominicans *o* Predicants) ‖ *smetti di fare il —!*, (*fam.*) stop sermonizing!.

predicatòrio, *ag.* predicatory; (*sentenzioso*) preachifying: *mi parlò in tono —*, he spoke to me in a preachifying tone.

predicazióne, *s.f.* preaching: *la — del Vangelo*, the preaching of the Gospel; *il ministero della —*, the office of a preacher; *si diede alla —*, he devoted himself to preaching.

predicòzzo, *s.m.* (*scherz.*) lecture, talking-to: *fare un — a qlcu.*, to give s.o. a lecture (*o* a talking-to).

predigeríto, *ag.* predigested.

predigestióne, *s.f.* **1.** (*fisiol.*) preliminary digestion **2.** (*chim.*) predigestion.

predilètto, *ag.* favourite; (*il più caro*) dearest: *i gialli sono la sua lettura prediletta*, thrillers are his favourite reading; *questo è il mio amico —*, this is my dearest friend ‖ *s.m.* pet, darling, favourite: *il — della mamma*, mother's pet (*o* darling); *era il — dell'insegnante*, he was the teacher's pet.

predilezióne, *s.f.* **1.** predilection, partiality, fondness: *a tutti nota la sua — per il jazz*, his partiality for jazz is known to everybody; *ha una — per questo genere di lettura*, he has a fondness for this kind of reading **2.** (*oggetto prediletto*) favourite.

predilígere, *v.t.* to prefer, to have a predilection for (s.o., sthg.); to like better (*fra due*); to like best (*fra molti*); (*aver più caro*) to hold dearer (*fra due*); to hold dearest (*fra molti*): *predilige l'architettura moderna*, he prefers (*o* has a predilection for) modern architecture; *l'amico che prediligo*, the friend I hold dearest; *amo entrambi i miei figli, ma prediligo il minore*, I love both my children but hold the younger dearer; *mi interessano tanto la prosa che la poesia, ma prediligo quest'ultima*, I am interested both in prose and in poetry, but I prefer the latter.

predimostrazióne, *s.f.* (*letter.*) previous demonstration.

prèdio, *s.m.* (*dir.*) property: — *rustico*, country property.

predíre, *v.t.* **1.** to foretell, to forecast, to predict, to prophesy: *si è avverato tutto ciò che hai predetto*, everything you prophesied has come true; — *una disgrazia*, to predict a misfortune; — *il futuro*, to foretell the future: — *il futuro a qlcu.*, to predict s.o.'s future: *crede che la zingara possa predirgli il futuro*, he believes that the gipsy can predict his future; — *il tempo*, to forecast the weather **2.** (*preannunziare*) to portend, to forebode: *questo vento predice pioggia*, this wind forebodes rain; *il volo di taluni uccelli predicava sciagure*, the flight of some birds portended misfortunes.

predispórre, *v.t.* **1.** to predispose; (*indurre*) to induce: *predisponilo in mio favore*, predispose him in my favour; *l'alcool predispone l'organismo alle malattie nervose*, alcohol predisposes the organism to nervous diseases; *questo libro ti predisporrà al sonno*, this book will put you to sleep **2.** (*provvedere in anticipo*) to prearrange, to arrange beforehand; (*progettare*) to plan: — *tutto per una spedizione*, to arrange everything for an expedition; — *un viaggio in America*, to plan a trip to America ‖ **predispórsi,** *v.r.* to prepare oneself: *si predispose con rassegnazione alla morte*, he prepared himself for death with resignation.

predisposizióne, *s.f.* **1.** (*med.*) (*diatesi*) predisposition, proneness: — *all'artrite*, proneness to arthritis **2.** (*inclinazione*) bent; tendency: *avere — alla musica*, to have a bent for music **3.** (*preparazione*) preparation, arrangement.

predispósto, *ag.* **1.** predisposed: — *in mio favore*, predisposed in my favour **2.** (*preparato*) arranged, prepared.

predizióne, *s.f.* prediction, prophecy.

predominànte, *ag.* predominant, predominating, prevalent, prevailing: *abitudine, opinione —*, prevalent (*o* prevailing) habit, opinion; *un colore —*, a predominant colour; *malattia — nel paese*, disease (that is) prevalent in the country.

predominànza, *s.f.* predominance, prevalence.

predominàre, *v.i.* to predominate, to prevail: *il diletto spesso predomina sull'utile*, pleasure often predominates (*o* prevails) over profit; *in lui predomina* *l'orgoglio*, pride is the predominant feature of his character; *in questa stanza predomina il rosso*, red predominates in this room; *gli occhi neri predominano nel sud*, black eyes prevail in the South ‖ *v.t.* (*sopraffare*) to overcome, to overwhelm: *l'ira lo predomina spesso*, he is often overcome by anger.

predomínio, *s.m.* **1.** predominance, prevalence; (*superiorità*) pre-eminence, superiority; (*preponderanza*) preponderance; (*supremazia*) supremacy: *il — della Chiesa in Italia nel secolo diciassettesimo*, the supremacy of the Church in Italy in the seventeenth century; *il — delle passioni*, the prevalence of passions; *soggetto al — straniero*, subject to foreign supremacy **2.** (*sovrabbondanza di una sostanza*): *acqua con — di sali*, (*chim.*) water in which salts predominate.

predóne, *s.m.* marauder, plunderer; (*ladrone*) robber.

preelèggere, *v.t.* to pre-elect: *il Signore preelesse Maria a essere madre del Salvatore*, the Lord pre-elected Mary to be the mother of Jesus Christ.

preelezióne, *s.f.* pre-election, predestination.

preesistènte, *ag.* pre-existent: *condizioni preesistenti alla guerra*, conditions existing before the war.

preesistènza, *s.f.* pre-existence.

preesistere, *v.i.* to pre-exist.

prefabbricáre, *v.t.* to pre-fabricate.

prefabbricáto, *ag.* pre-fabricated.

prefabbricazióne, *s.f.* pre-fabrication.

prefáto, *ag.* aforesaid.

prefázio, *s.m.* (*eccl.*) preface.

prefazióne, *s.f.* preface, introduction, foreword.

preferènza, *s.f.* **1.** preference: *non ho preferenze*, I have no preferences; *quell'attore gode le preferenze del pubblico*, that actor enjoys the favour of the public; *avere — per qlcu.*, *ql.co.*, to prefer s.o., sthg.; *dare la — a ql.co.*, to give sthg. the preference ‖ *a — di*, rather than (o in preference to): *io prenderei questo a — dell'altro*, I should prefer to take this one rather than the other ‖ *di —*, preferably (o mostly o generally): *di — vado al mare*, I generally go to the seaside **2.** (*parzialità*) partiality, favouritism: *gli usò troppe preferenze*, he was too partial to him.

preferenziále, *ag.* preferential: *tariffa —*, preferential tariff; *titoli*, *azioni preferenziali*, (*econ.*) preference stock (o shares); *un trattamento —*, a preferential treatment; *voto —*, preferential vote.

preferíbile, *ag.* preferable: *sarebbe — parlargli*, it would be better to speak to him.

preferibilménte, *av.* preferably, in preference.

preferíre, *v.t.* **1.** to prefer; to like better, to like more (*fra due*); to like best, to like most (*fra molti*): *ecco ciò che preferisco*, here is what I like most; *mio fratello preferisce il sidro al vino*, my brother prefers cider to wine (o likes cider better than wine); *Rosa preferisce stare a casa piuttosto che venire con te*, Rose prefers to stay at home rather than come with you; *noi preferiremmo andare piuttosto che restare*, we had (o we would) rather go than stay **2.** (*giudicare opportuno*) to choose, to like: *fate come preferite*, do as you like (o choose).

preferíto, *ag.* favourite ‖ *s.m.*, **preferíta**, *s.f.* favourite, pet, darling.

prefettízia, *s.f.* frock-coat.

prefettízio, *ag.* prefectorial, prefectoral; prefect (*attributivo*).

prefètto, *s.m.* (*st. amm. eccl.*) prefect: *— degli studi*, master responsible for discipline; *— di disciplina*, (*nei collegi cattolici*) prefect; *— di polizia*, prefect of police; *il — di Roma*, the prefect of Rome.

prefettúra, *s.f.* (*st. amm. eccl.*) prefecture.

prèfica, *s.f.* **1.** (*st. romana*) hired female mourner **2.** *fig.* (*persona piagnucolosa*) whimperer, whiner.

prefíggere, *v.t.* **1.** (*fissare*) to fix, to prefix: *— una data*, *un termine*, to fix a date, a term **2.** (*prestabilire*) to pre-establish, to establish beforehand; (*predisporre*) to pre-arrange, to arrange beforehand ‖ **prefíggersi**, *v.r.* to propose to oneself; to be determined, to be

resolved: *mi prefiggo di farlo*, I am determined (o resolved) to do it; *mi prefiggo di pagarlo domani*, I am determined to pay him tomorrow; *si prefisse grandi cose ma non riuscì in nessuna*, he intended great things but he was successful in none; *— uno scopo*, to propose an aim to oneself.

prefiggiménto, *s.m.* **1.** (*il fissare*) fixing **2.** (*il prestabilire*) pre-establishing; (*il predisporre*) pre-arranging **3.** (*proposito*) proposal, determination, resolve.

prefigurànte, *ag.* prefiguring.

prefiguràre, *v.t.* to prefigure.

prefiguráto, *ag.* prefigurate, prefigured.

prefigurazióne, *s.f.* prefiguration.

prefìsso, *ag.* **1.** (*prestabilito*) pre-established, pre-determinate; (*predisposto*) pre-arranged: *la meta prefissa*, the appointed goal; *avere uno scopo —*, to have an aim in view; *ha lo scopo — di lasciare il paese*, he intends to leave the country **2.** (*gram.*) prefixed: *particelle prefisse*, prefixed particles ‖ *s.m.* (*gram.*) prefix.

preflorazióne, *s.f.* (*bot.*) prefloration.

prefogliazióne, *s.f.* (*bot.*) prefoliation.

preformáre, *v.t.* (*letter.*) to preform.

preformazióne, *s.f.* (*letter.*) preformation.

pregàre, *v.t.* **1.** to pray: *andò in chiesa a —*, he went to church to pray; *— Dio*, to pray God ‖ *prega il Signore che io non ti veda*, pray God I won't see you **2.** (*domandare*) to ask, to beg; (*richiedere*) to request: *pregalo di venir dentro*, ask him (to come) in; *mi ha pregato di fargli un favore*, he asked me to do him a favour; *mi pregò di aspettarlo*, he asked me to wait for him; *mi pregò di non lasciarlo*, he begged me not to leave him; *siete pregati di essere puntuali*, you are requested to be punctual; *siete pregati di andarvene subito*, you are requested to go away (o to leave) at once; *ti prego di comportarti bene*, I beg you to behave well; *ti prego di venire al più presto*, please, come as soon as possible ‖ *lo fece senza farsi —*, he did it without much persuading; *si fa sempre — per venire*, it takes lot of persuading to get him to come; *vieni*, *non farti —*, come in, don't wait to be asked.

pregévole, *ag.* valuable: *quadro —*, valuable picture.

pregevolézza, *s.f.* value, valuableness.

preghièra, *s.f.* **1.** prayer: *preghiere del mattino*, *della sera*, morning, evening prayers; *— di ringraziamento*, prayer of thanksgiving; *in —*, in prayer; *libro di preghiere*, prayer-book; *dire le preghiere*, to say one's prayers **2.** (*domanda*, *richiesta*) request, entreaty: *— di aiuto*, request for help; *su — di qlcu.*, at s.o.'s request; *dopo molte preghiere decise di parteggiare per noi*, after many entreaties he decided to side with us; *rimanere sordo alle preghiere di qlcu.*, to remain deaf (o to close one's ears) to s.o.'s entreaties; *rivolgere una — a qlcu.*, to make a request to s.o.; *soddisfare le preghiere di qlcu.*, to satisfy s.o.'s requests.

pregiàbile, *ag.* valuable, worthy.

pregiabilità, *s.f.* valuableness, value.

pregiàre, *v.t.* **1.** (*stimare*, *apprezzare*) to esteem, to appreciate, to value: *pregio moltissimo la sua opinione*, I esteem his opinion very highly (o I hold his opinion in great esteem) **2.** (*lodare*) to praise ‖ **pregiàrsi**, *v.r.* to be honoured: *mi pregio della sua amicizia*, I have the honour of his friendship (o I consider it an honour to be his friend) ‖ *mi pregio comunicarvi che*, I am honoured (o I have the honour) to tell you that ‖ *mi pregio porgervi i miei distinti saluti*, I beg to remain yours faithfully...

pregiàto, *ag.* **1.** (*stimato*) esteemed ‖ *Pregiatissimo Signore*, (*come inizio di una lettera*) Dear Sir; *Pregiatissimo Signor Giuseppe Rossi*, (*negli indirizzi*) Giuseppe Rossi Esq.; *ho ricevuto la vostra pregiata del...*, (*comm.*) I have received your favour of... **2.** (*prezioso*) precious; (*di valore*) valuable: *vini pregiati*, vintage wines; *l'argento è meno — dell'oro*, silver is less valuable than gold.

prègio, *s.m.* **1.** (*stima*, *considerazione*) esteem, regard:

ho in gran — *le tue opinioni*, I set a high value on your opinion (*o* I hold your opinion in high esteem *o* I highly appreciate your opinion); *essere in gran* — *presso qlcu.*, to be held in high esteem by s.o. **2.** (*valore*) value, worth: *di* —, valuable; *di nessun* —, of no value; *porcellane di* —, valuable china; *statua di grande, poco* —, statue of great, little value (*o* worth) **3.** (*merito*) merit; (*buona qualità*) good quality: *l'inestimabile* — *della sincerità*, the inestimable quality of sincerity; *conosco i tuoi pregi*, I know your merits; *ha il* — *di essere breve*, it has the merit of being brief.

pregiudicànte, *ag.* prejudicial.

pregiudicàre, *v.t.* **1.** (*compromettere*) to prejudice; to jeopardize; to be prejudicial to (s.o., sthg.), to compromise; to undermine: *questo pregiudicherà la sua fede in altre cose*, this will undermine his faith in other things; *questo pregiudicherà la tua reputazione*, this will compromise (*o* undermine) your reputation; *la sua partenza pregiudicò moltissimo i miei programmi*, his departure was most prejudicial to my plans; *la sua posizione fu pregiudicata moltissimo da tutti i pettegolezzi sul suo passato*, his position was compromised very much by all the gossip about his past **2.** (*danneggiare*) to prejudice, to impair, to damage, to injure, to harm: *non devi* — *la tua salute*, you must not impair your health; *senza* — *i miei diritti*, without prejudicing my rights **3.** (*rar.*) (*giudicare prima del tempo*) to prejudge, to judge beforehand ‖ **pregiudicàrsi**, *v.r.* to harm one's reputation.

pregiudicàto, *ag.* **1.** (*già giudicato*) prejudged: *una opinione pregiudicata*, a prejudice **2.** (*pieno di pregiudizi*) full of prejudice: *ha una mente pregiudicata*, he is full of prejudice **3.** (*votato all'insuccesso*) bound to fail: *è un progetto* —, it is a project bound to fail ‖ *s.m.* (*dir.*) previous offender.

pregiudiziàle, *ag.* **1.** (*che pregiudica*) prejudicial **2.** (*dir.*) (*che precede il giudizio*) prejudicial ‖ *s.f.* (*dir.*) prejudicial question.

pregiudizialménte, *av.* **1.** prejudicially **2.** (*che precede il giudizio*) previously, preliminarily.

pregiudiziévole, *ag.* prejudicial, detrimental.

pregiudízio, *s.m.* **1.** prejudice, bias: *egli ha un* — *contro l'arte moderna*, he has a prejudice (*o* a bias) against modern art **2.** (*danno*) prejudice, damage, detriment: *a, con* — *di*, (*consapevolmente*) in prejudice of; (*inconsapevolmente*) to the prejudice of: *egli lavora moltissimo con* — *della sua salute*, he works very hard to the detriment of his health; *falsificò un assegno a* — *del principale*, he forged a cheque in prejudice of his employer; *uscì al freddo, a* — *della sua salute*, she went out in the cold to the prejudice of her health; *essere di* — *a*, to be prejudicial to **3.** (*giudizio anticipato*) prejudgement.

pregnànte, *ag.* **1.** pregnant **2.** (*denso di significato*) pregnant, weighty: *parola* —, weighty word; *risposta* —, pregnant answer.

prégno, *ag.* **1.** (*gravido*) pregnant **2.** (*fig. letter.*) (*pieno*) full; (*ricco*) rich (in sthg.); (*saturo*) saturated (with sthg.); (*impregnato*) impregnated (with sthg.): *aria pregna di umidità*, air saturated with moisture; *libro* — *di concetti*, book full of thought; *occhi pregni di lacrime*, eyes full of tears.

prègo[1], *s.m.* (*poet.*) prayer.

prègo[2], *inter.* (*risposta a* grazie) that's all right!, don't mention it!, not at all!; (*amer.*) you're welcome!.

pregustaménto, *s.m.* foretaste, anticipation.

pregustàre, *v.t.* to foretaste, to anticipate, to look forward to (sthg., doing): — *il piacere di fare ql.co.*, to anticipate the pleasure of doing sthg.; — *la vendetta*, to look forward to vengeance.

pregustatóre, *s.m.* **1.** foretaster **2.** (*st.*) taster.

pregustatríce, *s.f.* foretaster.

pregustazióne, *s.f.* foretaste, anticipation.

preindicàto, *ag.* above-mentioned.

preistòria, *s.f.* prehistory: *gli uomini della* —, prehistoric men.

preistòrico, *ag.* **1.** prehistoric: *età preistorica*, prehistoric age **2.** (*vecchissimo*) ancient.

prelatésco, *ag.* (*spreg.*) prelatish.

prelatízio, *ag.* prelatic(al): *abito* —, prelate's gown; *dignità prelatizia*, prelatic(al) dignity.

prelàto, *s.m.* (*eccl.*) prelate: — *maggiore*, major prelate; — *minore*, minor prelate.

prelatúra, *s.f.* (*eccl.*) prelacy, prelature.

prelazióne, *s.f.* (*dir.*) pre-emption.

prelevaménto, *s.m.* **1.** drawing: — *di sangue*, (*med.*) drawing of blood (*o* blood abstraction) **2.** (*comm.*) drawing, withdrawal; (*somma prelevata*) amount drawn: — *di un campione*, drawing of a sample; *ho fatto un* — *di 200.000 lire alla banca*, I have drawn 200,000 lire from the bank; *ottenuto da* — *dalle riserve*, obtained by drawing on the reserves; *addebitare il proprietario per i prelevamenti fatti a titolo privato*, to debit the proprietor for all the amounts drawn for his personal use.

prelevàre, *v.t.* **1.** to draw: — *il sangue*, (*med.*) to draw blood **2.** (*comm.*) to draw, to withdraw: — *un campione*, to draw a sample; — *denaro dalla banca*, to draw (*o* to withdraw) funds from the bank.

prelezióne, *s.f.* introductory lecture.

prelibàre, *v.t.* to have a foretaste of (sthg.), to foretaste.

prelibàto, *ag.* **1.** excellent; delicious; choice (*attributivo*): *nella loro cantina hanno dei vini prelibati*, they have choice wines in their cellar **2.** (*di argomento*) touched: *l'argomento, finora* —, *sarà trattato largamente*, the subject, only touched so far, will be dealt with in detail.

prelibazióne, *s.f.* prelibation, foretaste.

prelièvo, *V.* prelevaménto.

preliminàre, *ag.* preliminary: *un'introduzione* —, a preliminary introduction; *daremo anzitutto alcune notizie preliminari*, first of all we shall give some preliminary news ‖ *s.m.* **1.** (*premessa*) introduction; premise: *preliminari all'etica*, introduction to ethics **2.** (*primo accordo*) preliminary: *i preliminari della pace*, the preliminaries to peace.

preliminarménte, *av.* preliminarily.

prelodàto, *ag.* (*rar.*) above-mentioned.

prelúdere, *v.i.* **1.** to introduce (sthg.): *preluderà all'argomento con poche parole*, he will introduce the subject in few words **2.** (*preannunziare*) to prelude (sthg.); to foreshadow (sthg.): *il cielo prelude alla tempesta*, the sky forebodes a storm; *segni che preludono alla guerra*, signs which foreshadow war; *un terribile bombardamento preluse alla battaglia*, a terrible bombardment preluded the battle.

preludiàre, *v.i.* (*mus.*) to prelude.

prelúdio, *s.m.* **1.** (*mus.*) prelude: *il* — *di questa fuga è piuttosto difficile*, the prelude to this fugue is rather difficult; *mi piace molto il* — *di quell'opera*, I love the prelude to that opera **2.** (*segno precursore*) prelude; beginning: *quello fu il* — *della guerra*, that was the prelude to the war.

prematuraménte, *av.* prematurely: *morì* —, he died before his time.

prematúro, *ag.* premature, untimely: *morte prematura*, untimely death; *parto* —, premature birth; *era* — (*il*) *farlo*, it was too early to do it; *non prendere una decisione prematura*, don't make a hasty decision.

premeditàre, *v.t.* to premeditate; to design, to plan, to contrive: *avevano premeditato una fuga*, they had planned an escape; *sembra che abbia premeditato il delitto*, he appears to have premeditated the crime.

premeditataménte, *av.* premeditatedly, with premeditation.

premeditàto, *ag.* premeditated: *assassinio* —, premeditated (*o* wilful) murder.

premeditazióne, *s.f.* premeditation: *con* —, with

premeditation; *fu un delitto senza* —, it was an unpremeditated crime.

premènte, *ag.* 1. (*urgente*) pressing, urgent 2. *pompa* —, (*mec.*) force-pump.

prementovàto, *ag.* (*rar.*) above-mentioned.

prèmere, *v.t.* 1. to press: *premi il grilletto!*, press the trigger!; — *un bottone*, to press a button 2. (*stringere*) to pinch: *queste scarpe premono troppo il piede*, these shoes pinch my feet 3. (*spingere*) to press; (*incalzare*) to bear down on (s.o.): *la folla lo premeva da ogni lato*, the crowd pressed in upon him from all sides; *i nostri soldati premevano il nemico*, our soldiers bore down on the enemy ‖ *v.i.* 1. to press: *premi col dito sulla vena*, press your finger on the vein 2. (*pesare, gravare*) to press, to weigh: *se la scatola preme su ql.co. di leggero, lo schiaccia*, if the box weighs down on sth. lighter, it will crush it 3. (*insistere*) to press (sthg.), to insist: *non — su questo punto*, don't press (*o* don't insist on) this point 4. (*esercitare pressione morale*) to press (s.o.), to urge (s.o.): *premono su di lui perchè faccia testamento*, they are urging him to make his will 5. (*importare, stare a cuore*) to matter, to interest, to be of interest: *è il tuo avvenire che mi preme*, it is your future that matters to me; *mi preme che egli lo sappia subito*, I want him to know it at once; *mi preme di sapere se è arrivato bene*, I am anxious to know whether he has arrived safely; *la sua reputazione non gli preme affatto*, he holds his reputation very cheap; *i tuoi problemi mi premono assai*, I am very much concerned about your problems 6. (*essere urgente*) to be pressing, to be urgent: *questa faccenda preme*, this matter is pressing ‖ *preme!*, (*sulle lettere*) urgent (*o* for immediate delivery).

premèssa, *s.f.* 1. previous statement; introduction: *dopo alcune premesse affrontò il problema*, after some preliminary remarks he came to the problem; *farò una breve* —, I shall give a brief introduction ‖ *non fare tante premesse!*, (*scherz.*) don't beat about the bush! 2. (*fil.*) premise, premiss: — *maggiore, minore*, major, minor premise.

premèsso, *ag.* previous.

preméttere, *v.t.* 1. to premise: *avevo premesso che non ne sapevo assolutamente niente*, I had stated in advance I knew nothing at all about it; *bisogna che premetta*, I must state beforehand; *premetterò alcune considerazioni di carattere generale*, I shall premise a few general remarks; *premetto questi particolari*, I premise these details ‖ *ciò premesso*, that being stated ‖ *premesso che egli abbia torto*, granted that he is wrong 2. (*mettere prima*) to put before, to place before: *di solito in inglese l'aggettivo va premesso al nome*, in English an adjective is generally placed before the noun.

premiàbile, *ag.* 1. priz(e)able, deserving a prize 2. (*degno di ricompensa*) worthy of reward.

premiàndo, *ag.* deserving a prize ‖ *s.m.* person worthy of a reward.

premiànte, *ag.* 1. awarding a prize, giving a prize 2. (*che ricompensa*) rewarding.

premiàre, *v.t.* 1. to give a prize to (s.o., sthg.); to award a prize to (s.o., sthg.): *egli fu premiato*, he was given a prize; *fu premiato con una borsa di studio*, he was awarded a scholarship 2. (*ricompensare*) to reward, to repay; to recompense: *voglio — la sua sincerità*, I want to reward his truthfulness; — *la diligenza di qlcu.*, to reward s.o.'s diligence; — *qlcu. per la sua gentilezza*, to recompense (*o* to repay) s.o. for his kindness.

premiàto, *ag.* 1. given a prize, awarded a prize ‖ *i premiati*, the prize-winners 2. (*ricompensato*) rewarded.

premiatóre, *s.m.*, **premiatríce**, *s.f.* 1. (*chi dà un premio*) prize giver 2. (*chi dà una ricompensa*) rewarder.

premiazióne, *s.f.* prize-giving, awarding of prizes.

première, *s.f.* 1. (*prima rappresentazione*) first performance, première 2. (*prima lavorante in una sartoria*) forewoman (*pl.* forewomen).

premilitàre, *ag.* premilitary ‖ *s.m.* member of a junior training corps.

preminènte, *ag.* pre-eminent.

preminènza, *s.f.* pre-eminence; superiority, excellence: *aver la — su qlcu.*, to have pre-eminence over s.o.

prèmio, *s.m.* 1. prize, award: — *di consolazione*, consolation prize; — *in denaro*, cash-prize; *distribuzione dei premi*, prize-giving; *gli fu assegnato il primo* —, he was awarded the first prize; *ricevette un libro in* —, he received a book as a prize; *vinse un grosso* —, he won a big prize; *concedere, dare un* —, to award a prize; *vincere un — ad una mostra*, to win (o to carry off) a prize at an exhibition ‖ *Premio Nobel*, Nobel prize 2. (*ricompensa*) reward, recompense, premium: — *per buona condotta*, reward for good conduct; — *per i propri servizi*, reward for one's services; *ogni fatica merita un* —, every effort deserves recognition; *lavorare senza speranza di* —, to work without hope of reward (*o* recompense) 3. (*comm.*) premium: — *d'assicurazione*, insurance premium; — *per l'assicurazione in caso di morte*, life premium; *calcolare il — su...*, to calculate the premium on... 4. (*incoraggiamento dato dallo Stato a industria, commercio, ecc.*) bounty: — *d'esportazione*, bounty on exportation.

prèmito, *s.m.* 1. pressure 2. (*med.*) tenesmus.

premitúra, *s.f.* 1. pressing: — *dell'uva*, grape-pressing 2. (*sugo spremuto*) juice.

premolàre, *ag.s.m.* (*anat.*) premolar.

premoníre, *v.t.* to premonish, to forewarn.

premonitóre, *ag.* premonitory, (fore)warning ‖ *s.m.*, **premonitríce**, *s.f.* premonitor.

premonitòrio, *ag.* premonitory, (fore)warning.

premonizióne, *s.f.* premonition, forewarning.

premoriènza, *s.f.* (*dir.*) predecease.

premoríre, *v.i.* (*letter.*) to predecease (s.o.), to die before (s.o.).

premozióne, *s.f.* (*fil. teol.*) predetermination, preordination.

premuníre, *v.t.* 1. to fortify beforehand; to forearm: *la fortezza era stata premunita contro gli attacchi*, the fortress had been fortified in advance against attacks 2. *fig.* (*cautelare, preservare*) to preserve: *la prudenza ci ha premuniti*, caution has made us wary ‖ **premunírsi**, *v.r.* to secure oneself, to protect oneself: *la città si premunì contro le inondazioni*, the city secured itself against floods; *dovresti premunirti contro questa eventualità*, you should take protective measures against this eventuality; — *di una rivoltella*, to provide oneself with a revolver.

premunizióne, *s.f.* 1. premunition 2. *fig.* precaution.

premúra, *s.f.* 1. (*cura, sollecitudine*) care: *avrò — di fartelo sapere al più presto*, I shall take care to let you know as soon as possible; *dovresti lavorare con più* —, you should work more carefully; *ebbi — che tutto fosse fatto bene*, I took care that everything was done well; *ho — di sapere come sta*, I am anxious to know how he is; *non si è mai dato — di venirmi a trovare*, he has never troubled to come and see me 2. (*gentilezza*) kindness; (*attenzione*) attention: *è pieno di premure per me*, he is full of attention towards me; *ti ringrazio per tutta la tua* —, thank you for all your kindness; *le tue premure mi hanno veramente commosso*, your attentions have really touched me 3. (*fretta*) hurry, haste: *digli di finire il lavoro e fagli* —, tell him to hurry up and finish the job; *è un affare di* —, it is an urgent matter; *fagli — di venire*, tell him to hurry up and come; *ho — di andarmene*, I am in a hurry to go away; *ho molta* —, I am in a great hurry; *non c'è* —, there is no hurry; *fare ql.co. di* —, to do sthg. in haste.

premurosaménte, *av.* 1. (*con cura, sollecitudine*) attentively, with care, solicitously 2. (*gentilmente*) kindly, politely 3. (*con prontezza*) readily.

premuróso, *ag.* 1. (*sollecito*) thoughtful, attentive, solicitous 2. (*gentile*) kind, polite.

premúto, *ag.* pressed; *fig.* urged, driven.

prenarràre, *v.t.* to mention above.

prenàscere, *v.i.* to be born before (s.o.).

prèndere, *v.t.* **1.** to take; (*acchiappare*) to catch; (*afferrare*) to seize: *il gatto ha preso un topo,* the cat has caught a mouse; *hanno preso il ladro,* they have caught the thief; *ho preso due pesci, una lepre,* I've caught two fish, a hare; *le prese la mano,* he took her hand; *lo prese per il braccio e lo spinse fuori,* he seized him by the arm and pushed him out; *prendi questa lettera,* take this letter; *prendilo se lo vuoi,* take it if you want it; *prendo lezioni d'inglese,* I take English lessons; *prese la palla che gli gettai,* he caught the ball I threw him; *questa mattina non ero in tempo per — il treno delle nove,* this morning I was not in time to catch the nine o'clock train; *questo esempio è preso dalla Bibbia,* this example is taken from the Bible; *— un cavallo per le briglie,* to take (hold of) a horse by the bridle; *— d'assalto,* to take by storm (anche *fig.*); *— una fortezza,* to take (o to capture) a fortress; *— una laurea,* to take a degree; *— una medicina,* to take a medicine; *— le misure a qlcu.,* to take s.o.'s measure; *— per il collo qlcu.,* to seize s.o. by the throat; *fig.* to make s.o. pay through the nose; *— un premio,* to take (o to win) a prize; *— qlcu. fra le braccia,* to take s.o. in one's arms; *— qlcu. prigioniero,* to take s.o. prisoner; *— uno schiaffo,* to be slapped; *— una sgridata,* to be scolded (o to get a lecture); *— su,* to pick up: *prendi su quelle carte,* (*da terra*) pick up those papers; (*prendile con te*) take those papers with you; *— un taxi,* to take a taxi; *andare a —,* to fetch: *devo andarti a — un bicchiere d'acqua?,* shall I fetch you a glass of water?; *puoi andare a — tuo figlio a scuola?,* can you fetch my son from school?; *lasciarsi, farsi —* to let oneself be caught || *il cavallo gli prese la mano,* he lost control of the horse || *è uscito a — aria,* he has gone out to get some fresh air || *fu presa dalla collera,* she was seized with anger; *fu preso dalla paura,* he was seized with fright; *fu preso da malore,* he was taken ill || *fui preso in trappola,* I was caught in a trap || *lo presi per un inglese,* I took him for an Englishman || *non — freddo,* don't take cold || *non ha preso cibo da due giorni,* he hasn't eaten for two days || *non so come prenderlo, è sempre così nervoso,* I don't know how to handle him, he is always so irritable || *per chi mi prendi?,* who do you take me for? || *prendi questa strada,* take this road || *prendi tempo, non c'è fretta,* take your time, there's no hurry || *questo lavoro prende molto tempo,* this job takes a long time || *presi tanta pioggia,* I got soaking wet (o I got soaked to the skin) || *verrò a prenderti nel pomeriggio,* I'll call for you in the afternoon || *— a,* (*incominciare a*) to start (doing): *dopo la morte di suo figlio egli prese a bere,* after his son's death he took to drinking; *quando prende a parlare nessuno lo ferma,* when he starts talking nobody can stop him || *— un abbaglio, un granchio,* to slip up badly || *— l'abitudine di...,* to get into the habit of... || *— alla lettera,* to take literally || *— alloggio,* to take lodgings || *— a prestito,* to borrow || *— le armi,* to take up arms || *— atto di qlco.,* to take note of sthg. || *— attraverso i campi,* to strike out across the fields || *— un bagno,* to have (o to take) a bath || *— congedo da,* to take one's leave of || *— contatto con qlcu.,* to contact s.o. || *— coraggio,* to take heart || *— corpo,* to take shape || *— le cose come vengono,* to take things as they come || *— una cosa per un'altra,* to mistake one thing for another || *— dei pensionanti,* to take in boarders || *— di mira qlcu.,* to make s.o. the target of one's attacks || *— di petto,* to confront || *— fiato,* to take breath || *— una foto,* to take a photo || *— fuoco,* to catch (o to take) fire (anche *fig.*) || *— un impegno,* (*un appuntamento*) to make an appointment; *l'impegno di fare qlco.,* to pledge oneself to do sthg. || *— un impiego,* to take a job || *— in affitto,* to rent ||

— interesse a qlco., to take an interest in sthg. || *— il largo,* (*mar.*) to take to the open sea; *fig.* to make oneself scarce || *— una malattia, il raffreddore, la tosse,* to catch an illness, a cold, a cough || *— mano, pratica a,* (*impratichirsi di*) to get the knack of || *— marito, moglie,* to get married || *— nota di qlco.,* to take note of sthg. || *— note, appunti,* to take notes || *— o lasciare,* take it or leave it || *— un ordine,* (*comm.*) to book (o to take) an order || *— i pasti,* to have (o to take) one's meals || *— piede,* to catch on || *— qlco. a cuore,* to take sthg. to heart || *— qlco. in mala parte,* to take sthg. amiss || *— qlco. con le buone, con le cattive,* to handle s.o. with tact, to handle s.o. roughly || *— qlcu. in simpatia, antipatia,* to take a liking, a dislike to s.o. || *— una risoluzione,* to make a resolution || *— una bella sbornia,* to get as drunk as a lord || *— il sole,* to bask in the sun || *— un terno al lotto,* to have a stroke of luck || *— il toro per le corna,* to take the bull by the horns || *— il velo,* to take the veil || *prenderle,* to be beaten; (*di bambini*) to be smacked (o spanked): *il bambino le prese da suo padre,* the child was smacked by his father || *essere preso d'amore per...,* to fall in love with... **2.** (*assumere*) to take over, to assume; (*personale*) to engage: *abbiamo preso una cuoca, una dattilografa,* we engaged a cook, a typist; *— il comando,* to take over command; *— la direzione di una ditta,* to assume the management of a firm; *— la responsabilità di qlco.,* to take the responsibility for sthg. || *— delle informazioni,* to make inquiries || *— servizio,* to begin working **3.** (*cogliere, sorprendere*) to catch, to take: *lo presi mentre frugava nella mia scrivania,* I caught him while he was (o in the act of) rummaging in my desk; *— il nemico di sorpresa,* to take the enemy by surprise **4.** (*occupare*) to take up: *questa poltrona prende troppo posto,* this armchair takes up too much room **5.** (*comprare*) to buy, to get: *le devo — un soprabito nuovo,* I must buy (o get) a new coat for her **6.** (*ottenere, guadagnare*) to get: *dove prendesti quel denaro?,* where did you get that money?; *prende sempre brutti voti,* he always gets bad marks; *quanto prendi alla settimana?,* how much do you get (o earn) a week? **7.** (*far pagare*) to charge: *quanto prendi per lezione?,* how much do you charge for a lesson (o per lesson)? **8.** (*colpire*) to catch, to get, to hit: *lo presi sulla testa,* I caught him on the head; *prese il leone al primo colpo,* he got the lion first shot ♦ *v.i.* **1.** (*voltare*) to turn: *— a sinistra, a destra,* to turn (to the) left, (to the) right **2.** (*attecchire*) to take root: *questi fiori non prendono,* these flowers don't take root **3.** (*rappigliarsi*) to set: *il cemento non ha preso,* the cement has not set || **prèndersi,** *v.r.* **1.** (*prendere per sè*) to take: *non si prende mai nessuno svago,* he never takes time off; *se non lo vuoi me lo prendo io,* if you don't want it, I'll take it myself; *— la parte migliore di qlco.,* to take the best part of sthg.; *— una vacanza,* to take a holiday **2.** (*assumersi*) to assume: *mi sono preso l'impegno di curare i bambini,* I have promised to take care of the children; *— cura di,* to take care of; *— la responsabilità di qlco.,* to assume responsibility for sthg. **3.** (*Fraseologia*): *che ti prende?,* what's the matter with you? (o what's up?); *non prendertela!,* don't take on so!; *non prendertela con me,* don't be angry with me (o don't lay the blame on me); *se la prende comoda,* he takes it easy; *se la prende troppo per l'avvenire di suo fratello,* he is too concerned about his brother's future; *se la prese a cuore,* he took it to heart; *se l'è presa,* he has taken it amiss (o he has taken offence at it); *— delle libertà,* to take liberties; *— un malanno,* to catch an illness ♦ *v.r. reciproco: non sapevo che si erano presi a pugni,* I didn't know that they had come to blows; *si presero per i capelli, a pugni,* they went for each other.

prendíbile, *ag.* that may be taken; catchable.

prendisóle, *s.m.* sun-suit.

prenditóre, *s.m.,* **prenditríce,** *s.f.* **1.** receiver || *— del* *lotto*, receiver of money staked on a lottery 2. (*comm.*) (*di cambiale*) payee.

prenditoría, *s.f.* lottery office.

prenóme, *s.m.* prænomen (*pl.* prænomina).

prenominàto, *ag.* aforesaid, above-mentioned.

prenotàre, *v.t.* to book; to engage: — *una camera, un posto a teatro*, to book a room, a seat at the theatre || **prenotàrsi**, *v.r.* to book (sthg.).

prenotazióne, *s.f.* booking.

prenozióne, *s.f.* prenotion, foreknowledge.

prènsile, *ag.* prehensile: *coda* — prehensile tail.

prensióne, *s.f.* prehension: *organi di* —, (*di animali*) prehensile organs.

prenunziàre, *v.t.* to foretell, to prenunciate.

prenunziazióne, *s.f.* forenotice, prenunciation.

prenúnzio, *s.m.* (*letter.*) prediction.

preoccupàre, *v.t.* 1. to worry, to make anxious, to trouble: *c'è ql.co. che la preoccupa*, she has sthg. on her mind; *che cosa lo preoccupa?*, what is worrying him?; *quel che mi preoccupa è che...*, what troubles me is that...; *la sua salute mi preoccupa*, his health worries me; *il suo lavoro lo preoccupa molto*, his work worries him a great deal 2. (*arc.*) (*occupare prima*) to preoccupy || **preoccupàrsi**, *v.r.* to be worried (about s.o., sthg.); to be anxious (about s.o., sthg.); to worry (about s.o., sthg.): *egli si preoccupa per la salute di suo figlio*, he is worried about his son's health; *egli si preoccupa sempre della salute di suo figlio*, he worries about his son's health; *io mi preoccupo solo di riuscire*, I am only anxious to succeed; *non preoccuparti*, don't worry; *smetti di preoccuparti di queste piccole cose*, stop worrying about these little things || *non si è neppure preoccupato di farmelo sapere*, he hasn't even taken the trouble to let me know.

preoccupàto, *ag.* 1. worried (about s.o., sthg.), anxious (about s.o., sthg.), troubled (by sthg.): *era — di arrivare in tempo*, he was anxious to arrive in time; *sono — per queste notizie*, I am troubled by this news; *sono molto — per lui*, I am very worried about him 2. (*arc.*) (*occupato prima*) preoccupied.

preoccupazióne, *s.f.* 1. worry, care: *la — di un esame*, the worry of an examination; *è libero da tutte le preoccupazioni della vita quotidiana*, he is free from all the cares of everyday life; *la mia sola — è stata d'assicurare...*, my only care has been to ensure...; *la mia vita è sempre stata piena di preoccupazioni*, my life has always been full of worries; *quel ragazzo è una vera — per me*, that boy is a real worry to me 2. (*arc.*) (*occupazione precedente*) preoccupation 3. (*ret.*) (*prolessi*) prolepsis (*pl.* prolepses).

preopinànte, *s.c.* previous speaker.

preordinaménto, *s.m.* 1. prearrangement 2. (*predestinazione*) predestination.

preordinàre, *v.t.* 1. to prearrange, to predispose: *un piano preordinato*, a prearranged plan 2. (*predestinare*) to predestine.

preordinazióne, *s.f.* 1. prearrangement 2. (*predestinazione*) predestination.

preparàre, *v.t.* to prepare: — *un esame, una lezione, una medicina, un pranzo*, to prepare an examination, a lesson, a medicine, a dinner; — *qlcu. a una cattiva notizia*, to prepare s.o. for a piece of bad news; — *un ragazzo a un esame*, to coach a boy for an exam; — *la tavola*, to lay the table || *quel bambino sta preparando una birichinata*, that child is planning a piece of mischief || — *la strada*, *fig.* to pave the way || **preparàrsi**, *v.r.* to get ready, to prepare (oneself): *preparati se vuoi uscire*, get ready if you want to go out; *si sta preparando un temporale*, a storm is brewing.

preparatívo, *ag.* (*rar.*) preparatory || *s.m.* preparation: *i preparativi di guerra*, preparations for war; *i preparativi per la partenza*, preparations for leaving.

preparàto, *ag.* prepared; (*pronto*) ready: — *ad un esame*, prepared for an exam; *la tavola è preparata*, the table is laid || *s.m.* preparation: *preparati chimici*,

chemicals (*o chemical compounds o chemical preparations*); *preparati per lucidatura*, (*ind.*) polish; *è un ottimo* —, (*med.*) it is a very good preparation.

preparatóre, *s.m.* preparer.

preparatòrio, *ag.* preparatory.

preparatríce, *s.f.* preparer.

preparazióne, *s.f.* 1. preparation: *senza* —, without any (*o* with no) preparation; *la tua — per questo esame non è sufficiente*, you are not sufficiently prepared for this exam 2. (*tec.*) dressing, preparation: — *alla sbarbatura*, (*di ingranaggio*) preshaving; — *di uno stampo*, (*tip.*) make-ready; — *in piombo*, patenting; — *meccanica dei minerali*, ore dressing; — *per via umida*, wet dressing; *tempo di* —, (*mil.*) preparation time.

preponderànte, *ag.* preponderant, prevailing, predominant: *forza* —, preponderant strength; *motivo* —, predominant motif; *opinione* —, prevailing opinion; *partito* —, predominant party.

preponderanteménte, *av.* preponderantly.

preponderànza, *s.f.* preponderance, prevalence; (*maggioranza*) majority; (*superiorità*) superiority: — *della passione sulla riflessione*, preponderance of passion over reason; — *dei voti*, majority of votes; — *delle forze*, superiority of strength; — *straniera*, foreign domination.

preponderàre, *v.i.* to preponderate, to prevail, to predominate: *una ragione preponderò sopra tutte le altre*, one reason preponderated over all the others.

prepórre, *v.t.* 1. (*mettere davanti*) to put before, to place before: *questa pagina va preposta all'altra*, this page is to be placed before the other 2. (*preferire*) to prefer, to give preference to (s.o., sthg.): — *una persona a un'altra*, to prefer one person to another one 3. (*mettere a capo*) to appoint head, to put at the head: *fu preposto all'amministrazione*, he was put at the head of the management; *lo preposero al comando dell'esercito*, he was appointed head of the army.

prepositívo, *ag.* (*gram.*) 1. prepositive: *particella prepositiva*, prepositive particle 2. prepositional: *locuzione prepositiva*, prepositional phrase.

prepositúra, *s.f.* 1. (*ufficio di preposto*) office of parish priest; (*st.*) provostship 2. (*residenza del preposto*) parish priest's residence; (*st.*) provostry.

preposizióne, *s.f.* (*gram.*) preposition.

prepósto, *s.m.* (*eccl.*) parish priest; (*st.*) provost.

prepotènte, *ag.* 1. overbearing: *desiderio, bisogno* —, overbearing desire, need 2. (*di persona, arrogante*) domineering, overbearing, tyrannical || *s.m.* domineering fellow, overbearing fellow; (*fam.*) bully.

prepotenteménte, *av.* domineeringly, overbearingly.

prepotènza, *s.f.* 1. (*l'essere prepotente*) overbearingness, arrogance 2. (*azione da prepotente*) overbearing action.

preraffaellísmo, *s.m.* (*st. art.*) Pre-Raphaeli(ti)sm.

preraffaellíta, *ag.s.m.* (*st. art.*) Pre-Raphaelite, Preraphaelite.

prerogatíva, *s.f.* 1. prerogative: *le prerogative regie*, the king's prerogatives; *arrogarsi una* —, to assume (*o* to arrogate to oneself) a prerogative; *godere di una* —, to enjoy a prerogative 2. (*proprietà speciale*) quality, faculty; (*di cosa*) property: *la calamita ha la — di attrarre il ferro*, a magnet has the property of attracting iron.

présa, *s.f.* 1. (*il prendere*) taking; catching; seizing: — *di posizione*, taking up a position; *fig.* taking sides (*o* taking a stand): — *di possesso di una carica*, taking over an office; — *di possesso di una casa*, taking possession of a house || — *in giro*, leg-pull (*o* joke) 2. (*espugnazione, cattura*) seizure, capture: *la — di una città*, the capture (*o* taking) of a town; *la — di una fortezza*, the seizure of a fortress; *la — di un ladro*, the capture (*o* catching) of a thief 3. (*stretta*) grasp, hold, grip; (*nella lotta*) hold: *ha una — forte*, he has a firm grip (*o* grasp); *abbandonare la* —, to let go one's hold;

fig. to give in; *allentare la* —, to release one's hold ‖ *non ho* — *su di lui*, I have no hold over him ‖ *è alle prese con la giustizia*, he is up against the law; *venire alle prese 'con qlcu.*, *ql.co.*, to come to grips with s.o., sthg. **4.** *far* —: *non so se questa pianta farà* —, I don't know if this tree will take (root); *questo argomento non fa* — *sul pubblico*, this subject has no grip on (o hold over) the public; *il terreno è scivoloso e le ruote non fanno* —, the ground is slippery and the wheels cannot get a grip on it **5.** (*bottino di caccia*) bag ‖ *cane da* —, pointer (o setter) **6.** (*cine.*) take, shot: *macchina da* —, camera; *ripetere la* —, to retake **7.** (*di ancora*) grip: *l'ancora fece* —, the anchor held (o bit) **8.** (*d'acqua, aria*) intake; (*di gas*) outlet **9.** (*elett.*) tap: — *di corrente*, current-tap (o point o socket); — *di corrente a muro*, wall-plug (o wall-point o wall -socket); — *di corrente esterna, incassata*, surface point (o socket), flush point (o socket); — *di terra*, earth plate; *asta di* —, trolley pole **10.** (*tel.*) jack: — *di chiamata*, calling jack **11.** (*di cemento, ecc.*) set, setting: — *al contatto dell'aria*, air-hardening; — *lenta, rapida*, slow, quick setting; *far* —, to set **12.** (*pizzico*) pinch: *una* — *di sale, tabacco*, a pinch of salt, tobacco **13.** (*sporgenza, impugnatura*) grip **14.** (*mar.*) (*palo d'ormeggio*) bitt **15.** *fig.* (*appiglio, pretesto*) handle: *dar* — *alle calunnie*, to give a handle to (o for) calumny.

presàgio, *s.m.* omen, presage; (*presentimento*) presentiment; (*di calamità*) portent: — *di male*, presage of evil; *terribili presagi*, dire portents; *uccello di sinistro* —, bird of ill omen; *è di buon, cattivo* —, it is of good, ill omen; *il tuo* — *si è avverato*, your presage has become a reality; *avere* — *di ql.co.*, to have a presentiment of sthg.; *considerare ql.co. un buon* —, to take sthg. as a good omen.

presagíre, *v.t.* **1.** (*prevedere*) to foresee, to foretell, to predict; (*in base a ragionamento*) to forecast, to prognosticate: *avevo presagito ciò che sarebbe accaduto*, I had foreseen what would happen; *ha presagito un grande successo*, he has predicted a great success; *i meteorologi presagiscono cattivo tempo per domani*, the meteorologists forecast (o prognosticate) bad weather for to-morrow; *presagisco che perderemo*, I have a presentiment that we shall lose; — *il futuro*, to foretell the future **2.** (*essere presagio di*) to forebode, to presage; (*generalmente riferito a calamità*) to portend: *credono che le eclissi solari presagiscano disgrazia*, they believe that eclipses of the sun portend evil; *quelle nuvole scure presagiscono una tempesta*, those dark clouds forebode a storm.

presàgo, *ag.*: *essere* — *di*, (*prevedere*) to have a presentiment of; (*essere presagio di*) to presage (o to forebode): *quella madre era presaga della morte del figlio*, that mother had a presentiment of her son's death.

presàme, *s.m.* (*caglio*) rennet.

presbiopía, *s.f.* presbyopia; long-sightedness.

prèsbite, *ag.* presbyopic; long-sighted ‖ *s.c.* presbyope, presbyte; long-sighted person.

presbiteràle, *ag.* (*eccl.*) presbyterial.

presbiteràto, *s.m.* (*eccl.*) presbyterate.

presbiterianísmo, *s.m.* (*st. relig.*) Presbyterianism.

presbiteriàno, *ag. s.m.* (*st. relig.*) Presbyterian.

presbitèrio, *s.m.* presbytery.

presbitísmo, *s.m.* presbyopia; long-sightedness.

prescégliere, *v.t.* to choose, to select.

prescélto, *ag.* chosen, selected.

presciènte, *ag.* prescient.

presciènza, *s.f.* prescience.

prescíndere, *v.i.* to leave (sthg.) out of consideration: *a* — *da ciò*, leaving this out of consideration (o apart from this).

prescrittíbile, *ag.* (*dir.*) prescriptible.

prescrittívo, *ag.* (*dir.*) prescriptive.

prescrítto, *ag.* **1.** prescribed; (*stabilito*) established, fixed; (*obbligatorio*) compulsory: *libri di testo prescritti*, prescribed text-books; *medicine prescritte*, prescribed

medicines; *il modulo* —, the prescribed form ‖ *è* — *l'abito da sera*, evening dress (de rigueur) **2.** (*dir.*) prescribed ‖ *s.m.* prescript, ordinance.

prescrivènte, *ag.* prescribing.

prescrívere, *v.t.* **1.** to prescribe, to order: *il medico mi ha prescritto assoluto riposo*, the doctor said I should 'have absolute rest; *il medico mi ha prescritto una medicina*, the doctor has prescribed a medicine for me **2.** (*dir.*) to prescribe ‖ **prescríversi**, *v.r.* (*andare in prescrizione*) to prescribe.

prescrizióne, *s.f.* **1.** ordinance, regulation, precept: *le prescrizioni della Chiesa*, the precepts of the Church; *prescrizioni legali*, official instructions (o regulations); *contrario alle prescrizioni*, contrary to regulations **2.** (*med.*) prescription: *è una* — *del mio medico*, it is a prescription of my doctor; *il medico mi darà delle prescrizioni*, the doctor will prescribe for me **3.** (*dir.*) prescription: — *acquisitiva*, acquisitive (o positive) prescription; — *estintiva*, extinctive (o negative) prescription; *caduto in* —, invalidated by prescription.

presentàbile, *ag.* presentable.

presentabilità, *s.f.* presentability.

presentabilménte, *av.* presentably.

presentàre, *v.t.* **1.** to present; (*proporre*) to propose; (*inoltrare*) to send in: — *una cambiale*, (*in banca*) to present a bill; — *i conti*, to render accounts; — *una domanda, un documento*, to send in an application, a document; — *un progetto di legge*, to bring in (o to introduce) a bill; — *qlcu. come candidato*, to present (o to propose) s.o. as a candidate; — *un reclamo*, to put in a claim; — *un saldo a favore di qlcu.*, to show a balance in s.o.'s favour **2.** (*mostrare*) to present, to show; (*esibire*) to produce: *egli presentò i suoi documenti*, he showed (o produced) his documents; *la luna ci presenta sempre la stessa faccia*, the moon always shows us the same face; *mi presentò la lettera*, he showed me the letter; *questo caso presenta delle difficoltà*, this case presents some difficulties ‖ — *le armi*, (*mil.*) to present arms: *presentat'arm!*, (*mil.*) present arms! **3.** (*offrire*) to present, 'to offer: *il concerto era presentato da una grande società*, (*alla radio*) the concert was sponsored by a big firm; *le presentò un mazzo di fiori*, he offered her a bunch of flowers (o he presented her with a bunch of flowers) ‖ — *garanzie*, to offer securities; — *vantaggi*, to offer advantages ‖ — *i propri omaggi*, to pay one's respects; — *i propri complimenti, scuse*, to present one's compliments, apologies **4.** (*condurre al cospetto*) to present; (*far conoscere*) to introduce, to present: *gli presentò i prigionieri*, he presented the prisoners to him; *mi hai già presentato quel signore*, you have already introduced that gentleman to me; *presentami il tuo amico, per piacere*, please introduce me to your friend; *essere presentato a corte*, to be presented at court (o to go to court) **5.** (*uno spettacolo*) to present: — *un programma radiofonico*, to present a radio programme ‖ **presentàrsi**, *v.r.* **1.** to present oneself: *egli si presentò al giudice, al suo principale*, he presented himself to the judge, to his boss; *ella si presentò alla mia porta con un bambino fra le braccia*, she appeared at my door with a child in her arms; — *ad un esame*, to sit for (o to present oneself for o to go in for) an examination: *si presenterà all'esame il mese venturo*, he will sit for his exam next month; — *come candidato a ql.co.*, to run (o to offer oneself as a candidate o to come forward as a candidate) for sthg.: *quest'anno egli si presenterà come candidato alla presidenza*, this year he will run for the presidency; — *davanti al tribunale*, to appear in court (o to come before the court) ‖ *quella ragazza si presenta molto bene*, that girl looks very nice **2.** (*farsi conoscere*) to introduce oneself: *si presentò allo zio del suo amico*, he introduced himself to his friend's uncle **3.** (*offrirsi*) to offer; (*capitare*) to occur: *è la prima occasione che si presenta*, it is the first opportunity that has offered; *questa possibilità non mi si era mai* *presentata alla mente*, this possibility had never come into my mind before; *spero che un caso simile non si presenterà mai qui*, I hope that such a case will never occur here **4.** (*sembrare, apparire*) to seem, to appear: *il problema non si presenta difficile*, the problem doesn't seem to be difficult **5.** (*med.*) to present.

presentatóre, *s.m.* **1.** presenter **2.** (*rad. tv.*) announcer; (*di varietà, ecc.*) compère ‖ **presentatríce**, *s.f.* **1.** presenter **2.** (*rad. tv.*) (woman) announcer.

presentazióne, *s.f.* **1.** presentation: *la — di un programma radiofonico*, the presentation of a radio programme; *contro — di documenti*, upon production of documents (*o* against documents); *la — di un piatto contribuisce al buon esito di un pranzo*, the way in which the food is presented contributes towards the success of a meal; *il testo era preceduto da alcune pagine di —*, the text was preceded by a few pages of introduction (*o* introductory pages) ‖ *la Presentazione di Maria Vergine*, the Presentation of the Blessed Virgin Mary **2.** (*di una persona a un'altra*) introduction; (*a corte*) presentation: *una lettera di —*, a letter of introduction; *dovresti fare le presentazioni*, you should do the introducing **3.** (*med.*) presentation.

presènte[1], *ag.* **1.** present: *— mio padre*, in the presence of my father; *tutti i miei amici erano presenti al mio matrimonio*, all my friends were present at my wedding ‖ *—!*, here! **2.** (*nella mente*) present; clear: *è sempre — alla mia mente*, I always keep it in my mind; *aver —*, to bear (*o* to keep) in mind: *non ho — se egli ci fosse o no*, I can't remember whether he was there or not; *essere — nella memoria di qlcu.*, to be present in one's recollection ‖ *mio nonno è ancora molto —*, my grandfather is still very clear-minded **3.** (*attuale*) present, actual; current: *la — generazione*, the present generation; *il — mese*, the current month ‖ *il tempo —*, (*gram.*) the present tense **4.** (*questo*) this: *il — libro*, this book; *la — settimana*, this week ‖ *la — (lettera)*, (*comm.*) this letter; *con la —*, (*comm.*) herewith; *nella —*, (*comm.*) herein ‖ *s.m.* **1.** present, present time: *il — e il futuro*, the present and the future; *egli non vive nel —*, he does not live in the present ‖ *al —*, at present **2.** (*gram.*) present, present tense **3.** *pl.* those present: *fra i presenti non vi fu nessuno che lo seguì*, among the bystanders there was nobody who followed him; *tutti i presenti furono premiati*, all those who were present were given a prize; *tutti i presenti sono invitati*, all the present company are invited ‖ *i presenti esclusi*, present company excluded (*o* excepted).

presènte[2], *s.m.* present, gift: *mi ha fatto un grazioso —*, he has given me a nice present (*o* gift).

presenteménte, *av.* at present, now.

presentiménto, *s.m.* foreboding, presentiment.

presentíre, *v.t.* to have a foreboding of (sthg.); to have a presentiment of (sthg.); to have a premonition of (sthg.); to foresee: *avevo presentito ciò che sarebbe accaduto*, I had foreseen what would happen.

presènza, *s.f.* **1.** presence: *fu condotto alla — del re*, he was taken into the presence of the king; *in — dello zinco, l'acido solforico sviluppa idrogeno*, in the presence of zinc, sulphuric acid gives off hydrogen; *nessuno si era accorto della sua —*, nobody had noticed his presence; *posso avere l'onore della sua —?*, may I have the honour of your presence?; *la sua — ci salvò dal pericolo*, his presence saved us from danger ‖ *— d'animo, di spirito*, presence of mind ‖ *di —*, (*di persona*) in person (*o* personally) ‖ *fare atto di —*, to put in (*o* to make) an appearance **2.** (*aspetto fisico*) presence, appearance: *una ragazza di bella —*, a fine-looking girl; *una signora di nobile —*, a noble -looking lady ‖ *non aver —*, to be unimposing: *quell'uomo non ha —*, he is an unimposing man **3.** (*a scuola, in ufficio*) attendance: *la — è obbligatoria alla mia scuola*, attendance is compulsory at my school; *questa settimana ha solo due presenze*, this week his record shows only two attendances.

presenziàle, *ag.* (*rar.*) present, in person.

presenzialménte, *av.* (*rar.*) personally.

presenziàre, *v.t.* to attend: *— un'adunanza*, to attend a meeting ‖ *v.i.* to be present: *— ad un esame*, to be present at an examination.

presèpe, presèpio, *s.m.* crib.

preservàre, *v.t.* to preserve: *Dio ti preservi da questi mali!*, may God preserve you from these evils!.

preservatívo, *ag.s.m.* preservative.

preservatóre, *s.m.*, **preservatríce**, *s.f.* preserver.

preservazióne, *s.f.* preservation: *in buono stato di —*, in a good state of preservation.

presíccio, *ag.* fresh-killed, fresh-caught.

presidàto, *s.m.* (*rar.*) headship.

prèside, *s.m.* headmaster, principal ‖ *— di facoltà*, dean.

presidentàto, *s.m.* presidency, presidentship; chairmanship; (*presidato*) headship.

presidènte, *s.m.* **1.** president; (*di assemblea*) chairman: *— del consiglio di amministrazione*, chairman of the board of directors; *— onorario*, honorary president; *il vice — del comitato*, the vice-chairman of the committee; *il — chiuse l'assemblea*, the chairman closed the meeting **2.** (*pol.*) president; (*ul Parlamento inglese e americano*) speaker: *il — di una repubblica*, the president of a republic; *il Presidente del Consiglio*, the Premier (*o* the Prime Minister).

presidentéssa, *s.f.* presidentess.

presidènza, *s.f.* **1.** presidency: *durante la — di Truman*, during the presidency of Truman **2.** (*di una assemblea*) chair; chairmanship: *a quella riunione la — era al sig. B.*, at that meeting Mr. B. took the chair (*o* was the chairman) **3.** (*di società*) management; (*insieme dei direttori*) board of directors **4.** (*di scuola*) headship, headmastership; (*studio del preside*) head-master's study.

presidenziàle, *ag.* presidential.

presidiàle[1], *ag.* (*di presidio*) garrison (*attributivo*).

presidiàle[2], *ag.* (*di preside*) headmaster's, head's (*attributivo*).

presidiàre, *v.t.* (*mil.*) to garrison.

presidiàrio, *ag.* presidiary, garrison (*attributivo*).

presidiàto, *ag.* garrison (*attributivo*); garrisoned: *città presidiata*, garrison town.

presídio, *s.m.* **1.** (*mil.*) garrison: *comandante del —*, garrison-commander; *milizie di —*, garrison troops **2.** (*mil.*) (*luogo presidiato*) fortified place, strong place **3.** (*difesa, protezione*) defence, protection.

presièdere, *v.i.* **1.** to preside, to act as chairman: *— a un'assemblea*, to preside over (*o* at) a meeting; *— a una sessione parlamentare*, to preside at a session of Parliament **2.** (*vigilare, dirigere*) to be at the head (of sthg.): *— ai lavori stradali*, to be at the head of the road works.

préso, *ag.* **1.** caught; occupied; (*impegnato*) engaged: *le città prese furono rase al suolo*, the occupied towns were razed to the ground ‖ *— d'amore*, overwhelmed by love **2.** (*occupato, di posto, ecc.*) taken.

prèssa, *s.f.* **1.** (*mec.*) press: *— a banco inclinabile*, inclinable press; *— a bilanciere*, fly press; *— a braccio*, horning press; *— a eccentrico*, eccentric(-shaft) press; *— a frizione*, friction press; *— a ingranaggi*, geared press; *— a mano*, hand press; *— a piegare*, forming press; *— a riscaldamento interno*, hot-press; *— a vapore*, steam press; *— a vite*, screw press; *— centripeta*, centripetal press; *— da legatore*, (*tip.*) lying press; *— idraulica*, hydraulic forging press; *— multipla*, multiple press; *— per olio*, oil press; *— sbavatrice*, flash trimming press; *— verticale*, standing press **2.** (*folla*) crowd, throng: *far — intorno a ql.co., qlcu.*, to crowd round sthg., s.o. **3.** (*fretta*) hurry, haste: *in —*, in a hurry.

pressacàrte, *s.m.* paper-weight.

pressaforàggi, *s.f.* (*agr.*) forage-press, hay-press.

pressànte, *ag.* pressing, urgent.

pressanteménte, *av.* pressingly, urgently.

pressappòco, *av.* approximately, nearly, about: *erano — le tre quando venne,* it was about three o'clock when he came.

pressàre, *v.t.* **1.** to press: — *a freddo, a caldo, (mec.)* to cold-press, to hot-press **2.** *fig.* to press, to urge.

pressatúra, *s.f. (mec.)* pressing.

prèssi, *s.m.pl. (vicinanze)* neighbourhood (*sing.*); (*dintorni*) surroundings; (*sobborghi*) suburbs, outskirts, environs: *abito nei pressi di,* I live on the outskirts of.

pressióne, *s.f.* pressure: — *atmosferica, (fis.)* atmospheric pressure; — *cinetica, (mec.)* kinetic pressure; — *critica, (chim. fis.)* critical pressure; — *del sangue, (fisiol.)* blood-pressure; — *del vento,* wind load (*o* pressure); — *di alimentazione, (aer.)* boost (*o* manifold pressure); — *di arresto, (fis.)* dynamic (*o* stagnation *o* velocity *o* kinetic) pressure; — *di aspirazione, (mec.)* suction pressure; — *di bloccaggio, (mec.)* locking pressure; — *di frenatura, (mec.)* braking power (*o* brake pressure); — *elettrostatica, (elett.)* electrostatic pressure; — *normale, (di esercizio)* rated pressure; — *ridotta, (fis.)* reduced pressure; — *specifica,* specific pressure; — *totale, (mec.)* total head (*o* pressure); *a bassa —, (fis.)* low-pressure; *alta, bassa —,* high, low pressure; *aumento di —, (fis.)* pressure increase; *caduta di —, (fis.)* pressure drop (*o* fall in pressure); *prova di —, (ind.)* pressure test; *sotto —,* under pressure (anche *fig.*); *mantenere la —,* to keep up steam; *mettere in —,* to raise steam ‖ *sotto la — della povertà, fig.* under the pressure of poverty ‖ *fare — su qlcu., fig.* to put pressure on s.o.

prèsso, *av.* **nearby, near, near at hand, close at hand:** *lì — c'è un fiume,* there is a river nearby; *si fece più —, più da —,* he came closer (*o* nearer); *la sua casa è qui —,* his house is near (*o* not far off *o* not far from) here ‖ *a un di —,* about (*o* approximately): *c'erano a un di — venti persone,* there were about twenty people ‖ *da —,* closely (anche *fig.*); from close to: *sorvegliare qlcu. da —,* to watch s.o. closely; *vedere la morte da —,* to look death in the face (*o* to see death from close to) ‖ *prep.* **1.** (*vicino a, non lontano da, nei pressi di*) **near, not far from, in the vicinity of:** *la pianura di Maratona — Atene,* the plain of Marathon not far from Athens; *abito — Firenze,* I live near Florence; *Fiesole è una cittadina — Firenze,* Fiesole is a small town in the vicinity of Florence **2.** (*accanto a, a fianco di*) **beside, by; next to:** *abito — la chiesa,* I live by (*o* next to) the church; *sedette — suo marito,* she sat down beside (*o* by the side of) her husband; *sedeva — la finestra,* she was sitting by the window; *siedi — di me,* sit down by (*o* beside) me **3.** (*a casa di, nell'ufficio di*) **at; with;** (*negli indirizzi*) **care of** (abbr. c/o) : *abito — mia zia,* I live at my aunt's; *lavoro — una ditta svizzera,* I work with a Swiss firm; *lavoro — il Signor Rossi,* I work with (*o* for) Mr. Rossi; *non guadagnavo molto — la signora B.,* I didn't earn much at Mrs. B's ‖ *ambasciatore — la Santa Sede,* Ambassador to the Holy See **4.** (*fra*) **among:** *il sacrificio umano era diffuso — i popoli antichi,* human sacrifice was widespread among ancient peoples **5.** (*in senso morale*) **with; over:** *egli ha un grande ascendente — mio figlio,* he has a great hold over my son; *questi metodi non hanno successo — di me,* these methods have no success with me **6.** *presso a,* (*in confronto a*) in comparison (*o* compared) with; (*quasi*) almost: — *a sua cugina sembra bella,* compared with her cousin she looks beautiful; *è — a due anni che non lo vedo,* it's almost two years since I've seen him **7.** *pressappoco,* about (*o* more or less *o* approximately): *c'erano pressappoco cento persone,* there were approximately a hundred people; *sarà pressappoco mezzogiorno,* it is about twelve **8.** *essere — a fare ql.co.,* to be about to do (*o* to be on the point of doing) sthg.: *era — a partire,* he was on the point of going (*o* about to go *o* he was just going to start).

pressoché, prèsso che, *av.* **almost, nearly, close on:** *il mio lavoro è — finito,* my work is nearly completed; *la sua cultura è — nulla,* his culture is almost non-existent.

pressúra, *s.f. (rar.)* **1.** (*pressione*) pressure **2.** (*oppressione*) oppression.

prestabilíre, *v.t.* to pre-establish, to establish in advance, to fix in advance, to pre-arrange: *era tutto prestabilito,* everything was pre-arranged.

prestaménte, *av.* quickly, soon, readily.

prestanóme, *s.m.* dummy, man of straw.

prestànte, *ag.* **1.** good-looking: *è un uomo —,* he is a good-looking man **2.** (*che eccelle*) excellent, excelling.

prestanteménte, *av.* excellently, eminently.

prestànza, *s.f.* **1.** (*bell'aspetto*) fine appearance **2.** (*eccellenza*) excellence, superiority ‖ *le Prestanze Vostre,* (*titolo d'onore*) Your Honour.

prestàre, *v.t.* to lend: — *denaro a interesse,* to lend money on interest; — *denaro, un libro a qlcu.,* to lend money, a book to s.o. (*o* to lend s.o. money, a book) ‖ — *aiuto,* to lend a (helping) hand ‖ — *attenzione,* to pay attention ‖ — *fede a qlcu.,* to believe s.o. ‖ — *giuramento,* to take an oath ‖ — *obbedienza a qlcu.,* to obey s.o. ‖ — *omaggio,* to pay homage ‖ — *orecchio, ascolto,* to lend an ear (*o* to listen) ‖ — *la propria opera,* to give one's services ‖ *farsi — ql.co. da qlcu.,* to borrow sthg. from s.o. ‖ **prestàrsi,** *v.r.* **1.** to lend oneself, to favour (sthg.), to give countenance; (*acconsentire*) to consent, to countenance (sthg.): *egli non si presterebbe mai ad un inganno,* he would never lend himself to deception; *egli si prestò ai loro disonesti intrighi,* he lent himself to their dishonest plots; *non credo che egli si presterà a fare questo,* I do not think he will consent to do it; *questa frase si presta facilmente a un malinteso,* this sentence may easily cause a misunderstanding **2.** (*adoperarsi, dare aiuto*) to be useful, to help (s.o.): *vorrebbe —, ma arriva quando le cose sono già fatte,* he would like to help (*o* to be useful *o* to make himself useful), but he arrives when things are already done; *si presta molto per i poveri,* he likes helping the poor very much **3.** (*essere adatto*) to lend oneself; to be fit (for sthg., for doing): *questa stanza non si presta a sala da pranzo,* this room does not lend itself to dining-room; *questa stoffa non si presta per fare tende,* this material is not fit for making curtains; *questo palcoscenico non si presta per commedie del genere,* this stage is not fit for such plays.

prestatóre, *s.m.* **1.** lender: — *di denaro,* money-lender; — *su pegno,* pawnbroker ‖ — *di lavoro, d'opera,* (*dir.*) workman **2.** (*rar.*) (*usuraio*) money-lender.

prestazióne, *s.f.* **1.** (*tributo, tassa*) tribute, tax **2.** (*prestito*) loan ‖ — *d'opera,* (*dir.*) work done **3.** *pl.* (*servizi*) services: *le prestazioni di un dottore, di un avvocato,* the services of a doctor, of a lawyer **4.** (*di motore, di atleta*) performance.

prestézza, *s.f.* **1.** quickness **2.** (*di mente pronta*) alertness.

prestidigitatóre, *s.m.* conjurer, conjuror.

prestidigitazióne, *s.f.* prestidigitation, sleight-of-hand, legerdemain.

prestigiatóre, *s.m.* conjurer, conjuror.

prestígio, *s.m.* **1.** (*influenza, autorità*) prestige: *il — di una nazione, di una scuola, di un insegnante,* the prestige of a nation, of a school, of a teacher; *quell'uomo manca di —,* that man is lacking in prestige **2.** (*fascino*) glamour, magic: *il — della divisa,* the glamour of the uniform **3.** (*prestidigitazione*) prestidigitation, sleight-of-hand: *giochi di —,* conjuring tricks.

prestigióso, *ag.* **1.** (*che ha fascino*) glamorous **2.** (*ingannevole*) prestigious, deceptive, illusory.

prestinàia, *s.f.* bakeress; baker's wife.

prestinàio, *s.m.* baker.

prèstito, *s.m.* loan: — *a interesse,* loan at interest — *allo scoperto,* loan on overdraft (*o* unsecured loan)

— *a lunga, breve scadenza*, long-term, short-term loan; — *a premio*, loan at premium; — *a scadenza*, loan at notice; — *dello Stato*, Government loan; — *di denari, libri*, loan of money, books; — *di guerra*, war loan; — *forzoso*, forced loan; — *garantito*, secured loan; — *grazioso*, interest-free loan; — *ipotecario*, mortgage loan; — *pubblico*, public loan; — *su pegno*, loan on pawn: *agenzia di prestiti su pegni*, pawnshop; *emissione di un* —, issue of a loan; *contrarre un* —, to contract a loan; *dare un* —, to lend; *emettere un* —, to issue (o to raise o to float) a loan; *prendere ql.co. in* — *da qlcu.*, to borrow sthg. of (o from) s.o.; *rimborsare un* —, to redeem a loan; *sottoscrivere un* —, to subscribe to a loan.

prèsto, *av.* **1. soon, before long, in a short time:** *sarà qui* —, he will soon be here (o he will be here before long); *sarebbe arrivato* — *e così lo aspettai*, he was to arrive soon, and so I waited for him; *si farà buio* —, it will soon be dark; *il suo successo fu* — *evidente*, his success was soon evident ‖ — *o tardi*, sooner or later (o eventually) ‖ *al più* —, as soon as possible: *fatelo al più* —, do it as soon as possible; (*comm.*) do it at your earliest convenience; *verrò al più* —, I shall come as soon as possible (o as soon as I can) **2.** (*di buon'ora*) **early:** *al mattino* —, early in the morning; *arrivammo troppo* —, we got there too early; *non posso venire molto* —, I cannot come very early **3.** (*in fretta*) **quickly:** *fa* —, be quick (o hurry up o make haste); *fallo* —, do it quickly ‖ *si fa* — *a parlare*, easier said than done ‖ *inter.* **quick!, be quick!, hurry up!, come along!** ‖ *ag.* **1.** (*spedito, lesto*): — *di mano*, dext(e)rous **2.** (*letter.*) (*pronto, disposto*) prepared, ready: ... *alla Fortuna, come vuol, son* —, ...I am prepared for Fortune as she wills.

prèsule, *s.m.* prelate; (*vescovo*) bishop.

presúmere, *v.t.* **1.** to presume; (*immaginare*) to imagine; (*congetturare*) to conjecture; (*supporre*) to think: *egli presume di potermi far fare ciò che vuole*, he thinks he can make me do what he likes; *presumo che abbia ragione*, I presume he is right; *presumo che sarà in ritardo*, I expect he will be late; *ti conosco bene e posso* — *ciò che mi dirai*, I know you well and I can imagine what you will tell me ‖ *v.i.* to presume (on s.o., sthg.), to rely (on s.o., sthg.): *egli presume troppo delle sue forze*, he relies too much on his strength; — (*troppo*) *di se stesso*, to rely too much on oneself.

presumíbile, *ag.* presumable; (*probabile*) probable.

presumibilménte, *av.* presumably; (*probabilmente*) probably.

presuntivaménte, *av.* presumptively.

presuntívo, *ag.* **1.** presumptive **2.** (*preventivato*) estimated ‖ *s.m.* (*somma preventivata*) estimate.

presúnto, *ag.* **1.** presumed; (*supposto*) supposed: *il* — *colpevole*, the supposed (o alleged) culprit; *erede* —, (*dir.*) heir presumptive **2.** (*valutato*) estimated: *spesa presunta*, estimated expense.

presuntuosaménte, *av.* presumptuously, conceitedly.

presuntuosità, *s.f.* presumptuousness, presumption, conceit.

presuntuóso, *ag.* presumptuous, conceited: *è un giovane* —, he is a conceited youth ‖ *s.m.* presumptuous person; (*scherz.*) conceited ass.

presunzióne, *s.f.* **1.** (*ardire*) presumption, conceit: *ebbe la* — *di cimentarsi con me*, he had the presumption to compete with me; *perdonate la mia* —, forgive my presumption **2.** (*supposizione*) presumption, assumption: *era una semplice* —, it was a mere presumption.

presuppórre, *v.t.* **1.** to presuppose: *la sua condotta presuppone una debolezza di mente*, his behaviour presupposes a weakness of mind **2.** (*supporre*) to suppose: *presupponevo che egli fosse all'estero*, I supposed he was abroad.

presupposizióne, *s.f.* **1.** presupposition **2.** (*supposizione*) supposition.

presuppósto, *ag.* presupposed ‖ *s.m.* presupposition.

pretàglia, *s.f.* (*spreg.*) priestly rabble, priestery.

prète, *s.m.* **1.** priest: *chiamare il* —, to call the priest; *farsi* —, to take orders **2.** (*fam.*) (*telaio per scaldaletto*) wooden frame holding bed-warmer.

pretendènte, *s.m.* **1.** pretender; claimant: — *al trono*, pretender to the throne **2.** (*corteggiatore*) suitor.

pretèndere, *v.t.* **1.** (*sostenere*) to claim, to pretend, to profess: *pretende di essere un gentiluomo*, he professes to be a gentleman; *pretende di essere un grande artista*, he claims (o pretends) to be a great artist; *pretende di esserne il padrone*, he claims to be the owner of it; *pretendeva di aver ragione*, he claimed that he was right ‖ *una mistura che pretendeva di essere birra*, a mixture which pretended to be beer ‖ *pretenderla a*, (*atteggiarsi a*) to pose: *pretenderla a poeta, a letterato*, to pose as a poet, as a scholar **2.** (*esigere*) to expect; to claim, to lay a claim to (sthg.); to exact; to require, to demand, to want: *ma che cosa pretendi?*, what do you expect?; *pretende sempre più di quanto gli spetta*, he always wants more than his due (o than his fair share); *pretende prezzi esagerati*, he asks exorbitant prices; *pretendeva che andassi da lui a mezzanotte*, he expected me to go to his house at midnight; *pretendeva di poter spadroneggiare in casa mia*, he wanted to play the master in my house; *pretendo che mi dica la verità*, I want him to tell me the truth; *pretendo ubbidienza e onestà dai miei figli*, I exact obedience and honesty from my children; *pretendono una gran parte dell'eredità*, they have laid claim to a large part of the inheritance; *pretese che lo pagassi subito*, he demanded that I should pay him at once; *questo è* — *molto*, that's asking a lot; *si può* — *ubbidienza ma non devozione dai propri domestici*, one can exact obedience, but not devotion, from one's servants; — *l'impossibile*, to expect the impossible **3.** (*credere, ritenersi capace*) to think oneself capable (of doing): *pretende di farlo presto e bene*, he thinks he will be able to do it quickly and well; *pretendeva d'imparare il latino in pochi mesi*, he thought himself capable of learning Latin in a few months ‖ *v.i.* to pretend: — *alla mano di una fanciulla*, to pretend to a young lady's hand; — *a un trono*, to pretend to a throne.

pretensióne, *s.f.* **1.** pretension, claim: *accampare molte pretensioni*, to lay many claims **2.** (*presunzione*) pretension. pretence: *uomo di molta* —, pretentious man ‖ *senza pretensioni*, modestly **3.** (*prezzo richiesto*) price.

pretensióso, pretenzióso, *ag.* pretentious: (*arrogante*) arrogant; (*affettato*) affected; (*presuntuoso*) conceited: *un giovane* —, a conceited young man.

preterintenzionàle, *ag.* (*dir.*) unintentional.

preterintenzionalità, *s.f.* (*dir.*) unintentionality.

preteríre, *v.t.* (*rar.*) (*omettere*) to omit.

pretèrito, *ag.* preterit(e), past ‖ *s.m.* **1.** (*gram.*) preterit(e) (tense) **2.** (*fam.*) buttocks (*pl.*).

preterizióne, *s.f.* (*ret.*) preterition.

preteméttere, *v.t.* (*rar.*) to pretermit, to omit.

pretermissióne, *s.f.* (*rar.*) pretermission, omission.

preternaturàle, *ag.* preternatural.

pretésa, *s.f.* **1.** (*presunzione*) pretension, pretence: *aveva la* — *di essere il miglior scrittore del suo paese*, he claimed to be the best writer in his country; *non ha la* — *di essere bella*, she lays no claim to good looks; *non ho la* — *di esserti superiore*, I don't pretend (o claim) to be better than you; *non ho la* — *di vincere*, I don't expect to win; *questi mobili non hanno alcuna* — *di bellezza o di stile, ma sono molto pratici*, this furniture is without any pretence (o has no pretensions) to beauty or style, but is very practical; *ridevo della sua* — *di essere un grande poeta*, I used to laugh at his pretension of being a great poet ‖ *con la* —, under pretence: *venne con la* — *di insegnarmi la matematica*, he came under pretence of teaching me maths ‖ *senza* —, *pretese*, unpretentiously (o unpretendingly): *una persona senza pretese*, a person without pretence (o an unpretentious person) **2.** (*esigenza; richiesta; diritto*) claim, pretension, demand: *avanza delle pretese* *irragionevoli,* he makes unreasonable claims; *aveva la — che noi gli ubbidissimo,* he wanted us to obey him; *è di poche pretese e si accontenta di quello che ha,* he is very easy to please and is content with what he has; *ha molte pretese, preferisco non averlo come ospite,* he is very hard to please, I prefer not to have him as my guest; *sono costretto ad accettare le sue ingiuste pretese,* I am forced to accept his unjust demands; *le sue pretese non possono essere soddisfatte,* his demands cannot be satisfied; *avanzare delle pretese su ql.co.,* to claim rights over sthg.

pretésco, *ag.* (*spreg.*) priest-like; sanctimonious.

pretéso, *ag.* **1.** (*chiesto*) claimed **2.** (*supposto, ritenuto*) supposed, alleged: *un — errore,* an alleged mistake; *pretesa nobiltà,* self-styled nobility.

pretèsta, *s.f.* praetexta (*pl.* praetextae).

pretestàto, *ag.* wearing a praetexta.

pretèsto, *s.m.* **1.** pretext, pretence, excuse: *col — che doveva studiare,* under (o on *o* upon) the pretext that he had to study (o of studying); *col — di vedermi,* on the pretext of seeing me; *devo trovare un — plausibile per non andarci,* I must find a plausible excuse for not going **2.** (*occasione*) opportunity, occasion: *cogliere un —,* to seize an opportunity; *dar — a ql.co.,* to give occasion for sthg.

pretíno, *ag.* priest-like, priestly ‖ *s.m.* young priest.

pretísmo, *s.m.* (*spreg.*) bigotry.

pretónzolo, *s.m.* (*spreg.*) priestling.

pretóre, *s.m.* **1.** (police-) magistrate; (*giudice*) judge **2.** (*st. romana*) praetor.

pretoriàle, *ag.* (*st.romana*) praetorial.

pretoriàno, *ag. s.m.* (*st.romana*) praetorian (anche *fig.*).

pretòrio, *ag.* **1.** magisterial, magistratic(al), pertaining to a (police-)magistrate **2.** (*st. romana*) praetorial ‖ *s.m.* (*st. romana*) praetorium.

prettaménte, *av.* merely, purely, simply.

prètto, *ag.* pure; (*vero e proprio*) real: *in — inglese,* in pure English; *un vino —,* an unadulterated wine.

pretúra, *s.f.* **1.** police-court, magistrate's court **2.** (*st. romana*) praetorship.

prevalènte, *ag.* prevalent, prevailing: *una moda —,* a prevalent (o prevailing) fashion; *una moda — nel nostro paese,* a fashion prevailing in our country.

prevalenteménte, *av.* prevalently, prevailingly.

prevalènza, *s.f.* prevalence; (*supremazia*) supremacy: *avere la — su qlcu.,* to prevail over s.o.

prevalére, *v.i.* to prevail (against s.o., sthg.; over s.o., sthg.): *le sue ragioni prevalsero e io dovetti cedere,* his reasons prevailed and I had to yield; *il suo buon senso prevalse sulla passione,* his common sense prevailed over his passion ‖ **prevalérsi,** *v.r.* to avail oneself, to take advantage: *egli si prevalse della sua autorità per avere ciò che voleva,* he availed himself of his authority to get what he wanted.

prevaricàre, *v.i.* **1.** to prevaricate (anche *fig.*); (*abusare del proprio potere*) to abuse one's office: *— dalla fede,* to lapse from the faith **2.** (*uscir dai limiti*) to go beyond the limits.

prevaricatóre, *s.m.*, **prevaricatríce,** *s.f.* prevaricator.

prevaricazióne, *s.f.* prevarication (anche *fig.*); (*abuso di potere*) abuse of office.

prevedére, *v.t.* **1.** to foresee; to forecast; (*aspettarsi*) to expect, to anticipate: *avevo previsto ciò che sarebbe avvenuto,* I had foreseen what would happen; *i contadini prevedono un buon raccolto,* the farmers expect a rich harvest; *non posso prevederne le conseguenze,* I cannot forecast (o foresee) the consequences; *prevedo che sarà qui presto,* I expect he will be here soon; *potevi prevederlo,* you could have foreseen it **2.** (*di legge, contratto, ecc.*) to provide for (sthg.): *nel modo previsto dalla legge,* in the manner provided for by law; *il contratto prevede che l'inquilino paghi anticipatamente,* the contract provides that the tenant shall pay

in advance; *il legislatore ha previsto il caso,* the legislator has provided for the case.

prevedíbile, *ag.* foreseeable: *tutto ciò era —,* all this could be foreseen (o expected).

preveggènte, *ag.* foreseeing; provident.

preveggènza, *s.f.* foresight, prevision.

preveníre, *v.t.* **1.** (*precedere*) to precede, to forestall, to anticipate: *volevo telefonarti ma mi hai prevenuto,* I wanted to ring you up but you have forestalled me; *— un concorrente,* to forestall a competitor; *— una domanda,* to anticipate a request **2.** (*evitare*) to prevent, to ward off, to avert: *— una guerra, un pericolo,* to prevent a war, a danger; *— una malattia,* to prevent an illness **3.** (*avvertire prima*) to inform, to (fore)warn: *avreste dovuto prevenirmi,* you ought to have warned me (o you ought to have let me know); *non ho fatto in tempo a prevenirlo,* I was not in time to (fore)warn him; *— le autorità,* to give notice to the authorities.

preventivaménte, *av.* **1.** beforehand, in advance **2.** (*in modo preventivo*) preventively.

preventivàre, *v.t.* (*comm.*) to estimate: *— le entrate,* to estimate revenue (o income); *— le spese,* to estimate the expenditure.

preventivàto, *ag.* (*comm.*) estimated: *costo —,* estimated cost; *regolare le entrate in base alle spese preventivate,* to raise revenue to meet the estimated expenditure ‖ *s.m.* estimate: *il — della spesa,* the estimate of (o for) expenditure.

preventívo, *ag.* **1.** preventive, previous, precautionary: *avviso —,* previous notice; *giustizia preventiva,* (*dir.*) preventive justice; *medicina preventiva,* preventive medicine; *misure preventive,* preventive (o precautionary) measures ‖ *carcere —,* preventive detention **2.** (*comm.*) estimated: *bilancio —,* budget; *fattura preventiva,* proforma invoice ‖ *s.m.* (*comm.*) estimate: *— della spesa,* estimate of (o for) expenditure; *— dell'entrata,* revenue estimate; *un — prudente,* a conservative estimate.

preventòrio, *s.m.* **1.** (*med.*) preventive sanatorium **2.** (*riformatorio*) reformatory.

preventríglio, *s.m.* (*di uccello*) proventriculus (*pl.* proventriculi).

prevenúto, *ag.* **1.** prejudiced, biased: *egli è — contro di te,* he has a prejudice (o bias) against you **2.** (*preavvisato*) forewarned **3.** (*preoccupato*) worried ‖ *s.m.* (*dir.*) the accused.

prevenzióne, *s.f.* **1.** bias, prejudice: *giudizio senza —,* unprejudiced (o unbiased) judgement; *non ho prevenzioni contro di lui,* I have no prejudice against him; *parlare senza prevenzioni,* to speak without prejudice **2.** (*il prevenire*) prevention; (*misura preventiva*) precautionary measure: *— infortuni,* (*ind.*) accident prevention.

previaménte, *av.* previously.

previdènte, *ag.* provident, far-seeing, far-sighted: *amministrazione —,* provident administration; *uomo —,* far-sighted man.

previdenteménte, *av.* providently, far-sightedly.

previdènza, *s.f.* providence, foresight: *uomo di grande —,* very far-sighted man; *la sua — lo ha reso ricco,* his providence has made him rich ‖ *— sociale,* social security ‖ *fondo di —,* national insurance fund.

previdenziàle, *ag.* previdential: *oneri previdenziali,* social welfare contributions; *riforma —,* social security reform.

prèvio, *ag.* previous, prior ‖ *previa autorizzazione,* by authority received; *— avviso, accordo,* upon notice, agreement: *— consenso delle parti interessate,* subject to agreement of the interested parties; *— esame,* subject to examination; *— pagamento,* against payment.

previsióne, *s.f.* **1.** forecast, prevision; expectation: *previsioni del raccolto,* forecast for the harvest; *previsioni metereologiche,* weather-forecast; *ciò è contro le* *mie previsioni*, that is contrary to my expectations; *non posso fare nessuna* —, I cannot make any forecast; *il suo successo ha superato ogni* —, his success has gone beyond every expectation; *le tue previsioni erano tutte sbagliate*, your forecasts were all wrong **2.** *(comm.)* estimate: — *delle entrate, delle spese*, estimate of (the) revenue, of (the) expenditure; *fare la* — *delle entrate, delle spese*, to estimate revenue, expenditure.

prevísto, *ag.* **1.** foreseen, forecast: *avvenimento* —, foreseen event **2.** *(comm.)* estimated: *entrata prevista*, estimated income; *la spesa prevista è di due milioni di lire*, the estimated expenditure is two million lire **3.** *(di legge, contratto, ecc.)* provided (for): *caso* —, case provided for; *come è* — *nel contratto*, as provided in the contract ‖ *s.m.* what is expected: *le trattative durarono più a lungo del* —, the negotiations lasted longer than expected.

prevòsto, *s.m.* *(eccl.)* parish-priest; *(st.)* provost.

preziosaménte, *av.* preciously.

preziosísmo, *s.m.* *(letter.)* euphuism, preciosity.

preziosità, *s.f.* **1.** preciousness, costliness **2.** *(ricercatezza)* preciosity.

prezióso, *ag.* **1.** precious; *(costoso)* costly: *metalli preziosi*, precious metals; *pietra preziosa*, precious stone; *un quadro* —, a precious (o valuable) painting **2.** *fig.* precious, valued: *amico* —, valued friend; *il dono* — *della vita*, the precious gift of life; *un uomo, cittadino* —, a valued man, citizen; *la libertà è preziosa*, freedom is precious; *il suo aiuto, consiglio mi fu* —, his help, advice was invaluable to me ‖ *il Preziosissimo Sangue di Gesù*, the Precious Blood (of Jesus Christ) **3.** *(ricercato)* precious, affected: *uno stile, linguaggio* —, a precious (o affected) style, language **4.** *farsi, rendersi* —, to require much pressing ‖ *s.m.* jewel.

prezzàre, *v.t.* *(valutare)* to appraise, to value; *(avere in stima)* to value ‖ **prezzàrsi,** *v.r.* to value oneself.

prezzatóre, *ag.* appraising ‖ *s.m.* **prezzatríce,** *s.f.* valuer, appraiser.

prezzémolo, *s.m.* parsley ‖ *antico come il* —, as old as the hills (o as Methuselah).

prèzzo, *s.m.* **1.** price: — *a forfait*, price by the job; — *all'ingrosso*, wholesale price; — *al minuto, al dettaglio*, retail price; — *alto, basso*, high, low price; — *a respiro*, time (o account) price; — *compresa l'assicurazione e il trasporto*, cost, insurance, freight *(abbr. c.i.f.)*; — *corrente, del giorno*, current (o market o ruling) price; — *d'acquisto*, purchase price; — *dazio compreso, non compreso*, duty paid, unpaid; — *dell'offerta*, supply price; — *di apertura, chiusura*, opening, closing price; — *di calmiere*, state-controlled price; — *di compensazione*, making-up price; — *di compera, vendita*, buying, selling price; — *di costo*, cost price; — *di favore*, special price; — *di listino*, list price; — *di monopolio*, monopoly price; — *di stima*, estimated price; — *equo*, fair price: *te lo cederò a un* — *equo*, I'll let you have it at a fair price; — *fisso*, fixed price; — *imposto*, forced price; — *lordo, netto*, gross, net price; — *sotto costo*, under-cost price; *a* — *ridotto*, at a reduced price; *a caro, poco* —, at a high, low price; *a metà* —, at half price; *andamento, corso dei prezzi*, course of prices; *aumento, rialzo dei prezzi*, rise in prices; *diminuzione dei prezzi*, decline (o fall) in prices; *fluttuazioni dei prezzi*, fluctuations in prices; *listino dei prezzi*, price-list; *riduzione sul* —, reduction (o allowance) on the price; *ultimo, ultimissimo* —, bottom, rock-bottom price; *il* — *è a convenirsi*, the price is to be agreed upon; *i prezzi precipitano*, prices are tumbling; *i prezzi scendono, salgono*, prices are dropping (o falling), are rising; *i prezzi si sostengono*, prices are steady (o the market is steady); *i prezzi sono alti, bassi*, prices rule high, low; *i prezzi sono incerti*, prices are erratic; *i prezzi sono precipitati*, prices have sunk; *alzare i prezzi, (il mercato)* to bull the market; *aumentare, abbassare i prezzi*, to raise, to reduce prices; *calcolare i prezzi al minimo*, to cut prices close; *discutere*

il —, to bargain; *mantenere un* —, to keep up a price; *pagare a caro* — *ql.co.*, to pay dear for sthg. (anche *fig.*); *praticare buoni prezzi*, to charge fair (o moderate) prices; *tirare sul* —, to haggle about the price ‖ — *d'affezione*, fancy price ‖ — *del riscatto*, redemption price ‖ — *del silenzio*, hush-money ‖ *quell'oggetto non ha, è senza* —, that object is priceless (o beyond price) ‖ *fare il* —, *(stimare)* to value **2.** *(costo)* cost; *(tariffa)* fare: *i prezzi ferroviari furono aumentati il mese scorso*, train fares were raised last month ‖ *a* — *di grandi sacrifici*, at the cost of great sacrifices ‖ *a qualunque* —, at any cost **3.** *(valore)* value, worth: *oggetto di poco, di gran* —, object of little, great value; *dare un alto* — *a ql.co.*, to set a high value (up)on sthg. **4.** *pl.* *(condizioni)* terms; charges: *quali sono i vostri prezzi per vitto e alloggio?*, what are your terms for board and lodging?; *i vostri prezzi sono troppo alti*, your charges are too high **5.** *(stima, considerazione)* esteem, consideration: *far gran* — *di ql.co.*, to value sthg. highly; *tenere qlcu. in gran* —, to hold s.o. in great esteem.

prezzolàre, *v.t.* *(assoldare)* to hire; *(a scopo malvagio)* to bribe.

prezzolàto, *ag.* hired; *(mercenario)* mercenary: *sicari prezzolati*, hired assassins; *stampa prezzolata*, mercenary press.

prìa, *(poet.)* per **prìma.**

Prìamo, *no.pr.m.* *(lett.)* Priam.

priapísmo, *s.m.* *(med.)* priapism.

Prìapo, *no.pr.m.* *(mit.)* Priapus.

prigióne, *s.f.* **1.** prison, jail, gaol: *andare in* —, to go to prison (o to jail); *evadere dalla* —, to break prison (o to escape from prison); *mandare, mettere in* —, to send to prison (o to put into prison) ‖ *questa casa è una* —, this house is like a prison **2.** *(pena)* imprisonment: *cinque anni di* —, five years' imprisonment; *condannare alla* —, to sentence to prison **3.** *(mil.)* detention ‖ *s.m.* *(prigioniero)* prisoner.

prigionìa, *s.f.* imprisonment, captivity.

prigionièro, *ag.* imprisoned ‖ *s.m.* prisoner: — *di guerra*, prisoner of war; — *politico*, political prisoner (o state-prisoner); *fare, esser fatto* —, to take, to be taken prisoner.

prillàre, *v.t.i.* to twirl, to whirl (round).

prìllo, *s.m.* twirl, whirl.

prìma[1], *av.* **1.** before: *molto* —, long before; *poco* —, a short time (o shortly) before; *avresti dovuto dirmelo* —, you should have told me before; *ne so meno di* —, I know less than I did before; *ne so quanto* —, I know just as much as I did before; *non voglio incontrarla, partirò* —, I do not want to meet her; I shall leave before she comes ‖ *da* —, before: *lo conoscevo da* —, I knew him before **2.** *(in anticipo)* **beforehand: in advance:** *un'altra volta dimmelo* —, tell me in advance next time; *devi dirmi tutto* — *se vuoi che venga*, you will have to tell me everything beforehand, if you want me to come **3.** *(più presto)* **earlier, sooner:** *cercherò di venire qualche giorno* —, I shall try and come a few days earlier; *dovresti andare a letto* —, you should go to bed earlier; *non puoi venire* —?, can't you come earlier?; *vieni* —, *se puoi*, come sooner, if you can ‖ — *o poi*, sooner or later ‖ *quanto* —, *(presto)* soon (o presently o before long); *(il più presto possibile)* as soon as possible **4.** *(un tempo, una volta)* **once; formerly:** — *c'era un parco qui*, there was a park here formerly; — *vivevo a Roma*, I used to live in Rome (once) ‖ *di* —: *ai tempi di* '—, in the old days; *egli non è più quello di* —, he is not the man he was (o he is no longer his former self o he is but a shadow of his former self); *ora siamo più amici di* —, now we are closer (o better) friends than ever **5.** *(per prima cosa, davanti, per primo)* **first:** — *mangiamo, poi usciremo*, let us eat first, then go out; *egli entrò* —, *gli altri lo seguirono*, he came in first, the others followed (him) ‖ *prep.* before: — *delle 7*, before 7 (o'clock); — *di Cristo*, before Christ *(abbr. B.C.)*; — *di te*, before you; —

di tutto, first of all ‖ **príma di, che**, *l. cong.* **1. before:** — *che essi venissero*, before they came; — *che io nascessi*, before I was born; — *di partire, ti telefonerò*, I'll ring you up before leaving (*o* before I leave); *pensaci bene* — *di decidere*, think well before you decide **2.** (*piuttosto che*) **sooner than, rather than:** *vorrei* — *diventare povero che diventare ladro*, I would rather (*o* sooner) be poor than a thief.

príma[2], *s.f.* **1.** (*nell'ordinamento scolastico*) first class **2.** (*ferr.*) first-class: *viaggiare in* —, to travel first-class **3.** (*teat.*) first night; (*cine.*) " première " **4.** (*scherma*) basic position, initial position; (*ginnastica*) basic position **5.** (*eccl.*) prime **6.** — *di cambio*, (*comm.*) first of exchange **7.** *aiutante maggiore in* —, (*mil.*) regimental adjutant **8.** *sulle prime, a tutta* —, at first.

primaiuòla, *s.f.* primipara (*pl.* primiparae).

primaménte, *av.* (*letter.*) **1.** (*da principio*) at first **2.** (*principalmente*) chiefly **3.** (*prima di tutto*) in the first place, first of all.

primariaménte, *av.* primarily, chiefly.

primàrio, *ag.* primary: *le primarie autorità*, the primary authorities; *era primaria*, (*geol.*) primary age; *una questione di primaria importanza*, a matter of primary importance; *rocce primarie*, (*geol.*) primary rocks ‖ *medico* —, head physician ‖ *scuola primaria*, primary school ‖ *s.m.* head physician.

primàte, *s.m.* **1.** (*eccl.*) primate **2.** *pl.* notables, elders.

primàti, *s.m.pl.* (*zool.*) Primates.

primatíccio, *ag.* early.

primatísta, *s.c.* (*spor.*) record-holder.

primàto, *s.m.* **1.** primacy, pre-eminence; (*supremazia*) supremacy: — *navale, letterario, commerciale*, naval, literary, commercial supremacy; *avere, tenere il* —, to hold the supremacy **2.** (*spor.*) record: *battere il* —, to break (*o* to beat) the record.

primavèra, *s.f.* **1.** spring: *aria di* —, spring air; *l'arrivo della* —, the arrival of (the) spring; *equinozio di* —, vernal equinox; *in* —, in spring (*o* in springtime); *nei primi giorni della* —, in early spring ‖ *morì nella* — *della vita*, she died in the prime (*o* in the springtime) of life ‖ *quell'uomo deve aver visto molte primavere*, that man must have seen many winters ‖ *una rondine non fa* —, *prov.* one swallow does not make a summer **2.** (*bot.*) primula, woodland primrose.

primaveríle, *ag.* spring (*attributivo*); vernal; springlike: *aspetto* —, springlike aspect; *brezze, piogge primaverili*, spring breezes, rains; *erba* —, spring grass; *fiori primaverili*, spring (*o* vernal) flowers; *vestiti primaverili*, spring clothes.

primazía, *s.f.* (*eccl.*) primacy.

primaziàle, *ag.* (*eccl.*) primatial.

primeggiàre, *v.i.* to excel; to take the lead: *da ragazzo egli primeggiava in coraggio fra tutti i suoi amici*, as a boy he excelled all his friends in courage; *l'Italia ha sempre primeggiato nell'arte*, Italy has always taken the lead in art; — *in latino, al tennis*, to excel in Latin, at tennis.

primèvo, *ag.* primeval.

primièra, *s.f.* (*giuoco di carte*) primero.

primieraménte, *av.* **1.** (*per la prima volta*) for the first time **2.** (*anteriormente*) formerly; (*precedentemente*) previously **3.** (*in primo luogo*) primarily, firstly **4.** (*soprattutto*) above all.

primièro, *ag.* **1.** (*primo*) first **2.** (*anteriore*) former; (*precedente*) previous: *primiera usanza*, old custom ‖ *s.m.* (*prima parte di una sciarada*) the first.

primigènio, *ag.* primitive, primigenial.

primína, *s.f.* (*bot.*) primine.

primípara, *s.f.* primipara (*pl.* primiparae).

primitivaménte, *av.* primitively.

primitívo, *ag.* **1.** primitive; (*pristino*) pristine; (*primordiale*) primeval: *cultura, arte primitiva*, primitive culture, art; *età, religioni primitive*, primitive ages, religious; *freschezza e vigore primitivi*, pristine freshness

and vigour; *nome* —, (*gram.*) primitive (*o* radical) word; *popoli primitivi*, primitive peoples; *uomo* —, primitive man ‖ *i primitivi*, the primitives (anche *pitt.*) **2.** *fig.* (*rozzo*) crude, primitive: *ha modi primitivi*, he has crude manners; *vivere in modo* —, to live primitively.

primízia, *s.f.* **1.** early fruit; (*di verdura*) early vegetable **2.** (*novità*) novelty **3.** (*notizia recentissima*) brand-new piece of news.

prímo, *ag.num.ord.* **1.** **first**; (*tra due*) **former:** *il* — *di questa lunga fila*, the first of this long row; *il* — *di tutti*, the first of all; *il* — *mese dell'anno*, the first month of the year; *la prima persona*, (*gram.*) the first person; *il* — *piano*, the first floor (*o amer.* second floor); *il* — *re Tudor*, the first Tudor King; *di questi due libri preferisco il* —, of these two books I prefer the former; *fu tra i primi ad arrivare*, he was among the very first to arrive; *partirò domani col* — *treno*, I'll leave tomorrow by the first train; *Piero e Giovanni sono amici; il* —, *è avvocato, il secondo dottore*, Peter and John are friends; the former is a lawyer, the latter is a doctor; « *Preferisci Virgilio, Orazio o Lucrezio?* », « *Preferisco il* — », "Do you prefer Virgil, Horace or Lucretius?", "I prefer the first"; *riuscire* —, to come out first ‖ *il* — *nato*, the first-born ‖ *il* — *venuto*, the first comer ‖ *a prima vista*, (*dapprima*) at first (sight); (*di traduzione, esecuzione musicale*) at sight ‖ *Atto I, Scena II*, Act one, Scene two ‖ *Carlo* —, *Elisabetta prima, re Enrico* —, Charles the First, Elizabeth the First, King Henry the First ‖ *di prima mano*, first-hand ‖ *di prim'ordine*, first-class (*o* first-rate): *un mascalzone di prim'ordine*, a first-class scoundrel ‖ *in* — *luogo*, in the first place (*o* first of all) ‖ *in un* — *tempo*, at first ‖ *per prima cosa*, first thing: *fallo per prima cosa domani*, do it first thing tomorrow **2.** (*principale, più importante*) **chief, principal, main;** (*migliore*) **best:** *i primi cittadini del paese*, the leading (*o* first) citizens of the country; *appartiene ad una delle prime famiglie della città*, he belongs to one of the best families in town; *ecco la ragione prima per cui non vengo*, that's the main (*o* chief *o* principal) reason why I don't come ‖ *prima classe*, (*ferr.*) first class ‖ *prima donna*, (*teat.*) leading lady; (*opera*) prima donna ‖ *Primo Ministro*, Prime Minister (*o* Premier) ‖ *prima parte*, (*teat.*) lead; leading rôle (anche *fig.*) ‖ *violino, violoncello*, first violin (*o* leader), first cello **3.** (*iniziale; più lontano nel tempo*) **early:** *i primi Cristiani*, the early Christians; *i primi giorni della rivoluzione*, the early days of the revolution; *la prima infanzia, giovinezza*, early childhood, youth; *le prime leggende*, the earliest (*o* first) legends; *le prime ore del mattino*, the early hours of the morning; *la prima parte dell'anno, del secolo*, the early part of the year, of the century; *fin dalla sua prima età*, from a very early age; *nei primi mesi dell'anno*, in the early months of the year; *i nostri primi poeti*, our early poets; *uno dei primi Vittoriani*, an early Victorian ‖ *di* — *mattino, pomeriggio*, early in the morning, in the afternoon **4.** (*prossimo*) **next:** *glielo porterò la prima volta che andrò da lui*, I'll take it to him the next time I go to his house; *ho perso il treno delle dieci; prenderò il* — *in partenza*, I have missed the ten o'clock train; I'll get the next one **5.** (*passato, precedente*) **former:** *sta tornando alle sue prime abitudini*, he is getting back to his former (*o* old) habits ‖ *s.m.* **1.** first: *il* — *dell'anno*, New Year's Day; *il* — *di febbraio, di marzo*, the First of February, of March **2.** (*inizio*): *ai primi dell'Ottocento*, in the early nineteenth century; *ai primi del mese*, at the beginning of (*o* early in) the month **3.** (*più importante; migliore*) *è dei primi*, he is one of the best; *essere il* — *della classe*, to be top of the form.

primogènita, *s.f.* first-born.

primogènito, *ag.* first-born, eldest ‖ *s.m.* first-born.

primogenitóre, *s.m.* primogenitor ‖ **primogenitrice**, *s.f.* primogenitrix.

primogenitúra, *s.f.* primogeniture: *diritto di —,* (*st.*) right of primogeniture.

prímola, *s.f.* (*bot.*) primrose.

primordiàle, *ag.* primordial, primeval.

primordialménte, *av.* primordially.

primòrdio, *s.m.* beginning, origin: *i primordi della civiltà,* the dawn of civilization; *i primordi della letteratura italiana,* the beginnings of Italian literature.

prímula, *s.f.* (*bot.*) primrose.

princesse, *s.f.* (*abito intero da donna*) princess (dress), princess(e).

principàle, *ag.* principal, main, chief: *la città —,* the principal town; *i fiumi principali d'Italia,* the chief rivers of Italy; *linea —,* (*ferr.*) main line; *i miei interessi principali,* my chief interests; *il motivo — di un'azione,* the principle motive of an action; *le opere principali di un autore,* the main works of an author; *proposizione —,* (*gram.*) principal (*o* main) clause; *il punto — di un argomento,* the main point of an argument; *lo scopo —,* the main (*o* chief) object; *la sede — di una banca,* the head office of a bank; *la strada — di una città,* the main street of a town ‖ *s.m.* **1.** (*capo d'azienda*) principal; (*direttore*) manager; (*padrone*) master; (*datore di lavoro*) employer; (*fam.*) boss **2.** (*punto, argomento essenziale*) principal thing, main point: *il — è riuscire,* the principal (*o* great) thing is to succeed; *veniamo al —,* let's come to the main point.

principalménte, *av.* principally, mainly, chiefly.

principàto, *s.m.* **1.** (*territorio retto da un principe*) principality **2.** (*ufficio, dignità, giurisdizione di un principe*) princedom **3.** (*supremazia*) supremacy **4.** *pl.* (*gerarchia angelica*) principalities.

prìncipe, *s.m.* prince (anche *fig.*): *— consorte,* Prince Consort; *il — dei poeti, dei romanzieri, dei bugiardi,* the very prince of poets, of novelists, of liars; *— del sangue,* prince of the blood; *il Principe di Galles,* the Prince of Wales; *il Principe Edoardo,* Prince Edward; *— ereditario,* Crown Prince; *un — reale,* a royal prince; *il — reale,* the Prince Royal; *vivere da —,* to live like a prince ‖ *— degli apostoli,* Prince of the Apostles ‖ *della Chiesa,* Prince of the Church ‖ *— delle tenebre,* (*il demonio*) the prince of darkness.

principescaménte, *av.* in a princely manner.

principésco, *ag.* princely; princelike (*attributivo*): *aspetto —,* princely countenance; *modi principeschi,* princely (*o* princelike) manners.

principéssa, *s.f.* princess: *la Principessa Clara,* Princess Clara; *la — reale,* the Princess Royal.

principessìna, *s.f.* **1.** (*giovane principessa*) young princess **2.** (*figlia di un principe*) prince's daughter.

principiànte, *s.c.* beginner: *un lavoro da principianti,* a work for beginners.

principiàre, *v.t.i.* (*arc.*) to begin, to start, to commence: *principiò a cantare,* he began to sing; *— una discussione,* to start an argument; *— un lavoro,* to begin a work ‖ *a — da,* beginning with: *a — da oggi,* (as) from today; *tutti i cittadini, a — dal sindaco,* protestarono, all the citizens, beginning with the mayor, protested.

principìno, *s.m.* **1.** (*giovane principe*) young prince **2.** (*figlio di un principe*) prince's son.

principìo, *s.m.* **1.** beginning: *al — dell'anno, del mese,* at the beginning of (*o* early in) the year, the month; *al — del libro, della strada,* at the beginning of the book, of the road; *proprio dal —,* from the very beginning; *diede — al suo discorso dicendo...,* he began his speech by saying...; *incomincia dal —,* start from the beginning ‖ *da, in, al, sul —,* (*all'inizio*) at the beginning (*o* at first) ‖ *dal — alla fine,* from beginning to end **2.** (*legge, sistema, norma*) principle: *il — della continuità,* (*mat.*) the principle of continuity; *il — di Archimede,* (*fis.*) the principle of Archimedes; *— di uguaglianza,* principle of equality; *principi morali, religiosi,* moral, religious principles; *un uomo che non ha principi,* a man of no principles; *seguire un — di condotta,* to follow a line of conduct ‖ *per —,* on principle: *non ho accettato per —,* I have not accepted on principle; *fare ql.co. per —,* to make it a matter of principle to do sthg. (*o* to do sthg. on principle) ‖ *partire dal che...,* to start from the principle that... **3.** *pl.* (*elementi, rudimenti*) principles, rudiments: *gli mancano persino i principi della matematica, grammatica, ecc.,* he lacks even the rudiments of mathematics, grammar, etc. **4.** (*origine, causa*) origin, cause, principle: *i principi della civiltà,* the origins of civilization; *Dio, — dell'universo,* God, the prime cause of the universe; *quell'amicizia fu il — della sua rovina,* that friendship was the cause of his ruin ‖ *il — del bene, del male,* (*fil.*) the principle of good, of evil **5.** (*chim.*) principle: *— attivo,* active principle (*o* constituent).

princisbécco, *s.m.* pinchbeck: *ornamento di —,* pinchbeck ornament ‖ *restare di —,* to be taken aback.

prióra, *s.f.* (*eccl.*) prioress.

prioràle, *ag.* of a prior.

prioràto, *s.m.* priorship, priorate.

prióre, *s.m.* (*eccl. st.*) prior.

priòri, a, *l.av.* a priori.

prioría, *s.f.* (*eccl.*) **1.** (*chiesa*) priory **2.** (*ufficio di priore*) priorship, priorate.

priorità, *s.f.* priority: *diritto di —,* right of priority; *avere la —,* to have priority.

Prisciàno, *no.pr.m.* (*st.*) Priscian.

Priscílla, *no.pr.f.* Priscilla.

Prísco[1], *no.pr.m.* (*st.*) Priscus.

prísco[2], *ag.* (*letter.*) ancient, old.

prísma, *s.m.* (*geom. ott.*) prism: *— deflettore,* (*ott.*) deflecting prism; *— di rinvio,* (*ott.*) reflecting prism; *— raddrizzatore,* (*ott.*) erecting (*o* rectifying) prism.

prismàtico, *ag.* **1.** prismatic: *colori prismatici,* prismatic colours; *cristalli prismatici,* prismatic crystals **2.** *cassetta prismatica,* (*mec.*) box angle-plate.

prístino, *ag.* pristine, former; original: *pristina grandezza,* pristine greatness; *— stato,* former state; *— vigore,* pristine vigour ‖ *rimettere ql.co. in —,* to restore sthg. to its former state.

pritanèo, *s.m.* (*archeol.*) prytaneum.

prìtano, *s.m.* (*st. greca*) prytany.

privàre, *v.t.* to deprive; to bereave (*gener. fig.*); (*non concedere*) to deny: *fui privato dell'unica speranza che avevo,* I was bereft (*o* bereaved) of the only hope I had; *la guerra lo privò dei suoi due figli,* the war bereaved him of his two sons; *lo privarono di tutte le sue ricchezze,* they deprived (*o* stripped) him of all his possessions; *nessuno può privarmi di questa gioia,* nobody can deprive me of this joy; *perchè vuoi privarci della tua compagnia?,* why do you want to deprive us of (*o* to deny us) your company?; *spero di non essere privato del piacere della tua amicizia,* I hope I shall not be deprived of the pleasure of your friendship; *— della vista,* to deprive of sight; *— dell'onore,* to deprive of honour ‖ **privàrsi**, *v.r.* to deprive oneself; (*negarsi*) to deny oneself (sthg.), to give up (sthg.): *dovetti privarmi anche di questa soddisfazione,* I had to deny myself (*o* give up) even this satisfaction; *egli si priva di molte cose necessarie per mandare a scuola suo figlio,* he denies himself many necessary things to send his son to school; *egli si privò di tutto ciò che aveva,* he deprived himself of everything he had.

privataménte, *av.* privately, in private.

privatísta, *s.c.* external student, private student; (*agli esami*) external candidate: *una sessione per i privatisti,* a session for external candidates; *mio fratello è un —,* my brother is an external student.

privatíva, *s.f.* **1.** (*tabaccheria*) tobacconist's (shop); (*monopolio*) monopoly: *generi di —,* (State) monopolies **2.** (*esclusiva*) sole-right, patent, patent-right.

privativaménte, *av.* privatively.

privatívo, *ag.* privative: *alfa privativa,* alpha privative.

privàto, *ag.* **1.** private; (*personale*) personal: *affare, interesse* —, private business, interest; *una faccenda privata*, a personal matter; *lettera, scuola, banca, automobile privata*, private letter, school, bank, car; *insegnante* —, private teacher; *vita, proprietà, segretaria privata*, private life, property, secretary ‖ *in* —, in private **2.** (*privo*) deprived; bereft, bereaved (*gener. fig.*): — *di ogni speranza*, bereft of all hope ‖ *s.m.* private citizen, private person, private individual.

privazióne, *s.f.* **1.** (*azione del privare*) privation, deprivation; (*perdita*) loss: — *della libertà*, loss of liberty; — *dell'ufficio*, deprivation of office **2.** (*disagio*) privation, hardship: *vita di* —, life of hardship; *soffrire, subire severe privazioni*, to suffer, to undergo severe privations **3.** (*sacrificio*) sacrifice: *non tutti sanno fare delle privazioni*, not everybody can make sacrifices **4.** (*assenza, mancanza*) absence: — *di colpa*, absence of guilt (o of blame).

privilegiàre, *v.t.* **1.** to privilege **2.** (*dotare*) to gift, to endow: *la natura lo aveva privilegiato con doti particolari*, he had been endowed by nature with particular gifts.

privilegiàto, *ag.* **1.** privileged: *le classi privilegiate*, the privileged classes; *condizioni privilegiate*, privileged conditions ‖ *i privilegiati*, the privileged: *i pochi privilegiati*, the privileged few ‖ *altare* —, (*eccl.*) privileged altar **2.** (*comm.*) preferred, privileged, preferential; preference (*attributivo*): *azioni privilegiate*, preference shares; *credito* —, preferential (o preferred o privileged) credit; *titolo* —, preference (o preferential) stock.

privilègio, *s.m.* **1.** privilege: *i privilegi della nobiltà*, the privileges of the nobility; *è un* — *della vecchiaia*, that is a privilege (o a prerogative) of old age; *concedere, godere un* —, to grant, to enjoy a privilege; *violare i privilegi di qlcu.*, to invade s.o.'s privileges **2.** (*foglio, atto che concede un privilegio*) licence **3.** (*dir.*) lien ‖ — *del foro*, (*dir. eccl.*) privilege (o benefit) of clergy.

privo, *ag.* devoid, destitute; (*mancante*) lacking (in sthg.), wanting (in sthg.); — *di buon senso, di orgoglio, di malignità*, devoid of common sense, of pride, of malice; — *di energia*, wanting in energy; — *di entusiasmo*, lacking in enthusiasm; — *di genitori*, without parents; — *di interesse, di ogni probabilità*, devoid of interest, of all probability; — *di madre*, motherless; — *di mezzi*, destitute of means; — *di ogni senso della bellezza*, devoid of any sense of beauty; — *di padre*, fatherless; *sono* — *di sue notizie da due mesi*, I haven't heard from him for two months.

pro[1], *s.m.* (*giovamento, utilità*) advantage; profit; benefit; use: *a mio* —, to my advantage; *non mi viene nessun* — *da questo affare*, this business does not do me any good (o I don't get anything out of this business); *far* — *di ql.co.*, to take advantage of sthg. (o to turn sthg. to one's advantage) ‖ *a che* —?, what's the use of it? (*o fam.* what for?); *a che* — *lavorare tanto?*, what is the use of working so hard? ‖ *buon* — *gli faccia!*, much good may it do him!.

pro[2], *prep.* (*per, a favore di*) **for:** — *infanzia abbandonata*, for waifs and strays; *questi sono gli argomenti* — *e contro le tue proposte*, these are the arguments for and against your proposals ‖ — *bono pacis*, for the sake of peace; — *domo mea*, to my own advantage ‖ — *forma*, for form's sake (o pro forma) ‖ *s.m.* **pros** (*pl.*): *il* — *e il contro di una questione*, the pros and cons of a matter; *valutare il* — *e il contro*, to consider (o to weigh) the pros and cons.

proàva, *s.f.* great grandmother.

proàvo, *s.m.* **1.** great grandfather **2.** *pl.* ancestors, forefathers.

probàbile, *ag.* **1.** probable, likely: *molto* —, very probable; *poco* —, hardly probable (o unlikely): *è assai poco* —, it is most unlikely; « *Verrai allora?* », « *È poco* — », "Will you come then?", "I should hardly think so"; *la* — *origine di tutte queste complicazioni è*

che..., the probable origin of all these complications is that...; *è* — *che ci sia un temporale*, it is probable that there will be a storm (o there is likely to be a storm); *è* — *che egli parta per l'Inghilterra*, it is probable that he will leave (o he is likely to leave) for England; *è* — *che piova*, it is likely to rain (o it looks like rain); *è* — *che questo sia vero*, this is likely to be true; *è più che* —, it is more than likely (o fam. you bet) **2.** (*verosimile*) probable, likely: *una scusa poco* —, an unlikely story **3.** (*dimostrabile*) provable: *opinione* —, (*fil.*) provable opinion ‖ *s.m.* what is probable: *il* — *si può sempre dimostrare*, what is probable (o provable) can always be demonstrated.

probabilìsmo, *s.m.* (*fil. teol.*) probabilism.

probabilìsta, *s.m.* (*fil. teol.*) probabilist.

probabilità, *s.f.* probability, likelihood; chance: *al di là di ogni* —, beyond the bounds of probability; *con ogni* —, in all probability (o most likely o in all likelihood); *le* — *sono poche, ma egli spera ugualmente*, the probabilities (o chances) are few, but he hopes all the same; *c'è la* — *che...*, there is the probability that...: *c'è (la)* — *che parta per l'America*, there is the probability that he will leave (o he is likely to leave) for America; *c'è una* — *su cento*, there is one chance in a thousand; *che* — *ci sono?*, what are the probabilities? (o the chances?); *ha una buona* — *di vincere*, he has a good chance of winning; *non c'è* — *che guarisca, che venga*, there is no probability of his recovery, of his coming; *non ha nessuna* — *di riuscire*, he has no chance of success ‖ *calcolo delle* —, (*mat.*) calculus of probability.

probabilménte, *av.* probably, likely: *molto* —, very probably (o most probably o very likely); — *verrà in ritardo*, probably he will come late (o he is likely to come late).

probaménte, *av.* honestly, uprightly.

probànte, probatìvo, probatòrio, *ag.* probative, probatory.

probazióne, *s.f.* (*eccl.*) probation.

probità, *s.f.* probity, uprightness; integrity.

probivìri, *s.m.pl.* arbiters.

problèma, *s.m.* problem: *un* — *matematico*, a mathematical problem; *i problemi sociali, politici*, social, political problems; *risolvere un* —, to solve a problem; *il* — *è che...*, the problem (o question) is that... ‖ *questo ragazzo è un* —, this boy is a problem.

problematicaménte, *av.* problematically.

problemàtico, *ag.* **1.** (*difficile, complicato*) problematic(al): *carattere* —, problematical character **2.** (*incerto, dubbio*) problematic(al); uncertain: *un guadagno* —, an uncertain gain **3.** (*del problema*) of the problem.

pròbo, *ag.* upright.

proboscidàti, *s.m. pl.* (*zool.*) Proboscidea.

probòscide, *s.f.* trunk, proboscis (*pl.* proboscises, proboscides).

procàccia, *s.m.* **1.** (*postino*) postman (*pl.* postmen) **2.** (*corriere*) carrier.

procaccévole, *ag.* industrious.

procacciànte, *ag.* **1.** industrious, hardworking **2.** (*intrigante*) meddlesome ‖ *s.c.* busybody, meddler.

procacciàre, *v.t.* to procure, to get: *questo libro gli procacciò molti premi*, this book gained him many prizes; *ti procaccerò quel lavoro appena possibile*, I shall procure that job for you (o I shall get you that job) as soon as possible ‖ **procacciàrsi,** *v.r.* to procure (anche *fig.*); to get: *come si procaccia da vivere?*, how does he get his living?; *devo procacciarmi un lavoro*, I must get myself a job; — *la fiducia di qlcu.*, to gain s.o.'s confidence.

procàce, *ag.* **1.** (*sfacciato*) forward, petulant, saucy **2.** (*provocante*) provoking **3.** (*inverecondo*) immodest.

procaceménte, *av.* **1.** (*sfacciatamente*) impudently **2.** (*in modo provocante*) provokingly, provocatively **3.** (*in modo inverecondo*) immodestly.

procacità, *s.f.* **1.** (*sfacciataggine*) procacity, impudence 2. (*l'essere provocante*) provocativeness 3. (*inverecondia*) immodesty.

procedènte, *ag.* proceeding.

procedènza, *s.f.* proceeding; procession (anche *teol.*).

procèdere, *v.i.* 1. to proceed, to go on, to continue: *dopo una breve pausa l'oratore procedette*, after a short pause the orator went on; *il lavoro non procede*, the work does not proceed; *prima di — oltre*, before we proceed any further; *procedete!*, go on! (o proceed!); *procedevano in silenzio*, they went on in silence; *procedi oltre, questo non m'interessa*, go on, this does not interest me; — *cautamente*, to proceed cautiously; — *di buon passo*, to walk smartly 2. (*agire, comportarsi*) to act, to behave; (*trattare*) to deal: *dovresti — con più tatto con quell'uomo*, you should deal more tactfully with that man; *procedi onestamente*, behave honestly 3. (*dir.*) to proceed: — *contro qlcu.*, to proceed against s.o.; — *per vie legali contro qlcu.*, to take legal proceedings against s.o. ‖ *non luogo a —*, nonsuit (o no case): *sentenza di non luogo a —*, nonsuit judgement 4. (*derivare, aver origine*) to proceed, to originate: *da che procede questo fatto?*, what is this fact due to?; *tutti i suoi guai procedono dalla sua avventatezza*, all his troubles proceed from his rashness ‖ *il Figlio procede dal Padre*, (*teol.*) the Son proceeds from the Father 5. (*accingersi*) to start: *decisero di — alla perforazione del pozzo*, they decided to start the drilling of the well.

procèdere, *s.m.* 1. (*il progredire*) process: *il — del tempo*, the process of time; *col — del tempo*, as time goes on 2. (*condotta, comportamento*) conduct, behaviour, way of dealing: *non approvo il suo — verso quell'uomo*, I do not approve of his behaviour towards that man.

procedimènto, *s.m.* 1. (*comportamento*) behaviour, conduct: *questo è un — disonesto*, this is unfair behaviour 2. (*il procedere, il corso*) course: *il — storico dei fatti*, the historical development of the facts 3. (*dir.*) proceedings (*pl.*): *iniziare il — contro qlcu.*, to begin proceedings against s.o. 4. (*scient. tec.*) process; procedure: — *a matrice piana*, (*tip.*) planographic process; — *chimico*, chemical process; — *di un'analisi chimica*, procedure of a chemical analysis; — *di avvicinamento*, (*aer.*) approach procedure; — *di fabbricazione*, (*ind.*) manufacturing process; — *di malleabilizzazione della ghisa*, (*metal.*) mitis casting; — *di una operazione matematica*, process of a mathematical operation.

procedúra, *s.f.* (*dir.*) procedure: — *legale, civile, legal*, civil procedure; *codice di — penale*, code of criminal procedure; *errore di —*, error of procedure; *ordine, regole di —*, order, rules of procedure.

proceduràle, *ag.* (*dir.*) procedural, of procedure: *regole procedurali*, rules of procedure.

procedurísta, *s.m.* expert in procedure.

procèlla, *s.f.* (*poet.*) storm, tempest (anche *fig.*).

procellària, *s.f.* (*ornit.*) (stormy-)petrel.

procellosaménte, *av.* stormily, tempestuously (anche *fig.*).

procellóso, *ag.* stormy, tempestuous (anche *fig.*).

processàbile, *ag.* indictable, liable to prosecution.

processàre, *v.t.* to try: — *qlcu. per assassinio, furto*, to try s.o. for murder, theft ‖ *far —*, to bring to trial (o to prosecute): *far — qlcu. per un delitto*, to bring s.o. to trial for a felony; *far — qlcu. per una leggera infrazione*, to prosecute s.o. for a misdemeanour.

processionalménte, *av.* processionally, in procession.

processionàre, *v.i.* to go in procession, to procession.

processionària, *s.f.* (*entom.*) processionary.

processióne, *s.f.* 1. procession: *una — di formiche*, a procession of ants; *una — di visite*, a succession of visitors; — *religiosa*, religious procession; *andare, camminare in —*, to go, to walk in procession; *formare una —*, to form a procession 2. (*teol.*) procession, emanation: *la — dello Spirito Santo*, the procession of the Holy Ghost.

procèsso, *s.m.* 1. (*dir.*) action, trial, proceedings (*pl.*): — *civile*, lawsuit (o civil proceedings); — *penale*, criminal trial; *andò sotto — l'anno scorso*, he was tried last year; *ero presente al suo —*, I was present at his trial; *essere sotto — per ql.co.*, to be on trial for sthg.; *intentare un — a qlcu.*, to bring an action (o to institute proceedings) against s.o.: *intentò — di divorzio contro suo marito*, she instituted divorce proceedings against her husband; *mettere qlcu. sotto —*, to bring s.o. to trial; *perdere un —*, to lose a suit (o an action); *vincere il —*, to win one's case 2. — *verbale*, minutes (o procès-verbal) 3. (*corso*) course; (*stadio*) process: *il — di una malattia*, the course of an illness; — *di sviluppo*, process of growth; — *infiammatorio*, inflammatory process; *in — di formazione, di lavorazione, di costruzione*, in process of formation, of manufacture, of construction; *in — di tempo*, in the course of time 4. (*tec.*) (*metodo*) process: — *chimico*, chemical process; — *delle camere di piombo*, (*chim.*) chamber process; — *di isomerizzazione*, (*chim.*) isoforming (o isomerization); — *di laminazione*, (*metal.*) rolling process; — *Solvay*, (*chim. ind.*) ammonia-soda process 5. (*anat.*) process: *processi ciliari*, ciliary process.

processuàle, *ag.* (*dir.*) of a trial; trial (*attributivo*): *spese processuali*, costs.

pròci, *s.m.pl.* suitors.

procínto, *s.m.*: *essere in — di*, to be on the point of: *ero in — di partire*, I was going to leave (o I was on the point of leaving).

Procióne, *no.pr.m.* (*astr.*) Procyon ‖ **procióne**, *s.m.* (*zool.*) procyon.

proclàma, *s.m.* proclamation.

proclamàre, *v.t.* 1. to proclaim; (*promulgare*) to promulgate: *fu proclamato re*, he was proclaimed king; — *un decreto, una legge*, to promulgate a decree, a law 2. (*dichiarare*) to proclaim, to state, to declare: *proclamava continuamente la sua innocenza*, she constantly proclaimed her innocence.

proclamatóre, *ag.* proclaiming ‖ *s.m.*, **proclamatríce**, *s.f.* proclaimer.

proclamazióne, *s.f.* proclamation.

proclítico, *ag.* (*gram.*) proclitic.

proclíve, *ag.* inclined: *è — all'indulgenza, all'ozio*, he is inclined to be indulgent, lazy.

proclività, *s.f.* tendency, inclination, proclivity.

procombènte, *ag.* procumbent (anche *bot.*).

procómbere, *v.i.* to fall dead.

proconsolàre, *ag.* (*st. romana*) proconsular.

proconsolàto, *s.m.* (*st. romana*) proconsulate, proconsulship.

procónsole, *s.m.* (*st. romana*) proconsul.

Procòpio, *no.pr.m.* (*st.*) Procopius.

procrastinaménto, *s.m.* procrastination.

procrastinàre, *v.t.* to put off, to defer; to postpone, to adjourn; (*rar.*) to procrastinate: *l'adunanza fu procrastinata*, the meeting was postponed to the following day ‖ *v.i.* to procrastinate: *non mi piace — come fai tu*, I do not like to procrastinate as you do.

procrastinatóre, *ag.* procrastinatory, procrastinating ‖ *s.m.*, **procrastinatríce**, *s.f.* procrastinator.

procrastinazióne, *s.f.* procrastination.

procreàbile, *ag.* generable, that can be procreated.

procreaménto, *s.m.* procreation.

procreàre, *v.t.* to procreate, to generate.

procreatóre, *ag.* procreant, procreating, generating ‖ *s.m.*, **procreatríce**, *s.f.* procreator, parent.

procreazióne, *s.f.* procreation.

procúra, *s.f.* 1. power of attorney; proxy: — *generale*, full power of attorney; *avere la — di qlcu.*, to stand proxy for s.o. (o to be granted power of attorney by s.o.); *dare la — a qlcu.*, to accord (o to grant) power of attorney to s.o. (o to confer powers of attorney (up)on s.o.) ‖ *per —*, by proxy (o per procurationem) (*abbr.* p.p.): *firmare per —*, to sign per procurationem; *sposarsi, votare per —*, to marry, to vote by proxy **2.** (*documento di procura*) letter of attorney, procuratory **3.** (*ufficio, sede del procuratore*) solicitor's office.

procuràre, *v.t.* **1.** to procure, to get; (*causare*) to cause: *ci ha procurato i biglietti*, he has got the tickets for us; *ciò mi procurò molti guai*, this caused me much trouble; *mi ha procurato delle preziose informazioni*, he has got some valuable information for me ‖ *dove manca natura, arte procura*, *prov.* where nature is lacking, art provides **2.** (*cercare*) to try; to manage: *procura di farlo bene, di non farti male*, try to do it well, not to get hurt; *procura di saperlo al più presto*, try to find out as soon as possible; *procurerò di venire prima di sera*, I shall manage to come before evening ‖ **procuràrsi,** *v.r.* to get, to procure: *dobbiamo procurarci i soldi prima della fine della settimana*, we must raise the money before the end of the week; *si procura sempre delle noie*, he always gets into trouble; *— da vivere*, to get (*o* to make) a living ‖ *— un raffreddore*, to catch a cold.

procuratóre, *s.m.* **1.** attorney, proctor **2.** (*procuratore legale*) (*in Inghilterra*) solicitor (*sino al 1873*: attorney-at-law); (*negli Stati Uniti*) attorney-at-law ‖ *Procuratore Generale*, Attorney-General; (*in Scozia*) Lord Advocate; *Sostituto Procuratore*, Solicitor General **3.** *Procuratore del Re, della Repubblica*, (*in Inghilterra*) Public Prosecutor; (*negli Stati Uniti*) District Attorney; (*in Scozia*) Procurator Fiscal **4.** (*st. romana*) Procurator **5.** *Procuratore di San Marco*, (*st. veneziana*) Procurator of Saint Mark **6.** (*eccl.*) procurator.

procurazióne, *s.f.* procuration (anche *eccl.*).

Procúste, *no.pr.m.* (*mit.*) Procrustes.

pròda, *s.f.* **1.** (*sponda*) shore; (*di fiume*) bank **2.** (*margine*) edge, border: *un filare di alberi era sulla — del campo*, there was a row of trees at the edge of the field ‖ *la — del letto*, the bedside **3.** (*arc.*) (*prua*) prow.

pròde[1], *ag.* brave, valiant ‖ *s.m.* (*uomo valoroso*) brave man, valiant man.

pròde[2], *s.m.* (*arc.*) (*utilità*) good, profit.

prodeggiàre, *v.i.* (*mar.*) (*bordeggiare*) to tack; (*costeggiare*) to coast.

prodeménte, *ag.* bravely, valiantly.

prodézza, *s.f.* **1.** (*valore*) prowess, bravery **2.** (*atto di coraggio*) brave deed, exploit: *compiere delle prodezze*, to perform brave deeds (*o* great exploits) ‖ *che bella —!*, a fine feat indeed!.

prodière, prodièro, *ag.* forward; bow (*attributivo*) ‖ *s.m.* **1.** (*rematore di prua*) bow, bow-oar **2.** (*nave che funge da guida*) leading ship.

prodigalità, *s.f.* prodigality, lavishness; (*di denaro*) extravagance.

prodigalménte, prodigaménte, *av.* prodigally, lavishly; (*riguardo al denaro*) extravagantly.

prodigàre, *v.t.* to lavish, to be prodigal of (sthg.) (anche *fig.*): *— denaro*, to be (very) extravagant (*o fam.* to throw one's money around); *— lodi, affetto*, to lavish (*o* to be prodigal of) praise, affection ‖ **prodigàrsi,** *v.r.* to do all one can: *egli si prodigò per tutti loro*, he did all he could for them all.

prodígio, *s.m.* **1.** prodigy; (*meraviglia*) marvel, wonder: *i prodigi della scienza*, the prodigies of science; *è un — di sapienza*, he is a prodigy of learning ‖ *bambino —*, infant prodigy ‖ *fare, compiere prodigi*, to work wonders (*o* miracles) **2.** (*presagio*) omen, presage.

prodigiosaménte, *av.* prodigiously; (*meravigliosamente*) wonderfully.

prodigiosità, *s.f.* prodigiousness.

prodigióso, *ag.* prodigious; (*meraviglioso*) marvellous, wonderful: *memoria prodigiosa*, prodigious memory.

pròdigo, *ag.* prodigal, lavish; (*di denaro*) (very) extravagant: *essere — di lodi, cure*, to be prodigal (*o* lavish) of praise, care ‖ *il figliuol —*, the prodigal son ‖ *s.m.* prodigal, spendthrift, lavish person.

proditoriaménte, *av.* treacherously.

proditòrio, *ag.* treacherous.

pròdomo, *s.m.* (*arch.*) main door.

prodótto, *ag.* **1.** produced: *articolo — in serie*, a mass-produced article; *il cioccolato — in Svizzera è ottimo*, chocolate made in Switzerland is very good **2.** (*addotto*) exhibited, produced: *— in giudizio, in Tribunale*, produced in Court ‖ *s.m.* **1.** product; produce (*coll. con costruzione sing.*): *prodotti agricoli*, agricultural produce (*o* products); *prodotti chimici*, chemical products (*o* chemicals); *i prodotti della terra*, the produce of the land; *un — dell'industria, del genio*, a product of industry, of genius; *— derivato, secondario*, by-product; *prodotti di scarto*, waste products; *prodotti finiti*, finished goods; *prodotti industriali*, industrial products; *— manufatto*, manufactured article; *— nazionale, estero*, home, foreign product **2.** (*risultato, frutto*) fruit, result, product; produce (*coll. con costruzione sing.*): *il — delle mie fatiche*, the fruits of my labour; *questo è il — della tua pigrizia*, this is the result of your laziness; *quest'opera è il — di un anno di ricerche*, this work is the fruit (*o* product) of a year of research **3.** (*arit.*) product.

pròdromo, *s.m.* **1.** warning sign **2.** (*med.*) symptom.

producíbile, *ag.* producible.

producibilità, *s.f.* producibility.

prodúrre, *v.t.* **1.** (*generare, fruttare*) to produce; to yield, to bear; (*di miniera*) to produce, to yield: *quest'albero non produce frutti*, this tree doesn't bear (*o* yield) any fruit; *il XVI secolo produsse grandi artisti*, the 16th century produced a number of great artists; *questa miniera produce molto carbone*, this mine produces (*o* yields) a lot of coal; *— calore*, to generate heat **2.** (*causare, originare*) to cause, to give rise to (sthg.), to produce: *l'esplosione fu prodotta dalla temperatura troppo alta*, the explosion was caused by the excessive temperature; *la pioggia produsse gravi danni*, the rain caused great damage; *questo cattivo tempo produrrà molte malattie*, this bad weather will cause much illness; *la sua condotta produsse molti guai*, his behaviour gave rise to a lot of trouble; *— l'effetto contrario*, to produce the opposite effect; *— un'emozione*, to cause (*o* to give rise to) excitement (*o* an emotion); *— un'impressione favorevole*, to produce (*o* to create) a favourable impression **3.** (*fabbricare*) to produce, to make, to manufacture, to turn out: *questa fabbrica produce articoli di porcellana*, this factory produces (*o* makes *o* manufactures) china articles; *questa macchina può — centinaia di fogli di carta al minuto*, this machine can turn out hundreds of sheets of paper in a minute **4.** (*di scrittore, artista, produttore, ecc.*) to produce: *produce un romanzo all'anno*, he produces (*o* brings out) a novel every year; *questo scrittore ha prodotto poco in questi ultimi anni*, this writer has produced very little in the last few years; *— una commedia, un film*, to produce a play, a film **5.** (*mostrare, presentare*) to show, to produce: *— il biglietto, i documenti*, to show one's ticket, documents; *— un testimonio*, (*dir.*) to produce (*o* to call *o* to bring forward) a witness ‖ **prodúrsi,** *v.r.* **1.** to cause oneself; to inflict on oneself: *— una ferita*, to injure oneself **2.** (*teat.*): *egli si produsse nella parte di Amleto*, he played Hamlet; *— sulla scena*, to appear on the stage **3.** (*accadere*) to happen, to occur: *i mutamenti che si sono prodotti negli ultimi anni*, the changes that have come about in the last few years.

produttività, *s.f.* productiveness, productivity.

produttívo, *ag.* **1.** productive; fruitful: *capacità produttiva della terra*, productive power of the soil; *vigna produttiva*, productive (*o* fruitful) vineyard **2.** (*comm.*) (*che dà guadagno*) productive, yielding, bearing: *— d'interesse*, interest-bearing; *— di reddito*, revenue -bearing; *azioni produttive di un dividendo*, shares yielding a dividend; *imposta, tassa largamente produttiva*, highly productive duty (*o* tax).

produttóre, *ag.* **1.** productive, producing: *paesi pro-*

duttori, productive (*o* producing) countries **2.** (*che fabbrica*) manufacturing ‖ *s.m.*, **produttríce**, *s.f.* **1.** producer **2.** (*fabbricante*) manufacturer; maker.

produzióne, *s.f.* **1.** production; (*fabbricazione*) manufacture: — *artistica, letteraria*, artistic, literary production; *la — del formaggio, della seta*, the production of cheese, of silk; — *eccessiva, eccesso di —*, over-production; — *in massa*, mass-production; — *nazionale, estera*, home, foreign production; *articolo di — italiana*, Italian-made article; *articolo di — straniera*, article of foreign manufacture; *costi di —*, production costs (*o* costs of production); *spese di —*, production expenses (*o* expenses of production); *aumentare, diminuire la —*, to increase, to cut (*o* to slow) down (*o* to reduce) production ‖ *direttore di —*, (*cine.*) producer **2.** (*quantità prodotta in un dato tempo da macchine, industrie, ecc.*) output, production: *la — annua di una fabbrica, di una miniera*, the annual output (*o* production) of a factory, of a mine; *la — di quest'anno dell'industria vinicola*, this year's output in the wine industry; *la — giornaliera di una macchina*, the daily output of a machine; *capacità di —*, production-capacity (*o* capacity of output) **3.** (*presentazione*) exhibition: — *di documenti*, exhibition of documents; — *di un testimonio*, (*dir.*) production (*o* calling) of a witness.

proemiàle, *ag.* (*letter.*) proemial, prefatory.

proemialménte, *av.* (*letter.*) preliminarily.

proemiàre, *v.i.* (*letter.*) to compose a proem.

proèmio, *s.m.* (*letter.*) proem, preface, introduction ‖ *senza —*, (*preamboli*) without preamble.

profanaménte, *av.* profanely.

profanàre, *v.t.* **1.** to profane, to desecrate; (*violare*) to violate: — *un altare, una chiesa*, to profane (*o* to desecrate) an altar, a church; — *una tomba*, to violate a grave **2.** (*fare uso indegno di*) to profane; to misuse, to debase: *ha profanato il nome di patria*, he has debased his country's name; — *il nome di Dio*, to profane the name of God (*o* to take the name of God in vain).

profanàto, *ag.* **1.** profaned, desecrated; (*violato*) violated **2.** (*usato indegnamente*) profaned, debased.

profanatóre, *ag.* profaning, desecrating; (*che viola*) violating ‖ *s.m.*, **profanatríce**, *s.f.* profaner, desecrator; (*che viola*) violator.

profanazióne, *s.f.* profanation, desecration; (*violazione*) violation.

profanità, *s.f.* **1.** profanity, profaneness **2.** (*detto profano*) profanity.

profàno, *ag.* **1.** (*non sacro, mondano*) profane; secular: *autore —*, profane author; *letteratura, storia, musica profana*, profane (*o* secular) literature, history, music **2.** (*irriverente*) profane, irreverent: *linguaggio —*, profane language; *parole profane*, profane (*o* irreverent) words **3.** (*inesperto*) ignorant (of sthg.): *essere — in un'arte, in una scienza*, to be ignorant of an art, of a science ‖ *s.m.* **1.** the profane: *non confondere il sacro col —!*, do not confound things sacred and profane! **2.** (*persona inesperta*) layman (*pl.* laymen), outsider: *in fatto di medicina, filosofia sono solo un —*, as regards medicine, philosophy I am only a layman (*o* a bad judge); *sono un — in pittura*, I am only a layman so far as painting is concerned ‖ *i profani*, the laity.

profènda, *s.f.* (*razione di biada*) provender, fodder.

proferíbile, *ag.* utterable; mentionable: *parole non proferibili*, unmentionable words.

proferiménto, *s.m.* **1.** utterance **2.** (*rar.*) (*pronuncia*) pronunciation.

proferíre, *v.t.* **1.** to utter: *non proferì sillaba*, he did not utter (*o* speak) a word; *proferì alcune parole, poi uscì*, he uttered a few words, then he went out **2.** (*pronunciare*) to pronounce: *non può — bene certe lettere*, he has difficulty in pronouncing some letters **3.** (*pronunciare solennemente*) to pronounce: — *una sentenza*, (*dir.*) to pronounce a judgment **4.** *V.* **profferíre 1.**

professànte, *ag.* professing, practising: *cattolico —*, professed Catholic.

professàre, *v.t.* **1.** to profess: *professa grande ammirazione per Rossini*, he professes great admiration for Rossini; — *una religione, una dottrina politica*, to profess a religion, a political belief ‖ — (*i voti religiosi*), to profess **2.** (*esercitare*) to profess, to practise: — *la medicina, l'avvocatura*, to profess (*o* to practise) medicine, law ‖ **professàrsi**, *v.r.* to profess oneself: *si professava nostro amico*, he professed himself our friend; — *democratico*, to profess oneself a democrat.

professataménte, *av.* professedly.

professionàle, *ag.* professional: *malattie professionali*, occupational (*o* industrial) diseases; *scuole professionali*, vocational schools.

professióne, *s.f.* **1.** profession, calling: *la — dell'avvocato, del medico, dell'insegnante*, the profession of a lawyer, of a doctor, of a teacher; *che — esercita tuo fratello?*, what is your brother by profession? (*o* what is your brother's profession?); *esercitare una —*, to practise a profession; *scegliere una —*, to take up (*o* to choose) a profession ‖ *di —*, by profession: *è cantante, pittore di —*, he is a singer, a painter by profession (*o* he is a professional singer, painter) **2.** (*dichiarazione*) profession: — *di fede, di amicizia*, profession of faith, of friendship.

professionísta, *s.m.* **1.** professional man: *libero —*, professional man **2.** (*spor.*) professional ‖ *s.f.* **1.** professional woman **2.** (*spor.*) professional.

professo, *ag.* (*eccl.*) professed: *monaca professa*, professed nun ‖ *i professi*, the professed.

professoràle, *ag.* **1.** professorial **2.** (*iron.*) pedantic, donnish, professorial: *tono —*, professorial tone.

professoràto, *s.m.* professorship.

professóre, *s.m.* **1.** teacher; (school-)master; (*titolare di cattedra universitaria*) professor: — *di diritto, di medicina*, professor of law, of medicine; — *di disegno*, drawing master (*o* teacher); — *incaricato*, (*universitario*) lecturer (*o amer.* assistant professor); — *ordinario*, (*universitario*) professor ‖ *il Professor Brown*, (*ordinario di università*) Professor Brown; (*insegnante*) Mr. Brown ‖ *ne sa quanto un —*, (*scherz.*) he is a walking encyclopedia ‖ *non fare il —*, don't be pedantic **2.** (*mus.*) instrumentalist: *è un — d'orchestra del Covent Garden*, he is a member of the Covent Garden orchestra.

professoréssa, *s.f.* **1.** teacher; (*titolare di cattedra universitaria*) (lady) professor: — *incaricata*, (*universitaria*) lecturer; *è — di piano*, she teaches the piano **2.** (*iron.*) (*donna saccente*) blue-stocking.

professòrio, *V.* **professoràle 2.**

profèta, *s.m.* **1.** prophet: *il — Isaia*, the prophet Isaiah; *i profeti minori*, the minor prophets ‖ *il Profeta*, (*Maometto*) the Prophet **2.** (*chi prevede il futuro*) prophesier, prophet: — *di sventura*, prophet (*o* prophesier) of evil; *è stato buon —*, he has proved a true prophet (*o* he has prophesied right) ‖ *nessuno è — in patria*, *prov.* no man is prophet in his own country.

profetàre, *v.t.* to prophesy, to predict, to foretell: *profetò la sua futura grandezza*, she prophesied his future greatness.

profetéssa, *s.f.* prophetess.

profeticaménte, *av.* prophetically.

profètico, *ag.* prophetic(al).

profetizzàre, *V.* **profetàre.**

profettízio, *ag.* (*dir.*) profectitious.

profezía, *s.f.* prophecy: *le profezie si sono avverate*, the prophecies were fulfilled; *ella ha il dono della —*, she has the gift of prophecy.

profferíre, *v.t.* **1.** to proffer, to offer: — *cibo, aiuto, consigli*, to offer food, help, advice **2.** (*pronunciare*) to utter: *senza — parola*, without a word ‖ **profferírsi**, *v.r.* to offer oneself.

profferíto, *ag.* proffered, offered.

profferitóre, *s.m.*, **profferitríce**, *s.f.* (*rar.*) profferer.

profferta, *s.f.* **1.** offer: *accettò le mie profferte d'aiuto*, he accepted my offer of help **2.** (*comm.*) tender, bid,

proficiènte, *ag.s.m.* proficient.

profìcuaménte, *av.* profitably: *studia* —, he studies with profit.

profìcuo, *ag.* profitable, advantageous; useful: *affare* —, paying (o profitable) business; *una speculazione proficua*, a profitable speculation.

profilàre, *v.t.* **1.** (*ritrarre in profilo*) to draw in profile, to represent in profile, to profile; (*delineare*) to delineate **2.** (*orlare*, *filettare*) to edge, to border **3.** (*mec.*) to profile ‖ **profilàrsi**, *v.r.* to be outlined, to stand out (in profile): *le montagne si profilavano nell'azzurro del cielo*, the mountains stood out (o were outlined) against the blue sky; — *all'orizzonte*, to be outlined against the horizon: *il castello si profila all'orizzonte*, the castle is outlined against the horizon.

profilàssi, *s.f.* (*med.*) prophylaxis.

profilàto, *ag.* **1.** (*delineato in contorno*) outlined; (*affilato*) sharp: *naso* —, sharp nose; *viso* —, clear-cut features **2.** (*orlato*) edged, bordered, trimmed: — *d'oro*, edged with gold ‖ *s.m.* (*metal.*) section, section iron, structural shape: — *a bulbo*, bulb iron; — *a L*, angle iron (o angle); — *a doppio T*, H-beam (o I-beam); — *a T*, Tee; — *a U*, channel; — *di acciaio*, structural steel; — *leggero*, light section; — *normale*, standard section; — *per costruzioni navali*, shipbuilding section; — *speciale*, shape.

profilatríce, *s.f.* forming machine: — *a rulli*, roll forming machine.

profilàttico, *ag.* (*med.*) prophylactic.

profilatúra, *s.f.* **1.** (*orlatura per abito*) edging, bordering, trimming **2.** (*mec.*) profiling, forming: — *al tornio*, profile turning.

profìlo, *s.m.* **1.** (*linea di contorno*) outline, contour: *il* — *di una catena di montagne*, the outline of a mountain range **2.** (*volto visto di fianco*) profile: *un* — *delicato*, a delicate profile; *ella ha un bel* —, she has a beautiful profile ‖ *di* —, in profile: *vista di* — *sembra bella*, seen in profile she seems beautiful; *rappresentare*, *disegnare di* —, to represent, to draw in profile **3.** (*breve studio critico-biografico*) monograph, sketch: *ha pubblicato un bel* — *del Leopardi*, he published an excellent monograph on Leopardi **4.** (*arch.*) profile, section **5.** (*tec.*): — *ad evolvente*, (*mec.*) involute profile; — *alare*, (*aer.*) wing contour; — *della filettatura*, (*mec.*) thread form; — *dell'eccentrico*, cam track (o cam contour); — *longitudinale*, (*di teleferica*) longitudinal section **6.** (*ott.*) shadow.

profittàre, *v.i.* **1.** (*trar profitto*) to profit (from, by s.o., sthg.), to take advantage, to avail oneself; (*abusare*) to take undue advantage: *dovresti* — *di questa liquidazione*, you should take advantage of this sale; — *dell'amicizia*, to take (undue) advantage of friendship; — *dei consigli di qlcu.*, to profit by s.o.'s advice; — *di un'occasione*, to avail oneself of an opportunity **2.** (*progredire*) to progress, to make progress: — *negli studi*, to make progress in one's studies **3.** (*rar.*) (*essere utile*) to be useful: *quell'esempio gli profittò molto*, that example was very useful to him **4.** (*guadagnare*) to make profits: *con quel commercio profittava poco*, he made little profit in that business **5.** (*bot.*) (*allignare*) to thrive.

profittatóre, *s.m.*, **profittatríce**, *s.f.* exploiter; (*in tempo di guerra*) profiteer.

profittévole, *ag.* profitable.

profittevolménte, *av.* profitably: *lavora* —, he works with profit.

profìtto, *s.m.* **1.** profit, advantage, benefit: *egli sa trarre* — *da ogni circostanza*, he knows how to take advantage of any circumstance; *ha frequentato con* — *un corso di dizione*, he has profited from a course in elocution; *mettere a* — *ql.co.*, to turn sthg. to account (o profit): *metti a* — *la tua conoscenza dell'inglese*, make good use of your English; *studiare con* —, to study with profit; *trarre* — *da qlcu.*, *ql.co.*, to profit by s.o.,

sthg. **2.** (*guadagno*) profit, gain: — *lordo*, *netto*, net, gross profit; *il* — *deve essere adeguato al rischio*, profit must be adequate to the risk; *ha ricavato un buon* — *da quell'affare*, he made a good profit on (o out of) that transaction; *spera in un buon* —, he hopes to make a large profit; *vendere con* —, to sell at a profit **3.** *pl.* (*redditi*) profit(s): *profitti e perdite*, (*comm.*) profit and loss account; *compartecipazione ai profitti*, profit-sharing; *il ribasso dei salari rialza i profitti*, the lowering of wages raises profits; *l'ultimo sciopero ha diminuito i profitti dell'azienda*, the last strike has lowered the profits of the firm; *accertare i profitti di qlcu.*, to determine s.o.'s profits.

proflùvio, *s.m.* **1.** overflow **2.** (*med.*) discharge **3.** (*grande abbondanza*) flood, flow, spate, superabundance: *un* — *di lacrime*, *di parole*, a flood of tears, of words.

profondaménte, *av.* deeply, profoundly: — *addormentato*, sound (o fast) asleep; — *commosso*, deeply moved (o touched); — *grato*, deeply (o profoundly) grateful; *sono* — *interessato a quella nuova scoperta*, I am deeply interested in that new discovery; *dormire* —, to sleep soundly (o like a log); *odiare qlcu.* —, to hate s.o. intensely.

profondaménto, *s.m.* (*letter. rar.*) **1.** (*lo sprofondare*) sinking **2.** (*il rendere profondo*) deepening.

profondàre, *v.t.* **1.** (*rar.*) (*rendere profondo*) to deepen: — *un canale*, *un fosso*, to deepen a canal, a ditch **2.** (*affondare*) to sink: — *una nave*, to sink a ship ‖ *v.i.* (*rar.*) to sink: *il legno non profonda nell'acqua*, wood does not sink in water; *la nave profondò*, the ship sank ‖ **profondàrsi**, *v.r.* (*fig. rar.*) (*immergersi*) to become absorbed, to become immersed: *egli si profondò nei suoi pensieri*, he became absorbed in his thoughts.

profóndere, *v.t.* to lavish; (*denaro*, *scialacquarlo*) to squander: *quella madre profonde sollecitudine verso i suoi bambini*, that mother lavishes care on her children; — *il proprio denaro in divertimenti*, to squander one's money on pleasure; — *lodi*, *parole*, to lavish praise, words ‖ **profóndersi**, *v.r.* to be lavish (of, in sthg.), to be prodigal (of sthg.): *egli si profondeva sempre in lodi*, he was always lavish of (o in his) praise; *quando lo seppe si profuse in ringraziamenti per mezz'ora*, when he found out he thanked everybody for half an hour.

profondità, *s.f.* depth, deepness; profundity: *le* — *del mare*, the depths of the sea; *la* — *del suo sapere*, the depth (o profundity) of his knowledge; *la* — *del suo sentimento*, the deepness of his feeling; *la* — *di un fiume*, *pozzo*, the depth of a river, well; *la* — *di un suono*, *colore*, the depth of a sound, colour; *nella* — *della notte*, in the depth(s) of night; *questo stagno ha una* — *di dieci piedi*, this pond is ten feet deep.

profóndo, *ag.* **1.** profound, deep: *profonda conoscenza*, *malinconia*, profound knowledge, melancholy; — *dolore*, *interesse*, *pensiero*, *mistero*, deep (o profound) sorrow, interest, thought, mystery; — *pensatore*, deep (o profound) thinker; *colore* —, deep (o dark) colour; *un lago*, *fiume*, *mare* —, a deep lake, river, sea; *silenzio* —, deep (o profound) silence; *un sospiro*, *suono* —, a deep sigh, sound; *un uomo di profonda cultura*, a man of profound (o deep) learning; *voce profonda*, deep (o low) voice; *cadde in un sonno* —, he fell into a deep (o profound) sleep; *quell'acqua è profonda un metro*, that water is a metre deep **2.** (*che ha profonde radici*) deep-rooted: *una profonda antipatia*, a deep-rooted dislike; *un sentimento*, *amore* —, a deep-rooted feeling, love.

profóndo, *s.m.* depth: *nel* — *della notte*, at dead of night; *nel* — *del mio cuore*, at the bottom of my heart; *un mostro che veniva dal* — *del mare*, a monster which came from the depth(s) of the sea.

profóndo, *av.* deep, deeply; profoundly.

pròfuga, *s.f.*, **pròfugo**, *s.m.* refugee.

profumàre, *v.t.* **1.** to perfume; to scent; to spray scent on (s.o., sthg.): *il parrucchiere mi ha lutta profumata*, the hairdresser has sprayed scent all over me; *profumò la lettera prima di spedirla*, she put scent on the letter before sending it; — *una stanza, l'aria*, to scent a room, the air **2.** (*suffumigare coi disinfettanti*) to disinfect || **profumàrsi**, *v.r.* to put on scent; to spray scent on oneself: *non mi profumo mai*, I never use scent; *si sta profumando*, she is spraying herself with scent.

profumataménte, *av.* **1.** (*generosamente*) generously, liberally **2.** (*ad alto prezzo*) dearly, at a high price: *l'ho pagato* —, I have paid dearly for it.

profumàto, *ag.* **1.** sweet-smelling; (*impregnato di profumo*) scented, perfumed: *fazzoletto* —, scented handkerchief; *fiori profumati*, sweet-smelling flowers **2.** (*caro, costoso*) dear, expensive.

profumería, *s.f.* **1.** (*negozio del profumiere*) perfumery, perfumer's shop **2.** (*l'arte del profumiere*) perfumery *pl.* (*profumi*) perfumery articles (*pl.*); perfumes (*pl.*), scents (*pl.*).

profumière, *s.m.* perfumer: *negozio di* —, perfumer's (shop).

profúmo, *s.m.* perfume; scent; (*fragranza*) fragrance (anche *fig.*): *il* — *di un fiore*, the scent of a flower; *che buon* — *manda questo arrosto!*, how good this roast meat smells!; *che buon* — *manda questo fiore!*, how sweet this flower smells!; *fabbrica profumi*, he makes perfumes; *scritti che hanno un* — *di antichità*, *fig.* writings with a fragrance of antiquity.

profusaménte, *av.* **1.** profusely, abundantly **2.** (*diffusamente*) at (great) length; (*dettagliatamente*) in detail: *trattò* — *di questo argomento*, he spoke at length on this subject.

profusióne, *s.f.* profusion, over-abundance: *una* — *di doni, lodi, ringraziamenti*, a profusion of gifts, praise, thanks; *c'erano fiori a* —, there were flowers in profusion; *dare, comperare, ordinare, spendere a* —, to give, to buy, to order, to spend lavishly.

profúso, *ag.* profuse.

progeneràre, *v.t.* (*letter.*) to procreate.

progènie, *s.f.* progeny, issue, descendants (*pl.*).

progenitóre, *s.m.* ancestor, progenitor: *i nostri progenitori*, our ancestors.

progenitríce, *s.f.* ancestress, progenitress.

progettàre, *v.t.* **1.** to plan; to project: *sto progettando di partire per la Spagna*, I am planning to leave for Spain; — *una gita*, to plan a trip **2.** (*tec.*) to plan, to design: — *una casa*, to plan a house.

progettísta, *s.c.* **1.** (*tec.*) planner, designer **2.** (*rar.*) (*persona facile a idear piani*) schemer.

progètto, *s.m.* **1.** plan; project: *il* — *di una casa, una strada, un ponte*, the plan of a house, a road, a bridge; *il* — *governativo di mantenere l'attuale tariffa*, the government's plan to maintain the present tariff; *dimmi i tuoi progetti*, tell me your plans; *far progetti*, to make plans (o to plan) || — *di legge*, bill **2.** (*pianta della sistemazione di una fabbrica, negozio, ecc.*) lay -out **3.** (*cianografia*) blueprint.

prognatísmo, *s.m.* (*antropologia*) prognathism.

prognàto, *ag.* prognathous, prognathic.

Prògne, *no.pr.f.* (*mit.*) Progne || **prògne**, *s.f.* (*poet.*) progne, swallow.|

prògnosi, *s.f.* (*med.*) prognosis (*pl.* prognoses).

prognòstico, *e derivati, V.* **pronòstico**, *e derivati.*

progràmma, *s.m.* **1.** programme; (*amer.*) program; (*prospetto*) prospectus (*pl.* prospectuses): — *delle corse*, (*spor.*) race-card; — *scolastico*, syllabus; *il* — *del concerto è molto buono*, the programme of the concert is very good; *il* — *di latino della quinta classe è molto difficile*, the Latin syllabus of the fifth form is very hard; *che* — *hai per domani?*, what are your plans for tomorrow?; *desidereremmo ricevere il* — *della vostra scuola*, we should like to receive the prospectus of your school; *hai comperato un* —?, have you bought a programme?;

secondo il — *dovremmo essere già a Roma*, according to programme we should already be in Rome; *svolgere un* —, to carry out a programme || *non ho in* — *di partire domani*, I have no intention of leaving tomorrow **2.** (*pol.*) prcgram(me): *il* — *del nostro governo*, the programme of our government; — *elettorale*, electoral programme (o election platform).

programmàre, *v.t.* to program(me); to schedule; (*amer.*) to program.

programmàtico, *ag.* programmatic.

programmazióne, *s.f.* (*cine.*) programming.

progrediènte, *ag.* progressing, progressive.

progredíre, *v.i.* **1.** to advance: *i soldati progredivano lentamente verso le posizioni nemiche*, the soldiers were slowly advancing towards the enemy's positions **2.** *fig.* to get on, to go on, to progress; (*far progressi*) to make progress, to make headway: *il lavoro non progredisce*, the work is not getting on (o is not progressing); *il mio libro progredisce lentamente*, my book is getting on (o going on) slowly; — *verso la soluzione di un problema*, to make headway towards the solution of a problem.

progredíto, *ag.* **1.** advanced: *studi progrediti*, advanced studies **2.** (*civile*) civilized: *nazioni progredite*, civilized countries.

progressióne, *s.f.* progression: — *aritmetica, geometrica*, arithmetical, geometrical progression; — *ascendente*, (*mus.*) ascending progression.

progressísmo, *s.m.* progressism, progressionism.

progressísta, *ag.* progressive: *idee progressiste*, progressive ideas; *partito, politica* —, progressive party, policy || *s.m.* (*pol.*) progressive, progressist.

progressivaménte, *av.* progressively.

progressívo, *ag.* progressive: *ordine, sviluppo, aumento* —, progressive order, development, increase; *paralisi progressiva*, (*med.*) ascending (o creeping) paralysis; *tassa progressiva*, graduated tax.

progrèsso, *s.m.* progress (*solo sing.*); headway; (*perfezionamento*) improvement: *il* — *della civiltà, della scienza*, the progress of civilization, of science; *il* — *delle costruzioni*, the improvements in house-building; *il* — *di una malattia*, the progress of a disease; *non si è registrato alcun* —, no headway has been made; *credere nel* —, to believe in progress; *fare progressi in ql.co.*, to make progress (o headway) in sthg. (o to improve in sthg.): *fece pochi progressi in latino*, he made little progress in Latin || *in* — *di tempo*, in the course of time.

proibènte, *ag.* forbidding, prohibiting, prohibitory.

proibíre, *v.t.* **1.** to forbid; to prohibit: *gli fu proibito di parlare*, he was forbidden (o he was not allowed) to speak; *gli proibirono di fumare*, he was forbidden to smoke; *la legge proibisce l'importazione e la vendita di questi articoli*, the law prohibits the import and sale of these articles; *il medico mi ha proibito il vino*, the doctor has forbidden me (to drink) wine; *mi si proibisce di vederlo*, I am forbidden (o not allowed) to see him; *ti proibisco di uscire*, I forbid you to go out; — *l'accesso in casa propria a qlcu.*, to forbid s.o. the house || *proibito fumare*, no smoking (o smoking forbidden) **2.** (*impedire*) to prevent, to hinder; to debar: *i venti ci proibiscono di navigare*, the winds prevent us from sailing; — *la libertà dei movimenti*, to prevent freedom of movement.

proibitívo, *ag.* prohibitive: *prezzi proibitivi*, prohibitive prices.

proibíto, *ag.* forbidden: *armi proibite*, forbidden weapons; *frutto* —, forbidden fruit; *libri proibiti*, books on the Index (o forbidden books); *tempi proibiti*, (*eccl.*) forbidden times || *faccia proibita*, (*da galera*) look (o face) of a gallowsbird || — *come le pistole corte*, (*scherz.*) strictly forbidden.

proibitóre, *s.m.*, **proibitríce**, *s.f.* prohibiter.

proibitòrio, *ag.* prohibitory.

proibizióne, *s.f.* prohibition.

proibizionísmo, *s.m.* prohibitionism.

proibizioníota, *s.c.* prohibitionist.

proiettàre, *v.t.* **1.** to project, to cast, to throw: *ogni corpo proietta un'ombra*, every solid body throws (o projects) a shadow; *il sole proietta i suoi raggi sulla terra*, the sun projects (o casts) its beams on the earth; *il vulcano proietta lapilli*, the volcano ejects (o throws out) lapilli; — *la propria ombra sul marciapiede*, to throw one's shadow on the pavement **2.** (*cine.*) to show; to screen: *il film sarà proiettato la settimana ventura*, the film will be shown next week **3.** (*geom.*) to project: — *una figura*, to project a figure ǁ *v.i.* (*arch.*) to project, to protrude, to jut out ǁ **proiettàrsi**, *v.r.* **1.** to be projected, to be cast: *un'ombra si proiettava sul muro*, a shadow fell (o was cast) on the wall **2.** (*arch.*) to project, to protrude, to jut out.

proiettifício, *s.m* ammunition factory.

proièttile, *s.m.* projectile; shell; shot: — *a mitraglia*, canister (shot); — *a razzo*, rocket missile; — *atomico*, atomic shell; — *controllato a distanza*, guided missile; — *illuminante*, star shell; — *incendiario*, incendiary shell; — *inesploso*, dud; — *perforante*, armour-piercing shell; — *pieno*, solid shell; — *tracciante*, tracer-bullet (o shell).

proiettívo, *ag.* projective, projectional.

proiètto, *ag.* projected ǁ *s.m.* **1.** (*proiettile*) projectile **2.** (*arch.*) projection.

proiettóre, *s.m.* **1.** (*riflettore*) searchlight; (*a luce diffusa*) floodlight; (*radar*) projector; (*faro di automobile*) head lamp, headlight: — *aeronautico*, (*aer.*) aeronautical light; — *a lente metallica*, (*radar*) metal lens; — *di segnalazione del traffico aereo*, (*aer.*) air-traffic signal light; — *per la determinazione della quota delle nubi*, cloud searchlight; — *per retromarcia*, (*aut.*) back-up lamp; — *ultrasonoro*, (*strum. idrofonico*) supersonic oscillator **2.** (*cine.*) (motion-picture) projector, (movie) projector: — *per diapositive*, stereopticon.

proiezióne, *s.f.* **1.** projection: — *cilindrica, conica*, (*geog.*) cylindrical, conical projection; — *di una figura su un piano*, (*geom.*) the projection of a figure on a plane; *la* — *di un'ombra*, the projection of a shadow; — *gnomonica*, (*geog.*) gnomonic projection; — *ortogonale*, (*geom.*) orthogonal projection; — *prospettica*, (*geog. geom.*) perspective projection **2.** (*foto. cine. tv.*) projection: — *di fondo*, (*tv.*) background projection; *macchina da* —, (*cine.*) (motion-picture) projector; *sala di* —, projection room **3.** (*spettacolo cinematografico*) showing: *la* — *del film è stata rimandata*, the showing of the film has been postponed **4.** *pl.*: *conferenza con proiezioni*, lecture and film-show; *le nostre lezioni di geografia sono illustrate da proiezioni*, (*diapositive*) our geography lessons are illustrated by slides.

prolàsso, *s.m.* (*med.*) prolapse, prolapsus.

pròle, *s.f.* issue, offspring, progeny: *egli morì senza* —, he died without issue ǁ *come sta la tua* —?, how are your children?.

prolegàto, *s.m.* (*st. eccl.*) prolegate, prolegatus.

prolegòmeni, *s.m.pl.* (*lett.*) prolegomena.

prolèpsi, prolèssi, *s.f.* (*ret.*) prolepsis.

proletariàto, *s.m.* proletariat(e).

proletàrio, *ag.s.m.* proletarian.

proliferazióne, *s.f.* (*biol.*) proliferation.

prolífero, *ag.* prolific.

prolificàre, *v.i.* to procreate, to proliferate.

prolificazióne, *s.f.* prolification.

prolificità, *s.f.* prolificness, prolificacy, prolificity.

prolífico, *ag.* prolific (*anche fig.*): *animale* —, prolific animal; *autore* —, *fig.* prolific author.

prolissaménte, *av.* prolixly.

prolissità, *s.f.* prolixity, prolixness.

prolísso, *ag.* prolix: *un discorso, oratore* —, a prolix speech, speaker.

pròlogo, *s.m.* prologue: *il* — *dei « Canterbury Tales »*, the Prologue to the " Canterbury Tales ".

prolúdere, *v.i.* **1.** (*fare una prolusione*) to give an opening lecture; to give an opening address **2.** (*dare inizio*) to begin (sthg.), to open (sthg.): — *a un corso di lezioni*, to begin (o to open) a course of lectures.

prolúnga, *s.f.* **1.** (*mil.*) waggon **2.** (*grosso canapo*) prolonge **3.** (*mec. elett.*) extension.

prolungàbile, *ag.* **1.** prolongable, extendable **2.** (*prorogabile*) prolongable; (*differibile*) delayable, deferrable.

prolungaménto, *s.m.* **1.** prolongation, extension, lengthening: *il* — *di una linea, di un segmento*, the prolongation of a line, of a segment; — *di una linea ferroviaria*, extension of a railway line; — *di una sillaba*, (*gram.*) lengthening of a syllable; — *delle vacanze*, extension of the holidays **2.** (*continuazione*) continuation: *questa strada è il* — *della strada principale*, this road is the continuation of the main street.

prolungàre, *v.t.* **1.** to prolong, to extend; (*allungare*) to lengthen; (*protrarre*) to protract: — *una guerra*, to protract a war; — *una linea ferroviaria, un muro, uno steccato*, to extend a railway line, a wall, a fence; — *un soggiorno di due settimane*, to protract a stay for two weeks; — *una vacanza*, to extend (o to prolong) a holiday; — *una visita*, to prolong (o to extend) a visit **2.** (*prorogare*) to extend; (*differire*) to postpone, to delay, to defer: *il termine del concorso è stato prolungato*, the time-limit of the competition has been extended; — *un pagamento*, to delay a payment; — *una scadenza*, to extend a maturity ǁ **prolungàrsi**, *v.r.* **1.** (*continuare*) to continue, to extend: *il sentiero si prolunga fino al mare*, the path continues to the sea **2.** (*dilungarsi*) to dwell (on sthg.): *non prolungarti in chiacchiere*, do not waste your time in idle talk; — *su un argomento*, to dwell on a subject.

prolungataménte, *av.* at great length.

prolungazióne, *s.f.* **1.** prolongation, extension **2.** (*proroga*) extension; postponement, delay **3.** (*mus.*) holding (of a note).

prolusióne, *s.f.* opening address, opening lecture.

prolúvie, *s.f.* **1.** flood **2.** (*med.*) diarrhoea.

promanàre, *v.t.* to send forth ǁ *v.i.* to issue.

promemòria, *s.f.* memorandum (*pl.* memoranda, memorandums).

promèssa[1], *s.f.* promise: — *di matrimonio*, promise of marriage; *promesse vane*, empty promises; *belle, grandi promesse*, fair, great promises; *rottura di* — (*di matrimonio*), breach of promise; *si arrese sotto* — *di aver salva la vita*, he surrendered on the promise that his life would be spared; *essere impegnato da una* —, to be promise-bound; *fare una* —, to make a promise; *mancare alla* —, to break one's promise; *mantenere una* —, to keep a promise ǁ — *da marinaio*, dicer's oath ǁ *quel ragazzo è una* —, he is a boy of promise.

promèssa[2], *s.f.* (*fidanzata*) fiancée.

promèsso, *ag.* promised ǁ *la Terra Promessa*, (*Bibbia*) the Promised Land ǁ *i « Promessi Sposi »*, " The Betrothed " ǁ *s.m.* (*fidanzato*) fiancé.

Promèteo, *no.pr.m.* (*mit.*) Prometheus.

promettènte, *ag.* promising: *uno scrittore* —, a promising writer (o a writer of promise); *tempo* —, promising weather; *il raccolto sembra* —, the harvest looks promising.

promèttere, *v.t.* to promise: *mi promise un bel regalo*, he promised me a beautiful present; *mi promisero di tornare subito*, they promised me to come back at once (o they promised me they would be back at once); — *in moglie*, to promise in marriage; — *sul Vangelo*, to swear on the Bible ǁ *il cielo promette una tempesta*, a storm seems to be threatening ǁ — *mari e monti*, to promise heaven and earth (o great things) ǁ — *certo e venir meno sicuro*, *prov.* it is one thing to promise and another to perform (o saying and doing are different things) ǁ *v.i.* to promise: *la campagna promette bene*, the harvest is full of promise; *questo pittore promette bene*, this is a promising painter (o this is a painter of promise); *le vigne promettono*, the vines look promising ‖ **prométtersi**, *v.r.* **1.** to promise oneself: *mi promisi una bella vacanza*, I promised myself a nice holiday; — *dei piaceri nuovi*, to anticipate new pleasures **2.** (*fidanzarsi*) to become engaged.

promettitóre, *s.m.*, **promettitríce**, *s.f.* promiser.

prominènte, *ag.* prominent; jutting: *naso* —, prominent nose; *roccia* —, jutting rock; *zigomi prominenti*, prominent cheek-bones.

prominènza, *s.f.* prominence.

promiuístro, *s.m.* acting-minister.

promiscuaménte, *av.* promiscuously.

promiscuità, *s.f.* promiscuity, promiscuousness.

promíscuo, *ag.* **1.** mixed, promiscuous: *matrimonio* —, mixed marriage; *pubblico* —, mixed crowd; *scuola promiscua*, mixed (*o* co-educational) school **2.** (*gram.*) common: *genere* —, common gender.

promissàrio, *s.m.* (*dir.*) promisee.

promissióne, (*letter.*) per **proméssa**.

promissivaménte, *av.* (*letter.*) promissorily.

promissívo, *ag.* (*letter.*) promissive, promissory.

promissóre, *s.m.* (*letter.*) promiser.

promissòrio, *ag.* promissory: *giuramento* —, (*dir.*) promissory oath.

promontòrio, *s.m.* (*geog.*) promontory, headland: *Monaco sorge su un* — *roccioso*, Monaco stands on a rocky promontory.

promòsso, *ag.* **1.** successful: *studenti, candidati promossi*, successful students, candidates ‖ *i promossi*, successful candidates **2.** (*sostenuto*) promoted: *iniziativa promossa da un'impresa commerciale*, initiative promoted by a business enterprise.

promotóre, *ag.* promoting: *comitato* —, promoting committee ‖ *s.m.*, **promotríce**, *s.f.* promoter.

promovènte, *ag.* promoting.

promoviménto, *s.m.* promotion, preferment.

promovitóre, *ag.* promoting ‖ *s.m.*, **promovitríce**, *s.f.* promoter.

promozióne, *s.f.* **1.** promotion: *non credo che avrà la* — *perchè ha studiato troppo poco*, I do not think he will pass because he has studied too little **2.** (*avanzamento di grado*) promotion, advancement; (*spec. eccl.*) preferment: *ottenere una* —, to get a promotion; *ottenere la* — *a capitano*, to be promoted captain.

promulgaménto, *s.m.* promulgation, publication.

promulgàre, *v.t.* to promulgate, to publish: — *un decreto, una teoria*, to promulgate a decree, a theory.

promulgatóre, *s.m.*, **promulgatríce**, *s.f.* promulgator.

promulgazióne, *s.f.* promulgation, publication.

promuòvere, *v.t.* **1.** to promote, to further, to foster: — *la causa del popolo*, to promote the cause of the people; — *la cultura*, to promote learning; — *un'industria*, to encourage an industry; — *un progetto di legge*, to promote a bill; — *lo sviluppo di un paese arretrato*, to promote the growth of a backward country **2.** (*far avanzare di grado*) to promote: *fu promosso ufficiale*, he was promoted officer; — *qlcu. capitano*, to promote s.o. captain **3.** (*a scuola*) to pass: *non fu promosso*, he did not pass; *il professore non lo promosse*, the teacher did not pass him; — *uno studente*, to pass a student **4.** (*provocare*) to cause, to provoke: — *la traspirazione*, to provoke (*o* to cause) perspiration.

prònao, *s.m.* (*arch.*) pronaos (*pl.* pronaoi).

pronatóre, *s.m.* (*anat.*) pronator.

pronazióne, *s.f.* pronation.

pronipóte, *s.m.* **1.** (*di bisnonno*) great grandson, great grandchild; (*di prozio*) grand-nephew ‖ *i pronipoti*, (*maschi e femmine*) great grandchildren **2.** *pl.* (*discendenti*) descendants ‖ *s.f.* (*di bisnonno*) great grand -daughter, great grandchild; (*di prozio*) grand-niece.

pròno, *ag.* **1.** prone; (*prostrato*) prostrate: — *a terra*, prone on the ground **2.** (*incline*) prone, inclined: — *al vizio*, prone (*o* inclined) to vice; — *al*

volere ˈdella plebe, prone to the common people's will.

pronóme, *s.m.* (*gram.*) pronoun: — *dimostrativo, personale*, demonstrative, personal pronoun.

pronomiuàle, *ag.* (*gram.*) pronominal.

pronominalménte, *av.* (*gram.*) pronominally.

pronosticàre, *v.t.* **1.** to prognosticate, to forecast, to foretell: — *il futuro*, to foretell the future; — *malanni*, to prognosticate trouble; — *il tempo*, to forecast the weather; — *la vittoria della propria squadra*, to forecast (*o* to prognosticate) the victory of one's own team **2.** (*far prevedere*) to portend, to presage, to prognosticate: *queste nuvole pronosticano tempesta*, these clouds portend a storm; *questi strani fenomeni pronosticano sciagure*, these strange phenomena presage (*o* portend *o* herald) calamities.

pronosticatóre, *ag.* foretelling, prognosticating ‖ *s.m.*, **pronosticatríce**, *s.f.* foreteller, prognosticator.

pronosticazióne, *s.f.* foretelling, prognostication.

pronòstico, *s.m.* forecast, prediction, prognostic: *i pronostici dell'astrologo per il nuovo anno*, the astrologer's forecasts for the new year; *i pronostici sulle squadre vincenti*, prognostics about the winning teams; *i suoi pronostici si avverano sempre, prima o poi*, his predictions (*o* forecasts) always come true, sooner or later; *fare un* —, to make a forecast: *l'astrologo ha fatto un buon* — *per il nuovo anno*, the astrologer has cast a favourable horoscope for the new year; *l'indovina mi ha fatto un cattivo* —, the fortune-teller prophesied a bad future for me.

prontaménte, *av.* readily, quickly; (*subito*) at once, immediately; (*senza indugio*) promptly, without delay: *accorse* — *al richiamo*, he answered the appeal at once; *afferrava* — *il significato di ogni vocabolo*, he caught the meaning of every word immediately; *la fattura ancora scoperta deve essere pagata* —, the outstanding invoice must be promptly settled; *i vostri ordini saranno* — *eseguiti*, your orders will be promptly executed; *rispondere, ubbidire* —, to reply, to obey at once.

prontézza, *s.f.* readiness, quickness: — *di mente*, readiness of mind; — *di movimento*, quickness of movement; — *di spirito*, quickness of wit; *con* —, promptly; *la sua* — *nel rispondere meravigliava tutti i suoi insegnanti*, his readiness (*o* quickness) in answering surprised all his teachers.

prónto, *ag.* **1.** ready, prepared: — *all'azione*, ready for action; — *ad ogni evenienza*, ready (*o* prepared) for every eventuality; *la colazione è pronta*, lunch is ready; *l'automobile è pronta*, the car is ready; *la merce è pronta per la spedizione*, the goods are ready for shipment; *non sono ancora* —, I am not ready yet; *sei* — *per incominciare?*, are you ready to begin?; *sono* — *a fare ciò che vuoi*, I am ready to do what you want; *trovatevi pronti alle cinque precise*, be ready at five o'clock sharp; *tutto era* — *per il matrimonio*, everything was ready for the wedding; *tener* — *ql.co.*, to keep sthg. ready: *tieni* — *un ombrello*, keep an umbrella ready; *tenersi* — *! , (al* *telefono*) hallo! (*o* hullo)! ‖ *pronti!*, (*mil.*) (*a un ufficiale*) yes, Sir! ‖ *pronta cassa*, (*comm.*) ready cash; *a pronti*, (*comm.*) for cash; *pagamento a pronti*, cash payment (*o* ready cash *o* cash down) ‖ — *soccorso*, first aid ‖ *in* —, ready: *ogni cosa è in* —, everything is ready; *aver in* — *i denari, i documenti*, to have the money, the documents ready **2.** (*lesto, rapido*) prompt, quick, ready: — *nelle risposte*, ready in one's answers; *intelligenza pronta*, quick intelligence; *movimenti pronti*, quick movements; *un ragazzo* —, a quick (*o* alert) boy; *risposta pronta*, prompt answer; (*sollecita*) early answer ‖ *pronta consegna*, (*comm.*) prompt delivery; *pronta spedizione*, (*comm.*) speedy conveyance.

prontuàrio, *s.m.* handbook, book of reference: — *dei conti fatti*, (*comm.*) ready reckoner; — *di citazioni dantesche*, handbook of quotations from Dante.

prònuba, *s.f.,* **prònubo,** *s.m.* marriage-maker, match-maker; (*st. romana*) paranymph.

pronúncia, *s.f.* pronunciation: *difetto di* —, defect of pronunciation (*o* faulty articulation); *dizionario di* —, pronouncing dictionary.

pronunciàbile, *ag.* pronounceable.

pronunciaménto[1], *s.m.* pronunciation.

pronunciaménto[2], *s.m.* (*st.*) pronunciamento.

pronunciàre, *v.t.* **1.** to pronounce; (*proferire*) to utter: *cerca di* — *le parole staccandole bene,* try to utter each word distinctly; *egli non pronuncia correttamente l'inglese,* he does not pronounce English correctly; *non bisogna mai* — *il suo nome,* you must never mention him (*o* utter his name); *non pronunciò neppure una parola,* he did not utter a single word; *sentii* — *il mio nome,* I heard my name (mentioned); — *bene una parola,* to pronounce a word well; — *male,* to mis-pronounce (*o* to pronounce badly); — *una sentenza di morte,* to pronounce (*o* to pass) a sentence of death ‖ — *i voti,* (*eccl.*) to pronounce one's vows **2.** (*dire*) to say; (*recitare*) to deliver: *pronunciò una grande verità,* he exposed a great truth; — *un discorso,* to deliver a speech ‖ **pronunciàrsi,** *v.r.* to pronounce; (*dare la propria opinione*) to declare one's opinion, to give one's opinion: *nessuno si volle pronunciare,* nobody wanted to give his opinion; *si pronunciò in suo favore,* he declared himself in his favour; — *contro un progetto,* to declare oneself against a plan.

pronunciàto, *ag.* **1.** pronounced, uttered **2.** (*rilevato*) pronounced, marked, decided; (*forte, spiccato*) strong: *un* — *accento straniero,* a strong (*o* marked) foreign accent; *una pronunciata caratteristica,* a strong feature; *una pronunciata differenza,* a marked difference; *una pronunciata tendenza,* a pronounced tendency; *un mento* —, a protruding chin ‖ *s.m.* proposition.

pronunciatóre, *s.m.,* **pronunciatríce,** *s.f.,* pro-nouncer.

pronúnzia, *V.* **pronúncia.**

pronunziàbile, *ag.* pronounceable.

pronunziaménto, *s.m.* (*rar.*) pronunciation.

pronunziàre, *V.* **pronunciàre.**

pronunziatívo, *ag.* pronounceable; (*che pronunzia*) pronouncing.

pronunziàto, *V.* **pronunciàto.**

pronunziatóre, *s.m.,* **pronunziatríce,** *s.f.* pro-nouncer.

pronunziazióne, *s.f.* **1.** pronunciation **2.** (*dichiarazione*) declaration.

propagàbile, *ag.* propagable.

propagaménto, *s.m.* propagation.

propagànda, *s.f.* **1.** propaganda: *la* — *del partito socialista,* the Socialist Party propaganda; *cercherò di farti* —, I shall try to make you known; *queste nuove idee si diffusero attraverso la* — *nemica,* these new ideas spread through the enemy's propaganda; *far* — *per un'idea, un principio,* to disseminate (*o* to propagandize) an idea, a principle ‖ *la Congregazione di Propaganda Fide,* (*eccl.*) the Congregation of Propaganda **2.** (*comm.*) advertising: *quella ditta fa molta* — *all'estero,* that firm advertises largely abroad; *senza* — *non si vende niente,* you cannot sell any-thing without advertising.

propagandàre, *v.t.* **1.** to propagandize, to dissemi-nate, to propagate: *un'idea, una teoria,* to propagan-dize an idea, a theory **2.** (*comm.*) to advertise: — *la propria merce,* to advertise one's goods.

propagandísmo, *s.m.* propagandism.

propagandísta, *s.c.* **1.** propagandist **2.** (*comm.*) advertiser.

propagandístico, *ag.* propagandistic; (*comm.*) adver-tising: *stampa propagandistica,* (*pol.*) propaganda press; *fare una campagna propagandistica,* to run an adver-tising campaign.

propagàre, *v.t.* to propagate, to spread: *le mosche propagano malattie,* flies spread diseases; — *luce, ca-*lore, to propagate light, heat; — *notizie,* to propagate (*o* to spread) news ‖ **propagàrsi,** *v.r.* to spread, to propagate: *le erbacce si propagarono per tutto il campo,* the weeds spread all over the field; *la luce si propaga in linea retta,* light is propagated (*o* light travels) in straight lines; *la malattia si propagò in fretta,* the disease spread quickly; *i pettegolezzi si propagano facilmente,* gossip spreads easily; *queste idee si pro-pagano in tutta Europa,* these ideas are spreading all over Europe.

propagatóre, *s.m.,* **propagatríce,** *s.f.* propagator.

propagazióne, *s.f.* propagation: — *della fede, di un suono,* propagation of the faith, of a sound.

propagginaménto, *s.m.* (*agr.*) layering.

propagginàre, *v.t.* **1.** (*agr.*) to layer **2.** (*st.*) (*seppel-lire col capo all'ingiù*) to bury head downwards.

propagginazióne, *s.f.* **1.** (*agr.*) layering **2.** (*st.*) (*sep-pellimento col capo all'ingiù*) burying head downwards.

propàggine, *s.f.* **1.** (*agr.*) layer: *la vite si riproduce per* —, the vine is reproduced by layers **2.** (*ramifi-cazione*) ramification: *le propaggini delle Alpi,* the ramifications of the Alps **3.** (*discendente*) descendant; offspring (*invariato al pl.*); (*discendenza*) descent.

propalàre, *v.t.* to spread; (*divulgare*) to divulge: — *notizie,* to spread news; — *un segreto,* to divulge a secret.

propalatóre, *s.m.,* **propalatríce,** *s.f.* divulgator.

propalazióne, *s.f.* spreading, divulgation.

propàno, *s.m.* (*chim.*) propane.

proparalèssi, *s.f.* (*gram.*) paragoge.

proparossítono, *ag.* (*gram.*) proparoxytone.

propedèutica, *s.f.* propaedeutics.

propedèutico, *ag.* propaedeutic(al).

propellènte, *ag.* propellent, propelling.

propèllere, *v.t.* to propel.

propèndere, *v.i.* to incline, to lean, to be inclined, to be disposed, to tend: *egli propende sempre verso l'indulgenza,* he is always inclined to be indulgent; *egli propende verso il comunismo, verso destra,* he leans towards Communism, to the right; *io propendo a cre-dere che...,* I am inclined to believe that...; *riguardo alla sua proposta propendo per il no, per il sì,* as regards his proposal, I am rather against it, I have nothing against it.

propensióne, *s.f.* **1.** propensity, propension; (*ten-denza*) tendency; (*inclinazione*) inclination: *sembra avere una grande* — *allo studio,* he appears to have a great inclination (*o* propensity) towards study **2.** (*sim-patia*) attraction, liking.

propènso, *ag.* inclined, disposed, propense; (*favore-vole*) favourable; (*pronto*) ready: *è sempre* — *a con-traddirmi,* he is always ready to contradict me; *sono* — *crederlo,* I am inclined (*o* I incline) to believe it.

properispòmeno, *ag.* (*gram.*) properispomenon.

Propèrzio, *no.pr.m.* (*st. lett.*) Propertius.

propilèo, *s.m.* (*arch.*) propylaeum (*pl.* propylaea).

propína, *s.f.* examiner's fee.

propinàre, *v.t.* to give; (*somministrare*) to administer: — *il veleno,* to administer poison ‖ *v.i.* (*brindare*) to toast.

propinatóre, *s.m.,* **propinatríce,** *s.f.* giver.

propinquità, *s.f.* **1.** (*vicinanza*) propinquity, near-ness **2.** (*parentela*) propinquity; (*affinità*) affinity.

propínquo, *ag.* (*rar.*) **1.** (*vicino*) near, neighbour-ing **2.** (*congiunto*) related ‖ *s.m.* (*rar.*) **1.** (*vicino*) neigh-bour **2.** (*congiunto*) relation, relative, kinsman (*pl.* kinsmen).

propiziaménte, *av.* propitiously, favourably.

propiziànte, *ag.* propitiatory.

propiziàre, *v.t.* to propitiate; (*placare*) to appease: — *gli dei,* to propitiate the gods ‖ **propiziàrsi,** *v.r.* to propitiate; to gain s.o.'s favour: *riuscì a* — *il giu-dice,* he succeeded in gaining the judge's favour.

propiziatóre, *ag.* propitiatory ‖ *s.m.,* **propiziatríce,** *s.f.* propitiator.

propiziatòrio, *ag.* propitiatory ‖ *s.m.* (*relig.*) propitiatory, mercy-seat.

propiziazióne, *s.f.* propitiation ‖ *giorno di* —, (*relig. ebraica*) Day of Atonement (*o* Yom Kippur).

propízio, *ag.* **1.** propitious, gracious: *Dio è* — *agli umili*, God is gracious to the humble; *la fortuna mi fu propizia*, luck was kind to me; *rendersi propizi gli dei*, to propitiate the gods **2.** (*opportuno*) propitious, favourable; (*adatto*) right: *occasione propizia*, right (*o* propitious) occasion; *venti propizi*, favourable winds; *aspetto il momento* —, I am waiting for the right moment; *questa circostanza era propizia ai nostri piani*, this circumstance was propitious (*o* favourable) to our plans.

proponènte, *ag.* proposing, propounding ‖ *s.m.* proponent, propounder.

proponíbile, *ag.* proposable.

proponiménto, *s.m.* purpose, resolution, resolve: *faccio sempre buoni proponimenti ma non li mantengo mai*, I always make good resolutions but I never carry them out (*o fam.* I never stick to them) ‖ *far* — *di*, to resolve to: *fece* — *di non farlo più*, he resolved never to do it again.

propórre, *v.t.* to propose; (*suggerire*) to suggest: *l'insegnante mi ha proposto un argomento che non mi piace*, the teacher has suggested a subject (to me) I do not like; *io lo proporrò come preside*, I shall propose him for headmaster; *propongo che egli sia licenziato*, I propose (*o* suggest) that he should be dismissed; *propongo una soluzione diversa*, I propose a different solution; *proporrei di aspettare*, I should suggest waiting; — *a esempio*, to point out (*o* to hold up *o* to set up) as an example; — *a qlcu. un affare, un brindisi, una questione, condizioni favorevoli*, to propose an affair, a toast, a question, favourable terms to s.o.; — *un prezzo*, (*domandarlo*) to ask a price; (*offrirlo*) to offer a price; — *un progetto di legge*, to bring in a bill ‖ *l'uomo propone e Dio dispone*, *prov.* man proposes, God disposes ‖ **propórsi,** *v.r.* to purpose, to propose, to intend: *mi propongo di non andarci più*, I propose (*o* I purpose) never to go (*o* going) there again; *si era proposto grandi cose ma non ha fatto niente*, he had planned great things but he has done nothing; *si propose di mettere in risalto l'influsso francese*, he purposed to emphasize the French influence; *si propone di vederti prima di partire*, he intends to see (*o* seeing) you before leaving; — *un obiettivo*, to propose an object (*o* aim) to oneself.

proporzionàbile, *ag.* proportionable.

proporzionàle, *ag.* proportional: — *a*, proportional to; *grandezze direttamente proporzionali*, (*mat.*) proportional dimensions; *grandezze inversamente proporzionali*, (*mat.*) inversely proportional dimensions; *rappresentanza* —, (*pol.*) proportional representation.

proporzionalità, *s.f.* proportionality.

proporzionalménte, *av.* proportionally, in proportion: — *a quanto ho fatto avrei dovuto guadagnare di più*, in proportion (*o* according) to what I have done I should have earned more; *egli sarà ricompensato* —, he will be rewarded proportionally.

proporzionàre, *v.t.* to proportion: — *le spese ai guadagni*, to proportion one's expenditure to one's gains.

proporzionataménte, *av.* proportionately.

proporzionàto, *ag.* **1.** proportioned: *un edificio, un corpo ben* —, a well-proportioned building, body **2.** (*conforme, adeguato*) proportionate: *la punizione era proporzionata alla colpa*, the punishment was in proportion to the crime; *la ricompensa non è proporzionata allo sforzo*, the reward is not proportionate to the effort **3.** (*adatto*) fit (for sthg.), suitable (for sthg.).

proporzióne, *s.f.* **1.** proportion; (*rapporto*) ratio: *la* — *fra le nascite e le morti*, the ratio between births and deaths; *mancante di proporzioni*, lacking in proportion; *senza proporzioni*, out of proportion (*o* dispro-

portionate); (*senza confronto*) without comparison; *una sala di vaste proporzioni*, a hall of vast proportions (*o* a large hall); *le proporzioni di quella statua sono perfette*, the proportions of that statue are perfect; *non c'è* — *tra la pena e la colpa*, the punishment doesn't fit the crime; *la nostra spesa è, non è in* — *al nostro reddito*, our expenditure is in, out of proportion to our income **2.** (*mat.*) proportion, ratio: — *antecedente*, antecedent; — *armonica*, harmonic ratio; — *conseguente*, consequent; — *diretta, inversa*, direct, inverse ratio; *estremi, medi di una* —, extremes, means of a proportion; *termini della* —, terms of a proportion **3.** (*chim.*) proportion: *legge delle proporzioni costanti, multiple*, law of constant, multiple proportions.

propòsito, *s.m.* **1.** (*proponimento*) purpose; (*intenzione*) intention; (*disegno*) design: *onestà, fermezza di* —, honesty, firmness of purpose; *ho fatto il* — *di non uscire per qualche giorno*, I have decided not to go out for a few days; *i miei propositi sono sempre buoni, ma non riesco mai ad effettuarli*, my intentions are always good, but I never succeed in carrying them out; *non so che* — *abbia*, I do not know what his intentions are; *cambiare* —, to change one's mind; *essere debole, fermo di* —, to be weak, firm of purpose ‖ *di* —, on purpose (*o* intentionally); (*seriamente*) seriously (*o* in earnest): *l'hai fatto per caso o di* —?, did you do it by accident or on purpose?; *mettersi a studiare di* —, to begin studying seriously (*o* in earnest) ‖ *uomo, donna di* —, strong-willed man, woman **2.** (*scopo*) purpose, aim, object: *che cosa è il* — *di tutto ciò?*, what is the purpose of all this?; *il mio* — *era di diffondere queste notizie*, my aim (*o* object) was to spread this news; *questo non serve al mio* —, this does not answer my purpose ‖ *questo viene, capita proprio a* —, (*serve al mio scopo*) this suits my purpose perfectly **3.** (*tema, assunto*) subject: *per tornare al nostro* —..., to get back to the subject... ‖ *a* — *di*, with regard to (*o* in connection with *o* apropos of); *a questo* — *potrei dirti un mucchio di cose*, on this subject I could tell you a lot of things; *a questo* — *vorrei dirti che*..., with reference to this (*o* in this connection) I should like to tell you that... ‖ *fuori* —, (*di osservazione, ecc.*) out of place ‖ *a* —, *dove è andato tuo fratello?*, by the way, where has your brother gone? **4.** (*opportunità*) chance, opportunity: *ad ogni* — *mi ricorda che*..., he takes every chance (*o* opportunity) to remind me that... ‖ *ciò che disse era molto a* —, what he said was very much to the purpose (*o* to the point *o* relevant); *io conosco la persona a* —, I know the right person; *parlò molto a* —, he spoke very much to the point; *questo viene proprio a* —, (*al momento opportuno*) this comes just at the right time (*o* moment); *scegli delle espressioni a* —, choose appropriate expressions; *arrivare proprio a* —, to arrive in the nick of time; *fare ql.co. a* —, to do sthg. at the right moment (*o* time) ‖ *fuori* (*di*) —, *male a* —, ill-timed (*o* inopportune) (*ag.*); at the wrong moment (*o* time) (*av.*).

proposizióne, *s.f.* **1.** (*gram.*) sentence, clause: — *principale, subordinata*, main (*o* principal), subordinate clause; — *semplice, composta, interrogativa, esclamativa*, simple, compound, interrogative, exclamatory sentence **2.** (*ret. mat.*) proposition **3.** (*proposta*) proposition, proposal: — *di eleggere un arbitro*, proposal for the election of an arbitrator.

propósta, *s.f.* proposal: — *di matrimonio*, proposal (of marriage): *fare una* — *di matrimonio a una signorina*, to propose to a young lady; — *di pace*, peace proposal(s); *fare, accettare una* —, to make, to accept a proposal ‖ — *di legge*, (parliamentary) bill.

propósto, *ag.* proposed ‖ *s.m.* **1.** (*eccl.*) provost **2.** (*st.*) provost (first magistrate of a mediaeval town).

propretóre, *s.m.* (*st. romana*) propraetor.

propriaménte, *av.* **1.** (*con proprietà*) properly **2.** (*realmente*) really **3.** (*esattamente*) exactly, precisely: *quella è* — *la verità*, that is precisely the truth.

proprietà, *s.f.* **1.** property, ownership, possession: — *privata, pubblica*, private, public property; — *senza usufrutto*, ownership without usufruct; *diritto di* —, right of ownership; *nuda* —, bare ownership; *trasferimento di* —, transfer of property; *la fattoria è di* — *di mio padre*, the farm belongs to my father; *questa casa è di mia* —, this house is my property ‖ — *letteraria*, copyright **2.** (*possedimento*) property, estate: *ho comprato una* — *in campagna*, I have bought a property in the country; *la sua* — *era in una stupenda posizione*, his estate was in a wonderful position **3.** (*caratteristica*) property, characteristic: — *chimiche, fisiche*, chemical, physical properties; *le* — *del ferro, dell' oro*, the properties of iron, gold **4.** (*correttezza, decoro*) propriety, correctness: — *di linguaggio*, propriety of language; *ella veste con molta* —, she dresses very neatly; *parla con* —, he speaks very precisely.

proprietària, *s.f.* **1.** owner, proprietress **2.** (*di locanda, pensione*) landlady.

proprietàrio, *ag.* proprietary: *l'ente* — *di quell'edificio*, the society that owns that building ‖ *s.m.* **1.** owner, proprietor: *legittimo* —, lawful owner; — *terriero*, landowner; *piccolo* — *terriero*, small holder; *era* — *di un grande albergo*, he was the owner of a big hotel; *sono* — *di questa casa*, I am the owner of this house **2.** (*possidente*) man of property **3.** (*di locanda, pensione*) landlord.

pròprio, *ag.* **1.** (*con funzione di possessivo o come rafforzativo di possessivo*) own; one's; of one's own: *con le mie proprie orecchie*, with my own ears; *ha una teoria sua propria*, he has a theory of his own; *ogni uomo ha il* — *destino*, every man has his own destiny; *scritto di propria mano*, written in one's own hand; *avere una casa propria è il sogno di tutti*, to have a house of one's own is everybody's dream; *morire per il* — *paese*, to die for one's country ‖ *amor* —, self-esteem (o self-respect) ‖ *fare del* — *meglio*, to do one's best **2.** (*adatto, appropriato, opportuno*) proper (to s.o., sthg., to do), fit (for s.o., sthg., to do), fitting (s.o., sthg.), suitable, right (for s.o., sthg., to do); befitted (for s.o., sthg., to do) (*predicativo*), suited (*predicativo*): *divertimento* — *alla vecchiaia*, amusement fitting old age; *non è il momento* — *per parlare di denaro*, this is not a suitable (o a fitting) time to talk about money; *ogni cosa verrà a suo* — *tempo*, everything will come in its proper time; *la primavera è la stagione propria alle passeggiate in campagna*, spring is the right season for country walks; *questi termini non sono propri*, these terms are not suitable; *questo stile è pieno di espressioni proprie*, this style is full of apt phrases; *questo vestito è* — *all'occasione*, this dress is well-suited to the occasion ‖ *vero* —, real (o proper): *stavamo in un vero e* — *albergo*, we were staying at a real hotel; *vorrei avere una vera e propria casa invece di una catapecchia come questa*, I should like to have a proper (o real) house instead of a tumble-down hut like this **3.** (*letterale*) exact, literal: *il senso* — *di una parola*, the exact (o literal) sense of a word **4.** (*mat. gram.*) proper: *frazione propria*, (*mat.*) proper fraction; *nome* —, (*gram.*) proper noun **5.** (*decente, conveniente*) correct, decent; seemly: *un comportamento* —, a seemly behaviour; *è vestita in modo molto* —, she is dressed very correctly; *veste sempre abiti molto propri*, she is always very decently dressed **6.** (*caratteristico*) typical, characteristic; peculiar (to s.o., sthg.): *con quell'arroganza che gli è propria*, with his typical (o characteristic) arrogance; *la ragione è propria dell'uomo*, reason is peculiar to man ‖ *s.m.* **1.** one's own: *dare a ciascuno il* —, to give to each his due; *perderci del* —, to lose one's own money ‖ *in* —: *ha una ditta in* —, he has a business of his own; *commerciare, lavorare in* —, to trade, to work on one's own account **2.** (*qualità caratteristica*) characteristic: *la generosità è il suo* —, generosity is his chief characteristic **3.** *pl.* (*parenti, famiglia*): *aver cura dei propri*, to take care of one's own people (o family).

pròprio, *av.* **1.** (*esattamente*) just, exactly: — *allora, ora*, just then, now; — *così*, just like that: *si dice* — *così*, that's exactly what one says; *arrivò* — *in quel momento*, he arrived at that very moment; *hai comperato* — *ciò che volevo*, you have bought just what I wanted; *quello che volevo dirti è* — *questo*, that is just what I was going to tell you; *sono* — *dieci*, they are exactly ten **2.** (*veramente*) really, quite: *è* — *stupido*, he is really stupid; *ho* — *studiato*, I have really studied; *mi sento* — *male*, I do feel ill (o I feel really ill); *sei* — *tu?*, is it really you? ‖ — *?*, really? (o indeed?).

propugnàcolo, *s.m.* bulwark (anche *fig.*).

propugnàre, *v.t.* to support, to defend, to champion; to fight for (sthg.): — *una causa*, to defend (o to support) a cause; — *una dottrina politica*, to support a political doctrine; — *un ideale religioso*, to fight for a religious ideal.

propugnatóre, *s.m.* supporter, champion, defender.

propugnazióne, *s.f.* (*letter. rar.*) support, defence.

propulsióne, *s.f.* propulsion: — *ad accumulatori*, (*elett.*) storage-battery propulsion; — *a getto*, jet-propulsion; — *a razzo*, (*aer.*) rocket-propulsion; — *a reazione*, (*aer.*) jet-propulsion; — *turbo-elettrica*, (*ind. mec.*) turbo-electric propulsion; *a* — *autonoma*, (*mec.*) self-propelled.

propulsívo, *ag.* propulsive.

propulsóre, *ag.* propelling ‖ *s.m.* propeller.

propulsòrio, *ag.* propulsive, propellent, propelling.

pròra, *s.f.* prow, bow, head: — *diritta*, straight stem; — *rigonfia*, bluff bow; *a* —, at the bow; *albero di* —, foremast; *castello di* —, forecastle; *da* — *a poppa* fore and aft; *onda di* —, bow wave; *ruota di* —, stem (post); *vento di* —, head wind; *dirigere la* — *al largo*, to stand out (o off); *mettere la* — *in direzione opposta al vento*, to bear up.

pròroga, *s.f.* **1.** (*rinvio*) adjournment **2.** (*dilazione*) respite, extension: *concedere una* — *di cinque giorni*, to grant a respite of five days; *domandare una* — *di pagamento*, to ask for an extension of payment.

prorogàbile, *ag.* **1.** (*rinviabile*) adjournable, postponable, deferable **2.** (*prolungabile*) extendable.

prorogàre, *v.t.* **1.** (*rinviare*) to put off, to postpone to delay, to defer: *l'assemblea è prorogata fino al prossimo mese*, the meeting is put off until next month; *il processo è stato prorogato alla settimana prossima*, the trial has been postponed until next week **2.** (*prolungare*) to extend, to prolong: *l'esposizione è stata prorogata di dieci giorni*, the exhibition has been extended for ten days; *gli hanno prorogato la licenza fino alla fine del mese*, his leave has been extended until the end of the month; *il termine di consegna è stato prorogato fino al mese venturo*, the term of delivery has been extended until next month.

prorogazióne, (*rar.*) per **pròroga**.

prorompènte, *ag.* bursting out: *vi fu un applauso* —, there was a burst of applause.

prorómpere, *v.i.* **1.** to burst (out) (anche *fig.*); to break out (anche *fig.*): *proruppe in aspre parole*, he burst into abuse; *proruppe in una risata*, he burst out laughing; *allora i nostri proruppero dalle trincee*, then our soldiers burst out from the trenches; *il fuoco prorompeva da tutte le parti*, fire was breaking out all over; *il pubblico prorompe in lunghi applausi*, the audience burst into long applause; *il torrente prorompeva dal suo letto*, the torrent burst its banks; — *in bestemmie*, to burst out swearing; *la vidi* — *in pianto*, I saw her burst into tears **2.** (*di liquidi*) to gush out (of sthg.), to pour out (of sthg.): *il sangue gli proruppe dalle vene*, blood gushed out of his veins.

pròsa, *s.f.* **1.** prose: *poema in* —, prose-poem; *conosci le opere in* — *di Donne?*, do you know Donne's prose works?; *è una* — *che sembra poesia*, it is prose that is like poetry; *è una* — *così limpida e piacevole che si legge tutta d'un fiato*, it is such a pleasant and clear prose that is hard to put it down; *è una* — *robusta e* *densa di pensiero,* it is prose which is robust and packed with thought; *è una — troppo ampollosa per il mio gusto,* this prose is too bombastic for my liking; *sto leggendo una bella — di Leopardi,* I am reading a fine prose passage by Leopardi **2.** (*materialità, volgarità*) prose, commonplace: *la grigia — della vita quotidiana,* the monotony of everyday life; *sei molto cambiato, sei diventato tutta —,* you have altered a lot, you are extremely prosaic now **3.** (*teat.*): *compagnia di —,* dramatic company; *preferisco la — all'opera,* I enjoy a play better than an opera; *il teatro di — moderno rifugge dal monologo,* in modern drama monologue is avoided.

prosaicaménte, *av.* prosaically, in a prosaic manner.

prosaicísmo, *s.m.* prosaicism; prosaicness: *il suo — è nauseante,* his prosaicism is revolting.

prosàico, *ag.* **1.** prosaic; prose (*attributivo*): *componimento —,* prose work **2.** (*materiale, volgare*) prosaic; commonplace (*attributivo*); dull: *che vita prosaica !,* what a dull life!; *come sei —!,* how prosaic you are!; *ha uno stile —,* he has a prosaic style; *scusa se parliamo di cose prosaiche,* excuse us for talking about prosaic matters.

prosaísmo, *s.m.* (*rar.*) prosaism.

prosàpia, *s.f.* (*letter.*) race, stock, lineage: *— di eroi,* race of heroes; *— di re,* race of kings; *discendeva da nobile —,* he came of a noble line.

prosàstico, *ag.* prose (*attributivo*): *uso —,* prose usage.

prosatóre, *s.m.,* **prosatríce,** *s.f.* prose-writer.

proscènio, *s.m.* (*teat.*) proscenium (*pl.* proscenia); stage: *palco di —,* stage-box; *l'autore apparve sul —,* the author appeared on the stage.

prosciògliere, *v.t.* **1.** to free, to set free, to absolve, to release: *— da un obbligo,* to release from an obligation; *— qlcu. da un voto, una promessa, un giuramento, ecc.,* to free (*o* to absolve) s.o. from a vow, a promise, an oath, etc. **2.** (*dir.*) to acquit, to absolve: *— un imputato,* to acquit a defendant.

proscioglimènto, *s.m.* **1.** absolution, release **2.** (*dir.*) acquittal.

prosciòlto, *ag.* **1.** absolved, released **2.** (*dir.*) acquitted.

prosciugaménto, *s.m.* **1.** drying up; (*artificiale*) draining; (*bonifica*) reclamation: *— delle paludi,* draining (*o* reclamation) of the marshes **2.** (*med.*) drainage.

prosciugàre, *v.t.* to dry up; (*artificialmente*) to drain; (*bonificare*) to reclaim: *queste paludi saranno presto prosciugate,* these swamps will soon be drained; *stanno progettando di — tutta questa regione,* they are planning to reclaim all this area; *il vento prosciuga il terreno,* the wind dries up the ground ‖ *v.i.* to dry up: *il formaggio prosciuga,* cheese dries up ‖ **prosciugàrsi,** *v.r.* to dry up: *i torrenti si prosciugarono durante la calda estate,* the streams dried up during the hot Summer.

prosciútto, *s.m.* ham: *— cotto,* boiled (*o* smoked) ham; (*dolce*) baked ham ‖ *avere gli occhi foderati di —,* (*fam.*) to be blind to evidence.

proscrítto, *ag.* proscribed, banished, outlawed, exiled ‖ *s.m.* exile, outlaw.

proscrívere, *v.t.* **1.** to proscribe, to outlaw, to banish, to exile **2.** (*segregare*) to reject, to exclude.

proscrizióne, *s.f.* proscription, banishment.

prosecutóre, *s.m.* pursuer.

prosecuzióne, *s.f.* prosecution, continuation.

proseggiàre, *v.i.* **1.** to write in prose, to prose **2.** (*usare stile prosaico*) to prose.

proseggiatóre, *s.m.,* **proseggiatríce,** *s.f.* prose-writer.

prosegretàrio, *s.m.* **1.** assistant secretary **2.** (*eccl.*) pro-secretary.

proseguiménto, *s.m.* continuation ‖ *buon —!,* all the best to you!.

proseguíre, *v.t.* to continue, to keep up, to carry on, to pursue: *decise di — il suo lavoro,* he decided to continue his work; *non potè — gli studi,* he could not pursue his studies; *proseguì le sue ricerche,* he carried

on his research; *— il cammino,* to go on one's way; *— la lettura,* to go on reading (*o* to read on) ‖ *v.i.* to go on, to continue, to pursue: *non lo lasciarono — e dovette smettere di parlare,* they did not let him go on and he was obliged to stop talking; *proseguo per Milano,* I'm going on to Milan ‖ *far — una lettera a un nuovo indirizzo,* to forward a letter to a new address.

prosèlite, *V.* prosèlito.

proselitísmo, *s.m.* proselytism.

prosèlito, *s.m.* proselyte: *far proseliti,* to make proselytes (*o* to proselytize *o* to proselyte).

prosènchima, *s.f.* (*bot.*) prosenchyma.

Prosèrpina, *no.pr.f.* (*mit.*) Proserpina, Proserpine.

prosettóre, *s.m.* (*anatomista*) prosector.

prosíeguo, *s.m.* (*dir.*) course.

prosillogísmo, *s.m.* (*fil.*) prosyllogism.

prosíndaco, *s.m.* acting mayor, deputy mayor.

pròsit, *inter.* to your health!.

prosodía, *s.f.* prosody.

prosodíaco, *ag.* prosodic(al), prosodial.

prosodicaménte, *av.* prosodically.

prosòdico, *ag.* prosodic(al), prosodial.

prosopopèa, *s.f.* **1.** (*ret.*) prosopopoeia **2.** (*gravità affettata*) presumption; haughtiness: *ha molta —,* he is very haughty.

prosopopèico, *ag.* (*ret.*) prosopopoeic(al).

prosperaménte, *av.* prosperously.

prosperaménto, *s.m.* prospering, thriving.

prosperàre, *v.i.* to prosper, to thrive, to flourish, to do well: *i bambini prosperano in campagna,* children prosper in the country; *economicamente questo paese prospera,* economically this country is doing well; *i miei affari prosperano,* my business is prospering (*o* is thriving); *questi alberi prosperano in terreno umido,* these trees thrive in humid ground ‖ *v.t.* to prosper: *Dio vi prosperi !,* may God prosper you!.

prosperità, *s.f.* prosperity, prosperousness: *la — di una famiglia, un paese, un'industria,* the prosperity of a family, a country, an industry; *ondata di —,* (*econ.*) boom; *periodo di —,* period of prosperity ‖ *—!,* bless you!.

pròspero, *ag.* **1.** prosperous, thriving, flourishing: *azienda prospera,* flourishing (*o* prosperous) firm; *un paese —,* a prosperous (*o* thriving) country; *salute prospera,* very good health; *un secolo —,* a prosperous century **2.** (*favorevole*) happy, lucky, fortunate: *un — avvenimento,* a happy (*o* lucky) event; *un vento —,* a fair wind.

prosperosaménte, *av.* prosperously, thrivingly.

prosperóso, *ag.* **1.** prosperous, thriving **2.** (*florido, in salute*) healthy: *una ragazza prosperosa,* a buxom girl.

prospettàre, *v.t.* **1.** to show, to point out; to propose: *mi ha prospettato tutti i lati della faccenda,* he showed (*o* he pointed out to) me all sides of the question; *mi prospettò un affare,* he proposed a business deal to me; *— un'ipotesi,* to formulate a hypothesis **2.** (*guardare*) to look (out) on to (sthg.): *la casa prospetta al mare,* the house looks (out) on to the sea.

prospetticaménte, *av.* perspectively.

prospèttico, *ag.* perspective (*attributivo*).

prospettíva, *s.f.* **1.** perspective: *— aerea,* aerial perspective; *— rapida,* isometric projection; *disegno in —,* drawing in perspective; *i principi della —,* the principles of perspective; *quadro senza —,* picture out of perspective **2.** (*possibilità futura*) prospect, view: *a quel tempo avevo molto poco in —,* at that time I had very little in prospect (*o* view); *ha prospettive di successo,* he has prospects of success; *in quanto alla sua carriera ha delle belle prospettive,* as regards his career he has good prospects; *non è una bella —,* it is a dreary outlook; *non ha che la — dell'ospizio,* he has nothing but the poor-house before him; *non vi era alcuna — d'accordo,* there was no prospect of agreement; *questo mi apre nuove prospettive,* this opens new prospects to my mind; *vendette tutto ciò che aveva con la — di lasciare il paese*, he sold everything he had with a view to leaving the country.

prospettivaménte, *av.* perspectively.

prospettivísta, *s.m.* perspective painter.

prospètto, *s.m.* **1.** view; landscape; prospect: *un — di monti*, a mountain view **2.** *(fronte)* front: *figura di —*, front figure; *palco di —*, front box; *visto di —*, seen from the front; *se lo guardi di —...*, if you look at it from the front... **3.** *(specchietto)* prospectus programme; *(sommario)* summary.

prospettóre, *s.m.*, **prospettríce**, *s.f.* prospector.

prospezióne, *s.f.* *(miner.)* prospecting.

prospiciènte, *ag.* facing, looking on to (sthg.); opposite: *— il bosco*, looking on to the wood; *— la strada*, facing the street.

prossenèta, *s.m.* proxenet(e).

prossenetísmo, *s.m.* proxenetism.

prossèno, *s.m.* *(st. greca)* proxenus, proxenos *(pl.* proxeni).

prossimaménte, *av.* **1.** (very) soon, in a short time, in the near future, before long **2.** *(nelle programmazioni cinematografiche)* coming shortly ‖ *s.m.* *(sequenze di film proiettate a scopo reclamistico)* trailer.

prossimità, *s.f.* **1.** closeness, nearness, proximity: *la — della partenza non gli permise di accettare il mio invito*, the closeness (o imminence) of his departure prevented him from accepting my invitation; *uno dei vantaggi di questo albergo è la sua — al mare*, one of the hotel's advantages is its closeness (o nearness) to the sea ‖ *in — di*, in proximity to (o near): *in — della stazione*, near (o in proximity to) the station; *in — delle montagne*, near the mountains; *siamo in — delle vacanze*, the holidays are near (o approaching o at hand) **2.** *(stretta parentela)* close relationship **3.** *(somiglianza)* similarity, likeness: *— di gusti, di idee*, similarity of tastes, ideas.

pròssimo, *ag. superl.* **1. near, close;** *(solo predicativi)* **at hand, near-at-hand, close-at-hand:** *nel — futuro*, in the near future; *la sua fine è prossima*, his end is near (o is approaching); *le vacanze sono prossime*, the holidays are at hand (o near o getting close) ‖ *— a*, near, close to: *è — ai vent'anni*, he is nearly twenty; *l'ufficio postale è — alla scuola*, the post-office is close to the school; *essere — alla fine*, to be near the end; *fig.* to be near one's end ‖ *— a fare ql.co.*, on the point of doing sthg.: *ero — a rinunciare*, I was on the point of giving (it) up ‖ *parente —*, near (o close) relative **2.** *(seguente nel tempo e nello spazio)* next: *alla prossima occasione*, on the next occasion; *l'anno, il mese —*, next year, month; *nei prossimi mesi*, in the next few months; *camminiamo fino al — villaggio*, let us walk as far as the next village; *quando parte il — treno?*, when does the next train leave? ‖ *il 15 del mese —*, *(comm.)* on the 15th prox. **3.** *(gram.)*: *passato —*, present perfect; *trapassato —*, past perfect ‖ *s.m.* neighbour, fellow creature: *il nostro —*, our fellow creatures (o fellowmen); *amerai il — tuo come te stesso*, thou shalt love thy neighbour as thyself.

pròstata, *s.f.* *(anat.)* prostate (gland).

prostàtico, *ag.* prostatic: *ipertrofia prostatica*, *(patol.)* prostatic hypertrophy.

prostatíte, *s.f.* *(patol.)* prostatitis.

prostèndere, *v.t.* to stretch (out), to draw out, to extend ‖ **prostèndersi**, *v.r.* to stretch oneself ‖ *— in discorsi*, to lose oneself in verbosity.

prosternàre, *v.t.* to prostrate, to throw down ‖ **prosternàrsi**, *v.r.* to prostrate (oneself); to bow down.

prosternazióne, *s.f.* prostration.

pròstesi, *s.f.* *(gram.)* prosthesis.

pròstilo, *s.m.* *(arch.)* prostyle.

prostituíre, *v.t.* to prostitute: *— il proprio ingegno, i propri ideali*, to prostitute one's talent, one's ideals ‖ **prostituírsi**, *v.r.* **1.** to prostitute oneself **2.** *(vendersi vergognosamente)* to sell oneself, to debase oneself.

prostitúta, *s.f.* prostitute.

prostituzióne, *s.f.* prostitution.

prostraménto, *s.m.* prostration.

prostràre, *v.t.* **1.** to prostrate; to throw down **2.** *(fiaccare)* to prostrate, to exhaust; to overwhelm: *egli era prostrato dal dolore*, he was overwhelmed by grief; *la lunga malattia lo ha prostrato*, his long illness has prostrated him ‖ **prostràrsi**, *v.r.* to prostrate oneself; to bow down: *egli si prostrò davanti all'idolo*, he prostrated himself (o he bowed down) before the idol.

prostràto, *ag.* prostrate (with sthg.) *(anche fig.)*: *— dalle preoccupazioni, dal dolore*, prostrate with worries, with grief.

prostrazióne, *s.f.* prostration *(anche fig.)*.

prosuòcera, *s.f.* parent-in-law's mother.

prosuòcero, *s.m.* parent-in-law's father.

protagonísta, *s.c.* protagonist *(anche fig.)*.

Protàgora, *no.pr.m.* *(st. fil.)* Protagoras.

pròtasi, *s.f.* *(teat. gram.)* protasis *(pl.* protases).

protàtico, *ag.* *(gram.)* protatic.

protèggere, *v.t.* **1.** to protect, to defend (from, against s.o., sthg.); *(riparare)* to shelter: *devi — la ferita dall'aria*, you must protect your wound from the air; *questi occhiali ti proteggeranno gli occhi dal vento*, these goggles will protect your eyes from the wind; *una volta le mura proteggevano la città dal nemico*, formerly walls protected the town against the enemy; *— dal freddo, dalla pioggia*, to shelter from the cold, the rain **2.** *(tutelare, custodire)* to watch over (s.o., sthg.), to guard: *i cani proteggono le greggi*, sheep-dogs guard the flocks; *ci deve essere un angelo che protegge i bambini*, there must be an angel who watches over children; *siamo protetti dalla polizia e da sentinelle*, we are guarded by the police and by sentries ‖ *che Dio ti protegga!*, God keep you! **3.** *(favorire)* to favour; *(patrocinare)* to patronize; *(incoraggiare)* to protect, to encourage: *la fortuna protegge gli audaci*, fortune favours the brave; *— le arti, i giovani artisti*, to patronize the arts, young artists; *— il commercio, un'industria*, to protect (o to encourage o to foster) trade, an industry ‖ **protèggersi**, *v.r.* to protect oneself: *costruì un riparo per — dal vento*, he built a shelter to protect himself from the wind.

protèico, *ag.* *(chim. fisiol.)* proteinous, proteinic, proteinaceous; protein *(attributivo)*.

proteifórme, *ag.* protean; proteiform: *ingegno, natura —*, protean genius, nature.

proteína, *s.f.* *(chim. fisiol.)* protein.

protèndere, *v.t.* to stretch (out), to hold out: *— le braccia*, to stretch out one's arms; *— lo sguardo*, to gaze forth: *— lo sguardo nel vuoto*, to gaze into space ‖ **protèndersi**, *v.r.* to stretch oneself; *(in avanti)* to lean forward.

protensívo, *ag.* *(fil.)* protensive.

Pròteo, *no.pr.m.* *(mit.)* Proteus ‖ **pròteo**, *s.m.* *(zool.)* proteus.

proteolísi, *s.f.* *(biol. chim.)* proteolysis.

protervaménte, *av.* insolently; arrogantly.

protèrvia, *s.f.* insolence; arrogance.

protèrvo, *ag.* **1.** insolent; arrogant **2.** *(impetuoso)*: *vento —*, relentless wind.

pròtesi, *s.f.* **1.** *(chir.)* prosthesis: *— dentaria*, dental prosthesis **2.** *(gram.)* *(prostesi)* prosthesis.

Protesilào, *no.pr.m.* *(lett.)* Protesilaus.

protéso, *ag.* outstretched: *con le braccia protese*, with outstretched arms; *con le orecchie protese*, with pricked ears.

protèsta, *s.f.* **1.** protest: *una — formale*, a formal protest; *uno sciopero di —*, a protest strike; *ci furono molte proteste contro quella legge*, there were many protests against that law; *elevò una fiera — contro...*, he raised an energetic protest against...; *fare una —*, to make (o to set) a protest **2.** *(dichiarazione)* protestation: *— di amore*, protestation of love.

protestànte, *ag.* **1.** protestant **2.** *(st. relig.)* Protestant:

pastore —, (Protestant) minister (*o* parson) ‖ *s.c.* (*st. relig.*) Protestant.

protestantésimo, protestantísmo, *s.m.* (*st. relig.*) Protestantism.

protestàre, *v.i.* to protest: *quando egli fu ingiustamente punito, io protestai,* when he was unjustly punished I protested; *tutti protestarono contro le nuove misure,* everybody protested against the new measures ‖ *v.t.* **1.** to protest, to profess: *protestava la sua innocenza,* he protested his innocence (*o* that he was innocent); — *amicizia per qlcu.,* to make profession of friendship for s.o.; — *la propria lealtà, devozione,* to protest one's loyalty, devotion **2.** (*comm.*) to protest: — *una cambiale,* (*con protesto definitivo*) to protest a bill; (*con protesto preliminare*) to note a bill ‖ **protestàrsi,** *v.r.* to protest oneself, to profess oneself: *si protestava innocente,* he protested that he was innocent; *si protesta mio amico,* he professes himself a friend of mine.

protestàto, *ag.* **1.** protested **2.** (*di cambiale*) dishonoured.

protestatóre, *s.m.,* **protestatríce,** *s.f.* protester, protestor (anche *comm.*).

protestazióne, *s.f.* protestation: — *di affetto, di amicizia,* protestation of affection, of friendship.

protèsto, *s.m.* **1.** (*comm.*) protest; (*preliminare*) noting: — *per mancata accettazione,* protest for non -acceptance; — *per mancato pagamento,* protest for non-payment; *atto di* —, certificate of protest; *avviso di* —, notice of protest; *levare* — *a carico di una persona,* to serve a protest on a person ‖ *in* —, under protest: *cambiale in* —, bill under protest; *lasciar andare una cambiale in* —, to dishonour a bill **2.** (*protesta*) protestation.

protètta, *s.f.* protégée, favourite: *è la* — *di mia madre,* she is my mother's protégée.

protettívo, *ag.* protective.

protètto, *ag.* **1.** protected; (*riparato*) sheltered: *luogo* —, sheltered place; *un paese* —, a protected country ‖ *un'industria protetta,* (*econ.*) a protected industry **2.** (*custodito*) guarded **3.** (*favorito*) favoured; (*patrocinato*) patronized ‖ *s.m.* protégé, favourite: *il* — *del re,* the king's favourite; *era un* — *di Madame de Staël,* he was one of Madame de Staël's protégés.

protettoràto, *s.m.* **1.** (*ufficio di protettore*) protectorship **2.** (*pol.*) protectorate.

protettóre, *ag.* protector, protective; patronizing: *truppe protettrici,* protective troops ‖ *santo* —, patron saint ‖ *Società protettrice degli animali,* Society for the Prevention of Cruelty to Animals ‖ *s.m.* **1.** protector **2.** (*mecenate, patrono*) patron: — *dei malati,* patron of the sick; — *delle Arti,* patron of the Arts; *si diede delle arie da* —, he put on patronizing airs **3.** (*pol.*) Protector: *Cromwell fu il lord* — *dell'Inghilterra,* Cromwell was the Lord Protector of England.

protettríce, *s.f.* patroness ‖ *Protettrice degli afflitti,* (*la Madonna*) Protectress of the afflicted.

protezióne, *s.f.* **1.** protection: *la* — *dei deboli,* the protection of the weak; *questi Stati sono sotto la* — *britannica,* these States are under British protection; *il ragazzo era sotto la mia* —, the boy was under my protection ‖ *misure di* — *antiaerea,* air-raid precautions ‖ *opera di* — *dell'infanzia,* child-welfare association **2.** (*mecenatismo, patronato*) patronage: *chiedere la* — *di qlcu.,* to solicit s.o.'s patronage (*o* support); *guardare qlcu. con aria di* —, to look patronizingly at s.o.; *prendere qlcu. sotto la propria* —, to take s.o. under one's patronage: *la signora X li ha presi sotto la sua* —, Mrs. X has taken them under her patronage.

protezionísmo, *s.m.* (*econ.*) protectionism.

protezionísta, *s.m.* (*econ.*) protectionist.

protísti, *s.m.pl.* (*biol.*) Protista.

protistología, *s.f.* protistology.

pròto, *s.m.* (*tip.*) foreman (*pl.* foremen), overseer.

protocanònico, *ag.* (*eccl.*) protocanonical.

protocollàre, *ag.* protocol (*attributivo*).

protocollàre, *v.t.* to file, to record: *il contratto è stato protocollato,* the contract has been recorded; — *un atto,* to record a deed.

protocollísta, *s.m.* registrar, keeper of records.

protocòllo, *s.m.* **1.** (*prima stesura di trattato*) protocol: *firmare il* —, to sign the protocol **2.** (*registro, indice*) record, register: *essere a* —, to be on record; *mettere a* —, to record (*o* to file *o* to protocol) ‖ *formato* —, foolscap (size) **3.** (*ufficio*) record office, registry **4.** (*cerimoniale diplomatico*) protocol, ceremonial, political etiquette: *le esigenze del* —, the exigencies of etiquette (*o* protocol); *avere la precedenza secondo il* —, to have precedence according to the protocol.

protóne, *s.m.* (*fis.*) proton.

protonotariàto, *s.m.* (*eccl. st.*) prot(h)onotaryship.

protonotàrio, *s.m.* (*eccl. st.*) prot(h)onotary: — *apostolico,* Prot(h)onotary Apostolic(al).

protopàpa, *s.m.* (*eccl.*) protopapas, protopope.

protoplàsma, *s.m.* (*biol.*) protoplasm.

protoplàste, *s.m.* (*Causa Prima*) Protoplast.

protoplàsto, *ag.* protoplastic ‖ *s.m.* (*biol.*) protoplast.

protospatàrio, *s.m.* (*st. bizantina*) protospatharius.

protòssido, *s.m.* (*chim.*) protoxide.

protòttero, *s.m.* (*ittiol.*) protopterus (*invariato al pl.*).

protòtipo, *s.m.* prototype ‖ *è il* — *dello stupido,* he is a perfect idiot; *è il* — *dello svizzero,* he is a typical Swiss.

protozòi, *s.m. pl.* (*biol.*) Protozoa.

protozòico, *ag.* **1.** (*geol. paleont.*) protozoic **2.** (*biol.*) protozoan, protozoal, protozoic.

protràrre, *v.t.* **1.** to protract, to prolong: — *una discussione, una visita,* to protract a discussion, a visit **2.** (*differire*) to put off, to postpone, to defer: *ha protratto la partenza,* he has put off his departure.

protrazióne, *s.f.* **1.** protraction **2.** (*differimento*) putting off, deferment.

protuberànte, *ag.* protuberant, bulging, swelling out.

protuberànza, *s.f.* protuberance, prominence: — *ossea,* (*anat.*) apophysis; *protuberanze solari,* (*astr.*) solar prominences (*o* protuberances).

protutóre, *s.m.* (*dir.*) guardian ad litem.

pròva, *s.f.* **1.** (*dimostrazione*) proof; (*testimonianza*) evidence (*solo sing.*): — *a carico,* (*dir.*) evidence for the prosecution; — *addotta dalla pubblica accusa,* (*dir.*) evidence produced by the Public Prosecutor; (*in Gran Bretagna*) evidence for the Crown; — *a discarico,* (*dir.*) evidence for the defence; — *diretta,* (*dir.*) prima facie evidence; — *in contrario,* (*dir.*) evidence to the contrary; — *indiretta,* (*dir.*) circumstantial (*o* indirect *o* hearsay) evidence; — *testimoniale,* (*dir.*) evidence of witnesses; *assolto per insufficienza di prove,* (*dir.*) acquitted on the grounds of insufficient proof; *proscioglimento per insufficienza di prove,* (*dir.*) " not guilty "; *la* — *verte su...,* (*dir.*) the evidence bears on (*o* relates to)...; *diede* — *di essere un vero amico,* he proved to be a real friend; *ne abbiamo le prove scritte,* we have written evidence of it; *nessuno lo crederà se non puoi portare delle prove,* nobody will believe it, if you cannot prove it; *questa è una* — *della sua innocenza,* this is a proof of (*o* this proves) his innocence; *ti dò questo come* — *della mia amicizia,* I give you this as a proof (*o* a token) of my friendship; *ti racconto tutte queste cose a* — *delle mie assersioni,* I tell you all these things to support my assertions; *voglio la* — *di quanto hai detto,* I want proof of what you have said; *dare* — *di coraggio,* to give a proof of one's courage; *dare* — *d'intelligenza,* to give a proof of (*o* to show *o* to display) one's intelligence ‖ *fino a* — *contraria,* until one has proof to the contrary **2.** (*esperimento*) trial, test: — *ad alta tensione,* (*elett.*) high -voltage test; — *a fatica,* (*edil.*) fatigue test; — *a freddo,* (*di motori*) cold test; — *agli ormeggi,* (*mar.*) quay trial; — *al banco*, (*di motori*) bench test; (*di pompe, ecc.*) rig test; — *al freno*, (*di motori*) brake test; — *alla fiamma*, (*chim.*) flame test; — *all'urto*, (*edil.*) shock test; *prove a terra*, (*aer.*) ground tests; — *a trazione*, (*edil.*) tensile test; — *a tutta forza*, (*mar.*) full-power trial; — *conclusiva*, crucial test; — *dei filati*, (*ind. tessile*) yarn testing; — *di collaudo*, acceptance test; — *di durata*, (*mec.*) endurance test; (*spor.*) long distance trial; — *di durezza*, (*mec.*) hardness test; — *di elasticità*, (*fis.*) elasticity test; — *di pressione*, (*ind.*) pressure test; — *di resistenza*, (*spor.*) test of stamina; — *di rigidità*, (*elett.*) electric strength test; — *di sicurezza*, reliability test; — *di tiro*, (*artigl.*) range trial; — *di velocità*, speed test; — *in volo*, (*aer.*) flight trial; — *su strada*, road test; *apparecchio di* —, test set; *banco di* —, testing bench; *campo di* —, proving ground; *ordine di* —, (*comm.*) trial order; *stanza di* —, testing room; *volo di* —, trial flight; *farò un mese di* —, I shall be on probation for a month; *ho preso un'automobile in* —, I have taken a car on trial; *lo assumerò in* —, I shall give him a trial; *il nuovo impiegato è solo in* —, the new clerk is only on probation; *mettere una macchina in* —, to test a machine; *reggere alla* —, to stand the test; *superare una* —, to pass a test ‖ — *del fuoco*, ordeal (*o* trial) by fire (anche *fig.*) ‖ *a* — *di bomba*, bomb-proof; *a* — *di cannone*, shell-proof ‖ *un amico a tutta* —, a tried friend ‖ *lo so per* —, I know from experience ‖ *mettere qlcu. alla* —, to put s.o. to the test (*o* to test s.o. out *o* to try s.o. out) ‖ *alla* — *si scortica l'asino*, *prov.* the proof of the pudding is in the eating 3. (*esame*) test, examination: — *orale*, oral test (*o* examination); — *scritta*, written examination; *sostenere una* —, to take (*o* to sit for) an examination 4. (*tentativo*) try: *farò la* —, I shall try; *ho fatto quattro prove, ma non sono mai riuscito*, I have tried four times (*o* I have had four tries), but I've never been successful; *non so usare la macchina da cucire, ma lasciami fare una* —, I can't work a sewing-machine, but let me have a try (*o* a go) at it 5. (*sofferenza, sventura*) trial: *fu una dura* —, it was a severe trial; *la mia vita fu piena di prove*, my life was full of trials 6. (*risultato, riuscita*) result: *dare una buona* —, to give good results 7. (*di abito, durante la confezione*) fitting: *ho fatto tre prove per questo abito*, I've had three fittings for this dress; *mettere in* — *un abito*, to make a dress ready for a fitting 8. (*teat.*) rehearsal: — *generale*, dress rehearsal; *ogni giorno facciamo tre ore di* —, every day we rehearse for three hours 9. (*tip.*) (printing) proof: *foglio di* —, specimen page; *prima* —, galley (-proof); *seconda* —, revise; *terza* —, second revise; *correggere una* —, to correct a proof; *tirare una* —, to pull a proof 10. (*mat.*) proof: *fa' la* — *di questa addizione*, check this sum; *fare la* — *del nove*, to cast out the nines 11. *far* —, (*di piante*) to take root.

provàbile, *ag.* provable, demonstrable.
provabilità, *s.f.* provableness, demonstrability.
provànte, *ag.* probative, evidential.
provàre, *v.t.* 1. (*dimostrare*) to prove, to show, to demonstrate: *come si può* — *che Dio esiste?*, how can one prove that God exists?; *egli provò la verità delle sue asserzioni producendo documenti*, he proved (*o* he gave proof of) the truth of his assertions by producing documents; *non possiamo* — *la sua colpa*, we cannot prove his guilt; *quell'avvenimento provò che aveva ragione*, the event showed that he was right (*o* proved him right); *questo prova che egli l'ha fatto apposta*, this shows that he has done it on purpose; *questo non è ancora stato provato*, this remains to be proved; *si provò la falsità della sua relazione*, his report proved false 2. (*tentare, sperimentare*) to try: *fa* — *a me ora*, let me try (*o* let me have a try) now; *non l'ho mai fatto, ma proverò*, I have never done it, but I'll have a try (*o* a go); *proverò ad alzarmi alle sei*,

I shall try to get up at six; *provò a chiedere*, he tried to ask; *vorrei* — *la tua automobile*, I should like to try your car; — *una nuova medicina*, to try a new medicine ‖ *proviamo un po'*, let's have a try ‖ — *per credere*, (you) try and see 3. (*mettere alla prova*) to test, to try: *fu duramente provato dalle avversità*, he was severely tried by hardships; *prima di assumerla voglio* — *le sue capacità*, before engaging you, I want to test your abilities; *quell'uomo fu duramente provato dalla vita*, that man was sorely tried by life; *questo lavoro di precisione proverà la tua pazienza*, this work of precision will test (*o* try) your patience; *il suo coraggio fu duramente provato*, his courage was severely tried (*o* tested) 4. (*sentire*) to feel; (*conoscere per esperienza*) to experience: *ho provato quanto sia piacevole vivere in campagna*, I have experienced the pleasures of living in the country; *non ho mai provato una simile emozione, gioia*, I have never felt such an emotion, such joy; *provai un dolore alla schiena*, I felt a pain in my back; *provai una gran delusione*, I felt deeply disappointed; *provò pietà per lui*, he felt pity for him 5. (*abiti, ecc.*) to try on; (*abito in confezione*) to have a fitting: *devo andare dalla sarta a* —, I have to go to the dressmaker's for a fitting; — *un cappello, un paio di scarpe, un vestito*, to try on a hat, a pair of shoes, a dress 6. (*collaudare*) to test: *le nostre macchine vengono tutte provate prima di essere messe in vendita*, our machines are all tested before being put on sale 7. (*saggiare*) to try, to test: — *la purezza di un metallo*, to try (*o* to test) a metal for impurity 8. (*teat.*) to rehearse: *gli attori stanno provando*, the actors are rehearsing; — *una commedia*, to rehearse a play ‖ *v.i.* (*rar.*) (*attecchire*) to take (root) ‖ **provàrsi**, *v.r.* 1. to try: *egli si provò, ma non riuscì*, he tried, but he did not succeed; *provati a farlo*, try to do it ‖ *provati ad aprir bocca!*, you just try to open your mouth again! ‖ *provali e vedrai!*, you just try! 2. (*abiti, ecc.*) to try on; (*abito in confezione*) to have a fitting: *devo andare dal sarto a provarmi un abito*, I must go to the tailor for a suit fitting; — *un abito prima di comprarlo*, to try on a dress before buying it 3. — *con, contro qlcu.*, (*letter.*) to measure one's strength, one's ability with s.o.

provataménte, *av.* (*rar.*) 1. (*sperimentalmente*) by experiment 2. (*evidentemente*) evidently.
provàto, *ag.* 1. tried: *un amico* —, a tried friend; *un uomo* — *dalla vita, dalle sventure*, a man tried by life, by misfortune 2. (*evidente*) evident: *prova provata*, evident proof 3. (*mec.*) tested: — *al banco*, bench-tested.
proveniènte, *ag.* 1. coming: *merci provenienti dalla Francia*, goods coming from France 2. (*causato*) caused (by sthg.); proceeding (from sthg.): *dolore* — *da un'ammaccatura*, pain caused by a bruise; *malattia* — *dall'abuso di alcool*, illness caused by (*o* proceeding from) the abuse of alcool.
proveniènza, *s.f.* 1. origin, provenance: *di dubbia* —, of doubtful origin; *luogo di* —, place of origin; *quale è la* — *di queste merci?*, where do these goods come from? 2. (*fonte*) source: *la* — *di queste informazioni è inattendibile*, the source of this information is unreliable.
provenìre, *v.i.* 1. to come: *proveniamo dalla stessa città*, we come from the same town 2. *fig.* (*avere origine*) to originate (from sthg.), to be caused (by sthg.), to be brought about (by sthg.), to arise (from sthg.): *tutti questi inconvenienti provengono da un cattivo imballaggio*, all these troubles are caused by bad packing; *tutti i guai gli provengono dalla pigrizia*, all his troubles are brought about by his laziness.
provènto, *s.m.* proceeds (*pl.*); (*reddito*) income: *proventi dell'industria*, income deriving from industry; *i proventi di queste vendite non furono lauti*, the proceeds of these sales were not large.
Provènza, *no.pr.f.* (*geog.*) Provence.

provenzàle, *ag.s.c.* Provençal.

provenzaleggiànte, *ag.* in the Provençal style; of Provençal inspiration: *poesia* —, poetry of Provençal inspiration.

provenzaleggiàre, *v.i.* to imitate Provençal poets.

proverbiàle, *ag.* proverbial: *la sua avarizia è* —, his stinginess is proverbial (*o* is a proverb).

proverbialménte, *av.* proverbially.

provèrbio, *s.m.* proverb; (*adagio*) adage, saying: *per, in* —, proverbially; *come dice il* —, as the saying goes; *giocare ai proverbi*, to play proverbs; *passare in* —, to become a proverb (*o* a byword): *la sua pigrizia è passata in* —, he is a proverb for laziness ‖ *libro dei Proverbi, i Proverbi,* (*Bibbia*) (Book of) Proverbs ‖ *i proverbi sono la saggezza dei popoli,* proverbs are the wisdom of the people.

proverbióso, *ag.* full of proverbs.

proverbista, *s.c.* proverbialist; proverb-monger.

provése, *s.m.* (*mar.*) bow fast.

provétta, *s.f.* **1.** (*chim.*) test-tube: — *graduata,* graduated measuring tube **2.** (*mec.*) (*barretta per prove*) test-bar.

provètto, *ag.* **1.** (*maturo*) mature: *persona d'età provetta,* person of mature years **2.** (*esperto, abile*) experienced, skilled, skilful: *un operaio* —, a skilled workman; *uno scrittore* —, a clever writer.

providènza, *V.* **provvidènza.**

provincia, *s.f.* **1.** province: *vita di* —, provincial (*o* country) life; *venire dalla* —, to come from the provinces; *vivere in* —, to live in the provinces **2.** (*ogni circoscrizione amministrativa*) district **3.** (*paese, regione*) district, region, area: *viaggiare in lontane province,* to travel through remote districts **4.** (*eccl. st. romana*) province: *l'impero romano era diviso in province,* the Roman Empire was divided into provinces.

provinciàle, *ag.* provincial: *abitudini, gusti provinciali,* provincial customs, tastes; *ragazza* —, provincial (*o* small-town) girl; *strade provinciali,* provincial roads; *questa è una strada* —, this is a main road ‖ *padre* —, (*eccl.*) provincial ‖ *s.m.* **1.** provincial, small-towner **2.** (*eccl.*) provincial.

provincialismo, *s.m.* provincialism: *il* — *di certi scrittori,* the provincialism of certain writers; *questa prosa è piena di provincialismi,* this piece of prose is full of provincialisms.

provincialménte, *av.* provincially.

provino, *s.m.* **1.** (*campione*) sample **2.** (*chim.*) (*provetta*) test-tube **3.** (*teat.*) try-out **4.** (*cine.*) (*prova di un attore*) film-test, trial; (*sequenze di film proiettate a scopo reclamistico*) trailer.

provocàbile, *ag.* provokable, provocable.

provocànte, *ag.* **1.** provocative: *parole provocanti,* provocative words; *uno sguardo* —, a provocative glance **2.** (*irritante*) provoking, irritating, annoying **3.** (*invitante*) inviting.

provocanteménte, *av.* **1.** provocatively **2.** (*in modo irritante*) provokingly **3.** (*in modo invitante*) invitingly.

provocàre, *v.t.* **1.** to provoke, to cause, to give rise to (sthg.); (*eccitare*) to excite, to stir up: *la sua condotta provocò del malcontento fra il popolo,* his behaviour roused discontent among the people; *la sua morte fu provocata da un embolo,* his death was caused by an embolus; *le sue dichiarazioni provocarono molte lamentele,* his declarations gave rise to many complaints; — *la collera di qlcu.,* to excite s.o.'s anger; — *il riso,* to provoke laughter; — *una rissa,* to provoke a riot; — *il vomito,* to induce vomiting **2.** (*istigare; sfidare*) to provoke: *egli mi provocò ed io lo schiaffeggiai,* he provoked me and I hit him.

provocativo, *ag.* provocative.

provocatóre, *ag.* **1.** provocative **2.** (*irritante*) provoking ‖ *s.m.,* **provocatrice,** *s.f.* provoker.

provocatòrio, *ag.* provocative.

provocazióne, *s.f.* provocation: *va in collera alla minima* —, he gets angry on the slightest provocation.

provolóne, *s.m.* "provolone" (kind of cheese made in Southern Italy).

provòsto, *s.m.* (*eccl.*) parish-priest; (*st.*) provost.

provvedére, *v.t.* **1.** to provide, to supply, to furnish: *egli ci provvede il carbone tutti gli anni,* he supplies us with coal every year; *l'ho provveduto di viveri e libri per una settimana,* I provided (*o* supplied) him with victuals and books for a week; *mi ha sempre provveduto di tutto ciò di cui avevo bisogno,* he has always provided me with everything I needed **2.** (*preparare*) to get ready, to prepare: *è stato provveduto tutto per la partenza,* everything has been prepared for the departure ‖ *v.i.* **1.** to provide (for sthg.); to see (to sthg.), to see (about sthg.); to arrange (for sthg.): *a ciò provvederà lui,* he will see to it; *dobbiamo* — *ai bisogni del popolo,* we must provide for the needs of the people; *egli provvede ai bisogni della sua famiglia, all'educazione dei suoi figli,* he provides for his family, for his children's education; *ho provveduto a tutto per la tua partenza,* I have arranged everything for your departure; *non ho ancora provveduto al mio passaporto,* I have not seen (*o* done anything) about my passport yet; *provvederò anche a questo,* I shall arrange for this as well **2.** (*procurare*): *devi* — *che venga anche lui,* you must get him to come too; *dovresti* — *di arrivare molto presto,* you should arrange to arrive very early; *provvederò che abbia tutto ciò che gli occorre,* I shall see to it that he has everything he needs; *provvedi che le cose vadano meglio,* try to make things go better; *provvedi che il gatto non entri in casa,* take care the cat does not get in; *provvedi che non beva troppo,* see to it that he does not drink too much **3.** (*prendere cura*) to take care (of s.o., sthg.): *se dovessi morire chi provvederà ai miei figli?,* if I die who will take care of my children? **4.** (*prendere un provvedimento*) to take a decision: *qui bisogna* — *subito,* a quick decision must be taken ‖ **provvedérsi,** *v.r.* to provide oneself: *si era provvisto di una rivoltella,* he had provided himself with a revolver; — *di abiti, cibo, ecc.,* to provide oneself with clothes, food, etc.

provvediménto, *s.m.* **1.** (*rimedio, disposizione*) measure, action: — *amministrativo, legislativo,* administrative, legislative measure; — *disciplinare,* disciplinary action; *allo stato in cui sono arrivate le cose è inutile ogni* —, in the present state of things all measures are useless (*o* all action is useless); *prendere* (*severi*) *provvedimenti contro qlcu.,* to take (severe) measures (*o* action) against s.o. **2.** (*misura di previdenza*) precaution: *provvedimenti igienici, sanitari,* hygienic, sanitary precautions **3.** (*atto del provvedere*) provision.

provveditoràto, *s.m.* superintendent's office ‖ — *agli studi,* local education office ‖ — *generale dello Stato,* governmental stationery office.

provveditóre, *s.m.* **1.** (*soprintendente*) superintendent ‖ — *agli studi,* local director of education **2.** (*mil.*) (*chi provvede agli approvvigionamenti*) quarter-master general **3.** — *navale,* (*mar.*) ship-chandler.

provveduto, *ag.* **1.** provided (with sthg.), supplied (with sthg.) **2.** (*accorto*) wary: *il saggio e* — *lettore,* the wise and wary reader.

provvidaménte, *av.* providently, prudently.

provvidènte, *ag.* provident.

provvidenteménte, *av.* providently.

provvidènza, *s.f.* providence: *la Provvidenza ci aiuterà,* Providence will help us; *è un dono della Provvidenza,* it's a gift of Providence ‖ *essere una* —, to be providential: *quella eredità è stata una* — *per noi,* that inheritance was providential for us.

provvidenziàle, *ag.* providential: *aiuto* —, providential (*o* heaven-sent) help; *uomo* —, man sent by providence.

provvidenzialménte, *av.* providentially.

pròvvido, *ag.* provident; (*economo*) thrifty: *amministrazione, governo* —, wise administration, government; *consiglio* —, sound advice; *natura provvida,* provident nature; *uomo* —, provident (*o* thrifty) man.

provvigióne, *s.f.* **1.** (*comm.*) commission: *conto provvigioni*, commission account; *vendita a —*, sale on commission; *riceve una — del 4 % su quello che vende*, he receives a commission of 4 % on what he sells **2.** (*provvista*) supply.

provvisionàle, *ag.* (*dir.*) provisional ‖ *s.f.* (*dir.*) provisional clause.

provvisionàre, *v.t.* (*rar.*) to pay wages to (s.o.).

provvisióne, *s.f.* **1.** (*provvista*) provision: *provvisioni di guerra*, war-materials **2.** (*salario*) salary; wages (*pl.*) **3.** (*comm.*) commission: *— bancaria*, exchange; *addebitare una —*, to charge a commission; *concedere, riconoscere una —*, to allow a commission; *dedurre una —*, to deduct a commission.

provvisionière, *s.m.* provider; purveyor.

provvisoriaménte, *av.* provisionally, temporarily.

provvisorietà, *s.f.* temporariness: *la — della sua posizione*, the provisional character of his position.

provvisòrio, *ag.* temporary, provisional: *condizioni provvisorie*, temporary conditions; *esercizio —*, provisional duty; *governo, accomodamento —*, provisional government, arrangement; *in via provvisoria*, temporarily (*o* provisionally); *misure provvisorie*, temporary (*o* provisional) measures; *nomina provvisoria*, temporary appointment; *ponte —*, temporary bridge; *ho un lavoro —*, I have a temporary job; *stipularono un accordo —*, they laid down a provisional agreement.

provvìsta, *s.f.* **1.** supply, stock, provision: *provviste di merce*, stocks; *provviste militari, navali*, military, naval stores (*o* supplies); *andrò al mercato perchè le nostre provviste sono finite*, I shall go to the market because our provisions are finished; *dobbiamo fare — di vino*, we must buy (*o* get in) some wine; *ho una buona — di farina*, I have a good supply of flour (*o* I am well supplied with flour); *andare a fare provviste*, to go shopping; *far —*, to take (*o* to lay) in provisions; *mettere da parte provviste per l'inverno*, to lay in stores frat he winter **2.** *fig.* store: *ha una buona — di coraggio*, he has good store of courage.

provvìsto, *ag.* **1.** supplied (with sthg.), provided (with sthg.): *la cucina è ben provvista di utensili*, the kitchen is well supplied with utensils; *quel negozio è ben — di articoli di pelle*, that shop is well supplied with leather-goods (*o* that shop has a large supply of leather-goods); *sono — di tutto ciò che mi occorre*, I am provided with all I need **2.** *fig.* well-to-do, wealthy, well-off: *essere ben —*, to be well-off.

prozía, *s.f.* great-aunt.

prozío, *s.m.* great-uncle.

prúa, *s.f.* (*mar.*) prow, bow(s).

prudènte, *ag.* **1.** prudent, discreet: *un'azione, una risposta, una persona —*, a prudent action, answer, person **2.** (*cauto*) cautious, careful: *sii — nel guidare l'automobile*, be careful when you drive **3.** (*pauroso*) fearful, timorous.

prudenteménte, *av.* **1.** prudently, discreetly **2.** (*cautamente*) cautiously, carefully **3.** (*paurosamente*) fearfully, timorously.

prudènza, *s.f.* **1.** prudence, discretion: *la — è una virtù cardinale*, prudence is one of the cardinal virtues; *agire con —*, to use discretion **2.** (*cautela*) caution, care: *guida con —!*, drive with caution! (*o* care!) ‖ *—!*, be careful! (*o* caution!) ‖ *la — non è mai troppa*, safety first! **3.** (*precauzione*) precaution: *per — prenderò l'ombrello*, I shall take an umbrella as a precaution.

Prudènzia, *no.pr.f.* Prudence ‖ *dim.* Prue.

prudenziàle, *ag.* **1.** prudential: *per ragioni prudenziali*, for prudential reasons **2.** (*di cautela*) precautionary: *misure prudenziali*, precautionary measures.

prudenziálménte, *av.* prudentially.

prúdere, *v.i.* to itch: *la ferita mi prude*, my wound itches; *mi prudeva dappertutto*, I was itching all over; *non grattarti dove ti prude*, do not scratch yourself where you itch ‖ *mi ha toccato dove mi prude*, *fig.* he has touched me on the raw ‖ *mi prude la lingua dalla*

voglia di dirgli..., I have a good mind to tell him... ‖ *mi prudevano le mani dalla voglia di dargli uno schiaffo*, I was itching to box his ears.

pruderie, *s.f.* prudery.

prudóre, *s.m.* itch, irritation.

prueggiàre, *v.i.* (*mar.*) to luff.

pruéggio, *s.m.* (*mar.*) luffing.

prúgna, *s.f.* (*bot.*) plum: *— secca*, prune; *prugne cotte*, stewed prunes; *color —*, plum-coloured.

prúgno, *s.m.* (*bot.*) plum-tree.

prúgnola, *s.f.* (*bot.*) wild plum.

prugnuòlo, *s.m.* (*bot.*) agaric.

pruìna, *s.f.* **1.** (*letter.*) (*brina*) hoar-frost **2.** (*di frutti*) bloom (on fruit).

pruinóso, *ag.* **1.** (*letter.*) (*brinato*) frosty **2.** (*coperto di pruina*) pruinose.

prunàio, *s.m.* thicket of thorn-bushes ‖ *trovarsi in un —*, *fig.* to be in the mire (*o* in a mess).

prunèlla, *s.f.* (*bot.*) prunella.

prunéto, *s.m.* thicket of thorn-bushes.

prúno, *s.m.* **1.** (*cespuglio*) thorn-bush **2.** (*spina*) thorn, prickle.

prunóso, *ag.* thorny.

prurígine, *s.f.* **1.** itch, irritation **2.** (*med.*) prurigo.

pruriginóso, *ag.* **1.** itching, irritating **2.** *fig.* (*frizzante*) sparkling; (*appetitoso*) appetizing.

prurìto, *s.m.* itch (anche *fig.*); irritation: *ho — al braccio*, my arm itches.

Prússia, *no.pr.f.* (*geog.*) Prussia ‖ *blu di —*, Prussian blue.

prussiàno, *ag.s.m.* Prussian.

prussiàto, *s.m.* (*chim.*) prussiate: *— giallo di potassio*, yellow prussiate of potash; *— rosso*, red prussiate.

prússico, *ag.* (*chim.*) prussic: *acido —*, prussic acid.

psammòma, *s.m.* (*patol.*) psammoma (*pl.* psammomata, psammomas).

pseudoestesía, *s.f.* (*med.*) pseudaesthesia.

pseudomembràna, *s.f.* (*med.*) pseudomembrane.

pseudomòrfo, *ag.* (*min.*) pseudomorph.

pseudomorfòsi, *s.f.* (*min.*) pseudomorphism.

pseudònimo, *ag.* pseudonymous ‖ *s.m.* pseudonym, assumed name; (*di uno scrittore*) pen-name.

psicagogía, *s.f.* psychagogy.

psicagògico, *ag.* psychagogic.

psicagògo, *s.m.* psychagogue.

psicanàlisi, *s.f.* psycho-analysis.

psicanalítico, *ag.* psycho-analytic.

psicastenía, *s.f.* (*med.*) psychasthenia.

psíche[1], *s.f.* **1.** (*anima*) psyche **2.** (*entom.*) psyche.

Psíche[2], *no.pr.f.* (*mit.*) Psyche: *Amore e —*, Eros and Psyche.

psichiàtra, *s.c.* psychiatrist.

psichiatría, *s.f.* psychiatry.

psichiàtrico, *ag.* psychiatric(al): *ospedale —*, mental hospital.

psíchico, *ag.* **1.** psychic(al): *forze psichiche*, psychic forces **2.** (*mentale*) mental: *malattia psichica*, mental illness.

psichísmo, *s.m.* (*fil.*) psychicism.

psicodinàmica, *s.f.* psychodynamics.

psicofísica, *s.f.* psychophysics.

psicofisiología, *s.f.* psychophysiology.

psicofisiològico, *ag.* psychophysiological.

psicografía, *s.f.* psychography.

psicògrafo, *s.m.* psychograph.

psicogràmma, *s.m.* psychogram.

psicología, *s.f.* psychology.

psicologicaménte, *av.* psychologically.

psicològico, *ag.* psychologic(al) ‖ *guerra psicologica*, psychological warfare ‖ *momento —*, psychological moment.

psicologísmo, *s.m.* psychologism.

psicologísta, *s.c.* psychologist.

psicòloga, *s.f.*, **psicòlogo**, *s.m.* psychologist.

psicomanzía, *s.f.* psychomancy.

psicometría, *s.f.* psychometry.
psicopatía, *s.f. (med.)* psychopathy.
psicopàtico, *ag.s.m.* psychopathic.
psicopatología, *s.f.* psychopathology.
psicopatòlogo, *s.m.* psychopathologist.
psicòsi, *s.f.* psychosis *(pl.* psychoses).
psicosomàtico, *ag.* psychosomatic.
psicotècnica, *s.f.* psychotechnics.
psicoterapèutica, *s.f.* psychotherapeutics.
psicoterapía, *s.f.* psychotherapy.
psieròmetro, *s.m. (meteorologia)* psychrometer.
psittacòsi, *s.f. (patol.)* psittacosis.
psoríasi, *s.f. (patol.)* psoriasis.
psòrico, *ag.* psoric.
ptèride, *s.f. (bot.)* Pteris.
pterigoidèo, *ag. (anat.)* pterygoid.
pterodàttilo, *s.m. (paleont.)* pterodactyl.
pteròpo, *s.m. (zool.)* pteropus.
pteròpodi, *s.m.pl. (zool.)* Pteropoda.
pterosàuro, *s.m. (paleont.)* pterosaur.
ptialína, *s.f. (chim. biol.)* ptyalin.
ptialísmo, *s.m. (med.)* ptyalism.
ptomaína, *s.f. (chim.)* ptomaine.
ptòsi, *s.f. (med.)* ptosis.
pubblicàbile, *ag.* publishable, fit for publication.
pubblicaménte, *av.* publicly, in public.
pubblicàre, *v.t.* 1. to publish, to bring out, to issue: *il libro sarà pubblicato il mese venturo,* the book will be published next month; — *un giornale, una rivista,* to issue a newspaper, a magazine || *pubblicato a cura di...,* edited by... || *appena pubblicato,* just out (o just published) 2. *(leggi, decreti, ecc.)* to issue: — *un decreto, un bollettino,* to issue a decree, a bulletin 3. *(divulgare)* to publish, to spread abroad, to broadcast: *andar pubblicando gli altrui segreti,* to broadcast another person's secrets.
pubblicazióne, *s.f.* 1. publication: *la — di un libro,* the publication of a book; *il libro è in corso di —,* the book is in course of publication; *mi mandò alcune sue pubblicazioni,* he sent me a few of his publications 2. *(di leggi, decreti, ecc.)* issue: *la — di un decreto,* the issuing of a decree 3. *pl. (di matrimonio)* banns: *fare le pubblicazioni,* to publish (o to put up) the banns.
pubblicísta, *s.c.* 1. publicist 2. *(giornalista)* journalist.
pubblicità, *s.f.* 1. publicity: *la — di queste informazioni,* the publicity of this information; *odio la — e cerco di evitarla,* I hate publicity and try to avoid it || *sta' zitto, non far — !,* keep quiet about it, don't make it public! (o don't broadcast it!) 2. *(propaganda commerciale)* advertising: — *luminosa,* luminous signs; *agente di —,* advertising agent; *(al servizio di un attore, di un cantante, di un campione sportivo, ecc.)* publicity agent; *(chi si occupa di public relations)* public relations officer; *agenzia di —,* advertising agency; *piccola —,* small advertisements *(o fam.* small ads.); *specialista in —,* advertising expert *(o amer.* adman); *ufficio di —,* advertising office; *cercherò di far — al tuo libro,* I shall try to make your book known; *nessuno può vendere senza — al giorno d'oggi,* nobody can sell without advertising nowadays; *far — a un prodotto,* to advertise a product || *la — è l'anima del commercio,* advertising is the very soul of trade.
pubblicitàrio, *ag.* advertising: *agente, ufficio —,* advertising agent, office; *avviso —,* advertisement; *campagna pubblicitaria,* advertising campaign.
púbblico, *ag.* public; *(statale)* state *(attributivo):* — *funzionario,* civil servant; *biblioteca pubblica,* public library; *debito —,* National (o Public) Debt; *diritto —,* public law; *forza pubblica,* police-force (o civil police); *giardini pubblici,* public gardens; *istruzione pubblica,* state education; *lavori pubblici,* public works; *nemico —,* public enemy: *nemico — numero 1,* public enemy number 1; *notaio —,* notary public; *opinione, salute, vita pubblica,* public opinion, health, life; *questione di interesse —,* public matter; *(d'importanza nazionale)*

matter of national importance; *servizi pubblici,* public services; *scuola pubblica,* state school; *spese pubbliche,* public expense: *a spese pubbliche,* at public expense; *le conferenze sono pubbliche,* the lectures are public; *fare una pubblica protesta,* to make a public protest; *lavorare per il bene —,* to work for the common good; *tenere una pubblica riunione,* to have (o to hold) an open (o public) meeting || *render —,* to make public (o to broadcast) || *s.m.* 1. public: *il — dei lettori,* the reading public; *il — italiano,* the Italian public; *i gusti del —,* the tastes of the public; *l'opinione del —,* public opinion; *uno scrittore senza —,* a writer without a public; *il — è pregato di...,* the public is (o are) requested to...; *il — non è ammesso,* the public is (o are) not admitted || *in —,* in public: *mettere in —,* to make public (o to broadcast o to reveal o to disclose) 2. *(di un teatro, un concerto, una conferenza, ecc.)* audience: *il — non ha applaudito,* the audience did not applaud; *parlare a un — numeroso,* to speak to a large audience.
púbe, *s.m. (anat.)* pubis *(pl.* pubes).
pubertà, *s.f.* puberty.
pubescènte, *ag.* pubescent.
pubescènza, *s.f.* pubescence.
púbico, *ag. (anat.)* pubic.
pudibóndo, *ag.* modest, demure; *(con affettazione)* prudish, prim: *una ragazza pudibonda,* a demure (o modest) girl; *un sorriso —,* a demure smile; *non essere così —,* don't be so prudish.
pudicaménte, *av.* modestly, demurely.
pudicízia, *s.f.* modesty, demureness, pudency; *(con affettazione)* prudery.
pudíco, *ag. (modesto)* modest, demure; *(vergognoso)* bashful: *sorriso —,* bashful smile.
pudóre, *s.m.* modesty, decency; *(ritegno)* reserve: *offesa al —,* offence against decency; *oltraggio al —,* indecent behaviour; *il suo rossore non era — ma la coscienza della sua colpa,* her blush was not modesty but the consciousness of her guilt; *le sue parole offendono il —,* his words are an offence against decency; *il — le impediva di parlare,* her modesty prevented her from speaking || *senza —,* shameless *(ag.);* shamelessly *(av.).*
puericultúra, *s.f.* child-welfare.
pueríle, *ag.* childish; puerile: *giuochi puerili,* childish games; *voce —,* childish voice.
puerilità, *s.f.* childishness; puerility: *la — della sua domanda,* the childishness of his question; *le sue — mi danno ai nervi,* his childish behaviour gets on my nerves.
puerilménte, *av.* childishly; puerilely.
puerízia, *s.f.* childhood.
puèrpera, *s.f.* puerpera *(pl.* puerperae).
puerperàle, *ag.* puerperal: *febbre —,* puerperal fever.
puerpèrio, *s.m.* puerpery, confinement.
puf¹, *s.m.* 1. *(sgabello rotondo)* pouf 2. *(di vestiti)* pouf.
puf², *(voce onomatopeica riproducente un tonfo)* flop, plop.
puffíno, *s.m. (ornit.)* puffin.
pugilàto, *s.m. (spor.)* boxing, pugilism: *guanti da —,* boxing-gloves; *incontro di —,* boxing-match; *fare del —,* to box.
pugilatóre, púgile, *s.m. (spor.)* boxer, pugilist.
pugilística, *s.f. (spor.)* boxing, pugilism.
pugilístico, *ag.* boxing *(attributivo);* pugilistic: *incontro —,* boxing-match.
púglia, *s.f.* 1. *(gettone)* counter, fish 2. *(l'insieme dei gettoni)* pool.
Púglia, *no.pr.f. (geog.)* Apulia.
púgna, *s.f. (poet.)* fight, battle.
pugnàce, *ag.* pugnacious, bellicose.
pugnaceménte, *av.* pugnaciously.
pugnalàre, *v.t.* to stab: — *qlcu. alle spalle,* to stab s.o. in the back.
pugnalàta, *s.f.* 1. stab: *fu colpito con una —,* he

was stabbed **2.** (*colpo a tradimento*) a stab in the back **3.** *fig.* blow, shock: *questa notizia è stata per me una vera —*, this news was a great blow to me.

pugnalatóre, *s.m.* stabber.

pugnàle, *s.m.* dagger: *colpo di —*, stab ‖ *la notizia fu un colpo di — al cuore*, the news was a severe blow.

pugnàre, *v.i.* (*letter.*) to fight.

pugnatóre, *s.m.*, **pugnatríce,** *s.f.* (*letter.*) fighter.

pugnèllo, *s.m.* **1.** fistful **2.** (*impugnatura*) handle.

pugnitòpo, *s.m.* (*bot.*) butcher's broom, knee-holly.

púgno, *s.m.* **1.** (*mano chiusa*) fist: *mi colpì col —*, he struck me with his fist; *allargare, aprire il —*, to open one's fist; *colpire col —*, to punch; *mostrare i pugni a qlcu.*, to shake one's fist at s.o. (*o* to threaten s.o. with one's fist); *serrare, stringere il —*, to clench one's fist ‖ *a pugni stretti*, with clenched fists ‖ *di proprio —*, in one's own handwriting: *lo scrisse di suo —*, he wrote it himself; *questa lettera è scritta di suo —*, this letter is in his own handwriting ‖ *in —*, in one's hand: *avanzarono con la spada in —*, they advanced with their swords in their hands; *avevano la vittoria in —*, they had victory (*o* victory was) within their grasp; *li tiene in —*, he has them in his power ‖ *serrare le pugna*, (*arc.*) to die **2.** (*colpo*) punch, blow: *gli assestò un — alla mascella*, he gave him one on the jaw; *mi diede un — sul naso*, he punched me (*o* he struck me) on the nose; *mi tirò un — in un occhio*, he landed me one (*o* punched me) in the eye ‖ *essere un — in un occhio*, to be an eyesore: *il tuo vestito è un — in un occhio*, your dress is an eyesore ‖ *fare a pugni*, to fight (*o* to box); *fig.* to clash; (*contrastare*) to disagree, to contradict: *il colore della tua sciarpa fa a pugni col tuo vestito*, the colour of your scarf clashes with that of your dress; *dovemmo fare a pugni per passare*, we had to fight our way through; *i miei piani fanno a pugni coi suoi*, my plans clash with his; *questi due principi fanno a pugni*, these two principles are contradictory (*o* incompatible)‖ *venire a pugni*, to come to blows **3.** (*manciata*) fistful; handful (anche *fig.*): *un — di farina*, a handful of flour; *un — di soldati*, a handful of soldiers ‖ *rimanere con un — di mosche*, to remain empty-handed.

puh, *inter.* faugh!.

púla, *s.f.* chaff, husk: *il grano viene separato dalla — mediante la battitura o la trebbiatura*, grain is separated from the chaff (*o* husk) by beating or threshing.

púlce, *s.f.* flea: *— di mare*, water-flea; *— penetrante*, chigoe ‖ *una — in un orecchio*, a suspicion (*o* doubt): *mettere una — in un orecchio a qlcu.*, to raise (*o* to awaken) s.o.'s suspicions ‖ *color —, puce* ‖ *chi dorme coi cani si leva con le pulci*, *prov.* you cannot touch pitch without being defiled.

puleeséeca, *s.f.* (*pizzicotto*) pinch.

pulciàio, *s.m.* flea-pit, nest of fleas.

Pulcinèlla, *no.pr.m.* (*st. teat.*) Punch, Punchinello: *teatrino di —*, Punch and Judy show; *si mascherò da —*, he dressed up as Punch ‖ *il segreto di —*, open secret ‖ **pulcinèlla,** *s.m.* (*burattino, buffone*) buffoon; (*spreg.*) fool ‖ *fare il —*, to break one's promise.

pulcinellàta, *s.f.* piece of buffoonery.

pulcíno, *s.m.* chick ‖ *un — nella stoppa*, a helpless creature ‖ *bagnato come un —*, soaked to the skin.

pulcióso, *ag.* flea-ridden.

pulédra, *s.f.* filly.

pulédro, *s.m.* colt.

puléggia, *s.f.* (*mec.*) pulley: *— a diametro variabile*, expanding pulley; *— a fascia piana*, band-pulley (*o* wheel); *— fissa*, fast (*o* fixed) pulley; *— folle*, idler (*o* idle pulley *o* loose pulley); *— scanalata*, sheave.

púlica, púliga, *s.f.* air bubble (in glass).

pulíre, *v.t.* **1.** to clean; (*lavare*) to wash: *devo far — questo abito*, I must get this dress cleaned; *puliscigli il viso*, wash his face; *— ben bene il pavimento*, to scrub the floor; *— la casa, il giardino*, to clean (up) the house, the garden; *— un secchio, un lavandino, i vetri*

delle finestre, to clean a bucket, a sink, the windows ‖ *— il piatto*, *fig.* to lap up everything (*o* to lick the plate clean) **2.** (*lucidare*) to polish: *devo far — questo tavolo*, I must get this table polished; *— l'argento, un pavimento di legno, scarpe*, to polish the silver, a parquet-floor, shoes **3.** (*mondare*) to clean: *pulisci il riso prima di cuocerlo*, clean the rice before cooking it; *— un'aiuola dalle erbacce*, to weed a flower-bed ‖ *— uno scritto*, to polish a piece of writing ‖ **pulìrsi,** *v.r.* **1.** to clean oneself; (*lavarsi*) to wash (oneself): *— la bocca*, (*col tovagliolo*) to wipe one's mouth; *— i denti*, to clean (*o* to brush *o* to wash) one's teeth; *— le mani, la faccia, le gambe*, to wash one's hands, face, legs; *— il naso*, to blow one's nose; *— le unghie*, to clean one's nails **2.** *fig.* (*dirozzarsi*) to grow refined.

puliseioréechi, *s.m.* ear-pick.

puliseipénne, *s.m.* pen-wiper.

puliseipièdi, pulisciseàrpe, *s.m.* door-mat; (shoe-) scraper.

pulíta, *s.f.* cleaning: *dare una — a ql.co.*, to clean sthg.

pulitaménte, *av.* **1.** cleanly **2.** (*fam.*) (*come si deve*) properly, neatly.

pulitézza, *s.f.* **1.** cleanness (anche *fig.*); (*ordine*) neatness **2.** (*di stile*) neatness.

pulitíno, *ag.* tidy: *un bambino —*, a very tidy child.

pulíto, *ag.* clean; (*ordinato*) neat, tidy; *fig.* clear, clean: *casa pulita*, clean (*o* neat) house; *conversazione pulita*, clean conversation; *una coscienza pulita*, a clear conscience; *un vestito —*, a clean dress; *una vita pulita*, a clean life ‖ *osso —*, picked bone ‖ *scrittura pulita*, neat (*o* clear) handwriting ‖ *farla pulita*, to get off scot free ‖ *far piazza pulita*, (*mangiare tutto*) to eat up everything; (*portar via tutto*) to clean out everything: *l'epidemia fece piazza pulita di molta gente*, the epidemic swept away a lot of people ‖ *lasciar qlcu. —*, to clean s.o. out ‖ *s.m.* fair copy: *consegnare il —*, to hand in the fair copy; *mettere a —*, to make a fair copy.

pulíto, *av.* cleanly, neatly: *mangiare —*, to eat tidily.

pulitóre, *ag.* cleaning, cleansing ‖ *s.m.* cleaner.

pulitríce, *s.f.* **1.** cleaner **2.** (*mec.*) buffer, polishing -machine, buffing-machine: *— a nastro*, surface sand-papering machine; *disco per —*, polishing-disk (*o* -mop).

pulitúra, *s.f.* cleaning; (*lucidatura*) polishing.

pulizía, *s.f.* (*il pulire*) cleaning; (*l'essere pulito*) cleanliness, cleanness: *— urbana*, city cleaning; *ha la mania della —*, he has a mania for cleanliness; *in casa sua c'è una gran —*, his house is very clean ‖ *far —*, to do the cleaning (*o* to clean up); *fig.* to make a clean sweep:‖ *ho fatto una bella — di tutta quell'anticaglia*, I have cleaned out all that old stuff; *non ho ancora fatto —*, I have not done the cleaning yet.

pullman, *s.m.* **1.** (motor-)coach **2.** (*ferr.*) Pullman (-car).

pullover, *s.m.* pullover.

pullulaménto, *s.m.* (*rar.*) swarming, pullulation.

pullulànte, *ag.* **1.** pullulant: *i pullulanti arbusti*, the sprouting bushes **2.** *fig.* swarming (with s.o., sthg.), teeming (with s.o., sthg.), pullulating (with sthg.): *la città era — di spie*, the town was swarming with spies.

pullulàre, *v.i.* **1.** (*germogliare*) to pullulate, to sprout **2.** (*scaturire*) to spring up (anche *fig.*): *oggigiorno le case pullulano per tutta la città*, nowadays houses are springing up all over the city **3.** (*contenere in gran numero*) to swarm (with s.o., sthg.), to teem (with s.o., sthg.), to pullulate (with sthg.): *la sala pullulava di gente*, the hall was swarming with people.

pullulazióne, *s.f.* pullulation.

púlpito, *s.m.* pulpit ‖ *da che — viene la predica!*, look who's talking! ‖ *quell'uomo è noioso, gli piace montar sul —*, that man is a bore, he likes laying down the law.

pulsànte, *ag.* pulsating, beating; (*palpitante*) throbbing: *corrente —*, (*elett.*) pulsating current ‖ *s.m.* push

-button, plunger: — *a pera*, pear-push; — *da campanello*, bellpush; — *di scatto*, (*foto.*) shutter-release.

pulsàre, *v.i.* to pulsate, to beat (anche *fig.*); (*palpitare*) to throb: *mi sentivo — le vene*, I could feel my veins throbbing; *il suo cuore pulsa ancora*, his heart is still beating.

pulsàtile, *ag.* **1.** pulsatory; pulsatile: *vene pulsatili*, pulsatory veins **2.** *strumenti pulsatili*, (*mus.*) percussion instruments.

pulsazióne, *s.f.* **1.** pulsation, beat; (*palpito*) throb, throbbing: *pulsazioni cardiache*, pulsations (o heart-beats) **2.** (*mus.*) vibration.

pulsìmetro, *s.m.* (*med.*) pulsimeter.

pulverulènto, *ag.* dusty, pulverulent.

pulvinàre, *s.m.* **1.** (*st. romana*) pulvinar **2.** (*tribuna di stadio*) grandstand.

pulvíscolo, *s.m.* dust: — *atmosferico*, motes.

pulzèlla, *s.f.* maid ‖ *la Pulzella d'Orléans*, the Maid of Orléans.

pum, *inter.* bang!.

pùma, *s.m.* (*zool.*) puma.

pungènte, *ag.* **1.** thorny, prickly; stinging (*attributivo*): *un arbusto —*, a prickly shrub; *le ortiche sono pungenti*, nettles sting **2.** *fig.* biting; pungent; sharp: *critica —*, pungent (o biting) criticism; *gusto —*, sharp taste; *una lingua —*, a sharp tongue; *odore —*, pungent smell; *parole pungenti*, biting words; *vento, freddo —*, biting wind, cold.

pungenteménte, *av.* bitingly, pungently, sharply.

púngere, *v.t.* **1.** to prick; to sting: *il freddo mi pungeva la faccia*, the cold stung my face; *fui punto da una zanzara*, I was stung by a mosquito; *le ortiche, le vespe pungono*, nettles, wasps sting; *le rose pungono*, roses prick **2.** (*ferire, offendere*) to prick, to sting; to wound: *fu punto dal rimorso, dall'invidia*, he was stung (o pricked) with remorse, with envy; *mi pungeva la coscienza*, my conscience pricked (o stung) me; *il tuo sarcasmo lo punse*, your sarcasm stung him ‖ — *sul vivo*, to cut s.o. to the quick **3.** (*stuzzicare*) to tease, to provoke: *si divertiva a pungerla, ma lei taceva*, he delighted in provoking her, but she remained silent **4.** (*spronare*) to spur **5.** (*stimolare*): *mi punge la curiosità*, I am itching with curiosity; *mi punge il desiderio di vederlo*, I am itching to see him ‖ **púngersi,** *v.r.* to prick oneself; to sting oneself: *per acchiapparlo si punse la mano*, he pricked his hand catching it.

pungiglióne, *s.m.* sting.

pungitòpo, *s.m.* (*bot.*) butcher's broom, knee-holly.

pungolàre, *v.t.* to goad (anche *fig.*); (*incitare*) to spur on: — *il bestiame*, to goad the cattle; — *qlcu. a lavorare, a studiare*, to goad s.o. (o to spur s.o. on) to work, to study.

púngolo, *s.m.* goad; *fig.* (*stimolo*) prick; (*incitamento*) spur: *il — della coscienza*, the prick of conscience; *il — dell'ambizione*, the spur of ambition; *un — per spingere il bestiame*, a goad for driving cattle.

puníbile, *ag.* punishable.

punibilità, *s.f.* punishability.

puníceo, *ag.* puniceous, dark red.

púnico, *ag.* Punic: *le guerre puniche*, the Punic wars.

puníre, *v.t.* **1.** to punish: *i malfattori sono puniti dalla legge*, wrong-doers are punished by the law; — *un bambino per mancanza di sincerità*, to punish a child for telling lies **2.** (*vendicare*) to revenge: — *un torto, un'offesa*, to revenge a wrong, an insult.

puníto, *ag.* punitive: *spedizione punitiva*, (*mil.*) punitive expedition.

punitóre, *ag.* punishing, punitive: *giustizia punitrice*, punitive justice ‖ *s.m.*, **punitríce,** *s.f.* punisher.

punizióne, *s.f.* punishment: — *corporale*, corporal punishment; *la — di un delitto*, the punishment of a crime; — *grave, esemplare*, severe, exemplary punishment; — *lieve*, light punishment; *in — delle sue colpe*, as a punishment for his wrong-doings; *andare senza —* to go unpunished; *infliggere una — a qlcu.*, to inflict a punishment on s.o.

púnta, *s.f.* **1.** point: *la — di un ago, coltello, spillo*, the point of a needle, knife, pin; *la — di un bastone*, the end (o point) of a stick; *con la — all'insù*, point upwards; *ha la — troppo aguzza*, it is too pointed; *fare la — a una matita*, to sharpen a pencil ‖ *cappello a tre punte*, three-cornered hat ‖ *ora di —*, rush hour ‖ *parlare in — di forchetta*, to speak affectedly ‖ *prendere ql.co. di —*, to meet sthg. head on; *prendere qlcu. di —*, to clash with s.o. **2.** (*tec.*) (*di tornio*) centre; (*per perforazioni*) bit; (*da trapano*) drill: — *da registrazione*, (*elett.*) recording stylus; — *di diamante*, diamond point; — *per compassi*, compass-point **3.** (*estremità*) tip, end: — *del naso*, tip of the nose; — *del dito*, finger-tip; *camminare sulla — dei piedi*, to walk on the tips of one's toes (o to walk on tiptoe) ‖ *avere ql.co. sulla — delle dita*, to have sthg. at one's finger-tips; *avere ql.co. sulla — della lingua*, to have sthg. on the tip of one's tongue **4.** (*cima, sommità*) (*di albero, campanile, ecc.*) top; (*di monte*) peak **5.** (*promontorio*) headland, cape, promontory; (*con nomi propri geografici*) point, cape **6.** — (*d'avanguardia*), (*mil.*) point **7.** (*un po'*): *una — di sale*, a pinch of salt; *una — di zucchero, cannella*, (just) a bit of sugar, of cinnamon; *c'era una — d'invidia nelle sue parole*, there was a touch (o a slight tinge) of envy in his words; *questa salsa ha una — di acido*, this sauce is (just) a bit sour **8.** (*dolore, trafitta*) sharp pain, twinge: *ho una — nello stomaco*, I have a sharp pain (o twinge) in my stomach **9.** (*di vino, acidità*): *questo vino ha un po' di —*, this wine is slightly sour **10.** *cane da —*, pointer.

puntàle, *s.m.* **1.** metal point **2.** (*di bastone, ombrello, ecc.*) ferrule **3.** (*di stringa*) tag **4.** (*mec.*) push-rod **5.** (*mar.*) (*colonna tra ponte e ponte*) pillar, stanchion; (*altezza tra chiglia e coperta*) depth: — *di stiva*, depth of hold.

puntaménto, *s.m.* (*mil.*) aim, sighting, laying: — *a distanza*, remote control; — *diretto*, direct laying; — *indiretto*, indirect laying.

puntàre, *v.t.* **1.** (*dirigere, volgere*) to point; to direct (anche *fig.*); (*volgere e prendere la mira*) to point, to aim, to sight, to level: *devi — con cura prima di sparare*, you must take careful aim before shooting; *egli puntò alla lepre e sparò*, he aimed at the hare and fired; *mi puntò gli occhi addosso*, he fixed his eyes on me; *puntò il bastone verso di me*, he pointed the stick at me; *puntò il fucile contro la tigre*, he aimed (o levelled) his gun at the tiger; — *l'attenzione su ql.co.*, to direct one's attention to sthg.; — *un cannocchiale*, (*dirigerlo*) to point a pair of field-glasses; (*metterlo a fuoco*) to focus a pair of field-glasses; — *il dito verso qlcu.*, to point at (o to) s.o.; — *i propri sforzi su ql.co.*, to concentrate one's efforts on sthg. (o to direct one's efforts towards sthg. o to aim at sthg.) ‖ — *un orologio*, to set a clock **2.** (*spingere, appoggiare con forza*) to push: *puntò l'asta della bandiera in terra*, he pushed the flag-staff into the ground; *puntò il remo alla riva per allontanare la barca*, he pushed the boat away from the bank with the oar; *si alzò puntando le mani sulla tavola*, he got up pushing his hands on the table; — *i gomiti sulla tavola*, to put one's elbows on the table ‖ — *i piedi*, *fig.* to put one's foot down **3.** (*di cane*) to point: *il cane puntò, poi si scagliò sulla preda*, the dog pointed (o set) and then dashed on the prey; — *una lepre*, to point a hare **4.** (*scommettere*) to bet, to wager: *ho puntato cinquecento lire su quel cavallo*, I have bet (o put) five hundred lire on that horse **5.** — *le vele*, (*mar.*) to hoist the sails ‖ *v.i.* (*dirigersi*) to head; (*spingersi*) to press: *puntammo verso la città*, we pressed on towards the city; *puntavamo a nord*, we were heading north; *puntavano diritti su Londra*, they were heading straight for London.

puntàta, *s.f.* **1.** (*di uno scritto pubblicato periodica-*

mente) instalment: *pubblicato a puntate*, issued in instalments; *storia a puntate*, serial story **2.** (*al gioco*) stake, bet **3.** (*breve visita*) flying visit: *feci una — a Roma*, I paid a flying visit to Rome **4.** (*colpo*) thrust; stab **5.** (*il puntare del cane*) pointing **6.** (*aer.*) (*picchiata*) nose-dive **7.** (*mil.*): *— offensiva*, reconnaissance in force.

puntatóre, *s.m.* **1.** (*mil.*) layer, marksman (*pl.* marksmen): *— in direzione*, (*mar.*) trainer **2.** (*al giuoco*) better.

punteggiaménto, *s.m.* **1.** (*il punteggiare*) dotting **2.** (*punti*) dots (*pl.*).

punteggiàre, *v.t.* **1.** (*gram.*) to punctuate **2.** (*pitt.*) to dot.

punteggiàto, *ag.* **1.** (*gram.*) punctuated: *il tuo compito è — male*, your work is badly punctuated **2.** (*sparso di puntini*) dotted: *— di rosso*, dotted with red; *linea punteggiata*, dotted line.

punteggiatúra, *s.f.* **1.** (*gram.*) punctuation: *segni di —*, punctuation marks **2.** (*macchiettatura*) dotting.

puntéggio, *s.m.* **1.** (*gram.*) punctuation **2.** (*pitt.*) dotting **3.** (*spor.*) score: *la squadra totalizzò un buon —*, the team made a good score.

puntellàre, *v.t.* **1.** to prop (up), to buttress, to shore (up), to support: *— un muro*, to shore up (o to buttress) a wall; *— un ramo con un bastone*, to prop up (o to support) a branch with a stick **2.** *fig.* (*sostenere*) to back (up): *questa azienda è puntellata dalla banca*, this firm is backed by the bank ‖ **puntellàrsi**, *v.r.* **1.** to barricade oneself in **2.** *fig.* (*cercare appoggi*) to look for support.

puntellatúra, *s.f.* propping, buttressing, shoring; (*effetto del puntellare*) support: *— di sostegno*, (*edil.*) crib.

puntèllo, *s.m.* **1.** prop, buttress, shore, support, stay: *— di bacino*, (*mar.*) bilge-block; *— metallico allungabile*, pack-prop **2.** *fig.* (*appoggio, sostegno*) prop, support.

puntería, *s.f.* **1.** (*mec.*) tappet **2.** (*mil.*) laying (a gun).

punteruòlo, *s.m.* **1.** drift, (prick-)punch **2.** (*lesina*) awl **3.** (*entom.*) weevil.

puntíglio, *s.m.* punctilio (*pl.* punctilios); (*ostinazione*) obstinacy, stubbornness: *per —*, out of pique (o out of spite o in a fit of pique): *per — non si fece più vedere da noi*, out of pique he did not come to see us any more; *non si tratta che di un —*, it is nothing but obstinacy.

puntigliosaménte, *av.* punctiliously; (*ostinatamente*) obstinately.

puntiglióso, *ag.* punctilious; (*ostinato*) obstinate: *carattere —*, obstinate character (o disposition).

puntína, *s.f.* **1.** (*da grammofono*) (gramophone) needle **2.** (*da disegno*) drawing-pin **3.** (*mec.*) point: *— di candela*, spark-plug point.

puntíno, *s.m.* dot: *puntini di sospensione*, dots ‖ *a —*, precisely: *cotto a —*, done to a turn; *fare qlco. a —*, to do sthg. properly ‖ *mettere i puntini sugli i*, to dot one's i's (and cross one's t's).

púnto[1], *s.m.* **1.** point: *— cardinale*, cardinal point; *— cieco*, (*anat.*) blind spot; *— critico*, (*fis. geog. mar.*) critical point; *— di accensione*, (*chim. fis.*) fire (o burning) point; *— di appoggio*, (*edil.*) point of support; (*fis.*) fulcrum (*pl.* fulcra); *— di arresto*, (*fis.*) stop; *— di combustione*, (*fis.*) ignition-point; *— di congelamento*, (*fis.*) freezing-point; *— di contatto*, (*mec.*) point of contact; *— di cottura*, cooking-point; *— di ebollizione*, boiling-point; *— di equilibrio*, (*fis.*) balance -point; (*chim.*) end-point; *— di fusione*, melting-point; *— di intersezione*, intersection-point; *— di oro*, (*finanza*) gold-point; *— di presa*, (*foto. aer.*) camera-station; *— di riferimento*, reference-point; (*aer.*) check point (o leading-mark); (*toponomastica*) starting (o datum)-point; *— di rottura*, (*fis.*) breaking-point; *— di saturazione*, (*chim. fis.*) saturation-point; *— equinoziale, solstiziale*, (*astr.*) equinoctial, solstitial point; *punti lacrimali*, (*anat.*) lacrimal points; *— limite*, (*mat.*) limit-point; *— morto*, (*mil.*) dead angle; (*mec.*)

dead point (o centre); (*rad.*) dead spot; *messa a —*, set-up; (*ott.*) focus; *fig.* restatement: *messa a — di una questione*, restatement of a question; *mettere a —*, to set up; (*ott.*) to focus; *fig.* to restate: *mettere a — una questione*, to restate (o to formulate) a question ‖ *— debole*, weak point: *il nuoto è un mio — debole*, swimming is not one of my strong points ‖ *— di vista*, point of view (o viewpoint): *sotto tutti i punti di vista*, from all points of view (o in all respects); *non afferro il tuo —*, I don't catch your point ‖ *di tutto — : vestito di tutto —*, completely dressed; *l'appartamento è arredato di tutto —*, the flat is fitted out with everything **2.** (*argomento, questione*) point: *— è che dovresti lavorare di più*, the point is that you should work harder; *hai ragione su tutti i punti*, you are right on every point; *ne fa un — d'onore, di coscienza*, he makes it a point of honour, conscience; *questo è il —*, this is the point; *questo è il — da far rilevare*, this is the point to emphasize; *questo è il — principale dell'argomento*, this is the main point of the subject; *sta al —*, do not stray (o wander) from the point; *su questo — sono completamente d'accordo*, I quite agree on this point; *vieni al —*, come to the point; *chiarire un —*, to clear up a point **3.** (*dettaglio*) detail, point: *avevo trascurato questo —*, I had overlooked this detail (o point); *l'abbiamo considerato — per —*, we have considered it in detail (o point by point) **4.** (*momento*) point, moment: *a un certo —*, at a certain moment; *a questo — smise di parlare*, at this point he stopped talking; *siamo arrivati al — giusto*, we arrived at the right moment ‖ *alle 10 in —*, at ten o'clock sharp ‖ *in — di morte*, at the point of death ‖ *per un — non cadde nel fiume*, he almost (o he all but) fell into the river ‖ *essere sul — di fare qlco.*, to be on the point of doing (o to be about to do) sthg. **5.** (*luogo*) point, place, spot: situation: *— di arrivo*, point (o place) of arrival; *— di osservazione*, lookout-point; *— di partenza*, starting-point (o point of departure); *da questo — si ha una bellissima vista della baia*, from this point you get a wonderful view of the bay; *la villa è in un bellissimo —*, the villa is beautifully situated **6.** (*posizione*) position: *il — del sole all'orizzonte*, the sun's position on the horizon; *fare il —*, (*mar.*) to determine the ship's position (o to take the ship's bearings) ‖ *a che — è il tuo lavoro?*, how far have you got with your work?; *a che — siamo?*, where are we? (o where have we got to?); *l'affare è a questo —*, the business has got to this point; *al — in cui stanno le cose...*, as matters stand...; *le cose sono a buon —*, things are going on satisfactorily; *le cose sono al — di prima*, things stand as before; *sono a buon —*, I have made good progress **7.** (*grado*) degree, extent: *a tal — che...*, to such a pass (o pitch) that... (o to such a point that...); *fino a un certo —*, to a certain extent **8.** (*gram.*): *— e a capo*, full stop and new paragraph; *— esclamativo*, exclamation mark; *— e virgola*, semicolon; *punti di sospensione*, dots; *— fermo*, full stop; *— interrogativo*, question mark; *due punti*, colon; *mettere i punti sugli i*, to dot one's i's (anche *fig.*) ‖ *per un — Martin perdè la cappa*, for want of a nail the shoe is lost ‖ *fare —*, (*fermarsi*) to stop (o to come to a full stop) **9.** (*mus.*) dot **10.** (*al cucito e nella maglia*) stitch: *— a coste*, rib-stitch; *— a croce*, cross-stitch; *— a giorno*, hem-stitch; *— catenella*, chain-stitch; *— dritto, a legaccio*, plain -stitch; *— indietro*, back-stitch; *— nascosto*, blind -stitch; *— rammendo*, darning-stitch; *— rovescio*, back-stitch (o purl); *— smerlo*, buttonhole stitch; *crescere, calare un —*, to add, to slip a stitch; *lasciar cadere un —*, to drop a stitch; *mettere su i punti*, to cast on stitches ‖ *devo dare un — al mio vestito*, I must stitch up my dress ‖ *non sa dare neanche un —*, she cannot sew a stitch ‖ *un — in tempo ne salva cento*, *prov.* a stitch in time saves nine **11.** (*chir.*) stitch: *il chirurgo mi diede tre punti*, I had three stitches **12.** (*termine scolastico*) mark: *prende sempre* *cattivi punti*, he always gets bad marks **13.** (*al giuoco*) point; (*pl.*) (*punteggio*) score: *l'asso vale dieci punti*, the ace is worth ten points (*o* scores ten); *come stiamo a punti?*, what is the score?; *ho fatto cinque punti*, I have made five points (*o* I have scored five); *fare molti punti*, to make a good score; *vincere ai punti*, (*boxe*) to win on points ‖ *in matematica egli dà dei punti a chiunque*, in mathematics he gives points to anybody ‖ *questo ragazzo ha dei punti*, this boy has good points ‖ *la sua buona volontà è un — in suo favore*, his good will is a point in his favour **14.** (*comm.*) point: *le azioni sono salite di alcuni punti*, the shares have gone up a few points **15** (*tip.*) point **16.** (*passo di libro*) passage **17.** (*articolo, parte di trattato, ecc.*) head **18.** (*macchiolina*) dot: *la nave era come un — all'orizzonte*, the ship was like a dot on the horizon **19.** — *nero*, (*comedone*) comedo (*pl.* comedones) **20.** (*di colore*) shade, degree: *è un bel — di verde*, it's a nice shade of green.

púnto², *ag.* (*dial.*): *non... —*, not... any (*o* no): *non ho punta voglia di uscire con te*, I have no (*o* I haven't any) wish to go out with you ‖ *pron.* (*dial.*): *non... —*, not... any (*o* none): « *Hai dei libri?* », « *Non ne ho punti* », "Have you any books? ", " I have none " (*o* " I haven't any ") ‖ *av.: non... —*, not... at all (*o* not at all): *non l'ho visto —*, I haven't seen him at all; *non sono — soddisfatto di lui*, I am not at all satisfied with him ‖ *non è — nè poco*, nothing at all; *poco o —*, little or nothing (at all).

puntofrànco, *s.m.* **1.** (*territorio esente da imposte doganali*) duty-free area **2.** (*deposito doganale*) bonded warehouse.

puntóne, *s.m.* **1.** (*edil.*) strut; (*di capriata in legno*) principal rafter, strut: — *d'angolo*, hip-rafter; *falso —*, (common) rafter **2.** (*mil.*) (*formazione di battaglia a cuneo*) arrow-head formation; (*saliente*) salient.

puntuàle, *ag.* **1.** punctual: — *a consegnare, nei pagamenti*, punctual in delivery, in payments; *treno —*, punctual train **2.** (*rar.*) (*di cosa fatta con scrupolosità*) precise, exact: *lavoro —*, precise work.

puntualità, *s.f.* punctuality: — *abituale*, usual punctuality; — *nei pagamenti*, punctuality in payments; *richiedere —*, to exact punctuality.

puntualménte, *av.* punctually.

puntuazióne, *s.f.* (*rar.*) (*interpunzione*) punctuation.

puntúra, *s.f.* **1.** (*di insetto*) sting; bite; (*di spina, ago, ecc.*) prick: — *di pulce*, flea-bite; — *di vespa, di ape*, bee-sting, wasp-sting; — *velenosa*, poisonous sting **2.** (*iniezione*) injection: *fare una — a qlcu.*, to give s.o. an injection **3.** (*dolore acuto*) shooting pain: *sentì una — in una spalla*, he felt a shooting pain in one shoulder **4.** *fig.* pain: — *che gli trafisse il cuore*, pain which pierced his heart.

puntúto, *ag.* pointed.

punzecchiaménto, *s.m.* **1.** (*di insetti*) stinging; biting; (*di spina, ago, ecc.*) pricking **2.** *fig.* (*molestamento*) teasing.

punzecchiàre, *v.t.* **1.** (*di insetti*) to sting; to bite; (*di spina, ago*) to prick: *fui punzecchiato da una zanzara*, I was bitten by a mosquito; *una vespa, un'ape lo punzecchiò*, a wasp, a bee stung him; — *un dito*, to prick a finger **2.** *fig.* (*molestare*) to tease: *smettila di punzecchiarlo*, stop teasing him ‖ **punzecchiàrsi**, *v.r.* reciproco to tease each other (one another).

punzecchiatúra, *s.f.* **1.** (*di insetti*) stinging; biting; (*di spina, ago, ecc.*) pricking: *la — di un'ape, di una vespa*, the stinging of a bee, of a wasp; *la — di una zanzara, di una pulce*, the biting of a mosquito, of a flea **2.** (*traccia di puntura*) sting; bite; (*di spina, ago, ecc.*) prick: *mi sono svegliato con molte punzecchiature di zanzare*, I woke up with a lot of mosquito-bites **3.** *fig.* (*molestamento*) teasing.

punzonàre, *v.t.* (*mec.*) to punch, to stamp.

punzonatóre, *ag.* punching ‖ *s.m.* puncher.

punzonatríce, *s.f.* **1.** puncher **2.** (*macchina*) punch,

punching-machine, punching-press: — *a mano*, hand metal-punch; — *per occhielli*, eyelet-punch.

punzonatúra, *s.f.* (*mec.*) punching; (*fucinatura*) piercing: — *cava*, (*mec.*) trepanning.

punzóne, *s.m.* **1.** (*mec.*) drift, (prick-) punch, drift-pin; (*di fucinatrice*) header, heading-tool: — *a forare*, piercing-punch; — *a tranciare*, blanking-punch; — *di ricalcatura*, heading-tool (*o* punch); — *per incassare chiodi*, nail-punch **2.** (*oreficeria*) pusher: — *autocentrante*, self-centring pusher **3.** (*pugno*) punch.

punzonísta, *s.c.* punch-cutter, puncher.

púpa, *s.f.* **1.** (*di insetto*) pupa (*pl.* pupae) **2.** (*fam.*) (*bambina*) little girl; (*molto piccola*) baby **3.** (*ragazza*) doll.

pupàrio, *s.m.* (*scient.*) puparium (*pl.* puparia); (*bozzolo*) cocoon.

pupàttola, *s.f.* **1.** doll: *ha un viso di —*, she has a doll's face **2.** (*bambina piccola*) little girl.

pupazzettàre, *v.t.* **1.** (*caricaturare*) to caricature **2.** (*illustrare con pupazzetti*) to illustrate with sketches.

pupazzétto, *s.m.* sketch; caricature.

pupàzzo, *s.m.* puppet.

pupílla¹, *s.f.* (*anat.*) pupil ‖ *con le pupille asciutte*, with dry eyes (*o* dry-eyed) ‖ *essere la — degli occhi di qlcu.*, *fig.* to be the apple of s.o.'s eye.

pupílla², *s.f.* (*dir.*) female pupil, female ward.

pupillàre¹, *ag.* (*anat.*) pupillar(y).

pupillàre², *ag.* (*dir.*) pupillary.

pupíllo, *s.m.* (*dir.*) ward, pupil ‖ *essere fuori dei pupilli*, to be of age; *uscire dai pupilli*, to come of age ‖ *essere messo nei pupilli*, (*essere interdetto*) to be suspended.

púpo, *s.m.* **1.** puppet **2.** (*fam.*) (*bambino*) baby.

puraménte, *av.* **1.** purely **2.** (*semplicemente*) merely, simply **3.** (*solamente*) only.

purché, *cong.* **1.** provided (that), on condition that: — *tu mi faccia questo favore...*, provided you do me this favour...; *accetto, — possa un giorno fare altrettanto per te*, I accept, but only on condition that you will let me do the same thing for you one day **2.** (*ottativo*) if only: — *venga!*, if only he would come!.

purchessía, *ag.* any, any ... whatever; of any kind (*predicativo*): *un abito —*, (*fam.*) any old dress; *un colore —*, any colour (whatever); *in un modo —*, anyhow ‖ *av.* at random; (*fam.*) any old how: *è pettinata —*, her hair is anyhow (*o fam.* any old how); *sceglie i suoi abiti —*, she chooses her clothes at random.

púre¹, *av.* **1.** (*anche*) also, too; as well: *tu —*, you too; *come — sapevamo che..*, we also knew that...; *verrò io —*, I shall come too; *vidi lui —*, I saw him as well; *vi è — un giardino*, there is also a garden ‖ *non —*, (*non solo*) not only ‖ *quando —, se —*, even if: *se — me l'avessero detto, che cosa avrei potuto fare?*, even if they had told me, what could I have done? ‖ *pur studiando, ascoltava la radio*, while she was studying, she listened to the radio ‖ *dovessi pur rimetterci la vita, lo farò*, I'll do it, if it kills me (*o* if it is the last thing I do); *non lo vorrei fosse pur d'oro*, I wouldn't have it at any price **2.** (*tuttavia, eppure*) but, yet; still, however: *è molto povero, — non si lamenta mai*, he is very poor, but (*o* yet) he never complains; (*ma*) — *non posso crederci!*, however, I can't believe it!; *tutto questo è vero, — non credo che tu abbia ragione*, all this is quite true; however (*o* still) I don't think you are right **3.** (*con valore concessivo*) certainly, please, of course; as you like: *fa —*, please do (*o* certainly *o* of course *o* by all means); *faglielo — sapere, a me non importa*, tell him if you like, I don't care; *vieni, entra —*, please (*o* do) come in; *vieni — quando vuoi*, of course, come when you like **4.** (*enfatico, intensivo*): *bisogna pur campare*, you have got to live; *credi — che è un mascalzone*, believe me, he is a rascal; *è pur bello fare una passeggiata in campagna!*, how nice it is to go for a walk in the country!; *è pur vero che la Svizzera è un bel paese!*, how true it is that Switzerland is a beautiful country! || *senza pur fiatare*, without a word || **pur di**, *l. cong.* if only: — *di vederla, farebbe qualsiasi cosa*, he would do anything, if only he could see her; *farebbe qualsiasi cosa pur di riuscire gradito ai superiori*, he would do anything to ingratiate himself with his superiors.

purè[2], *s.m.* (*cuc.*) mash, purée; — *di patate*, mashed potatoes; *fare un — di verdura*, to mash vegetables.

purézza, *s.f.* purity, pureness: *la — dell'aria*, the pureness of the air; — *del cielo*, clearness of the sky; — *di propositi*, purity of purpose; — *di stile, linguaggio*, purity of style, of language.

púrga, *s.f.* laxative, purgative.

purgànte, *ag.s.m.* laxative, purgative.

purgàre, *v.t.* 1. to purge 2. (*purificare*) to purge; to purify: *purga la tua mente dai cattivi pensieri*, purge your mind of evil thoughts; — *l'anima, la mente dal male, dal peccato*, to purge one's soul, mind of evil, sin; — *l'aria, il sangue dalle impurità*, to purify the air, the blood; — *il linguaggio dai barbarismi*, to purge the language of barbarisms 3. (*eccl.*) (*espiare*) to expiate 4. (*scritti*) to expurgate: — *un libro*, to expurgate a book 5. (*nettare*) to clean; (*da erbacce*) to weed || **purgàrsi**, *v.r.* 1. to purge oneself 2. (*purificarsi*) to purge oneself, to purify oneself 3. (*giustificarsi*) to clear oneself: — *di un'accusa*, to clear oneself of a charge.

purgàta, *s.f.* purging; purge.

purgatézza, *s.f.* (*di stile, linguaggio*) purity.

purgatívo, *ag.* laxative, purgative: *pastiglie purgative*, laxative tablets.

purgàto, *ag.* 1. (*depurato*) purged 2. (*castigato, puro*) purified: *stile* —, purified style 3. (*di libro*) expurgated.

purgatòrio, *ag.* purgatorial || *s.m.* purgatory: *le anime del* —, the souls in purgatory.

purgazióne, *s.f.* 1. cleansing, purging 2. (*purificazione*) purgation, purification 3. (*eccl.*) (*espiazione*) expiation 4. (*dir.*) (*di ipoteche, debiti*) redemption.

purificàre, *v.t.* to purify, to cleanse, to purge (anche *fig.*): — *l'anima, il cuore, la mente dal peccato*, to purge one's soul, heart, mind of sin; — *l'aria di una stanza*, to purify the air of a room; — *il sangue, un liquido*, to purify the blood, a liquid || **purificàrsi**, *v.r.* to purify oneself (of sthg.).

purificatívo, *ag.* purifying, purificatory.

purificàto, *ag.* purified, cleansed, purged (anche *fig.*).

purificatóio, *s.m.* (*eccl.*) purificator.

purificatóre, *ag.* purificatory, purifying || *s.m.*, **purificatríce**, *s.f.* purifier.

purificazióne, *s.f.* 1. purification 2. *la Purificazione*, (*eccl.*) the Purification of the Blessed Virgin Mary (*o* Candlemas).

purísmo, *s.m.* purism.

purísta, *s.c.* purist.

purità, *s.f.* purity, pureness: — *d'animo*, purity of mind.

puritaneggiànte, *ag.* puritanical.

puritanésimo, puritanísmo, *s.m.* (*st. relig.*) Puritanism (anche *fig.*).

puritàno, *s.m.* (*st. relig.*) Puritan (anche *fig.*).

púro, *ag.* 1. pure: — *di mente*, pure in mind; *acqua, aria pura*, pure water, air; *alcool, oro* —, pure alcohol, gold; *anima, vita pura*, pure soul, life; *lana, seta pura*, pure wool, silk; *linguaggio, stile* —, pure language, style: *parla nel più — inglese*, he speaks the purest English; *razza pura*, pure breed; *scienza, arte, matematica pura*, pure science, art, mathematics; *vino, cognac* —, neat wine, brandy 2. (*casto*) chaste: *una ragazza pura*, a chaste girl 3. (*sgombro*) clear: *cielo* —, clear sky; *coscienza pura*, clear conscience 4. (*mero, semplice*) mere, sheer: *il — necessario*, what is strictly necessary; *pura pazzia*, sheer (*o* mere) madness; *la pura verità*, the plain truth; *per — caso*, by mere chance.

purosàngue, *s.m.* thoroughbred.

purpúreo, *ag.* deep red; purple: *manto* —, purple mantle.

purpúrico, *ag.* (*chim.*) purpuric.

purtròppo, *av.* unfortunately: — *è già andato via*, unfortunately he has already gone.

purulènto, *ag.* (*med.*) purulent.

purulènza, *s.f.* (*med.*) purulence, purulency.

pus, *s.m.* (*med.*) pus.

puseísmo, *s.m.* (*st.relig.*) Puseyism.

puseísta, *s.c.* (*st. relig.*) Puseyite.

pusillànime, *ag.* pusillanimous, faint-hearted, cowardly: *uomo* —, pusillanimous man || *s.m.* coward.

pusillanimaménte, *av.* pusillanimously, faint-heartedly.

pusillanimità, *s.f.* pusillanimity, faint-heartedness, cowardice.

pusillità, *s.f.* (*letter.*) 1. (*meschinità*) meanness 2. (*pusillanimità*) pusillanimity.

pusillo, *ag.* 1. (*meschino*) mean 2. (*pusillanime*) pusillanimous || *s.m.* (*letter.*) 1. (*persona meschina*) mean person 2. (*pusillanime*) coward.

pústa, *s.f.* "Puszta" (Hungarian prairie land).

pustèrla, *s.f.* (*st.*) postern.

pústola, *s.f.* (*med.*) pustule; pimple: — *maligna*, malignant pustule.

pustolóso, *ag.* (*med.*) pustulous; pimply.

putacàso, *cong.* suppose, supposing: — *non venisse* supposing he did not come.

putativaménte, *av.* putatively.

putatívo, *ag.* putative: *padre* —, putative father.

puteàle, *s.m.* (*archeol.*) puteal.

Putifàrre, *no.pr.m.* (*Bibbia*) Potiphar.

putifèrio, *s.m.* hubbub, uproar, row, shindy: *sollevare un* —, to make an uproar (*o fam.* to kick up a shindy *o* to kick up a row).

putíre, *v.i.* (*rar.*) to stink.

putrèdine, *s.f.* 1. rottenness, putridity, putridness (anche *fig.*) 2. (*cosa putrefatta*) rot.

putrefàre, *v.i.*, **putrefàrsi**, *v.r.* to putrify, to rot, to decay, to decompose, to go bad.

putrefàtto, *ag.* putrefied, rotten.

putrefazióne, *s.f.* putrefaction, decomposition: *in stato di avanzata* —, in an advanced state of decomposition.

putrèlla, *s.f.* (*edil.*) iron beam, steel beam.

putrescènte, *ag.* putrescent.

putrescènza, *s.f.* (*rar.*) putrescence.

putrescíbile, *ag.* putrescible.

putridità, *s.f.* putridity, putridness, rottenness.

pútrido, *ag.* 1. putrid, rotten (anche *fig.*): *acqua putrida*, putrid (*o* tainted) water 2. *fermentazione putrida*, (*chim.*) putrefactive fermentation || *s.m.* corruption: *vi è del — in questo paese*, something is rotten in this country.

putridúme, *s.m.* rot; filth (anche *fig.*).

puttàna, *s.f.* harlot, whore; (*sl.*) tart.

pútto, *s.m.* putto (*pl.* putti).

púzza, *V.* púzzo.

puzzàre, *v.i.* to stink, to smell bad, to have a bad smell: *puzza di acido, di marcio*, it smells sour, rotten; *questa carne puzza*, this meat stinks; — *di vino, aglio, naftalina*, to smell of wine, garlic, naphtaline (*o* to smell of a liquid); — *d'avaro*, to reek of avarice: *si sente dalla sua condotta puzza d'avaro*, judging by his behaviour, you can smell the miser in him || *a ognuno puzza essere deriso*, everybody dislikes being laughed at || *mi puzza*, (*ho il sospetto di ql.co.*) I smell a rat || *ti puzza la salute, il denaro?*, why do you waste your health, your money?.

púzzo, *s.m.* stink, stench, bad smell: *che* —*!*, what a horrible smell (*o* stench)!; *c'è — di pesce marcio*, there is a stench of rotten fish.

púzzola, *s.f.* (*zool.*) polecat, fitchet, fitchew.

puzzolènte, *ag.* stinking, bad-smelling.

puzzolenteménte, *av.* stinkingly.

puzzóne, *s.m.* (*volg.*) 1. stinking fellow; bad-smelling person 2. (*persona spregevole*) skunk 3. (*persona schizinosa*) fussy person, fastidious person.

Q

q, *s.f.m.* (*quindicesima lettera dell'alfabeto italiano*) q (*pl.* qs, q's) ‖ — *come Quarto*, (*tel.*) q for Queenie.

qua, *av.* **1.** here; (*rar.*) (*con movimento*) **hither:** — *e là*, here and there: *correvano — e là*, they ran here and there (*o rar.* they ran hither and thither); *eccomi* —, here I am; *vieni* —, come here; *voglio questo* —, I want this one (here) ‖ — *dentro, fuori*, in here, out here; — *giù, su*, down here, up here ‖ — *la mano*, let's shake hands ‖ *di* —, (over) here; (*da questa parte, da questo lato*) on this side: *vieni di — un momento*, come (over) here for a minute ‖ *di — di, al di — di*, on this side of: (*al*) *di — delle Alpi*, on this side of the Alps ‖ *il mondo di —*, this world ‖ *per di —*, this way: *prendete per di —*, go this way ‖ — *ti voglio!*, now I'll see what you are made of! ‖ *da'* —, give it to me ‖ *essere più di là che di —*, to be at one's last gasp **2.** (*in espressioni di tempo*): *da un anno in* —, for the last year (or so); *da un po' di tempo in* —, for some time now; *da quando in —?*, since when?.

quàcchera, quàcquera, *s.f.* (*st. relig.*) Quakeress. **quaccherísmo, quacquerísmo**, *s.m.* (*st. relig.*) Quakerism.

quàcchero, quàcquero, *s.m.* (*st. relig.*) Quaker. **quadèrna**, *V.* **quatèrna**.

quadernàccio, *s.m.* rough work book.

quadernàrio, *V.* **quaternàrio**.

quadèrno, *s.m.* **1.** exercise-book, copy-book **2.** (*nell'antica arte della stampa*) quire.

quàdra, *s.f.* **1.** (*mar.*) square sail: *alla* —, square-rigged **2.** (*astr.*) quadrant; fourth part of the meridian **3.** *dare la — a qlcu.*, (*metterlo in ridicolo*) to hold s.o. up to ridicule.

quadràbile, *ag.* quadrable.

quadragenàrio, *ag.s.m.* quadragenarian.

quadragèsima, *s.f.* (*eccl.*) Quadragesima: *domenica di* —, Quadragesima Sunday.

quadragesimàle, *ag.* (*rar.*) quadragesimal.

quadragèsimo, *ag.num.ord. s.m.* fortieth.

quadrangolàre, *ag.* quadrangular.

quadràngolo, *ag.* quadrangular ‖ *s.m.* (*geom.*) quadrangle.

quadrànte, *s.m.* **1.** (*geom. astr.*) quadrant **2.** (*di orologio*) dial; clock-face **3.** — (*solare*), sun-dial.

quadràre, *v.t.* **1.** (*geom.*) to square, to quadrate: — *il cerchio*, to square the circle **2.** (*adattare*) to square, to adjust: *non posso — le mie azioni ai tuoi principi*, I cannot square my actions to your principles **3.** (*formare*) to shape: *lo studio dell'aritmetica quadra la mente del bambino*, the study of arithmetics shapes the mind of a child ‖ *v.i.* **1.** (*convenire*) to suit (s.o., sthg.), to fit: *le mie teorie quadrano con le tue*, my theories fit in with yours; *quel nome non gli quadra affatto*, that name doesn't suit him at all **2.** (*piacere, garbare*) to like (*costruzione pers.*): *il suo modo di comportarsi non mi quadra*, I do not like the way he behaves.

quadratamènte, *av.* squarely.

quadràto, *ag.* **1.** square: *due miglia quadrate*, two square miles; *metro* —, square metre; *un pezzo di carta, un tavolo* —, a square piece of paper, table **2.** *radice quadrata*, (*mat.*) square root **3.** (*robusto*) square, square-built: *spalle quadrate*, square (-built) shoulders: *dalle spalle quadrate*, square-shouldered **4.** (*ben formato*) strong, sound: *un carattere* —, a strong (o sound) character; *mente quadrata*, strong mind: *dalla mente*

quadrata, strong-minded; *un uomo* —, a sound man ‖ *s.m.* **1.** (*geom.*) square: *un — ha quattro lati*, a square has four sides ‖ — *ufficiali*, (*mar.*) wardroom **2.** (*mat.*) square: *il — di un numero*, the square of a number; *espressione al* —, quadratic; *elevare un numero al* —, to square a number **3.** (*mil.*) square **4.** (*boxe*) ring **5.** (*tip.*) quad.

quadratúra, *s.f.* squaring; (*geom. astr.*) quadrature: *la — del circolo*, the squaring of the circle: *trovare la — del circolo*, *fig.* to square the circle ‖ *in* —, (*elett.*) wattless (o in quadrature).

quadrèllo, *s.m.*; *pl.f.* **quadrèlla** (*nel senso 5*); *pl.m.* **quadrèlli** (*negli altri sensi*) **1.** (*mattonella quadrata*) square tile **2.** (*ago da imballatore*) packing-needle **3.** (*arnese quadrangolare per rigare*) square ruler **4.** (*arch.*) quarrel **5.** (*poet.*) (*freccia, dardo*) quarrel.

quadrería, *s.f.* (*rar.*) (*pinacoteca*) picture gallery.

quadrettàre, *v.t.* to divide into squares; (*tessuti*) to chequer.

quadrettàto, *ag.* squared; (*di tessuti*) chequered.

quadricíclo, *s.m.* quadricycle.

quadricípite, *s.m.* (*anat.*) quadriceps.

quadricromía, *s.f.* (*foto. tip.*) four-colour process.

quadriennàle, *ag.* quadrennial.

quadriènnio, *s.m.* quadrennium (*pl.* quadrennia).

quadrifòglio, *ag.* four-leaved ‖ *s.m.* **1.** four-leaved clover **2.** (*stradale*) clover-leaf **3.** (*arch.*) quatrefoil.

quadrifórme, *ag.* quadriform.

quadrifrónte, *ag.* quadrifrons.

quadríga, *s.f.* quadriga (*pl.* quadrigae).

quadrigàrio, *s.m.* quadriga driver.

quadrigàto, *s.m.* (*moneta romana*) quadrigatus (*pl.* quadrigati).

quadrigèmino, *ag.* quadrigeminal, quadrigeminous ‖ *parto* —, delivery of quadruplets.

quadríglia, *s.f.* (*musica e danza*) quadrille.

quadrilàtero, *ag.* four-sided, quadrilateral ‖ *s.m.* (*geom. mil.*) quadrilateral.

quadrilíngue, *ag.* quadrilingual.

quadrilióne, *s.m.* **1.** (*secondo l'uso italiano, americano e francese, corrispondente a 1000⁵*) a thousand billion; (*amer.*) quadrillion **2.** (*secondo l'uso tedesco e inglese, corrispondente a 1000⁸*) quadrillion; (*amer.*) septillion.

quadrilobàto, *ag.* quadrilobate.

quadrilústre, *ag.* twenty years old (*predicativo*); twenty-year-old (*attributivo*).

quadrimèstre, *s.m.* period of four months.

quadrimotóre, *s.m.* (*aer.*) four-engined aircraft.

quadrinòmio, *s.m.* (*alg.*) quadrinomial.

quadripartíre, *v.t.* to divide into four parts.

quadripartíto, *ag.* divided into four parts; quadripartite: *un trattato* —, (*pol.*) a quadripartite treaty.

quadriplegía, *s.f.* (*patol.*) quadriplegia.

quadrirème, *s.f.* (*st. mar.*) quadrireme.

quadrisíllabo, *ag.* quadrisyllabic, tetrasyllabic ‖ *s.m.* (*poes.*) quadrisyllable, tetrasyllable.

quadrívio, *s.m.* **1.** cross-roads (*pl.*) **2.** (*nella scuola medioevale*) quadrivium (*pl.* quadrivia).

quàdro, *ag. V.* **quadràto** 1. 3. ‖ *s.m.* **1.** picture (anche *fig.*), painting; (*descrizione*) description: — *a olio*, oil-painting; *i quadri di Van Gogh*, Van Gogh's pictures; *quadri murali*, mural paintings (o murals); *galleria di quadri*, picture-gallery; *ha molti bei quadri*, he has many fine pictures; *mi fece un terribile — della situazione*, he gave me a terrible picture of the situation; *questo è il — della situazione*, this is how things are; *questo libro è un bellissimo — della vita del secolo scorso*, this book is a wonderful description of life in the last century; *dipingere un —*, to paint a picture ‖ *quadri plastici, viventi*, tableaux vivants **2.** (*figura quadrata*) square: *a quadri*, chequered: *vorrei un disegno a quadri*, I should like a check (pattern) **3.** (*vista, spettacolo*) sight: *che — commovente!*, what a moving sight! **4.** (*tabella*) table: *— riassuntivo*, summary; *— sinottico*, synoptic table **5.** (*teat. cine.*) scene **6.** (*mil.*) cadre: *i quadri dell'esercito*, the cadres of the army; *il — del reggimento*, the regimental cadre **7.** (*elett.*) board, panel; (*tv.*) frame, raster: *— a pulsanti*, (*elett.*) press-button board; *— degli interruttori*, (*elett.*) switch-board; *— degli strumenti*, (*aut.*) instrument board (*o* cluster) **8.** *pl.* (*carte*) diamonds **9.** *— di poppa*, (*mar.*) upper stern.

quadrúccio, *s.m.* (*finestra di proiettore cinematografico*) film-trap, film-gate.

quadrúmane, *ag.* (*zool.*) quadrumanous ‖ *s.m.* (*zool.*) quadruman(e) ‖ *i quadrumani*, the Quadrumana.

quadrumviràto, *s.m.* quadrumvirate, quadrivirate.

quadrúmviro, *s.m.* quadrumvir (*pl.* quadrumviri).

quadrúpede, *ag.s.m.* (*zool.*) quadruped.

quadruplicàre, *v.t.* to quadruple; to quadruplicate; to multiply by four ‖ **quadruplicàrsi**, *v.r.* to quadruple.

quadruplicazióne, *s.f.* quadruplication.

quadrúplice, *ag.* quadruple(x), fourfold ‖ *la Quadruplice Alleanza*, (*st.*) the Quadruple Alliance.

quadruplicità, *s.f.* quadruplicity.

quàdruplo, *ag.* quadruple ‖ *s.m.* quadruple; (*quattro volte tanto*) four times as much: *egli guadagna il — di me*, he earns four times as much as I do.

quàgga, *s.f.* (*zool.*) quagga.

quaggiú, *av.* **down here**: *siamo — in cantina*, we are down here in the cellar ‖ *le cose di —*, things of this world ‖ *— abbiamo avuto una bellissima estate*, here in the South we've had a lovely summer.

quàglia, *s.f.* (*ornit.*) quail.

quagliaménto, *s.m.* curdling.

quagliàre, *v.t.i.*, **quagliàrsi**, *v.r.* to curdle.

quagliàta, *s.f.* curds (*pl.*); (*giuncata*) junket.

quaglière, *s.m.* (*richiamo per le quaglie*) quail-pipe, quail-call.

quàglio, *s.m.* rennet.

quai, *s.m.* **1.** (*banchina lungo un fiume*) embarkment **2.** (*ferr.*) (*marciapiede*) platform **3.** (*mar.*) (*banchina di scarico*) quay, wharf.

quàlche, *ag.indef.* **1.** (*un certo numero di*) **a few; some** (*in proposizioni affermative; in proposizioni interrogative quando si attende risposta affermativa e nelle formule di cortesia*); **any** (*in proposizioni interrogative*): *— anno fa*, some (*o* a few) years ago; *— cosa*, *V.* **qualcòsa**; *— volta*, sometimes; *fra — minuto*, in a few minutes; *c'è — lettera per me?*, are there any letters for me?; *dàgli — consiglio, informazione*, give him some advice, some information; *hai avuto — difficoltà?*, have you had any difficulty?; *mi portò — libro*, he brought me a few (*o* some) books; *posso prendere — fiore?*, may I take some flowers?; *sono qui da — ora*, I have been here (for) a few (*o* some) hours; *starò qui — giorno*, I shall stay here a few (*o* some) days; *vuoi — rivista?*, do you want some magazines? **2.** (*una certa quantità di*) **some**, **a certain amount of**: *ci vuole — tempo per abituarcisi*, it takes a certain amount of (*o* some) time to get used to it; *non si vede da — tempo*, we have not seen him for some time **3.** (*quale che sia*) **some** (**...or other**) (*in proposizioni affermative; in proposizioni interrogative quando si attende risposta affermativa e nelle formule di cortesia*); **any** (*in proposizioni interrogative*): *— giorno*, some day: *verrò — giorno*, I shall come some day (*o* some-

time); *in — luogo*, somewhere (or other); anywhere: *deve esserci una bottiglia di whisky in — luogo*, there must be a bottle of whisky somewhere; *l'hai visto in — luogo?*, have you seen him anywhere?; *non l'ho già vista prima in — luogo?*, haven't I seen you before somewhere (*o* some place?); *in — altro luogo*, somewhere else; anywhere else; *in — modo*, somehow (or other); *troverò — pretesto, scusa*, I'll find some pretext, some excuse (or other).

qualchedúno, *V.* **qualcúno**.

qualcòsa, *pron. indef.* **1. something**: *— da mangiare, da bere*, something to eat, to drink: *andiamo a prendere — da bere*, let's go and have a drink; *— di nuovo, di bello, di strano*, something new, beautiful, strange; *qualcos'altro*, something else; *c'è — di errato in questa frase*, there is something wrong in this sentence; *dite —*, say something ‖ *mille e —*, a thousand odd ‖ *— mi dice che..*, something tells me that... ‖ *crede di essere —*, he thinks he is somebody ‖ *è — nella City*, he is something in the City ‖ *è già —!*, that's something! ‖ *è un ingegnere o — di simile*, (*fam.*) he is an engineer or something ‖ *meglio — che nulla*, *prov.* little is better than nothing **2.** (*in proposizioni interrogative, dubitative e condizionali*) **anything**; (*quando si attende risposta affermativa e nelle formule di cortesia*) **something**: *c'è — alla radio?*, is there anything on the wireless?; *c'è qualcos'altro?*, is there anything else?; *posso fare — per te?*, can I do something (anything) for you?; *posso offrirti — da bere?*, will you have something to drink?; *vuoi sentire — di buffo?*, shall I tell you something funny?

qualcúno, *pron. indef.* **1.** (*in proposizioni affermative o interrogative da cui si attenda risposta affermativa*) **somebody, someone**; (*partitivo*) **some**: *— ti chiama*, somebody is calling you; *— di noi rifiutò di andare*, some of us refused to go; *c'è — alla porta*, there is somebody at the door; *che belle rose!, dammene qualcuna*, what lovely roses!, give me some; *quanti libri hai! puoi prestarmene —?*, what a lot of books you've got! can you lend me some?; *se solo conoscessi — con cui parlare!*, if only I knew someone to talk to! ‖ *qualcun altro*, somebody else ‖ *crede d'essere —*, he thinks he is somebody ‖ *ne farà qualcuna delle sue*, he will get up to one of his usual larks (o pranks) **2.** (*in proposizioni interrogative, negative, dubitative*) **anybody, anyone**; (*partitivo*) **any**: *— di voi l'ha visto?*, has any of you seen him?; *c'è — che vorrebbe andarci?*, is there anybody (o anyone) who would like to go?; *hai visto — che conosciamo?*, have you seen anybody we know?; *non riesco a trovare — che lo possa fare*, I can't find anybody who can do it; *non potresti regalarmene qualcuna?*, couldn't you give me any?; *se — di loro lo vedesse*, if any of them should see him; *se — venisse, ditegli di aspettare*, if anybody comes, tell him to wait ‖ *qualcun altro*, anybody else **3.** (*alcuni, certi*) **some, some people**; (*alcuni, pochi*) **a few**: *— è del nostro parere, altri no*, some agree with us and some disagree; *di tutti quei quadri solo — aveva pregio*, of all those pictures, only a few were of any value.

quàle, *ag.* **1.** *interr.* (*riferito a un numero limitato di cose o persone*) **which**: *— libro vuoi? questo o quello?*, which book do you want? this one or that?; *quali studenti sono stati bocciati?*, which students have failed? **2.** *interr.* (*riferito a numero indeterminato di cose o persone*) **what**: *quali libri ti piacciono?*, what books do you like?; *quali novità ci sono?*, what news?; *non puoi immaginare in quali condizioni lo trovai*, you cannot imagine what condition I found him in **3.** (*correlativo di tale*) **as**: *è — io lo lasciai*, it is as I left it; *il risultato fu — speravamo*, the result was (just) what we hoped it would be; *la situazione era (tale) — io pensavo che fosse*, the situation was just as (o just what) I thought it would be; *è tale — sua sorella*, he is just like his sister; *è tutto suo padre tale e —*, he is the spit image of his father ‖ *qual madre, tal* *figlia, prov.* like mother, like daughter **4.** (*con valore esclamativo o enfatico*) *sing.* **what (a)**; *pl.* **what:** — *errore!,* what a mistake!; — *sciocchezza!,* what nonsense!; *quali tristi pensieri!,* what sad thoughts! **5.** *indef.* (*qualunque*) **whatever:** — (*che*) *sia stata l'importanza storica di questi scritti...,* whatever historical importance these writings may have had...; *quali* (*che*) *siano i suoi difetti so che è un uomo onesto,* whatever his faults may be I know him to be an honest man **6.** *indef.* (*correlativo di quale*) (*letter.*): *qual fior purpureo, qual vermiglio,* some purple flowers, some scarlet ones; *qual uomo andava a cavallo,* — *a piedi,* some went on horseback, others on foot **7.** (*pleonastico*): *c'era una certa qual amarezza nelle sue parole,* there was a certain bitterness in his words (*o* his words were somewhat bitter) **8.** *pronominale:* *il* — *padre Cristoforo...,* he, Father Christopher...; *dette le quali cose uscì,* having said this, he went out || *un lavoro non tanto per la* —, a rather scrappy piece of work; *è una persona per la* —, he is a very straight person || *pron.* **1.** *interr.* (*riferito a un numero limitato di cose o persone*) **which:** — *di questi quadri preferisci?,* which of these pictures do you like best?; — *è il tuo amico?,* which is your friend?; *non so* — *scegliere,* I don't know which to choose **2.** *interr.* (*riferito a numero indeterminato di cose o persone*) **what:** *qual è il prezzo di questa merce?,* what is the price of these goods?; *qual è lo scopo della tua vita?,* what is your aim in life?; *non so quali siano le sue intenzioni,* I don't know what his intentions are **3.** *rel.* (*riferito a persone*) *sogg.* **who, that;** *oggetto* **who(m), that;** *obliquo* **whom;** *poss.* **whose:** *c'era un uomo il* — *gentilmente mi indicò la strada,* there was a man that (*o* who) kindly showed me the way; *coloro i quali non amano la natura devono essere senza anima,* those who do not love nature must have no soul; *una donna della* — *tutti ammirano la virtù,* a woman whose virtue everybody admires; *ecco l'uomo del* — *parlavamo,* that is the man we were speaking of (*o* of whom we were speaking); *è un uomo sul* — *si può contare,* he is a man you can rely on (*o* on whom you can rely); *non conosco la signora della* — *intendi parlare,* I don't know the lady you are referring to **4.** *rel.* (*riferito a cose o animali*) *sogg. oggetto obliquo* **which, that;** *poss.* **of which, whose:** *dov'è l'uccello del* — *abbiamo udito il canto?,* where is the bird whose song we have just heard?; *il mondo nel* — *viviamo,* the world we live in (*o* in which we live); *quelle voci, le quali si fanno udire ogni notte, mi spaventano terribilmente,* those voices, which I hear every night, scare me to death; *questa è la casa della* — *parlavamo,* this is the house (which *o* that) we were talking about; *questo è il cappello col* — *uscii ieri,* this is the hat I went out with yesterday || *la qual cosa,* which: *egli ricorse alle vie legali, la qual cosa non approvai affatto,* he took legal action, which I didn't approve at all **5.** *indef.* (*correlativo di quale*) (*letter.*): *qual qui, qual là,* some here, some there; *a* — *dà, a* — *promette,* to some he gives, to others he promises || *s.m.* (*qualità*) **quality:** *non m'importa il* — *ma il quanto,* I don't mind about the quality, it's the quantity I'm interested in || *av.* **1.** (*in qualità di*) **as:** *sono venuto* — *rappresentante di mio fratello,* I have come as my brother's representative **2.** (*poet.*) (*nelle similitudini*) **like as:** *quali muovon le onde alla sassosa riva...,* like as the waves towards the pebbled shore....

qualífica, *s.f.* **1.** qualification: — *di idoneo all'insegnamento,* teaching qualification; *con la sua* — *di dottore in legge...,* with his legal qualification...; *non so se ha le qualifiche necessarie per occupare quel posto,* I don't know if he has the necessary qualifications for that post **2.** (*titolo*) title: *si merita la* — *di miglior giocatore di bridge dell'anno,* he deserves the title of best bridge-player of the year.

qualificàbile, *ag.* qualifiable.

qualificàre, *v.t.* **1.** to qualify: *il sapore piccante lo*

qualifica come droga, its pungent taste qualifies it as a spice **2.** (*definire*) to call, to qualify: — *qlcu. come un ciarlatano,* to call s.o. a quack.

qualificativo, *ag.* qualificative, qualifying: *aggettivo* —, (*gram.*) qualifying adjective.

qualificàto, *ag.* **1.** (*abilitato*) qualified: *medico* —, qualified doctor **2.** (*abile*) skilled, skilful: *operai qualificati,* skilled workers **3.** (*dir.*) (*aggravato*) aggravated: *furto* —, aggravated theft.

qualificatóre, *ag.* qualificatory, qualifying || *s.m.* **1.** qualifier **2.** (*eccl.*) qualificator.

qualificatrice, *s.f.* qualifier.

qualificazióne, *s.f.* qualification.

qualità, *s.f.* **1.** quality, nature; (*proprietà*) property: *la* — *del clima, del suolo,* the nature of the climate, of the soil; *articolo di buona* —, (good-) quality article; *vino di prima* —, *di* — *inferiore,* choice, inferior wine; *una* — *dei diamanti è la durezza,* one of the properties (*o* qualities) of diamonds is hardness; *mi importa più la* — *che la quantità,* I care for quality rather than quantity || *gente di* —, people of quality (*o* gentlefolk) **2.** *pl.* (*doti*) qualities: *ha delle* — *che la rendono simpatica,* she has endearing qualities; *non ha le* — *richieste per quel posto,* he has not the necessary qualities for that post **3.** (*sorta, specie*) kind, sort: — *di tè,* leaf grades (of tea); *gente di ogni* —, people of all kinds; *vini di diverse* —, wines of different sorts **4.** (*ufficio, carica*) capacity: *nella sua* — *di medico,* in his capacity of doctor (*o* as a doctor); *serviva in* — *di maggiordomo,* he served as a butler; *agire in* — *di tutore,* to act in one's capacity as guardian.

qualitativo, *ag.* qualitative.

qualménte, *av.* (*rar.*) per **cóme.**

qualóra, *cong.* **in case;** (*se*) **if, in case:** — *non si potesse avvertirlo in tempo...,* if (*o* in case) they can't advise him in time...; — *piova, non usciremo,* if it rains, we won't go out; — *tu desideri ulteriori informazioni,* if (*o* in case) you require further information (*o* should you require further information); *prenderò l'ombrello* — *dovesse piovere,* I'll take my umbrella in case it rains.

qualsíasi, qualsisía, qualsivòglia, qualúnque, *ag. indef.* **1. any:** *a* — *costo,* at any cost (*o* at all costs); *a* — *prezzo,* at any price; *in* — *caso,* in any case; — *sciocco sa farlo,* any fool can do that; *sa parlare* — *lingua,* he can speak any language || — *cosa,* anything || *in* — *modo,* anyhow || *uno* — *dei due fratelli,* either of the two brothers (*o* either brother); *uno* — *di noi,* any one of us; *uno* — *te lo potrebbe dire,* anyone could tell you that **2.** (*quale che sia*) **whatever;** (*riferito a numero limitato*) **whichever:** — *siano le sue proposte, non accettarle,* whatever his proposals may be, do not accept them; *da* — *parte si voltasse non vedeva che sabbia,* whichever way he turned, he saw nothing but sand || — *cosa,* whatever: — *cosa accada, non lasciarmi,* do not leave me, whatever happens; — *cosa dica, non credergli,* whatever he may say, do not believe him **3.** (*ogni*) **every, each:** — *persona io incontrassi,* every (*o* each) person I met || — *cosa,* everything: — *cosa io faccia, secondo te sbaglio,* everything I do is wrong according to you **4.** (*posposto, gener. spreg.*) **common, ordinary:** *un uomo* —, an ordinary man; *era una stanza* —, it was just an ordinary room; *era una vecchia casa* —, it was just a common old house; *non gli si può offrire un impiego* —, we can't give him an ordinary (*o* any odd) job || *pron. indef.* (*rar.*) per **chiúnque.**

quàndo, *av.* **1. when:** — *l'hai visto l'ultima volta?,* when did you see him last?; — *verrai?,* when will you come?; *ditemi* — *verrà,* tell me when he will come || *a* — ?, when?: *a* — *le nozze?,* when will the wedding be? (*o* when is the wedding?) || *da* —?, since when? (*o* how long?): *da* — *è malato?,* how long (*o* since when) has he been ill?; *da* — *lo conosci?,* how long have you known him?; «*È sposato*», «*Davvero? Ma da* —?», "He is married ", " Really? Since when? " || *di* —*?*: *di* — *è questo giornale?*, what is the date of this newspaper?; *sai di* — *è quel palazzo?*, do you know when that palace dates from? || *di* — *in* —, from time to time (*o* now and then *o* occasionally *o* every so often): *lo vedo di* — *in* —, I see him from time to time || *fino a* —*?*, how long? (*o* till when?): *fino a* — *starai qui?*, how long will you be here? (*o* till when will you stay here?) || *per* —*?*, when?: *per* — *è la riunione?*, when is the meeting? **2.** (*enfatico*): —, *la smetti, la finirai?*, when will you stop it? (*o* when will you have done?); — *mai verrà?*, whenever is he going to arrive (*o* to get here)?; — *si dice essere fortunati!*, talk about luck!; *da* — *in qua si usa entrare in un ufficio privato senza bussare?*, since when have people been going into private offices without knocking? || *cong.* **1.** **when:** — *arrivai, egli era già partito*, when I arrived, he had already left; — *ero a scuola*, when (I was) at school; *gliene parlerò* — *lo vedrò*, I'll mention it to him when I see him; *verrà un giorno* — *ti pentirai di ciò che hai fatto*, the day will come when you will regret what you have done || *da* —, since: *ho sempre lavorato con lui da* — *venni in Italia*, I have worked with him ever since I came to Italy; *molte cose sono accadute da* — *te ne andasti*, many things have happened since you went away || *di* —, of the time when: *questi sono ricordi di* — *eravamo in Inghilterra*, these are souvenirs of the time when we were in England || *fino a* —, till (*o* until): *da ora fino a* — *sarai partito*, from now till you leave **2.** (*mentre*) **while:** *leggo sempre il giornale della sera* — *mia moglie prepara la cena*, I always read the evening paper while my wife is getting the dinner **3.** (*ogni volta che*) **whenever:** — *la gente dice quel genere di cose, si sa che non le dice sul serio*, whenever people say that sort of thing, you know they don't mean it **4.** (*con valore condiz.*) **if:** — *non foss'altro, fallo per me*, do it for me, if for no other reason; *è inutile comperarlo* — *poi non lo adoperi*, it is no use buying it if you are not going to use it || *quand'anche*, even if (*o* even though): *quand'anche lo dicesse lui, non ci crederei*, even if he were to say so himself, I should not believe it **5.** (*con valore causale*) **since; if:** — *dico che è così!*, if (*o* since) I say so!; — *è così...*, if that is the case...; — *tutti lo vogliono...*, seeing that (*o* if) everybody wants it... **6.** (*con valore avversativo*) **when:** — *perchè va a piedi* — *potrebbe andare in automobile?*, why does he walk when he could go by car? **7.** (*nel corso di una narrazione, con riferimento a circostanza inattesa*): *lo avevamo appena nominato* — *apparve sulla soglia*, no sooner had we mentioned his name than he appeared on the doorstep || *quand'ecco*, when suddenly: *quand'ecco vedemmo un punto all'orizzonte*, when suddenly we saw a dot on the horizon **8.** (*correlativo*): *quando... quando*, sometimes... sometimes: *egli arrivava sempre tardi, — con una scusa, — con un'altra*, he was always late, sometimes with one excuse, sometimes with another || *s.m.* **when:** *il come e il* —, the how and the when.

quantità, *s.f.* **1.** quantity: *il concetto di* —, the idea of quantity; *per me la qualità è più importante della* —, for me quality is more important than quantity **2.** (*quantitativo*) quantity, amount; (*gran quantità, abbondanza*) abundance: — *necessaria*, required amount; — *trascurabile*, negligible quantity (*o* amount); *piccola, gran* —, small, large quantity (*o* amount): *in gran* —, in large quantities; (*in abbondanza*) in abundance; *in piccole* —, in small quantities; *la — di lavoro che una macchina può fare*, the amount of work that a machine is capable of || *una* (*grande*) — *di*, (*con s. al sing.*) a large quantity (*o* amount) of; a great (*o* a good) deal of; a lot of; lots of; (*con s. al pl.*) a great (*o* a good) many; a lot of; lots of: *beveva una — di birra*, he drank a great quantity of beer; *c'è una — di gente che...*, there are a lot of people who... (*o* there are a great many people who...); *c'era una — di gente*, there was a large crowd; *ha una — di lettere da scrivere*, he

has a lot of letters to write; *ho una — di amici*, I have got a great many friends; *vendiamo una — di questi libri*, we sell a great many of these books **3.** (*poes. mus. mat. fis.*) quantity: — *di elettricità*, quantity of electricity; — *di luce*, (*fis.*) quantity of light; — *di moto*, (*fis.*) momentum; — *di moto angolare*, (*mec.*) angular momentum; (*fis. atomica*) spin; — *negativa*, (*mat.*) negative (quantity); *la — di una vocale*, the quantity of a vowel.

quantitativaménte, *av.* quantitatively.

quantitativo, *ag.* **1.** quantitative: *analisi quantitativa*, (*chim.*) quantitative analysis **2.** (*gram.*): *aggettivo* —, adjective of quantity; *avverbio* —, adverb of degree || *s.m.* quantity, amount: — *disponibile*, available amount (*o* amount available); — *occorrente*, amount wanted (*o* needed); *ne abbiamo ancora un piccolo — in magazzino*, we still have a small quantity in stock (*o* on hand); *comperare, vendere in quantitativi*, to buy, to sell in large quantities (*o* in quantity *o* in bulk).

quànto, *ag.* **1.** *interr.* **how much;** *pl.* **how many:** — *carbone ti occorre?*, how much coal do you want?; *quante lezioni hai preso?*, how many lessons did you take?; *per quante settimane rimarrai qui?*, how many weeks will you stay here? **2.** *esclamativo* **what, what a lot of, how much;** *pl.* **what a lot of, how many:** — *carbone abbiamo consumato quest'inverno!*, what a lot of (*o* how much) coal we burnt last winter!; — *freddo, caldo ho patito!*, what cold, heat I suffered!; — *interesse ha suscitato!*, what (*o* what a lot of *o* how much) interest it aroused!; *quanti libri ha nella sua biblioteca!*, how many (*o* what a lot of) books he has in his library! **3.** *quanto tempo*, how long: — *tempo ci vuole?*, how long does it take?; — *tempo rimarrai qui?*, how long will you remain here? **4.** (*nel comp. di uguaglianza*) **as:** *ho tanti amici quanti ne ha lui*, I have as many friends as he has; *ho tanti amici quanti nemici*, I have as many friends as I have enemies; *ho tanto denaro — lui*, I have as much money as he has; *non ho tanti libri quanti ne ha lui*, I have not so many books as he has **5.** (*in espressioni ellittiche*): — *c'è da qui alla stazione?*, how far is the station from here?; — *costano queste pere al chilo?*, how much a kilo are these pears?; — *è passato!*, it was so long ago!; — *fa, costa?*, how much is it?; — *ha di febbre?*, what is his temperature?; *quanti ne abbiamo del mese?*, what day of the month is it? (*o* what is the date today?); — *rimarrai qui?*, how long will you be staying here?; *ha guadagnato — ha voluto*, he made as much as he wanted (to); *l'ho pagato — vale*, I paid what it was worth; *non so — impiegai ad arrivare qui*, I don't know how long it took me to get here || *pron.* **1.** (*ciò che*) **what, all; as much as:** — *ho è a tua disposizione*, what (*o* all) I have is at your disposal; *da — si vede...*, from what (*o* as far as) one can see...; *ha — gli occorre*, he has what (*o* all) he needs; *non credere a — ti ha detto*, don't believe what he has told you; *non dire a nessuno — sai*, don't tell anybody what you know; *questo è — so*, this is all (*o* as much as) I know || *le diede* — *aveva di meglio*, he gave her the best he had || *per — tu gli dica*, whatever you tell him **2.** *pl.* **all; as many as:** *ha detto di no a quanti gliel'hanno domandato*, he said no to all who asked him; *ne prese quanti ne volle*, he took all (*o* as many as) he wanted || *av.* **1.** **how, how much:** — *è lontana la chiesa?*, how far is the church?; — *hai fumato oggi?*, how much (*o* what a lot) you have smoked today!; — *sono felice!*, how happy I am! **2.** *tanto... quanto..., così... quanto...*, (*con ag. ed av.*) **as... as...** (*in proposizioni affermative e interrogative*); **so... as...** (*in proposizioni negative*): *non è così stupido — sembra*, he is not so stupid as he looks; *questa stanza è tanto grande — l'altra*, this room is as large as the other (one) **3.** (*tanto*) *quanto*, (*con verbi*) **as much as:** *impara (tanto)* — *può*, he learns as much as he can; *non impara (tanto)* — *potrebbe*, he does not learn as much as he could; *tu lavori (tanto)* — *lui*, you work as much as he does **4.** *tanto... quanto...*, **both... and...**: *venderò tanto l'automobile* — *il motoscafo*, I'll sell both my car and my speed-boat **5.** — *più...*, *tanto meno...*, the more..., the less...; the *...er...*, the less...; — *più...*, *tanto più...*, the more..., the *...er...*, the *...er...*: — *più facile è, tanto meno interessante lo trovo*, the easier it is, the less interesting I find it; — *più invecchia, tanto più diventa sordo*, the older he gets, the deafer he becomes; — *più lo vedo, tanto meno mi piace*, the more I see him, the less I like him; — *più si sa, tanto più si vorrebbe sapere*, the more one knows, the more one would like to know **6. (Fraseologia):** — *a*, as for; *(circa, intorno)* as to: — *a te*, as for you; — *agli altri non ne so nulla*, I don't know anything as to the others; — *a stare una settimana, non c'è nemmeno da parlarne*, as for staying a week it is out of the question ‖ — *mai*, as much as ever; *(molto)* very *(o awfully o extremely)*: *fu*—*mai gentile*, he was awfully kind; *ti amo* — *mai*, I love you as much as ever ‖ — *prima*, *(presto)* in a short time *(o before long o soon)*; *(al più presto)* as soon as possible; *(nella corrispondenza commerciale)* at your earliest convenience: *per favore fateci sapere la vostra decisione* — *prima*, please let us know your decision at your earliest convenience; *ti scriverò* — *prima*, I'll write to you soon; *ve lo faremo sapere* — *prima*, we will let you know as soon as possible ‖ *in* —, in that: *tu differisci da me in* — *ami la musica*, you are different from me in that you love music ‖ *per* —, however *(con ag. e av.)*; however much *(con s. e v.)*: *per* — *indaffarato tu sia dovresti telefonargli qualche volta*, however busy you are *(o you may be)* you should ring him up sometimes; *per* — *tu studi non sarà mai abbastanza*, however much you study it will never be enough.

quànto, *s.m. (fis.)* quantum *(pl.* quanta): *la teoria dei quanti*, quantum theory.

quantúnque, *av. (benchè)* though, although.

quarànta, *ag. num. card. s.m.* forty.

quarantamíla, *ag. num. card. s.m.* forty thousand.

quarantèna, *s.f.* quarantine: *essere in* —, to be in quarantine; *tenere in* —, to keep in quarantine.

quarantènne, *ag.* forty years old *(predicativo)*; forty-year-old *(attributivo)* ‖ *s.m.* forty-year-old man ‖ *s.f.* forty-year-old woman.

quarantènnio, *s.m.* period of forty years.

quarantèsimo, *ag. num. ord. s.m.* fortieth.

quarantína, *s.f.* about forty, some forty: *una* — *di bambini*, about forty children; *una* — *di minuti*, some forty minutes; *egli è sulla* —, he is about forty (years old); *ha passato la* —, he is in his forties.

quarantòtto, *ag. num. card. s.m.* forty-eight ‖ *il* —, *(st.)* the revolutionary year of 1848 ‖ *che* —!, what a mess! ‖ *mandar ql.co. a carte* —, to mess sthg. up; *mandare qlcu. a carte* —, to send s.o. to hell.

quarésima, *s.f. (eccl.)* Lent: *mezza* —, Mid-Lent: *domenica di mezza* —, Mid-Lent Sunday; *la prima domenica di* —, the first Sunday in Lent ‖ *faccia da* —, dismal *(o* Lenten) face ‖ *lungo come la* —, *(fam.)* as slow as a snail ‖ *fare* —, to keep Lent *(o* to fast during Lent); *rompere la* —, to break the Lenten fast *(o* to give up fasting during Lent).

quaresimàle, *ag.* Lent *(attributivo)*; Lenten ‖ *s.m. (eccl.)* Lent sermon.

quaresimalísta, *s.m. (eccl.)* Lent preacher.

quàrta, *s.f.* **1.** *(astr.)* quarter **2.** *(mar.)* rhumb **3.** *(aut.)* fourth gear ‖ *partì in* — *per descrivermi le sue avventure*, he threw himself headlong into the description of his adventures **4.** *(scherma)* quart, quarte, carte **5.** *(mus.)* fourth.

quartabuòno, *s.m. (falegnameria)* quarter round.

quartàle, *s.m. (teat.)* quarter of an actor's salary.

quartàna, *s.f. (med.)* quartan (fever), quartan ague.

quartàto, *ag.* **1.** *(membruto)* well-built, sturdy **2.** *(arald.)* quartered.

quartétto, *s.m. (mus.)* quartet.

---

quartière, *s.m.* **1.** *(di una città)* quarter; neighbourhood; *(rione amministrativo)* ward (of a town), district: *quartieri bassi*, slums; — *degli ebrei*, ghetto *(o* Jewish quarter); — *italiano*, Italian quarter; — *Latino*, Latin Quarter (in Paris); — *residenziale*, residential quarter; *noi viviamo in un bel* —, we live in a nice neighbourhood **2.** *(appartamento)* flat; *(amer.)* apartment; *(alloggio)* lodgings *(pl.)*: *un* — *ammobiliato*, a furnished flat **3.** *(mil.)* quarters *(pl.)*; *(caserma)* barracks *(pl.)*: — *d'inverno*, winter quarters: *ritirarsi nei quartieri d'inverno*, to go into winter quarters; — *generale*, headquarters: *gran* — *generale*, General Headquarters **4.** *(arald.)* quartering: *scudo a quartieri*, quartered shield **5.** *(posta)* postal district **6.** *(di scarpe)* quarter **7.** *dar* —, to give s.o. quarter; *domandare* —, to ask for quarter *(o* to cry quarter).

quartiermàstro, *s.m. (mil.)* quartermaster.

quartína, *s.f. (poes.)* quatrain.

quartíno, *s.m.* **1.** quarter of a litre; about half a pint **2.** *(mus.)* small clarinet.

quàrto, *ag.num.ord.* fourth: *la quarta dimensione*, the fourth dimension; *il* — *giorno del mese*, the fourth day of the month; *la quarta parte*, the fourth part; *arrivò* —, he arrived fourth; *abitare al* — *piano*, to live on the fourth floor ‖ *Pio Quarto*, Pius the Fourth ‖ *s.m.* **1.** quarter, fourth: *un* — *di pollo*, a quarter of a chicken; *un* — *della popolazione*, a fourth *(o* a quarter) of the population; *un* — *di secolo*, a quarter of a century; *il primo* — *di luna*, the first quarter of the moon; *ho letto un* — *di questo libro*, I have read a fourth *(o* a quarter) of this book; *lo posso avere per un* — *del suo prezzo*, I can buy it for a quarter of its price; *ne voglio solo un* —, I only want a quarter *(o* a fourth) of it; *dividere ql.co. in quarti*, to divide sthg. into quarters *(o* to quarter sthg.) ‖ *quarti di finale*, *(spor.)* quarter-finals ‖ *fare il* —, *(a carte, a tennis)* to make a fourth ‖ *tre quarti*, three-quarters, three-fourths: *i tre quarti del globo*, the three-quarters of the globe; *a tre quarti*, three-quarters *(o* three-fourths): *bottiglia a tre quarti vuota, piena*, bottle three-quarters empty, full **2.** *(nelle determinazioni di tempo)* quarter: *un* — *d'ora*, a quarter of an hour: *ho passato un brutto* — *d'ora*, fig. I went through a bad quarter of an hour; *tre quarti d'ora*, three quarters of an hour: *lo aspetto da tre quarti d'ora*, I have been waiting for him for three quarters of an hour; *questo orologio batte le mezze ore ma non i quarti*, this clock strikes the half-hours but not the quarters; *(sono) le due e un* —, (it is) a quarter past two; *(sono) le cinque e tre quarti*, (it is) a quarter to six; *(sono) le nove meno un* —, (it is) a quarter to nine **3.** *(tip.)* quarto: *edizione in* —, quarto edition **4.** *(arald.)* quarter.

quartodècimo, *ag.num.ord. s.m.* fourteenth.

quartogènito, *ag.* fourth born ‖ *s.m.* fourth child.

quartúccio, *V.* **quartíno 1.**

quartúltimo, *ag. s.m.* fourth from the end.

quarzífero, *(min.)* quartziferous.

quarzíte, *s.f. (min.)* quartzite; quartz-rock.

quàrzo, *s.m. (min.)* quartz: — *affumicato*, brown quartz; *lampada di* —, *(fis.)* quartz lamp.

quarzóso, *ag. (min.)* quartzy, quartzose.

quàsi, *av.* **1.** **almost; nearly; hardly** *(con significato negativo)*: — *sempre*, almost always; *egli* — *morì*, he nearly died; *era* — *pieno*, it was nearly full; *non ho* — *nessun amico*, I have hardly any friends *(o* almost no friends); *non lo vedo* — *mai*, I hardly ever see him; *non mi è rimasto* — *niente*, I have hardly anything *(o* almost nothing) left; *sono* — *le tre*, it is nearly *(o* almost) three o'clock; *sono qui da* — *mezz'ora*, I have been here for nearly *(o* almost) half an hour; *vennero* — *tutti*, almost *(o* nearly) all of them came ‖ *senza* —, certainly *(o* for sure) ‖ — *cadevo*, I nearly fell *(o* I all but fell) ‖ *ce ne sono cinquanta o* —, there are fifty of them or very nearly **2.** *(in alcuni composti)* **quasi:** — *contratto*, *(dir.)* quasi-contract; — *delitto*, (*dir.*) quasi-delict; — *onesto, buono,* quasi-honest,-good; — *pubblico,* quasi-public ‖ **quàsi (che),** *cong.* **as if:** *era molto preoccupato* — (*che*) *sapesse ciò che stava per accadere,* he was very worried, as if he knew what was going to happen; *mi parlò* — (*che*) *non mi avesse mai visto prima,* he spoke to me as if he had never met me before.

quàssia, *s.f.* (*bot. farm.*) quassia.

quassù, *av.* **up here:** *da* — *c'è una splendida vista,* from up here the view is splendid ‖ — *l'inverno è stato piuttosto rigido,* here in the North it has been rather a hard winter.

quatèrna, *s.f.* set of four numbers; (*vincita*) set of four winning numbers: *far* —, *vincere una* —, to win with a set of four numbers.

quaternàrio, *ag.* **1.** (*geol.*) Quaternary: *il periodo* —, the Quaternary period **2.** (*di quattro sillabe*) of four syllables; (*di quattro versi*) of four lines: *strofa quaternaria,* stanza of four lines (*o* quatrain); *verso* —, line of four syllables ‖ *s.m.* **1.** (*geol.*) Quaternary **2.** (*verso di quattro sillabe*) line of four syllables.

quaterniòni, *s.m. pl.* (*mat.*) quaternions.

quàtto, *ag.* squatting, crouching; (*per la paura*) cowering; (*silenzioso*) silent: *starsene* —, to keep quiet ‖ — —, very quietly: *svignarsela* — —, to slip away on the quiet.

quattordicènne, *ag.* fourteen years old (*predicativo*); fourteen-year-old (*attributivo*) ‖ *s.m.* fourteen-year-old boy ‖ *s.f.* fourteen-year-old girl.

quattordicèsimo, *ag. num. ord. s.m.* fourteenth.

quattórdici, *ag. num. card. s.m.* fourteen ‖ *sono le* —, it is two o'clock.

quattrinàio, *s.m.* moneyed man.

quattríno, *s.m.* farthing: *non ho il becco di un* —, I haven't got a farthing (*o* I am broke); *non vale un* —, it isn't worth a (brass) farthing; *sono senza un* —, I am penniless; *stai buttando via tempo e quattrini,* you are wasting time and money; *essere pieno di quattrini,* to be rolling in money; *fare quattrini,* to make money: *ha fatto un sacco di quattrini,* he has made a lot of money; *pagare fino all'ultimo* —, to pay to the last farthing; *star male a quattrini,* to be hard up.

quàttro, *ag. num. card. s.m.* four: *il* — *di gennaio,* the fourth of January; *alle* —, at four (o'clock) ‖ *a* — *remi,* four-oared: *barca a* — *remi,* four-oar; *a* — *ruote,* four-wheeled: *carrozza a* — *ruote,* four-wheeler; *tiro a* —, four-in-hand ‖ *a quattr'occhi,* in private (*o* in confidence) ‖ *in* — *e quattr'otto,* in less than no time (*o* in the twinkling of an eye) ‖ *gliene dirò* —, I'll give him a piece of my mind ‖ *fare* — *chiacchiere,* to have a chat ‖ *fare il diavolo a* —, (*far gran fracasso*) to kick up a shindy (*o* to make a hullabaloo); (*sforzarsi per ottenere*) to leave no stone unturned ‖ *fare* — *passi,* to take a stroll: *andare a fare* — *passi,* to go for a stroll ‖ *fare* — *salti,* to have a dance ‖ *farsi in* —, to do one's utmost ‖ *non dire* — *finchè non l'hai nel sacco, prov.* don't count your chickens before they're hatched.

quattròcchi, *s.m.* (*scherz.*) (old) four-eyes.

quattròcchi, a, *l.av.* privately, in confidence.

quattrocentésco, *ag.* 15th century (*attributivo*); (*art. lett. italiana*) quattrocento (*attributivo*).

quattrocentèsimo, *ag. num. ord. s.m.* four hundredth.

quattrocentísta, *s.m.* (*art.*) quattrocentist.

quattrocènto, *ag. num. card.* four hundred ‖ *s.m.* (*quindicesimo secolo*) fifteenth century; (*art. lett. italiana*) quattrocento.

quattromíla, *ag. num. card. s.m.* four thousand.

quégli, quéi, *pron. pers. dimostrativo m. sing. sogg.* (*letter.*) **he:** *e* — *rispose villanamente,* and he replied discourteously.

quéllo, *ag. dimostrativo* **1. that;** *pl.* **those:** *quella stessa sera,* that very evening (*o* that same evening);

quel tal libro, that book; *con quell'abito non potevo certo andare a teatro,* I certainly couldn't go to the theatre in that dress; *dammi quei libri,* give me those books; *quelle signore sono le zie di Lucia,* those ladies are Lucia's aunts ‖ *quel matto di tuo fratello,* that crazy brother of yours ‖ *ehi, quell'uomo!,* hey there! ‖ *in quel mezzo,* (*nel frattempo*) meanwhile (*o* in the meantime) **2.** (*in funzione di art. determinativo*) **the:** — *stesso uomo,* the same man; *quel poco che ho,* the little I have; *non tornò più in quella casa dove aveva trascorso la sua infanzia,* he never returned to the house where he had spent his childhood **3.** (*in espressioni ellittiche*): — *del latte, del gas,* the milkman, the gasman; *quelli di Roma,* the Romans ‖ *in quel di,* in; (*nelle vicinanze di*) in the neighbourhood (*o* vicinity) of: *che novità ci sono in quel di Monza?,* what's the latest (news) in Monza?; *è un grosso borgo in quel di Milano,* it is a large country-town in the neighbourhood of Milan ‖ *in quella,* at that moment (*o* minute); *in quella che...,* at the very moment that... (*o* as...) ‖ *ne ho udite di quelle!,* the things I have been told!; *ne ho viste di quelle da far rabbrividire!,* I have seen things that would make you shudder! ‖ *pron. dimostrativo* **1. that** (**one**); *pl.* **those:** — *davanti,* (*riferito a persona*) that person in front; (*riferito a cosa*) that one in front; — *lì,* that one (there); *quelle sono le mie amiche,* those are my friends; *lascio questa valigia e prendo quella,* I'll leave this suitcase and take that one; *non è* — *il libro che cercavo,* that's not the book I was looking for; *non voglio questi, voglio quelli,* I don't want these, I want those; *non voglio il tuo libro, ma* — *di tuo fratello,* I don't want your book, but your brother's; *prendi quei due,* take those two ‖ — *sì che è buono!,* that's really good! (*o* iron. he is a fine one!); — *sì che è vino!,* that's what you might call wine! ‖ *gran fortuna fu quella!,* that was a great piece of luck! **2.** (*al posto del nome che si dovrebbe ripetere*) **the one;** *pl.* **the ones:** — *con gli occhiali,* the one with the glasses; — *d'oro,* the gold one; *preferisco le commedie antiche a quelle moderne,* I prefer old plays to modern (ones); *questo è* — *che cercavi,* this is the one you were looking for; *scegliete quelli migliori,* choose the best ones **3.** (*seguito da pron. rel.*) (*con valore di* colui) **the one, the man;** (*con valore di* colei) **the woman;** *pl.* (*con valore di* coloro) **those, the people;** (*con valore di* chiunque) **whoever, anyone:** — *che l'ha rotto dovrà pagare,* the one who (*o* whoever) has broken it will have to pay; *quelli che non ti conoscono diranno che sei pazzo,* those who don't (*o* anyone who doesn't) know you will say you are crazy; *quella con cui parlaste è inglese,* the woman you spoke to is English **4.** (*con valore di* egli) **he;** (*ella*) **she;** (*essi, esse*) **they:** *quelli risposero...,* and they answered... **5.** — *che,* (*ciò che*) **what;** *tutto* — *che,* everything (*o* all) **6.** —*... questo,* (*per indicare il primo e il secondo di cose o persone già menzionate*) **the former... the latter:** *Maria e Margherita sono sorelle; quella è bruna, questa è bionda,* Maria and Margherita are sisters; the former is brunette, the latter is blonde; *i suoi allievi e i miei sono molto diversi; quelli sono studiosi e attenti, questi lenti e pigri,* his pupils and mine are very different; the former (*o* his) are studious and attentive, the latter (*o* mine) slow and lazy **7.** *questo... quello,* (*con valore di* l'uno... l'altro) one... one (*o* one... the other); (*con valore di* alcuni... altri) some... some (*o* some... others): *questo a piedi e* — *a cavallo,* one on foot, one (*o* the other) on horseback **8.** (*come pred. nominale*): *egli è sempre* —, he is still the same as he used to be; *egli non è più* —, he is not his old (*o* former) self.

quercéta, *s.f.,* **queréto,** *s.m.* oak-plantation; oak-grove.

quèrcia, *s.f.* oak(-tree): *forte come una* —, as strong as an oak.

querciuòlo, *s.m.* young oak, oakling.

querèla, *s.f.* **1.** (*lamentela*) complaint **2.** (*dir.*) action, lawsuit: *sporger* — *contro qlcu.*, to bring an action (o to proceed) against s.o.

querelànte, *ag.* complaining ‖ *s.c.* (*dir.*) plaintiff.

querelàre, *v.t.* (*dir.*) to bring an action against (s.o.), to proceed against (s.o.), to take legal proceedings against (s.o.), to prosecute ‖ **querelàrsi**, *v.r.* to complain.

querelàto, *ag.* (*dir.*) accused ‖ *s.m.* (*dir.*) defendant.

querimònia, *s.f.* (*letter.*) 1. complaint 2. *pl.* (*voci lamentose*) laments.

quèrulo, *ag.* (*letter.*) querulous; complaining; peevish.

quesìto, *ag.* (*dir.*) required: *diritti quesiti*, acquired rights ‖ *s.m.* 1. question, query: *porre un* —, to put a question; *risolvere un* —, to resolve a question 2. (*problema*) problem.

quésti, *pron. pers. dimostrativo m. sing. sogg.* (*letter.*) he; this man; (*quest'ultimo*) the latter.

questionàbile, *ag.* questionable; disputable.

questionàre, *v.i.* to quarrel; to dispute.

questionàrio, *s.m.* questionnaire, questionary; set of questions: *rispose solo a cinque domande del* —, he only answered five of the set of questions; *riempire un* —, to fill up a questionnaire.

questionatóre, *s.m.*, **questionatrìce**, *s.f.* disputant; quarreller; questioner.

questióne, *s.f.* 1. (*discussione, controversia*) question, issue; (*argomento, faccenda*) question, matter; (*punto della questione*) question, point: *questioni economiche, politiche*, economic, political questions (o matters); *la* — *è che...*, the point is that...; *è una* — *molto difficile da decidere*, it is a very difficult question (o matter) to decide; *non farne una* —*!*, don't make an issue of it!; *per me è* — *di sentimento*, for me it is a question of sentiment; *qui sta la* —, this is the point; *sollevare, risolvere una* —, to raise, to settle an issue (o a question) ‖ *in* —, in question (o at issue): *il libro, l'uomo in* —, the book, the man in question; *il punto in* —, the point at issue; *non chiamarmi in* —, don't drag me into the argument ‖ *il nocciolo della* —, the heart of the matter ‖ *è* — *di vita o di morte*, it is a matter of life and death ‖ *questa è una* — *di lana caprina*, this is a pointless question 2. (*pol.*) (*problema*) problem, question: *la* — *algerina, orientale*, the Algerian, Eastern problem (o question) 3. (*quesito*) question: *porre una* —, to put (o to pose) a question 4. (*dubbio*) doubt, question: *mettere in* — *che...*, to dispute that...: *i giornali mettono in* — *la solidità dell'alleanza*, the papers are casting doubts upon (o questioning) the strength of the alliance 5. (*lite*) quarrel; dispute: *ho avuto una* — *con lui*, I have had a quarrel with him; *vennero a* — *e si picchiarono*, they argued and came to blows 6. (*dir.*) (*azione legale*) action at law; lawsuit.

quésto, *ag. dimostrativo* 1. this; *pl.* these: *queste case*, these houses; *in* — *momento*, at this moment; *su* — *punto*, on (o about) this point; *mi disse queste medesime parole*, this is exactly what she told me (o these are her exact words); *non uscire con* — *freddo*, don't go out in this cold; *preferisco quest'altro vestito*, I prefer this other dress ‖ *quest'oggi*, today ‖ *dopo aver visitato* — *e quel luogo, ritornò*, after visiting various places he returned ‖ *l'ho visto con questi occhi*, I saw it with my own eyes 2. (*riferito a tempo*): *le vicende di questi venti anni*, the events of the last twenty years; *questa settimana sono stato a Torino*, I have been to Turin this week; *verrò da te quest'estate*, I'll come and stay with you this summer 3. (*in espressioni ellittiche*): *in questa*, at this moment (o minute); *questa è bella!*, that's a good one!; *questa non me l'aspettavo!*, I didn't expect this!; *che vergogna, esserti ridotto a* —*!*, what a disgrace that you should come to this!; *sentite questa!*, listen to this! ‖ *pron. dimostrativo* 1. this (one); *pl.* these: — *vicino a me*, this one near me; *questa è mia sorella*, this is my sister; *questi sono migliori dei tuoi*, these are better than yours; *nessuno di questi*

mi piace, I don't like any of them; *scelgo questa*, I choose this one ‖ *lo va dicendo a* — *e a quello*, she goes around telling everybody 2. (*con valore di* egli) he; (ella) she; (essi, esse) they: *chiamò sua figlia, ma questa non venne*, he called his daughter, but she did not come 3. (*con valore di ciò*) that, this: — *è quanto disse*, that's what he said; *in* — *non siamo d'accordo*, we don't agree about this; *tutto* — *è sbagliato*, this is all wrong; *per* — *ho rifiutato*, therefore I refused ‖ — *e altro*, all this, and more ‖ — *mai e poi mai!*, never, I tell you! ‖ *o* — *poi!*, go on! ‖ — *è quanto!*, that's all! ‖ *dirai* — *e quello...*, you'll say this and this... ‖ *e con* — *ti saluto*, and with that I leave you ‖ *guadagna un milione al mese, ma, con tutto* —, *i denari non gli bastano*, he gets a million lire a month, but he never has enough money ‖ *ho fatto un errore; e con* —*?*, *e per* —*?*, I've made a mistake; so what? 4. *quello... —*, (*per indicare il primo e il secondo di cose o persone già menzionate*) the former... the latter: *John e Charles sono due miei amici; quello è inglese, — è americano*, John and Charles are two friends of mine; the former is English, the latter is American.

questóre, *s.m.* 1. (*st. romana*) quaestor 2. (*capo di polizia di una provincia italiana*) questor.

quèstua, *s.f.* begging; (*in chiesa*) collection: *proibita la* —, no begging; *la* — *di oggi sarà a favore della costruzione di nuove chiese*, today the collection will be for the building of new churches; *andare alla* —, to go begging.

questuànte, *ag.* begging: *frate* —, begging friar ‖ *s.c.* beggar.

questuàre, *v.i.* to beg; to go begging; to seek alms.

questúra, *s.f.* 1. (*st. romana*) quaestorship 2. (*ufficio di pubblica sicurezza*) police-headquarters (*pl.*).

questurìno, *s.m.* policeman (*pl.* policemen).

quèto, *e derivati*, *V.* **quièto**, *e derivati*.

qui, *av.* 1. here; (*rar.*) (*con movimento*) hither: *da* — *a lì*, from here to there; *eccomi* —, here I am; *questo ragazzo* —, this boy (here); *di* — *non si passa*, you cannot get through here; *guarda* —, look here; *ho male* —, I have a pain here; *non lo sento da* —, I cannot hear it from here; *portalo* —, bring it here; *sono* —, I am here; *vieni* —, come here (*o rar.* come hither); *voglio questo* —, I want this one (here) ‖ — *dentro, fuori*, in here, out here; — *dirimpetto*, opposite here; — *sotto, sopra*, down here, up here; — *vicino*, near here (o close by) ‖ *nativo di* —, a native of these parts ‖ *per di* —, this way: *passate per di* —, go this way ‖ — *casca l'asino!*, there's the rub! ‖ — *ha torto*, this is where he is wrong ‖ — *ti voglio!*, now we'll see what you're made of! ‖ *di* — *consegue che...*, hence it follows that... ‖ *non si muoverebbe di* — *a lì, se potesse farne a meno*, he wouldn't stir an inch if he could help it 2. (*in espressioni di tempo*): *da* — *innanzi*, from now on (o henceforth); *di* — *a un anno*, a year from now; *di* — *a otto giorni*, a week today; *egli ha taciuto fin* —, so far he has said nothing ‖ *lo faccio* — *per* —, (*subito*) I'll do it here and now (o straightaway).

quid, *s.m.* (*lat.*) something: — *simile*, something like that; *c'è un* — *che non capisco*, there is something I do not understand.

quìdam, *s.m.* (*lat.*) quidam, a certain person.

quiddatívo, *ag.* (*fil.*) quiddative.

quiddità, *s.f.* (*fil.*) quiddity.

quiescènte, *ag.* quiescent.

quiescènza, *s.f.* 1. quiescence 2. (*collocamento a riposo*) retirement: *trattamento di* —, pension.

quietaménte, *av.* quietly.

quietànza, *s.f.* receipt, acquittance; (*per atto pubblico*) release ‖ *per* —, paid (o received) (in full).

quietanzàre, *v.t.* to receipt; to give a receipt for (sthg.); to acknowledge receipt of (sthg.).

quietàre, *v.t.* to quiet; (*calmare*) to calm; (*alleviare*) to soothe ‖ **quietàrsi**, *v.r.* to quiet(en) down; to calm down.

quiète, *s.f.* **1.** quiet, quietness; (*calma*) calm; (*tranquillità*) stillness; *fig.* tranquillity; (*pace*) peace; (*silenzio*) silence: *la — che precede la tempesta,* the calm before the storm; *la — dei boschi,* the stillness of the woods; *— della mente,* peace of mind; *la — della notte,* the still (o silence) of the night; *la — del mare,* the calm of the sea; *in tempi di —,* in times of quiet (o peace); *per mia —,* for my peace of mind; *ci fu una grande —,* there was a great calm; *dopo tanto rumore, un po' di — distende i nervi,* after so much noise, silence relaxes the nerves; *il paese godette molti anni di — dopo la guerra,* the country enjoyed many years of quiet (o peace) after the war; *vuole solo la —,* he would do anything for a quiet life; *turbare la — pubblica,* to disturb the peace || *l'ultima —,* one's last sleep **2.** (*contrapposta a moto*) rest; immobility: *passare dallo stato di — a quello di moto,* to pass from a state of rest to a state of motion **3.** (*riposo*) rest: *ha bisogno di un po' di —,* he needs (some) rest.

quietísmo, *s.m.* **1.** (*st. relig.*) quietism **2.** (*apatia, indifferenza*) apathy, indifference.

quietísta, *s.c.* (*st. relig.*) quietist.

quièto, *ag.* quiet; (*calmo*) calm; (*tranquillo*) still; *fig.* tranquil; (*pacifico*) peaceful; pacific; (*silenzioso*) silent: *la quieta bellezza del suo viso,* the tranquil beauty of her face; *l'aria quieta,* the calm air; *cavallo —,* quiet horse; *mare —,* calm sea: *un mare — come l'olio,* a sea as smooth as a millpond; *una mente quieta,* a tranquil mind; *una natura quieta,* a pacific nature; *notte quieta,* quiet (o still) night; *una strada quieta,* a quiet road; *fu una settimana molto quieta,* it was a very quiet week; *lo tenne — con delle promesse,* she fobbed him off with (false) promises; *non può restare —,* he can't keep still (o he is a fidget); *sta' —!, (taci!),* be (o keep) quiet!; (*non muoverti!*) keep still! (o don't move!); *dormire —,* to sleep in peace; *essere amante del — vivere,* to be fond of a quiet life || *— —,* very quietly (o softly): *se ne andò — —,* he crept (o he stole) silently away || *acqua quieta, fig.* little hypocrite: *è un'acqua quieta,* he looks as if butter wouldn't melt in his mouth; *le acque quiete rovinano i ponti, prov.* still (o smooth) waters run deep.

quinàrio, *ag.* **1.** (*composto di cinque elementi*) quinary **2.** (*di cinque sillabe*) of five syllables || *s.m.* (*verso di cinque sillabe*) line of five syllables.

quínci, *av.* (*letter.*) **from here; hence:** *— innanzi,* henceforth.

quineónce, *s.m.* (*agr.*) quincunx.

quindecemvibàto, *s.m.* (*st. romana*) quindecemvirate.

quindecèmviro, *s.m.* (*st. romana*) quindecemvir (*pl.* quindecemviri).

quindèna, *s.f.* (*eccl.*) quindene.

quíndi, *av.* **1.** (*perciò*) **therefore, hence:** *— bisogna decidersi,* therefore we must make up our minds **2.** (*poi*) **then, afterwards:** *e — disse che...,* and then he said that... **3.** (*letter.*) (*di qui*) **hence, from here:** *— innanzi,* henceforth.

quindicennàle, *ag.* **1.** (*che dura quindici anni*) lasting fifteen years **2.** (*che avviene ogni quindici anni*) recurring every fifteen years.

quindicènne, *ag.* fifteen years old (*predicativo*); fifteen-year-old (*attributivo*) || *s.m.* fifteen-year-old boy || *s.f.* fifteen-year-old girl.

quindicènnio, *s.m.* period of fifteen years.

quindicèsimo, *ag. num. ord. s.m.* fifteenth.

quíndici, *ag. num. card. s.m.* fifteen: *il — di gennaio,* the fifteenth of January: *verrò il — di gennaio,* I'll come on the fifteenth of January; *— giorni fa,* a fortnight ago (o *amer.* two weeks ago); *fra — giorni,* in a fortnight; *oggi a —,* today fortnight (o a fortnight today); *una vacanza di — giorni,* a fortnight's holiday; *mi pagano ogni — giorni,* I am paid fortnightly.

quindicimíla, *ag. num. card. s.m.* fifteen thousand.

quindicína, *s.f.* **1.** about fifteen; some fifteen: *una — di giorni fa,* about a fortnight ago; *fra una — di giorni,*

in about a fortnight; *c'era una — di persone,* there were about fifteen people; *ci vorrà una — di giorni,* it will take about a fortnight (o *amer.* two weeks) **2.** (*paga di quindici giorni*) a fortnight's wages (*pl.*)

quindicinàle, *ag.* fortnightly, bimonthly: *rivista —,* fortnightly magazine || *s.m.* fortnightly magazine.

quinquagenària, *s.f.* woman of fifty, fifty-year-old woman, quinquagenarian.

quinquagenàrio, *ag.* fifty years old (*predicativo*); fifty-year-old (*attributivo*); quinquagenarian || *s.m.* man of fifty, fifty-year-old man, quinquagenarian.

quinquagèsima, *s.f.* (*eccl.*) Quinquagesima (Sunday).

quinquagèsimo, *ag. num. ord. s.m.* fiftieth.

quinquemviràto, *s.m.* (*st. romana*) quinquemvirate.

quinquennàle, *ag.* quinquennial; five-year (*attributivo*): *piano —,* five-year plan.

quinquènne, *ag.* five years old (*predicativo*); five-year-old (*attributivo*) || *s.m.* five-year-old boy || *s.f.* five-year-old girl.

quinquènnio, *s.m.* five-year period; quinquennium (*pl.* quinquennia).

quinquerème, *s.f.* (*st. mar.*) quinquereme.

quínta, *s.f.* **1.** (*scuola*) fifth class; fifth form **2.** (*mus.*) fifth **3.** (*scherma*) quinte **4.** (*teat.*) wing || *dietro le quinte, fig.* behind the scenes; *operare tra le quinte, fig.* to work underhand.

quintàle, *s.m.* quintal (*misura di peso* = 220.46 lb.).

quintàna[1], *s.f.* (*bersaglio girevole e l'esercizio del colpirlo*) quintain.

quintàna[2], *s.f.* (*med.*) quintan.

quintería, *s.f.* (*agr.*) five-year rotation (of crops).

quintèrno, *s.m.* five sheets (*pl.*); (*rar.*) quinternion.

quintessènza, *s.f.* quintessence (anche *fig.*).

quintessenziàre, *v.t.* to quintessence, to extract the quintessence of (sthg.).

quintétto, *s.m.* (*mus.*) quintet(te), quintetto.

quintíle, *s.m.* (*astr.*) quintile.

Quintiliàno, *no.pr.m.* (*st. lett.*) Quintilian.

quintilióne, *s.m.* **1.** (*secondo l'uso italiano, americano e francese, corrispondente a 1000[6]*) trillion; (*amer.*) quintillion **2.** (*secondo l'uso tedesco e inglese, corrispondente a 1000[10]*) quintillion; (*amer.*) nonillion.

quintíno[1], *s.m.* fifth of a litre.

Quintíno[2], *no.pr.m.* Quintin, Quentin || *San —,* (*geog.*) St. Quentin.

quínto[1], *ag.num.ord.* fifth: *la quinta parte,* the fifth part; *il mio appartamento è al — piano,* my flat is on the fifth floor || *quinta colonna,* (*pol.*) fifth column || *Enrico Quinto,* Henry the Fifth || *s.m.* fifth: *un — del raccolto,* one fifth of the crop; *abbiamo mangiato un — della torta,* we have eaten a fifth of the cake; *dividere ql.co. in quinti,* to divide sthg. into fifths.

Quínto[2], *no.pr.m.* Quintus.

quintodècimo, *ag. num. ord. s.m.* fifteenth.

quintogènito, *ag.* fifth-born || *s.m.* fifth child.

quintúltimo, *ag.s.m.* fifth from the end.

quintuplicàre, *v.t.* to quintuplicate, to quintuple, to multiply by five.

quintuplicazióne, *s.f.* quintuplication.

quintúplice, *ag.* fivefold, quintuplicate.

quíntuplo, *ag.s.m.* quintuple.

quiproquò, *s.m.* **1.** (*equivoco, malinteso*) quid pro quo; misunderstanding **2.** (*errore*) mistake.

Quirinàle, *no.pr.m.* (*geog.*) Quirinal.

Quiríno, *no.pr.m.* (*mit.*) Quirinus.

Quiríti, *s.m. pl.* (*st. romana*) Quirites.

quisquília, *s.f.* trifle: *non perdetevi in quisquilie,* don't get lost in trifles.

quistióne, *V.* **questióne.**

quitànza, quitànzare, *V.* **quietànza, quietanzàre.**

quívi, *av.* (*letter.*) (*qui*) **here;** (*là*) **there.**

quiz, *s.m.* quiz (*pl.* quizzes).

quondam, *av.* (*lat.*) (*una volta*) formerly; one time || *ag.* (*lat.*) **1.** (*defunto*) late: *il — Signor Rossi,* the late Mr. Rossi **2.** (*di persona che un tempo aveva una ca-*

rica) quondam, former: *il — presidente*, the former (*o* quondam) president.

quòta, *s.f.* **1.** (*parte*) share; quota: *— d'abbonamento*, subscription (dues); — *d'iscrizione*, entrance-fee; *ho già versato la mia —*, I have already paid my share ‖ *— d'immigrazione*, immigration quota **2.** (*comm.*) instalment; quota; share: *— di ammortamento*, depreciation allowance; — *mensile*, monthly instalment **3.** (*aer.*) altitude, height: *— di volo*, flight altitude; *ad alta —*, at high altitude: *volare ad alta, bassa —*, to fly high, low; *perdita di —*, loss of altitude; *perdere —*, to lose height; *prendere —*, to climb (*o* to gain height) **4.** (*mar. mil.*) depth: *— periscopica*, periscope-depth **5.** (*topografia*) elevation, altitude: *— zero*, sea-level.

quotàre, *v.t.* **1.** (*Borsa*) to quote: *fu quotato 200 sterline*, it was quoted at £ 200; *questi titoli non sono quotati in Borsa*, these shares are not quoted on the Stock Exchange **2.** (*valutare*) to appreciate, to estimate ‖ **quotàrsi,** *v.r.* to subscribe (a figure): *ci quotammo per 1500 lire ciascuno*, we subscribed 1500 lire each.

quotàto, *ag.* **1.** (*Borsa*) quoted: *prezzo — sulla piazza*, price quoted (*o* ruling) on the market; *prezzo precedentemente —*, prior price; *prezzo ultimamente —*, up-to-date (*o* latest) price **2.** (*valutato, stimato*) esteemed, appreciated, valued; popular, well-liked: *una persona molto quotata*, a highly esteemed person; *è molto — da noi*, he is very popular with us; *è molto — fra i suoi colleghi*, he is well-liked among his colleagues ‖ *un operaio —*, an efficient worker.

quotazióne, *s.f.* (*Borsa*) quotation: *— di apertura*, opening quotation; *quotazioni di Borsa*, Stock Exchange quotations; *— di chiusura*, closing quotation; *— ufficiale*, official quotation.

quotidianaménte, *av.* daily, every day.

quotidiàno, *ag.* daily; quotidian: *malaria quotidiana*, (*patol.*) quotidian fever; *la vita quotidiana*, everyday life ‖ *dacci oggi il nostro pane —*, give us this day our daily bread ‖ *s.m.* daily (paper): *ci sono molti quotidiani in Inghilterra*, there are many dailies in England.

quòto, *s.m.* (*arit.*) quotient.

quoziènte, *s.m.* **1.** (*arit.*) quotient **2.** *— respiratorio*, (*fisiol.*) respiratory coefficient (*o* quotient).

R

r, *s.f.m.* (*sedicesima lettera dell'alfabeto italiano*) r (*pl.* rs, r's) ‖ — *come Roma*, (*tel.*) r for Robert.

rabàrbaro, *s.m.* (*bot.*) rhubarb.

rabattíno, *ag.* industrious; (*intraprendente*) enterprising ‖ *s.m.* industrious man.

rabballinàre, *v.t.* to roll up; to wrap up.

rabbaruffàre, *v.t.* (*scompigliare*) to ruffle: *il vento mi ha rabbaruffato i capelli*, the wind has ruffled my hair ‖ **rabbaruffàrsi**, *v.r.* (*litigare*) to quarrel; (*azzuffarsi*) to fight; to scuffle; (*venire alle mani*) to come to blows.

rabbaruffàto, *ag.* ruffled.

rabbàttere, *v.t.* to half-close, to leave ajar.

rabbatuffolàre, *v.t.* to reduce to a small ball.

rabbelliménto, *s.m.* embellishment.

rabbellíre, *v.t.* **1.** (*abbellire molto*) to embellish, to beautify **2.** (*abbellire di nuovo*) to embellish again, to beautify again ‖ **rabbellírsi**, *v.r.* **1.** (*diventare più bello*) to become more beautiful **2.** (*adornarsi*) to adorn oneself.

rabberciaménto, *s.m.* patching (up); botching.

rabberciàre, *v.t.* to patch (up); to botch: — *un lavoro*, to botch a piece of work; — *un vestito*, to patch (up) a dress.

rabberciàto, *ag.* patched (up); botched.

rabberciatóre, *s.m.* patcher; botcher.

rabberciatúra, *s.f.* patching (up); botching.

ràbbi, *s.m.* rabbi (*pl.* rabbis).

ràbbia, *s.f.* **1.** rage, anger, fury: *la* — *delle onde*, the fury of the waves; *in un momento di* —, in a fit of rage; *pieno di* —, filled with anger; *questo mi fa* —, this makes me angry; *essere preso dalla* —, to fly into a rage (*o* a fury); *schiumare di* —, to foam with rage **2.** (*idrofobia*) rabies, hydrophobia.

rabbínico, *ag.* rabbinical.

rabbinísmo, *s.m.* rabbinism.

rabbinísta, *s.m.* rabbinist.

rabbíno, *s.m.* rabbi (*pl.* rabbis) ‖ *il Gran Rabbino*, the Chief Rabbi.

rabbiosaménte, *av.* furiously, angrily; madly.

rabbióso, *ag.* **1.** furious, angry; (*di cose*) furious: *uno sguardo* —, a furious (*o* angry) look; *un vento* —, a furious wind ‖ *ho una fame rabbiosa*, I am starving (*o* I am ravenous) **2.** (*idrofobo*) rabid, hydrophobic.

rabboccàre, *v.t.* to fill up, to fill to the brim.

rabboccatúra, *s.f.* filling up, filling to the brim.

rabbonacciàre, *v.t.* **1.** to calm **2.** to pacify; (*riconciliare*) to reconcile ‖ *v.i.*, **rabbonacciàrsi**, *v.r.* **1.** to calm down, to quiet(en) down: *il mare* (*si*) *rabbonacciò*, the sea became calm **2.** *fig.* to become pacified; (*riconciliarsi*) to make it up, to make friends again.

rabboníre, *v.t.* to calm down, to pacify, to quiet down: *lo rabboni con la persuasione*, he persuaded him to calm (*o* quiet) down; *non lo rabbonirai con sole parole*, you will not calm him down only with words ‖ *v.i.*, **rabbonírsi**, *v.r.* to calm down, to quiet down.

rabbracciàre, *V.* riabbracciàre.

rabbreviàre, *v.t.* to shorten, to make shorter ‖ **rabbreviàrsi**, *v.r.* to shorten, to become shorter.

rabbriccicàre, *v.t.* **1.** to patch up, to mend: *gli rabbriccicò due vecchie maglie*, she mended (*o* patched up) two old vests for him **2.** *fig.* (*guadagnare a stento*) to scrape together, to scrape up: *rabbriccicò qualche soldo*, he scraped some money together.

rabbrividíre, *v.i.* (*di paura, ecc.*) to shudder; (*di freddo*) to shiver: *egli rabbrividì a quell'orribile vista*,

he shuddered at that horrible sight; *il freddo intenso mi fece* —, the intense cold made me shiver; *rabbrividii a quel pensiero*, I shuddered at the thought of it.

rabbrunàre, *v.t.* to make darker, to darken.

rabbruscàre, *v.i.*, **rabbruscàrsi**, *v.r.* **1.** (*rannuvolarsi*) to darken, to get overcast: *il cielo* (*si*) *rabbrusca*, the sky is darkening (*o* getting overcast) **2.** (*farsi più freddo*) to get colder: *l'aria* (*si*) *sta rabbruscando*, the air is getting colder **3.** *fig.* (*offuscarsi, di viso*) to darken; (*turbarsi, di persona*) to become sulky: *si rabbruscò e non volle più dire una parola*, he became sulky and didn't want to say a word.

rabbuffàre, *v.t.* **1.** to ruffle; (*mettere in disordine*) to disorder: *non rabbuffarmi i capelli!*, don't ruffle my hair!; *l'uccello rabbuffò le piume*, the bird ruffled (up) its feathers **2.** (*rimproverare*) to reprimand, to scold: *la rabbuffarono perché era pigra*, they scolded her for being lazy; — *qlcu. severamente*, to reprimand s.o. severely ‖ **rabbuffàrsi**, *v.r.* **1.** to become ruffled **2.** (*oscurarsi, del tempo*) to become overcast ‖ *v.r. reciproco* (*azzuffarsi*) to come to blows with each other (one another).

rabbuffàto, *ag.* (*di capelli, penne, ecc.*) ruffled; (*in disordine*) untidy, dishevel(l)ed.

rabbúffo, *s.m.* stern rebuke, reprimand: *fare un* — *a qlcu.*, to administer a rebuke to (*o* to reprimand) s.o.

rabbuiàre, *v.i.*, **rabbuiàrsi**, *v.r.* **1.** (*di tempo*) to darken, to become overcast; (*annottare*) to get dark, to grow dark: *il cielo* (*si*) *rabbuiò*, the sky darkened; *sta rabbuiando*, it is getting dark **2.** *fig.* (*offuscarsi, di viso*) to darken; (*turbarsi, di persona*) to get sulky: (*si*) *è rabbuiato in volto*, his face darkened.

rabdomànte, *s.c.* (water-)diviner, dowser: *bacchetta di* —, dowsing-rod (*o* divining-rod).

rabdomàntico, *ag.* (water-)divining, dowsing.

rabdomanzía, *s.f.* (water-)divining, dowsing.

rabelesiàno, *ag.* Rabelaisian.

rabescàme, *s.m.* arabesques (*pl.*).

rabescàre, *v.t.* to decorate with arabesques.

rabescàto, *ag.* arabesque(d), decorated with arabesques, ornamented with arabesques: *uno stipo* —, an arabesqued cabinet.

rabescatúra, *s.f.* arabesque: *una spada con fine* —, a sword with fine arabesques.

rabésco, *s.m.* **1.** arabesque: *disegnare, intagliare rabeschi*, to draw, to carve arabesques **2.** (*scrittura brutta, incomprensibile*) scrawl, scribble.

ràbido, *ag.* (*letter.*) rabid, furious.

rabottatríce, *s.f.* (*tip.*) edge-planing machine.

rabòtto, *s.m.* (*tip.*) edge-plane.

ràbula, *s.m.* (*azzeccagarbugli*) pettifogger.

raccapezzàre, *v.t.* **1.** (*raccogliere*) to gather, to put together, to collect: *vedrò di* — *i denari per il viaggio*, I'll try to get together the money for the journey **2.** *fig.* (*comprendere*) to understand; (*trovare*) to find out: *cerca di raccapezzarne il principio*, try to find out the beginning of it; *non ci raccapezzo nulla*, I cannot understand anything ‖ **raccapezzàrsi**, *v.r.* to see one's way: *a questo punto non mi raccapezzai più*, at this point I could not see my way any more; *quanto a questa faccenda non mi ci raccapezzo*, as to this matter I can't make it out (*o* I can't make head or tail of it).

raccapricciànte, *ag.* horrifying; (*terrificante*) blood-curdling, terrifying: *un racconto* —, a horrifying tale;

uno spettacolo —, a terrifying spectacle; *si udì un urlo* —, a terrifying (o blood-curdling) scream was heard.

raccapricciàre, *v.t.* **1.** to horrify; (*atterrire*) to terrify: *quello spettacolo mi raccapricciò*, that sight horrified me **2.** (*rar. letter.*) (*increspare*) to ripple ‖ *v.i.*, **raccapricciàrsi**, *v.r.* to shudder, to be horrified: (*si*) *raccapricciò alla vista del sangue*, she shuddered at the sight of blood.

raccapríccio, *s.m.* horror; (*terrore*) fear, terror: *un brivido di* —, a shudder; *scena che desta* —, horrifying scene; *un urlo di* — *partì dalla folla*, the crowd yelled with terror; *provare* — *ad un racconto, ad uno spettacolo*, to shudder (o to be horrified) at a tale, a sight.

raccattàre, *v.t.* **1.** to pick up: — *il bastone*, to pick up one's stick; — *un punto*, (*a maglia*) to pick up a stitch **2.** (*raccogliere, mettere insieme*) to collect: — *modi di dire*, to collect idiomatic expressions.

raccattatíccio, *s.m.* (*spreg.*) rubbish.

raccattàto, *ag.* **1.** picked up **2.** (*raccolto*) collected.

raccattatóre, *s.m.*, **raccattatríce**, *s.f.* collector.

raccattatúra, *s.f.* **1.** (*il raccattare*) picking up; (*cose raccattate*) things picked up (*pl.*) **2.** (*il raccogliere*) collecting; (*cose raccolte*) things collected (*pl.*), collection.

raccenciàre, *v.t.* to patch (up), to mend ‖ **raccenciàrsi**, *v.r.* **1.** (*vestirsi di cenci*) to dress in rags **2.** (*migliorare la propria posizione*) to improve one's position.

raccèndere, *v.t.* (*fuoco*) to relight, to rekindle; (*lampada*) to relight; (*speranza*) to revive.

raccentràre, *v.t.* to centralize.

raccerchiàre, *v.t.* to surround again.

raccertàre, *v.t.* to confirm ‖ **raccertàrsi**, *v.r.* to make sure.

racchetàre, *v.t.* to calm; (*dolore, rimorso*) to soothe ‖ **racchetàrsi**, *v.r.* to calm down.

racchétta[1], *s.f.* **1.** (*spor.*) racket, racquet: — *da neve*, racket (o snow-shoe); — *da ping-pong*, table-tennis bat; — *da tennis*, tennis-racket ‖ *racchette degli sci*, ski-sticks **2.** (*aut.*) (*del tergicristallo*) windscreen-wiper.

racchétta[2], *s.f.* (*razzo*) rocket.

racchettière, *s.m.* (*mil.*) soldier in charge of rocket signals.

ràcchio, *ag.* ugly ‖ *s.m.* (*racimolo*) small bunch of grapes.

racchiocciolàrsi, *v.r.* to curl up.

racchiúdere, *v.t.* to contain, to hold, to include; (*implicare*) to imply: *è un libro che racchiude idee nuove*, it is a book that contains new ideas; *questo cassetto racchiude importanti documenti*, this drawer contains important documents; *la sua domanda racchiude già la risposta*, his question already implies the answer.

racciabattàre, *v.t.* (*rabberciare*) to patch up, to mend ‖ *v.i.* (*trascinare le ciabatte*) to shuffle.

raccògliere, *v.t.* **1.** to pick up; (*fiori, cotone, ecc.*) to pick: *raccogli quel fazzoletto, quel pezzo di carta*, pick up that handkerchief, that piece of paper; *il treno si ferma per* — *i passeggeri*, the train stops to pick up passengers; — *cotone*, to pick cotton; — *i feriti, i naufraghi*, to pick up the wounded, the shipwrecked men; — *impulsi*, (*elett.*) to pick up impulses; — *un punto*, (*a maglia*) to pick up a stitch ‖ — *l'allusione*, to take the hint ‖ — *il guanto*, (*la sfida*) to pick (o to take) up the gauntlet **2.** (*radunare, mettere insieme*) to gather, to get together; to assemble, to collect: *devi* — *tutti gli studenti in questa sala*, you must assemble all the students in this hall; *egli raccolse una ventina di uomini*, he got together about twenty men (o he collected about twenty men); *ogni settimana raccolgo alcuni amici a casa mia*, every week I get a few friends together at my house; *raccolse le sue carte e se ne andò*, he gathered (up) his papers and went away; *speriamo di* — *almeno 50.000 lire*, we hope to collect 50,000 lire at least; — *i capelli in una crocchia*, to gather (up) one's hair into a knot; — *informazioni, notizie su qlco.*, to gather information, news about

sthg.; — *legna*, to gather wood ‖ — *le idee, le proprie energie*, to collect (o to gather) one's ideas, one's energies ‖ — *lodi*, to gain (o to win) praise **3.** (*collezionare*) to collect, to make a collection of (sthg.): — *francobolli, monete*, to collect stamps, coins **4.** (*ricevere*) to receive: *la proposta raccolse molti voti*, the proposal received many votes ‖ *raccolse molta simpatia*, he was well liked by everybody; *raccolse molta simpatia da noi*, he became very popular with us ‖ *l'eredità di qlcu.*, to inherit from s.o. **5.** (*aver come raccolto*) to reap, to harvest: *spero di* — *più dell'anno scorso*, I hope to reap more than last year ‖ — *il frutto del proprio lavoro*, to harvest the fruits of one's work ‖ *si raccoglie quel che si semina*, prov. as ye sow, so shall ye reap **6.** (*accogliere, dar rifugio a*) to take in, to shelter: *ospizio che raccoglie l'infanzia abbandonata*, institute which takes in (o shelters) abandoned children **7.** (*ripiegare*): — *le ali*, (*di uccello*) to fold its wings; — *le vele*, to furl the sails **8.** (*tirare a sè*): — *le reti*, to draw (o to pull) in the nets ‖ **raccògliersi**, *v.r.* **1.** to gather, to assemble: *si raccolsero tutti intorno a lui*, they all gathered around him **2.** (*concentrarsi*) to collect one's thoughts, to concentrate: *voglio raccogliermi un po' prima di incontrarlo*, I want to collect my thoughts before meeting him **3.** (*ammassarsi, di nuvole, ecc.*) to gather.

raccoglimènto, *s.m.* **1.** (*meditazione*) meditation **2.** (*concentrazione*) concentration: *ascoltare con il massimo* —, to listen with the greatest attention; *pregare con grande* —, to pray with great concentration.

raccogliticcio, *ag.* collected at random, taken at random; picked (up) haphazardly: *truppe raccoglititicce*, troops recruited at random ‖ *s.m.* assortment: *un* — *di gente della peggior specie*, an assortment of people of the worst type.

raccoglitóre, *ag.* collecting ‖ *s.m.* **1.** picker; gatherer: — *di cotone*, cotton-picker **2.** (*collezionista*) collector **3.** (*compilatore*) compiler **4.** (*cartella per documenti, ecc.*) file, folder.

raccoglitríce, *s.f.* **1.** picker; gatherer **2.** (*collezionista*) collector **3.** (*compilatrice*) compiler **4.** (*macchina per raccogliere grano*) picker.

raccòlta, *s.f.* **1.** (*il raccogliere*) (*grano, ecc.*) harvesting; (*uva*) grape-harvesting, vintaging; (*cotone, ecc.*) picking **2.** (*raccolto*) harvest, crop; (*dell'uva*) grape-harvest, vintage: *la* — *del grano quest'anno è stata buona*, the crop of wheat has been good this year; *fare la* — *del grano, del fieno*, to harvest the wheat, the hay **3.** (*epoca del raccolto*) harvest-time **4.** (*collezione*) collection: *una bella* — *di francobolli*, a fine collection of stamps; *fa la* — *di monete antiche*, he collects old coins; *pubblicare una* — *di poesie*, to publish a collection of poems **5.** (*adunanza*) gathering: *chiamare a* — *le truppe*, to gather (o to assemble) the troops; *suonare a* — *per la ritirata*, to sound the retreat ‖ *chiamare a* — *le proprie energie, idee*, to collect one's energies, ideas.

raccoltaménte, *av.* meditatively, intently: *pensare* —, to think intently; *pregare* —, to be intent on one's prayers.

raccòlto, *ag.* **1.** (*colto*) picked: *fiori raccolti*, picked flowers **2.** (*adunato*) collected, gathered: *gente raccolta in piazza*, people gathered in the square **3.** *fig.* (*pensoso*) absorbed, engrossed: *era* — *nella sua lettura*, he was engrossed in his reading; *era tutto* — *nei suoi pensieri*, he was deeply absorbed in his thoughts; *in chiesa devi stare* —, in church you must be silent and intent **4.** (*intimo*) cosy, snug: *stanza raccolta*, cosy little room **5.** (*rannicchiato*) curled up, crouching: *col corpo* —, with one's body curled up; *con le gambe raccolte*, with one's knees drawn up ‖ *s.m.* crop, harvest (anche *fig.*): *il* — *del grano*, the wheat-harvest; *il* — *di mele di quest'anno*, this year's crop of apples; *un buon* —, a good harvest (anche *fig.*); *epoca del* —, harvest-time.

raccomandàbile, *ag.* reliable, recommendable: *è una persona poco* —, he is an unreliable person; *questo* *albergo è* —, this hotel is recommendable (*o is to be recommended*).

raccomandàre, *v.t.* **1.** to recommend: *cercherò di raccomandarti presso il direttore,* I shall try to recommend you to the manager; *hai un buon insegnante da raccomandarmi?,* can you recommend me a good teacher?; *posso — questo prodotto,* I can recommend this product **2.** (*affidare*) to recommend, to commit, to entrust: *ti raccomando questo bambino,* look after (*o take care of*) this child for me ‖ — *l'anima a Dio,* to recommend (*o to commit*) one's soul to God **3.** (*esortare*) to exhort: *mi raccomandò che tutto fosse fatto bene,* he exhorted me to do everything properly **4.** (*lettere, pacchi, ecc.*) to register: — *una lettera,* to register a letter **5.** (*assicurare legando*) to fasten: — *a un albero,* to fasten to a tree ‖ **raccomandàrsi,** *v.r.* to implore (s.o.), to beg (s.o.): *egli si raccomandò a me perchè gli trovassi un posto,* he begged me to find him a job; *si raccomandò tanto perchè non lo dicessimo a nessuno,* he implored us not to tell anybody about it; *vieni presto, mi raccomando,* please come soon ‖ — *alle gambe,* to run away ‖ — *da sè,* to need no recommendation.

raccomandàta, *s.f.* **1.** registered letter: *fare una* —, to register a letter **2.** (*persona raccomandata*) person recommended.

raccomandatàrio, *s.m.* **1.** person to whom one is recommended **2.** (*mar.*) ship's agent.

raccomandàto, *ag.* **1.** recommended **2.** (*di lettera, pacchi, ecc.*) registered ‖ *s.m.* person recommended: *questo è il suo* —, this is the man he recommended.

raccomandatóre, *s.m.,* **raccomandatríce,** *s.f.* recommender.

raccomandazióne, *s.f.* **1.** recommendation: *lettera di* —, letter of introduction; *egli ha molte raccomandazioni,* he has many recommendations; *fare una* —, to make a recommendation **2.** (*di lettere, pacchi, ecc.*) registration **3.** (*esortazione*) exhortation; (*ammonizione*) warning; (*consiglio*) advice, recommendation: *la mamma gli fece mille raccomandazioni,* his mother gave him lots of advice.

raccomodaménto, *s.m.* repairing, mending.

raccomodàre, *v.t.* **1.** to repair, to mend: — *un orologio,* to repair a watch; — *un paio di scarpe,* to repair (*o to mend*) a pair of shoes; — *un vestito,* to mend a dress **2.** (*mettere in ordine*) to arrange, to put in order: *raccomodò i fiori nel vaso,* she arranged the flowers in the vase; — *la cravatta a qlcu.,* to straighten s.o.'s tie **3.** (*rimettere in sesto*) to revive, to set up: *quel vino mi ha raccomodato,* that wine has revived me.

raccomodatóre, *s.m.,* **raccomodatríce,** *s.f.* repairer, mender.

raccomodatúra, *s.f.* repairing, mending.

racconciaménto, *s.m.* mending, repairing.

racconciàre, *v.t.* **1.** (*raccomodare*) to mend, to repair: — *una strada,* to repair a road **2.** (*correggere migliorando*) to improve, to amend: — *un discorso,* to amend a speech ‖ **racconciàrsi,** *v.r.* **1.** (*rassettarsi*) to tidy oneself: — *i capelli,* to tidy one's hair **2.** (*riconciliarsi*) to become reconciled, to make it up **3.** (*del tempo, rasserenarsi*) to clear up **4.** (*risanarsi*) to recover.

racconciatúra, *s.f.* mending, repairing.

raccóncio, *ag.* **1.** (*riparato*) mended, repaired **2.** (*migliorato*) improved ‖ *s.m.* (*racconciatura*) mending, repairing.

racconsolàre, *v.t.* to console, to comfort ‖ **racconsolàrsi,** *v.r.* to console oneself, to comfort oneself.

raccontàbile, *ag.* fit to be told.

raccontafàvole, *s.m.* fibber, story-teller.

raccontàre, *v.t.* to tell, to relate, to recount, to narrate: *raccontami una storia,* tell me a story; *raccontano che...,* people say (*o it is said*) that...; *si racconta che egli sia molto ricco,* they say (that) he is very rich (*o he is said to be very rich*); *la storia non racconta di lui,* history does not mention him; *ti hanno raccontato la verità?,* were you told the truth? ‖ *a me*

la racconti?, tell it to the marines! ‖ *che cosa mi racconti!,* what are you telling me! ‖ *ringrazia Dio che questa la puoi* —, thank God you lived to tell the tale ‖ *raccontarne delle belle,* to spin yarns; *raccontarne delle belle sul conto di qlcu.,* to tell yarns about s.o. ‖ *va' a raccontarla altrove,* go and tell that to the marines ‖ — *per filo e per segno,* to narrate in detail.

raccontatóre, *s.m.,* **raccontatríce,** *s.f.* teller, narrator.

raccónto, *s.m.* **1.** story, tale; (*novella*) short story: — *di avventure,* tale of adventure; — *di fate,* fairy-tale; — *poliziesco,* detective-story; *libro di racconti,* story -book **2.** (*resoconto*) account, relation; (*relazione*) report; (*narrazione*) narration, narrative: *il* — *delle sue avventure,* the relation (*o account*) of his adventures; *mi fece un* — *dettagliato di quel che era accaduto,* he gave me a detailed report of what had happened.

raccorciaménto, *s.m.* shortening.

raccorciàre, *v.t.* to shorten ‖ **raccorciàrsi,** *v.r.* to grow shorter: *ora le giornate si raccorciano,* the days are growing shorter now.

raccordàre, *v.t.* **1.** to join together, to connect, to link together: — *due tubazioni,* to connect two pipes **2.** (*dare una curvatura di raccordo*) to radius; (*togliere gli spigoli vivi*) to blend **3.** (*ferr.*) to collect by siding ‖ **raccordàrsi,** *v.r.* to agree again.

raccòrdo, *s.m.* **1.** connection **2.** (*mec.*) union, connector: — *alla base del dente,* tooth-fillet; — *concavo di due superfici,* fillet; — *del cono,* cone radius; — *filettato,* nipple; — *orientabile,* banjo-union **3.** (*per tubazioni*) pipe-fitting: — *a tre pezzi,* pipe-union; — *a vite,* nipple; — *con diramazione,* branch; — *di fognatura,* house-sewer; — *per manichetta antincendio,* fire -hose connection **4.** (*ferr.*) siding, sidetrack, spur-track: — *insabbiato,* sanded siding; — *privato,* private siding (*o sidetrack*); *tronco di* —, feeder-line.

raccostaménto, *s.m.* **1.** (*avvicinamento*) approaching **2.** (*confronto*) comparison.

raccostàre, *v.t.* **1.** (*accostare*) to bring near, to approach, to push close **2.** (*confrontare*) to compare.

raccozzàre, *v.t.* to throw together ‖ **raccozzàrsi,** *v.r.* to get together, to meet.

racemífero, *ag.* (*bot.*) racemiferous.

racèmo, *s.m.* (*bot.*) raceme.

racemóso, *ag.* (*bot.*) racemose.

Rachèle, *no.pr.f.* Rachel.

rachialgía, *s.f.* (*med.*) rachialgia.

rachianestesía, *s.f.* (*med.*) rachianaesthesia.

rachicèntesi, *s.f.* (*med.*) rachicentesis.

ràchide, *s.f.* (*zool.bot.anat.*) r(h)achis (*pl.*r(h)achides).

rachidèo, *ag.* r(h)achidian.

rachítico, *ag.* **1.** rickety; (*rar.*) rachitic: *bimbo* —, rickety child **2.** (*stentato*) stunted: *una pianta rachitica,* a stunted plant.

rachítide, *s.f.,* **rachitísmo,** *s.m.* (*patol.*) rickets; (*rar.*) rachitis.

racimolàre, *v.t.* to scrape together, to gather, to collect; to pick (up); to glean (*anche fig.*): — *denaro,* to scrape money together; — *notizie,* to glean news ‖ *v.i.* (*agr.*) to glean a vineyard.

racimolatóre, *s.m.,* **racimolatríce,** *s.f.* **1.** collector; picker; gleaner (*anche fig.*): *quello è un* — *di idee altrui,* that man picks other people's brains **2.** (*agr.*) gleaner.

racimolatúra, *s.f.* **1.** (*il racimolare*) scraping together, gathering; picking (up); gleaning (*anche fig.*) **2.** (*ciò che si è racimolato*) scrapings (*pl.*); gleanings (*pl.*) (*anche fig.*) **3.** (*agr.*) (*il raccogliere racimoli*) gleaning; (*i racimoli raccolti*) the gleanings (*pl.*) of a vineyard.

racímolo, *s.m.* small bunch of grapes.

racquetàre, *v.t.* to calm down, to quieten down; to appease, to pacify ‖ **racquetàrsi,** *v.r.* to calm down.

racquistàre, *V.* **riacquistàre.**

ràda, *s.f.* (*mar.*) roadstead; roads (*pl.*).

Radamànto, *no.pr.m.* (*mit.*) Rhadamanthus.

radaménte, *av.* (*rar.*) rarely, seldom.

radància, *s.f.* (*mar.*) thimble.

ràdar, *s.m.* radar: — *ad onde persistenti,* continuous-wave radar; — *altimetrico,* height-finding radar; — *anticollisione e per avvistamento meteore,* cloud and collision warning radar; — *a risposta,* radar beacon (*o racon o secondary radar*); — *di controllo per aeroporti,* airfield-control radar; — *per intercettazione aerei,* aircraft-interception radar; — *portuale,* harbour-control radar; — *terrestre,* land-based radar; *contatto* —, radar contact; *nave attrezzata con* —, radar-fitted ship.

radarísta, *s.m.* radar controller.

radatúra, *s.f.* thinness.

radàzza, *s.f.* (*mar.*) swab.

radazzàre, *v.t.* (*mar.*) to swab.

raddensàbile, *ag.* capable of being thickened, condensable.

raddensaménto, *s.m.* thickening, condensation.

raddensàre, *v.t.* to thicken, to condense ‖ **raddensàrsi,** *v.r.* to thicken, to become thicker, to condense.

raddensatóre, *ag.* thickening, condensing ‖ *s.m.,* **raddensatríce,** *s.f.* thickener.

raddirizzàre, *e derivati,* V. **raddrizzàre,** *e derivati.*

raddobbàre, *v.t.* 1. to deck again, to adorn again 2. to repair, to refit (*anche mar.*).

raddòbbo, *s.m.* (*mar.*) repair, refit: *bacino di* —, dry-dock (*o graving-dock*).

raddoleàre, *v.i.* to become milder.

raddolciménto, *s.m.* 1. sweetening 2. *fig.* softening, appeasing; (*di dolore*) alleviation, mitigation.

raddolcíre, *v.t.* 1. to sweeten: — *una bibita,* to sweeten a drink 2. *fig.* to soften; to soothe: *lo raddolcì con un sorriso,* she softened (*o* pacified *o* mollified) him with a smile; *il successo gli ha raddolcito il carattere,* his success has softened his character; *lu tua presenza ha raddolcito la sua ira,* your presence has soothed his anger; — *un colore, un contrasto,* to tone down (*o* to soften) a colour, a contrast; — *un dolore,* to soothe (*o* to allay) a pain; — *la fatica di qlcu.,* to lighten s.o.'s toil; — *il tono della voce,* to subdue the tone of one's voice (*o* to soften one's voice) 3. (*metallo, acqua*) to soften ‖ **raddolcírsi,** *v.r.* 1. to soften; (*di dolore*) to be soothed, to be allayed 2. (*di tempo*) to become milder, to grow milder.

raddoppiaménto, *s.m.* 1. doubling: *il* — *di una linea,* (*ferr.*) the doubling of a line (*o* the laying of a second track) 2. (*gram.*) reduplication.

raddoppiàre, *v.t.* 1. to (re)double: *la linea verrà raddoppiata entro la fine dell'anno,* (*ferr.*) a second track will be laid before the end of the year; — *un numero,* to double a number; — *il proprio guadagno,* to double one's earnings; — *il proprio zelo, le proprie preoccupazioni,* to redouble one's zeal, one's worries 2. (*gram.*) to reduplicate ‖ *v.i.,* **raddoppiàrsi,** *v.r.* to (re)double.

raddoppiàta, *s.f.* 1. (re)doubling 2. (*equitazione*) gallop.

raddoppiataménte, *av.* doubly.

raddoppiàto, *ag.* 1. (re)doubled: *prese a scavare con ardore,* he started digging with redoubled zeal 2. (*gram.*) reduplicated.

raddoppiatúra, *s.f.* (re)doubling.

raddóppio, *s.m.* 1. (re)doubling: *binario di* —, (*ferr.*) switch-line 2. (*al biliardo*) double 3. (*equitazione*) gallop.

raddormentàre, *v.t.* to send to sleep (again) ‖ **raddormentàrsi,** *v.r.* to fall asleep (again).

raddossàre, *v.t.* to burden (again) (*anche fig.*).

raddrizzaménto, *s.m.* 1. straightening 2. (*correzione*) correction, redressing.

raddrizzàre, *v.t.* 1. to straighten, to make straight: *raddrizza quel quadro,* put that picture straight; — *una barra, una linea,* to straighten a bar, a line ‖ — *le gambe ai cani,* to wash a blackmoor white (*o* to labour in vain *o* to wash a donkey's ears) 2. (*correggere*) to correct; to redress; to revise: *dovresti* — *le tue idee su questo argomento,* you should revise your ideas on this matter; — *i torti,* to redress wrongs ‖ **raddrizzàrsi,** *v.r.* 1. to straighten oneself; (*mettersi eretto*) to draw oneself up 2. (*correggersi*) to correct oneself; (*migliorare*) to improve.

raddrizzatóre, *ag.* straightening ‖ *s.m.* 1. straightener 2. (*elett.*) rectifier.

raddrizzatríce, *s.f.* (*mec.*) straightener.

raddrizzatúra, *s.f.* straightening.

raddúrre, *v.t.* 1. to bring (back) 2. (*ridurre*) to reduce ‖ **raddúrsi,** *v.r.* to assemble.

radènte, *ag.* 1. shaving 2. (*che passa rasente*) grazing, skimming: *tiro* —, (*mil.*) grazing fire; *volo* —, (*aer.*) grazing flight ‖ *attrito* —, (*fis.*) rolling friction.

radènza, *s.f.* grazing movement.

ràdere, *v.t.* 1. to shave: *avete tempo di radermi?,* have you got time to shave me?; *mi avete rasato male,* you have shaved me badly; *questa mattina mi ha rasato il barbiere,* this morning I was shaved by the barber ‖ *farsi* —, to get a shave 2. (*abbattere*) to raze: *la città fu rasa al suolo dalle bombe,* the city was razed (to the ground) by the bombs 3. (*sfiorare*) to graze, to skim: *l'aeroplano rase il suolo,* the plane grazed (*o* skimmed) the ground; *un canale rade le mura,* a canal flows past the walls; *i proiettili radevano la nostra casa,* the bullets grazed our house; — *la superficie dell'acqua,* to skim the surface of the water 4. (*cancellare*) to erase ‖ **ràdersi,** *v.r.* to shave (oneself): *mi rado tutte le mattine,* I shave every morning; *ti radi da solo o vai dal barbiere?,* do you shave yourself or do you go to the barber's?.

radézza, *s.f.* 1. thinness; rareness; (*scarsità*) scarcity 2. (*intervallo*) interval: *gli alberi sono a una* — *di sei metri l'uno dall'altro,* the trees are arranged at intervals of six metres 3. (*successione a lunghi intervalli*) infrequency.

radiàle, *ag.* 1. (*anat.*) radial: *nervo* —, radial nerve 2. (*di raggio*) radial: *asse* —, radial axle; *turbina* —, (*mec.*) radial flow turbine.

radiànte, *ag.* 1. radiant: *calore* —, radiant heat 2. *fig.* radiant, beaming: *occhi radianti,* radiant eyes ‖ *s.f.* (*geom.*) radian.

radiàre¹, *v.i.* (*mandare raggi*) to radiate, to beam.

radiàre², *v.t.* 1. to expel; (*un nome*) to strike off: *fu radiato dalla scuola,* he was expelled from school; *lo radiarono dall'università,* he was sent down; *il suo nome fu radiato dalla lista,* his name was struck off the list ‖ — *un'ipoteca,* (*dir.*) to extinguish a mortgage 2. (*mar. mil.*) to condemn.

radiàti, *s.m.pl.* (*zool.*) Radiata.

radiàto¹, *ag.* radiate(d).

radiàto², *ag.* expelled; (*di nome*) struck off: — *da un'università,* sent down.

radiatóre, *s.m.* 1. (*aut. aer.*) radiator: — *a nido d'api,* (*aut.*) honeycomb radiator; — *anteriore,* (*aer.*) nose radiator; — *dell'olio,* (*aer.*) oil-cooler; *maschera per* —, (*aut.*) radiator-cowl; *tappo del* —, (*aut.*) radiator cap 2. (*termosifone*) radiator: — *ad alette,* gilled (*o* finned) radiator; — *a pannelli,* panel radiator; — *incassato,* recessed radiator.

radiazióne¹, *s.f.* (*fis.*) radiation: — *bianca,* white radiation; — *cosmica,* cosmic radiation; — *infrarossa,* infra-red radiation; — *nera,* full radiation; *caratteristica di* —, radiation pattern.

radiazióne², *s.f.* (*espulsione*) expulsion; (*di nome*) striking off.

ràdica, *s.f.* 1. (*legno*) briar (wood), brier (wood): *pipa di* —, brier (pipe) 2. (*radice*) root.

radicàle, *ag.* radical: *il partito* —, (*pol.*) the radical party; *una differenza* —, a radical difference; *segno, numero* —, (*mat.*) radical sign, number ‖ *s.m.* radical: — *acido,* (*chim.*) acid radical ‖ *s.f.* (*gram.*) root, radical: *la* — *di una parola,* the root of a word.

radicaleggiàre, *v.i.* (*pol.*) to favour the radical party.

radicalísmo, *s.m.* (*pol.*) radicalism.

radicalménte, *av.* **1.** radically **2.** (*completamente*) radically, completely, fundamentally: *sono due lingue — diverse,* they are two completely different languages.

radicaménto, *s.m.* radication, striking root.

radicàndo, *s.m.* (*mat.*) radical quantity.

radicàre, *v.i.* to root, to strike root, to take root, to radicate (anche *fig.*): *simili idee non radicano qui,* such ideas do not take root here ‖ **radicàrsi,** *v.r.* to root, to strike root, to take root.

radicàto, *ag.* deep(ly)-rooted, deep-seated (anche *fig.*): *una radicata antipatia,* a deep-rooted dislike.

radicazióne, *s.f.* rooting, radication.

radícchio, *s.m.* (*bot.*) chicory: — *bianco,* wild chicory.

radíce, *s.f.* **1.** root (anche *fig.*): *la — di un dente, della lingua, di un'unghia,* the root of a tooth, of the tongue, of a nail; *la — di una pianta,* the root of a plant; *la — di un polipo, di un callo,* (*med.*) the root of a polypus, of a corn; *la — di tutti i mali,* the root of all evil; *andare alla — delle cose,* to get to the root of things; *mettere, prendere —,* to take (*o* to strike) root (*spec. fig.*); *metter le radici al sole,* to up-root (*o* to root up) a plant **2.** (*rafano*) horse-radish **3.** (*mat. gram. mec.*) root: — *di un numero,* the root of a number; — *di una parola,* the root of a word; — *di un prigioniero,* (*mec.*) fast end (*o* root); — *quadrata, cubica,* (*mat.*) square, cube root; — *quadrata dei valore medi al quadrato,* (*elett.*) root-mean-square (*o* R.M.S.); *estrazione di —,* (*mat.*) extraction (*o* evolution) of root; *segno di —,* (*mat.*) radical sign.

radichétta, *s.f.* (*bot.*) radicle.

radicifórme, *ag.* (*bot.*) radiciform.

radicolíte, *s.f.* (*patol.*) radiculitis.

radiestesía, *s.f.* sensitivity to radiation.

ràdio[1], *s.m.* (*anat.*) radius (*pl.* radii).

ràdio[2], *s.m.* (*chim.*) radium: — *emanazione,* radium emanation.

ràdio[3], *s.f.* (*rad.*) **1.** radio, wireless; (*apparecchio*) radio(-set), wireless(-set), set: — *a galena,* crystal-set; — *a più valvole,* multi-valve set; — *grammofono,* radiogram; — *portatile,* portable radio: — *portatile ricevente e trasmittente,* walkie-talkie (*o* walky-talky); — *ricevente, trasmittente,* radio(-receiver), (radio-)transmitter; *impianto —,* (*aer.*) radio equipment; *ponte —,* radio-link; *c'è ql.co. alla radio?,* is there anything on the radio (*o* wireless)?; *ho comprato una nuova —,* I have bought a new radio (set); *ascoltare ql.co. alla —,* to listen to sthg. on the radio (*o* to listen in to sthg.); *cantare, parlare per —,* to sing, to talk on the wireless; *mandare un messaggio per —,* to send a message by radio; *trasmettere per —,* to broadcast **2.** (*sede*) radio: *è impiegato alla —,* he is on the radio staff.

radioamatóre, *s.m.,* **radioamatríce,** *s.f.* radio amateur; (*sl.*) radio ham.

radioattività, *s.f.* (*fis.*) radioactivity: — *indotta,* induced radioactivity; — *naturale,* natural radioactivity.

radioattívo, *ag.* (*fis.*) radioactive: *ferro —,* radio iron; *periodo —,* (*fis. atomica*) half-life; *pioggia radioattiva,* (*neol.*) fall-out; *zolfo —,* radio sulphur.

radioauditóre, *s.m.,* **radioauditríce,** *s.f.* listener; listener-in (*pl.* listeners-in).

radioaudizióne, *s.f.* listening; listening-in.

radiobiología, *s.f.* radiobiology.

radiobússola, *s.f.* (*mar. aer.*) radio-compass.

radiocanàle, *s.m.* radio channel.

radiocardiografía, *s.f.* radiocardiography.

radiochímica, *s.f.* radiochemistry.

radiocomandàre, *v.t.* to radio-control.

radiocomandàto, *ag.* radio-controlled.

radiocomàndo, *s.m.* radio control, wireless control.

radiocomunicazióne, *s.f.* wireless-communication, radio-communication.

radioconduttóre, *s.m.* radio-conductor.

radiocronísta, *s.c.* radio commentator.

radiodermíte, *s.f.* (*patol.*) radio-dermatitis.

radiodiffóndere, *v.t.* to broadcast.

radiodiffusióne, *s.f.* broadcasting; broadcast.

radiodilettànte, *s.c.* **1.** radio amateur **2.** (*chi costruisce radio*) amateur wireless-constructor.

radiofàro, *s.m.* radio-beacon: — *circolare, onnidirezionale,* (*aer. mar.*) omnidirectional radio-beacon (*abbr.* ORB); — *di avvicinamento,* (*aer.*) approach beacon; — *direttivo,* (*aer. mar.*) radio range beacon; — *di rotta,* (*mar.*) course-indicating beacon; — *di terra,* (*mar.*) ground radio-beacon; — *fisso,* (*aer. mar.*) directional radio-beacon; — *girevole,* (*aer. mar.*) rotating radio-beacon; — *per aviazione,* aviation beacon; *orientamento mediante —,* (*aer. mar.*) radio range orientation.

radiofonía, *s.f.* radiophony.

radiofònico, *ag.* radio, wireless (*attributivi*); radiophonic: *apparecchio —,* wireless- (*o* radio-) set; *stazione, trasmissione radiofonica,* wireless-station, wireless transmission.

radiòfono, *s.m.* (*fis.*) radiophone.

radiofonògrafo, *s.m.* radiogram(ophone).

radiofotografía, *s.f.* **1.** (*fotoradiogramma*) radiophotograph **2.** (*trasmissione di fotografie per radio*) radio-photography.

radiogoniometría, *s.f.* radiogoniometry.

radiogoniomètrico, *ag.* radiogoniometric.

radiogoniòmetro, *s.m.* radio-compass, radio direction-finder, wireless direction-finder.

radiografàre, *v.t.* to radiograph.

radiografía, *s.f.* **1.** radiograph, X-ray photograph, radiogram: *fare una — dello stomaco, del torace,* to take a radiograph of the stomach, of the chest **2.** (*radiologia*) radiography, X-ray photography.

radiogràmma, *s.m.* radiogram, radiotelegram.

radiogrammòfono, *s.m.* radiogram(ophone).

radiolàri, *s.m.pl.* (*biol.*) Radiolaria.

radiolocalizzatóre, *s.m.* radar apparatus.

radiolocalizzazióne, *s.f.* radar, radiolocation.

radiología, *s.f.* radiology; (*radioterapia*) X-ray treatment.

radiològico, *ag.* radiological.

radiòlogo, *s.m.* radiologist.

radiomessàggio, *s.m.* radio-message, wireless-message.

radiomètrico, *ag.* radiometric.

radiòmetro, *s.m.* radiometer.

radioónda, *s.f.* radio-wave: *radioonde a bassa frequenza, ad alta frequenza,* low-frequency, high-frequency radio-waves.

radioricevènte, *s.m.* radio-receiver, wireless-receiver, receiving set.

radioscopía, *s.f.* radioscopy.

radioscòpico, *ag.* radioscopic: *esame —,* X-ray examination.

radiosità, *s.f.* radiance, radiancy.

radióso, *ag.* radiant, beaming, bright, shining: *un — avvenire,* a bright future; *giornata radiosa,* bright day; *occhi radiosi,* shining (*o* bright) eyes; *viso —,* radiant face.

radiosónda, *s.f.* radiosonde.

radiotècnica, *s.f.* radiotechnology.

radiotelecomandàre, *v.t.* to radio-control.

radiotelèfono, *s.m.* radio-telephone.

radiotelegrafàre, *v.t.* to radio, to wireless.

radiotelegrafía, *s.f.* radio-telegraphy, wireless-telegraphy.

radiotelegraficaménte, *av.* by radio, by wireless.

radiotelegràfico, *ag.* wireless (*attributivo*), radio-telegraphic: *stazione radiotelegrafica,* wireless-station.

radiotelegrafísta, *s.m.* wireless-telegraphist.

radiotelegràmma, *s.m.* radiotelegram, wireless-telegram, Marconigram.

radioterapía, *s.f.* (*med.*) radiotherapy; radiotherapeutics; ray treatment.

radioteràpico, *ag.* (*med.*) radiotherapeutic.

radiotrasméttere, *v.t.* to broadcast; (*a una persona determinata*) to radio: *il concerto sarà radiotrasmesso domani,* the concert will be broadcast tomorrow; *mi radiotrasmisero le istruzioni,* they radioed the instructions to me.

radiotrasmettitóre, *s.m.* radio-transmitter.

radiotrasmissióne, *s.f.* broadcasting; broadcast: — *alla frequenza comune,* common-channel broadcasting; — *delle immagini,* photoradio ‖ — *a premi,* give-away show.

radiotrasmittènte, *ag.* broadcasting ‖ *s.f.* (radio) broadcasting station.

radiovisióne, *s.f.* television.

ràdo, *ag.* **1.** rare, thin, sparse: *barba rada,* sparse beard; *brodo —,* thin broth; *capigliatura rada,* thin hair; *case rade,* scattered houses; *foresta rada,* thin (*o* thinly-planted) forest; *nebbia rada,* thin (*o* light) fog; *tessuto —,* thin material **2.** (*non frequente*) infrequent; occasional: *rade apparizioni,* infrequent (*o* occasional) appearances ‖ *di —,* rarely (*o* seldom); *non di —,* often ‖ *s.m.* rareness, thinness.

ràdo, *av.* rarely, seldom.

ràdon, *s.m.* (*chim.*) radon.

radunàre, *v.t.* to assemble, to gather, to collect: *aveva radunato un gruzzolo,* he had gathered (*o* put together) a hoard; *raduna i tuoi libri e mettili qui,* gather your books and put them here; *gli studenti furono radunati nella sala,* the students were assembled (*o* collected) in the hall; — *gente, amici,* to gather people, friends ‖ **radunàrsi,** *v.r.* to assemble, to gather, to collect: *una gran folla si radunò intorno a lui,* a large crowd gathered (*o* assembled *o* collected) round him; — *in crocchi,* to gather in knots.

radunàta, *s.f.* **1.** (*il radunare*) assembling, gathering **2.** (*raduno*) assembly, gathering, collection: *una — di gente sulla piazza,* a gathering of people in the square; *far —,* to gather (*o* to assemble).

radùno, *s.m.* **1.** (*sportivo*) rally **2.** *V.* **radunàta.**

radùra, *s.f.* glade, clearing.

ràfano, *s.m.* (*bot.*) radish: — *tedesco,* horse-radish.

Raffaèle, *no.pr.m.* Raphael.

raffaellésco, *ag.* (*pitt.*) Raphaelesque: *profilo —,* fine (*o* delicate) profile; *stile —,* Raphaelesque style.

Raffaèllo, *no.pr.m.* (*st. pitt.*) Raphael.

raffazzonaménto, *s.m.* patching (up).

raffazzonàre, *v.t.* to patch up: *un discorso,* to patch up a speech ‖ **raffazzonàrsi,** *v.r.* (*acconciarsi alla meglio*) to dress up as best one can.

raffazzonatùra, *s.f.* patching (up): *il libro è una —,* the book is a patched-up job.

rafférma, *s.f.* **1.** (*conferma*) confirmation, reaffirmation **2.** (*rinnovo*) renewal **3.** (*mil.*) deferment of demobilization.

raffermàre, *v.t.* **1.** (*confermare*) to confirm, to reaffirm: — *una cosa detta,* to reaffirm something one has said; — *un impegno,* to confirm an engagement **2.** (*rinnovare*) to renew: — *un contratto,* to renew a contract **3.** (*riconfermare*) to re-engage: — *qlcu. in un ufficio,* to re-engage s.o. in an office **4.** (*rafforzare*) to strengthen **5.** (*mil.*) to defer (s.o.'s) demobilization ‖ **raffermàrsi,** *v.r.* (*solidificarsi*) to get hard, to harden.

raffèrmo, *ag.* stale: *pane —,* stale bread.

ràffica, *s.f.* **1.** squall; gust: — *di neve,* squall of snow; *il vento soffiava a raffiche,* the wind blew in gusts **2.** (*di armi da fuoco*) burst, volley: *una — di mitragliatrice,* a burst of machine-gun fire **3.** *fig.* hail, shower: *una — di colpi, di insulti,* a hail of blows, of insults.

raffiguràbile, *ag.* **1.** (*rappresentabile*) representable **2.** (*riconoscibile*) recognizable.

raffiguràre, *v.t.* **1.** (*rappresentare*) to represent **2.** (*riconoscere*) to recognize ‖ **raffiguràrsi,** *v.r.* (*immaginarsi*) to imagine; to picture to oneself: *me lo ero raffigurato alto e magro,* I had imagined him as a tall thin man;

mi piace raffigurarmi dove tu sei, I like to picture to myself the place where you are.

raffilàre, *v.t.* **1.** (*affilare*) to sharpen, to whet **2.** (*pareggiare tagliando*) to trim, to pare; (*un libro*) to shave.

raffilatóio, *s.m.* **1.** (*per affilare*) sharpener **2.** (*per pareggiare*) trimmer, clipper.

raffilatùra, *s.f.* **1.** (*affilatura*) sharpening, whetting **2.** (*pareggiamento*) paring, trimming; (*di libro*) shaving.

raffinaménto, *s.m.* **1.** refining: — *a fuoco,* (*ind.*) forge-refining; — *dello zucchero,* (*ind.*) sugar-refining **2.** *fig.* (*finezza*) refinement.

raffinàre, *v.t.* **1.** to refine (anche *fig.*); to purify: *leggi molto e cerca di — le tue espressioni,* read a lot and try to improve your speech; *vivere in mezzo alle cose belle raffina il gusto,* living among beautiful things refines one's taste; — *l'oro,* to purify gold; — *il sale,* to refine salt **2.** (*assottigliare*) to thin, to pare down: — *un bastone,* to thin down a stick ‖ **raffinàrsi,** *v.r.* to refine, to become refined (anche *fig.*): *con lo studio il gusto si raffina,* one's taste is refined by study; *l'oro si raffina nel fuoco,* gold is purified by melting.

raffinataménte, *av.* in a refined way, refinedly.

raffinatézza, *s.f.* refinement (anche *fig.*): *la — dell'arte,* the refinement of art; *la — della crudeltà,* the refinement of cruelty; *la — di un metallo,* the refinement of a metal; *è persona di grande —,* he is a very refined person; *sono raffinatezze che non capisco,* these are refinements I don't understand.

raffinàto, *ag.* refined (anche *fig.*): *arte raffinata,* refined art; *zucchero —,* refined sugar; *ha un'educazione raffinata,* he has refined manners; *sei di un'astuzia raffinata,* you are very subtle in your cunning ‖ *s.m.* refined person.

raffinatóio, *s.m.* (*metal.*) refining furnace.

raffinatóre, *ag.* refining: *arte raffinatrice,* refining art ‖ *s.m.,* **raffinatríce,** *s.f.* refiner.

raffinatùra, raffinazióne, *s.f.* refining.

raffinería, *s.f.* refinery: — *di petrolio,* oil-refinery; — *di zucchero,* sugar-refinery.

ràffio, *s.m.* grapnel, grappling-iron (*o* -hook).

raffittíre, *v.t.* **1.** to thicken, to make thicker: *ha intenzione di — il giardino,* he intends to put more plants in his garden **2.** (*rendere più frequente*) to make more frequent: *ha raffittito le sue gite a Como,* he has been going to Como more often ‖ **raffittírsi,** *v.r.* to thicken; (*di tessuti*) to shrink: *l'erba, dopo il primo taglio, si raffittisce,* grass thickens after the first cutting.

rafforzaménto, *s.m.* **1.** (*rinforzamento*) reinforcement **2.** *fig.* (*rinvigorimento*) strengthening.

rafforzàre, *v.t.* **1.** (*rinforzare*) to reinforce, to strengthen: — *le fondamenta,* to reinforce the foundations; — *un ponte,* to reinforce a bridge **2.** *fig.* (*rinvigorire*) to strengthen: *se vuoi riuscire nella vita, devi — la volontà,* if you want to be successful in life, you must strengthen your will; *la tua risposta ha rafforzato la mia decisione,* your answer has strengthened my decision **3.** (*mil.*) to fortify, to reinforce, to strengthen ‖ **rafforzàrsi,** *v.r.* to grow stronger, to get stronger, to increase in strength (anche *fig.*): *quel partito di sinistra si è recentemente rafforzato,* that left-wing party has grown stronger recently; *se vai in montagna per un po' di tempo, ti rafforzerai,* if you go to the mountains for some time, you will get stronger.

raffratellàre, *V.* **riaffratellàre.**

raffreddaménto, *s.m.* **1.** (*ind.*) cooling: — *ad acqua,* water-cooling; — *ad aria,* air-blast cooling; — *ad aria soffiata,* blown-air cooling; — *ad irraggiamento,* radiant cooling; — *entro stampo,* (*metal.*) die-quenching **2.** *fig.* (*di sentimenti*) coolness: *c'è un certo — fra di noi,* there is a certain coolness between us.

raffreddàre, *v.t.* **1.** to make cold; to cool: *questa nevicata ha raffreddato l'aria,* this snowfall has made the air cold; *raffredda bene questo vino prima di servirlo,* cool this wine well before serving it **2.** *fig.* to lessen, to diminish: *la distanza non ha raffreddato la loro amicizia*, distance has not lessened their friendship; *questo raffredderà il tuo entusiasmo, spero*, this, I hope, will lessen (*o damp*) your enthusiasm ‖ **raffreddàrsi,** *v.r.* **1.** to get cold, to become cold; to cool, to grow cool: *lascia che il tè si raffreddi un po'*, let your tea cool (down) a little; *questa stanza si raffredda subito*, this room soon gets quite cold **2.** *fig.* to die down, to wane: *i suoi entusiasmi si raffreddano facilmente*, his enthusiasms soon die down **3.** (*prendere un raffreddore*) to catch (a) cold, to get a cold: *se esci senza ombrello con questo tempo, ti raffredderai*, you will catch a cold if you go out without an umbrella in this weather.

raffreddàto, *ag.* **1.** cooled: *aria raffreddata*, cooled air; *questo vino va servito ben* —, this wine is to be well cooled before you serve it **2.** (*infreddato*): *è molto* —, he has a nasty cold.

raffreddatóio, *s.m.* (*ind. vetraria*) cooling chamber.

raffreddatóre, *ag.* cooling ‖ *s.m.* **1.** cooler: — *dell'olio,* (*aer.*) oil-cooler; — *in cascata*, cascade cooler; — *per olio vegetale*, (*ind. chim.*) vegetable-oil cooler **2.** (*metal.*) chill, chiller: — *inglobato*, internal chill.

raffreddatúra, *s.f.* (*raffreddore*) cold; (*leggera influenza*) chill.

raffreddóre, *s.m.* cold: — *di petto*, a cold in the chest; — *di testa*, a cold in the head; *aveva un forte* —, he had a heavy cold; *se non ti copri bene con questo freddo, ti buscherai un bel* —, if you don't wrap up well in this cold weather, you'll catch a nasty cold.

raffrenàbile, *ag.* restrainable.

raffrenàre, *v.t.* to restrain, to check, to curb, to control (anche *fig.*): *non sa* — *l'ira*, he cannot restrain (*o control*) his temper; *soltanto dopo gravi perdite è riuscito a* — *la passione per il giuoco*, only after heavy losses has he been able to check his passion for gambling; — *la lingua*, to check (*o* to curb) one's tongue ‖ **raffrenàrsi,** *v.r.* to restrain oneself, to control oneself (anche *fig.*): *raffrenati tutte le volte che stai per dire ql.co. di spiacevole*, restrain yourself every time you are going to say sthg. unpleasant.

raffrescaménto, *s.m.* cooling.

raffrescàre, *v.i.* to get cool, to grow cool; (*diventare più fresco*) to get cooler ‖ **raffrescàrsi,** *v.r.* to get cold: *sta' attento a non raffrescarti*, take care not to get cold.

raffrescàta, *s.f.* fall in temperature.

raffrettàre, *v.t.* to hasten, to hurry.

raffrontaménto, *s.m.* comparison.

raffrontàre, *v.t.* to compare, to collate: — *due testi*, to compare two texts ‖ *v.i.*, **raffrontàrsi,** *v.r.* to agree.

raffrónto, *s.m.* comparison, collation.

ràfia, *s.f.* (*bot.*) raffia.

ràgadi, *s.f.pl.* (*med.*) rhagades.

raganèlla, *s.f.* **1.** (*zool.*) tree-frog **2.** (*battola*) rattle, clapper.

ragàzza, *s.f.* **1.** girl: *una bella* —, a good-looking girl; — *sotto ai vent'anni*, teen-ager; *questo è il mio nome di* —, this is my maiden name ‖ — *squillo*, call-girl **2.** (*figlia*) daughter, girl **3.** (*innamorata*) sweetheart, girl-friend.

ragazzàglia, *s.f.,* **ragazzàme,** *s.m.* noisy crowd of boys, gang of boys, crowd of youngsters.

ragazzàta, *s.f.* **1.** childish trick, boyish trick, boyish prank: *è solo una* —, it's just a boy's prank **2.** (*opera immatura*) immature work.

ragàzzo, *s.m.* **1.** boy; youth; (*fam.*) lad: *un* — *di diciotto anni*, a youth of eighteen; *un* — *di dieci anni*, a boy of ten; *è un bravo* —, he is a good boy; *erano tutti ragazzi sotto ai vent'anni*, they were all teen-agers; *non fare il* —, don't act like a boy; *nonostante i suoi trent'anni è ancora un* —, he's still a boy, though he's over thirty ‖ *da* —, when a boy: *lo conosco fin da* —, I have known him since he was a boy **2.** (*figlio*) son, boy: *questo è il mio* —, this is my boy **3.** (*innamorato*) boy-friend, sweetheart **4.** (*garzone, fattorino*) boy, errand-boy, shop-boy; (*di ufficio*) office-boy: *il* — *del dro-*

ghiere, the grocer's boy; *il* — *dell'ascensore*, the lift-boy (*o amer.* the elevator-boy) **5.** (*fam.*) (*persona*) fellow, chap, boy; (*amer.*) guy: *che simpatico* —!, what a nice fellow!; *forza ragazzi!*, come on boys!.

ragazzóne, *s.m.* big boy: *quell'uomo è un vero* —, that man is just a great big boy.

ragazzòtto, *s.m.* lad, sturdy boy.

ragazzúme, *V.* **ragazzàglia.**

raggelàre, *v.i.,* **raggelàrsi,** *v.r.* to freeze.

raggentilíre, *v.t.* to refine; to teach good manners to (s.o.) ‖ **raggentilírsi,** *v.r.* to improve one's manners, to refine, to become refined.

raggiaménto, *s.m.* (*rar.*) radiation.

raggiànte, *ag.* radiant (with sthg.) (anche *fig.*); (*brillante*) shining (with sthg.); *fig.* beaming (with sthg.): — *di felicità*, radiant with happiness; *calore* —, (*fis.*) radiant heat; *le stelle raggianti*, the shining stars.

raggiàre, *v.i.* to radiate (with sthg.) (anche *fig.*); (*brillare*) to shine (with sthg.); *fig.* to beam (with sthg.): *raggiava di gioia*, he was beaming with joy; *il sole raggiava in cielo*, the sun was shining in the sky ‖ *v.t.* to radiate: *il suo volto raggiava gioia*, his face was radiant with joy; — *luce e calore*, to radiate light and heat.

raggiàto, *ag.* radiate, radial; radiated.

raggièra, *s.f.* aureole, radiant crown, radiant halo, halo (of rays) ‖ *a* —, radially.

ràggio, *s.m.* **1.** (*fis.*) ray; (*di luce*) ray, beam: — *alfa*, alpha ray; — *catodico*, cathode ray; — *cosmico*, cosmic ray; — *di luna*, moon-beam (*o* ray of moonlight); — *di sole*, sunbeam (*o* ray of sunlight); — *infracosmico*, infra-cosmic ray; — *infrarosso*, infra-red ray; — *luminoso*, ray of light; — *positivo*, positive (*o* canal) ray; — *röntgen*, röntgen ray; — *ultravioletto*, ultraviolet ray; — *X*, X-ray; *un debole* — *di luce*, a faint gleam of light; *fascio di raggi luminosi*, pencil of rays **2.** *fig.* ray, gleam: *un* — *di speranza*, a ray (*o* gleam) of hope **3.** (*scient.*) radius (*pl.* radii, radiuses): — *del cerchio inscritto*, (*geom.*) inradius; — *del cerchio primitivo*, (*mec.*) pitch-circle radius; — *del cono primitivo*, (*mec.*) cone distance; — *di curvatura*, (*scienza delle costruzioni*) bending radius; — *vettore*, (*mat. astr.*) radius vector **4.** (*area, campo*) radius (*pl.* radii, radiuses); range: *entro un* — *di cinque miglia*, within a radius (*o* a range) of five miles; *il mio* — *d'azione*, my range (*o* field) of action **5.** (*di ruota*) spoke.

raggiraménto, *s.m.* trick, cheat, swindle.

raggiràre, *v.t.* to trick, to cheat, to swindle: *si lasciava* — *da tutti*, he let everyone cheat him ‖ **raggiràrsi,** *v.r.* **1.** to wander about, to go about; to hang about **2.** (*trattare*) to handle (sthg.), to deal (with sthg.): *la discussione si raggirava su questo problema*, the discussion turned on this problem.

raggiràta, *s.f.* trick, cheat, swindle.

raggiratóre, *ag.* deceitful; swindling ‖ *s.m.,* **raggiratríce,** *s.f.* trickster, cheat, swindler.

raggirévole, *ag.* deceiving, deceitful, cheating.

raggíro, *s.m.* trick, cheat, deceit, subterfuge: *ottenere ql.co. con un* —, to obtain sthg. by a trick.

raggiróne, *s.m.* deceiver, cheat.

raggiúngere, *v.t.* **1.** to reach; to get to (s.o., sthg.); to arrive at (a place); to join: *li raggiungerò appena mi scriveranno*, I shall join them as soon as they write to me; *raggiunse la cima della montagna*, he reached (*o* got to) the top of the mountain; *la somma raggiunge i due milioni di lire*, the sum amounts to two million lire; *va' avanti, ti raggiungo presto*, go ahead, I'll soon catch up with you; — *un'automobile per la strada*, to overtake a car on the road **2.** (*conseguire*) to attain, to achieve: — *buoni risultati*, to achieve good results; — *il proprio scopo*, to attain (*o* to achieve) one's aim **3.** (*colpire*) to hit: *fu raggiunto da una pallottola*, a bullet hit him; — *il bersaglio*, to hit the target.

raggiungiménto, *s.m.* **1.** reaching **2.** (*conseguimento*) attainment, achievement.

raggiuntàre, *v.t.* to sew together, to join.

raggiustamènto, *s.m.* **1.** readjustment, repairing **2.** (*il riordinare*) rearrangement **3.** (*riconciliazione*) reconciliation.

raggiustàre, *v.t.* **1.** to readjust, to repair **2.** (*riordinare*) to rearrange, to set in order **3.** (*picchiare*) to strike, to beat ‖ **raggiustàrsi,** *v.r.* (*riconciliarsi*) to reconcile oneself (to s.o., sthg.; with s.o.) ‖ *v.r. reciproco* to become reconciled, to make (it) up.

ragglutinaménto, *s.m.* agglutination.

ragglutinàre, *v.t.* to agglutinate.

raggomitolàre, *v.t.* to roll up, to make into a ball ‖ **raggomitolàrsi,** *v.r.* to curl up, to roll oneself up.

raggranchiàre, raggranchíre, *v.t.* to benumb, to stiffen: *il freddo le aveva raggranchito le mani,* cold had benumbed his hands ‖ *v.i.* to become stiff: *sono tutto raggranchito,* I am stiff (*o* benumbed) with cold.

raggraneìllàre, *v.t.* to scrape together, to scrape up: — *un po' di soldi,* to scrape together some money.

raggrinzaménto, *s.m.* wrinkling (up), shrivelling up); crumpling.

raggrinzàre, raggrinzíre, *v.t.* to wrinkle (up), to shrivel (up); to crumple: *il caldo ha raggrinzito le foglie di queste piante,* the heat has shrivelled (up) the leaves of these plants; — *la fronte,* to frown (*o* to furrow one's brow); — *un vestito,* to crumple a dress ‖ *v.i.,* **raggrinzàrsi, raggrinzírsi,** *v.r.* to become wrinkled, to wrinkle, to shrivel: *le foglie si raggrinziscono al sole,* leaves shrivel in the sun; *il volto gli si è tutto raggrinzito,* his face has become all wrinkled.

raggrinzàto, raggrinzíto, *ag.* wrinkled, wrinkly, shrivelled: *una foglia raggrinzita,* a shrivelled leaf; *la sua faccia è tutta raggrinzita,* his face is all wrinkled.

raggroppàre, *v.t.* to knot ‖ **raggroppàrsi,** *v.r.* to knot, to become knotted.

raggrottàre, *v.t.* to knit: — *le ciglia,* to knit one's brows (*o* to frown).

raggrumàre, *v.t.i.,* **raggrumàrsi,** *v.r.* to clot; to coagulate, to curdle.

raggrumàto, *ag.* clotted; coagulated, curdled.

raggruppaménto, *s.m.* **1.** (*il raggruppare*) grouping **2.** (*gruppo*) group, assemblage: *un — di persone,* a group of people.

raggruppàre, *v.t.* to group, to assemble ‖ **raggruppàrsi,** *v.r.* to group, to assemble, to collect, to gather, to cluster: *i bambini si raggrupparono intorno alla nonna,* the children clustered (*o* gathered) round their grandmother; *molta gente si raggruppò intorno a lui,* many people assembled (*o* gathered *o* collected) round him.

raggruzzolàre, *v.t.* to scrape together ‖ **raggruzzolàrsi,** *v.r.* to curl up, to roll oneself up.

ragguagliàbile, *ag.* comparable.

ragguagliaménto, *s.m.* **1.** (*pareggiamento*) equalization; levelling **2.** (*paragone*) comparison.

ragguagliàre, *v.t.* **1.** (*pareggiare*) to equalize; to place on the same level; to level; to balance: — *le partite,* (*comm.*) to balance accounts **2.** (*paragonare*) to compare **3.** (*spianare*) to plane, to smooth, to make smooth **4.** (*informare*) to inform.

ragguagliataménte, *av.* **1.** (*comparativamente*) comparatively **2.** (*dettagliatamente*) in detail.

ragguàglio, *s.m.* **1.** (*pareggio*) equalization; levelling; balance **2.** (*paragone*) comparison **3.** (*informazione*) information; (*relazione*) report **4.** (*proporzione*) rate: *al — 2%,* at the rate of 2%.

ragguardévole, *ag.* **1.** considerable: *una quantità —* a considerable quantity **2.** (*importante*) notable.

ragguardevolézza, *s.f.* importance.

ragguardevolménte, *av.* considerably; notably.

ràgia, *s.f.* resin; rosin: *acqua —,* turpentine.

ragionaménto, *s.m.* **1.** reasoning, argument: *non fare tròppi ragionamenti,* don't reason too much; *il tuo — è giusto,* your reasoning is right; *persuadere col —,* to persuade by argument ‖ *bel —!,* (*iron.*) what

nonsense! **2.** (*discussione*) discussion **3.** (*discorso*) talk.

ragionàre, *v.i.* **1.** to reason (about, upon sthg.): *egli non sa —,* he cannot reason; — *su un argomento,* to reason about a subject **2.** (*discutere*) to argue (about sthg.): *ragionarono a lungo su questa faccenda ma non vennero a nessuna decisione,* they argued about this matter for a long time but they did not come to any decision **3.** (*parlare*) to talk over, to discuss (sthg.): *ne ragionerò con lui,* I shall talk it over with him.

ragionataménte, *av.* **1.** (*col ragionamento*) by reasoning **2.** (*ragionevolmente*) reasonably.

ragionàto, *ag.* **1.** reasoned: *una decisione ben ragionata,* a well-reasoned (*o* thought-out) decision **2.** (*razionale*) rational **3.** (*logico*) logical **4.** (*ragionevole*) reasonable.

ragionatóre, *s.m.,* **ragionatríce,** *s.f.* reasoner.

ragióne, *s.f.* **1.** reason: *l'età della —,* the years of discretion: *avere l'età della —,* to have come to the years of discretion; *l'uso della —,* the use of reason; *le disgrazie gli hanno turbato la —,* his misfortunes have unsettled his mind; *agire contro —,* to act contrary to all reason; *condurre alla —,* to bring to reason; *perdere il lume della —,* to lose one's reason (*o* to go mad) ‖ *— pura, pratica,* (*fil.*) pure, practical reason **2.** (*causa, motivo*) reason, motive: *per nessuna —,* for no reason (*o* on no account): *per nessuna — lo voglio vedere,* I don't want to see him for any reason (*o* on no account do I want to see him); *che — può avere avuto per fare ciò?,* what motive can he have had for doing that?; *dimmi la — per la quale l'hai fatto,* tell me the reason why you've done it; *ho qualche — di temere,* I have reason to fear; *non c'è — di pensarlo,* there is no reason to think so (*o* there are no grounds for thinking so); *non è una (buona) —,* that is no reason; *non so la — di tutto ciò,* I do not know the reason for all that; *chiedere la — di un'azione,* to ask the reason for an action ‖ *— di essere,* reason for existence (*o* raison d'être): *il suo sospetto non aveva più — d'essere,* her suspicion was no longer justified (*o* she no longer had any reason to be suspicious) ‖ *— di famiglia,* family reasons ‖ *— di più,* all the more reason: *è una — di più per licenziarlo,* that's another reason for dismissing him ‖ *— per cui,* that's why ‖ *— ultima delle cose,* (*fil.*) the first cause of things ‖ *assente per ragioni di salute,* absent on account of ill health ‖ *bella —!,* what nonsense! ‖ *dare, rendere — di ql.co.,* to give the reason for sthg. ‖ *darsi, farsi, rendersi —,* to resign oneself (*o* to accept the inevitable *o* to make the best of a bad job): *non so rendermi — di ciò che ho fatto,* I cannot explain why I did it; *non so rendermi — di tutto ciò,* I cannot understand the reason for all that **3.** (*argomentazione, prova*) reason, justification: *addurre le proprie ragioni,* to put forward one's reasons; *intendere —,* to listen to reason ‖ *a ragion veduta,* after due consideration ‖ *rendere di pubblica —,* to make manifest **4.** (*diritto*) right; reason: — *e torto,* right and wrong; *a — o a torto,* rightly or wrongly; *a — si preoccupa di ciò,* he has reason to worry about it; *ciò mi darà —,* this will prove (*o* show) I am right; *egli è dalla parte della —,* he is in the right; *non voleva darmi —,* he did not want to admit I was right; *questo gli apparteneva di —,* this belonged to him by right; *avere —,* to be right: *ho — da vendere,* I am absolutely right; *egli ha — di sgridarlo,* he is right in scolding him (*o* he has every reason to scold him); *hai non — ma ragionissima,* you're dead right; *io ho sempre —,* I am always right (*o fam.* heads I win, tails you lose); *avere mille ragioni,* to be quite right; *far valere le proprie ragioni,* to assert one's rights ‖ *— di Stato,* (*st.*) reason of State ‖ *a maggior, più forte —,* even more so ‖ *aver — di qlcu., ql.co.,* to get the better (*o* the upper hand) of s.o., sthg. ‖ *darle di santa — a qlcu.,* to give s.o. a good (*o* sound) beating (*o* thrashing *o* flogging) (*o fam.* to tan s.o.'s hide); *prenderle di santa —,* to get a good beating ‖

farsi — *da sè*, to take the law into one's hands ‖ *rendere* — *a qlcu.*, to do justice to s.o. ‖ *ricorrere a chi di* —, to apply to the proper person **5.** (*rapporto, proporzione*) ratio, proportion; (*tasso*) rate: — *diretta, inversa*, direct, inverse ratio; — *geometrica*, geometric ratio; *in* — *del 10 %*, at the rate of 10 %; *in* — *di tanto ognuno*, at the rate of so much a head **6.** (*comm.*): — *sociale*, style (*o* title *o* (trade) name) **7.** (*arc.*) quality; species.

ragionería, *s.f.* book-keeping; accountancy.

ragionévole, *ag.* **1.** reasonable; (*di buon senso*) sensible: *un essere* —, a reasonable (*o* rational) being; *un ragazzo* —, a sensible boy **2.** (*giusto, conforme a misura*) reasonable, just: *una pretesa* —, a reasonable claim; *prezzo* —, reasonable price.

ragionevolézza, *s.f.* reasonableness.

ragionevolménte, *av.* reasonably.

ragionière, *s.m.* accountant; book-keeper.

raglan, *s.m.* raglan: *maniche alla* —, raglan sleeves.

ragliaménto, *s.m.* braying.

ragliàre, *v.i.* to bray (anche *fig.*).

ragliàta, **ràglio**, *s.m.* bray, braying.

ràgna, *s.f.* **1.** (*rete per catturare uccelli*) bird net; (*agguato*) snare (anche *fig.*): *cader nella* —, to fall into a snare **2.** (*ragnatela*) cobweb **3.** (*parte logora di una stoffa*) threadbare patch, frayed place **4.** (*nuvoletta rada*) feathery cloud.

ragnàre, *v.i.*, **ragnàrsi**, *v.r.* **1.** (*di tessuto, logorarsi*) to fray, to become threadbare **2.** (*di cielo, coprirsi di nubi rade*) to be covered with feathery clouds.

ragnatéla, *s.f.*, **ragnatélo**, *s.m.* cobweb, (spider's) web: *stanza piena di ragnatele*, room full of cobwebs ‖ *sottile come una* —, as thin as a cobweb.

ragnàto, *ag.* (*di tessuto, logoro*) frayed, threadbare.

ragnatúra, *s.f.* **1.** (*parte logora di stoffa*) frayed place, threadbare patch **2.** (*nuvole rade*) feathery clouds (*pl.*).

ràgno, *s.m.* spider: *tela di* —, cobweb (*o* spider's web) ‖ *non saper cavare un* — *dal buco*, (*fam.*) to be good for nothing.

ragú, *s.m.* (*cuc.*) ragout.

raià, *s.m.* rajah.

raid, *s.m.* **1.** (*spor.*) race **2.** (*mil.*) raid.

Raimóndo, *no.pr.m.* Raymond.

ràion, *s.m.* (*ind. tessile*) rayon.

ràis, *s.m.* head fisherman.

rajà, rajah, *s.m.* rajah.

ralínga, *s.f.* (*mar.*) bolt-rope.

ràlla, *s.f.* (*mec.*) **1.** (*di porta*) pivot **2.** (*supporto di spinta*) thrustbearing, thrust-block **3.** (*per la rotazione di un piano orizzontale in un rimorchio*) fifth wheel.

rallegraménto, *s.m.* **1.** (*il rallegrarsi*) rejoicing **2.** (*gioia*) joy **3.** *pl.* congratulations: *molti rallegramenti*, many congratulations; *ti faccio i miei rallegramenti per esserci riuscito*, I congratulate you on your success.

rallegràre, *v.t.* to cheer (up), to make glad, to gladden: *questa notizia mi rallegra assai*, this news makes me very glad (*o* happy); *la sua presenza mi rallegra sempre*, his presence always cheers me up ‖ **rallegràrsi**, *v.r.* **1.** to rejoice (at sthg.), to be glad (about sthg.); to cheer up: *egli si rallegrò subito quando glielo dissi*, he cheered up at once when I told him; *mi rallegrai di quelle buone notizie*, I rejoiced at the good news; *mi rallegro di sapere che egli sta meglio*, I rejoice (*o* I am glad) to hear that he is better **2.** (*congratularsi*) to congratulate: — *con qlcu. per ql.co.*, to congratulate s.o. on sthg.: *mi rallegro con te per il tuo brillante successo*, I congratulate you on your brilliant success.

rallentaménto, *s.m.* **1.** (*di velocità*) slowing (down), slackening of speed, lessening of speed **2.** (*diminuzione*) slackening, slowing down, lowering, lessening: — *nella produzione*, slackening (*o* slowing down) of production.

rallentàndo, *s.m.* **1.** (*mus.*) rallentando **2.** (*cine.*) slow-motion,

rallentàre, *v.t.* (*allentare*) to slacken (anche *fig.*),

to relax (anche *fig.*); (*diminuire*) to slacken (anche *fig.*), to lessen (anche *fig.*): — *una corda*, to slacken a rope; — *la disciplina*, to relax discipline; — *il passo*, to slacken one's pace; — *la presa*, to relax (*o* to slacken) one's hold; — *la produzione*, to lessen production; — *i propri sforzi*, to relax (*o* to slacken) one's efforts; — *il tempo*, (*mus.*) to slacken the tempo; — *la velocità*, to slacken speed (*o* to slow down) ‖ *v.i.* **1.** (*di velocità*) to slow down, to slacken speed: *devi* — *in una zona abitata*, you must slow down (*o* slacken speed) in a built-up area **2.** (*diminuire*) to die down, to slacken; to grow less; to become fewer (*solo con sogg. al pl.*): *la produzione ha rallentato in questi ultimi anni*, production has slackened (*o* died down) in the last few years; *le sue visite rallentavano*, his visits became fewer; *il vento rallentò*, the wind died down (*o* slackened) ‖ **rallentàrsi**, *v.r.* to slacken, to get slack, to relax: *la disciplina si sta rallentando*, discipline is getting slack (*o* is being relaxed); *questa fune si è rallentata*, this rope has got slack; *le vendite si rallentano sempre in questa stagione*, sales always slacken at this time of year.

rallentatóre, *s.m.* **1.** (*mec.*) decelerator **2.** (*cine.*) slow-motion camera: *film proiettato col* —, film shown in slow-motion **3.** (*foto.*) restrainer.

rallignàre, *v.i.* to take root again (anche *fig.*).

rallíno, *s.m.* (*mec.*) pivot.

ràma, *s.f.* **1.** branch; (*molto piccola*) twig **2.** (*complesso dei rami*) ramage.

ramàccia, *s.f.* (*scopa*) broom.

ramadàn, *s.m.* (*relig. maomettana*) Ramadan.

ramàio, *s.m.* copper-smith.

ramaiolàta, *s.f.* ladleful.

ramaiuòlo, *s.m.* ladle.

ramanzína, *s.f.* telling-off, dressing-down, scolding: *fare una* — *a qlcu.*, to give s.o. a good telling-off.

ramàre, *v.t.* to copper, to cover with copper.

ramàrro, *s.m.* (*zool.*) green lizard.

ramàto, *ag.* **1.** (*coperto di rame*) copper-covered **2.** (*color di rame*) copper (*attributivo*); copper-coloured.

ramatúra, *s.f.* copperplating, coppering.

ramàzza, *s.f.* (*scopa*) broom.

ramazzàre, *v.t.* to sweep.

ràme, *s.m.* **1.** (*metal.*) copper: — *fuso*, casting copper; — *greggio, nero*, blister (*o* black) copper; — *in barre*, wirebar copper; *filo di* —, copper wire; *monete di* —, copper coins; *solfato di* —, (*chim.*) copper sulphate; *utensile di* —, copper utensil; *rivestire di* —, to copper **2.** *pl.* (*oggetti in rame*) copper (*solo sing.*): *il lunedì pulisco sempre i rami*, on Mondays I always polish the copper.

ramèico, *ag.* (*chim.*) cupric.

rameóso, *ag.* (*chim.*) cuprous.

ramerino, *s.m.* (*bot.*) rosemary.

ràmico, *ag.* (*chim.*) cupric.

ramiè, *s.m.* (*fibra tessile*) ramie.

ramière, *s.m.* copper-smith.

ramífero, *ag.* (*min.*) copper-bearing (*attributivo*), rich in copper: *filone* —, copper-bearing lode.

ramificàre, *v.i.*, **ramificàrsi**, *v.r.* to branch out, to ramify.

ramificàto, *ag.* branched, branching.

ramificazióne, *s.f.* ramification: *le ramificazioni di un fiume, di una società*, the ramifications of a river, of a society.

ramingàre, *v.i.* to rove, to roam, to wander.

ramíngo, *ag.* roving, wandering.

ramíno¹, *s.m.* (*vaso di rame*) copper jar.

ramíno², *s.m.* (*giuoco di carte*) rummy.

rammagliàre, *v.t.* to mend a run, to mend a ladder: *sai* — *una calza?*, do you know how to mend a ladder?.

rammagliatúra, *s.f.* mending (of a ladder).

rammarginàre, *V.* **rimarginàre**.

rammaricàre, *v.t.* to afflict ‖ **rammaricàrsi**, *v.r.* **1.** to regret (sthg.), to be sorry (about sthg.): *mi rammarico di non poterlo vedere*, I regret not being able (*o* I am sorry not to be able) to see him 2. (*lamentarsi*) to complain (of, about *sthg.*): *non fa che* —, he does nothing but complain.

rammàrico, *s.m.* regret, sorrow: *devo esprimere il mio — per quanto è accaduto*, I must express my regret for what happened; *penso a quel che ho fatto con molto —*, I think with sorrow of the things I have done.

rammassàre, *v.t.* to amass, to pile up.

rammemoràre, *V.* **rammentàre**.

rammendàre, *v.t.* to darn, to mend.

rammendatóre, *s.m.*, **rammendatríce**, *s.f.* darner, mender.

rammendatúra, *s.f.* 1. (*atto del rammendare*) darning, mending 2. (*effetto del rammendare*) darn, mend.

ramméndo, *s.m.* 1. (*atto del rammendare*) darning, mending: *palla da —*, darning-ball 2. (*effetto del rammendare*) darn, mend.

rammentàre, *v.t.* 1. to remember, to recall, to recollect; (*richiamare alla memoria*) to remind (s.o. of sthg.): *rammentami che devo andar via alle cinque*, remind me that I have to go at five; *mi rammenta suo padre*, he reminds me of his father; *non rammento questo libro*, I cannot remember this book; *non rammento il vostro nome*, I don't recollect (o recall o remember) your name; *qui tutto mi rammenta la mia gioventù*, everything here reminds me of my youth 2. (*menzionare*) to mention: *non — questo quando lui è qui*, don't mention this when he is here 3. (*teat.*) (*suggerire*) to prompt ‖ **rammentàrsi**, *v.r.* to remember, to recall, to recollect: *cercherò di rammentarmi ciò che ho visto*, I shall try to recollect (o remember) what I saw; *non mi rammento se lui c'era o no*, I cannot remember whether he was there or not; *non mi rammento il titolo*, I cannot recall (o remember) the title; *per quel che mi rammento*, as far as I can recollect ‖ *egli non si rammenta dal naso alla bocca!*, he can't even remember his own name!.

rammentatóre, *s.m.* 1. reminder 2. (*teat.*) (*suggeritore*) prompter.

rammolliménto, *s.m.* softening: *— cerebrale*, (*patol.*) softening of the brain.

rammollíre, *v.t.* 1. to soften (anche *fig.*), to make soft (anche *fig.*): *egli è rammollito dalla vita comoda*, easy living has made him soft; *quelle truppe sono rammollite dall'ozio*, those troops have been softened by idleness; *— la cera*, to soften wax 2. (*impietosire*) to move to pity ‖ **rammollírsi**, *v.r.* to soften (anche *fig.*), to go soft (anche *fig.*): *la cera si rammollisce al sole*, wax softens in the sun; *gli si è rammollito il cervello*, he has gone a bit soft in the head.

rammollíto, *ag.* soft (anche *fig.*); softened (anche *fig.*); (*effeminato*) effeminate: *un vecchio —*, an old man in his dotage; *non è così — come sembra*, he isn't as soft as he looks ‖ *s.m.* 1. (*imbecille*) imbecile 2. (*persona effeminata*) effeminate person; softling.

ràmo, *s.m.* 1. branch (anche *fig.*): *i rami di un albero*, the branches of a tree; *un — di una famiglia, di una scienza*, a branch of a family, of a science; *— d'ulivo*, olive-branch; *— piccolo*, twig; *— principale*, bough ‖ *avere un — di pazzia*, to have a touch of insanity; (*scherz.*) to be a bit dotty 2. (*campo di attività, di interessi*) branch, line: *— d'affari*, branch (o line) of business; *questo non è il mio —*, this is not my line 3. (*di fiume, lago, ecc.*) branch; arm: *— di un fiume*, di una catena di montagne, di una strada, a branch of a river, of a mountain-range, of a road; *il — di un lago*, the arm of a lake 4. (*filone di minerale*) vein 5. (*rampa di scale*) flight 6. (*delle corna*) antler: *i rami delle corna di un cervo*, the antlers of a stag.

ramolàccio, *s.m.* (*bot.*) radish.

ramoscèllo, *s.m.* twig.

ramosità, *s.f.* branchiness.

ramóso, *ag.* branched, branchy.

ràmpa, *s.f.* 1. (*ripida salita*) steep slope, ramp 2. (*di scale*) flight 3. (*zool. arald.*) paw.

rampànte, *ag.* 1. (*arald.*) rampant: *leone —*, lion rampant 2. (*che rampa*) climbing.

rampàre, *v.i.* (*rar.*) to climb ‖ *v.t.* to paw.

rampàta, *s.f.* 1. (*ripida salita*) steep slope 2. (*colpo di zampa*) blow with a paw.

rampicànte, *ag.* climbing; (*di pianta*) creeping: *pianta —*, creeper ‖ *s.m.* 1. (*ornit.*) climber 2. (*bot.*) creeper,

rampicàre, *v.i.*, **rampicàrsi**, *v.r.* to climb; (*di pianta*) to creep.

rampicatóre, *ag.* climbing ‖ *s.m.*, **rampicatríce**, *s.f.* (mountain) climber.

rampichíno, *s.m.* (*ornit.*) tree-creeper.

rampicóne, *s.m.* grapnel, grappling-iron.

rampinàre, *v.i.* (*mar.*) to grapple.

rampinàta, *s.f.* blow with a grapnel.

rampíno, *s.m.* (*di cavallo*): *piede —*, stub-toe ‖ *s.m.* 1. hook: *lo tirarono fuori dal pozzo con un —*, they pulled it out of the well with a hook ‖ *attaccarsi a tutti i rampini*, *fig.* to hang on tooth and nail ‖ *giocare di —*, *fig.* to steal 2. (*unghia di felino*) claw 3. (*rebbio di forchetta*) prong 4. (*mar.*) grapnel 5. (*fam.*) (*singolo segno di una scrittura irregolare o mal tracciata*) pothook.

rampógna, *s.f.* (*letter.*) reprimand, reproach: *aspre rampogne*, bitter reproaches.

rampognàre, *v.t.* (*letter.*) to reprimand, to reproach.

rampollàre, *v.i.* 1. (*di acqua*) to spring forth 2. (*di pianta*) to shoot (up) 3. (*sorgere*) to rise: *i pensieri rampollavano nella sua mente*, thoughts surged up in (o rose to) his mind.

rampóllo, *s.m.* 1. (*polla*) spring 2. (*di pianta*) shoot, scion 3. (*discendente*) offspring, scion 4. (*scherz.*) (*bambino*) brat, child.

rampóne, *s.m.* 1. (*mar.*) harpoon 2. (*da montagna*) crampon.

ramponière, *s.m.* (*mar.*) harpooner.

Ramsète, *no.pr.m.* (*st.*) Ram(e)ses.

ramúto, *ag.* (*rar.*) branched, branchy.

ràna, *s.f.* 1. frog ‖ *— pescatrice*, (*ittiol.*) frog-fish (o fishing frog) ‖ *gonfio come una —*, self-conceited ‖ *uomo —*, (*mar. mil.*) frogman 2. (*nuoto*) breast stroke: *nuotare a —*, to swim the breast stroke.

rànca, *s.f.* lame leg.

rancheggiàre, **ranchettàre**, *v.i.* to hobble, to limp.

rancía, *s.f.* (*mar.*) ration-list.

ranciàto, *ag.* orange (-coloured).

ràncico, *s.m.* sour taste in the mouth.

ranceóso, *ag.* rancid.

rancidaménte, *av.* rancidly.

rancidézza, *s.f.* rancidness, rancidity.

rancidíre, *v.i.* to become rancid.

rancidità, *s.f.* rancidity.

ràncido, *ag.* 1. rancid, rank: *burro —*, rancid butter 2. (*vecchio, ammuffito*) musty, trite: *stile —*, musty (o trite) style ‖ *s.m.* rancid taste, rancid smell: *questo burro sta prendendo il —*, this butter is getting rancid; *sapere di —*, to have a rancid (o rank) taste.

rancidúme, *s.m.* 1. rancidity 2. (*cose rancide*) rancid stuff 3. (*vecchiume*) stale; old-fashioned things (*pl.*).

ranchière, *s.m.* (*mil.*) (mess-)cook.

ràncio¹, *ag.* orange (coloured).

ràncio², *s.m.* (*mil.*) ration (*gener. pl.*), mess: *ora del —*, mess-time; *il — è stato scarso oggi*, the rations were poor today; *distribuire il —*, to distribute (o hand out) the rations.

rancóre, *s.m.* grudge, rancour: *senza —*, without malice (o without ill-feeling); *ci sono dei vecchi rancori tra di loro*, there is bad blood between them; *portare, serbare — a qlcu.*, to bear s.o. a grudge (o malice o ill-will): *non gli porto —*, I bear him no grudge; *soddisfare un — personale*, to gratify a private grudge.

rànda, *s.f.* 1. (*mar.*) spanker 2. (*rar.*) (*margine, estremità*) edge, extremity ‖ *a — a —*, closeby.

randàgio, *ag.* stray, wandering: *cane —*, stray dog.

randeggiàre, *v.i.* (*mar.*) to coast.

randellàre, *v.t.* to club, to cudgel, to bludgeon.

randellàta, *s.f.* blow with a club, blow with a cudgel, blow with a bludgeon.

randèllo, *s.m.* club, cudgel, bludgeon.

Randòlfo, *no.pr.m.* Randolph, Randal.

ranèlla, *s.f.* **1.** (*mec.*) washer **2.** (*zool.*) murex (*pl.* murices, murexes).

ranétta, *s.f.* (*varietà di mela*) rennet.

rànfìa, *s.f.* claw; (*di uccelli rapaci*) talon, claw.

ranfìgnàre, *v.t.* (*rar.*) to snatch away.

ranghinatóre, *s.m.* (*agr.*) side-delivery rake.

ràngo, *s.m.* **1.** rank, standing, place, station: *di alto* —, of high rank (*o* standing *o* degree); *avere il* — *di colonnello,* to hold the rank of colonel; *decadere dal proprio* —, to come down in the world; *occupare un* — *superiore, inferiore a qlcu.,* to rank above, below s.o.; *occupare un alto* — *sociale,* to be of high social standing **2.** (*mil.*) (*schiera, fila*) rank: *formare i ranghi,* to fall in(to) line; *mettere i soldati in due ranghi,* to draw up the men in two ranks; *rientrare nei ranghi,* to fall in again; *fig.* to return to the ranks; *rompere i ranghi,* to be dismissed (*o* to break away); *serrare i ranghi,* to close up (*o* to close the ranks); *uscire dai ranghi,* to break the ranks.

ràngola, *s.f.* (*rar.*) **1.** (*respiro affannoso*) panting **2.** *fig.* (*preoccupazione*) care, worry.

ranísta, *s.c.* (*spor.*) breast-stroke swimmer.

rannaiuòla, *s.f.* lyeing trough.

rannàta, *s.f.* lye washing.

ranneràre, *v.i.,* **ranneràrsi,** *v.r.* to cloud over.

ranneríre, *v.t.i.* to darken, to blacken.

rannestàre, *v.t.* to graft again.

rannlecchiàrsi, *v.r.* to crouch; to cuddle (up): — *dietro la porta,* to crouch behind the door; — *in un angolo,* to crouch in a corner; — *sotto le coperte,* to cuddle up under the blankets.

rannìdàre, *V.* annidàre.

rànno, *s.m.* lye ‖ *è perdere il* — *e il sapone,* it is wasted effort.

rannobìlíre, *v.t.* to ennoble, to make noble ‖ *v.i.* to become noble.

rannobìlíto, *ag.* ennobled.

rannodaménto, *s.m.* retying.

rannodàre, *v.t.* **1.** to retie **2.** *fig.* (*riprendere, riallacciare*) to renew: — *un'amicizia,* to renew friendship.

rannóso, *ag.* lye (*attributivo*).

rannuvolaménto, *s.m.* clouding over.

rannuvolàre, *v.i.* to become cloudy, to get cloudy, to cloud over: *in questa stagione spesso rannuvola,* in this season it often gets cloudy ‖ **rannuvolàrsi,** *v.r.* **1.** to become cloudy, to get cloudy, to cloud over: *il cielo si rannuvola,* the sky is clouding over (*o* is getting cloudy) **2.** *fig.* (*oscurarsi in volto*) to cloud over, to become gloomy, to darken: *a quelle parole si rannuvolò,* at those words he became gloomy.

rannuvolàta, *s.f.* clouding over: *una improvvisa* — *oscurò il cielo,* the sky suddenly became clouded over.

rannuvolàto, *ag.* **1.** clouded, cloudy, overcast: *cielo* —, clouded (*o* overcast) sky **2.** *fig.* (*accigliato*) gloomy: *volto* —, gloomy face.

ranòcchìa, *s.f.* frog.

ranocchiàia, *s.f.* **1.** place infested with frogs **2.** (*luogo paludoso*) swamp, marsh.

ranocchiàio, *s.m.* **1.** (*scherz.*) (*chi mangia ranocchie*) frog-eater **2.** (*chi vende ranocchie*) frog-seller.

ranocchiésco, *ag.* (*scherz.*) frog (*attributivo*).

ranòcchio, *s.m.* **1.** frog **2.** (*scherz.*) (*bambino*) brat.

rantolàre, *v.i.* **1.** to breathe heavily, to gasp for breath, to wheeze **2.** (*in punto di morte*) to have the death-rattle (in one's throat).

rantolìo, *s.m.* heavy breathing, gasping for breath.

ràntolo, *s.m.* **1.** heavy breathing, gasping for breath, wheezing **2.** (*della morte*) death-rattle.

rantolóso, *ag.* wheezing, gasping: *vecchio* —, wheezing old man.

rànula, *s.f.* (*patol.*) ranula.

ranuncolàcee, *s.f. pl.* (*bot.*) Ranunculaceae.

ranúncolo, *s.m.* (*bot.*) buttercup, ranunculus (*pl.* ranunculuses, ranunculi).

ràpa, *s.f.* (*bot.*) turnip ‖ *cime di* —, turnip-tops ‖ *testa di* —, *fig.* dunce (*o* blockhead) ‖ *voler cavar sangue da una* —, (*fam.*) to try to draw blood from a stone.

rapàccio, *s.m.* (*bot.*) rape.

rapàce, *ag.* **1.** rapacious, greedy: *uomo* —, greedy (*o* rapacious) man ‖ *sguardo* —, greedy eyes **2.** (*di animali*) predatory: *uccello* —, bird of prey.

rapaceménte, *av.* rapaciously, greedily.

rapacità, *s.f.* rapacity, greed.

rapàio, *s.m.* **1.** turnip field **2.** *fig.* (*confusione*) confusion, mess, muddle.

rapàre¹, *v.t.* to crop, to shear: *il barbiere mi ha rapato,* the barber has cropped my hair; — *qlcu. a zero,* to shave s.o.'s head.

rapàre², *v.t.* (*il tabacco*) to rasp, to grate.

rapàta, *s.f.* cropping.

rapàto¹, *ag.* cropped, shorn.

rapàto², *s.m.* (*tabacco da fiuto in polvere*) snuff.

rapè, *s.m.* (*tabacco grosso da fiuto*) rappee.

raperèlla, *s.f.* (*mec.*) washer.

raperíno, *s.m.* (*ornit.*) siskin.

raperónzolo, *s.m.* (*bot.*) rampion.

ràpida, *s.f.* rapid.

rapidaménte, *av.* rapidly.

rapidità, *s.f.* swiftness, rapidity, quickness, speed: *la* — *della corrente,* the swiftness (*o* rapidity) of the stream; *con la* — *del fulmine, del pensiero,* with the swiftness (*o* rapidity) of lightning, of thought; *camminare con grande* —, to walk very quickly.

ràpido, *ag.* swift, rapid, quick, speedy, fast: *rapida lettura,* quick (*o* speedy) reading; — *movimento,* swift movement; — *sguardo,* swift (*o* quick) glance; — *sviluppo,* rapid (*o* quick) growth; *una barca era trascinata lontana dalla rapida corrente,* a boat was being carried away by the rapid (*o* fast) current; *un delitto cui seguì una rapida vendetta,* a murder which was followed by a swift (*o* speedy) vengeance ‖ *s.m.* (*ferr.*) fast train, express (train): *il* — *delle 8,15,* the 8.15 express.

rapiménto, *s.m.* **1.** abduction; (*specialmente di bambino*) kidnapping: *non sono ancora stati scoperti gli autori del* — *del bambino,* the kidnappers of the child have not been discovered yet **2.** *fig.* (*estasi*) rapture, ecstasy: *ebbe alcuni istanti di* —, he was in ecstasy for a few moments.

rapína, *s.f.* **1.** robbery (with violence); (*saccheggio*) plunder: *la* — *è più grave del furto,* robbery with violence is more serious than theft; *commettere una* —, to commit a robbery ‖ — *a mano armata,* armed robbery ‖ *uccelli di* —, birds of prey ‖ *vivere di* —, to live by plunder **2.** (*cose rapite*) stolen goods (*pl.*); (*bottino*) plunder.

rapinàre, *v.t.i.* to rob; (*saccheggiare*) to plunder: *fu rapinato mentre rincasava a tarda notte,* he was robbed on his way back home late at night.

rapinatóre, *s.m.* robber; (*saccheggiatore*) plunderer.

rapíre, *v.t.* **1.** to abduct; (*specialmente bambini*) to kidnap; (*rubare*) to steal, to carry off: *il tesoro era stato rapito,* the treasure had been stolen (*o* carried off); — *un bambino,* to kidnap a child; — *una persona,* to abduct a person ‖ *rapito alla morte,* snatched from the jaws of death; *rapito dalla morte,* ravished by death **2.** *fig.* (*estasiare*) to ravish, to enrapture: *fummo rapiti dalla sua splendida voce,* we were ravished by her beautiful voice.

rapíto, *ag.* **1.** (*di persona*) abducted; (*specialmente di bambino*) kidnapped; (*rubato*) stolen: *il bimbo* — *è stato ritrovato,* the kidnapped child has been found; *i gioielli rapiti furono nascosti in una cantina,* the stolen jewels were hidden in a cellar **2.** *fig.* (*estasiato*) ravished, enraptured: *sguardo* —, ravished expression; *la guardava* —, he watched her enraptured.

rapitóre, *ag.* driving: *forza rapitrice delle acque,* driving force of the waters ‖ *s.m.,* **rapitríce,** *s.f.* abductor; *(specialmente di bambini)* kidnapper.

ràppa, *s.f.* 1. *(ciocca di pianticella)* tuft 2. *(mil.)* tassel.

rappaciàre, *V.* **rappacificàre.**

rappacificaménto, *s.m.* reconciliation.

rappacificàre, *v.t.* to reconcile, to pacify: — *due amici,* to reconcile (*o* to restore peace between *o* to pacify) two friends ‖ **rappacificàrsi,** *v.r.* reciproco to make peace, to become reconciled; to make it up; to make friends again: *dopo lunghe contese i due popoli si rappacificarono,* after a long conflict the two peoples became reconciled (*o* made peace); *finalmente si rappacificarono,* they made it up at last.

rappacificazióne, *s.f.* reconciliation.

rappallottolàre, *v.t.* to roll up into a ball.

rappattumàre, *V.* **rappacificàre.**

rappezzaménto, *s.m.* patching (up), mending: — *fatto alla meglio,* botching.

rappezzàre, *v.t.* 1. to patch (up), to mend: *rappezzami questa gonna,* please, patch this skirt for me; — *una camera d'aria,* to patch an inner tube 2. *fig.* (*mettere insieme*) to piece together: *ha frugato nella biblioteca per* — *questo articolo,* he has searched through the library to piece together this article.

rappezzatóre, *s.m.,* **rappezzatríce,** *s.f.* mender.

rappezzatúra, *s.f.* 1. patching (up) 2. *(parte rappezzata)* patch.

rappèzzo, *s.m.* 1. patch: *il suo vestito è pieno di rappezzi,* her dress is full of patches 2. *fig.* (*pretesto, scusa magra*) flimsy excuse, pretext; *(ripiego di poco effetto)* poor substitute: *questa scusa non è che un* —, this is merely a flimsy excuse.

rappianàre, *v.t.* to level.

rappiccàre, *V.* **riappiccàre.**

rappicciàre, *V.* **riappicciàre.**

rappicciníre, *v.t.* to make smaller.

rappicciolíre, rappiccolíre, *v.t.* to make smaller ‖ *v.i.,* **rappicciolírsi, rappiccolírsi,** *v.r.* to become smaller, to diminish.

rappigliaménto, *s.m.* (*rar.*) thickening; (*coagulamento*) coagulation; (*di latte*) curdling.

rappigliàre, *v.i.,* **rappigliàrsi,** *v.r.* to set, to thicken; to solidify; (*coagulare*) to coagulate; (*di latte*) to curdle.

rappisolàrsi, *v.r.* to drop off again (to sleep).

rapportàre, *v.t.* 1. to report, to relate, to tell: *rapportai il fatto alla polizia,* I reported the fact to the police 2. (*pettegolezzi, chiacchiere, ecc.*) to spread: *non fidarti delle persone che rapportano pettegolezzi maligni,* don't trust people who spread malicious gossip 3. (*aggiungere parte mancante*) to replace with another piece (*o* part) 4. (*pitt.*) to transfer, to reproduce ‖ **rapportàrsi,** *v.r.* to refer ‖ — *a qlcu.,* (*seguire il suo consiglio*) to take (*o* to follow) s.o.'s advice.

rapportatóre, *ag.* reporting, relating ‖ *s.m.* 1. reporter, relater; (*di pettegolezzi, ecc.*) spreader 2. (*topografia*) station-pointer 3. (*artigl.*) protractor: — *circolare,* circular protractor ‖ **rapportatríce,** *s.f.* reporter, relater; (*di pettegolezzi, ecc.*) spreader.

rappòrto, *s.m.* 1. (*relazione scritta o orale*) report; (*amm.*) statement: *il* — *mensile di una banca,* (*amm.*) the monthly statement of a bank; *il* — *ufficiale di un comitato al Parlamento,* the official report of a committee to Parliament; *fece un lungo e dettagliato* — *sulle sue ricerche,* he made a long and detailed report of his researches; *ho fatto un* — *contro di lui al suo direttore,* I reported him to his manager ‖ *andare a* — *da qlcu.,* to report to s.o.: *andò a* — *dal comandante,* he reported to his commanding officer ‖ *chiamare qlcu. a* —, to summon s.o.; (*mil.*) to tell s.o. to report 2. (*relazione, connessione*) relation, relationship; connection; intercourse: *rapporti commerciali, sociali,* business, social relations; *rapporti di amicizia,* friendly relations; *rapporti fra padre e figli,* father

-child relationship; *rapporti sessuali,* sexual intercourse; *i rapporti fra loro sono piuttosto tesi,* their relations are rather strained; *non c'è alcun* — *tra queste due cose,* there is no relation (*o* connection) between these two things; *le tue parole non hanno alcun* — *con questo problema,* what you say has no relation (*o* connection) with (*o* bears no relation to) this problem; *avere rapporti con qlcu.,* to have relations with s.o.: *ho avuto solo rapporti d'affari con lui,* I have had only business relations with him; *l'Italia non ha mai avuto nessun* — *con quel paese,* Italy has never had any relations with that country; *essere in buoni rapporti con qlcu.,* to be on good terms with s.o.; *mettere qlcu. in* — *con qlcu.,* to put s.o. in touch with s.o.; *mettersi in* — *con qlcu.,* to get in touch with s.o.; *rompere i rapporti,* to sever (*o* to break off) relations ‖ *in* — *a...,* in relation to... (*o* in connection with...) 3. (*riguardo*): *in* — *a,* in connection with (*o* with reference to); *sotto questo* —, in this respect; *sotto tutti i rapporti,* in every respect (*o* from all points of view) 4. (*mat. mec., ecc.*) ratio: — *di contrazione,* (*aer.*) contraction ratio; — *di funzionamento,* (*aer.*) slip function; — *di lavoro,* (*fis.*) work ratio; — *di riflusso,* (*chim.*) reflux ratio; — *di transformazione,* (*elett.*) ratio of transformation (*o* conversion); — *di trasmissione,* (*mec.*) gear; — *totale di trasmissione,* (*mec.*) overall gear ratio; — *tra il diametro e la lunghezza focale,* (*ott.*) aperture ratio; *nel* — *di cinque a quindici,* (*mat.*) in the ratio of five to fifteen 5. (*cucito*) appliqué.

rapprèndere, *v.i.,* **rapprèndersi,** *v.r.* (*coagulare, coagularsi*) to congeal, to coagulate; (*rassodare, rassodarsi*) to set; (*di latte*) to curdle: *questa gelatina (si) rapprende in fretta,* this jelly sets quickly; *il sangue (si) rapprende presto,* blood congeals (*o* coagulates) quickly.

rappresàglia, *s.f.* retaliation; reprisal: *atto di* —, act of retaliation; *per* —, in (*o* by way of) reprisal; *fare rappresaglie contro qlcu.,* to retaliate against s.o.

rappresentàbile, *ag.* performable: *questa commedia non è* —, this play is not performable.

rappresentànte, *ag.* 1. representing; (*descrivente*) describing 2. (*teat.*) performing ‖ *s.c.* representative; (*comm.*) agent: — *esclusivo,* sole agent.

rappresentànza, *s.f.* 1. representation (anche *pol.*); (*deputazione*) deputation: — *proporzionale,* (*pol.*) proportional representation; *agire in* — *di qlcu.,* to act on behalf of s.o. ‖ *spese di* —, entertainment expenses: *indennità per le spese di* —, entertainment allowance 2. (*comm.*) agency: — *esclusiva,* sole agency; *ha la* — *di una grande ditta,* he is agent for a big firm.

rappresentàre, *v.t.* 1. to represent: *la giustizia è rappresentata come una dea con in mano una bilancia,* Justice is represented as a goddess holding a pair of scales; *questo quadro rappresenta un paesaggio marino,* this picture represents a seascape; *i segni fonetici rappresentano i suoni,* phonetic symbols represent sounds 2. (*simboleggiare*) to symbolize, to represent, to stand for: *il leone rappresenta la forza,* the lion symbolizes strength; *in questo dramma il padre rappresenta la malvagità, il figlio la bontà,* in this drama the father represents (*o* symbolizes) wickedness, the son represents goodness 3. (*essere il rappresentante di*) to represent; to act for (s.o., sthg.); (*comm.*) to be agent for (s.o., sthg.): *il partito repubblicano era rappresentato da cinque uomini,* the Republican Party was represented by five men; *rappresento mio fratello,* I am acting for my brother; — *una ditta,* to be agent for a firm 4. (*teat.*) to perform, to act, to give; (*fam.*) to put on: — *una commedia,* to perform (*o* fam. to put on) a play ‖ — *una parte molto importante,* to play a very important part (anche *fig.*) 5. (*cine.*) to show (a film) 6. (*significare*) to mean: *le sue opinioni non rappresentano niente per me,* his opinions do not mean anything to me ‖ **rappresentàrsi,** *v.r.* to picture to oneself, to imagine.

rappresentativaménte, *ar.* representatively.

rappresentatívo, *ag.* representative.

rappresentatóre, *ag.* representing, representative; (*descrivente*) describing, descriptive ‖ *s.m.*, **rappresentatríce,** *s.f.* representer, representative.

rappresentazióne, *s.f.* **1.** representation; (*descrizione*) description: *ci diede una vivida — di quello che aveva sofferto,* he gave us a vivid description of his sufferings (*o* of what he had suffered); *questa è una — di un paesaggio russo,* this is a representation of a Russian landscape **2.** (*teat.*) performance: *la — di una commedia,* the performance of a play; *prima —,* first night (*o* première *o* first performance); *prima — assoluta,* world première ‖ *sacre rappresentazioni,* mysteries **3.** (*dir.*) representation: *ereditare per diritto di —,* to inherit by right of representation.

rappréso, *ag.* congéaled, coagulated; (*rassodato*) set; (*di latte*) curdled: *sangue —,* congealed blood.

rapsodía, *s.f.* rhapsody.

rapsodísta, *s.m.* rhapsodist.

rapsòdo, *s.m.* rhapsode, rhapsodist.

raraménte, *av.* seldom, rarely.

rarefacènte, *ag.* rarefactive, rarefying.

rarefàre, *v.t.* to rarefy ‖ **rarefàrsi,** *v.r.* to rarefy; to become rarefied.

rarefattíbile, *ag.* rarefiable.

rarefattívo, *ag.* rarefactive.

rarefàtto, *ag.* rarefied.

rarefazióne, *s.f.* rarefaction.

rarézza, *V.* **rarità 1. 3.**

rarificeàre, *v.t.* to rarefy.

rarità, *s.f.* **1.** rareness, rarity: *i diamanti sono molto costosi per la loro —,* diamonds are very expensive on account of their rarity **2.** (*cosa rara e pregevole*) rarity, curiosity; (*novità*) novelty: *questo oggetto è una —,* this object is a rarity (*o* curiosity) **3.** (*scarsezza*) scarceness, scarcity: *la — di certe piante,* the scarcity of certain plants **4.** (*rar.*) (*di tessuti, radezza*) thinness.

ràro, *ag.* **1.** rare; scarce; (*non comune*) uncommon, extraordinary: *libro, francobollo —,* rare book, stamp; *metalli rari,* rare (*o* precious) metals; *il buon senso è una delle cose più rare,* common sense is one of the rarest things; *era lodato per le sue rare virtù,* he was praised for his rare (*o* uncommon) virtues ‖ *come le mosche bianche,* as rare as can be ‖ *una bestia rara,* fig. an extraordinary person (*o* fam. a queer fish) **2.** (*infrequente*) rare; (*eccezionale*) exceptional; unusual: *un caso —,* an exceptional case; *le sue rare visite,* his rare visits; *è — che lo si veda,* it is unusual (*o* a rare thing) to see him ‖ *rare volte,* rarely (*o* seldom): *rare volte ho visto ql.co. di simile,* I have seldom seen such a thing **3.** (*rado*) thin; scanty: *nuvola rara,* thin cloud; *popolazione rara,* scanty population **4.** *terre rare,* (*chim.*) rare earths.

ras, *s.m.* ras.

rasàre, *v.t.* **1.** (*radere capelli, barba*) to shave: *il barbiere mi ha rasato,* the barber shaved me (*o* gave me a shave) **2.** (*pareggiare*) to smooth: *— un prato,* to mow a lawn; *— una siepe,* to trim (*o* to clip) a hedge ‖ **rasàrsi,** *v.r.* (*radersi*) to shave.

rasàto, *ag.* **1.** (*sbarbato*) shaven: *un mento ben —,* a clean-shaven chin **2.** (*liscio*) smooth **3.** (*simile a raso*) satin (*attributivo*): *carta rasata,* satin-paper; *tessuto —,* (*di seta*) satin; (*di lana*) clear-finished material.

rasatríce, *s.f.* (*ind. tessile*) shearing-machine.

rasatúra, *s.f.* **1.** (*di barba, capelli*) shaving, shave **2.** (*lisciatura*) smoothing; (*di siepe*) clipping; (*di prato*) mowing.

raschiaménto, *s.m.* **1.** scraping **2.** (*chir.*) curettage, curettement **3.** (*il tossicchiare*) clearing the throat.

raschiàre, *v.t.* to scrape, to scratch; (*cancellare*) to erase, to scratch out: *devi — via la vernice,* you must scrape away (*o* off) the paint; *egli raschiò l'intonaco dalla parete,* he scraped the plaster off the wall; *l'iscrizione fu raschiata via,* the inscription was scratched out ‖ *v.i.* (*tossicchiare*) to cough; to clear one's throat:

il raffreddore mi ha fatto — tutta la notte, my cold kept me coughing all night ‖ **raschiàrsi,** *v.r.*: *— la gola,* to clear one's throat.

raschiàta, *s.f.* scraping, scratching.

raschiatóio, *s.m.* scraper; (*metal.*) rabble.

raschiatóre, *ag.* scraping ‖ *s.m.*, **raschiatríce,** *s.f.* scraper.

raschiatúra, *s.f.* **1.** (*il raschiare*) scraping, scratching **2.** (*materia tolta raschiando*) scraping: *— di limone,* grated lemon-peel.

raschiétto, *s.m.* scraper; (*per cancellare*) eraser, erasing knife: *— piegato,* (*mec.*) hooked scraper; *finito a —,* (*mec.*) scrape-finished.

raschíno, *s.m.* erasing-knife.

ràschio¹, *s.m.* (*irritazione alla gola*) irritation in the throat, roughness of the throat.

raschío², *s.m.* scraping.

ràscia, *s.f.* **1.** (*tessuto di lana*) serge **2.** (*paramenti*) funeral hangings (*pl.*).

rasciugaménto, *s.m.* drying up.

rasciugàre, *v.t.* to dry: *— le lacrime, i panni,* to dry one's eyes (*o* tears), clothes ‖ *— una bottiglia,* to drain a bottle ‖ *— le tasche a qlcu.,* to clean s.o. out ‖ **rasciugàrsi,** *v.r.* to dry oneself: *— le mani, la faccia,* to dry one's hands, face.

rasciugatúra, *s.f.,* **rasciúgo,** *s.m.* drying, drying-up.

rasciútto, *ag.* dry, dried.

rasentàre, *v.t.* **1.** to graze, to graze by (s.o., sthg.), to graze past (s.o., sthg.), to skim past (s.o., sthg.), to shave: *l'autobus rasentò il muro,* the bus grazed (*o* shaved) the wall; *l'automobile ci rasentò mentre attraversavamo la strada,* the car grazed us (*o* skimmed past us) while we were crossing the street; *il proiettile mi rasentò la testa,* the bullet skimmed past my head; *l'uccello rasentò la superficie del lago,* the bird skimmed over the surface of the lake **2.** fig. (*confinare con*) to border on (sthg.): *ciò che ha detto rasenta l'idiozia,* what he said borders on the ridiculous; *rasenta la quarantina,* he is bordering on (*o* coming up to) forty; *— la pazzia,* to border on insanity ‖ *questa azione rasenta il codice penale,* this action just misses being illegal (*o* is just inside the law).

rasènte (a), *prep.* close to, very near: *— alla casa, al muro,* close to (*o* very near) the house, the wall; *— terra,* close to the ground; *passar —,* to skim (*o* to graze): *la palla passò — la rete,* the ball just skimmed the net.

rasièra, *s.f.* scraper.

ràso¹, *ag.* smooth; (*di barba*) shaven; (*di capelli*) shaven, close-cropped: *pelo —,* short hair ‖ *— al suolo,* razed to the ground ‖ *bicchiere —,* glass full to the brim; *misura rasa,* strike (*o* bare) measure ‖ *campagna rasa,* bare country ‖ *la mia mente è tabula rasa,* my mind is a blank ‖ *far tabula rasa,* to make a clean sweep.

ràso¹ (a), *prep.* close to: *camminava — al muro,* he was walking close to the wall.

ràso², *s.m.* satin: *un abito di —,* a satin dress.

rasoiàta, *s.f.* razor-slash.

rasóio, *s.m.* razor: *— elettrico,* electric razor; *— di sicurezza,* safety-razor; *il filo del —,* the razor's edge (*anche* fig.); *affilare il —,* to sharpen the razor.

ràspa, *s.f.* rasping-file, rasp.

raspaménto, *s.m.* rasping.

raspànte, *ag.* **1.** rasping **2.** (*di vino*) biting, rasping.

raspàre, *v.t.* **1.** (*levigare con la raspa*) to rasp, to file, to scrape: *— una superficie,* to rasp (*o* to file *o* to scrape) a surface **2.** (*irritare*) to rasp, to irritate: *queste sigarette raspano la gola,* these cigarettes irritate the throat **3.** (*grattare con le unghie*) to scratch: *il cane raspava la porta,* the dog was scratching at the door; *i polli raspavano nel cortile,* the chickens were scratching about in the courtyard **4.** (*di cavallo*) to paw: *— il terreno,* to paw the ground **5.** (*fam.*) (*rubare*) to pinch: *chi ha raspato il mio libro?,* who's pinched my book? **6.** (*produrre rumore*) to scratch, to rasp: *quella penna raspa quando scrivi*, that pen scratches when you write **7.** (*scrivere male*) to scribble: *scrivi chiaro, non — così!*, write clearly, don't scribble like that! **8.** (*frugare*) to search through: *non — nel mio cassetto*, don't go searching through my drawer.

raspatóio, *s.m.* (*agr.*) harrow.

raspatúra, *s.f.* **1.** rasping ‖ *— di gallina*, (*scherz.*) ugly handwriting **2.** (*ciò che si toglie raspando*) raspings (*pl.*); filings (*pl.*).

raspíno, *s.m.* rasper, scraper, smoothing-file.

raspío, *s.m.* rasping, rasping noise.

ràspo, *s.m.* **1.** (*graspo*) grape-stalk: *certe volte si fa il vino senza adoperare i raspi*, sometimes wine is made without using the grape-stalks **2.** (*vet.*) mange.

raspollàre, *v.t.* to glean ‖ *v.i.* to glean grapes.

raspollatúra, *s.f.* **1.** (*l'atto di raspollare*) grape -gleaning **2.** (*cose raspollate*) gleanings (*pl.*) (anche *fig.*): *raspollature critiche*, critical gleanings.

raspóllo, *s.m.* small bunch of grapes.

raspóso, *ag.* rough: *legno —*, rough wood.

rassegaménto, *s.m.* setting, solidification, solidifying.

rassegàre, *v.i.*, **rassegàrsi,** *v.r.* (*solidificarsi*) to set, to solidify: *il burro raffreddando si rassega*, butter solidifies when it cools; *lascia che il brodo rasseghi*, let the broth set.

rassegàto, *ag.* **1.** set, solidified **2.** *fig.* (*trito*) trite; (*stantio*) stale: *ormai è un affare —*, by now it is a stale matter.

rasségna, *s.f.* **1.** (*mil.*) (*rivista*) review; (*ispezione*) inspection; (*adunanza*) assembly, parade, muster: *il primo ministro fu presente alla — militare tenuta per l'anniversario della Liberazione*, the Prime Minister was present at the military review held on the anniversary of the Liberation; *tutti devono andare alla — delle 7*, all ranks will parade (o assemble o muster o go on parade) at 7 a. m.; *passare in —*, to inspect: *il generale passò in — la guardia d'onore*, the general inspected the guard of honour ‖ *quel soldato è sotto —*, they are considering that soldier's discharge from the service **2.** (*recensione*) review: *— teatrale*, theatrical review; *fare una — dei libri più recenti*, to review (o to criticise) the latest books **3.** (*esame su vasta scala*) survey: *— economica della nazione*, survey of the national economy **4.** (*periodico*) magazine, review: *una — letteraria*, a literary magazine (o review).

rassegnaménto, *s.m.* (*rar.*) reviewing, review.

rassegnàre, *v.t.* **1.** (*mil.*) to review; to inspect; to muster: *— i coscritti*, to inspect the recruits **2.** (*consegnare, presentare*) to hand in: *— le dimissioni*, to hand (o to send) in one's resignation; *ieri ha rassegnato le dimissioni dal comitato*, yesterday he resigned from the committee ‖ **rassegnàrsi,** *v.r.* **1.** to resign oneself: *è un gran dolore, ma bisogna —*, it is a great sorrow, but one must resign oneself to it; *mi rassegno alla vostra volontà*, I resign myself to your will; *mi sono rassegnato a lavorare con lui*, I have resigned myself to working with him; *si è finalmente rassegnato al suo destino*, he has at last resigned himself to his fate **2.** (*sottoscriversi*) *mi rassegno vostro devotissimo...*, I am (o remain) Yours faithfully....

rassegnataménte, *av.* resignedly.

rassegnàto, *ag.* resigned: *partì afflitto, ma —*, when he left he was sad but resigned; *si vede che è avvilito, ma —*, one can see he is discouraged, but resigned; *si vedeva che non era — a morire così presto*, one could see he was not resigned to dying so young.

rassegnazióne, *s.f.* resignation: *ci vuole —*, you must be resigned; *lo sopportò con — per mesi, ma poi perse la pazienza*, for months he endured it with resignation, but finally he lost his temper.

rassembràre[1], *v.i.* (*rar.*) (*somigliare*) to look like (s.o., sthg.); to be like (s.o., sthg.); to resemble (s.o., sthg.).

rassembràre[2], *v.t.* (*rar.*) (*raccogliere*) to gather, to collect ‖ **rassembràrsi,** *v.r.* to gather, to meet.

rasserenaménto, *s.m.* **1.** clearing up **2.** *fig.* (*il ritornare lieti*) cheering up.

rasserenàre, *v.t.* **1.** to clear (up), to brighten up: *il vento ha rasserenato il cielo*, the wind has cleared (up) the sky **2.** *fig.* (*far tornare lieto*) to cheer up: *quella notizia lo rasserenò*, that piece of news cheered him up ‖ *v.i.*, **rasserenàrsi,** *v.r.* **1.** to clear (up), to brighten up: *il cielo (si) rasserenò verso sera*, the sky cleared (up) towards evening; *partimmo che il tempo si era rasserenato*, when we left, the weather had brightened up (o cleared up) **2.** *fig.* (*tornare lieto*) to cheer up, to brighten up: *si è rasserenato dopo l'arrivo di suo figlio*, he cheered up after his son's arrival.

rasserenàto, *ag.* **1.** clear (again): *guardavo il cielo —*, I was looking at the sky, which had cleared up **2.** *fig.* cheerful (again): *quando mi guardò era —*, when he looked at me he was cheerful once again.

rasserenatóre, *ag.* **1.** clearing, brightening **2.** *fig.* (*che allieta*) cheerful: *dimmi una parola rasserenatrice*, tell me something cheerful.

rassestàre, *v.t.* to put in order, to arrange, to tidy (up).

rassettaménto, *s.m.* **1.** (*il rassettare*) tidying (up), arranging **2.** (*ordine*) tidiness, order, arrangement.

rassettàre, *v.t.* **1.** to arrange, to tidy (up); to put in order: *rassetta la tua camera, prima di uscire*, tidy (up) your room before going out **2.** (*riparare*) to mend, to repair: *gli rassettò i calzoni*, she mended his trousers **3.** (*riaccomodare*) to readjust **4.** (*correggere*) to correct, to emend ‖ **rassettàrsi,** *v.r.* to tidy oneself, to make oneself tidy: *rassettati un po' prima di venire a pranzo*, tidy yourself up a little before coming to dinner.

rassettatúra, *s.f.* **1.** (*il rassettare*) tidying (up), arranging **2.** (*ordine*) tidiness, order, arrangement.

rassicu-rànte, *ag.* reassuring; (*incoraggiante*) encouraging: *mi bastò la sua parola —*, his reassuring words were enough to help me.

rassicuràre, *v.t.* to reassure; (*incoraggiare*) to encourage: *cercai di rassicurarlo*, I tried to reassure him; *lo rassicurai nel miglior modo possibile*, I reassured him as well as I could ‖ **rassicuràrsi,** *v.r.* **1.** to be reassured, to recover confidence: *alle mie parole si rassicurò*, my words reassured him; *sembrò —*, he appeared reassured **2.** (*assicurarsi*) to make sure: *devi rassicurarti che la porta sia ben chiusa*, you must make sure the door is properly locked.

rassicuràto, *ag.* reassured.

rassicurazióne, *s.f.* assurance, reassurance: *nonostante le mie rassicurazioni*, in spite of my assurances.

rassodaménto, *s.m.* **1.** hardening, stiffening **2.** *fig.* strengthening, consolidation: *il — della nostra alleanza*, the consolidation of our alliance.

rassodàre, *v.t.* **1.** to harden: *la ginnastica rassoda i muscoli*, gymnastics hardens the muscles **2.** *fig.* to strengthen, to consolidate: *la sua visita rassodò i nostri legami di amicizia*, his visit strengthened the ties of our friendship ‖ *v.i.*, **rassodàrsi,** *v.r.* to harden: *il fango (si) rassodava al sole*, the mud was hardening in the sun; *questo cemento (si) rassoda molto velocemente*, this cement hardens (o sets) very quickly.

rassomigliànte, *ag.* like (s.o., sthg.), similar; alike (*predicativo*): *quei due fratelli sono molto rassomiglianti*, those two brothers are very much alike (o very similar); *è molto — a sua madre*, she is very like her mother.

rassomigliànza, *s.f.* likeness, resemblance, similarity: *non vedo nessuna — fra questi due*, I cannot see any likeness (o similarity) between these two.

rassomigliàre, *v.i.* to be like (s.o., sthg.), to resemble (s.o., sthg.); to be similar; (*solo nell'aspetto*) to look like (s.o., sthg.): *egli rassomiglia moltissimo a suo fratello*, he is very much like (o he looks very much like o he closely resembles o he is very much similar to) his brother ‖ *v.t.* (*rar.*) **1.** to be like; to be similar to (s.o., sthg.), to resemble; (*solo nell'aspetto*) to look like: *rassomiglia lo zio*, he looks like his uncle **2.** (*paragonare*) to compare: *lo rassomigliò a un demonio*, she compared him to a devil ‖ **rassomigliàrsi,** *v.r.* reciproco, to be similar, to be alike; to resemble each other (one another): *i due cugini si rassomigliano molto*, the two cousins are very similar (*o* very much alike *o* look very much alike) ‖ *si rassomigliano come due gocce d'acqua*, they are as like as two peas.

rassottigliaménto, *s.m.* **1.** thinning **2.** *fig.* (*il rendere più acuto*) sharpening.

rassottigliàre, *v.t.* **1.** to make thin **2.** *fig.* (*rendere più acuto*) to sharpen: *il bisogno rassottiglia la mente, l'ingegno*, necessity sharpens the mind, the wits ‖ **rassottigliàrsi,** *v.r.* **1.** to thin: *bisogna stare qui finchè la nebbia si rassottiglia*, we must stay here till the fog thins (out) **2.** *fig.* (*farsi più acuto*) to sharpen.

rastrellaménto, *s.m.* **1.** raking **2.** (*saccheggio*) ransacking, plundering **3.** (*mil.*) mopping up; (*di polizia*) combing **4.** (*di fondo di mare, fiume, lago*) dragging.

rastrellàre, *v.t.* **1.** to rake: — *il fieno*, to rake the hay **2.** (*saccheggiare, rubare*) to ransack, to plunder **3.** (*mil.*) to mop up; (*di polizia*) to comb: *la polizia ha rastrellato la città*, the police have combed the city; — *un paese occupato, un campo di battaglia*, to mop up an occupied country, a battle-field **4.** (*fondo di mare, fiume, lago*) to drag.

rastrellatúra, *V.* rastrellaménto.

rastrellièra, *s.f.* **1.** (*per il fieno*) hay-rack **2.** (*per i piatti*) plate-rack **3.** (*per fucili*) rifle-rack; (*per fucili da caccia*) gun-rack.

rastrèllo, *s.m.* **1.** rake **2.** (*rastrelliera per fucili*) rifle-rack; (*per fucili da caccia*) gun-rack **3.** (*cancello alle porte di una città*) portcullis.

rastremàre, *v.t.*, **rastremàrsi,** *v.r.* (*arch.*) to taper.

rastremazióne, *s.f.* (*arch.*) tapering.

ràta, *s.f.* instalment: *a rate*, by (*o* in) instalments (*o sl.* on the never-never); *pro, per* —, pro rata (*o* in proportion *o* proportionately).

ratafià, *s.m.* (*liquore*) ratafia, ratafee: — *di ciliegie*, cherry-brandy.

rateàle, *ag.* by instalments.

ratealménte, *av.* by instalments.

rateàre, *v.t.* to divide into instalments.

ràteo, *s.m.* (*comm.*) calculation of interest for a period of less than six months.

ratièra, *s.f.* (*ind. tessile*) dobby.

ratífica, *s.f.*(*dir.*) ratification, confirmation, approval: — *di una sentenza*, confirmation of a sentence.

ratificàre, *v.t.* **1.** (*dir.*) to ratify, to confirm, to approve: — *un trattato*, to ratify a treaty **2.** (*confermare*) to confirm: *ratifico quanto dissi ieri*, I confirm what I said yesterday.

ratificatóre, *ag.* (*dir.*) ratifying, confirming ‖ *s.m.*, **ratificatríce,** *s.f.* (*dir.*) ratifier, confirmer.

ratificazióne, *s.f.* (*dir.*) ratification, confirmation.

Ratisbóna, *no.pr.f.* (*geog.*) Ratisbon.

ratizzàre, *v.t.* to divide into instalments.

rat musqué, *s.m.* musk-rat, musquash.

rattaccàre, *v.t.* to re-attach, to re-fasten.

rattaménte, *av.* (*con rapidità*) swiftly, quickly.

rattemperàre, *v.t.* to temper, to mitigate, to moderate ‖ **rattemperàrsi,** *v.r.* to restrain oneself.

rattenére, *e derivati, V.* trattenére, *e derivati*.

rattepidíre, *v.t.* to cool (anche *fig.*) ‖ *v.i.*, **rattepidírsi,** *v.r.* to cool down (anche *fig.*).

rattézza, *s.f.* (*rapidità*) speed, rapidity, quickness.

rattiepidíre, *V.* rattepidíre.

rattína, *s.f.* (*panno cardato*) ratteen.

rattizzàre, *v.t.* to poke; to stir (up) (anche *fig.*): — *il fuoco*, to poke (*o* to stir) the fire.

ràtto¹, *s.m.* **1.** abduction; rape: *il* — *delle Sabine*, the rape of the Sabines **2.** (*di bambini*) kidnapping **3.** (*furto, rapina*) theft, robbery.

ràtto², *s.m.* (*zool.*) rat.

ràtto³, *ag.* (*rapido, veloce*) quick, swift ‖ *av.* (*rapidamente, velocemente*) quickly, swiftly.

rattoppàre, *v.t.* **1.** to patch (up), to mend: — *un vestito*, to patch up (*o* to mend) a dress; — *un paio di scarpe*, to mend a pair of shoes **2.** (*correggere*) to touch up: — *versi*, to touch up verses.

rattoppatúra, *s.f.* **1.** (*il rattoppare*) patching up, mending **2.** (*rattoppo*) patch.

rattòppo, *s.m.* patch.

rattrappiménto, *s.m.* (*contrazione*) contraction (of muscles); (*intorpidimento*) benumbing.

rattrappíre, *v.t.i.*, **rattrappírsi,** *v.r.* **1.** (*intorpidire*) to benumb: *il freddo mi ha rattrappito i piedi*, the cold has benumbed my feet; *mi si sono rattrappite le mani dal freddo*, my hands are benumbed (*o* stiff) with cold **2.** (*contrarre*) to contract.

rattrappíto, *ag.* **1.** (*intorpidito*) benumbed **2.** (*contratto*) contracted.

rattristaménto, *s.m.* **1.** (*il rattristarsi*) saddening **2.** (*tristezza*) sadness.

rattristànte, *ag.* saddening.

rattristàre, *v.t.* to sadden; to grieve ‖ **rattristàrsi,** *v.r.* **1.** (*divenire triste*) to become sad **2.** (*essere triste, spiacente*) to sorrow, to be sad; to be sorry; to grieve: *tutta la nazione si rattristò per la sua morte*, the whole nation grieved at (*o* for *o* over) his death.

rattristíre, *v.t.* to depress; to sadden ‖ **rattristírsi,** *v.r.* **1.** to become depressed; to become sad **2.** (*di fiori, languire*) to droop.

raucaménte, *av.* hoarsely.

raucèdine, *s.f.* hoarseness: *avere la* —, to have a hoarse voice.

ràuco, *ag.* hoarse: *suono* —, hoarse sound.

ravanèllo, *s.m.* (*bot.*) radish.

ravennàte, *ag.* of Ravenna ‖ *s.c.* inhabitant of Ravenna.

raviòli, *s.m.pl.* (*cuc.*) ravioli.

ravizzóne, *s.m.* (*bot.*) rape; cole: *olio di* —, rape-oil.

ravvaloràre, *v.t.* **1.** to increase; to add value to (s.o., sthg.): — *il credito*, to increase credit **2.** (*rafforzare*) to strengthen.

ravvedérsi, *v.r.* to reform, to mend one's ways: *spero che si ravveda*, I hope he will mend his ways.

ravvediménto, *s.m.* reformation; amendment.

ravvedúto, *ag.* reformed.

ravviaménto, *s.m.* **1.** (*il mettere in ordine*) tidying (up), putting in order **2.** (*il mettere sulla buona via*) putting on the right patch.

ravviàre, *v.t.* **1.** (*mettere in ordine*) to tidy (up), to put in order: — *una stanza*, to tidy up a room **2.** (*di fuoco, rattizzarlo*) to poke **3.** (*mettere sulla buona via*) to put on the right patch ‖ **ravviàrsi,** *v.r.* to tidy oneself: *ella si ravviò i capelli*, she tidied her hair; — *gli abiti*, to adjust (*o* to straighten) one's dress.

ravviàta, *s.f.* tidying (up): *darsi una* — *ai capelli*, to tidy (*o* to comb) one's hair.

ravvicinaménto, *s.m.* **1.** approach(ing), coming closer **2.** (*riconciliazione*) reconciliation **3.** (*confronto*) comparison.

ravvicinàre, *v.t.* **1.** to bring closer **2.** (*riconciliare*) to reconcile **3.** (*confrontare*) to compare ‖ **ravvicinàrsi,** *v.r.* **1.** to draw closer **2.** (*riconciliarsi*) to become reconciled (with s.o.), to make (it) up (with s.o.) ‖ *v.r.* reciproco to become reconciled, to make (it) up.

ravvisàbile, *ag.* recognizable.

ravvisàre, *v.t.* to recognize: *in questo quadro si ravvisa la mano del maestro*, in this picture we can recognize the hand of the master; *ti ravvisai subito*, I recognized you at once.

ravvivaménto, *s.m.* **1.** revivification; (*ritorno in uso, risveglio*) revival **2.** (*animazione*) animation.

ravvivànte, *ag.* reviving, revivifying.

ravvivàre, *v.t.* **1.** to revive (anche *fig.*); to revivify: *l'acqua ravviva i fiori*, water revives flowers; *ravviva il fuoco*, make up the fire; — *una persona svenuta*, to revive a fainting person; — *vecchie abitudini*, to revive (*o* to renew) old customs **2.** (*animare*) to animate, to enliven; (*rallegrare*) to brighten (up): *la gioia ravvivava il suo viso*, his face lit up with joy; *la stanza era ravvivata da molti mazzi di fiori*, the room was brightened up by many bunches of flowers ‖ **ravvivàrsi**, *v.r.* **1.** to revive: *le rose si ravvivarono subito nell'acqua*, the roses revived at once in the water **2.** (*animarsi*) to become animated; (*rallegrarsi*) to brighten up.

ravvivàto, *ag.* **1.** revived, revivified **2.** (*animato*) animated, enlivened; (*rallegrato*) brightened.

ravvivatóre, *s.m.*, **ravvivatríce**, *s.f.* **1.** reviver **2.** (*chi anima*) animator.

ravvòlgere, *e derivati, V.* **avvòlgere**, *e derivati.*

ravvoltolàre, *e derivati, V.* **avvoltolàre**, *e derivati.*

rayé, *ag.* (*rigato*) striped.

ràyon, *s.m.* rayon.

raziocinànte, *ag.* reasoning.

raziocinàre, *v.i.* to reason.

raziocinatívo, *ag.* ratiocinative.

raziocínio, *s.m.* **1.** (*ragione*) reason **2.** (*ragionamento*) reasoning; ratiocination **3.** (*buon senso, criterio*) common sense: *senza* —, without common sense.

razionàle, *ag.* rational: *un essere* —, a rational being; *meccanica* —, pure mechanics; *numero* —, rational number ‖ *s.m.* (*eccl.*) rational.

razionalísmo, *s.m.* (*fil.*) rationalism.

razionalísta, *s.c.* (*fil.*) rationalist.

razionalità, *s.f.* rationality.

razionalizzàre, *v.t.* to rationalize.

razionalizzazióne, *s.f.* rationalization.

razionalménte, *av.* rationally.

razionaménto, *s.m.* rationing.

razionàre, *v.t.* to ration.

razióne, *s.f.* **1.** ration, allowance: — *di pane, di burro*, bread, butter ration; *doppia* —, double ration; *mettere a* —, to put s.o. on short allowance (*o* rations) **2.** (*porzione*) portion, share.

ràzza[1], *s.f.* **1.** race, breed: *una* — *di bestiame*, a breed of cattle; *la* — *bianca, gialla*, the white, yellow race; — *canina*, breed of dogs; *la* — *semitica*, the Semitic race; *la* — *umana*, the human race; *di* — *incrociata*, cross-bred; *di* — *pura*, pure-bred; (*di bestiame, cani, ecc.*), pedigree; (*di cavallo*) thoroughbred: *un cavallo di* — (*pura*), a thoroughbred (horse); *odio di* —, race-hatred; *migliorare, incrociare le razze*, to improve, to cross the breeds **2.** (*stirpe*) race; (*discendenza*) descent, stock: *di nobile* —, of noble descent; *è di buona* —, he comes of sound stock **3.** (*genere, sorta*) kind, sort: *gente di tutte le razze*, all kinds of people; *che* — *di lavoro è?*, what kind of work is it? ‖ *che* — *di cretino!*, what an idiot!.

ràzza[2], *s.f.* (*delle ruote*) spoke.

ràzza[3], *s.f.* (*ittiol.*) ray, skate.

razzamàglia, *s.f.* (*marmaglia*) rabble, mob, riff-raff.

razzía, *s.f.* **1.** (*incursione a scopo di preda*) raid, foray: *fare* —, to sack (*o* to plunder) **2.** (*insetticida*) insect-powder, insecticide.

razziàle, *ag.* racial.

razziàre, *v.t.* to sack, to plunder.

razziatóre, *s.m.* sacker, plunderer.

razzísmo, *s.m.* racialism.

razzísta, *s.c.* racialist.

ràzzo, *s.m.* **1.** (*pirotecnico*) rocket, sky-rocket **2.** (*proiettile*) rocket; (*missile*) missile **3.** (*per segnalazioni luminose*) signal rocket; star shell; flare **4.** (*raggio di ruota*) spoke **5.** (*aer. mec.*): *aereo* —, (*aer.*) rocket-plane; *motore a* —, (*mec.*) rocket-motor (*o* rocket-engine); *propulsione a* —, (*mec.*) rocket-propulsion.

razzolàre, *v.i.* to scratch (about): *le galline razzolavano nel cortile*, the hens were scratching about in the yard ‖ *egli predica bene e razzola male*, he does not practise what he preaches ‖ *chi di gallina nasce convien che razzoli*, *prov.* the leopard cannot change his spots **3.** (*rovistare*) to rummage.

razzumàglia, *s.f.* (*marmaglia*) rabble, mob, riff-raff.

re[1], *s.m.* king: — *assoluto, costituzionale*, absolute, constitutional king; *il* — *degli animali*, the king of beasts; *il* — *dei cuochi*, the king of cooks; *il* — *del petrolio*, the oil-king; *il* — *di fiori, di cuori*, (*a carte*) the king of clubs, of hearts; *il* — *di Francia*, the king of France; *scacco al* —, (*negli scacchi*) check; *giurare fedeltà al proprio* —, to swear fidelity to one's king ‖ *i Re Magi*, the Magi (*o* the Three Kings) ‖ *il Re Sole*, the Sun-King (*o* le Roi-Soleil) ‖ *Cristo Re*, Christ the King.

re[2], *s.m.* (*mus.*) D, re.

reagènte, *ag.* reacting ‖ *s.m.* (*chim.*) reagent.

reagíre, *v.i.* to react (anche *chim.*): *sopportarono tutto ciò senza* —, they bore all this without reacting; — *alle passioni*, to wrestle with one's passions; — *violentemente a un'accusa*, to react violently against an accusation.

reàle[1], *ag.* **1.** real; (*vero*) true: *fatti reali*, real facts; *vantaggio* —, real advantage **2.** (*dir.*) real: *azione* —, real action; *diritti reali*, real rights **3.** (*mat.*) real: *numero* —, real number ‖ *s.m.* the real; (*realtà*) reality.

reàle[2], *ag.* royal: *famiglia* —, royal family; *un principe* —, a royal prince; *sangue* —, royal blood; *i reali*, the royal family.

reàle[3], *s.m.* (*moneta spagnola*) real.

realísmo, *s.m.* **1.** (*fil. lett. art.*) realism **2.** (*fedeltà all'originale*) realism: *riprodotto con sorprendente* —, reproduced with startling realism.

realísta[1], *s.c.* (*fil.*) realist.

realísta[2], *s.c.* (*persona monarchica*) royalist ‖ *essere più* — *del re*, to be more Catholic than the Pope.

realístico, *ag.* realistic; realist (*attributivo*).

realizzàre, *v.t.* **1.** to carry out, to realize; (*conseguire*) to achieve, to accomplish: — *un'idea, un progetto*, to carry out (*o* to realize) an idea, a plan **2.** (*convertire in denaro, riscuotere*) to realize: *delle azioni*, to realize (*o* to sell out) shares; — *un profitto*, to realize a profit; *quanto hai realizzato con la tua vecchia automobile?*, how much did your old car fetch? (*o* how much did you get for your old car?) ‖ **realizzàrsi**, *v.r.* to come true; to come off, to be realized; to be fulfilled: *i miei progetti si sono realizzati*, my plans have come off (*o* have been realized).

realizzazióne, *s.f.* **1.** carrying out, fulfilment, realization; (*conseguimento*) achievement: *la* — *delle sue speranze*, the fulfilment (*o* the realization) of his hopes; *la* — *del nostro scopo*, the achievement of our aim **2.** (*conversione in danaro*) realization **3.** (*teat.*) production; (*messa in scena*) staging.

realménte[1], *av.* really; (*veramente*) truly.

realménte[2], *av.* (*regalmente*) royally.

realtà, *s.f.* reality: *attenersi alla* —, to stick to realities (*o* to facts); *essere vicino alla* —, to be near the mark; *essere lontano dalla* —, to be wide of the mark ‖ *in* —, in reality (*o* really *o* as a matter of fact).

reàme, *s.m.* kingdom: *il* — *dei cieli*, the kingdom of heaven.

reàto, *s.m.* (*contravvenzione*) offence; (*delitto*) crime: — *di lesa maestà*, crime of lese-majesty; *commettere un* —, to commit a crime; *incolpare qlcu. di un* —, to charge s.o. with a crime.

reattíno, *s.m.* (*ornit.*) wren.

reattívo, *ag.* (*chim.*) reactive: *carta reattiva*, test paper ‖ *s.m.* (*chim.*) reagent.

reattóre, *s.m.* **1.** (*fis. atomica*) reactor: — *a catena*, chain reactor; — *nucleare*, nuclear reactor; *regione attiva del* —, reactor core **2.** (*elett.*) choke coil **3.** (*aeroplano a reazione*) jet (plane).

reazionàrio, *ag.* *s.m.* reactionary.

reazióne, *s.f.* reaction: — *a catena*, (*fis. atomica*) chain reaction; — *acida*, (*chim.*) acid reaction; — *acustica*, (*rad.*) acoustic feedback; — *basica*, (*chim.*) alkaline reaction; *aereo a* —, (*aer.*) jet(-plane); (*aereo*) *caccia a* —, (*aer.*) jet fighter(-plane); *motore a* —

(*mec.*) jet engine (*o* jet-motor *o* rocket-motor); *propulsione a* —, (*mec.*) jet-propulsion; *tempo di* —, (*psicologia*) reaction time.

rébbio, *s.m.* prong.

Rebècca, *no.pr.f.* Rebecca ‖ *dim.* Becky.

rèbus, *s.m.* **1.** rebus, picture-puzzle **2.** *fig.* riddle.

recalcitrànte, **recalcitràre**, *V.* **ricalcitrànte**, **ricalcitràre**.

recapitàre, *v.t.* to deliver: — *una lettera, un pacco*, to deliver a letter, a parcel.

recàpito, *s.m.* **1.** (*indirizzo*) address: *ha il* — *alla locanda*, he is generally to be found at the public -house **2.** (*consegna*) delivery: *pronto* —, prompt delivery; *la lettera non ha avuto* —, the letter was not delivered.

recàre, *v.t.* **1.** to bring; to bear (anche *fig.*); (*contenere*) to contain: *il giornale recava delle cattive notizie*, the newspaper contained (*o* gave) bad news; *il suo viso reca i segni della sofferenza*, his face bears the signs of his suffering; *la tavoletta recava un'iscrizione latina*, the tablet bore a Latin inscription; — *un'ambasciata*, to bring (*o* to carry) a message; — *conforto*, to bring comfort ‖ — *ad effetto*, to carry out: *non potè* — *ad effetto il suo piano*, he could not carry out his plan ‖ — *a mente*, to bear in mind: *reca a mente ciò che ti dico*, bear in mind what I tell you ‖ — *a perfezione*, to bring to perfection ‖ — *a termine*, to finish (off): *devi* — *a termine questo lavoro*, you must finish (off) this work **2.** (*cagionare, arrecare*) to bring about, to cause: *ciò mi recò molto danno*, this did me a lot of harm; *ciò mi recò una quantità di noie*, this caused me a lot of trouble; *non voglio recarti noia, disturbo*, I don't want to give you any trouble (*o* to trouble you); — *dolore*, to give (*o* to bring *o* to cause) sorrow; — *gioia a qlcu.*, to make s.o. happy; — *piacere a qlcu.*, to give s.o. pleasure **3.** (*volgere, tradurre*) to turn: — *in volgare*, to turn into the vulgar tongue **4.** (*considerare, interpretare*) to interpret: *il suo gesto gli fu recato a lode*, his gesture was interpreted in his favour ‖ **recàrsi**, *v.r.* **1.** to go: *mi recai alla stazione*, I went to the station **2.** — *a mente*, to call to mind.

recèdere, *v.i.* to recede, to withdraw; to withdraw (sthg.); (*rinunziare*) to give up (sthg.): — *da un contratto*, to withdraw from a contract; — *dalle proprie offerte, promesse*, to withdraw one's offers, promises; — *da una posizione*, to withdraw (*o* to back out of) a position; — *da una protesta*, to give up a claim.

recensióne, *s.f.* review: — *di un libro*, review of a book; *copia in* —, review copy; *fare la* — *di un libro*, to review a book.

recensíre, *v.t.* to review.

recensíto, *ag.* reviewed.

recensóre, *s.m.* reviewer.

recènte, *ag.* recent; late; (*nuovo*) new: *recenti avvenimenti, notizie*, recent events, news; *di data* —, of recent date; *negli anni recenti*, in recent (*o* in late) years; *un provvedimento* —, a new measure; *una scoperta, un'invenzione* —, a recent (*o* a new) discovery, invention ‖ *recentissime*, (*giornalismo*) latest news (*o* stop press) ‖ *di* —, recently.

recenteménte, *av.* recently.

rècere, *v.t.* (*letter.*) to vomit ‖ *far* —, to induce vomit; *fig.* to disgust.

recessióne, *s.f.* recession.

recèsso, *s.m.* **1.** recess (anche *fig.*): *i recessi di una montagna*, the recesses of a mountain; *gli intimi recessi del cuore*, the inmost recesses of the heart **2.** (*dir.*) renunciation; (*ritiro*) withdrawal **3.** (*il recedere*) receding, withdrawing, recession.

recettíbile, *ag.* receptible.

recettibilità, *s.f.* receptibility.

recettività, *s.f.* receptivity, receptiveness.

recettívo, *ag.* receptive.

recètto, *s.m.* shelter, retreat.

recezióne, *s.f.* **1.** (*rad.*) reception: — *a cardioide*, heart (*o* cardioid) reception; — *ad eterodina*, beat (*o* heterodyne) reception; — *differenziale*, diversity reception; *disturbare la* —, to blanket **2.** (*comm.*) receipt: *accusare* — *di ql.co.*, to acknowledge receipt of sthg.

recídere, *v.t.* to cut (off); (*chir.*) to amputate: — *un arto, un organo*, to amputate a limb, an organ; — *un ramo da un albero*, to cut off a branch from a tree; — *la testa di un animale*, to cut off an animal's head.

recidíva, *s.f.* **1.** (*dir.*) relapse (into crime) **2.** (*med.*) relapse.

recidivàre, *v.i.* to relapse.

recidività, *s.f.* **1.** (*dir.*) recidivism **2.** (*med.*) relapse.

recidívo, *ag.* **1.** (*dir.*) recidivous **2.** (*med.*) relapsing ‖ *s.m.* **1.** (*dir.*) recidivist; habitual criminal, old offender **2.** (*med.*) relapser.

recíngere, *v.t.* to surround, to encompass, to enclose: — *un giardino con un muro*, to surround a garden with a wall (*o* to fence in a garden).

recínto, *ag.* surrounded, enclosed ‖ *s.m.* **1.** enclosure, fence; (*per animali da cortile*) pen: — *in muratura*, walled enclosure; *muro di* —, enclosure -wall **2.** (*spor.*) ring.

reciòtto, *s.m.* "reciotto" (Italian sparkling red wine).

rècipe, *s.m.* (*med.*) prescription; (*arc.*) recipe: *per* —, by prescription.

recipiènte, *ag.* capacious ‖ *s.m.* container, vessel, receptacle; (*ind.*) kier, vat; (*di latta*) can, tin: — *graduato*, (*chim.*) graduate; — *metallico*, (*ind.*) kettle; — *per acqua lustrale*, (*arch.*) piscina; — *per generi alimentari*, food-container.

recíproca, *s.f.* (*mat.*) reciprocal.

reciprocaménte, *av.* reciprocally, mutually: *ci aiutiamo* —, we help each other (one another).

reciprocànza, *s.f.* reciprocity, reciprocality.

reciprocàre, *v.t.* to reciprocate.

reciprocazióne, *s.f.* **1.** reciprocation **2.** (*avvicendamento*) alternation.

reciprocità, *s.f.* reciprocity, reciprocality.

recíproco, *ag.* **1.** reciprocal, mutual: *amore* —, mutual love; *obblighi, vantaggi reciproci*, reciprocal (*o* mutual) obligations, benefits **2.** (*mat. gram.*) reciprocal: *in ragione reciproca*, (*mat.*) in inverse ratio; *verbi reciproci*, (*gram.*) reciprocal verbs.

recisaménte, *av.* resolutely.

recisióne, *s.f.* (*chir.*) excision; (*amputazione*) amputation.

recíso, *ag.* **1.** cut (off); (*chir.*) excised: *fiori recisi*, cut flowers **2.** (*risoluto*) resolute, determined: *una risposta recisa*, a flat answer.

rècita, *s.f.* **1.** (*rappresentazione*) performance: — *all'aperto*, out-door performance; — *di beneficenza*, charity performance **2.** (*recitazione*) recitation.

recitàbile, *ag.* **1.** suitable for recitation **2.** (*rappresentabile*) performable.

recitàre, *v.t.* **1.** to recite: *recitò un sonetto*, he recited a sonnet; — *una lezione*, to repeat a lesson; — *le preghiere*, to say one's prayers **2.** (*teat.*) to act, to play: *recitano tutti bene in questa commedia*, they all act well in this play; — *una parte*, to play a part; — *la parte di Re Lear*, to play (*o* to act) King Lear **3.** *fig.* (*fingere*) to act: *i suoi modi non erano spontanei, ha recitato tutto il tempo*, his manners were not spontaneous, he acted all the time; — *la commedia*, to play a part.

recitatívo, *ag.* (*mus.*) recitative ‖ *s.m.* (*mus.*) recitative, recitativo.

recitatóre, *s.m.*, **recitatríce**, *s.f.* reciter.

recitazióne, *s.f.* **1.** recitation: — *di una poesia*, recitation of a poem **2.** (*teat.*) acting: *scuola, insegnante di* —, drama school, drama teacher; *la* — *era buona, ma la messa in scena era mediocre*, the acting was good but the staging was poor.

reclamànte, *ag.* **1.** claiming **2.** (*che si lamenta*) complaining ‖ *s.m.* claimant, claimer.

reclamàre, *v.t.* to claim; to demand: — *un diritto,* to claim a right; — *il pagamento di un debito,* to demand the payment of a debt; — *il risarcimento dei danni,* to claim damages ‖ *v.i.* to complain; to protest: *egli fu il solo a —,* he was the only one to complain (*o* to protest).

réclame, *s.f.* **1.** (*pubblicità*) advertising: *fare della — a un prodotto,* to advertise a product **2.** (*avviso pubblicitario*) advertisement (*o fam.* ad).

reclamísta, *s.m.* advertiser, booster.

reclamístico, *ag.* advertising.

reclàmo, *s.m.* complaint: *inoltrare, respingere un —,* to make, to reject a complaint.

reclinàre, *v.t.* to bow, to incline, to bend: — *il capo,* to bow (*o* to bend) one's head ‖ *v.i.* to slope.

reclinàto, *ag.* bowed, inclined, bent: *parlò col capo —,* he spoke with his head bent (*o* bowed).

reclíno, *ag.* (*letter.*) bowed, inclined, bent.

reclusióne, *s.f.* **1.** seclusion: *nella — di questo luogo solitario,* in the seclusion of this solitary place ‖ *suore di —,* enclosed nuns **2.** (*dir.*) (*pena carceraria*) imprisonment, confinement: *cinque anni di —,* five years' imprisonment (*o* confinement); *fu condannato alla —,* he was condemned to imprisonment.

reclúso, *ag.* secluded ‖ *monache recluse,* enclosed nuns ‖ *s.m.* (*prigioniero*) prisoner.

reclusòrio, *s.m.* prison, gaol, jail.

rècluta, *s.f.* **1.** (*mil.*) recruit **2.** (*novizio*) novice: *è una — dell'arte,* he is a novice in the arts.

reclutaménto, *s.m.* (*mil.*) recruitment, enlistment.

reclutàre, *v.t.* (*mil.*) to recruit, to enlist.

recollètti, *s.m.pl.* (*eccl.*) Recollects.

recòndito, *ag.* hidden, concealed; (*profondo*) inmost, innermost: *luogo —,* hidden (*o* concealed) place; *pensieri reconditi,* inmost thoughts; *scopo, significato —,* hidden purpose, meaning ‖ *s.m.* inmost recess: *nei profondi reconditi dell'anima,* in the inmost recesses of the soul.

record, *s.m.* record: — *di velocità,* speed-record; *battere un —,* to break (*o* to beat) a record; *stabilire un —,* to set up a record.

recriminàre, *v.i.* **1.** to recriminate; to retort an accusation **2.** (*lamentarsi*) to complain: *allo stato delle cose non giova —,* as things stand there is no use in complaining.

recriminatóre, *ag.* **1.** recriminating **2.** (*che si lamenta*) complaining ‖ *s.m.,* **recriminatríce,** *s.f.* **1.** recriminator **2.** (*chi si lamenta*) complainer.

recriminazióne, *s.f.* **1.** recrimination **2.** (*lamentela*) complaint: *non perder tempo in inutili recriminazioni!,* don't waste your time in useless complaints!.

recrudescènza, *s.f.* recrudescence, fresh outbreak; return: — *di febbre,* recrudescence of fever; *una — di influenza,* a fresh outbreak of influenza; *c'è stata una — di cattivo tempo,* there has been a return of bad weather.

rècto, *s.m.* face; (*di foglio*) recto; (*di moneta, medaglia*) obverse: *sul — della cambiale,* on the face of the bill.

recuperàre, *V.* **ricuperàre.**

recuperatòrio, *ag.* (*dir.*) recuperatory.

redarguíre, *v.t.* to blame; (*rimproverare*) to scold, to reproach: — *aspramente,* to scold severely.

redàtto, *ag.* drawn up, compiled, written; (*da parte del redattore di un giornale*) subedited.

redattóre, *s.m.* **1.** (*compilatore*) drawer (up), compiler, drafter, writer: — *di un documento, di una relazione,* drawer (up) of an instrument, of a report **2.** (*nei giornali*) member of the editorial staff: *sono — di questo giornale,* I am on (*o* I belong to) the editorial staff of this newspaper; (*se unico*) I am the editor of this newspaper ‖ — *capo,* (chief) editor.

redazióne, *s.f.* **1.** drawing up; (*il compilare*) compiling **2.** (*di giornale*) editing: *la — di un giornale richiede molto lavoro,* the editing of a newspaper requires

a great deal of work **3.** (*insieme dei redattori*) editorial staff **4.** (*ufficio di redazione*) editorial office **5.** (*variante*) version.

redditízio, *ag.* profitable, paying, remunerative.

rèddito, *s.m.* income; revenue: *redditi commerciali, industriali,* commercial, industrial profits; — *derivato dal capitale,* capitalistic income; — *goduto,* income enjoyed; — *lordo, netto,* gross, net income; — *nazionale,* national income; — *professionale,* professional income; — *pubblico,* public revenue; *imposta sul —,* income-tax; *teoria del —,* income theory; *titoli a — fisso,* fixed-interest securities; *colpire qualsiasi forma di —,* to seize upon any source of revenue; *godere di un largo —,* to enjoy a large income; *spendere più del proprio —,* to exceed one's income; *vivere di —,* to live on one's income.

redènto, *ag.* **1.** redeemed: — *dal vizio,* redeemed from vice ‖ *i redenti,* (*teol.*) the redeemed **2.** (*riscattato*) ransomed.

redentóre, *ag.* redeeming; (*che riscatta*) ransoming ‖ *s.m.,* **redentríce,** *s.f.* redeemer ‖ *il Redentore,* the Redeemer.

redentorísta, *s.m.* (*eccl.*) Redemptorist.

redenzióne, *s.f.* redemption: — *del genere umano,* redemption of mankind; *senza —,* past redemption.

redibitòrio, *ag.* (*dir.*) redhibitory.

redibizióne, *s.f.* (*dir.*) redhibition.

redígere, *v.t.* (*compilare, scrivere*) to draw up, to draft, to compile, to write: *questo documento fu redatto davanti a un notaio,* this document was drawn up before a lawyer; — *un articolo,* to write an article; (*da parte del redattore di un giornale*) to subedit an article; — *un programma,* to draw up a programme.

redímere, *v.t.* to redeem; to ransom: *Cristo ci ha redenti dal peccato originale,* Christ has redeemed us from original sin; — *un'ipoteca,* to redeem a mortgage; — *uno schiavo,* to free a slave.

redimíbile, *ag.* redeemable; (*di peccato*) atonable: *prestito —,* redeemable loan.

redimibilità, *s.f.* redeemability, redeemableness.

redimibilménte, *av.* redeemably.

redimíre, *v.t.* (*letter.*) to crown; (*cingere*) to wreathe.

redimíto, *ag.* (*letter*) crowned; (*cinto*) wreathed.

redingote, *s.f.* frock-coat.

rèdini, *s.f.pl.* reins (anche *fig.*): *le — di un cavallo,* the reins of a horse; *con le — abbandonate,* with reins slack (*o* with a loose rein *o* with a slack rein); *abbandonare le —,* to drop the reins; *assumere le — della casa,* to assume the reins of the household; *lasciare a un cavallo le — sul collo,* to give a horse free rein; *tenere le —,* to hold the reins; *tirare le —,* to draw rein.

redivívo, *ag.* **1.** restored to life **2.** (*nuovamente incarnato*) new, second: *un Raffaello —,* a second Raphael.

rèdo, *s.m.* (*rar.*) sucking-calf; (*puledro*) foal.

rèdola, *s.f.* gravelled path, garden-path.

redolènte, *ag.* fragrant, scented.

redúce, *ag.* returning: *è — da un lungo viaggio,* he has just returned from a long journey; *è — da molte battaglie,* he has been through many a battle ‖ *s.m.* veteran; survivor: *i reduci della battaglia,* the survivors of the battle.

reduplicàre, *v.t.* to double, to duplicate.

reduplicazióne, *s.f.* (*gram.*) doubling, duplication.

réfe, *s.m.* thread, yarn: *matassa di —,* skein of yarn ‖ *cucire a — doppio,* fig. to play a double game ‖ *essere cuciti a — doppio, fig.* to be inseparable friends.

referendàrio, *s.m.* **1.** (*dir. eccl.*) referendary **2.** (*spreg.*) spy.

referèndum, *s.m.* referendum (*pl.* referendums, referenda).

referènza, *s.f.* reference, testimonial: *una cameriera con buone referenze,* a maid with good references; *ogni domanda deve essere accompagnata da referenze,* every application must be accompanied by testimonials.

refertàre, *v.i.* to report.

referto, *s.m.* report: — *medico,* medical report.

refettoriàle, *ag.* refectory (*attributivo*).

refettòrio, *s.m.* refectory.

refezióne, *s.f.* meal: — *scolastica,* school-meal.

refrain, *s.m.* (*mus.*) refrain.

refrattàrio, *ag.* 1. (*ind.*) refractory, fire-proof: *materiale* —, refractory material; *mattone* —, fire-brick; *terra refrattaria,* fire-clay 2. (*restio*) refractory; (*intrattabile*) unmanageable; (*ostinato*) obstinate: — *alla legge,* unwilling to accept the law; *un malato* — *alle cure,* a refractory patient; *un ragazzo* — *alla disciplina,* a refractory (o unmanageable) boy; *essere* — *a ql.co.,* to have no inclination for sthg. ‖ *prete* —, (*st.*) recalcitrant (o non-juring) priest 3. (*mil.*) (*renitente alla leva*) absentee.

refrigeránte, *ag.* 1. refrigerating, refrigerant, refrigerative: *cella* —, refrigerator; *miscela* —, freezing-mixture 2. (*rinfrescante*) cooling, refreshing: *bevanda* —, cooling drink ‖ *s.m.* 1. (*ghiacciaia*) refrigerator, ice-chest 2. (*med.*) refrigerant.

refrigeràre, *v.t.* 1. to refrigerate 2. (*rinfrescare*) to cool, to refresh 3. (*confortare*) to comfort, to console.

refrigerativo, *ag.* 1. refrigerative, refrigerant 2. (*rinfrescante*) cooling, refreshing.

refrigeràto, *ag.* 1. chilled; (*congelato*) frozen: *carne refrigerata,* chilled meat 2. (*confortato*) comforted.

refrigeratóre, *ag.* refrigeratory ‖ *s.m.* refrigerator; cooler.

refrigerazióne, *s.f.* refrigeration; cooling: — *ad acqua,* (*aut.*) water-cooling; — *dell'aria,* air-refrigeration.

refrigèrio, *s.m.* 1. refreshment; cool: *nel* — *dei boschi,* in the cool of the forest 2. (*sollievo*) relief; (*conforto*) comfort.

refurtíva, *s.f.* stolen goods (*pl.*), stolen property.

refusàre, *v.t.* (*tip.*) to misprint.

refusióne, *V.* **rifusióne.**

refúso, *s.m.* (*tip.*) misprint.

refutàre, *v.t.* (*rar.*) to refute.

regàglie, *s.f. pl.* (*cuc.*) giblets.

regalàbile, *ag.* 1. fit for a present 2. (*di persona, corruttibile*) bribable.

regalàre, *v.t.* 1. to present, to make a present of (sthg.), to give: *egli regalò un anello a sua sorella,* he gave his sister a ring (o he gave a ring to his sister); — *un mazzo di fiori a qlcu.,* to present s.o. with a bunch of flowers (o to give s.o. a bunch of flowers o to present a bunch of flowers to s.o.) ‖ *gli ha regalato un pugno in viso,* (*fam.*) he gave him one in the face 2. (*vendere a buon prezzo*) to sell cheap; (*fam.*) to give away ‖ **regalàrsi,** *v.r.* to grant oneself, to allow oneself: — *un sigaro,* to allow (o to permit) oneself a cigar.

regalàto, *ag.* 1. presented, given 2. (*venduto a buon prezzo*) cheap; (*fam.*) given away 3. (*squisito*) delicious.

regàle, *ag.* regal, kingly, royal: *abiti regali,* regal clothes; *accoglienza* —, royal welcome; *autorità* —, regal (o royal) authority; *corona* —, royal crown; *dignità* —, regal dignity; *portamento* —, kingly (o regal) bearing: *era un ospite* —, he was a royal host.

regalìa, *s.f.* 1. (*mancia*) gratuity 2. (*diritto regio*) royalty 3. *pl.* produce given by a tenant-farmer to his landlord.

regalità, *s.f.* royalty, regality, kingliness.

regalménte, *av.* royally, regally.

regàlo, *s.m.* present, gift: — *di nozze,* wedding-present; — *natalizio,* Christmas present; *in* —, as a present; *fare un* — *a qlcu.,* to make s.o. a present ‖ *mi fai un* — *se accetti la mia proposta,* I shall be very obliged to you if you accept my proposal.

règamo, *s.m.* (*cuc.*) origan, origanum; marjoram.

regàta, *s.f.* regatta: — *di panfili,* sailing-regatta.

rège, *s.m.* (*letter.*) king.

regèsto, *s.m.* (*arc.*) regest.

reggènte, *s.m.* regent: *il* — *di Spagna,* the regent of Spain; *principe* —, Prince Regent.

reggènza, *s.f.* regency.

règgere, *v.t.* 1. to bear, to support, to carry, to hold: *l'arco è retto da due pilastri,* the arch is supported by two pillars; *le gambe non mi reggono più,* my legs cannot carry me any longer; *lo reggeva per il braccio,* she was holding him up by the arm; *quattro pilastri reggono il tetto,* four pillars hold up (o support) the roof; *quella corda non lo reggerà,* that rope will not hold him; *questa carriola non regge più di così,* this wheelbarrow cannot carry more than that; *questa mensola non può* — *tanti libri,* this shelf won't hold so many books; *reggimi, sto per cadere,* hold me up, I am going to fall; — *un bimbo fra le braccia,* to hold a child in one's arms; — *un peso,* to bear a weight ‖ *non reggo bene il vino,* I can't take much wine ‖ — *l'anima coi denti,* to hang on to life ‖ — *i cordoni,* to be a pall-bearer ‖ — *il governo, la presidenza,* to hold the government, the presidency ‖ — *il mare,* to ride the sea well ‖ — *la prova,* to stand the test ‖ — *la spesa,* to stand the expense 2. (*tenere in mano*) to hold: *reggimi il bastone, il cappello,* hold my stick, my hat; — *il lume,* to hold the candle; *fig.* to play gooseberry 3. (*governare*) to rule (over): — *un impero,* to rule over an empire; — *un paese,* to rule a country 4. (*dirigere*) to manage; to run: — *un'azienda,* to manage a firm; — *una scuola,* to run a school 5. (*gram.*): *preposizione che regge l'accusativo,* preposition which governs (o takes) the accusative; *un verbo che regge l'infinito,* a verb which must be followed by (o which takes o which governs) the infinitive ‖ *v.i.* 1. (*resistere*) to hold (out): *il nemico non reggerà a lungo,* the enemy will not hold out long; *questa corda, questo ramo non regge,* this rope, this branch will not hold; *sono stanco, non reggo più,* I am tired, I cannot hold out any longer ‖ *non mi regge il cuore a vederlo così afflitto,* my heart breaks (o it breaks my heart) to see him so sad; *non mi regge il cuore di farlo,* I have not the heart to do it 2. (*stare in piedi*) to stand: *questo edificio reggerà almeno cent'anni,* this building will stand a hundred years at least ‖ *questo principio non regge,* this principle does not stand (o does not hold good); *le sue opinioni non reggono,* his opinions do not hold water 3. (*durare*) to last, to hold (out): *questo bel tempo non reggerà molto a lungo,* this fine weather will not hold out (o last) long; *la situazione non resse a lungo,* the situation did not last long 4. (*avere il dominio, il potere*) to be in power, to hold power, to hold sway: *in quel paese reggono i monarchici,* the monarchists are in power (o hold sway) in that country 5. (*sopportare*) to stand (sthg.), to bear (sthg.); (*resistere*) to resist (sthg.): *ditta che non reggerebbe alla concorrenza,* firm which could not stand competition; *non potè* — *a tanto male,* she could not stand (o bear) such pain; *questo materiale regge al fuoco,* this material is fireproof; — *ad un colpo,* to stand (o to bear o to withstand) a blow; — *al caldo, al freddo,* to stand the heat, the cold; — *alle fatiche,* to stand up to hard work; — *alle lusinghe, al denaro,* to resist flattery, money; — *alla prova,* to stand the test ‖ — *al confronto con...,* to bear comparison with... ‖ **règgersi,** *v.r.* 1. (*sostenersi*) to stand: *egli si regge in piedi, sulle gambe a fatica,* he can hardly stand; *ero così stanco che non mi reggevo più,* I was so tired that I could not hold out any longer; — *a galla,* to float; — *a una ringhiera,* to hold on to a railing ‖ *come posso reggermi in una tale situazione?,* how can I keep going in such a situation?; *con tante spese la ditta stenta a* —, with so much expense, the firm can hardly keep going (o keep on its feet) 2. (*governarsi*) to be ruled: *quel paese si regge a repubblica,* that country is a republic.

reggétta, *s.f.* iron hoop.

règgia, *s.f.* royal palace: *la sua casa sembra una —*, her house is like a palace.

reggiàno, *ag.* of Reggio Emilia (*predicativo*) ‖ *s.m.* **1.** native of Reggio **2.** (*formaggio grana*) Parmesan cheese.

reggibràca, *s.m.* hip-strap.

reggicatinélle, *s.m.* washstand.

reggifiàschi, *s.m.* bottle-stand.

reggilúme, *s.m.* lamp-stand; lamp-bracket.

reggiménto, *s.m.* **1.** (*mil.*) regiment: *— di fanteria*, infantry regiment **2.** (*folla*) regiments (*pl.*), crowd, large number: *un — di visitatori*, a large number (*o* a crowd) of visitors **3.** (*governo*) government: *— dispotico*, despotic government **4.** (*gram.*) regimen.

reggipància, *s.m.* **1.** body-belt **2.** (*di cavallo*) belly-band.

reggipénne, *s.m.* pen-rack; (*con calamaio*) inkstand.

reggipètto, *s.m.* **1.** brassière; (*fam.*) bra **2.** (*finimento per cavallo*) breast-band.

reggiséno, *s.m.* brassière, bra.

reggitèsta, *s.m.* head-rest.

reggitirèlle, *s.m.* trace-tug.

reggitóre, *ag.* **1.** ruling **2.** (*che amministra*) managing ‖ *s.m.* **1.** ruler, governor **2.** (*amministratore*) manager, director.

reggitríce, *s.f.* **1.** ruler **2.** (*amministratrice*) manageress, directress.

regía, *s.f.* **1.** régie, state monopoly (of salt and tobacco) **2.** (*cine.*) direction: *— di...*, directed by...; *la — di questo film è ottima*, the direction of this film is excellent **3.** (*teat.*) production: *— di...*, produced by....

regiaménte, *av.* regally, royally.

regicída, *ag.* regicidal ‖ *s.m.* regicide.

regicídio, *s.m.* regicide.

regíme, *s.m.* **1.** régime, regime; (*governo*) government: *il — attuale*, the present régime; *il nuovo, il vecchio — politico*, the new, the old political régime **2.** (*regole di igiene*) regimen; (*dieta*) diet: *essere a —*, to be on a diet **3.** (*mec.*) speed: *— continuo*, continuous running; *— di impatto*, (*aer.*) rate of catch; *— massimo, (di motori)* peak r.p.m.; *— permanente, transitorio*, (*elett. rad.*) steady, transient condition; *basso —*, slow running; *mancare di carburante ad alto —*, (*di motori*) to starve at high speed.

regína[1], *s.f.* queen: *— madre*, queen-mother; *— vedova*, queen-dowager; *la — Vittoria*, Queen Victoria; *Elisabetta, — d'Inghilterra*, Elizabeth, Queen of England ‖ *la Regina dei Cieli*, the Queen of Heaven ‖ *la — dei prati*, (*bot.*) meadow-sweet ‖ *la — della festa*, the belle of the ball ‖ *la — di picche*, the queen of spades ‖ *ape —*, (*entom.*) queen-bee ‖ *da —*, queenly (*o* queenlike).

Regína[2], *no.pr.f.* Regina.

Reginàldo, *no.pr.m.* Reginald ‖ *dim.* Reggie, Rex.

reginétta, *s.f.* queen: *— di bellezza*, beauty-queen.

règio, *ag.* **1.** royal: *la Regia Marina*, the Royal Navy; *Università Regia*, State University **2.** *acqua regia*, (*chim.*) aqua regia.

regionàle, *ag.* regional, provincial.

regionalísmo, *s.m.* **1.** regionalism, localism **2.** (*amministrazione regionale*) regional government.

regionalísta, *s.m.* regionalist.

regionalménte, *av.* regionally.

regióne, *s.f.* **1.** region, area; district: *le regioni artiche, tropicali*, the Artic, tropical regions; *la — dei laghi*, the lake district; *una — industriale, agricola*, an industrial, agricultural area; *una — montuosa*, a mountainous area (*o* district) **2.** (*divisione amministrativa*) district, province: *la Toscana è una delle più belle regioni d'Italia*, Tuscany is one of the most beautiful provinces in Italy **3.** (*anat.*) region: *la — lombare*, the lumbar region **4.** *fig.* province, realm: *nelle regioni dell'arte*, in the province (*o* realms) of art.

regísta, *s.m.* (*teat.*) producer; (*cine.*) director.

registràbile, *ag.* recordable, registrable.

registrànte, *ag.* recording, registering ‖ *s.m.* registrar, recorder.

registràre, *v.t.* **1.** to record, to register; (*comm.*) to enter, to book; (*protocollare*) to file: *— una domanda*, to file a petition; *— un fatto, una nascita, una morte, un testamento*, to register a fact, a birth, a death, a will; *— una fattura*, (*comm.*) to enter an invoice; *— un ordine*, to book an order; *— una somma su un libro di conti*, (*comm.*) to enter a sum in an account -book ‖ *far —*, to register (*o* to check): *devo far — il mio bagaglio*, I must have my luggage registered (*o* checked) **2.** (*segnare*) to record (anche *fig.*): *questo risultato deve essere registrato*, this result is worth recording; *la storia di questo paese registra molti esempi di eroismo*, the history of this country records many examples of heroism; *il termometro registrava una temperatura assai bassa*, the thermometer registered (*o* recorded) a very low temperature **3.** (*mus.*) to set: *— uno strumento musicale*, to set an instrument **4.** (*cine. con magnetofono*) to record, to tape-record **5.** (*mec.*) to adjust: *— le punterie*, (*aut.*) to adjust the valve-tappets ‖ *— un orologio*, to set a watch **6.** (*tip.*) to register.

registràto, *ag.* booked; registered, recorded.

registratóre, *s.m.* **1.** (*chi registra*) registrar **2.** (*apparecchio per registrare*) recorder, register: *— di cassa*, cash-register; *— di quota*, (*aer.*) altimeter (*o* altitude -recorder); *— di velocità*, speedometer (*o* speed-register); *— magnetico*, magnetic recorder; *— su nastro*, tape -recorder.

registratúra, *s.f.* recording.

registrazióne, *s.f.* **1.** registration, recording: *— a dischi*, disk-recording; *— automatica dei suoni*, automatic recording of sounds; *— indisturbata*, noiseless recording-booth; *— su nastro*, tape-recording; *cabina di — sonora*, monitor-room; *centrale di —*, recording -room **2.** (*comm.*) entry, recording, record: *— a giornale*, entry; *— composta*, compound entry; *— in fattura*, casting; *cancellare una —*, to cancel an entry; *controllare tutte le registrazioni a giornale*, to go over all entries; *fare — conforme*, to enter in conformity; *presentare un atto per la —*, to file a deed with the Registrar.

regístro, *s.m.* **1.** register: *— della parrocchia*, parish register; *— di classe*, class-register; *— di classificazione del Lloyd*, (*mar.*) Lloyd's register; *i registri di stato civile*, the registers of births, marriages and deaths; *— genealogico*, (*di cavalli*) stud-book **2.** (*comm.*) register, book; (*libro dei verbali*) minute-book: *— a matrice*, counterpart register; *— a molte colonne*, multi -column book; *— a una colonna*, single-column book; *— dei conti di corrispondenza*, draft-register; *— di magazzino*, warehouse-book; *essere a —*, to be on record; *mettere a —*, to enter (*o* to book) **3.** (*ufficio governativo*) Registrar's Office, Registry: *ha pagato una forte tassa di Registro*, he paid a heavy registration (fee) ‖ *— dello stato civile*, Registry Office ‖ *Pubblico Registro Aeronautico*, Air Registration Board; *Pubblico Registro Navale*, Register of Shipping **4.** (*mus.*) register: *— alto*, upper register; *— di organo*, stop (*o* register); *— medio*, middle register; *cambiar —*, to change register; *fig.* to change tune; (*cambiar vita*) to turn over a new leaf: *dopo le mie parole, cambiò —*, he changed his tune after my words **5.** (*mec.*) (*di orologio*) regulator; (*di freno*) brake-adjuster; (*valvola di regolazione per l'aria*) register: *— di bordo*, (*aer.*) log(-book); *— per ventilazione*, (*mec.*) ventilation-flap (*o* damper); *valvola di —*, (*mec.*) throttle-valve **6.** (*tip.*) register: *fuori —*, out of register; *in —*, in register.

regnànte, *ag.* **1.** reigning **2.** (*prevalente*) prevailing ‖ *s.m.* sovereign.

regnàre, *v.i.* **1.** to reign: *la Regina Vittoria regnò in Inghilterra per sessantaquattro anni*, Queen Victoria reigned over England for sixty-four years **2.** *fig.* to reign; (*comandare*) to rule: *in casa vorrebbe — su tutti*, he would like to rule over the whole household; *regna* *fra loro la perfetta armonia*, perfect harmony reigns between them; *regnava il disordine più assoluto in camera tua*, there was absolute chaos in your room **3.** (*prevalere*) to prevail: *in Toscana regna l'ulivo*, the olive prevails in Tuscany; *le nebbie regnano nelle valli*, fog prevails in the valleys **4.** (*durare*) to last: *in quel paese non può — la pace*, in that country peace cannot last; *questa moda non regnerà a lungo*, this fashion will not last long.

regnícolo, *ag.* native of a kingdom, born in a kingdom; living in a kingdom ‖ *s.m.* native of a kingdom; inhabitant of a kingdom.

régno, *s.m.* **1.** reign: *durante il — di Enrico VIII*, during (*o* in) the reign of Henry VIII; *fu un — glorioso*, it was a glorious reign ‖ *venga il Regno Tuo*, thy Kingdom come **2.** (*paese retto a monarchia*) kingdom: *il Regno Unito di Gran Bretagna*, the United Kingdom of Great Britain ‖ *il Regno dei Cieli*, the Kingdom of Heaven **3.** *fig.* kingdom; (*letter.*) realm: *il — animale, vegetale, minerale*, the animal, vegetable, mineral kingdom; *il — della poesia*, the realm of poetry; *la casa è il — della donna*, the home is the woman's kingdom; *quando si trova coi suoi amici, è nel suo —*, when he is with his friends, he is in his element **4.** (*autorità e dignità di re*) throne, kingship: *aspirare al —*, to aspire to the throne; *giungere al —*, to come to the throne; *rinunziare al —*, to renounce the throne.

règola, *s.f.* **1.** rule: *— catenaria*, (*mat.*) chain-rule; *le regole dell'etichetta*, the rules of etiquette; (*delle fasi*, (*chim.*) phase-rule; *la — del tre*, (*arit.*) the rule of three; *regole di grammatica*, rules of grammar; *le regole di un giuoco*, rules (*o* laws) of a game; *di —*, as a rule; *un'eccezione alla —*, an exception to the rule; *secondo la —*, according to the rule; *l'eccezione conferma la —*, the exception proves the rule; *conformarsi a una —*, to conform to a rule ‖ *per tua —*, for your information **2.** (*esempio, guida*) example: *la sua vita può servire di — a tutti*, his life might serve as an example to all **3.** (*misura, moderazione*) moderation: *dovresti avere più — nel mangiare e nel bere*, you should have more moderation in eating and drinking; *bere senza —*, to drink immoderately (*o* without moderation) **4.** (*eccl.*) rule; (*ordine*) order: *la — francescana*, the rule of St. Francis; (*ordine*) the Franciscan order **5.** (*consuetudine, usanza*) custom, habit: *è di — che la persona più giovane saluti per prima la più anziana*, it is the custom for the younger person to greet the older first **6.** (*dieta, regime*) diet: *stare alla —*, to be on a diet; *uscire dalla —*, to break a diet **7.** *in —*, in order: *le sue carte non sono in —*, his papers are not in order; *essere in — coi pagamenti*, to have effected all payments (*o* to be up-to-date with one's payments); *fare le cose in —*, to do things properly; *mettere ql.co. in —*, to put sthg. right (*o* in order); *tenere ql.co. in —*, to keep sthg. in order.

regolamentàre, *ag.* regulation (*attributivo*), prescribed: *misura, peso —*, regulation (*o* prescribed) size, weight; *velocità —*, regulation speed; *non è —*, it is not according to regulations (*o* it is against the rules).

regolamentarménte, *av.* according to the rules.

regolaménto, *s.m.* **1.** (*dir.*) rule, regulation: *— edilizio*, building code; *— ferroviario*, railway regulations; *— interno di una società*, (*dir. comm.*) articles of association; *il — scolastico*, school regulations; *— siradale*, rule of the road **2.** (*di conti*) settlement.

regolàre[1], *ag.* regular: *a intervalli regolari*, at regular intervals; *esercito —*, regular army; *grandezza, profilo —*, regular size, profile; *polso —*, regular pulse; *verbo —*, regular verb.

regolàre[2], *v.t.* **1.** to regulate; to adjust: *le leggi che regolano la concorrenza*, the rules which regulate competition; *— un orologio*, to set a watch; *— la propria condotta*, to regulate one's conduct; *— la temperatura, la velocità*, to regulate temperature,

speed **2.** (*controllare*) to control: *— il corso delle acque*, to check (*o* to control) the flow of water; *— le proprie spese*, to control one's expenses **3.** (*sistemare*) to settle: *— i conti*, to settle accounts; *— una questione*, to settle a matter **4.** (*guidare, governare*) to guide, to lead: *lasciati — da chi ha più esperienza di te*, let yourself be guided by those who have more experience than you **5.** (*mec.*) to adjust, to square **6.** (*rad.*) (*sintonizzare*) to tune (in) ‖ **regolàrsi,** *v.r.* **1.** to act: *non so come regolarmi*, I do not know which way to turn; *non so come regolarmi in questa faccenda*, I do not know how to manage (*o* how to act in) this matter; *regolati secondo il buon senso*, act according to common sense **2.** (*moderarsi, controllarsi*) to control oneself.

regolarità, *s.f.* **1.** regularity; (*di movimento, ritmo*) evenness: *prova di —*, (*aut.*) reliability trial **2.** (*puntualità*) punctuality: *— nel pagare i propri debiti*, punctuality in paying one's debts.

regolarizzàre, *v.t.* to regularize.

regolarizzazióne, *s.f.* regularization.

regolarménte, *av.* **1.** regularly: *veniva — a trovarci*, he came to see us regularly **2.** (*debitamente*) regularly, properly, duly: *ministri — designati*, duly (*o* regularly) appointed ministers **3.** (*puntualmente*) punctually.

regolataménte, *av.* **1.** regularly **2.** (*con moderazione*) moderately: *bere —*, to drink moderately.

regolatézza, *s.f.* (*sobrietà*) sobriety.

regolàto, *ag.* regular, steady; well-regulated; orderly: *in modo —*, in an orderly fashion; *vita regolata*, steady (*o* regular) life.

regolatóre, *ag.* regulating: *piano —*, town-plan; *principio —*, regulating principle ‖ *s.m.* **1.** (*chi regola*) regulator **2.** (*mec.*) (*di motori*) governor; (*elett.*) regulator: *— a induzione*, (*elett.*) induction regulator; *— automatico*, (*mec.*) automatic governor; *— centrifugo*, (*mec.*) centrifugal governor; *— dei punti*, (*di macchina da cucire*) stitch adjustment; *— della tensione*, (*elett.*) voltage regulator; *— del tempo*, (*di un orologio*) regulator; *— di amplificazione*, (*rad.*) gain control; *— di giri*, (*di un motore*) speed governor; *— di livello*, (*idraulica*) level control; *— di pressione*, (*di gas*) pressure regulator; *— di volume*, (*rad.*) volume control.

regolatríce, *s.f.* regulator.

regolazióne, *s.f.* **1.** regulation **2.** (*mec.*) adjustment; (*rad. elett.*) regulation: *— a zero*, zero adjustment; *— dei giri*, (*di un motore*) governing; *— della tensione*, (*elett.*) voltage regulation; *— di precisione*, (*elett. mec.*) micrometer adjustment; *vite di —*, (*mec.*) adjusting screw.

regolízia, *s.f.* (*pop.*) liquorice.

Règolo[1], *no.pr.m.* (*st.*) Regulus.

règolo[2], *s.m.* **1.** (*riga*) straight-edge; ruler, rule: *— calcolatore*, (*ing.*) slide rule; *— calcolatore dell'ampiezza visiva*, (*ott. med.*) visual field slide rule **2.** (*falegnameria*) list.

règolo[3], *s.m.* (*ornit.*) golden-crested wren.

regredíre, *v.i.* to go backwards, to regress.

regressióne, *s.f.* regression.

regressivaménte, *av.* regressively.

regressívo, *ag.* regressive: *forma regressiva*, (*biol.*) throw-back.

regrèsso, *s.m.* **1.** regress, regression: *progresso e —*, progress and regress **2.** (*mar.*) slip: *— apparente*, apparent slip; *— dell'elica*, screw slip; *— negativo*, negative slip **3.** (*ferr.*) switchback, back shunt **4.** (*biol.*) throw-back.

reiètto, *ag.* rejected: *era — da tutti*, he was rejected (*o* spurned) by everybody ‖ *moglie reietta*, repudiated wife ‖ *s.m.* outcast, castaway: *i reietti dalla fortuna*, the outcasts of fortune.

reiezióne, *s.f.* rejection.

reína, (*poet.*) per **regína.**

reincarnàre, *v.t.* to reincarnate ‖ **reincarnàrsi,** *v.r.* to be reincarnated.

reincarnazióne, *s.f.* reincarnation.

reintegraménto, *V.* **reintegrazióne.**

reintegràre, *v.t.* **1.** to reintegrate, to reinstate, to restore: — *il proprio patrimonio,* to restore one's patrimony; — *qlcu. nel suo ufficio,* to reinstate (*o* to reintegrate) s.o. in his office (*o* to restore s.o. to his office) **2.** (*risarcire*) to indemnify, to compensate: *voglio essere reintegrato dei danni,* I want to be indemnified for the damages.

reintegrazióne, *s.f.* **1.** reintegration, reinstatement, restoration **2.** (*risarcimento*) indemnification, compensation.

reità, *s.f.* **1.** (*colpevolezza*) guiltiness; (*colpa*) guilt **2.** (*malvagità*) wickedness.

reiteràbile, *ag.* repeatable.

reiteràre, *v.t.* to reiterate, to repeat.

reiterataméente, *av.* reiteratedly.

reiterazióne, *s.f.* reiteration, repetition.

relativaménte, *av.* **1.** comparatively, relatively: *è — a buon mercato,* it is comparatively cheap **2.** — *a,* with regard to (*o* as regards): — *a quella questione,* as regards that matter.

relativísmo, *s.m.* (*fil.*) relativism.

relativísta, *s.c.* (*fil.*) relativist.

relatività, *s.f.* relativity: *la — delle cose,* the relativity of things; *teoria della —,* (*fis.*) theory of relativity.

relatívo, *ag.* **1.** relative: *la capacità è relativa all'intelligenza,* capacity is relative to intelligence **2.** (*non assoluto*) relative, comparative: *periodo di riposo —,* period of comparative (*o* relative) rest; *lo disse con gentilezza relativa,* he said so with relative (*o* comparative) kindness; *tutto è — a questo mondo,* everything is relative in this world **3.** (*attinente*) pertinent, relevant: *con le relative prove,* with the relative proofs; *risposta relativa alla domanda,* answer pertinent (*o* relevant) to the question; *quanto dici non è — al nostro problema,* what you say is not pertinent (*o* relevant) to our problem **4.** (*rispettivo*) respective: *questa è la nota dei libri e dei relativi autori,* this is the list of the books and of their respective authors **5.** (*gram.*) relative: *pronome —,* relative pronoun; *proposizione relativa,* relative clause.

relatóre, *s.m.,* **relatríce,** *s.f.* **1.** bearer: — *di cattive notizie,* bearer of bad news **2.** (*di un comitato, commissione*) chairman (*pl.* chairmen) **3.** (*a un congresso*) rapporteur **4.** (*di una legge*) proposer of a bill.

relazióne, *s.f.* **1.** account, report: *fare una — dettagliata su ql.co.,* to make a detailed report on sthg. **2.** (*legame, nesso*) relation, connection, connexion: — *d'affari,* business connection (*o* relation): *avere, essere in — d'affari con qlcu.,* to have business relations (*o* dealings) with s.o.; *entrare in — d'affari con qlcu.,* to open up a business connection with s.o.; *relazioni d'amicizia,* friendly relations; *relazioni diplomatiche cordiali, tese,* cordial, strained diplomatic relations; *rompere, riallacciare le relazioni diplomatiche con qlcu.,* to break off, to resume diplomatic relations with s.o.; — *fra causa ed effetto,* relation (*o* connection) between cause and effect; — *stretta,* close connection: *questi fatti secondo me sono in stretta — tra di loro,* according to me these facts are closely bound up with one another; *non vedo alcuna — fra queste due idee,* I cannot see any connection between these two ideas; *avere — con ql.co.,* to be connected with sthg.; *stringere — con qlcu.,* to enter into relations with s.o. ‖ *in — a...,* in relation to...: *in — a quanto ho detto ieri,* in relation to (*o* regarding) what I said yesterday ‖ *essere in buone relazioni con qlcu.,* to be on good terms with s.o. **3.** (*contatto*) touch: *mettere qlcu. in — con qlcu.,* to put s.o. in touch with s.o.; *mettersi in — con qlcu.,* to get into touch with s.o. **4.** (*conoscenza*) acquaintance: *ha molte, poche, potenti relazioni,* he has many, few, powerful acquaintances **5.** (*relazione amorosa*) (love) affair.

relè, *s.m.* (*elett.*) relay: — *a bobina mobile,* moving

-coil relay; — *ad azione ritardata,* time-delay relay; — *a induzione,* induction relay; — *di binario,* track relay; — *di massima corrente,* over-current (*o* overload) relay; — *telegrafico,* telegraphic relay; — *termico,* thermal cut out (*o* temperature relay).

relegaménto, *s.m.* banishment, relegation.

relegàre, *v.t.* to banish, to relegate: — *ql.co. in soffitta,* to relegate (*o* to consign) sthg. to the attic; — *qlcu. in Corsica,* to banish s.o. to Corsica.

relegazióne, *s.f.* banishment, relegation.

religióne, *s.f.* **1.** religion: *la — cattolica,* the Catholic religion; — *di Stato,* established religion; *la — maomettana,* the Mahommedan religion; — *monoteistica, politeistica,* monotheistic, polytheistic religion; — *naturale, rivelata,* natural, revealed religion; *i dommi della —,* religious dogmas; *pratiche di —,* religious practices; *senza —,* unreligious (*o* without religion); *morì senza i conforti della —,* he died without the comfort of religion; *abbracciare una —,* to embrace a religion; *abiurare una —,* to abjure a religion ‖ *le guerre di —,* (*st.*) the wars of religion ‖ *il culto della bellezza è la sua —,* love of beauty is a religion with him **2.** (*culto*) worship, cult: *la — della patria,* worship (*o* cult) of one's country; *la — delle tombe,* the worship of the grave **3.** (*scrupolosità*) religious care: *egli cura il suo giardino con —,* he looks after his garden with religious care; *raccogliere i ricordi di famiglia con —,* to collect family souvenirs religiously **4.** (*ordine monastico*) religious order: *entrare in, nella —,* to enter a religious order (*o* to take the vows).

religiósa, *s.f.* (*eccl.*) religious; (*monaca*) nun.

religiosaménte, *av.* **1.** religiously **2.** (*scrupolosamente*) religiously, scrupulously.

religiosità, *s.f.* **1.** religiousness, piety **2.** (*scrupolosità*) scrupulousness.

religióso, *ag.* **1.** religious: *abito —,* religious habit; *matrimonio —,* church wedding; *ordini religiosi,* religious orders; *soggetti, libri religiosi,* religious subjects, books; *è un uomo molto —,* he is a very religious (*o* pious *o* devout) man **2.** (*scrupoloso*) religious, scrupulous ‖ *silenzio —,* blank silence ‖ *s.m.* religious; (*monaco*) monk; (*frate*) friar.

relíquia, *s.f.* relic: *le reliquie del passato,* the relics of the past; *conservare ql.co. come una —,* to keep sthg. as a relic (*o* to treasure sthg. up).

reliquiàrio, *s.m.* reliquary, shrine.

relítto, *s.m.* **1.** (*mar.*) wreckage (*coll. con concordanza sing.*); flotsam and jetsam (*pl.*); *un —,* a piece of wreckage; *vidi dei relitti galleggianti sul mare,* I saw some wreckage floating on the sea ‖ *un — della società,* an outcast of society **2.** (*geol.*) relict land.

remàre, *v.i.* to row; (*con palelle*) to paddle.

remàta, *s.f.* **1.** row: *farò una —,* I shall have (*o* I shall go for) a row **2.** (*colpo di remo*) stroke (of oar).

rematóre, *s.m.* rower, oarsman (*pl.* oarsmen): *un buon —,* a good oarsman (*o* oar) ‖ **rematríce,** *s.f.* rower, oarswoman (*pl.* oarswomen).

remeggiàre, *v.i.* **1.** to row **2.** (*di ali*) to flap.

reméggio, *s.m.* **1.** (*il remare*) rowing, oarage **2.** (*l'insieme dei remi*) oars (*pl.*) **3.** (*di ali*) flapping.

remigànte, *ag.* rowing ‖ *s.c.* rower.

remigànti, *s.f.pl.* (*penne delle ali di uccelli*) remiges: — *primarie, secondarie,* primary, secondary remiges.

remigàre, *v.i.* **1.** to row **2.** (*di ali*) to flap.

Remígio, *no.pr.m.* Remigius.

reminiscènza, *s.f.* reminiscence, memory: *la teoria platonica della —,* the Platonic doctrine of reminiscence.

remissìbile, *ag.* pardonable, remissible: *peccato —,* remissible sin.

remissióne, *s.f.* **1.** remission: — *di un'azione legale,* (*dir.*) remission (*o* abatement *o* abandonment) of an action; — *di un debito,* remission (*o* remitting) of a

737

debt; — *dei peccati*, remission (*o* forgiveness) of sins; — *di una rivendicazione*, (*dir.*) remission of a claim ‖ *senza* —, unremittingly **2.** (*indebolimento*) remission, diminution: — *della febbre*, remission (*o* subsidence) of the fever **3.** (*remissività*) submissiveness, meekness: — *d'animo*, weakness.

remissivaménte, *av.* submissively.

remissività, *s.f.* submissiveness.

remissívo, *ag.* **1.** submissive, yielding **2.** *clausola remissiva*, (*dir.*) saving clause.

remittènte, *ag.* (*med.*) remittent, abating: *febbre* —, remittent fever.

remittènza, *s.f.* remission, abatement, diminution.

Rèmo¹, *no.pr.m.* Remus.

rèmo², *s.m.* oar: — *a pala larga*, paddle; — *corto*, scull; *barca a due remi*, pair-oar; *barca a quattro remi*, four-oar; *colpo di* —, stroke; *pala di* —, oar-blade; *fornire di remi*, to supply (*o* to furnish) with oars.

remolíno, *s.m.* (*vortice di vento*) eddy, whirlwind.

rèmolo, *s.m.* (*vortice d'acqua*) eddy, whirlpool.

rèmora, *s.f.* **1.** (*impedimento*) impediment; obstacle **2.** (*indugio*) delay **3.** (*ittiol.*) remora.

remòto, *ag.* **1.** remote, distant: *un* — *antenato*, a remote ancestor; *remote conseguenze*, remote consequences; *una remota somiglianza*, a distant resemblance (*o* likeness); *età remote*, remote ages; *un luogo* — *e solitario*, a remote and lonely place **2.** (*appartato*) secluded: *una valle remota*, a secluded valley **3.** (*gram.*): *passato* —, past simple tense (*o* preterite); *trapassato* —, past perfect.

remuneràre, *e derivati*, *V.* **rimuneràre,** *e derivati*.

réna, *s.f.* sand; (*arenile*) sands (*pl.*) ‖ *fabbricare sulla* —, *fig.* to build one's house on sand ‖ *gettare i quattrini come* —, to throw money away ‖ *portare* — *al lido*, to carry coals to Newcastle.

renàccio, *s.m.* sand-bank.

renàio, *s.m.* **1.** (*cava di rena*) sand-pit **2.** (*banco di rena*) sand-bank.

renaiòlo, *s.m.* sand-digger.

renàle, *ag.* (*anat.*) renal: *colica* —, (*patol.*) renal colic.

Renània, *no.pr.f.* (*geog.*) Rhineland.

renàno, *ag.* Rhine (*attributivo*); Rhenish.

Renàta, *no.pr.f.* Renée.

Renàto, *no.pr.m.* René.

rèndere, *v.t.* **1.** to give back, to return; to restore: *glielo resi ieri*, I gave it back to him yesterday; *ho reso il cappello che avevo preso per sbaglio*, I have given back the hat I took by mistake; *non mi ha ancora reso il libro*, he has not yet returned the book to me; *rendimi i quattrini che ti ho prestato*, give me back the money I lent you; — *la libertà a qlcu.*, to set s.o. free (*o* to restore s.o. to liberty); — *la vista ai ciechi*, to make the blind see ‖ *Varo, rendimi le mie legioni!*, Varus, give me back my legions! ‖ — *l'anima a Dio*, *l'ultimo respiro*, to breathe one's last (*o* to give up the ghost) ‖ — *la parola a qlcu.*, to release s.o. from his word **2.** (*contraccambiare*) to render, to give, to repay: *all'occasione ti renderò il servizio*, when the opportunity arises I'll repay your kindness; — *il saluto a qlcu.*, to return s.o.'s greeting; — *una visita*, to return a visit ‖ *a buon* —, my turn next time ‖ *Dio te ne renda merito*, God bless you for it; *Dio te ne renderà merito*, you'll be rewarded for it ‖ *quello che è fatto è reso*, it's tit for tat ‖ — *bene per male*, to render good for evil ‖ — *pan per focaccia, la pariglia*, to give tit for tat **3.** (*produrre, fruttare*) to return; to produce, to yield: *il burro rende più della margarina*, butter goes farther (*o* further) than margarine; *il lavoro non mi rende*, my work is not very remunerative; *quell'affare non rese molto*, that business did not pay very well (*o* was not very profitable); *quell'investimento non ha reso nessun profitto*, that investment has returned no profit; *questa speculazione renderà due milioni di lire*, this speculation will yield two million

lire; *questo investimento rende il 7% di interesse*, this investment brings in (*o* yields) 7% interest; *questo terreno non rende*, this land produces nothing **4.** (*dare, fare*) to render, to give, to pay: — *un servizio a qlcu.*, to render s.o. a service (*o* to do s.o. a favour): *con tutti i servizi che ti ho reso...*, with all the favours I have done you...; — *un buono, un cattivo servizio a qlcu.*, to do s.o. a good, a bad turn; — *le estreme onoranze a qlcu.*, to pay the last honours to s.o.; — *giustizia a qlcu.*, to do s.o. justice; — *lode*, to praise (*o* to give praise); — *omaggio a qlcu.*, to pay homage to s.o.; — *gli onori militari*, to present arms; — *testimonianza*, to bear witness ‖ — *le armi*, to surrender (*o* to lay down one's arms); *fig.* to acknowledge oneself beaten ‖ — *conto di ql.co.*, to give account of (*o* to account for) sthg.: *devo* — *conto, ragione di tutto ciò che spendo*, I must account (*o* give reasons) for all that I spend ‖ — *grazie*, to give (*o* to render) thanks **5.** (*far diventare*) to render, to make: *l'amore rende felici*, love makes one happy; *ciò rese inutili i nostri sforzi*, this made our efforts useless; *l'incremento dell'industria rese necessaria la costruzione di nuove fabbriche*, the development of industry made (*o* rendered) the construction of new factories necessary; *il lavoro rende forti*, work makes men strong; *la notizia la rese felice*, the news made her happy; *queste notizie lo resero incapace di parlare*, this news left (*o* rendered) him speechless; — *di pubblica ragione*, to make public (*o* known *o* manifest) **6.** (*esprimere, riprodurre*) to render, to reproduce, to express: *gli attori resero tutti i personaggi molto bene*, the actors rendered all the characters very well; *il pittore ha reso bene i tuoi lineamenti*, the painter has rendered (*o* reproduced *o* portrayed) your features very well; *questo romanzo rende molto vividamente i problemi del nostro tempo*, this novel is a vivid picture of the problems of our times; — *un'immagine*, to represent (*o* to reproduce) an image; — *pensieri, sentimenti*, to express (*o* to convey) thoughts, feelings ‖ *rendo l'idea?*, do you see what I mean? **7.** (*tradurre*) to render, to translate: *è molto difficile* — *la poesia in una lingua straniera*, it is very difficult to render poetry in a foreign language ‖ **rèndersi,** *v.r.* **1.** to make oneself; to become: *non bisogna* — *schiavi delle abitudini*, one must not become a slave to one's habits; *se gli scrivo si rende inutile la mia visita*, if I write to him my visit becomes useless; *se lo fai ti renderai odioso a tutti*, if you do it you'll make yourself hateful to everybody; — *ridicolo*, to make oneself ridiculous ‖ — *conto*, to realize: *mi resi conto che studiavo da dieci ore*, I realized I had been studying ten hours; *non si rende conto di quanto sia sciocco*, he does not realize how silly he is; *non so rendermi conto di come l'ho fatto*, I cannot explain how I have done it **2.** (*arrendersi*) to surrender; to give in, to yield: — *prigioniero*, to give oneself up **3.** (*recarsi*) to go; to proceed: — *in un luogo*, to go (*o* to make one's way) to a place: — *in tutta fretta in un luogo*, to make all speed to a place.

rendíbile, *ag.* (*che si può rendere*) returnable; (*che si deve rendere*) to be returned (*predicativo*): *queste bottiglie sono rendibili*, these bottles are returnable.

rendicónto, *s.m.* statement, report: *rendiconti mensili*, monthly statements.

rendiménto, *s.m.* **1.** rendering: — *di conti*, rendering of account ‖ — *di grazie*, thanksgiving **2.** (*produzione*) yield, production; (*resa*) output: — *all'ora*, output per hour; — *di un anno*, returns during the year; — *di una fattoria, di un'azienda*, the yield of a farm, of a firm; *il* — *di un motore*, the efficiency of an engine; — *di un tipo di benzina*, the power of a brand of petrol; — *effettivo*, rating performance; *motore, benzina ad alto* —, high-efficiency engine, petrol; *un operaio di buon* —, an efficient workman; *lavorare a pieno* —, to work full time; *ottenere da una macchina il massimo del* —, to get the optimum performance from a machine.

rèndita, *s.f.* (*privata*) income; (*di pubbliche ammi-*

nistrazioni) revenue: *ha una — mensile di centomila lire*, he has a private income of a hundred thousand lire a month; *vivere di —*, to live on a private income.

rène, *s.m.* (*anat.*) kidney: *— mobile*, floating kidney.

renèlla, *s.f.* (*med.*) gravel.

renètta, *s.f.* (*mela*) rennet.

réni, *s.f.pl.* loins; back (*sing.*); (*arc.*) reins: *avere mal di —*, to have a pain in one's back; *rompere le — a qlcu.*, to break s.o.'s back; *voltare le —*, to turn one's back.

renifórme, *ag.* reniform, kidney-shaped.

rénio, *s.m.* (*chim.*) rhenium.

renitènte, *ag.* unwilling, reluctant || *soldato — alla leva*, (*mil.*) absentee; *essere — alla leva*, (*mil.*) to fail to appear at the call-up.

renitènza, *s.f.* unwillingness, reluctance || *— alla leva*, (*mil.*) absenteeism.

rènna, *s.f.* (*zool.*) reindeer (*invariato al pl.*): *un branco di renne*, a herd of reindeer; *femmina di —*, doe reindeer; *maschio di —*, buck reindeer.

Réno, *no.pr.m.* (*geog.*) Rhine: *vino del —*, Rhine wine.

renonce, *s.f.* (*a carte*) renounce.

Rènzo, *no.pr.m. dim. di* **Lorènzo**.

rèo, *ag.* **1.** (*colpevole*) guilty: *— di un furto*, guilty of a theft **2.** (*malvagio*) wicked, evil: *un pensiero —*, an evil (*o* wicked) thought; *un uomo —*, a wicked man || *s.m.* (*dir.*) culprit: *— confesso*, self-confessed criminal; *— presunto*, the accused (*o* the supposed criminal).

reòforo, *s.m.* (*elett.*) rheophore.

reògrafo, *s.m.* (*elett.*) rheograph.

reometría, *s.f.* (*elett.*) rheometry.

reòmetro, *s.m.* (*elett.*) rheometer.

reoseòpico, *s.m.* (*elett.*) rheoscopic.

reoscòpio, *s.m.* (*elett.*) rheoscope.

reostàtico, *ag.* (*elett.*) rheostatic.

reòstato, *s.m.* (*elett.*) rheostat: *— di avviamento*, starting-rheostat (*o* starting-resistance); *— di campó*, field rheostat; *— regolatore di velocità*, speed-regulating rheostat.

reòtomo, *s.m.* (*elett.*) rheotome.

reotropísmo, *s.m.* rheotropism.

repàrto, *s.m.* **1.** department, division: *— di un ospedale, di un negozio*, department of a hospital, of a shop; *— spedizioni*, (*comm.*) shipping and forwarding department; *capo —*, (*di uffici*) department head; (*di fabbrica*) foreman; (*di grandi magazzini*) shopwalker **2.** (*mil.*) party, detachment. *un — d'artiglieria*, an artillery detachment.

repellènte, *ag.* repellent, repulsive (anche *fig.*): *forza —*, (*fis.*) repulsive force; *un sapore —*, a repulsive taste; *un uomo davvero —*, a quite repellent (*o* repulsive) man.

repèllere, *v.t.* to repel, to repulse, to drive back.

repentàglio, *s.m.* risk, danger: *essere a —*, to be in danger; *mettere a — la vita*, to risk one's life.

repènte, *ag.* sudden: *ira —*, sudden rage || *di —*, suddenly (*o* all of a sudden) || *av.* suddenly, all of a sudden: *apparve —*, he appeared suddenly.

repenteménte, repentinaménte, *av.* suddenly, all of a sudden.

repentíno, *ag.* sudden, unexpected: *un cambiamento —*, an unexpected change.

reperíbile, *ag.* to be found (*predicativo*): *non è — da nessuna parte*, it is not to be found anywhere; *non so se è —*, I do not know whether it can be found anywhere.

reperíre, *v.t.* to find.

repertàre, *v.t.* (*dir.*) to find.

repertàto, *ag.* (*dir.*) found.

repèrto, *ag.* found || *s.m.* **1.** (*med.*) report: *il — dei dottori*, the doctors' report **2.** (*dir.*) evidence; (*corpo del reato*) exhibit.

repertòrio, *s.m.* **1.** inventory, catalogue **2.** (*teat.*) repertoire, repertory.

repletívo, *ag.* pleonastic; filling.

repléto, *ag.* (*rar.*) replete, full.

rèplica, *s.f.* **1.** (*risposta*) answer, reply: *una — spiritosa*, a repartee (*o* a witty retort); *ecco adesso la mia —*, and this is my answer to it **2.** (*obiezione*) objection: *bisognò ascoltarlo senza fare —*, we had to listen to him without raising any objection **3.** (*copia, facsimile*) replica, copy **4.** (*di lavoro teatrale*): *la commedia ebbe molte repliche*, the play had a long run; *la commedia ha avuto venti, sessanta repliche*, the play had a run of twenty nights, of two months; *questa è la novantesima — della commedia*, this is the ninetieth performance of the play **5.** (*ripetizione*) repetition.

replicàbile, *ag.* **1.** answerable **2.** (*obiettabile*) objectionable **3.** (*ripetibile*) repeatable.

replicàre, *v.t.* **1.** to reply, to retort: *gli replicai che non potevo farlo*, I replied that I couldn't do it; *replicai alla sua lettera dopo pochi giorni*, I answered his letter after a few days **2.** (*obiettare*) to object: *obbedire senza —*, to obey without question **3.** (*ripetere*) to repeat: *la commedia fu replicata quindici volte*, the play had a run of fifteen nights; *l'orologio replicò l'ora*, the clock repeated the hour; *— un esercizio*, to repeat an exercise.

replicataménte, *av.* repeatedly.

replicatívo, *ag.* repetitive.

reportage, *s.m.* report.

reprensíbile, *ag.* reprehensible.

reprensióne, *s.f.* reprehension.

repressióne, *s.f.* repression: *la rivolta fu seguita da un periodo di sanguinosa —*, the revolt was followed by a period of bloody repression.

repressívo, *ag.* repressive: *legge repressiva*, repressive law; *misure repressive*, repressive measures.

reprèsso, *ag.* repressed: *emozioni represse*, repressed emotions; *istinti repressi*, (*psichiatria*) repressed instincts; *rabbia repressa*, repressed rage.

repressóre, *ag.* repressing || *s.m.* represser.

reprimènda, *s.f.* reprimand; rebuke.

reprímere, *v.t.* to repress, to check, to restrain (anche *fig.*): *— un'emozione, un desiderio*, to repress an emotion, a desire; *— la fame*, to restrain one's hunger; *— la propria ira*, to repress (*o* to restrain *o* to check) one's anger; *— una sommossa*, to repress (*o* to put down) a riot || **reprímersi**, *v.r.* to restrain oneself.

rèprobo, *ag.s.m.* reprobate.

repúbblica, *s.f.* **1.** republic: *— democratica, oligarchica*, democratic, oligarchic republic; *il paese sceglierà fra monarchia e —*, the country will choose between the monarchy and a republic || *la — delle lettere*, the republic of letters || *la Repubblica Italiana, Francese*, the Italian, French Republic || *la Repubblica Romana*, (*st.*) the Roman Republic **2.** (*fam.*) (*confusione*) mess.

repubblicanaménte, *av.* in a republican way.

repubblicàno, *ag.* republican: *governo —*, republican government; *partito —*, republican party || *s.m.* republican.

repudiàre, *V.* **ripudiàre**.

repugnàre, *V.* **ripugnàre**.

repulísti, *s.m.*: *fare un — (di ql.co.)*, (*scherz.*) to make a clean sweep (of sthg.).

repúlsa, repulsióne, repulsívo, *V.* **ripúlsa, ripulsióne, ripulsívo**.

repulsóre, *s.m.* (*ferr.*) buffer; (*amer.*) bumper.

reputàre, *v.t.* **1.** to deem, to consider, to repute: (*pensare, ritenere*) to think, to believe: *reputai che sarebbe stato meglio andarci*, I thought (*o* deemed) it better to go there; *reputo che non lo sappia*, I think he does not know; *è reputato un bravo tenore*, he is considered (*o* reputed) (to be) a good tenor; *lo reputavo necessario*, I considered (*o* deemed) it necessary (*o* that it was necessary); *la reputo un po' matta*, I consider her (to be) a bit crazy; *queste sono le misure reputate necessarie*, these are the measures considered (*o* reputed) necessary **2**. (*stimare*) to have a high opinion of (s.o., sthg.), to deem: *non reputo molto quell'uomo*, I do not have a high opinion of (*o* I do not think much of) that man ‖ **reputàrsi**, *v.r.* to consider oneself: *si reputa molto intelligente*, he considers himself very intelligent; *si reputi licenziato*, consider yourself dismissed.

reputàto, *ag.* esteemed, well thought of: *quello scrittore è molto* —, that writer is highly esteemed.

reputazióne, *s.f.* reputation, repute: *ha la* — *di essere molto avaro*, he has the reputation of being very stingy (*o* he has a reputation for stinginess); *gode* (*di*) *un'ottima* —, he has (*o* enjoys) a high reputation (*o* he is very well thought of); *ha una cattiva* —, he is a man of evil repute; *acquistare la* — *di...*, to acquire the reputation of... (*o* a reputation for...).

rèquie, *s.f.* **1**. (*riposo*) rest; (*pace*) peace: *non ebbi* — *in tutto il giorno*, I had no rest all day long; *questo bambino non mi dà mai* —, this child never lets me rest; *trovai un po' di* — *in casa sua*, I found some peace at his house ‖ *senza* —, unceasingly **2**. (*riposo eterno*) eternal rest ‖ (*Messa di*) —, Requiem (Mass) **3**. (*fam.*) (*preghiera*) prayer for the dead.

rèquiem, *s.m.* **1**. eternal rest ‖ (*Messa di*) —, Requiem (Mass) **2**. (*preghiera*) prayer for the dead.

requisíre, *v.t.* to requisition, to commandeer: — *cavalli, cibo*, to requisition horses, food.

requisíto, *ag.* requisitioned, commandeered ‖ *s.m.* requisite, qualification: *avere tutti i requisiti necessari per un posto*, to have all the necessary qualifications for a post.

requisitòria, *s.f.* (*dir.*) (Public Prosecutor's) bill of indictment.

requisizióne, *s.f.* requisition.

résa, *s.f.* **1**. (*mil.*) (*capitolazione*) surrender: — *a discrezione*, surrender at discretion; *la* — *di una città, del nemico*, the surrender of a town, of the enemy; — *incondizionata*, unconditional surrender; *intimare la* —, to summon to surrender **2**. (*rendimento*) yield: — *di gas*, gas yield; — *elastica*, (*mec.*) rebound elasticity; *la* — *del carbone è maggiore di quella della legna*, coal has a higher heating power than wood; *la* — *di un tipo di benzina*, the power of a brand of petrol; *il burro ha una* — *maggiore della margarina*, butter goes farther (*o* further) than margarine; *questa lana ha una buona* —, this wool goes very far; *ottenere da una macchina il massimo della* —, to get the maximum output from (*o* amount of work out of) a machine **3**. (*restituzione*) return, restitution: *la* — *dei giornali invenduti*, the return of unsold newspapers **4**. — *dei conti*, (*comm.*) rendering of accounts ‖ *prima o poi ci sarà la* — *dei conti, fig.* sooner or later there will be accounts to render.

rescíndere, *v.t.* (*dir.*) to rescind, to annul, to cancel: — *un contratto*, to rescind (*o* to cancel) a contract.

rescindíbile, *ag.* (*dir.*) rescindable.

rescissióne, *s.f.* (*dir.*) rescission, annulment.

rescísso, *ag.* (*dir.*) rescinded, annulled, cancelled.

rescissòrio, *ag.* (*dir.*) rescissory.

rescrítto, *s.m.* (*st. eccl.*) rescript.

resecàre, *v.t.* **1**. to cut off: — *un ramo da un albero*, to cut off a branch from a tree **2**. (*chir.*) to resect.

resecàto, *ag.* **1**. cut off **2**. (*chir.*) resected.

resèda, *s.f.* (*bot.*) reseda: — *odorosa*, mignonette.

resezióne, *s.f.* (*chir.*) resection.

residènte, *ag.* resident, residing: — *all'estero*, resident abroad; *ditta* — *in Milano*, firm registered in Milan ‖ *s.m.* **1**. (*che risiede abitualmente in un luogo*) resident **2**. (*rappresentante diplomatico*) Resident.

residènza, *s.f.* **1**. residence: — *legale*, legal residence; *cambiamento di* —, change of address; *luogo di* —, place of residence; *obbligo di* —, residence is required; *essere di* — *in un luogo*, to have one's residence in a place; *fissare la propria* — *in un paese*, to take up one's residence in a country **2**. (*ufficio e sede di residente*) residency **3**. (*eccl.*) residence.

residenziàle, *ag.* **1**. residential: *quartiere* —, residential neighbourhood **2**. (*che richiede residenza*) requiring residence.

residuàle, *ag.s.m.* residual.

residuàre, *v.t.* to reduce gradually ‖ *v.i.* to be left.

residuàrio, *s.m.* residuary legatee.

residuàto, *ag.* residual ‖ *s.m.*: — *di guerra*, war surplus.

resíduo, *ag.* remaining, residual, residuary, surplus ‖ *s.m.* residue, remainder; (*fam.*) balance: — *attivo*, (*comm.*) residual asset; — *catramoso*, (*chim.*) tarry residue; — *della calcinazione*, (*chim.*) calx; *residui della combustione*, (*chim.*) residual combustion products; — *di scarto*, tailing; — *passivo*, (*comm.*) residual liability; *residui radioattivi*, radioactive waste.

resiliènza, *s.f.* (*mec.*) resilience, resiliency.

rèsina, *s.f.* resin, rosin: *resine al silicone*, silicon resins; *resine da colata*, casting resins; — *sintetica*, synthetic resin; *resine stratificanti*, laminating resins; *resine termoplastiche*, thermoplastic resins; *colla di* —, resin size.

resinífero, *ag.* resiniferous.

resinificàre, *v.t.*, **resinificàrsi**, *v.r.* to resinify.

resinificazióne, *s.f.* resinification.

resinóso, *ag.* resinous.

resipiscènte, *ag.* resipiscent.

resipiscènza, *s.f.* resipiscence.

resistènte, *ag.* **1**. resistant; proof (against sthg.): — *all'acqua*, waterproof; *materiale* — *al fuoco*, material resistant to fire (*o* fireproof material *o* fire-resistant material); *non è* — *alla fatica*, he cannot endure fatigue **2**. (*forte*) strong, tough; (*di colori*) fast: *metallo* —, tough metal; *una stoffa* —, a strong material; *un uomo* —, a strong man.

resistènza, *s.f.* **1**. resistance (anche *fig.*); (*capacità di sopportazione*) endurance: — *alle autorità*, resistance to authority; — *alle fatiche*, resistance against fatigue; — *attiva, passiva*, active, passive resistance; *una stoffa di molta* —, a hard-wearing material; *i soldati opposero un'eroica* —, the soldiers put up an heroic resistance; *ero alla fine della mia* —, I was at the end of my endurance; *la sua* — *al dolore mi sorprende*, his resistance to pain surprises me; *offrire scarsa* —, to offer a weak resistance; *vincere la* — *del nemico*, to break down the enemy's resistance ‖ *la Resistenza*, (*movimento partigiano*) the Resistance (Movement) **2**. (*elett. fis. ecc.*) resistance: — *aerodinamica* (*all'avanzamento*), (*fis.*) drag; — *anodica*, (*rad.*) plate resistance; — *autoregolatrice*, (*elett.*) ballast resistance; — *d'avviamento*, (*mec.*) starting resistance; (*elett.*) starting resistor; *la* — *dell'aria, dell'acqua a un corpo*, (*fis.*) the resistance of the air, of water to a body; — *di contatto*, (*elett.*) contact resistance; — *di dispersione*, (*rad. tv.*) bleeder (*o* bleeder resistor *o* bleeder resistance); — *di radiazione*, (*di antenna di radio*) radiation resistance; — *di terra*, (*elett.*) earth resistance; — *dinamica*, (*rad.*) dynamic resistance; — *indotta*, (*aer.*) induced drag; — *riduttrice di tensione*, (*elett.*) voltage-reducing resistance; *coefficiente di* —, (*fis.*) drag coefficient **3**. (*di apparecchio elettrico*) resistance(-coil); resistor.

resístere, *v.i.* **1**. to resist (s.o., sthg.) (anche *fig.*), to withstand (s.o., sthg.) (anche *fig.*); (*a lungo, ripetutamente*) to hold out (against s.o., sthg.) (anche *fig.*); (*sopportare*) to endure (sthg.): *il nemico resistette per venti giorni*, the enemy held out for twenty days; *non so* — *al desiderio di una tazza di caffè*, I cannot resist a cup of coffee; *la sua salute non resisterà a questo clima*, his health will not (with)stand this climate; *sono stanco morto, non resisto più*, I am dead tired, I cannot go on any longer; — *a un assedio*, to withstand a siege; — *a un attacco*, to hold out against an attack; — *al dolore, alla sfortuna*, to endure (*o* to bear up against) pain, misfortune; — *alle tentazioni*, to resist temptation; — *a una malattia, alla vecchiaia*, to resist a disease, old age **2**. (*non essere danneggiato, intaccato*) to be proof (against sthg.): *questa sostanza* *resiste al fuoco, agli acidi*, this substance is proof against fire (*o* fireproof), against acids (*o* acid-proof).

réso, *ag.* **1.** returned, given back **2.** (*divenuto*) rondered, made **3.** (*arreso*) surrendered.

Réso, *no.pr.m.* (*lett.*) Rhesus.

resocontísta, *s.m.* (*neol.*) reporter.

resocónto, *s.m.* report, relation.

respingènte, *s.m.* (*ferr.*) buffer; (*amer.*) bumper.

respíngere, *v.t.* **1.** to repel, to drive back: — *il nemico, un assalto,* to repel (*o* to drive back) the enemy, an assault ‖ — *una lettera, un pacco al mittente,* to return (*o* to send back) a letter, a parcel to the sender **2.** (*rifiutare*) to reject, to refuse, to decline: — *un'offerta,* to reject an offer; — *una richiesta, una proposta, un reclamo,* to reject a request, a proposal, a claim **3.** (*riprovare*) to reject; (*fam.*) to fail, to plough: — *un candidato ad un esame,* to reject a candidate in an examination (*o fam.* to fail a candidate in an examination) ‖ **respíngersi,** *v.r. reciproco* to repel each other: *le due cariche elettriche si respingeranno,* the two electric charges will repel each other.

respingiménto, *s.m.* **1.** repelling **2.** (*rifiuto*) rejection.

respínto, *ag.* **1.** repelled, driven back **2.** (*rifiutato*) rejected, refused **3.** (*riprovato*) rejected (*o fam.* failed).

respiràbile, *ag.* respirable, breathable.

respirabilità, *s.f.* respirability, respirableness.

respiràre, *v.t.i.* **1.** to breathe, to respire (anche *fig.*): *tutti gli esseri viventi respirano,* all living beings breathe; — *a pieni polmoni,* to breathe deeply; — *aria pura,* to breathe pure air **2.** (*prendere fiato*) to get one's breath: *lasciami —, poi ti racconto tutto,* let me get my breath (*o* take breath), then I shall tell you everything; *ora che ho finito il mio lavoro posso finalmente —,* now that I have finished my work I can breathe at last (*o* I can have some respite *at last*).

respiratóre, *s.m.* **1.** (*med.*) respirator, pulmotor **2.** (*apparecchio per la respirazione subacquea*) breathing mask **3.** (*respiratore d'ossigeno per il volo ad alta quota*) oxygen mask.

respiratòrio, *ag.* respiratory.

respirazióne, *s.f.* respiration, breathing: — *artificiale,* artificial respiration; — *cutanea,* porous respiration; — *vegetale,* plant respiration; *ha la — molto difficile,* he has great difficulty in breathing.

respíro, *s.m.* **1.** breath; (*sospiro*) sigh; (*il respirare*) breathing: — *di sollievo,* sigh of relief; *si udiva il suo —,* one could hear his breathing; *il suo — era affannoso,* he was breathing with difficulty; *dare l'ultimo —,* to breathe one's last; *tirare un profondo —,* to take (*o* heave) a deep breath; *trattenere il —,* to hold one's breath **2.** *fig.* (*requie*) respite, rest; breath: *dammi un po' di —, poi vengo,* let me get (*o* recover) my breath (*o* let me have some respite), then I'll come; *non ho avuto un momento di —,* I haven't had a moment's rest **3.** (*metal.*) (*sfiatatoio*) gas-vent.

responsàbile, *ag.* responsible (for sthg.), answerable (for sthg.), liable (for sthg.): — *di fronte alla pubblica opinione,* responsible before public opinion; *egli non è — delle sue azioni,* he is not responsible for his actions; *mi considero — verso di lui delle conseguenze,* I consider myself answerable to him for the consequences; *i ministri sono responsabili di fronte al Parlamento,* ministers are responsible to Parliament; *un padre è — dei debiti di suo figlio,* a father is liable for the debts of his son; *tu sei — di ciò che è accaduto,* you are responsible for what has happened; *essere — dei danni,* to be liable for damages ‖ *direttore — di una rivista, di un giornale,* editor of a magazine, of a newspaper.

responsabilità, *s.f.* responsibility: *grave —,* heavy responsibility; *un posto di —,* a post of responsibility; *sotto la mia —,* on my own responsibility; *mi assumo la —,* I take the responsibility upon myself; *non mi prendo la — di farlo,* I will not take the responsibility of doing it; *attribuire la — di ql.co. a qlcu.,* to hold s.o. responsible for sthg.; *declinare ogni —,* to decline

all responsibility for sthg.; *dividere la — con altri,* to share the responsibility with others ‖ — *civile,* (*dir.*) civil liability ‖ *società a — limitata,* limited-liability company.

responsabilménte, *av.* responsibly.

responsióne, *s.f.* (*st.*) responsion.

responsívo, *ag.* (*rar.*) in reply.

respònso, *s.m.* **1.** response; (*risposta*) answer, reply: *il — dei medici,* the opinion of the doctors; *il — dei periti,* the opinion of the experts; *il — dell'oracolo,* the response of the oracle ‖ *finalmente si è deciso a dare il suo —!,* (*iron.*) at last he has made up his mind to give us his reply! **2.** (*eccl.*) (*responsorio*) response, responsory.

responsòrio, *s.m.* (*eccl.*) responsory, response.

rèssa, *s.f.* **1.** crowd, throng: *c'era gran — in piazza,* there was a large crowd in the square; *far — intorno a ql.co., a qlcu.,* to crowd round sthg., round s.o. **2.** (*istanza importuna*) entreaty: *far —,* to entreat.

rèsta[1]**,** *s.f.* **1.** (*setola della gluma in alcune graminacee*) awn, beard **2.** (*lisca di pesce*) fish-bone.

rèsta[2]**,** *s.f.* (*treccia di agli e di cipolle*) string.

rèsta[3]**,** *s.f.* (*st.*) rest: *con la lancia in —,* with lance in rest; *il cavaliere mise la lancia in —,* the knight laid (*o* set) his lance in rest.

restàre, *e derivati,* V. **rimanére,** *e derivati.*

restauràbile, *ag.* restorable; (*riparabile*) repairable.

restauràre, *v.t.* to restore: — *la monarchia, l'ordine in un paese,* to restore the monarchy, order in a country; — *un vecchio edificio, un quadro,* to restore an old building, a picture.

restauratóre, *s.m.,* **restauratríce,** *s.f.* restorer.

restaurazióne, *s.f.* restoration: *la — della monarchia,* the restoration of the monarchy; *la — di una vecchia chiesa, un monumento,* the restoration of an old church, a monument ‖ *il periodo della Restaurazione,* the Restoration (period).

restàuro, *s.m.* restoration; (*riparazione*) repair: *il — di un quadro,* the restoration of a picture; *chiuso per restauri,* closed for repairs; *in —,* under repair.

restío, *ag.* **1.** (*di persone*) unwilling, loath, reluctant, averse: *egli è — a ogni genere di disciplina,* he is averse to every kind of discipline; *essere — a fare ql.co.,* to be unwilling (*o* loath *o* reluctant) to do sthg. **2.** (*di bestie da soma*) jibbing (at sthg.), refractory, restive ‖ *s.m.* restiveness.

restituíbile, *ag.* returnable.

restituíre, *v.t.* **1.** to return, to give back, to restore: *devo — questo libro alla biblioteca,* I must return this book to the library; *restituiscimi ciò che ti diedi,* give me back what I gave you; *si devono — le cose prese per sbaglio,* you must restore the things taken by mistake **2.** (*rimettere, reintegrare, richiamare*) to restore, to reinstate: *lo restituirono al suo ufficio,* they restored him to his office; *quella cura lo restituì alla vita,* that treatment restored him to life; *il colore, la forma,* to restore the colour, the form.

restituzióne, *s.f.* **1.** restitution, return **2.** (*reintegrazione*) restoration, reinstatement.

rèsto, *s.m.* **1.** remainder, rest: *il — della compagnia,* the rest of the company; *il — della vita,* the rest (*o* remainder) of one's life; *il — di loro rimase a casa,* the rest (*o* remainder) of them stayed at home; *egli ne prese due ed io presi il —,* he took two and I took the rest; *io l'ho fatto fin qui, egli farà il —,* I have done it up to here, he will do the rest; *oggi saranno esaminati venti studenti, il — può tornare domani,* twenty students will be examined today, the remainder can come tomorrow; *pensate voi a tutto il —,* I leave everything else to you; *questo è l'inizio della mia storia, domani ti racconterò il —,* this is the beginning of my story, tomorrow I'll tell you the rest; *pagare il — a rate,* (*comm.*) to pay the balance in instalments ‖ *del —,* (*inoltre*) moreover (*o* besides); (*per altro*) on the other hand; *è troppo tardi, e del — sono stanco,* it is too late; besides, I am tired ‖ *in quanto al* —, (as) for the rest **2.** (*mat.*) remainder: *il* — *di questa divisione è cinque*, the remainder of this division is five **3.** (*di una somma di denaro*) change: *eccovi il* —, here is your change; *devo darvi un* — *di 250 lire*, I must give you 250 lire change; *non ho da darle il* —, I cannot give you the change (*o* I have no change to give you); *tenga il* —, keep the change ‖ *egli ha avuto il suo* —, (*ciò che si meritava*) he got his deserts; *poi avrai il* — *del carlino*, (*ciò che ti spetta*) then you will get the rest of what is coming to you **4.** *pl.* (*avanzi*) remains; (*di un esercito*) remnant(s): *i resti di un pasto, di una casa, di una vecchia città*, the remains of a meal, a house, an old town ‖ *resti mortali*, mortal remains.

restringènte, *ag.s.m.* astringent; (*med.*) styptic.

restríngere, *v.t.* **1.** to narrow; (*contrarre*) to contract: *il freddo restringe i corpi*, the cold contracts objects; — *il campo*, (*foto.*) to narrow the field **2.** (*pigiare*) to squeeze; (*legare strettamente*) to fasten: *restringi un poco queste cose e vedrai che ci stanno tutte*, squeeze these things a bit more and you will see that they all get in **3.** (*vestiti, ecc.*) to take in, to tighten: *bisogna far* — *questo vestito*, this dress must be taken in **4.** *fig.* (*limitare*) to limit; to restrict; (*diminuire*) to lessen, to reduce: *ho ristretto il mio esame agli aspetti sociali del problema*, I have restricted my survey to the social aspects of the problem; — *le spese*, to reduce expenses **5.** (*med.*) (*costipare*) to constipate ‖ **restríngersi,** *v.r.* **1.** to narrow, to get narrower; (*contrarsi*) to contract: *la strada si restringe*, the road gets narrower ‖ — *nelle spalle*, to shrug one's shoulders **2.** (*farsi stretti*) to close up; *restringetevi, sta venendo altra gente*, close up, there are other people coming **3.** (*di tessuti*) to shrink: *questo tessuto non si restringe*, this material does not shrink **4.** (*limitarsi*) to limit oneself; to restrain oneself: — *a parlare solo di un argomento*, to limit oneself to speaking of one subject only; — *nelle spese*, to limit one's expenses.

restringiménto, *s.m.* **1.** narrowing; (*contrazione*) contracting **2.** (*di vestito*) tightening; (*di tessuto*) shrinking, shrinkage: — *della pupilla*, contraction of the pupil **3.** (*limitazione*) limitation; restriction; (*diminuzione*) lessening, reduction **4.** (*med.*) stricture: — *intestinale*, stricture of the intestine.

restrittivaménte, *av.* restrictively.

restrittívo, *ag.* restrictive.

restrizióne, *s.f.* restriction: *restrizioni alla libertà di stampa*, restriction of the freedom of the press; *restrizioni sul commercio dei vini*, restrictions no the wine trade; *consentire a ql.co. senza restrizioni*, to consent to sthg. unreservedly ‖ — *mentale*, mental reservation.

resultàre, *V.* risultàre.

resupíno, *ag.* (*letter.*) supine, on one's back.

resúrgere, *V.* risórgere.

resurrezióne, *s.f.* resurrection.

retàggio, *s.m.* heritage, inheritance (anche *fig.*).

retàre, *v.t.* (*pitt.*) to reticulate.

retàta, *s.f.* netful; catch, haul (anche *fig.*): *una buona* — *di pesci*, a good catch (*o* haul) of fish.

réte, *s.f.* **1.** net: — *a deriva*, drift-net; — *a strascico*, trawl-net; — *da pesca*, fishing-net; — *della bicicletta*, dress-guard; — *metallica*, wire (-netting); — *parasiluri*, (*mar.*) (anti)torpedo-net; — *per i bagagli*, (*ferr.*) luggage-rack; — *per capelli*, hair-net; — *per farfalle*, (butterfly) net; *gettare, tirare la* —, to cast, to haul the net; *prendere uccelli, pesci nella* —, to net birds, fish **2.** (*intreccio*) network: — *dei paralleli e dei meridiani*, grid of parallels and meridians; — *di antenne*, (*rad.*) aerial array; — *di binari*, rail network; — *di distribuzione*, (*elett.*) grid (system); — *di fognatura*, drainage system; — *di tubazioni*, pipe network (*o* piping *o* piping system); — *elettrica*, electric system; — *ferroviaria*, railway system; — *telefonica, telegrafica*, telephone, telegraph system **3.** *fig.* (*inganno*) net, snare, trap: *cadere, dare*

nella —, to fall into the net (*o* trap); *prendere nella* —, to catch in the net; *rimanere nella propria* —, to be caught in one's own trap (*o* to be hoist with one's own petard); *tendere una* —, to lay a snare **4.** (*tennis*) tennis-net: *gettare la palla in* —, to net the ball; *scendere a* —, to come up to the net **5.** (*calcio*) (*rete*) net; (*porta, punto*) goal: *la pallonata fu così forte che sfondò la* —, the shot was so hard that it went through the back of the net; *fare, segnare una* —, to score a goal **6.** (*borsa per la spesa*) shopping-net **7.** (*anat.*) (*omento*) omentum (*pl.* omenta) **8.** (*pitt.*) reticulate **9.** (*rad.*) network.

reticèlla, *s.f.* **1.** (*per capelli*) hair-net **2.** (*su treni, aeroplani, ecc.*) luggage-rack **3.** (*per becco a gas*) wire-gauze; (*per lampada a benzina*) mantle: — *a incandescenza*, incandescent mantle.

reticènte, *ag.* reticent.

reticènza, *s.f.* reticence.

Rètiche (Alpi), *no.pr.f.pl.* (*geog.*) Rhaetian Alps.

reticolàre, *ag.* reticular.

reticolàre, *v.t.* to reticulate.

reticolàto, *ag.* reticulate; (*arch.*) reticular ‖ *s.m.* **1.** (*rete metallica*) wire-netting **2.** (*tracciato di linee*) network **3.** (*mil.*) barbed-wire entanglement **4.** (*arch.*) reticulated work.

retícolo, *s.m.* **1.** (*cavità nello stomaco dei ruminanti*) reticulum (*pl.* reticula) **2.** (*ott.*) reticle **3.** — (*spaziale*), (*fis. chim.*) (space-)lattice.

retifórme, *ag.* retiform.

retìna¹, *s.f.* (*per capelli*) hair-net.

rètina², *s.f.* (*anat.*) retina (*pl.* retinae, retinas).

retiníte, *s.f.* (*patol.*) retinitis.

rètore, *s.m.* **1.** (*st.*) rhetor, rhetorician **2.** (*iron. spreg.*) rhetorician.

retòrica, *s.f.* rhetoric: *la* — *del patriottismo*, the rhetoric of patriotism; *studiare* —, to study rhetoric.

retoricaménte, *ag.* rhetorically.

retòrico, *ag.* rhetorical: *domanda retorica*, rhetorical question ‖ *figura retorica*, figure of speech.

retoricúme, *s.m.* (*spreg.*) pure rhetoric.

retràttile, *ag.* retractile, retractable.

retribuíre, *v.t.* to remunerate, to pay; (*ricompensare*) to reward, to recompense: *noi fummo ben retribuiti per il nostro lavoro*, we were well paid for our work.

retribuíto, *ag.* paid; (*ricompensato*) rewarded, recompensed: *un lavoro ben* —, a well-paid work.

retributóre, *ag.* rewarding ‖ *s.m.*, **retributríce,** *s.f.* rewarder.

retribuzióne, *s.f.* remuneration, payment; (*compenso*) reward.

retrívo, *ag.* **1.** (*reazionario*) reactionary; conservative **2.** (*tardivo*) backward.

rètro, *av.* behind ‖ *vedi* —, (*di pagina*) please turn over (*abbr.* P.T.O.) ‖ *s.m.* back: *sul* —, on the back.

retroattivaménte, *av.* retroactively, retrospectively.

retroattività, *s.f.* retroactivity, retrospective effect.

retroattivo, *ag.* retroactive, retrospective.

retroazióne, *s.f.* retroaction, retrospective effect.

retrobottèga, *s.f.* back-shop, back of the shop.

retrocàmera, *s.f.* back-room.

retrocàrica, *s.f.* breech-loading: *cannone a* —, breech-loader (*o* breech-loading gun).

retrocèdere, *v.t.* **1.** (*mil.*) to degrade, to reduce in rank, to reduce to a lower rank: *egli fu retrocesso per insubordinazione*, he was degraded for insubordination **2.** (*dir.*) to recede ‖ *v.i.* **1.** to retreat, to withdraw, to fall back, to recede (anche *fig.*): *l'esercito retrocesse fino ai piedi delle colline*, the army retreated as far as the foothills; *pensaci su bene, perchè non ti sarà possibile* —, think it over well because you will not be able to withdraw; — *da una decisione*, to go back on a decision; — *da una posizione, un contratto*, to withdraw from a position, a contract **2.** (*fare un passo indietro*) to step back.

retrocessióne, *s.f.* **1.** retrocession (anche *med.*) **2.** (*de-*

gradazione, abbassamento di grado) degradation: *prima della sua* —, before his being reduced in rank.

retrocèsso, *ag.* degraded, reduced in rank.

retrocucína, *s.f.* scullery, back-kitchen.

retrodatàre, *v.t.* to back-date.

retrodatàto, *ag.* back-dated.

retrogradàre, *v.i.* (*astr.*) to retrograde.

retrogradazióne, *s.f.* (*astr.*) retrogradation, retrograde motion.

retrògrado, *ag.* 1. retrograde: *movimento* —, (*astr.*) retrograde motion; *ordine* —, retrograde order 2. (*antiquato*) retrograde; out-of-date; (*reazionario*) reactionary: *idee, tendenze retrograde*, out-of-date ideas, tendencies; *persona retrograda*, out-of-date person; *politica retrograda*, retrograde (*o* reactionary) policy ‖ *s.m.* retrograde; out-of-date person; (*reazionario*) reactionary person.

retroguàrdia, *s.f.* rear-guard: *stare nella* —, to be in the rear-guard; *fig.* to hang back.

retromàrcia, *s.f.* 1. reverse gear: *innestare la* —, to go into reverse 2. (*movimento all'indietro*) backing: *andare in* —, to go in reverse (*o* to reverse).

retroscèna, *s.m.* 1. (*teat.*) back of the stage: *andare nel* —, to go backstage ‖ *rimanere nel* —, *fig.* to keep behind the scenes 2. (*maneggio*) underhand work, intrigue: *non conoscevo tutto questo* —, I did not know about all this underhand work (*o* intrigue).

retroscritto, *ag.* written on the back ‖ *s.m.* writing on the back.

retrospettívo, *ag.* retrospective.

retrostànte, *ag.* at the back, lying behind: *camera* —, room at the back (*o* back-room).

retrostànza, *s.f.* back-room.

retrotèrra, *s.f.* hinterland.

retroversióne, *s.f.* 1. retroversion (anche *med.*) 2. (*versione nella lingua originale di passo tradotto in altra lingua*) retranslation, back version.

retrovíe, *s.f.pl.* zone behind the front (*sing.*).

rètta[1], *s.f.* charge: *la* — *è di mille lire al giorno*, the charge is one thousand lire a day.

rètta[2], *s.f.* (*geom.*) straight line.

rètta[3], *s.f.*: *dar* — *a qlcu.*, to pay attention to s.o. (*o* to listen to s.o.).

rettàle, *ag.* (*anat.*) rectal.

rettaménte, *av.* 1.(*onestamente*) honestly 2. (*correttamente*) correctly; (*giustamente*) rightly.

rettangolàre, *ag.* (*geom.*) rectangular.

rettàngolo, *s.m.* (*geom.*) rectangle: *triangolo* —, right-angled triangle.

rettífica, *s.f.* 1. rectification, correction: *la* — *di un errore*, the correction (*o* rectification) of a mistake 2. (*di alcool*) rectification, purification 3. (*mec.*) grinding 4.: — *di una curva*, (*geom.*) rectification of a curve.

rettificàre, *v.t.* 1. to rectify, to correct: — *una inesattezza*, to correct an inaccuracy 2. (*alcool*) to rectify, to purify 3. (*mec.*) to grind, to reface: — *un cuscinetto, una valvola*, to reface a bearing, a valve.

rettificàto, *ag.* 1. corrected, rectified 2. (*di alcool*) rectified, purified 3. (*mec.*) ground, refaced.

rettificatóre, *ag.* rectifying ‖ *s.m.* 1. (*chi rettifica*) rectifier 2. (*rad.*) detector, rectifier: — *a cristallo*, crystal detector.

rettificatríce, *s.f.* 1. (*chi rettifica*) rectifier 2. (*mec.*) grinder, grinding machine: — *per ingranaggi*, gear-grinding machine; — *per rulli*, roll grinder; — *universale*, universal grinding machine.

rettificazióne, *s.f.* 1. rectification, correction 2. (*di alcool*) rectification, purification 3. (*rad.*) rectification, detection: — *integrale*, full-wave rectification 4. (*mec.*) grinding, refacing.

rettifílo, *s.m.* straight stretch; (*spor.*) straight.

rèttile, *ag. s.m.* reptile (anche *fig.*).

rettilíneo, *ag.* 1. rectilinear, rectilineal ‖ *poligono* —, rectilinear polygon 2. *fig.* (*onesto*) upright; (*corretto*)

correct: *condotta rettilinea*, upright behaviour ‖ *s.m.* straight stretch; (*spor.*) straight: — *d'arrivo*, (*spor.*) final straight.

rettitúdine, *s.f.* rectitude, uprightness, honesty, righteousness: — *di propositi*, rectitude (*o* righteousness) of purpose; *giudicare con* —, to judge with honesty.

rètto, *ag.* 1. straight: *linea retta*, straight line ‖ *la retta via*, the straight and narrow path 2. *fig.* (*leale, onesto*) honest, upright, straight: *condotta retta*, straight (*o* upright) conduct; *è un uomo* —, he is an honest (*o* upright) man 3. (*giusto, corretto*) right, correct: *la retta pronuncia, interpretazione*, the right (*o* correct) pronunciation, interpretation 4. (*geom.*) right: *angolo* —, right angle ‖ *s.m.* 1. (*il giusto, l'onesto*) right 2. (*geom.*) right angle 3. (*anat.*) rectum (*pl.* recta) 4. (*di pagina*) recto.

rettoràto, *s.m.* 1. (*eccl.*) rectorship, rectorate 2. (*di università*) chancellorship, rectorship.

rettóre, *s.m.* 1. (*eccl.*) rector 2. (*di università*) chancellor, rector ‖ *Magnifico Rettore*, Chancellor; (*di università tedesca*) Rector Magnificus.

retteréssa, *s.f.* chancellor's wife, rector's wife.

rettoría, *s.f.* (*eccl.*) rectorate, rectorship.

rettòrica, *s.f.* rhetoric.

rèuma, *s.m.* (*patol.*) rheumatism; (*fam.*) rheumatics.

reumatalgía, *s.f.* (*med.*) rheumatalgia.

reumàtico, *ag.* rheumatic(al): *dolori reumatici*, rheumatic pains ‖ *s.m.* rheumatic.

reumatísmo, *s.m.* (*patol.*) rheumatism; (*fam.*) rheumatics: — *articolare*, rheumatism in the joints (*o* rheumatoid arthritis); — *muscolare*, muscular rheumatism.

reumatizzàto, *ag.* rheumaticky; afflicted with rheumatism (*predicativo*) ‖ *s.m.* rheumatic.

revellènte, *ag.s.m.* (*farm.*) revulsive.

reverèndo, *ag.* 1. reverend 2. (*eccl.*) Reverend (*abbr.* Rev.): *molto* —, right (*o* most) reverend: *il molto* — *Vescovo di...*, the Right Rev. the Bishop of... ‖ *s.m.* reverend, clergyman (*pl.* clergymen); reverend gentleman.

reverènte, *ag.* reverent.

reverenteménte, *av.* reverently.

reverènza, *V.* riverènza.

reverenziàle, *ag.* reverential.

reveríre, *V.* riveríre.

reversàle, *s.f.* (*scontrino per ritirare merci spedite per ferrovia*) collection order.

reversíbile, *ag.* reversible.

reversibilità, *s.f.* reversibility: — *dello sterzo*, (*aut.*) caster action.

reversióne, *s.f.* reversion (anche *biol.*).

revisionàre, *v.t.* (*mec.*) to overhaul.

revisióne, *s.f.* 1. revision 2. (*dir.*) review: — *di un processo*, review of a trial 3. (*comm.*) audit: — *dei conti*, audit of accounts 4. (*mec.*) overhaul, overhauling: — *generale*, general (*o* complete) overhaul; — *valvole*, valve overhauling; *manuale di istruzione per la* —, overhaul manual (*o* handbook).

revisóre, *s.m.* 1. reviser ‖ — *di bozze*, proof-reader 2. (*comm.*) auditor: — *dei conti*, auditor of accounts.

reviviscènza, *s.f.* reviviscence.

rèvoca, *s.f.* revocation, repeal.

revocàbile, *ag.* revocable.

revocabilità, *s.f.* revocability.

revocaménto, *s.m.* revocation, repeal.

revocàre, *v.t.* 1. (*richiamare*) to recall 2. (*abrogare*) to revoke, to repeal: — *una legge*, to revoke a law.

revocatívo, *ag.* revocating, revocatory.

revocatòrio, *ag.* revocatory.

revocazióne, *s.f.* revocation, repeal.

revòlver, *s.m.* 1. (*rivoltella*) revolver 2. *tornio a* —, (*mec.*) turret lathe (*o* capstan lathe).

revolveràre, *v.t.* to shoot with a revolver.

revolveràta, *s.f.* revolver shot.

revulsióne, *s.f.* (*med.*) revulsion.

revulsívo, *ag.s.m.* (*farm.*) revulsive.

Rèzia, *no.pr.f.* (*geog. st.*) Rhaetia, Raetia.

reziàrio, *s.m.* (*st. romana*) retiarius (*pl.* retiarii).

rézzo, *s.m.* **1.** (*ombra*) shade **2.** (*lieve brezza*) light breeze; (*brezza fresca*) cool breeze.

riabbandonàre, *v.t.* to abandon again, to forsake again || **riabbandonàrsi,** *v.r.* **1.** to surrender again **2.** (*darsi interamente*) to indulge again (in sthg.).

riabbassàre, *v.t.* to lower again || **riabbassàrsi,** *v.r.* **1.** to lower oneself again **2.** (*umiliarsi di nuovo*) to stoop again.

riabbàttere, *v.t.* to beat down again; to demolish again || **riabbàttersi,** *v.r.* to meet (s.o.) again.

riabbellíre, *v.t.* to embellish again; to adorn again || **riabbellírsi,** *v.r.* to grow beautiful again.

riabbigliàre, *v.t.* to dress again, to attire again || **riabbigliàrsi,** *v.r.* to dress again, to attire oneself again.

riabbonàrsi, *v.r.* to subscribe again, to take out a new subscription, to renew one's subscription.

riabbottonàre, *v.t.* to button (up) again || **riabbottonàrsi,** *v.r.* to button oneself up again.

riabbracciàre, *v.t.*, **riabbracciàrsi,** *v.r.* reciproco to embrace again.

riabilitàre, *v.t.* **1.** (*abilitare di nuovo*) to re-qualify **2.** (*dir.*) (*mettere nei diritti di prima*) to reinstate, to restore: — *qlcu. nei propri diritti,* to reinstate s.o. in his rights **3.** (*rimettere in buona fama*) to rehabilitate; (*fam.*) to whitewash: *gli storici hanno riabilitato Riccardo III,* historians have rehabilitated Richard III || **riabilitàrsi,** *v.r.* to rehabilitate oneself; to recover one's reputation.

riabilitàto, *ag.* **1.** rehabilitated **2.** (*dir.*) reinstated || *s.m.* **1.** rehabilitated person **2.** (*dir.*) reinstated person.

riabilitatóre, *ag.* **1.** rehabilitating **2.** (*dir.*) reinstating || *s.m.,* **riabilitatríce,** *s.f.* **1.** rehabilitator **2.** (*dir.*) reinstater.

riabilitazióne, *s.f.* **1.** rehabilitation; (*fam.*) whitewashing **2.** (*dir.*) (*reintegrazione*) reinstatement.

riaccadére, *v.i.* to happen again.

riaccalappiàre, *v.t.* to ensnare again (anche *fig.*).

riaccampàre, *v.t.* to encamp again || **riaccampàrsi,** *v.r.* to camp again.

riaccasàre, *v.t.*, **riaccasàrsi,** *v.r.* to remarry.

riaccèndere, *v.t.* to relight, to light again || **riaccèndersi,** *v.r.* (*illuminarsi di nuovo*) to brighten again (anche *fig.*); (*prender fuoco di nuovo*) to catch fire again.

riaccennàre, *v.t.* to mention again.

riaccettàre, *v.t.* to accept again, to reaccept.

riacchiappàre, *v.t.* to catch again, to recapture.

riacciuffàre, *v.t.* to seize again, to catch again.

riaccògliere, *v.t.* to receive again.

riaccomodàre, *v.t.* to repair again, to mend again, to readjust **2.** (*sistemare*) to settle again: — *una faccenda,* to settle a matter again || **riaccomodàrsi,** *v.r.* reciproco (*venire di nuovo ad un accordo*) to come to an agreement again; (*riappacificarsi dopo un litigio*) to patch up a quarrel, to make it up after a quarrel.

riaccompagnàre, *v.t.* to take home: *egli mi riaccompagnò a casa,* he took me home || **riaccompagnàrsi,** *v.r.* reciproco to come together again; to become friends again.

riaccorciàre, *v.t.* to shorten again, to reshorten.

riaccordàre, *v.t.* **1.** (*concedere di nuovo*) to grant again **2.** (*metter d'accordo di nuovo*) to reconcile **3.** (*mus.*) to retune, to tune again || **riaccordàrsi,** *v.r.* **1.** (*mettersi d'accordo di nuovo*) to come to an agreement again, to become reconciled **2.** (*mus.*) to tune up again.

riaccostàre, *v.t.* to reapproach, to approach again || **riaccostàrsi,** *v.r.* **1.** to reapproach, to draw near again **2.** (*riconciliarsi*) to become reconciled || *v.r.* reciproco to draw near to each other (one another) again.

riaccozzàre, *v.t.* to mix together again.

riaccreditàre, *v.t.* **1.** (*comm.*) to credit again, to accredit again **2.** (*avvalorare*) to confirm again || **riaccreditàrsi,** *v.r.* to obtain new credit.

riaccréscere, *v.t.* to increase again.

riaccusàre, *v.t.* to accuse again; (*dir.*) to recharge.

riacquistàbile, *ag.* recoverable.

riacquistàre, *v.t.* **1.** to buy back **2.** (*ricuperare, riprendere*) to recover, to regain: — *coraggio,* to recover one's courage; — *la libertà, la salute,* to recover (o to regain) one's freedom, one's health || **riacquistàrsi,** *v.r.* to win back, to retrieve.

riacquísto, *s.m.* **1.** (*il ricomperare*) repurchase **2.** (*il ricuperare*) recovery.

riadagiàre, *v.t.* to lay down again, to replace || **riadagiàrsi,** *v.r.* to lie down again, to subside again.

riadattaménto *s.m.* readaptation, new adaptation.

riadattàre, *v.t.* to readapt, to adapt again || **riadattàrsi,** *v.r.* **1.** to readapt oneself, to adapt oneself again **2.** (*rassegnarsi di nuovo*) to resign oneself again.

riaddoloràre, *v.t.* to grieve again, to afflict again || **riaddoloràrsi,** *v.r.* to grieve again.

riaddormentàre, *v.t.* to send to sleep again || **riaddormentàrsi,** *v.r.* to fall asleep again.

riadoperàre, *v.t.* to re-use, to use again || **riadoperàrsi,** *v.r.* to busy oneself again, to exert oneself again.

riadornàre, *v.t.* to readorn, to adorn again.

riaffacciàre, *v.t.* to present again; to bring forward again || **riaffacciàrsi,** *v.r.* **1.** to come forward again, to reappear, to appear again, to come out again **2.** (*ripresentarsi*) to rise again, to arise again: *quell'idea mi si riaffacciò alla mente,* that idea struck me again; *si riaffacciò questo problema,* this problem arose again.

riaffermàre, *v.t.* **1.** to reaffirm, to affirm again **2.** (*confermare*) to confirm.

riafferràre, *v.t.* to grasp again, to seize again || **riafferràrsi,** *v.r.* to catch hold of (s.o., sthg.) again || *v.r.* reciproco to catch hold of each other (one another) again.

riaffezionàre, *v.t.* to endear again || **riaffezionàrsi,** *v.r.* to take a new liking.

riaffibbiàre, *v.t.* **1.** to refasten, to rebutton **2.** (*dare di nuovo*) to give again.

riaffilàre, *v.t.* to resharpen, to sharpen again.

riaffittàre, *v.t.* **1.** to relet **2.** (*subaffittare*) to sub-let.

riaffratellàre, *v.t.* **1.** to get (s.o.) to fraternize again; to reconcile || **riaffratellàrsi,** *v.r.* reciproco to fraternize again; to be reconciled.

riaffrontàre, *v.t.* **1.** to face again, to confront again || — *battaglia,* to engage battle again **2.** (*trattare di nuovo*) to deal with (s.o., sthg.) again **3.** (*riconfrontare*) to compare again || **riaffrontàrsi,** *v.r.* reciproco to face each other (one another) again.

riagganciàre, *v.t.* **1.** to (re-)hook, to clasp (again) **2.** (*ferr.*) to couple (again).

riaggiogàre, *v.t.* **1.** to yoke again **2.** (*sottomettere di nuovo*) to subjugate again.

riaggiustàre, *v.t.* **1.** to remend, to repair again **2.** (*mettere in ordine*) to put in order (again) **3.** — *i conti,* (*comm.*) to settle accounts **4.** (*dare una lezione a*) to re-arrange || **riaggiustàrsi,** *v.r.* to improve: *la situazione si è riaggiustata,* the situation has improved.

riaggravàre, *v.t.* to make worse again || **riaggravàrsi,** *v.r.* to become worse again.

riaggregàre, *v.t.* to aggregate again.

riaguantàre, *v.t.* to seize again.

riaguzzàre, *v.t.* to re-sharpen, to sharpen again.

riallacciàre, *v.t.* **1.** to fasten again, to tie (up) again **2.** (*riprendere*) to renew, to resume: — *una corrispondenza,* to resume a correspondence.

riallargàre, *v.t.* to widen again || **riallargàrsi,** *v.r.* to become wider again.

riallentàre, *v.t.* to slacken again, to loosen again.

riallettàre, *v.t.* to allure again.

riallungàre, *v.t.* to lengthen again || **riallungàrsi,** *v.r.* to stretch oneself again; (*ridiventar lungo*) to become longer again.

riàlto, *s.m.* **1.** rise, height **2.** (*ricamo in rilievo*) embroidery in relief **3.** (*arch.*) flight of steps (in front of a house, church) ‖ *il Ponte di Rialto,* the Rialto (Bridge).

rialzaménto, *s.m.* **1.** heightening, lifting up, raising **2.** (*rialzo*) height, rise.

rialzàre, *v.t.* **1.** to raise (again), to lift (up) (again): — *un macigno,* to lift a big stone; — *una nave sommersa,* to refloat (*o* to raise) a sunken ship; — *gli occhi,* to raise one's eyes again; — *i prezzi, i salari,* to raise (*o* to increase) prices, wages; — *la testa,* to look up (*o* to hold up one's head) again **2.** (*rendere più alto*) to make higher, to heighten: — *una casa,* to make a house higher ‖ *v.i.* to raise, to go up: *il barometro rialza,* the barometer is going up ‖ **rialzàrsi,** *v.r.* to rise again, to get up again: *dopo che fece bancarotta, impiegò due anni a —,* after he went bankrupt he took two years to get on his feet again.

rialzísta, *s.c.* (*chi provoca rialzi in Borsa*) bull.

riàlzo, *s.m.* **1.** rise: *un — nei prezzi,* a rise in prices; *mercato con tendenza al —,* (*Borsa*) rising (*o* bullish) market; *tendenza al —,* (*Borsa*) upward trend (*o* bullish tendency); *i prezzi sono in —,* prices are on the rise; *giocare al —,* (*Borsa*) to bull the market (*o* to speculate on a rise); *provocare un — fittizio,* (*Borsa*) to rig the market **2.** *pl.* (*delle scarpe*) supports.

riamàre, *v.t.* **1.** (*amare di nuovo*) to love again **2.** (*ricambiare l'amore di*) to return s.o.'s love, to reciprocate s.o.'s love: *egli era riamato,* his love was returned.

riamicàre, *v.t.* to reconcile ‖ **riamicàrsi,** *v.r.* reciproco, to make friends again, to become friends again.

riammalàrsi, *v.r.* to fall ill again.

riamméttere, *v.t.* to admit again, to readmit.

riammiccàre, *v.i.* to wink (at s.o.) again.

riammiràre, *v.t.* to admire again.

riammissíbile, *ag.* readmissible.

riammissióne, *s.f.* readmission.

riammobiliàre, *v.t.* to refurnish.

riammogliàre, *v.t.* to give in marriage again ‖ **riammogliàrsi,** *v.r.* to re-marry, to marry again.

riammollíre, *v.t.* to soften again.

riammoníre, *v.t.* to warn again, to admonish again.

riàndare, *v.i.* to go again, to return ‖ *v.t.* (*ricordare*) to recall: — *i bei tempi passati,* to recall the good old times.

rianimàre, *v.t.* **1.** to revive, to reanimate: — *la speranza, la collera di qlcu.,* to reawaken (*o* to rekindle) s.o.'s hope, anger **2.** (*rallegrare*) to cheer up, to enliven: *un po' di whisky rianimò la compagnia,* some whisky enlivened the company; *il suo arrivo la rianimò,* his arrival cheered her up; — *un'assemblea,* to put fresh life into a meeting ‖ **rianimàrsi,** *v.r.* **1.** (*riacquistare allegria*) to cheer up **2.** (*riprendere coraggio*) to take courage again.

rianimazióne, *s.f.* reviving, reanimation.

riannaffiàre, *v.t.* to water again, to sprinkle again.

riannebbiàre, *v.t.* to cloud again ‖ *v.i.* to get foggy again, to grow misty again, to become foggy again.

riannessióne, *s.f.* re-annexation.

riannèttere, *v.t.* to reannex.

riannodàre, *v.t.* **1.** to knot again, to tie again **2.** (*riallacciare*) to renew: — *un'amicizia,* to renew a friendship ‖ **riannodàrsi,** *v.r.* to reunite, to rejoin.

riannunziàre, *v.t.* to announce again.

riannuvolàre, *v.i.,* **riannuvolàrsi,** *v.r.* **1.** to become cloudy again, to cloud over again **2.** (*turbarsi, oscurarsi di nuovo*) to grow gloomy again.

riapertúra, *s.f.* reopening: — *dei corsi,* beginning of term; — *delle scuole,* reopening of schools.

riappacificàre, *v.t.* to reconcile again ‖ **riappacificàrsi,** *v.r.* to become reconciled; to make it up again, to make friends again.

riappaltàre, *v.t.* **1.** to contract again **2.** (*appaltare ad altri*) to subcontract.

riappaltatóre, *s.m.* sub-contractor.

riappàlto, *s.m.* sub-contract.

riapparecchiàre, *v.t.* to prepare again, to get ready again: — *la tavola,* to lay the table again.

riapparíre, *v.i.* to reappear.

riapparizióne, *s.f.* reappearance.

riappèndere, *v.t.* to hang again.

riappiccàre, *v.t.* **1.** (*riappendere*) to hang up again **2.** (*ricongiungere*) to rejoin **3.** — *il fuoco a,* to set fire again to.

riappiccicàre, *v.t.* to join again, to attach again ‖ **riappiccicàrsi,** *v.r.* to adhere again, to stick again.

riappioppàre, *v.t.* to give again.

riapplaudíre, *v.t.* **1.** to applaud again **2.** (*riapprovare*) to approve again.

riappoggiàre, *v.t.* **1.** to lean again, to rest again **2.** (*favorire, sostenere di nuovo*) to back again, to support again.

riapprovàre, *v.t.* **1.** to approve again **2.** (*riconfermare*) to reconfirm.

riappuntellàre, *v.t.* **1.** to shore up again **2.** (*sostenere*) to support again.

riapríre, *v.t.* to reopen, to open again: *riaprite il libro!,* reopen your book!; — *una porta,* to open again (*o* to reopen) a door ‖ — *una vecchia ferita,* to reopen an old wound ‖ **riaprírsi,** *v.r.* to reopen: *i negozi, le scuole si riapriranno lunedì,* the shops, the schools will reopen on Monday.

riàrdere, *v.t.* **1.** to burn again **2.** (*rendere secco*) to dry; (*rendere arso*) to burn.

riarginàre, *v.t.* **1.** to embank again, to dyke again **2.** (*porre freno di nuovo a*) to stem again.

riarmaménto, *s.m.* (*mil.*) rearmament.

riarmàre, *v.t.* **1.** (*mil.*) to rearm **2.** (*mar.*) to equip again, to fit out again **3.** (*edil.*) to renew the false-work **4.** (*arma da fuoco*) to recock **5.** (*mus.*) to re-string ‖ **riarmàrsi,** *v.r.* to rearm.

riàrmo, *s.m.* rearmament.

riarricchíre, *v.t.* **1.** to enrich again, to make rich again **2.** (*abbellire di nuovo*) to embellish again ‖ **riarricchírsi,** *v.r.* to enrich oneself again, to grow rich again.

riàrso, *ag.* dry, parched, arid: *gola riarsa,* parched throat; *terreno —,* dry (*o* parched) ground.

riascoltàre, *v.t.* to listen again to (s.o., sthg.).

riaspettàre, *v.t.* to wait for (s.o., sthg.) again.

riassaggiàre, *v.t.* to taste again, to savour again.

riassalíre, *v.t.* to attack again, to assault again; to assail again (*anche fig.*).

riassaporàre, *v.t.* **1.** to savour again, to relish again **2.** (*godere di nuovo*) to enjoy again.

riassediàre, *v.t.* to besiege again.

riassestaménto, *s.m.* readjustment.

riassestàre, *v.t.* to readjust ‖ **riassestàrsi,** *v.r.* to readjust oneself.

riassettàre, *v.t.* to rearrange, to put in order again, to tidy up again ‖ **riassettàrsi,** *v.r.* to make oneself tidy again, to put oneself in order again.

riassètto, *s.m.* rearrangement, readjustment; (*riorganizzazione*) reorganization.

riassicuràre, *v.t.* (*comm.*) to reinsure ‖ **riassicuràrsi,** *v.r.* to reinsure oneself.

riassicuratóre, *ag.* reinsuring ‖ *s.m.* reinsurer.

riassicurazióne, *s.f.* (*comm.*) reinsurance.

riassociàre, *v.t.* to associate again; to take into partnership again ‖ **riassociàrsi,** *v.r.* **1.** to associate oneself again **2.** (*abbonarsi*) to subscribe again.

riassopírsi, *v.r.* to fall asleep again.

riassorbiménto, *s.m.* reabsorption.

riassorbíre, *v.t.* to reabsorb.

riassúmere, *v.t.* **1.** to re-engage, to take on again: *dopo due mesi tutti gli operai furono riassunti,* two months later all the workmen were taken on again **2.** (*riepilogare*) to resume, to sum up, to summarize, to recapitulate, to epitomize: *una bella poesia non si può —,* a beautiful poem cannot be summarized; *cercherò di riassumerti il suo discorso,* I'll try to sum up his speech for you **3.** (*dir.*) (*riprendere, la trattazione*) to resume.

riassuntívo, *ag.* recapitulatory, summarizing: *capitolo* —, summarizing chapter; *cenni riassuntivi,* summary.

riassúnto, *ag.* re-engaged ‖ *s.m.* resumé, summary, summing up, recapitulation, epitome, précis.

riassunzióne, *s.f.* **1.** (*di impiegato*) re-engagement **2.** (*dir.*) (*ripresa della trattazione*) resumption.

riattaccaménto, *s.m.* **1.** sticking **2.** (*ripresa*) resumption.

riattaceàre, *v.t.* **1.** to reattach; (*con gomma, colla*) to stick again: *il francobollo si è staccato, riattaccalo,* the stamp has come off, stick it on again; *riattaccami questo bottone, per favore,* sew this button on for me, please **2.** (*i cavalli ad una carrozza*) to harness (the horses to a carriage) again **3.** (*riprendere*) to resume: — *a lavorare,* to resume work (*o* to begin to work again); — *a suonare, a piangere,* to start playing, crying (*o* to play, to cry) again; — *il discorso,* to resume the conversation; — *il sonno,* to go to sleep again **4.** (*mil.*) (*riassalire*) to attack again **5.** (*telefono*) to hang up, to replace (the receiver): *ha riattaccato senza rispondere,* he hung up without answering ‖ **riattaceàrsi,** *v.r.* **1.** to stick again, to adhere again **2.** (*riaffezionarsi*) to become attached again: — *alla vita,* to recover one's zest for life.

riattaménto, *s.m.* refit, repair, rearrangement.

riattàre, *v.t.* to refit, to repair, to rearrange: — *un abito,* to alter a dress; — *una strada,* to repair a road.

riattèndere, *v.t.* to wait again for (s.o., sthg.); to expect again.

riattíngere, *v.t.* to draw (out) again.

riattivàre, *v.t.* **1.** to re-establish, to restore, to bring into use again, to put in service again: — *la circolazione del sangue,* to stimulate the circulation of the blood; — *una rete ferroviaria,* to put a railway (network) into service again **2.** (*fis. chim.*) to reactivate.

riattizzàre, *v.t.* **1.** (*il fuoco*) to poke again, to stir **2.** *fig.* to stir up again.

riavallàre, *v.t.* (*comm.*) to guarantee again; to consign again.

riavàllo, *s.m.* (*comm.*) new guarantee; renewal (of guarantee).

riavére, *v.t.* **1.** to have again: *oggi ha riavuto la febbre,* he has had a high temperature again today; *riebbe voglia di mangiare,* he felt like eating again **2.** (*ricuperare*) to get back, to get again, to recover: *ho riavuto il mio denaro,* I've got my money back; *potè* — *il figlio,* he could have his son back again; — *la vista, l'udito,* to recover one's sight, hearing **3.** *far* —, to revive: *la rugiada fece* — *i fiori,* the dew revived the flowers; *far* — *qlcu.,* to revive s.o. ‖ **riavérsi,** *v.r.* to recover, to recover one's strength; (*tornare in sè*) to recover one's senses: — *da una malattia,* to recover from (*o* to get over) an illness.

riavvallàre, *v.i.,* **riavvallàrsi,** *v.r.* to sink again.

riavvàllo, *s.m.* depression, hollow.

riavvampàre, *v.t.* to burn again ‖ *v.i.* to blaze again, to flare up again (anche *fig.*).

riavventàre, *v.t.* to hurl again ‖ **riavventàrsi,** *v.r.* to throw oneself again, to hurl oneself again.

riavvertíre, *v.t.* **1.** (*avvertire di nuovo*) to warn again **2.** (*sentire di nuovo*) to feel again.

riavvezzàre, *v.t.* to reaccustom, to accustom again.

riavvicinaménto, *s.m.* **1.** reapproaching, renewed approach **2.** (*riconciliazione*) reconciliation.

riavvicinàre, *v.t.* **1.** to approach again, to reapproach **2.** (*riconciliare*) to reconcile ‖ **riavvicinàrsi,** *v.r.* **1.** to approach again **2.** (*riconciliarsi*) to become reconciled, to make (it) up: *si riavvicinarono dopo molti mesi,* they were reconciled after many months.

riavvíncere, *v.t.* **1.** to bind again, to tie up again **2.** *fig.* to captivate again, to enthral again.

riavvisàre, *v.t.* **1.** to give notice again to (s.o.) **2.** (*ammonire di nuovo*) to warn again.

riavvòlgere, *v.t.* **1.** (*riaggomitolare*) to re-wind **2.** (*riavviluppare*) to re-wrap.

riazzannàre, *v.t.* to seize with one's fangs again.

riazzuffàrsi, *v.r.* to come to blows again.

ribaciàre, *v.t.* to kiss again ‖ **ribaciàrsi,** *v.r.* reciproco to kiss (each other) again.

ribadiménto, *s.m.* **1.** clinching, riveting **2.** *fig.* confirmation; repetition.

ribadíre, *v.t.* **1.** to clinch, to nail down, to rivet: *martello a* —, snap, riveting hammer **2.** *fig.* to fix, to rivet, to impress: — *un'accusa,* to confirm an accusation; — *un argomento,* to go over and over a subject again; — *ql.co. nella mente a qlcu.,* to impress sthg. on s.o.'s mind.

ribaditóio, *s.m.* (*mec.*) riveting hammer.

ribaditríce, *s.f.* (*mec.*) clinching machine, riveter, riveting machine: — *ad aria compressa,* pneumatic riveter; — *a serraggio pneumatico,* pneumatic squeeze riveting machine; — *elettrica,* electric riveting machine; — *idraulica,* hydraulic riveting machine.

ribaditúra, *s.f.* clinching, riveting: — *a caldo, a freddo,* hot, cold riveting; — *a macchina,* power riveting.

ribagnàre, *v.t.* to wet again.

ribaldeggiàre, *v.i.* (*letter.*) to be a brigand.

ribaldería, *s.f.* **1.** rascality, wickedness: *la sua* — *è ben nota,* his rascality is notorious **2.** (*azione da ribaldo*) rascally action, rascally trick, wicked deed, rascality: *le sue ribalderie erano famose,* his wicked deeds were notorious **3.** (*opera, lavoro mal fatto*) inferior piece of work: *questa commedia è una vera* —, this play is a very inferior piece of work.

ribàldo, *s.m.* rascal, scoundrel, rogue.

ribàlta, *s.f.* **1.** (*teat.*) (*fila dei lumi di un palcoscenico*) footlights (*pl.*) **2.** (*teat.*) (*parte anteriore del palcoscenico*) front of the stage: *luci della* —, (*la notorietà*) limelight; *venire alla* —, to appear before the curtain; *fig.* to come on (to) the scene **3.** (*asse, sportello spostabile*) flap **4.** (*di una botola*) trap-door.

ribaltaménto, *s.m.* upsetting, capsizing.

ribaltàre, *v.t.* to upset, to capsize ‖ *v.i.,* **ribaltàrsi,** *v.r.* to upset; to overturn, to capsize: *la carrozzina si ribaltò,* the perambulator upset (*o* was upset).

ribaltóne, *s.m.* **1.** (*balzo*) jerk **2.** (*rovescio*) upset.

ribassàre, *v.t.* to lower, to reduce: — *i prezzi,* to reduce prices ‖ *v.i.* to fall, to drop, to go down: *le azioni sono ribassate,* shares have gone down.

ribassàto, *ag.* reduced: *prezzo* —, reduced price.

ribassísta, *s.c.* (*chi provoca ribassi in Borsa*) bear.

ribàsso, *s.m.* **1.** fall, decline, drop: *un* — *nei prezzi,* a fall in prices; *mercato con tendenza al* —, (*Borsa*) bear market; *i prezzi sono in* —, prices are on the fall; *giocare al* —, (*Borsa*) to bear ‖ *essere in* —, *fig.* to be getting lower and lower **2.** (*sconto*) discount, reduction: *ottenere un* —, to get a discount.

ribàttere, *v.t.* **1.** to beat again, to strike again; (*con martello*) to hammer again: *battere e* —, to beat and to beat again; — *un materasso,* to remake a mattress ‖ — *una costura,* (*stirarla*) to iron a seam **2.** (*ribadire*) to clinch, to rivet: — *un chiodo,* to clinch a nail **3.** (*mil.*) (*respingere*) to repel: — *l'assalto,* to repel the assault **4.** (*confutare*) to confute: *osò* — *le idee del padre,* he dared to confute his father's ideas **5.** (*fam.*) to say over and over again: — *le medesime cose,* to say the same things over and over again **6.** (*spor.*) to return: — *la palla,* to return the ball ‖ *v.i.* to insist.

ribattezzàre, *v.t.* to rebaptize, to rename: *ribattezzarono molte vie,* they renamed many streets.

ribattiménto, *s.m.* **1.** renewed beating **2.** (*ribadimento*) clinching, riveting **3.** (*confutazione*) confutation **4.** (*spor.*) return.

ribattíno, *s.m.* (*mec.*) rivet: — *a testa cilindrica,* flat-head rivet; — *a testa tonda,* round-head rivet.

ribattitóre, *s.m.,* **ribattitríce,** *s.f.* **1.** (*ribaditore*) riveter **2.** (*confutatore*) confuter **3.** (*spor.*) he (*o* she) who returns the service.

ribattitúra, *s.f.* **1.** (*ribadimento*) clinching, riveting **2.** (*orlatura*) fell.

ribattúta, *s.f.* (*spor.*) return (of the service): *egli fa delle belle ribattute*, he has a nice return.

ribèca, *s.f.* (*mus.*) rebeck.

ribellàre, *v.t.* to incite to revolt, to cause to rebel; (*sollevare*) to rouse ‖ **ribellàrsi**, *v.r.* to rebel (against s.o., sthg.), to rise (against s.o., sthg.), to revolt (against s.o., sthg.): *indussero i sudditi a — al re*, they induced the subjects to rise (*o* to revolt) against their king; *— al proprio destino*, to rebel against one's fate.

ribèlle, *ag.* **1.** rebellious; rebel (*attributivo*): *— all'autorità paterna*, rebellious to one's father's authority; *esercito —*, rebel army; *temperamento —*, rebellious character; *era — ad ogni disciplina*, he was unamenable to discipline ‖ *riccioli ribelli*, unruly locks ‖ *tela — all'ago*, cloth difficult to sew **2.** (*ostinato*) stubborn, obstinate: *febbre, malattia —*, persistent fever, disease ‖ *s.c.* rebel.

ribellióne, *s.f.* rebellion: *atto di —*, rebellious act; *in aperta —*, in open rebellion; *in stato di —*, in a state of rebellion; *reprimere una —*, to quell a rebellion.

ribenedíre, *v.t.* **1.** to bless again; (*riconsacrare*) to reconsecrate: *— una chiesa*, to reconsecrate a church **2.** (*perdonare*) to forgive: *— il figliolo*, to forgive one's son.

ríbes, *s.m.* (*bot.*) black-currant.

ribòbolo, *s.m.* Florentine popular witticism.

riboccànte, *ag.* overflowing (with sthg.): *cuore — di affetto*, heart overflowing with love.

riboccàre, *v.i.* to overflow (with sthg.), to be overflowing (with sthg.): *il suo cuore riboccava di gioia e di gratitudine*, his heart overflowed with joy and gratitude; *la piazza ribocca di gente*, the square is overflowing with people.

ribócco, *s.m.* overflow; super-abundance ‖ *a —*, in great quantity.

ribolliménto, *s.m.* **1.** ebullition, boiling **2.** *fig.* (*agitazione*) agitation: *sento un gran — di sdegno*, I am boiling over with indignation **3.** (*geol. chim.*) bubbling.

ribollío, *s.m.* **1.** continuous boiling **2.** *fig.* (*agitazione, fermento*) agitation, ferment.

ribollíre, *v.i.* **1.** to boil again; to boil (anche *fig.*): *il mare ribolliva*, the sea was boiling; *si sentì — il sangue nelle vene*, he felt his blood boiling in his veins; *— di rabbia, di sdegno*, to boil over with rage, with indignation **2.** (*fermentare*) to ferment: *il vino ribolle*, the wine is fermenting **3.** (*rampollare*) to surge: *cento pensieri gli ribollivano nel cervello*, many thoughts surged up in his mind ‖ *v.i.* to boil again.

ribollitúra, *s.f.* **1.** (*il ribollire*) reboiling **2.** (*cosa ribollita*) thing reboiled: *questa non è che una — di avanzi*, these are only reboiled left-overs.

ribòtta, *s.f.* junket, junketing, spree: *fare —*, to junket (*o* to go on a spree).

ribrézzo, *s.m.* disgust, horror: *fare —*, to disgust (*o* to horrify *o* to make sick); *sentire — di ql.co.*, to be disgusted (*o* to be horrified *o* to feel sick) at sthg.

ribussàre, *v.t.* to knock again.

ributtànte, *ag.* disgusting, shocking, hideous, repulsive.

ributtàre, *v.t.* **1.** (*gettare di nuovo*) to throw again: *io lo raccolsi ed egli lo ributtò in terra*, I picked it up, and he threw it to the ground again **2.** (*respingere con forza*) to repel, to repulse: *— un assalto*, to repel an assault; *— i nemici*, to repulse the enemy ‖ *v.i.* **1.** *fig.* (*ripugnare*) to disgust, to horrify, to repel **2.** (*agr.*) (*germogliare di nuovo*) to bud again ‖ **ributtàrsi**, *v.r.* **1.** (*buttarsi giù*) to throw oneself down, to lie down **2.** (*perdersi d'animo*) to lose heart.

ricacciàre, *v.t.* **1.** to drive back, to push back; (*respingere*) to repel, to force back: *fu ricacciato in fondo alla fila*, he was pushed back to the end of the queue; *lo ricacciò con sdegno*, he repelled him with disdain; *il nemico fu ricacciato al di là del fiume*, the enemy were

driven back across the river ‖ *— in gola un'ingiuria, una menzogna a qlcu.*, to make s.o. retract (*o* take back) an insult, a lie **2.** (*rimandare fuori*) to drive out again, to turn out again, to eject again; (*riesiliare*) to banish again: *tornarono, ma li ricacciò dalla sua casa*, they went back but he turned (*o* drove) them out of his house again; *tornò in patria dopo molti anni, ma fu ricacciato*, he returned to his country after many years but he was banished again **3.** (*ficcare di nuovo*) to thrust again ‖ **ricacciàrsi**, *v.r.* to plunge again, to thrust oneself again: *si ricacciò tra la folla*, he plunged into the crowd again; *ti sei ricacciato nei guai!*, you've got yourself into trouble again!.

ricadènte, *ag.* hanging: *la chioma — dei salici*, the hanging branches of the willows.

ricadére, *v.i.* **1.** (*cadere di nuovo*) to fall (down) again (anche *fig.*); (*cadere giù*) to fall back: *ricadde dalla bicicletta*, he fell from his bicycle again; *fece uno sforzo per sollevarsi, ma ricadde sul cuscino*, she made an effort to raise herself, but fell back on to the pillow; *sono ricaduti in potere del nemico*, they have fallen into the enemy's hands once again; *— nella povertà*, to fall into poverty once more ‖ *— ammalato*, to fall ill again **2.** (*avere una ricaduta*) to relapse (anche *fig.*): *pensavano fosse guarito ma poi ricadde*, they thought he had recovered but then he relapsed; *— in errore*, to relapse into error; *— in uno stato di depressione*, to relapse into a state of depression; *— nel vizio*, to relapse into vice **3.** (*pendere*) to hang (down): *un ciuffo di capelli le ricade sulla fronte*, a tuft of hair hangs over her forehead; *una stoffa che ricade bene*, a cloth that hangs well **4.** (*toccare, spettare*) to fall, to be placed: *tutte le colpe ricadono su di lui*, all the blame falls on him **5.** (*dir.*) to pass (to s.o., sthg.); to go (to s.o., sthg.): *le terre che possedeva ricaddero sui cugini di parte materna*, the land he owned passed (*o* went) to his cousins on his mother's side.

ricadúta, *s.f.* relapse (anche *fig.*): *una — potrebbe essergli fatale*, a relapse might be fatal to him; *le sue ricadute nell'errore sono indice di debolezza*, his relapses into error show his weakness; *fare una —*, to relapse (*o* to have a relapse).

ricalàre, *v.i.* to fall again, to drop again.

ricalàta, *s.f.* **1.** falling again, dropping again: *la — del pendolo*, the swing of the pendulum **2.** *fig.* (*rar.*) (*cantilena*) drawling: *la — della parlata veneziana*, the drawling of the Venetian dialect.

ricalcàbile, *ag.* (*di disegno*) transferable.

ricalcàre, *v.t.* **1.** to push down, to pull down: *ricalcò il cappello sugli occhi*, he pulled his hat down on his eyes ‖ *— le orme di qlcu.*, to tread (*o* to follow) in s.o.'s steps **2.** (*imitare*) to imitate **3.** (*un disegno*) to transfer **4.** (*mec.*) to cold-head; (*metal.*) to upset.

ricalcàto, *ag.* **1.** (*di disegno*) traced **2.** *fig.* imitated.

ricalcatóio, *s.m.* rammer.

ricalcatúra, *s.f.* **1.** (*di disegno*) transfer **2.** (*imitazione*) copy, imitation **3.** (*mec. metal.*) upsetting, heading.

ricalcitraménto, *s.m.* recalcitration.

ricalcitrànte, *ag.* recalcitrant.

ricalcitràre, *v.i.* **1.** (*di cavallo*) to kick (out) **2.** *fig.* (*far resistenza*) to recalcitrate (against sthg.), to be recalcitrant: *— alla volontà di qlcu.*, to recalcitrate against s.o.'s will.

ricalzàre, *v.t.* to put on again.

ricamàre, *v.t.* to embroider (anche *fig.*): *— in bianco*, to embroider household linen.

ricamàto, *ag.* **1.** embroidered: *una tovaglia ricamata*, an embroidered table-cloth **2.** (*simile a ricamo*) embroidery-like.

ricamatóre, *s.m.* embroiderer.

ricamatríce, *s.f.* embroideress.

ricamatúra, *s.f.* **1.** (*ricamo*) embroidery, needlework **2.** (*il ricamare*) embroidering.

ricambiàre, *v.t.* **1.** (*cambiare di nuovo*) to change again **2.** (*contraccambiare*) to return, to reciprocate:

non so come — questo favore, I do not know how to reciprocate this favour; *vi ringrazio degli auguri che ricambio cordialmente*, I thank you for your good wishes which I heartily reciprocate; — *una visita, un regalo, una cortesia*, to return a visit, a present, a courtesy ‖ **ricambiàrsi**, *v.r. reciproco* to exchange: — *i saluti*, to exchange greetings.

ricàmbio, *s.m.* **1.** replacement, substitution ‖ *di —*, spare: *pezzo di —*, *(aut.)* spare part; *ruota di —*, *(aut.)* spare wheel; *non ho abiti di —*, I have no spare clothes (*o* I have not a change of clothes) **2.** *(scambio)* exchange: — *di cortesie*, exchange of courtesies **3.** *(fisiol. biol.)* metabolism: *disturbi del —*, metabolic disturbances.

ricàmo, *s.m.* embroidery *(anche fig.)*; needle-work: *ricami in oro*, gold-lace embroidery.

ricancellàre, *v.t.* to cross out again, to erase again.

ricantàre, *v.t.* **1.** to sing again **2.** *(ripetere)* to repeat ‖ — *le lodi di qlcu.*, to sing s.o.'s praises ‖ — *su tutti i toni*, to repeat over and over again **3.** *(ritrattare)* to retract.

ricantazióne, *s.f.* retractation, recantation.

ricapitàre[1], *V.* **recapitàre.**

ricapitàre[2], *v.i.i.* **1.** to arrive again, to come again **2.** *(accadere di nuovo)* to happen again.

ricapitolàre, *v.t.* to sum up, to recapitulate; to summarize ‖ *ricapitolando*, *(detto alla fine di un discorso)* in short (*o* to make a long story short).

ricapitolazióne, *s.f.* recapitulation, summing-up, summary.

ricaricaménto, *s.m.* **1.** reloading **2.** *(elett.)* recharging **3.** *(di orologio)* rewinding.

ricaricàre, *v.t.* **1.** to reload: — *un autocarro, una nave*, to reload a lorry, a ship; — *un fucile*, to reload a rifle **2.** *(batteria)* to recharge **3.** *(orologio)* to rewind, to wind up again ‖ **ricaricàrsi**, *v.r.* to burden oneself again.

ricascànte, *V.* **ricadènte.**

ricascàre, *V.* **ricadére 1. 2. 3.**

ricascàta, *s.f.* **1.** *(ricaduta)* relapse **2.** *(di tendaggi, ecc.)* sweep: *una bella — di tende*, the curtains have a beautiful sweep.

ricàseo, *s.m.* **1.** *(arch.)* cove **2.** *(drappeggio)* drapery.

ricattàre, *v.t.* **1.** to blackmail **2.** *(ricuperare)* to recover ‖ **ricattàrsi**, *v.r.* **1.** *(vendicarsi)* to avenge oneself, to take revenge (for sthg.) **2.** *(rifarsi)* to recoup oneself.

ricattatóre, *s.m.*, **ricattatríce**, *s.f.* blackmailer.

ricattatòrio, *ag.* blackmailing.

ricàtto, *s.m.* blackmail(ing): *fu vittima di un —*, *subì un —*, he was blackmailed.

ricavàre, *v.t.* **1.** *(trarre)* to draw: *questa è la morale che ho ricavato da questo libro*, this is the moral I have drawn from this book **2.** *(ottenere)* to obtain, to get: *da certi scolari non si ricava un bel nulla*, you can get nothing at all out of some pupils; *questo vestito è stato ricavato da uno scampolo*, this dress has been made out of a remnant **3.** *(estrarre)* to extract: *questa essenza si ricava da un fiore esotico*, this essence is extracted from an exotic flower **4.** *(guadagnare)* to gain, to make (a profit): *ha ricavato più di quanto pensasse dalla vendita della sua casa*, he made a bigger profit than he thought (he would) from the sale of his house; *non ne ricaverai un grande utile*, you will not derive a large profit from it **5.** *(cavare di nuovo)* to draw again.

ricavàto, *ag.* **1.** *(tratto)* drawn **2.** *(ottenuto)* obtained **3.** *(estratto)* extracted **4.** *(guadagnato)* gained ‖ *s.m.* proceeds *(pl.)*; return: *il — della vendita*, the proceeds of the sale; *il — sarà devoluto ad opere di beneficenza*, the proceeds will be devoted to charity.

ricàvo, *s.m.* proceeds *(pl.)*; return: — *netto*, net proceeds; *dare un buon —*, to yield a good return.

riccaménte, *av.* richly, magnificently; luxuriously.

Riccàrdo, *no.pr.m.* Richard ‖ *dim.* Dick ‖ — *Cuor di Leone*, *(st.)* Richard the Lion-heart(ed).

ricchézza, *s.f.* **1.** wealth; riches *(pl.)*: — *nazionale*,

national wealth; *esibizione di —*, showing off of wealth (*o* riches); *divise le sue ricchezze con suo fratello*, he shared his wealth (*o* riches) with his brother; *è un uomo con una grande —*, he is a man of great wealth; *tutte le mie ricchezze sono all'estero*, all my wealth is (*o* all my riches are) abroad **2.** *(abbondanza)* abundance; plenty, wealth; — *di idee, di parole, di esempi*, wealth of ideas, words, examples; *questo paese ha — d'acqua*, this country has plenty (*o* an abundance) of water **3.** *(l'essere ricco)* richness, wealth: — *del sottosuolo*, the richness (*o* wealth) of the subsoil.

ricciàia, *s.f.* *(di ricci vuoti)* heap of chestnut husks; *(di ricci con castagne)* heap of chestnuts in the husk.

ricciarèllo, *s.m.* "ricciarello" (Sienese almond cake).

ricciatóio, *s.m.* curling-irons *(pl.)*, curling-tongs *(pl.)*.

ríccio[1], *ag.* curly: *c'era un bambino con i capelli ricci, ricci*, there was a little boy with very curly hair; *era un vecchio signore con una barba lunga e riccia*, it was an old gentleman with a long, curly beard ‖ *s.m.* **1.** curl; lock: *quando era bambina aveva molti ricci*, as a child, she had a lot of curls; *si faceva i ricci*, she curled her hair; *si faceva sempre fare i ricci da...*, she always had her hair curled at...; *tiene un — della sua nonna in una bella spilla antica*, she keeps a lock of her grandmother's in a beautiful old brooch ‖ — *del pastorale*, *(eccl.)* shepherd's crook **2.** *(di tessuto)* terry: — *di ordito*, warp pile; *tessuto a —*, terry cloth **3.** *(di film)* loop **4.** *(mec.)* burr.

ríccio[2], *s.m.* *(zool.)* hedgehog: — *di mare*, sea-urchin.

ríccio[3], *s.m.* *(bot.)* chestnut husk: *c'erano mucchi di castagne ancora nei loro ricci*, there were heaps of chestnuts still in their husks.

ricciolína, *s.f.* **1.** *(bot.)* curly endive **2.** *(ragazza ricciuta)* curly-headed girl.

rícciolo, *s.m.* **1.** curl; lock **2.** *(mec.)* burr.

ricciolùto, ricciùto, *ag.* curly: *un bambino tutto —*, a curly-headed child; *testa ricciuta*, curly head.

rícco, *ag.* **1.** rich, wealthy; well-off: *una ricca famiglia*, a rich family; *un paese —*, a rich (*o* wealthy) country; *un uomo —*, a rich (*o* wealthy) man (*o* a man of wealth); *essere —*, to be well-off ‖ *è — sfondato*, he is awfully rich (*o* he has pots of money) ‖ *chi è contento è —*, *prov.* he who is happy is rich **2.** *(grande, di valore)* rich; valuable: *un — dono*, a valuable (*o* a rich) gift; *una ricca eredità*, a large (*o* rich) inheritance **3.** *(sontuoso, sfarzoso)* rich, sumptuous: *ricche vesti*, sumptuous clothes **4.** *(abbondante)* rich (in sthg.), abounding (in sthg.), full: — *di fantasia*, rich in (*o* full of) imagination; — *di idee*, full of ideas; — *di risorse naturali*, rich in natural resources; *una parete ricca di ornamenti*, a richly-decorated wall; *terra ricca di minerali*, land rich in minerals ‖ *s.m.* rich man, wealthy man: *i ricchi*, the rich (*o* the wealthy); *un nuovo —*, a nouveau riche (*o* an upstart *o* a parvenu).

riccóne, *s.m.* nabob, crœsus: *è un —*, he has pots of money.

ricérca, *s.f.* **1.** search; quest: *la — dell'oro*, the quest for gold; *la — della merce rubata fu inutile*, the search for the stolen goods was in vain; *ordinò la — dei disertori*, he ordered a search for the deserters ‖ *alla — di*, in search of: *corsi alla — di un dottore*, I ran to find a doctor; *è sempre alla — dell'interesse personale*, he always has an eye to his own interest (*o* he is always in search of his own interest); *siamo alla — di ql.co.*, we are in search of sthg. (*o fam.* we are on the look-out for sthg.); *partire alla — di un tesoro*, to set off in quest (*o* in search) of a treasure **2.** *(il perseguire)* pursuit: *la — della felicità*, the pursuit of happiness; *la — del sapere*, the pursuit of knowledge; *la — della verità*, the search after truth ‖ *alla — di*, in pursuit of **3.** *(a carattere scientifico)* research: *ricerche nucleari*, nuclear researches; *ricerche scientifiche, storiche*, scientific, historical researches; *laboratorio di ricerche*, research laboratory; *lavoro di —*, research work; *dedicò tutta la sua vita alla — scientifica*, he devoted all his life to scientific research; *fece lunghe ricerche sulle cause di questo male*, he carried out a long research into the causes of this disease; *le sue ricerche non sono state fruttuose*, his researches have not been successful 4. (*indagine*) investigation, inquiries: *con ulteriori ricerche scoprì che...*, on further investigation he discovered that...; *fare delle ricerche su ql.co.*, to make inquiries about sthg. 5. (*richiesta*) demand: *c'è molta — di questo articolo*, there is great demand for this article.

ricercàre, *v.t.* 1. (*cercare di nuovo*) to look for (s.o., sthg.) again: *visto che non era in casa, andrò a ricercarlo questa sera*, as he was not in, I shall go and look for him again this evening 2. (*cercare con cura*) to seek, to seek for (s.o., sthg.), to search for (s.o., sthg.): *il ladro fu ricercato per tutta la città*, the thief was sought all over the city (*o* they searched for the thief all over the city); *quell'uomo è ricercato dalla polizia*, that man is wanted by the police; *— l'autore di un delitto*, to search for (*o* to make a search for) a murderer 3. (*perseguire*) to pursue, to seek after (sthg.): *— la felicità, i piaceri mondani*, to pursue (*o* to seek after) happiness, worldly pleasures 4. (*investigare, studiare*) to investigate, to inquire into (sthg.): *— le cause di un incidente*, to investigate the causes of an accident; *— l'origine della specie umana*, to inquire into the origins of the human species; *— la verità dei fatti*, to investigate the truth of facts 5. (*richiedere*) to want; to require; to demand: *ricerchiamo maggiore pazienza da parte vostra*, we want (*o* demand) more patience on your part; *se nessuno ricerca il mio aiuto, me ne andrò a casa*, if nobody wants my help I'm going home.

ricercataménte, *av.* 1. (*con raffinatezza*) refinedly 2. (*con affettazione*) affectedly: *parla —*, he speaks affectedly.

ricercatézza, *s.f.* 1. (*raffinatezza*) refinement: *è un ambiente di una certa —*, it is a place of a certain refinement; *non ha nessuna — nel vestire*, her clothes lack any refinement; *non mi piace l'eccessiva — del suo stile*, I do not like the preciosity of his style 2. (*parola, modo affettato*) affectation: *vorrei che la smettesse con le sue ricercatezze*, I wish he would drop his affectations.

ricercàto, *ag.* 1. (*richiesto*) sought-after: *è un chirurgo —*, he is a much sought-after surgeon (*o* he is in great demand as a surgeon); *è un testo molto —*, there is a great demand for this text; *questo non è un articolo —*, there is no demand for this article 2. (*raffinato*) refined: *è ricercata nel vestire*, she dresses in a refined style 3. (*affettato*) affected: *modi ricercati*, affected manners 4. (*fuori del consueto*) far-fetched: *espressione ricercata*, far-fetched expression.

ricercatóre, *ag.* searching (for s.o., sthg.), seeking (for s.o.): *critica ricercatrice del vero*, criticism searching for truth ‖ *s.m.*, **ricercatrìce**, *s.f.* 1. seeker, searcher: *è — di antichità*, he is always looking for antiques; *— della verità*, searcher after truth 2. (*chi fa ricerche scientifiche*) researcher, research-worker.

ricerchiàre, *v.t.* to re-hoop.

ricètta, *s.f.* 1. (*med.*) prescription 2. (*cuc.*) recipe: *mi ha dato una buona — per la torta di mele*, she gave me a good recipe for (making) an apple-tart 3. *fig.* formula: *nel suo sistema di vita aveva trovato la — della felicità*, in her way of life she had founded the formula for happiness (*o* the key to happiness).

ricettàcolo, *s.m.* 1. receptacle; repository: *questo porto è il — della peggior feccia del mondo*, all the scum of the earth finds its way to this port 2. (*bot.*) receptacle.

ricettaménto, *V.* **ricettazione**.

ricettàre, *v.t.* 1. (*ospitare*) to shelter, to harbour: *— un fuggiasco*, to shelter a fugitive 2. (*custodire roba rubata*) to receive.

ricettàrio, *s.m.* 1. (*med.*) prescription-book, book of prescriptions 2. (*cuc.*) recipe-book, book of recipes.

ricettàto, *ag.* 1. sheltered 2. *merce ricettata*, received stolen goods.

ricettatóre, *s.m.*, **ricettatrìce**, *s.f.* receiver (of stolen goods); (*sl.*) fence.

ricettazióne, *s.f.* (*dir.*) receiving of stolen goods; (*sl.*) fencing: *è accusato di —*, he is accused of receiving stolen goods.

ricettività, *s.f.* receptivity, receptiveness.

ricettìvo, *ag.* receptive.

ricètto, *s.m.* shelter: *dar —*, to give shelter.

ricevènte, *ag.* receiving ‖ *s.m.* 1. receiver 2. (*comm.*) consignee.

ricévere, *v.t.* 1. to receive: *ho ricevuto la tua lettera stamane*, I received your letter this morning; *questa stanza non riceve abbastanza luce*, this room does not receive enough light; *ricevette la merce giusto in tempo*, he received the goods just in time; *— un regalo, un favore, un'offesa, una notizia, visite*, to receive a present, a favour, an offence, a piece of news, visitors ‖ *— il battesimo*, to be baptized 2. (*accettare*) to accept; (*ammettere, accogliere*) to admit: *fu ricevuto nel nostro gruppo*, he was admitted into our group; *non dovevi — il suo denaro*, you should not have accepted money from him; *le sue idee non saranno ben ricevute nel nostro paese*, his ideas will not be well accepted in our country; *— uno come novizio*, to admit s.o. as a novice 3. (*prendere, avere*) to take, to have, to get: *ricevo 500 lire al giorno*, I get 500 lire a day; *— in cambio*, to take (*o* to receive) in exchange; *— in prestito*, to borrow 4. (*contenere, accogliere*) to admit: *il porto di Genova riceve grandi bastimenti*, the port of Genoa can admit big ships; *questa sala può — cento persone*, this hall can admit (*o* can hold) a hundred people 5. (*dare il benvenuto a, accogliere*) to receive, to welcome: *andremo alla stazione a riceverli*, we shall go to the station to welcome (*o* to meet) them; *mi ricevettero a braccia aperte*, they received me with open arms 6. (*ammettere nel proprio domicilio, studio, ecc.*) to receive, to be at home (to visitors): *il dottore riceve dalle 14 alle 16 pomeridiane*, the doctor receives patients from 2 to 4 p.m.; *mia madre riceve il venerdì*, my mother is at home on Fridays; *non ho ancora ricevuto quest'anno*, I have not given a party yet this year; *non ricevo mai quando la cameriera è fuori*, I never receive visitors when the maid is out; *non ricevo oggi*, I am not at home to anyone to-day 7. (*dare udienza*) to grant audience to (s.o.); to hold audience: *il ministro non riceve*, the minister does not hold audience.

ricevìbile, *ag.* receivable.

ricevibilità, *s.f.* receivability, receivableness.

riceviménto, *s.m.* 1. (*atto del ricevere*) receiving; receipt; reception: *al — della merce*, on receipt of the goods; *al — di queste notizie*, on receiving this news; *accusare — di ql.co.*, to acknowledge receipt of sthg. 2. (*ammissione*) admission: *— di un nuovo socio*, admission of a new member 3. (*trattenimento, festa*) reception; party: *— di nozze*, wedding-party; *sala di —*, reception-room; *andare ad un —*, to go to a party; *dare un —*, to give a party.

ricevitóre, *s.m.* receiver: *— acustico*, (*rad. elett.*) sounder; *— a galena*, (*rad.*) crystal-set; *— d'echi*, echo-receiver; *— delle imposte*, tax-collector; *— di ritorno*, (*rad.*) homing-receiver; *— Morse*, (*tel.*) Morse-receiver; *— telefonico*, (telephone) receiver ‖ *— del Registro*, registrar.

ricevitorìa, *s.f.* receiving-office ‖ *— del Registro*, registry.

ricevùta, *s.f.* 1. (*comm.*) receipt: *— a saldo*, receipt in full; *— sulla fiducia*, trust receipt; *raccomandata con — di ritorno*, registered letter with advice of receipt; *manca la —*, the receipt is missing; *accusare — di ql.co.*, to acknowledge receipt of sthg. 2. (*riconoscimento di debito*) I owe you (*abbr.* I.O.U.).

ricezióne, *V.* **recezione**.

richiamàre, *v.t.* 1. (*chiamare di nuovo*) to call again:

chiamai e richiamai, ma nessuno rispose, I called and called, but no one answered; *vuoi — più tardi?*, would you call again later? ‖ — *alle armi*, to recall for military service ‖ — *qlcu. in carica*, to recall s.o. to office 2. (*chiamare indietro, far tornare*) to call back, to recall: *gli affari lo richiamarono a Roma*, business called (*o* summoned) him back to Rome; *richiamalo, ho dimenticato di dirgli ql.co.*, call him back, I have forgotten to tell him sthg.; — *il cane*, to call off one's dog; — *un generale, un ambasciatore, un esiliato*, to recall a general, an ambassador, an exile ‖ — *un aeroplano*, to flatten out (*o* to level off) an aircraft ‖ — *all'ordine*, to call to order ‖ — *in vita*, to restore (*o* to bring back) to life ‖ — *ql.co. alla mente di qlcu.*, to recall sthg. to s.o.'s mind (*o* to remind s.o. of sthg.): *questa scena mi richiama alla mente ql.co. di molto triste*, this scene reminds me of sthg. very sad; *questo mi richiama alla mente la mia ultima visita qui*, this recalls to my mind my last visit here ‖ — *qlcu. ai dovere*, to recall s.o. to his duty 3. (*ritirare*) to withdraw: — *le truppe dalle posizioni occupate*, to withdraw the troops from the positions occupied 4. (*attirare*) to attract; to draw: *ella vestiva sempre di rosso per — l'attenzione*, she was always dressed in red to attract people's attention; *questa commedia richiamerà molti spettatori*, this play will draw large audiences; *voglio — la tua attenzione su questo fatto*, I want to call (*o* to draw) your attention to this fact (*o* I want to point out this fact to you) 5. (*rimproverare*) to rebuke, to reprimand: *lo richiamò aspramente*, he reprimanded him severely 6. (*rar.*) (*dir.*) (*chiamare in giudizio*) to summon ‖ **richiamàrsi**, *v.r.* 1. (*riferirsi*) to refer: *a un documento, a un'autorità*, to refer to a document, an authority 2. (*appellarsi*) to appeal: — *alla giustizia*, to appeal to the law 3. (*letter.*) (*dolersi*) to complain: — *di un'ingiuria*, to complain of a wrong 4. — *di qlcu.*, (*letter.*) (*sporgere querela*) to prosecute s.o.

richiamàto, *s.m.* soldier recalled to arms.

richiàmo, *s.m.* 1. recall: *fu necessario il — della flotta*, the recall of the fleet was necessary ‖ — *alle armi*, recall to arms ‖ — *all'ordine*, call to order 2. (*allettamento*) call: *il — della foresta, del mare*, the call of the wild, of the sea; *uccello da —*, decoy 3. *segno di —*, (*tip.*) cross-reference mark.

richiedènte, *s.c.* applicant, petitioner.

richièdere, *v.t.* 1. (*domandar di nuovo*) to ask for (sthg.) again; (*domandare in restituzione*) to ask for (sthg.) back: *richiese il suo libro*, he asked for his book back 2. (*domandare*) to ask; (*con insistenza*) to demand: *gli richiese aiuto*, he asked him for help (*o* his help); *questo articolo è molto richiesto*, this article is much in demand; — *a qlcu. nome e indirizzo*, to ask s.o. his name and his address; — *un favore a qlcu.*, to ask s.o. a favour (*o* to ask a favour of s.o.) 3. (*esigere*) to request; to demand: *egli richiede ciò che gli devi*, he requests what you owe him; *essi richiesero che egli pagasse tutto*, they demanded that he (should) pay for everything; *tu richiedi troppo*, you ask too much 4. (*necessitare*) to require, to need: *questo lavoro richiede molta pazienza*, this work requires a lot of patience.

richièsta, *s.f.* request; (*generalmente perentoria*) demand: *a —*, by request; *dietro — scritta*, on written application; *dietro vostra —*, at your request; *programma a —*, request-programme; *le richieste dei cittadini non furono accolte dal loro re*, the citizens' demands were not granted by their king; *c'è una gran — di questo articolo*, this article is in great demand (*o* much in demand); *c'è una gran — di stenografi*, there is a great demand for shorthand-writers; *far — di ql.co.*, to make a request for sthg.; *soddisfare le richieste di qlcu.*, to satisfy s.o.'s demands.

richièsto, *ag.* 1. requested; demanded: *articolo molto —*, article much in demand 2. (*necessario*) required, necessary: *titoli di studio richiesti*, necessary qualifica-

tions 3. (*conveniente*) suitable: *decoro — da un luogo*, decorum suitable to (*o* befitting) a place.

richiúdere, *v.t.* to close again, to reclose, to shut again ‖ **richiúdersi**, *v.r.* 1. (*di porte, finestre, ecc.*) to close again, to shut again 2. (*di ferita*) to heal (up).

ricíngere, *V.* **recíngere**.

ricíno, *s.m.* (*bot.*) ricinus: *olio di —*, (*farm.*) castor-oil.

ricògliere, *v.t.* to pick again, to gather again.

ricognitóre, *s.m.* 1. reconnoitrer 2. (*aer.*) scout, reconnaissance-aircraft, spotter-aircraft.

ricognizióne, *s.f.* 1. (*mil.*) reconnaissance: — *tattica*, land-reconnaissance; *aereo da —*, (air) scout (*o* reconnaissance-aircraft); *essere in —*, to be on a reconnaissance; *fare una —*, to reconnoitre (*o* to make a reconnaissance) 2. (*rar.*) (*riconoscimento*) recognition; (*di un debito*) acknowledgement: *atto di —*, (*dir.*) ascertainment.

ricollegàre, *v.t.* 1. (*legare di nuovo*) to link again; (*riunire*) to reunite 2. (*connettere*) to connect: *non riesco a — queste due idee*, I cannot connect these two ideas ‖ **ricollegàrsi**, *v.r.* 1. to be connected (with sthg.) 2. (*riconciliarsi*) to become reconciled (with s.o., to sthg.).

ricollocaménto, *s.m.* replacement, replacing; (*in una carica*) reappointment.

ricollocàre, *v.t.* to replace, to put back; (*in una carica*) to reappoint ‖ **ricollocàrsi**, *v.r.* (*riprendere marito*) to marry again.

ricolmàre, *v.t.* 1. to fill to the brim, to fill up 2. *fig.* to load; to overwhelm: — *qlcu. di gentilezze*, to load s.o. with kindness (*o* to heap kindness on s.o.).

ricolmatúra, *s.f.* filling up.

ricólmo, *ag.* 1. full; (*colmo fino all'orlo*) full to the brim, filled to the brim, brimful: *bicchiere —*, full glass 2. *fig.* loaded (with sthg.); overwhelmed (with sthg.): *partì — di benedizioni*, he went away loaded with blessings.

ricoloràre, ricoloríre, *v.t.* to colour again; to repaint; to give another coat of paint to (sthg.) ‖ **ricoloràrsi, ricolorírsi**, *v.r.* to colour again; to put on colour again.

ricoltivàre, *v.t.* to recultivate, to cultivate again (anche *fig.*); to farm again; to till again.

ricombàttere, *v.t.* to fight again, to struggle again.

ricombinàre, *v.t.* 1. to rearrange, to arrange again; (*rimettere insieme*) to recombine 2. (*progettare di nuovo*) to replan.

ricominciaménto, *s.m.* recommencement; recommencing.

ricominciàre, *v.t.i.* to begin again, to start again, to recommence: *dopo una breve pausa, ricominciò*, after a short pause he began (*o* started) again; — *a leggere*, to begin (*o* to start) to read (*o* reading) again ‖ *si ricomincia?*, (*per richiamare all'ordine*) are you at it again?.

ricomméttere, *v.t.* 1. to commit again: — *un errore*, to make a mistake again 2. (*riaffidare*) to entrust again: — *ql.co. a qlcu.*, to entrust s.o. with sthg. (*o* to entrust sthg. to s.o.) again 3. (*ricongiungere*) to join again, to put together again: — *i pezzi di un vaso rotto*, to join (*o* to put) together the fragments of a broken vase.

ricommettitúra, *s.f.* (*il ricongiungere*) joining: *la — di un osso*, the knitting of a bone.

ricomparíre, *v.i.* to reappear.

ricompàrsa, *s.f.* reappearance.

ricompènsa, *s.f.* reward, recompense; (*rar.*) requital: *la prigione fu la giusta — dei suoi delitti*, prison was a just reward (*o* requital *o* punishment) for his crimes ‖ *in —*, as a reward (*o* in return *o* in recompense): *in — dei vostri servizi*, as a reward (*o* in return) for your services.

ricompensàbile, *ag.* rewardable.

ricompensàre, *v.t.* to reward, to recompense; (*rar.*)

to requite: *le sue sofferenze saranno ricompensate,* his sufferings will be rewarded; — *qlcu. per i suoi servizi,* to reward (o to recompense) s.o. for his services.

ricompensatóre, *s.m.,* **ricompensatríce,** *s.f.* rewarder, recompenser.

ricomperàre, *V.* **ricompràre.**

ricompilàre, *v.t.* to compile again.

ricompórre, *v.t.* **1.** (*opera letteraria, musicale*) to rewrite: — *una sinfonia, una poesia,* to rewrite a symphony, a poem **2.** (*rimettere insieme*) to reassemble; (*tip.*) to reset, to recompose: — *una linea,* (*tip.*) to reset a line; — *una macchina,* to reassemble a machine **3.** (*riassestare*) to re-form, to form again, to recompose: — *un ministero,* to re-form a ministry **4.** — *il viso,* to recompose one's features ‖ **ricompórsi,** *v.r.* to recover oneself, to compose oneself.

ricomposizióne, *s.f.* **1.** (*di opera letteraria, musicale*) rewriting **2.** (*il rimettere insieme*) reassembling, reassembly; (*tip.*) resetting, recomposition: — *di un mosaico,* reassembling of a mosaic **3.** (*il riassestare*) re-formation, recomposition: — *di una società,* re-formation of a society.

ricompràre, *v.t.* **1.** to repurchase, to buy again; (*la stessa cosa che si era venduta*) to buy back: *ho ricomprato il quadro che avevo venduto tre anni or sono,* I have bought back the painting I sold three years ago **2.** (*spendere molto per cosa ricevuta in dono, eredità*) to spend more than the value of (sthg.): *ho ereditato quella casa, ma ci ho tanto speso che l'ho ricomprata,* I inherited that house, but I have spent more than its value on it **3.** (*riscattare*) to ransom; (*redimere*) to redeem: *Cristo ha ricomprato il genere umano dalla dannazione e dal peccato,* Christ redeemed mankind from damnation and sin; — *un prigioniero,* to ransom a prisoner.

ricomunicàre, *v.t.* **1.** to communicate again **2.** (*eccl.*) (*assolvere da scomunica*) to absolve from excommunication ‖ *v.i.* to communicate again ‖ **ricomunicàrsi,** *v.r.* (*eccl.*) to take Communion again.

riconciliàbile, *ag.* reconcilable.

riconciliaménto, *s.m.* reconciliation, reconcilement.

riconciliàre, *v.t.* to reconcile: — *due persone,* to reconcile one person to (o with) another ‖ **riconciliàrsi,** *v.r.* to become reconciled (to s.o.), to make (it) up (with s.o.): *si è riconciliato con sua madre,* he is now reconciled with his mother; *mi sono riconciliato con il mio destino,* I am reconciled to my fate ‖ — *con Dio,* (*eccl.*) to make one's peace with God ‖ *v.r. reciproco* to become reconciled, to be reconciled, to make (it) up, to make friends again: *litigammo aspramente ma ci siamo riconciliati,* we had a big quarrel but we have made friends again (o we have made it up).

riconciliatóre, *s.m.,* **riconciliatríce,** *s.f.* reconciler.

riconciliazióne, *s.f.* reconciliation, reconcilement.

ricondannàre, *v.t.* to condemn again.

ricondúrre, *v.t.* **1.** to take back; to bring back; to lead back; to lead again: *dei cattivi compagni lo ricondussero su una cattiva strada,* evil companions led him astray again; *lo ricondusse a vedere lo spettacolo,* he took him to see the show again; *riconducilo da me,* bring him back to my house; — *a casa,* to take home; — *la pace tra i popoli,* to bring back peace among the nations **2.** (*riconfermare in una carica*) to confirm in an office ‖ **ricondúrsi,** *v.r.* to go back again.

riconduzióne, *s.f.* **1.** taking back; bringing back; leading back **2.** (*dir.*) renewal.

riconférma, *s.f.* reconfirmation; confirmation.

riconfermàre, *v.t.* to reconfirm: — *qlcu. in una carica,* to reconfirm s.o. in an office ‖ **riconfermàrsi,** *v.r.* (*dimostrarsi di nuovo*) to prove oneself again.

riconfessàre, *v.t.* to reconfess.

riconficcàre, *v.t.* to drive in again, to reinsert.

riconfiscàre, *v.t.* to reconfiscate, to confiscate again.

riconfortàre, *v.t.* to recomfort, to comfort, to con-

sole, to cheer up: *le sue parole mi riconfortarono,* his words cheered me up (o recomforted me) ‖ **riconfortàrsi,** *v.r.* to take comfort, to cheer up.

ricongiúngere, *v.t.* to rejoin; to reunite ‖ **ricongiúngersi,** *v.r.* to join again (s.o., sthg.), to rejoin (s.o., sthg.): — *alla famiglia,* to rejoin one's family (o to join one's family again).

ricongiungiménto, *s.m.* rejoining; reunion; (*incontro*) meeting.

riconnèttere, *v.t.* to re-connect, to connect again.

riconoscènte, *ag.* grateful, thankful.

riconoscènza, *s.f.* gratitude, thankfulness.

riconóscere, *v.t.* **1.** to recognize: *era cambiato tanto che non lo riconobbi,* he had changed so much that I did not recognize him; — *qlcu. al passo, alla voce,* to recognize (o to know) s.o. by his walk, by his voice **2.** (*ammettere apertamente, ufficialmente, come legittimo*) to recognize, to acknowledge: *la legge non riconobbe i suoi diritti,* the law did not recognize his claims; *non la riconobbe come moglie,* he did not recognize her as his wife; *si rifiutarono di — il re,* they refused to acknowledge the king; — *un figlio,* to acknowledge a child; — *l'indipendenza di un paese,* to recognize the independence of a country; — *qlcu. come capo,* to acknowledge s.o. as one's leader **3.** (*ammettere*) to acknowledge, to admit, to own: *non volle — il suo errore,* he did not want to acknowledge (o to admit) his mistake; *riconosco che tu hai ragione,* I admit you are right; *riconosco che tutto questo è vero,* I acknowledge (o recognize) that all this is true; *riconosco di essermi sbagliato,* I own (o admit o confess) that I was mistaken; — *la propria colpa,* to acknowledge (o to admit) one's guilt **4.** (*comprendere, discernere*) to recognize, to know: *riconobbe subito il pericolo,* he recognized the danger immediately; *riconobbi in lui un talento eccezionale per la musica,* I recognized (o saw) that he had an exceptional talent for music **5.** (*considerare*) to recognize, to acknowledge: *i suoi servigi non furono riconosciuti,* his services were not recognized **6.** (*identificare*) to identify: *occorre un documento per farsi —,* a document is necessary to identify oneself (o to make oneself known) **7.** (*mil.*) to reconnoître ‖ **riconóscersi,** *v.r.* to recognize oneself, to acknowledge oneself: *egli si riconobbe colpevole,* he acknowledged that he was guilty; — *vinto,* to own oneself beaten (o to acknowledge defeat) ‖ *v.r. reciproco* to recognize each other (one another).

riconoscíbile, *ag.* recognizable.

riconoscibilménte, *av.* recognizably.

riconosciménto, *s.m.* **1.** recognition: *il — di una persona,* the recognition of a person **2.** (*riconoscimento formale, ufficiale*) recognition, acknowledg(e)ment: — *di un debito,* acknowledgment of a debt; (*comm.*) I owe you (*abbr. I.O.U.*); — *di un figlio naturale,* affiliation of an illegitimate child; *il — di un nuovo Stato,* the recognition of a new State **3.** (*ammissione*) admission, avowal: *il — di un errore,* the admission (o avowal) of an error **4.** (*identificazione*) identification: *segno di —,* identification mark **5.** (*compenso*) recognition: *un regalo in — di un servizio,* a present in recognition of a service.

riconoscitóre, *s.m.,* **riconoscitríce,** *s.f.* recognizer.

riconosciúto, *ag.* **1.** recognized **2.** (*ammesso*) acknowledged ‖ *feste riconosciute,* public and religious holidays.

riconquista, *s.f.* reconquest, recapture.

riconquistàre, *v.t.* to reconquer, to win back.

riconsacràre, *v.t.* to reconsecrate.

riconsacrazióne, *s.f.* reconsecration.

riconségna, *s.f.* redelivery, restitution, return.

riconsegnàre, *v.t.* to redeliver, to hand back.

riconsideràre, *v.t.* to reconsider.

riconsigliàre, *v.t.* to advise again ‖ **riconsigliàrsi,** *v.r.* to consult (s.o.) again.

riconsolàre, *v.t.* to recomfort, to comfort again, to console again ‖ **riconsolàrsi,** *v.r.* to be recomforted.

riconsolidàre, *v.t.* to reconsolidate.

ricontàre, *v.t.* to re-count, to count again.

riconvalidàre, *v.t.* to make valid again; to validate again.

riconveníre, *v.t.* (*dir.*) to bring a counter-charge against (s.o.), to bring a counter-claim against (s.o.).

riconvenziònàle, *ag.* (*dir.*) counter-claim (*attributivo*), countercharge (*attributivo*) ‖ *s.f.* (*dir.*) counter-claim, countercharge.

riconvenzióne, *s.f.* (*dir.*) counter-claim, countercharge.

riconversióne, *s.f.* reconversion.

riconvertíre, *v.t.* to reconvert ‖ **riconvertírsi,** *v.r.* to be reconverted, to be converted again.

riconvocàre, *v.t.* to convoke again, to resummon.

riconvocazióne, *s.f.* resummons.

ricopèrto, *ag.* **1.** covered (with sthg.): — *di argento,* silver-plated; — *di carta,* paper-covered; — *di pelle,* leather-covered ‖ *dente* —, covered tooth; *sedia ricoperta,* upholstered chair **2.** (*nascosto*) hidden.

ricopertúra, *s.f.* covering, cover; (*di metallo*) plating; (*di mobili*) cover: *la — di una poltrona,* the cover of an arm-chair.

ricòpia, *s.f.* **1.** second copy **2.** (*quadro copiato da una copia*) copy of a copy.

ricopiàre, *v.t.* **1.** to copy; (*copiare di nuovo*) to recopy, to copy again; (*copiare in bella copia*) to copy fair, to make a fair copy of (sthg.) **2.** (*dipingere*) to paint: — *dal vero,* to paint from nature.

ricopiatóre, *s.m.,* **ricopiatríce,** *s.f.* **1.** copyist, copier **2.** (*plagiatore*) plagiarist, plagiary.

ricopiatúra, *s.f.* **1.** (*il ricopiare*) copying, recopying **2.** (*copia*) copy.

ricopríbile, *ag.* coverable.

ricopríre, *v.t.* **1.** to cover; (*coprire di nuovo*) to re-cover, to cover again: *l'edera ricopre tutto il muro,* the wall is all covered with ivy; *la neve ricopriva la cima delle montagne,* the snow covered the tops of the mountains; — *un divano di cretonne,* to cover a sofa with cretonne; — *di fiori,* to cover with flowers; — *un libro,* to cover a book **2.** (*mil.*) (*difendere*) to cover: *la cavalleria ricoprì la ritirata,* the cavalry covered the retreat **3.** (*nascondere*) to hide, to conceal **4.** *fig.* (*colmare*) to load: — *qlcu. di regali, onori,* to load s.o. with gifts, honours **5.** (*ind.*) to coat: — *di piombo,* to coat with lead; — *galvanicamente,* to plate ‖ **ricoprírsi,** *v.r.* **1.** to cover oneself (with sthg.) (*anche fig.*): — *di vergogna,* to cover oneself with shame **2.** (*ripararsi*) to cover oneself (with sthg.): *si ricopriva dello scudo,* he protected himself with his shield ‖ — *della spesa,* (*comm.*) to cover one's expenses **3.** (*rimettersi il cappello*) to cover one's head.

ricopritóre, *ag.* covering ‖ *s.m.,* **ricopritríce,** *s.f.* coverer.

ricopritúra, *s.f.* (*agr.*) covering.

ricordàbile, *ag.* **1.** (*memorabile*) memorable; worth remembering **2.** (*che si può menzionare*) mentionable.

ricordànza, *s.f.* **1.** remembrance; recollection, memory: *una lieta, una vaga* —, a pleasant, a vague recollection (*o* memory)‖ *a — d'uomo,* (with)in living memory: *a — d'uomo non si è mai vista una cosa simile,* nothing like this has been seen in living memory **2.** *pl.* (*scritti commemorativi*) memoirs; memorials **3.** (*menzione*) mention; (*fama*) fame.

ricordàre, *v.t.* **1.** to remember: *non ricordo che egli abbia parlato così,* I do not remember his saying that; *non ricordo che me l'abbiate detto,* I do not remember your telling me so; *non ricordo il suo nome,* I cannot remember (*o* recall) his name; *per quanto ricordo,* as far as I remember; *ricordo bene che me l'avete detto,* I well remember your telling me; *ricordo d'averlo visto,* I remember seeing it; *ricordo di averlo già incontrato,* I remember having met him before (*o* that I have already met him); *ricordo molto bene ciò che accadde,*

I remember what happened very well **2.** (*richiamare alla propria memoria*) to recollect, to recall: *cercherò di — quel che mi disse,* I shall try to recollect what he told me; *non riesco a — il titolo di quel libro,* I cannot recall the title of that book **3.** (*chiamare alla memoria altrui*) to remind; to recall: *mi si ricordò la mia promessa,* I was reminded of my promise; *questo mi ricorda che...,* this reminds me that...; *ricordami che devo dargli due libri,* remind me that I must give him two books; *ricordami di comperare dei fiori,* remind me to buy some flowers; *si ricorda ai passeggeri che...,* passengers are reminded that...; *il suo stile ricorda Pope,* his style is reminiscent of Pope's; *ti ricorderò questo impegno,* I shall remind you of this engagement; *tutto qui mi ricorda la mia giovinezza,* everything here recalls my youth (*o* reminds me of my youth) ‖ *ricordami a tuo fratello,* remember me to your brother **4.** (*menzionare*) to mention: *anche Platone ricorda questo,* Plato, too, mentions (*o* refers to) this; *non avresti dovuto — queste cose a casa loro,* you should not have mentioned these things at their house; *ricordiamo come esempio,* let us mention as an example ‖ **ricordàrsi,** *v.r.* **1.** to remember (s.o., sthg.): *il bambino non si ricorda più di suo padre,* the child does not remember his father any longer; *mi ricordo che era molto pigro,* I remember he was very lazy; *mi ricordo che John disse che...,* I remember John saying that...; *non mi ricordo,* I do not remember; *ricordati di me,* remember me ‖ *me ne ricorderò per un pezzo!,* I shan't forget it in a hurry! ‖ *non si ricorda dal naso alla bocca, da qui a lì,* he can't even remember his own name (*o* he can't remember a thing from one minute to the next) **2.** (*richiamare alla propria memoria*) to recollect, to recall: *cerca di ricordarti come l'hai fatto,* try to recall how you did it.

ricordatívo, *ag.* **1.** memorative, commemorative **2.** (*degno di essere ricordato*) memorable.

ricordàto, *ag.* mentioned; (*rammentato*) recalled.

ricordévole, *ag.* **1.** (*memore*) mindful **2.** (*memorabile*) memorable.

ricordevolménte, *av.* (*memorabilmente*) memorably.

ricòrdo, *s.m.* **1.** memory; remembrance; recollection: *i ricordi della sua infanzia infelice lo ossessionavano,* he was haunted by the memories of his unhappy childhood; *il — di ciò che vidi mi rallegra ancora,* the recollection of what I saw still cheers me; *egli non è che un vago — per me,* he is only a faint memory to me; *i miei primi ricordi risalgono a quando avevo tre anni,* my earliest recollections go back to when I was three; *ne ho un — vago, confuso,* I have a vague, confused recollection of it; *non avevo alcun — di tutto questo,* I had no remembrance of all that; *quei fatti divennero solo un —,* the events became only a memory; *questo luogo risveglia tristi ricordi,* this place awakens sad memories; *avere, serbare un piacevole — di qlcu., ql.co.,* to have a pleasant recollection of s.o., sthg.: *serbo di lui un — dolcissimo,* his memory is dear to me; *conservare un — preciso di ql.co.,* to retain (*o* to have) a clear memory of sthg. ‖ *questo monumento fu costruito a — dei nostri soldati,* this monument was built as a memorial to our soldiers **2.** (*oggetto ricordo*) (*di luogo, avvenimento*) souvenir; (*di persona defunta*) memento (*pl.* mementos, mementoes); (*di persona assente, lontana*) keepsake: — *di famiglia,* heirloom; *ho comperato un — di Roma,* I have bought a souvenir of Rome; *lo tengo come — di mio padre,* I am keeping it as a memento of my father; *tienlo per —,* keep it as a memento (*o* hold it as a keepsake); *vi ho portato un piccolo —,* I have brought you a small souvenir ‖ *per — di,* in remembrance of (*o* in memory of) **3.** (*testimonianza*) record: *non abbiamo nessun — di quell'antica civiltà,* we have no record of that old civilization **4.** *pl.* (*memorie*) reminiscences; (*lett.*) memoirs: « *I miei ricordi* » *di M. D'Azeglio,* D'Azeglio's "Memoirs"; *lasciò ai nipoti un libro di ricordi,* he left his grandchildren a book of reminiscences.

ricoricàre, *v.t.* to lay down again ‖ **ricoricàrsi,** *v.r.* 1. to lie down again; (*ritornare a letto*) to go to bed again 2. (*tramontare ancora*) to set again.

ricoronàre, *v.t.* to crown again.

ricorrèggere, *v.t.* to correct again, to recorrect.

ricorrènte, *ag.* 1. (*anat.*) recurrent 2. (*che si ripete*) recurrent, recurring: *febbre* —, recurrent fever; *feste ricorrenti,* recurring feasts; *serie* —, (*mat.*) recurrent (*o recurring*) series 3. (*che avviene*) occurring ‖ *s.c.* (*dir.*) petitioner; claimant.

ricorrènza, *s.f.* 1. (*ritorno periodico*) recurrence 2. (*anniversario*) anniversary; (*festa*) festivity; (*occasione*) occasion; (*giorno*) day.

ricórrere, *v.i.* 1. (*correre di nuovo*) to run again; (*correre indietro*) to run back ‖ — *col pensiero al passato,* to cast one's mind back into the past 2. (*rivolgersi*) to apply; (*valersi*) to resort, to have recourse; (*valersi*) to resort, to have resort, to have recourse; (*fare appello*) to appeal: *se hai bisogno di ql.co. ricorri a me,* if you need sthg. apply to me; — *alla forza,* to resort to force; — *all'aiuto di qlcu.,* to have recourse to s.o. (*o* to apply to s.o. for help *o* to turn to s.o. for help); — *a uno stratagemma,* to resort (*o* to have resort) to a stratagem; — *alle vie legali,* to have recourse to legal proceedings 3. (*dir.*) to apply; (*appellarsi, a magistrato superiore*) to appeal: — *all'autorità,* to apply to the authorities; — *al Ministero,* to apply to the Ministry; — *contro una sentenza,* to appeal against a sentence; — *in appello,* to appeal (*o* to make an appeal) 4. (*ripetersi*) to recur: *questi elementi ricorrono nella letteratura di quel periodo,* these elements are often (to be) found (*o* often recur) in the literature of the period; *questo fenomeno ricorre tutti gli anni,* this phenomenon recurs every year 5. (*accadere*) to occur, to happen; (*di date*) to fall: *Natale ricorre il 25 dicembre,* Christmas-day falls on 25th December; *oggi ricorre il terzo anniversario del nostro matrimonio,* to-day is the third anniversary of our wedding.

ricorrezióne, *s.f.* new correction.

ricórso, *s.m.* 1. resort, recourse: *fare* — *a un amico,* to (have) resort to a friend 2. (*dir.*) petition; (*reclamo*) claim; (*a magistrato superiore*) appeal: — *in appello,* appeal: *fare* — *in appello,* to appeal (*o* to make an appeal); *su* — *di qlcu.,* on a petition by s.o. (*o* at s.o.'s petition); *fare un* —, to make a petition; *fare* — *contro una sentenza,* to appeal (*o* to make an appeal) against a sentence; *presentare un* — *a qlcu.,* to file (*o* to lodge) a petition with s.o. 3. (*ritorno periodico*) return, recurrence: *il* — *delle stagioni,* the return of the seasons ‖ *la teoria dei corsi e ricorsi storici,* the theory of the repetition of historical phenomena.

ricostituènte, *ag.* (*farm.*) reconstituent; tonic (*attributivo*) ‖ *s. m.* (*farm.*) tonic.

ricostituíre, *v.t.* 1. to reconstitute; (*ristabilire*) to re-establish; (*la salute*) to restore: — *una società,* to reconstitute a partnership 2. (*formare di nuovo*) to re-form, to form again: — *un governo,* to re-form a government ‖ **ricostituírsi,** *v.r.* 1. to be reconstituted; (*ristabilirsi in salute*) to recover (one's health) 2. (*formarsi di nuovo*) to re-form, to form again.

ricostituzióne, *s.f.* reconstitution; reconstruction; (*ristabilimento*) re-establishment.

ricostruíre, *v.t.* to rebuild, to reconstruct (*anche fig.*): — *i fatti, un delitto,* to reconstruct the facts, a crime; — *una casa,* to rebuild (*o* to reconstruct) a house ‖ — *un testo,* to restore a text.

ricostruttívo, *ag.* reconstructive.

ricostruttóre, *ag.* reconstructive ‖ *s.m.,* **ricostruttríce,** *s.f.* rebuilder, reconstructor.

ricostruzióne, *s.f.* rebuilding, reconstruction: — *di una casa,* rebuilding of a house.

ricòtta, *s.f.* 1. buttermilk curd ‖ *uomo di* —, milksop (*o* weakling) 2. (*metal.*) annealing.

ricottàio, *s.m.* 1. (*chi vende ricotta*) seller of buttermilk curd 2. (*scherz.*) (*chi mangia ricotta*) eater of buttermilk curd.

ricòtto, *ag.* 1. re-cooked, cooked again 2. (*metal.*) annealed, ann: — *completamente,* soft annealed; *rame* —, soft copper.

ricottúra, *s.f.* 1. re-cooking 2. (*metal.*) annealing: — *a bassa temperatura,* sub-critical annealing; — *completa,* full annealing; — *di distensione,* stress-relieving; — *di globulizzazione,* spheroidizing; — *di omogeneizzazione,* homogenizing; — *in bianco,* bright annealing; — *intermedia,* process annealing; *cassetta di* —, annealing box; *forno di* —, annealing furnace.

ricoveràre, *v.t.* to shelter, to give shelter to (s.o.): *ricoverò il pellegrino,* he gave shelter to the pilgrim; *il vecchio fu ricoverato,* the old man was taken to a charity home; — *in un ospedale,* to hospitalize; (*accettare in ospedale*) to admit (into hospital) ‖ **ricoveràrsi,** *v.r.* to take shelter.

ricoveràto, *s.m.* 1. (*in un istituto di carità*) inmate 2. (*in un ospedale*) patient: *tutti i ricoverati di questo padiglione sono gravi,* all the patients in this pavilion are seriously ill.

ricóvero, *s.m.* 1. sheltering: — *in ospedale,* hospitalization 2. (*rifugio*) shelter, refuge: *cercar* —, to seek refuge ‖ — *antiaereo,* air-raid shelter 3. (*orfanatrofio*) orphanage; (*ospizio per poveri*) poor people's home; (*ospizio per vecchi*) old people's home.

ricreaménto, *s.m.* recreation, amusement.

ricreàre, *v.t.* 1. (*creare di nuovo*) to re-create 2. (*dar sollievo a*) to relieve ‖ — *gli occhi,* to delight s.o.'s eyes; — *lo spirito,* to restore s.o.'s spirits ‖ **ricreàrsi,** *v.r.* to refresh oneself; to amuse oneself; to find recreation (in sthg.).

ricreatívo, *ag.* recreative; (*divertente*) amusing; (*piacevole*) pleasant: *lettura ricreativa,* light reading.

ricreatóre, *ag.* 1. that creates again 2. (*che dà sollievo*) relieving; refreshing: *un silenzio* —, a refreshing silence ‖ *s.m.* 1. person who re-creates 2. (*chi dà sollievo*) person who relieves; person who restores.

ricreatòrio, *ag.* (*rar.*) recreative, recreational ‖ *s.m.* recreational institute.

ricreatríce, *s.f.* 1. person who re-creates 2. (*chi dà sollievo*) person who relieves; person who restores.

ricreazióne, *s.f.* recreation: *devo prendermi un po' di* — *altrimenti mi stanco troppo,* I must take some recreation or I get too tired; *dopo una breve* — *riprese a lavorare,* after a short break he resumed work; *egli considera la lettura come una* —, he considers reading as a recreation ‖ *l'ora della* —, playtime (*o* break).

ricrédere, *v.t.* to believe again ‖ **ricrédersi,** *v.r.* to change one's mind: *lo credevo buono ma mi sono ricreduto,* I thought he was good but I have changed my mind.

ricrescènte, *ag.* growing again (*predicativo*).

ricrescènza, *V.* **escrescènza.**

ricréscere, *v.i.* to grow again, to increase; (*di prezzi*) to rise (again) ‖ *v.t.* to increase: — *una maglia,* to add a stitch.

ricrescimento, *s.m.* new growth, fresh growth; (*aumento*) new increase, fresh increase.

ricréscita, *s.f.* new growth, fresh growth; (*di prezzi*) new increase: — *delle erbe,* fresh growth of grass.

ricuciménto, *s.m.* sewing up; re-sewing.

ricucíre, *v.t.* 1. to re-sew, to sew (up) again 2. (*chir.*) to sew up: — *una ferita,* to sew up a wound.

ricucitúra, *s.f.* 1. sewing up; re-sewing 2. (*i punti*) seam.

ricuòcere, *v.t.* 1. to re-cook, to cook again: — *al forno,* to bake again 2. (*metal.*) to anneal.

ricuperàbile, *ag.* recoverable.

ricuperaménto, *s.m.* recovering; recovery; recuperation; (*mar.*) salvaging.

ricuperàre, *v.t.* to recover; (*mar.*) to salvage: *abbiamo ricuperato ciò che avevamo perduto,* we have recovered what we had lost; *ha ricuperato il suo denaro,* he has recovered his money; *le salme sono state ricuperate dopo tre ore di ricerche,* the corpses were recovered after a three-hour search; — *un carico da un naufragio,* to salvage a cargo from a wreck; — *un credito,* (*comm.*) to recover a credit; — *la salute,* to recover one's health; — *il tempo perduto,* to make up for lost time; — *la vista,* to recover one's sight.

ricuperatóre, *s.m.,* **ricuperatríce,** *s.f.* recuperator.

ricuperazióne, *V.* **ricuperaménto.**

ricúpero, *s.m.* **1.** recovery: — *dei danni,* recovery of damages; *il — di una cosa perduta,* the recovery of something lost **2.** (*salvamento*) rescue; (*mar.*) salvaging: *il — del carico,* the salvaging of the cargo; *servizi di —,* salvage-services **3.** (*dir.*) recovery: *diritto di —,* right of recovery **4.** (*cosa ricuperata*) thing recovered; (*mar.*) salvage: *i ricuperi dei campi di battaglia,* what has been rescued (*o* recovered) from the battle-fields.

ricurvàre, *v.t.* **1.** (*curvare*) to bend, to curve **2.** (*curvare di nuovo*) to bend again.

ricúrvo, *ag.* (*molto curvc*) bent, curved; (*ritorto*) crooked: — *sotto un fardello,* bent under a burden; *bastone* —, crook; *ramo* —, crooked branch; *spalle ricurve,* round shoulders; *un vecchio* —, a hunched-up old man.

ricúsa, *s.f.* **1.** refusal; denial **2.** (*dir.*) objection: — *dei giurati,* objection to the jury.

ricusàbile, *ag.* refusable; refutable.

ricusàre, *v.t.* **1.** to refuse; to reject; to deny: — *un favore a qlcu.,* to refuse (*o* to deny) s.o. a favour; — *una proposta,* to refuse (*o* reject) a proposal **2.** (*dir.*) to object to (s.o., sthg.): — *un giudice,* to object to a judge; — *un testimonio,* to object to a witness || *v.i.* (*mar.*) to slacken: *il vento ricusa,* the wind is slackening.

ricusazióne, *s.f.* (*dir.*) objection: — *di un giudice,* objection to a judge.

ridacchiàre, *v.i.* to giggle, to titter: *le ragazze ridacchiarono alle sue parole,* the girls giggled at his words.

ridanciàno, *ag.* jolly, jocular || *musa ridanciana,* (*poesia burlesca*) comic verse.

ridàre, *v.t.* **1.** (*dare di nuovo*) to give again: *bisogna ridargli la medicina,* you must give him the medicine again || — *fuori,* (*ripubblicare*) to republish **2.** (*restituire*) to give back, to return: *ridammi il mio denaro,* give me back my money; *ti ha ridato il libro che gli hai prestato?,* did he give you back (*o* did he return) the book you lent him? **3.** (*battere di nuovo*) to strike again, to hit again || *dagli e ridagli,* try and try again || *v.i.* **1.** — *fuori,* to reappear (*o* to come out again *o* to break out again): *gli ha ridato fuori l'eczema,* his eczema has reappeared **2.** — *giù,* to relapse: *sembrava guarito ma è ridato giù,* he seemed to have recovered, but he has had a relapse (*o* he has relapsed).

rídda, *s.f.* **1.** (*ballo in tondo*) round dance **2.** (*confusione*) turmoil, tumult, confusion: *una — di emozioni,* an emotional tumult (*o* a turmoil of emotions); *dovrai cacciarti in quella* —, you'll have to push through that noisy crowd.

riddàre, *v.i.* to dance in a ring.

ridènte, *ag.* **1.** smiling: *occhi ridenti,* smiling eyes **2.** (*piacevole*) pleasant: *vita* —, pleasant life **3.** (*ameno*) charming: *luogo* —, charming place **4.** (*luminoso*) bright: *cielo* —, bright sky.

rídere, *v.i.* **1.** to laugh (at s.o. sthg.): *è una cosa da* —, this will make you laugh; (*è un'inezia*) it's only a trifle; *mi fai sempre* —, you always make me laugh; *non c'è da* —, it is no laughing matter; *non ci vedo niente da* —, I cannot see anything to laugh at in that; *non ho voglia di* —, I'm in no mood for laughing; *non mi piace che si rida di me,* I do not like being laughed at; *non mi piace il suo modo di — dei mali altrui,* I do not like the way he laughs at other people's troubles; *rise fino alle lacrime,* she laughed till she cried; *ti farai — dietro da tutti,* you will be-

come a laughing stock; *tutti ridono alle sue spalle,* everybody laughs at him behind his back; *tutti ridono di lui,* everybody laughs at him; — *forzatamente,* to give a forced laugh; *scoppiare a* —, to burst out laughing (*o* to break into a laugh) || *commedia da* —, comedy || *un re da* —, a puppet king || *c'era da morire dal* —, it was terribly funny! (*o* you would have died laughing!) || *ha le scarpe che ridono,* (*scherz.*) his shoes are split || *lo disse solo per* —, (*per ischerzo*) he only said it for fun (*o* in jest) || *ma non farmi* —!, (*non dire sciocchezze*) don't make me laugh! (*o* don't talk nonsense!) || *quando la vede gli ridono gli occhi di gioia,* when he sees her his eyes sparkle with joy || *rideva in cuor suo,* he was laughing up his sleeve || *la speranza rideva nei suoi occhi,* hope was shining in her eyes || — *a crepapelle, sganghèratamente,* to split one's sides with laughter (*o* to roar with laughter); — *come un matto,* to laugh one's head off (*o* to laugh like a madman); — *di cuore,* to laugh heartily || — *in faccia a qlcu.,* to laugh in s.o.'s face || — *per non piangere,* to laugh bravely || — *sotto i baffi,* to laugh up one's sleeve || *far — i sassi, i polli, le panche,* to make a cat laugh || *prendere ql.co. in* —, to laugh sthg. off || *chi ride in venerdì, piange la domenica,* prov. laugh today and cry tomorrow || *ride bene chi ride ultimo,* prov. he who laughs last laughs longest **2.** (*arridere*) to smile (on s.o., sthg.): *la fortuna gli ride,* fortune smiles on him || **rídersi,** *v.r.* to laugh (at s.o., sthg.), to make fun (of s.o., sthg.): *egli se la rideva di noi,* he was laughing at (*o* making fun of *o* mocking) us; *me la rido della sua opinione,* I do not give a fig for his opinion; *me ne rido,* I laugh at it.

rídere, *s.m.* laughing, laughter: *ho sentito un gran* —, I heard a lot of laughing; *non ne potevo più dal gran* —, my sides were aching with laughing.

ridestàre, *v.t.* **1.** (*destare di nuovo*) to wake (up) again: *ci destò alle due e poi ci ridestò alle cinque,* he woke us up at two o'clock and then he woke us up again at five **2.** (*poet.*) (*destare*) to awaken: *il cinguettio degli uccelli lo ridestò all'alba,* the chirping of birds awakened him at daybreak **3.** (*ravvivare*) to rouse (again), to reawaken: — *sentimenti, ricordi,* to arouse (*o* to awaken) feelings, memories || **ridestàrsi,** *v.r.* **1.** (*destarsi di nuovo*) to wake (up) again, to awake again: *mi riaddormentai e non mi ridestai fino all'alba,* I fell asleep and I did not wake up again until daybreak **2.** (*poet.*) (*destarsi*) to awake: *la natura si ridesta al sorgere del sole,* nature awakes at daybreak **3.** (*ravvivarsi*) to reawaken; (*riaccendersi*) to be roused (again): *l'amore si ridestò in lei,* love reawakened in her; *sospetti che si ridestano ad ogni nuovo indizio,* suspicions that are roused at any new circumstance; *la sua collera si ridestò,* his anger was roused again.

ridétto, *ag.* repeated: *queste sono cose dette e ridette,* these things have been repeated over and over again.

ridévole, *ag.* **1.** (*che fa ridere*) laughable, risible; ridiculous, absurd **2.** (*di scherno, derisione*) contemptuous: *motto* —, contemptuous words.

ridevolménte, *av.* ridiculously, absurdly.

ridicíbile, *ag.* repeatable.

ridicitóre, *s.m.,* **ridicitríce,** *s.f.* (*rar.*) **1.** repeater **2.** (*spia*) informer.

ridicolàggine, *s.f.* **1.** (*cosa ridicola*) nonsense (*solo sing.*); absurdity: *quei pregiudizi sono ridicolaggini,* those prejudices are nonsense **2.** (*l'essere ridicolo*) ridiculousness.

ridicolaménte, *av.* ridiculously, absurdly: *era orgoglioso del suo piccolo successo,* he was ridiculously proud of his petty success.

ridícolo, *ag.* **1.** ridiculous, absurd: *ha un aspetto* —, he looks ridiculous; *non essere* —!, don't be absurd (*o* ridiculous)!; *sei tanto — quando parli così,* you are so ridiculous when you talk like that; *le sue pretese sono ridicole,* his claims are absurd; *veste in modo* —, she dresses absurdly **2.** (*meschino*) paltry: *uno stipendio*

—, a paltry salary ‖ *s.m.* **1.** ridicule: *il — è un'arma potente*, ridicule is a potent weapon ‖ *cadere nel —*, to fall into ridicule ‖ *gettare il — su qlcu., ql.co.*, to make a laughing-stock of s.o., sthg. ‖ *mettere in qlcu., ql.co.*, to ridicule s.o., sthg. (*o* to make fun of s.o., sthg. *o* to hold s.o., sthg. up to ridicule) **2.** (*ridicolaggine*) ridiculousness: *non ne vedo il —*, I can't see the ridiculous side of it; *non sentiva il — della situazione*, he did not see the ridiculousness of the situation.

ridimensionàre, *v.t.* **1.** to reshuffle: *— un problema*, to reshuffle a problem **2.** (*pol.*) to make a few changes in (a political programme) **3.** *— una ditta*, (*amm.*) to reorganize a firm.

ridimostràre, *v.t.* to demonstrate again.

ridipíngere, *v.t.* to repaint, to paint again.

ridíre, *v.t.* **1.** (*dire di nuovo*) to say again; to tell again: *dobbiamo dirglielo e ridirglielo*, we have to tell him over and over again **2.** (*riferire*) to repeat: *ridice tutto al maestro*, he repeats everything to the teacher; *— un segreto*, to tell a secret **3.** (*obiettare*) to object to (s.o., sthg.); to find fault with (s.o., sthg.); to find a blemish in (sthg.): *ha sempre da — su ciò che faccio*, he always finds fault with what I do; *non trovò niente da —*, he found nothing to object to; *trova da — sul mio vestito*, he objects to my dress.

ridiscéndere, *v.t.i.* to come down again; to go down again: *— il fiume*, to go down the river again.

ridisciògliere, *v.t.* to melt again.

ridiscórrere, *v.i.* to talk again.

ridisegnàre, *v.t.* to draw again, to re-design.

ridispórre, *v.t.* to set out again, to arrange again.

ridistèndere, *v.t.* to spread out again.

ridistrúggere, *v.t.* to destroy again.

ridiveníre, ridiventàre, *v.i.* to become again, to grow again, to turn again: *il tempo ridiventa freddo*, the weather is turning (*o* becoming) cold again; *— giovane*, to grow (*o* to become) young again.

ridivídere, *v.t.* to divide again.

ridolére, *v.i.* to ache again ‖ **ridolérsi,** *v.r.* to complain again.

ridomandàre, *v.t.* to ask again, to inquire again.

ridonàre, *v.t.* to give again; to give back.

ridonatóre, *s.m.*, **ridonatríce,** *s.f.* one who gives again.

ridondaménto, *s.m.* overflowing.

ridondànte, *ag.* redundant.

ridondànza, *s.f.* redundance, redundancy.

ridondàre, *v.i.* **1.** (*sovrabbondare*) to be redundant; to superabound (in, with sthg.), to overflow (with sthg.): *il suo stile ridonda di fronzoli*, his style is overloaded with frills **2.** (*di vento*) to become favourable **3.** (*tornare, risultare*) to redound: *ciò che fece ridonda a suo onore*, what he did redounds to his credit.

ridóppio, *s.m.*: *a —*, more than doubly; (*abbondantemente*) abundantly.

ridormíre, *v.i.* to sleep again.

ridòsso, *s.m.* (*luogo riparato*) shelter, sheltered place ‖ *a —*, close to (*o* very near *o* close at hand); (*alle spalle*) above: *la casa era a — delle rocce*, the house was close to the cliffs; *la città ha a — le montagne*, the city has the mountains at its back; *seduto a — della porta*, sitting close to the door; *avere qlcu. a —*, (*mantenerlo*) to have s.o. on one's hands.

ridótta, *s.f.* (*mil.*) redoubt.

ridótto, *ag.* reduced: *— al minimo*, reduced to the minimum; *frazione ridotta ai minimi termini*, a fraction reduced to its lowest terms; *in proporzioni ridotte*, on a small scale; *prezzo —*, reduced price: *biglietti a prezzo —*, cheap tickets ‖ *in cattive condizioni, mal —*, in a bad state (*o* in a sorry plight) ‖ *edizione ridotta*, abridged edition ‖ *s.m.* (*teat.*) foyer, lounge.

ridubitàre, *v.i.* to doubt again.

riducíbile, *ag.* reducible.

riducibilità, *s.f.* reducibility, reducibleness.

ridúrre, *v.t.* **1.** to reduce, to cut down; to curtail; to shorten: *— il capitale*, (*comm.*) to reduce the capital;

— *un discorso*, to cut down (*o* to shorten) a speech; — *il personale*, to cut down (*o* to reduce) the staff; — *il prezzo di un articolo*, (*comm.*) to reduce (*o* to lower *o* to bring down) the price of an article; — *le spese, lo stipendio*, to reduce expenses, wages; — *una vacanza*, to curtail a holiday; — *la velocità*, to reduce speed ‖ — *un'opera letteraria*, to abridge a literary work ‖ — *la velatura*, (*mar.*) to shorten (*o* to take in) sail **2.** (*trasformare, convertire*) to reduce; to turn: *ridussero a scuola quel convento*, they turned that convent into a school: — *il ferro in acciaio*, to reduce iron to (*o* to turn iron into) steel; — *frazioni ai minimi termini*, (*mat.*) to reduce fractions to their lowest terms; — *in moneta italiana*, to turn into Italian money; — *in pezzi*, to break to pieces; — *in polvere*, to reduce to dust; — *le yarde al sistema metrico*, to reduce English yards to metres; — *un ossido*, (*chim.*) to reduce an oxide; — *ql.co. in briciole*, to crumble sthg. up; — *le sterline in scellini*, to reduce pounds to shillings **3.** (*adattare*) to adapt: — *per lo schermo*, (*cine.*) to adapt for the screen; — *un testo per le scuole*, to adapt (*o* to simplify) a text for schools; — *un vestito da uomo*, to cut down a suit **4.** (*mus.*) to adapt, to arrange: — *una sinfonia per pianoforte*, to arrange a symphony for the piano **5.** (*tradurre*) to translate: — *in francese*, to translate into (*o* to turn into) French **6.** (*portare, costringere*) to drive, to reduce; (*far diventare*) to drive: *questo rumore mi riduce nevrastenico*, this noise drives me mad; — *alla disperazione*, to reduce (*o* to drive) to despair; — *alla miseria*, to reduce to poverty; — *alla rovina*, to bring to ruin; — *al silenzio, all'obbedienza, alla disciplina*, to reduce to silence, obedience, discipline; — *qlcu. in fin di vita*, to bring s.o. to the brink of death (*o* to reduce s.o. to his last gasp); *essere ridotto a fare ql.co.*, to be reduced to doing sthg.: *fu ridotto a rubare, a mendicare*, he was reduced (*o* driven) to stealing, to begging ‖ — *a mal partito*, to bring to a sorry plight **7.** (*ricondurre*) to bring back, to take back: — *il gregge all'ovile*, to bring back the sheep to the fold ‖ — *alla memoria*, to recall (*o* to bring back) to memory ‖ — *alla ragione*, to bring to reason **8.** (*chir.*) (*frattura, ecc.*) to reduce ‖ **ridúrsi,** *v.r.* **1.** to reduce oneself, to come (down): *non volevo ridurmi a questo*, I didn't want to come to this; *si ridusse a vendere i suoi mobili*, he was reduced to selling his furniture; *le spese si riducono a poco*, the expenses come (down) to very little; *tutta la difficoltà si riduce a sapere se...*, the whole difficulty reduces itself (*o* comes down) to the question whether...; — *allo stretto necessario*, to confine oneself to what is strictly necessary **2.** (*diventare*) to be reduced, to become: *si è ridotto a pelle e ossa*, he was reduced to skin and bone (*o* to a skeleton) **3.** (*restringersi*) to shrink: *questa stoffa non si riduce*, this material does not shrink **4.** (*ritirarsi*) to retire: *si ridusse a vita privata*, he retired into private life; *si ridusse a vivere in campagna*, he retired and went to live in the country.

riduttóre, *ag.* reducing: *agente —*, (*chim.*) reducing agent ‖ *s.m.* **1.** reducer **2.** (*mec.*) reducer; reduction-gear, reduction-unit: — *di pressione, di velocità*, pressure-, speed-reducer **3.** (*foto.*) adapter ‖ **riduttríce,** *s.f.* reducer.

riduzióne, *s.f.* **1.** reduction, cut: — *dei prezzi*, reduction in prices; — *dei salari*, cut in wages (*o* wage-cut); — *di capitale*, writing down (*o* reduction) of capital; — *di pena*, reduction of sentence **2.** (*sconto*) discount: *fare una —*, to give (*o* to grant) a discount **3.** (*adattamento*) adaptation **4.** (*mus.*) arrangement **5.** (*chim. mec.*) reduction **6.** (*chir.*) reducting, setting.

rieccitàre, *v.t.* to excite again; to stir again; to stimulate again ‖ **rieccitàrsi,** *v.r.* to get excited again.

riècco, *inter.* here (s.o., sthg.) is again, here is (s.o., sthg.) again; here (s.o., sthg.) are again, here are (s.o., sthg.) again: *rieccoci a Natale*, here we are at Christmas again; *rieccola qui*, here she is again.

riecheggiàre, *v.i.* to re-echo: *i loro canti riecheggiavano nella valle*, their songs re-echoed through the valley.

riedificàbile, *ag.* rebuildable.

riedificàre, *v.t.* to rebuild, to reconstruct.

riedificatóre, *s.m.*, **riedificatríce**, *s.f.* rebuilder.

riedificazióne, *s.f.* rebuilding; reconstruction.

rieducàre, *v.t.* to re-educate: — *i centri nervosi dopo una paralisi*, to re-educate nerve-centres after (a) paralysis.

rieducazióne, *s.f.* re-education.

rielèggere, *v.t.* to re-elect.

rieleggíbile, *ag.* re-elegible.

rieleggibilità, *s.f.* re-elegibility.

rielètto, *ag.* re-elected ‖ *s.m.* re-elected person.

rielezióne, *s.f.* re-election.

riemèrgere, *v.i.* to re-emerge, to emerge again.

riemersióne, *s.f.* re-emergence, re-emersion.

riempíbile, *ag.* refillable.

riempiménto, *s.m.* filling (up); refilling; stuffing.

riempíre, *v.t.* 1. to fill (up) (anche *fig.*); to stuff: *mi ha riempito le tasche di caramelle*, he filled (o stuffed) my pockets with sweets; *il suo arrivo mi riempì di gioia*, his arrival filled me with joy; *ti ha riempito la testa di sciocchezze*, he has stuffed your head with nonsense; — *i bicchieri*, to fill the glasses; (*nei brindisi*) to charge the glasses; — *uno scaffale di libri*, to fill a shelf with books; — *un pollo prima di cucinarlo*, to stuff a chicken before cooking it; — *una stanza di mobili*, to fill (o to crowd) a room with furniture; — *i vuoti*, to refill the empties 2. (*scrivere in spazi vuoti*) to fill in (sthg.): — *un modulo*, to fill in a form ‖ **riempírsi**, *v.r.* 1. to fill (up) (with sthg.), to fill oneself (with sthg.), to be filled (with sthg.): *la piazza si riempì presto di gente*, the square (was) soon filled with people; *la stanza si riempì di fumo*, the room filled with smoke 2. (*fam.*) (*rimpinzarsi*) to stuff oneself (with sthg.), to cram oneself (with sthg.): *mi sono riempito di maccheroni*, I have stuffed (o crammed) myself with macaroni.

riempíta, *s.f.* filling (up).

riempitívo, *ag.* filling ‖ *s.m.* 1. (*pleonasmo*) pleonasm 2. (*cosa che riempie*) filling; (*cuc.*) stuffing.

riempitóre, *s.m.*, **riempitríce**, *s.f.* filler.

riempitúra, *s.f.* filling (up); stuffing.

rientràbile, *ag.* 1. (*foto.*) collapsible 2. (*aer.*) retractable.

rientraménto, *s.m.* 1. re-entry 2. (*rientranza*) recess; (*di costa*) indentation.

rientrànte, *ag.* re-entering; receding, hollow: *guance rientranti*, hollow cheeks; *superficie* —, concave surface; *torace* —, hollow chest ‖ *s.m.* (*mil.*) re-entering angle; re-entrant.

rientrànza, *s.f.* recess; (*di costa*) indentation.

rientràre, *v.i.* 1. (*entrare di nuovo*) to re-enter (sthg.), to enter (sthg.) again; (*tornare*) to return (to sthg.); to go back (to sthg.); to come back (to sthg.): *è ora di* — (*a casa*), it is time to return (o to go) home; *non rientrò più in quella casa*, he never entered that house again; *quando rientrò in Italia era ricco*, when he returned to Italy he was a rich man; — *alla base*, (*mil.*) to return to base; — *in collegio*, to go back to school; — *in porto*, (*mar.*) to return to port; — *nell'esercito*, to go back into the army ‖ — *in giuoco*, to return to the game ‖ — *in lizza*, to return to the fray ‖ — *in possesso di qlco.*, to recover sthg.; — *in sè*, to return to one's senses ‖ — *nelle grazie di qlcu.*, to regain s.o.'s favour 2. (*teat.*) to re-enter: *rientra Macbeth*, re-enter Macbeth 3. (*far parte*) to form part (of sthg.), to be part (of sthg.), to be included (in sthg.), to come into (sthg.); to fall within (sthg.), to come within (sthg.): *questo non rientra nei miei doveri*, this isn't (o doesn't form) part of my duties; *questo non rientra nel mio campo*, this doesn't fall (o come) within my province; *questo non rientra nel nostro programma*, this doesn't

form part of (o come into o is not included in) our programme; *questo rientra in un'altra questione*, that doesn't come into the question (o that is quite a different matter) 4. (*restringersi*) to shrink 5. (*piegare in dentro*) to recede.

rientràta, *s.f.* 1. re-entry, re-entrance 2. (*ritorno*) return.

rientràto, *ag.* 1. returned 2. (*cavo, infossato*) hollow: *guance rientrate*, hollow cheeks 3. (*fallito*) failed, vanished: *speranza rientrata*, vanished hope 4. (*foto.*) collapsed: *obiettivo* —, collapsed lens.

riéntro, *s.m.* 1. re-entry 2. (*rientranza*) recess: *un* — *nel muro*, a recess in the wall 3. (*di stoffa*) shrinkage 4. (*astronautica*) re-enter: *problema del* —, re-enter problem.

riepilogaménto, *V.* riepílogo.

riepilogàre, *v.t.* to recapitulate, to summarize, to sum up; (*fam.*) to recap: *adesso riepiloghiamo*, let us now recapitulate (o sum up o (fam.) have a recap) — *il discorso, i fatti*, to summarize the speech, the facts.

riepilogazióne, *s.f.*, **riepílogo**, *s.m.* recapitulation, summing up; (*fam.*) recap.

riesàme, *s.m.* re-examination.

riesaminàre, *v.t.* to re-examine, to examine again ‖ — *un processo*, to reopen a trial.

riescíre, *V.* riuscíre.

riesercitàre, *v.t.* to exercise, to re-exercise, to exercise again; to train, to train again: — *un arto paralizzato*, to exercise a paralysed limb ‖ **riesercitàrsi**, *v.r.* to train (oneself) again, to go into training again; to practise (sthg., doing) again: — *nel nuoto*, to practise swimming again.

riesiliàre, *v.t.* to exile again.

riesploràre, *v.t.* to re-explore, to explore again.

riespórre, *v.t.* to re-expound, to expound again: — *una dottrina*, to expound a doctrine again.

riesportàre, *v.t.* (*comm.*) to re-export.

riesportazióne, *s.f.* (*comm.*) re-exportation.

riespugnàre, *v.t.* to recapture.

rièssere, *v.i.* to be again: *spero di* — *con voi domani*, I hope to be with you again tomorrow ‖ *ci risiamo con queste sue lamentele!*, there he goes again with his grumbling!.

rievocàre, *v.t.* 1. to recall, to evoke (again); to conjure up (again): — *il passato*, to recall the past; — *lo spirito dei morti*, to conjure up the spirits of the dead 2. (*commemorare*) to commemorate.

rievocazióne, *s.f.* 1. recalling 2. (*commemorazione*) commemoration.

rifabbricàbile, *ag.* rebuildable.

rifabbricàre, *v.t.* to rebuild: *dopo la guerra hanno rifabbricato la città esattamente come prima*, after the war the city was rebuilt just as it had been before.

rifaciménto, *s.m.* 1. remaking 2. (*ricostruzione*) reconstruction 3. (*di opera letteraria*) rifacimento (*pl.* rifacimenti), re-writing; (*adattamento*) adaptation: *il* — *del Berni dell'« Orlando Innamorato »*, Berni's rifacimento of "The Orlando Innamorato" 4. (*dir.*) (*rifusione dei danni*) compensation, indemnification.

rifacitóre, *ag.* for remaking (*predicativo*) ‖ *s.m.*, **rifacitríce**, *s.f.* 1. remaker 2. (*di opera letteraria*) adapter.

rifalciàre, *v.t.* to mow again.

rifallíre, *v.i.* to fail again; to go bankrupt again.

rifàre, *v.t.* 1. to do again; to make again, to remake: *bello quel passo di danza, rifallo!*, that dance step is fine, do it again!; *è tutto da* —, the whole thing must be done again; *non ho ancora rifatto il mio letto*, I have not yet made my bed ‖ *un bel quadro rifà una stanza*, a fine picture makes a room — *un esame*, to take an exam(ination) again ‖ — *la pace*, to make it up again 2. (*ricostruire*) to rebuild: *l'antica chiesa fu rifatta nel XVIII secolo*, the ancient church was rebuilt in the 18th century 3. (*rileggere*) to re-elect: — *qlcu.*

presidente, to re-elect s.o. president (*o* chairman) **4.** (*ripercorrere*) to retrace: *ha dovuto — la strada fino al semaforo*, he had to retrace his steps as far as the traffic-lights **5.** (*riparare*) to repair: *devo far — questo divano*, I must have this sofa repaired **6.** (*imitare*) to imitate, to ape: *— i gesti, le mosse di qlcu.*, to ape (*o* to imitate) s.o.'s gestures, movements **7.** (*imitare fraudolentemente*) to forge: *— la firma di qlcu.*, to forge s.o.'s signature **8.** (*indennizzare*) to indemnify, to make good: *vi rifarò dei danni*, I will make your damages good; *— qlcu. delle spese*, to reimburse s.o. ‖ **rifàrsi**, *v.r.* **1.** to make up: *voleva — del denaro perduto*, he wanted to make up (*o* he wanted to recover) the money he had lost; *— del tempo perduto*, to make up for lost time ‖ *dopo che fece bancarotta ci mise tre anni a —*, after he went bankrupt he took three years to get on his feet again ‖ *ho perso tutto il mio denaro ed ora devo rifarmi da capo*, I have lost all my money and now I must start again from scratch **2.** (*riprendere forza, salute*) to recover: *si è rifatto bene*, he has made a good recovery; *— in salute*, to recover (one's health) **3.** (*vendicarsi*) to get even (with s.o.); to revenge oneself: *egli voleva — su di loro degli insulti ricevuti*, he wanted to get even with them (*o* to revenge himself on them) for the insults he had received **4.** (*risalire*) to go back: *rifacciamoci al principio del Medio Evo*, let's go back to the beginning of the Middle Ages **5.** (*seguire, imitare*) to follow: *qui l'autore si rifà a un metodo classico*, here the author is following a classical method.

rifasciàre, *v.t.* to rebandage; (*neonato*) to swaddle again: *gli rifasciò il braccio*, she rebandaged his arm; *rifasciò il bambino*, she swaddled the baby again.

rifàscio, a, *l.av.* (*alla rinfusa*) in confusion; (*in abbondanza*) in profusion ‖ *andare a —*, (*in rovina*) to go to rack and ruin.

rifattíbile, *ag.* **1.** remakeable **2.** (*ricostruibile*) rebuildable **3.** (*restaurabile*) restorable.

rifàtto, a, *ag.* **1.** remade; redone: *ho visto che il mio letto è —*, I see my bed has been remade; *la mia stanza non è rifatta*, my room has not been done ‖ *villano —*, upstart **2.** (*restaurato*) restored.

rifavoríre, *v.t.* to favour again.

rifazióne, *s.f.* (*dir.*) indemnity: *— dei danni*, indemnity for damages.

riferènte, *s.c.* relater, relator.

riferíbile, *ag.* **1.** referable **2.** (*raccontabile*) fit to be told: *è una storiella che non è —*, it is a story which is not fit to be told.

riferiménto, *s.m.* **1.** reference: *con — alla nostra lettera*, (*comm.*) referring to our letter; *segno di —*, reference mark; *ha fatto — a ql.co. che non ho ben capito*, he referred to something which was not quite clear to me (*o* I didn't quite understand); *nelle sue lettere ci sono molti riferimenti a persone interessanti*, there are many references to interesting people in his letters ‖ *punto di —*, landmark **2.** (*aer.*) datum (*pl.* data): *linea di —*, datum-line; *piano di —*, datum-level (*o* plane); *punto di —*, datum-point.

riferíre, *v.t.* **1.** to report, to tell, to relate, to refer: *la Commissione riferì al Ministro*, the Commission reported to the Minister; *devi — tutto ciò che vedi*, you must report everything you see; *non avresti dovuto riferirgli queste cose*, you should not have told him these things; *non gli si può dir nulla, che lo va subito a —*, you can't tell him anything without his reporting it straight away; *riferiscimi le sue precise parole*, tell me his precise words **2.** (*attribuire*) to refer; to ascribe, to attribute: *riferiscono i suoi successi alle sue molte amicizie altolocate*, they attribute (*o* ascribe) his success to his many influential friends; *riferiva la poca volontà di lavorare di suo figlio alla sua salute delicata*, he ascribed his son's scarce inclination to work to his delicate health; *riferiva il suo insuccesso al destino*, he ascribed his failure to fate (*o* he blamed fate for

his failure) ‖ **riferírsi**, *v.r.* **1.** (*rapportarsi*) to refer, to make reference: *mi riferisco a quello che ho già detto ieri*, I refer to what I said yesterday **2.** (*aver relazione*) to relate, to refer; to concern (s.o., sthg.), to apply, to have reference: *a chi si riferisce quella allusione?*, who(m) does that allusion refer to?; *la mia osservazione si riferisce direttamente a...*, my remark directly concerns...; *i regolamenti si riferiscono solo ai bambini*, the regulations apply (*o* refer) only to children **3.** (*rimettersi*) to appeal, to have recourse: *— al giudizio di un arbitro*, to appeal to the judgement of an umpire.

riferitóre, *s.m.*, **riferitríce**, *s.f.* reporter.

rifermàre, *v.t.* **1.** (*fermare di nuovo*) to fix again: *riferma l'uscio, per favore*, will you please fix the door again? **2.** (*confermare*) to confirm: *fu rifermata al suo posto*, she was confirmed in her position.

riferràre, *v.t.* (*un cavallo*) to re-shoe.

ríffa[1], *s.f.* (*lotteria*) raffle.

ríffa[2], *s.f.* violence ‖ *di — o di raffa*, by hook or by crook.

riffóso, *ag.* violent, rough.

rifiancàre, *v.t.* to add new support to (sthg.).

rifiàtare, *v.i.* **1.** (*respirare*) to breathe (anche *fig.*) **2.** (*dir parola*) to speak a word.

rificcàre, *v.t.* to thrust again; to drive in again ‖ **rificcàrsi**, *v.r.* **1.** to get oneself (into sthg.) again; to thrust oneself (into sthg.) again **2.** (*rimettersi*) to thrust back: *si rificcò il cappello in testa e se ne andò*, he thrust his hat back on his head and off he went.

rifilàre, *v.t.* **1.** to spin again **2.** (*tagliare a filo, orlare*) to trim, to edge: *— un lembo di stoffa*, to trim a piece of cloth **3.** (*riferire*) to report, to repeat: *rifilò a sua madre tutto quel che avevamo detto*, he repeated everything we said to his mother **4.** (*menare*) to deal: *gli rifilò due ceffoni*, he slapped him twice (*o* he gave him a couple of slaps); *— un colpo*, to deal (*o* to strike) a blow **5.** (*appioppare*) to palm off: *il panettiere mi ha rifilato del pane vecchio*, the baker has palmed off some stale bread on me.

rifilatóre, *ag.* tell-tale (*attributivo*) ‖ *s.m.* tell-tale ‖ **rifilatríce**, *s.f.* **1.** tell-tale **2.** (*metal.*) trimmer.

rifilatúra, *s.f.* **1.** (*il rifilare*) trimming **2.** (*profilatura*) border.

rifiniménto, *s.m.* finishing touch; finishing; finish.

rifiníre, *v.t.* **1.** to finish, to give the finishing touch to (sthg.) **2.** (*ridurre in cattivo stato*) to finish off: *quel colpo mi ha quasi rifinito*, that blow almost finished me off **3.** (*soddisfare*) to satisfy: *il suo lavoro non mi rifinisce*, his work does not quite satisfy me **4.** (*cessare*) to finish, to cease, to stop: *non rifinisce mai di ripetere le stesse cose*, he never stops repeating the same things.

rifinitézza, *s.f.* **1.** finish **2.** (*spossatezza*) fatigue, exhaustion **3.** (*languore di stomaco*) hunger.

rifiníto, a, *ag.* **1.** (*finito con cura*) well-finished: *un vestito, lavoro ben —*, a well-finished dress, piece of work **2.** (*esausto*) finished off; worn out; exhausted.

rifinitóre, *s.m.*, **rifinitríce**, *s.f.* finisher.

rifinitúra, *s.f.* finishing touch; final touches (*pl.*).

rifiorènte, *ag.* flourishing again; *fig.* (*di cose*) thriving again: *questa industria è —*, this industry is thriving again.

rifioriménto, *s.m.* **1.** reflourishing; *fig.* (*rinascimento, risveglio*) revival **2.** *pl.* (*ornamenti*) flourishes: *ci sono troppi rifiorimenti nel tuo tema*, there are too many flourishes in your composition.

rifioríre, *v.i.* **1.** to blossom again, to bloom again, to flower again: *questi fiori rifioriranno fra due mesi*, these flowers will blossom again in two months' time **2.** *fig.* (*tornare in ottime condizioni*) to flourish again; (*di salute*) to recover: *il bimbo rifiorisce ora che è passato il freddo*, the child is flourishing (*o* doing well) again now that the cold weather has ended; *rifiorirono le arti*, the fine arts flourished again; *la sua azienda sta rifio-*

rendo, his business is flourishing (*o* thriving) again 3. (*tornare a mente*) to come back to one's mind: *un vago ricordo mi rifiorì nella memoria*, a vague memory came into my mind 4. (*ricoprirsi di macchie di muffa*) to get covered with musty stains ‖ *v.t.* 1. to embellish, to adorn, to make beautiful: *la gioia rifioriva il suo viso*, joy made her face beautiful; — *una composizione letteraria*, to embellish a literary composition 2. (*inghiaiare*) to gravel: — *una strada*, to gravel a road.

rifioríta, *s.f.* new blooming, new blossoming.

rifioríto, *ag.* 1. blooming again, in blossom again: *le siepi rifiorite dopo l'inverno*, the hedges in blossom again after the winter 2. (*tornato in ottime condizioni*) flourishing again 3. (*ristabilito in salute*) recovered.

rifioritúra, *s.f.* 1. reflorescence; new blossom 2. (*abbellimento*) embellishment 3. (*ret. mus.*) flourish 4. (*riapparizione di una macchia*) re-appearance of a stain 5. (*ghiaia*) gravel.

rifischiàre, *v.i.* to whistle again, to hiss again ‖ *v.t.* (*riferire*) to report.

rifischióna, *s.f.*, **rifischióne**, *s.m.* tell-tale, tale-bearer.

rifiutàbile, *ag.* refusable.

rifiutàre, *v.t.* 1. to refuse; (*respingere*) to reject; (*declinare*) to decline: — *un invito*, to decline an invitation; — *un'offerta*, to refuse (*o* to decline *o* to reject) an offer; — *una proposta*, to refuse (*o* to reject) a proposal; — *un regalo, un lavoro*, to refuse a present, a job 2. (*non concedere*) to refuse, to deny; to withhold: *non puoi rifiutargli la libertà*, you cannot deny him his freedom; *perchè gli rifiuti la tua approvazione?*, why do you withhold your consent from him?; — *l'aiuto, un favore a qlcu.*, to deny s.o. help, a favour; — *obbedienza a qlcu.*, to refuse obedience to s.o. 3. (*non riconoscere come proprio*) to disown: *rifiutò tutte le sue poesie giovanili*, he disowned all his youthful poems 4. (*ippica*) to refuse: *il cavallo rifiutò la siepe*, the horse refused the fence.

rifiutatóre, *ag.* of refusal (*predicativo*) ‖ *s.m.*, **rifiutatríce**, *s.f.* refuser.

rifiúto, *s.m.* 1. refusal: *al suo — di arrendersi sparò*, on his refusing to surrender, he fired; *oppose un —*, he refused; *il suo — mi sorprende*, his refusal surprises me ‖ *materiale, merce di —*, waste material, goods 2. (*cosa rifiutata*) thing refused; *pl.* waste (*sing.*), rubbish (*sing.*): *cassetta dei rifiuti*, waste-basket ‖ *i rifiuti della società*, the dregs of society.

riflessaménte, *av.* by reflection; indirectly.

riflessìbile, *ag.* reflexible.

riflessibilità, *s.f.* reflexibility.

riflessióne, *s.f.* 1. (*fis.*) reflection, reflexion: — *del terreno*, (*radar*) background return; — *di immagine, di luce, di suono*, reflection of image, of light, of sound; — *multipla del suono*, sound-reverberation; — *regolare*, (*ott.*) regular reflection; — *spuria*, (*radar*) spurious (*o* parasitic) reflection; — *totale*, total reflection; *angolo di —*, angle of reflection 2. (*meditazione*) reflection, meditation; (*considerazione*) consideration, deliberation: *dopo lunga —*, after long deliberation; *dopo matura —*, on thinking it over (*o* everything considered *o* after lengthy deliberation); *una persona senza —*, an inconsiderate (*o* thoughtless) person 3. (*osservazione*) reflection, remark: *intelligenti riflessioni sulla storia*, intelligent reflections upon history; *fece alcune utili riflessioni*, he made a few useful remarks.

riflessivaménte, *av.* thoughtfully, pensively.

riflessívo, *ag.* 1. thoughtful, reflective: *ha una mente molto riflessiva*, he has a very thoughtful cast of mind 2. (*gram.*) reflexive: *verbo —*, reflexive verb.

riflèsso, *ag.* 1. reflex (anche *fig.*); reflected: *calore —*, reflected heat; *influenza riflessa*, reflex influence; *luce riflessa*, reflected light: *brillare di luce riflessa*, to shine with reflected light 2. (*fisiol.*) reflex: *azione riflessa, movimento —*, reflex action, movement ‖ *s.m.* 1. reflection: — *del ghiaccio*, ice-blink; *il — dell'acqua*, the

reflection of the water; *i riflessi della luce, del calore*, the reflections of light, of heat; *il — della luna sul lago*, the reflection of the moon in the lake 2. *fig.* influence, reflection, effect: *i riflessi dell'opinione pubblica*, the influence of public opinion; *le leggi dovrebbero essere un — della volontà del popolo*, laws should be a reflection of the people's will ‖ *di —*, as a consequence: *lo vidi fermarsi improvvisamente e lo seguii di —*, I saw him stop suddenly and I did the same automatically ‖ *per —*, indirectly: *sapere ql.co. per —*, to hear of sthg. indirectly (*o* in a roundabout way) 3. (*sfumatura di colore*) tint, hue: *il suo abito ha riflessi cangianti*, her dress has ever-changing hues; *i suoi capelli hanno riflessi dorati*, her hair has golden tints 4. (*fisiol.*) reflex: — *del ginocchio*, knee-jerk; *il dottore mi provò i riflessi*, the doctor tested my reflexes; *ha riflessi pronti*, he has quick reflexes.

riflettènte, *ag.* reflecting, reflective.

riflèttere, *v.t.* 1. to reflect: *lo specchio riflette le immagini*, a mirror reflects images; — *la luce, il calore*, to reflect light, heat 2. *fig.* (*rispecchiare*) to reflect, to mirror: *le sue opere riflettono la sua epoca*, his works mirror his times; *i suoi occhi riflettono ciò che pensa*, her eyes reflect what she thinks ‖ *v.i.* to reflect, to ponder (sthg.; on, upon sthg.), to consider (sthg.). to weigh (sthg.): *devo — prima di prendere questa decisione*, I must think it over before making up my mind; *dopo aver molto riflettuto*, after much thought; *non ho mai riflettuto su questa faccenda*, I have never reflected upon (*o* thought about) this matter; *riflettete bene!*, think it over!; *senza —*, inconsiderately (*o* thoughtlessly) ‖ **riflèttersi**, *v.r.* 1. to be reflected (anche *fig.*): *gli alberi si riflettono nel lago*, the trees are reflected (*o* are mirrored) in the lake; *l'invidia si riflette sul suo volto*, envy is reflected in his face; *le luci si riflettono nell'acqua*, the lights are reflected in the water 2. (*ripercuotersi*) to be reflected; to have repercussions: *l'aumento dei salari si rifletterà sul costo della vita*, the wage-increase will have repercussions on the cost of living.

riflettóre, *s.m.* searchlight; reflector: — *ad arco*, (*cine.*) kleig light; — *angolare*, (*radar*) corner reflector; — *lenticolare*, (*elett.*) spot (light); — *parabolico*, (*radar*) parabolic reflector (*o* dish); — *per palcoscenico*, stage floodlight; *raggio di —*, searchlight beam; *essere illuminato dai riflettori*, to be flood-lit.

rifluíre, *v.i.* 1. (*fluire indietro*) to flow back 2. (*fluire di nuovo*) to flow again, to reflow: *tutte le merci rifluiscono sul mercato*, all the goods are flowing on to the market again.

riflússo, *s.m.* ebb, reflux, refluence: *flusso e — del mare*, ebb and flow (*o* flux and reflux) of the tides.

rifocillaménto, *s.m.* refreshment.

rifocillàre, *v.t.* to give refreshment to (s.o.) ‖ **rifocillàrsi**, *v.r.* to take refreshment.

rifóndere, *v.t.* 1. (*rimborsare*) to refund, to reimburse: *pagalo, poi ti rifonderò*, pay him, then I shall reimburse you; — *le spese a qlcu.*, to refund s.o.'s expenses 2. (*fondere di nuovo*) to remelt, to melt again 3. (*versare di nuovo*) to refill, to replenish, to top up: — *olio alla lampada*, to refill the lamp.

rifondíbile, *ag.* 1. refundable, reimbursable 2. (*che può fondere di nuovo*) capable of being remelted 3. (*riempibile*) refillable, replenishable.

riforbíre, *v.t.* to refurbish: — *le armi*, to refurbish one's arms.

rifórma, *s.f.* 1. reform; reformation: *la — del calendario, di una legge*, the reform of the calendar, of a law; *proporre riforme radicali*, to propose sweeping reforms ‖ *la Riforma*, (*st. relig.*) the Reformation 2. (*mil.*) rejection (from military service).

riformàbile, *ag.* 1. reformable 2. (*mil.*) rejectable (from military service).

riformàre, *v.t.* 1. to reform, to amend: *dovrebbe — la sua condotta, i suoi modi*, he should reform (*o* amend) his conduct, his manners; — *una legge*, to reform (*o* to amend) a law **2**. (*mil.*) to declare unfit for military service, to reject **3**. (*trasformare*) to transform, to change: — *con un pugno i connotati a qlcu.*, to smash s.o.'s face in.

riformatívo, *ag*. reformative, reformatory.

riformàto, *ag*. **1**. reformed, amended **2**. (*mil.*) (declared) unfit for military service || *s.m.* **1**. (*mil.*) man unfit for military service; rejected conscript **2**. *pl.* (*eccl.*) reformed monks: *i Minori riformati*, reformed friars minor **3**. *pl.* (*i Protestanti*) Reformed Churches.

riformatóre, *s.m.* reformer, amender.

riformatòrio, *s.m.* reformatory.

riformatríce, *s.f.* reformer, amender.

riformazióne, *s.f.* reformation.

riformísmo, *s.m.* reformism.

riformísta, *s.c.* reformist.

riforniménto, *s.m.* **1**. (*il rifornire*) supplying (with sthg.), providing (with sthg.); (*aer. aut.*) refuelling: — *in volo*, (*aer.*) refuelling in flight; *stazione, posto di* —, (*aut.*) filling-station; (*amer.*) gas-station **2**. (*scorta*) supply; stock: *i rifornimenti non sono ancora arrivati*, the supplies have not yet arrived; *ha un buon* — *di candele*, he has a large supply (*o* stock) of candles; *fare* — *di benzina*, to fill up the tank.

rifornìre, *v.t.* to supply, to provide: *l'ho rifornito di tutto ciò di cui può aver bisogno*, I have supplied him with everything he may need; — *le truppe di armi e di viveri*, to supply (*o* to provide) the troops with arms and victuals || **rifornìrsi**, *v.r.* to supply oneself (with sthg.), to provide oneself (with sthg.), to take in a supply (of sthg.): *mi sono rifornito di sigari*, I supplied (*o* I provided) myself with cigars; — *di acqua*, (*mar.*) to take on water; — *di benzina*, to fill up (*o* to take on petrol).

rifornitóre, *s.m.* **1**. (*chi rifornisce*) supplier, provider, purveyor **2**. (*ferr.*) water-crane.

rifornitríce, *s.f.* supplier, provider, purveyor.

rifràngere, *v.t.* (*fis.*) to refract: *l'acqua rifrange la luce*, water refracts light || **rifràngersi**, *v.r.* to be refracted.

rifrangíbile, *ag*. (*fis.*) refrangible.

rifrangibilità, *s.f.* (*fis.*) refrangibility.

rifrangiménto, *s.m.* (*fis.*) refraction.

rifràtto, *ag*. (*fis.*) refracted.

rifrattòmetro, *s.m.* (*fis.*) refractometer.

rifrattóre, *ag*. refracting || *s.m.* (*astr.*) refractor.

rifrazióne, *s.f.* (*fis.*) refraction: — *atmosferica*, atmospheric refraction; — *sismica*, (*geotecnica*) seismic refraction; *angolo di* —, (*ott.*) angle of refraction (*o* refractive angle); *indice di* —, (*ott.*) index of refraction; *relativo alla* —, refractive.

rifréddo, *s.m.* (*vivanda fredda*) cold dish.

rifríggere, *v.t.* **1**. to refry, to fry again **2**. (*ripetere*) to harp on (sthg.); to keep on repeating: *tu friggi e rifriggi sempre le stesse cose*, you keep on repeating (*o* you keep harping on) the same things || *v.i.* to fry too long (in too much fat): *il pesce è lì che rifrigge*, the fish is getting soggy after frying so long in all that fat.

rifrítto, *ag*. **1**. refried, fried again **2**. *fig.* (*trito*) stale, trite: *idee fritte e rifritte*, stale ideas; *mi dice sempre le stesse storie fritte e rifritte*, he is always harping on the same stories || *s.m.* smell of stale fried fat: *sa di* —, it tastes of stale fat.

rifrittúme, *s.m.*, **rifrittúra**, *s.f.* (*spreg.*) rehash (anche *fig.*).

rifrugàre, *v.t.* to search through (sthg.) again.

rifrustàre, *v.t.* **1**. (*frustare di nuovo*) to whip again, to thrash again **2**. (*rovistare*) to rummage in (sthg.), to go through (sthg.): *rifrustò tutti i vecchi giornali che aveva in casa*, he went through all the old newspapers he had in the house **3**. (*perlustrare*) to search: *rifrustò tutte le osterie per trovarvi il vino che voleva*, he searched all the inns in order to find the wine he

wanted **4**. (*rivangare*) to redig, to dig up again: *non sono cose da* — *ora*, it is not the sort of thing you should dig up now.

rifrútto, *s.m.* (*comm.*) usury.

rifuggíre, *v.i.* **1**. (*fuggire di nuovo*) to escape again, to flee again: *il prigioniero è rifuggito*, the prisoner has escaped again **2**. (*rifugiarsi fuggendo*) to escape: *erano rifuggiti tutti sulla montagna*, they had all escaped to the mountains **3**. (*essere alieno*) to shun (s.o., sthg.), to shrink (from s.o., sthg.), to avoid (s.o., sthg.): *rifugge dal parlar di sè*, he shrinks from talking about himself; *rifugge dal pettegolezzo di qualsiasi genere*, she shuns gossip in any form; *rifuggiva dalla vendetta*, he was against revenge; *non rifugge da nessun mezzo pur di riuscire*, he does not shrink from any means in order to be successful || *v.t.* (*scansare*) to shun, to avoid, to shrink from (s.o., sthg.): *rifugge la fatica*, she avoids fatigue; *rifugge la gente*, she shuns people's company; *rifuggiva ogni responsabilità*, he avoided (*o* shrank from) every responsibility.

rifugiàrsi, *v.r.* **1**. to shelter, to take shelter, to take cover, to take refuge: *corremmo a rifugiarci nella capanna*, we rushed to take shelter in the hut; *si rifugiarono come meglio poterono*, they sheltered as well as they could; *si rifugiò in solaio per paura di prenderle*, he hid (himself) in the attic as he was afraid of getting a good thrashing **2**. (*cercare conforto*) to take refuge, to seek refuge, to seek comfort: *si rifugiò nella religione*, he sought comfort in religion.

rifugiàto, *s.m.* refugee: *rifugiati politici*, political refugees.

rifúgio, *s.m.* **1**. shelter, refuge: — *antiaereo*, air-raid shelter; — *antiatomico*, A-shelter; — *sotterraneo*, dug-out; *cercò un* — *per ripararsi dalla pioggia*, he looked for (a) shelter from the rain; *non trovò un* — *sicuro*, he could not find a safe refuge; *dare* — *a qlcu.*, to shelter s.o. (*o* to give shelter to s.o.) **2**. *fig.* refuge, shelter; (*conforto*) comfort: *il* — *della fede*, the comfort of faith; *il suicidio è l'ultimo* — *della disperazione*, suicide is the last refuge of despair.

rifulgènte, *ag*. shining, bright, refulgent.

rifúlgere, *v.i.* **1**. to shine brightly (with sthg.), to glow (with sthg.): *il sole rifulgeva*, the sun was shining brightly; *il suo viso rifulgeva di felicità*, his face was glowing with happiness **2**. (*essere preminente*) to be conspicuous, to shine: *la sua gloria rifulge ancora*, his glory still shines (*o* is still unfaded).

rifusióne, *s.f.* **1**. (*nuova fusione*) remelting; recasting **2**. (*rimborso*) repayment, reimbursement: — *dei danni*, indemnification.

rifúso, *ag*. **1**. (*fuso di nuovo*) remelted **2**. (*rimborsato*) refunded, reimbursed.

ríga, *s.f.* **1**. line: *le righe di una pagina*, the lines of a page; — *diritta*, straight line; — *spettrale*, (*fis.*) spectrum-line; *l'ultima* — *di un paragrafo*, (*tip.*) break (-line); *fare una* — *a maglia*, to knit a round; *tirare una* — *col lapis*, to draw a line with a pencil || *scrivimi due righe*, drop me a line || *leggere fra le righe*, to read between the lines **2**. (*regolo*) rule(r): *a* T, T-square; — *da disegno*, drawing rule; — *in acciaio*, steel rule; — *per modellisti*, (*mec.*) contraction (*o* shrink)-rule **3**. (*fila*) row: *su una* —, in a row; *mettersi in* —, (*mil.*) to line up: *i soldati si misero in* —, the soldiers lined up; *rompere le righe*, to disperse (*o* to break the ranks); (*mil.*) to dismiss || — *dest(ra)*, *sinist(ra)!*, (*mil.*) right, left dress! || *un bugiardo di prima* —, a consummate (*o* an out and out) liar; *è un furfante di prima* —, he is an arrant knave (*o* a villain of the deepest dye) || *mettersi in* — *con qlcu.*, *fig.* to get into line with s.o. || *rimettere in* — *qlcu.*, *fig.* to put s.o. on the right path (*o* to make s.o. behave properly) || *stare in* —, *fig.* to toe the line (*o* to behave properly) || *uscire fuori dalla* —, *fig.* to rise from the ranks (*o* to make one's name) **4**. (*striscia*) stripe: *calze, pantaloni a righe*, striped socks, trousers; *una stoffa a righe rosse*, a cloth with red stripes; *tessuto a righe*, striped material 5. (*scriminatura*) parting: — *in mezzo*, parting in the middle; *farsi la — a sinistra*, to part one's hair on the left 6. (*mus.*) stave, staff (*pl.* staves).

rigàglia, *s.f.* 1. floss silk 2. (*soprappiù*) surplus.

rigàglie, *s.f.pl.* (*cuc.*) giblets.

rigàgnolo, *s.m.* 1. rivulet, brook 2. (*rivoletto che corre lungo i marciapiedi*) gutter.

rigalleggiàre, *v.i.* to refloat, to be afloat again.

rigàme, *s.m.* (*arch.*) flute.

rigàre, *v.t.* 1. to rule: — *un foglio di carta*, to rule a sheet of paper 2. — *diritto, fig.* to behave well (*o fam.* to go straight) 3. (*solcare*) to furrow: *le lacrime le rigavano il viso*, tears furrowed her face 4. (*un'arma da fuoco, provvederla di scanalatura*) to rifle.

rigatíno, *s.m.* (*tessuto*) striped cloth.

rigàto, *ag.* 1. ruled: *carta rigata*, ruled paper 2. (*a strisce*) striped: *portava un abito —*, she wore a striped dress 3. (*solcato*) furrowed: — *di pianto*, furrowed by tears 4. (*di arma da fuoco*) rifled 5. (*arch.*) fluted 6. *vento —*, (*mar.*) strong wind.

rigatóni, *s.m.pl.* (*cuc.*) "rigatoni" (large macaroni).

rigatóre, *s.m.*, **rigatríce**, *s.f.* 1. regulator, adjuster 2. (*di carta*) ruler.

rigattería, *s.f.* 1. second-hand dealer's (shop) 2. (*ciarpame*) rubbish, trash.

rigattière, *s.m.* second-hand dealer.

rigatúra, *s.f.* 1. (*su un foglio di carta*) ruling 2. (*di arma da fuoco*) rifling: — *a passo costante*, uniform-twist rifling.

rigeneràre, *v.t.* 1. to regenerate: *la grazia di Dio lo ha rigenerato*, God's grace has regenerated him 2. (*riparare*) to repair: — *un cuscinetto*, (*mec.*) to repair a bearing; — *un pneumatico*, to retread a tire || **rigeneràrsi**, *v.r.* to regenerate.

rigeneratóre, *ag.* regenerating, regenerative || *s.m.* 1. (*chi rigenera*) regenerator 2. — *dei capelli*, hair-restorer 3. (*ind.*) heat-exchanger.

rigeneratríce, *s.f.* regenerator.

rigenerazióne, *s.f.* regeneration (anche *fig.*): *la — delle ossa*, regeneration of the bones; *la — morale di un popolo*, the moral regeneration of a people.

rigènte, *ag.* (*poet.*) (*intirizzito*) frozen stiff.

rigermogliàre, *v.i.* 1. to resprout; to bud again 2. *fig.* (*rinascere*) to spring up again; to be born again.

rigettàbile, *ag.* rejectable.

rigettàre, *v.t.* 1. to throw again; to throw back: — *una palla*, to throw back (*o* to return) a ball; — *un pesce nell'acqua*, to throw (*o* to cast) a fish back into the water 2. (*respingere*) to reject; to repel: *relitti rigettati dal mare*, wreckage thrown (*o* cast) up by the sea; — *il nemico oltre il fiume*, to drive the enemy back across the river; — *un'offerta*, to reject an offer 3. (*vomitare*) to vomit; to throw up 4. (*rigermogliare*) to shoot (up) again, to resprout, to put out fresh shoots; to bud again 5. (*rifondere*) to cast again || **rigettàrsi**, *v.r.* to fall back.

rigètto, *s.m.* 1. (*rifiuto*) rejection, refusal 2. (*geol.*) throw: — *orizzontale*, heave; — *stratigrafico*, (dip-)slip.

righèllo, *s.m.* ruler: — *graduato*, scale.

righettàre, *v.t.* to stripe; to rule.

righettàto, *ag.* striped; ruled.

rigidaménte, *av.* 1. rigidly, stiffly 2. (*severamente*) strictly, sternly, severely; rigorously, rigidly.

rigidézza, *s.f.* 1. (*rigidità*) stiffness, rigidity 2. *fig.* (*rigorosità, severità*) strictness, severity; rigour: *la — della legge*, the rigour (*o* severity) of the law; *la — dei suoi principi*, the rigour of his principles.

rigidità, *s.f.* 1. stiffness, rigidity: — *cadaverica*, (*med.*) rigor mortis; — *muscolare*, stiffness of the muscles 2. (*di clima*) rigours (*pl.*): *la — del clima*, the rigours of the climate 3. *fig.* (*severità*) severity, strictness 4. (*elett.*) (electrical) strength.

rígido, *ag.* 1. rigid, stiff: *cartone, collo —*, stiff cardboard, collar; *una verga rigida*, a rigid rod; *ho le mani*

rigide dal freddo, my hands are stiff with cold (*o* are frozen stiff) 2. (*freddissimo*) rigorous, harsh, severe: *clima —*, rigorous climate; *inverno —*, harsh (*o* severe) winter 3. *fig.* (*rigoroso, severo*) strict, severe, stern; rigorous, rigid: *rigida disciplina*, rigid discipline; *il mio insegnante è molto —*, my teacher is very strict (*o* very severe) || *s.m.* severe cold; rigours (*pl.*).

rigiraménto, *s.m.* turning round; going round.

rigiràre, *v.t.* 1. to turn round; to turn again: — *la chiave*, to turn the key again; — *ql.co. tra le mani*, to turn sthg. over in one's hands 2. (*circondare*) to surround; (*andare intorno a*) to go round: *un fiume rigira tutta la città*, a river completely surrounds the city; — *la montagna*, to go round the mountain 3. (*deviare*) to turn, to change: — *il discorso*, to change the subject; — *una frase*, to recast a sentence 4. (*ingannare*) to trick, to dupe, to take in 5. (*comm.*) to employ: — *un capitale*, to employ capital || *v.i.* (*andare e venire*) to go up and down; to walk (about): — *per la città*, to walk about the town || *gira e rigira alfine l'ho trovato*, by dint of searching at last I found him; *gira e rigira siamo ancora qui*, after such a lot of walking we are back here again || **rigiràrsi**, *v.r.* to turn round; (*aggirarsi*) to wander (about, around); to walk (about): *in questa stanza non c'è spazio da —*, (*fam.*) there isn't room to swing a cat here; *rigirati, voglio vedere il dietro del vestito*, turn round, I want to see the back of your dress || *rigirarsela*, to manage (one's affairs): *se la rigirino come meglio possono*, let them manage as well as they can; *rigirarsela bene*, to get on well.

rigíro, *s.m.* 1. turning round; winding: *dopo giri e rigiri, si arrivò*, after a lot of winding in and out we got there; *non c'è posto per il — del carro*, there is no room to turn the cart round 2. (*comm.*) employment 3. *fig.* (*raggiro*) trick; underhand dealing 4. *fig.* (*garbuglio di parole*) involved expression: *con grandi rigiri di parole non ha detto nulla*, he went round and round in circles and said nothing.

rigiuràre, *v.t.i.* to reswear, to swear again.

rígo, *s.m.* 1. line: *scrivere un —*, to drop a line 2. (*mus.*) stave, staff (*pl.* staves).

rigóglio, *s.m.* 1. luxuriance; vigour, bloom (anche *fig.*): *in pieno —*, in full bloom (*o* vigour); *nel — della giovinezza*, in the bloom (*o* vigour) of youth 2. (*gorgoglio*) bubbling.

rigogliosaménte, *av.* luxuriantly; vigorously.

rigoglióso, *ag.* luxuriant; vigorous, blooming, flourishing (anche *fig.*): *industrie rigogliose*, flourishing industries; *crescere —*, to be thriving (*o* flourishing *o* blooming).

rigògolo, *s.m.* (*ornit.*) oriole.

rigolétto, *s.m.* (*danza*) round.

rigonfiaménto, *s.m.* blowing up, inflation, swelling.

rigonfiàre, *v.t.* to blow up, to inflate, to swell, to puff up; (*pneumatici*) to pump up: *il vento rigonfiava le vele*, the wind swelled the sails; — *un pallone*, to blow up a balloon || *v.i.*, **rigonfiàrsi**, *v.r.* to swell (up), to rise: *il riso nell'acqua rigonfia*, rice swells up in water; *le vele si rigonfiarono*, the sails swelled out.

rigónfio, *ag.* inflated (with sthg.), swollen (with sthg.), puffed up (with sthg.): — *d'orgoglio*, puffed up (*o* swollen) with pride || *s.m.* swelling.

rigóre, *s.m.* 1. rigours (*pl.*); severity: — *dell'inverno*, rigours of winter; *il — del tempo, del clima*, the severity of the weather, of the climate 2. (*severità*) rigour, strictness; — *della disciplina*, strictness of discipline; *applicherà la legge in tutto il suo —*, he will apply the full rigour of the law; *punire, trattare col massimo —*, to punish, to treat with the utmost severity || *di —*, compulsory: *in questo teatro è di — l'abito da sera*, at this theatre evening-dress is compulsory || *arresto di —*, (*mil.*) close arrest; *cella di —*, (*mil.*) cell 3. (*spor.*): *area di —*, penalty-area; *calcio di —*, penalty-kick 4. (*esattezza*) rigour, exactitude, exactness: *trattava il suo argomento col massimo*

—, he handled his subject with the utmost exactitude ‖ *a* —, according to the rule: *a — di logica*, according to the rules of logic; *a — di termini*, in the strict sense 5. (*rar.*) (*rigidità, durezza*) rigidity, stiffness: *il — di una sbarra di ferro*, the rigidity of an iron bar.

rigorísmo, *s.m.* rigo(u)rism.

rigorísta, *s.c.* rigo(u)rist.

rigorosaménte, *av.* 1. (*severamente*) rigorously, severely, strictly 2. (*esattamente*) strictly, exactly: — *parlando,* strictly speaking.

rigorosità, *s.f.* 1. (*severità*) rigorousness, rigour, strictness 2. (*esattezza*) strictness, preciseness 3. (*rigorismo*) rigo(u)rism.

rigoróso, *ag.* 1. (*rigido*) rigorous, severe: *clima* —, severe climate 2. (*severo*) rigorous, severe, strict: *disciplina rigorosa*, strict discipline; *insegnante* —, strict (*o* severe) teacher 3. (*esatto*) strict, exact: *ragionamento* —, strict reasoning; *è molto — nelle sue affermazioni*, he is very scrupulous (*o* exact) in his statements.

rigovernàre, *v.t.* 1. (*stoviglie*) to wash up: *hai finito di — in cucina?*, have you finished washing up in the kitchen? 2. (*cavalli*) to curry 3. (*governare di nuovo*) to govern again.

rigovernatúra, *s.f.* 1. (*di stoviglie*) washing-up: *acqua di* —, dish-water 2. (*di cavalli*) currying.

riguadagnàre, *v.t.* 1. (*guadagnare di nuovo*) to earn again 2. (*ricuperare*) to win back, to regain, to recover: — *il favore, la fiducia di qlcu.*, to win back s.o.'s favour, confidence; — *il tempo perduto*, to make up for lost time; — *terreno*, to regain ground 3. (*raggiungere di nuovo*) to regain: — *la riva*, to regain the shore.

riguardànte, *ag.* (*concernente*) concerning, regarding.

riguardàre, *v.t.* 1. to look at (s.o., sthg.) (again); (*con attenzione*) to examine: *ho riguardato il tuo lavoro e mi pare sia soddisfacente*, I have examined your work and it seems to be satisfactory; *non ho trovato nessun errore, comunque lo riguarderò*, I haven't found any mistakes, however I shall look at it again; — *un conto*, to examine (*o* to check) an account 2. (*considerare*) to regard, to consider; to look on (s.o., sthg.): *lo riguardano come un capolavoro*, they regard it as a masterpiece (*o* they consider it a masterpiece *o* they look on it as a masterpiece) 3. (*concernere*) to regard, to concern: *per quanto riguarda questa faccenda*, as regards this matter (*o* as far as this matter is concerned); *per quel che mi riguarda*, as far as I am concerned (*o* as for me); *questo non ti riguarda*, this does not concern you (*o* this is no concern of yours) ‖ *v.i.* 1. (*mirare*) to aim (at s.o., sthg.): *riguarda ad un solo ed unico scopo nella vita*, he has one aim and object in life 2. (*essere volto*) to overlook (sthg.), to look on (to sthg.); to face (sthg.): *la casa riguarda a sud*, the house faces south; *la mia camera riguarda la piazza*, my room overlooks (*o* looks on to) the square ‖ **riguardàrsi,** *v.r.* 1. (*proteggere la propria salute*) to take care of oneself, to look after oneself; to protect oneself (against sthg.): *egli deve — dal freddo*, he must protect himself against the cold; *egli si riguarda molto*, he takes great care of himself; *riguardati*, take care of yourself (*o* take care of yourself); *riguardati dalle correnti d'aria*, keep away (*o* protect yourself) from draughts 2. (*stare in guardia*) to beware (of s.o., sthg.).

riguardàta, *s.f.* look, glance: *dare una — a ql.co.*, to have a look at sthg.

riguardàto, *ag.* wary: *stare* —, to take care of oneself.

riguardévole, *ag.* 1. (*considerevole*) considerable, remarkable: *somma* —, considerable sum 2. (*importante*) important: *una persona* —, an important person.

riguàrdo, *s.m.* 1. (*cura, attenzione*) care: *abbi — di non fare troppo rumore*, be careful (*o* take care) not to make too much noise; *abbiti* —, take care of yourself (*o* look after yourself); *egli si ha tutti i riguardi*, he takes great care of himself; *non ha alcun — per la sua sa-*

lute, he does not take any care of his health; *maneggiare con* —, to handle with care 2. (*rispetto, considerazione*) regard, consideration, respect: *una persona di* —, a person of consequence; *devi aver — della sua età*, you must have respect for his age; *ha molto — delle cose altrui*, he is very careful with other people's things; *lo farò per — a suo padre*, I shall do it out of regard for his father; *mi mancò di* —, he was disrespectful (*o* rude) to me; *non ha avuto alcun — per i miei sentimenti*, he had no regard (*o* consideration) for my feelings; *per — alla sua età non glielo abbiamo detto*, out of consideration for his age we have not told him ‖ *non aver — di prendere ciò che ti occorre*, don't hesitate to take what you need ‖ *parlare senza riguardi*, (*francamente*) to speak openly (*o* frankly); (*senza rispetto*) to speak disrespectfully 3. (*relazione, attinenza*) regard, respect: — *a me*, as far as I am concerned (*o* as for me); — *a questo*, with regard to this; — *a questo problema*, as regards this problem (*o* as to this problem); *a questo* —, in this connection; *sotto ogni* —, in every respect; *sotto questo* —, in this respect; *voglio precise informazioni al* —, I want precise information on this matter.

riguardosaménte, *av.* 1. (*rispettosamente*) respectfully, considerately 2. (*con cautela*) carefully.

riguardóso, *ag.* 1. (*rispettoso*) respectful (to s.o.); considerate: — *dei diritti altrui*, respectful of other people's rights; *essere — con una signora*, to be respectful to a lady 2. (*cauto*) careful.

rigurgitaménto, *s.m.* 1. (*di acque*) flowing back; (*straripamento, traboccamento*) overflowing 2. (*di stomaco*) regurgitation, repeating; (*negli infanti*) breaking wind; (*fam.*) burping 3. (*gorgo d'acqua*) eddy, whirlpool.

rigurgitànte, *ag.* 1. (*traboccante*) overflowing 2. (*brulicante*) swarming: — *di gente*, swarming with people.

rigurgitàre, *v.i.* 1. (*di acque*) to gush back; to flow back; (*straripare, traboccare*) to overflow 2. (*di stomaco*) to regurgitate, to repeat; (*negli infanti*) to break wind; (*fam.*) to burp 3. (*brulicare*) to swarm (with s.o.), to be crowded (with s.o.), to overflow (with s.o.): *le strade rigurgitano di gente*, the streets are swarming (*o* are crowded) with people; *i treni rigurgitavano di gente*, the trains were packed with people 4. (*abbondare*) to abound (in sthg.): *negozi che rigurgitano di merce*, shops chock-full of goods (*o* crammed with goods); *la sua casa rigurgita di libri*, his house is full to overflowing with books (*o* is full of books).

rigúrgito, *s.m.* 1. (*straripamento, traboccamento*) overflow, overflowing 2. (*di stomaco*) regurgitation, repeating; (*negli infanti*) breaking wind; (*fam.*) burping 3. (*travaso*) extravasation: — *di sangue*, extravasation of blood 4. (*gorgo d'acqua*) eddy, whirlpool.

rigustàre, *v.t.* 1. to taste again 2. (*godere di nuovo*) to relish again.

rilanciàre, *v.t.* 1. to throw again; to hurl again; to fling again 2. (*ad un'asta*) to raise: — *l'offerta*, to raise the bidding.

rilàncio, *s.m.* 1. (*nuovo lancio*) new throw 2. (*ad un'asta*) raising.

rilasciaménto, *s.m.* 1. release, discharge, dismissal: *il — dei prigionieri*, the release (*o* discharge) of prisoners 2. (*concessione, cessione*) granting; issue, issuing: *il — di un passaporto*, the issuing of a passport 3. (*med.*) (*di tessuto muscolare*) prolapse, prolapsus.

rilasciàre, *v.t.* 1. (*lasciare di nuovo*) to leave again 2. (*mettere in libertà*) to release, to set free, to discharge: — *un paziente*, to discharge a patient; — *un prigioniero*, to release (*o* to discharge) a prisoner (*o* to set a prisoner free) 3. (*cedere, concedere, dare*) to grant, to give; to issue: — *un certificato, un passaporto*, to issue a certificate, a passport; — *una parte del proprio stipendio*, to give part of one's wages; — *un permesso*, to grant permission; — *una ricevuta*, to give (*o* to issue) a receipt 4. (*allentare*) to relax, to slacken, to loosen ‖ **rilasciàrsi,** *v.r.* 1. (*allentarsi*) to 'relax, to slacken, to become loose: *questa corda si rilascia*, this rope is getting slack (*o* loose) **2.** (*med.*) (*di tessuto muscolare*) to prolapse.

rilàscio, *s.m.* **1.** release, discharge, dismissal **2.** (*concessione, cessione*) granting; issue, issuing.

rilassaménto, *s.m.* **1.** relaxation, slackening: — *della disciplina*, relaxation (*o* slackening) of discipline; — *di una corda*, slackening of a rope **2.** (*med.*) (*di tessuto muscolare*) prolapse, prolapsus.

rilassàre, *v.t.* (*allentare*) to slacken, to loosen; (*distendere*) to relax: *questa musica rilassa* (*i nervi*), this music relaxes the nerves; — *le corde di un violino*, to slacken (*o* to loosen) the strings of a violin; — *la disciplina*, to relax discipline; — *i muscoli*, to relax one's muscles; — *i propri sforzi*, to slacken one's efforts ‖ **rilassàrsi,** *v.r.* **1.** (*allentarsi*) to slacken; to become loose: *la morale si è rilassata*, morals have become loose; *la sua severità si è rilassata*, his severity has relaxed **2.** (*distendere i nervi*) to relax: *vado a rilassarmi sul divano*, I am going to relax on the sofa **3.** (*med.*) (*di tessuto muscolare*) to prolapse.

rilassataménte, *av.* slackly, loosely.

rilassatézza, *s.f.* laxity, looseness: *la — della morale*, laxity (*o* looseness) of morals (*o* moral laxity).

rilassativo, *ag.* **1.** relaxing **2.** (*farm.*) (*lassativo*) laxative.

rilassàto, *ag.* **1.** relaxed: *muscoli rilassati*, relaxed muscles **2.** (*allentato*) loose, slack **3.** (*detto dei costumi*) loose, lax: *disciplina rilassata*, lax discipline.

rilavàre, *v.t.* to wash again, to re-wash.

rilavoràre, *v.t.* to work again.

rilegàre, *v.t.* **1.** to retie, to tie again; to bind again **2.** (*libri*) to bind: — *un libro in pelle*, to bind a book in leather **3.** (*incastonare*) to set, to mount.

rilegàto, *ag.* bound: *un libro — in pelle*, a book bound in leather (*o* a leather-bound book).

rilegatóre, *s.m.*, **rilegatrìce,** *s.f.* book-binder.

rilegatùra, *s.f.* (*di libri*) binding, bookbinding: — *in pelle*, leather-binding.

rilèggere, *v.t.* to read again, to reread: *dovresti — questo libro*, you should read this book again; *ho letto e riletto questo passaggio*, I have read this passage over and over again.

rilènto, a, *l.av.* slowly: *andare a —*, to go slow(ly).

rilevaménto, *s.m.* **1.** (*topografia*) survey: — *delle altitudini*, survey of heights; — *di un piano quotato*, contouring; — *geofisico*, (*miner.*) geophysical prospecting; — *sotterraneo*, (*miner.*) underground survey **2.** (*mar.*) bearing; observation: — *ad incrocio*, cross bearing; — *alla bussola*, compass bearing; — *astronomico*, astronomical observation; — *idrofonico*, (*mil.*) hydrophone bearing; — *polare*, relative (*o* polar) bearing **3.** (*sporgenza*) prominence, projection **4.** (*mil.*) (*cambio*) relieving: — *di una sentinella*, relieving of a sentry.

rilevànte, *ag.* **1.** (*che ha rilievo*) prominent **2.** (*importante*) important; (*considerevole*) considerable: *un — numero di uomini*, a large number of men.

rilevàre, *v.t.* **1.** to take off again, to take away again **2.** (*rialzare*) to raise (*anche fig.*): *lo rilevò da terra*, she raised him from the ground; *quelle parole rilevarono le sue speranze*, those words raised his hopes **3.** (*notare*) to notice; (*mettere in evidenza*) to point out; (*esaminare*) to survey: *dovresti — questi aspetti del problema*, you should point out these aspects of the problem; *non l'avevo rilevato*, I had not noticed it; *volevo farti — alcuni errori*, I wanted to point out a few mistakes to you; — *la situazione internazionale*, to survey the international situation **4.** (*prendere*) to take: — *il calco, la maschera di un cadavere*, to take a death-mask; — *un'impronta digitale*, to take a finger-print **5.** (*topografia*) to survey, to plot: — *un tratto di terra*, to survey a tract of land **6.** (*mar.*) to take the bearing of (*sthg.*) **7.** (*sostituire*) to relieve: *andrò a rilevarlo dopo la lezione*, I shall go and relieve him (*o* take his place) after the lesson **8.** (*comm.*) to take

over: — *una ditta, un negozio*, to take over a firm, a shop **9.** (*andare a prendere per accompagnare*) to call for (s.o.): *verrò a rilevarti alle otto*, I shall call for you at eight o'clock **10.** (*apprendere*) to learn: *ho rilevato quella notizia dal giornale*, I learnt that piece of news from the newspaper ‖ *v.i.* (*cuc.*) to rise ‖ **rilevàrsi,** *v.r.* **1.** (*rialzarsi*) to rise again, to stand up again **2.** (*riprendersi*) to recover.

rilevatàrio, *s.m.* **1.** (*comm.*) purchaser **2.** (*dir.*) (*cessionario*) transferee.

rilevàto, *ag.* (*in rilievo*) in relief; (*sporgente*) prominent, projecting, protruding.

rilevatùra, *s.f.* (*sporgenza*) prominence, projection.

rilièvo, *s.m.* **1.** relief: *un bel — di marmo*, a beautiful marble relief; *carta in —*, (*geog.*) relief map; *profilo in —*, profile in relief; *mise le figure in —*, he brought the figures into relief; *l'ombreggiatura dà — al dipinto*, the shading gives relief to the drawing; *lavorare di —*, to make reliefs **2.** (*importanza*) importance, stress: *cosa di —*, important thing (*o* matter); *mettere in —*, *dare — a*, to point out (*o* to emphasize *o* to stress): *l'autore ha dato particolare — a questo problema*, the author has laid special stress on this problem; *non avrei messo così in — queste cose*, I should not have emphasized these things so much; *vorrei mettere in — questi particolari*, I should like to point out these details; *occupare una posizione di —*, to hold a prominent position (*o* to be a public figure) **3.** (*osservazione*) remark: *fare un —*, to make a remark **4.** (*topografia*) survey: — *topografico*, plotting; *prendere rilievi di un tratto di terra*, to survey (*o* to plot) a tract of land **5.** (*comm.*) taking over: *il — di un'azienda*, the taking over of a business **6.** *pl.* (*avanzi di cibo*) scraps, leavings.

rilucènte, *ag.* shining; glittering.

rilucentézza, *s.f.* brilliancy; shine; glitter.

rilúcere, *v.i.* to shine; to glitter; to glisten ‖ *non è tutto oro quello che riluce*, *prov.* all that glitters (*o* glistens) is not gold.

riluttànte, *ag.* reluctant.

riluttànza, *s.f.* reluctance: *lo fece con —*, he did it with reluctance (*o* reluctantly); *non mostrò alcuna — ad andarci*, he showed no reluctance to go there.

riluttàre, *v.i.* to reluct (at sthg., at doing), to rebel (against sthg., against doing), to oppose (sthg., doing).

rìma[1], *s.f.* rhyme; (*rar.*) rime: *rime alternate*, alternate rhymes; — *leonina*, double rhyme; — *piana, tronca*, feminine, masculine rhyme; *ottava —*, ottava rima; *terza —*, terza rima; *poesia a rime obbligate*, poem with set rhymes; *essere a — baciata*, to rhyme in pairs; *far —*, to rhyme; *mettere in —*, to put into rhyme (*o* verse); *scrivere in —*, to write in rhyme ‖ *rispondere per le rime*, to give a sharp answer (*o fam.* to give tit for tat).

rìma[2], *s.f.* **1.** (*anat.*) rima (*pl.* rimae): — *boccale*, rima oris; — *palpebrale*, rima palpebrarum **2.** (*mar.*) (*falla*) leak.

rimacinàre, *v.t.* to grind again.

rimagliàre, rimagliatúra, *V.* **rammagliàre, rammagliatùra.**

rimandàre, *v.t.* **1.** (*mandare di nuovo*) to send again **2.** (*restituire*) to give back, to return; to send back: *rimandò tutti i regali che aveva ricevuto*, she sent back all the presents she had received; *quando mi rimanderai l'ombrello che ti ho prestato?*, when will you give me back the umbrella I lent you? **3.** (*far tornare*) to send back: *fu rimandato al paese d'origine*, he was sent back to his native village; *l'ho rimandato a comprare il giornale*, I have sent him back to buy a paper ‖ — *da Erode a Pilato*, to send from pillar to post **4.** (*posporre*) to postpone, to defer, to put off: *la lezione è stata rimandata di una settimana*, the lesson has been postponed (*o* deferred) for a week; — *un dibattito*, to put off (*o* to postpone) a debate ‖ *non — mai a domani ciò che può essere fatto oggi*, never put off till to-morrow what can be done to-day **5.** (*mandare ad altra prova d'esame*) to make (s.o.) repeat (an exam): *fu rimandato a ottobre in tre materie*, he had to repeat three subjects in October **6.** (*mil.*) (*dichiarare rivedibile*) to declare temporarily unfit **7.** (*fare riferimento*) to refer: — *ad un libro, una pagina, ecc.*, to refer to a book, to a page, etc.

rimàndo, *s.m.* **1.** sending back; returning ‖ *di* —, in return **2.** (*differimento*) postponement, putting off; adjournment: — *di un dibattito*, adjournment of a debate **3.** (*spor.*) (*di palla*) throw-in **4.** (*tip.*) (*richiamo*) reference (-mark): *in questo dizionario ci sono molti rimandi*, in this dictionary there are many reference-marks.

rimaneggiaménto, *s.m.* **1.** (*riordinamento*) rearrangement, readjustment: — *di una commedia*, readaptation (*o* rearrangement) of a play **2.** (*modifica*) adjustment, change: — *delle tasse*, tax adjustment **3.** (*pol.*) (*rimpasto*) shuffle: — *del gabinetto*, cabinet-shuffle.

rimaneggiàre, *v.t.* **1.** (*riordinare*) to rearrange, to reorganize **2.** (*modificare*) to adjust, to change, to alter **3.** (*pol.*) (*rimpastare*) to shuffle: — *il gabinetto*, to shuffle the cabinet.

rimanènte, *ag.* remaining: *gli scolari rimanenti*, the remaining pupils ‖ *s.m.* remainder, rest: *il* — *della vita*, the remainder (*o* rest) of one's life; *venti persone entrarono e i rimanenti rimasero fuori*, twenty people came in and the remainder stayed outside ‖ *del* —, (*del resto, comunque*) however; (*inoltre*) moreover.

rimanènza, *s.f.* remainder, remnant: *la* — *del denaro*, the remainder of the money; *la* — *sarà venduta a buon mercato*, the remnant(s) will be sold cheap.

rimanére, *v.i.* **1.** to remain, to stay: *ho premura, non posso* —, I am in a hurry, I cannot stay; *rimani lì*, remain (*o* stay) there; *rimarrò solo alcuni giorni in Germania*, I shall remain (*o* stay *o* stop) in Germany only a few days; *rimase a casa a curare il bambino*, she stayed (*o* remained) at home to look after the child; *rimasero dentro perchè fuori faceva freddo*, they stayed in because it was cold outside; *rimasi alzato fino a mezzanotte*, I stayed up till midnight; *il treno partì e io rimasi a terra*, the train started and I was left behind; — *a cena*, to stay to dinner; — *a guardare*, to watch; — *a letto*, to stay in (*o* to keep one's) bed; — *fuori di casa*, to be left outside; (*rimanere assente*) to stay (*o* to be) away ‖ *dove sono rimasto?*, where did I leave off? ‖ *ho voluto provare e ci rimasi*, (*ne fui scottato*) I wanted to try and I paid for it ‖ *ti ho raccontato tutto, ma rimanga fra noi*, I have told you everything, but don't breathe a word of it ‖ — *a bocca aperta*, to gape (*o* to stand gaping) ‖ — *all'asciutto, al verde*, to be left penniless ‖ — *con un palmo di naso*, to feel done (*o* disappointed) ‖ — *d'accordo con qlcu.*, to agree with s.o.: *rimanemmo d'accordo che essi sarebbero partiti prima e io li avrei raggiunti dopo due giorni*, we agreed that they would leave before and I should join them after two days ‖ — *di stucco*, to be taken aback ‖ — *in asso*, to be left in the lurch ‖ — *indietro*, to remain behind (*o* to get behind *o* to fall behind): *non voglio* — *indietro col lavoro*, I do not want to get behind with my work; *questo ragazzo rimarrà indietro dai suoi compagni*, this boy is bound to fall behind (*o* cannot keep pace with) the rest of the class; *se vengo con te, il mio lavoro rimane indietro*, if I come with you, I shall fall behind in my work; *tutti se ne andarono ed io rimasi indietro*, everybody left and I remained behind ‖ — *in dubbio*, to be in doubt ‖ — *male*, (*deluso*) to be disappointed; (*prendere in mala parte*) to take (sthg.) badly ‖ — *meravigliato*, to be astonished ‖ — *morto sul colpo*, to be struck dead on the spot; — *ucciso, ferito*, to be killed, wounded ‖ — *orfano*, to be left an orphan; — *vedovo*, to become a widower ‖ — *soddisfatto*, to be satisfied ‖ — *sullo stomaco*, (*di cibo*) not to agree with (s.o.); *fig.* to rankle: *la cotoletta di maiale che*

ho mangiato a colazione mi è rimasta sullo stomaco, (*fam.*) the pork chop I had for lunch did not agree with me; *mi piacciono le uova ma mi rimangono sullo stomaco*, (*fam.*) I like eggs but they don't like me; *i suoi insulti mi sono rimasti sullo stomaco*, *fig.* his insults still rankle **2.** (*avanzare*) to remain, to be left: *dopo il terremoto, rimase ben poco della città*, after the earthquake very little remained of the city; *mi rimangono solo tre giorni di vacanza*, I have only three days left of my holiday; *mi rimanevano solo pochi soldi*, I had very little money left; *non gli rimase nulla*, he had nothing left; *non rimangono che cinque biglietti*, only five tickets are left; *rimane ben poco da fare, da dire*, very little remains to be done, to be said; *se si sottrae 8 da 10 rimane 2*, if you subtract 8 from 10, 2 remains **3.** (*durare*) to remain, to last: *il pericolo rimane*, the danger persists (*o* is still there); — *in carica*, to stay in office **4.** (*essere situato*) to be (located *o* situated): *dove rimane la chiesa?*, where is the church (located *o* situated)? **5.** (*mantenersi*) to remain, to keep: *rimanete insieme*, keep together; *rimani calmo, tranquillo*, keep calm, still; *rimase un buon amico*, he remained a good friend; — *fedele, onesto*, to remain faithful, honest **6.** (*essere sorpreso*) to be greatly surprised, to be astonished: *al vederlo rimasi*, I was greatly surprised to see (*o* at seeing) him; *a udire queste cose io rimasi*, I was astonished at hearing these things **7.** (*spettare*) *ciò rimane a te*, (*è affar tuo*) this is your (own) business; *rimane a te la decisione*, it rests with you to decide **8.** (*letter.*) (*cessare*) to stop.

rimangiàre, *v.t.* to eat again ‖ **rimangiàrsi**, *v.r.* to take back: *dovette* — *quel che aveva detto*, he had to eat his words; — *la parola*, to take back one's word.

rimànte, *ag.* rhyming ‖ *s.c.* rhymist.

rimarcàre, *v.t.* **1.** (*marcare di nuovo*) to mark again **2.** (*notare*) to notice.

rimarchévole, *ag.* remarkable.

rimàrco, *s.m.* remark.

rimàre, *v.t.* to versify, to put into rhyme, to rhyme: — *un sonetto*, to rhyme a sonnet ‖ *v.i.* to rhyme: *queste parole non rimano*, these words do not rhyme.

rimarginàre, *v.t.* to heal (anche *fig.*): *il tempo rimargina le piaghe dell'anima*, time heals all sorrows ‖ *v.i.*, **rimarginàrsi**, *v.r.* to heal (up).

rimàrio, *s.m.* rhyming dictionary; book of rhymes.

rimaritàre, *v.t.*, **rimaritàrsi**, *v.r.* to remarry, to marry again.

rimasticàre, *v.t.* **1.** to chew again **2.** *fig.* to chew (upon, over sthg.), to ruminate (sthg.; on, over sthg.).

rimàsto, *ag.*: — *al verde, all'asciutto*, penniless; — *fuori*, (*escluso, omesso*) left out (*o* omitted); *un attore* — *senza lavoro*, an actor out of work; *un'espressione rimasta celebre*, an expression which has become famous; *coi pochi soldi rimasti non arriveremo alla fine del mese*, with the little cash we have left we shall not get by till the end of the month ‖ *i rimasti*, those left behind: *s'allontanò tra lo stupore dei rimasti*, he went off to the amazement of those left behind.

rimasùglio, *s.m.* remainder, residue; remains (*pl.*): *i rimasugli di un pranzo*, the remains of a dinner.

rimàto, *ag.* rhymed: *parole rimate*, rhymed words.

rimatóre, *s.m.* rhymer, poet; (*spreg.*) rhymester.

rimatrìce, *s.f.* rhymer, poetess; (*spreg.*) rhymester.

rimbaccuccàre, *v.t.* to muffle up, to wrap up ‖ **rimbaccuccàrsi**, *v.r.* to muffle oneself up, to wrap oneself up.

rimbandalzíre, *v.i.*, **rimbaldanzírsi**, *v.r.* to grow bold (again), to recover one's self-assurance.

rimballàre, *v.t.* to repack ‖ *v.i.* to bob (up and down).

rimbalzàre, *v.i.* **1.** to rebound, to bound back, to bounce: *la palla rimbalzò contro la rete*, the ball rebounded against the net; *la palla rimbalzò verso di lui*, the ball bounded back to him; *questa palla non rimbalza bene*, this ball does not bounce well **2.** (*detto di* *proiettile*) to ricochet: *le pallottole rimbalzarono,* the bullets ricocheted (upwards).

rimbalzèllo, *s.m.* ducks and drakes: *giocare a —,* to play ducks and drakes.

rimbalzíno, *s.m.* pitch-and-toss.

rimbàlzo, *s.m.* rebound ‖ *di —,* on (*o* at) the rebound; *fig.* in retort.

rimbambiménto, *s.m.* dotage.

rimbambiníre, *v.i.,* **rimbambinírsi,** *v.r.* (*rar.*) to grow childish.

rimbambíre, *v.i.* to reach one's dotage.

rimbambíto, *ag.* in one's dotage (*predicativo*); (*stupido*) stupid ‖ *s.m.* dotard.

rimbarbogíre, *v.i.* to become a dotard.

rimbarcàre, *v.t.* to re-embark; (*comm.*) to re-ship ‖ **rimbarcàrsi,** *v.r.* **1.** to re-embark, to go to sea again **2.** (*di legname, incurvarsi*) to warp; to bend.

rimbàrco, *s.m.* re-embarkation; (*comm.*) re-shipment.

rimbastíre, *v.t.* to baste again.

rimbeccàre, *v.t.* to retort to (s.o., sthg.); to answer back.

rimbécco, *s.m.* retort, sharp answer ‖ *di —,* in retort: « *Non verrò mai più qui »,* rispose *di —,* " I shall never come here again ", he retorted.

rimbecillimento, *s.m.* softening of the brain; growing stupid.

rimbecillíre, *v.i.* to grow stupid; (*di vecchi*) to be in one's dotage; to reach one's dotage.

rimbellíre, *v.t.* to embellish, to make more beautiful ‖ *v.i.,* **rimbellírsi,** *v.r.,* to become more beautiful: (*si*) *è molto rimbellita,* her looks have improved greatly.

rimbiancàre, rimbianchíre, *v.t.* to whiten again, to whitewash again ‖ *v.i.* to grow white again.

rimbiondíre, *v.i.,* **rimbiondírsi,** *v.r.* to become fairer.

rimboccaménto, *s.m.* tucking up; turning up; (*di lenzuola*) turning down.

rimboccàre, *v.t.* **1.** to tuck (up); to turn up; (*lenzuola*) to turn down: *gli rimboccò le coltri,* she tucked him up in bed **2.** (*rar.*) (*abboccare di nuovo*) to fill (up) again: — *una bottiglia,* to fill (up) a bottle again ‖ *il vento rimboccò il fumo nel camino,* the wind drove the smoke back down the chimney ‖ **rimboccàrsi,** to tuck (up); to turn up: *si rimboccò i calzoni,* he turned up his trousers; — *le maniche,* to tuck up (*o* to roll up) one's sleeves.

rimboccatúra, *s.f.* **1.** (*il rimboccare*) tucking up; turning up; (*di lenzuolo*) turning down **2.** (*parte rimboccata*) tuck; turn-up.

rimbócco, *s.m.* turn-down; (*di calzoni*) turn-up; (*di manica*) turned-up cuff.

rimbombànte, *ag.* **1.** thundering, booming: *voce —,* thundering voice **2.** *fig.* high-sounding, bombastic: *discorso —,* bombastic speech.

rimbombàre, *v.i.* to thunder, to roar; to resound: *i cannoni rimbombavano,* the cannon roared; *il tavolato rimbombava sotto i loro passi,* the footbridge resounded with their footsteps.

rimbómbo, *s.m.* boom, roar: *il — del cannone,* the roar (*o* boom) of the cannon.

rimborsàbile, *ag.* repayable, reimbursable, refundable.

rimborsaménto, *V.* rimbórso.

rimborsàre, *v.t.* **1.** to repay, to reimburse, to refund: *mi hanno rimborsato,* I got my money back; — *le spese a qlcu.,* to repay (*o* to reimburse) s.o.'s expenses: *ti rimborserò le spese del viaggio,* I shall refund (*o* reimburse) your travelling expenses **2.** (*rimettere nella borsa*) to replace in one's bag ‖ **rimborsàrsi,** *v.r.* to get one's money back.

rimbórso, *s.m.* repayment, reimbursement, refund: — *del dazio,* toll refund; *avviso di —,* notice for reimbursement; *ottenere il — fiscale,* to get a tax refund.

rimboscaménto, *s.m.* reafforestation.

rimboscàre, *v.t.* to reafforest ‖ **rimboscàrsi,** *v.r.* to take to the woods, to take to the forest.

rimboschiménto, *s.m.* reafforestation.

rimboschíre, *v.t.* to reafforest ‖ *v.i.,* **rimboschírsi,** *v.r.* to become wooded again.

rimbottàre, *v.t.* to recask.

rimbrattàre, *v.t.* to dirty again.

rimbrodolàre, *v.t.* **1.** to dirty again **2.** (*coprire malamente di vernice*) to redaub.

rimbrottàre, *v.t.* to scold, to reproach, to rebuke; (*fam.*) to give (s.o.) a lecture.

rimbròtto, *s.m.* reproach, rebuke; (*fam.*) lecture.

rimediàbile, *ag.* remediable.

rimediàre, *v.t.* (*racimolare*) to scrape up, to scrape together; (*guadagnare*) to earn: *spero di — un po' di denaro,* I hope to scrape some money together ‖ *v.i.* **1.** to remedy (sthg.); to find a remedy for (sthg.), to cure (sthg.); to make up for (sthg.): *dobbiamo — a quello che abbiamo fatto,* we must make up for what we have done; *questi sono mali a cui non si rimedia,* these are evils which cannot be cured; — *a un inconveniente,* to find a remedy for (*o* to remedy) a defect **2.** (*provvedere*) to take steps (to do sthg.); to do (sthg.) about (sthg.): *oggi non c'è nulla da mangiare: come si rimedia?,* we have not got anything to eat today: what shall we do about it?.

rimedicàre, *v.t.* to re-dress, to dress again.

rimédio, *s.m.* remedy; (*cura*) cure: *ho trovato un — a questo inconveniente,* I have found a remedy for this defect; *non c'è —,* there is nothing to be done about it; *non c'è — per questa malattia,* there is no cure for this disease; *questo è un buon — per il mal di testa,* this is a good remedy for headache; *il riposo è il miglior —,* rest is the best cure ‖ *a estremi mali, estremi rimedi,* prov. desperate ills demand desperate remedies.

rimeditàre, *v.t.* to remeditate, to meditate again.

rimembrànza, *s.f.* remembrance; memory: *una dolce —,* a sweet memory ‖ *parco delle rimembranze,* memorial park (*o* garden).

rimembràre, *v.t.i.* to remember.

rimenàre, *v.t.* **1.** (*ricondurre*) to take back; to bring back; to lead back **2.** (*mescolare*) to stir; (*agitare*) to shake.

rimenàta, *s.f.* **1.** stir: *dare una — alla minestra,* to give the soup a stir **2.** (*fam.*) (*rimprovero*) scolding.

rimenío, *s.m.* (*il mescolare*) stirring; (*l'agitare*) shaking.

rimeritàre, *v.t.* to reward, to recompense.

riméscere, *v.t.* to pour out again.

rimescolaménto, *s.m.* **1.** mixing; stir **2.** (*di carte*) shuffle; shuffling **3.** (*confusione*) confusion **4.** (*turbamento, emozione*) shock; feeling of confusion.

rimescolàre, *v.t.* **1.** (*mescolare*) to mix (up); to stir; (*mescolare di nuovo*) to remix, to mix up again; to restir, to stir again: — *la minestra,* to stir the soup **2.** (*carte*) to shuffle; (*mescolare di nuovo*) to reshuffle **3.** (*frugare, rovistare*) to rummage among (sthg.): *ho rimescolato questi vecchi documenti ma non ho trovato niente,* I have rummaged among these old documents but I have not found anything **4.** (*turbare, agitare*): *gli si rimescolò il sangue per la rabbia,* his blood boiled; *quella vista mi ha fatto — il sangue,* that sight has made my blood curdle; *sentirsi — per lo spavento,* to feel one's blood run cold ‖ **rimescolàrsi,** *v.r.* **1.** (*turbarsi*) to be upset; to be shocked **2.** (*immischiarsi*) to meddle (with sthg.); to interfere.

rimescolàta, *s.f.* **1.** mixing; stir: *dare una — alla minestra,* to stir the soup **2.** (*di carte*) shuffle; shuffling: *dare una — alle carte,* to shuffle the cards.

rimescolío, *s.m.* **1.** constant mixing; changing about **2.** (*confusione*) confusion **3.** (*turbamento, emozione*) shock; feeling of confusion: *a quella orribile vista mi sono sentito uno strano —,* my blood curdled (*o* ran cold) at that horrible sight.

riméssa, *s.f.* **1.** (*il rimettere*) replacing; (*la cosa rimessa*) replacement: *la — a posto di un osso,* (*chir.*) the setting of a bone ‖ — *della palla,* (*tennis, ecc.*)

return; — *in giuoco*, *(calcio, ecc.)* throw-in **2.** *(per automobili)* garage; *(per carrozze)* coach-house: *dietro la casa c'è una — per automobili*, there is a garage behind the house **3.** *(riserva)* store, reserve: *quest'anno abbiamo una buona — di grano*, this year we have a good reserve of corn **4.** *(comm.)* *(di denaro)* remittance; *(di merci)* consignment: *— di fondi*, remittance of funds; *le rimesse degli emigrati sono state particolarmente alte quest'anno*, remittances made by emigrants have been particularly high this year; *attendo una — di libri*, I am waiting for a consignment of books; *il mese scorso Vi abbiamo fatto una — di un milione*, last month we remitted the sum of one million lire to you **5.** *(comm.)* *(perdita)* loss: *nel vendere quella merce ho avuto una forte —*, I suffered a heavy loss on the sale of those goods || *vendere a —*, to sell at a loss **6.** *(germoglio)* sprout, shoot; *(il rimettere germogli)* sprouting: *le rose si potano perchè facciano una migliore —*, roses are pruned so that they will put out more shoots.

rimessaménte, *av.* **1.** submissively: *rispondeva —*, he answered submissively **2.** *(fiaccamente)* half-heartedly.

rimessitíccio, *s.m. (germoglio, virgulto)* shoot.

rimésso, *ag.* **1.** that has been put back || *dente —*, false tooth || *orlo —*, false hem **2.** *(ristabilito)* fit again, well again: *mi sento completamente —*, I feel completely fit again **3.** *(perdonato)* forgiven, remitted: *peccato —*, forgiven sin **4.** *(umile)* meek || *s.m.* **1.** *(intarsio)* inlay **2.** *(ritocco)* touching up **3.** *(ripiegatura d'orlo)* hem.

rimestàre, *v.t.* **1.** to stir; *(mestare di nuovo)* to restir, to stir again: *— la minestra*, to stir the soup **2.** *fig.* to stir up; to raise again: *perchè vuoi — questi vecchi rancori?*, why do you want to stir up these old grudges?.

rimestatóre, *ag.* stirring up || *s.m.*, **rimestatríce,** *s.f.* agitator.

rimestío, *s.m.* continuous stirring.

riméttere, *v.t.* **1.** to put again; to put back: *devo — questi fiori sul tavolo?*, shall I put these flowers back on the table?; *rimettilo a posto*, put it back in its place; *rimettilo dove l'hai trovato*, put it back where you found it; *— il cappello*, to put one's hat on again; *— i denti*, to cut one's second teeth; *— in discussione* to bring up for discussion again; *— in giuoco, (spor.)* to throw in; *fig. (rimettere in ballottaggio)* to risk; *— in marcia,* (aut.) to restart; *— in uso, in funzione*, to bring into use again; *— un libro al suo posto*, to replace a book; *— a posto un osso*, to set a bone; *— la spada nel fodero*, to sheathe one's sword; *— sul trono*, to restore to the throne || *— a nuovo*, to do up: *far — a nuovo una casa*, to have a house done up || *— bocca*, *(intervenire di nuovo)* to intervene again; *— mano a ql.co.*, to get on with sthg. || *— l'orologio*, to put a watch right || *— piede*, to set foot again: *non rimetterò mai più piede in questa casa*, I shall never set foot in this house again || *— lo stomaco*, to put one's stomach right: *quel cognac mi ha rimesso lo stomaco*, that brandy has put my stomach right (*o* has settled my stomach) **2.** *(restituire)* to give back, to return: *gli rimisi ciò che mi aveva prestato*, I gave him back what he had lent me **3.** *(mandare)* to remit; *(consegnare)* to hand, to deliver: *la citazione fu rimessa stamane proprio a lui*, the summons was delivered into his hands this morning; *prego rimetterci la somma al più presto*, please remit us the amount as soon as possible; *— denaro a qlcu.*, to remit money to s.o.; *— un dispaccio a qlcu.*, to hand (*o* to deliver) a message to s.o.; *— documenti a qlcu.*, to lodge documents with s.o. **4.** *rimetterci*, to lose; to ruin: *ci ho rimesso un paio di scarpe*, I ruined a new pair of shoes; *ci rimetterai la salute*, you will ruin your health; *ci si rimette il fiato a parlare con lui*, it is a waste of breath talking to him; *in questo affare ci ho rimesso molto denaro*, I have lost a lot of money in this business; *se non ci guadagna non ci rimette*, if he doesn't gain anything, at least

he won't lose anything; *rimetterci di decoro, reputazione*, to lose face, one's reputation || *rimetterci le penne*, *(denaro)* to go broke **5.** *(rimandare)* to put off, to postpone, to defer: *l'incontro è stato rimesso a un altro giorno*, the meeting has been put off to another day; *non si può — ciò a più tardi?*, can't we leave that till later?; *— un affare al domani*, to put off (*o* to defer) a matter till the morrow; *— una causa di una settimana*, to postpone (*o* to remand) a case for a week **6.** *(recuperare)* to recover: *— il sonno perduto*, to catch up on lost sleep **7.** *(perdonare)* to remit, to forgive: *un'offesa*, to pardon an offence; *— un peccato*, to remit a sin || *rimetti a noi i nostri debiti come noi li rimettiamo ai nostri debitori*, forgive us our trespasses, as we forgive them that trespass against us **8.** *(affidare)* to refer; to leave; to submit: *dovreste — questa faccenda a un esperto*, you should refer (*o* submit) this matter to an expert; *rimettiamo a te la decisione*, we will leave the decision (*o* we will leave it) to you; *rimetto a te questo problema*, I leave this problem to you (*o* in your hands); *— un affare al giudizio di qlcu.*, to refer a matter to s.o.'s judgement; *— un prigioniero alla giustizia*, to hand a prisoner over to justice; *— la propria sorte nelle mani di qlcu.*, to put one's fate in s.o.'s hands || *— l'anima a Dio*, to commit one's soul to God **9.** *(vomitare)* to bring up, to vomit, to throw up: *rimise tutto ciò che aveva mangiato*, he brought up all that he had eaten; *mi viene da —*, I feel sick; *questa medicina mi fa venire da —*, this medicine makes me feel sick ◊ **rimettersi,** *v.r.* **1.** *(mettersi di nuovo)*: *mi sono rimesso in una situazione difficile*, I have put myself in a difficult situation again; *rimettiti le scarpe*, put your shoes on again; *si rimise a lavorare*, he started working (*o* set to work) again (*o* he resumed work); *— a sedere*, to sit down again; *— in viaggio*, to set out (*o* off forth) again **2.** *(rasserenarsi)*: *il tempo si sta rimettendo*, it is clearing up (*o* the weather is improving) **3.** *(ristabilirsi)* to recover: *egli non si è ancora rimesso*, he has not yet recovered; *— da un colpo, da uno spavento*, to recover from a shock, from a fright; *— in forze, in salute*, to recover one's strength, one's health || *— in sesto*, to recover one's position: *dopo che fece bancarotta ci mise due anni per — in sesto*, after going bankrupt he took two years to get on his feet again **4.** *(affidarsi)* to rely on (s.o., sthg.): *devi rimetterti al parere del tuo medico*, you must put yourself in your doctor's hands; *mi rimetto alla tua discrezione*, I rely on your discretion; *mi rimetto a te per la decisione*, I leave it to you to decide.

rimettitíccio, *s.m. (virgulto)* shoot.

rimettitúra, *s.f.* **1.** replacing, replacement **2.** *(ind. tessile)* looming.

rimiràre, *v.t.* to gaze at (s.o., sthg.); to stare at (s.o., sthg.): *rimiravano stupiti le vetrine illuminate*, they stared at the lighted windows; *rimirava la sua opera con visibile soddisfazione*, he was gazing at his work with evident satisfaction ◊ **rimiràrsi,** *v.r.* to contemplate oneself; to admire oneself, to look at oneself with complacence: *indossò l'abito nuovo e si rimirò a lungo allo specchio*, she put on her new dress and admired herself in the mirror for a long time.

rimissióne, *V.* **remissióne.**

rimmelensíre, *v.i.* to grow duller.

rimminchioníre, *v.i. (volg.)* **1.** to become stupid **2.** *(divenire smemorato)* to grow forgetful.

rimodellàre, *v.t.* to remodel.

rimodernaménto, *s.m.* **1.** modernization, modernizing; renovation; remodelling **2.** *(miglioria)* improvement.

rimodernàre, *v.t.* to modernize; to renovate; to remodel: *— un abito, un cappello*, to remodel a dress, a hat (*o* to give a dress, a hat a new look); *— un appartamento, una casa*, to modernize a flat, a house || **rimodernàrsi,** *v.r.* to become up-to-date, to bring oneself up-to-date.

rimodernatóre, *s.m.*, **rimodernatríce**, *s.f.* modernzer.

rimodernatúra, *s.f.* **1.** modernization, modernizing; remodelling: — *di un abito*, remodelling of a dress; *ha speso un capitale per la* — *del salotto*, she spent a lot of money on giving her drawing-room a new look **2.** (*miglioria*) improvement: *le rimodernature non rendono nuovo un vecchio edificio*, improvements do not make an old building new.

rimondàre, *v.t.* to clean (again), to clean out (again): *dobbiamo* — *gli alberi del frutteto*, we'll have to prune the trees in the orchard; — *una fossa*, to clean out (*o* clear out) a ditch.

rimondatúra, *s.f.* **1.** cleaning **2.** (*mondiglia*) rubbish (*solo sing.*), refuse (*solo sing.*).

rimóndo, *ag.* cleaned, cleared: *fossa rimonda*, cleared ditch; *ramo* —, pruned branch.

rimónta, *s.f.* **1.** (*mil.*) remount **2.** (*di scarpe*) vamping: *queste vecchie scarpe hanno bisogno di una buona* —, these old shoes want a good vamping.

rimontàre, *v.i.* **1.** (*risalire*) to remount: — *a cavallo, in sella*, to remount; — *in automobile, in carrozza*, to get into a car, a coach again **2.** *fig.* to go back, to date back: *queste tradizioni rimontano al Medioevo*, these traditions date (*o* go) back to the Middle Ages ‖ *v.t.* **1.** (*risalire*) to go up: — *la corrente*, to sail upstream; (*in mare*) to stem (the current); — *un fiume*, to go up a river **2.** (*ricomporre*) to reassemble: — *una macchina*, to reassemble a machine **3.** (*rimettere a nuovo*): — *un cappello*, to remodel a hat; — *un paio di scarpe*, to vamp a pair of shoes **4.** (*mil.*) to remount: — *una squadra di cavalleria*, to remount a squadron of cavalry.

rimontatúra, *s.f.* **1.** (*di una macchina*) reassemblng **2.** (*di scarpe*) vamping; (*di cappelli*) remodelling.

rimorchiàre, *v.t.* to tow: — *un'automobile*, to tow a car; — *una barca*, to tow a boat; — *una nave*, to tow a ship ‖ — *qlcu.*, (*fam.*) to get s.o. to come: *cerca di* — *anche lui*, try to get him to come too; *lasciarsi* —, (*fam.*) to get oneself taken along (*o* to let oneself be taken in tow).

rimorchiatóre, *ag.* towing ‖ *s.m.* (*mar.*) tug(-boat): — *a vapore*, steam-tug.

rimòrchio, *s.m.* **1.** tow: *cavo, corda da* —, tow -rope (*o* towline); *gancio di* —, tow-hook; *andare a* —, to be towed; *avere, prendere a* —, to have, to take in tow; *entrare in porto a* —, (*mar.*) to be towed into port **2.** (*veicolo*) trailer; (*mar.*) tow: — *con guida*, (*ferr.*) control trailer; — *stradale*, trailer-truck.

rimòrdere, *v.t.* **1.** (*mordere di nuovo*) to bite again; (*mordere chi ha morso*) to bite back **2.** *fig.* to prick: *gli rimorde la coscienza*, his conscience pricks him; *quel ricordo lo rimorde ancora*, that memory still hurts him.

rimordiménto, *s.m.* (*rimorso*) remorse; regret.

rimoríre, *v.i.* to die again: *ogni inverno la natura rimuore*, every winter nature dies again.

rimormoràre, *v.t.i.* **1.** to murmur again; to whisper again **2.** (*brontolare*) to moan again.

rimòrso, *ag.* **1.** that has been bitten again **2.** (*pentito*) repentant; remorseful ‖ *s.m.* remorse; regret: — *di coscienza*, remorse (*o* pang of conscience); *ho* — *di quel che ho fatto*, I feel remorse for (*o* I regret) what I have done; *lo ha fatto senza alcun* —, he did it without remorse.

rimòsso, *ag.* removed: *un magistrato* — *dal suo ufficio*, a magistrate removed from his office; *un ostacolo per sempre* —, an obstacle removed for ever.

rimostrànte, *ag.s.c.* remonstrant.

rimostrànza, *s.f.* remonstrance, protest, expostulation, complaint: *fare le proprie rimostranze*, to remonstrate (*o* to protest *o* to complain *o* to expostulate): *gli feci le mie rimostranze per il modo in cui mi avevano trattato*, I remonstrated with him about (*o* I complained to him about) the way I had been treated.

rimostràre, *v.t.* to show again ‖ *v.i.* to remonstrate, to protest, to expostulate, to complain.

rimòto, *V.* **remòto**.

rimovíbile, *ag.* removable.

rimoviménto, *s.m.* removal.

rimovitóre, *ag.* removing ‖ *s.m.*, **rimovitríce**, *s.f.* remover.

rimozióne, *s.f.* **1.** removal: — *di un oggetto, di un dubbio*, removal of an object, of a doubt **2.** (*destituzione*) dismissal, removal.

rimpaciàre, *v.t.* to reconcile ‖ **rimpaciàrsi**, *v.r.* to get reconciled: *mi son rimpaciato con lui*, I am reconciled (*o* I have made it up) with him.

rimpadronírsi, *v.r.* to take possession again; to seize (sthg.) again.

rimpaginàre, *v.t.* (*tip.*) to re-page, to page again.

rimpaginatúra, *s.f.* (*tip.*) re-paging, new paging.

rimpagliàre, *v.t.* to re-cover with straw; (*imbottire di nuovo di paglia*) to re-stuff with straw.

rimpagliatóre, *s.m.*, **rimpagliatríce**, *s.f.* person who covers (sthg.) with straw.

rimpagliatúra, *s.f.* (*copertura*) new straw covering; (*imbottitura*) new straw stuffing.

rimpàllo, *s.m.* (*al biliardo*) counterblow.

rimpaludàre, *v.i.* to become swampy again.

rimpanàre[1], *v.t.* (*cuc.*) to bread again, to bread -crumb again.

rimpanàre[2], *v.t.* (*mec.*) to re-thread.

rimpanatúra[1], *s.f.* (*cuc.*) re-breading, re-covering with bread-crumbs.

rimpanatúra[2], *s.f.* (*mec.*) re-threading.

rimpannucciàre, *v.t.* to give some new clothes to ‖ — *qlcu.*, *fig.* to improve s.o.'s financial position ‖ **rimpannucciàrsi**, *v.r.* **1.** to wear better clothes **2.** *fig.* to improve one's financial position, to become better off: *si è rimpannucciato*, he is better off than before; *si sta rimpannucciando*, he is improving his financial position.

rimpantanàrsi, *v.r.* **1.** to get muddy again; to stick in the mud again **2.** *fig.* to get entangled again, to get mixed up again: *si è rimpantanato con quei mascalzoni*, he has got entangled (*o* mixed up) with those rascals again.

rimparàre, *v.t.* to re-learn, to learn again.

rimpastàre, *v.t.* **1.** to knead again; to mix again **2.** (*raffazzonare*) to rearrange, to reshuffle **3.** (*pol.*) (*rimaneggiare*) — *un ministero*, to shuffle a cabinet.

rimpasticciaménto, *s.m.* new mess, another mess.

rimpasticciàre, *v.t.* **1.** to bungle again, to make a mess of (sthg.) again **2.** *fig.* to grope for (sthg.): *rimpasticciava qualche scusa per la sua assenza*, he groped for some excuse to explain his absence.

rimpàsto, *s.m.* **1.** kneading again; mixing again **2.** (*raffazzonatura*) rearrangement, reshuffling **3.** (*pol.*) (*rimaneggiamento*) shuffle: — *ministeriale*, cabinet -shuffle.

rimpatriàre, *v.t.* to repatriate, to send back to s.o.'s country ‖ *v.i.* to repatriate, to return to one's country.

rimpatriàto, *s.m.* repatriate.

rimpàtrio, *s.m.* repatriation: *dopo tre anni ottenne il* —, after waiting three years, he was repatriated.

rimpettíre, *v.i.*, **rimpettírsi**, *v.r.* to swell with pride.

rimpettíto, *ag.* haughty, arrogant.

rimpètto, *av.* face to face; **opposite**: *la casa* —, the house opposite ‖ **rimpètto a**, *l.prep.* **1. opposite**; (*in presenza di*) face to face: *la casa* — *a noi*, the house opposite ours **2.** (*in confronto a*) **in comparison with**.

rimpiallacciàre, *v.t.* to veneer again.

rimpiallacciatúra, *s.f.* veneering: *foglio sottile per* —, scale-board.

rimpiàngere, *v.t.* **1.** to mourn, to lament, to bewail: *si rimpiangerà molto la sua perdita*, his loss will be much lamented; — *la morte di qlcu.*, to lament (*o* to mourn *o* to bewail) s.o.'s death **2.** (*provare disap-*

punto) to regret: *rimpiango di non esserci andato*, I regret not having gone.

rimpiànto, *ag.* regretted ‖ *s.m.* regret: *non ho alcun — per quel che ho fatto*, I have no regrets for what I have done.

rimpiastràre, *v.t.* to re-plaster; to daub again.

rimpiastricciàre, *v.t.* 1. to daub again 2. *fig.* (*raccomodare alla peggio*) to botch up.

rimpiattàre, *v.t.* to hide, to conceal ‖ **rimpiattàrsi**, *v.r.* to hide (oneself), to conceal oneself.

rimpiattíno, *s.m.* hide-and-seek: *giocare a —*, to play hide-and-seek.

rimpiazzàre, *v.t.* to replace.

rimpiàzzo, *s.m.* replacement.

rimpiccioliménto, *s.m.* lessening, decrease.

rimpicciolíre, rimpiccolíre, *v.t.* to make smaller, to lessen, to decrease ‖ *v.i.*, **rimpicciolírsi, rimpiccolírsi**, *v.r.* to become smaller, to lessen, to decrease.

rimpiegàre, *v.t.* to re-employ.

rimpiègo, *s.m.* re-employment.

rimpinguàre, *v.t.* 1. to fatten (up) 2. (*arricchire*) to enrich ‖ *v.i.*, **rimpinguàrsi**, *v.r.* 1. to fatten, to grow fat 2. (*arricchirsi*) to grow rich.

rimpinzaménto, *s.m.* stuffing, cramming.

rimpinzàre, *v.t.* to fill, to stuff, to cram: *non — quel bambino di dolci*, don't stuff that child full of cakes ‖ **rimpinzàrsi**, *v.r.* to stuff oneself: *si è rimpinzato di pane*, he has stuffed himself with bread.

rimpolpàre, *v.t.* 1. (*ingrassare*) to fatten (up), to make fat 2. (*arricchire*) to enrich, to make rich ‖ **rimpolpàrsi**, *v.r.* 1. to get fat, to put on weight 2. (*arricchirsi*) to become rich.

rimpossessàrsi, *v.r.* to take possession again, to re-possess oneself.

rimproveràbile, *ag.* reprehensible, reproachable; (*biasimevole*) blamable, blameworthy.

rimproveràre, *v.t.* 1. to reproach, to upbraid; to reprove, to rebuke; (*ufficialmente*) to reprimand; (*sgridare*) to scold, to tell off, to chide: *dovrebbe essere rimproverato per la sua pigrizia*, he ought to be rebuked for his laziness; *il maestro lo rimproverò perchè non aveva fatto il compito*, the teacher reproved (*o* scolded) him for not having done his homework; *la mamma ti rimproverà, quando vedrà che ti sei sporcato il vestito*, mother will scold you when she sees you have made your dress dirty (*o fam.* mother will tell you off when she sees you' ve got your dress dirty); *mia madre mi rimproverò perchè non avevo avuto maggior cura di me stesso*, my mother reproached me for (*o* with) not having taken better care of myself; *l'ufficiale fu rimproverato in pubblico*, the officer was reprimanded in public 2. (*biasimare, riprovare*) to blame, to criticize, to censure: *gli si rimproverò la sua cattiva condotta*, he was much blamed (*o* criticized) for his bad behaviour 3. (*rinfacciare*) to grudge: *gli rimprovera anche quel misero tozzo di pane che gli dà*, he grudges him even the poor crust of bread he gives him; *— un beneficio fatto a qlcu.*, to grudge s.o. a service rendered ‖ **rimproveràrsi**, *v.r.* 1. to reproach oneself (with sthg., with doing); (*biasimarsi*) to blame oneself (for sthg., for doing): *egli non ha nulla da —*, he has nothing to reproach himself with (*o* to blame himself for) 2. (*pentirsi di*) to regret (sthg., doing); to repent (of sthg., of doing): *non mi sono mai rimproverato la mia fiducia nella gente*, I have never regretted my trust in people.

rimpròvero, *s.m.* reproach; reproof, rebuke; (*ufficiale*) reprimand; (*sgridata*) scolding: *un amaro —*, a bitter reproach; *un aspro —*, a sharp rebuke (*o* reprimand); *uno sguardo di —*, a look of reproach; *ricevette un bel — da sua madre*, he got a frightful scolding from his mother (*o fam.* he got a frightful telling-off from his mother); *muovere un — a qlcu.*, to reproach (*o* to scold *o* to rebuke *o* to reprove) s.o.

rimuginàre, *v.t.* 1. (*frugare*) to rummage; to rummage through 2. (*agitare nella mente*) to brood over

(sthg.), to turn over in one's mind: *che cosa stai rimuginando?*, what are you turning over in your mind?.

rimuneràre, *v.t.* to remunerate; *fig.* to reward, to recompense: *questo lavoro non viene rimunerato*, this work is not remunerated; *la virtù sarà rimunerata*, virtue will be rewarded; *— qlcu. per ql.co.*, to recompense (*o* to reward) s.o. for sthg.

rimuneratívo, *ag.* remunerative; (*che dà profitto*) profitable: *lavoro —*, profitable work.

rimuneràto, *ag.* remunerated; rewarded, recompensed.

rimuneratóre, *s.m.* remunerator; rewarder, recompenser.

rimuneratòrio, *ag.* remunerative.

rimuneratríce, *s.f.* remunerator; rewarder, recompenser.

rimunerazióne, *s.f.* remuneration; reward, recompense.

rimuòvere, *v.t.* 1. to remove (anche *fig.*): — *una causa, un dubbio, un timore*, to remove a cause, a doubt, a fear; *— una pietra*, to remove a stone 2. (*deporre, destituire*) to remove, to displace: *— qlcu. dal suo ufficio*, to remove s.o. from office 3. (*distogliere*) to deter; (*dissuadere*) to dissuade: *cercherò di rimuoverlo dal suo proposito*, I shall try to dissuade him from his purpose 4. (*scavare*) to dig: *— il terreno*, to dig the ground ‖ **rimuòversi**, *v.r.* to move, to budge: *non vuole — da quello che ha detto*, he won't move (*o* budge) from what he said.

rimutaménto, *s.m.* further change.

rimutàre, *v.t.* 1. to change again 2. (*far cambiare opinione a*) to make (s.o.) change his mind ‖ **rimutàrsi**, *v.r.* (*cambiare idea*) to change one's mind.

rinacerbíre, *v.t.* to embitter: *il dolore l'ha rinacerbito*, sorrow has embittered him ‖ *v.i.*, **rinacerbírsi**, *v.r.* 1. to become embittered 2. (*di dolore*) to become sharper, to become harsher.

Rinàldo, *no.pr.m.* Reginald, Ronald, Reynold ‖ *dim.* Reg, Reggie, Rex, Ronnie.

rinarràre, *v.t.* to re-tell, to tell again, to narrate again.

rinascènte, *ag.* renascent, reviving, returning.

Rinascènza, *V.* **Rinasciménto**.

rinàscere, *v.i.* to revive (anche *fig.*); (*rigermogliare*) to spring up again; (*nascere di nuovo*) to be born again: *i fiori rinascono nell'acqua*, flowers revive in water; *quando lo vidi mi rinacque la speranza*, when I saw him my hope revived; *questa è una tradizione che non può —*, this is a tradition which cannot be revived; *quest'erba rinascerà in primavera*, this grass will grow again in the spring; *questo fatto fece — in lui vecchi rancori*, this fact revived old grudges in him; *rinacquero le arti*, there was a revival of the arts ‖ *mi sento —*, (*mi sento un altro uomo*) I feel a new man.

Rinasciménto, *s.m.* (*st. art. lett.*) Renaissance, Renascence: *il — italiano, francese*, the Italian, French Renaissance; *architettura, mobili —*, Renaissance architecture, furniture.

rinàscita, *s.f.* 1. rebirth 2. *fig.* revival: *la — celtica*, the Celtic revival (*o* renaissance); *la — delle lettere, della cultura, di vecchi costumi*, the revival of letters, of learning, of old customs.

rinàto, *ag.* 1. reborn 2. *fig.* revived: *mi sento —*, I feel a new man.

rinavigàre, *v.t.i.* to sail again.

rincagnàrsi, *v.r.* to frown, to scowl.

rincagnàto, *ag.* pug (*attributivo*): *viso, naso —*, pug-face, pug-nose.

rincalcàre, *v.t.* to press down; to pull down, to push down: *rincalcò il cappello fino agli orecchi*, he pulled (*o* pushed) his hat down over his ears.

rincalzaménto, *s.m.* 1. (*agr.*) earthing up 2. (*rimboccamento*) tucking in 3. (*di mobile*) propping up.

rincalzàre, *v.t.* 1. (*agr.*) to earth up: *— una pianta*, to earth up a plant ‖ *andare a — i cavoli*, *fig.* to go and push up daisies **2.** (*rimboccare*) to tuck in: — *il letto, le coperte*, to tuck in the bed-sheets **3.** (*assicurare l'equilibrio di*) to prop up: — *un mobile*, to prop up a piece of furniture; — *un palo con sassi*, to prop a stake with stones.

rincalzàta, *s.f.* **1.** (*agr.*) single earthing up **2.** (*rimboccata*) tucking in **3.** (*di mobile, ecc.*) propping up: *dare una* — *ad un tavolo*, to prop up a table.

rincalzatóre, *s.m.* (*agr.*) ridging plow, ridger.

rincalzatúra, *s.f.* (*agr.*) earthing up.

rincàlzo, *s.m.* **1.** (*agr.*) earthing up **2.** (*rinforzo*) reinforcement, support, help ‖ *a* —, in support: *a* — *di ciò che ti ho già detto*, in support of what I have already told you ‖ *di* —: *truppe di* —, supporting troops (*o* reinforcements); *ed egli di* — *disse...*, he supported his statement by saying....

rincamminàrsi, *v.r.* to start walking again.

rincantàre, *v.t.* to charm again.

rincantucciàre, *v.t.* to put in a corner; to drive into a corner ‖ **rincantucciàrsi,** *v.r.* to hide (oneself) in a corner, to creep into a corner: *appena mi vide corse a* —, as soon as he saw me he ran into a corner.

rincappellàre, *v.t.*: — *il vino*, to add old wine to grape-must.

rincaràre, rincaríre, *v.t.* to raise, to raise the price of: *hanno rincarato lo zucchero*, they have raised the price of sugar; — *i prezzi*, to raise prices ‖ — *la dose*, to increase the quantity; to aggravate the situation: *egli rincarò la dose raccontando cose non vere*, he aggravated the situation telling things which were not true ‖ *v.i.* to become more expensive, to go up, to rise: *i generi alimentari stanno rincarando*, foodstuffs are getting more expensive; *i prezzi rincarano*, price are rising: *la vita rincara*, the cost of living is going up.

rincarnàre, *v.t.* to fatten, to make fat ‖ *v.i.* **1.** to get fat, to put on weight **2.** (*di ferite*) to heal ‖ **rincarnàrsi,** *v.r.* to get fat, to put on weight.

rincarnazióne, *s.f.* reincarnation.

rincàro, *s.m.* (*comm.*) rise in prices, price rise.

rincartàre, *v.t.* to wrap in paper again.

rincasàre, *v.i.* to go back home; to come back home; to return home ‖ *v.t.* (*arc.*) (*ricondurre a casa*) to take back home, to bring home again.

rincassàre, *v.t.* **1.** (*rimettere in cassa*) to pack again, to put in a crate again **2.** (*riscuotere di nuovo*) to cash again, to collect again.

rincatenàre, *v.t.* to chain up again.

rincattivíre, *v.i.*, **rincattivírsi,** *v.r.* to grow crosser, to become angrier.

rincavàre, *v.t.* to hollow out again.

rincentràre, *v.t.* to re-centre.

rinchinàrsi, *v.r.* (*umiliarsi*) to humiliate oneself.

rinchiúdere, *v.t.* to shut in, to shut up: *fu rinchiuso in una stanza*, he was shut (up) in a room ‖ **rinchiúdersi,** *v.r.* to shut oneself up; *fig.* to retire into one's shell: *egli si rinchiuse in se stesso, e non volle parlare a nessuno*, he retired into his shell and did not want to speak to anybody.

rinchiúso, *ag.* shut in, shut up ‖ *s.m.* enclosure, enclosed place ‖ *saper di* —, to have a musty smell.

rinciampàre, *v.i.* **1.** to stumble again (over sthg.) **2.** (*incontrare di nuovo*) to meet (s.o.) again.

rincitrullíre, *v.t.* to make silly; to make stupid; to drive silly ‖ *v.i.*, **rincitrullírsi,** *v.r.* to grow silly; to grow stupid.

rinciuchíre, *v.i.* to become more ignorant; to become sillier.

rinciviliménto, *s.m.* civilization.

rincivilíre, *v.t.* to civilize; (*raffinare*) to refine ‖ *v.i.*, **rincivilírsi,** *v.r.* to become (more) civilized; (*raffinarsi*) to become (more) refined.

rincòfori, *s.m.pl.* (*entom.*) Rhynchophora.

rincollàre, *v.t.* to paste again, to glue again ‖ **rincollàrsi,** *v.r.* (*di acque*) to become obstructed.

rincolleríre, *v.i.* to get angry again.

rincòllo, *s.m.* (*di acque*) obstruction.

rincomineiàre, *V.* **ricominciàre.**

rincontràre, *v.t.*, **rincontràrsi,** *v.r.* to meet again.

rincóntro[1], *s.m.* **1.** meeting, encounter **2.** (*paragone*) comparison **3.** *a, di* —, in front.

rincóntro[2], *av.* (*dirimpetto*) opposite ‖ **rincóntro a,** *l. prep.* opposite, in front of: *abita* — *a noi*, he lives opposite us.

rincoraggiàre, *v.t.* to encourage (again).

rincoraménto, *s.m.* encouragement.

rincoràre, *v.t.* to encourage; to comfort; to cheer up ‖ **rincoràrsi,** *v.r.* to pluck up courage; to cheer up.

rincorporàre, *v.t.*, **rincorporàrsi,** *v.r.* to incorporate again.

rincórrere, *v.t.* to run after (s.o., sthg.); (*inseguire*) to chase, to pursue: *il gatto sta rincorrendo un topo*, the cat is chasing a mouse ‖ **rincórrersi,** *v.r. reciproco* to run after each other (one another); (*inseguirsi*) to chase each other (one another).

rincórsa, *s.f.* run-up: *prendere la* —, to take a run -up; *saltare senza* —, to jump from a standing position.

rincòti, *s.m.pl.* (*entom.*) Rhynchota.

rincréscere, *v.i.* **1.** to be sorry (for, about s.o., sthg.), to regret (s.o., sthg.): *me ne rincresce*, I regret it; *mi rincresce di non poterlo fare*, I am sorry I can't do it (*o* I regret not being able to do it); *mi rincresce molto del suo insuccesso*, I deeply regret (*o* I am very sorry about) his failure; *questo avvenimento è una cosa che rincresce*, this is a regrettable event **2.** (*arrecar noia*) to mind (*costruzione pers.*): *ti rincrescerebbe aprire la finestra?*, would you mind opening the window?.

rincrescévole, *ag.* **1.** (*spiacevole*) disagreeable, unpleasant **2.** (*noioso*) annoying.

rincrescevolménte, *av.* regrettably.

rincresciménto, *s.m.* regret: *con mio* —, to my regret; *con molto* —, with much regret.

rincrescióso, *ag.* **1.** regrettable; (*spiacevole*) disagreeable, unpleasant **2.** (*noioso*) annoying.

rincrudelíre, *v.t.* to make crueller ‖ *v.i.* to become crueller.

rincrudiménto, *s.m.* aggravation, worsening: *il* — *di una malattia*, the aggravation (*o* worsening) of an illness; *ci fu un* — *del freddo*, it got colder (*o* the weather became colder).

rincrudíre, *v.t.* to aggravate; (*esacerbare*) to embitter: *il dolore lo ha rincrudito*, sorrow has embittered him ‖ *v.i.*, **rincrudírsi,** *v.r.* to get worse, to worsen: *il tempo (si) è rincrudito*, the weather has got worse.

rinculàre, *v.i.* **1.** to recoil, to draw back, to move back **2.** (*artigl.*) to recoil.

rincúlo, *s.m.* (*artigl.*) recoil: *il* — *di un cannone*, the recoil of a gun.

rinduríre, *v.t.* to harden again ‖ *v.i.*, **rindurírsi,** *v.r.* to harden; (*indurirsi di più*) to grow harder.

rinettàre, *v.t.* to clean again, to re-clean.

rinfacciàre, *v.t.* to throw (it) in s.o.'s face, to fling (it) in s.o.'s face: *sa che sono stato sgarbato e me lo rinfaccia sempre*, he knows that I have been rude and he always throws it in my face (*o* in my teeth).

rinfagottàre, *v.t.* **1.** (*fare un fagotto*) to bundle up, to make up into a bundle **2.** (*avvolgere come un fagotto*) to wrap up: *faceva molto freddo ed eravamo tutti rinfagottati*, it was very cold and we were all wrapped up **3.** (*vestire senza eleganza*): *è sempre rinfagottata in vestiti ridicoli*, she always wears ridiculous dresses ‖ **rinfagottàrsi,** *v.r.* to dress badly.

rinfanciullíre, *v.i.* to become childish, to grow childish, to enter one's second childhood.

rinfantocciàre, *v.t.* to dress as a puppet.

rinfervoràre, *v.t.* to enliven, to animate: — *la discussione*, to animate the discussion ‖ **rinfervoràrsi,** *v.r.* to liven up (again), to become animated (again).

rinfiammàre, *v.t.* to rekindle ‖ **rinfiammàrsi,** *v.r.* **1.** to burst into flame again: *il fieno si rinfiammò subito*, the hay burst into flame again at once **2.** (*ec-*

citarsi di nuovo) to kindle again, to excite again: — *d'ira*, to kindle with anger again.

rinfiancàre, *v.t.* to prop; to support (anche *fig.*): *rinfiancò l'accusa con nuove prove*, he supported the accusation with new evidence.

rinfiànco, *s.m.* prop; support (anche *fig.*).

rinfierìre, *v.i.* 1. (*infierire di nuovo*) to rage again 2. (*divenire più vigoroso, più fiero*) to become stronger.

rinfittìre, *v.t.* 1. to thicken, to make thicker 2. (*rendere più frequenti*) to make more frequent: *il medico ha rinfittito le visite*, the doctor has made his visits more frequent || *v.i.*, **rinfittìrsi**, *v.r.* 1. to thicken; to become thicker 2. (*di lana*) to shrink.

rinfocàre, *V.* **rinfiammàre**.

rinfocolaménto, *s.m.* 1. poking 2. *fig.* rekindling; reviving.

rinfocolàre, *v.t.* 1. (*riattizzare*) to poke 2. *fig.* (*riaccendere, fomentare*) to rekindle, to kindle again, to excite again, to stir up again; to revive: *ciò ha rinfocolato l'interesse per queste cose*, this has stirred up interest in these things again; — *un vecchio rancore*, to stir up an old grudge.

rinfoderàre, *v.t.* to sheathe (again) || **rinfoderàrsi**, *v.r.* to withdraw into one's shell.

rinforzaménto, *s.m.* strengthening, reinforcement.

rinforzàre, *v.t.* 1. to strengthen, to make stronger: *questa medicina ti rinforzerà*, this medicine will make you stronger; — *i muscoli*, to strengthen the muscles; — *la voce*, to strengthen the voice || — *la concentrazione di una soluzione*, (*chim.*) to strengthen a solution 2. (*mil.*) to reinforce: — *le truppe*, to reinforce the troops 3. (*accrescere la stabilità di*) to reinforce, to strengthen, to back; (*con contrafforti*) to prop up: — *agli appoggi*, (*edil.*) to reinforce at bearings; — *un muro*, to back (o to reinforce) a wall; — *le vele, gli alberi*, (*mar.*) to strengthen the sails, the masts 4. (*foto.*) to intensify 5. (*mec.*) to stiffen 6. *fig.* (*ribadire, avvalorare*) to support, to back: — *i propri argomenti, le proprie ragioni*, to support one's arguments, reasons || *v.i.* 1. to strengthen 2. (*di pioggia*) to become heavier; (*di vento*) to grow stronger || **rinforzàrsi**, *v.r.* to become stronger; to make oneself stronger.

rinforzàto, *ag.* 1. strengthened, reinforced 2. (*mil.*) reinforced 3. (*edil. mar.*) strengthened; (*con contrafforti*) propped up 4. (*mec.*) stiffened 5. *fig.* strengthened, supported, backed.

rinfòrzo, *s.m.* 1. strengthening, reinforcement 2. *rinforzi, truppe di* —, (*mil.*) reinforcements: *sono stati mandati rinforzi al fronte*, reinforcements have been sent to the front 3. (*edil.*) reinforcement, strengthening, bracing, backing; (*con contrafforti*) propping up: — *d'angolo*, angle-brace 4. (*foto.*) intensification 5. (*mec.*) stiffener; (*di gomma*) chafing strip 6. (*per calzature*) support 7. *fig.* (*aiuto, sostegno*) help, support.

rinfrancàre, *v.t.* (*incoraggiare*) to re-invigorate; to reanimate; to encourage: *la loro buona accoglienza lo rinfrancò*, their welcome encouraged him || **rinfrancàrsi**, *v.r.* 1. (*riprendere coraggio*) to pluck up courage again, to take heart again 2. (*migliorare*) to improve (sthg.): *starò in Inghilterra un anno per rinfrancarmi in inglese*, I shall stay in England a year to improve my English.

rinfràngere, *V.* **infràngere**.

rinfrescaménto, *s.m.* 1. cooling 2. *fig.* refreshing.

rinfrescànte, *ag.* cooling; refreshing: *bibita* —, refreshing drink || *s.m.* gentle laxative.

rinfrescàre, *v.t.* 1. to cool, to make cooler: *il temporale ha rinfrescato l'aria*, the storm has cooled the air; — *il vino*, to cool the wine 2. (*ristorare*) to refresh: *ho rinfrescato i cavalli*, I have refreshed the horses 3. (*mettere a nuovo*) to do up, to renovate; (*ritoccare*) to restore: *devo far* — *la mia casa quest'anno*, I must have my house done up this year; — *un qua-*

dro, to restore a picture || *far* — *un abito*, to renovate a dress 4. *fig.* (*rinnovare*): — *la battaglia*, to renew the battle; — *la memoria*, to refresh one's memory 5. (*agr.*) to plough: — *un campo*, to plough a field || *v.i.* 1. to cool: *alla sera l'aria rinfresca*, in the evening the air cools 2. (*di vento che diventa più gagliardo*) to freshen || **rinfrescàrsi**, *v.r.* to refresh oneself: *ci fermeremo a rinfrescarci lungo la strada*, we shall stop on the way to take some refreshments; *vorrei rinfrescarmi con qualche bevanda, con una bella doccia*, I should like to refresh myself with a drink, with a nice shower.

rinfrescèata, *s.f.* 1. (*diminuzione di temperatura*) cooling: *starò in campagna fino alle prime rinfrescate*, I shall stay in the country till the weather gets cooler 2. *darsi una* —, to freshen oneself up: *mi darò solo una* — *alle mani*, I shall just wash my hands.

rinfrescatìvo, *ag.* refreshing.

rinfrèsco, *s.m.* 1. refreshments (*pl.*): *il* — *era piuttosto meschino*, the refreshments were rather scanty 2. (*ricevimento*) cocktail party: *invitare per un* —, to invite to a cocktail party.

rinfronzìre, *v.i.* to put out new leaves || **rinfronzìrsi**, *v.r.* (*agghindarsi*) to titivate oneself.

rinfronzolàrsi, rinfronzolìrsi, *v.r.* to titivate oneself, to deck oneself out.

rinfùsa, àlla, *l.av.* in confusion: *carico alla* —, (*mar.*) loaded in bulk.

ringabbiàre, *v.t.* 1. to cage again 2. *fig.* (*imprigionare di nuovo*) to imprison again.

ringagliardiménto, *s.m.* strengthening.

ringagliardìre, *v.t.* to reinvigorate, to strengthen || *v.i.*, **ringagliardìrsi**, *v.r.* to become more vigorous.

ringalluzzàre, ringalluzzìre, *v.t.* to elate; to make cocky, to make jaunty: *il successo lo ha ringalluzzito*, his success has made him cocky (o jaunty) || *v.i.*, **ringalluzzàrsi, ringalluzzìrsi**, *v.r.* to become cocky, to get cocky, to become jaunty, to get jaunty, to become elated: *quando parla della sua giovinezza ringalluzzisce tutto*, when he talks about his youth he becomes elated.

ringalluzzìto, *ag.* cocky, jaunty, elated, proud.

ringambàre, *v.t.* to strengthen || *v.i.* to become stronger.

ringentilìre, *v.t.* to refine, to make more refined: *l'arte ringentilisce l'animo*, art refines the soul; *il vivere con quella persona lo ha ringentilito*, living with that person has made him more refined || *v.i.*, **ringentilìrsi**, *v.r.* to become (more) refined.

ringhiàre, *v.i.* to growl, to snarl (anche *fig.*).

ringhièra, *s.f.* railings (*pl.*); (*della scala*) banisters (*pl.*): *afferrarsi alla* —, to hold on to the banisters.

rìnghio, *s.m.* growl, snarl (anche *fig.*).

ringhiosaménte, *av.* with a growl, with a snarl (anche *fig.*).

ringhióso, *ag.* snarling; *fig.* (*che brontola*) snappish: *un vecchio* —, a snappish old man.

ringhiottìre, *v.t.* to swallow again.

ringinocchiàre, *v.i.* to kneel (down) again.

ringiovanìre, *v.t.* 1. to make young (again); to rejuvenate: *la gioia lo ha ringiovanito*, joy has made him young again; *quella cura lo ha ringiovanito*, that treatment has rejuvenated him 2. (*far sembrare più giovane*) to make (s.o.) look younger: *il colore di questo abito ti ringiovanisce*, the colour of this dress makes you look younger || *v.i.* 1. to grow young again 2. (*sembrare più giovane*) to look younger: *più diventa vecchia più ringiovanisce*, the older she gets, the younger she looks 3. (*riacquistare vigore*) to recover one's vigour 4. (*di albero*) to put out new leaves.

ringiovanìto, *ag.* young again, rejuvenated: *sembrare* —, to seem rejuvenated; *sentirsi* —, to feel young again.

ringoiàre, *v.t.* 1. to swallow again 2. (*ritrattare*) to withdraw: *ringoiò tutte le sue ingiurie*, he withdrew all his insults ‖ **ringoiàrsi**, *v.r.* (*ritrattare*) to withdraw.

ringolfàrsi, *v.r.* **1.** (*immergersi di nuovo*) to plunge again (into sthg.) **2.** *fig.* (*impelagarsi di nuovo*) to get entangled again.

ringollàre, *v.t.* **1.** to swallow again **2.** *fig.* (*trattenere*) to hold back, to check: — *il pianto*, to hold back one's tears.

ringorgàre, *v.i.* **1.** to be obstructed, to be blocked **2.** (*formar gorghi*) to form whirlpools **3.** (*rigurgitare*) to overflow, to flood.

ringórgo, *s.m.* **1.** overflowing **2.** (*gorgo*) whirlpool.

ringrandíre, *v.t.* to make larger, to enlarge ‖ *v.i.* to become larger.

ringraziaménto, *s.m.* **1.** thanks (*pl.*): *lettera di —*, letter of thanks; *i miei migliori ringraziamenti a tutti voi*, my best thanks to all of you; *moltissimi ringraziamenti per quello che hai fatto*, very many thanks for what you have done; *esprimere il proprio —*, to express one's thanks; *fare i propri ringraziamenti a qlcu.*, to thank s.o. **2.** (*eccl.*) thanksgiving.

ringraziàre, *v.t.* **1.** to thank: *devi — solo te stesso per questo*, you have only yourself to thank for it; *— di cuore, sentitamente*, to thank heartily, sincerely; *— qlcu. per ql.co.*, to thank s.o. for sthg. ‖ *sia ringraziato il cielo!*, thank heavens! **2.** (*declinare*) to decline: *volevano fargli festa, ma egli ringraziò*, they wanted to give a party in his honour, but he declined.

ringrullíre, *v.i.* to grow stupid, to become stupid.

ringuainàre, *v.t.* to sheathe (again): — *la spada*, to sheathe one's sword (again).

riníte, *s.f.* (*patol.*) rhinitis.

rinnegaménto, *s.m.* disowning, repudiation, recantation; disavowal; (*di fede*) denial, abjuration.

rinnegàre, *v.t.* to disown, to repudiate, to recant; to disavow; to deny: *Pietro rinnegò Cristo tre volte*, Peter denied Christ thrice; — *gli amici*, to repudiate one's friends; — *il proprio partito*, to disown (o to deny) one's party; — *la propria religione*, to deny one's religion.

rinnegàta, *s.f.* renegade.

rinnegàto, *ag.* renegade: *cristiano —*, renegade Christian ‖ *s.m.* renegade.

rinnegatóre, *s.m.*, **rinnegatríce**, *s.f.* denier, disowner, renegade.

rinnegazióne, *V.* **rinnegaménto**.

rinnervàrsi, *v.r.* to regain strength.

rinnestàre, *v.t.* **1.** (*agr.*) to graft again, to regraft **2.** (*med.*) to revaccinate **3.** (*ricongiungere*) to rejoin **4.** (*mec.*) to re-engage: —'*una marcia*, to re-engage a gear.

rinnèsto, *s.m.* **1.** (*agr.*) new grafting, regrafting **2.** (*med.*) revaccination.

rinnobilíre, *v.t.* to ennoble (anche *fig.*).

rinnovàbile, *ag.* renewable.

rinnovaménto, *s.m.* **1.** renewal **2.** (*rinascita*) revival.

rinnovàre, *v.t.* **1.** to renew: — *un assalto*, to renew an attack; — *una cambiale, un contratto*, (*comm.*) to renew a bill, a contract; — *una conoscenza*, to renew an acquaintance; — *una richiesta*, to renew (o to repeat) a request; — *i ringraziamenti a*, to thank again: *voglio rinnovarti i miei ringraziamenti*, I want to thank you again; — *le scuse*, to apologize again; — *gli sforzi*, to renew one's efforts **2.** (*ridestare*) to renew, to rouse again: — *un dolore*, to renew a sorrow; — *la pietà, l'entusiasmo*, to renew pity, enthusiasm **3.** (*cambiare*) to renew, to change: — *l'aria in una stanza*, to change the air in a room (o to let fresh air into a room o to air a room); — *la casa*, to redecorate (o to do up) one's house; — *il guardaroba*, to renew one's wardrobe; — *il personale di servizio*, to make a complete change of servants (o to renew one's staff) **4.** (*rinvigorire*) to invigorate: — *la vite, l'ulivo*, to strengthen the vine, the olive ‖ **rinnovàrsi**, *v.r.* to happen again,

to be repeated: *spero che ciò non si rinnovi*, I hope this will not happen again.

rinnovatóre, *s.m.*, **rinnovatríce**, *s.f.* renewer.

rinnovazióne, *s.f.* renewal, renovation.

rinnovellàre, *v.t.* (*letter.*) to renew: *ciò rinnovella il mio dolore*, this renews my sorrow ‖ **rinnovellàrsi**, *v.r.* (*letter.*) to be renewed.

rinnòvo, *s.m.* renewal: — *dell'atto di citazione*, (*dir.*) renewal of the writ of summons; *il — di una cambiale*, the renewal of a bill; *avviso di —*, renewal notice.

rinobilitàre, *v.t.* to ennoble again, to dignify again.

rinocerónte, *s.m.* rhinoceros (*pl.* rhinoceros, rhinoceroses).

rinofonìa, rinolalìa, *s.f.* rhinophonia, rhinolalia.

rinolaringíte, *s.f.* (*patol.*) rhinolaryngitis.

rinologìa, *s.f.* (*med.*) rhinology.

rinomànza, *s.f.* renown, fame, celebrity.

rinomàre, *v.t.* **1.** to repeat the name of (s.o., sthg.) **2.** (*render celebre*) to make famous, to make celebrated.

rinomàto, *ag.* renowned, famous.

rinominàre, *v.t.* **1.** to name again **2.** (*designare di nuovo*) to reappoint **3.** (*rieleggere*) to re-elect.

rinoplastìa, rinoplàstica, *s.f.* (*chir.*) rhinoplasty.

rinorragìa, *s.f.* (*patol.*) rhinorrhagia.

rinorrèa, *s.f.* (*patol.*) rhinorrhœa.

rinoscopìa, *s.f.* (*med.*) rhinoscopy.

rinoscòpio, *s.m.* (*med.*) rhinoscope.

rinotificàre, *v.t.* to notify again.

rinquadràre, *v.t.* **1.** to reframe **2.** (*mil.*) to regroup.

rinquattrinàre, *v.t.* to give more money to (s.o.), to supply money to (s.o.) ‖ **rinquattrinàrsi**, *v.r.* to provide oneself with money again.

rinsaccaménto, *s.m.* repacking, packing again.

rinsaccàre, *v.t.* to repack, to pack again ‖ *v.i.*, **rinsaccàrsi**, *v.r.* to shrug one's shoulders.

rinsaldaménto, *s.m.* **1.** (*l'inamidare di nuovo*) starching again **2.** *fig.* (*consolidamento*) strengthening, consolidating.

rinsaldàre, *v.t.* **1.** (*inamidare di nuovo*) to starch again **2.** *fig.* (*consolidare*) to strengthen, to consolidate: *in questi ultimi anni egli ha rinsaldato la sua posizione in quella ditta*, in recent years he has consolidated his position in that firm; *la sua risposta rinsaldò la mia opinione*, his answer strengthened my opinion.

rinsanguàre, *v.t.* **1.** to supply with new blood, to transfuse new blood into (s.o.), to reinvigorate **2.** *fig.* (*ridare vigore a*) to give new strength to (s.o., sthg.), to give new life to (s.o. sthg.) ‖ **rinsanguàrsi**, *v.r.* **1.** to recover, to become stronger **2.** *fig.* (*rifornirsi di denaro*) to re-establish one's financial condition.

rinsanguinàre, *v.t.* to stain with blood again ‖ **rinsanguinàrsi**, *v.r.* to become blood-stained again.

rinsaníre, *v.i.* **1.** to recover (one's health) **2.** (*rinsavire*) to recover one's wits, to return to reason.

rinsaviménto, *s.m.* return to reason: *dopo il suo —*, after he recovered his wits.

rinsavíre, *v.i.* to recover one's wits, to return to reason, to come to one's senses, to become sane again.

rinselvàre, *v.t.* (*rar.*) to reafforest ‖ **rinselvàrsi**, *v.r.* to become forested again.

rinselvatichíre, *v.i.* to grow wild again.

rinserràre, *v.t.* to shut up again ‖ **rinserràrsi**, *v.r.* to shut oneself up.

rinsudiciàre, *v.t.* to soil again ‖ **rinsudiciàrsi**, *v.r.* to become soiled again, to get soiled again.

rinsuperbíre, *v.i.* to become proud again; to become more arrogant.

rintàllo, *s.m.* (*bot.*) superfluous thallus.

rintanàrsi, *v.r.* **1.** to shut oneself up **2.** (*nascondersi*) to hide oneself: *dov'è andato a —?*, where has he gone and hidden himself?.

rintasàre, *v.t.* to clog again, to choke up again.

rintaseàre, *v.t.* to pocket again.

rintavolàre, *v.t.* **1.** (*a scacchi*) to set (chessmen) on the board again **2.** *fig.* (*incominciare di nuovo*) to start again.

rintegràre, *e derivati*, *V.* **reintegràre**, *e derivati*.

rinteneríre, *v.t.* **1.** to soften again **2.** *fig.* to move again || **rintenerírsi**, *v.r.* to be moved, to be affected.

rintepidíre, *v.i.* to become lukewarm (*anche fig.*).

rinterraménto, *s.m.* filling up (with earth).

rinterràre, *v.t.* to fill up (with earth).

rintèrro, *s.m.* filling up (with earth).

rinterzàre, *v.t.* **1.** (*triplicare*) to triplicate, to treble **2.** (*dividere in tre parti*) to divide into three parts.

rintiepidíre, *v.i.* to become lukewarm (*anche fig.*).

rintoccàre, *v.i.* **1.** (*di orologio*) to strike; (*di campana*) to toll **2.** (*risonare*) to echo.

rintócco, *s.m.* (*di orologio*) stroke; (*di campana*) toll, tolling: *i rintocchi di una campana*, the tolling of a bell; — *funebre*, knell.

rintonacàre, *v.t.* to plaster again.

rintònaco, *s.m.* new plaster.

rintonàre, *v.t.* to intone again.

rintontíre, *v.i.*, **rintontírsi**, *v.r.* to be stupefied again.

rintorpidíre, *v.t.* to make torpid again || **rintorpidírsi**, *v.r.* to become torpid, to grow torpid.

rintracciàbile, *ag.* traceable; (*trovabile*) findable.

rintracciaménto, *s.m.* tracing; (*il trovare*) finding.

rintracciàre, *v.t.* **1.** to trace; to track: — *le cause di un fatto*, *le origini di una famiglia*, to trace the causes of a fact, the origins of a family; — *un ladro*, to trace a thief; — *una lepre*, to track a hare **2.** (*trovare*) to find (out): *ho rintracciato quel libro*, I have found that book; *l'influsso di questo filosofo si rintraccia nelle opere dei suoi contemporanei*, the influence of this philosopher is to be found in the works of his contemporaries; *non hanno ancora rintracciato chi ne è responsabile*, they have not yet found out who is responsible (for it).

rintrecciàre, *v.t.* to intertwine.

rintristíre, *v.i.* to droop again.

rintrodúrre, *v.t.* to reintroduce.

rintronaménto, *s.m.* (*rimbombo*) boom; booming.

rintronàre, *v.t.* **1.** (*assordire*) to deafen; (*stordire*) to stun: *la sua voce mi rintronò gli orecchi*, his voice almost deafened me **2.** (*scuotere*) to shake || *v.i.* to boom; to resound: *i cannoni rintronavano nella notte*, the guns were booming in the night.

rintròno, *s.m.* (*rar.*) boom.

rintuòno, *s.m.* faint boom; faint booming.

rintuzzaménto, *s.m.* **1.** blunting **2.** (*repressione*) repressing, repression; abating **3.** (*il ribattere*) retorting.

rintuzzàre, *v.t.* **1.** (*spuntare*) to blunt **2.** (*reprimere*) to repress; to abate: — *le speranze di qlcu.*, to abate s.o.'s hopes **3.** (*ribattere*) to retort, to fling back: — *un'accusa*, to retort (*o* to fling back) an accusation.

rinúncia, **rinúnzia**, *s.f.* renunciation, renouncement; (*dir.*) release.

rinunziaménto, *s.m.* renouncement, renouncing.

rinunziànte, *ag.* renouncing || *s.c.* renouncer.

rinunziàre, *v.t.i.* **1.** to renounce, to give up; to for(e)go: — (*a*)*i divertimenti*, to forgo amusements; — *al piacere di fare ql.co.*, to give up the pleasure of doing sthg.; — *al trono*, to renounce the throne || — (*a*) *un diritto*, to waive a right **2.** (*abbandonare*) to relinquish: — (*al*)*la speranza*, to relinquish hope **3.** (*dir.*) to release.

rinunziatàrio, *s.m.* (*dir.*) releasee.

rinunziatóre, *ag.* renouncing || *s.m.*, **rinunziatríce**, *s.f.* renouncer; (*dir.*) releasor.

rinvangàre, *V.* **rivangàre**.

rinveleníre, *v.t.* to embitter (again) || **rinvelenírsi**, *v.r.* to become embittered again.

rinveníbile, *ag.* recoverable, retraceable.

rinveniménto, *s.m.* **1.** (*scoperta*) discovery, recovery **2.** (*il ricuperare i sensi*) recovery, coming to one's senses.

rinveníre, *v.t.* **1.** (*trovare*) to find: — *un libro raro*, to find a rare book **2.** (*scoprire*) to discover, to find out: — *un nuovo congegno*, to discover a new device || *v.i.* **1.** (*ricuperare i sensi*) to recover one's senses, to come to oneself: *ella svenne, ma rinvenne dopo pochi minuti*, she fainted but she came to herself after a few minutes **2.** (*riprendere morbidezza*) to soften; to become flexible again; (*riprendere freschezza*) to revive: *i fiori rinvengono se messi nell'acqua*, flowers revive when placed in water; *questo cuoio rinviene ungendolo*, this leather becomes flexible again on being greased; *l'uva passa rinviene facilmente nell'acqua tiepida*, raisins soften easily in lukewarm water.

rinverdíre, *v.t.* **1.** to make green again **2.** (*ravvivare*) to reawaken, to rekindle: — *le speranze di qlcu.*, to reawaken s.o.'s hopes || *v.i.* **1.** (*tornare verde*) to grow green again, to turn green again **2.** (*ravvivarsi*) to revive, to take on new life.

rinverniciàre, *v.t.* (*con tinta trasparente*) to revarnish; (*con tinta opaca*) to repaint.

rinverzàre, *v.t.* to plug, to block up.

rinverzicàre, *V.* **rinverdíre**.

rinvestiménto, *s.m.* **1.** (*comm.*) reinvestment **2.** (*dei fiaschi*) re-covering with straw.

rinvestíre, *v.t.* **1.** (*rimettere in possesso*) to restore to the possession of (sthg.): *fu rinvestito di tutti i suoi titoli*, he was restored to the possession of all his titles (*o* all his titles were restored to him) **2.** (*comm.*) to reinvest.

rinvestitúra, *V.* **rinvestiménto**.

rinviàre, *v.t.* **1.** to put off, to postpone, to defer, to adjourn: *ho rinviato il mio arrivo*, I have put off (*o* deferred *o* postponed) my arrival; *l'incontro fu rinviato di una settimana*, the meeting was adjourned for a week; *la lezione fu rinviata alla settimana seguente*, the lesson was put off until the following week; — *ad altra data*, to defer (sthg.) to a later date; — *una causa*, (*dir.*) to adjourn a case; — *il pagamento di una somma*, to postpone the payment of a sum **2.** (*mandare indietro*) to return, to send back: — *la palla*, (*spor.*) to return the ball.

rinvigoriménto, *s.m.* strengthening, reinvigoration.

rinvigoríre, *v.t.* to reinvigorate; to instil new life into (s.o.): *esercizio che rinvigorisce il corpo*, exercise that reinvigorates the body; — *i soldati*, to instil new life into the soldiers || *v.i.*, **rinvigorírsi**, *v.r.* to become reinvigorated; to regain strength: *mi sento rinvigorito*, I feel another person.

rinvílio, *s.m.* drop, fall (in price).

rinvilíre, *v.t.* to lower, to reduce: — *i prezzi*, to lower (*o* to reduce) prices || *v.i.* to fall (in price), to become cheaper: *lo zucchero rinvilisce*, sugar is becoming cheaper (*o* falling in price).

rinviluppàre, *v.t.* to rewrap, to wrap up again.

rinvío, *s.m.* **1.** postponement, deferment, adjournment: *il — di una causa*, (*dir.*) the adjournment of a case; *il — di una partenza*, the postponement of a departure **2.** (*il rimandare indietro*) returning, sending back.

rinvispíre, *v.i.* to become lively again.

rinvitàre[1], *v.t.* to re-invite, to invite again || **rinvitàrsi**, *v.r. reciproco*, to invite each other (one another) again.

rinvitàre[2], *v.t.* (*avvitare di nuovo*) to screw (up) again.

rinvivíre, *v.i.* to revive: *i fiori rinvivíscono nell'acqua*, flowers revive in water.

rinvogliàre, *v.t.* to entice again; (*allettare di nuovo*) to allure again.

rinvòlgere, *v.t.* to rewrap, to wrap up again || **rinvòlgersi**, *v.r.* to wrap oneself up (again).

rinvoltàre, *v.t.* to wrap up again.

rinvòlto, *s.m.* (*rar.*) parcel.

rinvoltolàre, *V.* **avvoltolàre**.

rinvoltúra, *s.f.* **1.** wrapping **2.** (*tela per la mer-*

canzia) canvas (for covering goods) **3.** (*intreccio*) plot (of a play) **4.** (*ret.*) (*eufemismo*) euphemism.

rinzaccheràre, *v.t.* to make muddy again, to be-mire again ‖ **rinzaccheràrsi,** *v.r.* to get muddy again.

rinzaffàre, *v.t.* **1.** to bung again **2.** (*edil.*) to rough in, to give a first coat of plaster to (sthg.).

rinzaffatúra, *s.f.*, **rinzàffo,** *s.m.* (*edil.*) roughing-in (coat).

rinzeppàre, *v.t.* to cram, to stuff ‖ **rinzeppàrsi,** *v.r.* to cram (oneself), to stuff (oneself).

rinzeppatúra, *s.f.* **1.** (*zeppa*) wedge **2.** (*il rinzep-pare*) cramming, stuffing.

rinzolfàre, *v.t.* to treat with sulphur again.

río[1], *s.m.* **1.** (*poet.*) rivulet; brook, stream **2.** (*a Ve-nezia*) canal.

río[2], *ag.* (*malvagio*) wicked, bad, evil.

rioccupàre, *v.t.* to reoccupy ‖ **rioccupàrsi,** *v.r.* to occupy oneself again.

rioccupazióne, *s.f.* reoccupation.

Río délle Amàzzoni (il), *no.pr.* (*geog.*) the (river) Amazon.

rioffèndere, *v.t.* to reoffend, to offend again.

rioffríre, *v.t.* to reoffer, to offer again.

rionàle, *ag.* ward (*attributivo*): *mercato* —, local market.

rióne, *s.m.* ward; district, quarter; neighbourhood: *ufficio postale del* —, local post-office.

rionoràre, *v.t.* to rehonour, to honour again.

rioperàre, *v.t.* (*chir.*) to reoperate: — *qlcu.*, to op-erate (up)on s.o. again ‖ *v.i.* to act again, to have an effect again: *medicina che riopera,* medicine that has a repeated effect.

riordinaménto, *s.m.* **1.** rearrangement: — *di una biblioteca,* rearrangement of a library; *lavoro di* —, work of rearrangement **2.** (*riorganizzazione*) reorgani-zation: — *dell'esercito,* reorganization of the army.

riordinàre, *v.t.* **1.** to (re)arrange, to put in order again; to tidy up, to retidy: *devo* — *le mie carte sulla scrivania,* I must tidy up my papers on the desk; *dovresti* — *un po' le idee,* you should try to arrange your ideas a little; *riordina almeno la tua stanza,* tidy up your room at least **2.** (*riorganizzare*) to reor-ganize: *riordinò le finanze mediante un sistema rigidis-simo di tassazione,* he reorganized the finances by a very strict system of taxation; *riordinò la scuola con principi moderni,* he reorganized the school according to modern principles **3.** (*comandare di nuovo*) to reorder, to order again: *il carbone non è arrivato, riordinalo,* the coal has not arrived, will you order it again? ‖ **rior-dinàrsi,** *v.r.* to tidy oneself up, to put oneself in order: *devo riordinarmi prima di uscire,* I must tidy myself up before going out; *perchè non ti riordini i capelli prima di pranzo?,* why don't you tidy up your hair before dinner?.

riordinatóre, *s.m.*, **riordinatríce,** *s.f.* **1.** rearrang-er **2.** (*chi riorganizza*) reorganizer.

riordinazióne, *s.f.* **1.** rearrangement **2.** (*riorganiz-zazione*) reorganization **3.** (*nuova ordinazione*) new order **4.** (*eccl.*) new ordination.

riórdino, (*rar.*) per **riordinaménto.**

riordíre, *v.t.* **1.** to reweave **2.** *fig.* to rehatch.

riorganizzàre, *v.t.* to reorganize: *riorganizzò l'eser-cito,* he reorganized the army ‖ **riorganizzàrsi,** *v.r.* to reorganize oneself: *il partito si sta riorganizzando,* the party is getting reorganized.

riorganizzatóre, *s.m.*, **riorganizzatríce,** *s.f.* reor-ganizer.

riorganizzazióne, *s.f.* reorganization.

riosservàre, *v.t.* to reobserve, to observe again.

riottosaménte, *av.* **1.** quarrelsomely, turbulent-ly **2.** (*indocilmente*) intractably.

riottóso, *ag.* **1.** quarrelsome, turbulent **2.** (*indocile*) indocile, intractable.

riotturàre, *v.t.* to stop again; to refill: *ieri mi sono fatto* — *un dente,* I had a tooth refilled yesterday.

rípa, *s.f.* **1.** (*riva*) bank ‖ -*uccelli di* —, riparian birds **2.** (*luogo scosceso*) escarpment.

ripacificàre, *V.* **rappacificàre.**

ripagàre, *v.t.* **1.** (*pagare di nuovo*) to pay again: *ho perso la ricevuta e ho dovuto ripagare,* I lost my receipt and had to pay again **2.** (*ricompensare*) to repay, to reward; to requite: *ha ripagato le mie gentilezze con l'ingratitudine più nera,* he has repaid my kind-ness with the blackest ingratitude; *non ripagherai mai abbastanza i tuoi genitori di tutto quello che hanno fatto per te,* you will never repay your parents enough for what they have done for you **3.** (*risarcire*) to replace: *questo vaso l'hai rotto tu, e tu lo ripagherai,* this vase was broken by you and you shall have to replace it.

ripalpàre, *v.t.* **1.** to feel again, to touch again **2.** (*med.*) to palpate again.

riparàbile, *ag.* reparable, emendable.

riparàre[1], *v.t.* **1.** (*proteggere*) to shelter, to protect; to shield, to screen: — *dal freddo, dal sole, dalla piog-gia, dal vento,* to shelter from the cold, from the sun, from the rain, from the wind; *quegli alberi riparano la casa dal vento,* those trees shield (o screen) the house from the wind; *questi occhiali riparano gli occhi dal bagliore della neve,* these goggles shield your eyes from the glare of the snow **2.** (*aggiustare*) to repair, to mend; (*mec.*) to repair, to fix; (*mar.*) to refit: *la casa deve essere riparata,* the house needs putting in order; — *un motore,* to recondition a motor; — *un muro, una rottura,* to repair a wall, a break; — *una scarpa,* to repair (o to mend) a shoe; — *un vestito,* to mend a dress **3.** (*risarcire*) to redress, to make amends for (sthg.): — *un danno, un torto,* to redress an injury, a wrong; — *un'ingiustizia,* to rectify (o to make good) an injustice; — *una malefatta,* to undo a piece of mischief ‖ — *il tempo perduto,* to make up for lost time **4.** (*rimediare*) — *un esame,* to repeat an examination **5.** (*parare*) to parry, to ward off: — *un colpo,* to parry a blow ‖ *v.i.* (*porre rimedio*) to remedy (sthg.), to make up (for sthg.); to redress (sthg.): — *ad un inconveniente,* to remedy (o to put right) a defect; — *ad un maldestro,* to make good a piece of damage; — *ad una perdita,* to make up for a loss ‖ **riparàrsi,** *v.r.* (*difendersi*) to protect oneself: *porto il cappotto per ripararmi dal freddo,* I wear an overcoat to protect myself from the cold.

riparàre[2], *v.i.* (*rifugiarsi*) to take shelter, to take refuge; to repair (to a place): *ripararono in una ca-verna,* they took shelter (o cover) in a cave; *ripararono in Francia,* they repaired to France ‖ **riparàrsi,** *v.r.* to take shelter, to take cover.

riparàto, *ag.* sheltered.

riparatóre, *ag.* repairing, restoring ‖ *s.m.*, **ripara-tríce,** *s.f.* repairer, mender.

riparazióne, *s.f.* **1.** repairing; repair, reparation; (*mec.*) repair, fixing; (*mar.*) refit: *in* —, under repair: *una casa in* —, a house under repair; *strada in* —, road up; *devo far fare una* — *a queste scarpe,* I must have these shoes repaired; *questo vestito ha bisogno di qualche* —, this dress needs some repairing; *fare delle riparazioni,* to do some repairs **2.** *fig.* reparation, atonement; amends (*pl.*), redress: *riparazioni di guerra,* war reparations; *in* — *di un torto,* in reparation of (o in atonement for o as amends for) a wrong; *esigere una* —, to demand reparation ‖ *esame di* —, exam done (o repeated) at the October session.

ripàrio, *ag.* riparian: *uccello* —, riparian bird.

riparlàre, *v.i.* to speak again; (*discutere*) to talk over again: *riparlammo di quella questione, ma non riuscii a convincerlo,* we talked that matter over again, but I did not manage to persuade him ‖ *ne riparleremo,* we shall see about it; (*lasciamo ca-dere il discorso*) let's drop the subject ‖ **riparlàrsi,** *v.r. reciproco* (*rappacificarsi*) to become reconciled: *ci riparliamo nonostante tutto,* we are again on speaking terms in spite of everything.

ripàro, *s.m.* **1.** shelter, cover: *dovresti mettere questa pianta al — dai venti,* you should shelter this plant from the wind; *eravamo finalmente al — dalla pioggia torrenziale,* we were at last sheltered from the torrential rain; *non poterono trovare un — sicuro,* they could not find a safe shelter **2.** (*schermo*) protection, defence: *farsi —,* to protect (*o* to shield) oneself **3.** (*rimedio*) remedy, cure: *bisognerà correre ai ripari,* we shall have to do something about it; *non c'è — a questo,* there is no remedy for this; *trovare un — a ql.co.,* to find a remedy for sthg. ‖ *senza —,* irreparably (*o* irretrievably) **4.** (*mec.*) guard: *— contro gli spruzzi di olio,* oil-splash guard; *— della cinghia,* belt safety-guard; *— di protezione del mandrino,* chuck guard **5.** (*mil.*) shelter: *— trasversale di una trincea,* traverse.

ripartíbile, *ag.* (*divisibile*) divisible; (*distribuibile*) distributable.

ripartiménto, *s.m.* **1.** (*divisione*) division; (*distribuzione*) distribution, sharing out **2.** (*scompartimento*) compartment.

ripartíre[1], *v.t.* (*dividere*) to divide, to parcel out; to distribute; (*distribuire*) to share: *il denaro fu ripartito fra di noi,* the money was divided (*o* shared) among us; *il suo latifondo fu ripartito in tante fattorie,* his large estate was parcelled out into so many farms; *il suo patrimonio fu ripartito fra gli eredi,* his estate was shared among his heirs.

ripartíre[2], *v.i.* (*partire di nuovo*) to leave again, to start again, to set out again; (*mec.*) to start again ‖ *far —,* (*mec.*) to restart: *far — una macchina,* to get a car to start again.

ripartitaménte, *av.* in lots; separately.

ripartizióne, *s.f.* (*divisione*) division; (*distribuzione*) distribution, allotment, sharing out: *una — diseguale della ricchezza,* an unequal distribution of wealth; *opportuna — delle spese,* proper allotment of expenses.

ripàrto, *s.m.* **1.** repartition, distribution **2.** (*comm.*) allotment: *fare un — di azioni,* to allot shares; *rinunciare al —,* to renounce one's claim to allotment **3.** (*scompartimento*) compartment.

ripassàre, *v.t.* **1.** (*attraversare di nuovo*) to cross again, to recross: *— un fiume, l'oceano,* to cross a river, the ocean again **2.** (*far passare di nuovo*) to strain again, to re-strain: *il caffè,* to percolate coffee again; *— i pomodori,* to strain tomatoes again **3.** (*dare di nuovo*) to pass again, to hand again: *puoi ripassarmi quel libro?,* can you pass (*o* hand) me that book again? **4.** (*rivedere*) to revise; (*rileggere*) to read over again, to look over again; to have a look at (sthg.), to go through (sthg.): *ho ripassato il suo lavoro e non ho trovato errori,* I have gone through his work and have not found any mistakes; *vorrei — questo libro per trovare quel nome,* I should like to go through this book to find that name; *— i conti,* to review the accounts; *— una lezione,* to revise a lesson **5.** (*ritoccare*) to give a finishing touch to (sthg.); (*mec.*) to overhaul: *dissi al verniciatore di — questa porta,* I told the decorator to give this door a fresh coat of paint; *— al trapano,* (*mec.*) to redrill; *— un cuscinetto,* (*mec.*) to reface a bearing; *—una macchina, un motore,* (*mec.*) to overhaul a car, an engine (*o* a motor); *— le sedi delle valvole,* (*mec.*) to regrind the valve seats **6.** (*percuotere*) to give a (sound) thrashing to (s.o.): *gli hanno ripassato ben bene le costole,* they gave him a sound thrashing (*o* a good licking) ‖ *v.i.* to pass again (through a place); to call again (on s.o.): *ripasserò da Milano la settimana ventura,* I shall be passing through Milan again next week; *ripasserò da te domani,* I'll call on you again tomorrow; *ripasserò di qui fra poco,* I shall come this way again before long.

ripassàta, *s.f.* **1.** (*il passare di nuovo*) *mi vedrai alla mia,* you will see me when I come back this way **2.** (*scorsa*) another look: *dare una — a una lezione,* to look (*o* to read) over a lesson again (*o* to go

through a lesson again) **3.** (*pulita*) clean(ing); (*mec.*) (*revisione*) overhaul(ing): *dare una — ad un motore,* to give an engine an overhaul(ing); *dare una — ad una stanza,* to give a room a clean(ing); *dare una — ad un vestito,* to spruce up a dress; *dare una — al tavolo,* to give the table a wipe over **4.** (*mano*): *dare una — di vernice a ql.co.,* to give sthg. a new coat of paint **5.** (*rabbuffo*) scolding, telling-off: *gli ho dato una buona —,* I gave him a jolly good scolding.

ripasseggiàre, *v.i.* to walk again.

ripàsso, *s.m.* **1.** (*ritorno*) return **2.** (*revisione*) revision: *esercizi di —,* revision (*o* recapitulation) exercises; *stiamo facendo il — del programma di inglese,* we are going through our English programme again.

ripàtico, *s.m.* river port, fluvial port.

ripeggioràre, *v.t.* to worsen again, to make worse again; to make worse and worse ‖ *v.i.* to worsen again.

ripensaménto, *s.m.* reflection.

ripensàre, *v.i.* **1.** to think of (sthg.) again; to think (sthg.) over: *ci ripenserò,* I shall think it over; *lascia che ci ripensi,* let me think it over; *non ci ho mai ripensato,* I have never thought of it again; *ora che ci ripenso...,* now that I think of it... **2.** (*cambiar parere*) to change one's mind: *ci ho ripensato, non lo voglio più,* I have changed my mind, I don't want it any more ‖ *v.t.* (*letter.*) to recall, to evoke.

ripènse, *ag.* (*letter.*) riverside (*attributivo*).

ripentírsi, *e derivati, V.* **pentírsi,** *e derivati.*

ripercórrere, *v.t.* to run over (sthg.) again, to run through (sthg.) again; to travel over (sthg.) again.

ripercòssa, *s.f.* repercussion.

ripercòsso, *ag.* **1.** beaten again **2.** (*riflesso*) reflected.

ripercotiménto, *s.m.* continuous beating.

ripercuòtere, *v.t.* to strike again, to beat again ‖ **ripercuòtersi,** *v.r.* **1.** to reverberate, to re-echo: *il suono si ripercuoteva nella caverna,* the sound reverberated (*o* re-echoed) in the cave **2.** *fig.* to influence (s.o., sthg.): *la sua influenza si ripercuote su tutti i suoi contemporanei,* his influence is to be found in all his contemporaries.

ripercussióne, *s.f.* repercussion (anche *fig.*): *i recenti avvenimenti politici avranno ripercussioni anche nel campo degli affari,* the recent political events will have repercussions in the field of business too.

ripercussívo, *ag.* repercussive.

ripèrdere, *v.t.* to lose again.

riperdonàre, *v.t.* to forgive again.

ripesàre, *v.t.* to reweigh, to weigh again.

ripescàre, *v.t.* **1.** to fish up; to fish out, to catch again: *questa trota era sfuggita, ma poi la ripescai,* this trout had got away, but then I caught it again; *— un cadavere,* to fish out a body **2.** (*ritrovare*) to find again, to get hold of (s.o., sthg.): *non so dove ripescarlo,* I do not know where to get hold of him again; *ripescai quella lettera tra vecchi libri,* I found (*o* came across) that letter again among some old books.

ripésco, *s.m.* (*intrigo*) intrigue.

ripéstare, *v.t.* to pound again; to regrind.

ripetènte, *ag.* repeating ‖ *s.c.:* *in questa classe ci sono tre ripetenti,* in this class there are three students repeating the course they did last year; *mio fratello è —,* my brother is repeating a year at school.

ripètere, *v.t.* **1.** (*rifare*) to repeat: *— un esperimento, un errore, un esame,* to repeat an experiment, a mistake, an examination; *— una classe a scuola,* to repeat a year at school **2.** (*ridire*) to repeat, to say again: *ascoltalo bene perchè non ripete mai quello che ha detto,* listen to him carefully because he never repeats what he has said; *una cosa che si ripete spesso,* a thing that is said over and over again; *glielo ho ripetuto tante volte,* I have told him over and over again; *non — quello che t'ho detto,* don't repeat what I told you; *— una domanda,* to repeat a question; *— una poesia,* to repeat (*o* to practise reciting) a poem ‖ *non me lo farò — due volte,* I shall not need to be told twice ‖ *far — la lezione a qlcu.*, to hear s.o.'s lesson 3. (*derivare da*) to spring from (sthg.), to be derived from (sthg.): *la mitologia romana ripete quella greca*, Roman mythology was derived from that of the Greeks 4. (*teat.*) to rehearse 5. (*dir.*) to ask back, to claim back ‖ **ripètersi**, *v.r.* to repeat oneself: *cura di non ripeterti*, try not to repeat yourself; *la storia si ripete*, history repeats itself.

ripetitóre, *s.m.* 1. repeater: — *d'impulsi*, (*tel.*) impulse repeater; — *di segnali*, (*ferr.*) signal repeater; — *girostatico*, (*mar.*) repeater 2. (*a scuola*) coach, private tutor; (*fam.*) crammer.

ripetizióne, *s.f.* 1. (*rifacimento*) repetition: — *di un esperimento, di un fatto*, repetition of an experiment, of a fact; *è una pura — di quanto è già stato fatto*, it is a mere repetition of what has already been done 2. (*ripasso*) revision: *una — generale della materia alla fine di un trimestre*, a general revision of the subject at the end of a term 3. (*lezione privata*) private lesson: *andare a — da qlcu.*, to take private lessons from s.o. (*o* to get coaching from s.o.); *dare ripetizioni a qlcu.*, to coach s.o. (*o* to give private lessons to s.o.) 4. (*mec.*): *fucile a —*, repeating rifle (*o* repeater); *orologio a —*, repeater (watch) 5. (*mus.*) practice; (*teat.*) rehearsal 6. (*dir.*) claiming back: — *d'indebito*, recovery of payment made by mistake.

ripetutaménte, *av.* repeatedly, again and again, over and over again: *gliel'ho detto —*, I have told him over and over again.

ripetúto, *ag.* repeated.

ripiallàre, *v.t.* to re-plane, to plane again.

ripianàre, *v.t.* to level.

ripiàngere, *v.i.* to cry again, to weep again.

ripiàno, *s.m.* 1. (*scaffale*) shelf 2. (*pianerottolo*) landing 3. (*terreno pianeggiante*) level ground, terrace.

ripiantàre, *v.t.* to replant, to plant again.

ripicchiàre, *v.t.* to beat again, to hit again, to strike again ‖ *v.i.* (*alla porta*) to knock again.

ripicchiàta, *s.f.* 1. another beating 2. (*alla porta*) renewed knocking.

ripícco, *s.m.* spite, pique: *fare ql.co. per —*, to do sthg. out of spite.

ripidaménte, *av.* steeply.

ripidézza, *s.f.* steepness.

ripído, *ag.* steep: *discesa ripida*, steep descent.

ripiegaménto, *s.m.* 1. folding; bending 2. (*mil.*) retreat, withdrawal: — *di forze*, withdrawal of forces.

ripiegàre, *v.t.* 1. to bend again 2. (*piegare*) to fold (up): — *un giornale*, to fold up a newspaper; — *un lenzuolo*, to fold back a sheet 3. (*abbassare*) to lower: — *la bandiera*, to lower the flag ‖ — *le ali*, to fold one's wings (anche *fig.*) 4. (*abbattere*) to overthrow 5. (*rimediare*) to find a remedy for (sthg.): *cercherò di ripiegarla*, I shall try to find a remedy for it ‖ *v.i.* 1. (*dirigersi*) to turn, to bend: *la strada ripiega verso la montagna*, the road bends towards the mountains 2. (*mil.*) (*ritirarsi*) to withdraw, to give ground, to retire: *le nostre truppe furono costrette a —*, our troops were forced to give ground (*o* to retire) ‖ *ripiegò sulla sua precedente posizione*, he retired to his former position ‖ **ripiegàrsi**, *v.r.* to bend: *i rami si ripiegavano sotto il peso dei frutti*, the branches were bending under the weight of the fruit ‖ — *in se stesso*, to retire into oneself.

ripiegàta, *s.f.* folding; bending.

ripiegatúra, *s.f.* 1. (*piega*) fold 2. (*curva*) turn, bend 3. (*il ripiegare*) folding; bending.

ripiègo, *s.m.* (*espediente*) expedient, device; shift, makeshift; (*rimedio*) remedy: *abito di —*, makeshift dress; *un meschino —*, a poor expedient; *ricorrere a un —*, to resort to an expedient; *vivere di ripieghi*, to live on one's wits.

ripienézza, *s.f.* fullness, repletion.

ripièno, *ag.* 1. full; replete (with sthg.): *una bottiglia ripiena d'acqua*, a bottle full of water; *una stanza ripiena di gente*, a room crowded with people 2. (*riem-pito, infarcito*) stuffed (with sthg.): — *di segatura*, stuffed with sawdust; *pollo —*, stuffed chicken 3. (*pervaso*) full; overflowing (with sthg.): — *di contentezza*, overflowing with gladness ‖ *s.m.* 1. filling; (*cuc.*) stuffing: — *di rigaglie*, stuffing of giblets 2. (*trama*) woof, weft 3. (*gonfiezza di stomaco*) fullness, repletion 4. (*cosa, persona che serve a far numero*) make-weight: *qui io ci sono per —*, I am here as a make-weight.

ripigiàre, *v.t.* to re-press, to press again.

ripigliàre, *V.* **riprèndere**.

ripiglíno, *s.m.* (*giuoco infantile*) cat's cradle.

ripiombàre, *v.i.* (*cadere di nuovo*) to fall (down) again; to plunge back: — *sul nemico*, to fall on the enemy once more ‖ *v.t.* 1. (*ricoprire di piombo*) to recover with lead 2. (*far cadere di nuovo*) to plunge back: *la morte di suo padre lo ripiombò nella disperazione*, his father's death plunged him back into despair.

riplasmàre, *v.t.* to remould, to remodel.

ripopolaménto, *s.m.* repeopling, repopulating.

ripopolàre, *v.t.* to repeople, to repopulate: — *una riserva di caccia*, to restock a hunting preserve.

ripòrgere, *v.t.* to hand again, to offer again.

ripórre, *v.t.* 1. to put back, to replace: *ho preso il libro ma l'ho riposto subito*, I took the book but I put it back at once; — *la spada nel fodero*, to sheathe one's sword 2. (*mettere via*) to put away: *quando avrai finito di giocare riponi i tuoi giocattoli*, put your toys away when you have finished playing; *riponi queste carte*, put these papers away; — *un abito per l'inverno*, to put a dress away for the winter; — *il raccolto*, to get the harvest in; — *il vino nelle botti*, to barrel the wine 3. (*collocare*) to place, to put: — *la fiducia, le proprie speranze in qlcu.*, to place confidence, one's hopes in s.o. 4. (*nascondere*) to hide, to conceal ‖ **ripórsi**, *v.r.* 1. (*riprendere*) to resume (sthg.), to start again: — *a lavorare*, to resume work (*o* to start working again *o* to set to work again) 2. (*nascondersi*) to hide (oneself): — *in agguato*, to lie in wait.

riportàre, *v.t.* 1. to bring again; to take again; (*portare indietro*) to bring back; to take back; to carry back: *dai suoi viaggi riportò molte cose*, he brought back a great many things from his travels; *lo riportarono a casa tutto malconcio*, they took (*o* carried) him home in a terrible state; *riportalo qui*, bring it here again; *ti riporterò il libro appena l'ho letto*, I shall bring you back the book as soon as I have read it; — *un lavoro*, to deliver a piece of work 2. (*riferire*) to report, to relate; (*citare*) to quote: *devi — tutto ciò che vedi*, you must report all (that) you see; *ha riportato i minimi dettagli*, he reported every detail; *questo scrittore riporta spesso passi di autori greci*, this writer often quotes passages from Greek authors; *tutti i giornali riportarono la notizia*, all the (news)papers carried the news; — *l'opinione di una persona autorevole*, to quote the opinion of an authority; — *la verità*, to report the truth 3. (*ricevere, conseguire*) to get, to receive; to carry off; (*subire*) to suffer: — *una buona impressione*, to get a good impression; — *un danno*, to suffer damage; — *gravi ferite*, to suffer serious injury (*o* to be seriously injured); — *una leggera ferita*, to be slightly wounded (*o* injured); — *un premio*, to get (*o* to receive *o* to carry off) a prize; — *la vittoria*, to carry off the victory 4. (*arit.*) to carry; (*amm.*) to carry forward: *scrivo 9 e riporto 3*, I write 9 and carry 3; — *una somma alla pagina seguente*, to carry the total forward to the next page 5. (*Borsa*) to carry over, to contango 6. (*disegno*) to transfer ‖ **riportàrsi**, *v.r.* 1. (*tornare*) to go back (anche *fig.*): *dovete riportarvi al quinto secolo*, you must go back to the fifth century; *mi riportai a Roma*, I went back to Rome; *riportati a destra*, move to the right (again) 2. (*rimettersi*) to rely (on sthg.): *mi riporto al suo savio giudizio*, I rely on his wise judgement 3. (*riferirsi*) to refer: *mi riporto a cose che sapete già*, I refer to things you already know; — *alle teorie già esposte,* to refer to the above-mentioned theories.

riportatóre, *s.m.,* **riportatríce,** *s.f.* reporter.

ripòrto, *s.m.* **1.** bringing back ‖ *cane da* —, gun-dog **2.** (*arit.*) amount to be carried **3.** (*borsa*) contango, carry over **4.** (*ornamento*) appliqué (work).

riposànte, *ag.* **1.** restful: *una persona, vita* —, a restful person, life **2.** (*calmante*) soothing **3.** (*piacevole*) pleasant, agreeable.

riposàre, *v.t.* **1.** to rest: *cessò di cantare per* — *la voce,* he stopped singing to rest his voice; *questa luce riposa gli occhi,* this light rests (*o* soothes) the eyes; — *la mente,* to rest the mind **2.** (*posare di nuovo*) to place back, to replace, to put back, to lay down again: *riposa il libro sul tavolo,* put the book back on the table ‖ *v.i.* **1.** to rest, to have a rest, to take a rest; (*dormire*) to sleep: *hai riposato bene?,* have you had a nice rest?; *riposa da due ore,* he has been resting (*o* sleeping) for two hours; *voglio* — *un poco,* I want to rest a little (*o* to have a little rest) ‖ — *sugli allori,* to rest on one's laurels **2.** (*essere sepolto*) to rest, to lie (buried): *egli riposa in questo cimitero,* he rests (*o* lies) in this churchyard **3.** (*poggiare, reggersi*) to rest, to be supported by (sthg.), to be built: *le fondamenta riposano sulla roccia,* the foundations rest (*o* are built) upon rock **4.** (*fidarsi*) to rely upon (s.o., sthg.), to put one's trust in (s.o., sthg.): — *in qlcu.,* to rely on s.o. **5.** (*di terreno*) to rest, to lie fallow: *lasciare* — *la terra,* to let a piece of ground rest (*o* lie fallow) **6.** (*di liquido*) to settle ‖ **riposàrsi,** *v.r.* to rest, to have a rest, to take a rest; (*sdraiarsi*) to lie down: *perchè non ti riposi?,* why don't you take a rest?; *quando mi sento stanco, mi riposo per dieci minuti,* when I feel tired I lie down for ten minutes; *vorrei riposarmi prima di riprendere a lavorare,* I should like to rest before resuming work.

riposàta, *s.f.* **1.** (*riposo*) rest **2.** (*pausa*) pause.

riposataménte, *av.* quietly; peacefully.

riposàto, *ag.* **1.** rested; (*ristorato*) refreshed; (*fresco*) fresh: *mente riposata,* fresh mind **2.** (*tranquillo*) quiet, calm; (*indisturbato*) undisturbed **3.** (*di liquido*) settled: *vino* —, settled wine.

ripòso, *s.m.* **1.** rest, repose: *in* —, at rest: *stare in* —, to be at rest (*o* to rest); *il* — *è necessario,* rest is necessary; *abbiamo avuto due giorni di* —, we have had two days of rest; *faccio sempre un* — *dopo colazione,* I always have a rest after lunch; *mi sono preso un po' di* —, I have taken a little rest; *oggi è un giorno di* —, to-day is a day of rest ‖ —*!,* (*mil.*) stand at ease! ‖ *buon* —*!,* have a nice rest! (*o* sleep well!) ‖ *stasera* —, (*teat.*) no performance to-night ‖ *andare a* —, to retire; *mettere qlcu. a* —, (*per malattia*) to put s.o. on the sick-list; (*per raggiunti limiti di età*) to superannuate s.o. **2.** (*tranquillità, calma*) tranquillity, peace, quiet: *il paese, dopo tante guerre, chiedeva solo* —, the country, after so many wars, wanted only peace **3.** (*di terreno*) fallowing: *terra in* —, fallow land; *stare in* —, to lie fallow **4.** (*mus.*) pause, hold.

ripossedére, *v.t.* to own again, to re-own, to repossess.

ripósta, *s.f.* (*provvista*) provision, supply.

ripostaménte, *av.* secretly, hiddenly.

ripostíglio, *s.m.* **1.** cupboard; storeroom, lumber-room **2.** (*nascondiglio*) hiding-place.

ripósto, *ag.* hidden; (*segreto*) secret: *intenzioni riposte,* secret intentions; *pensieri riposti,* secret thoughts.

ripotàre, *v.t.* to reprune, to prune again, to lop again.

ripranzàre, *v.i.* to dine again.

ripregàre, *v.t.* to pray again; to ask again, to beg again.

ripremiàre, *v.t.* to reward again: to give (s.o.) another prize.

riprèndere, *v.t.* **1.** (*prendere di nuovo*) to retake, to take again; (*riacchiappare*) to catch again: *riprendi il*

tuo posto!, sit down again! (*o* take a seat again!); *devo* — *la medicina?,* shall I take my medicine again?; *ha ripreso l'abitudine di fumare,* he has got into the habit of smoking again; *temo di aver ripreso il raffreddore,* I am afraid I have caught a cold again (*o* I have caught another cold); — *le armi,* to take up arms again; — *il cammino,* to take to the road again: *riprese il cammino verso casa,* he set out for home again ‖ *lo ha ripreso la febbre, la gotta,* he has (had) another bout of fever, another attack of gout ‖ — *coraggio,* to take courage again; — *fiato,* to take breath ‖ — *un punto,* (*nel lavoro a maglia*) to pick up a stitch ‖ — *quota,* (*aer.*) to regain height **2.** (*riassumere*) to resume; (*personale*) to re-engage: *ripresi il servo che avevo licenziato,* I re-engaged (*o* took on again) the servant I had dismissed; — *il comando della nave,* to resume the command of the ship **3.** (*ricominciare*) to begin again, to resume; (*un discorso*) to go on; to reply: « *Dimmi* », *riprese,* « *a che ora sei arrivato?* », "Tell me", he went on, "what time did you arrive?"; — *a scrivere, a lavorare,* to begin writing, working again; — *il lavoro, la lettura,* to resume work, reading **4.** (*ricatturare, riconquistare*) to retake, to recapture: *riprendemmo il prigioniero fuggito,* we recaptured the escaped prisoner; — *una fortezza, una città,* to retake (*o* to recapture) a fortress, a town **5.** (*riavere*) to take back, to get back; (*ricuperare*) to recover: *riprendi queste carte,* take these papers back; *la casa editrice riprese le copie invendute del libro,* the publishing house took back the unsold copies of the book; *quando posso* — *i miei libri?,* when can I take (*o* get) back my books?; *sono andata a* — *l'ombrello che avevo dimenticato,* I went to recover (*o* to collect) the umbrella I had forgotten; — *un dono,* to take a gift back; — *forza,* to recover strength; — *i sensi,* to recover consciousness **6.** (*rimproverare*) to reprove, to find fault with (s.o.): *egli mi riprende sempre,* he always finds fault with me; — *severamente qlcu.,* to reprove s.o. sharply **7.** (*sartoria*) to take in: *questo vestito deve essere ripreso sulle spalle,* this dress must to taken in on the shoulders **8.** (*teat.*) to revive: *questa commedia è stata ripresa dopo venti anni,* this play has been revived after twenty years **9.** (*cine.*) to take, to shoot ‖ *v.i.* to recover; to revive: *i fiori riprendono nell'acqua,* flowers revive in water; *il vecchio riprende lentamente,* the old man is slowly recovering ‖ *la vita riprende,* things are looking up again ‖ **riprèndersi,** *v.r.* **1.** (*da malattia*) to recover; (*da turbamento*) to collect oneself: *datemi il tempo di riprendermi,* give me time to collect myself; *dopo la morte di suo padre, non si riprese più,* after his father's death he was no longer his former self; *dopo la malattia si riprese lentamente,* after his illness he recovered slowly ‖ *dopo aver fatto bancarotta, non si riprese più,* after he went bankrupt he never got on his legs again **2.** (*correggersi*) to correct oneself: *fece un errore madornale, ma si riprese subito,* he made a huge mistake but he corrected himself at once.

riprensíbile, *ag.* reprehensible, blamable.

riprensibilménte, *av.* reprehensibly.

riprensióne, *s.f.* reprehension, reproof, blame.

riprensívo, riprensòrio, *ag.* reprehensive; corrective: *misure riprensive,* corrective measures.

riprésa, *s.f.* **1.** (*ricominciamento*) restarting, renewal; resumption: — *dell'attività,* renewal of activity; *la* — *del lavoro, di un processo,* the resumption of work, of a trial; — *delle ostilità,* renewal of hostilities ‖ *a diverse riprese,* at different times; *a due riprese,* twice over; *a più riprese,* on several occasions (*o* many times *o* again and again): *fare ql.co. a più riprese,* to do sthg. in successive stages **2.** (*rinascita*) revival: — *di antiche tradizioni,* revival of old traditions **3.** (*riconquista*) recapture: *la* — *della città fu sanguinosa,* the recapture of the town caused much blood-shed **4.** (*da* *malattia, emozioni*) recovery: *la sua — fu molto lenta*, his recovery was very slow ‖ *— negli affari*, business recovery **5.** (*teat.*) revival: *la — di quella commedia ebbe molto successo*, the revival of that play was very successful **6.** (*cine.*) shot, take, shooting: *— col rallentatore*, slow-motion shot; *— di un interno*, interior shooting; *— inclinata*, angle shot (*o* view); *— muta*, mute shot; *trucchi di —*, shooting tricks **7.** (*aut.*) acceleration: *la mia automobile ha una buona —*, my car has a good acceleration **8.** (*registrazione*) recording: *sistema di — ottica e sonora sulla stessa pellicola*, single recording system **9.** (*pugilato, lotta*) round; (*scherma*) bout; (*calcio, pallacanestro, ecc.*) second half (of game) **10.** (*mus.*) repeat.

ripresentàre, *v.t.* to present again, to re-present ‖ **ripresentàrsi,** *v.r.* to present oneself again: *quando si ripresenterà l'occasione*, when the opportunity arises again.

ripréso, *ag.* **1.** retaken **2.** (*riassunto*) resumed; (*di personale*) re-engaged **3.** (*rimproverato*) reproved.

riprestàre, *v.t.* to lend again, to re-lend.

riprincipiàre, *v.t.* to begin again, to re-begin.

ripristinàbile, *ag.* restorable, renewable.

ripristinaménto, *V.* **riprístino.**

ripristinàre, *v.t.* to restore; (*rimettere in vigore*) to re-establish: *— una legge*, to bring a law into force again; *— una linea ferroviaria*, to restore a railway line; *— la pace, l'ordine in un paese*, to restore peace, order in a country; *— una vecchia usanza*, to re-establish an old custom; *— un vecchio edificio*, to restore an old building.

ripristino, *s.m.* restoration; (*il rimettere in vigore*) re-establishment: *il — dell'ordine*, the restoration of order; *il — di un binario ferroviario*, the restoration of a railway line; *il — di un edificio*, the restoration of a building; *il — di una legge*, the re-establishment of a law; *piano di —*, (*econ.*) rehabilitation plan.

ripristinàto, *ag.* restored; (*rimesso in vigore*) re-established.

riproducìbile, *ag.* reproduceable, reproducible.

riprodúrre, *v.t.* to reproduce: *— un disegno*, to reproduce a drawing; *— un pensiero in parole*, to translate a thought into words; *— un suono, un'immagine*, to reproduce a sound, an image ‖ **riprodúrsi,** *v.r.* to reproduce: *certe piante si riproducono per gemmazione*, some plants reproduce by gemmation.

riproduttività, *s.f.* reproductivity, reproductiveness.

riproduttìvo, *ag.* reproductive.

riproduttóre, *ag.* reproducing ‖ *s.m.* **1.** parent **2.** (*tec.*): *— acustico*, (*di radiogrammofono, ecc.*) pick-up; *— fonografico*, (*per radiotrasmittente*) turn-table.

riproduttrìce, *s.f.* parent.

riproduzióne, *s.f.* reproduction: *la — della specie*, (*biol.*) the reproduction of the species; *la — di una parte del corpo*, (*biol.*) the reproduction of a part of the body; *questa è la — di un bellissimo quadro*, this is a reproduction of a very beautiful painting.

riprométtere, *v.t.* to promise again ‖ **riprométtersi,** *v.r.* **1.** to propose, to intend: *mi ripromettevo di farlo al più presto*, I proposed (*o* I intended) to do (*o* doing) it as soon as possible **2.** (*sperare*) to hope; (*aspettarsi*) to expect: *mi ripromettevo di fare in tempo*, I hoped to be in time; *mi riprometto un grande successo*, I expect great success.

ripropórre, *v.t.*, **ripropórsi,** *v.r.* to re-propose.

ripròva, *s.f.* **1.** (fresh) proof; new evidence; (*conferma*) confirmation: *a — di ciò che dissi*, as a proof of what I said **2.** (*mat.*) proof.

riprovàre, *v.t.* **1.** (*provare, tentare di nuovo*) to try again: *non sono riuscito, ma riproverò*, I have not succeeded but I shall try again **2.** (*sentire, sperimentare di nuovo*) to feel again, to experience again **3.** (*disapprovare*) to criticize, to reprove: *i suoi modi sono riprovati da tutti*, his manners are criticized (*o* re-

proved) by everybody **4.** (*respingere agli esami*) to fail: *ho riprovato due studenti*, I have failed two students ‖ *essere riprovato*, to fail: *fui riprovato in inglese e in latino*, I failed in English and in Latin ‖ **riprovàrsi,** *v.r.* to try again.

riprovàto, *ag.* (*respinto agli esami*) failed, unsuccessful, rejected ‖ *s.m.* unsuccessfull candidate.

riprovatóre, *s.m.*, **riprovatrìce,** *s.f.* critic.

riprovazióne, *s.f.* criticism, reprobation; *incontrare la — generale*, to meet with general reprobation.

riprovévole, *ag.* **1.** blamable, blameworthy, censurable **2.** (*vergognoso*) shameful **3.** (*spregevole*) despicable, contemptible.

riprovevolménte, *av.* **1.** blamably **2.** (*vergognosamente*) shamefully **3.** (*spregevolmente*) despicably, contemptibly.

riprovvedére, *v.t.* to supply with (sthg.) again ‖ *v.i.* to provide for (sthg.) again; to see to (sthg.) again; to arrange for, about (sthg.) again ‖ **riprovvedérsi,** *v.r.* to provide oneself with (sthg.) again.

ripuàrio, *ag.* **1.** (*letter.*) riparian; riverside (*attributivo*) **2.** (*st.*) Ripuarian.

ripubblicàre, *v.t.* to republish.

ripudiàbile, *ag.* that can be repudiated.

ripudiàre, *v.t.* **1.** to repudiate, to disown; (*respingere*) to reject: *un figlio*, to disown a son; *— la moglie*, to repudiate one's wife; *— i propri scritti*, to disown one's writings **2.** (*dir.*) to renounce, to relinquish: *— una eredità*, to renounce an inheritance.

ripudiatóre, *s.m.*, **ripudiatrìce,** *s.f.* repudiator.

ripúdio, *s.m.* repudiation.

ripugnànte, *ag.* **1.** (*disgustoso*) disgusting, horrible: *un gusto —*, a disgusting taste; *un viso —*, a horrible face **2.** (*contrario*) repugnant: *le sue proposte sono ripugnanti ai miei principi morali*, his proposals are repugnant to my moral principles.

ripugnànza, *s.f.* **1.** repugnance; disgust; dislike: *ho — a farlo*, I am loath to do it; *non so superare la mia — per gli scarafaggi*, I cannot overcome my repugnance for cockroaches; *sento — per questo modo di pensare*, this way of thinking is repugnant to me; *la sua — a scrivere era nota a tutti*, his dislike of writing was known to everybody **2.** (*riluttanza*) reluctance: *ho — a parlare in pubblico*, I am reluctant to speak in public.

ripugnàre, *v.i.* **1.** (*essere contrario*) to be repugnant, to be contrary: *ciò che dice ripugna ai miei principi*, what he says is repugnant to my principles; *ciò ripugna alla logica*, this is contrary to logic **2.** (*disgustare*) to disgust: *mi ripugna l'idea di aiutare un uomo disonesto*, I loathe (*o* I detest) the idea of helping a dishonest man; *le sue idee mi ripugnano*, his ideas disgust me; *questo odore mi ripugna*, this smell disgusts me.

ripuliménto, *s.m.* **1.** cleaning; recleaning **2.** (*il dirozzare*) polishing up.

ripulìre, *v.t.* **1.** (*pulire di nuovo*) to clean again **2.** (*pulire*) to clean (up); (*mettere in ordine*) to tidy (up): *— la casa*, to clean the house; *— un campo dalle erbacce*, to weed a field (*o* to clear a field of weeds); *— un paio di scarpe*, to clean a pair of shoes; *— una stanza*, to clean up (*o* to tidy up) a room **3.** (*dirozzare, perfezionare*) to polish (up): *— il proprio stile, le proprie maniere*, to polish (up) one's style, one's manners **4.** (*svuotare di ogni bene*) to ransack: *il ladro gli ripulì la casa*, the thief ransacked his house of everything **5.** (*vincere al giuoco*) to clean out: *— qlcu. al giuoco*, to clean s.o. out **6.** (*mangiare tutto*) to eat up: *ripulì tutto ciò che c'era sulla tavola*, he ate up everything on the table ‖ **ripulìrsi,** *v.r.* **1.** to clean oneself, to tidy oneself, to make oneself tidy: *devo ripulirmi prima di uscire*, I must tidy myself before going out **2.** (*dirozzarsi*) to refine oneself, to polish (up) one's manners.

ripulìsti, *V.* **repulìsti.**

ripulìta, *s.f.* **1.** (*il ripulire*) clean, cleaning: *dare* *una* — *a ql.co.*, to clean up sthg. (*o* to give sthg. a clean); *darsi una* —, to tidy oneself up ‖ *ha fatto una* — *di quello che era in tavola*, he ate up everything on the table **2.** (*eliminazione*) clean sweep: *il direttore della fabbrica ha fatto una* — *generale*, the manager of the factory has made a clean sweep.

ripulíto, *ag.* **1.** clean **2.** (*in ordine*) tidy; in order (*predicativo*).

ripulitóre, *s.m.*, **ripulitríce**, *s.f.* cleaner.

ripulitúra, *s.f.* **1.** cleaning **2.** (*rifinitura di opera d'arte, ecc.*) finishing touch.

ripullulàre, *v.i.* **1.** to spring up again **2.** (*bot.*) to pullulate again (anche *fig.*).

ripúlsa, *s.f.* refusal; repulse: *ricevere una* —, to meet with a repulse.

ripulsàre, *v.t.* to refuse; to repulse.

ripulsióne, *s.f.* **1.** repulsion, repugnance, aversion: *sentire* — *per qlcu.*, to feel repugnance for s.o. **2.** (*fis.*) repulsion.

ripulsívo, *ag.* **1.** repulsive, repellent; (*disgustoso*) disgusting, loathsome **2.** (*fis.*) repulsive.

riputàre, *e derivati*, *V.* **reputàre**, *e derivati*.

riquadràre, *v.t.* **1.** to square (anche *mat.*) **2.** (*una stanza*) to decorate.

riquadratóre, *s.m.* (*decoratore*) decorator.

riquadratúra, *s.f.* **1.** squaring **2.** (*decorazione*) decoration **3.** (*spazio quadro*) square.

riquàdro, *s.m.* square; (*su parete, soffitto*) panel.

rirómpere, *v.t.*, **rirómpersi**, *v.r.* to break again.

risàcca, *s.f.* surf.

risàia, *s.f.* rice-field.

risaiuòla, *s.f.*, **risaiuòlo**, *s.m.* rice-weeder.

risaldaménto, *s.m.* resoldering.

risaldàre, *v.t.* to resolder.

risaldatúra, *s.f.* resoldering.

risalíre, *v.t.* **1.** to re-ascend; to go up again, to climb (up) again: — *la collina, la montagna*, to climb up the hill, the mountain again; — *le scale*, to go upstairs again **2.** (*nuotare, navigare contro corrente*) to go up; (*di pesce*) to run up: *la barca risalì il fiume*, the boat went up the river; — *la corrente*, to go upstream; *fig.* to stem the current: *il ragazzo risalì la corrente a nuoto*, the boy swam upstream ‖ *v.i.* **1.** to re-ascend; to go up again, to climb (up) again: *risali da lui, per piacere*, please, go up to his room again; *risali subito nella tua camera e non scendere finché non ti chiamo*, go upstairs at once to your room and don't come down till I call you ‖ — *sul trono*, to re-ascend the throne **2.** *fig.* to go up again, to rise again: *le nostre azioni sono risalite*, (*comm.*) our shares have gone up again; *i prezzi risalgono*, prices are rising (*o* going up) again; *la temperatura risale*, the temperature is rising (*o* going up) again **3.** (*rimontare nel tempo*) to go back, to date back, to trace back: *dovete* — *al Medioevo per trovare le origini di questa leggenda*, you must go back to the Middle Ages to find the origins of this legend; *le origini della sua famiglia risalgono al XIII secolo*, the origins of his family date back to the thirteenth century; *la sua antipatia per le ciliege risale ad un'indigestione*, his dislike for cherries traces back to an attack of indigestion.

risalíto, *s.m.* upstart, parvenu, nouveau riche.

risaltàre, *v.i.* to jump again, to leap again: *il cavallo risaltò*, the horse jumped again; — *un muro*, to leap a wall again; — *una siepe*, to jump over a hedge again ‖ *v.i.* **1.** (*spiccare*) to show up, to catch the eye: *il grigio scuro non risalta sul blu*, dark grey does not stand out against blue; *questo colore risalta poco*, this colour does not show up very well; *la sua cicatrice risalta di più quando è abbronzato*, his scar shows up more when he is sunburnt ‖ *far* —, to show up (*o* to enhance): *il blu fa* — *la sua bella carnagione*, blue shows up her lovely complexion **2.** (*di persona*) to stand out **3.** (*arch.*) to jut out.

risàlto, *s.m.* **1.** prominence; relief; (*enfasi*) emphasis: *la guglia della chiesa si ergeva con gran* — *contro il cielo*, the spire of the church rose in full relief against the sky; *questi colori mancano di* —, these colours lack vividness; *dar* — *a ql.co.*, to give prominence to sthg. (*o* to make sthg. stand out *o* to make sthg. prominent *o* to make sthg. conspicuous); (*dare enfasi*) to lay emphasis on (*o* to emphasize) sthg.: *nel suo discorso diede particolare* — *a questa idea*, in his speech he put special emphasis on this idea; *non è dato* — *sufficiente alla parte del figlio*, the son's part is not given enough emphasis (*o* prominence) ‖ *far* —, to stand out: *i suoi capelli neri fanno* — *sulla carnagione chiara*, her dark hair stands out against her fair complexion **2.** (*rimbalzo*) rebound **3.** (*arch.*) relief **4.** (*mec.*) projection, projecting part.

risalutàre, *v.t.* to greet again ‖ **risalutàrsi**, *v.r.* reciproco, to greet each other (one another) again.

risanàbile, *ag.* **1.** curable; (*rar.*) healable **2.** (*bonificabile*) reclaimable.

risanaménto, *s.m.* **1.** curing, healing; (*guarigione*) recovery **2.** (*di costumi, ecc.*) reformation **3.** (*bonifica*) reclamation **4.** — *di quartieri popolari*, slum-clearance **5.** (*comm.*) balancing (of the accounts).

risanàre, *v.t.* **1.** to cure, to heal, to restore to health: *il soggiorno in campagna lo ha risanato*, his stay in the country has cured him (*o* restored him to health) **2.** (*bonificare*) to reclaim: — *un terreno paludoso*, to reclaim a marsh **3.** — *un quartiere popolare*, to clear a slum **4.** (*comm.*) to balance (the accounts) ‖ *v.i.* to recover.

risanatóre, *ag.* healing ‖ *s.m.*, **risanatríce**, *s.f.* healer.

risanguinàre, *v.i.* to bleed again.

risapére, *v.t.* to know, to come to know, to get to know, to hear of (sthg.): *non ricordo da chi lo riseppi*, I do not remember who I heard it from (*o* who told me) ‖ *è risaputo che egli è un disonesto*, it is well-known that he is a dishonest man.

risarcíbile, *ag.* (*comm.*) that can be indemnified.

risarciménto, *s.m.* **1.** (*comm.*) compensation, indemnity; damages (*pl.*): — *dei danni*, compensation for damages; *domanda di* —, claim for damages; *infortunio rimasto senza* —, an accident which has not been compensated; *aggiudicare il* — *dei danni*, to award damages; *avere diritto al* — *dei danni*, to be entitled to an indemnity (*o* to damages); *domandare il* — *dei danni*, to claim damages; *essere obbligato al* —, to be bound to pay an indemnity **2.** (*riparazione*) repair.

risarcíre, *v.t.* **1.** (*comm.*) to indemnify, to compensate: *ho diritto ad essere risarcito della perdita subìta*, I am entitled to be indemnified for the loss suffered; — *qlcu. dei danni*, to pay compensation for damages **2.** (*riparare*) to restore, to repair.

risàta, *s.f.* laughter, laugh, burst of laughter: *una* — *beffarda*, a sneer; *una* — *fragorosa*, a guffaw (*o* a horse-laugh); *una* — *grassa*, a hearty laugh; *una* — *omerica*, homeric laughter; *fare una bella* —, to have a good laugh; *provocare una* — *generale*, to raise a general laugh; *scoppiare in una* —, to burst out laughing (*o* to break into a laugh).

riscaldaménto, *s.m.* **1.** heating: — *ad acqua calda*, hot water heating; — *ad aria calda*, hot blast heating; — *a pannelli radianti*, panel heating (*o* radiant heating); — *a vapore*, steam heating; *impianto di* —, heating system: *impianto di* — *a termosifone*, hot water heating system; *impianto di* — *centrale*, central heating plant; *pagare il supplemento per il* —, to pay a supplement for the heating **2.** (*alterazione febbrile*) feverishness **3.** (*eruzione cutanea*) prickly heat.

riscaldàre, *v.t.* **1.** to warm, to heat: *la casa è riscaldata per mezzo di termosifoni*, the house is heated by means of radiators; *riscalda i vestiti del bambino, prima di metterglieli*, warm the child's clothes before putting them on him; *il sole ha riscaldato l'aria*, the sun has warmed the air; — *in anticipo*, to preheat ‖

— *le reni a qlcu.*, to thrash s.o. **2.** (*scaldare di nuovo*) to warm up, to heat up, to warm again: — *una minestra, il latte*, to warm up a soup, milk **3.** (*eccitare*) to warm up, to stir up, to excite: *l'indignazione l'aveva riscaldato tutto*, indignation had stirred him up; *quel libro aveva riscaldato la sua immaginazione*, that book had excited (*o* stirred up) his imagination; — *i sentimenti di qlcu.*, to stir (*o* to excite) s.o.'s feelings **4.** (*med.*) to inflame ‖ **riscàldarsi**, *v.r.* **1.** to warm oneself, to warm up, to get warm: *lascia che mi riscaldi le mani al fuoco*, let me warm my hands at the fire; *vorrei fare un po' di moto per riscaldarmi*, I should like to take some exercise to warm up; — *per attrito*, (*fis.*) to run hot; — *vicino al fuoco*, to warm oneself near the fire **2.** (*di fieno, grano che fermenta*) to get hot, to ferment **3.** (*di animali*) to rut; to be in heat **4.** *fig.* (*infervorarsi*) to warm up, to get excited: *egli si riscaldava man mano che parlava*, he warmed up as he went on speaking; *non c'era ragione di — tanto*, there was no reason to get so excited; — *nella discussione*, to get excited in a discussion.

riscaldàta, *s.f.* warm; warming up: *da' una — a questo latte*, warm up this milk; *datti una — vicino al fuoco*, have a warm by the fire.

riscaldatívo, *ag.* inflammatory, heating.

riscaldàto, *ag.* **1.** heated, warm: *casa riscaldata*, heated house **2.** (*eccitato*) excited; (*arrabbiato*) angry **3.** (*di cibo*) warmed up: *minestra riscaldata*, warmed up soup; *sa di —*, it tastes as if it has been warmed up.

riscaldatóre, *s.m.* heater, radiator: — *a getto di vapore*, stream-jet blower; — *a raggi infrarossi*, infra-red heater; — *a resistenza*, resistance heater.

riscaldatúra, *s.f.* heating, warming up.

riscàldo, *s.m.* (*med.*) **1.** (*arrossamento*) inflammation, irritation **2.** (*eruzione cutanea*) heat-spots (*pl.*).

riscappàre, *v.i.* to escape again.

riscattàbile, *ag.* redeemable, ransomable.

riscattàre, *v.t.* **1.** to ransom, to redeem: — *da ipoteca*, to reedem from mortgage; — *un oggetto impegnato*, to redeem a pawned object; — *un prigioniero, uno schiavo*, to ransom (*o* to redeem) a prisoner, a slave **2.** *fig.* (*redimere*) to redeem ‖ **riscattàrsi**, *v.r.* **1.** (*redimersi*) to redeem oneself **2.** (*vendicarsi*) to avenge oneself, to take revenge.

riscéndere, *v.t.i.* to redescend, to descend again.

rischiaraménto, *s.m.* **1.** illumination, brightening, lighting up **2.** *fig.* lighting up, brightening.

rischiaràre, *v.t.* **1.** to illuminate, to light (up): *il sole rischiarava la pianura*, the sun illuminated (*o* lighted) the plain; *la stanza era rischiarata da una lampada a olio*, the room was illuminated by an oil-lamp **2.** *fig.* (*illuminare*) to light up, to brighten (up); (*la mente*) to enlighten; (*render chiaro*) to clear (up): *la gioia gli rischiarava il viso*, joy lit up (*o* brightened) her face; — *la mente di qlcu.*, to enlighten s.o.'s mind; — *i propri pensieri*, to clear one's thoughts; — *la vita di chi soffre*, to brighten the lives of those who suffer ‖ — *la voce*, to clear one's voice ‖ *v.i.* (*albeggiare*) to dawn ‖ **rischiaràrsi**, *v.r.* **1.** (*illuminarsi*) to light up; to brighten (up): *al vederla il suo viso si rischiarò*, when he saw her his face brightened **2.** (*acquistare chiarezza, limpidezza*) to get clearer (*anche fig.*); (*di cielo*) to clear up: *si sta rischiarando*, it is clearing up; *la situazione non si rischiara*, the situation is not getting clearer.

rischiàre, *v.t.* to risk, to expose to risk, to venture: — *la propria vita, salute*, to risk (*o* to venture) one's life, health ‖ *v.i.* to run the risk: *egli rischiò di essere licenziato*, he ran the risk of being dismissed.

rischiaríre, *V.* **rischiaràre**.

ríschio, *s.m.* risk: *a — del destinatario*, (*comm.*) at the customer's (*o* buyer's) risk; *a — di perdere la vita*, at the risk of losing one's life; *per conto e — di qlcu.*, (*comm.*) for s.o.'s account and risk; *non c'è —*

di sbagliare, there is no risk (*o* danger) of making a mistake; *voglio proporlo anche a — di ricevere un rifiuto*, I want to propose this even at the risk of meeting with a refusal; *correre il — di perdere del denaro*, to run the risk of losing some money; *mettere a — ql.co.*, to risk (*o* to venture) sthg.; *mettere a — qlcu.*, to expose s.o. to a risk.

rischióso, *ag.* **1.** risky; (*pericoloso*) dangerous **2.** (*audace*) audacious, daring.

risciacquaménto, *s.m.* rinsing.

risciacquàre, *v.t.* to rinse ‖ **risciacquàrsi**, *v.r.* to rinse: — *la bocca, le mani*, to rinse one's mouth, one's hands.

risciacquàta, *s.f.* **1.** rinse, rinsing: *dare una — a ql.co.*, to give sthg. a rinse (*o* to rinse sthg.) **2.** *fig.* (*sgridata*) scolding, rebuke; (*fam.*) lecture.

risciacquatúra, *s.f.* **1.** (*il risciacquare*) rinsing **2.** (*l'acqua in cui sono risciacquati i piatti*) dish-water: *piatto che sa di —*, dish that tastes of washing-up water.

risciàcquo, *s.m.* **1.** culvert, gutter **2.** (*med.*) mouth-wash.

risciò, *s.m.* ricksha(w), jinricksha, jinrikisha.

risciògliere, *v.t.* **1.** to solve again **2.** (*sciogliere cosa annodata*) to untie again.

riscontàre, *v.t.* (*comm.*) to rediscount.

riscónto, *s.m.* (*comm.*) rediscount.

riscontràbile, *ag.* **1.** (*che può essere controllato*) that may be checked **2.** (*che può essere trovato*) that may be found.

riscontràre, *v.t.* **1.** (*controllare*) to check, to verify: — *una citazione*, to check a quotation; — *dei conti*, to check (*o* to verify) accounts **2.** (*trovare*) to find: to notice: — *un errore*, to find a mistake **3.** (*confrontare*) to compare, to collate: — *una cosa con un'altra*, to compare one thing with another; — *due edizioni di un libro*, to collate two editions of a book ‖ **riscontràrsi**, *v.r.* **1.** (*incontrarsi*) to meet **2.** (*corrispondere*) to tally; to match: *i loro resoconti non si riscontrano*, their reports do not tally.

riscóntro, *s.m.* **1.** (*controllo*) checking, control, verification: *il — dei conti*, the checking (*o* audit) of accounts; *fare il — di ql.co.*, to check sthg. **2.** (*confronto*) comparison, collation: *ho fatto il — di questa traduzione con l'originale*, I have compared this translation with the original; *queste cose non hanno — nella storia*, these things are not to be found in history; *il suo coraggio non ha —*, nobody can match him for courage; *mettere a —*, to compare **3.** (*corrispondenza simmetrica*) pendant: *questo quadro fa — all'altro*, this picture makes a pendant to the other one **4.** (*risposta*) reply: *in — alla vostra lettera*, in reply to your letter **5.** (*corrente d'aria*) draught **6.** (*passamano su giubba*) breast-strap.

riscoppiàre, *v.i.* **1.** to burst (out) again; to explode again **2.** (*di piante*) to sprout again; to bud again **3.** (*di guerra, epidemia*) to break out again.

riscopríre, *v.t.* to discover again; to find out again.

riscòssa, *s.f.* **1.** (*insurrezione*) revolt, insurrection **2.** (*riconquista*) recovery: *andare, muovere alla —*, to counter-attack **3.** (*riscatto*) redemption.

riscossióne, *s.f.* collection: (*fatta in una giornata*) day's takings (*pl.*): — *delle imposte*, collection of taxes.

riscòsso, *ag.* **1.** collected **2.** (*liberato*) freed, liberated.

riscotíbile, *ag.* collectable.

riscotitóre, *s.m.*, **riscotitríce**, *s.f.* collector.

riscrívere, *v.t.i.* **1.** to rewrite, to write again **2.** (*scrivere di rimando*) to write back.

riscuòtere, *v.t.* **1.** (*ricevere in pagamento*) to collect; to receive; to draw; to cash; to get: *cercherò di — quel denaro*, I shall try to collect that money; *non ho ancora riscosso*, I have not got my money yet; *vorrei — i soldi che mi dovete*, I should like to collect the money you owe me; — *un assegno*, to cash a cheque; — *denaro da una banca*, to draw money from a bank; — *lo stipendio*, to draw (*o* to collect) one's salary **2.** (*con-*

seguire) to earn; to win: *egli riscuote molte simpatie*, he is well liked by everybody; — *approvazioni, lodi*, to win (*o* to earn) approbation, praise; — *la stima generale*, to enjoy general esteem 3. (*scuotere*) to shake; to rouse (anche *fig.*): *non ho potuto riscuoterlo dalla sua pigrizia*, I have not been able to rouse him from (*o* to shake him out of) his laziness 4. (*riscattare*) to redeem; to ransom; (*liberare*) to free: — *un pegno al Monte di Pietà*, to redeem a pledge at the pawnbroker's ‖ **riscuòtersi**, *v.r.* 1. (*trasalire*) to start: *a quel grido mi riscossi*, I started at that cry 2. (*riprendere i sensi*) to recover consciousness; to come to, to come round: — *dal torpore*, to shake off one's torpor 3. (*liberarsi*) to free oneself.

risecàre, *v.t.* to cut off; to cut away ‖ — *le spese*, to cut down expenses.

riseccàre, *v.t.*, **riseccàrsi**, *v.r.* to dry up.

risecchíre, *v.i.* to get dry; to wither: *questa pianta è risecchita presto*, this plant has withered quickly; *questo pane risecchisce facilmente*, this bread gets stale (*o* dry) quickly.

risécco, *ag.* dry, dried up: *pelle risecca*, dry skin.

risedére, *v.i.* 1. to sit down again 2. (*risiedere*) to reside, to be resident, to dwell: *risiede all'estero*, he resides (*o* he lives) abroad 3. (*essere situato*) to be situated: *la città risiede ai piedi del monte*, the town is situated at the foot of the mountain.

riséga, *s.f.* 1. (*arch.*) offset, set-back 2. (*della pelle*) fold.

risegàre, *v.t.* to saw again.

risegnàre, *v.t.* to re-mark, to re-sign.

riselciàre, *v.t.* to re-pave, to pave again.

riseminàre, *v.t.* to resow, to sow again.

risentiménto, *s.m.* resentment; grudge: *con* —, resentfully; *il* — *del popolo verso il governo*, the people's resentment against the Government; *egli nutriva un profondo* — *verso di me*, he harboured a deep grudge against me; *non ho del* — *verso di lui*, I bear no grudge against him.

risentíre, *v.t.* 1. (*udire di nuovo*) to hear again, to re-hear; (*sentire di nuovo*) to feel again: *vorrei* — *quella sinfonia*, I should like to hear that symphony again 2. (*sentire, provare*) to feel; (*subire*) to suffer: *egli risente le conseguenze della sua disonestà*, he is suffering the consequences of his dishonesty; *risento ora gli effetti di quella medicina*, I can feel the effects of that medicine now; *non ho mai più risentito quel dolore*, I have never felt that pain again ‖ *v.i.* 1. to show traces; (*di persona, portar le conseguenze*) to feel the effect: *benché sia passato attraverso molte difficoltà, il suo carattere non ne risente*, although he has suffered many hardships, his character does not show any trace of it; *egli risente della sua severa educazione*, he feels the effects of his strict education; *le opere di questo scrittore risentono delle sue umili origini*, the works of this writer show traces of his humble origins 2. (*echeggiare, risuonare*) to resound (with sthg.), to echo (sthg.): *la valle risentì delle sue grida*, the valley resounded with his cries ‖ **risentírsi**, *v.r.* 1. to resent (sthg.), to take offence (at sthg.): *egli potrebbe risentirsene*, he might take offence at it (*o* he might take it amiss); *egli si risentì delle mie parole*, he resented my words (*o* he took offence at my words) 2. (*tornare in sè*) to recover one's senses; (*destarsi*) to awaken 3. (*sentire le conseguenze*) to feel the effects: *spesso si risente della vecchia piaga*, he often feels the effects of his old wound.

risentitaménte, *av.* resentfully; angrily.

risentíto, *ag.* 1. (*sdegnato*) resentful; angry: *parole risentite*, resentful words; *sguardo* —, angry look; *egli me lo disse molto* —, he told me so very angrily 2. (*sentito di nuovo*) heard again: *musica sentita e risentita*, music heard over and over again 3. (*gagliardo*) vigorous: *trotto* —, vigorous trot.

riseppelliménto, *s.m.* reburial, reinterment.

riseppellíre, *v.t.* 1. to rebury, to bury again, to reinter 2. (*nascondere di nuovo*) to hide again.

risequestràre, *v.t.* (*dir.*) to reconfiscate.

riserbàre, *v.t.* 1. to keep again 2. (*riservare*) to reserve, to save.

riserbatézza, riserbàto, *V.* **riservatézza, riservàto**.

risèrbo, *s.m.* reserve; (*discrezione*) discretion; (*ritegno*) self-restraint: *apprezzo il suo* —, I appreciate his discretion; *si comportò con molto* —, he behaved with great discretion; (*con ritegno*) he behaved with great self-restraint.

risería, *s.f.* (*ind.*) rice-factory.

riserràre, *v.t.* to close, to shut; to shut again, to reshut, to close again, to reclose.

risèrva, *s.f.* 1. reserve (anche *fig.*); supply, stock: — *di farina*, stock of flour; — *monetaria, bancaria, aurea, statutaria*, monetary, bank, gold, statutory reserve; *fondo di* —, (*comm.*) reserve fund; *merci in* —, goods in stock; *pezzi di* —, spare parts; *le nostre riserve di grano si stanno esaurendo*, our wheat supplies are running out; *avere in* —, to have in reserve (anche *fig.*): *ho una buona* — *di argomenti, energia*, I have a good reserve of arguments, energy 2. (*restrizione*) reserve, reservation: *con le debite riserve*, with due reservation; *senza riserve*, without reserve (*o* reservation); *accetto con qualche* —, I accept with some reservations; *fare qualche* —, to make some reservations ‖ — *mentale*, mental reservation 3. (*riserbo*) reserve: *me lo confidò con gran* —, he told me with the greatest reserve; *agire con* —, to act with reserve 4. (*mil. spor.*) reserve: *le riserve*, (*mil. spor.*) the reserves; *truppe di* —, (*mil.*) reserves (*o* supporting troops); *chiamare la* —, (*mil.*) to call up the reserves 5. (*di caccia, pesca*) preserve: *ha una vasta* —, he has a large game-preserve; *cacciare in* —, to shoot over a preserve.

riservàre, *v.t.* 1. to reserve, to keep: *ho riservato due stanze a questo albergo*, I have reserved (*o* booked) two rooms at this hotel; *riserva le tue energie per più tardi*, reserve (*o* keep) your energy for later on; *ti ho riservato una grande sorpresa*, I have reserved a great surprise for you; *ti ho riservato un pezzo di torta*, I have kept a piece of cake for you 2. (*differire*) to put off: *riservo questa decisione a domani*, I will put off this decision to to-morrow (*o* I will reserve this decision for to-morrow) ‖ **riservàrsi**, *v.r.* 1. to reserve oneself: *mi riservo per lavori più importanti*, I am saving my energy for more important works; *mi riservo questo diritto*, I reserve this right to myself 2. (*ripromettersi*) to intend: *mi riservo di dirtelo la settimana ventura*, I shall tell you next week; *mi riservo di farlo domani*, I intend to do it to-morrow 3. (*med.*): — *la diagnosi*, to refuse to formulate a definite diagnosis: *il medico si riservò la diagnosi*, the physician refused to express his opinion.

riservataménte, *av.* reservedly.

riservatézza, *s.f.* reserve, reservedness; prudence, circumspection ‖ — *di stile*, restrained style.

riservàto, *ag.* 1. reserved: *posto* —, reserved seat; *sala riservata*, reserved room ‖ *caccia riservata*, game-preserve ‖ *caso* —, (*teol.*) reserved case ‖ *prognosi riservata*, (*med.*) reserved prognosis 2. (*chiuso, circospetto*) reserved, restrained: *carattere* —, reserved character; *persona riservata*, reserved person; *è molto* — *nel parlare*, he is very discreet 3. (*segreto*) private: *lettera riservata*, private (*o* confidential) letter.

riservíre, *v.t.* to serve again.

riservísta, *s.m.* (*mil.*) reservist.

risíbile, *ag.* ridiculous, laughable.

risicàre, *v.t.* to risk, to venture ‖ *v.i.* to run a risk: *ha risicato di morire*, he risked death ‖ *chi non risica non rosica*, *prov.* nothing ventured, nothing gained.

rísico, *s.m.* (*rar.*) risk: *andare a* — *di*, to run the risk of.

risicoltóre, *s.m.* (*agr.*) rice-grower.

risicoltúra, *s.f.* (*agr.*) rice-growing.

risicóso, *ag.* (*rar.*) **1.** risky **2.** (*audace*) audacious, daring.

risièdere, *v.i.* to reside (anche *fig.*): *egli risiede a Roma,* he resides (o lives) in Rome; *l'intelligenza risiede nel cervello,* intelligence is located in the brain; *ogni potere risiede nell'imperatore,* all power resides in the emperor.

risigillàre, *v.t.* to re-seal, to seal again.

risípola, *s.f.* (*patol.*) erysipelas.

rísma, *s.f.* **1.** ream **2.** (*spreg.*) (*qualità*) kind, sort, quality: *sono tutti della stessa —,* they are all of a kind.

ríso[1], *s.m.* **1.** laugh, laughter: *un — amaro, aperto,* a bitter, a hearty laugh; *— beffardo,* sneer; *— e pianto,* laughter and tears; *un — sardonico, sprezzante,* a sardonic, a scornful laugh; *uno scoppio di risa,* a burst of laughter; *è oggetto di — fra i suoi compagni di scuola,* he is the laughing-stock of his school-fellows; *strappò le risa dell'auditorio,* he drew a laugh from the audience; *esser preso da un accesso di — irrefrenabile,* to be overcome with laughter; *frenare il —,* to check one's laughter ‖ *prendere ql.co. in —,* to make light of sthg. ‖ *sbellicarsi dalle risa,* to split one's sides with laughter ‖ *il — abbonda sulle labbra degli stolti,* prov. laughter abounds in the mouths of fools ‖ *il — fa buon sangue,* prov. laugh and grow fat **2.** (*gioia*) smile: *il — della primavera,* (*poet.*) the smile of spring.

ríso[2], *s.m.* (*bot.*) rice: *— al latte,* (*cuc.*) rice-milk; *— brillato,* husked rice; *— soffiato,* puffed rice; *acqua di —,* rice-water; *budino di —,* rice-pudding; *farina di —,* rice-flour; *minestra di —,* rice-soup.

risognàre, *v.t.i.* to dream again.

risolàre, *v.t.* to (re)sole.

risolatúra, *s.f.* (re)soling.

risolíno, *s.m.* little laugh, giggle.

risollevaménto, *s.m.* **1.** lifting; raising **2.** (*miglioramento*) improvement.

risollevàre, *v.t.* **1.** to lift up again; to raise again: *— una questione,* to raise a question again **2.** (*incrementare*) to better, to improve: *— l'industria,* to better industry **3.** (*confortare*) to cheer: *ciò mi ha risollevato lo spirito,* this has cheered me up.

risòlto, *ag.* solved, resolved: *un problema —,* a problem (re)solved.

risolúbile, *ag.* solvable, resolvable.

risolutaménte, *av.* resolutely.

risolutézza, *s.f.* resolution, resoluteness: *con —,* resolutely (o with resolution).

risolutívo, *ag.* resolutive: *condizione risolutiva,* (*dir.*) resolutive condition; *formula risolutiva,* (*mat.*) resolutive solution; *rimedio —,* (*med.*) resolutive remedy.

risolúto, *ag.* **1.** (*deciso*) resolved, resolute, determined: *uomo —,* resolute man; *sono — a sapere tutto,* I am determined (o resolved) to know everything **2.** (*disciolto*) melted.

risolutóre, *s.m.,* **risolutríce,** *s.f.* solver.

risoluzióne, *s.f.* **1.** resolution; decision: *una coraggiosa —,* a courageous resolution; *ho preso la — di studiare le lingue,* I resolved (o I decided) to study languages; *prendere una —,* to take a decision (o to make up one's mind) **2.** (*risolutezza*) resolution: *con molta —,* with great resolution; *la sua — meravigliò tutti,* his resolution surprised everybody **3.** (*mat.*) solution: *la — di un problema,* the solution of a problem **4.** (*dir.*) dissolution; cancellation: *la — di un contratto,* the cancellation of a contract; *la — di una società,* the dissolution of a company **5.** (*med.*) resolution.

risolvènte, *ag.* **1.** solving **2.** (*med.*) resolvent ‖ *s.m.* (*med.*) resolvent.

risòlvere, *v.t.* **1.** to solve, to work out; to resolve: *— un dubbio, una difficoltà,* to resolve a doubt, a difficulty; *— un problema, un'equazione, un indovinello,* to solve (o to work out) a problem, an equation, a riddle **2.** (*definire, comporre*) to settle, to resolve: *— una questione,* to settle a question **3.** (*de-*

cidere) to resolve, to decide: *risolse di farlo lui stesso,* he resolved (o decided) that he would do it (o to do it) himself; *risolsi di partire,* I resolved (o I decided) to leave **4.** (*rescindere*) to rescind, to annul, to cancel: *— un contratto,* to rescind a contract **5.** (*dissipare*) to disperse: *— la nebbia, il fumo,* to disperse the fog, the smoke **6.** (*chim.*) to resolve, to break down, to reduce: *nubi che il freddo ha risolto in pioggia,* clouds that the cold has resolved into rain; *— un composto nei suoi elementi,* to break a compound down into (o to reduce a compound to) its elements **7.** (*med.*) to resolve: *— un ascesso,* to resolve an abscess ‖ **risòlversi,** *v.r.* **1.** (*decidersi*) to decide; to make up one's mind: *non so risolvermi,* I cannot make up my mind; *si risolse a farlo,* he resolved to do it **2.** (*tramutarsi*) to change into (sthg.), to turn into (sthg.): *la nebbia si risolse in pioggia,* the fog turned into rain; *tutto si risolse in bene, in male,* everything turned out well, badly; *tutto si risolse in nulla,* it all came to nothing (o fizzled out) **3.** (*di malattia*) to clear up: *non è niente di grave, si risolverà in pochi giorni,* it's nothing serious, it will clear up in a few days.

risolvíbile, *ag.* **1.** solvable, soluble, resolvable **2.** (*dir.*) annullable, rescindable.

risolvibilità, *s.f.* solvability, solubility, resolvability.

risommàre, *v.t.* to sum up again.

risonànte, *ag.* resonant, resounding: *note risonanti,* resonant notes; *voce —,* resonant (o resounding) voice.

risonànza, *s.f.* **1.** resonance; sonority: *— del periodo,* sonority of phrasing **2.** (*suono*) sound **3.** (*eco*) echo: *la sua teoria ebbe molta —,* the echo of his theory spread far and wide.

risonàre, *v.i.* to resound, to echo; to ring (out): *dolci canti risuonavano nel bosco,* sweet songs resounded (o echoed) through the wood; *risuonavano grida di guerra,* war-cries rang out; *la sua fama risuona per tutto il mondo,* his fame resounds all over the world; *non ho udito — che lodi,* I have heard nothing but praise; *le sue parole risuonano ancora nei miei orecchi,* his words are still ringing in my ears ‖ *v.t.* (*il campanello*) to ring again; (*strumento, testo musicale*) to play again: *devo — questo pezzo di Mozart?,* shall I play this piece of Mozart again?; *se nessuno apre la porta, risuona il campanello,* if nobody opens the door, ring the bell again.

risórgere, *v.i.* **1.** to rise again; (*ravvivarsi*) to revive: *la città risorse dalle ceneri,* the town rose (again) from its ashes; *le nostre speranze risorsero,* our hopes revived; *— a nuova vita,* to take (on) a new lease of life ‖ *la patria è risorta,* our country has regained its freedom **2.** (*risuscitare*) to resurrect, to rise again (from the dead): *Cristo è risorto!,* Christ is risen! **3.** (*rifiorire*) to revive, to flourish again: *le arti risorsero,* the arts revived; *l'industria è risorta,* industry has revived (o is flourishing again) ‖ *far —,* to revive, to resurrect.

risorgiménto, *s.m.* revival, renaissance: *il — delle arti, della cultura,* the revival of the arts, of learning ‖ *il Risorgimento,* (*st. italiana*) the Risorgimento.

risórsa, *s.f.* **1.** resource: *risorse naturali,* natural resources **2.** (*espediente*) expedient; resource: *un uomo di risorse,* a man of resource.

risórto, *ag.* **1.** risen again; (*ravvivato*) revived **2.** (*risuscitato*) resurrected **3.** (*rifiorito*) revived.

risospíngere, *v.t.* to push again, to drive again: *mi risospinse contro il muro,* he pushed me against the wall.

risotterràre, *v.t.* to rebury, to bury again.

risòtto, *s.m.* (*cuc.*) "risotto" (an Italian dish of rice).

risottométtere, *v.t.* to subdue again.

risovvenírsi, *v.r.* (*letter.*) to remember, to recollect.

risparmiàre, *v.t.* **1.** to save: *la lavatrice mi fa — mollissimo tempo,* the washing-machine saves me a lot of time; *— denaro,* to save money; *— per la vecchiaia,* to save for one's old age; *— tempo, fiato,* *energia*, to save one's time, breath, energy 2. (*evitare*) to save; to spare: *per me puoi — di venire*, as far as I am concerned you need not come; *puoi — di farlo*, you need not do it (*o* you can save yourself the trouble of doing it); *questo gli risparmierà il disturbo*, this will save (*o* spare) him the trouble; — *l'imbarazzo a qlcu.*, to spare s.o.'s embarrassment 3. (*preservare*) to spare: *che il Signore risparmi la vita dei nostri figli*, may the Lord spare our children's lives 4. (*avere riguardo di*) to spare: *la morte non risparmia nessuno*, death spares nobody; *la sua ironia non risparmia nessuno*, his irony does not spare anybody 5. (*non affaticare*) to spare, not to tire: — *un cavallo*, to spare a horse ‖ **risparmiàrsi**, *v.r.* to spare oneself: *non si risparmia*, he doesn't spare himself.

risparmiatóre, *ag.* thrifty ‖ *s.m.*, **risparmiatríce**, *s.f.* saver; (*persona economa*) thrifty person.

rispàrmio, *s.m.* 1. saving: *capacità di —*, saving-power; *lo faccio per — di tempo*, I do it to save time; *senza —*, lavishly (*o* profusely) 2. (*denaro risparmiato*) savings (*pl.*): *cassa di —*, *banca di piccolo —*, savings-bank (*o* penny-bank); *deposito a —*, savings deposit; *libretto di —*, savings-book; *vivere dei propri risparmi*, to live on one's savings.

rispecchiàre, *v.t.* 1. to reflect: *la superficie dell'acqua rispecchia le case sulla riva*, the surface of the water reflects the houses on the shore 2. *fig.* to reflect, to mirror: *le sue azioni rispecchiano i suoi sentimenti*, his actions reflect his feelings ‖ **rispecchiàrsi**, *v.r.* to be reflected: *gli alberi si rispecchiano nell'acqua*, the trees are reflected in the water.

rispedíre, *v.t.* 1. (*spedire di nuovo*) to send again; (*comm.*) (*specialmente per mare*) to ship again; (*per terra*) to reforward 2. (*spedire indietro*) to send back; (*comm.*) to ship back 3. (*far proseguire per altro indirizzo*) to forward; to send on.

rispedizióne, *s.f.* sending back; (*specialmente per mare*) reshipping; (*per terra*) reforwarding.

rispettàbile, *ag.* 1. respectable: *una persona —*, a respectable person ‖ *il — pubblico è pregato di...*, members of the public are requested kindly to... 2. (*considerevole*) considerable: *un'età —*, a considerable age; *un reddito —*, a considerable income; *aveva un naso —*, (*scherz.*) he had a large nose.

rispettabilità, *s.f.* respectability.

rispettàre, *v.t.* 1. to respect; (*onorare*) to honour: *— il padre e la madre*, to honour one's father and mother; *— la vecchiaia*, to respect old age ‖ *— la propria firma, una cambiale*, to honour one's signature, a bill: *non ha rispettato la sua firma*, he has not honoured his signature ‖ *farsi —*, to make oneself respected (*o* to command respect): *è un uomo che sa farsi —*, he is a man who makes himself respected (*o* who commands respect) ‖ *bisogna — l'albero per la sua ombra*, *prov.* honour the tree that gives you shelter 2. (*osservare*) to respect, to observe, to comply with (*sthg.*): *non ha rispettato la legge*, he has broken the law; *non ha rispettato questa clausola del contratto*, he has not complied with (*o* respected) this clause of the contract; *— i gusti, i desideri, i diritti di qlcu.*, to respect s.o.'s tastes, wishes, rights; *— la tradizione*, to be respectful of tradition ‖ *far — la legge*, to enforce the law ‖ **rispettàrsi**, *v.r.* to respect oneself: *mi rispetto troppo per far ciò*, I am above doing that (*o* I have too much self-respect to do that).

rispettivaménte, *av.* respectively: *essi sono — suo padre, suo cugino e suo fratello*, they are her father, her cousin and her brother respectively ‖ *— a*, considering; (*in confronto a*) in comparison with: *ha fatto molta strada — alle sue origini umili*, he has come a long way, considering his humble origins.

rispettívo, *ag.* respective: *i loro nomi erano sulla lista secondo le loro rispettive capacità*, their names were on the list according to their respective capacities.

rispètto, *s.m.* 1. respect: *il — della legge*, the observ-

ance of the law; *il —' di se stesso*, self-respect; *col massimo —*, with the utmost respect; *è una persona che incute, ispira —*, he is a person who commands respect; *la salutò col dovuto —*, he greeted her with all due respect (*o* reverence); *quell'insegnante è tenuto in gran —*, that teacher is held in great respect (*o* is much respected); *avere — per qlcu., ql.co.*, to have respect for s.o., sthg.; *fare ql.co. per — a qlcu.*, to do sthg. out of respect for s.o.; *mancare di — a qlcu.*, to be lacking in respect towards (*o* to be disrespectful to) s.o.; *parlare con —*, to speak respectfully; *portare — a qlcu.*, to respect s.o.; *trattare qlcu. con —*, to treat s.o. with respect (*o* deference): *è trattato con gran — da tutti*, he is looked up to by everybody (*o* everybody treats him with respect) ‖ *— umano*, respect for public opinion: *non ha alcun — umano*, he has no respect for public opinion (*o* he doesn't care what people think) ‖ *con — parlando*, if you'll excuse my saying so (*o* saving your reverence) ‖ *i miei rispetti*, my respects (*o* regards): *presentate i miei rispetti a vostra madre*, please give my respects to your mother ‖ *tenere qlcu. a —*, to keep s.o. at a respectful distance ‖ *la morte non porta — a nessuno*, *prov.* death is no respecter of persons 2. (*aspetto, relazione*) respect: *sotto molti, tutti i rispetti*, in many, in all respects ‖ *— a*, as regards (*o* as to): *— a quella faccenda non so che dirli*, as regards (*o* as to) that matter, I do not know what to tell you ‖ *a, in, per — di*, in comparison with (*o* compared with): *è molto poco in — di quel che mi aspettavo*, it is very little in comparison (*o* compared) with what I expected 3. (*mar.*) spare part: *àncora, vela di —*, spare anchor, sail.

rispettosaménte, *av.* respectfully.

rispettóso, *ag.* respectful: — *verso qlcu.*, respectful to s.o.; *a rispettosa distanza*, at a respectful distance.

rispiegàre, *v.t.* 1. to re-explain, to explain again 2. (*distendere di nuovo*) to unfold again.

risplendènte, *ag.* bright, shining, sparkling; (*luccicante*) glittering; resplendent: *occhi risplendenti*, shining (*o* bright) eyes; *sole —*, bright sun; *stelle risplendenti*, glittering (*o* bright) stars; *viso —*, bright face.

risplendenteménte, *av.* brightly; sparkingly; resplendently.

risplendènza, *s.f.* brightness; resplendence; splendour.

risplèndere, *v.i.* to shine; (*scintillare*) to sparkle; (*luccicare*) to glitter: *risplende il sole*, the sun is shining; *le stelle risplendevano*, the stars were glittering; *i suoi gioielli risplendevano nel buio*, her jewels were glittering in the darkness; *il suo viso risplendeva di gioia*, his face was shining with joy; *— di bellezza*, to shine with beauty ‖ *il suo nome risplenderà nei secoli*, his name will be famous through the centuries.

rispogliàre, *v.t.* 1. to undress again 2. (*privare di nuovo*) to deprive again; (*depredare di nuovo*) to re-plunder, to plunder again ‖ **rispogliàrsi**, *v.r.* 1. to undress again 2. (*privarsi di nuovo*) to deprive oneself again.

rispolveràre, *v.t.* 1. to dust (again) 2. *fig.* (*rinfrescare*) to brush up: *— le proprie conoscenze d'inglese*, to brush up one's knowledge of English.

rispondènte, *ag.* in keeping (with sthg.); answering (sthg., to sthg.); in harmony (with sthg.); (*in conformità*) in conformity (with sthg.): *ciò non è — ai miei bisogni*, this does not answer (to) my needs; *le colonne della facciata non sono rispondenti a quelle delle ali*, the pillars of the façade are not in harmony with those of the wings; *le sue azioni non sono rispondenti alle sue parole*, his actions are not in keeping with his words.

rispondènza, *s.f.* correspondence; (*accordo*) agreement; (*armonia*) harmony: *non c'è alcuna — fra i suoi ideali e la sua condotta*, there is no correspondence between his ideals and his conduct.

rispóndere, *v.i.* 1. to answer (s.o., sthg.), to reply

un'eco ci rispose dalla grotta, an echo replied to us from the grotto; *mi rispose che non poteva venire*, he answered that he could not come; *non ho ancora risposto alla sua lettera*, I have not answered (*o* replied to) his letter yet; — *a una domanda*, to answer (*o* to reply to) a question; — *a un invito*, to reply to (*o* to answer) an invitation; — *al fuoco del nemico*, to reply to the enemy's fire; — *all'appello*, to answer the roll; *fig.* to answer the call; — *al saluto di qlcu.*, to return (*o* to acknowledge) s.o.'s greeting; — *a voce*, to give a verbal answer; — *con un cenno del capo*, to nod (*o* to reply with a nod); — *con una risata*, to answer with a laugh; — *di sì, di no*, to answer yes, no; — *per iscritto*, to answer (*o* to reply) in writing ‖ *non rispose verbo*, he did not answer a word ‖ — *al nome di*, to answer to the name of ‖ — *a mezza bocca*, to answer reluctantly ‖ — *a rovescio*, to reply irrelevantly ‖ — *a tono*, to give a reasonable (*o* logical) answer ‖ — *per le rime*, to give a sharp answer ‖ — *secco secco*, to give a terse answer **2.** (*rimbeccare*) to answer back: *quando lo rimprovero risponde sempre*, when I scold him he always answers back **3.** (*essere responsabile*) to answer (for s.o., sthg.); to be responsible (for s.o., sthg.): *io non rispondo delle sue azioni*, I do not answer for his actions; *ne risponderai personalmente*, you will answer for it personally; *rispondo io della sua obbedienza*, I will answer for his obedience; *ritornerà, ne rispondo io*, he will come back, I assure you (*o* you take my word for it) **4.** (*corrispondere*) to answer (sthg., *o* to sthg.): *ciò risponde al mio scopo*, this answers my purpose; *egli non rispondeva alle mie speranze*, he did not answer to my hopes; *parole che non rispondono al pensiero*, words that do not correspond with one's thoughts; *questo arnese non risponde all'uso*, this tool is not suitable for the work; *questo non risponde ai miei bisogni*, this does not answer to my needs; *questo quadro non risponde alla descrizione che ho udito di esso*, this picture does not answer to the description I had of it; — *all'attesa di qlcu.*, to come up to (*o* to satisfy *o* to be equal to) s.o.'s expectations **5.** (*obbedire*) to respond: *i nervi rispondono a stimoli*, nerves respond to stimuli; *questo cavallo, questo motore non risponde*, this horse, this motor does not respond **6.** (*guardare*) to give on (to sthg.): *queste finestre rispondono sul cortile*, these windows give on to the courtyard **7.** (*a carte*) to reply ‖ *v.t.* **1.** to answer: — *poche parole*, to say a few words in reply; — *poche righe*, to write a few words in reply **2.** (*a carte*) to reply: *ho chiamato cuori e ha risposto quadri*, I called hearts and he replied diamonds ‖ — *picche*, to refuse flatly ‖ **rispóndersi**, *v.r. reciproco* to correspond: *le due ali dell'edificio non si rispondono*, the two wings of the building do not correspond.

rispondièro, *ag.* (*rar.*) (*impertinente*) impertinent, pert, saucy.

responsàbile, *V.* **responsàbile**.

responsióne, *s.f.* responsion.

risp- onsívo, *ag.* responsive.

risposàre, *v.t.*, **risposàrsi**, *v.r.* to remarry, to marry again.

rispósta, *s.f.* **1.** answer, reply: — *secca*, terse (*o* sharp) answer; *in* — *a*, in reply to; *in attesa di una sollecita* —..., hoping (*o* waiting) for an early reply...; *è stata data una* — *alla sua lettera?*, has his letter been answered (*o* replied to)?; *non ho avuto* — *alla mia lettera*, I have had no answer (*o* reply) to my letter; *questa è una domanda senza* —, this is an unanswerable question; *per tutta* — *scoppiò in lacrime*, her only answer was to burst into tears; *il suo appello restò senza* —, there was no response to his appeal; *dare una* — *a qlcu.*, to give s.o. an answer; *lasciare una lettera senza* —, to leave a letter unanswered; *trovare una* — *a tutto*, to find an answer for everything **2.** (*scherma*) riposte: *botta e* —, thrust and counterthrust (anche *fig.*) **3.** (*responso*) response.

risprèmere, *v.t.* to squeeze again, to re-press.

rispuntàre, *v.t.* **1.** (*spuntare di nuovo*) to blunt again; (*capelli, baffi*) to retrim; (*alberi, rami*) to lop again, to re-lop **2.** (*comm.*) to re-check **3.** *fig.* (*vincere, superare di nuovo*) to overcome again ‖ **rispuntarla**, (*averla vinta di nuovo*) to have one's way again ‖ *v.i.* **1.** (*riapparire*) to reappear; (*di astri*) to rise again **2.** (*di rami, germogli*) to sprout again ‖ **rispuntàrsi**, *v.r.* (*perdere la punta, smussarsi*) to get blunt.

ríssa, *s.f.* **1.** fight; brawl, affray; riot **2.** (*polemica*) polemic; controversy, disputation.

rissànte, *s.c.* brawler; rioter.

rissàre, *v.i.* to fight; to brawl; to riot.

rissatóre, *s.m.*, **rissatríce**, *s.f.* brawler; rioter.

rissóso, *ag.* quarrelsome.

ristabiliménto, *s.m.* **1.** re-establishment; restoration **2.** (*recupero della salute*) recovery.

ristabilíre, *v.t.* to re-establish; to restore: *le cure e il riposo valgono a* — *la salute*, treatment and rest can restore one's health; — *la monarchia*, to restore the monarchy; — *l'ordine, la pace*, to restore order, peace ‖ **ristabilírsi**, *v.r.* **1.** (*stabilirsi di nuovo*) to resettle, to settle again **2.** (*rimettersi*) to recover, to get well again: — *in salute*, to recover (one's health).

ristagnaménto, *s.m.* **1.** (*di sangue*) sta(u)nching **2.** (*di acque*) stagnation.

ristagnàre[1], *v.t.* (*far cessare di sgorgare*) to sta(u)nch: *ristagnarono il sangue che gli usciva dal naso*, they staunched the blood flowing from his nose ‖ *v.i.* **1.** (*impaludarsi*) to stagnate, to be stagnant: *le acque ristagnarono nella valle*, the waters stagnated in the valley **2.** (*languire*) to be at a standstill; (*comm.*) to be slack: *gli affari ristagnano*, business is dull (*o* slack).

ristagnàre[2], *v.t.* **1.** (*ricoprire di stagno*) to cover with tin again; to tin-plate again **2.** (*saldare di nuovo*) to resolder, to solder again.

ristagnatúra, *s.f.* tin-plating; re-tinning.

ristàgno, *s.m.* **1.** (*di sangue*) sta(u)nching **2.** (*di acque*) stagnation **3.** (*inerzia*) dullness; (*comm.*) slackness: — *negli affari, nel commercio*, slackness in business, in trade; *c'è un* — *negli affari*, business is slack.

ristàmpa, *s.f.* reprint; reprinting; (new) impression: *sesta* —, sixth impression (*o* sixth printing); *questo libro è in* —, this book is reprinting.

ristampàre, *v.t.* to reprint.

ristàre, *v.i.* **1.** to stay again **2.** (*cessare*) to stop, to cease: *non ristette dal correre*, he did not stop running **3.** (*letter.*) (*rimanere*) to remain: *ristetti in ascolto*, I stopped and listened ‖ **ristàrsi**, *v.r.* (*astenersi*) to refrain: — *dal fare ql.co.*, to refrain from doing sthg.

ristauràre, *e derivati*, *V.* **restauràre**, *e derivati*.

ristillàre, *v.t.* to drip again.

ristoràbile, *ag.* restorable.

ristoraménto, *s.m.* **1.** refreshment **2.** (*restaurazione*) restoration.

ristorànte, *ag.* restorative, refreshing ‖ *s.m.* restaurant; (*di stazione*) refreshment-room, buffet.

ristoràre, *v.t.* **1.** to refresh, to restore (anche *fig.*): *un po' di riposo, di cibo ti ristorerà*, some rest, food will restore you; *quella tazza di tè mi ha ristorato*, that cup of tea has put me right; — *le proprie forze*, to restore one's strength **2.** (*letter.*) (*compensare*) to compensate: — *di ogni danno*, to compensate for any loss ‖ **ristoràrsi**, *v.r.* to refresh oneself: *ci fermammo per ristorarci*, we stopped and took some refreshments; *si ristorarono in una locanda prima di ripartire*, they refreshed themselves at an inn before setting out again.

ristoratívo, *ag.* restorative, refreshing ‖ *s.m.* refreshment.

ristoratóre, *ag.* restorative, refreshing: *pioggia ristoratrice*, refreshing rain; *sonno* —, refreshing sleep ‖ *s.m.* **1.** restorer **2.** (*ristorante*) restaurant.

ristoratríce, *s.f.* restorer.

ristorazióne, *s.f.* **1.** restoration **2.** (*risarcimento*) compensation.

ristornàre, *v.i.* to rebound: *il sasso battè nel muro e ristornò*, the stone hit the wall and rebounded.

ristórno, *s.m.* rebound ‖ *di* —, on the rebound.

ristóro, *s.m.* **1.** relief, solace: *la cura portò* —, the treatment brought relief; *trovar* — *in gl.co.*, to find solace in sthg. **2.** (*bevanda*, *cibo*) refreshment ‖ *luogo di* —, refreshment-room **3.** (*risarcimento*) compensation.

ristrettaménte, *av.* **1.** narrowly, restrictedly **2.** (*poveramente*) in straightened circumstances; poorly.

ristrettézza, *s.f.* **1.** narrowness **2.** (*meschinità*) meanness: — *di idee*, narrow-mindedness **3.** (*insufficienza*) lack: — *di mezzi*, lack of means ‖ *in ristrettezze finanziarie*, in straightened circumstances (*o* hard up).

ristrétto, *ag.* **1.** narrow: *passaggio* —, narrow passage **2.** (*gretto*, *meschino*) narrow, mean: *idee ristrette*, narrow ideas; *mente ristretta*, narrow mind: *persona dalla mente ristretta*, narrow-minded (*o* mean) person; *fare una vita ristretta*, to lead a narrow life **3.** (*limitato*) narrow, limited, restricted; (*scarso*) scanty, poor: *un* — *campo d'azione*, a restricted (*o* limited *o* narrow) range of action; *un* — *cerchio di conoscenze*, a narrow circle of acquaintances; *mezzi ristretti*, scanty (*o* poor) means; *nel senso più* —, in the narrowest sense; *la mia conoscenza dell'inglese è molto ristretta*, my knowledge of English is very limited (*o* poor) **4.** (*condensato*) condensed: *idea ristretta in poche parole*, idea condensed into a few words ‖ *brodo* —, consommé **5.** (*comm.*) reduced: *vendere a prezzo* —, to sell at a reduced price.

ristríngere, *v.t.* to tighten again: *mi ristrinse la mano*, he shook hands with me again.

ristuccàre, *v.t.* **1.** (*edil.*) to replaster, to plaster (up) again, to stucco again **2.** (*nauseare*) to surfeit **3.** (*annoiare*) to bore.

ristuccatúra, *s.f.* (*edil.*) replastering: *queste pareti hanno bisogno di diverse ristuccature*, these walls need to be replastered in several places.

ristucchévole, *ag.* cloying; tiring, wearying.

ristúcco, *ag.* sick, tired; (*fam.*) fed up: *sono* — *di lui*, I am sick (*o* tired) of him; *sono* — *di tutti questi pettegolezzi*, I am fed up with all this gossip(ing).

ristudiàre, *v.t.* to study again.

ristuzzicàre, *v.t.* to poke again; to prod again (anche *fig.*).

risucchiàre, *v.t.* to suck again.

risúcchio, *s.m.* **1.** (*vortice*) eddy; whirlpool **2.** (*metal.*) pipe, piping.

risucciàre, *v.t.* **1.** to suck again **2.** *fig.* (*sopportare di nuovo*) to put up with (sthg.) again.

risultànte, *ag.* resulting, consequent, resultant ‖ *s.f.* (*fis.*) resultant.

risultànza, *s.f.* result, issue; outcome (*invariato al pl.*): *secondo le risultanze del processo*, according to the outcome of the trial.

risultàre, *v.i.* **1.** to result; to come out; to turn out; to follow, to ensue; (*avere origine*) to spring; (*apparire*) to appear: *risultò che la causa dell'esplosione era diversa*, it turned out that the cause of the explosion was different; *risultò che la moneta era falsa*, he coin turned out to be false; *ciò risulterà dall'inchiesta*, this will come out in the enquiry; *ciò risultò da varie circostanze*, this resulted from many circumstances; *dall'autopsia risultò che era morto di morte naturale*, it resulted (*o* turned out) from the autopsy that he had died a natural death; *dalle sue parole risulta che...*, from his words it appears that...; *da tutto ciò risultò molto scontento*, it all caused a great deal of dissatisfaction; *ne risulta che...*, consequently ...(*o* the result is that...); *non so immaginare che cosa ne risulterà*, I cannot imagine what the result of it will be; *la sua innocenza risultò da molte circostanze*, many circumstances pointed to his innocence ‖ *risulta chiaro che...*, it is clear (*o* evident) that... **2.** (*essere noto*): *mi risulta che sia un buon lavoratore*, I am told

he is a good worker; *questo non mi risulta*, I do not know anything about that.

risultàto, *s.m.* result; outcome (*invariato al pl.*): *risultati di una elezione*, results of an election (*o* election results); — *di un'operazione aritmetica*, result of an arithmetical operation; — *di parità*, (*spor.*) draw (*o* tie); *eccone il* —, that is what it led to; *l'esperimento ha dato ottimi risultati*, the experiment has given (*o* yielded) excellent results; *questo fu il* — *della sua pigrizia*, this was the result (*o* outcome) of his laziness.

risuonàre, *V.* risonàre.

risurrezióne, *s.f.* resurrection ‖ *la Risurrezione*, the Resurrection.

risuscitaménto, *s.m.* **1.** resuscitation **2.** *fig.* revival.

risuscitàre, *v.t.* **1.** to resuscitate, to revive: — *i morti*, to raise the dead **2.** *fig.* to revive: *questo cognac mi ha risuscitato*, this brandy has put new life into me; — *dall'oblìo*, to rescue from oblivion; — *una vecchia tradizione*, to revive an old tradition ‖ *v.i.* to rise again, to resuscitate, to revive, to come to life again: *Cristo risuscitò da morte*, Christ rose again from the dead.

risuscitàto, *ag.* resuscitated, revived ‖ *mi sento* —, I feel a new man (*o* I feel another person).

risuscitatóre, *ag.* resuscitating, resuscitative, reviving ‖ *s.m.*, **risuscitatríce**, *s.f.* reviver.

risvegliaménto, *s.m.* (re)awakening.

risvegliàre, *v.t.* **1.** to awake(n), to wake (up), to rouse: *fui risvegliato dal rumore di un'automobile*, I was awakened (*o* roused) by the noise of a car ‖ *la primavera risveglia la natura*, spring awakens nature **2.** *fig.* to awake(n), to rouse, to revive: *vorrei* — *il suo interesse su questo soggetto*, I should like to awake his interest in this subject; — *la memoria*, to revive the memory; — *ricordi*, to stir up (*o* to rouse) memories; — *vecchie passioni*, to stir up (*o* to rouse *o* to wake) old passions ‖ **risvegliàrsi**, *v.r.* **1.** to wake (up), to rouse (up): *mi risvegliai da un sonno agitato*, I woke out of (*o* from) a troubled sleep; *quando si risvegliò era troppo tardi*, when he woke up it was too late ‖ *la natura si risveglia in primavera*, nature wakes (*o* comes to life) in spring **2.** *fig.* to revive, to be (a)roused: *i miei antichi dubbi si risvegliarono*, my old doubts were roused; *la sua gelosia si risvegliò*, his jealousy was aroused afresh; *il suo coraggio si risvegliò*, his courage revived.

risvéglio, *s.m.* **1.** (re)awakening: *al mio* — *trovai che...*, when I woke up (*o* on awaking) I found that... **2.** *fig.* revival: — *della cultura*, revival of learning.

risvòlta, *V.* risvòlto.

risvoltàre, *v.t.* (*svolgere di nuovo*) to unwrap again ‖ *v.i.* (*mutare di nuovo direzione*) to turn again.

risvòlto, *s.m.* (*della giacca*) lapel; (*delle maniche*) cuff; (*della tasca*) flap; (*dei pantaloni*) turn-up; (*amer.*) cuff.

Rita, *no.pr.f.* dim. di **Margherita**.

ritagliàre, *v.t.* to cut out; to cut (off): — *un annuncio pubblicitario*, *un articolo da un giornale*, to clip (*o* to cut out) an advertisement, an article from a newspaper; — *una figura*, to cut out a picture.

ritagliatóre, *ag.* cutting ‖ *s.m.*, **ritagliatríce**, *s.f.* cutter.

ritàglio, *s.m.* **1.** (*taglio di stoffa*) length; (*scampolo*) remnant ‖ *vendere a* —, (*al minuto*) to sell retail (*o* to retail) **2.** *pl.* (*avanzi di stoffa*) remnants, cuttings **3.** (*di giornale*) (newspaper) clipping, cutting **4.** (*parte*, *porzione minima*): *ritagli di tempo*, odd moments; *lo farò appena avrò un* — *di tempo*, I shall do it as soon as I have some spare time (*o* a moment to spare).

ritardàbile, *ag.* delayable.

ritardàre, *v.t.* **1.** to delay, to hold up, to retard: *ciò ha ritardato il suo sviluppo mentale*, this has retarded his mental development; *la nostra partenza fu ritardata dall'inatteso arrivo di due ospiti*, our departure was delayed (*o* held up) by the unexpected arrival of two guests; — *il movimento di una ruota*, to retard the motion of a wheel; — *il progresso*, to retard progress 2. (*differire*) to defer, to put off, to postpone: *devo — il mio arrivo*, I must defer (*o* put off) my arrival ‖ *v.i.* to delay, to be late: *non so perchè egli ritardi tanto*, I do not know why he is so late; *perchè hai ritardato tanto a pagare?*, why have you waited so long before paying? ‖ *il mio orologio ritarda*, my watch is slow.

ritardatàrio, *s.m.* late-comer; (*nel pagare*) defaulter.

ritardàto, *ag.* delayed.

ritardatóre, *ag.* delaying, retardative ‖ *s.m.*, **ritardatríce,** *s.f.* delayer, retarder.

ritàrdo, *s.m.* **1.** delay: *un — di due ore*, a delay of two hours; *senza ulteriore —*, without further delay; *l'aeroplano aveva mezz'ora di —*, the plane was half an hour late; *ci fu un — di un mese nella consegna del lavoro*, there was a time-lag of one month in the delivery of the work; *questo orologio ha un — di dieci minuti*, this watch is ten minutes slow ‖ *in —*, late: *sono in —?*, am I late?; *il treno è in —*, the train is late ‖ *riguadagnare il —*, to make up (for lost) time **2.** (*mus.*) retardation.

ritassàre, *v.t.* to tax again.

ritégno, *s.m.* **1.** (*riserbo*) reserve, reservedness: *senza —*, without reserve (*o* unreservedly): *parlare senza —*, to speak one's mind (*o* to speak out); *il suo — si avvicina alla freddezza*, his reserve is close to coldness; *parlare con molto —*, to speak very reservedly (*o* with much reserve) **2.** (*freno*) restraint; (*riluttanza*) reluctance: *senza ritegni*, unrestrainedly (*o* without restraint); *ha — a parlare della sua famiglia*, he is reluctant to speak (*o* he shrinks from speaking) of his family; *mostrò — a farlo*, he showed reluctance to do it; *non aver — a domandarmi quello che ti occorre*, do not hesitate to ask me for what you need **3.** (*difesa, freno*) stop, check: *asta di —*, (*mec.*) check-rod; *valvola di —*, (*mec.*) check-valve (*o* non-return valve) **4.** (*argine*) dam, damming: *c'era una diga a — del fiume*, there was a dam to keep back the river.

ritemperàre, *v.t.* to resharpen, to sharpen again.

ritempràre, *v.t.* **1.** to strengthen, to fortify, to restore: *la campagna mi ha ritemprato le forze*, the country has restored my strength; *— il coraggio*, to fortify one's courage; *— lo spirito*, to strengthen one's spirit **2.** (*metalli*) to harden again, to retemper ‖ **ritempràrsi,** *v.r.* to get stronger, to acquire new strength, to recruit one's health: *è andato al mare per —*, he has gone to the seaside to recruit his health; *si è ritemprato nella lotta quotidiana*, the daily struggle has made a man of him.

ritenére, *v.t.* **1.** to hold, to detain, to stop, to retain, to keep (*anche fig.*): *egli non può — il cibo*, he cannot hold his food; *— le lacrime*, to keep back (*o* to hold back *o* to check) one's tears; *— il nemico*, to hold the enemy back; *— qlcu. prigioniero*, to keep s.o. prisoner **2.** (*ricordare*) to remember: *non so — quello che leggo*, I cannot remember what I read; *questo bambino non ritiene niente*, this child cannot keep a thing in his head; *— ql.co. a memoria*, to remember sthg. by heart **3.** (*conservare*) to keep, to maintain: *— il posto*, to keep one's place **4.** (*comm.*) (*trattenere*) to hold back **5.** (*credere*) to think, to deem, to believe; (*considerare*) to consider, to regard: *ho ritenuto di far bene*, I believed I was doing right; *ho ritenuto necessario dirglielo*, I deemed it necessary to tell him; *non lo ritengo possibile*, I do not think it possible; *non lo ritengo un uomo onesto*, I do not consider him an honest man; *tutti lo ritengono una vittima*, everybody regards him (as) a victim ‖ **ritenérsi,** *v.r.* **1.** (*trattenersi*) to restrain oneself, to control oneself: *— dal ridere*, to restrain one's mirth **2.** (*considerarsi*) to regard oneself, to consider oneself.

ritenimėnto, *s.m.* **1.** (*ritegno*) restraint **2.** (*trattenuta*) deduction **3.** (*il trattenere*) holding.

ritenitíva, *s.f.* (*facoltà di ricordare*) retentiveness of memory).

ritentàre, *v.t.* **1.** to try again, to retry **2.** (*sottoporre a nuova tentazione*) to tempt again.

ritentíva, *s.f.* (*facoltà di ritenere*) retentiveness.

ritenúta, *s.f.* (*comm.*) deduction: — *sullo stipendio*, deduction from one's wages (*o* stoppage of pay).

ritenutaménte, *av.* reservedly, with reserve.

ritenutézza, *s.f.* reservedness, reserve.

ritenúto, *ag.* **1.** reserved: *siate ritenuti nel parlare*, be cautious when you speak **2.** (*trattenuto*) deducted.

ritenzióne, *s.f.* **1.** (*med.*) retention: — *urinaria*, retention of urine **2.** (*comm.*) (*trattenuta*) deduction.

ritèssere, *v.t.* **1.** to weave again, to reweave **2.** *fig.* (*rifare*) to recompose: *ho dovuto — tutto il romanzo*, I had to recast the whole novel.

ritessitúra, *s.f.* **1.** new weaving, reweaving **2.** *fig.* (*rifacimento*) recasting.

ritíngere, *v.t.* to dye again; to re-dye.

ritínto, *ag.* re-dyed.

ritiràre, *v.t.* **1.** (*tirare indietro*) to withdraw, to draw back, to take back, to retract: *ritiro ciò che ho detto*, I take back what I said; *ritirò velocemente la mano e non fu colpito*, he drew back his hand very quickly and so he was not hurt; — *la candidatura*, to withdraw one's candidature (*o* to stand down); — *una moneta*, to call in a currency; — *un'offerta, una promessa, un'affermazione*, to withdraw (*o* to take back) an offer, a promise, a statement; — *la parola data*, to take back one's word; — *il proprio favore a qlcu.*, to withdraw one's favour from s.o.; — *ql.co. dalla circolazione*, to withdraw sthg. from circulation; — *una querela, un'accusa*, to withdraw an action, an accusation; — *le truppe*, to withdraw the troops **2.** (*riscuotere*) to draw, to withdraw; (*farsi consegnare*) to collect: *passerà poi qlcu. a — i biglietti*, somebody will come later to collect the tickets; — *della merce, un pacco*, to collect (*o* to pick up) goods, a parcel; — *denaro da una banca*, to draw money from (*o* to take money out of) a bank; — *il proprio salario*, to draw one's salary; — *un vaglia*, to cash a money-order ‖ *egli stava copiando, e allora gli ritirai il foglio*, he was cribbing and so I cancelled his paper **3.** (*sparare di nuovo*) to shoot again, to fire again **4.** (*tip.*) (*ristampare*) to reprint ‖ *v.i.* (*restringersi*) to shrink: *questa stoffa ritira facilmente*, this material shrinks very easily ‖ **ritiràrsi,** *v.r.* **1.** to retire, to withdraw: *egli si ritirò subito dopo cena perchè aveva molto sonno*, he retired immediately after supper because he was very sleepy; *ora che ho promesso non posso ritirarmi*, now that I have promised I cannot take back my word; *uno dei candidati si ritira*, one of the candidates is dropping out; — *a vita privata*, to retire into private life; — *da un esame*, to withdraw from an examination; — *dagli affari, dalla politica*, to retire from (*o* to give up) business, politics; — *dalla lotta*, to retire from the field (*o* to withdraw from the fight); — *in buon ordine*, to retire in good order; — *in campagna*, to retire into the country; — *in un paese di campagna*, to retire to a country village; — *in se stesso*, to retire into oneself ‖ *la Corte si ritira*, the Court is adjourned (*o* the Court will rise) **2.** (*di acque*) to fall, to subside; (*di mare*) to recede; (*di marea*) to ebb: *a tre giorni dall'inondazione le acque si ritirarono*, after three days the flood-waters began to subside; *il mare si ritira in questo punto*, the sea is receding at this point; *la marea incominciò a —*, the tide began to ebb (*o* to go out) **3.** (*di truppe*) to retreat; to retire: *le truppe si ritirarono*, the troops retreated (*o* retired) **4.** (*di stoffa, restringersi*) to shrink: *questa stoffa non si ritira*, this cloth does not shrink.

ritiràta, *s.f.* **1.** retreat: *una prudente —*, a prudent retreat (*anche fig.*); *fecero una — che pareva una fuga*, they retreated but seemed to be put to flight; *battere in —*, to beat a retreat (*anche fig.*); *essere in —*, to be in retreat; *proteggere una —*, to cover a retreat; *suonare la —*, to sound the retreat; *tagliare una —*, to cut off (o to intercept) a retreat || — *strategica*, strategic retreat 2. (*in caserma*) tattoo: *suonare la* —, to beat (o to sound) the tattoo 3. (*latrina*) lavatory, toilet; (*amer.*) rest-room 4. (*fortificazione*) inner fortification 5. (*scusa, pretesto*) pretext.

ritirataménte, *av.* secludedly, in retirement: *vivere* —, to live in retirement (o to lead a retired life).

ritiratézza, *s.f.* seclusion, retirement.

ritiràto, *ag.* 1. retired; secluded; sequestered: — *dal mondo*, retired from the world; *valle ritirata*, secluded valley; *vita ritirata*, retired life; *vivere* —, to live in retirement (o seclusion) 2. (*pensionato*) retired; pensioned 3. (*ristretto*) shrunk(en): *indumento* —, shrunken garment 4. (*non sporgente*) non-projecting.

ritìro, *s.m.* 1. (*il ritirare*) withdrawal: — *di truppe, di un ragazzo da scuola, di ql.co. dalla circolazione*, withdrawal of troops, of a boy from school, of sthg. from circulation 2. (*il farsi consegnare*) collection 3. (*luogo appartato*) retreat: *un* — *in cima ad una montagna*, a retreat at the top of a mountain 4. (*il ritirarsi*) retirement, retreat; seclusion; (*dagli affari*) retirement, retiring: *ufficiale in* —, a retired officer || — *spirituale*, (spiritual) retreat 5. (*edil.*) shrinkage.

ritmàre, *v.t.* to mark: — *il passo*, to set the pace; — *il tempo*, to mark the time.

ritmàto, *ag.* measured; rhythmical: *passo* —, measured step.

rítmica, *s.f.* (*mus. poes.*) rhythmic(s).

ritmicaménte, *av.* rhythmically.

rítmico, *ag.* rhythmic(al); measured: *movimento* —, rhythmical movement; *prosa ritmica*, rhythmical prose.

rítmo, *s.m.* rhythm.

ríto, *s.m.* 1. rite: *il* — *ambrosiano, anglicano, romano*, the Ambrosian, Anglican, Roman rite; *riti nuziali, funebri*, nuptial, burial rites; *secondo il nostro* —, according to our rite 2. (*fam.*) (*usanza*) custom, use: — *togliersi il cappello*, it is the custom to take off one's hat; *queste sono cose di* —, these are customary things.

ritoccaménto, *V.* ritoccatúra.

ritoccàre, *v.t.* 1. to retouch, to touch up: — *un quadro, uno scritto*, to retouch (o to touch up) a picture, a piece of writing 2. (*comm.*) to re-adjust: — *le tariffe*, to re-adjust the prices 3. (*foto.*) to retouch.

ritoccàta, *s.f.* touching up: *devo dare qualche* — *a questo quadro, prima di venderlo*, I must touch up this picture before selling it.

ritoccàto, *ag.* 1. retouched, touched up: *una parte ritoccata*, a retouched part 2. (*comm.*) re-adjusted.

ritoccatóre, *s.m.*, **ritoccatríce**, *s.f.* (*pitt. foto.*) retoucher.

ritoccatúra, *s.f.* retouching, touching up: *se guardi bene questo disegno, noterai che ci sono alcune ritoccature*, if you look at this drawing carefully, you will notice it has been touched up.

ritocchíno, *s.m.* 1. slight touching up 2. (*fam.*) (*spuntino*) snack.

ritócco, *s.m.* 1. additional touch, final touch, fresh touch; (*variazione*) slight alteration; (*correzione*) repair: *con qualche* —, *questo ritratto sarà molto bello*, with some additional touches this portrait will be very fine; *devo fare qualche* — *a questa composizione*, I must touch up this composition 2. (*pitt. foto.*) retouching.

ritògliere, *v.t.* 1. to take off again, to take away again: *lo tolse, lo rimise e lo ritolse*, he took it off, put it back and took it off again 2. (*riappropriarsi di*) to take back: *mi ritolse ciò che mi aveva dato*, he took back what he had given me 3. — *moglie, marito*, (*risposarsi*) to remarry, to marry again: *rimasto vedovo ritolse moglie*, as his wife had died he married a second time || **ritògliersi**, *v.r.* 1. to take off again, to take away again: *si ritolse il cappello*, he took off his hat again 2. (*riappropriarsi di*) to take back: *si ritolse ciò che mi aveva donato*, he took back what he had given me.

ritondàre¹, *v.t.* (*arrotondare*) to make round.

ritondàre², *v.t.* (*tosare*) to crop || — *i capelli a qlcu.*, to crop s.o.'s hair.

ritóndere, *v.t.* to shear again; to clip again; to crop.

ritòrcere, *v.t.* 1. (*torcere di nuovo*) to twist again, to retwist; (*con forza*) to wring (out) again: *raccolse il fazzoletto che era caduto di nuovo nell'acqua e lo ritorse*, she picked up the handkerchief that had fallen back into the water and wrung it out again 2. (*ind. tessile*) to twist, to twine: — *filo, cotone*, to twist thread, cotton 3. *fig.* (*rilanciare*) to retort: — *un'accusa, un affronto contro qlcu.*, to retort an accusation, an affront upon s.o. || **ritòrcersi**, *v.r.* to become twisted, to get twisted: *la corda si è tutta ritorta*, the string has got all twisted.

ritorciménto, *s.m.* 1. (*il ritorcere*) twisting (again); (*con forza*) wringing out (again) 2. *fig.* retorting.

ritorcitúra, *s.f.* (*ind. tessile*) twisting, cabling.

ritornàre, *v.i.* 1. to return; (*andare indietro*) to go back; (*venire indietro*) to come back: *l'ho incontrato ritornando dalla chiesa*, I met him on my way back (o on my way home) from church; *mi fece segno di* —, he waved me back; *non ritornerò mai più in quel paese*, I shall never go back (o return) to that country again; *ritorna presto*, come back soon; *ritorneremo su questo argomento*, we shall come back to this subject; — *a casa*, to return (o to go back o to come back) home; — *ad una vecchia abitudine*, to return to an old habit || — *in sé*, to come to one's senses (o to come to o to come round); (*rinsavire*) to come to one's senses 2. (*ricorrere*) to recur: *questa situazione non ritorna spesso nella storia del nostro paese*, this situation does not often recur in the history of our country 3. (*ridiventare*) to become again: *dopo una bella lavata la camicia ritornò nuova*, after a good washing the shirt became like new again || *v.t.* 1. (*restituire*) to return, to give back: *gli ho già ritornato quel denaro*, I have already returned that money to him (o given him that money back) 2. (*far ritornare*) to bring back, to restore: *lo ritornò in vita*, he brought him back (o he restored him) to life; *ritornò il palazzo all'antico splendore*, he restored the palace to its ancient splendour || **ritornàrsi, ritornàrsene**, *v.r.* to return; (*andar indietro*) to go back; (*venire indietro*) to come back: *se ne ritornò a casa*, he went back home.

ritornèllo, *s.m.* (*poet. mus.*) refrain, chorus: *canticchiava il* — *di una canzone popolare*, he was humming the chorus (o refrain) of a popular song || *ripetere sempre lo stesso* —, *fig.* to be always harping on the same string.

ritórno, *s.m.* 1. return; (*ad intervalli più o meno regolari*) recurrence: *il* — *della primavera*, the return of spring; *al mio* —, on my return; *dopo il suo* — *dall'Inghilterra*, after his return from England; *biglietto di andata e* —, return ticket; *viaggio di* —, return journey; (*per mare*) return voyage; *il* — *della febbre è un grave sintomo*, the return (o recurrence) of the fever is a serious symptom; *ci fermeremo al* —, we shall stop here on our way back (o when coming back); *farò* — *appena possibile*, I shall come (o go) back as soon as I can; *essere di* —, to be back; *partita di* —, (*spor.*) return match || *gli domandai: « Quando posso rivederti? », ed egli di* —: « *La settimana prossima* », I asked him: " When shall I see you again? ", " Next week ", he replied 2. (*mec.*) (*di molla*) recovery; (*di pistone*) reversal; (*di pezzo metallico dopo piegatura*) spring back: — *di fiamma*, backfire (o flash-back) 3. (*lv.*) flyback; (*rad.*) return, echo 4. (*comm.*): *carico di* —, homeward cargo; *conto di* —, redraft account; *merci di* —, returns (o returned goods); *nolo di* —, homeward freight; *spese di* —, return charges; *vuoti di* —, empties.

ritorsióne, *s.f.* 1. (*di accusa, insulto, ecc.*) retortion; retort 2. (*rappresaglia*) retaliation.

ritòrta, *s.f.* 1. (*ramoscello flessibile*) withe, withy 2. *fig.* (*vincolo*) chain, bond: *spezzate le ritorte, il popolo riac-*

quistò la libertà, breaking their bonds, the people reconquered their freedom.

ritòrto, *ag.* twisted: *filo* —, twisted thread.

ritòrtola, *s.f.* (*ramoscello flessibile*) withe, withy.

ritradúrre, *v.t.* **1.** (*tradurre di nuovo*) to translate again, to retranslate: *ritradusse il brano per renderne meglio il senso*, he translated the passage a second time to make its meaning clearer **2.** (*riportare nella lingua originale*) to retranslate, to translate back: *traducete l'esercizio 15 dall'inglese in italiano e poi ritraducetelo in inglese*, translate exercise No. 15 from English into Italian and then translate it back into English.

ritrasformàre, *v.t.* to transform again || **ritrasformàrsi,** *v.r.* to transform oneself again, to be transformed again, to turn (oneself) back.

ritràrre, *v.t.* **1.** to withdraw, to draw back: — *la mano, il piede*, to withdraw (*o* to draw back) one's hand, foot **2.** (*distogliere*) to divert, to turn away, to turn aside: *ritrasse lo sguardo da quell'orribile vista*, he turned his eyes away from the horrible sight; — *uno da un'impresa*, to divert s.o. from an enterprise **3.** (*ricavare*) to get, to derive, to obtain: *ho ritratto un buon profitto da quell'impresa*, I made a good profit on that deal; — *vantaggio, beneficio da ql.co.*, to derive advantage, benefit from sthg. **4.** (*rappresentare, riprodurre*) to represent, to reproduce, to portray, to depict: *non è facile* — *su una tela il suo enigmatico sorriso*, it is not easy to reproduce his enigmatic smile on canvas; *questo quadro ritrae una veduta marina*, this picture represents a sea-scape; *volle farsi* — *a cavallo*, he wanted to be portrayed on horseback; — *a memoria*, to draw from memory **5.** (*dedurre*) to deduce; to understand: *dalla tua lettera ritraggo che hai nostalgia della tua casa*, from your letter I understand that you feel homesick || *v.i.* (*somigliare*) to take after (s.o.): *ritrae da suo padre*, he takes after his father || **ritràrsi,** *v.r.* **1.** to withdraw, to retire: *la chiocciola si ritrasse nel suo guscio*, the snail withdrew into its shell; *si ritrasse più in fretta che potè*, he withdrew as quickly as he could **2.** (*liberarsi, sottrarsi*) to withdraw, to get out (of sthg.): *ora che hai promesso non puoi più ritrarti*, now that you have promised you can't get out of it **3.** (*rappresentarsi*) to represent oneself.

ritrattàre[1], *v.t.* **1.** (*trattare di nuovo*) to treat again, to deal with (sthg.) again: — *un argomento*, to deal with a subject again **2.** (*disdire*) to retract, to withdraw, to take back: — *un'accusa*, to withdraw (*o* to take back) an accusation; — *un'affermazione*, to retract (*o* to withdraw) a statement; — *le proprie parole*, to retract (*o* to withdraw *o* to take back) one's words || **ritrattàrsi,** *v.r.* to recant, to retract: *egli fu costretto a* —, he was compelled to recant; *egli lo disse, ma subito si ritrattò*, he said it, but took back his words at once.

ritrattàre[2], *v.t.* (*raffigurare*) to portray, to depict, to draw || **ritrattàrsi,** *v.r.* (*raffigurarsi*) to draw oneself.

ritrattazióne, *s.f.* **1.** (*nuova trattazione*) new treatment; rehandling **2.** (*il disdire*) retraction, withdrawal: — *delle proprie opinioni*, the retraction of one's opinions; — *di un'accusa*, withdrawal of an accusation; — *di un'affermazione*, retraction of a statement.

ritrattìsta, *s.c.* portrait-painter, portraitist: *questo pittore è un eccellente* —, this painter is an excellent portraitist.

ritràtto, *ag.* **1.** (*tratto indietro*) drawn back, withdrawn: *con gli aculei ritratti*, with quills drawn back **2.** (*rappresentato, figurato*) portrayed, depicted, drawn: *ben* —, well-drawn; *un viso ben* —, a well-drawn face; *personaggio fedelmente* —, faithfully-portrayed character || *s.m.* **1.** portrait: — *a olio*, portrait in oils; — *in miniatura*, miniature; — *somigliante*, faithful (*o* lifelike) portrait; *mi ha regalato il suo* —, she gave me her portrait; *il pittore gli ha fatto un bel* —, the painter painted a good portrait of him; *lo scrittore ne fece il fedele* — *nel suo romanzo*, the

writer drew a faithful portrait of her character in his novel; *farsi fare il* —, to have one's portrait painted **2.** (*fedelissima immagine*) picture, image: *ella è il* — *di sua madre*, she is the very (*o fam.* the spit) image of her mother; *pare il* — *della salute*, he looks the picture of health; *quest'uomo è il* — *dell'avarizia*, this man is the soul of avarice.

ritraversàre, *v.t.* to recross, to cross again.

ritrazióne, *s.f.* retraction.

ritrécine, *s.f.* (*rete da pesca*) sweep-net.

ritrinceràre, *v.t.* to entrench again || **ritrinceràrsi,** *v.r.* to entrench oneself again, to dig oneself in again.

ritríto, *ag.* (*ripetuto*) stale, hackneyed: *è una storia ritrita*, it is an old story || *trito e* —, stale (*o* hackneyed): *un argomento trito e* —, a hackneyed subject.

ritroncàre, *v.t.* to cut off again, to truncate again.

ritrósa, *s.f.* **1.** (*per pesci*) (fish-)creel **2.** (*per uccelli*) (*gabbia*) fowling-cage; (*rete*) fowling-net **3.** (*vortice*) whirl; vortex (*pl.* vortices) **4.** (*dial.*) (*di capelli*) obstinate lock.

ritrosàggine, *s.f.* (*rar.*) per **ritrosia**.

ritrosaménte, *av.* **1.** (*con riluttanza*) reluctantly, unwillingly **2.** (*con timidezza*) shyly, bashfully; (*specialmente di fanciulla*) coyly.

ritrosìa, *s.f.* **1.** (*riluttanza*) reluctance, unwillingness; (*avversione*) aversion: *la sua* — *a mostrarsi in pubblico era nota a tutti*, his reluctance to be seen (*o* aversion to being seen) in public was well-known **2.** (*timidezza*) shyness, bashfulness; (*specialmente di fanciulla*) coyness: *la sua* — *gli ha impedito di farsi degli amici*, his shyness (*o* bashfulness) has prevented him from making friends.

ritrosità, *s.f.* (*rar.*) per **ritrosia**.

ritróso, *ag.* **1.** (*retrogrado*) backward; (*che torna indietro*) retreating: *movimento* —, backward movement; *onde ritrose*, retreating waves || *a* —, backwards; (*contro*) against: *a* — *della corrente*, against the current; *camminare a* —, to go backwards **2.** (*riluttante*) reluctant, unwilling; averse: *è* — *ad accettare i nostri consigli*, he is reluctant to accept our advice; *è* — *a frequentare cattivi compagni*, he is unwilling (*o* reluctant) to associate with bad company **3.** (*scontroso*) farouche; (*timido*) shy, bashful; (*specialmente di fanciulla*) coy: *è* — *per natura*, he is naturally shy || *non fare la ritrosa!*, don't be coy! || *s.m.* mouth of a net.

ritrovàbile, *ag.* **1.** that can be found **2.** (*ricuperabile*) recoverable.

ritrovaménto, *s.m.* **1.** finding again **2.** (*invenzione*) invention; (*scoperta*) discovery: *il* — *della bussola*, the invention of the compass || — *della Santa Croce*, the finding of the True Cross **3.** (*teat.*) discovery scene.

ritrovàre, *v.t.* **1.** to find again: *bada di non farti* — *qui un'altra volta!*, don't let me find you here again!; *la chiave è stata ritrovata*, the key has been found; *devo averlo lasciato sulla panchina, ma spero di ritrovarlo*, I must have left it on the bench but I hope to find it again; *ha ritrovato la sua strada*, he has found his way again **2.** (*recuperare*) to recover: *il tempo perduto non si ritrova più*, lost time can never be made up; — *il coraggio, la parola*, to recover one's courage, one's power of speech **3.** (*scoprire*) to discover, to find: *ha ritrovato un'isola sconosciuta*, he has discovered an unknown island; *ha ritrovato un rimedio contro quella malattia*, he has discovered a remedy for that disease **4.** (*incontrare di nuovo*) to meet again; (*far visita a*) to visit, to call (up)on (s.o.): *andiamo a ritrovarlo*, let's go and see him; *lo ritrovai ad un congresso*, I met him again at a congress **5.** (*riconoscere*) to recognize: *è difficile* — *il suo stile in quel romanzo*, his style is hardly recognizable in that novel; *non lo ritrovo in questa fotografia*, I cannot recognize him in this photo || **ritrovàrsi,** *v.r.* **1.** to find oneself: *ci ritrovammo ben presto in cima alla montagna*, we soon found ourselves at the top of the mountain; *si ritrovarono allo stesso punto*, they found themselves once again in the same position **2.** (*incontrarsi di nuovo*) to meet again: *ci ritroveremo quest'estate al mare*, we shall meet again at the seaside this summer 3. (*raccapezzarsi*) to see one's way, to make (sthg.) out: *accompagnami a casa, perchè qui non mi ci ritrovo*, take me home, I do not know the way (o I have lost my bearings) || *mi ci trovo con questa gente*, I feel at ease with these people.

ritrovàta, *s.f.* 1. (*il ritrovare*) finding again 2. (*invenzione*) invention; (*scoperta*) discovery.

ritrovàto, *s.m.* 1. (*invenzione*) invention; (*scoperta*) discovery 2. (*espediente*) expedient; device, contrivance; (*fam.*) gadget.

ritrovatóre, *s.m.* (*inventore*) inventor; (*scopritore*) discoverer.

ritròvo, *s.m.* 1. meeting-place; (*di criminali*) haunt 2. (*riunione*) reunion, gathering.

rìtta, *s.f.* right hand.

rìtto, *ag.* 1. upright, erect; (*diritto*) straight: *a coda ritta*, with tail erect; *capelli ritti per lo spavento*, hair standing on end with fright; *mettere un palo —*, to set a pole upright; *stare —*, to stand upright (o erect o up straight) || *— come un fuso*, as straight as a post 2. (*destro*) right: *volgersi a mano ritta*, to turn to the right || *s.m.* 1. (*di stoffe*) right side 2. (*puntello*) upright, support; (*miner.*) pit-prop.

rituàle, *ag.* 1. ritual 2. (*conforme alle consuetudini*) customary || *s.m.* 1. (*eccl.*) ritual, ceremonial 2. (*cerimoniale, galateo*) ceremonial.

ritualìsmo, *s.m.* (*st. relig.*) ritualism.

ritualìsta, *s.m.* (*st. relig.*) ritualist.

ritualménte, *av.* ritually.

rituffàre, *v.t.*, **rituffàrsi**, *v.r.* to replunge.

rituràre, *v.t.* to stop again, to replug.

riudìre, *v.t.* to hear again.

riumiliàre, *v.t.* to humble again, to mortify again.

riúngere, *v.t.* 1. to oil again; to grease again 2. (*adulare di nuovo*) to flatter again || **riúngersi**, *v.r.* (*rifar quattrini*) to make money again.

riunióne, *s.f.* reunion, gathering, meeting; (*fam.*) get-together: *— di atletica leggera, di corse*, (*spor.*) athletics-meeting, race-meeting; *— di famiglia*, family reunion; *— di vecchi compagni di scuola*, college reunion; *— mondana*, social gathering; *prendere parte ad una —*, to attend a meeting; *tenere una —*, to hold a meeting.

riunìre, *v.t.* 1. to re-unite: *— i pezzi di ql.co.*, to put together the pieces of sthg. 2. (*adunare*) to gather; to collect together: *riunisci i tuoi libri sul tavolo*, collect your books together on the table; *— alcuni amici*, to gather together a few friends; *— una assemblea*, to convene an assembly 3. (*unire*) to join together; to combine: *questa soluzione riunisce molti vantaggi*, this solution combines (o unites) a number of advantages 4. (*riconciliare*) to reconcile, to bring together again: *il dolore ci ha riuniti*, grief has brought us together again 5. (*equitazione*) to gather: *— un cavallo*, to gather a horse || **riunìrsi**, *v.r.* 1. to re-unite, to come together again: *dopo una lunga separazione si riunirono*, after a long separation they came together again 2. (*unirsi, allearsi*) to unite; (*adunarsi*) to gather, to meet: *riuniamoci e saremo più forti*, let us unite and we shall be stronger; *ci riunivamo in un bar di Via Veneto ogni settimana*, we used to meet every week in a bar on the Via Veneto; *domani si riunisce il Parlamento*, Parliament will meet to-morrow; *— intorno al fuoco*, to gather round the fire 3. (*essere insieme, trovarsi*) to combine, to be combined: *molte buone qualità si riunivano in lui*, many good qualities were combined in him.

riunìto, *ag.* 1. re-united 2. (*adunato*) gathered 3. (*messo insieme*) joined, combined.

riúnto, *ag.* 1. re-oiled, oiled again; greased again 2. (*arricchito*) parvenu (*attributivo*): *villano —*, nouveau riche (o upstart).

riuscíre, *v.i.* 1. to succeed (in doing); to manage;

(*essere capace*) to be able: *non riuscii a saperlo*, I did not manage to get to know it (o to find it out); *non riuscii a vederlo*, I was not able to see him; *non riuscimmo a superare l'esame*, we failed to pass our examination; *non riesco a capire perchè*, I cannot understand why; *non sono mai riuscito a farlo venire*, I have never been able (o I have never managed) to get him to come; *riuscii a dominare la mia collera*, I managed to master my anger; *riuscì a finire il lavoro*, he succeeded in finishing his work 2. (*aver buon esito*) to succeed (in sthg., in doing), to be successful (in sthg., in doing); to manage (sthg.); to turn out well: *come avvocato non riuscì*, he did not succeed as a lawyer; *tutti i miei piani riuscirono*, all my plans succeeded (o my plans were all successful); *i nostri piani non riuscirono*, our plans failed (o were unsuccessful); *il pranzo, l'esperimento riuscì bene*, the dinner, the experiment turned out well; *penso di riuscirci*, I think I can manage it; *questo dolce è riuscito molto bene*, this cake has turned out very well; *— negli affari*, to succeed in business || *(non) — bene in fotografia*, (not) to come out very well 3. (*avere attitudine, capacità*) to be good at (sthg., doing); to be clever at (sthg., doing): *egli riesce bene in matematica, in disegno*, he is good (o clever) at mathematics, at drawing 4. (*apparire, risultare*) to be; (*dimostrarsi*) to prove: *ciò mi riesce nuovo*, this is new to me; *egli riesce simpatico a tutti*, everybody likes him; *riuscì un completo fallimento*, it was a complete failure; *messo alla prova, egli riuscì il più bravo*, when put to the test he proved to be the cleverest; *il lavoro non mi riusciva gradito*, I did not like my work very much; *tutto gli riusciva intollerabile*, everything was unbearable to him 5. (*giungere*) to come (to a place), to arrive (at, in a place); (*sboccare*) to lead (to a place): *per quella strada si riesce sulla piazza*, if you go down that street you come to the square; *il sentiero riesce sulla strada*, the path leads to the main road 6. (*andare a parare*) to drive (at sthg.): *chi sa a che cosa vuol — con queste parole*, I wonder what he is driving at with these words 7. (*uscire di nuovo*) to go out again: *tornò a casa, ma riuscì subito*, he came home but went out again at once.

riuscìta, *s.f.* (*risultato*) issue, result; (*successo*) success: *la — di ciò dipende solo da te*, the success of this depends entirely on you; *queste scarpe hanno fatto una buona —*, these shoes have worn well; *cattiva —*, lack of success: *l'esperimento ha fatto una cattiva —*, the experiment was a failure (o did not come off well); *qualunque sia la — dell'impresa*, whatever the outcome of the undertaking may be.

riuscíto, *ag.* successful: *un abito, un dolce ben —*, a well-made dress, cake: *un'impresa riuscita*, a successful undertaking; *mal —*, unsuccessful.

rìva, *s.f.* 1. (*di mare, lago*) shore: *sulla — del mare*, on the seashore; *città sulla — del mare*, seaside town; *mantenersi a —*, to keep close to the shore; *toccare la —*, to set foot on shore 2. (*di fiume, canale*) bank.

rivaccinàre, *v.t.* to revaccinate.

rivaccinazióne, *s.f.* revaccination.

rivàle, *ag.* rival (*attributivo*): *le potenze rivali*, the rival powers || *s.c.* rival, competitor: *rivali in amore*, rivals in love; *rivali in commercio*, business rivals.

rivaleggiàre, *v.i.* to rival (s.o.), to vie, to compete: *— con qlcu. in amore*, to be s.o.'s rival in love; *— con qlcu., con ql.co. in bellezza*, to compete (o to vie) in beauty with s.o., with sthg.

rivalérsi, *v.r.* 1. to make good one's losses, to make up for one's losses: *credo che non potrò rivalermi con nessuno*, I don't think I shall be able to recover my money at all; *egli non ha il diritto di — su di me*, he has no right to make good his losses at my expense; *— di un danno su qlcu.*, to make up for a loss at s.o.'s expense 2. (*valersi di nuovo*) to make use again: to avail oneself again.

rivalicàre, *v.t.* to cross again, to recross.

rivalità, *s.f.* rivalry.

rivàlsa, *s.f.* **1.** (*rivincita*) revenge: *prendersi la — su qlcu.*, to take one's revenge on s.o. **2.** (*risarcimento*) compensation; reimbursement ‖ *— cambiaria*, (*comm.*) redraft.

rivalutàre, *v.t.* **1.** to revalue: *— uno scrittore*, to revalue a writer **2.** (*di valuta*) to revalue: *— una valuta*, to revalue a currency **3.** (*elevare*) to raise: *— gli stipendi*, to raise salaries.

rivalutazióne, *s.f.* **1.** revaluation **2.** (*di valuta*) revaluation **3.** (*aumento*) rise; (*amer.*) raise.

rivangàre, *v.t.* to dig up again (anche *fig.*): *non — il passato*, let bygones be bygones (*o* don't dig up the past).

rivedére, *v.t.* **1.** (*vedere, incontrare di nuovo*) to see again; to meet again: *lo rividi dopo una settimana*, I saw him again after a week; *non l'ho mai più rivisto*, I have never met him again ‖ *chi non muore si rivede*, *prov.* those who do not die, come back **2.** (*un luogo, ritornarci*) to return, to come back, to go back: *— la patria*, to come back to one's country **3.** (*correggere*) to correct, to revise; (*verificare*) to check: *— le bozze*, to proof-read (*o* to proof-correct); *— i conti*, to check the accounts; (*se da specialista chiamato ufficialmente*) to audit the accounts; *— l'edizione di un libro, una traduzione*, to revise the edition of a book, a translation **4.** (*ripassare*) to look over again: *— la lezione*, to look over one's lesson again ‖ *— le costole, il pelo a uno*, to give s.o. a good hiding (*o* to give s.o. a thrashing) **5.** (*passare in rivista*) to review; (*ispezionare*) to inspect: *— le fortificazioni*, to inspect the fortifications; *— le truppe*, to review the troops **6.** (*affilare, arrotare*) to whet, to sharpen: *— il filo di una spada*, to sharpen a sword ‖ **rivedérsi,** *v.r. reciproco*, to see each other (one another) again; to meet again ‖ *a rivederci*, au revoir (*o* good-bye *o* see you soon) ‖ *ci rivedremo a Filippi*, we shall meet again (*o* letter. thou shalt meet me) at Philippi.

rivedíbile, *ag.* **1.** revisable **2.** (*mil.*) temporarily unfit.

rivedtóre, *ag.* revising: *commissione riveditrice del bilancio*, commission revising the balance-sheet ‖ *s.m.*, **riveditríce,** *s.f.* reviser, revisor.

rivedúta, *s.f.* look, glance: *ho dato una — alla sua tesi*, I've had a look (*o* glance) at his thesis.

rivedúto, *ag.* revised; (*corretto*) corrected; (*verificato*) checked: *bozze rivedute*, corrected proofs; *edizione riveduta*, revised edition.

rivelàbile, *ag.* revealable.

rivelàre, *v.t.* **1.** to reveal, to disclose: *— le proprie intenzioni*, to reveal (*o* to disclose) one's intentions; *— un segreto*, to reveal (*o* to disclose) a secret **2.** (*dar prova di, mostrare*) to reveal, to show, to display: *egli rivelò tutta la sua intelligenza in questo lavoro*, he displayed all his intelligence in this work; *il lavoro rivelò le sue qualità*, the work revealed his qualities **3.** (*teol.*) to reveal: *— il dogma della Trinità*, to reveal the dogma of the Trinity ‖ **rivelàrsi,** *v.r.* to reveal oneself, to show oneself: *egli si rivelò un vero amico*, he showed (*o* revealed) himself to be a real friend.

rivelàto, *ag.* revealed: *religioni rivelate*, (*teol.*) revealed religions.

rivelatóre, *ag.* revealing: *sguardo —*, revealing (*o* tell-tale) glance ‖ *s.m.* **1.** revealer **2.** (*rad.*) (*rettificatore*) detector; (*coesore*) coherer: *— a campo frenante*, retarding field detector (*o* reverse-field detector); *— a cristallo*, crystal detector; *— a eterodina*, heterodyne detector **3.** (*chim. foto.*) developer.

rivelatríce, *s.f.* revealer.

rivelazióne, *s.f.* **1.** revelation: *è una vera — per me*, it is a real revelation to me **2.** (*teol.*) revelation: *la divina —*, divine revelation **3.** (*fis. rad.*) detection.

rivellino, *s.m.* (*mil.*) (*opera di fortificazione*) ravelin.

rivéndere, *v.t.* **1.** to resell, to sell again: *se ti di-* *spiace di avermelo venduto, te lo rivendo*, if you are sorry you sold it to me, I'll resell it to you (*o* I'll sell it back to you) **2.** (*vendere al dettaglio*) to sell retail, to retail **3.** (*superare*) to surpass: *in filosofia li rivende tutti*, in philosophy he surpasses everybody.

rivendíbile, *ag.* resalable.

rivendicàre, *v.t.* to claim; (*dir.*) to vindicate: *— il diritto di fare ql.co.*, to claim the right to do sthg.; *— la libertà perduta*, to claim lost freedom; *— la priorità*, to claim priority; *— ql.co. a qlcu.*, to claim sthg. from s.o. ‖ **rivendicàrsi,** *v.r.* to revenge oneself (on s.o., for sthg.).

rivendicatóre, *ag.* **1.** claiming **2.** (*vendicatore*) revenging ‖ *s.m.*, **rivendicatríce,** *s.f.* **1.** claimant, claimer **2.** (*chi vendica di nuovo*) revenger.

rivendicazióne, *s.f.* claim; vindication.

rivéndita, *s.f.* **1.** (*il rivendere*) resale; reselling **2.** (*negozio*) shop.

rivenditóre, *s.m.*, **rivenditríce,** *s.f.* **1.** (*al minuto*) retailer; (*piccolo negoziante*) small shopkeeper **2.** (*rigattiere*) second-hand dealer.

rivendúgliolo, *s.m.* (*spreg.*) small shopkeeper.

riveníre, *v.i.* **1.** to come again, to return, to come back **2.** (*rinvenire*) to come to, to recover one's senses.

riverberaménto, *s.m.* (*di suono*) reverberation; (*di luce, calore*) reflection.

riverberàre, *v.t.* (*di suono*) to reverberate, to re-echo; (*di luce, calore*) to reverberate, to reflect ‖ *v.i.*, **riverberàrsi,** *v.r.* (*di suono*) to be re-echoed (anche *fig.*); (*di luce, calore*) to be reflected (anche *fig.*): *la sua gloria si riverbera sull'intera famiglia*, his glory is reflected on the whole family.

riverberazióne, *s.f.* (*di suono*) reverberation; (*di luce, calore*) reflection.

rivèrbero, *s.m.* (*di suono*) reverberation; (*di luce, calore*) reflection; (*bagliore*) glare: *— della luce, del calore*, reflection of light, of heat; *forno a —*, (*metal.*) reverberatory furnace; *lume a —*, reverberator; *proteggiti gli occhi dal —*, protect your eyes from the glare ‖ *di —*, indirectly: *colpire di —*, to hit indirectly.

riverènte, *ag.* reverent; (*rispettoso*) respectful.

riverenteménte, *av.* reverently; (*rispettosamente*) respectfully.

riverènza, *s.f.* **1.** reverence; (*rispetto*) respect: *— verso Dio*, reverence before God; *la — che si deve ai vecchi*, the respect due to old people; *trattare qlcu. con —*, to treat s.o. with reverence (*o* reverently) ‖ *con —*, (*con rispetto parlando*) with (all) due respect (*o* saving your presence) **2.** (*inchino*) bow; (*fatto da donna*) curtsey: *fare una —*, to drop a curtsey (*o* to bow) ‖ *far la —*, (*scherz.*) (*appisolarsi*) to nod **3.** (*ossequio*) regard.

riverenziàle, *ag.* reverential: *timore —*, reverential fear.

riveríre, *v.t.* **1.** (*venerare*) to revere; (*rispettare*) to respect; (*onorare*) to honour: *— i propri genitori*, to respect one's parents **2.** (*ossequiare*) to pay one's respects to (s.o.): *riverite per me vostro padre*, give my respects to your father; *quando arriverà dovrò andarlo a —*, when he arrives I shall have to go and pay my respects to him.

riveríto, *ag.* revered; (*stimato*) esteemed; (*rispettato*) respected: *— da tutti*, respected by all; *Riverito Signore*, (*iniziando una lettera*) Dear Sir; *la vostra riverita lettera*, your esteemed letter ‖ *—, signor mio!*, my regards, sir ‖ *ho i miei riveriti dubbi*, (*iron.*) I have grave doubts.

riverniciàre, *v.t.* to repaint; (*con lacca*) to revarnish.

riverniciatúra, *s.f.* repainting; (*con lacca*) revarnishing.

riversaménto, *s.m.* (out)pouring.

riversàre, *v.t.* **1.** to pour (again), to pour out (again): *riversami da bere*, pour me out another glass; *riversò l'acqua nella bottiglia*, he poured the water back into the bottle **2.** (*versare*) to pour: *questo fiume riversa le* *sue acque nel mare*, this river flows into the sea **3.** (*attribuire*) to throw: — *la colpa su qlcu.*, to throw (*o* to lay) the blame on s.o. ‖ **riversàrsi**, *v.r.* **1.** to flow: *le acque di questo fiume si riversano nel lago*, the waters of this river flow into the lake **2.** *fig.* to pour: *tutti si riversarono nella grande sala*, everybody poured (*o* rushed) into the big hall.

riversíbile, *ag.* reversible.

riversibilità, *s.f.* reversibility.

riversióne, *s.f.* (*dir. biol.*) reversion.

rivèrso, *ag.* on one's back: *cadere* —, to fall on one's back ‖ *s.m.* (*arc.*) **1.** (*di pioggia*) shower **2.** (*rovina*) disaster.

rivestiménto, *s.m.* covering; (*interno*) lining: *il* — *di un muro*, the facing of a wall; — *di pelle*, leather covering: *con un* — *di pelle*, leather-covered; *la scatola ha un* — *di velluto*, the box has a velvet lining.

rivestíre, *v.t.* **1.** (*vestire di nuovo*) to dress again, to reclothe **2.** (*provvedere di vestiti*) to clothe: *ha bisogno di essere completamente rivestito*, his wardrobe needs to be completely renewed **3.** (*ricoprire*) to cover; (*foderare*) to line: — *con mattonelle*, (*edil.*) to tile; — *con pannelli*, (*edil.*) to panel; — *di pelle, di legno*, to line (*o* to cover) with leather, wood **4.** (*miner.*) (*un pozzo*) to tub **5.** *fig.* to hold: — *una carica, un grado*, to hold a position, a rank: *rivestiva la carica di sindaco*, he held office of mayor ‖ **rivestírsi**, *v.r.* to dress (oneself) again; to clothe oneself (with sthg.) (anche *fig.*): *la natura si riveste di fiori*, nature clothes (*o* bedecks) herself with flowers.

rivestíto, *s.m.* **1.** dressed (in sthg.): — *a festa*, in one's Sunday clothes ‖ *villano* —, upstart (*o* parvenu) **2.** (*ricoperto*) covered (with sthg.); (*foderato*) lined (with sthg.).

rivestítúra, *V.* **rivestiménto**.

rivétto, *s.m.* (*mec.*) rivet: — *a maschio*, screw-rivet; — *a testa fresata piana*, countersunk-head rivet; — *spaccato*, split rivet; — *tubolare*, tubular rivet.

rivièra, *s.f.* coast ‖ *la Riviera italiana*, the Italian Riviera.

rivieràsco, *ag.* coast (*attribulivo*) ‖ *s.m.* coast-dweller.

rivíncere, *v.t.* **1.** to win again **2.** (*ricuperare vincendo*) to win back.

rivíncita, *s.f.* **1.** (*mil.*) reconquest **2.** (*spor.*) return match; (*al giuoco*) return game: *dare, volere la* —, to give, to want a chance of revenge **3.** *fig.* (*vendetta*) revenge: *prendersi la* —, to take one's revenge.

rivisitàre, *v.t.* to revisit, to visit again.

rivísta, *s.f.* **1.** revising, revision: *dare una* — *a ql.co.*, to revise sthg. **2.** (*mil.*) review; (*parata*) parade: *la grande* — *per la festa nazionale*, the great parade for the national festival; *passare in* — *le truppe*, to review the troops ‖ *passare in* — *il proprio passato*, to pass one's past in review **3.** (*periodico*) review; (*rotocalco*) magazine: — *di moda*, fashion magazine; — *letteraria, scientifica*, literary, scientific review; — *trimestrale*, quarterly (review); *giornali e riviste*, newspapers and magazines **4.** (*teat.*) revue: — *di varietà*, variety show.

rivívere, *v.t.* to live again, to relive: *non vorrei quei momenti*, I should not like to relive those moments; *se io potessi* — *la mia vita*, if I could live my life over again ‖ *v.i.* **1.** to live again, to relive, to revive: *i fiori rivivono al fresco*, flowers revive in the cool; *in noi rivivono le qualità dei nostri nonni*, the qualities of our ancestors live again in us (*o* relive in us) **2.** (*ritornare in vita*) to come to life again: *mi sento* —, (*mi sento un altro uomo*) I feel (like) a new man; *rivisse la cultura, rivissero le antiche tradizioni*, there was a revival of learning, of the old traditions ‖ *fare* — *qlcu.*, to bring s.o. to life again.

rivivificàre, *v.t.* to revivify, to revive.

rivivíscènza, *s.f.* reviviscence.

rívo, *s.m.* brook; stream (anche *fig.*): *un* — *di san-*

gue, di lacrime, di lava, a stream of blood, tears, lava.

rivolére, *v.t.* **1.** to want again **2.** (*volere indietro*) to want back.

rivòlgere, *v.t.* **1.** to turn: — *gli occhi al cielo*, to turn one's eyes to heaven; — *i propri pensieri, sforzi, interessi a ql.co.*, to turn one's thoughts, efforts, interests to sthg. **2.** (*indirizzare*) to address: *a chi sono rivolte queste parole?*, who are these words addressed to?; *mi rivolse la parola in inglese*, he addressed me in English; *non mi ha neppure rivolto la parola*, he has not even spoken to me; — *una preghiera a qlcu.*, to address a prayer to s.o. **3.** — *ql.co. nella mente*, to brood over sthg.: *sta ancora rivolgendo nella mente le stesse cose*, he is still brooding over the same things **4.** (*rovesciare*) to turn upside-down: *rivolse la borsa con l'apertura all'ingiù*, he turned the bag upside down **5.** (*distogliere*) to turn away; (*dissuadere*) to dissuade: *lo rivolgemmo da quella cattiva azione*, we dissuaded him from that evil action; *rivolsi lo sguardo da quella scena*, I turned my eyes away from that sight **6.** (*girare*) to turn: — *la chiave nella toppa*, to turn the key in the lock ‖ **rivòlgersi**, *v.r.* **1.** to turn; (*parlando*) to address (s.o.): *mi rivolgo solo a coloro che vogliono ascoltarmi*, I am only addressing those who want to listen to me; *"Va bene", disse rivolgendosi verso di me*, "All right", he said turning to me **2.** (*ricorrere*) to apply, to refer; (*per conforto*) to turn: *rivolgiti a lui per qualsiasi cosa tu abbia bisogno*, apply to him for anything you may need; *si rivolse alla madre perchè la confortasse*, she turned to her mother for comfort ‖ — *alla religione*, to turn to religion ‖ *per ulteriori informazioni* — *a...*, for further information apply to... **3.** (*essere indirizzato*) to apply, to be addressed: *questa osservazione non si rivolge a te*, this remark does not apply to you; *queste parole si rivolgono a te*, these words are addressed to you **4.** (*dirigersi*) to make for (a place): *ci rivolgemmo verso casa*, we made for home **5.** (*ribellarsi*) to rebel, to revolt: *gli indigeni si rivolsero contro il viceré*, the natives rebelled against the viceroy **6.** (*girare*) to turn.

rivolgiménto, *s.m.* **1.** upheaval, (*fig.* upheaval, disturbance: *i rivolgimenti della crosta terrestre*, the upheavals of the earth's crust; — *politico*, political disturbance; — *sociale*, social upheaval **2.** (*rivoluzione*) revolution; (*cambiamento*) change: — *nelle arti*, change in the arts.

rivòlta, *s.f.* **1.** revolt, rebellion: *domare una* —, to put down a rebellion **2.** (*mar. mil.*) mutiny **3.** (*giro*) turn **4.** (*risvolto, di guanto, ecc.*) turn-up.

rivoltànte, *ag.* revolting, disgusting.

rivoltàre, *v.t.* **1.** to turn over again; to turn round again: *voltò e rivoltò quelle pagine*, he turned those pages over and over again **2.** (*rovesciare*) to turn (over); (*con l'interno all'esterno*) to turn inside out; (*capovolgere*) to turn upside-down: *rivolta quel bicchiere*, turn that glass upside-down; — *la frittata*, to turn (over) the omelette; *fig.* to change one's tune; — *il materasso*, to turn the mattress; — *un vestito*, to turn a dress: *questo vestito è stato rivoltato*, this dress has been turned; — *le zolle*, to turn the soil ‖ *far* — *un vestito*, to have a dress turned **3.** (*mescolare*) to mix: — *l'insalata*, to mix a salad **4.** *fig.* (*sconvolgere*) to upset: *questo odore mi rivolta lo stomaco*, this smell upsets my stomach ‖ **rivoltàrsi**, *v.r.* **1.** (*dall'altra parte*) to turn round; (*rigirarsi*) to turn over: *ella si rivoltò per salutarmi*, she turned round to wave to me; *quel malato non può neppure* — *nel letto*, that patient cannot even turn over in bed; *si è rivoltato nel letto per tutta la notte*, he tossed about in his bed the whole night long **2.** (*ribellarsi*) to revolt, to rebel: *egli si rivoltò contro di me come una vipera*, he turned on me like a viper; *il mio senso dell'onore si rivolta ad una simile proposta*, my sense of honour revolts at (*o* against) such a proposal; *si rivoltarono contro il loro re*, they revolted (*o* rebelled) against their king **3.** *fig.*

(*sconvolgersi*) to turn: *quando vidi quel sangue mi si rivoltò lo stomaco*, when I saw that blood my stomach turned.

rivoltàta, *s.f.* turning over.

rivoltatúra, *s.f.* turning (inside out).

rivoltàto, *ag.* turned; turned out; (turned) inside out: *abito —*, turned dress; *con le tasche rivoltate*, with his pockets inside out ‖ *giubba rivoltata*, *fig.* turncoat.

rivoltèlla, *s.f.* revolver: *— a sei colpi*, six-chambered revolver (*o* six-shooter); *— automatica*, automatic revolver.

rivoltellàta, *s.f.* revolver shot.

rivòlto, *V.* risvòlto.

rivoltolaménto, *s.m.* turning over; rolling over.

rivoltolàre, *v.t.* 1. to turn (over); to roll (over): *rivollolava della carta fra le mani*, he was turning some paper in his hands 2. (*mettere sossopra*) to turn upside-down, to turn topsyturvy: *— la biancheria nel cassetto*, to turn the linen in the drawer upside down (*o* topsyturvy) ‖ **rivoltolàrsi**, *v.r.* to roll over; to roll about; to wallow: *— nel letto*, to roll about in (*o* to toss on) one's bed; *— nel fango*, to wallow in mud.

rivoltolío, *s.m.* turning (over).

rivoltolóne, *s.m.* somersault: *fare un —*, to turn a somersault ‖ *a rivoltoloni*, somersaulting.

rivoltóso, *ag.* rebellious ‖ *s.m.* rebel, rioter.

rivoluzionàre, *v.t.* to revolutionize.

rivoluzionàrio, *ag.s.m.* revolutionary: *teorie rivoluzionarie*, revolutionary theories.

rivoluzionarìsmo, *s.m.* revolutionism.

rivoluzióne, *s.f.* 1. revolution: *la — francese, russa*, the French, Russian revolution; *allo scoppio della —*, on the outbreak of the revolution; *le sue idee portarono una completa — nelle scienze naturali*, his ideas brought about a complete revolution in the natural sciences 2. (*scient.*) revolution: *la — di una ruota*, the revolution of a wheel; *la — della Luna intorno alla Terra*, (*astr.*) the revolution of the Moon round the Earth 3. (*confusione*) mess: *che —!*, what a mess!.

rivulsióne, *s.f.* (*med.*) revulsion.

rivulsìvo, *ag.* (*med.*) revulsive.

rizòma, *s.m.* (*bot.*) rhizome.

rízza, *s.f.* (*mar.*) 1. lashing 2. *pl.* gripes.

rizzàre, *v.t.* 1. to raise, to erect: *— la bandiera, una vela*, to hoist the flag, a sail; *— le orecchie*, to prick up one's ears (anche *fig.*) (*o fig.* to strain one's ears); *— la testa*, to raise one's head ‖ *è una storia che fa — i capelli*, it is a story which makes one's hair stand on end ‖ *— la cresta*, to grow proud (*o* insolent); (*darsi delle arie*) to put on airs 2. (*erigere*) to erect, to raise; (*costruire*) to build: *— un monumento*, to raise (*o* to erect) a monument; *— un muro*, to build a wall 3. (*mar.*) to lash, to frap ‖ **rizzàrsi**, *v.r.* to stand up: *gli ordinai di —*, I ordered him to stand straight ‖ *a quelle parole mi si rizzarono i capelli*, those words made my hair stand on end.

rizzatúra, *s.f.* (*mar.*) gripes (*pl.*).

roàno, *ag.s.m.* roan.

ròba, *s.f.* stuff; things (*pl.*): *— di casa*, household articles (*o* stuff); *che cos'è questa —?*, what is this stuff? (*o* what is this?); *ho della — da farti vedere*, I have sthg. (*o* some stuff) to show you; *ho portato della — da mangiare*, I have brought sthg. to eat; *ho solo vecchia da vendere*, I only have old things to sell; *non mi piace questo genere di —*, I do not like this sort of thing (*o* stuff); *questo abito è fatto di — a buon mercato*, this dress is made of cheap stuff; *questa è nostra*, this belongs to us (*o* this is ours *o* this is our stuff); *la vostra — non è ancora arrivata*, your stuff has not arrived yet ‖ *— da matti, da chiodi!*, nonsense! (*o* rubbish! *o* fantastic!) ‖ *bella —!*, (*iron.*) a fine thing (indeed!) ‖ *che —!*, what rubbish! ‖ *non desiderare la — d'altri*, (*Bibbia*) thou shalt not covet thy neighbour's goods.

robàccia, *s.f.* rubbish, poor stuff.

ròbbia, *s.f.* (*bot.*) madder.

Robèrta, *no.pr.f.* Roberta.

Robèrto, *no.pr.m.* Robert ‖ *dim.* Bob, Bobby.

robínia, *s.f.* (*bot.*) locust-tree, false acacia, robinia.

robiòla, *s.f.* "robiola" (kind of Italian soft cheese).

robivècchio, *s.m.* rag-and-bone-man (*pl.* rag-and-bone-men).

robòt, *s.m.* robot.

robustaménte, *av.* robustly, strongly, sturdily.

robustézza, *s.f.* 1. robustness, strength, sturdiness: *— di membra*, sturdiness of limb 2. *fig.* (*vigore*) vigour.

robústo, *ag.* 1. robust, strong; hardy, sturdy: *colpo —*, strong (*o* sturdy) blow; *un giovane —*, a robust (*o* sturdy) young man 2. (*vigoroso*) vigorous: *una mente robusta*, a strong mind; *stile —*, vigorous style.

rocàggine, *s.f.* hoarseness, raucousness.

rocambolésco, *ag.* (*letter.*) extraordinary, fantastic.

rocaménte, *av.* hoarsely.

ròcca[1], *s.f.* 1. (*fortezza*) stronghold (anche *fig.*); fortress, fort: *assalire la —*, to assail (*o* to attack) the fortress 2. (*roccia*) rock: *cristallo di —*, rock-crystal 3. (*del camino*) chimney-pot.

ròcca[2], *s.f.* (*conocchia*) distaff.

roccafòrte, *s.f.* stronghold (anche *fig.*); fortress, fort: *Ginevra fu la — del Calvinismo*, Geneva was the stronghold of Calvinism.

roccétto, *s.m.* (*eccl.*) rochet.

rocchétto[1], *s.m.* 1. reel; (*bobina*) bobin: *— di filo*, reel of thread 2. (*elett.*) coil: *— d'induzione*, induction coil; *— di Ruhmkorff*, Ruhmkorff spark-coil 3. (*cine.*) spool: *— a denti*, claw; *— avvolgitore*, take-up spool; *— svolgitore*, delivery spool 4. (*mec.*): *— a denti*, sprocket-wheel; *— a denti conduttore*, driving sprocket; *— d'accensione*, (*aut.*) ignition coil 5. (*foto.*) roll.

rocchétto[2], *s.m.* (*eccl.*) rochet.

ròcchio, *s.m.* 1. (*di tronco d'albero*) log; (*di colonna*) drum 2. (*rotolo*) roll 3. (*pezzo tondeggiante*) round: *— di manzo*, round of beef.

ròccia, *s.f.* rock; (*picco montano*) crag; (*scogliera*) cliff: *una città costruita sulla —*, a town built on rock; *stare al sole sulle rocce*, to lie in the sun on the rocks; *tuffarsi da una —*, to dive from a rock ‖ *fare della —*, to rock-climb: *non ho ancora fatto della — quest'anno*, I haven't done any rock-climbing yet this year.

rocciatóre, *s.m.* rock-climber; cragsman (*pl.* cragsmen).

roccióso, *ag.* rocky ‖ *le Montagne Rocciose*, the Rocky Mountains (*o* the Rockies).

ròcco, *s.m.* (*a scacchi*) castle, rook.

ròccolo, *s.m.* nets with decoy for attracting birds (*pl.*).

rochézza, *s.f.* hoarseness, raucousness.

ròco, *ag.* hoarse, raucous: *voce roca*, hoarse voice.

rococò, *ag.s.m.* rococo: *mobili —*, rococo furniture; *stile —*, rococo (style).

rodàggio, *s.m.* (*aut.*) running in: *in —*, "running in": *un'automobile in —*, a car being run in.

Ròdano, *no.pr.m.* (*geog.*) Rhone.

ròdere, *v.t.* 1. to gnaw; (*rosicchiare*) to nibble: *i topi hanno roso un pezzo di questo libro*, the mice have gnawed away a piece of this book; *— un osso*, to gnaw (at) a bone ‖ *un osso duro da —*, a hard nut to crack ‖ *— il freno*, to chafe under restraint (*o* to champ the bit) 2. (*scherz.*) (*mangiare*) to eat: *vorrei ql.co. da —*, I'd like a bite (*o* I'd like sthg. to eat) 3. (*corrodere*) to corrode, to eat into (sthg.), to bite into (sthg.): *gli acidi rodono i metalli*, acids eat (*o* bite) into metals; *questa sbarra è stata rosa dalla ruggine*, this bar has been corroded by rust 4. *fig.* (*tormentare*) to gnaw at (sthg.); to torture: *le preoccupazioni le rodevano il cuore*, worries gnawed at her heart; *questi insulti lo rodono*, these insults are wearing him out ‖ **ròdersi**, *v.r.* to worry, to be worried; to wear oneself out, to be consumed, to pine (away): *egli si rode per niente*, he is wearing himself out for nothing; *se fossi in te non mi roderei tanto*, if I were you I shouldn't worry so much (o I shouldn't be so worried); — *d'invidia, di gelosia*, to be consumed with envy, jealousy; — *di rabbia*, to chafe (o to be consumed) with rage || — *il fegato, il cuore*, to eat one's heart out.

Rodèsia, *no.pr.f.* (*geog.*) Rhodesia.

Ròdi, *no.pr.f.* (*geog.*) Rhodes.

rodiménto, *s.m.* **1.** (*il rodere*) gnawing **2.** (*erosione*) erosion **3.** *fig.* (*cruccio*) anxiety, worry: *non voleva mostrare il suo* —, he did not want to show his anxiety.

ròdio, *s.m.* (*chim.*) rhodium.

roditóre, *ag.* gnawing || *s.m.* (*zool.*) rodent || *i roditori*, Rodentia.

rododèndro, *s.m.* (*bot.*) rhododendron (*pl.* rhododendra, rhododendrons).

Rodòlfo, *no.pr.m.* Rudolph, Rudolf || *dim.* Rolf.

rodomontàta, *s.f.* rodomontade.

rodomónte, *s.m.* rodomont; braggart.

rodomontésco, *ag.* rodomontade, boastful, bragging.

Rodrígo, *no.pr.m.* Roderick.

rogàre, *v.t.* (*dir.*) to draw up: — *un atto*, to draw up a deed.

rogatòria, *s.f.* (*dir.*) request: *per* —, by request.

rogazióne, *s.f.* **1.** (*st. romana*) rogation **2.** *pl.* (*eccl.*) rogations.

ròggia, *s.f.* irrigation ditch.

rògito, *s.m.* (*dir.*) deed; instrument: *stendere un* —, to draw up a deed.

rógna, *s.f.* **1.** (*scabbia*) scabies; (*di cani, pecore*) mange **2.** *fig.* (*briga fastidiosa*) nuisance; trouble: *non voglio darti delle rogne*, I do not want to give you any trouble; *questo lavoro è una vera* —, this work is a real nuisance; *cercar rogne*, to be looking for trouble.

rognapièdi, *s.m.* paring-knife.

rognóne, *s.m.* (*cuc.*) kidney.

rognóso, *ag.* **1.** scabby; (*di cani, pecore*) mangy **2.** *fig.* (*fastidioso*) troublesome.

rògo[1], *s.m.* **1.** (*supplizio del fuoco*) stake: *condannare, mandare al* —, to condemn, to send to the stake **2.** (*pira*) funeral-pyre **3.** (*falò*) (bon)fire.

rógo[2], *s.m.* (*bot.*) bramble.

Rolàndo, *no.pr.m.* Roland.

rolíno, *s.m.* roll.

rollàre, *v.i.* (*mar.*) to roll || *v.t.* to roll (up): — *le tende*, to roll up the curtains.

rollàta, *s.f.* (*mar.*) rolling: — *improvvisa*, lurch.

rollío, *s.m.* roll, rolling.

rollòmetro, *s.m.* (*mar.*) oscillometer.

Róma, *no.pr.f.* (*geog.*) **1.** Rome || — *non fu fatta in un giorno*, Rome was not built in a day || *non si può andare a* — *e stare a casa*, one cannot have one's cake and eat it || *tutte le strade conducono a* —, all roads lead to Rome **2.** (*autorità papale*) Rome: *separarsi da* —, to separate from Rome; *sottomettersi a* —, to submit to Rome.

romagnòlo, *ag.* of Romagna, from Romagna || *s.m.*, **romagnòla**, *s.f.* inhabitant of Romagna.

romàico, *ag.s.m.* Romaic.

romanaménte, *av.* in the Roman way, after the Roman fashion; like a Roman.

romàncio, *ag.s.m.* Romans(c)h.

romanésco, *ag.* of modern Rome || *s.m.* Roman dialect.

Romanía, *no.pr.f.* (*geog.*) Rumania.

romànico, *ag.* **1.** (*arch.*) Romanesque: *una cattedrale romanica*, a Romanesque cathedral **2.** (*romanzo*) Romanic; Romance (*attributivo*): *lingue romaniche*, Romance (o Romanic) languages.

romanísmo, *s.m.* idiom of the Roman dialect.

romanísta, *s.m.* **1.** (*dotto nel diritto romano*) Romanist **2.** (*dotto nelle lingue romanze*) Romanist, specialist in the Romance languages.

romanità, *s.f.* Roman spirit.

romàno, *ag.* **1.** Roman: *la Chiesa romana*, the Roman Church; *l'impero* —, the Roman Empire; *numeri romani*, Roman numbers (o numerals) || *carattere* —,

(*tip.*) Roman type || *carciofi alla romana*, (*cuc.*) artichauts à la Romaine || *fare allu romana*, to pay one's own share **2.** (*romanzo*) Romanic; Romance (*attributivo*): *lingue romane*, Romance (o Romanic) languages **3.** (*arch.*) (*romanico*) Romanesque: *stile* —, Romanesque style || *s.m.*, **romàna**, *s.f.* Roman.

romanteaménte, *av.* romantically.

romanticheria, *s.f.* romanticism: *quella signora e piena di romanticherie*, that lady is full of romantic attitudes; *questo racconto non è che una* —, this tale is nothing but romantic nonsense.

romanticísmo, *s.m.* (*st. lett.*) Romanticism.

romàntico, *ag.* romantic: *ideali romantici*, romantic ideals; *è inguaribilmente romantica*, she is incurably romantic || *età romantica*, Romantic Age.

romanticúme, *s.m.* romantics (*pl.*).

romantizzàre, *v.t.* to romanticize.

romànza, *s.f.* **1.** (*poes.*) romance **2.** (*mus.*) romance; (*di melodramma*) aria.

romanzàre, *v.t.* (*dare carattere di romanzo a*) to romanticize: — *la realtà*, to make a romance out of reality.

romanzùto, *ag.* romanticized: *storia romanzata*, romanticized history.

romanzatóre, *s.m.*, **romanzatríce**, *s.f.* romancer.

romanzeseaménte, *av.* romantically.

romanzésco, *ag.* romantic: *avventure romanzesche*, romantic adventures; *una storia romanzesca*, a romantic story (o a romance); *la sua vita è una realtà romanzesca*, his life seems pure fiction.

romanzétto, *s.m.* **1.** (*breve romanzo*) short novel, novelette **2.** (*storia fantastica*) romance: *ci ha fabbricato tutto un* —, he has made a romance of it all **3.** (*relazione amorosa*) love affair, romance.

romanzière, *s.m.* novelist.

romànzo[1], *ag.* Romance: *lingue romanze*, Romance languages.

romànzo[2], *s.m.* **1.** novel: — *a fumetti*, strip cartoon story; — *a puntate*, serial (story); — *a tesi*, novel with a message; — *d'avventure*, adventure story; — *di cappa e spada*, cloak and dagger novel; — *fiume*, saga novel; — *giallo, poliziesco*, detective novel (o thriller o murder story); — *nero*, Gothic novel; — *picaresco*, picaresque novel; — *psicologico*, psychological novel; *Walter Scott scrisse romanzi storici*, Walter Scott wrote historical novels **2.** (*componimento medioevale*) romance: *i romanzi cavallereschi del Medioevo*, the romances of the Middle Ages, *i romanzi della Tavola Rotonda*, the romances of the Round Table (o the Arthurian cycle) **3.** (*storia incredibile*) romance: *c'era un'aria di* — *in quella casa*, there was an air of romance in that house; *la sua vita fu tutta un* —, all his life was a romance **4.** (*novellistica*) fiction: *il* — *americano è molto letto*, the American novel is much read.

rómba, *s.f.* roar; rumble: *la* — *del traffico*, the rumble of the traffic; *la* — *del vento*, the roar of the wind.

rombànte, *ag.* roaring; rumbling; (*tuonante*) thundering.

rombàre, *v.i.* to roar; to rumble; (*tuonare*) to thunder: *i cannoni rombavano in lontananza*, the guns were thundering in the distance; *il tuono rombava minacciosamente*, the thunder rumbled threateningly.

rómbico, *ag.* (*geom.*) rhombic.

rómbo[1], *s.m.* **1.** (*geom.*) rhomb; rhombus (*pl.* rhombuses, rhombi) **2.** (*la trentaduesima parte della rosa dei venti*) point, rhumb: *dare il* —, (*mar.*) to give the course.

rómbo[2], *s.m.* (*ittiol.*) rhombus (*pl.* rhombuses, rhombi); brill: — *chiodato*, turbot.

rómbo[3], *s.m.* roar; rumble; (*tuono*) thunder: *il* — *dei cannoni*, the thunder of the guns; — *dell'elica*, propeller noise; — *del vento*, the roar of the wind.

romboèdrico, *ag.* rhombohedral.

romboèdro, *s.m.* (*geom.*) rhombohedron (*pl.* rhombohedra, rhombohedrons).

romboidàle, *ag.* rhomboid(al).

rombòide, *ag.* rhomboid(al) || *s.m.* rhomboid.

romèno, *ag. s.m.* Rumanian || **romèna**, *s.f.* Rumanian.

romèo[1], *s.m.* pilgrim (going to Rome).

Romèo[2], *no.pr.m.* Romeo.

rómice, *s.f.* (*bot.*) rumex.

romitàggio, *s.m.* 1. hermitage 2. (*casa solitaria*) solitary house, isolated house.

romitàno, *ag.* 1. (*solitario*) solitary 2. (*rozzo*) rough, coarse || *s.m.* hermit.

romítico, *ag.* hermitic.

romíto, *ag.* lonely, solitary: *un luogo* —, a solitary place || *s.m.* hermit: *una vita da* —, a solitary life.

romitòrio, *s.m.* hermitage.

Ròmolo, *no.pr.m.* (*st.*) Romulus.

romóre, *e derivati*, *V.* **rumóre**, *e derivati*.

rómpere, *v.t.* to break: *il fiume romperà presto gli argini*, the river will soon break its banks; — *un bicchiere, un piatto*, to break a glass, a plate; — *in due, in tre*, to break in two (*o* half), in three; — *un ramo, un bastone*, to snap a bough, a stick in two || *se non la pianti, ti rompo il muso!*, (*fam.*) if you don't stop it, I'll bash your face in! || *voglio romperla con quell'uomo*, I want to break with him || — *l'amicizia*, to break the ties of friendship || — *la calca*, to elbow one's way through the crowd || — *la consegna*, to break bounds || — *un esercito*, to disrupt (*o* to scatter) an army || — *la fede data*, to break faith || — *un fidanzamento*, to break off an engagement || — *il ghiaccio, fig.* to break the ice || — *l'incantesimo, l'incanto*, to break the spell (*o* the charm) || — *gli indugi*, to burst into action || — *una lancia in favore di qlcu.*, to take up the cudgel for s.o. || — *le linee nemiche*, to break the enemy's lines || — *la pace*, to break the peace || — *il passo*, (*mil.*) to break step || — *i ponti con qlcu.*, to fall out with s.o. || — *una promessa, un contratto, il digiuno*, to break a promise, a contract, one's fast || — *le righe*, (*mil.*) to break ranks: *rompete le righe!*, dismiss! || — *le scatole, gli stivali, le tasche a qlcu.*, (*volg.*) to get s.o.'s goat || — *il silenzio*, to break the silence || — *il terreno*, to break up the ground || — *la testa a qlcu., fig.* to drive s.o. crazy || *v.i.* 1. to break: *la nave ruppe sulle rocce*, the ship broke on the rocks 2. (*proromvere*) to burst: — *in pianto*, to burst into tears || **rómpersi**, *v.r.* 1. to break: *questa porcellana si rompe facilmente*, this china breaks easily; *se fai cadere il bicchiere, si romperà*, if you drop the glass, it will break to pieces; — *un braccio, una gamba*, to break one's arm, one's leg; — *il collo, l'osso del collo*, to break one's neck || *non romperti la testa su quell'indovinello*, don't rack (*o* cudgel) your brains over that riddle 2. (*di vena, vescica*) to rupture, to burst: *gli si ruppe una vena*, he burst a vein.

rompíbile, *ag.* breakable.

rompicàpo, *s.m.* 1. worry, trouble 2. (*indovinello*) puzzle, riddle.

rompicòllo, *s.m.* 1. (*persona scapestrata*) reckless fellow, dare-devil, madcap 2. (*luogo pericoloso*) dangerous place || *a* —, headlong (*o* at breakneck speed).

rompighiàccio, *s.m.* 1. (*mar.*) ice-breaker 2. (*per alpinisti*) ice-axe.

rompiménto, *s.m.* breaking.

rompiscàtole, *s.c.* (*volg.*) nuisance, bore.

rompitóre, *ag.* breaking || *s.m.*, **rompitríce**, *s.f.* breaker.

rompitútto, *s.c.* (*fam.*) destructive person.

rónca, *s.f.* pruning-knife, pruning-hook, bill-hook.

roncàre, *v.t.* to prune; (*sarchiare*) to weed.

roncatúra, *s.f.* pruning; (*sarchiatura*) weeding.

ronchétto, *s.m.* small sickle.

roncíglio, *s.m.* hook.

Roncisvàlle, *no.pr.f.* (*geog.*) Roncesvalles.

rónco[1], *s.m.* blind alley || *essere nel* —, *fig.* to be up a blind alley.

rónco[2], *s.m.* (*med.*) rhonchus (*pl.* rhonchi).

róncola, *s.f.* pruning-knife, pruning-hook, bill-hook.

róncolo, *s.m.* gardening-knife || *gambe a* —, bow-legs.

roncóne, *s.m.* sickle.

rónda, *s.f.* (*mil.*) rounds (*pl.*); (*pattuglia*) patrol: *passa la* —, the patrol is going the rounds; *essere di* —, to be on patrol; *fare la* —, to go (*o* to make) the rounds (*o* to be on patrol); (*di poliziotto*) to be on one's beat || *fare la* — *a una ragazza*, to hang round a girl.

rondèlla, *s.f.* (*mec.*) washer: — *aperta*, open (*o* slip) washer; — *circolare*, round washer; — *di sicurezza*, lock-washer.

rondèllo, *s.m.* (*mus. poes.*) rondel.

róndine, *s.f.* (*ornit.*) swallow || *rondinella di mare*, (*ittiol.*) flying gurnard || *a coda di* —, swallow-tailed: *giacca a coda di* —, swallow-tailed coat || *una* — *non fa primavera*, *prov.* one swallow does not make a summer.

rondò, *s.m.* 1. (*mus.*) rondo 2. (*poes.*) rondel.

rondóne, *s.m.* (*ornit.*) swift.

ronfaménto, *s.m.* snoring.

ronfàre, ronfiàre, *v.i.* to snore.

rónfio, *s.m.* snoring.

ronzaménto, *s.m.* buzzing, humming.

ronzàre, *v.i.* 1. to buzz, to hum: *le api, le vespe ronzano*, bees, wasps buzz (*o* hum) || *cosa ti ronza per il capo?*, what is going on in your head? || *mi ronzano gli orecchi*, my ears are buzzing 2. (*girare*) to hang: *egli ronza sempre intorno a mia sorella*, he is always hanging round my sister.

Ronzinànte, *no.pr.m.* (*lett.*) Rosinante || **ronzinànte**, *s.m.* (*ronzino*) jade, broken-down horse.

ronzíno, *s.m.* jade, broken-down horse.

ronzío, *s.m.* buzzing, humming; drone: — *alle orecchie*, buzzing in the ears; (*med.*) tinnitus.

ronzóne, *s.m.* 1. (*moscone*) bluebottle 2. (*corteggiatore*) suitor.

ròrido, *ag.* (*rugiadoso*) dewy; (*bagnato*) wet; (*umido*) moist, damp.

ròsa[1], *ag.s.m.* pink: *il* — *antico*, rose; *un abito* —, pink dress; *il* — *è un bellissimo colore*, pink is a very nice colour || *s.f.* 1. (*bot.*) rose: — *canina*, dogrose; — *damascena*, damask-rose; — *del Giappone*, camellia; — *di Gerico*, rose of Jericho; — *di macchia*, wild rose; — *di Natale*, Christmas rose; — *muschiata*, musk-rose; — *muschiosa*, moss-rose; — *tea*, tea-rose; *acqua di* —, rose-water; *un bottone di* —, a rosebud; *legno di* —, rosewood || *fresco come una* —, as fresh as a daisy || *la guerra delle due Rose*, (*st. inglese*) the Wars of the Roses || *un socialista all'acqua di rose*, (*fam.*) a moderate socialist; *una punizione all'acqua di rose*, (*fam.*) a mild punishment || *non sono tutte rose*, it is not all roses || *se son rose fioriranno*, the proof of the pudding is in the eating || *essere su un letto di rose*, to be on a bed of roses || *vedere il mondo color di* —, to view the world (*o* to see things) through rose-coloured spectacles || *non c'è* — *senza spine*, *prov.* there is no rose without a thorn 2. (*coccarda*) rose, rosette: *ella fece una* — *con un mazzo di nastri*, she made a rosette out of a bunch of ribbons 3. (*arch.*) (*rosone*) rose-window, wheel-window 4. (*mus.*) sound-hole 5. (*di diamante*) rose-diamond, rose-cut diamond 6. — *dei venti*, compass-card 7. *pl.* (*letter.*) (*guance rosee*): *le rose del suo volto*, the roses in her cheeks.

Ròsa[2], *no.pr.f.* Rose, Rosa.

rosàcee, *s.f.pl.* (*bot.*) Rosaceae.

rosàceo, *ag.* rosaceous; rosy; pinkish.

rosàio, *s.m.* 1. rose-bush; rose 2. (*roseto*) rosery.

Rosalía, *no.pr.f.* Rosalia, Rosalie.

Rosalínda, *no.pr.f.* Rosalind.

Rosamúnda, *no.pr.f.* Rosamund, Rosamond.

rosàrio, *s.m.* (*eccl.*) rosary: *dire il* —, to say the rosary || *la Madonna del Rosario*, Our Lady of the Rosary.

rosàto, *ag.* 1. (*che contiene essenza di rose*) rose (*attributivo*): *acqua rosata*, rose-water; *miele* —, rose

-hip syrup **2.** (*roseo*) rosy (anche *fig.*): *sogni rosati,* rosy dreams ‖ *vino* —, vin rosé.

rosbíffe, *s.m.* (*cuc.*) roast-beef.

ròseo, *ag.* rose-coloured; rosy (anche *fig.*): *guance rosee,* rosy cheeks; *speranze, prospettive rosee,* rosy hopes, prospects; *non è tutto — come pensi tu,* all is not so rosy as you think; *veder tutto —,* to see everything through rose-coloured spectacles.

roseola, *s.f.* **1.** (*patol.*) roseola; (*specie di morbillo*) German measles (*pl.*) **2.** *fig.* (*rossore*) blush, flush.

roséto, *s.m.* rose-garden, rosery, rosary.

rosétta, *s.f.* **1.** (*ornamento a forma di rosa*) rosette **2.** (*diamante tagliato a rosa*) rose(-diamond), rose -cut diamond **3.** (*mec.*) washer.

rosicànte, *ag. s.m.* (*zool.*) rodent.

rosicàre, *v.t.* to nibble; (*rodere*) to gnaw ‖ *chi non risica non rosica, prov.* one who never tries never succeeds.

rosicchiaménto, *s.m.* nibbling; gnawing.

rosicchiàre, *v.t.* to nibble; (*rodere*) to gnaw: *i topi hanno rosicchiato un pezzetto di formaggio,* the mice have gnawed off a bit of cheese; *— un osso,* to gnaw (at) a bone; *— un pezzo di pane,* to nibble a piece of bread.

rosicchio, rosicchiolo, *s.m.* dry crust (of bread).

rosignuòlo, *s.m.* (*ornit.*) nightingale.

Rosina, *no.pr.f.* dim. di **Ròsa**.

rosmaríno, *s.m.* (*bot.*) rosemary.

Rosmúnda, *no.pr.f.* Rosamund, Rosamond.

róso, *ag.* **1.** (*corroso*) corroded **2.** (*rosicchiato*) nibbled; gnawed; eaten.

rosolàccio, *s.m.* (*bot.*) corn poppy, field poppy.

rosolàre, *v.t.* (*cuc.*) to brown: — *la carne,* to brown the meat ‖ **rosolàrsi,** *v.r.* **1.** (*detto di carne*) to get brown **2.** *fig.* (*al sole*) to bask (in the sun); (*al fuoco*) to toast oneself.

rosolía, *s.f.* (*patol.*) rubeda; German measles (*pl.*).

rosòllo, *s.m.* rosolio.

rosóne, *s.m.* **1.** (*arch.*) rose-window; (*ornamento*) rosette **2.** (*elett.*) rosette: — *da soffitto,* ceiling-rose.

róspo, *s.m.* **1.** (*zool.*) toad ‖ *ingoiare un* —, (*tollerare ql.co. di increscioso*) to swallow a bitter pill **2.** (*spreg.*) (*persona poco socievole*) unsociable person.

Rossàna, *no.pr.f.* Roxana.

rossàstro, rosseggiànte, *ag.* reddish, ruddy.

rosseggiàre, *v.i.* **1.** to be reddish **2.** (*diventare rosso*) to redden, to turn red.

rossétto, *s.m.* **1.** (*per le labbra*) lipstick: *devo ancora darmi il* —, I still have to put on my lipstick; *non si dà mai il* —, she never wears lipstick; *si mette troppo* —, she uses too much lipstick **2.** (*per le guance*) rouge.

rossézza, *s.f.* redness.

rossíccio, *ag.* reddish, ruddy.

rossígno, *ag.* russet, reddish.

rósso, *ag.* red: — *di rabbia,* red with anger; *capelli rossi,* red hair: *una donna dai capelli rossi,* a redhead (o a red-haired woman); *diventar* —, (*per eccitazione, rabbia*) to go red in the face (o to flush); (*per vergogna, imbarazzo*) to blush (o to flush); *la fanciulla diventò rossa,* the girl blushed ‖ — *come un gambero, un peperone,* as red as a beetroot ‖ *l'Armata Rossa,* the Red Army; *la bandiera rossa,* the Red Flag; *idee rosse,* (*fam.*) red (o bolshy) ideas ‖ *le camicie rosse,* the Red Shirts ‖ *la Croce Rossa,* the Red Cross ‖ *avere il sangue — nelle vene,* to have red blood in one's veins (o to be red-blooded) ‖ *s.m.* red: — *chiaro, scuro,* light, dark red; — *ciliegia,* cerise; (*metal.*) cherry-red; — *corallo,* coral red; — *cupo,* (*metal.*) dull red; — *di Venezia,* Venetian red; — *d'uovo,* yolk (of egg); — *inglese,* (*chim.*) (*per pittura*) English red; — *mattone,* brick-red; *ho dipinto le pareti di* —, I have painted the walls red; *vestire di* —, to dress in red ‖ *i rossi,* (*pol.*) the Reds ‖ *vedere* —, to see red ‖ — *di sera, buon tempo si spera, prov.* red sky at night, shepherd's delight.

rossóre, *s.m.* **1.** flush; (*per vergogna, imbarazzo*) blush, flush: *un — di gioia, di eccitazione,* a flush of joy, of excitement; *quella vista le fece salire il — alle guance,* that sight made her blush **2.** (*vergogna*) shame: *persona senza* —, shameless person; *quell'uomo non ha* —, that man has no shame; *avere, sentire — di ql.co., qlcu.,* to be ashamed of sthg., s.o.: *non ebbe — di dirmi tutto,* he was not ashamed to tell me everything **3.** (*med.*) (*arrossamento*) redness; red spot.

ròsta, *s.f.* (*arch.*) fan-window.

rosticcère, *s.m.* owner of a rotisserie; ⌐cook-shop keeper.

rosticceria, *s.f.* rotisserie; cook-shop.

rosticcio, *s.m.* (*metal.*) dross.

rostràle, *ag.* (*archeol. zool.*) rostral.

rostràto, *ag.* **1.** (*zool.*) billed; beaked; rostrate(d) **2.** (*archeol.*) rostrate(d); (*rostrale*) rostral: *colonna rostrata,* rostral column.

ròstro, *s.m.* **1.** rostrum (*pl.* rostrums, rostra); bill; beak **2.** *pl.* (*archeol.*) rostra.

ròta, *V.* **ruòta**.

rotàbile, *ag.* carriageable; carriage (*attributivo*): *strada* —, road suitable for vehicles.

rotacísmo, *s.m.* (*fonet.*) rhotacism.

rotàia, *s.f.* **1.** (*ferr.*) rail: — *corta,* make-up rail; — *per gru,* crane-rail; — *per tranvia,* tram-rail; *terza* —, third (o contact) rail; *essere fuori dalle rotaie,* to be off the rails (anche *fig.*); *uscir dalle rotaie,* to leave (o to go off) the rails (anche *fig.*) **2.** (*solco lasciato da ruote*) wheel-track; rut.

rotànte, *ag.* rotating, rotary, revolving.

rotàre, *v.i.* to rotate; (*astr.*) to revolve; (*roteare*) to wheel: *un cilindro che ruota intorno al suo asse,* a cylinder which rotates on its own axis; *la Terra ruota intorno al Sole,* the Earth revolves round the Sun ‖ *v.t.* to rotate, to revolve; (*gli occhi*) to roll: — *gli occhi,* to roll one's eyes ‖ *far* —, to wheel.

rotatíva, *s.f.* (*tip.*) rotary machine, rotary press.

rotatívo, *ag.* rotative, rotary.

rotatòrio, *ag.* rotating, rotatory, rotary, rotative: *moto, movimento* —, rotating motion, movement; *muscolo* —, (*anat.*) rotator.

rotazióne, *s.f.* **1.** rotation: — *del flusso dell'elica,* (*aer.*) race rotation; *la — di un corpo sul suo asse,* the rotation of a body on its axis; — *in senso antiorario,* anticlockwise rotation; — *in senso orario,* clockwise rotation; *asse di* —, axis of rotation; *direzione di* —, direction of rotation; *la — della Terra produce il giorno e la notte,* the rotation of the Earth produces night and day ‖ — *degli incarichi,* rotation in office (o of offices) **2.** (*agr.*) rotation: — *dei raccolti,* rotation of crops.

roteaménto, *s.m.* (*letter.*) rotating; (*di uccelli*) wheeling; (*di occhi*) rolling.

roteàre, *v.t.* to swing; (*gli occhi*) to roll: *egli roteava le braccia,* he was swinging his arms ‖ *v.i.* to wheel: *un falco roteava nell'aria,* a hawk was wheeling in the air.

rotèlla, *s.f.* **1.** small wheel; (*fissata alle gambe di un mobile*) castor: *pattini a rotelle,* roller-skates ‖ *avere una — fuori posto,* to have a screw loose **2.** (*anat.*) (*rotula*) knee-cap, knee-pan **3.** (*st.*) (*scudo rotondo*) round shield.

rotíferi, *s.m.pl.* (*zool.*) Rotifera.

rotísmo, *s.m.* (*mec.*) wheelwork: — *a ingranaggi cilindrici,* spur gearing; — *epicicloidale,* epicyclic train; *rotismi moltiplicatori,* step-up wheels.

rotocàlco, *s.m.* rotogravure process: *rivista a* —, illustrated magazine.

rotocalcografía, *s.f.* printing by a rotogravure process.

rotocalcogràfico, *ag.* rotogravure (*attributivo*): *riproduzione rotocalcografica,* rotogravure reproduction.

rotoláménto, *s.m.* rolling.

rotolàre, *v.t.* **1.** to roll: — *una botte, un sasso,* to roll a barrel, a stone ‖ — *le scale*, to fall down the stairs **2.** (*arrotolare*) to roll up: — *un pezzo di carta*, to roll up a piece of paper ‖ *v.i.* to roll: *la palla rotolava giù per la discesa*, the ball was rolling down the slope ‖ **rotolàrsi**, *v.r.* to roll, to wallow: — *nel fango*, to wallow in the mud; — *sull'erba*, to roll on the grass.

ròtolo, *s.m.* **1.** roll: *un* — *di carta, di monete, di tela*, a roll of paper, of coins, of cloth; — *di corda*, coil of rope ‖ *andare a rotoli*, to go to rack and ruin; *mandare a rotoli*, to ruin **2.** (*foto.*) roll of film, cartridge.

rotolóne, *s.m.* tumble, fall.

rotolóne, rotolóni, *av.*: *cadere, venir giù rotoloni*, to tumble down ‖ *mandare* (*a*) *rotoloni*, to ruin.

rotonàve, *s.f.* (*mar.*) rotor-ship.

rotónda, *s.f.* **1.** (*edificio rotondo*) rotunda **2.** (*di stabilimento balneare*) terrace.

rotondaménte, *av.* roundly.

rotondàre, *v.t.* to make round, to round ‖ — *un podere*, to enlarge a farm ‖ — *una somma, lo stipendio*, to round off a sum, one's wages.

rotondeggiànte, *ag.* roundish.

rotondeggiàre, *v.i.* to have a roundish shape ‖ *v.t.* to make round; to make roundish.

rotondézza, rotondità, *s.f.* roundness, rotundity: *la rotondità di una frase, fig.* the roundness of a sentence; *la rotondità della Terra*, the rotundity of the Earth.

rotóndo, *ag.* **1.** round: *una finestra rotonda*, a round window; *piatto* —, round plate; *la palla è rotonda*, the ball is round ‖ *la Tavola Rotonda*, the Round Table **2.** (*grassoccio*) plump, round, rotund: *una figura piuttosto rotonda*, a rather plump figure; *guance rotonde*, plump (*o* round) cheeks **3.** (*ampio, sonoro*) sonorous, full(-toned); deep: *stile* —, sonorous style; *voce rotonda*, full(-toned) voice.

rotóre, *s.m.* (*aer. elett.*) rotor: — *ad anelli*, (*elett.*) slip-ring rotor; — *anticoppia*, (*aer.*) auxiliary rotor; — *di coda*, (*aer.*) tail rotor; — *di elicoplano*, (*aer.*) paddle-wheel rotor; — *radiale*, (*aer.*) radial rotor.

ròtta¹, *s.f.* **1.** (*rottura di argine*) breach: *il Po minaccia una* — *degli argini*, the Po threatens to break its banks (*o* a breach in its banks) ‖ *a* — *di collo*, (*precipitosamente*) headlong; (*di cosa che va male*) to rack and ruin: *andare a* — *di collo.* (*precipitosamente*) to go at breakneck speed (*o* headlong); (*andar male*) to go to rack and ruin ‖ *essere in* — *con qlcu.*, to be on bad terms with s.o.; *venire alle rotte con qlcu.*, to break off relations (*o* a friendship) with s.o. (*o* to fall out with s.o.) **2.** (*grave sconfitta*) rout, retreat: *il nemico era in* —, the enemy was in (full) retreat; *mettere in* —, to put to rout.

ròtta², *s.f.* (*mar. aer.*) route, course: — *lossodromica*, (*mar.*) loxodromic course (*o* rhumb-line); — *magnetica*, (*mar. aer.*) magnetic course; *linea di* —, (*mar.*) rhumb line; *fate* — *verso nord*, (*mar.*) steer north(wards); *la nave fa* — *verso Napoli*, the ship is bound for Naples; *la nave fa* — *verso sud*, the ship's course is due south; *la nave non era sulla sua* —, the ship was off course; *cambiare* —, to change one's course; *tenere una* —, to hold a course.

rottàme, *s.m.* **1.** wreck (anche *fig.*): *è un* — *umano*, he is a (physical) wreck **2.** *pl.* (*cose in rovina*) scraps; bits; rubbish (*sing.*): *rottami di ferro*, scrap-iron; *rottami di naufragio*, wreckage.

ròtto, *ag.* **1.** broken: *finestra, scarpa rotta*, broken window, shoe; *gamba rotta*, broken leg; *un piatto* —, a broken dish ‖ *con voce rotta*, in a broken voice; *voce rotta dai singhiozzi*, voice broken by (*o* with) sobs ‖ *ho le gambe, le ossa rotte dalla fatica*, my legs, my bones are aching with tiredness; *sentirsi tutto* —, to be aching all over **2.** (*sciolto*) broken; broken off (*predicativo*): *un fidanzamento* —, a broken engagement; *un voto* —, a broken vow **3.** (*stracciato*) torn: *un vestito* —, a torn dress **4.** (*dato, dedito*) given, addicted: — *al bere*, addicted to drinking; — *al vizio*, given to vice **5.** (*avvezzo*) accustomed: — *alla fatica*, untirable;

egli è — *a questo lavoro*, he is an old hand at this work ‖ *s.m.* **1.** break, fracture ‖ *per il* — *della cuffia*, by the skin of one's teeth: *salvarsi per il* — *della cuffia*, to escape by the skin of one's teeth **2.** *pl.* (*spiccioli*) (small) change (*sing.*): *duemila lire e rotti*, two thousand lire odd.

rottúra, *s.f.* **1.** (*in un vetro, una rete, ecc.*) hole; (*in una parete*) breach; breakage: *mi diedero diecimila lire per le eventuali rotture*, they gave me ten thousand lire for possible breakages **2.** *fig.* (*scioglimento, cessazione*) break; breaking off; rupture: *la* — *di un accordo*, the breaking off (*o* rupture) of an agreement; *la* — *di un fidanzamento*, the breaking off of an engagement; *ci fu una* — *nella loro amicizia*, there was a break in their friendship.

ròtula, *s.f.* (*anat.*) knee-cap, patella (*pl.* patellae), rotula.

rotúleo, *ag.* (*anat.*) rotular.

roulette, *s.f.* roulette.

roulotte, *s.f.* caravan, trailer.

routine, *s.f.* routine.

rovàio, *s.m.* north wind.

rovàno, *ag.* **1.** (*di cavallo*) roan **2.** (*color ruggine*) rust-coloured.

rovèllo, *s.m.* rage, anger.

rovènte, *ag.* red-hot; fiery, scorching (anche *fig.*): *discorso* —, fiery speech; *ferro* —, red-hot iron.

róvere, *s.m.* (*bot.*) oak: *tavolo di* —, oak table.

roveretàno, *ag.* of Rovereto, from Rovereto ‖ *s.m.* native of Rovereto, inhabitant of Rovereto.

roveréto, *s.m.* oak-wood.

rovèscia, *s.f.* (*risvolto di manica*) cuff; (*risvolto di giacca*) lapel.

rovesciaménto, *s.m.* **1.** upsetting, overturning; reversal: — *della situazione*, the reversal of the situation **2.** (*di governo, ecc.*) overthrowing.

rovesciàre, *v.t.* **1.** to upset, to overturn; (*capovolgere*) to turn upside down: *il bambino ha rovesciato la sua tazza di latte*, the child upset (*o* to overturned) his cup of milk; *rovescia una carta*, turn up a card; *rovescia quel bicchiere*, (*capovolgilo*) turn the glass upside down; — *una barca*, to upset (*o* to capsize) a boat ‖ — *una situazione*, to reverse a situation **2.** (*gettare*) to throw: *la forza dell'esplosione mi rovesciò a terra*, the force of the explosion threw me to the ground; *rovesciarono proiettili sul nemico*, they rained bullets on the enemy ‖ *rovesciò il capo indietro e rise*, he threw back his head and laughed **3.** (*rivoltare*) to turn inside out: — *una manica, un paio di guanti*, to turn a sleeve, a pair of gloves inside out **4.** (*versare*) (*intenzionalmente*) to pour; (*accidentalmente*) to spill: *cerca di non* — *il latte, il vino sulla tovaglia*, try not to spill milk, wine on the table-cloth; *rovesciaci su dell'acqua bollente*, pour some hot water on it **5.** *fig.* (*abbattere*) to overthrow: — *un governo*, to overthrow a government **6.** (*vuotare*) to empty: — *la borsetta*, to empty one's bag; — *il sacco*, (*fam.*) to make a clean breast of it ‖ **rovesciàrsi**, *v.r.* **1.** to overturn, to be overturned; (*capovolgersi*) to capsize: *la barca si rovesciò*, the boat overturned (*o* capsized); *l'automobile si rovesciò dopo lo scontro*, the car overturned after the collision **2.** (*riversarsi*): *la folla si rovesciò nello stadio*, the crowd poured into the stadium; *una pioggia di lapilli si rovesciò sulla città*, a hail of stones fell upon the town; *un violento temporale si rovesciò su di noi*, a violent storm burst over us.

rovesciàta, *s.f.* (*calcio*) back-kick.

rovèscio, *ag.* **1.** (*capovolto*) upside down; (*con l'interno all'esterno*) inside out ‖ *a* —, *alla rovescia*, (*capovolto*) upside down; (*con l'interno all'esterno*) inside out; (*col davanti dietro*) back to front (*o* wrong way round); *fig.* wrongly; badly: *prese la mia osservazione alla rovescia*, he took my remark the wrong way; *quel quadro è appeso alla rovescia*, that picture is hanging upside down; *ti sei messo il pullover a* —, you have put your pullover on inside out; you have put your pullover on back to front; *tutto va alla rovescia*, everything is going badly; *capire ql.co. alla rovescia*, to misunderstand sthg. ‖ *punto* —, (*lavoro a maglia*) purl stitch **2.** (*supino*) supine: *le bottiglie di certi vini vanno tenute rovesce*, some bottles of wine have to be kept horizontal; *cadere, giacere* —, to fall, to lie on one's back ‖ *s.m.* **1.** reverse, reverse side, other side, back: *il* — *della medaglia*, the reverse (*o* the other side) of the medal (anche *fig.*); *il* — *di una busta, di un foglio*, the back of an envelope, of a sheet of paper; *il* — *di una stoffa*, the reverse side of a cloth ‖ *ogni cosa ha il suo* —, there are two sides to everything **2.** (*opposto*) opposite: *egli è proprio il mio* —, he is just the opposite of me; *fa sempre il* — *di quello che gli dico*, he always does the opposite of what I tell him **3.** (*di pioggia, ecc.*) heavy shower; *fig.* rain, hail: *un* — *di critiche*, a hail of criticism; *un* — *d'ingiurie*, a rain of insults; *un* — *di pioggia*, a heavy shower (of rain); *un* — *di sassi*, a volley of stones **4.** (*tennis*) backhand: *è stato un bel* —, that was a good backhand (stroke); *ha un buon* —, he has a good backhand; *tirare di* —, to play a backhand (stroke); *tirare sul* — *di qlcu.*, to play on s.o.'s backhand **5.** (*grave danno*) set-back, reverse: — *finanziario*, financial set-back; *ebbe molti rovesci di fortuna*, he suffered many reverses (*o* many set-backs).

rovesciòne, *s.m.* (*manrovescio*) back-hander.
rovescióne, rovescióni, *av.* on one's back.
rovéto, *s.m.* bramble-bush, clump of briars.
rovína, *s.f.* **1.** (*il rovinare*) collapse, fall: *il ponte minaccia* —, the bridge is threatening to collapse **2.** (*cosa rovinata, rudere*) ruin: *le rovine di un tempio, di una città*, the ruins of a temple, of a town; *andare, cadere in* —, to go to ruin **3.** (*sfacelo, causa di rovina*) ruin, downfall: *il bere fu la sua* —, drinking was his ruin (*o* ruined him); *la sua* — *fu causata dal giuoco*, his downfall was caused by gambling; *tu sarai la mia* —, you will be my ruin (*o* the ruin of me); *andare, cadere in* —, to go to rack and ruin; *mandare in* —, to ruin **4.** (*violenza*) violence: *la piena travolse tutto nella sua* —, the flood carried away everything in its violence.
rovinàre, *v.t.* **1.** to ruin; (*guastare, danneggiare*) to spoil: *il bere lo ha rovinato*, drinking has ruined him; *il cattivo tempo ha rovinato le mie vacanze*, the bad weather has spoiled my holidays; *egli ha rovinato tutti i miei piani*, he has spoilt (*o* upset) all my plans; *il fumo rovina l'appetito*, smoking spoils one's appetite; *la grandine ha rovinato i fiori*, the hail ruined the flowers; *il leggere troppo rovina gli occhi*, too much reading ruins the eyes **2.** (*abbattere, demolire*) to demolish, to pull down: — *una fortezza*, to demolish a fortress ‖ *l'acqua cheta rovina i ponti*, *prov.* still waters run deep ‖ *v.i.* to crash; to fall with a crash; to collapse: *l'aeroplano rovinò contro le rocce*, the plane crashed against the rocks; *la casa rovinò a terra*, the house collapsed; *il masso rovinò giù dal monte*, the boulder crashed down the mountain-side ‖ **rovinàrsi,** *v.r.* to ruin oneself, to be ruined: *egli si rovinò col bere*, he ruined himself drinking; — *l'appetito*, to spoil one's appetite; — *la salute*, to ruin one's health.
rovinàto, *ag.* ruined: *quell'uomo è* —, that man is ruined (*o* done for); *la sua salute è rovinata*, he is broken down in health (*o* his health is ruined).
rovinío, *s.m.* **1.** downfall **2.** (*rumore*) crash.
rovinosaménte, *av.* **1.** ruinously **2.** (*violentemente*) violently, furiously.
rovinóso, *ag.* **1.** (*apportatore di rovina*) ruinous: *spese rovinose*, ruinous expenses **2.** (*violento, furioso*) violent, furious: *un temporale* —, a violent storm.
rovistàre, *v.t.i.* to ransack (sthg.); to search (sthg.): — *in un cassetto*, to ransack a drawer; — *nella propria memoria*, to search one's memory.
róvo, *s.m.* (*bot.*) blackberry bush.

rózza, *s.f.* jade.
rozzaménte, *av.* roughly, coarsely (anche *fig.*); (*goffamente*) clumsily: *trattava* —, his manners were coarse (*o* rough).
rozzézza, *s.f.* roughness, coarseness (anche *fig.*); (*goffaggine*) clumsiness.
rózzo, *ag.* **1.** rough, coarse: *lavorazione rozza*, rude (*o* rough) workmanship; *pietre rozze*, rough stones; *stoffa rozza*, rough material **2.** (*grossolano*) rough, coarse, uncouth; (*impacciato, goffo*) clumsy; (*rude*) rude: *rozza semplicità*, rude simplicity; *linguaggio* —, coarse language; *modi rozzi*, coarse (*o* rough) manners; *stile* —, rough style; *uomo* —, rude (*o* uncouth) man.
rúba, *s.f.* (*rar.*) plunder, robbery: *mettere a* —, (*saccheggiare*) to pillage ‖ *andare a* —, to be sold off rapidly (*o* to meet with a ready sale *o* to sell like hot cakes).
rubacchiaménto, *s.m.* petty thieving, pilfering.
rubacchiàre, *v.t.* to pilfer.
rubacuòri, *ag.* fetching, bewitching: *sguardo* —, bewitching glance ‖ *s.m.* lady-killer ‖ *s.f.* flirt.
rubàre, *v.t.* **1.** to steal: *mi hanno rubato il portafogli*, they have stolen my wallet (*o* I have had my wallet stolen); — *un bambino*, to kidnap a child ‖ *mi hai rubato la parola*, you've taken the words out of my mouth ‖ *un muro che ruba la vista*, a wall that hides the view ‖ *per studiare devo* — *ore al sonno*, I must steal the time for study from my sleep ‖ — *a man salva*, to plunder ‖ — *un bacio, un segreto*, to steal a kiss, a secret ‖ — *il cuore, il mestiere a qlcu.*, to steal s.o.'s heart, s.o.'s job ‖ — *un'idea*, to steal an idea ‖ — *nel giuoco*, to cheat ‖ — *il sonno a qlcu.*, to deprive s.o. of sleep ‖ — *sul peso*, to give short measure ‖ — *il tempo a qlcu.*, to take up s.o.'s time **2.** (*derubare*) to rob: — *i pellegrini*, to rob the pilgrims.
rubàto, *ag.* stolen: *merce rubata*, stolen goods ‖ *s.m.* (*mus.*) rubato.
rubefacènte, *ag.* (*med.*) rubefacient.
rubefazióne, *s.f.* (*miner.*) ferrugination.
rubèola, *s.f.* (*patol.*) rubeola; German measles (*pl.*).
rubería, *s.f.* theft: *questa è una* —, this is a theft (*o* this is stealing); *commettere ruberie*, to steal; *vivere di ruberie*, to live by stealing.
rubicóndo, *ag.* ruddy, rubicund: *guance rubiconde*, ruddy cheeks; *viso* —, rubicund face.
Rubicóne, *no.pr.m.* (*geog.*) Rubicon: *passare il* —, to cross the Rubicon (anche *fig.*).
rubídio, *s.m.* (*min.*) rubidium.
rubinétto, *s.m.* tap, cock; (*amer.*) faucet: — *del gas*, gas-tap (*o* cock); — *dell'acqua*, water-tap; — *di decompressione*, (*mec.*) compression relief tap; *aprire un* —, to turn a tap on; *chiudere un* —, to turn a tap off.
rubino, *s.m.* (*min.*) ruby.
rubízzo, *ag.* (*florido, sano*) hale.
rúblo, *s.m.* rouble.
rubríca, *s.f.* **1.** (*in un periodico*) survey; (*in un giornale*) column: — *letteraria*, literary survey; — *teatrale*, theatre column **2.** (*indice alfabetico*) index (*pl.* indexes, indices); (*libretto, quaderno con indice alfabetico*) index-book; (*per indirizzi*) address-book: — *telefonica*, list of telephone numbers **3.** (*st. eccl.*) rubric **4.** (*min.*) red ochre; (*arc.*) rubric.
rubricàre, *v.t.* to index.
rubricísta, *s.c.* (*eccl.*) rubricist, rubrician.
rúbro, *ag.* (*letter.*) red.
rúca, ruchétta, rúcola, *s.f.* (*bot.*) rocket.
rúde, *ag.* **1.** (*rozzo*) rough; (*brusco, aspro*) harsh, rough; (*severo*) severe, harsh: *carattere* —, rough character; *educazione* —, severe (*o* harsh) upbringing; *modi rudi*, rough (*o* unpolished *o* unrefined) manners; *parole rudi*, rough (*o* harsh) words; *punizioni rudi*, harsh punishments; *risposta* —, rough answer; *sistemi rudi*, rough methods; *uomo* —, rough man **2.** (*duro*) hard: *un* — *colpo*, a hard blow; *un* — *lavoro*, a hard work.
rudeménte, *av.* **1.** (*rozzamente*) roughly; (*aspramente*)

harshly; (*severamente*) severely, harshly 2. (*duramente*) hard.

rúdere, rúdero, *s.m.* 1. ruin: *i ruderi di un tempio,* the ruins of a temple 2. *fig.* ruin, wreck: *quell'uomo è un* —, that man is a wreck.

rudézza, *s.f.* (*rozzezza*) roughness; (*asprezza*) harshness: *la — dei modi,* roughness of manners.

rudimentàle, *ag.* 1. rudimentary, rough: *disegno* —, rough drawing; *tavolo* —, rudimentary table; *tecnica* —, rudimentary technique 2. (*non bene sviluppato*) rudimentary: *organo* —, rudimentary organ.

rudiménto, *s.m.* 1. rudiment: *i rudimenti della matematica,* the rudiments (*o* first elements *o* first principles) of mathematics 2. (*di un organo*) rudiment: *avere un — di ali,* to have rudimentary wings.

ruffiàna, *s.f.* procuress.

ruffianeggiàre, *v.i.* to procure.

ruffiàno, *s.m.* procurer.

Rúfo, *no.pr.m.* (*st.*) Rufus.

rúga, *s.f.* 1. wrinkle: *un viso solcato da rughe,* a face furrowed (with wrinkles) (*o* a wrinkled face) 2. (*piega di abito*) crease, wrinkle: *fare rughe,* to crease.

rugàre, *v.t.* (*volg.*) (*annoiare, seccare*) to bother: *non rugarmi,* don't bother me (*o* stop worrying me).

rugàto, *ag.* (*pieno di rughe*) wrinkled, furrowed.

ruggènte, *ag.* roaring.

Ruggèro, *no.pr.m.* Roger.

rugghiàre, e derivati, *V.* **ruggíre, e derivati.**

rúggine, *ag.* rust (*attributivo*): *color* —, rust-coloured || *mela* —, russet (apple) || *s.f.* 1. rust: *prendere, fare la* —, to get rusty (*o* to rust) 2. (*agr.*) blight, rust 3. (*rancore*) grudge, ill-feeling, bad blood: *c'è una vecchia — fra di loro,* there is bad blood (*o* an old grudge) between them; *avere della — con qlcu.,* to have a grudge against (*o* an ill-feeling towards) s.o.

rugginóso, *ag.* rusty (anche *fig.*): *ferro* —, rusty iron; *memoria rugginosa,* rusty memory.

ruggíre, *v.i.* to roar (anche *fig.*): *i leoni ruggiscono,* lions roar; *il vento ruggisce,* the wind is roaring.

ruggíto, *s.m.* roar, roaring (anche *fig.*).

rugiàda, *s.f.* 1. dew (anche *fig.*): *coperto, umido di* —, dewy; *goccia di* —, dew-drop 2. *— del sole,* (bot.) sundew.

rugiadóso, *ag.* dewy (anche *fig.*).

rugliàre, *v.i.* 1. (*di cane*) to growl 2. (*rumoreggiare sordamente*) to roar.

rugosità, *s.f.* 1. (*di viso*) wrinkledness 2. (*scabrosità*) roughness; (*di terreno*) ruggedness.

rugóso, *ag.* 1. wrinkled, lined: *viso* —, wrinkled face 2. (*scabro*) rough; (*di terreno*) rugged 3. (*di foglie*) rugose.

ruína, e derivati, *V.* **rovina, e derivati.**

rullàre, *v.i.* 1. to roll: *i tamburi rullavano,* the drums rolled 2. (*mar.*) to roll: *la nave rullava nella tempesta,* the ship was rolling in the storm 3. (*di aeroplano*) to taxi || *v.t.* to roll: *— una strada,* to roll a road.

rullío, *s.m.* 1. roll, rolling: *il — di un tamburo,* the roll of a drum 2. (*mar.*) roll, rolling.

rúllo, *s.m.* 1. (*di tamburo*) roll: *il — dei tamburi,* the roll of the drums 2. (*tec.*) roller; roll; (*per rimozione di macchine pesanti*) dolly; (*di macchina da stampa*) roller; (*di macchina da scrivere*) platen: *— a filettare,* (*mec.*) thread roller; *— cilindrico, conico,* straight, conical roller; *— compressore,* (*mec.*) steam-roller; *— dentato,* (*cine.*) sprocket; *— di guida,* (*cine.*) (*di proiettore*) guide roller; *— di pellicola,* (*foto.*) roll of film; *— di trazione,* (*ind. tessile*) drawing-frame roller; *— per filigranare,* (*ind. carta*) dandy roll (*o* dandy roller); *— portacingolo,* (*mec.*) track roller; *— pressore, tensore,* (*cine.*) (*di proiettore*) pressure, tension roller; *— spianatore,* (*mec.*) jockey (*o* straightening roll); *catena a rulli,* (*mec.*) roller-chain; *cuscinetto a rulli,* (*mec.*) roller-bearing.

rum, *s.m.* rum.

rúmba, *s.f.* (*danza, musica*) rumba.

rumèno, *ag.s.m.* Ro(u)manian.

ruminànte, *ag.s.m.* ruminant.

ruminàre, *v.i.* to ruminate, to chew the cud (anche *fig.*) || *v.t.* 1. to ruminate 2. (*rimuginare*) to ruminate, to ponder: *che cosa rumini?,* what are you pondering (over)?.

ruminazióne, *s.f.* rumination (anche *fig.*); pondering.

rúmine, *s.m.* (*di ruminante*) rumen.

rumóre, *s.m.* 1. noise, din: *— assordante, forte, sordo,* deafening, loud, dull noise; *— metallico,* clang; *il — era insopportabile,* the noise was unbearable (*o fam.* enough to wake the dead); *fare* —, to make a noise || *fare molto* —, *fig.* to arouse great interest: *il libro fece molto* —, the book aroused great interest (*o* caused a stir); *la sua avventura fece molto* —, his adventure was much talked about 2. (*tumulto*) uproar, din, clamour: *la folla si levò a* —, the crowd was in an uproar; *un gran — si levò nella sala,* a great uproar arose in the hall; *gli studenti facevano un terribile* —, the students were making a terrible din || *lontano dai rumori del mondo,* far from the madding crowd || *mettere il campo a* —, to give the alarm 3. (*notizia vaga*) rumour, talk: *correvano rumori di guerra,* there was a rumour that war would break out.

rumoreggiaménto, *s.m.* 1. rumbling; noise 2. (*tumulto*) uproar.

rumoreggiànte, *ag.* rumbling; (*rumoroso*) noisy.

rumoreggiàre, *v.i.* 1. to make a noise; to rumble: *il tuono rumoreggiava,* the thunder was rumbling 2. (*tumultuare*) to make a noise; to be in an uproar: *la folla rumoreggiava,* the crowd was in an uproar 3. (*spargere voce*) to rumour.

rumoreggiatóre, *ag.* rumbling; noisy || *s.m.,* **rumoreggiatríce,** *s.f.* 1. noisy person 2. (*chi fa tumulti*) rioter 3. (*maldicente*) slanderer.

rumorío, *s.m.* noise.

rumorosaménte, *av.* noisily; loudly.

rumoróso, *ag.* noisy; (*sonoro*) loud: *musica rumorosa,* noisy music; *persona, casa rumorosa,* noisy person, house; *quartiere* —, noisy neighbourhood; *voce, risata rumorosa,* loud voice, laugh.

rúna, *s.f.* rune.

rúnico, *ag.* runic: *caratteri runici,* runic letters.

ruòlo, *s.m.* 1. roll, list: *ruoli dell'equipaggio, dell'esercito,* muster-roll; *i ruoli del Ministero,* the list of Ministry employees; *i ruoli del personale insegnante,* the list of state teachers; *essere cancellato dai ruoli, essere iscritto nei ruoli,* to be struck from the list, to be put on the list (*o* roll) || *personale di* —, *fuori* —, permanent, temporary staff || *la causa fu rinviata a nuovo* —, (*dir.*) the case was held over; *mettere a — una causa,* (*dir.*) to enter a case for trial 2. (*teat.*) (*parte*) part, rôle (anche *fig.*): *ha recitato nel — di Adelchi,* he played the rôle of Adelchi; *avere il — principale,* to play the leading rôle.

ruòta, *s.f.* wheel: *ruote anteriori, posteriori,* (*aut.*) front, rear wheels; *— a pale,* (*mar.*) paddle-wheel; *a raggi,* (*mec.*) spoked wheel; *— del mulino,* mill-wheel; *— del timone,* (*mar.*) helm (*o* wheel); *— del vasaio,* potter's wheel; *— dentata,* (*mec.*) cog-wheel (*o* toothed-wheel); *— di frizione,* (*mec.*) friction wheel; *— di ingranaggio,* (*mec.*) gear-wheel; *— di scorta,* (*aut.*) spare wheel; *— motrice,* (*mec.*) driving-wheel; *un giro di* —, a turn of the wheel; *veicolo a due, quattro ruote,* two-wheeled, four-wheeled vehicle; *fu messo al supplizio della* —, he was broken on the wheel; *le ruote affondavano nel terreno,* the wheels sank in the ground; *le ruote girano a vuoto,* the wheels are idling || *la — della fortuna,* the wheel of fortune || *la Sacra Romana Rota,* (*eccl.*) the Sacred Roman Rota || *il pavone fa la* —, the peacock spreads its tail; *il tacchino fa la* —, the turkey struts; *fare la* —, *fig.* to strut (like a turkey) || *essere l'ultima — del carro,* (*fam.*) to count for nothing || *mettere i bastoni fra le ruote a qlcu.,* to put a spoke in s.o.'s wheel || *ungere le ruote*, *fig*. to grease the wheels.

rúpe, *s.f.* cliff, rock.

rupèstre, *ag*. (*letter*.) rocky; rock (*attributivo*): *un paesaggio* —, a rocky landscape; *piante rupestri*, rock -plants; *pino* —, rock-pine.

rúpia[1], *s.f.* (*patol*.) rupia.

rupía[2], *s.f.* (*moneta d'argento dell'India*) rupee.

ruràle, *ag*. rural; country (*attributivo*): *economia* —, rural economy; *popolazione* —, rural population; *scuola* —, country school; *zona* —, rural district || *i rurali*, country people.

ruralizzàre, *v.t.* to ruralize.

ruscellétto, *s.m.* brooklet, streamlet; (*poet*.) rivulet, rill.

ruscèllo, *s.m.* brook, stream.

rúsco, *s.m.* (*bot*.) butcher's broom.

rúspa, *s.f.* 1. (*agr*.) scraper 2. (*il razzolare*) scratching about 3. (*cerca di castagne*) chestnut gathering: *andare alla* —, to go chestnut gathering.

ruspàre, *v.i.* 1. (*agr*.) to transport earth with a scraper 2. (*razzolare*) to scratch about 3. (*cercare castagne dopo il raccolto*) to gather chestnuts.

rúspo, *ag*. rough: *sasso* —, rough stone || *moneta ruspa*, new coin || *s.m.* 1. (*zecchino*) sequin 2. (*ciò che si trova ruspando*) scrapings (*pl*.), pickings (*pl*.) || *uccelli di* —, poultry.

russaménto, *s.m.* snoring.

russàre, *v.i.* to snore.

Rússia, *no.pr.f.* (*geog*.) Russia || *che russia!*, (*fam*.) what a mess! || *cuoio di* —, Russia leather || *la Piccola* —, (*geog*.) the Ukraine.

rússo, *ag.s.m.* Russian || **rússa**, *s.f.* Russian.

russofilía, *s.f.* Russophilism.

russòfilo, *ag.s.m.* Russophil(e).

russofobía, *s.f.* Russophobia.

russòfobo, *ag.s.m.* Russophobe.

rusticàggine, *s.f.* rusticity, roughness.

rusticàle, *ag*. rustic: *poemetti rusticali*, short rustic poems.

rusticalménte, *av*. (*letter*.) rustically.

rusticaménte, *av*. rustically, roughly.

rusticàno, *ag*. rustic.

rustichézza, *s.f.* rusticity, roughness: *ci accolse con la sua cordiale* —, he welcomed us with his rough cordiality.

rusticità, *s.f.* 1. rusticity: *mi piace la* — *di questa casetta*, I like the rusticity of this little house 2. (*rozzezza*) roughness, rusticity: — *di modi*, roughness of manner.

rústico, *ag*. 1. country (*attributivo*); rustic, rural: *casa rustica*, rustic house; *danze rustiche*, country -dances; *facciata rustica*, rustic façade; *gente rustica*, country-folk; *mobili di stile* —, furniture in farmhouse style; *piaceri rustici*, rural pleasures; *scene, tradizioni rustiche*, rural scenes, customs; *semplicità rustica*, rustic simplicity; *vita rustica*, country life || *alla rustica*, simply: *trattamento alla rustica*, rough and ready treatment 2. (*rozzo*) rustic, rough, unrefined, uncouth: *modi rustici*, rustic (o rough) manners; *ha un'aria rustica*, he has an unrefined (o uncouth) air 3. (*ritroso*) unsociable: *è un bambino* —, he is an unsociable child || *s.m.* 1. peasant, rustic 2. (*casa di contadini*) outhouse.

rúta, *s.f.* (*bot*.) rue: — *di muro*, wall-rue.

rutàcee, *s.f.pl*. (*bot*.) Rutaceae.

Rutènia, *no.pr.f.* (*geog*.) Ruthenia.

rutènio, *s.m.* (*chim*.) ruthenium.

rutèno, *ag. s.m.* Ruthenian, Ruthene.

Ruth, *no.pr.f.* Ruth.

rutilànte, *ag*. (*poet*.) shining, glowing, rutilant.

rutilàre, *v.i.* (*rar*.) to shine, to glow.

rútilo, *s.m.* (*min*.) rutile.

ruttàre, *v.i.* to belch.

rútto, *s.m.* belch.

ruttóre, *s.m.* (*elett*.) contact-breaker, trembler: *molla, puntine del* —, contact-breaker spring, points.

ruvidaménte, *av*. 1. roughly, coarsely 2. (*scortesemente*) roughly, coarsely; rudely.

ruvidézza, ruvidità, *s.f.* 1. roughness, coarseness 2. (*scortesia*) roughness, coarseness; rudeness.

rúvido, *ag*. 1. rough, coarse: *mani ruvide*, rough hands; *stoffa ruvida*, rough (o coarse) cloth 2. *fig*. (*scortese*) rough, coarse; rude: *modi ruvidi*, rude (o rough o coarse) manners; *uomo* —, rough man.

rúzza, *s.f.* (*screzio*) difference, variance; (*litigio*) quarrel: *c'è un po' di* — *fra loro*, they are at variance.

ruzzàre, *v.i.* (*fam*.) to romp.

ruzzolàre, *v.i.* 1. (*cadere rotolando*) to tumble down: — *giù per le scale*, to tumble down the stairs 2. (*rotolare*) to roll: *le palline ruzzolano sul pavimento*, the marbles are rolling (about) on the floor || *v.t.* (*far rotolare*) to roll: — *un sasso*, to roll a stone.

ruzzolàta, *s.f.* tumble, heavy fall.

ruzzolóne, *s.m.* tumble, heavy fall: *fare un brutto* —, to have a nasty tumble; *fig*. to come down in the world.

ruzzolóni (a), *l.av.*: *cadere, venire giù a* — to tumble down.

S

s, *s.f.m.* (*diciassettesima lettera dell'alfabeto italiano*) s (*pl.* ss, s's) ‖ — *come Savona*, (*tel.*) s for sugar ‖ *a forma di S*, S (*attributivo*); S-shaped: *curva ad S*, S-bend; *un divano a (forma di) S*, an S-sofa.

Sàba, *no.pr.f.* (*geog. st.*) Sheba: *la Regina di —*, the Queen of Sheba.

sabàtico, *ag.* sabbatic(al): *anno —*, sabbatical year.

sabatíno, *ag.* Saturday (*attributivo*).

sàbato, *s.m.* Saturday: *verrà —*, he is coming on Saturday ‖ *— santo*, (*eccl.*) Holy Saturday ‖ *Dio non paga il —*, prov. the mills of God grind slowly.

sabàudo, *ag.* Savoyard; of Savoy.

sàbba, *s.f.* (*mit. nordica*) witches' Sabbath.

sàbbia, *s.f.* 1. sand; (*spiaggia*) sands (*pl.*): *un grano di —*, a grain of sand; *banco di —*, sandbank; *cava di —*, sand-pit; *i bambini giocavano sulla —*, the children were playing on the sand; *costruire sulla —*, *fig.* to build on sand; *seminare nella —*, *fig.* to plough the sands 2. (*med.*) urinary sand.

sabbiàre, *v.t.* to sand; (*mec.*) to sand-blast.

sabbiatríce, *s.f.* (*mec.*) sand-blasting machine, sander.

sabbiatúra, *s.f.* 1. (*mec.*) sand-blasting 2. (*med.*) (hot) sand-bath.

sabbièra, *s.f.* sand-box.

sabbióne, *s.m.* sandy soil.

sabbióso, *ag.* sandy.

sabeísmo, *s.m.* (*st. relig.*) Sabaism; star-worship.

sabelliàno, *ag.s.m.* (*st. relig.*) Sabellian.

sabèllico, *ag.s.m.* (*st. romana*) Sabellian.

sabèllo, *ag.s.m.* (*st. romana*) Sabellian.

sabèo, *ag.s.m.* Sab(a)ean.

sabína[1], *s.f.* (*bot.*) savin(e).

Sabína[2], *no.pr.f.* Sabina, Sabine.

sabíno, *ag.s.m.* Sabine ‖ **sabína**[3], *s.f.* Sabine (woman) ‖ *il ratto delle Sabine*, the rape of the Sabine women.

sabotàggio, *s.m.* sabotage: *atto di —*, act of sabotage.

sabotàre, *v.t.* to sabotage.

sabotatóre, *s.m.*, **sabotatríce**, *s.f.* saboteur.

saburràle, *ag.* (*med.*) saburral.

sàcca, *s.f.* 1. bag; satchel: *— da viaggio*, travelling -bag; (*di un soldato, marinaio*) kit-bag 2. (*mil.*) pocket 3. *— d'aria*, (*aer.*) air-pocket 4. (*insenatura di mare*) sea-inlet, bay.

saccaràto, *s.m.* (*chim.*) saccharate.

saccarífero, *ag.* (*chim.*) sacchariferous.

saccarificàre, *v.t.* (*chim.*) to saccharify.

saccarificazióne, *s.f.* (*chim.*) saccharification.

saccarimetría, *s.f.* (*chim.*) saccharimetry.

saccarímetro, *s.m.* (*chim.*) saccharimeter.

saccarína, *s.f.* (*chim.*) saccharin(e).

saccaròide, *ag.* saccharoid(al).

saccaromicèti, *s.m. pl.* (*bot.*) Saccharomyces.

saccaròsio, *s.m.* (*chim.*) saccharose.

saccàta, *s.f.* sackful, bagful.

saccàto, *ag.* (*med.*) saccate.

saccènte, *ag.* pedantic; (*presuntuoso*) conceited: *donna —*, bluestocking ‖ *s.c.* pedant; sciolist, wiseacre: *fare il —*, to air one's knowledge.

saccenteménte, *av.* pedantically; sciolistically; (*presuntuosamente*) conceitedly.

saccentería, *s.f.* pedantry; (*presunzione*) conceit.

saccheggiaménto, *s.m.* 1. (*il saccheggiare*) sacking, pillaging, plundering, looting 2. (*saccheggio*) sack, pillage.

saccheggiàre, *v.t.* to sack, to pillage, to plunder to loot: *— una città*, to sack a town ‖ *— un autore*, to pillage an author.

saccheggiatóre, *s.m.*, **saccheggiatríce**, *s.f.* pillager, plunderer, looter.

sacchéggio, *s.m.* sack, pillage.

sacchétta, *s.f.* (*per cavalli*) nose-bag.

sàcco[1], *s.m.* 1. sack; bag: *— a pelo*, sleeping-bag; *— a terra*, (*mil.*) sand-bag; *— da montagna*, rucksack; *— da viaggio*, travelling-bag; *un — di patate*, a sack of potatoes; *un — di tela*, a cloth bag; *— postale*, mail-bag; *tela da sacchi*, sackcloth ‖ *abito a —*, loose dress (o sack dress) ‖ *colazione al —*, picnic ‖ *credo non sia tutta farina del suo —*, I think s.o. else had a finger in the pie ‖ *agire con la testa nel —*, to act recklessly (o thoughtlessly o rashly) ‖ *essere un — d'ossa*, to be a bag of bones ‖ *essere colto con le mani nel —*, to be caught red-handed ‖ *mettere qlcu. nel —*, to take s.o. in (o to cheat s.o. o to trick s.o. o to swindle s.o.) ‖ *tenere il — a qlcu.*, to aid and abet s.o. ‖ *vestire il — della penitenza*, to wear sackcloth and ashes ‖ *vuotare il —*, to speak out (o to speak one's mind) ‖ *non dir quattro finchè non lo hai nel —*, prov. don't count your chickens before they are hatched 2. (*grande quantità*) a lot: *un — di preoccupazioni, lavoro*, a lot of worries, work; *egli ha un — di soldi*, he has pots of money 3. (*anat. bot.*) sac: *— lacrimale*, lachrymal sac 4. pocket (*misura di peso per aridi = 76,2 kg*).

sàcco[2], *s.m.* (*letter.*) (*saccheggio*) sack, pillage: *mettere a — una città*, to sack a town.

saccòccia, *s.f.* pocket.

saccomànno, *s.m.* 1. (*saccheggiatore*) sacker, plunderer, pillager 2. (*saccheggio*) sack, plunder, pillage.

saccóne, *s.m.* palliasse, paillasse, straw mattress.

sàcculo, *s.m.* (*anat.*) saccule.

sacèllo, *s.m.* sacellum (*pl.* sacella): *— mortuario*, mortuary chapel.

sacerdotàle, *ag.* sacerdotal, priestly, priestlike.

sacerdotalménte, *av.* sacerdotally.

sacerdòte, *s.m.* priest ‖ *un — delle arti*, a devotee of the arts.

sacerdotéssa, *s.f.* priestess.

sacerdòzio, *s.m.* priesthood; ministry: *assumere il —*, to enter the Church (o to go into the Church).

sacràle, *ag.* (*anat.*) sacral.

sacralgía, *s.f.* (*med.*) sacralgia.

sacramentàle, *ag.* 1. sacramental: *atti, riti sacramentali*, sacramental acts, rites 2. (*solenne*) solemn.

sacramentàli, *s.m.pl.* (*eccl.*) sacramentals.

sacramentalménte, *av.* sacramentally.

sacramentàre, *v.t.* (*eccl.*) to administer the sacraments to (s.o.) ‖ *v.i.* 1. (*giurare*) to take (an) oath, to swear 2. (*bestemmiare*) to swear; to blaspheme; to curse ‖ **sacramentàrsi**, *v.r.* to receive the sacraments.

sacramentàrio[1], *s.m.* (*eccl. st.*) sacramentary.

sacramentario[2], *s.m.* (*st.*) (*eretico*) Sacramentarian.

sacramentàto, *ag.*: *Gesù —*, Jesus in the Most Holy Sacrament of the Altar.

sacraménto, *s.m.* 1. (*teol.*) sacrament: *il Santissimo Sacramento*, the Holy (o Blessed) Sacrament; *i sette sacramenti*, the seven sacraments; *accostarsi al Sacramento*, to partake of the Sacrament; *dare, prendere i sacramenti*, to administer, to receive the sacraments 2. (*giuramento*) oath 3. (*bestemmia*) swear-word, oath, curse.

sacràre, *v.t.* **1.** to consecrate; to dedicate **2.** (*volg.*) (*bestemmiare*) to swear, to curse ‖ **sacràrsi**, *v.r.* to devote oneself, to devote one's life.

sacràrio, *s.m.* **1.** shrine; sanctuary ‖ *rifugiarsi nel — della famiglia*, to take refuge in the bosom of one's family **2.** (*archeol.*) sacrarium (*pl.* sacraria).

sacràto, *ag.* **1.** (*consacrato*) consecrated: *ostia sacrata*, consecrated host **2.** (*che ha preso i voti*) professed: *monaca sacrata*, professed nun ‖ *s.m. V.* **sagràto**.

sacrestàno, **sacrestía**, *V.* **sagrestàno**, **sagrestía**.

sacrificaménto, *s.m.* (*rar.*) **1.** (*il sacrificare*) sacrificing **2.** (*sacrificio*) sacrifice.

sacrificàre, *v.t.* to sacrifice: *— la propria vita alla patria, alla causa della giustizia*, to sacrifice (*o* to lay down) one's life for one's country, in the cause of justice; *— vittime agli dei*, to sacrifice victims to the gods ‖ *v.i.* to offer sacrifices, to make offerings ‖ **sacrificàrsi**, *v.r.* to sacrifice oneself, to sacrifice one's life.

sacrificàto, *ag.* sacrificed.

sacrificatóre, *s.m.*, **sacrificatríce**, *s.f.* sacrificer.

sacrifício, **sacrifízio**, *s.m.* sacrifice: *il — della Messa*, the sacrifice of the Mass; *egli ha fatto molti sacrifici per i suoi figli*, he has made many sacrifices for his children; *fu ucciso un bue in —*, an ox was killed as a sacrifice; *fare un — agli dei*, to make a sacrifice (*o* an offering) to the gods; *offrire in —*, to offer in sacrifice ‖ *— di sè*, self-sacrifice ‖ *il Santo Sacrificio*, (*la Messa*) the (Holy) Mass.

sacrilegaménte, *av.* sacrilegiously.

sacrilègio, *s.m.* sacrilege (*anche fig.*).

sacrílego, *ag.* sacrilegious: *atti sacrileghi*, sacrilegious acts ‖ *è una lingua sacrilega*, he has an evil tongue ‖ *s.m.* impious person.

sacripànte, *s.m.* blusterer; swashbuckler; bully.

sacrísta, *s.m.* sacristan; sacrist; sexton.

sàcro, *ag.* **1.** sacred, holy: *un — diritto*, a sacred right; *il — nome di Gesù*, the sacred name of Jesus; *le Sacre Scritture*, the Holy Scriptures; *luogo —*, holy (*o* sacred) place; *musica sacra*, sacred music; *ordini sacri*, holy orders; *storia sacra e profana*, sacred and profane history; *vestimenti sacri*, sacred vestments; *nell'antico Egitto il bue era un animale —*, in ancient Egypt the ox was a sacred animal; *il ricordo di lui è — per me*, the memory of him is sacred to me; *considerare sacra una promessa*, to hold a promise sacred ‖ *la Sacra Famiglia*, the Holy Family ‖ *Sacra Maestà*, His Sacred Majesty ‖ *il Sacro Romano Impero*, the Holy Roman Empire **2.** *osso —*, (*anat.*) sacrum (*pl.* sacra).

sacrosantaménte, *av.* **1.** (*indiscutibilmente*) indisputably **2.** (*meritatamente*) deservedly.

sacrosànto, *ag.* **1.** sacrosanct, sacred: *un diritto — a* sacred right **2.** (*indiscutibile*) absolute, indisputable: *questa è la verità sacrosanta*, this is the absolute (*o* indisputable) truth **3.** (*meritato*) well-deserved: *una punizione sacrosanta*, a well-deserved punishment.

sadducèo, *ag.* (*st. ebraica*) Sadducean ‖ *s.m.* (*st. ebraica*) Sadducee.

sàdico, *ag.* sadistic ‖ *s.m.* sadist.

sadísmo, *s.m.* sadism.

saétta, *s.f.* **1.** arrow **2.** (*fulmine*) thunderbolt; (*lampo*) flash (of lightning) **3.** (*di orologio*) hand **4.** (*geom.*) sagitta (*pl.* sagittae) **5.** (*artig.*) bit **6.** (*fam.*) (*bambino irrequieto*) imp.

saettaménto, *s.m.* shooting (*anche fig.*).

saettànte, *ag.* shooting; darting; speeding.

saettàre, *v.t.* **1.** (*lanciare saette a*) to shoot arrows at (s.o., sthg.) **2.** *fig.* to shoot; to dart: *mi saettò uno sguardo di rimprovero*, he darted a look of reproof at me; *il sole saettava i suoi raggi*, the sun was shooting its rays ‖ *v.i.* (*guizzare*) to dart; to shoot: *la meteora saettò nel cielo*, the meteor shot across the sky.

saettatóre, *ag.* shooting ‖ *s.m.* archer; bowman (*pl.* bowmen).

saettatríce, *s.f.* archer.

saettière, *s.m.* archer; bowman (*pl.* bowmen).

saettifórme, *ag.* arrow-shaped.

saettóne, *s.m.* (*arch.*) strut.

safèna, *s.f.* (*anat.*) saphena.

sàffica, *s.f.* (*poes.*) Sapphic verse.

sàffico, *ag.* (*poes.*) Sapphic: *strofa saffica*, Sapphic verse; *verso —*, Sapphic line.

Sàffo, *no.pr.f.* (*st. lett.*) Sappho.

safranína, *s.f.* (*chim.*) safranin(e).

sàga, *s.f.* (*lett.*) saga.

sagàce, *ag.* sagacious, shrewd, wise.

sagaceménte, *av.* sagaciously, shrewdly, wisely.

sagàcia, **sagacità**, *s.f.* sagacity, shrewdness, wisdom.

sagapèno, *s.m.* (*bot.*) sagapenum.

sagèna, *s.f.* (*rete da pesca*) seine.

saggézza, *s.f.* wisdom.

saggiaménte, *av.* wisely, judiciously.

saggiàre, *v.t.* (*analizzare*) to assay; to test: *— oro, argento*, to assay gold, silver; *— una soluzione chimica*, to test a chemical solution.

saggiatóre, *s.m.* **1.** assayer; tester **2.** (*bilancia per saggiare l'oro*) assay balance; scales (*pl.*) for gold.

saggiatúra, *s.f.* assaying; testing.

saggina, *s.f.* (*bot.*) sorghum, (Indian) millet.

sagginàle, *ag.* sorghum (*attributivo*); millet (*attributivo*) ‖ *s.m.* sorghum-stalk, millet-stalk.

sagginàre, *v.t.* to fatten.

sagginóto, *ag.* roan: *cavallo —*, roan (horse).

sàggio[1], *ag.* wise; sage; (*prudente*) prudent; (*di buon senso*) sensible: *una saggia decisione*, a wise decision; *saggi consigli*, sage advice; *un uomo —*, a wise man; *questo fu molto — da parte tua*, that was very sensible of you ‖ *s.m.* wise man, sage ‖ *i Sette Saggi*, the Seven Sages (*o* the Seven Wise Men).

sàggio[2], *s.m.* **1.** (*lett.*) essay **2.** (*di oro, argento, ecc.*) assay: *il — di un metallo*, an assay of a metal **3.** (*nelle scuole*): *— ginnico, musicale*, gym-(nastic) display, school concert **4.** (*campione*) sample **5.** (*prova*) example, instance: *questo è un — delle mie capacità*, this is an example of my capacities; *dare un — delle proprie abilità*, to give a show of one's abilities **6.** (*comm.*) (*tasso*) rate: *— di sconto*, rate of discount.

saggísta, *s.m.* essayist.

saggístico, *ag.* essay (*attributivo*).

saggiuòlo, *s.m.* **1.** (*campione*) sample (of wine, oil) **2.** (*bottiglietta*) small bottle **3.** (*bilancia*) scale (for weighing coins).

sagittàle, *ag.* **1.** (*di saetta*) arrow-shaped; arrow (*attributivo*) **2.** (*anat.*) sagittal: *sutura —*, sagittal suture **3.** (*di foglia*) sagittate(d).

sagittàrio, *s.m.* archer; bowman (*pl.* bowmen) ‖ *il Sagittario*, (*astr.*) the Sagittarius.

sagittàto, *ag.* (*di foglia*) sagittate(d).

sàgo, *s.m.* sago (*pl.* sagos): *palma del —*, sago palm.

sàgola, *s.f.* (*mar.*) line.

sàgoma, *s.f.* **1.** (*forma*) shape, outline, profile: *la — di un edificio*, the outline of a building **2.** (*modello*) pattern; mould **3.** *— limite del carico*, (*ferr.*) loading -gauge **4.** *quell'uomo è una bella —!*, (*fam.*) that man is quite a character!.

sagomàre, *v.t.* to mould, to shape.

sagomàto, *ag.* shaped: *ben —*, finely-shaped.

sàgra, *s.f.* festival: *— del villaggio*, village festival.

sagramentàre, **sagràre**, *v.i.* (*volg.*) (*bestemmiare*) to curse, to swear.

sagràto, *s.m.* **1.** parvis, church-square **2.** (*cimitero presso la chiesa*) churchyard **3.** (*volg.*) (*bestemmia*) oath, curse.

sagrestàno, *s.m.* sacristan, sacrist; sexton.

sagrestía, *s.f.* sacristy, vestry.

sagrí, *s.m.* shagreen.

sagrinàto, *ag.* shagreened; shagreen (*attributivo*).

sagrísta, *s.m.* sacristan, sacrist; sexton.

sàgro, *s.m.* (*st. mil.*) falcon.

sagú, *s.m.* sago (*pl.* sagos): *palma del —*, sago palm.

Sahàra, *no.pr.m.* (*geog.*) Sahara.

sàia, *s.f.* (*tessuto*) serge.

sàica, saìca, *s.f.* (*mar.*) saic, saick, saique.

sàio, *s.m.* **1.** (*di soldato romano*) sagum (*pl.* saga) **2.** (*veste medievale*) doublet **3.** (*tonaca monacale*) habit.

sàla¹, *s.f.* hall; room: — *caldaie*, boiler room; — *cinematografica*, cinema hall; — *da ballo*, dance-hall; — *da biliardo*, billiard-room; — *da giuoco*, card-room; — *da pranzo*, dining-room; — *d'attesa*, waiting-room; — *dei banchetti*, banquet-hall; — *di lettura*, reading-room; — *macchine*, engine-room; — *nautica*, chart-room; — *operatoria*, operating theatre; — *parto*, delivery room; — *per concerti*, concert-hall; (*in casa privata*) music-room; *in questo cinema, teatro c'è sempre la — piena*, at this cinema, theatre there is always a full house; *tutte le sale del castello erano piene di gente*, all the halls of the castle were full of people.

sàla², *s.f.* (*mec.*) axle(-tree).

salàeca, *s.f.* (*ittiol.*) pilchard.

salàce, *ag.* **1.** (*lascivo*) salacious **2.** (*pungente*) spicy.

salacità, *s.f.* **1.** (*l'essere lascivo*) salacity **2.** (*l'essere pungente*) spiciness.

Saladíno, *no.pr.m.* (*st.*) Saladin.

salagióne, *s.f.* salting, pickling; curing.

salamàndra, *s.f.* (*zool.*) salamander.

salàme, *s.m.* **1.** (*cuc.*) salame (*pl.* salami) **2.** (*fam. fig.*) silly goose.

salameceàre, *v.t.* (*scherz.*) to salaam to (s.o.).

salamelèceo, *s.m.* (*scherz.*) salaam: *fare salamelecchi*, to bow and scrape.

Salamína, *no.pr.f.* (*geog.*) Salamis.

salamòia, *s.f.* pickle: *aringhe in —*, pickled herrings; *cipolline in —*, onion pickles; *verdure in —*, pickles (*o* vegetables in pickle); *mettere in —*, to pickle.

salamoiàre, *v.t.* to pickle.

salàre, *v.t.* to salt; (*per conservare*) to corn || — *la scuola*, (*marinarla*) to play truant.

salariàre, *v.t.* to give a salary to (s.o.).

salariàto, *ag.* wage-earning || *s.m.* **1.** wage-earner **2.** (*operaio*) workman (*pl.* workmen); (*impiegato*) office-worker.

salàrio, *s.m.* wages (*gener. pl.*); pay: *ha un buon —*, he gets good wages (*o* good pay).

salassàre, *v.t.* to bleed (anche *fig.*).

salàsso, *s.m.* **1.** (*med.*) bleeding **2.** *fig.* extortion.

salàta, *s.f.* salting: *da' una — alla minestra*, put some salt in the soup.

salatíno, *s.m.* salt bisquit: — *al formaggio*, cheese bisquit.

salàto, *ag.* **1.** salt, salty: *questa minestra è troppo salata*, this soup is too salt || *il Gran Lago Salato*, Great Salt Lake **2.** (*conservato nel sale*) salt, salted, corned: *carne salata*, salted meat; *mandorle salate*, salted almonds; *manzo —*, salt (*o* corned) beef; *pesce —*, salt fish **3.** (*costoso*) expensive, dear, costly: *pagar —*, to pay through one's nose **4.** (*salace*) keen, biting; (*piccante*) spicy: *un epigramma —*, a biting epigram; *uno scherzo —*, a spicy joke || *raccontarne di salate*, to tell spicy stories **5.** (*severo*) stiff, severe || *s.m.* salt pork.

salatóio, *s.m.* salting-room.

salatúra, *s.f.* salting.

sàlce, salcéto, *V.* **sàlice, salicéto.**

salcíccia, *s.f.* sausage.

salcígno, *ag.* **1.** (*di legno*) knotty, gnarled **2.** (*di carne*) tough **3.** (*di persone*) stubborn; hard.

sàlcio, *V.* **sàlice.**

salciuòlo, *s.m.* withe, withy.

sàlda¹, *s.f.* starch-water.

sàlda², *s.f.* (*campo a pascolo*) grazing-ground, pasture.

saldaménte, *av.* firmly; solidly; steadily (anche *fig.*).

saldaménto, *s.m.* **1.** (*metal.*) soldering; welding **2.** (*comm.*) settlement in full.

saldàre, *v.t.* **1.** (*metal.*) to solder; to weld: — *a dolce, a stagno*, to soft-solder (*o* to braze); — *a gas*, to gas-weld; — *a pressione*, to pressure

-weld; — *a punti*, to spot-weld; — *a scintillio*, to flash-weld; — *autogeno*, to (gas-)weld; — *tubazioni di piombo*, to wipe **2.** (*comm.*) to settle, to square up; to pay: — *i conti*, to settle one's accounts **3.** (*ossa, fratture, ecc.*) to join || **saldàrsi**, *v.r.* (*di ferite*) to heal; (*di ossa*) to knit.

saldatívo, *ag.* **1.** (*metal.*) soldering; welding **2.** (*comm.*) settling.

saldatóio, *s.m.* soldering-iron, soldering-copper, copper-bolt: — *a martello*, soldering-hammer.

saldatóre, *s.m.* solderer; welder.

saldatríce, *s.f.* (*mec.*) welder, welding machine: — *ad arco*, arc-welding machine (*o* welding set).

saldatúra, *s.f.* soldering; welding: — *ad arco*, arc-welding; — *a dolce, a stagno*, soft-soldering; — *a fuoco*, forge-welding; — *a gas*, gas-welding; — *a pressione*, pressure-welding; — *a punti*, spot-welding; — *a rilievo*, projection-welding; — *a scintillio*, flash-welding; — *automatica*, automatic welding; — *continua*, seam welding; — *del legno*, woodwelding; — *elettrica*, electric welding; — *forte*, hard-soldering: *lega per — forte*, hard solder; — *provvisoria*, tack-welding.

saldézza, *s.f.* firmness; steadiness; strength (anche *fig.*): — *di mente*, strength of mind; — *di principi*, strength (*o* firmness) of principle.

sàldo, *ag.* **1.** firm, solid, steady: *un muro —*, a solid wall; *tenersi —*, to stand firm **2.** (*forte*) strong: *avere le braccia salde*, to have strong arms **3.** *fig.* firm, steadfast, staunch: *una salda amicizia*, a staunch (*o* constant) friendship; *essere — nei propri principi*, to be resolute (*o* firm) in one's principles || *s.m.* (*comm.*) **1.** (*pareggiamento di partite, conti*) balance: — *attivo, passivo*, credit, debit balance **2.** (*pagamento*) settlement: *a — del nostro conto*, in settlement of our account || *ricevuta a —*, receipt in full **3.** (*liquidazione*) (clearance) sale: *prezzi di —*, bargain prices.

sàle, *s.m.* **1.** salt: *sali (aromatici)*, (*farm.*) smelling-salts; — *basico*, (*chim.*) basic salt; *sali da bagno*, bath-salts; — *da cucina*, kitchen-salt; — *da tavola*, table-salt; — *grosso*, (*ind.*) coarse salt; — *inglese, amaro*, (*farm.*) Epsom-salts; *un pizzico di —*, a pinch of salt || *restare di —*, to be dumbfounded **2.** (*buon senso*) common-sense, mother-wit: *è un uomo che ha — in zucca*, he's got plenty of common-sense || *prendere ql.co. con un grano di —*, to take sthg. with a pinch of salt **3.** (*letter.*) (*arguzia*) piquancy, wit || — *attico*, Attic wit (*o* Attic salt).

salesiàno, *ag. o s.m.* Salesian.

salgèmma, *s.m.* rock-salt.

saliàre, *ag.* (*st. romana*) Salian.

saliceàcee, *s.f.pl.* (*bot.*) Salicaceae.

saliceàstro, *s.m.* (*bot.*) wild willow.

sàlice, *s.m.* (*bot.*) willow, willow-tree: — *piangente*, weeping-willow (anche *fig.*).

salicéto, *s.m.* willow-grove, willow-wood.

salicilàto, *s.m.* (*chim.*) salicylate.

salicílico, *ag.* (*chim.*) salicylic.

salicína, *s.f.* (*chim.*) salicin.

sàlico, *ag.* Salic: *legge salica*, (*st.*) Salic law.

saliènte, *ag.* **1.** (*importante*) important; salient; noteworthy, outstanding: *i fatti più salienti*, the most important facts; *punti, caratteristiche salienti*, salient points, characteristics **2.** (*sporgente*) projecting; prominent **3.** (*crescente*) rising; growing: *la marea —*, the rising tide || *s.m.* (*arch. mil.*) salient.

salièra, *s.f.* salt-cellar.

salífero, *ag.* saliferous, salt-bearing.

salificàbile, *ag.* (*chim.*) salifiable.

salificàre, *v.t.* (*chim.*) to salify.

salificazióne, *s.f.* (*chim.*) salification.

salígno, *ag.* salty, saltish.

sàlii¹, *s.m.pl.* (*tribù franca*) Salians.

sàlii², *s.m.pl.* (*sacerdoti romani*) Salii.

salína, *s.f.* **1.** (*di sale marino*) salt-works (*pl.*); salt-pan, salt-pit, saline **2.** (*di salgemma*) salt-mine.

salinàio, salinatóre, *s.m.* salter.

salinità, *s.f.* salinity, saltness.

salíno, *ag.* saline; salty, salt (*attributivo*): *soluzione salina*, saline solution; *sorgente salina*, salt spring.

salíre, *v.i.* to rise; to climb (sthg.); to go up (sthg.); to come up (sthg.); to get on (sthg.); to mount (sthg.); to ascend (sthg.): *l'aeroplano saliva lentamente*, the plane was climbing slowly; *il calore, il fumo sale*, heat, smoke rises; *il fiume è salito di un metro*, the river has risen a metre; *le lacrime le salirono agli occhi*, tears rose to her eyes (o tears welled up in her eyes); *non salii perchè l'ascensore era rotto*, I did not go up because the lift was not working; *non salì perchè non voleva vedermi*, he did not come up because he did not want to see me; *non — su quel ramo perchè potrebbe rompersi*, do not get on that branch because it might break; *il pallone salì diritto e poi scoppiò*, the balloon went (o rose) straight up, then it burst; *i prezzi salgono*, prices are rising (o going up); *salì a cavallo e scomparve nel bosco*, he mounted (his horse) and disappeared into the wood; *la strada sale*, the road rises (o climbs o goes uphill); *la temperatura, la marea sale*, the temperature, the tide is rising; *— a bordo di una nave*, to go on board a ship; *— in tutta fretta*, to hasten up; *— su un albero*, to climb a tree; *— su un monte*, to climb (o to go up) a mountain; *— su una scala*, to climb (up) (o to mount) a ladder; *— su una sedia*, to climb (o to get) on a chair; *— su un tram, un treno*, to get on a tram, a train ‖ *— al trono*, to ascend the throne ‖ *— socialmente*, to rise socially ‖ *far — qlcu. nella propria automobile*, to give s.o. a lift ‖ *v.t.* to go up, to ascend; to come up; to mount: *— un monte*, to climb (o to go up o to ascend) a mountain; *— le scale*, to go up the stairs.

Salisbúrgo, *no.pr.f.* (*geog.*) Salzburg.

saliscéndi, *s.m.* latch ‖ *i — della fortuna*, the ups and downs of fortune.

salíta, *s.f.* **1.** slope, ascent: *una ripida —*, a steep slope; *fare una —*, to climb (a slope) (o to go uphill) **2.** (*il salire*) ascent: *la — della montagna fu molto dura*, the ascent of the mountain was very difficult ‖ *— in candela*, (*aer.*) zooming **3.** (*aumento*) rise, increase: *una — dei prezzi, della temperatura*, a rise (o an increase) in prices, in temperature **4.** (*ferr.*) gradient, slope: *forte —*, steep gradient.

salíva, *s.f.* saliva, spit, spittle.

salivàle, salivàre[1], *ag.* salivary.

salivàre[2], *v.i.* to salivate.

salivatòrio, *ag.* salivary.

salivazióne, *s.f.* salivation.

Sallústio, *no.pr.m.* (*st. lett.*) Sallust.

sàlma, *s.f.* corpse; (*resti mortali*) remains (*pl.*).

salmàstro, *ag.* brackish; saltish ‖ *s.m.* salty taste.

salmeggiaménto, *s.m.* psalm-singing, psalmody.

salmeggiàre, *v.i.* to sing psalms.

salmeggiatóre, *s.m.* psalm-singer, psalmodist.

salmería, *s.f.* (*mil.*) baggage-train.

salmí, *s.m.* (*cuc.*) salmi, ragout: *lepre in —*, jugged hare.

salmísta, *s.m.* **1.** psalmist **2.** (*salterio*) psalter.

sàlmo, *s.m.* psalm.

salmodía, *s.f.* psalmody.

salmodiàre, *v.i.* to sing psalms.

salmòdico, *ag.* psalmodic.

salmóne, *s.m.* (*ittiol.*) salmon (*invariato al pl.*): *piccolo —*, samlet.

salmonèlla, *s.f.* (*biol.*) salmonella (*pl.* salmonellae).

salnitràle, *ag.* (*chim.*) saltpetre (*attributivo*).

salnítro, *s.m.* (*chim.*) saltpetre, nitre, potassium nitrate.

salnitróso, *ag.* (*chim.*) saltpetrous.

salòlo, *s.m.* (*farm.*) salol.

Salomè, *no.pr.f.* (*Bibbia*) Salome.

Salomóne, *no.pr.m.* (*Bibbia*) Solomon ‖ *Isole —*, (*geog.*) Solomon Islands.

salomònico, *ag.* Solomonic.

salóne, *s.m.* hall; large hall; reception-room ‖ *vettura —*, (*ferr.*) Pullman-car.

Salonícco, *no.pr.f.* (*geog.*) Salonika.

salottésco, *ag.* (*spreg.*) drawing-room (*attributivo*).

salottièro, *ag.* drawing-room (*attributivo*): *modi salottieri*, drawing-room manners ‖ *s.m.* man-about-town (*pl.* men-about-town); (*fam.*) lounge-lizard.

salottíno, *s.m.* parlour; sitting-room.

salòtto, *s.m.* sitting-room; (*salotto dove si riceve*) drawing-room; (*stanza di soggiorno*) living-room; (*salottino*) parlour: *conversazione da —*, drawing-room conversation ‖ *compreremo un —*, we shall buy a drawing-room suite.

salpàre, *v.i.* to (set) sail; to set out: *la nave salperà domani*, the ship will sail tomorrow ‖ *v.t.:* *— l'àncora*, to weigh anchor.

salpínge, *s.f.* (*anat.*) salpinx (*pl.* salpinges).

salpingíte, *s.f.* (*patol.*) salpingitis.

sàlsa, *s.f.* sauce: *— di pomodoro*, tomato sauce; *— piccante*, piquant sauce; *— verde*, parsley sauce ‖ *in tutte le salse*, in all ways.

salsamentàrio, *s.m.* seller of delicatessen.

salsaparíglia, *s.f.* (*bot.*) sarsaparilla.

salsèdine, *s.f.* **1.** (*il sapere di sale*) saltiness; (*il contenere sale*) saltness **2.** (*sale marino*) salt.

salsedinóso, *ag.* salt (*attributivo*); salty.

salsíccia, *s.f.* sausage.

salsicciàio, *s.m.* **1.** (*chi fabbrica salsicce*) sausage maker **2.** (*chi vende salsicce*) sausage seller.

salsiccióne, salsicciòtto, *s.m.* large sausage.

salsièra, *s.f.* sauce-boat.

sàlso, *ag.* salt (*attributivo*); salty: *acqua salsa*, salt-water.

salsoiòdico, *ag.* iodine (*attributivo*): *acqua salsoiodica*, iodine water.

salsúme, *s.m.* salted meat.

saltabécca, *s.f.* (*entom.*) grasshopper.

saltabeccàre, saltabellàre, *v.i.* to hop, to gambol.

saltaleóne, *s.m.* (*molla*) spring.

saltamartíno, *s.m.* **1.** (*giocattolo*) jumping toy **2.** (*pop.*) (*grillo*) cricket; (*cavalletta*) grasshopper **3.** *fig.* (*bambino vivace*) imp.

saltàre, *v.i.* **1.** to jump, to spring, to leap: *il cane mi saltò addosso*, the dog jumped (o sprang) at me; *il chiodo saltò subito via*, the nail sprang out at once; *egli saltò due metri*, he jumped more than six feet; *— a cavallo*, to vault onto one's horse; *— al collo di qlcu.*, to fling one's arms round s.o.'s neck (o to hug s.o.); *— alla pertica*, to pole-vault; *— fuori dal letto*, to spring (o to jump) out of bed; *— giù, su, di qua e di là*, to jump down, up, about; *— in piedi*, to jump (o to spring) to one's feet; *— su un piede solo*, to hop ‖ *il bottone è saltato*, the button has come off; *è saltata una molla*, a spring has broken ‖ *che cosa mai ti salta in mente?*, what on earth are you thinking of?; (*cosa stai facendo?*) what on earth do you think you're doing? (o you're up to?); *questo non mi è neanche saltato in mente*, that has never crossed my mind ‖ *è un colore che salta agli occhi*, it is a colour that catches one's eye ‖ *mi saltò addosso con un mucchio d'insulti*, he assailed me with a lot of insults ‖ *saltò su a dire che...*, he interrupted, saying that...; *saltò su con delle sciocche osservazioni*, he broke in with some silly remarks ‖ *— di gioia*, to jump for joy ‖ *— di palo in frasca, da un argomento all'altro*, to jump from one subject to another ‖ *far — un bambino sulle ginocchia*, to dandle a child on one's knee ‖ *far — il banco*, (*al giuoco*) to break the bank ‖ *far — qlcu.*, (*licenziarlo*) to give s.o. the sack ‖ *far — una serratura*, to break a lock ‖ *far — il tappo di una bottiglia*, to make the cork of a bottle pop ‖ *farsi — le cervella*, to blow one's brains out **2.** (*esplodere*) to explode; to blow up: *il radiatore saltò in aria*, the radiator exploded; *sono saltate le valvole*, the fuses have blown; *tutte le case saltarono in aria*, all the houses were blown up ‖ *v.t.* to jump, to leap, to jump over (sthg.), to leap over (sthg.); to skip (anche *fig.*): *il cavallo saltò l'ostacolo*, the horse jumped the obstacle; — *la corda*, to skip; — *delle pagine, un capitolo*, to skip some pages, a chapter; — *un muro, uno steccato*, to jump (over) a wall, a fence ‖ — *una classe*, to skip a class ‖ — *una difficoltà*, to get round a difficulty ‖ — *un giro di danza*, to sit out a dance ‖ — *il pasto*, to skip (*o* to miss) a meal.

saltarèllo, *s.m.* "saltarello" (Italian popular dance).

saltàto, *ag.* (omesso) skipped, omitted: *due righe saltate*, two lines omitted.

saltatóia, *s.f.*, **saltatóio,** *s.m.* (*posatoio*) perch; roost.

saltatóre, *ag.* jumping, leaping ‖ *s.m.*, **saltatríce,** *s.f.* **1.** jumper **2.** (*ostacolista*) hurdler **3.** (*acrobata*) acrobat.

saltellaménto, *s.m.* tripping; hopping; skipping.

saltellànte, *ag.* tripping; hopping; skipping.

saltellàre, *v.i.* to trip; to hop; to skip: *i passeri si avvicinarono saltellando*, the sparrows came hopping up to us.

saltèllo, *s.m.* hop; skip ‖ *a saltelli*, hopping.

saltellóne, saltellóni, *av.* leaping, jumping.

salterellàre, *v.i.* to hop about; to skip about.

salterèllo, *s.m.* (*fuoco artificiale*) cracker.

saltèrio, saltèro, *s.m.* **1.** (*antico strumento musicale*) psaltery **2.** (*strumento musicale moderno*) zither **3.** (*libro dei salmi*) psalter, Book of Psalms **4.** (*libretto d'argomento religioso su cui si imparava a leggere*) primer.

saltimbànco, *s.m.* **1.** acrobat, tumbler **2.** (*ciarlatano*) charlatan, mountebank.

saltimbócca, *s.m.* (*cuc.*) "saltimbocca" (fried veal with ham).

saltimpàlo, *s.m.* (*ornit.*) stonechat.

sàlto, *s.m.* jump, leap, spring, bound: — *con l'asta*, (*spor.*) pole-jump (*o* -vault); — *in alto, in lungo*, (*spor.*) high, long jump; *a salti*, by jumps; *a gran salti*, by leaps and bounds; *in un —*, in one bound; *fig.* in the twinkling of an eye; *fare un —*, to take a jump (*o* to make a leap); *fare un — mortale*, to turn a somersault ‖ *un — nei prezzi*, a rise in prices ‖ *un — nel buio*, *fig.* a leap in the dark ‖ *un — nella temperatura*, (*diminuzione*) a drop in the temperature ‖ *farò un — a Milano*, I shall pop over to Milan; *fare un — da un amico*, to drop in on a friend ‖ *fare quattro salti*, (*danzare*) to have a dance.

saltuariaménte, *av.* at intervals, now and then; irregularly, desultorily.

saltuàrio, *ag.* desultory, irregular: *lettura saltuaria*, desultory reading; *visite saltuarie*, irregular visits.

salubèrrimo, *ag.* (*superl. di salubre*) very healthy.

salúbre, *ag.* healthy, salubrious; wholesome: *aria —*, wholesome air; *clima —*, healthy climate.

salubreménte, *av.* healthily; wholesomely.

salubrità, *s.f.* healthiness; wholesomeness.

salumàio, *V.* salumière.

salúme, *s.m.* salted meat.

salumería, *s.f.* **1.** delicatessen (*pl.*) **2.** (*negozio*) delicatessen shop.

salumière, *s.m.* pork-butcher; (*amer.*) delicatessen seller.

salumifício, *s.m.* delicatessen factory.

salutànte, *ag.* cheering: *folla —*, cheering crowd.

salutàre[1], *v.t.* **1.** to greet; to salute; to hail; to say hallo to (s.o.): *canti popolari salutano il turista al suo ingresso nel paese*, folk-songs greet the tourist as he enters the village; *lo salutai, ma fece finta di non sentire*, I said hallo to him, but he pretended not to hear; *mi salutò con un cenno*, he gave me a nod; *mi salutò con la mano*, he waved to me (*o* he gave me a wave); *il suo ingresso fu salutato da un lungo applauso*, his appearance was greeted with prolonged applause ‖ *passar via senza — qlcu.*, to cut s.o. ‖ *distintamente vi salutiamo*, (*comm.*) we are (*o* we remain) Yours

faithfully (*o* Yours truly) ‖ *saluta tua madre per me*, give my regards to your mother (*o* remember me to your mother); *ti saluto cordialmente, Giovanni*, (*in fine di lettera*) kind regards, Yours John **2.** (*mil.*) to salute **3.** (*con inchino*) to bow (to s.o.) **4.** (*dare il benvenuto a*) to welcome **5.** (*congedarsi da*) to say good-bye to (s.o.).

salutàre[2], *ag.* **1.** healthy; wholesome **2.** *fig.* beneficial.

salutarménte, *av.* **1.** healthily **2.** *fig.* beneficially.

salutazióne, *s.f.* salutation, greeting ‖ *la Salutazione angelica*, the Angelical Salutation.

salúte, *s.f.* **1.** health: — *cagionevole*, poor health; — *cattiva*, bad health; — *di ferro*, perfect health; *cura la tua —*, take care of your health; *è delicato di —*, his health is delicate; *questo ti fa bene alla —*, this is good for your health; *godere ottima —*, to be in perfect health ‖ — *!*, bless you! ‖ *alla tua —!*, good health! (*o* cheerio!); *bere alla — di qlcu.*, to drink (to) s.o.'s health ‖ *biscotti della —*, digestive biscuits ‖ *casa di —*, nursing-home **2.** (*salvezza, sicurezza*) safety: *la — della patria*, the safety of one's country; *la — pubblica*, public welfare (*o* public well-being) ‖ *porto di —*, haven **3.** (*spirituale*) salvation.

salutífero, *ag.* beneficial, salutary (anche *fig.*).

salutísta, *s.c.* **1.** hygienist **2.** (*membro dell'Esercito della Salvezza*) member of the Salvation Army, Salvationist.

salúto, *s.m.* **1.** greeting; salute; salutation: *cenno di —*, nod: *fare un cenno di — a qlcu.*, to give s.o. a nod; *scambiare un —*, to exchange a greeting; *togliere il — a qlcu.*, to cut s.o. ‖ *distinti, cordiali saluti*, (*in fine di lettera*) Yours faithfully (*o* Yours truly) ‖ *porta i miei saluti a tua madre*, give my regards to your mother **2.** (*mil.*) salute **3.** (*con un inchino*) bow: *fare un profondo — a qlcu.*, to give s.o. a low bow.

sàlva, *s.f.* salvo (*pl.* salvoes, salvos); volley (anche *fig.*): *una — di applausi*, a volley (*o* round) of applause; *una — di insulti*, a volley of insults; *una — di pallottole, di frecce*, a volley of bullets, of arrows; *ci fu una — come saluto al nuovo re*, there was a salvo as a salute to the new king ‖ *colpo a —, a salve*, blank (shot); *sparare a —, a salve*, to fire blanks; (*per saluto*) to fire salvoes.

salvacondótto, *s.m.* safe-conduct.

salvadanàio, salvadanàro, *s.m.* money-box.

salvagènte, *s.m.* **1.** (*ciambella di salvataggio*) life-buoy, life-belt; (*cintura di salvataggio*) life-jacket **2.** (*per il traffico stradale*) traffic island.

salvaguardàre, *v.t.* to safeguard, to guard, to protect: — *i propri interessi, la propria reputazione*, to safeguard one's interests, one's reputation.

salvaguàrdia, *s.f.* safeguard, protection.

salvaménto, *s.m.* **1.** (*il salvare*) saving, rescuing **2.** (*salvezza, sicurezza*) safety; (*salvataggio*) rescue: *trarre, portare a —*, to rescue (*o* to bring to safety).

salvapúnte, *s.m.* (*di matita*) pencil-cap, pencil-top.

salvàre, *v.t.* **1.** to save (anche *fig.*): — *l'anima*, to save one's soul; — *le apparenze*, to save (*o* to keep up) appearances; — *la faccia*, to save one's face; — *la pelle*, to save one's skin; — *una situazione*, to save a situation; — *la vita a qlcu.*, to save s.o.'s life ‖ *Dio salvi il re!*, God save the king! **2.** (*trarre in salvo*) to rescue: — *qlcu. da un pericolo incombente*, to rescue s.o. from an impending danger; *andare a — qlcu.*, to go to s.o.'s rescue **3.** (*mettere in serbo*) to save, to lay aside, to put aside: *ho salvato un pezzo di torta per te*, I have saved a piece of cake for you ‖ **salvàrsi,** *v.r.* **1.** to save oneself **2.** (*rifugiarsi*) to take shelter.

salvatàcco, *s.m.* heel-tap.

salvatàggio, *s.m.* **1.** rescue: *correre a — di qlcu.*, to go to s.o.'s rescue **2.** (*mar.*) salvage, salvaging, salving: *cintura di —*, life-jacket (*o* life-belt); *scialuppa di —*, life boat; *società di —*, salvage company.

salvatóre[1], *ag.* saving, redeeming; rescuing ‖ *s.m.* saviour, redeemer; rescuer; saver.

Salvatóre[2], *no.pr.m.* Salvador.

salvatríce, *s.f.* saver, rescuer.

salvazióne, *s.f.* salvation.

sàlve, *inter.* hail.

salveregína, *s.f.* (*preghiera*) Salve Regina.

salvézza, *s.f.* **1.** salvation: — *dell'anima,* salvation of the soul; — *spirituale,* spiritual salvation; *la lettura è la mia* —, reading is my salvation; *trovare la propria* — *in ql.co.,* to find one's salvation in sthg. || *àncora di* —, *fig.* sheet-anchor || *Esercito della Salvezza,* Salvation Army **2.** (*sicurezza*) safety: *la* — *della patria,* the safety of one's country **3.** (*scampo*) escape: *non c'è via di* —, there is no escape (*o* way out).

sàlvia, *s.f.* (*bot.*) sage.

Salviàno, *no.pr.m.* (*st. lett.*) Salvianus.

salviétta, *s.f.* **1.** (*tovagliolo*) (table-)napkin, serviette **2.** (*asciugamano*) towel.

sàlvo, *ag.* **1.** safe, unhurt, unscathed: *la sua vita è salva,* his life is safe; *il tuo onore è* —, your honour is safe || *arrivare sano e* —, to arrive safe and sound (*o* safely) **2.** (*al sicuro*) secure: — *da pericoli,* secure from danger || *essere in* —, to be in a safe place (*o* to be safe); *mettere ql.co. in* —, to put sthg. in a safe place; (*da parte*) to put sthg. aside (*o* by); *mettere qlcu. in* —, to bring s.o. to safety.

sàlvo, *prep.* except (for), excepting, save; excepted: — *avviso contrario da parte vostra,* failing your advice to the contrary; — *caso di forza maggiore,* Acts of God excepted; — *correzioni,* subject to correction; — *errore od omissione,* errors and omissions excepted; — *imprevisti,* barring accidents; — *ulteriori informazioni,* unless further information should be given; *egli è dappertutto,* — *dove dovrebbe essere,* he is everywhere excepting where he ought to be; *sono tutti rotti,* — *due,* they are all broken except two; *tutto è perduto,* — *l'onore,* all is lost save honour; *vennero tutti,* — *Peter,* they all came except (for) Peter || **sàlvo che,** *l. cong.* except that; (*a meno che*) unless: — *che venga,* unless he comes; *la tua composizione è buona,* — *che è troppo corta,* your composition is good except that it is too short.

sàmara, *s.f.* (*bot.*) samara.

samàrio, *s.m.* (*chim.*) samarium.

samaritàno, *ag. s.m.* Samaritan: *il buon* —, (*Bibbia*) the good Samaritan.

sàmba, *s.f.* (*musica, danza*) samba: *ballare la* —, to samba.

sambúca, *s.f.* (*mus. mil.*) sambuca.

sambúco[1], *s.m.* (*bot.*) elder(-tree).

sambúco[2], *s.m.* (*mar.*) dhow, dow.

Sàmo, *no.pr.f.* (*geog.*) Samos || *portar vasi a* —, to carry coals to Newcastle.

samoièdo, *ag.s.m.* Samoyed(e).

Samotràcia, *no.pr.f.* (*geog. st.*) Samothrace.

samovàr, *s.m.* samovar.

Samuèle, *no.pr.m.* Samuel || *dim.* Sam(my).

samurài, *s.m.* Samurai (*invariato al pl.*).

san, *ag.* Saint (*abbr.* St.).

sanàbile, *ag.* curable, healable; (*rimediabile*) remediable: *male* —, remediable ill (*o* harm).

sanabilità, *s.f.* curability.

sanaménte, *av.* **1.** healthily; wholesomely **2.** (*rettamente*) honestly; morally; (*con buon senso*) sanely.

sanàre, *v.t.* **1.** (*ferita aperta*) to heal (*anche fig.*); (*da malattie, ecc.*) to cure (*anche fig.*): *il tempo sana tutti i dolori,* time heals all (sorrows); — *una ferita,* to heal a wound || — *un luogo,* to make a place healthy || — *terre paludose,* to reclaim marshy land **2.** (*correggere*) to rectify, to put right.

sanatívo, *ag.* healing, curative, sanative.

sanatóre, *ag.* healing || *s.m.,* **sanatríce,** *s.f.* healer.

sanatòrio, *s.m.* sanatorium (*pl.* sanatoria).

sanbeníto, *s.m.* (*st.*) sanbenito.

San Bernàrdo, *no.pr.m.* (*geog.*) Saint Bernard: *Gran, Piccolo* —, Great, Little Saint Bernard || **sanbernàrdo,** *s.m.* (*cane*) Saint Bernard.

Sàncio, *no.pr.m.* Sancho.

sancíre, *v.t.* to sanction; (*ratificare*) to ratify: — *una legge, un trattato,* to ratify a law, a treaty.

sancíto, *ag.* sanctioned; (*ratificato*) ratified: — *dall'uso,* sanctioned by custom; *diritti sanciti,* sanctioned rights.

sancta sanctorum, *s.m.* **1.** (*nel tempio di Salomone a Gerusalemme*) Holy of Holies **2.** (*tabernacolo*) tabernacle **3.** (*scherz.*) sanctum (sanctorum), den.

sanctus, *s.m.* (*eccl.*) Sanctus: *suonare il* —, to ring the Sanctus bell.

sanculòtto, *s.m.* (*st. francese*) sansculotte.

sàndalo[1], *s.m.* (*bot.*) **1.** (*albero*) sandalwood (tree), sandal **2.** (*legno*) sandalwood, sandal.

sàndalo[2], *s.m.* (*calzatura*) sandal.

sàndalo[3], *s.m.* (*mar.*) punt.

sandolíno, *s.m.* (*mar.*) small canoe.

San Domíngo, *no.pr.m.* (*geog.*) Santo Domingo: *la Repubblica di* —, the Dominican Republic.

Sàndro, *no.pr.m. dim.* di **Alessàndro.**

sandràcca, *s.f.* (*ind. chim.*) sandarac(h).

sanforizzàre, *v.t.* (*ind. chim.*) to sanforize.

sanforizzàto, *ag.* (*ind. chim.*) sanforized.

sangiaccàto, *s.m.* (*st.*) sanjak.

sangiàcco, *s.m.* (*st.*) sanjakbeg, sanjakbey.

sàngue, *s.m.* **1.** blood: *analisi del* —, blood-test; *animale a* — *caldo, freddo,* warm-,cold-blooded animal; *avvelenamento del* —, blood-poisoning; *donatore di* —, blood-donor; *gruppi del* —, blood-groups; *macchiato di* —, blood-stained; *occhi iniettati di* —, bloodshot eyes; *perdita di* —, bleeding; *rosso* —, blood-red (*o* sanguine); *sacrificio di* —, blood-sacrifice; *spargimento di* —, bloodshed; *temperatura del* —, blood-heat; *trasfusione di* —, blood-transfusion; *vittoria senza spargimenti di* —, bloodless victory; *cavar* —, to let blood; *cavar* — *a qlcu.,* to bleed s.o. (anche *fig.*); *perdere* — *dal naso,* to bleed at (*o* from) the nose; *picchiare* (*qlcu.*) *a* —, to beat (s.o.) till one draws blood; *versare* —, to shed blood: *versare il proprio* — *per la patria,* to shed one's blood for one's country || — *di drago,* (*tipo di resina*) dragon's blood || — *freddo, fig.* coolness (*o* self-possession *o* composure *o* courage): *a* — *freddo,* in cold blood || *al* —, (*di carne*) underdone || *assetato di* —, bloodthirsty || *un mezzo* —, (*di cavallo*) a half-bred; *un puro* —, a thoroughbred (*o* a blood-horse) || *il* — *gli montò al viso,* the blood rushed to his face (*o* he flushed up) || *il* — *non è acqua,* blood is thicker than water || *c'è del cattivo* — *fra loro,* there is bad (*o* ill) blood between them || *ciò mi fa agghiacciare il* —, this makes my blood curdle (*o* run cold); *una vista che agghiaccia il* —, a blood-curdling sight || *me lo sentivo nel* —, I had a presentiment (*o* foreboding) of it || *mi ribolle il* —, my blood is up; *mi sento ribollire il* — *nelle vene,* I feel my blood boil || *non farti cattivo* — *per me,* don't bother your head about me || *non ha* — *nelle vene,* he is very cold-blooded || *quella persona non mi va a* —, I do not like that person at all || *il suo* — *ricadrà su di voi,* his blood shall be on your head || *avere la musica nel* —, to have music in one's blood || *avere il* — *caldo,* to be hot-blooded || *cavar* — *da una rapa,* to get blood out of a stone || *farsi buon* —, to laugh heartily (*o* to have a good laugh); *farsi cattivo* —, *guastarsi il* — *per ql.co.,* to worry (*o* to fret and fume) over (*o* about) sthg. || *sudare, sputare* —, to sweat, to spit blood || *buon* — *non mente,* prov. blood will tell **2.** (*famiglia, stirpe, origine*) blood; family, stock; origin, extraction: — *blu,* blue blood; — *reale,* blood royal; *principe del* —, prince of the blood; *un uomo di* — *plebeo,* a man of humble origin (*o* extraction); *la voce del* —, the call of blood (*o* of kinship); *è di* — *nobile,* he comes of a noble family (*o* of noble stock); *egli è del mio* —, he is my own flesh and blood.

sanguífero, *ag.* sanguiferous.

sanguificàre, *v.i.* to produce blood; to sanguify.

sanguificatóre, *ag.* haemopoietic.

sanguificazióne, *s.f.* sanguification; blood-making.

sanguígna, *s.f.* **1.** (*pitt.*) sanguine **2.** (*min.*) blood-stone.

sanguígno, *ag.* **1.** (*anat.*) sanguineous; blood (*attributivo*): *plasma, vaso* —, blood plasma, vessel **2.** (*di temperamento*) sanguine, full-blooded **3.** (*di colore*) blood-red ‖ *diaspro* —, (*min.*) bloodstone.

sanguinàccio, *s.m.* blood-sausage; (*se già cotto*) black-pudding, blood-pudding.

sanguinànte, *ag.* bleeding (anche *fig.*).

sanguinàre, *v.i.* to bleed (anche *fig.*): *il mio cuore sanguina per te*, my heart bleeds for you; *è una ferita che sanguina ancora*, *fig.* the wound still rankles; *mi sanguina il naso*, my nose is bleeding.

sanguinària, *s.f.* (*bot.*) blood-wort; bloody dock.

sanguinàrio, *ag.* sanguinary, bloody; (*crudele*) blood-thirsty: *passioni sanguinarie*, bloody passions; *temperamento* —, sanguinary disposition; *uomo* —, blood-thirsty man.

sànguine, *s.m.* (*bot.*) (red) dogwood; wild cornel.

sanguinèlla, *s.f.* (*bot.*) blood-wort; bloody dock.

sanguineo, *ag.* **1.** (*insanguinato*) bloody **2.** (*di color sangue*) blood-coloured **3.** (*pletorico*) sanguine, sanguineous: *temperamento* —, sanguine temperament.

sanguinolènte, sanguinolènto, *ag.* **1.** (*sanguinante*) bleeding **2.** (*grondante sangue*) dripping with blood; (*di carne*) very underdone **3.** (*insanguinato*) bloody, bloodstained **4.** (*misto a sangue*) sanguinolent.

sanguinosaménte, *av.* **1.** bloodily, sanguinarily **2.** *fig.* (*violentemente*) mortally.

sanguinóso, *ag.* **1.** bloody, sanguinary: *sanguinosa battaglia*, bloody (o sanguinary) battle **2.** *fig.* (*mortale*) mortal: *ingiuria sanguinosa*, mortal (o deadly) insult.

sanguisùga, *s.f.* **1.** (*zool.*) leech **2.** *fig.* extortioner; (*fam.*) blood-sucker, leech.

sànie, *s.f.* (*letter.*) (*pus*) sanies.

sanificàre, *v.t.* **1.** to sanify **2.** (*terre paludose*) to reclaim.

sanità, *s.f.* **1.** (*qualità di sano*) soundness: — *di corpo e di mente*, soundness of body and mind; *la* — *di una dottrina*, the soundness of a doctrine ‖ — *mentale*, sanity **2.** (*salute*) health ‖ — *marittima*, port medical office ‖ *Ministero della Sanità*, Ministry of Health ‖ *truppe di* —, Medical Corps ‖ *ufficio di* —, health office.

sanitàrio, *ag.* sanitary: *cordone* —, sanitary cordon; *corpo* —, (*mil.*) Medical Corps; *ispettore* —, sanitary inspector; *misure sanitarie*, sanitary measures; *ottime condizioni sanitarie*, excellent sanitary conditions; *servizi sanitari*, medical (o health) services; *ufficiale* —, health officer ‖ *s.m.* physician.

sannìta, *s.c.* Samnite.

sannìtico, *ag.* Samnite.

sàno, *ag.* **1.** (*esente da malattia, difetto*) sound; (*che appare in buona salute*) healthy, wholesome: *un aspetto* —, a healthy (o wholesome) appearance: *un bambino* —, a healthy child; *carnagione sana*, healthy complexion; *costituzione sana*, sound constitution; *frutto* —, sound fruit; *essere* — *di corpo*, to be sound in wind and limb ‖ *i sani*, the healthy ‖ — *come un pesce*, as sound as a bell ‖ — *di mente*, sane (o of sound mind o sound of mind); (*dir.*) of sound disposing mind ‖ — *e salvo*, safe and sound ‖ *mente sana in corpo* —, a sound mind in a sound body ‖ *chi va piano va* — *e va lontano*, *prov.* slow but sure **2.** (*salubre*) healthy, healthful, wholesome: *aria sana*, healthy (o healthful) air; *cibo* —, wholesome (o healthful) food; *clima* —, healthy (o wholesome) climate **3.** (*saggio, giusto*) sound: *sani consigli*, sound (o wholesome) advice; *sane dottrine*, sound doctrines; *sana morale*, sound morals; *sana politica*, sound policy; *sani principi*, sound principles **4.** (*non corrotto*) healthy: *affetti sani*, healthy affections; *la borghesia era ancora sana*, the middle class was still healthy **5.** (*intero, intatto*) intact: *non*

c'è un piatto — *in tutta la casa*, there isn't a dish intact in the whole house **6.** (*intero, completo*) whole: *sono stato un anno* — *senza vederti*, I have not seen you for a whole year ‖ *di sana pianta*, from scratch: *ha riorganizzato la ditta di sana pianta*, he has re-organized his firm from scratch; *te lo sei inventato di sana pianta*, you've made it all up.

sanrocchíno, *s.m.* pilgrim's cape.

sànsa, *s.f.* husk: — *di olive*, olive husk; *olio di* —, husk oil.

sanscritìsta, *s.m.* Sanskritist, Sanskrit scholar.

sànscrito, *ag.s.m.* Sanskrit.

Sansóne, *no.pr.m.* (*Bibbia*) Samson ‖ **sansóne,** *s.m.* (*uomo fortissimo*) Samson.

santabàrbara, *s.f.* (*mar. mil.*) (powder-)magazine.

santaménte, *av.* holily; (*piamente*) piously; (*devotamente*) devoutly: *morire* —, to die a godly death.

santarèlla, *s.f.*, **santarèllo,** *s.m.* (*iron.*) goody-goody.

Sant'Èlena, *no.pr.f.* (*geog.*) Saint Helena (Island).

santèlmo, *s.m.*: *fuoco di* —, St. Elmo's fire (o corposant).

santificaménto, *s.m.* (*rar.*) sanctification.

santificànte, *ag.* sanctifying: *grazia* —, (*teol.*) sanctifying grace.

santificàre, *v.t.* **1.** (*canonizzare*) to canonize **2.** (*consacrare*) to sanctify, to consecrate ‖ *sia santificato il Tuo Nome*, hallowed be Thy Name ‖ — *le feste*, to keep (o to observe) holy days.

santificatívo, *ag.* sanctifying.

santificatóre, *ag.* sanctifying ‖ *s.m.*, **santificatríce,** *s.f.* sanctifier.

santificazióne, *s.f.* sanctification ‖ — *delle feste*, observance (o keeping) of holy days.

santimònia, *s.f.* **1.** sanctity, saintliness **2.** (*iron.*) sanctimony, sanctimoniousness.

santimoniàle, *ag.* **1.** holy, saintly **2.** (*iron.*) sanctimonious.

santíno, *s.m.* (*immaginetta sacra*) small holy picture.

Santíppe, *no.pr.f.* Xant(h)ippe ‖ **santíppe,** *s.f.* (*moglie bisbetica*) Xant(h)ippe.

santíssimo, *ag.* most holy, most sacred ‖ *il Santissimo (Sacramento)*, the Blessed (o Holy) Sacrament.

santità, *s.f.* holiness; (*di persona*) saintliness; (*di legge, voto, ecc.*) sanctity ‖ *Sua Santità*, His Holiness.

sànto, *ag.* **1.** holy ‖ *la Santa Alleanza*, (*st.*) the Holy Alliance; *Santa Comunione*, Holy Communion; *Santa Croce*, Holy Cross; *Santa Messa*, Holy Mass; *il Santo Padre*, the Holy Father; *la Santa Sede*, the Holy See; *il Sant'Uffizio*, the Holy Office; *acqua santa*, holy water; *anno* —, Holy Year; *la Città Santa*, the Holy City; *giovedì* —, Maundy (o Holy) Thursday; *guerra santa*, holy war; *olio* —, holy oil; *settimana santa*, Holy Week; *sabato* —, Holy Saturday; *Spirito Santo*, Holy Spirit (o Holy Ghost); *Terra Santa*, Holy Land; *venerdì* —, Good Friday ‖ *in santa pace*, in peace ‖ *tutti i santi giorni*, every single day ‖ *tutto il* — *giorno*, all day long (o *fam.* the whole blessed day) ‖ *gliele diede di santa ragione*, he beat him soundly **2.** (*seguito da nome proprio*) Saint (abbr. St.): *Santo Stefano*, Saint Stephen; *Santa Teresa*, Saint Teresa **3.** (*pio*) pious, godly: *santi pensieri*, pious thoughts **4.** (*da santo*) saintly: *vita santa*, saintly life ‖ *s.m.* saint: — *patrono*, patron saint; *giorno di tutti i Santi*, All Saints' Day; *pazienza da* —, saintly patience; *la pazienza di un* —, the patience of a saint; *che* — *è oggi?*, what saint's day is it today?; *questo sarebbe sufficiente a far perdere la pazienza a un* —, this would be enough to provoke a saint (o this would try the patience of a saint); *festeggiare il proprio* —, to keep one's saint's day (o name-day) ‖ *il Santo dei Santi*, the Holy of Holies (o Sanctum Sanctorum) ‖ *a dispetto dei santi*, at any cost ‖ *compreriamolo e qualche* — *aiuterà*, let's buy it and hope for the best ‖ *avere un* — *dalla propria parte*, (*essere molto fortunato*) to have a guardian angel; (*avere qualche forte protezione*) to have protection in high places ‖

non saper più a che — votarsi, to be at one's wits' end ‖ *non v'è — che sia senza peccato, prov.* it is a good horse that never stumbles ‖ *passata la festa gabbato lo —, prov.* once on shore we pray no more (*o* the river is passed and God forgotten) ‖ *scherza coi fanti e lascia stare i santi, prov.* don't mix up the sacred with the profane.

santocchiería, *s.f.* bigotry, sanctimoniousness.

santòcchio, *s.m.* bigot.

santofílla, *s.f.* (*chim. biol.*) xanthophyll.

sàntola, *s.f.* (*dial.*) godmother.

sàntolo, *s.m.* (*dial.*) godfather.

santóne, *s.m.* **1.** (*presso i maomettani*) santon, marabout **2.** (*bigotto*) bigot.

santonína, *s.f.* (*chim. farm.*) santonin.

santopsía, *s.f.* (*med.*) xanthopsia.

santoréggia, *s.f.* (*bot.*) savory.

santuàrio, *s.m.* **1.** sanctuary **2.** *fig.* sanctuary, shrine.

sanzionàre, *v.t.* to ratify; to sanction; to approve: *— una legge,* to ratify a law.

sanzióne, *s.f.* **1.** sanction: *sanzioni contro un paese,* sanctions against a country **2.** (*ratificazione, approvazione*) ratification; sanction; approval ‖ *la Prammatica Sanzione,* (*st.*) the Pragmatic Sanction.

sapére, *v.t.* **1.** to know: *egli non sa comportarsi,* he does not know how to behave; *egli sa quello che vuole,* he knows what he wants (*o* he knows his own mind); *egli sa il suo mestiere,* he knows his job (*o* business); *ella sa sempre la lezione molto bene,* she always knows her lesson very well; *non lo so,* I do not know; *non sapevo come dirtelo,* I did not know how to tell you; *non so che dirti,* I do not know what to say to you; *per quanto ci è dato —,* as far as we know; *suo zio sa tre lingue straniere,* his uncle knows three foreign languages; *vorrei —,* I'd like to know; *non — che fare, che dire,* to be at a loss what to do, what to say ‖ *bisogna saperci fare con lui,* you have to know how to handle him ‖ *un certo non so che,* a certain "je ne sais quoi" ‖ *che ne so io?,* how should (*o* do) I know? ‖ *chi sa!,* who knows!; *chi sa se verrà,* I wonder whether he will come ‖ *egli è un uomo che sa vivere,* he is a man who knows how to enjoy life ‖ *egli ha saputo la miseria e il dolore,* he has known poverty and sorrow ‖ *egli non sa niente di niente,* he is absolutely ignorant (*o* he does not know anything) ‖ *egli non sa quello che si dice,* he is talking through his hat ‖ *egli sa di musica e di letteratura,* he is well-versed in music and literature ‖ *egli sa fare con la gente,* he knows how to treat people ‖ *egli vende vestiti, cappelli, scarpe e che so io,* he sells clothes, hats, shoes and what not ‖ *è morto di non so quale malattia,* he died of some disease or other ‖ *Iddio sa quando tornerò,* Heaven knows when I shall come back ‖ *in gennaio, si sa, fa freddo,* everybody knows that it is cold in January ‖ *non si sa mai,* you never know ‖ *non voglio più saperne di lui, di ciò,* I do not want to have anything more to do with him, with it ‖ *sappiate bene che...,* you can rest assured that... ‖ *se lo viene a —...,* if he gets to know (*o* to hear) of it... ‖ *un uomo che sa,* a learned man ‖ *— a memoria,* to know by heart ‖ *saperla lunga,* to know a thing or two ‖ *— ql.co. per filo e per segno,* to know sthg. like the back of one's hand ‖ *— vita e miracoli di qlcu.,* to know everything about s.o. ‖ *buono a sapersi,* that's worth knowing ‖ *far — ql.co. a qlcu.,* to let s.o. know sthg.; (*per iscritto*) to drop s.o. a line about sthg.; (*mandare a dire*) to send (s.o.) word of sthg.: *ti farò — quando verrò,* I shall let you know when I'm coming **2.** (*essere capace di*) can (to do); to be able (to do); to know how (to do): *egli sa fare qualunque cosa,* he can do anything; *egli sa ottenere ciò che vuole,* he knows how to get what he wants; *un giorno saprò parlare il russo,* one day I shall be able to speak Russian; *non me lo seppe dire,* he could not tell me; *non sa fare niente,* he is quite useless; *non saprei dire perchè,* I couldn't say why; *non so farlo,* I do not know how to do it; *non so parlare fran-*

cese, I cannot speak French; *sai nuotare?,* can you swim? **3.** (*essere consapevole di*) to know, to be aware of (sthg.): *non sapevo di questi intrighi,* I wasn't aware of these intrigues; *so dei suoi meriti,* I know (*o* I am aware) of his merits; *so il rischio che corro,* I am aware of the risk I am running **4.** (*essere a conoscenza di*) to know; to be acquainted with (sthg.): *non so niente di tutto questo,* I know nothing about all this; *sapevo che sarebbe venuto,* I knew he would come; *sapevo già di questi fatti due anni fa,* I was already acquainted with these facts two years ago; *se avessi saputo!,* if only I had known!; « *Suo fratello è arrivato ieri* », « *Lo so* », "His brother arrived yesterday", "I know" **5.** (*venire a conoscenza di*) to learn; to hear, to get to know: *come hai saputo queste notizie?,* how did you hear these tales?; *ho saputo che...,* it has come to my knowledge that...; *ho saputo di un malinteso tra voi due,* I have heard of a misunderstanding between you; *presto o tardi si sa tutto,* everything comes out sooner or later; *questo è quanto ho saputo,* that is what I heard; *ricordo come lo seppi,* I remember how I heard about it; *si seppe che...,* it was known that... ‖ *v.i.* **1.** (*aver sapore*) to taste; (*aver odore*) to smell: *questa minestra sa di aglio,* this soup tastes of garlic; *sa di bruciato,* it tastes burnt; *sa di niente,* it is tasteless; *la sua stanza sapeva di fumo,* his room smelt of smoke ‖ *mi sa di poco di buono,* it seems to me that he is no good ‖ *una ragazza che non sa di niente,* an insipid girl **2.** (*avere sentore, pensare*): *mi sa che egli sia malato,* I think he must be ill; *mi sa che sia rimasto a letto,* I bet he's stayed in bed.

sapére, *s.m.* **1.** (*scibile*) knowledge: *il — umano,* human knowledge **2.** (*cultura*) learning, erudition, scholarship: *un uomo di gran —,* a man of great learning.

sapidità, *s.f.* sapidity, savouriness (anche *fig.*).

sàpido, *ag.* sapid, savoury (anche *fig.*).

sapiènte, *ag.* **1.** (*saggio*) wise **2.** (*colto*) learned, erudite ‖ *s.m.* **1.** (*uomo saggio*) wise man, sage **2.** (*uomo colto*) scholar, learned man ‖ *s.f.* **1.** (*donna saggia*) wise woman **2.** (*donna colta*) scholar, learned woman.

sapienteménte, *av.* **1.** (*saggiamente*) wisely **2.** (*con sapienza*) learnedly.

sapientóne, *s.m.* **1.** sage **2.** (*iron.*) wiseacre.

sapiènza, *s.f.* **1.** (*saggezza*) wisdom ‖ *libro di —,* (*Bibbia*) Book of Wisdom **2.** (*cultura*) learning, erudition, scholarship **3.** (*sapere*) knowledge.

sapienziàle, *ag.* sapiential.

saponàceo, *ag.* soapy, saponaceous.

saponàio, *s.m.* **1.** (*chi fabbrica sapone*) soap-maker **2.** (*chi vende sapone*) soap-seller.

saponària, *s.f.* (*bot.*) soapwort, soap-plant.

saponàrio, *ag.*: *radica saponaria,* soap-root.

saponàta, *s.f.* **1.** lather; soap-suds (*pl.*) **2.** (*sudore del cavallo*) lather **3.** (*adulazione*) soft soap.

sapóne, *s.m.* soap: *— da barba,* shaving-soap; (*in bastoncino*) shaving-stick; *— da bucato, da bagno,* washing-soap, bath-soap; *— liquido, tenero,* liquid, soft soap; *bolla di —,* soap-bubble ‖ *dare del — a qlcu., fig.* to soft-soap s.o.

saponétta, *s.f.* **1.** cake of soap **2.** (*orologio*) hunter.

saponièra, *s.f.* soapbox.

saponificàre, *v.t.* to saponify.

saponificatóre, *ag.* saponifying ‖ *s.m.,* **saponificatríce,** *s.f.* saponifier.

saponificazióne, *s.f.* saponification.

saponifício, *s.m.* soap-works (*pl. con costruzione sing.*).

saponína, *s.f.* (*chim.*) saponin.

saponóso, *ag.* soapy.

sapóre, *s.m.* **1.** taste, flavour: *questa carne non ha —,* this meat has no taste **2.** *fig.* flavour, savour, relish: *il rischio dà — ad ogni impresa,* risk gives relish to any enterprise.

saporíre, *v.t.* to flavour; to season.

saporitaménte, *av.* savourily, tastily, toothsomely: *condito* —, highly seasoned || *dormire* —, to sleep soundly || *pagare ql.co.* —, to pay through the nose for sthg.; *si fa pagare* —, he asks very high prices || *ridere* —, to laugh heartily (*o* with gusto).

saporìto, *ag.* **1.** savoury, tasty, toothsome: *un piatto molto* —, a very tasty dish **2.** (*salato*) salty: *la minestra era un po' saporita*, the soup was a little too salty **3.** (*arguto*) witty; (*piccante*) racy: *aneddoto* —, racy anecdote; *osservazioni saporite*, witty remarks; *risposta saporita*, tart (*o* sharp) answer **4.** (*costoso*) expensive, dear: *conto* —, excessive bill **5.** (*di sonno, profondo*) sound.

saporosaménte, *av.* tastily, savourily.

saporosità, *s.f.* tastiness, savouriness.

saporóso, *ag.* tasty, savoury.

saprofitísmo, *s.m.* (*bot.*) saprophytism.

saprofíto, *s.m.* (*bot.*) saprophyte.

sapúta, *s.f.* knowledge || *per* —, by hearsay.

saputaménte, *av.* **1.** knowingly; (*con consapevolezza*) consciously **2.** (*in modo saccente*) with a pretence of knowledge.

saputèlla, *s.f.* wiseacre.

saputèllo, saputíno, *s.m.* wiseacre, sciolist, pretended scholar: *fare il* —, to show off one's knowledge (*o* to give oneself airs of wisdom).

sapúto, *ag.* **1.** (*colto*) learned: *un uomo* —, a learned man **2.** (*noto*) well-known: *una cosa saputa e risaputa*, a well-known thing || *s.m. V.* **saputèllo.**

Sàra, *no.pr.f.* Sara(h) || *dim.* Sadie, Sal, Sallie.

sarabacchíno, *s.m.* wagonette.

sarabànda, *s.f.* (*musica, danza*) saraband.

saràceo, *s.m.* (*strum. artig.*) rip-saw.

saracèno, *ag.* Saracen, Saracenic || *grano* —, Saracen corn (*o* buckwheat) || *s.m.* Saracen || **saracèna,** *s.f.* Saracen.

saracinésca, *s.f.* **1.** (*di negozio*) rolling shutter **2.** (*chiusa*) sluice-gate **3.** (*di castello, fortezza, ecc.*) portcullis **4.** (*di porta*) (door-)latch.

saracinésco, *ag.* Saracen, Saracenic.

saracíno, *ag.* Saracen(ic) || *grano* —, Saracen corn (*o* buckwheat) || *s.m.* **1.** Saracen || *bestemmiare come un* —, to swear like a trooper **2.** (*fantoccio della quintana*) quintain || **saracína,** *s.f.* Saracen.

Saragòzza, *no.pr.f.* (*geog.*) Saragossa.

sarcàsmo, *s.m.* sarcasm.

sarcasticaménte, *av.* sarcastically.

sarcàstico, *ag.* sarcastic.

sarchiaménto, *s.m.* hoeing, weeding.

sarchiàre, *v.t.* to hoe, to weed.

sarchiatóre, *ag.* hoeing, weeding || *s.m.* hoer, weeder.

sarchiatríce, *s.f.* **1.** hoer, weeder **2.** (*mec. agr.*) weeder, weeding machine.

sarchiatúra, *s.f.* hoeing, weeding.

sarchiellàre, *v.t.* to hoe, to weed.

sarchièllo, sàrchio, *s.m.* hoe.

sàrcina[1], *s.f.* (*biol.*) sarcina (*pl.* sarcinae).

sarcína[2], *s.f.* (*chim.*) hypoxanthine, sarcine.

sarcíte, *s.f.* (*patol.*) sarcitis.

sarcocàrpo, *s.m.* (*bot.*) sarcocarp.

sarcocòlla, *s.f.* sarcocolla.

sarcòde, *s.m.* (*biol.*) sarcode.

sarcòfaga, *s.f.* (*entom.*) blowfly, flesh-fly.

sarcòfago, *s.m.* sarcophagus (*pl.* sarcophagi).

sarcolèmma, *s.m.* (*anat.*) sarcolemma.

sarcolíte, *s.f.* (*min.*) sarcolite.

sarcología, *s.f.* sarcology.

sarcòma, *s.m.* (*patol.*) sarcoma (*pl.* sarcomata).

sarcomatòsi, *s.f.* (*patol.*) sarcomatosis.

sarcoplàsma, *s.m.* sarcoplasm.

sarcòtico, *ag.* (*anat.*) sarcous.

sàrda[1], *s.f.* (*ittiol.*) sardine; sardelle.

sàrda[2], *s.f.* (*min.*) sard(ine).

sardanapalésco, *ag.* Sardanapalian.

Sardanapàlo, *no.pr.m.* (*st.*) Sardanapalus.

Sardégna, *no.pr.f.* (*geog.*) Sardinia.

sardegnuòlo, *ag.* Sardinian.

sardèlla, sardína, *s.f.* sardine: *sardine in scatola*, tinned sardines || *pigiati come sardine*, packed like sardines.

sàrdo, *ag.s.m.* Sardinian || **sàrda,** *s.f.* Sardinian.

sardònica, *s.f.* (*min.*) sardonyx.

sardonicaménte, *av.* sardonically.

sardònico, *ag.* sardonic.

sargàsso, *s.m.* (*bot.*) sargasso; gulf-weed || *Mare dei Sargassi,* (*geog.*) Sargasso Sea.

sàri, *s.m.* (*indumento indiano*) sari, saree.

sàriga, *s.f.* (*zool.*) sarigue.

saríssa, *s.f.* (*st. mil.*) sarissa (*pl.* sarissæ).

sarmàtico, *ag. s.m.* Sarmatian.

Sarmàzia, *no.pr.f.* (*geog. st.*) Sarmatia.

sarmentàceo, *ag.* (*bot.*) sarmentaceous.

sarménto, *s.m.* (*bot.*) **1.** runner; sarmentum (*pl.* sarmenta) **2.** (*di vite*) vine-shoot; vine-branch.

sarmentóso, *ag.* (*bot.*) sarmentous, sarmentose.

saròng, *s.m.* (*indumento malese*) sarong.

sarrocchíno, *s.m.* pilgrim's cape.

Sarpèdone, *no.pr.m.* (*lett.*) Sarpedon.

sarrussòfono, *s.m.* (*mus.*) sarrusophone.

sàrta, *s.f.* dressmaker, tailoress.

sàrtia, *s.f.* (*mar.*) shrouds (*pl.*).

sartiàme, *s.m.* (*mar.*) rigging; shrouds (*pl.*).

sartína, *s.f.* grisette.

sàrto, *s.m.* tailor: — *da donna*, ladies' tailor (*o* dressmaker).

sartoría, *s.f.* **1.** (*da uomo*) tailor's; (*da donna*) dressmaker's **2.** (*casa di moda*) fashion-house, couture-house || *abito di* —, model dress.

sartòrio, *s.m.* (*anat.*) sartorius.

sassafràsso, *s.m.* (*bot. farm.*) sassafras.

sassàia, *s.f.* **1.** (*argine di sassi*) barrier of stones **2.** (*luogo sassoso*) stony place; (*strada sassosa*) stony road.

sassai(u)òla, *s.f.* **1.** (*pioggia di sassi*) shower of stones, volley of stones **2.** (*battaglia a sassate*) stone-fight.

sassaiuòlo, *ag.*: *colombo* —, (*ornit.*) rock-pigeon.

sassànide, *ag.* Sassanian || *s.c.* Sassanid || *i Sassanidi,* Sassanidae.

sassàta, *s.f.* blow with a stone: *prendere a sassate qlcu.*, to pelt s.o. with stones; *tirare sassate a qlcu.*, to throw stones at s.o.

sassèlla, *s.m.* "sassella" (kind of red wine produced in Northern Italy).

sasséto, *s.m.* stony ground.

sassificàre, *v.t.* (*rar.*) to petrify.

sassífraga, *s.f.* (*bot.*) saxifrage, stone-break.

sàsso, *s.m.* **1.** stone: *duro come un* —, as hard as stone; *tirare un* — *a qlcu.*, to throw a stone at s.o. || *a un tiro di* — *da…*, within a stone's throw of… || *faceva pietà ai sassi*, it was enough to make the stones weep || *avere un cuore di* —, to have a heart of stone || *rimanere di* —, to be dumbfounded || *tirare sassi in piccionaia*, to harm oneself while trying to harm others **2.** (*ciottolo, sassolino*) pebble **3.** (*pietra sepolcrale*) tombstone **4.** (*pietra, roccia*) stone, rock: *una casa di* —, a house of stone; *costruito sul* —, built on rock.

sassofonísta, *s.c.* saxophonist.

sassòfono, *s.m.* (*mus.*) saxophone.

sassofràsso, *s.m.* (*bot. farm.*) sassafras.

sàssola, *s.f.* (*mar.*) bail.

sassolíno, *s.m.* (*piccolo sasso*) pebble.

sassolíte, *s.f.* (*min.*) sassolite.

sàssone, *ag.s.c.* Saxon: *genitivo* —, Saxon genitive.

Sassònia, *no.pr.f.* (*geog.*) Saxony.

sassóso, *ag.* stony, full of stones, covered with stones.

Sàtana, *no.pr.m.* Satan.

Satanàsso, *no.pr.m.* Satanas || **satanàsso,** *s.m.* **1.** (*demonio*) devil **2.** (*persona prepotente*) bully.

satànico, *ag.* satanic, diabolical, devilish: *un piano* —, a devilish plot || *scuola satanica,* (*st. lett.*) Satanic school.

satanísmo, *s.m.* (*st. lett.*) satanism.

satèllite, *ag.* satellitic; satellite (*attributivo*): *stato* —, satellite state ‖ *s.m.* satellite:' — *artificiale*, artificial satellite.

satin, *s.m.* (*tessuto*) satin.

satinàre, *v.t.* to glaze, to satin.

satinàto, *ag.* glazed, satined; satin (*attributivo*): *carta, pelle satinata*, glazed paper, leather.

sàtira, *s.f.* satire: — *personale*, lampoon.

satireggiàre, *v.t.* to satirize: — *la propria epoca*, to satirize one's own times.

satirescaménte, *av.* satyrically.

satìreseo, *ag.* satyric(al): *dramma* —, satyric drama.

satiríasi, *s.f.* (*med.*) satyriasis.

satiricaménte, *av.* satirically.

satírico, *ag.* satiric(al): *poesia satirica*, satirical poetry; *stile, scrittore* —, satirical style, writer ‖ *s.m.* **1.** (*scrittore satirico*) satirist **2.** (*genere satirico*) satire.

satirizzàre, (*rar.*) per **satireggiàre**.

sàtiro, *s.m.* **1.** (*mit.*) Satyr **2.** (*uomo lascivo*) satyr.

satívo, *ag.* cultivable, tillable.

satólla, *s.f.* (*scorpacciata*) fill, bellyfull.

satollàre, *v.t.* to satiate, to sate, to fill up ‖ **satollàrsi**, *v.r.* to eat one's fill, to eat to repletion.

satóllo, *ag.* satiated, sated.

satrapéssa, *s.f.* (*st.*) satrapess.

satrapía, *s.f.* (*st.*) satrapy.

sàtrapo, *s.m.* (*st.*) satrap.

saturàbile, *ag.* saturable.

saturabilità, *s.f.* saturability.

saturàre, *v.t.* to saturate; to glut: — *l'atmosfera*, to saturate the atmosphere; — *un liquido di sale*, to saturate a liquid with salt; — *il mercato*, to glut the market; — *il proprio appetito*, to glut one's appetite ‖ — *la mente di fatti storici*, to fill up (o to saturate) the mind with historical events ‖ **saturàrsi**, *v.r.* to become saturated, to reach saturation; to glut oneself.

saturazióne, *s.f.* saturation: — *magnetica*, (*elett.*) magnetic saturation; *punto di* —, saturation point.

saturnàle, *ag.* (*st.*) Saturnalian ‖ *s.m. pl.* (*st.*) Saturnalia (anche *fig.*).

satúrnia, *s.f.* (*entom.*) emperor-moth.

saturníno, *ag.* **1.** (*di Saturno*) Saturnine **2.** (*malinconico*) saturnine, gloomy **3.** (*med.*) saturnine.

satúrnio, *ag.* Saturnian ‖ *verso* —, (*poes.*) Saturnian verse.

saturnísmo, *s.m.* (*patol.*) lead-poisoning, saturnism.

Satúrno, *no.pr.m.* (*astr. mit.*) Saturn ‖ **satúrno**, *s.m.* (*alchimia*) (*piombo*) Saturn.

sàturo, *ag.* **1.** saturated (with sthg.): *atmosfera, soluzione satura*, saturated atmosphere, solution **2.** (*ripieno*) full: — *di invidia*, full of envy.

saudíto, *ag.* Saudi: *Arabia Saudita*, Saudi Arabia ‖ *s.m.*, **saudíta**, *s.f.* Saudi Arabian.

Sàul, *no.pr.m.* (*Bibbia*) Saul.

sàuri, *s.m.pl.* (*zool.*) Sauria.

sàuro, *ag.* sorrel ‖ *s.m.* sorrel (horse).

sauròpodi, *s.m.pl.* (*zool.*) Sauropoda.

sauté, *ag.* (*cuc.*) sauté, sautéed.

savàna, *s.f.* (*geog.*) savanna(h).

Savèrio, *no.pr.m.* Xavier.

saviaménte, *av.* wisely, sensibly.

saviézza, *s.f.* wisdom, (good) sense.

sàvio, *ag.* **1.** wise, sensible: *savi consigli*, wise advice; *savia decisione*, wise (o sensible) decision **2.** (*buono*) good: *un bambino* —, a good child; *sii* —, be good ‖ *s.m.* wise man, sage ‖ *i Sette Savi*, the Seven Sages.

Savòia, *no.pr.f.* (*geog.*) Savoy.

savoiàrdo, *ag.* Savoyard ‖ *s.c.* Savoyard ‖ *s.m.* (*biscotto*) Savoy (biscuit).

saziàbile, *ag.* satiable.

saziabilità, *s.f.* satiability.

saziàre, *v.t.* **1.** to satisfy, to sate, to glut; to satiate: *aveva tanta fame che non sapevo come saziarlo*, he was so hungry that I didn't know how to satisfy

his appetite; — *la curiosità, l'ambizione, il desiderio di vendetta*, to satisfy (o to gratify) one's curiosity, one's ambition, one's desire for revenge; — *il proprio appetito*, to sate (o to glut) one's appetite; — *la sete di qlcu.*, to satisfy (o to quench) s.o.'s thirst **2.** (*stuccare*) to fill: *questo è un cibo che sazia molto*, this food is very filling ‖ **saziàrsi**, *v.r.* **1.** to satisfy one's appetite, to gratify one's appetite; to become satiated, to get full: *mi sazio subito di patate*, I soon get full with potatoes **2.** (*stancarsi*) to get tired: *non mi sazio mai di leggere*, I never get tired of reading.

sazietà, *s.f.* satiety, surfeit: *la* — *elimina il desiderio*, satiety removes desire; *bere a* —, to drink one's fill; *mangiare a* —, to eat one's fill (o to eat to repletion o to eat to surfeit) ‖ *ne ho a* —, *fig.* I have (had) more than enough of it.

saziévole, *ag.* **1.** filling **2.** (*noioso*) boring, tiresome.

sàzio, *ag.* **1.** replete; (*fam.*) full (up): *non posso mangiare nient'altro, sono* —, I cannot eat anything else, I am full (up) **2.** (*saturo*) satiate(d) (with sthg.), sated (with sthg.): — *di lodi*, sated with praises **3.** (*stanco*) tired, sick; (*sl.*) fed up (with sthg.): — *di queste lamentele*, tired of these complaints.

sbaccanàre, *v.i.* to make a great noise; (*fam.*) to kick up a din, to kick up a shindy.

sbaccanío, *s.m.* din, row; (*fam.*) shindy.

sbaccellàre, *v.t.* to shell: — *i piselli*, to shell peas.

sbaccellatúra, *s.f.* shelling.

sbacchettàre, *v.t.* to beat: — *tappeti*, to beat carpets.

sbacchettàta, *s.f.* beating: *abbiamo dato una bella* — *al tappeto*, we gave the carpet a good beating.

sbacchettatúra, *s.f.* beating.

sbacchiaménto, *s.m.* banging; (*specialmente di porta*) slamming.

sbacchiàre, *v.t.* to bang; (*specialmente una porta*) to slam: *sbacchiò il libro sul tavolo*, she banged (o slammed) the book (down) on the table; — *la porta*, to slam (o to bang) the door ‖ *v.i.* to bang; (*specialmente di porta*) to slam: *la porta sbacchiò*, the door slammed.

sbaciucchiaménto, *s.m.* kissing; (*sl. amer.*) necking.

sbaciucchiàre, *v.t.* to smother with kisses; (*sl. amer.*) to neck ‖ **sbaciucchiàrsi**, *v.r. reciproco* to smother each other with kisses.

sbaciucchío, *s.m.* kissing; (*sl. amer.*) necking.

sbadacchiàre, *v.t.* (*edil.*) to prop up.

sbadacchiatúra, *s.f.* (*edil.*) propping.

sbadàcchio, *s.m.* (*miner.*) stull.

sbadatàggine, *s.f.* (*noncuranza*) carelessness, heedlessness; (*sconsideratezza*) thoughtlessness; (*inavvertenza*) inadvertence: *per* —, through carelessness (o heedlessness); through thoughtlessness; through inadvertence; *commettere una* —, to blunder through carelessness.

sbadataménte, *av.* (*trascuratamente*) carelessly, heedlessly; (*sconsideratamente*) thoughtlessly; (*inavvertitamente*) inadvertently.

sbadàta, *s.f.* scatter-brain.

sbadàto, *ag.* (*noncurante*) careless, heedless; (*sconsiderato*) thoughtless; (*sventato*) scatter-brained: *risposta sbadata*, thoughtless answer ‖ *alla sbadata*, (*trascuratamente*) carelessly (o heedlessly); (*sconsideratamente*) thoughtlessly; (*inavvertitamente*) inadvertently ‖ *s.m.* scatter-brain.

sbadigliaménto, *s.m.* yawning.

sbadigliàre, *v.i.* to yawn: — *fino a rompersi le mascelle*, to yawn one's head off.

sbadíglio, *s.m.* yawn; (*lo sbadigliare*) yawning: *un gran* —, a big yawn; *lo* — *è contagioso*, yawning is catching.

sbafàre, *v.t.* (*fam.*) (*scroccare*) to scrounge, to cadge: — *un pranzo*, to scrounge a dinner.

sbafatóre, *s.m.*, **sbafatríce**, *s.f.* scrounger, cadger.

sbàfo, *s.m.* scrounging, cadging ‖ *vivere a* —, to scrounge a living.

sbagliàre, *v.t.* to mistake, to make a mistake in (sthg.), to go wrong in (sthg.), to do wrong: — *un calcolo*, to miscalculate (*o* to be out in one's reckoning) (*anche fig.*); — *il colpo*, to miss the target; — *l'ora*, to mistake the time; — *strada*, to mistake the way (*o* to take the wrong way); — *treno*, to take the wrong train ‖ — *il passo*, to be (*o* to fall) out of step ‖ *v.i.*, **sbagliàrsi**, *v.r.* to make a mistake, to be mistaken, to be wrong, to go wrong; to err: *la casa è la terza a destra*, *non puoi sbagliarti*, the house is the third on the right, you can't miss it; *chiunque può —*, everybody can make mistakes; *hai sbagliato nel riportare i numeri*, you have made a mistake in carrying the numbers forward; *mi potrei sbagliare*, *ma credo che sia questo*, I may be wrong, but I think it is this; (*ti*) *sbagli*, *non è così*, you are mistaken, it isn't so; *ti sbagli troppo spesso*, you make too many mistakes; *riconoscere di aver sbagliato*, to acknowledge one's mistake(s) ‖ *sbaglia anche il prete all'altare*, to err is human ‖ — *di grosso*, to make a blunder (*o* to blunder) ‖ *mi hai fatto sbagliare*, you made me make a mistake.

sbagliàto, *ag.* wrong, mistaken; (*erroneo*) erroneous: *calcolo —*, wrong calculation; *idee, opinioni sbagliate*, wrong ideas, opinions; *interpretazione, pronuncia sbagliata*, wrong interpretation (*o* misinterpretation), wrong pronunciation (*o* mispronunciation); *nozioni sbagliate*, mistaken notions; *osservazione sbagliata*, erroneous observation; *l'uso — di una parola*, the wrong use of a word; *il suo compito era tutto —*, his homework was all wrong; *comporre un numero telefonico —*, to dial the wrong number; *interpretare una parola in senso —*, to take a word in the wrong sense.

sbàglio, *s.m.* mistake, error; (*passo falso*) slip; (*sproposito*) blunder: *gli sbagli della giovinezza*, the errors of youth; *per —*, by mistake; *lo — fu suo*, it was his fault; *vi sono alcuni sbagli nel tuo dettato*, there are a few mistakes in your dictation; *fare uno —*, to make a mistake (*o* an error *o* a slip *o* a blunder); *riconoscere i propri sbagli*, to acknowledge one's mistakes.

sbaldanzíre, *v.t.* to cow; to daunt ‖ *v.i.*, **sbaldanzírsi**, *v.r.* to be cowed; to be daunted.

sbalestraménto, *s.m.* (*divagamento*) digression.

sbalestràre, *v.t.* **1.** to send; to drive: — *qlcu. da un luogo a un altro*, to drive s.o. from pillar to post **2.** (*turbare*) to upset: *quel conto ha sbalestrato le mie condizioni finanziarie*, that bill has upset my budget ‖ *v.i.* **1.** (*non colpire nel segno*) to miss the mark **2.** (*divagare*) to wander, to digress ‖ **sbalestràrsi**, *v.r.* **1.** (*fare bancarotta*) to go bankrupt **2.** (*turbarsi*) to be upset **3.** (*di cavallo*) to rear.

sbalestràto, *ag.* **1.** (*squilibrato*) unbalanced **2.** (*sconsiderato*) reckless, rash, foolhardy.

sballàre, *v.t.* **1.** to unpack **2.** (*sgonfiare*) to brag, to boast; (*fam.*) to talk big ‖ *sballarle grosse*, to tell tall stories.

sballàto, *ag.* **1.** unpacked **2.** (*squilibrato*) unbalanced; (*disordinato*) untidy, disorderly: *mente sballata*, unbalanced mind ‖ *impresa sballata*, rash (*o* foolhardy) enterprise **3.** (*inventato*) made up: *è una storia sballata*, it is a made-up story.

sballatúra, *s.f.* **1.** unpacking **2.** (*esagerazione*) exaggeration.

sballóna, *s.f.* (*fam.*) story-teller; boaster, braggart.

sballonàta, *s.f.* (*fam.*) tall story; boast.

sballóne, *s.m.* (*fam.*) story-teller; boaster, braggart.

sballottaménto, *s.m.* jolting, tossing; (*di un bambino*) dandling.

sballottàre, *v.t.* to jolt (about), to toss (about); to push (about): *l'aeroplano era sballottato dal forte vento*, the plane was tossed (about) by the strong wind; *l'automobile ci ha sballottati per tutta la strada*, the car has jolted us (about) all the way; *la barca era sballottata dalle onde*, the boat was tossed by the waves; *essere sballottato dalla folla*, to be pushed about in the crowd ‖ *non mi piace essere sballottato da una*

destinazione all'altra, I don't like being driven from pillar to post ‖ — *un bambino*, to dandle a child.

sbalordiménto, *s.m.* amazement, astonishment; (*confusione*) bewilderment.

sbalordíre, *v.t.* **1.** to amaze, to astonish; to dumbfound; (*confondere*) to bewilder **2.** (*tramortire*) to stun, to flabbergast.

sbalorditàggine, *s.f.* piece of stupidity, piece of silliness.

sbalorditívo, *ag.* amazing, astonishing; dumbfounding; (*che confonde*) bewildering.

sbalordíto, *ag.* **1.** amazed, astonished; dumbfounded; (*confuso*) bewildered **2.** (*tramortito*) stunned.

sbalzaménto, *s.m.* **1.** (*lo sbalzare*) throwing; (*il rimbalzare*) bouncing **2.** (*destituzione*) dismissal, removal.

sbalzàre, *v.t.* **1.** to throw, to toss, to fling: *il cavallo lo sbalzò di sella*, the horse tossed him from the saddle; *fu sbalzato da cavallo*, he was thrown from his horse; — (*fuori*) *da ql.co.*, to throw (*o* to toss *o* to fling) out of sthg.: *fu sbalzato dall'automobile*, he was thrown out of the car **2.** (*rimuovere*) to dismiss: — *qlcu. dal suo ufficio*, to dismiss s.o. (from his position) (*o fam.* to give s.o. the sack) ‖ — *un governo*, to overthrow a government **3.** (*artig.*) to emboss ‖ *v.i.* to spring, to leap; (*rimbalzare*) to bounce.

sbalzàto, *ag.* (*artig.*) embossed.

sbalzatóre, *s.m.*, **sbalzatríce**, *s.f.* (*artig.*) embosser.

sbalzellàre, *v.t.i.* to bump, to jolt.

sbalzellío, *s.m.* bumping, jolting.

sbalzellóne, *s.m.* jolt, jerk ‖ *a sbalzelloni*, jerkily (*o* in jumps).

sbàlzo, *s.m.* **1.** bound, jump, leap; bounce ‖ *a sbalzi*, by fits and starts (*o* in spurts *o* desultorily) **2.** (*cambiamento*) change: *sbalzi di temperatura*, changes of temperature ‖ *sbalzi della fortuna*, ups and downs **3.** *lavoro a —*, (*in rilievo*) embossed work.

sbancàre, *v.t.* to break; (*fam.*) to leave broke; to bankrupt: *mi sbancò*, (*al giuoco*) he left me broke (*o fam.* cleaned me out); *sbancò la cassa del casinò*, he broke the bank at the casino.

sbandaménto, *s.m.* **1.** (*di gente*) dispersal; disbanding **2.** (*mar.*) list; listing, heeling (over); (*aer.*) sideslip; sideshipping; (*aut.*) skid; skidding.

sbandàre, *v.t.* **1.** to disperse, to break up; to disband: — *la folla*, to disperse the crowd **2.** (*mar.*) to cause to heel (over), to cause to list; (*aer.*) to cause to sideslip; (*aut.*) to cause to skid ‖ *v.i.* (*mar.*) to heel (over), to list; (*aer.*) to sideslip; (*aut.*) to skid: *la nave sbanda a destra*, *a sinistra*, the ship lists (*o* has a list) to starboard, to port ‖ **sbandàrsi**, *v.r.* to disperse, to break up; to disband: *la folla si sbandò per le strade*, the crowd dispersed in the streets; *le truppe si sbandarono*, the troops disbanded.

sbandàta, *V.* **sbandaménto**.

sbandataménte, *av.* in confusion.

sbandàto, *ag.* dispersed, broken up; disbanded ‖ *s.m.* straggler.

sbandieraménto, *s.m.* **1.** flag-waving **2.** (*ostentazione*) display; (*spreg.*) show, parade.

sbandieràre, *v.i.* to wave flags, to wave a flag ‖ *v.t.* (*ostentare*) to display; (*spreg.*) to parade, to make a show of (sthg.), to make a display of (sthg.).

sbandieràta, *s.f.* flag-waving; (*ostentazione*) display of flags.

sbandiménto, *s.m.* banishment.

sbandíre, *v.t.* to banish.

sbandòmetro, *s.m.* (*aer.*) turn and bank indicator.

sbagliaménto, *s.m.* rout, routing, dispersal.

sbaragliàre, *v.t.* to rout, to put to rout ‖ **sbaragliàrsi**, *v.r.* to turn into a rout.

sbaraglíno, *s.m.* (*giuoco*) backgammon.

sbaràglio, *s.m.* **1.** (*rotta*) rout **2.** (*rischio*) risk; (*pericolo*) danger, jeopardy: *si buttò allo —*, he threw himself into the fight; *essere allo —*, to be in danger (*o* in jeopardy); *mandare le truppe allo —*, to send the troops into the fight; *mettere allo — la propria vita,* to jeopardize (*o* to endanger) one's life; *mettersi allo —,* to expose oneself to danger.

sbarazzàre, *v.t.* to clear (up); to rid: *vorrei poterti — di queste noie,* I wish I could rid you of these troubles; — *la mente di qlcu. dal sospetto,* to clear s.o.'s mind of suspicion; — *una stanza,* to clear up (*o* to tidy up) a room; — *la tavola,* to clear the table ‖ **sbarazzàrsi,** *v.r.* to rid oneself, to get rid: *vorrei sbarazzarmi di questa merce,* I should like to get rid of these goods; — *di un debito,* to rid oneself of a debt; — *di qlcu.,* to get rid of s.o.

sbarazzína, *s.f.* little scamp.

sbarazzinàta, *s.f.* prank, trick.

sbarazzíno, *ag.* free and easy; easy going; unconventional ‖ *s.m.* little scamp; little rogue; street urchin.

sbarbàre, *v.t.* 1. (*radere*) to shave ‖ *farsi —,* to get a shave 2. (*mec.*) to shave 3. (*svellere*) to uproot ‖ **sbarbàrsi,** *v.r.* (*radersi*) to shave (oneself), to have a shave.

sbarbatèllo, *s.m.* (*iron.*) (young) colt.

sbarbàto, *ag.* 1. (*rasato*) shaven 2. (*imberbe*) beardless 3. (*sradicato*) uprooted.

sbarbatríce, *s.f.* 1. (*mec.*) shaving-machine: — *per ingranaggi,* gear shaving-machine 2. (*agr.*) hummeler.

sbarbatúra, *s.f.* (*mec.*) shaving: — *bombata,* crown (*o* elliptoid) shaving; — *cilindrica,* "roto shave"; — *diagonale,* diagonal (*o* underpass) shaving; — *normale,* conventional (*o* crossed-axe) shaving.

sbarbicaménto, *s.m.* uprooting, eradication, extirpation.

sbarbicàre, *v.t.* to uproot, to eradicate, to extirpate.

sbarbificàre, *v.t.* (*scherz.*) to shave ‖ **sbarbificàrsi,** *v.r.* (*scherz.*) to shave (oneself).

sbarcàre, *v.t.* to disembark, to land, to put ashore, to set ashore; (*merci*) to unload, to discharge: — *un carico,* to unload (*o* to discharge *o* to land) a cargo; — *passeggeri,* to land passengers ‖ — *il lunario,* to make both ends meet ‖ *v.i.* to land, to disembark; (*temporaneamente*) to go ashore: *sbarcai a Genova,* I landed at Genoa.

sbarcàto, *ag.* unloaded, discharged ‖ *marinaio —,* (*riformato*) discharged sailor.

sbarcatóio, *s.m.* quay, wharf; landing-stage, pier.

sbàrco, *s.m.* 1. (*di passeggeri*) landing; (*di merci*) discharge, unloading: *lo — dei Padri Pellegrini in America,* the landing of the Pilgrim Fathers in America; *ponte di —,* gangway; *lo — del carico richiese tre ore,* the unloading (*o* discharge of the cargo) took three hours; *non c'era nessuno ad aspettarmi allo —,* there was nobody waiting for me when I landed ‖ *compagnia da —,* (*mar. mil.*) landing-party; *mezzo da —,* (*mar. mil.*) landing-craft; *truppe da —,* (*mar. mil.*) landing -force 2. (*sbarcatoio*) quay, wharf; landing-stage, pier.

sbàrra, *s.f.* 1. bar: — *a bilico,* (*di passaggio a livello*) (bascule) barrier; *una — da un lato all'altro della strada,* a bar (*o* barrier) across the road; — *di controllo,* (*fis. atomica*) control-rod; *una — di ferro,* an iron bar; *le sbarre di una prigione,* the bars of a prison; — *di sicurezza,* (*fis. atomica*) safety-rod; — *spaziatrice,* (*di macchina da scrivere*) space-bar 2. (*del timone*) tiller 3. (*ginnastica*) bar 4. (*mus.*) bar(-line) 5. (*dir.*) bar: *venire, presentarsi alla —,* to appear at the bar 6. (*arald.*) bar 7. (*ortografia*) cross(-bar): *la — di una t,* the cross(-bar) of a t.

sbarraménto, *s.m.* 1. barricade, obstruction 2. (*di acque*) barrage; dam; weir 3. (*mil.*) barrage, defence; (*di porto*) boom: — *antiaereo,* anti-aircraft barrage; — *di mine,* mine-field; — *di palloni,* (*aer. mil.*) balloon barrage; — *retale,* net; *tiro di —,* (artillery) barrage 4. (*lo sbarrare*) barring (up), stopping; (*di porto*) blocking; (*di valle*) damming; (*di via*) closing 5. (*in miniera,* *per ventilazione*) brattice; stopping.

sbarràre, *v.t.* 1. to bar; to block (up), to obstruct; (*acque*) to dam: *ci sbarrarono la strada e perciò dovemmo tornare indietro,* they barred the way and therefore we

were obliged to come back; — *l'entrata,* to block the entrance; *sbarrarono l'entrata del parco,* they closed the entrance to the park; — *il cammino a qlcu.,* to obstruct s.o.'s path (anche *fig.*); — *porte e finestre,* to bar doors and windows; — *una strada,* to block (up) a road 2. (*spalancare*) to open wide: — *gli occhi,* to open one's eyes wide 3. — *un assegno,* (*comm.*) to cross a cheque 4. (*cancellare*) to cross out, to strike out: — *una parola,* to cross out a word.

sbarràto, *ag.* 1. (*di strada*) blocked ‖ *strada sbarrata,* (*nei cartelli*) road blocked (*o* no thoroughfare) 2. (*di porta, finestra*) barred; closed 3. (*di occhi*) wide open 4. (*di assegno*) crossed.

sbarrétta, *s.f.* (*tip.*) bar.

sbassàre, *e derivati,* V. **abbassàre,** *e derivati.*

sbatacchiaménto, *s.m.* 1. (*atto*) banging, slamming 2. (*effetto*) bang, slam.

sbatacchiàre, *v.t.* 1. to bang, to slam: *lo sbatacchiò contro il muro,* he banged him against the wall; *mi sbatacchiò l'uscio in faccia,* he slammed the door in my face 2. (*sbattere con forza ripetutamente*) to rattle, to bang to and fro: *il vento sbatacchiava le imposte,* the wind was rattling the shutters (*o* was banging the shutters to and fro); — *le ali,* to flap its wings ‖ *v.i.* to bang, to slam: *c'è una finestra che sbatacchia,* there is a window banging ‖ **sbatacchiàrsi,** *v.r.* to toss about.

sbatacchiàta, *s.f.* bang, slam.

sbatacchío, *s.m.* banging, slamming; tossing about.

sbàttere, *v.t.* 1. (*urtare contro*) to knock, to bang; to beat: — *ql.co. contro un muro,* to knock (*o* to bang) sthg. against a wall ‖ *non so dove — la testa,* I don't know which way to turn (*o* I am at my wits' end) ‖ — *la testa contro il muro, fig.* to beat one's head against a brick-wall 2. (*chiudere violentemente*) to slam, to bang: *uscì sbattendo la porta,* he went out slamming the door; — *la porta in faccia a qlcu.,* to slam the door in s.o.'s face (anche *fig.*) 3. (*gettare*) to throw: *queste vecchie case saranno sbattute giù,* these old buildings will be knocked down; *sbattè le carte sul tavolo,* he threw the cards on the table; — *giù un vaso,* to throw down a vase; — *via un paio di scarpe,* to throw away a pair of shoes ‖ *l'hanno sbattuto in un paesino di campagna,* they have sent him to a country village ‖ *se non taci ti sbatto fuori dalla stanza,* if you don't shut up, I'll throw you out of the room ‖ — *in prigione,* to fling into prison ‖ — *via denaro, tempo,* to waste money, time 4. (*agitare, scuotere*) to shake; to toss: *il vento sbatteva i rami,* the wind was shaking (*o* tossing) the branches; — *le ali,* to flap its wings; — *il contenuto di una bottiglia,* to shake the contents of a bottle; — *un tappeto, una coperta fuori dalla finestra,* to shake a carpet, a blanket out of the window ‖ — *la panna,* to whip cream; — *le uova,* to beat eggs ‖ *v.i.* 1. (*di porte, finestre*) to bang, to slam: *c'è una porta che sbatte,* there is a door banging 2. (*di vele, di ali*) to flap 3. (*mec.*) (*di valvola*) to clatter, to chatter, to rattle ‖ **sbàttersi,** *v.r.* to toss, to toss about: *egli si sbatteva in preda al dolore,* he was tossing about in pain.

sbattezzàre, *v.t.* to force to abjure Christianity ‖ **sbattezzàrsi,** *v.r.* to abjure Christianity.

sbattighiàccio, *s.m.* (cocktail) shaker.

sbattiménto, *s.m.* 1. (*di porte, finestre*) banging, slamming 2. (*scuotimento*) shaking, tossing; (*di panna*) whipping; (*di uova*) beating 3. (*di corpo libero al vento*) flapping 4. (*mec.*) (*di cinghia*) flapping; (*di valvola*) clattering, chattering, rattling 5. (*aer.*) (*vibrazione aeroelastica*) flutter 6. (*aut.*) (*lubrificazione*) (wheel-) clearance.

sbattitúra, V. **sbattiménto** 1. 2. 3.

sbattúta, *s.f.* shake, shaking.

sbattúto, *ag.* 1. (*abbattuto*) depressed; worn-out; harassed-looking ‖ *occhi sbattuti,* dull (*o* lifeless) eyes; *viso —,* tired face 2. *uovo —,* beaten egg.

sbavàggio, *s.m.* (*tip.*) blur.

sbavagliàre, *v.t.* to ungag.

sbavàre, *v.i.* 1. to dribble; to slaver, to slobber 2. (*tip.*)

to smudge, to blur **3.** (*di colore*) to run; (*di penna*) to smudge ‖ *v.t.* **1.** to dribble over **2.** (*metal.*) to clean, to trim, to snag ‖ **sbavàrsi,** *v.r.* to dribble all down (oneself); to slobber all down (oneself).

sbavàto, *ag.* **1.** covered with dribble; covered with slobber **2.** (*tip.*) smudged **3.** (*di pittura, ecc.*) blurred.

sbavatúra, *s.f.* **1.** (*bava*) dribble; slobber, slaver **2.** (*di lumaca*) slime **3.** (*tip.*) blur, smudge **4.** (*di carta*) uncut edge **5.** (*metal.*) trimming: *molatrice per* —, snag-grinder.

sbavóna, *s.f.,* **sbavóne,** *s.m.* slobberer; dribbler.

sbeccucciàre, *v.t.* to chip.

sbeccucciàto, *ag.* chipped.

sbeffàre, sbeffeggiàre, *e derivati, V.* **beffàre, beffeggiàre,** *e derivati.*

sbellicàrsi, *v.r.:* — *dalle risa,* to split one's sides (with laughter) (*o* to roar with laughter).

sbellicatamѐnte, *av.* side-splittingly.

sbendàre, *v.t.* to unbandage, to remove the bandages from (s.o., sthg.) ‖ **sbendàrsi,** *v.r.* to remove one's bandages.

sberciàre, *v.i.* **1.** (*mancare il bersaglio*) to miss the mark **2.** (*fare sberleffi*) to make grimaces **3.** (*gridare*) to bawl (out).

sberlèffo, *s.m.* grimace: *fare sberleffi,* to make grimaces; *fare uno* — *a qlcu.,* to make a face at s.o.

sberrettàrsi, *v.r.* to take off one's cap, to raise one's cap.

sbertàre, sberteggiàre, *V.* **beffàre, beffeggiàre.**

sbertucciàre, *v.t.* **1.** (*schernire*) to mock; to sneer at (s.o.); to jeer at (s.o.); to deride **2.** (*sgualcire*) to crumple; to wrinkle; to crease.

sbevacchiàre, *v.i.* to tipple; (*fam.*) to booze.

sbevazzamѐnto, *s.m.* tippling; (*fam.*) boozing.

sbevazzàre, *v.i.* to tipple; (*fam.*) to booze.

sbevazzatóre, *s.m.,* **sbevazzatríce,** *s.f.* tippler, drunkard; (*fam.*) boozer.

sbiadíre, *v.t.* to fade: *il sole ha sbiadito le tende,* the sun has faded the curtains ‖ *v.i.* to fade, to grow pale: *colori che non sbiadiscono,* fast colours; *questo colore sbiadisce facilmente,* this colour fades easily.

sbiadíto, *ag.* **1.** (*scolorito*) faded **2.** (*pallido*) pale **3.** *fig.* dull, uninteresting: *un racconto* —, a dull story.

sbiànca, *s.f.* (*ind. tessile, cartaria*) bleaching.

sbiancamѐnto, *s.m.* **1.** (*foto.*) whitening **2.** (*ind. tessile, cartaria*) bleaching.

sbiancàre, *v.t.* to bleach (*anche ind.*): — *una tela al sole,* to bleach linen in the sun ‖ *v.i.,* **sbiancàrsi,** *v.r.* **1.** to turn white **2.** (*impallidire*) to go pale, to grow pale **3.** (*sbiadire*) to fade.

sbiancàto, *ag.* white; pale.

sbicchieràre, *v.i.* **1.** to sell wine by the glass **2.** (*bere in compagnia*) to have a drink together.

sbicchieràta, *s.f.* drinking together, drinking in company.

sbiecàre, *v.t.* **1.** (*mettere di sbieco*) to slant, to put aslant **2.** (*raddrizzare*) to straighten **3.** (*guardare torvamente*) to look askance at (s.o., sthg.) **4.** (*orlare*) to border, to edge, to trim ‖ *v.i.,* **sbiecàrsi,** *v.r.* to slant, to be aslant.

sbièco, *ag.* (*inclinato*) sloping, slanting; aslant (*predicativo*); (*obliquo*) oblique ‖ *appendere ql.co. di* —, to hang sthg. askew (*o* awry); *guardare qlcu. di* —, *fig.* to look askance at s.o.; *tagliare una stoffa di* —, to cut a cloth on the bias ‖ *s.m.* (*orlo, bordo per guarnire un abito*) border, edge; trimming.

sbigottimѐnto, *s.m.* **1.** dismay **2.** (*stupore*) bewilderment; (*meraviglia*) astonishment, amazement.

sbigottíre, *v.t.* **1.** to dismay: *fui sbigottito alla notizia dell'incidente,* I was dismayed at the news of the accident **2.** (*rendere attonito*) to bewilder; (*per meraviglia*) to astonish, to amaze, to dumbfound, to flabbergast: *egli fu sbigottito alla vista di ciò,* he was astonished at the sight of it **3.** (*terrificare*) to terrify ‖ *v.i.,* **sbigottírsi,** *v.r.* **1.** to be dismayed **2.** (*rimanere attonito*) to be bewildered; (*per meraviglia*) to be as-

tonished, to be amazed, to be dumbfounded **3.** (*per timore*) to be frightened.

sbigottíto, *ag.* **1.** dismayed **2.** (*attonito*) bewildered; (*meravigliato*) astonished **3.** (*impaurito*) frightened.

sbilanciamѐnto, *s.m.* **1.** loss of balance; unsettling **2.** derangement.

sbilanciàre, *v.t.* **1.** to unbalance; to put out of balance; to unsettle: *questo acquisto mi ha sbilanciato,* this purchase has almost ruined me **2.** (*disturbare*) to disturb; to derange ‖ **sbilanciàrsi,** *v.r.* to lose one's balance ‖ *non si sbilancia mai troppo,* (*nello spendere*) he is never lavish in spending his money; (*nel parlare*) he always weighs his words.

sbilàncio, *s.m.* **1.** (*squilibrio*) lack of balance **2.** (*sproporzione*) disproportion, lack of proportion **3.** (*perdita*) loss **4.** (*eccesso*) excess **5.** (*deficit*) deficit.

sbilènco, *ag.* **1.** crooked; distorted; misshapen; awry (*predicativo*): *un vecchio* —, a misshapen old man **2.** (*dalle gambe storte*) bow-legged, bandy(-legged).

sbirciàre, *v.t.i.* **1.** (*guardare di traverso*) to cast a sidelong glance; to cast sidelong glances at (s.o., sthg.) **2.** (*guardare attentamente*) to eye; to scan: *lo sbirciò con molta attenzione,* he eyed him very carefully.

sbirciàta, *s.f.* (*sidelong*) glance: *dare una* — *a ql.co.,* to glance at sthg. ✍

sbirràglia, *s.f.* (*spreg.*) police; (*fam.*) cops (*pl.*).

sbírro, *s.m.* **1.** (*spreg.*) policeman (*pl.* policemen); (*fam.*) cop **2.** (*mar.*) selvagee.

sbizzarrírsi, *v.r.* to satisfy one's whims.

sbloccamѐnto, *V.* **sblòcco.**

sbloccàre, *v.t.* **1.** (*mil.*) to raise the blockade of (sthg.) **2.** (*mec.*) to release the brake of (sthg.) **3.** (*ferr.*) to clear **4.** — *gli affitti,* to decontrol rents.

sblòcco, *s.m.* **1.** (*mil.*) raising the blockade **2.** (*mec.*) releasing the brake **3.** (*ferr.*) clearing **4.** (*econ.*) decontrol: — *degli affitti,* decontrol of rents; — *dei prezzi,* unfreezing (of prices).

sbòbba, sbòbbia, *s.f.* (*pop.*) bad soup; sloppy soup.

sboccamѐnto, *s.m.* **1.** (*deflusso*) outflow **2.** (*foce*) mouth, outfall.

sboccàre, *v.i.* **1.** (*di corso d'acqua*) to flow, to debouch: *quel fiume sbocca nel mare,* that river flows into the sea **2.** (*di strada*) to lead (to a place); to come out (at a place): *dove sbocca questa strada?,* where does this road come out? *va' avanti diritto e sboccherai in una piazza,* go straight on and you will come to a square **3.** (*irrompere*) to break: *la folla sboccò nel giardino,* the crowd broke into the garden **4.** (*traboccare*) to overflow, to brim over ‖ *v.t.* **1.** (*piatti, tazze, ecc.*) to chip: *ho sboccato questo vaso per sbaglio,* I have accidentally chipped this vase **2.** — *una bottiglia di vino,* to skim the oil from a bottle of wine.

sboccatàggine, *s.f.* coarseness.

sboccataménte, *av.* coarsely.

sboccàto, *ag.* **1.** (*detto di vaso, bottiglia, ecc.*) chipped **2.** *fig.* coarse: *linguaggio* —, coarse language; *persona sboccata,* foul-mouthed person.

sboccatúra, *s.f.* (*di fiume*) mouth.

sbocciamѐnto, *s.m.* **1.** (*di fiori*) blossoming, blooming **2.** *fig.* blossoming.

sbocciàre, *v.i.* **1.** to open; to blossom, to bloom: *queste rose sboccheranno domani,* these roses will open tomorrow **2.** *fig.* (*nascere*) to be born, to start, to begin: *la loro amicizia sbocciò l'anno scorso,* their friendship started last year ‖ *v.t.* (*al giuoco delle bocce*) to hit.

sbòccio, *s.m.* blooming, blossoming: *lo* — *dei fiori,* the blossoming of flowers; *in pieno* —, in full bloom; *sul primo* —, *fig.* in the bloom of youth.

sbócco, *s.m.* **1.** outlet **2.** (*uscita*) exit, way out **3.** (*di fiume*) mouth.

sbocconcellàre, *v.t.* **1.** to nibble: — *un pezzo di pane,* to nibble (at) a piece of bread **2.** (*spezzettare*) to cut into small pieces, to divide into small parts **3.** (*piatti, tazze, ecc.*) to chip.

sbocconcellàto, *ag.* 1. (*di pane, ecc.*) half-eaten 2. (*di piatto, tazza, ecc.*) chipped.

sbocconcellatúra, *s.f.* 1. (*di pane, ecc.*) nibble 2. (*di piatto, tazza, ecc.*) chip.

sbòffo, *s.m.* puff.

sbollàre, *v.t.* to unseal.

sbollíre, *v.i.* 1. to cease boiling; to go off the boil 2. *fig.* (*calmarsi*) to cool down.

sbolognàre, *v.t.* (*fam.*) to palm off: — *ql.co. a qlcu.*, to palm off sthg. on s.o.

sbombàre, *v.i.* (*fam.*) to tell tall stories.

sbombazzàre, sbombettàre, *v.i* .(*bere smodatamente*) to drink immoderately, to drink to excess; (*fam.*) to soak.

sbonzolàre, *v.i.* (*spenzolare*) to hang down, to dangle.

sbòrnia, *s.f.* 1. drunkenness: *avere la* —, to be (blind-) drunk; *prendere la* —, to get (blind-)drunk 2. *fig.* (*infatuazione*) infatuation.

sborniàre, *v.t.* to make drunk ‖ **sborniàrsi**, *v.r.* to get drunk.

sborniàto, *ag.* (blind-)drunk.

sborniòna, *s.f.*, **sbornióne**, *s.m.* drunkard.

sborsaménto, *s.m.* disbursement, paying out.

sborsàre, *v.t.* to disburse, to pay, to pay out, to spend: *senza* — *niente*, without spending a penny.

sbórso, *s.m.* 1. (*lo sborsare*) disbursement, payment 2. (*somma sborsata*) outlay.

sboscàre, *e derivati*, *V.* **diboscàre**, *e derivati*.

sbottàre, *v.i.* to burst out: — *in pianto, in riso*, to burst out crying, laughing.

sbottàta, *s.f.*, **sbòtto**, *s.m.* outburst.

sbottonàre, *v.t.* to unbutton ‖ **sbottonàrsi**, *v.r.* 1. to undo one's buttons: — *il soprabito*, to unbutton one's overcoat 2. (*fam.*) (*confidarsi*) to disclose one's feelings (to s.o.), to unbosom oneself (to s.o.); to open one's heart (to s.o.); (*sl. amer.*) to unbutton one's lips (to s.o.).

sbottonatúra, *s.f.* 1. unbuttoning 2. (*fam.*) (*il confidarsi*) unbosoming.

sbottoneggiàre, *v.i.* to banter, to malign.

sbozzaménto, *V.* **sbozzatúra**.

sbozzàre, *v.t.* 1. to sketch out, to outline 2. (*scult.*) to rough-hew.

sbozzatóre, *s.m.*, **sbozzatríce**, *s.f.* 1. sketcher 2. (*scult.*) rough-hewer.

sbozzatúra, *s.f.* 1. sketch, outline 2. (*scult.*) rough -hewing, rough-cast.

sbozzimàre, *v.t.* (*ind. tessile*) to size-break.

sbozzimatríce, *s.f.* (*ind. tessile*) size-breaking machine.

sbozzíno, *s.m.* (*falegnameria*) jack-plane.

sbòzzo, *s.m.* rough sketch, draft.

sbozzolàre, *v.i.* 1. (*levare i bozzoli dalle frasche*) to take the cocoons from the branches 2. (*uscire dal bozzolo*) to come out of the cocoon.

sbozzolatúra, *s.f.* taking the cocoons from the branches.

sbracàre, *v.t.* to unbreech; (*sl.*) to debag ‖ **sbracàrsi**, *v.r.* to take off one's breeches; to take off one's trousers‖ — *dalle risa*, to split one's sides (with laughter).

sbracataménte, *av.* 1. (*spensieratamente*) carelessly 2. (*sguaiatamente*) unbecomingly: *ridere* —, to split one's sides (with laughter).

sbracàto, *ag.* 1. (*con gli abiti in disordine*) with (one's) clothes in disorder 2. (*spensierato*) care-free: *vita sbracata*, care-free life 3. (*sguaiato*) unseemly, unbecoming; vulgar: *modi sbracati*, unseemly manners.

sbracciàre, *v.t.* to take (sthg.) off one's arm ‖ *v.i.* to gesticulate ‖ **sbracciàrsi**, *v.r.* 1. (*rimboccarsi le maniche*) to roll up one's sleeves, to turn up one's sleeves 2. *fig.* (*darsi da fare*) to strive, to struggle, to make efforts.

sbracciàto, *ag.* with bare arms.

sbracería, *s.f.* (*millanteria*) swaggering, boasting.

sbraciàre, *v.t.* to stir, to poke: — *il fuoco*, to poke (o to stir) the fire.

sbraciatóio, *s.m.* poker.

sbraitaménto, *s.m.* shouting, bawling.

sbraitàre, *v.i.* to shout, to bawl.

sbraitío, *s.m.* shouting, bawling.

sbraitóna, *s.f.*, **sbraitóne**, *s.m.* shouter, bawler.

sbranaménto, *s.m.* tearing to pieces.

sbranàre, *v.t.* to tear to pieces: *l'agnello fu sbranato dal lupo*, the lamb was torn to pieces and devoured by the wolf.

sbrancaménto, *s.m.* separation from the flock.

sbrancàre, *v.t.* 1. (*togliere dal branco*) to take from the flock, to separate 2. (*disperdere*) to disperse, to scatter ‖ **sbrancàrsi**, *v.r.* 1. (*di animali*) to stray from the flock 2. (*di persone*) to disperse, to scatter.

sbrandellàre, *v.t.* to tear (in)to shreds.

sbrandellàto, *ag.* torn, ragged.

sbràno, *s.m.* tear, rent.

sbrattàre, *v.t.* 1. (*pulire*) to clean 2. (*sgombrare*) to clear.

sbrattàta, *s.f.* 1. (*il pulire*) cleaning 2. (*lo sgombrare*) clearing.

sbràtto, *s.m.* 1. (*pulitura*) cleaning 2. (*sgombero*) clearing: *stanza di* —, box-room.

sbravazzàre, *v.i.* (*millantare*) to brag, to boast.

sbravazzóne, *s.m.* (*millantatore*) braggart, boaster.

sbreccàre, *v.t.* to chip: — *l'orlo di una tazza*, to chip the edge of a cup.

sbrendolàre, *v.i.* to hang (down) in rags; (*pendere giù*) to dangle.

sbréndolo, *s.m.* tatter, shred, rag.

sbrendellóne, *V.* **sbrindellóne**.

sbriciolaménto, *s.m.* crumbling.

sbriciolàre, *v.t.* to crumble: — *pane*, to crumble bread ‖ **sbriciolàrsi**, *v.r.* to crumble: *una torta che si sbriciola facilmente*, a cake that crumbles easily.

sbriciolatúra, *s.f.* 1. (*briciole*) crumbs (*pl.*) 2. (*lo sbriciolare*) crumbling.

sbrigàre, *v.t.* to finish off, to dispatch, to expedite; to get through (sthg.); (*sl.*) to knock off: *in pochi minuti sbrigò ogni cosa*, in a few minutes he dealt with (o fixed) everything; — *affari*, to dispatch business; — *una gran quantità di lavoro*, to get through a great deal of work; — *un lavoro*, to finish off a piece of work ‖ — *qlcu.*, (*mandarlo all'altro mondo*) to finish s.o. off (o to dispatch s.o. o to settle s.o. o to settle s.o.'s hash); (*mandarlo via*) to deal with s.o. (o to get rid of s.o. quickly) ‖ — *una questione*, (*risolverla*) to settle a matter ‖ **sbrigàrsi**, *v.r.* to hurry up, to hasten, to make haste: *sbrigati, è ora di andare*, hurry up (o be quick), it is time to go ‖ — *di qlcu.*, to get rid of s.o.

sbrigativaménte, *av.* expeditiously, quickly.

sbrigatívo, *ag.* expeditious, quick, hasty, speedy: *il modo più* —, the most expeditious way; *una persona sbrigativa*, a person who deals with things quickly; *risposta sbrigativa*, hasty answer.

sbrigliaménto, *s.m.* unbridling.

sbrigliàre, *v.t.* 1. to unbridle 2. *fig.* (*sfrenare*) to unbridle, to let loose, to loosen: — *la fantasia*, to give free rein to one's imagination (o to let one's fancy rove) ‖ *v.i.* to pull the bridle ‖ **sbrigliàrsi**, *v.r.* 1. to free oneself of the bridle 2. *fig.* (*sfrenarsi*) to throw off all restraint.

sbrigliàta, *s.f.* 1. tug at the bridle 2. *fig.* (*rimprovero*) rebuke.

sbrigliataménte, *av.* without restraint, freely.

sbrigliatézza, *s.f.* unruliness.

sbrigliàto, *ag.* 1. (*di cavallo*) unbridled 2. *fig.* (*sfrenato*) unbridled, unrestrained, unchecked 3. (*indisciplinato*) unruly.

sbrindellàre, *v.t.* to tear to pieces ‖ *v.i.* to hang (down) in rags; (*pendere giù*) to dangle.

sbrindèllo, *s.m.* tatter, shred, rag.

sbrindellóne, *s.m.* **1.** (*straccione*) tatterdemalion, ragamuffin **2.** (*persona vestita sciattamente*) slovenly person.

sbroccàre, *v.t.* **1.** (*ind. serica*) to cleanse **2.** (*brucare*) to browse on (sthg.).

sbroccatúra, *s.f.* (*ind. serica*) cleansing.

sbròcco, *s.m.* (*ind. serica*) floss-silk.

sbroccolàre, *v.t.* (*brucare*) to browse on (sthg.).

sbrodolaménto, *s.m.* soiling, staining.

sbrodolàre, *v.t.* **1.** to soil: *ho sbrodolato il vestito di latte*, I have spilt milk on my dress **2.** — *un lungo discorso*, to make a prolix speech ‖ **sbrodolàrsi**, *v.r.* to spill sthg. on one's clothes.

sbrodolatúra, *s.f.* **1.** (*macchia*) stain **2.** (*discorso senza senso*) rigmarole.

sbrodolóna, *s.f.*, **sbrodolóne**, *s.m.* **1.** slovenly eater **2.** (*chi parla confusamente*) babbler, gabbler.

sbrogliaménto, *s.m.* disentanglement; extrication.

sbrogliàre, *v.t.* **1.** to disentangle, to unravel; to extricate: — *una matassa*, to disentangle a skein; — *qlcu. da una difficoltà*, to extricate s.o. from a difficulty **2.** (*sgombrare*) to clear: — *la tavola*, to clear the table ‖ **sbrogliàrsi**, *v.r.* to extricate oneself: *mi sono sbrogliato senza il suo aiuto*, I managed without his help.

sbrogliàto, *ag.* (*sgombro*) clear.

sbronciàre, **sbroncíre**, *v.i.* (*imbronciarsi*) to pout.

sbrónza, *V.* **sbòrnia**.

sbrucàre, *v.t.* to browse (on).

sbruffàre, *v.t.* **1.** (*spruzzare*) to besprinkle **2.** (*corrompere*) to bribe ‖ *v.i.* (*ingannare con vanterie*) to bluff, to brag.

sbruffàta, *s.f.* **1.** (*spruzzata*) sprinkling **2.** (*smargiassata*) bluff.

sbrúffo, *s.m.* **1.** (*spruzzo*) sprinkle **2.** (*denaro dato per ottenere ql.co. illegalmente*) bribe.

sbruffóne, *s.m.* (*dial.*) braggart, boaster.

sbucàre, *v.i.* **1.** to come out (of a place): *da dove è sbucata la talpa?*, where did the mole come out of? **2.** *fig.* to spring: *da dove sei sbucato?*, where have you sprung (*o* come) from? ‖ *v.t.* (*rar.*) to drive out, to dislodge.

sbucciapatàte, *s.m.* potato-peeler.

sbucciàre, *v.t.* **1.** to peel: — *un'arancia*, to peel an orange; — *una mela, una pera, una patata*, to peel an apple, a pear, a potato **2.** (*sgranare*) to shell: — *piselli, fagioli*, to shell peas, beans **3.** (*togliere la loppa a*) to husk ‖ **sbucciàrsi**, *v.r.* **1.** to graze oneself: — *un ginocchio*, to graze a knee **2.** (*cambiare la pelle*) to slough one's skin, to cast one's skin: *i serpenti si sbucciano*, snakes slough their skins.

sbucciatúra, *s.f.* **1.** (*lo sbucciare*) peeling; (*lo sgusciare*) shelling **2.** (*le pelli tolte di mele, pere, ecc.*) peelings (*pl.*); (*i gusci di piselli, ecc.*) pods (*pl.*): — *di patate*, potato peelings **3.** (*il togliere la loppa*) husking **4.** (*scalfittura*) scratch.

sbuccióna, *s.f.*, **sbuccióne**, *s.m.* (*fam.*) (*scansafatiche*) idler.

sbudellaménto, *s.m.* **1.** disembowelling **2.** (*di polli*) drawing **3.** (*di pesci*) gutting **4.** (*l'uccidere con pugnalata*) stabbing (to death).

sbudellàre, *v.t.* **1.** to disembowel **2.** (*polli*) to draw **3.** (*pesci*) to gut **4.** (*uccidere con pugnalata*) to stab (to death) ‖ **sbudellàrsi**, *v.r.* to disembowel oneself ‖ — *dal ridere*, (*pop.*) to split one's sides with laughter ‖ *v.r. reciproco* to stab each other (one another).

sbuffànte, *ag.* puffing.

sbuffàre, *v.i.* **1.** (*ansimare*) to pant, to puff: *egli sbuffava*, he was puffing and blowing **2.** (*per ira, noia*) to snort; to fume **3.** (*detto di vento*) to blow **4.** (*gettare buffi di fumo*) to puff away: *la locomotiva sbuffava*, the engine was puffing away; *il vapore sbuffava dalla pentola*, the steam was puffing out of the pot ‖ *v.t.* to blow out.

sbuffàta, *s.f.* **1.** puff **2.** (*per ira, noia*) snort.

sbúffo, *s.m.* **1.** puff; (*di vento*) gust: *uno — di fumo*, a puff of smoke ‖ *maniche a sbuffo*, puff(ed) sleeves **2.** (*per ira, noia*) snort.

sbugiardàre, *v.t.* to give the lie to (s.o.).

sbullonàre, *v.t.* to unbolt.

sburràre, *v.t.* (*scremare*) to skim.

sburràto, *ag.* (*scremato*) skimmed.

sbuzzàre, *V.* **sbudellàre**.

scàbbia, *s.f.* **1.** (*patol.*) scabies, itch, psora **2.** (*delle pecore*) mange.

scabbióso, *ag.* scabby, scabbed.

scabíno, *s.m.* (*st.*) echevin.

scabrézza, *s.f.* roughness, ruggedness (anche *fig.*).

scàbro, *ag.* rough, rugged (anche *fig.*): *stile* —, rough (*o* rugged) style; *strada scabra*, rough (*o* bumpy) road; *superficie scabra*, rough (*o* rugged *o* uneven) surface.

scabrosaménte, *av.* roughly, ruggedly.

scabrosità, *s.f.* **1.** roughness, ruggedness **2.** *fig.* difficulty: *limare le* —, to eliminate the difficulties.

scabróso, *ag.* **1.** rough, rugged: *pietra scabrosa*, rough stone **2.** *fig.* difficult, scabrous, delicate, awkward: *argomento* —, scabrous (*o* delicate) subject; *domanda scabrosa*, delicate (*o* awkward) question.

scaccàto, **scaccheggiàto**, *ag.* chequered, checkered.

scàcchi, *V.* **scàcco 2. 3.**.

scacchièra, *s.f.* (*per gli scacchi*) chess-board; (*per la dama*) draught-board.

scacchière, *s.m.* **1.** (*mil.*) (*zona*) zone **2.** (*st.*) *Scacchiere*, Exchequer: *Cancelliere dello Scacchiere*, Chancellor of the Exchequer; *Corte dello Scacchiere*, Court of Exchequer. **3.** *V.* **scacchièra**.

scacchista, *s.c.* chess-player.

scacchístico, *ag.* chess (*attributivo*).

scàccia, *s.m.* (*nella caccia*) (*battitore*) beater.

scacciacàni, *s.m.* dummy pistol.

scacciafúmo, *s.m.* (*mil.*) air blast.

scacciaménto, *s.m.* driving away; driving out.

scacciamósche, *s.m.* fly-flap, fly-whisk, fly-killer.

scacciapensièri, *s.m.* **1.** recreation, pastime: *questo libro è un buon* —, this book helps to pass the time away **2.** (*strumento musicale*) Jew's harp.

scacciàre, *v.t.* to drive away; to drive out, to dispel; (*espellere*) to expel: *il lavoro scaccia la noia*, work dispels boredom; *il vento scacciò tutte le nuvole*, the wind drove away all the clouds; — *dubbi, timori, preoccupazioni*, to dispel (*o* to drive away) doubts, fears, worries; — *le mosche*, to drive away the flies; — *il nemico dalla città*, to drive the enemy out of the town; — *un ragazzo da scuola*, to expel a boy from school ‖ *chiodo scaccia chiodo*, *prov.* one pain drives out another.

scacciàta, *s.f.* driving away; driving out; (*espulsione*) expulsion.

scacciàto, *ag.* (*espulso*) expelled ‖ *s.m.* (*esule*) exile.

scaccíno, *s.m.* church-cleaner.

scàcco, *s.m.* **1.** (*quadratino di scacchiera*) square **2.** *pl.* (*disegno su tessuti, ecc.*) check (*sing.*): *disegno a scacchi*, check pattern ‖ *vedere il sole a scacchi*, *fig.* to be behind bars **3.** *pl.* (*giuoco*) chess (*sing.*): *il giuoco degli scacchi*, the game of chess; *pezzi degli scacchi*, chess-men; *fare una partita a scacchi*, to play (*o* to have) a game of chess; *giuocare a scacchi*, to play (at) chess ‖ — *matto*, checkmate; *dare* — *a qlcu.*, to check s.o. (*o* to frustrate s.o.'s plans); *dare* — *matto*, to checkmate (anche *fig.*); *dare lo* — *matto in tre mosse*, to checkmate the king in three moves (*o* to mate in three); *tenere qlcu. in* —, to hold (*o* to keep) s.o. in check **4.** (*sconfitta*) loss; (*insuccesso*) check, set-back: *subire uno* —, to suffer a loss; (*un insuccesso*) to suffer a check (*o* set-back).

scadènte, *ag.* **1.** poor, shoddy; of inferior quality: *cibo* —, poor food; *merce* —, goods of inferior quality; *stoffa* —, shoddy cloth **2.** (*comm.*) (*che scade*) falling due.

scadènza, *s.f.* (*comm.*) maturity; (*di contratto*) expiry: — *a giorno fisso*, maturity on a fixed day; — *a vista*, maturity at sight; — *indeterminata*, maturity at will; — *lontana, prossima*, distant, near maturity; — *media*, average maturity; *alla — della cambiale*, on maturity of the bill (*o* on the bill falling due); *in ordine di* —, in reference to maturity; *prolungare la* —, to extend maturity ‖ *a* —, on term: *acquisto a* —, purchase on term (*o* time bargain) ‖ *a breve, lunga* —, at short, long maturity: *cambiale a breve, lunga* —, short-, long-dated bill; *effetti a lunga* —, long-run effects; *programma, attività a lunga* —, long-term programme, activity; *lo farò a breve* —, I'll do it in a short time.

scadenzàrio, *s.m.* (*comm.*) (discount) bill-book; (*amer.*) tickler.

scadenzière, (*rar.*) per **scadenzàrio**.

scadére, *v.i.* 1. to expire: *il contratto, il periodo di prova scade oggi*, the contract, the trial-period expires today; *il termine è scaduto il...*, the term expired on... 2. (*di cambiali, pagamenti, ecc.*) to become due, to fall due, to mature, to be due: *la cambiale è scaduta da due giorni*, the bill has been due two days (*o* is two days overdue); *questa cambiale scade fra un mese*, this bill will fall due in a month's time 3. (*peggiorare*) to fall off; (*diminuire*) to go down, to decrease: *la qualità della vostra merce è scaduta in questi ultimi anni*, the quality of your goods has fallen off these last few years; — *di valore*, to decrease in value ‖ *egli mi è molto scaduto*, he has sunk very much in my estimation.

scadiménto, *s.m.* decline, decay, falling off.

scadúto, *ag.* 1. expired: *il mese appena* —, the month just expired (*o* elapsed) 2. (*comm.*) due; overdue: *interessi scaduti*, interest due 3. (*decaduto*) deteriorated: *bellezza scaduta*, faded beauty.

scafàndro, *s.m.* diving-suit.

scafàrda, *s.f.* (*mar.*) small rowing-boat.

scaffalàre, *v.t.* to shelve.

scaffalatúra, *s.f.* 1. shelving 2. *V.* **scaffàle**.

scaffàle, *s.m.* shelf (*pl.* shelves); (*per libri*) book -shelf (*pl.* book-shelves); (*di magazzino*) stand: — *a rastrelliera*, rack.

scàfo, *s.m.* (*mar. aer.*) hull, body: — *ad ala portante*, (*mar.*) hydrofoil hull; — *esterno*, (*di sottomarino*) outer casing; — *resistente alla pressione*, (*mar.*) pressure -hull; — *saldato*, (*mar.*) welded hull; *longitudinalmente allo* —, (*mar.*) fore and aft; *trasversalmente allo* —, (*mar.*) athwartship.

scafocefalìa, *s.f.* (*med.*) scaphocephaly.

scafocèfalo, *ag.* (*med.*) scaphocephalic, scaphocephalous ‖ *s.m.* (*med.*) scaphocephaloid.

scafòide, *s.m.* (*anat.*) scaphoid.

scagionàre, *v.t.* to acquit; to exculpate; (*scusare*) to excuse; (*giustificare*) to justify ‖ **scagionàrsi**, *v.r.* to exculpate oneself; (*scusarsi*) to excuse oneself; (*giustificarsi*) to justify oneself.

scàglia, *s.f.* 1. flake; chip; scale: *le scaglie di un'armatura*, the scales of a piece of armour; — *di ferro*, scale of iron (*o* forge scale); — *di legno*, chip (*o* splinter *o* sliver) of wood; — *di pietra, diamante*, chip of stone, of diamond; *una* — *di sapone*, a flake of soap ‖ *sapone in scaglie*, soap-flakes 2. (*di rettili, pesci*) scale.

scagliàbile, *ag.* throwable.

scagliaménto, *s.m.* flinging, hurling; throwing.

scagliàre[1], *v.t.* to fling, to hurl; to throw; to shy: — *bombe*, to throw bombs; (*sganciarle*) to drop bombs; — *insulti, minacce a qlcu.*, to hurl insults, threats at s.o.; — *sassi contro qlcu.*, to fling stones at s.o. ‖ **scagliàrsi**, *v.r.* to hurl oneself, to throw oneself, to dash, to rush; to assail (s.o., sthg.): *le onde si scagliano sulla scogliera*, the waves dash against the cliffs; *si scagliò avanti*, he rushed forward; *si scagliò contro di me con un mucchio di insulti*, he assailed me with a string of insults; *si scagliò verso il nemico*, he hurled himself at (*o* against) the enemy.

scagliàre[2], *v.t.* (*togliere scaglie a*) to scale.

scagliatóre, *s.m.*, **scagliatrice**, *s.f.* thrower.

scagliatúra, *s.f.* scaling.

scagliétta, *s.f.* (*di pietra*) splinter.

scagliòla, *V.* **scagliuòla**.

scaglionaménto, *s.m.* (*mil.*) arrangement in echelons.

scaglionàre, *v.t.* 1. to divide into groups 2. (*mil.*) to echelon.

scaglióne, *s.m.* 1. (*gruppo*) group: *a scaglioni*, in groups 2. (*mil.*) echelon 3. (*ampio gradino*) large step 4. (*di monte*) mountain-terrace.

scagliòso, *ag.* scaly.

scagliuòla, *s.f.* 1. (*min.*) scagliola 2. (*bot.*) canary -grass.

scagnòzzo, *s.m.* 1. (*prete povero*) poor priest 2. (*lavoratore maldestro*) bungler, botcher 3. (*tirapiedi*) hanger-on, understrapper: *gira sempre accompagnato dai suoi scagnozzi*, (*fam.*) he always goes around surrounded by his gang.

scàla, *s.f.* 1. staircase, stairway; stairs (*pl.*); (*trasportabile*) ladder: — *a chiocciola*, spiral (*o* winding *o* corkscrew) staircase; — *a due rampe*, staircase with two flights; — *a pioli*, (rung-)ladder; — *da pompieri*, fireman's ladder; — *di comando, di fuori banda*, (*mar.*) accomodation-ladder; — *di corda*, rope-ladder; — *di servizio*, backstairs; — *di sicurezza*, fire-escape; — *esterna*, perron; — *mobile*, moving staircase; — *pieghevole*, folding ladder; — *porta, da aggiuntare*, extension ladder; — *portatile a libretto*, step-ladder (*o* pair of steps); *una rampa di scale*, a flight of stairs; *la tromba delle scale*, the stair-well; *questa casa ha due scale*, this house has two staircases; *montare su una* — (*trasportabile*), to mount (*o* to climb) a ladder; *ruzzolare dalle scale*, to fall downstairs; *salire le scale*, to go upstairs (*o* to climb the stairs); *scendere le scale*, to go downstairs; *salire, scendere le scale di corsa*, to run upstairs, downstairs (*o* to run up, down the stairs) 2. (*scala graduata*) scale: — *decimale, logaritmica*, decimal, logarithmic scale; — *dei venti*, wind-scale; — *mobile*, (*econ.*) sliding scale; — *parlante*, (*rad.*) tuning-dial; — *telemetrica*, (*di cannoni*) range scale; — *ticonica*, diagonal scale; — 1:1, 1:2, 1:4, full-, half-, quarter- scale; *disegno in* —, scale drawing; *questa carta è alla* — *dell'uno a mille*, this map is drawn to a scale of one to a thousand; *esercitarsi a fare le scale al pianoforte*, to practise scales on the piano 3. (*proporzione*) scale: *su vasta* —, on a vast scale 4. (*al poker*) straight: — *reale*, straight flush.

scalaménto, *s.m.* 1. scaling, climbing 2. (*aer.*) (*delle ali*) stagger 3. (*riduzione*) reduction, scaling-down.

scalandróne, *s.m.* (*mar.*) foot-board, gang-board.

scalappiàre, *v.t.* to free from a snare; to disentangle ‖ **scalappiàrsi**, *v.r.* to free oneself from a snare; to disentangle oneself.

scalàre[1], *ag.* gradual; graduated; proportional ‖ *interesse* —, (*econ.*) scaled (*o* diminishing) interest.

scalàre[2], *v.t.* 1. to climb (up), to scale; (*st. mil.*) to escalade: — *una montagna*, to climb a mountain; — *un muro*, to scale a wall 2. (*diminuire*) to scale down: — *un debito*, to scale down a debt 3. (*a maglia*) to decrease.

scalàta, *s.f.* climbing, scaling; (*st. mil.*) escalade: *dare la* — *a*, to climb (*o* to scale); *dare la* — *al potere*, to climb to power.

scalàto, *ag.* graduated.

scalatóre, *s.m.*, **scalatríce**, *s.f.* climber; (*rocciatore*) rock-climber.

scalcagnàre, *v.i.* to walk heel and toe ‖ *v.t.* 1. to wear down the heels of (one's shoes) 2. (*maltrattare*): — *qlcu.*, to walk all over s.o. (*o* to trample on s.o.).

scalcagnàto, *ag.* 1. down-at-heel 2. (*sciatto*) down -at-heel, shabby, seedy.

scalcàre, *v.t.* to carve.

scalciàre, *v.i.* to kick (out).

scalciàta, *s.f.* kick; kicking out.

scalcinàre, *v.t.* to scrape the plaster off (sthg.), to remove the plaster from (sthg.) ‖ **scalcinàrsi**, *v.r.* to peel.

scalcinàto, *ag.* 1. (*privato d'intonaco*) unplastered 2. (*sciatto*) shabby.

scalcinatúra, *s.f.* removal of plaster.

scàlco, *s.m.* **1.** (*chi trincia vivande*) carver **2.** (*lo scalcare*) carving: *coltello da* —, carving-knife.

scaldabàgno, *s.m.* geyser; water-heater.

scaldacòlla, *s.m.* glue-warming apparatus.

scaldalètto, *s.m.* warming-pan, bed-warmer.

scaldamàni, **scaldamàno**, *s.m.* hand-warmer.

scaldaménto, *s.m.* heating, warming.

scaldapànche, *s.m.* lazy-bones, lazy-boots; (*amer.*) chair-warmer.

scaldapiàtti, *s.m.* dish-warmer, chafing-dish.

scaldapièdi, *s.m.* foot-warmer.

scaldàre, *v.t.* to heat; (*moderatamente*) to warm (anche *fig.*): *notizia che scalda il cuore*, news that warms the heart; — *l'aria di una stanza*, to warm the air of a room; — *dell'acqua*, to heat some water; — *l'immaginazione*, to fire the imagination; — *le mani vicino al fuoco*, to warm one's hands at the fire; — *una minestra*, to warm up a soup ‖ **scaldàrsi**, *v.r.* **1.** to warm oneself; to heat (up); to get warm, to warm up (anche *fig.*): *l'acqua si scalda*, the water is heating; — *al fuoco, al sole*, to warm oneself at the fire, in the sun **2.** (*eccitarsi*) to get excited; (*arrabbiarsi*) to get angry: — *per niente*, to get excited over nothing.

scaldasèggiole, *s.m.* lazy-bones, lazy-boots; (*amer.*) chair-warmer.

scaldàta, *s.f.* warming (up): *dare una* — *alla minestra*, to warm up the soup.

scaldavivànde, *s.m.* dish-warmer, chafing-dish.

scaldíno, *s.m.* hand-warmer.

scaldíglia, *s.f.* (*strumento termico*) heater.

scàldo, *s.m.* (*st.*) (*bardo*) scald, skald.

scalèa, *s.f.* flight of steps; flight of stairs; staircase.

scalèno, *ag.* **1.** (*geom.*) scalene: *triangolo* —, scalene triangle **2.** *muscolo* —, (*anat.*) scalene muscle (*o* scalenus).

scalenoèdro, *s.m.* (*geom.*) scalenohedron.

scalèo, *s.m.* double ladder.

scalettàre, *v.t.* **1.** to terrace **2.** (*rubrica, registro*) to provide with a thumb-index.

scalettàto, *ag.* **1.** terraced **2.** (*di rubrica, registro*) (provided) with a thumb-index.

scalfaròtto, **scalferòtto**, *s.m.* fur-lined slipper.

scalfíre, *v.t.* to scratch: — *il vetro*, to cut glass ‖ **scalfírsi**, *v.r.* to get scratched: — *un dito*, to scratch one's finger.

scalfit(t)úra, *s.f.* scratch.

scalímetro, *s.m.* (*disegno*) draftsman's scale.

scalinàta, *s.f.* flight of steps; steps (*pl.*); staircase; stairs (*pl.*).

scalíno, *s.m.* **1.** step (anche *fig.*); (*di scala a pioli*) rung **2.** (*miner.*) bench.

scalmàna, *s.f.* **1.** (*med.*) cold; chill **2.** (*infatuazione*) (passing) fancy, fad: *prendere una* — *per ql.co.*, to take a fancy to sthg.

scalmanàrsi, *v.r.* **1.** to catch a cold; to catch a chill **2.** (*agitarsi eccessivamente*) to get excited, to get worked up: *non scalmanarti per così poco*, don't get excited about such a trifle **3.** (*darsi da fare*) to bustle (about sthg.).

scalmanàta, *s.f.* rush.

scalmanàto, *ag.* **1.** out of breath, breathless **2.** (*eccitato*) excited.

scalmanatúra, *V.* scalmàna.

scalmièra, *s.f.* (*mar.*) rowlock.

scàlmo, *s.m.* **1.** (*mar.*) rowlock **2.** (*costruzioni navali*) futtock, timber: — *di cubia*, hawse timber; *primo, secondo* —, first, second futtock.

scalmòtto, *s.m.* (*mar.*) bulwark stay.

scàlo, *s.m.* **1.** (*aer. mar.*) (*luogo, fermata per carico e scarico*) call: — *intermedio*, (*aer.*) intermediate landing (*o* call); (*mar.*) intermediate port (*o* call); *porto di* —, port of call; *fare* — *a*, (*aer.*) to land (*o* to call) at; (*mar.*) to put in (*o* to call) at; *volo senza* —, non-stop flight **2.** (*ferr.*) goods-station; (*amer.*) freight-yard **3.** (*mar.*) (*impalcatura di sostegno per navi*):

— *di alaggio*, slip (*o* slipway); — *di costruzione*, building-slip (*o* stocks); *una nave allo* —, a ship on the stocks.

scalógna[1], *s.f.* (*bot.*) sha(l)lot, scallion.

scalógna[2], *s.f.* (*fam.*) (*sfortuna*) bad luck, ill luck.

scalognàto, *ag.* (*fam.*) (*sfortunato*) unlucky.

scalóne, *s.m.* great staircase.

scalòppa, **scaloppína**, *s.f.* (*cuc.*) veal cutlet.

scalpellàre, *v.t.* **1.** to chisel; to engrave; to chip **2.** (*cancellare, distruggere con scalpello*) to chisel off.

scalpellatóre, *s.m.*, **scalpellatríce**, *s.f.* engraver.

scalpellatúra, *s.f.* engraving; chiselling.

scalpellinàre, *V.* scalpellàre.

scalpellíno, *s.m.* stone-cutter, stone-dresser.

scalpèllo, *s.m.* **1.** chisel; (*miner.*) bit; (*chir.*) scalpel: — *a caldo, a freddo*, hot, cold chisel; — *ad alette*, wing-bit; — *a punta di diamante*, diamond chisel (*o* diamond-pointed bit); — *da calafato*, chinsing-iron; — *da falegname*, woodwork chisel; — *da fonderia*, flogging chisel; — *da marmista*, double-facet cape chisel; — *da muratore*, stone chisel; — *da sbozzo*, boaster; — *da tornitore*, turning chisel; — *tondo*, gouge **2.** *fig.* (*scultore*) sculptor **3.** *fig.* (*scultura*) sculpture.

scalpicciaménto, *V.* scalpiccío.

scalpicciàre, *v.i.* **1.** (*di animale*) to paw (the ground) **2.** (*di persona*) to shuffle; to shuffle along; to slouch along.

scalpiccío, *s.m.* **1.** (*di animale*) pawing (the ground) **2.** (*di persona*) shuffling.

scalpitaménto, *s.m.* (*di cavallo*) pawing (the ground).

scalpitànte, *ag.* **1.** (*di cavallo*) pawing (the ground) **2.** *fig.* (*di persona*) stamping.

scalpitàre, *v.i.* **1.** (*di cavallo*) to paw (the ground) **2.** *fig.* (*di persona*) to stamp.

scalpitío, *s.m.* **1.** (*di cavallo*) pawing (the ground) **2.** *fig.* (*di persona*) stamping.

scalpóre, *s.m.* fuss; noise: *per che cosa è tutto questo* —?, what is all this fuss about?; *fare molto* —, to make (*o* to kick up) a great fuss (about sthg.): *questo fatto fece molto* —, this fact was much talked about.

scaltraménte, *av.* shrewdly; (*spreg.*) cunningly, slyly, artfully, craftily.

scaltrézza, *s.f.* shrewdness; (*spreg.*) cunning, slyness, artfulness, craftiness.

scaltríre, *v.t.* to sharpen s.o.'s wits ‖ **scaltrírsi**, *v.r.* **1.** to become sharp, to become cunning; (*fam.*) to become crafty **2.** (*diventare esperto*) to become an expert.

scaltríto, *ag.* **1.** shrewd, sharp; (*spreg.*) cunning, sly, artful, crafty **2.** (*esperto*) experienced.

scàltro, *ag.* shrewd, sharp; (*spreg.*) cunning, sly, artful, crafty.

scalzacàne, **scalzacàni**, *s.m.* **1.** down-and-out; tramp **2.** (*incompetente*) botcher, bungler.

scalzaménto, *s.m.* **1.** taking off (s.o.'s) shoes and socks **2.** (*agr.*) hoeing **3.** (*lo smuovere alla base*) undermining (anche *fig.*).

scalzàre, *v.t.* **1.** (*togliere calze e scarpe a*) to take s.o.'s shoes and socks off **2.** (*agr.*) to hoe; to bare the roots of (a tree) **3.** (*smuovere alla base*) to undermine (anche *fig.*): *l'acqua del fiume sta scalzando questo muro*, the water of the river is undermining this wall; — *l'autorità di qlcu.*, to undermine s.o.'s authority; — *qlcu. dal suo ufficio*, to oust s.o. from (his) office ‖ **scalzàrsi**, *v.r.* **1.** to take one's shoes and socks off **2.** (*di dente*) to get loose.

scalzàto, *ag.* **1.** undermined (anche *fig.*) **2.** (*di cavallo*) unshod.

scàlzo, *ag.* barefoot, bare-footed: *essere, camminare* —, to be, to walk barefoot (*o* bare-footed) ‖ *Carmelitani Scalzi*, (*eccl.*) Barefooted (*o* Discalced) Carmelites.

Scamàndro, *no.pr.m.* (*geog. mit.*) Scamander.

scambiaménto, *s.m.* **1.** exchanging; (*scambio*) exchange **2.** (*per errore*) mistaking.

scambiàre, *v.t.* **1.** to exchange: — *parole, saluti*, to exchange words, greetings **2.** (*per errore*) to mistake :

— *una persona, una cosa per un'altra*, to mistake one person, one thing for another 3. (*barattare*) to barter ‖ **scambiàrsi**, *v.r. reciproco* to exchange; (*fam.*) to swap: *ci scambiamo dei francobolli*, we swap postage stamps; *ci siamo scambiati delle lettere*, there has been some correspondence between us; — *delle informazioni*, to exchange information.

scambiàto, *ag.* 1. wrong: *l'ombrello —*, the wrong umbrella 2. *occhi scambiati*, (*strabici*) squinting eyes.

scambiatóre, *s.m.* exchanger: — *di calore*, (*fis.*) heat exchanger; — *di ioni*, (*chim. fis.*) ion exchanger.

scambiétto, *s.m.* (*passo di danza*) entrechat; (cross-) caper.

scambiévole, *ag.* reciprocal, mutual.

scambievolézza, *s.f.* reciprocity, mutuality.

scambievolménte, *av.* reciprocally, mutually.

scàmbio, *s.m.* 1. exchange: — *di favori, di lettere, di prigionieri*, exchange of favours, of letters, of prisoners; *in — di ql.co.*, in exchange for sthg.; *c'era stato uno — di colpi*, there had been an exchange of blows (*o blows had been exchanged*); *fare uno —*, to make an exchange: *avevano fatto uno — di cappelli*, they had exchanged hats 2. (*comm.*) exchange; barter: *valore di —*, value in exchange (*o exchangeable value*) ‖ *libero —*, (*econ.*) free trade 3. (*ferr.*) points (*pl.*); (*amer.*) switch: — *doppio*, two-way frog; (*amer.*) three-throw (*o double*) switch; — *automatico*, self-acting turn-out; — *normale*, standard points 4. (*chim. fis.*) exchange: — *di base*, (*chim.*) exchange of base; — *di calore*, (*fis.*) heat-exchange (*o heat-transfer*) 5. — *aereo*, (*di filobus*) aerial-frog (*o trolley-frog*) 6. — *elettronico*, (*rad.*) electronic switching system.

scambista, *s.m.* 1. (*ferr.*) pointsman (*pl.* pointsmen); shunter; (*amer.*) switchman (*pl.* switchmen) 2. (*libero*) —, (*econ.*) free-trader.

scamiciàrsi, *v.r.* to take one's jacket off; to be in one's shirtsleeves.

scamiciàto, *ag.* shirt-sleeved (*attributivo*); in one's shirtsleeves (*predicativo*) ‖ *s.m.* 1. (*zotico*) oaf (*pl.* oafs, oaves), lout 2. (*sovversivo*) revolutionary: *teorie da —*, subversive political ideas.

scamonèa, *s.f.* (*bot. farm.*) scammony.

scamosciàre, *v.t.* to chamois.

scamosciàto, *ag.* shammy (*attributivo*); chamois (*attributivo*); suède (*attributivo*): *guanti scamosciati*, chamois (*o suède*) gloves; *pelle scamosciata*, shammy (*o wash*)-leather; *scarpe scamosciate*, suède shoes.

scamosciatúra, *s.f.* (*ind.*) oil tanning.

scamòscio, (*rar.*) *per* **scamosciàto**.

scamozzàre, *v.t.* to lop (off), to pollard.

scamozzatúra, *s.f.* lopping, pollarding.

scampafórca, *s.m.* gallows-bird; jail-bird.

scampagnàre, *v.i.* to go for a trip in the country.

scampagnàta, *s.f.* trip into the country.

scampanaménto, *s.m.* 1. chiming; pealing; bell-ringing 2. (*mec.*) (*difetto di motore*) piston slap.

scampanàre, *v.i.* 1. to chime; to peal 2. (*di gonna*) to flare, to flute 3. (*mec.*) (*di motore difettoso*) to slap 4. (*fonderia*) to rap.

scampanàta, *s.f.* chime; chiming; peal; ringing.

scampanatúra, *s.f.* 1. (*svasatura di gonna*) bell-mouth, flaring 2. (*fonderia*) rapping.

scampanellàre, *v.i.* to ring long and loudly.

scampanellàta, *s.f.* loud long ring.

scampanellío, *s.m.* long loud ring(ing).

scampanío, *s.m.* pealing (of bells).

scampàre, *v.t.* 1. (*salvare*) to save, to rescue, to deliver: *lo scampai dalla rovina*, I saved him from ruin ‖ *Dio ci scampi!*, God forbid! 2. (*evitare*) to avoid; to escape: — *un pericolo*, to escape a danger ‖ *l'hai scampata bella*, you've had a narrow escape (*o a narrow squeak o a close shave*) ‖ *v.i.* 1. to escape (sthg.): — *alla punizione*, to escape punishment; — *da morte*, to escape death; — *per miracolo*, to have a miraculous escape 2. (*rifugiarsi*) to take refuge.

scampàto, *ag.* 1. saved, rescued, delivered 2. (*evitato*) avoided; escaped.

scàmpo[1], *s.m.* escape, safety: *dobbiamo trovare uno —*, we must find a way of escape; *non c'è (via di) —*, there is no escape (*o there is no way out*); *cercare, trovare — nella fuga*, to seek, to find safety in flight.

scàmpo[2], *s.m.* (*zool.*) nephrop ‖ *scampi*, (*cuc.*) scampi.

scàmpolo, *s.m.* remnant, fent: *vendita di scampoli*, remnant sale ‖ — *di tempo*, spare moment.

scanalàre, *v.t.* 1. to groove, to channel 2. (*arch.*) to flute, to channel 3. (*mec.*) to groove, to spline.

scanalàto, *ag.* 1. grooved, channelled 2. (*arch.*) fluted, channelled 3. (*mec.*) grooved, splined: *albero —*, splined shaft.

scanalatúra, *s.f.* 1. groove; grooving 2. (*arch.*) flute; fluting 3. (*mec.*) spline; groove: — *per guarnizione*, packing groove; — *per lubrificazione*, oil groove.

scancellàre, *V.* **cancellàre**.

scancío, *s.m.*: *di, a, per —*, askew, awry; askance: *guardare di —*, to look askance.

scandagliàre, *v.t.* 1. to sound: — *un canale*, to sound a channel 2. *fig.* to sound, to fathom: — *i sentimenti di qlcu.*, to sound s.o.'s feelings.

scandagliàta, *s.f.* sounding.

scandagliatóre, *s.m.* leadsman (*pl.* leadsmen), sounder.

scandàglio, *s.m.* (*mar.*) 1. sounding-lead, sounding-line, plummet, sounding-rod: — *acustico*, echo sounder (*o sonic depth finder*); — *di profondità*, bathometer; — *meccanico*, sounding machine; — *ultrasonoro*, supersonic sounding set; *gettare lo —*, to heave the lead 2. (*lo scandagliare*) sounding: *fare gli scandagli*, to take soundings 3. *fig.* sounding.

scandalísmo, *s.m.* scandal-mongering.

scandalísta, *s.c.* scandal-monger.

scandalístico, *ag.* scandal-mongering.

scandalizzàre, *v.t.* to scandalize, to shock ‖ **scandalizzàrsi**, *v.r.* to be scandalized, to be shocked: — *per nulla*, to be shocked at nothing.

scandalizzatóre, *ag.* scandalizing, shocking ‖ *s.m.*, **scandalizzatríce**, *s.f.* scandalizer.

scàndalo, *s.m.* scandal: *libro che fa —*, book that shocks the public; *evitare uno —*, to avoid a public scandal; *dar —*, to scandalize; *fare uno —*, to stir up a scandal; *sollevare uno —*, to give rise to a scandal ‖ *pietra dello —*, (chief) culprit ‖ *gridare allo —*, to cry shame.

scandalosaménte, *av.* scandalously, disgracefully.

scandalóso, *ag.* scandalous, shocking, disgusting, shameful, disgraceful: *notizia scandalosa*, shocking news; *è — che non abbia ancora pagato i suoi debiti*, it is disgraceful that he has not yet paid his debts.

scandènte, *ag.* (*bot.*) (*rampicante*) rambling, climbing.

scàndere, *V.* **scandíre**.

Scandinàvia, *no.pr.f.* (*geog.*) Scandinavia.

scandínavo, *ag. s.m.* Scandinavian.

scàndio, *s.m.* (*chim.*) scandium.

scandíre, *v.t.* 1. to scan: — *un verso*, to scan a line 2. (*mus.*) to stress 3. (*parole, sillabe*) to syllabize.

scannabécco, *s.m.* (*coltello da macellaio*) butcher's knife.

scannapagnòtte, scannapàne, *s.m.* (*buono a nulla*) good-for-nothing.

scannàre[1], *v.t.* 1. to cut s.o.'s throat, to slit s.o.'s throat; (*un maiale*) to stick 2. (*uccidere crudelmente*) to butcher, to slaughter 3. (*far pagare eccessivamente*) to fleece, to skin; (*rovinare*) to ruin: *locandiere che scanna gli avventori*, inn-keeper who fleeces his customers.

scannàre[2], *v.t.* (*ind. tessile*) to unwind, to unroll.

scannatóio, *s.m.* slaughter-house, abattoir.

scannatóre, *s.m.* 1. cut-throat; slaughterer 2. (*strozzino*) usurer.

scannatúra, *s.f.* slaughtering.

scannellaménto, *V.* **scannellatúra**.

scannellàre, *v.t.* **1.** (*scanalare*) to groove, to channel **2.** (*arch.*) to flute, to channel **3.** (*ind. tessile*) (*svolgere dal cannello*) to unwind, to unroll.

scannellàto, *ag.* **1.** (*scanalato*) grooved, channelled **2.** (*arch.*) fluted, channelled **3.** (*ind. tessile*) unwound, unrolled.

scannellatúra, *s.f.* **1.** (*scanalatura*) groove; grooving **2.** (*arch.*) flute; fluting **3.** (*ind. tessile*) unwinding, unrolling.

scannèllo, *s.m.* (*macelleria*) rump-steak.

scànno, *s.m.* **1.** seat; (*di coro*) stall **2.** (*mar.*) sand-bank.

scanonicàre, *v.t.* to deprive of the status of canon.

scansafatíche, *s.m.* lazy-bones, lazy-boots.

scansaménto, *s.m.* avoiding, shunning; escaping (sthg., from sthg.).

scansàre, *v.t.* to avoid; to shun; to escape (sthg., from sthg.): *tutti lo scansano*, everybody shuns him; — *un pericolo, un ostacolo*, to avoid a danger, an obstacle ‖ — *un colpo*, to ward off a blow ‖ **scansàrsi**, *v.r.* to step aside, to side-step.

scansía, *s.f.* shelves (pl.); (*per libri*) book-case.

scansióne, *s.f.* **1.** (*di versi*) scansion **2.** (*mus.*) stressing **3.** (*di parole, sillabe*) syllabification; (*il compitare*) spelling **4.** (*tv.*) scanning.

scànso, *s.m.* avoidance ‖ *a* — *di*, (in order) to avoid: *a* — *di equivoci*, to avoid misunderstandings.

scantinàre, *v.i.* **1.** (*mus.*) (*andare fuori tempo*) to go out of tune **2.** *fig.* (*deviare dalla retta via*) to go astray.

scantinàto, *s.m.* basement.

scantonaménto, *s.m.* **1.** (*il levare gli spigoli*) rounding (off) (corners) **2.** (*l'evitare*) avoiding.

scantonàre, *v.t.* **1.** (*levare gli spigoli a*) to round off; to remove corners from (sthg.) **2.** (*evitare*) to avoid ‖ *v.i.* **1.** (*voltare l'angolo*) to turn the corner **2.** (*menare il can per l'aia*) to beat about the bush.

scantucciàre, *v.t.* (*pane*) to cut the crust off (bread).

scanzonàto, *ag.* free and easy, unconventional.

scapaccióne, *s.m.* slap, smack: *dare uno* — *a qlcu.*, to give s.o. a slap (o to box s.o.'s ears).

scapàre, *v.t.* to cut off the head of (a fish) ‖ **scapàrsi**, *v.r.* (*lambiccarsi il cervello*) to rack one's brains.

scapatàggine, *s.f.* **1.** recklessness, heedlessness **2.** (*azione da scapato*) reckless action.

scapataménte, *av.* recklessly, heedlessly.

scapàto, *ag.* reckless, heedless ‖ *alla scapata*, recklessly (o heedlessly) ‖ *s.m.* reckless man.

scapecchiàre, *v.t.* (*lino*) to hackle.

scapecchiatóio, *s.m.* flax-comb, (flax-)hackle.

scapestratàggine, *s.f.* **1.** (*avventatezza*) recklessness, rashness; (*sfrenatezza*) dissoluteness; wildness **2.** (*azione da scapestrato*) reckless action, rash action; wild action.

scapestrataménte, *av.* (*avventatamente*) recklessly, rashly; (*senza freno*) dissolutely; wildly.

scapestràto, *ag.* (*avventato*) reckless, rash, madcap (*attributivo*); (*sfrenato*) dissolute; wild ‖ *alla scapestrata*, (*avventatamente*) recklessly (o rashly); (*senza freno*) dissolutely (o wildly) ‖ *s.m.* madcap, scapegrace, dare-devil.

scapezzaménto, *s.m.* pollarding, lopping.

scapezzàre, *v.t.* to pollard, to lop.

scapézzo, *s.m.* pollarding, lopping.

scapigliàre, *v.t.* to dishevel: — *qlcu.*, to ruffle s.o.'s hair ‖ **scapigliàrsi**, *v.r.* to become dishevelled.

scapigliàto, *ag.* **1.** dishevelled, ruffled **2.** *fig.* disorderly, unruly, irregular, loose; (*di persona*) unconventional, free and easy: *vita scapigliata*, disorderly (o unruly o loose) life ‖ *s.m.* Bohemian.

scapigliatúra, *s.f.* loose living; unconventionality, Bohemianism ‖ *Scapigliatura*, "Scapigliatura" (late 19th Century Milanese literary movement).

scapitàre, *v.i.* **1.** to lose (sthg.); to suffer loss: *in questo affare ci scapito*, I lose by this business **2.** (*perdere nella reputazione*) to lose one's credit.

scàpito, *s.m.* **1.** damage, loss: *vendere a* —, to sell at a loss **2.** *fig.* detriment, prejudice: *con mio grave* —, to my great prejudice; *egli lavora troppo, a* — *della*

sua salute, he works too hard to the detriment of his health; *questo andrà a* — *della mia reputazione*, this will be prejudicial to my reputation.

scapitozzàre, *v.t.* to pollard.

scàpo, *s.m.* **1.** (*arch.*) scape, scapus (pl. scapi) **2.** (*bot.*) scape.

scàpola, *s.f.* (*anat.*) shoulder-blade, scapula (pl. scapulae).

scapolàre[1], *ag.* (*anat.*) scapular ‖ *s.m.* (*eccl.*) scapular.

scapolàre[2], *v.t.i.* (*scampare*) to escape: *l'hai scapolata bella*, you have escaped by the skin of your teeth.

scàpolo, *ag.* single, unmarried ‖ *s.m.* bachelor.

scappaménto, *s.m.* **1.** (*di gas, vapore*) escape **2.** (*di motori*) exhaust: *tubo, valvola di* —, exhaust pipe, valve **3.** (*ferr.*) blast pipe **4.** (*di orologio*) escapement.

scappàre, *v.i.* **1.** to escape, to run away, to flee: *scappa!*, run away! (o get away quickly!); *i nemici scapparono*, the enemy fled; — *di prigione*, to escape from prison ‖ *a scappa e fuggi*, (*in gran fretta*) in a tearing hurry ‖ *di qui non si scappa*, there is no escape (o getting away) from here ‖ *ho molta fretta, devo* —, I am in a great hurry, I must run off ‖ *mi scappa spesso la pazienza*, I often lose my patience (o temper) ‖ *i suoi vestiti gli sono scappati di misura*, he has grown out of his clothes ‖ — *a gambe levate*, to take to one's heels ‖ *far* — *qlcu.*, to help s.o. to escape **2.** (*sfuggire*): *mi lasciai* — *una bella occasione*, I missed a good opportunity; *la penna mi è scappata di mano*, the pen slipped from my fingers; *scrivilo, altrimenti ti scappa di mente*, write it down, otherwise you will forget it **3.** (*non potersi trattenere*): *mi scappò da ridere*, I could not help laughing **4.** (*saltar fuori*): *gli scappò una parola*, a word escaped him; *mi scappò detto che l'avevo*, without meaning to, I happened to say that I had it.

scappàta, *s.f.* **1.** (*fuga*) escape, flight **2.** (*breve visita*) call; short visit: *fare una* — *da qlcu.*, to pay s.o. a short visit (o to call on s.o.); *fare una* — *in un luogo*, to go somewhere for a short visit **3.** (*atto di leggerezza*) escapade: *in gioventù fece le sue scappate*, he sowed his wild oats in his youth **4.** (*motto, frizzo*) witty remark.

scappatóia, *s.f.* loop-hole, way out; subterfuge, shift: *cercare delle scappatoie*, to look for a way out; *trovare una* —, to find a loop-hole (o a way out).

scappavía, *s.f.* **1.** (*uscita segreta*) secret exit **2.** (*scappatoia*) subterfuge; loop-hole **3.** (*mar.*) (*iole*) gig.

scappellàre, *v.t.* (*mar.*) to unrig, to strip (mast, yard) ‖ **scappellàrsi**, *v.r.* (*levarsi il cappello*) to take off one's hat; (*per salutare*) to raise one's hat.

scappellàta, *s.f.* raising of one's hat: *fare scappellate a qlcu.*, to raise one's hat to s.o.

scappellottàre, *v.t.* to slap, to smack.

scappellòtto, *s.m.* slap, smack: *dare uno* — *a qlcu.*, to give s.o. a slap (o smack o to box s.o.'s ears); *prendere a scappellotti qlcu.*, to slap (o to smack) s.o.

scappucciàre[1], *v.t.* to take off s.o.'s hood, to unhood ‖ **scappucciàrsi**, *v.r.* to take off one's hood.

scappucciàre[2], *v.i.* **1.** (*inciampare*) to stumble **2.** *fig.* (*commettere un errore*) to make a blunder.

scappúccio, *s.m.* **1.** (*l'inciampare*) stumble **2.** (*errore*) blunder.

scapricciàre, scapriccíre, *v.t.*: — *qlcu.*, to cure s.o. of his whims ‖ **scapricciàrsi, scapriccírsi**, *v.r.* to satisfy one's whims.

scarabàttola, *s.f.* **1.** (*cristalliera*) glass cabinet **2.** *pl.* (*cose di nessun valore*) paraphernalia; (*spreg.*) rubbish (*sing.*).

scarabèidi, *s.m.pl.* (*entom.*) Scarabaeidae.

scarabèo, *s.m.* (*entom.*) scarab, scarabaeus (pl. scarabaeuses, scarabaei).

scarabocchiàre, *v.t.* to scribble, to scrawl.

scarabocchiatóre, *s.m.*, **scarabocchiatríce**, *s.f.* scribbler, scrawler.

scarabocchiatúra, *s.f.* scribbling, scrawling.

scarabòcchio, *s.m.* **1.** scribble, scrawl: *la tua firma* è uno —, your signature is a scrawl **2.** (*macchia d'inchiostro*) blot **3.** *fig.* scribbling: *questi non sono quadri, sono scarabocchi infantili*, these are not pictures, but a child's scribblings **4.** (*persona mal fatta*) runt.

scarabocchióne, *ag.* scribbling, scrawling‖ *s.m.*, **scarabocchióna**, *s.f.* scribbler, scrawler.

scaracchiàre, *v.i.* (*volg.*) to spit.

scaràcchio, *s.m.* (*volg.*) spit.

scaracchióne, *s.m.* (*volg.*) spitter.

scarafàggio, *s.m.* cockroach, black-beetle.

scaramanzía, *s.f.* **1.** superstitious practice: *facciamo scaramanzie perchè non venga!*, let's cross our fingers, in the hope that he will not come! (*o* let's touch wood lest he should come!); *toccare ferro per —*, to touch wood for luck **2.** (*atto, gesto magico*) piece of sorcery, piece of magic.

scaramàzzo, *ag.*: *perla scaramazza*, irregular (*o* deformed) pearl.

scaramúccia, *s.f.* skirmish: *— letteraria*, literary skirmish.

scaramucciàre, *v.i.* to skirmish.

scaraventàre, *v.t.* to hurl, to fling: *— pietre contro qlcu.*, to hurl (*o* to fling) stones at s.o. ‖ **scaraventàrsi**, *v.r.* to hurl oneself, to fling oneself, to dash: *— nella mischia*, to hurl oneself into the fray.

scarceraménto, *s.m.* release (from prison).

scarceràre, *v.t.* to release (from prison), to set free.

scarcerazióne, *s.f.* release (from prison).

scardàre, *v.t.* to husk.

scardassàre, *v.t.* (*ind. tessile*) to card, to comb.

scardassatóre, *s.m.*, **scardassatríce**, *s.f.* (*ind. tessile*) carder, comber.

scardassatúra, *s.f.* (*ind. tessile*) carding, combing.

scardàsso, *s.m.* (*ind. tessile*) combing-card.

scardinàre, *v.t.* to unhinge.

scàrica, *s.f.* **1.** (*di armi da fuoco*) discharge, volley; (*di proiettili, frecce, ecc.*) volley, shower (anche *fig.*): *una — di artiglieria, di fucileria*, a salvo of artillery, a volley of rifle-fire; *— di frecce*, discharge (*o* volley *o* shower) of arrows; *— di insulti*, shower of insults; *una — di proiettili, di sassi*, a volley (*o* a shower) of bullets, of stones; *una — di pugni*, a shower of blows **2.** (*elett.*) discharge, flashover; (*tra elettrodi*) jump spark: *— a bagliore*, glow discharge; *— a fiocco*, brush discharge; *— di accumulatore*, discharge of battery; *— oscillante*, oscillatory discharge **3.** (*rad.*) (*disturbo nella ricezione*) atmospheric disturbance: *— a scatto*, impulse flashover **4.** (*evacuazione del ventre*) movement, clearing.

scaricabaríli, *s.m.*: *fare a —*, to lay the blame on s.o. else (*o* to blame s.o. else *o fam.* to pass the buck).

scaricaménto, *s.m.* unloading, discharging, discharge: *piano di —*, (*ferr.*) unloading platform.

scaricàre, *v.t.* **1.** to discharge: *le nuvole scaricano elettricità nell'aria*, the clouds discharge their electricity into the air; *questi tubi scaricano l'acqua in un serbatoio*, these pipes discharge the water into a tank; *— il fucile*, to fire (*o* to discharge) a gun; (*toglierne la carica*) to unload a gun; *— ingiurie su qlcu.*, to heap insults on s.o.; *— la responsabilità, la colpa su qlcu.*, to lay the responsibility, the blame on s.o. **2.** (*deporre*) to discharge: *le merci furono presto scaricate*, the goods were soon discharged (*o* unloaded); *— passeggeri*, to discharge passengers **3.** (*liberare del carico*) to discharge, to unload: *— una nave*, to discharge (*o* to unload) a ship ‖ *— qlcu. di una responsabilità*, to free s.o. from a responsibility ‖ *— la coscienza di ql.co.*, to get sthg. off one's conscience **4.** (*mec.*): *— una molla*, to release a spring; *— l'olio*, to drain the oil (off); *— il vapore*, to blow off steam **5.** (*evacuare*) to evacuate, to discharge: *— il ventre*, to clear one's bowels ‖ **scaricàrsi**, *v.r.* **1.** to relieve oneself; to free oneself (from sthg.): *— di un peso*, to relieve oneself of a burden (anche *fig.*); *— di una responsabilità*, to free oneself of a responsibility; *— di un segreto*, to relieve oneself of a

secret **2.** (*perdere la carica*) to run down: *il mio orologio si è scaricato*, my watch has run down **3.** (*sfociare*) to discharge (itself), to flow: *il Nilo si scarica nel Mediterraneo*, the Nile flows into the Mediterranean **4.** (*di fulmini*) to discharge electricity.

scaricatóio, *s.m.* **1.** (*scalo*) wharf **2.** (*tubo di scarico*) waste-pipe, drain-pipe.

scaricatóre, *s.m.* **1.** unloader: *— di porto*, docker **2.** (*tubo di scarico*) waste-pipe, drain-pipe **3.** (*elett.*) discharger, arrester.

scaricatúra, *s.f.* unloading, discharge.

scàrico, *ag.* **1.** unloaded, discharged: *un carretto —*, an unloaded cart; *una nave scarica*, an unloaded (*o* a discharged) ship ‖ *capo —*, (*buontempone*) wag (*o* scatter brain) **2.** (*di arma da fuoco*) unloaded; (*di orologio, batteria, ecc.*) run-down: *una batteria scarica*, a run-down battery; *un fucile —*, an unloaded gun; *l'orologio è —*, the clock has run down **3.** (*leggero*) light; (*sbiadito*) faded: *colore —*, faded colour; *vino —*, light wine **4.** (*limpido, sereno*) clear, unclouded: *cielo —*, clear (*o* unclouded) sky ‖ *s.m.* **1.** discharge, unloading: *lo — della merce, di una nave*, the discharge (*o* unloading) of the goods, of a ship; *— in mare*, (*mar.*) jettison; *— rapido*, (*aer.*) jettison; *acqua di —*, waste water; *luogo di —*, dump (*o* dumping-place) ‖ *a — di qualsiasi responsabilità*, to avoid any responsibility **2.** (*materiale di rifiuto*) waste **3.** (*comm.*): *libro di —*, stock book; *numero di —*, (*somma*) paying out number; (*materiale*) going out number **4.** (*mec.*) (*di motore*) exhaust: *anticipo allo —*, exhaust opening before bottom dead centre; *collettore di —*, (*aer.*) exhaust ring; *cono di —*, exhaust cone; *resistenza allo —*, exhaust back pressure; *tubo di —*, exhaust pipe **5.** (*edil.*): *— d'acqua* (*piovana*), drain; *— di terra*, earth dump; *— in fogna*, sink; *tubo di —*, waste-pipe (*o* drain-pipe) **6.** (*giustificazione*) defence: *a suo — dobbiamo dire che egli non sapeva nulla*, in his defence we must say that he did not know anything ‖ *a — di coscienza*, to free one's conscience ‖ *testimone di —*, (*dir.*) witness for the defence.

scarificàre, *v.t.* (*chir. agr.*) to scarify.

scarificatóre, *s.m.* (*chir. agr.*) scarifier.

scarificatúra, scarificazióne, *s.f.* (*chir. agr.*) scarification.

scarlattína, *s.f.* (*patol.*) scarlet fever, scarlatina.

scarlàtto, *ag. s.m.* scarlet.

scarmigliàre, *e derivati*, *V.* **scapigliàre**, *e derivati*.

scarnàre, *v.t.* **1.** to unflesh, to remove flesh from (sthg.) **2.** (*conceria*) to flesh ‖ **scarnàrsi**, *v.r.* (*dimagrire*) to grow thin, to lose flesh.

scarnascialàre, *v.i.* to revel.

scarnascialàta, *s.f.* revels (*pl.*); revelling.

scarnicciàre, *v.t.* (*conceria*) to flesh.

scarnificàre, *v.t.* to take flesh off (s.o., sthg.); to tear flesh off (s.o., sthg.): *— un osso*, to take the flesh off a bone; *— un'unghia incarnata*, to remove an ingrowing nail ‖ **scarnificàrsi**, *v.r.*: *mi sono scarnificato un dito col rasoio*, I cut my finger to the bone with my razor.

scarníre, *V.* **scarnificàre** ‖ **scarnírsi**, *v.r.* (*dimagrire*) to grow thin.

scarníto, scàrno, *ag.* **1.** thin, lean, emaciate(d) **2.** (*scarso*) scanty, poor.

scarógna, scarognàto, *V.* **scalógna²**, **scalognàto**.

scàrpa, *s.f.* **1.** shoe: *scarpe alte*, (*stivali*) boots (*o amer.* shoes); *scarpe a punta*, pointed shoes; *scarpe a punta quadra*, square-toed shoes; *scarpe basse*, shoes (*o amer.* low shoes); (*col tacco basso*) low-heeled shoes; *scarpe col tacco*, high-heeled shoes; *scarpe con la para*, rubber-soled shoes; *scarpe con stringhe*, lace-up shoes; *scarpe da ballo*, dancing-shoes; *scarpe da sera*, evening shoes; *scarpe da tennis*, tennis-shoes; *scarpe di tela*, canvas shoes; *scarpe ortopediche*, (*med.*) orthopaedic shoes; (*tipo di scarpe da donna*) wedge heeled shoes; *scarpe sfondate*, worn-out shoes; *lucido da scarpe*, shoe polish (*o* cream); *un paio di scarpe*, a pair of shoes; *suolatura di —*, shoe soling (*o sole laying*); *mettersi, togliersi le scarpe,* to put on, to take off one's shoes ‖ — —, on foot: *se ne andava — — lungo la strada,* he was plodding along the street ‖ *non gli rassomiglia neanche nella suola delle scarpe,* he could not be more different from him ‖ *non esser degno di lustrar le scarpe a qlcu.,* not to be fit to tie s.o.'s shoe-laces ‖ *morire con le scarpe ai piedi, (di morte violenta)* to die with one's boots on; *(di morte improvvisa)* to die suddenly **2.** *(pendio di muro, di terrapieno)* scarp: — *del terreno,* slope; *muro di* —, *(edil.)* scarp wall ‖ *a* —, *(in pendio)* sloping **3.** *(di ruota)* skid **4.** *a* —, *(tec.) (a sdrucciolo)* mitre *(attributivo)* **5.** — *dell'ancora, (mar.)* anchor fluke chock.

scarpàio, scarpàro, *s.m.* **1.** *(venditore ambulante di scarpe e pianelle)* pedlar of shoes and slippers **2.** *(dial.) (calzolaio)* shoemaker.

scarpàta, *s.f.* scarp, escarp; slope.

scarpíno, *s.m.* pump.

scarpóne *s.m.* **1.** boot; hobnailed boot; *(per alpinismo)* climbing-boot; *(da sci)* ski(ing)-boot **2.** *fig.* *(soldato alpino)* mountain soldier.

scarroceiàre, *v.i.* *(mar.)* to make leeway.

scarròccio, *s.m.* *(mar.)* leeway.

scarrozzàre, *v.t.* to drive about (in a carriage); to take for a drive (in a carriage) ‖ *v.i.* to drive about (in a carriage); to go for a drive (in a carriage).

scarrozzàta, *s.f.* drive (in a carriage): *fare una* —, to go for a drive.

scarrucolaménto, *s.m.* running (of a rope) over a pulley; lowering with a pulley.

scarrucolàre, *v.t.* **1.** *(liberare, il canapo)* to disentangle (the rope) from the pulley **2.** *(lasciar cadere)* to release suddenly.

scarrucolío, *s.m.* **1.** running of a pulley **2.** *(rumore)* sound of a running pulley.

scarsaménte, *av.* scarcely, barely; *(insufficientemente)* insufficiently: *è* — *sufficiente,* it is scarcely sufficient; *ha risposto* —, he has answered insufficiently.

scarseggiàre, *v.i.* to be lacking (in sthg.); to be short; to be scarce: *egli scarseggia di buon senso,* he is lacking in common sense; *io scarseggio di denari,* I am short of money; *scarseggiava l'acqua,* water was lacking (o scarce).

scarsèlla, *s.f.* **1.** purse; (money-)bag **2.** *(fam.) (tasca)* pocket.

scarsézza, scarsità, *s.f.* **1.** scarcity, shortage; *(mancanza)* lack, want: — *di acqua, frutta,* scarcity (o shortage) of water, fruit; — *di ingegno,* lack of intelligence **2.** *(taccagneria)* stinginess, niggardliness.

scàrso, *ag.* scarce, scanty; poor; *(insufficiente)* short; *(mancante)* lacking (in sthg.): — *di intelletto,* lacking in wit; *misura scarsa,* short measure; *peso* —, short weight; *provvista scarsa,* poor (o scanty) supply; *raccolto* —, scanty (o poor) crop; *reddito* —, poor income; *vista scarsa,* poor sight; *qui i buoni alberghi sono scarsi,* here good hotels are scarce; *il cibo è* —, food is scarce (o scanty) ‖ *annata scarsa,* lean year.

scartabellàre, *v.t.* to look through (sthg.); *(velocemente)* to skim through (sthg.): — *un dizionario,* to thumb through a dictionary.

scartafàccio, *s.m.* note-book; scribbling-pad.

scartaménto[1], *s.m.* *(lo scartare)* rejection; discarding.

scartaménto[2], *s.m.* *(ferr.)* gauge: — *normale, ridotto, variabile,* standard, narrow, variable gauge: *ferrovia a* — *ridotto,* narrow-gauge railway.

scartàre[1], *v.t.* **1.** to unwrap; to unpack: *scarta quei libri,* unwrap those books **2.** *(rifiutare scegliendo)* to reject; to discard, to cast off: *le copie difettose vennero scartate,* the defective copies were rejected; — *un'ipotesi,* to discard a hypothesis; — *una proposta,* to reject a proposal; — *un soprabito vecchio, un paio di scarpe,* to discard (o to cast off) an old overcoat, a pair of shoes ‖ — *una carta, (al giuoco)* to discard (o to throw away) a card ‖ — *qlcu. alla leva,* to reject s.o. for military service.

scartàre[2], *v.i.* *(deviare bruscamente a lato)* to swerve: *il cavallo, l'automobile scartò a destra,* the horse, the car swerved to the right.

scartàta[1], *s.f.* *(lo scartare)* rejection; discarding.

scartàta[2], *s.f.* **1.** *(brusca deviazione laterale)* swerve **2.** *(fam.) (ramanzina)* scolding: *fare una* — *a qlcu.,* to give s.o. a lecture.

scartàto, *ag.* discarded, cast off, rejected: *abiti scartati,* cast-off (o discarded) clothes ‖ *s.m.* *(mil.)* reject.

scàrto[1], *s.m.* **1.** *(lo scartare)* discarding; *(la cosa scartata)* discard: *articoli di* —, discarded (o rejected) articles; *roba di* —, refuse (o waste matter) ‖ — *di leva, (mil.)* rejected conscript **2.** *(alle carte, lo scartare e la carta scartata)* discard.

scàrto[2], *s.m.* **1.** *(brusca deviazione laterale)* swerve **2.** *(differenza)* disparity; difference **3.** *(spor.)* dribble; dribbling.

scartoceiàre, *v.t.* **1.** to unwrap; to unpack; to unfold **2.** — *granoturco,* to strip maize.

scartoceiatúra, *s.f.* **1.** unwrapping; unpacking; unfolding **2.** *(di granoturco)* stripping.

scartòccio, *s.m.* **1.** paper-bag **2.** *(per lumi a petrolio)* lamp-chimney **3.** *(arch.)* cartouche.

scartòffie, *s.f.pl.* *(spreg.)* **1.** heap of papers *(sing.)* **2.** *(pratica d'ufficio)* paper work *(sing.):* *ho molte* — *da esaminare,* I have a lot of paper work to do; *lascia le tue* — *e vieni a prendere un po' d'aria,* tear yourself away from your desk and come and get some fresh air.

scasàre, *v.i.* to move, to move house: *scaseremo questa settimana,* we are moving (house) this week ‖ *v.t.* *(sfrattare)* to evict.

scàssa, *s.f.* *(mar.)* step.

scassàre[1], *v.t.* **1.** *(togliere da una cassa)* to unpack **2.** *(aprire con forza)* to force open.

scassàre[2], *v.t.* *(pop.) (cancellare)* to rub out.

scassàre[3], *v.t.* **1.** *(agr.) (dissodare)* to break up; to plough up **2.** *(fam.) (rompere, sfondare)* to smash.

scassatúra[1], *s.f.* *(il togliere da una cassa)* unpacking.

scassatúra[2], *s.f.* *(pop.) (cancellatura)* rubbing out.

scassinaménto, *s.m.* breaking open.

scassinàre, *v.t.* to force open; to pick the lock of (sthg.); to break open: — *una porta,* to force a door open.

scassinatóre, *s.m.* thief *(pl.* thieves*)*; *(di casa) (di giorno)* house-breaker; *(di notte)* burglar; *(di banca)* bank-robber; *(di negozio)* shop-breaker.

scassinatúra, *s.f.* breaking open.

scàsso, *s.m.* **1.** *(di serratura)* lock-picking; *(di casa)* house-breaking ‖ *furto con* —, *(in casa) (di giorno)* house-breaking; *(di notte)* burglary; *(in banca)* bank-robbery; *(in negozio)* shop-breaking **2.** *(agr.)* trenching.

scatafàscio, a, *V.* catafàscio.

scatarràre, *v.i.* to cough and splutter.

scatenaceiàre, *v.t.i.* to unbolt.

scatenaménto, *s.m.* **1.** unchaining **2.** *fig.* *(furia prorompente)* bursting (forth), outburst; outbreak.

scatenàre, *v.t.* **1.** *(togliere la catena a)* to unchain; to let loose **2.** *(aizzare)* to stir up: — *il popolino contro qlcu.,* to stir up the mob against s.o. **3.** *(suscitare)* to rouse: — *l'ilarità generale,* to set everyone laughing (o to raise a storm of laughter); — *l'indignazione, l'odio di qlcu.,* to rouse s.o.'s indignation, hatred **4.** *(causare)* to cause: *la sua ambizione scatenò la guerra,* his ambition caused the war **scatenàrsi,** *v.r.* **1.** *(liberarsi dalla catena)* to break loose **2.** *(prorompere, scoppiare)* to break out; to burst forth: *si scatenò una rivolta, un grande incendio,* a revolt, a great fire broke out; *a quelle parole la sua ira si scatenò,* at those words his anger burst forth ‖ *si scatenò contro di me,* he assailed me.

scatenàto, *ag.* **1.** unchained; chainless **2.** *(sfrenato)* unrestrained: *furia scatenata,* unchecked fury; *da piccolo era* —, as a child he was completely out-of-hand; *è* —, nothing will stop him.

scàtola, *s.f.* **1.** box; *(di latta)* tin; *(amer.)* can: *una*

— *di biscotti, di cioccolatini*, a box of biscuits, of chocolates; *una — di carne, di piselli*, a tin of meat, of peas; *una — di fiammiferi*, a box of matches; *una — di spilli*, a box of pins; *mangiò un'intera — di cioccolatini*, he ate a whole box of chocolates ‖ *la — armonica*, sound-box ‖ *la — cranica*, (anat.) the skull ‖ *a lettere di —*, in huge letters: *titolo a lettere di —*, huge (o *fam.* screaming) head-line; *dire a lettere di —*, *fig.* to speak out one's mind ‖ *in —*, tinned: *carne, minestra, frutta in —*, tinned meat, soup, fruit ‖ *rompere le scatole a qlcu.*, (*volg.*) to get s.o.'s goat **2.** (*mec.*) box; case; housing: *— a muro*, wall-box; *— del differenziale*, (*aut.*) differential (gear) carrier; *— di connessione*, (*elett.*) junction-box; *— di derivazione*, (*elett.*) connector-block; *— per film*, film-case.

scatolàio, *s.m.* **1.** box-maker **2.** (*chi vende scatole*) box-seller.

scatolàme, *s.m.* **1.** tins (*pl.*); (*amer.*) cans (*pl.*) **2.** (*cibi in scatola*) tinned food; (*amer.*) canned food.

scatolifìcio, *s.m.* box-factory.

scatología, *s.f.* scatology.

scatològico, *ag.* scatological.

scattàre, *v.i.* **1.** to be released; to go off: *premendo il grilletto, il percussore scatta*, when the trigger is pressed the firing-pin is released; *la trappola non scattò*, the trap did not go off (o did not work) ‖ *— a vuoto*, (*di arma da fuoco*) to misfire ‖ *far —*, to release: *far — una molla*, to release a spring **2.** *fig.* (*balzare*) to spring (up): *al segnale i corridori scattarono*, on the starting -signal the runners sprang forward ‖ *— come una molla*, to spring up ‖ *— in piedi*, to spring to one's feet ‖ *— sull'attenti*, (*mil.*) to spring to attention **3.** *fig.* (*adirarsi*) to lose one's temper, to fly into a rage: *scatta ad ogni minima contrarietà*, he flies into a rage at the slightest thing.

scattìno, *s.m.* (*di orologio*) catch, release.

scàtto, *s.m.* **1.** (*di meccanismo*) click: *— a vuoto*, (*di arma da fuoco*) misfire; *lo — della serratura lo fece sobbalzare*, the click of the lock made him start **2.** (*pezzo meccanico*) release: *— automatico*, automatic release; *lo — del percussore nel fucile*, the release of the firing -pin in a rifle; *serratura a —*, spring-lock **3.** *fig.* (*balzo*) spring: *fu in piedi con uno —*, he sprang to his feet (like a Jack-in-the-box) ‖ *a scatti*, in jerks: *camminare a scatti*, to walk jerkily; *parlare a scatti*, to talk in jerks ‖ *di —*, suddenly: *si alzò di —*, he sprang up **4.** (*moto d'ira*) fit of temper, outburst of rage; (*impulso*) impulse: *— di generosità*, generous impulse; *ebbe uno — d'ira*, he had an outburst of rage; *non tollero i tuoi scatti*, I cannot put up with your fits of temper **5.** (*di anzianità*) increase (according to seniority).

scaturìgine, *s.f.* **1.** spring **2.** *fig.* (*origine*) source.

scaturìre, *v.i.* **1.** to spring: *l'acqua scaturisce dal suolo*, water springs from the earth **2.** (*in gran quantità*) to gush (out, forth); to spout: *le lacrime scaturirono dai suoi occhi*, tears gushed from her eyes; *il petrolio scaturiva in gran quantità*, the oil was gushing out (o forth) in great quantity; *il sangue scaturiva dalla ferita*, blood spouted (o issued) from the wound **3.** (*aver origine, derivare*) to originate; to result; to derive; to ensue: *il fuoco scaturì da sotto il pavimento*, the fire originated under the floor; *un grave danno ne scaturì*, much harm resulted from this; *tutti i miei malanni scaturirono da un malinteso*, all my troubles derived from a misunderstanding.

scavalcàre, *v.t.* **1.** (*gettare da cavallo*) to unhorse, to dismount: *— un cavaliere*, to unhorse (o to dismount) a rider **2.** *fig.* (*soppiantare*) to supplant, to oust: *fu scavalcato dal suo rivale*, he was supplanted by his rival; *— qlcu. in un posto*, to oust s.o. from his post **3.** (*passare avanti a, sorpassare*) to excel: *studiò molto e scavalcò tutti in latino*, he studied hard and excelled everybody in Latin **4.** (*passare sopra a*) to step over (sthg.); (*arrampicandosi*) to climb over (sthg.); (*saltando*) to jump over (sthg.): *— un muro*, to climb over a wall (o to

scale a wall); *— un ruscello*, to step over a brook; *— uno steccato*, to climb over a fence (o to jump over a fence) ‖ *v.i.* to dismount, to alight (from one's horse), to get off one's horse.

scavallàre, *v.i.* **1.** (*correre qua e là*) to frolic about, to frisk about **2.** (*correre a cavallo*) to ride about.

scavaménto, *s.m.* digging up, excavation.

scavàre, *v.t.* **1.** to dig; to excavate; to hollow (out); (*in una miniera*) to mine: *scavarono un grosso buco nel terreno per le fondamenta*, they excavated a big hole in the ground for the foundations; *è difficile — il terreno quando è gelato*, it is difficult to dig the ground when it is frozen hard; *questo buco fu scavato dall'acqua*, this hole was hollowed out by the water; *— con la draga*, to dredge; *— un fosso*, to dig a ditch (o to ditch); *— un pozzo*, to sink a well; *— una trincea*, to dig a trench; *— un tunnel*, to bore a tunnel ‖ *si scavò la fossa con le sue mani*, *fig.* he cut his own throat **2.** (*cose sepolte, riportarle alla luce*) to excavate: *— antiche rovine*, to excavate ancient ruins; *— una città sepolta*, to excavate a buried city; *— un tesoro*, to dig up a treasure **3.** *fig.* to dig up: *scavò strani argomenti, strane teorie*, he dug up strange ideas, strange theories **4.** (*fare lo scollo ad abito, ecc.*) to widen, to enlarge: *— il collo di un vestito*, to enlarge the collar of a dress; *— le maniche*, to widen the sleeves.

scavàto, *ag.* **1.** dug out, excavated: *quel canale è poco —*, that canal is not very deep **2.** (*incavato*) hollow: *guance scavate*, hollow cheeks.

scavatóre, *s.m.* digger ‖ **scavatríce**, *s.f.* **1.** digger **2.** (*macchina*) excavator, digger: *— a cucchiaia*, power-shovel; *— per fossi*, ditching-machine; *— pneumatica*, pneumatic digger.

scavatúra, *s.f.* **1.** (*lo scavare*) digging; excavation **2.** (*scollo*) hole: *— del collo, della manica*, neck -hole, arm-hole.

scavezzacòllo, *s.m.* **1.** headlong fall ‖ *a —*, at breakneck speed; *fig.* rashly, recklessly: *andare a —*, to go at breakneck speed; *correre a —*, to run at full speed **2.** *fig.* (*rompicollo*) dare-devil, reckless fellow.

scavezzàre[1], *v.t.* (*tagliare i rami a*) to pollard, to lop off ‖ **scavezzàrsi**, *v.r.* to break: *si è scavezzato una gamba*, he broke a leg.

scavezzàre[2], *v.t.* (*levare la cavezza a*) to unbridle.

scavèzzo, *ag.* shortened.

scàvo, *s.m.* **1.** (*lo scavare*) digging out, excavating; excavation; (*in una miniera*) mining: *— di estrazione*, (*min.*) stope; *sezione di —*, (*min.*) working-face; *iniziare uno —*, to break ground **2.** (*archeol.*) excavation: *scavi archeologici*, archaeological excavations; *gli scavi di Pompei*, the excavations of Pompeii **3.** (*incavatura*) hole: *lo — del collo, della manica*, the neck-hole, the arm-hole.

scazónte, *ag.* (*poes.*) scazontic ‖ *s.m.* scazon.

scazzottàre, *v.t.* (*volg.*) to punch.

scégliere, *v.t.* **1.** to choose, to pick, to select; (*fare una scelta*) to make a choice of (sthg.): *non ho ancora scelto*, I haven't chosen yet; *non ho ancora scelto le migliori composizioni*, I haven't yet selected the best compositions; *non so quale libro —*, I don't know which book to choose; *quale sceglieresti fra questi?*, which of these would you choose (o pick)? ‖ *non c'è da —*, there is no choice ‖ *— una carriera*, to choose a career ‖ *— il minore dei due mali*, to choose the lesser of (the) two evils **2.** (*tirar fuori*) to pick out, to sort out: *egli fu scelto come il migliore studente*, he was picked out as the best student; *scegli i libri inglesi e mettili tutti qui*, sort out the English books and put them all here; *scegli le pesche più grosse e portale qui*, pick out the biggest peaches and bring them here ‖ *— il campo*, (*spor.*) to toss for ends.

sceglimento, *V.* **scélta**.

sceglitóre, *s.m.*, **sceglitríce**, *s.f.* selector, chooser.

sceicco, *s.m.* sheik(h).

scelleràggine, **scelleratàggine**, *V.* **scelleratézza**.

scelleratamὲnte, *av.* **1.** wickedly **2.** *fig.* terribly (badly): *leggere* —, to read terribly (badly).

scelleratézza, *s.f.* **1.** wickedness, evil **2.** (*atto scellerato*) misdeed, crime.

scelleràto, *ag.* **1.** wicked, evil: *uomo, pensiero* —, evil (*o* wicked) man, thought **2.** *fig.* (*pessimo*) awful, terrible: *tempo* —, awful (*o* terrible) weather ‖ *s.m.* scoundrel, wicked person.

scellíno, *s.m.* shilling (*abbr. s.*): *mezzo* —, sixpence; *moneta da due scellini,* two-shilling piece (*o* florin).

scélta, *s.f.* **1.** choice, choosing: *non ho possibilità di* —, I have no choice; *fare una* —, to make a choice; *fare la propria* —, to take one's choice ‖ *la* — *della lana, del caffè,* the sorting of wool, of coffee ‖ *merce di prima* —, choice (*o* first-quality) goods ‖ *frutta o dolce a* —, choice of fruit or sweet **2.** (*selezione*) selection, choice: *una* — *di poesie,* a selection of poems; *una buona* — *di colori,* a good choice of colours.

sceltaménte, *av.* choicely; elegantly.

sceltézza, *s.f.* choiceness; elegance.

scélto, *ag.* choice; select(ed); carefully chosen, hand-picked: *frutta scelta,* choice fruit; *poesie scelte,* selected poems; *ufficiali scelti a uno a uno,* hand-picked officers; *rivolgersi ad un pubblico* —, to address a chosen few.

scemaménto, *s.m.* diminution, falling, reduction, abatement ‖ — *della luna,* (*astr.*) waning of the moon.

scemàre, *v.t.* to diminish, to reduce, to lessen, to lower, to abate; to shorten: — *il dolore,* to lessen the pain; — *il prezzo di ql.co.,* to reduce (*o* to lower) the price of sthg.; — *la superbia di qlcu.,* to lower s.o.'s pride ‖ *v.i.* to diminish, to lessen, to abate, to decrease, to go down, to fall, to wane: *il dolore scemava,* the pain was diminishing (*o* abating); *la sua gloria sta scemando,* his glory is waning; *la temperatura sta scemando,* the temperature is falling (*o* going down).

scemènza, *s.f.* **1.** stupidity, silliness **2.** (*detto da scemo*) folly, stupidity: *non dire scemenze,* don't talk nonsense.

scémo, *ag.* **1.** stupid, silly **2.** (*non pieno*) not full; half-empty **3.** (*mancante*) lacking (in sthg.) ‖ *s.m.* idiot, fool.

scempiὰggine, *V.* **scemènza.**

scempiaménte, *av.* **1.** stupidly, foolishly **2.** (*non doppiamente*) singly.

scempiaménto, *s.m.* (*sdoppiamento*) halving.

scempiàre, *v.t.* (*sdoppiare*) to halve.

scempiatàggine, *V.* **scemènza.**

scémpio[1], *ag.* **1.** stupid, foolish, silly **2.** (*non doppio*) single: *filo* —, single thread.

scémpio[2], *s.m.* (*sterminio*) havoc; (*strage*) slaughter: *fare* — *di ql.co.,* to make havoc of sthg.

scèna, *s.f.* **1.** scene: *la* — *del fantasma nell'« Amleto »,* the ghost scene in "Hamlet"; — *muta,* dumb scene: *fece* — *muta all'esame,* he didn't utter a single word at the exam; *cambiamento di* —, change of scene; *la* — *del primo atto è a Roma,* the scene of the first act is in Rome; *il primo atto è diviso in quattro scene,* the first act is divided into four scenes ‖ *colpo di* —, stage-effect; *fig.* unexpected event ‖ *chi è di* —?, whose turn is it? **2.** (*palcoscenico*) stage; (*scena dipinta*) scenery, scene: *dietro le scene,* behind the scenes (anche *fig.*); *direttore di* —, stage-director; *egli ha dipinto le scene per la commedia,* he has painted the scenery for the play; *cambiare le scene,* to change the scenes; *entrare in* —, to enter (the scene); *fig.* to interfere: *non voglio entrare in* —, I don't want to interfere ‖ *messa in* —, mise-en-scène (*o* staging); *fig.* showing off: *è solo una messa in* —, it is merely showing off ‖ *andare in* —, to be performed (*o* to be staged) ‖ *calcare le scene,* to be an actor (*o* to tread the boards) ‖ *mettere in* — *una commedia,* to stage (*o* to put on) a play ‖ *scomparire dalle scene,* to leave the stage (anche *fig.*) **3.** *fig.* (*teatro*) theatre, stage: *una commedia nuova per le scene francesi,* a novelty for the French stage ‖ *darsi alle scene,* to go on the stage **4.** (*vista, spettacolo*

di vita) scene; view: *scene della vita militare,* scenes of military life; *scene di dolore,* scenes of grief; *la* — *politica,* the political scene; (*il mondo politico*) the political world; *che bella* —!, what a lovely view! ‖ *fare* —, to make an impression (*o* to make a sensation) **5.** (*litigio*) scene, row: *fare una* —, to make a scene; *hanno avuto una* — *terribile stamattina,* they had a terrible row this morning.

scenàrio, *s.m.* **1.** (*teat.*) scenery (anche *fig.*): *lo* — *è grandioso,* the scenery is imposing **2.** (*canovaccio di commedia, pellicola, ecc.*) scenario (*pl.* scenarios).

scenarísta, *s.c.* (*cine.*) scenarist, scenario-writer.

scenàta, *s.f.* scene, row: *fare una* —, to make a scene (*o fam.* to kick up a row).

scéndere, *v.t.* **1.** to go down, to come down, to descend: — *un colle, una collina,* to go down a hill; — *le scale,* (*andare giù*) to go downstairs; (*venire giù*) to come downstairs: — *correndo le scale,* to run down the stairs (*o* to run downstairs) **2.** (*dial.*) (*far scendere*) to take down, to bring down, to carry down: *scendi il bagaglio,* bring (*o* carry *o* take) down the luggage ‖ *v.i.* **1.** to go down, to come down, to descend: *l'angelo scese dal cielo,* the angel descended from Heaven; *fermati, scendo subito,* stop there, I'll come down at once; *i fiumi scendono verso il mare,* rivers flow down to the sea; *non è ancora sceso,* he is not down yet; *scendi da quella scala,* get down of that ladder; *scendo un momento dal cartolaio,* I am just going down to the stationer's for a moment; *scesi al fiume,* I went down to the river; — *a valle,* to go downhill; (*venire a valle*) to come downhill; — *da un albero,* to climb down a tree; — *da un monte,* to come down a mountain; — *in cantina,* to go down to the cellar; — *in fretta, con rumore,* to hurry (*o* to hasten) down, to clatter down ‖ *fallo* —!, (*mandalo giù*) send him down!; (*chiamalo giù*) call him down! ‖ *le sue parole mi scesero al cuore,* his words touched my heart ‖ — *ai minimi particolari,* to enter into the smallest (*o* minutest) details ‖ — *in basso,* *fig.* to go to the bad ‖ — *in campo, in lizza,* to enter the field, the lists ‖ — *nella scala sociale,* to sink in the social scale **2.** (*da un veicolo*) to get off (sthg.); to get out (of sthg.): *devo* — *alla prossima stazione,* I must get off at the next station; *in genere scendo qui,* this is where I usually get off; — *a terra,* (*da una nave*) to (go on) land; — *da un'automobile,* to get out of a car; — *da cavallo,* to dismount from a horse (*o* to get off a horse); — *dal tram,* to get off a tram; — *da un treno,* to get off (*o* to get out of) a train ‖ — *ad un albergo,* to put up at an hotel: *a che albergo sei sceso?,* what hotel are you staying (*o* have you put up) at? **3.** (*declinare*) to slope down(wards), to run down, to descend: *la montagna scende verso il mare,* the mountain slopes down towards the sea; *la scogliera scendeva a picco sul mare,* the cliff fell sheer to the sea; *il sentiero scende ripidamente,* the path descends steeply; *la strada scende verso la valle,* the road runs down to the valley **4.** (*di astri*) to sink, to go down: *la luna sta scendendo,* the moon is going down; *il sole scendeva verso ovest,* the sun was sinking in the west **5.** (*abbassarsi, cadere*) to fall, to drop: *il barometro era sceso,* the barometer had fallen (*o* dropped); *il livello del terreno è sceso un po',* the level of the ground has fallen a little; *non puoi* — *col prezzo?,* couldn't you bring your price down a little?; *i prezzi scendono,* prices are falling; *scende la notte,* night is falling; *il silenzio scese sul villaggio,* silence fell on the village; *la temperatura è scesa molto in questi ultimi giorni,* the temperature has fallen a lot in the last few days **6.** (*abbassarsi, umiliarsi*) to stoop, to lower oneself: *non scendo a trattare con gente simile,* I wouldn't stoop to dealing with people like that; — *a patti con qlcu.,* to come to terms with s.o. **7.** (*cadere, pendere*) to fall; to come down, to hang down: *la barba gli scendeva sul petto,* his beard came down to his chest; *i capelli le scendevano sulle spalle,* her hair fell (*o* hung down) to her shoulders; *il vestito mi scendeva fino alle caviglie*, my dress came down to my ankles 8. (*avere origine*) to descend, to be descended; to come (of s.o., sthg.); (*di fiume*) to rise (in a place): *il Po scende dalle Alpi*, the Po rises in the Alps; *la sua famiglia scende dai Normanni*, his family is descended from (o goes back to) the Normans; *scende da una stirpe di contadini*, he comes of peasant stock.

scendibàgno, *s.m.* bath-mat.

scendíbile, *ag.* descendable.

scendilètto, *s.m.* bedside carpet.

sceneggiàre, *v.t.* 1. (*teat.*) to arrange into scenes 2. (*ridurre a forma drammatica*) to dramatize: — *un romanzo*, to dramatize a novel.

sceneggiatóre, *s.m.*, **sceneggiatríce,** *s.f.* (*cine.*) scenarist, scenario-writer.

sceneggiatúra, *s.f.* 1. arrangement of scenes 2. (*cine.*) scenario.

scenicaménte, *av.* scenically.

scènico, *ag.* scenic(al): *effetti scenici*, stage effects.

scenografía, *s.f.* scene-painting, scenography.

scenogràfico, *ag.* scenographic(al).

scenògrafo, *s.m.* scene-painter, scenographer.

scèpsi, *s.f.* (*fil.*) scepsis, skepsis.

sceríffo[1]**,** *s.m.* sheriff.

sceríffo[2]**,** *s.m.* (*discendente di Maometto*) shereef, sherif, sharif.

scèrnere, *v.t.* 1. (*scegliere*) to choose, to select, to sort out: *scerni tra queste cose le migliori*, choose the best from among these things 2. (*rar.*) (*discernere*) to discern.

scerniménto, *s.m.* 1. (*scelta*) selection 2. (*discernimento*) discernment.

scerpellàto, scerpellíno, *ag.* (*med.*) red-rimmed: *occhi scerpellati*, red-rimmed eyes.

scerpellóne, *s.m.* blunder, error.

scervellàre, *v.t.* to drive mad: *mi ha scervellato con le sue chiacchiere*, she has driven me mad with her chattering ‖ **scervellàrsi,** *v.r.* to rack one's brains: *mi scervellai tutto il giorno su quel problema*, I racked my brains all day over that problem.

scervellàto, *ag.* brainless, hare-brained ‖ *s.m.* brainless person, hare-brained person.

scésa, (*poet.*) per **discésa.**

scéso, *ag.* descended ‖ *gente scesa*, (*decaduta socialmente*) people who have come down in the world.

scetticaménte, *av.* sceptically; (*amer.*) skeptically.

scetticísmo, *s.m.* scepticism; (*amer.*) skepticism.

scèttico, *ag.* sceptical; (*amer.*) skeptical; (*fil.*) sceptic(al): *filosofo* —, sceptic(al) philosopher; *persona scettica*, sceptical person; *principi scettici*, (*fil.*) sceptic(al) principles; *sorriso* —, sceptical smile ‖ *s.m.* sceptic; (*amer.*) skeptic: *è uno* —, he is a sceptic.

scettràto, *ag.* sceptred.

scèttro, *s.m.* sceptre (anche *fig.*): *deporre lo* —, to lay down the crown (o to abdicate); *tenere lo* —, to hold the sceptre; *usurpare lo* —, to usurp the throne.

sceveraménto, *s.m.* separation, severance.

sceveràre, *v.t.* to discern, to distinguish, to separate: — *il bene dal male*, to distinguish good from evil.

sceviòtte, *s.m.* (*ind. tessile*) cheviot.

scévro, *ag.* exempt, free: — *da imperfezioni*, free from faults; *ipotesi non scevra di fondamento*, a hypothesis not without foundation.

schèda, *s.f.* 1. card; (*di schedario*) index-card, filing-card 2. (*elettorale*) voting-paper, ballot-paper: *il computo delle schede*, count.

schedàre, *v.t.* to file, to catalogue.

schedàrio, *s.m.* card-index.

schéggia, *s.f.* splinter, chip: *una* — *di legno, metallo, vetro*, a splinter of wood, metal, glass.

scheggiàre, *v.t.* 1. to chip: *bada a non* — *il tavolo*, be careful not to chip the table 2. (*ridurre in schegge*) to splinter, to shatter: *il sasso scheggiò il vetro della*

finestra, the stone splintered the window-pane ‖ **scheggiàrsi,** *v.r.* to splinter, to chip: *è un legno che non si scheggia facilmente*, it is a wood that does not chip easily; *in quell'incidente si scheggiò due denti*, he had two teeth broken in the accident.

scheggiàto, *ag.* chipped, splintered: *dente* —, broken tooth; *mobile, vaso* —, chipped piece of furniture, vase; *vetro* —, splintered glass.

scheggiatúra, *s.f.* 1. splintering, chipping 2. (*parte scheggiata*) part chipped off 3. (*schegge*) splinters (*pl.*).

scheggióso, *ag.* splintery.

Schèlda, *no.pr.f.* (*geog.*) Scheldt.

schelètrico, *ag.* 1. skeleton-like, skeletal 2. *fig.* skeleton (*attributivo*): *prosa scheletrica*, poor prose; *riassunto* —, skeleton outline.

scheletríre, *v.t.* to reduce to a skeleton; *fig.* to cut down to the bare bones ‖ **scheletrírsi,** *v.r.* to be reduced to a skeleton: *si è quasi scheletrita*, she is only skin and bones now.

scheletríto, *ag.* reduced to a skeleton, emaciated ‖ *alberi scheletriti*, bare trees.

schèletro, *s.m.* 1. skeleton: *trovarono uno* — *ben conservato*, a well-preserved skeleton was found ‖ *è uno* —, she is a living skeleton; *è ridotta a uno* —, she is reduced to a skeleton; *quel vecchio pare uno* —, that old man is only skin and bones 2. (*intelaiatura, ossatura*) skeleton, framework: *lo* — *di quell'edificio è antico*, the frame of that building is very old; *si trattava dello* — *di una nave romana*, it was the skeleton of a Roman ship 3. (*schema*) skeleton, outline, scheme: *lo* — *di una conferenza*, the schome of a lecture; *lo* — *di una poesia*, the outline of a poem.

schèma, *s.m.* 1. scheme, plan; (*traccia, piano*) outline, scheme: *lo* — *generale di un libro*, the general outline of a book; *ci tracciò uno* — *di lavoro per il periodo successivo*, he gave us a scheme of work for the following period; *non hanno accettato il suo* —, his plan was not accepted 2. (*schizzo*) sketch: *fammi uno* — *di quella casa*, draw me a sketch-plan of that house 3. (*tec.*) diagram: — *di avvolgimento*, (*elett.*) winding diagram; — *di connessione*, (*elett.*) wiring diagram; — *di montaggio*, (*elett.*) circuit diagram: — *di montaggio di un circuito di radio*, hook-up 4. (*comm.*) scheme.

schematicaménte, *av.* schematically.

schemàtico, *ag.* schematic: *diagramma* —, schematic diagram.

schematísmo, *s.m.* schematism.

scheràno, *s.m.* cut-throat.

schérma, *s.f.* 1. fencing: *gara di* —, fencing match; *maestro di* —, fencing master; *sala di* —, fencing room; *gioca di* —, he fences; *tira bene di* —, he fences well; *tirava bene di* —, he used to play a good stick 2. *gener. pl.* (*letter.*) polemic; (*schermaglia*) skirmish.

schermàglia, *s.f.* 1. scrimmage, scuffle, skirmish 2. *fig.* (*discussione polemica*) skirmish, discussion, polemic.

schermàre, *v.t.* 1. (*munire di schermo*) to screen 2. (*elett. rad. fis.*) to shield.

schermàto, *ag.* 1. (*munito di schermo*) screened 2. (*elett. rad. fis.*) shielded.

schermidóre, *s.m.* fencer.

schermíre, *v.i.* (*tirare di scherma*) to fence ‖ **schermírsi,** *v.r.* to defend oneself, to protect oneself (anche *fig.*): *sa* — *molto bene da situazioni imbarazzanti*, he knows how to get out of awkward situations very well; — *da un colpo*, to parry (o to fend off o to ward off) a blow; — *da domande imbarazzanti*, to parry embarrassing questions.

schermístico, *ag.* fencing.

schermitóre, *s.m.*, **schermitríce,** *s.f.* fencer.

schérmo, *s.m.* 1. protection, defence: *la luce era così forte che dovevo farmi* — *agli occhi*, the light was so bright that I had to protect my eyes against it ‖ *farsi* — *dell'autorità di qlcu.*, *fig.* to hide oneself behind s.o.'s. authority: *ti sei fatto* — *della mia autorità*, you have screened yourself behind my authority 2. (*cine. tv.*) screen: — *argentato*, silver screen; — *di tela*, cloth screen; — *panoramico*, cinemascope screen; — *paraluce*, dowser; — *televisivo*, television screen (*o* telescreen); — *trasparente*, translucent screen; *proiettare sullo* —, to screen ǁ *l'arte dello* —, cinema; *artisti dello* —, film stars; *commedia per lo* —, screen play; *adattare per lo* —, to adapt for the screen 3. (*foto.*) filter: — *giallo*, yellow filter 4. (*fis.*) shield: — *termico*, thermal shield 5. (*elett.*) shield, screen: — *magnetico*, magnetic shielding (*o* screen) 6. (*mec.*) baffle.

schernévole, *ag.* 1. sneering, mocking: *parole schernevoli*, mocking words 2. (*sprezzante*) scornful, contemptuous 3. (*degno di scherno*) contemptible.

schernevolménte, *av.* 1. sneeringly 2. (*con sprezzo*) scornfully, contemptuously: *parlava di lui* —, she spoke scornfully of him.

scherníre, *v.t.* to sneer at (s.o., sthg.), to scoff at (s.o., sthg.), to jeer at (s.o., sthg.), to laugh at (s.o., sthg.), to mock at (s.o., sthg.): — *la religione*, to sneer (*o* to scoff) at religion.

schernìto, *ag.* derided.

schernitóre, *ag.* sneering, mocking, scoffing ǁ *s.m.*, **schernitríce**, *s.f.* sneerer, mocker, scoffer.

schérno, *s.m.* 1. sneer, mockery, derision: *parole di* —, sneering words; *sorriso, espressione di* —, sneer 2. (*oggetto di scherno*) laughing-stock, butt: *era lo* — *di tutta la città*, he was the laughing-stock of the whole town.

scherzàre, *v.i.* 1. to joke (at, about s.o., sthg.), to jest (at, about s.o., sthg.): *gli piace* — *su tutto*, he likes to make fun of everything; *non ha fatto che* — *tutto il pomeriggio*, he has done nothing but joke all the afternoon; *scherzi o dici sul serio?*, are you joking or are you in earnest?; *tu scherzi!*, are you joking! (*o amer.* are you kidding!) 2. (*prendere, considerare con leggerezza*) to trifle (with s.o., sthg.), to joke (about s.o., sthg.), to make light of (s.o., sthg.): *non bisogna* — *su queste cose*, one must not joke about these things; *non* — *con questa malattia*, do not make light of this illness; *non si scherza coi sentimenti altrui*, one must not trifle with the feelings of others ǁ *c'è poco da* —, it is no joke ǁ *con lui non si scherza*, he is not a man to be trifled with ǁ *non* — *col fuoco*, do not play with fire ǁ — *con l'amore*, to trifle with love ǁ — *con la morte*, to gamble with death 3. (*trastullarsi*) to play: *i bambini scherzano tutto il giorno*, children play all day long; *il gatto scherzava col gomitolo*, the cat was playing with the ball ǁ *la brezza scherzava fra i fiori, sull'acqua*, the breeze was playing among the flowers, on the water ǁ *non* — *con l'orso se non vuoi esser morso*, *prov.* you can't play with fire without being burnt.

scherzeggiàre, (*rar.*) *per* **scherzàre**.

scherzévole, **scherzevolménte**, *V.* **scherzóso**, **scherzosaménte**.

schérzo, *s.m.* 1. joke, jest; (*tiro*) trick: *uno* — *di cattivo genere*, a bad joke; *era solo uno* —, it was only a joke; *non sa stare allo* —, he cannot take a joke; *fare un brutto* — *a qlcu.*, to play a bad trick on s.o.; *fare scherzi*, to make jokes (*o* to joke *o* to jest); *fare uno* — *a qlcu.*, to play a joke on s.o.; *spingere lo* — *troppo oltre*, to carry the joke too far; *volgere ql.co. in* —, to laugh a thing off ǁ *scherzi a parte*, joking aside ǁ *gli scherzi della fortuna*, the tricks of fortune ǁ — *di natura*, freak of nature (*o* sport) ǁ *per* —, for fun (*o* in jest *o* for a joke): *fare, dire ql.co. per* —, to do, to say sthg. in sport (*o* for a joke *o* in jest) ǁ *a carnevale ogni* — *vale*, *prov.* at carnival anything goes 2. *pl.* (*effetti*) effects, works: *scherzi d'acqua*, water-works; *scherzi di colori*, colour effects; *scherzi di immagini*, imagery; *scherzi di luce*, (*teat.*) lighting effects; *questi sono gli scherzi del vino*, these are the effects of wine 3. (*mus.*) scherzo (*pl.* scherzos).

scherzosaménte, *av.* playfully, jokingly, facetiously.

scherzóso, *ag.* playful, jocose, humorous, facetious: *vento, getto d'acqua* —, playful wind, jet of water.

schettinàre, *v.i.* to roller-skate.

schèttino, *s.m.* roller-skate.

schiàccia, *s.f.* 1. trap 2. (*per capelli*) curling-tongs (*pl.*) 3. (*per cialde, ecc.*) tongs (*pl.*).

schiaccialimóni, *s.m.* lemon-squeezer.

schiacciaménto, *s.m.* 1. crushing, squashing, squeezing 2. (*di pneumatico*) deflection: — *normale*, normal deflection; — *totale*, maximum deflection.

schiaccianóci, *s.m.* nut-cracker; nut-crackers (*pl.*).

schiacciànte, *ag.* (*decisivo*) overwhelming: *prova* —, decisive (*o* overwhelming) proof.

schiacciapatàte, *s.m.* potato masher.

schiacciàre, *v.t.* 1. to crush; to squash; (*calpestare*) to tread on (sthg.): *fu schiacciato da un tram*, he was run over by a tram; *hai schiacciato il mio cappello, la frutta, i fiori*, you have squashed my hat, the fruit, the flowers; *mi hai schiacciato un piede*, you have trod on my toes; *molta gente morì schiacciata tra la folla*, many people were crushed to death in the crowd; *quella folla mi schiacciava*, I was being crushed by the crowd; — *una noce*, to crack a nut; — *patate, verdure*, to mash potatoes, vegetables; — *un ragno*, to crush (*o* to tread on) a spider ǁ — *un moccolo*, (*bestemmiare*) to let fly an oath ǁ — *un sonnellino*, to have a nap 2. (*annientare*) to crush, to overwhelm: *fu schiacciato sotto il peso della fatica*, he was overwhelmed by fatigue; *fu schiacciato da una serie di sventure*, he was crushed by a series of misfortunes; — *un avversario*, to crush (*o* to overwhelm) an enemy; — *con argomenti, prove, ecc.*, to overwhelm with arguments, proofs, etc. ǁ — *qlcu. a un esame*, to fail s.o. at an exam ǁ **schiacciàrsi**, *v.r.* to get squashed; to get crushed: *le pesche si sono tutte schiacciate*, the peaches are all squashed; — *un dito*, to crush one's finger.

schiacciasàssi, *s.m.* steam-roller.

schiacciàto, *ag.* 1. squashed 2. (*piatto*) flat: *naso* —, flattened (*o* squashed) nose ǁ *arco* —, (*arch.*) flattened arch.

schiacciatúra, *s.f.* crushing; squashing; cracking.

schiacciuòla, *s.f.* (*per capelli*) curling tongs (*pl.*).

schiacciàta, *s.f.* 1. squeezing, squeeze 2. (*focaccia*) flat bread.

schiaffàre, *v.t.* (*fam.*) to hurl, to fling: *ho schiaffato tutti i libri in un angolo*, I have thrown all the books into a corner; *lo schiaffò fuori dalla porta*, she bundled him out of the house.

schiaffeggiàre, *v.t.* to slap, to smack, to cuff.

schiàffo, *s.m.* 1. slap, smack; box on the ear: *dare uno* —, to give a box on the ear (*o* a smack *o* a slap); *prendere a schiaffi qlcu.*, to box s.o.'s ear(s) ǁ *faccia da schiaffi*, impudent-looking face 2. (*affronto*) affront, insult, slap in the face: *la promozione del suo più giovane collega fu uno* — *per lui*, his younger colleague being promoted was a slap in the face for him ǁ — *morale*, insult (*o* slap in the face).

schiamazzàre, *v.i.* 1. to make a din 2. (*di galline*) to squawk; (*di oche*) to cackle.

schiamazzatóre, *s.m.*, **schiamazzatríce**, *s.f.* roisterer, rowdy.

schiamàzzo, *s.m.* din, uproar; (*fam.*) shindy: *che* —!, what a din (*o* noise)!; *fu accusato di schiamazzi notturni*, he was accused of rowdiness at night; *fare* —, to make (*o* to create) a din.

schiantàre, *v.t.* to break (*anche fig.*): *quella notizia gli schiantò il cuore*, that piece of news broke his heart; *il vento ha schiantato diversi rami*, the wind has broken (off) several branches ǁ **schiantàrsi**, *v.r.* to break (*anche fig.*); to snap; (*abbattersi*) to crash: *l'albero si schiantò al suolo*, the tree crashed to the ground; *a quella vista mi si schiantò il cuore*, that sight broke my heart; *la fune si schiantò*, the rope snapped (*o* broke).

schiànto, *s.m.* 1. crash: *lo* — *di un albero*, the crash of a falling tree (o the crashing down of a tree) ‖ *di —*, suddenly (o all of a sudden) **2.** (*dolore*) pang: *uno — al cuore*, a pang in one's heart ‖ *è uno — il vederlo*, it breaks one's heart to see him.

schiàppa, *s.f.* **1.** (*scheggia*) splinter **2.** (*spreg.*) (*persona inesperta*) duffer, dunce; (*fam.*) wash-out, dead -loss: *— in latino*, a duffer (o *fam.* a wash-out) at Latin; *è una — al tennis*, he is a wash-out (o a dead-loss) at tennis (o as a tennis player he is a good cook).

schiaràre, (*letter.*) per **rischiaràre.**

schiariménto, *s.m.* **1.** clearing up **2.** (*spiegazione*) explanation: *mi diede ampi schiarimenti*, he gave me a full explanation.

schiaríre, *v.t.* **1.** to make clear, to clear; (*capelli*) to bleach; (*ravvivare, rendere brillante*) to brighten (up): *vorrei — questa stanza con una tappezzeria più vivace*, I would like to brighten up this room with gayer wall-paper; *farsi — i capelli*, to have one's hair bleached **2.** (*delucidare, chiarire*) to make clear, to clear (up), to clarify: *questo libro ti schiarirà le idee*, this book will make your ideas clear **3.** (*sbiadire*) to fade: *il sole schiarisce i colori*, the sun fades (o bleaches) colours ‖ *v.i.* **1.** to clear (up); (*del giorno*) to break: *il giorno schiarisce*, day is breaking; *il tempo schiarisce*, the weather is clearing up **2.** (*sbiadire*) to fade: *il blu schiarisce facilmente*, blue fades easily ‖ **schiarírsi**, *v.r.* (*diventar chiaro*) to clear (up), to grow clear; to grow light(er); (*sbiadirsi*) to fade; (*decolorarsi i capelli*) to bleach; (*diventar vivo, brillante*) to brighten (up), to light up: *il cielo rannuvolato si schiarì verso sera*, the cloudy sky cleared towards evening; *le si sono schiariti i capelli*, her hair has grown lighter; *si è schiarita i capelli*, she has bleached her hair; *il suo volto si schiarì quando mi vide*, his face brightened up (o lit up) when he saw me; *— la voce*, to clear one's voice (o throat).

schiaríta, *s.f.* **1.** clearing: *ci fu una — verso le sei*, the sky cleared a little towards six o'clock **2.** *fig.* (*miglioramento*) improvement: *abbiamo notato una — nei rapporti fra le due nazioni*, we have noticed an improvement in the relations between the two nations.

schiàtta, *s.f.* **1.** stock, family: *di nobile —*, of noble stock **2.** (*razza*) race **3.** (*discendenti*) descendants (*pl.*); offspring, issue.

schiattàre, *v.i.* to burst; *— di rabbia*, to burst with rage.

schiattíre, *v.i.* (*di cani da caccia*) to give tongue.

schiàva, *s.f.* slave woman, slave girl.

schiavésco, *ag.* slavish.

schiavína, *s.f.* **1.** (*veste dei pellegrini*) pilgrim's gown **2.** (*coperta di panno grosso*) coarse blanket.

schiavísta, *s.c.* **1.** (*sostenitore della schiavitù*) anti -abolitionist: *stati schiavisti*, slave States **2.** (*mercante di schiavi*) slave-trader.

schiavitú, *s.f.* slavery (anche *fig.*): *la — di un vizio*, the slavery of a vice; *abolizione della —*, abolition of slavery; *la — fu praticata in tutte le parti del mondo*, slavery was carried on in all parts of the world: *alcuni popoli sono ancora in —* some peoples are still in slavery; *odio la — di un orario di ufficio*, I hate having to be subjected to office hours.

schiàvo, *ag.* slave (*attributivo*) (anche *fig.*); enslaved, subject: *— dei suoi, del bere, del fumo*, a slave to his family, to drink, to tobacco; *un paese —*, a subject country; *una popolazione schiava*, an enslaved population; *è diventata schiava dei suoi bambini*, she has become a slave to her children ‖ *s.m.* slave: *lo — di Petronio*, the slave of Petronius; *commercio degli schiavi*, slave -trade (o slave-traffic); *mercante di schiavi*, slave-trader; *mercato di schiavi*, slave market.

schiavóne, *ag. s.m.* (*st.*) Slavonian.

schiccheràre¹, *v.t.* **1.** (*scribacchiare*) to scribble **2.** (*disegnare in fretta*) to sketch **3.** (*spifferare*) to blurt out, to blab: *schiccherò tutto quel che sapeva*, he blurted out (o blabbed) everything he knew.

schiccheràre², *v.t.i.*, **schiccheràrsi**, *v.r.* (*bere avidamente*) to tipple.

schidionàre, *v.t.* (*rar.*) (*cuc.*) to spit, to put (sthg.) on a spit.

schidionàta, *s.f.* (*infilacciata*) spitful.

schidióne, *s.m.* (*spiedo*) spit.

schièna, *s.f.* **1.** back: *dietro la —*, behind one's back; *colpire qlcu. alla —*, to stab s.o. in the back (anche *fig.*); *curvare la —*, to bend one's back; *fig.* to bow one's neck; *essere disteso sulla —*, to be lying on one's back; *portare ql.co. sulla —*, to carry sthg. on one's back; *rompere la — a qlcu.*, to break s.o.'s back; *rompersi la —*, to break one's back (anche *fig.*): *non ti rompi certo la — per il troppo lavoro!*, you don't overwork (o strain) yourself!; *vedere qlcu. di —*, to have a back-view of s.o. ‖ *a — di mulo, d'asino*, (*di strada*) cambered; (*di ponte, tetto*) hog-backed (o hump -backed) ‖ *lavoro di —*, back-breaking work ‖ *avere molti anni sulla —*, to have many years on one's shoulders (o to be a person of many summers) **2.** (*di monte*) ridge.

schienàle, *s.m.* **1.** back: *sedia dall'alto —*, high -backed chair **2.** (*midollo spinale di bue macellato*) spinal marrow.

schièra, *s.f.* **1.** formation: *una — di soldati*, a formation of soldiers; *in —*, in formation: *mettersi in —*, to fall in; *procedere a schiere*, to proceed in formation **2.** (*gruppo di persone*) group; (*masnada, compagnia*) band; (*di ragazzi di una scuola*) crocodile: *una — di malviventi*, a band of rogues; *la — degli scioperanti avanzava lentamente*, the group of strikers proceeded slowly.

schieraménto, *s.m.* **1.** (*il disporre a schiere*) marshalling, arrayment **2.** (*disposizione a schiere*) array: *— di battaglia*, battle array.

schieràre, *v.t.* to marshal, to draw up, to array: *— truppe*, to marshal (o to draw up) troops ‖ **schieràrsi**, *v.r.* **1.** to draw up: *si schierarono lungo la strada*, they drew up along the road; *le truppe si schierarono in ordine di combattimento*, the troops drew up in battle order **2.** (*parteggiare*) to side (with s.o.), to take sides (with s.o.): *egli si schierò dalla nostra parte*, he sided with us.

schiettaménte, *av.* **1.** (*lealmente*) frankly, openly, sincerely **2.** (*semplicemente*) simply.

schiettézza, *s.f.* **1.** (*purità*) purity: *— di lingua*, purity of language **2.** (*lealtà*) frankness, openness, sincerity.

schiètto, *ag.* **1.** (*genuino*) pure, unadulterated, genuine: *acqua schietta*, pure water; *oro —*, pure gold; *vino —*, undiluted (o neat) wine **2.** *fig.* (*puro*) pure: *lingua schietta*, pure language **3.** (*leale, franco*) frank, open, sincere: *una persona schietta*, a frank person; *fui molto — con lui*, I was very frank (o open) with him ‖ *a dirla schietta*, to speak frankly (o to tell the truth) **4.** (*sano*) sound: *pesche schiette*, sound peaches **5.** (*di ramo*) smooth: *ramo —*, smooth branch **6.** (*arch.*) (*non lavorato*) plain, blank: *pannello —*, plain panel ‖ *av.* frankly, openly: *parlare —*, to speak frankly.

schifàre, *v.t.* (*avere a schifo*) to loathe: *egli schifa la carne di maiale*, he loathes pork ‖ **schifàrsi**, *v.r.* to feel disgust (at sthg., at doing sthg.), to feel repugnance (to sthg., to doing sthg.).

schifézza, *s.f.* **1.** (*l'essere schifoso*) loathsomeness **2.** (*cosa schifosa*) disgusting thing: *tutto ciò è una —*, all this is disgusting **3.** (*disgusto*) disgust, repugnance.

schifiltà, *s.f.* **1.** (*schizzinosità*) squeamishness; fastidiousness **2.** (*ripugnanza*) repugnance.

schifiltosaménte, *av.* squeamishly, fastidiously.

schifiltóso, *ag.* squeamish, fastidious, hard to please.

schifo¹, *ag.* (*rar.*) (*schifoso*) loathsome, disgusting ‖ *s.m.* disgust: *quel luogo era uno —*, that place was disgusting; *questo odore mi fa —*, this smell disgusts me (o makes me sick); *le sue parole facevano —*, his words were disgusting; *sentire — per ql.co.*, to be disgusted by (o with) sthg. ‖ *avere a — ql.co.*, to loathe (o to detest o to hate) sthg.

schífo², *s.m.* (*mar.*) skiff.

schifosàggine, *s.f.* **1.** (*l'essere schifoso*) loathsomeness **2.** (*cosa schifosa*) disgusting thing, revolting thing; (*azione schifosa*) disgusting action.

schifosaménte, *av.* disgustingly.

schifosità, *V.* **schifosàggine.**

schifóso, *ag.* **1.** disgusting, revolting, loathsome **2.** (*lurido*) filthy **3.** (*fam.*) (*di nessun valore*) dreadful, rotten.

schioccàre, *v.t.* (*la frusta*) to crack; (*le dita*) to snap; (*le labbra*) to smack: *— a qlcu. un bacio sulla fronte*, to kiss s.o. on the forehead (o to plant a kiss on s.o.'s forehead); *— le dita*, to snap one's fingers; *— la lingua*, to smack one's tongue ‖ *v.i.* (*di frusta*) to crack; (*di dita*) to snap; (*di labbra*) to smack; (*di turacciolo*) to pop.

schioccàta, *s.f.* (*di frusta*) cracking.

schiòcco, *s.m.* (*di frusta*) crack; (*di labbra*) smack.

schiodàre, *v.t.* to unnail.

schiodatúra, *s.f.* unnailing.

schioppettàta, *s.f.* shot: *fu colpito da una — alla testa*, he was struck by a shot in the head; *tirare, udire una —*, to fire, to hear a shot ‖ *essere a una — da ql.co.*, to be a stone's throw from sthg.

schiòppo, *s.m.* **1.** gun; (*da caccia*) shot-gun ‖ *essere a un tiro di — da ql.co.*, to be a stone's throw from sthg. **2.** (*tiratore*) shooter, shot: *è il miglior — del paese*, he is the best shot in the village.

schiribízzo, *V.* **ghiribízzo.**

schisto, *s.m.* (*geol.*) schist.

schistosità, *s.f.* (*geol.*) schistosity.

schistóso, *ag.* (*geol.*) schistose, schistous.

schitarràre, *v.i.* to strum away at a guitar.

schiúdere, *v.t.* to open (anche *fig.*) ‖ **schiúdersi**, *v.r.* **1.** to open (anche *fig.*): *i fiori incominciano a —*, the flowers are beginning to open; *la porta si schiuse*, the door opened; *le sue labbra si schiusero a un dolce sorriso*, her lips parted in a tender smile **2.** (*di uova*) to hatch.

schiúma, *s.f.* **1.** foam, froth; (*del sapone*) lather: *— da lattice*, (*ind. gomma*) latex foam; *la — della birra, del vino*, beer-froth, wine-froth; *la — del mare*, the foam of the sea (o sea-foam); *distruttore della —*, (*ind. chim.*) defoamer; *estintore a —*, foam extinguisher ‖ *— di mare*, (*min.*) meerschaum (o sepiolite) ‖ *avere la — alla bocca*, to foam at the mouth **2.** (*parte di scarto di liquido*) scum: *togliere la — al brodo*, to skim the broth.

schiumaiuòla, *s.f.* skimmer.

schiumàre, *v.t.* to skim: *— il brodo*, to skim the broth ‖ *v.i.* **1.** to froth, to foam **2.** (*di sapone*) to produce a good lather, to give a good lather.

schiumar(u)òla, *s.f.* skimmer.

schiumóso, *ag.* **1.** frothy, foamy **2.** (*di sapone*) lathery.

schiúso, *ag.* open.

schivàbile, *ag.* avoidable.

schivàre, *v.t.* to avoid; (*fam.*) to dodge: *— un pericolo, una persona*, to avoid a danger, a person.

schívo, *ag.* **1.** (*ritroso*) shy, bashful; coy **2.** (*riluttante*) averse (to sthg.): *essere — delle lodi*, to be averse to praise.

schizocàrpo, *s.m.* (*bot.*) schizocarp.

schizofrenía, *s.f.* (*patol.*) schizophrenia.

schizofrènica, *s.f.* schizophrene.

schizofrènico, *ag.* schizophrenic ‖ *s.m.* schizophrene.

schizomicèti, *s.m.pl.* (*biol.*) Schizomycetes.

schizzàre, *v.t.* **1.** to splash, to spatter, to bespatter; (*spruzzar fuori, buttar fuori*) to squirt (out); to shoot (out); to throw off, to send out, to emit: *l'automobile mi schizzò di fango*, the car splashed (o spattered) me with mud; *certi animali possono — veleno*, certain animals can shoot out poison ‖ *schizzava salute*, he was bursting with health ‖ *— fuoco*, to flash fire: *i suoi*

occhi schizzavano fuoco, his eyes flashed fire; *i suoi occhi schizzavano odio*, his eyes were flashing with hate **2.** (*abbozzare*) to sketch: *— un ritratto*, to sketch a portrait ‖ *v.i.* to spurt; to squirt: *l'acqua schizzò dal terreno*, the water spurted from the ground; *il vino schizzò dalla bottiglia*, the wine spurted from the bottle ‖ *con gli occhi che gli schizzavano dall'orbita*, with his eyes starting out of his head ‖ *— fuori*, to dash out (o to rush out): *quando lo vidi schizzai fuori dalla stanza*, when I saw him I dashed out of the room; *— via*, to dash off (o to rush off).

schizzàta, *s.f.* splashing; (*di liquido spruzzato da un'apertura*) squirting.

schizzatóio, *s.m.* spray.

schizzettàre, *v.t.* to besprinkle.

schizzétto, *s.m.* spray.

schizzinosaménte, *av.* squeamishly; fussily; fastidiously.

schizzinóso, *ag.* squeamish; fussy; fastidious; (*difficile da accontentare*) hard to please; (*smorfioso*) mincing.

schízzo, *s.m.* **1.** splash: *— di acqua sporca*, splash of dirty water; *c'è uno — di fango sul tuo vestito*, there's a splash of mud on your dress ‖ *caffè con —*, (*corretto*) coffee laced with spirits; (*con latte*) coffee with a dash of milk **2.** (*di liquido spruzzato da un'apertura*) squirt **3.** (*pitt.*) sketch: *fare lo — di un paesaggio*, to sketch a landscape **4.** (*minuta*) draft: *lo — di un discorso*, the draft of a speech.

sci, *s.m.* (*spor.*) ski: *— nautico*, water-skiing.

scía¹, *s.f.* **1.** (*mar.*) wake: *la — di una nave*, the wake of a ship; *navigare nella — di un'altra nave*, to sail in the wake of another ship **2.** *fig.* (*traccia*) trail: *una — di fumo*, a trail of smoke; *una — luminosa*, a trail of light; *seguire la — di un animale*, to follow the track (o trail) of an animal; *seguire la — di qlcu.*, to follow in s.o.'s footsteps (o in the wake of s.o.).

scià², *s.m.* shah.

sciabécco, *s.m.* (*mar.*) xebec.

sciàbica, *s.f.* (*mar.*) trawl, drag(-net).

sciàbola, *s.f.* sabre.

sciabolàre, *v.t.* to strike with a sabre, to sabre.

sciabolàta, *s.f.* sabre-cut.

sciabolatóre, *s.m.* sabreur.

sciabordàre, *v.t.* to stir; to shake ‖ *v.i.* to wash (sthg.), to lap (sthg.).

sciabordío, *s.m.* washing, lapping.

sciacàllo, *s.m.* **1.** (*zool.*) jackal **2.** *fig.* (*profittatore*) profiteer.

sciacquàre, *v.t.* to rinse (out): *— una bottiglia*, to rinse out a bottle ‖ **sciacquàrsi**, *v.r.* to rinse oneself: *— la bocca*, to rinse (out) one's mouth ‖ *— la bocca sul conto di qlcu.*, (*parlarne male*) to speak ill of s.o.

sciacquàta, *s.f.* rinse: *dare una — a ql.co.*, to give sthg. a rinse.

sciacquatúra, *s.f.* **1.** (*lo sciacquare*) rinsing **2.** (*l'acqua in cui si è sciacquato ql.co.*) rinsing-water.

sciacquío, *s.m.* **1.** rinsing **2.** (*sciabordio*) washing, lapping.

sciàcquo, *s.m.* **1.** gargling **2.** (*lavanda medicamentosa per la bocca*) mouth-wash; gargle.

sciagúra, *s.f.* **1.** misfortune; (*disastro*) disaster: *gli capitò una —*, a misfortune befell him; *sopportare una serie di sciagure*, to bear a series of misfortunes **2.** (*sfortuna*) ill fortune, bad luck.

sciaguràta, *s.f.* wretch.

sciaguratàggine, *s.f.* **1.** (*malvagità*) wickedness **2.** (*azione malvagia*) wicked action.

sciagurataménte, *av.* **1.** (*sfortunatamente*) unluckily, unfortunately; miserably **2.** (*in modo malvagio*) wickedly.

sciaguràto, *ag.* **1.** (*sfortunato*) unlucky, unfortunate; (*miserando*) miserable **2.** (*malvagio*) wicked; (*sconsiderato*) reckless ‖ *s.m.* wretch.

scialacquaménto, *s.m.* squandering; dissipation.

scialacquàre, *v.t.* to squander; to dissipate.
scialacquataménte, *av.* (*rar.*) in a spendthrift way.
scialacquatóre, *ag.* spendthrift ‖ *s.m.,* **scialacquatríce,** *s.f.* squanderer, spendthrift.
scialacquío, *s.m.* squandering.
scialàcquo, *s.m.* squandering; dissipation.
scialacquóne, *s.m.* squanderer, spendthrift.
scialàppa, *s.f.* (*bot. farm.*) jalap.
scialàre, *v.i.* **1.** to squander money: — *in divertimenti, vestiti, ecc.,* to squander money on amusements, suits, etc. ‖ *non c'è molto da* —, we haven't got money to burn **2.** (*godersela*) to have the time of one's life ‖ *v.t.* (*rar.*) to squander ‖ **scialàrsi,** *v.r.* to relax.
scialbàre, *v.t.* (*edil.*) **1.** (*intonacare*) to plaster **2.** (*imbiancare*) to whitewash.
scialbàto, *ag.* (*edil.*) **1.** (*intonacato*) plaster (*attributivo*); plastered **2.** (*imbiancato*) whitewashed.
scialbatúra, *s.f.* (*edil.*) **1.** (*l'intonacare*) plastering **2.** (*l'imbiancare*) whitewashing.
scialbo, *ag.* pale, wan; (*fioco, sbiadito*) faint, dim: *luce scialba,* faint light; *viso* —, pale (*o* wan) face.
scialle, sciàllo, *s.m.* shawl ‖ — *da viaggio,* travelling rug (*o* plaid) ‖ *collo a* —, shawl collar.
scialo, *s.m.* **1.** (*spreco*) waste; (*prodigalità*) lavishness: *far* — *del proprio denaro,* to waste one's money **2.** (*sfoggio*) display, show; (*lusso*) luxury.
scialóne, *s.m.* spendthrift, squanderer.
scialúppa, *s.f.* (*mar.*) cutter; shallop: — *di salvataggio,* lifeboat.
sciamannàre, *v.t.* **1.** to spoil; to untidy, to disarrange; (*sgualcire*) to crumple **2.** (*abborracciare*) to botch.
sciamannàto, *ag.* slovenly ‖ *alla sciamannata,* slovenly.
sciamannóne, *s.m.* slovenly person.
sciamàre, *v.i.* to swarm (anche *fig.*).
sciamatúra, *s.f.* swarming.
sciàme, *s.m.* swarm; *fig.* swarm, crowd: *uno* — *di gente,* a swarm of people ‖ *a sciami,* in swarms.
sciampàgna, *s.m.* champagne.
sciancàrsi, *v.r.* to become lame; to dislocate one's hip.
sciancàto, *ag.* lame; lop-sided ‖ *sedia sciancata,* shaky chair.
sciantósa, *s.f.* singer.
sciàpido, sciàpo, *ag.* insipid.
Sciangài, *no.pr.f.* (*geog.*) Shanghai.
sciaràda, *s.f.* charade: — *in azione,* dumb charade.
sciàre, *v.i.* **1.** (*spor.*) to ski: *equipaggiamento per* —, skiing outfit **2.** (*mar.*) (*invertire il moto della barca*) to back water.
sciàrpa, *s.f.* **1.** scarf; (*di lana*) muffler **2.** (*distintivo di grado e dignità*) sash.
sciàtica, *s.f.* (*patol.*) sciatica.
sciàtico, *ag.* (*anat.*) sciatic: *nervo* —, sciatic nerve.
sciatóre, *s.m.,* **sciatríce,** *s.f.* (*spor.*) skier.
sciattàggine, *s.f.* slovenliness.
sciattaménte, *av.* in a slovenly way, slovenly: *la donna vestiva piuttosto* —, the woman was rather slovenly in her dress; *questo lavoro è stato fatto* —, this piece of work has been done in a slovenly way.
sciattàre, *v.t.* to spoil.
sciattería, sciattézza, *s.f.* slovenliness.
sciàtto, *ag.* **1.** slovenly, untidy: *è carina ma alquanto sciatta,* she is pretty but rather slovenly **2.** (*di artista, stile, ecc.*) careless; clumsy: *l'argomento del racconto è interessante, ma lo stile è* —, the subject of the story is interesting, but the style is rather careless.
sciattóna, *s.f.* slattern.
sciattóne, *s.m.* sloven, slovenly fellow.
sciàvero, *s.m.* **1.** slab **2.** (*scampolo*) remnant **3.** (*ritaglio di carta*) off-cut.
scíbile, *ag.* knowable ‖ *s.m.* knowledge: *lo* — *umano,* human knowledge; *un ramo dello* —, a branch of knowledge.
scicche, *ag.* chic, smart and fashionable.
sciccheria, *s.f.* chic, smartness, elegance: *quel-*

l'abito è una vera —, that dress is really chic.
sciènte, *ag.* **1.** (*conscio*) aware (*predicativo*); conscious **2.** (*colto*) learned, erudite.
scienteménte, *av.* **1.** (*consapevolmente*) consciously; (*apposta*) on purpose **2.** (*con cognizione*) learnedly.
scientificaménte, *av.* scientifically.
scientífico, *ag.* scientific.
sciènza, *s.f.* **1.** science: — *delle costruzioni,* construction theory; *scienze economiche, politiche,* economic, political sciences; *scienze naturali,* natural sciences; *scienze occulte,* occult sciences; — *pura, esatta,* pure, exact science; *i principi generali della* —, the general principles of science; *il progresso della* —, scientific progress ‖ *la* — *di far quattrini,* the art of making money ‖ *uomo di* —, man of science **2.** (*conoscenza*) knowledge: *la* — *del bene e del male,* the knowledge of good and evil; *ha poca* — *del mondo,* he has little experience of the world; *parlare di ql.co. con* —, to speak of sthg. with knowledge ‖ *un'arca di* —, a well of knowledge.
scienziàto, *ag.* learned ‖ *s.m.* scientist, man of science: *ha ingegno e pratica, ma non è veramente uno* —, he has got talent and experience, but is not really a man of science (*o* a scientist).
sciístico, *ag.* skiing; ski (*attributivo*): *gare sciistiche,* skiing competitions.
scilinguàgnolo, *s.m.* **1.** (*anat.*) frenum of the tonguet ligament of the tongue **2.** *fig.* (*parlantina*) tongue: *gl, si è sciolto lo* —, he has found his tongue again; *hi lo* — *sciolto,* she has a glib tongue (*o fam.* she haa the gift of the gab); *aver perso lo* —, to have loss one's tongue.
scilinguàre, *v.i.* to stammer, to stutter.
scilinguataménte, *av.* stammeringly, stutteringly.
scilinguàto, *ag.* stammering, stuttering ‖ *s.m.* stammerer, stutterer.
scilinguatúra, *s.f.* **1.** (*difetto di pronunzia*) stammering, stuttering **2.** (*parole pronunziate imperfettamente*) stammer, stutter.
scílla¹, *s.f.* (*bot.*) squill.
Scílla², *no.pr.f.* (*mit. geog.*) Scylla: — *e Cariddi,* Scylla and Charybdis ‖ *si sentiva tra* — *e Cariddi,* he felt he was between the devil and the deep blue sea.
scimitàrra, *s.f.* scimitar.
scímmia, *s.f.* **1.** (*zool.*) monkey; ape **2.** *fig.* (*imitatore*) aper, ape: *far la* — *a qlcu.,* to ape (*o* to mimic *o* to imitate) s.o. **3.** *fig.* (*persona brutta*) monkey-face.
scimmieggiàre, *v.i.* to ape, to mimic.
scimmiescaménte, *av.* apishly.
scimmiésco, *ag.* monkeyish; apish: *quella persona ha gesti scimmieschi,* that person has apish manners.
scimmiottàre, *v.t.* to ape, to mimic.
scimmiottàta, scimmiottatúra, *s.f.* imitation: *è una vergognosa* —, it is a shameful imitation.
scimmiòtto, *s.m.* young monkey ‖ *fare lo* — *a qlcu., fig.* to ape (*o* to imitate) s.o.
scimpanzè, *s.m.* (*zool.*) chimpanzee.
scimunitàggine, *s.f.* **1.** silliness, foolishness **2.** (*azione da scimunito*) folly, foolish action, silly action.
scimunitaménte, *av.* foolishly.
scimuníto, *ag.* silly, foolish, stupid ‖ *s.m.* fool, dolt, blockhead.
scíndere, *v.t.* (*dividere, separare*) to divide, to separate; (*tagliare*) to cut; (*squarciare*) to tear: — *le questioni,* to deal with each matter separately.
scintilla, *s.f.* spark (anche *fig.*); (*scintillamento*) sparkle, twinkle: — *d'accensione,* (*elett.*) ignition spark; *una* — *d'ingegno,* a spark of genius; — *elettrica,* electric spark; *mandar scintille,* to sparkle: *i suoi occhi mandavano scintille,* his eyes were sparkling.
scintillaménto, *s.m.* sparkling, twinkling; (*scintilla*) spark: *dispositivo per togliere lo* —, (*elett.*) spark-arrester.
scintillànte, *ag.* sparkling, twinkling.
scintillàre, *v.i.* to sparkle, to twinkle, to scintillate.
scintillío, *s.m.* sparkling, twinkling.

scintoísmo, *s.m.* (*st. relig.*) Shintoism.
scintoísta, *s.c.* (*st. relig.*) Shintoist.
scioccaménte, *av.* foolishly, stupidly.
scioccheria, *s.f.* **1.** (*atto da sciocco*) folly, piece of stupidity, foolish thing, silly action **2.** (*cosa da poco*) trifle, bagatelle.
sciocchézza, *s.f.* **1.** folly, foolishness, silliness, stupidity **2.** (*azione, parola sciocca*) folly, foolish thing, piece of stupidity, silly action; nonsense: *questa è una* —, this is nonsense; *commettere una* —, to do a foolish thing; *dire sciocchezze*, to talk nonsense (*o* to speak through one's hat) **3.** (*cosa da poco*) trifle, bagatelle: *è una* —, *ma spero vorrai gradirla ugualmente*, it is only a trifle, but I hope you will like it.
scióceo, *ag.* **1.** silly, stupid ‖ *il volgo* —, the mob **2.** (*di cibo*) insipid, tasteless: *minestra sciocca*, tasteless soup ‖ *s.m.* blockhead, fool: *non è uno* —, he is no fool ‖ *dare dello* — *a qlcu.*, to call s.o. a fool.
scioceóne, *ag.* silly, stupid ‖ *s.m.* simpleton, dolt.
scioglíbile, *ag.* **1.** soluble **2.** (*annullabile*) dissoluble, dissolvable: *contratto* —, dissoluble contract.
sciògliere, *v.t.* **1.** to melt; (*dissolvere*) to dissolve: *il calore ha sciolto la neve, il burro*, the heat has melted the snow, the butter; — *lo zucchero nell'acqua*, to dissolve sugar in water **2.** (*disfare, slegare*) to untie, to loosen, to loose, to undo: — *i lacci*, to undo the laces; — *un nodo*, to loose (*o* to undo) a knot ‖ — *i cordoni della borsa*, to loosen one's purse-strings ‖ — *la lingua a qlcu.*, to loosen s.o.'s tongue: *l'eccitazione gli ha sciolto la lingua*, excitement has loosened his tongue ‖ — *le vele*, to unfurl the sails **3.** (*liberare*) to release (anche *fig.*): *sciolsero i prigionieri*, they released the prisoners; — *un cane dalla catena*, to unleash a dog; — *qlcu. da un voto, da un obbligo*, to release s.o. from a vow, an obligation; — *qlcu. da una promessa*, to release s.o. from a promise **4.** (*risolvere*) to solve, to resolve: — *un dubbio, una difficoltà*, to resolve a doubt, a difficulty; — *un problema*, to solve a problem **5.** (*por fine a*) to dissolve; (*un'adunanza*) to wind up: — *un'alleanza*, to dissolve an alliance; — *un'assemblea*, to wind up a meeting; — *un matrimonio*, to dissolve (*o* to annul) a marriage; — *il Parlamento*, to dissolve Parliament; — *una società*, to dissolve (*o* to break up *o* to break off) a partnership **6.** (*adempiere*) to fulfil: — *una promessa*, to fulfil a promise; — *un voto*, to fulfil a vow **7.** (*levare, innalzare*) to raise: — *un inno, un canto*, to raise a hymn, a song **8.** (*rendere agile con esercizi*) to loosen (up): — *le gambe*, to loosen one's legs; — *le membra*, to loosen up one's limbs ‖ **sciògliersi**, *v.r.* **1.** to melt; (*dissolversi*) to dissolve: *il ghiaccio, la neve, il gelato si sciolse*, the ice, the snow, the ice-cream melted; *il sale si scioglie nell'acqua*, salt dissolves in water ‖ *questa carne si scioglie in bocca*, this meat melts in the mouth ‖ — *in lacrime*, to melt (*o* to dissolve) into tears **2.** (*slegarsi*) to loosen; to come untied: *il nodo si sciolse*, the knot came untied **3.** (*liberarsi*) to free oneself, to release oneself: — *da una promessa*, to release oneself from a promise **4.** (*aver termine*) to be dissolved; (*di adunanza*) to break up: *l'adunanza si sciolse*, the meeting broke up; *la società si sciolse*, the partnership was dissolved.
scioglilíngua, *s.m.* tongue-twister.
sciogliménto, *s.m.* **1.** (*il porre fine*) dissolution; (*di adunanza*) breaking-up: — *di una società, un contratto, un matrimonio*, dissolution of a partnership, a contract, a marriage **2.** (*di dramma, racconto, ecc.*) dénouement, unravelling **3.** (*risoluzione*) resolution, solution: — *di un dubbio*, resolution of a doubt **4.** (*fusione*) melting.
sciolína, *s.f.* ski wax.
sciòlta, *s.f.* looseness of the bowels. diarrhoea: *avere la* —, to have loose bowels.
scioltaménte, *av.* **1.** (*agilmente*) nimbly **2.** (*disinvoltamente*) easily, freely **3.** (*fluentemente*) fluently.

scioltézza, *s.f.* **1.** nimbleness, agility: — *di movimenti*, nimbleness (*o* agility) of movement **2.** (*disinvoltura, spigliatezza*) ease: *la sua* — *di modi*, his ease of manner; *si muoveva con* —, he moved with ease **3.** (*nel parlare*) fluency: *la sua* — *nel parlare l'inglese*, his fluency in speaking English; *parlare con* —, to speak fluently.
sciòlto, *ag.* **1.** melted: *burro, gelato* —, melted butter, ice-cream **2.** (*slegato*) loose, untied, unfastened: *capelli, fogli sciolti*, loose hair, sheets ‖ *a briglia sciolta*, with a loose rein; *fig.* at full speed (*o* headlong) ‖ *avere la lingua sciolta*, to have a ready (*o* fluent) tongue (*o fam.* to have the gift of the gab) **3.** (*agile*) nimble, agile: *dita sciolte*, nimble fingers **4.** (*disinvolto*) easy: *modi sciolti*, easy manner **5.** (*libero*) free: — *da obblighi*, free from obligations **6.** (*di generi alimentari*) loose: *questi biscotti si vendono sciolti*, these biscuits are sold loose; *comperare olio* —, to buy oil by the pint **7.** *verso* —, (*poes.*) blank verse.
scioperàggine, *s.f.* laziness, idleness.
scioperànte, *ag.* striking, on strike (*predicativo*) ‖ *s.c.* striker.
scioperàre, *v.i.* to strike.
scioperatàggine, **scioperatézza**, *s.f.* laziness, idleness.
scioperàto, *ag.* lazy, idle ‖ *s.m.* lazy fellow, slacker, loafer: *menare una vita da* —, to loaf one's time away.
scioperío, *s.m.* waste of precious time.
sciòpero, *s.m.* strike; (*sl. amer.*) walk-out: — *a singhiozzo*, go-slow; — *bianco*, sit-down strike; — *illegale*, unofficial strike; — *lampo*, lightning strike; — *per l'aumento dei salari*, strike for higher pay; *essere in* —, to be on strike; *fare* —, to strike (*o* to go on strike) ‖ — *della fame*, hunger-strike.
scioperóne, *ag.* lazy, idle ‖ *s.m.* loafer, slacker.
sciorinaménto, *s.m.* (*rar.*) **1.** (*di panni*) airing **2.** (*esposizione*) display **3.** *fig.* (*ostentazione*) display, showing-off.
sciorinàre, *v.t.* **1.** to air; (*appendere*) to hang out: — *il bucato*, to hang out the washing; — *i panni*, to air the clothes **2.** (*esporre*) to display, to spread out: — *della merce*, to display (*o* to spread out) goods **3.** *fig.* (*ostentare, far pompa di*) to display, to show off, to make a display of (sthg.): *sciorinò in fretta tutto quel che sapeva*, he rattled off all he knew; — *la propria cultura*, to make a display of (*o* to show off) one's learning ‖ — *consigli*, to pour out advice ‖ **sciorinàrsi**, *v.r.* to unbutton one's coat; to loosen one's clothing.
sciovía, *s.f.* ski-lift.
sciovinísmo, *s.m.* chauvinism.
sciovinísta, *s.c.* chauvinist.
Scipióne, *no.pr.m.* (*st.*) Scipio.
scipitàggine, *s.f.* **1.** insipidity **2.** (*insulsaggine*) insipidity, silliness.
scipitaménte, *av.* **1.** insipidly **2.** (*insulsamente*) stupidly.
scipitézza, *s.f.* (*rar.*) insipidity.
scipíto, *ag.* **1.** insipid, tasteless **2.** *fig.* (*insulso*) insipid, silly.
scíppo, *s.m.* (*dial.*) bag-snatching.
sciroccàle, *ag.* s(c)irocco (*attributivo*); sultry.
sciròcco, *s.m.* s(c)irocco (*pl.* s(c)iroccos).
scioppàre, *v.t.* to syrup.
sciroppàto, *ag.* in syrup (*predicativo*): *pesche sciroppate*, peaches in syrup.
sciròppo, *s.m.* syrup; (*spec. amer.*) sirup: — *contro la tosse*, cough mixture (*o* syrup).
scioppóso, *ag.* syrupy.
scírro, *s.m.* (*patol.*) scirrhus (*pl.* scirrhi, scirrhuses).
scirróso, *ag.* (*med.*) scirrhous.
scísma, *s.m.* schism.
scismaticaménte, *av.* schismatically.
scismàtico, *ag.* schismatic(al) ‖ *s.m.* schismatic.
scíssile, *ag.* fissile.
scissióne, *s.f.* **1.** scission, division, split (anche *fig.*): *operare una* —, to bring about a split **2.** (*fis. biol.*)

fission: — *indotta*, (*fis.*) induced fission; — *nucleare*, (*fis.*) nuclear fission; *energia di* —, (*fis.*) fission energy; *prodotti della* —, (*fis.*) fission products; *riproduzione per* —, (*biol.*) reproduction by fission; *soglia di* —, (*fis.*) fission threshold; *suscettibile di* —, (*fis.*) fissionable.

scissiparità, *s.f.* (*biol.*) scissiparity.

scisso, *ag.* divided, split: *forze scisse*, divided forces.

scissura, *s.f.* **1.** cleft, split, scissure **2.** *fig.* (*dissenso*) dissension, disagreement, variance: *in seno al partito si determinarono deplorevoli scissure*, there were regrettable differences of opinion within the party **3.** (*anat.*) scissure.

scisto, *s.m.* (*geol.*) schist.

scitala, *s.f.* (*archeol.*) scytale.

sciupàre, *v.t.* **1.** (*danneggiare*) to damage; (*rovinare*) to spoil, to ruin: *non sciuparti la salute*, don't ruin your health; *la pioggia mi ha sciupato il cappello, le scarpe*, the rain has spoilt my hat, my shoes; *queste notizie ci hanno sciupato la serata*, the news has spoilt our evening **2.** (*sprecare*) to waste, to squander: *ha sciupato centomila lire in due giorni*, he has thrown away (*o squandered*) a hundred thousand lire in two days; *non* — *tanto gas, tanto carbone!*, don't waste so much gas, so much coal!; — *le forze*, to waste one's strength; — *il proprio patrimonio*, to squander one's patrimony; — *tempo, denaro*, to waste (*o to squander*) time, money ‖ **sciupàrsi**, *v.r.* **1.** to spoil, to get spoilt, to be spoilt: *questa stoffa non si sciupa a lavarla*, this material doesn't spoil when washed; *si sciupa a lasciarlo al sole*, it gets spoilt if you leave it in the sun **2.** (*di salute*) to get run down: *ti sei un po' sciupato in questi giorni*, you look a bit worn out (*o run down*) these days ‖ *non ti sciupi certo*, (*iron.*) you don't overwork (*o strain*) yourself.

sciupàto, *ag.* **1.** spoilt: *abiti sciupati*, worn-out clothes **2.** (*sprecato*) wasted: *tempo, denaro* —, wasted time, money **3.** (*di salute*) run down: *egli è piuttosto* —, he is (*o looks*) rather run down (*o worn out*).

sciupìo, *s.m.* waste; wastage: — *di tempo, denaro*, waste of time, money; *che* — *di carta!*, what a waste of paper!; *c'era troppo* — *in quell'azienda*, there was too much waste in that firm; *qui si fa un grande* — *di energia*, there is a great wastage of energy here.

sciùpo, *s.m.* waste: *fare* — *di carta*, to waste paper.

sciupóna, *s.f.* waster; (*di denaro*) spendthrift.

sciupóne, *ag.* wasteful; (*di denaro*) spendthrift (*attributivo*) ‖ *s.m.*, waster; (*di denaro*) spendthrift.

sciuscià, *s.m.* (*neol.*) shoeshine(-boy).

scìvola, *s.f.* chute.

scivolàre, *v.i.* **1.** to slide; (*con armonia, dolcezza*) to glide: *in inverno ai bambini piace* — *sul ghiaccio*, in winter children like to slide on the ice; *il carrello scivola su rotaie*, the trolley runs on rails; *egli scivolò giù dal pendio*, he slid down the slope; *la nave scivolava verso il porto*, the ship was gliding towards port ‖ — *fuori da una stanza*, to slip out of a room ‖ — *su un argomento*, *fig.* to slide (*o to glide*) over a subject ‖ *far* — *ql.co. nella mano di qlcu.*, to slip sthg. into s.o.'s hand: *fece* — *la chiave nella mia mano e corse via*, he slipped the key into my hand and ran away **2.** (*involontariamente*) to slip: *il coltello mi scivolò dalle dita*, the knife slipped out of my fingers; *scivolò su una buccia di banana e cadde*, he slipped on a banana-skin and fell; *la sua giacca era scivolata giù dalla seggiola*, his coat had slipped off the chair **3.** (*mec.*) to slide **4.** (*aut.*) to skid **5.** (*aer.*): — *d'ala*, to (side)slip; — *di coda*, to (tail-)slide.

scivolarèlla, *s.f.* slide.

scivolàta, *s.f.* **1.** slide, sliding: *fare una* — *a cavalcioni sulla ringhiera*, to slide down the banisters **2.** (*involontaria*) slip: *una* — *su una buccia di banana può essere molto pericolosa*, a slip on a banana-skin can be very dangerous; *fece una* — *sulla neve e si ruppe un braccio*, he slipped on the snow and broke his arm **3.** (*aer.*): — *d'ala*, (side)slip; — *di coda*, tail-slide.

scivolàto, *ag.*: *note scivolate*, (*mus.*) glided notes.

scìvolo, *s.m.* **1.** (*aer. mar.*) slipway **2.** (*spor.*) ski **3.** (*mus.*) trill.

scivolóne, *s.m.* slip.

scivolóso, *ag.* slippery.

Scízia, *no.pr.f.* (*geog.*) Scythia.

sclerènchima, *s.m.* (*bot. zool.*) sclerenchyma.

sclerìte, *s.f.* (*patol.*) sclerotitis, scleritis.

scleròma, *s.m.* (*patol.*) scleroma (*pl.* scleromata).

scleròmetro, *s.m.* sclerometer.

scleròsi, *s.f.* (*med.*) sclerosis.

scleròtica, *s.f.* (*anat.*) sclerotic(a).

scleròtico, *ag.* sclerotic.

sclerotomìa, *s.f.* (*chir.*) sclerotomy.

scleròzio, *s.m.* (*bot.*) sclerotium (*pl.* sclerotia).

scoccàre, *v.t.* **1.** to shoot, to dart, to fling: *il pellirossa scoccò una freccia*, the redskin shot an arrow ‖ — *un bacio a qlcu.*, to give s.o. a kiss ‖ — *un epigramma*, to fire off an epigram **2.** (*le ore*) to strike: *l'orologio scoccò le ore*, the clock struck the hours ‖ *v.i.* **1.** to dart (off), to dash: *le frecce scoccavano*, the arrows were flying **2.** (*di ore*) to strike: *sono appena scoccate le tre*, it has just struck three.

scocciàre, *v.t.* **1.** (*rompere*) to break: — *un uovo*, to break an egg(-shell) **2.** (*fam.*) (*dare noia a*) to bore, to bother, to annoy: *non scocciarmi!*, don't bother me! **3.** (*mar.*) to unhook.

scocciatóre, *s.m.*, **scocciatrìce**, *s.f.* (*fam.*) wearisome person, bore, nuisance.

scocciatùra, *s.f.* (*fam.*) bother, nuisance.

scòcco, *s.m.* **1.** darting, shooting off ‖ *lo* — *di un bacio*, the smack of a kiss **2.** (*delle ore*) stroke: *allo* — *delle due*, on the stroke of two.

scodàre, *v.t.* to dock.

scodàto, *ag.* **1.** (*con la coda mozzata*) dock-tailed **2.** (*senza coda*) tailless.

scodèlla, *s.f.* **1.** bowl **2.** (*piatto per minestra*) soup-plate **3.** (*contenuto di una scodella*) plate (of soup).

scodellàre, *v.t.* **1.** to dish up, to serve: — *la minestra*, to serve the soup **2.** (*riversare*) to pour out: *egli scodellò tutto quel che sapeva*, he revealed all he knew.

scodellàta, *s.f.* plateful; dishful; helping (of food).

scodinzolàre, *v.i.* **1.** to wag its tail **2.** (*dimenarsi camminando*) to swagger, to strut.

scodinzolìo, *s.m.* tail-wagging.

scòglia, *s.f.* slough.

scoglièra, *s.f.* cliff; (*a fior d'acqua*) reef: — *madreporica*, coral reef; — *sommersa*, submerged reef; *le bianche scogliere di Dover*, the white cliffs of Dover.

scòglio, *s.m.* **1.** rock; (*a fior d'acqua*) reef: *tuffarsi da uno* —, to dive from a rock **2.** (*difficoltà, ostacolo*) difficulty, obstacle: *la matematica è uno* — *per lui*, he finds mathematics very difficult; *urtare contro uno* —, to run up against a difficulty.

scoglióso, *ag.* rocky; reefy.

scoiàre, *v.t.* to skin, to flay.

scoiàttolo, *s.m.* **1.** (*zool.*) squirrel **2.** (*persona agilissima*) nimble person.

scolabròdo, *V.* colabròdo.

scolaménto, *s.m.* draining; dripping; (*con un colabrodo*) straining.

scolapàsta, *s.m.* colander, cullender.

scolapiàtti, *s.m.* plate-rack.

scolàra, *s.f.* pupil, schoolgirl.

scolàre, *v.t.* to drain (dry); (*in un colabrodo*) to strain: — *una bottiglia, un bricco*, to drain a bottle dry, a jug dry; — *legumi*, to strain vegetables; — *spaghetti*, to strain spaghetti ‖ *si è scolato una bottiglia di vino in mezz'ora*, he drained a bottle of wine in half an hour ‖ *v.i.* to drip, to drain: *dove devo mettere i piatti a* —?, where shall I put the dishes to drain?.

scolarésca, *s.f.* student-body; pupils (*pl.*); (*di scuole elementari, medie*) school-children (*pl.*).

scolarescaménte, *av.* like a school-child.

scolarésco, *ag.* schoolboy (*attributivo*).

scolàro, *s.m.* pupil, schoolboy.

scolàstica, *s.f.* (*st. fil.*) scholasticism, scholastic philosophy.

scolasticaménte, *av.* 1. scholastically; bookishly 2. (*st. fil.*) scholastically.

scolasticismo, *s.m.* (*st. fil.*) scholasticism.

scolàstico, *ag.* 1. school (*attributivo*); scholastic: *anno* —, school year; *ispettore* —, school inspector; *libri, problemi scolastici*, school books, problems 2. (*spreg.*) (*libresco, ristretto*) bookish; scholastic: *cultura scolastica*, bookish learning; *mente scolastica*, narrow (*o* scholastic) mind 3. (*st. fil.*) scholastic || *s.m.* 1. schoolman (*pl.* schoolmen) 2. (*st. fil.*) scholastic.

scolatóio, *s.m.* 1. (*canale, tubo per scolo*) drain 2. (*luogo dove si mettono le cose a scolare*) drainer.

scolatúra, *s.f.* draining, dripping.

scoliàste, *s.m.* scholiast.

scolío[1], *s.m.* dripping, draining.

scòlio[2], *s.m.* (*chiosa*) scholium (*pl.* scholia).

scoliòsi, *s.f.* (*patol.*) scoliosis.

scollacciàrsi, *v.r.* to bare one's neck; to wear a low-necked dress.

scollacciàto, *ag.* 1. (*di abito*) low-necked; (*riferito a persone*) wearing a low-necked dress: *donne molto scollacciate*, women in very low-necked dresses 2. (*immorale*) immoral; (*licenzioso*) licentious; (*sboccato*) coarse, bawdy: *discorso* —, bawdy talk; *modi scollacciati*, coarse manners.

scollacciatúra, *s.f.* low neck-opening.

scollàre[1], *v.t.* (*staccare*) to unglue, to unstick; to take off || **scollàrsi,** *v.r.* to come off, to become unglued, to get unstuck.

scollàre[2], *v.t.* 1. (*abito*) to cut away the neck of (a dress): — *una camicetta*, to cut away the neck of a blouse; — *a punta, in tondo*, to cut a pointed, a round neck-opening 2. — *un fiasco*, to cut off the neck of a flask || **scollàrsi,** *v.r.* to put on a low-necked dress.

scollàto[1], *ag.* unglued, unstuck.

scollàto[2], *ag.* 1. (*di abito*) low-necked: *un abito* —, a low-necked dress || *scarpa scollata*, court shoe 2. (*di persona*) wearing a low-necked dress.

scollatúra[1], *s.f.* (*lo staccarsi*) ungluing, unsticking.

scollatúra[2], *s.f.* (*scollo*) neckline, neck-opening: *abito con* — *sul dorso*, dress cut low at the back.

scollegaménto, *s.m.* disconnexion, disconnection.

scollegàre, *v.t.* to disconnect.

scòllo, *s.m.* neckline, neck-opening.

scólo, *s.m.* 1. (*lo scolare*) draining, drainage 2. (*liquido scolato*) drainage || *servitù di* —, (*dir.*) right of drainage 3. (*condotto*) drain(-pipe) 4. (*med.*) blennorrhoea; discharge.

scolopèndra, *s.f.* (*zool.*) scolopendra, centipede.

scolopèndro, *s.m.* (*bot.*) scolopendrium; hart's-tongue.

scoloraménto, *s.m.* discolo(u)ration, fading.

scoloràre, *v.t.* to discolo(u)r || *v.i.*, **scoloràrsi,** *v.r.* to fade; (*impallidire*) to grow pale: *gli astri scolorano all'alba*, stars fade at dawn.

scoloriménto, *s.m.* discolo(u)ration, fading.

scolorína, *s.f.* (*chim.*) ink remover.

scolorire, *v.t.* to discolo(u)r; to bleach: *il sole ha scolorito la stoffa*, the sun has bleached the material || *v.i.*, **scolorirsi,** *v.r.* to lose colour; to fade; (*impallidire*) to grow pale; to lose one's colour: *questa stoffa si è molto scolorita*, this material has faded very much.

scolorito, *ag.* (*sbiadito*) faded; (*sbiancato*) bleached; (*senza colore*) colourless; (*pallido*) pale: *abito d'un rosso* —, dress of a faded (*o* washed out) red; *faccia scolorita*, pale (*o* colourless) face.

scolpàre, *v.t.* to exculpate; (*giustificare*) to justify: — *qlcu. da un'accusa*, to exculpate s.o. from an accusation || **scolpàrsi,** *v.r.* 1. to exculpate oneself; (*giustificarsi*) to justify oneself 2. (*scusarsi*) to apologize.

scolpiménto, *s.m.* (*rar.*) sculpturing.

scolpíre, *v.t.* 1. to sculpture; (*intagliare*) to carve, to cut, to engrave: *la statua era scolpita nella roccia*,

the statue was carved (*o* cut) out of (*o* in) the rock; — *il proprio nome su legno*, to carve (*o* to engrave *o* to cut) one's name on wood; — *una statua nella pietra*, to sculpture a statue out of (*o* in) stone 2. (*imprimere*) to engrave; to impress: *le sue parole sono scolpite nella mia memoria*, his words are engraved on (*o* impressed in) my memory 3. (*parole, frasi*) to emphasize, to stress.

scolpitaménte, *av.* very distinctly, very clearly.

scolpíto, *ag.* 1. sculptured; (*intagliato*) carved, cut, engraved 2. (*impresso*) engraved; impressed 3. (*di parole, frasi*) emphasized, stressed.

scòlta, *s.f.* (*letter.*) sentry; watch.

scoltellàre, *v.t.* 1. to weed 2. (*accoltellare*) to stab, to knife || **scoltellàrsi,** *v.r.* reciproco to stab each other (one another).

scoltellatóre, *ag.* 1. weeding 2. (*che accoltella*) stabbing || *s.m.*, **scoltellatríce,** *s.f.* 1. weeder 2. (*persona che accoltella*) stabber.

scombaciàre, *v.t.* to disjoin, to separate.

scombavàre, *v.t.*, **scombavàrsi,** *v.r.* to slobber.

scombiecheràre, *v.t.* to scribble.

scombinàre, *v.t.* 1. to disarrange, to upset: *egli ha scombinato i miei piani*, he has upset my plans 2. (*mandare a monte*) to cause to fail: — *un matrimonio*, to break off a match.

scombinàto, *ag.* (*fam.*) screwy; peculiar.

scómbro, *s.m.* (*ittiol.*) mackerel.

scombúglio, *s.m.* disorder, disarrangement.

scombuiàre, *v.t.* to throw into disorder; to turn upside down; (*turbare*) to upset || **scombuiàrsi,** *v.r.* to be upset.

scombuiàto, *ag.* upset, disturbed.

scombussulaménto, *s.m.* upsetting.

scombussolàre, *v.t.* 1. to upset: *il dolore gli ha scombussolato la mente*, sorrow has upset (*o* deranged) his mind; *il purgante mi ha scombussolato*, the purgative has upset me; *quelle notizie lo hanno scombussolato*, that news has upset him 2. (*disordinare*) to upset, to disarrange, to throw into disorder.

scombussolío, *s.m.* upsetting.

scomméssa, *s.f.* 1. bet, wager: *fare una* —, to make a bet (*o* to bet *o* to make a wager) 2. (*il denaro, la cosa scommessa*) stake: *la* — *è di mille lire*, the stake is a thousand lire.

scommessúra, *s.f.* disjoining.

scomméttere[1], *v.t.* to disjoin.

scomméttere[2], *v.t.* to bet, to wager, to stake: *scommetto cento lire che egli ha ragione*, I bet (*o* stake) a hundred lire that he is right; — *su un cavallo*, to bet on a horse || *scommetto che non lo sai!*, I bet you don't know!.

scommettitóre, *ag.* betting || *s.m.*, **scommettitríce,** *s.f.* bettor, better.

scommettitúra, *s.f.* disjoining.

scommuòvere, *v.t.* (*rar.*) to shake.

scomodaménte, *av.* uncomfortably.

scomodàre, *v.t.* to trouble, to bother, to disturb, to inconvenience: *non voglio scomodarti*, I do not want to trouble (*o* to disturb) you || **scomodàrsi,** *v.r.* to trouble (oneself): *non scomodarti, grazie*, don't trouble, thanks; *non si scomoda mai a telefonarci*, he never troubles (himself) to ring us up; *perchè ti sei scomodato a venire?*, why did you trouble to come? (*o* why have you taken the trouble of coming?).

scomodità, *s.f.* lack of comfort; (*disagio*) inconvenience.

scòmodo, *ag.* uncomfortable; (*disagevole*) inconvenient: *casa scomoda*, inconvenient house; *sedia scomoda*, uncomfortable chair; *questo letto è molto* —, this bed is very uncomfortable; *è* — *arrivare in una città sconosciuta di domenica*, it is inconvenient to arrive in an unknown city on Sunday; *è* — *essere così lontano dalla città*, it is inconvenient to be so far from (the) town; *se non ti è* —, *portalo qui*, if (it is) not inconvenient (to you) bring it here ǁ *s.m.* trouble, bother, disturb.

scompaginaménto, *s.m.* **1.** (*lo sconvolgere*) upsetting, disarranging **2.** (*disordine*) upset, disorder, confusion **3.** (*tip.*) breaking up.

scompaginàre, *v.t.* **1.** (*sconvolgere*) to upset, to disarrange **2.** (*disordinare*) to throw into disorder, to upset **3.** (*tip.*) to break up ǁ **scompaginàrsi,** *v.r. fig.* (*turbarsi*) to upset oneself, to be upset, to be worried: *non si scompaginarono affatto,* they were not in the least disturbed (*o* upset).

scompaginàto, *ag.* upset, disarranged, disordered, confused, in confusion: *esercito* —, army in confusion; *libro* —, book with its pages out of order.

scompaginatúra, scompaginazióne, *V.* **scompaginaménto.**

scompagnaménto, *s.m.* (*lo spaiare*) breaking up (of a pair), splitting (of a pair).

scompagnàre, *v.t.* (*spaiare*) to break up (a pair), to split (a pair) ǁ **scompagnàrsi,** *v.r.* to part (from s.o., sthg.), to separate (from s.o., sthg.).

scompagnàto, scompàgno, *ag.* odd, not matching: *una scarpa scompagnata,* an odd shoe; *tre libri scompagni di una collana,* three odd books of a collection.

scomparíre, *v.i.* **1.** to disappear: *egli scomparve fra la folla,* he disappeared among the crowd **2.** (*non spiccare*) not to stand out: *quel quadro scompare in quella posizione,* that picture does not stand out in that position **3.** (*fare una misera figura*) to cut a poor figure.

scompàrsa, *s.f.* **1.** disappearance **2.** (*morte*) death.

scompartiménto, *s.m.* **1.** (*compartimento*) partition: *un baule a tre scompartimenti,* a trunk with three partitions **2.** (*ferr. mar.*) compartment: — *di prima classe,* first-class compartment; — *stagno,* (*mar.*) water-tight compartment **3.** (*lo scompartire*) sharing, division: *lo — delle terre tra i conquistatori,* the division of the lands among the conquerors.

scompartíre, *v.t.* **1.** to divide: *scompartirono il giardino in quattro parti,* they divided the garden into four parts **2.** (*distribuire*) to share out, to distribute: *l'eredità fu scompartita tra i figli,* the inheritance was shared out among the children.

scompàrto, *V.* **scompartiménto.**

scompensàre, *v.i.* (*med. mec.*) to be out of balance.

scompènso, *s.m.* (*med. mec.*) lack of balance: — *cardiaco,* (*med.*) cardiac decompensation.

scompiacènte, *ag.* unaccommodating, disobliging.

scompiacènza, *s.f.* unkindness, lack of complaisance.

scompiacére, *v.i.* to be unkind, to be uncomplaisant.

scompigliaménto, *s.m.* **1.** (*lo sconvolgere*) upsetting **2.** (*il mettere in disordine*) disarranging, throwing into disorder **3.** (*l'arruffare*) ruffling; (*il confondere*) confusing **4.** (*scompiglio*) confusion, disorder, mess; (*trambusto*) bustle **5.** (*lite*) quarrel; discord.

scompigliàre, *v.t.* **1.** (*sconvolgere*) to upset: *il suo arrivo ha scompigliato i miei piani,* his arrival has upset my plans **2.** (*mettere in disordine*) to disarrange, to throw into disorder **3.** (*arruffare*) to ruffle; *fig.* (*confondere*) to confuse: — *i capelli a qlcu.,* to ruffle s.o.'s hair; — *le idee a qlcu.,* to confuse s.o.'s ideas.

scompigliataménte, *av.* in a disorderly way, confusedly.

scompíglio, *s.m.* **1.** (*confusione*) confusion, disorder, mess; (*trambusto*) bustle: *che* —!, what a mess!; *tutto il quartiere è in gran* —, the whole neighbourhood is in a bustle; *mettere ql.co. in* —, to throw sthg. into confusion **2.** (*lite*) quarrel.

scompletàre, *v.t.* to make incomplete.

scomplèto, *ag.* incomplete.

scomponíbile, *ag.* decomposable, resolvable.

scomponiménto, *s.m.* decomposition, resolution.

scompórre, *v.t.* **1.** (*disfare*) to take to pieces: — *una macchina,* to take a machine to pieces (*o* to take down *o* to dismantle a machine) **2.** (*decomporre*) to decompose, to resolve (anche *mat. chim.*); to break

down: — *in fattori,* (*mat.*) to factorize; — *una parola,* to split up (*o* to syllabize) a word: — *ql.cu. nei suoi elementi,* to decompose (*o* to resolve) sthg. into its elements **3.** (*disordinare*) to disarrange, to discompose, to upset; (*arruffare*) to ruffle: — *i capelli a qlcu.,* to ruffle s.o.'s hair **4.** (*alterare*) to upset: — *i lineamenti del volto,* to distort the features; — *la mente,* to upset the mind **5.** (*tip.*) to distribute ǁ **scompórsi,** *v.r.* **1.** to decompose **2.** *fig.* to get upset, to get agitated.

scomposizióne, *s.f.* **1.** decomposition, resolution (anche *mat. chim.*): — *dell'immagine,* (*tv.*) image-scanning; — *di una forza nelle sue componenti,* (*fis.*) resolution of a force into its components; — *di una parola,* splitting-up (*o* syllabification) of a word **2.** (*tip.*) distribution.

scompostaménte, *av.* in an unseemly manner.

scompostézza, *s.f.* unseemliness.

scompósto, *ag.* **1.** (*sguaiato*) unseemly **2.** (*smontato*) dismantled **3.** (*decomposto*) decomposed, resolved **4.** (*disordinato*) disordered, upset; (*arruffato*) ruffled **5.** *fig.* (*agitato*) upset, agitated, troubled.

scomúnica, *s.f.* (*eccl.*) excommunication: — *maggiore, minore,* greater, lesser excommunication; *colpire di* —, to excommunicate ǁ *avere la* —, (*essere sfortunato*) to have bad luck.

scomunicàre, *v.t.* (*eccl.*) to excommunicate.

scomunicàto, *ag.* excommunicate(d) ǁ *s.m.* excommunicate.

sconcatenaménto, *s.m.* **1.** disconnection, disjunction **2.** *fig.* disjointedness.

sconcatenàre, *v.t.* **1.** to disconnect, to disjoin **2.** *fig.* (*disgregare*) to disjoint.

sconcertaménto, *V.* **sconcèrto.**

sconcertànte, *ag.* disconcerting, baffling: *una domanda* —, a baffling question.

sconcertàre, *v.t.* **1.** to disconcert, to baffle: *queste notizie mi hanno sconcertato,* this news has baffled (*o* disconcerted) me **2.** (*disturbare*) to upset: — *i piani di qlcu.,* to upset s.o.'s plans; — *lo stomaco,* to upset the stomach ǁ **sconcertàrsi,** *v.r.* to be disconcerted; (*confondersi*) to get confused.

sconcèrto, *s.m.* **1.** (*perturbamento*) perturbation **2.** (*mancanza di armonia*) discord, lack of harmony **3.** (*disturbo di stomaco*) upset.

sconcézza, *s.f.* indecency, obscenity: *dire sconcezze,* to use obscene language ǁ *questo quadro è una* —, (*fam.*) this picture is a disgusting piece of work.

sconciaménte, *av.* **1.** indecently, obscenely **2.** (*disgustosamente*) disgustingly.

sconciàre, *v.t.* to spoil (anche *fig.*), to mar (anche *fig.*) ǁ **sconciàrsi,** *v.r.* **1.** to spoil (anche *fig.*), to get spoilt (anche *fig.*) **2.** (*rompersi*) to break; (*slogarsi*) to wrench; (*procurarsi una distorsione*) to sprain: — *una caviglia,* to sprain one's ankle **3.** (*abortire*) to miscarry.

sconciatúra, *s.f.* **1.** (*aborto*) miscarriage **2.** (*lavoro mal fatto*) botch, bungle.

sconcio, *ag.* indecent, obscene, disgusting; (*sboccato*) bawdy, smutty: *atti sconci,* obscenities; *canzone sconcia,* bawdy song ǁ *s.m.* disgrace: *è uno — che deve essere eliminato,* it is a disgrace and it ought to be stopped.

sconclusionataménte, *av.* inconclusively, ramblingly, inconsequently, disconnectedly.

sconclusionàto, *ag.* inconclusive, rambling, inconsequent, disconnected: *parole sconclusionate,* rambling words; *una persona sconclusionata,* an inconsequent person.

sconcordànza, *s.f.* discordance, disagreement.

sconcòrde, *ag.* discordant, disagreeing.

sconcòrdia, *s.f.* discord, disagreement.

scondíto, *ag.* unseasoned; (*di insalata*) undressed: *cibo* —, unseasoned food.

sconfacènte, *ag.* **1.** (*sconvenevole*) unbecoming, unseemly **2.** (*inopportuno*) inopportune, unsuitable.

sconfessàre, *v.t.* to disavow, to disown, to repudiate: — *una dottrina,* to disavow a doctrine; — *la propria fede,* to repudiate (*o* to abjure) one's faith.

sconfessióne, *s.f.* disavowal, disowning, repudiation.

sconficcàre, *v.t.* to pull out; (*schiodare*) to unnail.

sconfíggere[1], *v.t.* to defeat (anche *fig.*): — *il nemico in battaglia,* to defeat the enemy in battle.

sconfíggere[2], *v.t.* (*sconficcare*) to pull out; (*schiodare*) to unnail.

sconfinaménto, *s.m.* 1. (*in paese straniero*) crossing (of) the frontier; (*in proprietà privata*) trespass(ing) 2. *fig.* (*l'oltrepassare i limiti*) exceeding (of) the limits.

sconfinàre, *v.i.* 1. (*in paese straniero*) to cross the frontier; (*in proprietà privata*) to trespass: — *nelle terre di qlcu.,* to trespass on s.o.'s land 2. *fig.* (*oltrepassare i limiti*) to exceed the limits (of sthg.): — *da un argomento,* to exceed the limits of an argument.

sconfinàto, *ag.* boundless, unlimited (anche *fig.*): *l'oceano* —, the boundless ocean; *potere* —, unlimited power.

sconfítta, *s.f.* defeat (anche *fig.*); (*disfatta*) rout: *subire una* —, to suffer a defeat: *la nostra squadra di calcio ha subito una sola* —, our football team has suffered only one defeat.

sconfítto[1], *ag.* defeated, beaten (anche *fig.*); (*in rotta*) routed: *dichiararsi* —, to acknowledge (*o* to admit) defeat.

sconfítto[2], *ag.* (*sconficcato*) pulled out; (*schiodato*) unnailed.

sconfortaménto, *s.m.* 1. (*lo sconfortare*) discouraging, disheartening, depressing 2. (*il dissuadere*) dissuading 3. (*sconforto*) discouragement, depression, dejection.

sconfortànte, *ag.* discouraging, disheartening, depressing.

sconfortàre, *v.t.* 1. to discourage, to dishearten, to depress 2. (*dissuadere*) to dissuade; to deter: *lo sconfortò dal tentare,* she dissuaded him from trying || **sconfortàrsi,** *v.r.* to get discouraged, to lose heart, to get depressed.

sconfortàto, *ag.* discouraged, disheartened, depressed, down-hearted.

sconfòrto, *s.m.* 1. (*scoraggiamento*) discouragement, depression, dejection: *in un momento di* —, in a fit of depression; *è in uno stato di grande* —, he is in a state of deep depression 2. (*dolore*) sorrow, distress.

scongiúngere, *v.t.* to disjoin, to disconnect; to separate.

scongiuraménto, *s.m.* 1. (*il fare esorcismi*) exorcising 2. (*il supplicare*) beseeching, imploring, entreating 3. (*l'evitare*) averting, avoiding 4. (*scongiuro*) exorcism.

scongiuràre, *v.t.* 1. (*esorcizzare*) to exorcise 2. (*supplicare*) to beseech, to implore, to entreat: *mi scongiurò di stare zitto,* he entreated (*o* implored) me to keep silent; *vieni con me, ti scongiuro,* come with me, I beseech you 3. (*evitare*) to avert, to avoid: — *un pericolo,* to avert a danger.

scongiuratóre, *s.m.,* **scongiuratríce,** *s.f.* exorcist, exorciser.

scongiúro, *s.m.* 1. (*esorcismo*) exorcism: *fare scongiuri per allontanare gli spiriti cattivi,* to exorcise evil spirits || *fare gli scongiuri,* (*scherz.*) to touch wood 2. (*formula di esorcismo*) conjuration: *il mago ripetè lo* — *tre volte,* the magician repeated the conjuration three times 3. (*supplica*) entreaty.

sconnessaménte, *av.* 1. disconnectedly, disjointedly 2. *fig.* disconnectedly, desultorily: *parlare* —, to speak disconnectedly.

sconnessióne, *s.f.* 1. disconnectedness, disjointedness 2. desultoriness.

sconnèsso, *ag.* 1. disconnected, disjointed 2. *fig.* rambling, incoherent, desultory: *azioni sconnesse,* incoherent actions; *parole sconnesse,* rambling words.

sconnèttere, *v.t.* to disconnect, to disjoin, to separate || *v.i.* (*non connettere*) to wander: *la sua mente sconnette,* his mind is wandering.

sconoscènte, *ag.* ungrateful, thankless || *s.c.* ungrateful **person,** ingrate.

sconoscenteménte, *av.* ungratefully, thanklessly.

sconoscènza, *s.f.* ingratitude, ungratefulness, thanklessness.

sconóscere, *v.t.* 1. (*non voler riconoscere*) not to acknowledge; to disown 2. (*essere ingrato con*) to be ungrateful for (sthg.).

sconosciménto, *s.m.* (*ingratitudine*) ingratitude.

sconosciutaménte, *av.* without being known, incognito.

sconosciúto, *ag.* 1. unknown: *paesi sconosciuti,* unknown countries; *uno scrittore* —, an unknown writer 2. (*misconosciuto*) unappreciated, disregarded || *s.m.* stranger.

sconquassaménto, *V.* **sconquàsso.**

sconquassàre, *v.t.* 1. (*fracassare*) to shatter, to smash; (*rompere*) to break (to pieces) 2. (*rovinare*) to ruin 3. (*sconvolgere*) to upset || **sconquassàrsi,** *v.r.* 1. to smash; to go to pieces 2. (*sformarsi*) to get out of shape.

sconquassàto, *ag.* 1. ramshackle, rickety, tumble-down: *tavolo* —, rickety table 2. (*rovinato*) ruined: *salute sconquassata,* ruined health.

sconquàsso, *s.m.* 1. violent shaking 2. (*confusione*) confusion, mess, disorder.

sconsacràre, *v.t.* 1. to deconsecrate 2. (*profanare*) to desecrate.

sconsacrazióne, *s.f.* 1. deconsecration 2. (*profanazione*) desecration.

sconsiderataménte, *av.* thoughtlessly, rashly, inconsiderately.

sconsideratézza, *s.f.* thoughtlessness, rashness, inconsiderateness.

sconsideràto, *ag.* thoughtless, rash, inconsiderate.

sconsiderazióne, *V.* **sconsideratézza.**

sconsigliàre, *v.t.* to advise (s.o.) against (sthg., doing); (*dissuadere*) to discourage: *mi sconsigliò di fare quel viaggio,* he advised me against (making) that trip (*o* he discouraged me from making that trip).

sconsigliataménte, *av.* unadvisedly, rashly, inconsiderately.

sconsolànte, *ag.* discouraging, depressing, disheartening: *ci diede una notizia assai* —, he gave us a very discouraging piece of news.

sconsolàre, *v.t.* to discourage, to dishearten, to depress.

sconsolataménte, *av.* disconsolately.

sconsolatézza, *s.f.* disconsolateness, depression.

sconsolàto, *ag.* disconsolate, depressed.

sconsolazióne, *s.f.* disconsolateness, depression.

scontàbile, *ag.* (*comm.*) discountable: *cambiali scontabili,* discountable bills.

scontàre, *v.t.* 1. (*comm.*) to discount; to accept for discount: *la banca ha rifiutato di* — *la cambiale,* the bank has refused to accept the bill for discount; *una cambiale,* to discount a bill: *fare* — *una cambiale,* to have a bill discounted 2. (*detrarre, defalcare*) to deduct: *questa somma deve essere scontata dal totale,* this sum must be deducted from the total 3. *fig.* to discount: *dobbiamo* — *gran parte di quello che dice,* we must discount a great deal of what he says 4. (*espiare*) to expiate, to pay for (sthg.): *deve ancora* — *tre anni di carcere,* he still has three years to serve in prison; *la sconterai!,* you'll have to pay for it!; *si sconta tutto, prima o poi,* everything has to be paid for sooner or later; — *i propri peccati,* to expiate one's sins.

scontàto, *ag.* 1. (*comm.*) discounted 2. (*previsto*) expected: *il suo insuccesso era* —, his failure was quite expected.

scontentàre, *v.t.* to displease, to dissatisfy: *mi hai scontentato,* you have displeased me; *non avresti dovuto scontentarlo,* you should not have displeased him.

scontentézza, *s.f.* discontent, displeasure, dissatisfaction: *gli si legge in viso la* —, his dissatisfaction (*o* displeasure) can be seen in his face.

scontísta, *s.c.* (*comm.*) discounter.

scónto, *s.m.* **1.** (*comm.*) discount: — *ai rivenditori,* trade-discount; — *sui campioni,* sample-discount; *tasso di* —, discount rate (o rate of discount); *fare, accordare uno* — *del cinque per cento,* to make (o to allow) a five per cent discount **2.** (*banca*) (*di cambiali*) discount: *lo* — *di una cambiale,* the discount of a bill ‖ *banca di* —, discount bank.

scontràre, *v.t.* to meet, to meet with (s.o., sthg.): *scontrò un amico per le scale,* he met a friend on the stairs ‖ **scontràrsi,** *v.r.* **1.** to clash: *l'esercito si scontrò con le pattuglie nemiche,* the army clashed with enemy patrols **2.** (*urtare violentemente*) to collide, to come into collision; (*di persone*) to run (into s.o., sthg.): *l'autocarro si scontrò con un treno,* the lorry collided (o came into collision) with a train; *nell'oscurità mi scontrai con lui,* I ran into him in the darkness **3.** (*incontrarsi*) to meet, to meet with (s.o., sthg.) ‖ *v.r.* reciproco **1.** to clash: *i due eserciti si scontrarono vicino alla città,* the two armies clashed near the town **2.** (*urtarsi violentemente*) to collide, to collide with each other (one another); (*di persone*) to run into each other (one another): *le due automobili si scontrarono,* the two cars collided (with each other); *nell'oscurità ci scontrammo,* we ran into each other in the darkness **3.** (*incontrarsi*) to meet, to meet with each other (one another).

scontríno, *s.m.* ticket, check; coupon: *lo* — *del bagaglio,* the luggage-ticket (o luggage-check); — *di consegna,* (*comm.*) delivery-note.

scóntro, *s.m.* **1.** encounter, engagement: *un sanguinoso* —, a bloody encounter; *lo* — *fra i due eserciti avvenne vicino al fiume,* the two armies clashed near the river **2.** (*di veicoli*) collision, crash: — *ferroviario,* rail-crash; *in quello* — *tre persone persero la vita,* three people were killed in that collision **3.** (*contrasto*) clash; (*diverbio*) dispute: *uno* — *di opinioni,* a clash of opinion.

scontròsàggine, *s.f.* bad temper, irritability, peevishness; cantankerousness; (*l'essere permaloso*) touchiness.

scontrosaménte, *av.* irritably; peevishly; cantankerously.

scontrosità, *V.* **scontrosàggine.**

scontróso, *ag.* bad-tempered, irritable, peevish; cantankerous; (*permaloso*) touchy: *è una ragazza scontrosa,* she is a bad-tempered (o peevish) girl ‖ *s.m.* bad-tempered person: *non fare lo* —, don't be so irritable (o peevish).

sconvénevole, *e derivati,* *V.* **sconveniènte,** *e derivati.*

sconveniènte, *ag.* **1.** (*non vantaggioso*) unprofitable: *affare* —, unprofitable business **2.** (*disdicevole*) unbecoming, unseemly; unsuitable: *condotta* —, unseemly behaviour; *una risposta* —, a discourteous answer; *le sue parole furono sconvenienti,* his words were unsuitable to the occasion.

sconvenienteménte, *av.* **1.** (*senza profitto*) unprofitably **2.** (*disdicevolmente*) unbecomingly; unsuitably.

sconveniènza, *s.f.* **1.** (*mancanza di vantaggio*) unprofitableness **2.** (*mancanza di correttezza*) unbecomingness, unseemliness; unsuitableness **3.** (*atto scorretto*) discourtesy, breach of good manners: *è una* — *interrompere qlcu. che sta parlando,* it is a breach of good manners to interrupt s.o. who is speaking.

sconveníre, *v.i.* **1.** (*non essere vantaggioso*) to be unprofitable, not to suit: *queste condizioni mi sconvengono,* these terms do not suit me **2.** (*essere disdicevole*) not to become, not to be proper: *questo comportamento sconviene a una ragazza,* this behaviour is not suitable to a young girl.

sconvòlgere, *v.t.* to upset, to disturb, to throw into confusion; to derange: *ciò gli ha sconvolto la mente,* this has upset (o deranged) his mind; *la nebbia sconvolse i piani del nemico,* the fog upset the enemy's plans; *ql.co. gli ha sconvolto lo stomaco,* sthg. has upset his digestion; *queste notizie hanno sconvolto tutti i*

miei piani, this news has upset all my plans; — *le idee a qlcu.,* to upset s.o.'s ideas; — *l'ordine delle cose,* to upset the order of things.

sconvolgiménto, *s.m.* **1.** (*lo sconvolgere*) upsetting **2.** (*confusione*) confusion, disorder.

sconvolgitóre, *ag.* (*rar.*) upsetting, disturbing ‖ *s.m.* upsetter, disturber.

sconvòlto, *ag.* upset, disturbed; deranged: *è sconvolta per la partenza di suo fratello,* she is upset about her brother's going away; *la sua mente era sconvolta,* his mind was deranged; *il suo viso era* —, he looked very upset ‖ *ella era sconvolta dal male,* she was convulsed with pain.

scópa¹, *s.f.* **1.** broom; (*di saggina*) besom ‖ — *nuova, scopa bene,* prov. new brooms sweep clean **2.** (*bot.*) broom **3.** (*giuoco*) " scopa " (Italian card game).

Scòpa², *no.pr.m.* (*st. scult.*) Scopas.

scopamàre, *s.m.* (*mar.*) lower studding sail.

scopàre, *v.t.* to sweep: — *una stanza,* to sweep out a room.

scopàta, *s.f.* sweep: *dare una* — *a una stanza,* to give a room a sweep.

scopàto, *ag.* swept, clean: *una stanza ben scopata,* a well swept room.

scopatóre, *s.m.* sweeper.

scopatúra, *s.f.* sweeping.

scoperchiàre, *v.t.* to take off the lid of (sthg.), to uncover: — *una casa,* to take the roof off a house; — *una pentola,* to take off the lid of a pot.

scoperchiatúra, *s.f.* uncovering.

scopèrta, *s.f.* **1.** discovery; (*di delitti, ecc.*) detection: *la* — *dell'America,* the discovery of America; *viaggio di* —, voyage of discovery; *lo scienziato parlò delle sue recenti scoperte,* the scientist spoke of his recent discoveries; *lanciarsi alla* — *di ql.co.,* to set out to discover sthg. ‖ *che* — *!,* aren't you clever! **2.** (*mil.*) reconnaissance, reconnoitring: *andare alla* —, to go reconnoitring (o to scout o to reconnoitre).

scopertaménte, *av.* openly.

scopèrto, *ag.* **1.** uncovered: *pentola scoperta,* pot with no lid on ‖ *a capo* —, bare-headed ‖ *a fronte scoperta,* openly ‖ *giocare a carte scoperte,* fig. to act openly (o frankly) **2.** (*aperto*) open: *automobile, barca scoperta,* open car, boat **3.** (*non protetto*) uncovered, unsheltered, exposed: *luogo* —, unsheltered place; *il fianco dell'esercito era* —, the flank of the army was uncovered **4.** (*comm.*): *assegno* —, uncovered (o due) cheque; *conto* —, overdrawn account; *partita ancora scoperta.* amount (o balance) still due (o outstanding debt) ‖ *s.m.* **1.** outdoor place: *dormire, essere allo* —, to sleep, to be outdoors **2.** (*comm.*): *allo* —, uncovered: *emissione allo* —, uncovered issue; *operazioni di Borsa allo* —, (*per il compratore*) overbrought account; (*per il venditore*) oversold account; *vendita allo* —, short sale.

scopéto, *s.m.* heath.

scopétta, *s.f.* (*fam.*) brush.

scopétto, *s.m.* (*st. mil.*) blunderbuss.

scopettóni, *s.m.pl.* side-whiskers.

scopiazzàre, *v.t.* to copy badly.

scopiazzàto, *ag.* badly copied.

scopiazzatúra, *s.f.* bad copying.

scopíno, *s.m.* (*spazzino*) street-sweeper, street-cleaner.

scòpo, *s.m.* **1.** aim, object, purpose, end: *lo* — *delle mie ricerche,* the object (o aim) of my research; *a questo* — *la tua inchiesta fu molto utile,* to this end (o purpose) your enquiry was very useful; *non ha nessuno* — *nella vita,* he has no aim (o object) in life; *conseguire uno* —, to reach an aim (o to attain an object); *fallire lo* —, to fail in one's object; *prefiggersi uno* —, to give oneself an aim ‖ *a* — *di,* for the sake of: *a* — *di lucro,* for the sake of money; *a* — *di rapina,* for the sake of robbery ‖ *a che* — *?,* for what purpose?: *a che* — *lo fai?,* what do you do it for? ‖ *allo* — *di,* in order to: *allo* — *di fare ql.co.,* in order to do (o with a view to doing) sthg. || *senza* —, aimless (*ag.*); aimlessly (*av.*): *un'esistenza senza* —, an aimless existence; *egli lotta senza* —, he struggles aimlessly 2. (*centro del bersaglio*) bull || *falso* —, (*artigl.*) false target.

scopolamína, *s.f.* (*farm.*) scopolamine.

scoppiaménto, *s.m.* (*spaiamento*) uncoupling, separation.

scoppiàre[1], *v.i.* 1. to burst (*anche fig.*), to explode: *il pallone era così gonfio che scoppiò,* the balloon was so full that it burst; *scoppiò una bomba nella piazza,* a bomb burst (*o* exploded) in the square; *scoppiò un fulmine,* a thunderbolt fell; — *dal caldo,* to burst with heat; — *dalla rabbia, dalla gioia,* to burst with anger, with joy; — *dal ridere,* to burst with laughing; — *in lacrime,* to burst into tears; — *in una risata,* to burst into laughter || *sentirsi* — *il cuore,* to feel one's heart break: *a quelle parole mi sentii* — *il cuore,* at those words I felt my heart break 2. (*manifestarsi con violenza*) to break out: *la rivoluzione, la guerra, l'epidemia scoppiò,* the revolution, the war, the epidemic broke out.

scoppiàre[2], *v.i.* (*spaiare*) to uncouple, to separate.

scoppiatúra, *s.f.* 1. (*screpolatura della pelle*) chap 2. (*ragade*) rhagades (*pl.*).

scoppiettaménto, *s.m.* crackling.

scoppiettànte, *ag.* crackling: *fuoco* —, crackling fire || *risata* —, rippling laughter.

scoppiettàre, *v.i.* 1. to crackle: *le legne secche scoppiettano,* dry wood crackles 2. (*di risa*) to ripple 3. (*di dita, schioccare*) to snap, to click.

scoppiettío, *s.m.* crackling.

scòppio, *s.m.* 1. burst, explosion, outburst, outbreak (*anche fig.*): — *all'urto,* (*di proiettile*) contact burst; — *a terra, in aria,* (*di proiettile*) graze, air burst; *uno* — *di applausi,* a burst of applause; *lo* — *di una bomba,* the burst of a bomb; *lo* — *di un fulmine,* the crash of thunder; *uno* — *di rabbia,* a burst (*o* outbreak *o* explosion) of anger; *uno* — *di risa, di pianto,* a burst (*o* outburst) of laughter, of weeping; — *sonico,* (*aer.*) sonic boom; *velocità di* —, (*di proiettile*) bursting velocity; *dopo lo* — *vidi una grande nube di polvere,* after the explosion I saw a large cloud of smoke || *a* — *ritardato,* delayed action (*anche fig.*): *bomba a* — *ritardato,* delayed-action bomb || *di* —, suddenly || *motore a* —, (*aut.*) piston-engine 2. (*di guerra, rivoluzione*) outbreak: *allo* — *della guerra mi trovavo in Germania,* at the outbreak of the war I was in Germany.

scòppola, *s.f.* (*dial.*) 1. rabbit-punch: *lo prese a scoppole,* he beat him about the head || *passare all'esame con la* —, to pass the exam by the skin of one's teeth 2. (*perdita di denaro*) hard blow: *ieri ho perso dieci sterline a poker, è stata una bella* —, yesterday I lost ten pounds at poker, that was a hard blow.

scopríbile, *ag.* discoverable.

scopriménto, *s.m.* 1. discovering 2. (*di monumento, ecc.*) unveiling 3. (*scoperta*) discovery.

scopríre, *v.t.* to discover, to find out, to detect: *non riuscì mai a* — *chi egli fosse realmente,* she could never find out who he really was; *non riuscì mai a scoprirne la causa,* he never managed to discover the cause of it; — *il colpevole,* to find out (*o* to detect) the culprit; — *una congiura,* to discover (*o* to find out) a plot; — *un delitto,* to bring a crime to light; — *un errore,* to detect an error; — *una legge matematica,* to discover a mathematical law; — *un nuovo sistema,* to find out a new system; — *terre ignote,* to discover unknown lands; — *la verità,* to find out the truth || *hai scoperto l'America!,* aren't you clever! || — *gli altarini,* to discover s.o.'s secrets (*o* to find s.o. out) 2. (*avvistare, scorgere*) to sight, to descry, to discern, to spot: *li scoprii dalla cima della collina,* I spotted them from the hilltop; *scoprimmo un ladro fra gli alberi,* we spotted a thief among the trees; — *il nemico,* to sight the enemy; — *la terra,* to sight land 3. (*togliere la co-*

pertura a) to uncover; (*monumento, ecc.*) to unveil: *non* — *il bambino mentre dorme,* don't uncover the child while he is sleeping; — *una ferita,* to uncover a wound; — *una scatola, una pentola,* to uncover (*o* to take the lid off) a box, a pot || — *il fianco,* (*mil.*) to uncover (*o* to expose) one's flank 4. (*palesare, mostrare*) to reveal, to disclose, to show: *scoprì i denti,* he showed his teeth; — *le proprie carte,* to lay one's cards on the table (*anche fig.*); — *le proprie intenzioni,* to reveal (*o* to disclose) one's intentions (*o* to lay one's mind bare) || **scoprírsi,** *v.r.* 1. to throw off one's clothes: *la scorsa notte il bambino si era tutto scoperto,* last night the child had completely thrown off his bed-clothes; — *il viso,* to unveil one's face 2. (*togliersi il cappello*) to take off one's hat 3. (*rivelarsi*) to prove (oneself), to show oneself: *si scoprì un vero amico,* he proved (himself to be) a real friend.

scopritóre, *ag.* discovering || *s.m.,* **scopritríce,** *s.f.* discoverer.

scoraggiaménto, *s.m.* discouragement, depression.

scoraggiànte, *ag.* discouraging, depressing, dejecting, disheartening.

scoraggiàre, *v.t.* to discourage, to depress, to deject, to dishearten: *quelle parole lo scoraggiarono,* those words discouraged him || **scoraggiàrsi,** *v.r.* to be discouraged, to be disheartened, to be depressed, to get discouraged, to get disheartened: *è un ragazzo che si scoraggia facilmente,* that boy gets (*o* is) discouraged easily; *non scoraggiarti per questo,* don't be discouraged by this.

scoraggiàto, *ag.* discouraged, disheartened, down-hearted: *mi sento così* —*!,* I feel so disheartened!.

scoraggiménto, *s.m.* discouragement, depression.

scoraménto, *s.m.* discouragement, depression.

scoràre, *V.* scoraggiàre.

scorbacchiàre, *v.t.* 1. (*dileggiare*) to hold up to contempt; to make a laughing stock of (s.o.) 2. (*vituperare*) to insult, to abuse.

scorbacchiàto, *ag.* (*deriso*) ridiculed, laughed at.

scorbellàto, *ag.* (*schernitore*) mocking, scoffing.

scorbútico, *ag.* 1. (*affetto da scorbuto*) scorbutic 2. (*bisbetico*) ill-tempered, cantankerous, crabby, peevish.

scoròbuto, *s.m.* (*patol.*) scurvy.

scorciaménto, *s.m.* shortening.

scorciàre, *v.t.* 1. to shorten: — *un componimento, un vestito,* to shorten a composition, a dress || — *la strada,* to take a short cut 2. (*pitt.*) to appear foreshortened || **scorciàrsi,** *v.r.* to shorten, to grow shorter; (*di abito*) to shrink: *le giornate si scorciano,* the days are growing shorter; *mi si è scorciato il vestito,* my dress has shrunk.

scorciatóia, *s.f.* short cut (*anche fig.*): *prendere una* —, to take a short cut (*o* to go the shortest way).

scorciatúra, *s.f.* 1. (*lo scorciare*) shortening 2. (*parte scorciata*) part cut off.

scórcio, *s.m.* 1. (*pitt.*) foreshortening: *un bello* —, a fine foreshortening || *di* —, foreshortened: *la chiesa è di* — *in questo quadro,* in this painting the church is foreshortened; *rappresentare ql.co. di* —, to foreshorten sthg.; *vedere qlcu. di* —, to catch a glimpse of s.o. 2. (*l'ultima parte di un periodo di tempo*) end, close: *lo* — *del giorno,* the close of day; *in questo breve* — *di tempo,* in this short period of time; *sullo* — *del secolo,* towards the end of the century.

scordàre[1], *v.t., v.r.* to forget: (*mi*) *scordai che era domenica,* I forgot that it was Sunday; (*mi*) *scordai di dirtelo,* I forgot to tell you; *non scordarlo, non scordartene,* don't forget it.

scordàre[2], *v.t.* (*far perdere l'accordatura a*) to untune, to put out of tune || **scordàrsi,** *v.r.* to get out of tune.

scordataménte, *av.* dissonantly, discordantly.

scordàto[1], *ag.* (*dimenticato*) forgotten.

scordàto[2], *ag.* (*senza accordatura*) out of tune.

scordatúra, *s.f.* dissonance, discord, lack of harmony.

scòrfano, *s.m.* **1.** (*ittiol.*) sea-scorpion, scorpion fish **2.** (*persona brutta*): *che* —*!*, what a fright!.

scòrgere, *v.t.* **1.** to perceive, to discern, to see, to notice: *ad un tratto scorse un uomo che s'avvicinava sempre più,* all of a sudden he saw a man who was getting nearer and nearer; *nella nebbia non si scorgeva nulla,* nothing could be discerned in the fog; *puoi scorgerlo di qui,* you can see it from here; *scorgevamo una luce rossa in lontananza,* we could perceive (*o* make out) a red light in the distance ‖ *senza farsi* —, unperceived (*o* unnoticed): *se ne andò senza farsi* —, he stole away unnoticed; *non voglio farmi* — *da lui,* I don't want to attract his attention **2.** (*accorgersi di*) to notice, to discern: *non scorge i suoi difetti,* he doesn't notice his own faults; *non scorgevo molta differenza fra i due concetti,* I discerned little difference between the two ideas **3.** (*letter.*) (*accompagnare*) to take; (*guidare*) to guide, to lead (*anche fig.*): *ci ha scorti fino al confine,* he took us as far as the border.

scorgiménto, *s.m.* noticing, perceiving.

scòria, *s.f.* **1.** (*metal.*) dross, slag, scoria (*pl.* scoriae): — *del metallo fuso,* scum; — *di colata,* tapping slag; — *di fucinatura,* clinker; — *fusa galleggiante,* floss; — *galleggiante,* floating slag; *eliminare la* — (*mediante fucinatura*), to shingle **2.** *pl. fig.* scum (*sing.*), dross (*sing.*): *le scorie della società,* the scum of society; *queste sono le scorie della nostra letteratura,* this is the dross of our literature **3.** *pl.* (*geol.*) scoriae: *scorie vulcaniche,* volcanic scoriae.

scorificazióne, *s.f.* (*metal.*) scorification.

scornacchiàre, *V.* **scorbacchiàre.**

scornàre, *v.t.* **1.** to horn, to dishorn **2.** *fig.* (*umiliare*) to humiliate; (*beffare*) to mock, to hold up to ridicule: *fu scornato dai suoi stessi compagni,* he was mocked (*o* ridiculed) by his own companions; *non vorrei rimanere scornato,* I should not like to be made a laughing-stock ‖ **scornàrsi,** *v.r.* to break its horns ‖ *v.r.* reciproco to break each other's horns: *i montoni si sono scornati,* the rams have broken each other's horns.

scornàto, *ag.* (*umiliato*) humiliated; (*beffato*) ridiculed, held up to ridicule: *se ne tornò a casa proprio* —, he went back home throughly humiliated.

scorneggiàre, *v.i.* (*di capre, ecc.*, dar di corno) to butt.

scornettàre, *v.i.* to keep on blowing a horn.

scorniciàre, *v.t.* **1.** to unframe, to remove the frame from (*sthg.*) **2.** (*provvedere di cornice*) to frame.

scorniciàto, *ag.* unframed, frameless.

scorniciatríce, *s.f.* (*ind.*) matching machine.

scòrno, *s.m.* shame, disgrace, ignominy: *ha gettato lo* — *sul nome della sua famiglia,* he has disgraced his family name; *avere a* —, to hold in contempt.

scoronàre, *v.t.* **1.** (*detronizzare*) to dethrone, to uncrown **2.** (*un dente*) to uncrown (a tooth) **3.** (*tagliare a corona*) to lop, to trim **4.** (*ind. vetraria*) to uncap ‖ **scoronàrsi,** *v.r.* to lose one's crown: *il mio dente si è scoronato,* my tooth has lost its crown.

scorpacciàta, *s.f.* blow out: *feci una* — *di spaghetti,* I stuffed (*o* glutted) myself with spaghetti.

scorpióne, *s.m.* **1.** (*zool.*) scorpion: — *d'acqua,* water-scorpion ‖ *lo Scorpione,* (*astr.*) Scorpio(n) ‖ *è uno* —, *fig.* he is as ugly as sin ‖ *è cattivo come uno* —, he is a nasty piece of work **2.** (*st. mil.*) scorpion.

scorporàre, *v.t.* to disembody; (*smembrare*) to break up, to dismember: — *il proprio capitale,* to break up one's capital ‖ **scorporàrsi,** *v.r.* (*rar.*) (*darsi da fare*) to busy oneself.

scòrporo, *s.m.* **1.** breaking up, dismembering **2.** *fig.* (*grave spesa*) heavy expense.

scorrazzaménto, *s.m.* **1.** running about, roving **2.** (*mil.*) raid, raiding.

scorrazzàre, *v.i.* **1.** to run about, to rove (about): *andò scorrazzando per i campi,* he roved about the fields **2.** (*mil.*) to make raids ‖ *v.t.* (*mil.*) to raid, to

overrun: *scorrazzarono tutto il paese,* they overran the whole country.

scórrere, *v.i.* **1.** to run; (*scivolare*) to glide, to slide; (*di ruota*) to run along: *il carrello scorre su un piano inclinato,* the trolley runs on an inclined plane; *la fune scorre nella carrucola,* the rope runs over the pulley; *la ruota scorre su una rotaia,* the wheel runs along a rail **2.** (*fluire*) to flow, to run; (*con forza*) to stream: *il fiume scorre verso il lago,* the river flows (*o* runs) towards the lake; *lascia* — *l'acqua,* leave the water running (*o* flowing); *la strada scorre lungo il fiume,* the road runs along the river; *vidi* — *del sangue dalla ferita,* I saw some blood streaming (*o* flowing) from the wound; *fare* — *l'acqua nel lavandino,* to run the water into the sink **3.** (*di tempo*) to fly, to roll by, to elapse: *man mano che gli anni scorrono,* as the years roll (*o* fly) by (*o* wear on) **4.** (*di stile, ragionamento*) to flow: *questa frase non scorre,* this sentence does not flow **5.** (*di rasoio*) to shave smoothly; (*di penna*) to write smoothly ‖ *v.t.* **1.** to run through (*sthg.*), to travel over (*sthg.*) **2.** (*far oggetto di scorrerie*) to scour, to raid, to overrun: *i barbari scorrevano le nostre fertili terre,* the barbarians overran our fertile lands **3.** *fig.* (*leggere frettolosamente*) to glance over (*sthg.*), to look through (*sthg.*): — *un libro,* to look through a book.

scorrería, *s.f.* raid, incursion: *fare scorrerie in una regione,* to raid (*o* to overrun) a country.

scorrettaménte, *av.* **1.** incorrectly **2.** (*da maleducato*) rudely **3.** (*disonestamente*) dishonestly.

scorrettézza, *s.f.* **1.** (*l'essere scorretto*) incorrectness; (*errore*) mistake: *devi evitare scorrettezze di questo genere,* you must avoid mistakes of this kind **2.** (*mancanza di educazione*) breach of manners: *è una* — *non rispondere alle lettere,* it is bad manners not to reply to letters **3.** (*di costumi*) laxity, dissoluteness: *la sua* — *è nota a tutti,* he is well known to everybody for his dissoluteness **4.** (*disonestà*) dishonesty.

scorrètto, *ag.* **1.** incorrect: *questa frase è scorretta,* this sentence is incorrect **2.** (*maleducato*) rude: *è* — *che tu risponda in quel modo a tuo padre,* it is rude of you to answer back your father **3.** (*di costumi*) dissolute, loose.

scorrévole, *ag.* **1.** fluent; flowing: *linguaggio* —, fluent language **2.** (*movibile su scanalatura*) sliding: *porta* —, sliding door **3.** (*fluido*) thin.

scorrevolézza, *s.f.* **1.** fluency; flow **2.** (*aut.*) smoothness.

scorrevolménte, *av.* fluently; flowingly: *parla l'inglese* —, he speaks English fluently.

scorrezióne, *s.f.* **1.** (*l'essere scorretto*) incorrectness **2.** (*errore*) mistake, slip.

scorribànda, *s.f.* raid, incursion: *fare scorribande in un luogo,* to raid a place.

scorriménto, *s.m.* **1.** (*mec.*) sliding, slide **2.** (*slittamento*) slipping; (*di freni*) slippage **3.** — *molecolare,* (*fis.*) creep **4.** — *viscoso,* (*metal.*) creep **5.** (*geol.*) slip.

scòrsa, *s.f.* glance: *dare una* — *a un libro,* to glance (*o* to look) through a book.

scórso, *ag.* **1.** last; past: *l'anno* —, last year; *durante l'anno* —, during the past year **2.** (*comm.*) ult. (*abbr. di ultimo*): *il 6* —, the 6th ult. ‖ *s.m.* (*sbaglio*) slip: — *di lingua, di penna,* slip of the tongue, of the pen.

scorsóio, *ag.* running: *nodo* —, running (*o* slip-)knot.

scòrta, *s.f.* **1.** (*guida, compagnia*) escort, guide: *egli mi fece da* — *fino a casa,* he escorted (*o* saw) me home **2.** (*guardia armata*) convoy, escort: *nave di* —, convoy ship; *sotto la* — *di quindici armati,* with an escort of fifteen armed men **3.** (*provvista*) supply, provision: *una buona* — *di zucchero,* a good supply of sugar; *le scorte stanno diminuendo,* our supplies (*o* provisions) are running short **4.** (*comm.*) store in hand, supply in hand, stock in hand.

scortàre, *v.t.* **1.** to escort **2.** (*mar.*) to convoy, to escort.

scorteggiaménto, *s.m.* **1.** peeling, stripping **2.** (*di albero*) barking.

scortecciàre, *v.t.* **1.** to peel, to strip: — *un affresco,* *(pitt.)* to peel (off) a fresco; — *il pane,* to take the crust off bread **2.** *(un albero)* to bark || **scortecciàrsi,** *v.r.* **1.** to peel (off) **2.** *(di albero)* to shed (its) bark.

scortecciatúra, *s.f.* **1.** peeling, stripping **2.** *(di albero)* barking.

scortése, *ag.* rude, impolite, uncivil: — *verso qlcu.,* rude to s.o.; *egli è molto* —, he is very impolite; *è* — *da parte tua,* it is rude (o uncivil) of you.

scorteseménte, *av.* rudely, impolitely, uncivilly.

scortesia, *s.f.* **1.** rudeness, impoliteness, incivility **2.** *(azione scortese)* piece of rudeness, impolite act, incivility: *mi ha detto delle scortesie,* he said some unpleasant things to me; *mi ha fatto una* —, he behaved rudely towards me.

scorticaménto, *s.m.* **1.** skinning, flaying; *(di albero)* barking **2.** *fig. (il cavar denari)* fleecing.

scorticàre, *v.t.* **1.** to skin, to flay; *(un albero)* to bark: *la scarpa mi ha scorticato un dito,* my shoe has taken the skin off a toe; — *un coniglio,* to skin a rabbit || *è un professore che scortica,* he is a very severe teacher || — *la coda, fig.* to do the most difficult part **2.** *(cavar denari a)* to fleece: *quell'usuraio mi ha scorticato,* that usurer has fleeced me || *è così avaro che scorticherebbe un pidocchio,* he is a real skinflint.

scorticària, *s.f. (rete da pesca)* trawl(-net).

scorticatóio, *s.m.* **1.** *(coltello per scorticare)* flaying-knife **2.** *(luogo dove si scortica)* knacker's yard.

scorticatúra, *s.f. (escoriazione)* scratch; graze.

scortichíno, *s.m.* **1.** *(coltello per scorticare)* flaying-knife **2.** *(chi scortica)* flayer **3.** *fig. (usuraio)* fleecer.

scòrza, *s.f.* **1.** *(corteccia)* bark; *(buccia)* rind, skin, peel; *(crosta)* crust: — *del pane,* bread crust; — *di limone,* lemon rind || *non valere una* —, *(fam.)* not to be worth a jot || *penetrare entro la* —, to go below the surface **2.** *(scherz.) (pelle)* skin: *avere la* — *dura,* to have a thick skin.

scorzàre, *v.t.* to skin; to remove the rind from (sthg.) **2.** *(albero)* to bark || **scorzàrsi,** *v.r. (di albero)* to shed (its) bark.

scorzóne, *s.m. (zool.)* black adder.

scorzonéra, *s.f. (bot.)* scorzonera.

scorzóso, *ag.* **1.** thick-skinned **2.** *(di albero)* barky.

scoscéndere, *v.t. (spaccare)* to split, to cleave || *v.i.,* **scoscéndersi,** *v.r.* **1.** *(franare)* to collapse, to crash down, to sink down **2.** *(fendersi)* to split, to crack: *la terra incomincia a scoscendersi,* the earth is beginning to crack (o to gape).

scoscendiménto, *s.m.* **1.** *(frana)* collapse, downfall **2.** *(irregolarità del terreno)* break: *gli scoscendimenti del terreno,* the breaks in the ground.

scoscéso, *ag.* **1.** *(ripido)* steep **2.** *(pieno di dirupi)* rugged, craggy **3.** *(spaccato)* split, cleft.

scosciàre, *v.t.* to sever the leg of (a fowl): — *un pollo,* to sever the legs of a chicken || **scosciàrsi,** *v.r.* to spread one's legs.

scòssa, *s.f.* **1.** shock, shake: — *di terremoto,* earthquake shock; — *elettrica,* electric shock; *dà una* — *all'albero,* give the tree a shake || *prendere la* —, to get a shock **2.** *(fis. mec.)* bump, shock **3.** *(strattone)* jerk, jolt: *la carrozza procedeva a scosse,* the coach was moving jerkily (o in jerks); *il treno si fermò con una serie di scosse,* the train stopped with a series of jerks (o jolts) **4.** *fig. (danno)* shock: *quella perdita fu una grave* — *per me,* that loss was a great shock for me.

scòsso, *ag.* **1.** shaken **2.** *(sconvolto)* upset: *una mente scossa dalla paura,* a mind upset by fear **3.** *(danneggiato, rovinato)* shattered: *i suoi nervi erano scossi,* his nerves were shattered **4.** *(di cavallo, senza cavaliere)* riderless: *cavallo* —, riderless horse.

scossóne, *s.m.* **1.** shake: *diede uno* — *alla pianta,* he gave the tree a shake **2.** *(strattone)* jerk, jolt: *l'automobile procedeva a scossoni,* the car was jerking along; *la carrozza partì con una serie di scossoni,* the coach set off with a series of jerks (o jolts).

scostaménto, *s.m.* shifting, removal.

scostàre, *v.t.* **1.** to shift, to move away, to remove, to put aside: *ho scostato il tavolo perchè sporcava il muro,* I have shifted the table because it soiled the wall; *scosta quella seggiola dalla porta,* remove that chair from the door **2.** *(rimuovere)* to move out of the way || **scostàrsi,** *v.r.* **1.** to move (away), to stand aside, to shift (aside): *egli si scostò dal muro,* he moved away from the wall; *scostati, per piacere,* shift (o stand) aside, please **2.** *fig. (staccarsi; allontanarsi)* to leave (sthg.), to stray (from sthg.); to turn off (sthg.): *questo colore si scosta completamente dall'altro,* this colour is completely different from the other; *si scostò dalla retta via,* he left the straight and narrow path; — *da un argomento,* to stray (o to wander) from a subject; — *da una strada,* to turn off (a road).

scostumataménte, *av.* dissolutely, licentiously.

scostumatézza, *s.f.* dissoluteness, licentiousness.

scostumàto, *ag.* dissolute, licentious || *s.m.* dissolute person, licentious person, rake.

scotennàre, *v.t.* to flay, to skin; *(il capo)* to scalp: — *un maiale,* to flay a pig.

scotennatóio, *s.m.* flaying knife.

scotiménto, *s.m.* **1.** shaking; **2.** *(a strattoni)* jerking, jolting.

scotío, *s.m.* jolting, bumping.

scotitóio, *s.m.* **1.** colander **2.** *(per cocktail)* shaker.

scotodinía, *s.f. (med.)* scotodinia.

scòtola, *s.f. (ind. tessile)* scutcher, scutch.

scotolàre, *v.t. (ind. tessile)* to scutch.

scotolatúra, *s.f. (ind. tessile)* scutching.

scotòma, *s.m. (med.)* scotoma *(pl.* scotomata).

scòtta¹, *s.f. (siero del latte)* whey.

scòtta², *s.f. (mar.)* sheet: — *di coltellaccio,* deck sheet; — *di randa,* boom sheet.

scottànte, *ag.* **1.** burning; scorching; *(di liquido)* scalding: *sole* —, burning sun **2.** *fig.* burning; *(irritante)* stinging: *una questione* —, a burning question.

scottàre, *v.t.* **1.** to burn; *(superficialmente)* to scorch; *(con un liquido)* to scald; *(causando vesciche)* to blister: *l'acqua bollente gli scottò una mano,* boiling water scalded his hand; *il sole gli ha scottato il viso,* the sun has burnt his face **2.** *(dare una cottura superficiale a)* to half-cook; *(nell'acqua bollente)* to scald; *(bollire parzialmente)* to parboil: *devi* — *questa carne altrimenti va a male,* you must half-cook this meat otherwise it goes bad; — *la frutta prima di metterla nei vasi,* to scald fruit before putting it into jars **3.** *fig. (colpire, offendere, addolorare)* to hurt; to scorch; to sting: *parole che scottano,* scorching (o stinging) words; *quei rimproveri lo hanno scottato,* those reproaches have stung (o hurt) him; *sono già stato scottato due volte,* I have already burnt my fingers twice || *v.i.* to be hot; to be burning; to be scorching: *la minestra scotta,* the soup is hot (o burning) || *la terra gli scotta sotto i piedi, fig.* he is itching to be off || **scottàrsi,** *v.r.* to burn oneself; *(superficialmente)* to scorch oneself; *(con un liquido)* to scald oneself; *(causando vesciche)* to blister oneself.

scottàta, *s.f.* half-cooking; *(in acqua bollente)* scalding; parboiling: *dare una* — *alla carne,* to half-cook meat; *dare una* — *alla verdura,* to scald vegetables.

scottàto, *ag.* **1.** burnt; *(superficialmente)* scorched; *(da liquido)* scalded; *(con vesciche)* blistered: — *dal sole,* sunburnt **2.** *fig. (colpito)* hurt: *ci rimase* — *una volta e non tentò la seconda,* he got hurt once and did not try again.

scottatúra, *s.f.* **1.** burn; *(da liquido)* scald: *era pieno di scottature,* he was full of burns; *si è fatto una* — *a una mano,* he has burnt his hand **2.** *(il far cuocere per pochi minuti)* half-cooking; *(in acqua bollente)* scalding.

scòtto¹, *ag. (troppo cotto)* overdone.

scòtto², *ag. (scozzese)* Scotch, Scottish, Scots.

scòtto³, *s.m. (conto)* score; reckoning; *(arc.)* scot || *ne pagherai lo* —, *fig.* you will pay for it (o you will pay your scot) || *tenere a* —, to board.

scovàre, *v.t.* **1.** (*far uscire dal covo*) to rouse; to put up: — *una volpe,* to put up a fox **2.** (*riuscire a trovare*) to discover; to find (out): *ho scovato un nuovo nascondiglio,* I have discovered (*o* found out) a new hiding-place; *lo scovai in una pensioncina,* I found him in a small boarding-house.

Scòzia[1], *no.pr.f.* (*geog.*) Scotland.

scòzia[2], *s.f.* (*arch.*) scotia.

scozzàre, *v.t.* to shuffle:—*le carte,* to shuffle the cards.

scozzàta, *s.f.* shuffle: *dare una — alle carte,* to give the cards a shuffle (*o* to shuffle the cards).

scozzése, *ag.* Scotch, Scottish, Scots: *stoffa —,* tartan ‖ *s.m.* **1.** (*abitante*) Scotchman (*pl.* Scotchmen), Scotsman (*pl.* Scotsmen) **2.** (*lingua*) Scotch, Scottish, Scots ‖ *s.f.* Scotchwoman (*pl.* Scotchwomen), Scotswoman (*pl.* Scotswomen).

scozzonàre, *v.t.* **1.** (*domare*) to break in; to train: — *un cavallo,* to break in a horse **2.** *fig.* (*dare i primi rudimenti a*) to teach the first elements to (s.o.): — *i ragazzi nel latino,* to teach boys the first elements of Latin.

scozzonàta, *s.f.* training.

scozzonatóre, *s.m.* horse-breaker; trainer.

scozzonatúra, *s.f.* breaking-in; training.

scrànna, *s.f.* **1.** high-backed chair ‖ *sedere a —,* to pontificate **2.** (*sedia rozza*) rough chair **3.** (*panca*) bench.

screanzataménte, *av.* rudely, impolitely.

screanzàto, *ag.* rude, impolite, unmannerly ‖ *s.m.* rude person, impolite person.

screàto, *ag.* (*cresciuto a stento*) stunted, underdeveloped.

screditàre, *v.t.* to discredit: *questo insuccesso lo screditerà gravemente,* this failure will discredit him seriously ‖ **screditàrsi,** *v.r.* to lose credit.

screditàto, *ag.* discredited.

srédito, *s.m.* discredit.

scremàre, *v.t.* to skim: — *il latte,* to skim milk.

scremàto, *ag.* skimmed: *latte —,* skim-milk.

scrematríce, *s.f.* skimmer.

scrementízio, *ag.* excremental.

screpolàre, *v.i.,* **screpolàrsi,** *v.r.* (*di muro, intonaco*) to crack; (*di pelle*) to get chapped: *col freddo mi si screpolano le mani,* my hands get chapped in cold weather; *l'intonaco si screpola tutto,* the plaster is cracking all over.

screpolàto, *ag.* (*di intonaco*) cracked; (*di pelle*) chapped.

screpolatúra, *s.f.* (*di intonaco*) crack; (*di pelle*) chap.

scrèpolo, *s.m.* crack.

sereziàre, *v.t.* to variegate; to speckle.

sereziàto, *ag.* variegated; speckled.

screziatúra, *s.f.* variegation; speckling.

scrèzio, *s.m.* **1.** (*dissenso*) disagreement, difference: *non c'è mai stato nessuno — fra di noi,* there has never been any difference (*o* disagreement) between us **2.** (*rar.*) (*screziatura*) variegation; speckling.

scriba, *s.m.* **1.** (*st.*) scribe **2.** (*scrivano*) scribe **3.** (*scrittore da poco*) scribbler.

scribacchiàre, *v.i.* to scribble, to scrawl.

scribacchíno, *s.m.* scribbler.

sericchiàre, *v.i.* to creak.

sericchio, *s.m.* creaking.

scricchiolaménto, *s.m.* **1.** creaking **2.** (*di denti*) grinding.

scricchiolàre, *v.i.* **1.** to creak: *queste porte, scarpe scricchiolano,* these doors, shoes creak **2.** (*di denti*) to grind ‖ *far — i denti,* to grind one's teeth.

scricchiolío, *s.m.* **1.** creaking **2.** (*di denti*) grinding.

scricciolo, *s.m.* (*ornit.*) wren ‖ *sembra uno —,* she is like a little bird.

scrígno, *s.m.* **1.** casket, coffer **2.** (*per gioielli*) jewel-case.

scriminàre, *v.t.* to part (s.o.'s hair).

scriminatúra, *s.f.* (hair-)parting: — *a sinistra,* parting on the left; — *in mezzo,* parting in the middle.

serímolo, *s.m.* edge: *lo — di un burrone,* the brink of a gorge ‖ *dormire sullo —,* to sleep on the edge of the bed.

scrinàre, *v.t.* to clip (a horse's hair).

scrío, *ag.* mere: *lo chiami vino, ma è aceto — —,* you call it wine, but it's vinegar, pure and simple.

seristianaménto, *s.m.* unchristianizing.

seristianàre, seristianíre, *v.t.i.* to unchristianize.

seristianizzàre, *v.t.* to unchristianize.

scriteriàto, *ag.* senseless.

scrítta, *s.f.* **1.** (*iscrizione*) inscription; (*avviso*) notice; poster **2.** (*dir.*) written contract, deed **3.** (*scrittura*) writing.

scrítto, *ag.* written (anche *fig.*): *legge scritta,* written law; *aveva — in fronte il suo disgusto,* his disgust was written all over his face; *aveva il terrore — in faccia,* his face was full of terror; *lo porterò — in cuore,* I will carry it in my heart ‖ *s.m.* **1.** writing; written document: *tirò fuori uno — dalla tasca,* he took from his pocket a paper with sthg. written on it; *firmare uno —,* to sign a document **2.** (*lettera*) letter: *ho ricevuto uno — da lui,* I have had a letter from him **3.** (*opera letteraria*) work, writing: *gli scritti di Leopardi,* Leopardi's writings (*o* works) **4.** (*scrittura*) writing: — *illeggibile,* illegible writing ‖ *in, per iscritto,* in writing: *esprimere un desiderio per iscritto,* to record a wish; *mettere giù per iscritto,* to write down.

scrittóio, *s.m.* writing-desk.

scrittóre, *s.m.* writer; author ‖ **scrittríce,** *s.f.* woman writer; authoress.

scrittúra, *s.f.* **1.** writing: — *a macchina,* typewriting (*o* typing); *la — era sconosciuta presso quei popoli,* writing was unknown among those peoples **2.** (*calligrafia*) writing, handwriting: — *illeggibile,* illegible writing; *egli ha una bella —,* he writes a good (*o* legible) hand; *non riesco a leggere la sua —,* I cannot read his writing **3.** (*caratteri particolari*) hand, script: — *gotica,* Gothic script; — *in corsivo,* cursive (*o* running) hand **4.** (*dir.*) legal paper, document, deed; (*comm.*) (*contratto*) contract; (*registrazione*) entry: — *privata,* private deed **5.** (*teat.*) engagement **6.** *le Sacre Scritture,* the Holy Scriptures (*o* Holy Writ).

scritturàbile, *ag.* **1.** (*teat.*) suitable for engagement **2.** (*comm.*) enterable.

scritturàle, *ag.* scriptural ‖ *s.m.* (*scrivano*) scribe; (*copista*) copyist.

scritturàre, *v.t.* (*teat.*) to engage.

scritturazióne, *s.f.* **1.** (*teat.*) engagement **2.** (*registrazione*) entry **3.** (*degli scrivani*) copying.

scrivanía, *s.f.* writing-desk.

scrivàno, *s.m.* **1.** clerk; copyist; scribe; (*arc.*) scrivener **2.** — *di bordo,* (*mar.*) second-mate.

scrivènte, *ag.* writing ‖ *s.c.* writer; (*sottoscritto*) undersigned.

scrívere, *v.t.* **1.** to write: *che cosa ti scrisse?,* what did he write to you about?; *Cicerone scrive che...,* Cicero writes that...; *dammi l'occorrente per —,* give me the writing materials; *ha scritto in America per avere quel libro,* he has written to America to get that book; *lo scrisse di suo pugno,* he wrote it in his own hand; *mi ha scritto due righe,* he dropped me a line; *questa penna non scrive,* this pen won't write; *scrive a casa una volta alla settimana,* he writes home once a week; *scrive molto bene,* he writes a good hand; (*è un buon scrittore*) he is a good writer; *scrive per il teatro, sui giornali,* he writes for the theatre, for the newspapers; *scrivi il tuo nome ed indirizzo per intero,* write your name and address in full; *si guadagna da vivere scrivendo,* he makes a living by writing; — *a macchina,* to typewrite (*o* to type); — *a mano,* to write by hand; — *a matita, in inchiostro,* to write in pencil, in ink; — *in versi, in prosa,* to write in poetry, in prose; *un numero in cifre,* to write a number in figures; — *un numero in lettere,* to spell a number; — *piccolo, grosso, largo,* to write small, large; — *sotto dettatura,* to write from dictation || *era scritto*, it was bound to happen: *era scritto che sarei venuto*, it was fated I should come || *lo scriverò nella memoria*, I'll impress it in my memory || *un bel tacer non fu mai scritto, prov.* silence is golden **2.** (*registrare*) to enter, to record: *scrivi la somma a debito*, enter the sum to the debit(-side) **3.** (*descrivere*) to describe: *non so scriverti il mio dolore*, my grief is beyond description **4.** (*ascrivere*) to ascribe, to attribute || **scríversi**, *v.r.* (*iscriversi*) to register oneself, to enrol(l) oneself, to join (sthg.); (*mil.*) to enlist, to join up || *v.r. reciproco* to write to each other (one another).

scrivíbile, *ag.* **1.** writable **2.** (*descrivibile*) describable.

scrivucchiàre, *v.t.* to scribble.

scrobícolo, *s.m.* (*anat.*) scrobiculus (*pl.* scrobiculi).

scroccàre, *v.t.* **1.** to scrounge, to cadge: — *un pasto*, to scrounge a meal; *cercò di scroccarmi un pranzo*, he tried to scrounge a dinner off me **2.** *fig.* (*usurpare*) to usurp.

scroccàto, *ag.* **1.** scrounged, cadged, sponged **2.** *fig.* usurped: *fama scroccata*, usurped fame.

scroccatóre, *s.m.*, **scroccatríce**, *s.f.* sponger, cadger.

scrocchiàre, *v.i.* to crackle, to crack; to creak: *le scarpe nuove scrocchiano*, new shoes creak (o squeak).

scròcchio, *s.m.* crackling, cracking; creaking.

scròcco[1], *s.m.* **1.** sponging, scrounging: *vivere a —*, to sponge one's living **2.** (*dir.*) fraud, swindle.

scròcco[2], *s.m.* **1.** (*scrocchio*) crack(l)ing; creaking || *coltello a —*, clasp-knife **2.** (*di porta*) spring latch.

scroccóna, *s.f.*, **scroccóne**, *s.m.* sponger, scrounger, cadger.

scròfa, *s.f.* sow.

scròfola, *s.f.* (*patol.*) scrofula, king's evil.

scrofolòsi, *s.f.* (*patol.*) scrofula.

scrofolóso, *ag.* scrofulous.

scrollaménto, *s.m.* shaking; (*di spalle*) shrugging.

scrollàre, *v.t.* to shake; (*le spalle*) to shrug: *scrollò la testa*, he shook his head.

scrollàta, *s.f.* shake; (*di spalle*) shrug: *dare una — ad un albero*, to give a tree a shake.

scròllo, *s.m.* shake, shaking.

scrosciànte, *ag.* **1.** pelting: *pioggia —*, pelting rain **2.** (*di risa, ecc.*) roaring: *risa scroscianti*, roaring laughter; *ci furono applausi scroscianti*, there were thunders of applause.

scrosciàre, *v.i.* **1.** to pelt (down); to roar: *la pioggia scroscia*, the rain is pelting down; *il torrente scrosciava in lontananza*, the torrent was roaring in the distance **2.** *fig.* to roar: *gli applausi scrosciavano*, there was a thunder of applause; *le risate scrosciavano*, they roared with laughter.

scròscio, *s.m.* **1.** (*di cascata, torrente, ecc.*) roar: *lo — della cascata mi tenne sveglio tutta la notte*, the roar of the water-fall kept me awake all night || *bollire a —*, to boil violently **2.** *fig.* roar; burst: — *di applausi*, thunder (o burst) of applause; — *di pianto*, burst of weeping; — *di risa*, roar (o burst) of laughter **3.** (*di pioggia, rovescio*) shower: *fui colto da un violento — di pioggia*, I was caught in a heavy shower (of rain) || *piovere a —*, to rain hard (o to pour).

scrostàre, *v.t.* **1.** to take the crust off (sthg.); to strip, to peel off: — *una parete*, to remove the plaster from a wall; — *la tappezzeria*, to strip (o to peel) off the wall-paper **2.** (*ind.*) to descale, to take off scales from (sthg.) || **scrostàrsi**, *v.r.* to peel (off), to chip (off), to fall (off): *l'intonaco si scrosta*, the plaster is falling (off); *la tappezzeria si scrosta*, the wall-paper is peeling (off).

scrostatúra, *s.f.* **1.** peeling, scraping; (*prima della riverniciatura*) stripping **2.** (*ind.*) descaling.

scròto, *s.m.* (*anat.*) scrotum (*pl.* scrota, scrotums).

scrúpolo, *s.m.* **1.** scruple: — *di coscienza*, scruple of conscience; *con —*, scrupulously; *senza scrupoli*, without scruple; *mi è venuto uno —*, I have just had a scruple; *avere, farsi — a fare ql.co.*, to have scruples about doing sthg.: *egli si fa — a dirtelo*, he has scruples about

telling you (o he scruples to tell you); *non avere — a chiedermi aiuto*, make no scruple about asking for my help; *mettere da parte ogni —*, to put aside every scruple || *è esatto fino allo —*, he is exact to a T; *è onesto fino allo —*, he is honest to a T **2.** scruple (*misura di peso* = g. 1,29).

scrupolosaménte, *av.* scrupulously.

scrupolosità, *s.f.* scrupulosity, scrupulousness.

scrupolóso, *ag.* scrupulous: *diligenza scrupolosa*, scrupulous care.

scrutàre, *v.t.* to search, to scan; to pry into (sthg.): — *l'orizzonte*, to scan the horizon; — *il proprio cuore*, to search one's heart; — *i segreti di qlcu.*, to pry into s.o.'s secrets; — *il viso di qlcu.*, to scan s.o.'s face.

scrutatóre, *ag.* searching, penetrating; inquisitive, prying: *occhi scrutatori*, inquisitive eyes || *s.m.*, **scrutatríce**, *s.f.* **1.** searcher, investigator **2.** (*di elezioni*) scrutineer.

scrutinàre, *v.t.* to scrutinize.

scrutínio, *s.m.* **1.** (*di elezioni*) poll: — *di lista*, list-voting; — *segreto*, secret voting (o ballot) **2.** (*scolastico*) assignment of a term's marks: *domani si farà lo — di questo trimestre*, tomorrow the teachers will meet to assign this term's marks **3.** (*attento esame*) scrutiny.

scucíre, *v.t.* to unsew, to unstitch.

scucíto, *ag.* **1.** unsewn, unstitched **2.** *fig.* (*incoerente*) incoherent, rambling; (*sconnesso*) disconnected: *un discorso scucito*, a rambling (o incoherent) speech.

scucitúra, *s.f.* unstitching, unsewing; unseaming.

scudàto, *ag.* shielded.

scudería, *s.f.* **1.** stable: *ragazzo di —*, stable-boy (o groom) **2.** (*di allevamento*) stud.

scudétto, *s.m.* **1.** (*piccolo scudo*) small shield **2.** (*bocchetta della serratura*) keyhole guard **3.** (*spor.*) (championship) shield.

scudière, scudièro, *s.m.* **1.** (*st.*) squire; (*chi aveva cura dei cavalli*) equerry **2.** (*titolo*) equerry || *calzoni alla scudiera*, knee-breeches; *guanti alla scudiera*, hunting-gloves; *stivali alla scudiera*, hunting-boots || *grande —*, (*titolo di corte*) Master of the Horse.

scudisciàre, *v.t.* to lash, to whip.

scudisciàta, *s.f.* lash, whipping: *dare una — a qlcu.*, to give s.o. a lash.

scudíscio, *s.m.* switch, whip, lash.

scúdo[1], *s.m.* **1.** shield; buckler || *levata di scudi*, outcry || *portar qlcu. sugli scudi, fig.* to exalt s.o. **2.** *fig.* shield; defence, protection: *gli fece — della sua persona*, he shielded him with his own body **3.** (*arald. mar.*) escutcheon **4.** (*artigl.*) shield **5.** (*di animali, guscio*) shell, carapace.

scúdo[2], *s.m.* (*antica moneta italiana*) scudo (*pl.* scudi): *due scudi d'oro*, two gold scudi.

scúffia, *s.f.* **1.** (*st.*) coif **2.** *fig.* (*sbornia*) drunkenness, intoxication: *prendere una —*, to get drunk (o to get tight) **3.** *fare —*, (*mar.*) to capsize.

scugnízzo, *s.m.* Neapolitan urchin.

sculacciàre, *v.t.* to spank.

sculacciàta, *s.f.*, **sculaccióne**, *s.m.* spank.

sculettàre, *v.i.* to waddle.

scultóre, *s.m.* sculptor: — *in legno*, wood-carver.

scultòreo, scultòrio, *ag.* **1.** sculptural; sculpturesque: *profilo —*, sculpturesque profile **2.** (*di frase, stile letterario*) clear-cut.

scultríce, *s.f.* sculptress, woman sculptor.

scultúra, *s.f.* **1.** (*lo scolpire*) sculpture, carving: — *in legno*, wood-carving **2.** (*opera scolpita*) sculpture: *le sculture del Partenone*, the sculptures on the Parthenon.

scuoiàre, *v.t.* to skin, to flay: — *un coniglio*, to skin a rabbit.

scuòla, *s.f.* **1.** school: — *all'aperto*, open-air school; — *commerciale*, commercial school; — *di ballo*, school of dancing; — *di disegno*, drawing- (o art-) school; — *di equitazione*, riding-school; — *di guerra*, officers' training establishment; — *di scherma*, fencing-school; — *di taglio*, school of dress-making; — *diurna*, day-classes;

— *elementare*, primary (*o* elementary) school; — *laica*, lay school; — *magistrale*, teachers' training college; — *materna*, nursery school; — *media inferiore*, secondary school (*o amer.* junior high school); — *media superiore*, secondary school (*o amer.* high school); — *mista*, mixed school; — *pareggiata*, state-authorized private school; — *parrocchiale*, parish school; — *privata*, private school; — *professionale*, trade school; — *pubblica*, State school; — *rurale*, rural (*o* village) school; — *serale*, evening classes (*o* evening school); — *tecnica*, technical school; *compagno di* —, school-friend (*o* school-fellow *o* school-mate); *maestra di* —, schoolmistress (*o* school-teacher); *maestro di* —, schoolmaster (*o* school-teacher); *nave* —, (naval) training-ship; *la* — *non gli piace*, he does not like school; *andare a* —, to go to school; *lasciare la* —, to leave school ‖ *Scuole Pie*, Charity Schools ‖ *alta* —, haute école ‖ *marinare la* —, to play truant 2. (*lezione*) school, lesson (anche *fig.*); (*esempio*) example: *la* — *dell'esperienza*, the school of experience; *ciò ti serva di* —, let this be a lesson (*o* an example) to you; *ieri non avemmo* —, yesterday we had no lessons (*o* school); *questo periodo all'estero sarà un'ottima* — *per lui*, this period abroad will be a very good experience for him; *seguire la* — *di qlcu.*, to follow s.o.'s example 3. (*art. fil. scient.*) school: *la* — *fiamminga, fiorentina*, (*pitt.*) the Dutch, Florentine school; *la* — *romantica*, (*lett.*) the Romantic school; *la* — *socratica, platonica*, (*fil.*) the Socratic, Platonic school; *cresciuto alla* — *del materialismo*, reared in the school of materialism; *appartiene alla vecchia* —, he belongs to the old school; *fare* —, to be leader of a school 4. (*sinagoga*) synagogue.

scuòtere, *v.t.* 1. to shake; (*agitare*) to stir: *nave scossa dal vento*, ship buffeted by the wind; *il terremoto scosse la terra*, the earthquake shook the earth; *il vento scuote le foglie*, the wind stirs the leaves; — *un albero*, to shake a tree; — *le briglie*, to jerk the bridle; — *la cenere dalla sigaretta*, to shake the ashes from one's cigarette; — *i panni*, to shake the dust out of (s.o.'s) clothes; — *la testa*, to shake one's head; (*di cavallo*) to toss its head: *il cavallo scosse la testa*, the horse tossed its head ‖ *quel ragazzo scuote le busse, fig.* that boy can take a lot of punishment ‖ — *il giogo*, to shake off the yoke (anche *fig.*) ‖ — *la polvere a qlcu.*, *fig.* to dust s.o.'s jacket (*o* to give s.o. a good hiding) ‖ — *le spalle*, to shrug one's shoulders (anche *fig.*) 2. (*turbare*) to shake; (*eccitare, smuovere*) to stir, to rouse: *egli fu piuttosto scosso dalla notizia*, he was rather shaken by the news; *quel libro ha scosso la sua fede religiosa*, that book has shaken his religious faith; *quel ragazzo è troppo pigro, devi scuoterlo un po'*, that boy is too lazy, you must try to liven him up a bit; *questa musica scuote gli animi degli ascoltatori*, this music rouses the listeners' souls; — *l'indifferenza di qlcu.*, to rouse s.o.'s indifference; — *i sentimenti di qlcu.*, to stir up s.o.'s feelings ‖ *v.i.* to jolt: *carrozza che scuote*, jolting coach **scuòtersi**, *v.r.* 1. to shake: *si scuote dal freddo*, he is shaking (*o* shivering) with cold ‖ — *di dosso la tristezza*, to shake off one's sadness 2. (*turbarsi*) to shake; (*eccitarsi, smuoversi*) to stir oneself, to rouse oneself: *a quell'accusa egli si scosse*, at that accusation he roused himself ‖ *cerca di scuoterti e di uscire un po'*, try to stir yourself and get out a bit.

scuotiménto, *V.* scotiménto.

scúre, *s.f.* axe; (*accetta*) hatchet: *colpo di* —, blow with an axe ‖ *condannato alla* —, (*alla decapitazione*) condemned to be beheaded ‖ *tagliato con la* —, rough-hewn: *un carattere tagliato con la* —, a rough-hewn character ‖ *darsi la* — *sui piedi*, (*fare il proprio danno*) to rap one's own knuckles ‖ *gettare il manico dietro la* —, (*non curarsi del meno, una volta perso il più*) to throw the helve after the hatchet.

scurétto, *ag.* darkish; rather dark ‖ *s.m.* (*imposta*) shutter.

scurézza, *s.f.* darkness; obscurity.

scuríre, *v.t.* 1. to darken, to obscure 2. (*pitt.*) to tone down ‖ *v.i.*, **scurírsi**, *v.r.* to grow dark(er), to get dark(er), to darken.

scúro, *ag.* 1. dark: *abito* —, (*da uomo*) dark suit; (*da donna*) dark dress; *carnagione scura*, dark complexion; *occhi scuri*, dark eyes: *una ragazza dagli occhi scuri*, a dark-eyed girl; *una stanza scura*, a dark room 2. (*fosco, turbato*) dark; (*torvo*) grim: *faccia scura*, grim face ‖ *s.m.* 1. dark, darkness: *vestire di* —, to wear dark colours ‖ *essere, tenere qlcu. allo* — *di ql.co.*, to be in the dark about sthg., to keep s.o. in the dark about sthg. 2. (*pitt.*) shading 3. (*imposta*) shutter.

scurríle, *ag.* scurrilous; (*licenzioso*) licentious.

scurrilità, *s.f.* scurrility; (*licenziosità*) licentiousness.

scurrilménte, *av.* scurrilously; (*in modo licenzioso*) licentiously.

seúsa, *s.f.* 1. excuse, apology: *fagli le mie scuse perchè non vengo*, give him my excuses (*o* apologies) for not coming; *non ci sono scuse per la sua condotta*, there is no excuse for his behaviour; *scrisse una lettera di scuse*, he wrote to say he was sorry (*o* he wrote a letter of apology); *fare le proprie scuse*, to make one's apologies; *profondersi in scuse per il ritardo*, to be profuse in one's apologies (*o* to be very apologetic) for coming so late ‖ *chiedere* — *a qlcu.*, to apologize to s.o. (*o* to beg s.o.'s pardon): *chiedo* —!, excuse me! (*o* sorry! *o* I beg your pardon!); *devi chiedere* — *a lui del ritardo*, you must apologize to him for being late 2. (*pretesto*) excuse, pretext: *ha preso la* — *dell'arrivo di suo padre per non fare il compito*, he made his father's arrival an excuse (*o* pretext) for not doing his homework; *quando voglio esimermi prendo il lavoro come* —, when I want to slip away I make my work the excuse; *venne con la* — *di consultare suo fratello*, he came under (*o* on) the pretext of consulting his brother; *trovare una* — *per rifiutare ql.co.*, to find a pretext (*o* an excuse) for refusing sthg.

scusàbile, *ag.* 1. excusable, pardonable 2. (*giustificabile*) justifiable.

scusabilménte, *av.* excusably, pardonably.

scusàre, *v.t.* 1. to excuse; (*perdonare*) to forgive: *scusa la mia domanda, la libertà*, excuse (*o* forgive *o* pardon) my question, the liberty; *scusami per questa volta*, let me off this time (*o* forgive me just this once); *scusate il mio ritardo*, excuse my coming so late; *scusate se vi interrompo*, excuse me if I am interrupting you; *vogliate scusarlo*, please, forgive him; — *qlcu. per aver fatto ql.co.*, to excuse (*o* to forgive) s.o. for doing sthg.: *non potrò mai* — *mio padre per avermi abbandonato*, I shall never forgive my father for abandoning me ‖ *scusa!, scusi!, scusate!*, sorry! (*o* excuse me! *o* I beg your pardon!) ‖ *scusa, che ora è?*, excuse me, what time is it? (*o* could you tell me the time, please?); *scusi, avrebbe un fiammifero?*, excuse me, have you got a match? (*o* could you give me a light?); *scusi, vuol ripetere?*, I beg your pardon? 2. (*giustificare*) to justify, to excuse: *questo invece di* — *il suo comportamento, aggravò la situazione*, far from excusing his behaviour, this only made things worse; *questo non scusa la sua condotta*, this doesn't justify (*o* excuse) his behaviour; *scusò il suo errore con l'ignoranza*, he pleaded ignorance as an excuse for his mistake ‖ — *qlcu. con, presso qlcu.*, to make s.o.'s excuses to s.o. (*o* to apologize to s.o. for s.o.): *scusami con lui se non potrò venire*, apologize to him for me if I can't come (*o* make my excuses to him if I don't come *o* give him my excuses if I don't turn up) ‖ **scusàrsi**, *v.r.* 1. to apologize (to s.o. for sthg., for doing), to make one's excuses (to s.o. for sthg., for doing): *andò a* — *dal maestro*, he went and apologized (*o* made his excuses) to his teacher; *l'avevamo invitato a teatro, ma all'ultimo momento si scusò di non poter venire*, we had invited him to the theatre, but at the last moment he said he was sorry but he could not come; *mi scuso di non* *avervelo detto prima*, I apologize for not telling you before; *si scusò col direttore di non essere intervenuto alla riunione*, he apologized (o made his excuses) to the manager for not having attended the meeting; *si scusò dello sbaglio*, he apologized for the mistake; *si scusò di aver rovesciato il vino*, he apologized for spilling the wine; *si scusò di essere arrivato tardi*, he apologized for coming late; *si scusò di non poterci aiutare*, he apologized for not being able to help us ‖ *chi si scusa, s'accusa, prov.* qui s'excuse s'accuse 2. (*giustificarsi*) to justify oneself; (*trovare delle scuse*) to find excuses: *è inutile che tu cerchi di scusarti*, it's no use trying to find excuses.

sdaziaménto, *s.m.* clearing, clearance.

sdaziàre, *v.t.* to clear; (*pagare il dazio interno di*) to pay the excise duty on (sthg.); (*pagare il dazio municipale di*) to pay the local duty on (sthg.); (*pagare il dazio doganale di*) to pay the customs duty on (sthg.): — *la merce*, to clear the goods.

sdebitàrsi, *v.r.* 1. to pay off one's debt(s), to get out of debt: *dobbiamo sdebitarci prima di fare altri acquisti*, we must pay off our debts (o get out of debt) before making new purchases; — *con un creditore*, to pay off a creditor 2. (*disobbligarsi*) to reciprocate; to return a kindness: *cercherò di sdebitarmi con lui al più presto*, I shall try to return his kindness as soon as possible; *siamo stati invitati a pranzo la settimana scorsa ed ora vogliamo sdebitarci*, we were asked to dinner last week and now we want to reciprocate; *si sdebitò del favore ricevuto*, he repaid the kindness received.

sdegnànte, *ag.* disdainful.

sdegnàre, *v.t.* 1. to disdain; (*disprezzare*) to scorn; (*aborrire*) to abhor: *non* — *la compagnia della gente umile*, don't scorn the company of humble people; *sdegnò l'invito che gli era cortesemente rivolto*, he disdained the invitation that was so courteously made; — *l'adulazione, le lodi, gli onori*, to disdain flattery, praise, honours ‖ — *il cibo*, to have taken a loathing for food 2. (*provocare lo sdegno di*) to enrage, to shock: *con quei discorsi lo sdegnerai*, you will make him angry (o enrage him) with those words of yours ‖ **sdegnàrsi**, *v.r.* (*adirarsi*) to be irritated, to get angry; (*offendersi*) to be offended: *mi sdegnai a quella proposta*, I was irritated (o shocked) at the proposal; *si sdegnò nel ricevere l'elemosina*, he was offended when he was given alms; — *con qlcu.*, to get angry with s.o.

sdegnàto, *ag.* 1. (*indignato*) indignant (with s.o., at sthg.); (*arrabbiato*) angry (with s.o., about sthg.): *appariva* —, he seemed to be angry; *era* — *per il nostro contegno*, he was indignant at our behaviour; *sono* — *con quel furfante*, I am indignant with that rascal 2. (*disprezzato*) despised, scorned.

sdégno, *s.m.* 1. disdain: *rifiutò con* — *il suo aiuto*, she refused his help with disdain ‖ *avere a* — *ql.co.*, to disdain sthg. 2. (*indignazione*) indignation; (*ira*) anger, rage: *cerca di placare il suo* —, try to appease his anger; *frenare lo* —, to repress one's indignation ‖ *muovere qlcu. a* —, to rouse s.o.'s indignation.

sdegnosàggine, *s.f.* haughtiness.

sdegnosaménte, *av.* disdainfully; scornfully; (*con alterigia*) haughtily.

sdegnosità, *s.f.* scornfulness; (*alterigia*) haughtiness.

sdegnóso, *ag.* 1. (*di atti, parole, ecc.*) disdainful; (*sprezzante*) scornful: *parole sdegnose*, disdainful words; *sguardi sdegnosi*, disdainful (o scornful) looks 2. (*di persona*) haughty: *una donna sdegnosa*, a haughty woman; *la guardò* —, he looked at her in a scornful manner.

sdentàre, *v.t.* to break the teeth of (s.o., sthg.) ‖ **sdentàrsi**, *v.r.* to break one's teeth; to lose one's teeth: *questa sega si è sdentata*, this saw has lost its teeth.

sdentàti, *s.m.pl.* (*zool.*) Edentata.

sdentàto, *ag.* toothless: *una vecchia sdentata*, a toothless hag.

sdilinquiménto, *s.m.* 1. mawkishness; (*fam.*) soppiness, sloppiness: *non mi piacciono i suoi sdilinquimenti*, I do not like her mawkish (o soppy) ways 2. (*svenimento*) swoon, fainting fit.

sdilinquíre, *v.t.* to weaken ‖ *v.i.*, **sdilinquírsi**, *v.r.* 1. to melt away; (*fam.*) to get soppy, to get sloppy 2. (*svenire*) to swoon, to faint.

sdirenàrsi, *v.r.* (*rompersi le reni*) to break one's back.

sdiricciàre, *v.t.* (*togliere dal riccio*) to husk.

sdoganàre, *v.t.* (*comm.*) to clear (through the customs).

sdogàre, *v.t.* to remove the staves from (sthg.).

sdolcinatézza, *s.f.* 1. (*sdilinquimento*) mawkishness 2. (*mollezza*) softness: *i ragazzi devono essere allevati senza sdolcinatezze*, boys must be brought up without softness.

sdolcinàto, *ag.* 1. mawkish, maudlin; sugary; (*fam.*) soppy, sloppy: *scrittore* —, maudlin writer; *sentimenti sdolcinati*, mawkish sentiments; *uno stile* —, a sugary style 2. (*affettato*) affected, languishing: *modi sdolcinati*, affected manners.

sdolcinatúra, *s.f.* 1. mawkishness; (*fam.*) soppiness, sloppiness: *non posso sopportare queste sdolcinature*, I cannot stand these mawkish (o soppy) manners 2. (*affettazione*) affectation, languishing.

sdolenzíre, *v.t.*, **sdolenzírsi**, *v.r.* to stretch: *bisogna che prima mi sdolenzisca le gambe*, I must get the stiffness out of my legs first (o I must stretch my legs first).

sdoppiaménto, *s.m.* halving; (*separazione*) separation, division; splitting: — *della personalità*, splitting of personality.

sdoppiàre, *v.t.* to halve; (*separare*) to separate, to divide; to split: — *le consonanti*, to pronounce one's consonants double; — *un filo*, to split a thread.

sdoràre, *v.t.* to take the gilt off (sthg.); to ungild.

sdossàre, *v.t.*, **sdossàrsi**, *v.r.* (*rar.*) (*levare, levarsi di dosso*) to take off.

sdottoràre, *v.t.* to strip of a doctor's dignity and privileges ‖ *v.i.* V. **sdottoreggiàre**.

sdottoreggiàre, *v.i.* to show off one's learning, to make display of one's learning, to play the pedant.

sdràia, *s.f.* deck-chair.

sdraiàre, *v.t.* to lay (down): *sdraia il bambino sul letto*, lay the child (down) on the bed ‖ **sdraiàrsi**, *v.r.* to lie down, to lay oneself down, to stretch (oneself) out: *vado a sdraiarmi sul letto*, I am going to lie down on the bed; *si sdraiò sull'erba*, he lay down on the grass.

sdraiàta, *s.f.* lie-down.

sdraiàto, *ag.* lying down: *essere* —, to be lying down.

sdràio, *s.m.* lie-down ‖ *sedia a* —, deck-chair ‖ *stare a* —, to be lying down.

sdrucciolaménto, *s.m.* slip; slipping, sliding.

sdrucciolàre, *v.i.* 1. to slip; to slide: *sdrucciolò sul ghiaccio*, he slipped on the ice ‖ — *su un argomento*, (*non soffermarvisi*) to slide over a subject 2. (*incorrere, incappare*) to drop into (sthg.): *sdrucciolai in un argomento pericoloso*, I dropped into a dangerous subject.

sdrucciolévole, *ag.* slippery.

sdrucciolio, *s.m.* slipping.

sdrúcciolo, *ag.* 1. (*scorrevole*) fluid; fluent 2. (*fonet.*) proparoxytone: *parola sdrucciola*, proparoxytone 3. (*poes.*) dactylic: *verso* —, dactylic verse ‖ *s.m.* 1. (*sdrucciolamento*) slip; slipping, sliding 2. (*forte pendio*) steep slope.

sdrucciolóne, *s.m.* slip; slipping, sliding: *ho fatto uno* — *su una buccia di arancia*, I slipped on an orange peel ‖ *venir giù a sdruccioloni*, to slide down.

sdrucciolóso, *ag.* slippery.

sdrúcio, *s.m.* 1. tear, rent, rip 2. (*ferita profonda*) deep wound.

sdrucíre, *v.t.* 1. (*strappare*) to tear, to rend, to rip: *ho sdrucito il vestito contro un chiodo*, I have torn my dress on a nail 2. (*scucire*) to unstitch ‖ **sdrucírsi**, *v.r.* 1. (*strapparsi*) to tear, to get torn: *mi si è sdrucito* *il soprabito,* my overcoat has (got) torn 2. *(scucirsi)* to (be)come unstitched.

sdrucíto, *ag.* 1. *(strappato)* torn, rent 2. *(scucito)* unstitched, unseamed 3. *(logoro)* worn out; *(sbrindellato)* ragged.

sdrucitúra, *s.f.* 1. *(strappo)* rent, tear, rip 2. *(scucitura)* unstitching.

sdruscíre, *e derivati, V.* **sdrucíre,** *e derivati.*

se¹, *cong.* 1. *(condizionale)* if: — *avrò tempo, verrò,* if I have time, I shall come; — *fossi ricco, comprerei una bella villa in campagna,* if I were rich, I should buy a fine house in the country; — *non avesse piovuto, avremmo fatto prima,* if it had not rained (o had it not rained) we should have been here sooner; — *non mi sbaglio,* if I'm not mistaken; — *non riuscirò a vederlo, gli manderò un telegramma,* if I don't (o I should not) see him, I'll send him a telegram; — *piove, non uscirò,* I shall not go out, if it rains; — *si può,* — *è possibile,* if possible: *rimandalo subito,* — *è possibile,* send it back at once, if possible; *sarebbe arrivata prima,* — *non avesse perso il treno,* she would have been here sooner, if she hadn't missed the train; *staremmo volentieri a casa,* — *piovesse,* we should be quite content to stay at home, if it turned out wet 2. *(dubitativo)* **whether, if:** *mi domando* — *sia una buona idea,* I wonder whether (o if) it is a good idea; *non so* — *dovrei dirglielo o no,* I don't know whether (o if) I should tell him or not (o I wonder whether or not I should tell him); *non so* — *sia arrivato,* I do not know whether (o if) he has arrived 3. *(concessivo)* **if:** — *ho taciuto, non è perchè credessi di aver torto,* if I was silent it was not because I thought I was wrong; *mi lamento, è perchè ne ho ben motivo,* if I complain it is because I have good reason 4. *(ottativo)* **if only:** — *potessi andare!,* if only I could go!; — *solo avessi saputo!,* if only I had known! (o if I had only known! o had I but known!) 5. **(Fraseologia):** — *mai, (nel caso che)* if, in case; *(in tal caso)* in that case: — *mai, tornerò prima,* in that case, I'll come back earlier; *fammi sapere* — *mai dovesse ritornare prima delle sette,* let me know if he should happen to return before seven; *prendi l'ombrello,* — *mai dovesse piovere,* take an umbrella, in case it rains ‖ — *no, if not (o otherwise): dammi retta,* — *no te ne pentirai,* listen to me, if you don't (o otherwise you'll) regret it ‖ — *non altro, if only; at least;* if nothing else: *non era proprio ammalato, ma chiamò il dottore,* — *non altro per tranquillizzarsi,* he wasn't exactly ill, but he called in the doctor if only to set his mind at rest; *sapevo che non avevo probabilità di superare l'esame, ma,* — *non altro, è stata un'esperienza,* I knew I hadn't a chance of passing the exam, but at least it was an experience; *sono proprio sicuro che non mi divertirò; ma,* — *non altro, mi riposerò,* I'm sure I shan't really enjoy myself, but it will be a rest if nothing else ‖ — *non che,* except that (o but for the fact that): *dovrei temere il peggio,* — *non che so che posso contare sul suo aiuto,* I should fear the worst, but for the fact that I know I can count on his help; *il tuo tema è fatto bene,* — *non che è un po' lungo,* your essay is quite good, except that it is a bit too long ‖ — *poi, if:* — *poi non vuoi farlo, tanto peggio per te,* if you don't want to do it, so much the worse for you ‖ — *pure, anche,* — *(quand'anche)* even if; *(sebbene)* even though: — *pure, anche* — *perdesse tutto, sarebbe capace di tirare avanti,* even if he lost everything, he would still be able to carry on; *anche* — *fosse un re, non lo saluterei,* I wouldn't take my hat off to him, even if he were a king; *anche* — *sono stanca, non voglio rinunciare a quella festa,* even though I'm tired, I don't want to miss the party ‖ *come* — *, as if (o as though): come* — *non si sapesse che...,* as if it weren't common knowledge that...; *si comportava come* — *nulla fosse accaduto,* she behaved as though (o as if) nothing had happened ‖ — *non fosse che l'ho visto io*

stesso..., but for the fact that I saw it for myself...; — *non fosse per i miei reumatismi, verrei con te,* if it weren't (o were it not) for my rheumatism, I should come with you; — *non fosse stato per lui,* but for him (o if it had not been for him) ‖ *Dici che non c'era? Ma* — *l'ho visto io con i miei occhi!,* He wasn't there, you say? But I saw him with my own eyes! ‖ *e* — *provassimo?,* suppose we try?; *e* — *si facesse una partita a bridge?,* what do you say to (o what about) a game of bridge? ‖ *immagina* — *ero furioso!,* you can imagine how angry I was!; *tu sai bene* — *ti amo!,* you know how much I love you! ‖ *s.m.* **if:** *a furia di* — *e di ma non si combinò nulla,* what with all the ifs and buts, nothing got done.

sé², *pron.pers.r. 3ª persona m.f. sing. pl. oggetto e obliquo* 1. **one(self); him(self); her(self); it(self); them(selves):** *ognuno per* —, every man for himself; *vuole sempre qualcuno con* —, he always wants someone with him; *egli porta sempre un ombrello con* —, he always carries an umbrella (with him); *non ha mai denaro con* —, he never has any money on him; *prese il bimbo con* —, she took the child with her; *quella donna parla solo di* —, that woman only speaks about herself; *si preoccupano solo di* — *(stessi),* they only worry about themselves; *trasse a* — *il bimbo,* she drew the child to her; *vide* — *stesso nello specchio,* he saw himself in the mirror; *fare ql.co. da* —, to do sthg. (by) oneself; *pensare a* —, to think of oneself: *non pensa che a* —, he thinks of (o cares for) no one but himself ‖ *un uomo pieno di* —, a conceited man; *un uomo sicuro di* —, a man who is sure of himself (o a self-confident man); *diceva tra* — *e* —, she was saying to herself ‖ *essere fuori di* —, to be beside oneself: *è fuori di* — *dal dolore,* he is beside himself with grief ‖ *tornare in* —, to come to (o to recover) consciousness; *uscire di* —, to be beside oneself 2. *espressioni con il sé si traducono spesso in inglese facendo ricorso alle forme composte con* **self-:** *amore di* —, selfishness (o self-love); *padronanza di* —, self-control (o self-possession); *una porta che si chiude da* —, a self-closing door; *rispetto di* —, self-respect; *sicurezza di* —, self-assurance; *stima di* —, self-esteem; *un uomo che si è fatto da* —, a self-made man; *un uomo sicuro di* —, a self-confident man; *un uomo soddisfatto di* —, a self-satisfied man; *verità che si dimostra da* —, self-evident truth.

sebàcco, *ag.* sebaceous: *ghiandole sebacee, (anat.)* sebaceous glands.

sebàceo, *ag. (chim.)* sebacic.

Sebastiàno, *no.pr.m.* Sebastian.

Sebastòpoli, *no.pr.f. (geog.)* Sevastopol.

sebbène, *cong.* **though, although:** — *siamo parenti, non l'ho mai visto,* (al)though we are relations, I have never seen him; — *sia povero, è generoso,* (al)though (he is) poor, he is generous.

sèbo, *s.m. (chim. biol.)* sebum.

secànte, *ag.* 1. cutting 2. *(geom.)* secant ‖ *s.m. (geom.)* secant.

secàre, *v.t.* 1. to cut 2. *(geom.)* to intersect.

sécca, *s.f.* 1. shoal, shallow: — *di corallo,* coral shoal; — *di sabbia,* sand-bank; *dare in una* —, to run aground ‖ *abbandonar qlcu. sulle secche, fig.* to leave s.o. in the lurch ‖ *trovarsi sulle secche, fig.* to be on the rocks 2. *(dial.) (siccità)* drought.

seccaménte, *av.* 1. dryly 2. *(freddamente)* coldly.

seccànte, *ag.* 1. *(che secca)* drying 2. *(irritante)* annoying, irritating, troublesome; *(noioso)* tiresome, boring: *una cosa, persona* —, a nuisance (o a bore).

seccàre, *v.t.* 1. to dry (up); *(frutta, ecc., per conservarla)* to desiccate, to dry: *il vento aveva seccato il terreno,* the wind had dried (up) the ground; — *fichi,* to desiccate (o to dry) figs 2. *(irritare)* to annoy, to irritate; *(disturbare)* to bother, to trouble; *(annoiare)* to bore, to weary: *non seccarmi con le tue domande sciocche,* don't bother me with your silly questions ‖

v.i. to dry (up): *mettere i funghi a — al sole*, to put mushrooms to dry in the sun ‖ **seccàrsi,** *v.r.* **1.** (*diventar secco*) to dry (up): *la mia ferita si è seccata*, my wound has dried up; *il pozzo si è seccato*, the well has dried up **2.** (*sentir noia*) to get bored (with s.o., sthg., doing), to grow tired (of s.o., sthg., doing); (*irritarsi*) to get irritated (with s.o., at sthg., at doing), to get annoyed (with s.o., at sthg., at doing): *mi sono seccato per quello che mi ha detto*, I got angry at what he said to me.

seccàta, *V.* **seccatúra.**

seccatíccio, *ag.* dryish; (*risecchito*) dried up ‖ *s.m.* (*persona magra*) lean person, skinny person.

seccatívo, *ag.* drying (*attributivo*); siccative; (*che essicca frutta, ecc., per conserva*) desiccative.

seccàto, *ag.* **1.** (*secco*) dried **2.** (*irritato*) annoyed (with s.o., at sthg.), irritated (with s.o., at sthg.); (*annoiato*) bored (with s.o., sthg.), tired (of s.o., sthg.), weary (of s.o., sthg.): *era molto — per quanto ho fatto*, he was very annoyed (o irritated) at what I had done; *sono — di far sempre lo stesso lavoro*, I am tired of always doing the same kind of work.

seccatóio, *s.m.* **1.** drying-room, drying-oven **2.** (*mar.*) squeegee.

seccatóre, *s.m.*, **seccatríce,** *s.f.* bother, nuisance, bore.

seccatúra, *s.f.* **1.** (*noia*) bother, nuisance, bore: *che —!*, what a bother! (o what a nuisance!) **2.** (*essiccamento*) drying; (*di frutta, ecc., per conserva*) desiccation.

secchézza, *s.f.* **1.** dryness (anche *fig.*): *— di spirito, di stile*, dryness of spirit, style **2.** (*magrezza*) thinness.

sécchia, *s.f.* **1.** pail, bucket **2.** (*contenuto di una secchia*) pail(ful), bucket(ful): *una mezza — di latte*, half a pail of milk ‖ *a secchie*, in bucketfuls ‖ *piovere a secchie rovesce*, (*fam.*) to rain cats and dogs **3.** (*gergo studentesco*) swot.

secchiàta, *s.f.* bucketful.

sécchio, *s.m.* pail, bucket: *— del latte*, milk-pail; *— per il carbone*, coal-scuttle.

secchióne, *s.m.* (*gergo studentesco*) swot.

séccia, *s.f.* (*agr.*) stubble.

sécco, *ag.* **1.** dry: *caldo —*, dry heat; *clima, tempo —*, dry climate, weather; *frutta secca*, dry fruit; *legno —*, seasoned wood; *pane —*, dry bread; *terreno —*, dry (o arid) ground ‖ *tosse secca*, dry cough ‖ *vini secchi*, dry wines ‖ *avere la gola secca*, to be thirsty (o to feel dry) **2.** (*dissecato*) dried; (*appassito*) withered: *fagioli, fichi, piselli secchi*, dried beans, figs, peas; *uva secca*, raisins; *butta via quei fiori, ormai sono secchi*, throw those flowers away, now they are withered **3.** (*magro*) thin, skinny: *era un uomo alto è —*, he was a tall thin man ‖ *— come un chiodo*, as thin as a rake **4.** (*asciutto, brusco*) sharp; (*di stile*) bald; (*freddo, compassato*) cold, stiff: *modi secchi*, cold (o stiff) manners; *mi diede una risposta secca*, he gave me a sharp reply **5.** (*risoluto, repentino*): *gli è venuto un accidente —*, (*fam.*) he popped off; *lo spaccò con un colpo —*, he split it at a single blow; *mi diede un no —*, he refused point-blank ‖ *s.m.* **1.** (*parte secca*) dry part **2.** (*clima asciutto*) dry climate; (*siccità*) drought **3.** (*persona magra*) thin person: *i grassi ed i secchi*, the fat and the thin **4.** (*mar.*): *nave in —*, ship aground; *tirare una barca in —*, to beach a boat ‖ *lasciare ql.cu. in —*, *fig.* to leave s.o. in the lurch ‖ *rimanere al —*, *fig.* to be left penniless.

sécco, *av.* **1.** dryly: *lavatura a —*, dry-cleaning; *lavare a —*, to dry-clean ‖ *essere a —*, to be short of money **2.** (*recisamente*) sharply: *rispose — —*, he replied sharply.

seccóre, *s.m.* dryness.

seccúme, *s.m.* **1.** (*cose secche*) dry things (*pl.*) **2.** (*foglie secche*) dry leaves (*pl.*).

secentènne, *ag.* recurring every six hundred years.

secentèsimo, *ag.num.ord.s.m.* six hundredth.

secentísmo, *s.m.* (*art. lett.*) **1.** seventeenth century style; (*in Italia*) "Seicento" style **2.** (*preziosità*) preciosity.

secentísta, *s.m.* (*art. lett.*) seventeenth century artist.

secentístico, *ag.* (*art. lett.*) seventeenth century (*attributivo*), of the seventeenth century.

secènto, *V.* **seicènto.**

secèrnere, *v.t.* to secrete.

secessióne, *s.f.* secession: *guerra di —*, war of secession; (*st. americana*) Civil War.

secessionísta, *s.c.* secessionist.

séco, *pron. pers. m.f.* 3ª *persona sing.pl. obliquo* (*con lui*) **with him;** (*con lei*) **with her;** (*con loro*) **with them:** *lo portarono —*, they brought him with them; *lo prese —*, he, she took it with him, with her.

secolàre, *ag.* **1.** secular, age-old; centuries old (*predicativo*); age-long (*attributivo*): *alberi secolari*, secular (o age-old) trees; *esperienza —*, age-long experience; *tradizione —*, age-old (o time-honoured) custom; *la mia casa è —*, my house is centuries old **2.** (*che si rinnova ogni secolo*) secular: *giuochi secolari*, secular games **3.** (*laico*) secular, lay; temporal: *educazione —*, secular education ‖ *braccio —*, secular arm ‖ *clero —*, secular clergy ‖ *s.m.* layman (*pl.* laymen) ‖ *i Secolari*, the laity.

secolarésco, *ag.* secular; worldly.

secolarizzàre, *v.t.* to secularize ‖ **secolarizzàrsi,** *v.r.* to return to the world.

secolarizzazióne, *s.f.* secularization.

sècolo, *s.m.* **1.** century: *a un — dalla sua morte*, a century after his death; *la fine, il principio del —*, the end, the beginning of the century; *fino al XV —*, up to the XV century; *nel nostro —*, in our century; *per tre secoli*, for three centuries; *siamo nel XX —*, we are in the twentieth century ‖ *nel corso dei secoli*, in the course of ages ‖ *sembra un — che...*, (*fam.*) it seems ages since... ‖ *sono secoli, è un — che non lo vedo*, I have not seen him for ages ‖ *andare col —*, to be born at the beginning of the century **2.** (*tempo, epoca*) age, epoch, time: *il — delle macchine*, the machine age; *il grande — di Augusto in Roma*, the great Augustan Age in Rome; *il — di Luigi XIV*, the age of Louis XIV; *le meraviglie del nostro —*, the wonders of our age; *il — in cui viviamo*, the age (o century) we live in ‖ *il — d'oro delle arti*, the Golden Age of Art ‖ *dal principio dei secoli*, from time immemorial ‖ *fino alla fine dei secoli*, to the end of time ‖ *nella notte dei secoli*, in remote antiquity ‖ *per tutti i secoli dei secoli*, world without end **3.** (*mondo, cose mondane*) world; things mundane (*pl.*): *ritirarsi dal —*, to withdraw from the world (o worldly life) ‖ *al —*, in the world: *Padre Pietro, al — John Brown*, Father Peter, in the world John Brown.

secónda, *s.f.* **1.** (*anat.*) afterbirth **2.** (*aut.*) second gear **3.** (*ferr.*) second class **4.** (*termine scolastico*) second year **5.** (*scherma*) seconde **6.** *— di cambio*, (*comm.*) second of exchange.

secónda, a, *l. av.*: *andare a —*, (*mar.*) to go downstream ‖ *tutto gli va —*, *fig.* everything is going well with him ‖ **a secónda di,** *l. prep.* according to : *a — delle circostanze*, according to circumstances; *a — del merito*, according to (o on) s.o.'s merits.

secondàre, *v.t.* **1.** to gratify; to indulge; to countenance: *egli seconda tutti i capricci di suo figlio*, he indulges (o gratifies) all his son's whims; *non capisco come ella potesse — la sua condotta*, I do not understand how she could countenance his conduct **2.** (*favorire*) to favour: *la fortuna lo seconda*, fortune favours him **3.** (*rar.*) (*seguire*) to follow.

secondariaménte, secondly; in the second place.

secondàrio, *ag.* **1.** secondary: *educazione secondaria*, secondary education; *era secondaria*, (*geol.*) secondary epoch **2.** (*minore, accessorio*) secondary, subordinate, minor: *accento —*, secondary accent (o stress); *circuito —*, (*fis.*) secondary circuit; *intreccio —*, (*teat.*) sub-plot; *linea secondaria*, (*ferr.*) branch line; *pianeta —*, secondary planet; *questione secondaria*, question of minor (o secondary) interest (o side-issue); *questa è* *una cosa secondaria,* this is a trifling matter (*o a trifle*); *avere una parte secondaria,* to play a minor part ‖ *di secondaria importanza,* of minor importance.

secondíno, *s.m.* warder.

secóndo, *ag.* **1.** *num. ord.* second: — *piano,* second floor (*o amer.* first floor); *Carlo II,* Charles the Second; *egli è* — *in graduatoria,* he is the second best; *arrivare* —, to come (in) second ‖ — *cugino,* second cousin ‖ — *violino,* second violin ‖ *di seconda mano,* second -hand: *libri di seconda mano,* second-hand books; *comperare di seconda mano,* to buy second-hand ‖ *in* — *luogo,* in the second place ‖ *il primo..., il* —..., the former..., the latter...: *Gianni e Carlo sono fratelli: il primo è ingegnere, il* — *è dentista,* John and Charles are brothers, the former is an engineer, the latter is a dentist **2.** (*nuovo, altro*) second: *seconda natura,* second nature; *seconde nozze,* second marriage; *egli è un* — *Galileo,* he is a second (*o a new o another*) Galileo ‖ *secondi fini,* ulterior motives **3.** (*inferiore*) second: *merce di seconda scelta,* seconds; *non è* — *a nessuno,* he is second to none ‖ —, *ufficiale in seconda,* (*mar.*) executive officer **4.** (*favorevole*) favourable, propitious: *venti secondi,* favourable winds ‖ *s.m.* **1.** (*minuto secondo*) second: *aspetta un* —, wait a second **2.** (*mar.*) (*ufficiale in seconda*) executive officer **3.** (*padrino in duello*) second.

secóndo, *prep.* **1. according to, in accordance with, in conformity with:** — *certi autori,* according to certain authors; — *me, lui, ecc.,* according to me, to him, etc. (*o in my, his, etc.* opinion *o* to my, his, etc. mind); — *il mio modo di vedere,* to my way of thinking; — *le tue istruzioni,* according to (*o* in accordance with *o* in conformity with) your instructions; — *l'ora che arrivi,* according to when you arrive; — *quel che farò,* according to what I shall do ‖ *dare a ciascuno* — *il merito,* to give everybody their due **2.** (*seguendo*): *ella veste* — *la moda italiana,* she dresses in the Italian way; *andare* — *il vento,* to sail with the wind; *fig.* to follow the crowd ‖ *av.* **1.** (*secondariamente*) second: *non si può, primo perchè..., — perchè...,* you can't, first because..., second because... **2.** (*a seconda dei casi*): « *Lo farai?* », « *Secondo* », "Will you do it?", "It depends" ‖ **secóndo che,** *l.cong.* **according to whether:** — *che mi piaccia o no,* according to whether I like it or not.

secondogènita, *s.f.* second(-born) daughter.

secondogènito, *ag.* second-born ‖ *s.m.* second(-born) son.

secrétaire, *s.m.* secretaire, writing-desk.

secretívo, *ag.* (*fisiol.*) secretory.

secréto, *ag.* (*fisiol.*) secreted ‖ *s.m.* (*fisiol.*) secretion.

secretóre, *ag.* (*fisiol.*) secretory.

secretòrio, *ag.* (*fisiol.*) secretory.

secrezióne, *s.f.* (*fisiol.*) secretion.

securtà, *s.f.* safety; security.

sèdano, *s.m.* (*bot.*) celery.

sedàre, *v.t.* to soothe; to calm: — *la fame,* to appease one's hunger; — *l'ira,* to soothe one's anger; — *la sete,* to quench (*o* to assuage) one's thirst; — *una tempesta,* to calm a storm; — *un tumulto,* to put down a riot.

sedatívo, *ag.s.m.* sedative.

sède, *s.f.* **1.** seat, centre: *una* — *di antiche tradizioni,* a seat of old traditions; *in Italia, Milano è la* — *principale del commercio e Roma è la* — *del governo,* in Italy, Milan is the chief seat of commerce and Rome is the seat of government; *questa scuola è* — *di esami,* this school is an examination centre; *questo disturbo ha* — *nello stomaco,* this trouble has its seat in the stomach **2.** (*residenza*) residence: *aver* —, to have residence; *cambiar* —, to change one's residence **3.** (*eccl.*) see: — *vescovile,* see (*o diocesan centre*) ‖ *la Santa Sede,* the Holy See **4.** (*edificio in cui risiedono pubblici uffici*) office: — *centrale,* head office; *egli non è in* —, he is not in the office **5.** (*sessione*) session, sitting: *in* — *di esami,* during the examinations (*o* at exami-

nation time) ‖ *in separata* —, in a special session; (*in privato*) in private **6.** (*mec.*) (*di valvola*) seat, seating; (*di cuscinetto*) housing: — *conica,* conical seat; — *di bloccaggio,* lock slot; — *di rotolamento,* race; — *di valvola riportata,* valve insert; — *piana,* flat seat; *ripassare le sedi delle valvole,* to grind (*o* to re-cut) the valve seats.

sedentàrio, *ag.* sedentary: *lavoro* —, sedentary work; *vita sedentaria,* sedentary life ‖ *s.m.* sedentary man.

sedére, *v.i.* **1.** (*essere seduto*) to sit, to be sitting, to be seated: *egli sedeva in poltrona vicino alla finestra,* he was sitting (*o* he sat *o* he was seated) in an armchair near the window; *quando tutti sedevano a tavola...,* when everybody was seated at (the) table...; *alzarsi da* —, to rise (*o* to get up) (from one's seat); *mettere qlcu. a* —, to seat s.o. ‖ *posti a* —, seats ‖ — *in Parlamento,* to sit in Parliament; — *sul trono,* to sit on the throne **2.** (*mettersi a sedere*) to sit, to sit down, to take a seat: *egli sedette vicino a me,* he sat down near me; *il malato si alzò a* — *sul letto,* the sick man sat up in bed; *possiamo* — *a tavola senza aspettarlo,* we can sit down at table without waiting for him; *sedete, prego!,* please, sit down! (*o* be seated! *o* take a seat!) ‖ **sedérsi,** *v.r.* to sit, to sit down, to take a seat: *non voglio sedermi qui,* I do not want to sit here; *siediti!,* sit down!.

sedére, *s.m.* bottom, behind.

sèdia, *s.f.* chair: — *a dondolo,* rocking-chair; — *a sdraio,* deck-chair; — *di paglia,* straw-bottomed chair; — *pieghevole,* folding chair; — *elettrica,* electric chair (*o amer.* hot chair) ‖ — *gestatoria,* (*eccl.*) gestatorial chair.

sediàrio, *s.m.* (*persona addetta al trasporto della sedia gestatoria*) gestatorial chair carrier.

sedicènne, *ag.* sixteen years old (*predicativo*); sixteen-year-old (*attributivo*): *un ragazzo* —, a sixteen-year -old boy ‖ *s.m.* sixteen-year-old boy ‖ *s.f.* sixteen-year -old girl.

sedicènte, *ag.* self-styled, would-be.

sedicèsimo, *ag. num. ord.* sixteenth ‖ *s.m.* **1.** sixteenth **2.** (*tip.*) sextodecimo (*abbr.* 16mo).

sédici, *ag. num. card. s.m.* sixteen.

sedíle, *s.m.* **1.** seat, chair: — *anteriore,* (*aut.*) front seat; — *catapultabile,* (*aer.*) ejection (*o* ejector-) seat; — *girevole,* swivel chair (*o* revolving chair); — *pieghevole,* folding seat (*o* camp-stool); — *posteriore,* (*aut.*) back seat **2.** (*panca*) bench.

sedimentàrio, *ag.* (*geol.*) sedimentary.

sedimentazióne, *s.f.* (*geol.*) sedimentation.

sediménto, *s.m.* (*chim. geol.*) sediment, deposit; dregs (*pl.*).

sedimentóso, *ag.* (*geol.*) sedimentary.

sedi(u)òlo, *s.m.* (*carrozzino a un posto*) sulky.

sedizióne, *s.f.* sedition; (*ammutinamento*) mutiny.

sediziosaménte, *av.* seditiously.

sedizióso, *ag.* seditious ‖ *s.m.* agitator.

seducènte, *ag.* **1.** seductive; enticing, alluring **2.** (*che tenta*) tempting: *offerta* —, tempting offer **3.** (*affascinante*) charming, fascinating: *una donna* —, a charming (*o* fascinating) woman; *sorriso* —, fetching smile.

seducíbile, *ag.* seducible.

sedúrre, *v.t.* **1.** to seduce; to entice, to allure: — *una donna,* to seduce a woman **2.** (*tentare*) to tempt **3.** (*affascinare*) to charm, to fascinate.

sedúta, *s.f.* **1.** sitting, session (anche *pol. dir.*); meeting: — *di una corte, di una commissione,* sitting (*o* session) of a court, of a commission; — *segreta,* secret session; *aprire, chiudere, rinviare una* —, to open, to close, to adjourn a meeting; *essere in* —, to be sitting (*o* in session) ‖ — *stante,* (*durante la seduta*) during the sitting; (*immediatamente*) immediately (*o* at once) **2.** (*lo stare a sedere*) sitting, session: *durante le sue sedute mattutine dal barbiere,* during his morning sessions at the barber's; *questo ritratto richiese parecchie sedute,* this portrait required several sittings.

sedúto, *ag.* sitting; seated: *state seduti,* sit down

(o don't stand up o *formale* keep your seats); *essere* —, to be sitting.

seduttóre, *s.m.*, **seduttríce**, *s.f.* seducer.

seduzióne, *s.f.* 1. seduction; enticement, allurement; (*attrazione*) attraction: *la città e le sue seduzioni*, the city and its attractions 2. (*tentazione*) temptation 3. (*fascino*) charm, fascination.

séga, *s.f.* 1. saw: — *a caldo*, (*metal.*) hot saw; — *a mano*, hand-saw: — *a mano da falegname*, bucksaw; — *a mano per tronchi*, pitsaw (o whipsaw o two-man saw); — *a nastro*, belt saw; — *a telaio*, frame saw; — *chirurgica*, amputation saw; — *cilindrica*, cylinder saw; — *circolare*, circular saw (o disk saw); — *da macellaio*, butcher's saw; — *meccanica*, sawing machine; — *multipla*, gang saw; — *per metalli*, hack-saw; *a denti di* —, serrated (o saw-toothed); *a forma di* —, serriform; *lama della* —, saw-blade 2. *pesce* —, (*ittiol.*) saw-fish.

ségala, **ségale**, *s.f.* (*bot.*) rye: — *cornuta*, ergot (o spurred rye); *pane di* —, rye-bread.

segalígno, *ag.* 1. (*di segala*) rye (*attributivo*) 2. (*di persona*) wiry.

segaménto, *s.m.* sawing.

segantíno, *s.m.* sawyer.

segàre, *v.t.* 1. to saw: — *un tronco*, to saw a trunk 2. (*mietere*) to mow 3. (*tagliare*) to cut 4. (*stringere fortemente*) to cut into (sthg.): *questo elastico gli sega la gamba*, this elastic cuts into his leg.

segatóre, *s.m.* 1. sawyer 2. (*mietitore*) mower.

segatúra, *s.f.* 1. (*il segare*) sawing 2. (*detriti di legno segato*) sawdust 3. (*mietitura*) mowing.

seggétta, *s.f.* close-stool.

sèggio, *s.m.* 1. chair; seat: *un* — *in parlamento*, a parliamentary seat; *il* — *presidenziale*, the president's chair ‖ *il* — *di S. Pietro*, the papacy ‖ — *elettorale*, poll (o polling station o voting station); (*commissione scrutatrice*) board of scrutineers: *andare al* — *elettorale*, to go to the poll ‖ *balzare, togliere qlcu. di* —, to remove s.o. from office 2. (*sede vescovile*) see 3. (*stallo*) stall: *seggi dei canonici*, cathedral stalls; *seggi dei senatori*, senators' places.

sèggiola, *V.* **sèdia**.

seggiolàio, *s.m.* 1. (*chi fabbrica seggiole*) chair-maker 2. (*chi aggiusta seggiole*) chair-mender 3. (*chi vende seggiole*) chair-seller.

seggiolóne, *s.m.* 1. (*grande sedia*) big chair 2. (*per bambini*) high-chair.

seggiovía, *s.f.* chair-lift.

seghería, *s.f.* saw-mill.

seghétta, *s.f.* 1. (*piccola sega*) small saw 2. (*morsa che si applica alle froge dei cavalli*) barnacles (*pl.*).

seghettàto, *ag.* serrated, serrate, saw-toothed: *foglia seghettata*, serrate leaf.

segmentazióne, *s.f.* (*biol. geom.*) segmentation.

segménto, *s.m.* 1. (*biol. geom.*) segment 2. (*di motori*) piston-ring; (*per freni*) brake-lining.

segnacàrte, *s.m.* book-mark.

segnacàso, *s.m.* (*gram.*) prepositional particle.

segnàcolo, *s.m.* (*letter.*) (*simbolo*) symbol; ensign.

segnalàre, *v.t.* 1. to signal: — *un ordine, un messaggio*, to signal an order, a message 2. (*additare, far notare*) to signalize, to point out: *mi ha segnalato i libri che preferisce*, he has pointed out the books he likes best to me; *questo risultato è meritevole di essere segnalato*, this result is worth recording; — *una difficoltà a qlcu.*, to call s.o.'s attention to a difficulty; — *ql.co. all'attenzione di ql.cu.*, to point out sthg. to s.o. (o to draw s.o.'s attention to sthg.); — *qlcu., ql.co. alla polizia*, to report s.o., sthg. to the police ‖ **segnalàrsi**, *v.r.* to distinguish oneself: *si segnalò per la sua assidua diligenza*, he distinguished himself by his painstaking diligence; — *all'attenzione di qlcu.*, to catch s.o.'s eye.

segnalataménte, *av.* signally, remarkably.

segnalàto, *ag.* 1. indicated, marked: *una curva ben segnalata*, a well-marked curve 2. (*insigne*) signal, remarkable, conspicuous, noteworthy, eminent; (*grande*) great: *un* — *favore*, a great favour; *poeti segnalati*, well-known poets; *virtù segnalata*, signal virtue.

segnalatóre, *ag.* signalling ‖ *s.m.* 1. signaller, signalman (*pl.* signalmen) 2. (*apparecchio per trasmettere segnali*) signaller: — *di sbandamento*, (*mar.*) heeling gear.

segnalazióne, *s.f.* 1. (*il segnalare*) signalling: — *a lampi*, (*mil.*) flash signalling; — *con bandiera*, (*mar.*) flag signalling; — *in codice*, (*mil.*) coding; —*ottica*, (*mil.*) visual signalling 2. (*segnale*) signal: *segnalazioni stradali*, traffic signals; *cabina, servizio di* —, (*ferr.*) signal box, service.

segnàle, *s.m.* signal; (*aer.*) marker: — *acustico*, sound signal; — *a disco*, (*ferr.*) disc signal; — *d'aiuto*, *di pericolo*, (*rad.*) distress, danger signal; — *di allarme*, alarm signal; (*ferr.*) emergency brake; — *di immagine*, (*tv.*) picture signal; — *di linea libera*, (*tel.*) (*prima di comporre il numero*) dialling tone; (*dopo composto il numero*) ringing tone; — *di occupato*, (*tel.*) engaged tone; — *d'ostacolo*, (*aer.*) obstruction marker; — *di passaggio a livello*, (*ferr.*) level-crossing signal; — *di riconoscimento*, (*mil.*) recognition signal; — *fumogeno*, (*mil.*) smoke signal; — *orario*, (*rad. tel.*) time-signal; — *stradale*, road sign; *codice dei segnali*, code of signals; *fare segnali con una bandiera*, to make signals with a flag.

segnalíbro, *s.m.* book-mark.

segnalínee, *s.m.* (*spor.*) linesman (*pl.* linesmen).

segnàre, *v.t.* 1. to mark; (*col marchio*) to brand: *aveva segnato alcuni passi del libro*, he had marked a few passages of the book; *ha segnato gli errori in rosso*, he has marked the mistakes in red; *il ruscello segna i limiti della nostra proprietà*, the stream marks the boundary of our estate; *il suo viso era segnato dal vaiolo*, his face was pock-marked (o pitted with smallpox); — *il bestiame*, to brand the cattle; — *i colli*, (*comm.*) to mark the packages 2. (*scalfire*) to scratch: *non* — *il banco!*, don't scratch your desk! 3. (*prendere nota di*) to record, to note, to mark; (*registrare*) to enter: *ha segnato le cose da ricordare*, he noted down the things to be remembered; *segna il nome, l'ora dell'appuntamento*, note down the name, the time of the appointment; — *il prezzo delle merci*, to mark the prices of the goods; — *i punti*, (*al giuoco*) to keep the score; — *le spese*, to keep a record of (o to write down) one's expenses ‖ — *nella mente*, to impress on one's memory 4. (*indicare*) to indicate, to show; (*col dito*) to point at (s.o., sthg.): *il contatore segna...*, the meter reads...; *l'orologio segna le ore*, the clock tells the time; *l'orologio segna le tre*, the clock says (o points to) three o'clock; *un palo segna la strada*, a sign-post indicates the road; *il punto preciso è segnato sulla carta*, the exact point is shown on the map; *il termometro segna 10 gradi*, the thermometer registers (o stands at) 10 degrees ‖ — *qlcu. a dito, fig.* to point a scornful finger at s.o. 5. — *il passo*, (*mil.*) to mark time (anche *fig.*) 6. (*firmare*) to sign: — *un documento*, to sign a document ‖ **segnàrsi**, *v.r.* to cross oneself; to make the sign of the cross ‖ *non c'è neanche il tempo di* —, (*dial.*) there's not even time to breathe.

segnataménte, *av.* mainly, especially, chiefly.

segnatària, *s.f.* signatory.

segnatàrio, *ag.s.m.* signatory.

segnatàsse, *s.m.* unpaid-postage-stamp.

segnàto, *ag.* 1. marked; (*col marchio*) branded ‖ — *da Dio*, ill-favoured person ‖ *pecora segnata*, branded sheep 2. (*scalfito*) scratched 3. (*annotato*) recorded, noted, marked 4. (*indicato*) indicated, shown 5. (*benedetto col segno della croce*) blessed.

segnatóio, *s.m.* (*strum. artig.*) marking tool.

segnatóre, *ag.* marking; branding ‖ *s.m.*, **segnatríce**, *s.f.* marker; brander; (*al giuoco*) scorer.

segnatúra, *s.f.* 1. (*il segnare*) marking 2. (*tip.*) signature **3.** (*numero di collocazione*) press-mark; (*amer.*) callnumber **4.** (*eccl.*) " Segnatura " (highest Papal court).

ségno, *s.m.* **1.** mark, sign; (*macchia*) spot, stain; (*graffiatura*)scratch; (*cicatrice*) scar: *i segni della pioggia, d'una malattia, della vecchiaia,* the signs of the rain, of a disease, of old age; *ha un grosso — sul viso,* he has a big scar on his face; *i segni su questa porta furono probabilmente fatti con un coltello,* the scratches on this door were probably made with a knife ‖ *segni caratteristici,* special peculiarities; — *di riconoscimento,* sign of recognition ‖ *per filo e per —,* in all details ‖ *— di croce,* sign of the cross: *farsi il — della croce,* to make the sign of the cross (*o* to cross oneself); *fare un — di croce su ql.co., fig.* to wash one's hands of sthg. ‖ *non dare — di vita,* to give (*o* to show) no sign of life ‖ *perdere il — in un libro,* to lose one's place in a book **2.** (*traccia*) mark; *fig.* trace; (*vestigia*) vestige: *i segni dei suoi piedi sulla neve,* his footprints in the snow; *i segni di una triste esperienza, di una vecchia civiltà,* the traces of a sad experience, of an old civilization; *il suo viso portava impressi i segni della sofferenza,* she bore marks of suffering on her face **3.** (*ortografico*) mark; (*mat. astr. mus.*) sign: *segni algebrici,* algebraic signs (*o* symbols); *segni astronomici,* astronomic signs (*o* symbols); *i segni dello zodìaco,* the signs of the Zodiac; *segni ortografici,* punctuation marks; — *positivo,* — *negativo,* positive (*o* plus) sign, negative (*o* minus) sign **4.** (*indizio*) sign, indication; *sintomo*) symptom: — *ammonitore,* warning sign; *l'improvviso abbassarsi del barometro è un — di pioggia,* the sudden fall of the barometer is an indication (*o* a sign) of rain; *dare segni di stanchezza,* to show signs of weariness **5.** (*prova*) mark, token: *come — della sua amicizia, del suo amore,* as a token of his friendship, of his love; *è — di buon carattere,* it is a mark of good character **6.** (*gesto*) sign, gesture; (*colla testa*) nod; (*con la mano*) wave: *mi fece — con la mano,* he waved his hand to me; *mi fece un — con la testa,* he nodded to me; *mi fece — di avvicinarmi,* he made a sign to me to come nearer; *fare — di sì,* to nod in agreement **7.** (*bersaglio*) target: *tiro a —,* target-practice; (*il luogo*) shooting-gallery; *colpire il —,* to hit the target; *sbagliare il —,* to miss the target ‖ *dare, cogliere nel —, fig.* to hit the mark (*o* to guess right) ‖ *essere fatto — a,* to be the butt (*o* target) of: *essere fatto — al ridicolo, agli scherzi,* to be the butt for jokes, for ridicule **8.** (*limite*) limit; (*grado, misura*) degree: *all'ultimo —,* to the utmost; *sino a un certo —,* to a certain degree; *passare il —,* to overstep the mark **9.** (*simbolo*) symbol: *la colomba è — di pace,* the dove is a symbol of peace **10.** (*segnale*) signal: *fare segni con una luce rossa,* to make signals with a red light.

ségo, *s.m.* tallow.

ségolo, *s.m.* pruning-knife.

segóso, *ag.* tallowy, tallowish.

segregaménto, *s.m.* segregation, isolation.

segregàre, *v.t.* to segregate, to isolate: — *un malato,* to isolate a sick man ‖ **segregàrsi,** *v.r.* to segregate oneself; to withdraw; to sequester oneself: — *dal mondo,* to withdraw from the world.

segregàto, *ag.* segregated, isolated; sequestered: *una vita segregata,* a sequestered life; *vivere —,* to live a secluded (*o* to lead a sequestered) life.

segregazióne, *s.f.* segregation, isolation ‖ — *cellulare,* solitary confinement.

segréta, *s.f.* **1.** dungeon **2.** (*eccl.*) Secret.

segretaménte, *av.* secretly, covertly, in secret.

segretària, *s.f.* (lady) secretary.

segretariàle, *ag.* secretarial.

segretariàto, *s.m.* secretariat(e); secretaryship.

segretàrio, *s.m.* **1.** secretary: — *comunale,* town -clerk; — *d'ambasciata,* embassy secretary; — *d'università,* registrar; — *privato,* private secretary; *ti farò da —,* (*scherz.*) I'll be your secretary ‖ *Segretario di*

Stato, Secretary of State ‖ — *galante,* secretary of gallantry **2.** (*ornit.*) secretary-bird.

segretería, *s.f.* **1.** (*ufficio*) secretariat(e), secretary's office **2.** (*il personale*) secretariat(e), secretarial staff ‖ *Segreteria di Stato,* Secretariat of State **3.** (*scrivania*) writing-desk.

segretézza, *s.f.* secrecy: *confido nella tua —,* I rely on your secrecy ‖ *in tutta —,* in all secrecy.

segréto, *ag.* **1.** secret: *colloquio —,* secret talk; *fondi segreti,* (*dello Stato*) secret funds; *matrimonio —,* secret marriage; *passaggio —,* secret passage; *pensieri, sentimenti segreti,* inmost (*o* secret) thoughts, feelings; *porta segreta,* secret door; *scrutinio —,* secret vote; *servizio —,* (*polizia*) secret police; (*informazione militare*) secret service; *società segreta,* secret society; *tener —,* to keep secret: *tieni segreta questa notizia,* keep this news close (*o* secret) **2.** (*discreto*) discreet: *è un uomo —,* he is a discreet man ‖ *s.m.* **1.** secret: *il — della confessione,* the secret of the confessional; *i segreti della natura,* the secrets of nature; *il — del successo, della felicità,* the secret of success, of happiness; — *di fabbricazione,* secret of manufacture; *mi confidò un —,* he entrusted me with a secret; *custodire, mantenere un —,* to keep a secret; *lasciarsi sfuggire un —,* to let the cat out of the bag; *non aver segreti per nessuno,* to have no secrets for anybody; *partecipare un — a qlcu.,* to let s.o. into a secret; *rivelare un —,* to disclose a secret; *tradire un —,* to betray a secret ‖ *un — di Pulcinella,* an open secret ‖ — *epistolare,* secrecy of correspondence; — *professionale,* professional secrecy; *violazione del — professionale,* breach of professional secrecy ‖ *in —,* in secrecy (*o* confidentially): *ciò mi fu detto in —,* I was told about it confidentially; *dire ql.co. a qlcu. in (gran) —,* to tell s.o. sthg. as a (great) secret ‖ *strappare un — di bocca a qlcu.,* to make s.o. reveal a secret **2.** (*intimità*) secrecy: *nel — della propria stanza,* in the secrecy of one's room **3.** (*parte recondita, interna*) depth: *nel — del bosco,* in the depth (*o* thick) of the forest **4.** (*l'intimo*) depths (*pl.*): *nel — del cuore,* in the depths of one's heart; *nel — della propria coscienza,* in the depths of one's conscience; *sembrava sereno, ma nel — soffriva,* he seemed happy, but in his heart he was suffering **5.** (*congegno di cassaforte*) combination.

seguàce, *ag.* (*rar. poet.*) following; (*flessibile*) flexible, pliable, supple: *l'edera —,* the supple ivy ‖ *s.c.* follower, supporter, adherent; (*discepolo*) disciple: *un — della filosofia platonica,* a follower of Platonic philosophy; *un — di Cristo,* a disciple (*o* follower) of Christ; *il principe e i suoi seguaci,* the prince and his followers.

seguènte, *ag.* following; next; subsequent, ensuing: *il giorno —,* the following (*o* next day); *nei mesi seguenti,* during the ensuing months; *le pagine seguenti,* the following pages; *il treno —,* next train; *gli avvenimenti seguenti dimostrarono che aveva torto,* subsequent events showed that he was wrong.

seguènza, (*arc.*) per **sequènza.**

segúgio, *s.m.* **1.** (*zool.*) (blood)hound **2.** (*investigatore, poliziotto*) bloodhound, detective.

seguíre, *v.t.* **1.** to follow (*anche fig.*): *il cane segue il padrone,* the dog follows his master; *la crisi che seguì la guerra,* the crisis which followed the war; *lo seguì con lo sguardo fino al fiume,* his eyes followed him to the river; *non riesco a — quello che dici,* I cannot follow what you are saying; *seguì la professione del padre,* he followed his father's profession; — *la corrente,* to go down stream; *fig.* to go with the stream; — *l'esempio di qlcu.,* to follow the example of s.o.; — *le orme di qlcu., fig.* to follow in s.o.'s footsteps; — *una pista, fig.* to follow up a clue; — *un processo sul giornale,* to follow a case in the newspaper; — *la moda,* to follow the fashion **2.** (*pedinare*) to follow, to shadow: *l'agente seguì il ladro,* the policeman shadowed the thief **3.** (*procedere per*) to follow, to proceed along (sthg.), to go (on): *lascio che le cose seguano il loro* *corso*, I let things run their course; *segui la tua via e non dare ascolto a nessuno*, go your own way and don't listen to anybody; *se segui questa via arriverai fra dieci minuti*, if you keep to (o follow) this road you will arrive in ten minutes **4.** (*sorvegliare, sovrintendere*) to supervise, to oversee: *vi erano sempre parecchi ingegneri a — il lavoro degli operai*, there were always several engineers to supervise (o to oversee) the workmen's work ‖ *l'ho seguito per l'esame di latino*, I have coached him for his Latin examination **5.** (*frequentare regolarmente*) to attend (regularly): *seguo i concerti della « Scala »*, I attend the concerts at "La Scala" **6.** (*attenersi a, eseguire*) to follow; to conform to (sthg.): *segui le istruzioni*, follow the instructions; *— il consiglio di qlcu.*, to follow (o to take) s.o.'s advice ‖ *v.i.* **1.** to follow: *scrivi quanto segue*, write down what follows; *seguì un periodo di benessere*, a period of well-being followed ‖ *segue lettera*, letter will follow **2.** (*continuare*) to follow, to continue: *segue al prossimo numero*, to be continued in our next issue; *segue a tergo*, please turn over (*abbr.* P.T.O.) **3.** (*risultare*) to follow, to result: *da quanto dici, segue che è colpa sua*, from what you say it follows that it is his fault **4.** (*accadere*) to happen, to occur: *mi domando che cosa seguirà*, I wonder what will happen.

seguitàbile, *ag.* followable.

seguitaménte, *av.* uninterruptedly.

seguitàre, *v.t.* (*rar.*) to follow: *seguitava le mie orme*, he followed (in) my tracks ‖ *v.i.* **1.** to go on (doing), to keep on (doing), to continue (doing, to do): *seguita, per piacere*, go (o keep) on, please; *seguitò a parlare*, he went on (o continued) speaking (o he continued to speak) **2.** (*venir dopo*) to follow (sthg.), to ensue: *al male seguita il rimorso*, remorse follows evil.

seguitatóre, *ag.* following ‖ *s.m.*, **seguitatríce**, *s.f.* follower.

séguito, *s.m.* **1.** (*corteo, scorta*) retinue, suite, train: *un — di ammiratori*, a train of admirers; *il re e il suo —*, the king and his retinue; *essere al — di un ambasciatore*, to be among an ambassador's suite **2.** (*seguaci, ammiratori*) followers (*pl.*): *Aristotele e il suo —*, Aristotle and his followers **3.** (*sequela, successione*) series, succession; sequence, train: *un — di idee, di eventi*, a succession of ideas, of events; *un — di pensieri*, a train of thought; *un — di vittorie, di disavventure*, a series of victories, of misadventures ‖ *di —*, in succession; (*senza interruzione*) uninterruptedly (o without interruption) ‖ *e così di —*, and so on (o and so forth) ‖ *in —*, later on (o afterwards) ‖ *in — a*, in consequence of (o owing to o on account of): *in — a questo*, owing to this; *la ditta fallì in — a sbagliate speculazioni*, the firm went bankrupt owing to mistaken speculations **4.** (*continuazione*) continuation: *il — di un articolo, di una storia*, the continuation of an article, of a story ‖ *il — al prossimo numero*, to be continued (in our next issue) ‖ *dar — a ql.co.*, to carry out sthg. ‖ *far — a ql.co.*, to follow up sthg. **5.** (*aderenza, favore*) following: *ha molto — nell'assemblea*, he has a large following in the assembly **6.** (*comm.*): *a — della vostra lettera*, following up your letter; *a — di quanto sopra*, as a consequence of the above; *facendo — alla nostra lettera del...*, further to (o with further reference to) our letter of the....

sèi, *ag.num.card.s.m.* six: *il — di agosto*, on the sixth of August; *il — di cuori*, the six of hearts; *alle — del mattino*, at six in the morning; *un bambino di — anni*, a six-year-old child.

Seiàno, *no.pr.m.* (*st.*) Sejanus.

seicènto, *ag.num.card.* six hundred ‖ *s.m.* (*diciassettesimo secolo*) the seventeenth century.

seimíla, *ag. num. card.* six thousand.

seísmo, *s.m.* seismism.

selàci, *s.m.pl.* (*ittiol.*) Selachii.

sélce, *s.f.* (*min.*) flint, flint-stone: *una scure di —*, a flint axe.

selciàio, *s.m.* paver, paviour.

selciàre, *v.t.* to pave: *— una strada*, to pave a road.

selciàto, *s.m.* pavement.

selciatóre, *s.m.* paver, paviour.

selciatúra, *s.f.* paving.

selcióso, *ag.* (*min.*) flinty.

Selène, *no.pr.f.* (*mit.*) Selene.

selènico, *ag.* **1.** (*chim.*) selenic **2.** (*letter.*) (*lunare*) lunar.

selènio, *s.m.* (*min.*) selenium.

selenìta, *s.c.* inhabitant of the moon, selenite.

selenìte, *ag.* (*letter.*) lunar ‖ *s.f.* (*min.*) selenite.

selenítico, *ag.* (*min.*) selenitic.

selenografía, *s.f.* selenography.

selenogràfico, *ag.* selenographic(al).

selenògrafo, *s.m.* selenographer.

selettività, *s.f.* selectivity (anche *rad.*).

selettívo, *ag.* selective (anche *rad.*).

selettóre, *ag.* selective ‖ *s.m.* selector: *— di banda*, (*rad.*) band-selector; *— di canale*, (*tv.*) channel-selector; *— di distanza*, (*radar*) range selector; *— di onda*, (*rad.*) wave-selector.

Selèucia, *no.pr.f.* (*geog. st.*) Seleucia.

Selèucidi, *s.m.pl.* (*st.*) Seleucidae.

Selèuco, *no.pr.m.* (*st.*) Seleucus.

selezionàre, *v.t.* to select, to choose, to pick out.

selezióne, *s.f.* **1.** selection, choice: *— artificiale*, artificial selection; *— del personale*, personnel selection; *— naturale*, natural selection; *una buona — di libri*, a good selection of books **2.** (*rad.*) (*selettività*) selectivity.

sèlla, *s.f.* **1.** saddle: *— all'inglese*, hunting-saddle; *— da amazzone*, side-saddle; *cavallo da —*, saddle-horse; *far cadere di — qlcu.*, to unsaddle (o to unhorse) s.o.; *montare in —*, to mount; *rimettersi in —*, to get into the saddle again; *fig.* to get on one's legs again; *togliere la — ad un cavallo*, to unsaddle a horse ‖ *stare bene in —*, to ride well (o to have a good seat) **2.** (*di animale macellato*) saddle: *— di montone*, saddle of mutton **3.** (*valico*) saddle **4.** *— turcica*, (*anat.*) sella turcica.

sellàio, *s.m.* saddler, harness-maker.

sellàre, *v.t.* to saddle.

sellàto, *ag.* saddled.

sellería, *s.f.* **1.** (*bottega del sellaio*) saddlery **2.** (*ripostiglio dei finimenti in una scuderia*) harness-room.

sellíno, *s.m.* saddle: *— di bicicletta*, bicycle saddle.

Sèlma, *no.pr.f.* Selma.

seltz, *s.m.* soda, soda-water, seltzer: *sifone di —*, soda-siphon; *whisky e —*, whisky and soda.

sélva, *s.f.* **1.** wood; forest **2.** *fig.* mass, great quantity: *— di capelli*, mass of hair; *una — di errori*, an enormous number of mistakes.

selvàggia, *s.f.* savage.

selvaggiaménte, *av.* savagely; wildly.

selvaggína, *s.f.* game.

selvàggio, *ag.* **1.** (*non civilizzato, primitivo*) savage, uncivilized, primitive: *paese —*, primitive (o uncivilized) country; *popolo —*, uncivilized (o primitive) people; *tribù selvagge*, savage tribes; *vita selvaggia*, primitive life **2.** (*selvatico, incolto*) wild: *animali selvaggi*, wild beasts; *fiore, arbusto —*, wild flower, shrub; *luogo —*, wild place **3.** *fig.* wild; (*primitivo*) untamed, primitive; (*rozzo*) rough: *animo —*, primitive (o untamed) soul; *grida selvagge*, wild cries; *modi selvaggi*, rough manners **4.** (*scontroso*) unsociable: *è un ragazzo —*, he is an unsociable boy ‖ *s.m.* savage.

selvaticaménte, *av.* wildly.

selvatichézza, *s.f.* **1.** wildness **2.** (*mancanza di socievolezza*) unsociableness, unsociability **3.** (*mancanza di finezza*) roughness.

selvàtico, *ag.* **1.** wild: *animale, fiore —*, wild animal, flower **2.** (*non socievole*) unsociable: *uomo —*, unsociable man **3.** (*rude*) rough.

selvaticùme, *s.m.* wildness.

selvicoltóre, *s.m.* forester, sylviculturist.
selvicoltúra, *s.f.* forestry, sylviculture.
selvóso, *ag.* wooded, woody, well-wooded.
Sem, *no.pr.m.* (*Bibbia*) Shem.
semafòrico, *ag.* semaphoric; semaphore (*attributivo*).
semaforísta, *s.m.* (*ferr.*) signalman (*pl.* signalmen).
semàforo, *s.m.* **1.** traffic-lights (*pl.*), traffic-signals (*pl.*): *le automobili devono arrestarsi quando il —
è rosso,* cars must stop when the traffic-lights are at red **2.** (*ferr.*) (railway-)signal: *ala, braccio del —,* signal-arm **3.** (*mar.*) signal-station.
semàio, *s.m.* **1.** silkworm-breeder **2.** (*venditore di semi*) seedsman (*pl.* seedsmen); (*venditore di semi abbrustoliti*) seller of pumpkin-seeds.
semàntica, *s.f.* **1.** semantics **2.** (*semeiotica*) semeiotics.
semàntico, *ag.* semantic.
semasiología, *s.f.* semasiology.
semasiològico, *ag.* semasiological.
semasiòlogo, *s.m.* semasiologist.
semàta, *s.f.* barley-water.
sembiànte, *s.m.* (*letter.*) **1.** (*fattezze*) countenance, face; features (*pl.*): *onesto —,* honest face; *il suo dolce —,* her sweet countenance **2.** (*apparenza*) semblance, resemblance, appearance: *aver — di ql.co.,* to look like sthg.: *ha — di vetro,* it looks like glass (*o* it has the appearance of glass) ‖ *in sembianti,* apparently ‖ *far —,* to pretend (*o* to feign).
sembiànza, *s.f.* (*letter.*) **1.** (*fattezze*) countenance, face; features (*pl.*): *un giovane di belle sembianze,* a good-looking young man **2.** (*apparenza*) appearance, resemblance: *aver — di, essere in — di,* to look like (*o* to have the appearance of): *ha — di gentiluomo,* he looks like a gentleman.
sembràre, *V.* **parére 1. 2.**
séme, *s.m.* **1.** seed: *— di anice,* aniseed; *— di lino,* flax-seed (*o* linseed); *semi di zucca,* pumpkin-seeds; *semi oleosi,* oleiferous seeds; *grano da —,* seed-corn; *olio di semi,* seed-oil ‖ *semi di bachi,* silkworm eggs **2.** (*di mela, pera, ecc.*) pip: *senza semi,* pipless: *un'arancia senza semi,* a pipless orange **3.** *fig.* (*origine, causa*) cause, seed, germ: *il — della discordia,* the seed of discord; *il — della virtù, del vizio,* the seed of virtue, of vice; *questo fu il — di molti mali,* this was the cause of many evils **4.** (*letter.*) (*discendenza*) seed: *il — di Abramo,* the seed of Abraham **5.** (*delle carte da giuoco*) suit: *carte dello stesso —,* cards of the same suit.
semeiòtica, *s.f.* semeiotics.
Sèmele, *no.pr.f.* (*mit.*) Semele.
seménta, *s.f.* **1.** (*semi*) seeds (*pl.*) **2.** (*il seminare*) sowing: *hanno dato inizio alla —,* they have begun sowing **3.** (*tempo della semina*) sowing-season, seed-time.
sementàre, *v.t.* to sow.
sementatóre, *s.m.,* **sementatríce,** *s.f.* sower.
seménte, *s.f.* (*semi*) seeds (*pl.*): *gettare la —,* to sow.
semènza, *s.f.* **1.** seeds (*pl.*): *il contadino ripone la — per l'autunno,* the farmer puts seeds aside for the autumn **2.** (*semi di zucca abbrustoliti*) pumpkin-seeds (*pl.*) **3.** *fig.* (*origine, causa*) cause, seed, germ: *la — del vizio,* the seed of vice **4.** (*letter.*) (*progenie*) progeny, offspring; (*discendenza*) descent.
semenzàio, *s.m.* **1.** seed-bed, seed-plot; nursery (*anche fig.*) **2.** (*venditore di semi*) seedsman (*pl.* seedsmen).
semestràle, *ag.* half-yearly (*attributivo*); semi-annual (*attributivo*); six-monthly (*attributivo*): *una rivista —,* a magazine that comes out twice a year; *una visita —,* a six-monthly visit.
semestralménte, *av.* half-yearly, semi-annually, six-monthly: *questa rivista esce —,* this magazine comes out twice a year.
semèstre, *s.m.* **1.** half-year, six-month period; (*scolastico*) semester: *nel primo — del 1960 la produzione è aumentata,* production increased in the first half (*o* first six months) of 1960 **2.** (*rata semestrale*) six-monthly instalment; (*compenso semestrale*) six months' pay.

semiacèrbo, *ag.* half-ripe, unripe.
semiapèrto, *ag.* half-open.
semiàsse, *s.m.* **1.** (*geom.*) semi-axis (*pl.* semi-axes) **2.** (*aut.*) axle-shaft, drive-shaft.
semibàrbaro, *ag.* semi-barbarous, semi-barbarian ‖ *s.m.* semi-barbarian.
semibrève, *s.f.* (*mus.*) semibreve.
semibústo, *s.m.* half-bust.
semicadènza, *s.f.* (*mus.*) semi-cadence.
semicérchio, *s.m.* (*geom.*) semicircle.
semichiúso, *ag.* half-closed.
semicircolàre, *ag.* semicircular: *canali semicircolari,* (*anat.*) semicircular canals.
semicírcolo, *s.m.* (*geom.*) semicircle.
semicirconferènza, *s.f.* (*geom.*) semi-circumference.
semicolònna, *s.f.* half-column.
semiconsonànte, *s.f.* (*fonet.*) semi-consonant.
semicopèrto, *ag.* half-covered.
semicròma, *s.f.* (*mus.*) semiquaver.
semicúpio, *s.m.* hip-bath.
semidènso, *ag.* semi-thick.
semidiàfano, *ag.* semi-diaphanous.
semidiàmetro, *s.m.* (*geom.*) semi-diameter.
semidifettívo, *ag.* (*gram.*) semi-defective.
semidío, *s.m.* demigod.
semidóppio, *ag.* (*bot.*) semi-double ‖ *s.m.* (*eccl.*) semi-double.
semidòtto, *ag.* half-educated ‖ *s.m.* half-educated man.
semiellíssi, *s.f.* (*geom.*) semi-ellipse.
semifilòsofo, *s.m.* (*scherz.*) pseudo-philosopher.
semifinàle, *s.f.* (*spor.*) semifinal.
semifinalista, *s.c.* (*spor.*) semifinalist.
semifluído, *ag.* (*fis.*) semifluid.
semifréddo, *ag.* half-cold ‖ *s.m.* "semifreddo" (kind of Italian ice-cream).
semigòtico, *ag.* semi-Gothic.
semigratúito, *ag.* half-price (*attributivo*).
semilavoràto, *ag.* semi-finished, semi-manufactured.
semilíbero, *ag.* half-free ‖ *s.m.* half-free man.
semilibertà, *s.f.* half-freedom.
semilunàre, *ag.* semilunar: *valvola —,* (*anat.*) semilunar valve.
semilúnio, *s.m.* period of the half-moon.
semimínima, *s.f.* (*mus.*) crotchet.
semimòrto, *ag.* **1.** half-dead **2.** (*di luce*) dim **3.** (*di vocabolo*) obsolete.
semimpermeàbile, *ag.* semi-impermeable.
semimúto, *ag.s.m.* semi-mute.
sémina, *s.f.* sowing: *stagione della —,* sowing-season (*o* seed-time).
seminàbile, *ag.* fit to be sown (*predicativo*).
seminagióne, *s.f.* **1.** sowing **2.** (*tempo della semina*) sowing season, seed-time.
seminàle, *ag.* seminal.
seminàre, *v.t.* **1.** to sow: *è troppo presto per —,* it is too soon to sow yet; *— un campo a frumento,* to sow a field with wheat; *— frumento,* to sow wheat ‖ *si raccoglie quel che si semina,* as a man sows, so shall he reap ‖ *chi semina vento raccoglie tempesta, prov.* sow the wind and reap the whirlwind **2.** *fig.* (*diffondere*) to sow; (*spargere*) to spread, to scatter: *le mosche seminano le malattie,* flies spread disease; *— il malcontento, l'odio tra i cittadini,* to sow seeds of discontent, of hatred among the citizens; *— il terrore,* to sow (*o* to spread) terror **3.** (*disseminare*) to scatter, to strew: *non — la tua roba!,* don't scatter (*o* strew) your things around!.
seminàrio, *s.m.* **1.** (*eccl.*) seminary **2.** (*di università*) seminar **3.** (*semenzaio*) seed-bed.
seminarísta, *s.m.* seminarist.
seminàta, *s.f.* (*semina*) sowing.
seminatívo, *ag.* fit to be sown (*predicativo*).
seminàto, *ag.* sown (with sthg.); *fig.* spread (with sthg.), strewn (with sthg.): *cielo — di stelle,* sky strewn

with stars; *sentiero — di fiori*, path strewn with flowers; *terreno — a frumento*, land sown with wheat ‖ *s.m.* sown land, sown field ‖ *uscire dal —, fig.* to wander from the subject (*o* point).

seminatóio, *s.m.* seed-drill.

seminatóre, *ag.* sowing ‖ *s.m.* sower.

seminatríce, *s.f.* **1.** sower **2.** (*mec.*) sowing-machine.

seminatúra, *s.f.* **1.** sowing **2.** (*tempo della semina*) sowing season, seed-time.

seminfermità, *s.f.* partial infirmity: *— mentale*, partial insanity.

seminúdo, *ag.* half-naked, semi-nude.

semiologìa, *s.f.* semeiology, semeiotics.

semionciàle, *ag.* semi-uncial.

semiopàco, *ag.* semi-opaque.

semioscurità, *s.f.* half-darkness; half-light.

semiovàle, *ag.* semi-oval.

semipagàno, *ag.s.m.* semi-pagan.

semiparàbola, *s.f.* (*geom.*) semiparabola.

semipoèta, *s.m.* (*spreg.*) poetaster.

semipoètico, *ag.* half-poetic.

semipúbblico, *ag.* semi-public.

Semiràmide, *no.pr.f.* (*st.*) Semiramis.

semirígido, *ag.* semi-rigid; semi-flexible: *dirigibile —*, (*aer.*) semi-rigid airship; *stivali semirigidi*, semi-flexible boots.

semisecolàre, *ag.* **1.** (*che ricorre ogni mezzo secolo*) semi-centennial **2.** (*che dura da mezzo secolo*) half a century old (*predicativo*); fifty years old (*predicativo*); half-century-old (*attributivo*); fifty-year-old (*attributivo*).

semiselvàggio, *ag.* half-savage: *la popolazione semi-selvaggia di quell'isola*, the half-savage population of that island.

semisèrio, *ag.* half-serious; serio-comic: *faccia, espressione semiseria*, half-serious face, look; *opera semiseria*, (*teat.*) serio-comic opera; *me lo disse in tono —*, he told me so in a half-serious tone.

semisfèra, *s.f.* hemisphere, half-sphere.

semisfèrico, *ag.* hemispheric(al).

semispènto, *ag.* **1.** half-burnt; half-extinguished: *carboni semispenti*, half-burnt coals **2.** (*fievole, smorto*) faint; lifeless: *occhi semispenti*, lifeless eyes; *voce semispenta*, faint voice.

semìta, *s.c.* Semite.

semítico, *ag.* Semitic.

semitìsmo, *s.m.* Semitism.

semitìsta, *s.m.* Semitist, Semitic scholar.

semitonàto, *ag.* (*mus.*) semitonic, semitonal.

semitóndo, *ag.* half-round, semicircular.

semitòno, *s.m.* (*mus.*) semitone.

semitrasparènte, *ag.* semitransparent.

semitropicàle, *ag.* semitropical.

semiuffìciàle, *ag.* semi-official.

semivestíto, *ag.* half-dressed.

semivívo, *ag.* half-alive; half-dead.

semivocàle, *s.f.* (*fonet.*) semivowel.

semivocàlico, *ag.* (*fonet.*) semivocalic.

semivolàta, *s.f.*, **semivólo,** *s.m.* (*a pallacorda*) half-volley.

sémola[1], *s.f.* **1.** (*crusca*) bran **2.** (*efelide*) freckle.

sémola[2], *s.f.* (*dial.*) (*fior di farina*) (fine) flour: *pane di —*, super-fine bread.

semolàta, *s.f.* drench.

semolíno, *s.m.* semolina.

semolóso, *ag.* **1.** bran (*attributivo*): *pane —*, bran bread **2.** (*lentigginoso*) freckly, freckled: *pelle semolosa*, freckly skin.

semovènte, *ag.* self-moving; self-propelled, self-propelling; (*automatico*) automatic: *cannone —*, self-propelled gun.

semovènza, *s.f.* self-movement, self-propulsion.

Sempióne, *no.pr.m.* (*geog.*) Simplon.

sempitèrno, *ag.* everlasting ‖ *in —*, everlastingly.

sémplice, *ag.* **1.** simple; single: *corpo —*, simple body; *equazione, frazione —*, simple equation, fraction; *fiore —*, single bloom; *nodo —*, single knot; *tempo —*, (*gram.*) simple tense ‖ *bancarotta —*, bankruptcy ‖ *furto —*, (*dir.*) simple theft ‖ *partita —*, (*comm.*) single entry ‖ *regola del tre —*, (*mat.*) rule of three ‖ *voti semplici*, (*eccl.*) simple vows **2.** (*solo*) simple; mere; sheer: *la verità pura e —*, the plain truth (*o* the truth pure and simple); *la — descrizione dei fatti la fece piangere*, the mere description of the facts made her cry; *la — prudenza vuole che...*, ordinary (*o* elementary) prudence demands that...; *è follia pura e —*, it is sheer madness; *è un ladro puro e —*, he is an out and out thief; *è una truffa pura e —*, this is cheating pure and simple; *fu condannato in base a un — sospetto*, he was condemned on a mere suspicion; *l'ho visto per la — ragione che passava*, I saw him for the simple reason that he was passing by; *stare alla — parola di qlcu.*, to take s.o. at his word **3.** (*non ricercato*) simple, plain; (*senza malizia*) simple-hearted: *un'anima —*, a simple soul; *cibo, mobilia —*, plain food, furniture; *gente —*, plain (*o* homely) people; *parole semplici*, plain words; *un uomo —*, a plain man; *vestito —*, plain (*o* simple) dress; *la vita —*, the simple life; *è una ragazza —*, she is a simple girl; *avere gusti semplici*, to have simple tastes ‖ *alla —*, simply (*o* plainly) **4.** (*facile*) simple, easy: *una domanda —*, an easy question; *metodo —*, simple (*o* easy) method; *il mio compito è piuttosto —*, my task is quite easy **5.** (*mil. mar.*) ordinary, common: *marinaio —*, ordinary seaman; *soldato —*, private (soldier).

semplicemènte, *av.* **1.** simply, plainly: *ci ricevette —*, he received us simply; *vivere —*, to live a simple life **2.** (*solamente*) simply, only, merely: *ho fatto — rilevare che...*, I merely (*o* simply) observed that... **3.** (*senza malizia*) artlessly; frankly.

semplicétto, *ag.* naïve, ingenuous.

sémplici, *s.m.pl.* (*rar.*) (*erbe medicinali*) simples.

sempliciàrio, *s.m.* herbal, simple-gathering book.

semplicióne, *s.m.* simpleton, naïve person: *è un —*, he is easily taken in (*o* he'll swallow anything).

semplicioneria, *s.f.* **1.** simple-mindedness, naïveté **2.** (*facilóneria*) easy-going attitude.

sempliciòtto, *s.m.* simpleton: *che —!*, what a simpleton!; *è un —*, he is a simpleton.

semplicìsmo, *s.m.* superficiality, over-simplified attitude.

semplicìsta[1], *ag.* over-simplified: *dottrina —*, over-simplified doctrine ‖ *s.m.* (*persona superficiale*) superficial person.

semplicìsta[2], *s.m.* **1.** (*erborista*) herbalist **2.** (*sempliciario*) herbal.

semplicità, *s.f.* simplicity.

semplicizzàre, **semplificàre,** *v.t.* to simplify: *ciò semplifica le cose*, this makes things easier; *— una frazione*, (*mat.*) to reduce a fraction to its lowest terms.

semplificàto, *ag.* simplified.

semplificatóre, *ag.* simplifying ‖ *s.m.*, **semplificatríce,** *s.f.* simplifier, simplificator.

semplificazióne, *s.f.* simplification.

sèmpre, *av.* **1.** **always**; (*rar.*) **ever**: *arriva — tardi*, he is always late; *brontola —*, he is always grumbling; *non — tu hai ragione*, you are not always right; *non sarà — così!*, it won't always be like that!; *si sente — stanco*, he always feels tired ‖ *— avanti!*, ever onward! ‖ *— meglio*, better and better; *— meno*, less and less: *è — meno gentile con me*, she is always less and less kind to me; *— peggio*, worse and worse: *mi tratta — peggio*, she treats me worse and worse; *— più*, more and more: *mi piace — più*, I like it more and more; *saliva — più*, he went up and up; *si fa — più scuro*, it is getting darker and darker ‖ *— vostro*, (*in chiusa di lettera*) yours ever (*o* ever yours) ‖ *— usual*: *mi sorrise col suo sorriso di —*, he gave me his usual smile ‖ *ora e —*, now and for ever ‖ *per —*, for ever (*o fam.* for good): *addio per —*, farewell (*o* good-bye).

for ever; *una volta per* —, once (and) for all; *è partito per* —*?*, has he gone for good? || *quasi* —, nearly always: *è quasi* — *fuori*, she is nearly always out || *i ragazzi sono* — *ragazzi*, boys will be boys 2. (*con ag. nell'uso attributivo*) **ever**: *occhi* — *sorridenti*, ever-smiling eyes; *esercita un'influenza* — *crescente su di lui*, she exercises an ever-growing influence on him 3. (*ancora*) still: *c'è* — *tempo, non ti allarmare!*, there is still time, don't panic!; *è venuto tardi, ma* — *in tempo*, he came late, but still in time; *sei* — *in collera con me?*, are you still angry with me?; *il suo stato è grave, ma c'è* — *speranza*, his condition is dangerous, but there is still hope for him; *vive* — *qui?*, does he still live here? 4. (*in ogni caso, tuttavia*) **always, anyhow, nevertheless**: *anche se ti offre solo cinque sterline, è* (*pur*) — *qualcosa*, even if he offers you five pounds, it's (always) something; *è* (*pur*) — *vero che...*, it is nevertheless true that...; *posso* — *tentare*, I can always try (o anyhow, I can try); *resta* — *il fatto che la vidi*, the fact remains that I saw her || **sèmpre che**, *l. cong.* **provided** (**that**): *lo farò,* — *che tu lo voglia*, I'll do it provided (that) you want me to; *verremo,* — *che non piova*, we shall come provided (that) it doesn't rain.

sempreverde, *ag.s.m.* (*bot.*) **evergreen**.

semprevivo, *s.m.* (*bot.*) **houseleek**.

Sempronio, *no.pr.m.* **Sempronius** || *Tizio, Caio e* —, Tom, Dick and Harry.

sèna, *s.f.* (*bot.*) **senna**.

sènapa, *s.f.* (*bot. cuc.*) **mustard**.

senapàto, *ag.* **mustard** (*attributivo*): *impiastro* —, (*med.*) mustard-plaster (o mustard-poultice).

sènape, *s.f.* (*bot. cuc.*) **mustard**.

senapièra, *s.f.* **mustard-pot**.

senapísmo, *s.m.* (*med.*) **mustard-plaster, mustard -poultice**.

senàrio, *ag.* (*poes.*) (*di sei sillabe*) **of six syllables**; (*di sei piedi*) **of six feet** || *s.m.* (*poes.*) (*verso di sei sillabe*) **line of six syllables**; (*verso di sei piedi*) **senarius** (*pl.* senarii).

senàto, *s.m.* 1. **senate** || — *accademico*, senatus academicus || *Palazzo del Senato*, Senate-house 2. (*st. romana*) **senate**.

senatoconsúlto, *s.m.* (*dir. romano*) **senatus-consultum** (*pl.* senatus-consulta).

senatoràto, *s.m.* **senatorship**.

senatóre, *s.m.* **senator**.

senatoriàle, senatòrio, *ag.* **senatorial**.

Sèneca, *no.pr.m.* (*st. lett.*) **Seneca**.

Senegàl, *no.pr.m.* (*geog.*) **Senegal**.

senegalése, *ag.* **Senegalese** || *s.c.* Senegalese (*invariato al pl.*).

senescènza, *s.f.* **senescence**.

senése, *ag.* **Sienese** || *s.c.* Sienese (*invariato al pl.*).

seníle, *ag.* **senile**: *decadenza* —, **senile decay**.

senilità, *s.f.* **senility**.

senilménte, *av.* **senilely, in a senile way**.

senióre, *ag.s.m.* **senior**.

sènna[1], *s.f.* (*bot.*) **senna**.

Sènna[2], *no.pr.f.* (*geog.*) **Seine**.

sennino, *s.m.* (*fanciullo assennato*) **clever child**.

sénno[1], *s.m.* **sense**; **judgement**; **wisdom**: *un uomo di* —, a man of sense (o of good judgement); *non hai proprio* —*!*, you've got no sense at all!; *questa è cosa fatta con* —, this has been done sensibly || *da* —, seriously: *parli da* —*?*, are you serious? (o in earnest?) || *lo ha fatto a suo* —, he did it according to his own judgement (o good sense) || *essere fuori di* —, to be out of one's senses (o wits); *essere in* —, to be in one's (right) senses; *far tornare in* — *qlcu.*, to bring s.o. to his senses; *perdere il* —, to lose one's wits (o to go mad); *tornare in* —, to come to one's senses || *far* —, to reach the age of discretion || *del* — *di poi son piene le fosse*, *prov.* it's easy to be wise after the event.

sennò[2], *cong.* **otherwise**: *obbedisci,* — *te ne pentirai*, do what I tell you, otherwise you'll be sorry.

sennonché, *cong.* **except that, but for the fact that**.

séno[1], *s.m.* 1. **breast**; **bosom** (anche *fig.*): *ella lo strinse al* —, she pressed him to her breast (o bosom); *nascose la lettera in* —, she hid the letter in her bosom; *allattare un bimbo al* —, to breast-feed (o to suckle) a baby || *in* — *a*, in the bosom of: *in* — *alla Chiesa, alla famiglia*, in the bosom of the church, of the family; *in* — *alla commissione*, within the committee; *in* — *al partito*, within the party || *scaldare una serpe in* —, to nourish (o to nurse) a viper in one's bosom 2. (*grembo, viscere*) **womb**: *il* — *della terra*, the bosom (o the bowels) of the earth; *portare un figlio in* —, to carry a child in one's womb || *benedetto il frutto del* — *tuo*, blessed is the fruit of thy womb 3. (*cuore, animo*) **breast, bosom**: *la fiamma che gli arde in* —, the flame burning in his breast 4. (*anat. patol.*) **sinus** (*pl.* sinuses, sinus): — *fistoloso*, sinus 5. (*geog.*) **inlet, bay, cove**.

séno[2], *s.m.* (*trigonometria*) **sine** (*abbr.* sin).

Senòfane, *no.pr.m.* (*st. fil.*) **Xenophanes**.

senofobìa, *s.f.* **xenophobia**.

senòfobo, *s.m.* **xenophobe**.

Senofónte, *no.pr.m.* (*st. lett.*) **Xenophon**.

sensàle, *s.m.* **broker**; **middleman** (*pl.* middlemen); (*marittimo*) **ship-broker**.

sensataménte, *av.* **sensibly**; **judiciously**.

sensatézza, *s.f.* **good sense**; **judgement**; **wisdom**.

sensàto, *ag.* **sensible**; **judicious**: *una persona sensata*, a sensible person; *il suo ragionamento è molto* —, there is a lot of sense in what he says.

sensazionàle, *ag.* **sensational**; **exciting**; **thrilling**: *romanzo* —, thriller; *la stampa* —, (*spreg.*) the yellow (o gutter) press; *la commedia ebbe un successo* —, the play was a great hit (o a great success).

sensazióne, *s.f.* 1. **sensation**; **feeling**: *dare, provare una* — *di caldo, freddo, dolore*, to give, to have a sensation of warmth, cold, pain 2. (*scalpore*) **sensation**: *la scoperta fece grande* —, the discovery made a great sensation || *a* —, sensational 3. (*idea*) **feeling**: *ho la* — *che tu abbia ragione*, I have a feeling you are right.

senserìa, *s.f.* 1. **broking** 2. (*mercede del sensale*) **brokerage**.

sensìbile, *ag.* 1. **sensitive**: — *al calore, al freddo, all'umidità*, sensitive to heat, to cold, to moisture; — *alle sofferenze altrui, al rimprovero*, sensitive to other people's sufferings, to reproof; *mercato* —, (*econ.*) responsive market; *pellicola* —, (*foto.*) sensitive film; *un ragazzo* —, a sensitive boy; *temperamento* —, sensitive nature; *un termometro molto* —, a very sensitive thermometer; *il mondo degli affari è molto* — *ai cambiamenti politici*, the business world is very sensitive to political changes; *questa bilancia è* — *al milligrammo*, this balance is sensitive to a milligramme; *avere la pelle* —, to have a sensitive skin (o fam. to be thin-skinned); *essere* — *al dolore*, to be very sensitive (o susceptible) to pain; *essere* — *alla gentilezza di qlcu.*, to appreciate s.o.'s kindness (o to be sensible of s.o.'s kindness) 2. (*percepito dai sensi*) **notable, sensible**; **tangible**: *un* — *aumento*, a notable (o sensible) increase; *una* — *differenza*, a notable (o sensible) difference; *danni sensibili*, serious damage; *fenomeni sensibili*, sensible phenomena; *mondo* —, tangible world.

sensibilità, *s.f.* 1. **sensitiveness**; (*delicatezza*) **delicacy**: *non volevo offendere la tua* —, I didn't mean to hurt your feelings 2. (*scient.*) **sensitivity**: *la* — *di un termometro, una pellicola*, the sensitivity of a thermometer, a film; — *di variazione*, (*rad. tv.*) variational sensitivity; — *luminosa*, (*tv.*) luminous sensitivity.

sensibilizzàre, *v.t.* (*foto.*) to **sensitize**.

sensibilizzatóre, *s.m.* (*foto.*) **sensitizer**.

sensibilizzazióne, *s.f.* (*foto.*) **sensitization**.

sensibilménte, *av.* 1. **sensitively** 2. (*notevolmente*) **notably, sensibly, considerably**.

sensísmo, *s.m.* (*st. fil.*) **sensism**.

sensísta, *s.m.* (*st. fil.*) **sensist**.

sensitíva, *s.f.* **1.** (*sensibilità*) sensitiveness **2.** (*bot.*) sensitive plant ‖ *essere una* —, *fig.* to be very sensitive.

sensitivà, *s.f.* sensitivity.

sensitívo, *ag.* **1.** (*che percepisce sensazioni*) sensory, sensorial: *organo* —, sensory organ **2.** (*sensibile*) sensitive: *un temperamento* —, a sensitive nature.

sènso, *s.m.* **1.** sense: *il — dell'udito*, the sense of hearing; *i cinque sensi*, the five senses; *errore dei sensi*, errors of sense; *gli organi dei sensi*, the sense-organs; *i piaceri dei sensi*, the pleasures of the senses ‖ *sesto* —, sixth sense ‖ *— dell'orientamento*, sense of locality (o direction) ‖ *— del tempo*, sense of time ‖ *perdere i sensi*, to lose consciousness; *ricuperare i sensi*, to recover consciousness (o to come to) **2.** (*sensazione*) sensation, feeling; (*coscienza*) sense; (*sentimento*) feeling, sentiment: *— del dovere, dell'onore, di responsabilità*, sense of duty, of honour, of responsibility; *— di compassione*, feeling of pity; *un — di freddo, di caldo, di dolore*, a feeling (o sensation) of cold, of warmth, of pain; *— di gratitudine*, feeling of gratitude; *— di paura*, sensation of fear; *un — di piacere, gioia, compassione*, a feeling of pleasure, joy, pity ‖ *— morale, pratico*, moral, practical sense ‖ *fare —*, (*disgusto*) to disgust; (*orrore*) to horrify **3.** (*significato*) sense, meaning: *— proprio, figurato di una parola*, literal, figurative sense of a word; *doppio* —, double meaning; *non riesco a capire il — di questa frase*, I cannot understand the meaning of this sentence; *non so in che — egli usa questo idiotismo*, I do not know in what sense he uses this idiom; *quel che dice non ha* —, what he is saying does not make sense (o he is talking nonsense) ‖ *ai sensi di legge*, according to the law ‖ *in un certo* —, in one sense; *in ogni* —, in every sense ‖ *ripetere a* —, to resume (o to repeat in one's own words) **4.** (*direzione, verso*) direction, way: *— unico*, one-way only; *— vietato*, no entry; *in — giusto*, the right way (o in the right direction); *in — opposto*, the opposite way (o in the opposite direction); *in ogni* —, in all directions; *va' in quel* —, go that way **5.** (*modo*) way, manner: *risposta in — affermativo*, answer in the affirmative (o affirmative answer); *dovete scrivere in questo* —, you must write in these terms; *si può fare in questo o quel* —, you can do it (in) this or that way.

sensòrio, *ag.* sensory, sensorial; sense (*attributivo*): *nervi sensori*, (*anat.*) sensory nerves; *organo* —, (*anat.*) sense-organ ‖ *s.m.* sense; sense-organ.

sensuàle, *ag.* sensual ‖ *s.c.* sensualist.

sensualísmo, *s.m.* **1.** sensualism **2.** (*st. fil.*) sensualism.

sensualísta, *s.m.* **1.** sensualist **2.** (*st. fil.*) sensualist.

sensualístico, *ag.* **1.** sensualistic **2.** (*st. fil.*) sensualistic.

sensualità, *s.f.* sensuality.

sensualménte, *av.* sensually.

sentènza, *s.f.* **1.** (*dir.*) sentence; judg(e)ment; award; decision: *cassare una* —, to quash a sentence; *emanare una* —, to deliver (o to pass o to give) judgement; *pronunziare una* —, to pass sentence: *pronunziare una — di morte contro qlcu.*, to sentence s.o. to death; *ricorrere in appello contro una* —, to appeal against a decision **2.** (*opinione*) opinion: *sono della vostra stessa* —, I share your opinion ‖ *sputar sentenze*, to play the wiseacre **3.** (*massima*) saying; maxim; (*aforisma*) aphorism.

sentenziàle, *ag.* containing maxims: *libro* —, book of maxims.

sentenziàre, *v.i.* **1.** (*dir.*) to judge, to deliver a judgement; to hold: *la corte sentenziò che era colpevole*, the court held that he was guilty **2.** (*pronunciarsi*) to pronounce; (*sputar sentenze*) to talk sententiously ‖ to play the wiseacre.

sentenziosaménte, *av.* sententiously.

sentenzióso, *ag.* sententious.

sentièro, *s.m.* path (anche *fig.*); pathway, footpath; track: *il — della gloria*, the path of glory; *uscire dal — battuto*, to go off the beaten track.

sentimentàle, *ag.* sentimental: *di valore* —, of

sentimental value; *natura* —, sentimental nature; *fare il* —, to be sentimental.

sentimentalísmo, *s.m.* sentimentalism.

sentimentalísta, *s.c.* sentimentalist.

sentimentalità, *s.f.* sentimentality.

sentimentalménte, *av.* sentimentally.

sentiménto, *s.m.* **1.** sentiment; (*moto dell'animo*) feeling: *un — di pietà, di orgoglio*, a feeling (o sentiment) of pity, pride; *il — religioso*, religious sentiment; *donna di nobili sentimenti*, woman of lofty feelings; *persona di gran* —, good-hearted person; *ciò ha molta presa sui miei sentimenti*, this appeals to my feelings very much; *ho offeso i suoi sentimenti*, I have hurt his feelings; *questo film trabocca di* —, this film has too much sentiment; *esprimere, controllare i propri sentimenti*, to express, to control one's feelings **2.** (*facoltà, disposizione spirituale*) feeling: *— estetico*, aesthetic feeling **3.** (*opinione*) sentiment, opinion: *esprimere i propri sentimenti su ql.co.*, to express one's sentiments (o opinion) on sthg. **4.** *pl.* (*sensi*) senses: *con tutti i sentimenti*, in one's full senses; *perdere i sentimenti*, to lose one's senses.

sentína, *s.f.* **1.** (*mar.*) bilge **2.** *fig.* (*ricettacolo*) sink: *una — di malvagità*, a sink of iniquity.

sentinèlla, *s.f.* sentry, sentinel: *dare il cambio alla* —, to relieve the sentry; *essere di* —, to be on sentry -go; *montare la* —, to mount guard ‖ *— perduta*, outlying sentry ‖ *fare la — davanti alla porta di qlcu.*, (*scherz.*) (*aspettarlo*) to do sentry-go before s.o.'s door.

sentíre, *v.t.* **1.** to feel (anche *fig.*): *hai sentito il peso di questo pacco?*, have you felt the weight of this parcel?; *senti quanta umidità c'è in questa stanza*, feel how damp this room is; *sento un bruciore allo stomaco*, I've got heartburn; *sento che ha bisogno di me*, he needs me, I feel it; *sento che ha ragione*, I feel he is right; *sento la forza delle sue convinzioni*, I feel the force of his convictions; *— caldo, freddo*, to feel warm, cold; *— il caldo, il freddo*, to feel the heat, the cold; *— compassione per qlcu.*, to feel pity for s.o.; *— fame, sete*, to feel hungry, thirsty; *— la fatica*, to feel the strain; *— la frusta*, to feel the whip; *— un male alla schiena*, to feel a pain in one's back; *— la mancanza di qlcu., ql.co.*, to feel the lack of (o to miss) s.o., sthg.; *— i morsi della fame*, to feel the pangs of hunger; *— il morso*, to feel the bit; *— l'obbligo*, to feel obliged; *— un prurito*, to feel an itch; *— il solletico*, to be ticklish ‖ *è un egoista che non sente nulla*, he is an egoist without feelings ‖ *è un uomo schietto, le dice come le sente*, he is an outspoken man, he speaks as he feels ‖ *il freddo incomincia a farsi* —, the cold is beginning to make itself felt ‖ *non sento più le gambe*, I can hardly stand ‖ *non tutti la sentono allo stesso modo*, not everyone feels the same way ‖ *gli uomini hanno gli anni che sentono, le donne quelli che dimostrano*, *prov.* men are as old as they feel, women as old as they look **2.** (*tastare*) to feel: *senti come è ruvido*, feel how rough it is; *senti il mio polso*, feel my pulse; *senti se è abbastanza caldo*, feel whether it is warm enough **3.** (*gustare*) to taste: *senti questo caffè*, taste this coffee; *senti se ti piace questa salsa*, taste this sauce and see if you like it; *sento ql.co. di strano in questo dolce*, I can taste sthg. strange in this cake **4.** (*odorare*) to smell: *il cane l'ha sentito al fiuto*, the dog has scented it; *l'ho sentito dall'odore*, I smell it; *senti questa rosa*, smell this rose; *sento odore di cipolla, di gas, di bruciato*, I smell onions, gas, sthg. burning **5.** (*udire*) to hear: *fui così felice di — che avevi vinto il premio*, I was so happy to hear you had won the prize; *ho sentito dire che non è in città*, I have heard that he is not in town; *ho sentito un rumore*, I heard a noise; *lo sentii io dire questo*, I heard him say(ing) this myself; *mi pare ancora di — la sua voce*, I still seem to be able to hear his voice; *non l'ho mai sentito cantare*, I have never heard him sing; *non ne ho mai sentito parlare*, I have never heard of it; *non se ne* *sentì più parlare,* no more was heard of it; *non voglio sentirne più parlare,* I do not want to hear any more about (*o* of) it; *si sente il treno,* you can hear the train; *si sentiva un gran baccano,* you could hear a rumpus ‖ *a quel che sento,* from what I hear ‖ *ne sentirete delle belle,* you won't half get (*o* catch) it ‖ *non sente nemmeno le cannonate,* he sleeps like a log ‖ *se ne sentono di tutti i colori!,* the things you hear! (*o* that happen!) ‖ *farsi* —, to make oneself heard: *fatti* —!, speak up for yourself!; *non ti far* — *a piangere,* don't let them hear you crying **6.** (*ascoltare*) to listen to (s.o., sthg.): *senti il tuo avvocato,* go and see your lawyer; *senti!, volevo dirti...,* look!, I wanted to tell you...; *sentiamo!,* let's hear it; — *una commedia,* to listen to a play; — *una conferenza,* to listen to a lecture; — *la lezione a un bambino,* to make a child repeat his lesson; — *la radio,* to listen to the radio; *stammi a* —, listen to me ‖ *non sente altro che l'interesse,* he doesn't do anything for nothing ‖ — *la messa,* to be at (*o* to attend) mass ‖ *v.i.* **1.** (*udire*) to hear: *egli non sente, è sordo,* he cannot hear, he is deaf ‖ *da quell'orecchio non ci sente,* he is deaf in that ear; *fig.* he is turning a deaf ear **2.** (*avere gusto*) to taste: — *di buono,* to taste good; — *di pesce,* to taste of fish **3.** (*avere odore*) to smell: — *di buono,* to smell good; — *di muffa,* to smell musty **3.** (*stimare*) *egli sente rettamente,* he has worthy feelings; *sente troppo di sè,* he is too self-conscious ‖ **sentírsi,** *v.r.* **1.** to feel; to feel up to (sthg., doing); to feel like (sthg., doing): *non mi sento di mangiare, uscire,* I do not feel like eating, going out; *non mi sento in grado di fare una cosa così difficile, una passeggiata così lunga,* I do not feel up to doing such a difficult thing, to going for such a long walk; *non mi sento in grado di fare molto,* I do not feel up to doing much; *si sentiva morire,* he felt he would die; — *offeso, grato, obbligato,* to feel hurt, grateful, obliged; — *rinato,* to feel reborn ‖ *non me la sento,* I do not feel like (*o* up to) it **2.** (*stare*) to feel, to be: *come ti senti?,* how do you feel? (*o* how are you feeling?); *mi sento come se fossi su un aeroplano,* I feel as if I were in a plane; *non mi sento completamente bene,* I do not feel quite myself; — *a proprio agio,* to feel at ease (*o* at home) — *bene, male, stanco, depresso,* to feel well, ill, tired, depressed; — *svenire,* to feel faint.

sentíre, *s.m.* (*sentimento*) feeling: *uomo di alto* —, man of worthy feelings.

sentitaménte, *av.* heartily, sincerely: *vi ringraziamo* —, we heartily thank you.

sentíto, *ag.* **1.** heart-felt, sincere: *sentita simpatia, gioia,* heart-felt sympathy, joy; *i miei sentiti ringraziamenti,* my best thanks; *i miei più sentiti auguri,* my very best (*o* sincerest *o* hearty deal) wishes **2.** (*udito*) heard ‖ *per* — *dire,* by hearsay **3.** (*influente*) influential: *è una persona molto sentita,* he is very influential.

sentóre, *s.m.* **1.** (*vago sospetto*) inkling: *ho* — *di un complotto,* I suspect a plot; *non avevo* — *di quel che stava per accadere,* I had no inkling of what was happening **2.** (*arc. poet.*) (*odore*) smell, scent.

senussíta, *s.m.* (*relig. pol.*) Senussi (*invariato al pl.*).

sènza, *prep.* **1.** without: — *camicia,* without a shirt; *fig.* (*al verde*) broke; — *scarpe,* barefoot(ed); — *soldi,* without (*o* with no) money; — *un soldo,* penniless; *uomo* — *scrupoli,* unscrupulous man; *sono rimasto* — *pane,* I haven't any bread left; *sono uscito* — *cappello,* I went out without a hat ‖ *senz'altro,* (*subito*) at once (*o* with no further delay); (*certamente*) certainly; — *dubbio,* — *forse,* without (*o* with no) doubt (*o* undoubtedly); — *fallo,* without fail ‖ — *confronto,* unrivalled ‖ — *fine,* endlessly (*av.*); endless (*ag.*) ‖ — *numero,* innumerable (*o* countless) ‖ *senz'ombra di...,* without a trace of... ‖ — *spese,* no charge ‖ — *tanti discorsi, complimenti,* without mincing one's words: *me l'ha detto* — *tanti discorsi, complimenti,* he told me without

mincing his words‖ — *testa,* thoughtlessly (*av.*); thoughtless (*ag.*) ‖ *non* —, (*letter.*) not without: *si lamentò, non* — *lacrime,* he grieved not without tears ‖ *fare* — *di ql.co.,* to do (*o* to go) without sthg. **2.** (*eccettuato, oltre a*) without counting, excluding: *sono 600 km* — *il tratto da qui all'autostrada,* it is 600 kms. excluding the stretch from here to the motorway ‖ **sènza, sènza che,** *cong.* without (doing): *uscì* — *che gli dicessimo nulla,* he went out without our saying anything; — *parlare,* without speaking.

senzapàtria, *s.c.* unpatriotic person.

senzatétto, *s.c.* homeless person.

senziènte, *ag.* sentient.

sepaiuòla, *s.f.* (*ornit.*) wren.

sèpalo, *s.m.* (*bot.*) sepal.

separàbile, *ag.* separable.

separabilità, *s.f.* separability, separableness.

separaménto, *V.* separazióne.

separàre, *v.t.* **1.** to separate, to divide; to part: *ho separato i miei libri dai tuoi,* I have separated my books from yours; — *i buoni dai cattivi,* to separate the good from the bad; — *due litiganti,* to part two people quarrelling; — *il sale da una soluzione,* (*chim.*) to separate the salt from a solution **2.** (*tener diviso*) to separate, to divide; to keep apart: *le due montagne sono separate da una valle,* the two mountains are separated by a valley; *la lite separò i due amici,* the quarrel kept the two friends apart; *l'oceano separa l'Europa dall'America,* the ocean divides Europe from America; *un tavolo lo separava dalla porta,* there was a table between him and the door **3.** *fig.* (*distinguere*) to distinguish: *la ragione separa l'uomo dagli animali,* reason distinguishes man from beasts ‖ **separàrsi,** *v.r.* to separate; (*allontanarsi*) to part: *chiacchierarono un poco poi si separarono,* they talked for a while and then they parted; *vissero insieme per cinque anni poi si separarono,* they lived together for five years then separated; — *amichevolmente,* to part friends.

separataménte, *av.* separately.

separatísmo, *s.m.* (*pol.*) separatism.

separatísta, *ag.* (*pol.*) separatist: *movimento* —, separatist movement ‖ *s.c.* (*pol.*) separationist, separatist.

separatívo, *ag.* separative, separating.

separatóre, *ag.* separatory, separating ‖ *s.m.* separator: — *centrifugo,* (*ind.*) centrifugal separator; — *di polvere,* (*ind.*) dust trap; — *magnetico,* (*miner.*) magnetic separator.

separazióne, *s.f.* **1.** separation, division (anche *dir.*): — *dei poteri, dei beni,* division of powers, of property; — *di letto e di mensa,* (*dir.*) separation from bed and board; — *legale,* (*dir.*) judicial separation **2.** (*lo stare lontano*) separation; (*il separarsi*) parting: *dopo una lunga* — *dalla sua famiglia,* after a long separation from his family; *fu una triste* —, it was a sad parting.

sepiolíte, *s.f.* (*min.*) sepiolite, meerschaum.

sepolcràle, *ag.* sepulchral (anche *fig.*); *pietra* —, sepulchral stone; *voce* —, sepulchral voice.

sepolcréto, *s.m.* burial-ground, cemetery.

sepólcro, *s.m.* sepulchre, tomb, grave: — *di famiglia,* family-vault; — *marmoreo,* marble tomb ‖ — *imbiancato,* whited sepulchre ‖ *il Santo Sepolcro,* the Holy Sepulchre: *Cavaliere del Santo Sepolcro,* Knight of the Holy Sepulchre ‖ *visita dei Sepolcri,* devotion of the seven churches ‖ *condurre qlcu. al* —, (*farlo morire*) to drive s.o. to the grave ‖ *scendere nel* —, to go to one's last resting place.

sepólto, *ag.* **1.** buried: — *vivo,* buried alive; *città sepolte,* buried cities ‖ *morto e* —, dead and buried **2.** *fig.* buried; (*sprofondato*) sunk; (*perso*) lost: — *nel dolore, nel sonno,* sunk in grief, in sleep; — *nell'oblio,* lost (*o* buried) in oblivion.

sepoltúra, *s.f.* **1.** (*il seppellire*) burial: *intervenire alla* — *di qlcu.,* to attend s.o.'s burial; *privare della* — *ecclesiastica,* to deny Christian burial **2.** (*sepolcro*) sepulchre, tomb, grave.

seppelliménto, *s.m.* burial.

seppellíre, *v.t.* **1.** to bury: *il cane aveva seppellito l'osso nel giardino*, the dog had buried the bone in the garden; *la capanna fu completamente sepolta sotto la neve*, the hut was completely buried by the snow; *lo seppellirono vivo*, they buried him alive; — *un morto*, to bury a dead man; — *un tesoro*, to bury a treasure ‖ *ci seppellirà tutti*, he will outlive us all ‖ — *l'ascia di guerra*, to bury the hatchet **2.** *fig.* to bury; (*nascondere*) to hide: *seppellì un documento in un vecchio armadio*, he hid a document in an old cupboard; — *la pratica*, to file the case (*o* the papers) away; — *un ricordo*, to bury a memory ‖ **seppellírsi**, *v.r.* to bury oneself: — *fra i libri*, to bury oneself in one's books; — *in campagna*, to bury oneself in the country.

seppellitóre, *s.m.* grave-digger.

séppia, *s.f.* (*zool.*) cuttle-fish: *osso di* —, cuttle-fish bone ‖ *nero di* —, (*pitt.*) sepia.

seppúre, *cong.* (*quand'anche*) **even if**; (*sebbene*) **even though**: — *fossi arrivato prima, non saresti riuscito a vederlo*, even if you had come earlier, you would not have been able to see him; — *sono stanca, non voglio rinunciare a quella festa*, even though I am tired, I don't want to miss the party.

sèpsi, *s.f.* (*med.*) sepsis.

sepsína, *s.f.* (*chim. biol.*) sepsine.

sequèla, *s.f.* **series** (*invariato al pl.*), **sequence, succession, train**: *una* — *di idee*, a sequence (*o* a train) of ideas; *una* — *di tristi avvenimenti*, a series (*o* a succession) of sad events.

sequènza, *s.f.* **1.** series (*invariato al pl.*), sequence, succession, train: *una* — *di disastri*, a succession of disasters **2.** (*cine. carte*) sequence: *una* — *di cuori*, (*a carte*) a sequence of hearts **3.** (*eccl.*) sequence.

sequestràbile, *ag.* sequestrable.

sequestràre, *v.t.* (*dir.*) **1.** to sequestrate, to sequester, to attach; (*generalmente per debiti*) to distrain upon (sthg.); to distress: *i suoi beni furono sequestrati dal magistrato*, his property was sequestrated by the magistrate; — *i mobili di qlcu.*, to distrain upon s.o.'s furniture **2.** (*portar via*) to confiscate, to take away: *il maestro sequestrò il libro allo scolaro*, the teacher confiscated (*o* took away) the book from the pupil **3.** (*confiscare*) to sequestrate, to seize: to confiscate: — *un'arma*, to confiscate a weapon; — *un giornale*, to confiscate (*o* to sequestrate) a newspaper **4.** — *una persona*, to restrain a person unlawfully.

sequèstro, *s.m.* (*dir.*) **1.** sequestration, attachment; (*generalmente per debiti*) distress, distraint: — *dei beni del debitore all'inizio della procedura fallimentare*, distraint (*o* distress) levied after the commencement of bankruptcy; *esente da* —, exempt from attachment (*o* sequestration); *ordine di* —, writ of distress (*o* attachment); *sotto* —, under distress (*o* attachment): *nave sotto* —, distrained ship; *fare un* —, to levy a distraint; *mettere ql.co. sotto* —, to distrain upon sthg. (*o* to place sthg. under distraint); *ordinare il* — *di ql.co.*, to order the attachment (*o* sequestration) of sthg. **2.** (*confisca*) sequestration, seizure, confiscation: — *di un film, di un libro*, sequestration of a film, of a book **3.** — *di persona*, unlawful restraint.

sequòia, *s.f.* (*bot.*) sequoia.

séra, *s.f.* evening; night: *abito da* —, evening dress; *l'altro ieri* —, the evening before last; *buona* —, good-evening: *dare la buona* —, to say good-evening; *da mane a* —, from morning to night; *di* —, in the evening; *domani* —, tomorrow evening (*o* tomorrow night); *ieri* —, yesterday evening (*o* last night); *questa* —, this evening (*o* tonight); *tre sere fa*, three evenings ago; *verso* —, at dusk; *arrivai lunedì* —, I arrived on Monday evening; *cala la* —, *si fa* —, it is growing dark; *ho una* — *libera ogni due settimane*, I have a night off every other week; *passai una bella* — *da loro*, I spent a nice evening at their house; *sul calare, sul fare della* —, at nightfall ‖ *l'ultima* —, (*la morte*) one's last end.

seràcco, *s.m.* serac.

seràfico, *ag.* seraphic ‖ *l'ordine* —, the Franciscan order.

serafíno, *s.m.* (*relig.*) seraph (*pl.* seraphim, seraphs).

seràle, *ag.* evening (*attributivo*); night (*attributivo*): *scuola* —, evening- (*o* night-) school.

seralménte, *av.* every evening.

serapèo, *s.m.* (*archeol.*) Serapeum.

Seràpide, *no.pr.m.* (*mit. egizia*) Serapis.

seraschière, *s.m.* (*st. turca*) seraskier.

seràta, *s.f.* **1.** evening: *non so come passare la* —, I don't know how to spend the evening; *avere una* — *di svago*, to have a night off **2.** (*ricevimento serale*) party; reception: *lo incontrai a una* — *in casa di sua sorella*, I met him at a party at his sister's **3.** (*rappresentazione teatrale*) evening performance: — *d'addio*, farewell performance; — *di beneficenza*, charity performance; — *di gala*, gala evening.

seratànte, *s.m.* artist for whom (a) benefit (performance) is held.

serbàre, *v.t.* **1.** (*mettere in serbo*) to put aside, to lay aside, to lay by: *serbava le mele per l'inverno*, she used to put aside apples for the winter; — *il denaro per la vecchiaia*, to lay aside money for one's old age **2.** (*conservare, mantenere*) to keep: *serbami il posto, torno subito*, keep my seat, please, I'll be back in a moment; *serbo un magnifico ricordo di lui*, I cherish a wonderful memory of him; — *fede*, to keep faith; — *un segreto*, to keep a secret **3.** (*nutrire in sè*) to nourish: — *odio, rancore a qlcu.*, to nourish hatred, rancour for s.o. ‖ **serbàrsi**, *v.r.* to keep, to remain: — *fedele*, to remain faithful; — *in buona salute*, to keep in good health.

serbatóio, *s.m.* **1.** reservoir, tank; (*di penna stilografica*) barrel: — *a caduta, a gravità*, (*mec.*) gravity tank; — *a scarico rapido*, (*aer.*) jettisonable tank; — *d'acqua*, water reservoir; — *d'aria*, (*ind.*) air receiver; — *del carburante*, (*aut. aer.*) fuel tank; — *del cilindro del freno*, (*ferr.*) brake cylinder tank; — *della benzina*, (*aut.*) petrol tank (*o amer.* gasoline tank); — *dell'olio*, (*aer. mec.*) oil tank; (*elett.*) oil conservator; — *di acqua dolce*, (*mar.*) fresh-water tank; — *di alimentazione*, feed tank; — *di compensazione*, (*idraulica*) surge tank; — *di livello*, (*idraulica*) gauge tank; — *di sviluppo*, (*cine.*) developing tank; — *in acciaio inossidabile per reazioni chimiche*, stainless steel reaction vessel; — *piezometrico*, (*idraulica*) standpipe; — *sganciabile*, (*aer.*) drop tank **2.** (*di arma da fuoco*) magazine.

Sèrbia, *no.pr.f.* (*geog.*) Serbia.

sèrbo[1], *ag.* Serbian ‖ *s.m.* Serb, Serbian.

sèrbo[2], *s.m.* keeping, custody, reserve: *mettere in* —, to put aside; *tenere in* —, to keep aside (*o* in reserve).

sèrbo-[3], (*prefisso*) Serbo-: — *croato*, Serbo-Croat (*o* Serbo-Croatian).

seréna, *s.f.* (*meteorologia*) serein.

serenaménte, *av.* serenely.

serenàre, (*poet.*) per **rasserenàre**.

serenàta, *s.f.* serenade: *fare, cantare una* — *a qlcu.*, to play, to sing s.o. a serenade (*o* to serenade s.o.).

serenèlla, *s.f.* (*bot. pop.*) lilac.

sereníssimo, *ag.* (*titolo dato ai dogi, a principi*) Serene Highness: *Sua, Vostra Altezza Serenissima*, His, Your Serene Highness.

serenità, *s.f.* **1.** serenity: *la* — *del cielo*, the serenity (*o* clearness) of the sky; *la* — *del mare*, the serenity (*o* calmness) of the sea **2.** (*tranquillità, calma*) serenity, calmness: *la* — *del suo sguardo*, the serenity of his expression: *affrontare la vita con* —, to face life with serenity **3.** (*titolo dato a principi*) Serenity: *Vostra Serenità*, Your Serenity.

seréno, *ag.* **1.** serene, clear: *cielo* —, clear (*o* serene) sky; *giornata serena*, clear day; *notte serena*, clear night ‖ *un fulmine a ciel* —, a bolt from the blue **2.** (*lieto*) serene; (*tranquillo*) tranquil, quiet: *animo* —, serene soul; *sguardo, sorriso* —, serene look, smile; *vita serena,* quiet (o tranquil) life ‖ *giudizio* —, objective (o unbiased) judgement ‖ *s.m.* clear sky: *torna il* —, it is clearing up again ‖ *al* —, in the open air (o outdoors).

sergènte, *s.m.* 1. sergeant: — *maggiore,* sergeant -major 2. (*strum. artig.*) carpenter's clamp.

Sèrgio, *no.pr.m.* Sergius.

seriaménte, *av.* seriously, earnestly; (*gravemente*) gravely: — *ammalato,* seriously ill; *parlo* —, I am speaking seriously (o I am in earnest).

seríceo, *ag.* (*poet.*) silken; silky, sericeous.

sericína, *s.f.* (*ind. tessile*) sericin, silk gelatin, silk glue.

sèrico, *ag.* silk (*attributivo*); silky: *industria serica,* silk industry.

seríeolo, *ag.* sericultural.

sericoltóre, *s.m.* sericulturist, silkgrower; silkworm breeder.

sericoltúra, *s.f.* sericulture.

sèrie, *s.f.* 1. series (*invariato al pl.*); (*successione*) succession; sequence: *la* — *degli imperatori romani,* the succession of Roman emperors; *una* — *di insuccessi,* a series (o succession) of failures; *una* — *di sventure,* a series of misfortunes (o a chapter of accidents); *le calamità vengono in* —, misfortunes never come singly (o it never rains but it pours); *quell'editore ha iniziato una nuova* — *di pubblicazioni scientifiche,* that publisher has begun a new series of scientific publications; *commettere una* — *di gaffes,* to commit a series of blunders ‖ *fuori* —, special: *modello fuori* —, special model (o amer. custom-built model) ‖ *in* —, mass-produced: *automobili, abiti in* —, mass-produced cars, clothes; *fabbricazione, produzione in* —, mass-production ‖ *modello di* —, production model 2. (*complesso, assieme*) set: *una* — *di chiavi,* a set of keys; *una* — *di francobolli, monete,* a set of stamps, coins 3. (*fila*) row, range: *una* — *di case,* a row of houses 4. (*chim. mat. elett.*) series: — *armonica,* (*mat.*) harmonic series; — *del metano,* (*chim.*) methane series; *accoppiamento in* —, connection in series.

serietà, *s.f.* seriousness; (*gravità*) gravity: *la* — *della situazione,* the gravity of the situation; *la* — *di una ditta,* the reliability of a firm; *agire con molta* —, to act in all seriousness.

sèrio, *ag.* serious, earnest; (*grave*) grave; (*pensieroso*) thoughtful: *un* — *lavoratore,* a serious (o an earnest) worker; *seria malattia, situazione,* serious illness, situation; *ditta seria,* reliable firm; *guai seri,* serious troubles; *una persona seria,* a serious person; *è un affare* —, it is a serious matter; *perchè sei così* —?, why are you so serious? (o thoughtful?) ‖ *s.m.* seriousness: *parlare tra il* — *e il faceto,* to talk half-seriously (o half-jokingly) ‖ *sul* —, seriously (o in earnest); (*davvero*) really: *è bello sul* —, it is really beautiful; *prendere ql.co. sul* —, to take sthg. seriously.

serménto, *e derivati,* V. **sarménto**, *e derivati.*

sermonàre, *v.i.* to sermonize, to preach.

sermóne, *s.m.* 1. sermon: *fare un* —, to deliver a sermon 2. (*rimprovero*) lecture, talking-to: *fare un* — *a qlcu.,* to give s.o. a lecture (o a good talking-to o a telling-off).

sermoneggiàre, *v.i.* to sermonize, to preach.

seròtino, *ag.* 1. evening (*attributivo*): *la brezza serotina,* the evening breeze 2. (*tardivo*) tardy, late 3. (*che matura tardi*) backward, late: *frutti serotini,* backward fruit.

sèrpa, *s.f.* (*sedile del vetturino sulle diligenze*) coach -box: *montare in* —, to get on the box.

serpàio, *s.m.* nest of snakes.

serpàro, *s.m.* snake-charmer.

sèrpe[1], *s.f.* (*zool.*) snake, serpent ‖ *a* —, (*serpeggiando*) winding ‖ *fatto a* —, (*a spirale*) coiled ‖ *allevare, scaldarsi una* — *in seno,* to nurse (o to nourish) a viper in one's bosom.

sèrpe[2], *s.f.* (*sedile del vetturino sulle diligenze*) coach -box.

serpeggiaménto, *s.m.* 1. winding; meandering 2. (*ferr.*) hunting.

serpeggiànte, *ag.* winding; meandering.

serpeggiàre, *v.i.* 1. to wind; to meander: *il fiume serpeggia nella valle,* the river meanders through the valley; *il sentiero sale serpeggiando sulla collina,* the path winds up the hill 2. (*strisciare*) to creep 3. (*insinuarsi*) to spread: *il malcontento serpeggiava tra i soldati,* discontent was spreading among the soldiers.

serpentària, *s.f.* (*bot.*) serpentaria, serpentary.

serpentàrio, *s.m.* (*ornit.*) secretary-bird ‖ *il Serpentario,* (*astr.*) the Serpentarius.

serpènte, *s.m.* 1. (*zool.*) snake (anche *fig.*); serpent (anche *fig.*): — *a sonagli,* rattlesnake; — *dagli occhiali,* cobra; *un* — *tra l'erba,* (*un'insidia nascosta*) a snake in the grass ‖ *il Serpente,* (*astr.*) the Serpent 2. — *di Faraone,* (*chim.*) Pharaoh's serpent.

serpentèllo, *s.m.* 1. small snake 2. (*bambino cattivo*) imp, little devil.

serpentína, *s.f.* 1. (*tubo a spirale*) coil 2. (*mec.*) worm-wheel 3. (*chim.*) (*storta*) retort 4. (*strada a giravolte*) winding road 5. (*min.*) serpentine 6. (*artigl.*) serpentine 7. (*aer.*) snaking.

serpentíno, *ag.* serpentine, snakelike, snaky; fig. (*velenoso*) venomous: *danza serpentina,* serpentine dance; *lingua serpentina,* venomous tongue ‖ *s.m.* 1. (*min.*) serpentine: — *nobile,* noble (o precious) serpentine 2. (*tubo a spirale*) coil.

serpígine, *s.f.* (*patol.*) serpigo (*pl.* serpigines, serpigoes).

serpiginóso, *ag.* serpiginous.

serpígno, *ag.* (*letter.*) snake (*attributivo*).

sérqua, *s.f.* 1. (*dozzina*) dozen 2. (*gran quantità*) a large number, a lot, lots (*pl.*).

sèrra, *s.f.* 1. greenhouse, glasshouse; (*se unita a un edificio*) conservatory; (*se riscaldata*) hothouse: — *per palme,* palm house; — *per viti,* vinery; *fiore di* —, hothouse flower (anche *fig.*) ‖ *sei stato allevato in una* —, you are a hothouse plant 2. (*sbarramento fluviale*) dike 3. (*gola montana*) gorge ‖ *s.m.: un* — — —, a large crowd (o a crush).

serrabòzze, *s.m.* (*mar.*) shank painter.

serrafíla, serrafile, *s.m.* 1. (*mil.*) rear-rank man, serrefile, serafile 2. (*mar.*) rear-ship.

serrafílo, *s.m.* (*elett.*) clamping-screw, terminal-screw.

serràglio[1], *s.m.* 1. (*per bestie feroci*) menagerie 2. (*barricata*) barricade, barrier 3. (*luogo chiuso, rinserrato*) enclosure 4. (*arch.*) (*chiave di volta*) keystone.

serràglio[2], *s.m.* (*nel palazzo del sultano*) seraglio (*pl.* seragli, seraglios).

serramànico, a, *l. av.: coltello a* —, jack-knife.

serràme, *s.m.* lock; bolt; fastening.

serraménto, *s.m.* 1. (*il serrare*) locking; bolting 2. (*serrame*) lock; bolt; fastening 3. *pl.* fastenings; (*usci*) doors; (*finestre*) windows; (*persiane*) shutters.

serrànda, *s.f.* 1. (*saracinesca di negozio*) shutter; (*a maglia*) grill 2. — *di una chiusa,* (*idraulica*) lock-gate.

serràre, *v.t.* 1. (*chiudere*) to shut, to close; (*a chiave*) to lock: — *la porta,* to lock the door ‖ — *bottega,* to close down (o to shut up shop) ‖ — *un dolore nel cuore,* to lock a grief in one's heart ‖ — *la stalla quando sono fuggiti i buoi, prov.* to lock the stable door after the horse has bolted 2. (*stringere*) to tighten; (*con le mani, tra le braccia*) to clasp; (*pugni, denti*) to clench; (*labbra*) to set: *serrò il bicchiere nella mano,* he clasped the glass in his hand; — *il laccio intorno al collo di qlcu.,* to tighten the noose around s.o.'s neck (anche *fig.*); — *le braccia al petto,* to clasp one's breast; — *la mano a qlcu.,* to clasp s.o.'s hand; — *gli occhi,* to screw up one's eyes; (*morire*) to close one's eyes ‖ *il pianto le serrava la gola,* she was choked by sobs ‖ — *le file,* (*mil.*) to close the ranks 3. (*circondare*) to surround: *li serrava un cerchio di fuoco,* they were surrounded by a ring of fire 4. (*concludere*) to conclude: — *un patto,* to conclude a pact 5. (*incalzare*) to press hard upon (s.o.): — *il nemico*, to press hard upon the enemy **6.** (*sbarrare*) to block: — *il letto del fiume*, to block (*o* to stop up) a river; — *una strada*, to block a road **7.** (*mar.*): — *le vele*, to take in (*o* to shorten) the sails; — *il vento*, to haul the wind ‖ *v.i.* **1.** (*chiudere*) to close: *questa finestra non serra bene*, this window does not close well **2.** (*stringere*) to be tight: *queste maniche serrano troppo al gomito*, these sleeves are too tight at the elbows ‖ **serràrsi**, *v.r.* **1.** (*chiudersi*) to lock oneself: *si serrò in camera*, he locked himself in his room **2.** (*stringersi*) to tighten; (*di denti, pugni*) to clench: *la mano mi si serrò intorno al bicchiere*, his hand tightened about the glass; *le sue labbra si serrarono*, his lips tightened ‖ *a pensarci mi si serra il cuore*, the thought wrings my heart **3.** (*avvicinarsi, accostarsi*) to press, to hug (sthg.); (*accalcarsi*) to press, to crowd; (*appiattirsi contro*) to flatten oneself against (sthg.): — *alla costa*, (*mar.*) to hug the coast; — *addosso a qlcu.*, (*per assalirlo*) to close in on s.o.; — *intorno a qlcu.*, to press (*o* to crowd) around s.o.; — *al muro*, to hug the wall; (*appiattirsi contro*) to flatten oneself against the wall ‖ *v.r. reciproco* to close up; (*per paura, freddo, ecc.*) to huddle together: *la folla si serrò per fargli posto*, the crowd closed up to make room for him.

serraschière, *s.m.* (*st. turca*) seraskier.

serràta, *s.f.* **1.** (*sbarramento contro l'acqua*) dike, dam **2.** (*steccato intorno a edificio in costruzione*) hoarding **3.** (*sospensione di lavoro*) lock-out.

serrataménte, *av.* closely; (*in modo conciso*) concisely.

serràto, *ag.* **1.** (*chiuso*) closed, shut: *finestre, porte serrate*, closed windows, doors **2.** (*stretto*) close: *maglie serrate*, close stitches; *lo tenne* — *come in una morsa*, he held him in a vice-like grip; *avere la pronunzia serrata*, to have a close pronunciation ‖ *in file serrate*, in serried ranks **3.** (*conciso*) close; (*compatto*) compact: *ragionamento* —, close argument (*o* reasoning); *stile* —, compact (*o* concise) style **4.** (*rapido*) quick: *trotto* —, quick trot.

serratúra, *s.f.* lock: — *a cilindri*, Yale (cylinder) lock; — *a nottolini*, lever tumbler lock; — *con risalti corrispondenti agli intagli della chiave*, warded lock; — *con scatto a molla*, latch; — *di sicurezza*, safety lock; *buco della* —, keyhole; *forzare una* —, to force a lock.

Sèrse, *no.pr.m.* (*st.*) Xerxes.

sèrto, *s.m.* (*poet.*) garland, wreath.

Sertòrio, *no.pr.m.* (*st.*) Sertorius.

sèrva, *s.f.* maid-servant (*pl.* maid-servants); woman-servant (*pl.* women-servants).

servàggio, *s.m.* bondage; serfdom; thraldom: *libertà dal* — *dello straniero*, freedom from foreign bondage.

servènte, *ag.* serving ‖ *cavalier* —, cavalier (*o* lady's escort) ‖ *s.m.* **1.** servant **2.** (*mil.*) gunner **3.** (*in ospedale*) male nurse ‖ *s.f.* maid-servant (*pl.* maid-servants).

serventése, *s.m.* (*poes.*) sirvente.

servétta, *s.f.* **1.** young maid **2.** (*teat.*) soubrette.

servíbile, *ag.* usable.

servidoràme, *s.m.* (*spreg.*) servants (*pl.*).

servígio, *s.m.* service, favour: *mi hai reso un gran* —, you have done me a great service (*o* favour); *render servigi alla patria*, to render services to one's country.

servíle, *ag.* **1.** servile, slavish: *catena* —, slave's chain ‖ *opere servili*, (*eccl.*) servile works ‖ — (*st. romana*) servile war **2.** (*basso, vile, pedissequo*) servile, slavish, obsequious: *adulazione, obbedienza* —, servile (*o* obsequious) flattery, obedience; *imitazione* —, slavish imitation; *timore* —, servile fear **3.** (*gram.*) servile: *verbo* —, servile verb.

servilísmo, *s.m.*, **servilità**, *s.f.* servility; (*grettezza*) meanness: — *d'animo, di ingegno*, servility of spirit, meanness of spirit.

servilménte, *av.* servilely; (*grettamente*) meanly.

servíre, *v.t.* **1.** to serve: — *una causa, la patria*, to serve a cause, one's country; — *Dio, il demonio*, to serve God, the devil; — *il Signore*, to serve the Lord ‖ — *messa*, to serve at mass **2.** (*prestare un servizio a*) to serve; to attend to (s.o.): *in che posso servirla?*, can I help you? (*o* what can I do for you?); *la stanno servendo?*, are you being seen to?; *la mia sarta mi serve molto bene*, I am very satisfied with my dressmaker; *quel negozio serve molta gente*, that shop has many customers; — *un cliente*, to serve a customer ‖ « *È lei il signor X?* », « *Per servirla* », "Are you Mr. X?", "At your service" ‖ *ora ti servirò a dovere*, I'll sort you out ‖ — *di barba e capelli*, *fig.* to wait hand and foot on s.o. **3.** (*di persone di servizio*) to wait (up)on (s.o.): *a quel pranzo eravamo serviti da tre camerieri*, at that dinner we were waited on by three servants; *aveva due cameriere che la servivano*, she had two maids to wait upon her; *lo servo da dieci anni*, I have been in his service for ten years ‖ — *due padroni*, to serve two masters **4.** (*offrire, presentare, cibi, ecc.*) to serve; to help (s.o. to sthg.): *devo* —, *signora?*, shall I serve dinner, Madam?; *il pranzo è servito*, dinner is served; *servono sempre patate bollite con la carne*, they always serve boiled potatoes with meat; *ti servo un po' di gelato?*, shall I help you to some ice-cream?; — *da bere a qlcu.*, to give s.o. sthg. to drink; — *ql.co. di caldo*, to serve up sthg. hot **5.** (*fare il proprio ufficio*) to serve: *gli occhi non lo servivano più*, his eyes did not serve him any more; *la sua memoria l'ha mal servito*, his memory served him badly (*o* played him false) **6.** (*le carte*) to deal ‖ *essere servito*, (*al poker*) to stand pat **7.** — *un pezzo*, (*mil.*) to serve a gun ‖ *v.i.* **1.** (*prestar servizio*) to serve: *aveva servito sotto Napoleone*, he had served under Napoleon; *ella era stanca di* — *in quella famiglia*, she was tired of being a maid in that family; *in quale arma hai servito?*, what were you in?; — *come autista*, to work as a driver; — *nell'esercito, nella marina*, to serve in the army, in the navy **2.** (*a tavola*) to wait, to serve: *non sa* — *a tavola*, she doesn't know how to wait (*o* to serve) at table **3.** (*giovare, essere utile*) to serve, to be of use: *a che serve lavorare tanto?*, what's the use (*o* the good) of working so hard?; *a che serve questo utensile?*, what do you use this tool for?; *ciò non serve che a irritarlo*, it only irritates him; *il cloro serve a sbiancare*, chlorine is used for bleaching; *la lettura serve di distrazione*, reading serves to pass the time; *non serve a niente*, it is no use (*o* it is useless); *non serve ripeterglielo*, it's no use telling him again; *quel libro gli è servito molto*, that book has been of great use to him; *questo libro servirà a fartelo capire*, this book will help you to understand it; — *allo scopo*, to serve the purpose **4.** (*far l'ufficio, le veci di*) to serve: *mi servì di guida*, he acted as my guide; *questo asse ci servirà da tavolo*, this board will serve us for a table; — *di norma, di scusa, di pretesto*, to serve as a rule, as an excuse, as a pretext **5.** (*al tennis, ecc.*) to serve: *chi serve, a chi tocca* —?, whose serve (*o* service) is it? **6.** (*occorrere*): *le serve nulla?*, can I help you? ‖ **servírsi**, *v.r.* **1.** (*usare*) to use (sthg.), to make use (of sthg.): *egli si servì del mio nome*, he used my name; *ha una magnifica macchina fotografica, ma non se ne sa servire*, he has got a wonderful camera, but he doesn't know how to use it; *mi servii della tua macchina da scrivere*, I used your typewriter; *non so se me ne servirò*, I don't know whether I shall use (*o* make use of) it **2.** (*a tavola*) to help oneself (to sthg.): *serviti*, help yourself; *serviti di piselli*, help yourself to the peas **3.** (*fornirsi*): *dove ti servi per la carne?*, where do you buy (*o* get) your meat?; *mi servo da una bravissima sarta*, I have a very good dressmaker; *non mi sono mai servita da lui*, I have never bought anything from him.

servíta, *s.m.* (*eccl.*) Servite.

servíto, *ag.* served (*predicativo*) ‖ *s.m.* **1.** (*servizio*) service **2.** (*portata*) course: *un pranzo con tre serviti*, a three-course meal.

servitoràme, *s.m.* (*spreg.*) servants (*pl.*).

servitóre, *s.m.* **1.** servant: — *in livrea*, liveried servant || — *di Dio*, servant of God || *vostro — umilissimo*, your obedient (o humble) servant **2.** (*carrello per vivande*) serving trolley.

servitorésco, *ag.* servile.

servitú, *s.f.* **1.** servitude, slavery, bondage: *liberarsi dalla —*, to free oneself from slavery (o bondage) || — *della gleba*, (*st.*) serfdom **2.** (*legame*) slavery: *la — dell'orario*, the slavery of a time-table **3.** (*personale di servizio*) servants (*pl.*): *bisogna trattar bene la —*, one must treat one's servants well **4.** (*dir.*) servitude: — *personale, prediale*, personal, praedial servitude.

serviziàle, *s.m.* (*med.*) enema (*pl.* enemas, enemata).

serviziévole, *ag.* obliging.

servizievolménte, *av.* obligingly.

servízio, *s.m.* **1.** (*di domestici*) service: *donna a mezzo —*, charwoman (o part-time maid); *donna di —*, maid; *andare a —*, to go into service; *aver vent'anni di —*, to have served twenty years; *essere a —*, to be in service; *prendere — presso qlcu.*, to take service with s.o.; *prendere al proprio —*, to take into one's service || *porta, scala di —*, back (o service) door, stairs || *il — in questo albergo è piuttosto scadente*, the service in this hotel is rather poor; *il — non è incluso nel prezzo*, the service is not included in the price **2.** (*mil.*) service; duty: — *di guardia*, guard duty; — *militare*, national (o military) service; — *obbligatorio*, compulsory military service; *ufficiale di —*, orderly officer; *essere in — attivo*, to be on active service **3.** (*lavoro*) work: *in, fuori —*, on, off duty; *turno di —*, shift; *ha dieci anni di — presso quella ditta*, he has been with that firm for ten years; *lasciare il —*, (*per sempre*) to resign (from) one's post; (*provvisoriamente*) to stop work: *lasciò il — per una settimana*, he stopped work for a week; *riprendere il —*, to take up one's work again **4.** (*prestazione, funzione*): *i servizi di un avvocato*, the services of a lawyer; *un autobus pronto al —*, a bus in running order; *l'ascensore è fuori —*, the lift is out of use; *l'autobus non fa — la domenica*, the bus does not run on Sundays; *quest'ufficio non fa — il pomeriggio*, this office is not open in the afternoon; *metter un autobus in —*, to put a bus into service || *stazione di —*, service station || *fare un viaggio e due servizi*, to kill two birds with one stone **5.** (*favore*) favour; (*azione*) turn: *egli mi ha fatto un grandissimo —*, he has done me a very big favour; *mi hai reso un cattivo —*, you have done me a bad turn **6.** (*reparto*) department: — *acquisti, impianti, trasporti*, purchase (o purchasing), planning, transport department **7.** (*istituzione di pubblica utilità*) service: — *aereo, ferroviario*, air, railway service; — *assistenza stradale*, road service; — *consolare, diplomatico, sanitario*, consular, diplomatic, health service; — *di autobus*, bus service; — *informazioni*, information service; (*mil.*) intelligence secret service; — *postale, telefonico*, postal, telephone service; *servizi pubblici*, public services **8.** (*resoconto giornalistico*) service **9.** (*tennis, ecc.*) serve, service **10.** (*eccl.*) service: — *divino*, divine service; — *funebre*, burial (o funeral) service **11.** (*insieme di oggetti adibiti a un determinato uso*) service, set: — *da caffè*, coffee-service; — *da tavola, di piatti*, dinner -service (o -set); — *da tè*, tea-service (o -set); — *di posate*, set of cutlery; — *per toilette*, toilette-set.

sèrvo, *ag.* (*letter.*) servile || *s.m.* **1.** (*servitore*) servant: *fui introdotto dal —*, I was shown in by the servant || — *della gleba*, (*st.*) serf || — *di Dio*, servant of God || — *muto*, (*carrello portavivande*) dumb-waiter **2.** (*schiavo*) slave: — *del denaro*, slave to money; — *di una passione*, slave of (o to) a passion; — *di pregiudizi*, slave of prejudice.

servocomàndo, *s.m.* (*aer.*) servo control.

servofréno, *s.m.* (*mec. aut.*) brake booster.

servomotóre, *s.m.* (*mec. aer.*) servomotor.

servostèrzo, *s.m.* (*aut.*) power steering.

sèsamo, *s.m.* (*bot.*) sesame: *olio di —*, oil of sesame (o sesame oil) || — *apriti!*, open sesame!.

sesamòide, *ag.* (*anat.*) sesamoid.

sesquiòssido, *s.m.* (*chim.*) sesquioxide.

sesquipedàle, *ag.* sesquipedalian.

sessagenàrio, *ag.s.m.* sexagenarian.

sessagèsima, *s.f.* (*eccl.*) Sexagesima.

sessagèsimo, *ag.num.ord. s.m.* sixtieth.

sessànta, *ag.num.card. s.m.* sixty.

sessantènne, *ag.* sixty years old (*predicativo*); sixty -year-old (*attributivo*) || *s.c.* sixty-year-old person.

sessantèsimo, *ag.num.ord. s.m.* sixtieth.

sessantína, *s.f.* about sixty, some sixty: *una — di persone*, about sixty people; *un uomo sulla —*, a man in his sixties.

sessennàle, *ag.* sexennial.

sessènne, *ag.* six years old (*predicativo*); six-year-old (*attributivo*) || *s.c.* six-year-old child.

sessènnio, *s.m.* period of six years.

sèssile, *ag.* (*bot.*) sessile.

sessióne, *s.f.* session: — *di esami*, examination session (o session of examinations); — *estiva, autunnale*, summer, autumn session; — *invernale, primaverile della Corte d'Assise*, winter, spring Assizes.

sessitúra, *s.f.* tuck.

sèsso, *s.m.* **1.** sex: *bambino di — maschile, femminile*, male child, female child; *d'ambo i sessi*, of both sexes; *senza —*, sexless || *il — debole*, the weaker sex; *il — forte*, the stronger sex; *il bel, gentil —*, the fair, gentle sex **2.** (*organi genitali*) genitals (*pl.*).

sèssola, *s.f.* (*mar.*) skeet.

sessuàle, *ag.* sexual; sex (*attributivo*).

sessualità, *s.f.* sexuality.

sèsta, *s.f.* **1.** (*eccl.*) sext **2.** (*mus.*) sixth **3.** (*compasso*) compass, pair of compasses.

sestànte, *s.m.* sextant: — *a bolla d'aria*, (*aer.*) bubble sextant; — *aeronautico*, air sextant.

sestàrio, *s.m.* sextary.

sèste, *s.f.pl.* **1.** (*compasso*) compasses || *parlare con le —*, (*con affettazione*) to speak affectedly **2.** (*scherz.*) (*gambe lunghe*) long legs.

sestèrzio, *s.m.* (*moneta romana*) sesterce; sestertius (*pl.* sestertii).

sestétto, *s.m.* (*mus.*) sextet.

sestière, *s.m.* **1.** district; ward: *viveva in un vecchio — di Genova*, he lived in an old district of Genoa **2.** (*misura di capacità*) sextary.

sestíle, *ag.s.m.* (*astr.*) sextile.

sestína, *s.f.* **1.** (*canzone di sei stanze*) sestina **2.** (*stanza di sei versi*) six-line stanza **3.** (*formato di carta da lettera*) letter-paper of small size.

sèsto[1]**,** *ag.num.ord. s.m.* sixth.

sèsto[2]**,** *s.m.* **1.** (*ordine*) order: *mettere le cose in —*, to put things in order **2.** (*arch.*) curve (of an arch): — *acuto, ogive*: *arco a — acuto*, pointed (o ogival) arch; *a tutto —*, round **3.** (*tip.*) format.

sèsto[3]**,** *no.pr.m.* (*st.*) Sextus.

sestúltimo, *ag.* last but five.

sestuplicàre, *v.t.* to multiply by six, to sextuple.

sestúplice, sèstuplo, *ag.* sextuple, sixfold.

séta, *s.f.* silk: — *artificiale*, artificial silk; — *candeggiata*, bleached silk; — *floscia*, slack silk; — *grezza*, raw silk; — *pura*, pure silk; — *ritorta*, net silk; — *vegetale*, vegetable silk; *baco da —*, silkworm; *cascami di —*, silk waste; *matassa di —*, skein of silk; *indossava un vestito di —*, she was wearing a silk dress || *quella ragazza ha capelli di —*, that girl has silky hair || *camminare sopra un filo di —*, to tread warily.

setàccio, *s.m.* sieve.

setàceo, *ag.* silky.

setaiuòlo, *s.m.* **1.** (*chi lavora la seta*) silk worker, silk weaver **2.** (*chi conduce un setificio*) silk manufacturer **3.** (*chi commercia in seta*) silk dealer, silk merchant.

séte, *s.f.* thirst (anche *fig.*): — *ardente, tormentosa,* burning thirst; — *di vendetta, di sapere,* thirst for revenge, knowledge; — *di vino,* thirst for wine; *è un cibo che mette* —, it is a food that makes you thirsty; *muoio di* —, I am dying of thirst (o I am parched); *avere* —, to be thirsty: *avere* — *di sangue,* to be bloodthirsty; *placare la propria* —, to quench one's thirst.

setería, *s.f.* 1.(*setificio*) silk-factory 2. (*negozio di seta*) silk shop 3. *pl.* (*articoli di seta*) silk goods, silks.

setifício, *s.m.* silk-factory, silk-mill.

sétola, *s.f.* bristle; (*crine*) hair: *le setole del maiale,* pig's bristles; *pennello di* —, bristle-brush.

setolàre, *v.t.* to brush.

setolinàio, *s.m.* brush maker.

setolinàre, *v.t.* to brush.

setolíno, *s.m.* (bristle-)brush.

setolóso, setolúto, *ag.* bristly.

setóne, *s.m.* (*vet.*) seton.

sètta, *s.f.* sect: — *religiosa,* religious sect.

settàngolo, *ag.* (*geom.*) heptagonal ‖ *s.m.* (*geom.*) heptagon.

settànta, *ag.num.card. s.m.* seventy.

settantènne, *ag.* seventy years old (*predicativo*); seventy-year-old (*attributivo*) ‖ *s.c.* seventy-year-old person.

settantèsimo, *ag.num.ord. s.m.* seventieth.

settantína, *s.f.* about seventy, some seventy: *essere presso la* —, to be nearly seventy (years old).

settàrio, *ag.s.m.* sectarian.

settarísmo, *s.m.* sectarianism.

settatóre, *s.m.,* **settatríce,** *s.f.* (*letter.*) follower; partisan.

sètte, *ag.num.card. s.m.* seven: *i* — *peccati capitali,* the seven deadly sins; *le* — *virtù,* the seven virtues; *ho preso* — *in latino,* I have got seven out of ten in Latin ‖ — *bello,* (*a carte*) seven of diamonds ‖ *i Sette Dormienti,* the Seven Sleepers ‖ *la guerra dei* — *anni,* (*st.*) the Seven Years' War ‖ *farsi un* — *nei calzoni,* to rip one's trousers ‖ *levare qlcu. ai* — *cieli,* to praise s.o. to the skies.

settecentésco, *ag.* eighteenth century (*attributivo*): *letteratura settecentesca,* eighteenth century literature; *secondo la moda settecentesca...,* after the eighteenth century fashion....

settecentèsimo, *ag.num.ord. s.m.* seven hundredth.

settecentísta, *s.c.* (*art. lett.*) eighteenth century author; eighteenth century artist.

settecènto, *ag.num.card.* seven hundred ‖ *s.m.* (*diciottesimo secolo*) eighteenth century.

settèmbre, *s.m.* September.

settembríno, *ag.* September (*attributivo*): *aria settembrina,* September air.

settemíla, *ag.num.card. s.m.* seven thousand.

settèmplice, *ag.* sevenfold, septuple.

settenàrio, *ag.* septenary ‖ *s.m.* (*poes.*) septenarius (*pl.* septenarii).

settennàle, *ag.* septennial.

settennàto, *s.m.* septennate.

settènne, *ag.* seven years old (*predicativo*); seven-year-old (*attributivo*) ‖ *s.c.* seven-year-old child.

settènnio, *s.m.* septennium (*pl.* septennia).

settentrionàle, *ag.* 1. Northern; North (*attributivo*): *Africa, America* —, North Africa, America; *Asia, Irlanda* —, Northern Asia, Ireland; *l'emisfero* —, the northern hemisphere; *l'Italia* —, North(ern) Italy; *vento* —, north wind 2. (*volto a settentrione*) northerly: *lato* —, northerly side ‖ *s.c.* northerner.

settentrióne, *s.m.* north: *casa esposta a* —, house facing (the) north; *nel* — *d'Italia,* in the north of Italy; *vento del* —, north wind.

settenviràto, *s.m.* (*st.*) septemvirate.

settènviro, *s.m.* (*st.*) septemvir (*pl.* septemviri, septemvirs).

setticemía, *s.f.* (*patol.*) septicaemia.

setticèmico, *ag.* septicaemic.

settícida, *ag.* (*rar. bot.*) septicidal.

sèttico, *ag.* (*med.*) septic: *ferita settica,* septic wound.

settifórme, *ag.* septiform.

sèttima, *s.f.* 1. (*mus.*) seventh 2. (*med.*) (*settimana*) week; (*giorno di crisi*) seventh-day crisis.

settimàna, *s.f.* 1. week: *una* — *di vacanza,* a week's holiday; *la* — *ventura, scorsa,* next, last week; *di* — *in* —, from week to week; *ogni due settimane,* every other week (o every two weeks); *ogni tre settimane,* every third week (o every three weeks); *in* — *non è mai in casa,* he is never at home during the week ‖ *Settimana Santa,* (*eccl.*) Holy Week ‖ *fine* —, week-end: *passeremo la fine* — *in campagna,* we are going to spend the week-end in the country ‖ *essere di* —, to be on duty (for the week) 2. (*paga settimanale*) week's pay; week's wages (*pl.*).

settimanàle, *ag.* weekly: *pubblicazione* —, weekly publication; *ha una paga* — *di 12.000 lire,* he has a weekly pay of 12,000 lire ‖ *s.m.* 1. (*giornale settimanale*) weekly, weekly magazine: — *illustrato,* picture magazine 2. (*paga settimanale*) week's pay; week's wages (*pl.*).

settimanalménte, *av.* weekly.

settimèllo, *ag.* of seven months (*predicativo*) ‖ *s.m.* seven months' child.

settimèstre, *ag.* (*rar.*) of seven months (*predicativo*).

settimíno, *s.m.* 1. (*mus.*) septet 2. (*bambino nato di sette mesi*) seven months' child.

Settímio, *no.pr.m.* (*st.*) Septimius.

sèttimo, *ag.num.ord.s.m.* seventh ‖ *essere al* — *cielo,* to be in one's seventh heaven.

settína, *s.f.* a group of seven.

settizònio, *s.m.* (*st. astr.*) the seven heavens (*pl.*).

sètto, *s.m.* (*anat.*) septum (*pl.* septa): — *nasale,* nasal septum.

settóre, *s.m.* 1. (*geom.*) sector: — *sferico,* sector of a sphere 2. (*di aula semicircolare*) block of seats ‖ *approvazione da tutti i settori della Camera,* approbation from all parts of the Chamber 3. (*mil.*) sector, area: — *di tiro,* firing area 4. (*campo*) field: *si è fatto molto in questo* —, much has been done in this field 5. (*chi seziona i cadaveri*) dissector: *perito* —, forensic surgeon.

settuagenàrio, *ag.* septuagenary; seventy years old (*predicativo*); seventy-year-old (*attributivo*) ‖ *s.m.* septuagenarian, seventy-year-old man.

settuagèsima, *s.f.* (*eccl.*) Septuagesima.

settuagèsimo, *ag.num.ord. s.m.* seventieth.

settuplicàre, *v.t.* to multiply by seven, to septuple ‖ **settuplicàrsi,** *v.r.* to increase seven times, to septuple.

sèttuplo, *ag. s.m.* sevenfold, septuple.

severaménte, *av.* severely; (*austeramente*) sternly.

severità, *s.f.* severity, strictness; (*austerità*) sternness.

sevèro[1], *ag.* severe, strict; (*austero*) stern: *aspetto, sguardo* —, severe (o stern) look; *costumi severi,* strict habits; *disciplina severa,* strict discipline; *un giudice* —, a severe judge; *un insegnante* —, a strict teacher; *punizione, sentenza severa,* severe (o harsh) punishment, sentence; *stile* —, severe style.

Sevèro[2], *no.pr.m.* (*st.*) Severus.

seviziàre, *v.t.* to torture; to torment (anche *fig.*).

sevízie, *s.f.pl.* torture (*sing.*): *usare* — *contro qlcu.,* to torture s.o.

sèvo[1], *ag.* (*arc.*) cruel.

sévo[2], *s.m.* tallow.

sezionaménto, *s.m.* dissection.

sezionàre, *v.t.* to dissect.

sezionàto, *ag.* dissected.

sezióne, *s.f.* 1. section: — *aerea,* (*aer.*) aircraft section; — *alare,* (*aer.*) wing section; — *aurea,* (*mat.*) golden section; — *d'urto,* (*fis. atomica*) cross section; — *d'urto per diffusione,* (*fis. atomica*) scattering cross section; — *orizzontale, parziale, ribaltata,* (*disegno*) horizontal, part, revolved section; — *rilevamento vampa,* (*artigl.*) flash-spotting section; — *tampone,* (*ferr.*), stopped section; — *trasversale, verticale, (disegno)* cross, vertical section **2.** (*reparto*) department; (*di stabilimento*) department, division; (*di miniera*) panel: — *chirurgia,* surgical department; — *di commissariato,* Police station; — *di lingue straniere,* foreign languages department; — *motori,* engine division **3.** (*di scuola, indirizzo*) side: — *classica,* classical side; — *scientifica,* scientific side **4.** (*dissezione*) dissection: — *cadaverica,* post-mortem examination (*o sectio cadaveris*).

sfaccendàre, *v.i.* to bustle about, to be busy: *bisogna vedere come sfaccenda per casa,* you should see how hard she works in the house; *il mattino ho sempre da —,* in the morning I am always bustling about.

sfaccendàto, *ag.* idle ‖ *s.m.* loafer, idler.

sfaccettàre, *v.t.* to facet, to cut facets on (sthg.): — *un diamante,* to cut a diamond.

sfaccettatúra, *s.f.* **1.** (*lo sfaccettare*) faceting **2.** (*le faccette*) facets (*pl.*).

sfacchinàre, *v.i.* to drudge, to toil.

sfacchinàta, *s.f.* drudgery, heavy piece of work: *è stata una vera* — *il nostro trasloco,* our moving to the new house has really been hard work.

sfacciatàggine, *s.f.* impudence, cheek(iness); insolence: *con la massima* —, with the utmost impudence; *basta con la tua* — *!,* I've had enough of your cheek!; *ebbe la* — *di rispondermi,* he had the effrontery to answer me back.

sfacciataménte, *av.* impudently, cheekily; insolently; (*senza vergognarsi*) shamelessly.

sfacciatézza, *s.f.* **1.** impudence, cheek; insolence **2.** (*di colori*) gaudiness **3.** (*di luce*) glare.

sfacciàto, *ag.* **1.** impudent, cheeky, saucy; insolent; (*che non si vergogna*) shameless: *una menzogna sfacciata,* a brazen lie; *hai dato a tua madre una risposta molto sfacciata,* you have given your mother a very insolent answer; *non essere così* — *!,* don't be so cheeky!; *questa è adulazione sfacciata,* this is shameless flattery **2.** (*di colori*) gaudy: *non mi piace quel vestito, ha dei colori sfacciati,* I don't like that dress, its colours are too gaudy **3.** (*di luce*) dazzling, glaring: *c'era una luce così sfacciata che mi dava fastidio agli occhi,* there was such a glaring light that it hurt my eyes ‖ *s.m.* impudent person; shameless individual ‖ *sei uno sfacciatello,* you are a cheeky imp.

sfacèlo, *s.m.* **1.** break-up, ruin (anche *fig.*): *lo* — *dell'impero, the break-up of the empire; è una famiglia in* —, it is a family which is breaking up; *quella casa è in pieno* —, that house is falling to pieces; *andare in* —, to go to rack and ruin; *mandare in* —, to bring to rack and ruin **2.** (*di organi*) sphacelation.

sfaciménto, *s.m.* decay; ruin.

sfagliàre[1], *v.t.* (*carte*) to discard, to throw away.

sfagliàre[2], *v.i.,* **sfagliàrsi,** *v.r.* to flake (off), to scale.

sfàglio, *s.m.* (*di carte*) discard: *sta' attento allo* — *del tuo compagno,* pay attention to your partner's discard.

sfàgno, *s.m.* (*bot.*) sphagnum (*pl.* sphagna).

sfàlcio, *s.m.* (*agr.*) mowing.

sfàlda, *s.f.* flake, scale: *si disfà a sfalde,* it is flaking (off).

sfaldàbile, *ag.* flaky, scaly.

sfaldàre, *v.t.* to flake, to scale ‖ **sfaldàrsi,** *v.r.* to flake (off, away), to scale (off): *la vernice si sfalda dal muro,* the paint on the wall is flaking (off).

sfaldatúra, *s.f.* **1.** flaking (off), scaling (off) **2.** (*geol.*) cleavage: *piano di* —, cleavage plane.

sfalsaménto, *s.m.* (*aer.*) stagger.

sfalsàre, *v.t.* (*mec. edil.*) to stagger, to offset.

sfamàre, *v.t.* to appease s.o.'s hunger, to satisfy s.o.'s hunger: *questa roba basterebbe a* — *un esercito,* there's enough here to feed an army ‖ **sfamàrsi,** *v.r.* to appease one's hunger: *non hanno da* —, they haven't enough to eat.

sfamàto, *ag.* full up (*predicativo*); satiated.

sfangàre, *v.t.* to clean the mud off (sthg.); to sweep the mud off (sthg.); to brush the mud off (sthg.) ‖

v.i. **1.** to splash through mud **2.** (*uscire dal fango*) to come out of the mud **3.** *fig.* (*uscire da un imbroglio*) to get out of trouble, to get out of difficulty ‖ **sfangàrsi,** *v.r.:* sfangarsela, to get out of a scrape.

sfàre, *v.t.* **1.** to undo **2.** (*sciogliere*) to melt ‖ **sfàrsi,** *v.r.* **1.** to melt, to dissolve **2.** (*indebolirsi*) to weaken **3.** (*liberarsi*) to get rid (of s.o., sthg.).

sfarfallaménto, *s.m.* **1.** (*lo svolazzare*) flitting about (anche *fig.*) **2.** (*cine.*) flicker **3.** — *delle ruote anteriori, (aut.)* front-wheel wobble.

sfarfallàre, *v.i.* **1.** to emerge from the cocoon **2.** (*svolazzare*) to flutter about; *fig.* to flit to and fro **3.** (*dire spropositi*) to talk idle nonsense.

sfarfallatúra, *s.f.* emergence from the cocoon.

sfarfallóne, *s.m.* blunder.

sfarinàbile, *ag.* pulverizable.

sfarinaménto, *s.m.* pulverizing, pulverization.

sfarinàre, *v.t.* to pulverize ‖ **sfarinàrsi,** *v.r.* to crumble.

sfàrzo, *s.m.* pomp, magnificence; (*ostentazione*) ostentation, display: *abbigliato con* —, gorgeously dressed.

sfarzosaménte, *av.* sumptuously, gorgeously.

sfarzosità, *s.f.* sumptuousness, gorgeousness.

sfarzóso, *ag.* sumptuous, gorgeous, splendid, magnificent: *sfarzose decorazioni,* gorgeous decorations; *ricevimento* —, magnificent reception.

sfasaménto, *s.m.* **1.** (*mec. elett.*) phase-displacement, phase-difference: — *del comando,* (*aer.*) control-advance; *angolo di* —, (*elett.*) phase (displacement) angle **2.** *fig.* (*sconclusionatezza*) inconsequence; (*incoerenza*) inconsistency.

sfasàre, *v.t.* (*elett.*) to dephase, to displace the phase of (sthg.) ‖ *v.i.* **1.** (*mec. elett.*) to be out of phase **2.** (*elett.*) (*abbassare il fattore di potenza*) to lower the power factor.

sfasàto, *ag.* **1.** (*elett.*) out of phase; (*di motori a combustione interna*) with faulty timing **2.** *fig.* (*sconclusionato*) inconsequent; (*incoerente*) inconsistent: *una mente sfasata,* an inconsequent mind.

sfasciaménto[1], *s.m.* unbinding, unbandaging.

sfasciaménto[2], *s.m.* (*rovina*) breakdown, ruin; collapse.

sfasciàre[1], *v.t.* to unbandage: — *un bambino,* to remove the swaddling clothes from a baby; — *una ferita,* to remove the bandages from (*o* to unbandage) a wound.

sfasciàre[2], *v.t.* (*rompere*) to shatter, to smash; (*demolire*) to demolish, to dismantle: — *una nave,* to break up (*o* to dismantle) a ship; — *una sedia,* to smash a chair ‖ **sfasciàrsi,** *v.r.* to fall to pieces, to get smashed; (*crollare*) to collapse: *alla morte dell'imperatore l'impero si sfasciò,* when the emperor died the empire collapsed; *l'automobile si sfasciò contro un albero,* the car crashed into a tree.

sfasciàto[1], *ag.* unbandaged, unswathed; (*di bambino*) unswaddled.

sfasciàto[2], *ag.* **1.** (*rotto*) in pieces (*predicativo*); smashed **2.** (*di corpo troppo grasso*) flabby, bloated.

sfasciatúra, *s.f.* unswathing, unbandaging; (*di un bambino*) unswaddling: *per la* — *è meglio aspettare il dottore,* it's better to wait for the doctor to have the bandages removed.

sfàscio, *s.m.* breakdown, ruin; collapse.

sfasciúme, *s.m.* wreck; ruin: *quell'uomo non era che uno* —, that man was nothing but a wreck.

sfataménto, *s.m.* discrediting, disproving: — *di una leggenda, di una teoria,* discrediting of a legend, of a theory.

sfatàre, *v.t.* to discredit, to disprove: *fu così sfatata la sua fama di dotto,* that is how he lost his reputation for learning; — *una leggenda,* to discredit a legend; — *una teoria,* to discredit (*o* to disprove) a theory.

sfatàto, *ag.* discredited, disproved.

sfaticàto, *ag.* lazy, idle ‖ *s.m.* idler, loafer, lazybones, slacker: *è uno* —, he is an idler.

sfàtto, *ag.* **1.** undone, unmade: *il letto era* —, the bed was unmade **2.** (*troppo cotto*) overcooked **3.** (*eccessivamente grasso*) flabby.

sfavillaménto, *s.m.* shine; (*per luce riflessa*) sparkle.

sfavillàre, *v.i.* to shine; (*per luce riflessa*) to sparkle: *la neve sfavillava al sole,* the snow sparkled in the sunshine; *il sole sfavilla sulle montagne,* the sun is shining on the mountains; *i suoi occhi sfavillavano di gioia,* his eyes sparkled with joy.

sfavillío, *s.m.* shining; (*per luce riflessa*) sparkling.

sfavóre, *s.m.* disfavour, disapproval; (*discredito*) discredit: *lo — del popolo,* the disapproval (*o* disfavour) of the people; *quello che fece andò naturalmente a suo* —, what he did naturally brought discredit on him.

sfavorévole, *ag.* unfavourable; (*contrario*) contrary, adverse: *parere* —, unfavourable opinion; *le condizioni ci sono sfavorevoli,* conditions are against us.

sfavorevolménte, *av.* unfavourably.

sfavoríre, *v.t.* to treat unfairly; (*avversare*) to oppose.

sfebbràre, *v.t.* to bring s.o.'s temperature down ‖ *v.i.,* **sfebbràrsi,** *v.r.: si è sfebbrato,* his temperature has fallen.

sfebbràto, *ag.* without a temperature (*predicativo*).

sfegatàrsi, *v.r.* to wear oneself out (shouting), to shout oneself hoarse: *mi sono sfegatato per tentare di farglielo capire,* I wore myself out trying to make him understand what I was saying.

sfegatataménte, *av.* fanatically; (*appassionatamente*) passionately.

sfegatàto, *ag.* fanatic(al); (*appassionato*) passionate: *amici sfegatati,* close friends; *è uno — lettore di libri gialli,* he is a passionate reader of thrillers; *è uno — wagneriano,* he is a fanatical Wagnerite.

sfenòide, *s.m.* (*anat.*) sphenoid.

sfèra, *s.f.* **1.** (*geom. astr.*) sphere: — *celeste,* celestial sphere; — *retta, parallela,* right, parallel sphere; — *terrestre,* globe (*o* orb *o* earth) ‖ *la musica delle sfere,* the music of the spheres **2.** *fig.* (*ambiente, cerchia*) sphere, circle; (*campo*) sphere: — *d'azione,* sphere of action; *nelle alte, basse sfere,* in the upper, lower spheres **3.** (*di orologio*) hand **4.** (*mec.*) ball: *sfere macinanti,* (*ind.*) grinding balls; *cuscinetto a sfere,* ball-bearings ‖ *penna a* —, ball-point (pen).

sfericaménte, *av.* spherically.

sfericità, *s.f.* sphericity.

sfèrico, *ag.* spherical.

sferistèrio, *s.m.* spheristerion.

sferoidàle, *ag.* spheroidal.

sferòide, *s.m.* spheroid.

sferòmetro, *s.m.* (*strum. scient.*) spherometer.

sferràre, *v.t.* **1.** (*un cavallo*) to unshoe **2.** (*tirare con forza*) to land, to deliver: — *un colpo in faccia a qlcu.,* to land a blow in s.o.'s face ‖ — *un attacco,* to launch (*o* to deliver) an attack ‖ **sferràrsi,** *v.r.* **1.** (*di cavallo*) to lose a shoe **2.** (*scatenarsi*) to break loose **3.** (*mar.*) to drag.

sferruzzàre, *v.i.* to knit.

sfèrza, *s.f.* whip; lash (anche *fig.*): *la — della critica,* the lash of criticism; *la — del sole,* the burning rays of the sun; *la — del vento,* the lashing of the wind.

sferzàre, *v.t.* **1.** to whip; to lash; to flog; to scourge; to thrash: *la pioggia sferzava i vetri,* the rain lashed against the window-panes **2.** *fig.* to reprimand.

sferzàta, *s.f.* **1.** lash **2.** *fig.* sharp rebuke.

sfiaccolàre, *v.i.* to flare; (*risplendere*) to shine.

sfiaccolàto, *ag.* worn out, jaded.

sfiancàre, *v.t.* to wear out, to exhaust; (*fam.*) to knock out: *questa lunga arrampicata mi ha sfiancato,* this long climb has knocked me out ‖ **sfiancàrsi,** *v.r.* to tire oneself out, to exhaust oneself.

sfiancàto, *ag.* worn out; (*fam.*) knocked out.

sfiatàre, *v.i.* (*di gas, aria*) to leak; to escape ‖ **sfiatàrsi,** *v.r.* to talk oneself hoarse: *mi sono sfiatato per spiegarglielo,* I talked myself hoarse explaining it to him.

sfiatàto, *ag.* (*senza fiato*) out of breath (*predicativo*); breathless: *un cantante* —, a singer who hasn't got much of a voice.

sfiatatóio, *s.m.* vent, airhole; (*mec.*) breather; (*edil.*) ventilation opening.

sfibbiàre, *v.t.,* **sfibbiàrsi,** *v.r.* to unbuckle; to unfasten: — *la cintura,* to unfasten one's belt.

sfibraménto, *s.m.* weakening, enfeeblement.

sfibrànte, *ag.* enervating, wearying; exhausting.

sfibràre, *v.t.* **1.** (*indebolire*) to weaken, to enervate, to enfeeble **2.** (*spossare*) to wear out: *questo lavoro mi sfibra,* this work is wearing me out **3.** (*ind. cartaria*) to break; (*il legno*) to grind.

sfibràto, *ag.* **1.** (*indebolito*) weakened, enfeebled **2.** (*spossato*) worn-out **3.** (*di legno*) de-fibred.

sfìda, *s.f.* challenge (anche *fig.*); defiance (anche *fig.*): *è una — al buon senso,* it is a challenge to common sense; *accogliere, raccogliere la* —, to accept the challenge; *lanciare una* —, to issue a challenge: *lanciò una — al nemico,* he shouted defiance at the enemy; *mandare la — a qlcu.,* to send s.o. a challenge ‖ *cartello di* —, cartel ‖ *in tono di* —, defiantly.

sfidànte, *ag.* challenging; defying ‖ *s.m.* challenger; defier: *i padrini dello* —, the challenger's seconds.

sfidàre, *v.t.* **1.** to challenge (anche *fig.*); to dare; to defy (anche *fig.*): *lo sfidai a duello,* I challenged him to a duel; *mi sfidò in combattimento,* he dared me to fight; — *qlcu. a fare, dire ql.co.,* to dare (*o* to defy *o* to challenge) s.o. to do, to say sthg.: *ti sfido a fare questo lavoro in un'ora,* I defy you to do this work in one hour *sfido!, sfido io!,* I quite believe it! (*o* to be sure! *o* of course!) ‖ — *il tempo, i secoli,* to defy time, the centuries **2.** (*affrontare*) to brave, to face, to dare: — *la morte,* to face death; — *il pericolo,* to dare danger; — *la tempesta,* to brave the storm ‖ **sfidàrsi,** *v.r. reciproco* to challenge each other: *si sfidarono a duello,* they challenged each other to a duel.

sfidàto, *ag.* challenged; defied (*predicativo*) ‖ *s.m.* (*gener. spor.*) defender: *lo — e lo sfidante,* the defender and the challenger.

sfidatóre, *s.m.,* **sfidatríce,** *s.f.* challenger (anche *fig.*); defier (anche *fig.*).

sfidúcia, *s.f.* mistrust, distrust; lack of confidence: *aver — di se stesso,* to be lacking in (*o* to have no) self-confidence; *aver — di, verso qlcu.,* to mistrust s.o. ‖ *voto di* —, (*pol.*) vote of no-confidence.

sfiduciàre, *v.t.* to discourage, to dishearten: *ogni piccola cosa lo sfiducia,* any mere trifle disheartens him ‖ **sfiduciàrsi,** *v.r.* to become discouraged, to become disheartened, to become downhearted: *non sfiduciarti al primo insuccesso,* do not get (*o* do not be) disheartened at the first failure.

sfiduciàto, *ag.* discouraged, disheartened, downhearted: *appariva stanco e* —, he looked tired and disheartened; *era — ed aveva bisogno di conforto,* he was in low spirits and needed consolation; *sono — dopo tanti insuccessi,* I feel disheartened (*o* discouraged) after so many failures.

sfígmico, *ag.* (*med.*) sphygmic.

sfigmografía, *s.f.* (*med.*) sphygmography.

sfigmògrafo, *s.m.* (*med.*) sphygmograph.

sfigmomanòmetro, *s.m.* (*med.*) sphygmomanometer.

sfiguràre, *v.t.* to disfigure; to spoil: *una modifica sgraziata può — un bel quadro,* a clumsy modification may spoil a fine painting; *il vaiuolo lo ha sfigurato,* smallpox has disfigured him ‖ *v.i.* to cut a poor figure; (*essere fuori posto*) to look out of place: *non vuole — all'esame,* he does not want to cut a poor figure at the examination; *questo tappeto sfigura in un salotto così elegante,* this carpet looks shabby in such a fine drawing-room; *se indosserai questo bel vestito mi farai* —, if you wear this fine dress of yours you'll make me cut a poor figure ‖ **sfiguràrsi,** *v.r.* to disfigure oneself.

sfiguràto, *ag.* disfigured: *un viso* —, a disfigured face.

sfigurito, *ag.* (*rar.*) disfigured.

sfilàccia, *s.f.* 1. (*fili sdruciti*) ravellings (*pl.*) 2. (*ind. tessile*) bast: — *di lino*, lint; — *di lino e canapa*, harl.

sfilacciàre, *v.t.i.*, **sfilacciàrsi**, *v.r.* to fray; (*ind. tessile*) to unravel: *questa stoffa si sfilaccia facilmente*, this material frays easily.

sfilacciàto, *ag.* frayed: *orlo* —, frayed hem.

sfilacciatúra, *s.f.* fraying.

sfilaccicàre, *V.* **sfilacciàre**.

sfilàccio, *s.m.* (*rar.*) threads (*pl.*); frayed edge.

sfilàre, *v.t.* 1. to unthread; (*perle, ecc.*) to unstring: — *un ago*, to unthread a needle; — *una collana di perle*, to unstring beads; — *dallo spiedo un arrosto, tordi*, to unspit a roast, thrushes || — *il portafogli di tasca a qlcu.*, to slip a wallet out of s.o.'s pocket || — *il rosario*, fig. to speak ill of s.o. 2. (*togliere i fili a*) to pull threads out of (sthg.), to take threads from (sthg.): — *la tela per ricamarla*, to pull threads out of linen in order to embroider it 3. (*guastare il taglio a*) to blunt the edge of (sthg.): *bada a non* — *il rasoio*, be careful not to blunt the edge of the razor || *v.i.* to parade; to march past; to file: *i soldati sfilavano davanti al re*, the soldiers were parading before (*o* marching past) the king || **sfilàrsi**, *v.r.* 1. to (be)come unthreaded; to become unstrung: *l'ago si è sfilato*, the thread has come out of the needle; *le perle si sono sfilate*, the beads have come unstrung 2. (*togliersi di dosso*) to slip off: *si sfilò i calzoni*, he slipped off his trousers; — *i guanti, le calze*, to slip (*o* to take) off one's gloves, socks.

sfilàta, *s.f.* 1. (*passaggio*) passing; (*di soldati*) march past; (*parata*) parade: *la* — *di una processione*, the passing of a procession; *assisteremo alla* — *dopo la rivista*, we'll watch the parade (*o* march past) after the review; *ho ricevuto un invito per la* — *di moda*, I've received an invitation to the fashion-show 2. (*serie, fila*) line, string: *una* — *di nomi*, a long string (*o* list) of names; *c'era una* — *di automobili davanti ai cancelli*, there was a line of cars in front of the gates.

sfilàto, *ag.* 1. (*di ago*) unthreaded; (*di perle, ecc.*) unstrung: *conserva le perle sfilate in una scatola*, keep your unstrung beads in a box 2. (*di tessuto*) unwoven 3. (*di lama*) blunt || *s.m.* hemstitch.

sfilatúra, *s.f.* 1. unthreading; (*di perle, ecc.*) unstringing 2. (*l'estrarre fili da un tessuto*) extraction of threads.

sfínge, *s.f.* 1. (*mit. scult.*) Sphinx 2. fig. (*persona impenetrabile*) sphinx: *volto di* —, sphinx-like mask; *è una vera* —, he is a real sphinx 3. (*entom.*) sphinx.

sfiniménto, *s.m.* exhaustion; extreme weakness; (*svenimento*) swoon, faint; (*collasso*) breakdown: — *di forze*, exhaustion.

sfiníre, *v.t.* to exhaust, to wear out: *il troppo lavoro l'ha sfinito*, overwork has worn him out || *v.i.* (*svenire*) to faint.

sfinitézza, *s.f.* exhaustion, extreme weakness.

sfiníto, *ag.* worn out, exhausted; — *dalla fatica*, worn out (with fatigue); *mi sento* —, I feel worn out.

sfintère, *s.m.* (*anat.*) sphincter.

sfioccàre, *v.t.* to fray (out); to unravel || **sfioccàrsi**, *v.r.* to fray, to become unravelled.

sfiòcco, *s.m.* fraying out, unravelling.

sfiocinàre, *v.t.* to remove stones and skin from (grapes).

sfiondàre, *v.t.* 1. to sling: — *un sasso*, to sling a stone 2. fig. (*lanciare*) to throw, to hurl: — *insulti*, to throw insults around.

sfioraménto, *s.m.* 1. grazing, skimming; touching (anche fig.) 2. (*lo spogliare dei fiori*) taking flowers off 3. (*lo scremare*) skimming.

sfioràre, *v.t.* 1. to graze, to skim, to touch lightly: *l'aereo sfiorò l'erba*, the plane skimmed the grass; *la palla sfiorò il muro*, the ball grazed the wall; *la rondine sfiorò l'acqua*, the swallow skimmed (over) the water; — *la rete*, (*tennis*) to touch the net 2. fig. (*toccare di sfuggita*) to touch on (sthg.): *ho già sfiorato*

questi argomenti, I have already touched on these subjects; — *la verità*, to touch on the truth 3. (*spogliare dei fiori*) to take flowers off (sthg.): *il vento ha sfiorato il rosaio*, the wind has stripped the rose of its flowers 4. (*scremare*) to skim: — *il latte*, to skim milk 5. (*rar.*) (*prendere il meglio di, una mercanzia*) to take the best of (sthg.).

sfioràto, *ag.* touched (on) (*predicativo*) (anche fig.): *un argomento appena* —, a subject hardly touched on.

sfioratóio, **sfioratóre**, *s.m.* 1. (*mec.*) spillway: — *a stramazzo*, weir 2. (*miner.*) baffle-board.

sfioríre, *v.i.* to wither, to fade (anche fig.): *le gardenie sfioriscono presto*, gardenias soon fade; *quelle rose sono sfiorite*, those roses have withered; *la sua giovinezza sfioriva*, her youth was fading; *il tempo ha fatto* — *la sua bellezza*, time has withered her beauty.

sfioríto, *ag.* faded (anche fig.), withered (anche fig.).

sfioritúra, *s.f.* fading (anche fig.), withering (anche fig.).

sfittàre, *v.t.* to vacate.

sfítto, *ag.* vacant: *quell'appartamento è rimasto* —, that flat has remained vacant.

sfocàre, *v.t* (*foto.*) to put out of focus.

sfocàto, *ag.* (*foto.*) out of focus.

sfociaménto, *s.m.* debouchment.

sfociàre, *v.t.* to widen the mouth of (a river) || *v.i.* to flow, to debouch: *il Po sfocia nell'Adriatico*, the Po flows into the Adriatic Sea.

sfoderaménto, *s.m.* 1. unlining 2. (*lo sguainare*) unsheathing 3. (*ostentazione*) display, showing off.

sfoderàre, *v.t.* 1. to unline; to remove the lining of (sthg.), to take out the lining of (sthg.): — *una giacca*, to take out the lining of a jacket 2. (*sguainare*) to unsheathe, to draw: — *la spada*, to draw (*o* to unsheathe) one's sword (anche fig.) 3. (*ostentare*) to display, to show off: — *la propria cultura*, to display one's learning.

sfoderàto, *ag.* 1. unlined: *scarpe sfoderate*, unlined shoes 2. (*sguainato*) unsheathed, drawn.

sfogàre, *v.t.* to give vent to (sthg.), to vent (anche fig.); to let out: *apri la finestra per* — *questo fumo*, open the window and let this smoke out; *aprirono una cataratta per* — *l'acqua*, they opened a lock to let the water out; *il chirurgo fece un'incisione per* — *il pus*, the surgeon made an incision to let the pus out; — *la gioia, l'odio*, to give vent to joy, to hate; — *la propria collera, la propria indignazione*, to give vent to one's anger, one's indignation: *sfogò la sua collera su di me*, he vented his anger on me; — *il proprio dolore*, to tell one's sorrow: *avevo bisogno di* — *il mio dolore con qlcu.*, I needed to tell my sorrow to s.o. || *far* — *il fumo*, to let the smoke out; *far* — *una malattia*, to let a disease take its course; *far* — *qlcu.*, to let s.o. say his fill: *fatelo* — *finché è giovane*, let him run wild while he is young; *lo feci* — *finché si calmò*, I let him say his fill until he calmed down || *v.i.* to come out; to go out; fig. to burst: *il fumo è sfogato dalla finestra*, the smoke went out of the window; *la piaga sfoga*, the pus is coming out (of the wound); *il suo dolore sfogò in lacrime*, he gave vent to his pain in tears || **sfogàrsi**, *v.r.* 1. to relieve one's feelings, to get a load off one's chest; (*con collera*) to give vent to one's feelings: — *con qlcu.*, to open one's heart (*o* to unburden oneself) to s.o.; — *in lacrime*, to weep out one's sorrow 2. (*levarsi la voglia*) to take one's fill: *lascia che si sfoghi a mangiare cioccolata*, let him eat his fill of chocolates.

sfoggiaménto, *s.m.* showing off, flaunting, display.

sfoggiàre, *v.t.i.* to show off, to flaunt: — (*in*) *abiti*, (*in*) *erudizione*, to show off one's clothes, one's learning.

sfoggiataménte, *av.* flauntingly.

sfòggio, *s.m.* show, display, parade, ostentation: *v'era un grande* — *di ricchezza*, there was a great display of wealth; *fare* — *di erudizione*, to show off one's learning.

sfòglia, *s.f.* 1. (*lamina di metallo*) foil 2. (*pasta spianata per tagliolini, ecc.*) sheet of pastry; (*dolce*) puff: *pasta* —, puff pastry 3. (*ittiol.*) (*sogliola*) sole.

sfogliàre[1], *v.t.* to thin out the leaves of (sthg.); (*un fiore*) to pluck the petals off (sthg.): — *pannocchie di granoturco,* to husk corn-cobs; — *un ramoscello,* to strip the leaves off a twig ‖ **sfogliàrsi,** *v.r.* 1. to lose leaves, to shed leaves; (*di fiore*) to shed petals: *questi fiori si sfogliano,* these flowers are shedding their petals 2. (*sfaldarsi*) to flake off.

sfogliàre[2], *v.t.* to turn over the pages of (sthg.); (*dare un'occhiata a*) to glance through (sthg.), to skim through (sthg.), to dip into (sthg.).

sfogliàta[1], *s.f.* (*cuc.*) puff-pastry.

sfogliàta[2], *s.f.* glance: *dare una* — *ad un libro,* to glance (*o* to skim) through a book.

sfogliatríce, *s.f.* (*agr.*) husker.

sfogliatúra, *s.f.* 1. stripping of leaves 2. (*di metalli*) scaling, exfoliation, flaking.

sfógo, *s.m.* 1. vent, outlet (anche *fig.*): *apertura di* —, vent-hole; *le acque trovano uno* — *attraverso la diga,* the waters find a vent through the dike; *fece uno* — *con l'amico,* he unbosomed himself to his friend; *la sua energia ha bisogno di uno* —, his energy wants an outlet; *aprire uno* — *al fumo,* to provide an outlet for smoke; *dare* — *alla propria collera, al proprio risentimento,* to give vent to one's anger; *dare* — *alla propria immaginazione,* to give free play to one's imagination 2. (*med.*) eruption, rash 3. — *di un arco,* (*arch.*) height of an arch.

sfogoraménto, *s.m.* blazing.

sfolgorànte, *ag.* blazing, flaming; flashing: — *di bellezza,* ablaze with beauty.

sfolgoràre, *v.i.* 1. to blaze; to flash: *il sole, la luce sfolgorava,* the sun, the light was blazing; *i suoi occhi sfolgoravano,* her eyes were flashing 2. (*rar.*) (*muoversi rapidamente*) to flash.

sfolgoràto, *ag.* 1. (*arc.*) blazing; flashing 2. (*sontuoso*) sumptuous, luxurious; (*smoderato*) excessive.

sfolgoreggiaménto, *s.m.* blazing; flashing.

sfolgoreggiàre, *v.i.* to blaze; to flash.

sfolgorío, *s.m.* blaze; flashing: *uno* — *di luci, di gioielli,* a blaze of lights, of jewels.

sfollagènte, *s.m.* truncheon; (*amer.*) night-stick.

sfollaménto, *s.m.* 1. dispersal 2. (*mil.*) evacuation.

sfollàre, *v.t.* to disperse: *i vigili sfollarono la gente dalla sala,* the policemen dispersed the people out of the hall ‖ *v.i.* 1. to disperse: *dopo il comizio la gente sfollò in varie direzioni,* after the meeting the people dispersed in different directions 2. (*mil.*) to evacuate (sthg.): — *da una città,* to evacuate a city.

sfollàta, *s.f.* evacuee.

sfollàto, *ag.* (*di luogo*) evacuated ‖ *s.m.* evacuee.

sfondaménto, *s.m.* breaking (anche *fig.*): *lo* — *delle linee nemiche,* the breaking of the enemy's lines.

sfondàre, *v.t.* 1. (*rompere il fondo a*) to break the bottom of (sthg.); to knock the bottom out of (sthg.); to smash in: *sfondò la scatola,* he smashed in the box; — *una barca,* to stave in a boat 2. (*rompere passando*) to break through; to break down: *sfondò la porta,* he broke the door down ‖ — *una porta aperta,* to explain what is obvious ‖ — *lo stomaco,* (*riferito a cibo*) to be heavy; (*riferito a discorso*) to be boring 3. (*mil.*) to break through, to pierce: — *le linee nemiche,* to break through the enemy lines ‖ *v.i.* 1. (*aver successo*) to have success; to make one's way: *lavora da due anni come avvocato ma non ha ancora sfondato,* he has been working two years as a lawyer but he hasn't made his way yet 2. (*sprofondare*) to sink, to give way: *gli è sfondata la terra sotto i piedi,* the ground gave way under his feet ‖ **sfondàrsi,** *v.r.* to break at the bottom; to burst at the bottom; to be smashed in.

sfondastòmaco, *ag.* boring ‖ *s.c.* (*persona noiosa*) bore.

sfondàto, *ag.* 1. (*senza fondo*) without a bottom

(*predicativo*); bottomless: *un vaso* —, a pot without a bottom ‖ *scarpe sfondate,* worn-out shoes ‖ *è ricco* —, (*fam.*) he is rolling in it 2. (*insaziabile*) insatiable, voracious ‖ *s.m.* 1. (*ghiottone*) glutton 2. (*rar.*) (*sfondo*) background.

sfondatúra, *s.f.* (*il rompere passando*) breaking through; (*il rompere spalancando*) breaking open; (*l'abbattere*) breaking down; (*il fare a pezzi*) smashing.

sfóndo, *s.m.* 1. (*pitt.*) background: *lo* — *di un quadro,* the background of a picture ‖ *sullo* —, in the background 2. (*ambiente*) background; setting: *è un'opera a* — *sociale,* it is a work with a social setting; *fa da* — *a quest'opera la New York del diciottesimo secolo,* the setting of this novel is the eighteenth-century New York; *le vicende del protagonista hanno per* — *la guerra civile spagnola,* the adventures of the hero take place against the background of the Spanish Civil War.

sforacchiàre, *V.* **foracchiàre.**

sforbiciàre, *v.t.* to cut (with scissors).

sformàre, *v.t.* 1. to pull out of shape, to deform: — *un cappello,* to pull a hat out of shape 2. (*togliere dalla forma*) to remove from the mould: — *un budino,* to remove a table cream from the mould (*o* to dish up a table cream) ‖ **sformàrsi,** *v.r.* to lose one's shape, to get out of shape.

sformàto, *ag.* shapeless: *queste scarpe sono sformate,* these shoes have lost their shape ‖ *s.m.* (*cuc.*) pudding; table cream.

sfornàre, *v.t.* 1. to take out of the oven 2. (*produrre*) to bring out: *egli sforna un romanzo ogni due mesi,* he brings out (*o* he turns out) a novel every two months.

sforníre, *v.t.* to deprive, to strip ‖ **sfornírsi,** *v.r.* to deprive oneself: *non posso sfornirmi di tutto il necessario,* I cannot deprive myself of all that is necessary.

sforníto, *ag.* 1. destitute, deprived, lacking (in sthg.): — *di denaro,* destitute of money; *è completamente* — *di buon senso,* he is completely destitute of (*o* lacking in) common sense 2. (*mil.*) undefended.

sfortúna, *s.f.* ill luck, bad luck; (*disgrazia*) misfortune: *la mia solita* —!, just my luck!; *perseguitato dalla* —, pursued by ill luck; *questa fu una vera* —!, that was a real piece of bad luck!.

sfortunataménte, *av.* unfortunately, unluckily.

sfortunàto, *ag.* unlucky, unfortunate: *una persona, avventura sfortunata,* an unlucky person, adventure; *sono sempre* — *al giuoco,* I am never lucky at gambling.

sforzàre, *v.t.* 1. to strain, to force: — *la mente di un bambino,* to force a child's mind; — *gli occhi, la voce,* to strain one's eyes, one's voice 2. (*scassinare*) to force: — *una serratura, una porta,* to force a lock, a door 3. (*costringere*) to force: — *qlcu. a fare ql.co.,* to force s.o. to do sthg. ‖ **sforzàrsi,** *v.r.* to strive, to try hard: *egli si sforzò di farsi capire,* he strove (*o* tried hard) to make himself understood.

sforzataménte, *av.* 1. (*con grande sforzo*) with much effort; with a great effort 2. (*in modo forzato*) forcedly.

sforzàto, *ag.* 1. (*costretto*) forced, compelled 2. (*artificioso*) forced; false: *posa sforzata,* false attitude; *sorriso* —, forced smile 3. (*più veloce del normale*) very fast, very quick: *passo* —, very fast pace 4. (*detto di vino*) rich.

sforzatúra, *s.f.* 1. (*lo sforzare*) straining, forcing: *quel tuo dolore al braccio è effetto di una* —, that pain in your arm is (due to) your having strained it 2. (*lo scassinare*) forcing: *la* — *di una porta,* the forcing of a door 3. (*cosa sforzata*) far-fetched thing, exaggeration: *nel romanzo ci sono molte sforzature,* in the novel there are many exaggerations.

sfòrzo, *s.m.* 1. effort; strain; exertion: — *di attenzione,* strain on one's attention; — *di volontà,* effort of will; *dopo molti sforzi,* after much effort; *malgrado tutti i miei sforzi,* in spite of all my efforts (*o* exertions); *senza* —, without effort; *feci ogni* — *per aiutarlo,* I made every effort to help him; *non fare sforzi*, don't strain yourself; *non mi costa nessuno* —, it is no effort for me; *questo lavoro richiede troppo* —, this work is too much of a strain (*o* requires too much effort); *fare uno* —, to make an effort; *fare sforzi disperati*, to make desperate efforts; *sostenere lo* —, to stand (*o* to bear) the strain ‖ *bello* —*!*, a good effort! **2.** (*conato*): — *di stomaco*, retch **3.** (*mec.*) stress, strain: — *di flessione*, bending stress; — *di taglio*, shearing stress; — *di torsione*, torsional stress; — *di trazione ai cerchioni*, (*ferr.*) tractive effort at the periphery of the driving-wheel; — *totale di trazione*, (*ferr.*) gross tractive effort; *mettere sotto* —, (*mec.*) to put under stress.

sfóttere, *v.t.* (*pop.*) to take it out of (s.o.), to pull s.o.'s leg.

sfracassàre, *V.* **fracassàre**.

sfracellàre, *v.t.* to smash; to shatter: *le sfracellò il cranio*, it smashed her head in ‖ **sfracellàrsi**, *v.r.* to crash; to smash: *l'aeroplano si sfracellò contro la montagna*, the aeroplane crashed against the mountain; *l'automobile andò a* — *contro un muro*, the car smashed into a wall.

sfrangiàre, *v.t.* to undo to form a fringe ‖ **sfrangiàrsi**, *v.r.* to fray.

sfrangiàto, *ag.* **1.** (*sfilacciato*) frayed **2.** (*ornato di frangia*) fringed.

sfrangiatúra, *s.f.* **1.** (*sfilacciatura*) fraying **2.** (*frangiatura*) fringing.

sfratàre, *v.t.* to dismiss from a monastic order ‖ **sfratàrsi**, *v.r.* to leave a monastic order.

sfrattàre, *v.t.* **1.** to turn out, to evict: *la padrona di casa lo ha sfrattato*, his landlady has turned him out **2.** (*espellere*) to expel.

sfràtto, *s.m.* **1.** turning out, eviction: *dare, ricevere lo* —, to give, to receive notice to quit **2.** (*espulsione*) expulsion.

sfregaménto, *s.m.* rubbing, friction.

sfregàre, sfregàta, *V.* **fregàre 1.**, **fregàta 1.**

sfregatúra, *s.f.* **1.** (*sfregamento*) rubbing, friction **2.** (*graffiatura*) scratch; mark.

sfregiàre, *v.t.* **1.** to deface; to disfigure; (*con oggetto tagliente*) to slash: *le sfregiò il viso*, he disfigured her face **2.** (*offendere nell'onore*) to disgrace; to tarnish, to sully.

sfrégio, *s.m.* **1.** slash; (*cicatrice*) scar **2.** (*offesa*) disgrace; (*affronto*) affront; (*insulto*) insult.

sfrenàre, *v.t.* to unbridle; to let loose; to give free play to (sthg.): — *la propria immaginazione*, to give free play to one's imagination; — *la propria lingua*, to unbridle one's tongue ‖ **sfrenàrsi**, *v.r.* to get loose.

sfrenataménte, *av.* **1.** wildly; unrestrainedly: *piangere* —, to cry without restraint **2.** (*dissolutamente*) licentiously; dissolutely.

sfrenatézza, *s.f.* **1.** wildness; unrestraint **2.** (*dissolutezza*) licentiousness; dissoluteness; profligacy.

sfrenàto, *ag.* **1.** wild; unbridled; unrestrained: *ambizione, passione sfrenata*, unbridled ambition, passion; *una corsa sfrenata*, a headlong rush; *un ragazzo* —, a wild (*o* boisterous *o* unruly) boy; *riso, pianto* —, unrestrained laughter, crying **2.** (*dissoluto*) licentious.

sfríggere, sfrig(g)olàre, *v.i.* to sizzle; to hiss.

sfri(g)golío, *s.m.* sizzling; hissing.

sfringuellàre, *v.i.* **1.** to twitter; to warble **2.** (*parlare senza competenza*) to talk big ‖ *v.t.* (*spifferare*) to blab.

sfrisàre, *v.t.* **1.** (*sfiorare*) to graze; (*graffiare*) to scratch **2.** (*al biliardo*) to make to kiss.

sfríso, *s.m.* (*al biliardo*) kissing.

sfrittellàre, *v.i.* (*cuc.*) to make fritters ‖ **sfrittellàrsi**, *v.r.* to get spattered with grease.

sfrombolàre, *v.t.* (*scagliare con la fionda*) to sling.

sfrondaménto, *s.m.* **1.** stripping of leaves **2.** *fig.* cutting, curtailing; curtailment.

sfrondàre, *v.t.* **1.** (*togliere le fronde a*) to strip of leaves **2.** (*togliere il soverchio a*) to cut, to curtail: — *un discorso, un racconto*, to cut (*o* to curtail) a speech, a report ‖ **sfrondàrsi**, *v.r.* to shed its leaves.

sfrontatàggine, *s.f.* effrontery; impudence; shamelessness; (*fam.*) cheek, nerve.

sfrontataménte, *av.* with effrontery, impudently.

sfrontatézza, *s.f.* effrontery; impudence; shamelessness; (*fam.*) cheek, nerve: *ebbe la* — *di dirlo!*, he had the impudence to say it!; *ebbe la* — *di scrivermi ancora*, he had the cheek (*o* nerve) to write to me again.

sfrontàto, *ag.* brazen; impudent; shameless; (*fam.*) cheeky: *risposta sfrontata*, impudent reply; *è una menzogna sfrontata!*, it's a brazen (*o* barefaced) lie! ‖ *s.m.* impudent fellow; shameless fellow: *è uno* —*!*, he is an impudent fellow! (*o fam.* he's got a nerve *o* a cheek!).

sfrottolàre, *v.i.* to tell fibs.

sfruconàre, *v.t.* (*rovistare con ferro, bacchella*) to poke; to prod.

sfrusciàre, *v.i.* to rustle; to hiss.

sfruscío, *s.m.* rustling; hissing.

sfruttaménto, *s.m.* exploitation: — *di una miniera*, exploitation of a mine.

sfruttàre, *v.t.* **1.** to overwork; to exploit: — *il terreno*, to overwork land ‖ — *gli operai, i lavoratori*, to exploit (*o* to sweat) the workers **2.** (*approfittare di*) to exploit; to abuse; to take advantage of (s.o., sthg.), to profit by (s.o., sthg.): *sfruttò la sua dabbenaggine, la sua generosità*, he exploited (*o* abused) his simple-mindedness, his generosity; *cercherò di* — *al massimo le mie vacanze*, I shall try to make the most of my holidays; *non lasciarti* — *da lui*, don't let him take advantage of you; — *una situazione*, to take advantage of a situation; — *un successo*, to take the greatest possible advantage of a success.

sfruttatóre, *ag.* exploiting ‖ *s.m.*, **sfruttatríce**, *s.f.* **1.** exploiter **2.** profiteer; speculator.

sfuggènte, *ag.* **1.** receding: *fronte, mento* —, receding forehead, chin **2.** *fig.* elusive: *sguardo* —, elusive look.

sfuggévole, *ag.* fleeting, transitory, transient.

sfuggevolézza, *s.f.* fleetingness, transitoriness.

sfuggevolménte, *av.* fleetingly, transitorily.

sfuggíre, *v.i.* **1.** to escape (s.o., sthg.), to slip (sthg.): *mi è sfuggito il suo nome*, his name has slipped my mind; *mi sfuggì di mano*, it slipped out of my hands; *non lasciarti* — *quest'occasione*, don't miss this opportunity (*o* don't let this opportunity slip); *nulla sfugge alla sua perspicacia*, nothing escapes his penetration; — *alla morte, a un castigo*, to escape death, a punishment; — *all'attenzione di qlcu.*, to escape s.o.'s notice (*o* to pass unnoticed) ‖ — *a una promessa*, to break a promise ‖ — *per un pelo*, to escape by the skin of one's teeth (*o* to have a narrow escape) **2.** (*di parola, scappar di bocca*) to escape (s.o.): *gli sfuggirono cose che non avrebbe dovuto dire*, he let out (*o* blurted out) things he should not have said; *non gli è sfuggita una sola parola*, not a single word escaped him (*o* he didn't let out a single word) **3.** (*di paesaggio, degradare*) to recede ‖ *v.t.* to avoid; to shun: — *il pericolo*, to avoid danger.

sfuggíta, di, *l.av.* quickly, hastily: *vedere qlcu. di* —, to have a glimpse of s.o.

sfumàre, *v.i.* **1.** to evaporate **2.** (*andare in fumo*) to vanish; to end in smoke, to come to nothing: *speranze che sfumano*, vanishing hopes; *il mio viaggio in America è sfumato*, my journey to America has come to nothing **3.** (*di colori*) to shade: *un blu che sfuma sul viola*, a blue shading into violet ‖ *v.t.* **1.** (*pitt.*) to shade: — *un colore*, to tone down a colour; — *un disegno*, to shade a drawing; — *un'ombra*, to soften a shadow **2.** (*un suono*) to diminish gradually **3.** (*far evaporare*) to steam.

sfumàto, *ag.* **1.** (*svanito*) vanished: *un progetto* —, a vanished project **2.** (*di colori, luci*) soft; shaded.

sfumatúra, *s.f.* **1.** (*lo sfumare*) shading **2.** (*tono, gradazione*) shade, nuance (anche *fig.*): — *di significato*, shade of meaning (*o* nuance); *le sfumature del verde*, the shades of green; *questa è solo una* —, this is only a nuance.

sfumíno, *s.m.* (*pitt.*) stump.

sfuriàre, *v.t.* to vent: — *la propria collera*, to vent (*o* to give vent to) one's rage ‖ *v.i.*, **sfuriàrsi,** *v.r.* to rage, to give vent to one's rage.

sfuriàta, *s.f.* **1.** outburst (of anger); fit of passion; (*rimprovero*) tirade: *fa spesso sfuriate, ma si calma subito*, he often flies into a passion but he calms down quickly; *mi fece una — perchè ero arrivato tardi*, he told me off (*o fam.* he blew me up) because I had arrived late ‖ *— di vento, di pioggia*, gust of wind, of rain **2.** (*cosa fatta in fretta*) rush.

sgabbiàre, *v.t.* to uncage, to take out of the cage.

sgabellàre, *v.t.* (*sdoganare*) to clear ‖ **sgabellàrsi,** *v.r.* (*liberarsi*) to get rid: — *di qlcu., ql.co.*, to get rid of s.o., sthg. ‖ *sgabellarsela*, to get off.

sgabèllo, *s.m.* stool; (*per appoggiarvi i piedi*) foot -stool ‖ *farsi — di qlcu.*, (*sfruttarlo*) to exploit s.o.

sgabuzzíno, *s.m.* closet.

sgagliardàre, sgagliardíre, *v.t.* to weaken, to enfeeble ‖ **sgagliardàrsi, sgagliardírsi,** *v.r.* to weaken.

sgaidàre, *v.t.* (*tagliar di sbieco*) to cut obliquely.

sgallàre, *v.t.i.* (*far venir vesciche*) to blister.

sgallettàre, *v.i.* (*mettersi in mostra*) to show off.

sgallettío, *s.m.* (*il mettersi in mostra*) showing-off.

sgambàre, *v.t.* (*rompere il gambo a*) to break the stalk of (sthg.) ‖ *v.i.* to walk fast; (*camminare a lunghi passi*) to stride ‖ **sgambàrsi,** *v.r.* to get footsore.

sgambàta, *s.f.* (*lunga passeggiata*) long walk; (*corsa*) run.

sgambàto, *ag.* **1.** (*senza gambo*) stalkless **2.** (*stanco*) footsore **3.** *calze sgambate*, short socks (*o* ankle-socks).

sgambettàre, *v.i.* **1.** (*dimenare le gambe*) to kick (one's legs) about **2.** (*camminare con passi corti e rapidi*) to trip (along), to scurry (along), to scuttle (along).

sgambétto, *s.m.* **1.** trip: *mi fece lo — e caddi per terra*, he tripped me and I fell to the ground ‖ *dare lo — a qlcu.*, *fig.* to oust s.o. (from an office) (*o* to supplant s.o.) **2.** (*piccolo passo*) trip.

sganasciaménto, *s.m.* dislocation (of s.o.'s jaw).

sganasciàre, *v.t.* **1.** to dislocate (s.o.'s jaw) **2.** (*sfasciare*) to break: — *un mobile*, to break a piece of furniture ‖ — *un libro*, to break the back of a book ‖ **sganasciàrsi,** *v.r.* to dislocate one's jaw ‖ — *dalle risa*, to split one's sides with laughter.

sganasciàta, *s.f.* **1.** dislocation (of s.o.'s jaw) **2.** (*riso sgangherato*) guffaw.

sganciàre, *v.t.* to unhook; (*vetture ferroviarie*) to uncouple, to disconnect; (*bombe*) to release (bombs), to drop (bombs) ‖ **sganciàrsi,** *v.r.* **1.** to be unhooked; to come unhooked; (*di vetture ferroviarie*) to come uncoupled **2.** (*mil.*) to lose touch (with s.o.): *la III divisione si è sganciata dal nemico*, the 3rd Division lost touch with the enemy **3.** (*liberarsi*) to get away: — *da una persona noiosa*, to get away from a bore.

sganciaménto, *s.m.* **1.** unhooking; (*di vetture ferroviarie*) uncoupling; (*di bombe*) releasing, dropping **2.** (*mil.*) loss of touch.

sgangheraménto, *s.m.* **1.** unhinging **2.** (*sfasciamento*) breaking.

sgangheràre, *v.t.* **1.** to unhinge: *se continui a sbattere la porta in quel modo la sganghererai*, if you go on banging the door like that you'll have it off its hinges **2.** (*sfasciare*) to break; (*slogare*) to dislocate.

sgangheratàggine, *s.f.* **1.** (*l'essere sconquassato*) ricketiness **2.** (*sguaiataggine*) boisterousness.

sgangheratamếnte, *av.* (*sguaiatamente*) boisterously, coarsely: *ridere —*, to split one's sides with laughter.

sgangheràto, *ag.* **1.** unhinged **2.** (*sconquassato*) ramshackle, rickety, tumble-down: *una carrozza, sedia sgangherata*, a ramshackle coach, chair **3.** (*sguaiato*) boisterous, wild: *riso —*, wild laughter **4.** (*spossato*) worn out.

sgarbatàggine, *V.* **sgarbería.**

sgarbatamếnte, *av.* rudely, impolitely.

sgarbatézza, *V.* **sgarbería.**

sgarbàto, *ag.* rude, impolite, unmannerly, ill-mannered: *uomo —*, rude man; *non essere — con tua sorella!*, don't be rude to your sister!.

sgarbería, *s.f.*, **sgàrbo,** *s.m.* **1.** (*l'essere sgarbato*) rudeness, impoliteness, incivility **2.** (*parola, atto sgarbato*) piece of rudeness, offence: *ricevetti molte sgarberie da lui*, I was treated rudely (*o* impolitely) by him several times; *dire delle sgarberie*, to say rude things; *fare una — a qlcu.*, to be rude to s.o.

sgargiànte, *ag.* gaudy, showy: *colori sgargianti*, gaudy colours; *vestito —*, showy dress; *era tutta —*, she was very showily dressed.

sgargiàre, *v.i.* **1.** (*ringalluzzirsi*) to get cocky **2.** (*far pompa di eleganza vistosa*) to show off.

sgarràre, *v.i.* **1.** to be wrong, to be mistaken; to make a mistake, to make an error **2.** (*di orologio*) (*se è avanti*) to gain; (*se è indietro*) to lose: *il mio orologio sgarra cinque minuti al giorno*, my watch gains (*o* loses) five minutes every day ‖ *egli non sgarra mai un minuto*, he is always dead on time.

sgàrza, *s.f.* (*zool.*) heron.

sgattaiolàre, *v.i.* **1.** to slip away, to steal away: *egli sgattaiolò via senza che lo vedessimo*, he stole (*o* slipped) away without our seeing him **2.** (*cavarsi d'impaccio*) to wriggle out (of sthg.): *non potei — da quella difficoltà*, I could not wriggle out of that difficulty.

sgavazzàre, *v.i.* (*far baldoria*) to revel, to make merry.

sgelàre, *v.t.i.*, **sgelàrsi,** *v.r.* to thaw, to melt.

sghémbo, *ag.* oblique, crooked, slant(ing): *linee sghembe*, oblique lines ‖ *a —*, obliquely (*o* crookedly *o* slantingly): *andare a —*, to walk crookedly ‖ *tagliato di —*, cut on the bias ‖ *s.m.* obliquity.

sgheronàto, *ag.* flared.

sghèrro, *s.m.* bravo (*pl.* bravoes, bravos), hired ruffian, hired assassin.

sghiacciàre, *v.t.i.*, **sghiacciàrsi,** *v.r.* to thaw, to melt.

sghignazzaménto, *s.m.* **1.** (*lo sghignazzare*) scornful laughing **2.** (*risata schernitrice*) scornful laugh.

sghignazzàre, *v.i.* to laugh scornfully.

sghignazzàta, *s.f.* scornful laugh.

sghimbèscio, *ag.* oblique, crooked, slant(ing) ‖ *a, di —*, awry (*o* aslant): *aveva il cappello di —*, his hat was awry ‖ *mettere a —*, to put aslant.

sghiribizzo, *s.m.* whim, caprice, fancy.

sghiribizzóso, *ag.* whimsical, capricious.

sgobbàre, *v.i.* (*lavorar molto*) to work hard, to toil; (*fam.*) to slog; (*studiare sodo*) to swot.

sgòbbo, *s.m.* drudgery.

sgobbóne, *s.m.* hard worker; (*fam.*) slogger; (*in gergo studentesco*) swot.

sgocciolaménto, *s.m.* **1.** dripping, trickling **2.** (*difetto di verniciatura*) runs (*pl.*), tears (*pl.*).

sgocciolàre, *v.t.* to drip, to trickle: — *il fiasco*, to drain the flask (to the last drop) ‖ *v.i.* to drip, to trickle: *dal crepaccio sgocciolava acqua*, water trickled through the crevice; *le foglie sgocciolano*, the leaves are dripping; *la pioggia sgocciola dalle foglie*, the rain is dripping from the leaves ‖ *far —*, to pour drop by drop: *far — dell'olio in una padella*, to pour oil drop by drop into a pan.

sgocciolatóio, *s.m.* (*edil.*) drip, drip-stone.

sgocciolatúra, *s.f.* **1.** dripping **2.** (*pl.*) (*ultime gocce*) last drops: *bere tutte le sgocciolature dei bicchieri*, to drink the dregs left in the glasses.

sgocciolío, *s.m.* dripping, trickling: *lo — di quel rubinetto mi rende nervoso*, the dripping of that tap is getting on my nerves.

sgócciolo, *s.m.* **1.** (*lo sgocciolare*) dripping; trickling **2.** (*ultima goccia*) last drop ‖ *essere agli sgoccioli*, (*detto di energie, finanze, ecc.*) to be at the end of one's tether; (*stare per morire*) to be at one's last gasp; (*essere alla fine di ql.co.*) to be at the end of sthg.

sgolàrsi, *v.r.* to shout oneself hoarse.

sgomberàre, *e derivati*, *V*. **sgombràre**, *e derivati*.

sgombràre, *v.t.* to clear (anche *fig.*); (*portar via*) to clear away: *sgombra tutte queste cose inutili*, clear away all these useless things; — *un luogo da ql.co.*, to clear a place of sthg.: *sgombra il tavolo, la stanza dai tuoi libri*, clear the table, the room of your books; — *la mente dal sospetto*, to clear one's mind of suspicion; — *il passo a qlcu.*, to make way for s.o. ‖ — *la fronte*, (*mar.*) to clear the decks for action ‖ — *una posizione*, (*mil.*) to abandon (*o* to give up) a position ‖ — *un appartamento*, to move out of a flat ‖ *v.i.* **1.** to clear out, to clear off: *sgombra al più presto se non vuoi esser visto*, clear off (*o* out) as soon as possible if you don't want to be seen **2.** (*traslocare*) to move (out): *sgombrarono in settembre*, they moved out in September.

sgombràto, *ag.* cleared.

sgombratóre, *ag.* clearing (*attributivo*) ‖ *s.m.* furniture-remover; removal-man (*pl.* removal-men).

sgombratúra, *s.f.* **1.** clearing **2.** (*trasloco*) removal.

sgómbro[1], *ag.* **1.** clear (of sthg.), free (from sthg.) (anche *fig.*): *animo — di sospetti*, mind free from suspicion **2.** (*vuoto*) empty ‖ *s.m.* (*trasloco*) removal.

sgómbro[2], *s.m.* (*ittiol.*) mackerel.

sgomentàre, *v.t.* to dismay, to daunt, to frighten: *la notizia li sgomentò*, the news dismayed them ‖ **sgomentàrsi**, *v.r.* to be frightened, to get frightened; to be dismayed, to be daunted: *non ti sgomentare, non è poi così difficile*, don't be dismayed (*o* frightened), it isn't so hard after all.

sgoménto, *ag.* dismayed, daunted, frightened ‖ *s.m.* dismay, fright: *non ti far prendere dallo —*, don't be dismayed (*o* frightened).

sgominàre, *v.t.* to rout; to defeat.

sgominío, *s.m.* confusion, disorder.

sgomitolàre, *v.t.*, **sgomitolàrsi**, *v.r.* to unwind.

sgommàre, *v.t.* to ungum.

sgommatúra, *s.f.* (*ind. tessile*) degumming, scouring.

sgonfiaménto, *s.m.* deflation.

sgonfiàre, *v.t.* **1.** to deflate: — *un pallone, un pneumatico*, to deflate a balloon, a tyre **2.** (*far svanire*) to bring down: — *l'orgoglio di qlcu.*, to bring down s.o.'s pride **3.** (*annoiare, seccare*) to annoy, to bother ‖ **sgonfiàrsi**, *v.r.* **1.** to deflate: *il pallone si sgonfiò*, the balloon deflated **2.** (*med.*) to go down: *il livido si è sgonfiato*, the bruise has gone down.

sgonfiàto, *ag.* **1.** deflated ‖ *pallone —*, *fig.* pricked (*o* punctured) balloon **2.** (*med.*) gone down (*predicativo*).

sgonfiatúra, *s.f.* **1.** deflation **2.** (*seccatura*) bother.

sgónfio, *ag.* **1.** deflated: *pneumatico —*, deflated tyre **2.** (*med.*) gone down (*predicativo*) ‖ *s.m.* (*rigonfio di maniche*) puff.

sgonfiòtto, *s.m.* **1.** (*cuc.*) "sgonfiotto" (kind of Italian soufflé) **2.** (*rigonfio di maniche*) puff.

sgonnellàre, *v.i.* **1.** (*dimenarsi camminando*) to wiggle **2.** (*andare in giro per mettersi in mostra*) to gad about **3.** (*affaccendarsi in casa*) to fuss about.

sgórbia, *s.f.* (*strum. artig. chir.*) gouge: — *triangolare*, corner chisel.

sgorbiàre, *v.t.* **1.** (*scarabocchiare*) to scrawl **2.** (*macchiare*) to stain, to blot.

sgorbiatúra, *s.f.* scrawl.

sgòrbio, *s.m.* **1.** scrawl: *non riesco a leggere i suoi sgorbi*, I cannot read his scrawl **2.** (*macchia*) stain, blot **3.** (*pittura mal fatta*) daub: *questo non è un quadro, è uno —*, this is not a picture, it is a daub **4.** (*uomo deforme*) deformed man.

sgorgaménto, *s.m.* gushing out, spouting, spurting.

sgorgàre, *v.i.* **1.** to gush (out), to spout, to spurt: *l'acqua, il petrolio sgorgò dal tubo*, the water, the oil gushed from the pipe; *le lacrime le sgorgano dagli occhi*, tears are flowing from her eyes; *il sangue sgorgava dal taglio*, blood was spouting (*o* spurting) from the cut ‖ *parole di affetto le sgorgarono dal cuore*, loving words sprang from her heart **2.** (*sfociare*) to

flow: *il Po sgorga nell'Adriatico*, the Po flows into the Adriatic Sea.

sgorgatóio, *s.m.* outlet.

sgórgo, *s.m.* gush, spout ‖ *a —*, in profusion.

sgottàre, *v.t.* (*mar.*) to bail.

sgovernàre, *v.t.* to misgovern.

sgovèrno, *s.m.* misgovernment.

sgozzàre, *v.t.* **1.** to cut s.o.'s throat, to slaughter, to butcher **2.** (*strozzar con l'usura*) to fleece.

sgozzatúra, *s.f.* slaughter.

sgozzíno, *s.m.* (*strozzino*) usurer.

sgradévole, *ag.* unpleasant, disagreeable.

sgradevolménte, *av.* unpleasantly, disagreeably.

sgradíre, *v.t.* (*rar.*) to dislike.

sgradíto, *ag.* unpleasant, disagreeable; (*male accetto*) unwelcome: *un sapore —*, an unpleasant (*o* disagreeable) taste; *visita sgradita*, unwelcome visit.

sgràffa, *s.f.* (*tip.*) accolade.

sgraffiàre, *e derivati*, *V*. **graffiàre**, *e derivati*.

sgraffignàre, *v.t.* (*rubare*) to pilfer; to pinch.

sgrammaticàre, *v.i.* to make grammatical mistakes.

sgrammaticàto, *ag.* grammatically wrong, ungrammatical: *parla, scrive in modo —*, he speaks and writes ungrammatically.

sgrammaticatúra, *s.f.* grammatical mistake: *questa lettera è piena di sgrammaticature*, this letter is full of grammatical mistakes.

sgranaménto, *s.m.* (*di piselli, fagiuoli, ecc.*) shelling, hulling; (*di granoturco*) husking; (*di cotone*) ginning.

sgranàre, *v.t.* **1.** (*piselli, fagiuoli, ecc.*) to shell, to hull; (*granoturco*) to husk; (*cotone*) to gin ‖ — *gli occhi*, to open one's eyes wide ‖ — *il rosario*, to say the rosary (*o* to tell one's beads) **2.** (*mangiare avidamente*) to devour, to eat (up) ‖ **sgranàrsi**, *v.r.* (*sbriciolarsi*) to crumble.

sgranatríce, *s.f.* (*per granoturco*) husker; (*per cotone*) cotton-gin.

sgranatúra, *s.f.* (*di piselli, fagiuoli, ecc.*) shelling, hulling; (*di granoturco*) husking; (*di cotone*) ginning.

sgranchíre, *v.t.*, **sgranchírsi**, *v.r.* to stretch: — *le gambe*, to stretch one's legs.

sgranocchiàre, *v.t.* to munch: — *un biscotto*, to munch a biscuit.

sgrassàre, *v.t.* to take the grease off (sthg.); to remove the fat from (sthg.): — *il brodo*, to skim the grease from the broth.

sgravàre, *v.t.* **1.** (*alleggerire*) to lighten **2.** *fig.* to relieve, to ease, to free: *mi hai sgravato da una grande preoccupazione*, you have relieved (*o* eased) me of a great worry; — *la popolazione da una tassa*, to relieve (*o* to ease) the population of a tax ‖ **sgravàrsi**, *v.r.* **1.** to relieve oneself (of sthg.): *voleva — la coscienza*, he wanted to ease his conscience **2.** (*partorire*) to be delivered of a child; (*di animali*) to bring forth.

sgràvio, *s.m.* **1.** (*alleggerimento*) lightening, unloading **2.** *fig.* relief, alleviation: — *delle imposte*, reduction in taxation ‖ *a, per — di coscienza*, for conscience sake **3.** (*giustificazione*) justification, excuse: *per suo — devo dire che non lo sapeva*, in his justification I must say that he did not know it **4.** (*med.*) evacuation.

sgraziataménte, *av.* **1.** awkwardly, ungracefully, clumsily **2.** (*arc.*) (*disgraziatamente*) unfortunately.

sgraziàto, *ag.* **1.** awkward, ungraceful, clumsy: *movimenti sgraziati*, clumsy (*o* awkward) movements; *un ragazzo è spesso più — di una ragazza*, a boy is often clumsier than a girl **2.** (*arc.*) (*disgraziato*) unfortunate.

sgretolaménto, *s.m.* pounding, shattering.

sgretolàre, *v.t.* **1.** to pound, to smash to pieces, to shatter, to crumble: *il gelo sgretola le rocce*, frost splits rocks; — *il vetro*, to shatter glass **2.** (*sotto i denti*) to crumble, to crunch: *il cane stava sgretolando un osso*, the dog was crunching a bone; — *il pane*, to crunch one's bread ‖ **sgretolàrsi**, *v.r.* to crumble, to fall to pieces: *il legno si sgretolò in polvere*, the wood crumbled into dust; *la terra si sgretola al sole*, the soil turns to dust in the sun.

sgretolío, *s.m.* crumbling.

sgrícciolo, *s.m.* (*ornit.*) wren.

sgridàre, *v.t.* to rebuke, to scold, to chide; (*fam.*) to give a lecture to (s.o.), to tell off: *non sgridatemi, non ne ho colpa!*, don't scold me, it isn't my fault!; — *un alunno perchè pigro*, to chide (*o* to scold *o* to rebuke) a pupil for being lazy.

sgridàta, *s.f.* rebuke, scolding; (*fam.*) lecture: *dare una — a qlcu.*, to scold (*o* to chide) s.o.

sgrillettàre, *v.i.* (*di cose che friggono*) to hiss.

sgrínfia, *s.f.* claw (anche *fig.*).

sgrondàre, *v.t.i.* (*sgocciolare*) to drip, to trickle.

sgroppàre[1], *v.t.* (*sciogliere*) to untie.

sgroppàre[2], *v.i.* (*di cavallo*) to buck ‖ *v.t.* (*un animale*) to break the back of (an animal).

sgroppàta, *s.f.* bucking, buckjump.

sgropponàre, *v.i.* 1. (*di cavallo*) to buck (jump) 2. (*sgobbare*) to drudge, to fag.

sgropponàta, *s.f.* buckjump.

sgrossaménto, *s.m.* (*sbozzo*) rough-shaping.

sgrossàre, *v.t.* 1. (*sbozzare*) to rough(-shape) 2. (*dirozzare*) to refine.

sgrossatúra, *s.f.* (*sbozzatura*) rough-shaping.

sgrovigliàre, **sgrovigliolàre**, *v.t.* to unravel.

sgrugnàre, *v.t.* to strike in the face; to smash s.o.'s face ‖ **sgrugnàrsi**, *v.r. reciproco* to smash each other's (one another's) face.

sgrugnàta, *s.f.*, **sgrúgno**, **sgrugnóne**, *s.m.* blow in the face.

sgrumàre, *v.t.* to scrape tartar from (sthg.).

sgruppàre, *v.t.* (*sciogliere*) to untie.

sguaiatàggine, *s.f.* uncomeliness, unseemliness; (*volgarità*) coarseness.

sguaiatamènte, *av.* unbecomingly, unseemly; (*volgarmente*) coarsely: *ridere —*, to laugh coarsely.

sguaiàto, *ag.* unbecoming, unseemly, uncomely; (*volgare*) coarse: *linguaggio —*, coarse language; *persona sguaiata*, coarse (*o* rough) person; *posa sguaiata*, unbecoming posture; *riso —*, coarse laughter ‖ *s.m.* coarse person.

sguainàre, *v.t.* to unsheathe: — *la spada*, to draw (*o* to unsheathe) one's sword.

sgualcíre, *v.t.* to rumple; to wrinkle; to crease ‖ **sgualcírsi**, *v.r.* to crease: *questa stoffa si sgualcisce facilmente*, this material creases easily.

sguància, *s.f.* (*equitazione*) bit-strap.

sguanciàre, *v.t.* to dislocate s.o.'s jaw; to break s.o.'s jaw.

sguancio, *s.m.*: *a —*, awry.

sguàrdia, *s.f.* (*tip.*) fly-leaf.

sguàrdo, *s.m.* 1. look, glance; (*ammirato*) gaze; (*fisso*) stare: *uno — amoroso, penetrante*, a loving, piercing glance; *uno — interrogativo, triste*, a questioning, sad look; *uno — vitreo*, a glassy stare; *esposto agli sguardi*, exposed to view; *distolse lo — da lei*, he looked away from her; *mi lanciò uno — furioso*, he glared at me; *mi soffermai con lo — su un quadro di Cézanne*, I let my eye dwell upon a picture by Cézanne; *attirare gli sguardi (di qlcu.)*, to attract (s.o.'s) attention; *cercare qlcu. con lo —*, to look round for s.o.; *dare uno — a ql.co.*, to have (*o* to take) a look (*o* glance) at sthg.; *gettare uno —, lanciare uno — a qlcu., ql.co.*, to cast a glance at s.o., sthg.; *sfuggire agli sguardi di qlcu.*, to escape (*o* to slip) s.o.'s notice; *volgere lo —*, to turn one's eyes ‖ *al primo —*, at first sight ‖ *occhi senza —*, dull eyes 2. (*vista di un luogo*) view: *bello —*, fine view.

sguarníre, *v.t.* 1. to untrim; to strip the trimmings from, off (sthg.) 2. (*mil.*) to dismantle: — *un fortino, un presidio*, to dismantle a fort, a garrison.

sguàttera, *s.f.* scullery-maid.

sguàttero, *s.m.* scullery-boy.

sguazzàre, *v.i.* 1. to wallow (anche *fig.*): *ai bambini piace — nel fango*, children like to wallow in mud;

— *nella ricchezza*, to wallow (*o* to roll) in riches 2. (*in indumenti*) to be lost: — *nel vestito, nel soprabito*, to be lost in one's suit, overcoat ‖ *v.t.* (*scialacquare*) to squander, to waste.

sgúbbia, *s.f.* (*strum. artig.*) gouge.

sguercíre, *v.i.* 1. to ruin one's eyes 2. (*rar.*) (*aguzzare la vista*) to squint.

sguerníre, *V.* **sguarníre**.

sguinzagliàre, *v.t.* to unleash, to let loose: *gli sguinzagliarono dietro la polizia, i cani*, they set the police, the dogs on him; — *un cane*, to unleash (*o* to let loose) a dog.

sguisciàre, *v.i.* to wriggle; to slip away: *l'anguilla mi sguisciò dalle dita*, the eel wriggled out of my fingers.

sguizzàre, **sguízzo**, *V.* **guizzàre**, **guízzo**.

sgusciàre[1], *v.i.* to slip away, to steal away: *lo afferrai per la manica, ma sgusciò via*, I caught him by the sleeve, but he slipped away.

sgusciàre[2], *v.t.* (*levare dal guscio*) to shell, to hull.

sgusciatríce, *s.f.* (*agr.*) hulling machine.

sgusciatúra, *s.f.* shelling, hulling.

si[1], *pron. r. m.f.* 3ª *persona sing. pl. oggetto e obliquo* 1. oneself; himself; herself; itself; themselves: — *è tagliato questa mattina mentre si faceva la barba*, he cut himself this morning while he was shaving; *egli — fermò*, he stopped; *essi — lavarono alla fontana*, they washed (themselves) at the pump; *la fanciulla — guardò nello specchio*, the girl looked at herself in the mirror; *quando — alzò...*, when he got up... 2. (*coi riflessivi impropri, quando ha funzione di compl. di termine, dà luogo all'ag. poss. corrispondente*): — *lavò le mani*, he washed his hands; — *mise le mani in tasca*, he put his hands in his pockets; — *tolse il cappello*, he took off his hat 3. (*coi riflessivi pronominali non si traduce*): — *dimenticò di chiudere la porta*, he forgot to close the door; — *ricordarono di me*, they remembered me; — *stupirono della sua intelligenza*, they were amazed at her intelligence ‖ *pron. reciproco* (*fra due*) **each other**; (*fra più di due*) **one another**: — *guardarono negli occhi*, they looked into each other's eyes; *non — parlano più*, they don't speak to each other any more; *i tre amici — parlarono per due ore*, the three friends talked to one another for two hours ‖ *pron. indef.* **one**; **they**; **people**; **we**; **you**; **man**; **men**: — *dice*, people (*o* they) say; — *direbbe che...*, one might (*o* would) say that...; — *è deboli*, men are weak; — *vede che sei felice*, one can see you are happy; *come — arriva a Torino?*, how does one get to Turin?; *mi — dice...*, I am told (*o* I hear *o* they tell me)...; *non — deve dimenticare che è molto giovane*, we must not forget that she is very young; *non — può*, you can't (*o* you mustn't *o* it is not allowed *o* it is forbidden); *non — sa mai*, one never can tell ‖ *particella* 1. (*passivante*): — *fanno bei cappelli ad Alessandria*, fine hats are made at Alessandria; *qui — parla inglese*, English (is) spoken (here) 2. (*pleonastica*): *non sa quel che — dice*, he doesn't know what he is talking about; *poco mancò che egli non — morisse in quell'incidente*, he was all but killed in the accident.

si[2], *s.m.* (*mus.*) si, B.

si[3], *particella di affermazione* yes: *è vero — o no?*, is it true, yes or no?; « *Lo vuoi?* », « *Sì* », " Do you want it? ", " Yes, I do "; *non rispondeva nè — nè no*, she wouldn't say yes, and she wouldn't say no; *se c'è lui non vengo, altrimenti —*, if he is there I will not come, otherwise I will; « *Sono felici?* », « *Pare di —, credo di —* », " Are they happy? ", " It seems so, I think so "; *dire di —*, to say yes; *fare cenno di —*, to nod; *rispondere di —*, to answer yes ‖ — *certo, davvero, ma — certo (che) —*, (yes) certainly ‖ *e — che*, (and) yet: *e — che di pazienza ne ho tanta!*, and yet I am a very patient man!; *e — che te l'avevo detto!*, but I did tell you! ‖ *forse (che) —, forse (che) no*, maybe yes, maybe no ‖ *uno — e uno no*, every other one ‖ *s.m.* 1. yes: *un — deciso*, an emphatic yes ‖ *essere tra il — e il no*, to be uncertain (*o* to hesitate *o* to be unable tó make up one's mind) ‖ *pronunziare il —*, *(degli sposi)* to say "I will" 2. *(voto positivo)* ay *(pl.* ayes): *i — e i no erano pari*, the ayes and the noes were even.

sí[4], *av.* (*letter.*) (*così*) so: *un uomo — intelligente*, so intelligent a man (*o* such an intelligent man); *è — bello!*, it is so beautiful! ‖ — ... —, (*tanto ... quanto*): *egli era pieno — d'ignoranza — di superbia*, he was as ignorant as he was proud ‖ — *che*, — *da: fece — che lo persuase*, he managed to persuade him; *fece — da accontentarlo*, he managed to satisfy him ‖ — ... *che*, — ... *da*, so ... that, so ... as (+ *inf.*): *era — contento che ...*, he was so satisfied that...; *era una giornata — bella che...*, it was such a lovely day that... ‖ — *come: fece — com'egli volle*, he did just what he wanted.

sía ... sía, *cong.* 1. (*l'uno o l'altro*) **whether ... or, either ... or:** — *per modestia — per pigrizia, non ha mai scritto niente*, whether (*o* either) out of modesty or laziness, he never wrote anything ‖ *sia che... sia che*, whether (*o* if)... or: — *che arrivino presto — che arrivino tardi...*, if (*o* whether) they arrive early or late...; — *che tu venga — che non venga, io ci andrò*, I will go there whether (*o* if) you come or not 2. (*entrambi*) **both ... and:** — *tu — io abbiamo torto*, both you and I are wrong; *è — ricco — generoso*, he is both rich and generous.

Síam, *no.pr.m.* (*geog.*) Siam.

siamése, *ag.* Siamese: *gatto —*, Siamese cat ‖ *fratelli siamesi*, Siamese twins ‖ *s.c.* Siamese (*invariato al pl.*).

Síbari, *no.pr.f.* (*geog. st.*) Sybaris.

sibaríta, *s.c.* 1. Sybarite 2. (*persona di costumi molto raffinati*) sybarite.

sibariticaménte, *av.* sybaritically.

sibarítico, *ag.* sybaritic(al).

Sibèria, *no.pr.f.* (*geog.*) Siberia: *clima da —*, Siberian weather.

siberiàno, *ag.s.m.* Siberian.

sibèrico, *ag.* Siberian: *freddo —*, Siberian cold.

sibilànte, *ag.* 1. hissing, sibilant: *un suono —*, a hissing sound 2. (*fonet.*) sibilant ‖ *s.f.* (*fonet.*) sibilant.

sibilàre, *v.i.* to whistle; to hiss: *la pallottola sibilò nell'aria*, the bullet whistled through the air; *il serpente alzò il capo e cominciò a —*, the snake raised its head and began to hiss; *il vento sibilava tra le foglie*, the wind was whistling among the leaves.

sibilatóre, *ag.* hissing ‖ *s.m.*, **sibilatríce,** *s.f.* whistler.

sibílla[1], *s.f.* sibyl.

Sibílla[2], *no.pr.f.* Sibyl, Sibil ‖ *dim.* Sib.

sibillíno, *ag.* 1. sibylline: *i libri sibillini*, (*st.*) the Sibylline Books 2. (*misterioso*) mysterious, sibylline: *discorso, sorriso —*, mysterious speech, smile.

síbilo, *s.m.* hiss, hissing sound; whistling, whistle: *il — del vento*, the whistling of the wind; *il — di una sirena*, the wail of a siren.

sic, *av.* (*lat.*) sic.

sicàno, *ag.* (*letter. rar.*) Sicilian.

sicàrio, *s.m.* hired assassin, cut-throat, bravo (*pl.* bravos, bravoes): *il delitto fu commesso da un —*, the crime was committed by a hired assassin.

sicché, *cong.* 1. (*cosicché*) so... that: *era forte — nessuno poteva vincerlo*, he was so strong that nobody could beat him 2. (*perciò*) so; (*formale e letter.*) therefore: *sei tornato a casa — ho deciso di non partire più*, you have come home, so I have decided not to leave 3. (*insomma, allora*) then, well: —, *vieni o non vieni?*, well, are you coming or not? (*o* are you coming or not, then?).

siccità, *s.f.* drought; dry weather.

siccóme, *av.* as: *chiaro — il sole*, as clear as the sun; *ho fatto — volevi tu*, I did as you wished ‖ *cong.* **as, since, because:** — *sapevo che sarebbe venuto, rimasi a casa*, as (*o* since) I knew he would come, I stayed at home (*o* I stayed at home because I knew he would come).

Sicília, *no.pr.f.* (*geog.*) Sicily.

siciliàna, *s.f.* (*musica, danza*) siciliana.

siciliàno, *ag.s.m.* Sicilian ‖ **siciliàna,** *s.f.* Sicilian (woman).

síelo, *s.m.* (*antica moneta*) shekel.

sicofànte, *s.m.* sycophant.

sicomòro, *s.m.* (*bot.*) sycamore.

sicònio, *s.m.* (*bot.*) syconium.

sicòsi, *s.f.* (*patol.*) sycosis.

sículo, *ag.* Sicilian.

sicumèra, *s.f.* presumption; (*ostentazione*) ostentation.

sicúra, *s.f.* safety-catch.

sicuraménte, *av.* 1. (*certamente*) certainly: *verrà —*, certainly he will come (*o* he will come for certain) 2. (*senza pericoli*) safely, in safety: *navigare —*, to sail safely.

sicurézza, *s.f.* 1. (*certezza*) certainty: *avevo la — di riuscire*, I was sure of success; *non posso dirtelo con —*, I cannot tell you with certainty; *rispondere con —*, to answer without hesitation (*o* with assurance) 2. (*immunità da pericoli*) safety, security: *la — di un luogo*, the safety of a place; *dispositivo di —*, safety device; *guardia di pubblica —*, policeman; *lampada di —*, safety-lamp; *misura di —*, precautionary (*o* safety) measure; *per maggior —*, for safety's sake; *rasoio di —*, safety-razor; *serratura di —*, safety-lock; *spilla di —*, safety-pin; *uscita di —*, emergency door (*o* exit); *valvola di —*, (*mec.*) safety-valve ‖ *la Pubblica Sicurezza*, the Police 3. (*fiducia*) trust, confidence: — *nell'avvenire*, trust in the future; *ispirare —*, to inspire confidence.

sicúro, *ag.* 1. (*certo*) sure, certain: *guadagno —*, certain (*o* assured) income; *notizia sicura*, certain news; *ne sono —*, I am sure of it; *ormai la vittoria è sicura*, now our victory is certain; *sono — della sua sincerità, di ciò che dice*, I am sure of his sincerity, of what he says; *sono — di averlo visto*, I am sure I saw him; *sta' —*, be sure; *essere — di riuscire*, to be sure of succeeding (*o* of success); *salvare da sicura morte*, to save from certain death ‖ — *di sè*, self-confident 2. (*immune da pericoli*) safe, secure; (*ben difeso*) sheltered; (*protetto*) protected: — *da rischio, pericolo*, safe from risk, danger; *un luogo —*, a safe place; *una strada, guida, politica sicura*, a safe road, guide, policy; *qui sono —*, here I am safe; *il tempo è —*, the weather has settled 3. (*che non sbaglia*) unerring, unfailing; (*saldo*) steady, firm: *arma sicura*, accurate arm; (*che non presenta pericoli*) safe arm; *cavallo —*, (*non ombroso*) quiet horse; (*sl. sportivo*) dead cert (horse); *colpo d'occhio —*, unerring glance; *gusto —*, discerning taste; *mano sicura*, steady hand ‖ *a colpo —*, without fail (*o* for certain) 4. (*tranquillo*) calm, quiet: *con animo —*, with calm courage: *affrontare un pericolo con animo —*, to face a danger with calm courage; *passare — in mezzo a un tumulto*, to pass calmly through a tumult 5. (*esperto*) skilful, skilled, expert; clever: — *nel maneggio delle armi*, skilful (*o* skilled *o* expert) in handling weapons; *un tiratore —*, a good shot; *nell'ortografia è poco —*, his spelling is rather shaky 6. (*fidato*) reliable, trustworthy, trusty: *persona, fonte sicura*, reliable person, source; *mettere il proprio danaro in mani sicure*, to entrust one's money to safe hands; *puoi essere — di lui*, you can rely on him ‖ *s.m.* safety; (*luogo sicuro*) safe place: *essere al —*, to be in safety (*o* safe); *mettere al —*, to put in a safe place (*o* to put away safely); (*iron.*) (*in carcere*) to put out of harm's way ‖ *di —*, certainly: *di — pioverà*, it will certainly rain.

sicúro, *av.* certainly, of course: «*Vuoi proprio partire?*», «*Sicuro*», "Do you really want to leave?", "Certainly".

sicurtà, *s.f.* 1. (*sicurezza*) security 2. (*assicurazione*) assurance 3. (*cauzione, garanzia*) guarantee.

sideràle, *ag.* sidereal.

sidèreo, *ag.* sidereal: *luce siderea*, sidereal light.

sideríte, *s.f.* (*min.*) siderite.

siderografía, *s.f.* (*artig.*) siderography.

siderolíte, *s.f.* (*min.*) siderolite.

sideroscòpio, *s.m.* (*fis.*) sideroscope.

siderurgía, *s.f.* metallurgy of iron.

siderúrgico, *ag.* iron (*attributivo*): *industria siderurgica*, iron and steel industry; *stabilimento* —, ironworks ‖ *s.m.* iron worker;

Sidóne, *no.pr.f.* (*geog. st.*) Sidon.

sídro, *s.m.* cider, cyder.

siepàglia, siepàia, *s.f.* overgrown hedge.

sièpe, *s.f.* 1. hedge: — *morta, viva*, dead, quickset hedge ‖ *corsa con siepi*, (*spor.*) steeplechase ‖ *ogni pruno fa* —, *prov.* every little counts 2. (*barriera*) hedge, wall, barrier: *una* — *di baionette*, a hedge of bayonets.

sièro, *s.m.* 1. (*fisiol.*) serum (*pl.* sera, serums) 2. (*del latte*) whey.

sierósa, *s.f.* (*anat.*) serous membrane.

sierosità, *s.f.* serosity.

sieróso, *ag.* serous.

sieroterapèutico, *ag.* serotherapeutic.

sieroterapía, *s.f.* (*med.*) serotherapy.

sieroteràpico, *ag.* serotherapeutic.

sièrra, *s.f.* (*geog.*) sierra.

sièsta, *s.f.* siesta; (*pisolino*) nap: *fare la* —, to have a nap.

siffattaménte, *av.* in such a way, in such a manner.

siffàtto, *ag.* (*letter.*) such: *se si va con siffatta gente ci si rimette la reputazione*, if you go around with such people you will lose your reputation.

sifìlide, *s.f.* (*patol.*) syphilis.

sifilítico, *ag. s.m.* syphilitic.

sifóne, *s.m.* siphon, syphon: — *per il seltz*, soda-water siphon.

sigaràia, *s.f.*, **sigaràio**, *s.m.* 1. (*chi fa sigari*) cigar-maker 2. (*chi vende sigari*) cigar-seller.

sigarétta, *s.f.* cigarette.

sígaro, *s.m.* cigar.

Sigfrído, *no.pr.m.* Siegfried, Sigurd.

sigillàre, *v.t.* 1. to seal: — *con cera*, to seal with wax; — *una lettera, una bottiglia, ecc.*, to seal a letter, a bottle, etc. ‖ — *una porta*, (*dir.*) to affix an official seal to a door 2. (*chiudere ermeticamente*) to seal up, to close hermetically: *queste scatolette vengono sigillate*, these tins are closed hermetically (*o* sealed up).

sigillàrio, *s.m.* (*rar.*) craftsman who makes seals.

sigillatóre, *s.m.*, **sigillatríce**, *s.f.* sealer.

sigillatúra, *s.f.* sealing.

sigíllo, *s.m.* seal: — *di Stato*, State seal; *sotto* —, under seal; *mettere il proprio* — *su un documento*, to set (*o* to put) one's seal to a document ‖ *sotto il* — *della confessione, del silenzio*, under the seal of confession, of silence ‖ *ho il* — *sulle labbra*, my lips are sealed ‖ *apporre i sigilli* (*su una porta*), (*dir.*) to affix an official seal (to a door) ‖ *mettere ql.co. sotto sette sigilli*, to close sthg. hermetically.

sigillografía, *s.f.* (*sfragistica*) sphragistics.

Sigismóndo, *no.pr.m.* Sigismund, Siegmund.

sigízia, *s.f.* (*astr.*) syzygy.

sígla, *s.f.* abbreviation; (*monogramma*) monogram ‖ — *automobilistica*, initials of place of registration.

siglàre, *v.t.* to initial.

siglàrio, *s.m.* collection of abbreviations.

sígma, *s.m.* (*lettera dell'alfabeto greco*) sigma.

sigmoidèo, *ag.* (*anat.*) sigmoid(al).

sigmoidíte, *s.f.* (*patol.*) sigmoiditis.

signífero, *ag.* standard-bearing ‖ *s.m.* standard-bearer.

significànte, *ag.* significant, meaningful; expressive: *il tuo silenzio è* —, your silence is significant.

significàre, *v.t.* 1. (*voler dire*) to mean, to signify: *che cosa significa questa parola?*, what does this word mean?; *ciò non significa che...*, this doesn't mean (*o* signify) that...; *la sua devozione significava moltissimo per me*, his devotion meant a great deal to me; *il tuo mal di testa significa che il tempo sta per cambiare*, your headache means (*o* signifies) that the weather is going to change 2. (*comunicare con scritto, parole*)

to signify, to make known: *significò la sua approvazione con un cenno del capo*, he signified his approval with a nod 3. (*simboleggiare*) to symbolize, to be the symbol of (sthg.), to represent: *la violetta significa modestia*, the sweet violet is the symbol of modesty.

significativaménte, *av.* significantly, meaningfully.

significatívo, *ag.* significant, meaningful; expressive: *discorso* —, meaningful speech; *sguardo* —, significant (*o* expressive) look.

significàto, *s.m.* 1. meaning, sense, purport: *il* — *di una frase, di un modo di dire*, the sense (*o* meaning) of a sentence, of an idiom; *il* — *di una parola*, the meaning (*o* sense) of a word 2. (*valore*) import, significance: *egli non capisce il* — *di quello che sto facendo*, he does not understand the import (*o* significance) of what I am doing.

significazióne, *s.f.* 1. significance, meaning 2. (*valore*) import, significance.

signóra, *s.f.* 1. lady; woman (*pl.* women): *quella* — *è ancora bella*, that lady in still beautiful 2. (*seguito da cognome*) Mrs.: *la* —, Mrs. Rossetti 3. (*vocativo*) Madam; (*accompagnato dal cognome*) Mrs.; (*accompagnato da titoli non si traduce*): *Signora Contessa* (*Rossi*), Countess (Rossi); *Signora Sindachessa*, Mayoress; *buon giorno,* —*!*, good morning, Madam!; *come sta,* — *Rossi?*, how do you do, Mrs. Rossi? 4. (*padrona*) mistress; (*proprietaria*) owner, mistress: *è inglese la tua* —*?*, is your mistress English?; *quella vedova è* — *di questa proprietà*, that widow is the owner of this estate ‖ *Nostra Signora*, Our Lady ‖ *Venezia era la* — *dei mari*, Venice was the Mistress of the Seas 5. (*donna ricca*) rich lady; (*di rango*) lady, gentlewoman (*pl.* gentlewomen): *una vera* —, a real lady; *fare una vita da* —, to live like a duchess 6. (*moglie*) wife: *il signor Rossetti e* —, Mr. and Mrs. Rossetti; *arrivederla, signor Rossi, i miei migliori saluti alla sua* —*!*, Good bye, Mr. Rossi, give my best regards to your wife (*o* to Mrs. Rossi).

signóre, *s.m.* 1. gentleman (*pl.* gentlemen); man: *quei signori sono amici miei*, these gentlemen are friends of mine 2. (*seguito da cognome*) Mr.: *il* — *Rossi*, Mr. Rossi; *i signori Smith*, (*i coniugi Smith*) Mr. and Mrs. Smith 3. (*vocativo*) Sir; (*accompagnato dal cognome*) Mr.; (*accompagnato da titoli*) Mr.; (*con titolo nobiliare non si traduce*): *Signor Conte* (*Rossetti*), Count (Rossetti); *Signor Presidente*, Mr. President; *Signor Sindaco*, Mr. Mayor; *caro* —, dear Sir; *Lei,* —, *non mi ha ancora risposto*, you, Sir, have not yet answered me ‖ *signore e signori!*, Ladies and Gentlemen! 4. (*padrone*) master; (*proprietario*) owner, master: *il* — *non è in casa*, the master is not in; *io conosco il* — *di quella proprietà*, I know the owner of that estate 5. (*uomo ricco*) lord; (*di rango*) gentleman (*pl.* gentlemen): *egli è un vero* —, he is a real gentleman; *darsi arie da gran* —, to act the lord ‖ *vivere da* —, to live like a lord 6. (*st.*) (*reggitore*) Prince 7. *Signore*, (*Dio*) God; Lord: *con l'aiuto del Signore*, with God's help; *il giorno del Signore*, the Lord's Day; *la pace del Signore*, the peace of God.

signoreggiànte, *ag.* dominant; ruling; domineering.

signoreggiàre, *v.t.* 1. to rule; to dominate: — *un paese*, to rule a country 2. (*dominare, tenere a freno*) to dominate; to master: — *la mente*, to dominate one's mind; — *le proprie passioni*, to master (*o* to dominate) one's passions 3. (*sovrastare*) to dominate, to overhang; to tower above (sthg.): *un castello signoreggiava il paesaggio*, a castle towered above (*o* dominated) the landscape; *le montagne signoreggiano la valle*, the mountains dominate (*o* rise above) the valley ‖ *v.i.* to rule; to domineer: *gli piace* — *su tutti*, he likes to domineer over everybody; — *su un paese*, to rule over a country.

signoría, *s.f.* 1. (*potestà, dominio*) domination, dominion (*anche fig.*): *la Spagna sotto la* — *dei Mori*, Spain under the domination of the Moors; *essere in* — *di ql.co., qlcu., fig.* to be ruled (*o* dominated) by sthg., s.o.; è in — delle passioni, he is dominated by his passions || mettersi in —, to put on airs 2. (st.) seign(i)ory 3. Signoria, (titolo) (rivolto a uomo) Lordship; (rivolto a donna) Ladyship.

signoríle, ag. 1. (riferito a uomo) gentlemanly, gentlemanlike, courtly; (riferito a donna) ladylike: modi signorili, (di donna) ladylike manners; uomo dal portamento —, man with a gentlemanly bearing 2. (elegante, raffinato) luxury (attributivo); high-class (attributivo): un appartamento —, a luxury flat; una strada —, a high-class (o exclusive) street; trattamento —, first-class treatment.

signorilità, s.f. 1. courtliness, urbanity, distinction 2. (eleganza, raffinatezza) luxury, high class.

signorilménte, av. (riferito a uomo) in a courtly (o gentlemanly) way; (riferito a donna) in a ladylike way.

signorína, s.f. 1. young lady; girl: una — di Roma, a young lady from Rome 2. (seguito da nome o cognome) Miss: la — Anna, Miss Ann; la — Maria Rossi, (se primogenita) Miss Rossi; (se non primogenita) Miss Maria Rossi; le signorine Brown, the Misses Brown (o the Miss Browns) 3. (vocativo) Madam; Miss; (accompagnato da nome o cognome) Miss; (accompagnato da titoli non si traduce): — contessa Rossetti, Countess (Rossetti); — dottoressa (Rossetti), doctor Rossetti; sì, —, yes ma'am (o pop. yes, miss) 4. (padroncina) young mistress: la mia — è gentile, my young mistress is kind 5. (donna non sposata) unmarried woman; (nubile) spinster 6. (figlia) daughter: i miei saluti alla sua —, my regards to your daughter.

signoríno, s.m. 1. Master: il — Giovanni, Master John 2. (giovinetto) young gentleman.

signoróne, s.m. very wealthy man.

signoròtto, s.m. squire: — di campagna, country gentleman.

Silèno, no.pr.m. (mit.) Silenus.

silènte, ag. (letter.) silent, quiet.

silenziàrio, s.m. (eccl. st.) silentiary.

silenziatóre, s.m. 1. (aut.) silencer, muffler 2. (di arma) silencer.

silènzio, s.m. 1. silence: — assoluto, blank (o unbroken o dead) silence; il — della notte, the silence (o stillness o hush) of the night; in —, in silence: soffrire in —, to suffer in silence; mantenere il —, to keep silent; stare in —, to remain silent || —!, silence! (o hush! o quiet! o fam. shut up!) || — glaciale, di tomba, icy, deathlike silence || fare —, to keep quiet (o to be silent): fa' —!, keep quiet! (o stop talking!) || mettere ql.co. in —, to hush sthg. up || passare ql.co. sotto —, to pass sthg. over in silence (o not to mention sthg.): queste cose sono passate sotto —, these things have been passed over in silence || ridurre al —, to silence (o to reduce to silence) || vivere in —, to live obscurely || il — è d'oro, prov. silence is golden 2. (mil.) lights-out: suonare il —, to sound lights-out.

silenziosaménte, av. silently, quietly; noiselessly.

silenzióso, ag. 1. silent, quiet: rimase — tutto il pomeriggio, he remained silent all through the afternoon 2. (senza rumori) noiseless: stanza, strada silenziosa, noiseless room, street.

sílfide, s.f. (mit.) sylph (anche fig.).

sílfo, s.m. (mit.) sylph.

silicàto, s.m. (min. chim.) silicate: — di potassio, potassium silicate; — di soda, soda silicate.

sílice, s.f. (min.) silica.

silíceo, ag. siliceous, silicious.

silícico, ag. silicic.

silício, s.m. (min.) silicon.

silicòsi, s.f. (patol.) silicosis.

siliqua, s.f. (bot.) siliqua (pl. siliquae).

Silla, no.pr.m. (st.) Silla.

síllaba, s.f. syllable: — lunga, breve, long, short syllable; divisione in sillabe, division into syllables (o syllabi(fi)cation); parola di tre sillabe, three-syllabled

word || non proferì una —, he did not utter a syllable || non raccontare neppure una — di quanto hai udito, don't utter a syllable (o don't breathe a word) about what you have heard || non sapeva una — di..., he didn't know the first thing about....

sillabàre, v.t. to syllabicate, to syllabify, to syllabize.

sillabàrio, s.m. spelling-book, primer.

sillabazióne, s.f. syllabication, syllabification.

sillàbico, ag. syllabic: accento —, syllabic accent || canto —, (mus.) syllabic singing.

síllabo, s.m. 1. syllabus (pl. syllabi, syllabuses), summary, index (pl. indexes, indices) 2. (eccl.) syllabus (pl. syllabi, syllabuses).

sillèpsi, sillèssi, s.f. (gram.) syllepsis (pl. syllepses).

sílloge, s.f. (lett.) collection, compilation, sylloge.

sillogísmo, s.m. (fil.) syllogism.

sillogística, s.f. (fil.) syllogistics.

sillogisticaménte, av. (fil.) syllogistically.

sillogístico, ag. (fil.) syllogistic.

sillogizzàre, v.t.i. to syllogize.

sílo, s.m. silo (pl. silos): — di minerale, (min.) ore bin; — di sterile, (min.) waste-bin; immagazzinamento nei sili, ensilage; mettere nei sili, to ensile (o to silo).

silòfago, s.m. (entom.) xylophagan.

silofonísta, s.c. xylophonist.

silòfono, s.m. (mus.) xylophone.

silografía, s.f. (artig.) xylograph(y).

silogràfico, ag. (artig.) xylographic.

silògrafo, s.m. (incisore in legno) xylographer.

silòide, ag. xyloid.

silolíte, s.f. artificial wood.

silología, s.f. (scient.) xylology.

siluétta, s.f. silhouotto.

silumín, s.m. (metal.) silumin.

siluraménto, s.m. torpedoing.

silurànte, s.f. (mar.) torpedo boat.

siluràre, v.t. 1. to torpedo (anche fig.): — un piano, un progetto, to torpedo a plan, a project 2. fig. (licenziare) to fire, to give the sack to (s.o.); (mil.) to cashier: hanno silurato il colonnello, they have cashiered the colonel.

siluriàno, ag.s.m. (geol.) Silurian.

silurifício, s.m. (mil.) torpedo-factory.

siluripèdio, s.m. (mil.) torpedo firing-range.

silurísta, s.m. (mil.) torpedoman (pl. torpedomen), torpedoist.

silúro, s.m. 1. (ittiol.) torpedo (pl. torpedoes), electric ray 2. (mil.) torpedo (pl. torpedoes): — a baffi, whiskered torpedo; — acustico, acoustic torpedo; — aereo, (aer.) aerial torpedo; — elettrico, magnetico, electric, magnetic torpedo; camera siluri, (mar.) torpedo compartment; rete di protezione contro i siluri, (mar.) torpedo-net.

silvàno¹, ag. sylvan, silvan: divinità silvane, sylvan deities || s.m. sylvan deity, faun.

Silvàno², no.pr.m. Silvanus.

silvèstre, ag. 1. sylvan, silvan 2. (selvatico) wild.

Silvèstro, no.pr.m. Silvester || la notte di S. —, New Year's Eve.

Sílvia, no.pr.f. Sylvia, Silvia || dim. Syl, Sylvie.

Sílvio, no.pr.m. Sylvius, Silvius.

silvicoltóre, s.m. forester, sylviculturist.

silvicoltúra, s.f. forestry, sylviculture.

síma, s.f. (geol.) sima.

simbiónte, s.m. (biol.) symbion(t).

simbiòsi, s.f. (biol.) symbiosis.

simboleggiàre, v.t. to symbolize: l'ulivo simboleggia la pace, the olive-tree symbolizes peace.

simbolicaménte, av. symbolically.

simbòlico, ag. 1. symbolic(al) 2. (nominale) nominal: prezzo —, nominal price; paga un affitto puramente —, he pays a purely nominal rent.

simbolísmo, s.m. (lett. art.) symbolism.

simbolísta, s.m. (lett. art.) symbolist.

símbolo, *s.m.* **1.** symbol: *la croce è — della fede cristiana,* the cross is the symbol of the Christian faith; *il verde è — di speranza,* green is a symbol of hope ‖ *il — degli Apostoli,* (*teol.*) the Apostles' Creed **2.** (*mat. chim. astr.*) symbol: *simboli matematici, chimici,* mathematical, chemical symbols.

simbología, *s.f.* symbology.

Simeóne, *no.pr.m.* Simeon.

similàre, *ag.* similar.

similarità, *s.f.* similarity.

símile, *ag.* **1.** like (s.o., sthg.), similar; alike (*predicativo*): *quantità simili,* like quantities; *egli è — a suo padre,* he is like his father; *per quel che riguarda la scuola egli è — a te,* as regards school (*o* as far as school is concerned), he is like (*o* similar to) you; *quei due fratelli sono molto simili,* those two brothers are very much alike; *il ritratto è — all'originale,* the portrait is like the original; *sono simili nel colore,* they are similar in colour; *il tuo caso è — al mio,* your case is similar to (*o* like) mine ‖ *e (cose) simili,* and the like; *egli si interessa di economia, politica e (cose) simili,* he is interested in economics, politics and the like ‖ *sono simili come due gocce d'acqua,* they are as like as two peas (in a pod) **2.** (*tale*) such: *cose simili sembrano impossibili,* such things seem impossible; *hai mai visto una cosa —, niente di —?,* have you ever seen such a thing (*o* the like of that)?; *non ho detto niente di —,* I said nothing of the sort (*o* no such thing) **3.** (*geom.*) similar: *rettangoli, triangoli simili,* similar rectangles, triangles ‖ *s.m.* **1.** *non va mai coi suoi simili,* he never goes with people like himself ‖ *ogni — ama il suo —, prov.* birds of a feather flock together **2.** (*prossimo*) fellow, fellow-creature, fellow-man (*pl.* fellow-men): *dobbiamo amare i nostri simili,* we must love our fellows **3.** *il —: auguro il — a te,* the same to you; *io sto bene e il — spero di voi,* I am well and I hope you are, too.

similitúdine, *s.f.* **1.** likeness, similitude: *Dio creò l'uomo a sua —,* God created man in His likeness **2.** (*ret.*) simile: *la poesia di Omero è ricca di similitudini,* Homer's poetry is rich in similes.

similménte, *av.* (*lo stesso*) the same, likewise; (*in modo simile*) in a similar way, similarly: *avrei agito —,* I should have done the same (*o* likewise); *si sono comportati —,* they behaved in a similar way.

similòro, *s.m.* (*metal.*) pinchbeck, tombac(k), Dutch metal.

simmetría, *s.f.* symmetry: *edificio senza—,* unsymmetrical building; *piano di —,* (*geom.*) plane of symmetry.

simmetricaménte, *av.* symmetrically.

simmètrico, *ag.* symmetric(al).

símo, *ag.* (*letter.*) simous.

Simóne, *no.pr.m.* Simon.

simonía, *s.f.* simony: *peccato di —,* simony.

simoníaco, *ag.* simoniac(al): *frate —,* simoniac friar ‖ *s.m.* simoniac.

Simònide, *no.pr.m.* (*st.*) Simonides.

simpatía, *s.f.* **1.** liking; (*attrazione*) attraction: *ha la — di tutti,* he is well-liked by everybody (*o* he is very popular with everybody); *ho molta — per lui,* I like him very much; *non ha alcuna — per cose simili,* he has no liking for such things (*o* he doesn't like this sort of thing at all); *le sue simpatie e antipatie dipendono dal suo umore,* his likes and dislikes depend on his mood; *provare una — per qlcu.,* to take (*o* to feel attracted) to s.o. **2.** (*med.*) sympathy.

simpaticaménte, *av.* nicely; (*piacevolmente*) pleasantly, agreeably.

simpàtico, *ag.* **1.** nice; (*amabile*) likeable; (*piacevole*) pleasant, agreeable; (*di modi, maniere, cattivante*) taking, winning: *una persona simpatica,* a nice (*o* pleasant *o* agreeable) person; *una serata, una sorpresa simpatica,* a pleasant (*o* an agreeable) evening, surprise; *una voce simpatica,* a pleasant (*o* an agreeable) voice; *egli è molto —,* he is very nice; *ha dei*

modi simpatici, he has very taking (*o* winning) ways; *mi è molto simpatica,* I like her very much; *non è facile incontrare persone simpatiche,* one does not often meet likeable people; *non fosti molto — con lui,* you were not very nice (*o* kind) to him; *non l'ho trovato —,* I did not think he was very nice; *riuscì — a tutti,* he was liked by everybody **2.** *il gran simpatico,* (*anat.*) the sympathetic nerve **3.** *inchiostro —,* sympathetic ink.

simpatizzànte, *ag.* sympathizing ‖ *s.c.* sympathizer.

simpatizzàre, *v.i.* **1.** to sympathize; (*tra due*) to take a liking to each other; (*tra molti*) to take a liking to one another: *i due ragazzi simpatizzarono,* the two boys took a liking to each other; *essi non simpatizzarono,* they didn't like one another; *— con una persona,* to sympathize with a person **2.** (*riuscir simpatico*) to inspire sympathy (in s.o.): *egli simpatizzò moltissimo con tutti,* he was very popular with everybody.

Simplício, *no.pr.m.* Simplicius.

simposíaco, *ag.* (*letter.*) symposiac.

simposiàrea, simposiàreo, *s.m.* symposiarch.

simpòsio, *s.m.* **1.** symposium (*pl.* symposia, symposiums) **2.** (*piccolo congresso*) symposium, conference.

simulàcro, *s.m.* **1.** simulacre, simulacrum (*pl.* simulacra), sacred image: *un — di pietra,* a stone simulacrum **2.** *fig.* simulacrum (*pl.* simulacra); (*ombra*) shadow; (*finzione*) sham, mere pretence: *un — di antichi splendori,* a mere shadow of ancient splendours; *un — di battaglia,* a sham fight.

simulaménto, *s.m.* simulation.

simulàre, *v.t.* to simulate, to feign, to sham: *— fedeltà,* to simulate faithfulness; *— una malattia,* to feign (*o* to sham) sickness (*o sl. mil.* to malinger); *— un sentimento di gratitudine,* to feign gratitude ‖ *v.i.* to pretend, to sham, to dissemble: *non —!,* don't pretend!.

simulatamente, *av.* feignedly.

simulàto, *ag.* simulated, feigned, fake, sham, false: *acquisto —,* fictitious purchase; *indignazione simulata,* feigned indignation; *malattia simulata,* feigned (*o* sham) illness; *matrimonio, titolo —,* fake marriage, title ‖ *s.m.* (*simulazione*) falsehood.

simulatóre, *s.m.,* **simulatríce,** *s.f.* simulator, faker, shammer; (*chi mente*) liar; (*chi inganna*) deceiver, cheat(er); (*ipocrita*) hypocrite.

simulatòrio, *ag.* simulated, feigned, fake, sham.

simulazióne, *s.f.* simulation, feigning, shamming: *— di reato,* (*dir.*) simulation of a crime; *inarrivabile nell'arte della —,* unbeatable in the art of simulation.

simultànea, *s.f.* simultaneous translation.

simultaneaménte, *av.* simultaneously.

simultaneità, *s.f.* simultaneity, simultaneousness.

simultàneo, *ag.* simultaneous (with sthg.).

simún, *s.m.* (*vento dei deserti africani*) simoom, simoon.

sinagòga, *s.f.* **1.** synagogue **2.** *fig.* (*luogo di confusione*) babel.

Sínai, *no.pr.m.* (*geog.*) Sinai.

sinalèfe, *s.f.* (*gram.*) synaloepha.

sinallagmàtico, *ag.* (*dir.*) synallagmatic.

sinartròsi, *s.f.* (*med.*) synarthrosis.

sincàrpio, *s.m.* (*bot.*) syncarp.

sincàrpo, *ag.* (*bot.*) syncarpous.

sinceraménte, *av.* sincerely, frankly, honestly, openly: *— non so che cosa dirgli,* honestly, I don't know what to tell him.

sinceràre, *v.t.* to convince; (*assicurare*) to assure ‖ **sinceràrsi,** *v.r.* to make sure: *— di una cosa,* to make sure of sthg.: *sincerati che la porta sia chiusa,* make sure that the door is locked; *sono quasi certo, ma voglio sincerarmene,* I am almost certain, but I want to make sure.

sincerità, *s.f.* sincerity, frankness, honesty, candour: *in tutta —,* in all sincerity.

sincèro, *ag.* **1.** sincere, honest, true, open, frank: *— rincrescimento,* sincere regret; *dolore —,* genuine sorrow; *una persona sincera*, a sincere (*o* an honest) person; *sentimenti sinceri*, sincere feelings **2.** (*di vino, olio*) pure, unadulterated: *vino* —, unadulterated wine.

sínchisi, *s.f.* (*gram. ret. patol.*) synchysis.

sincípite, *s.m.* (*anat.*) sinciput.

sincipitàle, *ag.* (*anat.*) sincipital.

sinclinàle, *ag.* (*geol.*) synclinal.

sincopàre, *v.t.* (*gram. mus.*) to syncopate.

sincopàto, *ag.* (*gram. mus.*) syncopated.

síncope, *s.f.* **1.** (*med.*) syncope **2.** (*mus. gram.*) syncopation.

sincrètico, *ag.* (*fil.*) syncretic.

sincretísmo, *s.m.* (*fil.*) syncretism.

sincretísta, *s.m.* (*fil.*) syncretist.

sincrociclotróne, *s.m.* (*fis. nucleare*) synchrocyclotron.

sincronía, *s.f.* synchrony.

sincronísmo, *s.m.* synchronism.

sincronístico, *ag.* synchronistic, synchronous.

sincronizzàre, *v.t.* to synchronize.

sincronizzatóre, *s.m.* (*mec. cine. aer.*) synchronizer.

sincronizzazióne, *s.f.* synchronization: — *preventiva,* (*cine.*) prescoring.

sincrono, *ag.* synchronous: *alternatore* —, (*elett.*) synchronous alternator.

sincrotróne, *s.m.* (*fis. nucleare*) synchrotron.

sindacàbile, *ag.* **1.** (*controllabile*) checkable, controllable; (*verificabile*) verifiable **2.** (*censurabile*) censurable; (*biasimabile*) blamable; (*criticabile*) criticizable.

sindacàle, *ag.* **1.** (*del sindaco di una città*) of the mayor; (*del sindaco di un'azienda*) auditorial: *l'autorità* —, the mayor's authority **2.** (*di sindacato*) trade-union (*attributivo*): *azione* —, trade-union action ‖ *Camera Sindacale degli agenti di cambio,* Stock Exchange Committee.

sindacalísmo, *s.m.* (*movimento sindacalista*) trade-unionism; (*sindacalismo rivoluzionario, movimento mirante alla conquista del potere economico da parte dei sindacati*) syndicalism.

sindacalísta, *s.c.* trade-unionist; (*fautore del sindacalismo rivoluzionario*) syndicalist.

sindacaménto, *s.m.* **1.** (*controllo*) control, check; (*verifica*) verification; (*ispezione*) inspection; (*di conti*) audit **2.** (*censura*) censure; (*biasimo*) blame.

sindacàre, *v.t.* **1.** (*controllare*) to control, to check; (*verificare*) to verify; (*ispezionare*) to inspect; (*conti*) to audit **2.** (*censurare*) to censure; (*biasimare*) to blame; (*criticare*) to criticize: — *la condotta di qlcu.,* to censure s.o.'s behaviour.

sindacàto, *s.m.* **1.** (*ufficio di sindaco*) mayoralty **2.** (*revisione dei conti*) audit; (*controllo*) control, check **3.** (*associazione industriale*) syndicate; association, trust; pool: — *carbosiderurgico,* coal and steel pool; — *del carbone,* coal trust; — *industriale,* manufacturing trust **4.** (*associazione di lavoratori*) trade-union.

síndaco, *s.m.* **1.** mayor; (*in alcune città inglesi*) Lord Mayor **2.** (*comm.*) auditor: — *effettivo, supplente,* standing, substitute auditor.

sindèresi, *s.f.* (*fil.*) synteresis (*pl.* syntereses).

sindesmología, *s.f.* syndesmology.

síndone, *s.f.* shroud, sindon ‖ *la Santa Sindone,* the Holy Shroud.

síndrome, *s.f.* (*med.*) syndrome.

sinechía, *s.f.* (*med.*) synechia.

sinecúra, *s.f.* (*eccl.*) sinecure.

sinèddoche, *s.f.* (*ret.*) synecdoche.

sinèdrio, *s.m.* (*st. ebraica*) Sanhedrim, Sanhedrin.

sinèresi, *s.f.* (*gram.*) synaeresis.

sinergía, *s.f.* (*med.*) synergy.

sinergísmo, *s.m.* (*med.*) synergy.

sinestèsi, *s.f.* syn(a)esthesia (*pl.* syn(a)esthesiae).

sinfonía, *s.f.* symphony.

sinfònico, *ag.* symphonic; symphony (*attributivo*): *concerto* —, symphony concert; *musica sinfonica,* symphonic music; *orchestra sinfonica,* symphony orchestra.

sinfonísta, *s.c.* symphonist.

sinforòsa, *s.f.* **1.** (*cappello*) Dolly Varden **2.** (*vecchia che vuol fare la giovane*) old flirt.

singalése, *ag.* Cingalese, Sin(g)halese ‖ *s.c.* Cingalese (*invariato al pl.*); Sin(g)halese (*invariato al pl.*).

Singapóre, *no.pr.f.* (*geog.*) Singapore.

singenèsia, *s.f.* (*bot.*) Syngenesia.

singhiozzàre, *v.i.* **1.** (*avere il singhiozzo*) to hiccup **2.** (*piangere a singhiozzi*) to sob: *il povero bambino non cessava di* —, the poor child did not stop sobbing.

singhiózzo, *s.m.* **1.** hiccup: *avere il* —, to have the hiccups **2.** (*sussulto di pianto*) sob.

singolàre, *ag.* **1.** (*gram.*) singular **2.** (*strano*) singular, peculiar, strange, unusual; (*bizzarro*) odd, queer; quaint; eccentric: *un carattere* —, a peculiar character; *un caso* —, a singular case; *gusti singolari,* queer tastes **3.** (*eccellente, raro*) remarkable, rare, singular: *bellezza, ingegno* —, remarkable beauty, talent; *virtù* —, rare virtue **4.** (*singolo*) single: *singolar tenzone,* single combat ‖ *s.m.* **1.** (*gram.*) singular **2.** (*tennis*) singles (*pl.*): — *femminile, maschile,* women's, men's singles.

singolareggiàre, *v.i.* to excel, to stand out.

singolarità, *s.f.* **1.** (*stranezza, originalità*) singularity, peculiarity, strangeness, oddity, queerness: *la* — *del caso occorsogli,* the singularity (*o* strangeness) of the case which had occurred to him **2.** (*eccellenza, rarità*) remarkableness, rarity.

singolarménte, *av.* **1.** (*a uno a uno*) singly, separately, individually: *comunicò la notizia* — *ai membri dell'associazione,* he told the news to the members of the association separately **2.** (*segnatamente*) particularly: *fatto* — *grave,* particularly serious event **3.** (*specialmente*) especially: *attendere* — *a ql.co.,* to attend to sthg. especially.

síngolo, *ag.* single, individual: *ogni* — *libro, giorno, membro,* every single book, day, member; *non puoi basarti su un caso* —, you cannot base your argument on a single case ‖ *s.m.* **1.** (*individuo, uomo*) individual: *gli interessi del* —, the interests of the individual ‖ *per* —, singly (*o* separately *o* individually) **2.** (*spor.*) single; (*tennis, golf*) singles (*pl.*): *facciamo un* —, let's play a singles.

singúlto, *V.* **singhiózzo.**

siníbbio, *s.m.* blizzard.

siniscalcàto, *s.m.* (*st.*) **1.** (*ufficio*) seneschalship **2.** (*area di giurisdizione*) seneschalsy.

siniscàlco, *s.m.* (*st.*) seneschal.

sinístra, *s.f.* **1.** (*mano sinistra*) left, left hand: *molti scrivono con la* —, many people write with the left hand **2.** (*parte sinistra*) left, left-hand side: *la* — *di un fiume,* the left bank of a river; *alla mia* —, on my left; *la prima strada a* —, the first street on the left; *il suo vicino di* —, his left-hand neighbour; *girate a* —, turn to the left ‖ *tutto a* —!, (*mar.*) hard aport! **3.** (*pol.*) left: *estrema* —, extreme left; *uomo di* —, left winger.

sinistraménte, *av.* **1.** (*in modo ostile*) sinisterly, grimly; (*in modo infausto*) ominously **2.** (*malamente*) badly, in a hostile manner.

sinistràto, *ag.* **1.** (*di edificio, bombardato*) bomb-damaged **2.** (*menomato fisicamente*) injured ‖ *s.m.* **1.** (*senzatetto*) homeless person **2.** (*chi ha subìto una menomazione fisica*) injured person.

sinístro, *ag.* **1.** left; left-hand (*attributivo*): *ala sinistra,* left wing; *lato* —, left side (*o* left-hand side) **2.** (*minaccioso, ostile*) sinister, grim; (*infausto*) ominous: *un aspetto* —, a sinister (*o* grim) appearance; *espressione sinistra,* sinister (*o* grim) expression; *occhiata sinistra,* sinister glance; *segni, presentimenti sinistri,* sinister (*o* ominous) signs, presentiments ‖ *s.m.* **1.** (*disgrazia*) accident, mishap: *assicurazione contro i sinistri,* insurance against damage (*o* accident insurance) **2.** (*boxe*) left: *gli vibrò un* —, he landed him a straight left.

sinistròrso, *ag.* sinistrorse, sinistrorsal.

sinizèsi, *s.f.* (*gram. med.*) synizesis (*pl.* synizeses).

síno, *V.* **fino 1.**

sinodàle, *ag.* (*eccl.*) synodal.
sinodalménte, *av.* (*eccl.*) synodically.
sinòdico, *ag.* (*eccl. astr.*) synodic, synodical.
sínodo, *s.m.* (*eccl. astr.*) synod.
sinología, *s.f.* Sinology.
sinològico, *ag.* Sinological.
sinòlogo, *s.m.* Sinologue, Sinologist.
sinonimía, *s.f.* synonymy.
sinonímico, *ag.* synonymic.
sinònimo, *ag.* synonymous || *s.m.* synonym.
sinòpia, *s.f.* sinopite, ruddle.
sinóra, *V.* finóra.
sinòssi, *s.f.* synopsis (*pl.* synopses).
sinòttico, *ag.* synoptic(al): *tavole sinottiche,* synoptic tables || *Vangeli sinottici,* Synoptic Gospels.
sinòvia, *s.f.* (*anat.*) synovia.
sinoviàle, *ag.* (*anat.*) synovial.
sinovíte, *s.f.* (*patol.*) synovitis.
sintàssi, *s.f.* syntax.
sintatticaménte, *av.* syntactically.
sintàttico, *ag.* syntactic(al).
síntesi, *s.f.* synthesis (*pl.* syntheses).
sinteticaménte, *av.* synthetically.
sintètico, *ag.* **1.** synthetic(al): *gomma, resina sintetica,* synthetic rubber, resin **2.** (*conciso*) concise.
sintetizzàre, *v.t.* to synthetize, to synthesize.
sintoísmo, *s.m.* (*st. relig.*) Shintoism.
sintomàtico, *ag.* symptomatic.
sintomatología, *s.f.* symptomatology.
síntomo, *s.m.* **1.** symptom: *i sintomi di una malattia,* the symptoms of an illness **2.** *fig.* (*indizio*) symptom, sign, token: *questo ritardo è un — di pigrizia,* this delay is a symptom (o sign) of laziness.
sintonía, *s.f.* (*rad.*) syntony, tuning: *— acuta,* sharp tuning; *acutezza di —,* tuning sharpness; *indicatore di —,* tuning indicator.
sintònico, *ag.* (*rad.*) syntonic.
sintonizzàbile, *ag.* (*rad.*) tunable: *non —,* non-tunable.
sintonizzàre, *v.t.* (*rad.*) to syntonize, to tune in.
sintonizzatóre, *s.m.* (*rad.*) syntonizer, tuner: *— a due circuiti,* two-circuit tuner; *— multiplo,* multiple tuner.
sintonizzazióne, *s.f.* (*rad.*) syntonization, tuning: *— di antenna in parallelo,* parallel antenna tuning; *— doppia,* double-spot tuning; *— ottima,* fine tuning.
sinuosaménte, *av.* sinuously, tortuously.
sinuosità, *s.f.* sinuosity; winding: *la — di un sentiero, di un fiume,* the winding of a path, of a river.
sinuóso, *ag.* sinuous, tortuous; winding: *fiume, sentiero —,* winding river, path.
sinusíte, *s.f.* (*patol.*) sinusitis.
sinusòide, *s.f.* (*geom.*) sinusoid.
sionísmo, *s.m.* (*pol.*) Zionism.
sionísta, *s.c.* (*pol.*) Zionist.
sionístico, *ag.* Zionist.
sipàrio, *s.m.* curtain, drop-curtain: *cala il —,* the curtain falls (o is lowered); *si alza il —,* the curtain rises (o is raised).
Siracúsa, *no.pr.f.* (*geog.*) Syracuse.
siracusàno, *ag. s.m.* Syracusan || **siracusàna,** *s.f.* Syracusan.
síre, *s.m.* Sire.
siréna¹, *s.f.* (*mit.*) mermaid; siren (anche *fig.*): *canto di —,* siren song.
siréna², *s.f.* (*acu.*) siren, hooter: *— da nebbia,* (*mar.*) foghorn; *la — di una fabbrica,* factory hooter (o factory whistle); *la — di una nave,* ship's siren; *— elettrica,* electric siren.
Síria, *no.pr.f.* (*geog.*) Syria.
siríaco, *ag. s.m.* Syriac: *chiesa, lingua siriaca,* Syriac church, language.
siriàno, *ag. s.m.* Syrian || **siriàna,** *s.f.* Syrian.
sirínga, *s.f.* **1.** (*mus.*) syrinx (*pl.* syringes): *la — di Pan,* Pan's syrinx **2.** (*med.*) syringe: *— ipoder-*

mica, hypodermic syringe **3.** (*med.*) (*catetere*) catheter **4.** (*mec.*) syringe: *— per grasso,* grease gun; *— per lubrificazione,* oil gun; *— per olio,* oil syringe **5.** (*bot.*) syringa
siringàre, *v.t.* to syringe; (*iniettare*) to inject.
siringatúra, *s.f.* syringing.
sirínge, *s.f.* (*formazione laringea degli uccelli*) syrinx (*pl.* syringes).
siringíte, *s.f.* (*patol.*) syringitis.
siringotomía, *s.f.* (*chir.*) syringotomy.
siringòtomo, *s.m.* (*chir.*) syringotome.
Sírio, *no.pr.m.* (*astr.*) Sirius, Dogstar.
siròcchia, *s.f.* (*arc.*) sister.
sírte, *s.f.* **1.** quicksand; syrtis (*pl.* syrtes) || *la Gran Sirte, la Piccola Sirte,* (*geog.*) Syrtis Major, Syrtis Minor **2.** *fig.* (*insidia*) snare, trap.
sirventése, *s.m.f.* (*poes.*) sirvente.
Sísifo, *no.pr.m.* (*mit.*) Sisyphus || *la fatica di —,* the labour of Sisyphus.
sísmico, *ag.* seismic.
sismografía, *s.f.* seismography.
sismògrafo, *s.m.* seismograph.
sismogràmma, *s.m.* seismogram.
sismología, *s.f.* seismology.
sismòlogo, *s.m.* seismologist.
sissignóra, *av.* yes, madam.
sissignóre, *av.* yes, sir.
sistèma, *s.m.* **1.** system: *— aritmico,* (*tel.*) start-stop (system); *— automatico,* (*tel.*) automatic system; *— di diffusione sonora,* (*acu. rad.*) public-address system; *— filosofico,* philosophical system; *— metrico decimale,* metric system; *— muscolare, nervoso,* (*anat.*) muscular, nervous system; *— orografico, idrografico,* (*geog.*) orographic, hydrographic system; *— planetario, solare,* (*astr.*) planetary, solar system; *— tolemaico, copernicano,* (*astr.*) Ptolemaic, Copernican system **2.** (*metodo*) system, method; (*modo*) way; (*abitudine*) custom: *— di governo,* system of government; *— di vita,* way of life; *devi cambiar — se vuoi riuscire,* you must change your ways if you want to be successful; *non è mio — lasciare le cose a metà,* it is not my custom to leave things unfinished; *non ha — nel suo lavoro,* he has no system (o method) in his work; *questo è il suo — di fare le cose,* this is his way of doing things; *fare ql.co. con —,* to do sthg. methodically; *lavorare senza —,* to work without method.
sistemàre, *v.t.* **1.** (*ridurre a sistema*) to systematize **2.** (*mettere in ordine*) to arrange: *sistemali in ordine alfabetico,* arrange them in alphabetical order; *— i libri in uno scaffale,* to arrange books on a shelf || *lo sistemerò io!,* I'll fix him! **3.** (*definire, regolare*) to settle: *— un conto,* to settle an account (o a bill); *— una lite,* to make up a quarrel **4.** (*collocare*): *ho sistemato i figli da mia madre,* I have left my children at my mother's; *l'ho sistemato presso la ditta di un mio amico,* I have found him a job (o I have fixed him up with a job) in the firm of a friend of mine || **sistemàrsi,** *v.r.* **1.** to settle (down): *egli si sistemò vicino a Roma,* he settled near Rome; *siamo sistemati nella nostra nuova casa,* we have settled down in our new home **2.** (*trovar lavoro*) to find a job: *mi sono sistemata bene,* I have found a very good job.
sistemàtica, *s.f.* systematics.
sistematicaménte, *av.* systematically, methodically, with method: *lavorare —,* to work methodically; *ordinare ql.co. —,* to arrange sthg. systematically.
sistemàtico, *ag.* **1.** systematic **2.** (*metodico*) systematic, methodical: *contraddizione sistematica,* systematic opposition; *persona sistematica,* methodical person.
sistemazióne, *s.f.* **1.** (*ordine, assetto*) arrangement, placing; (*collocazione di macchinari, impianti*) layout: *la — del mobilio è solo provvisoria,* the arrangement of the furniture is only a temporary one (o this is only a temporary arrangement of the furniture); *voglio cambiare la — di quei libri,* I want to change the

arrangement (*o placing*) of those books **2.** (*il sistemare, il sistemarsi*) settlement; settling; (*fam.*) fixing-up: *la — dei propri interessi*, the settlement of one's own interests; *la — del contratto richiese più giorni*, the settlement (*o fam.* fixing-up) of the contract took several days; *hai provveduto alla — del conto?*, have you settled (*o paid*) the bill? (*o* have you seen to the settlement of the bill?); *la mia — qui a Roma è definitiva*, I have now settled down in Rome for good (*o* my settling in Rome is permanent) **3.** (*posto, lavoro*) job; position; post: *ha trovato una buona — come segretaria*, she has found a good position as a secretary; *suo figlio ha finalmente trovato una buona —*, his son has found a good job at last **4.** (*messa a punto, di macchine, strumenti*) setting.

sístilo, *ag.* (*arch.*) systyle.

Sísto, *no.pr.m.* Sistus.

sístole, *s.f.* (*fisiol.*) systole.

sístro, *s.m.* (*mus.*) sistrum (*pl.* sistra).

sitibóndo, *ag.* (*letter.*) **1.** very thirsty, parched **2.** *fig.* (*avido*) thirsting (for, after sthg.), eager (for sthg.): *— di vendetta, di gloria*, thirsting for vengeance, for glory; *essere — di sangue*, to thirst for blood.

síto¹, *ag.* situated, placed, located: *la casa è sita su un colle*, the house is situated on a hill ‖ *s.m.* **1.** place, spot; site: *il — di una città, di un monumento*, the site of a town, of a monument; *il più bel — del giardino*, the nicest spot (*o place*) in the garden **2.** (*poet.*) (*contrada*) place, country: *in lontani siti*, in far away countries.

síto², *s.m.* (*tanfo di muffa*) musty smell.

sitofobia, *s.f.* sit(i)ophobia.

situàre, *v.t.* **1.** to site, to place **2.** (*costruire*) to build.

situazióne, *s.f.* **1.** situation, location, site: *questa città è in una bella —*, this town has a fine location (*o* is in a fine spot) **2.** (*condizione*) situation, position: *la — economica, politica*, the economic, political situation; *la — è molto cambiata*, the situation has changed a great deal; *essere in una — imbarazzante*, to be in an awkward situation (*o position*).

Síva, *no.pr.m.* (*relig. indù*) Siva, Shiva.

Sivíglia, *no.pr.f.* (*geog.*) Seville.

sizígia, *s.f.* (*astr.*) syzygy.

sízza, *s.f.* north wind; bitterly cold wind.

ski, *s.m.* (*spor.*) ski.

slabbràre, *v.t.* **1.** to chip the rim of (sthg.); to break the rim of (sthg.): *— un vaso*, to break the rim (*o* brim *o* lip) of a vase ‖ *v.i.* **1.** to overflow; to flow over; to brim over: *il latte slabbra*, the milk is brimming over **2.** (*di ferita*) to gape; to open.

slabbràto, *ag.* **1.** chipped: *una tazza slabbrata*, a cup with a chipped rim **2.** (*di ferita*) gaping, open.

slabbratúra, *s.f.* **1.** chipping **2.** (*orlo rotto*) chipped edge **3.** (*mec.*) burr: *prova di —*, flanging test.

slacciàre, *v.t.* to unlace, to undo, to untie; (*sbottonare*) to unbutton: *slacciami le scarpe*, unlace my shoes ‖ **slacciàrsi,** *v.r.* to come unlaced, to come undone, to come untied; (*sbottonarsi*) to come unbuttoned: *mi si sono slacciate le scarpe*, my shoelaces have come undone; *slacciati la giacca*, unbutton your jacket; *— la cintura*, to undo one's belt.

sladinàre, *v.t.* (*mec.*) to run in.

sladinatúra, *s.f.* (*mec.*) running in.

slalom, *s.m.* (*spor.*) slalom.

slamàre, *v.t.* to make slide, to make slip ‖ *v.i.* to slide, to slip.

slanciaménto, *s.m.* hurling, flinging.

slanciàre, *v.t.* to hurl, to fling, to throw ‖ **slanciàrsi,** *v.r.* **1.** to hurl oneself, to rush, to dash: *si slanciarono fuori*, they rushed (*o* dashed) out; *si slanciò contro di me*, he hurled himself upon (*o* at) me **2.** *fig.* (*avventurarsi*) to venture, to engage: *si slanciò in quella pazza impresa*, he engaged in that crazy undertaking.

slanciàto, *ag.* **1.** (*snello*) slim, slender **2.** (*ardimentoso*) bold.

slàncio, *s.m.* **1.** rush; impetus; (*salto*) jump: *entrò nella stanza con —*, he came into the room with a rush (*o* he rushed into the room); *se prendi più —, riuscirai a saltare quel muro*, if you gather more impetus in running up, you'll manage to jump that wall; *i soldati si gettarono di — sul nemico*, the soldiers made a rush (*o* a dash) at the enemy ‖ *di primo —*, at the first go **2.** *fig.* (*energia*) energy, ardour; (*fam.*) go; (*entusiasmo*) enthusiasm; (*impulso*) impulse: *in uno — di entusiasmo, di generosità*, in a fit (*o* burst) of enthusiasm, of generosity; *agire di —*, to act on impulse; *essere pieno di —*, to be full of energy (*o* go) **3.** (*mar.*) rake: *— del dritto di prua*, rake of the stem.

slargàre, *e derivati*, *V.* **allargàre,** *e derivati.*

slatinàre, *v.i.* (*iron.*) to show off one's knowledge of Latin.

slattaménto, *s.m.* weaning.

slattàre, *v.t.* to wean.

slavàto, *ag.* **1.** (*di colore*) washed out; (*di colorito*) pale, colourless, wan **2.** *fig.* (*sbiadito*) dull; uninteresting; insipid: *un racconto —*, a dull story.

slavína, *s.f.* landslide; (*di neve*) snowslide.

slavísmo, *s.m.* Slavism.

slàvo, *ag.* **1.** Slav **2.** (*di lingua*) Slav(ic). Slavonic ‖ *s.m.* **1.** Slav **2.** (*lingua*) Slavonic ‖ **slàva,** *s.f.* Slav.

slavòfilo, *ag.s.m.* Slavophil(e).

slavòfobo, *ag.s.m.* Slavophobe.

sleàle, *ag.* disloyal, unfaithful; unfair: *concorrenza —*, unfair competition; *giuoco —*, foul play; *persona —*, disloyal (*o* unfaithful) person.

slealménte, *av.* disloyally, unfaithfully; unfairly.

slealtà, *s.f.* disloyalty, unfaithfulness, unfairness.

slegaménto, *s.m.* untying, undoing, unfastening, loosening.

slegàre, *v.t.* to untie, to undo, to unfasten, to loosen: *gli slegò le mani*, he untied (*o* unbound) his hands; *— un nodo*, to untie a knot ‖ **slegàrsi,** *v.r.* to untie oneself, to get untied, to get undone; to loosen.

slegataménte, *av.* loosely.

slegàto, *ag.* **1.** untied, undone, loose **2.** (*non rilegato*) unbound: *un libro —*, an unbound book **3.** (*di discorso, ecc.*) disconnected, incoherent: *parole slegate*, disconnected words.

slegatúra, *s.f.* untying, undoing, loosening.

slembàre, *v.i.* to hang down.

slentàre, *v.i.* (*rar.*) to slacken.

Slèsia, *no.pr.f.* (*geog.*) Silesia.

slítta, *s.f.* **1.** sleigh, sledge: *cane da —*, sledge-dog (*o* husky); *andare in —*, to sleigh (*o* to sledge); *trasportare i viveri in —*, to sledge one's provisions **2.** (*artigl.*) chassis **3.** (*mec.*) slide; (*di pressa*) ram; (*di tornio*) saddle: *— portafresa*, cutter slide; *— portautensile*, toolslide (*o* cutter slide); *— trasversale*, cross slide.

slittaménto, *s.m.* **1.** skidding; sliding; (*aut.*) skid; (*aer.*) side slip: *indicatore di —*, (*ferr.*) wheel slip indicator **2.** (*mec.*) (*scorrimento*) slipping **3.** (*cine.*) (*di pellicola*) slippage.

slittàre, *v.i.* **1.** (*scivolare*) to skid, to slide; to slip: *l'automobile slittò sul ghiaccio*, the car skidded on the ice **2.** (*andare in slitta*) to sleigh, to sledge **3.** (*mec.*) (*di cinghia*) to slip.

slogaménto, *s.m.* dislocation.

slogàre, *v.t.,* **slogàrsi,** *v.r.* to dislocate: *si slogò un polso*, he dislocated his wrist.

slogàto, *ag.* dislocated.

slogatúra, *s.f.* dislocation.

sloggiàre, *v.t.* to dislodge, to drive out: *— il nemico*, to dislodge the enemy ‖ *v.i.* **1.** to clear out: *sloggia se non vuoi metterti nei pasticci*, clear out if you don't want to get into trouble **2.** (*mil.*) to decamp.

slombàre, *v.t.* **1.** to break s.o.'s back (*anche fig.*) **2.** *fig.* (*estenuare*) to wear out, to knock up, to knock out: *il peso di questa valigia mi ha slombato*, the weight of this suitcase has broken my back ‖ **slombàrsi,** *v.r.* to break one's back (anche *fig.*): *mi sono quasi slombato a portare questo pacco*, I have almost broken my back carrying this parcel.

Slovàcchia, *no.pr.f.* (*geog.*) Slovakia.

slovàceo, *ag.s.m.*, **slovàcca**, *s.f.* Slovak.

slovèno, *ag.* Slovenian ‖ *s.m.*, **slovèna**, *s.f.* Slovene, Slovenian.

slungàre, *v.t.* **1.** to prolong **2.** (*indumento*) to let down.

smaccàre, *v.t.* (*rar.*) to shame, to put to shame.

smaccàto, *ag.* sickly-sweet (anche *fig.*): *adulazioni smaccate*, sickening adulation; *vino* —, sickly-sweet wine.

smacchiàre, *v.t.* to clean, to remove the stains from (sthg.): — *un vestito*, to clean a dress.

smacchiatóre, *s.m.* stain-remover, spot-remover: — *a secco*, dry-cleaner.

smacchiatúra, *s.f.* cleaning: — *a secco*, dry-cleaning.

smàceo, *s.m.* mortification, let-down; (*fam.*) slap in the face: *il suo rifiuto fu un vero* — *per me*, his refusal was a real mortification (*o* let-down *o fam.* slap in the face) for me; *subire uno* —, to have a let -down.

smagliànte, *ag.* dazzling (anche *fig.*); shining: *colori smaglianti*, brilliant colours; *la sua* — *bellezza*, her dazzling beauty; *un sorriso* —, a dazzling smile.

smagliàre, *v.t.* **1.** to unravel; (*una catena*) to break the links of (a chain) **2.** (*togliere dalle maglie della rete*) to disentangle (a fish) **3.** (*arc.*) (*scoraggiare*) to discourage, to dishearten ‖ **smagliàrsi**, *v.r.* to break; (*di calze*) to ladder: *mi si è smagliata una calza*, I have got a ladder (*o amer.* a run) in my stocking; *questa catena si è smagliata*, this chain has broken; *queste calze si smagliano facilmente*, these stockings ladder easily.

smagliatúra, *s.f.* **1.** (*lacerazione delle maglie di una calza*) ladder; (*amer.*) run **2.** (*lesione della cute*) vibex (*pl.* vibices).

smagnetizzàre, *v.t.* (*elett.*) to demagnetize.

smagnetizzazióne, *s.f.* (*elett.*) demagnetization.

smagràre, **smagríre**, *V.* **dimagràre**.

smaliziàre, *v.t.* **1.** (*scaltrire*) to smarten up: *dobbiamo smaliziarlo, è troppo ingenuo per la sua età*, we must try and sharpen him up a bit, he is too ingenuous for his age **2.** (*rendere edotto, specialmente in materia sessuale*) to put (s.o.) wise to (sthg.).

smaliziàto, *ag.* **1.** (*scaltrito*) cunning, crafty, shrewd: *è* — *e non ha bisogno di consigli*, he is shrewd enough, he doesn't need any advice **2.** (*edotto, specialmente in materia sessuale*): *quella ragazza è troppo smaliziata per la sua età*, that girl is too knowing for her age.

smallàre, *v.t.* (*levare il mallo a, noci*) to shell (walnuts).

smaltàre, *v.t.* **1.** to enamel; (*ind. ceramica*) to glaze: — *a vetrino*, (*ind. ceramica*) to glaze; — *il ferro*, to enamel iron **2.** (*foto.*) (*lucidare*) to glaze: — *copie fotografiche*, to glaze prints **3.** *fig.* (*coprire*) to cover: *molti fiori rossi e gialli smaltavano il prato*, many red and yellow flowers covered the meadow ‖ **smaltàrsi**, *v.r.* to paint: — *le unghie*, to paint one's nails.

smaltatóre, *ag.* (*artig.*) enamelling ‖ *s.m.*, **smaltatríce**, *s.f.* (*artig.*) enameller, enamellist.

smaltatúra, *s.f.* **1.** enamelling; (*ind. ceramica*) glazing: — *a vetrino*, (*ind. ceramica*) glazing; *la* — *di questo pezzo è difettosa*, the enamelling of this piece is defective **2.** (*foto.*) (*lucidatura*) glazing.

smaltería, *s.f.* enamel factory.

smaltiménto, *s.m.* **1.** (*digestione*) digestion **2.** (*vendita*) sale; (*il disfarsi*) getting rid (of sthg.).

smaltíre, *v.t.* **1.** (*digerire*) to digest; *fig.* to swallow: *non riusciva a* — *il pasto sostanzioso*, he could not digest the substantial meal; *sono insulti che non si possono* —, such insults cannot be swallowed; — *la collera*, to get over one's anger ‖ — *la sbornia*, to get over one's drunkenness: *aveva la sbornia, ma la smaltì durante la notte*, he got drunk but he slept it off over-

night **2.** (*vendere*) to sell; to sell off; (*disfarsi di*) to get rid of (sthg.): *smaltì in poco tempo i fondi di magazzino*, he sold off his old stock quickly; — *una partita di olio, zucchero*, to sell off a lot of oil, sugar **3.** (*sfogare*) to drain: — *acque*, to drain water.

smaltísta, *s.m.* (*artig.*) enamellist, enameller.

smaltitóio, *s.m.* drain.

smàlto, *s.m.* **1.** enamel; (*ind. ceramica*) glaze: — *sintetico*, synthetic enamel; *lo* — *usato in ceramica*, the glaze used in ceramics; *metallo rivestito di* —, metal coated with enamel; *pentole di* —, enamelware; *vernice a* —, enamel paint; *verniciatura a* —, enamel painting ‖ — *da unghie*, nail-polish (*o* nail-varnish) **2.** (*oggetto smaltato*) enamel-work: *un pregevole* — *antico*, a valuable old piece of enamel **3.** (*anat.*) enamel: *lo* — *dei denti*, the enamel of the teeth **4.** (*calcestruzzo*) concrete.

smammolàrsi, *v.r.* to have a wonderful time ‖ — *dalle risa*, to split one's sides with laughing.

smancería, *s.f.* mawkishness: *non fare smancerie!*, don't be so mawkish!.

smanceróso, *ag.* mawkish.

smangiàre, *v.t.* to corrode; to eat away, to wear away, to eat into (sthg.): *gli acidi smangiano i metalli*, acids corrode (*o* eat into) metals; *l'acqua ha smangiato l'argine*, the water has eaten (*o* worn) the bank away; *le mie suole sono smangiate con tutto questo camminare*, my soles are worn out with all this walking ‖ **smangiàrsi**, *v.r.* (*fam.*) to fret, to worry ‖ — *il fegato*, to fret one's guts out.

smangiàto, *ag.* corroded; worn out: *queste suole sono smangiate*, these soles are worn out.

smània, *s.f.* **1.** great desire (for sthg.), longing (for sthg.), craving (for sthg.), eagerness (for sthg.): *ha una grande* — *di imparare l'inglese*, he is very eager to learn English; *ha* — *di successo, gloria, denaro*, he is eager (*o* thirsting *o* craving *o* longing) for success, glory, money; *ho una grande* — *di vederlo*, I have a great desire (*o* I am longing) to see him; *la sua* — *di ricchezza lo ha rovinato*, his thirst (*o* craving *o* desire) for riches has ruined him **2.** (*frenesia, agitazione*) frenzy: *ho avuto la* — *per tutta la notte*, I was restless (*o* tossing and turning) all night; *ho una* — *per tutto il corpo*, I am all on edge; *andare in smanie*, to get into a frenzy.

smaniàre, *v.i.* **1.** to yearn (for sthg.), to long (for sthg.), to crave (for sthg.): *egli smania di cambiare lavoro*, he is craving (*o* longing) for a new job; *smania sempre di parlare*, he is eager (*o* longing) to speak **2.** (*essere in agitazione*) to be restless; to chafe, to fret: *egli smania prima di addormentarsi*, he is always restless (*o* he always tosses about) before going to sleep; *non ho dormito molto, ho smaniato tutta la notte*, I didn't sleep much, I was tossing (and turning) about all night (*o* I was restless all night) ‖ *far* — *qlcu.*, to cause s.o. to rave.

smaniosaménte, *av.* eagerly.

smanióso, *ag.* **1.** eager (for sthg.), craving (for sthg.), thirsting (for, after sthg.): *è* — *di ricchezza*, he is eager (*o* craving *o* thirsting) for wealth; *sono* — *di vederlo*, I am eager to see him **2.** (*agitato*) restless.

smantellaménto, *s.m.* dismantling, dismantlement.

smantellàre, *v.t.* to dismantle: — *una fortezza, un naviglio*, to dismantle a fortress, a ship.

smargiassàre, *v.i.* to brag, to swagger.

smargiassàta, *s.f.* brag(ging), rodomontade, swagger.

smargiàsso, *s.m.* braggart, bully, blusterer, swashbuckler: *non fare lo* —, stop bragging.

smarginàre, *v.t.* to trim the edge of (sthg.); (*tip.*) to drop.

smarriménto, *s.m.* **1.** loss; (*disguido*) miscarriage: *lo* — *del pacco ha dato origine a grandi complicazioni*, the miscarriage of the parcel caused great complications **2.** (*confusione*) bewilderment; (*sbigottimento*) dismay **3.** (*svenimento*) fainting fit, swoon.

smarríre, *v.t.* **1.** to mislay: — *un ombrello, una*

penna, i guanti, to mislay an umbrella, a pen, one's gloves ‖ — *i sensi,* to lose one's senses ‖ — *lu strada,* to lose one's way 2. *(confondere, turbare)* to bewilder; *(sbigottire)* to dismay ‖ **smarrírsi,** *v.r.* 1. *(perdere la strada)* to lose one's way: *egli si smarrì fra i campi,* he lost his way (*o* got lost) among the fields 2. *(di lettera, pacco)* to miscarry 3. *(confondersi, turbarsi)* to be bewildered; *(sbigottirsi)* to be dismayed; *(confondersi)* to get confused: *a quella domanda egli si smarrì,* at that question he got confused; *a quella vista egli si smarrì,* when he saw that he got bewildered 4. *fig.* *(uscire dalla retta via)* to go astray, to stray 5. *(di colori, sbiadirsi)* to fade.

smarríto, *ag.* 1. mislaid; lost ‖ *pecorella smarrita, fig.* lost sheep ‖ *ufficio oggetti smarriti,* lost property office 2. *(sbigottito)* bewildered; *(spaventato)* dismayed, frightened: *aveva un'aria smarrita quando lo vidi,* he looked bewildered when I saw him.

smascellaménto, *s.m.* dislocation of the jaw.

smascellàrsi, *v.r.* to dislocate one's jaw ‖ — *dalle risa,* to split one's sides with laughter.

smascheraménto, *s.m.* unmasking.

smascheràre, *v.t.,* **smascheràrsi,** *v.r.* to unmask (anche *fig.*): *smascherò l'impostore,* he unmasked the impostor.

smatassàre, *v.t.* to unwind, to wind off.

smattonàre, *v.t.* to remove the bricks of (sthg.).

smelàre, *v.t.* to remove the honey from (the honey-combs).

smelensíto, *ag.* stupid, imbecile, weak-minded; *(di vecchio)* doting.

smembraménto, *s.m.* dismemberment (anche *fig.*): — *di una nazione,* dismemberment of a nation.

smembràre, *v.t.* to dismember (anche *fig.*), to split up (anche *fig.*): — *un paese,* to split up a country ‖ **smembràrsi,** *v.r.* to get dismembered, to split up: *la famiglia si è smembrata,* the family has split up.

smemoràre, *v.i.* (rar.) 1. *(perdere la memoria)* to lose one's memory 2. *(diventare stupido)* to become stupid.

smemoratàggine, *s.f.* 1. *(mancanza di memoria)* lack of memory, forgetfulness 2. *(dimenticanza)* lapse of memory.

smemoràto, *ag.* 1. forgetful; *(distratto)* absent-minded 2. *(stupido, insensato)* stupid.

smentíre, *v.t.* to deny; to disprove; to belie, to give the lie to (s.o.): *egli smentì tutto quel che aveva detto,* he denied all he had said; *i fatti lo smentirono,* facts gave him the lie; *le sue azioni smentiscono le sue parole,* his actions belie his words; — *una notizia,* to deny a piece of news ‖ — *se stesso,* to be untrue to oneself ‖ **smentírsi,** *v.r.* 1. to contradict oneself, to give oneself the lie: *egli si smentì senza volerlo,* he gave himself the lie without wishing to 2. *(venir meno)* to be untrue to oneself: *egli non si è mai smentito,* he has never been untrue to himself.

smentíta, *s.f.* denial; refutation: *i fatti diedero una* — *a quel che aveva detto,* the facts disproved what he had said; *dare una* — *a qlcu.,* to give s.o. the lie.

smeraldíno, *ag.* emerald green.

smeràldo, *s.m.* 1. emerald 2. *(colore)* emerald (green).

smerciàbile, *ag.* saleable, sellable.

smerciàre, *v.t.* *(vendere)* to sell; *(sbolognare)* to sell off: — *merce rubata,* to sell stolen goods.

smèrcio, *s.m.* sale: *trovare, avere* —, to sell: *questo articolo non trova facile* —, this article doesn't sell easily.

smèrgo, *s.m.* *(ornit.)* merganser.

smerigliàre, *v.t.* to polish with emery; *(mec.)* to grind, to lap; *(microfinire)* to hone: — *a nastro,* to linish; — *le valvole,* to grind the valves; — *il vetro,* to frost glass.

smerigliàto, *ag.* emery *(attributivo)*; *(mec.)* ground, lapped; *(carta smerigliata,* emery paper; *superficie smerigliata,* lapped surface; *vetro* —, frosted glass.

smerigliatríce, *s.f.* 1. *(macchina utensile)* lapping

machine; grinder; *(microfinitrice)* honing machine; *(a nastro)* linisher, linishing machine 2. *(macchina per la finitura del legno)* sanding machine, sander, sand-papering machine; *(a nastro)* belt sander, belt sanding machine 3. *(per pellicola)* film polishing machine.

smerigliatúra, *s.f.* 1. polishing with emery; *(mec.)* lapping, grinding; *(microfinitura)* honing: — *a getto di acqua,* vapour blasting; — *a nastro,* linishing; — *degli ingranaggi,* gear lapping 2. *(carpenteria)* sanding, sandpapering.

smeríglio, *s.m.* *(min.)* emery: *lima a* —, emery stick; *mola a* —, emery wheel; *polvere di* —, emery dust; *tela* —, emery cloth.

smerlàre, *v.t.* to border with scallops; to scallop.

smerlatúra, *s.f.* scallop-edging.

smerlettàre, *v.t.* to scallop.

smèrlo, *s.m.* scallop: *punto a* —, buttonhole stitch.

smésso, *ag.* cast off: *abito* —, cast-off dress.

sméttere, *v.t.* to stop, to leave off; to give up: *devi — di fumare,* you must give up smoking; *smetti di raccontare fandonie,* stop telling fibs; *smetti di scherzare, di piangere,* stop joking, crying; *smetto di lavorare alle cinque,* I stop (*o* leave off) work at five o'clock ‖ *smettila!,* stop it! (*o* leave off!) ‖ — *casa,* to give up one's house ‖ — *un vestito,* to cast off a dress.

smezzaménto, *s.m.* halving.

smezzàre, *v.t.* 1. to halve, to cut in half: — *un panino,* to cut a roll in half 2. *(interrompere)* to interrupt.

smidollàre, *v.t.* to take the marrow out of (sthg.): — *un osso,* to take the marrow out of a bone ‖ **smidollàrsi,** *v.r.* to lose one's strength, to grow weak.

smidollàto, *ag.* 1. *(cavo)* hollow 2. *(di persona, fiacco, imbelle)* spineless.

smilitarizzàre, *v.t.* *(una zona)* to demilitarize; *(una persona)* demobilize; *(fam.)* to demob.

smilitarizzazióne, *s.f.* *(di zona)* demilitarization; *(di persona)* demobilization; *(fam.)* demob.

smilzo, *ag.* thin, lean: *ragazzo* —, thin boy.

sminchioníre, *v.i.* *(volg.)* to come to one's wits, to stop acting the fool.

sminuíre, *v.t.* to diminish, to lessen: *quell'azione sminuì la sua fama,* that action diminished his fame ‖ **sminuírsi,** *v.r.* to belittle oneself: *non ti* —!, don't belittle yourself!.

sminuzzaménto, *s.m.* mincing, cutting into little pieces.

sminuzzàre, *v.t.* *(tritare)* to mince, to hash; *(tagliuzzare)* to chop up; *(sbriciolare)* to crumble; to break up.

Smírne, *no.pr.f.* *(geog.)* Smyrna.

smirniòta, *ag.s.c.* Smyrnean, Smyrniote.

smistaménto, *s.m.* 1. clearing: *ospedale di* —, clearing hospital; *posto di* —, *(mil.)* clearing station 2. *(ferr.)* shunting; *(amer.)* switching: *stazione di* —, shunting station 3. *(di corrispondenza)* sorting.

smistàre, *v.t.* 1. to sort (out): — *le lettere,* to sort (out) letters 2. *(ferr.)* to shunt; *(amer.)* to switch 3. *(mil.)* to post: — *un reggimento,* to post a regiment.

smisuratamónte, *av.* beyond measure; immeasurably; immensely, enormously, hugely.

smisuratézza, *s.f.* immeasurability, immeasurableness; immensity; enormousness, hugeness.

smisuràto, *ag.* immeasurable, unbounded; immense; enormous, huge; *(smoderato)* inordinate: *ambizione smisurata,* unbounded ambition; *orgoglio* —, inordinate pride.

smobiliàre, *v.t.* to remove the furniture from (a place).

smobiliàto, *ag.* unfurnished.

smobilitàre, *v.t.* *(mil.)* to demobilize; *(fam.)* to demob.

smobilitazióne, *s.f.* *(mil.)* demobilization; *(fam.)* demob.

smocciàre, *v.t.* to wipe s.o.'s nose.

smoccolàre, *v.t.* to snuff: — *una candela,* to snuff a candle ‖ *v.i.* *(fam. scherz.)* to swear.

smoccolatóio, *s.m.* snuffers *(pl.)*.

smoccolatúra, *s.f.* **1.** (*parte di candela già arsa*) snuff **2.** (*lo smoccolare*) snuffing.

smodàre, *v.i.* to exceed, to go beyond the limit: — *nel lavorare*, to overwork; — *nel mangiare*, to overeat.

smodataménte, *av.* immoderately, excessively.

smodàto, *ag.* immoderate, excessive.

smoderataménte, *av.* immoderately, excessively.

smoderatézza, *s.f.* immoderateness, immoderation, excessiveness; excess; exaggeration; intemperance: *beve con* —, he drinks to excess; *la* — *delle sue pretese*, the immoderateness of his demands.

smoderàto, *ag.* immoderate, excessive.

smoking, *s.m.* dinner-jacket; (*amer.*) tuxedo.

smonacàre, *v.t.* to dismiss from a monastic order || **smonacàrsi,** *v.r.* to leave a monastic order.

smontàggio, *s.m.* (*mec.*) disassembly: — *di motori*, disassembly of engines; — *generale*, strip(ping).

smontaménto, *s.m.* (*mec.*) disassembly.

smontàre, *v.t.* **1.** (*far scendere*) (*da cavallo*) to unhorse, to unseat; (*da un'automobile*) to drop: *puoi smontarmi qui*, you can drop me here **2.** (*scomporre in parti*) to take down, to take to pieces; (*una porta*) to unhang, to unhinge; (*una gemma*) to unset; (*mec.*) to disassemble, to dismantle: — *un diamante*, to unset a diamond; — *l'impianto di pompaggio*, (*min.*) to pull the well; — *un motore*, to dismantle an engine; — *un orologio*, to take a watch to pieces **3.** *fig.* (*deprimere, scoraggiare*) to dishearten, to discourage; to cool; to damp: *avevo molta speranza, ma questo insuccesso mi ha smontato*, I had great hopes but this failure had disheartened me; *è molto presuntuoso, cercherò di smontarlo*, he is very self-conceited, I shall try to take him down a peg; *lavora con tanta fiducia che non ho il coraggio di smontarlo*, he works with so much confidence that I have not the courage to dishearten him; *non si lascia — facilmente*, he isn't easily discouraged (*o* disheartened); *quando ha deciso ql.co. non è facile smontarlo*, when he has decided sthg. it is not easy to discourage him; — *l'orgoglio di qlcu.*, to cool s.o.'s pride; — *la speranza di qlcu.*, to dampen s.o.'s hopes; — *lo zelo di qlcu.*, to dampen s.o.'s zeal || *v.i.* **1.** (*da un treno, autobus, tram, ecc.*) to get off, to alight (from sthg.); (*da un'automobile*) to get out (of sthg.); (*da cavallo*) to dismount || — *dal servizio*, to go off duty **2.** (*sbiadire*) to fade: *questi colori non smontano*, these colours do not fade || **smontàrsi,** *v.r.* to cool down: *si eccita facilmente, ma poi si smonta subito*, he easily gets excited but then he cools down at once.

smontatúra, *s.f.* (*mec.*) disassembly.

smórfia, *s.f.* **1.** grimace, wry face: *fare una* —, to make a grimace (*o* a face) (*o* to pull a wry face); *fare smorfie a qlcu.*, to pull (*o* to make) faces at s.o.; *fare una — di dolore*, to wince with pain || *perchè tante smorfie?*, (*svenevolezze*) why so much mincing?; (*storie*) why so much fuss? || *non fare troppe smorfie a questo bambino, se non vuoi viziarlo*, don't pet this child too much if you don't want to spoil him **2.** (*dial.*) "smorfia" (book for the interpretation of dreams).

smorfiosaménte, *av.* affectedly, mincingly.

smorfióso, *ag.* affected, mincing.

smòrto, *ag.* pale, wan; colourless: — —, deadly pale: *diventò* — —, he grew deadly pale; *colore* —, pale (*o* dead) colour; *viso* —, pale face; *egli era molto* —, he was very pale.

smorzaménto, *s.m.* **1.** (*attenuamento*) (*di luce*) shading; dimming; (*di colori*) toning down; (*di suoni*) deadening, lowering; (*di sete*) quenching **2.** *fig.* (*di passioni, sentimenti*) quenching, appeasing; damping **3.** (*spegnimento*) putting out; extinguishing.

smorzàre, *v.t.* **1.** (*attenuare*) (*luce*) to shade; to dim; (*colori*) to tone down; (*suoni*) to deaden, to lower: *in questo quadro i rossi vanno smorzati*, in this picture the reds must be toned down; *per — questa luce violenta devi chiudere le imposte*, in order to soften this harsh light you must close the shutters; — *l'appetito*, to

lessen the appetite; — *la sete*, to quench one's thirst; — *un suono*, to deaden a sound; — *la voce, il tono di voce*, to lower one's voice **2.** (*passioni, sentimenti*) to quench, to appease; to damp: — *l'ira, la collera di qlcu.*, to appease s.o.'s anger; — *le speranze*, to damp hopes **3.** (*spegnere*) to put out; to extinguish: — *il fuoco*, to put out (*o* to quench) the fire; — *un incendio*, to extinguish a fire; — *il lume, la luce*, to put out the light || — *la calce*, to slake lime **4.** (*fis.*) to damp(-en) || **smorzàrsi,** *v.r.* **1.** (*attenuarsi*) to grow fainter; to die away, to fade (away): *il colore del cielo si smorzava*, the colour of the sky was dying away; *la luce si smorza*, the light is growing fainter; *il rumore si smorzò*, the noise grew fainter **2.** (*di passioni, sentimenti*) to be appeased, to fade: *la sua ira si è smorzata*, his anger has been appeased; *le sue speranze si smorzeranno a questa notizia*, his hopes will fade at this news; *il suo entusiasmo si smorzò a quelle parole*, those words damped his enthusiasm **3.** (*spegnersi*) to go out: *il fuoco si è smorzato*, the fire has gone out.

smorzatúra, *s.f.* (*di colori*) toning down; (*di suoni*) deadening, lowering.

smòrzo, *s.m.* (*mus.*) damper, mute.

smòsso, *ag.* **1.** shifted, displaced: *oggetti smossi*, displaced things || *terra smossa*, turned soil **2.** (*malfermo, tentennante*) loose: *denti smossi*, loose teeth.

smòtta, *s.f.*, **smottaménto,** *s.m.* landslip, landslide.

smottàre, *v.i.* to slip, to slide down.

smottatúra, *s.f.* landslip, landslide.

smozzàre, *v.t.* to cut off, to lop off.

smozzicaménto, *s.m.* **1.** pitting; tearing to pieces; hacking to pieces **2.** (*di parole*) swallowing; (*di discorsi*) mumble.

smozzicàre, *v.t.* **1.** to pit; to tear to pieces; to hack to pieces: *i muri erano smozzicati dalle granate*, the walls were pitted by shrapnels; *il suo viso era smozzicato dal vaiuolo*, his face was pitted by the smallpox; *usa un coltello più affilato, stai smozzicando la torta!*, use a sharper knife, you are hacking the cake to pieces! **2.** (*parole*) to swallow; (*discorsi*) to mumble: — *le parole*, to swallow one's syllables.

smozzicàto, *ag.* **1.** pitted; torn to pieces; hacked to pieces: *mura smozzicate*, pitted walls **2.** (*di parole, discorsi*) broken.

smozzicatúra, *s.f.* **1.** pitting; tearing to pieces; hacking to pieces **2.** (*di parole*) swallowing; (*di discorsi*) mumble.

smúngere, *v.t.* **1.** *fig.* to fleece; (*esaurire*) to bleed dry: — *i cittadini con le tasse*, to bleed the citizens dry with taxes; — *denaro a qlcu.*, to fleece s.o. **2.** (*prosciugare*) to drain, to dry up.

smúnto, *ag.* (*pallido*) pale, wan; (*emaciato*) emaciated, lean: *colori smunti*, pale (*o* dead) colours; *viso* —, pale (*o* wan) face; (*emaciato*) emaciated face.

smuòvere, *v.t.* **1.** to shift, to displace; to move: *hanno smosso l'armadio per imbiancare la parete*, they shifted the cupboard to whitewash the wall; *non riuscirono a — il masso*, they could not move (*o* shift) the boulder; *questi arnesi non devono essere smossi*, this equipment must not be moved || — *l'intestino*, to loosen the bowels || — *il terreno*, to turn the ground **2.** *fig.* (*dissuadere*) to dissuade, to deter, to move: *non riuscimmo a smuoverlo dal suo proposito*, we could not move him from his determination; *se ha deciso, è difficile smuoverlo*, once he has made up his mind it is difficult to dissuade (*o* to deter) him **3.** *fig.* (*commuovere*) to move, to affect, to touch: *le vostre preghiere non lo smuoveranno*, your prayers will not move (*o* touch) him || **smuòversi,** *v.r.* **1.** to move: *per quanti sforzi facessero, il macigno non si smosse*, despite their efforts the boulder would not move **2.** *fig.* (*mutar proposito*) to change one's mind, to be diverted: *non si smosse dalla sua decisione*, he did not change his mind (*o* he was not diverted from his resolution) **3.** *fig.* (*commuoversi*) to be moved, to be touched, to be affected: *non si smosse alle loro lacrime*, he was not moved by their tears.

smuràre, *v.t.* to unwall.

smussaménto, *s.m.* **1.** rounding off, blunting, bevelling **2.** *fig.* (*attenuazione*) softening, smoothing.

smussàre, *v.t.* **1.** to round off, to blunt, to bevel: — *gli angoli*, to round off the corners **2.** *fig.* (*attenuare*) to soften, to smooth ‖ **smussàrsi**, *v.r.* (*di lame*) to get blunt.

smussàto, *ag.* **1.** blunted, bevelled; (*rotondo*) round **2.** *fig.* (*attenuato*) softened, smoothed.

smussatúra, *s.f.*, **smússo**, *s.m.* blunting, bevelling.

snaturaménto, *s.m.* **1.** change of nature; (*in senso deteriore*) perversion **2.** (*cambiamento*) change.

snaturàre, *v.t.* **1.** to pervert the nature of (s.o., sthg.): *dottrine che snaturano l'uomo*, doctrines which pervert the nature of man **2.** *fig.* (*alterare*) to change, to alter, to pervert: — *un fatto*, to misrepresent a fact ‖ **snaturàrsi**, *v.r.* to degenerate.

snaturaménte, *av.* cruelly, inhumanly.

snaturatézza, *s.f.* cruelty, inhumanity.

snaturàto, *ag.* **1.** unnatural, inhuman, heartless: *una madre snaturata*, an unnatural mother **2.** (*alieno dalla propria natura*) perverted.

snazionalizzàre, *v.t.* to denationalize.

snazionalizzazióne, *s.f* denationalization.

snebbiàre, *v.t.* **1.** to dispel the fog from (a place), to clear (a place) of fog **2.** *fig.* to clear: — *la mente*, *le idee*, to clear the mind, one's ideas ‖ **snebbiàrsi**, *v.r.* to clear (up): *il cielo si snebbiò*, the sky cleared (up).

snellaménte, *av.* **1.** (*slanciatamente*) slenderly **2.** (*agilmente*) nimbly.

snellézza, *s.f.* **1.** (*l'essere slanciato*) slenderness, slimness **2.** (*agilità*) nimbleness, agility.

snèllo, *ag.* **1.** (*slanciato*) slender, slim: *una colonna snella*, a slender column; *è una ragazza piuttosto snella*, she is a rather slim (o slender) girl **2.** (*agile*) nimble, agile: *dita snelle*, nimble fingers **3.** (*di stile*) easy.

snellìre, *v.t.* **1.** to make slender **2.** *fig.* (*semplificare*) to simplify ‖ **snellìrsi**, *v.r.* to grow slender, to grow slim.

snervaménto, *s.m.* enervation.

snervànte, *ag.* enervating; exhausting: *clima* —, enervating climate; *un lavoro* —, an exhausting work.

snervàre, *v.t.* to enervate, to debilitate, to enfeeble; (*esaurire*) to exhaust, to wear out: *un clima che snerva*, an enervating climate; *il lavoro mi ha snervato*, work has worn me out ‖ **snervàrsi**, *v.r.* to be enervated; (*esaurirsi*) to get exhausted.

snervataménte, *av.* weakly, feebly; (*fiaccamente*) wearily.

snervatézza, *s.f.* enervation, weakness, feebleness; (*fiacchezza*) weariness.

snervàto, *ag.* enervate(d), weak, feeble; (*fiacco*) weary; (*esaurito*) exhausted, worn out.

snidàre, *v.t.* to flush; to drive out, to dislodge (anche *fig.*): — *un animale*, to flush (o to put up) an animal; — *il nemico*, to dislodge the enemy.

snob, *s.c.* snob.

snobìsmo, *s.m.* snobbery, snobbishness.

snocciolàre, *v.t.* **1.** to stone, to remove the stone from (sthg.): — *le ciliegie*, to stone cherries **2.** *fig.* (*sborsare*) to pay out: *dovetti* — *un mucchio di denaro*, I had to pay out a lot of money **3.** *fig.* (*spiattellare*) to tell, to speak: — *tutta la verità*, to tell the whole truth **4.** (*pronunciare di seguito*): — *le preghiere*, to say one's prayers; — *il rosario*, to say the Rosary.

snodaménto, *s.m.* untying, unbinding.

snodàre, *v.t.* **1.** (*disfare il nodo di, sciogliere*) to untie; to loosen; to unbind ‖ — *la lingua*, to loosen one's tongue **2.** (*rendere agile*) to make supple: *è un movimento per* — *le giunture*, it is an exercise for loosening stiff joints; — *le membra*, to make one's limbs more supple ‖ **snodàrsi**, *v.r.* **1.** to get untied; to get unbound **2.** (*di strada*) to wind: *la strada si snoda lungo la valle*, the road winds along the valley.

snodàto, *ag.* **1.** supple: *dita, giunture snodate*, supple fingers, joints **2.** (*da potersi piegare, articolare* jointed: *una bambola snodata*, a jointed doll.

snodatúra, *s.f.* (*articolazione delle giunture*) joint.

snudàre, *v.t.* **1.** (*denudare*) to bare, to lay bare **2.** (*sguainare*) to unsheathe, to draw: — *la spada*, to draw one's sword.

soàve, *ag.* sweet, soft, gentle: *colori soavi*, soft colours; *musica* —, soft music; *odore* —, sweet smell; *sguardo* —, gentle look; *vino* —, sweet wine; *voce* —, sweet (o gentle) voice.

soaveménte, *av.* sweetly, softly, gently.

soavità, *s.f.* sweetness, softness, gentleness.

soavizzàre, *v.t.* to soften, to sweeten.

sobbalzàre, *v.i.* **1.** to jerk, to jolt: *la carrozza procedeva sobbalzando*, the coach was jerking (o jolting) along; *la macchina sobbalzò nel fermarsi*, the car stopped with a jerk **2.** (*trasalire*) to start: *sobbalzai al suono della sua voce*, I started at the sound of his voice; *sobbalzò di paura quando lo vide*, he started with fear when he saw him ‖ *il cuore mi sobbalzò dalla gioia*, my heart leapt up with joy.

sobbàlzo, *s.m.* **1.** jerk, jolt: *il treno si fermò con un* —, the train stopped with a jerk; *procedere a sobbalzi*, to jerk (o to jolt) along **2.** (*sussulto*) start ‖ *di* —, with a start: *svegliarsi di* —, to wake up with a start.

sobbarcàrsi, *v.r.* to take (it) upon oneself, to undertake: *non posso sobbarcarmi all'impegno di farlo*, I cannot take it upon myself to do it (o I can't undertake to do it); *si è sobbarcato alle spese di tutto*, he has taken it upon himself to pay for everything.

sobbolliménto, *s.m.* simmer; simmering (anche *fig.*).

sobbollìre, *v.i.* to simmer (anche *fig.*).

sobbórgo, *s.m.* suburb: *vivo nei sobborghi di Parigi*, I live in the suburbs of Paris.

sobillaménto, *s.m.* stirring up, instigation, incitement.

sobillàre, *v.t.* to stir up, to instigate, to incite: — *il popolo alla rivolta*, to stir up (o to incite) the people to rebellion.

sobillatóre, *s.m.*, **sobillatríce**, *s.f.* instigator.

sobriaménte, *av.* soberly, moderately (anche *fig.*).

sobrietà, *s.f.* sobriety, moderation (anche *fig.*): — *di parole*, sobriety (o moderation) of words.

sòbrio, *ag.* **1.** sober, moderate (anche *fig.*): *colori sobri*, sober colours; *è un uomo* —, he is a sober (o temperate) man **2.** (*semplice*) simple, sober: *gusti sobri*, simple tastes; *vita sobria*, simple life.

socchiúdere, *v.t.* **1.** (*chiudere non completamente*) to half-close **2.** (*aprire un po'*) to half-open, to leave ajar.

socchiúso, *ag.* half-open, half-closed; (*detto di porta, finestra, ecc.*) ajar: *con gli occhi socchiusi*, with half-open eyes; *la finestra era socchiusa*, the window was ajar.

sòccida, *s.f.* (*dir.*) agistment.

sòccio, *s.m.* agistor.

sòcco, *s.m.* (*st. teat.*) sock ‖ *calzare il* —, to write plays.

soccómbere, *v.i.* **1.** to succumb, to give way; to be overcome (by sthg.): — *al dolore, alle tentazioni*, to succumb to grief, to temptation; — *alla forza del nemico*, to yield to (o to be overcome by) the strength of the enemy **2.** (*morire*) to die, to succumb.

soccórrere, *v.t.* **1.** to succour, to assist, to help, to relieve: — *i feriti*, to succour the wounded; — *i poveri*, to assist (o to relieve) the poor **2.** (*mandare rinforzi a*) to succour, to reinforce: — *gli assediati*, to reinforce (o to succour) the besieged ‖ *v.i.* (*letter.*) (*venire alla mente*) to occur, to come to mind: *mi soccorse il ricordo di lei*, the memory of her came to my mind; *non mi soccorse il nome*, the name did not occur to me ‖ **soccórrersi**, *v.r. reciproco* to succour each other (one another), to assist each other (one another).

soccorrévole, *ag.* helpful; helping; (*caritatevole*) charitable: *una mano* —, a helping hand.

soccorrevolménte, *av.* helpfully; *(caritatevolmente)* charitably.

soccorritóre, *s.m.,* **soccorritríce,** *s.f.* succourer.

soccórso, *s.m.* **1.** help, aid, succour, assistance, relief: *invocazione di* —, call for help; *andare al* — *di qlcu.,* to go to s.o.'s rescue; *domandare* —, to ask for help; *gridare al* —, to call (*o* to cry) for help; *portare* —, to bring help (*o* to give *o* to lend assistance) ‖ *uscita di* —, emergency door (*o* emergency exit) **2.** (*med.*) aid: *primo* —, first aid; *pronto* —, *posto di pronto* —, first aid station **3.** (*rinforzo*) reinforcement: *andare in* — *di un battaglione, una nave,* to go in support of a battalion, of a ship; *attendere i soccorsi,* to wait for reinforcements **4.** (*sovvenzione*) (financial) assistance: — *ai poveri,* poor assistance ‖ *società di mutuo* —, friendly society.

soccòscio, *s.m.* rump.

sociàbile, *ag.* (*letter.*) sociable.

sociabilità, *s.f.* (*letter.*) sociability.

sociabilménte, *av.* (*letter.*) sociably.

socialdemocràtico, *ag.* (*pol.*) socialdemocratic ‖ *s.m.* (*pol.*) social democrat.

socialdemocrazia, *s.f.* (*pol.*) socialdemocratic party.

sociàle, *ag.* **1.** social: *assistente* —, social worker; *ceto* —, social standing; *classi sociali,* social classes; *contratto* —, social contract; *ordine* —, social order; *relazioni sociali,* social relations; *scienze sociali,* social sciences; *l'uomo è un animale* —, man is a social animal ‖ *le guerre sociali,* (*st. romana*) the Social Wars **2.** (*comm.*) of the firm, of the company, registered: *anno* —, company's (trading) year; *capitale* —, registered capital; *proprietà* —, corporate property; *ragione* —, style of the firm (*o* of the company); *sede* —, head office; *statuto* —, articles of association.

socialísmo, *s.m.* (*pol.*) Socialism.

socialísta, *s.m.* (*pol.*) Socialist.

socialístico, *ag.* (*pol.*) Socialist, Socialistic: *dottrine socialistiche,* Socialist doctrines.

socialistòide, *s.m.* near-socialist.

socialità, *s.f.* sociality.

socializzàre, *v.t.* to socialize.

socializzazióne, *s.f.* socialization.

socialménte, *av.* socially.

società, *s.f.* **1.** society, community: *la* — *moderna,* modern society; *la* — *umana,* human society; *certi costumi offendono l'intera* —, certain customs are repugnant to the whole of society; *ogni individuo ha dei doveri verso la* —, everyone has duties towards society (*o* the community); *essere in lotta con la* —, to be at war with society; *essere tagliato fuori dalla* —, to be cut off from society; *vivere ai margini della* —, to live on the fringe of society ‖ *la* — *elegante,* the fashionable world; *l'alta* —, high society ‖ *la* — *operaia,* the working class ‖ *i rifiuti della* —, the outcasts of society **2.** (*associazione*) society, association: — *filantropica, letteraria,* philanthropic, literary society; — *per la protezione degli animali,* Society for the Prevention of Cruelty to Animals; — *segreta,* secret society; — *sportiva,* sports society ‖ *Società delle Nazioni,* (*st.*) League of Nations **3.** (*comm.*) company; partnership: — *anonima,* joint-stock company: — *anonima a responsabilità illimitata,* joint-stock company with unlimited liability; — *anonima a responsabilità limitata al capitale,* limited (liability) company; *costituire una* — *anonima,* to form a joint-stock company; — *cooperativa,* cooperative society; — *d'assicurazione,* insurance company: — *d'assicurazione contro gli incendi,* fire-insurance company; — *d'assicurazione sulla vita,* life-assurance company; — *di navigazione, ferroviaria,* shipping, railway company; — *edilizia,* building society; — *in accomandita,* limited partnership; — *in nome collettivo,* general partnership; — *per azioni,* joint-stock company; *entrare in* — *con qlcu.,* to enter into partnership with s.o.; *formare, sciogliere, liquidare una* —, to form, to dissolve, to wind up a partnership;

ritirarsi da una —, to withdraw from a partnership ‖ *fare* —, (*fam.*) to share **4.** (*riunione, ritrovo elegante*) society: *abito da, di* —, evening dress; (*da uomo*) (*smoking*) dinner jacket (*o amer.* tuxedo); (*frac*) evening dress; *giuochi di* —, parlour games; *vita di* —, social life; *non mi trovo a mio agio in* —, I don't feel at ease in society; *frequentare la* —, to move in society.

societàrio, *ag.* (*comm.*) social.

sociévole, *ag.* sociable, companionable, social: *una persona molto* —, a good mixer; *l'uomo è un animale* —, man is a social animal.

socievolézza, *s.f.* sociability, sociableness.

socievolménte, *av.* sociably.

socinianísmo, *s.m.* (*st. relig.*) Socinianism.

sociniàno, *ag.s.m.* (*st. relig.*) Socinian.

sòcio, *s.m.* **1.** member: — *a vita,* life member; — *onorario,* honorary member; *un vecchio* — *del Club,* an old member of the Club; *farsi* — *di un circolo,* to become a member of a club **2.** (*di una società scientifica, accademia*) fellow: *un* — *dell'Accademia Reale,* a fellow of the Royal Academy **3.** (*comm.*) partner, associate: — *accomandante,* special (*o* limited) partner; — *accomandatario,* unlimited partner; — *anziano,* senior partner; — *di industria,* working partner; — *entrante,* incoming partner; — *nominale,* nominal partner; — *occulto,* sleeping (*o* silent *o* dormant) partner; — *ordinario,* active (*o* ordinary) partner; *fui suo* — *in varie iniziative,* I was his associate in several undertakings; *entrare come* — *in una ditta,* to enter a firm as a partner.

sociología, *s.f.* sociology.

sociologicaménte, *av.* sociologically.

sociològico, *ag.* sociological.

sociòlogo, *s.m.* sociologist.

Sòcrate, *no.pr.m.* (*st. fil.*) Socrates.

socraticaménte, *av.* (*fil.*) Socratically.

socràtico, *ag.* (*fil.*) Socratic(al): *ironia socratica,* Socratic irony; *metodo* —, Socratic method ‖ *s.m.* (*fil.*) Socratic.

sòda, *s.f.* **1.** (*chim.*) soda; (*carbonato di sodio*) sodium carbonate: — *caustica,* caustic soda (*o* sodium hydroxide); — *per lavare,* washing soda; *acqua di* —, soda(-water); *bicarbonato di* —, sodium bicarbonate (*o* bicarbonate of soda) **2.** (*min.*) natron.

sodàglia, *s.f.* unbroken ground.

sodàle, *s.m.* (*letter.*) companion, fellow-member.

sodalízio, *s.m.* **1.** (*società*) society, association **2.** (*confraternita*) brotherhood, confraternity: *pio* —, sodality.

sodaménte, *av.* (*fortemente*) hard.

sodàre, *v.t.* **1.** (*consolidare*) to consolidate; *rafforzare*) to strengthen **2.** (*ind. tessile*) to full.

sodatríce, *s.f.* (*ind. tessile*) fuller.

soddisfacènte, *ag.* satisfactory: *i progressi di quello studente sono soddisfacenti,* that pupil's progress is satisfactory.

soddisfacenteménte, *av.* satisfactorily.

soddisfaciménto, *s.m.* **1.** satisfaction; gratification **2.** (*adempimento*) fulfilment, discharge.

soddisfàre, *v.t.* **1.** to satisfy; to gratify: *è difficile* — *tutti,* it is difficult to please everybody; *non devi* — *tutti i suoi capricci,* you must not gratify all his whims; *questo lavoro non mi soddisfa,* this work does not satisfy me; *spero di* — *le tue speranze, aspettative,* I hope to fulfil your hopes, expectations; — *i desideri, la curiosità di qlcu.,* to satisfy (*o* to gratify) s.o.'s wishes, curiosity; — *la propria fame,* to satisfy one's hunger **2.** (*adempiere, far fronte a*) to fulfil, to meet, to discharge: *non poteva* — *i suoi debiti,* he was unable to discharge his debts; *siamo dolenti di non poter* — *i vostri desideri,* we are sorry not to be able to meet your wishes; — *un conto,* to meet a bill; — *un creditore,* to satisfy (*o* to pay off) a creditor; — *un debito,* to discharge a debt; — *una domanda,* to comply with a request; — *un obbligo,* to fulfil (*o* to discharge) an obligation **3.** (*riparare*) to make amends for (sthg.) ‖

v.i. to fulfil (sthg.), to discharge (sthg.): — *a un dovere,* to discharge (o to fulfil) a duty || **soddisfàrsi,** *v.r.* to be satisfied; to satisfy oneself.

soddisfàtto, *ag.* **1.** satisfied (with s.o., sthg.); pleased (with s.o., sthg.), contented (with sthg.); content (with sthg.) (*predicativo*): *sorriso —,* pleased smile; *aveva uno sguardo —,* he had a contented look (o he looked contented); *non ne sono —,* I am not pleased (o content) with it; *non sono soddisfatta della tua spiegazione,* I am not satisfied with your explanation; *non sono — del mio lavoro,* I am not pleased (o content) with my work; *sarebbe molto — di essere lasciato a casa,* he would be quite satisfied to be left at home; *sono molto — di lui,* I am very pleased (o satisfied) with him || *mal —,* dissatisfied **2.** (*pagato*) paid up: *debito —,* paid up debt.

soddisfazióne, *s.f.* satisfaction: *la — dei propri desideri,* the satisfaction (o gratification) of one's wishes; *con mia grande —,* to my great satisfaction; *ciò fu di grande — per me,* this was a great satisfaction to me; *ho provato molta — nel farlo,* I have found great satisfaction in doing it; *quel bambino è di grande — per sua madre,* that child is a great comfort to his mother; *questo mi dà molta —,* this gives me great satisfaction || *dare —,* (*in una contesa*) to give satisfaction; *domandare — per un'offesa,* to demand satisfaction for an offence.

sodézza, *s.f.* **1.** (*solidità*) solidity, firmness; consistency; (*durezza*) hardness; (*compattezza*) compactness **2.** (*densità*) thickness **3.** (*serietà*) seriousness, soundness; (*ponderatezza*) consideration.

sòdico, *ag.* (*chim.*) sodic; sodium (*attributivo*).

sòdio, *s.m.* (*chim.*) sodium: *bicarbonato di —,* sodium bicarbonate (o bicarbonate of soda); *cianuro di —,* sodium cyanide; *cloruro di —,* sodium chloride; *nitrato di —,* sodium nitrate; *perborato di —,* perborax; *silicato di —,* sodium silicate (o soluble glass o water-glass).

sodisfàre, e derivati, V. **soddisfàre, e derivati.**

sòdo, *ag.* **1.** (*solido*) solid, firm; (*duro*) hard; (*massiccio*) massive; (*compatto*) compact: *carni sode,* firm flesh; *muro —,* massive wall; *muscoli sodi,* firm muscles; *uova sode,* hard-boiled eggs; *questo budino non è abbastanza —,* this pudding is not hard enough || *star —,* (*non cedere*) to stand firm **2.** (*di terreno non lavorato*) unbroken **3.** (*denso*) thick: *minestra troppo soda,* soup which is too thick **4.** (*forte*) strong; heavy: *gli diede un pugno —,* he gave him a heavy (o vigorous) blow || *darle sode a qlcu.,* to strike s.o. hard **5.** *fig.* (*serio, fondato*) sound, well-grounded: *sode qualità,* sound (o sterling) qualities; *cultura soda,* sound knowledge; *è un uomo —,* he is a sound man || *s.m.* (*terreno sodo*) firm ground: *posare sul —,* to stand on firm ground (*anche fig.*) || *sul —,* (*seriamente*) in earnest (o seriously) || *venire al —,* (*venire ai fatti*) to come to the point.

sòdo, *av.* (*fortemente*) hard: *lo picchiò —,* he hit him hard; *dormir —,* (*profondamente*) to sleep soundly; *mangiar —,* (*fare un buon pasto*) to have a hearty (o substantial) meal; (*mangiare molto per abitudine*) to be a good eater; *studiare, lavorare —,* (*con accanimento*) to study, to work hard.

Sòdoma, *no.pr.f.* (*st. biblica*) Sodom.

sodomía, *s.f.* sodomy.

sodomìta, *s.m.* sodomite.

sodomítico, *ag.* sodomitic(al).

sofà, *s.m.* sofa, divan.

sofferènte, *ag.* **1.** suffering: *è — di cuore, di reni,* he suffers from heart trouble, from kidney trouble; *egli è molto —,* he suffers a great deal; *il malato non è più —,* the patient does not suffer any more **2.** (*malaticcio*) poorly: *è — da molto tempo,* he has been poorly for a long time **3.** (*tollerante*) tolerant: *è — del freddo,* he stands the cold very well.

sofferènza, *s.f.* **1.** suffering, pain: *le sofferenze dei poveri, di un malato,* the sufferings of the poor, of a

sick man; *il vederlo è una vera —,* it's really painful to see him **2.** (*tolleranza*) endurance, long-suffering **3.** (*comm.*) (*ritardo*) delay: *cambiale in —,* unpaid bill.

sofferíre, (*arc.*) per **soffríre.**

soffermàre, *v.t.* to bring to a stop, to stop: — *il passo,* to come to a stop (o to stop a little) || **soffermàrsi,** *v.r.* to stop (a little), to pause, to linger: *si soffermò a guardare la vetrina,* she paused (o stopped a little) to look at the shop-window || — *su un argomento,* to dwell upon (o to linger over) a subject.

soffermàta, *s.f.* stop, pause.

soffèrto, *ag.* suffered, endured || *s.m.* (*dir.*) term (of imprisonment) already undergone.

soffiàggio, *s.m.* (*metal.*) blow: — *finale,* after-blow.

soffiaménto, *s.m.* blowing.

soffiànte, *s.m.* (*mec.*) blower: — *di una fucina,* fan blower.

soffiàre, *v.i.* **1.** to blow, to blow (sthg.): *il vento soffia forte stasera,* the wind is blowing hard tonight; — *su una candela,* (*spegnendola*) to blow out a candle; — *sul caffè,* to blow one's coffee; — *nel fuoco,* to blow the fire; *fig.* to stir up trouble **2.** (*ansare, sbuffare*) to blow, to puff; (*di gatto*) to spit: *le scale lo fanno —,* the stairs make him puff and blow || — *come un mantice,* to blow (o to puff) like a grampus || *v.t.* **1.** to blow: — *aria in q1.co.,* to blow air into sthg.; — *il fumo in faccia a qlcu.,* to puff smoke into s.o.'s face || — *una cosa nell'orecchio a qlcu.,* to whisper sthg. in someone's ear || — *il vetro,* to blow glass **2.** (*portar via*) to blow off; (*a dama, agli scacchi*) to huff: *il vento mi ha soffiato via il cappello,* the wind has blown my hat off; — *una pedina,* to huff a man (o a piece) || *mi ha soffiato il portafoglio,* he has relieved me of my pocket-book || — *il posto a qlcu.,* to supplant s.o. **3.** (*spifferare*) to report, to tell: *appena lo vide gli soffiò ogni cosa,* as soon as he saw him, he blurted out everything || **soffiàrsi,** *v.r.:* — *il naso,* to blow one's nose; — *sulle dita,* to blow on one's fingers.

soffiàta, *s.f.* puff.

soffiàto, *ag.: grano —,* puffed maize (o *amer.* pop-corn); *riso —,* puffed rice.

soffiatóio, *s.m.* bellows (*pl.*).

soffiatóre, *ag.* blowing || *s.m.* **1.** (*per locomotive*) blower **2.** (*chi soffia il vetro*) glass-blower.

soffiatríce, *s.f.:* — *per anime,* (*mec.*) core blowing machine.

soffiatúra, *s.f.* blowing: — *del vetro,* (*ind.*) glass-blowing, — *sottocutanea,* (*metal.*) subcutaneous blow-hole.

sòffice, *ag.* soft: *materasso —,* soft mattress.

sofficeménte, *av.* softly.

soffieria, *s.f.* (*metal.*) furnace bellows (*pl.*).

soffiétto, *s.m.* **1.** bellows (*pl.*); (*per spargere insetticidi*) powder-bellows: *il — della mia macchina fotografica è rotto,* the bellows in my camera are broken || *a —,* folding **2.** (*di carrozza*) hood **3.** — *intercomunicante,* (*ferr.*) gangway **4.** (*in un giornale, articolo laudativo*) puff: — *editoriale,* blurb.

sóffio, *s.m.* **1.** puff, whiff; (*violento*) blast, gust; (*alito*) breath: *un — d'aria, di fumo, di vapore,* a puff (o whiff) of air, smoke, steam; *un — di vento,* a breath of wind; (*violento*) a gust of wind; *il — gelato del nord,* the icy blast from the north; *con un —,* with a puff: *spegnere una candela con un —,* to blow (o to puff) out a candle; *non un — d'aria, di vento,* not a breath of air; *un — d'aria calda entrò dalla finestra aperta,* a puff of warm wind came in through the open window || *in un —,* (*in un attimo*) in an instant (o in a flash o in the twinkling of an eye); (*sottovoce*) in a whisper: *parola mormorata in un —,* word uttered in a whisper **2.** (*verso del gatto*) spitting **3.** (*ispirazione*) inspiration: *il — divino, poetico,* divine, poetic inspiration **4.** (*med.*) murmur, puff: — *al cuore,* murmur of the heart (o cardiac murmur); *un leggero — polmonare,* a veiled puff.

soffióne, *s.m.* **1.** (*canna per soffiare nel fuoco*) blow-pipe; (*mantice*) bellows (*pl.*) **2.** (*geol.*) fumarole **3.** (*bot.*) dandelion **4.** *fig.* (*spia*) spy.

soffitta, *s.f.* attic; (*abbaino*) garret.

soffitto, *s.m.* ceiling: — *a cassettoni*, lacunar ceiling; — *a graticcio di canne*, cane-mesh ceiling; — *a rete*, (wire-) mesh ceiling; — *a ricasco*, cove; — *a travi di legno*, wooden-beam ceiling; — *a volta*, arched ceiling; — *in cemento armato*, reinforced-concrete ceiling; — *in mattoni*, brick ceiling.

soffocaménto, *s.m.* choking, stifling; suffocation: *morì per* —, he was choked to death.

soffocànte, *ag.* choking, stifling, suffocating: *caldo* —, stifling (*o* suffocating) heat; *clima* —, sultry climate.

soffocàre, *v.t.* **1.** to choke, to stifle, to suffocate, to smother: *l'edera soffocherà l'albero*, the ivy will choke the tree; *ero soffocato dal fumo, dalla polvere*, I was stifled (*o* choked) by the smoke, by the dust; *fu quasi soffocato da un nocciolo di prugna*, he was almost choked by a plum-stone; *lo soffocò con un cuscino*, he suffocated him (*o* smothered him to death) with a pillow; *parlò con voce soffocata dai singhiozzi*, she spoke in a voice choked with sobs ‖ — *un bambino di baci*, to smother a child with kisses **2.** (*reprimere, attutire*) to stifle, to repress: — *la collera*, to choke down (*o* to stifle *o* to smother) one's anger; — *un fuoco*, to choke (*o* to stifle) a fire; — *i propri sentimenti*, to stifle one's feelings; — *una rivolta nel sangue*, to put down a rebellion; — *uno sbadiglio, una risata, un grido*, to stifle a yawn, a burst of laughter, a cry; — *uno scandalo*, to hush up (*o* to stifle) a scandal ‖ *v.i.* to choke, to stifle, to suffocate: *il bambino stava per* —, the child was going to choke; *mi sento* —, I have a choking (*o* stifling *o* suffocating) feeling; *qui si soffoca*, it is suffocating (*o* stifling) here; — *dall'indignazione*, to choke with indignation.

soffocazióne, *s.f.* choking, stifling; suffocation.

sòffoco, *s.m.* sultriness, heavy heat.

soffregaménto, *s.m.* (slight) rubbing.

soffregàre, *v.t.* to rub (gently).

soffrìbile, *ag.* bearable, endurable, sufferable.

soffribilménte, *av.* bearably, endurably, sufferably.

soffrìggere, *v.t.i.* to fry slightly, to brown.

soffrire, *v.t.* **1.** to suffer: — *la fame*, to suffer (the pangs of) hunger; (*per un lungo periodo*) to go hungry; — *insulti, il martirio, una perdita*, to suffer insults, martyrdom, a loss; — *la sete*, to suffer thirst **2.** (*sopportare*) to bear, to stand, to endure, to put up with (s.o., sthg.): *l'orecchio non soffre i suoni troppo acuti*, the ear cannot bear extremely sharp sounds; *nessuno poteva* — *quella persona*, nobody could bear (*o* stand *o* endure *o* put up with) that person; *non posso* — *di vederti trattato così*, I cannot bear to see you treated like that; *non posso* — *che egli ti insulti*, I cannot allow him to insult you ‖ *v.i.* to suffer: *è malato ma non soffre*, he is ill but does not suffer; *ha mólto sofferto per la morte del suo amico*, his friend's death was a great sorrow for him; *la sua reputazione, la sua salute, il suo lavoro ne soffrirà*, his reputation, his health, his work will suffer by it; *le vigne hanno sofferto per il gelo*, the vines have suffered from the frost; — *di mal di mare*, to suffer from seasickness; — *di mal di cuore, di reumatismi*, to suffer from heart -disease, from rheumatism.

soffritto, *s.m.* (*cuc.*) browned onions (*pl.*): *preparare un* —, to brown some onions.

soffùso, *ag.* suffused (with sthg.); (*cosparso*) spread (with sthg.): — *di luce*, suffused with light; — *di sudore*, suffused with perspiration.

Sofia[1], *no.pr.f.* Sophia, Sophie, Sophy.

Sòfia[2], *no.pr.f.* (*geog.*) Sofia.

sofìsma, *s.m.* (*fil.*) sophism.

sofìsta, *s.m.* (*fil.*) sophist.

sofìstica, *s.f.* (*fil.*) sophistry.

sofisticaménte, *av.* sophistically.

sofisticàre, *v.i.* to quibble, to split hairs; to sophisticate: *sofisticò molto su questo argomento*, he quibbled a lot about this matter ‖ *v.t.* (*alterare, una sostanza*) to adulterate: — *il burro*, to adulterate butter.

sofisticazióne, *s.f.* adulteration: *la* — *delle sostanze alimentari è punita a norma di legge*, the adulteration of food-stuffs is punished by law.

sofistichería, *s.f.* sophistry; (*pedanteria*) hair-splitting, quibbling.

sofìstico, *ag.* **1.** sophistical **2.** (*fil.*) sophistic.

sòfo, *s.m.* (*letter. scherz.*) wise man; sage.

Sòfocle, *no.pr.m.* (*st. lett.*) Sophocles.

sofoclèo, *ag.* (*lett.*) Sophoclean.

Sofonìsba, *no.pr.f.* (*st.*) Sophonisba.

soggettàre, *e derivati*, *V.* assoggettàre, *e derivati*.

soggettìsta, *s.c.* (*cine.*) scenario writer.

soggettivaménte, *av.* subjectively.

soggettivìsmo, *s.m.* **1.** (*fil.*) subjectivism **2.** (*art.*) subjectivity, subjectiveness.

soggettivìsta, *s.c.* **1.** (*fil.*) subjectivist **2.** (*art.*) subjective artist: *questo scrittore è un* —, he is a subjective writer.

soggettività, *s.f.* subjectivity, subjectiveness.

soggettìvo, *ag.* subjective.

soggètto[1], *ag.* **1.** (*sottoposto, sottomesso*) subject: *esistono ancora molti stati soggetti al dominio dello straniero*, there still exist many states subject to foreign rule; *siamo tutti soggetti alle leggi di natura*, we are all subject to the laws of nature **2.** (*esposto, incline*) subject, liable; prone: — *a penalità, a tassa*, liable to penalty, to tax; *persone soggette all'invidia, a un male*, persons subject (*o* prone) to envy, to an illness **3.** (*dipendente*) dependant (on sthg.): *questo è* — *alla tua approvazione*, this is subject to (*o* dependant on) your approval ‖ *s.m.* (*suddito*) subject.

soggètto[2], *s.m.* **1.** (*argomento, tema*) subject (-matter), topic, theme: *il* — *della lezione di oggi*, the subject of to-day's lesson; *il* — *della nostra conversazione*, the topic (*o* subject) of our conversation; *il* — *di un esperimento medico*, the subject of a medical experiment; *il* — *di un libro*, the subject (-matter) of a book; *il* — *di un pittore*, the subject of a painter ‖ *allontanarsi dal* —, to wander off (*o* to get away from) the subject; *cambiare* —, to change subject; *scegliere un* — *infelice*, to make an unhappy choice of subject **2.** (*med.*) subject: — *anemico, isterico*, anemic, hysterical subject **3.** (*spreg. scherz.*) subject, fellow: — *pericoloso*, dangerous subject (*o* fellow); *cattivo* —, nasty (*o* unpleasant) character; *ma sai che sei un bel* —!, you are a rogue, you know! **4.** (*gram. fil.*) subject: *il* — *e l'oggetto*, the subject and the object.

soggezióne, *s.f.* **1.** (*sottomissione*) subjection: *vivere in* —, to live in subjection (*o* in bondage) **2.** (*timore, rispetto*) awe, respect; (*timidezza*) shyness, bashfulness; (*imbarazzo*) uneasiness, embarrassment: *egli mi incute, mi mette* —, he makes me feel uneasy (*o* awkward); *ho* — *di lui*, I feel uneasy with him.

sogghignàre, *v.i.* to sneer; to grin.

sogghígno, *s.m.* sneer; grin.

soggiacére, *v.i.* **1.** (*essere sottoposto*) to be subjected: — *alle prepotenze di qlcu.*, to be subjected to s.o.'s insults **2.** (*essere soggetto, esposto*) to be subject, to be liable: — *alle ingiurie del tempo*, to be subject to the ravages of time **3.** (*morire*) to succumb, to die.

soggiaciménto, *s.m.* subjection.

soggiogaménto, *s.m.* subjugation, subjection.

soggiogàre, *v.t.* to subjugate, to bring into subjection; to subdue (*anche fig.*): — *nemici, natura, terra incolta*, to subdue enemies, nature, waste land; — *un paese*, to subjugate a country (*o* to bring a country into subjection); — *le proprie passioni*, to subdue one's passions.

soggiornàre, *v.i.* **1.** to stay **2.** (*dimorare*) to live.

soggiórno, *s.m.* **1.** stay: *dopo un breve* —, after a short stay: *imposta di* —, visitors' tax; *permesso di*

—, permission to stay; (*documento*) residence permit 2. (*stanza di*) —, living-room.

soggiúngere, *v.t.* to add ‖ *v.i.* 1. to add 2. (*rispondere*) to answer.

soggiuntívo, *ag.s.m.* (*gram.*) subjunctive, conjunctive: *modo* —, subjunctive (*o* conjunctive) mood.

soggólo, *s.m.* 1. (*di monaca*) wimple 2. (*di cavallo*) throat-band, throat-latch 3. (*di berretto militare*) chin-strap.

sogguardàre, *v.t.* to look stealthily at (s.o., sthg.).

sòglia, *s.f.* threshold (anche *fig.*): *la* — *della vita, del successo*, the threshold of life, of success; *sulla* —, on the threshold; *varcare la* —, to cross the threshold.

sòglio, *s.m.* throne: — *regio, pontificio*, royal, papal throne.

sògliola, *s.f.* (*ittiol.*) sole.

sognàbile, *ag.* (*immaginabile*) imaginable; (*concepibile*) conceivable.

sognànte, *ag.* 1. dreaming 2. (*che sembra sognare*) dreamy: *occhi sognanti*, dreamy eyes.

sognàre, *v.t.i.* to dream: *egli sogna felicità e ricchezza*, he dreams of happiness and riches; *non sogno mai*, I never dream; *sognai di essere in America*, I dreamt I was in America; — (*di*) *qlcu., ql.co.*, to dream of (*o* about) s.o., sthg.; *passare il tempo sognando*, to dream away one's time ‖ — *a occhi aperti*, to have day-dreams (*o* to day-dream) ‖ **sognàrsi**, *v.r.* (*immaginare*) to dream; to imagine, to fancy: *come avrei potuto sognarmelo?*, how could I have imagined such a thing?; *deve esserselo sognato*, he must have dreamt of it; *non mi sognavo proprio che sarebbe arrivato*, I little dreamt that (*o* I never imagined) he would arrive; *non potrei neanche sognarmi di farlo*, I couldn't even dream of doing it; *non sognartelo neppure*, don't even dream of it; *non sognarti che io possa accettare una cosa simile*, don't imagine that I can accept such a thing.

sognatóre, *ag.* 1. dreaming 2. (*che sembra sognare*) dreamy ‖ *s.m.*, **sognatríce**, *s.f.* dreamer.

sógno, *s.m.* 1. dream (anche *fig.*): *un* — *ad occhi aperti*, a day-dream; *il mondo dei sogni*, the land of dreams (*o* dreamland); *è passato come un* —, it passed like a dream; *ella era un vero* — (*tanto era bella*), she looked a real dream; *la felicità è solo un* —, happiness is only a dream; *il mio* — *sarebbe di vivere in campagna*, my dream would be to live in the country; *il nostro viaggio fu un* —, our trip was like a dream; *ti ho visto in* —, I saw you in a dream; *fare un bel, brutto* —, to have a pleasant, bad dream ‖ *buona notte, sogni d'oro!*, good-night, sweet dreams! ‖ *neanche per* —!, by no means!: «*Faresti tu una cosa simile?*», «*Neanche per* —!», "Would you do such a thing?", "I wouldn't dream of it!" 2. (*fantasticheria*) fancy, reverie.

sòia, *s.f.* (*bot.*) soya(-bean).

sol, *s.m.* (*mus.*) sol, G.

solàio, *s.m.* 1. (*soffitta*) attic; (*se reso abitabile*) garret 2. (*edil.*) floor: — *a travicelli*, joisted floor; — *a travi di legno*, wooden-beam floor; — *con isolamento acustico*, sound-proof floor; — *incastrato*, fixed floor; — *misto in cemento armato e laterizio*, tile-lintel floor.

solaménte, *av.* 1. only; (*unicamente*) solely 2. (*semplicemente*) merely.

solanàcee, *s.f.pl.* (*bot.*) Solanaceae.

solanína, *s.f.* (*chim.*) solanin(e), solanina.

solàno, *s.m.* (*bot.*) Solanum.

solàre[1], *ag.* 1. solar; sun (*attributivo*): *anno, giorno, ora* —, solar year, day, time; *eclisse* —, solar eclipse; *luce* —, sunlight; *macchia* —, sunspot; *orologio* —, sun-dial; *raggio* —, sunbeam (*o* ray of sunlight); *sistema* —, solar system ‖ *plesso* —, (*anat.*) solar plexus 2. (*radioso*) radiant, sunny, bright 3. (*evidente, chiarissimo*) evident, obvious, clear: *una dimostrazione* —, a clear demonstration 4. (*magnifico*) august, glorious, divine.

solàre[2], *v.t.* to sole; (*risolare*) to resole.

solàrio, *s.m.* solarium (*pl.* solaria).

solàta, *s.f.* sunstroke.

solatío, *ag.* sunny ‖ *s.m.* (*rar.*) sunny place.

solatúra, *s.f.* soling; (*risolatura*) resoling.

soleàbile, *ag.* ploughable.

soleàre, *v.t.* to plough; to furrow (anche *fig.*): *una fronte solcata di rughe*, a furrowed brow; *il bosco era solcato da numerosi sentieri*, the wood was crossed by numerous paths; *in estate il cielo è spesso solcato da stelle cadenti*, in summer the sky is often streaked with falling stars; *le lacrime le solcavano le guance*, tears were running down her cheeks; *la nave solcava le onde*, the ship was ploughing the waves; *la sua fronte era solcata dal dolore*, his brow was furrowed by sorrow; — *un campo*, to plough a field.

solcatúra, *s.f.* 1. ploughing; furrowing 2. (*mec.*) grooving.

sólco, *s.m.* 1. (*agr.*) furrow; (*sottile*) drill: *l'aratro scava dei solchi nel terreno*, the plough cuts furrows in the ground; *seminare il grano nei solchi*, to sow the corn in drills ‖ *seguire il* — *di qlcu.*, to follow in the wake of s.o. (*o* in s.o.'s footsteps) ‖ *uscire dal* —, to go astray 2. (*ruga*) furrow, wrinkle 3. (*di nave*) wake; (*di ruota sul terreno*) rut, track; (*scia luminosa*) streak, trail 4. (*mec. anat.*) groove 5. (*metal.*) (*di colata*) runner.

soleòmetro, *s.m.* (*mar.*) log: — *a barchetta*, log-chip; — *a elica*, patent log; *tamburo del* —, log-reel.

soldàno, *s.m.* sultan.

soldatàglia, *s.f.* soldiery; (*truppe mercenarie*) mercenary troops (*pl.*), mercenaries (*pl.*).

soldatésca, *s.f.* soldiery; (*esercito*) army.

soldatescaménte, *av.* in a soldierly manner, in military fashion.

soldatésco, *ag.* soldierly, soldierlike, military: *modi soldateschi*, soldierly (*o* military) manners.

soldatíno, *s.m.* 1. young soldier 2. (*giocattolo*) toy-soldier: — *di piombo*, tin soldier.

soldàto, *s.m.* soldier: — *di artiglieria*, artilleryman; — *di cavalleria*, cavalryman (*o* horse-soldier *o* trooper); — *di fanteria*, infantryman (*o* foot-soldier); — *di ventura*, soldier of fortune; — *semplice*, private (soldier); — *veterano*, old soldier; *andare* —, to enlist (*o* to join the army *o* to go for a soldier); *fare il* —, to be (*o* to serve) in the army ‖ — *da capo a piedi*, every inch a soldier ‖ — *del papa*, (*scherz.*) harmless soldier ‖ — *di Cristo*, soldier of Christ.

sòldo, *s.m.* 1. penny, halfpenny, farthing; copper, coin: *affare da quattro soldi*, twopenny-halfpenny business; *una cosa da pochi soldi*, a worthless thing; *medico da pochi soldi*, twopenny-halfpenny doctor; *aveva in mano qualche* —, he had a few coppers (*o* coins) in his hand; *non avrei dato due soldi per la sua vita*, I wouldn't have given a farthing for his chance of living; *non ha un* —, he hasn't got a penny (*o* he is penniless); *non vale un* —, he is not worth a farthing 2. *pl.* (*denaro*) money (*sing.*): *soldi per i minuti piaceri*, pocket-money; *l'ho comperato per pochi soldi*, I got it for next to nothing (*o* very cheap); *avere molti soldi*, to have a lot of money; *essere a corto di soldi*, to be short of money; *fare soldi*, to make money; *lasciare qlcu. senza soldi*, to leave s.o. penniless (*o* destitute) 3. (*st.*) (*ventesima parte della lira*) soldo (*pl.* soldi) 4. (*salario*) pay; wages (*pl.*): *essere al* — *di qlcu.*, to be in s.o.'s pay.

sóle, *s.m.* 1. (*splendore, calore del sole*) sunshine: *al* —, in the sun; *abbronzato dal* —, sun-tanned (*o* sunburnt); *bagno di* —, sun-bathing; (*med.*) sun-bath: *il medico mi ha ordinato dei bagni di* —, the doctor told me to take sun-baths; *questa mattina voglio fare un bel bagno di* —, I want to do some sun-bathing this morning; *cappello da* —, sun-hat; *colpo di* —, (touch of) sunstroke; *una giornata piena di* —, a sunny day; *giornata senza* —, sunless day; *in pieno* —, in bright sunshine; *levata, sorgere del* —, sunrise; *luce del* —, sunlight; *luogo senza* —, sunless spot; *niente* — *oggi*, no sunshine to-day; *occhiali da* —, sun-glasses; *ombrellino da* —, sun-shade (*o* parasol); *orologio a* —, sun-dial; *un posto al* —, a place in the sun (anche *fig.*);

raggio di —, sunbeam (*o* ray of sunlight); *scottato dal* —, sunburnt; *scottatura da* —, sunburn; *tramonto del* —, sunset; *il* — *sorge, tramonta,* the sun rises, sets; *non abbiamo* — *da due giorni,* we have had no sunshine for two days; *splende il* —, the sun is shining; *alzarsi col* —, to rise with the sun; *fare la cura del* —, to sunbathe (*o* to take a sun-bath); *prendere il* —, to take the sun (*o* to lie *o* to sit in the sun) ‖ *il* — *di mezzanotte,* the midnight sun ‖ *bello come il* —, as beautiful as the morning star (*o* divinely beautiful) ‖ *niente di nuovo sotto il* —, nothing new under the sun ‖ *è chiaro come il* —, it is as clear as daylight ‖ *aprire gli occhi al* —, (*nascere*) to see the light of day (*o* to be born) ‖ *andare a vedere il* — *a scacchi,* (*andare in prigione*) to be put behind bars (*o* to go to prison) ‖ *avere ql.co. al* —, to own a bit of land ‖ *fare ql.co. alla luce del* —, to do sthg. openly **2.** (*poet.*) (*giorno, anno*) sun.

solecísmo, *s.m.* solecism.

solecizzàre, *v.i.* to solecize.

soleggiàre, *v.t.* to sun-dry, to dry in the sun.

soleggiàto, *ag.* sunny: *stanza soleggiata,* sunny room.

solènne, *ag.* **1.** solemn, grave; (*formale*) formal; (*impressionante*) impressive: *giuramento, promessa, festa* —, solemn oath, promise, feast; *maniere solenni,* solemn (*o* grave) manners; *messa* —, solemn high mass; *momento* —, solemn moment; *parole solenni,* solemn (*o* grave) words **2.** (*fam.*) first-rate, terrific: *una* — *sgridata,* a terrific scolding; *un* — *mascalzone,* a first-rate (*o* perfect) scoundrel.

solennemènte, *av.* solemnly, gravely; (*formalmente*) formally; (*in modo impressionante*) impressively.

solennità, *s.f.* solemnity; (*cerimonia*) ceremony: *la* — *del Natale,* the solemnity of Christmas.

solennizzàre, *v.t.* to solemnize.

solenòide, *s.m.* (*elett.*) solenoid.

solére, *v.i.* to use (*usato solo nel passato; nel presente si ricorre all'uso esclusivo del verbo dipendente, spesso accompagnato da* usually): *come si suol dire,* as they say; *egli suole alzarsi di buon'ora,* he (usually) gets up early; *lavora di più di quanto soleva fare due anni fa,* he works more than he used to two years ago; *solevo andare da lui ogni giorno,* I used to go to his house every day; *solevo studiare molto,* I used to study a great deal.

solèrte, *ag.* diligent, industrious; (*zelante*) zealous.

solertemènte, *av.* diligently, industriously; (*con zelo*) zealously.

solèrzia, *s.f.* diligence, industry; (*zelo*) zeal.

solètta, *s.f.* **1.** (*di calza*) sole, stocking-sole **2.** (*di scarpa*) insole **3.** (*edil.*) slab.

solètto, *ag.* alone (*predicativo*): *solo* —, all alone.

sòlfa, *s.f.* **1.** (*mus.*) scale, sol-fa **2.** *fig.* old story: *è sempre la stessa* —, it is always the same old story.

solfanèllo, *s.m.* match ‖ *piglia fuoco come un* —, he is inclined to flare up.

solfàra, *s.f.* sulphur mine.

solfàre, *v.t.* (*agr.*) to sulphur, to sulphurize.

solfatàra, *s.f.* (*geol.*) solfatara.

solfàto, *s.m.* (*chim.*) sulphate: — *di calcio,* calcium sulphate; — *di calcio anidro,* anhydrite; — *di magnesio,* magnesium sulphate (*o* Epsom salts); — *di rame,* copper (*o* cupric) sulphate; — *ferroso,* ferrous sulphate.

solfatúra, *s.f.* (*agr.*) sulphuring.

solfeggiàre, *v.t.* (*mus.*) to sol-fa, to solmizate.

solféggio, *s.m.* (*mus.*) solfeggio (*pl.* solfeggi, solfeggios).

solferíno, *ag.* solferino (*attributivo*).

solfidràto, *s.m.* (*chim.*) sulphydrate.

solfídrico, *ag.* (*chim.*) sulphydric.

solfíto, *s.m.* (*chim.*) sulphite.

sólfo, *V.* zólfo.

solfocianúro, *s.m.* (*chim.*) sulphocyanide.

solfonàto, *ag.* (*chim.*) sulphonated.

solfonazióne, *s.f.* (*chim.*) sulphonation.

solfònico, *ag.* (*chim.*) sulphonic.

solforàre, *v.t.* (*chim.*) to sulphurize, to sulphurate.

solforàto, *ag.* (*chim.*) sulpherized, sulphurated: *idrogeno* —, hydrogen sulphide.

solforazióne, *s.f.* (*chim.*) sulphuration.

solfòrico, *ag.* (*chim.*) sulphuric.

solforíle, *s.m.* (*chim.*) sulphuryl: *cloruro di* —, sulphuryl chloride.

solforóso, *ag.* (*chim.*) sulphurous.

solfúro, *s.m.* (*chim.*) sulphide: — *di ammonio,* ammonium sulphide; — *di carbonio,* carbon disulphide.

solidàle, *ag.* **1.** solid (for s.o.): *il popolo era pienamente* — *con il Ministro,* the country was solid for the Minister **2.** (*dir.*) joint and several; jointly liable, jointly responsible: *responsabilità* —, joint and several liability; *essere* —, to be jointly liable.

solidalmènte, solidariamènte, *av.* **1.** solidly **2.** (*dir.*) jointly and severally: *obbligarsi* —, to bind oneself jointly and severally.

solidarietà, *s.f.* **1.** solidarity: — *nazionale,* national solidarity **2.** (*dir.*) joint and several obligation, joint and several liability.

solidàrio, *ag.* **1.** (*dir.*) jointly liable, joint and several: *debitore* —, jointly liable debtor **2.** (*solidale*) solid (for s.o.).

solidézza, *V.* solidità.

solidificàre, *v.t.,* **solidificàrsi,** *v.r.* to solidify.

solidificazióne, *s.f.* (*fis.*) solidification.

solidità, *s.f.* **1.** solidity (anche *fig.*): — *di una dottrina,* solidity of a doctrine; — *di un muro,* solidity of a wall **2.** (*di colori*) fastness.

sòlido, *ag.* **1.** solid: *corpi solidi,* solid bodies; *geometria solida,* solid geometry **2.** (*stabile*) solid: *costruzione solida,* solid construction; *fondamenta solide,* solid foundations; *governo* —, solid government **3.** (*di colori*) fast **4.** *fig.* (*saldo*) sound: *argomento* —, sound argument; *reputazione solida,* sound reputation **5.** *fig.* (*degno di fiducia*) solid, reliable: *ditta solida,* solid (*o* reliable) firm ‖ *s.m.* **1.** solid (anche *geom.*): *i solidi e i liquidi,* solids and liquids; *il cubo è un* —, a cube is a solid **2.** *in* —, (*dir.*) jointly and severally.

solilòquio, *s.m.* soliloquy.

Solimàno, *no.pr.m.* (*st.*) Solyman, Suleiman.

solíngo, *ag.* lonely; solitary; alone (*predicativo*): *luogo* —, solitary spot; *vita solinga,* solitary life; *era tutto* —, he was all alone; *mi sento* —, I feel lonely.

solíno, *s.m.* (detached) collar: —*duro,* starched collar.

solípede, *ag.* (*zool.*) soliped, solipedous.

solipsísmo, *s.m.* (*fil.*) solipsism.

solísta, *s.c.* (*mus.*) soloist.

solitamènte, *av.* usually, generally.

solitariamènte, *av.* solitarily.

solitàrio, *ag.* solitary; lonely; alone (*predicativo*): *luogo* —, solitary (*o* lonely) place: *vita solitaria,* solitary life ‖ *verme* —, tapeworm ‖ *s.m.* **1.** hermit; solitary **2.** (*gioco a carte*) patience, solitaire **3.** (*brillante*) solitaire.

sòlito, *ag.* usual, customary: *le solite cose,* the usual things; *la solita vita,* the usual life; *le sue solite abitudini,* his usual (*o* customary) habits ‖ *essere* —, to be used to (doing): *è* — *venire presto,* he usually comes early; *ero* — *andarci tutti i giorni,* I used to go there every day (*o* I would go there every day); *non sono* — *fare queste cose,* I am not used (*o* accustomed) to doing these things ‖ *s.m.* **1.** (*la solita cosa*) the usual: *fecero il* —, they did the usual **2.** (*abitudine, costume*): *come al* —, as usual; *di* —, usually (*o* as a rule); *prima del* —, earlier than usual; *secondo il suo* — *mi disse una bugia,* as usual, he told me a lie.

solitúdine, *s.f.* **1.** solitude; loneliness: *in* —, in solitude; *soffrire di* —, to suffer from loneliness **2.** (*luogo disabitato*) solitude, lonely spot: *rifugiarsi nella* —, to take refuge in a lonely spot.

solívo, *ag.* sunny.

sollazzamènto, *s.m.* amusement; entertainment; recreation; (*passatempo*) pastime.

sollazzànte, *ag.* amusing; entertaining.

sollazzàre, *v.t.* to amuse; to entertain ‖ **sollazzàrsi,** *v.r.* to amuse oneself; to enjoy oneself.

sollazzévole, *ag.* amusing; entertaining: *compagnia* —, entertaining company; *gioco* —, amusing game.

sollazzevolménte, *av.* amusingly; entertainingly.

sollàzzo, *s.m.* 1. amusement; entertainment; recreation; (*passatempo*) pastime 2. (*zimbello*) laughing-stock: *essere il* — *di tutti,* to be a general laughing-stock.

sollecitaménte, *av.* 1. (*prontamente*) promptly; quickly, speedily 2. (*premurosamente*) carefully; diligently.

sollecitaménto, *s.m.* 1. (*il fare premura, il chiedere con urgenza*) urging, pressing 2. (*il chiedere con insistenza, richiesta insistente*) solicitation 3. (*l'affrettare*) hastening.

sollecitàre, *v.t.* 1. (*fare premura a; chiedere con urgenza*) to urge, to press: *lettera che sollecita pagamento,* dunning letter; *mi sollecitò a dare una precisa risposta, ad andare da lui,* he urged (*o* pressed) me to give a precise answer, to go to him; *sollecitai mio fratello perché mi mandasse il denaro,* I urged my brother to send me the money; — *la consegna di ql.co.,* to press for the delivery of sthg.; — *riforme,* to press for reforms 2. (*brigare, chiedere con insistenza*) to solicit: — *un incarico, un piacere,* to solicit an appointment, a favour; — *insistentemente ordinazioni,* to tout for orders; — *un pagamento di ql.co.,* to solicit payment for sthg. 3. (*affrettare*) to hurry up, to hasten: — *il proprio lavoro,* to hurry up (*o* to hasten) one's work ‖ **sollecitàrsi,** *v.r.* to hurry up, to make haste, to hasten.

sollecitatóre, *s.m.* petitioner.

sollecitatòria, *s.f.* 1. urgent (written) request 2. (*di pagamento*) dunning letter.

sollecitatòrio, *ag.* soliciting: *lettera sollecitatoria,* soliciting letter.

sollecitatríce, *s.f.* petitioner.

sollecitazióne, *s.f.* solicitation; (*preghiera*) entreaty: *una* — *di pagamento,* a request for payment; *lettera di* —, dunning letter; *egli non cedette alle mie sollecitazioni,* he did not yield to my entreaties.

sollécito, *ag.* 1. (*rapido*) prompt, speedy, quick: *una sollecita reazione,* a prompt reaction; *una sollecita risposta,* a prompt (*o* an early) reply; — *a fare ql.co.,* prompt to do sthg. 2. (*preoccupato, ansioso*) solicitous (about s.o., sthg.): — *della salute,* solicitous about one's health; — *dell'educazione dei figli,* solicitous about one's children's education; *troppo* — *degli onori,* too eager for honours 3. (*premuroso, gentile*) obliging ‖ *s.m.* solicitation: *fare un* —, to solicit.

sollecitúdine, *s.f.* 1. (*rapidità*) promptness, speed, quickness, dispatch: *fare ql.co. con* —, to do sthg. with dispatch; *rispondere con* —, to answer promptly ‖ *con cortese* —, (*comm.*) at your earliest convenience 2. (*interessamento*) concern, care, solicitude: *ha mostrato molta* — *verso di me,* he has shown great concern for me 3. (*gentilezza*) kindness, attention: *le sollecitudini di cui mi ha circondato,* the attentions he has showered on me.

solleóne, *s.m.* dog-days (*pl.*).

solleticaménto, *s.m.* 1. tickling 2. (*stimolo*) tickling; stimulus (*pl.* stimuli), spur, incitement.

solleticànte, *ag.* 1. (*appetitoso*) appetizing: *cibo, odore* —, appetizing food, smell 2. (*allettante*) alluring.

solleticàre, *v.t.* 1. to tickle: *solleticava il bambino con una piuma,* she tickled the child with a feather 2. (*eccitare, stimolare*) to tickle; to spur on; to stimulate, to excite: *lo solleticò con la speranza di successo,* he spurred him on with the hope of success; *quel cibo solletica il mio palato,* that food tickles my palate; *prospettive che solleticano,* alluring (*o* attractive) prospects; — *l'ambizione, la vanità di qlcu.,* to tickle s.o.'s ambition, vanity; — *l'appetito di qlcu.,* to tempt s.o.'s appetite; — *la curiosità di qlcu.,* to excite (*o* to stimulate *o* to stir) s.o.'s curiosity.

solletico, *s.m.* 1. tickle; tickling: *fare il* — *a qlcu.,* to tickle s.o.; *patire, soffrire il* —, to be ticklish 2. *fig.*

(*desiderio*) itch: *sentire il* — *di fare ql.co.,* to be itching to do sthg.

sollevàbile, *ag.* that may be lifted, liftable; that may be raised (*anche fig.*); that may be hoisted.

sollevaménto, *s.m.* 1. lifting; raising; hoisting: *capacità, meccanismo di* —, (*mec.*) lifting-power, lifting -gear ‖ — *pesi,* (*spor.*) weight-lifting 2. (*aer.*) take -off 3. (*rivolta*) rising, revolt 4. (*sollievo*) relief, comfort.

sollevàre, *v.t.* 1. to lift; to raise: *lo sollevò dal letto,* he lifted him out of bed; *lo sollevò da terra come una piuma,* he lifted it as if it were a feather; *l'automobile sollevò una nuvola di polvere,* the motor-car raised a cloud of dust; *questa cassa è troppo pesante perché io possa sollevarla,* this box is too heavy for me to lift; *questa gru può* — *20 tonnellate,* this crane can lift 20 tons; *sollevalo attentamente,* lift it carefully; *sollevò il bambino per fargli vedere la processione,* he lifted the child up so he could see the procession; *sollevò il bicchiere per un brindisi agli amici lontani,* he raised his glass in a toast to absent friends; — *il capo, gli occhi, le braccia,* to raise one's head, one's eyes, one's arms; — *un coperchio,* to lift (*o* to raise) a lid; — *un peso, una pietra, un pacco,* to lift a weight, a stone, a parcel 2. (*issare*) to hoist: *le macchine venivano sollevate sul ferry-boat da una gru,* the cars were hoisted onto the ferry-boat by a crane 3. *fig.* (*levare, alzare, innalzare*) to raise: — *qlcu. dalla miseria,* to raise s.o. from poverty; — *grida,* to raise cries; — *un'obiezione,* to raise an objection; — *una preghiera a Dio,* to raise a prayer to God; — *proteste contro un provvedimento,* to raise protests against a measure 4. (*far sorgere, far nascere*) to raise: *egli sollevò un gran disordine tra la folla,* he raised hell among the crowd; — *dubbi, una difficoltà,* to raise doubts, a difficulty; — *un putiferio,* to raise a riot; — *una questione, un problema,* to raise a question, a problem; — *una rivolta,* to raise a revolt 5. (*far insorgere*) to raise, to stir up: — *a tumulto,* to rouse to violence; — *il paese, il popolo contro qlcu.,* to stir up (*o* to raise) the country, the people against s.o. 6. (*dar sollievo a, alleviare*) to relieve, to comfort: *questa notizia mi ha sollevato molto,* this news has been a great relief to me; *la tua compagnia riesce sempre a sollevarmi,* your company always brings me relief; — *gli afflitti, gli infermi,* to comfort the afflicted, the sick; — *la miseria di qlcu.,* to relieve s.o.'s poverty ‖ **sollevàrsi,** *v.r.* 1. to rise; to arise (*gener. fig.*): *il pallone si sollevò in aria,* the balloon rose into the air; *questo pane non si è sollevato,* this bread has not risen; *si sollevò una disputa,* a quarrel arose; *si sollevò una fitta nebbia,* a thick fog rose; *si sollevò un gran rumore,* a great noise arose; *si sollevò una nube di polvere, di fumo,* a cloud of dust, of smoke rose; *il vento si sollevò improvvisamente,* the wind rose ‖ *egli si sollevò dall'estrema miseria,* he rose from beggary 2. (*insorgere*) to rise: *l'intero paese si era sollevato,* the whole country had risen; *i soldati si sollevarono contro il loro comandante,* the soldiers rose against their leader 3. (*riaversi, riprendersi*) to recover, to get over (sthg.): *dopo la morte di suo padre non si sollevò più,* he never got over his father's death; *egli non si sollevò più da quella malattia,* he never recovered from (*o* got over) that illness; *hai bisogno di sollevarti un po',* you need cheering up a bit; — *da un duro colpo,* to recover from a hard blow.

sollevàto, *ag.* (*rasserenato*) relieved, cheered up.

sollevatóre, *ag.* lifting; raising; hoisting ‖ *s.m.* 1. lifter ‖ — *di pesi,* (*spor.*) weight-lifter 2. (*mec.*) lift(er); hoist: — *elettromagnetico,* magnet-lifter; — *idraulico,* (*aut.*) hydraulic hoist; (*mec. agr.*) hydraulic power-lift; — *meccanico,* (*mec. agr.*) mechanical power lift 3. (*agitatore*) agitator, ringleader 4. (*confortatore*) reliever, comforter 5. (*anat.*) elevator ‖ **sollevatríce,** *s.f.* lifter.

sollevazióne, *s.f.* 1. (*rivolta*) rising, revolt 2. (*il sollevare*) lifting; raising (*anche fig.*); hoisting.

sollièvo, *s.m.* relief; (*conforto*) comfort: *con mio* *gran* —, to my great relief; *fu un gran* — *per me ricevere la tua lettera,* it was a great relief to me to receive your letter; *mi è di gran* — *il sapere che mi sei vicino,* it is a great comfort to me to know that you are near; *portare* — *a una pena,* to relieve a pain; *portare* — *a qlcu.,* to bring relief to s.o.

sollúcchero, *s.m.* rapture: *andare in* —, to go into raptures; *mandare in* —, to send (s.o.) into raptures.

solo, *ag.* **1.** alone (*predicativo*): *devi lasciarmi* —, you must leave me alone; *verremo noi soli e i bambini,* we'll come, just us and the children; *vive (da)* —, he lives on his own (o alone); *vive troppo* —, he lives too much alone ‖ — *soletto,* all (o quite) alone ‖ *da* —, by oneself (o on one's own o alone): *l'ha fatto da (sè)* —, he has done it by himself; *sapresti farlo da* —?, could you do it by yourself (o on your own o alone)? ‖ *da* — *a* —, in private (o tête à tête) ‖ *le disgrazie non vengono mai sole, prov.* troubles never come singly **2.** (*unico*) only: *il* — *superstite,* the only survivor; *con un letto* —, with one bed; *una sola volta,* just once; *un figlio* —, an only son; *la mia sola speranza,* my only hope; *il suo* — *e unico desiderio,* his one and only wish; *un uomo con un occhio* —, a one-eyed man; *è la sola cosa che so,* it is the only thing I know; *mi basta un cenno* — *per farmi capire,* just a nod is enough to make myself understood **3.** (*soltanto*): *egli* — *avrebbe potuto dirlo,* he alone (o only he) could have said it; *mi ha dato cento lire sole,* he only gave me a hundred lire ‖ *Dio* — *lo sa!,* God only knows! ‖ *ho due braccia sole,* I've only got one pair of hands ‖ *l'uomo non vive di* — *pane,* man does not live by bread alone **4.** (*esclusivo*) sole: *il* — *proprietario,* the sole owner; *il* — *rappresentante della ditta,* the sole agent of the firm ‖ *s.m.* **1.** (*unico*) only one: *sono il* — *a farlo,* I am the only one that does it **2.** (*mus.*) solo (*pl.* solos): *un (a)* —, a solo.

sólo, *av.* **only:** — *lui mancava,* he was the only one missing; *ho* — *questo,* I have only got this; *non* — *lo rimproverai, ma anche lo castigai,* I not only scolded him, but I punished him too ‖ *se* — *potessi vederlo!,* if only I could see him! ‖ **sólo che,** *l. cong.* **1.** (*ma*) **only, but:** *lo farebbe,* — *che deve partire,* he would do it, only (o but) he has to leave **2.** (*purché*) **if only:** *lo farei subito* — *che ne avessi la possibilità,* I'd do it straight away, if only I had the chance.

Solóne, *no.pr.m.* (*st.*) Solon.

solstiziàle, *ag.* (*astr.*) solstitial.

solstízio, *s.m.* (*astr.*) solstice: — *d'estate, d'inverno,* summer, winter solstice.

soltànto, *V.* **solaménte.**

solúbile, *ag.* soluble: — *in acqua,* (*chim.*) soluble in water; *problema* —, soluble problem.

solubilità, *s.f.* solubility.

solutívo, *ag.* (*chim.*) solvent.

soluzióne, *s.f.* **1.** (*chim.*) solution: — *anticongelante,* (*aut.*) antifreeze; — *satura,* saturated solution; — *tamponata,* buffered solution; *aumentare la concentrazione di una* —, to strengthen a solution; *diluire la concentrazione di una* —, to dilute a solution **2.** (*spiegazione, scioglimento*) (re)solution, solving: — *di un dubbio, di un problema,* solution of a doubt, of a problem **3.** — *di continuità,* (*med.*) solution of continuity (anche *fig.*).

solvènte, *ag.* (*chim. comm.*) solvent ‖ *s.m.* (*chim.*) solvent.

solvènza, *s.f.* (*comm.*) solvency.

solvíbile, *ag.* (*comm.*) solvent.

solvibilità, *s.f.* (*comm.*) solvency.

sòma, *s.f.* **1.** load, burden: — *molto pesante,* very heavy load; *bestia da* —, beast of burden (o pack-animal); *cavallo da* —, pack-horse **2.** *fig.* (*peso*) burden.

Somàlia, *no.pr.f.* (*geog.*) Somaliland, Somalia.

sòmalo, *ag.* Somaliland (*attributivo*) ‖ *s.m.,* **sòmala,** *s.f.* Somali (*pl.* Somalis, Somali).

somàra, *s.f.* she-ass.

somaràggine, *s.f.* **1.** stupidity, doltishness **2.** (*atto, detto stupido*) piece of stupidity.

somaràta, *s.f.* piece of stupidity.

somàro, *s.m.* ass, donkey (anche *fig.*).

somàtico, *ag.* somatic: *caratteri somatici,* somatic types; *cellule somatiche,* somatic cells.

somatología, *s.f.* somatology.

sombrèro, *s.m.* sombrero (*pl.* sombreros).

someggiàre, *v.t.* to transport by pack-animal.

somière, somièro, *s.m.* (*letter.*) pack-animal.

somigliànte, *ag.* alike (*predicativo*); like (s.o., sthg.), resembling (s.o., sthg.); (*simile*) similar: *è un caso* — *al tuo,* it is a case similar to (o resembling) yours; *era un animale* — *ad uno scoiattolo,* it was an animal looking like a squirrel; *questo ritratto non è* —, this portrait is not like him (her); *sono molto somiglianti,* they are very much alike.

somigliantemént, *av.* in like manner, likewise; (*similmente*) similarly.

somigliànza, *s.f.* likeness, resemblance: *stretta* —, close resemblance; *non vedo la minima* — *tra lui e suo fratello,* I see no likeness whatever between him and his brother; *se guardi meglio, c'è una certa* — *fra i due,* if you look closer, there is a certain resemblance between the two ‖ *l'uomo fu fatto ad immagine e* — *di Dio,* man was made in God's own image and likeness.

somigliàre, *v.t.* **1.** to be like, to look like, to resemble: *questo è un ritratto che non somiglia l'originale,* this portrait is not a good likeness; *somiglia molto lo zio,* he looks very much like his uncle **2.** (*paragonare*) to compare: *molti somigliano l'uomo a un viandante,* man is often compared to a pilgrim ‖ *v.i.* to be like (s.o., sthg.), to look like (s.o., sthg.), to resemble (s.o., sthg.): *gli somigli nella voce,* you have a voice like his; *somiglia moltissimo a sua sorella,* she is the (living) image of her sister; *il tuo caso somiglia al mio,* your case is like (o resembles) mine ‖ **somigliàrsi,** *v.r.* **reciproco** to be like each other (one another), to look like each other (one another), to resemble each other (one another): *le due sorelle si somigliano,* the two sisters resemble each other; *si somigliano come due gocce d'acqua,* they are as like as two peas.

sómma, *s.f.* **1.** (*arit.*) addition (sum); (*risultato di un'addizione*) sum, total: *fare una* —, to do an addition (sum) ‖ *tirare le somme, fig.* to sum up (sthg.): *se tiriamo le somme del suo discorso...,* if we sum up (the points of) his speech...; *tirando le somme...,* everything considered... (o after all... o taking everything into account...) **2.** (*di denaro*) sum (of money), amount of money: *una grossa* — *di denaro,* a large sum (o a large amount of money); *la* — *ammonta a un centinaio di sterline,* the total amounts to a hundred pounds; *pagare una forte* —, to pay a large sum; *spendere una* — *folle di denaro,* (*fam.*) to spend a mint of money **3.** (*conclusione*) conclusion: *la* — *delle sue lamentele è...,* the conclusion of his complaint is... **4.** (*rar.*) (*compendio*) epitome ‖ *la Somma Teologica di S. Tommaso d'Aquino,* the Summa Theologica of St. Thomas Aquinas ‖ *in* —, in short (o briefly).

sommamént, *av.* **1.** (*estremamente*) extremely, exceedingly **2.** (*altamente*) highly, in the highest degree.

sommàre, *v.t.* **1.** to add; to sum up: *somma dieci a venti e avrai trenta,* add ten to twenty and you get thirty; — *dei numeri,* to add up (o to sum up) figures **2.** (*calcolare*) to consider, to reckon: *se ci sommi anche i rischi, vedrai che non è un buon affare,* if you also consider the risks, you will realize it is not a good bargain ‖ *tutto sommato,* everything considered (o after all): *ha un carattere difficile, ma, tutto sommato, è un buon uomo,* he is not very easy to get on with, but everything considered, he is a good man ‖ *v.i.* (*ammontare*) to amount (to sthg.), to come to (sthg.): *i feriti sommano a sei,* casualties amount to six.

sommariamént, *av.* summarily; (*in breve*) briefly.

sommàrio, *s.m.* **1.** summary, brief: *una spiegazione sommaria,* a brief explanation; *esporrò in modo* —, I shall be brief in my account; *voglio solo una relazione* *sommaria*, I only want a short report ?. *(dir.)* summary; *giustizia sommaria*, summary justice; *fu un procedimento —*, it was a summary procedure ‖ *s.m.* **1.** summary, brief account **2.** *(indice)* index: *— di un trattato*, index of a treaty.

sommatòria, *s.f. (mat.)* summation.

sommèrgere, *v.t.* **1.** to submerge; *(inondare)* to flood: *i campi furono sommersi dalle acque del fiume*, the fields were flooded with the water of the river **2.** *fig. (colmare)* to overwhelm: *mi sommerge di gentilezze tutte le volte che vado da lei*, she overwhelms me with kindness whenever I go and stay with her ‖ **sommèrgersi**, *v.r.* **1.** to sink: *la nave si sommerse*, the ship sank **2.** *(di sottomarino)* to submerge, to dive.

sommergíbile, *ag.* submersible ‖ *s.m. (mar. mil.)* submarine: *— a controcarena*, saddle-tank submarine; *— atomico*, nuclear-powered submarine; *— attrezzato per il lancio di missili*, missile launching submarine; *— di lunga carena*, fleet submarine, *— di media crociera*, sea-going submarine; *— posamine*, mine laying submarine.

sommergibilista, *s.m. (mar. mil.)* submariner, member of a submarine crew.

sommersióne, *s.f.* submersion.

sommèrso, *ag.* submerged: *trovarono un paese —*, they found a submerged village.

sommessaménte, *av.* **1.** submissively, humbly **2.** *(a bassa voce)* softly, in a low voice, in a subdued tone.

sommésso, *ag.* **1.** submissive, docile; subdued; *(umile)* humble, meek: *è poco — alla mamma*, he does not listen to his mother; *venne da me tutto umile e —*, he came to me all meek and humble **2.** *(di voce)* low, subdued, soft: *parlava a voce sommessa*, she spoke in a low subdued voice.

somministràre, *v.t.* to administer, to give: *mi hanno somministrato una medicina molto amara*, I was given a very bitter medicine; *oggi gli hanno somministrato l'Estrema Unzione*, he was administered Extreme Unction to-day ‖ *— a qlcu. una buona dose di schiaffi*, to give s.o. a jolly good hiding.

somministratóre, *s.m.*, **somministratríce**, *s.f.* giver; administrator; minister.

somministrazióne, *s.f.* **1.** *(il somministrare)* giving; administration; supply, provision **2.** *(la cosa somministrata)* supply, provision.

sommissióne, *V.* sottomissióne.

sommità, *s.f.* summit, top (anche *fig.*): *la — dell'arte, del sapere*, the summit of art, of knowledge; *la — di un monte*, the top of a mountain.

sómmo, *ag. superl.* highest; *fig.* supreme, superlative; *(grande)* great: *il — bene, male*, the supreme good, evil; *somma bontà*, supreme (*o* superlative) goodness; *le somme cime delle Alpi*, the highest peaks of the Alps; *somma felicità, gloria*, supreme happiness, glory; *somma pazienza, intelligenza*, great patience, intelligence; *un — poeta, artista*, a great poet, artist; *è di una somma bellezza*, it is supremely (*o* extremely) beautiful; *tenere qlcu. in — disprezzo*, to hold s.o. in supreme contempt ‖ *il Sommo Pontefice*, the Supreme Pontiff ‖ *al, in — grado*, to, in the highest degree ‖ *per sommi capi*, briefly (*o* summarily) ‖ *s.m.* summit, top: *il — del monte*, the top of the mountain; *al — della scala*, at the top of the stairs ‖ *al — del successo*, at the peak of his success; *il — della sua ambizione era...*, the height of his ambition was... ‖ *al —*, *(sommamente)* extremely (*o* superlatively).

sommòssa, *s.f.* rising, rebellion: *scoppiò una —*, a rising broke out; *reprimere una — nel sangue*, to put down a rising (*o* a rebellion) with bloodshed.

sommòsso, *ag.* **1.** *(agitato)* troubled, excited (anche *fig.*): *acque sommosse*, troubled waters; *animi sommossi*, troubled (*o* excited) spirits **2.** *(commosso)* moved: *alle preghiere*, moved by entreaties.

sommoviménto, *s.m.* **1.** *(il sommuovere)* stirring, agitating (anche *fig.*) **2.** *(movimento)* movement; *(agitazione)* agitation, disturbance.

sommozzatóre, *s.m. (mar. mil.)* frogman (*pl.* frogmen); *(nuotatore subacqueo)* skin-diver.

sommuòvere, *v.t.* **1.** to stir up: *— la melma in uno stagno*, to stir up the mud in a pond **2.** *fig. (eccitare)* to stir up, to rouse, to excite: *— le passioni di qlcu.*, to stir up (*o* to rouse *o* to excite) s.o.'s passions; *— il popolo*, to stir up (*o* to rouse) the people.

sonàbile, *ag.* playable.

sonaglièra, *s.f.* collar with bells.

sonàglio, *s.m.* harness-bell; *(giocattolo)* rattle ‖ *serpente a sonagli*, rattlesnake.

sonànte, *ag.* *(che risuona)* resounding; *(sonoro)* sonorous ‖ *denaro —*, ready money (*o* cash).

sonàre, *v.t.* **1.** to sound; *(campane, campanello)* to ring: *credevo che tu avessi sonato (il campanello)*, I thought you had rung; *devo — per chiamare la cameriera?*, shall I ring for the maid?; *— l'allarme*, to sound the alarm; *— il clacson*, to sound the horn (*o* to hoot); *— una nota*, to sound a note; *— la ritirata*, *(mil.)* to sound the retreat; *— la sveglia*, *(mil.)* to sound reveille ‖ *sonarle a qlcu.*, *(fam.)* to give s.o. a good thrashing **2.** *(eseguire, musica)* to play: *l'organo sonava la marcia nuziale*, the organ was playing the wedding march; *— un pezzo di musica*, to play a piece of music; *— il piano*, to play the piano; *— ql.co. al piano*, to play sth. on the piano; *— il violino, il flauto*, to play the violin, the flute **3.** *(di orologio)* to strike: *l'orologio della chiesa ha appena sonato mezzogiorno*, the church-clock has just struck noon; *questo orologio suona le ore*, this clock strikes the hours ‖ *v.i.* **1.** to sound; *(di campane, campanelli)* to ring: *il campanello suona*, the bell is ringing; *le campane suonano a festa*, the festive bells are ringing (*o* chiming); *egli ordinò di — a festa*, he ordered the festive bells to be rung; *questo fischietto, questa tromba non suona*, this whistle, this trumpet does not play (*o* blow); *— a martello*, to sound the alarm; *— a morto*, to toll for the dead **2.** *(eseguire musica)* to play: *egli suona in un'orchestra sinfonica*, he plays in a symphony orchestra; *— a orecchio*, to play by ear **3.** *(scoccare)* to strike: *le dodici sono sonate qualche minuto fa*, twelve o'clock struck some minutes ago; *non è ancora sonata mezzanotte*, it has not struck midnight yet; *sono appena sonate le sei*, it has just struck six **4.** *(risonare)* to ring, to resound (anche *fig.*): *il giardino sonava di allegre grida*, the garden was ringing with cheerful cries; *il suo nome sonerà per tutto il mondo*, his name will resound all over the world **5.** *(di periodo, versi, ecc.)* to sound: *mi suona sbagliato, strano*, it sounds wrong, strange to me; *questa frase non suona bene*, this sentence does not sound well (*o* right).

sonàta, *s.f.* **1.** *(il sonare del campanello)* ring: *ci fu una lunga —*, there was a long ring **2.** *(mus.)* sonata: *una — di Beethoven*, a sonata by Beethoven; *una — per violino e pianoforte*, a sonata for violin and piano ‖ *fammi una — prima che me ne vada*, play something for me before I go away **3.** *(scherz.) (imbroglio)* swindle: *non andrò più in quel negozio, ho avuto una bella —!*, I'll never go to that shop again, I've been done!; *dare una — a qlcu.*, to take s.o. in; *prendere una —*, to be taken in.

sonàto, *ag.* **1.** *(scoccato)*: *sono le tre sonate*, it is past three (o'clock) ‖ *ha quarant'anni sonati*, he is well over forty **2.** *rimanere sonati*, *(fam.)* to be taken in.

sonatóre, *s.m.*, **sonatríce**, *s.f.* player: *— di violino*, violin player (*o* violinist) ‖ *buonanotte, suonatori!* that's that!

Sónda[1], *no.pr.f. (geog.)* Sunda: *Isole della —*, Sunda Islands.

sónda[2], *s.f.* **1.** *(mar.)* sounding line, line and plummet **2.** *(med.)* probe **3.** *(mec.)* feeler **4.** *(miner.)* drill: *— a percussione*, percussion (*o* churn) drill; *— a rotazione*, rotary drill; *— campionatrice*, core drill (*o* sampler) **5.** *pallone —*, *(meteorologia)* sounding balloon.

sondàbile, *ag. (rar.)* soundable.

sondàggio, *s.m.* **1.** sounding (anche *mar.*) **2.** (*med.*) probing **3.** (*miner.*) drilling, boring: — *a percussione,* percussive boring; — *con fango misto ad aria,* aerated -mud drilling; — *sottomarino,* offshore (*o* submarine) drilling; *impianto di* —, rig.

sondàre, *v.t.* **1.** to sound (anche *fig.*): *cercherò di sondarlo su questa faccenda,* I shall try to sound him on this matter **2.** (*med.*) to probe.

soneria, *s.f.* **1.** (*meccanismo di orologio*) striking -mechanism: *caricare la* —, to wind up the striking -mechanism **2.** (*congegno di segnalazione*) bell: — *d'allarme,* alarm(-bell); — *elettrica,* electric bell; — *telefonica,* telephone bell.

sonettista, *s.m.* sonneteer.

sonétto, *s.m.* (*poes.*) sonnet.

sonio, *s.m.* prolonged unpleasant sound.

sonnacchiàre, *v.i.* to doze.

sonnacchiosaménte, *av.* drowsily, sleepily.

sonnacchióso, *ag.* **1.** drowsy, half-asleep, sleepy **2.** *fig.* (*torpido*) torpid: *spirito* —, torpid spirit.

sonnàmbula, *s.f.* sleep-walker, somnambulist.

sonnambulismo, *s.m.* sleep-walking, somnambulism.

sonnàmbulo, *s.m.* sleep-walker, somnambulist.

sonnecchiàre, *v.i.* to doze.

sonnellino, *s.m.* nap, doze: *fare un* —, to take (*o* to have) a nap.

sonnifero, *ag.* **1.** somniferous, soporific **2.** *fig.* (*noioso*) boring: *libro* —, boring book ǁ *s.m.* **1.** sleeping drug, sleeping draught, soporific: *prendere un* —, to take a sleeping draught **2.** *fig.* (*cosa noiosa*) bore: *questo libro è un* —, this book is a bore.

sonnilòquio, *s.m.* somniloquy.

sonnìloquo, *s.m.* somniloquist.

sónno, *s.m.* sleep: — *profondo, leggero,* sound, light sleep; *nel primo* —, in one's first sleep; *faccio sempre il* — *dopo colazione,* I always have a nap after lunch; *ho fatto un lungo* —, I had a long sleep; *la sua voce mi mette* —, his voice makes me sleepy; *avere* —, to be sleepy; *essere in un* — *profondo,* to be fast asleep; *parlare nel* —, to talk in one's sleep; *perdere il* —, to lose one's sleep; *prendere* —, to fall asleep; *rompere il* —, to wake ǁ *malattia del* —, sleeping-sickness ǁ *dormire il* — *del giusto,* to sleep the sleep of the just ǁ *morire, cascare dal* —, to be ready to drop with sleep.

sonnolènto, *ag.* **1.** drowsy, sleepy, somnolent **2.** *fig.* (*lento*) torpid: *acque sonnolente,* torpid waters.

sonnolènza, *s.f.* drowsiness, sleepiness, somnolence.

sonòmetro, *s.m.* (*mus.*) sonometer.

sonoraménte, *av.* sonorously ǁ *gliele ho date* —, I gave him a sound thrashing.

sonorità, *s.f.* sonority, sonorousness, resonance: — *della voce,* the sonority of the voice; *questa stanza ha molta, poca* —, this room has good, bad acoustics.

sonorizzàre, *v.t.* (*cine.*) to post-score, to add a sound-track to (sthg.).

sonorizzazióne, *s.f.* (*cine.*) post-scoring.

sonòro, *ag.* **1.** (*risonante*) resonant, sonorous: *metalli sonori,* sonorous metals; *nota sonora,* resonant note; *voce sonora,* sonorous (*o* resonant) voice **2.** (*rumoroso*) loud: *fischi, risa sonore,* loud laughters, whistles **3.** (*cine.*) sound (*attributivo*): *colonna sonora,* sound -track; *complesso* —, sound equipment; *effetto* —, sound -effect; *film* —, sound-film (*o* talking-picture *o* talkie); *schermo* —, sound-screen **4.** (*fonet.*) sonant, voiced **5.** *onde sonore,* (*fis.*) sound-waves.

sontuóso, *e derivati, V.* **suntuóso,** *e derivati.*

soperchiàre, *e derivati, V.* **soverchiàre,** *e derivati.*

sopiménto, *s.m.* drowsiness, dozing.

sopire, *v.t.* **1.** (*assopire*) to make drowsy **2.** (*calmare*) to calm, to soothe; to appease: — *la collera di qlcu.,* to calm (*o* to appease) s.o.'s anger; — *un dolore,* to soothe a pain; — *i sensi,* to dull one's senses.

sopóre, *s.m.* **1.** drowsiness, doze **2.** (*patol.*) sopor.

soporifero, *ag.* **1.** soporific, soporiferous **2.** *fig.* (*di persona*) boring; (*di cosa*) soporific, boring.

sopperire, *v.i.* **1.** (*provvedere*) to provide: — *ai bisogni della propria famiglia,* to provide for the needs of one's family **2.** (*supplire*) to make up: *egli sopperisce con la bontà alla sua mancanza di intelligenza,* he makes up for his lack of intelligence with his goodness.

soppesàre, *v.t.* **1.** to weigh in one's hand **2.** *fig.* (*considerare*) to weigh, to consider carefully: — *i pro e i contro,* to weigh the pros and cons.

soppéso, di, *l.av.* bodily: *alzare qlcu. di* —, to lift s.o. bodily.

soppiantàre, *v.t.* to supplant, to oust: *egli fu soppiantato dal suo più caro amico,* he was supplanted by his dearest friend; — *qlcu. nel suo ufficio,* to oust s.o. from his office.

soppiàtto, di, *l.av.* stealthily, secretly, on the sly: *uscire, entrare di* —, to steal out, to steal in.

sopportàbile, *ag.* bearable, endurable, tolerable.

sopportabilità, *s.f.* bearableness, endurableness.

sopportabilménte, *av.* bearably, endurably.

sopportaménto, *V.* **sopportazióne.**

sopportàre, *v.t.* **1.** to support, to tolerate, to bear, to endure, to stand, to put up with (s.o., sthg.), to suffer: *una pianta che non sopporta gli sbalzi di temperatura,* a plant which cannot support (*o* tolerate *o* stand) changes of temperature; *non posso* — *quell'uomo,* I cannot bear (*o* stand *o* tolerate *o* put up with *o* endure *o* suffer) that man; *non potevo* — *di vederlo soffrire tanto,* I could not bear (*o* stand) to see him suffer so much; *non sopporto che egli ti tratti così,* I cannot suffer him to treat you like that; *non sopporto che egli spadroneggi in casa mia,* I cannot bear (*o* stand *o* put up with) him lording it in my house; *sa* — *il dolore con molto coraggio,* he bears (*o* endures *o* supports) his pain with great courage; — *un peso, una responsabilità,* to bear a burden, a responsibility **2.** (*sostenere*) to support: *queste colonne non potranno* — *il terrazzo,* this columns will not support the balcony.

sopportatóre, *s.m.* bearer, endurer, sufferer.

sopportazióne, *s.f.* **1.** endurance: *dimostrò molta* — *durante la marcia,* he showed great endurance on the march **2.** (*pazienza*) tolerance, patience.

soppressa, *s.f.* press; (*per asciugare panni*) mangle.

soppressàre, *v.t.* to press; (*panni bagnati*) to mangle.

soppressatúra, *s.f.* pressing; (*di panni bagnati*) mangling.

soppressióne, *s.f.* **1.** suppression (anche *med.*): — *di una rivolta, di un desiderio,* the suppression of a revolt, of a desire **2.** (*abolizione*) abolition: *la* — *di una legge,* the abolition of a law.

sopprìmere, *v.t.* **1.** to suppress, to do away with (sthg.): — *un'insurrezione, un desiderio,* to suppress an insurrection, a desire **2.** (*abolire*) to abolish: *queste abitudini dovrebbero essere soppresse,* these habits should be done away with; — *una legge,* to abolish a law **3.** (*uccidere*) to kill: — *un rivale,* to kill a rival.

sópra, *prep.* **1.** (*nel caso di sovrapposizione con contatto*) on, upon: *una statua* — *un'alta colonna,* a statue on a tall column; *la bomba cadde* — *un ospedale,* the bomb fell on a hospital; *la ciurma si trovava* — *coperta,* the crew were on deck; *scrivici* — *l'indirizzo,* write the address on it; *si gettarono* — *di lui,* they flung themselves upon him; *il suo ragionamento era fondato* — *false premesse,* his reasoning was based on false premises; *mettere delle monete una* — *l'altra,* to put coins one on top of the other; *stendere la coperta* — *il letto, la tovaglia* — *la tavola,* to spread the blanket on the bed, the table-cloth on the table (*o* to put the cloth on); *versare inchiostro* — *il tappeto,* to spill ink on the carpet **2.** (*nel caso di sovrapposizione senza contatto e quando sia implicito il concetto di dominio, superiorità, protezione, difesa, rivestimento*) over: *l'aeroplano volava* — *Parigi,* the plane was flying over Paris; *era chino* — *il suo lavoro,* he was bending over his work; *ha l'abitazione* — *il negozio,* he lives over his shop; *metti il cappotto* — *il tailleur,* put your coat over your suit; *la minaccia di un licenziamento pende — il suo capo*, the threat of dismissal is hanging over his head; *mise uno scialle — le spalle*, she put a shawl over her shoulders; *regna — molti popoli*, he reigns over many peoples; *avere un vantaggio — qlcu.*, to have an advantage over s.o.; *essere, stare — a qlcu.*, *(essergli superiore)* to be over s.o. **3.** *(al di sopra di, più in alto di)* **above**: *l'aeroplano volava alto — la città, le nubi*, the plane was flying high above the city, above the clouds; *una montagna si elevava — il lago*, a mountain rose above the lake; *il ritratto della nonna era appeso — il caminetto*, grandmother's portrait hung above (o over) the fireplace ‖ *— tutto*, above all: *e — tutto non parlarne con nessuno*, and above all, don't talk to anybody about it ‖ *— zero*, above zero ‖ *lo ama — tutti*, she loves him more than anyone else **4.** *(oltre)* **over**: *egli è — la trentina*, he is over thirty; *il prezzo di questo vaso è — le diecimila lire*, the price of this vase is over ten thousand lire **5.** *(intorno a)* **on**: « *Saggio — l'intelletto umano* », "Essay on Human Understanding" **6.** *(dopo)*: *disgrazie — disgrazie*, one misfortune after another; *Bolzano è un po' — Trento sulla linea del Brennero*, Bolzano is a little above Trento on the Brenner line; *fa debiti — debiti*, he runs up one debt after another; *non dovresti bere vino — il latte*, you'd better not drink wine on top of milk **7.** **(Fraseologia)**: *ci dormirò —*, I'll sleep on it; *ne ho fin — i capelli, (sono molto occupato)* I'm up to my eyes in it; *(ne sono stufo)* I'm sick and tired of it; *pensaci —*, think it over; *contare, fare assegnamento — qlcu., ql.co.*, to count on s.o., on sthg.; *essere — pensiero*, to be thoughtful (o to be deep in thought); *metterci una pietra —*, to let bygones be bygones; *passar — a ql.co.*, to overlook sthg.; *prendere ql.co. — di sè, (assumersene la responsabilità)* to take sthg. on oneself ‖ *av.* **above**; *(al piano di sopra)* **upstairs**: *le circostanze — enunciate*, the above (-mentioned) circumstances; *da quanto —*, from the foregoing; *come abbiamo detto —*, as we said above; *è d'oro soltanto —*, it is only gold on the surface; *mi chiamò da —*, he called me from upstairs ‖ *mettilo nel baule, — —*, put it in the trunk, at the very top; *scavare il terreno — —, (in superficie)* to turn over the surface of the ground ‖ *s.m.* upper part, top: *il — del coperchio era smaltato*, the top of the lid was enamelled (o the lid had an enamel top) ‖ **di sópra**, V. **disópra**.

soprabbondàre, e derivati, V. **sovrabbondàre, e derivati**.

sopràbito, *s.m.* overcoat.

sopraccàpo, *s.m.* *(preoccupazione)* worry, care, trouble, anxiety.

sopraccaricàre, e derivati, V. **sovraccaricàre, e derivati**.

sopraccàrta, *s.f.* *(busta)* envelope, cover.

sopraccennàto, V. **sopraddétto**.

sopracciglio, *s.m.* eyebrow.

sopracciliàre, *ag.* superciliary.

soprac(c)itàto, V. **sopraddétto**.

sopraccopèrta¹, *s.f.* **1.** bedspread, counterpane, coverlet **2.** *(di libro)* cover, (dust)-jacket.

sopraccopèrta², *av.* *(mar.)* on deck.

sopraddétto, *ag.* above-mentioned *(attributivo)*, aforesaid *(attributivo)*.

sopraddòte, *s.f.* additional dowry.

sopradescritto, *ag.* described above *(predicativo)*.

sopraelevàre, *v.t.* **1.** *(edil.)* to increase the height of (sthg.): *sopraelevarono l'edificio di due piani*, they increased the height of the building by two stories **2.** *(strade, rotaie ferroviarie, ecc.)* to bank ‖ **sopraelevàrsi**, *v.r.* to rise (above sthg.).

sopraelevazione, *s.f.* **1.** *(edil.)* raising **2.** *(di strade, rotaie ferroviarie, ecc.)* superelevation, cant **3.** *— di tensione*, *(elett.)* voltage rise.

sopraffàre, *v.t.* to overwhelm, to overcome: *essi furono sopraffatti dal nemico*, they were overwhelmed

by the enemy; *fu sopraffatto dall'imponenza delle Alpi*, he was overwhelmed by the grandeur of the Alps; *fui sopraffatto dal timore, dal dolore*, I was overcome by fear, by grief.

sopraffazióne, *s.f.* overwhelming, overpowering; *(abuso)* abuse.

sopraffilàre, *v.t.* to overcast.

sopraffilo, *s.m.* *(sopraggitto)* overcast(ing).

sopraffine, V. **sopraffino**.

sopraffinèstra, *s.f.* *(arch.)* fan-light.

sopraffino, *ag.* **1.** first-rate, first-class: *merce, qualità sopraffina*, first-rate goods, quality; *pranzo —*, first-class (o first-rate) dinner **2.** *fig.* superfine; *(estremo)* extreme; *(esperto)* expèrt, masterly: *col suo tatto —*, with his extreme tact; *di sopraffina intelligenza*, of extreme (o exceptional) intelligence; *ingegno —*, superfine intelligence; *un ladro —*, an expert (o a masterly) thief; *pazienza sopraffina*, extreme patience; *la sua abilità sopraffina*, his masterly skill; *il suo gusto —*, his superfine taste; *è un cuoco —*, he is an expert (o a masterly) cook.

sopraffusióne, *s.f.* *(fis.)* superfusion, supercooling.

sopraggittàre, *v.t.* to overcast.

sopraggitto, *s.m.* overcast(ing): *cucire a —*, to overcast.

sopraggiúngere, *v.i.* **1.** *(arrivare)* to arrive: *stavo studiando quando sopraggiunsero i miei amici*, I was studying when my friends arrived **2.** *(accadere)* to happen, to occur: *dobbiamo rimandare la decisione perchè è sopraggiunto ql.co. di nuovo*, we must put off our decision because sthg. new has come up.

sopraggiúnta, *s.f.* addition ‖ *di, per —*, moreover (o besides o in addition): *per — a quel che ho già detto*, over and above what I have already said (o in addition to what I have already said).

sopraggravàre, *v.t.* to overload, to surcharge, to overburden ‖ **sopraggravàrsi**, *v.i.* to overload oneself, to overburden oneself.

sopraggràvio, *s.m.* new load, new burden.

sopraindicàto, V. **sopraddétto**.

sopraintèndere, V. **soprintèndere**.

sopraluògo, *s.m.* *(dir.)* investigation on the spot.

soprammànica, *s.f.* over-sleeve.

soprammàno, *s.m.* *(sopraggitto)* overcast(ing).

soprammentovàto, soprammenzionàto, V. **sopraddétto**.

soprammercàto, per, *l.av.* moreover, besides, on top of that.

soprammettere, *v.t.* to place (up)on, to put (up)on.

soprammòbile, *s.m.* knick-knack, nick-nack.

soprammòdo, *av.* *(oltremodo)* exceedingly, extremely.

soprammontàre, *v.i.* **1.** to overlap: *il collo non soprammonta bene*, the collar does not fit well **2.** *(rar.)* *(sovrabbondare)* to be excessive; to superabound.

soprannaturàle, *ag.* **1.** supernatural: *fenomeni soprannaturali*, supernatural phenomena **2.** *(grandissimo)* extreme: *gentilezza —*, extreme kindness ‖ *s.m.* supernatural.

soprannóme, *s.m.* nickname.

soprannominàre, *v.t.* to nickname; *(chiamare)* to call, to dub.

soprannominàto, *ag.* **1.** nicknamed; *(chiamato)* called, dubbed **2.** *(nominato sopra)* above-mentioned *(attributivo)*, mentioned above *(predicativo)*.

soprannumeràrio, *ag.* supernumerary: *impiegato —*, extra employee; *osso —*, supernumerary bone.

soprannúmero, *s.m.* excess, surplus: *un — di venti persone*, an excess of twenty people ‖ *in —*, in excess (o extra o supernumerary): *dieci operai in —*, ten extra workers; *ci sono dieci pagine in —*, there are ten pages in excess.

sopràno, *s.m.* *(mus.)* soprano *(pl.* sopranos, soprani): *voce di —*, soprano (o treble) voice ‖ *mezzo —*, mezzo-soprano.

sopraornàto, *s.m.* *(arch.)* entablature.

sopraòsso, *V.* **sopròsso.**

soprappàga, *s.f.* extra pay.

soprappagàre, *v.t.i.* to overpay.

soprappàrto, *av.* (*vicina al parto*) in labour.

soprappassàggio, *s.m.* overbridge: — *della ferrovia,* railway overbridge.

soprappensièro, *av.* **1.** lost in thought: *ero* —, I was lost in thought (*o* I was miles away) **2.** (*distrattamente*) absent-mindedly: *lo disse* —, he said it absent-mindedly.

soprappéso, *s.m.* overweight.

soprappiú, *s.m.* extra, addition; surplus: *questo è un* —, *non è incluso nel bilancio familiare,* this is an extra, it is not included in the family budget ‖ *in, per* —, in addition (*o* besides *o* as well): *avere ql.co. in* —, to have a surplus of sthg. ‖ *av.* (*inoltre*) besides, as well.

soprappórre, *e derivati, V.* **sovrappórre,** *e derivati.*

soprapprèzzo, *s.m.* **1.** increase in price: *questi terreni hanno avuto un* —, this land has increased in price **2.** (*ciò che si paga in più*) surcharge, extra charge: *pagammo un* —, we paid an extra charge.

soprapprofítto, *s.m.* excess profit; extra profit.

soprar(r)iferíto, *V.* **sopraddétto.**

soprarriscaldaménto, *s.m.* overheating.

soprarrivàre, *V.* **sopraggiúngere.**

soprascàrpa, *s.f.* galosh, overshoe.

soprascrítta, *s.f.* **1.** (*indirizzo*) address **2.** (*iscrizione*) inscription.

soprascrítto, *ag.* above-written (*attributivo*), above-mentioned (*attributivo*).

soprasensíbile, *ag.* (*fil.*) supersensible.

sopraspésa, *s.f.* extra expenditure.

soprassàlto, *s.m.* start, jerk, jump ‖ *di* —, all of a sudden (*o* with a start).

soprassàta, *s.f.* " soprassata " (kind of sausage).

soprassaturazióne, *s.f.* (*chim.*) supersaturation.

soprassedére, *v.i.* to wait: *soprassediamo qualche giorno,* let's wait for a few days ‖ — *a ql.co.,* (*differirla*) to put sthg. off (*o* to delay *o* to postpone sthg.).

soprassèllo, *s.m.* additional burden ‖ *per* —, in addition (*o* into the bargain).

soprassòglio, *s.m.* (*arch.*) architrave, lintel.

soprassòldo, *s.m.* extra pay.

soprastallía, *s.f.* (*mar. comm.*) demurrage: *giorni di* —, demurrage days.

soprastànte, *s.m.* supervisor: *il* — *ai lavori,* the works supervisor.

soprastàre, *v.i.* **1.** *V.* **sovrastàre 2.** (*soprintendere*) to supervise **3.** (*indugiare*) to wait.

soprastruttúra, *s.f.* superstructure (anche *fig.*).

soprat(t)àceo, *s.m.* heel-tap.

soprattàssa, *s.f.* extra tax, additional tax.

soprattassàre, *v.t.* to surtax, to levy an extra tax on (sthg.).

soprattútto, *av.* above all; (*specialmente*) mostly, especially, chiefly: *desidero* — *che tu sia buono,* above all I want you to be good; *nevica* — *in montagna,* it snows especially in the mountains.

sopravanzàre, *v.t.* (*superare*) to surpass, to exceed ‖ *v.i.* **1.** (*sporgere*) to jut out, to stand out, to stick out, to project: *c'è un asse che sopravanza,* there is a board jutting (*o* sticking) out **2.** (*pendere*) to show: *ti sopravanza il vestito,* your dress is showing **3.** (*avanzare*) to be left over, to remain over: *con la stoffa che ci sopravanza, mi farò fare una gonna,* I shall get (*o* have) a skirt made with the material left over; *non ci sopravanza molto tempo,* we have not much time left.

sopravànzo, *s.m.* (*eccedenza*) surplus; (*rimanenza*) remainder: *ce n'è di* —, there is more than enough (*o* there is a surplus); *comprare dei libri col* — *di una somma,* to buy some books with the remainder of a sum ‖ *di* —, (*in aggiunta*) in addition.

sopravvalutàre, *v.t.* to overrate, to over-estimate, to overvalue.

sopravvegliàre, *v.t.* (*rar.*) (*sorvegliare*) to watch (over).

sopravveniènte, *ag.* sudden, unexpected: *febbre* —, sudden fever.

sopravveniènza, *s.f.* sudden occurrence, unexpected event.

sopravveníre, *v.i.* **1.** (*di persona*) to turn up, to appear: *in quel momento sopravvenne il maestro e la baldoria finì come per incanto,* the master appeared and the din stopped all of a sudden; *stava per fuggire, quando sopravvennero le guardie,* he was going to escape, when the Police turned up **2.** (*di cose*) to crop up, to come about, to spring up: *se qualcosa di inaspettato dovesse* —, if anything unexpected should crop up; *sopravvenne una lunga serie di guai,* a long series of troubles cropped up.

sopravvènto, *s.m.* **1.** (*mar.*) windward: *barra* —, weather helm; *la barca passò a* —, the boat passed to windward **2.** *fig.* upper hand, superiority; (*vantaggio*) advantage: *l'ira ebbe il* — *su di lui,* anger overwhelmed (*o* got the upper hand of) him; *il nemico ebbe il* — *sui nostri soldati,* the enemy got the upper hand of our soldiers.

sopravvèste, *s.f.* overall.

sopravvissúto, sopravvivènte, *ag.* surviving ‖ *s.m.* survivor.

sopravvivènza, *s.f.* survival, surviving; outliving.

sopravvívere, *v.i.* to survive (s.o., sthg.); to outlive (s.o., sthg.): *il marito sopravvisse alla moglie tre anni,* the husband outlived his wife three years; *non potè* — *alla sciagura,* he did not manage to survive the disaster; *solo pochi sopravvissero al terribile terremoto,* only few survived the terrible earthquake.

sopravvòlta, *s.f.* double vault.

sopredificàre, *v.t.* to superstruct.

soprelevàre, *V.* **sopraelevàre.**

soprelevazióne, *V.* **sopraelevazióne.**

sopressàre, *v.t.* to press; (*panni bagnati*) to mangle.

sopressàta, *s.f.* "sopressata" (kind of sausage).

soprintendènte, *s.m.* superintendent: — *ai lavori pubblici,* Superintendent of Public Works.

soprintendènza, *s.f.* superintendence.

soprintèndere, *v.i.* to superintend (s.o., sthg.), to supervise (s.o., sthg.): *è incaricato di* — *ai lavori,* he is charged with the supervision of the works (*o* it is his job to superintend the works).

sopròsso, *s.m.* **1.** (*patol.*) exostosis (*pl.* exostoses) **2.** (*vet.*) splint **3.** (*rar.*) (*noia, fastidio*) trouble.

soprumeràle, *s.m.* (*st.*) superhumeral.

soprúso, *s.m.* abuse of power: *è un vero e proprio* —, it is a real abuse of power; *non tollero soprusi,* I am not going to be taken advantage of; *fare un* — *a qlcu.,* to take advantage of s.o.; *ricevere un* —, to be abused.

soqquadràre, *v.t.* (*rar.*) (*mettere sottosopra*) to turn upside down, to muddle.

soqquadràto, *ag.* (*messo sottosopra*) muddled, upside down, chaotic, topsyturvy.

soqquàdro, *s.m.* (*scompiglio*) confusion, muddle: *a* —, topsyturvy (*o* in utter confusion *o* in a mess): *ha messo a* — *tutti i cassetti,* she has turned everything upside down in all the drawers.

sòrba, *s.f.* **1.** (*bot.*) sorb, sorb-apple ‖ *col tempo e con la paglia maturano le sorbe,* *prov.* all things come to him who waits **2.** (*percossa*) thrashing (*solo sing.*): *gli hanno dato molte sorbe,* they have given him a good thrashing.

sorbettàre, *v.t.* (*gelare*) to freeze ‖ **sorbettàrsi,** *v.r.* (*sorbirsi*) to put up with (s.o., sthg.): *mi sono dovuto* — *quel noioso per tutta la serata,* I had to put up with that bore the whole evening.

sorbettièra, *s.f.* ice-cream machine, ice-cream box.

sorbétto, *s.m.* sherbet; (*gelato*) ice-cream ‖ *sto diventando un* —, I am turning into a block of ice.

sorbíre, *v.t.* to sip: *stava sorbendo il caffè,* he was sipping his coffee ‖ **sorbírsi,** *v.r.* *fig.* (*sopportare*) to put up with (s.o., sthg.); to swallow: *dovette* — *i loro* *insulti*, he had to swallow their insults; — *un discorso noioso*, to put up with a boring talk.

sòrbo, *s.m.* (*bot.*) sorb, service-tree.

Sorbóna, *no.pr.f.* (*Università di Parigi*) Sorbonne.

sorcíno, *ag.* mouse-grey, mouse-coloured.

sórcio, *s.m.* (*zool.*) mouse (*pl.* mice).

sórcolo, *s.m.* (*bot.*) graft.

sordàggine, *s.f.* (slight) deafness.

sordaménte, *av.* 1. dully, with a dull sound: *cadde* —, it fell with a thud 2. (*nascostamente*) secretly, on the sly, underhandedly.

sordàstro, *ag.* hard of hearing.

sordidaménte, *av.* 1. filthily, dirtily 2. (*da avaro*) sordidly, meanly.

sordidézza, *s.f.* 1. filthiness, dirtiness 2. (*avarizia*) sordidness, meanness.

sórdido, *ag.* 1. filthy, dirty ‖ *avarizia sordida*, mean (*o* vile) avarice 2. (*avaro*) sordid, mean.

sordína, *s.f.* (*mus.*) mute, sordino (*pl.* sordini), sordine: *mettere la* — *a un violino*, to mute a violin ‖ *alla* —, (*di soppiatto*) on the sly (*o* slyly *o* underhandedly) ‖ *suonare in* —, to play in a minor key.

sordità, *s.f.* deafness: — *temporanea*, temporary deafness ‖ —, *verbale*, (*patol.*) word deafness.

sórdo, *ag.* 1. deaf: — *da un orecchio*, deaf in one ear ‖ — *come una campana*, as deaf as a (door-) post ‖ *fare il* —, to turn a deaf ear (to sthg.) ‖ *non c'è peggior* — *di chi non vuol udire*, prov. none so deaf as those that won't hear 2. *fig.* (*insensibile*) deaf; insensible: *egli fu* — *a tutti i miei ammonimenti*, he was deaf to all my warnings 3. (*di suono, rumore*) dull, hollow: *colpo* —, dull (*o* muffled) blow; *rumore* —, dull (*o* hollow) noise; *suono* —, dull sound; *voce sorda*, dull (*o* hollow) voice; *cadde con un colpo* —, it fell with a thump (*o* thud) ‖ *sala sorda*, non-echoing (*o* echo-proof) room 4. (*di dolore*) dull 5. (*nascosto, subdolo*) underhand, sly: *opposizione sorda*, underhand opposition; *ostilità sorda*, veiled hostility ‖ *s.m.* deaf person.

sordomutismo, *s.m.* deaf-mutism, deaf-dumbness.

sordomúto, *ag.* deaf-and-dumb ‖ *s.m.* deaf-mute: *alfabeto per sordomuti*, deaf-and-dumb alphabet.

sorèlla, *s.f.* 1. sister: — *germana, carnale*, sister-german (*o* full sister); — *maggiore*, elder sister ‖ — *di latte*, foster-sister ‖ *navi, nazioni sorelle*, sister ship, nations ‖ *le nove sorelle*, (*mit.*) the Muses; *le tre sorelle*, (*mit.*) the Fates (*o* the Three Sisters) 2. (*suora*) sister: *sorelle della Carità*, Sisters of Charity.

sorellànza, *s.f.* 1. sisterhood 2. (*rapporto*) relationship: *la* — *delle lingue romanze*, the relationship of the Romance languages.

sorellàstra, *s.f.* (*con uno dei genitori in comune*) half-sister; (*con tutti e due i genitori diversi*) step-sister.

sorgènte, *ag.* rising: *la luna* —, the rising moon ‖ *s.f.* 1. spring; source: *le sorgenti di un fiume*, the sources (*o* the head) of a river; — *di petrolio*, oil-spring; *sorgenti minerali*, mineral springs; — *termale*, hot (*o* thermal) spring; *acqua di* —, spring-water 2. (*origine*) source, origin; (*causa*) cause: — *di dolori, di ricchezza*, source of troubles, of wealth.

sórgere, *v.i.* 1. to rise: *a che ora sorge il sole?*, what time does the sun rise?; *là dove sorge la luna…*, there where the moon rises…; *la nebbia sorgeva dal lago*, the mist was rising from the lake; *vidi* — *il sole*, I saw the sun rise ‖ *quando lo videro tutti sorsero in piedi*, when they saw him, they all rose to their feet (*o* stood up) 2. (*elevarsi, ergersi*) to rise; to stand: *in lontananza sorge un vecchio castello*, in the distance rises an old castle; *le montagne sorgevano di fronte a noi*, the mountains were rising before us 3. (*assurgere*) to rise (to sthg.); (*giungere*) to attain (to sthg.): *quello scrittore sorse a gran fama*, that writer rose to great fame 4. (*scaturire, nascere*) to rise (anche *fig.*); *fig.* to arise, to spring out (of sthg.): *da qui sorse una gran discussione, un dubbio*, a great discussion, a doubt

(a)rose from this; *dove sorge il Nilo?*, where does the Nile rise?; *il Reno sorge dalle Alpi*, the Rhine rises in the Alps 5. (*insorgere*) to rise; to revolt, to rebel: *tutti sorsero contro di lui*, everybody rose against him.

sorgiva, *s.f.* (*acqua di vena*) spring-water.

sorgivo, *ag.* spring (*attributivo*): *acqua sorgiva*, spring-water.

sórgo, *s.m.* (*bot.*) sorghum, Indian millet.

soriàno, *ag.* Syrian ‖ *gatto* —, tabby cat.

soríte, *s.m.* (*fil.*) sorites.

sormontàre, *v.t.* 1. to surmount; (*di acque*) to overflow: *le acque sormontarono gli argini*, the water overflowed the banks 2. (*superare, vincere*) to overcome, to surmount: — *una difficoltà*, to overcome (*o* to surmount) a difficulty.

sorníone, *ag.* sly, sneaking: *modi sornioni*, sneaking ways; *una persona sorniona*, a sly person; *uno sguardo* —, a sly glance ‖ *s.m.* sly person.

sororàle, *ag.* sororal, sisterly.

sororicída, *s.c.* sororicide.

sorpassàre, *v.t.* 1. (*oltrepassare*) to overtake, to pass; (*spor.*) to outrun: — *un'automobile*, to overtake (*o* to pass) a car; — *la velocità limite*, to exceed the speed limit 2. (*sopravanzare*) to surpass, to go beyond; to outdo, to excel: *ciò sorpassa le mie speranze*, this surpasses (*o* goes beyond) my hopes; — *qlcu. in ql.co.*, to outdo (*o* to excel) s.o. in sthg.

sorpassàto, *ag.* old-fashioned, out-of-date: *idee sorpassate*, old-fashioned ideas.

sorpàsso, *s.m.* (*aut.*) passing, overtaking: *divieto di* —, (*segnalazione stradale*) no passing.

sorprendènte, *ag.* surprising, astonishing.

sorprèndere, *v.t.* 1. (*cogliere inaspettatamente*) to catch; to overtake: *fummo sorpresi dal temporale*, we were caught in the storm; *lo sorpresi mentre fumava*, I caught him smoking; *la pioggia, la notte lo sorprese mentre passava il fiume*, the rain, the night overtook him while he was crossing the river; — *qlcu. in flagrante*, to catch s.o. in the act (*o* red-handed) ‖ *egli sorprese la mia buona fede*, he took advantage of my confidence in him 2. (*meravigliare*) to surprise: *fui sorpreso di vederlo fare una cosa simile*, I was surprised to see him doing such a thing; *tu mi sorprendi*, I am surprised at you ‖ **sorprèndersi**, *v.r.* 1. to catch oneself: *mi sono sorpreso a sbadigliare*, I caught myself yawning 2. (*meravigliarsi*) to be surprised: *non c'è da sorprendersene*, (there is) nothing to be surprised at (*o* it is no wonder); *non mi sorprenderebbe che egli lo facesse*, I should not be surprised at his doing it.

sorprésa, *s.f.* surprise: *una piacevole* —, a pleasant surprise; *ciò fu una grande* — *per me*, it was a great surprise to me; *con mia grande* —, to my great surprise; *ho una* — *per lui*, I have a surprise for him; *la sua* — *era molto evidente*, his surprise was very evident; *fare una* — *a qlcu.*, to give s.o. a surprise ‖ *di* —, by surprise: *attacco di* —, sudden attack; *visita di* —, surprise visit; *prendere di* —, to take by surprise.

sorrèggere, *v.t.* to support, to prop (up) (anche *fig.*): *egli è sorretto dalla speranza, dalla fede*, he is supported by hope, by faith; *le pareti sono sorrette da lunghi pali*, the walls are supported (*o* propped up) by long poles; — *un bambino che cammina a stento*, to hold up a child who can hardly walk.

sorridènte, *ag.* smiling: *un viso* —, a smiling face.

sorrídere, *v.i.* 1. to smile (anche *fig.*): *la fortuna gli sorride*, fortune smiles on him; *mi sorrise*, he smiled at me; *non l'ho mai visto* —, I have never seen him smile; *la vita ti sorride*, life is smiling before you; — *artificiosamente*, to simper 2. (*piacere, attrarre*) to make (s.o.) happy; to appeal: *mi sorride l'idea di andare in America*, the idea of going to America makes me happy; *quel progetto non mi sorrideva*, that plan did not appeal to me.

sorríso, *s.m.* smile (anche *fig.*): *un* — *affettato*, a simper; *i sorrisi della fortuna*, the smiles of fortune; *il — della natura*, the smile of nature; *un — ironico*, an ironical smile; *un leggero —*, a faint smile; *un — le sfiorò le labbra*, a smile hovered on her lips; *aveva un — enigmatico*, she smiled an enigmatic smile; *lo accolsi con il — sulle labbra*, I received him with a smile on my lips; *trattenere un —*, to keep down a smile.

sorsàta, *s.f.* gulp; draught; sip.

sorseggiàre, *v.t.* to sip.

sórso, *s.m.* **1.** gulp; draught; sip: *un — di whisky*, a snip of whisky; *bere a lunghi sorsi*, to take long draughts; *bere a piccoli sorsi*, to take small sips; *bere a sorsi*, to sip; *bere in un —*, to drink at one gulp (o draught) **2.** *(piccola quantità)* drop: *vorrei un — di acqua*, I should like a drop of water.

sòrta, *s.f.* kind, sort: *libri di ogni —*, books of all kinds (o all kinds of books); *ogni — di gente*, all kinds of people; *è un imbroglione della peggior —*, he is a swindler of the worst description; *me ne fa di tutte le sorte*, he plays all kinds (o sorts) of tricks on me; *questi ragazzacci sono tutti della stessa —*, these bad boys are all of a kind; *dirne di tutte le sorte a qlcu.*, to call s.o. all sorts of names; *lo offese dicendogliene di tutte le sorte*, he offended him by calling him all sorts of names ‖ *senza spesa di —*, without any expense; *non c'è difficoltà di —*, there is no difficulty.

sòrte, *s.f.* **1.** destiny, fate, fortune, lot; *(caso)* chance: *— favorevole, sfavorevole*, good, bad fortune; *i tiri della —*, the tricks of fortune; *dobbiamo accettare la nostra —*, we must accept our lot; *è in balia della —*, he is at the mercy of fate; *ognuno è schiavo della propria —*, every man is a slave to his own destiny (o fate); *essere favorito dalla —*, to be favoured by fortune; *meritare una — migliore*, to deserve a better fate ‖ *per buona, cattiva —*, luckily, unluckily: *per buona — c'era un medico*, fortunately (o luckily) there was a doctor ‖ *gli toccò in — una buona moglie*, he had the fortune to have a good wife; *mi è toccato in — di rimanere qui*, it has fallen to my lot to remain here ‖ *estrarre a — ql.co.*, to draw (o to cast) sthg. by lot ‖ *far buon viso a cattiva —*, to make the best of a bad bargain ‖ *gettare le sorti*, to cast lots ‖ *tentare la —*, to tempt fate ‖ *tirare a —*, to draw (o to cast) lots **2.** *(avvenire)* future, destiny: *le sorti di una nazione*, the destiny (o the future) of a nation; *ha in mano le sorti del paese*, he has the destiny of his country in his hands **3.** *(condizione)* state, lot: *non mi lamento della mia —*, I don't complain of my lot; *sono inquieto circa la sua —*, I am very anxious about his fate **4.** *(ventura)* chance: *ho avuto la — di incontrarlo*, I happened to meet him **5.** *(dir.)* capital: *perdette gli interessi e la —*, he lost both interest and capital.

sorteggiàre, *v.t.* to draw (lots) for (sthg.), to cast lots for (sthg.), to draw by lot: *incominciarono a — i premi*, they began to draw (lots) for the prizes; *— un nome*, to draw a name (by lot).

sortéggio, *s.m.* draw, drawing: *fare il —*, to draw (o to cast lots).

sortilègio, *s.m.* witchcraft, sorcery: *fare sortilegi*, to practice witchcraft.

sortìlego, *s.m.* sorcerer.

sortìre[1], *v.t.* *(letter.)* to get; to be endowed by nature with (sthg.): *egli sortì un vero talento per la musica*, he was endowed by nature with a real talent for music; *non sortì quel che si aspettava*, he did not get what he expected.

sortìre[2], *v.i.* **1.** *(essere sorteggiato)* to come out, to be drawn: *sono sortiti questi nomi*, these names have come out **2.** *(mil.)* to sally (forth) **3.** *(uscire)* to go out.

sortìta, *s.f.* **1.** *(mil.)* sally, sortie **2.** *(trovata spiritosa)* sally, witty remark.

sorvegliànte, *s.m.* overseer; *(sovrintendente)* superintendent, supervisor; *(ispettore)* inspector; *(guardiano)* keeper, caretaker, watchman *(pl.* watchmen): *— di notte*, night watchman (o guard).

sorvegliànza, *s.f.* overseeing, surveillance, watch; *(sovrintendenza)* superintendence, supervision; *(vigilanza)* care; *(ispezione)* inspection: *sotto —*, under surveillance (o observation): *per quanto riguarda il suo lavoro egli è sotto la mia —*, as regards his work he is under my supervision; *tienlo sotto —*, keep a close watch on him.

sorvegliàre, *v.t.* **1.** to oversee, to supervise, to superintend; *(un macchinario)* to attend to (sthg.): *— i lavori*, to oversee the works **2.** *(tener d'occhio)* to watch, to look after (s.o., sthg.), to mind: *non preoccuparti, lo sorveglio io*, don't worry, I'll watch over (o look after) him; *puoi — i bambini mentre sono fuori?*, can you watch (o look after o keep an eye on o mind) the children while I am out?; *— il gregge*, to watch the sheep.

sorvolàre, *v.t.* **1.** to fly over (sthg.): *l'aeroplano sorvolò la valle*, the plane flew over the valley **2.** *(passar sopra)* to pass over (sthg.): *sorvoliamo su questo punto*, let's pass over this point; *— sulle difficoltà*, to pass over difficulties.

sòsia, *s.m.* double: *egli è il tuo —*, he is your double.

sospèndere, *v.t.* **1.** *(attaccare, appendere)* to suspend, to hang (up): *— una lampada al soffitto*, to hang a lamp from the ceiling; *— ql.co. con una corda*, to hang sthg. by a rope **2.** *(chim. fis.)* to suspend **3.** *(impiccare)* to hang: *fu sospeso a un albero*, he was hanged on a tree **4.** *(interrompere, rimandare)* to suspend, to defer, to adjourn, to interrupt: *l'affare fu sospeso a causa della sua partenza*, the business was adjourned owing to his departure; *i lavori furono sospesi per due settimane*, the works were stopped for two weeks; *— una cura per alcuni giorni*, to stop (o to interrupt) a treatment for a few days; *— le ostilità*, to suspend hostilities; *— i pagamenti, le consegne*, to suspend payment, deliveries; *— un processo*, to adjourn a trial; *— la pubblicazione*, to suspend publication; *— una seduta per una settimana*, to adjourn a sitting for a week; *— una sentenza*, to suspend a judgement; *— un servizio*, to suspend a service **5.** *(per punizione)* to suspend: *— a divinis*, *(eccl.)* to suspend (from the exercise of sacred functions); *— qlcu. da un ufficio*, to suspend s.o. from an office; *— uno studente*, to suspend a student.

sospendìbile, *ag.* suspensible.

sospensióne, *s.f.* **1.** *(incertezza)* suspension: *— d'animo*, suspension **2.** *(interruzione; dilazione)* suspension, interruption: *— dei pagamenti, consegne*, *(comm.)* suspension of payment, deliveries; *— del lavoro*, stoppage of work; *— delle ostilità*, suspension of hostilities; *— di una seduta*, adjournment of a sitting; *istanza di —* *(dir.)* motion to stay ‖ *puntini di —*, dots (o suspension points) **3.** *(privazione di carica, impiego, ecc.)* suspension: *— da una carica*, suspension from an office; *— di uno studente, un funzionario*, suspension of a student, an official **4.** *(chim. fis. mec.)* suspension: *— anteriore*, *(aut.)* front-wheel suspension; *— cardanica*, *(mec.)* gimbals; *— elastica*, *(mec.)* elastic suspension; *— rigida*, *(ferr. elett.)* rigid suspension; *bracci della —*, *(mec.)* suspension arms; *molla di —*, suspension spring; *particelle in —*, suspended particles; *ponte, lampada a —*, suspension bridge, lamp.

sospensìva, *s.f.* **1.** *(sospensione)* suspension **2.** *(proroga)* extension.

sospensìvo, *ag.* **1.** suspensive ‖ *punti sospensivi*, suspension points **2.** *(dubbio)* doubtful, uncertain.

sospensòrio, *ag.* suspensory ‖ *s.m.* *(anat.)* suspensory (muscle); *(legamento)* suspensory ligament.

sospéso, *ag.* **1.** hanging, suspended: *— all'occhiello*, hanging from the buttonhole; *una lampada sospesa al soffitto*, a lamp hanging from the ceiling; *ponte —*, suspension bridge **2.** *(interrotto)* suspended, interrupted: *i lavori sono sospesi da una settimana*, the works have been interrupted for a week **3.** *(punito)* suspended: *— a divinis*, *(eccl.)* suspended a divinis; *un alunno —*, a suspended pupil **4.** *(trepidante)* in suspense *(predica-*

tivo); (*preoccupato*) worried; (*indeciso*) undecided: *non te-nerlo così* —, don't keep him in suspense like that; *siamo ancora con l'animo* —, we are still in suspense; *sono sempre con l'animo* — *quando viaggia in aeroplano*, I am always worried when he takes a plane ‖ *sistemare una questione in* —, to settle a matter pending.

sospettàbile, *ag.* liable to suspicion.

sospettaménte, *av.* suspectedly.

sospettàre, *v.t.* to suspect: *lo sospettano di tradimento*, they suspect him of treason; *non mi meraviglia perchè lo sospettavo da tempo*, I am not surprised, for I suspected it long ago (*o fam.* for I smelled a rat long ago); *sospettano che egli sia un ladro*, they suspect him of being a thief; *sospettano che l'abbia fatto*, they suspect him of having done it (*o* they suspect he has done it); — *un pericolo, un'inganno, un'insidia*, to suspect a danger, a trick, a snare ‖ *v.i.* to suspect (s.o., sthg.); to distrust (s.o., sthg.): *l'uno sospettava dell'altro*, they distrusted each other; *non puoi* — *della sua onestà*, you cannot question his honesty; — *di ql.co.*, to question sthg.; — *di qlcu.*, to distrust s.o.

sospètto, *ag.* **1.** (*che suggerisce sospetto*) suspicious: *aria sospetta*, suspicious air; *con un'occhiata sospetta*, with a suspicious glance; *in circostanze sospette*, in suspicious circumstances; — (*discutibile*) suspect (*predicativo*); questionable: *affermazioni sospette*, questionable statements; *la sua buona fede è sospetta*, his good faith is suspect (*o* questionable) ‖ *s.m.* **1.** suspicion: *al di sopra di ogni* —, above suspicion; *ciò mi mise in* —, this made me suspicious; *guardava con* —, he was looking with suspicion; *ho il* — *che egli sia un ladro*, I have a suspicion (*o* I suspect) (that) he is a thief (*o* I suspect him to be a thief); *cadere in* —, to fall under suspicion; *destare* —, to rouse suspicion **2.** (*persona oggetto del sospetto altrui*) suspect: *la polizia arrestò i sospetti*, the police arrested the suspects.

sospettosaménte, *av.* suspiciously.

sospettóso, *ag.* suspicious, distrustful.

sospingere, *v.t.* to push, to drive (anche *fig.*): *la fame lo sospinse a quel delitto, alla disperazione*, hunger drove him to that crime, to despair; *la zattera era sospinta dalle correnti*, the raft was driven by the currents; — *lo sguardo verso ql.co.*, to look towards sthg. ‖ *a ogni piè sospinto*, at every moment.

sospiràre, *v.i.* **1.** to sigh: *lo udii* — *nel sonno*, I heard him sigh in his sleep; *perchè sospiri?*, why are you sighing? ‖ — *di sollievo*, to sigh with relief: *sospirai di sollievo alla notizia*, I sighed with relief at the news ‖ — *per il dolore*, to sigh with grief: *piangeva e sospirava per il dolore*, she sighed and wept with grief **2.** *fig.* (*struggersi*) to pine, to sigh: — *per qlcu., ql.co.*, to pine (*o* to sigh) for s.o., sthg.: *da anni sospira per lui*, she has been pining for him for years; *sospira per il figlio perduto*, she sighs for her lost child; *sospira per la lontananza dell'amico*, she sighs over the separation from her friend ‖ *far* — *qlcu.*, to make s.o. suffer: *il figlio l'ha fatto tanto* —, his son has caused him much suffering ‖ *v.t.* to long for (sthg.), to pine for (s.o., sthg.), to sigh for (s.o., sthg.), to crave for (sthg.), to yearn for (sthg.): — *la patria*, to long (*o* to pine *o* to yearn) for one's native land; — *il ritorno di qlcu.*, to long for s.o.'s return; — *le vacanze*, to long (*o* to crave) for holidays ‖ *far* — *ql.co. a qlcu.*, to keep s.o. longing for sthg.; (*far attendere ql.co. a qlcu.*) to keep s.o. waiting for sthg.: *mi ha fatto* — *a lungo la risposta*, he kept me longing for an answer a long time; *ti ha fatto* — *i soldi*, he kept you waiting a long time for the money ‖ *farsi* —, to keep s.o. waiting (a long time): *ti sei fatto* —!, you have kept us waiting a long time!.

sospiràto, *ag.* (*desiderato*) longed for, craved for: *la tanto sospirata pace*, the much longed for peace; *finalmente fu servita la sospirata colazione*, the lunch they craved for was brought in at last.

sospirévole, *ag.* (*letter.*) sighing: *con voce* —, in a sighing voice.

sospìro, *s.m.* sigh (anche *fig.*): — *di rammarico*, sigh of regret (anche *fig.*): *si congedò dagli amici con un* — *di rammarico*, he parted from his friends with a sigh of regret; — *di sollievo*, sigh of relief (anche *fig.*): *alla notizia della promozione trasse un* — *di sollievo*, at the news of his promotion he drew (*o* breathed) a sigh of relief; *profondo* —, deep (*o* heavy) sigh; *emettere un* —, to give (*o* to breathe) a sigh; *trarre un lungo* —, to draw (*o* to heave) a long sigh ‖ *a sospiri*, at (long) intervals: *pagare a sospiri*, to pay at (long) intervals ‖ *il Ponte dei Sospiri*, the Bridge of Sighs ‖ *rendere l'ultimo* —, to breathe one's last.

sospirosaménte, *av.* sighingly, with sighs; (*lamentosamente*) plaintively.

sospiróso, *ag.* (*letter.*) **1.** sighing **2.** *fig.* (*lacrimoso*) plaintive: *poesia sospirosa*, plaintive poem.

sossópra, *V.* sottosópra.

sòsta, *s.f.* **1.** (*fermata*) stop, halt: *è in programma una - - a Lodi*, a stop at Lodi is scheduled; *il treno fece una* — *di venti minuti*, the train stopped for twenty minutes; *vi sono ancora due soste prima di Roma*, there are still two stops before Rome ‖ *divieto di* —, (*aut.*) no parking **2.** (*pausa*) pause; (*interruzione*) interruption, break; (*tregua militare*) truce: *sono molto stanco, avrei bisogno di una* — *di dieci minuti*, I am very tired, I need ten minutes' rest; *vi è una* — *di un'ora per la colazione*, there is an hour's break for lunch **3.** (*requie*) rest, quiet, peace: *il mal di testa non gli dà* —, his headache gives him no rest **4.** (*mec.*) dwell, tarry.

sostantivaménte, *av.* substantively, substantivally.

sostantivàre, *v.t.* (*gram.*) to substantivize: — *un aggettivo*, to use an adjective as a noun.

sostantìvo, *ag.* (*gram.*) substantive: *il verbo* —, the substantive verb ‖ *s.m.* substantive, noun.

sostànza, *s.f.* **1.** (*essenza*) substance, essence: — *materiale, spirituale*, material, spiritual substance; — *e forma sono opposti*, substance and form are opposites; *bada alla* — *e non alla forma delle cose*, mind the substance and not the form of things; *sono simili nella forma ma diversi nella* —, they are alike in form but different in essence (*o* in substance); *sacrificare la* — *per la forma*, to sacrifice the substance for the shadow ‖ *in* —, (*essenzialmente*) in substance (*o* essentially); (*in breve*) in short **2.** (*materia*) substance, matter, material, stuff: — *alimentare*, food-stuff; — *bituminosa*, (*edil.*) bituminous material; — *corrosiva*, (*chim.*) corroding substance (*o* mordant); *sostanze grasse, oleose*, fatty, oily substances; *sostanze liquide, solide*, liquid, solid substances; — *medicinale*, drug; — *radioattiva*, radiator; — *tossica*, toxicant; *la* — *di cui è fatta una cosa*, the substance (*o* matter) of which a thing is made **3.** (*argomento; parte essenziale di discorso, ecc.*) substance, gist, point: *la* — *di un articolo, di un discorso*, the gist (*o* the substance) of an article, of a speech; *questo è la* — *di quanto disse*, this is the point (*o* the gist) of what he said **4.** (*nutrimento*) *cibo di poca* —, unsubstantial food; *piatto di* —, substantial dish; *questo cibo ha poca* —, this food is not very nourishing (*o* substantial); *dar* —, to nourish **5.** (*patrimonio*) substance, patrimony, property; fortune: *ha dissipato la* — *di suo padre*, he has squandered his father's substance; *ha ereditato tutte le sostanze paterne*, he has inherited the whole of his father's fortune; *possedeva una piccola* —, he had a small patrimony; *accumulare sostanze*, to amass riches.

sostanziàle, *ag.* substantial, essential: *una differenza* —, a substantial (*o* an essential) difference; *la parte* — *del discorso*, the essential part (*o* the gist) of the speech ‖ *s.m.* (*sostanza*) substance.

sostanzialità, *s.f.* substantiality.

sostanzialménte, *av.* substantially.

sostanziàre, *v.t.* to reduce to substance ‖ **sostanziàrsi**, *v.r.* (*ridursi*) to boil down (to sthg.): *il suo discorso si sostanzia in questo*, his speech boils down to this.

sostanzióso, *ag.* **1.** (*nutriente*) substantial, nourishing, nutritious: *cibo* —, substantial (*o* nourishing) food **2.** (*di terreno*) rich: *un terreno* —, a rich soil **3.** (*che dà giovamento allo spirito*) which feeds the spirit: *un libro* —, a book which feeds the spirit.

sostàre, *v.i.* to stop, to pause, to halt: *sostò qui per circa due ore,* he stopped here for about two hours; — *dal fare ql.co.,* to stop doing sthg.

sostégno, *s.m.* **1.** support, prop (anche *fig.*): — *morale,* moral support; *un* — *teneva in piedi il muro,* a support (*o* prop) kept the wall standing; *era il solo* — *della sua vecchiaia,* she was the sole support of his old age; *parlò in* — *delle sue teorie,* he spoke in support of his theories; *questo muro ha bisogno di un* —, this wall needs to be propped up; *tu sei il* — *della tua famiglia,* you are the support of your family **2.** (*tec. edil.*) support; (*puntone*) strut; (*mec.*) support, brace, standard; (*elett.*) standard; (*chim.*) stand: — *del timone,* (*mar.*) rudder arm; — *di grondaia,* (*edil.*) gutter bearer; — *per lampada,* (*per illuminazione stradale*) lamp-post; — *per provette,* (*chim.*) test-tube rack.

sostenére, *v.t.* **1.** to support, to hold up, to sustain: *l'ho sostenuto col braccio,* I supported him with my arm; *il muro è sostenuto da lunghi pali,* the wall is supported (*o* propped up) by long poles; *se non lo sostieni cadrà,* if you don't hold him up he will fall; *tutto il peso era sostenuto da una grossa corda,* the entire weight was supported by a big rope ‖ *la speranza ci sostiene,* hope gives us strength ‖ *sai* — *una conversazione in inglese?,* can you carry on a conversation in English?; — *la conversazione,* to keep the conversation going (*o fam.* to keep the ball rolling) **2.** (*portare*) to carry: *questo ponte non può* — *più di dieci tonnellate,* this bridge cannot carry more than ten tons **3.** (*appoggiare*) to back (up), to support, to uphold: *l'accusa è stata sostenuta da prove convincenti,* the accusation was backed up by convincing evidence; *fu sostenuto da suo padre in tutti i modi,* he was backed (up) by his father in every way; *questa società è sostenuta da un miliardario americano,* this company is backed by an American millionaire; *questa teoria è sostenuta dall'esperienza e dai fatti,* this theory is supported by experience and by facts; *sono pronto a* — *il mio punto di vista,* I am ready to uphold (*o* to defend) my point of view; *spero che egli sosterrà le mie teorie,* I hope he will back up my theories; — *un amico,* to support a friend; — *una causa, una dottrina,* to uphold (*o* to support *o* to defend) a cause, a doctrine; — *un partito,* to support a party; (*con finanziamenti*) to back a party; — *la verità,* to uphold the truth **4.** (*affermare*) to maintain: *l'ho detto e lo sostengo,* I said it and I maintain it; *sostiene d'averlo visto,* he maintains (*o* asserts) that he saw it; — *la propria innocenza,* to maintain that one is innocent (*o* to assert one's innocence): *sostenne fino all'ultimo la sua innocenza,* he maintained to the last that he was innocent **5.** (*tener alto*) to keep up (anche *fig.*): *dobbiamo* — *il buon nome della scuola, la reputazione della nostra famiglia,* we must keep up the good name of the school, the reputation of the family; *egli non potrà* — *quel livello di vita,* he will not be able to keep up that standard of life; — *i prezzi,* to keep prices up **6.** (*mil.*) (*resistere a*) to resist; to withstand: — *un attacco nemico,* to resist an enemy attack; — *il fuoco nemico,* to withstand the enemy's fire **7.** (*sopportare*) to stand, to bear, to endure: *non potè* — *il dolore,* he couldn't bear (*o* stand) the pain; *non sostenne bene la prova,* he did not stand the test very well; — *la concorrenza,* to stand up to (*o* to meet) competition; — *il confronto con...,* to stand (*o* to bear) comparison with...; — *le spese di ql.co.,* to bear the cost of sthg. ‖ *non sostiene l'alcool,* he can't hold his drink ‖ — *il mare,* (*di nave, ecc.*) to ride well; (*di persona*) to be a good sailor **8.** (*subire*) to sustain, to suffer: — *un attacco,* (*mil.*) to sustain (*o* to suffer) an attack; — *il martirio,* to suffer martyrdom; — *una*

perdita, to sustain (*o* to suffer) a loss **9.** (*provvedere al mantenimento di*) to support: — *la propria famiglia,* to support one's family **10.** (*esercitare*) to hold: — *la presidenza,* to hold the presidency **11.** — *una parte,* (*teat.*) to act (*o* to sustain) a rôle **12.** — *un esame,* to take (*o* to sit for) an examination **13.** — *una nota,* (*mus.*) to hold a note **14.** (*trattenere*) to hold: — *l'acqua,* (*di argine*) to contain the waters; — *le lacrime,* to hold back one's tears; — *qlcu. in carcere,* to hold (*o* to keep) s.o. in prison ‖ **sostenérsi,** *v.r.* **1.** (*stare in piedi*) to stand (up) (anche *fig.*); (*appoggiandosi a qlcu., ql.co.*) to support oneself (against s.o., sthg.); to lean (on s.o., sthg.): *cammina sostenendosi con un bastone,* he walks leaning on a stick; *è un'ipotesi che non si sostiene,* it's a hypothesis that won't stand up; *le tue opinioni sono assurde e non si sostengono,* your opinions are absurd and do not hold water **2.** (*sostentarsi*) to sustain oneself, to keep up one's strength: *egli deve* — *con cibi molto nutrienti,* he must sustain himself (*o* keep up his strength) with nourishing food **3.** (*mantenersi*) to support oneself (by sthg., by doing), to keep oneself (by sthg., by doing): *guadagna appena il necessario per* —, he hardly makes enough to keep himself.

sosteníbile, *ag.* **1.** sustainable, supportable **2.** (*di idee, opinioni*) tenable, maintainable: *opinione poco* —, untenable opinion (*o* opinion that cannot be maintained) **3.** (*sopportabile*) bearable, endurable: *la situazione non è più* —, the situation is no longer bearable.

sostenibilità, *s.f.* **1.** supportability, supportableness **2.** (*di idee, opinioni*) tenability, tenableness **3.** (*sopportabilità*) bearableness, endurability.

sosteniménto, *s.m.* **1.** (*sostegno*) support (anche *fig.*) **2.** (*sostentamento*) sustenance.

sostenitóre, *ag.* supporting ‖ *s.m.* supporter.

sostenitríce, *s.f.* supporter, supportress.

sostentaménto, *s.m.* **1.** maintenance, sustenance, sustentation: *egli provvede al* — *della sua famiglia,* he supports (*o* maintains) his family **2.** *resistenza, forza di* —, (*aer.*) wing resistance.

sostentàre, *v.t.* to support, to maintain: *egli sostenta la sua famiglia col suo lavoro,* he supports (*o* maintains) his family with his work ‖ **sostentàrsi,** *v.r.* to sustain oneself: *si sostenta di sola frutta e verdura,* he sustains himself on fruit and vegetables only.

sostenutézza, *s.f.* stiffness, reserve, stand-offishness.

sostenúto, *ag.* **1.** stiff, distant, reserved: *una espressione sostenuta,* a distant expression; *modi sostenuti,* distant (*o* stiff) manners; *era piuttosto* —, he was rather stiff; *non fare il* —, don't be stand-offish **2.** (*comm.*) (*che si mantiene alto*) steady: *cambi sostenuti,* steady rates of exchange; *prezzi sostenuti,* steady prices **3.** (*mus.*) sustained.

sostituíbile, *ag.* replaceable.

sostituíre, *v.t.* **1.** (*rimpiazzare*) to replace, to substitute: *i tram saranno sostituiti da autobus,* trams will be replaced by buses; — *i brillanti con pezzi di vetro,* to substitute brilliants by pieces of glass (*o* pieces of glass for brilliants) **2.** (*prendere il posto di*) to take the place of (s.o.), to replace, to substitute for (s.o.): *egli fu sostituito da un suo amico,* he was replaced by a friend of his; *lo sostituii durante la sua assenza,* I took his place during his absence **3.** (*dir.*) to substitute in remainder.

sostitutívo, *ag.* substitutive.

sostitúto, *s.m.* substitute, deputy: *mandare un* —, to send a substitute.

sostituzióne, *s.f.* **1.** replacement; substitution; (*cambiamento*) change: *la* — *di un elemento sconvolge tutto il sistema,* the change of an element upsets the whole system; *la* — *di un vecchio insegnante,* the replacement of an old teacher ‖ *in* — *di,* in place of (*o* as a substitute for): *ho comperato questo libro in* — *di quello che ho perso,* I have bought this book in place of the one I lost **2.** (*dir.*) substitution: — *testamentaria,* substitution in remainder **3.** (*chim.*) substitution.

sostràto, *s.m.* substratum (*pl.* substrata): *è rozzo ma in lui c'è un — di sostanziale bontà,* he is rough but he has a substratum of substantial goodness; *in questo terreno c'è un — d'argilla,* this soil has a substratum of clay.

sottacére, *v.t.* to omit (to say): *— ql.co. a qlcu.,* to keep sthg. from s.o.

sottacéti, *s.m.pl.* (*cuc.*) pickles.

sottàcqua, *av.* under water: *nuotare —,* to swim under water ‖ *lavorare —, (non agire con franchezza)* to play an underhand game (*o* to do sthg. on the sly).

sottàna, *s.f.* **1.** (*sottoveste*) petticoat **2.** (*gonna*) skirt ‖ *sempre cucito alla — della mamma,* always tied to his mother's apron-strings **3.** (*veste talare*) cassock, soutane **4.** (*scherz.*) (*donna*) woman (*pl.* women): *quando ci si mettono le sottane..., (quando entrano in ballo le donne...)* when women set to it....

sottécchi, *av.* stealthily; by stealth: *guardare —,* to look stealthily.

sottèndere, *v.t.* (*geom.*) to subtend.

sottentraménto, *s.m.* replacement.

sottentràre, *v.i.* to take the place (of s.o., sthg.), to replace (s.o., sthg.): *all'amore sottentrò l'odio,* love turned to (*o* was replaced by) hate; *egli sottentrò a suo fratello,* he took his brother's place.

sotterfúgio, *s.m.* subterfuge, trick; shift: *ricorrere a un —,* to resort to a subterfuge ‖ *di —,* stealthily: *vedersi di —,* to see one another by stealth.

sottèrra, *l. av.* underground: *tesoro nascosto —,* treasure hidden underground; *uscito di —,* coming from underground ‖ *avrei voluto nascondermi —, (per la vergogna)* I wished the earth would open and swallow me up.

sotterraménto, *s.m.* burial, burying, interment.

sotterràneo, *ag.* underground (*attributivo*); subterranean: *ferrovia sotterranea,* underground (railway) (*o amer.* subway); *passaggio —,* underground passage (*o* subway); *prigioni sotterranee,* dungeons ‖ *s.m.* (*scantinato*) cellar; (*di basilica*) vault, crypt; (*di castello*) dungeon.

sotterràre, *v.t.* **1.** to bury; to inter; (*agr.*) to earth up: *— i semi,* to earth up the seeds; *— un tesoro,* to bury a treasure ‖ *ne ha sotterrati parecchi, fig.* he has outlived many of his friends ‖ *andare a farsi —, fig.* to hide one's head: *può andare a farsi —,* he may as well go and hide his head **2.** (*investire male*) to sink: *in quell'impresa ha sotterrato un patrimonio,* he has sunk a fortune in that undertaking.

sotterràto, *ag.* buried (anche *fig.*): *— nelle faccende,* buried in one's work; *morto e —,* dead and buried.

sottigliézza, *s.f.* **1.** thinness; fineness: *la — di un filo metallico,* the fineness of a wire **2.** (*magrezza*) slenderness, thinness **3.** (*acutezza*) subtlety; sharpness: *— di un ragionamento,* subtlety of an argument **4.** (*cavillo*) quibble: *queste sono sottigliezze,* these are quibbles.

sottíle, *ag.* **1.** thin; fine; (*tenue*) tenuous: *filo —,* fine thread; *lavoro —,* fine (*o* delicate) work; *polvere —,* fine dust; *profumo —,* pervasive scent; *punta —,* fine (*o* sharp) point; *strato —,* thin layer; *voce —,* thin voice ‖ *aria —,* thin air ‖ *udito, orecchio —,* keen hearing **2.** (*magro*) slender, thin: *gambe sottili,* thin (*o* slender) legs; *ragazza —,* slender girl **3.** (*penetrante*) subtle; (*acuto*) sharp: *distinzione, osservazione —,* subtle distinction, remark; *malizia —,* subtle malice; *mente —,* subtle (*o* sharp) mind ‖ *il Dottor Sottile,* the Subtle Doctor ‖ *mal —,* consumption **4.** (*astuto*) shrewd, sly, cunning ‖ *s.m.: il —,* thin part ‖ *guardare troppo per il —,* to split hairs.

sottilizzàre, *v.i.* to split hairs, to subtilize.

sottilménte, *av.* **1.** (*finemente*) finely; (*minutamente*) minutely; in detail: *— lavorato,* finely wrought; *esaminare —,* to examine in detail **2.** (*accuratamente*) carefully: *studiare — una questione,* to study a question carefully **3.** (*con acutezza*) subtly; sharply **4.** (*con astuzia*) shrewdly, cunningly.

sottintèndere, *v.t.* to imply, to understand: *e con questo che cosa vuoi —?,* and what do you understand (*o* imply) by that?.

sottintéso, *ag.* understood, implied: *idea sottintesa,* understood idea; *è — che tu verrai con me,* it is understood that you will come with me; *qui il verbo è —,* here the verb is (to be) understood (*o* implied) ‖ *s.m.* (*allusione*) implicit meaning, allusion: *non capisco i suoi sottintesi,* I don't understand his allusions; *parlare senza sottintesi,* to speak plainly (*o* openly).

sótto, *prep.* **1.** under; (*al di sotto, più in basso*) below; beneath, underneath: *— il letto, il tavolo,* under the bed, the table; *— la pelle,* under the skin; *— il vestito,* under one's dress; *abita — a, di noi,* he lives below (*o* under) us; *l'acqua scorre — questa crosta di ghiaccio,* water flows under(neath) this ice-crust; *lo nascose — la tovaglia,* he hid it under(neath) the tablecloth; *portava un libro — il braccio,* he was carrying a book under his arm; *la processione passò — le mie finestre,* the procession passed below my windows; *si mise al riparo — un albero,* he took shelter under a tree; *stava proprio — la mia finestra,* she was standing right (*o* just) under my window; *passare — un ponte,* to pass under a bridge; *vivere — lo stesso tetto,* to live under the same roof; *volare — le nubi,* to fly below (*o* under *o* beneath) the clouds ‖ *sott'acqua,* underwater ‖ *— il livello del mare,* below sea level ‖ *sott'olio, sott'aceto,* in oil, in vinegar ‖ *— la pari,* (*comm.*) below par **2.** *fig.* under: *— le armi,* under arms; *— l'azione di una droga,* under the effects of a drug; *— la bandiera italiana,* under the Italian flag; *— la direzione, la guida di...,* under the management, the guidance of...; *— il fuoco nemico,* under enemy fire; *— un giogo,* under a yoke; *— giuramento,* on oath; *— un'impressione,* under an impression; *— un impulso improvviso,* on a sudden impulse; *— il nome di,* under the name of; *— l'obbligo di fare ql.co.,* under an obligation to do sthg.; *— pena di morte,* under sentence of death; *— il pretesto di...,* on (*o* with) the pretext of...; *— processo,* on trial; *il regno di,* under the reign of; *una rigida disciplina,* under strict discipline; *— gli Stuart,* under the Stuarts; *glielo impose — minaccia di morte,* he forced him to do it on pain of death; *studia — un buon maestro,* she studies with a good teacher; *avere — il proprio dominio,* to have under one's dominion (*o* in one's power); *avere qlcu. — la propria tutela,* to have s.o. under one's guardianship; *essere nato — Saturno,* to be born under Saturn **3.** (*inferiore a*) under: *— la media,* under (*o* below) average; *— le mille lire,* under a thousand lire; *— i vent'anni,* under twenty (years of age); *— zero,* under (*o* below) zero; *è di poco — il quintale,* it's just under a hundred kilos **4.** (*in espressioni di tempo*): *— Natale, Pasqua,* at Christmas, Easter time; *siamo ormai — la vendemmia, gli esami,* we are now getting close to the grape-harvest, the exams **5.** (*Fraseologia*): *un lupo — la veste di agnello,* a wolf in sheep's clothing; *paese a tre miglia — Firenze,* a village three miles south of Florence; *— questo aspetto la faccenda non mi piace,* from that point of view I don't like the business; *andare — una macchina,* to get run over by a car; *avere ql.co. — il naso,* to have sthg. (right) under one's nose; *dare — a qlcu.,* to crack the whip (at s.o.); *mettere ql.co. — i denti,* to have a bite to eat; *mettere qlcu. — i piedi,* to treat s.o. like a door-mat; *passare ql.co. — silenzio,* to pass over sthg. in silence (*o* to say nothing about sthg. *o* to keep quiet) ‖ *av.* underneath; below, beneath; (*al piano di sotto*) downstairs: *i nomi — menzionati,* the names below; *qui, lì —,* under here, there; *aveva un pesante soprabito ma, — solo un vestito di seta,* she was wearing a heavy overcoat, but only a silk dress underneath it; *ti aspetto —,* I'll wait for you downstairs; *va sopra o —?,* does it go on top or underneath?; *vedevamo — la pianura,* we could see the plain below (*o* beneath); *— —, (di nascosto)* on the quiet: *cercava — — di rovinarmi,* he tried to ruin me on the quiet ‖ —, *ragazzi, al lavoro!*, come on, lads, get on with it! ‖ *ci dev'essere ql.co.* —, there must be sthg. behind it ‖ *andar* —, (*sommergersi*) to submerge (*o* to go down); (*tramontare*) to set (*o* to go down) ‖ *farsi* —, to push oneself forward ‖ *guardare qlcu. di* — *in sù*, to look s.o. up and down ‖ *s.m.* underside: *il* — *del coperchio*, the underside (*o* the inside) of the lid.

sottoascèlla, *s.f.* dress-shield.

sottobànco, *l.av.* under-the-counter: *vendita* —, under-the-counter sale; *mettere una cosa* —, to hush sthg. up.

sottobicchière, *s.m.* saucer.

sottobòsco, *s.m.* undergrowth, underbrush.

sottobottíglia, *s.m.* saucer.

sottocàlcio, *s.m.* (*di fucile*) toe of rifle butt.

sottocàlza, *s.f.* under-stocking.

sottocàpo, *s.m.* assistant-manager; vice-director: — *cannonniere*, gunner's mate; — *timoniere*, coxswain's mate.

sottòcchio, *av.*: *ho* — *la tua lettera*, I have your letter in front of me (*o* before me); *guardare* — *qlcu.*, *ql.co.*, to look at s.o., sthg. stealthily; *tenere ql.co.* —, to keep an eye on sthg.

sottochiàve, *av.* under lock and key: *essere, mettere, tenere* —, to be, to put, to keep under lock and key ‖ *tenere le figlie* —, to lock up one's daughters (*o* to keep one's daughters under lock and key).

sottocóda, *s.m.* crupper.

sottocommissióne, *s.f.* sub-commission: *ci sono quattro sottocommissioni di esami*, there are four examination sub-commissions.

sottocomitàto, *s.m.* subcommittee.

sottocopèrta, *s.f.* **1.** undercover **2.** (*mar.*) below deck: *andare, scendere* —, to go below.

sottocòppa, *s.f.* saucer.

sottocuòco, *s.m.* undercook.

sottocutàneo, *ag.* subcutaneous: *iniezione sottocutanea*, subcutaneous injection.

sottodivisióne, *s.f.* subdivision.

sottodominànte, *ag.s.f.* (*mus.*) subdominant.

sottoespósto, *ag.* (*foto.*) underexposed.

sottofàscia, *s.m.* printed matter posted in wrapper.

sottofóndo, *s.m.* (*edil.*) foundation: — *del pavimento*, floor rough (*o* floor foundation); — *di strada*, road foundation.

sottogàmba, *av.*: *prendere ql.co.* —, to make light of sthg.: *la sua malattia non dev'essere presa* —, his illness must not be made light of; *prendere qlcu.* —, to attach no importance to s.o.

sottogóla, *V.* soggólo.

sottolineàre, *v.t.* **1.** to underline **2.** *fig.* (*mettere in rilievo*) to lay stress on (sthg.), to emphasize.

sottolineàto, *ag.* **1.** underlined **2.** *fig.* (*messo in rilievo*) emphasized, stressed ‖ *s.m.* underlined part of a manuscript.

sottolineatúra, *s.f.* underlining.

sottolinguàle, *ag.* sublingual.

sottolunàre, *ag.* sublunary.

sottomàno, *av.* **1.** (*di nascosto*) underhand, underhandedly: *agire di* —, to act underhand(edly) **2.** (*a portata di mano*) at hand, within easy reach: *avere ql.co.* —, to have sthg. at hand (*o* within easy reach).

sottomàre, *s.m.* sea bottom.

sottomaríno, *ag.* submarine ‖*s.m.* submarine: — *atomico*, atomic sub(marine) (*o* A-submarine).

sottomascellàre, *ag.* submaxillary.

sottomésso, *ag.* **1.** (*soggiogato*) subdued, subject: *un popolo* —, a subject people **2.** (*obbediente*) submissive, obedient; (*rispettoso*) respectful: *ragazzo* —, obedient (*o* submissive) boy.

sottométtere, *v.t.* **1.** to subject; to subdue (anche *fig.*): — *una nazione*, to subject a nation; — *le proprie passioni*, to subdue one's passions **2.** (*presentare*) to submit: — *un caso al giudizio di qlcu.*, to submit a

case to s.o.'s judgement ‖ **sottométtersi,** *v.r.* to submit: — *all'autorità di qlcu.*, to submit to s.o.'s authority.

sottomissióne, *s.f.* **1.** (*il sottomettere, la conquista*) subdual, subjugation; subjection; conquest **2.** (*l'essere sottomesso*) submission **3.** (*rispetto, obbedienza*) submissiveness, obedience.

sottomúltiplo, *ag.s.m.* (*mat.*) submultiple.

sottopància, *s.m.* belly-band, girth.

sottopassàggio, *s.m.* subway, underground passage, underpass; (*ferr.*) subway.

sottopiède, *s.m.* **1.** (*per lo sprone*) foot-strap **2.** (*nelle scarpe*) cork sole.

sottopórre, *v.t.* **1.** (*assoggettare*) to subject, to subjugate: — *molte province*, to subject many provinces (*o* to bring many provinces into subjection) **2.** (*presentare*) to submit: *l'architetto sottopose i suoi piani al consiglio municipale*, the architect submitted his plans to the city council; — *un caso alla corte*, to submit a case to the court; — *una questione al giudizio di qlcu.*, to submit a question to s.o.'s judgment **3.** (*far subire*) to subject: *fu sottoposto ad un esame rigoroso*, he was subjected to a rigorous examination; *fu sottoposto a molte prove*, he underwent many trials; *fui sottoposto ad una rigida disciplina*, I was subjected to strict discipline (*o* I came under strict discipline); *furono sottoposti a molte e gravi umiliazioni* they were subjected to many and great humiliations; *essere sottoposto ad un'operazione*, to have (*o* to undergo) an operation **4.** (*esporre*) to expose: *ciò era sottoposto a molte critiche*, it was subjected to much criticism; — *qlcu. a rischi*, to expose s.o. to risks ‖ **sottopórsi,** *v.r.* to submit: — *alla volontà di Dio*, to submit to God's will; — *ad una operazione*, to have (*o* to undergo) an operation.

sottoposizióne, *s.f.* submission; subjection; subjugation.

sottopósto, *ag.* **1.** submitted (*predicativo*); subjected (*predicativo*) **2.** (*esposto*) exposed: — *a pericoli, rischi, tentazioni*, exposed to dangers, risks, temptations ‖ *s.m.* subordinate.

sottoprefètto, *s.m.* subprefect.

sottoprefettúra, *s.f.* subprefecture.

sottoprodótto, *s.m.* by-product.

sottórdine, *s.m.* (*bot. zool.*) suborder ‖ *essere, passare in* —, *fig.* to be, to become subordinate.

sottoscàla, *s.m.* cupboard under the stairs.

sottoscapolàre, *ag.* subscapular.

sottoscrítto, *ag.* undersigned; subscribed: *capitale, prestito* —, subscribed capital, loan; *domanda sottoscritta*, undersigned request ‖ *s.m.* undersigned: *il* — *dichiara che...*, the undersigned declares that....

sottoscrittóre, *ag.* signatory ‖ *s.m.*, **sottoscrittríce,** *s.f.* signer, subscriber.

sottoscrívere, *v.t.* to sign; (*comm.*) to underwrite: — *una dichiarazione, una lettera*, to sign a declaration, a letter; — *obbligazioni, azioni*, to underwrite bonds, shares; — *una polizza d'assicurazione*, to underwrite an insurance policy ‖ *v.i.* to subscribe: — *a un periodico*, to subscribe to a periodical; — *a un prestito*, to subscribe to a loan; — *a una proposta*, to assent to a proposal; — *per una forte somma a pro di un'istituzione di carità*, to subscribe (*o* to donate) a large sum to a charitable institution ‖ **sottoscríversi,** *v.r.* to sign ‖ *mi sottoscrivo vostro devotissimo*, I beg to remain yours faithfully (*o* I remain yours faithfully).

sottoscrizióne, *s.f.* **1.** signature **2.** (*raccolta di firme di aderenti*) subscription: *aprire una* — *ad un fondo*, to open a subscription to a fund; *fare una* — *per...*, to raise a subscription for....

sottosegnàre, *v.t.* **1.** to sign **2.** (*sottolineare*) to underline.

sottosegretariàto, *s.m.* under-secretaryship.

sottosegretàrio, *s.m.* under-secretary ‖ — *di Stato*, Under-Secretary of State.

sottosópra, *av.* **1.** upside down: *rivoltò — tutti i bicchieri*, he turned all the glasses upside down **2.** (*in disordine*) topsy-turvy, upside down: *essere —*, to be in confusion; *tutto il mondo è —*, the whole world has turned topsy-turvy; *mettere — ql.co.*, to turn sthg. topsy-turvy: *la casa fu messa —*, the house was turned upside down; *quel fatto ci mise tutti —*, that event threw us into utter confusion ‖ *s.m.* confusion, disorder, mess: *con questo — non ci si raccapezza affatto*, one can't make head or tail of it with this confusion.

sottospècie, *s.f.* subspecies (*invariato al pl.*).

sottosquàdro, *s.m.* (*di uno stampo*) undercut, back-draft.

sottostànte, *ag.* **1.** below (*predicativo*); beneath (*predicativo*): *la pianura —*, the plain below **2.** (*inferiore*) lower.

sottostàre, *v.i.* **1.** (*essere sotto*) to be below, to be under **2.** (*essere soggetto*) to be subjected: *— a molte critiche*, to be subjected to much criticism **3.** (*sottomettersi*) to submit; to yield: *non voglio — alle sue imposizioni*, I don't want to submit to his impositions; *— ai capricci di qlcu.*, to endure s.o.'s whims.

sottosuòlo, *s.m.* subsoil: *esplorare il —*, to explore the subsoil.

sottotenènte, *s.m.* second lieutenant; (*aer.*) pilot -officer: *— di vascello*, (*mar.*) sub-lieutenant.

sottotèrra, *av. s.m.* underground.

sottotítolo, *s.m.* sub-title.

sottovalutàre, *v.t.* to undervalue, to underestimate.

sottovàso, *s.m.* saucer (for flower-pot).

sottovènto, *s.m.* (*mar.*) lee: *costa di —*, lee-shore ‖ *av.* leeward ‖ *Isole Sottovento*, (*geog.*) Leeward Islands.

sottovèste, *s.f.* **1.** petticoat; slip **2.** (*panciotto*) waistcoat.

sottovíta, *s.f.* (*copribusto*) bodice.

sottovóce, *av.* in a low voice, in an undertone, under one's breath, in a whisper.

sottraèndo, *s.m.* (*arit.*) subtrahend.

sottràrre, *v.t.* **1.** (*arit.*) to substract: *— quattro da dieci*, to substract four from ten **2.** (*portar via*) to take away, to withdraw; (*rubare*) to steal, to purloin: *aveva sottratto diecimila lire dalla cassaforte*, he had stolen ten thousand lire from the safe; *— un documento, una lettera*, to purloin a document, a letter **3.** (*liberare, salvare*) to deliver; to preserve: *lo sottrassero alla morte, al pericolo*, they delivered him from death, from danger; *— qlcu. alla vendetta di qlcu.*, to put s.o. out of reach of s.o.'s revenge; *— qlcu. all'ira della folla*, to protect s.o. from the anger of the mob **4.** (*detrarre*) to deduct: *— le spese*, to deduct expenses ‖ **sottràrsi**, *v.r.* to get out (of sthg.); to avoid (sthg.), to evade (sthg.), to elude (sthg.): *non posso sottrarmi al mio dovere*, I can't evade my duty; *non riuscirà a — alla giustizia*, he will not be able to evade justice; *— ad un obbligo*, to back out of an obligation; *— alla morte, al castigo*, to escape death, punishment; *— al pericolo*, to get out of danger; *— alla vigilanza di qlcu.*, to escape from s.o.'s vigilance.

sottràtto, *ag.* **1.** (*arit.*) subtracted: *il numero —*, the subtracted number **2.** (*rubato*) stolen: *il denaro —*, the stolen money; *il documento —*, the purloined document.

sottrattóre, *s.m.* **1.** (*chi sottrae*) thief, purloiner **2.** (*arit.*) subtrahend.

sottrattríce, *s.f.* thief, purloiner.

sottrazióne, *s.f.* **1.** (*arit.*) subtraction: *fare una —*, to make a subtraction **2.** (*portar via*) taking away, withdrawal; theft: *— di documenti*, abstraction of documents **3.** (*detrazione*) deduction.

sottufficiàle, *s.m.* non-commissioned officer; (*mar. mil.*) petty officer, warrant officer.

soubrette, *s.f.* (*teat.*) soubrette.

souvenir, *s.m.* souvenir.

sovènte, *av.* often, frequently: *di —*, often; *lo vedo —*, I often (o frequently) see him; *vorrei che ci vedessimo più —*, I wish we could meet more often.

soverchiaménte, *av.* excessively, immoderately.

soverchiànte, *ag.* overwhelming: *la forza — del nemico*, the overwhelming strength of the enemy.

soverchiàre, *v.t.* **1.** to overflow: *il fiume soverchiò gli argini*, the river overflowed its banks **2.** (*essere migliore di*) to surpass, to outdo, to excel: *nessuno lo poteva — in destrezza*, nobody could surpass (o outdo o excel) him in skill **3.** (*sopraffare, opprimere*) to overwhelm, to overcome; to crush: *ci ha soverchiato di gentilezze*, he has overwhelmed us with kindness; *fu soverchiato da una serie di disgrazie*, he was crushed by a series of misfortunes; *non lasciarti — dalla tentazione*, don't let yourself be overcome by temptation ‖ *v.i.* (*sovrabbondare*) to be over, to be left over.

soverchiatóre, *ag.* overbearing: *nazione soverchiatrice*, oppressor nation ‖ *s.m.*, **soverchiatríce**, *s.f.* oppressor.

soverchiería, *s.f.* browbeating, bullying; oppression; abuse of power: *commettere, subire soverchierie*, to be guilty of oppression, to suffer oppression.

sovèrchio, *ag.* excessive: *soverchia precisione, cura*, excessive precision, care; *soverchi scrupoli*, excessive scruples ‖ *s.m.* excess: *pretende il —*, he is asking too much ‖ *averne di —*, to have more than enough ‖ *il — rompe il coperchio*, *prov.* too much is too much.

sóvero, (*rar.*) per **súghero**.

sovesciàre, *v.t.* (*agr.*) to plough in.

sovèscio, *s.m.* (*agr.*) green manure.

sovièt, *s.m.* soviet: *Soviet Supremo*, Supreme Soviet (o Council).

soviètico, *ag.* soviet: *Russia sovietica*, Soviet Russia.

sóvra, (*poet.*) per **sópra**.

sovrabbondànte, *ag.* superabundant.

sovrabbondanteménte, *av.* superabundantly.

sovrabbondànza, *s.f.* superabundance, excess: *— di parole*, verbosity (o flood of words).

sovrabbondàre, *v.i.* to superabound, to overabound.

sovraccaricàre, *v.t.* to overload; to overburden: *— qlcu. di lavoro*, to overload s.o. with work.

sovraccàrico, *ag.* overloaded, overburdened: *— di lavoro*, **overloaded** (o overburdened) with work; *questa automobile è sovraccarica*, this car is overloaded ‖ *s.m.* **1.** overload, overloading; additional load, additional burden; excessive load, excessive burden: *— momentaneo*, (*elett. mec.*) momentary overload; (*rad. tv.*) blast **2.** (*spor.*) (*di cavalli*) weight-handicap.

sovraeccitàre, *e derivati*, *V.* **sovreccitàre**, *e derivati*.

sovraespósto, *ag.* **1.** (*suddetto*) above-mentioned **2.** (*foto.*) overexposed.

sovraffollàre, *v.t.* to overcrowd.

sovraffollàto, *ag.* overcrowded; packed: *la sala era sovraffollata*, the hall was packed full.

sovràna, *s.f.* **1.** sovereign; (*regina*) queen **2.** (*antica moneta*) sovereign **3.** (*sterlina*) pound.

sovranaménte, *av.* **1.** royally, sovereignly, regally **2.** (*supremamente*) supremely.

sovraneggiàre, *v.i.* to rule, to reign; to domineer (anche *fig.*): *— su un paese*, to rule (o to reign) over a country; *— tra i colleghi*, to domineer (o to lord it) over one's colleagues.

sovranità, *s.f.* **1.** sovereignty: *aver diritto di — sopra un territorio*, to have sovereign rights over a territory **2.** (*supremazia*) supremacy: *la — della legge*, the supremacy of the law; *la — dell'ingegno*, the supremacy of genius.

sovràno, *ag.* **1.** sovereign: *potere —*, sovereign power: *principe —*, sovereign prince **2.** (*supremo*) sovereign, supreme: *— disprezzo*, sovereign (o supreme) contempt; *bellezza sovrana*, sovereign beauty; *onore —*, supreme honour **3.** (*che sta sopra*) impending: *rupe sovrana*, impending crag ‖ *s.m.* sovereign; (*re*) king: *alla presenza del —*, in the king's presence ‖ *— di sè stesso*, master of oneself ‖ *il disordine regna —*, disorder reigns.

sovrannaturàle, *V.* **soprannaturàle**.

sovrappopolàre, *v.t.* to overpeople, to overpopulate.

sovrappopolàto, *ag.* overpeopled, overpopulated.

sovrappórre, *v.t.* to put (sthg.) on (sthg.); to lay (sthg.) on (sthg.); to place (sthg.) on (sthg.); to superimpose: — *due triangoli,* (*geom.*) to superimpose two triangles; — *un'immagine a un'altra,* to superimpose one image on another (o to put *o* to lay *o* to place) one image (up)on another ‖ **sovrappórsi,** *v.r.* 1. (*mettersi sopra*) to be placed one upon another; to be superimposed: *le immagini si sovrappongono,* the images are superimposed (o are placed one upon another) 2. (*rendersi superiore*) to get the upper hand (of s.o., sthg.); to get the better (of s.o., sthg.): *è un codardo e gli piace — ai deboli,* he is a coward and likes to get the better of weak people.

sovrapposizióne, *s.f.* superimposition; (*mec. rad.*) overlap.

sovrappósto, *ag.* laid upon, placed upon; superimposed: *i mattoni sono sovrapposti l'uno all'altro,* the bricks are laid one upon the other.

sovrapproduzióne, *s.f.* overproduction.

sovrastànte, *ag.* overhanging, impending (anche *fig.*): *pericolo* —, impending danger; *la scogliera — la spiaggia,* the cliffs overhanging the beach.

sovrastàre, *v.i.* 1. to dominate (sthg.); to overhang (over sthg.): *la montagna sovrasta alla valle,* the mountain dominates the valley 2. *fig.* (*essere imminente*) to hang (over s.o., sthg.); to impend (over s.o., sthg.): *ignaro della sciagura che lo sovrasta,* unaware of the impending calamity; *molti pericoli ci sovrastano,* many dangers are hanging (o are impending) over us 3. (*essere superiore*) to be superior (to s.o., sthg.): *egli sovrasta di molto a tutti gli altri competitori,* he is much superior to all the other competitors ‖ *v.t.* to surpass, to excel, to outdo: *egli sovrasta tutti in astuzia,* he surpasses (o excels) everybody in cunning.

sovreccedènte, *ag.* superabundant ‖ *s.m.* surplus, excess, superfluity.

sovreccedènza, *s.f.* excess, surplus.

sovreccèdere, *v.t.i.* to exceed greatly.

sovreccitàbile, *ag.* overexcitable.

sovreccitabilità, *s.f.* overexcitability.

sovreccitaménto, *s.m.* overexcitement.

sovreccitànte, *ag.* overexciting.

sovreccitàre, *v.t.* to overexcite ‖ **sovreccitàrsi,** *v.r.* to become overexcited; to get overexcited.

sovreccitàto, *ag.* overexcited.

sovreccitazióne, *s.f.* overexcitement.

sovrimpórre, *v.t.* to impose again: — *una tassa,* to impose an extra tax (o to surtax).

sovrimpósta, *s.f.* additional tax.

sovrintèndere, *e derivati,* V. **soprintèndere,** *e derivati.*

sovrumanaménte, *av.* superhumanly.

sovrumàno, *ag.* superhuman (anche *fig.*): *gli angeli sono spiriti sovrumani,* angels are superhuman spirits; *sforzi sovrumani,* superhuman efforts.

sovveniménto, *s.m.* (*rar.*) 1. (*aiuto*) help, assistance 2. (*ricordo*) recollection.

sovvenire, *v.t.* (*aiutare*) to help, to assist ‖ *v.i.* 1. (*venire in aiuto*) to help (s.o.): *sovvieni ai miei mali,* help me in my misfortunes 2. *far* —, to remind (s.o., sthg.): *fammi — che devo mandargli un libro,* remind me that I must send him a book ‖ **sovvenírsi,** *v.r.* (*ricordarsi*) to remember (s.o., sthg.); (*venire alla mente*) to occur: *non mi sovvengo del tuo nome,* I do not remember your name; *non mi sovvenne che dovevamo incontrarci,* it did not occur to me that we were to meet.

sovventóre, *s.m.,* **sovventríce,** *s.f.* helper.

sovvenzionàre, *v.t.* to subsidize.

sovvenzióne, *s.f.* subsidy, subvention.

sovversióne, *s.f.* overthrow, subversion: — *di un governo,* overthrow (o subversion) of a government.

sovversivaménte, *av.* subversively.

sovversivísmo, *s.m.* tendency to subversion.

sovversívo, *ag.* subversive ‖ *s.m.* subverter.

sovvertiménto, *s.m.* overturning; subversion, overthrow.

sovvertíre, *v.t.* to overthrow, to subvert: — *il governo,* to overthrow the government.

sovvertitóre, *s.m.,* **sovvertitríce,** *s.f.* subverter.

sozzaménte, *av.* filthily, foully (anche *fig.*).

sozzézza, *s.f.* filthiness, foulness (anche *fig.*).

sózzo, *ag.* filthy, foul (anche *fig.*).

sozzúme, *s.m.,* **sozzúra,** *s.f.* filth, filthiness, foulness (anche *fig.*).

spaccalégna, *s.m.* wood-cutter.

spaccaménto, *s.m.* splitting, cleaving.

spaccamontàgne, *s.m.* (*spaccone*) braggard, boaster.

spaccapiètre, *s.m.* stone-breaker.

spaccàre, *v.t.* to split, to cleave; (*rompere*) to break: *ha spaccato il tavolo,* he broke the table; *ha spaccato il vetro con un sasso,* he broke the glass with a stone; — *un pezzo di legno,* to split (o to cleave) a piece of wood ‖ *c'era un sole che spaccava le pietre,* the sun was blazing down ‖ *quest'orologio spacca il minuto,* this watch is dead right ‖ — *un capello in quattro,* to split hairs ‖ **spaccàrsi,** *v.r.* to split, to cleave; (*rompersi*) to break: *il ghiaccio si spacca,* the ice is breaking up; *un legno che si spacca facilmente,* wood that cleaves easily; *per l'urto si è spaccato un vetro,* a glass broke in the collision.

spaccàta, *s.f.* (*ginnastica*) splits (*pl.*): *fare la* —, to do the splits.

spaccàto, *ag.* split, cleft; (*rotto*) broken: *legna spaccata,* chopped wood ‖ *un milanese* —, a Milanese through and through ‖ *è suo padre* —, he is exactly like his father ‖ *s.m.* (*arch.*) vertical section.

spaccatúra, *s.f.* split, cleft, cleavage, fissure; (*incrinatura*) crack: — *a caldo, a freddo,* (*metal.*) hot, cold crack.

spacchettàre, *v.t.* to unpack; to undo: *ho spacchettato i libri,* I have unpacked the books; — *un pacchetto,* to undo a parcel.

spacciàre, *v.t.* 1. (*vendere, liquidare*) to sell 2. (*divulgare*) to spread, to give out; (*mettere in circolazione*) to circulate: — *moneta falsa,* to circulate counterfeit money; — *notizie,* to spread (o to give out) news 3. (*far credere*) to make (s.o.) believe (sthg.): *me lo voleva — per oro,* he wanted to make me believe that it was gold ‖ — *fandonie,* to tell fibs 4. (*sbrigare*) to dispatch: — *una faccenda,* to dispatch a matter 5. (*uccidere*) to kill, to dispatch: *lo spacciò con un colpo di rivoltella,* he shot him (dead) with a revolver 6. *i dottori l'hanno spacciato,* the doctors have given him up ‖ **spacciàrsi,** *v.r.* to give oneself out (to be), to set (oneself) up as: *egli si spaccia per un grande scienziato,* he gives himself out to be (o he sets himself up as) a great scientist.

spacciàto, *ag.* done for: *egli è* —, he is done for (o it is all up with him).

spacciatóre, *s.m.* 1. (*venditore*) seller 2. (*divulgatore*) spreader, divulger 3. (*chi mette in circolazione*): — *di monete false,* forger.

spàccio, *s.m.* 1. (*vendita*) sale 2. (*negozio*) shop: — *aziendale,* factory shop; — *di sale e tabacchi,* shop for the sale of salt and tobacco.

spàceo, *s.m.* 1. split, cleft, fissure; (*incrinatura*) crack 2. (*apertura di vestito*) vent.

spacconàta, *s.f.* braggadocio (*pl.* braggadocios): *è stata solo una* —, it was only a piece of braggadocio.

spaccóne, *s.m.* boaster, braggart.

spàda, *s.f.* 1. sword: — *alla mano,* sword in hand; — *da scherma, da terreno,* fencing sword; *duello alla* —, duel with swords; *battersi con la* —, to sword-fight; *brandire la* —, to brandish one's sword; *cingere la* —, to gird a sword; *incrociare la — con qlcu.,* to measure (o to cross) swords with s.o.; *sguainare, rinfoderare la* —, to draw, to sheathe one's sword; *tirare di* —, to fence ‖ *la — della giustizia,* the Sword of Justice ‖ *la — di Damocle,* the sword of Damocles ‖ *egli è una* *ottima* —, he is an excellent swordsman (*o* fencer) ǁ *difendere a* — *tratta*, to defend with all one's might ǁ *passare qlcu. a fil di* —, to run s.o. through (with one's sword) **2.** *pl.* (*carte*) spades **3.** *pesce* —, (*ittiol.*) swordfish **4.** *pera* —, (*bot.*) spade pear.

spadaccíno, *s.m.* **1.** swordsman (*pl.* swordsmen), fencer **2.** (*attaccabrighe*) quarrelsome person.

spadàio, spadàro, *s.m.* sword-maker.

spàdice, *s.m.* (*bot.*) spadix (*pl.* spadices).

spadíno, *s.m.* court-sword.

spadísta, *s.c.* fencer.

spadóna, *s.f.* (*bot.*) spade pear.

spadóne, *s.m.* broadsword.

spadronàre, spadroneggiàre, *v.i.* to lord it, to domineer: *non lasciarlo* — *in casa tua*, don't let him lord it in your house.

spaesàto, *ag.* **1.** (*fuori del proprio paese*) out of one's country **2.** (*smarrito, turbato*) lost, out of one's element: *mi sento* — *senza di te*, I feel lost without you.

spaghétti, *s.m.pl.* (*cuc.*) spaghetti (*solo sing.*): *questi* — *sono molto buoni*, this spaghetti is very nice.

spaghétto, *s.m.* **1.** string **2.** (*fam.*) (*paura*) fear.

spaginàre, *v.t.* to alter the paging of (a book).

spagliaménto, *s.m.* removal of straw.

spagliàre[1], *v.t.* to take the straw off (sthg.), to remove the straw from (sthg.) ǁ *v.i.* (*rar.*) **1.** to live on straw **2.** (*vivere a spese altrui*) to sponge: *è un mese che spaglia a casa mia*, he has been sponging at our house for a month now ǁ **spagliàrsi**, *v.r.* to lose its straw: *questa seggiola si spaglia*, this chair is losing its straw.

spagliàre[2], *v.i.*, **spagliàrsi**, *v.r.* to overflow: *il fiume si è spagliato nella pianura*, the river overflowed into the plain.

spagliatóre, *s.m.*, **spagliatríce,** *s.f.* (*chi scrocca*) sponger, scrounger.

spagliatúra, *s.f.* removal of straw.

spàglio, *s.m.* **1.** (*di acque*) flooding ǁ *seminare a* —, to sow broadcast **2.** (*di cavallo*) swerve.

Spàgna, *no.pr.f.* (*geog.*) Spain ǁ *cera di* —, sealing -wax ǁ *erba spagna* (*bot.*) purple medick (*o* lucerne).

spagnolàta, *s.f.* (*millanteria*) bragging, boasting, bravado (*pl.* bravado(e)s).

spagnoleggiàre, *v.i.*, to affect Spanish manners.

spagnolésco, *ag.* **1.** Spaniardlike **2.** (*borioso*) boastful; bragging.

spagnolétta, *s.f.* **1.** (*su cui si avvolge filo*) spool **2.** (*di finestra*) sash-bolt **3.** (*sigaretta*) cigarette **4.** (*fam.*) (*nocciolina americana*) peanut, ground-nut.

spagnolísmo, *s.m.* **1.** Hispanicism **2.** (*moda spagnola*) Spanish fashion.

spagn(u)òlo, *ag.* Spanish ǁ *s.m.* **1.** (*abitante*) Spaniard **2.** (*lingua*) (the) Spanish (language) ǁ **spagn(u)òla,** *s.f.* **1.** Spaniard, Spanish woman (*pl.* Spanish women) **2.** (*patol.*) Spanish influenza.

spàgo, *s.m.* **1.** string; twine, pack-thread: *un gomitolo di* —, a ball of string; *un pezzo di* —, a bit of string ǁ *dar* — *a uno, fig.* to get s.o. talk **2.** (*fam.*) (*paura*) fear, funk.

spài, *s.m.* (*mil.*) spahi, spahee.

spaiaménto, *s.m.* uncoupling, unmatching.

spaiàre, *v.t.* to uncouple, to unmatch.

spaiàto, *ag.* odd, unmatched, unpaired: *una scarpa spaiata*, an odd shoe.

spalancaménto, *s.m.* opening wide, throwing open.

spalancàre, *v.t.* to open wide, to throw open: — *le braccia, gli occhi*, to open one's arms, one's eyes wide; — *una porta, una finestra*, to fling open a door, a window ǁ **spalancàrsi**, *v.r.* to burst open, to be thrown open: *si spalancò la finestra*, the window burst open.

spalancàto, *ag.* wide open: *con la bocca spalancata*, agape; *con gli occhi spalancati*, with wide-open eyes: *lo guardò con gli occhi spalancati per la sorpresa*, he looked at him in wide-eyed surprise.

spalàre[1], *v.t.* **1.** to shovel away; to sweep away:

— *la neve*, to shovel the snow away **2.** — *i remi*, (*mar.*) to feather the oars.

spalàre[2], *v.t.* (*togliere pali a*) to unprop.

spalàta, *s.f.* shovelling.

spalatóre, *s.m.*, **spalatríce,** *s.f.* shoveller.

spalatúra, *s.f.* shovelling.

spalcàre, *v.t.* **1.** to remove scaffolding from (sthg.) **2.** (*tagliar rami a*) to lop off boughs from (a tree) ǁ *v.i.* (*primeggiare*) to excel, to stand first.

spàlco, *s.m.*: *di* —, first-class (*attributivo*): *un attore di* —, an excellent (*o* a first-rate) actor; *un cantante di* —, a first-class singer.

spàldo, *s.m.* bastion.

spàlla, *s.f.* **1.** shoulder; *pl.* (*dorso, schiena*) back (*sing.*): *una pugnalata alle spalle*, a stab in the back (anche *fig.*); *ha una* — *più alta dell'altra*, he has one shoulder higher than the other one; *il tuo vestito è troppo stretto sulle spalle*, your dress is too narrow across the shoulders; *avere le spalle larghe*, to have broad shoulders (anche *fig.*); *portare il fucile a* —, to carry one's rifle on one's shoulder; *portare ql.co. sulle spalle*, to carry sthg. on one's back; *scrollare le spalle*, to shrug one's shoulders; *volgere le spalle a qlcu.*, to turn one's back to s.o.; *fig.* to turn one's back on s.o.; (*fuggire*) to flee; (*mil.*) to take the flight ǁ — *a* —, shoulder to shoulder ǁ *la* — *di un attore*, (*attore che suggerisce le battute ad un comico*) the straight man (*o* the feed) ǁ *violino di* —, (*mus.*) second violin ǁ *accarezzare le spalle a qlcu.*, (*percuoterlo*), to give s.o. a good thrashing (*o* to dust a person's jacket) ǁ *attaccare il nemico alle spalle*, to attack the enemy in the rear ǁ *avere una famiglia numerosa sulle spalle*, to have a large family on one's hands ǁ *avere la testa sulle spalle*, to have a head on one's shoulders ǁ *dire ql.co. dietro le spalle di qlcu.*, to say sthg. behind s.o.'s back ǁ *mettere qlcu. con le spalle al muro*, to put s.o. with his back to the wall ǁ *prendersi una responsabilità sulle spalle*, to take a responsibility upon oneself ǁ *ridere alle spalle di qlcu.*, to laugh at s.o. behind his back ǁ *vivere alle spalle di qlcu.*, to live on s.o. **2.** (*tip.*) shoulder **3.** — *del timone*, (*mar.*) rudder bow.

spallàre, *v.t.* to dislocate s.o.'s shoulder ǁ **spallàrsi,** *v.r.* to dislocate one's shoulder.

spallàta, *s.f.* **1.** push with the shoulder: *fece cadere lo steccato con una* —, he knocked the fence down with his shoulder **2.** (*alzata di spalle*) shrug (of one's shoulders).

spalleggiaménto, *s.m.* backing, supporting.

spalleggiàre, *v.t.* to back, to support: *era spalleggiato da suo padre*, he was backed (up) by his father ǁ **spalleggiàrsi,** *v.r. reciproco* to back each other (one another); to support each other (one another).

spalleggiàto, *ag.* backed, supported.

spallétta, *s.f.* parapet.

spallièra, *s.f.* **1.** (*di seggiola, divano, ecc.*) back **2.** (*testata del letto*) head of the bed; (*ai piedi del letto*) foot of the bed **3.** (*di piante*) espalier.

spallína, *s.f.* **1.** (*mil.*) epaulet(te) ǁ *si guadagnò le spalline*, he won his epaulet(te)s **2.** (*di vestito, sottoveste femminile*) shoulder-strap.

spallóne, *s.m.* (*dial.*) (*contrabbandiere*) smuggler.

spallúccia, *s.f.* narrow shoulder ǁ *far spallucce*, to shrug one's shoulders.

spallucciàta, *s.f.* shrug (of the shoulders): *rispose a spallucciate*, he replied shrugging his shoulders.

spalmàre, *v.t.* to spread; to smear: — *il burro su una fetta di pane*, to butter a slice of bread (*o* to spread butter on a slice of bread); — *del grasso su una superficie*, to smear (*o* to spread) grease on a surface ǁ **spalmàrsi,** *v.r.* to smear oneself (with sthg.): *spalmarsi il viso di crema*, to smear one's face with cream.

spalmàta, *s.f.* smearing: *dare una* — *di cera sul pavimento*, to smear some wax on the floor.

spalmatúra, *s.f.* smearing; spreading.

spàlmo, *s.m.* (*mar.*) spreading.

spàlto, *s.m.* (*edil. mil.*) glacis.

spampanaménto, *s.m.* **1.** (*il togliere le foglie alle viti*) stripping (of a vine) **2.** (*il perdere le foglie, di viti*) shedding (of vine leaves) **3.** (*di fiori*) opening out.

spampanàre, *v.t.* (*togliere le foglie a, una vite*) to strip (a vine) of its leaves ‖ **spampanàrsi,** *v.r.* **1.** (*di vite*) to shed its leaves; (*di fiore*) to open out its petals: *questi fiori si stanno spampanando,* these flowers are opening out their petals **2.** — *dal ridere,* fig. to laugh helplessly.

spanàre, *v.t.* **1.** (mec.) to strip, to break the thread of (sthg.) **2.** (agr.) to remove the earth from the roots of (sthg.).

spanàto, *ag.* (mec.) stripped.

spanciàre, *v.t.* to gut ‖ *v.i.* (*di muro*) to bulge ‖ **spanciàrsi,** *v.r.*: — *dal ridere,* to split one's sides with laughter.

spanciàta, *s.f.* **1.** (*urto con la pancia*) belly-flop: *prendersi una* —, to do a belly-flop **2.** (*scorpacciata*) bellyful: *fece una — di uva,* he stuffed himself with grapes.

spàndere, *v.t.* **1.** to spread: *l'albero spande i rami,* the tree spreads its branches; *la lampada spandeva la luce su tutta la stanza,* the lamp spread its light all over the room; — *il terrore,* to spread terror **2.** (*divulgare*) to spread, to divulge: — *notizie allarmanti,* to spread alarming news **3.** (*versare*) to shed: — *lacrime, sangue,* to shed tears, blood ‖ — *acqua,* (*orinare*) to make water **4.** (*scialacquare*) to squander: *durante le vacanze spende e spande,* during his holidays he squanders his money ‖ **spàndersi,** *v.r.* to spread: *i pettegolezzi si spandono facilmente in questa città,* gossip spreads easily in this town; *la popolazione si spandeva per le strade,* the people spread through the streets.

spandiménto, *s.m.* **1.** spreading **2.** (*il versare*) shedding.

spanditóre, *ag.* spreading ‖ *s.m.,* **spanditríce,** *s.f.* spreader.

spanditúra, *s.f.* **1.** spreading **2.** (*il versare*) shedding.

spaniàre, *v.t.* to remove (a bird) from bird-lime ‖ **spaniàrsi,** *v.r.* **1.** to escape from bird-lime **2.** fig. (*liberarsi da un impaccio*) to get out of a tight spot.

spanieràre, *v.t.* to take (sthg.) out of a basket.

spànna, *s.f.* span ‖ *alto una* —, tiny.

spannàre, *v.t.* **1.** to skim: — *il latte,* to skim milk **2.** (*nettare*) to clean.

spannatóia, *s.f.* skimmer.

spannatúra, *s.f.* skimming.

spannocchiàre, *v.t.* to husk, to strip.

spantanàre, *v.t.,* **spantanàrsi,** *v.r.* to get out of the mire (anche fig.).

spànto, *ag.* **1.** (*sparso*) spread **2.** fig. (*pomposo*) inflated.

spappagallàre, *v.i.* **1.** (*cianciare*) to chatter, to prattle **2.** (*ripetere come un pappagallo*) to repeat like a parrot.

spappolàre, *v.t.* to pulp ‖ **spappolàrsi,** *v.r.* **1.** to become mushy: *la pasta si è tutta spappolata,* the spaghetti has become all mushy ‖ — *dalla risa,* to split one's sides with laughter **2.** fig. (*prender gusto*) to take pleasure (in sthg.).

spappolàto, *ag.* mushy.

sparagèlla, *s.f.* (bot.) wild asparagus.

sparagiàia, *s.f.* asparagus bed.

spàragio, *s.m.* (bot.) asparagus.

sparagnàre, *v.t.* (dial.) to spare; to save.

sparàgno, *s.m.* (dial.) sparing; saving; (*denaro risparmiato*) savings (pl.).

sparaménto, *s.m.* shooting.

sparapàne, *s.m.* (*mangiapane*) loafer.

sparàre[1], *v.t.* to shoot, to fire; to discharge: *sparò due cartucce senza colpirlo,* he shot (off) (o discharged) two cartridges without getting him; *mi ordinò di* —, he ordered me to fire; — *a un leone, un bersaglio, un soldato,* to fire (o to shoot) at a lion, a target, a soldier; — *a salve,* to fire in salvoes; — *un colpo,* to fire a shot; — *un fucile, una rivoltella,* to shoot (off) a rifle, a revolver ‖ — *un calcio,* (*di cavallo, ecc.*) to lash out (a kick) ‖ *spararle grosse,* to talk big (o to tell tall

stories o to draw the long bow) ‖ **spararsi,** *v.r.* to shoot oneself.

sparàre[2], *v.t.* (*squartare*) to split: — *un pesce,* (*per ripulirlo dalle interiora*) to gut a fish; — *un pollo,* to draw a chicken ‖ **sparàrsi,** *v.r.* (*farsi in quattro*): — *per qlcu.,* to go to any length of trouble for s.o.

sparàre[3], *v.t.* (*togliere i paramenti a*) to take down hangings from (a church).

sparàta, *s.f.* **1.** discharge, volley **2.** (*spacconata*) brag; braggadocio (pl. braggadocios).

sparàto, *ag.* **1.** shot **2.** (*tagliato in due*) split ‖ *s.m.* shirt-front.

sparatóre, *ag.* shooting, firing ‖ *s.m.* shooter, firer.

sparatòria, *s.f.* shooting; exchange of shots.

sparecchiaménto, *s.m.* clearing (the table).

sparecchiàre, *v.t.* **1.** to clear: — *la tavola,* to clear the table **2.** (*trangugiare*) to guzzle: *sparecchiò tutto in pochi minuti,* he guzzled everything up in a few minutes.

sparéggio, *s.m.* **1.** disparity, inequality; (*deficit*) deficit **2.** (spor.) deciding game; deciding set; deciding match; (*a carte*) rubber game.

spàrgere, *v.t.* **1.** to scatter, to strew: — *fiori,* to strew flowers: — *fiori su una tomba,* to strew a grave with flowers; — *semi, ghiaia,* to scatter seed, gravel; — *zucchero, sale,* to sprinkle sugar, salt ‖ — *denari a piene mani,* to throw money around **2.** (*divulgare*) to spread: — *notizie,* to spread news; — *un segreto,* to spread a secret around ‖ — *ai quattro venti,* to throw to the winds ‖ — *una voce,* to spread a rumour ‖ — *zizzania,* fig. to spread discord **3.** (*versare*) to shed: — *lacrime, sangue,* to shed tears, blood **4.** (*luce*) to shed: *il lume spargeva una luce fioca,* the lamp shed a dim light ‖ **spàrgersi,** *v.r.* **1.** to scatter, to disperse, to spread: *si sparsero per la campagna,* they scattered (o dispersed) through the countryside **2.** (*diffondersi*) to spread: *la notizia si sparse in un baleno,* the news spread like wildfire; *si sparse la voce che...,* the rumour spread that....

spargiménto, *s.m.* **1.** spreading **2.** (*versamento*) shedding: — *di sangue,* bloodshed.

spargisàle, *s.m.* salt-cellar.

sparigliàre, *v.t.* to unmatch.

sparìre, *v.i.* **1.** to disappear: *egli sparì in un baleno,* he disappeared in a twinkle; *le frutta appena messe in tavola sparirono,* the fruit disappeared as soon as it was put on the table; *gli è sparito il portafogli,* his wallet has disappeared; *il gruzzolo sparì in pochi mesi,* the savings disappeared in a few months; *il sole sparì dietro una nuvola,* the sun disappeared behind a cloud; *sparì tra la folla,* he disappeared into the crowd; *le sue rughe sono sparite,* her wrinkles have disappeared **2.** (*morire*) to pass away.

sparizióne, *s.f.* disappearance.

sparlàre, *v.i.* to run (s.o., sthg.) down, to speak badly: *sparlò di me,* he talked behind my back.

sparnazzaménto, *s.m.* **1.** (*lo sparpagliare*) scattering **2.** fig. (*scialacquamento*) squandering.

sparnazzàre, *v.t.* **1.** to scatter **2.** fig. (*scialacquare*) to squander.

spàro[1], *s.m.* shot, report, detonation: *lo — di un fucile,* a rifle-shot (o the report of a rifle).

spàro[2], *s.m.* (ittiol.) sparus (pl. spari).

sparpagliaménto, *s.m.* scattering, spreading.

sparpagliàre, *v.t.* to scatter, to spread: *sparpagliò le carte sul tavolo,* he scattered the cards on the table ‖ **sparpagliàrsi,** *v.r.* to scatter, to disperse: *la gente si sparpagliò nel parco,* the people scattered through the park.

sparpagliataménte, *av.* scatteredly; (*in disordine*) in disorder.

sparpàglio, *s.m.* scattering; (*disordine*) disorder.

sparsaménte, *av.* here and there, scatteredly.

spàrso, *ag.* **1.** (*versato*) shed: *sangue* —, shed blood **2.** (*sciolto*) loose: *capelli, fogli sparsi,* loose hair, sheets ‖ *in ordine* —, (mil.) in open order.

Spàrta, *no.pr.f.* (*geog. st.*) Sparta.

Spàrtaco, *no.pr.m.* (*st.*) Spartacus.

spartaménte, *av.* here and there, scatteredly.

spartanaménte, *av.* Spartanly, in Spartan fashion: *vivere* —, to lead a Spartan life.

spartàno, *ag.* Spartan (anche *fig.*): *educazione spartana*, Spartan (o rigid) education ‖ *alla spartana*, Spartanwise ‖ *s.m.* Spartan ‖ spartàna, *s.f.* Spartan.

sparteìna, *s.f.* (*chim.*) sparteine.

spartiàcque, *s.m.* watershed; (*amer.*) divide.

spartìbile, *ag.* divisible.

spartiménto, *s.m.* (*il dividere*) dividing; (*divisione*) division.

spartinéve, *s.m.* snow-plough; (*amer.*) snowplow.

spartíre, *v.t.* 1. (*separare*) to separate: — *i litiganti*, to separate quarellers 2. (*distribuire*) to divide, to share out: *i briganti spartirono il bottino*, the brigands shared out the loot; *il guadagno verrà spartito fra noi quattro*, the profit will be shared (o divided) among us four ‖ *non ho nulla da* — *con lui*, I have nothing to do with him 3. (*mus.*) to score, to orchestrate.

spartitaménte, *av.* separately.

spartíto, *ag.* divided, shared: *patrimonio* —, divided patrimony ‖ *s.m.* (*mus.*) score: — *per pianoforte*, piano score.

spartitóre, *s.m.*, spartitríce, *s.f.* divider, sharer.

spartitràffico, *s.m.* traffic island.

spartizióne, *s.f.* 1. division, sharing; partition ‖ *la* — *della Polonia*, the partition of Poland 2. (*scriminatura*) parting.

spàrto, *s.m.* (*bot.*) esparto (grass).

sparutézza, *s.f.* leanness, spareness, haggardness.

sparúto, *ag.* lean, spare, haggard: *dal viso* —, haggard-faced.

sparvière, sparvièro, *s.m.* 1. (*ornit.*) sparrow-hawk 2. (*edil.*) mortar-board.

spasimànte, *ag.* 1. suffering, tortured, racked with pain 2. (*innamorato*) lovesick ‖ *s.m.* wooer, lover: *dice di avere molti spasimanti*, she says she has many wooers ‖ *fare lo* —, to spoon.

spasimàre, *v.i.* 1. to suffer agonies, to suffer terribly, to be racked with pain: *ho spasimato per questo dente*, I have suffered agonies with this tooth; — *di caldo, di sete*, to suffer the agonies of heat, of thirst 2. *fig.* to yearn, to long: *spasimava di poterlo rivedere*, she was yearning to see him again; — *d'amore per qlcu.*, to be head over heels in love with s.o.

spasimataménte, *av.* 1. painfully 2. *fig.* ardently.

spàsimo, *s.m.* 1. pang (anche *fig.*): — *atroce*, atrocious pang; *spasimi d'amore*, pangs of love; *gli spasimi della gelosia*, the pangs of jealousy; *gli spasimi della morte*, the pangs of death; *sentire gli spasimi della fame*, to feel the pangs of hunger 2. (*med.*) (*spasmo*) spasm, pang.

spasimóso, *ag.* (*rar.*) painful: *ricordi spasimosi*, painful memories; *sogno* —, painful dream.

spàsmo, *s.m.* (*med.*) spasm, spasmus: — *facciale*, facial spasm; — *nittitante*, spasmus nictitans.

spasmodicaménte, *av.* spasmodically.

spasmòdico, *ag.* (*med.*) spasmodic: *contrazione spasmodica*, spasmodic contraction.

spasmofilía, *s.f.* (*patol.*) spasmophilia.

spassàre, *v.t.* to amuse, to entertain, to divert: *le sue storielle ci spassavano*, his jokes amused us ‖ *far* — *qlcu.*, to amuse (o to entertain o to divert) s.o. ‖ spassàrsi, *v.r.* to amuse oneself, to enjoy oneself ‖ *spassarsela*, to have a very good time (o to have the time of one's life): *quel ragazzo se la spassa tutto il giorno invece di studiare*, that boy amuses himself all day instead of studying; *ve la siete spassata al mare?*, did you have a good time at the seaside?.

spasséggio, *e derivati, V.* passéggio, *e derivati.*

spassionataménte, *av.* dispassionately, impartially: *ve lo dico* —, I tell you dispassionately; *vorrei che giudicaste* — *chi di noi ha ragione*, I should like you to judge impartially which of us is right.

spassionatézza, *s.f.* dispassionateness, impartiality.

spassionàto, *ag.* dispassionate, impartial, unbias(s)ed, disinterested: *animo* —, unbias(s)ed mind; *giudizio* —, impartial (o unbiassed) judgement.

spàsso, *s.m.* 1. (*divertimento*) amusement, entertainment; (*passatempo*) pastime: *concedersi, prendersi qualche* —, to have some fun ‖ *che* —*!*, what fun! (o how amusing!) ‖ *per* —, as a joke: *lo stuzzicava per* —, he badgered him as a joke (o for a joke) ‖ *prendersi* — *di qlcu.*, to make fun of s.o. 2. (*passeggio*): *andare a* —, to go for a walk ‖ *essere a* —, (*essere disoccupato*) to be out of work; *mandare qlcu. a* —, (*liberarsene*) to get rid of s.o.; (*licenziarlo*) to dismiss s.o.

spassóso, *ag.* funny, amusing: *che tipo* —*!*, what an amusing character!; *è una storia spassosa*, it is a funny story.

spàstico, *ag.* (*med.*) spastic.

spastoiàre, *v.t.* 1. to unshackle 2. *fig.* (*liberare*) to release, to set free ‖ spastoiàrsi, *v.r.* to get out (of sthg.) (anche *fig.*).

spàta, *s.f.* (*bot.*) spathe.

spàtico, *ag.* (*min.*) spathic.

spàto, *s.m.* (*min.*) spar: — *d'Islanda*, Iceland spar; — *fluore*, fluor-spar; — *pesante*, barytes (o heavy spar).

spàtola, *s.f.* 1. spatula, spatule 2. (*per decoratori*) broad knife, putty knife.

spatriàre, *e derivati, V.* espatriàre, *e derivati.*

spauràcchio, *s.m.* 1. scarecrow: *il contadino pose uno* — *nel suo campo*, the peasant put a scarecrow in his field 2. *fig.* bugbear, bugaboo: *la matematica è il suo* —, mathematics is his bugbear (o bugaboo).

spauràre, (*letter.*) per spaurìre.

spauriménto, *s.m.* fright.

spaurìre, *v.t.* to frighten: *non bisogna* — *i bambini*, children should not be frightened ‖ spaurìrsi, *v.r.* to get frightened: *si spaurì e non volle uscir solo*, he got frightened and did not want to go out alone.

spaurìto, *ag.* frightened: *il bambino guardò suo padre con occhi spauriti*, the child looked at his father with fear in his eyes.

spavaldaménte, *av.* boldly, arrogantly, defiantly.

spavaldería, *s.f.* 1. boldness, arrogance, defiance: *lo disse per* —, he said it out of defiance 2. (*bravata*) boast: *le sue spavalderie mi danno ai nervi*, his boasts get on my nerves.

spavàldo, *ag.* bold, arrogant, defiant: *modi spavaldi*, bold (o arrogant o defiant) manners; *lo guardò con aria spavalda*, she looked at him haughtily ‖ *s.m.* bold fellow, arrogant fellow, braggart: *smetti di fare lo* —, stop this bragging.

spaventapàsseri, *s.m.* scarecrow (anche *fig.*).

spaventàre, *v.t.* to frighten, to scare: *quel rumore mi ha spaventato*, that noise has frightened me; *le tue minacce non mi spaventano*, your threats don't frighten me ‖ spaventàrsi, *v.r.* to be frightened, to get frightened, to be scared, to get scared: *non spaventarti*, don't be frightened; *si spaventò a morte*, he was scared to death.

spaventàto, *ag.* frightened, scared: *fuggì via tutto* —, he ran away thoroughly frightened.

spaventévole, *ag.* 1. fearful, dreadful, appalling: *vista, minaccia* —, fearful sight, threat; *ha un viso* —, he has a terrible face 2. *fig.* (*enorme*) huge, enormous: *difficoltà, ignoranza* —, enormous difficulty, ignorance.

spaventevolménte, *av.* 1. frightfully, dreadfully, awfully 2. (*enormemente*) enormously.

spavènto, *s.m.* fright; fear; terror: *tremava di* —, he was trembling with fear; *fare* — *a qlcu.*, to give s.o. a fright (o to frighten s.o.) ‖ *essere uno* —, to be a fright: *questo quadro è un vero* —, this picture is really awful ‖ *morire dallo* —, to die of fright (o to be scared to death).

spaventosaménte, *av.* dreadfully, fearfully, terribly.

spaventóso, *ag.* dreadful, frightful, terrible: *uno* —

delitto, a dreadful crime; *una spaventosa minaccia*, a terrible threat; *una ferita spaventosa*, a frightful wound.

spaziàle, *ag.* spatial; space (*attributivo*): *capsula —*, space capsule; *conquista —*, space achievement; *pilota —*, space-pilot; *sonda —*, space probe; *velocità —*, space-velocity.

spaziàre, *v.t.* to space (anche *tip.*) ‖ *v.i.*, **spaziàrsi**, *v.r.* to range, to rove: *la sua mente spaziava liberamente nel passato*, his mind ranged (o roved) freely in the past; *i suoi occhi spaziavano sul mare*, his eyes were roving over the sea.

spazieggiàre, *v.t.* to space (anche *tip.*).

spazieggiatúra, *s.f.* (*tip.*) spacing.

spazientírsi, *v.r.* to lose (one's) patience.

spàzio, *s.m.* 1. (*estensione non limitata*) space: *— a quattro dimensioni*, space-time continuum; *la concezione di — e tempo*, the conception of space and time; *uomo nello —*, man in space; *gravitare nello —*, to gravitate in space 2. (*estensione limitata*) space; (*posto*) room; (*distanza*) distance: *— di frenatura*, (di veicoli) braking-distance; *— interplanetario*, interplanetary space; *— interstellare*, interstellar space; *lo — percorso*, the distance run; *le due case erano separate da uno — di dieci metri*, the two houses were separated by a space of ten metres; *non c'è — qui per questa seggiola*, there is no space (o room) here for this chair; *non ti scrivo altro per mancanza di —*, I won't write any more for lack of space; *questo armadio occupa troppo —*, this wardrobe takes up too much room (o space) ‖ *— esplosivo*, (*elett.*) spark-gap ‖ *— nocivo*, (*mec.*) clearance (volume) ‖ *— vitale*, living-space 3. (*di tempo*) period, space: *nello — di due ore, di un anno*, in the space (o period) of two hours, of a year 4. (*tip. mus.*) space: *— da 4*, (*tip.*) 4-em space; *— finissimo*, (*tip.*) hair-space; *— in bianco*, (*tip.*) blank (space); (*tra caratteri*) pigeon-hole.

spaziosaménte, *av.* spaciously.

spaziosità, *s.f.* spaciousness, roominess; (*ampiezza*) width, breadth.

spazióso, *ag.* spacious, roomy; (*ampio*) wide, broad: *un appartamento —*, a spacious (o roomy) apartment; *fronte spaziosa*, broad forehead; *una porta, una strada spaziosa*, a wide door, road.

spazzacamíno, *s.m.* chimney-swęep(er).

spazzafórno, *s.m.* 1. (*arnese*) oven-rake, oven-brush 2. (*persona*) oven-man (*pl.* oven-men).

spazzaménto, *s.m.* sweeping; cleaning.

spazzamíne, *s.m.* (*mar.*) mine-sweeper.

spazzanéve, *s.m.* snow-plough; (*amer.*) snowplow.

spazzàre, *v.t.* to sweep; (*spazzar via*) to sweep away (anche *fig.*): *spazza via questa carta straccia*, sweep this waste paper away; *la civiltà spazza via i pregiudizi*, civilization sweeps away prejudice; *il ponte fu spazzato da un'onda*, the deck was swept by a wave; *i proiettili spazzavano il terreno davanti alle trincee*, bullets swept the area in front of the trenches; *il vento ha spazzato le foglie*, the wind has swept the leaves away; *— la neve*, to sweep the snow away; *— una stanza, una strada*, to sweep a room, a street ‖ *scopa nuova spazza bene, prov.* a new broom sweeps clean.

spazzàta, *s.f.* sweep; sweeping: *dà una bella — alla cucina*, give the kitchen a good sweep; *dà una bella — a queste foglie morte*, make a clean sweep of these dead leaves.

spazzatúra, *s.f.* 1. (*azione dello spazzare*) sweeping 2. (*rifiuti*) sweepings (*pl.*); garbage, rubbish: *bidone della —*, dust-bin; *carro della —*, dustcart; *mucchio di —*, rubbish-heap; *ho trovato una spilla nella —*, I found a brooch among the sweepings.

spazzaturàio, *s.m.* dust-man (*pl.* dust-men).

spazzíno, *s.m.* 1. (*di strade*) road-sweeper 2. (*spazzaturaio*) dust-man (*pl.* dust-men).

spàzzola, *s.f.* brush: *— per abiti*, clothes-brush; *— per capelli*, hair-brush; *— per scarpe*, shoe-brush ‖ *capelli a —*, crew-cut.

spazzolàre, *v.t.* to brush ‖ **spazzolàrsi**, *v.r.* to brush (oneself): *— le scarpe, il vestito*, to brush one's shoes, suit.

spazzolàta, *s.f.* brush: *dà una bella — a questi abiti*, give these clothes a good brush.

spazzolatúra, *s.f.* brushing.

spazzolíno, *s.m.* (small) brush: *— da denti*, tooth-brush; *— da unghie*, nail-brush.

specchiàio, *s.m.* 1. (*chi fabbrica specchi*) mirror-maker 2. (*chi ripara specchi*) mirror-repairer.

specchiàrsi, *v.r.* 1. to look at oneself (in a mirror): *essa non fa che —*, she does nothing but look at herself in the mirror 2. (*riflettersi*) to be reflected, to be mirrored: *le montagne si specchiano nel mare*, the mountains are reflected (o mirrored) in the sea ‖ *— in qlcu.*, to model oneself on s.o. (o to take example from s.o.).

specchiàto, *ag.* 1. (*integro*) honest, upright: *un uomo —*, an upright man 2. (*senza macchia*) spotless, pure: *specchiata onestà*, spotless honesty.

specchièra, *s.f.* looking-glass; (*toilette*) dressing-table.

specchiétto, *s.m.* 1. hand-mirror, (small) looking-glass: *— retrovisore*, (*aut.*) driving-mirror (o rear-vision-mirror o rearview-mirror) ‖ *— per le allodole*, lark-mirror; *fig.* allurement (o flattery o enticement) 2. (*tavola riassuntiva*) scheme, table.

spècchio, *s.m.* 1. mirror (anche *fig.*); looking-glass: *— elicoidale*, (*tv.*) mirror-screw; *— frontale*, (*med.*) forehead-mirror; *— parabolico*, (*cine.*) parabolic mirror (o reflector); *— retrovisivo, retrovisore*, (*aut.*) driving-mirror (o rear-vision-mirror o rearview-mirror); *— riflettente*, (*ott.*) reflecting substage mirror; *— riflettore*, (*cine.*) reflecting mirror; *— rinoscopico*, (*med.*) rhinoscopic mirror; *— ustorio*, burning-glass; *armadio a —*, mirror wardrobe; *gli occhi sono lo — dell'anima*, the eyes are the mirror (o the windows) of the soul; *non fa che stare allo —*, she does nothing but look at herself in the mirror; *questo romanzo è lo — dei tempi*, this novel is a mirror of the times; *guardarsi allo —*, to look at oneself in the mirror ‖ *— d'acqua*, sheet of water; *essere a — dell'acqua*, to be on the shore; *il castello è a — del mare*, the castle is on the seashore ‖ *galleria degli specchi*, hall of mirrors ‖ *scrittura a —*, mirror-writing: *Leonardo scriveva a —*, Leonardo used (to do) mirror-writing ‖ *essere liscio come uno —*, to be as smooth as a mirror ‖ *essere pulito come uno —*, to be as clean as a new pin 2. (*prospetto*) prospectus, register; (*amm.*) schedule: *— delle assenze*, register of absences; *— delle ore lavorate da ogni singolo operaio*, time-table; *lo — degli esami*, the time-table of the exams 3. (*esempio*) pattern, model, example: *è uno — di integrità, di virtù*, he is a model of integrity, of virtue; *farsi — di qlcu.*, to take one's example from s.o. (o to model oneself on s.o.) 4. *— di poppa*, (*mar.*) transom.

speciàle, *ag.* 1. special, particular: *in un modo —*, in a special way; *predilezione —*, special predilection; *provvedimento —*, special provision; *treni speciali*, special trains; *ho ql.co. di — per te*, I have sthg. special for you; *questo è un caso —*, this is a particular case ‖ *in special modo*, especially (o particularly) 2. (*particolare, strano*) peculiar, singular: *ha un carattere —*, he has a peculiar character 3. (*scelto, di prima qualità*) first-class; choice (*attributivo*), first-quality (*attributivo*): *frutta —*, choice fruit; *olio —*, first-quality oil.

specialísta, *s.c.* specialist.

specialità, *s.f.* speciality, specialty: *la — di questo oggetto è il suo colore*, the speciality (o peculiarity) of this object is its colour; *è una — farmaceutica*, it is a pharmaceutical speciality; *la letteratura tedesca è la sua —*, German literature is his special subject (o specialty); *la neurologia è la sua —*, nervous diseases are his speciality (o he is a specialist in nervous diseases); *questa è una delle più conosciute — della nostra casa*, this is one of the most popular speciality of the house; *tutte le nostre specialità sono in vetrina,* all our specialties are in the shop-window.

specializzàre, *v.t.,* **specializzàrsi,** *v.r.* to specialize.

specializzazióne, *s.f.* specialization.

specialménte, *av.* especially, particularly.

spècie, *s.f.* **1.** kind, sort: *gente di ogni — e di ogni razza,* people of every kind and description; *c'erano libri di ogni —,* there were books of all kinds; *che — di uomo è costui?,* what kind of man is he?; *hanno fatto una — di accordo fra di loro,* they have come to a sort of agreement; *mi fecero vedere una — di violino che non avevo mai visto,* I was shown a kind of violin I had never seen before ‖ *in —,* especially (*o* in particular): *tutti, ma lui in —,* everybody, but he in particular **2.** (*scient.*) species (*invariato al pl.*): *la — umana,* the human species (*o* mankind); *l'origine di una —,* the origin of a species; *secondo la teoria dell'evoluzione, ogni — si sviluppa da — preesistenti,* according to the theory of evolution, every species develops from pre-existing species **3.** (*teol.*) species (*invariato al pl.*): *l'Eucaristia sotto le — del pane e del vino,* the Eucharist under the species of bread and wine **4.** *far —, (far meraviglia)* to surprise (*o* to impress): *mi fa — che tu parli a questo modo,* it surprises me that you should speak like that; *non fatevene —, è un uomo fatto così,* don't be surprised, he is like that; *non mi farebbe — se...,* I shouldn't be surprised if....

spècie, *av.* especially, particularly: *in quella casa sono tutti pazzi, — i figlioli,* everybody is raving mad in that house, especially the children.

specìfica, *s.f.* (*comm.*) detailed list, detailed bill, detailed note: *mandatemi una —,* will you send me a detailed list?.

specificàbile, *ag.* specifiable.

specificaménte, *av.* specifically, precisely; (*particolarmente*) particularly.

specificàre, *v.t.* to specify, to define: *bisognerebbe che tu specificassi un po' meglio ciò che intendi dire,* you should define your meaning more accurately; *non è prudente — troppo,* it is not advisable to enter into too many details; *voglio — come avvennero i fatti,* I want to make clear how it happened; *— i motivi delle proprie lagnanze,* to specify the grounds of one's complaints.

specificataménte, *av.* specifically, precisely; (*particolarmente*) particularly: *indicare —,* to state precisely.

specificatìvo, *ag.* specifying.

specificàto, *ag.* specified, defined.

specificazióne, *s.f.* specification ‖ *complemento di —,* (*gram.*) genitive case.

specìfico, *ag.* **1.** specific: *caratteri specifici,* specific characters; *differenze specifiche,* specific variations; *non vi è distinzione specifica tra una lingua e un dialetto,* there is no specific distinction between a language and a dialect **2.** (*precisato*) specific, precise, explicit, definite: *sono venuto qui con uno scopo —,* I have come here with a precise object **3.** (*fis.*) specific: *peso —,* specific gravity **4.** (*med.*) specific: *rimedio —,* specific remedy ‖ *s.m.* (*med.*) specific.

specillàre, *v.t.* (*chir.*) to probe.

specìllo, *s.m.* (*chir.*) probe.

speciosaménte, *av.* speciously.

speciosità, *s.f.* speciousness, speciosity.

specióso, *ag.* specious: *un pretesto —,* a specious excuse; *mi sembra un argomento — il tuo,* your argument is specious in my opinion.

spèco, *s.m.* (*letter.*) (*antro*) cave, cavern; den.

spècola, *s.f.* (*osservatorio astronomico*) observatory.

spècolo, *s.m.* (*chir.*) speculum (*pl.* specula).

speculàre[1]**,** *ag.* specular, mirror-like.

speculàre[2]**,** *v.t.* **1.** to examine (with a speculum) **2.** (*indagare con l'intelletto*) to speculate upon, about (sthg.); to meditate upon (sthg.): *— le leggi della natura,* to speculate upon the laws of nature ‖ *v.i.* (*comm.*) to speculate (on, for sthg.): *— al rialzo, al ribasso,*

(*Borsa*) to speculate for the advance, for the fall; *— in Borsa,* to speculate on the Stock Exchange; *— su un articolo,* to speculate in an article; *— sulle differenze,* to speculate for differences.

speculataménte, *av.* (*rar.*) (*consideratamente*) on consideration, on reflection.

speculatìva, *s.f.* speculativeness.

speculativaménte, *av.* speculatively.

speculatìvo, *ag.* **1.** speculative: *mente speculativa,* speculative mind; *scienze speculative,* speculative sciences **2.** (*comm.*) speculative: *affare —,* speculative bargain.

speculatóre, *ag.* **1.** speculative: *una mente speculatrice,* a speculative mind **2.** (*comm.*) speculative ‖ *s.m.,* **speculatrìce,** *s.f.* **1.** speculator: *uno — del vero,* a speculator on the truth **2.** (*comm.*) speculator: *— al rialzo, al ribasso,* bull, bear (speculator); *— di borsa,* jobber; *— in grano,* speculator in corn.

speculazióne, *s.f.* **1.** speculation: *è molto portato alla —,* he is much given to speculation; *le sue speculazioni lo condussero alla conclusione che Dio non esiste,* his speculations led him to the conclusion that God does not exist **2.** (*comm.*) speculation: *— fortunata, rischiosa,* lucky, risky speculation; *lanciarsi in una —,* to launch into a speculation; *partecipare ad una —,* to join (*o* to share) in a speculation.

spedàle, *e derivati, V. ospedàle, e derivati.*

spedìre, *v.t.* **1.** to send, to mail, to dispatch; (*via mare*) to ship; (*via terra*) to forward: *ha spedito le merci a mezzo corriere,* he has sent the goods through a forwarding agent; *spedirò il pacco in America,* I'll ship the parcel to America; *— a mezzo piroscafo,* to ship by steamer; *— a piccola, grande velocità,* to send by slow, fast train; *— come campione,* to send by sample -post; *— contro assegno,* to send collection on delivery; *— in busta aperta,* to send by book-post; *— per ferrovia,* to send by rail; *— per pacco postale,* to send by parcel-post; *— per posta,* to send by post (*o* to post *o* to mail); *— sotto fascia,* to send under cover ‖ *— qlcu. all'altro mondo,* to send s.o. to the other world **2.** (*sbrigare*) to dispatch, to finish off; to settle: *vorrei — questa faccenda prima di partire,* I should like to settle this matter before leaving ‖ *— una causa,* (*dir.*) to enter a case for trial **3.** (*nel linguaggio della Curia, compilare, stendere*) to compile, to draw up, to write down: *— una bolla,* to draw up a bull ‖ **spedìrsi,** *v.r.* (*affrettarsi*) to hasten, to make haste, to be quick.

speditaménte, *av.* **1.** expeditiously, quickly, speedily, promptly: *camminare —,* to walk quickly **2.** (*correntemente*) fluently: *parlare, leggere —,* to speak, to read fluently.

speditézza, *s.f.* **1.** expedition, quickness, promptness, dispatch: *fare ql.co. con —,* to do sthg. with dispatch **2.** (*nel parlare, scrivere*) fluency.

speditìvo, *ag.* expeditious, quick, speedy, prompt.

spedìto, *ag.* **1.** quick, prompt: *essere — nel fare ql.co.,* to be quick (*o* prompt) in doing sthg. ‖ *avere la lingua troppo spedita,* to talk too much ‖ *essere dato per — dal proprio medico,* to be given up by one's doctor **2.** (*nel parlare, scrivere*) fluent: *ha una pronuncia spedita,* he has a fluent pronunciation ‖ *av. V.* **speditaménte.**

speditóre, *ag.* forwarding, sending, shipping (*attributivi*) ‖ *s.m.,* **speditrìce,** *s.f.* forwarder, sender, shipper.

spedizióne, *s.f.* **1.** (*comm.*) consignment, forwarding; (*via mare*) shipment; (*di lettere, pacchi*) dispatch: *— per via aerea,* airfreight; *— per ferrovia,* carriage by rail; *avviso di —,* advice-note; *bollettino, foglio di —,* consignment-note; *casa di spedizioni,* forwarding-agency; *istruzioni per la —,* forwarding (*o* shipping) instructions; *libro spedizioni,* shipping (-sales) book; *norme per le spedizioni,* forwarding (*o* shipping) regulations; *ricevuta di —,* consignment-receipt; *spese di —,* forwarding (*o* shipping) charges; *la — delle lettere, dei pacchi, dei telegrammi fu ritardata,* the dispatch of letters, parcels, telegrams was delayed; *fare una* —, to send a consignment: *fare una* — *di cinquanta sacchi di carbone*, to ship fifty sacks of coal **2.** (*scient. mil.*) expedition: — *archeologica*, archaeological expedition; — *di soccorso*, (*mil.*) relief expedition (*o relieving force*); — *militare*, military expedition; — *punitiva*, (*mil.*) punitive expedition; *corpo di* —, (*mil.*) expeditionary force; *i risultati della* — *al polo sud*, the results of the expedition to the South Pole; *organizzare una* —, to organize an expedition **3.** (*mar.*) clearing papers (*pl.*) **4.** *pl.* (*nella fattura di un vestito*) tailoring expenses.

spedizionière, *s.m.* forwarding-agent, shipping-agent, carrier.

spègnere, *v.t.* **1.** to extinguish; (*fuoco*) to put out; (*gas, luce, radio*) to turn out; (*con interruttore*) to switch off: — *una candela con un soffio*, to blow out (*o* to put out) a candle; — *il gas*, to turn off the gas; — *la luce*, to put out (*o* to turn off *o* to switch off) the light; — *la radio*, to switch off (*o* to turn off) the radio **2.** (*estinguere*) to kill, to stifle: — *le proprie ambizioni, passioni*, to stifle one's ambitions, passions; — *l'amore di qlcu.*, to kill s.o.'s love; — *un debito*, to pay off a debt; — *la sete*, to quench one's thirst ‖ — *la calce viva*, to slake (*o* to quench) lime ‖ **spègnersi,** *v.r.* **1.** (*di luce, fuoco*) to be extinguished, to go out, to die out; (*di fuoco*) to burn out: *la candela si spegne*, the candle is going out; *il fuoco si spense*, the fire burnt (*o* went) out **2.** *fig.* (*scomparire*) to die down; to fade (away): *la speranza si spense nei suoi occhi*, hope faded from his eyes; *la sua collera va spegnendosi*, his anger is cooling down; *il suo sorriso si spense*, his smile faded away **3.** (*morire*) to pass away; (*estinguersi*) to die out: *si spense due giorni fa*, he passed away two days ago.

spegníbile, *ag.* extinguishable.

spegniménto, *s.m.* **1.** extinction, extinguishment **2.** (*metal.*) blowing-out; (*fis. atomica*) shutdown: — *immediato di un reattore nucleare*, (*fis. atomica*) scram.

spegnitóio, *s.m.* extinguisher, snuffer.

spegnitóre, *ag.* (*rar.*) extinguishing ‖ *s.m.* extinguisher, snuffer.

spegnitúra, *s.f.* candle-snuffing.

spelacchiaménto, *s.m.* tearing the hair out.

spelacchiàre, *v.t.* to tear out the hair of (sthg.): *perchè hai spelacchiato così il tuo orsacchiotto?*, why have you torn your teddy-bear's hair out like that? ‖ **spelacchiàrsi,** *v.r.* to lose (its) hair: *la mia pelliccia si è tutta spelacchiata*, my fur-coat is covered with worn patches.

spelacchiàto, *ag.* scanty-haired; (*di stoffe, pellicce*) worn(-out); *un cane* —, a bare dog; *una pelliccia spelacchiata*, a worn-out (*o* shabby) fur-coat.

spelagàre, *v.t.* **1.** to fish (sthg.) up, to fish (sthg.) out **2.** *fig.* (*levare da impicci*) to help out of a difficulty.

spelàre, *v.t.* **1.** (*togliere il pelo a*) to unhair **2.** *fig.* (*cavar denari a*) to fleece ‖ *v.i.*, **spelàrsi,** *v.r.* to lose its hair: *la tua pelliccia (si) spela*, your fur-coat is losing its hair.

spelàto, *ag.* hairless; (*di stoffe, pellicce*) worn(-out); threadbare: *i polsi di quella pelliccia sono spelati*, the cuffs of that fur-coat are worn; *un soprabito dal collo* —, an overcoat with a threadbare collar.

spelatúra, *s.f.* **1.** (*lo spelare*) unhairing **2.** (*parte spelata*) hairless patch, worn patch.

speleología, *s.f.* speleaology.

speleòlogo, *s.m.* spelaeologist.

spellàre, *v.t.* **1.** to skin, to flay: — *una lepre*, to skin a hare **2.** *fig.* (*carpire denaro a*) to skin, to fleece: *essere spellato da uomini disonesti*, to be fleeced by dishonest men ‖ **spellàrsi,** *v.r.* to skin, to get skinned; to peel: *mi si spella il naso*, my nose is peeling; *mi sono spellato un ginocchio*, I have grazed my knee.

spellatúra, *s.f.* **1.** (*lo spellare*) skinning, flaying **2.** (*abrasione*) abrasion, graze, excoriation.

spellicciàre, *v.t.* **1.** to skin **2.** *fig.* (*malmenare*) to ill-treat, to ill-use.

spelliicciàta, *s.f.* **1.** skinning **2.** *fig.* (*rimprovero acerbo*) dressing-down, telling-off.

spelluzzicàre, *V.* **spilluzzicàre.**

spelónca, *s.f.* **1.** cave, cavern **2.** *fig.* (*luogo squallido; ricetto di malandrini*) den.

spèlta, *s.f.* (*bot.*) spelt.

speluzzàre, *V.* **spelacchiàre.**

spème, (*poet.*) per **sperànza.**

spendacción a, *s.f.*, **spendaccióne,** *s.m.* spendthrift.

spèndere, *v.t.* **1.** to spend (anche *fig.*): *spese 50.000 lire per una collana*, she spent 50,000 lire on a necklace; *spese la sua giovinezza in questo lavoro*, he spent his youth on this work; *è un uomo che spende*, he likes to spend his money; *ha speso 20.000 lire in libri*, he spent 20,000 lire on books; *quanto ti hanno fatto* —?, how much have they charged you?; *se lo comperi, avrai speso bene il tuo denaro*, if you buy it, you will have spent your money wisely; — *denaro, tempo*, to spend money, time; — *un patrimonio*, to spend a fortune ‖ *è un uomo che spende e spande*, he throws his money around ‖ *chi più spende meno spende*, prov. cheapest is dearest **2.** (*giovarsi di*) to make use of (s.o., sthg.): *spendi pure il mio nome*, make use of my name if you like.

spenderéccio, *ag.* lavish, prodigal.

spendíbile, *ag.* spendable.

spendibilità, *s.f.* spendability.

spendicchiàre, *v.t.i.* to spend a little at a time.

spèndita, *s.f.* spending.

spenditóre, *s.m.*, **spenditríce,** *s.f.* spender.

spendolàre, *v.i.* to hang; to dangle.

spenducchiàre, *v.t.i.* to spend a little at a time.

spèngere, *V.* **spègnere.**

spennacchiaménto, *s.m.* **1.** plucking **2.** *fig.* fleecing, skinning.

spennacchiàre, *v.t.* **1.** to pluck: — *un pollo, un volatile*, to pluck a chicken, a fowl **2.** *fig.* (*carpire denaro a*) to fleece, to skin ‖ **spennacchiàrsi,** *v.r.* to lose its feathers; (*mutare le penne*) to moult.

spennacchiàto, *ag.* plucked.

spennacchièra, *s.f.* plume, panache.

spennàcchio, *s.m.* plume, crest.

spennàre, *V.* **spennacchiàre.**

spennellàre *e derivati, V.* **pennellàre,** *e derivati.*

spensieratàggine, *s.f.* thoughtlessness.

spensierataménte, *av.* thoughtlessly.

spensieratézza, *s.f.* thoughtlessness.

spensieràto, *ag.* **1.** thoughtless: *gioventù spensierata*, thoughtless youth **2.** (*senza preoccupazioni*) care-free: *fa una vita spensierata*, he leads a care-free life.

spènto, *ag.* **1.** extinguished; out (*predicativo*): *a luci spente*, with the lights out; *il fuoco è* —, the fire is out; *la luce è spenta*, the light is out **2.** (*estinto, scomparso*) extinct: *civiltà spenta*, dead civilization; *vulcano* —, extinct volcano **3.** (*scialbo, smorto*) dull, dead: *colori spenti*, dull (*o* dead) colours; *occhi spenti*, dull (*o* dead *o* lifeless) eyes.

spenzolàre, *v.i.* to hang; to dangle.

spenzolóni, a, *l.av.* hanging, dangling.

spèra, *s.f.* **1.** (*letter.*) sphere: *le spere celesti*, the celestial spheres **2.** (*specchio*) (small round) mirror **3.** — *di sole*, (*raggio di sole*) sun-beam; (*macchia luminosa che fa un raggio battendo su un corpo*) patch of sunlight.

speràbile, *ag.* to be hoped (for): *ciò è* —, this is to be hoped for; *è* — *che...*, it is to be hoped that....

sperànza[1]**,** *s.f.* hope: *il color della* —, the colour of hope; *nella* — *di ricevere presto una vostra risposta*, hoping to hear from you soon; *oltre ogni* —, past (*o* beyond) all hope; *raggio di* —, gleam of hope; *senza* —, hopeless (*ag.*); hopelessly (*av.*); *una vaga* —, a lingering hope; *egli è pieno di* —, he is very hopeful; *ho buone speranze che torni presto*, I have good hopes (*o* strong hopes) that he will soon come back; *non* *ho* —, I have no hope; *quel ragazzo era la* — *di suo padre*, that boy was his father's hope; *abbandonare la* —, to give up hope; *cullarsi in vane speranze*, to cherish vain hopes; *deludere le speranze di qlcu.*, to disappoint s.o.'s expectations; *esprimere la ferma* — *che...*, to express the confident hope that...; *nutrire* — *di fare ql.co.*, to set one's hopes on doing sthg.; *riporre le proprie speranze in ql.co.*, *in qlcu.*, to set one's hopes on sthg., on s.o. (*o* to rest one's hopes in sthg., in s.o. *o* to pin one's faith on sthg., on s.o.); *vivere di* —, to live on hope; *vivere nella* — *di fare ql.co.*, to live in hope of doing sthg. ‖ *un ragazzo di belle speranze*, a promising boy (*o* a boy full of promise) ‖ *finchè c'è vita c'è* —, while there is life there is hope.

Speрànza[2], *no.pr.f.* Hope.

speranzosaménte, *av.* hopefully.

speranzóso, *ag.* hopeful.

speràre, *v.t.* **1.** to hope for (sthg.): *spera un po' di aiuto da suo padre*, he hopes for some help from his father; *sperava di riuscire*, he hoped to succeed (*o* he would succeed); *speriamo che tutto vada bene*, let us hope all goes well; *spero che tu guarisca presto*, I hope you (will) soon recover; *spero di no*, I hope not; *spero di sì, lo spero*, I hope so; *spero di vederlo presto*, I hope to see him soon; *questo non è il risultato che speravo*, this is not the result I had hoped for **2.** (*aspettarsi*) to expect: *non speravo che sarebbe venuto*, I did not expect him to come; — *il peggio per l'avvenire*, to expect the worst for the future ‖ *v.i.* to hope (for sthg., in s.o.): *egli spera ancora*, he is still hoping; — *in bene*, to hope for the best; — *in Dio*, to hope in God; — *negli amici*, to hope in friends; — *nel futuro*, to hope in the future; — *nella guarigione, nel ritorno di qlcu.*, to hope for s.o.'s recovery, for s.o.'s return; *continuare a* —, to hope on.

spèrdere, *v.t.* (*rar.*) **1.** (*disperdere*) to disperse, to scatter **2.** (*smarrire*) to lose ‖ **spèrdersi**, *v.r.* **1.** (*smarrirsi*) to lose oneself, to get lost, to go astray **2.** (*dileguarsi*) to disappear, to vanish.

sperdiménto, *s.m.* dispersal, dispersion.

sperdúto, *ag.* **1.** dispersed, scattered; (*vagante*) wandering **2.** (*isolato*) secluded; (*selvaggio*) wild: *vive in un luogo* — *delle Alpi*, he lives in a secluded place in the Alps **3.** (*smarrito*) lost (anche *fig.*): — *nella foresta*, lost in the forest; *mi sento* — *senza di te*, I feel lost without you **4.** *fig.* (*a disagio*) uncomfortable, ill at ease: *si sentì* — *in loro compagnia*, he felt uncomfortable (*o* ill at ease) in their company.

sperequazióne, *s.f.* disproportion; inequality: *degli stipendi*, inequality of pay.

spergiuràre, *v.i.* to perjure oneself, to swear falsely, to forswear oneself: *giurò e spergiurò che non era vero*, he swore again and again that it was not true ‖ *v.t.* to swear falsely: — *il nome di Dio*, to swear falsely in the name of God; — *il vero*, to swear falsely.

spergiuratóre, *s.m.*, **spergiuratríce**, *s.f.* perjurer.

spergiúro, *ag.* perjured ‖ *s.m.* **1.** (*chi giura il falso*) perjurer **2.** (*giuramento falso*) perjury.

spericolàto, *ag.* **1.** (*temerario*) reckless, daring **2.** (*timoroso*) timid ‖ *s.m.* **1.** (*temerario*) reckless fellow, daring fellow **2.** (*timoroso*) timid soul.

sperimentàle, *ag.* experimental: *prezzo* —, testing price; *scuola, teatro* —, experimental school, theatre.

sperimentalménte, *av.* experimentally.

sperimentàre, *v.t.* to experiment with (sthg.), to try, to test, to essay: — *un nuovo metodo*, to try a new method; — *un prodotto chimico*, to test a chemical product; — *nuovi metodi di insegnamento*, to experiment with new methods of teaching.

sperimentàto, *ag.* **1.** (*esperto*) experienced **2.** (*provato*) tried: *di sperimentata onestà*, of tried integrity.

sperimentatóre, *s.m.*, **sperimentatríce**, *s.f.* experimenter.

spèrma, *s.m.* (*fisiol.*) sperm.

spermacèti, *s.m.* spermaceti.

spermàtico, *ag.* (*fisiol.*) spermatic.

spermatísmo, *s.m.* (*fisiol.*) spermatism.

spermatocèle, *s.m.* (*patol.*) spermatocele.

spermatogènesi, *s.f.* (*fisiol.*) spermatogenesis, spermatogeny.

spermatorrèa, *s.f.* (*med.*) spermatorrh(o)ea.

spermatozòo, *s.m.* (*biol.*) spermatozoon (*pl.* spermatozoa).

spermòfilo, *s.m.* (*zool.*) spermophile.

spermogònio, *s.m.* (*bot.*) spermogonium (*pl.* spermogonia).

speronàre, *v.t.* (*mar.*) to ram.

speronàta, *s.f.* (*mar.*) ramming.

speróne, *s.m.* **1.** spur **2.** (*mar.*) ram.

sperperaménto, *s.m.* squandering, dissipation; wasting.

sperperàre, *v.t.* to squander, to dissipate; to waste: — *il proprio denaro, un patrimonio*, to squander one's money, to dissipate a fortune.

sperperatóre, *s.m.*, **sperperatríce**, *s.f.* squanderer, waster.

spèrpero, *s.m.* dissipation, squandering; waste: *in quella casa c'è uno* — *straordinario*, in that house there is a lot of waste.

spèrso, *V.* sperdúto.

sperticatolaménte, *av.* excessively, exaggeratedly.

sperticàto, *ag.* excessive, exaggerated: *lodi sperticate*, excessive praise.

spésa, *s.f.* **1.** expense; expenditure, outlay; (*carico*) charge; (*costo*) cost (*gener. sing.*): *spese a carico del destinatario*, charges forward; *spese accessorie*, incidental expenses (*o* incidental charges); *spese di bollo*, stamp dues; *spese di dogana*, customs expenses (*o* customs charges); *spese di gestione*, overheads; *spese di guerra*, war expenses; *spese di imballaggio*, packing charges (*o* packing expenses); *spese di magazzinaggio*, storing expenses (*o* storing charges); *spese di manutenzione*, maintenance charges; *spese di rappresentanza*, entertainment expenses; *spese di registro*, registration dues; *spese di riparazione*, cost of repairs (*o* charge for repairs); *spese di trasporto*, transport expenses (*o* transport charges); *spese di viaggio*, travelling expenses; *spese impreviste*, unforeseen expenses; *spese legali*, costs; *spese minute*, petty expenses; *spese postali*, postage (*o* postal charges); *spese preventivate*, estimated cost; *spese straordinarie*, extra expenses; *spese varie*, sundry expenses; *spese vive*, out-of-pocket expenses; *a proprie spese*, at one's expense; *fig.* to one's cost: *imparare a proprie spese*, to learn to one's cost; *a spese altrui*, at other people's expense (anche *fig.*); *a spese pubbliche*, at public expense; *comprese le spese*, charges included (*o* inclusive of charges); *escluse le spese*, charges excluded (*o* exclusive of charges); *esente da spese*, free of charge (*o* no charge); *ci fu una* — *di cinquanta milioni di lire per nuove attrezzature*, there was an expenditure (*o* outlay) of fifty million lire on (*o* for) new fittings; *egli non bada alle spese*, he spares no expense (*o* money is no object to him); *sta facendo delle grandi spese*, he is spending a lot of money; *coprire le spese*, to cover the cost; *far fronte a una* —, to meet an expense; *incorrere in grandi spese*, to incur great expenditure; *ridurre le spese*, to cut down one's expenses; *sostenere le spese di ql.co.*, to bear the cost of (*o* to pay for) sthg. ‖ *essere sulle spese*, to support (*o* to keep) oneself **2.** (*compera*) shopping; purchase: *spese di Natale*, Christmas shopping; *questo mobile è stato una bella* —, this piece of furniture was a good buy; *andare a far spese*, to go shopping.

spesàre, *v.t.* to pay expenses for (s.o.); to maintain, to keep: to pay for s.o.'s keep.

spesàto, *ag.*: *essere* —, to have (all) expenses paid.

spéso, *ag.* spent: *denaro ben* —, money well spent; *tempo* — *male*, wasted time.

spesseggiàre, *v.t.* to repeat ‖ *v.i.* to be frequent; to become frequent.

spessíre, *v.t.* to thicken ‖ **spessírsi**, *v.r.* to thicken.

spésso, *ag.* **1.** (*fitto*) thick; (*denso*) dense; (*compatto*) compact: *nebbia spessa*, dense (*o* thick) fog; *ho bisogno di un legno più* —, I need a more compact wood **2.** (*grosso*) thick: *un muro* — *30 cm.*, a wall thirty centimetres thick **3.** (*frequente*) frequent: *spessi errori*, frequent mistakes ‖ *spesse volte*, often (*o* frequently) ‖ *av.* **often, frequently:** *accade* — *che...*, it often happens that...; *ci vado* —, I often (*o* frequently) go there ‖ — *e volentieri*, very often.

spessóre, *s.m.* **1.** thickness: *la porta ha lo* — *di circa cinque centimetri*, the door is about two inches thick **2.** (*tec.*) thickness; (*aut.*) (*di freni*) lining; (*edil.*) (*per livellamento*) shim: — *circolare*, (*mec.*) circular thickness; — *cordale*, (*mec.*) chordal thickness; — *dell'ala*, (*aer.*) wing thickness; — *di una volta*, (*edil.*) thickness of a vault; — *per freni*, (*aut.*) brake lining; — *relativo*, (*aer.*) thickness ratio.

spettàbile, *ag.* respectable, honourable ‖ *Spettabile Ditta Monti*, Messrs. Monti.

spettabilità, *s.f.* respectability.

spettàcolo, *s.m.* **1.** spectacle, sight, scene: *uno* — *commovente*, a touching sight (*o* spectacle); *che* — *!*, what a sight!; *le cascate del Niagara sono uno dei più meravigliosi spettacoli che abbia mai visto*, Niagara Falls are one of the most wonderful sights I have ever seen ‖ *dare* — *di sè*, to make a spectacle of oneself **2.** (*teat.*) performance: *sala di* —, theatre; *tassa sugli spettacoli*, entertainment tax; *ci sono tre spettacoli al giorno*, there are three performances a day; *la fine dello* — *è a mezzanotte*, the performance ends at midnight.

spettacolosaménte, *av.* spectacularly; imposingly; impressively.

spettacolóso, *ag.* spectacular; (*imponente*) imposing; impressive: *una spettacolosa manifestazione pirotecnica fu organizzata per l'arrivo della diva*, a spectacular display of fireworks was arranged for the arrival of the star.

spettànte, *ag.* due.

spettànza, *s.f.* **1.** concern: *questo non è di mia* —, this is not my concern (*o* this is no concern of mine) **2.** *pl.* (*denaro dovuto*) dues; (*onorario*) fee (*sing.*): *ho ricevuto le mie spettanze*, I have received my dues.

spettàre, *v.i.* to be (for s.o.), to be up; to be one's concern: *spetta a lui pensare a tutto questo*, it is for him (*o* it is up to him) to think of all these things; *non spetta a te giudicare queste cose*, it is no concern of yours to judge these things; *questa volta spetta a te decidere*, this time it's your turn to decide ‖ *quell'eredità non gli spetta*, that inheritance does not belong to him by right.

spettatóre, *ag.* onlooking ‖ *s.m.*, **spettatríce**, *s. f.* **1.** spectator; onlooker; *pl.* (*di cinema, teatro, ecc.*) audience (*sing.*): — *di un incontro di calcio*, spectator at a football match; — *in piedi*, (*amer.*) stander; *attori e spettatori*, actors and audience; *uno* — *cominciò a fischiare*, a member of the audience began to boo **2.** (*testimone*) witness; bystander: — *di un incidente*, accident-witness; *è stata spettatrice di tutti questi avvenimenti*, she lived through (*o* she witnessed) all these events; *nessuno potè testimoniare perchè non c'era stato nessuno* — *per la strada*, nobody could act as witness because there had been no bystander in the street.

spettegolàre, *v.i.* to gossip.

spettinàre, *v.t.* to ruffle s.o.'s. hair: *il vento ti ha spettinato*, the wind has ruffled your hair ‖ **spettinàrsi**, *v.r.* to ruffle one's hair: *come hai fatto a spettinarti in quel modo?*, how did you manage to get your hair so ruffled?.

spettinàto, *ag.* unkempt, uncombed: *sei troppo* —, your hair is too untidy.

spettoràre, *v.t.i.* to expectorate ‖ **spettoràrsi**, *v.r. rar.*) to bare one's chest; to bare one's bosom.

spettràle, *ag.* **1.** ghostly, ghost-like, spectral, ghastly: *ha un aspetto* —, he looks perfectly ghastly **2.** (*fis.*) spectral: *analisi* —, spectral (*o* spectrum) analysis.

spèttro, *s.m.* **1.** ghost, spectre: *dice di aver visto uno* —, he says he saw a ghost ‖ *sembrare uno* —, to look like a ghost **2.** (*fis.*) spectrum: — *di assorbimento*, absorption spectrum; — *di scintilla*, spark spectrum; — *infrarosso*, infrared spectrum; — *solare*, solar spectrum; — *ultravioletto*, ultraviolet spectrum; — *visibile*, visible (*o* ocular) spectrum.

spettrografía, *s.f.* (*fis.*) spectrography: — *di massa*, mass spectrography.

spettrogràfico, *ag.* (*fis.*) spectrographic.

spettrògrafo, *s.m.* (*fis.*) spectrograph: — *a cristallo*, (*radiologia*) crystal spectrograph; — *a raggi X*, (*radiologia*) X-ray spectrograph; — *di massa*, (*fis. atomica*) mass spectrograph; — *nel, a vuoto*, (*radiologia*) vacuum spectrograph.

spettrología, *s.f.* spectrology.

spettrometría, *s.f.* (*fis.*) spectrometry.

spettromètrico, *ag.* (*fis.*) spectrometric.

spettròmetro, *s.m.* (*fis.*) spectrometer: — *a raggi X*, (*radiologia*) X-ray spectrometer; — *di massa*, (*fis. atomica*) mass spectrometer.

spettromicroscòpio, *s.m.* (*fis.*) spectromicroscope.

spettroscopía, *s.f.* (*fis.*) spectroscopy: — *di massa*, (*fis. atomica*) mass spectroscopy.

spettroscopicaménte, *av.* (*fis.*) spectroscopically.

spettroscòpico, *ag.*(*fis.*) spectroscopic(al): *binario* —, spectroscopic binary; *microscopio* —, spectromicroscope.

spettroscòpio, *s.m.* (*fis.*) spectroscope: — *a raggi catodici*, (*elettronica*) cathode-ray spectroscope; — *a reticolo*, (*ott.*) diffraction spectroscope.

speziàle, *s.m.* **1.** (*chi vende spezie*) grocer **2.** (*farmacista*) chemist, apothecary.

spèzie, *s.f.pl.* spices.

speziería, *s.f.* **1.** (*drogheria*) grocery, grocer's shop **2.** (*farmacia*) apothecary's shop, chemist's shop **3.** (*spezie*) spices (*pl.*).

spezzàbile, *ag.* breakable.

spezzaménto, *s.m.* breaking.

spezzàre, *v.t.* **1.** to break (anche *fig.*): *ciò mi spezza il cuore*, this breaks my heart; — *ql.co. in due*, to break sthg. in two; — *un ramo*, to break a branch ‖ — *una lancia in favore di qlcu.*, to take up the cudgel for s.o. **2.** (*interrompere*) to break, to interrupt: — *un viaggio*, to break a journey ‖ **spezzàrsi**, *v.r.* to break (anche *fig.*): *la corda si spezzò ed egli cadde*, the rope broke and he fell; *mi si spezza il cuore a pensarci*, it breaks my heart to think of it (*o* my heart aches at the thought of it); — *un braccio*, to break one's arm.

spezzataménte, *av.* **1.** (*pezzo per pezzo*) bit by bit, piecemeal **2.** (*con irregolarità*) by fits and starts.

spezzatíno, *s.m.* (*cuc.*) stew: — *di vitello*, veal stew.

spezzàti, *s.m.pl.* (*denari spiccioli*) small change.

spezzàto, *ag.* broken: *un ramoscello* —, a broken twig.

spezzatúra, *s.f.* **1.** (*lo spezzare*) breaking **2.** (*volume scompagnato*) odd volume.

spezzettaménto, *s.m.* breaking to bits, cutting in small pieces, chopping.

spezzettàre, *v.t.* **1.** to break (sthg.) to bits. to cut (sthg.) in small pieces, to chop: — *legna, verdura*, to chop wood, vegetables **2.** (*tritare*) to mince, to hash.

spezzettatúra, *s.f.* breaking to bits, chopping.

spezzóne, *s.m.* **1.** (*mil.*) incendiary bomb **2.** (*metal.*) (*di lamiera, di profilato*) cut-down size, crop end; (*pezzo da forgiare*) forging stock; (*billetta*) billet.

spía, *s.f.* **1.** spy; (*riferito a bambini*) telltale, sneak: *egli fa sempre la* — *all'insegnante*, he always sneaks to the teacher; *è una* — *della polizia*, he is a police informer (*o sl.* he is a copper's nark *o* nose); *fare la* —, to play the spy (*o* to inform) **2.** (*indizio, cenno*) evidence; proof: *questo mozzicone di sigaretta è la* — *che tu sei stato qui*, this cigarette end is the evidence that you have been here 3. (*di porta, di prigione*.) Judas-hole; (*di convento*) grill; (*di collegio*) guichet; (*di botte, ecc.*) peephole, inspection hole 4. (*elett. aut.*): — *luminosa*, warning light; — *olio*, oil window; *lampada a* —, pilot lamp.

spiaccicàre, *v.t.* to squash || **spiaccicàrsi**, *v.r.* to get squashed.

spiacènte, *ag.* 1. (*dispiaciuto*) sorry: *sono* — *di doverti dire che...*, I am sorry to have to tell you that... 2. (*spiacevole*) unpleasant.

spiacére, *V.* **dispiacére**.

spiacévole, *ag.* 1. unpleasant, disagreeable 2. (*che causa delusione*) disappointing.

spiacevolézza, *s.f.* unpleasantness, disagreeableness.

spiacevolménte, *av.* unpleasantly, disagreeably.

spiàggia, *s.f.* beach; (*riva*) (sea)shore: — *sabbiosa*, sandy beach; — *sassosa*, pebbly beach; *la* — *era gremita di bagnanti*, the beach was crowded with bathers; *la corrente lo spingeva lentamente verso la* —, the current was slowly driving him towards the shore; *andare alla* —, to go to the beach; *essere alla* —, to be on the beach.

spiaménto, *s.m.* spying.

spianaménto, *s.m.* 1. levelling; (*il rendere liscio*) smoothing: *lo* — *della strada, del terreno*, the levelling of the road, of the ground 2. (*il radere al suolo*) razing (to the ground): — *di una fortezza*, razing to the ground of a fortress 3. (*spiegazione*) explanation.

spianàre, *v.t.* 1. to level, to make level; (*rendere liscio*) to smooth: *in questo tratto la strada non è stata spianata*, along this stretch the road has not been levelled; — *a livello*, (*mec.*) to flush; — *con rulli*, (*mec.*) to roll; — *una lamiera*, (*mec.*) to straighten out (o to flatten) a sheet; — *mediante pressione*, (*mec.*) to flatten; — *il terreno*, to level the ground; — *le costure di un vestito*, to smooth down the seams of a dress; — *la pasta*, to roll out the dough || — *le costure a qlcu.*, *fig.* to give s.o. a good hiding || — *la fronte*, to smooth one's brow || — *il fucile contro qlcu.*, to level one's gun at s.o. 2. (*radere al suolo*) to raze (to the ground): — (*al suolo*) *una fortezza, una città*, to raze a fortress, a town (to the ground) 3. (*appianare*) to smooth (away): — *il cammino, la strada a qlcu.*, to smooth (o to pave) the way for s.o.; — *una difficoltà, un ostacolo*, to smooth away a difficulty, an obstacle 4. (*spiegare*) to explain: — *un testo*, to explain a text || *v.i.* 1. (*pianeggiare*) to be level, to be flat: *qui la strada spiana*, the road is level here 2. (*posare in piano*) to be steady; to be level: *questo tavolo non spiana*, this table is not steady || **spianàrsi**, *v.r.* *fig.* to become smooth, to smooth down: *la sua fronte si spianò*, his brow became smooth.

spianàta, *s.f.* 1. (*lo spianare*) levelling; (*il rendere liscio*) smoothing: *dare una* — *al terreno*, to level out a piece of ground; *dare una* — *alle costure di un vestito*, to smooth down the seams of a dress 2. (*luogo spianato*) flat space, open space; (*in un bosco*) clearing; (*mil.*) esplanade.

spianàto, *ag.* level; levelled, flattened; (*liscio*) smooth: *strada spianata*, levelled road || *fronte spianata*, smooth brow || *fucile* —, levelled rifle: *avanzarono coi fucili spianati*, they advanced with levelled rifles || *s.m.* flat space, open space; (*in un bosco*) clearing; (*mil.*) esplanade.

spianatóia, *s.f.* rolling-board.

spianatóio, *s.m.* rolling-pin.

spianatóre, *ag.* levelling; smoothing (anche *fig.*) || *s.m.* leveller; smoother.

spianatrìce, *s.f.* 1. leveller; smoother 2. (*mec.*) flattening machine, straightening machine.

spianatúra, *s.f.* levelling; (*il rendere liscio*) smoothing.

spiàno, *s.m.* 1. levelling; (*il rendere liscio*) smoothing 2. (*largo piano*) open space; (*in un bosco*) clearing || **a tútto spiàno**, *l.av.* profusely; uninterruptedly: *lavorare a tutto* —, to work all out (o to work non-stop); *spendere a tutto* —, to spend furiously.

spiantaménto, *s.m.* 1. (*lo svellere*) uprooting; pulling out 2. (*rovina*) ruin.

spiantàre, *v.t.* 1. (*svellere*) to uproot; to pull out: — *un albero*, to uproot a tree; — *un palo*, to pull out a pole 2. (*rovinare*) to send to one's ruin: *le liti spiantano le famiglie*, quarrels send families to their ruin; *queste spese mi hanno spiantato*, these expenses have brought me to my ruin || **spiantàrsi**, *v.r.* (*andare in rovina*) to go to ruin: *in pochi mesi si sono spiantati*, they have gone to ruin in a few months.

spiantàto, *ag.* (*in miseria*) penniless, ruined: *un nobile* —, a penniless (o ruined) nobleman || *s.m.* penniless person, pauper: *non darà sua figlia a uno* —, he will not marry his daughter to a pauper.

spiànto, *s.m.* ruin, destruction; *dare lo* — *a ql.co.*, to send sthg. to rack and ruin.

spiàre, *v.t.* 1. to spy upon (s.o., sthg.): — *qlcu.*, *i movimenti di qlcu.*, to spy upon s.o., upon s.o.'s movements: *spiava i nostri movimenti*, he was spying upon us 2. (*cercare, indagare*) to try to judge: *spiava sul viso di lei le impressioni delle sue parole*, he tried to judge the effect of his words by the expression on her face 3. (*aspettare con ansia*) to watch for (sthg.): *spiava il momento migliore per andarsene*, he was watching for the best moment to steal away; — *il momento opportuno per parlare*, to watch for the right moment to speak.

spiatóre, *s.m.*, **spiatrìce**, *s.f.* (*letter.*) spy.

spiattellàre, *v.t.* 1. to blab (out): *spiattellò tutto*, he blabbed (o blurted) it all out 2. (*dire apertamente*) to speak out, to say flatly.

spiattellataménte, *av.* openly, plainly, flatly: *dire* —, to blab (o to blurt) out.

spiazzàta, *s.f.*, **spiàzzo**, *s.m.* open space; (*in un bosco*) clearing.

spíca, (*rar. poet.*) per **spíga**.

spiccànte, *ag.* striking; showy: *colore* —, striking colour; *vestito* —, showy dress.

spiccàre, *v.t.* 1. to pick, to pluck; (*disgiungere*) to detach, to cut off: — *un fiore, una foglia, un grappolo d'uva*, to pick a flower, a leaf, a bunch of grapes; — *la testa dal busto a qlcu.*, to sever s.o.'s head from his shoulders 2. to enunciate distinctly: — *le parole*, to enunciate one's words distinctly; *egli spicca bene le parole*, he enunciates his words very distinctly 3. — *un salto*, to take a leap; — *un volo*, to fly up; *fig.* to take (to) flight: *l'uccello spiccò il volo*, the bird flew up || — *il bollore*, to begin to boil 4. (*dir.*) to issue: — *un ordine, un mandato di cattura*, to issue an order, a warrant of arrest 5. — *una tratta*, (*comm.*) to draw a bill || *v.i.* to stand out: *egli spicca fra gli altri per la sua altezza*, he stands out from among the others for his height; *il rosso è un colore che spicca*, red is a colour that catches the eye.

spiccataménte, *av.* distinctly, clearly: *mentalità* — *occidentale*, distinctly Western mentality; *una pronuncia* — *lombarda*, a distinctly Lombard pronunciation.

spiccàto, *ag.* 1. strong, marked, striking: *una spiccata inclinazione per la musica*, a marked inclination for music; *spiccata pronuncia toscana*, marked (o strong) Tuscan accent; *una spiccata somiglianza*, a strong (o striking) resemblance 2. (*nitido, distinto*) distinct, clear: *contorni spiccati*, clear outlines; *pronunzia ben spiccata*, distinct (o clear) pronunciation.

spícchio, *s.m.* 1. (*di agrumi*) segment; (*di frutta in genere*) slice, quarter; (*di aglio*) clove (of garlic) || *a spicchi*, sliced 2. (*geom.*) sector of a sphere) 3. (*arch.*) gore 4. (*eccl.*) segment of a biretta.

spicciàre¹, *v.i.* (*sgorgare con forza*) to gush, to spurt.

spicciàre², *v.t.* 1. to dispatch: — *una faccenda*, to dispatch a piece of business || — *un cliente*, to attend to (o to serve) a customer quickly 2. (*cambiare in spiccioli*) to change: *puoi spicciarmi una sterlina?*, can you change me a pound-note? || **spicciàrsi**, *v.r.* to hurry up, to make haste: *speravo di spicciarmi prima*, I 'hoped to get through before; *spicciati o perderai il treno*, hurry up or you'll miss the train; — *a rientrare*, to hurry home.

spicciatívo, *ag.* quick, swift, hasty, prompt: *modi spicciativi*, straightforward (*o* forthright) ways; *persona spicciativa*, go-ahead person; *è molto — nel fare le cose*, he is very quick in doing things.

spiccicàre, *v.t.* to detach, to unstick, to unglue: — *un foglio di carta incollata*, to detach a glued sheet of paper ‖ *non sa ancora — una parola*, he cannot utter a word yet ‖ **spiccicàrsi**, *v.r.* to detach oneself ‖ *non riesco a spiccicarmelo di torno*, I cannot get rid of him.

spíccio, *ag.* **1.** quick, prompt, swift: *modi spicci*, straightforward (*o* forthright) ways ‖ *andare per le spicce*, to go straight to the point (*o* not to beat about the bush) **2.** (*libero*) free: *sarò — alle quattro*, I'll be free at four **3.** (*di moneta*) small: *moneta spiccia*, small change.

spicciolàre[1], *v.t.* **1.** (*frutta*) to pick off: — *l'uva*, to pick off grapes **2.** (*fiori*) to pluck off.

spicciolàre[2], *v.t.* (*cambiare in spiccioli*) to change: — *un biglietto di banca*, to change a bank-note.

spicciolàta, àlla, *l.av.* few at a time: *arrivarono alla —*, they arrived a few at a time.

spicciolataménte, *av.* few at a time.

spícciolo, *ag.* **1.** small: *moneta spicciola*, small change: *hai diecimila lire spicciole?*, have you got the change of ten thousand lire? ‖ *dillo in moneta spicciola*, put it plainly **2.** (*semplice, comune*) simple, common: *lettori, spettatori spiccioli*, common readers, audience ‖ *s.m.* change (*invariato al pl.*): *hai qualche —?*, have you got any small change?; *ho bisogno di spiccioli*, I need some small change; *non ho uno —*, I am penniless.

spícco, *s.m.*: *fare —*, to stand out (*o* to catch the eye): *faceva — per la sua brillante conversazione*, he stood out because of his brilliant conversation; *il rosso è un colore che fa —*, red is a colour which catches the eye.

spicilègio, *s.m.* (*letter.*) **1.** spicilege, collection, anthology **2.** (*spigolatura*) gleaning.

spider, *s.m.* (*aut.*) two-seater sports car.

spidocchiàre, *v.t.* to delouse ‖ **spidocchiàrsi**, *v.r.* to delouse oneself.

spièdo, *s.m.* **1.** spit: *arrosto allo —*, roast on the spit; *mettere un pollo allo —*, to put a chicken on the spit (*o* to spit a chicken) **2.** (*st.*) (*picca*) hunting-spear, pike.

spiegàbile, *ag.* explainable, explicable.

spiegacciàre, *V.* spiegazzàre.

spiegaménto, *s.m.* **1.** spreading out **2.** (*mil.*) deployment: — *di truppe*, deployment of troops.

spiegàre, *v.t.* **1.** to explain, to expound; (*interpretare*) to interpret: *non so come — la poesia*, I don't know how to interpret this poem; *spiegami come lo fai*, explain to (*o* tell) me how you do it; *spiegami perchè l'hai fatto*, explain to me why you have done it; — *un problema, il significato di ql.co.*, to explain (*o* to expound) a problem, the meaning of sthg.; — *una sciarada*, to explain a charade **2.** (*stendere*) to unfold, to spread out; to lay out: *egli spiegò la coperta perchè la vedessi*, he spread out the blanket for me to see ‖ — *le ali, il volo*, to spread (*o* to unfold) one's wings (anche *fig.*) ‖ — *le vele*, to unfurl the sails ‖ — *la voce*, to project one's voice **3.** (*mil.*) to deploy: — *le truppe*, to deploy the troops **4.** (*mostrare*) to display, to show; to exhibit: *egli spiega molto ingegno*, he displays great talent ‖ **spiegàrsi**, *v.r.* **1.** to explain oneself, to make oneself understood: *egli si spiega bene in inglese*, he can make himself understood in English; *non sapevo spiegarmi*, I did not know how to explain myself; *spieghiamoci*, let's get it straight ‖ *mi spiego?*, do you see what I mean? (*o* have I made myself clear?) ‖ *non so se mi spiego!*, I do not know if you see what I mean! **2.** (*stendersi*) to unfold, to spread out; (*aprirsi*)

to open out: *le bandiere si spiegavano al vento*, the flags were waving in the wind.

spiegataménte, *av.* openly, clearly.

spiegatívo, *ag.* explanatory.

spiegàto, *ag.* open, spread out: *bandiere spiegate al vento*, flags waving in the wind; *vele spiegate*, unfurled sails ‖ *a voce spiegata*, in a loud voice.

spiegatúra, *s.f.* spreading out, unfolding.

spiegazióne, *s.f.* explanation: — *del problema*, explanation of the problem; — *del Vangelo*, explanation of the Gospel; *dare una — di ql.co.*, to give an explanation of (*o* to account for) sthg.; *domandare una — a qlcu.*, to call s.o. to account ‖ *avere una — con qlcu.*, to have it out with s.o.

spiegazzaménto, *s.m.* crumpling; creasing, rumpling.

spiegazzàre, *v.t.* to crumple (up); to crease, to rumple: — *un foglio, un giornale*, to crumple (up) a sheet of paper, a newspaper; — *una stoffa, un vestito*, to crease (*o* to rumple) a piece of material, a dress.

spieggiàre, *V.* spiàre.

spietataménte, *av.* pitilessly, ruthlessly, mercilessly.

spietàto, *ag.* pitiless, ruthless, merciless: — *contro qlcu.*, merciless towards s.o.; *parole spietate*, ruthless words ‖ *le faceva una corte spietata*, he would not take no for an answer.

spifferàre, *v.t.* (*riferire, raccontare senza discrezione*) to blurt out ‖ *v.i.* **1.** (*suonare il piffero*) to pipe **2.** (*del vento, fischiare*) to whistle.

spifferàta, *s.f.* piping.

spíffero, *s.m.* (*corrente d'aria*) draught.

spifferóne, *s.m.* (*chiacchierone*) telltale.

spíga, *s.f.* (*infiorescenza*) spike; (*infruttescenza*) ear: — *di frumento*, ear of wheat ‖ *disegno a —*, herring-bone pattern ‖ *mattonato a —*, herring-boned brick-work ‖ *tessuto a —*, twilled-cloth.

spigàre, *v.i.* to ear: *questo frumento non spiga bene*, this wheat does not ear well.

spigàto, *ag.* herring-bone (*attributivo*).

spigatúra, *s.f.* **1.** (*lo spigare*) earing **2.** (*il periodo della spigatura*) earing time.

spighétta, *s.f.* (*nastro, cordoncino*) braid.

spigionàrsi, *v.r.* to remain vacant.

spigionàt..., *ag.* vacant: *casa spigionata*, vacant house.

spigliataménte, *av.* **1.** easily, freely: *conversare —*, to talk in a free and easy manner **2.** (*agilmente*) nimbly.

spigliatézza, *s.f.* **1.** ease: *mi rispose con —*, he answered me in a free and easy manner **2.** (*agilità*) nimbleness.

spigliàto, *ag.* **1.** easy, free and easy: *modi spigliati*, free and easy ways **2.** (*agile*) nimble.

spignoràre, *v.t.* to redeem.

spígo *s.m.* (*bot.*) lavender.

spígola, *s.f.* (*ittiol.*) bass.

spigolàre, *v.t.* to glean (anche *fig.*): — *un campo*, to glean a field; — *fatti, notizie*, to glean facts, news.

spigolatóre, *s.m.*, **spigolatríce**, *s.f.* gleaner (anche *fig.*).

spigolatúra, *s.f.* **1.** (*lo spigolare*) gleaning **2.** *pl. fig.* (*fatterelli, notizie*) gleanings.

spígolo, *s.m.* **1.** edge; corner: — *vivo*, sharp corner; *ho battuto il ginocchio contro lo — del tavolo*, I hit my knee against the corner of the table ‖ *smussare gli spigoli, fig.* to patch things up **2.** (*geom.*) edge, arris **3.** (*arch.*) edge, arris; (*smussato*) chamfer.

spigonàrdo, *s.m.* (*bot.*) lavender.

spigríre, *v.t.* to shake (s.o.) out of (his) laziness ‖ **spigrírsi**, *v.r.* to shake off one's laziness.

spílla, *s.f.* **1.** (*spillo*) pin: — *di sicurezza*, safety-pin **2.** (*gioiello*) brooch.

spillaccheràre, *v.t.* to brush the mud off (sthg.) ‖ **spillaccheràrsi**, *v.r.* to brush oneself.

spillàre, *v.t.* **1.** to broach, to tap, to pierce; (*attingere spillando*) to draw: *spillò un bicchiere di vino*, he drew a glass of wine out of a barrel; — *una botte*, to broach (o to tap o to pierce) a cask **2.** *fig.* (*cavare astutamente*) to worm (sthg. out of s.o.): *mi ha spillato un mucchio di quattrini*, he has got (o wormed) a lot of money out of me ‖ *v.i.* to drip.

spillàtico, *s.m.* pin-money.

spillatúra, *s.f.* broaching, tapping, piercing.

spìllo, *s.m.* **1.** pin: — *da cravatta*, tie-pin; — *di sicurezza*, *da balia*, safety-pin; *capocchia di* —, pin-head; *cuscinetto per spilli*, pin-cushion; *foro di* —, pinhole; *fermare ql.co. con spilli*, to pin sthg. down ‖ *colpo di* —, *fig.* pin-prick **2.** (*mec.*) plunger, valve core: *valvola a* —, needle valve **3.** (*stilo per forare botti*) broach, piercer **4.** (*zampillo*) jet: — *d'acqua*, jet of water.

spillóne, *s.m.* **1.** (*gioiello*) brooch **2.** (*spillo per cappello*) hat-pin; (*per sciarpa*) scarf-pin.

spilluzzicaménto, *s.m.* nibbling.

spilluzzicàre, *v.t.* **1.** to nibble, to peck at (sthg.) **2.** (*rubacchiare*) to lay one's hands on (sthg.): *è riuscito a — un po' di soldi*, he succeeded in laying his hands on some money.

spilluzzichína, *s.f.*, **spilluzzichíno**, *s.m.* nibbler.

spillúzzico, *s.m.* nibbling ‖ *a* —, little by little (o a little at a time).

spiloreria, *s.f.* stinginess, niggardliness, meanness.

spilòrcia, *s.f.* miser, close-fisted person, stingy person.

spilòrcio, *ag.* stingy, niggardly, mean, close-fisted, miserly ‖ *s.m.* miser, close-fisted person, stingy person.

spiluccàre, *V.* **piluccàre**.

spilungóna, *s.f.* lanky girl, lanky woman.

spilungóne, *s.m.* lanky fellow, lanky man; (*fam.*) spindle-shanks.

spína, *s.f.* **1.** thorn: *le spine di una rosa*, the thorns of a rose ‖ *corona di spine*, crown of thorns ‖ *un letto di spine*, a bed of thorns ‖ *questa è la mia —*, this is my torment ‖ *la vita è irta di spine*, life is fraught with difficulties ‖ *avere una — nel cuore*, to have an aching pain in one's heart ‖ *stare sulle spine*, to be on tenter-hooks ‖ *togliere a qlcu. una — dal cuore*, to take a thorn out of s.o.'s pillow ‖ *non c'è rosa senza spine*, prov. there's no rose without thorns **2.** (*lisca*) fishbone ‖ *a — di pesce*, herring-bone: *disegno a — di pesce*, herring-bone pattern; *tessuto a — di pesce*, twill (o twilled o herring-bone cloth) **3.** (*elett.*) (electrical) plug: — *con interruttore*, switch plug; — *di contatto*, connecting plug; — *di prova*, test plug; — *tripolare*, three-pin plug **4.** (*mec.*) pin, peg: — *ad occhio*, eye pin; — *cilindrica*, parallel-pin; — *conica*, taper pin; — *di riferimento*, dowel; — *di sicurezza*, shear (o break) pin; — *di torsione*, torque pin **5.** (*mar.*) eye-bolt **6.** (*di botte*) bung-hole **7.** — *dorsale*, (*anat.*) backbone (o spine).

spinàce, spinàcio, *s.m.* spinach (solo sing.); spinage (solo sing.): *questi spinaci sono molto buoni*, this spinach is very nice.

spinàio, *s.m.* (*pruneto*) thicket of thorn-bushes.

spinàle, *ag.* (*anat.*) spinal: *midollo* —, spinal marrow.

spinapésce, a, *l.av.* herring-bone (*attributivo*).

spinàre, *v.t.* (*un pesce*) to bone.

spinarèllo, *s.m.* (*ittiol.*) stickleback.

spinàto, *ag.* **1.** (*a spina di pesce*) herring-bone (*attributivo*): *tessuto* —, herring-bone (o twilled) cloth (o twill) **2.** *filo* —, barbed wire.

spinèllo[1], *s.m.* (*min.*) spinel: — *nobile*, ruby spinel.

spinèllo[2], *s.m.* (*ittiol.*) stickleback.

spinéto, *s.m.* (*pruneto*) thicket of thorn-bushes.

spinétta, *s.f.* (*mus.*) spinet.

spingàrda, *s.f.* (*st. mil.*) **1.** springal(d) **2.** (*archibugio*) musket.

spingere, *v.t.* **1.** to push, to shove; (*ficcare*)! to drive, to thrust: *non —, non spingete!*, don't push! (o don't shove!); *spingi la poltrona contro la parete*, push (o shove) the armchair against the wall; *spinse la vanga nel terreno*, he thrust (o drove) the spade into the ground; *spinsero i tronchi nel fiume*, they pushed the

logs into the river; *il vento spinse la barca verso la riva*, the wind drove the boat towards the shore; — *qlcu., ql.co. fuori, avanti, dentro, indietro*, to push s.o., sthg. out, on (o forward), in, back ‖ —, (*sulle porte*) push ‖ *non spingo fin là le mie ambizioni*, I don't carry my ambitions as far as that; *non spingo la mia antipatia fino a volerlo veder soffrire*, I don't carry my dislike for him to the point of wanting to see him suffer; *non spingono a tanto la loro amicizia*, they don't carry their friendship to such lengths; *spingeva la sua antipatia fino all'odio*, she carried her dislike to the point of hatred; *spinse il suo amore fino al ridicolo*, she carried her love to ridiculous extremes ‖ — *un attacco a fondo*, to push (o to thrust o to drive) an attack home ‖ — *uno scherzo oltre i limiti*, to carry a joke too far ‖ — *lontano lo sguardo*, to strain one's eyes into the distance **2.** (*condurre*) to drive; (*indurre, persuadere*) to induce; (*istigare*) to egg on; to incite; (*stimolare*) to urge: *che cosa mai lo spinse a partire così presto?*, what on earth induced him to leave so soon?; *la disperazione lo spinse al suicidio*, despair drove him to suicide; *la fame lo spinse a farlo*, hunger drove him to do it; *la miseria lo spinse a mendicare*, poverty drove him to beg; *quel tuo amico ti spinge sempre a fare ciò che non dovresti*, your friend is always egging you on to do things that you ought not to do; *spinse gli operai a scioperare*, he incited the men to strike; *suo padre lo spingeva a studiare di più, ma egli non voleva saperne*, his father urged him to study harder, but he wouldn't listen to him; *temo che qlcu. spinga la ciurma all'ammutinamento*, I am afraid s.o. might incite the crew to mutiny ‖ **spingersi**, *v.r.* **1.** to push: *ci spingemmo fino a Parigi*, we pushed on as far as Paris; *in due giorni l'esercito si spinse fino a...*, in two days the army pushed as far as...; *non volevamo spingerci troppo lontano*, we did not want to go too far (anche *fig.*); *si spinse tra la folla*, he pushed (his way) through the crowd (o he thrust his way through the crowd); — *avanti*, to push forward (o to thrust oneself forward) **2.** (*gettarsi*) to throw oneself: *egli si spinse in un'impresa rischiosa*, he threw himself into a risky enterprise.

spiníte, *s.f.* (*patol.*) spinal meningitis.

spíno[1], *s.m.* **1.** (*spina*) thorn: *punto da uno* —, pricked by a thorn **2.** (*pruno*) thorn-bush, bramble.

spíno[2], *ag.*: *porco* —, porcupine (o hedgehog); *uva spina*, gooseberry.

spinóne, *s.m.* **1.** (*cane*) griffon **2.** (*tessuto*) herring-bone cloth.

spinosità, *s.f.* **1.** thorniness, spinosity **2.** (*difficoltà*) difficulty; (*scabrosità*) ticklishness.

spinóso, *ag.* **1.** thorny, prickly, spiny **2.** (*scabroso, difficile*) thorny, ticklish: *un argomento* —, a thorny subject; *una questione spinosa*, a ticklish question ‖ *persona spinosa*, surly person **3.** (*doloroso*) sorrowful: *vita spinosa*, sorrowful life ‖ *s.m.* (*zool.*) hedgehog.

spínta, *s.f.* **1.** push; (*violenta*) shove, thrust: *dare una — a ql.co.*, to give a push (o shove o thrust) to sthg. **2.** *fig.* (*aiuto*) push, helping-hand: *ha bisogno di una — per riuscire*, he needs a helping-hand if he is to succeed; *senza la tua — non avrei ottenuto questo posto*, I should not have got this post if you had not pushed me **3.** *fig.* (*incentivo, stimolo*) incentive, spur, stimulus: *una — a ben operare*, a stimulus (o an incentive) to act well **4.** (*mec. edil.*) thrust: — *al decollo*, (*aer.*) take-off thrust; — *aerostatica*, (*aer.*) aerostatic lift; — *assiale*, (*mec.*) axial thrust; — *della terra*, (*edil.*) earth pressure (o thrust); — *dell'elica*, (*aer. mar.*) screw propeller thrust; — *del vento*, (*edil.*) wind pressure; — *orizzontale*, (*di arco*) drift; *cuscinetto di* —, (*mec.*) thrust bearing **5.** — *di galleggiamento*, (*mar.*) buoyancy.

spínte o spònte, *l.av.* willy-nilly: *deve venire* —, he must come whether he likes it or not.

spinterògeno, *s.m.* (*aut.*) (battery) coil ignition.

spínto, *ag.* **1.** pushed; driven (anche *fig.*): — *avanti, indietro,* pushed forward, back; — *dalla collera,* driven by anger; — *dalla necessità,* under the pressure of necessity; — *dalla pietà,* prompted (*o* driven) by pity; — *da motivi segreti,* impelled by secret motives; — *da un compagno cadde e si ruppe un braccio,* pushed over by his companion, he fell and broke his arm; *si sentì* — *a prendere la parola,* he felt an impulse to speak || — *agli estremi,* pushed to the extreme: *questo era un esempio di onestà spinta agli estremi,* that was an example of honesty pushed to the extreme **2.** (*eccessivo*) excessive, exaggerated: *il suo orgoglio* —, his excessive pride **3.** (*audace*) risky, risqué: *discorsi spinti,* risqué talk; *idee spinte,* daring ideas.

spintóne, *s.m.* violent push, shove: *farsi avanti a forza di spintoni,* to elbow one's way forward.

spiombàre, *v.t.* to unseal, to take the leaden seals off (sthg.), to unplumb || *v.i.* **1.** to weigh as heavy as lead **2.** (*pendere*) to lean.

spionàggio, *s.m.* espionage, spying.

spioncíno, *s.m.* peep-hole; spy-hole, judas-hole.

spióne, *s.m.* spy; (*fam.*) telltale.

spiovènte, *ag.* drooping, falling; sloping: *un paio di baffi spioventi,* a pair of drooping moustaches; *spalle spioventi,* stooping shoulders; *un tetto* —, a sloping roof || *s.m.* **1.** (*arch.*) slope: *a* —, weathered **2.** (*geog.*) watershed.

spiòvere, *v.i.* **1.** to stop raining: *prima di uscire aspetta che spiova,* wait for it to stop raining before you go out **2.** (*ricadere*) to come down; to droop: *i capelli le spiovono sulle spalle,* her hair comes down to her shoulders **3.** (*scorrere*) to flow.

spippolàre, *v.t.* **1.** to pick off **2.** *fig.* (*spiattellare*) to declare openly.

spíra, *s.f.* **1.** coil; (*spirale*) spiral: *una* — *di fumo,* a curl of smoke; *spire inattive,* (*elett. rad.*) dead turns; *le spire di una molla,* (*mec.*) the coils of a spring; *spire morte,* (*elett. rad.*) dead-end turns; *spire utili,* (*mec.*) active coils; *fatto a spire,* forming a spiral **2.** (*di serpente*) coil: *il serpente lo serrò fra le sue spire,* the serpent crushed him in its coils **3.** (*arch.*) scroll, volute.

spiràglio, *s.m.* **1.** small opening; air-hole, vent: *aprire uno* — *in un muro,* to make a small hole in a wall **2.** (*filo d'aria*) breath (of air); (*di luce*) gleam (of light) **3.** *fig.* (*barlume*) gleam: *uno* — *di speranza,* a gleam of hope **4.** (*mar.*) skylight.

spiràle, *ag.* spiral || *s.f.* **1.** (*geom.*) spiral **2.** (*molla*) spring; (*di orologio*) hairspring.

spiralménte, *av.* spirally.

spiraménto, *s.m.* blowing.

spiràre, *v.i.* **1.** (*soffiare*) to blow: *un forte vento spirava dal sud,* a strong wind was blowing from the south; *non spirava un alito di vento,* there wasn't a breath of air || *spira aria di burrasca, fig.* there is a storm in the air (*o* the atmosphere is stormy) **2.** (*morire*) to pass away, to breathe one's last: *egli spirò ieri sera,* he passed away last night **3.** (*scadere*) to expire: *il termine spira domani,* the term expires tomorrow **4.** (*emanare*) to emanate, to proceed: *una fraganza spirava dal giardino,* a fragrance emanated from the garden **5.** (*poet.*) (*respirare*) to breathe || *v.t.* **1.** (*emanare*) to breathe out, to exhale, to send off: — *fumo, fragranza,* to exhale smoke, fragrance || *i suoi occhi spirano dolcezza,* her eyes are beaming with sweetness || — *l'anima,* to breathe one's last **2.** (*poet.*) (*ispirare*) to inspire **3.** (*poet.*) (*respirare*) to breathe.

spiràto, *ag.* **1.** (*trascorso*) expired **2.** (*morto*) dead.

spirèa, *s.f.* (*bot.*) spiraea.

spiríllo, *s.m.* (*biol.*) spirillum (*pl.* spirilla).

spiritàle, *ag.* (*poet.*) spiritual.

spiritaménto, *s.m.* being possessed.

spiritàre, *v.i.,* **spiritàrsi,** *v.r.* **1.** to be possessed **2.** *fig.* (*essere fuori di sè*) to be beside oneself: — *dalla paura,* to be out of one's wits with fear.

spiritataménte, *av.* insanely, madly.

spiritàto, *ag.* **1.** possessed: *un giovane che si sospettava fosse* — *fu portato in chiesa,* a young man who was supposed to be possessed was taken to the church **2.** (*spaventato*) frightened, terrified: *mi guardò con occhi spiritati,* he looked at me with frightened eyes || *s.m.* possessed man: *urlava come uno* —, he was shouting as if he were possessed.

spiritèllo, *s.m.* **1.** sprite; (*folletto buono*) elf (*pl.* elves); (*folletto cattivo*) goblin **2.** (*ragazzo vivace*) imp **3.** (*letter.*) (*spirito vitale*) élan vitale.

spirítico, *ag.* spiritualist(ic): *seduta spiritica,* spiritualist séance.

spiritísmo, *s.m.* spiritualism, spiritism.

spiritísta, *s.c.* spiritualist, spiritist.

spiritístico, *ag.* spiritualistic, spiritistic.

spírito, *s.m.* **1.** (*ente spirituale*) spirit: *Dio è puro* —, God is pure spirit; *il regno degli spiriti,* the realm of spirits || — *folletto,* sprite || *lo Spirito Maligno,* the Evil One || *lo Spirito Santo,* the Holy Ghost (*o* the Holy Spirit) **2.** (*afflato vitale*) spirit; (*anima*) soul: *gli spiriti animali,* the animal spirits; — *vitale,* vital spirit; *esalare lo* —, to breathe one's last (*o* to give up one's spirit) **3.** (*fil.*) (*contrapposto a materia*) spirit: *i valori dello* —, spiritual values; *sono con lui in* —, I am with him in spirit **4.** (*fantasma*) spirit; ghost; phantom: *in questa casa vi sono degli spiriti,* this house is haunted; *credere negli spiriti,* to believe in ghosts **5.** (*mente, intelligenza*) mind: *presenza di* —, presence of mind || — *profetico,* prophetic spirit **6.** (*persona di spiccate doti intellettuali*) mind: *uno* — *eletto,* a master-spirit; *i grandi spiriti,* the great minds; *uno dei migliori spiriti del suo paese,* one of the leading spirits of his country **7.** (*tendenza informatrice, atteggiamento spirituale*) spirit; attitude: *lo* — *dell'epoca,* the spirit of the age; — *di contraddizione, osservazione, sacrificio,* spirit of contradiction, observation, sacrifice; — *materno,* maternal attitude; *egli fu lo* — *della rivoluzione,* he was the leading spirit of the revolution || — *di corpo,* esprit de corps; — *di parte,* partisan spirit; — *di squadra,* team-spirit || — *pubblico,* public feeling **8.** (*significato essenziale*) spirit, (inner) meaning; sense: *bisognerebbe sempre seguire lo* — *piuttosto che la lettera della legge,* one should always go by the spirit of the law rather than by the letter **9.** (*arguzia*) wit; (*umorismo*) humour: *motto di* —, witticism; *persona di* —, witty person; *non mi sembra ci sia molto* — *in quello che dice,* I do not see much humour in what he says; *quell'uomo è pieno di* —, that man is full of wit || *fare dello* —, to be witty: *fa dello* — *di patata,* (*fam.*) he is trying to be funny **10.** (*vivacità*) life; liveliness: *dovresti mettere un po' più di* — *in quello che fai,* you ought to put a little more life into what you are doing **11.** (*gram. greca*) breathing: — *aspro, dolce,* rough, smooth breathing **12.** (*chim.*) (*alcool*) alcohol: — *di legno,* wood-spirit; *lampada a* —, spirit-lamp.

spiritosàggine, *s.f.* witticism; (*spreg.*) would-be witticism, attempt at wit: *con le sue insulse spiritosaggini,* with his tasteless witticisms.

spiritosaménte, *av.* wittily, with humour.

spiritosità, *s.f.* wittiness; (*detto, atto spiritoso*) witticism; (*scherz.*) poor humour.

spiritóso, *ag.* **1.** witty: *discorso, uomo* —, witty speech, man; *risposta spiritosa,* witty reply (*o* retort); *vuol fare lo* — *e non ci riesce,* he tries to be witty, but he can't quite make it **2.** (*alcoolico*) alcoholic: *bevanda spiritosa,* alcoholic drink.

spirituàle, *ag.* spiritual: *godimento* —, spiritual delight; *letture spirituali,* spiritual readings; *vita* —, spiritual life || *canti spirituali negri,* (negro) spirituals || *esercizi spirituali,* spiritual exercises || *padre* —, Father confessor.

spiritualísmo, *s.m.* (*fil.*) spiritualism, spiritism.

spiritualísta, *s.c.* (*fil.*) spiritualist, spiritist.

spiritualístico, *ag.* (*fil.*) spiritualistic, spiritistic.

spiritualità, *s.f.* spirituality.

spiritualizzàre, *v.t.* to spiritualize.

spiritualménte, *av.* spiritually.

spíro, *s.m.* (*poet.*) **1.** spirit, soul **2.** (*soffio*) breath: *uno — d'aria,* a breath of air.

spiròmetro, *s.m.* spirometer.

spírto, *s.m.* (*poet.*) spirit.

spiumacciàre, *v.t.* to shake up.

spiumacciàta, *s.f.* shaking up: *dà una — al cuscino,* shake up the cushion.

spiumàre, *v.t.* **1.** to pluck: *— un pollo,* to pluck a chicken **2.** *fig.* (*togliere quattrini a*) to fleece: *l'ha spiumato ben bene,* he fleeced him of everything he had (*o* he cleaned him out) ‖ **spiumàrsi,** *v.r.* to moult.

spizzicàre, *v.t.* to nibble.

spízzico, a, *l.av.* little by little, bit by bit: *pagare a —,* to pay a little at a time.

splancnología, *s.f.* (*scient.*) splanchnology.

splenalgía, *s.f.* (*med.*) splenalgia, splenalgy.

splendènte, *ag.* bright, shining, resplendent, brilliant: *occhi splendenti,* bright eyes; *sole —,* bright sunshine.

splendenteménte, *av.* brightly, shiningly, resplendently, brilliantly.

splèndere, *v.i.* to shine (anche *fig.*); (*scintillare*) to glitter, to sparkle, to glisten; (*luccicare*) to gleam: *il sole splendeva nel cielo,* the sun was shining in the sky; *la sua armatura splendeva al sole,* his armour was gleaming in the sunshine; *i suoi occhi splendevano di gioia,* his eyes were shining with joy.

splendidaménte, *av.* **1.** wonderfully, splendidly: *dipinge —,* he paints splendidly **2.** (*sfarzosamente*) magnificently, gorgeously, splendidly: *casa — arredata,* magnificently furnished house **3.** (*generosamente*) generously.

splendidézza, *s.f.* **1.** (*splendore, lucentezza*) splendour, brightness **2.** (*magnificenza, sfarzo*) magnificence, gorgeousness, splendour, sumptuousness: *la — della Corte,* the magnificence of the Court.

splèndido, *ag.* **1.** wonderful, splendid: *uno — dipinto,* a wonderful painting; *una splendida giornata,* a splendid (*o* glorious) day; *una splendida idea, occasione,* a splendid idea, opportunity; *uno — lavoro,* a wonderful piece of work; *un romanzo —,* an excellent (*o* a wonderful) novel; *quel ragazzo ha fatto una splendida riuscita,* that boy had a splendid success; *fare uno — matrimonio,* to make a splendid marriage **2.** (*sfarzoso*) magnificent, gorgeous, splendid: *splendide vesti,* gorgeous robes; *la coda splendida del pavone,* the gorgeous tail of the peacock; *ricevimento —,* magnificent party; *palazzo —,* splendid (*o* magnificent) mansion **3.** (*generoso, munifico*) munificent, very generous, very liberal: *è una persona splendida,* he is a very generous (*o* very liberal *o* munificent) person **4.** (*splendente*) bright, shining: *la luce splendida della luna,* the bright moonlight.

splendóre, *s.m.* **1.** splendour (anche *fig.*), brightness (anche *fig.*): *lo — dell'arte, dell'ingegno,* the splendour of art, of genius; *lo — del sole,* the splendour (*o* brightness) of the sun **2.** (*sfarzo*) magnificence, splendour, sumptuousness: *lo — della Corte,* the splendour (*o* magnificence) of the Court ‖ *vivere in seno agli splendori,* to live in the lap of luxury **3.** (*bellezza*) beauty: *che — di casa!,* what a wonderful house!; *che — di ragazza!,* what a beautiful girl!.

splène, *s.m.* (*anat.*) spleen, milt.

splenectomía, *s.f.* (*chir.*) splenectomy.

splenètico, *ag.s.m.* splenetic.

splènico, *ag.* splenic.

splènio, *s.m.* (*anat.*) splenius.

spleníte, *s.f.* (*patol.*) splenitis.

Splúga (Pàsso déllo), *no.pr.m.* (*geog.*) Splugen Pass.

spodestaménto, *s.m.* (*da proprietà*) dispossession; (*da posizione di autorità*) dethronement.

spodestàre, *v.t.* (*da proprietà*) to dispossess; (*da po-*

sizione di autorità) to dethrone, to deprive (s.o.) of power: *i nobili francesi furono spodestati dalle loro terre,* the French nobles were dispossessed of their lands: — *un re,* to dethrone a king.

spoetizzàre, *v.t.* to disenchant, to deprive (s.o.) of poetic illusion; to shock: *ci sono cose che spoetizzano,* there are things which disenchant one; *non ti dico la verità perchè non voglio spoetizzarti,* I will not tell you the truth as I do not want to deprive you of your poetic illusions (*o* to disenchant you); *il suo parlare sboccato spoetizza veramente,* his coarse language is really shocking.

spòglia, *s.f.* **1.** (*di animale*) skin, hide; (*di rettile*) slough: *la serpe buttò la sua —,* the serpent cast its slough **2.** (*veste*) dress (*invariato al pl.*), clothes (*pl.*): *spoglie regali,* regal dress; *spoglie sacerdotali,* priestly vestments ‖ *spoglie mortali,* mortal remains ‖ *sotto mentite spoglie,* in disguise **3.** *pl.* (*bottino*) spoils; booty (*sing.*): *dividere le spoglie,* to divide the spoils ‖ *spoglie opime,* spolia opima **4.** *pl.* (*bot.*) (*di alberi, di granoturco*) leaves; (*di bulbi, cipolle, ecc.*) layers, coats **5.** (*mec.*) (*di utensile da taglio*) rake; (*di stampo, modello*) draft.

spogliaménto, *s.m.* **1.** (*atto dello spogliare*) undressing **2.** (*depredazione*) spoliation, despoilment **3.** (*saccheggio*) plunder, pillage.

spogliàre, *v.t.* **1.** to strip: — *un albero, una pianta delle proprie foglie,* to strip (*o* to denude *o* to bare) a tree of its leaves; — *un giardino di tutti i fiori,* to strip a garden of all its flowers; (*raccoglierli*) to pluck all the flowers in a garden ‖ — *un osso,* (*spolparlo*) to take the flesh off a bone ‖ — *il riso,* (*brillarlo*) to husk (*o* to polish) rice **2.** (*svestire*) to undress: to strip: — *un bambino,* to undress a child ‖ — *l'abito,* (*abbandonare un ordine religioso*) to renounce (*o* to give up) one's vows **3.** (*privare*) to strip, to deprive, to divest, to despoil: *lo spogliarono di ogni autorità,* they deprived (*o* stripped) him of all authority; — *qlcu. d'ogni bene,* to despoil (*o* to deprive) s.o. of all his possessions (*o* of all his property) **4.** (*depredare*) to rob; (*saccheggiare*) to plunder, to pillage: — *una casa, una città,* to plunder a house, a town; — *i nemici vinti, uccisi,* to despoil conquered, dead enemies **5.** (*fare lo spoglio di*) to go through (sthg.): — *la corrispondenza,* to go through the mail; — *le schede,* to count (*o* go through) the voting (*o* ballot) papers ‖ **spogliàrsi,** *v.r.* **1.** (*svestirsi*) to undress; to strip: *si spogliò da capo a piedi,* he stripped from head to foot **2.** (*di alberi, fiori, ecc.*) to shed (sthg.), to lose (sthg.): *ormai gli alberi si spogliano delle foglie,* the trees are losing their leaves **3.** (*privarsi, rinunciare*) to strip oneself, to give up (sthg.), to divest oneself: *si spogliò di ogni suo avere per darlo ai poveri,* he stripped (*o* divested) himself of all his possessions to give them to the poor; — *di un diritto, del dominio,* to give up a right, power **4.** (*depositare le impurità*) to clear: *il vino si è spogliato,* wine has cleared **5.** (*di rettile*) to cast its slough, to slough its skin: *la serpe comincia a — dagli occhi,* a snake begins to cast its slough at the eyes.

spogliarèllo, *s.m.* strip-tease.

spogliatóio, *s.m.* dressing-room; (*di teatro, ecc.*) cloak-room: — *per signore,* ladies' cloak-room.

spogliatóre, *s.m.* (*saccheggiatore*) plunderer, pillager.

spogliazióne, *V.* spoliazióne.

spòglio, *ag.* **1.** (*svestito*) undressed **2.** (*nudo*) bare: *albero —,* bare tree ◇ *s.m.* **1.** (*computo*) counting; (*esame*) scrutiny, perusal, examination: — *di voti,* counting of votes; *lo — di tutte le sue carte richiese molto tempo,* the perusal of his papers required a long time; *ho fatto lo — di tutte queste riviste, tutti questi documenti,* I have gone all through these reviews, these documents; *fare lo — della corrispondenza,* to go through the mail **2.** (*vestito che si smette*) cast -off: *lasciò tutti gli spogli al cameriere,* he left all his cast-offs to his man-servant.

spòla, *s.f.* (*ind. tessile*) shuttle; (*bobina di filato*

avvolta sulla spola) cop; (*supporto della bobina di filato*
spool: *macchina a fare* —, winding machine; *ricambio
automatico delle spole*, automatic cop changing ‖ *far
la* —, to go to and fro (*o* to go backwards and forwards): *fare la* — *fra un luogo e un altro*, to ply between one place and another.

spolétta, *s.f.* **1.** (*per avvolgere filo*) spool **2.** (*artigl.*)
fuse: — *a tempo*, time fuse; — *di fondello*, base fuse;
radio —, proximity fuse (*o* variable time fuse).

spolettièra, *s.f.* (*ind. tessile*) winding machine,
winding frame.

spoliazióne, *s.f.* **1.** (*atto dello spogliare*) undressing **2.** (*depredazione*) spoliation; (*saccheggio*) plunder,
pillage.

spoliticàre, *v.i.* to talk politics.

spollonàre, *v.t.* to trim, to prune.

spollonatúra, *s.f.* vine-trimming, vine-pruning.

spolmonàrsi, *v.r.* to talk oneself hoarse, to shout
oneself hoarse: *mi sono spolmonato per convincerlo*, I
have talked myself hoarse to convince him.

spolpaménto, *s.m.* **1.** taking the flesh off (sthg.) **2.** *fig.*
(*lo spogliare d'ogni denaro*) skinning, bleeding, fleecing.

spolpàre, *v.t.* **1.** to take the flesh off (sthg.), to
strip the flesh off (sthg.) ‖ *la malattia lo ha spolpato*,
his illness has reduced him to skin and bone **2.** *fig.*
(*spogliare d'ogni denaro*) to skin, to bleed white, to
fleece: *quell'usuraio mi spolpa*, that usurer is skinning
me (*o* bleeding me white).

spoltríre, spoltroníre, *v.t.* to cure (s.o.) of laziness:
suo padre lo spoltrì, his father cured him of laziness ‖
spoltrírsi, spoltronírsi, *v.r.* to shake off one's laziness.

spolveràre, *v.t.* **1.** to dust; (*vestiti, tappeti*) to
beat the dust from (sthg.); (*spazzolare*) to brush:
— *un tavolo*, to dust a table; — *un vestito*, to brush
a dress ‖ *i ladri spolverarono la casa*, the thieves made
a clean sweep of the house ‖ — *le spalle a qlcu.*, to dust
s.o.'s jacket (*o* s.o.'s coat) **2.** (*mangiare ingordamente*)
to eat up: *aveva molta fame e spolverò tutto in cinque
minuti*, he was very hungry and ate up everything
in five minutes **3.** (*pitt.*) to pounce **4.** (*aspergere con
sostanza in polvere*) to dust, to sprinkle: — *di zucchero
un dolce*, to dust a cake with sugar ‖ **spolveràrsi,**
v.r. to dust oneself; (*spazzolarsi*) to brush oneself.

spolveràta, *s.f.* **1.** dust; dusting; (*spazzolata*) brush;
brushing: *dare una* — *a un mobile*, to give a piece of
furniture a dusting **2.** (*l'aspergere con sostanza in polvere*) dusting, sprinkling: *dare una* — *di zucchero a
una torta*, to dust a cake with sugar.

spolveratóre, *s.m.* duster.

spolveratríce, *s.f.* **1.** (*aspiratore elettrico*) vacuum
cleaner **2.** (*chi spolvera*) duster.

spolveratúra, *s.f.* **1.** dusting **2.** *fig.* (*infarinatura*)
smattering: *una* — *di inglese*, a smattering of English.

spolverína, *s.f.* dust-coat, overall; (*amer.*) duster.

spolveríno, *s.m.* **1.** feather duster **2.** (*polverino*)
sand-box.

spolverío, *s.m.* **1.** cloud of dust **2.** (*scherz.*) (*grande
mangiata*) blow-out.

spolverizzàre, *v.t.* **1.** (*ridurre in polvere*) to pulverize, to powder **2.** (*aspergere*) to dust, to sprinkle: —
un dolce di zucchero, to dust (*o* to sprinkle) a cake
with sugar **3.** (*pitt.*) to pounce.

spolverizzatóre, *s.m.* pulverizer.

spolverízzo, *s.m.* (*pitt.*) pounce.

spólvero, *s.m.* **1.** dusting **2.** (*pitt.*) perforated pattern;
(*spolverizzo*) pounce **3.** (*farina sottile*) fine flour **4.** *fig.*
(*infarinatura*) smattering: — *di conoscenza*, smattering
of knowledge.

spomiciàre, *v.t.* to pumice.

spónda, *s.f.* **1.** (*orlo*) edge, margin; (*di abisso*) brink;
— *di un letto*, edge of a bed; — *di un precipizio*, edge
(*o* brink) of a precipice ‖ *tirare di* —, (*biliardo*) to shoot
from the cushion **2.** (*riva*) bank, side: *sulla* — *del
fiume*, by the side of the river **3.** (*parapetto*) parapet:
— *di un ponte*, parapet of a bridge.

spondàico, *ag.* (*poes.*) spondaic: *esametro* —, spondaic
hexameter.

spondèo, *s.m.* (*poes.*) spondee.

spondilíte, *s.f.* (*patol.*) spondylitis.

spòndilo, *s.m.* (*anat.*) spondyl.

spongifórme, *ag.* spongiform.

spongína, *s.f.* (*chim. biol.*) spongin.

spongiosità, *s.f.* sponginess.

spongióso, *ag.* spongy.

spongiuòla, *s.f.* (*bot.*) spongiole.

sponsàle, *ag.* nuptial ‖ *s.m.pl.* nuptials; wedding (*sing.*).

spontaneaménte, *av.* spontaneously: *quelle piante
crescono* —, those plants grow spontaneously.

spontaneità, *s.f.* spontaneity, spontaneousness.

spontàneo, *ag.* spontaneous: *combustione spontanea*,
(*chim.*) spontaneous combustion; *generazione, produzione spontanea*, (*biol.*) spontaneous generation; *offerta
spontanea*, spontaneous offer; *stile* —, spontaneous
style.

spopolaménto, *s.m.* depopulation.

spopolàre, *v.t.* to depopulate ‖ **spopolàrsi,** *v.r.* to
become depopulated, to depopulate.

spopolàto, *ag.* depopulated; (*deserto*) deserted.

spoppaménto, *s.m.* weaning.

spoppàre, *v.t.* to wean.

spoppatúra, *s.f.* weaning.

spòra, *s.f.* (*bot. biol.*) spore.

Spòradi, *no.pr.f.pl.* (*geog.*) Sporades.

sporadicaménte, *av.* sporadically.

sporadicità, *s.f.* sporadicity.

sporàdico, *ag.* sporadic: *casi sporadici*, sporadic
cases.

sporàngio, *s.m.* (*bot.*) sporangium (*pl.* sporangia).

sporcacciàre, *v.t.* (*pop.*) to dirty, to soil, to foul.

sporcaccióna, *s.f.* dirty woman, filthy woman.

sporcaccióne, *ag.* dirty, filthy ‖ *s.m.* dirty man,
filthy man, pig.

sporcaménte, *av.* dirtily, filthily.

sporcàre, *v.t.* **1.** to dirty, to soil, to foul; *ho sporcato il vestito di fango*, I have soiled (*o* dirtied) my
dress with mud **2.** *fig.* (*deturpare*) to soil, to sully, to
stain: — *la propria fama*, to stain one's reputation ‖
sporcàrsi, *v.r.* **1.** to dirty oneself, to get dirty: *questo
vestito si sporca facilmente*, this dress gets dirty easily
(*o* soils easily); — *il viso*, to dirty one's face **2.** *fig.*
(*insudiciarsi*) to soil: *non voglio sporcarmi le mani
in questa faccenda*, I do not want to soil my hands
in this business.

sporcàto, *ag.* **1.** dirty, foul **2.** *fig.* soiled, sullied.

sporchería, *s.f.* **1.** dirt, filth **2.** *fig.* dirty action.

sporchézza, *s.f.* dirtiness, filthiness, foulness.

sporcízia, *s.f.* **1.** dirt, filth **2.** *fig.* (*parola turpe*) dirty
word; (*azione turpe*) dirty action, filth.

spòrco, *ag.* **1.** dirty, soiled, filthy, foul: *bambino* —,
dirty child; *biancheria sporca*, soiled linen; *mani sporche di fango*, hands dirty with mud ‖ *lingua sporca*,
furred tongue ‖ *avere la fedina penale sporca*, (*dir.*) to
have a black record **2.** *fig.* (*turpe*) dirty; (*disonesto*)
dishonest; (*volgare*) coarse: *azioni sporche*, dishonest
actions; *coscienza sporca*, guilty conscience; *parola
sporca*, coarse (*o* dirty) word; *è un affare* —, it's a
dirty (*o* low-down) business ‖ *me l'ha fatta sporca*, he
has played me a dirty trick ‖ *adottare una politica
sporca*, to crawl.

sporgènte, *ag.* jutting (out), protruding, projecting; (*protuberante*) protuberant, bulging: *denti, labbra
sporgenti*, protruding teeth, lips; *occhi sporgenti*, bulging (*o* protuberant) eyes.

sporgènza, *s.f.* protrusion, projection, protuberance:
la — *di quel balcone*, the protrusion of that balcony;
il muro è pieno di sporgenze, the wall is full of protru-
sions (*o* juts).

spòrgere, *v.i.* to jut out, to stick out, to project,
to protrude: *la mensola sporge di circa trenta centimetri*, the shelf sticks out about one foot; *una trave*

che sporge dal muro, a beam jutting out of the wall; — *sopra ql.co.,* to overhang sthg.: *delle rocce sporgevano sopra il torrente,* cliffs overhung the stream ‖ *v.t.* to put out, to lean out, to stretch out, to hold out, to stick out, to put forward: *sporse il capo dalla finestra,* he put his head out of the window; — *la mano,* to stretch out one's hand ‖ — *querela contro qlcu.,* (*dir.*) to sue s.o. (*o* to take action against s.o.) ‖ **spòrgersi,** *v.r.* to lean out: *è pericoloso — dal finestrino,* it is dangerous to lean out of the window.

sport, *s.m.* sport: — *estivi, invernali,* summer, winter sports; *egli fa molti —,* he practises many sports ‖ *fare ql.co. per —,* to do sthg. for fun.

spòrta, *s.f.* basket, shopping basket, hamper: *una — di patate,* a basket of potatoes ‖ *un sacco e una —,* (*fam.*) a great quantity: *gliene ho dette un sacco e una —,* I have given him a piece of my mind (*o* I have given him a good dressing-down).

sportèllo, *s.m.* **1.** door: *gli sportelli dei vagoni ferroviari,* the carriage doors; *lo — di un'automobile, di una gabbia,* the door of a car, of a cage **2.** (*di portone*) wicket **3.** (*di uffici postali, banche*) counter (window); (*di biglietteria*) ticket window.

sportíva, *s.f.* sportswoman (*pl.* sportswomen).

sportivaménte, *av.* sportingly.

sportívo, *ag.* sporting; sports (*attributivo*); sportsmanlike, sportsmanly: *edizione sportiva,* (*di un giornale*) sporting (*o* sports) edition (of a newspaper); *giornale —,* sporting newspaper; *qualità sportive,* sportsmanlike qualities; *redattore —,* sporting (*o* sports) editor; *i risultati sportivi,* the sporting results; *spirito —,* sporting spirit; *vestiti sportivi,* sports clothes; *egli fa una vita sportiva,* he goes in for sports a lot ‖ *s.m.* sportsman (*pl.* sportsmen).

spòrto, *ag.* leaning out (of sthg.) (*predicativo*); (*proteso*) outstretched: *col capo — dal finestrino,* with his head leaning out of the window; *con le mani sporte,* with outstretched hands ‖ *s.m.* (*arch.*) projection.

spòsa, *s.f.* bride; (*letter.*) spouse; (*moglie*) wife (*pl.* wives): *vestito da —,* wedding-dress; *ho visto una — vestita di bianco,* I have seen a bride dressed in white.

sposalízio, *s.m.* wedding; (*letter.*) nuptials (*pl.*).

sposàre, *v.t.* **1.** to marry, to get married to (s.o.): *le chiese di sposarlo,* he proposed to her; *sposò un uomo molto ricco,* she married a very rich man **2.** (*unire in matrimonio*) to marry, to join in marriage: *li sposò un prete di Roma,* a priest from Rome married them **3.** (*dare in matrimonio*) to marry (off), to give in marriage: *sposò sua figlia a un cugino di sua moglie,* he gave his daughter in marriage (*o* he married his daughter) to a cousin of his wife's **4.** (*unire*) to wed, to unite: — *la virtù alla bellezza,* to wed virtue to beauty **5.** (*abbracciare*) to embrace, to espouse: — *una causa, un partito,* to embrace a cause, a party ‖ **sposàrsi,** *v.r.* to get married, to marry: *non si è ancora sposato,* he has not got married yet; *si è sposata con un inglese,* she married an Englishman; *si sposeranno domani,* they will get married tomorrow.

sposàto, *ag.* **1.** married: *donna sposata,* married woman; *uomo —,* married man **2.** *fig.* (*congiunto, unito*) wedded: *uno stile felicemente — al contenuto,* a style happily wedded to the content.

spòso, *s.m.* bridegroom; (*letter.*) spouse; (*marito*) husband ‖ *gli sposi,* the married couple (*o* husband and wife) ‖ « *Promessi Sposi »,* (*lett.*) "the Betrothed".

spossaménto, *V.* **spossatézza.**

spossànte, *ag.* exhausting; (*stancante*) wearing; (*snervante*) enervating: *un clima —,* an enervating climate.

spossàre, *v.t.* to exhaust; (*stancare*) to tire out, to wear out; (*snervare*) to enervate: *questo lavoro mi ha spossato,* this work has tired (*o* worn) me out.

spossatézza, *s.f.* exhaustion; (*stanchezza*) weariness, tiredness; (*fatica*) fatigue.

spossàto, *ag.* tired out, weary.

spossessàre, *v.t.* to dispossess, to deprive, to oust.

spostaménto, *s.m.* **1.** moving, shifting, displacement **2.** (*cambiamento*) change **3.** (*mar. chim.*) displacement.

spostàre, *v.t.* **1.** to move, to shift, to displace: — *l'accento,* to shift the accent; — *un letto, una sedia,* to move a bed, a chair; — *una parola,* to change the position of a word; — *il proprio interesse su un altro argomento,* to shift one's interest to another subject ‖ — *un impiegato,* to transfer (*o* to move) an employee **2.** (*cambiare*) to change: *vorrei — l'orario delle mie lezioni,* I should like to change my lesson hours ‖ — *di tono,* (*mus.*) to change tone **3.** (*dissestare*) to ruin, to get into financial trouble: *tutte queste spese mi hanno spostato,* all these expenses have ruined me **4.** (*chim.*) to displace ‖ **spostàrsi,** *v.r.* **1.** to move, to shift, to change one's place: *non fa che — da un luogo all'altro,* he does nothing but shift from one place to another **2.** (*rovinarsi*) to be ruined.

spostàto, *ag.* **1.** out of its place (*predicativo*) ‖ *ora spostata,* unusual time: *viene a trovarmi a ore spostate,* he comes to see me at unusual (*o* inconvenient) times **2.** (*dissestato*) ill-adjusted ‖ *s.m.* ill-adjusted person; misfit.

spostatúra, *s.f.* **1.** moving, shifting, displacing **2.** (*cosa spostata*) thing out of place.

sprànga, *s.f.* **1.** bar, cross-bar; (*catenaccio*) bolt **2.** (*fibbia*) buckle.

sprangàre, *v.t.* to bar; (*con catenaccio*) to bolt: — *una porta, finestra,* to bar a door, window.

sprangatúra, *s.f.* barring; (*con catenaccio*) bolting.

spràzzo, *s.m.* **1.** (*di liquidi*) splash: — *d'acqua, di fango,* splash of water, of mud **2.** (*baleno*) flash: — *d'ingegno,* brain-wave; — *di luce, di speranza,* flash of light, of hope.

Sprèa, *no.pr.f.* (*geog.*) Spree.

sprecàre, *v.t.* to waste; (*scialacquare*) to squander: — *il fiato,* to waste one's breath; — *il proprio denaro,* to waste (*o* to squander) one's money; — *il tempo,* to waste time.

sprèco, *s.m.* waste: — *di denaro, tempo, energia,* waste of money, time, energy; *c'è — di tutto in questa casa,* there is waste of everything in this house; *fare — di ql.co.,* to waste sthg.

sprecóna, *s.f.,* **sprecóne,** *s.m.* waster, wastrel, squanderer.

spregévole, *ag.* despicable, contemptible, mean: *è un essere —,* he is a mean fellow.

spregevolménte, *av.* despicably, contemptibly, meanly.

spregiàre, *v.t.* to despise, to scorn; (*sdegnare*) to disdain.

spregiatívo, *ag.* scornful, disdainful, disparaging.

spregiatóre, *s.m.,* **spregiatríce,** *s.f.* despiser, scorner.

sprègio, *s.m.* contempt, disdain, scorn: *con —,* with contempt (*o* disdain); *in —,* in contempt; *sorriso di —,* contemptuous smile; *avere a — qlcu.,* to hold s.o. in contempt; *mostrare il proprio —,* to show one's contempt (*o* disdain *o* scorn).

spregiudicataménte, *av.* **1.** open-mindedly **2.** (*imparzialmente*) impartially.

spregiudicatézza, *s.f.* **1.** open-mindedness, freedom from prejudice **2.** (*imparzialità*) impartiality.

spregiudicàto, *ag.* **1.** unprejudiced, open-minded **2.** (*imparziale*) impartial ‖ *s.m.* unprejudiced person, open-minded person.

sprèmere, *v.t.* to squeeze (anche *fig.*); (*torcere*) to wring out: — *un'arancia fino all'ultima goccia,* to squeeze an orange dry; — *un limone, il sugo di un limone,* to squeeze a lemon, the juice out of a lemon; — *panni bagnati,* to wring out wet clothes; — *qualche lacrima,* to squeeze out a tear; (*costringere a piangere*) to wring tears (from s.o.); — *una spugna, l'acqua da una spugna,* to squeeze a sponge, to squeeze the water out of a sponge ‖ — *denaro da qlcu.*, to squeeze (*o* to wring) money out of s.o. ‖ **sprèmersi**, *v.r.*: — *un foruncolo*, to squeeze the matter out of a boil ‖ — *il cervello*, to cudgel (*o* to rack) one's brains.

spremilimóni, *s.m.* lemon-squeezer.

spremitóio, *s.m.* squeezer.

spremitúra, *s.f.* **1.** squeezing; (*di panni bagnati*) wringing **2.** (*succo*) juice.

spremúta, *s.f.* squash: — *di limone, di arancia*, lemon, orange squash.

spremúto, *ag.* squeezed; (*di panni*) wrung: *arancia, limone* —, squeezed orange, lemon ‖ *essere un limone* —, to be a squeezed orange.

spretàre, *v.t.* to unfrock ‖ **spretàrsi**, *v.r.* to renounce one's priesthood.

spretàto, *ag.* unfrocked.

sprezzànte, *ag.* scornful, contemptuous; disdainful: — *del pericolo*, scornful of danger; *con aria di* — *indifferenza*, with an air of contemptuous indifference; *modi sprezzanti*, disdainful ways; *sguardo* —, scornful (*o* contemptuous) look.

sprezzanteménte, *av.* scornfully, contemptuously, disdainfully.

sprezzàre, (*rar.*) per **disprezzàre**.

sprezzatóre, *ag.* scornful, contemptuous ‖ *s.m.*, **sprezzatríce**, *s.f.* despiser, scorner.

sprezzatúra, *s.f.* studied carelessness.

sprèzzo, (*rar.*) per **disprèzzo**.

sprigionaménto, *s.m.* **1.** exhalation; (*violento*) bursting out, bursting forth; (*di liquidi*) gushing out: *lo* — *di un gas*, the exhalation of a gas **2.** (*rar.*) (*scarceramento*) release, releasing.

sprigionàre, *v.t.* **1.** to emit, to give off; to exhale: — *gas, fumo, vapore*, to give off (*o* to exhale *o* to emit) gas, smoke, steam; — *calore, luce*, to emit (*o* to give off) heat, light **2.** (*rar.*) (*scarcerare*) to release, to set free ‖ **sprigionàrsi**, *v.r.* to be emitted, to be given off; (*con violenza*) to burst out, to burst forth; (*di liquidi*) to gush out; *fig.* to burst forth: *si sprigionarono scintille*, sparks were emitted (*o* were given off); *si sprigionò un getto di vapore*, a jet of steam burst out (*o* forth).

sprillàre, *v.i.* to squirt; to spout; to spurt.

sprillo, *s.m.* spout, spurt.

sprimacciàre, *v.t.* to shake up: *ella sprimacciò il materasso*, she shook up the mattress.

springàre, *v.i.* (*letter.*) to spring, to kick.

sprizzàre, *v.t.i.* to squirt; to spout; to spurt: *sprizzò acqua dalla roccia*, water spurted from the rock; — *sangue*, to spurt blood; — *scintille*, to spit (out) sparks ‖ *sprizzava gioia da tutti i pori*, she was bursting with joy.

sprizzo, *s.m.* **1.** spout, spurt **2.** *fig.* (*lampo*) flash: *uno* — *di ingegno*, a brainwave.

spròcco, *s.m.* (*bot.*) shoot, twig.

sprofondaménto, *s.m.* sinking; (*di nave*) foundering; (*crollo*) collapse; (*cedimento*) subsidence; giving way.

sprofondàre, *v.t.* (*rar.*) **1.** to sink, to founder: — *una nave*, to sink (*o* to founder) a ship **2.** (*far cadere*) to cause to collapse: *la neve ha sprofondato il tetto*, the snow has caused the roof to collapse ‖ *v.i.*, **sprofondàrsi**, *v.r.* **1.** to sink; (*di nave*) to founder; (*andare a fondo*) to go to the bottom; (*crollare*) to collapse; (*cedere, di pavimento, ecc.*) to subside, to give way; (*cadere*) to fall: *egli* (*si*) *sprofondava nella palude*, he was sinking into the bog; *la nave sprofondò*, the ship foundered (*o* sank *o* went to the bottom); *nel terremoto alcune case sono sprofondate*, some houses collapsed in the earthquake; *il pavimento* (*si*) *sprofondò sotto l'enorme peso*, the floor subsided (*o* gave way) under the heavy weight; *sprofondarono nel baratro*, they fell into the abyss ‖ — *in una poltrona*, to sink into an armchair **2.** *fig.* (*immergersi*) to sink; to be absorbed: *quando si sprofonda nei suoi pensieri non*

sente niente, when he is absorbed in his thoughts he does not hear anything **3.** *fig.* (*profondersi*): — *in ringraziamenti*, to thank profusely; — *in scuse*, to excuse oneself profusely.

sprofondàto, *ag.* **1.** sunk, sunken; (*di nave*) foundered ‖ — *in una poltrona*, sunk in an armchair **2.** (*profondo*) deep **3.** (*arc.*) (*senza fondo*) bottomless ‖ *è ricco* —, he is fabulously rich **4.** *fig.* (*immerso*) sunk, absorbed.

sprolòquio, *s.m.* long rigmarole, long rambling speech.

spronàio, *s.m.* spurrier, spur-maker.

spronàre, *v.t.* **1.** to spur (anche *fig.*): *l'ambizione lo spronò a tutto questo*, ambition spurred him to all this; *devo spronarlo continuamente per farlo studiare*, I have to urge him continually to make him study; — *un cavallo*, to spur a horse; — *qlcu. a fare ql.co.*, to goad s.o. into doing sthg. **2.** (*edil.*) to buttress **3.** — *le scarpe*, (*andare a piedi*) to go on shank's pony.

spronàta, *s.f.* spurring (anche *fig.*).

spronatóre, *ag.* spurring, goading.

spróne, *s.m.* **1.** spur: *gli sproni di un cavaliere*, a rider's spurs ‖ *a spron battuto*, at full speed ‖ *dar di* — *a un cavallo*, to spur a horse **2.** *fig.* (*incitamento, stimolo*) spur, stimulus: *lo* — *dell'ambizione*, the spur (*o* stimulus) of ambition; *lo* — *della fame*, the goad (*o* spur) of hunger **3.** (*zool. bot.*) spur **4.** (*arch.*) scarp, buttress **5.** (*mar.*) ram (of warship).

sproporzionàle, *ag.* disproportionate, unproportional, out of proportion.

sproporzionalità, *s.f.* disproportion.

sproporzionàre, *v.t.* (*rar.*) to disproportion.

sproporzionataménte, *av.* disproportionately.

sproporzionàto, *ag.* disproportionate, out of proportion (to, with sthg.): *è un prezzo* — *al valore reale di quel quadro*, it is a price out of proportion to (*o* with) the actual value of that painting; *ha la testa sproporzionata al resto del corpo*, his head is out of proportion to (*o* with) the rest of his body.

sproporzióne, *s.f.* disproportion: *c'è una certa* — *fra le varie parti dell'opera*, there is a certain disproportion between the different parts of the work; *c'è una* — *enorme fra quello che guadagna e quello che spende*, there is a great disproportion between what he earns and what he spends.

spropositàre, *v.i.* to blunder, to make mistakes: *hai tradotto spropositando*, there are some blunders in your translation; *non parla senza* —, he cannot speak without blundering.

spropositataménte, *av.* **1.** blunderingly **2.** (*enormemente*) enormously, hugely, disproportionately: *mangia* —, she eats enormously.

spropositàto, *ag.* **1.** full of blunders: *scrive certe lettere spropositate che ci fanno morir dal ridere*, he writes letters so full of blunders that make us roar with laughter **2.** (*enorme*) enormous, huge: *ha un naso* —, he has such a huge nose; *ha un prezzo così* — *che non vale la pena di comprarlo*, it costs such an enormous price that it is not worth (while) buying.

spropòsito, *s.m.* **1.** blunder, mistake, error: *ha fatto uno* — *a sposare quella donna*, he has made a gross mistake in marrying that woman; *non fa una cosa che non sia uno* —, he never does anything without putting his foot in it ‖ *era così disperato che i suoi temettero facesse uno* —, he was so desperate that his people feared that he would do sthg. silly ‖ *gli fai una domanda, e ti risponde a* —, you ask him a question and his answer is off the point ‖ *non mi far dire uno* —, (*fam.*) don't make me say what I don't want to **2.** (*errore grammaticale o sintattico*) blunder, mistake, howler: *nel compito hai fatto uno* — *madornale*, you have made a howler in your exercise **3.** (*fam.*) (*eccesso*) excess, huge quantity: *di dolci, poi, ne mangia uno* —, (*fam.*) as for sweets he eats huge quantities of them ‖ *costa uno* —, it is frightfully expensive.

spropriàre, *v.t.* to expropriate, to dispossess, to

deprivo: *hanno spropriato lo zio di tutto ciò che aveva*, they have deprived uncle of everything he had ‖ **spropriàrsi**, *v.r.* to deprive oneself: *non posso spropriarmi per lui*, I cannot deprive myself of what I have for his sake.

spropriazióne, *s.f.* expropriation, dispossession.

spròprio, *s.m.* 1. expropriation, dispossession 2. (*spesa eccessiva*) waste of money, squandering: *come posso sopportare questo —?*, how can I put up with this waste of money?.

sprovvedére, *v.t.* to leave (s.o.) unprovided ‖ **sprovvedérsi**, *v.r.* to deprive oneself: *si è sprovveduto del necessario*, he has deprived himself of the necessaries of life.

sprovvedutaménte, *av.* 1. (*incautamente*) incautiously 2. (*inaspettatamente*) unexpectedly.

sprovvedúto, *ag.* 1. (*incauto*) incautious, unwary 2. *V.* **sprovvísto**.

sprovvísto, *ag.* 1. devoid, destitute; unprovided (with sthg.), lacking (sthg.): *la casa era sprovvista di tutto*, the house was completely unprovided (o was out of everything o lacked everything); *completamente — di buon senso*, completely lacking (o devoid of) common sense 2. (*impreparato*) unprepared, unready ‖ *alla sprovvista*, unawares: *cogliere qlcu. alla sprovvista*, to catch s.o. unawares.

spruzzàglia, *s.f.* 1. spray 2. (*pioggia fine*) drizzle.

spruzzaménto, *s.m.* 1. (*lo spruzzare*) spraying; sprinkling 2. (*spruzzo*) spray 3. (*fis.*) sputtering: *— catodico*, cathodic sputtering.

spruzzàre, *v.t.* 1. to spray; to sprinkle, to besprinkle: *— ql.co. di acqua*, to sprinkle (o to spray) sthg. with water 2. (*inzaccherare*) to splash.

spruzzàta, *s.f.* 1. (*spruzzo*) spray; sprinkling 2. (*breve pioggia*) light shower.

spruzzàto, *ag.* sprinkled; sprayed; (*chiazzato*) speckled, spotted.

spruzzatóre, *s.m.* 1. (*chi spruzza*) sprayer; sprinkler 2. (*arnese per spruzzare*) spray 3. (*aut.*) jet: *— compensatore*, auxiliary jet.

spruzzatúra, *s.f.* spraying; sprinkling: *— (di vernice) a caldo*, hot spraying; *— (di vernice) a freddo*, cold spraying.

sprúzzo, *s.m.* 1. spray (*invariato al pl.*); sprinkling: *uno — d'acqua*, a sprinkling of water; *verniciatura a —*, spray painting; *gli spruzzi delle onde arrivavano fino alla strada*, the spray (of the waves) reached the road 2. (*di liquido sporco*) splash.

spruzzolàre, *v.t.* (*spruzzare*) to sprinkle; to spray ‖ *v.i.* (*piovigginare*) to drizzle.

spruzzolàta, *s.f.* 1. (*lo spruzzare*) sprinkling; spraying 2. (*pioggerella*) light shower.

spruzzolàto, *ag.* sprinkled; sprayed; (*chiazzato*) speckled, spotted.

spudorataménte, *av.* shamelessly, impudently; (*fam.*) cheekily.

spudoratézza, *s.f.* shamelessness, impudence; (*fam.*) cheekiness: *che —!*, what cheek!.

spudoràto, *ag.* shameless, impudent, brazen; (*fam.*) cheeky ‖ *s.m.* shameless fellow, impudent fellow.

spúgna, *s.f.* 1. sponge: *pescatore di spugne*, sponge diver; *cancellare ql.co. con la —*, to sponge (o to rub) sthg. off; *fig.* to expunge sthg.; *passare la — sopra ql.co.*, to pass the sponge over sthg.; *fig.* to let bygones be bygones ‖ *quell'uomo è una —*, that man is a soak (o a sponge); *bere come una —*, to drink like a fish ‖ *gettare la —*, to throw up the sponge (o to throw in the towel) 2. (*tessuto spugnoso*) sponge-cloth: *accappatoio di —*, bath-wrap; *asciugamano di —*, bath-towel 3. *— di platino*, (*chim.*) platinum sponge 4. (*metal.*) ball.

spugnàre, *v.t.* to sponge up, to mop (up).

spugnàta, *s.f.* sponge, sponging.

spugnatúra, *s.f.* sponge down.

spugnòla, *s.f.*, **spugnòlo**, *s.m.* (*bot.*) morel.

spugnosità *s.f.* sponginess.

spugnóso, *ag.* spongy: *platino —*, (*chim.*) spongy platinum.

spulàre, *v.t.* (*agr.*) to winnow, to fan.

spulatúra, *s.f.* (*agr.*) winnowing, fanning.

spulciàre, *v.t.* 1. to look for fleas on (s.o.) 2. (*esaminare attentamente*) to scrutinize, to examine very carefully ‖ *— dati, informazioni*, to gather data, information here and there ‖ **spulciàrsi**, *v.r.* to look for fleas on oneself.

spulciatúra, *s.f.* scrutiny, close examination.

spulezzàre, *v.i.* (*fuggir via*) to run away, to flee.

spulézzo, *s.m.* (*fuga*) flight.

spulíre, *v.t.* (*rar.*) to polish: *— un vetro*, (*smerigliarlo*) to grind a glass.

spulizzíre, *v.t.* (*rar.*) (*pulire*) to clean.

spúma, *V.* **schiúma**.

spumànte, *ag.* foaming, frothing: *vino —*, sparkling wine ‖ *— di rabbia*, fuming with rage ‖ *s.m.* sparkling wine, champagne-type wine.

spumàre, *v.i.* to foam, to froth.

spumeggiànte, *ag.* foaming, frothing.

spumeggiàre, *v.i.* to foam, to froth: *il torrente spumeggiava*, the torrent was foaming.

spumóne, *s.m.* " spumone " (kind of ice cream).

spumosità, *s.f.* frothiness, foaminess.

spumóso, *ag.* frothy, foamy; (*di vino*) sparkling.

spuntàre, *v.t.* 1. (*rompere, guastare la punta di*) to blunt; to break the point of (sthg.): *— un ago, una spada*, to blunt a needle, a sword 2. (*tagliare la punta a*) to cut the tip off (sthg.); to trim: *— una siepe*, to trim a hedge; *— un sigaro*, to cut (the tip of) a cigar ‖ *farsi — i capelli*, to have one's hair trimmed 3. (*staccare, cosa appuntata*) to unpin: *— un nastro*, to unpin a ribbon 4. (*controllare*) to check: *— un conto, la merce*, to check an account, the goods 5. *fig.* (*vincere, superare*) to overcome: *— una difficoltà*, to overcome a difficulty ‖ *spuntarla*, to succeed (o to win one's way): *fu difficile, ma la spuntammo*, it was difficult, but we made it ‖ *v.i.* 1. (*incominciare a sorgere, nascere*) (*di sole, ecc.*) to rise; (*di alberi, fiori, ecc.*) to sprout; (*di capelli, ecc.*) to begin to grow: *gli è spuntato il primo dente*, he has cut his first tooth; *incominciano a spuntargli i capelli*, his hair is beginning to grow; *quando spunta il giorno*, when day breaks; *il sole, la luna spunta*, the sun, the moon rises; *spuntano le prime foglie*, the first leaves are sprouting ‖ *gli spuntarono le lacrime agli occhi*, tears rose to (o welled up in) his eyes (o his eyes filled with tears) ‖ *un timido sorriso gli spuntò sulle labbra*, he smiled shyly (o he gave a shy smile) 2. (*apparire*) to appear; to come out: *lo vidi — all'angolo della via*, I saw him appearing round the corner; *il nemico spuntò da dietro un colle*, the enemy appeared from behind a hill; *spuntarono da dietro alla siepe*, they came out from behind the hedge; *spuntava solo la sua testa*, only his head was sticking out ‖ **spuntàrsi**, *v.r.* 1. (*perdere la punta*) to get blunt, to lose its point: *questa spada si è spuntata*, this sword has got blunt; *si è spuntata la matita*, the pencil has got blunt (o has lost its point) 2. (*staccarsi*) to come unpinned 3. *fig.* (*svanire*) to die down: *la sua collera si spuntò quando gli dissero che ciò non era vero*, his anger died down when they told him it wasn't true.

spuntàre, *s.m.* (*nascita, apparizione*) breaking; (*di alberi, fiori, ecc.*) sprouting: *allo — del giorno*, at daybreak (o at dawn); *allo — del sole*, at sunrise.

spuntàto, *ag.* blunt, pointless: *matita spuntata*, pointless pencil; *una spada spuntata*, a blunt sword.

spuntatríce, *s.f.* 1. (*mec.*) chamfering machine 2. (*ind. tessile*) snipping machine, snipper.

spuntatúra, *s.f.* 1. blunting 2. cutting off the tip; trimming ‖ *spuntature di sigari*, cigar-ends (o cigar-tips o stumps) 3. (*controllo*) checking, control 4. (*metal.*) crop(-end); cropping 5. (*mec.*) chamfering 6. (*ind. tessile*) snipping.

spuntellàre, *v.t.* (*levare i puntelli a*) to remove the props from (sthg.), to unprop.

spuntíno, *s.m.* snack: *fare uno —,* to have a snack.

spúnto, *s.m.* **1.** (*acidità del vino*) sourness: *questo vino ha preso lo —,* this wine has got a little sour **2.** (*teat.*) cue: *gli diedi lo —, poi continuò da solo,* I gave him the cue, then he went on by himself **3.** (*suggerimento*) cue, hint **4.** (*punto di partenza*) starting point: *prese lo — da questa osservazione per esporre il suo caso,* he took this remark as a starting point for presenting his case; *questo fu lo — di un lungo discorso,* this was the starting point of a long speech **5.** (*mus.*) entry.

spuntóne, *s.m.* **1.** (*st. mil.*) pike, halberd **2.** (*grossa punta di ferro*) spike.

spunzecchiàre, *V.* punzecchiàre.

spunzonàre, *v.t.* **1.** to push; (*dare gomitate a*) to elbow **2.** *fig.* (*incitare*) to spur: — *qlcu. a fare ql.co.,* to spur s.o. to do sthg.

spunzóne, *s.m.* **1.** (*punta di ferro*) spike: *gli spunzoni del cancello,* the spikes of the gate **2.** (*grossa spina*) big thorn **3.** (*gomitata*) push with one's elbow: *farsi largo tra la folla a spunzoni,* to elbow one's way through the crowd.

spurgaménto, *s.m.* **1.** (*il pulire*) cleaning; purging: *lo — delle fogne,* the cleaning of sewers **2.** (*med.*) (*lo spurgare*) discharging; (*spurgo*) discharge **3.** (*l'espettorare*) expectorating.

spurgàre, *v.t.* **1.** (*pulire*) to clean; to purge: — *un fosso,* to clean a ditch **2.** (*med.*) to discharge: — *materia,* to discharge matter || *v.i.,* **spurgàrsi,** *v.r.* (*espettorare*) to expectorate, to spit.

spúrgo, *s.m.* **1.** (*lo spurgare*) discharging; (*l'espettorare*) expectorating **2.** (*ciò che viene espulso*) discharge: — *di pus,* discharge of pus.

spúrio, *ag.* **1.** (*illegittimo*) illegitimate: *figlio —,* illegitimate son **2.** (*falso, apocrifo*) spurious **3.** *costole spurie,* (*med.*) false ribs.

sputacchiàre, *v.i.* to spit || *v.t.* to spit at (s.o., sthg.).

sputacchièra, *s.f.* spittoon.

sputàcchio, *s.m.* spittle, spit.

sputapépe, *s.m.* (*persona petulante*) petulant person; snarler.

sputàre, *v.t.i.* to spit (anche *fig.*): *è vietato —,* spitting prohibited; *sputò il nocciolo della ciliegia,* he spat out the cherry-stone; *il vulcano sputava fiamme,* the volcano spat fire; — *addosso a qlcu.,* to spit at (o on) s.o.; — *su ql.co.,* to spit at (o on) sthg. || *questo lavoro mi ha fatto — sangue,* this work has made me spit blood || *sputa fuori!,* spit it out! || — *sentenze,* to play the wiseacre || *sputa sempre veleno,* he has a venomous tongue.

sputasénno, *s.m.,* **sputasentènze,** *s.m.* wiseacre.

sputàto, *ag.* that has been spat out || *questo ragazzo è suo padre nato e —,* (*fam.*) this boy is the dead spit of his father.

sputnik, *s.m.* (*astronautica*) sputnik.

spúto, *s.m.* spit, spittle.

squadernàre, *v.t.* **1.** to turn over the leaves of (a book) **2.** (*dire apertamente*) to say openly; to tell openly; (*mostrare apertamente*) to show openly **3.** (*spalancare*) to open (sthg.) wide.

squàdra, *s.f.* **1.** (*da disegno*) (set) square: — *a cappello,* back square; — *a 45°,* mitre square; — *a T, doppia,* T-square; — *di legno, metallo,* wooden, metal square; — *esagonale,* hexagonal square; — *falsa,* bevel (square); *essere a —,* to be at right angles; *essere fuori —,* to be out of square; *fig.* to be out of sorts; *uscire di —,* to be out of line; *fig.* to go astray **2.** (*mil.*) (*drappello sotto un graduato*) squad; (*mar.*) squadron: *una — di soldati,* a squad of soldiers; *a squadre,* in (o by) squads || — *del buon costume,* anti-vice squad || — *mobile, volante,* flying squad **3.** (*spor.*) team: *compagno di —,* team-mate; *spirito di —,* team spirit; *la — dei calciatori giuoca bene,* the football team is playing well **4.** (*di operai*) gang; (*di persone che lavo-*

rano in modo organizzato) team: *capo —,* foreman (*o* ganger); *lavoro a squadre,* team-work; *una — di operai stava lavorando sulla ferrovia,* a gang of workmen were working on the railway **5.** (*mec.*) plate, square: — *di attacco,* (*di travatura metallica*) connecting plate (*o* joint plate); — *di precisione,* precision square; — *fissa,* try square.

squadràre, *v.t.* **1.** to square **2.** (*guardare da capo a piedi*) to look (s.o.) up and down: *la squadrò un attimo,* he looked her up and down for a moment.

squadratúra, *s.f.* squaring.

squadríglia, *s.f.* (*mar. aer.*) squadron.

squàdro, *s.m.* **1.** squaring **2.** (*topografia*) square.

squadróne, *s.m.* (*mil.*) squadron; company.

squagliaménto, *s.m.* **1.** melting; liquefying; (*di ghiaccio*) thaw(ing) **2.** (*fam.*) (*lo svignarsela*) clearing off; stealing away.

squagliàre, *v.t.* to melt (down); to liquefy || **squagliàrsi,** *v.r.* **1.** to melt; to liquefy; (*di ghiaccio*) to thaw **2.** (*fam.*) (*svignarsela*) to steal away; to make off; to clear off.

squalífica, *s.f.* disqualification.

squalificàre, *v.t.* to disqualify.

squallidézza, *s.f.* dreariness, bleakness.

squàllido, *ag.* dreary, bleak.

squallóre, *s.m.* dreariness, bleakness.

squàlo, *s.m.* (*ittiol.*) squalus (*pl.* squali), shark.

squàma, *s.f.* **1.** (*di pesci, rettili, pelle*) scale **2.** (*lamina di metallo*) flake.

squamàre, *v.t.* (*togliere le squame a*) to scale || **squamàrsi,** *v.r.* **1.** (*perdere le squame*) to scale **2.** (*sfaldarsi*) to flake (off).

squamóso, *ag.* **1.** scaly **2.** (*che si sfalda*) flaky.

squarciagóla, a, *l.av.* at the top of one's voice.

squarciaménto, *s.m.* tearing, rending, ripping up.

squarciàre, *v.t.* **1.** to tear, to rend, to rip up: — *un pezzo di stoffa,* to tear a piece of cloth; — *le vesti a qlcu.,* to rend s.o.'s garments **2.** *fig.* to dispel: *il sole squarciò le nubi,* the sun dispelled the clouds; — *il velo del mistero,* to dispel a mystery (*o* to tear aside the veil of mystery) || **squarciàrsi,** *v.r.* to be torn, to be rent: *le nubi si squarciarono,* there was a rift in the clouds; *la vela si squarciò,* the sail was rent.

squàrcio, *s.m.* **1.** gash, laceration: *aveva uno — in un braccio,* he had a gash in his arm **2.** (*di stoffa, vesti*) rent, gash, tear: *avere uno — nel vestito,* to have a tear in one's dress **3.** (*la parte squarciata*) shred **4.** (*passo di libro, scritto*) passage.

squartaménto, *s.m.* quartering.

squartàre, *v.t.* to quarter; to cut to pieces, to cut up.

squartatóio, *s.m.* (*coltello da beccaio*) butcher's cleaver.

squartatúra, *s.f.* quartering.

squassaménto, *s.m.* (violent) shaking, jolting.

squassàre, *v.t.* to shake violently, to jolt.

squàsso, *s.m.* violent shake, jolt.

squattrinàre, *v.t.* to leave (s.o.) penniless; to reduce (s.o.) to penury || *v.i.* to squander one's money || **squattrinàrsi,** *v.r.* to be left penniless.

squattrinàto, *ag.* penniless || *s.m.* penniless person.

squèro, *s.m.* (*mar.*) boat-house, boat-shed.

squilibràre, *v.t.* **1.** to throw out of balance, to unbalance **2.** (*facoltà mentali*) to derange || **squilibràrsi,** *v.r.* to lose one's balance.

squilibràto, *ag.* **1.** unbalanced **2.** (*pazzo*) mad, insane || *s.m.* madman, lunatic.

squilíbrio, *s.m.* **1.** lack of balance; (*rar.*) disequilibrium **2.** — *mentale,* derangement.

squílla[1]**,** *s.f.* **1.** ringing **2.** (small) bell; (*di mucche*) cow-bell; (*di pecore*) sheep-bell.

squílla[2]**,** *s.f.* (*bot. zool.*) squill.

squillànte, *ag.* shrill, sharp; (*di trombe*) blaring; (*di campane*) pealing: *voce —,* shrill voice.

squillàre, *v.i.* to ring; (*di trombe*) to blare; (*di campane*) to peal.

squíllo, *s.m.* sharp sound; (*di trombe*) blare; (*di campane*) peal; (*di campanelli*) ring ‖ *ragazza* —, call-girl.

squíncio, *ag.* oblique, slanting ‖ *di* —, askance: *lo guardò di* —, he looked at him askance.

squinternàre, *v.t.* **1.** (*sconnettere*) to ruin, to spoil **2.** (*squadernare*) to thumb through (sthg.) **3.** (*scombussolare, mandare sossopra*) to throw into disorder, to disarrange; *fig.* to upset, to discompose.

squisitaménte, *av.* exquisitely.

squisitézza, *s.f.* exquisiteness; (*di cibo, sapore*) deliciousness.

squisìto, *ag.* **1.** exquisite; of rare quality (*predicativo*): *di squisita forma,* of exquisite form; *di squisita lavorazione,* of exquisite workmanship; *la sua casa mostra il suo gusto* —, his house shows his exquisite taste **2.** (*di cibo, sapore*) delicious: *questo dolce è* —, this cake is delicious.

squittinàre, *v.t.* (*rar.*) (*scrutinare*) to scrutinize.

squittíre, *v.i.* **1.** (*di topi e simili*) to squeak; (*di uccelli*) to cheep; (*del bracco quando leva la preda*) to yelp **2.** (*di persone*) to yelp.

sradicaménto, *s.m.* uprooting; eradication (anche *fig.*), extirpation (anche *fig.*).

sradicàre, *v.t.* to uproot (anche *fig.*); to eradicate, to extirpate (anche *fig.*): *le abitudini contratte da molto tempo sono difficili da* —, long-established habits are hard to uproot; *il vento sradicò gli alberi,* the wind uprooted the trees; — *un male, i pregiudizi,* to extirpate an evil, prejudices; — *la povertà,* to eradicate poverty.

sragionaménto, *s.m.* false reasoning; nonsense.

sragionàre, *v.i.* to reason falsely; to talk nonsense: *non ti ascolto perchè stai sragionando,* I won't listen to you because you are talking nonsense.

sragionévole, *V.* **irragionévole.**

sregolataménte, *av.* **1.** disorderly; immoderately, intemperately; *bere* —, to drink immoderately; *vivere* —, to lead a disorderly life **2.** (*dissolutamente*) dissolutely.

sregolatézza, *s.f.* **1.** disorderliness; intemperance **2.** (*dissolutezza*) dissoluteness, profligacy: *la* — *dei costumi del nostro tempo,* the dissolute morals of the day.

sregolàto, *ag.* **1.** disorderly; immoderate, intemperate: *una condotta sregolata,* a disorderly conduct **2.** (*dissoluto*) dissolute, profligate.

srugginíre, *v.t.* to remove the rust from (sthg.), to de-rust.

stabaccàre, *v.i.* to take snuff.

stabbiàre, *v.t.* (*concimare*) to manure.

stàbbio, *s.m.* **1.** (*recinto per animali*) pen; (*per maiali*) (pig)sty **2.** (*concime*) manure.

stabbiuòlo, *s.m.* (pig)sty.

stàbile, *ag.* **1.** stable, steady, firm: *fondamenta stabili,* steady (o firm o stable) foundations ‖ *beni stabili,* real estate ‖ *colori stabili,* fast colours ‖ *governo* —, stable government ‖ *in pianta* —, on the permanent staff: *personale in pianta* —, permanent staff ‖ *naviglio* —, steady ship **2.** (*permanente*) permanent, durable, lasting: *compagnia* —, (*teat.*) permanent company; *impiego* —, permanent job; *pace* —, enduring (o lasting) peace; *residenza* —, permanent residence **3.** (*costante*) stable, steady, constant: *carattere* —, stable (o steady) character; *tempo* —, stable weather ‖ *s.m.* house, building.

stabiliménto, *s.m.* **1.** factory, plant; works (*pl.* spesso con costruzione *sing.*): — *chimico,* chemical plant; — *metallurgico,* metallurgical works; *uno* — *siderurgico,* an iron works; *il direttore di uno* —, a factory manager; *lo* — *chiude alle sei,* the works close at six **2.** (*edificio pubblico*) establishment: — *balneare,* bathing establishment ‖ — *penale,* prison **3.** (*lo stabilire*) establishment: *lo* — *di una nuova repubblica,* the establishment of a new republic.

Stabiliménti (déllo Strétto, *no.pr.m.pl.* (*geog.*) Straits Settlements.

stabilíre, *v.t.* **1.** to establish, to fix: *devi* — *i prezzi delle merci,* you must quote (o fix) the prices of the goods; *resta da* — *il giorno della partenza,* the departure date remains to be settled (o fixed o decided upon); — *una data,* to fix a date **2.** (*accertare*) to establish, to ascertain: *prima di tutto devo* — *se questo è vero o no,* first of all I must ascertain whether this is true or not; — *un fatto,* to establish a fact **3.** (*decidere*) to decide: *stabilì di partire subito,* he decided to leave at once **4.** (*assegnare*) to assign, to allot: *stabilirono due case in dote alla ragazza,* they allotted the girl two houses as a dowry **5.** (*mar.*) to set: — *le vele,* to set the sails ‖ **stabilírsi,** *v.r.* to settle, to establish oneself: *si stabilirono a Milano,* they settled in Milan.

stabilità, *s.f.* stability, steadiness, firmness: — *chimica,* chemical stability; — *di un edificio,* stability of a building; — *d'idee,* steadiness of ideas; — *dei prezzi,* steadiness of prices; — *di una tavola,* firmness (o stability) of a table; — *del terreno,* soil stability.

stabilizzàre, *v.t.* to stabilize.

stabilizzatóre, *s.m.* (*aer. mar.*) stabilizer: — *automatico,* automatic stabilizer; — *giroscopico,* gyro -stabilizer; — *girostatico,* gyrostatic stabilizer.

stabilizzazióne, *s.f.* stabilization: — *di una unità monetaria,* stabilization of a monetary unit.

stabilménte, *av.* firmly.

stabulàrio, *s.m.* (*canile municipale*) dog-pound.

stabulazióne, *s.f.* stalling (of cattle).

staccàbile, *ag.* detachable: *foglio* —, loose leaf.

staccaménto, *s.m.* detachment.

staccàre, *v.t.* **1.** to take off; to take out; to detach; to cut off; (*strappare*) to tear off, to pull off; to tear out, to pull out; (*tirar giù*) to take down: *gli staccarono la testa,* they cut off his head; — *un assegno dal libretto,* to tear a cheque out of the cheque-book; (*emetterlo*) to issue a cheque; — *un bottone,* to take off a button; — *una cedola da,* to detach a coupon from...; — *un fiore da una pianta,* to pick (o to pluck) a flower from a plant; — *una pagina,* to tear out a page; — *un pezzo da ql.co.,* to cut (o to break) a piece off sthg.; — *un pezzo di ql.co.,* to detach (o to cut off o to break off) a piece of sthg.; — *un quadro dal muro,* to take a picture down; — *una tenda,* to take down a curtain; — *la tappezzeria,* to tear (o to pull) the paper off the wall ‖ *non posso* — *gli occhi da...,* I cannot take my eyes off... ‖ — *le parole,* to enunciate carefully ‖ — *un vestito,* to cut (off) a dress-length **2.** (*sciogliere, slegare*) to loosen, to unfasten; to untie, to unbind, to (un)loose; (*sganciare*) to unhook: — *una barca,* to untie a boat; — *i buoi,* to unyoke the oxen; — *un cane dalla catena,* to let a dog off its chain; — *i cavalli da una carrozza,* to unharness the horses from a coach; — *un rimorchio,* to unhook a trailer; — *una vettura,* (*ferr.*) to uncouple a coach **3.** (*scostare*) to move away: — *un tavolo dal muro,* to move a table away from the wall **4.** (*separare*) to separate: *staccarono il bambino dalla madre,* they separated the child from its mother; — *una questione dall'altra,* to separate one question from the other ‖ *v.i.* **1.** (*spiccare, risaltare*) to stand out: *quella figura non stacca bene dal fondo,* that figure does not stand out very well (against its background); *il rosso stacca bene sul nero,* red stands out well against black **2.** (*fam.*) (*cessare il lavoro*) to knock off; to down tools: *gli operai staccano alle cinque,* the men knock off (o down tools) at five ‖ **staccàrsi,** *v.r.* **1.** to come off, to break off; to come out; to get detached: *quel francobollo non si stacca,* that stamp won't come off; *questo chiodo si sta staccando,* this nail is coming out; *un ramo si staccò dall'albero,* a branch broke off the tree; *s'è staccato un bottone,* a button has come off; *la tappezzeria si era staccata in più punti,* the wall-paper had come off in several places **2.** (*sciogliersi, slegarsi*) to break loose, to break away; (*sganciarsi*) to get unhooked, to come unhooked: *il cane è riuscito a* — *dalla catena,* the dog è ccmged to break loose from the chain; *la nave si anaoriata dall'ormeggio*, the ship broke loose from her aomstngs; *il rimorchio si è staccato*, the trailer broke away (*o came unhooked*) **3.** (*scostarsi*) to get away, to move away: *staccati dal muro*, get (*o* move) away from the wall **4.** (*separarsi*) to leave (s.o., sthg.), to part: *quando arrivò il treno, non sapeva — da sua madre*, when the train arrived, he could hardly bring himself to leave (*o* to part from) his mother **5.** (*abbandonare, allontanarsi*) to detach oneself; (*da vizi, ecc.*) to give up (s.o., sthg.): *non sa — da questa abitudine*, he cannot give up (*o* break himself of) this habit; — *dai piaceri del mondo*, to detach oneself from wordly pleasures (*o* to turn one's back on the world) **6.** (*distaccare*) to pull ahead (of s.o., sthg.): *tre cavalli si staccarono dal gruppo*, three horses pulled ahead of the group **7.** (*essere differente*) to differ, to be different: *la riproduzione si stacca molto dall'originale*, the reproduction differs greatly from the original.

staccataménte, *av.* at intervals; separately.

stacciàio, *s.m.* **1.** (*chi fabbrica stacci*) sieve-maker **2.** (*chi vende stacci*) sieve-seller.

stacciàre, *v.t.* to sieve, to sift.

stacciàta, *s.f.* **1.** (*lo stacciare*) sieving, sifting **2.** (*quantità di farina che si mette nello staccio*) sieveful.

stacciatúra, *s.f.* **1.** (*lo stacciare*) sieving, sifting **2.** (*quanto resta della farina setacciata*) siftings (*pl.*).

stàccio, *s.m.* sieve.

staccionàta, *s.f.* (wooden) fence.

stàceo, *s.m.* **1.** separation, detachment || *fare —*, *fig.* to stand out **2.** — *d'abito*, cut of cloth (for a suit).

stadèra, *s.f.* steelyard: — *a ponte*, (*mec.*) weigh-bridge.

stàdio, *s.m.* **1.** (*antica misura greca*) stadium (*pl.* stadia) **2.** (*campo di giuoco*) (*nell'antichità*) stadium (*pl.* stadia); (*in età moderna*) stadium (*pl.* stadiums), sports ground **3.** (*fase*) stage, phase, period; (*di malattia*) stage, stadium (*pl.* stadia): *nella mia vita passai per diversi stadi*, my life went through different phases.

stàffa, *s.f.* **1.** stirrup: *perse la —*, his feet came out of the stirrups; *mettere i piedi nelle staffe*, to put one's feet in the stirrups || *perdere le staffe*, *fig.* to lose one's self-control || *tenere il piede in due staffe*, to run with the hare and hunt with the hounds **2.** (*anat.*) stirrup-bone **3.** (*mec. edil.*) stirrup, bracket; (*per appendere*) (*mec.*) hanger: — *a U*, (*mec.*) U-bolt; —*centrale*, (*mec.*) spring band; — *per grondaie*, strap **4.** (*metal.*) flask, moulding box.

staffàle, *s.m.* foot-rest of a spade.

staffétta, *s.f.* courier; (*mil.*) dispatch rider || *corsa a —*, relay race || *macchina —*, (*ferr.*) pilot engine.

staffière, *s.m.* footman (*pl.* footmen), groom.

staffilàre, *v.t.* to whip, to lash, to flog: — *un cavallo*, to whip (*o* to flog) a horse; — *un ragazzo*, to whip a boy.

staffilàta, *s.f.* **1.** lash, stroke of the whip **2.** *fig.* (*critica acerba*) cruel taunt.

staffile, *s.m.* **1.** whip, lash, scourge, thong **2.** (*di staffa*) stirrup-strap.

stafilocòcco, *s.m.* (*biol.*) Staphylococcus (*pl.* Staphylococci).

stafilòma, *s.m.* (*patol.*) staphyloma.

stàggia, *V.* **stàggio**.

staggiàre, *v.t.* (*agr.*) to prop.

stàggio, *s.m.* **1.** shaft: *i due staggi di una scala a pioli*, the two shafts of a ladder **2.** (*di sedia*) back leg (of a chair) **3.** (*di rete da uccellare*) bar.

staggíre, *v.t.* (*dir.*) to seize, to levy a seizure on (sthg.).

stagionàle, *ag.* seasonal: *la migrazione — degli uccelli*, the seasonal migration of birds.

stagionaménto, *s.m.* seasoning.

stagionàre, *v.t.i.* to season: — *legname, vino*, to season timber, wine.

stagionàto, *ag.* **1.** seasoned: *legno, vino —*, seasoned wood (*o* timber), wine **2.** *fig.* (*scherz.*) (*attempato*) elderly: *un uomo —*, a man of many winters.

stagionatóre, *ag.* seasoning || *s.m.*, **stagionatrice**, *s.f.* seasoner.

stagionatúra, *s.f.* seasoning.

stagióne, *s.f.* **1.** season: *la bella, la brutta —*, the summer, the winter months; *le quattro stagioni dell'anno*, the four seasons of the year || *mezza —*, between-season (*o* mid-season): *vestito da mezza —*, in-between-season garment **2.** (*tempo, periodo*) season, time: *la — delle pesche*, the peach season; *la — delle piogge*, the rainy season; *la — del raccolto*, harvest-time (*o* the harvest season); *frutta di —*, fruit in season; *frutta fuori —*, fruit out of season; *prezzi di alta —*, high-season charges; *prezzi di bassa —*, off-season (*o* low season) charges; *è la — dei fichi d'India*, prickly-pears are in season; *si è aperta, chiusa la — della caccia*, it is the open, close season for game || — *morta*, dead (*o* dull *o* off) season **3.** (*teat.*) season: — *lirica, concertistica, teatrale*, opera, concert, theatrical season **4.** (*tempo atmosferico*) weather: *abbiamo avuto una — molto cattiva*, we have had very bad weather **5.** (*arc.*) (*momento, opportunità*) (proper) time, opportunity.

Stagíra, *no.pr.f.* (*geog. st.*) Stagyra.

stagliàre, *v.t.* to hack, to mangle || **stagliàrsi**, *v.r.* to stand out.

stagliàto, *ag.* sheer: *roccia stagliata*, sheer cliff.

stàgna, *s.f.* tin.

stagnàio, *s.m.* tin-smith, tinman (*pl.* tinmen).

stagnaménto, *s.m.* stagnation.

stagnànte, *ag.* stagnant: *acqua —*, stagnant water.

stagnàre[1], *v.t.* **1.** (*metal.*) to tin; to tin-plate; (*saldare*) to solder **2.** (*rendere impermeabile*) to waterproof: — *un barile*, to waterproof a barrel.

stagnàre[2], *v.i.* (*di liquido*) to stagnate (anche *fig.*) || *v.t.* to sta(u)nch: — *il sangue*, to stanch blood.

stagnàta, *s.f.* **1.** (*stagnatura*) tinning **2.** (*padella di stagno*) tin pan.

stagnatúra, *s.f.* tinning.

stagníno, *s.m.* tin-smith, tinman (*pl.* tinmen).

stàgno[1], *s.m.* (*min.*) tin || *saldare a —*, to solder.

stàgno[2], *ag.* water-tight: *compartimento —*, water-tight compartment.

stàgno[3], *s.m.* (*bacino d'acqua ferma*) pond, pool.

stagn(u)òla, *s.f.* tin-foil.

stàio, *s.m.*, *pl. m.* **stài** (*nei sensi* 1. 2.); *pl. f.* **stàia** (*nel senso* 3.) **1.** (*misura di capacità*) bushel: *uno — di grano*, a bushel of corn **2.** (*recipiente*) bushel || *cappello a —*, (*scherz.*) top hat **3.** (*contenuto di uno staio*) bushelful || *a staia*, in great quantity.

stalagmíte, *s.f.* (*geol.*) stalagmite.

stalagmítico, *ag.* stalagmitic.

stalattíte, *s.f.* (*geol.*) stalactite.

stalattítico, *ag.* stalactitic, stalactic.

Stalingràdo, *no.pr.f.* (*geog.*) Stalingrad.

stàlla, *s.f.* stable; (*per bestiame*) cowshed, cowhouse; (*per pecore*) sheepfold; (*per maiali*) pigsty: *garzone, mozzo di —*, stable-boy; (*di scuderia*) stable-lad; *maestro di —*, head-lad || *ha una casa che pare una —*, *fig.* his house is like a pigsty || *avere una ricca —*, to have a fine herd of cattle; (*di cavalli*) to have a fine string of horses || *chiudere la — quando sono fuggiti i buoi*, *prov.* to lock the stable door after the horse has bolted.

stallàggio, *s.m.* **1.** stabling **2.** (*costo dello stallaggio*) stabling fee.

stallàta, *s.f.* stable; (*di bestiame*) herd; (*di pecore*) flock.

stallàtico, *s.m.* **1.** (*concime*) dung, manure **2.** (*luogo dove si danno a nolo bestie da traino*) livery-stable **3.** *V.* **stallàggio**.

stallie, *s.f.pl.* (*comm. mar.*) lay-days.

stallière, *s.m.* stable-boy, stable-man (*pl.* stable-men); groom.

stallíno, *ag.* stalled, stall-fed: *cavallo —*, stalled horse || *s.m.* small stable.

stallívo, *ag.* stalled, stall-fed.

stàllo, *s.m.* **1.** seat; stall **2.** *(aer.)* stall: *indicatore di —,* stall indicator **3.** *(a scacchi)* stalemate **4.** *(arc.) (stanza)* room.

stallóne, *s.m.* stallion.

stallúccio, *s.m. (piccola stalla per maiali)* pigsty.

stamàne, stamàni, stamattína, *av.* this morning: *una notizia di —,* a fresh piece of news; *— mi sono alzato presto,* I got up early this morning; *ci vado —,* I am going there this morning.

stambécco, *s.m. (zool.)* steinbock, ibex.

stambèrga, *s.f.* hovel.

stambúgio, *s.m.* hole; small dark room: *non so come possa stare in quello —,* I don't know how he can live in that hole.

stamburaménto, *s.m.* drumming (anche *fig.*).

stamburàre, *v.i.* to drum, to beat the drum ‖ *v.t. fig.* to boast about (sthg.): *— qlcu.,* to praise s.o. (*o* to sing s.o.'s praises) ‖ *— le proprie qualità,* to blow one's own trumpet.

stamburàta, *s.f.* drumming.

stàme, *s.m.* **1.** *(bot.)* stamen **2.** *(parte fine della lana)* fine carded wool ‖ *lo — della vita,* (*poet.*) the thread of life.

stamígna, stamína, *s.f.* bunting, tamin(e).

staminàle, *s.m. (mar.)* futtock.

stàmpa, *s.f.* **1.** print (anche *foto.*): *— chiara, grande, piccola,* clear, large, small print; *bozze di —,* printer's proofs; *errore di —,* misprint (*o* printing-error) ‖ *stampe, (nelle spedizioni postali)* printed matter **2.** *(arte, atto dello stampare)* printing (anche *foto.*): *— in rilievo,* relief-printing; *la — fu inventata nel XV secolo,* printing was invented in the fifteenth century; *il libro è in corso di —,* the book is printing (*o* is in the press) ‖ *dare alle stampe,* to send to press **3.** *fig. (periodici, giornali, ecc.)* press: *— a grande tiratura,* mass circulation press; *la — estera, locale, periodica, politica, religiosa,* the foreign, local, periodical, political, religious press; *agenzia di —,* news-agency; *campagna di —,* press-campaign; *libertà di —,* freedom of the press; *ritagli di —,* press-cuttings; *la — lo criticò moltissimo,* the press criticized him a great deal ‖ *la — gialla,* the yellow press ‖ *conferenza —,* press-conference ‖ *avere una buona —,* to have a good press **4.** *(riproduzione)* print, engraving: *ho comperato due stampe dell'Ottocento,* I have bought two nineteenth-century prints; *le pareti sono piene di vecchie stampe,* the walls are covered with old prints **5.** *(stampo)* print, stamp, die (*pl.* dies) **6.** *(genere)* kind, sort, stamp; *un uomo della vecchia —,* a man of the old stamp; *di quegli uomini se n'è perduta la —,* they don't make men like that any more; *essere della stessa —,* to be of the same stamp.

stampàbile, *ag.* printable, fit to print: *romanzo —,* printable novel.

stampàggio, *s.m. (mec.)* pressing; (*a mano*) swaging: *— a caldo,* hot-pressing (*o* press-forging); *— con maglio* (*a caldo*), drop-forging; *— dei pezzi circolari,* circle-stamping; *— di piega per lamiere,* forming; *— profondo,* deep-drawing; *matrice per — a caldo,* swaging-die; *polvere di —,* (*ind.*) moulding-powder.

stampàre, *v.t.* **1.** *(imprimere)* to stamp, to print: *un'orma sulla neve,* to make a footprint in the snow ‖ *— un bacio in fronte a qlcu.,* to plant a kiss on s.o.'s forehead ‖ *far — il proprio nome su articoli di pelle,* to have one's name stamped on leather-goods **2.** *(tip. foto.)* to print: *— a mano,* to print by hand; *— un giornale, un libro,* to print a newspaper, a book; *— un'incisione,* to print an engraving **3.** *fig. (pubblicare)* to publish; to print: *stampa un romanzo all'anno,* he publishes a novel every year; *— un articolo,* to print an article **4.** *(coniare)* to coin, to strike: *— medaglie, monete,* to coin medals, coins ‖ *— una bugia,* to invent a lie **5.** *(tec.) (con pressa)* to press; (*con maglio*) to drop-forge; (*a mano*) to swage: *— a caldo* (*con pressa*), to hot-press (*o* to press-forge) ‖ **stampàrsi,** *v.r. fig.: — in mente ql.co.,* to impress sthg. firmly on one's mind:

stampati bene in mente queste parole!, impress these words firmly on your mind!.

stampatèllo, *s.m.* block letters (*pl.*), capital letters (*pl.*): *non sa fare lo —,* he can't write in block letters ‖ *a, in —,* in block letters: *col titolo in, a —,* with the title in block letters.

stampàto, *ag.* printed: *foglio —,* printed sheet of paper; *tessuto —,* printed material; *un vestito (di tessuto) —,* a print dress ‖ *alla macchia,* printed secretly ‖ *parlare come un libro —,* (*fam.*) to talk like a book ‖ *s.m.* **1.** printed matter: *l'affrancatura degli stampati,* the postage for printed matter **2.** *(modulo)* (printed) form: *siamo sprovvisti di stampati,* we have run out of forms.

stampatóre, *ag.* printing ‖ *s.m.* **1.** *(tip.)* printer, typographer **2.** *(mec.)* hammerman (*pl.* hammermen)

stampatríce, *s.f. (macchina)* printing-machine, printing-press: *— per film sonoro,* sound-film printing-machine.

stampèlla, *s.f.* crutch: *camminare con le stampelle,* to go on crutches.

stampería, *s.f.* printing-works, printing-house.

stampíglia, *s.f.* **1** *(foglio volante)* fly-sheet **2.** *(forma per imprimere)* rubber-stamp.

stampigliàre, *v.t.* to stamp.

stampigliatúra, *s.f.* stamping.

stampíno, *s.m.* **1.** stencil(-plate) ‖ *i suoi quadri sembrano fatti con lo —,* his pictures look as if they have been mass-produced **2.** *(punteruolo)* punch.

stàmpo, *s.m.* **1.** die (*pl.* dies); stamp; mould: *— abbozzatore,* blocker (*o* blocking-die); *— a bugna,* bulge-die; *— a caldo,* swage; *— aperto,* open die; *— a pozzo,* block-mould; *— di piega,* forming-die; *— finitore,* finishing-die; (*per il vetro*) blow-mould; *— fisso,* stationary die; *— formatore,* blank mould; *— mobile,* moving die; *— per bordare,* curling-die; *— per budini,* mould for puddings; *— per chiodi,* rivet-set (*o* riveting-die); *— per finitura,* finishing-die; *— per ghiaccio,* ice-can (*o* ice-mould); *— per punzonatura,* piercing-die; *lo — per una statua,* the mould for a statue; *impronta dello —,* die-impression; *incisione dello —,* die-sinking; *macchina per lavorare stampi,* die-sinking machine **2.** *(uccello da richiamo)* decoy **3.** *(genere, tipo)* kind, sort, stamp: *una signora di antico —,* a lady of the old stamp; *sono tutti dello stesso —,* they are all of the same stamp.

stanàre, *v.t.* to drive out (anche *fig.*); to rouse: *hanno stanato la volpe,* they have started the fox; *sta sempre in casa ed è difficile stanarlo,* he is always at home, and it is difficult to dig him out (*o* to get him to go out).

staneaménte, *av.* wearily: *andare, camminare, — to plod: *se ne andava — verso casa,* he was plodding his way home.

stancàre, *v.t.* **1.** to tire, to fatigue, to weary: *questo lavoro mi stanca,* this work tires me; *— i cavalli,* to tire the horses ‖ *— la pazienza di qlcu.,* to exhaust s.o.'s patience ‖ *— un pezzo di terra,* to exhaust a piece of ground **2.** *(infastidire, annoiare)* to vex, to annoy; to bore: *le sue continue richieste mi stancavano terribilmente,* his continual importunities annoyed me no end ‖ **stancàrsi,** *v.r.* **1.** to tire, to get tired, to grow weary; *(annoiarsi)* to get bored: *il bambino si stancò presto del suo giuoco,* the child soon tired of his game; *mi stanco terribilmente in campagna,* in the country I get bored stiff (*o* bored to death); *non ci si stanca di ascoltarlo,* one never tires (*o* wearies) of listening to him; *— a forza di parlare, di correre,* to talk, to run oneself tired; *— gli occhi a fare ql.co.,* to strain one's eyes (in) doing sthg.

stanchévole, *ag.* tiring, tiresome, wearing, wearisome: *un lavoro —,* a tiresome job; *una salita —,* a wearing ascent.

stanchézza, *s.f.* tiredness, weariness: *— fisica, morale,* physical, moral tiredness; *vinto dalla —,* overcome by tiredness; *avere, sentire —,* to feel (*o* to be) tired (*o* weary); *dare —,* to tire: *questo lavoro mi dà una grande —,* this work wears me out.

stànco, *ag.* **1.** tired, weary: — *del mondo*, tired of the world (*o* world-weary); — *morto*, dead tired (*o* tired to death *o* tired out); *sono, mi sento* —, I am, I feel tired; *sono* — *di aspettare*, I am tired of waiting; *essere* — *di ql.co., qlcu.*, to be tired of sthg., s.o. (*o* to be sick of sthg., s.o.) **2.** (*di terreno*) exhausted, worn out: *terreno* —, exhausted (*o* worn out) soil.

stàndard, *s.m.* standard.

standardizzàre, *v.t.* to standardize.

standardizzàto, *ag.* standardized; (*prodotto in serie*) mass-produced.

standardizzazióne, *s.f.* standardization; (*fabbricazione in serie*) mass-production.

stànga, *s.f.* **1.** (*barra*) bar **2.** (*di passaggio a livello*) (level crossing) barrier **3.** (*di carro, carrozza*) shaft; (*di aratro*) beam **4.** (*di ghiaccio*) ice block.

stangàre, *v.t.* **1.** (*sbarrare*) to bar: — *l'uscio*, to bar the door **2.** (*percuotere*) to thrash.

stangàta, *s.f.* (*colpo con una stanga*) blow with a bar.

stanghétta, *s.f.* **1.** (*piccola stanga*) small bar **2.** (*di serratura*) bolt **3.** (*mus.*) bar **4.** (*di occhiali*) bar, arm: *occhiali a* —, spectacles.

stangóne, *s.m.* **1.** long bar **2.** (*persona molto alta*) lanky person, lengthy person.

Stanislào, *no.pr.m.* Stanislas.

stannìto, *s.f.* (*chim.*) stannite: — *di sodio*, sodium stannite.

stanòtte, *av.* **1.** tonight, to-night **2.** (*la notte scorsa*) last night.

stànte[1], *ag.*: *acqua* —, (*stagnante*) stagnant water; *a sè* —, apart (*o* by the way): *questa è una faccenda a sè* —, this matter is apart; *il mese* —, (*corrente*) current month ‖ *seduta* —, during the sitting; during the meeting; (*subito*) at once (*o* immediately *o* straight away).

stànte[2], *prep.* owing to, because of, on account of: — *il cattivo tempo*, owing to the bad weather ‖ **stànte che**, *l.cong.* as, since: — *che non volete venire*, as (*o* since) you don't want to come.

stantìo, *ag.* **1.** stale (anche *fig.*): *notizie stantie*, stale news; *pane, uova stantie*, stale bread, eggs; *sapere di* —, to taste stale **2.** (*fuori moda*) old-fashioned: *una acconciatura stantia*, an old-fashioned hair-style.

stantùffo, *s.m.* (*mec.*) **1.** (*di motore*) piston: — *a disco*, flat piston; — *a mantello*, skirt type piston; — *a pattino*, (*di macchina a vapore*) slipper piston; — *di compensazione*, balance piston; — *flottante*, floating piston; *corsa dello* —, piston stroke; *fascia elastica dello* —, piston ring; *stelo di* —, (*di macchina a vapore*) piston rod **2.** (*di pompa, pressa idraulica, ecc.*) plunger.

stànza, *s.f.* **1.** room: — *ammobiliata*, furnished room (*o* apartment); — *attigua*, next room; — *da bagno*, bathroom; — *da letto*, bedroom; *stanze da affittare*, rooms to let; *stanze interne*, inner rooms; — *mortuaria*, mortuary; *un appartamento con cinque stanze*, a flat with five rooms (*o* a five-roomed flat); *questa* — *è vicino alla tua*, this room is next to yours ‖ *Stanze Vaticane*, Vatican Stanze **2.** (*dimora*) stay: *qui potrà avere comoda* —, here you will be able to have a comfortable stay; *essere di* — *in un luogo*, (*mil.*) to be stationed in a place; *prendere, avere* — *in un luogo*, to settle down in a place **3.** (*poes.*) stanza: *le stanze dell'Ariosto*, Ariosto's stanzas **4.** — *di compensazione*, (*comm.*) clearing-house.

stanziàle, *ag.* permanent.

stanzialménte, *av.* permanently.

stanziaménto, *s.m.* appropriation: — *di fondi, di una somma*, appropriation of funds, of a sum.

stanziàre, *v.t.* to appropriate, to set apart: — *una somma per la costruzione di una scuola*, to appropriate a sum for the building of a school ‖ *v.i.* **1.** (*decretare*) to decree, to deliberate **2.** (*mil.*) to be quartered.

stapèdio, *s.m.* (*anat.*) stapedius (muscle).

stappàre, *v.t.* to uncork: — *una bottiglia di spumante*, to uncork a bottle of champagne.

stàre, *v.i.* **1.** to stay, to remain; (*in piedi*) to stand:

devo — *con te?*, shall I stay with you?; *è stato via tre settimane*, he stayed away three weeks; *non* — *sotto la pioggia*, don't stay out in the rain; *perchè non stai con me?*, why don't you stay with me?; *questi fiori devono* — *fuori di notte*, these flowers must be left out at night; *sta' al sole, all'ombra*, stay in the sun, in the shade; *sta' dove sei*, stay where you are; *sta' fermo*, stand still; *stai qui finchè ritorno*, stay here till I come back; *starò solo dieci minuti*, I'll only stay ten minutes; *stette alla finestra ad osservarmi*, she stayed at the window watching me; *sto da mia zia per alcuni giorni*, I'm staying at my aunt's for a few days ‖ — *a chiacchierare*, to stand chattering; — *a letto*, to stay in bed; — *alzato*, to stay up; — *diritto*, to stand up straight; (*sedendo*) to sit up straight; — *in casa*, to stay indoors; — *indietro*, to stand back; — *in disparte*, to stand aside; — *in piedi*, to stand; — *in poltrona*, to sit in an armchair; — *saldo*, to stand firm (*o* fast) (anche *fig.*); — *seduto*, to remain seated; — *sdraiato*, to be lying down; — *sveglio*, to stay awake **2.** (*abitare*) to live: *quando stavo a Milano*, when I lived (*o* I used to live) in Milan; *sta in campagna sei mesi all'anno*, he lives in the country six months a year; *sto uscio a uscio con lui*, I live next door to him **3.** (*essere*) to be: *le cose stanno così*, it's like this; *così sta scritto*, thus it is written; *la mia casa sta a quattro miglia da Genova, dal confine*, my house is four miles from Genoa, from the frontier (*o* the border); *quell'albergo sta in cima a una collina, in riva al lago*, the hotel is (*o* stands) on a hilltop, on the shore of the lake; *qui sta la difficoltà*, this is the difficulty; *sta' attento, buono, tranquillo*, be careful, good, quiet; *stando così le cose...*, things being as they are...; *sta' sicuro che verrà*, you may be sure he will come; *stava su questo tavolo*, it was on this table; *sta' zitto!*, be (*o* keep) quiet!; (*sl.*) shut up!; *stavo studiando*, I was studying ‖ — *a dieta*, to be on a diet; — *alla cassa, a servizio*, to be at the cash-desk, in service; — *per fare ql.co.*, to be going (*o* about) to do sthg. (*o* to be on the point of doing sthg.): *stavo per venire da te*, I was about to come to you **4.** (*dipendere*) to depend: *se stesse in me l'avresti già*, if it depended on me, you would already have it; *tutto sta se si può arrivare in tempo*, everything depends on whether we get there in time **5.** (*spettare, toccare*) to be up; to be for (s.o.); to be one's turn: *non sta a te giudicare ciò*, it is not for you to judge this matter; *questa volta sta a te dirglielo*, this time it is your turn to tell him; *se stesse a me decidere...*, if it were up to me to decide...; *sta a me fare le carte*, it is my turn to deal; *sta a te il pensar queste cose*, it is up to you to think of these things; *sta a lui decidere questa faccenda*, it is up to him (*o* it is his business *o* it is his job) to decide these matters **6.** (*parteggiare*) to side: *con chi sta il tuo amico?* who does your friend side with?; — *coi repubblicani*, to side with the Republicans; *se non stai con noi, stai contro di noi*, if you are not with us, you are against us **7.** (*andare*) to be: *sono stato a Londra l'anno scorso*, I went to London last year; *sono stato dal dottore, dalla sarta*, I went to see my doctor, I went to the dressmaker's **8.** (*durare*) to stand, to last: *questo monumento starà nei secoli*, this monument will stand for centuries **9.** (*attenersi*): *devi* — *a quel che ti dicono di fare*, you must do as they tell you; *io sto al suo consiglio*, I follow his advice **10.** (*mat.*) to be: *20 sta a 40 come 50 sta a 100*, 20 is to 40 as 50 is to 100 **11.** (*al giuoco, non volere altre carte*) to stick: *sto!*, stick! **12.** (*Fraseologia*): *a quanto sta ora lo zucchero?*, what is the price of sugar now? (*o* what does sugar cost now?) ‖ *come mi sta questo cappello?*, how does this hat suit me? ‖ *come sta tuo padre?*, how is your father (getting on)?; *come stai?*, how are you? ‖ *come stiamo a soldi?*, how do we stand for money? ‖ *fatto sta che...*, the fact is, that... ‖ *non mi* — *a dire che sei ammalato perchè non ti credo*, don't tell me you are ill because I don't believe you ‖ *non può — senza fumare,* he can't do without smoking ‖ *non sta più in sè dalla curiosità, dalla gioia,* he is beside himself with curiosity, with joy ‖ *si starà a vedere come si metteranno le cose,* we shall see how things turn out; *sta a vedere,* wait and see ‖ *stai fresco se non sei di ritorno prima di mezzanotte!,* if you don't come back before midnight, you'll be for it! ‖ *stammi a sentire,* listen! ‖ *stando a quel che si dice...,* according to what they say... ‖ *starà poco a piovere,* it is going to rain; *starà poco a tornare,* he'll soon be back ‖ *stava un po' sulle sue,* he was rather reserved ‖ *— a cuore: mi sta molto a cuore saperlo,* I am very anxious to know; *mi sta molto a cuore il tuo futuro,* I have your future at heart ‖ *— alla larga da ql.co., qlcu.,* to give sthg., s.o. a wide berth ‖ *— all'erta,* to be on the alert (o on one's guard) ‖ *— allo scherzo,* to take sthg. in good part ‖ *— a occhi aperti,* to keep one's eyes open ‖ *— al paragone,* to stand comparison; *— alla prova,* to stand the test ‖ *— ai patti,* to keep (to) an agreement; *— a una promessa,* to keep a promise ‖ *— bene, male, (in salute)* to be well, not to be well; *(finanziariamente)* to be well off, badly off; *(di abito)* to suit, not to suit; *(addirsi)* to be fitting, to be unbecoming: *non sta bene che si comporti così,* it is unbecoming of him to behave like that; *non sta bene che una signora dica queste cose,* it is not fitting for (o it does not become) a lady to say these things; *questo vestito non ti sta bene,* this dress does not suit you; *sta bene!, (mantienti in buona salute)* take care of yourself!; *(va bene, d'accordo)* all right! (o very well!); *sto abbastanza bene,* I am pretty (o fairly) well; *ti sta bene, ben ti sta!,* it serves you right! ‖ *— con l'acqua alla gola,* to be up to one's neck (in sthg.) ‖ *— con la bocca aperta,* to stand open-mouthed ‖ *— con le mani in mano,* to idle one's time away ‖ *— dietro a qlcu.,* to dog s.o.'s footsteps; *(sorvegliarlo)* to keep an eye on s.o. ‖ *— in forse,* to be in doubt ‖ *— sulle generali,* to keep (o to stick) to generalities ‖ *starci, (esserci spazio): in questo cinema ci sta molta gente,* there is room for a great many people in this cinema; *non ci sta più niente,* there is no more room; *non riesco a farcene — di più,* I can't get any more in; *se non ci sta, mettilo qui,* if there isn't room for it, put it here ‖ *starci, (accettare): ci stai?,* is it all right with you? ‖ *lasciar —, (non infastidire; non toccare)* to leave (s.o., sthg.) alone; *(non agitare)* to let (sthg.) stand: *bisogna lasciar — questo vino per un po' di tempo prima di berlo,* we must let this wine stand a bit before drinking it; *lascia — il gatto,* leave the cat alone; *lascia — i miei libri,* leave my books alone (o don't touch my books); *lascialo —, perchè non ne ha colpa,* leave him alone: it isn't his fault; *lasciami —,* leave me alone ‖ **stàrsi,** *v.r.* **1.** *se ne stava solo soletto,* he was all alone; *statevene tranquilli,* keep calm; *(non preoccupatevi)* don't worry **2.** *(astenersi)* to refrain (from doing): *se ne stette dal rispondere,* he refrained from giving any answer; *stattene dal fare ciò,* don't do that.

stàrna, *s.f.* (*ornit.*) gray partridge.

starnazzàre, *v.i.* to flutter; to flap its wings.

starnutaménto, *s.m.* sneezing.

starnutàre, *v.i.* to sneeze.

starnutatòrio, *ag.* sternutatory, sternutative ‖ *s.m.* sternutatory.

starnutìglia, *s.f.* (*farm.*) sternutatory, errhine.

starnutìre, *v.i.* to sneeze.

starnùto, *s.m.* sneeze, sneezing, sternutation: *fare uno —,* to sneeze.

stasàre, *v.t.* to unclog, to unstop, to open: *— un lavandino,* to unclog a sink.

staséra, *av.* this evening, tonight, to-night.

stàsi, *s.f.* **1.** (*med.*) stasis (*pl.* stases) **2.** (*arresto*) stoppage, standstill: *il commercio è in un periodo di —,* business is at a standstill.

statàle, *ag.* state (*attributivo*); of the state: *banca,*

scuola, impiegato —, state bank, school, employee ‖ *s.m.* state employee; (*in Gran Bretagna*) Civil Servant.

statalizzàre, *v.t.* (*pol. econ.*) to nationalize, to put (sthg.) under state control.

statalizzazióne, *s.f.* (*pol. econ.*) nationalization.

statàrio, *ag.* (*dir.*) summary.

stàte, (*poet.*) per **estàte.**

statère, *s.m.* (*antica moneta*) stater.

stàtica, *s.f.* statics.

stàtico, *ag.* static: *momento —,* (*scienza delle costruzioni*) static moment.

statìsta, *s.m.* statesman (*pl.* statesmen); (*arc.*) statist.

statìstica, *s.f.* **1.** statistics: *la — è una scienza molto importante,* statistics is a very important science **2.** (*calcolo statistico*) statistical table; statistics (*pl.*): *— della popolazione,* statistics of the population; *le statistiche dicono che la popolazione è in continuo aumento,* statistics show that there is a continual increase in population.

statìstico, *ag.* statistical: *tavole statistiche,* statistical tables (o statistics).

statizzàre, *V.* **statalizzàre.**

statizzazióne, *V.* **statalizzazióne.**

stàto, *s.m.* **1.** state, condition: *— d'animo,* mood; *lo — delle cose,* the state of things; *— di salute,* state of health; *— solido, liquido, (fis.)* solid, liquid state; *in buono —,* in good condition; *in cattivo —,* in bad condition; *nel mio —,* in my condition; *guarda in che — è!,* look what a state he is in! ‖ *— d'assedio,* state of siege; *— d'emergenza,* state of emergency ‖ *— di grazia,* state of grace ‖ *essere in — interessante,* to be pregnant (o to be with child) **2.** (*posizione sociale*) (social) condition; rank: *farsi uno —,* to make a position (o place) for oneself (in society) **3.** (*dir.*) status: *— civile,* civil status; *— coniugale, libero,* married, single status; *ufficiale di — civile,* Registrar; *ufficio di — civile,* registry (o register) office **4.** *Stato,* (*pol.*) State: *lo Stato Pontificio,* the Papal State; *scuola, università, prigione, impiegato di Stato,* State school, university, prison, employee ‖ *colpo di Stato,* coup d'Etat ‖ *ragione di Stato,* reason of State ‖ *uomo di Stato,* statesman **5.** *Stato* (*mil.*): *Stato Maggiore,* General Staff; *ufficiale di Stato Maggiore,* Staff Officer ‖ *gli Stati Generali,* (*st.*) the States General ‖ *il Terzo Stato,* (*st.*) the Third Estate.

statolder, *s.m.* (*st. olandese*) stadtholder, stadholder.

statóre, *ag.* stator (*attributivo*) ‖ *Giove Statore,* (*mit.*) Jupiter Stator ‖ *s.m.* (*elett.*) stator: *protezione a persiana sullo —,* (*mec.*) louver stator guard (o cover).

statoscòpio, *s.m.* (*aer.*) statoscope.

stàtua, *s.f.* statue: *— votiva,* votive statue; *decretare una —,* to decree a statue; *fare, innalzare una —,* to raise a statue; *sembrare una —,* to look like a statue ‖ *fare la —,* to stand like a statue.

statuària, *s.f.* statuary.

statuàrio, *ag.* **1.** statuesque: *bellezza statuaria,* statuesque beauty; *posa statuaria,* statuesque posture **2.** (*per fare statue*) statuary: *marmo —,* statuary marble.

statuétta, *s.f.* statuette.

statuìre, *v.t.i.* to decree, to ordain.

statunitènse, *ag.* United States (*attributivo*): *economia —,* United States economy ‖ *s.c.* American, United States citizen.

statùra, *s.f.* height, stature; size: *la — di un uomo,* the height of a man; *di media —,* of middle height; *essere di bassa —,* to be short of stature; *essere di grande —,* to be very tall ‖ *— morale,* moral stature.

statutàrio, *ag.* statutory, statute (*attributivo*).

statùto, *s.m.* **1.** (*pol. st.*) statute; (*costituzione*) constitution: *gli articoli dello —,* the articles of the statute **2.** (*dir.*) statute, ordinance; articles (*pl.*): *gli statuti dell'Accademia Navale,* the statutes of the Naval Academy; *— dell'Università,* University statutes; *— di una corporazione,* statute (o ordinance) of a corporation; *— di una società,* statute of a company.

stavòlta, *av.* this time.

stàza, *V.* **stàzza**.

Stàzio, *no.pr.m.* (*st. lett.*) Statius.

stazionàre, *v.i.* 1. to stand, to stay, to stop 2. (*di vetture*) to be parked.

stazionàrio, *ag.* stationary (anche *med.*): *barometro* —, steady barometer; *malattie stazionarie*, stationary diseases; *temperatura stazionaria*, stationary temperature; *nave stazionaria*, (*mar. mil.*) guard-ship ‖ *pianeta* —, (*astr.*) stationary planet ‖ *s.m.* (*mar. mil.*) guard-ship.

stazióne, *s.f.* 1. station: — *capolinea*, terminus (station); — *clandestina*, (*rad.*) illicit station; — *degli autobus*, bus station; *una* — *di carrozze, di auto pubbliche*, a carriage, a cab, a taxi rank; — *di direzione del tiro*, (*mar. mil.*) fire control station; — *di raccordo*, (*ferr.*) tran(s)shipping station; — *di rifornimento*, (*aut.*) filling station (o *amer.* gas station); — *di smistamento*, (*ferr.*) shunting station; — *di testa*, (*ferr.*) terminal station; — *emittente*, (*rad.*) broadcasting station; — *ferroviaria*, railway station; — *locale*, (*rad.*) spot station; — *meteorologica*, weather (o meteorological) station; — *principale, intermedia, di transito*, main, intermediate, transit station; — *trasmittente*, (*rad.*) transmitting station; *capo* —, (*ferr.*) station master ‖ *le numerose stazioni commerciali dei Fenici*, the many Phoenician trading stations; *una potente* — *navale*, a powerful naval station 2. (*fermata*) stop: *fare* — *in un posto*, to stop in a place 3. (*sede di un distaccamento*) post, station: — *dei carabinieri*, carabinieri post; — *di polizia*, police station 4. (*luogo di villeggiatura*) resort: — *balneare*, seaside resort; — *estiva, invernale*, summer, winter resort 5. (*eccl.*) station: *le stazioni della Via Crucis*, the stations of the Cross; *oggi la* — *è a S. Giovanni Laterano*, the station today is at St. John Lateran's.

stàzza, *s.f.* (*mar.*) tonnage: *la* — *di una nave*, the tonnage of a ship; — *lorda, netta*, gross, net tonnage; *ponte di* —, tonnage deck.

stazzàre, *v.t.* (*mar.*) 1. to have a tonnage of (sthg.): *una nave che stazza 13.000 tonnellate*, a ship with a tonnage of 13,000 tons; *quanto stazza questa nave?*, what is the tonnage of this ship? 2. (*misurare con la stazza*) to gauge, to measure.

stazzatóre, *s.m.* (*mar.*) gauger, measurer.

stazzatúra, *s.f.* (*mar.*) tonnage, measurement.

stazzonaménto, *s.m.* 1. (*lo spiegazzare*) crumpling, creasing 2. (*il maneggiare con mal garbo*) clumsy handling.

stazzonàre, *v.t.* 1. (*spiegazzare*) to crumple, to crease 2. (*maneggiare con mal garbo*) to handle clumsily.

steapsìna, *s.f.* (*chim. biol.*) steapsin.

steàrico, *ag.* (*chim.*) stearic.

stearìna, *s.f.* (*chim.*) stearin.

steatìte, *s.f.* (*min.*) steatite, soapstone.

stécca, *s.f.* 1. (small) stick 2. (*di ombrello, ventaglio*) rib 3. (*da biliardo*) cue 4. (*di persiana alla veneziana*) slat; (*di persiana con avvolgibile*) louver-board 5. (*med.*) (*per arti rotti*) splint 6. (*di busto o altri indumenti*) whale-bone 7. (*mus.*) (*nota falsa*) false note: *fare una* —, (*cantando*) to sing a false note; (*suonando*) to play a false note 8. (*di sigarette*) pack 9. (*ferr.*) fish-plate: — *angolare*, angle fishplate.

steccadènte, *s.m.* tooth-pick.

steccàia, *s.f.* mill-dam.

steccàre, *v.t.* 1. (*chiudere con steccato*) to fence in 2. (*cuc.*) (*lardellare*) to dress with bacon-fat 3. (*med.*) (*fasciare con stecche*) to put in splints ‖ *v.i.* (*mus.*) (*cantando*) to sing a false note; (*suonando*) to play a false note.

steccàto, *s.m.* 1. fence 2. (*intorno a edificio in costruzione*) hoarding 3. (*alle corse dei cavalli*) rails (*pl.*).

stecchétto, *s.m.* small stick ‖ *stare a* —, to live on short rations (o commons): *deve stare a* — *se vuole dimagrire*, she must cut down her food, if she wants to slim; *ho pochi soldi e devo stare a* — *fino alla fine*

del mese, I have little money left and I have to do with what I have until the end of the month; *tenere a* —, (*di cibo*) to keep s.o. on short commons; (*di danaro*) to keep s.o. on a short allowance: *il dottore ha detto di tenerlo a* —, the doctor has ordered to keep him on a strict diet; *ha un padre molto severo che lo tiene a* —, he has a very strict father who keeps him short of money.

stecchìno, *s.m.* 1. small stick 2. (*stuzzicadenti*) tooth-pick.

stecchìre, *v.t.* to kill on the spot: *con una pugnalata al cuore la stecchì*, he killed her outright with a stab in her heart ‖ **stecchìrsi**, *v.r.* 1. (*seccare*) to dry up 2. (*dimagrire molto*) to become as thin as a rake.

stecchìto, *ag.* 1. dried up: *c'era solo un povero albero* —, there was only one bare dried up tree 2. (*magrissimo*) skinny, emaciated: *secco* —, as thin as a rake; *il povero bambino è così* — *che fa pena vederlo*, the poor child is only skin and bones, he is a pitiful sight 3. (*morto*) stone dead: *i suoi lo trovarono* — *il mattino seguente*, his family found him stone dead next morning.

stécco, *s.m.* 1. stick; (*ramoscello secco*) dry twig: *era là che raccoglieva stecchi per il fuoco*, she was there gathering sticks for the fire; *fissale insieme con uno* —, fix them together with a stick ‖ *campa con uno* — *unto*, *fig.* he lives on a pittance ‖ (*persona magra*) bag of bones: *quel povero ragazzo è ridotto uno* —, that poor boy is reduced to skin and bones (o is a bag of bones).

steccònàia, *s.f.* stockade, paling.

steccònàre, *v.t.* to fence in.

steccònàta, *s.f.*, **steccònàto**, *s.m.* stockade, paling; (*recinto*) enclosure.

steccóne, *s.m.* stake, post.

Stefània, *no.pr.f.* Stephanie.

Stéfano, *no.pr.m.* Stephen.

stégola, *s.f.* plough-handle.

stégolo, *s.m.* wheel-shaft, sail-axle.

stèla, stèle, *s.f.* stele (*pl.* stelae).

Stélla[1], *no.pr.f.* Stella, Estella.

stélla[2], *s.f.* 1. star: — *cadente*, shooting-star (o falling-star); — *cometa*, comet; — *del mattino, della sera*, morning, evening star; *stelle doppie, fisse*, double, fixed stars; *un cielo senza stelle*, a starless sky; *arrivammo a casa alla luce delle stelle*, we got back home by starlight; *il cielo era pieno di stelle*, the sky was full of stars ‖ *la* — *polare*, (*astr.*) the north star (o the pole star); *le sette stelle dell'Orsa Maggiore*, (*astr.*) the Big Dipper (o the Great Bear o Ursa Major); *le sette stelle dell'Orsa Minore*, (*astr.*) the Little Dipper (o the Little Bear o Ursa Minor) ‖ — *di mare*, (*zool.*) starfish ‖ — *filante*, streamer ‖ *a forma di* —, *fatto a* —, starlike: *un gioiello a forma di* —, a star-shaped jewel ‖ *ha due occhi che sembrano delle stelle*, her eyes are like stars ‖ *i prezzi erano alle stelle*, prices were sky-high ‖ *quella bambina sembra una* —, that little girl is really lovely ‖ *portare qlcu. alle stelle*, to praise s.o. to the skies ‖ *vedere le stelle*, to see stars: *ho visto le stelle quando mi colpì sul naso*, I saw stars when he hit me on the nose 2. (*destino, fato*) star, fate: *così vogliono le stelle*, fate wills it; *è nato sotto una buona, una cattiva* —, he was born under a lucky, an unlucky (o evil) star; *è perseguitato dalla sua cattiva* —, he is hounded by fate; *può ringraziare la sua buona* — *se ci è riuscito*, he can thank his lucky star if he has succeeded; *la sua* — *è tramontata*, his sun has set; *la sua* — *sale*, his star is rising (o is in the ascendant); *seguire la propria* —, to follow one's star (o destiny) 3. (*diva*) star: — *del cinema*, film-star; — *della televisione*, television-star 4. (*di cavallo*) blaze, star 5. (*rotella dello sperone*) rowel 6. (*asterisco*) star, asterisk: *è segnato con due stelle*, *stellette*, it is marked with two stars 7. (*ind. tessile*) swift 8. (*mec.*) row: *a* — *semplice*, single-row; *a doppia* —, double-row.

stellànte, *ag.* **1.** starry: *notti stellanti,* starry nights **2.** (*lucente*) starry, bright, shining: *occhi stellanti,* starry eyes.

stellàre, *ag.* **1.** stellar; star (*attributivo*): *luce* —, stellar light **2.** (*a forma di stella*) star-shaped: *figura* —, star-shaped figure.

stellàre, *v.t.* **1.** to spangle with stars **2.** (*ornare a guisa di stelle*) to stud, to sprinkle ‖ **stellàrsi**, *v.r.* to fill with stars: *il cielo cominciò a* —, the sky began to fill with stars.

stellàto, *ag.* starry, starred; starlit: *cielo* —, starry sky; *notte stellata,* starry night ‖ *la bandiera stellata,* the Stars and Stripes ‖ *s.m.* (*mar.*) wedgelike: — *di poppa,* run; — *di prua,* entrance.

stelleggiàre, *v.t.* to spangle with stars.

stellétta, *s.f.* **1.** asterisk **2.** (*mil.*) star: *perdere le stellette,* to be demoted.

stellettàre, *v.t.* (*tip.*) to star, to mark with an asterisk.

stellionàto, *s.m.* (*dir.*) stellionate.

stellióne, *s.m.* (*zool.*) stellion.

stelloncíno, *s.m.* short paragraph (in a newspaper).

stellóne, *s.m.* **1.** (*solleone*) extreme heat **2.** *lo* — (*d'Italia*), the lucky star of Italy.

stèlo, *s.m.* **1.** stalk, stem **2.** (*peduncolo di fiore*) stalk, peduncle **3.** (*mec.*) stem; (*di utensile*) shank; (*di rotaia*) web: — *a espansione,* expanding mandrel; — *della valvola,* valve-stem (*o* spindle); — *dello stantuffo,* piston-rod.

stèmma, *s.m.* coat-of-arms, armorial bearings, escutcheon.

stemmàto, *ag.* armorial, blazoned.

stemperaménto, *s.m.* **1.** mixing; dissolving, melting **2.** (*di metalli*) untempering.

stemperàre, *v.t.* **1.** to mix; to dissolve, to melt: — *i colori,* to mix colours; — *la farina nel latte,* to mix flour with milk; — *una pastiglia nel caffè,* to melt a tablet in coffee **2.** *fig.* (*diluire*) to spin out: — *un discorso,* to spin out (*o* to draw out) a speech; — *il proprio pensiero,* to lose oneself in verbiage **3.** (*togliere la tempera a, metalli*) to untemper **4.** (*far perdere la punta a*) to blunt ‖ **stemperàrsi**, *v.r.* **1.** to melt, to dissolve: — *in lacrime,* to dissolve in(to) tears **2.** (*perdere la punta*) to get blunt.

stemperataménte, *av.* (*rar.*) immoderately, intemperately.

stemperàto, *ag.* **1.** immoderate, intemperate; *vita stemperata,* disorderly life **2.** (*diluito*) dissolved, diluted.

stemperatúra, *V.* **stemperaménto.**

stempiàrsi, *v.r.* to lose one's hair at the temples; to go bald.

stempiàto, *ag.* **1.** bald at the temples; going bald: *è così giovane ed è già* —, he is so young but he is already going bald **2.** (*rar.*) (*enorme*) huge, enormous.

stendardière, *s.m.* standard-bearer; (*mil.*) ensign.

stendàrdo, *s.m.* **1.** standard, banner, flag: *sotto lo* —, under the colours **2.** (*bot.*) standard, vexillum (*pl.* vexilla), banner.

stèndere, *v.t.* **1.** (*spiegare*) to spread (out); to lay out; (*appendere*) to hang out: *stese il giornale sul tavolo,* (*per leggerlo*) he spread the newspaper on the table; (*per riparare il tavolo*) he spread the newspaper over the table; *stese tutta la sua merce sul pavimento,* he laid out all his goods on the floor; *stesero le reti sulla sabbia,* they spread the nets on the sand; — *le ali,* to spread one's wings; — *il bucato, i panni,* to hang out the washing, the clothes; — *il bucato sull'erba,* to spread out the washing on the grass; — *un tappeto,* to lay a carpet; — *la tovaglia,* to put the cloth on **2.** (*distendere, allungare*) to stretch (out): *stendete bene le gambe,* stretch your legs out; *egli stese la mano per prenderlo,* he stretched out his hand to seize it; *il medico lo fece* — *sul lettino,* the doctor made him lie on the couch; — *le braccia,* to stretch out one's arms ‖

— *la mano,* (*chiedere l'elemosina*) to extend one's hand (*o* to hold one's hand out) ‖ — *il passo,* to lengthen one's stride **3.** (*spalmare*) to spread: *fate attenzione a* — *bene la vernice,* make sure you spread the paint evenly; — *il burro su una fetta di pane,* to spread butter on a slice of bread; — *olio su di una bruciatura,* to spread oil on a burn **4.** (*scrivere, mettere per iscritto*) to draw up, to draft: — *un contratto,* to draw up a contract; — *una relazione,* to draft a report **5.** (*spianare, metalli*) to hammer out **6.** (*rilassare*) to relax: — *i muscoli, i nervi,* to relax the muscles, the nerves **7.** (*allentare*): — *l'arco,* to unstring a bow **8.** (*ind. tessile*) to tenter ‖ **stèndersi**, *v.r.* **1.** (*estendersi*) to stretch: *il bosco si stende sino al fiume,* the wood stretches as far as the river; *da ogni parte si stende un vasto deserto,* a vast desert stretches away on every side; *il suo regno si stendeva da un mare all'altro,* his kingdom stretched from sea to sea; *la valle si stende verso sud,* the valley stretches to the south ‖ *fin dove si stende l'occhio,* as far as the eye can see **2.** (*allungarsi*) to stretch oneself out; (*sul letto*) to lie down: *dopo colazione devo stendermi per almeno venti minuti,* after lunch I must lie down for at least twenty minutes; — *per terra,* to stretch oneself out on the ground.

stendiménto, *s.m.* **1.** (*lo spiegare*) spreading; laying out **2.** (*l'allungare*) stretching out **3.** (*lo spalmare*) spreading **4.** (*stesura*) drawing up, drafting.

stenebràre, *v.t.* **1.** to dispel darkness from (sthg.) **2.** (*illuminare*) to enlighten: — *la mente,* to enlighten the mind.

stenocardìa, *s.f.* (*patol.*) stenocardia.

stenodattilògrafa, *s.f.*, **stenodattilògrafo**, *s.m.*, shorthand-typist.

stenògrafa, *s.f.* shorthand-writer, stenographer.

stenografàre, *v.t.* to take down in shorthand, to write down in shorthand: — *un discorso,* to take a speech down in shorthand.

stenografàto, *ag.* (written in) shorthand.

stenografìa, *s.f.* shorthand, stenography.

stenograficaménte, *av.* in shorthand.

stenogràfico, *ag.* shorthand, stenographic: *metodo* —, shorthand method; *resoconto* —, stenographic report; *scrittura stenografica,* shorthand (-writing).

stenògrafo, *s.m.,* shorthand-writer, stenographer.

stenòsi, *s.f.* (*med.*) stenosis (*pl.* stenoses).

stenotipìa, *s.f.* stenotypy, stenotyping.

stenotipìsta, *s.c.* stenotypist.

stentacchiàre, *v.i.* to be in straitened circumstances.

stentàre, *v.i.* **1.** to find it hard, to have difficulty (in doing); to be hardly able: *stenta a farsi capire,* he is hardly able to make himself understood; *stentai ad arrivare in fondo,* I found it hard to reach the end of it; *stenta un poco a camminare,* he has some difficulty in walking; *stentava a crederlo,* he could hardly believe it ‖ — *a fare una cosa,* (*farla di malavoglia*) to be slow in doing sthg.: *stenta sempre a pagare,* he is always slow in paying (*o* he always keeps people waiting for their money) **2.** (*mancare del necessario*) to be in need, to be in want ‖ *v.t.* — *la vita,* to be hard up.

stentataménte, *av.* **1.** with difficulty: *scrive* —, he writes with difficulty **2.** in poverty.

stentatézza, *s.f.* **1.** difficulty: — *nel camminare, parlare,* difficulty in walking, speaking **2.** (*povertà*) poverty, narrow circumstances.

stentàto, *ag.* **1.** hard, difficult; laboured: *uno stile* —, a laboured style; *una vita stentata,* a hard (*o* difficult) life **2.** (*cresciuto a stento*) stunted, scrubby: *una pianta stentata,* a scrubby (*o* stunted) tree ‖ *s.m.* difficulty.

Stenterèllo, *no.pr.m.* (*st. teat.*) Stenterello ‖ **stenterèllo**, *s.m.* (*persona magra e goffa*) lean clumsy fellow.

stentíno, *ag.* sickly, ailing; frail.

stènto, *ag.* *V.* **stentàto** ‖ *s.m.* **1.** privation: *subire molti stenti,* to suffer many privations; *vivere negli stenti,* to live in poverty **2.** *(sforzo, fatica)* effort, difficulty, hard work: *capire la sua scrittura è un vero —,* understanding his writing is real hard work ‖ *a —,* hardly (*o* with difficulty): *cammina a —,* he has some difficulty in walking; *lo capivo a —,* I could hardly understand him.

Stèntore, *no.pr.m.* *(mit.)* Stentor.

stentòreo, *ag.* stentorian: *una voce stentorea,* a stentorian voice.

stentucchiàre, *v.i.* to be in straitened circumstances.

stepidíre, *v.t.,* **stepidírsi,** *v.r.* to warm (up).

stéppa, *s.f* steppe.

stèreo, *s.m.* dung, excrement.

stercoràceo, stercoràrio, *ag.* stercorary, stercoral, stercoraceous: *scarabeo —,* *(entom.)* dung-beetle.

stereòbate, *s.m.* *(arch.)* stereobate.

stereofonía, *s.f.* stereophony.

stereofònico, *ag.* stereophonic.

stereografía, *s.f.* *(geom.)* stereography.

stereogràfico, *ag.* *(geom.)* stereographic, stereographical.

stereògrafo, *s.m.* *(foto.)* stereograph.

stereometría, *s.f.* *(geom.)* stereometry.

stereomètrico, *ag.* *(geom.)* stereometric, stereometrical.

stereoscopía, *s.f.* *(ott.)* stereoscopy.

stereoscòpico, *ag.* *(ott.)* stereoscopic(al).

stereoscòpio, *s.m.* *(ott.)* stereoscope.

stereotipàre, *v.t.* to stereotype.

stereotipàto, *ag.* stereotyped (anche *fig.*).

stereotipía, *s.f.* **1.** *(arte, metodo)* stereotypy, stereotype **2.** *(lastra per stereotipare)* stereotype.

stereotipísta, *s.c.* stereotyper.

stereòtipo, *ag.* stereotyped (anche *fig.*).

stereotomía, *s.f.* *(geom.)* stereotomy.

stèrile, *ag.* **1.** sterile, barren, unfruitful: *animale, pianta —,* sterile animal, plant; *terra —,* barren (*o* sterile *o* unfruitful) land **2.** *fig.* *(infecondo)* sterile, barren; *(inutile)* useless, sterile: *discorso, mente —,* sterile (*o* barren) speech, mind; *discussione —,* useless (*o* sterile) argument.

sterilíre, *v.t.* to make sterile, to make barren (anche *fig.*) ‖ *v.i.,* **sterilírsi,** *v.r.* to become sterile, to become barren (anche *fig.*).

sterilità, *s.f.* **1.** sterility, barrenness, unfruitfulness; unproductiveness **2.** *fig.* *(infecondità)* sterility, barrenness; *(inutilità)* uselessness, sterility.

sterilizzàre, *v.t.* to sterilize.

sterilizzatóre, *ag.* sterilizing ‖ *s.m.* sterilizer.

sterilizzazióne, *s.f.* sterilization.

sterilménte, *av.* **1.** barrenly, unfruitfully; unproductively **2.** *fig.* barrenly; *(inutilmente)* uselessly, in vain.

sterlína, *ag.* sterling: *lira —,* pound (sterling) ‖ *s.f.* pound (sterling).

sterminàre, *v.t.* to exterminate; *(distruggere)* to destroy; *(annientare)* to wipe out: *abbiamo sterminato i parassiti di queste piante,* we have exterminated the pests on these plants; *l'esercito fu sterminato,* the army was wiped out.

sterminataménte, *av.* immensely, enormously.

sterminatézza, *s.f.* immensity; enormity; vastness.

sterminàto, *ag.* **1.** exterminated; *(distrutto)* destroyed; *(annientato)* wiped out **2.** *(smisurato)* immense; enormous; vast; huge.

sterminatóre, *ag.* exterminating; destroying ‖ *s.m.,* **sterminatríce,** *s.f.* exterminator; destroyer.

stermínio, *s.m.* **1.** extermination; *(distruzione)* destruction; *(strage)* slaughter: *la battaglia finì in uno —,* the battle turned into a slaughter **2.** *(fam.)* *(enorme quantità)* huge quantity: *c'era uno — di gente,* there was a huge crowd of people.

stèrno, *s.m.* *(anat.)* breast-bone; sternum *(pl.* sterna).

sternutàre, e derivati, *V.* **starnutàre, e derivati.**

stèro, *s.m.* *(unità di capacità corrispondente al metro cubo)* stere, cubic metre.

sterpàglia, *s.f.,* brushwood.

sterpàia, *s.f.,* **sterpàio,** *s.m.* scrub.

sterpàme, *s.m.* (heap of) brushwood.

sterpàre, *v.t.* **1.** *(rar.)* *(togliere gli sterpi a)* to weed **2.** *(sradicare)* to uproot; *fig.* to eradicate.

sterpéto, *s.m.* scrub.

stèrpo, *s.m.* *(ramo secco)* dry twig, dry shoot; *(pruno)* thorn; thorn-bush; *(ceppo)* tree-stump: *terreno pieno di sterpi,* undergrowth.

sterpóso, *ag.* full of tree-stumps; covered in dry twigs; full of dry twigs.

sterquilínio, *s.m.* *(letter.)* dunghill.

sterraménto, *s.m.* digging up; excavation (anche *archeol.*).

sterràre, *v.t.* to dig up; to excavate (anche *archeol.*).

sterratóre, *s.m.* navvy, digger.

stèrro, *s.m.* **1.** *(lo sterrare)* digging up (anche *archeol.*) **2.** *(terra scavata)* excavated earth; loose earth.

stertóre, *s.m.* stertorous breathing.

stertoróso, *ag.* stertorous.

sterzàre[1], *v.t.* *(dividere in tre parti)* to divide into three ‖ *— un bosco,* to thin out a wood ‖ *— tabacchi,* to blend different qualities of tobacco.

sterzàre[2], *v.i.* *(aut.)* to steer.

sterzàta, *s.f.* *(aut.)* sudden turn.

stèrzo, *s.m.* *(aut.)* steering-gear, steering-wheel.

Stesícoro, *no.pr.m.* *(st. lett.)* Stesichorus.

stéso, *ag.* **1.** *(spiegato)* spread (out); *(appeso)* hanging: *il bucato era — al sole,* the washing was hanging in the sun; *c'era una bella tovaglia stesa sul tavolo,* there was a fine cloth spread on the table; *c'erano molte bandiere stese alle finestre,* there were a lot of flags hanging from the windows **2.** *(allungato)* stretched out; *(sul letto)* lying; *(teso)* outstretched: *col braccio —, con la mano stesa,* with outstretched arm, hand; *era — per terra,* he was stretched out on the ground; *lo trovai — sul letto,* I found him lying on the bed **3.** *(spalmato)* spread: *colori stesi male,* unevenly spread colours **4.** *(redatto)* drawn up **5.** *(rilassato)* relaxed.

stèssere, *v.t.* to unweave.

stésso, *ag.* **1.** *(medesimo)* same: *la città era ancora la stessa dopo vent'anni,* the town was still the same after twenty years; *diede la stessa risposta di prima,* he gave the same answer as before; *è la stessa persona che hai visto ieri a casa mia,* he is the same person you saw yesterday at my house; *è proprio lo — negozio dove andavo io,* it is the very same shop where I used to go; *nacquero entrambi nello — giorno e nella stessa città,* they were both born on the same day and in the same town; *non è più lo — uomo dopo la malattia,* he is not the same man since his illness **2.** *dimostrativo (con valore intensivo):* *io —,* I myself, I... myself; *tu —,* you yourself, you... yourself; *egli —,* he himself, he... himself; *ella stessa,* she herself, she... herself; *esso —,* it itself, it... itself; *noi stessi,* we ourselves, we... ourselves; *(pl. di maestà)* we ourself, we... ourself; *voi stessi,* you yourselves, you... yourselves; *essi stessi,* they themselves, they... themselves; *ci andai io —,* I went there myself; *ciò è descritto dall'autore —,* that is described by the author himself; *io — lo vidi,* I myself saw it; *lo disse ella stessa,* she said it herself; *noi stessi dovremmo fare questo,* we ought to do this ourselves ‖ *la bontà stessa,* she is kindness itself **3.** *dimostrativo (intensivo con pronomi riflessivi)* -self *(pl.* -selves) *(suffisso a formare in inglese i pronomi riflessivi):* *me —,* myself; *te —,* yourself; *(poet.)* thyself; *se —,* himself; itself; *(indef.)* oneself; *se stessa,* herself; *noi stessi,* ourselves; *(pl. di maestà)* ourself; *voi stessi,* yourselves; *loro stessi,* themselves; *conosci te —,* know thyself; *egli ama se — più di ogni altra cosa,* he loves himself above everything; *non si deve pensare solo a se stessi*, one should not think of oneself alone; *sii fedele a te —*, be true to yourself ‖ *di per se —*, in itself **4.** *dimostrativo (con valore di* proprio, esattamente; perfino) **very:** *in quel momento —*, at that very moment; *oggi —*, this very day; *quella sera stessa*, that very evening; *sua madre stessa rifiuta di aiutarlo*, his very mother refuses to help him; *troverai il negozio che cerchi in questa stessa via*, you'll find the shop you are looking for in this very street ‖ *s.m.* **same:** *anche lui dirà lo —*, he will say the same too (*o* as well); *quando faccio qualcosa, lui fa lo —*, when I do something, he does the same; «*Vuoi parlare con me o con lui?*», «*È lo —*», "Do you want to speak to me or to him?", "It's the same (*o* It's all the same to me)" ‖ *av.* **the same;** (*in ogni modo*) **all the same, anyway:** *lo farò lo —*, I'll do it all the same (*o* anyway); *sta press'a poco lo — di ieri*, he is much the same as yesterday.

stesúra, *s.f.* **1.** drawing up, drafting: *la — del contratto richiese un'ora*, the drawing up of the contract took one hour **2.** (*redazione*) draft: *la prima — di un romanzo, di un verbale*, the first draft of a novel, of a charge.

stetoscopía, *s.f.* (*med.*) stethoscopy.

stetoscòpico, *ag.* (*med.*) stethoscopic.

stetoscòpio, *s.m.* (*med.*) stethoscope.

Stettíno, *no.pr.f.* (*geog.*) Stettin.

stía, *s.f.* hen-coop.

stíbico, *ag.* (*chim.*) stibic.

stibína, *s.f.* (*min.*) stibnite.

stíbio, *s.m.* (*chim.*) antimony.

sticometría, *s.f.* (*tip.*) stichometry.

sticomitía, *s.f.* (*teat. greco*) stichomythia.

stiffèlius, *s.m.* (*abito maschile da cerimonia*) frock -coat.

Stíge, *no.pr.m.* (*geog. mit.*) Styx.

stígio, *ag.* (*mit.*) Stygian (anche *fig.*).

stigliàre, *v.t.* (*togliere il tiglio a, lino, canapa, ecc.*) to hackle.

stigliatóre, *ag.* hackling (*attributivo*) ‖ *s.m.* hackler ‖ **stigliatríce,** *s.f.* **1.** hackler **2.** (*mec.*) hackling -machine.

stigliatúra, *s.f.* hackling.

stígma, *s.m.; pl.m.* **stígmi** (*nel senso* **2.**); *pl.f.* **stígmate** (*negli altri sensi*) **1.** (*marchio*) stigma (*pl.* stigmas), brand, mark (anche *fig.*): *egli ha lo — del delinquente*, he has the brand of the criminal **2.** (*zool.*) stigma (*pl.* stigmata); (*bot.*) stigma (*pl.* stigmas) **3.** (*med.*) stigma (*pl.* stigmata): *le stigmate del vaiolo, della degenerazione mentale*, the stigmata of small-pox, of mental degeneration **4.** *pl.* (*eccl.*) stigmata: *le stigmate di S. Francesco*, the stigmata of St. Francis.

stigmatizzàre, *v.t.* to stigmatize.

stilàre, *v.t.* to draw up, to draft: *— un contratto*, to draft a contract.

stíle, *s.m.* **1.** style: *— barocco, gotico, romanico*, Baroque, Gothic, Romanesque style; *—disadorno, conciso, bare*, concise style; *lo — di un tennista*, the style of a tennis-player; *— novecento*, twentieth -century style; *mobili — Impero*, Empire furniture; *nello, secondo lo — di Rubens*, in the style of Rubens (*o* after the manner of Rubens); *non mi piace il suo — nello scrivere*, I do not like his style of writing ‖ *con —*, stylishly (*o* in style): *gioca, si veste con —*, he plays, dresses stylishly; *far le cose con —*, to do things in style ‖ *in grande —*, on a grand scale (*o* in grand style) ‖ *una persona di —*, a stylish person ‖ *aver —*, to be stylish: *quella ragazza ha molto —*, that girl is very stylish **2.** (*usanza, consuetudine*) habit: *lamentarsi è il suo —*, it is his habit to complain **3.** (*verghetta per scrivere*) style; stylus (*pl.* styli, styluses) **4.** (*modo di computare il tempo negli anni*) style: *Vecchio, Nuovo —*, Old, New Style **5.** (*stiletto*) stiletto (*pl.* stilettoes, stilettos), stylet.

stilettàre, *v.t.* to stab.

stilettàta, *s.f.* stab (anche *fig.*): *ho sentito una — al fianco*, I felt a stabbing pain in my side.

stilétto, *s.m.* stiletto (*pl.* stilettoes, stilettos), stylet.

Stilicóne, *no.pr.m.* (*st.*) Stilicho.

stilísta, *s.c.* stylist.

stilística, *s.f.* stylistics.

stilizzàre, *v.t.* to stylize.

stilizzàto, *ag.* stylized: *arti stilizzate*, stylized arts.

stílla, *s.f.* drop: *a — a —*, drop by drop.

stillàre, *v.t.i.* to exude, to ooze, to drip: *dalla ferita stilla sangue*, blood is oozing from the wound; *i pini stillano resina*, pines exude resin; *— lacrime*, to shed tears ‖ **stillàrsi,** *v.r.:* *— il cervello*, to rack (*o* to cudgel) one's brains.

stillicídio, *s.m.* dripping ‖ *servitù dello —*, (*dir.*) right of drip.

stílo, *s.m.* **1.** (*verghetta per scrivere*) style; stylus (*pl.* styli, styluses): *disegnare con lo —*, to draw with a stylus **2.** (*ferro aguzzo per intagliare*) stylet, style **3.** (*braccio della stadera*) beam; (*indice di bilancia*) needle **4.** (*di meridiana*) style, gnomon **5.** (*stiletto*) stiletto (*pl.* stilettoes, stilettos) **6.** (*bot.*) style **7.** (*edil.*) circular section wooden pole **8.** (*per registrazione di dischi*) stylus; (*per incisione*) recording-stylus, cutting -stylus.

stilòbate, *s.m.* (*arch.*) stylobate.

stilogràfico, *ag.* stylographic(al): *inchiostro —*, fountain-pen ink; *penna stilografica*, fountain-pen.

stíma, *s.f.* **1.** (*valutazione*) estimate, valutation, appraisement, appraisal: *— catastale*, cadastral survey; *fare la — di ql.co.*, to make an estimate of sthg. (*o* to estimate *o* to appraise sthg.) **2.** (*buona opinione*) esteem, estimation: *abbiamo molta — di voi*, we hold you in high esteem (*o* estimation); *egli gode la — di tutti*, he enjoys general esteem; *questo merita tutta la mia —*, this deserves all my esteem; *perdere la — di qlcu.*, to lose s.o.'s esteem (*o* estimation); *tenere qlcu. in molta, poca —*, to think highly, little of s.o. ‖ *successo di —*, succès d'estime **3.** (*mar.*) reckoning: *— delle distanze*, range estimation.

stimàbile, *ag.* estimable, respectable.

stimabilità, *s.f.* estimableness, respectability.

stimàre, *v.t.* **1.** (*valutare*) to estimate, to value, to appraise: *egli stimò questa proprietà quattro milioni*, he valued this property at four millions; *non stimi abbastanza le sue qualità*, you underestimate his qualities; *questa casa fu stimata al di sopra, sotto del suo valore*, this house was overestimated, underestimated; *— un danno*, to appraise a damage; *— una distanza*, to calculate a distance; *— il valore di ql.co.*, to estimate (*o* to appraise) the value of sthg. ‖ *far — un gioiello*, to have a jewel valued (*o* appraised) **2.** (*tenere in alta considerazione*) to esteem: *è molto stimato per la sua sincerità*, he is highly esteemed for his sincerity; *lo stimo moltissimo*, I hold him in high esteem (*o* I think very highly of him *o* I esteem him very much) **3.** (*ritenere*) to consider, to think: *lo stimo un imbroglione*, I consider him a swindler; *non lo stimo necessario*, I do not think it necessary ‖ **stimàrsi,** *v.r.* **1.** (*giudicarsi*) to consider oneself: *non mi stimo capace di farlo*, I do not consider myself able to do it; *— fortunato*, to think (*o* to deem) oneself lucky (*o* to account oneself lucky) **2.** (*tenersi in alta considerazione*) to rate oneself highly: *egli si stima moltissimo*, he has a very high opinion of himself.

stimàto, *ag.* esteemed: *articolo molto —*, highly esteemed article.

stimatóre, *ag.* valuing, estimating, appraising ‖ *s.m.*, **stimatríce,** *s.f.* valuer, estimator, appraiser.

stímma, *V.* **stígma.**

stimmatizzàre, *v.t.* to stigmatize.

stimolànte, *ag.* stimulating ‖ *s.m.* (*med.*) stimulant.

stimolàre, *v.t.* **1.** to goad: *— i buoi*, to goad oxen **2.** *fig.* to stimulate, to spur, to incite: *è stimolato dall'ambizione*, he is stimulated (*o* spurred) by ambition; *la ne-*

cessità lo stimolò a fare ciò, necessity spurred (*o* drove *o* incited) him to do that; — *l'appetito*, to whet the appetite 3. (*med.*) to stimulate: *una bevanda che stimola i centri nervosi*, a beverage that stimulates the nervous centres.

stimolatívo, *ag.* stimulative.

stimolatóre, *ag.* stimulating ‖ *s.m.*, **stimolatríce,** *s.f.* stimulator, inciter.

stímolo, *s.m.* 1. goad 2. *fig.* stimulus (*pl.* stimuli), goad, spur, incentive: *il bisogno è un grande — al lavoro*, necessity is a great spur to work; *ha bisogno di uno — per andare avanti*, he needs a stimulus to go ahead; *sentire lo — della fame*, to begin to feel the pangs of hunger 3. (*med.*) stimulant.

stínco, *s.m.* (*anat.*) shin, shin-bone ‖ *non era uno — di santo*, he was far from being a saint.

stíngere, *v.t.i.*, **stíngersi,** *v.r.* to fade, to discolour: *questi colori (si) stingono facilmente*, these colours fade easily ‖ *non stinge*, non-fading.

stintignàre, *v.i.* to hesitate.

stínto, *ag.* faded, discoloured.

stípa, *s.f.* (*fuscelli e simili per far fuoco*) brushwood.

stipàre[1], *v.t.* (*togliere la stipa da*) to clear away the brushwood from (a place).

stipàre[2], *v.t.* (*ammassare*) to cram, to crowd, to pack closely: *li stiparono tutti in una stanza*, they packed (*o* crowded) them all together into a room; — *un cassetto di carte*, to cram a drawer with papers.

stipàto[1], *ag.* (*netto di stipa*) free from brushwood.

stipàto[2], *ag.* (*ammassato*) crowded (with s.o., sthg.), packed (with s.o., sthg.): *gente stipata in una sala*, people crowded (*o* packed *o* crammed) in a hall; *un teatro —*, a crowded (*o* packed) theatre.

stipendiàre, *v.t.* to pay a salary to (s.o.): *dovresti stipendiarlo se vuoi che lavori di più*, you should pay him a salary if you want him to work more; *dovrò — un'altra persona*, I shall have to take on another person.

stipendiàto, *ag.* salaried ‖ *s.m.* salaried worker.

stipèndio, *s.m.* salary, stipend: *avere qlcu. al proprio —*, to have s.o. as one's employee; *essere agli stipendi di qlcu.*, to be s.o.'s employee.

stipéto, *s.m.* (*terreno cosparso di stipe*) scrub.

stipettàio, *s.m.* (*chi fa stipi*) cabinet-maker.

stípite, *s.m.* 1. jamb, (side-)post: — *di finestra*, window-post; — *di porta*, door-post 2. (*bot.*) (*tronco*) trunk 3. (*stirpe*) stock, strain.

stípo, *s.m.* cabinet.

stípola, *s.f.* (*bot.*) stipule.

stípsi, *s.f.* (*med.*) constipation, costiveness.

stípula, *s.f.* (*bot.*) stipule.

stipulànte, *ag.* stipulating ‖ *s.c.* stipulator, stipulating party.

stipulàre, *v.t.* to stipulate: *stipularono che entrambi avrebbero seguito le decisioni dell'assemblea*, they stipulated that both of them should follow the decisions of the assembly; *stipularono l'immediata consegna della merce*, they stipulated an immediate delivery of the goods; — *che tutte le spese siano a carico del locatario*, to stipulate that the tenant should be responsible for all repairs; — *un contratto di matrimonio*, to draw up a marriage-contract; — *un matrimonio*, to arrange a marriage.

stipulàto, *ag.* stipulated.

stipulazióne, *s.f.* stipulation: — *di un contratto*, stipulation (*o* drawing up) of a contract.

stiracchiaménto, *s.m.* 1. stretching, pulling, tugging 2. (*il softisticare*) distorting, twisting 3. (*il mercanteggiare*) bargaining, haggling.

stiracchiàre, *v.t.* 1. to stretch, to pull, to tug: — *le gambe, braccia*, to stretch one's legs, arms 2. (*sofisticare su*) to distort, to twist: — *il significato di una frase*, to twist (*o* to distort) the meaning of a sentence 3. (*mercanteggiare*) to bargain over (sthg.),

to haggle about (sthg.): — *il prezzo di ql.co.*, to bargain over (the price of) sthg.

stiracchiataménte, *av.* with an effort, with difficulty: *egli fu promosso molto —*, he passed with great difficulty; *riuscì a provarne la verità molto —*, he had great difficulty in proving the truth of it.

stiracchiàto, *ag.* forced: *un sorriso —*, a forced smile ‖ *una dimostrazione stiracchiata*, an unconvincing demonstration; *ragionamento —*, forced argument.

stiracchiatúra, *s.f.* 1. stretching 2. (*interpretazione stiracchiata*) forced interpretation.

stiraménto, *s.m.* 1. stretching 2. (*col ferro*) ironing; pressing.

stiràre, *v.t.* 1. to stretch: — *le braccia, le gambe*, to stretch one's arms, legs 2. (*col ferro caldo*) to iron; to press: — *biancheria, una camicia*, to iron linen, a shirt; — *un vestito*, to press (*o* to iron) a suit ‖ **stiràrsi,** *v.r.* to stretch (oneself).

stiràto, *ag.* ironed, pressed.

stiratóio, *s.m.* 1. (*asse da disegno*) drawing-board 2. (*panno che ricopre l'asse per stirare*) ironing-board cover.

stiratóra, *s.f.* ironer.

stiratoría, *s.f.* (*rar.*) ironing-shop.

stiratríce, *s.f.* ironer.

stiratúra, *s.f.* ironing.

stirería, *s.f.* ironing-shop.

Stíria, *no.pr.f.* (*geog.*) Styria.

stíro, *s.m.*: *ferro da —*, iron.

stirpàre, *e derivati*, *V.* **sterpàre**, *e derivati*.

stírpe, *s.f.* 1. birth, descent, stock; (*razza*) race: *una — di guerrieri*, a race of warriors; *persona di nobile —*, person of noble birth (*o* descent *o* stock *o* extraction) 2. (*prole*) offspring, issue.

stiticaménte, *av.* 1. costively 2. (*in modo avaro*) niggardly; (*fam.*) stingily.

stitichézza, *s.f.* 1. constipation, costiveness 2. (*avarizia*) niggardliness; (*fam.*) stinginess.

stítico, *ag.* 1. constipated, costive 2. (*avaro*) niggardly; (*fam.*) stingy.

stiúma, *e derivati*, *V.* **schiúma**, *e derivati*.

stíva[1], *s.f.* 1. (*mar.*) hold: — *cisterna*, deep tank; — *per carbone*, bunker (*o* coal-hold); — *refrigerata*, refrigerated hold; *mettere nella —*, to stow.

stíva[2], *s.f.* (*manico dell'aratro*) plough-handle.

stivàggio, *s.m.* (*mar.*) stowage.

stivàle, *s.m.* boot: *stivali alla scudiera*, top-boots; *mettersi, togliersi gli stivali*, to put on, to take off one's boots ‖ *lo Stivale*, "*lo Stivale*" (Italy) ‖ *ingegnere dei miei stivali*, (*iron.*) engineer, my foot! ‖ *lustrare a uno gli stivali*, to lick s.o.'s boots ‖ *rompere gli stivali a uno*, (*fam.*) to bore s.o. stiff.

stivalería, *s.f.* boot factory.

stivalétto, *s.m.* ankle-boot.

stivàre, *v.t.* (*mar.*) to stow.

stivatóre, *s.m.* (*mar.*) stevedore, longshoreman (*pl.* longshoremen).

stízza, *s.f.* anger; irritation: *cercherò di calmare la sua —*, I shall try to calm down his anger; *mi fece venire la —*, it made me angry; *se gli prende la —*, if he gets angry; *si rodeva di —*, he was fretting with irritation; *provar — per ql.co.*, to be angry about sthg.

stizzíre, *v.t.* to irritate, to vex: *non stizzirlo!*, don't irritate (*o* vex) him! ‖ *far — qlcu.*, to make s.o. angry (*o* cross) ‖ **stizzírsi,** *v.r.* to get angry, to get cross, to lose one's temper: *si è stizzito sul serio*, he was really angry; *si stizzisce subito*, it doesn't take much to make him angry (*o* he loses his temper easily).

stizzíto, *ag.* cross, angry: *rispose —*, he replied angrily.

stizzosaménte, *av.* irritably, peevishly.

stizzóso, *ag.* irritable, peevish: *parole stizzose*, peevish words; *è troppo —*, he is too irritable.

stòa, *s.f.* (*st.*) stoa (*pl.* stoae, stoas).

stoccafísso, *s.m.* stockfish ‖ *sembrare uno —*, to be as thin as a lath.

Stoccàrda, *no.pr.f.* (*geog.*) Stuttgart.

stoccàta, *s.f.* **1.** (*colpo di pugnale, ecc.*) thrust, stab **2.** (*parola mordace*) thrust, gibe: *lanciare una — a qlcu.*, to gibe at s.o. **3.** (*richiesta di denaro*) sudden request for money.

stoccheggiàre, *v.t.* (*ferire con uno stocco*) to wound with a rapier ‖ *v.i.* (*star sulle parate*) to parry.

stòcco¹, *s.m.* rapier: *bastone a, con lo —,* sword-stick.

stòcco², *s.m.* (*stollo del pagliaio*) pole (of haystack).

Stoccólma, *no.pr.f.* (*geog.*) Stockholm.

stòffa, *s.f.* **1.** material, cloth; fabric: *— di seta, cotone, lana,* silk, cotton, woollen cloth; *— in pezza,* cloth in the piece; *— per abiti,* dress-material; *due metri di —,* two metres of cloth; *che genere di — è?,* what material (*o* what sort of cloth) is it?; *ho comperato una — molto pesante, buona,* I have bought some very heavy, good material **2.** *fig.* stuff: *in lui c'è della —,* there is good stuff in him; *non ha la — dell'artista,* he is not the stuff artists are made of; *questi ragazzi sono tutti della stessa —,* these boys are all of the same kind (*o* of the same stamp); *suo fratello è di un'altra —,* his brother is made of different stuff.

stòia, *V.* **stuòia.**

stoiàre, *v.t.* (*rar.*) to cover with mats.

stoiàta, *s.f.* (*arch.*) lath and plaster ceiling.

stoicaménte, *av.* stoically: *sopportare — il dolore,* to support pain stoically.

stoicísmo, *s.m.* **1.** (*st. fil.*) Stoicism **2.** *fig.* stoicism: *sopportò il colpo con vero —,* he bore the blow with real stoicism.

stòico, *ag.* **1.** (*st. fil.*) Stoic: *filosofia stoica,* Stoic philosophy **2.** *fig.* stoic(al): *animo —,* stoical mind ‖ *s.m.* **1.** (*st. fil.*) Stoic: *gli stoici,* the Stoics **2.** *fig.* stoic: *è uno —,* he is a stoic.

stoíno, *s.m.* door-mat.

stòla, *s.f.* **1.** stole: *— di ermellino, visone,* ermine, mink stole **2.** (*eccl.*) stole **3.** (*st. romana*) stole.

stolidàggine, *s.f.* stolidity; stupidity.

stolidaménte, *av.* stolidly; stupidly.

stolidézza, *s.f.,* **stolidità,** *s.f.* stolidity; stupidity.

stòlido, *ag.* stolid; stupid ‖ *s.m.* stolid person; stupid person.

stòllo, *s.m.* (*agr.*) pole (of haystack) ‖ *pare uno —,* (*fam.*) he's as long as a bean-pole.

stolóne, *s.m.* (*bot.*) stolon.

stoltaménte, *av.* foolishly, stupidly.

stoltézza, *s.f.* foolishness, stupidity, silliness.

stoltilòquio, *s.m.* stupid speech.

stoltízia, *s.f.* (*rar.*) foolishness, stupidity, silliness.

stólto, *ag.* foolish, stupid, silly ‖ *s.m.* fool.

stòma, *s.m.* (*bot.*) stoma (*pl.* stomata).

stomacàggine, *s.f.* sickness, nausea.

stomacàle, *ag.* stomachal; stomach (*attributivo*).

stomacànte, *ag.* sickening, nauseating (*anche fig.*).

stomacàre, *v.t.i.* to sicken, to nauseate (*anche fig.*): *questo cibo mi stomaca,* this food nauseates (*o* sickens) me; *la sua adulazione mi stomaca,* his flattery sickens me (*o* makes me sick) ‖ **stomacàrsi,** *v.r.* to be nauseated (by sthg.).

stomacàto, *ag.* sickened, nauseated (*anche fig.*).

stomachévole, *av.* sickening, nauseating (*anche fig.*): *odore —,* nauseating (*o* sickening) smell.

stomachevolménte, *av.* sickeningly, nauseatingly.

stomàchico, *ag.* (*farm.*) stomachic.

stòmaco, *s.m.* **1.** stomach: *a — pieno,* on a full stomach; *a — vuoto,* on an empty stomach; *mal di —,* stomach-ache; *ha uno — debole, forte,* he has a weak, strong stomach ‖ *sforzo di —,* retching ‖ *le cipolle mi stanno sullo —,* onions lie on my stomach; *ho ancora la colazione sullo —, la colazione mi è rimasta sullo —,* I haven't yet digested my lunch; *la sua arroganza mi sta sullo —, fig.* I cannot stomach his arrogance ‖ *ha uno — di struzzo,* he has the digestion of an ostrich ‖ *mi sento un vuoto nello —,* (*fam.*) I am faint with hunger ‖ *dare allo — a qlcu.,* to sicken (*o* to nau-

seate) s.o. ‖ *dare di —,* to vomit (*o* to throw up) **2.** *fig.* (*coraggio*) courage; (*fam.*) guts (*pl.*); (*sfrontatezza*) effrontery, nerve, cheek: *ebbe lo — di leggere tutti quei libri noiosi,* he had the courage (*o* guts) to read all those boring books; *ha avuto lo — di dirmelo,* he had the nerve (*o* effrontery) to tell me.

stomacóso, *V.* **stomachévole.**

stomàtico, *ag.* **1.** (*dello stomaco*) stomachic; stomach (*attributivo*) **2.** (*rar.*) (*della bocca*) stomatic.

stomatíte, *s.f.* (*patol.*) stomatitis.

stomatología, *s.f.* (*med.*) stomatology.

stomatològico, *ag.* (*med.*) stomatologic(al).

stomatoscòpio, *s.m.* (*med.*) stomatoscope.

stomía, *s.f.* (*chir.*) anastomosis.

stonacàre, *v.t.* to unplaster.

stonàre, *v.i.* **1.** (*cantando*) to be out of tune, to sing out of tune; (*suonando*) to be out of tune, to play out of tune; (*uscire dal tono*) to fall out of tune **2.** *fig.* to be out of place; (*di colori*) to clash, to jar: *le sue osservazioni stonarono in quel momento,* his remarks were out of place at that moment; *il verde stona coll'azzurro,* green clashes with blue ‖ *v.t.* (*turbare*) to upset: *queste notizie mi hanno stonato,* this news has upset me ‖ *il lungo viaggio mi ha stonato,* the long journey has put me out of sorts.

stonàta, *V.* **stonatúra.**

stonàto, *ag.* **1.** out of tune; (*di nota*) false: *un violino —,* an out-of-tune violin; *egli è molto —,* he cannot sing in tune **2.** *fig.* out of place: *tutto quel che diceva era —,* everything he said was out of place **3.** (*turbato*) upset ‖ *sono sempre — dopo un lungo viaggio,* I am always out of sorts after a long journey.

stonatúra, *s.f.* false note (*anche fig.*): *nel suo discorso c'era qualche —,* there were a few false notes in his speech; *quel tappeto in questo salotto è una —,* that carpet is a false note (*o* is out of place) in this drawing-room.

stóppa, *s.f.* tow: *— da calafato,* (*mar.*) (caulking) oakum ‖ *carne che sembra —,* stringy (*o* tough) meat ‖ *ha i capelli biondo —,* she has tow-coloured hair ‖ *essere un pulcino tra la —,* to be like a fish out of water.

stoppabúchi, *s.c.* (*fam.*) stop-gap.

stoppàccio, *s.m.* **1.** wad; wadding **2.** (*miccia*) tinder; blasting-fuse, (quick) match.

stoppaccióso, *ag.* towy; (*di carne*) tough, stringy.

stoppàre¹, *v.t.* to stop with tow; to plug; (*mar.*) (*calafatare*) to caulk.

stoppàre², *v.t.* (*giuoco del calcio*) to stop.

stoppatóre, *s.m.* (*mar.*) (*calafato*) caulker.

stóppia, *s.f.* (*agr.*) stubble.

stoppinièra, *s.f.* wick-holder; taper-holder.

stoppíno, *s.m.* **1.** (*di candela*) wick **2.** (*miccia*) tinder; blasting-fuse **3.** (*ind. tessile*) rove.

stoppóso, *ag.* towy; (*di carne*) tough, stringy.

stòrcere, *v.t.* **1.** to twist; to wrench: *— un braccio a qlcu.,* to twist s.o.'s arm; *— un lenzuolo bagnato,* to wring out a wet sheet ‖ *— la bocca,* to twist one's mouth ‖ *— gli occhi,* to roll one's eyes ‖ *— il significato di una frase, fig.* to twist the meaning of a sentence **2.** (*disfare la torsione di*) to untwist ‖ **stòrcersi,** *v.r.* **1.** to twist; to writhe: *egli si storceva dal male,* he writhed in pain ‖ *— dal ridere,* to split one's sides with laughter **2.** (*lussarsi, slogarsi*) to twist, to wrench: *— una caviglia, un polso,* to twist (*o* to wrench) one's ankle, one's wrist.

storcicòllo, *V.* **torcicòllo.**

storcilèggi, *s.m.* (*spreg.*) pettifogger.

storciménto, *s.m.* twist; wrench.

stordiménto, *s.m.* **1.** dizziness, giddiness: *questo — è dovuto al colpo che hai ricevuto,* this dizziness is caused by the blow you received; *avere uno —,* to feel giddy **2.** (*sbalordimento, meraviglia*) stupefaction; bewilderment.

stordíre, *v.t.* **1.** (*con un colpo*) to stun, to daze: *il* *poliziotto lo stordì con un colpo alla testa*, the police-man stunned (*o* dazed) him with a blow on the head 2. (*di vino, liquori*) to dull (s.o.'s senses) 3. (*di rumore*) (*assordare*) to deafen; (*innervosire*) to drive crazy: *rumore che stordisce*, deafening noise; *quel bambino mi stordisce*, that child is driving me crazy 4. *fig.* (*sbalordire*) to stun, to stupefy: *quella notizia l'aveva stordito*, that piece of news had stupefied (*o* stunned) him ‖ **stordìrsi**, *v.r.* to dull one's senses: *cercava di — col bere*, he tried to dull his senses with drink.

storditàggine, *s.f.* 1. absent-mindedness, heedlessness; carelessness 2. (*stupidità*) foolishness, silliness, stupidity 3. (*errore sciocco*) foolish mistake, blunder; (*detto sciocco*) foolish remark: *questa è stata una vera —*, this was a really foolish mistake.

storditaménte, *av.* 1. absent-mindedly, heedlessly 2. (*scioccamente*) foolishly.

storditézza, *s.f.* 1. absent-mindedness, heedlessness; carelessness 2. (*stupidità*) foolishness.

stordìto, *ag.* 1. stunned, dazed; giddy: *era — per il colpo*, he was left stunned (*o* dazed) by the blow; *mi sento — in tutto questo traffico*, I feel dazed in all this traffic 2. (*sbalordito*) bewildered: *aveva un'aria stordita*, he looked bewildered 3. (*sbadato, sventato*) absent-minded, heedless 4. (*sciocco*) foolish, silly ‖ *s.m.* fool: *è uno —*, he is a fool.

stòria, *s.f.* 1. history: *— antica, medievale, moderna*, ancient, mediæval, modern history; *— dell'arte*, history of art; *— della letteratura italiana*, history of Italian literature; *— delle dottrine economiche*, history of economic doctrines; *— d'Italia*, history of Italy; *— greca, romana*, Greek, Roman history; *— naturale*, natural history; *lezione, esame di —*, history lesson, examination; *libro di —*, history-book ‖ *la — della mia vita*, the story of my life ‖ *la — sacra*, sacred history 2. (*racconto*) story, tale: *storie di avventure*, tales of adventure (*o* adventure-stories); *una — di fate*, a fairy-tale (*o* fairy-story); *è una lunga —!*, it's a long story!; *raccontami una —*, tell me a story ‖ *è sempre la stessa —!*, it is always the same (old) story! 3. (*bugia*) story, fib: *fece circolare delle storie sul mio conto*, he spread stories about me; *non raccontare storie!*, don't tell stories (*o* fibs)! ‖ *storie!*, nuts! (*o* go on! *o* get away!) 4. (*obiezione*) objection; (*pretesto*) pretext: *non far tante storie!*, don't make so much fuss!; *se dovesse fare delle storie, fammelo sapere*, if he should raise any objections, let me know.

storiàre, *v.t.* to storiate.
storicaménte, *av.* historically.
storicìsmo, *s.m.* 1. (*fil.*) historicism, historism 2. (*metodo storico nella critica*) historical method.
storicità, *s.f.* historicity.
stòrico, *ag.* 1. historical: *critica storica, metodo —*, historical criticism, method; *romanzo —*, historical novel; *scuola storica*, (*econ.*) historical school; *verità storica*, historical truth 2. (*gram.*) historic: *presente —*, historic present 3. (*vero, esatto*) true ‖ *s.m.* historian.
storièlla, *s.f.* 1. little story 2. (*frottola*) fib, story, lie 3. (*barzelletta*) funny story, joke.
storiografìa, *s.f.* historiography.
storiogràfico, *ag.* historiographic(al).
storiògrafo, *s.m.* historiographer.
storióne, *s.m.* (*ittiol.*) sturgeon.
stormìre, *v.i.* to rustle.
stórmo, *s.m.* 1. flight, flock: *uno — di uccelli*, a flight (*o* flock) of birds; *uno — di aeroplani*, a flight of aeroplanes ‖ *a stormi*, in flocks (anche *fig.*) 2. *fig.* (*frotta, moltitudine*) crowd, swarm: *uno — di gente*, a crowd (*o* swarm) of people ‖ *suonare a —*, to ring the tocsin.
stornàre, *v.t.* to avert, to ward off; to divert, to turn aside: *— l'attenzione di qlcu. da ql.co.*, to divert (*o* to turn) s.o.'s attention from sthg.; *— un pericolo*, to avert (*o* to ward off) a danger ‖ *— un contratto*,

(*romperlo*) to break a contract ‖ *— una somma*, to transfer a sum of money.
stornellàre, *v.i.* to sing stornelli; to sing ditties.
stornèllo[1], *s.m.* (*lett. mus.*) stornello (*pl.* stornelli); ditty.
stornèllo[2], *s.m.* (*ornit.*) starling.
stórno[1], *ag.* dapple-grey ‖ *s.m.* (*ornit.*) starling.
stórno[2], *s.m.* (*amm.*) transfer.
storpiaménto, *s.m.* 1. crippling, maiming 2. *fig.* mangling.
storpiàre, *v.t.* 1. to cripple, to maim: *fu storpiato in guerra*, he was crippled (*o* maimed) in the war; *fu storpiato da una caduta da cavallo*, he was crippled by a fall from his horse 2. (*rovinare, massacrare*) to mangle: *— un nome*, (*scrivendolo*) to misspell a name; (*pronunciandolo*) to garble a name; *— le parole*, to mangle one's words; *— un pezzo di musica*, to mangle a piece of music ‖ *— una ragazza*, to find a bad husband for a girl ‖ *il troppo storpia*, *prov.* too much is too much.
storpiataménte, *av.* badly, wrongly: *pronunciare una parola —*, to mispronounce a word.
storpiàto, *ag.* 1. crippled, maimed 2. *fig.* mangled.
storpiatùra, *s.f.* 1. crippling, maiming 2. *fig.* mangling 3. (*lavoro mal fatto*) botch, bungled work.
stórpio, *ag.* crippled ‖ *s.m.* cripple.
stòrta, *s.f.* 1. twist; (*ad un'articolazione*) sprain: *ho preso una — a un piede*, I have sprained my ankle 2. (*chim.*) retort.
stortaménte, *av.* crookedly (anche *fig.*).
stortàre, *V.* stòrcere.
stortézza, *s.f.* crookedness.
stòrto, *ag.* 1. twisted; (*piegato*) crooked: *una bacchetta storta*, a crooked stick; *bocca storta*, twisted mouth; *gambe storte*, bandy legs; *un naso —*, a crooked nose; *un quadro —*, a picture hung crooked ‖ *occhi storti*, squinting eyes: *uomo dagli occhi storti*, cross-eyed man 2. (*storpio*) crippled 3. (*falso, sbagliato*) false; wrong: *idee storte*, wrong ideas ‖ *s.m.* cripple.
stortùra, *s.f.* 1. deformity 2. (*idea sbagliata*) wrong idea; (*errore*) mistake, error.
stovaìna, *s.f.* (*farm.*) stovaine.
stovigliàio, *s.m.* 1. (*commerciante in stoviglie*) dealer in earthenware and crockery 2. (*vasaio*) potter.
stovìglie, *s.f.pl.* kitchenware (*sing.*); crockery (*sing.*); earthenware (*sing.*).
stoviglierìa, *s.f.* crockery (solo *sing.*).
stozzàccio, *s.m.* iron dross.
stozzaménto, *s.m.* (*mec.*) slotting.
stozzàre, *v.t.* (*mec.*) to slot.
stozzatrìce, *s.f.* (*mec.*) slotter.
stozzatùra, *s.f.* (*mec.*) slotting.
stòzzo, *s.m.* (*mec.*) slot-milling tool.
strabalzaménto, *s.m.* (*traballamento*) jolting, tossing about.
strabalzàre, *v.i.* (*traballare*) to jolt, to toss about.
stràbico, *ag.* squinting; squint-eyed, cross-eyed: *egli è —*, he squints ‖ *s.m.* squinter, cross-eyed person.
strabiliànte, *ag.* amazing, astonishing.
strabiliàre, *v.i.*, **strabiliàrsi**, *v.r.* to be amazed, to be astonished ‖ *far strabiliare*, to amaze, to astonish.
strabìsmo, *s.m.* (*med.*) squint, squinting; strabismus: *essere affetto da —*, to squint.
straboccaménto, *s.m.* 1. overflowing 2. *fig.* (*gran quantità*) superabundance.
straboccànte, *ag.* 1. overflowing 2. *fig.* (*eccessivo*) superabundant.
straboccàre, *v.i.* 1. to overflow 2. *fig.* (*abbondare*) to abound.
strabocchévole, *ag.* 1. overflowing 2. *fig.* (*eccessivo*) superabundant; excessive.
strabocchevolménte, *av.* superabundantly.
strabócco, *s.m.* overflowing.
Strabóne, *no.pr.m.* (*st. lett.*) Strabo.

strabuzzàre, *v.t.*: — *gli occhi*, to roll one's eyes.

stracanàrsi, *v.r.* (*lavorare come un cane*) to work like a slave.

stracannàre, *v.t.* (*ind. tessile*) to rewind.

stracannatúra, *s.f.* (*ind. tessile*) rewinding.

stracàrico, *ag.* overloaded (with sthg.), overburdened (with sthg.).

stràcca, *s.f.* fatigue, tiredness, weariness ‖ *alla* —, wearily.

straccàre, *v.t.* to fatigue, to tire out ‖ **straccàrsi**, *v.r.* to get tired (out).

straccería, *s.f.* rags (*pl.*), tatters (*pl.*).

stracchézza, *s.f.* tiredness, fatigue, weariness.

stracchíno, *s.m.* "stracchino" (kind of soft cheese made in Lombardy).

stracciàbile, *ag.* tearable.

stracciàio, **stracciaiuòlo**, *s.m.* **1.** rag-and-bone -man (*pl.* rag-and-bone-men) **2.** (*ind. tessile*) comber.

stracciaménto, *s.m.* **1.** tearing; rending **2.** (*ind. tessile*) combing.

stracciàre, *v.t.* **1.** to tear; (*rar.*) to rend: *ho stracciato il vestito*, I have torn my dress; — *una lettera*, to tear up a letter; — *un pezzo di carta*, to tear a piece of paper **2.** (*ind. tessile*) to comb ‖ **stracciàrsi**, *v.r.* to tear, to get torn: *questa carta si straccia facilmente*, this paper tears easily.

stracciàto, *ag.* **1.** torn; ragged: *vestiti stracciati*, torn (*o* ragged) clothes **2.** (*di persona*) in rags; in tatters **3.** *fig.* (*dilaniato*) torn.

stracciatúra, *V.* **stracciaménto**.

stràccio, *ag.* torn; in rags ‖ *carta straccia*, waste paper ‖ *s.m.* **1.** rag; tatters (*pl.*): *un mucchio di vecchi stracci*, a heap of old rags; *gli stracci si usano per fare carta*, rags are used for making paper; *era vestito di stracci*, he was dressed in rags (*o* tatters) ‖ *era ridotta uno* —, she was worn out ‖ *non ha trovato uno* — *di marito*, she hasn't been able to get even the poorest of husbands ‖ *gli stracci vanno sempre all'aria*, *prov.* the weakest goes to the wall **2.** (*panno, cencio*) cloth: — *per la polvere*, duster; — *per le scarpe*, shoe-cloth **3.** (*strappo*) tear, rent **4.** (*ind. tessile*) noil; combings (*pl.*).

stracciòna, *s.f.*, **stracciòne**, *s.m.* ragamuffin, tatterdemalion.

stràcco, *ag.* **1.** very tired, tired out, exhausted ‖ — *morto*, dead tired **2.** *fig.* (*fiacco*) weak; lukewarm: *amore* —, lukewarm love; *promesse stracche*, weak promises **3.** (*di terreno*) impoverished; exhausted, worn out.

stracontènto, *ag.* overjoyed; very happy.

stracòtto, *ag.* overdone ‖ *s.m.* (*cuc.*) stew.

stràda, *s.f.* **1.** road; (*di città, fiancheggiata da case*) street: — *a fondo cattivo*, uneven (*o* bad) road; — *alpestre*, mountain road; — *a due corsie*, dual carriage-way; — *a senso unico*, one-way street; — *asfaltata*, asphalt road; — *carreggiabile*, cartway; — *carrozzabile*, carriage-way; — *cieca*, cul-de-sac (*o* blind alley); — *di campagna*, country road; — *di circonvallazione*, by-pass; — *ferrata*, railway; — *ghiaiata*, gravel road; — *in costruzione*, road under construction; — *in macadam*, macadamized road; — *lastricata, selciata*, paved road; — *maestra*, main road (*o* highroad *o* highway); — *mulattiera*, mule-track (*o* bridle-path); — *principale*, main highway (*o* road); — *provinciale*, country road; *una* — *romana*, a Roman road; — *sbarrata*, road blocked (*o* no thoroughfare); — *sdrucciolevole*, slippery road; — *secondaria*, by-road (*o* side street); — *sotterranea*, tunnel; — *statale*, state road; — *traversa*, (*scorciatoia*) short-cut; *all'angolo della* —, at the street corner; *bivio della* —, road fork; *colmo della* —, crown of the road; *dall'altra parte della* —, across (*o* on the other side of) the road (*o* street); *in mezzo alla* —, in the middle of the street (*o* road); *manutenzione delle strade*, road maintenance; *regolamento della* —, rule of the road; *il traffico nelle strade*, the traffic in the streets; *abito in una* — *molto tranquil-*

la, I live in a very quiet street (*o* road); *a quest'ora è già in* —, by now he is on the road; *l'ho incontrato per la* —, I have met him in the street; *la mia finestra dà sulla* —, my window opens out (*o* looks out) on the street; *questa* — *è molto battuta*, this is a very busy road; *attraversare la* —, to cross the street (*o* the road); *fare, aprire una* —, to build, to open a road ‖ *bandito di* —, highway bandit ‖ *ragazzo di* —, street -arab ‖ *l'uomo della* —, the man in the street ‖ *tutta la* — *è sua*, he thinks he owns the road ‖ *darsi, gettarsi alla* —, to become a highway bandit ‖ *mettere qlcu. sulla* —, to reduce s.o. to poverty ‖ *tutte le strade conducono a Roma*, *prov.* all roads lead to Rome **2.** (*via, cammino*) way (anche *fig.*): — *facendo*, on the way; *la* — *più breve da qui alla stazione*, the shortest way from here to the station; *a un'ora di* —, (*camminando*) an hour's walk away; *un luogo fuori* —, an out-of-the -way place; *è un giovane che farà* —, he is a young man who will go a long way; *ha trovato la* — *fatta*, he had everything done for him (*o* he had everything on a plate); *ho perso la* —, I have lost my way; *io faccio* —, I'll lead the way; *non ha ancora trovato la sua* —, *fig.* he hasn't found his way yet; *non so che* — *prendere*, I don't know which way to go; *fig.* I don't know which way to turn; *non so trovare la* — *per andare a casa*, I can't find my way home; *per ottenere quell'impiego bisogna che trovi la* — *giusta*, he must find the right way to get that job; *sei fuori* —, *fig.* you are on the wrong track; *si è fatto* — (*nel mondo*), he has made his way (in the world); *si fece* — *fra la folla*, he pushed his way through the crowd; *si vide chiusa ogni* —, *fig.* he realized every possibility was closed to him; *va' per la tua* —, go your own way; *cambiar* —, to change direction; *domandare la* —, to ask the way; *essere, mettere su una buona, cattiva* —, to be, to put on the right, wrong track; *fare, rifare la* — *a piedi*, to walk, to walk back; *fare la* — *con qlcu.*, to go, to come with s.o.; *farsi una* — *in mezzo alla neve*, to clear a way through the snow; *fermarsi per la* —, to stop on the way; *indugiare per la* —, to loiter on the way; *tagliare la* — *a qlcu.*, to cross the road in front of s.o.; *fig.* to stand in s.o.'s way **3.** (*astr.*) (*orbita*) orbit.

stradàle, *ag.* road (*attributivo*); of the road (*predicativo*): *attraversamento* —, road crossing; *codice* —, highway code; *fondo* —, road-bed; *incidente* —, road accident; *lavori stradali*, roadworks; *manutenzione* —, upkeep of the roads; *piano* —, roadway; *regolamento* —, rule of the road ‖ *s.m.* (*strada*) road; (*viale*) avenue.

stradàre, *v.t.* **1.** (*mettere sulla buona strada*) to put on the right road, to direct **2.** *fig.* (*avviare a carriera, studi*) to start ‖ **stradàrsi**, *v.r.* (*avviarsi*) to set out (for a place).

stradàrio, *s.m.* road-map.

stradíno, *s.m.* road-mender.

stradísta, *s.m.* road-racing cyclist.

stradivàrio, *s.m.* Stradivarius, Stradivari (*abbr.* Strad).

stradóne, *s.m.* large road; (*viale*) avenue.

stradóppio, *ag.* more than double.

stradotàle, *ag.* (*dir.*) extradotal, paraphernal.

strafalcióne, *s.m.* blunder: *composizione piena di strafalcioni*, composition full of blunders.

strafàre, *v.i.* to overdo.

strafàtto, *ag.* **1.** (*troppo maturo*) overripe **2.** (*stracotto*) overdone.

strafelàrsi, *v.r.* **1.** (*perdere il respiro*) to gasp for breath **2.** (*stancarsi*) to get tired out, to tire oneself out.

strafelàto, *ag.* **1.** (*ansante*) breathless, panting, out of breath **2.** (*stanco*) tired out.

strafíne, *ag.* superfine, very fine.

strafóro, *s.m.* (*traforo*) fretwork: *lavorare di* —, to cut out a fretwork ‖ *di* —, (*di nascosto*) secretly; (*furtivamente*) on the sly (*o* on the quiet); (*di sfuggita*) stealthily: *lo potrei avere di* —, I could get it on the quiet; *si vedono di* —, they see each other stealthily.

strafottènte, *ag*. 1. (*noncurante*) unconcerned, regardless of other people's feelings 2. (*arrogante*) arrogant; (*sfrontato*) impudent.

strafottènza, *s.f.* 1. (*noncuranza*) carelessness, disregard for other people's feelings; (*arroganza*) arrogance 2. (*sfrontatezza*) effrontery, impudence: *non mi piace la sua —*, I don't like his impudence.

strafóttersi, *v.r.* (*volg.*) not to care a damn (about sthg.): *me ne strafotto*, I don't care a damn about it (*o* I couldn't care less about it).

stràge, *s.f.* 1. (*eccidio*) slaughter; massacre; carnage: *fare una —*, to slaughter (*o* to massacre) ‖ *la — degli innocenti*, the slaughter of the innocents ‖ *il colera ha fatto — tra gli abitanti di quella zona*, cholera decimated the population of that area ‖ *fecero — di selvaggina*, they slaughtered a great deal of game 2. (*distruzione, danno*) destruction; havoc; damage: *il terremoto causò una — di case e persone*, the earthquake caused great damage and loss of life 3. (*grande quantità*) large quantity; mass: *una — di fiori*, a mass of flowers.

stragiudiziàle, *ag*. (*dir.*) extrajudicial.

stragiudizialménte, *av*. (*dir.*) extrajudicially.

stràglio, *s.m.* (*mar.*) stay, brace.

stragodére, *v.i.* to enjoy (sthg.) to the full.

stragónfio, *ag*. extremely swollen, excessively swollen.

stragrànde, *ag*. enormous, huge: *una — maggioranza*, an enormous majority.

stralciàre, *v.t.* 1. (*agr.*) to prune 2. *fig.* (*togliere via*) to take off; to take out; to take away: *una partita da un conto*, (*comm.*) to remove an item from an account 3. (*comm.*) (*liquidare*) to liquidate, to wind up 4. (*rar.*) (*sbrigare*) to settle.

stràlcio, *s.m.* 1. (*agr.*) pruning 2. *fig.* (*il togliere via*) removal 3. (*estratto*) extract 4. (*ritaglio di giornale*) newspaper cutting 5. (*comm.*) (*liquidazione*) liquidation, winding up: *vendere ql.co. a —*, to sell sthg. off.

stràle, *s.m.* dart; arrow: *gli strali d'Amore*, Cupid's darts.

stràllo, *s.m.* (*mar.*) stay, brace.

stralodàre, *v.t.* to overpraise; to praise highly.

stralucènte, *ag*. very shiny, glossy.

stralunaménto, *s.m.* rolling of the eyes; (*lo sbarrare gli occhi*) opening wide of the eyes.

stralunàre, *v.t.* to roll; (*sbarrare*) to open wide: *— gli occhi*, to roll one's eyes; (*sbarrarli*) to open one's eyes wide.

stralunàto, *ag*. 1. (*di occhi*) rolling; wild; (*sbarrato*) wide open; staring: *con gli occhi stralunati*, with staring eyes 2. (*di viso*) troubled; (*di persona*) upset: *era tutto —*, he was very upset.

stramaledíre, *v.t.* to curse heartily.

stramatúro, *ag*. overripe.

stramàre, *v.t.* to forage: *— i buoi*, to forage the oxen.

stramazzàre, *v.t.* to knock down ‖ *v.i.* to fall heavily; to collapse: *il cavallo stramazzò al suolo*, the horse fell heavily to the ground.

stramazzàta, *s.f.* heavy fall.

stramàzzo, *s.m.* straw mattress.

stramazzóne, *s.m.* 1. (*lo stramazzare*) falling heavily, collapsing 2. (*caduta*) heavy fall.

strambaménte, *av*. oddly, queerly, strangely.

strambería, *s.f.* oddity, eccentricity, queerness.

stràmbo, *ag*. 1. (*stravagante*) odd, eccentric, queer, strange, funny: *idee strambe*, eccentric (*o* funny *o* strange) ideas; *una persona stramba*, an odd (*o* eccentric *o* queer) person 2. (*storto*) (*di occhi*) squinting; (*di gambe*) bandy; crooked.

strambòtto, *s.m.* (*poes.*) "strambotto" (rustic love-song).

stràme, *s.m.* 1. (*per foraggio*) fodder 2. (*per lettiera*) litter, straw.

stramònio, *s.m.* (*bot. farm.*) stramonium.

strampalàto, *ag*. odd, queer, strange, eccentric:

condotta strampalata, odd (*o* eccentric) behaviour; *idee strampalate*, queer (*o* odd *o* strange) ideas ‖ *s.m.* strange person, odd person, eccentric.

stranaménte, *av*. strangely, oddly, queerly.

stranézza, *s.f.* 1. strangeness, oddity, queerness 2. (*atto strano, parola strana*) oddity, eccentricity.

strangolaménto, *s.m.* strangling; choking.

strangolàre, *v.t.* to strangle, to throttle; to choke: *questa cravatta mi strangola*, this tie is choking me.

strangolatóre, *s.m.* strangler.

stranguglióne, *s.m.* 1. (*patol.*) tonsil(l)itis 2. (*vet.*) strangles.

strangúria, stranguría, *s.f.* (*patol.*) strangury.

straniàre, *v.t.* to alienate, to estrange: *il suo comportamento lo ha straniato dalla famiglia*, his behaviour has estranged him from his family ‖ **straniàrsi**, *v.r.* to drift apart: *si strania da tutti*, he is drifting apart from everybody.

stranièro, *ag*. foreign: *lingua straniera*, foreign language ‖ *s.m.* foreigner: *ho conosciuto molti stranieri l'estate scorsa*, I met a lot of foreigners last summer.

stràno, *ag*. strange, odd, queer, funny; eccentric: *uno — caso*, a strange (*o* an odd *o* a queer *o* a funny) case; *uno — modo di camminare*, a queer (*o* a strange *o* an odd *o* a funny) way of walking; *che — !*, how odd!; *che strana idea!*, what a funny idea!; *che — tipo!*, what an odd kind of person!; *le sue strane abitudini*, his queer (*o* strange) habits.

straordinariaménte, *av*. 1. extraordinarily 2. (*insolitamente*) unusually, uncommonly 3. (*grandemente*) enormously, immensely.

straordinarietà, *s.f.* extraordinariness.

straordinàrio, *ag*. 1. extraordinary ‖ *lavoro —*, overtime (work) 2. (*insolito*) unusual, uncommon 3. (*enorme*) enormous, immense.

strapagàre, *v.t.* to overpay.

straparlàre, *v.i.* 1. (*dire sciocchezze*) to talk nonsense, to talk rubbish 2. (*vaneggiare*) to rave, to ramble 3. (*sparlare*) to talk slander; to gossip.

strapazzaménto, *s.m.* 1. ill-treatment 2. (*l'affaticarsi troppo*) overworking.

strapazzàre, *v.t.* 1. to ill-treat, to ill-use, to maltreat; (*sgridare*) to scold: *lo sta sempre strapazzando, povero bambino*, she is always scolding him, poor little fellow ‖ *— un lavoro*, to bungle (*o* to botch) a piece of work ‖ *— un pezzo di musica*, to mangle a piece of music ‖ *— uno scrittore*, to misinterpret a writer 2. (*trattare senza cura*) to ill-use, to use carelessly: *— i vestiti*, to take no care of one's clothes 3. (*far lavorare troppo*) to overwork: *— un cavallo*, to overwork a horse ‖ **strapazzàrsi**, *v.r.* to overwork oneself; to tire oneself out: *non strapazzarti*, don't overwork yourself (*o* don't overdo it).

strapazzàta, *s.f.* 1. scolding, telling-off: *gli diedi una bella —*, I gave him a good scolding (*o* a good telling-off) 2. (*fatica eccessiva*) overwork, over-exertion.

strapazzàto, *ag*. 1. (*maltrattato*) ill-treated, ill-used, maltreated 2. (*affaticato*) overworked 3. *uova strapazzate*, (*cuc.*) scrambled eggs.

strapàzzo, *s.m.* overwork, over-exertion: *non dovrebbe fare questi strapazzi*, he shouldn't over-exert himself like that; *sarebbe uno — per lui camminare per due miglia*, it would be too much for him walking two miles ‖ *abiti da —*, working-clothes ‖ *scrittore da —*, hack(-writer).

strapazzóso, *ag*. fatiguing, tiring.

strapèrdere, *v.i.* to lose heavily.

strapiantàre, *v.t.* to transplant.

strapièno, *ag*. full up, chock-full; (*traboccante*) overflowing.

strapiombàre, *v.i.* 1. to be out of the perpendicular; to lean: *il muro strapiomba a sinistra*, the wall leans to the left 2. (*scendere in perpendicolo*) to fall perpendicularly: *il precipizio strapiombava sul mare*, the precipice fell perpendicularly to the sea.

strapiómbo, *s.m.* **1.** projection **2.** (*di roccia*) precipice || *a* —, sheer (*o* vertically *o* perpendicularly): *la scogliera cade a* — *nel mare,* the cliff falls sheer to the sea.

strapotènte, *ag.* very powerful.

strapotènza, *s.f.* great power.

strappaménto, *s.m.* **1.** tearing **2.** pulling; ripping; wrenching; snatching.

strappàre, *v.t.* **1.** (*stracciare*) to tear: *ho strappato il vestito,* I have torn my dress; — *un pezzo di carta,* to tear a piece of paper **2.** (*togliere*) to pull up; to pull out; to pull away; (*con forza*) to tear up (anche *fig.*); to rip (anche *fig.*); to wrench (anche *fig.*); (*velocemente, di colpo*) to snatch (anche *fig.*); *fig.* to wring: *chi ha strappato la copertina di questo libro?,* who has pulled away (*o* torn off) the cover of this book?; *fu strappato alla morte da una nuova medicina,* he was snatched from death by a new medicine; *gli strappai una confessione, il segreto prima che morisse,* I wrung a confession, the secret from him just before he died; *gli strappai il libro di mano,* I snatched the book from (*o* out of) his hands; *la guerra lo strappò dagli studi,* the war snatched him from his studies; *le strapparono la figlia dalle braccia,* they tore her daughter from her arms; *mi strappò la chiave di mano,* he snatched the key from me (*o* out of my hands); *perchè hai strappato quel fiore? avresti dovuto tagliarlo,* why have you pulled that flower up? you should have cut it; *queste cose mi strappano il cuore,* these things break my heart; *strappò alcune pagine dal libro,* he tore a few pages out of the book (*o* he ripped a few pages out of the book); *la sua storia mi strappò le lacrime,* his story wrung tears from me (*o* moved me to tears); — *le cattive erbe,* to pull up the weeds: — *le cattive erbe da un campo,* to weed a field; — *un dente,* to pull out a tooth; — *un favore a qlcu.,* to wring a favour from (*o* out of) s.o.; — *un palo dal terreno,* to wrench a pole out of the ground; — *le penne a un uccello,* to pluck a bird; — *una pianta,* to pull up (*o* to tear up *o* to uproot) a plant || — *il pane, la vita,* to scrape a living || *farsi* — *un dente,* to have a tooth (pulled) out || **strappàrsi,** *v.r.* **1.** to tear, to get torn: *questa copertina si strapperà presto,* this cover will soon get torn; *questa stoffa si strappa facilmente,* this material tears easily || *a quelle parole mi si strappò il cuore,* those words broke my heart || — *i capelli,* to tear (*o* to rend) one's hair **2.** (*allontanarsi*) to tear oneself away: *non riesce a* — *dalla sua famiglia,* he cannot tear himself away from his family.

strappàta, *s.f.* **1.** pull, tug; snatch: *diede una* — *al campanello,* he gave the bell a pull (*o* tug) **2.** (*tortura*) strappado.

stràppo, *s.m.* **1.** tear, rent: (*si*) *fece uno* — *nei pantaloni,* he tore his trousers; *il suo soprabito era pieno di strappi,* his overcoat was full of tears **2.** (*strappata*) pull, tug; snatch; (*strattone*) jerk: *il cane con uno* — *ruppe la catena,* with a jerk the dog broke his chain; *diede uno* — *e il chiodo si staccò,* he gave a pull and the nail came away || *a strappi,* in jerks **3.** (*infrazione*) breach, infraction, infringement: — *alla legge,* infringement of the law; *uno* — *alle regole,* a breach of the rules **4.** (*muscolare*) sprain.

strapuntìno, *s.m.* gangway-seat.

strapúnto, *s.m.* quilt.

strarícco, *ag.* immensely rich.

straripaménto, *s.m.* overflow, overflowing.

straripàre, *v.i.* to overflow.

Strasbúrgo, *no.pr.f.* (*geog.*) Strasbourg.

strascicaménto, *s.m.* trailing, dragging; (*di piedi*) shuffling; (*di parole*) drawling.

strascicàre, *v.t.* to trail, to drag; (*i piedi*) to shuffle; (*le parole*) to drawl: *strascicava un cagnolino di legno con una corda,* he was trailing a little wooden dog on a string; *strascicava per terra un sacco di carbone,* he was dragging a sack of coal along the ground; *strascicava suo figlio per la mano,* he was dragging his

son by the hand || — *le gambe,* (*per debolezza, malattia*) to drag one's feet || — *un lavoro,* to do a job slowly and unwillingly || — *le parole,* to drawl (one's words) || *v.i.,* **strascicàrsi,** *v.r.* to drag oneself (along); to shuffle (along): *poteva* — *a malapena,* he could hardly drag himself along.

strascichío, *s.m.* trailing, dragging; (*di piedi*) shuffling; (*di parole*) drawling.

stràscico, *s.m.* **1.** (*di veste*) train: *lo* — *del suo vestito era più di tre metri,* the train of her dress was over three metres long **2.** (*residuo; sequela*) after-effect, sequel; train: *gli strascichi di una guerra, di malattie, di debiti, di guai,* the after-effects of a war, of illness, of debts, of troubles; *una guerra con una terribile pestilenza come* —, a war with a terrible pestilence in its train **3.** (*atto dello strascicare*) trailing, dragging; (*di parlata*) drawling: *parlare con lo* —, to speak with a drawl **4.** (*di lumaca*) trail **5.** (*rete per pesca*) trawl, drag-net **6.** (*caccia alla volpe*) drag-hunt.

strascicóni, a, *l.av.* dragging one's feet: *camminava a* —, he dragged his feet as he walked.

strascinaménto, *s.m.* trailing, dragging.

strascinàre, *V.* trascinàre.

stràscino[1], *s.m.* **1.** (*mar.*) drag-net, trail-net **2.** (*per uccelli*) draw-net, clap-net **3.** (*agr.*) bush-harrow, brush-harrow.

strascíno[2], *s.m.* (*macellaio*) butcher.

strasecolàre, *v.i.* to be amazed.

strass, *s.m.* strass.

stratagèmma, *s.m.* stratagem, trick; (*fam.*) dodge: *escogitare uno* —, to devise a stratagem; *ottenere ql.co. con uno* —, to obtain sthg. by trickery (*o* by a trick); *ricorrere ad uno* —, to have recourse to a stratagem.

stratèga, *s.c.* strategist.

strategìa, *s.f.* strategy, strategics.

strategicaménte, *av.* strategically.

stratègico, *ag.* strategic(al): *linea, ritirata strategica,* strategic line, retreat; *punto* —, strategic point.

stratègo, *s.m.* strategist.

stratificàre, *v.t.* to stratify || *v.i.,* **stratificàrsi,** *v.r.* to become stratified.

stratificàto, *ag.* stratified.

stratificazióne, *s.f.* **1.** (*geol.*) stratification, bedding **2.** (*di metalli*) stratification.

stratifórme, *ag.* (*geol.*) stratiform.

stratigrafìa, *s.f.* (*geol.*) stratigraphy.

stràto, *s.m.* **1.** layer, stratum (*pl.* strata); (*di rivestimento*) coat: *uno* — *bituminoso di copertura,* bitumen sheeting; — *di ghiaccio,* sheet of ice; — *di mattoni,* a layer of bricks; — *di polvere,* layer of dust; — *di vernice,* coat of paint; — *elettronico,* (*fis. atomica*) shell; — *filtrante,* (*ind. edil.*) filter bed; — *finale,* (*di vernice*) finishing coat; — *laminare,* laminar layer; — *limite,* (*mec.*) boundary layer; — *vorticoso,* vortex sheet; *a strati,* in layers: *una torta a strati,* a layer-cake || *gli strati della società,* the social strata (*o* the classes of society) **2.** (*geol.*) stratum (*pl.* strata): *affioramento superficiale di uno* —, outcrop **3.** (*meteorologia*) stratus (*pl.* strati) **4.** (*foto.*) layer: — *sensibile,* sensitive surface (*o* layer) **5.** (*di miniera*) vein, seam.

Stratóne, *no.pr.m.* (*st. fil.*) Strato.

stratosfèra, *s.f.* stratosphere.

stratosfèrico, *ag.* stratospheric.

stràtta, *s.f.* pull, jerk || *a stratte,* by fits and starts.

strattagèmma, *V.* stratagèmma.

strattóne, *s.m.* pull, wrench, jerk: *con un improvviso* — *il prigioniero si liberò dalla stretta delle guardie,* with a sudden jerk (*o* wrench) the prisoner got free of the guards' grasp; *dare uno* — *a ql.co., a qlcu.,* to give sthg. s.o. a pull || *a strattoni,* (*a strappi*) jerkily; (*a intervalli*) by fits and starts: *la carrozza procedeva a strattoni,* the coach was jerking along.

stravagànte, *ag.* odd, queer, strange: *comportamento* —, strange behaviour; *tempo* —, changeable weather || *s.m.* odd fellow, strange fellow; character.

stravaganteménte, *av.* oddly, queerly, strangely.

stravagànza, *s.f.* **1.** (*bizzarria*) oddness, queerness, strangeness, eccentricity **2.** (*azione bizzarra*) oddity, eccentricity: *non posso giustificare tutte le sue stravaganze,* I cannot account for all her eccentricities.

stravècchio, *ag.* very old.

stravedére, *v.i.* to see badly, to see wrongly ‖ — *per qlcu.,* to be crazy about s.o. (*o* to admire s.o. blindly).

stravíncere, *v.t.* to crush: *egli stravinse tutti i suoi avversari,* he crushed all his opponents ‖ *v.i.* to win all along the line; (*abusare della vittoria*) to abuse one's victory.

straviziàre, *v.i.* to be intemperate; (*bere troppo*) to drink to excess, to overdrink; (*mangiare troppo*) to eat to excess, to overeat.

stravízio, *s.m.* excess (in drinking and eating), intemperance: *questa è la conseguenza dei suoi stravizi,* this is the consequence of his excesses; *fare stravizi nel mangiare, nel bere,* to overeat, to overdrink.

stravòlgere, *v.t.* **1.** (*storcere*) to twist: *stravolse gli occhi,* he rolled his eyes **2.** (*volgere con violenza*) to rock, to shake: *il vento stravolgeva le navi,* the wind rocked the ships **3.** (*torcere di significato*) to twist, to wrench, to distort: — *i fatti,* to twist (*o* to wrench *o* to distort) facts.

stravolgiménto, *s.m.* **1.** (*lo storcere*) twisting: — *degli occhi,* rolling of the eyes **2.** (*il volgere con violenza*) rocking, shaking **3.** (*il torcere di significato*) twisting, wrenching, distorting.

stravòlto, *ag.* **1.** (*storto, contorto*) twisted: *il suo viso era* — *dal dolore,* his face was twisted with pain ‖ *con gli occhi stravolti,* with rolling eyes (*o* with one's eyes popping out of one's head) **2.** (*turbato*) upset, agitated, troubled: *una mente stravolta,* an upset (*o* deranged) mind; *era stravolta per le notizie che aveva ricevuto,* she was upset at the news she had received **3.** (*torto di significato*) twisted, wrenched, distorted: *una verità stravolta,* a twisted truth.

straziànte, *ag.* tormenting (anche *fig.*), torturing (anche *fig.*); *fig.* heart-rending: *un dolore* —, a torturing pain; (*morale*) a heart-rending grief; *un grido* —, a heart-rending cry.

straziàre, *v.t.* to tear (apart), to lacerate, to torture, to torment: *il nostro paese fu straziato dalla guerra,* our country was torn apart by the war; *queste canzoni mi straziano gli orecchi,* these songs are torture to my ears; *questo dolore mi strazia il cuore,* this grief tears my heart; *le sue suppliche straziano il cuore,* his entreaties are heart-rending; *il suo corpo fu straziato da una bomba,* his body was torn to pieces (*o* lacerated) by a bomb; — *un lavoro,* to bungle a piece of work; — *un pezzo di musica, una poesia,* to mangle a piece of music, a poem; — *il proprio patrimonio,* to squander one's patrimony.

straziàto, *ag.* torn, tormented: — *dai rimorsi,* tormented by remorse; *una famiglia straziata dall'odio,* a family torn by hatred.

stràzio, *s.m.* torment, torture: *è uno* — *il vederlo in quelle condizioni,* it is a torture to see him in those conditions; *i corvi fecero* — *del suo corpo,* the crows tore his body to pieces; *fecero* — *di tutto ciò che trovarono,* they played havoc with all they found; *fare* — *del proprio patrimonio,* to play havoc with one's patrimony.

strebbiàccio, *s.m.* (*rar.*) uncultivated land.

strebbiàre, *v.t.* to trample down.

strecciàre, *v.t.* to unplait.

stréga, *s.f.* **1.** witch; sorceress: *bruciare una* —, to burn a witch **2.** (*donna brutta, maligna*) witch, hag: *sua moglie è una* —, his wife is a hag.

stregaménto, *s.m.* bewitchment.

stregàre, *v.t.* to bewitch.

stregàto, *ag.* bewitched.

stregheria, *s.f.* (*rar.*) witchcraft; sorcery.

stregonàre, *v.t.* (*rar.*) to bewitch.

stregóne, *s.m.* wizard; sorcerer.

stregoneria, *s.f.* witchcraft; sorcery.

strégua, *s.f.* standard, rate: *alla tua* —, according to your standard; *a questa* —, at this rate ‖ *alla stessa* —, in the same way.

strelízzo, *s.m.* (*st. mil.*) strelitz.

stremàre, *v.t.* to exhaust, to tire out: *questo lavoro mi ha stremato le forze,* this work has exhausted me (*o* tired me out).

stremàto, *ag.* exhausted, tired out: *mi sentivo* — I felt exhausted.

stremenzire, *V.* **striminzire.**

stremíre, *v.t.* to frighten.

strèmo, *ag.* extreme; utmost: *strema miseria,* extreme distress ‖ *s.m.* extreme; utmost.

strènna, *s.f.* gift, present: — *di Natale,* Christmas present (*o* gift).

strenuaménte, *av.* bravely, valiantly, courageously.

strenuità, *s.f.* (*letter.*) bravery, valour, courage.

strènuo, *ag.* brave, valiant, courageous.

strepènte, *ag.* (*poet.*) clamorous.

strèpere, (*poet.*) per **strepitàre.**

strepitàre, *v.i.* **1.** to make a din, to make an uproar **2.** (*urlare*) to rave: *devo* — *per farmi intendere,* I have to shout to make myself understood; *smetti di* — *perchè non ti danno ugualmente ascolto,* stop raving, because they will not listen to you anyhow.

strepitío, *s.m.* din, uproar.

strèpito, *s.m.* **1.** din, uproar: *lo* — *cessò appena entrai nella stanza,* the din stopped as soon as I entered the room; *nella classe c'era un tale* — *che non si poteva quasi udire la voce dell'insegnante,* in the class there was such a din (*o* uproar) that the teacher's voice could hardly be heard ‖ *quel film ha fatto* —, that film was a hit **2.** (*clamore*) clamour: *lo* — *della folla,* the clamour of the crowd.

strepitosaménte, *av.* **1.** noisily; uproariously **2.** (*clamorosamente*) clamorously, boisterously.

strepitóso, *ag.* **1.** noisy; uproarious: *un riso* —, an uproarious laughter (*o* a roar of laughter); *ci furono applausi strepitosi,* there was a roar of applause **2.** (*clamoroso*) clamorous, boisterous: *un successo* —, a striking success.

streptocòcco, *s.m.* (*biol.*) streptococcus (*pl.* streptococci).

streptomicina, *s.f.* (*farm.*) streptomycin.

strétta, *s.f.* **1.** grasp, hold, grip, clasp: *la sua* — *quasi mi soffocava,* his hold was almost choking me; *allentare la* —, to release one's hold (*o* grasp) ‖ — *di mano,* handshake: *dare una* — *di mano a qlcu.,* to shake hands with s.o. ‖ *provare una* — *al cuore,* to feel a pang in one's heart **2.** (*calca*) press: *fu preso nella* — *della folla,* he was caught in the press **3.** (*gola*) gorge, pass ‖ *essere alle strette,* to be in dire straits: *era alle strette,* he was in dire straits (*o* he was between the devil and the deep blue sea *o* the knife was at his throat); *mettere alle strette,* to put s.o. with his back against the wall **4.** (*mus.*) stretta, stretto.

strettaménte, *av.* **1.** tight(ly); fast: *lo teneva* —, he held him fast; *legare qlco.* —, to bind sthg. tight-(ly) **2.** (*rigorosamente*) strictly: — *parlando,* strictly speaking; *osservare le regole* —, to observe the rules strictly.

strettézza, *s.f.* **1.** narrowness; tightness: — *di mente,* *fig.* narrow-mindedness **2.** (*povertà, ristrettezza*) straitened circumstances, financial difficulties: *essere in strettezze,* to be hard up **3.** (*difficoltà*) distress, hardship **4.** (*di amicizia*) closeness.

strettíre, *v.t.* to take in: — *una veste,* to take in a dress.

strétto, *ag.* **1.** narrow: *uno* — *passaggio, vicolo, corridoio,* a narrow passage, alley, corridor; — *di spalle,* (*di persona*) narrow in the shoulders; *fessura stretta,* narrow fissure; *foro* —, small hole; *spalle strette,* narrow shoulders; *strada stretta,* narrow road ‖ *entro stretti* *limiti*, within narrow limits **2.** (*di abiti, ecc.*) narrow; (*piccolo*) tight: *scarpe strette*, tight shoes; *scarpe strette in punta*, shoes narrow at the toe(s) (*o* pointed shoes); *quest'anno vanno di moda i pantaloni stretti*, this year narrow trousers are fashionable; *questa giacca è un po' stretta di spalle*, this jacket is a bit tight in (*o* across) the shoulders; *queste maniche sono così strette che non posso alzare le braccia*, these sleeves are so tight that I can't raise my arms ‖ *devo essere ingrassata, quest'abito mi va un po' — quest'anno*, I must have put on weight, this dress is a bit tight on me this year ‖ *essere di manica stretta*, to be very strict **3.** (*serrato*) tight, fast; (*di denti, ecc.*) clenched: *un nodo —*, a tight knot; *pugni stretti*, clenched fists; *chiudilo —*, close it tight; *col pugnale — in pugno, si avvicinò all'avversario*, he advanced on his adversary with a knife gripped in his hand; *legalo — al palo*, make it fast to the pole; *portarono un prigioniero — in catene*, they brought in a prisoner bound with chains; *questo pacchetto è stato legato troppo —*, this package has been wrapped too tight; *teneva — il bambino per la mano*, he held the child fast by the hand ‖ *a denti stretti*, with clenched teeth ‖ *avere il cuore —*, to be sad at heart (*o* to have a heavy heart) ‖ *essere — in una morsa*, *fig.* to be hemmed in on all sides ‖ *tenere qlcu. — in pugno*, to hold (*o* to have) s.o. in the palm of one's hand **4.** (*rigoroso*) strict, close: *stretta disciplina, osservanza*, strict discipline, observance; *stretta sorveglianza*, close supervision; *la stretta verità*, the strict truth; *digiuno —*, strict fast; *obbligo —*, firm obligation; *regola stretta*, strict rule ‖ *— necessario*, that which is strictly necessary; *generi di stretta necessità*, essential goods **5.** (*intimo*) close: *amici, parenti stretti*, close friends, relatives; *amicizia, parentela stretta*, close friendship, relationship; *essere in stretti rapporti con qlcu.*, to be in close relations with s.o. **6.** (*preciso*) exact, precise: *lo — significato di questa frase*, the exact (*o* precise) meaning of this sentence; *me ne renderai — conto*, you will account for it exactly **7.** (*chiuso*) close: *pronunzia, vocale stretta*, close pronunciation, vowel **8.** (*pigiato*) packed: *eravamo molto stretti nell'automobile*, we were quite packed in the car ‖ *s.m.* (*geog.*) strait: *lo — di Gibilterra*, the Straits of Gibraltar; *lo — di Magellano*, the Magellan Straits; *lo — di Messina è largo tre chilometri*, the Straits of Messina are three kilometres wide.

strettóia, *s.f.* **1.** (*benda*) bandage **2.** (*circostanza difficile*) difficulty, difficult situation: *ci troviamo in una —*, we are in difficulties.

strettóio, *s.m.* (*mec.*) press.

stría, *s.f.* **1.** stripe, streak **2.** (*arch.*) stria (*pl.* striae).

striàre, *v.t.* to streak, to stripe, to striate.

striàto, *ag.* streaked, striped, striated: *— di nero*, striped with black.

striatúra, *s.f.* streaking, striping, striation.

strienína, *s.f.* (*farm.*) strychnin(e).

stridènte, *ag.* **1.** shrill, sharp, strident; jarring: *lo — rumore delle cicale*, the strident noise of the cicadas; *il rumore — dei freni*, the screeching of the brakes; *una voce —*, a shrill (*o* sharp) voice **2.** (*discordante*) jarring, clashing; striking: *uno — contrasto*, a striking contrast; *colori stridenti*, clashing colours; *una nota —*, a jarring note.

strídere, *v.i.* **1.** to creak, to screech, to jar; (*di insetti*) to chirp, to chirr: *le cicale, i grilli stridono*, cicadas, crickets chirr; *le civette stridono*, owls screech; *quel cancello stride perchè ha bisogno di essere oliato*, that gate creaks because it needs oiling; *questo freno stride ogni volta che lo adopero*, this brake screeches (*o* jars) every time I use it **2.** (*contrastare, urtare*) to jar, to clash: *colori che stridono*, jarring (*o* clashing) colours.

stridío, *s.m.* creaking, screeching, jarring; chirping, chirring.

stridíre, (*letter.*) per **strídere**.

strído, *s.m.* scream, shriek; (*di animali*) screech, squeak; (*di insetti*) chirp, chirr: *acute strida*, shrill shrieks; *diede uno —*, he gave a scream; *le sue strida si alzavano al cielo*, his screams rose to the sky.

stridóre, *s.m.* creaking, screeching, jarring; (*di insetti*) chirping, chirring: *lo — dei freni*, the screeching of the brakes; *lo — di una porta, sega*, the creaking of a door, saw ‖ *lo — dei denti*, the gnashing of teeth.

stridulàre, *v.i.* to chirp.

stridulazióne, *s.f.* chirping.

strídulo, *ag.* shrill, piercing: *suono —*, shrill sound; *voce stridula*, shrill voice; *nota stridula*, jarring note.

strigàre, *v.t.* to unravel, to disentangle (*anche fig.*) ‖ **strigàrsi**, *v.r.* to get out of trouble.

stríge, *s.f.* (*ornit.*) screech-owl.

strígile, *s.m.* (*archeol.*) strigil.

stríglia, *s.f.* curry-comb.

strigliàre, *v.t.* **1.** to curry: *— un cavallo*, to curry a horse **2.** (*criticare aspramente*) to rebuke, to scold, to reprimand.

strigliàta, *s.f.* **1.** currying **2.** (*rimprovero*) scolding, rebuke, lecture: *gli diedi una bella —*, I gave him a good scolding (*o* lecture).

strigliatóre, *s.m.* groom.

strillàre, *v.i.* to scream, to shriek: *il bambino strilla da due ore*, the baby has been screaming for two hours ‖ *v.t.* (*rar.*) to scream, to shout: *strillava ' aiuto! '*, she was screaming for help.

strillo, *s.m.* scream, shriek, cry: *mandare uno —*, to give a scream (*o* shriek) ‖ *quanti strilli al suo ritorno!*, what a to-do there was when he came back!.

strillóne, *s.m.* newspaper boy; news-boy; news-man.

striminzire, *v.t.* **1.** (*rar.*) (*rendere stretto*) to tighten **2.** (*impedire la crescita di*) to stunt ‖ **striminzírsi**, *v.r.* (*stringersi*) to squeeze oneself: *per quanto si striminzisca nel busto, si vede che è grassa*, in spite of her squeezing herself into a corset, you can see she is fat.

striminzíto, *ag.* **1.** stunted, cramped: *era un povero albero —*, it was a poor stunted tree **2.** (*di persona*) thin, lean, shrunken: *aveva un viso così — che faceva pena*, his thin face was a pitiful sight ‖ *se ne stava lì tutto — per il freddo*, he was standing there shrinking with cold.

strimpellaménto, *s.m.* strumming, thrumming: *basta con questo —*, I've had enough of your strumming.

strimpellàre, *v.t.* to strum, to thrum, to scrape: *strimpella il pianoforte dalla mattina alla sera*, he strums the piano from morning to night; *strimpellava la chitarra per ore e ore senza preoccuparsi per i suoi vicini di casa*, he strummed (on) the guitar for hours without the least consideration for his neighbours; *— il violino*, to scrape (on) the violin.

strimpellàta, *s.f.* strumming, thrumming.

strimpellatóre, *s.m.*, **strimpellatríce**, *s.f.* strummer, thrummer.

strimpellatúra, *s.f.* strumming, thrumming.

strimpellío, *s.m.* strumming, thrumming.

strimpèllo, *s.m.* strumming, thrumming.

strimpellóne, *ag.* strumming, thrumming ‖ *s.m.*, **strimpellóna**, *s.f.* strummer, thrummer.

strinàre, *v.t.* to singe: *— i capelli*, to singe hair.

strinàto, *ag.* singed: *un pollo strinato*, a singed chicken ‖ *è secco —*, *fig.* he is as thin as a rake ‖ *s.m.* singeing: *puzzo di —*, smell of singeing.

strinatúra, *s.f.* singeing, singe.

strínga, *s.f.* lace: *comperami un paio di stringhe nere, per favore*, will you buy me a pair of black laces, please?; *devo cambiare le stringhe di questo busto*, I must change the laces of this corset.

stringàio, *s.m.* **1.** (*chi fa stringhe*) lace-manufacturer, lace-maker **2.** (*chi vende stringhe*) lace seller.

stringàre, *v.t.* **1.** to lace tightly, to fasten tightly **2.** (*rendere conciso*) to condense.

stringataménte, *av.* concisely, condensedly: *scrive davvero molto* —, he writes in a very concise manner indeed.

stringàto, *ag.* 1. laced, fastened 2. (*attillato*) close-fitting, tight 3. (*di stile*) concise, condensed, terse.

stringènte, *ag.* 1. urgent, pressing: *affari stringenti,* urgent business; *bisogni stringenti,* pressing needs 2. (*convincente*) cogent, persuasive: *è il solo argomento* —, it is the only persuasive argument.

stríngere, *v.t.* 1. (*serrare*) to press, to squeeze: *mi strinse la mano per mostrarmi la sua gratitudine,* he pressed my hand in gratitude; *non* — *quel pulcino a quel modo,* don't squeeze that chick like that; — *le labbra,* to press one's lips together; — *la mano a qlcu.,* to shake hands with s.o.; — *i pugni,* to clench one's fists ǁ *stringi, stringi,* in conclusion ǁ *questa vista mi stringe il cuore,* this sight wrings my heart ǁ *queste scarpe mi stringono in punta,* these shoes are tight at the toe; *questo vestito mi stringe in vita,* this dress is too tight for me at the waist ǁ — *d'assedio,* to besiege ǁ — *i denti,* to grind one's teeth ǁ *chi troppo abbraccia, nulla stringe,* prov. grasp all, lose all 2. (*restringere*) to tighten: *devo far* — *questo vecchio vestito,* I must have this old dress taken in; — *la cinghia,* to tighten one's belt (anche *fig.*); — *i freni,* to brake; *fig.* to tighten the reins; — *un nodo,* to tighten a knot 3. (*abbracciare*) to embrace, to hug, to clasp: *strinse suo figlio tra le braccia,* she clasped her son in her arms 4. (*impugnare*) to clasp, to grasp; to clutch; to grip: — *ql.co. in mano,* to grasp (*o* to grip) sthg. in one's hand; — *la spada,* to grasp the sword 5. (*concludere*) to make: — *un'alleanza,* to make (*o* to form) an alliance; — *amicizia con qlcu.,* to make friends with s.o.; — *un contratto, trattato,* to make a contract, a treaty 6. (*indurre*) to persuade; (*costringere*) to compel; (*urgere*) to press: *lo strinsi a chiederti scusa,* I persuaded him to apologize to you; *la miseria mi strinse a chiedergli del denaro,* need compelled me to ask him for money ǁ *il tempo stringe,* time presses (*o* time is running short) 7. (*avvitare*) to tighten, to screw tight: — *una vite,* to tighten a screw 8. (*mus.*) (*accelerare*) to quicken: — *il passo,* (*nel ballo*) to quicken the step; — *i tempi,* to quicken the tempo; *fig.* to conclude ǁ *v.i.* to be tight: *questo soprabito stringe,* this overcoat is tight ǁ **stríngersi,** *v.r.* 1. to press (against s.o., sthg.): *il bambino si stringeva alla madre,* the child was pressing against his mother ǁ — *nelle spalle,* to shrug one's shoulders ǁ — *nelle spese,* to reduce (*o* to cut) expenses 2. (*far spazio*) to squeeze oneself, to squeeze up: *potete stringervi un poco ancora?,* could you squeeze up a little more?

stringiménto, *s.m.* 1. pressing, squeezing ǁ *uno* — *al cuore,* a pang at one's heart 2. (*il legare, l'avvitare*) tightening 3. (*l'impugnare*) clasp, grasp 4. (*conclusione*) conclusion.

stríscia, *s.f.* 1. strip: *una* — *di carta, pelle, stoffa, terra,* a strip of paper, leather, cloth, land 2. (*riga*) stripe: *le strisce della zebra,* the stripes of a zebra; *una stoffa a strisce rosse e nere,* a cloth with red and black stripes ǁ *a strisce,* striped 3. (*scia*) streak, trail: *una* — *di luce,* a streak of light; *una* — *di lumaca,* the trail of a snail; *una* — *di sangue,* a trail of blood 4. (*coramella*) razor-strop.

strisciaménto, *s.m.* 1. creeping, crawling 2. (*il trascinare*) dragging 3. (*scivolando*) grazing, skimming 4. *fig.* (*adulazione*) fawning, grovelling.

strisciànte, *ag.* 1. crawling, creeping 2. *fig.* (*servile*) fawning, obsequious: *modi striscianti,* obsequious (*o* fawning) manners.

strisciàre, *v.t.* 1. to drag; to shuffle: *non* — *questa sedia perchè lascia un segno sul pavimento,* don't drag this chair because it leaves a mark on the floor; — *i piedi,* to shuffle one's feet ǁ — *una riverenza,* to bow low 2. (*radere*) to graze; to skim: *la palla strisciò il muro,* the ball grazed the wall; *la rondine strisciò*

l'acqua, the swallow skimmed the water 3. *fig.* (*adulare*) to fawn upon (s.o.); to grovel before (s.o.): — *i ricchi,* to fawn on the rich ǁ *v.i.* 1. to creep, to crawl: *egli strisciò lungo la parete,* he crept along the wall; *i serpenti strisciano per terra,* snakes crawl on the ground; — *ventre a terra,* to creep along the ground 2. (*scivolare*) to glide, to slide; to slip 3. *fig.* (*umiliarsi*) to grovel: *per far soldi quell'uomo strisce-rebbe,* that man would grovel to make money ǁ **strisciàrsi,** *v.r.* 1. to creep, to crawl: *si strisciò fino alla porta,* he crawled to the door 2. (*sfregarsi*) to rub oneself: *il gatto si strisciò contro la gamba del tavolo,* the cat rubbed itself against the leg of the table.

strisciàta, strisciatúra, *s.f.* 1. dragging; creeping, crawling 2. (*sfregatura*) rub, rubbing.

stríscio, *s.m.* graze: *di* —, grazingly: *il sasso lo colpì di* —, the stone just grazed him.

striscióne, *s.m.* 1. large stripe; large band: — *d'arrivo,* (*traguardo*) finishing-line 2. *fig.* (*adulatore*) flatterer; coaxer.

striscióni, a, *l.av.* draggingly, shufflingly: *camminare a* —, to shuffle (*o* to drag oneself) along.

stritolàbile, *ag.* that can be crushed.

stritolaménto, *s.m.* crushing, smashing (anche *fig.*).

stritolàre, *v.t.* to crush, to smash (anche *fig.*): *stritolò gli avversari con le sue argomentazioni,* he crushed his opponents with his arguments; *egli fu stritolato dalla folla,* he was crushed by the crowd; *il treno gli stritolò una gamba,* the train crushed his leg; — *il nemico,* to smash the enemy ǁ *vorrei essere là per poterlo* —, I should like to be there to make mincemeat of him ǁ **stritolàrsi,** *v.r.* to crush, to smash.

stritolàto, *ag.* crushed, smashed.

stritolatóre, *ag.* crushing, smashing ǁ *s.m.,* **stritolatríce,** *s.f.* crusher, smasher.

stritolatúra, *s.f.* crushing.

strizzàre, *v.t.* 1. to squeeze, to squash: — *un limone,* to squeeze a lemon ǁ — *l'occhio,* to wink (at s.o.) 2. (*torcere*) to wring: — *i panni,* to wring clothes.

strizzàta, *s.f.* 1. squeeze ǁ — *d'occhio,* wink: *dare una strizzatina d'occhio a qlcu.,* to wink at s.o. 2. (*il torcere*) wring: *dare una* — *a un lenzuolo bagnato,* to give a wring to a wet sheet.

strizzóne, *s.m.* 1. squeeze 2. (*dolore acuto*) sharp pain, stab of pain.

stròbilo, *s.m.* 1. (*bot.*) strobile, strobilus (*pl.* strobili) 2. (*zool.*) strobile, strobila (*pl.* strobilae).

stroboscòpico, *ag.* (*scient.*) stroboscopic.

stroboscòpio, *s.m.* (*scient.*) stroboscope.

stròfa, *s.f.* 1. (*poes.*) stanza, strophe 2. (*ret. greca*) (*prima parte del periodo lirico*) strophe.

strofantína, *s.f.* (*farm.*) strophantin.

strofànto, *s.m.* (*bot.*) strophantus.

stròfe, *V.* **stròfa.**

stròfico, *ag.* (*poes.*) stanzaic; strophic.

strofinàccio, *s.m.* duster; (*per asciugare piatti*) tea-cloth; (*per lavare pavimenti*) floor-cloth.

strofinaménto, *s.m.* rubbing.

strofinàre, *v.t.* to rub: — *un tavolo,* to rub a table ǁ **strofinàrsi,** *v.r.* to rub oneself: *il cane si strofinava contro di lui,* the dog was rubbing itself against him ǁ — *a qlcu.,* (*adularlo*) to fawn on s.o.

strofinàta, *s.f.* rub: *dare una* — *a ql.co.,* to give sthg. a rub.

strofinío, *s.m.* continuous rubbing.

strofinóni, *av.* rubbing oneself.

strogolàre, *v.i.* 1. to root, to rout 2. (*spreg.*) (*mangiare avidamente*) to gorge, to glut.

strogolóna, *s.f.,* **strogolóne,** *s.m.* (*spreg.*) glutton.

strologàre, *v.t.* 1. to foretell, to predict, to prophesy: — *il futuro,* to foretell the future; — *il tempo,* to study the weather ǁ *farsi* —, to have one's fortune told 2. (*almanaccare*) to day-dream, to build fantasies ǁ *v.i.* to cast horoscopes.

strología, *s.f.* (*pop.*) astrology.

stròlogo, *s.m.* (*pop.*) astrologer; fortune-teller.

stròma, *s.m.* (*fisiol.*) stroma (*pl.* stromata).

strombàre, *v.t.* (*rar. arch.*) to splay.

strombatúra, *s.f.* (*arch.*) splay.

strombazzaménto, *s.m.* trumpeting, puffing.

strombazzàre, *v.t.* to trumpet, to puff; to boost: *non fa che — la sua bravura,* he does nothing but blow his own trumpet; *strombazzano tanto la loro merce, ma nessuno la compera,* they puff their goods very much but nobody buys them; *— una notizia,* to trumpet (*o* to cry) a piece of news; *— uno scrittore,* to boost a writer ‖ *v.i.* **1.** (*suonar la tromba*) to sound a trumpet, to trumpet **2.** (*suonare il clacson*) to toot, to honk.

strombazzàta, *s.f.* **1.** (*suonata di tromba*) trumpeting **2.** (*lode sperticata*) boast.

strombazzàto, *ag.* trumpeted, puffed; boosted.

strombazzatóre, *s.m.,* **strombazzatríce,** *s.f.* (*chi loda in modo sperticato*) braggart, booster.

strombettàre, *v.i.* to blow the trumpet (badly) ‖ *v.t.* (*lodare in modo sperticato*) to trumpet, to puff.

strombettàta, *s.f.* **1.** trumpeting **2.** (*sperticata lode pubblica*) boast, brag.

strombettatóre, *s.m.,* **strombettatríce,** *s.f.* **1.** trumpeter **2.** (*chi loda in modo sperticato*) braggart, booster.

strombettío, *s.m.* continuous trumpeting.

strómbo[1], *s.m.* (*arch.*) splay.

strómbo[2], *s.m.* (*zool.*) stromb.

stroménto, *V.* **struménto.**

stroncaménto, *s.m.* **1.** breaking off **2.** (*critica spietata*) harsh criticism, slashing criticism.

stroncàre, *v.t.* **1.** to break off, to cut off: *— un ramo,* to break off a branch ‖ *— una resistenza,* to break down resistance **2.** *fig.* (*demolire*) to slate, to maul, to demolish: *il suo libro fu stroncato completamente dalla critica,* his book was completely demolished by the critics ‖ **stroncàrsi,** *v.r.* to break: *si stroncò un braccio,* he broke his arm.

stroncàto, *ag.* **1.** broken off, cut off **2.** *fig.* (*demolito*) slated, mauled.

stroncatóre, *ag. fig.* (*demolitore*) slating, mauling ‖ *s.m.* slashing critic.

stroncatòrio, *ag. fig.* (*atto a demolire*) slating, mauling, demolishing.

stroncatúra, *s.f.* (*aspra critica*) harsh criticism, slashing criticism.

stróneo, *ag.* maimed, crippled ‖ *s.m.* cripple.

strònzio, *s.m.* (*min.*) strontium.

stropicciaménto, *s.m.* **1.** rubbing; (*dei piedi*) shuffling **2.** (*lo sgualcire*) creasing, crumpling, wrinkling.

stropicciàre, *v.t.* **1.** to rub; (*i piedi*) to shuffle: *— due pietre l'una contro l'altra,* to rub two stones together; *— i piedi,* to shuffle one's feet **2.** (*sgualcire*) to crease, to crumple: *non — quel pezzo di carta,* don't crease (*o* crumple) that piece of paper ‖ **stropicciàrsi,** *v.r.* **1.** to rub oneself: *si stropicciava il braccio,* he was rubbing his arm; *— gli occhi,* to rub one's eyes ‖ *me ne stropiccio!,* I don't care a fig! **2.** (*sgualcirsi*) to crease, to get creased: *mi si è tutto stropicciato il vestito,* my dress has got all creased; *questa stoffa si stropiccia facilmente,* this material creases easily.

stropicciàta, *s.f.* rub.

stropicciatúra, *s.f.* **1.** rubbing; (*dei piedi*) shuffling **2.** (*lo sgualcire*) creasing, crumpling, wrinkling.

stropiccío, *s.m.* **1.** rubbing; (*dei piedi*) shuffling **2.** (*lo sgualcire*) creasing, crumpling, wrinkling.

stroppiàre, *V.* **storpiàre.**

stròppo, *s.m.* (*mar.*) strop, strap.

stròscio, *e derivati, V.* **scròscio,** *e derivati.*

stròzza, *s.f.* (*anat.*) throat, wind-pipe; (*fam.*) throttle, gullet: *prendere uno alla —,* to seize s.o. by the throat.

strozzaménto, *s.m.* **1.** (*lo strangolare*) strangling, throttling **2.** (*lo stringere sin quasi a chiudere*) obstructing; (*med.*) strangulating **3.** (*restringimento*) narrow

passage, narrowing **4.** (*il soffocare*) choking, stifling, smothering, suffocating **5.** (*il prestar denaro a usura*) fleecing.

strozzàre, *v.t.* **1.** (*uccidere strangolando*) to strangle, to throttle: *il povero uomo fu strozzato da un ladro,* the poor man was strangled (*o* throttled) by a thief **2.** (*stringere sin quasi a chiudere*) to obstruct; (*med.*) to strangulate: *uno scoglio strozza il passaggio,* a rock obstructs the passage **3.** *fig.* (*soffocare*) to choke, to stifle, to suffocate, to smother: *la rabbia lo strozzava,* he was choking with anger **4.** *fig.* (*prestar danaro a usura a*) to fleece, to skin: *egli fu strozzato da un usuraio,* he was fleeced by a usurer **5.** *— le colate,* (*metal.*) to choke runners.

strozzàto, *ag.* **1.** strangled, throttled: *egli morì —,* he was strangled **2.** (*soffocato*) choked: *con voce strozzata,* in a choked (*o* choking) voice **3.** (*di recipiente, che ha strettoie*) narrow-necked; (*di passaggi, tubazioni*) with narrow passages, with narrowings: *vaso —,* narrow-necked vase **4.** (*med.*) strangulated: *ernia strozzata,* strangulated hernia **5.** (*stretto*) tight: *veste strozzata,* tight dress.

strozzatóio, *ag.* strangling ‖ *s.m.* (*mar.*) compressor.

strozzatúra, *s.f.* **1.** (*lo strangolare*) strangling, throttling **2.** (*il soffocare*) choking, stifling **3.** (*lo stringere*) obstructing; (*med.*) strangulating **4.** (*restringimento*) (*di recipienti*) narrow neck; (*di passaggi, tubazioni*) narrow passage, narrowing **5.** (*il prestar denaro a usura*) fleecing **6.** (*usura*) usury.

strozzinàggio, *s.m.* usury.

strozzíno, *s.m.* usurer.

strubbiàre, *v.t.* (*rar.*) (*sciupare*) to spoil; to wear out quickly; to waste.

strucinàre, *v.t.* (*rar.*) (*sciupare*) to spoil; to waste.

strudel, *s.m.* (*cuc.*) strudel.

strúggere, *v.t.* **1.** to melt: *— il grasso, la cera,* to melt fat, wax **2.** (*consumare*) to wear out, to consume; to waste, to squander: *il rimorso lo struggeva,* remorse was wearing him out; *— il proprio patrimonio,* to waste (*o* to squander) one's patrimony **3.** (*distruggere*) to destroy: *— la città,* to destroy the town ‖ **strúggersi,** *v.r.* **1.** to melt: *la neve si strugge al sole,* snow melts in the sun ‖ *— in lacrime,* to melt into tears **2.** (*affliggersi*) to be distressed, to distress oneself: *egli si strugge di non poterlo rivedere,* he is distressed not to be able to see him again; *non struggerti, c'è ancora speranza!,* don't worry too much, there is still some hope! **3.** (*languire di passione, desiderio*) to be consumed (with sthg.); to pine (away) (with sthg., for s.o., sthg.): *ella si struggeva di tornare a casa,* she was pining to go back home; *— di gelosia, invidia, desiderio, dolore,* to be consumed with jealousy, envy, desire, grief.

struggicuòre, *s.m.* (*tormento*) heartache.

struggiménto, *s.m.* **1.** (*tormento*) torment, torture: *è uno — il sentirlo raccontare quelle cose,* it is a torture to hear him talking about those things **2.** (*desiderio intenso*) longing: *il suo — per tornare a casa,* his longing for home.

struggitóre, *ag.* destroying ‖ *s.m.,* **struggitríce,** *s.f.* destroyer.

strumentàle, *ag.* (*gram. mus.*) instrumental: *caso —,* instrumental case; *musica —,* instrumental music.

strumentalménte, *av.* instrumentally.

strumentàre, *v.t.* **1.** (*mus.*) to instrument **2.** (*dir.*) to draw up: *— un documento,* to draw up an instrument.

strumentatúra, *s.f.* (*mus.*) instrumentation, scoring.

strumentazióne, *s.f.* (*mus.*) instrumentation.

struménto, *s.m.* **1.** tool, implement; instrument: *strumenti agricoli,* farm implements; *strumenti chirurgici, astronomici,* surgical, astronomical instruments; *gli strumenti di un falegname, elettricista, idraulico, giardiniere, ecc.* the tools of a carpenter, an electrician, a plumber, a gardener, etc.; *strumenti di guerra,* instruments of war **2.** (*mus.*) instrument: *— a corda,* stringed instrument; *— a fiato,* wind instrument; *— a* *percussione*, percussion instrument **3.** *fig. (mezzo)* instrument, tool: *egli fu solo lo — di quel delitto*, he was only the instrument of that crime **4.** *(dir.)* instrument; *(atto)* deed.

strusciàre, *v.t.* **1.** *(strofinare)* to rub **2.** *fig. (adulare)* to adulate; to fawn on (s.o.) **3.** *(logorare)* to wear out; *(stazzonare)* to crumple, to crease ‖ **strusciàrsi**, *v.r.* **1.** *(strofinarsi)* to rub oneself: *non strusciarti contro il muro*, don't rub against the wall **2.** *(adulare)* to fawn (on s.o.).

strusciàta, *s.f.* rub.

struscióne, *s.m.* **1.** *(sciupone)* waster **2.** *(persona sciatta)* slovenly person **3.** *(adulatore)* flatterer; *(fam.)* crawler.

strútto, *ag.* **1.** *(sciolto)* melted: *cera strutta*, melted wax **2.** *(distrutto)* destroyed **3.** *(consumato)* consumed ‖ *s.m. (cuc.)* lard.

struttúra, *s.f.* structure: *— ad anello, (chim.)* ring structure; *— atomica, (fis.)* atomic structure; *la — del corpo umano*, the structure of the human body; *la — del periodo*, the structure of a sentence; *— in ferro, (edil.)* steel construction; *— lamellare, (geol.)* sheeting; *— portante, (edil. ind.)* carrying structure.

strutturàle, *ag.* structural.

strúzzo, *s.m. (ornit.)* ostrich ‖ *avere uno stomaco di —, fig.* to have the digestion of an ostrich.

stuccàre, *v.t.* **1.** to stucco, to coat with stucco, to plaster; *(masticiare)* to putty; *(la carrozzeria di automobile)* to stopper **2.** *(turare con stucco)* to fill: *— un buco*, to fill up a hole; *— un dente*, to fill a tooth **3.** *(saziare)* to surfeit; *(nauseare)* to sicken: *uva troppo dolce che stucca*, over-sweet grapes that make you sick **4.** *(annoiare)* to bore: *i suoi complimenti mi stuccano*, his compliments bore me stiff ‖ **stuccàrsi**, *v.r.* **1.** *(stancarsi)* to get tired; *(annoiarsi)* to get bored; to get sick.

stuccatóre, *s.m.* plasterer; stucco-worker.

stuccatúra, *s.f.* plastering; stucco-work.

stucchèvole, *ag.* **1.** *(di cibo) (che sazia)* filling; *(nauseante)* sickening: *il riso è —*, rice is filling **2.** *(noioso)* boring, tedious, tiresome: *discorso —*, boring speech.

stucchevolézza, *s.f.* tedium.

stucchevolménte, *av.* tediously, tiresomely.

stucchinàio, *s.m.* **1.** *(chi fabbrica figurine di stucco)* maker of plaster figurines **2.** *(chi vende figurine di stucco)* seller of plaster figurines.

stucchìno, *s.m.* plaster figurine, plaster statuette.

stúcco¹, *ag. (infastidito)* bored; sick; annoyed; *(fam.)* fed up (with sthg.): *sono — di mangiar sempre pesce*, I am sick of always eating fish; *sono — di tante domande*, I am bored by (o fed up with) so many questions.

stúcco², *s.m.* **1.** stucco *(pl. stuccoes)*, plaster; *(per i vetri)* putty **2.** *(decorazione di stucco)* stucco *(pl. stuccoes)*; stucco-work ‖ *rimanere di —*, to be dumb-founded.

stuccóso, *V.* **stucchévole**.

studènte, *ag.* studying ‖ *s.m.* student: *— di medicina, legge*, medical, law student.

studentésca, *s.f.* students *(pl.)*.

studentésco, *ag.* students' *(attributivo)*, student *(attributivo)*, school *(attributivo)*: *gergo —*, students' slang; *vita studentesca*, school life.

studentéssa, *s.f.* girl student.

studiacchiàre, *v.t.* to study fitfully, to study without enthusiasm.

studiàre, *v.t.* **1.** to study; *(parlando di studi universitari)* to read, to study: *ha studiato con un ottimo professore per cinque anni*, he studied under a very good professor for five years; *studia all'università di Roma, a Brera*, he is studying at Rome University, at Brera; *studia medicina*, he is reading (o studying) medicine (o he is studying to be a doctor); *— latino, storia, inglese*, to study Latin, history, English; *— legge, filosofia*, to read (o to study) law, philosophy; *— molto poco, sodo, di mala voglia*, to study very little, hard, very unwillingly; *— il violino*, to study

the violin ‖ *— le parole, (per non offendere o non compromettersi)* to weigh one's words **2.** *(esaminare)* to examine, to study: *— il carattere di una persona*, to study the character of a person; *— il modo di fare, di ottenere una cosa*, to try to work out how to do, to get sthg.; *— la situazione, un problema*, to examine (o to study) the situation, a problem ‖ **studiàrsi**, *v.r. (cercare, sforzarsi)* to try, to endeavour: *mi studierò di farlo come vuoi tu*, I shall try to do it as you want me to; *si studia di accontentarlo in tutti i modi*, she tries to please him in every way; *si studia sempre di piacere*, she always tries to please.

studiataménte, *av.* **1.** *(di proposito)* on purpose, deliberately **2.** *(affettatamente)* affectedly.

studiàto, *ag.* **1.** studied: *discorso —*, set speech; *una risposta studiata*, a studied answer **2.** *(affettato)* affected, artificial: *modi studiati*, affected manners; *sorriso —*, affected smile.

stúdio, *s.m.* **1.** study: *lo — della geografia, del greco, delle lingue*, the study of geography, of Greek, of languages; *studi irregolari*, irregular studies; *studi scientifici, classici*, scientific, classical studies; *corso, programma di studi*, course of study (o curriculum); *fece i suoi studi a Pavia*, he studied at Pavia; *ha fatto studi universitari?*, did he have a university education?; *non è molto amante dello —*, he doesn't like studying very much; *non ha fatto studi regolari*, he has not followed a regular course of study (o he hasn't studied regularly); *vuole dedicarsi allo — dell'economia*, he wants to devote himself to the study of economics; *incominciare, continuare, finire gli studi*, to begin, to continue, to finish one's studies ‖ *a bello —*, on purpose ‖ *uomo di studi*, studious man ‖ *essere allo —, (di progetto, legge, ecc.)* to be under consideration: *la proposta è allo — della commissione*, the proposal is under the consideration of (o is being considered by) the committee **2.** *(composizione musicale, critica; bozzetto)* study: *— di nudo*, study from the nude; *— per violino*, violin study; *ha pubblicato uno — su Dante*, he has published a study on Dante; *ho visto uno — di testa di Leonardo*, I have seen a study of a head by Leonardo; *suonò uno — di Chopin*, he played a study by Chopin **3.** *(progetto)* plan: *— per un nuovo impianto*, plan for a new plant; *— per un ponte*, plan for a bridge **4.** *(università)* university **5.** *(stanza da studio)* study: *lo troverai nel suo —*, you will find him in his study; *il suo — è sempre in disordine*, his study is always in disorder **6.** *(ufficio di professionista)* office; *(di pittore, fotografo, ecc.)* studio *(pl. studios)* **7.** *(cine. tv.)* studio *(pl. studios)* **8.** *(zelo, cura)*: *egli mette grande — in tutto quello che fa*, he takes great pains in everything he does.

studiosaménte, *av.* **1.** studiously; *(diligentemente)* diligently **2.** *(intenzionalmente)* on purpose, deliberately, intentionally.

studióso, *ag.* studious, fond of study: *un ragazzo —*, a studious boy ‖ *s.m.* scholar; student: *uno — di archeologia*, a student of archeology; *egli è uno —*, he is a scholar.

stuèllo, *s.m. (med.)* tent, dossil.

stúfa, *s.f.* **1.** stove: *— a carbone*, coal stove; *— ad acqua, (chim.)* stove with water jacket; *— ad aria, (chim.)* air-bath; *— a gas*, gas-stove; *— a petrolio*, oil-stove; *— elettrica*, electric stove; *— termostatica, (med.)* incubator (o thermostatic stove); *tubo da —*, stovepipe **2.** *(serra)* hothouse, greenhouse.

stufàre, *v.t.* **1.** *(cuc.)* to stew **2.** *(fam.) (stancare)* to bore: *mi ha stufato a morte con tutte le sue lamentele*, he's bored me to death with all his complaints ‖ **stufàrsi**, *v.r.* to get tired, to get weary; to grow bored (with s.o., sthg. with doing): *— di fare ql.co.*, to get tired of doing sthg.; *— di ql.co.*, to get tired (o weary) of sthg.

stufàto, *s.m. (cuc.)* stew, stewed meat.

stúfo, *ag.* tired; *(fam.)* fed up (with s.o., sthg., with doing); (fam.) sick: sono — da morire, I am bored to death; sono — di lui, di questo, I am tired (o sick) of him, of this (o fam. I am fed up with him, with this); sono — di lavorare, I am tired (o sick) of working (o fam. I am fed up with working).

stuòia, s.f. mat: una — di paglia, a straw mat; stuoie sottopiatto, table mats; ho bisogno di alcune stuoie per la mia casa, I need some matting for my house.

stuòlo, s.m. group, crowd, swarm, band: uno — di gente, a crowd (o swarm o lot) of people; uno — di studenti, a crowd (o band) of students.

stupefacènte, ag. stupefying; amazing, astonishing ‖ s.m. drug narcotic; (fam.) dope: spacciatore di stupefacenti, dealer in drugs (o fam. dope pedlar).

stupefàre, v.t. to stupefy; to amaze, to astonish ‖ stupefàrsi, v.r. to be stupefied; to be amazed, to be astonished.

stupefàtto, ag. stupefied; amazed, astonished.

stupefazióne, s.f. stupefaction; amazement, astonishment.

stupendaménte, av. wonderfully, marvellously.

stupèndo, ag. wonderful, marvellous: che — discorso!, what a wonderful speech!.

stupidàggine, s.f. 1. stupidity; foolishness: la — di alcune persone non ha limiti, there is no limit to some people's stupidity 2. (azione stupida) stupid trick; (errore stupido) stupid mistake; (cosa, parola stupida) piece of nonsense: mi rispose con una —, he gave me a stupid (o a foolish) answer; non dire stupidaggini, don't talk nonsense; questa è una delle sue solite stupidaggini, this is one of his usual stupid tricks 3. (cosa da poco) trifle.

stupidaménte, av. stupidly; foolishly.

stupidíre, v.t. to make stupid; (stordire) to stun, to daze: stupidito dal dolore, stunned (o dazed) by grief ‖ v.i. to become stupid; (essere stordito) to be stunned, to be dazed.

stupidità, s.f. stupidity; foolishness; la sua — è al di sopra di ogni comprensione umana, his stupidity passes all human understanding.

stúpido, ag. stupid; (fam.) dumb; (sciocco) foolish, silly: idee stupide, stupid (o idiotic) ideas; uno sguardo —, a stupid look; vita stupida, stupid (o aimless) life; egli è —, he is stupid ‖ s.m. fool, stupid person, blockhead: è uno —, he is a fool (o he is stupid); non fare lo —, don't be a fool.

stupíre, v.t. to astonish, to amaze: ciò mi stupisce, this amazes me ‖ v.i., stupírsi, v.r. to be astonished, to be amazed: mi stupisco di ciò che mi hanno detto, I am astonished at what they have told me.

stupóre, s.m. 1. astonishment, amazement: ero pieno di —, I was quite astonished; fa — il vederlo in quelle condizioni, it is astonishing to see him in such conditions; essere preso da —, to be seized with astonishment 2. (med.) (intorpidimento) stupor.

stupràre, v.t. to violate, to rape, to ravish.

stúpro, s.m. rape, violation.

stúra, s.f. (di bottiglie) uncorking; (di botti) unbunging: dare la — a una bottiglia, to uncork a bottle ‖ dare la — alle chiacchiere, to begin gossiping.

sturaménto, s.m. (di bottiglie) uncorking; (di botti) unbunging.

sturàre, v.t. (bottiglie) to uncork; (botti) to unbung ‖ — gli orecchi a qlcu., to give s.o. a piece of one's mind.

sturbàre, (rar.) per disturbàre.

stuzzicadènti, s.m. tooth-pick.

stuzzicaménto, s.m. 1. (il punzecchiare) prodding, poking; (il frugare) picking 2. (sfregamento) rubbing 3. (il molestare) teasing, provocation 4. (lo stimolare) exciting, whetting.

stuzzicànte, ag. appetizing: cibo —, appetizing food.

stuzzicàre, v.t. 1. (punzecchiare) to prod, to poke; (frugare) to pick: smettila di stuzzicarmi con quella penna, stop prodding (o poking) me with that pen; — i denti, to pick one's teeth ‖ — il fuoco, to poke the fire 2. (sfregare) to rub: non — gli occhi, don't rub your eyes 3. (molestare) to tease, to provoke: non — il gatto!, don't tease the cat!; non stuzzicatelo!, don't tease him! ‖ non — il can che dorme, prov. let sleeping dogs lie 4. (stimolare) to excite, to whet: ciò stuzzica la mia curiosità, this excites (o whets) my curiosity; — l'appetito di qlcu., to whet (o to stimulate) s.o.'s appetite 5. (toccare) to finger, to touch: i bambini continuano a — ogni cosa, children keep fingering everything.

stuzzichino, s.m. 1. (fam.) teaser 2. (dial.) (spuntino) snack.

su, prep. 1. (nel caso di sovrapposizione con contatto) on, upon; (direzione) onto: una macchia sul pavimento, a stain on the floor; la lettera era sul tavolo, the letter was (up)on the table; lo misi sulla sedia, I put it on the chair; il suo diritto alla fama poggia solo — queste basi, his claim to fame rests on this basis (o only on this basis); uscì sul balcone, he stepped onto the balcony 2. (nel caso di sovrapposizione senza contatto e quando sia implicito il concetto di dominio, superiorità, protezione, difesa, rivestimento) over: la lampada sospesa sul tavolo, the lamp hanging over the table; il ponte sul fiume, the bridge over the river; c'era una coltre di nubi sulla città, there was a blanket of clouds over the city; mettiti uno scialle sulle spalle, put a shawl over your shoulders; siamo ora — Londra, we are now over London; si tirò il cappello sugli occhi, he drew his hat down over his eyes; avere un grande vantaggio — qlcu., to have a great advantage over s.o.; avere potere — qlcu., to have power over s.o.; regnare — un paese, to rule over a country 3. (al di sopra di, più in alto di) above: cinquecento metri sul livello del mare, five hundred metres above sea-level; volavamo alto sulla città, we were flying high above the city 4. (lungo) on; (affacciato su) onto: sul lungomare, on the sea-front; una casa, una città — un fiume, a house, a town on a river; un negozio sulla Quinta Strada, a shop on the Fifth Avenue; il mio appartamento guarda sulla strada, my flat looks onto the street; questa porta dà sul giardino, this door opens out onto the garden 5. (verso, circa) about: sul far della sera, about dusk; sul mezzogiorno, about noon; un ragazzo sui dieci anni, a boy of about ten (o a boy about ten years old); egli è sulla trentina, he is about thirty 6. (verso) towards, to; (contro) on; at: marciavano — Napoli, they were marching on Naples; si diressero — Roma, they went towards (o they headed for) Rome; puntare il fucile — ql.co., to aim one's gun at sthg. 7. (intorno a) on, about: una conferenza sull'arte greca, a lecture on Greek art; — che cosa è la conferenza?, what is the lecture about?; so tutto — di lui, I know everything about him 8. (Fraseologia): sui due piedi, on the spot (o there and then); sull'istante, on the spot; dipinto — legno, tela, painted on wood, canvas; fatto — misura, made-to-measure; nove volte — dieci, nine times out of ten; sul momento non capii, at first I didn't understand (o I didn't understand at once); essere sul punto di fare ql.co., to be about (o going) to do sthg. (o to be on the point of doing sthg.); fare sul serio, to be in earnest (o serious); far debiti — debiti, to run up debt after debt; star sulle sue, to keep oneself to oneself ‖ av. 1. up; (ai piani superiori) upstairs: là —, up there; qui —, up here; alzati —, stand up; guarda —, look up; saltò —, he sprang up; tira — quel pezzo di carta, pick up that piece of paper; vieni — subito, come upstairs at once; andar —, to go up; to go upstairs: andar — per la collina, to go up the hill ‖ — e giù, up and down (o to and fro) ‖ — per giù, more or less (o about o roughly o approximately): ci sono — per giù trenta persone, there are thirty people more or less (o there are about thirty people) ‖ in —: da cento lire in —, from a hundred lire upwards; da

Foligno in — il treno rallenta, from Foligno onwards the train slows down; *non sa contare da dieci in —*, he doesn't know how to count from ten onwards; *non va nè in — nè in giù*, it doesn't go up or down; *andare in —*, to go upwards ‖ *più —*, up; *(più oltre)* further up: *tre case più —*, three houses further up *(o further along)*; *abita due piani più —*, he lives two floors up *(o above this)* ‖ *a mezzanotte era ancora —*, *(alzato)* he was still up at midnight ‖ *questo bambino viene — bene*, *(cresce bene)* this child is growing well; *viene — dal nulla*, he has come from nothing ‖ *ti ha messo — contro di me*, he turned you against me ‖ *essere — di giri*, to feel on top of the world ‖ *metter — casa*, to set up house ‖ *tirar — un bambino*, *(allevarlo)* to bring up a child ‖ *tirarsi —*, *(in salute)* to recover *(o* to pick up)*; *(finanziariamente)* to get on one's feet again **2.** *(indosso)* **on:** *aveva — un paio di scarpe nuove*, he had a pair of new shoes on *(o* he was wearing a pair of new shoes); *metti — il soprabito*, put your coat on ‖ *sta mettendo — arie*, he is putting on airs **3.** *(esortativo)*: *— con la vita!*, cheer up!; *—, andiamo*, come on, let's go; *—, bambini, fate in fretta*, come on, children, hurry up; *di' — (quello che sai)!*, *(fam.)* spit it out!.

suaccennàre, *v.t.* to mention above.

suaccennàto, *ag.* above mentioned, aforesaid.

suadènte, *ag. (letter.)* persuasive; winning.

suadére, *(letter.)* per **persuadére.**

suasìvo, *ag. (letter.)* suasive, persuasive; winning: *modi suasivi*, suasive ways.

subàcido, *ag. (chim.)* subacid.

subàcqueo, *ag.* underwater *(attributivo)*; subaqueous: *pesca subacquea*, underwater fishing.

subaffittàre, *v.t.* to sublet, to sublease.

subaffitto, *s.m.* **1.** sublease, sublet **2.** *(il subaffittare)* subletting.

subaffittuària, *s.f.*, **subaffittuàrio,** *s.m.* sublessee, subtenant.

subalpìno, *ag.* subalpine.

subaltèrno, *ag.* subordinate; *(spec. log.)* subaltern: *grado, posizione subalterna*, subordinate rank, position; *personale —*, subordinate staff; *proposizione subalterna*, *(log.)* subaltern proposition; *ufficiale —*, *(mil.)* subaltern ‖ *s.m.* subordinate; *(mil.)* subaltern.

subappaltàre, *v.t.* to give in subcontract.

subappaltatóre, *s.m.*, **subappaltatríce,** *s.f.* subcontractor.

subappàlto, *s.m.* subcontract.

súbbia, *s.f. (strum. artig.)* firmer chisel.

subbiàre, *v.t.* to chisel.

súbbio, *s.m. (strum. artig.)* (weaver's) beam: *— dell'ordito*, warp beam; *— del tessuto*, cloth beam.

subbissàre, *V.* **subissàre.**

subbúglio, *s.m.* confusion, turmoil; *(scompiglio)* disorder, mess: *che —!*, what a confusion!; *la casa era in —*, the house was in utter confusion *(o* in a turmoil); *non mettere in — le mie carte*, don't throw my papers into disorder *(o* don't make a mess of my papers); *il suo arrivo mise in — gli studenti*, his arrival caused a stir *(o* turmoil) among the students.

subcònscio, *s.m.* subconscious.

subcontràrio, *ag. (fil.)* subcontrary.

subcosciènte, *ag.* subconscious: *sensazioni subcoscienti*, subconscious sensations ‖ *s.m.* subconscious, subconscious mind.

subcosciènza, *s.f.* subconsciousness.

subdolaménte, *av.* underhand, underhandedly: *lavorava — per screditare i suoi avversari politici*, he worked underhand to discredit his political rivals.

súbdolo, *ag.* underhand, sly; *(sfuggente)* shifty: *arti subdole*, underhand tricks; *non fidarti di lui, è un uomo —*, don't trust him, he is a sly man; *non lasciarti ingannare dalle sue maniere subdole*, don't be taken in by his shifty manners.

subentràre, *v.i.* to take the place (of s.o., sthg.),

to succeed (s.o., sthg.); to replace (s.o., sthg.), to take over (from s.o.): *l'amore subentrò all'odio*, love replaced hatred; *egli subentrò a suo fratello nella direzione dell'azienda*, he took the place of *(o* he succeeded) his brother in the management of the firm *(o* he took over the management of the firm from his brother).

subiètto, *e derivati, V.* **soggètto,** *e derivati.*

subìre, *v.t.* **1.** to undergo: *— una condanna*, to be condemned; *— un'operazione, un cambiamento, una prova*, to undergo an operation, a change, a trial **2.** *(patire)* to suffer: *— una perdita, un danno, un insulto, il martirio*, to suffer a loss, a damage, an insult, martyrdom; *— una sconfitta*, to suffer a defeat.

subissàre, *v.t.* **1.** *(sprofondare)* to sink **2.** *(mandare in rovina)* to ruin **3.** *fig. (ricoprire)* to overwhelm: *egli mi subissa di gentilezze, di lodi*, he overwhelms me with kindness, with praise ‖ *v.i.* **1.** *(sprofondare)* to sink **2.** *(andare in rovina)* to fall into ruin.

subìsso, *s.m.* **1.** *(rovina)* ruin: *andare in —*, to fall into ruin *(o* to be ruined); *mandare in —*, to ruin: *mandare in — il proprio patrimonio*, to squander one's patrimony **2.** *(gran quantità)* shower: *un — di applausi*, a roar of applause; *un — di insulti*, a shower of insults; *un — di inviti, lettere, regali*, a shower of invitations, of letters, of presents.

subitaménte, *av.* **1.** *(immediatamente)* immediately, at once **2.** *(all'improvviso)* suddenly.

subitaneaménte, *av.* suddenly, all at once, all of a sudden.

subitaneità, *s.f.* suddenness.

subitàneo, *ag.* **1.** sudden: *prendere una subitanea decisione*, to make *(o* to take) a sudden decision **2.** *(istintivo)* instinctive: *moto —*, instinctive movement.

súbito¹, *ag.* sudden: *subita morte*, sudden death.

súbito², *av.* **1. at once, immediately, directly, right away, straight away**; *(presto)* **soon:** *ritorno —*, I'll be right back; *si stancò — del suo lavoro*, he soon got tired of his work *(o* he got tired of his work in no time); *vieni —*, come at once *(o* right away) ‖ *— dopo*, *av.* immediately afterwards; *prep.* immediately after *(o* just after): *— dopo mezzanotte*, immediately *(o* just) after midnight; *arrivò — dopo*, he arrived immediately afterwards; *partì — dopo colazione*, he left immediately *(o* directly *o* straight) after lunch ‖ *— prima*, just before: *— prima della guerra*, just before the war; *— prima di partire, venne a trovarmi*, just before he left *(o* leaving), he came to see me **2.** *(rar.) (improvvisamente)* **suddenly, all of a sudden** ‖ *di —*, *(arc.)* on a sudden.

sublimàre, *v.t.* to sublimate, to sublime (anche *chim.*).

sublimàto, *s.m. (chim.)* sublimate: *— corrosivo*, corrosive sublimate.

sublimazióne, *s.f.* sublimation (anche *chim.*).

sublìme, *ag.* sublime, lofty: *altezza —*, sublime *(o* lofty) height; *eroismo —*, sublime heroism ‖ *che idea —!*, *(iron.)* what a bright idea! ‖ *s.m.* the sublime.

sublimeménte, *av.* sublimely, loftily.

sublimità, *s.f.* sublimity, sublimeness.

sublinguàle, *ag.* sublingual: *ghiandola sublinguale*, *(anat.)* sublingual gland.

sublocàre, *v.t.* to sublet.

sublocatària, *s.f.*, **sublocatàrio,** *s.m.* subtenant.

sublocazióne, *s.f.* subletting.

sublunàre, *ag.* sublunar, sublunary.

subodoràre, *v.t.* to sense; to suspect: *avevo subodorato ql.co. di sospetto*, I had some suspicions *(o* fam. I had smelt a rat); *— un complotto*, to suspect a plot.

subordinaménto, *s.m.* subordination.

subordinàre, *v.t.* to subordinate: *egli subordina ogni cosa al proprio interesse*, he subordinates everything to his own interest.

subordinàta, *s.f. (gram.)* subordinate clause.

subordinataménte, *av.* subordinately.

subordinàto, *ag.* subordinate: *proposizione subordinata*, *(gram.)* subordinate clause ‖ *s.m.* subordinate.

subordinazióne, *s.f.* subordination.

subornàre, *v.t.* to suborn: *tentò di — un testimone,* he tried to suborn a witness.

subornatóre, *s.m.,* **subornatríce,** *s.f.* suborner.

subornazióne, *s.f.* subornation.

subsònico, *ag.* (*aer.*) subsonic.

substràto, *s.m.* substratum (*pl.* substrata) (anche *fig.*): *un — di verità,* a substratum of truth; *un — roccioso,* a substratum of rock.

suburbàno, *ag.* suburban: *piazza, strada suburbana,* suburban square, street.

suburbicàrio, *ag.* (*eccl.*) suburbicarian.

subúrbio, *s.m.* suburb (*spec. pl.*): *il — di Firenze,* the suburbs of Florence; *le scuole del —,* suburban schools.

subúrra, *s.f.* **1.** (*archeol.*) "suburra" (district of ill-fame in ancient Rome) **2.** (*quartiere malfamato*) slums (*pl.*): *la — di Milano,* the slums of Milan.

succedàneo, *ag.* (*rar.*) succedaneous || *s.m.* succedaneum (*pl.* succedanea): *— del caffè,* coffee substitute; *— del chinino,* quinine succedaneum.

succèdere, *v.i.* **1.** to succeed (*v.i.,* to sthg.): *egli succedette al padre negli affari,* he succeeded his father in the business; *Vittorio Emanuele III succedette a Umberto I,* Vittorio Emanuele III succeeded Umberto I; *— al trono,* to succeed to the throne **2.** (*seguire*) to follow: *le carestie spesso succedono alle guerre,* famines often follow wars; *un tuono succedette al lampo,* a roll of thunder followed the lightning **3.** (*accadere*) to happen, to occur, to befall (s.o.): *che cosa è successo?,* what has happened?; *che cosa ti succede?,* what's the matter with you?; *mi è successa una serie di disgrazie,* a series of misfortunes has befallen me; *qualsiasi cosa succeda,* whatever may happen; *sono cose che succedono,* these things happen || **succèdersi,** *v.r.* to follow one another; to follow one upon the other: *le rivoluzioni si succedettero ininterrottamente,* revolutions followed one upon the other without a break; *le stagioni si succedono,* the seasons follow one another.

succèdere, succèdersi, *s.m.* succession: *il — degli avvenimenti,* the course of events; *fu un — di insuccessi,* it was a succession of failures.

successióne, *s.f.* **1.** succession: *— al trono,* succession to the throne || *le guerre di —,* the Wars of Succession || *tassa di —,* succession duty **2.** (*seguito, serie*) succession: *— di avvenimenti,* course (o train) of events; *la sua vita è stata una — di errori,* his life was a succession of errors.

successivaménte, *av.* **1.** subsequently, afterwards: *approvò il nostro progetto ma — cambiò opinione,* he approved of our plan but subsequently (o afterwards) changed his mind **2.** (*in ordine successivo*) successively.

successívo, *ag.* following, subsequent: *il capitolo —,* the following (o the next) chapter; *gli avvenimenti successivi confermarono i nostri sospetti,* subsequent events confirmed our suspicions; *tornò il giorno, il lunedì, il mese —,* he came back the following day, Monday, month.

succèsso, *s.m.* **1.** (*esito favorevole*) success: *avrà molto — nella vita,* he will be a great success (o he will be very successful) in life; *ebbe un — completo,* he was entirely successful; *ebbe una serie di successi e di insuccessi,* he had a series of successes and failures; *ho cercato di farlo, ma senza —,* I have tried to do it but with no success; *la sua impresa ebbe —,* his enterprise met with success; *i suoi tentativi non ebbero alcun —,* his attempts failed completely || *aver — con le donne,* to be popular with women **2.** (*successo discografico, teatrale, ecc.*) hit: *i più grandi successi del 1960,* the biggest hits of 1960 **3.** (*esito*) outcome: *buon, cattivo —,* good, bad outcome.

successóre, *ag.* successive || *s.m.* successor.

successòrio, *ag.* successional.

succhiaménto, *s.m.* sucking.

succhiàre, *v.t.* **1.** to suck: *succhiò il veleno dalla sua*

ferita, he sucked the poison from his wound; *le api succhiano il nettare dai fiori,* bees suck nectar from flowers; *il bambino ha succhiato tutto un limone,* the child has sucked a lemon dry; *un'arancia,* to suck an orange; *— il latte,* to suck milk || *— il sangue a uno, fig.* to suck the life-blood out of s.o. **2.** (*assorbire*) to absorb, to suck in, to suck up: *le piante succhiano l'acqua dalla terra,* plants absorb (o suck in o suck up) water from the soil **3.** (*bere centellinando*) to sip: *— il caffè,* to sip coffee **4.** (*sopportare rassegnatamente*) to put up with (s.o., sthg.), || **succhiàrsi,** *v.r.*: *— il pollice,* to suck one's thumb.

succhiàta, *s.f.* sucking; suck.

succhiatóio, *s.m.* (*di insetti*) proboscis (*pl.* proboscises, proboscides).

succhiatóre, *ag.* sucking || *s.m.,* **succhiatríce,** *s.f.* sucker.

succhiellaménto, *s.m.* (*artig.*) boring, drilling.

succhiellàre, *v.t.* (*artig.*) to bore, to drill.

succhièllo, *s.m.* (*strum. artig.*) gimlet, auger.

súcchio, *s.m.* (*bot.*) sap.

succhióne, *s.m.* **1.** (*bot.*) young shoot **2.** *fig.* (*parassita*) parasite.

succiacàpre, *s.m.* (*ornit.*) goatsucker.

succiamèle, *s.m.* (*bot.*) broomrape.

succiàre, *V.* **succhiàre.**

succídere, *v.t.* (*rar.*) **1.** (*tagliare alla base*) to cut (sthg.) down to the root **2.** (*potare*) to prune, to lop.

succínico, *ag.* (*chim.*) succinic.

succiníte, *s.f.* (*min.*) succinite.

súccino, *s.m.* (*min.*) succinum.

succintaménte, *av.* **1.** scantily: *vestita —,* scantily dressed **2.** (*concisamente*) succintly, concisely, briefly.

succínto, *ag.* **1.** (*di abiti*) scanty: *(rialzato alla cintura*) tucked up **2.** (*conciso*) succint, concise, brief || *in —,* succinctly (o concisely o briefly).

succintòrio, *s.m.* (*eccl.*) succinctory; succintorium (*pl.* succintoria).

súcciola, *s.f.* boiled chestnut || *andare in brodo di succiole,* to go mad with joy.

succisióne, *s.f.* **1.** (*taglio alla base*) cutting down at the root **2.** (*potatura*) pruning, lopping.

succitàto, *ag.* above-mentioned, mentioned above.

succlàvio, *ag.* (*anat.*) subclavian, subclavicular.

súcco, *s.m.* **1.** juice: *— d'arancia, di limone, di pomodoro,* orange, lemon, tomato juice || *— gastrico,* (*fisiol.*) gastric juice **2.** *fig.* (*essenza*) gist, pith, essence, point: *il — di un discorso, di un libro,* the gist (o pith) of a speech, of a book; *il — di una questione,* the point of a matter.

succosaménte, *av.* pithily, concisely.

succosità, *s.f.* **1.** juiciness **2.** *fig.* (*ricchezza di contenuto*) pithiness, conciseness.

succóso, *ag.* **1.** juicy **2.** *fig.* (*ricco di contenuto*) pithy, concise.

súccuba, *s.f.* woman entirely dominated by s.o.

súccubo, *ag.* (*entirely*) dominated (by s.o.): *egli è — di sua moglie,* he is entirely dominated by his wife || *s.m.* **1.** man entirely dominated by s.o. **2.** (*spirito maligno*) succubus (*pl.* succubi); succuba (*pl.* succubae).

succulènto, *ag.* **1.** (*succoso*) succulent, juicy: *frutta succulenta,* juicy (o succulent) fruit **2.** (*gustoso, sostanzioso*) rich: *cibo —,* rich food; *pasto —,* copious repast.

succursàle, *ag.* (*comm.*) branch (*attributivo*): *sede —,* branch office || *s.f.* **1.** (*comm.*) branch, branch office, branch house: *la nostra banca ha molte succursali in Italia ed all'estero,* our bank has many branches in Italy and abroad; *questa ditta ha aperto una — nella vostra città,* this firm has opened a branch in your town **2.** (*eccl.*) chapel of ease.

succutàneo, *V.* **sottocutàneo.**

súcido, *V.* **súdicio.**

sud, *s.m.* south: *casa esposta a —,* house looking (o facing) south; *ho viaggiato a lungo nel — dell'Europa,* I have travelled a lot in the south of Europe (o in

South Europe); *l'Inghilterra è a — della Scozia*, England lies to the south of Scotland; *Roma è a — di Firenze*, Rome is to the south of Florence; *venire dal —*, to come from the south; *vivere al —*, to live in the south ‖ *— est*, *— ovest*, south-east, south-west ‖ *l'America del Sud*, *la Carolina del Sud*, South America, South Carolina; *Polo Sud*, South Pole ‖ *del —*, southern; south (*attributivo*): *abitanti del —*, southerners (*o* southern people); *i paesi del —*, southern countries; *vento del —*, south wind ‖ *verso a, —*, southward(s) (*o* south): *la nave è diretta a —*, the ship is heading south(wards); *percorse tre miglia ci dirigemmo a —*, after travelling three miles we turned south; *navigare, viaggiare verso —*, to sail, to travel south.

sudacchiàre, *v.i.* to perspire slightly.

sudafricàno, *ag.* South-African; (*boero*) African(d)er.

sudaménto, *s.m.* (*rar.*) sweating, perspiring.

sudàmina, *s.f.* (*med.*) sudamina (*pl.*).

Sudàn, *no.pr.m.* (*geog.*) Sudan: *— Anglo Egiziano*, (*st.*) Anglo-Egyptian Sudan.

sudànte, *ag.* sweating: *giunsero trafelati e sudanti*, they arrived sweating and out of breath.

sudàre, *v.i.* **1.** to sweat, to perspire: *sudo molto durante l'estate*, I perspire a great deal in Summer; *— per il caldo, per la fatica*, to sweat with heat, with fatigue; *— profusamente, abbondantemente*, to sweat (*o* to perspire) profusely ‖ *— freddo*, to be in a cold sweat: *quella vista mi ha fatto — freddo*, that sight made my blood run cold (*o* put me in a cold sweat) ‖ *— sangue*, to sweat blood ‖ *far — qlcu.*, to make s.o. sweat: *questo calore mi fa —*, this heat makes me sweat; *questa arrampicata mi ha fatto —*, this climb has made me sweat **2.** *fig.* to toil; (*fam.*) to sweat: *ha sudato molto su questo lavoro*, she has toiled hard at this work; *— sui libri*, to pour over one's books ‖ *— sette camicie*, to toil hard: *abbiamo sudato sette camicie per questo lavoro*, we have toiled hard at this work; *ho sudato sette camicie per convincerlo*, I worked hard to convince him ‖ *quel problema mi ha fatto —*, that problem made me rack my brains **3.** (*trasudare*) to sweat; (*stillare*) to exude moisture; (*gocciolare*) to ooze: *gli alberi sudano quando fa molto caldo*, trees exude moisture when it is very hot; *dalle foglie sudava un liquido biancastro*, a whitish liquid was oozing from the leaves; *i vetri delle finestre sudano quando fa molto freddo fuori*, window panes steam up when it is very cold outside ‖

sudàrsi, *v.r.*: *— ql.co.*, to get sthg. by the sweat of one's brow; *— il pane*, to get a living by the sweat of one's brow.

sudàrio, *s.m.* sudarium (*pl.* sudaria).

sudàta, *s.f.* sweat: *dovresti fare una bella — per guarire il raffreddore*, you should have a good sweat to cure your cold; *ho fatto una gran —*, I have sweated a great deal.

sudatìccio, *ag.* moist: *freddo e —*, clammy; *mani sudaticce*, moist hands (*o* clammy hands) ‖ *s.m.* slight perspiration.

sudàto, *ag.* **1.** wet with perspiration, sweaty: *mani sudate*, sweaty hands; *ha la fronte sudata*, his brow is wet with perspiration; *essere tutto —*, to be in a sweat (*o* to be all of a sweat): *ho corso e sono tutta sudata*, I have run and I am in a sweat; *sono tutta sudata per lo spavento*, I am all of a sweat with fear **2.** *fig.* hard-earned: *denaro, pane —*, hard-earned money, bread.

suddétto, *ag.* above-mentioned, aforesaid.

suddiaconàto, *s.m.* (*eccl.*) subdeaconate, subdeaconry.

suddiàcono, *s.m.* (*eccl.*) subdeacon.

suddistinzióne, *s.f.* subdistinction.

súddita, *s.f.* subject.

sudditànza, *s.f.* subjection; (*cittadinanza*) citizenship.

súddito, *ag. s.m.* subject.

suddivídere, *v.t.* to subdivide.

suddivisíbile, *ag.* subdivisible.

suddivisióne, *s.f.* subdivision.

Sudèti (Mónti), *no.pr.m.pl.* (*geog.*) Sudetes Mountains.

sudicería, *s.f.* **1.** dirtiness, filthiness, foulness **2.** (*cosa sudicia*) dirty thing; foul thing; (*oscenità*) obscenity: *dice sempre delle sudicerie*, he is always using foul language.

sudiciaménte, *av.* dirtily, filthily, foully.

súdicio, *ag.* **1.** dirty, filthy, foul: *un bambino —*, a dirty child; *una casa sudicia*, a dirty (*o* filthy) house; *un viso, un vestito —*, a dirty face, dress ‖ *colore —*, dirty (*o* muddy) colour **2.** *fig.* dirty, filthy, foul: *coscienza sudicia*, unclean conscience; *discorsi sudici, azioni sudicie*, filthy talk, actions; *guadagni sudici*, filthy lucre ‖ *s.m.* dirt, filth (anche *fig.*).

sudicióna, *s.f.* slattern, slut (anche *fig.*).

sudicióne, *s.m.* dirty fellow, filthy person (anche *fig.*).

sudiciúme, *s.m.* dirt, filth (anche *fig.*).

sudísta, *ag.* (*st. amer.*) Southern ‖ *s.c.* (*st. amer.*) Southerner.

sudóre, *s.m.* **1.** sweat, perspiration: *gocce di —*, beads of perspiration; *madido di —*, streaming with (*o* bathed in) perspiration; *il caldo provoca il —*, heat induces perspiration; *quella medicina provoca il —*, that medicine brings on perspiration; *grondare —, andare in —*, to be running with sweat (*o* to be bathed in perspiration) ‖ *un — freddo*, a cold sweat: *a quella vista mi vennero i sudori freddi*, *fig.* at that sight my blood ran cold (*o* I broke out into a cold sweat) **2.** *fig.* toil, labours (*pl.*): *il frutto dei miei sudori*, the fruits of my labours; *quanto — mi è costato quel lavoro!*, how much hard work that job has cost me! ‖ *col — della fronte*, by the sweat of one's brow: *guadagnarsi da vivere col — della fronte*, to earn one's living by the sweat of one's brow.

sudorífero, *ag.* sudorific, sudatory; sudoriferous: *farmaco — (farm.)*, sudatory (*o* sudorific) drug; *glandole sudorifere*, (*anat.*) sudoriferous glands ‖ *s.m.* (*med. farm.*) sudorific, sudatory.

sudorífico, *ag.* sudorific, sudatory.

sudoríparo, *ag.* sudoriferous; sudorific, sudatory.

Súez, *no.pr.f.* (*geog.*) Suez: *il Canale di —*, the Suez Canal.

sufficiènte, *ag.* **1.** sufficient; enough: *una quantità —*, a sufficient quantity; *abbiamo pane, vino — per venti persone*, we have enough bread, wine for twenty people; *credi che questa carne sia —?*, do you think that this meat is enough?; *ho denaro più che —*, I have more than enough money (*o* I have money enough and to spare); *il mio reddito è appena — per la mia famiglia*, my income is hardly sufficient for my family; *non credo che questo sarà —*, I do not think that this will suffice; *non ho tempo — per fermarmi qui*, I haven't time enough (*o* enough time) to stop here ‖ *grazia —*, (*teol.*) sufficient grace ‖ *ragion —*, (*fil.*) sufficient reason **2.** (*altezzoso*) self-sufficient, self-important, conceited: *parlava in tono —*, he spoke with a conceited air ‖ *s.m.* **1.** sufficient: *ha il — per vivere*, he has enough to live (on) **2.** (*termine scolastico*) pass mark **3.** (*persona altezzosa*) haughty person: *fare il —*, to give oneself airs (*o* to assume a superior air).

sufficienteménte, *av.* sufficiently, enough: *questa stanza non è — riscaldata*, this room is not sufficiently heated (*o* heated enough).

sufficiènza, *s.f.* **1.** sufficiency ‖ *a —*, sufficiently (*o* enough): *ho denaro a —*, I have enough money; *ho lavorato più che a —*, I have worked more than enough; *ne hai comprato a —?*, have you bought enough? **2.** (*termine scolastico*) pass mark: *ha una — scarsa*, he has just passed **3.** (*alterigia*) self-sufficiency, self-importance, conceit: *aria di —*, superior air (*o* self-importance *o* self-important manner).

sufficit, *inter.* (*lat.*) that's enough.

suffísso, *s.m.* (*gram.*) suffix.

suffragàre, *v.t.* **1.** to support, to back: *egli non volle — il mio piano,* he would not back my plan; *questi sono i fatti che suffragano la mia teoria,* these are the facts that support my theory **2.** *(eccl.)* to pray for (s.o.): *— i morti,* to pray for the dead.

suffragatóre, *ag.* supporting, backing ‖ *s.m.* supporter.

suffragétta, *s.f.* suffragette.

suffràgio, *s.m.* **1.** *(pol.)* suffrage, vote: *i suffragi del popolo,* the suffrages of the people; *— universale,* universal suffrage; *diritto di —,* right of suffrage; *dare il proprio —,* to give one's suffrage (o vote) **2.** *(approvazione)* approval: *il suo piano non ebbe il — di tutti,* his plan was not approved by everybody **3.** *(eccl.)* suffrage: *una preghiera di — per i morti,* a prayer for the souls of the dead; *far dire una messa di — per i defunti,* to have a mass said for the souls of the dead.

suffragista, *s.m.* suffragist ‖ *s.f.* suffragette.

suffrútice, *s.m.* *(bot.)* suffrutex *(pl.* suffrutices).

suffumigàre, *v.t.* to suffumigate.

suffumígio, *s.m.* suffumigation.

suffusióne, *s.f.* *(med.)* suffusion.

súga, *ag.* *(pop.)*: *carta —,* blotting-paper.

sugànte, *ag.* drying, absorbent: *carta —,* blotting-paper.

sugàre, *V.* **asciugàre.**

suggellaménto, *s.m.* sealing.

suggellàre, *v.t.* to seal (anche *fig.)*: *queste esperienze in comune suggellarono la nostra amicizia,* these common experiences sealed our friendship; *il suo destino era già suggellato,* his fate was already sealed; *— una lettera,* to seal a letter.

suggèllo, *s.m.* seal (anche *fig.)*: *il suo viso portava il — della sofferenza,* his face bore the seal of suffering.

súggere, *V.* **succhiàre.**

suggeriménto, *s.m.* **1.** suggestion, hint, indication: *fallo secondo i suoi suggerimenti,* do it according to his suggestions; *gli diedi alcuni suggerimenti sul come farlo,* I gave him a few hints on how to do it; *gli diedi il — di cercare di incontrarlo,* I suggested he should try to meet him; *ho seguito il tuo —,* I have followed your suggestion ‖ *dietro — di qlcu.,* as suggested by s.o. **2.** *(imbeccata)* prompt; prompting: *l'attore non riusciva a sentire il —,* the actor couldn't hear the prompt.

suggerìre, *v.t.* **1.** to suggest; to advise: *il dottore suggerì una nuova terapia,* the doctor suggested (o advised) a new treatment; *gli suggerii di non venire,* I advised him not to come (o I suggested that he should not come); *mi suggerì come si doveva fare,* he suggested how it should be done; *— una risposta,* to suggest an answer **2.** *(dare come imbeccata a)* to prompt (anche *teat.)*: *non suggerite!,* no prompting; *il nostro insegnante non vuole che noi suggeriamo ai nostri compagni,* our teacher doesn't want us to prompt our school fellows; *— una parola ad un attore,* to prompt an actor with a word.

suggeritóre, *s.m.* *(teat.)* prompter (anche *fig.)*: *buca del —,* prompt-box; *non ho bisogno di suggeritori,* I need no prompters.

suggestionàbile, *ag.* **1.** easily influenced, impressionable **2.** *(med.)* suggestible.

suggestionabilità, *s.f.* **1.** impressionability **2.** *(med.)* suggestibility.

suggestionàre, *v.t.* **1.** to work on (s.o.); *(influenzare)* to influence: *lo suggestionò tanto che finì per crederci,* he worked on him to such an extent that he ended by believing it; *non cercare di suggestionarmi,* don't try to influence me; *non suggestionarlo, deve decidere da solo,* don't influence him, he must decide for himself; *— qlcu. a fare ql.co.,* to influence s.o. to do sthg. **2.** *(med.)* to suggestionize ‖ **suggestionàrsi,** to will oneself (to do sthg.).

suggestióne, *s.f.* **1.** suggestion (anche *med.)*: *— ipnotica,* hypnotic suggestion: *un ammalato per —,*

a hypochondriac; *potere di —,* power of suggestion; *soffrire un male per —,* to suffer from a psychosomatic ailment **2.** *(dir.)* undue influence.

suggestivaménte, *av.* **1.** evocatively **2.** *(in modo da suggestionare)* suggestively.

suggestívo, *ag.* **1.** evocative: *atmosfera, canzone, scena suggestiva,* evocative atmosphere, song, scene **2.** *(che suggestiona)* suggestive: *domande suggestive,* leading questions.

súghera, *s.f.* *(bot.)* cork-tree, cork-oak.

sugheréto, *s.m.* cork-plantation; cork-forest.

sugherifício, *s.m.* cork-factory.

súghero, *s.m.* cork; *(albero)* cork-tree, cork-oak: *— granulato,* granulated cork; *giacca di —, (salvagente)* cork-jacket; *ricoperto di —,* covered with cork.

sugheróso, *ag.* corky.

súgna, *s.f.* pork fat.

súgo, *s.m.* **1.** juice: *— d'arancia,* orange-juice; *— di limone,* lemon-juice; *questi pomodori non hanno —,* these tomatoes have no juice ‖ *il — dell'uva,* the juice of the grape **2.** *(cuc.)* *(di carne)* gravy; *(di pomodoro)* sauce: *spaghetti col sugo,* spaghetti with tomato-sauce; *dammi un pezzetto di carne senza —,* give me a bit of meat without gravy **3.** *fig.* *(sostanza)* gist, essence: *il — di un discorso, di un libro,* the essence (o gist) of a speech, of a book; *senza —,* without rhyme or reason: *un discorso senza —,* an empty speech.

sugosaménte, *av.* *fig.* pithily, concisely.

sugosità, *s.f.* **1.** juiciness **2.** *fig.* *(vigore, sostanza)* pithiness.

sugóso, *ag.* **1.** juicy: *un'arancia sugosa,* a juicy orange **2.** *fig.* *(vigoroso, sostanzioso)* pithy: *un discorso —,* a pithy speech.

suicida, *ag.* suicidal: *mania —,* suicidal mania ‖ *s.c.* suicide.

suicidàrsi, *v.r.* to commit suicide, to kill oneself.

suicìdio, *s.m.* suicide: *commettere —,* to commit suicide.

suindicàto, *ag.* above-mentioned.

suíno, *ag.* swine *(attributivo)*, of swine: *carne suina,* pork ‖ *s.m.* swine *(invariato al pl.)*, hog.

suite, *s.f.* *(mus.)* suite.

sulfamídico, *ag.* *(farm.)* sulphamidic ‖ *s.m.* *(farm.)* sulphonamide, sulphamide.

sulfúreo, *ag.* **1.** *(chim.)* sulphureous **2.** *fig.* *(infiammabile)* easily excited: *temperamento —,* inflammable temperament.

sullodàto, *ag.* already praised.

Sulpício, *no.pr.m.* *(st. romana)* Sulpicius.

sultàna, *s.f.* sultana.

sultanàto, *s.m.* sultanate.

sultanína, *s.f.* *(bot.)* sultana.

sultàno, *s.m.* sultan ‖ *il Gran Sultano,* the Grand Turk.

summenzionàto, *ag.* above-mentioned, aforesaid.

summúltiplo, *ag.s.m.* *(arit.)* submultiple.

súnna, *s.f.* *(relig. maomettana)* Sunna(h).

sunníta, *s.c.* Sunnite.

sunnominàto, *ag.* above-mentioned, above named.

sunteggiàre, *v.t.* to sum up, to summarize.

súnto, *s.m.* summary, résumé: *sunti di letteratura italiana,* summaries of Italian literature; *fare un —,* to make a summary; *fare il — di un racconto,* to sum up a story.

suntuàrio, *ag.* *(dir.)* sumptuary: *legge suntuaria,* sumptuary law.

suntuosaménte, *av.* sumptuously, luxuriously; magnificently.

suntuosità, *s.f.* sumptuousness, luxuriousness; magnificence.

suntuóso, *ag.* sumptuous, luxurious, magnificent: *una casa suntuosa,* a magnificent house; *vestito, ricevimento —,* sumptuous dress, reception.

súo, *ag. poss.* **1.** *(riferito a persone)* his *(di lui)*; her *(di lei)*; *(riferito a cose o ad animali di sesso non specificato)* its; *(suo proprio)* his own; her own; its own:

l'albero e i suoi frutti, the tree and its fruits; *la grande città e le sue attrattive*, the big city and its attractions; *quel — orgoglio*, that pride of his, of hers; *l'uomo e il — cane*, the man and his dog; *egli era con un — amico*, he was with one of his friends (*o* with a friend of his); *ha una casa sua?*, has he got a house of his own?; *non è affar —*, it is no business of his, hers; *non mi piace quella sua cugina*, I don't like that cousin of hers; *Roma ha un — fascino particolare*, Rome has a charm of its own; *la signora e — figlio vennero da me ieri*, the lady and her son came to my house yesterday || *Sua Eminenza*, His Eminence; *Sua Maestà*, His, Her Majesty; *Sua Santità*, His Holiness || *in vece sua*, instead of him, her (*o* in his, her stead) || *ogni cosa a — tempo*, there is a time for everything || *è venuto con la — Maria*, he has come with Mary || *lo fece per amor —*, he did it for love of him, of her (*o* for his, her sake) || *ormai ha i suoi sessant'anni suonati*, he is now past (*o* over) sixty || *sta prendendo il — caffè*, he is having his coffee 2. (*formula di cortesia*) **your**: *La ringraziamo della Sua lettera del 21 c.m.*, thank you for your letter of the 21st inst. || *Suo Giuseppe Rossi*, yours sincerely Giuseppe Rossi 3. (*come pred. nominale*) **his**; **hers**; (*rar.*) **its**: *il libro che ti ho prestato è —*, the book I have lent you is his, hers; *queste riviste sono sue*, these magazines are his, hers 4. (*con valore indef.*) **one's**; (*suo proprio*) **one's own**: *fare il — proprio comodo*, to do what one likes; *fare a — modo*, to do things one's own way 5. (*in forme ellittiche*): *con riferimento alla Sua pregiata (lettera) del 6 febbraio*, with reference to your letter (*o* to yours) of the 6 th February; *egli crede che io sia dalla sua (parte)*, he thinks I am on his side; *egli stava sulle sue*, he kept himself to himself; *ha un santo dalla sua*, he has an angel to look after him; *ne ha fatta una delle sue*, he has been up to his old (*o* usual) tricks; *ognuno ha le sue*, everyone has his own troubles; *vuol sempre dir la sua*, she always wants to have her say || **pron. poss.** (*riferito a persone*) **his** (*di lui*); **hers** (*di lei*): *dice che questo libro non è il —*, he says this book is not his; *non avevo fazzoletto, e lei me ne ha prestato uno dei suoi*, I had no handkerchief and she lent me one of hers; *questo è il tuo cappello, quello è il —*, this is your hat, that one is his, hers; *ti ha reso la penna e ora rendigli la sua*, he has given you back your pen, now give him his back || **s.m. 1.** *egli campa del —*, he lives on his income; *egli spende del —*, he spends his own money || *a ciascuno il —*, prov. to each one his own 2. (*partitivo*): *qualcosa, niente di —*, something, nothing of his own, her own 3. *pl.*: *i suoi*, his, her family (*o* his, her relatives *o fam.* his, her folks; his, her people); (*partigiani, seguaci*) his, her supporters.

suòcera, *s.f.* mother -in-law || *non fare la —!*, (*fam.*) don't nag at me!.

suòcero, *s.m.* father-in-law.

suòla, *s.f.* 1. sole: *— di gomma*, rubber sole; *— di para*, rubber sole; *— interna*, inner sole; *scarpe a — doppia*, double-soled shoes 2. (*di forno*) hearth, sole, bottom: *— acida*, acid bottom 3. (*miner.*) floor 4. (*di rotaia*) flange 5. (*mar.*) sole.

suòlo, *s.m.* 1. soil, ground: *— fertile, povero*, fertile, poor soil; *cadere al —*, to fall to the ground; *radere al —*, to raze to the ground || *il — patrio, nativo*, one's native soil 2. (*strato*) layer; bed: *un — di cemento*, a layer of cement; *un — di crema*, a layer of cream.

suonàre, *e derivati*, *V.* **sonàre**, *e derivati*.

suòno, *s.m.* 1. sound: *il — del pianoforte, del violino*, the sound of a piano, of a violin; *un — gradevole, stridulo, lamentoso*, a pleasant, shrill, mournful sound; *direttore del —*, sound director; *la fisica del —*, the physics of sound; *mandare un —*, to emit (*o* to give out) a sound; *udire un —*, to hear a sound || *barriera del —*, sound barrier || *lo accolsero a suon di fischi*, they greeted him with boos; *lo fecero ubbidire a suon di*

bastonate, they beat him into doing it 2. (*musica*) music: *con suoni e canti*, with music and songs 3. (*fonet.*) sound: *— vocalico*, vowel sound.

suòra, *s.f.* nun; sister: *suore di Carità*, Sisters of Charity; *Suor Maria*, Sister Mary; *ella parlava con una —*, she was talking to a nun.

superàbile, *ag.* surmountable.

superabilità, *s.f.* superability.

superalimentazióne, *s.f.* superalimentation, supernutrition.

superaménto, *s.m.* overcoming, surmounting; getting over; (*di esame*) getting through.

superàre, *v.t.* 1. (*oltrepassare, sorpassare*) to exceed; to be over (*sthg.*); (*aspettative*) to surpass, to exceed; (*riferito a persona*) to surpass, to excel: *l'allievo ha superato il maestro*, the pupil surpassed his master; *questa nave non supera i quindici nodi orari*, this ship cannot exceed fifteen knots; *il risultato ha superato tutte le nostre speranze*, the outcome exceeded all our hopes; *se non supera le dieci sterline, compralo pure*, buy it if it is not over (*o* more than) ten pounds; *la sua recitazione ha superato le mie aspettative*, his performance exceeded my expectations; *superò tutti i rivali*, he excelled all his rivals; *— in altezza, lunghezza*, to be higher, longer (*o* to exceed in height, in length); *— in numero, in peso*, to exceed in number, weight; *— in velocità*, to exceed in speed (*o* to be faster): *la mia macchina supera in velocità qualunque altra*, my car is faster than any other; *— qlcu. di x punti*, (*durante la partita*) to be x points ahead of s.o.; (*come risultato finale*) to score x points more than s.o.; *— qlcu. in ql.co.*, to excel s.o. in (*o* at) sthg. (*o* to surpass s.o. in sthg.): *lo supera in intelligenza, dottrina, astuzia*, he surpasses him in intelligence, learning, cunning || *— ogni primato*, to break all records || *— se stesso*, to surpass oneself 2. (*passare al di là di*) to get over (*sthg.*); (*attraversare*) to cross; (*oltrepassare un veicolo*) to pass: *mi superò in curva*, he passed me on a bend; *— un fiume, un burrone*, to cross a river, a ravine; *— un muro*, to get over a wall; *— una vetta*, to climb over a mountain-summit 3. (*vincere, sormontare*) to overcome, to surmount; to get over (*sthg.*); (*passare*) to get through (*sthg.*), to pass: *— una difficoltà, un ostacolo*, to overcome (*o* to surmount) a difficulty, an obstacle; *— un esame*, to get through (*o* to pass) an examination; *— una malattia*, to get over an illness; *— il nemico*, to overcome the enemy; *— un pericolo*, to overcome a danger; *— un periodo critico*, to get over (*o* to overcome) a critical period; *— la prova*, to pass the test || *— il concetto di patria*, to overcome nationalistic feelings.

superbaménte, *av.* 1. arrogantly; proudly; haughtily 2. (*magnificamente*) splendidly, superbly.

superbia, *s.f.* arrogance; pride; haughtiness: *montare in —*, to put on airs.

superbiosaménte, superbióso, *V.* **superbaménte, supèrbo**.

superbìre, *v.i.* to become arrogant, to grow arrogant, to put on airs.

supèrbo, *ag.* 1. arrogant; proud; haughty: *risposta superba*, arrogant (*o* haughty) answer; *un tono —*, a haughty (*o* arrogant) tone; *è giustamente — di suo figlio*, he is rightly proud of his son; *egli è molto —*, he is very arrogant (*o* self-conceited); *è troppo — per venire con noi*, he is too proud to come with us 2. (*altissimo*) lofty, sublime: *superbe vette*, lofty heights 3. (*magnifico*) splendid, superb: *superbi tesori d'arte*, splendid art treasures; *una casa superba*, a superb house; *un successo —*, a splendid success.

superdònna, *s.f.* paragon: *si crede una —*, she thinks she is a paragon.

supererogatòrio, *ag.* supererogatory: *opere supererogatorie*, works of supererogation.

supererogazióne, *s.f.* supererogation.

superfetazióne, *s.f.* (*med.*) superfetation.
superficiàle, *ag.* **1.** superficial (anche *fig.*): *l'aspetto — delle cose,* the superficial aspect of things; *cultura —,* superficial culture; *ferita —,* superficial wound; *persona —,* superficial person; *strato —,* superficial layer; *ho solo una conoscenza — di questo argomento,* I only have a superficial knowledge (*o* a smattering) of this subject **2.** (*geom.*) plane: *figure superficiali,* plane figures.
superficialità, *s.f.* superficiality.
superficialménte, *av.* superficially.
superficie, *s.f.* **1.** surface (anche *fig.*): *la — dell'acqua,* the surface of the water; *— liscia, ruvida,* smooth, rough surface; *— non lucida,* matting; *— piana, sferica,* plane, spherical surface; *— soggetta ad usura,* (*di una strada*) wearing surface; *— superiore,* top face; *— tirata a gesso,* (*pitt.*) gesso; *a — accidentata,* lumpy; *egli non va mai al di là della — delle cose,* he never goes beyond the surface of things; *è un uomo che in fatto di cultura è rimasto alla —,* he is a man whose culture is only superficial (*o* only skin-deep); *ferita che non va oltre la —,* wound which is only superficial **2.** (*geom.*) area: *misure di —,* square measures; *calcolare la — di un rettangolo,* to calculate the area of a rectangle; *misurare la — di una stanza,* to measure the area of a room **3.** *— bagnata,* (*mar.*) wet surface **4.** (*mec.*) (*di scorrimento*) way, surface: *— d'appoggio,* supporting surface; *— del pezzo,* work surface; *— di lavoro,* (*di un calibro*) gauging surface; *— portante,* bearing surface; *— smerigliata,* lapped surface.
superfluaménte, *av.* superfluously, unnecessarily.
superfluità, *s.f.* superfluity.
supèrfluo, *ag.* superfluous, unnecessary, needless: *parole, osservazioni superflue,* superfluous words, remarks; *spesa superflua,* unnecessary expense ‖ *s.m.* surplus.
superióra, *s.f.* (*eccl.*) Mother Superior.
superióre, *ag.* **1.** (*in senso assoluto*) **superior:** *un essere —,* a superior being; *una mente —,* a superior brain; *una persona —,* a highly-gifted person; *qualità —,* superior quality ‖ *ha sempre un'aria —,* (*di superiorità*) he always has a superior air (*o* an air of superiority) **2.** (*con valore comparativo*) **superior:** *è — a tutti noi in virtù e buon senso,* he is superior to us all in virtue and common-sense; *fummo travolti da una forza —,* we were overwhelmed by a superior force; *i nemici erano superiori in numero,* the enemy were superior in number; *questa merce è — alla tua,* these goods are superior to yours **3.** (*più alto, più elevato*) **higher:** *un grado —,* a higher degree; *prezzo, temperatura, velocità —,* higher price, temperature, speed; *una somma —,* a larger amount **4.** (*sovrastante*) **upper:** *le classi superiori,* the upper classes; *labbro, mascella, arto —,* upper lip, jaw, limb; *i piani superiori di una casa,* the upper floors of a house; *le regioni superiori dell'atmosfera,* the upper atmosphere; *abita al piano —,* he lives on the floor above; (*di una casa a due piani*) he lives on the upper floor ‖ *la parte — di un fiume,* (*a monte*) the upper part of a river **5.** (*al di sopra*) **above:** *— alla media,* above-average; *egli è — a ogni sospetto, critica, lode,* he is above suspicion, criticism, praise; *egli è — a queste meschinità,* he is above (*o* superior to) such meanness; *è un prezzo — alle mie possibilità,* it's a price above my possibilities **6.** (*di grado superiore*) **senior:** *le classi superiori di questa scuola,* the senior classes in this school; *dirigente —,* senior manager; *scuola secondaria —,* senior high-school; *ufficiale —,* senior officer **7.** (*più avanzato*) **advanced:** *istruzione —,* advanced education; *matematica —,* advanced mathematics; *scuola — di disegno,* advanced school of drawing; *studi superiori,* advanced studies ‖ *s.m.* **1. superior:** *rispettoso con i superiori,* respectful to one's superiors; *fu chiamato dal suo —,* he was called by his superior; *un ufficiale deve ubbidire ai superiori,* an officer must obey his superiors (in rank) **2.** (*eccl.*) *il* (*Padre*) *Superiore,* Father Superior **3.** *pl.*

(*autorità*) authorities: *con licenza dei superiori,* by permission of the authorities.
superiorità, *s.f.* superiority: *— di grado,* superiority of rank; *— di numero,* superiority in numbers; *la — della sua forza è evidente,* the superiority of his strength is evident ‖ *complesso di —,* (*psicologia*) superiority complex ‖ *la sua aria di — mi dà ai nervi,* his air of superiority gets on my nerves.
superiorménte, *av.* **1.** superiorly **2.** (*nella parte superiore*) on the upper part, on the upper side **3.** (*antecedentemente*) above: *— menzionato,* above-mentioned.
superlativaménte, *av.* superlatively.
superlatívo, *ag.* superlative: *bellezza, bontà superlativa,* superlative beauty, goodness; *grado —,* (*gram.*) superlative degree ‖ *s.m.* (*gram.*) superlative: *— assoluto, relativo,* absolute, relative superlative; *un aggettivo al —,* an adjective in the superlative.
supernaménte, *av.* (*letter.*) celestially; divinely.
supèrno, *ag.* (*letter.*) **1.** (*supremo, divino*) supernal; celestial, heavenly; divine: *le cose superne,* celestial things; *la volontà superna,* the Divine Will **2.** (*superiore*) superior: *grado —,* superior degree.
supernutrizióne, *s.f.* supernutrition.
súpero, *ag.* (*letter.*) celestial ‖ *i superi,* the Celestials (*o* the Gods).
supersònico, *ag.* supersonic: *velocità supersonica,* supersonic speed.
supèrstite, *ag.* surviving: *figli superstiti,* surviving children ‖ *s.m.* survivor: *i soli superstiti dell'alluvione,* the only survivors of the flood.
superstizióne, *s.f.* superstition.
superstiziosaménte, *av.* superstitiously.
superstizióso, *ag.* superstitious.
superuòmo, *s.m.* superman (*pl.* supermen).
supervisióne, *s.f.* supervision.
supervisóre, *s.m.* supervisor.
supinaménte, *av.* **1.** supinely (anche *fig.*) **2.** (*servilmente*) servilely.
supíno, *ag.* **1.** supine; *giacere, cadere —,* to lie, to fall on one's back **2.** *fig.* (*servile*) servile; (*inerte*) supine: *obbedienza supina,* servile obedience; *rassegnazione supina,* supine resignation ‖ *ignoranza supina,* crass ignorance ‖ *s.m.* (*gram.*) supine.
suppellèttile, *s.f.* **1.** furnishings (*pl.*); (*tec. mil.*) equipment: *la — archeologica di un museo,* the archeological treasures of a museum; *le suppellettili di casa,* household furnishings; *le suppellettili di una chiesa,* the furnishings of a church; *la — di un gabinetto di fisica,* the equipment of a physics laboratory; *le suppellettili di una scuola,* the furnishings of a school; *le suppellettili di un ufficio,* the furnishings of an office; *— militare,* military equipment; *furono scoperte due tombe con ricca —,* they discovered two richly-furnished tombs **2.** *fig.* (*capitale di cognizioni*) store of knowledge.
suppergiú, *av.* (*circa*) about, approximately, roughly; (*quasi*) almost, nearly, practically: *è — la stessa cosa,* it's practically (*o* roughly) the same thing; *hanno — la stessa età,* they are about the same age.
supplementàre, *ag.* supplementary, additional, extra: *aiuto —,* additional help; *angolo —,* (*geom.*) supplementary angle (*o* supplement); *compenso — per lavoro straordinario,* extra pay for overtime; *edizione —,* supplementary edition; *ore supplementari* (*di lavoro*), overtime: *due ore supplementari,* two hours of overtime; *spesa —,* additional charge; *tassa —,* supplementary tax (*o* surtax); *treno —,* relief-train.
suppleménto, *s.m.* **1.** supplement; (*appendice*) appendix (*pl.* appendices, appendixes); (*spesa supplementare*) extra (charge), additional charge; (*di biglietto ferroviario*) excess fare: *— di prezzo,* extra charge; *il — di una rivista, di un giornale,* the supplement to a magazine, to a newspaper; *ci sarà un — di duemila lire,* there will be an additional charge (*o* an extra) of two thousand lire; *posso avere un — di dolce?,* may I have some more cake?; *pagare il —,* (*ferr.*)

to pay the excess fare **2.** (*geom.*) supplement: *il — di quell'angolo è di settanta gradi*, the supplement of that angle is seventy degrees.

supplènte, *ag.* temporary: *un professore —*, a temporary teacher ‖ *s.c.* substitute, temporary teacher; (*di scuole elementari*) supply-teacher.

supplènza, *s.f.* temporary post: *avevo una — in una scuola statale*, I had a temporary post in a state school; *fare una —*, to act as substitute.

suppletívo, suppletòrio, *ag.* supplementary.

súpplica, *s.f.* petition; supplication, entreaty: *cedetti alle sue suppliche*, I yielded to his entreaties; *presentarono una — al re*, they presented a petition to the king.

supplicànte, *ag.* suppliant: *atteggiamento —*, suppliant attitude ‖ *s.c.* petitioner, suppliant.

supplicàre, *v.t.* to beg, to implore, to entreat, to beseech, to supplicate: *mi supplicò di non farlo*, he begged (*o* implored) me not to do it; *— qlcu. per ottenere ql.co.*, to supplicate s.o. for sthg. (*o* to implore sthg. of s.o.).

supplicatóre, *s.m.* petitioner, suppliant.

supplicatòrio, *ag.* supplicatory.

supplicazióne, (*rar.*) per **súpplica.**

súpplice, *ag.s.c.* suppliant.

supplichévole, *ag.* imploring, supplicating, suppliant, entreating: *voce —*, imploring voice; *la guardò con aria —*, he looked at her beseechingly.

supplichevolménte, *av.* imploringly, supplicatingly, entreatingly.

supplíre, *v.i.* **1.** (*compensare*) to make up for (sthg.): *— alla mancanza di ql.co.*, to make up for the lack of sthg.; *egli supplisce con la diligenza alla mancanza d'ingegno*, he makes up for his lack of talent with hard work **2.** (*sostituire*) to replace (s.o., sthg.), to substitute (for s.o.): *supplirò all'insegnante assente*, I shall substitute for the absent teacher ‖ *v.t.* to take the place of (s.o., sthg.), to replace, to substitute for (s.o.): *lo supplirò per una settimana*, I shall take his place (*o* substitute for him) for a week.

suppliziàre, *v.t.* to torture, to rack.

supplízio, *s.m.* **1.** torture, torment: *il — della fustigazione*, the torture (*o* torment) of the lash; *i supplizi delle popolazioni primitive*, the tortures of primitive peoples ‖ *il — di Tantalo*, the torment of Tantalus (anche *fig.*): *far patire il — di Tantalo a qlcu.*, to tantalize s.o. ‖ *l'ultimo —*, capital punishment (*o* the extreme penalty) ‖ *andare al —*, to go to the gallows (*o* to the scaffold) **2.** *fig.* (*tormento, pena*) torment, anguish, agony: *che — udirlo parlare!*, what a torment to hear him speak!; *lo stare con lui è un vero —*, being with him is real agony (*o* torture).

supponíbile, *ag.* supposable, assumable.

suppórre, *v.t.* **1.** to suppose, to assume; to guess; (*immaginare*) to imagine: *supponendo che egli non te lo dica, che cosa farai?*, supposing he shouldn't tell you, what will you do?; *supponete di essere a Roma*, imagine yourself in Rome; *suppongo che egli venga*, I assume (*o* I suppose *o* I guess *o* I imagine) he will come; *suppongo di sì*, I suppose so; *supponiamo che le cose stiano così*, let us assume that such is the case **2.** (*rar.*) (*porre sotto*) to place under **3.** (*dir.*) (*sostituire*) to substitute.

suppòrto, *s.m.* support; (*di un utensile, pezzo*) rest; (*mec.*) (*boccola*) journal box; (*mec. edil.*) (*staffa*) bracket; (*di motore aereo*) mounting; (*mec.*) (*di albero*) bearing, journal box, pillow block; (*foto.*) (*di pellicola*) support; (*ferr.*) (*di rotaia*) chair: *— a muro*, (*mec.*) wall bearing; *— antenna radio*, (*aer.*) mast-antenna; *— antivibrante*, (*mec.*) shock-isolating mounting; *— da formatore*, (*metal.*) chaplet (*o* staple); *— del differenziale*, (*aut.*) differential-carrier (*o* axle-casing); *— del fuso*, (*ind. tessile*) splindle-bearing; *— della valvola*, (*rad.*) tube -socket; *— del perno*, (*mec.*) journal-bearing; *— magnetico*, (*mec.*) magnetic stand; *— per tubi*, pipe-stand; *cappello del —*, (*mec.*) bearing-cap.

suppositívo, *ag.* hypothetical, suppositional.

suppositízio, *ag.* supposititious; supposed; putative.

suppositòrio, *s.m.* (*farm.*) suppository.

supposizióne, *s.f.* **1.** supposition, assumption, conjecture: *una — infondata*, an unfounded supposition; *questa è solo una —*, this is only a supposition; *fare una —*, to make a supposition **2.** *— d'infante*, (*dir.*) setting-up of a supposititious child.

suppósta, *s.f.* (*farm.*) suppository.

suppósto, *ag.* supposed, assumed: *il — ladro*, the alleged thief; *il — nemico*, the supposed enemy ‖ *s.m.* supposition ‖ **suppósto che,** *l. cong.* suppose, supposing: *— che non venga*, supposing he should not come.

suppuraménto, *s.m.* suppuration.

suppuràre, *v.i.* to suppurate, to fester.

suppuratívo, *ag.* suppurative ‖ *s.m.* (*farm.*) suppurative.

suppurazióne, *s.f.* suppuration: *l'ascesso viene a —*, the abscess is suppurating.

supremaménte, *av.* **1.** supremely **2.** (*straordinariamente*) extraordinarily.

supremazía, *s.f.* supremacy: *— commerciale, industriale, navale*, commercial, industrial, naval supremacy; *la — della Repubblica Veneta sui mari*, the naval supremacy of the Republic of Venice ‖ *Atto di Supremazia*, (*st. inglese*) Act of Supremacy.

suprèmo, *ag.* **1.** (*sommo, altissimo*) supreme: *suprema felicità*, supreme bliss; *l'autorità suprema*, the supreme authority; *il bene —*, the supreme good; *il Capo — della Chiesa*, the Supreme Pontiff; *il Capo — dello Stato*, the Head of State ‖ *il Comandante Supremo*, (*mil.*) the commander-in-chief; *comando —*, (*mil.*) headquarters (*abbr.* H.Q.) ‖ *il Consiglio Supremo*, the Supreme Council ‖ *la Corte Suprema*, the Supreme Court of Justice ‖ *l'Ente Supremo*, the Supreme Being **2.** (*principale*) prime, chief: *la suprema ragione*, the prime reason **3.** (*straordinario*) extraordinary: *di suprema bellezza*, of extraordinary (*o* extreme) beauty **4.** (*massimo*) great(est), highest: *con — disprezzo del pericolo*, with the greatest (*o* utmost) contempt for danger; *con — sforzo*, with great effort; *con mia suprema soddisfazione*, to my great satisfaction; *è cosa di suprema importanza*, it is a matter of the highest (*o* of the utmost *o* of the paramount) importance; *giunse a un grado — di felicità*, he reached the highest degree of happiness **5.** (*ultimo, estremo*) last: *il — addio*, the last farewell; *il — conforto della fede*, the last consolation of one's faith; *l'ora suprema*, one's last hour; *il suo sforzo —*, his crowning effort ‖ *il Giudizio Supremo*, the Last Judgement.

súra¹, *s.f.* (*capitolo del Corano*) sura.

súra², *s.f.* (*arc. anat.*) **1.** (*polpaccio*) calf (of the leg) **2.** (*fibula*) fibula (*pl.* fibulae, fibulas).

suràle, *ag.* (*arc. anat.*) sural: *vena —*, sural vein.

surgelaménto, *s.m.* (*neol.*) deep-freeze.

surgelàre, *v.t.* (*neol.*) to deep-freeze.

surménage, *s.m.* overwork.

surplus, *s.m.* surplus.

surrealísmo, *s.m.* (*st. art.*) surrealism.

surrealísta, *ag.s.m.* (*st. art.*) surrealist: *il movimento —*, the surrealist movement.

surrealisticaménte, *av.* (*st. art.*) surrealistically.

surrealístico, *ag.* (*st. ari.*) surrealistic.

surrenàle, *ag.* (*anat.*) suprarenal: *ghiandole surrenali*, suprarenal bodies (*o* capsules *o* glands).

surrettiziaménte, *av.* (*dir.*) surreptitiously.

surrettízio, *ag.* (*dir.*) surreptitious.

surriferíto, *ag.* above-mentioned: *l'ordine —*, (*comm.*) the above-mentioned order (*o* the order mentioned above).

surriscaldaménto, *s.m.* **1.** overheating **2.** (*fis.*) superheating, superheat: *— di vapore*, superheating.

surriscaldàre, *v.t.* **1.** to overheat **2.** (*fis.*) to superheat ‖ *v.i.*, **surriscaldàrsi,** *v.r.* to overheat, to get overheated: *il motore si è surriscaldato*, the engine has got overheated.

surriscaldàto, *ag.* **1.** overheated: *motore —*, overheated engine **2.** (*fis.*) superheated: *vapore —*, superheated steam.

surrogàbile, *ag.* replaceable.

surrogaménto, *s.m.* substitution, replacement.

surrogàre, *v.t.* **1.** to replace, to substitute: *dobbiamo surrogarlo con una persona più competente*, we must replace him with a more competent person; *— un prodotto con uno più economico*, to substitute one product with (*o* by) a more economical one **2.** (*prendere il posto di*) to replace, to substitute for (s.o.), to take the place of (s.o.): *sono stato chiamato a — l'insegnante assente*, I was called to substitute for the absent teacher.

surrogàto, *s.m.* substitute, surrogate: *— (del caffè)*, coffee surrogate (*o* substitute).

surrogazióne, *s.f.* **1.** substitution, replacement **2.** (*dir.*) subrogation: *— convenzionale*, conventional subrogation; *— di diritto*, subrogation established by (the) law.

Susànna, *no.pr.f.* Susan ‖ *dim.* Sue, Suky, Susie, Susy.

suscettíbile, *ag.* **1.** susceptible: *— di grandi sviluppi*, admitting of important developments; *— di miglioramento*, susceptible of improvement; *un testo — di molte interpretazioni*, a text susceptible of many interpretations **2.** (*permaloso*) touchy: *come sei —!*, how touchy you are!.

suscettibilità, *s.f.* **1.** susceptibility **2.** (*permalosità*) touchiness: *non intendevo urtare la sua —*, I did not mean to hurt his feelings.

suscitaménto, *s.m.* (*il provocare*) provoking, causing; (*l'eccitare*) exciting.

suscitàre, *v.t.* (*provocare*) to provoke, to cause, to give rise to (sthg.); to excite, to stir up: *ciò suscitò molte lamentele*, this gave rise to (*o* provoked) many complaints; *quella legge ingiusta susciterà sicuramente una rivolta*, that unjust law will certainly provoke (*o* cause) a riot; *il suo comportamento suscitò ovunque molta ammirazione*, his behaviour excited admiration everywhere; *— discordia*, to stir up discord; *— emozioni, passioni*, to stir up emotions, passions; *— indignazione*, to cause indignation; *— le ire di qlcu.*, to excite s.o.'s anger; *— malcontento, odio*, to stir up discontent, hatred; *— il riso*, to provoke laughter; *— uno scandalo*, to provoke (*o* to give rise to) a scandal.

susina, *s.f.* (*bot.*) plum.

susíno, *s.m.* (*bot.*) plum-tree.

suspicióne, *s.f.* (*dir.*) suspicion.

susseguènte, *ag.* subsequent, following: *eventi susseguenti*, subsequent events; *nei giorni susseguenti*, in the following days.

susseguenteménte, *av.* subsequently, later on, afterwards.

susseguíre, *v.i.* to follow (s.o., sthg.); to succeed: *all'esplosione susseguì un grande fragore*, a great roar followed the explosion; *i tuoni si susseguivano l'un l'altro ininterrottamente*, the rolls of thunder followed one another without a break.

sussidiàre, *v.t.* **1.** to support, to back; (*di governo*) to subsidize: *le ferrovie sono sussidiate dal governo*, the railways are subsidized by the government; *una grande ditta americana sussidia queste ricerche*, a large American firm is backing (*o* supporting) this research **2.** (*aiutare*) to help, to aid.

sussidiariaménte, *av.* subsidiarily; supplementarily.

sussidiàrio, *ag.* subsidiary: *armi sussidiarie*, subsidiary arms; *mezzi sussidiari*, subsidiary means; *truppe sussidiarie*, reserve troops.

sussídio, *s.m.* **1.** subsidy; (*rar.*) subvention: *il governo concede sussidi alle industrie*, the government grants subsidies to industry **2.** (*aiuto*) aid, help: *mandò i soldati in — della città*, he sent his soldiers to help the town.

sussiègo, *s.m.* haughtiness: *il suo — mi mette a disagio*, his haughtiness makes me feel uneasy; *trattare qlcu. con —*, to treat s.o. condescendingly.

sussistènte, *ag.* existing; existent; subsisting.

sussistènza, *s.f.* **1.** existence **2.** (*sostentamento*) subsistence, livelihood: *mezzi di —*, means of subsistence; *ha appena il sufficiente per la sua —*, he has hardly enough to live on; *i suoi mezzi di — sono molto scarsi*, his means of subsistence are very scanty; *guadagnare la propria —*, to earn one's living **3.** (*mil.*) (*il corpo*) Catering Corps; (*le provvigioni*) army provisions (*pl.*): *l'organizzazione della —*, the organization of the Catering Corps; *sussistenze militari*, military supplies; *le sussistenze erano insufficienti*, the army provisions were insufficient.

sussístere, *v.i.* **1.** to exist; to subsist: *legge che ancora sussiste in molte regioni*, law that still subsists in many countries; *queste speranze esist only in the minds of fools* **2.** (*esser valido, reggere*) to hold good; to hold water: *le sue ragioni non sussistono*, his arguments do not hold water.

sussultàre, *v.i.* **1.** to start, to give a start: *egli sussultò al suono del campanello*, he started (*o* he gave a start) at the sound of the bell; *mi hai fatto —*, you made me jump; *il mio cuore sussultava*, my heart was beating violently; *— di paura*, to start with fright ‖ *far — qlcu.*, to startle s.o. **2.** (*di cose*) to shake: *il ponte sussultò per il terremoto*, the bridge was shaken by the earthquake; *la terra sussultò*, the earth shook.

sussúlto, *s.m.* **1.** start, jump: *mi svegliai con un —*, I woke up with a start; *il mio cuore ebbe un —*, my heart leapt; *avere un — di gioia*, to leap for joy **2.** (*del suolo*) tremor.

sussurràre, *v.t.i.* **1.** to whisper; to murmur; (*di foglie*) to rustle: *il ruscello sussurrava fra gli alberi*, the brook was murmuring among the trees; *il vento sussurrava fra i rami*, the wind was whispering among the branches; *— una parola*, to whisper a word **2.** (*criticare, accusare a bassa voce*) to murmur; to speak badly (of s.o.): *egli sussurra contro di me*, he speaks badly of me; *il popolo sussurrava contro il governo*, the people were murmuring against the government **3.** (*di api, ronzare*) to buzz.

sussurratóre, *s.m.*, **sussurratríce**, *s.f.* **1.** whisperer **2.** (*maldicente*) murmurer; backbiter.

sussurrío, *s.m.* whispering (*anche fig.*); murmuring (*anche fig.*); (*di foglie*) rustling.

sussúrro, *s.m.* whisper; murmur; (*di foglie*) rustling; rustle: *il — di un ruscello, delle api*, the murmur of a brook, of bees; *il — del vento*, the whisper of the wind; *la sua voce era un —*, his voice was a whisper.

sussurróne, *s.m.* **1.** whisperer **2.** (*maldicente*) murmurer; backbiter **3.** (*persona che fa chiasso*) rowdy person, noisy person.

sutúra, *s.f.* (*anat. chir.*) suture.

suturàre, *v.t.* (*chir.*) to suture.

svagaménto, *s.m.* diversion, recreation.

svagàre, *v.t.* **1.** to distract s.o.'s attention, to divert: *cerchiamo di distrarlo e fargli dimenticare il suo dolore*, we try to distract his thoughts (*o* mind *o* attention) and make him forget his sorrow; *non è difficile svagarlo dal lavoro*, it is not difficult to divert him from his work; *tutti questi rumori mi svagano*, all these noises distract my attention **2.** (*divertire*) to amuse, to divert, to entertain: *la lettura è la cosa che lo svaga di più*, reading is the thing that amuses him most ‖ **svagàrsi**, *v.r.* **1.** to distract one's mind, to divert one's mind, to be diverted: *cerco di svagarmi ma non posso dimenticare quello che ho visto*, I try to distract (*o* divert) my mind but I cannot forget what I saw; *egli si svaga facilmente*, he is easily diverted **2.** (*divertirsi*) to amuse oneself, to enjoy oneself: *lavori troppo, hai bisogno di svagarti un po'*, you work too much, you need to amuse (*o* to enjoy) yourself a little.

svagatàggine, *s.f.* **1.** liking for amusement **2.** (*distrazione*) absent-mindedness, abstraction.

svagatézza, *s.f.* absent-mindedness, abstraction.

svagàto, *ag.* absent-minded ‖ *s.m.* absent-minded person.

svàgo, *s.m.* **1.** relaxation, diversion, amusement; (*passatempo*) hobby: *il giardinaggio è uno dei miei svaghi preferiti*, gardening is one of my favourite diversions; *ho bisogno di un po' di* —, I need some relaxation (*o* amusement); *raccoglie francobolli per* —, he collects postage-stamps as a hobby; *concedersi, prendersi un po' di* —, to enjoy oneself a little **2.** (*divertimento*) amusement, entertainment: *questa città non offre molti svaghi*, there are not many entertainments (*o* amusements) in this town.

svaligiaménto, *s.m.* robbery; plundering; (*di una casa*) burglary, house-breaking.

svaligiàre, *v.t.* **1.** to rob; to plunder; (*una casa*) to burgle: *i ladri hanno svaligiato la casa*, the thieves burgled the house; — *un treno, una banca*, to rob a train, a bank **2.** (*togliere dalla valigia*) to unpack.

svaligiatóre, *s.m.* robber; plunderer; (*di case*) burglar, house-breaker.

svalutàre, *v.t.* **1.** to devalue, to depreciate: — *la sterlina*, to devalue the pound **2.** (*sottovalutare*) to undervalue, to underrate: *non devi* — *tutto ciò che ti dà*, you must not undervalue everything he gives you; *questo articolo è svalutato sui vostri mercati*, this article is undervalued (*o* underrated) in your markets.

svalutazióne, *s.f.* devaluation, depreciation.

svampàre, *v.i.* **1.** (*mandare vampe*) to burst out: *il vapore svampò*, the steam burst out **2.** *fig.* (*esaurirsi, calmarsi*) to calm down, to quieten down: *la sua ira svampò presto*, his anger soon died down.

svaniménto, *s.m.* **1.** (*lo sparire*) disappearance, disappearing; (*di luce, colori, ecc.*) fading (away) **2.** *fig.* (*il dileguarsi*) vanishing **3.** (*il placarsi*) calming **4.** (*il perdere forza*) weakening.

svanìre, *v.i.* **1.** (*sparire*) to disappear; (*di luce, colori, ecc.*) to fade (away): *il ladro svanì nella nebbia*, the thief disappeared into the fog; *la luce svaniva lentamente*, the light was slowly fading; *la visione svanì*, the vision faded **2.** *fig.* (*andare in fumo, dileguarsi*) to vanish, to fade, to be lost: *le mie speranze svanirono presto*, my hopes soon vanished (*o* soon faded *o* were soon lost); *i ricordi svaniscono*, memories fade; *il suo progetto svanì*, his plan came to nothing **3.** (*placarsi*) to calm down: *la sua ira svanì*, his anger calmed down **4.** (*perdere forza*) to lose strength, to grow weaker: *quell'odore è già svanito*, that smell has already grown weaker (*o* fainter); *questo vino è svanito*, this wine has lost its strength.

svanìto, *ag.* **1.** (*sparito*) disappeared **2.** *fig.* (*andato in fumo, dileguato*) vanished **3.** (*calmato*) calmed down: *sogno* —, vanished dream **4.** (*che ha perso forza*) weakened: *un odore* —, a lingering smell; *un vino* —, a wine which has lost its strength ‖ — *di mente*, feeble-minded ‖ *egli è sempre* —, he is always in the clouds.

svantàggio, *s.m.* **1.** disadvantage, drawback: *gli svantaggi della tirannia sono molti*, many are the drawbacks (*o* disadvantages) of tyranny; *questa soluzione ha molti svantaggi*, this solution has many disadvantages (*o* drawbacks.) ‖ *la squadra australiana aveva due punti di* —, the Australian team were two points behind **2.** (*danno*) detriment: *a* — *della sua salute*, to the detriment of his health; *un giudizio a suo* —, a judgement to his detriment.

svantaggiosaménte, *av.* disadvantageously, unfavourably.

svantaggióso, *ag.* **1.** disadvantageous, unfavourable: *in una posizione svantaggiosa*, in a disadvantageous (*o* an unfavourable) position **2.** (*dannoso*) detrimental, prejudicial.

svaporàbile, *ag.* evaporable.

svaporaménto, *s.m.* evaporation.

svaporàre, *v.i.* **1.** to evaporate **2.** *fig.* (*svanire*) to evaporate, to vanish: *la sua passione era già svaporata da un pezzo*, his passion had already evaporated some time before; *il suo cervello svapora*, he is worn out mentally **3.** (*perdere forza*) to lose strength: *l'etere svapora se la boccettina non è ben chiusa*, ether loses its strength if the mouthpiece is not properly closed.

svaporazióne, *s.f.* evaporation.

svariaménto, *s.m.* (*variazione*) variation, change.

svariàre, *v.t.i.* (*variare*) to vary.

svariataménte, *av.* (*variamente*) variously: *sciarpe* — *colorate*, variously coloured scarves.

svariatézza, *s.f.* (*varietà*) variety: — *dei colori*, variety of colours.

svariàto, *ag.* varied, various: *svariati colori, forme, oggetti*, varied (*o* various) colours, shapes, things; *svariate ragioni*, various reasons; *spettacolo* —, varied show.

svàrio, *s.m.* **1.** (*differenza*) variation **2.** (*errore*) mistake, blunder.

svarióne, *s.m.* (*grave errore*) blunder.

svasàre[1], *v.t.* (*mettere in altro vaso*) to re-pot.

svasàre[2], *v.t.* (*mec.*) to flare; (*un foro per l'alloggiamento di una vite*) to countersink.

svasàto, *ag.* **1.** (*di abito*) bell-shaped **2.** (*mec.*) countersunk.

svasatùra[1], *s.f.* (*il cambiar di vaso*) re-potting.

svasatùra[2], *s.f.* **1.** (*di abito*) bell-shaping **2.** (*mec.*) (*lo svasare*) flaring, belling; (*apertura svasata*) countersink (hole) **3.** — *muraria*, (*edil.*) embrasure.

svàstica, *s.f.* (*croce uncinata*) swastika.

svecchiaménto, *s.m.* renewal; modernization.

svecchiàre, *v.t.* to renew; to modernize, to bring (sthg.) up to date.

svedése, *ag.* Swedish ‖ *s.c.* Swede ‖ *s.m.* (*lingua*) (the) Swedish (language).

svéglia, *s.f.* **1.** early call: *domani* — *alle quattro*, tomorrow I want an early call (*o* to be called) at four **2.** (*orologio*) alarm-clock: *caricare la* — *per le sette*, to set the alarm for seven o' clock **3.** (*mil.*) reveille: *suonare la* —, to sound the reveille.

svegliàre, *v.t.* **1.** to wake (up), to rouse, to awake: *a che ora ti devo* —?, at what time shall I wake you (up)?; *il canto degli uccelli lo svegliò all'alba*, the birds' singing awoke him at dawn; *dissi che non dovevo essere svegliato*, I said I was not to be woken; *fui svegliato dal suono della sveglia*, I was woken up (*o* roused) by the sound of the alarm-clock; *non lo sveglierebbero nemmeno le cannonate*, it would take a bomb to wake him up; *non svegliarlo*, don't wake him (up) ‖ *non* — *il can che dorme*, *prov.* let sleeping dogs lie **2.** (*sveltire*) to wake up, to rouse; (*animare, scuotere*) to liven up: *è indifferente a tutto, cerca di svegliarlo un po'*, he is indifferent to everything, try to liven him up a little (*o* a bit); *le nuove esperienze l'hanno svegliato*, his new experiences have woken him up (*o* have roused him) **3.** (*risvegliare*) to awaken, to arouse, to rouse: *cercherò di* — *il suo interesse, la sua curiosità in questa materia*, I shall try to awaken his interest in, his curiosity about this subject; — *l'appetito di qlcu.*, to arouse s.o.'s appetite; — *l'intelligenza di un bambino*, to arouse (*o* to awaken) a child's intelligence; — *l'invidia, il sospetto*, to arouse envy, suspicion; — *il senso del dovere in qlcu.*, to awaken s.o. to a sense of duty ‖ **svegliàrsi,** *v.r.* **1.** to wake (up), to awake: *mi sveglio sempre alle cinque*, I always wake (up) at five; *quando mi svegliai vidi che erano già le dieci*, I woke up and found it was already ten o' clock; *si sveglia ad ogni minimo rumore*, he wakes at the slightest sound; *si svegliò di soprassalto*, he woke with a start ‖ *svegliati!*, wake up! **2.** *fig.* (*risvegliarsi*): *il loro odio si svegliò ancora*, their hatred was rekindled (*o* roused again); *la sua coscienza finalmente si svegliò*, his conscience was roused at last; *tutta la natura si sveglia in primavera*, all nature reawakens in spring **3.** (*di* *vento, levarsi*) to rise: *si sta svegliando la tramontana*, the north wind is rising **4.** (*sveltirsi*) to rouse, to wake up: *si è molto svegliato da quando lo vidi l'ultima volta*, he has roused himself since I saw him last.

svegliaríno, *s.m.* **1.** (*orologio a sveglia*) alarm -clock **2.** (*mezzo per richiamare la memoria*) reminder **3.** (*fervorino, rimprovero*) reproach.

svegliatézza, *s.f.* alertness, quickness, wideawakeness: — *di mente*, readiness (*o* quickness) of mind.

svegliàto, *ag.* awake (*predicativo*).

svéglio, *ag.* **1.** awake (*predicativo*): *completamente —*, wide-awake; *sei già —?*, are you already awake? **2.** *fig.* (*pronto d'ingegno*) wide-awake (*predicativo*); alert, quick, quick-witted, smart: *un ragazzo —*, a quick(-witted) (*o* smart) boy; *come è sveglia questa bambinetta!*, how alert this little girl is!.

svelaménto, *s.m.* revelation, disclosure.

svelàre, *v.t.* **1.** to reveal, to disclose: — *un complotto*, to reveal a plot; — *un nome*, to reveal a name; — *i propri sentimenti*, to disclose (*o* to reveal) one's feelings; — *un segreto*, to reveal (*o* to disclose) a secret **2.** (*togliere il velo a*) to unveil: — *una statua*, to unveil a statue || **svelàrsi,** *v.r.* to reveal oneself.

svelataménte, *av.* openly.

svelatóre, *s.m.*, **svelatríce,** *s.f.* revealer.

svelenàre, sveleníre, *v.t.* to unpoison; *fig.* to remove the sting from (sthg.) || **svelenàrsi, svelenírsi,** *v.r.* (*sfogarsi*) to let out steam, to vent one's anger.

svèllere, *v.t.* to extirpate, to eradicate, to root out (anche *fig.*).

sveltaménte, *av.* quickly.

sveltézza, *s.f.* **1.** (*rapidità*) quickness, speed, dispatch, despatch: *fa tutto con grande —*, he does everything quickly; *vorrei che fosse fatto con —*, I should like it to be done with dispatch (*o* quickly) || — *di mano*, quickness of hand **2.** (*prontezza*) quickness, promptness, readiness: *la sua — d'ingegno mi sorprese*, his quickness of wit (*o* his readiness of mind) surprised me **3.** (*forma slanciata*) slimness.

sveltíre, *v.t.* **1.** to make quicker, to quicken; (*rendere snello*) to slim; (*rendere più agile*) to make nimbler; (*rendere più elastico*) to make suppler: *la lettura sveltisce la mente, l'intelligenza*, reading quickens the mind, the understanding; *la pratica l'ha sveltito nel lavoro*, experience has taught him to work quickly; — *la figura*, to slim; — *il passo*, to quicken one's pace (*o* to hurry up); — *la produzione*, to speed up production; — *i propri movimenti*, to make one's movements more agile (*o* suppler); — *il traffico*, to speed up the traffic **2.** (*rendere disinvolto*) to make polished; (*svegliare*) to wake up, to rouse: *la tua compagnia l'ha sveltito*, your company has polished his manners; *i tuoi viaggi all'estero ti hanno sveltito*, your journeys abroad have roused you (*o* woken you up) **3.** (*abbreviare*) to shorten: — *un romanzo*, to shorten a novel **4.** (*semplificare*) to simplify: — *una procedura*, to simplify a procedure || **sveltírsi,** *v.r.* **1.** to become quick(er); (*diventare più agile*) to become nimbler; to become suppler: — *nel fare ql.co.*, to become quicker in doing sthg. **2.** (*diventare più disinvolto*) to polish one's manners; (*svegliarsi*) to rouse, to wake up.

svèlto[1], *ag.* **1.** (*pronto, lesto*) quick: *è molto — nel capire, nel fare le cose*, he is very quick in understanding, in doing things || *è — di lingua*, he's always got an answer; — *di mano*, quick-handed || *alla svelta*, quickly: *l'ho fatto molto alla —*, I have done it very quickly **2.** (*intelligente*) quick-witted, sharp-witted, smart, alert: *un ragazzo —*, a quick-witted (*o* smart) boy **3.** (*slanciato*) slender: *un campanile —*, a slender steeple; *ha una figura svelta*, she has a slender (*o* slim) figure || *av.* fast, quick, quickly: *fa' —!*, hurry up!; *vai troppo —!*, you go too fast!.

svèlto[2], *ag.* extirpated, eradicated.

svenàre, *v.t.* **1.** to open s.o.'s veins, to sever s.o.'s

veins **2.** *fig.* (*estorcere denaro a*) to bleed || **svenàrsi,** *v.r.* to cut one's veins, to sever one's veins.

svéndere, *v.t.* (*comm.*) to undersell, to sell at a loss, to sell below cost: *fui costretto a — un'intera partita di merce*, I was compelled to undersell a whole lot of goods.

svéndita, *s.f.* (*comm.*) clearance sale.

svenevolàggine, *s.f.* lackadaisicalness; (*fam.*) soppiness.

svenévole, *ag.* maudlin, languishing, lackadaisical; (*fam.*) soppy: *modi svenevoli*, mawkish (*o* lackadaisical manners); *una signora molto —*, a very sentimental lady.

svenevolézza, *s.f.* lackadaisicalness; sentimentality; (*fam.*) soppiness.

svenevolménte, *av.* lackadaisically; sentimentally; (*fam.*) soppily.

svènia, *s.f. spec. pl.* (*svenevolezza*) simpering; (*fam.*) sloppiness.

sveniménto, *s.m.* faint, fainting fit, swoon: *essere colto da —*, to faint away.

svveníre, *v.i.* to swoon, to faint: — *di gioia*, to swoon with joy; — *di paura*, to faint with fear.

sventagliàre, *v.t.* to fan || **sventagliàrsi,** *v.r.* to fan oneself.

sventagliàta, *s.f.* **1.** fanning **2.** (*colpo di ventaglio*) blow with a fan **3.** (*scarica di mitraglia*) burst.

sventàre, *v.t.* **1.** to baffle, to foil, to thwart, to balk, to frustrate: — *i piani del proprio avversario*, to baffle (*o* to foil) the plans of one's opponent || — *una mina*, to uncover a mine **2.** (*mar.*) to spill.

sventatàggine, sventatézza, *s.f.* **1.** thoughtlessness, heedlessness, recklessness, rashness **2.** (*atto sventato*) thoughtless action, oversight.

sventàto, *ag.* **1.** thwarted, foiled, frustrated: *una trama sventata*, a foiled plot **2.** (*sbadato*) thoughtless|| heedless, reckless; (*fam.*) light-headed, scatter-brained , *s.m.*, heedless person; (*fam.*) scatter-brain, harum -scarum: *sei proprio uno —!*, you are a regular harum -scarum.

svèntola, *s.f.* **1.** (*pop.*) fire-fan **2.** (*fam.*) (*scapaccione*) slap.

sventolaménto, *s.m.* waving, fluttering: — *di bandiere*, flag-waving.

sventolàre, *v.t.* to wave, to flutter: — *una bandiera*, to wave a flag; — *un fazzoletto*, to wave a handkerchief || *v.i.* to wave, to flutter: *la bandiera sventola*, the flag is waving; *i panni sventolavano al vento*, the clothes were fluttering in the wind || **sventolàrsi,** *v.r.* to fan oneself.

sventolío, *s.m.* waving, fluttering.

sventraménto, *s.m.* **1.** disembowelment; (*di pesce, uccello*) gutting; (*di pollame*) drawing **2.** (*demolizione dei quartieri malsani*) demolition of the slums (of a town).

sventràre, *v.t.* **1.** to disembowel to eviscerate; (*pesci, uccelli*) to gut; (*pollame*) to draw **2.** (*demolire la parte vecchia di*) to demolish the old part of (sthg.); to demolish the slums of (sthg.): — *una città*, to demolish the slums of a town || *v.i.* (*arc.*) (*mangiare a crepapelle*) to eat like a horse || **sventràrsi,** *v.r.* to disembowel oneself, to commit hara-kiri.

sventràto, *ag.* **1.** disembowelled; eviscerated; (*di pesce, uccello*) gutted; (*di pollo*) drawn **2.** (*pop.*) (*mai sazio*) very greedy, insatiable.

sventúra, *s.f.* **1.** (*sfortuna*) bad luck, misfortune: *provato dalla —*, tried by misfortune; *la — lo perseguita*, he is persecuted by bad luck; *portare —*, to bring bad luck; *predire la —*, to foretell misfortune **2.** (*disavventura*) misfortune; mishap; (*grave sciagura*) catastrophe, calamity: *una serie di sventure*, a series of misfortunes; *ha la — di non aver più i genitori*, he is unfortunate in having lost his parents; *la sua morte fu una — per tutti noi*, his death was a calamity for all of us || *per —*, unluckily (*o* unfortunately): *per mia —*, unluckily for me || *per colmo di —*, to crown it all: *ero stanco e affamato e, per colmo di —, persi la valigia*, I was tired and hungry and to crown it all I lost my suit-case.

sventuràto, *ag.* unfortunate, unlucky: *giorno —*, unlucky day; *uomo —*, unlucky (*o* unfortunate) man ‖ *s.m.*, unlucky person, unfortunate person, wretch.

svenùto, *ag.* in a faint (*predicativo*), in a swoon (*predicativo*); unconscious.

sverginaménto, *s.m.* defloration, deflowering.

sverginàre, *v.t.* to deflower.

svergognàre, *v.t.* to shame, to put to shame: *fu svergognato in faccia a tutti*, he was shamed in front of everybody; *voglio svergognarlo di fronte ai suoi amici*, I want to shame him in front of his friends.

svergognataménte, *av.* shamelessly; impudently.

svergognatézza, *s.f.* shamelessness; impudence.

svergognàto, *ag.* **1.** shameless; impudent: *un imbroglione —*, a shameless (*o* an impudent) swindler **2.** (*confuso, imbarazzato*) abashed.

svergolaménto, *s.m.* **1.** (*aer.*) twisting, warping **2.** (*mec.*) twisting, twist **3.** (*metal.*) (*di un getto*) warping.

svergolàre, *v.i.* **1.** (*aer.*) to twist; to warp **2.** (*mec.*) to twist.

sverlàre, *v.i.* to twitter, to chirp.

svernaménto, *s.m.* wintering.

svernàre, *v.i.* to winter, to spend the winter.

svèrza, *s.f.* **1.** (*scheggia*) splinter **2.** (*rar.*) (*verza*) savoy (cabbage).

svesciàre, *v.t.* to blab.

svescicàre, *v.t.*, **svescicàrsi,** *v.r.* to blister.

svescicatúra, *s.f.* blistering.

svesciόne, *s.m.* blabber, tale-teller.

svestíre, *v.t.* to undress ‖ **svestírsi,** *v.r.* to undress, to undress oneself.

Svetònio, *no.pr.m.* (*st. lett.*) Suetonius.

svettaménto, *s.m.* lopping.

svettàre, *v.t.* to lop ‖ *v.i.* (*innalzarsi a mo' di vetta*) to stand out (against sthg.).

svettatóio, *s.m.* pruning-shears (*pl.*).

svettatúra, *s.f.* **1.** lopping **2.** (*rami tagliati*) lopped branches.

Svèvia, *no.pr.f.* (*geog.*) Swabia.

svèvo, *ag. s.m.* Swabian.

Svèzia, *no.pr.f.* (*geog.*) Sweden.

svezzaménto, *s.m.* weaning.

svezzàre, *v.t.* to wean.

sviaménto, *s.m.* **1.** deviation, diversion, turning aside; (*di un colpo*) warding off **2.** (*distrazione*) distraction, diversion **3.** (*lo sviare*) leading astray; (*lo sviarsi*) going astray **4.** (*ferr.*) derailment.

sviàre, *v.t.* **1.** to divert, to turn aside, to deflect; to ward off: *— un colpo*, to ward off a blow; *— un corso d'acqua*, to divert a stream; *— il discorso*, to change the subject; *— i sospetti*, to divert suspicion **2.** (*distrarre*) to distract, to divert: *cerca di sviarlo dai suoi tristi pensieri*, try to distract him from his sad thoughts; *quel rumore mi svia*, that noise distracts me; *— l'attenzione di qlcu. da ql.co.*, to distract (*o* to divert) s.o.'s attention from sthg. **3.** (*traviare*) to lead astray: *i cattivi compagni lo sviano*, his bad companions are leading him astray ‖ *v.i.* to be deflected, to be diverted ‖ **sviàrsi,** *v.r.* **1.** to move apart, to diverge **2.** (*traviarsi*) to go astray; to be deflected; to be diverted: *non sviarti dalla linea di condotta che hai deciso di seguire*, don't be diverted from the line of conduct you have decided on; *— dallo studio*, to be diverted from one's studies; *— dalla verità*, to deviate from the truth.

sviàto, *ag.* led astray (*predicativo*), misguided.

svicolàre, *v.i.* **1.** to turn the corner **2.** (*svignarsela*) to slink away.

svignàre, *v.i.*, **svignàrsela,** *v.r.* to slink away, to slip off, to sneak away.

svigoríre, *v.t.* to weaken, to enfeeble; to attenuate: *il troppo lavoro lo ha svigorito*, too much work has

weakened him ‖ *v.i.*, **svigorírsi,** *v.r.* to grow weak, to become weak; to lose one's vigour; to become enfeebled; to deteriorate.

sviliménto, *s.m.* depreciation.

svilíre, *v.t.* to depreciate.

svillaneggiàre, *v.t.* to insult; to abuse.

sviluppàbile, *ag.* capable of development, developable.

sviluppàre, *v.t.* **1.** (*disfare, sciogliere*) to untie, to undo, to loosen; (*liberare da un viluppo*) to loosen, to free: *la sviluppò dalle spire del serpente*, he loosened (*o* freed) her from the serpent's coils; *— un nodo*, to untie (*o* to undo *o* to loosen) a knot **2.** (*invigorire*) to strengthen, to develop: *la lettura sviluppa la mente*, reading develops the mind; *lo sport sviluppa le membra*, sport strengthens the limbs **3.** (*incrementare*) to develop, to expand: *— un'azienda*, to develop (*o* to expand) a business; *— le risorse naturali di un paese*, to develop the natural resources of a country **4.** (*svolgere, elaborare*) to develop, to work out: *— un argomento, un'idea*, to develop a subject, an idea; *— un progetto*, to work out a plan **5.** (*produrre*) to generate, to develop, to produce: *questo motore sviluppa 200 cavalli vapore*, this motor develops two hundred horse-power; *— calore, elettricità*, to generate heat, electricity **6.** (*foto. mat.*) to develop: *— un'equazione*, (*mat.*) to develop an equation; *— una lastra, una pellicola*, (*foto.*) to develop a plate, a film ‖ **sviluppàrsi,** *v.r.* **1.** to develop: *un bocciolo si sviluppa e diventa un fiore*, a bud develops into a flower; *la farfalla si sviluppa dal bozzolo*, the butterfly develops from a cocoon; *i frutti si sviluppano dai semi*, fruits develop from seeds **2.** (*crescere*) to grow; (*invigorirsi*) to strengthen, to develop: *la mente si sviluppa con la lettura*, the mind develops with reading; *quella pianta si sviluppa molto bene*, that plant is growing very well; *questo ragazzo si è molto sviluppato dall'ultima volta che lo vidi*, this boy has grown a lot since I saw him last **3.** (*ricevere incremento, espandersi*) to expand, to develop: *la città si sviluppa verso nord*, the city is expanding northwards; *il commercio internazionale si è molto sviluppato*, international trade has expanded a great deal; *la sua azienda si è molto sviluppata recentemente*, his business has developed (*o* expanded) a lot recently **4.** (*scoppiare*) to break out: *si è sviluppata un'epidemia*, an epidemic has broken out; *si è sviluppato un incendio*, a fire has broken out.

svilúppo, *s.m.* **1.** undoing; loosening **2.** (*accrescimento*) development, growth; (*rafforzamento*) strengthening: *— fisico, morale*, physical, moral development; *è nell'età dello —*, he is at the age of development; *ha raggiunto il pieno —*, he has reached full growth; *sta attraversando un periodo di rapido —*, he is going through a period of rapid growth **3.** (*espansione*) development, expansion, growth: *— di un'azienda*, the development (*o* expansion) of a business; *lo — di una città, del commercio*, the growth (*o* expansion) of a city, of trade; *arrestare lo — di ql.co.*, to check the development of sthg. ‖ *gli sviluppi di una situazione*, the developments of a situation **4.** (*elaborazione*) development, working out **5.** (*sprigionamento*) generation: *— di gas, elettricità*, generation of gas, electricity **6.** (*foto. mat.*) development.

svinàre, *v.t.* to rack (off) (wine), to draw (the wine) from a vat.

svinatúra, *s.f.* **1.** racking **2.** (*tempo dello svinare*) racking-time.

svincolaménto, *V.* **svíncolo.**

svincolàre, *v.t.* **1.** (*liberare*) to release, to free, to disengage: *— qlcu. da un obbligo*, to free s.o. from an obligation; *— qlcu. da una promessa*, to release s.o. from a promise **2.** (*riscattare*) to redeem: *— una proprietà ipotecata*, to redeem a mortgaged property **3.** (*sdaziare, sdoganare*) to clear; (*ritirare dalla stazione*) to collect: *— il bagaglio*, to collect one's luggage; —

merce dalla dogana, to clear goods from the customs ‖
svincolàrsi, *v.r.* to free oneself, to get free: — *dalla stretta di qlcu.*, to get free from s.o.'s grasp; — *dal fare ql.co.*, to get out of doing sthg.

svíncolo, *s.m.* **1.** (*il liberare*) release, freeing, disengaging **2.** (*riscatto*) redemption **3.** (*sdoganamento*) clearance.

sviolinàre, *v.t.* (*scherz.*) to fawn on (s.o.), to flatter.

sviolinàta, *s.f.* (*scherz.*) fawning, flattery.

svisaménto, *s.m.* **1.** (*lo sfregiare*) disfigurement **2.** (*il travisare*) distortion, twisting.

svisàre, *v.t.* **1.** (*sfregiare il viso a*) to disfigure **2.** (*travisare*) to distort, to twist: — *i fatti*, to twist the facts; — *il significato di una frase*, to twist the meaning of a sentence; — *la verità*, to distort the truth.

svisceraménto, *s.m.* **1.** (*il togliere le viscere*) evisceration, disembowelling **2.** *fig.* (*studio profondo*) dissection, thorough examination.

svisceràre, *v.t.* **1.** (*togliere le viscere a*) to eviscerate, to disembowel; (*un pollo*) to draw; (*pesci, uccelli*) to gut **2.** *fig.* (*studiare a fondo*) to dissect, to examine thoroughly, to go deeply into (sthg.): — *un argomento*, to dissect a subject ‖ **svisceràrsi**, *v.r.* to be consumed (with sthg.): — *d'amore per qlcu.*, to be consumed with love for s.o.

sviscerataménte, *av.* **1.** passionately, ardently **2.** (*affezionatamente*) devotedly, affectionately.

svisceratézza, *s.f.* strength, depth: *la — della sua passione*, the strength of his passion.

svisceràto, *ag.* **1.** passionate, ardent: *amore —*, passionate (*o* ardent) love **2.** (*molto affezionato*) devoted, very affectionate: *un amico —*, a devoted friend.

svísta, *s.f.* oversight.

svitaménto, *s.m.* unscrewing.

svitàre, *v.t.* to unscrew.

svitàto, *ag.* unscrewed ‖ *è un tipo —*, (*gergo*) he has a screw loose (*o* he is a bit barmy).

svitatúra, *s.f.* unscrewing.

sviticchiàre, *v.t.* to disentangle, to untwine, to disentwine ‖ **sviticchiàrsi**, *v.r.* to free oneself, to disentangle oneself (anche *fig.*).

Svízzera, *no.pr.f.* (*geog.*) Switzerland.

svízzero, *ag.* Swiss: *il confine —*, the Swiss border ‖ *le guardie svizzere*, the Swiss Guards ‖ *s.m.* **1.** (*abitante*) Swiss (*invariato al pl.*) **2.** (*st.*) (*mercenario*) Swiss mercenary, Switzer **3.** (*portiere gallonato*) commissionaire ‖ **svízzera**, *s.f.* Swiss (*invariato al pl.*).

svogliàre, *v.t.* to distract: *i divertimenti lo hanno svogliato dai suoi studi*, pleasure has robbed him of all desire to study ‖ **svogliàrsi**, *v.r.* to lose one's interest (in sthg.), to lose one's taste (for sthg.).

svogliatàggine, *V.* svogliatézza.

svogliataménte, *av.* **1.** unwillingly; listlessly: *fa tutto —*, he does everything listlessly **2.** (*pigramente*) lazily.

svogliatézza, *s.f.* **1.** unwillingness; listlessness, indifference **2.** (*pigrizia*) laziness.

svogliàto, *ag.* **1.** unwilling; listless, indifferent: — *al cibo*, unwilling to eat; *scolaro —*, unwilling pupil; *sentirsi —*, to feel listless **2.** (*pigro*) lazy ‖ *s.m.* slacker; lazy-bones.

svolazzaménto, *s.m.* **1.** flying about, flying here and there; (*di api, pipistrelli*) flitting; (*di farfalle*) fluttering **2.** (*l'essere agitato dal vento*) flapping, fluttering.

svolazzànte, *ag.* **1.** flying about; (*di api, pipistrelli*) flitting; (*di farfalle*) fluttering **2.** (*mosso dal vento*) flapping, fluttering; (*di capelli*) wind-swept.

svolazzàre, *v.i.* **1.** to fly about, to fly here and there; (*di api, pipistrelli*) to flit; (*di farfalle*) to flutter: *i passeri svolazzavano tra i rami degli alberi*, sparrows were flying about among the boughs of the trees **2.** (*essere agitato dal vento*) to flap, to flutter: *i suoi capelli svolazzavano al vento*, her hair was flying in the wind; *il suo vestito svolazzava al vento*, her dress was flapping (*o* fluttering) in the wind.

svolàzzo, *s.m.* **1.** (*lo svolazzare*) flapping, fluttering **2.** (*tratto di penna come ornato*) flourish **3.** *pl.* (*ornamenti eccessivi*) excessive ornamentation (*sing.*).

svòlgere, *v.t.* **1.** to unwind; to unroll: — *un gomitolo di lana*, to unwind a ball of wool; — *un libro*, to turn over the pages of a book; — *una pellicola, una pezza di stoffa, un rotolo di carta*, to unroll a film, a piece of cloth, a roll of paper **2.** (*trattare*) to develop, to treat; (*mettere in opera*) to carry out: *svolge un'intensa attività*, he carries on an intense activity; *svolse la sua tesi in un lungo articolo*, he developed his argument in a long article; *abbiamo già svolto il nostro programma di storia*, we have already gone through (*o* carried out) our history programme; *non ho ancora svolto il tema per lunedì*, I have not yet done my composition for Monday; — *un programma di lavoro*, to carry out a programme of work **3.** (*rar.*) (*dissuadere*) to dissuade, to divert ‖ **svòlgersi**, *v.r.* **1.** to unwind; to unroll **2.** (*svilupparsi*) to develop **3.** (*accadere*) to happen, to occur, to take place; (*procedere*) to go (on), ⸢to go off: *dimmi come si sono svolte le cose*, tell me how things went; *quando si svolse tutto questo?*, when did all this happen (*o* occur)?; *la scena si svolge a Roma*, the scene is laid (*o* takes place) in Rome; *tutto si svolse secondo i piani*, everything went (off) according to plan.

svolgiménto, *s.m.* **1.** unwinding, unrolling **2.** (*trattazione*) treatment, development: *lo — di un argomento*, the treatment of a subject **3.** (*sviluppo*) development; (*andamento*) course: *lo — degli eventi*, the course of events.

svòlta, *s.f.* **1.** (*lo svoltare*) turning: *fece una — a sinistra*, he turned to the left ‖ *divieto di — a sinistra*, no left turning **2.** (*punto in cui la strada svolta*) turn, bend: *una — stretta nella strada*, a sharp turn (*o* bend) in the road; *lo troverai alla prima —*, you will find it at the first turn **3.** (*curva di fiume*) winding **4.** *fig.* turning-point: *una — della storia*, a turning-point of history; *ero arrivato a una — della mia carriera*, I had come to a turning point in my career.

svoltàre, *v.t.* (*svolgere*) to unroll ‖ *v.i.* to turn: — *a sinistra, a destra*, to turn (to the) left, (to the) right.

svoltàta, *s.f.* **1.** (*lo svoltare*) turning **2.** (*svolta*) turn, bend.

svoltatúra, *s.f.* unrolling.

svòlto, *ag.* **1.** unrolled: *pacco —*, open package **2.** (*trattato, sviluppato*) treated, developed.

svoltolaménto, *s.m.* rolling.

svoltolàre, *v.t.* to roll ‖ **svoltolàrsi**, *v.r.* to roll about; to wallow: *i ragazzi si svoltolavano nella sabbia*, the boys were rolling about on the sand; — *nel fango*, to wallow in the mud.

svotàre, *v.t.* **1.** to empty **2.** *fig.* to deprive: — *una frase del suo contenuto*, to deprive a sentence of its meaning.

T

t, *s.f.m.* (*diciottesima lettera dell'alfabeto italiano*) t (*pl.* ts, t's) ‖ — *come Torino,* (*tel.*) t for Tommy ‖ *T a bulbo,* (*ind. metal.*) bulb-tee; (*raccordo a*) *T a 90°,* (*tubazioni*) 90° tee ‖ *fatto a T,* T-shaped; *ferro a T,* T-iron; *squadra a T,* tee square.

tabaccàia, *s.f.,* **tabaccàio,** *s.m.* tobacconist.

tabaccàre, *v.i.* to snuff, to take snuff.

tabaccheria, *s.f.* tobacco shop, tobacconist's shop.

tabacchièra, *s.f.* snuff-box.

tabàcco, *s.m.* tobacco (*pl.* tobaccos): — *da fiuto,* snuff; — *da fumo,* smoking tobacco; — *da masticare,* chewing tobacco; — *da pipa,* pipe-tobacco; — *trinciato,* cut tobacco; *borsa per il* —, tobacco pouch; *color* —, tobacco-colour: *stoffa color* —, tobacco-coloured material; *presa di* —, pinch of snuff; *fiutar* —, to snuff (*o* to take snuff) ‖ *Manifattura Tabacchi,* the (State) Tobacco Agency.

tabaccóne, *s.m.* snuffer, snuff-taker.

tabaccóso, *ag.* snuffy.

tabacòsi, *s.f.* (*patol.*) tabacosis.

tabagísmo, *s.m.* (*patol.*) tabagism, tabicism.

tabarin, *s.m.* night-club.

tabàrro, *s.m.* cloak; (*arc.*) tabard.

tàbe, *s.f.* (*patol.*) tabes: — *dorsale,* dorsal tabes.

tabèlla[1]**,** *s.f.* **1.** (*lista*) list; (*prospetto*) schedule; (*modulo*) form; (*quadro*) board: — *dei prezzi,* price-list; — *dell'orario ferroviario,* time-table; — *della febbre,* fever chart; — *delle ore di presenza* (*p. e. di lavoratori*), time sheet; — *di numerazione,* (*cine.*) number board (*o* slate); — *indice,* key plan; — *luminosa,* (*tv.*) (studio) light board **2.** (*votiva*) votive tablet.

tabèlla[2]**,** *s.f.* (*battola*) clapper ‖ *suonare le tabelle dietro qlcu.,* (*beffeggiarlo*) to jeer at s.o.

tabellièra, *s.f.* **1.** (*per cartellini di presenza di lavoratori*) timecard rack **2.** (*per utensili da officina*) tool board.

tabellióne, *s.m.* (*st. dir.*) tabellion.

tabellóne, *s.m.* notice board.

tabernàcolo, *s.m.* **1.** (*Bibbia*) tabernacle ‖ *la Festa dei Tabernacoli,* the Feast of Tabernacles **2.** (*ciborio*) tabernacle **3.** (*cappelletta*) shrine, sanctuary.

tabescènte, *ag.* tabescent.

tabètico, *ag.* (*med.*) tabetic.

tabí, *s.m.* (*antico tessuto*) tabby.

tàbico, *ag.* (*med.*) tabic.

tablíno, *s.m.* (*archeol.*) tablinum (*pl.* tablina).

tablòide, *s.m.* (*farm.*) tabloid.

tabòga, *s.m.* (*spor.*) toboggan.

Tàbor (Mónte), *no.pr.m.* (*geog.*) (Mount) Tabor.

taborétto, *s.m.* (*ind. legno*) router.

tabú, *s.m.* taboo: *questi argomenti sono* —, these topics are taboo; *dichiarare* — *ql.co.,* to taboo sthg.

tàbula, *s.f.* (*tavoletta per scrittura presso gli antichi*) tabula ‖ — *rasa,* tabula rasa: *la mia memoria è una* — *rasa,* my memory is a tabula rasa (*o* a complete blank); *fare* — *rasa di ql.co.,* (*sbarazzarsene*) to make a clean sweep of sthg. (*o* to sweep sthg. away); *ha fatto* — *rasa di tutto quel che c'era in cucina,* he has eaten up everything there was in the kitchen.

tabulàrio, *s.m.* (*archeol.*) tabularium (*pl.* tabularia).

tabulatóre, *s.m.* (*dispositivo di macchina per scrivere*) tabulator.

tàcca, *s.f.* **1.** (*piccola incisione*) notch, hack, cut; (*mec.*) notch, gate; (*tip.*) nick **2.** (*statura*) height, size **3.** (*qualità, condizione*) quality, condition, rank, state **4.** (*difetto*) blemish, flaw, defect, fault **5.** (*contrassegno*) tally.

taccagnería, *s.f.* stinginess; meanness; niggardliness.

taccàgno, *ag.* stingy; mean; miserly; niggardly ‖ *s.m.* miser; niggard; stingy person.

taccamàcca, *s.f.* (*bot.*) tacamahac, tacamahaca.

taccàta, *s.f.* (*mar.*) keelblock, bilge block: — *di bacino,* docking block.

taccheggiàre, *v.t.* **1.** (*rubare in un negozio fingendosi un cliente*) to shop-lift **2.** (*tip.*) to interlay, to underlay.

taccheggiatóre, *s.m.,* **taccheggiatrice,** *s.f.* shop-lifter.

tacchéggio, *s.m.* **1.** (*il rubare in un negozio fingendosi un cliente*) shop-lifting **2.** (*tip.*) interlaying, underlaying.

tacchettàre, *v.i.* to tap one's heels.

tacchétto, *s.m.* (*mar.*) cleat.

tacchína, *s.f.* turkey(-hen).

tacchino, *s.m.* turkey(-cock) ‖ *sembra un* — *quando fa la ruota,* he looks as proud as a peacock.

tacchinòtto, *s.m.* young turkey, turkey-pullet.

tàccia, *s.f.* **1.** (*cattiva fama*) bad reputation: *ha la* — *di avaro,* he has a reputation for stinginess (*o* he has the reputation of being stingy *o* a miser) **2.** (*accusa*) charge, imputation.

tacciàre, *v.t.* to tax, to charge, to accuse: *lo tacciano di disonestà,* they tax him with dishonesty.

tàcco, *s.m.* **1.** heel: *tacchi a spillo,* stiletto heels; *scarpe coi tacchi alti,* high-heeled shoes; *mettere i tacchi a,* to heel ‖ *alzare, battere il* —, to take to one's heels (*o* to run away *o* to show a clean pair of heels) ‖ *girare i tacchi,* to turn on one's heel **2.** (*tip.*) interlay, underlay **3.** (*rialzo, puntello*) prop stand **4.** *pl.* (*costruzioni navali*) blocks; (*aer.*) chocks.

tàccola[1]**,** *s.f.* **1.** (*piccolo difetto*) flaw, fault, blemish **2.** (*bazzecola*) trifle.

tàccola[2]**,** *s.f.* (*ornit.*) jackdaw.

taccolàre, *v.i.* (*chiacchierare*) to prattle, to chat.

taccolàta, *s.f.* **1.** (*inezia*) trifle **2.** (*chiacchierata*) chatter(ing), chit-chat, prating.

tacconàre, *v.t.* **1.** (*rappezzare*) to patch (anche *fig.*) **2.** (*impuntire*) to stitch: — *la suola di una scarpa,* to stitch the sole of a shoe.

taccóne, *s.m.* **1.** (*grosso tacco*) big heel ‖ *battere il* —, to take to one's heels (*o* to show a clean pair of heels) **2.** (*pezza, rattoppo*) patch (anche *fig.*) **3.** (*metal.*) scab: — *a coda di topo,* rat-tail scab; — *a fibbia,* buckle scab; — *a pelli di nero,* blacking scab; — *a scatola,* — *falso,* expansion scab.

taccuino, *s.m.* **1.** note-book, memorandum-book **2.** (*arc.*) (*almanacco, lunario*) almanac.

tacére, *v.i.* to be silent, to keep silent, to hold one's tongue: *egli tacque tutto il giorno,* he was silent all day through; *sa* —, he knows when to keep silent; *tacete!,* be (*o* keep) quiet! (*o* hold your tongue! *o sl.* shut up! *o* dry up!) ‖ *far* — *qlcu., ql.co.,* to silence s.o., sthg. (*o* to reduce s.o., sthg. to silence): *far* — *un bambino,* to hush a child (*o* to keep a child quiet); *far* — *il cannone nemico,* to silence the enemy's guns;

944

far — *la voce della coscienza*, to silence the voice of conscience ‖ *chi tace acconsente, prov.* silence means consent **2.** (*stare quieto, non far rumore*) to be still: *tutto tace*, all is still ‖ *v.t.* **1.** to be silent about (sthg.), to keep silent about (sthg.); to say nothing about (sthg.): *egli tacque tutto questo*, he said nothing about all this **2.** (*tralasciare, non dire*) to leave out, to omit; to pass over in silence: — *un nome*, to leave out a name ‖ *mettere in* — *uno scandalo*, to hush up a scandal.

tacére, *s.m.* silence ‖ *un bel tacer non fu mai scritto, prov.* silence is often the best answer.

tacheografía, *s.f.* tachygraphy.

tacheògrafo, *s.m.* tachygrapher.

tacheometría, *s.f.* tacheometry, tachymetry.

tacheomètrico, *ag.* tacheometric, tachymetric.

tacheòmetro, *s.m.* tacheometer, tachymeter.

tachicardía, *s.f.* (*patol.*) tachycardia.

tachifagía, *s.f.* tachyphagia.

tachifrasía, *s.f.* tachyphrasia.

tachigrafía, *s.f.* (*specialmente nell'antichità*) tachygraphy; shorthand.

tachìgrafo, *s.m.* **1.** (*specialmente nell'antichità*) tachygraph; shorthand writer **2.** (*aut.*) tachograph.

tachímetro, *s.m.* (*aut.*) tachometer, speedometer; (*di bicicletta*) ciclometer: — *a radiolocalizzazione*, (*per polizia stradale*) electromatic speedometer; — *centrifugo, elettrico, magnetico*, centrifugal, electric, magnetic tachometer; — *registratore*, tachograph; *flessibile per* —, (*aut.*) speedometer cable.

tachipnèa, *s.f.* (*med.*) tachypnea.

tacitaménte, *av.* **1.** (*in modo non espresso*) tacitly **2.** (*silenziosamente*) silently; (*senza rumore*) noiselessly.

tacitaménto, *s.m.* **1.** (*di uno scandalo*) hushing up **2.** (*di un creditore*) paying off.

tacitàre, *v.t.* (*far tacere*) to silence; to hush up: *denaro per* —, hush-money; — *un creditore*, to pay off a creditor; — *qlcu.*, to silence s.o.; — *uno scandalo*, to hush up a scandal; — *un testimone*, (*corromperlo*) to bribe a witness.

tacitiàno, *ag.* (*lett.*) Tacitean.

tàcito[1], *ag.* **1.** (*non espresso, sottinteso*) tacit: — *accordo, consenso, rimprovero*, tacit agreement, consent, reproof; *tacita intesa*, tacit understanding **2.** (*silenzioso*) silent; in silence: *guardava* — *quel che accadeva*, he was looking at what was happening in silence **3.** (*quieto*) still: *una tacita notte*, a still (*o* silent) night.

Tàcito[2], *no.pr.m.* (*st. lett.*) Tacitus.

taciturnaménte, *av.* taciturnly.

taciturnità, *s.f.* taciturnity.

tacitúrno, *ag.* taciturn, silent; reserved, uncommunicative: *è oltremodo* —, he is by no means loquacious.

Taddèo, *no.pr.m.* Thadd(a)eus ‖ *dim.* Thad(d)y.

tafanàrio, *s.m.* (*volg.*) back.

tafàno, *s.m.* (*entom.*) gad-fly, horse-fly.

taffería, *s.f.* round wooden board (for polenta).

tafferúglio, *s.m.* brawl, scuffle, scrimmage, tussle.

taffettà, *s.m.* **1.** (*tessuto*) taffeta **2.** (*cerotto*) sticking-plaster, court-plaster.

tafofobía, *s.f.* (*patol.*) taphephobia, taphophobia.

tàglia, *s.f.* **1.** (*prezzo del riscatto*) ransom **2.** (*indennità di guerra*) war-indemnity, tribute: *imporre una* — *su una città*, to levy a tribute on a city **3.** (*ricompensa a chi consegna un malfattore alla giustizia*) price, reward: *mettere una* — *su qlcu.*, to set a price on s.o.'s head **4.** (*tacca di contrassegno*) tally **5.** (*edil.*) (hoisting) tackle **6.** (*statura*) height; (*misura*) size: *un vestito della mia* —, a dress of my size; *era un uomo di mezza* —, he was a man of middle height; *qual è la tua* —?, what is your size?

tàglia-àcqua, *s.m.* (*edil.*) nosing.

tagliàbile, *ag.* that can be cut.

tagliabórse, *s.m.* cutpurse, pickpocket.

tagliabòschi, *V.* taglialégna.

tagliacàrta, *s.f.* (*ind. cartaria*) paper cutting machine: — *a ghigliottina*, guillotine (cutting machine).

tagliacàrte, *s.m.* paper-knife.

tagliafíli, *s.m.* wire cutter.

tagliafuòco, *s.m.* (*edil.*) fire stop, fire barrier.

taglialégna, *s.m.* wood-cutter; woodman (*pl.* woodmen); lumberman (*pl.* lumbermen).

tagliamàre, *s.m.* (*mar.*) break-water.

tagliaménto, *s.m.* cutting, cut.

tagliàndo, *s.m.* coupon.

tagliapiètra, tagliapiètre, *s.m.* stone-cutter.

tagliàre, *v.t.* **1.** to cut: *il bambino tagliò una fetta di torta*, the child cut a slice of cake; — *a fette*, to slice; — *a pezzetti della legna*, to chop some wood; — *un albero*, to cut down a tree; — *i capelli a zero a qlcu.*, to crop s.o.'s hair; — *la carne prima di servirla*, to carve meat before serving it; — *la carne prima di tritarla*, to cut up (*o* to chop) meat before mincing it; — *una ciocca di capelli a qlcu.*, to snip off a lock of s.o.'s hair; — *una mela, il grano, le pagine di un libro*, to cut an apple, corn, the pages of a book; — *ql.co. a pezzi*, to cut sthg. in(to) pieces; — *ql.co. in due, in tre, ecc.*, to cut sthg. in two, in three, etc.; — *una siepe*, to clip (*o* to trim) a hedge; — *la testa a qlcu.*, to cut s.o.'s head off (*o* to behead s.o.); — *un vestito*, to cut out a dress; — *via ql.co.*, to cut sthg. away (*o* off *o* out) ‖ *un vento che taglia la faccia*, a biting wind ‖ — *la corda*, to make off (*o* to cut and run) ‖ — *le gambe a qlcu.*, to stop s.o.'s way (*o* to baffle s.o.'s plans) ‖ — *i panni addosso a qlcu.*, to tear s.o.'s character to rags (*o* pieces) ‖ — *la testa al toro*, to cut the matter short ‖ *farsi* — *i capelli*, to have one's hair cut **2.** (*attraversare*) to cut across, to cross, to intersect: *una linea che ne taglia un'altra*, a line that intersects another; *sentiero che taglia una strada*, path that cuts across a road **3.** (*interrompere; togliere*) to cut off; to interrupt; to stop: *era tagliato fuori dalla società*, he was cut off from society; *hanno tagliato alcuni paragrafi*, they have cut out a few paragraphs; — *la ritirata al nemico*, to cut off the enemy's retreat; — *la strada a qlcu.*, to cut s.o. off (*o* to bar s.o.'s way); (*in automobile*) to cut in; — *i viveri a qlcu.*, to cut off s.o.'s supplies **4.** (*vini*) to blend **5.** (*a carte*) to cut ‖ *v.i.* to cut: *poiché eravamo in ritardo tagliammo per il bosco*, as we were late we cut across the wood ‖ — *corto*, to cut short ‖ **tagliàrsi,** *v.r.* to cut, to get cut: *la seta si taglia facilmente nelle pieghe*, silk gets easily cut in the folds; — *un dito, le unghie*, to cut one's finger, one's nails.

tagliaréte, *s.m.* (*mar. mil.*) net cutter.

tagliastràcci, *s.m.* (*ind. cartaria*) rag cutter, rag chopper.

tagliàta, *s.f.* cut, cutting; (*di erba*) mowing: — *dei capelli*, hair-cut.

tagliatèlle, *s.f.pl.* (*cuc.*) noodles.

tagliatíni, *s.m.pl.* (*cuc.*) thin noodles.

tagliàto, *ag.* **1.** cut: *cristallo* —, cut glass; *questo vestito è* — *a suo dosso*, this dress fits her well ‖ — *all'antica*, old-fashioned ‖ — *con l'accetta*, roughly made (*o* hacked out) ‖ — *fuori*, cut out (*o* off) **2.** (*inclinato, disposto*) cut out, fit: *essere* — *per ql.co.*, to be cut out (*o* fit) for sthg.: *è* — *per il comando*, he is cut out for a leader; *non è tagliata per la musica*, she has no talent for music.

tagliatóre, *s.m.* cutter.

tagliatríce, *s.f.* **1.** cutter **2.** (*mec.*) cutting machine.

tagliatúra, *s.f.* cutting, cut.

taglieggiàre, *v.t.* to tax; to levy taxes on (s.o., sthg.); to extort money from (s.o.).

tagliènte, *ag.* cutting, sharp (anche *fig.*); *fig.* harsh: *coltello* —, sharp knife; *freddo* —, sharp (*o* biting) cold; *lingua* —, sharp (*o* biting) tongue; *voce* —, harsh voice.

taglienteménte, *av.* cuttingly; sharply (anche *fig.*); *fig.* harshly.

taglière, *s.m.* trencher.

taglierína, *s.f.* (*ind. cartaria*) cutter.

taglieríni, *s.m.pl.* (*cuc.*) thin noodles.

tàglio, *s.m.* **1.** cut; (*di vite, bullone*) slot; (*azione*) cutting: — *cesareo,* (*chir.*) caesarean section (*o* operation); — *del fieno,* hay-harvest; — *dei capelli,* hair-cut; — *della testa,* beheading; — *del vetro,* cutting; *un* — *di carne,* a cut of meat; — *di una foresta,* cutting (*o* chopping down *o* felling) of the trees of a forest; — *di stoffa,* cut; *un* — *in un dito,* a cut in a finger: *mi son fatto un* — *in un dito,* I have cut my finger; *un* — *in faccia,* a cut on one's face; *lezioni di* —, dressmaking classes; *pietra da* —, ashlar (*o* freestone); *mi piace il* — *dei tuoi capelli,* I like the cut of your hair; *non mi piace il* — *della tua sarta,* I don't like the way your dressmaker cuts; *quel vestito ha un bel* —, that dress has a nice cut; *fare un* — *in un articolo, discorso, film,* to make a cut in an article, a speech, a film **2.** (*di vini*) blending **3.** (*di titoli, cartamoneta*) denomination: *un biglietto* (*di banca*) *di grosso, piccolo* —, a large, small bank-note **4.** (*parte tagliente*) edge: *il* — *di un coltello, di una lama, di una spada,* the edge of a knife, of a blade, of a sword; *armi da* —, edged weapons | *arma a doppio* —, *fig.* double-edged weapon || *per* —, edgewise **5.** (*margine*) edge: *il* — *dorato di un libro,* the gilt edge of a book **6.** (*taglia, dimensione*) size: *un cane di piccolo* —, a small-sized dog **7.** (*occasione, opportunità*) opportunity: *questo viene proprio a* —, this comes just at the right time **8.** (*scienza delle costruzioni*) shear, shearing stress: *resistenza al* —, resistance to shearing stress **9.** (*tennis*) chop.

tagliolíni, *s.m.pl.* (*cuc.*) thin noodles.

tagliòlo, *s.m.* **1.** (*pezzetto*) bit, piece **2.** (*scalpello*) chisel: — *a caldo, a freddo,* hot, cold chisel.

taglióne, *s.m.* talion, retaliation: *legge del* —, law of retaliation (*o* law of an eye for an eye): *applicare a qlcu. la legge del* —, to retaliate on s.o.

tagliuòla, *s.f.* trap, snare (*anche fig.*).

tagliuzzaménto, *s.m.* mincing.

tagliuzzàre, *v.t.* to cut into small pieces, to chop (up), to shred, to mince, to hash (up): — *carne, verdura,* to chop (up) (*o* to mince) meat, vegetables; — *un pezzo di carta, stoffa,* to shred a piece of paper, cloth.

Tàgo, *no.pr.m.* (*geog.*) Tagus.

tàguan, *s.m.* (*zool.*) taguan.

Tàide, *no.pr.f.* (*lett.*) Thais.

tàiga, *s.f.* taiga.

tailleur, *s.m.* costume.

Taíti, *no.pr.f.* (*geog.*) Tahiti.

talacimànno, *s.m.* muezzin.

talalgía, *s.f.* (*med.*) talalgia.

talamíta, *s.m.* (*st.*) thalamite.

tàlamo, *s.m.* **1.** (*letto nuziale*) nuptial bed: *condurre al* —, (*sposare*) to lead to the altar (*o* to marry) **2.** (*archeol.*) thalamus (*pl.* thalami) **3.** (*bot. anat.*) thalamus (*pl.* thalami): — *ottico,* (*anat.*) optic thalamus.

talàre, *ag.* (*lungo fino ai talloni*) reaching to the ankles, talaric || *abito* —, canonicals: *il rispetto dovuto all'abito* —, the respect due to the cloth.

talàri, *s.m.pl.* (*mit.*) talaria, heel-wings.

talàssico, *ag.* thalassic(al).

talassínidi, *s.m.pl.* (*zool.*) Thalassinidea.

talassòcrate, *s.m.* thalassocrat.

talassocrazía, *s.f.* thalassocracy.

talassofobía, *s.f.* (*patol.*) thalassophobia.

talassografía, *s.f.* thalassography, oceanography.

talassogràfico, *ag.* thalassographic.

talassògrafo, *s.m.* thalassographer.

talassometría, *s.f.* thalassometry.

talassòmetro, *s.m.* thalassometer.

talassoterapía, *s.f.* (*med.*) thalassotherapy.

talché, *cong.* so that: *fu molto educato questa volta,* — *dimenticai la sua maleducazione di un tempo,* he was very polite this time so that I forgot his past rudeness.

tàlco, *s.m.* (*min.*) talc || — *borato,* talcum powder.

talcose(h)ísto, *s.m.* (*min.*) talc-schist.

talcóso, *ag.* (*min.*) talcose, talcous.

tàle, *ag.* **1. such:** *una* — *cosa,* such a thing; *tali cose,* such things; *ho avuto un* — *dispiacere che non posso dimenticarlo,* I felt such sorrow that I cannot forget it; *la forza dell'esplosione fu* — *che...,* such was the force of the explosion that...; *la situazione non è* — *da causare preoccupazione,* the situation is not such as to cause worry **2.** (*se indica identità*) **like:** — *la madre,* — *la figlia,* like mother, like daughter || — *e quale,* exactly like (*seguito da s.*); exactly as (*seguito da verbo*): *egli è* — *e quale suo fratello,* he is exactly like his brother; *la situazione è* — *e quale come quando c'eri tu,* the situation is exactly as it was when you were here **3.** (*per indicare ql.co. o qlcu. in modo indeterminato*) **such and such:** *il* — *giorno, alla* — *ora,* on such and such a day, at such and such a time; *il* — *pagamento fu fatto alla* — *persona,* such and such a payment was made to such and such a person **4.** (*sopraddetto, summenzionato*) **above-mentioned, aforesaid; such; above:** *tali prezzi franco bordo Genova,* the above prices free on board Genoa; *se entro* — *data non ci sarà pervenuta alcuna notizia...,* if within such (*o* the aforesaid) date no news has reached us... || *pron. indef.* **someone, a certain man, a fellow:** *un* — *mi disse che...,* someone told me that...; *un* — *che conosco mi ha dato questo suggerimento,* a Johnny I know has given me this tip; *c'è un* — *che vuol parlarti,* there is someone (*o* a man *o* a fellow) who wants to speak to you || *quel* —, that fellow: *non mi parlare di quel* —, don't talk to me about that fellow || *il Signor Tal dei Tali,* Mr. What's his name (*o* Mr. What d'ye call him *o* Mr. So and So).

talèa, *s.f.* (*bot.*) scion.

taléggio, *s.m.* "taleggio" (kind of Lombard cheese).

talentàre, *v.i.* to please (s.o.); to suit (s.o.), to be to one's liking: *faccio come mi talenta,* I do as I like; *se non ti talenta, non farlo,* if it doesn't suit you, don't do it.

talènto, *s.m.* **1.** talent, intelligence; skill: *una persona di gran* —, a person of great talent (*o* a very talented person); *senza* —, talentless **2.** (*disposizione*) talent, gift, aptitude: *non ha* — *per il disegno,* he has no talent (*o* gift) for drawing **3.** (*volontà*) will: *a* —, at will **4.** (*peso, moneta antica*) talent || *la parabola dei talenti,* (*Bibbia*) the parable of the talents.

Talète, *no.pr.m.* (*st. fil.*) Thales.

Talía, *no.pr.f.* (*mit.*) Thalia.

talismàno, *s.m.* talisman, amulet, charm.

tàllero, *s.m.* (*antica moneta*) thaler.

tàllio, *s.m.* (*chim.*) thallium.

tallíre, *v.i.* (*bot.*) to sprout.

tàllo, *s.m.* (*bot.*) **1.** thallus (*pl.* thalli, thalluses) **2.** (*germoglio*) sprout || *rimettere il* —, *fig.* (*rinvigorire*) to regain strength (*o* to revive).

tallòfite, *s.f.pl.* (*bot.*) Thallophytes.

talloneíno, *s.m.* coupon, ticket, slip.

tallóne, *s.m.* **1.** heel || — *d'Achille,* Achilles' heel **2.** (*di aratro*) landside.

talménte, *av.* **1.** (*con ag. e av.*) so: *è* — *brutto che non posso guardarlo,* it is so ugly that I can't bear to look at it; *sto* — *bene ora, che dimentico di essere stato malato,* I am so well now that I forget I have been ill; *suonava* — *bene che eravamo tutti incantati,* she played so well that we were all spellbound **2.** (*con verbi*) **so much, in such a way, to such an extent, to such a degree:** *non credevo che quel libro potesse interessarmi* —, I did not think that book would interest me to such an extent (*o* so much) || **talménte che,** *l. cong.* **so much, to such an extent:** *gridava* — *che tutti credevano che fosse pazzo,* he was shouting so loudly that everybody thought he was mad; *quello spettacolo mi è piaciuto* — *che voglio rivederlo,* I liked the performance so much that I want to see it again; *ti odio* — *che ti ucciderei,* I hate you to such an extent that I could kill you.

Talmúd, *s.m.* (*st. ebraica*) Talmud.

talmúdico, *ag.* Talmudic.

talmudísta, *s.m.* Talmudist.

talòccia, *s.f.* (*pialletto per intonaci*) float.

talóra, *av.* sometimes; now and then; at times: — *ella è piuttosto nervosa,* now and then she is rather nervous; — *mi capita di balbettare,* sometimes I happen to stammer.

tàlpa, *s.f.* 1. (*zool.*) mole: *cieco come una* —, as blind as a mole; *grigio* —, mole grey 2. (*persona tarda, ottusa*) blockhead; dullard.

talúno, *ag. indef.* some, certain: *nel tuo compito ci sono taluni errori,* in your homework there are some mistakes; *per taluni aspetti questo intreccio ricorda quello di « Otello »,* in some aspects this plot resembles that of " Othello " ‖ *pron. indef.* someone, somebody (*riferiti a persona*); *pl.* some people, certain people (*riferiti a persona*); some (*riferito a persone e cose*); (*con partitivo*) some: — *potrebbe obiettare che...,* someone might object that...; *vi sono taluni che credono che Omero non sia mai esistito,* there are some people who think that Homer never existed.

talvòlta, *V.* talóra.

tamaríce, *s.f.* (*bot.*) tamarisk.

tamaríndo, *s.m.* 1. (*albero*) tamarind-tree 2. (*frutto, bevanda*) tamarind.

tamarísco, *s.m.* (*bot.*) tamarisk.

tambellóne, *s.m.* 1. (*edil.*) large brick 2. (*scimunito*) dullard; blockhead.

tamburàio, *s.m.* drum-maker.

tamburàre, *v.i.* to drum ‖ *v.t.* (*battere*) to beat.

tambureggiaménto, *s.m.* drumming.

tambureggiànte, *ag.* drumming: *fuoco* —, (*artigl.*) drum-fire.

tambureggiàre, *v.i.* to drum.

tamburèllo, *s.m.* (*mus.*) tambourine; (*arc.*) timbrel.

tamburinàre, *v.i.* to drum; (*con le dita*) to thrum.

tamburíno, *s.m.* (*suonatore di tamburo*) drummer.

tamburlàno, *s.m.* (*tosta-caffè*) coffee-roaster.

tambúro, *s.m.* 1. (*mus.*) drum: — *maggiore,* drum major; *bacchette per* —, drum-sticks; *suonatore di* —, drummer; *i tamburi rullavano,* the drums rolled; *battere, suonare il* —, to beat, to play the drum (*o* to drum); *tendere la pelle di un* —, to brace a drum ‖ *pesce* —, (*ittiol.*) drumfish ‖ *a* — *battente,* immediately (*o* at once) 2. (*mec.*) drum, cylinder; (*di rivoltella*) cylinder; (*di argano, orologio*) barrel: — *per freni anteriori, posteriori,* (*aut.*) front-brake, rear-brake drum 3. (*mar.*) (*di ruota a pale*) box 4. (*anat.*) eardrum 5. (*telaietto per ricamo*) tambour 6. (*arch.*) tambour.

tameríce, *s.f.* (*bot.*) tamarisk.

Tamerlàno, *no.pr.m.* (*st.*) Tamerlane, Tamburlaine.

Tamígi, *no.pr.m.* (*geog.*) Thames.

tampòco, *av.* (*rar.*) (*in frasi negative*) even: *non si degna* — *di scrivere,* he doesn't even condescend to write ‖ *non* —, neither... nor: *non è bello nè* — *ricco,* he is neither handsome nor rich.

tamponaménto, *s.m.* 1. plugging, stopping up, padding 2. (*med.*) tamponment, tamponage.

tamponàre, *v.t.* to stop up, to pad; (*med.*) to tampon: — *una ferita,* to plug (*o* to tampon) a wound; — *con argilla,* (*metal.*) to lute.

tamponatúra, *V.* tamponaménto.

tampóne, *s.m.* 1. plug, stopper, wad, pad 2. (*tip.*) (inking-)pad; (*per tirare bozze*) proof planer 3. (*di carta assorbente*) blotter 4. (*med.*) tampon 5. (*metal.*) bod, bott.

tamtàm, *s.m.* tam-tam.

tàna, *s.f.* 1. den; hole: *la* — *di un coniglio,* the burrow of a rabbit; *la* — *di un leone,* the lair of a lion; *la* — *di una tigre,* the den of a tiger; *la* — *di un topo,* the hole of a mouse; *la* — *della volpe,* the fox's earth 2. *fig.* den, hole: *in quale orribile, piccola* — *egli vive!,* what a wretched, little hole he lives in!.

tanàglia, *V.* tenàglia.

tanagliàre, *v.t.* to pincer.

tanàgra, *s.f.* (*archeol.*) tanagra.

tananàï, *s.m.* (*pop.*) (*frastuono*) hubbub, hullabaloo.

tanatofobìa, *s.f.* (*patol.*) thanatophobia.

tanatologìa, *s.f.* thanatology.

tanatomanìa, *s.f.* (*patol.*) thanatomania.

Tancrédi, *no.pr.m.* (*st.*) Tancred.

tàndem, *s.m.* tandem.

tanè, *ag.* tawny; tan (*attributivo*) ‖ *s.f.* tan-colour.

tanfàta, *s.f.* whiff of nasty smell.

tànfo, *s.m.* 1. (*cattivo odore*) stench 2. (*odore di muffa*) mouldy smell, fusty smell.

Tanganíca, *no.pr.m.* (*geog.*) Tanganyika.

tangènte, *ag.* 1. (*geom.*) tangent, tangential 2. (*rar.*) (*spettante*) due ‖ *s.f.* 1. (*geom.*) tangent ‖ *partire per la* —, (*fam.*) to fly off at a tangent (*o* to dodge the question) 2. (*rar.*) (*quota*) share, quota, portion.

tangènza, *s.f.* (*geom.*) tangency: — *a punto fisso,* (*aer.*) hovering ceiling; — *pratica,* (*aer.*) service ceiling; — *statica,* (*aer.*) static ceiling; — *teorica,* (*aer.*) absolute ceiling; *punto di* —, (*geom.*) tangential point.

tangenziàle, *ag.* (*geom.*) tangential.

tàngere, *v.t.* (*arc.*) 1. (*toccare*) to touch 2. (*riguardare*) to concern.

Tàngeri, *no.pr.f.* (*geog.*) Tangier.

tanghéggio, *s.m.* (*mar.*) pitching.

tànghero, *s.m.* boor, lout.

tangíbile, *ag.* tangible.

tangibilità, *s.f.* tangibility, tangibleness.

tangibilménte, *av.* tangibly.

tàngo, *s.m.* (*musica, danza*) tango (*pl.* tangos): *ballare il* —, to dance the tango (*o* to tango).

tanguíno, *s.m.* (*bot.*) tanghin, tanguin.

tank, *s.m.* (*mil.*) tank.

tannàto, *s.m.* (*chim.*) tannate.

tànnico, *ag.* (*chim.*) tannic.

tanníno, *s.m.* (*chim.*) tannin.

tantafèra, tantaferàta, *s.f.* (*sproloquio*) rigmarole.

tantàlio, *s.m.* (*chim.*) tantalum.

tantalíte, *s.f.* (*min.*) tantalite.

tàntalo[1], *s.m.* (*ornit.*) woodstork.

Tàntalo[2], *no.pr.m.* (*mit.*) Tantalus ‖ *far soffrire il supplizio di* — *a qlcu.,* to tantalize s.o.

tantíno, *s.m.* (little) bit, tiny bit; (*di liquidi*) drop: *un* — *d'acqua,* a (little) drop of water; *con un* — *di fortuna,* with a (little) bit of luck; *fammi un* — *di posto,* give me a little room; « *Vuoi ancora un po' di dolce?* », « *Solo un* — », "Would you like a little more cake? ", " Just a tiny bit " ‖ **un tantíno,** *l.av.* 1. a little (bit): *un* — *difficile,* a little (bit) difficult; *è un* — *arrabbiato con me,* he is a little (bit) angry with me; *essere un* — *indisposto,* to be rather (*o* slightly) out of sorts 2. (*riferito a tempo*) a moment: *aspetta un* —, wait a moment (*o fam.* a jiffy); *è arrivato un* — *prima, dopo,* he arrived a moment before, after (*o* the minute before, after).

tànto, *ag.* 1. (*di quantità*) so much; so great; *pl.* so many: *ha* — *denaro da poter comperare queste cose,* he has so much money as to be able to buy these things; *ho tanti libri che non so dove metterli,* I have so many books that I don't know where to put them; *ho* — *lavoro che non potrò venire,* I have so much work that I shall not be able to come; *non sapevo che tu avessi* — *denaro,* I did not know you had so much money; *non so come tu possa leggere con* — *rumore,* I don't know how you can read with so much noise; *sono lieto che la tua fiducia in me sia tanta,* I am glad your faith in me is so great 2. (*nei comp. di eguaglianza*) as much (*in proposizioni positive*), so much (*in proposizioni negative*); *pl.* as many (*in proposizioni positive*), so many (*in proposizioni negative*): *ho tanti amici quanti egli ha nemici,* I have as many friends as he has enemies; *ho* — *denaro quanto lui,* I have as much money as he has; *non ho tanti amici quanti (ne ha) lui,* I have not so many friends as he has (*o fam.* as him); *non ho* — *lavoro quanto ne hai tu,* I have not so much work as you ‖ *tanti partiti, tanti programmi,* so many parties, so many programmes **3.** *ogni tanti, ogni tante,* **every so many:** *ogni tante settimane,* every so many weeks ‖ *av.* **1.** (*con ag. ed av.*) **so:** *è — gentile,* he is so kind; *è — pallido che sembra malato;* he is so pale that he looks ill; *sia — gentile da portarmi quelle carte,* will you be so kind as to bring me those papers? **2.** (*con verbi*) (*così tanto*) **such a lot; so much;** (*molto*) **a lot;** (*very*) **much:** *hai lavorato — ieri,* you worked a lot yesterday; *ho lavorato — per lui!,* I have worked such a lot for him!; *lavora — che non ha tempo di riposarsi,* he works so much that he has no time to rest **3.** *tanto... quanto...,* (*con aggettivi ed avverbi*) **as... as...** (*in proposizioni affermative ed interrogative*); **so... as...** (*in proposizioni negative*): *ella è — alta quanto sua sorella,* she is as tall as her sister; *ella è — buona quanto bella,* she is as good as she is beautiful; *non è — alta quanto sua sorella,* she is not so tall as her sister; *non è — onesto quanto abile,* he is not so honest as he is clever; *non è — onesto quanto sembra,* he is not so honest as he seems **4.** *tanto... quanto...,* (*con sostantivi*) **both... and...:** *voglio vendere — questa casa quanto quella in campagna,* I want to sell both this house and the one in the country **5.** *tanto quanto...,* (*con verbi*) **as much as...:** *lavora — quanto può,* he works as much as he can; *lavora — quanto suo fratello,* he works as much as his brother; *non lavora — quanto dovrebbe,* he does not work as much as he should; *non lavora — quanto suo fratello,* he does not work as much as his brother **6.** *quanto più... tanto meno...,* the more... the less...; the... -er... the less...; *quanto più... tanto più...,* the more... the more...; the... -er... the... -er...: *quanto più ascoltava, — meno parlava,* the more he listened, the less he spoke; *quanto più fai, — meglio è,* the more you do, the better; *quanto più leggo, — più mi interesso al libro,* the more I read, the more I get interested in the book **7.** (*soltanto*) **just:** *— per cambiare,* just for a change; *— per far ql.co.,* just to do sthg. ‖ *per una volta —,* just for once **8.** (*con valore temporale*) **so long:** *ti ho aspettato —,* I have been waiting for you so long ‖ *di — in —,* from time to time (*o occasionally*): *viene a trovarci di — in —,* he drops in occasionally ‖ *una volta ogni —,* once in a while (*o* once in a blue moon) **9.** (*con valore moltiplicativo*) **as much:** *due, tre volte —,* two, three times as much **10.** (*in ogni modo*) **anyhow:** *se vuoi, puoi darglielo, — devo comprarne un altro,* you may give it to him, if you like, I must buy another one anyhow **11.** (Fraseologia): *— meglio,* so much the better ‖ *— meno,* least of all: *nessuno dovrebbe lamentarsi, — meno lui,* no one has cause to complain, he least of all; *se tu non vai, — meno andrò io,* if you don't go, no more will I ‖ *— peggio,* so much the worse ‖ *— più che...,* all the more that... ‖ *— vale, varrebbe che...,* one might as well...: *se intendi farlo in malo modo, — vale che tu non lo faccia affatto,* if you intend to do it that way, you might as well not do it at all ‖ *pron. s.m.* **1.** (*così tanto*) **so much;** *pl.* **so many:** *mai — fu fatto per tanti da così pochi,* never was so much done for so many by so few **2.** (*molto*) **a lot; much;** *pl.* **many (people); a lot of people** (*riferito a persone*); **many** (*riferito a cose e persone e con partitivo*): *tanti credono che non sia vero,* many people think it is not true **3.** (Fraseologia): *con — di pelliccia di visone,* arrayed in a mink coat; *rimase con — di naso,* he was completely baffled ‖ *mio padre gli dà un — alla settimana,* my father gives him a certain amount a week; *ricevo un — al mese dai miei genitori,* I get a monthly allowance from my parents ‖ *per quel — che ne so,* as far as I know ‖ *suo padre gliene diede tante,* his father gave him a good thrashing ‖ *vostra figlia me ne dice tante che non le credo più,* your daughter tells me so many tall stories that I don't believe her any more ‖ **tànto che,** *l. cong.* **so (that):** *non si udiva nulla, — che credevo che non ci fosse nessuno in casa,* one could

not hear anything, so I thought no one was at home ‖ **tànto è véro che,** *l. cong.* **so much so that.**

tàntra, *s.m.* (*relig. indù*) tantra.

tantrísmo, *s.m.* (*relig. indù*) tantrism.

taoísmo, *s.m.* (*st. relig.*) Taoism.

taoísta, *ag.* (*st. relig.*) Taoistic ‖ *s.c.* (*st. relig.*) Taoist.

tapinàre, *v.i.* (*letter.*) to live wretchedly, to live miserably, to lead a wretched life ‖ **tapinàrsi,** *v.r.* **1.** (*affliggersi*) to grieve, to be distressed **2.** (*irritarsi*) to worry.

tapíno, *ag.* wretched, miserable ‖ *s.m.* wretch.

tapiòca, *s.f.* (*cuc.*) tapioca.

tapíro, *s.m.* (*zool.*) tapir.

tapis roulant, *s.m.* escalator, moving staircase.

tàppa, *s.f.* **1.** (*luogo dove ci si ferma*) halting-place (anche *mil.*); (*fermata, sosta*) halt, stop, stay **2.** (*parte di un viaggio o percorso*) stage, leg: *la prima — del viaggio,* the first leg of the journey ‖ *le tappe della civiltà,* the stages in the progress of civilization **3.** (*di una corsa*) lap.

tappàre, *v.t.* **1.** to stop (up), to plug; to cork; to bung: *— una botte,* to bung a barrel; *— una bottiglia,* to cork a bottle; *— un buco,* to stop (up) (*o* to plug *o* to block up) a hole; *— una falla,* to stop a leak ‖ *— la bocca a qlcu., fig.* to shut s.o. up **2.** (*mec.*) to plug, to blank ‖ **tappàrsi,** *v.r.* **1.** (*naso, orecchie, ecc.*): *— il naso,* to hold one's nose; *— le orecchie,* to plug one's ears (*o* to refuse to hear) **2.** (*rinchiudersi*) to shut oneself **3.** (*imbacuccarsi*) to muffle oneself up.

tapparèlla, *s.f.* rolling shutter.

tappéto, *s.m.* **1.** carpet, rug: *— alto, rasato,* long-pile, short-pile carpet; *— da bagno,* bath-mat; *— da tavolo,* table cover; *un — di fiori, di muschio,* a carpet of flowers, of moss; *— erboso,* lawn (*o poet.* greensward); *— persiano,* Persian carpet; *— verde,* (*di tavolo da giuoco*) green baize; *fig.* (*bisca*) gambling-den (*o* -house); *mettere un — sul pavimento,* to carpet the floor ‖ *portare un problema sul —,* to bring up (*o* forward) a problem **2.** (*mar. mil.*) pattern: *— di disturbo,* distracting pattern; *— distruttivo,* destructive pattern **3.** *bombardamento a —,* (*aer.*) carpet (*o* pattern) bombing **4.** (*tec.*): *— di un forno di riscaldo,* (*ind. vetraria*) belt; *— stradale,* carpet.

tappezzàre, *v.t.* **1.** (*con carta*) to paper; (*con stoffa*) to hang with tapestry **2.** (*coprire*) to cover: *i muri sono tappezzati di manifesti pubblicitari,* the walls are covered (*o* plastered over) with posters **3.** (*foderare*) to upholster: *— un divano di damasco,* to upholster a sofa with damask **4.** (*parare*) to hang.

tappezzería, *s.f.* **1.** (*di carta*) wall-paper; (*di stoffa*) tapestry; (*paramenti*) hangings (*pl.*) ‖ *fare — in un ballo,* to be a wallflower **2.** (*arte del tappezziere*) upholstery.

tappezzière, *s.m.* **1.** (*chi riveste pareti*) paperhanger **2.** (*chi fodera poltrone, ecc.*) upholsterer.

tàppo, *s.m.* **1.** plug, stopper; (*zipolo*) bung; (*capsula per bottiglie*) cap; (*di sughero*) cork: *il — di una bottiglia del latte,* the cap of a milk-bottle; *— di scarico,* drain (*o* outlet) plug; *un vino che sa di —,* a wine which tastes of cork; *mettere il — a una bottiglia di vino,* to cork a bottle of wine **2.** (*tec.*): *— di un radiatore,* (*aut.*) cap; *— a corona,* crown cap; *— a vite,* (*mec.*) screw plug; *— a sfiatatoio,* (*elett.*) vent plug; *— dello snodo del tirante di sterzo,* (*aut.*) steering joint plug; *— di scarico dell'olio,* (*mec.*) oil drain plug; *— di volata,* (*artigl.*) tampion **3.** (*fam.*) (*persona bassa, tarchiata*) short and thickset fellow.

tàra, *s.f.* **1.** tare: *per sapere il peso netto dobbiamo fare la —,* to know the net weight we must ascertain the tare ‖ *devi fare la — di quello che dice,* you mustn't give too much credit to what he says **2.** (*pecca, difetto*) defect, blemish, fault ‖ *— ereditaria,* hereditary vice (*o* taint).

tarabúso, *s.m.* (*ornit.*) bittern.

tarantèlla, *s.f.* (*musica, danza*) tarantella, tarantelle.

tarantísmo, *s.m.* (*patol.*) tarantism.

Tàranto, *no.pr.f.* (*geog.*) Taranto; (*st.*) Tarentum.

taràntola, *s.f.* **1.** (*grosso ragno*) tarantula (*pl.* tarantulas, tarantulae) **2.** (*rettile*) gecko (*pl.* gecko(e)s).

tarantolàto, *ag.* (*patol.*) affected with tarantism.

tarantolísmo, *s.m.* (*patol.*) tarantism.

taràre, *v.t.* **1.** (*comm.*) to tare, to ascertain the tare of (sthg.) **2.** (*calibrare*) to calibrate **3.** (*mec.*) to set, to adjust.

taràto, *ag.* **1.** tared **2.** (*calibrato*) calibrated **3.** (*mec.*) set, adjusted **4.** (*difettoso*) defective, faulty: *un brillante* —, an impure diamond **5.** (*di persona con tara ereditaria*) with an hereditary vice **6.** (*moralmente*) corrupted.

taratóre, *s.m.* (*rar.*) one who tares.

taratúra, *s.f.* **1.** calibration **2.** (*mec.*) setting.

tàrchia, *s.f.* (*mar.*) sprit-sail.

tarchiàto, *ag.* thickset, sturdy, stout.

tardaménte, *av.* slowly, tardily.

tardànza, *s.f.* (*rar.*) delay.

tardàre, *v.i.* **1.** to delay, to be late, to be long: *l'aeroplano tardò due ore a causa della nebbia,* the plane was delayed two hours because of the fog; *egli non tardò a rendersi conto che aveva fatto un errore,* he soon realized that he had made a mistake; *egli tardò per il pranzo,* he was late for dinner; *il nostro aiuto tardò ed egli fu perduto,* our help arrived late and he was lost; *tardai a risponderti perchè pensavo che sarei venuto io stesso,* I was late in (o I put off) answering you because I expected to come myself; *non* —, *vieni subito,* don't be long (o don't delay), come at once ‖ *come mi tarda che egli arrivi!,* (*letter.*) how I long for his arrival! ‖ *v.t.* to delay, to defer, to put off: — *un pagamento,* to delay (o to defer o to put off) a payment.

tardézza, *s.f.* **1.** (*lentezza*) slowness **2.** (*di mente*) dullness, denseness.

tàrdi, *av.* late: *presto o* —, sooner or later; *arrivò* —, he arrived late; *arrivò più* — *di me,* he arrived later than I; *si fa* —, it is getting late; *te lo dirò più* —, I'll tell you later on; *fare* —, to be late; (*stare alzato fino a tarda ora*) to sit up late ‖ *al più* —, at the latest ‖ *sul* —, late in the day: *arrivò la sera sul* —, he arrived late in the evening ‖ *meglio* — *che mai,* *prov.* better late than never.

tardígrado, *ag.s.m.* (*zool.*) tardigrade (anche *scherz.*) ‖ *i tardigradi,* Tardigrada.

tardivaménte, *av.* tardily.

tardívo, *ag.* **1.** (*lento a svilupparsi*) backward, late: *bambino* —, backward child; *frutta tardive,* backward (o late) fruits **2.** (*che viene tardi*) tardy, belated: *ammende, scuse tardive,* tardy amends, excuses; *ricompensa tardiva,* tardy reward; *sviluppo* —, tardy development.

tàrdo, *ag.* **1.** (*lento*) slow; tardy; (*pigro*) sluggish; lazy: — *nei movimenti,* sluggish in movement; — *nel rispondere,* slow in answering; *egli è* — *nel fare le cose,* he is slow in doing things **2.** (*ottuso d'intelletto*) dull, slow-witted **3.** (*che viene tardi*) tardy: — *pentimento,* tardy repentance **4.** (*di tempo*) late: *a ora tarda,* at a late hour; *a tarda notte, sera,* late in the night, in the evening ‖ *morì a tarda età,* he died very old; *a causa della sua tarda età,* owing to his old age.

tàrga, *s.f.* **1.** (*di pietra*) slab; (*di metallo*) plate: — *automobilistica,* number-plate (o license-plate); — *di porta,* name-plate (o door-plate); — *di riconoscimento,* number-plate; *dati di* —, (*mec. elett.*) rating **2.** (*arc.*) (*scudo*) shield **3.** (*dial.*) (*grossa fetta*) slab.

targàre, *v.t.* (*aut.*) to give a number-plate to (a car): *un'automobile targata MI 549151,* a car with the license-plate MI 549151.

tarìffa, *s.f.* tariff, rate; (*tabella dei prezzi*) price-list, scale of charges: — *doganale,* customs tariff; *tariffe ferroviarie,* railway rates (o fares); — *passeggeri,* passenger tariff; — *postale,* postal rates; *quale è la vostra* — *per una stanza a un letto?,* how much do you charge for a single room?.

tarlàre, *v.i.,* **tarlàrsi,** *v.r.* to get worm-eaten.

tarlatàna, *s.f.* (*tessuto*) tarlatan.

tarlàto, *ag.* worm-eaten: *un mobile* —, a worm-eaten piece of furniture.

tarlatúra, *s.f.* **1.** worm-hole **2.** (*polvere di legno prodotta dal tarlo*) dust of worm-eaten wood.

tàrlo, *s.m.* **1.** (*entom.*) wood-worm: *roso dai tarli,* worm-eaten **2.** *fig.* gnawings (*pl.*): *il* — *della coscienza,* the gnawings of conscience.

tàrma, *s.f.* (*entom.*) moth.

tarmàre, *v.i.,* **tarmàrsi,** *v.r.* to be moth-eaten; to get moth-eaten.

tarmàto, *ag.* moth-eaten.

taroccàre, *v.i.* **1.** (*brontolare stizzosamente*) to grumble **2.** (*a carte*) to play one's trump card.

taròcco, *s.m.* taroc, tarot: *giocare ai tarocchi,* to play at tarots (o tarocs).

taròzzo, *s.m.* (*mar.*) futtock staff.

tarpàno[1], *ag.* (*rozzo*) rough, coarse.

tarpàno[2], *s.m.* (*zool.*) tarpan.

tarpàre, *v.t.* to clip (anche *fig.*): — *le ali a un uccello,* to clip a bird's wings; — *le ali a qlcu.,* to clip s.o.'s wings.

Tarpèa, *no.pr.f.* (*mit.*) Tarpeia.

tarpèo, *ag.* Tarpeian ‖ *Rupe Tarpea,* (*st.*) Tarpeian Rock.

Tarquínia, *no.pr.f.* (*geog. st.*) Tarquinia.

Tarquínio, *no.pr.m.* (*st.*) Tarquin ‖ — *il Superbo,* Tarquin the Proud.

tarsàle, *ag.* (*anat.*) tarsal.

tarsalgía, *s.f.* (*med.*) tarsalgia.

tarsìa, *s.f.* (*artig.*) marquetry, tarsia.

tarsiàre, *v.t.* to inlay.

tàrso[1], *s.m.* (*anat.*) tarsus (*pl.* tarsi).

Tàrso[2], *no.pr.m.* (*geog. st.*) Tarsus.

tartagliaménto, *s.m.* stutter, stuttering; stammer, stammering.

tartagliàre, *v.i.* to stutter; to stammer ‖ *v.t.* to stammer out ‖ — *il francese,* to speak broken French.

tartaglióna, *s.f.,* **tartaglióne,** *s.m.* stutterer; stammerer.

tartàna, *s.f.* (*mar.*) tartan.

tartàreo, *ag.* Tartarean.

tartaréseo, *ag.* Tartar, Tartarian ‖ *s.m.* (*lingua*) Tartar.

Tartaría, *no.pr.f.* (*geog.*) Tartary.

tartàrico, *ag.* (*chim.*) tartaric.

tàrtaro[1], *ag.s.m.* Tartar, Tatar.

tàrtaro[2], *s.m.* (*chim.*) tartar: *cremor di* —, cream of tartar.

Tàrtaro[3], *no.pr.m.* (*geog. mit.*) Tartarus.

tartaróso, *ag.* (*chim.*) tartaric.

tartarúga, *s.f.* **1.** tortoise; (*di mare*) turtle: *brodo di* —, turtle soup; *pettine di* —, tortoise-shell comb; *scudo di* —, tortoise-shell ‖ *andare a passo di* —, to go at a snail's pace **2.** (*persona lenta, impacciata*) sluggard.

tartassàre, *v.t.* **1.** to harass: *la città fu tartassata da molte incursioni aeree,* the town was harassed by many air-raids; — *uno studente,* to put a student through an exhaustive examination; — *un testimonio di domande,* to harass a witness with questions **2.** (*trattar male*) to maltreat, to ill-treat, to bully.

tartìna, *s.f.* (*cuc.*) canapé.

tartràto, *s.m.* (*chim.*) tartrate: — *di potassio,* potassium tartrate.

tartufàia, *s.f.* truffle-ground.

tartufàio, *s.m.* truffle seller.

tartufàto, *ag.* truffled.

tartúfo[1], *s.m.* truffle.

tartúfo[2], *s.m.* (*ipocrita*) sanctimonious hypocrite; Tartuf(f)e.

tàsca, *s.f.* **1.** pocket: — *interna, esterna,* inner, outer pocket; *coltello da* —, pocket-knife; *con le mani in* —, with one's hands in one's pockets; *edizioncina da* —, pocket edition; *orologio da* —, pocket watch; *aver le tasche vuote,* (*essere senza soldi*) to have empty pockets (*o to be penniless*); *mettere in — ql.co.*, to pocket sthg.; *mettere mano alla —*, (*essere pronto a pagare*) to be ready to pay; *mettere le mani in —*, to put one's hands in one's pockets; *pagare di — propria*, to pay out of one's own pocket (*anche fig.*); *rivoltare le tasche*, to turn out one's pockets ‖ *a me non viene niente in —*, I don't get anything out of it (o I have nothing to gain from it) ‖ *ho lavorato come un negro, ma ora ne ho piene le tasche*, (*fam.*) I have worked like a nigger but now I am sick of (o fed up with) it ‖ *non rompermi le tasche!*, (*volg.*) don't bother me! ‖ *conoscere ql.co. come le proprie tasche*, to know sthg. like the back of one's hand (o to know sthg. through and through) ‖ *mettersi l'orgoglio in —*, to pocket one's pride 2. (*borsa*) satchel 3. (*marsupio*) pouch 4. (*geol. min.*) nest.

tascàbile, *ag.* pocket (*attributivo*): *coltello —*, pocket-knife; *dizionario, libro —*, pocket-dictionary, pocket-book; *formato —*, pocket-size; *macchina fotografica —*, pocket-camera.

tascapàne, *s.m.* haversack.

tasceàta, *s.f.* pocketful.

taschíno, *s.m.* small pocket; (*del panciotto*) waistcoat pocket; (*per l'orologio*) fob.

Tasmània, *no.pr.f.* (*geog.*) Tasmania.

tàso, *s.m.* tartar; dregs (*pl.*).

tàssa, *s.f.* 1. (*dir. amm.*) tax, duty: *— di bollo*, stamp duty; *— di circolazione*, Road Fund Tax; *— di esercizio*, trade-licence tax; *— di ricchezza mobile*, income tax; *— di scambio*, purchase tax; *— di soggiorno*, visitors' tax (o non-resident tax); *— di successione*, inheritance tax; *— di zavorra*, (*mar.*) ballastage; *— sugli spettacoli* entertainment tax; *— sui cani*, dog licence; *tasse e imposte*, taxes and duties; *esente da tasse*, tax-free (o duty-free); *ricevitore delle tasse*, tax-collector; *soggetto a —*, liable to tax (o taxable); *imporre una — su ql.co.*, to levy a tax on sthg.; *pagare le tasse*, to pay one's taxes 2. (*per iscrizioni a scuola, ecc.*) fee: *— d'esame*, examination fee; *— di frequenza*, tuition fee; *— d'iscrizione*, entrance fee; *tasse scolastiche*, school fees.

tassàbile, *ag.* taxable, liable to tax, subject to a tax.

tassabilità, *s.f.* taxability, taxableness.

tassàmetro, *s.m.* (*aut.*) taximeter: *— di parcheggio*, parking meter.

tassàre, *v.t.* to tax, to charge (with duty), to levy a tax on (s.o., sthg.), to assess: *— gli articoli di lusso*, to tax luxury articles; *— duramente gli industriali*, to tax industrialists heavily (o to lay heavy taxes on industrialists).

tassativaménte, *av.* peremptorily; specifically, precisely.

tassatívo, *ag.* peremptory, compulsory: *un ordine —*, a peremptory order.

tassatóre, *s.m.* (*amm.*) assessor.

tassazióne, *s.f.* taxation, assessment: *— progressiva*, (*finanza*) graduated taxation.

tassellàre, *v.t.* 1. to dowel 2. (*fare un tassello in*) to wedge: *— una forma di cacio*, to take a wedge of cheese 3. (*lavorare d'intarsio*) to inlay.

tassellàto, *ag.* tessellated: *pavimento —*, tessellated pavement.

tassèllo, *s.m.* 1. dowel, plug: *mettere un —*, to wedge (o to plug) in a dowel 2. (*per decorazione*) inlay 3. (*pezza*) patch 4. (*metal.*) loose piece 5. (*edil.*) nag 6. (*mar.*) graving piece.

tassétto, *s.m.* (*piccola incudine*) stake.

tassí, *s.m.* taxi, taxi-cab.

tassidermía, *s.f.* taxidermy.

tassína, *s.f.* (*chim.*) taxine.

tassísta, *s.m.* taxi-driver, taxi-man (*pl.* taxi-men).

tàsso[1], *s.m.* (*zool.*) badger ‖ *dormire come un —*, to sleep like a log.

tàsso[2], *s.m.* (*bot.*) yew (-tree).

tàsso[3], *s.m.* (*incudine*) stake.

tàsso[4], *s.m.* (*econ. comm.*) rate: *— di interesse,*

interest rate; *— di scambio*, rate of exchange; *— di sconto*, discount rate: *— di sconto corrente*, market rate of discount.

tassonomía, *s.f.* taxonomy.

tassonòmico, *ag.* taxonomic(al).

tastaménto, *s.m.* touching; feeling; fingering.

tastàre, *v.t.* 1. (*toccare*) to touch; to feel; (*con la mano*) to finger: *— il polso a qlcu.*, to feel s.o.'s pulse (*anche fig.*) 2. (*scandagliare*) to sound, to probe ‖ *— il terreno*, *fig.* to feel one's way (o to explore the situation).

tastàta, *s.f.* touching; feeling; fingering.

tasteggiàre, *v.t.* (*mus.*) to touch the keys of (an instrument).

tastièra, *s.f.* keyboard.

tàsto, *s.m.* 1. (*di strumento musicale, macchina per scrivere, ecc.*) key: *— d'ascolto*, (*tel. mil.*) talking key; *— di ritorno*, (*di macchina per scrivere*) back-spacer (o return key); *— Morse*, Morse tapper; *— spaziatore*, (*di macchina per scrivere*) spacing bar; *battere i tasti di una macchina per scrivere*, to tap the keys of a typewriter ‖ *questo è un — piuttosto difficile da toccare*, *fig.* this subject is rather difficult to deal with ‖ *battere un falso*, *fig.* to strike a false note (o to hit on a delicate matter) 2. (*tatto*) touch; feel: *riconoscere ql.co. solamente al —*, to recognize sthg. only by the feel of it.

tastóni (a), *l.av.* gropingly: *procedere a — nel buio*, to grope one's way in the dark.

tàttica, *s.f.* 1. (*mil.*) tactics 2. *fig.* tactics (*pl.*): *la tua — è sbagliata*, your tactics are wrong.

tatticaménte, *av.* tactically.

tàttico, *ag.* tactical ‖ *s.m.* tactician.

tatticóne, *s.m.* (*persona astuta, accorta*) sly fellow.

tàttile, *ag.* tactile.

tattilità, *s.f.* tactility.

tàtto, *s.m.* 1. touch: *morbido, ruvido al —*, soft, rough to the touch; *il senso del —*, the sense of touch; *conoscere al —*, to know by feel (o by the touch) 2. *fig.* tact: *una persona di —*, a tactful person; *una persona senza —*, a tactless person; *devi domandarglielo con molto —*, you must ask him very tactfully; *si deve avere molto — per questo genere di lavoro*, one must have a great deal of tact for this kind of work; *mancare di —*, to show a want of tact.

tatuàggio, *s.m.* 1. tattoo, tattooed design 2. (*la pratica di tatuarsi*) tattooing.

tatuàre, *v.t.* to tattoo ‖ **tatuàrsi**, *v.r.* (*farsi tatuare*) to have oneself tattooed: *— un braccio*, to have one's arm tattooed.

tatuàto, *ag.* tattooed.

taumaturgía, *s.f.* thaumaturgy.

taumatúrgico, *ag.* thaumaturgic(al).

taumatúrgo, *s.m.* thaumaturge, thaumaturgist.

taurína, *s.f.* (*chim. biol.*) taurine.

tauríno, *ag.* taurine; bull-like (*attributivo*): *un uomo dal collo —*, a bull-necked man.

tauromachía, *s.f.* tauromachy, bull-fight(ing).

tautología, *s.f.* (*log.*) tautology.

tautològico, *ag.* (*log.*) tautologic(al).

tavèlla, *s.f.* (*edil.*) hollow flat block, hollow flat tile.

tavèrna, *s.f.* tavern, inn.

tavernière, *s.m.* tavern-keeper, inn-keeper.

tàvola, *s.f.* 1. table: *— allungabile*, draw-leaf table; *— da biliardo*, billiard table; *— da cucina*, kitchen table; *— da giuoco*, gaming-table; *— da pranzo*, dinner table; *— operatoria*, operating table; *— pieghevole*, gate-legged table; *biancheria da —*, table-linen; *cucchiaio da —*, table-spoon; *a —!*, dinner's ready (o fam. grub up!); *il pranzo è in —*, dinner is served; *alzarsi da —*, to rise from (o to leave) the table; *andare a —*, to go to table; *apparecchiare, sparecchiare la —*, to lay, to clear the table; *essere a — *, to be at table; *sedersi a —*, to sit down to dinner; *servire a —*, to wait at table ‖ *— calda*, snack bar ‖ *i piaceri della —*, the pleasures of the table; *amare la —*, to be fond of eating ‖ *mettere le carte in* —, *fig.* to lay one's cards on the table ‖ *tenere* — *imbandita*, (*essere molto ospitali*) to keep open house ‖ *la Tavola Rotonda*, (*lett.*) the Round Table **2.** (*tabella, prospetto; raccolta*) table: *tavole astronomiche*, astronomical tables; *tavole dei logaritmi*, (*mat.*) tables of logarithms; *tavole dei pesi e misure*, tables of weights and measures; — *di tiro*, (*artigl.*) firing (*o* gunnery) table; — *ottometrica*, (*med.*) Snellen test; — *pitagorica*, (*arit.*) multiplication table ‖ *le Tavole Amalfitane*, (*st.*) the Tables of Amalfi **3.** (*asse, assicella*) board; plank; (*di marmo*) slab: — *da stiro*, ironing board; — *per disegno*, drawing-board; *le tavole del palcoscenico*, the boards; — *di salvezza*, safety plank (anche *fig.*) ‖ *le Tavole della Legge*, (*Bibbia*) the Tables of the Law ‖ *le Dodici Tavole*, (*st. romana*) the Twelve Tables **4.** (*illustrazione di libro*) plate **5.** — *reale*, (*giuoco con dadi e pedine*) backgammon.

tavolàccio, *s.m.* (*per detenuti, soldati*) plank-bed.

tavolàta, *s.f.* table; dinner party: *una* — *di ragazzi allegri*, a table of merry boys; *che bella* —*!*, what a spread!.

tavolàto, *s.m.* **1.** (*di pavimento*) wood floor, plank floor; (*di muri*) boarding **2.** (*geog.*) table-land, plateau **3.** (*mar.*) planking: — *del ponte*, deck planking.

tavoleggiànte, *s.m.* (*rar.*) (*cameriere*) waiter.

tavolétta, *s.f.* **1.** tablet: *una* — *di cioccolata*, a tablet of chocolate **2.** (*assicella*) small board: — *di numerazione*, (*cine.*) number board ‖ — *votiva*, votive tablet **3.** (*edil.*) (*frattazzo*) float, plastering trowel **4.** — *pretoriana*, (*geodesia*) plane table.

tavolière, *s.m.* **1.** (*scacchiera*) chess-board, draught-board; (*per la tavola reale*) backgammon-board **2.** (*tavolino da giuoco*) gaming-table, card-table **3.** (*geog.*) (*altipiano*) table-land, plateau; (*bassopiano*) lowland.

tavolíno, *s.m.* small table; (*scrivania*) writing-table, writing-desk; — *abbassabile*, (*specialmente di scompartimento ferroviario*) drop-table; — *da giuoco*, gaming- (*o* card-)table; — *da notte*, bed-side table (*o* night -table) ‖ *è stato a* — *tutto il giorno*, he has spent all the day over his books.

tàvolo, *s.m.* table: — *anatomico*, (*med.*) anatomic table; — *da disegno*, drawing table (*o* desk); — *di lavoro*, work-table; — *di montaggio*, (*cine.*) splicing table.

tavolòzza, *s.f.* palette (anche *fig.*).

taxi, *s.m.* taxi, taxi-cab.

tàzza, *s.f.* **1.** cup: — *da caffè*, coffee-cup; — *da tè*, tea-cup **2.** (*contenuto*) cup(ful): *una* — *di caffè*, a cup of coffee; *una* — *di tè*, a cup of tea **3.** (*di fontana*) basin.

te[1], *pron. pers. m. f.* 2ª *persona sing.* **1.** *obliquo e oggetto* **you**; (*te stesso*) **yourself**: — *l'avevo detto*, I'd told you so; *abita sempre con* — *tua sorella?*, is your sister still living with you?; *chiudi il cancello dietro di* —, close the gate behind you; *deve dartelo*, he must give it (to) you; *devi decidere da* —, you must decide for yourself; *lo so che non* — *ne importa nulla*, I know it is all the same to you (*o fam.* I know you couldn't care less); *non ama che* —, you are the only person he loves; *non si preoccupa affatto di* —, he doesn't worry about you; *parlava sempre di* —, he was always talking about you; *volevano proprio* —, it was you they wanted; *vorrei dartene di più*, *ma non posso*, I should like to give you more, but I can't ‖ *guai a* —*!*, woe betide you! ‖ *per* —, *in quanto a* —, as for you (*o* as far as you are concerned) ‖ *tutto per* — (*solo*), all to yourself: *vorresti avere una casa tutta per* —*?*, would you like to have a house all to yourself? ‖ *ecco l'uomo che fa per* —, that is the man you need ‖ *non saper nè di me nè di* —, (*di cose*) to be insipid; (*di cibo*) to be tasteless (*o* insipid); (*di persona*) to be colourless (*o* insipid) ‖ *tocca a* —, it's your turn **2.** *sogg.* (*in proposizioni comparative e in funzione di predicato*) **you**: *beato, povero* —*!*, lucky, poor you!; *è molto più furbo di* —, he is a lot smarter than you are; *farei come* — *se potessi*, I should do the same as you if I could; *se io fossi* —, if I were you.

tè[2], *s.m.* tea: — *cinese, indiano*, China, Indian tea; — *leggero, forte*, weak, strong tea; — *pomeridiano*, afternoon tea; *casa da* —, tea-house; *dolce per il* —, tea-cake; *ora del* —, tea-time; *pastine da* —, tea biscuits; *sala da* —, tea-room; *servizio da* —, tea-service (*o* tea-set); *egli venne per il* —, he came to tea; *lo invitammo per il* —, we asked him to tea; *prendiamo il* — *alle cinque*, we have tea at five.

tèa, *ag.*: *rosa* —, tea-rose ‖ *s.f.* (*bot.*) tea.

teatíno, *ag. s.m.* (*eccl.*) Theatine.

teatràle, *ag.* theatrical (anche *fig.*).

teatralità, *s.f.* theatricality, theatricalism.

teatralménte, *av.* theatrically.

teatrànte, *s.m.* **1.** actor, comedian comic **2.** (*spreg.*) second-rate actor **3.** (*chi parla declamando*) tub-thumper.

teàtro, *s.m.* **1.** theatre; (*amer.*) theater; (*palcoscenico*) stage, scene: — *all'aperto*, open-air theatre; — *di posa*, (*cine.*) studio; — *di prosa*, (*edificio*) playhouse; *il cinema e il* —, the screen and the stage; *frequentatore di teatri*, theatre-goer; *ho visto l'* « *Amleto* » *a* —, I saw "Hamlet" on the stage; *questo argomento non è adatto per il* —, this subject is not fit for the stage; *andare a* —, to go to the theatre; *fare del* —, to be on the stage; *ritirarsi dal* —, to give up the stage; *scrivere per il* —, to write for the stage ‖ — *esaurito*, full house **2.** (*pubblico*) audience: *quando il violinista finì di suonare*, *il* — *applaudì per dieci minuti*, when the violinist finished playing, the audience clapped for ten minutes **3.** (*opere teatrali*) theatre; plays (*pl.*): *il* — *di Shakespeare*, Shakespeare's plays; *il* — *greco, moderno*, the Greek, modern theatre **4.** (*anfiteatro universitario*) theatre: — *anatomico*, anatomical theatre **5.** (*luogo d'azione*) theatre: *questi luoghi furono* — *di guerra*, these places were a theatre of war.

tebàico, *ag.* (*chim.*) thebaic.

Tebàide, *no.pr.f.* (*geog. st.*) Thebaid ‖ **tebàide**, *s.f.* solitude, hermitage: *vivere, ritirarsi in una* —, to live, to withdraw far from the madding crowd.

tebaína, *s.f.* (*chim.*) thebaine.

Tebàldo, *no.pr.m.* Theobald, Tybald.

tebàno, *ag.* Theban, Thebaic ‖ *s.m.* Theban.

Tèbe, *no.pr.f.* (*geog. st.*) Thebes.

tèca, *s.f.* **1.** casket; (*reliquario*) shrine **2.** (*anat.*) theca (*pl.* thecae).

Tècla, *no.pr.f.* Thecla.

tècnica, *s.f.* **1.** technique: — *applicata*, technique; *non conosco la nuova* — (*di guida*), I do not know the new technique (of driving); *quel pianista ha una* — *perfetta*, that pianist has a perfect technique **2.** (*tecnologia*) technics (*pl.*): — *elettronica*, (*rad.*) electronics; — *mineraria*, mining engineering.

tecnicaménte, *av.* technically.

tecnicísmo, *s.m.* technicality.

tècnico, *ag.* technical: *per motivi d'ordine* —, out of technical reasons; *scuola tecnica*, technical school; *termine* —, technical term: *ufficio* —, technical office ‖ *s.m.* technician, technicist; engineer: — *aeronautico*, qualified aircraft engineer; — *del collaudo*, (*ind.*) testing engineer; — *del suono*, (*cine.*) sound engineer.

tecnígrafo, *s.m.* universal drafting device.

tecnocrazía, *s.f.* technocracy.

tecnografía, *s.f.* technography.

tecnogràfico, *ag.* technographic.

tecnología, *s.f.* technology.

tecnològico, *ag.* technological.

tecnòlogo, *s.m.* technologist.

tèco, *pron.pers.* (*letter.*) **with you**; (*poet. arc.*) **with thee**.

tèda, *s.f.* (*letter.*) torch: *la* — *nuziale*, the bridal torch.

Teddy-boy, *s.m.* Teddy-boy.

tedescaménte, *av.* in a German manner.

tedescheggiàre, *v.i.* to Germanize.

tedeschería, *s.f.* (*spreg.*) (*i tedeschi*) Boches (*pl.*).

tedeschizzàre, *v.t.* to Germanize.

tedésco, *ag.* German ‖ *s.m.* **1.** German **2.** (*lingua*) (the) German (language) ‖ **tedésca**, *s.f.* German.

tedescòfilo, *s.m.* Germanophil.

tedescofobía, *s.f.* Germanophobia.

tedescòfobo, *s.m.* Germanophobe.

Te Deum, *s.m.* (*eccl. mus.*) Te Deum.

tediàre, *v.t.* to bore, to weary, to tire; (*infastidire*) to bother: *ci tedia a morte con i suoi racconti*, he wearies (o bores) us to death with his stories; *non tediarmi con domande sciocche!*, don't bother me with silly questions!; *questo libro mi tedia*, this book bores me.

tèdio, *s.m.* tedium, tediousness, wearisomeness, boredom.

tediosaménte, *av.* tediously, tiresomely, wearisomely.

tediosità, *s.f.* tediousness, tiresomeness, wearisomeness.

tedióso, *ag.* tedious, tiresome, wearisome, boring; (*ingrato*) irksome: *un lavoro —*, an irksome work; *un libro —*, a tedious (o boring) book; *una persona tediosa*, a boring person (o a bore).

tef, *s.m.* (*bot.*) tef, teff.

tegamàta, *s.f.* (*contenuto di un tegame*) panful.

tegàme, *s.m.* **1.** pan, saucepan ‖ *uova al —*, fried eggs **2.** (*tegamata*) panful: *un — di piselli*, a panful of peas.

téglia, *s.f.* baking-pan, baking-tin, pie-dish.

tégola, *s.f.* **1.** (roofing) tile: *— ad incastro*, interlocking tile; *— curva*, bent tile; *— di cemento*, cement roofing tile; *— di colmo (di un tetto)*, ridge tile; *copertura con tegole*, tile covering; *fabbricazione delle tegole*, tile-making; *posa in opera di tegole*, tiling; *tetto di tegole*, tile roof; *coprire un tetto di tegole*, to tile a roof ‖ *chi ha tegole di vetro, non tiri sassi al vicino*, *prov.* those who live in glass houses should not throw stones **2.** *fig.* blow: *che —!*, what a blow!.

tegolàia, *s.f.* (*fabbrica di tegole*) tilery, tile-kiln.

tegolàio, *s.m.* tiler.

tegolàto, *s.m.* tiling.

tégolo, *V.* tégola.

tegumentàle, tegumentàrio, *ag.* tegumental, tegumentary.

teguménto, *s.m.* tegument.

teièra, *s.f.* tea-pot: *copri- —*, tea-cosy.

teína, *s.f.* (*chim.*) theine.

teísmo, *s.m.* (*fil.*) theism.

teísta, *s.m.* (*fil.*) theist.

teístico, *ag.* (*fil.*) theistic(al).

tek, *s.m.* (*albero, legno*) teak.

téla, *s.f.* **1.** cloth: *— cerata*, oilcloth; *— da asciugamani*, towelling; *— da camicie*, shirting; *— da imballaggio*, pack-cloth; *— da lenzuola*, sheeting; *— da materassi*, ticking; *— da sacco*, sackcloth; *— di cotone*, cotton cloth; *— di juta*, jute cloth (o jute canvas); *— di lino*, linen; *— d'Olanda*, Dutch cloth; *— di pneumatico*, ply (o warp); *— gommata*, rubberized canvas; *— grezza*, unbleached linen; *— grezza di canapa*, (per vele, quadri, imballaggio) canvas; *— impermeabilizzata*, waterproof cloth; *— metallica*, wire gauze; *— olona*, olona cloth (o duck cloth o canvas); *— per aeroplani*, aeroplane fabric; *— per borsette, valigie*, bagging; *— per sedili*, (di treni, ecc.) seat webbing; *applicazione delle tele*, (a pneumatici) plying; *copertura di —*, canvas covering; *una pezza di —*, a roll of cloth; *rilegatura in —*, cloth binding; *imbiancare la —*, to bleach cloth ‖ *— di ragno*, cobweb ‖ *— di Penelope*, *fig.* web of Penelope (o never-ending task)‖ *far —*, (gergo) (*svignarsela*) to make oneself scarce **2.** (*teat.*) curtain: *cala la —*, the curtain falls; *si alza la —*, the curtain rises **3.** (*cine.*) screen **4.** (*pitt.*) painting, picture: *una — di Botticelli*, a painting by Botticelli **5.** (*trama, intreccio*) plot: *la — di un romanzo*, the plot of a novel ‖ *— giudiziaria*, judicial proceeding(s).

telàggio, *s.m.* (*qualità della tela*) quality (of cloth); (*tessuto della tela*) texture (of cloth).

telàio, *s.m.* **1.** loom: *— a mano*, hand loom; *— a pedali*, treadle loom; *— meccanico*, power loom; *— per maglieria*, knitter; *— per maglieria automatico*, self-acting knitter; *— per maglieria circolare*, circular knitter; *— per tappeti*, carpet loom **2.** (*ossatura, armatura, cornice*) frame; (*di automobile*) chassis (*pl.* chassis); car frame; (*scorrevole, di finestra*) sash; (*da ricamo*) tambour: *il — di una finestra, di un ombrello, di una porta*, the frame of a window, of an umbrella, of a door **3.** (*tip.*) chase.

Telamóne, *no.pr.m.* (*lett.*) Telamon ‖ **telamóne**, *s.m.* (*arch.*) telamon (*pl.* telamones).

telangettasía, *s.f.* (*patol.*) telangiectasia, telangiectasis.

telàre, *v.i.* (*gergo*) (*svignarsela*) to make oneself scarce.

telchíni, *s.m.pl.* (*mit.*) Telchines.

teleàrmi, *s.f.pl.* guided weapons.

teleautografía, *s.f.* (*tel.*) telautography.

teleautògrafo, *s.m.* (*tel.*) telautograph.

teleautogràmma, *s.m.* (*tel.*) telautogram.

teleaviazióne, *s.f.* guided flight.

teleavviatóre, *s.m.* (*elett.*) contactor starter, solenoid starter.

telebómba, *s.f.* guided missile.

telecàmera, *s.f.* (*tv.*) telecamera, television camera: *— portatile*, portable television apparatus (o fam. creepie-peepie); *carrello per —*, camera dolly.

telecomandàre, *v.t.* to radio-control.

telecomandàto, *ag.* radio-controlled.

telecomàndo, *s.m.* radio-control.

telecompositríce, *s.f.* teletypesetter.

telecomunicazióni, *s.f.pl.* telecommunications.

telecrònaca, *s.f.* television news(-reel): *ci sarà una — della partita*, the match will be televised.

telefèrica, *s.f.* cableway, aerial ropeway, telpherage: *— a va e vieni*, to-and-fro aerial ropeway (o jig-back).

telefèrico, *ag.* telpher (*attributivo*).

teleferísta, *s.m.* telpherman (*pl.* telphermen).

telefonàre, *v.t.* (*comunicare per telefono*) to telephone, to phone; (*chiamare per telefono*) to ring up: *mi telefonò la notizia che aspettavo*, he phoned me the news I was expecting; *ti telefonerò*, I'll give you a ring (o a call).

telefonàta, *s.f.* (telephone) call: *— intercomunale, interurbana*, trunk- (o long-distance) call; *— internazionale*, international trunk-call; *— urbana*, local call.

telefonía, *s.f.* telephony: *— senza fili*, wireless telephony (o radiotelephony).

telefonicaménte, *av.* by telephone, telephonically.

telefònico, *ag.* telephone (*attributivo*); telephonic: *apparecchio —*, telephone; *cabina telefonica*, telephone booth; *centralino —*, telephone exchange; *elenco —*, telephone directory; *rete telefonica*, telephone system; *servizio, ufficio —*, telephone service, office.

telefonísta, *s.m.* telephone operator, telephonist ‖ *s.f.* telephonist, telephone-girl.

telèfono, *s.m.* telephone; phone: *— automatico*, dial (o automatic) telephone; *— duplex*, party-line telephone; *— interno*, extension telephone (o interphone); *— senza fili*, wireless telephone; *abbonato al —*, (telephone) subscriber: *essere abbonato al —*, to be on the phone; *campanello del —*, telephone bell; *colpo di —*, (*fam.*) call: *dammi un colpo di —*, ring me up; *fili del —*, telephone wires; *numero di —*, telephone number; *ricevitore, trasmettitore del —*, telephone receiver, transmitter; *avere il —*, to have a phone; *chiamare qlcu. al —*, to ring (o to call) s.o. up; *essere desiderato al —*, to be wanted on the phone; *parlare al —*, to speak on the phone; *parlare per —*, to speak by telephone.

telefòto, *s.f.* **1.** (*telefotogramma*) telephoto **2.** (*abbr.*) di **telefotografía**.

telefotografàre, *v.t.* to telephotograph.

telefotografía, *s.f.* **1.** telephotography **2.** (*copia telefotografica*) telephotograph.

telefotogràfico, *ag.* telephotographic.
telefotogràmma, *s.m.* telephotograph.
telegènico, *ag.* telegenic.
telegiornàle, *s.m.* television news(-reel); (*fam.*) news.
telegrafàre, *v.t.* to telegraph, to wire; (*con cavo sottomarino*) to cable: — *un messaggio,* to telegraph a message; — *a Roma, a qlcu.,* to cable Rome, s.o.
telegrafía, *s.f.* telegraphy: — *senza fili,* wireless telegraphy.
telegraficaménte, *av.* by telegraph; telegraphically; (*con cavo sottomarino*) by cable.
telegràfico, *ag.* telegraphic; telegraph (*attributivo*): *cavo* —, telegraph-cable; *filo* —, telegraph-wire; *indirizzo* —, telegraphic address; *linea telegrafica,* telegraph line; *messaggio* —, telegraphic message; *palo* —, telegraph-pole (o -post); *ufficio* —, telegraph-office; *vaglia* —, telegraphic money-order.
telegrafìsta, *s.c.* telegraphist, telegraph operator; (*spec. amer.*) telegrapher.
telègrafo, *s.m.* **1.** telegraph: — *campale,* (*mil.*) field telegraph; — *Morse,* Morse telegraph; — *senza fili,* wireless telegraphy; *cavo del* —, telegraph-cable; *fattorino del* —, telegraph messenger; *filo del* —, telegraph-wire; *palo del* —, telegraph-pole (o -post) **2.** (*ufficio telegrafico*) telegraph-office.
telegràmma, *s.m.* telegram; wire; (*per cavo sottomarino*) cable(-gram): — *cifrato,* code telegram; — *con precedenza assoluta,* priority telegram; — *con risposta pagata,* pre- (o reply-) paid telegram; *un* — *da New York,* a cable from New York; — *lettera,* lettergram (o day letter); — *per l'interno, per l'estero,* inland, foreign telegram; — *urgente,* urgent telegram; *per* —, by wire; (*per cavo sottomarino*) by cable; *fare un* —, to wire; (*per cavo sottomarino*) to cable; *mandare un* — *a qlcu.,* to wire (to) s.o.; *mandare un* — *per chiamare qlcu.,* to wire for s.o.
Telèmaco, *no.pr.m.* (*lett.*) Telemachus.
telemeccànica, *s.f.* telemechanics.
telemeccànico, *ag.* telemechanic.
telemetría, *s.f.* telemetry.
telemètrico, *ag.* telemetric(al).
telemetrìsta, *s.m.* telemetrist; (*mil.*) range-taker.
telèmetro, *s.m.* telemeter; (*per arma da fuoco, strumento fotografico*) rangefinder.
teleobbiettìvo, *s.m.* (*foto.*) telephoto lens.
teleología, *s.f.* (*fil.*) teleology.
teleològico, *ag.* (*fil.*) teleologic(al).
teleòstei, *s.m.pl.* (*ittiol.*) Teleostei.
telepatía, *s.f.* telepathy: *per* —, by telepathy.
telepaticaménte, *av.* by telepathy, telepathically.
telepàtico, *ag.* telepathic.
telería, *s.f.* linen and cotton goods (*pl.*); soft goods (*pl.*): *commerciante in telerie,* linen draper; *negozio di* —, draper's shop.
teleruttóre, *s.m.* (*elett.*) remote control switch; (*interruttore elettromagnetico*) electromagnetic switch: — *di avviamento,* solenoid starter.
teleschérmo, *s.m.* (*tv.*) telescreen.
telescopicaménte, *av.* by telescope, telescopically.
telescòpico, *ag.* telescopic: *forcella a molleggio* —, (*mec.*) telescopic fork; *mirino* —, (*foto.*) telescopic finder; *osservazioni telescopiche,* telescopic observations.
telescòpio, *s.m.* telescope: — *a riflessione,* reflecting telescope; — *a rifrazione,* refracting telescope; — *equatoriale,* equatorial (telescope); — *girevole sull'asse orizzontale,* transit instrument; *stelle visibili al* —, stars visible through telescope.
telescrivènte, *s.f.* teletype, teletypewriter.
teleselezióne, *s.f.* (*tel.*) direct dialing.
telesísmico, *ag.* teleseismic.
telesísmo, *s.m.* teleseism.
telespettatóre, *s.m.* televiewer, viewer.
telestesía, *s.f.* tel(a)esthesia.
teletrasmèttere, *v.t.* to televise, to telecast.

teletrasmettitóre, *s.m.* telecaster.
teletrasmissióne, *s.f.* telecast.
telétta[1]**,** *s.f.* thin linen fabric; thin cotton fabric.
telétta[2]**,** *V.* **toilette.**
televisióne, *s.f.* **1.** television: — *a colori,* colour television; — *a gettone,* coin-free (o pay-as-you-see) television (*o amer.* fee television); — *in bianco e nero,* black-and-white television; *alla* —, on television; *per* —, by television: *trasmettere per* —, to televise **2.** (*televisore*) television set; televisor, television receiver.
televisívo, *ag.* televisional, televisionary; television (*attributivo*): *programma* —, television program(me); *trasmissione televisiva,* telecast.
televisóre, *s.m.* televisor; television set.
tellína, *s.f.* (*zool.*) cockle.
tellúrico, *ag.* telluric.
tellúrio, *s.m.* (*chim.*) tellurium.
télo[1]**,** *s.m.* (*pezzo di stoffa*) breadth of cloth; sheet: — *mimetico,* (*mil.*) camouflaged sheet; *un abito fatto di due teli,* a dress made with two lengths of material.
tèlo[2]**,** *s.m.* (*arc. letter.*) javelin, dart; (*freccia*) arrow.
telóne, *s.m.* (*teat.*) curtain.
téma[1]**,** *s.f.* (*paura*) fear: *per* — *di uno scontro,* for fear of a collision ‖ *non si fermò per* — *di arrivare in ritardo,* he did not stop lest he should be late; *per* — *che egli non venisse,* lest he should not come.
tèma[2]**,** *s.m.* **1.** (*argomento*) theme, subject, topic: — *d'attualità,* topic of the day; *il* — *di una conversazione,* the topic of a conversation; *il* — *di un discorso,* the theme of a speech; *uscire di* —, to wander from the subject ‖ *fuori* —, off the point **2.** (*scolastico*) composition: *svolgere un* —, to write a composition **3.** (*glottologia*) stem, theme: *il* — *di una parola,* the stem of a word **4.** (*mus.*) theme.
temàtico, *ag.* thematic.
temènza, *s.f.* (*rar.*) awe, dread.
temerariaménte, *av.* temerariously; rashly, recklessly; (*arrogantemente*) arrogantly.
temerarietà, *s.f.* temerity, rashness, recklessness; (*arroganza*) arrogance; (*folle audacia*) foolhardiness.
temeràrio, *ag.* temerarious, rash, reckless; (*arrogante*) arrogant: *un giudizio* —, a rash judgement; *scioccamente* —, foolhardy; *una persona temeraria,* a rash (o reckless) person ‖ *Carlo il Temerario,* (*st.*) Charles the Bold.
temére, *v.t.* **1.** (*avere timore di*) to fear, to be afraid of (s.o., sthg.); to dread: *accadde proprio quel che temevo,* it happened just as I feared; *non teme niente,* he fears nothing; *non temo di incontrarmi con lui,* I am not afraid of meeting him (o I do not fear to meet him); *non temo quell'uomo,* I am not afraid of that man; *temo che egli sia morto,* I fear he is dead; *temo che sia troppo tardi,* I fear it is too late; *temo di non riuscire,* I am afraid I might not succeed; — *Dio, la morte,* to fear (o to dread) God, death; — *il peggio,* to fear the worst **2.** (*rifuggire da*) to shrink from (sthg.): *quella bestia teme l'acqua,* that animal shrinks from water **3.** (*patire*) not to stand: *questa pianta teme il caldo, il freddo,* this plant cannot stand the heat, the cold ‖ *teme l'umidità, il caldo,* to be kept dry, cool ‖ *v.i.* to fear: *non temete di nulla!,* never fear!; *temo di no, temo di sì,* I fear not, I fear so; *temo per la sua salute,* I fear for his health; — *per la propria vita,* to go about in terror of one's life ‖ *non* —, *metterò io le cose a posto,* don't worry, I shall put things right.
temerità, *V.* **temerarietà.**
Tèmi, *no.pr.f.* (*mit.*) Themis.
temìbile, *ag.* dreadful; awe-inspiring.
Temìstocle, *no.pr.m.* (*st.*) Themistocles.
tempàccio, *s.m.* nasty weather, foul weather.
Tèmpe, *no.pr.f.* (*geog. st.*) Tempe.
tempellóne, *s.m.* (*rar.*) (*persona indecisa*) waverer.
tèmpera, *s.f.* **1.** (*metall.*) hardening; (*per immersione*) quenching; (*ind. vetraria*) tempering: — *di profondità,*

through hardening; — *in bianco*, bright hardening; — *localizzata*, selective quenching; *bagno di* —, quenching bath; *una lama di buona* —, a well tempered blade **2.** (*pitt.*) distemper, tempera: *disegno a* —, wash drawing; *dipingere a* —, to distemper **3.** (*mus.*) tone, timbre.

temperamatíte, *s.m.* pencil-sharpener.

temperaménto, *s.m.* **1.** temperament, disposition, temper: — *allegro, generoso*, cheerful, generous disposition; — *artistico, poetico*, artistic, poetic temperament; *un* — *collerico, nervoso, sanguigno*, a choleric, nervous, sanguine temperament; *un* — *dolce*, a sweet disposition (*o* temper); *pigro per* —, constitutionally lazy **2.** (*alleviamento*) mitigation **3.** (*espediente*) expedient **4.** (*accomodamento*) arrangement; (*compromesso*) compromise.

temperànte, *ag.* temperate, moderate.

temperateménte, *av.* temperately, moderately.

temperànza, *s.f.* temperance, moderation; sobriety; self-control: — *nel bere, nel mangiare*, temperance in eating, in drinking.

temperàre, *v.t.* **1.** (*mitigare*) to temper, to mitigate, to moderate: — *un castigo*, to mitigate a punishment; — *la giustizia con la clemenza*, to temper justice with mercy; — *la propria collera*, to moderate one's anger **2.** (*appuntare*) to sharpen: — *una matita*, to sharpen a pencil **3.** (*pitt.*) to temper: — *colori*, to temper colours **4.** (*metal.*) to temper, to harden; (*per immersione*) to quench; (*ind. vetraria*) to temper **5.** (*mus.*) to tone.

temperataménte, *av.* temperately, moderately; mildly.

temperàto, *ag.* temperate, moderate (anche *fig.*): — *nel mangiare, nel bere*, temperate (*o* self-controlled) in eating, drinking ‖ *clima* —, (*geog.*) temperate climate; *zona temperata*, (*geog.*) temperate zone.

temperatúra, *s.f.* **1.** temperature: — *ambiente*, room temperature; — *assoluta*, (*chim. fis.*) absolute temperature; — *critica*, (*chim. fis.*) critical temperature; — *del punto di rugiada*, (*fis.*) dew-point temperature; — *di accensione*, (*di un liquido combustibile*) (*chim.*) fire point; — *di accensione spontanea*, (*chim.*) fire point; — *di autoaccensione*, (*chim.*) spontaneous ignition temperature (*abbr.* S.I.T.); — *di colata*, (*fonderia*) tapping temperature; — *di combustione*, (*chim.*) combustion temperature; — *di condensazione*, (*fis. chim.*) dew point; — *di congelamento*, (*fis.*) freezing temperature; — *di dissociazione*, (*chim.*) dissociation temperature; — *di ebollizione*, (*fis.*) boiling temperature; — *di miscibilità*, (*chim. fis.*) mixibility temperature; — *di riferimento*, (*termica*) reference temperature; — *effettiva*, (*termica*) effective temperature; — *equivalente*, (*termica*) equivalent temperature; — *minima assoluta ottenibile*, nadir; — *minima*, (*saldatura*) interpass temperature; — *risultante*, (*termica*) resulting temperature; — *totale*, (*termica*) total temperature ‖ *abbassamento di* —, (*termica*) fall of temperature; *a* — *e pressione normali*, (*chim. fis.*) standard temperature and pressure; *bassa* —, (*termica*) low temperature; *misuratore di* —, (*scient.*) temperature gauge; *elevare la* —, (*termica*) to increase the temperature **2.** (*alterazione febbrile*) temperature, fever: *avere un po' di* —, to have (*o* to run) a temperature; *prendere la* — *a qlcu.*, to take s.o.'s temperature.

temperíno, *s.m.* penknife (*pl.* penknives), pocket-knife (*pl.* pocket-knives).

tempèsta, *s.f.* storm (anche *fig.*); tempest (anche *fig.*); *fig.* (*moltitudine di cose che cadono*) shower: *una* — *di applausi*, a storm of applause; *una* — *di colpi, frecce, proiettili*, a shower of blows, arrows, bullets; — *di grandine*, hail-storm; — *di neve*, snow-storm; — *di pioggia*, rain-storm; — *di vento*, wind-storm; *una* — *in un bicchiere d'acqua*, a storm (*o* a tempest) in a teacup; *battuto dalle tempeste*, storm-beaten; *bloccato dalla* —, storm-bound; *centro della* —, storm-centre (anche

fig.); *mare in* —, stormy sea; *sballottato dalla* —, storm-tossed; *segnale di* —, storm-signal; *zona delle tempeste*, storm-belt; *c'era aria di* —, there was a stormy atmosphere; *ci fu una violenta* —, there was a violent storm; *sollevare una* —, *fig.* to stir up a storm ‖ «*La tempesta*», (*lett.*) "The Tempest" ‖ *dopo la* — *viene il sereno*, *prov.* after the storm comes the calm.

tempestàre, *v.i.* to storm, to be stormy; (*grandinare*) to hail; (*infuriare*) to rage ‖ *v.t.* **1.** *fig.* (*importunare con insistenza*) to annoy, to harass: — *qlcu. di domande*, to harass s.o. with questions **2.** (*bombardare*) to bomb, to assail (anche *fig.*): — *il nemico di proiettili*, to bomb the enemy with shells (*o* to shell the enemy); — *qlcu. di insulti*, to assail s.o. with insults ‖ — *una porta di calci*, to kick a door furiously **3.** (*ornare*) to stud; to adorn; (*cospargere*) to strew.

tempestàto, *ag.* **1.** (*battuto*) beaten **2.** (*ornato*) studded; (*cosparso*) strewn: — *di perle, stelle*, studded with pearls, stars; *un prato* — *di fiori*, a lawn strewn with flowers.

tempestivaménte, *av.* at the right time, opportunely, seasonably.

tempestívo, *ag.* timely, opportune, seasonable: *provvedimenti tempestivi*, timely measures.

tempestosaménte, *av.* stormily, tempestuously; violently; (*tumultuosamente*) boisterously.

tempestóso, *ag.* stormy (anche *fig.*), tempestuous: *mare* —, stormy sea; *umore* —, stormy mood.

tèmpia, *s.f.* (*anat.*) temple.

tèmpio, *s.m.* temple: — *ebraico*, Jewish temple (*o* synagogue); *un* — *greco*, a Greek temple.

tempísta, *s.c.* **1.** time-keeper; (*mus.*) musician who keeps time well **2.** *fig.* person who does the right thing at the right time **3.** (*cronometrista*) checker.

templàre, *s.m.* (*st.*) (*Cavaliere*) —, (Knight) Templar.

tèmpo, *s.m.* **1.** time: — *assoluto, relativo*, absolute, relative time; — *del raccolto, di guerra*, harvest time, wartime; — *fa*, some time ago; *il* — *presente*, the present time; *a* — *di record*, in record time; *allo stesso* —, at the same time; *col passare del* —, in the long run; *da* — *immemorabile*, from time immemorial; *di* — *in* —, from time to time (*o* every now and then *o* once in a while); *due giorni di* —, two days' time; *fino a quel* —, up to that time; *fra qualche* —, within some time; *in breve* —, in a short time; *in metà* —, in half the time; *in un primo* —, at first; *logoro dal* —, time-worn; *molto* — *prima, dopo*, long before, after; *proprio al* — *giusto*, in the very nick of time ‖ *il* — *passa, vola*, time passes (*o* goes by), flies; *un* — *veniva qui spesso*, once he used to come here often; *andiamo, è* — *!*, let's go, time is up!; *ci vuole molto* — *per farlo bene*, it takes a lot of time to do it well; *col* — *le cose si metteranno a posto*, time will put things to rights; *è* — *che tu cambi, che tu volti pagina*, it is high time for you to turn over a new leaf; *è* — *che tu vada*, it is time you were going; *ella studia tutto il* —, she studies all the time; *lascialo decidere al* —, let time decide; *l'avevo detto a suo* —, I had said it some time before; *non ha resistito al collaudo del* —, it did not resist the test of time; *non lo vedevo da qualche* —, I had not seen him for some time; *questo lavoro mi prese molto* —, this work took me a lot of time ‖ *essere a* — *per fare ql.co.*, to be in time to do sthg.; *passare, trascorrere il proprio* —, to spend one's time ‖ *a* — *debito, in* — *utile*, in due time ‖ *a* — *perso, nei ritagli di* —, in one's spare time ‖ *per* —, early ‖ *non ho* — *da perdere*, I have no time to lose; *non metter* — *in mezzo*, don't lose time; *prendi* —, *pensaci su*, take your time, think it over ‖ *quello scrittore ha fatto il suo* —, that writer has had his day ‖ *ammazzare il* —, to kill time ‖ *dare* — *al* —, to take one's time ‖ *darsi bel* —, to have a good time (*o* to enjoy oneself) ‖ *guadagnar* —, to gain time ‖ *perdere, sprecare il proprio* —, to waste one's time ‖ *riguadagnare il — perduto*, to make up for lost time ‖ *il — è denaro*, *prov.* time is money ‖ *il — è galantuomo*, *prov.* murder will out ‖ *chi ha — non aspetti —*, *prov.* make hay while the sun shines **2.** (*epoca, età*) times (*pl.*), days (*pl.*), age: *al — dei Romani*, in the times of the Romans (*o* in Roman times); *ai miei tempi*, in my times; *a, in quei tempi*, in those times; *a, in quel —*, at that time; *in questi ultimi tempi*, of late (*o* lately) ‖ *al — che Berta filava*, in days gone by ‖ *il buon — antico*, the good old days (*o* times) ‖ *coi tempi che corrono*, as times go ‖ *marciare coi tempi*, to keep up with the times ‖ *precorrere i tempi*, to be ahead of (*o* to be born before) one's times **3.** (*atmosferico*) weather: *— bello*, nice (*o* fine) weather; *— brutto*, bad weather; *— da cani*, nasty (*o* foul *o* horrible) weather; *— piovoso*, rainy weather; *col brutto o col bel —*, rain or shine; *il — si mette al bello*, the weather is getting fine; *il — sta per cambiare*, the weather is going to change; *che — fa oggi?*, how is the weather today?; *non uscire con questo —!*, don't go out in such nasty weather!; *non venne a causa del —*, owing to the weather he could not come **4.** (*mus.*) time; tempo (*pl.* tempos, tempi); (*parte di composizione musicale*) movement; (*misura*) measure; (*battuta*) beat: *— di minuetto*, tempo di minuetto (*o* minuet-time); *i quattro tempi di una sinfonia*, the four movements of a symphony; *battere, tenere il —*, to beat, to keep time; *essere a, fuori —*, to be in, out of time; *perdere il —*, to go out of time; *battere in quattro tempi*, to beat four to the bar **5.** (*gram.*) tense: *— presente, passato, futuro*, present, past, future tense **6.** (*fase, parte*) stage, phase, part: *esercizio in tre tempi*, (*ginnastica*) exercise in three motions; *l'operazione fu eseguita in due tempi*, the operation was performed in two stages; *il secondo — sta per cominciare*, (*cine.*) the second part is going to begin.

Tèmpora, *s.f.pl.* (*eccl.*) Ember Days.

temporàle[1], *ag.* temporal; (*eccl.*) temporal, secular: *interessi temporali*, secular interests; *il potere — del Papa*, the temporal power of the Pope.

temporàle[2], *ag.* (*anat.*) temporal: *osso —*, temporal (bone).

temporàle[3], *s.m.* storm: *il — è cessato*, the storm is over; *ci fu un —*, there was a storm.

temporaléso, *ag.* stormy (*anche fig.*): *aria temporalesca*, stormy air.

temporalità, *s.f.* temporality.

temporalménte, *av.* temporally; (*eccl.*) temporally, secularly.

temporaneaménte, *av.* temporarily; transitorily.

temporaneità, *s.f.* temporariness; transitoriness.

temporàneo, *ag.* temporary; transitory: *una situazione temporanea*, a temporary situation.

temporeggiaménto, *s.m.* temporization, temporizing.

temporeggiàre, *v.i.* to temporize.

temporeggiatóre, *s.m.* temporizer ‖ *Fabio Massimo, il Temporeggiatore*, Fabius Maximus the Cunctator.

tèmpra, *s.f.* **1.** temper; (*metal.*) hardening; (*per immersione*) quenching; (*ind. vetraria*) tempering: *— di profondità*, through hardening; *— in bianco*, bright hardening; *— localizzata*, selective quenching; *bagno di —*, quenching bath; *una lama di buona —*, a well-tempered blade; *un metallo di buona —*, a well-tempered metal **2.** *fig.* character, fibre, temperament; disposition: *una persona della sua —*, a person of his character (*o* fibre *o* temperament); *un uomo di — robusta*, a man of strong fibre (*o* character) **3.** (*di suono*) timbre.

tempràre, *v.t.* **1.** (*metal.*) to temper, to harden; (*per immersione*) to quench: *— l'acciaio*, to temper steel **2.** *fig.* (*fortificare*) to strengthen; (*plasmare*) to form, to mould: *le difficoltà temprano l'animo*, hardships strengthen the soul; *la disciplina tempra il carattere*, discipline forms (*o* moulds) the character; *è temprato a tutte le difficoltà che dovrà affrontare*, he is inured to all the difficulties he will have to face.

tenàce, *ag.* **1.** tenacious; (*viscoso*) viscous, adhesive: *argilla —*, tenacious clay; *filo —*, tenacious (*o* strong) thread; *presa —*, tenacious hold; *memoria —*, tenacious (*o* retentive) memory **2.** (*fermo, perseverante*) persevering, persistent, tenacious, firm: *— nelle sue opinioni*, tenacious of his opinion; *fede —*, firm faith; *sforzi tenaci*, persistent efforts; *un uomo —*, a persevering man **3.** (*ostinato*) obstinate, stubborn, dogged.

tenaceménte, *av.* tenaciously; (*con perseveranza*) perseveringly; firmly; (*con ostinazione*) stubbornly.

tenàcia, *s.f.* tenacity, tenaciousness; (*perseveranza*) perseverance, firmness; (*ostinazione*) stubbornness.

tenacità, *s.f.* **1.** *V.* **tenàcia 2.** (*scient.*) tenacity **3.** (*metal.*) toughness.

tenàglia, *s.f.* **1.** *gener. pl.* tongs (*pl.*), pincers (*pl.*); (*pinze*) nippers (*pl.*); (*per curvare*) pliers (*pl.*): *— da fabbro*, blacksmith's tongs; *— da forgia*, anvil (*o* forge) tongs; *— da rilegatore*, band nippers; *— da rotaie*, rail tongs; *— da saldatore*, welder's tongs; *— da tappezziere*, upholsterer's pincers **2.** *gener. pl.* (*di crostacei*) pincers (*pl.*) **3.** (*mar.*) kevel **4.** (*fortificazione*) tenail(le).

tènda, *s.f.* **1.** curtain: *— per doccia*, shower curtain; *tirare le tende*, to draw the curtains **2.** (*da sole o per riparare la coperta delle navi*) awning **3.** (*da campo*) tent; (*grande padiglione*) marquee: *levare le tende*, to strike camp; *mettere, piantare le tende in un luogo*, to pitch one's tents in a place.

tendàle, *s.m.* awning.

tendènte, *ag.* tending: *blu — al verde*, blue tending to green; *un colore — al giallo, al verde*, a yellowish, greenish colour; *prezzi tendenti al ribasso*, prices tending to drop.

tendènza, *s.f.* **1.** tendency, trend: *la — della poesia moderna*, the trend of modern poetry; *le tendenze artistiche moderne*, the modern trends in art; *— verso l'alto, il basso*, tendency upwards, downwards **2.** (*attitudine, inclinazione*) tendency, bent, inclination, propensity, disposition: *— all'invidia*, disposition to envy; *— all'obesità*, tendency to fatness; *la — dell'uomo al male*, man's tendency to evil; *la sua — ad alterare la verità*, his propensity to distort the truth; *ha una speciale — al disegno*, he has a special bent for drawing.

tendenziosaménte, *av.* tendentiously.

tendenziosità, *s.f.* tendentiousness.

tendenzióso, *ag.* tendentious, tendential.

tènder, *s.m.* (*ferr.*) tender.

tèndere, *v.t.* **1.** (*porgere, protendere*) to stretch (out), to hold out: *egli tese la mano e lo acchiappò*, he stretched out his hand and caught it; *egli vi tese la mano*, he held out his hand to you; *— le braccia per prendere ql.co.*, to stretch out one's arms for sthg.; *— il collo*, to stretch one's neck ‖ *— gli orecchi*, to prick up one's ears **2.** (*mettere in tensione*) to tighten, to strain, to pull out, to bend: *— l'arco*, to bend the bow; *— una corda*, to pull a cord taut; *— una fune fino a romperla*, to strain a rope until it breaks; *— le funi, le redini*, to tighten the ropes, the reins; *— la pelle d'un tamburo*, to brace a drum; *— le vele di una nave*, to set the sails of a ship **3.** (*distendere*) to lay: *— la corda del bucato*, to put up a clothes line; *— un tappeto*, to lay a carpet ‖ *— un'insidia, una trappola*, to lay a snare ‖ *— le reti*, to cast the nets ‖ *v.i.* **1.** (*essere inclinato*) to tend, to trend, to incline, to be inclined: *l'arte moderna tende ad allontanarsi dalla tradizione*, modern art is tending away from tradition; *egli tende a esagerare ogni cosa*, he tends to exaggerate everything; *egli tende a ingrassare*, he is inclined to grow fat (*o* he inclines to fatness); *i salari tendono ad aumentare*, wages are tending to increase; *tendo a credergli*, I am inclined (*o* I incline) to believe him ‖ *un colore che tende al rosso*, a reddish colour; *questa salsa tende all'acido*, this sauce is almost sour **2.** (*mirare*) to aim (at sthg., doing): *egli tende a farsi conoscere*, he aims at being known; *il suo discorso tendeva a ql.co.*, his speech was aiming at sthg.

tendína, *s.f.* curtain.

tèndine, *s.m.* (*anat.*) tendon, sinew: — *d'Achille* Achilles tendon.

tendinóso, *ag.* (*anat.*) tendinous.

tenditóio, *s.m.* **1.** (*cavalletto per stendere*) clothes -horse **2.** (*luogo per stendere il bucato*) drying-room.

tenditóre, *s.m.* (*mec.*) turnbuckle.

tendóne, *s.m.* **1.** awning **2.** (*sipario*) curtain.

tènebre, *s.f.pl.* **1.** dark (*sing.*), darkness (*sing.*), obscurity (*sing.*): *col favore delle* —, under cover of darkness; *nelle* — *dell'ignoranza*, *fig.* in the darkness of ignorance; *vagare nelle* —, to wander in the dark ‖ *il Re delle* —, the Prince of Darkness **2.** (*eccl.*) tenebrae.

tenebrosaménte, *av.* **1.** darkly, murkily, gloomily **2.** (*misteriosamente*) mysteriously.

tenebrosità, *s.f.* **1.** darkness, murkiness, gloom; obscurity **2.** (*mistero*) mysteriousness.

tenebróso, *ag.* **1.** dark, murky, gloomy; sombre, obscure: *un carattere* —, a gloomy character; *un luogo* —, a gloomy (*o* dark *o* murky) place; *una notte tenebrosa*, a dark (*o* murky) night **2.** (*misterioso*) mysterious, sinister.

tenènte, *ag.* keeping; holding ‖ *s.m.* (*mil. mar.*) lieutenant: — *colonnello*, lieutenant-colonel; — *di vascello*, lieutenant; — *generale*, lieutenant-general.

teneraménte, *av.* tenderly, fondly.

tenére, *v.t.* **1.** (*mantenere, conservare, serbare*) to keep (*anche fig.*); (*tenere in mano, tenere saldo, trattenere, sostenere*) to hold (*anche fig.*): *l'amore li tiene insieme*, love holds them together; *ci ha tenuto in piedi per due ore*, he kept us standing for two hours; *due colonne tengono su il soffitto*, two pillars hold up the ceiling; *due vigili tenevano indietro la gente*, two policemen were keeping (*o* holding) the people back; *è mio padre che tiene la chiave di questa stanza, credo che la tenga nella sua scrivania*, it is my father who holds the key of this room, I think he keeps it in his desk; *egli teneva la mano di sua madre*, he was holding his mother's hand; *essi tennero il forte per venti giorni*, they held the fort for twenty days; *ho tenuto in casa il bambino*, I have kept the child in; *in questo negozio non teniamo margarina*, in this shop we don't keep margarine; *lo tennero in vita con una trasfusione di sangue*, they kept him alive by a blood transfusion; *posso* — *i guanti?*, may I keep my gloves on?; *posso tenerlo o devo darlo indietro?*, may I keep it or shall I give it back?; *puoi* — *questo posto per me?*, can you keep this seat for me?; *questo bimbo è così vivace che non so come tenerlo*, this child is so lively that I don't know how to hold him; *uno spillo tiene insieme le carte*, a pin holds the papers together; *tiene un cane ed un pappagallo*, he keeps a dog and a parrot ‖ *tientela per te*, keep it under your hat ‖ — *un'adunanza*, to hold a meeting ‖ — *a mente ql.co.*, to keep sthg. in mind ‖ — *la cassa*, (*comm.*) to have charge of the cash; — *i conti*, (*comm.*) to keep accounts ‖ — *un cuoco, una cameriera*, to keep a cook, a maid ‖ — *in debita considerazione ql.co.*, to hold sthg. in due consideration; — *qlcu. in grande considerazione*, to hold s.o. in great esteem ‖ — *un diario*, to keep a diary ‖ — *un discorso*, to deliver a speech ‖ — *fede a qlcu.*, to keep faith with s.o. ‖ — *il fiato*, to hold one's breath ‖ — *in mano ql.co.*, to keep sthg. in one's hands ‖ — *le lacrime*, to restrain one's tears ‖ — *una lezione*, to give a lecture ‖ — *le mani in tasca*, to keep one's hands in one's pocket ‖ — *nascosto ql.co. a qlcu.*, to keep sthg. from s.o. ‖ — *gli occhi chiusi*, to keep one's eyes shut ‖ — *le parti di qlcu.*, to side with s.o. ‖ — *presente ql.co.*, to bear sthg. in mind ‖ — *una promessa*, to keep a promise ‖ — *ql.co. in ordine*, to keep sthg. in order ‖ — *qlcu. all'oscuro di ql.co.*, to keep s.o. in the dark about sthg. ‖ — *qlcu. informato di ql.co.*, to keep s.o. informed about sthg. ‖ — *qlcu. per il braccio*, to hold s.o. by the arm ‖ — *un segreto*, to keep a secret ‖ — *su la testa*, to hold one's head up ‖ — *su il morale della gente*, to

bolster the people's moral **2.** (*prendere*) to take: *tieni questo libro*, take this book **3.** (*occupare*) to take up: *questa scrivania tiene troppo posto*, this desk takes up too much room **4.** (*contenere*) to hold, to contain: *questa bottiglia tiene un litro*, this bottle holds (*o* contains) a litre **5.** (*seguire*) to follow, to keep to (sthg.): *in Inghilterra i veicoli tengono la sinistra*, in England traffic keeps to the left; *non so che strada* —, *fig.* I do not know which course to follow; *tieni questa strada fino alla stazione*, follow this street as far as the station **6.** (*di nave, veicolo, ecc.*): *una nave che tiene il mare*, a seaworthy vessel; *questa automobile tiene bene la strada*, this car is very stable **7.** (*considerare*) to consider, to regard, to hold: — *caro ql.co.*, to hold sthg. dear; *l'ho sempre tenuto per un buon ragazzo*, I have always considered him to be (*o* regarded him as) a good boy; — *una notizia per vera*, to take news as true ‖ *se lo tenne per detto*, he took the lesson to heart **8.** (*liquido, gas, non lasciarlo passare*) to hold: *barile che tiene l'acqua*, barrel that holds water (*o* that is watertight); *questa stoffa tiene l'acqua*, this material is waterproof **9.** (*dirigere*) to keep: — *un negozio*, to keep a shop; — *una pensione*, to keep a boarding -house; — *una scuola*, to keep (*o* to run) a school ‖ *v.i.* **1.** (*somigliare*) to take after (s.o.): — *del padre, della madre*, to take after one's father, one's mother **2.** (*resistere*) to hold: *questa corda non terrà a lungo*, this rope will not hold long; *tieni duro, non cedere*, hold on, don't give in ‖ *non c'è scusa che tenga*, (*fam.*) there is no excuse for it **3.** (*ambire a, desiderare*) to like: *egli tiene che tutti lo sappiano*, he likes everybody to know; *egli tiene molto ai suoi titoli*, he is very proud of his titles; *non ci tengo*, I don't care (for it); *terrei molto a incontrarlo*, I should like very much to meet him ‖ **tenérsi,** *v.r.* **1.** to keep oneself, to hold oneself; to stand: *tienti alla ringhiera*, hold on to the banister; *tienti fermo*, hold (*o* keep) yourself still; *tienti fuori dalle loro discussioni*, keep out of their discussions; *tienti lontano da questi luoghi*, keep away from these places ‖ *egli si tenne sulle sue*, he was rather reserved (*o* stiff) ‖ — *in contatto con qlcu.*, to keep in touch with s.o. ‖ — *in esercizio*, to keep one's hand in: *ho studiato il francese molto tempo fa, ma mi tengo in esercizio leggendo*, I studied French a long time ago but I keep my hand in by reading ‖ — *indietro*, to stand back; — *in piedi*, to keep on one's feet; — *pronto*, to keep ready ‖ — *la pancia dal ridere*, (*fam.*) to hold one's sides with laughter **2.** (*considerarsi*) to hold oneself, to consider oneself: *non mi tengo responsabile di ciò*, I do not hold myself responsible for it **3.** (*trattenersi*) to help (doing): *non posso tenermi dal pensarci*, I cannot help thinking of it **4.** (*seguire*) to follow: *egli si tiene ai suoi principi*, he follows (*o* sticks to) his principles; *tienti alle sue istruzioni*, follow his instructions; *tienti al testo*, stick to the text.

tenerézza, *s.f.* **1.** tenderness, fondness, love, affection: *con* —, tenderly (*o* fondly) **2.** *pl.* (*carezze*) caresses.

Teneríffa, *no.pr.f.* (*geog.*) Tenerife, Teneriffe.

tènero, *ag.* **1.** (*molle*) tender, soft: *carne, frutta tenera*, tender meat, fruit; *pelle tenera*, tender (*o* sensitive) skin **2.** (*piccolo, delicato*) tender, delicate: *tenera pianticella*, tender little plant ‖ *tenera età*, tender age: *fin dalla sua più tenera età*, from his earliest youth **3.** *fig.* tender, loving, affectionate: *cuore* —, tender heart: *avere il cuore* —, to be tender- (*o* soft-)hearted; *un padre* —, a loving father; *uno sguardo* —, a loving look **4.** (*di parole, modi*) fond: *parole tenere*, fond words ‖ *s.m.* **1.** (*parte tenera*) tender part: — *delle foglie*, the tender (*o* soft) part of leaves **2.** (*affetto*) affection; sympathy: *c'è del* — *fra di loro*, there is a sympathy between them; *avere del* — *per qlcu.*, (*fam.*) to have a soft place (*o* spot) in one's heart for s.o.

tenerúme, *s.m.* **1.** (*parte tenera*) soft (*o* tender) part **2.** (*cartilagine*) cartilage, gristle **3.** (*sdolcinatezza*) mawkishness, sentimentality 4. (*smancerie*) slobbering: *coprire qlcu. di —*, to slobber over s.o.

tenèsmo, *s.m.* (*med.*) tenesmus.

tènia, *s.m.* (*zool.*) tapeworm; taenia (*pl.* taeniae).

teníbile, *ag.* tenable: *la posizione militare non era più —*, the military position was now untenable.

tenitóre, *s.m.* holder, keeper.

tènnis, *s.m.* (*spor.*) tennis: *— su prato*, lawn-tennis; *gara di —*, tennis match; *una partita di —*, a game of tennis; *giocare a —*, to play tennis.

tennísta, *s.c.* tennis-player.

tennístico, *ag.* tennis (*attributivo*): *gara tennistica*, tennis match.

tènno, *s.m.* (*st. giapponese*) Tenno.

tenodèsi, *s.f.* (*anat.*) tenodesis.

tenóre, *s.m.* 1. (*maniera*) tenor; way: *il — di vita degli italiani migliora*, the Italian standard of living (*o* living standard) is improving; *il suo — di vita è molto dispendioso*, the tenor of his life is very expensive; *devi cambiare —, se vuoi riuscire negli affari*, you must change your ways if you want to succeed in business; *questo è il mio — di vita*, this is the tenor of my life 2. (*di scritto, discorso, ecc.*) tenor; contents (*pl.*): *il — di un discorso*, the tenor of a speech; *il — di una lettera*, the tenor (*o* contents) of a letter; *la lettera è del seguente —*, the letter reads as follows 3. *a — di*, (*dir.*) according to: *a — dell'art. 2*, according to art. 2; *a — di legge*, according to the law 4. (*mus.*) tenor: *— drammatico, lirico*, dramatic, lyric tenor.

tenoreggiàre, *v.i.* to sing tenor.

tenoríle, *ag.* (*mus.*) tenor (*attributivo*): *voce —*, tenor voice.

tenoríno, *s.m.* (*mus.*) tenorino.

tenotomía, *s.f.* (*chir.*) tenotomy.

tensióne, *s.f.* 1. tension: *— arteriosa*, (*fisiol.*) arterial tension; *la — di una corda, di un muscolo*, the tension of a string, of a muscle; *— nervosa*, nervous tension (*o* strain) 2. *fig.* tension, strain: *la — fra due rivali*, the tension between two rivals 3. (*fis. elett.*) tension, voltage: *— anodica*, anode voltage (*o* plate voltage); *— di griglia*, grid voltage; *— di linea*, line voltage; *— di placca*, plate voltage; *— di sublimazione*, sublimation pressure; *— di vapore*, vapor pressure (*o* tension); *a — bassa*, low tension: *linea a — bassa*, low-tension line; *ad alta —*, high-tension: *linea ad alta —*, high-tension line ‖ *elevare la —*, to boost.

tensóre, *s.m.* (*anat.*) tensor.

tènta, *s.f.* (*chir.*) probe.

tentàbile, *ag.* 1. attemptable; open to trial 2. (*che può essere indotto in tentazione*) temptable, open to temptation.

tentacolàre, *ag.* tentacular.

tentàcolo, *s.m.* tentacle: *munito di tentacoli*, tentacled.

tentàre, *v.t.* 1. to try, to attempt, to make an attempt; (*con sforzo*) to endeavour: *devi —, se vuoi riuscire*, you have to endeavour if you want to succeed; *ho già tentato diverse volte di entrare*, I have already made several attempts to go in; *ho tentato, ma senza successo*, I have tried but with no success; *tenterò di convincerlo*, I shall try to convince him ‖ *— la fortuna*, to try one's luck ‖ *— non nuoce*, *prov.* there is no harm in trying 2. (*indurre in tentazione*) to tempt: *non tentarmi, non ho tempo di venire*, don't tempt me, I have no time to come; *quel dolce mi tenta*, that cake is tempting me; *Sant'Antonio fu tentato dal demonio*, St. Anthony was tempted by the devil; *sono tentato di andare a vedere*, I am tempted to go and see 3. (*tastare, toccare*) to touch, to feel: *— le corde di un violino*, to touch the strings of a violin 4. (*chir.*) to probe.

tentatívo, *s.m.* attempt; endeavour: *— d'evasione*, attempt to escape; *— di violenza, di resistenza*, attempt at violence, at resistance; *un — inutile*, a useless attempt; *un felice —*, a successful attempt; *fare un —*, to make an attempt (*o* endeavour).

tentatóre, *ag.* tempting ‖ *s.m.* tempter.

tentatríce, *s.f.* temptress.

tentazióne, *s.f.* temptation: *le tentazioni di una grande città*, the temptations of a big city; *ho la — di dirglielo*, I am tempted to tell him; *ho ceduto alla — di andare a spasso*, I yielded to the temptation to go for a walk; *indurre qlcu. in —*, to lead s.o. into temptation; *resistere alla —*, to resist temptation.

tentènna, *s.m.* waverer, hesitating person, irresolute person.

tentennaménto, *s.m.* 1. (*scuotimento*) shaking 2. (*traballamento*) tottering, staggering 3. (*oscillazione*) swinging 4. (*esitazione*) hesitation.

tentennàre, *v.t.* (*scuotere*) to shake: *— la testa*, to shake one's head ‖ *v.i.* 1. (*traballare*) to totter, to stagger, to be unsteady: *egli camminava tentennando*, he was staggering along; *il palo tentennò e cadde*, the post tottered and fell 2. (*oscillare*) to swing, to oscillate 3. (*esitare*) to hesitate, to waver: *— fra due decisioni*, to waver between two decisions; *non —, questa è la via giusta*, don't hesitate, this is the right way.

tentennío, *s.m.* shaking.

tentennóne, *V.* tentènna.

tentóni, *V.* tastóni.

tènue, *ag.* 1. (*sottile*) thin, slender, fine: *un — filo di luce*, a thin thread of light; *un — stelo*, a slender stem 2. (*piccolo*) small: *— guadagno, spesa*, small profit, expense; *— speranza*, small (*o* slender) hope 3. (*lieve*) slight: *un — tocco*, a slight touch 4. (*leggero, delicato*) soft: *— nuvoletta, pioggerella*, soft cloud, rain; *color —*, soft colour; *aveva gli occhi d'un — azzurro*, she had soft blue eyes 5. *intestino —*, (*anat.*) small intestine.

tenueménte, *av.* (*debolmente*) weakly; (*lievemente*) slightly.

tenuiròstri, *s.m.pl.* (*ornit.*) Tenuirostres.

tenuità, *s.f.* 1. (*sottigliezza*) thinness, tenuity, slenderness 2. (*piccolezza*) smallness 3. (*levità*) slightness 4. (*delicatezza, leggerezza*) softness.

tenúta, *s.f.* 1. (*azienda agricola*) estate, farm; (*amer.*) ranch: *ha una bellissima — vicino a Roma*, he has a very beautiful farm (*o* estate) near Rome 2. (*uniforme*) uniform: *— militare*, military uniform; *alta —*, (*mil.*) full dress; *in — di lavoro*, in working clothes; *in — sportiva*, in sport clothes 3. (*capacità*) capacity: *la — di un serbatoio*, the capacity of a tank 4. (*tec.*) seal: *— a liquido*, (*di gasometro*) wet seal; *— a secco*, (*di gasometro*) dry seal; *— di olio*, (*mec.*) oil seal; *— di strada*, (*aut.*) road-holding (*o* roadability); *— idraulica*, seal; *a — d'acqua*, (*ind.*) watertight; *a — d'aria*, (*ind.*) airtight; *a — d'olio*, (*mec.*) oiltight; *guarnizione di —*, (*mec.*) seal 5. *— dei libri*, (*comm.*) book-keeping.

tenutàrio, *s.m.* holder.

tenúto, *ag.* 1. (*obbligato*) obliged, bound; (*riconoscente*) obliged: *— a pagare*, obliged to pay; *non sono — a dirtelo*, I am not bound to tell you; *vi sono molto — per questo favore*, I am much obliged to you for this kindness 2. (*coltivato*) planted (with sthg.): *campo — a grano, patate*, field planted with corn, potatoes 3. (*conservato*) kept: *un libro ben —*, a well-kept book 4. (*ritenuto*) considered: *egli è — in gran conto*, he is highly considered.

tenzonàre, *v.i.* 1. to strive, to dispute, to combat, to battle 2. *fig.* to dispute, to debate.

tenzóne, *s.f.* 1. (*letter.*) combat, contest: *singolar —*, single combat 2. (*st. lett.*) tenson, poetic contest.

Teobàldo, *no.pr.m.* Theobald.

teobròma, *s.m.* (*bot.*) theobroma.

teobromína, *s.f.* (*chim.*) theobromine.

teocraticaménte, *av.* theocratically.

teocràtico, *ag.* theocratic(al).

teocrazía, *s.f.* theocracy.

Teòcrito, *no.pr.m.* (*st. lett.*) Theocritus.

teodicèa, *s.f.* (*teol.*) theodicy.

teodolíte, teodolíto, *s.m.* (*geodesia*) theodolite.

Teodòra, *no.pr.f.* Theodora.

Teodoríco, *no.pr.m.* (*st.*) Theodoric.

Teodòro, *no.pr.m.* Theodore.
Teodòsia, *no.pr.f.* (*st.*) Theodosia.
Teodòsio, *no.pr.m.* (*st.*) Theodosius.
teofanía, *s.f.* (*teol.*) theophany.
Teòfilo, *no.pr.m.* Theophilus.
Teofràsto, *no.pr.m.* (*st. lett.*) Theophrastus.
teogonía, *s.f.* theogony.
teogònico, *ag.* theogonic.
teologàle, *ag.* theological: *le tre virtù teologali,* the three theological virtues.
teologalménte, *av.* theologically.
teologàre, *v.i.* to theologize.
teologàstro, *s.m.* (*spreg.*) theologaster.
teología, *s.f.* theology: — *dommatica,* dogmatic theology; — *naturale,* natural theology; — *rivelata,* revealed theology; — *sistematica,* systematic theology.
teologicaménte, *av.* theologically.
teològico, *ag.* theological.
teologizzàre, *v.i.* to theologize.
teòlogo, *s.m.* theologian.
teomanía, *s.f.* (*patol.*) theomania.
teorèma, *s.m.* theorem.
teoremàtico, *ag.* theorematic(al).
teorètica, *s.f.* speculative philosophy.
teoreticaménte, *av.* theoretically.
teorètico, *ag.* theoretic(al).
teoría[1]**,** *s.f.* theory: *la* — *dell'evoluzione,* the theory of evolution; *la* — *e la pratica,* theory and practice; *in* —, in theory (*o* theoretically); *è della* — *che...,* he holds the theory that....
teoría[2]**,** *s.f.* (*processione, fila, sfilata*) procession, long series, long line, string: *una* — *di pellegrini,* a procession (*o* string) of pilgrims.
teòrica, *s.f.* theoretics; theory, system.
teoricaménte, *av.* theoretically, in theory.
teòrico, *ag.* theoretic(al) ‖ *s.m.* theorist, theoriser, theoretician.
teorizzàre, *v.i.* to theorize.
teosofía, *s.f.* theosophy.
teosòfico, *ag.* theosophic(al).
teòsofo, *s.m.* theosopher, theosophist.
tèpalo, *s.m.* (*di fiore*) tepal.
tepènte, *ag.* (*poet.*) lukewarm, tepid.
tepidàrio, *s.m.* (*archeol.*) tepidarium (*pl.* tepidaria).
tepidézza, *s.f.* lukewarmness, tepidity, tepidness (anche *fig.*).
tèpido, *ag.* lukewarm, tepid (anche *fig.*).
tepóre, *s.m.* lukewarmness, tepidity, tepidness (anche *fig.*).
téppa, *s.f.* mob, rabble, scum; dregs (*pl.*).
teppísmo, *s.m.* hooliganism, ruffianism.
teppísta, *s.m.* rough; hooligan, ruffian.
terapèuta, *s.c.* therapeutist.
terapèutica, *s.f.* therapeutics.
terapèutico, *ag.* therapeutic(al).
terapía, *s.f.* 1. (*cura*) therapy: — *curativa,* curative therapy; — *radiologica,* radiation (*o* X-ray) therapy 2. (*terapeutica*) therapeutics.
teratología, *s.f.* teratology.
teratològico, *ag.* teratologic(al).
tèrbio, *s.m.* (*chim.*) terbium.
tercína, *s.f.* (*di fiore*) tercine.
terebène, *s.m.* (*chim.*) terebene.
terebentína, *s.f.* (*chim.*) turpentine.
terebínto, *s.m.* (*bot.*) terebinth.
tèrebra, *s.f.* (*zool.*) terebra (*pl.* terebras, terebrae).
terebrànte, *ag.* piercing: *un dolore* —, a piercing pain.
terèdine, *s.f.* (*zool.*) teredo (*pl.* teredos, teredines).
terenziàno, *ag.* (*lett.*) Terentian.
Terènzio, *no.pr.m.* (*st. lett.*) Terence.
Terèo, *no.pr.m.* (*mit.*) Tereus.
Terèsa, *no.pr.f.* T(h)eresa.
tergàle, *ag.* tergal.
tèrgere, *v.t.* 1. (*asciugare*) to wipe (off), to dry:

— *le proprie lacrime,* to dry one's tears 2. (*pulire*) to clean 3. (*lucidare*) to polish.
tergicristàllo, *s.m.* (*aut.*) windscreen wiper.
tergiversàre, *v.i.* to hesitate; (*fam.*) to beat about the bush.
tergiversazióne, *s.f.* hesitation.
tèrgo, *s.m.* back (anche *fig.*): *a* — *di un foglio,* on the back of a sheet; *volgere il* — *a qlcu.,* to turn one's back on s.o. ‖ *da* —, from behind ‖ *segue a* —, please turn over (*abbr.* P.T.O.).
teriàca, *s.f.* (*farm.*) theriac, theriaca.
teriacàle, *ag.* (*farm.*) theriacal.
termàle, *ag.* thermal: *acqua* —, thermal water; *sorgente* —, thermal (*o* hot) spring.
tèrme, *s.f.pl.* 1. thermal baths, hot baths, hot springs; (*stazione termale*) spa (*sing.*) 2. (*archeol.*) thermae.
termestesía, *s.f.* (*med.*) thermesthesia.
tèrmico, *ag.* thermic: *condizioni termiche,* thermic conditions; *raggi termici,* thermic rays.
termidoriàno, termidorísta, *ag.s.m.* (*st. francese*) Thermidorian.
termidòro, *s.m.* (*st. francese*) Thermidor.
terminàbile, *ag.* terminable.
terminàle, *ag.* terminal.
terminànte, *ag.* ending, finishing, terminating: *una parola* — *in « s »,* a word ending in " s ".
terminàre, *v.t.* to end, to finish, to terminate: *terminò i propri giorni in campagna,* he ended his days in the country; — *di fare ql.co.,* to finish doing sthg: *terminò di studiare a 24 anni,* he finished studying at 24; — *un lavoro,* to finish a work ‖ *v.i.* 1. to end, to finish, to terminate; to come to an end, to be over: *la commedia termina in modo triste,* the play has a sad ending; *le parole che terminano in « f »,* the words ending (*o* terminating) in " f "; *il sentiero termina nel bosco,* the path ends in the wood 2. (*confinare*) to border (upon, on sthg.); to bound (sthg.): *ad occidente la California termina con l'Oceano Pacifico,* on the West California borders on the Pacific Ocean.
terminàto, *ag.* accomplished; finished, ended.
terminazióne, *s.f.* 1. (*desinenza*) ending, termination 2. (*fine*) end.
tèrmine[1]**,** *s.m.* 1. (*limite, confine*) limit (anche *fig.*); boundary; (*erma*) term, terminus: *il* — *di un campo,* the boundary of a field; *c'è un* — *a tutto,* there is a limit to everything; *porre un* — *a ql.co.,* to set a limit to sthg.; *rimanere entro i termini,* to remain within limits 2. (*limite di tempo, data*) term, date, time: — *di una cambiale,* date of a bill; *contratto a* —, (*comm.*) time-contract; *il* — *per la presentazione della domanda scadrà domani,* the time for sending in the application expires tomorrow; *il lavoro deve essere finito entro il* — *convenuto,* the work must be finished within the term agreed upon; *fissare un* —, to fix a term (*o* date); *prolungare il* —, to extend the time 3. (*compimento, fine*) end, close: *al* — *della riunione,* at the close of the meeting; *la lezione avrà* — *alle quattro,* the lesson will end at four; *condurre ql.co. a* —, to bring sthg. to an end (*o* to a close); *giungere a un* —, to come to an end; *mettere, porre* — *a ql.co.,* to put an end to sthg.; *portare a* — *un affare,* to conclude a bargain 4. (*condizione, norma*) term (anche *fig.*): *i termini di un contratto,* the terms of a contract; *a* — *dell'articolo 49,* by the terms of Article 49; *a* — *di legge,* legally; *non posso accettare i suoi termini,* I cannot accept his terms; *quali sono i vostri termini?,* what are your terms? ‖ *essere in buoni termini con qlcu.,* to be on good terms with s.o. 5. (*parola, espressione*) term, word: — *scientifico, tecnico,* scientific, technical term; *contraddizione in termini,* contradiction in terms; *in altri termini,* in other words; *una lettera nei seguenti termini,* a letter reading as follows; *egli parlò di te nei termini più favorevoli,* he spoke about you in the most favourable terms; *pesare i termini,* to weigh one's words ‖ *a rigor di termini,* strictly speaking ‖ *non ci*

adatteremo mai ai mezzi termini!, never shall we resort to compromise! **6.** (*mat. log.*) term: *i termini di una espressione matematica*, the terms of a mathematical expression; *i termini di un paragone*, the terms of a comparison; *ridurre una frazione ai minimi termini*, to reduce a fraction to its lowest terms **7.** *complemento di —*, (*gram.*) indirect object.

Tèrmine[2], *no.pr.m.* (*mit.*) Terminus.

terminología, *s.f.* terminology.

termitàio, *s.m.* termitarium, termitary.

tèrmite[1], *s.f.* (*entom.*) termite, white ant.

termíte[2], *s.f.* (*chim.*) thermite.

termitòfilo, *ag.* termitophilous.

termoanestesía, *s.f.* (*med.*) thermanesthesia, thermo-anesthesia.

termobaròmetro, *s.m.* (*fis.*) thermobarometer.

termocautèrio, *s.m.* (*chir.*) thermocautery.

termochímica, *s.f.* thermochemistry.

termochímico, *ag.* thermochemical.

termoinètica, *s.f.* (*fis.*) thermokinetics.

termoconvettóre, *s.m.* convector.

termocòppia, *s.f.* (*elett.*) thermocouple.

termocròsi, *s.f.* (*fis.*) thermochrosy.

termodinàmica, *s.f.* thermodynamics.

termodinàmico, *ag.* thermodynamic.

termoelettricità, *s.f.* thermoelectricity.

termoelèttrico, *ag.* thermoelectric(al).

termoelettròmetro, *s.m.* (*elett.*) thermoelectrometer.

termoestesía, *s.f.* (*med.*) thermo-esthesia.

termoestesiòmetro, *s.f.* (*med.*) thermesthesiometer.

termofobía, *s.f.* (*patol.*) thermophobia.

termòforo, *s.m.* heat pad, warming pad.

termogalvanòmetro, *s.m.* (*elett.*) thermogalvanometer.

termogènesi, *s.f.* thermogenesis.

termogenètico, *ag.* thermogenetic.

termògeno, *ag.* thermogenic.

termografía, *s.f.* thermography.

termògrafo, *s.m.* thermograph.

termoindurènte, *ag.* (*chim.*) thermosetting: *materia plastica —*, thermosetting composition.

termoióne, *s.m.* (*fis.*) thermion.

termoiònico, *ag.* (*fis.*) thermionic: *corrente termoionica*, thermionic current; *valvola termoionica*, thermionic tube (*o* valve).

termòlisi, *s.f.* (*chim.*) thermolysis.

termología, *s.f.* (*fis.*) thermology.

termològico, *ag.* (*fis.*) thermologic(al).

termomagnètico, *ag.* (*fis.*) thermomagnetic.

termomagnetísmo, *s.m.* (*fis.*) thermomagnetism.

termometría, *s.f.* thermometry.

termomètrico, *ag.* thermometric(al).

termòmetro, *s.m.* thermometer: *— ad alcool*, spirit thermometer; *— a massima, a minima*, maximum, minimum thermometer; *— a resistenza*, resistance thermometer; *— centigrado*, centigrade thermometer; *— differenziale*, differential thermometer; *— elettrico*, electric thermometer; *— medico*, clinical thermometer; *— metallico*, metallic thermometer; *il — sale, scende*, the temperature is rising, is dropping; *il — segna 70°*, the thermometer stands at 70°.

termomotóre, *s.m.* thermomotor.

termonucleàre, *ag.* thermonuclear.

termopíla, *s.f.* (*fis.*) thermopile.

Termòpili, *no.pr.f.pl.* (*geog. st.*) Thermopylae.

termoplàstico, *ag.* (*fis.*) thermoplastic.

termoreattóre, *s.m.* (*fis.*) thermoreactor.

termoregolatóre, *s.m.* (*fis.*) thermoregulator.

termoregolazióne, *s.f.* (*fis.*) thermoregulation.

tèrmos, *s.m.* thermos (bottle), vacuum-bottle.

termoscòpico, *ag.* thermoscopic(al).

termoscòpio, *s.m.* (*med.*) thermoscope.

termosifóne, *s.m.* **1.** (*radiatore*) radiator: *riscaldamento a —*, central heating plant **2.** (*fis.*) thermosiphon.

termostàtica, *s.f.* thermostatics.

termostaticaménte, *av.* thermostatically.

termostàtico, *ag.* thermostatic.

termòstato, *s.m.* thermostat, thermo-switch.

termotècnica, *s.f.* thermotechnics, heat technology.

termoterapía, *s.f.* (*med.*) thermotherapy; thermotherapeutics.

termotropísmo, *s.m.* thermotropism.

tèrna, *s.f.* **1.** tern **2.** (*triade*) triad.

ternàrio, *ag.* (*chim. mat.*) ternary.

tèrno, *s.m.* (*giuoco del lotto*) tern ‖ *vincere un — al lotto*, (*avere un colpo di fortuna*) to win the jackpot.

terpène, *s.m.* (*chim.*) terpene.

tèrra, *s.f.* **1.** (*il globo; l'opposto di cielo; materia non rocciosa della crosta terrestre*) earth: *terre alcaline*, alkaline earths; *— rara*, rare earth; *il cielo e la —*, Heaven and Earth; *le gioie della —*, earthly joys; *il miglior uomo sulla —*, the best man on earth; *la Terra è uno sferoide*, earth is a spheroid; *la Terra ruota sul suo asse e gira intorno al sole*, the earth rotates on its axis and revolves round the sun; *i vermi vivono nella —*, worms live in the earth; *riempire un secchio di —*, to fill a bucket with earth ‖ *— —*, earth bound ‖ *scendere a —*, (*smetterla di fantasticare*) to come back to earth **2.** (*massa solida del globo opposta alla massa acquea; proprietà terriera; terra arabile*) land: *armata di —*, (land-) army; *lingua di —*, (*geog.*) land-bridge; *proprietario di terra*, landowner; *una striscia, un pezzo di —*, a strip, a piece of land; *sulla — e sul mare*, on land and at sea; *trasporto via —*, land-carriage; *egli possiede molta —*, he owns a great deal of land; *è la — che nutre gli uomini*, man lives on the land; *la nave si avvicinava alla —*, the ship was approaching land; *non andai per —, ma per mare*, I didn't go by land but (I went) by sea; *avvistare la —*, to sight land; *costeggiare la —*, to keep close to shore; *scendere a —*, (*mar.*) to go ashore; *viaggiare per — e per mare*, to travel over land and sea ‖ *— in vista!*, (*mar.*) land ho! **3.** (*terreno*) ground; (*suolo*) soil: *una — fertile*, a fertile soil; *una — ricca di sali minerali*, a soil rich in minerals; *un buco nella —*, a hole in the ground; *cadere per —*, to fall to the ground (*o* to the floor); *dormire per —*, to sleep on the ground; *lavorare, scavare la —*, to till, to dig the ground ‖ *senza di te mi manca la — sotto i piedi*, I feel lost without you ‖ *filo di terra*, (*elett.*) ground wire; *presa a —*, earth terminal ‖ *essere a —*, (*finanziariamente*) to be broke; (*moralmente*) to be in low spirits (*o* to feel low) ‖ *raso —*, to the ground: *tagliare un albero raso —*, to cut a tree to the ground; *volare raso —*, to fly close to the ground ‖ *essere a —*, (*di pneumatico*) to have a puncture (*o* to have had a blow out) **4.** (*mondo*) world: *su questa —*, in this world **5.** (*regione, paese*) land, country: *in terre lontane*, in distant lands; *la propria — natia*, one's native country ‖ *— di nessuno*, (*mil.*) no-man's-land ‖ *la Terra Promessa*, the Promised Land **6.** (*varie sostanze naturali impiegate nell'industria e nell'artigianato*) loam; clay: *— d'ombra*, umber; *— inglese*, rotten-stone; *— da pipe*, pipe-clay; *— da porcellana*, kaolin; *— di Siena*, raw Sienna; *— di Siena bruciata*, burnt Sienna.

terracòtta, *s.f.* **1.** baked clay; terra-cotta: *vasellame di —*, earthenware **2.** (*oggetto in terracotta*) terra cotta.

terrafèrma, *s.f.* dry land, terra-firma.

terràglia, *s.f.* pottery; earthenware (*invariato al pl.*).

terràgno, *ag.* **1.** (*fatto di terra*) earth (*attributivo*), earthen **2.** (*che sta sotto terra*) underground (*attributivo*) **3.** (*che striscia per terra*) creeping.

terràgnolo, *ag.* **1.** (*che striscia per terra*) creeping **2.** (*che sta sotto terra*) underground (*attributivo*).

terramàra, *s.f.* (*agr. archeol.*) terramara.

terramicína, *s.f.* (*chim.*) terramycin.

Terranòva, *no.pr.f.* (*geog.*) Newfoundland ‖ **terranòva,** *s.m.* (*cane*) Newfoundland dog.

terrapièno, *s.m.* **1.** embankment, bank, earth platform, terrace, level surface: *costruire un —*, to embank **2.** (*mil.*) terreplain, rampart.

terràqueo, *ag.* terraqueous.

Terrasànta, *no.pr.f.* (*geog.*) Holy Land, Palestine.

terràtico, *s.m.* land rent.

terràzza, *s.f.* terrace: *questo appartamento ha una grande —,* this flat has a large terrace ‖ *collivazione a terrazze,* terrace-cultivation ‖ *giardino a terrazze,* terraced garden.

terrazzière, *s.m.* digger.

terràzzo, *V.* **terràzza.**

terremòto, *s.m.* **1.** earthquake: *una scossa di —,* an earthquake shock ‖ *entrò nella stanza come un —,* he came into the room as a whirlwind **2.** (*bambino chiassoso*) romp.

terréno, *ag.* **1.** earthly, worldly: *gioie, cose terrene,* earthly joys, things; *piaceri terreni,* worldly pleasures; *vita terrena,* earth life **2.** *piano —,* ground-floor ‖ *s.m.* **1.** ground; (*suolo*) soil: *— fertile, ricco, sabbioso,* fertile, rich, sandy soil; *— fabbricabile,* building site; *— ricco di minerali,* soil rich in minerals; *un buco nel —,* a hole in the ground; *guadagnare, perdere —,* to gain, to lose ground; *scavare il —,* to dig the ground ‖ *preparare il — a qlcu., fig.* to pave the way for s. o. **2.** (*proprietà terriera; terra arabile*) land: *possiede molto —,* he owns a great deal of land **3.** (*campo*) field: *i calciatori scesero sul —,* the footballers took the field.

tèrreo, *ag.* **1.** earthy **2.** (*di colorito*) wan, sallow, ashen, pallid.

terrèstre, *ag.* terrestrial; earthly: *l'asse, l'orbita —,* the earth's axis, orbit; *magnetismo —,* terrestrial magnetism; *trasporto —,* land transport ‖ *il paradiso —,* the Earthly Paradise.

terríbile, *ag.* terrible, awful, dreadful; frightful, fearful: *un temporale —,* a dreadful thunder-storm.

terribilità, *s.f.* terribleness, awfulness, dreadfulness.

terribilménte, *av.* terribly, awfully, dreadfully.

terríccio, *s.m.* mould.

terricciuòla, *V.* **terrúcola.**

terrier, *s.m.* (*cane*) terrier ‖ *fox- —,* fox-terrier.

terrièro, *ag.* land (*attributivo*): *proprietà terriera,* landed property; *proprietario —,* land-owner.

terrificànte, *ag.* terrific, terrifying, appalling.

terrificàre, *v.t.* to terrify, to appal, to frighten.

terrífico, *ag.* terrific, appalling.

terrígeno, *ag.* terrigenous.

terrígno, *ag.* **1.** earthy **2.** (*di colore*) yellowish; (*di colorito*) wan, sallow, ashen **3.** (*che sta sotto terra*) underground (*attributivo*).

terrína, *s.f.* tureen.

territoriàle, *ag.* territorial: *acque, diritti territoriali,* territorial waters, rights; *giurisdizione, governo —,* territorial jurisdiction, government ‖ *s.m.* (*mil.*) non-combattant.

territorialità, *s.f.* territoriality.

territòrio, *s.m.* territory.

terróne, *s.m.* (*fam.*) (*nativo dell'Italia meridionale*) South Italian.

terróre, *s.m.* terror, dread: *il — della morte,* the dread of death; *era il — del paese,* he was the terror of the countryside; *quell'uomo è il mio —,* that man is my bugbear; *avere — di ql.co.,* to have a holy terror (o dread) of sthg.; *avere — di qlcu.,* to go in terror of s.o.; *essere preso da —,* to be struck with terror; *incutere — a qlcu.,* to strike s.o. with terror (o to strike terror into s.o.'s heart) ‖ *il Terrore,* (*st. francese*) the Terror: *il periodo del Terrore,* the Reign of Terror.

terrorísmo, *s.m.* terrorism.

terrorísta, *s.m.* terrorist.

terrorístico, *ag.* terroristic.

terrorizzàre, *v.t.* to terrorize.

terróso, *ag.* earthy.

terrúcola, *s.f.* **1.** (*villaggio*) hamlet **2.** (*terreno magro*) poor soil.

Tertulliàno, *no.pr.m.* (*st. lett.*) Tertullian.

tersaménte, *av.* clearly; (*di stile*) tersely.

tersézza, *s.f.* clearness; (*di stile*) terseness.

Tersícore, *no.pr.f.* (*mit.*) Terpsichore.

Tersíte, *no.pr.m.* (*lett.*) Thersites.

tèrso, *ag.* clear; (*di stile*) terse: *cielo —,* clear sky.

tèrza, *s.f.* **1.** (*nell'ordinamento scolastico*) third form, third class; (*amer.*) third grade: *uno scolaro di —,* a third form pupil (o a third former) **2.** (*ferr.*) third class: *viaggiare in —,* to travel third class **3.** (*scherma*) tierce **4.** (*mus.*) third **5.** (*eccl.*) tierce.

terzàna, *s.f.* (*febbre*) —, (*patol.*) tertian, tertian fever, tertian ague.

terzaruòlo, *s.m.* (*mar.*) reef.

terzàvola, *s.f.* great-great-grandmother.

terzàvolo, *s.m.* great-great-grandfather.

terzétto, *s.m.* **1.** (*mus.*) terzetto (*pl.* terzetti), triplet; trio (*pl.* trios) **2.** (*gruppo di tre cose, persone*) triplet; trio (*pl.* trios).

terziàrio, *ag.* (*geol. eccl.*) tertiary: *era terziaria,* tertiary period ‖ *s.m.* (*eccl.*) tertiary.

terzíglio, *s.m.* "terziglio" (an Italian card-game).

terzína, *s.f.* (*poes. mus.*) tercet.

terzíno, *s.m.* (*calcio*) full back: *— destro, sinistro,* right, left back.

tèrzo, *ag.num.ord.* third: *la terza classe,* the third (class); *Giorgio Terzo,* George the Third; *in — luogo,* thirdly (o in the third place); *abitare al — piano,* to live on the third floor; *arrivare —,* to arrive third ‖ *terza rima,* (*poes.*) terza rima ‖ *il — Stato,* the Third Estate ‖ *sottoporre un prigioniero al — grado,* to put a prisoner through the third degree ‖ *fare il — incomodo,* to play gooseberry ‖ **1.** (*terza parte*) third: *il — del suo patrimonio,* the third of his estate; *tre terzi fanno un intero,* three thirds make a whole **2.** (*terza persona*) third person; *pl.* third party (*gener. sing.*): *in mano di terzi,* in possession of a third party; *per conto di terzi,* on behalf of a third party; *abbiamo bisogno di un — per poter giocare,* we need a third person to be able to play; *lascia giudicare a un —,* let a third person judge; *vendere a terzi,* to sell to outside parties.

terzogènito, *ag.s.m.* third-born.

terzúltimo, *ag.s.m.* antepenultimate; antepenult; last but two.

terzuòlo, *s.m.* **1.** (*ornit.*) tercel **2.** (*agr.*) third-cut hay **3.** (*mar.*) reef.

tésa, *s.f.* **1.** (*di cappello*) brim; (*di berretto*) visor: *cappello a larghe tese,* broad-brimmed hat **2.** (*il tendere le reti*) cast (of the nets).

tesàre, *v.t.* (*mar.*) to stretch, to put under tension.

tesatúra, *s.f.* (*elett.*) stretching.

tesaurizzàre, *v.i.* to hoard (up) ‖ *v.t.* to treasure (up).

tèschio, *s.m.* skull.

Tesèo, *no.pr.m.* (*mit.*) Theseus.

tèsi, *s.f.* **1.** thesis (*pl.* theses); dissertation: *— di laurea,* graduation thesis (o dissertation); *scrivere una —,* to write a thesis **2.** (*asserzione, pensiero*) thesis (*pl.* theses); proposition, argument: *romanzo a —,* thesis novel; *sostenere una —,* to support (o uphold) a thesis **3.** (*poes.*) thesis (*pl.* theses).

tesína, *s.f.* paper: *scrivere una —,* to write a paper.

tesmofòrie, *s.f.pl.* (*st. greca*) thesmophoria.

tesmotèta, *s.m.* (*st. greca*) thesmothete.

téso, *ag.* tight, taut, strained, stretched: *una corda tesa,* a tight (o taut) string; *nervi tesi,* overstrung nerves: *avere i nervi tesi,* to have one's nerves on edge; *essere in rapporti tesi con qlcu.,* to be on strained terms with s.o.

tesoreggiàre, *v.i.* to hoard (up) ‖ *v.t.* to hoard (up), to treasure (up).

tesorería, *s.f.* (*amm.*) treasury, exchequer.

tesorière, *s.m.* treasurer.

tesorizzàre, *v.i.* to hoard (up) ‖ *v.t.* to treasure (up), to hoard (up).

tesòro, *s.m.* **1.** treasure (anche *fig.*): *tesori d'arte,* art treasures; *— sepolto,* buried treasure; *i pirati rubavano i tesori,* pirates used to steal treasures ‖ *— mio!,* my darling!; *tu sei il mio —!,* (*fam.*) you are my darling! ‖ *è un — di marito,* (*fam.*) he is a paragon of a husband || *fare — di ql.co.*, *fig.* to avail oneself of sthg. (*o* to bear sthg. in mind) || *un buon amico è un —, prov.* a good friend is a treasure **2.** (*tesoreria*) treasury: *il Tesoro (dello Stato)*, the Treasury: *buono del —*, Treasury bill; *Ministro del Tesoro*, (*in Gran Bretagna*) Chancellor of the Exchequer; (*negli Stati Uniti*) Secretary of the Treasury; (*altrove*) Treasury Minister **3.** (*letter.*) thesaurus: *il « Tesoro » di Brunetto Latini*, the "Thesaurus" by Brunetto Latini.

Tèspi, *no.pr.m.* (*st. teat.*) Thespis.

Tessàglia, *no.pr.f.* (*geog.*) Thessaly.

tessàlico, *ag.* Thessalian.

tèssalo, *ag.s.m.* Thessalian.

Tessalònica, *no.pr.f.* (*geog. st.*) Thessalonica.

tèssera, *s.f.* **1.** card, ticket; pass: *— annonaria*, ration card; *— di iscrizione* (*a un partito, associazione, ecc.*), membership card; *— di riconoscimento*, identity card; *— ferroviaria*, railway pass; *— tranviaria*, street-car pass (*o* card) **2.** (*di mosaico*) tessera (*pl.* tesserae) **3.** (*archeol.*) tessera (*pl.* tesserae): *— militare*, tessera militaris.

tesseraménto, *s.m.* **1.** rationing: *— del burro*, butter rationing **2.** (*arruolamento*) enrolment.

tesseràre, *v.t.* **1.** to ration: *— il burro, lo zucchero*, to ration butter, sugar **2.** (*iscrivere a un partito, associazione, ecc.*) to give a membership card to (s.o.); (*arruolare*) to enrol.

tesseràto, *ag.* rationed: *carne tesserata*, rationed meat || *s.m.* (*membro di un partito, associazione, ecc.*) member; holder of a membership card.

tèssere, *v.t.* to weave (anche *fig.*): *molti hanno tessuto romanzi intorno a questo strano caso*, many have woven (*o* made up) romances around this strange case; *il ragno ha tessuto la sua tela*, the spider has woven its web; *— una congiura*, to weave a plot; *— una ghirlanda*, to weave a garland; *— una stoffa*, (*ind. tessile*) to weave a cloth; *— in diagonale*, (*ind. tessile*) to twill.

tèssile, *ag.* textile: *fibre tessili*, textile fibres; *industria —*, textile industry || *s.m.pl.* **1.** (*prodotti tessili*) textiles **2.** (*tessitori*) weavers: *sciopero dei tessili*, strike in the textile trades.

tessitóre, *s.m.*, **tessitrice,** *s.f.* weaver.

tessitoría, *s.f.* weaving-mill.

tessitúra, *s.f.* (*ind. tessile*) weaving; (*disposizione dei fili*) texture: *— della lana*, wool weaving; *— meccanica*, power-loom weaving; *attitudine alla —*, weavability.

tessúto, *s.m.* **1.** (*ind. tessile*) cloth, fabric, material, stuff: *— a maglia*, knitted fabric; *— a quadretti*, checked fabric; *— a righe*, striped fabric; *un — costoso*, an expensive material; *— di cotone, lana, seta*, cotton, woollen, silk fabric; *— fantasia*, fancy cloth (*o* fabric); *— fantasia in lana* (*tweed*), tweed; *— felpato*, plush fabric; *— ingualcibile*, crease-resisting fabric; *— misto*, (*lana e cotone*) union; *— per fodere*, lining fabric; *— per scarpe*, (*ind. gomma*) shoe fabric; *— per soprabiti*, overcoating; *— pettinato*, worsted fabric; *— spigato*, twill (weave); *fabbrica di tessuti*, cloth mill; *fabbricante di tessuti*, cloth manufacturer; *negozio di tessuti*, draper's shop; *negoziante di tessuti*, draper **2.** (*disposizione dei fili*) texture **3.** (*biol.*) tissue: *— connettivo, epiteliale, muscolare*, connective, epithelial, muscular tissue **4.** *fig.* tissue, web: *un — di menzogne*, a tissue (*o* web) of lies.

tèsta, *s.f.* **1.** head: *la — mi duole terribilmente*, my head aches dreadfully (*o* I have a splitting headache); *mi gira la —*, I feel giddy; *sono più alto di lui di tutta la —*, I am taller than he by a head; *avere il cappello in —*, to be wearing one's hat; *cadere con la — in giù*, to fall headlong (*o* head first); *chinare la —*, to bend one's head; *scrollare, sollevare la —*, to raise one's head; *tagliare la — a qlcu.*, to cut s.o.'s head off (*o* to behead s.o.) || *— di legno*, (*re, ministro senza potere*) figurehead (*o* man of straw); *— di rapa*, (*persona ottusa*) blockhead (*o* dolt *o* ass); *— dura*,

(*persona ostinata*) stubborn person; *— quadrata*, (*persona equilibrata*) well-balanced person; *— vuota*, empty skull || *cinquanta lire a —*, fifty liras a head || *un colpo di —*, a rash act || *voce di —*, (*mus.*) first voice || *affondare la — nella sabbia*, *fig.* to bury one's head in the sand; *agire con la — nel sacco*, to act like a fool || *andare alla —*, (*di vino, del successo*) to go to one's head || *avere la — sulle spalle*, to have one's (*o* a good) head on one's shoulders; *avere una bella —*, (*essere molto intelligente*) to have a fine brain || *avere debiti, lavoro fin sopra la —*, to be up to the eyes (*o* to be head over heels) in debt, in work || *fare la — come un pallone a qlcu.*, (*stordire con chiacchiere*) to talk s.o.'s head off || *fare di propria —*, to go (*o* to take) one's way || *giocare a — o croce*, to toss (up) a coin || *levarsi un'idea dalla —*, to put (*o* to get) an idea out of one's head; *mettere un'idea in — a qlcu.*, to put an idea into s.o.'s head; *mettersi un'idea in —*, to take an idea into one's head || *non avere la — a posto*, to be off one's head || *perdere la —*, to lose one's head || *piegare la — di fronte all'evidenza*, to bow to evidence || *rompersi la — per ricordare ql.co.*, to rack one's brains to remember sthg. || *tenere la — a posto*, to keep one's head || *tenere — a qlcu.*, (*stordire con chiacchiere*) to make head against s.o. || *uscirne con la — rotta*, to have the worst of it **2.** (*di cose*) head: *la — del letto*, the bed-head; *la — di un chiodo, spillo, martello*, the head of a nail, pin, hammer; *— di ponte*, bridge-head; *— di sbarco*, (*mil.*) beachhead **3.** (*posizione di guida, di comando*): *andare in —*, to lead the way; *essere alla — di un corteo*, to be heading a procession; *essere alla — di un esercito, di impresa commerciale*, to be at the head of an army, of a business; *essere alla — di un partito*, to be the leader of a party; *essere in — a tutti*, to be ahead of everybody.

testàbile, *ag.* (*dir.*) testable.

testàcei, *s.m.pl.* (*zool.*) Testacea.

testàceo, *ag.s.m.* (*zool.*) testacean.

testamentàrio, *ag.* testamentary: *esecutore —*, (*dir.*) testamentary executor.

testaménto, *s.m.* will, testament: *— olografo*, holograph will; *fare —*, to make one's will; *lasciare ql.co. per — a qlcu.*, to bequeath (*o* to will) sthg. to s.o. || *il Vecchio, il Nuovo Testamento*, (*Bibbia*) the Old, the New Testament.

testardàggine, *s.f.* stubbornness, obstinacy.

testardaménte, *av.* stubbornly, obstinately.

testàrdo, *ag.* stubborn, obstinate, headstrong.

testàre, *v.i.* (*dir.*) to make one's will.

testàta, *s.f.* **1.** head: *la — di un letto, di un ponte*, the head of a bed, of a bridge; *— di una trave*, headpiece of a beam **2.** (*intestazione*) heading **3.** (*colpo con la testa*) butt.

testàtico, *s.m.* (*dir.*) capitation, poll-tax, head-tax.

testatóre, *s.m.* (*dir.*) testator.

testatríce, *s.f.* (*dir.*) testatrix (*pl.* testatrices).

tèste[1], *s.c.* (*dir.*) witness: *— d'accusa*, witness for the prosecution; *— a difesa*, exculpatory witness (*o* witness for the defence).

testé[2], *av.* (*letter.*) just now: *egli è arrivato —*, he has just arrived.

testícolo, *s.m.* (*anat.*) testicle.

testièra, *s.f.* **1.** (*del letto*) bed-head **2.** (*parte di finimenti di cavallo*) crownpiece **3.** (*forma per modellare cappelli, ecc.*) block **4.** (*st. mil.*) battering ram.

testificàre, *v.t.* (*dir.*) to testify, to declare.

testificazióne, *s.f.* (*dir.*) testification.

testimòne, *s.c.* (*dir.*) witness: *— oculare*, eye-witness; *banco dei testimoni*, witness-box; *deporre come —*, to testify as witness; *far da — contro qlcu.*, to witness against s.o.; *far da — in favore di qlcu.*, to witness for (*o* to bear witness to) s.o.

testimoniàle, *ag.* (*dir.*) witness (*attributivo*), of the witness(es): *esame —*, witness examination || *s.m.* (*dir.*) witnesses (*pl.*): *il — d'accusa*, the witnesses for the prosecution.

testimoniànza, *s.f.* **1.** testimony, witness (anche *dir.*): *secondo la — degli storici,* according to the testimony of the historians; *questo sta a — di ciò che accadde,* this stands in witness of what happened; *fare —,* to bear witness; *portare falsa —,* to bear false witness **2.** (*prova*) evidence; proof: *in — del mio amore,* as a token of my love; *questa è una — della sua innocenza,* this is proof of his innocence.

testimoniàre, *v.t.* to testify; to witness: *egli testimoniò che l'automobile veniva da sinistra,* he testified that the car was coming from the left; *questo testimonia la mia buona volontà,* this witnesses my good will; *— il falso,* to give false testimony ‖ *v.i.* to witness, to bear witness: *egli testimoniò della mia onestà,* he bore witness to my honesty; *— in favore di, contro qlcu.,* to witness for, against s.o.

testimònio, *s.m.* **1.** (*testimone*) witness: *fare da —,* to act as a witness **2.** (*testimonianza, prova*) evidence, proof: *la sua sorpresa è — della sua innocenza,* his surprise is proof (o evidence) of his innocence **3.** (*ad un matrimonio*) best man.

testína, *s.f.* (*cuc.*) calf's head.

tèsto, *s.m.* text: *il — originale,* the original text; *errore di —,* textual error; *libro di —,* text-book; *attenersi al —,* to stick to the text; *restaurare un — antico,* to restore an ancient text ‖ *egli fa — in questo campo,* he is an authority in this field.

testolína, *s.f.* **1.** little head **2.** (*bambino sventato, bambina sventata*) light-minded child.

testóne, *s.m.* **1.** (*testa grossa*) big head **2.** (*stupido*) blockhead, dolt **3.** (*testardo*) stubborn fellow, obstinate fellow.

testosteróne, *s.m.* (*chim. biol.*) testosterone.

testuàle, *ag.* **1.** verbatim; (*preciso*) exact, precise: *le sue testuali parole,* his exact words; *una traduzione —,* a verbatim translation **2.** (*del testo*) textual.

testualménte, *av.* **1.** verbatim, word by word: *una storia raccontata —,* a story told verbatim; *riportare — un discorso,* to report a speech verbatim **2.** (*in modo preciso*) exactly, precisely.

testúggine, *s.f.* **1.** tortoise; (*di mare*) turtle **2.** (*st. mil.*) testudo (*pl.* testudines).

tetànico, *ag.* (*patol.*) tetanic.

tètano, *s.m.* (*patol.*) tetanus.

tête-à-tête, *l. av.* tête-à-tête: *ero — con lui,* I was tête-à-tête with him ‖ *s.m.* tête-à-tête: *un — per il caffè,* (*servizio da caffè per due*) a tête-à-tête coffee-set; *avere un — con qlcu.,* to have a tête-à-tête with s.o.

Tèti, Tètide, *no.pr.f.* (*mit.*) Thetis.

tetracòrdo, *s.m.* (*mus.*) tetrachord.

tetradimíte, *s.f.* (*min.*) tetradymite.

tetraèdrico, *ag.* (*geom.*) tetrahedral.

tetraèdro, *s.m.* (*geom.*) tetrahedron.

tetraetíle, *s.m.* (*chim. ind.*) tetraethyl lead.

tetràggine, *s.f.* gloom, dismalness, darkness.

tetragonàle, *ag.* (*geom.*) tetragonal.

tetràgono, *ag.* **1.** (*geom.*) tetragonal, four-sided **2.** *fig.* firm, steadfast, unyielding, unflinching ‖ *s.m.* (*geom.*) tetragon.

tetralogía, *s.f.* (*teat.*) tetralogy.

tetraménte, *av.* gloomily, dismally.

tetràmetro, *s.m.* (*poes.*) tetrameter.

tetràrca, *s.m.* (*st. romana*) tetrarch.

tetrarcàto, *s.m.* (*st. romana*) tetrarchate.

tetrarchía, *s.f.* (*st. romana*) tetrarchy.

tetràstico, *ag.s.m.* (*poes.*) tetrastich.

tetràstilo, *ag.s.m.* (*arch.*) tetrastyle.

tetravalènte, *ag.* (*chim.*) tetravalent.

tètro, *ag.* gloomy, dismal: *atmosfera, persona tetra,* gloomy atmosphere, person; *luogo —,* gloomy (o dismal) place; *umore —,* gloom (o despondency); *viso —,* gloomy face.

tétto, *s.m.* **1.** roof (anche *fig.*): *— a capanna, a due falde,* saddle roof; *— apribile,* (*specialmente di automobile*) reversible roof; *— ad abbaino,* mansard roof;

— a due falde su timpano, gable roof; *— ad una falda,* lean-to roof; *— gradinata,* stepped roof; *— a guglia,* spire roof; *— a lucernario,* lantern roof; *— a padiglione,* hip roof; *— terrazza,* platform (o flat) roof; *— d'ardesia, di tegole, di paglia,* slated, tiled, thatched roof; *il — di una casa,* the roof of a house; *— scorrevole,* sliding roof ‖ *sotto il proprio —,* under one's roof; *dormire sotto lo stesso —,* to sleep under the same roof ‖ *il — del mondo,* the roof of the world **2.** (*casa*) home, house: *egli non ha un —,* he has no home (o he is homeless).

tettóia, *s.f.* shed; (*sporgente da un muro*) penthouse; (*sovrastante una piattaforma*) platform roofing.

tettònica, *s.f.* tectonics.

tettònico, *ag.* tectonic.

tettríce, *s.f.* (*penna di uccello*) tectrix (*pl.* tectrices).

tettúccio, *s.m.* **1.** (*piccolo tetto*) small roof **2.** (*aer.*) canopy.

tèucrio, *s.m.* (*bot.*) Teucrium.

tèucro, *ag.s.m.* Teucrian.

teurgía, *s.f.* theurgy.

teúrgico, *ag.* theurgic(al).

teúrgo, *s.m.* theurgist.

tèutone, *ag.* Teutonic ‖ *s.m.* Teuton.

teutònico, *ag.* Teutonic: *l'ordine —,* (*st.*) the Teutonic Order.

Tévere, *no.pr.m.* (*geog.*) Tiber.

Thailàndia, *no.pr.f.* (*geog.*) Thailand.

thèrmos, *V.* **tèrmos.**

thulíte, *s.f.* (*min.*) thulite.

ti, *pron. pers. m.f.* 2ª *persona sing.* **1.** oggetto you; (*arc. poet.*) thee: *— amo,* I love you; *Ti veneriamo, o Dio,* we worship Thee, o God; *voglio vederti domani,* I want to see you tomorrow **2.** obliquo you, to you; (*arc. poet.*) thee, to thee: *— affido i miei figli,* I entrust you with my children (o I entrust my children to you); *Ti affido il mio spirito,* to Thee I commend my spirit; *ho deciso di dirti la verità,* I have decided to tell you the truth **3.** (*coi verbi riflessivi*) yourself (*talvolta omesso*); (*arc. poet.*) thyself: *non — stancare troppo, mi raccomando,* be careful not to tire yourself out; *pensavo che — saresti trovato male là,* I thought you wouldn't feel at home there; *va' a lavarti,* go and wash (yourself).

tialísmo, *s.m.* (*patol.*) ptyalism.

tiàra, *s.f.* tiara.

Tiberíade, *no.pr.f.* (*geog. st.*) Tiberias.

tiberíno, *ag.* Tiberine.

Tibèrio, *no.pr.m.* (*st.*) Tiberius.

Tibet, *no.pr.m.* (*geog.*) Tibet, Thibet.

tibetàno, *ag.s.m.* Tibetan.

tíbia, *s.f.* **1.** (*anat.*) shin-bone; tibia (*pl.* tibiae, tibias) **2.** (*mus.*) tibia (*pl.* tibiae, tibias).

tibiàle, *ag.* (*anat.*) tibial.

tibícina, *s.f.,* **tibícine,** *s.m.* (*mus.*) tibia-player, piper, flutist.

Tibúllo, *no.pr.m.* (*st. lett.*) Tibullus.

tiburtíno, *ag.* Tiburtine ‖ *s.m.* (*pietra*) travertin(e).

tic, *s.m.* (*contrazione nervosa dei muscoli*) tic.

ticchettàre, *v.i.* to tick.

ticchettío, *s.m.* ticking.

tícchio, *s.m.* **1.** *V.* tic **2.** (*ghiribizzo*) whim, fancy: *mi è saltato il — di fare una passeggiatina,* I have a fancy for a walk.

tictàc, *s.m.* (*voce onomatopeica riproducente il battito dell'orologio*) tick-tack.

tictòc, *s.m.* (*voce onomatopeica riproducente il battito del cuore*) pit-a-pat.

Tidèo, *no.pr.m.* (*mit.*) Tydeus.

tiepidézza, tiepidità, *s.f.* lukewarmness, tepidity, tepidness (anche *fig.*).

tièpido, *ag.* lukewarm, tepid (anche *fig.*).

Tièste, *no.pr.m.* (*lett.*) Thyestes.

tifàcee, *s.f.pl.* (*bot.*) Typhaceae.

Tifèo, *no.pr.m.* (*mit.*) Typhoeus.

tiflíte, *s.f.* (*patol.*) typhlitis.

tífo, *s.m.* **1.** (*patol.*) typhus: *— ambulatorio,* typhus ambulatorius; — *esantematico*, typhus exanthema-ticus 2. (*spor.*) fanaticism: *fare il — per una squadra di calcio*, to be a football team fan.

tifòide, *ag.* (*patol.*) typhoid.

tifoidèa, *s.f.* (*patol.*) typhoid fever.

tifóne[1], *s.m.* typhoon: *il — « Donna »*, the typhoon " Donna ".

Tifòne[2], *no.pr.m.* (*mit.*) Typhon.

tifóso, *ag.* (*patol.*) typhous || *s.m.* 1. (*patol.*) typhus patient 2. (*spor.*) fan, fanatic: *un — del calcio*, a foot-ball fan.

tight, *s.m.* (*abito maschile da cerimonia*) morning coat.

tíglio, *s.m.* 1. (*bot.*) lime, lime-tree: *infuso di —*, lime-blossom tea 2. (*fibra*) bast, fibre.

tiglióso, *ag.* (*fibroso*) fibrous; (*di carne*) tough.

tígna, *s.f.* (*patol.*) tinea, ring-worm; porrigo.

tignóso, *ag.* 1. (*patol.*) affected with ring-worm 2. *fig.* (*avaro*) stingy 3. *fig.* (*ostinato*) stubborn.

tignuòla, *s.f.* (*entom.*) moth; (*del grano*) weevil.

tigràto, *ag.* striped, streaked: *cavallo —*, black -spotted horse; *gatto —*, tabby (cat).

tígre, *s.f.* (*maschio*) tiger; (*femmina*) tigress.

tigrésco, *ag.* tigerish (anche *fig.*); *istinto, movimento —*, tigerish instinct, motion.

Tígri, *no.pr.m.* (*geog.*) Tigris.

tigròtto, *s.m.* (*zool.*) young tiger, tiger cub.

tilde, *s.m.* (*segno ortografico*) tilde.

tillíte, *s.f.* (*geol.*) tillite.

timbàllo, *s.m.* 1. (*mus.*) kettledrum, timbal 2. (*cuc.*) (*sformato*) timbale.

timbràre, *v.t.* to stamp, to postmark: *— a secco*, to emboss; *— un documento*, to stamp a document; *— una lettera*, to postmark a letter.

timbratríce, *s.f.* (*mec.*) marking machine.

timbratúra, *s.f.* stamping; (*di lettere*) postmarking.

timbro, *s.m.* 1. stamp: *— a secco*, embossed stamp; *— di gomma*, rubber stamp; *— d'ufficio*, office stamp; *— postale*, postmark 2. (*di voce, di strumento*) timbre.

Timbuctú, *no.pr.f.* (*geog.*) Timbuktu.

timidaménte, *av.* shyly, timidly; (*con fare vergo-gnoso*) bashfully; (*con fare schivo*) diffidently.

timidézza, timidità, *s.f.* shyness, timidity; (*ver-gogna*) bashfulness; (*ritrosia*) diffidence: *liberarsi dal-la propria —*, to throw off one's shyness.

tímido, *ag.* shy, timid, bashful; (*schivo*) diffident: *un ragazzo dall'aspetto —*, a shy-looking boy.

tímo, *s.m.* 1. (*bot.*) thyme 2. (*anat.*) thymus.

timóne[1], *s.m.* (*mar.*) rudder, helm (anche *fig.*); (*aer.*) rudder: *barra del —*, tiller; *ruota del —*, steering wheel; *dare un colpo di —*, to put the tiller hard over; *essere al — di una nave*, to steer a ship; *prendere il —*, to take the helm (anche *fig.*).

Timóne[2], *no.pr.m.* (*st.*) Timon.

timonèlla, *s.f.* (*carrozza leggera a due posti*) buggy, four-wheeled gig.

timonería, *s.f.* (*mar.*) steering compartment, wheel-house, pilothouse.

timonière, *s.m.* helmsman (*pl.* helmsmen); steersman (*pl.* steersmen); (*di piccola imbarcazione*) coxswain.

timoràto, *ag.* 1. respectful, fearful, timorous: *— di Dio*, God fearing 2. (*scrupoloso, retto*) scrupulous: *una coscienza timorata*, an over-scrupulous conscience.

timóre, *s.m.* dread, fear; (*misto a rispetto, soggezione*) fear, awe: *— di Dio*, fear of God (*o* of the Lord); *timor panico*, panic (terror); *per — di un malinteso*, for fear of a misunderstanding; *non aver — !*, don't be afraid!; (*non preoccuparti*) don't worry !; *non ho — di affron-tare la realtà*, I do not fear to face reality; *questi timori non hanno ragione di essere*, these fears have no grounds; *questo è proprio ciò di cui avevo —*, this is just what I dreaded; *avere —*, to fear (*o* to be afraid); *incutere — a qlcu.*, to strike (*o* to inspire) s.o. with fear || *per — di, che*, lest: *per — che tu non venissi*, lest you should not come.

timorosaménte, *av.* timorously, fearfully, timidly.

timoróso, *ag.* timorous, fearful, timid: *essere — di ql.co.*, to fear sthg. (*o* to be afraid of sthg).

Timòteo, *no.pr.m.* Timothy || *dim.* Tim.

timpànico, *ag.* (*anat.*) tympanic: *membrana limpa-nica*, tympanic membrane.

timpanísmo, *s.m.* (*patol.*) tympanites, tympanism.

timpanísta, *s.c.* (*mus.*) kettle-drummer, tympanist.

timpaníte, *s.f.* (*patol.*) 1. (*timpanismo*) tympanites, tympanism 2. (*infiammazione del timpano*) tympanitis.

tímpano, *s.m.* 1. (*anat.*) eardrum, tympanum || *rom-pere i timpani a qlcu.*, to burst s.o.'s eardrums. 2. (*mus.*) kettle-drum, timbal 3. (*arch.*) tympanum; gable.

tinàia, *s.f.* vat-room.

tínca, *s.f.* (*ittiol.*) tench.

tincóne, *s.m.* (*patol.*) bubo (*pl.* buboes).

Tíndaro, *no.pr.m.* (*mit.*) Tyndareus.

tinèllo, *s.m.* 1. (*stanza dove si mangia*) breakfast -room 2. (*piccolo tino*) small vat.

tíngere, *v.t.* 1. to dye: *— un vestito di nero*, to dye a dress black || *farsi — i capelli*, to have one's hair dyed 2. (*colorare lievemente*) to tinge 3. (*dipingere, truccare*) to make up: *— le labbra a qlcu.*, to paint s.o.'s lips 4. (*colorare*) to colour 5. (*macchiare*) to stain: *— l'acqua di sangue*, to stain water with blood || **tíngersi**, *v.r.* 1. to dye: *— i capelli*, to dye one's hair 2. (*colorarsi lievemente*) to tinge: *il cielo si tinge di rosso*, the sky is tinged with red 3. (*dipingersi, truccarsi*) to make up: *— le labbra*, to paint one's lips 4. (*macchiarsi*): *— le mani nel sangue di qlcu.*, to stain one's hands in s.o.'s blood.

tingitúra, *s.f.* dyeing.

tinníre, *V.* **tintinnàre**.

tinníto, *V.* **tintínno**.

tínnulo, *ag.* (*letter. rar.*) tinkling; jingling; clinking, chinking; trilling.

tíno, *s.m.* 1. vat; tub 2. (*metal.*) shaft.

tinòzza, *s.f.* tub; (*vasca, bagno*) bath-tub; (*recipiente per fare il bucato*) wash-tub.

tínta, *s.f.* 1. (*materia colorante*) dye; dyeing stuff: *mescolare due tinte*, to mix two dyes 2. (*tingitura*) dyeing: *la — non è riuscita bene*, the dyeing has not turned out well 3. (*colore*) colour, hue; (*delicata*) tint, tinge; (*sfumata*) shade: *— morbida*, soft colour; *mezza — vague colour; (*pitt.*) mezzotint; *la — delle montagne è troppo scura*, the colour (*o* hue) of the mountains is too dark; *questa è una bella —*, this is a nice colour || *una — di invidia*, a touch of envy || *romanzo a tinte forti*, sensational novel || *descrivere ql.co. a tinte fosche*, to paint sthg. in dark colours.

tintarèlla, *s.f.* (*fam.*) (*abbronzatura*) sun-tan: *pren-dere la —*, to get sun-tanned.

tinteggiàre, *v.t.* to paint, to tint, to tinge; (*edil.*) to distemper.

tinteggiatúra, *s.f.* painting, tinting: *— a calce*, (*edil.*) colour-wash painting; *— a tempera*, (*edil.*) distemper.

tintinnàbolo, *s.m.* (*letter.*) tintinnabulum (*pl.* tin, tinnabula).

tintinnaménto, *s.m.* tinkling; (*di campanelli*) jingling; (*di bicchieri*) clinking, chinking.

tintinnàre, *v.i.* to tinkle; (*di campanelli*) to jingle; (*di bicchieri*) to clink, to chink.

tintinnío, *s.m.* tinkling; jingling; clinking, chinking.

tintinníre, *V.* **tintinnàre**.

tintínno, *s.m.* (*letter. rar.*) tinkling; jingling; clinking, chinking.

tínto, *ag.* 1. dyed: *capelli tinti*, dyed hair; *un ve-stito — di verde*, a dress dyed green 2. (*dipinto, truccato*) painted, made up: *un viso —*, a painted face 3. (*mac-chiato*) stained (with sthg.): *— di inchiostro*, stained with ink; *mani tinte di sangue*, bloodstained hands.

tintóre, *s.m.* dyer; (*chi esegue anche lavature a secco*) cleaner: *portare un abito dal —*, to take a dress to the cleaners'.

tintoría, *s.f.* **1.** dye-works (*pl.*); (*impianto industriale*) dyeing plant; (*negozio ove si eseguono lavature a secco*) cleaners' (shop) **2.** (*l'arte del tingere*) dyeing.

tintúra, *s.f.* **1.** (*farm.*) tincture: — *di iodio,* tincture of iodine **2.** *V.* **tínta 1. 2.**

tiòrba, *s.f.* (*mus.*) theorbo.

tiorbísta, *s.c.* (*mus.*) theorbist.

tipàccio, *s.m.* rogue, rascal, nasty fellow, scoundrel.

tipétto, *s.m.*: *quella ragazza è un bel* —, that girl is a pretty little thing.

tipicaménte, *av.* typically.

típico, *ag.* typical.

tipificàre, *v.t.* to typify.

típo, *s.m.* **1.** type: *un uomo di* — *meridionale,* a man of the southern type; *egli è il* — *dell'eroe,* he is the typical hero (*o* he is a real hero) **2.** (*fam.*) (*individuo*) chap, fellow: *che strano* —!, *che bel* —!, what a funny chap!, what a queer fellow!; *è un* — *strano,* he is an odd (*o* a queer) sort of person **3.** (*modello*) model, pattern; standard: *oro* —, standard gold **4.** (*genere*) kind, sort: *diversi tipi di gente,* several kinds of people **5.** (*tip.*) type.

tipografía, *s.f.* **1.** (*l'arte dello stampare*) typography **2.** (*stamperia*) printing office, printing house.

tipograficaménte, *av.* typographically.

tipogràfico, *ag.* typographic(al).

tipògrafo, *s.m.* printer, typographer.

tipolitografía, *s.f.* typolithography.

tipòmetro, *s.m.* (*tip.*) type scale, type gauge.

tiptología, *s.f.* typtology.

tirabàci, *s.m.* lovelock, kiss-curl.

tirabòzze, *s.m.* (*tip.*) proof press.

tirabràce, *s.m.* baker's rake.

tiràggio, *s.m.* draught, draft.

tiralínee, *s.m.* drawing-pen.

tiramàntici, *s.m.* organ blower (anche *mec.*).

tiraménto, *s.m.* drawing; (*verso di sè*) pulling; (*il trascinare*) dragging.

tiranneggiaménto, *s.m.* tyrannizing.

tiranneggiàre, *v.t.* to tyrannize (s.o., over s.o.), to oppress: *quell'uomo tiranneggia la sua famiglia,* that man tyrannizes his family.

tirannescaménte, *av.* tyrannically, tyrannously, despotically, oppressively.

tirannésco, *ag.* tyrannical, tyrannous; despotical; oppressive.

tirannía, *s.f.* tyranny; despotism; oppression: *la* — *della moda,* the tyranny of fashion.

tirannicaménte, *av.* tyrannically; despotically; oppressively.

tirannicída, *ag.* tyrannicidal || *s.m.* tyrannicide.

tirannicídio, *s.m.* tyrannicide.

tirànnico, *ag.* tyrannical, tyrannous; despotical; oppressive; overpowering.

tirànnide, *s.f.* tyranny; despotism; oppression.

tirànno, *ag.* tyrannical; despotic || *s.m.* tyrant; despot; oppressor: *fare il* —, to play the tyrant.

tirànte, *s.m.* **1.** (*mec.*) connecting rod, tie-rod, stay -rod: — *del freno,* brake rod **2.** (*arch.*) tie-beam **3.** (*tiraggio*) draught, draft **4.** *pl.* (*bretelle*) braces.

tirapièdi, *s.m.* **1.** hangman's assistant **2.** *fig.* hanger -on, understrapper.

tirapúgni, *s.m.* knuckle-duster.

tiràre, *v.t.* **1.** to draw; to pull: *carrozza tirata da quattro cavalli,* coach drawn by four horses; *lo tirava per mano,* he was pulling him by the hand; *mi ha tirato per i capelli,* he has pulled my hair; *tira in là la seggiola,* move the chair; *tirò il tavolo vicino al muro,* he drew the table near the wall; *tirò il vaso verso di sè,* he drew the vase towards him || — *l'acqua al proprio mulino,* to bring grist to one's mill; — *a sorte,* to cast lots (*o* to choose by lots); — *il campanello con forza,* to pull the bell violently; — *il collo a qlcu.,* to wring s.o.'s neck; — *una conclusione,* to draw a conclusion; — *una corda,* to pull a rope; — *in ballo un argomento,*

to bring up a subject; — *una linea,* to draw a line; — *gli orecchi a qlcu.,* to pull s.o.'s ears; *fig.* to reproach s.o.; — *qlcu. per la manica,* to pluck s.o.'s sleeve; — *profitto da ql.co.,* to draw profit from sthg.; — *le reti,* to haul in the nets; — *un respiro,* to draw a breath; — *una somma,* to make an addition; — *le somme,* to sum up (anche *fig.*); — *un sospiro,* to give a sigh; — *le tende,* to draw the curtains || — *dentro,* to draw in: *tira dentro la lingua,* draw in your tongue || — *in disparte,* to draw aside || — *fuori,* to draw out: *non è facile tirargli fuori le sue impressioni,* it is not easy to draw out his impressions from him; *tirò fuori un libro dalla borsa,* he drew out a book from his bag || — *giù,* to pull down: *quell'influenza mi ha tirato giù,* that flu has pulled me down || — *indietro,* to draw back || — *su,* (*sollevare*) to hitch (up); (*prender su*) to take up; (*allevare*) to bring up: — *su le maniche,* to tuck up one's sleeves; — *su la testa,* to raise one's head || — *via,* to pull out (*o* to draw *o* to pull off *o* to pull away): *hanno tirato via l'etichetta,* they have pulled off (*o* away) the label; *il dentista gli tirò via il dente,* the dentist pulled out (*o* drew) his tooth; *tirò via un chiodo,* he drew a nail || — *a lustro,* to polish: *essere tirato a lustro, fig.* to be dolled up || — *la cinghia, fig.* to tighten one's belt || — *le cuoia,* to breathe one's last || — *da,* to be in the style of || — *un pavimento a cera,* to polish a floor **2.** (*trascinare*) to drag: *abbiamo dovuto tirarlo qui,* we had to drag him here; *il bambino tirava il suo cavallino,* the child was dragging his toy-horse; *egli tirava un sacco pesante,* he was dragging a heavy sack; — *in secco una barca,* to beach a boat || — *in lungo una storia,* to drag out (*o* to lengthen out) a story **3.** (*scagliare, lanciare*) to throw: — *una freccia,* to shoot an arrow; — *ql.co. fuori dalla finestra,* to throw sthg. out of the window; — *un sasso a un cane,* to throw a stone at a dog || — *i dadi,* to cast dice || — *moccoli,* to swear (*o* to curse) **4.** (*attirare*) to draw, to attract: *attore che tira tutta Londra,* actor who draws the whole of London; *questo manifesto tira molta gente,* this advertisement draws many people; *lo zucchero tira le mosche,* sugar attracts flies; — *qlcu. in un agguato,* to draw s.o. into a snare **5.** (*stampare*) to print: — *1000 copie di un libro,* to print 1000 copies of a book || *v.i.* **1.** to draw; to pull: *cavallo che tira bene,* horse that pulls well || *non mi piace questo lavoro, ma tiro avanti ugualmente,* I do not like this work, but I go on all the same; *non so come faccia a* — *avanti con così pochi soldi,* I do not know how he manages to get on with so little money || *tira via, queste sono piccolezze,* do not be fussy, these are only trifles; *egli tirò via sui dettagli perchè aveva premura,* he passed over the details because he was in a hurry **2.** (*di vestiti*) to be skin -tight: *questo vestito tira sui fianchi,* this dress is too tight on the hips **3.** (*sparare*) to shoot; (*far fuoco*) to fire: *egli sa* — *bene,* he is a good shot; *ordinò loro di* —, he ordered them to fire; — *a qlcu.,* to shoot (*o* to fire) at s.o. **4.** (*mirare*) to aim: *tira ai quattrini,* he aims at money **5.** (*soffiare*) to blow: *tira vento,* the wind is blowing (*o* it is windy) || *tira aria di tempesta, fig.* a storm is in the air (*o* there is a stormy atmosphere) **6.** (*aut.*) to run: *questa automobile tira bene,* this car runs well **7.** (*di strada*) to go uphill, to run uphill **8.** (*far passare il fumo*) to draw, to vent: *questo cammino tira bene,* this chimney draws well; *la tua sigaretta non tira,* your cigarette doesn't draw **9.** (*aver somiglianza*) to take after (s.o.): *tira dalla nonna,* she takes after her grandmother **10.** (*tendere, di colore*) to approach, to tend: *blu che tira al verde,* greenish blue; *un colore che tira al blu,* a bluish colour **11.** (*scherma*) to fence **tiràrsi,** *v.r.* to draw; to drag: *la bimba, intimorita, si tirò prontamente da parte,* the child, frightened, drew to one side hastily; *tirati vicino alla tavola,* draw near the table || — *addosso,* to draw on oneself: *si è tirato addosso molto odio,* he has drawn much hatred on himself || — *dietro,* to draw after (*o* to pull after); (*portarsi dietro*) to drag after: *devo sempre tirarmi dietro mio fratello*, I always have to drag my brother after me; *si tirò dietro la porta*, he pulled the door after him ‖ — *indietro*, to draw back ‖ — *lontano*, to draw away ‖ — *su*, (*alzarsi*) to draw oneself up: *egli si tirò su quando mi vide*, he drew himself up (*o* stood up) when he saw me ‖ — *via*, to take off: — *via il soprabito*, to take off one's overcoat ‖ — *la cinghia*, to tighten one's belt.

tirastivàli, *s.m.* boot-jack.

tiràta, *s.f.* **1.** pull; draw: *dare una* — *a una fune*, to give a pull at a rope; *dare una* — *d'orecchi a qluc.*, to pull s.o.'s ears; *fig.* to give s.o. a lecture **2.** (*tratto*): *egli lo fece in una* — *sola*, he did it at a stretch **3.** (*invettiva*) tirade: *il suo discorso era una lunga* — *contro gli oppositori*, his speech was a tirade against his opponents.

tiràto, *ag.* **1.** drawn: *con i lineamenti tirati*, with drawn features **2.** *V.* **tirchio.**

tiratóre, *s.m.* shooter: — *di scherma*, fencer; *un* — *provetto*, a sharp shooter; — *scelto*, marksman; *franco* —, sniper; *è un buon* —, he is a good shot.

tiratúra, *s.f.* **1.** (*il tirare*) drawing; pulling **2.** (*tip.*) printing; (*il numero delle copie stampate*) circulation: — *delle bozze*, proof-pulling; *questo giornale ha una* — *di più di 200.000 copie*, this newspaper has a circulation of more than 200,000; *questa rivista ha una* — *molto forte*, this review has a very wide circulation; *si farà una* — *di 500 copie*, 500 copies will be printed.

tirchierìa, *s.f.* stinginess, closeness, close-fistedness, niggardliness.

tìrchio, *ag.* stingy, close, close-fisted, niggardly.

tirèlla, *s.f.* (*finimento per cavalli*) trace.

tiremmòlla, *s.m.* (*fam.*) **1.** (*tergiversazione*) tergiversation, wavering **2.** (*persona indecisa*) wavering person.

Tirèsia, *no.pr.m.* (*mit.*) Tiresias.

tirétto, *s.m.* drawer.

tiritèra, *s.f.* rigmarole: *è sempre la solita* —, (*fam.*) it is always the same old story.

tìro[1], *s.m.* **1.** (*trazione*) draught: *bestie da* —, draught animals; *cavallo da* —, draught-horse **2.** (*muta*) team: — *a quattro*, four-in-hand **3.** (*lancio*) throw, cast: — *con l'arco*, archery; *un* — *di dadi*, a throw of dice; *a un* — *di sasso*, within a stone's throw; *questo fu un bel* —, this was a good throw ‖ *se mi viene a* — *lo arrangio io*, if I can get hold of him (*o* get my hands on him) I'll fix him **4.** (*di arma da fuoco*) shot, fire; (*lo sparare*) shooting: — *al piccione*, pigeon shooting; — *a segno*, target-firing; — *di sbarramento*, barrage-fire; *a un* — *di schioppo*, within gunshot (*o* rifle-shot); *poligono di* —, shooting-range; *scuola di* —, shooting school; *udii qualche* —, I heard some shots; *aprire il* —, to open fire **5.** (*scherzo*) trick: *giocare un brutto* — *a qlcu.*, to play a bad trick on s.o. **6.** (*di sigaro, ecc.*) puff: *posso fare un* — *dalla tua sigaretta?*, may I take (*o* have) a puff at your cigarette?.

Tìro[2], *no.pr.f.* (*geog. st.*) Tyre.

tirocinànte, *s.m.* apprentice, beginner; tyro (*pl.* tyros, tyroes); tiro (*pl.* tiro, tiroes).

tirocìnio, *s.m.* apprenticeship, novitiate.

tiròide, *s.f.* (*anat.*) thyroid.

tiroidectomìa, *s.f.* (*chir.*) thyroidectomy.

tiroidèo, *ag.* thyroid.

tiroidìna, *s.f.* (*farm.*) thyroidin.

tiroidìsmo, *s.m.* (*patol.*) thyroidism.

tiroidìte, *s.f.* (*patol.*) thyroiditis.

tirolése, *ag.* Tyrolese ‖ *s.c.* Tyrolese (*invariato al pl.*) ‖ *s.f.* (*danza*) tyrolienne.

Tiròlo, *no.pr.m.* (*geog.*) Tyrol, Tirol.

tironiàno, *ag.* Tironian: *note tironiane*, Tironian notes.

tirrèno, *ag.* Tyrrhene, Tyrrhenian ‖ **Tirrèno (il),** *no.pr.m.* (*geog.*) the Tyrrhenian Sea.

tìrso, *s.m.* thyrsus (*pl.* thyrsi) (*anche bot.*).

Tirtèo, *no.pr.m.* (*st. lett.*) Tyrtaeus.

tisàna, *s.f.* infusion, (herb) tea, ptisan, tisane.

tisanòtteri, *s.m.pl.* (*entom.*) Thysanoptera.

Tisbe, *no.pr.f.* (*mit.*) Thisbe.

tìsi, *s.f.* (*patol.*) consumption, phthisis: — *al secondo stadio*, phthisis confirmata.

tisichézza, *s.f.* **1.** (*patol.*) consumption **2.** (*estrema debolezza*) extreme weakness.

tìsico, *ag.* **1.** (*patol.*) consumptive, phthisical **2.** (*stentato, di piante*) stunted ‖ *s.m.* consumptive.

Tisìfone, *no.pr.f.* (*mit.*) Tisiphone.

tisiologìa, *s.f.* (*med.*) phthisiology.

tisiòlogo, *s.m.* phthisiologist.

titanàto, *s.m.* (*chim.*) titanate.

Titània, *no.pr.f.* (*mit.*) Titania.

titànico[1], *ag.* titanic: *sforzi titanici*, titanic efforts.

titànico[2], *ag.* (*chim.*) titanic: *acido* —, titanic acid.

titanìfero, *ag.* titaniferous.

titànio, *s.m.* (*chim.*) titanium.

titanìsmo, *s.m.* (*neol.*) Titanism.

titanìte, *s.f.* (*min.*) titanite.

Titàno, *no.pr.m.* (*mit.*) Titan.

titillaménto, *s.m.* titillation, tickling.

titillàre, *v.t.* to titillate, to tickle.

titillatóre, *s.m.* (*mec.*) tickler.

titillazióne, *s.f.* titillation, tickling.

Tìto, *no.pr.m.* (*st.*) Titus.

titolàre, *ag.* (*che ha un titolo e relativo ufficio*) regular; (*che ha solo il titolo*) titular: *insegnante* —, regular teacher; *cardinale* —, titular cardinal ‖ *s.m.* **1.** (*detentore*) regular holder; (*proprietario*) owner, proprietor; (*capo, di scuola, ecc.*) principal; (*il responsabile*) the man in charge: *un* — *di cattedra*, a full professor; *egli è il* — *di questo reparto*, he is in charge of this department **2.** (*eccl.*) titular.

titolàre, *v.t.* **1.** to title: — *un articolo, un libro*, to title an article, a book **2.** (*dare un titolo nobiliare a*) to confer a title upon (s.o.) **3.** (*chiamare*) to call **4.** (*chim.*) to titrate, to determine the strength of (sthg.) **5.** (*ind. tessile*) to number.

titolàto, *ag.* titled ‖ *s.m.* titled gentleman.

titolétto, *s.m.* (*tip.*) running head, current head.

tìtolo, *s.m.* **1.** title; (*testata*) headline: *il* — *di un libro, di un giornale*, the title of a book, of a newspaper; *a titoli cubitali*, in block type ‖ *a* — *di favore, premio, prestito*, as a favour, prize, loan; *a* — *gratuito*, free of charge (*o* as a present) **2.** (*onorifico, nobiliare, accademico*) title: *titoli ereditari, acquisiti*, hereditary acquired titles; *gli fu conferito il* — *di cavaliere*, a Knighthood was conferred on him (*o* he was knighted); *non ha alcun* — *accademico*, he has no academic title ‖ *gli appioppò dei brutti titoli*, (*fam.*) he called him names **3.** (*diritto*) title, right, claim; (*ragione*) reason: *a che* — *fai ciò?*, by what right are you doing this?; *non ho alcun* — *per questo posto, questa proprietà*, I have no title (*o* claim) to this post, this property; *questo è un altro* — *per esserci grati*, this is another reason for us to be thankful to you **4.** (*qualifica*) qualification: *quali sono i suoi titoli?*, what are his qualifications? **5.** (*documento*) document: *elenco dei titoli*, list of documents **6.** (*pubblicazione presentata ai concorsi accademici*) publication **7.** (*comm.*) security; (*obbligazione*) bond, security; (*azione*) stock, share: — *al portatore*, stock to bearer; — *di credito*, instrument of credit; — *di stato*, state bond (*o* government security); — *nominativo*, registered (*o* inscribed) stock; — *privilegiato*, preferred stock; *titoli sicuri*, gilt-edged securities **8.** (*chim.*) titre, strength **9.** (*grado di purezza di un tessuto*) count.

titolóne, *s.m.* (*tip.*) banner, banner head, banner line.

Titòne, *no.pr.m.* (*mit.*) Tithonus.

Tìtta, *no.pr.m.* *dim.* di **Battìsta.**

titubànte, *ag.* hesitant, hesitating, irresolute, faltering: *egli è ancora* —, he is still hesitating; *parlò con voce* —, he spoke in a faltering voice.

titubànza, *s.f.* hesitancy, irresoluteness, irresolution, perplexity.

titubàre, *v.i.* to hesitate, to falter, to waver.

tixotropía, *s.f.* (*fis.*) thixotropy.

tixotròpico, *ag.* (*fis.*) thixotropic.

tizianésco, *ag.* **1.** (*pitt.*) Titianesque **2.** (*di capelli*) titian, reddish-yellow.

Tiziàno, *no.pr.m.* (*st. pitt.*) Titian.

tízio, *s.m.* fellow: *c'era un — che avevo già incontrato,* there was a fellow I had already met ‖ *Tizio Caio e Sempronio,* Tom, Dick and Harry.

tízzo, tizzóne, *s.m.* brand, fire-brand; ember.

to', *inter.* (*prendi*) take it; (*guarda*) look at that: *—, è venuto anche lui,* look here, he has come too; *—, metti il libro a posto,* take this book and put it back in its place.

Tobìa, *no.pr.m.* Tobias, Tobiah ‖ *dim.* Toby.

tobòga, *s.m.* (*spor.*) toboggan.

toccàbile, *ag.* touchable.

toccaménto, *s.m.* touching.

toccànte, *ag.* touching.

toccàre, *v.t.* **1.** to touch; (*tastare*) to finger; (*maneggiare*) to handle: *egli toccò le corde dell'arpa,* he touched the strings of the harp; *lo toccò con la mano,* he touched it with his hand; *non —!,* don't touch!; *— il fondo,* to touch the bottom (anche *fig.*); *— la frutta,* to finger the fruit: *si prega di non — la frutta,* please do not handle the fruit; *— la mano,* (*stringerla*) to shake hands; *— il polso di qlcu.,* to take (o to feel) s.o.'s pulse; *fig.* (*sondarne le intenzioni*) to sound s.o. ‖ *chi tocca i fili muore!,* danger of death! ‖ *Dio me l'ha data, guai a chi me la tocca!,* this was given to me by God, and Heaven help who touches it! ‖ *egli vuole sempre — con mano quel che gli si dice,* he always wants to have proof of what he is told about; *ti farò — con mano l'errore delle tue affermazioni,* I shall make you realize how wrong your statements are ‖ *tocca ferro!,* touch wood! ‖ *— l'avversario,* (*scherma*) to touch one's opponent ‖ *— i bicchieri,* (*brindare*) to clink (o to touch) glasses ‖ *— cibo,* to touch food: *egli non tocca cibo, vino da cinque giorni,* he has not been touching food, wine for five days ‖ *guardare e non — è una cosa da imparare,* it is difficult to keep one's hands off sthg. ‖ *chi tocca la pece s'imbratta,* touch pitch and you will be defiled **2.** (*urtare, colpire*) to strike, to hit: *— nel segno,* to hit the mark (anche *fig.*); *— uno scoglio,* to strike a reef **3.** (*ferire*) to hurt, to touch: *guai a chi le tocca i figli!,* there is trouble in store for anyone who touches (o lays a finger on) her children!; *ho toccato il suo orgoglio,* I have touched his pride; *non bisogna toccarlo nei suoi sentimenti religiosi,* we must not hurt his religious feelings; *il suo sarcasmo non mi tocca,* his sarcasm does not touch me; *— qlcu. sul vivo,* to touch s.o. to the quick (o on a tender spot) **4.** (*commuovere*) to touch; to move: *quelle parole mi toccarono il cuore,* those words touched my heart; *la sua storia mi toccò profondamente,* his story touched (o moved) me deeply **5.** (*suonare*) to play: *— l'organo,* to play the organ ‖ *non devi — questo tasto,* you must not harp on that string **6.** (*raggiungere, arrivare a*) to reach; to touch: *era tanto alto che toccava il soffitto,* he was so tall that he could touch the ceiling; *la sua gonna toccava terra,* her skirt swept the ground; *le montagne sembrano — il cielo,* the mountains seem to touch the sky; *quella signora toccherà i quaranta anni,* that lady is fortyish; *— la meta,* to reach one's goal (anche *fig.*); *— terra,* to touch land ‖ *— il cielo con un dito, fig.* to be in the seventh heaven **7.** (*fare scalo a*) to call at (a place); to touch: *la nave tocca Genova e Napoli,* the ship calls at Genoa and Naples **8.** (*argomento, ecc.*) to touch on (sthg.): *toccò appena la questione,* he hardly touched on the question **9.** (*busse*): *ne toccò duramente,* (*fam.*) he got a good hiding ‖ *v.i.* **1.** (*capitare, accadere*) to fall; to happen: *la maggior parte del lavoro toccò a me,* most of the work fell on me; *mi toccò una grave responsabilità,* a serious responsibility fell to me; *sono spia-*

cente per ciò che è toccato a quel poveretto, I am sorry for what has happened to that poor fellow; *tocca sempre pagare a me,* I am always the one to pay ‖ *a chi tocca, tocca,* (*fam.*) if it is your turn, then you are in for it ‖ *— in sorte a qlcu.,* to fall to s.o.'s lot **2.** (*spettare, competere*) to concern; to fall: *a me toccarono due premi,* two prizes fell to me; *mi toccherebbe una vacanza,* I should have a right to a holiday; *mi toccò solo un pezzetto di torta,* I only got a bit of cake; *non gli toccò quasi nulla,* he hardly got anything; *questo non tocca a me,* that does not concern me; *tocca a te andare, fare le carte,* it is your turn to go, to shuffle the cards; *tocca a voi aiutarlo,* it is your duty (o it is up to you) to help him ‖ *a chi tocca?,* whose turn is it?; *tocca a te,* it is your turn; (*a dama, a scacchi*) it is your move ‖ *— in eredità,* to fall to s.o.'s share ‖ **toccàrsi,** *v.r.* to touch: *egli si toccò la mano,* he touched his hand ‖ *v.r. reciproco,* to touch each other (one another): *le due case si toccano,* the two houses touch each other *gli estremi si toccano, prov.* extremes meet.

toccasàna, *s.m.* cure-all, panacea.

toccàta, *s.f.* **1.** touch; touching **2.** (*mus.*) toccata (*pl.* toccate).

toccàto, *ag.* (*pazzoide*) touched.

tócco[1], *ag.* **1.** moved: *— dall'ira,* moved with anger **2.** (*pazzoide*) touched: *quell'uomo è un po' —,* that man is slightly touched ‖ *s.m.* **1.** touch: *il minimo — può romperlo,* the slightest touch may break it; *sentii un — sulle spalle,* I felt a touch on my shoulders **2.** (*di pianista, pittore*) touch: *egli ha un bellissimo — al piano,* he has a very fine touch on the piano; *il quadro ha bisogno di alcuni tocchi di rifinitura qua e là,* the painting needs a few finishing touches here and there; *sa fare un quadro con solo alcuni tocchi di pennello,* he can make a painting with only a few strokes of the brush; *si vede il — di un grande artista,* you can see the touch of a great artist **3.** (*colpo alla porta*) knock: *sentimmo tre tocchi alla porta,* we heard three knocks on the door **4.** (*rintocco di campana*) stroke; (*a morto*) toll, tolling, knell, knelling ‖ *al —,* at one o'clock.

tócco[2], *s.m.* piece: *un bel — di carne,* a nice piece of meat ‖ *un bel — di ragazza,* (*gergo*) a fine strapping girl.

tócco[3], *s.m.* (*berretta*) toque.

tòco, *s.m.* (*ornit.*) toco.

tocología, *s.f.* (*med.*) tocology, tokology.

tòdo, *s.m.* (*ornit.*) tody.

tòfi, *s.m.pl.* (*med.*) tophi.

tòga, *s.f.* **1.** toga (*pl.* togas, togae): *— candida, pretesta, virile,* toga candida, praetexta, virilis **2.** (*di magistrato, professore universitario*) gown.

togàto, *ag.* **1.** togaed, togated ‖ *commedia togata* (*st. teat.*) comoedia togata **2.** (*di magistrato, professore universitario*) wearing a gown **3.** *fig.* (*magniloquente*) bombastic: *stile —,* bombastic style.

tògliere, *v.t.* **1.** to take away, to take off; to remove; to take: *cerca di — questa macchia,* try to remove this stain; *egli non tolse mai gli occhi dal libro,* he never took his eyes off his book; *egli tolse un fiore dal mazzo,* he took a flower from the bunch; *la tolse in moglie,* he took her to wife; *questa frase è tolta da una poesia,* this sentence is taken from a poem; *questo non è il suo posto, toglilo di qui!,* this is not its place, take it away from here!; *togli il cappotto al bambino,* take off the child's coat; *togli le mani di tasca,* take your hands out of your pockets; *togli il vaso dal tavolo,* remove the vase from the table; *— un dubbio dalla mente di qlcu.,* to remove a doubt from s.o.'s mind; *— un'idea dalla testa a qlcu.,* to get an idea out of s.o.'s head ‖ *dovremmo — di mezzo queste difficoltà,* we should do away with these difficulties; *lo vogliono — di mezzo perchè è troppo pigro,* they want to get rid of him because he is too lazy ‖ *è onesto, ma ciò non toglie che sia uno stupido,* he is honest but this does prevent him from being a fool ‖ — *il saluto a qlcu.*, (*fam.*) to cut s.o. **2.** (*detrarre*) to take, to take off: *togli dieci lire dal totale*, take off ten liras from the total; *togli quattro da dieci*, take four from ten **3.** (*rubare*) to steal (anche *fig.*): — *qualche ora allo studio*, to steal a few hours from one's studies **4.** (*liberare da*) to free, to relieve, to rescue: *ciò mi toglie ogni responsabilità*, it relieves me of all responsibility; *mi ha tolto da un grave pericolo*, he has rescued me from a serious danger; *mi hai tolto un gran peso*, you have relieved me of a great burden; — *un'ipoteca da una proprietà*, to free a property from mortgage; — *qlcu. alla morte, dalla povertà*, to rescue s.o. from death, from poverty ‖ **tògliersi**, *v.r.* to get away, to get out: *togliti!*, get off! (*o* take yourself off! *o* make yourself scarce!); *togliti da quella seggiola!*, get off that chair!; *togliti dai piedi!*, (*fam.*) get out of the way!; — *dagli impicci*, to get out of trouble; — *i guanti*, to take off one's gloves; — *un'idea dalla testa*, to put an idea out of one's head; — *la soddisfazione di*, to give oneself the satisfaction of ‖ — *la vita*, to commit suicide (*o* to kill oneself).

toh, *V.* to'.

toilette, *s.f.* **1.** (*l'acconciarsi*) toilet: *perde molto tempo per la sua* —, she spends a lot of time on her toilet; *fare* —, to get dressed (*o* to make one's toilet) **2.** (*mobile*) dressing-table, toilet-table **3.** (*vestito*) toilette, toilet: *le piace mettere in mostra le sue toilettes*, she likes to display her toilettes (*o* toilets) **4.** (*gabinetto*) toilet-room, lavatory; (*amer.*) toilet.

tokài, *s.m.* (*vino ungherese*) Tokay.

Tòkio, *no.pr.f.* (*geog.*) Tokyo.

tòla, *s.f.* (*dial.*) (*latta*) tin ‖ *faccia di* —, cheek (*o* brazen face): *che (faccia di)* —*!*, what a cheek!.

tòlda, *s.f.* (*mar.*) deck.

tolemàico, *ag.* Ptolemaic ‖ *sistema* —, Ptolemaic system.

tolétta, *V.* toilette.

tolleràbile, *ag.* tolerable, endurable.

tollerabilménte, *av.* **1.** tolerably **2.** (*discretamente*) fairly.

tolle, rànte, *ag.* **1.** tolerant; (*indulgente*) indulgent **2.** (*che sopporta*) enduring.

tollerànza, *s.f.* **1.** tolerance; (*indulgenza*) indulgence: *il nostro governo ha sempre dato prova di grande* —, our government has always shown great tolerance ‖ *casa di* —, brothel **2.** (*capacità di sopportare il male*) endurance **3.** (*comm.*) allowance: — *sul peso*, allowance on weight.

tolleràre, *v.t.* to tolerate, to bear, to endure, to suffer, to put up with (sthg.): *ho tollerato la tua insolenza per un'ora*, I have put up with your insolence for an hour; *non posso* — *quell'uomo*, I can't bear (*o* put up with) that man; *non tollero che egli ti tratti così*, I can't tolerate (*o* suffer) his treating you like that; *non tollero di essere disturbato*, I cannot bear to be disturbed; — *un male, un insulto*, to endure (*o* to bear) a pain, an insult ‖ *non tollera le uova*, eggs don't agree with him.

tolomàico, *ag.* Ptolemaic.

Tolomèo, *no.pr.m.* (*st.*) Ptolemy.

Tolóne, *no.pr.f.* (*geog.*) Toulon.

Tolósa, *no.pr.f.* (*geog.*) Toulouse.

tolstoiàno, *ag.s.m.* Tolstoyan, Tolstoyist.

tolstoìsmo, *s.m.* Tolstoyism.

toltèchi, *s.m.pl.* Toltecs.

tòlto, *ag.* taken off ‖ *s.m.*: *il mal* —, ill-gotten gains.

tolú, *s.m.* (*farm.*) tolu.

toluène, *s.* (*chim.*) toluene.

toluòlo, *s.m.* (*chim.*) toluol.

tomàia, *s.f.*, **tomàio**, *s.m.* upper, vamp.

Tomàso, *V.* Tommàso.

tómba, *s.f.* grave, tomb: — *di famiglia*, family vault; *le tombe romane lungo la via Appia*, the Roman tombs along the Appian Way ‖ *dalla culla alla* —, from the cradle to the grave ‖ *segreto come una* —,

as close as a grave ‖ *una voce di* —, a sepulchral voice *ciò lo farebbe rivoltare nella* —, it's enough to make him turn in his grave ‖ *avere un piede nella* —, to have one foot in the grave ‖ *discendere nella* —, to go down into the tomb.

tombàcco, *s.m.* (*metal.*) tombac, tomback.

tombàle, *ag.* grave (*attributivo*), tomb (*attributivo*): *pietra* —, grave-stone (*o* tomb-stone).

tombíno, *s.m.* manhole, gully-hole.

tómbola, *s.f.* **1.** (*giuoco*) tombola; (*amer.*) bingo: *giocare a* —, to play tombola **2.** (*caduta*) tumble, fall: *fare una* —, to tumble down (*o* to fall): *egli fece una brutta* —, he had a nasty tumble.

tombolàre, *v.i.* to tumble down; (*col capo all'ingiù*) to fall headlong.

tombolàta, *V.* tómbola **2.**

tómbolo[1], *s.m.* **1.** (*cuscino per fare merletti*) lace pillow: *merletto a* —, pillow lace **2.** *V.* tómbola **2.**

tómbolo[2], *s.m.* (*persona grassoccia*) fatty.

tombolóne, *V.* tómbola **2.**

tombolòtto, *s.m.* (*persona grassoccia*) fatty.

tomìsmo, *s.m.* (*fil.*) Thomism.

tomìsta, *s.m.* (*fil.*) Thomist.

tomìstico, *ag.* (*fil.*) Thomistic(al).

Tommàso, *no.pr.m.* Thomas ‖ *fare come San* —, to be a doubting Thomas ‖ *dim.* Tom, Tommy.

tòmo, *s.m.* **1.** tome, volume **2.** (*tipo buffo*): *che bel* —*!*, (*fam.*) what a funny chap!.

tònaca, *s.f.* (*di frate*) frock, cowl; (*di prete*) soutane ‖ *gettare la* — (*alle ortiche*), to give up the frock ‖ *vestire la* —, to become a friar; (*di monaca*) to take the veil.

tonàle, *ag.* tonal.

tonalità, *s.f.* (*di suoni, colori*) tonality.

tonànte, *ag.* thundering: *dare ordini con voce* —, to thunder out an order ‖ *Giove Tonante*, the Thunderer.

tonàre, *v.i.* **1.** *imp.* to thunder: *aveva paura perchè tonava*, he was scared because it was thundering **2.** *fig.* (*di cannone, ecc.*) to sound like thunder; to thunder, to boom: (*parlare con veemenza*) to thunder out: *il cannone tuonò*, the cannon thundered; — *contro qlcu.*, to thunder out against s.o.

tónchio, *s.m.* (*entom.*) weevil.

tonchióso, *ag.* (*di grano, ecc.*) weevilled, weevilly.

tondàre, *v.t.* to round (off), to make round.

tondeggiaménto, *s.m.* **1.** (*rotondità*) roundness **2.** (*il tondeggiare*) rounding.

tondeggiànte, *ag.* roundish.

tondeggiàre, *v.i.* to be roundish ‖ *v.t.* to round (off), to make round.

tondèllo, *s.m.* **1.** round: — *di manzo*, (*cuc.*) round of beef **2.** (*rocchio di paglia per chiudere ql.co.*) stopper.

tóndere, *v.t.* (*letter.*) **1.** (*tosare*) to shear **2.** (*potare*) to lop, to prune; to trim.

tondétto, *ag.* roundish.

tondézza, *s.f.* roundness.

tondíno, *s.m.* **1.** (*piattino*) saucer **2.** (*arch.*) astragal **3.** (*di ferro*) iron rod.

tóndo, *ag.* **1.** round: *faccia tonda*, round face; *guance tonde*, round cheeks; *piatto* —, round plate ‖ *cifra tonda*, round figure ‖ *rimasi là due ore tonde*, I remained there two full hours ‖ *parlare chiaro e* —, to speak openly (*o* clearly *o* frankly): *gli dissi chiaro e* — *quello che pensavo*, I told him what I thought very clearly (*o* I told him my mind) **2.** (*tip.*) Roman ‖ *s.m.* **1.** round **2.** (*cerchio*) circle, ring: *ballare in* —, to dance in a circle (*o* in a ring) **3.** (*piatto*) plate **4.** (*pitt. scult.*) tondo (*pl.* tondi **5.** (*tip.*) Roman type.

tónfano, *s.m.* (*pop.*) pot-hole.

tonfàre, *v.i.* to splash.

tónfo, *s.m.* splash.

tònica, *s.f.* (*mus.*) tonic, key-note.

tonicità, *s.f.* tonicity.

tònico, *ag.* **1.** (*mus. med.*) tonic **2.** *accento* —, (*gram.*) tonic accent ‖ *s.m.* (*med. farm.*) tonic.

tonificànte, *ag.s.m.* tonic: *aria* —, bracing air.

tonificàre, *v.t.* to tone up, to brace, to invigorate.

Tonìno, Tònio, *no.pr.m. dim.* di **Antònio.**

tonnàra, *s.f.* 1. (*reti*) tunny-fishing nets (*pl.*) 2. (*luogo ove si pesca il tonno*) tunny-fishing grounds (*pl.*).

tonnaròtto, *s.m.* tunny fisherman (*pl.* tunny fishermen).

tonnàto, *ag.* (*cuc.*) with tunny sauce, in tunny sauce.

tonneggiàre, *v.t.* (*mar.*) to warp, to tow.

tonnéggio, *s.m.* (*mar.*) 1. (*il tonneggiare*) warping, towing 2. (*cavo da tonneggio*) warp, tow-line, tow-rope.

tonnellàggio, *s.m.* (*mar.*) tonnage.

tonnellàta, *s.f.* (*metrica*) (metric) ton (*misura di peso* = 2,204.6 lb.); (*in Gran Bretagna*) (long *o* gross *o* shipper's) ton (= kg. 1.016); (*negli Stati Uniti, nel Canada, in Sud-Africa*) (short) ton (= kg. 907,2).

tonnìna, *s.f.* pickled tunny-back.

tónno, *s.m.* (*ittiol.*) tunny; (*amer.*) tuna, tuna fish: *pesca del* —, tunny-fishing.

tòno, *s.m.* 1. tone: — *alto, basso, dolce, aspro,* high, low, sweet, harsh tone; *il* — *di una scuola,* the tone of a school; — *di voce,* tone of voice; *in* — *di supplica,* in an imploring tone; *in* — *scherzoso,* in a joking tone; *parlava con* — *arrabbiato, conciliativo,* he was speaking in an angry, a conciliatory tone; *la sua presenza dava* — *al ricevimento,* his presence gave the tone to the party; *cambiare* —, to change one's tone; *dare un* — *alla conversazione* ‖ to give the tone to (*o* to steer) the conversation ‖ *darsi* —, to give oneself airs ‖ *rispondere a* —, to answer to the point 2. (*mus.*) tone; key: *intervallo di due toni,* two-tone interval; — *maggiore, minore,* major, minor key 3. (*accordo, armonia*) tune: *quello che fa non è in* — *coi suoi principi,* what he does is not in keeping with his principles; *questi colori non sono in* —, these colours do not match; *dare il* — *a uno strumento,* to tune an instrument; *essere in* —, *fuori* —, (*mus.*) to be in, out of tune (anche *fig.*).

tonometría, *s.f.* (*fis. med.*) tonometry.

tonòmetro, *s.m.* (*fis. med.*) tonometer.

tonsílla, *s.f.* (*anat.*) tonsil.

tonsillàre, *ag.* (*anat.*) tonsillar.

tonsillectomía, *s.f.* (*chir.*) tonsillectomy.

tonsillíte, *s.f.* (*patol.*) tonsillitis.

tonsúra, *s.f.* (*eccl.*) tonsure.

tonsuràre, *v.t.* (*eccl.*) to tonsure.

tontína, *s.f.* (*assicurazioni*) tontine.

tónto, *ag.* dull, slow, dense, stupid ‖ *s.m.* dunce, simpleton.

topàia, *s.f.* 1. rats' nest 2. *fig.* hovel.

topàto, *ag.* mouse-coloured.

topàzio, *s.m.* (*min.*) topaz.

topéseo, *ag.* mousy.

topiària, *s.f.* topiary.

tòpica, *s.f.* 1. (*ret.*) topic 2. *fare una* —, *fig.* to drop a brick (*o* to make a blunder).

tòpico, *ag.* topical.

topinambùr(o), *s.m.* (*bot.*) Jerusalem artichoke.

topíno, *ag.* (*di colore*) mousy ‖ *s.m.* mouslet.

tòpo, *s.m.* mouse (*pl.* mice); (*ratto*) rat: — *acquaiolo,* water-rat; — *campagnolo,* harvest-mouse (*o* field-mouse); — *di chiavica,* brown (*o* Norway) rat; — *muschiato,* musk-rat ‖ — *d'albergo, fig.* hotel thief ‖ — *di biblioteca, fig.* bookworm ‖ *grigio* —, mouse-colour ‖ *fare la fine del* —, *essere presi come topi in trappola,* to be caught like a rat in a trap.

topografía, *s.f.* topography.

topograficaménte, *av.* topographically.

topogràfico, *ag.* topographic(al).

topògrafo, *s.m.* topographer.

Topolína, *no.pr.f.* (*personaggio di Walt Disney*) Minnie.

topolíno[1], *s.m.* 1. (*piccolo topo*) small mouse (*pl.* small mice) 2. (*aut.*) "topolino" (baby car).

Topolíno[2], *no.pr.m.* (*personaggio di Walt Disney*) Mickey Mouse.

toponimía, *s.f.* toponymy.

topònimo, *s.m.* place-name.

toponomàstica, *s.f.* toponymy.

toporàgno, *s.m.* (*zool.*) shrew-mouse (*pl.* shrew-mice).

tòppa[1], *s.f.* (*rappezzo*) patch: — *a caldo,* (*per camera d'aria*) heat patch; *mettere una* —, to patch up (anche *fig.*).

tòppa,[2] *s.f.* 1. (*serratura*) lock 2. (*buco della serratura*) keyhole.

toppàre, *v.t.* (*rar.*) to patch.

toppè, *s.m.* toupet.

tòppo, *s.m.* stump.

toppóne, *s.m.* 1. draw-sheet; (*nel lettino di un bimbo*) child's clout 2. (*calzoleria*) stiffening tip.

toràce, *s.m.* (*anat.*) thorax (*pl.* thoraces, thoraxes).

toracèntesi, *s.f.* (*chir.*) thoracentesis.

toràcico, *ag.* (*anat.*) thoracic.

toracoplàstica, *s.f.* (*chir.*) thoracoplasty.

toracotomía, *s.f.* (*chir.*) thoracothomy.

tórba, *s.f.* peat.

torbidaménte, *av.* turbidly; gloomily; confusedly.

torbidézza, torbidità, *s.f.* turbidity, turbidness; gloominess; confusedness; cloudiness.

tórbido, *ag.* 1. (*non limpido*) turbid, cloudy, muddy: *un fiume* —, a turbid (*o* muddy) river; *liquido* —, cloudy liquid; *pensieri torbidi,* turbid thoughts 2. (*fosco*) gloomy: *un'espressione torbida,* a gloomy expression 3. (*inquieto, turbato*) troubled: *tempi torbidi,* troubled times ‖ *s.m.* 1. (*disordine pubblico*) disorder, disturbance, trouble: *ci furono dei torbidi,* there was some disorder 2. (*situazione, circostanza equivoca*): *c'è del* — *qui,* there is something fishy here; *pescare nel* —, to fish in troubled waters.

torbièra, *s.f.* peat-bog, peat-moss.

tórbo, (*dial.*) per **tórbido.**

torbóso, *ag.* peaty.

tòrcere, *v.t.* 1. to wring: — *il collo a qlcu.,* to wring s.o.'s neck; — *panni bagnati,* to wring wet clothes ‖ *non gli ho torto un capello,* I haven't hurt him in the least 2. (*storcere*): — *la bocca, il viso,* to make a wry mouth, face; — *il naso,* to turn up one's nose; — *gli occhi,* to roll one's eyes 3. (*attorcigliare*) to twist: — *fili, corde,* to twist threads, strings; — *lana, cotone,* to twist wool, cotton; — *seta,* to twist (*o* to throw) silk ‖ *quel ragazzo mi diede del filo da* —, that boy gave me a lot of trouble; *questo lavoro mi dà del filo da* —, this work is a hard nut to crack 4. (*curvare*) to bend: — *un ramo, un'asta,* to bend a branch, a bar ‖ **tòrcersi,** *v.r.* to twist, to writhe: *si torceva dal dolore,* he was twisting about (*o* writhing) in pain; *si torceva dal ridere,* he was splitting his sides with laughter; *si torse una caviglia,* he twisted (*o* sprained) his ankle.

torchiàre, *v.t.* (*agr.*) to press.

torchiatúra, *s.f.* (*agr.*) pressing.

torchiètto, *s.m.* (*tip.*) printing frame.

tòrchio, *s.m.* press: — *calcografico,* (*tip.*) copperplate; — *da uva,* wine-press; — *idraulico,* (*agr. ind.*) hydraulic press; — *tipografico,* (printing-)press; — *tirabozze,* (*tip.*) proof press; *essere sotto i torchi,* (*tip.*) to be in the press ‖ *far gemere i torchi,* to get sthg. printed.

tòrcia, *s.f.* 1. torch 2. (*candela*) candle; taper.

torcibudèllo, *s.m.* (*fam.*) volvulus.

torcicòllo, *s.m.* 1. stiff neck 2. (*ornit.*) wryneck 3. *fig.* hypocrite; bigot.

torcièra, *V.* **torcière** 1.

torcière, *s.m.* 1. (*grande candeliere*) candelabrum (*pl.* candelabra) 2. (*portatore di torcia*) torch-bearer.

torciménto, *s.m.* 1. (*il torcere*) twisting; wringing 2. (*torsione*) twist; wring.

torcinàso, *s.m.* (*di cavalli*) barnacles (*pl.*).

torcióne, *s.m.* wiper, dish-cloth.

torcitóio, *s.m.* (*ind. della seta*) throwing machine.

torcitóre, *s.m.* twister; (*ind. della seta*) throwster.

torcitríce, *s.f.* 1. twister; (*ind. della seta*) throwster 2. (*mec.*) jack.

torcitúra, *s.f.* twisting, twist; (*ind. della seta*) throwing ‖ — *supplementare,* (*ind. cordame*) hardening

torcolière, *s.m.* (*tip.*) pressman (*pl.* pressmen).

tordèlla, *s.f.* (*ornit.*) missel, missel bird, missel thrush.

tórdo, *s.m.* **1.** (*ornit.*) thrush **2.** (*fig. rar.*) ninny, simpleton.

torèllo, *s.m.* **1.** young bull **2.** (*mar.*) garboard. garboard strake.

torèo, *s.m.* bullfight.

torèro, *s.m.* torero (*pl.* toreros), bullfighter.

torèutica, *s.f.* (*arte di cesellare*) toreutics.

torína, *s.f.* (*chim.*) thoria.

torinése, *ag.* Torinese ‖ *s.c.* Torinese (*invariato al pl.*).

Toríno, *no.pr.f.* (*geog.*) Turin.

tòrio, *s.m.* (*min.*) thorium.

toríte, *s.f.* (*min.*) thorite.

tórlo, *V.* **tuórlo.**

tórma, *s.f.* **1.** (*di animali*) herd **2.** (*di persone*) crowd, swarm, throng: *a torme,* in swarms.

tormalína, *s.f.* (*min.*) tourmalin(e): *— nera,* schorl.

torménta, *s.f.* snow-storm, blizzard: *una — politica,* *fig.* a political storm.

tormentàre, *v.t.* to torment, to torture; (*molestare*) to annoy, to worry, to vex, to aggravate, to fret: *è tormentato dalla tosse,* he is racked with a cough; *un forte mal di denti lo tormenta da due giorni,* a bad toothache has been tormenting him for two days; *mi tormenta sempre con un mucchio di domande,* he always worries (*o* annoys *o* torments) me with a lot of questions; *non — quel cane,* don't vex that dog ‖ **tormentàrsi,** *v.r.* to fret, to torment oneself, to worry, to be worried: *non tormentarti pensando a pericoli inesistenti,* don't fret by thinking of unexisting dangers.

tormentatívo, *ag.* tormentative.

tormentàto, *ag.* **1.** tormented, tortured: *— dal rimorso,* tortured by remorse **2.** (*inquieto*) restless: *anima tormentata,* restless soul.

tormentatóre, *s.m.* tormentor.

tormentatríce, *s.f.* tormentress.

tormentílla, *s.f.* (*bot.*) tormentil, tormentilla.

torménto, *s.m.* torment, torture: *i tormenti dei dannati,* the torments (*o* tortures) of the damned; *che — vederlo in quella condizione!,* what a torture to see him in that condition!; *quel ragazzo è il mio —,* that boy is the torment of my life; *questo mal di testa è un —,* this headache is a torment (*o* a torture).

tormentosaménte, *av.* tormentingly; (*con molestia*) vexingly.

tormentóso, *ag.* tormenting; (*molesto*) vexing, worrying.

tòrmini, *s.m.pl.* (*med.*) tormina.

tornacónto, *s.m.* profit, advantage, benefit: *il — non è molto alto,* the profit is not very high; *non gli venne nessun —,* it profited him nothing; *non lo faccio perchè non c'è —,* I don't do it because it doesn't pay; *fare ql.co. per —,* to do sthg. for profit.

tornàdo, *s.m.* tornado (*pl.* tornadoes).

tornànte, *ag.* returning ‖ *s.m.* bend, turning: *il — della strada,* the bend of the road.

tornàre, *v.i.* **1.** to return; (*andare di nuovo*) to go back; (*venire di nuovo*) to come back: *quando tornerai in America?,* when will you go back to America?; *torna indietro!,* come back!; *torna presto!,* come back soon!; *tornava da scuola,* he was coming back from school; *tornò dai suoi genitori,* he went back to his parents; *fare segno a qlcu. di —,* to wave (*o* to beckon) s.o. back; *— a casa,* to return (*o* to go *o* to come) home: *egli torna sempre a casa a tarda ora,* he always comes home late; *— alla mente,* to come back to one's mind: *il suo nome non mi torna alla mente,* I do not recall his name; *far — ql.co. alla mente di qlcu.,* to recall sthg. to s.o. (*o* to make s.o. remember sthg.); *— al mondo,* to return (*o* to come back) to the world; *— al punto di partenza,* to come full circle (*o* to come back where one started); *— in patria,* to go back home; *— in tutta fretta,* to hasten back; *— sano e salvo,* to return safe and sound; *— sui propri passi,* to turn back (*o* to retrace one's steps *o* to turn back on one's own tracks) ‖ *ho promesso di aiutarlo e non tornerò indietro,* I have promised to help him and I'll not draw back ‖ *lozione che fa — i capelli,* hair restorer ‖ *mi ritornano le forze,* I am recovering my strength ‖ *il passato non torna,* time that is passed will never come again ‖ *questo si chiama torna...,* (*fam.*) let me have this back... ‖ *si torna alle gonne corte,* we are going back to short skirts ‖ *torniamo a noi, a bomba,* let's go back to our subject ‖ *— a galla,* *fig.* to bob (*o* to come) up again ‖ *— a gola,* (*di cibi*) to repeat ‖ *— alla carica,* *fig.* to make a fresh attempt ‖ *— su una decisione,* to go back on a decision ‖ *— sul passato,* to go back (*o* to revert) to the past **2.** (*ridiventare*): *questa gonna è tornata nuova,* this skirt has come back like new; *— sano,* to recover one's health **3.** (*volgersi*) to turn: *il suo sorriso tornò in pianto,* his smile turned to tears **4.** (*riuscire, risultare*): *ciò mi torna nuovo,* this is new to me; *ciò torna a tuo credito,* this redounds to your credit; *non lo faccio perchè non mi torna conto,* I don't do it because it is not worth while (*o* it does not pay); *— comodo a qlcu.,* to be convenient for s.o.: *non andai perchè non mi tornava comodo,* I did not go because it was not convenient for me **5.** (*riuscire giusto, esatto*): *il conto torna,* the account is correct: *vedrai che il conto torna,* you'll see that things will work out; *questa somma non torna,* this sum is not correct; *vestito che torna,* well-fitting dress: *quel vestito non ti torna,* that dress does not fit you.

tornasóle, *s.m.* (*chim.*) litmus: *cartina di —,* litmus paper.

tornàta, *s.f.* **1.** (*ritorno*) return **2.** (*seduta*) session.

tornàto, *ag.* returned.

torneaménto, *s.m.* tournament, tourney, jousting.

torneàre, *v.i.* **1.** to tourney, to joust **2.** (*girare intorno*) to wheel round.

torneatóre, *s.m.* jouster, tourneyer.

tornèllo, *s.m.* (*strum. artig.*) (weaver's) warp-beam.

tornèo, *s.m.* tournament, tourney, jousting.

tornése, *s.m.* (*moneta antica*) " tornese ".

tornichétto, *s.m.* (*congegno per contare le persone che entrano in un museo, ecc.*) turnstile.

tórnio, *s.m.* (*mec.*) lathe, turning lathe: *— a copiare,* duplicating lathe (*o* copying lathe); *— automatico,* automatic lathe; *— da banco,* bench lathe; *— da legno,* wood-turning lathe; *— frontale,* end (*o* face) lathe; *— motorizzato,* motor-driven lathe; *— verticale,* boring mill.

torníre, *v.t.* **1.** (*mec.*) to turn: *— a spoglia,* to back off (on the lathe) **2.** *fig.* to polish; to shape: *egli tornisce i suoi versi molto bene,* he polishes his lines very well.

torníto, *ag.* **1.** (*mec.*) turned **2.** (*rotondeggiante*) round, rounded; (*ben fatto*) well-shaped **3.** *fig.* polished: *versi ben torniti,* well-polished lines.

tornitóre, *s.m.* turner.

tornitúra, *s.f.* **1.** (*mec.*) turning **2.** (*trucioli*) turnings (*pl.*).

tórno, *s.m.* **1.** *in quel —,* thereabouts: *dieci metri o in quel —,* ten metres or thereabouts; *in quel — di tempo,* at about that time; *egli vive a Brighton o in quel —,* he lives at Brighton or thereabouts **2.** *— —,* all round, round about **3.** *levarsi qlcu. di —,* to get rid of s.o.

tòro[1]**,** *s.m.* bull: *quel ragazzo è forte come un —,* that boy is as strong as a bull ‖ *prendere il — per le corna,* *fig.* to take the bull by the horns ‖ *tagliare la testa al —,* to cut the Gordian knot ‖ *Toro,* (*astr.*) Bull (*o* Taurus).

tòro[2]**,** *s.m.* **1.** (*letto matrimoniale*) wedding bed **2.** (*matrimonio*) marriage.

tòro[3]**,** *s.m.* (*arch. geom.*) torus (*pl.* tori), tore.

torpedinàre, *v.t.* to torpedo.

torpèdine, *s.f.* **1.** (*ittiol.*) torpedo (*pl.* torpedoes), cramp-fish, numb-fish **2.** (*mar. mil.*) (*mina subacquea*) submarine mine; (*siluro*) torpedo (*pl.* torpedoes).

torpedinièra, *s.f.* (*mar. mil.*) torpedo-boat.

torpèdo, *s.f.* (*aut.*) torpedo (*pl.* torpedoes).

torpedóne, *s.m.* (*aut.*) (motor-)coach.

torpidaménte, *av.* **1.** torpidly (anche *fig.*) **2.** (*lentamente*) sluggishly, very slowly.

torpidézza, torpidità, *s.f.* **1.** torpidness, torpidity (anche *fig.*) **2.** (*lentezza*) sluggishness, slowness.

tòrpido, *ag.* **1.** torpid (anche *fig.*) **2.** (*tardo*) sluggish, slow, dull.

torpóre, *s.m.* **1.** torpor (anche *fig.*) **2.** (*lentezza*) sluggishness, slowness, dullness.

torrai(u)òlo, *ag.*: *piccione* —, rock-pigeon.

tórre, *s.f.* **1.** tower: — *campanaria,* bell-tower (*o* belfry); — *merlata,* tower with battlements; — *pendente,* leaning tower ‖ *la Torre di Babele,* the Tower of Babel; *fig.* babel ‖ *la Torre di Londra,* the Tower of London **2.** (*mec.*) tower; (*rad.*) tower: — *di raffreddamento,* (*ind.*) cooling tower; — *di sondaggio,* (*miner.*) derrick; — *di trivellazione,* (*miner.*) derrick; — *primaria,* (*ind. chim.*) primary tower; — *serbatoio,* (*ferr.*) water tower; *gambe della* — *di trivellazione,* (*miner.*) derrick platform **3.** (*mil.*) (*batteria di nave da guerra*) battery: — *di grosso calibro,* main battery **4.** (*aer. mar.*) tower: — *di comando,* conning-tower; — *di controllo,* control tower **5.** (*scacchi*) castle, rook.

torrefàre, *v.t.* to torrefy: — *il caffè,* to roast coffee-beans.

torrefazióne, *s.f.* **1.** torrefaction; (*di caffè*) roasting **2.** (*negozio*) coffee store.

torreggiàre, *v.i.* to tower: *il castello torreggia sopra la vallata,* the castle towers over the valley.

torrènte, *s.m.* torrent, stream; (*flusso, profluvio*) flood: — *di fuoco,* stream of fire; *un* — *di lacrime,* a flood of tears; — *di montagna,* mountain stream (*o* hill-torrent); *un* — *di parole,* a flood (*o* torrent) of words; *torrenti di pioggia,* torrents of rain; *piovere a torrenti,* to rain in torrents (*o* to rain cats and dogs).

torrentízio, *ag.* torrent-like (*attributivo*): *fiume a regime* —, torrent-like river.

torrenziàle, *ag.* torrential: *piogge torrenziali,* torrential rains.

torrétta, *s.f.* **1.** small tower **2.** (*mil. mar.*) turret.

tòrrido, *ag.* torrid; scorching: *clima* —, torrid climate; *zona torrida,* (*geog.*) torrid zone.

torrière, *s.m.* tower-keeper.

torrióne, *s.m.* tower, keep, donjon, dungeon.

torróne, *s.m.* nougat.

torsèllo, *s.m.* **1.** (*cuscinetto per spilli*) pin-cushion **2.** (*cuscinetto che si pone sul capo per trasportar pesi*) pad **3.** (*conio per monete*) minting die.

torsióne, *s.f.* torsion; twisting: *bilancia di* —, torsion-balance; *sollecitazione di* —, (*edil.*) torsional stress.

tórso, *s.m.* **1.** (*di persona*) trunk **2.** (*di statua*) torso (*pl.* torsos) **3.** *V.* **tórsolo.**

tórsolo, *s.m.* (*di verdura*) stump; (*di frutta*) core ‖ *lanciar torsoli a qlcu., prendere qlcu. a torsoli,* to throw bad eggs (*o* rotten tomatoes) at s.o.

tórta, *s.f.* cake; pie; (*crostata*) tart: — *di mele,* apple pie, apple tart; — *di noci,* nut cake; — *di patate,* potato pie; *ho fatto una* —, I have made a cake ‖ *mangiare la* — *in capo a qlcu., superarlo in statura*) to overtop s.o.; (*in valore*) to excel s.o.

tortellini, *s.m.pl.* (*cuc.*) "tortellini" (ringlets of dough filled with seasoned minced meat).

tortèllo, *s.m.* (*cuc.*) **1.** (*fritto*) fritter; (*di pasta frolla*) (jam) tart **2.** *pl.* "tortelli" (sort of ravioli).

tortíccio, *ag.* (*mar.*) cable-laid, hawser-laid ‖ *s.m.* hawser-laid rope.

tortièra, *s.f.* baking-pan, baking-dish, baking-tin.

tortiglióne, *s.m.* twist ‖ *a* —, spirally.

tòrto[1], *ag.* (*curvo*) bent; (*obliquo*) crooked; (*ritorto*) twisted.

tòrto[2], *s.m.* **1.** wrong: *la differenza fra la ragione e il* —, the difference between right and wrong; *ha subito molti torti,* he has suffered many wrongs; *avere* —, to be wrong; *avere* — *marcio,* to be quite (*o* dead) wrong; *dare* — *a qlcu.,* to decide against s.o. (*o* to lay the blame on s.o.); *essere dalla parte del* —, to be in the wrong; *fare un* — *a qlcu.,* to wrong s.o. (*o* to do s.o. wrong) ‖ *a* —, wrongly (*o* wrongfully): *a* — *o a ragione,* rightly or wrongly; *egli fu punito a* —, he was punished wrongfully **2.** (*colpa*) fault: *riconoscere i propri torti,* to acknowledge one's faults.

tórtora, *s.f.* (*ornit.*) turtle-dove.

tortoreggiàre, *v.i.* to coo; (*di innamorati*) to bill and coo.

tortuosaménte, *av.* **1.** tortuously **2.** *fig.* crookedly.

tortuosità, *s.f.* **1.** tortuosity, tortuousness **2.** *fig.* tortuousness; (*slealtà*) crookedness.

tortuóso, *ag.* **1.** tortuous, winding; (*di fiume, strada*) meandering **2.** *fig.* tortuous; (*poco leale*) crooked: *mezzi tortuosi,* crooked means; *ragionamento* —, tortuous argument.

tortúra, *s.f.* torture (anche *fig.*): *strumento di* —, instrument of torture; *mettere qlcu. alla* —, to put s.o. to (the) torture; *stare con lui è una* —, to stay with him is a torture.

torturàre, *v.t.* to torture ‖ **torturàrsi,** *v.r.* to torment oneself, to worry: *è inutile* — *quando non c'è rimedio,* it is no use worrying when there is no remedy; — *il cervello,* to rack (*o* to cudgel) one's brains.

torvaménte, *av.* grimly, sternly, surlily.

tórvo, *ag.* grim, stern, surly: *sguardo* —, grim look.

tosàre, *v.t.* **1.** to shear, to clip: — *pecore,* to shear sheep ‖ *farsi* —, (*scherz.*) to have one's hair cut **2.** (*potare*) to prune **3.** (*monete*) to clip **4.** (*pelare, levar denari a*) to fleece.

tosatóre, *s.m.* shearer.

tosatríce, *s.f.* (*macchinetta per tosare*) clippers (*pl.*); (*per il prato*) lawn-mower.

tosatúra, *s.f.* shearing.

Toscàna, *no.pr.f.* (*geog.*) Tuscany.

toscanaménte, *av.* in the Tuscan way.

toscaneggiàre, *v.i.* (*parlare alla toscana*) to speak like the Tuscans; (*scrivere alla toscana*) to write like the Tuscans.

toscàno, *ag.* Tuscan: *ordine* —, (*arch.*) Tuscan order; *vini toscani,* Tuscan wines ‖ *s.m.* **1.** Tuscan **2.** (*tipo di sigaro*) "Toscano".

tósco[1], *ag.* (*letter.*) Tuscan.

tòsco[2], *s.m.* (*veleno*) poison, toxic, venom.

tosóne, *s.m.* (*vello*) fleece ‖ *l'Ordine del Toson d'Oro,* the Order of the Golden Fleece.

tósse, *s.f.* cough: *una* — *grassa, secca,* a loose, dry cough; *accesso di* —, fit of coughing; *avere la* —, to have a cough.

tossicchiàre, *v.i.* to cough slightly.

tossicità, *s.f.* toxicity.

tòssico, *ag.* toxic, poisonous: *sostanza tossica,* toxic substance ‖ *s.m.* poison, toxic, venom: *amaro come il* —, as bitter as aloes.

tossicologìa, *s.f.* toxicology.

tossicològico, *ag.* toxicological.

tossicòlogo, *s.m.* toxicologist.

tossicomanìa, *s.f.* (*med.*) toxicomania.

tossìna, *s.f.* (*chim. biol.*) toxin.

tossìre, *v.i.* to cough: *tossì per avvertirmi,* he gave a cough to warn me; *tossì tutto il giorno,* he coughed all day through; — *sangue,* to cough up blood.

tostapàne, *s.m.* toaster.

tostàre, *v.t.* to toast; (*caffè*) to roast.

tostàto, *ag.* toasted; (*di caffè*) roast (*attributivo*): *pane* —, toasted bread (*o* toast).

tostatúra, *s.f.* toasting; (*del caffè*) roasting.

tostíno, *s.m.* coffee-roaster.

tòsto[1], *ag.* **1.** (*duro*) hard: *questo pane è —*, this bread is hard **2.** *faccia tosta*, cheek, brazen face, impudence: *che faccia tosta!*, what (a) cheek! **3.** *V.* **tostàto** ‖ *s.m.* toast (*solo sing.*).

tòsto[2], *av.* (*letter.*) (*subito*) **at once**, **immediately**, **promptly**: *sortì —*, he went out at once; *venne —*, he came at once ‖ *ag.* (*arc.*) (*rapido*) quick, speedy ‖ **tòsto che**, *l.cong.* **as soon as**: *— che la vide, si innamorò di lei*, as soon as he saw her, he fell in love with her.

tot, *ag.* so many: *un conto di — lire*, a bill of so many liras.

totàle, *ag.* total, complete, entire, utter, whole; absolute: *una — fiducia*, an absolute trust; *distruzione —*, total destruction; *eclissi —*, total eclipse; *importo —*, total amount; *inabilità —*, total disability ‖ *s.m.* total: *un — di 2500 lire*, a total of 2500 lire ‖ *in —*, in the aggregate (o in all).

totalità, *s.f.* **1.** totality, entirety, whole: *preso nella sua —*, taken as a whole **2.** (*numero complessivo*) mass, whole body: *la — degli impiegati*, the whole body of employees (o all the employees).

totalitàrio, *ag.* **1.** (*totale, assoluto*) total, absolute **2.** (*pol.*) totalitarian: *regime —*, totalitarian regime.

totalitarìsmo, *s.m.* (*pol.*) totalitarianism.

totalizzàre, *v.t.* to totalize; (*spor.*) to score: *— 20 punti*, to score 20 points.

totalizzatóre, *s.m.* **1.** adding machine **2.** (*ippica*) totalisator, pari-mutuel.

totalizzazióne, *s.f.* totalization.

totalménte, *av.* totally, completely, entirely, utterly, wholly; absolutely.

tòtano, *s.m.* (*zool.*) cuttle-fish.

tòtem, *s.m.* totem.

totemìsmo, *s.m.* totemism.

totocàlcio, *s.m.* football pool.

toupet, *V.* **tuppè**.

tour de force, *s.m.* feat of strength.

tournée, *s.f.* tour (*anche teat.*).

tovàglia, *s.f.* **1.** (table-)cloth: *stendere la —*, to lay the cloth **2.** (*eccl.*) altar-cloth.

tovagliolíno, *s.m.* (*per bambini*) bib; (*piccolo tovagliuolo*) small napkin.

tovagliuòlo, *s.m.* napkin.

tòzzo[1], *ag.* squat, stocky, stumpy, thickset, dumpy: *una costruzione tozza*, a squat building; *un uomo —*, a squat (o stocky o thickset) man.

tòzzo[2], *s.m.* piece: *un — di pane*, a crust of bread; *un — di pan fresco*, a piece of fresh bread ‖ *accattare tozzi*, to beg for alms ‖ *comperare, vendere ql.co. per un — di pane*, to buy, to sell sthg. very cheap; *guadagnarsi un — di pane*, to make a living.

tra, *V.* **fra**[1].

trabàcca, *s.f.* hut, shanty, shed.

trabàccolo, *s.m.* (*mar.*) small fishing boat, lugger.

traballaménto, *s.m.* (*barcollamento, vacillamento*) staggering, lurching, reeling, tottering; (*di veicoli*) jolting, jerking, bumping, shaking, tossing.

traballànte, *ag.* (*barcollante, vacillante*) staggering, tottering; (*di veicoli*) shaking, tossing.

traballàre, *v.i.* **1.** (*barcollare, vacillare*) to stagger, to lurch, to reel, to totter; (*di bambini*) to toddle: *entrò, uscì traballando*, he staggered in, out; *quel palo traballa*, that pole is tottering; *gli ubriachi traballano mentre camminano*, drunkards stagger (o lurch) while walking; *procedere traballando*, to stagger (o to totter o to reel) along **2.** (*di veicoli*) to jolt, to jerk, to bump, to shake, to toss: *l'automobile procedeva traballando*, the car was jolting (o jerking o bumping) along.

traballío, *V.* **traballaménto**.

traballóne, *s.m.* **1.** (*di persona*) stagger, lurch: *camminare a tralloni*, to stagger (o to lurch) along **2.** (*di veicoli*) jolt, jerk, bump: *l'automobile procedeva a tralloni*, the car was jolting (o jerking o bumping) along; *il treno si fermò con un —*, the train stopped with a jerk.

trabultùre, *v.i.* (*di veicoli*) to capsize.

trabalzàre, *v.i.* (*di veicoli*) to jolt, to jerk, to bump.

trabalzóne, *s.m.* (*di veicoli*) jolt, jerk, bump.

tràbea, *s.f.* (*toga romana*) trabea (*pl.* trabeae).

trabeàto, *ag.* (*vestito di trabea*) trabeated.

trabeazióne, *s.f.* (*arch.*) trabeation.

trabiccolàio, *s.m.* person who sells or repairs rickety things.

trabíccolo, *s.m.* **1.** (*telaio per scaldaletto*) wooden frame holding bed-warmer **2.** (*mobile sgangherato*) rickety piece of furniture; (*veicolo sgangherato*) ramshackle vehicle.

traboccaménto, *s.m.* overflow, overflowing.

traboccànte, *ag.* overflowing: *— di gioia*, overflowing with joy.

traboccàre, *v.i.* to overflow (with sthg.), to flow over, to brim over: *il fiume è traboccato*, the river has overflowed its banks; *il lago sta per —*, the lake is going to overflow (o to flow over); *il latte è traboccato*, the milk has boiled over; *il mio cuore trabocca di felicità*, my heart is overflowing with happiness; *gli occhi le traboccavano di lacrime*, her eyes were filled with tears; *la pentola trabocca*, the pan is brimming over; *la sua rabbia traboccò*, his anger burst out ‖ *questo fu la goccia che fece — il vaso*, *fig.* this was the last straw.

trabocchétto, *s.m.* pitfall; snare, trap (*anche fig.*): *la sua proposta non è altro che un —*, his proposal is merely a trap; *cadere in un —*, to fall into a trap; *gettare i malfattori nel —*, to push criminals down into the pitfall.

trabocchévole, *ag.* overflowing, superabundant; excessive.

trabocchevolménte, *av.* overflowingly, superabundantly; excessively.

trabócco, *s.m.* **1.** overflow, overflowing **2.** (*st. mil.*) trebuchet, trebucket.

tracagnòtto, *ag.* squat, stocky, thickset, sturdy, dumpy ‖ *s.m.* squat person, dumpy person.

tracannàre, *v.t.* to gulp down: *— un bicchiere di birra*, to gulp down a glass of beer (o to empty a glass of beer at one gulp).

tracannatóre, *s.m.*, **tracannatríce**, *s.f.* gulper.

tracapéllo, *s.m.* (*bot.*) epithyme.

tracapíre, *v.t.i.* to misunderstand.

traceagnòtto, *V.* **tracagnòtto**.

traccheggiàre, *v.t.* (*tenere in sospeso*) to dally with (sthg.) ‖ *v.i.* (*tirare in lungo*) to dally, to temporize.

tracchéggio, *s.m.* dallying.

tràccia, *s.f.* **1.** trace, trail, track; (*di persona*) footsteps (*pl.*); footprints (*pl.*); (*di animale*) spoor; (*segno*) mark: *tracce lasciate da un'automobile, da una belva*, tracks left by a car, by a wild animal; *il leone ferito lasciò tracce di sangue*, the injured lion left a trail of blood; *la polizia non riuscì a trovare — del ladro*, the police could not find any trace of the thief; *le sue dita hanno lasciato una — sul mio libro*, his fingers have left a mark on my book; *il suo viso portava le tracce delle sue tristi esperienze*, his face bore the traces of his sad experiences; *trovarono le tracce di un'antica città*, they found the traces of an ancient town; *un uomo lasciò le sue tracce sulla neve*, a man left his footprints in the snow; *perdere, ritrovare la —*, (*a caccia*) to lose, to pick up the trail; *seguire le tracce di qlcu.*, to follow in s.o.'s tracks (o s.o.'s footsteps) **2.** (*schema, linea generale*) outline, general plan: *la — di una lezione, di un discorso*, the outline of a lecture, of a speech; *la — di un libro*, the general plan of a book; *sulla — seguita da...*, along the lines followed by....

tracciaménto, *s.m.* tracing; (*di strade*) layout: *— di curve di livello*, contouring; *eseguire il —*, (*sul terreno*) to layout.

tracciànte, *ag.* tracing: *proiettile —*, (*mil.*) tracer shell.

tracciàre, *v.t.* **1.** to trace (out), to mark out, to map out, to draw (anche *fig.*); (*discorso, ecc.*) to sketch out: *devi seguire la strada che ti ha tracciato*, you must follow the course he has traced out for you; — *a grandi linee*, to outline; — *un arco*, to describe an arc; — *un campo ricreativo, una strada*, to mark out a play-ground, a road; — *i confini (di una proprietà)*, to trace out the boundaries (of a property); — *una linea*, to draw a line; — *una linea di condotta*, to trace tout) a course of action; — *un modello su una stoffa*, oo trace a pattern on a cloth; — *un itinerario*, to map aut a route; — *il piano di un discorso*, to sketch out (speech; — *il piano di un edificio*, to trace out the plan of a building; — *lo schema di un romanzo, ecc.*, to sketch out a novel, etc. **2.** (*rar.*) (*seguire le tracce di*) to trace: — *un animale*, to trace an animal.

tracciàto, *s.m.* **1.** tracing; layout: *il — di una strada*, the layout of a street; *seguire il —*, to follow the tracing **2.** (*abbozzo*) sketch, plan.

tracciatóio, *s.m.* tracer.

tracciatóre, *s.m.* **1.** (*elemento radioattivo*) tracer **2.** (*operaio meccanico*) scriber.

tracciatúra, *s.f.* marking.

tràce, *ag.s.m.* Thracian.

trachèa, *s.f.* (*anat.*) windpipe; trachea (*pl.* tracheae).

tracheàle, *ag.* (*anat.*) tracheal, trachean.

tracheàti, *s.m.pl.* (*entom.*) Tracheata.

trachèidi, *s.m.pl.* (*bot.*) tracheids.

tracheíte, *s.f.* (*patol.*) tracheitis.

tracheotomìa, *s.f.* (*chir.*) tracheotomy.

trachíte, *s.f.* (*min.*) trachyte.

trachítico, *ag.* (*min.*) trachytic: *rocce trachitiche*, trachytic rocks.

trachíttero, *s.m.* (*ittiol.*) Trachypterus.

Tràcia, *no.pr.f.* (*geog. st.*) Thrace.

tracimàre, *v.i.* to overflow.

tràcio, *ag.s.m.* Thracian.

tracòlla, *s.f.* shoulder-belt, baldric: *a —*, (*mil.*) baldricwise; *borsetta a —*, long-strap bag; *portare ql.co. a —*, to carry sthg. across one's back.

tracollàre, *v.i.* **1.** (*perdere l'equilibrio*) to lose one's balance **2.** (*crollare, cadere*) to collapse, to fall down || *far — la bilancia*, to turn the scale (anche *fig.*).

tracòllo, *s.m.* collapse, breakdown, downfall, ruin (anche *fig.*); (*di prezzi, azioni, titoli, ecc.*) crash: — *della salute*, breakdown in health; *il — del mercato, della lira*, the collapse of the market, of the lira; *il — di tutte le mie speranze*, the collapse of all my hopes; *dopo il loro — andarono a vivere all'estero*, after their downfall they went to live abroad; *il nuovo aspetto della questione diede il —*, the new aspect of the matter turned the scale; *quella perdita diede il — ed egli fu rovinato per sempre*, that loss was the last straw and he was ruined for ever; *portare qlcu. al —*, to bring s.o. to ruin.

tracòma, *s.m.* (*patol.*) trachoma.

tracomatóso, *ag.* (*patol.*) trachomatous.

tracotànte, *ag.* overbearing, arrogant, overweening, haughty: *era troppo — per abbassarsi a una cosa simile*, he was too haughty to stoop to such a thing.

tracotànza, *s.f.* arrogance, haughtiness.

tradescànzia, *s.f.* (*bot.*) tradescantia.

tradiménto, *s.m.* **1.** treason: *alto —*, high treason: *fu condannato a morte per alto —*, he was condemned to death for high treason **2.** (*atto da traditore*) betrayal: *il suo — sarà punito molto severamente*, his betrayal will be punished very severely **3.** (*slealtà*) treachery || *a —*, by treachery (o treacherously): *un attacco a —*, a treacherous attack (o a stab in the back); *mi strapparono il consenso a —*, I was tricked into consenting || *questo è un —!*, (*fam.*) this is a dirty trick! || *mangiare pane a —*, to eat unearned bread.

tradíre, *v.t.* to betray (anche *fig.*); (*ingannare*) to deceive; (*essere infedele a*) to be unfaithful to (s.o., sthg.): *la sua eccitazione tradiva il suo timore*, his

excitement betrayed his fear; *le sue parole hanno tradito il suo pensiero, egli non intendeva dire questo*, his words have failed to express his thought, he did not mean to say this; *tu mi hai tradito*, you have deceived me; — *la moglie, il marito*, to be unfaithful to one's wife, one's husband; — *la patria, la famiglia, gli ideali, una causa*, to betray one's country, one's family, one's ideals, a cause; — *un segreto*, to betray a secret || **tradírsi**, *v.r.* to betray oneself: *con quelle parole si tradì*, with those words he betrayed himself.

traditóre, *ag.* treacherous: *sabbie traditrici*, treacherous sands; *sorriso —*, treacherous smile; *vino —*, treacherous wine || *s.m.* traitor, betrayer: — *della patria*, traitor to (o betrayer of) his country; *abbasso i traditori!*, down with traitors!.

traditríce, *s.f.* traitress, betrayer.

tradizionàle, *ag.* traditional, traditionary.

tradizionalísmo, *s.m.* traditionalism.

tradizionalísta, *s.c.* traditionalist.

tradizionalménte, *av.* traditionally.

tradizióne, *s.f.* tradition: *fondato sulla —*, based on tradition; *per —*, by tradition (o traditionally); *in quella famiglia è una — che il primogenito faccia il medico*, in that family it is a tradition for the eldest son to be a doctor; *mantenere una —*, to keep up a tradition; *spezzare una —*, to break a tradition.

tradótta, *s.f.* (*mil.*) troop-train, leave-train.

traducíbile, *ag.* translatable.

tradúrre, *v.t.* **1.** to translate: — *da una lingua in un'altra*, to translate from one language into another: *questo romanzo fu tradotto dall'inglese*, this novel was translated from the English **2.** (*esprimere*) to express: — *il pensiero di qlcu.*, to express s.o.'s thoughts **3.** — *in atto, in pratica ql.co.*, to bring (o to carry) sthg. into effect: — *in atto un piano*, to carry out a plan **4.** — *in carcere*, to take to prison **5.** (*trasformare*) to turn.

traduttóre, *s.m.*, **traduttríce**, *s.f.* translator.

traduzióne, *s.f.* translation: *una — dall'italiano in inglese*, a translation from Italian into English; *fare una —*, to do a translation.

traènte, *s.m.* (*comm.*) drawer.

trafelàre, *v.i.* (*rar.*) to pant, to be out of breath, to gasp for breath.

trafelàto, *ag.* panting, breathless, out of breath, gasping for breath: *alla fine della corsa erano trafelati*, they were breathless, when they stopped running.

trafèrro, *s.m.* (*elett.*) air gap.

trafficàbile, *ag.* (*vendibile*) saleable; (*negoziabile*) negotiable.

trafficànte, *s.m.* dealer, trader, trafficker; (*spreg.*) busybody: — *di armi*, trafficker in arms; — *di bestiame*, cattle dealer; — *di stupefacenti*, drug trafficker.

trafficàre, *v.i.* **1.** to deal, to trade, to traffic: — *con l'America*, to trade with America; — *in seta, in elettro-domestici*, to deal (o to trade) in silk, in electric appliances **2.** (*affaccendarsi*) to bustle about, to busy oneself: *non fa che — in cucina*, she does nothing but bustle about in the kitchen.

tràffico, *s.m.* **1.** traffic: — *aereo, ferroviario, stradale*, air, railway, road traffic; *linea di grande —*, line with heavy traffic; *le ore di — intenso*, the rush hours; *ore di — ridotto*, slack hours; *non c'è neppure un vigile per controllare il —*, there is not even a policeman to control the traffic **2.** (*comm.*) trade, trading: *il — delle pellicce*, the fur trade.

trafìggere, *v.t.* to transfix, to stab, to pierce through (anche *fig.*): *ebbe il cuore trafitto da un giavellotto*, he was pierced through the heart by a javelin; *lo trafisse con la spada*, he ran him through with his sword; *le sue parole mi hanno trafitto il cuore*, his words have pierced me to the heart.

trafiggiménto, *s.m.* transfixion, piercing through.

trafíla, *s.f.* **1.** (*procedura*) procedure, proceeding, routine: *una lunga — di azioni legali*, a long series of legal actions; *dovrai passare attraverso la normale — burocratica*, you will have to go through the normal bureaucratic procedure 2. (*mec.*) die-plate, draw-plate.

trafilàre, *v.t.* (*metal.*) to draw, to wiredraw: — *a caldo*, to hot-draw; — *a freddo*, to cold-draw.

trafilétto, *s.m.* paragraph; (*satirico*) lampoon.

trafìtta, *s.f.* **1.** (*dolore fisico, morale*) pang, sting: *sentì una — di dolore*, he felt a pang **2.** (*ferita*) wound.

trafìtto, *ag.* transfixed, stabbed, pierced; *fig.* broken: *cuore —*, broken heart.

traforàre, *v.t.* **1.** to bore, to drill, to pierce; (*con una galleria*) to tunnel; (*perforare*) to perforate: — *un'asse*, to bore (*o* to drill) a plank; — *una montagna*, to bore (*o* to tunnel) a mountain; — *un pezzo di carta*, to perforate a piece of paper; — *il terreno*, to drill the ground **2.** (*ricamare a traforo*) to embroider with open-work.

traforàto, *ag.* **1.** perforated **2.** (*ricamato a traforo*) open-work (*attributivo*).

traforatrìce, *s.f.* (*mec.*) fret-sawing machine.

traforazióne, *V.* **trafóro** 1.

trafóro, *s.m.* **1.** (*traforazione*) boring, drilling, piercing; (*perforazione*) perforation **2.** (*galleria in una montagna*) tunnel **3.** (*falegnameria*) fretwork: *sega da —*, fretsaw.

trafugaménto, *s.m.* stealing, purloining, filching.

trafugàre, *v.t.* to steal, to purloin, to filch.

trafugataménte, *av.* stealthily, by stealth.

tragèdia, *s.f.* tragedy (*anche fig.*): *l'«Amleto» di Shakespeare è una grande —*, Shakespeare's "Hamlet" is a great tragedy; *la morte di suo padre fu una —*, his father's death was a tragedy.

tragediògrafo, *s.m.* dramatist, dramaturge; tragedian.

traghettàre, *v.t.* to ferry: — *un fiume*, to ferry across a river; — *qlcu.* (*al di là di un fiume*), to ferry s.o. (across a river).

traghettatóre, *s.m.* ferryman (*pl.* ferrymen).

traghétto, *s.m.* **1.** (*luogo*) ferry; (*il traghettare*) ferrying **2.** (*nave*) ferry-boat.

tragicaménte, *av.* tragically.

tragicità, *s.f.* tragicalness.

tràgico, *ag.* tragic(al): *attore —*, tragic actor (*o* tragedian); *avvenimento —*, tragic event; *fine tragica*, tragic end ‖ *s.m.* **1.** (*scrittore*) dramatist; tragedian **2.** (*attore*) tragedian.

tragicòmico, *ag.* tragicomic.

tragicommèdia, *s.f.* tragicomedy.

tragittàre, *V.* **traghettàre.**

tragìtto, *s.m.* **1.** (*strada, percorso*) way: *il — è lungo da qui alla fattoria*, it is a long way from here to the farm; *feci una parte del — in aereo*, I flew part of the way; *lungo il —*, on the way; *qual è il — più breve?*, which is the shortest way? **2.** (*viaggio*) journey; (*per mare*) passage, crossing: *un — di due ore*, a two-hour crossing.

tràglia, *s.f.* (*mar.*) tackle, hoisting tackle.

tràgo, *s.m.* (*anat.*) tragus (*pl.* tragi).

traguardàre, *v.t.* (*guardare di sottecchi*) to look askance at (s.o., sthg.).

traguàrdo, *s.m.* **1.** (*punto d'arrivo nelle corse*) finishing post, winning post **2.** *fig.* (*meta*) goal, aim, end **3.** (*di strumento ottico, arma*) level, back-sight.

Traiàno, *no.pr.m.* (*st.*) Trajan.

traiettàre, *v.t.* to traject.

traiettòria, *s.f.* trajectory: — *di volo*, flight path.

trainàre, *v.t.* to drag, to haul, to draw, to tow: *la locomotiva trainava venticinque vagoni*, the locomotive was hauling twenty-five trucks.

tràino, *s.m.* **1.** (*il trainare*) dragging, haulage, drawing **2.** (*carro da trasporto*) truck; (*senza ruote*) sledge **3.** (*carico*) load.

tralasciaménto, *s.m.* **1.** (*omissione*) omission **2.** (*interruzione*) interruption.

tralasciàre, *v.t.* **1.** (*omettere*) to omit, to leave out: *ho tralasciato di dirtelo per tema che ti arrabbiassi*, I

did not tell you lest you should get cross; *nella sua relazione ha tralasciato le cose più importanti*, in his report he left out (*o* omitted) the most important things; — *i dettagli*, to leave out (*o* to omit) details; — *di fare ql.co.*, to omit doing (*o* to do) sthg. **2.** (*interrompere*) to interrupt, to break; (*desistere*) to give up: — *gli studi*, to interrupt one's studies.

tràlcio, *s.m.* (*di vite*) vine-shoot, vine branch; (*di altre piante*) shoot.

tralìccio, *s.m.* **1.** (*tela grossa per materassi e cuscini*) ticken, ticking; (*per sacchi*) sackcloth **2.** (*struttura metallica o in legno per costruzioni*) trellis, trellis-work, lattice-work: — *di ferro*, iron framework.

tralìce, in, *l.av.* obliquely, askance: *guardare qlcu. in —*, to look askance at s.o.

tralignaménto, *s.m.* degeneration, degeneracy.

tralignàre, *v.i.* to degenerate.

tralucènte, *ag.* **1.** (*trasparente*) transparent, translucent, translucid **2.** (*brillante*) shining.

tralùcere, *v.i.* **1.** (*trasparire*) to shine through, to shine forth **2.** (*brillare*) to shine (with sthg.): *gli occhi le tralucevano di gioia*, her eyes were shining with joy.

tram, *s.m.* tram, tram-car; (*amer.*) street-car, trolley-car.

tràma, *s.f.* **1.** (*di stoffa*) weft, woof, filling **2.** (*macchinazione, congiura*) plot, conspiracy: *oscure trame di fuorusciti*, secret conspiracies of exiles; *ordire una —*, to hatch (*o* to lay) a plot **3.** (*intreccio*) plot, plan: *la — di una commedia*, the plot (*o* plan) of a play.

tramàglio, *s.m.* (*mar.*) trammel (net), drag-net.

tramandàre, *v.t.* to hand down, to hand on, to transmit: *questa tradizione fu tramandata da padre in figlio*, this tradition was handed on from father to son; — *ai posteri*, to hand down to posterity.

tramàre, *v.t.* **1.** to weave **2.** *fig.* to plot, to intrigue: — *contro la sicurezza dello stato*, to conspire against the security of the State; — *un delitto*, to plot a crime.

trambùsto, *s.m.* bustle, turmoil, confusion: *siamo tutti in —*, we are all in a bustle; *aver l'animo in —*, to be upset.

tramenàre, *v.t.* **1.** (*portare qua e là*) to move about **2.** (*mettere sossopra*) to turn topsyturvy ‖ *v.i.* to bustle about, to be very busy.

tramenìo, *s.m.* bustle, fuss.

tramescolaménto, *s.m.* mixing, blending.

tramescolàre, *v.t.* to mix up, to blend.

tramestàre, *v.t.i.* to rummage.

tramestìo, *s.m.* rummaging.

tramèzza, *s.f.* **1.** (*divisione*) partition **2.** (*di scarpe*) slipsole.

tramezzàre, *v.t.* **1.** (*dividere*) to partition (off) **2.** (*interporre*) to interpose; (*con fogli*) to interleave.

tramezzìno, *s.m.* **1.** (*panino imbottito*) sandwich **2.** (*chi porta cartelli pubblicitari*) sandwich-man (*pl.* sandwich-men).

tramèzzo, *s.m.* **1.** partition; (*muro divisorio*) partition wall, curtain wall **2.** (*intervallo*) interval.

tramèzzo a, *l. prep.* *V.* **fra**[1].

tramischiàre, *V.* **frammischiàre.**

tràmite, *s.m.* **1.** (*sentiero*) path ‖ *per il — più sicuro*, *fig.* through the safest way **2.** (*per il*) — (*di*), through: — *un'agenzia*, through an agency; (*per*) — *nostro*, through us.

tramòggia, *s.f.* **1.** (*edil. ind.*) hopper : *carro a —*, (*miner.*) hopper ore car **2.** (*mar.*) hopper (-barge).

tramontàna, *s.f.* **1.** (*vento*) north wind **2.** (*settentrione*) north ‖ *perdere la —*, *fig.* to lose one's head (*o* to lose one's bearings).

tramontàno, *ag.* **1.** (*situato oltre i monti*) beyond the mountains, tramontane **2.** (*settentrionale*) north, northerly.

tramontàre, *v.i.* **1.** to set: *il sole sta tramontando*, the sun is setting **2.** (*venir meno, svanire*) to fade, to wane: *la sua bellezza è tramontata*, her beauty has faded; *la sua popolarità tramontò presto*, his popularity soon waned; *la sua stella è tramontata*, his star has (o is) set.

tramónto, *s.m.* **1.** (*di astri in generale*) setting; (*del sole*) sunset: *al* —, at sunset **2.** (*declino*) decline, end, wane: *il* — *dell'impero*, the decline of the empire; *la sua gloria è al* —, his glory is on the wane.

tramortiménto, *s.m.* swoon, faint, fainting fit.

tramortíre, *v.t.* to stun, to shock: *lo tramortì con un colpo in testa*, he stunned him with a blow on the head ‖ *v.i.* (*svenire*) to faint, to swoon.

tramortíto, *ag.* **1.** stunned **2.** (*svenuto*) fainted, senseless, inanimate.

trampolière, *s.m.* (*ornit.*) stilt-bird; wader.

trampolíno, *s.m.* spring-board, diving-board: *fare un salto dal* —, to jump off the spring-board.

tràmpolo, *s.m.* stilt: *camminare sui trampoli*, to walk on stilts ‖ *ragionamento che si regge sui trampoli*, unsteady reasoning.

tramutàre, *v.t.* **1.** (*cambiare, convertire*) to change, to convert, to transform, to transmute: — *il calore in energia*, to transform heat into energy **2.** (*travasare*) to decant **3.** (*trapiantare*) to transplant **4.** (*trasferire*) to transfer ‖ **tramutàrsi**, *v.r.* to change (into sthg.), to be converted (into sthg.), to be transformed (into sthg.).

tramutazióne, *s.f.* **1.** (*mutamento*) transmutation; change **2.** (*travasamento*) decanting **3.** (*trapianto*) transplantation.

tramutío, *s.f.* transmutation; change.

tramvài, *V.* tram.

tramvía, *V.* tranvía.

tramviàrio, *V.* tranviàrio.

trance, *s.m.* (*spiritismo*) trance: *cadere in* —, to fall into a trance; *mandare qlcu. in* —, to send s.o. into a trance.

trància, *s.f.* **1.** (*mec.*) shearing machine; shears (*pl.*): — *a ghigliottina*, guillotine shears; — *da banco*, bench shears **2.** (*taglierina per carta, cartoni*) cutter **3.** (*miner.*) slice: — *inclinata*, rill slice **4.** (*fetta*) slice: *una* — *di pane*, a slice of bread; *una* — *di pancetta*, a slice (o rasher) of bacon.

tranciàre, *v.t.* (*mec.*) to shear.

tranèllo, *s.m.* snare, trap: *cadere in un* —, to be caught in a snare.

trangugiàre, *v.t.* to gulp down, to bolt, to swallow; (*con avidità*) to wolf (down): — *un bicchiere d'acqua*, to gulp down a glass of water; — *un boccone amaro*, *fig.* to pocket an affront; — *un insulto*, to swallow an insult; — *un panino*, to bolt a sandwich.

trànne, *prep.* but, save, except: *tutti* — *me*, all but (o except) me; *erano tutti presenti* — *mia sorella*, everyone was present except (o save) my sister; *il tuo lavoro va bene* — *che per alcuni dettagli*, your work is good except for a few details.

tranquillaménte, *av.* calmly, quietly, peacefully, restfully, tranquilly: *egli ha dormito* —, he has had a quiet sleep.

tranquillànte, *ag.* tranquillizing, reassuring ‖ *s.m.* (*farm.*) tranquillizer.

tranquillàre, *V.* tranquillizzàre.

tranquillità, *s.f.* quiet, calm, peacefulness, peace; (*immobilità*) stillness; (*in senso morale*) tranquillity: *la* — *del mare*, the calmness of the sea; *la* — *della sera*, the stillness (o quiet) of the night; — *di spirito*, peace of mind; *turbare la* — *pubblica*, to disturb the peace.

tranquillizzàre, *v.t.* **1.** to tranquillize; (*calmare*) to calm (down), to quiet; (*placare*) to soothe: — *la popolazione, l'animo*, to tranquillize the population, the mind **2.** (*rassicurare*) to reassure: *le sue parole mi hanno tranquillizzato*, his words have reassured me ‖ **tranquillizzàrsi**, *v.r.* to calm oneself: *tranquillizzati, non c'è ragione di eccitarsi tanto*, calm yourself, there is no reason for getting so excited.

tranquíllo, *ag.* quiet, calm, peaceful; (*immobile*) still; (*in senso morale*) tranquil: *animo* —, quiet mind;

luogo —, peaceful (o restful) place; *mare* —, calm sea; *sonno* —, calm sleep; *un uomo* —, a quiet man; *vita tranquilla*, tranquil life; *andrà tutto bene, sta'* —, everything will be all right, do not worry; *era molto* — *prima dell'esame*, he was very calm before the examination; *lasciami* —!, leave me alone!; *non può stare* —, he cannot keep still; *tieni* — *il bambino*, keep the child quiet.

transalpíno, *ag.* transalpine.

transatlàntico, *ag.* transatlantic ‖ *s.m.* liner.

transàtto, *ag.* (*dir.*) settled, composed: *una lite transatta*, a settled controversy.

transazióne, *s.f.* **1.** arrangement, adjustment, compromise: *la faccenda fu sistemata con una* —, the matter was settled by an arrangement; *accettare una* —, to agree to a compromise; *venire a* — *con la propria coscienza*, to come to a compromise with one's conscience **2.** (*dir.*) transaction **3.** (*comm.*) composition: *fare una* — *con i propri creditori*, to make a composition with one's creditors **4.** *pl.* (*operazioni commerciali*) transactions: *transazioni di banca*, bank's transactions; *transazioni di Borsa*, Stock Exchange transactions.

transcèndere, *V.* trascèndere.

transcórrere, *V.* trascórrere.

transeat, *l.* (*lat.*) let it go.

transènna, *s.f.* (*arch.*) transenna (*pl.* transennae).

transètto, *s.m.* (*arch.*) transept.

transeúnte, *ag.* transient, fleeting.

trànsfuga, *s.m.* **1.** deserter, runaway, fugitive **2.** (*apostata*) apostate.

transiberiàno, *ag.* trans-Siberian: *ferrovia transiberiana*, trans-Siberian Railroad.

transigènte, *ag.* (*rar.*) tolerant.

transígere, *v.i.* **1.** (*venire a un accomodamento, a un compromesso*) to reach an agreement, to compromise; (*scendere a patti*) to come to terms; (*cedere*) to yield: — *in fatto di onore, di onestà*, to falter with one's honour, honesty; *non* —, to be adamant **2.** (*dir.*) to come to a transaction, to reach a transaction **3.** (*comm.*) to compound: — *con i propri creditori*, to compound with one's creditors ‖ *v.t.* (*dir.*) to compromise: — *una lite*, to compromise a dispute.

transilluminatóre, *s.m.* (*med.*) diaphanoscope.

transilluminazióne, *s.m.* (*med.*) diaphanoscopy.

Transilvània, *no.pr.f.* (*geog.*) Transylvania.

transístor, *s.m.* (*elett.*) transistor.

transitàbile, *ag.* practicable.

transitabilità, *s.f.* practicability: *stato di* —, condition of a road; *mettere una strada in stato di* —, to fit a road for traffic.

transitànte, *ag.* in transit: *merci transitanti*, goods in transit.

transitàre, *v.i.* to pass (through a place).

transitivaménte, *av.* (*gram.*) transitively.

transitívo, *ag.* (*gram.*) transitive.

trànsito, *s.m.* transit: *bolletta di* —, transit certificate; *in* —, in transit ‖ *vietato il* —, no thoroughfare ‖ — *interrotto*, road closed; (*per lavori stradali*) road up.

transitoriaménte, *av.* transitorily, temporarily; (*fugacemente*) transiently.

transitorietà, *s.f.* transitoriness, temporariness; (*fugacità*) transience, transiency.

transitòrio, *ag.* transitory, temporary; (*fugace*) transient, fleeting.

transizióne, *s.f.* transition: *periodo di* —, period of transition.

translúcido, *ag.* translucent, translucid.

translucidità, *s.f.* translucence, translucency.

transmaríno, *ag.* transmarine; oversea (*attributivo*).

transoceànico, *ag.* transoceanic.

transònico, *ag.* (*aer.*) transonic.

transpadàno, *ag.* transpadane.

transumànte, *ag.* transhumant.

transumànza, *s.f.* (*trasferimento di animali da un pascolo ad un altro*) transhumance.

transúnto, *s.m.* (*rar.*) summary.

transustanziàre, *v.t.*, **transustanziàrsi**, *v.r.* (*teol.*) to transubstantiate.

transustanziazióne, *s.f.* (*teol.*) transubstantiation.

transvolàre, *V.* **trasvolàre**.

trantràn, *s.m.* (*fam.*) routine: *il nostro solito —*, our humdrum life.

tranvài, *V.* **tram**.

tranvía, *s.f.* tramway, tramline; (*amer.*) street-car -line: *— elettrica*, electric tramway; *— urbana*, urban tramway.

tranviàrio, *ag.* tram (*attributivo*), tramway (*attributivo*): *linea tranviaria*, tram-line; *servizio —*, tramway service.

tranvière, *s.m.* 1. (*manovratore*) tram-driver; (*amer.*) street-car operator 2. (*bigliettario*) tram-conductor.

trapanaménto, *s.m.* **trapanazióne**.

trapanàre, *v.t.* 1. to drill, to bore 2. (*chir.*) to trephine, to trepan.

trapanatríce, *s.f.* (*mec.*) drilling machine, drill.

trapanatúra, *s.f.* drilling, boring.

trapanazióne, *s.f.* 1. drilling, boring 2. (*chir.*) trephination, trepanning, trepanation.

tràpano, *s.m.* 1. drill; (*falegnameria*) auger: *— ad aria compressa*, air drill; *— a mano*, hand drill; *— a petto*, breast drill; *— motorizzato*, power drill 2. (*chir.*) trepan, trepanning saw, trepline; (*odontoiatrico*) drill: *— indolore*, painless drill.

trapassàre, *v.t.* 1. (*attraversare*) to cross: *— un confine*, to cross a boundary 2. (*passare da parte a parte*) to pierce through, to run through; to transfix: *il proiettile gli trapassò il cuore*, the bullet pierced his heart through; *trapassò l'avversario con la spada*, he ran his opponent through 3. (*passare oltre*) to pass beyond || *v.i.* 1. (*passare*) to pass: *l'eredità trapassò da padre in figlio per parecchie generazioni*, the inheritance was handed down from father to son for several generations 2. (*morire*) to pass away, to die: *egli trapassò la notte scorsa*, he passed away (o died) last night.

trapassàto, *ag.* (*morto*) dead, deceased || *s.m.* (*gram.*) past perfect, pluperfect (tense).

trapàsso, *s.m.* 1. (*passaggio*) passage; (*l'attraversare*) crossing 2. (*morte*) passing away, death, decease 3. (*transizione*) transition 4. (*dir. comm.*) transfer.

trapelàre, *v.i.* to leak out, to ooze out (anche *fig.*); (*venire reso noto*) to come to be known: *dalle sue parole trapelò che era stato in prigione*, from his words it came to be known that he had been in prison; *lasciò — il segreto*, he let the secret (leak) out; *niente trapelò dalle sue parole*, nothing came to be known from his words; *la verità, la notizia trapelò*, the truth, the news leaked out.

trapèzio, *s.m.* 1. (*geom. anat.*) trapezium (*pl.* trapeziums, trapezia) 2. (*ginnastica*) trapeze.

trapezoidàle, *ag.* trapezoidal.

trapezòide, *s.m.* (*geom.*) trapezoid.

trapiantàbile, *ag.* transplantable.

trapiantaménto, *s.m.* transplantation.

trapiantàre, *v.t.* to transplant (anche *fig.*) || **trapiantàrsi**, *v.r.* 1. to be transplanted 2. (*stabilirsi*) to settle 3. (*emigrare*) to emigrate (to a place): *i miei cugini si trapiantarono negli Stati Uniti*, my cousins emigrated to the United States.

trapiantatóio, *s.m.* 1. (*agr.*) garden trowel 2. (*mec. agr.*) (*trapiantatrice*) transplanting apparatus, transplanting machine.

trapiantatóre, *s.m.* transplanter.

trapiantatríce, *s.f.* 1. transplanter 2. (*mec. agr.*) transplanting apparatus, transplanting machine.

trapiànto, *s.m.* 1. transplantation 2. (*chir.*) graft, grafting, transplantation: *— della cornea*, cornea grafting; *— osseo*, bone grafting.

trappísta, *s.m.* (*eccl.*) Trappist.

tràppola, *s.f.* trap, snare (anche *fig.*): *— per topi*, mouse-trap (o rat-trap); *il coniglio fu preso in —*, the rabbit was caught in a snare; *il topo fu preso in —*, the rat was caught in a trap; *attirare il nemico in una —*, to ambush the enemy; *cadere in una —*, to fall into a trap (anche *fig.*); *essere attirato in una —*, to be lured into a trap (anche *fig.*); *mettere una — per un animale*, to set a trap (o to lay a snare) for an animal; *prendere in — un topo*, to trap a rat.

trappolàre, *v.t.* 1. to trap, to entrap, to ensnare (anche *fig.*) 2. (*ingannare*) to dupe, to deceive.

trappolatóre, *s.m.* 1. (*chi pone trappole*) trapper 2. (*imbroglione*) swindler, cheat.

trappolería, *s.f.* (*inganno*) trick, trickery.

trappolíno, (*rar.*) per **trampolíno**.

trappolóne, *s.m.* (*imbroglione*) swindler, cheat.

trapúnta, *s.f.* quilt.

trapuntàre, *v.t.* 1. to quilt; to stitch through and through 2. (*ricamare*) to embroider.

trapuntàto, *ag.* 1. quilted 2. (*ricamato*) embroidered.

trapúnto, *ag.* 1. quilted || *cielo — di stelle*, starry sky 2. (*ricamato*) embroidered || *s.m.* 1. quilting 2. (*ricamo*) embroidery.

tràrre, *v.t.* 1. to draw (anche *fig.*): *egli trasse a sè la sedia e si sedette*, he drew the chair towards him and sat down; *lo trassi d'inganno*, I undeceived him; *mi trasse d'impaccio*, he got me out of the difficulty; *trae ispirazione dalla natura*, he draws his inspiration from nature; *trasse il denaro di tasca*, he drew the money from his pocket; *— a riva*, to pull to the shore; *— a salvamento*, to rescue; *— una conclusione*, to draw a conclusion; *— qlcu. in disparte*, to draw s.o. aside; *— la spada*, to draw (o to unsheathe) one's sword || *trae origine da una nobile famiglia*, he originates from a noble family || *— a sorte*, to draw lots || *— dal nulla*, to make out of nothing || *— in inganno*, to deceive || *— la seta*, to spin silk || *— un sospiro*, to heave a sigh || *— la vita*, to draw one's life (o days) || *— (ottenere)* to get, to derive: *non ne traggo alcun vantaggio, piacere*, I don't get (o derive) any benefit, pleasure from it || *— il miglior partito da ql.co.*, to make the best of sthg. 3. (*condurre*) to lead: *la curiosità lo trasse qui*, curiosity led him here; *— qlcu. al supplizio*, to take s.o. to be executed || *— a fine*, to bring to a close: *— ql.co. a buon fine*, to bring sthg. to a successful conclusion 4. (*gettare*) to throw: *— i dadi*, to throw (o to cast) the dice 5. (*comm.*) to draw: *— a vista*, to draw at sight; *— una cambiale*, to draw a bill || *v.i.* 1. (*andare*): *tutti traevano a vedere il miracolo*, all went to see the miracle; *— a piedi, a cavallo*, to make one's way on foot, on horseback 2. *— di scherma*, to fence || **tràrsi**, *v.r.* to draw: *— in disparte, indietro*, to draw aside, back: *è molto timida, si trae sempre indietro*, *fig.* she is very shy, she is always very retiring (o reserved) || *— da un impiccio*, to get out of a scrape.

trasalíre, *v.i.* to start, to startle, to be startled: *quando mi vide, trasalì*, when he saw me, he startled; *trasalì sentendo picchiare alla porta*, he gave a gasp on hearing a knock || *far —*, to startle.

trasandàre, *v.t.* to neglect: *— gli studi, il lavoro*, to neglect one's studies, work.

trasandàto, *ag.* neglectful, neglected, careless; slovenly, sloppy, shabby, seedy: *una casa, una stanza trasandata*, a shabby house, room; *essere — nella persona*, to have a shabby appearance.

trasbordàre, *v.t.* 1. (*mar.*) to tranship: *— un carico*, to tranship a cargo 2. (*ferr.*) to transfer: *— i passeggeri da un treno all'altro*, to transfer passengers from one train to another || *v.i.* (*cambiare treno, nave, ecc.*) to change.

trasbordatóre, *s.m.* (*carrello*) —, (*ferr.*) transfer table, traverser.

trasbórdo, *s.m.* 1. (*mar.*) transhipment 2. (*ferr.*) transfer 3. (*traghetto*) ferrying, ferrying across.

trascégliere, *V.* **scégliere**.

trascendentàle, *ag.* **1.** (*fil.*) transcendental **2.** (*eccezionale*) extraordinary, supernatural.

trascendentalísmo, *s.m.* (*fil.*) transcendentalism.

trascendentalménte, *av.* transcendentally.

trascendènte, *ag.* **1.** (*fil.*) transcendent **2.** (*mat.*) transcendental.

trascendènza, *s.f.* transcendence, transcendency.

trascèndere, *v.t.* to transcend; to surpass, to go beyond, to be beyond: *queste cose trascendono le mie capacità intellettive*, these things are beyond my understanding; *la sua generosità trascende le mie aspettative*, his generosity goes beyond my expectations; — *i limiti umani*, to transcend human limits ‖ *v.i.* to let oneself go, to go too far, to lose one's control, to go to excess, to run to excess: *egli non trascende mai*, he never lets himself go; *egli non trascende mai a queste meschinità*, he never stoops to these trivialities; — *ad atti villani*, to lower oneself to rude action.

trascicàre, *V.* **strascicàre**.

trascinàre, *v.t.* **1.** to drag (anche *fig.*); to trail: *il bimbo trascinava il suo cavalluccio di legno*, the child was trailing his wooden horse; *non — quella seggiola per terra!*, don't drag that chair along the floor!; — *la gamba, il piede*, to drag one's feet (*o* to shuffle); — *qlcu. nel fango*, *fig.* to drag s.o. (*o* s.o.'s name) through the mud (*o* mire) ‖ — *una vita di miseria*, to lead a wretched life **2.** (*condurre a forza*) to drag: *trascinarono il ladro alla polizia*, they dragged the thief to the police **3.** (*affascinare*) to fascinate: *trama, conversazione che trascina*, plot, conversation that fascinates ‖ **trascinàrsi**, *v.r.* to drag oneself along: *era molto vecchio e poteva — a malapena*, he was very old and could hardly drag himself along ‖ *la faccenda si trascinò per diversi anni*, the matter dragged on for several years ‖ *le ore si trascinano pesantemente*, time drags heavily by (*o* the heavy hours drag on *o* time hangs heavy) ‖ — *sulle ginocchia davanti a qlcu.*, to go on one's knees to s.o.

trascoloraménto, *s.m.* discoloration, discolourment, change of colour.

trascoloràre, *v.i.*, **trascoloràrsi**, *v.r.* **1.** to change one's colour **2.** (*impallidire*) to grow pale.

trascórrere, *v.t.* **1.** (*passare, consumare*) to spend, to pass: *trascorsi tre anni in America*, I spent three years in America; — *il tempo*, to spend one's time: — *il tempo nell'ozio*, to spend one's time in idleness (*o* to idle one's time away) **2.** (*percorrere*) to go about, to roam, to wander about: — *un paese*, to go (*o* to wander) about a country (*o* to ramble over a country) **3.** (*leggere rapidamente*) to go through: — *un libro*, to go through a book ‖ *v.i.* **1.** to pass, to elapse: *quei due anni trascorsero molto velocemente*, those two years passed (*o* elapsed) very swiftly **2.** (*non soffermarsi*) to pass (over sthg.): *trascorriamo sui dettagli dell'argomento*, let's pass over the details of the matter **3.** (*trascendere*): *non l'animo, soltanto la lingua ha trascorso*, not the mind, but the tongue alone was guilty of excess.

trascorrévole, *ag.* transient.

trascórso, *ag.* past: *gli anni trascorsi*, the past years ‖ *s.m.* (*piccolo errore, colpa lieve*) fault, slip, lapse: *gli perdonò alcuni trascorsi di gioventù*, he forgave him a few slips of youth.

trascrítto, *ag.*: *un documento —*, a transcript.

trascrittóre, *s.m.*, **trascrittríce**, *s.f.* transcriber, copyist.

trascrívere, *v.t.* **1.** to transcribe: — *in bella copia*, to write out a fair copy of **2.** (*dir.*) to register **3.** (*elett. acu.*) to transfer.

trascrizióne, *s.f.* **1.** transcription **2.** (*trapasso*) transfer: — *di titoli*, (*dir. comm.*) transfer of securities **3.** (*dir.*) registration.

trascuràbile, *ag.* negligible.

trascuràggine, **trascurànza**, *s.f.* carelessness, negligence, oversight: *per —*, through an oversight.

trascuràre, *v.t.* **1.** to neglect: — *di fare ql.co.*, to neglect to do (*o* doing) sthg. (*o* to fail to do sthg. *o* to omit to do sthg.): *non trascurate di scrivermi subito*, don't fail to write me at once; — *la propria famiglia, il proprio lavoro*, to neglect one's family, one's work **2.** (*tenere in poco conto*) to disregard, to slight.

trascuratàggine, *V.* **trascuràggine**.

trascurataménte, *av.* carelessly, negligently.

trascuratézza, *s.f.* **1.** carelessness, negligence: *biasimò la tua —*, he blamed your carelessness **2.** (*svista*) oversight, slip **3.** (*sciatteria*) slovenliness.

trascuràto, *ag.* **1.** (*negligente*) careless, negligent: — *nel lavoro*, negligent in one's work; *è molto — in ogni cosa che fa*, he is very careless in everything he does; *è — nella persona*, he is careless of his person **2.** (*non curato*) neglected: *un'influenza trascurata*, a neglected 'flu **3.** (*indifferente*) indifferent, casual: *è — verso i suoi amici*, he is indifferent towards his friends **4.** (*sciatto*) slovenly, sloppy.

trasecolaménto, *s.m.* amazement, astonishment.

trasecolàre, *v.i.* to be amazed, to be astonished, to be startled, to be bewildered.

trasentíre, *v.t.* to overhear.

trasferíbile, *ag.* transferable.

trasferiménto, *s.m.* transfer: *il — del governo da Firenze a Roma*, the transfer of the government from Florence to Rome; — *di domicilio*, change of address; — *di una proprietà, di un diritto*, (*dir.*) the transfer (*o* demise) of a property, right; *il — di un soldato da un reggimento a un altro*, the transfer of a soldier from one regiment to another.

trasferíre, *v.t.* to transfer, to remove: *egli fu trasferito in un altro stabilimento*, he was transferred to another factory; *la sede centrale fu trasferita a Roma*, the head office was transferred to Rome; *spera di essere trasferito a Milano*, he hopes to be transferred to Milan; — *un diritto a qlcu.*, (*dir.*) to transfer a right to s.o.; — *una proprietà*, (*dir.*) to convey an estate; — *le truppe in un'altra zona*, to remove the troops to another zone ‖ **trasferírsi**, to (re)move: *si è trasferito da Milano a Venezia*, he (re)moved from Milan to Venice; — *in campagna*, to (re)move into the country.

trasfèrta, *s.f.* **1.** transfer: *è in — per la sua ditta*, he is travelling on transfer for his firm's business ‖ *partita in —*, (*spor.*) out match **2.** (*indennità di trasferta*) travelling allowance; travelling expenses (*pl.*).

trasfiguraménto, *s.m.* transfiguration.

trasfiguràre, *v.t.* to transfigure ‖ **trasfiguràrsi**, *v.r.* to become transfigured, to undergo a transfiguration, to change one's aspect: *il suo viso si trasfigurò*, her face became transfigured.

trasfiguràto, *ag.* transfigured.

trasfigurazióne, *s.f.* transfiguration ‖ *la Trasfigurazione di Nostro Signore*, the Transfiguration of Christ on the Mount.

trasfóndere, *v.t.* **1.** to transfuse **2.** *fig.* to instil.

trasfondíbile, *ag.* transfusible, transferable.

trasformàbile, *ag.* **1.** transformable **2.** (*aut.*) convertible.

trasformabilità, *s.f.* transformability.

trasformàre, *v.t.* to transform, to change, to turn: — *l'acqua in ghiaccio*, to turn water into ice ‖ **trasformàrsi**, *v.r.* to transform oneself, to be transformed, to change (into sthg.): *il bruco si trasforma in farfalla*, the caterpillar changes into a butterfly.

trasformatívo, *ag.* transformative.

trasformatóre, *s.m.* (*elett.*) transformer: — *bifase*, two-phase transformer; — *di alta, bassa frequenza*, high-, low-frequency transformer; — *di corrente*, current transformer; — *riduttore* (*di tensione*), step-down transformer.

trasformazióne, *s.f.* transformation.

trasformísmo, *s.m.* (*biol.*) transformism.

trasformísta, *s.m.* **1.** (*biol.*) transformist **2.** (*teat.*) quick-change artist.

trasfusióne, *s.f.* transfusion: — *di sangue,* blood transfusion.

trasfúso, *ag.* transfused.

trasgrediménto, *s.m.* infringement, transgression.

trasgredíre, *v.t.i.* to infringe (sthg.); to transgress (sthg.); to break (sthg.); to violate (sthg.): — *una legge,* to infringe a law; — (*a*) *un ordine,* to disobey an order.

trasgreditóre, *s.m.* transgressor, trespasser.

trasgressióne, *s.f.* infringement, transgression.

trasgressóre, *s.m.* transgressor, trespasser.

traslataménte, *av.* figuratively, metaphorically.

traslàto, *ag.* figurative, metaphoric || *s.m.* (*ret.*) metaphor.

traslatóre, *s.m.* (*tel.*) repeater, translator: — *telegrafico,* (*elett.*) telegraphic repeater.

traslazióne, *s.f.* **1.** (*trasferimento*) transfer: — *di una salma,* transporting of a body **2.** (*fis.*) translation: *movimento di* —, motion (*o* movement) of translation **3.** (*dir.*) transferring, conveyance: *la* — *di una proprietà,* the conveyance of a property **4.** (*eccl.*) translation: *la* — *di un vescovo,* the translation of a bishop.

traslocaménto, *s.m.* removal.

traslocàre, *v.t.i.* to move, to remove: *abbiamo traslocato in un appartamento più grande,* we have moved into a larger flat; — *un negozio, un ufficio,* to move a shop, an office.

traslòco, *s.m.* removal: *furgone per traslochi,* removal van; *fare* —, to move out.

traslucidità, *s.f.* translucence, translucency.

traslúcido, *ag.* translucent, translucid.

trasmaríno, *ag.* transmarine.

trasméttere, *v.t.* to transmit, to pass on, to convey: *l'eredità fu trasmessa al figlio,* the inheritance was conveyed (*o* transferred) to his son; *trasmetti i miei saluti a tua madre,* give your mother my best regards || — *il caldo, il freddo,* (*fis.*) to transmit heat, cold; — *un dispaccio,* to transmit a dispatch; — *un'ordinazione,* to pass (*o* to remit) an order; — *per filo,* (*rad. tel.*) to pipe; — *per radio, per televisione,* to transmit by radio, by television (*o* to broadcast, to telecast); — *un programma registrato,* (*rad.*) to transcribe; — *sentimenti, sensazioni, informazioni,* to convey feelings, sensations, information.

trasmettitóre, *s.m.* (*rad. tel.*) transmitter: — *ripetitore,* (*rad.*) rebroadcasting set (*o* relay transmitter).

trasmigràre, *v.i.* to transmigrate (anche *fig.*).

trasmigrazióne, *s.f.* transmigration (anche *fig.*).

trasmissìbile, *ag.* transmissible, transmittable.

trasmissibilità, *s.f.* **1.** transmissibility **2.** (*dir.*) transferability: — *di diritti,* transferability of rights.

trasmissióne, *s.f.* **1.** (*biol.*) transmission: — *dei caratteri ereditari,* transmission of hereditary characters **2.** (*rad. tel.*) transmission: — *radiofonica,* broadcast; — *televisiva,* telecast || — *a premi,* giveaway show **3.** (*mec. aut.*) shafting: — *ad alberi,* (*mec.*) shafting; — *anteriore,* (*aut.*) front-wheel drive (*o* front drive); *albero di* —, (*aut.*) driving shaft **4.** (*dir.*) transfer(ence), conveyance, descent: — *di un bene per successione,* descent of an estate.

trasmissívo, *ag.* transmissive.

trasmissóre, *s.m.* transmitter.

trasmitténte, *ag.* (*rad. tel.*) transmitting: *apparecchio, stazione* —, transmitting set, station || *s.m.* (*rad. tel.*) transmitter.

trasmodaménto, *s.m.* excess.

trasmodàre, *v.i.* to exceed, to go beyond the limit: — *nel bere, nel mangiare,* to overdrink, to overeat.

trasmodataménte, *av.* excessively, immoderately, exceedingly.

trasmodàto, *ag.* excessive, immoderate, exceeding.

trasmutàbile, *ag.* transmutable.

trasmutabilità, *s.f.* transmutability.

trasmutaménto, *s.m.* (*rar.*) transmutation, transformation.

trasmutàre, *v.t.* to transmute, to transform, to

change: *tu devi* — *le tue abitudini di vita,* you'll have to change your habits of life || **trasmutàrsi,** *v. r.* to be transformed, to change: *quel ragazzo si è molto trasmutato,* that boy has changed a lot.

trasmutazióne, *s.f.* transmutation, transformation.

trasmutévole, *ag.* transmutable.

trasognàre, *v.i.* (*sognare a occhi aperti*) to indulge in day-dreams, to be lost in reverie.

trasognàto, *ag.* **1.** dreamy, lost in reverie, far-away: *uno sguardo* —, a far-away look **2.** (*stupefatto*) dazed.

traspadàno, *ag.* transpadane.

trasparénte, *ag.* transparent || *s.m.* (*oggetto trasparente*) transparency.

trasparènza, *s.f.* transparence, transparency.

trasparíre, *v.i.* **1.** to shine through (sthg.); to gleam through (sthg.); (*palesarsi*) to appear through (sthg.): *dai suoi occhi traspariva la gioia,* his eyes were shining with joy; *la luce traspariva dalle finestre,* the light was gleaming through the windows; *la luna traspariva fra le nuvole,* the moon was shining through the clouds; *il sole trasparì tra le nuvole,* the sun appeared among (*o* through) the clouds **2.** *lasciar, far* —, *fig.* to betray: *la sua condotta non lasciava* — *niente di strano,* his behaviour did not betray anything strange **3.** (*essere trasparente*) to be transparent: *il vetro trasparisce,* glass is transparent.

traspiràbile, *ag.* perspirable.

traspiràre, *v.i.* **1.** to perspire **2.** (*bot.*) to transpire **3.** *fig.* to transpire, to leak out, to come to light: *non traspirò nulla del suo segreto,* nothing of his secret transpired.

traspirazióne, *s.f.* **1.** perspiration **2.** (*bot.*) transpiration.

trasponiménto, *s.m.* transposition.

traspórre, *v.t.* to transpose: — *una parola in un periodo,* to transpose a word in a sentence.

trasportàbile, *ag.* transportable.

trasportàre, *v.t.* **1.** to transport, to carry, to convey: *devo* — *tutte queste cose nel nostro nuovo appartamento,* I must carry all these things to our new flat; — *merce, bagaglio, passeggeri,* to transport (*o* to carry *o* to convey) goods, luggage, passengers; — *qlcu. all'ospedale,* to carry (*o* to convey *o* to take) s.o. to hospital **2.** (*trasferire*) to transfer: *tutto il reparto fu trasportato a Roma,* all the department was transferred to Rome **3.** (*rinviare*) to postpone, to defer: *la festa è stata trasportata,* the festival has been postponed **4.** *fig.* to transport, to carry away: *essere trasportato dall'entusiasmo, dalla gelosia,* to be carried away by one's enthusiasm, one's jealousy; *lasciarsi* — *dall'ira,* to fly into a rage **5.** (*dir.*) to transfer, to make over, to assign to (s.o.) **6.** (*mat. mus.*) to transpose || **trasportàrsi,** *v.r.* to go; (*all'indietro*) to go back; (*in avanti*) to go forward: *trasportiamoci a destra,* let's go to the right; — *col pensiero ai tempi della giovinezza,* to cast one's mind back to the days of one's youth; — *nel futuro,* to cast one's mind into the future.

trasportatóre, *s.m.* **1.** (*mec.*) conveyer, conveyor, carrier: — *a catena,* chain conveyor; — *aereo,* overhead conveyer; — *a nastro,* belt conveyer (*o* belt carrier); — *a rulli,* roller conveyer; — *a tazze,* bucket conveyer (*o* skip hoist); *addetto al* —, conveyorman **2.** (*strumento*) —, (*mus.*) transposing instrument.

traspòrto, *s.m.* **1.** transport, conveyance, carriage: — *aereo,* transportation by air; — *al destinatario,* carriage forward; — *di corrispondenza,* transport of mail; — *di merci,* conveyance (*o* transport *o* carriage) of goods; — *di passeggeri, bagagli,* conveyance of passengers, luggage; — *pagato,* carriage free (*o* carriage paid); — *per terra, per mare,* transport by land, by sea; *mezzi di* —, means of transportation (*o* conveyance); *nave da* —, cargo (boat); *spese di* —, carriage; (*con carri*) cartage; (*per mare*) freight; *ufficio trasporti,* forwarding office **2.** *fig.* transport: *trasporti di gioia, amore, ira,* transports of joy, love, anger; *accogliere* *una notizia con —,* to receive news with transports of delight; *lavorare con —,* to work with enthusiasm.

traspositóre, *s.m.* transposer.

trasposizióne, *s.f.* transposition.

trassàto, *s.m.* (*comm.*) drawee.

trassinàre, *v.t.* to mishandle.

tràsso, *s.m.* (*tufo vulcanico*) trass.

trasteveríno, *ag. s.m.* Transtiverine, Transtiberine.

tràstola, *s.f.* (*dial.*) (*inganno*) trick, cheat.

trastúlla, *ag.: pascere qlcu. di erba —,* to feed s.o. with vain hopes.

trastullaménto, *s.m.* amusement.

trastullàre, *v.t.* to amuse: *passò la giornata trastullando i nipotini,* he spent his day amusing his grandchildren ‖ **trastullàrsi,** *v.r.* **1.** (*divertirsi*) to amuse oneself: *i bambini si trastullano con poco,* children amuse themselves with very little ‖ *— di qlcu.,* to make fun of s.o. **2.** (*giocare*) to play, to toy: *il bambino si trastullava con i suoi giocattoli,* the child was playing with his toys; *il gatto si trastullava con una pallina,* the cat was playing with a small ball **3.** (*scherzare*) to trifle: *non trastullarti con queste cose serie,* don't trifle with these serious matters.

trastullatóre, *s.m.,* **trastullatríce,** *s.f.* amuser.

trastullévole, *ag.* amusing.

trastúllo, *s.m.* **1.** plaything: *il cane è il — dei bimbi,* children make a plaything of a dog **2.** (*divertimento, passatempo*) amusement, sport, pastime **3.** (*zimbello*) laughing stock.

trastullóne, *s.m.* playful person.

trasudaménto, *s.m.* transuding; (*di sudore*) perspiration; (*volg.*) sweating; (*di liquidi, umidità, ecc.*) oozing.

trasudàre, *v.i.* to transude; (*sudore*) to perspire; (*volg.*) to sweat; (*umidità*) to sweat out, to ooze: *le piante trasudano quando non hanno abbastanza aria,* plants sweat when they haven't enough air ‖ *tutto il suo discorso trasudava ipocrisia,* his whole speech was shot through with hypocrisy ‖ *v.t.* to ooze with (sthg.): *i muri trasudavano umidità,* the walls were oozing with dampness.

trasumanàre, *v.i.* to be transhumanized.

trasumanazióne, *s.f.* transhumanation.

trasversàle, *ag.* transverse, transversal; cross (*attributivo*): *galleria —,* cross-gallery; *muro —,* partition-wall; *muscolo —,* (*anat.*) transverse (muscle); *piano —,* (*mar.*) athwartship plane; *trave —,* cross-girder; *via —,* cross-street (*o* side-street) ‖ *in senso —,* transversely (*o* crosswise *o* athwart); (*mar.*) athwartship ‖ *s.f.* **1.** (*linea*) transversal line **2.** (*via*) cross-street (*o* side-street).

trasversalménte, *av.* transversally, transversely, crosswise, athwart; (*mar.*) athwartship.

trasvèrso, *V.* **trasversàle.**

trasviàre, (*rar.*) per **traviàre.**

trasvolànte, *ag.* flying across; passing over (anche *fig.*).

trasvolàre, *v.t.* to fly across (sthg.): *— l'oceano,* to fly across the ocean ‖ *v.i.* to pass over (sthg.) (anche *fig.*): *— su un argomento,* to pass over a subject.

trasvolàta, *s.f.* flight across: *— atlantica,* flight across the Atlantic (*o* Atlantic flight).

trasvolatóre, *s.m.,* **trasvolatríce,** *s.f.* flyer.

tràtta, *s.f.* **1.** (*tirata, strattone*) pull, tug **2.** (*tratto*) distance; (*ferr.*) section, stretch **3.** (*periodo*) period, interval **4.** (*traffico*) trade: *— dei negri,* slave trade; *— delle bianche,* white-slave trade; *— di donne e bambini,* traffic in women and children **5.** (*comm.*) draft: *— a certo tempo data,* draft at a certain time after (*o* from) date; *— a certo tempo vista,* draft at a certain time after (*o* from) sight; *— a data fissa,* draft on a fixed date; *— allo scoperto,* overdraft; *— a vista,* sight draft; *— bancaria,* banker's bill; *avviso di —,* advice of draft; *la vostra — scade il 2 marzo,* your draft falls due on March 2nd; *accettare una —,* to accept a draft; *onorare, disonorare una —,* to honour, to

dishonour a bill; *pagare una —,* to pay a draft; *spiccare una — su qlcu. per 20 sterline,* to draw upon s.o. for twenty pounds **6.** (*rete da pesca*) seine.

trattàbile, *ag.* **1.** (*di argomento*) that can be dealt with; (*rar.*) dealable: *questo argomento non è —,* this subject is not to be dealt with (*o* cannot be dealt with) **2.** (*di persone*) docile, reasonable, tractable, manageable **3.** (*chim.*) treatable, tractable.

trattabilità, *s.f.* (*docilità, arrendevolezza*) tractability, tractableness, manageability, manageableness.

trattaménto, *s.m.* **1.** treatment: *il — dei carcerati è migliorato sensibilmente,* the treatment of prisoners has greatly improved; *il — in questo albergo è eccellente,* the treatment in this hotel is excellent; *fanno un buon —,* they keep a good table; *ricevere un buon —,* to be treated well **2.** (*cura*) treatment, cure: *il — di una malattia,* the treatment of a disease **3.** (*paga, stipendio*) pay; wage (*gener. pl.*), salary: *il — in quella ditta è soddisfacente,* salaries in that firm are satisfactory **4.** (*cine.*) treatment **5.** (*tec.*): *— ad aria calda,* (*ind. gomma*) hot-air treatment; *— a freddo,* (*metal.*) cold treating; *— limite,* (*chim. ind.*) threshold treatment; *— per immersione,* (*mec.*) dipping; *— preventivo,* (*ind.*) preliminary treatment; *— protettivo,* inhibiting; *— termico,* (*fis.*) heat treatment.

trattàre, *v.t.* **1.** to treat, to use, to deal with (s.o.), to behave to(wards) (s.o.): *in questo albergo trattano molto bene,* in this hotel they treat you very well; *la tratta come una bambina,* he treats her as (if she were) a little girl; *mi ha trattato molto gentilmente,* he behaved very kindly to me; *— bene qlcu.,* to use s.o. well; *— male qlcu.,* to use s.o. badly (*o* to ill-treat *o* to ill-use s.o.) ‖ *— qlcu. coi guanti,* to handle s.o. with kid gloves: *non mi ha trattato coi guanti,* he handled me without gloves **2.** (*maneggiare*) to handle: *devi — bene i tuoi libri,* you must handle your books with care **3.** (*curare*) to treat, to cure: *c'è un nuovo metodo di — la polmonite,* there is a new method of treating pneumonia **4.** (*chim.*) to treat: *— col vapore,* to steam; *— con amido,* to starch; *con ammoniaca,* to ammoniate; *— galvanicamente,* to plate; *— un metallo con acido,* to treat a metal with an acid; *— termicamente,* to heat-treat **5.** (*commerciare*) to deal in (sthg.): *— lana, seta,* to deal in wool, silk **6.** (*argomento, problema*) to deal with (sthg.), to treat, to handle: *ha sempre da — cose importanti,* he has always to deal with serious matters; *trattò la leggenda di S. Giorgio e il drago in una serie di dieci quadri,* he treated the legend of St. George and the dragon in a series of ten pictures **7.** (*discutere*) to discuss; (*negoziare*) to negotiate: *non voglio — un argomento così delicato,* I do not want to discuss such a delicate subject; *— un affare,* to transact (*o* to discuss) a business; *— le condizioni di resa,* to discuss the terms of surrender; *— la pace, un prestito,* to negotiate peace, a loan ‖ *v.i.* **1.** to deal, to treat: *non è facile — con gente permalosa,* it is not easy to deal with touchy people; *non ho mai potuto — con quella ditta,* I could never deal with that firm **2.** (*di argomento*) to deal with (sthg.), to be about (sthg.): *la sua conferenza trattava dei suoi viaggi,* his lecture dealt with (*o* was about) his travels ‖ **trattàrsi,** *v. imp.* to be a question of (sthg.), to be a matter of (sthg.): *la merce di cui si tratta,* the goods in question; *non si tratta di questo,* this is not the question; *il problema di cui si tratta,* the problem in hand; *quando si tratta di tradurre ql.co. di difficile si rifiuta di farlo,* when it comes to translating sthg. difficult he refuses to do it; *si tratta dei miei interessi,* my own interests are at stake (*o* involved); *si tratta di un caso speciale,* it is a particular case; *si tratta di cose ben più importanti,* the matter in hand is far more important; *si tratta di decidere se devo farlo o no,* the question is whether I must do it or not; *si tratta di vita o di morte,* it is a matter of life and death; *si tratta solo di aspettare un po',* it is only a question of time; *si tratta solo* *di premere un bottone,* it is only a question of pressing a button ‖ *v.r.:* — *bene,* (*non lasciarsi mancar nulla*), to treat oneself very well (*o* to take very good care of oneself).

trattàrio, *s.m.* (comm.) drawee.

trattatìsta, *s.c.* writer of treatises, treatiser.

trattatíva, *s.f.* negotiation: *trattative in corso,* pending negotiations; *trattative per l'acquisto di una casa,* negotiations for the purchase of a house; *le trattative sono state condotte dal mio segretario,* the negotiations have been carried on by my secretary ‖ *essere in trattative con qlcu. per ql.co.,* to be negotiating with s.o. for sthg.; *iniziare le trattative con qlcu.,* to enter into negotiations with s.o.

trattàto, *s.m.* **1.** (*accordo, patto*) treaty: *un — di pace,* a peace treaty; *ratificare un —,* to ratify a treaty **2.** (*scritto, libro*) treatise: *scrivere un — filosofico,* to write a philosophical treatise.

trattazióne, *s.f.* treatment: *la — di un argomento,* the treatment of a subject.

tratteggiùre, *v.t.* **1.** (*abbozzare*) to sketch, to outline (anche *fig.*) **2.** (*disegnare a trattini*) to dash; (*ombreggiare*) to hatch; (*cartografia*) to hachure **3.** (*descrivere*) to describe **4.** (*rappresentare*) to represent.

tratteggiàto, *ag.* **1.** (*abbozzato*) sketched, outlined **2.** (*disegnato a tratti*) dashed **3.** (*descritto*) described **4.** (*rappresentato*) represented.

trattéggio, *s.m.* **1.** (*il tratteggiare*) sketching, outlining **2.** (*abbozzo*) sketch, outline **3.** (*disegno a tratti*) dash; (*ombreggiatura*) hatch; (*cartografia*) hachure **4.** (*descrizione*) description **5.** (*rappresentazione*) representation.

trattenére, *v.t.* **1.** (*tenere, far rimanere*) to keep, to detain, to retain: *ci trattenne nel suo ufficio per due ore,* he kept us in his office for two hours; *fu trattenuto a scuola,* he was detained at school; *il mio lavoro mi tratterrà qui per qualche giorno,* my work will detain me here for a few days; *mi trattenne a cena,* he kept me for supper; *trattenne per sè due sterline,* he kept two pounds for himself; *— il respiro,* to hold one's breath **2.** (*frenare*) to hold back, to keep (back), to restrain, to check, to repress: *cerca di — la tua collera,* try to restrain (*o* to check *o* to repress) your anger; *non potei trattenerlo dall'uscire,* I could not keep him from going out; *non so cosa mi trattenne dal farlo,* I don't know what held me back (*o* restrained me) from doing it; *— le lacrime, il pianto,* to refrain one's tears **3.** (*dedurre*) to deduct: *tratteniamo le spese di trasporto dalla somma dovutavi,* we deduct the carriage from the amount we owe you **4.** (*intrattenere*) to entertain: *trattieni gli ospiti mentre mi preparo,* entertain the guests while I get ready ‖ **trattenérsi,** *v.r.* **1.** (*rimanere*) to stop, to stay, to remain: *mi tratterrò a Roma due giorni,* I shall stop in Rome two days; *trattieniti ancora un po' con noi,* stay (*o* remain) with us a little longer **2.** (*frenarsi*) to restrain oneself, to refrain oneself, to hold oneself back: *non potè — e scoppiò in lacrime,* she could not restrain herself and burst into tears **3.** (*fare a meno*) to help (doing); to avoid (doing); to keep oneself: *non potei trattenermi dal dirgli tutto,* I could not help telling him everything; *non poterono — dal ridere quando lo videro,* they could not help laughing on seeing him.

trattenimént o, *s.m.* **1.** (*festa, divertimento*) entertainment, party: *come è stato il —?,* how was the party?; *dà molti trattenimenti quando è qui,* he gives many parties when he is here; *devo andare a un —,* I must go to a party **2.** (*indugio*) delay ‖ *fare una guerra di—, fig.* to play a waiting game.

trattenúta, *s.f.* deduction: *una — sullo stipendio,* a deduction of pay.

trattíno, *s.m.* **1.** (*nelle parole composte*) hyphen: *unire con —,* to hyphenate **2.** (*per separare frasi subordinate*) dash.

tràtto, *s.m.* **1.** (*tirata*) pull, tug: *un — di corda,*

(*tortura*) a strappado ‖ *dare il — alla bilancia,* to turn the scale **2.** (*colpo*) stroke: *un — di matita, di penna, di pennello,* a stroke of the pencil, the pen, the brush **3.** (*linea*) line, outline: *— d'unione,* hyphen; *disegnare ql.co. a grandi tratti,* to draw sthg. in outline (*o* to outline sthg.) **4.** (*frazione di spazio, di tempo*) way, distance; tract, stretch: *un — di terra,* a tract (*o* stretch *o* strip) of land; *l'ultimo — del viaggio,* the last leg of the journey; *per un breve — di tempo,* for a short while; *abbiamo fatto un bel — di strada insieme,* we have gone a long way together; *c'è un lungo — da qui alla chiesa,* it is a long way (*o* distance) from here to the church; *la seguii per un lungo —,* I followed her a long way ‖ *ad un —, tutto d'un —, d'un —,* all of a sudden (*o* suddenly); *di — in —, — —,* now and then (*o* from time to time); *a tratti,* at intervals **5.** (*differenza*) difference: *c'è un gran — da questo a quello,* there is a great difference from this to that one ‖ *dal detto al fatto c'è gran —, prov.* there's many a slip 'twixt the cup and the lip **6.** (*passo di libro*) passage: *ho letto un — del secondo capitolo,* I have read a passage from the second chapter **7.** (*gesto, azione*) gesture: *— di spirito,* witticism (*o* witty remark *o* joke); *fu un — generoso, amichevole,* that was a generous, friendly gesture **8.** (*caratteristica*) trait, feature: *un — tipico del tuo carattere,* a typical trait of your character **9.** (*lineamento*) feature: *un viso dai tratti regolari,* a face with regular features **10.** (*modo di comportarsi*) address, bearing; manners (*pl.*); way of dealing: *un uomo con un — molto piacevole,* a man of very pleasing address; *mi piace il suo —,* I like his way of dealing with people; *il suo — simpatico lo rese molto popolare,* his nice bearing (*o* manners) made him very popular.

trattóre[1], *s.m.* **1.** (mec.) tractor: *— a cingoli,* (agr.) caterpillar (tractor) (*o* track-laying tractor); *— agricolo,* farm tractor; *— ferroviario,* railway tractor; *far funzionare un —,* to operate a tractor **2.** (*chi trae la seta dal bozzolo*) silk-spinner.

trattóre[2], *s.m.* (*oste*) inn-keeper, landlord; restaurant-keeper.

trattorìa, *s.f.* inn, tavern; restaurant.

trattríce, *V.* **trattóre** **1.**

trattúro, *s.m.* cattle-track.

tràuma, *s.m.* (med.) trauma (*pl.* traumata, traumas)

traumàtico, *ag.* (med.) traumatic.

traumatìsmo, *s.m.* (med.) traumatism.

traumatología, *s.f.* (med.) traumatology.

travagliàre, *v.t.* to torment, to afflict, to harass, to trouble: *il mal di denti lo travaglia,* his toothache torments him ‖ **travagliàrsi,** *v.r.* to worry (oneself), to toil.

travagliàto, *ag.* **1.** troubled, tormented; (*infelice*) unhappy: *esistenza travagliata,* unhappy existence **2.** (*difficile*) hard, troublous: *vita travagliata,* hard life.

travàglio, *s.m.* **1.** (*fatica*) toil, labour, travail **2.** (*del parto*) labour **3.** (*fastidio, cruccio*) trouble ‖ *avere — di stomaco,* to feel sick **4.** (*congegno per immobilizzare un cavallo che non voglia lasciarsi ferrare*) trave.

travaglióso, *ag.* toilsome, troublesome.

travalicàre, *v.t.* (letter.) to pass over (sthg.), to cross: *— i monti,* to cross the mountains.

travalicaménto, *s.m.* passing over.

travasaménto, *V.* **travàso.**

travasàre, *v.t.* to pour off, to decant: *— vino,* to decant wine.

travàso, *s.m.* **1.** pouring off, decanting **2.** (med.) effusion: *— di bile,* bilious attack; *fig.* fit of bad temper; *— di sangue,* extravasation of blood.

travàta, travatúra, *s.f.* (edil.) truss, trellis, lattice, girder: *— di un ponte,* bridge girder (*o* bridge truss); *— semplice,* king(-post) truss.

tràve, *s.f.* beam, girder, rafter: *— composta,* built-up beam (*o* truss-beam); *— di chiglia,* (mar.) bar keel; *— di coda,* (aer.) tail boom (*o* tail girder); *— di colmo* (*di un tetto*), ridgepole (*o* rooftree); *— in aggetto,* (scienza delle costruzioni) overhanging beam; *— maestra,* main girder; — *portante*, (*ferr.*) body bolster || *d'ogni fuscello fare una* —, to make mountains out of molehills || *si vede la scheggia nell'occhio altrui e non si vede la — nel proprio*, you see the mote in your brother's eye but not the beam in your own.

travedére, *v.i.* 1. (*ingannarsi*) to be mistaken 2. (*prendere una cosa per un'altra*) to mistake one thing for another || *v.t.* 1. (*vedere di sfuggita*) to catch a glimpse of (s.o., sthg.) 2. (*vedere indistintamente*) to see dimly, to see indistinctly.

travéggole, *s.f.pl.*: *avere le* —, to see double (o to mistake one thing for another): *credo che tu abbia le* —, I think you cannot see straight.

travèrsa, *s.f.* 1. (*sbarra*) cross-bar, cross-piece 2. (*ferr.*) sleeper; (*amer.*) tie 3. (*del letto*) underblanket 4. (*via*) side-road, cross-road 5. (*mar.*) deck girder.

traversàle, traversalménte, *V.* **trasversàle, trasversalménte**.

traversàre, *V.* **attraversàre**.

traversàta, *s.f.* (*di mare, fiume*) crossing, passage: *abbiamo fatto una bella* —, we have had a nice crossing.

traversía, *s.f.* 1. (*disavventura*) misfortune; mishap, accident, hardship 2. (*mar.*) strong side wind, prevailing wind.

traversína, *s.f.* (*ferr.*) sleeper; (*amer.*) tie.

traversíno, *s.m.* (*mar.*) breast band, breast rope: — *di maglia*, link stud.

travèrso, *ag.* 1. transverse, cross, crosswise: *una strada traversa*, a cross- (o side-) road || *per vie traverse*, *fig.* by underhand (o shady) methods 2. (*obliquo*) oblique, slanting: *uno sguardo* —, a slanting look || *s.m.* 1. (*estensione di un corpo nella sua larghezza*) width: *di* —, askance (o askew o awry): *l'hai appeso di* —, you have hung it askew; *il mio piano andò di* —, my plan went awry; *andare di* —, (*di cibo*) to go the wrong way; *avere il cappello di* —, to have one's hat on askew; *guardare qlcu. di* —, *fig.* to look askance at s.o. || *andare per* —, *fig.* to go wrong (with s.o.): *gli va tutto per* —, everything goes wrong with him 2. (*mar.*) side of a ship; beam: *al* —, on the beam (o abeam); *per il* — *di*, athwart.

traversóne, *s.m.* 1. cross-piece 2. (*mar.*) north-easterly gale 3. (*calcio*) diagonal shot.

travertíno, *s.m.* (*geol.*) travertine.

travestiménto, *s.m.* 1. disguise 2. (*parodia*) parody, travesty.

travestíre, *v.t.* 1. to disguise 2. (*parodiare*) to parody, to travesty 3. (*trasformare*) to alter, to transform || **travestírsi**, *v.r.* to disguise oneself (as s.o., sthg.): *si travestì da donna*, he disguised himself as a woman.

travestíto, *ag.* 1. disguised, in disguise: — *da diavolo*, disguised as a devil; *andò da loro* —, he went to them in disguise 2. (*parodiato*) parodied.

travétto, *s.m.* 1. (*piccola trave*) rafter, small beam 2. (*pop.*) (*impiegatuccio*) pen-pusher.

traviaménto, *s.m.* 1. deviation, going astray 2. (*perversione*) corruption, perversion.

traviàre, *v.t.* 1. to mislead, to lead astray: *egli fu traviato da un cattivo compagno*, he was misled (o led astray) by a bad companion 2. (*corrompere*) to corrupt; (*pervertire*) to pervert || **traviàrsi**, *v.r.* to go astray, to stray.

traviàto, *ag.* 1. misled, led astray 2. (*perverso*) corrupted, perverted.

traviatóre, *ag.* misleading; corruptive || *s.m.* misleader; corrupter.

travicèllo, *s.m.* joist, small beam, batten || *Re Travicello*, King Log.

travisaménto, *s.m.* alteration, distortion; misinterpretation; misrepresentation.

travisàre, *v.t.* to alter, to distort; to misinterpret; to misrepresent: — *un fatto*, to distort (o to twist o to misrepresent) a fact; — *il significato di una frase*, to distort (o to twist o to alter) the meaning of a sentence.

travolgènte, *ag.* sweeping, overwhelming, overpo-

wering: *emozione* —, sweeping emotion; *entusiasmo* —, overwhelming enthusiasm; *passione* —, overpowering passion.

travòlgere, *v.t.* 1. (*trascinar via*) to sweep away, to carry away: *l'alluvione travolse tutto*, the flood swept (o carried) away everything; *la casa fu travolta da una frana*, the house was swept away by a landslide 2. (*sopraffare*) to overwhelm, to rout, to crash: — *il nemico*, to overwhelm (o to rout o to crash) the enemy 3. (*investire*) to run over (s.o., sthg.): *fu travolto da un autobus*, he was (o got) run over by a bus 4. (*mettere sottosopra*) to overthrow, to overturn, to upset, to turn topsyturvy.

travolgiménto, *s.m.* 1. sweeping away, carrying away 2. (*capovolgimento*) overturning, overthrow, upsetting.

trazióne, *s.f.* (*mec. fis. med.*) traction: — *elettrica, a vapore*, electric-, steam-traction; *diverticolo da* —, (*med.*) traction diverticulum; *organi di* — *e repulsione centrali*, (*ferr.*) centre buffer coupler.

tre, *ag.num.card. s.m.* three: — *per cento*, (*comm.*) three per cent; — *quarti*, three quarters; — *volte*, three times (o *rar.* thrice); — *volte tanto*, three times as much; *regola del* —, rule of three: *eravamo in* —, we were three; *sono le* —, it is three o'clock || *un uomo* — *volte stupido*, a fool of fools.

treàlberi, *s.m.* (*mar.*) three-masted ship; three-master.

trébbia, *s.f.* 1. (*trebbiatura*) thrashing, threshing 2. (*trebbiatrice*) thrasher, thresher, thrashing machine; (*arc.*) flail.

trebbiàre, *v.t.* to thrash, to thresh; (*arc.*) to flail.

trebbiatóre, *s.m.* thrasher, thresher.

trebbiatríce, *s.f.* 1. thrasher, thresher 2. (*macchina per trebbiare*) thrashing machine, threshing machine.

trebbiatúra, *s.f.* thrashing, threshing.

trécca, *s.f.* (*spreg.*) market woman.

tréccia, *s.f.* 1. plait, braid: — *di capelli, di paglia*, plait (o braid) of hair, of straw; *ella porta le trecce*, she wears her hair in pigtails; *farsi le trecce*, to plait one's hair 2. (*tec.*) plait: — *di rame*, (*elett.*) copper plait; *conduttore a* —, (*elett.*) plaited conductor.

trecentésco, *ag.* (*art. lett.*) fourteenth century (*attributivo*); (*in Italia*) trecento (*attributivo*): *lingua, arte trecentesca*, trecento language, art.

trecentèsimo, *ag.num.ord.* three hundredth.

trecentísta, *s.m.* (*art. lett.*) fourteenth century writer, fourteenth century artist; (*italiano*) trecentist.

trecentístico, *V.* **trecentésco**.

trecènto, *ag.num.card.* three hundred: — *lire*, three hundred lire || *s.m.* (*quattordicesimo secolo*) fourteenth century; (*art. lett. italiana*) trecento.

tredicènne, *ag.* thirteen years old (*predicativo*); thirteen-year-old (*attributivo*) || *s.m.* thirteen-year-old boy || *s.f.* thirteen-year-old girl.

tredicèsimo, *ag.num.ord. s.m.* thirteenth.

trédici, *ag.num.card. s.m.* thirteen || *ore* —, one o'clock (o one p.m.).

tréfolo, *s.m.* strand: — *centrale*, core strand; *macchina per fare trefoli*, stranding machine; *avvolgere i trefoli*, to twist strands.

tregènda, *s.f.* 1. witches' sabbath: *notte di* —, Walpurgis night; (*notte tempestosa*) stormy night 2. (*pandemonio, confusione*) pandemonium.

tréggia, *s.f.* drag.

trégua, *s.f.* 1. truce: *una* — *di due ore*, a two hours' truce || *la Tregua di Dio*, (*st.*) the Truce of God 2. (*riposo*) rest, respite: *il dolore non gli dà* —, the pain gives him no rest || *senza* —, unrelentingly: *lavorare senza* —, to work incessantly.

tremacuòre, *s.m.* 1. (*palpitazione*) palpitation 2. (*trepidazione*) trepidation; (*ansietà*) anxiety.

tremànte, *ag.* shaking, trembling; (*di freddo*) shivering; (*di eccitazione, paura*) quivering; (*di orrore, repugnanza*) shuddering.

Tremànti, *s.m.pl.* (*Quaccheri*) Quakers.

tremàre, *v.i.* to shake (with sthg.), to tremble (with sthg.); (*di freddo*) to shiver (with sthg.); (*di eccitazione, paura*) to quiver (with sthg.), to quake (with sthg.); (*di orrore, repugnanza*) to shudder (with sthg.): *le foglie tremavano al vento,* the leaves were quivering in the wind; *gli tremano le mani,* his hands shake; *le tremavano le labbra,* her lips quivered; *la terra tremava,* the earth was quaking; *la voce gli tremò dalla gioia,* his voice trembled with joy; *tremo a pensarci,* I tremble (o I shudder) to think of it; *tremo per lui,* I tremble for him; — *di freddo,* to shiver (o to shake) with cold; — *di paura,* to tremble (o to quake) with fear; — *come una foglia,* to tremble like a leaf; — *tutto,* to tremble all over (o *fam.* to be all of a tremble).

tremarèlla, *s.f.* (*fam.*) shivers (*pl.*): *mi viene la* — *se solo ci penso,* I get the shivers if I think of it; *avere la* —, to be in a funk (o to shake in one's shoes); *far venire la* — *a qlcu.,* to give s.o. the shivers.

tremàtòdi, *s.m.pl.* (*zool.*) Trematoda.

tremebóndo, *ag.* trembling.

tremendaménte, *av.* **1.** awfully, terribly; tremendously; (*terribilmente*) dreadfully **2.** (*fam.*) (*straordinariamente*) awfully: *è* — *carina,* she is awfully nice.

tremèndo, *ag.* **1.** awful, terrible; tremendous; (*terribile*) dreadful **2.** (*fam.*) (*straordinario*) awful: *ho preso un* — *raffreddore,* I've caught an awful cold.

trementína, *s.f.* (*chim.*) turpentine: *essenza di* —, oil of turpentine.

tremíla, *ag.num.card.* three thousand.

tremillèsimo, *ag.num.ord.s.m.* three thousandth.

trèmito, *s.m.* shake, tremble, trembling; tremor; (*di freddo*) shiver, shivering; (*di eccitazione, paura*) quiver, quivering, quake; (*di orrore, repugnanza*) shudder, shuddering: *aveva un* — *di gioia, di pianto nella voce,* he had a tremor of joy, of tears in his voice; *fu preso dal* —, he started trembling (o shivering).

tremolànte, *ag.* shaking, trembling; (*di luce*) flickering; (*di stelle*) twinkling; (*di foglie*) quivering; (*di voce*) faltering: *mani tremolanti,* shaking hands; *voce* —, faltering (o trembling) voice.

tremolàre, *v.i.* (*di luce*) to flicker; (*di stelle*) to twinkle; (*di foglie*) to quiver: *le foglie tremolavano al vento,* the leaves were quivering in the wind; *una luce che tremola,* a flickering light.

tremolío, *s.m.* (*di luce*) flickering; (*di stelle*) twinkle, twinkling; (*di foglie*) quiver, quivering.

trèmolo, *ag.* trembling, tremulous; (*di luce*) flickering; (*di foglie*) quivering: *parlò con voce tremola,* he spoke in a trembling voice ‖ *s.m.* **1.** (*mus.*) tremolo **2.** (*bot.*) trembling poplar.

tremóre, *s.m.* **1.** (*med.*) tremor: — *alcoolico,* tremor potatorum **2.** *V.* **trèmito.**

tremòto, (*pop.*) per **terremòto.**

trèmulo, *V.* **trèmolo.**

trenàggio, *s.m.* training.

trèno[1], *s.m.* **1.** train: — *a breve percorso, locale,* local train; — *accelerato,* slow train; — *a lungo percorso,* mainline train; — *a vagoni intercomunicanti,* corridor train; — *bestiame,* cattle train; — *blindato,* armoured train; — *dai dintorni al capoluogo,* up train; — *dal capoluogo ai dintorni,* down train; — *del mattino,* morning train; *il* — *delle 9,45,* the 9.45 train; — *di lusso,* luxury train; — *direttissimo,* fast train; — *diretto,* through (o fast) train; — *di soccorso,* breakdown train; — *festivo,* excursion train; — *locale,* local train; — *merci,* goods train (o *amer.* freight train); — *militare,* troop train; — *omnibus,* stopping train (o slow train o *amer.* accomodation train); — *passeggeri,* passenger train; — *rapido,* express (train); *arrivo di un* — train arrival; *attenti al* — *!,* look out for locomotive!; *composizione di un* —, train composition; *formazione di un* —, making-up of a train; *in* —, in the train; *movimento dei treni,* train traffic; *partenza di un* —, train departure; *passaggio di un* —, running through of a train; *scomposizione dei treni,* splitting up of trains; *viaggio in* —, train journey; *il* — *è in orario,* the train is in good (o schedule) time; *andare in* —, to go by train; *dare la partenza a un* —, to despatch a train; *dare via libera al* —, to let the train run through; *perdere un* —, to miss a train; *pranzare in* —, to have dinner on the train; *prendere un* —, to catch a train; *salire in* —, to get into the train; *scendere dal* —, to get off (o out of) the train **2.** (*seguito, scorta*) train, retinue: *arrivò con il suo* — *di attendenti,* he arrived with his train of attendants **3.** (*tenore*) way of living, routine: *ha un* — *di vita molto strano,* he has a very strange way of living; *sono stanco del mio* — *di vita,* I am tired of my routine.

trèno[2], *s.m.,* **trenodía,** *s.f.* lamentation ‖ *i treni di Geremia,* (*Bibbia*) the lamentations of Jeremiah.

trénta, *ag.num.card.s.m.* thirty ‖ — *e quaranta,* (*giuoco di carte*) trente et quarante ‖ *i Trenta Tiranni,* (*st.*) the Thirty Tyrants ‖ *la Guerra dei Trent'Anni,* (*st.*) the Thirty Years' War ‖ *chi ha fatto* — *può far trentuno,* (*fam.*) if you have done so much, you might as well go the whole hog.

trentaduèsimo, *ag.num.ord.* thirty-second ‖ *s.m.* (*tip.*) thirty-twomo, 32mo: *un libro in* —, a thirty-twomo (o 32mo) book.

trentamíla, *ag.num.card.* thirty thousand.

trentaseièsimo, *s.m.* (*tip.*) thirty-sixmo. 36mo.

trentatré, *ag.num.card.s.m.* thirty-three ‖ *dica* —, (*med.*) say ninety-nine.

trentènne, *ag.* thirty years old (*predicativo*); thirty-year-old (*attributivo*) ‖ *s.m.* thirty-year-old man ‖ *s.f.* thirty-year-old woman.

trentènnio, *s.m.* period of thirty years.

trentèsimo, *ag.num.ord.s.m.* thirtieth.

trentína, *s.f.* about thirty, some thirty: *una* — *di uomini,* about (o some) thirty men; *aver passato la* —, to be in one's thirties; *essere sulla* —, to be about thirty.

Trentíno, *no.pr.m.* (*geog.*) Trentino.

Trènto, *no.pr.f.* (*geog.*) Trent, Trento ‖ *il Concilio di* —, (*st.*) the Council of Trent.

trentunèsimo, *ag.num.ord.s.m.* thirty-first.

trentúno, *ag.num.card.s.m.* thirty-one.

trepestío, *s.m.* stamping.

trepidaménte, *av.* tremblingly, anxiously, timorously.

trepidànte, *ag.* trembling, anxious, timorous.

trepidàre, *v.i.* to tremble, to be anxious, to be worried; to be in a flutter: *trepidava nell'attesa di notizie,* she was all in a flutter while waiting for the news; — *per qlcu., ql.co.,* to tremble for (o to be anxious about o to be worried about) s.o., sthg.

trepidazióne, *s.f.* trepidation, anxiety, timorousness, worry.

trèpido, *ag.* trembling, anxious, timorous.

treppiède, *s.m.* **1.** (*sostegno per pentole*) trivet **2.** (*di macchina fotografica*) tripod **3.** (*sgabello*) three-legged stool.

trequàrti, *s.m.* (*chir.*) trocar.

trésca, *s.f.* **1.** intrigue: — *amorosa,* affair (o intrigue) **2.** (*danza popolare*) "tresca" (country dance).

trescàre, *v.i.* **1.** to intrigue, to plot; (*avere una tresca amorosa*) to have an affair **2.** (*ballare la tresca*) to dance a country dance.

trescóne, *s.m.* "trescone" (country dance).

tréspolo, *s.m.* **1.** trestle **2.** (*veicolo malandato*) rickety vehicle, broken-down vehicle.

tressètte, *s.m.* "tressette" (card game).

Trèviri, *no.pr.f.* (*geog. st.*) Trier.

trèvo, *s.m.* (*mar.*) course.

triàca, *s.f.* (*farm.*) theriac(a).

triaeàle, *ag.* (*farm.*) theriacal, therial.

triaeisottaèdro, *s.m.* (*min. geom.*) triakisoctahedron.

tríade, *s.f.* triad (anche *mus.*).

triàndria, *s.f.pl.* (*bot.*) Triandria.

triangolàre, *ag.* triangular, three-cornered.

triangolarità, *s.f.* triangularity.

triangolarménte, *av.* triangularly.

triangolàto, *ag.* triangled.

triangolazióne, *s.f.* triangulation.

triàngolo, *s.m.* (*geom. mus.*) triangle: — *delle forze*, (*scienza delle costruzioni*) triangle of forces; — *equilatero, isoscele, ottuso, rettangolo, scaleno*, equilateral, isosceles, obtuse-angled, right-angled, scalene triangle; *i lati di un* —, the sides of a triangle.

triarchía, *s.f.* (*st.*) triarchy.

triàrii, *s.m.pl.* (*st.mil.*) triarii.

trías, *s.m.* (*geol.*) trias.

triàssico, *ag.* (*geol.*) triassic.

triatòmico, *ag.* (*chim.*) triatomic.

tríbade, *s.f.* tribade.

tribadísmo, *s.m.* tribadism.

tribàle, *ag.* tribal.

tribàsico, *ag.* (*chim.*) tribasic.

tribo-elettricità, *s.f.* (*elett.*) triboelectricity.

tribolaménto, *V.* **tribolazióne**.

tribolàre, *v.i.* **1.** (*faticare*) to toil, to have a lot of trouble: *tribolai molto per trovarlo*, I had a lot of trouble to find it **2.** (*soffrire*) to suffer (from sthg.), to be tormented (by sthg.): *tribola per i reumatismi*, he suffers from (*o* is afflicted with) rheumatism; *ha tribolato tutta la vita*, his life has been full of hardship ‖ *finalmente ha finito di* —, (*è morto*) at last death put an end to his sufferings ‖ *v.t.* to vex, to harass, to trouble, to disturb, to torment, to afflict, to worry: *la carestia tribolava il paese*, a famine vexed (*o* harassed) the country; *smetti di* — *tua sorella!*, stop tormenting (*o* worrying) your sister!.

tribolàto, *ag.* vexed, harassed, troubled, tormented, worried (by sthg.); afflicted (with sthg.): *una vita tribolata*, a hard life (*o* a life full of troubles).

tribolazióne, *s.f.* tribulation, suffering, affliction: *sopportò coraggiosamente le sue tribolazioni*, he endured his sufferings bravely (*o* with courage).

tríbolo, *s.m.* **1.** tribulation, trouble, suffering, worry: *la vita è piena di triboli*, life is full of troubles **2.** (*poet.*) (*rovo*) thorn, bramble, briar.

tribórdo, *s.m.* (*mar.*) starboard: *barra a* —!, starboard the helm!; *tutto a* —!, hard-a-starboard!.

tríbraco, *s.m.* (*poes.*) tribrach.

tribù, *s.f.* tribe: *le dodici* — *d'Israele*, the twelve tribes of Israel; *membro di* —, tribesman; *vita in* —, tribal life ‖ *una* — *di figli*, (*fam.*) a tribe of children; *sono una* —!, (*fam.*) they are a crowd!.

tribúna, *s.f.* **1.** (*per oratori*) tribune, platform **2.** (*per uditori*) gallery: *la* — *della stampa*, the press gallery **3.** (*spor.*) stand: — *centrale*, grand-stand **4.** (*arch.*) apse.

tribunàle, *s.m.* court (of justice), law-court, court of law; tribunal (anche *fig.*): — *civile*, civil court; — *dei minorenni*, juvenile court; *il* — *della coscienza, dell'opinione pubblica*, *fig.* the tribunal of conscience, of public opinion; — *militare*, court martial; — *penale*, criminal court; *aula di* —, court-room; *palazzo del* —, court-house (*o* Law Courts); *comparire in* —, to come before the court; *trascinare qlcu. in* —, to bring s.o. to court.

tribunalésco, *ag.* (*spreg.*) pettifogging: *questione tribunalesca*, pettifogging matter.

tribunàto, *s.m.* (*st. romana*) tribuneship, tribunate.

tribunésco, *ag.* (*spreg.*) flowery: *discorso* —, flowery address.

tribunízio, *ag.* (*da, di tribuno*) tribunicial, tribunitial, tribunitian.

tribúno, *s.m.* (*st. romana*) tribune: *tribuni della plebe*, tribunes of the people.

tributàre, *v.t.* to bestow, to grant, to give, to pay: — *grandi onori a qlcu.*, to bestow great honours upon

s.o.; — *omaggio al genio di un poeta*, to pay homage to the genius of a poet.

tributàrio, *ag.* **1.** (*che dà tributo*) tributary: *fiume, paese* —, tributary river, country **2.** (*fiscale*) fiscal: *polizia tributaria*, fiscal police; *sistema* —, system of taxation ‖ *s.m.* tributary.

tribúto, *s.m.* tribute (anche *fig.*): *imporre un* — *ad un paese*, to lay a country under tribute; *pagare il proprio* — *alla natura*, (*morire*) to pay the debt of nature; *pagare il proprio* — *di sangue a una causa*, to pay one's tribute of blood to a cause.

trichèco, *s.m.* (*zool.*) walrus (*pl.* walruses, walrus).

trichíasi, *s.f.* (*med.*) trichiasis.

trichína, *s.f.* (*zool.*) trichina (*pl.* trichinae).

trichinòsi, *s.f.* (*patol.*) trichinosis.

tricíclo, *s.m.* tricycle: — *a motore*, motor-tricycle.

tricípite, *ag.* **1.** three-headed: *aquila* —, three-headed eagle **2.** (*anat.*) triceps (*attributivo*) ‖ *s.m.* (*anat.*) triceps.

triclínio, *s.m.* (*archeol.*) triclinium (*pl.* triclinia).

triclíno, *ag.* (*min.*) triclinic.

tricofitiàsi, *s.f.* (*patol.*) trichophytosis.

tricología, *s.f.* trichology.

tricolóre, *ag.* tricolour, tricoloured; (*amer.*) tricolor, tricolored ‖ *s.m.* tricolour; (*amer.*) tricolor ‖ *il Tricolore*, the Italian flag.

tricòma, *s.m.* (*med.*) trichoma.

tricoptilòsi, *s.f.* trichoptilosis.

tricòrde, *ag.* (*mus.*) trichord.

tricòrne, *ag.* tricorn.

tricòrno, *s.m.* tricorn (hat).

tricòsi, *s.f.* (*patol.*) trichosis.

tricromía, *s.f.* **1.** (*processo di riproduzione zincografica a colori*) trichromatism **2.** (*riproduzione zincografica a colori*) trichromatic printing.

trictràc, *s.m.* (*giuoco*) trick-track.

tricuspidàle, *ag.* tricuspidal, tricuspidate.

tricúspide, *ag.* tricuspid.

tridentàto, *ag.* **1.** (*a tre punte*) tridental, tridentate **2.** (*armato di tridente*) tridented.

tridènte, *s.m.* **1.** (*di Poseidone*) trident (of Poseidon) **2.** (*per il fieno*) hayfork.

tridentíno, *ag.* Tridentine: *il Concilio Tridentino*, the Council of Trent.

tridimensionàle, *ag.* tridimensional; (*fis.*) three-dimensional.

tridimensionalità, *s.f.* tridimensionality; (*fis.*) three-dimensionality.

tríduo, *s.m.* (*eccl.*) triduum; (*rar.*) triduo.

trièdro, *ag.* trihedral ‖ *s.m.* trihedron.

trielína, *s.f.* (*chim.*) trichloroethylene.

triennàle, *ag.s.f.* triennial ‖ *la Triennale di Milano*, the Triennial of Milan.

triennalménte, *av.* triennially, every three years.

triènne, *ag.* **1.** (*triennale*) triennial **2.** (*di tre anni*) three years old (*predicativo*); three-year-old (*attributivo*).

triènnio, *s.m.* period of three years; triennium.

trieràrca, *s.m.* (*st.*) trierarch.

trierarchía, *s.f.* (*st.*) trierarchy.

Trièste, *no.pr.f.* (*geog.*) Trieste.

trifàse, *ag.* (*elett.*) three-phase (*attributivo*): *circuito* —, three-phase circuit; *convertitore* —, three-phase converter; *corrente* —, three-phase current.

trifàsico, *ag.* (*elett.*) three-phase (*attributivo*): *sistema* —, three-phase system.

trifenilmetàno, *s.m.* (*chim.*) triphenylmethane.

trifído, *ag.* (*bot. zool.*) trifid; three-cleft, tripartite.

trifogliàto, *ag.* (*bot.*) trifoliate, trifoliated.

trifòglio, *s.m.* **1.** (*bot.*) clover, trefoil, shamrock: *l'emblema nazionale irlandese è il* —, the national emblem of Ireland is the shamrock **2.** (*arch.*) trefoil.

trífola, *s.f.* (*dial.*) (*tartufo*) truffle.

trífora, *s.f.* (*arch.*) three-mullioned window, mullioned window with three lights.

triforcàrsi, *v.r.* to trifurcate.

triforcàto, triforcúto, *ag.* trifurcate, trifurcated.

trifórme, *ag.* triform, triformed.

trigèmino, *ag.* **1.** trigeminous: *parto —,* birth of triplets **2.** (*anat.*) trigeminal ‖ *s.m.* (*anat.*) trigeminal (nerve).

trigèsimo, *ag.num.ord.* thirtieth ‖ *s.m.: nel — della morte del Signor X,* on the thirtieth day after Mr. X's death.

tríglia, *s.f.* (*ittiol.*) red mullet ‖ *occhi di —, fig.* dull (lifeless) eyes; *fare l'occhio di — a qlcu.,* to cast amorous glances at s.o. (*o* to make sheep's eyes at s.o.).

tríglifo, *s.m.* (*arch.*) triglyph.

trigonàle, *ag.* trigonal.

trigono, *ag.* trigonal ‖ *s.m.* **1.** (*mar.*) lateen sail **2.** (*st. mus.*) trigon, trigonon.

trigonometría, *s.f.* trigonometry: *— piana,* plane trigonometry; *— sferica,* spherical trigonometry.

trigonometricaménte, *av.* trigonometrically.

trigonomètrico, *ag.* trigonometric.

trilateràle, *ag.* trilateral.

trilàtero, *ag.s.m.* (*geom.*) trilateral.

trilineàre, *ag.* trilinear.

trilíngue, *ag.* trilingual.

triliόne, *s.m.* **1.** (*secondo il sistema italiano, americano, francese, corrispondente a 1000⁴*) billion; (*amer.*) trillion **2.** (*secondo il sistema tedesco e inglese, corrispondente a 1000⁶*) trillion; (*amer.*) quintillion.

trillànte, *ag.* ringing: *campanelli trillanti,* ringing bells.

trillàre, *v.i.* to trill; (*squillare*) to ring: *trillò un campanello,* a bell rang; *il canarino trilla nella gabbia,* the canary is trilling in its cage.

trilleggiàre, *v.i.* to trill repeatedly.

tríllo, *s.m.* (*mus.*) trill.

trilobàto, *ag.* trilobate, trilobed, trilobated.

trilobíte, *s.m.* (*paleont.*) trilobite.

trilòbo, *ag.s.m.* (*arch.*) trilobe.

trilogía, *s.f.* (*st. teat.*) trilogy: *la — del « Wallenstein » di Schiller può essere considerata il suo capolavoro,* Schiller's "Wallenstein" trilogy may be considered his masterpiece.

trilústre, *ag.* (*letter.*) fifteen years old (*predicativo*); fifteen-year-old (*attributivo*).

trimestràle, *ag.* quarterly, trimensual, trimestrial: *pagamento —,* quarterly payment; *rivista —,* quarterly review.

trimestralménte, *av.* quarterly.

trimèstre, *s.m.* **1.** quarter; (*scolastico*) term **2.** (*assegno, paga trimestrale*) quarterage, quarter's salary.

trimètrico, *ag.* (*min.*) trimetric(al).

trímetro, *s.m.* (*poes.*) trimeter: *— giambico,* jambic trimeter; *— trocaico,* trochaic trimeter.

trimotóre, *s.m.* (*aer.*) three-engined aeroplane, trimotor: *— da bombardamento,* three-engined bomber.

trimpellàre, *v.i.* **1.** (*strimpellare*) to strum **2.** (*vacillare*) to stagger, to reel **3.** (*esitare*) to hesitate.

trimpellío, *s.m.* **1.** (*strimpellìo*) strum, strumming **2.** (*vacillamento*) staggering, reeling about **3.** (*esitazione*) hesitation.

Trimúrti, *s.f.* (*relig. indù*) Trimurti.

trína, *s.f.* lace, lace-work: *un colletto di —,* a lace collar.

trinàia, *s.f.* lace-maker.

trinàre, *v.t.* to trim with lace.

trínca, *s.f.* (*mar.*) gammon(ing) ‖ *nuovo di —,* (*fam.*) brand new.

trincàre¹, *v.t.* (*mar.*) to gammon, to woold.

trincàre², *v.t.* (*fam.*) to gulp; to swill.

trincaríno, *s.m.* (*mar.*) stringer: *— di coperta,* deck stringer.

trincàta, *s.f.* (*fam.*) draught, gulp: *in una sola —,* at one gulp.

trincatúra, *s.f.* (*mar.*) gammoning.

trincèa, *s.f.* **1.** (*mil.*) trench; dug-out: *guerra di —,* trench war **2.** (*ferr.*) cutting **3.** *— d'accesso,* (*miner.*) approach cutting.

trinceraménto, *s.m.* entrenchment.

trinceràre, *v.t.* to entrench: *il generale trincerò le sue truppe lungo il fiume,* the general had his men dig themselves in along the river ‖ **trinceràrsi,** *v.r.* to entrench oneself (*anche fig.*): *— dietro un pretesto,* to entrench oneself behind (*o* in) a pretext.

trincétto, *s.m.* (*strum. artig.*) paring knife, shoemaker's knife.

trinchettína, *s.f.* (*mar.*) fore topmast staysail.

trinchétto, *s.m.* (*mar.*): (*albero di*) *—,* foremast; *vela di —,* foresail.

trinciànte, *ag.* carving, sharp ‖ *s.m.* carver, carving knife.

trinciaforàggi, *s.f.* (*mec. agr.*) fodder-cutter.

trinciapàglia, *s.m.* (*agr.*) hay-cutter.

trinciàre, *v.t.* to cut (up), to hash (up); (*carne*) to carve: *— la paglia,* to cut up straw; *— un pollo,* to carve a chicken ‖ *— giudizi su ql.co.,* to judge sthg. rashly (*o* to express rash judgements about sthg.) ‖ *— i panni addosso a qlcu.,* to speak ill of s.o.

trinciàto, *ag.* cut up, hashed up; (*di carne*) carved ‖ *s.m.* cut tobacco, pipe-tobacco.

trinciatóre, *ag.* carving (up) ‖ *s.m.* carver, cutter.

trinciatríce, *s.f.* (*mec. agr.*) hay-cutter.

trinciatúra, *s.f.* cutting up, hashing up; (*di carne*) carving.

trincóne, *s.m.* (*ubriacone*) drunkard.

trinità, *s.f.* trinity ‖ *la Santissima Trinità,* the Trinity.

trinitàrio, *ag.* (*teol.*) trinitarian.

trinitrotoluène, *s.m.* (*chim.*) trinitrotoluene.

tríno, *ag.* trine.

trinomiàle, *ag.* (*mat.*) trinomial.

trinòmio, *s.m.* (*mat.*) trinomial.

trío, *s.m.* (*mus.*) trio (*pl.* trios).

tríodo, *s.m.* (*elett.*) triode.

trionfàle, *ag.* triumphal: *arco, carro, corona —,* triumphal arch, car, crown.

trionfalménte, *av.* triumphantly, in triumph.

trionfànte, *ag.* triumphant, exulting: *grida trionfanti,* triumphant shouts; *voce —,* triumphant voice ‖ *Chiesa Trionfante,* Church Triumphant.

trionfàre, *v.i.* **1.** to triumph (over s.o., sthg.); (*essere trionfante*) to be triumphant: *Cesare trionfò sui Galli,* Caesar triumphed over the Gauls; *— del proprio nemico,* to triumph over one's enemy; *la sua anima trionfa ora in cielo,* now his soul is triumphant in heaven **2.** (*aver ragione*) to overcome (s.o., sthg.), to get over (sthg.): *— di una difficoltà,* to overcome a difficulty.

trionfatóre, *ag.* triumphing ‖ *s.m.,* **trionfatríce,** *s.f.* triumpher.

trionfo, *s.m.* **1.** triumph, success: *il — della verità,* the triumph of truth; *arco di —,* triumphal arch; *fu ricevuto in —,* he was received in triumph; *ottenere molti trionfi,* to achieve many triumphs; *portare qlcu. in —,* to carry s.o. shoulder-high **2.** (*a carte*) trump **3.** (*alzata da tavola*) centre-piece.

triόni, *s.m.pl.* (*astr.*) Triones, Charles's Wain.

tripanosòma, *s.m.* (*zool.*) trypanosome.

tripartíre, *v.t.* to divide into three (parts).

tripartíto, *ag.* tripartite: *un patto —,* a tripartite agreement.

tripartizióne, *s.f.* tripartition.

tripètalo, *ag.* (*bot.*) tripetalous.

trípla, *s.f.* (*mus.*) triple measure, triple time.

triplàno, *s.m.* (*aer.*) triplane.

triplicàre, *v.t.* to treble, to triplicate: *— uno stipendio,* to treble (*o* to triplicate) a salary.

triplicataménte, *av.* triply; (*rar.*) trebly.

triplicàto, *ag.* trebled, triplicated ‖ *in —,* in triplicate.

triplicazióne, *s.f.* triplication.

tríplice, *ag.* threefold, treble, triple ‖ *la Triplice Alleanza,* (*st.*) the Triple Alliance.

triplicemènte, *av.* threefoldly, trebly, triply.

triplicità, *s.f.* triplicity.

tríplo, *ag.* triple, treble, threefold: *un — mento,* a triple chin; *in — tempo,* in three times the time; *con una corda tripla,* with a threefold string ‖ *s.m.* triple: *egli guadagna il — del mio stipendio,* he earns treble my salary; *questo costerà il —,* this will cost three times as much; *sei è il — di due,* six is the triple of two; *volle il — di quanto gli dovevo,* he wanted three times as much as I owed him.

trípode, *s.m.* **1.** (*archeol.*) tripod **2.** (*anat.*) tripod.

tripodía, *s.f.* (*poes.*) tripody.

tripoli¹, *s.m.* (*min.*) tripoli, rottenstone.

Trípoli², *no.pr.f.* (*geog.*) Tripoli.

tripolíno, tripolitàno, *ag.s.m.* Tripolitan.

trípolo, *s.m.* (*min.*) tripoli, rottenstone.

tríppa, *s.f.* **1.** (*cuc.*) tripe **2.** (*volg.*) (*pancia*) belly, paunch, corporation ‖ *metter su —,* to put on weight.

trippàio, *s.m.* tripe-seller, tripe-dealer.

trippería, *s.f.* tripery, tripe-shop.

trippóne, *s.m.* (*scherz.*) pot-bellied man.

tripsína, *s.f.* (*chim. biol.*) trypsin.

tripudiàre, *v.i.* to exult, to make merry; (*rar.*) to tripudiate: *la folla tripudiò all'annuncio della vittoria,* the crowd went wild with joy at the news of the victory.

tripúdio, *s.m.* **1.** (*esultanza*) exultation, exultancy, jubilation **2.** (*st.*) tripudium (*pl.* tripudia).

trirégno, *s.m.* (*eccl.*) (Pope's) tiara.

trirème, *s.f.* (*st. mar.*) trireme.

trisàgio, *s.m.* (*eccl.*) Trisagion.

trisàvola, *s.f.* great-great-grandmother.

trisàvolo, *s.m.* great-great-grandfather.

trisezióne, *s.f.* (*geom.*) trisection.

trisillàbico, *ag.* trisyllabic.

trisíllabo, *ag.* trisyllabic: *parola trisillaba,* trisyllabic word ‖ *s.m.* trisyllable.

trísma, *s.m.* (*med.*) thrismus; (*pop.*) lockjaw.

tristaménte, *av.* **1.** (*malvagiamente*) wickedly; (*con cattiveria*) badly **2.** (*meschinamente*) meanly, poorly **3.** (*tristemente*) sadly **4.** *— famoso,* notorious.

Tristàno, *no.pr.m.* Tristram ‖ *— e Isotta,* Tristram and Iseult.

tristanzuòlo, *ag.* **1.** (*misero, sparuto*) dejected-looking **2.** (*tristo*) ill-disposed.

tríste, *ag.* **1.** sad (about sthg.); sorrowful (of sthg.); (*addolorato*) grieved (at, over, of sthg.): *un — caso,* a sad case; *notizia —,* sad news; *sguardo —,* sorrowful look; *è — per la morte del suo diletto amico,* he is grieved at (o of o over) the death of his dearest friend; *egli è sempre molto —,* he is always very sad; *aver l'aria —,* to look sad **2.** (*cupo*) gloomy; (*deprimente*) depressing: *un luogo —,* a gloomy place.

tristeménte, *av.* sadly, sorrowfully.

tristézza, *s.f.* **1.** sadness, sorrow; (*dolore*) grief **2.** (*cupezza*) gloominess.

tristízia, *s.f.* **1.** (*malvagità*) wickedness, wretchedness **2.** (*tristezza*) sadness, sorrow.

trísto, *ag.* **1.** (*malvagio*) wicked; (*cattivo*) bad: *un omaccio —,* a wicked man **2.** (*meschino*) mean, poor ‖ *fare una trista figura,* to cut a poor figure **3.** (*disgraziato*) wretched **4.** (*triste*) sad ‖ *s.m.* wicked fellow, villain, rogue: *fare la fine del —,* to come to a bad end.

trisúleo, *ag.* (*poet.*) three-pointed, trifid, three-cleft.

tritàbile, *ag.* triturable.

tritacàrne, *s.m.* (*cuc.*) mincer, mincing machine.

tritaménto, *V.* tritatúra.

tritàre, *v.t.* **1.** to mince, to hash (up): *— carne,* to mince (o to hash up) meat **2.** (*pestare*) to pound.

tritàto, *ag.* minced, hashed: *carne tritata,* minced (o hashed) meat.

tritatúra, *s.f.* **1.** mincing, hashing **2.** (*pestatura*) pounding.

tritatútto, *s.m.* (*cuc.*) mincer, mincing machine.

tritèllo, *s.m.* (*agr.*) pollard, bran.

tríto, *ag.* **1.** (*tritato*) minced, hashed: *carne trita,* minced (o hashed) meat **2.** (*logoro*) worn out: *un vestito —,* a worn-out dress **3.** (*notissimo, comune*) trite, worn-out, stale, commonplace, hackneyed: *idee trite,* trite (o stale) ideas; *parole trite,* hackneyed words.

tritolàre, *v.t.* **1.** (*schiacciare*) to crush **2.** *V.* tritàre.

tritòlo¹, *s.m.* little bit, scrap.

tritòlo², *s.m.* (*chim.*) trinitrotoluene, trinitrotoluol (*abbr.* T.N.T. o TNT).

Tritóne, *no.pr.m.* (*mit.*) Triton ‖ **tritóne,** *s.m.* (*zool.*) **1.** (*mollusco*) triton **2.** (*varietà di anfibio*) newt.

tríttico, *s.m.* (*art.*) triptych.

Trittolèmo, *no.pr.m.* (*mit.*) Triptolemus, Triptolemos.

trittòngo, *s.m.* (*fonet.*) triphthong.

tritúme, *s.m.* (*briciole*) crumbs (*pl.*); (*pezzetti*) scraps (*pl.*); bits (*pl.*).

trituraménto, *s.m.* trituration.

trituràre, *v.t.* to triturate.

triturazióne, *s.f.* trituration.

triumviràle, *ag.* (*st. romana*) triumviral.

triumviràto, *s.m.* (*st. romana*) triumvirate.

triúmviro, *s.m.* (*st. romana*) triumvir (*pl.* triumvirs, triumviri).

trivalènte, *ag.* (*chim.*) trivalent.

trivalènza, *s.f.* (*chim.*) trivalence, trivalency.

trivèlla, *s.f.* **1.** (*falegnameria*) auger: *— ad elica,* screw auger; *— a sgorbia,* pod auger; *— a tortiglione,* screw auger **2.** (*miner.*) drill: *— a granaglia,* shot drill (o calyx drill); *— a percussione,* percussion drill (o churn drill).

trivellaménto, *V.* trivellatúra.

trivellàre, *v.t.* to bore, to drill: *— un pozzo petrolifero,* to drill an oil well.

trivellatúra, trivellazióne, *s.f.* (*min.*) drilling, boring, sinking: *— a getto (d'acqua, d'aria),* jetting; *— a rotazione,* rotary drilling; *— profonda,* deep drilling; *— sottomarina,* offshore drilling (o submarine drilling); *torre di —,* derrick.

trivèllo, *s.m.* (*mec.*) gimlet.

triviàle, *ag.* vulgar, low, coarse: *linguaggio —,* vulgar (o coarse) language.

trivialità, *s.f.* **1.** vulgarity, coarseness: *la — del suo contegno mi disgustò,* the vulgarity of his behaviour disgusted me **2.** (*espressione triviale*) coarse expression: *dire —,* to use coarse language.

trivialménte, *av.* vulgarly, coarsely.

trívio, *s.m.* **1.** (*crocicchio di strade*) cross-roads ‖ *gente da —,* vulgar (o low) people; *linguaggio da —,* coarse language **2.** (*nella scuola medioevale*) trivium (*pl.* trivia).

trocàico, *ag.* (*poes.*) trochaic.

trocantère, *s.m.* (*anat.*) trochanter: *il grande —,* the great trochanter (o trochanter major); *il piccolo —,* the lesser trochanter (o trochanter minor).

trochèo, *s.m.* (*poes.*) trochee.

trocísco, *s.m.* (*farm.*) troche, trochisk.

tròclea, *s.f.* (*anat.*) trochlea (*pl.* trochleae).

trocleàre, *ag.* (*anat.*) trochlear.

trofèo, *s.m.* trophy: *— di guerra,* trophy of war.

tròfico, *ag.* (*fisiol.*) trophic.

troglodíta, *s.c.* troglodyte (anche *fig.*).

troglodítico, *ag.* troglodytic(al).

troglodítismo, *s.m.* troglodytism.

trògolo, *s.m.* trough.

tròia¹, *s.f.* (*scrofa*) sow.

Tròia², *no.pr.f.* (*geog. st.*) Troy.

troiàno, *ag.s.m.* Trojan.

tròica, *s.f.* troika.

Tròilo, *no.pr.m.* (*lett.*) Troilus.

trómba, *s.f.* **1.** trumpet: *— acustica,* ear trumpet; *squillo di —,* trumpet blast; *suonare la —,* to sound (o to blow) the trumpet ‖ *la — del giudizio,* the last trump **2.** (*buccina*) bugle: *le trombe suonavano,* the bugles were blowing **3.** (*anat.*) tube: *— di Eustachio,*

Eustachian tube 4. (*proboscide*) trunk 5. (*pompa*) pump: — *idraulica*, hydraulic pump 6. (*delle scale, dell'ascensore*) well 7. (*meteorologia*): — *d'aria*, tornado (*pl.* tornadoes); — *marina*, water-spout.

trombàio, *s.m.* 1. (*chi fabbrica trombe*) trumpet-maker 2. (*idraulico*) plumber.

trombàre, *v.t.* 1. (*decantare*) to decant 2. (*fam.*) (*respingere, bocciare*) to reject; (*sl.*) to plough.

trombatúra, *s.f.* 1. (*travasamento*) decanting 2. (*fam.*) (*bocciatura*) rejection; (*sl.*) plough.

trombétta, *s.f.* 1. trumpet 2. (*arc.*) trumpeter.

trombettière, *s.m.* 1. (*mil.*) trumpeter 2. (*di buccina*) bugler.

trómbo, *s.m.* (*med.*) thrombus (*pl.* thrombi).

trombóne, *s.m.* 1. (*mus.*) trombone: *suonatore di* —, trombonist 2. (*schioppo con canna corta*) blunderbuss: *in quei tempi i banditi erano armati di* —, in those days bandits were armed with blunderbusses.

trombòsi, *s.f.* (*patol.*) thrombosis.

troncàbile, *ag.* 1. that can be cut off 2. *fig.* that can be broken off, interrupted.

troncaménto, *s.m.* 1. cutting off 2. breaking off.

troncàre, *v.t.* 1. to cut off; (*rar.*) to truncate: — *un ramo*, to cut off a branch; — *la testa a qlcu.*, to cut off s.o.'s head (*o* to behead s.o.) 2. *fig.* to break off, to cut short, to interrupt: *la sua carriera fu troncata da una grave malattia*, his career was ruined by a serious illness; — *un fidanzamento*, to break off an engagement; — *una conversazione*, to break off (*o* to interrupt) a conversation; — *le relazioni con qlcu.*, to break off relations with s.o.; — *il respiro a qlcu.*, to cut s.o.'s breath ‖ — *la strada a qlcu.*, to block s.o.'s way.

troncatúra, *s.f.* 1. cutting off 2. breaking off; (*metal.*) sprueing; (*ind. mec.*) cropping.

tronchesíno, *s.m.*, **tronchétti**, *s.m.pl.* cutting nippers (*pl.*).

trónco, *ag.* 1. truncate(d), cut off; broken (off); (*mutilato*) mutilated, maimed: *parlava con parole tronche*, he was speaking in broken words; *un uomo con le gambe tronche*, a man with his legs cut off ‖ *lasciare un lavoro in* —, to leave a work unfinished ‖ *licenziare in* —, to sack on the spot 2. (*gram.*) accented on the last syllable ‖ *s.m.* 1. trunk: *il* — *di un albero*, the trunk of a tree; *il* — *di un corpo umano*, the trunk of a human body 2. (*di albero abbattuto*) log: *alcuni tronchi d'albero galleggiavano sull'acqua*, a few logs were floating on the water 3. (*mozzicone d'albero ancora radicato nel terreno*) stump 4. — *ferroviario*, railway-section; (*diramazione*) branch line 5. (*geom.*) frustum (*pl.* frusta, frustums).

troncóne, *s.m.* stump: *il* — *di un albero, di una gamba*, the stump of a tree, of a leg.

troneggiàre, *v.i.* 1. to dominate (sthg.); (*con autorità*) to lord it (over s.o., sthg.): *troneggiava nel salotto*, she was dominating the drawing-room 2. (*torreggiare*) to tower (over s.o., sthg.) 3. (*spiccare*) to stand out.

tronfiàre, *v.i.* (*arc.*) 1. (*andare pavoneggiandosi*) to strut 2. (*ansimare*) to pant.

tronfièzza, *s.f.* 1. conceitedness 2. (*di stile*) pompousness.

trónfio, *ag.* 1. puffed up, conceited: *se ne andava* —, he was strutting along 2. (*di stile*) pompous.

tròno, *s.m.* 1. throne: *deporre un re dal* —, to dethrone a king; *salire al* —, to come to the throne (*o* to ascend the throne); *rinunciare al* —, to renounce the throne 2. *i Troni*, (*eccl.*) the Thrones.

tropicàle, *ag.* tropical.

tròpico, *s.m.* tropic: — *del Cancro, del Capricorno*, (*geog. astr.*) Tropic of Cancer, of Capricorn.

tropísmo, *s.m.* (*scient.*) tropism.

tròpo, *s.m.* (*ret.*) trope.

tropología, *s.f.* tropology.

tropologicaménte, *av.* tropologically.

tropològico, *ag.* tropological.

troposfèra, *s.f.* (*geol.*) troposphere.

tròppo, *ag.* too many; *pl.* too many: *troppi amici*, too many friends; — *amore*, too much love; *troppa gente*, too many people; — *lavoro*, too much work; *troppi libri*, too many books; *questo è* —*!* (*o* this has gone too far!); *questo dolore è* — *per sopportarlo da soli*, this sorrow is too much for one person to bear alone ‖ — *tempo*, too long (*o* too much time): *rimasi là* — *tempo*, I remained there too long; *l'ospite rimase* — *tempo*, the guest overstayed his welcome ‖ *av.* 1. (*con ag. ed av.*) too: — *bello per essere vero*, too good to be true; — *buono*, too good; — *gentile*, too kind; — *interessante*, too interesting: — *interessante per lasciarselo sfuggire*, too interesting to be missed; — *poco*, too little ‖ *anche* —, only too: *anche* — *lieto di aiutarti*, only too pleased to help you; *proprio* —, much too (*o* far too); all too: *le vacanze sono state proprio* — *corte*, the holidays have been all too short 2. (*con verbi*) too much: *lavora* —, he works too much; *mangia* —, he eats too much ‖ *tu lavori proprio* —, you work much too much 3. (*con valore temporale*) too long: *abbiamo aspettato* —, we have waited too long ‖ *pron.* too much; *pl.* too many (people) (*riferito a persone*) too many (*riferito a cose*) (*con partitivo*) too many: *troppi lo pensano*, too many (people) think so; *me ne hai dati troppi*, you have given me too many ‖ *il* — *stroppia*, too much is too much ‖ *me ne hai dato uno di* —, you have given me one too many ‖ *essere di* —, to be in the way (*o* to be unwelcome): *eravamo di* —, we were not wanted; *non sei di* —, you may as well stay.

tròta, *s.f.* (*ittiol.*) trout (*invariato al pl.*): — *salmonata*, salmon-trout (*o* sea-trout); *la pesca delle trote*, trout fishing.

trottàre, *v.i.* 1. to trot ‖ *far* — *un cavallo*, to trot a horse 2. *fig.* (*fam.*) to run: *mi fece* — *tutto il giorno*, he made me run around all day long; *sono in ritardo e dovrò* — *per arrivare in tempo*, I am late and I shall have to run to get there in time.

trottàta, *s.f.* 1. trot: *andare a fare una* —, to go for a trot 2. (*fam.*) run: *mi ha fatto fare una* — *per la città*, he drove me round the town.

trottatóia, *s.f.* carriage-way (in a cobbled street).

trottatóio, *s.m.* riding-ground, riding-field.

trottatóre, *s.m.* (*cavallo*) trotter.

trotterellàre, *v.i.* 1. to trot along 2. (*scherz.*) (*di persona*) to trot about; (*di bambini, di vecchi*) to toddle: *il bimbo trotterellava per la casa*, the child was toddling about the house.

tròtto, *s.m.* trot: *al gran* —, at a steady trot; *scuola di* —, riding-school; *mettere un cavallo al* —, to trot a horse; *procedere al piccolo* —, to proceed at a jog-trot.

tròttola, *s.f.* top.

trottolàre, *v.i.* to spin round, to whirl round.

trottolíno, *s.m.* (*fam.*) 1. (*bambino che cammina appena*) toddler 2. (*bambino vivacissimo*) restless child.

troupe, *s.f.* (*teat.*) troupe.

trousse, *s.f.* 1. evening bag 2. (*per attrezzi*) tool roll, tool kit.

trovàbile, *ag.* findable.

trovadóre, *s.m.* (*st. lett.*) troubadour.

trovadòrico, *ag.* troubadour (*attributivo*).

trovàre, *v.t.* 1. to find: *ho trovato il libro che avevo smarrito*, I have found the book I had lost; *trovai scritto nel giornale che era morto*, I saw in the paper that he was dead; *trovammo buona accoglienza presso i nostri amici*, we had a good welcome from our friends (*o* our friends gave us a hearty welcome); *trovò il cappotto nel baule*, he found his coat in the trunk ‖ *come trovi quel libro?*, how do you like that book?; *egli trovò pane pei suoi denti*, he got what was coming to him; *il genio civile trovò che la casa era in pericolo*, the surveyor's department found the house in a dangerous condition; *lo trovai alzato, a letto*, I found him up, in bed; *non lo trovai in casa*, I did not find him in; *non trovo più gli occhiali*, I cannot find my spectacles; *non trovo la strada per andare a casa*, I cannot find my way home; *non trovo il tempo per leggere*, I cannot find time to read; *sono lieto di trovarla in buone condizioni di salute*, I am pleased to find you in such good health; *l'ultima volta che lo vidi lo trovai ammalato*, (the) last time I saw him I found him ill ‖ — *l'espressione giusta*, to hit (*o* to chance) upon the right phrase; — *freddo, gelato, bello*, to find cold weather, freezing, good weather; — *pietà*, to find mercy; — *ql.co. errato*, to find sthg. wrong; — *ql.co. superbo*, to find sthg. magnificent; — *una scusa per ql.co.*, to find an excuse for sthg. ‖ — *da ridire su tutto*, to find fault with everything ‖ *non — colpa in alcuno*, to find fault with no one ‖ *chi cerca trova, prov.* seek and ye shall find (*o* who seeks finds) 2. (*scoprire*) to find (out): *ha trovato un nuovo sistema di farlo*, he has found a new system of doing it; *trovarono il colpevole*, they found out the culprit 3. (*incontrare*) to meet; to meet with (sthg.): *trovai molte difficoltà nel farlo*, I met with many difficulties in doing it; *il mio amico trovò la morte in un incidente aereo*, my friend met his death in an air-crash 4. (*sorprendere*) to catch: *furono trovati insieme*, they were found together; *lo trovai che rovistava in questo cassetto*, I caught him rummaging in this drawer 5. (*far visita a*) to see: *verrò a trovarti domani*, I shall come and see you to-morrow 6. (*pensare*) to think: *trovo che non dovresti farlo*, I think you should not do it ‖ **trovàrsi**, *v.r.* 1. to find oneself: *mi trovai nel giardino*, I found myself in the garden 2. (*essere*) to be; to be situated, to lie: *si trovano ancora cannibali nell'interno dell'Africa*, there are still cannibals in the heart of Africa; *ora mi trovo alla stazione*, now I am at the station; *il paese si trova a settentrione*, the village lies to the north; — *in buone, cattive condizioni finanziarie*, to be well, badly off; — *in una situazione difficile*, to be in an awkward situation 3. (*sentirsi*) to feel: *mi trovo molto bene in questo albergo*, I feel very comfortable in this hotel; — *a proprio agio*, to feel at ease; — *come a casa propria*, to feel at home 4. (*incontrarsi*) to meet: *ci trovavamo sempre vicino al ponte*, we used to meet near the bridge.

trovaròbe, *s.m.* (*teat.*) property-man (*pl.* property -men).

trovàta, *s.f.* trick, invention; (*espediente*) expedient, shift: *fu una bella —*, that was a clever trick; — *pubblicitaria*, publicity stunt.

trovatèllo, *s.m.* foundling: *ospizio per trovatelli*, foundling hospital.

trovàto, *s.m.* (*invenzione*) invention; (*scoperta*) discovery.

trovatóre, *s.m.* (*st. lett.*) troubadour.

trovièro, *s.m.* (*st. lett.*) trouvère, trouveur.

tròzza, *s.f.* (*mar.*) parrel.

truccàre, *v.t.* 1. to make up 2. (*spor.*) to fix: — *una partita*, to fix a match ‖ **truccàrsi**, *v.r.* to make (oneself) up: *gli attori si truccano sempre prima di recitare*, actors always make (themselves) up before acting; *ella si trucca troppo*, she is too much made up; — *il viso*, to make up one's face.

truccàto, *ag.* 1. made-up 2. (*spor.*) fixed: *incontro —*, fixed fight 3. *fotografia truccata*, trick photograph.

truccatóre, *s.m.*, **truccatríce**, *s.f.* (*teat.*) maker-up, make-up expert.

truccatúra, *s.f.* (*teat.*) make-up.

trúcco, *s.m.* 1. trick: *i trucchi di un prestigiatore*, the tricks of a conjurer; *questo è solo un —*, this is only a trick 2. (*inganno*) deceit 3. make-up: *darsi il —*, to make up one's face.

truccóne, *s.m.* faker, cheat.

trúce, *ag.* grim; (*minaccioso*) threatening; (*crudele*) fierce, cruel: *sguardo —*, grim look.

trucemènte, *av.* grimly; (*minacciosamente*) threateningly; (*crudelmente*) fiercely, cruelly.

trucidàre, *v.t.* to slay; (*assassinare*) to murder.

trucidatóre, *s.m.* slayer; (*assassino*) murderer.

truciolàre, *v.t.* (*rar.*) to chip.

trúciolo, *s.m.* chip, shaving: *trucioli per imballaggio*, wood-shavings.

trucolènto, truculènto, *ag.* truculent, cruel.

trúffa, *s.f.* cheat; swindle; trick: *è una volgare —*, it's a nasty trick.

truffaldíno, *ag.* nasty ‖ *s.m.* cheat, cheater; swindler.

truffàre, *v.t.* to cheat; to swindle: *mi ha truffato circa cento sterline*, he cheated me out of about a hundred pounds; *quell'uomo ha truffato parecchi commercianti*, that man has cheated (*o* swindled *o* taken in) several businessmen.

truffatóre, *s.m.*, **truffatríce**, *s.f.* cheat, cheater; swindler.

truffería, *s.f.* cheat; swindle; trick.

truísmo, *s.m.* (*neol.*) truism.

trullàggine, trullería, *s.f.* 1. silliness 2. (*cosa sciocca*) silly thing.

trúllo[1], *ag.* silly.

trúllo[2], *s.m.* (*abitazione a copertura conica, caratteristica della Puglia*) trullo (*pl.* trulli).

truògolo, *s.m.* trough.

trúppa, *s.f.* 1. (*mil.*) troop: *truppe aviotrasportate*, airborne troops; *truppe da sbarco*, landing force; *truppe d'assalto*, assault troops; *truppe di copertura*, covering troops; *truppe trasportate via mare*, seaborne troops; *uomo di —*, private (soldier); *arrivarono le truppe*, the troops arrived 2. troop, band: *una — di studenti*, a troop (*o* band) of students; *in —*, in a troop.

truschíno, *s.m.* (*tec.*) surface gauge.

tse-tsè, *s.f.* tsetse: *mosca —*, tsetse-fly.

tu, *pron.pers.m.f.* 2ª *persona sing.* 1. *sogg.* you; (*arc. poet.*) **thou**: — *devi partire subito*, you have to leave at once; *sei stato — a dirmi che sarebbe venuto*, it was you who told me he would come (*o* you were the one who told me he was coming) ‖ — *stesso*, *proprio —*, you yourself, you... yourself; (*arc.*) thou thyself, thou... thyself: *devi farlo proprio —*, you have to do it yourself ‖ *a — per —*, face to face: *si trovò a — per — con la morte*, he found himself face to face with death ‖ *contento —*, *contenti tutti*, if you are satisfied we all are ‖ *dare del — a qlcu.*, to address s.o. as "tu" (using 2nd person singular); (*essere in termini confidenziali*) to be on first-name terms with s.o.; (*rar.*) to thou s.o. 2. (*come pred. nominale*): *dopo quella disgrazia non sembri più —*, you have never been the same since the accident.

túba, *s.f.* 1. (*mus.*) tuba (*pl.* tubas, tubae): — *di basso*, bass-tuba 2. (*anat.*) tuba (*pl.* tubas, tubae) 3. (*cappello a cilindro*) top-hat.

tubàggio, *s.m.* (*miner.*) tubbing.

tubàre, *v.i.* to coo (anche *fig.*).

tubàrico, *ag.* (*anat.*) tubal: *gravidanza tubarica*, tubal pregnancy.

tubatúra, tubazióne, *s.f.* piping; pipes (*pl.*); pipe -line.

tuberàcee, *s.f.pl.* (*bot.*) Tuberaceae.

tubercolàre, *ag.* tubercular.

tubercolína, *s.f.* (*med.*) tuberculin.

tubèrcolo, *s.m.* 1. (*med.*) tubercle 2. (*bot.*) tuber.

tubercolosàrio, *s.m.* sanatorium (*pl.* sanatoria, sanatoriums).

tubercolòsi, *s.f.* (*patol.*) tuberculosis: — *ossea*, tuberculosis of the bones; — *polmonare*, (pulmonary) consumption.

tubercolóso, tubercolòtico, *ag.* tuberculous ‖ *s.m.* consumptive.

tubercolúto, *ag.* tuberculate(d), tubercled.

túbero, *s.m.* (*bot.*) tuber.

tuberósa, *s.f.* (*bot.*) tuberose.

tuberosità, *s.f.* tuberosity, tuberousness.

tuberóso, *ag.* tuberous, tuberose.

tubíno, *s.m.* bowler-hat; (*fam.*) billycock.

t ubísta, *s.m.* plumber.

túbo, *s.m.* 1. pipe, tube: — *a raggi catodici*, (*elett.*) cathode-ray tube; — *collettore*, header; — *da saggio*, (*chim.*) test-tube; — *dell'acqua*, water-pipe; — *del gas*, gas-pipe; — *della stufa*, stovepipe; — *di scappamento*, (*aut.*) exhaust-pipe; — *di scarico*, (*idraulica*) draining pipe (*o* drain-pipe *o* waste-pipe); — *lanciamine*, (*mar. mil.*) mine-shaft; — *lanciasiluri*, (*mar. mil.*) torpedo-tube; — *per fognatura*, sewer pipe; *giunzione di tubi*, pipe connection; *messa in opera di tubi*, pipelaying 2. (*anat.*) canal, duct: — *digerente*, alimentary canal.

tubolàre, *ag.* tubular ‖ *s.m.* (*pneumatico per bicicletta*) tubular tire.

tucàno, *s.m.* (*ornit.*) toucan ‖ **Tucàno**, *no.pr.m.* (*astr.*) Toucan.

Tucídide, *no.pr.m.* (*st. lett.*) Thucydides.

tucúl, *s.m.* "tucul" (Abyssinian circular hut).

tufàceo, *ag.* (*geol.*) tufaceous.

tuffàre, *v.t.* to plunge; to dip: — *la testa nell'acqua*, to plunge one's head into the water ‖ **tuffàrsi**, *v.r.* to plunge (anche *fig.*), to dive (anche *fig.*): *il caccia si tuffò sul nemico*, the fighter dived down on the enemy; *egli si tuffò nel lago*, he dived into the lake; — *in un argomento*, to plunge into a subject ‖ — (*in un'impresa*), to take the plunge.

tuffàta, *s.f.* plunge, dive, dip.

tuffatóre, *s.m.*, **tuffatríce**, *s.f.* diver.

túffo, *s.m.* 1. dive, plunge: — *ad angelo*, swallow dive (*o* swan dive); *fare un* —, to take a plunge (*o* to plunge *o* to dive) ‖ *ebbi un* — *al cuore*, *fig.* my heart gave a throb 2. (*picchiata di aereo*) dive.

túffolo, *s.m.* (*ornit.*) diver.

túfo, *s.m.* (*geol.*) tufa: — *vulcanico*, tuff.

tufóso, *ag.* (*geol.*) tufaceous.

túga, *s.f.* (*mar.*) bridge-house.

tugúrio, *s.m.* hovel, dog-hole: *vivevano in un* — *alla periferia della città*, they lived in a hovel on the outskirts of the town.

túia, *s.f.* (*bot.*) thuya.

tularemía, *s.f.* (*patol.*) tularemia, tularaemia.

túlio, *s.m.* (*chim.*) thulium.

tulipàno, *s.m.* tulip.

tulipína, *s.f.* (*farm.*) tulipine.

túlle, *s.m.* tulle.

Túllia, *no.pr.f.* Tullia.

tulliàno, *ag.* (*ciceroniano*) Tullian.

Túllio, *no.pr.m.* (*st. lett.*) (*Cicerone*) Tully.

tumefàre, *v.t.*, **tumefàrsi**, *v.r.* to tumefy.

tumefàtto, *ag.* tumefied, swollen.

tumefazióne, *s.f.* tumefaction, swelling.

tumidézza, **tumidità**, *s.f.* tumidity, tumidness.

túmido, *ag.* 1. tumid, swollen 2. (*di stile*) pompous.

túmolo, *s.m.* tumulus (*pl.* tumuli); (*tomba*) grave.

tumóre, *s.m.* (*patol.*) tumour: — *maligno*, malignant (*o* cancerous) tumour.

tumulàre, *ag.* tumulary, sepulchral: *pietra* —, tombstone (*o* gravestone).

tumulàre, *v.t.* to bury, to inter, to entomb.

tumulazióne, *s.f.* burial, interment, burying.

túmulo, *s.m.* tumulus (*pl.* tumuli); (*tomba*) grave.

tumúlto, *s.m.* 1. (*confusione*) tumult, uproar, turmoil 2. (*sommossa*) riot: *in Milano si ebbero violenti tumulti per l'aumento del pane*, violent riots broke out in Milan for the increase in the price of bread 3. *fig.* tumult: *il* — *delle passioni*, the tumult of passions; *ho l'animo in* —, my mind is in (a) tumult.

tumultuànte, *ag.* tumultuary, riotous, uproarious: *vita tumultuante*, stormy life ‖ *s.c.* rioter.

tumultuàre, *v.i.* to riot: *la folla tumultuava nelle strade*, the mob was rioting in the streets.

tumultuariaménte, *av.* tumultuarily, riotously, uproariously.

tumultuàrio, *ag.* tumultuary, riotous, uproarious.

tumultuosaménte, *av.* tumultuously, riotously, uproariously.

tumultuóso, *ag.* tumultuous, riotous, uproarious: *un'assemblea tumultuosa*, an uproarious session.

túndra, *s.f.* tundra.

tungstèno, *s.m.* (*chim.*) tungsten: *acciaio al* —, tungsten steel.

túnica, *s.f.* tunic (anche *anat. bot.*).

tunicàto, *ag.* (*anat. bot.*) tunicate.

tunicàti, *s.m.pl.* (*zool.*) Tunicata.

Túnisi, *no.pr.f.* (*geog.*) Tunis.

Tunisía, *no.pr.f.* (*geog.*) Tunisia.

tunisíno, *ag.s.m.* Tunisian.

tunnel, *s.m.* tunnel.

túo, *ag.poss.* 1. your; (*arc. poet.*) thy; (*tuo proprio*) your own: *i tuoi amici*, your friends; *il* — *libro*, your book; *un* — *libro*, one of your books (*o* a book of yours); — *padre e tua madre*, your father and mother; *questi tuoi quadri*, these pictures of yours; *hai una casa tua?*, have you got a house of your own?; *me l'ha detto tua figlia*, your own (*o* your very) daughter told me so; *nelle Tue mani rimetto l'anima mia*, into Thy hands I commend my spirit; *sia fatta la Tua volontà*, Thy will be done ‖ *in vece tua*, instead of you (*o* in your stead) ‖ *lo feci per amor* —, I did it for the love of you (*o* for your sake) 2. (*come pred. nominale*) yours: *questa penna è tua*, this pen is yours; *questi dischi non sono tuoi*, these records are not yours (*o* do not belong to you) 3. (*in espressioni ellittiche*): *la tua del mese scorso*, (*lettera*) your letter of last month; *anche tu hai avuto le tue* (*disgrazie*), you had your difficulties too; *egli è sempre dalla tua* (*parte*), he is always on your side; *ne hai fatta ancora una delle tue*, you have been up to your old tricks again (*o* up to one of your tricks); *stai sempre sulle tue*, you always keep yourself to yourself; *vuoi sempre dir la tua*, you always want to have your say ‖ *pron.poss.* yours; (*arc. poet.*) thine: *il mio appartamento è più piccolo del* —, my flat is smaller than yours; *mia sorella è uscita con la tua*, my sister has gone out with yours; *questo è il* —, *non il mio*, this is yours, not mine ‖ *s.m.* 1. *devi distinguere tra il mio e il* —, you must distinguish between what's mine and what's yours; *so che hai perso tutto il* —, I know you lost all your possessions 2. (*partitivo*): *qualcosa, niente di* —, something, nothing of your own 3. *pl.*: *i tuoi*, your family (*o* your relatives *o fam.* your folks *o* your people); (*partigiani, seguaci*) your supporters.

tuonàre, *V.* **tonàre**.

tuòno, *s.m.* 1. thunder: *forti tuoni annunciarono l'avvicinarsi del temporale*, loud peals of thunder announced the approaching of the storm 2. (*artigl.*) boom, roar: *si sentiva di lontano il* — *dei cannoni*, the boom of cannons was heard from afar.

tuòrlo, *s.m.* yolk: — *d'uovo*, yolk of egg.

tuppè, *s.m.* 1. toupet; tuft of hair 2. (*faccia tosta*) cheek, impudence, effrontery: *che* —!, what a cheek!; *ebbe il* — *di venire*, he had the cheek (*o* the sauce) to come.

turabúchi, *s.m. fig.* stop-gap.

tura-búco, *s.m.* (*gergo giornalistico*) filler.

turàcciolo, *s.m.* stopper; (*di sughero*) cork: *provvisto di* —, corked; *mettere il* — *a una bottiglia*, to cork a bottle.

turàre, *v.t.* to stop, to plug; to fill up: — *un buco*, to stop (up) (*o* to fill up) a hole; — *un dente*, to stop a tooth; — *una falla*, to stop a leak [— *la bocca a qlcu.*, to stop s.o.'s mouth (*o* to silence s.o.) ‖ turàrsi, *v.r.* 1. to stop: — *gli orecchi, il naso*, to stop one's ears, one's nose 2. (*chiudersi*) to shut oneself up: — *in casa*, to shut oneself up at home.

túrba, *s.f.* rabble, crowd, throng: *una* — *di gente*, a horde (*o* crowd) of people.

turbaménto, *s.m.* (*agitazione*) perturbation, agitation; (*eccitamento*) excitement; (*sconvolgimento*) upsetting: *il — dell'ordine pubblico*, the breach of the peace; *la notizia che il nemico era a due miglia provocò grande —*, the news that the enemy were two miles away caused great excitement.

turbànte, *s.m.* **1.** turban **2.** (*mar.*) turk's-head.

turbàre, *v.t.* **1.** to upset, to trouble, to disturb, to perturb: *ella era tutta turbata*, she was all in a flutter; *quella vista l'ha molto turbato*, that sight has upset him very much; *quel pensiero lo turbò per molto tempo*, that thought troubled (*o* disturbed) him for a long time; *venne a — la pace della nostra famiglia*, he came to disturb the peace of our family; *— il silenzio*, to break the silence **2.** (*agitare intorbidando*) to make cloudy, to make muddy, to muddy: *— le acque*, to muddy the waters ‖ **turbàrsi,** *v.r.* to get upset, to become agitated, to become uneasy: *egli si turbò assai quando lo seppe*, he got very upset when he knew it.

turbàto, *ag.* upset, troubled, disturbed, agitated, uneasy: *mente turbata*, upset mind; *sonno — da tristi pensieri*, sleep disturbed by sad thoughts.

turbatóre, *ag.* disturbing, perturbating, agitating ‖ *s.m.*, **turbatríce,** *s.f.* disturber, agitator.

turbína, *s.f.* (*mec.*) turbine: *— a reazione*, reaction turbine; *— a vapore*, steam turbine.

turbinàre, *v.i.* to whirl, to eddy (anche *fig.*): *le foglie turbinavano nel vento*, the leaves were whirling in the wind; *quei pensieri mi turbinano nella testa*, these thoughts whirl through my head; *il vapore turbinante vorticosamente nell'aria*, the vapour eddying wildly in the air.

túrbine, *s.m.* **1.** whirl, eddy (anche *fig.*): *un — di idee*, a whirl of ideas; *un — di polvere*, a whirl (*o* an eddy) of dust; *— di sabbia*, dust devil; *— di vento*, whirlwind; *la mia mente è in un —*, my mind is in a whirl **2.** (*uragano*) hurricane.

turbinío, *s.m.* whirling, eddying: *un — di gente*, a restless throng of people.

turbinosaménte, *av.* stormily.

turbinóso, *ag.* **1.** whirling: *velocità turbinosa*, dazzling speed; *vento —*, whirling wind (*o* whirlwind) **2.** (*tempestoso*) stormy: *cadde nelle turbinose acque del fiume*, he fell into the stormy river **3.** (*tumultuoso*) tumultuous: *un — accorrere di gente*, a tumultuous rushing of people.

turboalternatóre, *s.m.* (*elett.*) turboalternator.

turbocistèrna, *s.f.* (*mar.*) turbine-driven tanker.

turbocompressóre, *s.m.* (*mec. ind.*) multistage centrifugal blower.

turbodínamo, *s.f.* (*mec. elett.*) turbodynamo, turbogenerator.

turboèlica, *s.f.* (*mec. aer.*) turbo-propeller engine, propeller turbine engine.

turbogeneratóre, *s.m.* (*mec.*) turbogenerator.

turbogètto, *s.m.* (*mec. aer.*) turbojet engine.

turbolenteménte, *av.* turbulently; (*in modo sfrenato*) boisterously.

turbolènto, *ag.* **1.** turbulent, tumultuous; riotous; (*sfrenato*) boisterous, unruly: *un bambino —*, a boisterous (*o* unruly) child; *plebaglia turbolenta*, turbulent mob ‖ *i turbolenti*, riotous fellows **2.** (*agitato*) stormy: *una vita turbolenta*, a stormy life.

turbolènza, *s.f.* **1.** turbulence; (*sfrenatezza*) unruliness **2.** (*fis.*) turbulence ‖ *camera di —*, swirl chamber.

turbomotóre, *s.m.* (*mec.*) turbine engine.

turbonàve, *s.f.* (*mar.*) turbine steamship.

turboreattóre, *s.m.* (*aer.*) **1.** (*motore*) turbojet engine **2.** (*aeroplano*) turbojet.

túrca, àlla, *l.av.*: *caffè alla —*, Turkish coffee; *divano alla —*, ottoman; *sedere alla —*, to sit cross-legged.

turcàsso, *s.m.* quiver.

turcheggiàre, *v.i.* to make oneself Turkish in manners.

turchésco, *ag.* Turkish: *grano —*, Turkey corn ‖ *s.m.* (*lingua turca*) Turkish.

turchése, *s.f.* (*min.*) turquoise.

turchétto, *s.m.* (*ornit.*) pouter pigeon.

Turchía, *no.pr.f.* (*geog.*) Turkey.

turchinétto, *ag.* bluish ‖ *s.m.* washerwoman's blue.

turchíno, *ag.* deep blue: *cielo —*, deep blue sky ‖ *s.m.* cobalt blue.

turcimànno, *s.m.* dragoman (*pl.* dragomans, dragomen).

túrco, *ag.* Turkish ‖ *s.m.* **1.** Turk ‖ *bestemmiare come un —*, to swear like a trooper ‖ *fumare come un —*, to smoke like a chimney **2.** (*lingua*) (the) Turkish (language) ‖ *non parlo —*, (*parlo chiaro*) I speak plain English ‖ **túrca,** *s.f.* Turk.

Turènna, *no.pr.f.* (*geog.*) Touraine.

turgescènte, *ag.* turgescent, swelling.

turgidaménte, *av.* **1.** turgidly **2.** (*con stile enfatico*) turgidly, pompously, bombastically.

turgidézza, turgidità, *s.f.* **1.** turgidity **2.** (*stile enfatico*) turgidity, pompousness, bombast.

túrgido, *ag.* **1.** turgid **2.** (*di stile*) turgid, pompous, bombastic.

turgóre, *s.m.* **1.** turgidity **2.** (*stile enfatico*) turgidity, pompousness, bombast.

turíbolo, *s.m.* (*eccl.*) thurible, censer.

turiferàrio, *s.m.* (*eccl.*) thurifer; *fig.* incensor.

Turíngia, *no.pr.f.* (*geog.*) Thuringia.

turísmo, *s.m.* tourism: *ufficio del —*, travel (*o* tourist) agency; *gran —*, long-distance touring; *il — si è molto sviluppato in questi ultimi tempi*, tourism has increased greatly in the last few years.

turísta, *s.c.* **1.** tourist; (*fam.*) tripper: *l'Italia d'estate è invasa dai turisti*, every summer Italy is swarming with tourists **2.** (*visitatore di una città*) sight-seer.

turístico, *ag.* tourist (*attributivo*); touristic: *agenzia, classe turistica*, tourist agency, class; *visita turistica*, sight-seeing.

turlupinàre, *v.t.* to cheat, to swindle, to take in: *fu malamente turlupinato*, he was badly taken in.

turlupinatóre, *s.m.* cheat, swindler.

turlupinatúra, *s.f.* cheat, swindle, swindling.

túrno, *s.m.* **1.** turn: *a —*, in turn; *aspetto il mio —*, I am waiting for my turn; *chi è di —?*, (*a chi tocca?*) whose turn is it?; *è il tuo — di parlare*, it is your turn to speak; *faremo dei turni*, we shall take turns; *non è il tuo — ancora*, it is not your turn yet; *non venire se non è il tuo —*, do not come out of (your) turn; *venite a —*, come in turn; *lavorare a turni*, to work by turns **2.** (*servizio*) duty: *il medico di —*, the doctor on duty; *chi è di —?*, (*chi è di servizio?*), who is on duty?; *era di —*, he was on duty.

túrpe, *ag.* base, vile, disgraceful; filthy: *azioni turpi*, base (*o* vile) actions; *condotta —*, disgraceful behaviour; *pensiero —*, filthy thought.

turpeménte, *av.* basely, vilely, disgracefully; filthily.

turpilòquio, *s.m.* coarse language, obscene language.

turpitúdine, *s.f.* turpitude, baseness.

turríto, *ag.* turreted: *castello —*, turreted castle.

tussòr, *s.m.* (*bombice selvatico del Bengala e organzino di seta che se ne ricava*) tussore.

túta, *s.f.* overalls (*pl.*).

tutèla, *s.f.* **1.** (*dir.*) guardianship, tutelage: *diritto di —*, right of tutelage; *sotto —*, under guardianship; *avere la — di un bambino*, to have the guardianship (*o* tutelage) of a child **2.** (*protezione*) protection; (*difesa*) defence: *i cittadini sono sotto la — della legge*, citizens are under the protection of the law; *prendere qlcu. sotto la propria —*, to take s.o. under one's wing.

tutelàre, *ag.* tutelar, tutelary; guardian (*attributivo*): *angelo —*, guardian angel; *nume —*, protective deity; *fig.* guardian angel.

tutelàre, *v.t.* to guard, to protect, to defend: *la legge tutela i cittadini contro l'ingiustizia*, the law

protects citizens from injustice; — *la propria reputazione,
i propri diritti,* to guard one's reputation, one's rights.

tutóre, *s.m.* guardian.

tutòrio, *ag.* (dir.) tutorial, tutelary: *autorità tutoria,*
tutelary authority.

tuttavía, *av.cong.* yet, **nevertheless:** *l'amo, e — la
disprezzo,* I love her, and yet I despise her; *piove,
— credo sia meglio portare a spasso il bimbo,* it is raining, neverthless I think it is better to take the child
for a walk; *non mi fido di te, — voglio provare a darti
del lavoro,* I don't trust you, still I want to try and
give you a job.

tútto, *ag.* **1.** all, whole: *— il giorno,* all day: *per
— il giorno,* all day long; *tutta Italia,* all (o the whole
of) Italy: *in tutta Italia,* all over Italy; *per tutta Italia,*
throughout Italy; *tutta la notte,* all night: *per tutta
la notte,* all through the night; *con tutta coscienza,* in
all conscience; *in — il mondo,* all over the world;
per — il mondo, throughout the world; *per tutta la
casa,* all over (o throughout) the house; *tutta la casa
era in fiamme,* the whole house (o all the house) was
on fire; *— il mondo era in guerra,* the whole world
(o all the world) was at war; *devi dirmi tutta la verità,*
you must tell me the whole truth; *passai tutto il
tempo con loro,* I spent all time (o the whole time)
with them **2.** *pl.* all; (con valore di ogni) **every** (con
sostantivo e verbo al sing.): *tutti i libri di questo
autore,* all the books by this author; *tutti gli uomini
del Re,* all the King's men; *tutti gli allievi hanno
una penna,* every pupil has a pen; *tutti gli uomini
sono uguali,* all men are equal; *noi andiamo a scuola tutti i giorni,* we go to school every day ‖ *tutti
e due,* both: *andammo tutti e due,* both of us (o we
both) went; *andarono tutti e due,* they both (o both
of them) went; *tutti e tre, tutti e quattro,* all three,
all four ‖ *noi tutti,* we all (o all of us); *voi tutti,* you
all (o all of you) **3.** (con valore avverbiale) **all:** *— felice,*
as happy as a king (o as happy as a lark); *— sorrisi,*
wreathed in smiles; *è tutta colpa mia,* it is all my
fault; *è — sbagliato,* it is all wrong; *questo ragazzo è
— braccia e gambe,* this boy is all arms and legs **4.** (preceduto dalla prep. con con valore di nonostante) **for all:**
con — questo non fu capace di farlo, for all that he was
not able to do it; *con — il suo denaro non è felice,*
for all his money he is not happy ‖ *pron.* **1.** *sing.* **all,
everything:** *— è finito,* all is over; *— è perduto,* all

is lost; *diede — ciò che aveva,* he gave all he had (o
he gave everything he had); *si sa — !,* all (o everything) is known!; *se tu sapessi — !,* if you knew everything! (o if you but knew!) **2.** *pl.* **all; everybody, everyone** (con verbo al sing.): *l'opinione di tutti,* everybody's
opinion; *tutti dicono,* everybody says; *tutti partirono,*
they all left; *tutti mi hanno abbandonato,* everybody
has left me ‖ *s.m.* **whole:** *il — e le sue parti,* the whole
and its parts; *considerandolo come un —,* taken as
a whole ‖ *il Tutto,* the World: *l'infinita vanità del
Tutto,* the infinite vanity of the World ‖ (**Fraseologia**): *tutt'al più,* at the most ‖ *tutt'altra cosa,* an
entirely different matter ‖ *tutt'altro!,* on the contrary!
(o by no means! o anything but!); *è tutt'altro che
onesto,* he is anything but honest; *fa tutt'altro che
lavorare,* he does anything but work ‖ *tutt'intorno,*
all around: *tutt'intorno alla casa,* all around the
house ‖ *tutt'uno:* è *tutt'uno col suo capo,* he is hand
in glove with his boss; *è tutt'uno col suo lavoro,* he is
completely devoted to (o absorbed in) his work ‖ *a
tutta prova,* perfectly safe ‖ *a — spiano, a — andare,*
at full blast (o like a house on fire); *a tutta velocità,*
at full speed ‖ *a tutt'oggi,* up to the present (o until
today); *a — il 20 agosto,* up to and including August
20th ‖ *del —, in — e per —,* quite (o completely o wholly
o through and through): *è un mascalzone in — e per
—,* he is a scoundrel through and through; *è del —
sbagliato,* it is quite wrong ‖ *dopo —,* after all ‖ *in
—,* in all: *sette in —,* seven in all ‖ *prima di —,* (per
prima cosa) first of all; (in primo luogo) in the first
place; (soprattutto) above all: *prima di — devi far questo,* first of all you must do this; *prima di — non devi
dimenticare che è straniero,* in the first place you must
not forget he is a foreigner; *questo prima di —, sii
fedele a te stesso,* this above all, to yourself be
true ‖ *sono tutt'orecchi,* I am all ears ‖ *giocare il —
per —,* to risk everything on a single throw.

tuttoché, *cong.* (rar.) **albeit, though, although:** *— non
sia una bellezza è una ragazza graziosa,* albeit she is
not a beauty she is a pretty girl.

tuttodí, *av.* **1.** (continuamente) continually; (sempre)
always **2.** (tutto il giorno) all day long.

tuttóra, *av.* still: *è — in prigione,* he is still in prison.

túzia, *s.f.* (chim.) tutty.

tze-tzè, *s.f.* tsetse: *mosca —,* tsetse-fly.

tzigàno, *ag.s.m.* tzigano.

U

u, *s.f.m.* (*diciannovesima lettera dell'alfabeto italiano*) u (*pl.* us, u's) ‖ — *come Udine*, (*tel.*) u for uncle.

uàdi, *s.m.* wadi, wady.

ubbìa, *s.f.* **1.** whim, fad, crotchet: *tirati via queste ubbie dalla testa*, get these silly ideas out of your head **2.** (*pregiudizio*) prejudice: *è pieno di ubbie*, he is riddled with prejudice **3.** (*superstizione*) superstition: *ha l'— di credere negli spiriti*, he is superstitious enough to believe in ghosts **4.** (*timore ingiustificato*) groundless fear; (*mania*) mania: *ha l'— di essere perseguitato*, he suffers mildly from persecution mania.

ubbidiènte, *ag.* obedient; submissive; docile: *un bambino* —, an obedient child.

ubbidienteménte, *av.* obediently; submissively.

ubbidiènza, *s.f.* obedience; (*ai genitori, maestri, superiori*) dutifulness; (*all'autorità legale*) submission; (*al sovrano*) allegiance: — *passiva*, passive obedience; *in* — *agli ordini, alle regole*, in obedience to (*o* in accordance with *o* in compliance with) the orders, the rules; *dovere* — *a qlcu.*, to owe s.o. obedience; *giurare* — *al re*, to swear allegiance to the king.

ubbidìre, *v.i.* (*nel passivo ammette costruzione attiva*) **1.** to obey (s.o., sthg.), to comply (with s.o., sthg.): *ubbidisce alla forza di gravità*, it obeys the force of gravity; *voglio essere ubbidito*, I want to be obeyed; — *a un ordine*, to obey an order; *farsi* — *da qlcu.*, to compel (*o* to enforce) obedience from s.o. **2.** (*cedere, sottomettersi*) to yield, to submit: — *alla forza*, to yield to force.

ubbriàco, *e derivati*, *V.* **ubriàco**, *e derivati*.

ubertà, *s.f.* (*letter.*) fertility, fruitfulness; (*abbondanza*) abundance.

Ubèrto, *no.pr.m.* Hubert.

ubertosaménte, *av.* fruitfully; (*abbondantemente*) richly, abundantly.

ubertóso, *ag.* fertile, fruitful; (*abbondante*) rich, abundant: *suolo* —, fertile (*o* fruitful) soil.

ubicàre, *v.t.* to locate, to place, to set.

ubicàto, *ag.* located, situated, placed: *una casa ubicata in via Manzoni*, a house situated in via Manzoni.

ubicazióne, *s.f.* location, situation, site: *l'— di una casa*, the location of a house.

ubiquità, *s.f.* ubiquity, omnipresence: *avere il dono dell'—*, to have the gift of ubiquity.

ubriacàre, *v.t.* to make drunk, to intoxicate (anche *fig.*); (*inebriare*) to inebriate: *era ubriacato dal suo successo*, he was intoxicated by (*o* with) his success (*o* his success had gone to his head); *lo ubriacò per farlo parlare*, he made him drunk (*o* intoxicated him) to make him speak ‖ **ubriacàrsi**, *v.r.* to get drunk, to get intoxicated (anche *fig.*); (*inebriarsi*) to get inebriated: *si ubriaca tutte le sere*, he gets drunk every night.

ubriacatúra, *s.f.* **1.** intoxication (anche *fig.*): *prendere un'—*, to get drunk **2.** (*cotta*) crush: *ha preso un'— per l'amico di suo fratello*, she has a crush on her brother's friend.

ubriachézza, *s.f.* drunkenness; (*ebbrezza*) inebriety: *in uno stato di* —, in a drunken state; *la sua* — *mi disgusta*, his drunkenness disgusts me; *smaltire l'— dormendo*, to sleep off one's drunkenness (*o* to sleep oneself sober).

ubriàco, *ag.* drunk (with sthg.); intoxicated (with sthg.) (anche *fig.*): — *fradicio*, dead (*o* blind) drunk

(*o* as drunk as a lord); *è* — *di acquavite*, he is drunk (*o* intoxicated) with brandy; *è* — *di felicità*, he is drunk (*o* intoxicated) with happiness ‖ — *di fatica*, worn out with fatigue (*o* dead tired) ‖ *s.m.* drunk man.

ubriacóna, *s.f.*, **ubriaeóne**, *s.m.* drunkard.

ucàse, *s.m.* ukase (anche *fig.*).

uccellagióne, *s.f.* **1.** (*rar.*) (*caccia*) fowling **2.** (*selvaggina di penna*) feathered game.

uccellàia, *s.f.* (*uccellanda*) fowling place; fowl-run.

uccellàio, *s.m.* bird-seller, seller of birds.

uccellànda, *s.f.* fowling place; fowl-run.

uccellàre, *v.i.* to fowl, to go fowling ‖ *v.t.* (*imbrogliare*) to cheat, to dupe, to gull, to deceive.

uccellatóio, *s.m.* fowling place.

uccellatóre, *s.m.* **1.** fowler **2.** (*ingannatore*) cheater.

uccellièra, *s.f.* aviary, large bird-cage.

uccèllo, *s.m.* bird; fowl (*spec. coll.*): *uccelli acquatici*, water fowl(s); — *da gabbia*, cage bird; — *del paradiso*, bird-of-paradise; — *di passo*, bird of passage; — *di rapina*, bird of prey; — *migratore*, migrant bird; — *mosca*, humming-bird; *uccelli selvatici*, wild fowl(s) (*o* wild birds) ‖ *uccel di bosco*, fugitive (*o* runaway): *farsi uccel di bosco*, to take to the bush ‖ *vista a volo di—*, bird's-eye-view ‖ *vispo come un —*, as brisk as a bird ‖ *a ogni — il suo nido è bello*, *prov.* there is no place like home.

uccídere, *v.t.* to kill; (*assassinare*) to murder; (*trucidare*) to slay; (*massacrare*) to massacre, to slaughter; (*macellare*) to butcher, to slaughter; (*a pugnalate*) to stab to death; (*con arma da fuoco*) to shoot: *egli fu ucciso in un incidente di auto*, he was killed in a car accident; *egli lo uccise*, he killed him; *il freddo la uccise*, the cold killed her; *ha ucciso una volpe*, he has shot a fox; *Lincoln fu ucciso da un fanatico*, Lincoln was murdered by a fanatic; *il macellaio uccide le bestie una volta alla settimana*, the butcher slaughters once a week; — *qlcu. sparandogli alla testa*, to shoot s.o. through the head ‖ **uccídersi**, *v.r.* **1.** (*rimaner ucciso*) to get killed, to be killed: *si è ucciso in macchina*, he got killed in a car-crash **2.** (*suicidarsi*) to kill oneself, to commit suicide, to take one's own life: *quel giovane si uccise per disperazione*, that young man committed suicide in despair.

uccisióne, *s.f.* killing; (*assassinio*) murder; (*massacro*) slaughter.

uccíso, *ag.* killed; (*assassinato*) murdered; (*trucidato*) slain; (*massacrato*) massacred, slaughtered; (*a pugnalate*) stabbed to death; (*macellato*) butchered, slaughtered; (*con arma da fuoco*) shot ‖ *s. m.* dead man; victim: *gli uccisi*, the victims (*o* the dead *o* the slain).

uccisóre, *s.m.* killer; (*assassino*) murderer; (*trucidatore*) slayer; (*massacratore*) slaughterer.

Ucràina, *no.pr.f.* (*geog.*) Ukraine.

udíbile, *ag.* audible.

udibilità, *s.f.* (*acu.*) audibility, audibleness.

udiènza, *s.f.* **1.** audience, hearing; (*colloquio*) interview: *concedere un'—*, to grant an audience (*o* an interview); *dare* — *a qlcu.*, to give audience to s.o. (*o* to give s.o. a hearing) **2.** (*dir.*) hearing, sitting, session, court: — *a porte aperte*, sitting in open court; — *a porte chiuse*, sitting in camera; *l'— è fissata per domani*, the case will be heard to-morrow (*o* the case comes up for hearing to-morrow); *l'— fu rimandata al giorno seguente*, the hearing (*o* sitting) was adjourned to the next day; *ci fu un'— ieri*, they had a hearing yesterday; *andare a un'*—, to go to a hearing; *chiudere l'*—, to close the session (o the sitting).

udíre, *v.t.* to hear; *(ascoltare)* to listen (to s.o., sthg.): *egli non vuole udirmi*, he doesn't want to listen to me; *l'hai mai udito cantare?*, have you ever heard him sing?; *l'ho appena udito cantare nel giardino*, I heard him singing in the garden just now; *lo si udì dire queste cose*, he was heard to say these things; *non ne ho mai udito parlare*, I never heard of it; *non vuole neppure udirne parlare*, he doesn't even want to hear; *udii dare l'ordine*, I heard the order given; — *un rumore, un suono*, to hear a noise, a sound.

udítivo, *ag.* auditive, auditory: *canale, meato* —, *(anat.)* auditory canal, meatus.

udito, *s.m.* hearing: *il senso dell'*—, the sense of hearing; *egli ha perso l'*—, he has lost his hearing; *avere un* — *fino*, to be quick of hearing (o to have a keen sense of hearing); *essere tardo di* —, to be hard (o dull) of hearing.

uditoràto, *s.m.* *(dir.)* auditorship.

uditóre, *s.m.* **1.** *(ascoltatore)* listener, hearer: *gli uditori*, the audience **2.** *(a scuola)* auditor **3.** *(dir.)* auditor.

uditòrio[1], *ag.* auditory.

uditòrio[2], *s.m.* audience; listeners *(pl.)*; hearers *(pl.)*: *l'* — *era composto da molti stranieri*, the audience was made up of a large number of foreigners; *la maggior parte dell'* — *era composta da stranieri*, most of the listeners were foreigners; *avere un vasto* —, to have a large audience.

uditríce, *s.f.* **1.** *(ascoltatrice)* listener, hearer **2.** *(a scuola)* auditress **3.** *(dir.)* auditress.

udizióne, *(rar.)* per **audizióne**.

uff, *inter.* ugh!, blow!: —, *quel bambino!*, what a nuisance (o bore) that child is!.

ufficiàle[1], *ag.* official; formal: *dovere, invito, notizia, rappresentante* —, official duty, invitation, news, representative; *gazzetta* —, official gazette; *visita* —, formal call.

ufficiàle[2], *s.m.* officer *(anche mil.)*; official: — *ai rifornimenti*, quarter master; — *del genio*, engineer officer; — *dell'areonautica, dell'esercito, di marina*, air force, army, naval officer; — *dell'Esercito della Salvezza*, officer in the Salvation Army; — *di dogana*, customs officer; — *di giornata*, orderly; — *di polizia*, police officer; — *di rotta*, navigator; — *di Stato*, officer of State; — *di stato civile*, registrar; — *di stato maggiore*, staff officer; — *effettivo*, regular officer; — *giudiziario*, law officer (o bailiff); — *governativo*, government official; — *postale*, postal official; — *pubblico*, public officer; — *in seconda*, executive officer; *(mar.)* mate; — *sanitario*, health officer; — *subalterno*, junior officer; — *superiore*, field officer, *primo* —, *(mar.)* first mate.

ufficialità[1], *s.f.* officialism, official character: *l'* — *della notizia era discussa*, the official character of the news was in question.

ufficialità[2], *s.f.* coll. *(ufficiali)* officers *(pl.)*; officials *(pl.)*.

ufficialménte, *av.* officially.

ufficiànte, *s.m.* *(eccl.)* officiator.

ufficiàre, *v.i.* *(eccl.)* to officiate.

uffício, *s.m.* **1.** *(amm.)* office, bureau; *(amer.)* agency; *(reparto)* department: — *acquisti*, purchasing department (o buying office); — *assunzione mano d'opera*, labour office; — *brevetti*, *(dir.)* patent office; — *cassa*, cash office; — *collocamento*, employment agency; — *commerciale*, sales office (o sales department); — *contabilità*, accounting department; — *di stato civile*, registry office; — *informazioni*, information bureau; — *mobilitazione*, *(mil.)* mobilization office; — *oggetti smarriti*, lost property office; — *personale*, personnel department; — *postale, telegrafico*, post-, telegraph -office; — *prenotazioni*, booking office; — *principale*, head office; — *pubblicità*, advertising office; — *redazione*, editorial office; — *relazioni sociali*, public-relation department; — *segreteria*, secretary's office; —

succursale, branch office; — *telefonico pubblico*, public call-office; — *vendite estero*, foreign sales department; *capo* —, head clerk (o head of a department); *mobili per* —, office furniture; *orario d'* —, office hours; *l'* — *chiude a mezzogiorno*, the office closes at noon; *devo andare in* —, I must go to my office; *andare in* — *in macchina*, to go to the office by car (o to drive to the office) **2.** *(carica)* office: *l'* — *di presidente è pieno di responsabilità*, the office of chairman is full of responsibility; *accettare, coprire, rifiutare un* —, to accept, to hold, to refuse an office **3.** *(dovere)* duty: *adempiere al proprio* —, to do one's duty **4.** *(funzione)* function: *non è* — *di un insegnante dire queste cose*, it is not a teacher's business to say these things; *qual è il tuo* — *qui?*, what is your function here? **5.** *buoni uffici*, good offices: *per merito dei suoi buoni uffici ottenni questo posto*, thanks to his good offices I got this post **6.** *d'* —, officially: *gli scriverò d'* —, I shall write him an official letter; *glielo domanderò d'* —, I shall ask him in virtue of my office; *mi metterò in contatto con lui d'* —, I shall get in touch with him officially ‖ *nominato d'* —, *(dir.)* appointed by the Court **7.** *(eccl.)* *V.* **uffízio**.

ufficiosaménte, *av.* unofficially, semi-officially, officiously.

ufficióso, *ag.* **1.** officious, unofficial, semi-official: *una dichiarazione ufficiosa*, a semi-official statement **2.** *(premuroso)* obliging **3.** *bugia ufficiosa*, white lie.

uffiziàle, *V.* **ufficiàle**.

uffízio, *s.m.* *(eccl.)* office, service: *l'* — *dei defunti*, the Office for the Dead; — *sacro*, divine office ‖ *dire gli uffizi*, to say one's offices ‖ *il Santo Uffizio*, *(st. relig.)* the Holy Office.

úfo, a, *l.av.* gratis, without paying: *mangiare a* —, *(fam.)* to cadge a meal.

Ugànda, *no.pr.f.* *(geog.)* Uganda.

ugèllo, *s.m.* *(mec.)* nozzle; *(di un altoforno)* tuyerre.

úggia, s.f.* **1. *(noia)* boredom, annoyance, dislike: *il mio lavoro mi è venuto in* —, I have grown tired of my work; *questo libro mi dà l'* —, this book bores me; *questo tempo piovoso mi mette l'* — *addosso*, this rainy weather gives me the blues ‖ *avere, prendere in* —, to have (o to grow) a dislike for **2.** *(ombra)* shadow: *tutti questi alberi danno uggia ai fiori*, all these trees overshadow the flowers.

uggiolaménto, *s.m.* whining, yelping.

uggiolàre, *v.i.* to whine, to yelp.

uggiolío, *s.m.* whining, yelping.

uggiosaménte, *av.* boringly, tiresomely, wearisomely, tediously; irksomely.

uggiosità, *s.f.* tiresomeness, wearisomeness, tediousness; irksomeness; dullness; *(di tempo)* gloominess.

uggióso, *ag.* boring, tiresome, wearisome, tedions; irksome, dull; *(di tempo)* gloomy: *giornata uggiosa*, gloomy (o dull) day; *lettura uggiosa*, boring (o dull) reading; *una persona uggiosa*, a boring (o tiresome) person; *tempo* —, gloomy (o dull) weather.

ùggire, *v.t.* to overshadow.

úgna, e derivati, *V.* **únghia, e derivati.

**ugnatúra, s.f.* *(artig.)* chamfer, bevel.

Úgo, *no.pr.m.* Hugh.

úgola, s.f.* **1. *(anat.)* uvula *(pl. uvulae, uvulas)* ‖ *rinfrescarsi l'* —, to have a drink **2.** *(voce di cantante)* voice: *che magnifica* — *!*, what a wonderful voice!.

ugonottísmo, *s.m.* *(st. relig.)* Huguenotism.

ugonòtto, *s.m.* *(st. relig.)* Huguenot.

uguagliaménto, *s.m.* equalization, equalizing; *(livellamento)* levelling down.

uguagliànza, *s.f.* equality: — *di diritti, doveri*, equality of rights, duties; *comparativo di* —, *(gram.)* comparative of equality; *segno di* —, *(arit.)* sign of equality; *su una base di* — *con qlcu.*, on a footing of equality with s.o.; *predicare l'* — *degli uomini*, to preach the equality of men.

uguagliàre, *v.t.* **1.** (*essere uguale a*) to equal; to be equal to (s.o., sthg.): *non potrai mai uguagliarlo in virtù,* you will never be able to equal him in virtue; *la sua onestà non uguaglia il suo talento,* his honesty is not equal to his talent (o he is not so honest as he is talented) **2.** (*rendere uguale*) to equalize, to make equal; (*livellare*) to level: *la morte eguaglia tutti gli uomini,* death makes all men equal; — *un pezzo di terreno,* to level (o to smooth down o to even up) a piece of ground ‖ — *redditi, tasse,* (*amm.*) to equalize incomes, taxes ‖ *v.i.* (*rar.*) (*essere uguale*) to be equal ‖ **uguagliàrsi,** *v.r.* (*paragonarsi*) to compare oneself.

uguàle, *ag.* **1.** equal, same; like; alike (*predicativo*): *uguali diritti, uguali doveri,* equal rights, equal duties; *di* — *grandezza,* of equal size; *due parti uguali,* two equal parts; *due più due è* — *a quattro,* two times two makes (o is equal to) four; *ho un'automobile* — *alla sua,* I have a car like his; *queste due cose sono uguali tra loro,* these two things are equal to each other (o like each other); *questi due vestiti sono esattamente uguali,* these two dresses are exactly alike (o exactly the same); *la situazione è sempre* —, the situation is always the same ‖ *per me è* —, it is all the same to me **2.** (*uniforme*) uniform; (*similare*) similar: *queste traduzioni hanno errori uguali,* these translations have similar mistakes; *la temperatura in questa stanza è sempre* —, the temperature in this room is always uniform ‖ *s.m.* equal: *non troverò mai più il suo* —, I shall never find his equal (o like) again; *trattare qlcu. come un proprio* —, to treat s.o. as one's equal.

ugualménte, *av.* **1.** equally: *sono tutti* — *sciocchi,* they are all equally silly; *trattali tutti* —, treat them all equally (o in the same way) **2.** (*lo stesso*) all the same: *l'ho fatto* —, I have done it all the same.

uh, *inter.* ah!, oh!.

uhm, *inter.* hum, h'm.

uístiti, *s.m.* (*zool.*) marmoset.

ukàse, *s.m.* ukase (anche *fig.*).

ulàno, *s.m.* (*mil.*) uhlan.

úlcera, *s.f.* (*patol.*) ulcer; ulcus (*pl.* ulcera): — *gastrica,* gastric ulcer; — *peptica,* peptic ulcer; — *venerea, molle,* syphilitic ulcer.

ulceraménto, *s.m.* ulceration.

ulceràre, *v.t.,* **ulceràrsi,** *v.r.* to ulcerate.

ulcerativo, *ag.* ulcerative.

ulceràto, *ag.* ulcerated, ulcered.

ulcerazióne, *s.f.* ulceration.

ulceróso, *ag.* ulcerous.

ulèma, *s.m.* ulema.

ulígine, *s.f.* (*letter.*) moisture.

uliginóso, *ag.* (*letter.*) uliginous, uliginose.

Ulìsse, *no.pr.m.* Ulysses.

ulíte, *s.f.* (*patol.*) ulites.

ulíva, ulívo, *e derivati,* *V.* **olíva, olívo,** *e derivati.*

ulivèlla, *s.f.* (*edil.*) lewis.

Úlma, *no.pr.f.* (*geog.*) Ulm.

ulmàcee, *s.f.pl.* (*bot.*) Ulmaceae.

ulmàto, *s.m.* (*chim.*) ulmate.

úlmico, *ag.* (*chim.*) ulmic: *acido* —, ulmic acid.

ulmína, *s.f.* (*chim.*) ulmin.

úlna, *s.f.* (*anat.*) ulna (*pl.* ulnae, ulnas).

ulnàre, *ag.* (*anat.*) ulnar.

ulorragía, *s.f.* (*patol.*) ulorrhagia.

Ulríca, *no.pr.f.* Ulrica.

Ulríco, *no.pr.m.* Ulric.

ulterióre, *ag.* further, ulterior; subsequent, later: *ulteriori istruzioni,* further instructions; *fino a* — *avviso,* till further notice; *senza* — *perdita di tempo,* without further loss of time; *chiedere un* — *credito,* to ask for further credit ‖ *Gallia Ulteriore,* (*st.*) Further Gaul.

ulteriorménte, *av.* ulteriorly, further on, later on.

ultimaménte, *av.* **1.** (*recentemente*) lately, recently, of late, not long ago: — *non abbiamo avuto sue notizie,*

we have not heard from him lately; *che cosa hai fatto* —?, what have you been doing lately? **2.** (*da ultimo*) at last.

ultimàre, *v.t.* to finish, to bring to an end, to conclude, to complete: — *un lavoro,* to finish a piece of work.

ultimàto, *ag.* finished, concluded, completed: *a lavoro* —, when the work is finished.

ultimàtum, *s.m.* ultimatum (*pl.* ultimatums, ultimata): *presentare un* — *a un paese,* to present an ultimatum to a country.

ultimazióne, *s.f.* finishing, conclusion, completion, termination.

último, *ag.* **1.** (*in ordine di successione*) last: *gli ultimi capitoli di un libro,* the last chapters of a book; — *ma non meno importante,* last but not least; *l'ultima volta che lo vidi era molto pallido,* the last time I saw him (o when I saw him last) he was very pale; *la mia ultima settimana al mare,* my last week at the seaside; *la mia ultima speranza, parola,* my last hope, word; *nelle ultime due file,* in the last two rows; *la sua ultima lettera,* his last letter; *ha resistito fino all'*—, he has held on to the last; *lo tengo per* —, I keep it till the end; *oggi è l'*— *giorno,* to-day is the last day; *questa è l'ultima volta che te lo dico,* this is the last time I shall tell you ‖ *in* —, at the end ‖ *dare l'*— *tocco a un quadro,* to give the finishing touch to a painting **2.** (*il più recente*) latest, newest: *l'ultima moda,* the latest fashion; *gli ultimi modelli,* the latest models; *le ultime notizie sono nell'ultima edizione del giornale,* the latest news is in the latest edition of the newspaper ‖ *sai l'ultima di mio fratello?,* have you heard my brother's latest? **3.** (*estremo*) utmost: *gli ultimi confini della terra,* the utmost limits of the earth **4.** (*il più basso, il meno importante*) the lowest: *l'*— *degli ultimi,* the lowest of the low; *l'*— *prezzo,* the lowest price ‖ *essere l'ultima ruota del carro,* to be the least important person **5.** (*fondamentale, finale*) ultimate: *l'ultima causa,* the ultimate cause.

ultimogènito, *ag.* last-born (*attributivo*) ‖ *s.m.* last-born (child).

ultóre, *ag.* (*letter.*) avenging ‖ *s.m.* (*letter.*) avenger.

ultra, *av.* (*lat.*) **1.** extremely, in the highest degree; (*come prefisso*) ultra(-): — *accademico,* ultra-academic; — *arbitrario,* ultra-arbitrary; — *buono,* ultragood (o extremely good); — *conservatore,* ultra-conservative; — *critico,* ultra-critical; — *democratico,* ultrademocratic; — *saggio,* wise in the highest degree **2.** *non plus* —, *V.* **nonplusúltra.**

ultramaríno, *ag.* ultramarine.

ultramieròmetro, *s.m.* ultramicrometer.

ultramieroscòpico, *ag.* ultramicroscopic(al).

ultramieroscòpio, *s.m.* (*ott.*) ultramicroscope.

ultramontàno, *ag.s.m.* ultramontane.

ultraràpido, *ag.* ultrarapid.

ultraròsso, *ag.* (*ott.*) ultra-red, infra-red.

ultrasensíbile, *ag.* ultrasensitive.

ultrasònico, *ag.* (*acu.*) ultrasonic, supersonic: *onda ultrasonica,* supersonic wave; *volo* —, (*aer.*) supersonic flight.

ultrasuòno, *s.m.* (*acu.*) ultra-sound.

ultraviolétto, *ag.* (*fis.*) ultra-violet: *raggi ultravioletti,* ultra-violet rays.

ultravólo, *s.m.* (*aer.*) supersonic flight.

ululàre, *v.i.* to howl, to ululate; (*di sirena*) to hoot: *i lupi ululavano nella notte,* the wolves were howling in the night; *il vento ululava,* the wind was howling.

ululàto, úlulo, *s.m.* howl, howling; (*di sirena*) hoot: *l'*— *del lupo, del vento,* the howl(ing) of the wolf, of the wind.

úlva, *s.f.* (*bot.*) Ulva.

ulvàceo, *ag.* (*bot.*) ulvaceous.

umanaménte, *av.* **1.** (*da uomo*) humanly: *questo non è* — *possibile,* this is not humanly possible (o this goes beyond human possibilities); *agire, parlare,* *ragionare* —, to act, to speak, to reason humanly 2. (*benignamente*) humanely: *trattare qlcu.* —, to treat s.o. humanely.

umanàre, *v.t.* to humanize; to make human ‖ **umanàrsi,** *v.r.* to become human.

umanazióne, *s.f.* 1. humanization 2. (*teol.*) Incarnation.

umanésimo, umanísmo, *s.m.* (*st. lett.*) humanism.

umanísta, *s.m.* humanist.

umanità, *s.f.* 1. (*razza umana*) humanity, mankind: *le miserie dell'*—, the miseries of mankind (*o* humanity) 2. (*bontà, indulgenza*) humanity, humaneness: *trattàre qlcu. con* —, to treat s.o. with humanity 3. (*natura umana*) humanity: *ci fu chi negò l'*— *di Cristo*, there were those who denied the human nature of Christ 4. *pl.* (*gli studi letterari*) the humanities.

umanitàrio, *ag.* humanitarian: *tendenze umanitarie,* humanitarian tendencies.

umanitarísmo, *s.m.* humanitarianism.

umanizzàre, *V.* **umanàre.**

umàno, *ag.* 1. (*dell'uomo*) human: *corpo* —, human body; *un essere* —, a human being; *miseria, fragilità umana,* human misery, frailty; *la natura umana,* human nature 2. (*comprensivo, indulgente*) humane: *una persona umana,* a humane person; *ha modi molto umani,* he has very humane manners 3. *umane lettere,* humanities (*o* humane letters *o* humane studies) ‖ *s.m.* 1. human (being) 2. (*natura umana*) human nature.

umazióne, *s.f.* burial, burying, interment.

umbèlla, *s.f.* (*bot.*) umbel.

umbellàto, *ag.* (*bot.*) umbellate, umbellated.

umbellífero, *ag.* (*bot.*) umbelliferous.

Umbèrto, *no.pr.m.* Humbert.

umbílíco, *e derivati,* *V.* **ombelíco.** *e derivati.*

umbràtile, *ag.* (*letter.*) 1. (*ombroso*) shady 2. (*oscuro*) dark, dim 3. (*immaginario*) imaginary.

Úmbria, *no.pr.f.* (*geog.*) Umbria.

úmbro, *ag.* Umbrian ‖ *la Scuola Umbra,* (*st. pitt.*) the Umbrian School.

umeràle, *ag.* (*anat.*) humeral ‖ *s.m.* (*eccl.*) humeral veil.

umettàre, *v.t.* to moisten, to damp, to wet, to humidify, to humectate, to humect ‖ *linguetta da* —, adhesive flap.

umettatóre, *s.m.* (*ind.*) dampener, damper: — *a spazzola,* dampener brush.

umettazióne, *s.f.* moistening, damping, dampening, wetting, humectation: — *delle pelli,* damping up.

umidézza, *s.f.* damp, dampness, humidity, moisture.

umidíccio, *ag.* dampish.

umidificatóre, *s.m.* humidifier; (*ind. tessile*) conditioner: — *elettrico,* (*elettrodomestico*) electric evaporator.

umidità, *s.f.* dampness, moisture, moistness, wetness; humidity: — *assoluta, relativa,* (*fis.*) absolute, relative humidity; *l'*— *del suolo,* the moisture of the soil; *l'*— *di una casa,* the dampness of a house; *grado di* —, degree of humidity; *macchie di* —, mildew (*o* mold); *questa casa è piena di* —, this house is very damp; *questi muri trasudano* —, these walls send out moisture ‖ *teme l'*—, to be kept dry.

úmido, *ag.* damp, moist, wet; humid: *abiti umidi,* damp clothes; *casa umida,* damp house; *clima* —, damp climate; *corridoio scuro e* —, dark damp passage; *occhi umidi di pianto,* eyes moist with tears; *straccio* —, damp cloth; *tempo caldo* —, muggy weather; *tempo freddo e* —, raw weather; *terra umida,* moist earth; *vento* —, moist wind ‖ *s.m.* 1. (*umidità*) dampness, moisture 2. (*cuc.*) stew, stewed meat: *patate in* —, stewed potatoes; *cuocere in* —, to stew.

umidóre, *s.m.* (*letter.*) dampness, moisture.

úmile, *ag.* humble; (*modesto*) modest; (*sottomesso*) meek: — *di cuore,* humble of heart (*o* humble-hearted); *umili richieste,* modest demands; *di* — *nascita,* of humble birth; *modi umili,* humble manners; *è molto* — *verso di me,* he is very humble towards me; *ha un contegno*

—, he has a meek manner ‖ *il Vostro umilissimo servitore,* Your very humble servant.

umiliànte, *ag.* humiliating, humiliatory, mortifying: *una proposta, una condizione* —, a humiliating proposal, condition.

umiliàre, *v.t.* to humble, to humiliate, to mortify; to bring low, to abase: *non devi umiliarlo così,* you must not humiliate (*o* mortify) him like that; — *i propri avversari,* to humble one's opponents ‖ **umiliàrsi,** *v.r.* to humble oneself, to humiliate oneself, to abase oneself; to stoop: *devi essere rispettoso ma non devi umiliarti,* you must be respectful but you must not humble yourself; *egli si umiliò fino a chiedere l'elemosina,* he stooped to begging; — *di fronte a qlcu.,* to humble oneself before s.o. (*o* to cringe to s.o.).

umiliàto, *ag.* humbled, humiliated, mortified; abased: *era tutto* —, he was deeply mortified.

umiliazióne, *s.f.* humiliation; mortification; abasement: *egli subì molte umiliazioni,* he suffered much humiliation; *subire una* —, to suffer an affront.

umilménte, *av.* humbly; (*modestamente*) modestly.

umiltà, *s.f.* 1. humbleness; (*modestia*) modesty; (*sottomissione*) meekness: *l'*— *della sua origine,* the humbleness of his birth 2. (*virtù dell'essere umile*) humility: — *di cuore,* humility of heart; *in tutta* —, with all humility.

umoràle, *ag.* humoral: *patologia* —, humoral patology.

umóre¹, *s.m.* 1. (*di corpo animale, vegetale*) humour: — *acqueo, vitreo,* aqueous, vitreous humour 2. (*umidità*) moisture 3. (*stato d'animo*) humour, temper, mood; spirits (*pl.*): *cerco sempre di secondare i suoi umori,* I always try to humour him (*o* to comply with his whims); *ha un* — *molto instabile,* he is very moody; *essere di buon* —, to be in a good humour (*o* temper *o* mood); *essere di cattivo* —, to be in a bad mood (*o* humour *o* temper *o* to be out of temper *o* to feel depressed); *essere di ottimo* —, to be in high spirits.

umóre², umorísmo, *s.m.* humour: *l'*— *di Shaw,* Shaw's humour; *senso dell'*—, sense of humour; *le sue osservazioni sono piene di* —, his remarks are full of humour.

umorísta, *s.c.* humorist.

umorístico, *ag.* humorous; (*divertente*) funny: *giornale* —, humorous paper; *osservazione umoristica,* humorous remark; *pagina umoristica,* (*di un giornale*) humorous page; *scrittore* —, humorous writer; *storiella umoristica,* funny story.

un, úna, *V.* **úno, úna.**

unànime, *ag.* unanimous: *approvazione, voto* —, unanimous approval, vote; *tutti furono unanimi nel disapprovarlo,* they were all unanimous in disapproving him.

unanimeménte, *av.* unanimously, by one consent.

unanimità, *s.f.* unanimity: *assoluta* —, absolute unanimity; *eletto a* — *di voti,* elected with a unanimous vote; *la sua proposta fu accettata all'*—, his proposal was unanimously accepted.

uncinàre, *v.t.* 1. to hook 2. *fig.* (*rubare*) to steal.

uncinàto, *ag.* hooked, uncinate: *un becco* —, a hooked bill; *ferro* —, hooked iron ‖ *croce uncinata,* swastika.

uncinétto, *s.m.* crochet-hook: *lavoro all'*—, crochet work; *lavorare all'*—, to crochet.

uncíno, *s.m.* hook: *afferrare con un* —, to hook (*o* to seize with a hook) ‖ *attaccarsi a tutti gli uncini,* (*cercare tutti i cavilli*) to split hairs.

undècimo, *ag. num. ord.* eleventh.

undicènne, *ag.* eleven years old (*predicativo*); eleven-year-old (*attributivo*) ‖ *s.m.* eleven-year-old boy ‖ *s.f.* eleven-year-old girl.

undicèsimo, *ag.num.ord. s.m.* eleventh.

úndici, *ag.num.card.s.m.* eleven: *l'*— *di gennaio,* the eleventh of January.

undicimíla, *ag.num.card. s.m.* eleven thousand.

ungàrico, *ag.* Hungarian.

úngaro, *ag.s.m.* Hungarian.

úngere, *v.t.* **1.** to grease, to oil, to smear; (*macchiare*) to dirty: *ho unto la tovaglia*, I have dirtied the table -cloth; — *con una pomata*, to smear with an ointment; — *la lama di un coltello, le ruote di un carro*, to grease (*o* to oil) the blade of a knife, the wheels of a cart ‖ — *le ruote*, *fig.* to grease the wheels **2.** (*eccl.*) to anoint: *fu unto re la notte di Natale*, he was anointed king on Christmas Night **3.** *fig.* (*adulare*) to flatter, to square ‖ **úngersi,** *v.r.* to grease oneself, to smear oneself: *mi sono unto il vestito*, I have smeared my dress.

ungherése, *ag.s.c.* Hungarian ‖ *s.m.* (*lingua*) Hungarian: *egli parla l'*—, he speaks Hungarian.

Ungheria, *no.pr.f.* (*geog.*) Hungary.

únghero, *ag.s.m.* Hungarian.

únghia, *s.f.* **1.** nail: — *incarnata*, ingrowing nail; *unghie dei piedi*, toe-nails; *forbicine per unghie*, nail -scissors (*o* clippers); *limetta per unghie*, nail-file; *smalto per unghie*, nail-polish; *spazzolino per unghie*, nail-brush; *mordersi le unghie*, to bite one's nails; *tagliarsi le unghie*, to cut one's nails ‖ *un'*— *di spessore*, a hair('s)-breadth; *grande come un'*—, a mere speck (*o* a flea-bite) ‖ *avere le unghie lunghe*, *fig.* to be light -fingered; *mettere le unghie su ql.co.*, *fig.* to lay hands on sthg. ‖ *mettere fuori le unghie*, *fig.* to show fight **2.** (*artiglio*) claw; (*di uccello da preda*) talon ‖ *si vede l'*— *del leone*, *fig.* by his mark you know him **3.** (*zoccolo*) hoof (*pl.* hoofs, hooves): *le unghie del cavallo*, the hoofs of a horse **4.** *pl.* (*grinfie*) clutches: *cadere nelle unghie di qlcu.*, to get into s.o.s clutches **5.** (*mar.*) peak, bill, pea **6.** (*arch.*) groin **7.** (*taglio*) bevel cut, chamfer cut.

unghiàta, *s.f.* scratch: *dare un'*— *a qlcu.*, to scratch s.o.

unghiàto, *ag.* clawed.

unghiatúra, *s.f.* (*legatoria*) guard.

unghióne, *s.m.* claw; (*di uccello da preda*) talon.

unghiúto, *ag.* **1.** clawed **2.** (*ladro*) rapacious.

ungiménto, *s.m.* greasing; (*lubrificazione*)lubrication.

ungitóre, *s.m.* greaser.

ungitúra, *s.f.* greasing; (*lubrificazione*) lubrication.

unguentàre, *v.t.* to spread with ointment, to rub with ointment.

unguentàrio, *ag.* unguentary: *vaso* —, (*archeol.*) unguentarium ‖ *s.m.* **1.** (*chi prepara, vende unguenti*) unguentary **2.** (*vaso unguentario*) unguentarium (*pl.* unguentaria).

unguentière, *s.m.* unguentary.

unguènto, *s.m.* ointment, unguent.

ungulàto, *ag.* hoofed, ungulate ‖ *s.m.* ungulate ‖ *gli ungulati*, (*zool.*) Ungulata.

uníbile, *ag.* unitable, joinable.

unibilità, *s.f.* unitiveness.

unicaménte, *av.* only, solely, uniquely, merely.

unicameralísmo, *s.m.* (*pol.*) unicameralism.

unicellulàre, *ag.* (*biol.*) unicellular.

unicità, *s.f.* uniqueness, uniquity, oneness, singleness: *con* — *di intenti*, with singleness of purpose.

único, *ag.* **1.** only, one; (*solo, esclusivo*) sole: — *agente, concessionario, rappresentante*, sole agent, grantee, representative; — *erede*, sole heir; *esemplare* —, only copy extant; *la mia unica speranza*, my only hope; *il mio solo e* — *desiderio*, my one and only wish; *la sua unica ragione*, his sole reason; *è figlio* —, he is an only child; *egli è il mio* — *amico*, he is my only friend; *questa è l'unica cosa che potrei fare*, this is the one (*o* only) thing I could do; *siamo gli unici a saperlo*, we are the only people that know it ‖ *strada a senso* —, one -way road (*o* street) ‖ *fare un fronte* —, to present a united front **2.** (*singolo*) single: *binario* —, single track; *un numero* —, (*pubblicazione*) a single number; *una strada con un'unica corsia*, a road with a single lane **3.** (*senza uguale*) unique: *egli è* — *nel leggere Shakespeare*, he is unique in reading Shakespeare;

questo libro è — *nel suo genere*, this book is unique in its kind.

unicòrno, *ag.* unicorn, single-horned ‖ *s.m.* (*mit.*) Unicorn ‖ *l'*— *ed il leone*, the Unicorn and the Lion.

unificàbile, *ag.* unifiable.

unificàre, *v.t.* **1.** to unify: — *i codici*, to unify the codes **2.** (*dir. comm.*) (*consolidare*) to consolidate: — *debiti*, to consolidate debts **3.** (*uniformare*) to standardize: *i recipienti di alluminio furono unificati*, the aluminium containers were standardized.

unificatívo, *ag.* unifying.

unificàto, *ag.* **1.** unified **2.** (*dir. comm.*) consolidated **3.** (*uniformato*) standardized.

unificatóre, *ag.* unifying ‖ *s.m.*, **unificatríce,** *s.f.* unifier.

unificazióne, *s.f.* **1.** unification **2.** (*dir. comm.*) consolidation **3.** (*uniformazione*) standardization.

uniformàre, *v.t.* **1.** to conform: — *la propria condotta ai propri ideali*, to conform one's conduct to one's ideals **2.** (*rendere uniforme*)to make uniform, to standardize ‖ **uniformàrsi,** *v.r.* to conform, to comply (with sthg.), to abide (by sthg.): — *alla legge*, to abide by the law; — *alla volontà di qlcu.*, to conform to (*o* to comply with) s.o.'s will.

uniformazióne, *s.f.* standardization.

unifórme, *ag.* uniform; unvarying, regular; even: *colore* —, uniform (*o* even) colour; *misura, movimento, temperatura, velocità* —, uniform size, motion, temperature, speed; *passo* —, even (*o* uniform *o* unvarying) pace; *terreno* —, even ground; *vita* —, regular (*o* uniform *o* unvarying) life ‖ *s.f.* uniform: *l'*— *di un vigile urbano*, the uniform of a policeman; — *militare*, regimentals (*o* military uniform); *in alta* —, (*mil.*) in full (-dress) uniform (*o* in full regimentals); *indossare l'*—, (*mil.*) to become a soldier (*o* to enlist *o* to join up).

uniformeménte, *av.* uniformly; unvaryingly; evenly.

uniformità, *s.f.* uniformity; sameness; evenness: — *di* — *condotta*, uniformity (*o* consistency) of conduct; *di movimento*, evenness of motion; *l'*— *di un paesaggio*, the sameness of a landscape; — *di stile*, uniformity of style; — *di vedute*, uniformity (*o* identity) of viewsy

unigènito, *ag.* only-begotten, only: *figlio* —, onl.. child ‖ *s.m.* only child ‖ *l'Unigenito di Dio*, the Only -Begotten of the Father.

unilabiàto, *ag.* (*bot.*) unilabiate(d).

unilateràle, *ag.* unilateral, one-sided: *contratto, giudizio* —, unilateral (*o* one-sided) contract, judgement.

unilateralità, *s.f.* unilaterality, one-sidedness.

uniloculàre, *ag.* (*bot.*) unilocular, uniloculate, one -celled.

unimetallísmo, *s.m.* (*econ.*) monometallism.

uninominàle, *ag.* uninominal: *collegio* —, single -member constituency; *votazione* —, uninominal voting.

unióne, *s.f.* **1.** union; junction; combination: *l'*— *di due elementi*, the combination of two elements; *l'*— *di due fiumi*, the junction of two rivers **2.** (*di suoni, colori*) blending **3.** (*coalizione*) coalition: *l'*— *delle sinistre*, the left-wing coalition **4.** (*federazione, associazione, lega*, union: *Unione delle Repubbliche Socialiste Sovietiche*, Union of Socialist Soviet Republics; *Unione Doganale*) Customs Union; *Unione operaia*, Trade Union; *Unione Postale Universale*, Universal Postal Union; *Unione Sudafricana*, Union of South Africa **5.** (*matrimonio*) union, match: *la loro felice* —, their happy union (*o* match) **6.** *fig.* (*armonia, concordia*) union, unity, agreement, concord: *vivono e lavorano in perfetta* —, they live and work in perfect union ‖ *l'*— *fa la forza*, *prov.* unity is strength (*o* united we stand, divided we fall).

unionísmo, *s.m.* (*pol.*) unionism.

unionísta, *s.m.* (*pol.*) unionist.

uníparo, *ag.* (*biol.*) uniparous.

unipètalo, *ag.* (*bot.*) unipetalous.

unipolàre, *ag.* (*fis.*) unipolar; (*elett.*) unipolar, homopolar, single-pole.

unipolarità, *s.f.* (*fis.*) unipolarity.

unire, *v.t.* **1.** to unite, to join (together), to combine; (*allacciare*) to link, to connect: *le due isole sono unite da un ponte,* the two islands are joined by a bridge; *la loro comune sventura li unì,* their common misfortune united them; *non possiamo sempre unire il lavoro al piacere,* we can't always combine work with pleasure; *una rete ferroviaria unisce Parigi a tutte le grandi città,* a system of railways connects (*o* links up) Paris with all the large towns; — *due pezzi di corda,* to join two pieces of string (together); — *le forze,* to join forces; — *in matrimonio,* to join in marriage **2.** (*aggiungere*) to add: — *l'interesse al capitale,* to add the interest to the capital **3.** (*suoni, colori*) to blend **4.** (*accludere*) to enclose: *uniamo l'importo che vi dobbiamo,* we enclose the amount we owe you ‖ **unirsi,** *v.r.* to unite (with sthg.), to join (with s.o., sthg.), to join (s.o., sthg.), to join (in sthg.), to combine (with sthg.), to connect (with sthg.), to link on (to s.o., sthg.), to link up (with s.o., sthg.), to link in (with s.o., sthg.): *i due fiumi si uniscono a dieci miglia dal mare,* the two rivers join at ten miles from the sea; *elementi, partiti che si uniscono,* elements, parties that combine; *mia madre si unisce a me nel mandarvi molti auguri,* my mother joins me in sending you many wishes; *posso unirmi alla vostra compagnia, al giuoco?,* may I join your party, in the game?; *quegli stati si unirono qualche anno fa,* those states united a few years ago; *si unì in matrimonio con una donna più vecchia di lui,* he married a woman older than he; *le strade laterali si uniscono alle arterie principali,* side-streets connect with the main arteries; *uniamoci per combattere la povertà,* let us unite in fighting (*o* to fight) poverty.

unisessuàle, *ag.* (*bot.*) unisexual, unisexed.

unisessualità, *s.f.* (*bot.*) unisexuality.

unisillàbico, *ag.* monosyllabic.

unisillabo, *s.m.* monosyllable.

unisonànza, *s.f.* (*rar.*) unisonance.

unìsono, *ag.* unisonous, unisonal, unisonant ‖ *s.m.* unison; (*armonia*) harmony, concord, agreement: *un* — *perfetto,* a perfect unison; *essere, cantare all'*—, to be, to sing in unison.

unità, *s.f.* **1.** unity: — *di azione, di luogo, di tempo,* unity of action, of place, of time; *l'*— *di Dio,* (*teol.*) the unity (*o* the oneness) of God; — *di ideali,* unity of ideals; *l'*— *di una nazione,* the unity of a nation; *le* — *drammatiche,* the dramatic unities **2.** (*mil.*) unit: — *da superficie,* (*mar.*) surface vessel; — *tattica,* tactical unit; *alcune* — *della nostra flotta, del nostro esercito furono distrutte,* a few units of our fleet, of our army were destroyed **3.** (*misura, valore*) unit: — *assoluta,* (*fis.*) absolute unit; — *Curie,* (*fis.*) Curie; — *di assorbimento acustico,* (*fis.*) sabin; — *di calore,* (*fis.*) thermal unit; — *di lunghezza, peso, tempo, volume,* unit of length, weight, time, volume; — *di velocità di trasmissione telegrafica,* (*tel.*) baud; — *elettrica,* electric unit; — *elettromagnetica,* electromagnetic unit; — *monetaria,* monetary unit **4.** (*mat.*) unity; unit: *la colonna delle* —, the units column; *ridurre un coefficiente all'*—, to reduce a coefficient to unity.

unitaménte, *av.* **1.** unitedly **2.** — *a,* together with: *ti spedirò il libro* — *alla lettera,* I'll send you the book together with the letter.

unitàrio, *ag.* **1.** unitary: *sistema* —, unitary system; *prezzo* —, (*comm.*) unit-price **2.** (*pol. st. relig.*) unitary, unitarian ‖ *s.m.* (*st. relig.*) Unitarian.

unitarísmo, *s.m.* (*st. relig.*) Unitarianism.

unitézza, *s.f.* **1.** (*compattezza*) compactness **2.** (*uniformità*) uniformity.

unitìvo, *ag.* (*rar.*) unitive, uniting.

unìto, *ag.* **1.** united: *è una famiglia molto unita,* it is a very united family; *rimanete uniti!,* remain together! ‖ *Regno Unito,* United Kingdom ‖ *gli Stati Uniti d'America,* the United States of America **2.** (*ag-*

giunto) added **3.** (*accluso*) enclosed **4.** (*uniforme*) even: *tinta unita,* even colour.

univàlve, *ag.* (*zool.*) univalve.

universàle, *ag.* universal, general: *approvazione* —, general approval; *cultura* —, universal culture; *lingua* —, universal language; *principio, regola* —, universal principle, rule; *suffragio* —, universal suffrage ‖ *il Diluvio Universale,* the Deluge ‖ *erede* —, sole heir ‖ *il Giudizio Universale,* the Last Judgement ‖ *s.m.* (*letter.*) the totality of men.

universaleggiàre, *V.* **universalizzàre.**

universalità, *s.f.* universality: *l'*— *di Leonardo,* Leonardo's universality; *l'*— *degli italiani,* all Italians, (*o* the whole Italian nation).

universalizzàre, *v.t.* to universalize, to make universal, to render universal.

universalménte, *av.* universally: *è* — *risaputo che...,* it is universally acknowledged that....

università, *s.f.* university: — *di stato, privata,* state, private university; *aveva studiato all'*—, he had had a university education (*o* he had been through university *o fam.* he had been to college).

universitàrio, *ag.* university (*attributivo*): *professore, studente* —, university professor, student; *vita universitaria,* university life ‖ *s.m.* university student, undergraduate.

univèrso[1], *ag.* (*letter.*) (*intero*) whole: *l'*— *mondo,* the whole world.

univèrso[2], *s.m.* universe: *i misteri dell'*—, the mysteries of the universe; *per tutto l'*—, all over the world; *il mio* — *è molto limitato,* my universe is very limited.

univocaménte, *av.* univocally.

univoco, *ag.* univocal.

Únni, *s.m.pl.* (*st.*) Huns.

úno, un, úna, *art. indeterminativo* **1. a, an:** *un artista,* an artist; *un buco,* a hole; *una donna,* a woman; *un erede,* an heir; *un europeo,* a European; *un libro,* a book; *un onore,* an honour; *un'ora lieta,* a happy hour; *un'unione,* a union; *un uomo onesto,* an honest man ‖ *una cinquantina di persone,* some (*o* about) fifty people **2.** (*circa*): *un tre o quattro giorni,* (*fam.*) some (*o* about) three or four days.

úno, *ag.num.card.s.m.* one: — *contro cinque,* one to five; *un giorno o due,* one day or two; — *per cento,* one per cent; *un terzo,* one third; *un uomo con un solo occhio,* a one-eyed man; *un uomo su mille,* one man in a thousand; *nemmeno* —, not a single one; *numero* —, number one; *fig.* (*l'esponente più rappresentativo*) the star; the best (*o* most important) man: *un asino numero* —, (*fam.*) an egregious ass; *abbiamo due occhi, un naso, una bocca,* we have two eyes, one nose, one mouth; *ce n'era solo* —, there was only one; *ci volle una settimana esatta,* it took just one week; *ho solamente un libro,* I have only one book; *scrivi* —, write one; *contare per* —, to count by ones; *scrivere* — *e riportare cinque,* to write down one and carry five ‖ *a* — *a* —, one by one.

úno, úna, *pron. indef.* **1.** one: — *di noi, di voi, di loro,* one of us, of you, of them; — *di questi giorni,* one of these days; — *non può dire se sia vero o no,* one cannot tell whether it is true or not; *non voglio questo vestito, dammene* — *più scuro,* I don't want this dress, give me a darker one ‖ *uno..., l'altro...,* one..., the other...: *ha due figli,* — *è molto alto, l'altro è molto basso,* he has two sons, one is very tall, the other is very short ‖ *dall'* — *all'altro,* from one to the other ‖ *l'* — *vale l'altro,* one is as good as the other ‖ *uno..., un altro..., another...: i bimbi giocavano in giardino,* — *con la palla, un altro con la trottola,* the children were playing in the garden, one with a ball, another with a top ‖ *l'* — *e l'altro,* (*entrambi*) both; *gli uni e gli altri,* (*tutti*) they all; (*obliquo*) them all: *dammi l'una e l'altra matita,* give me both pencils; *ho letto l'* — *e l'altro,* I have read both of them (*o* them both); *partirono gli uni e gli* *altri*, they all left; *scrissi agli uni e agli altri*, I wrote to them all ‖ *l' — o l'altro*, either: *dammi l' — o l'altro*, give me either ‖ *nè l' — nè l'altro*, neither; *(in presenza di altra negazione)* either: *non voglio nè l' — nè l'altro*, I want neither (*o* I don't want either) ‖ *nè l' — ..., nè l'altro...* neither the one,...nor the other...; *(in presenza di altra negazione)* either the one..., or the other...: *nè l' — studiava nè l'altro leggeva*, neither was the one studying nor was the other reading ‖ *l'un l'altro, (reciproco)* each other *(generalmente fra due)*; one another *(generalmente fra molti)*: *si aiutano l'un l'altro*, they help each other ‖ *ne ha fatta una delle sue*, he has been up to one of his usual tricks; *ne ha fatta una grossa!*, he has done something very foolish! ‖ *ne vuoi sentire una?*, shall I tell you something? ‖ *non gliene va bene, male una*, everything goes wrong, well with him **2.** *(qualcuno)* **someone**; *(un tale)* **a fellow, a man**; *(una tale)* **a woman**: *c'era — che voleva parlarti*, there was someone (*o* a fellow *o* a man) who wanted to speak to you; *incontrai una che mi parlò assai bene di te*, I met a woman who spoke very well of you **3.** *(ciascuno)*: *facciamo un po' per —*, let's do a part each (*o* let's all do a share); *paghiamo metà per —*, let's go fifty-fifty.

untàre, *v.t.* to oil, to grease, to smear; *fig.* to flatter.

únto, *ag.* **1.** greasy, oily, smeary; *(macchiato)* dirty: *mani unte*, greasy (*o* dirty) hands; *un soprabito — e bisunto*, an all greasy overcoat **2.** *(eccl.)* anointed ‖ *l'Unto del Signore*, the Lord's Anointed ‖ *s.m.* grease; *(grasso alimentare)* fat: *— di maiale*, pork fat; *— per le ruote di un veicolo*, axle grease; *macchia d'—*, grease-spot; *dare dell'— a una ruota*, to grease a wheel; *macchiare d'— gli abiti*, to soil one's clothes with grease (*o* to grease one's clothes) ‖ *dare l'—, (adulare)* to butter up ‖ *dare dell'— a qlcu., (corromperlo)* to oil (*o* to grease) s.o.'s palm (*o* to bribe s.o.).

untóre, *s.m. (st.)* plague-spreader.

untúme, *s.m.* grease, greasy stuff; *(di grasso alimentare)* fat: *egli può scivolare facilmente con tutto questo — per terra*, he can easily slip with all this grease (*o* greasy stuff) on the floor; *non mi piace tutto questo — nella minestra*, I don't like all this fat on my soup.

untuosaménte, *av. fig.* unctuously, oilily, soapily: *parlò —*, he spoke unctuously.

untuosità, *s.f.* **1.** greasiness, fatness, oiliness **2.** *fig.* greasiness, oiliness, unctuousness, soapiness: *la sua — mi disgustava*, his soapiness disgusted me.

untuóso, *ag.* **1.** greasy, fat, oily **2.** *fig.* oily, unctuous, soapy: *modi untuosi*, oily (*o* unctuous *o* soapy) manners.

unzióne, *s.f.* unction (anche *fig.*): *predicare con —*, to preach with unction ‖ *Estrema Unzione, (eccl.)* Extreme Unction.

uòmo, *s.m.* **1.** man *(pl.* men): *— d'affari*, businessman; *un — da nulla*, a nobody (*o* a mere cipher); *l'— della strada*, the man in the street; *l'— delle caverne*, cave-man; *l'— del momento*, the man of the hour; *— di campagna*, countryman; *— di cuore*, kind-hearted man; *— di legge*, man of law; *— di lettere*, man of letters; *— di mare*, seaman; *un — di mezzi*, a well-to-do man; *un — di mondo*, a world-wise man; *un — d'ingegno*, a clever man; *— di paglia*, *fig.* man of straw (*o* figurehead); *un — di parola*, a trustworthy man; *un — di poche parole*, a man of few words; *— di scienza*, scientist; *— di società*, a man about town; *— di stato*, statesman; *— di studio*, scholar; *— d'onore*, man of honour; *— fatto*, grown-up man; *un — fidato*, a reliable man; *un — grande e grosso*, *un pezzo d'—*, a big man (*o* fellow); *un — onesto*, an honest man; *un — povero*, a poor man; *un — sportivo*, a sportsman; *un bell'—*, a good-looking (*o* handsome) man; *un grand'—*, a great man; *un pover'—*, a poor fellow; *la vita dell'—*, man's life; *l'— è mortale*, man is mortal; *gli uomini sono deboli*, men are weak; *Dio si fece —*, God was made man; *quello è il tuo —*, *l'— che fa al caso tuo*, that is your man (*o* the man for you); *sii — e non*

aver paura, be a man and don't be afraid; *sopportare ql.co. da —*, to bear sthg. like a man ‖ *l'— adatto nel posto adatto*, the right man in the right place ‖ *l'— nero*, the bogey(man) ‖ *un — nuovo*, an upstart; *a memoria d'—*, within the memory of men ‖ *a passo d'—*, at a walking pace ‖ *bene, caro il mio —!*, well, my dear fellow! ‖ *come un sol —*, as one man ‖ *da — a —*, as man to man ‖ *i diritti dell'—*, the rights of man ‖ *fino all'ultimo —*, to the last man ‖ *un — che sa quello che vuole*, a man who knows what he is about ‖ *è già un — fatto*, he is quite a man already; *farsi —*, to grow up ‖ *è un mezzo —*, he is only half a man ‖ *— avvisato mezzo salvato*, *prov.* (a man) forewarned is forearmed ‖ *l'— propone e Dio dispone*, *prov.* man proposes, God disposes **2.** *(marito)* husband: *il suo —*, her husband (*o* man).

uòpo, *s.m.*: *questo fa proprio al mio —*, this is just what I need (*o* this meets my needs) ‖ *all'—*, if necessary: *all'— ve lo faremo sapere*, if necessary we shall let you know ‖ *far, essere d'—*, to be necessary: *è, fa d'— che io lo veda subito*, it is necessary for me to see him at once (*o* I must see him at once); *non è, fa d'—*, it is not necessary: *non è, fa d'— che tu venga*, you need not come (*o* it is not necessary for you to come).

uòsa, *s.f.* legging, gaiter.

uòvo, *s.m.* egg: *uova affogate, in camicia*, poached eggs; *uova alla coque*, boiled eggs; *uova all'ostrica*, prairie oysters; *uova al prosciutto*, ham and eggs; *uova bazzotte, sode*, soft-boiled, hard-boiled eggs; *uova da bere*, new-laid eggs; *— di anatra, di gallina*, duck's, hen's egg; *— di baco da seta*, silkworm's egg; *— di Pasqua*, Easter egg; *uova guaste*, bad eggs; *uova strapazzate*, scrambled eggs; *bianco, chiara d'—*, white of egg; *guscio d'—*, egg-shell; *rosso d'—*, yolk: *devo farti un rosso d'— sbattuto?*, shall I whip the yolk of an egg for you?; *la gallina ha fatto l'—*, the hen has laid an egg; *covare uova*, to brood eggs ‖ *accomodare le uova nel paniere*, *fig.* to feather one's nest (*o* to arrange things according to one's convenience) ‖ *camminare sulle uova*, *fig.* to tread on eggs ‖ *cercare il pelo nell'—*, to split hairs ‖ *rompere le uova nel paniere a qlcu.*, *fig.* to upset s.o.'s plans ‖ *meglio un uovo oggi che una gallina domani*, *prov.* a bird in the hand is worth two in the bush.

úpupa, *s.f. (ornit.)* hoopoe.

úraco, *s.m. (anat.)* urachus.

uragàno, *s.m.* hurricane (anche *fig.*): *un — di applausi*, a hurricane of applause.

Uràli (gli), *no.pr.m.pl. (geog.)* (the) Ural (mountains).

uràngo, *s.m. (zool.)* orang-outang.

Urània, *no.pr.f. (mit.)* Urania.

urànico, *ag. (chim.)* uranic.

urànio, *s.m. (chim.)* uranium.

Uràno, *no.pr.m. (mit. astr.)* Uranus.

uranografía, *s.f. (astr.)* uranography.

uranogràfico, *ag. (astr.)* uranographic.

uranògrafo, *s.m.* uranographer.

uranología, *s.f. (astr.)* uranology.

uranometría, *s.f. (astr.)* uranometry.

uranoscopía, *s.f. (astr.)* uranoscopy.

uràto, *s.m. (chim.)* urate.

urbanaménte, *av.* urbanely, courteously, civilly, politely.

urbanésimo, urbanísmo, *s.m.* urbanism.

urbanística, *s.f.* town-planning.

urbanità, *s.f.* urbanity, courtesy, civility, politeness.

urbanizzàre, *v.t.* to urbanize.

urbanizzazióne, *s.f.* urbanization.

urbàno[1], *ag.* **1.** urban; city *(attributivo)*; town *(attributivo)*: *popolazione urbana*, urban population **2.** *(cortese)* urbane, courteous, civil, polite: *modi urbani*, polite manners.

Urbàno², *no.pr.m.* Urban.

úrbe, *s.f.* (*letter.*) city: *l'Urbe*, the Eternal City (*o* Rome).

urèa, *s.f.* (*chim. biol.*) urea.

urèdine, *s.f.* (*ruggine delle graminacee*) uredo.

uredinèe, *s.f.pl.* (*bot.*) Uredinales.

uremía, *s.f.* (*patol.*) uraemia.

urèmico, *ag.* (*patol.*) uraemic.

urènte, *ag.* (*letter.*) burning.

ureteràle, *ag.* (*anat.*) ureteral.

uretère, *s.m.* (*anat.*) ureter.

ureteríte, *s.f.* (*patol.*) ureteritis.

urètra, *s.f.* (*anat.*) urethra.

uretràle, *ag.* (*anat.*) urethral.

uretríte, *s.f.* (*patol.*) urethritis.

uretrotomía, *s.f.* (*chir.*) urethrotomy.

urgènte, *ag.* urgent, pressing: *affare* —, urgent (*o* pressing) business; *bisogno* —, urgent need; *lettera* —, urgent (*o* pressing) letter; *messaggio* —, urgent message.

urgenteménte, *av.* urgently, pressingly.

urgènza, *s.f.* urgency: *un affare di molta* —, a business of great urgency; *con molta* —, with great urgency; *lettera d'*—, urgent (*o* pressing) letter; *ho* — *di vederlo*, I must see him as soon as possible (*o* at once) ‖ *d'*—, urgently.

úrgere, *v.i.* to be urgent, to be pressing: *fa questo prima di tutto perchè urge*, do this first of all because it is urgent; *urge aiuto*, help is urgently required; *urge che lo facciate immediatamente*, it is absolutely necessary that you should do it immediately; *urge che lo veda subito*, it is essential for me to see him at once.

urí, *s.f.* (*vergine del paradiso maomettano*) houri.

Uría, *no.pr.m.* (*Bibbia*) Uriah.

uricemía, *s.f.* (*patol.*) uricaemia.

uricèmico, *ag.* (*patol.*) uricaemic.

úrico, *ag.* (*biol.*) uric: *acido* —, uric acid.

Urièle, *no.pr.m.* (*lett.*) Uriel.

urína, *e derivati, V.* **orína,** *e derivati.*

urlànte, *ag.* shouting, howling, yelling; shrieking: *una donna* —, a shrieking (*o* yelling) woman; *una folla* —, a shouting (*o* yelling) crowd.

urlàre, *v.i.* to shout, to yell, to bawl, to howl; to scream; (*strillare*) to shriek: *il bimbo urlava perchè aveva fame*, the baby was screaming because it was hungry; *il cane urlò in giardino per tutta la notte*, the dog howled in the garden all night; *il ferito urlava per lo spasimo*, the injured man was yelling with agony; *la folla urlava consigli all'arbitro*, the crowd were yelling (*o* bawling *o* shouting) advice to the referee; *non* — *così, ti odono ugualmente!*, don't shout like that, they can hear you!; *quei maledetti bambini dei vicini urlano tutto il giorno*, those wretched children next door are shouting and screaming all day long; *quel bambino è talmente viziato che incomincia a* — *quando non può fare quello che vuole*, that child is so spoilt that he starts crying (*o* howling *o* bawling) whenever he cannot get his own way; *urlava di dolore*, he was screaming (*o* howling) with pain; *urlò di orrore alla vista del topo*, she shrieked with horror at the sight of the mouse; *il vento urlava nel bosco*, the wind was howling in the wood.

urlàta, *s.f.* (*di derisione*) hoot.

urlatóre, *ag.* shouting, yelling, bawling, howling ‖ *scimmia urlatrice*, (*zool.*) howling monkey ‖ *s.m.*, **urlatríce,** *s.f.* **1.** shouter, bawler, howler **2.** (*neol.*) (*cantante*) pop-singer whose style is based on gimmicks and interpolated shouts and cries.

urlío, *s.m.* shouting, yelling, howling; shrieking: *l'* —*dei bambini*, the shouting (*o* yelling) of the children; *l'* — *dei lupi*, the howling of the wolves; *l'* — *della tempesta*, the howling (*o* roaring) of the storm.

úrlo, *s.m.* cry, shout, yell; shriek; scream: *le urla della folla*, the shouts (*o* roar) of the crowd; *l'* — *del*

---

vento, del lupo, del cane, the howl of the wind, of the wolf, of the dog; *un* — *di dolore*, a howl (*o* cry) of pain; *urla di gioia*, shouts of joy; *un* — *di indignazione*, a cry of indignation; *un* — *di terrore*, a shriek of terror; *mandare un* —, to give a cry (*o* shriek).

urlóne, *s.m.* shouter, howler, bawler.

úrna, *s.f.* **1.** urn: — *cineraria*, cinerary urn; *antiche urne romane*, ancient Roman urns; *seppellimento in urne*, urn burial **2.** (*recipiente in cui si raccolgono i voti*) ballot-box ‖ *apertura delle urne*, opening of the polls; *andare alle urne*, to go to the polls; *attendere il responso delle urne*, to wait for the votes to be returned.

úro, *s.m.* (*paleont.*) urus (*pl.* uri, uruses), aurochs.

urobilína, *s.f.* (*biol.*) urobilin.

urocèle, *s.m.* (*patol.*) urocele.

urocíste, *s.f.* (*patol.*) urocyst, urocystis.

urocròmo, *s.m.* (*biol.*) urochrome.

urodèlo, *s.m.* (*zool.*) urodele.

urogàllo, *s.m.* (*ornit.*) grouse (*invariato al pl.*).

urolitíasi, *s.f.* (*patol.*) urolithiasis.

urolíto, *s.m.* urolith, urolite.

urología, *s.f.* urology.

urològico, *ag.* urological.

uròlogo, *s.m.* urologist.

uròmetro, *s.m.* (*med.*) urometer.

uroniàno, *ag.* (*geol.*) Huronian.

uropígio, *s.m.* uropygium.

uroscopía, *s.f.* (*med.*) uroscopy.

urotropína, *s.f.* (*farm.*) urotropine.

urrà, *inter.* hurrah!, hurray!.

urtànte¹, *ag.* (*che infastidisce*) irritating, vexing, annoying: *un contegno* —, an irritating behaviour.

urtànte², *s.m.* (*mar.*) keelblock, bilge block.

urtàre, *v.t.* **1.** to knock; to knock against, into (s.o., sthg.); to bump; to bump into, against (s.o., sthg.); to strike against (s.o., sthg.); to hit on, against (s.o., sthg.); (*inciampare in*) to stumble over (s.o., sthg.), to stub one's toe against (s.o., sthg.): *lo urtai ed egli cadde*, I bumped into (*o* against) him and he fell down; *urtai un gradino e per poco non cadevo*, I stumbled over a step and almost fell; — *qlcu. per la strada*, to run into (*o* to jostle against *o* to collide with *o* to bump into) s.o. in the street **2.** (*infastidire*) to irritate, to vex, to annoy; (*offendere i sentimenti di*) to hurt, to shock, to offend: *non urtarlo*, don't irritate him; *questo rifiuto mi urta molto*, this refusal annoys me very much; *le sue parole urtarono i sentimenti di suo fratello*, his words hurt (*o* offended) his brother's feelings ‖ *il suo modo di parlare mi urta i nervi*, his way of speaking gets (*o* jars) on my nerves ‖ *v.i.* to knock; to stumble (over s.o., sthg.); to strike; to hit: *l'aereo urtò contro la collina*, the plane crashed into the hill; *la nave urtò contro uno scoglio*, the ship hit against a rock; *urtai contro una radice e caddi*, I stumbled against (*o* over) a root and fell; *urtai contro la seggiola*, I bumped into (*o* against) the chair ‖ **urtàrsi,** *v.r.* to get cross: *si urta per un nonnulla*, he gets cross at anything ‖ *v.r.* *reciproco* (*entrare in collisione*) to collide: *le due automobili si urtarono*, the two cars collided; *i due montoni si urtarono frontalmente*, the two rams ran full butt into each other; *le due navi si urtarono*, the two ships collided (*o* ran foul of one another).

urtàta, *s.f.* knock; (*spinta*) push, shove.

urtíca, *V.* **ortíca.**

urticària, *s.f.* (*patol.*) nettle-rash, urticaria.

úrto, *s.m.* **1.** (*spinta*) push, shove: *mi diede un tale* — *che per poco non caddi*, he gave me such a push that I almost fell; *si faceva largo tra la folla a forza di urti*, he pushed his way through the crowd **2.** (*scontro*) collision, impact: *l'* — *delle due automobili fece due vittime*, the collision of the two cars caused two victims **3.** (*attacco*) attack: *si preparano contro l'* — *del nemico*, they are getting ready for the enemy's attack **4.** (*contrasto*) clash, collision, conflict: *un* — *di* *idee, vedute,* a clash (*o* conflict) of ideas, views; *un — di interessi,* a conflict of interests; *questi colori sono in —,* these colours clash; *queste teorie sono in — con i nostri principi,* these theories are not in accord with our principles; *essere in — con qlcu.,* to be at variance with s.o.; *mettersi in — con qlcu.,* to fall out with s.o. ‖ *prendere qlcu. in —,* to take a dislike to s.o. **5.** *— di vomito,* retch.

urtóne, *s.m.* shove, knock: *dare un — a qlcu.,* to give s.o. a shove.

usàbile, *ag.* usable.

usànza, *s.f.* **1.** usage, custom: *secondo l'—,* according to custom; *è l'— del paese,* it is the custom of the country; *è un'antica — tedesca,* it is an ancient German custom; *non conosco le usanze della vostra famiglia,* I don't know the customs of your family; *ogni popolo ha le sue usanze,* every people has its own customs ‖ *paese che vai usanze che trovi, prov.* when in Rome, do as the Romans do **2.** (*abitudine*) habit: *secondo la mia —,* as is my habit (*o* as it is my wont *o* according to my wont); *è mia — alzarmi alle sette,* it is my habit to get up at seven; *avere l'— di fare ql.co.,* to be in the habit (*o* to make a habit) of doing sthg. (*o* to be accustomed to doing sthg).

usàre, *v.t.* to use, to make use of (sthg.); to employ: *all'esame non possiamo — il vocabolario,* at the examination we are not allowed to use our dictionaries; *dovresti — meglio il tuo denaro,* you should make better use of your money; *egli ci permise di — il suo nome,* he allowed us to use his name; *io uso la lana per pulire l'argento,* I use wool to polish silver; *non sa come — il suo tempo,* he doesn't know how to employ (*o* how to make use of) his time; *non uso mai il burro in cucina,* I never use butter in my cooking; *posso — la tua penna?,* may I use your pen?; *se non trovi il tuo libro, usa il mio,* if you can't find your book, use mine; *usate più astuzia, più attenzione,* use more cunning, more care (*o* be more cunning, more careful); *usò ogni artificio, ogni occasione per ottenerlo,* he used every artifice, every opportunity to get it; *— la forza,* to use force ‖ *egli mi usò la cortesia di darmi il suo posto,* he was kind enough to offer me his seat; *egli mi usò molte cortesie,* he showed me many kindnesses (*o* he heaped *o* showered kindnesses on me); *vogliate usarmi la cortesia di farmelo sapere subito,* please do me the favour of letting me know at once ‖ *— maniere gentili, sgarbate con qlcu.,* to treat s.o. kindly, rudely ‖ *— pietà verso qlcu.,* to show mercy to s.o. ‖ *v.i.* **1.** (*essere solito*) to use (*solo al pass.*); to be accustomed, to be used: *da giovani usavamo vederci spesso,* when young we used to see each other often: *due secoli fa gli uomini usavano portare la parrucca,* two centuries ago it used to be customary for a man to wear a wig; *ella usava telefonarmi solo quando aveva bisogno,* she would ring me up only when she was in need; *in Giappone si usa mangiare seduti sul pavimento,* in Japan it is customary (*o* it is the custom) to eat sitting on the floor; *usavo andare a teatro ogni sera,* I used to go (*o* I was accustomed to going) to the theatre every evening; *uso alzarmi alle sette,* I am accustomed to get up at seven; *io non uso fare così,* I am not accustomed to do (*o* used to doing) so **2.** (*essere di moda*) to be fashionable, to be in fashion: *il modello di quel vestito non si usa più,* the model of that dress is no longer fashionable (*o* is out of fashion); *quest'anno si usa molto il rosso,* red is very fashionable this year **3.** (*fare uso*) to make use, to use (sthg.): *— del nome di qlcu.,* to use s.o.'s name; *— del proprio diritto,* to take advantage of one's own right **4.** (*accompagnarsi*) to frequent (s.o.): *egli usa con cattivi compagni,* he frequents bad companions; *non ho mai usato con gente simile,* I have never had anything to do with such people.

usàto, *ag.* **1.** (*non nuovo*) second-hand; (*logoro*) worn-out: *libri, mobili usati,* second-hand books, fur-

niture; *vestiti usati,* second-hand clothes; *questo vestito è troppo —,* this dress is too worn-out **2.** (*abituato*) used, accustomed, inured: *— ai sacrifici, alle avversità,* inured to sacrifices, to hardships; *— al pericolo,* used to danger; *non sono — a queste cose,* I am not used (*o* accustomed) to these things **3.** (*abituale*) customary, usual: *la sua usata imprudenza,* his usual imprudence **4.** (*in uso*) in use; *parola non usata,* obsolete word (*o* word out of use); *procedimenti ancora usati,* proceedings still in use ‖ *s.m.* (*il solito, l'ordinario*): *cose fuori dell'—,* unusual things; *lo fece meglio dell'—,* he did it better than usual.

usbèrgo, *s.m.* **1.** hauberk **2.** *fig.* (*protezione*) protection, defence, shield: *sotto l'— della fede,* under the shield of faith.

uscènte, *ag.* **1.** (*che lascia una carica*) retiring: *presidente —,* retiring president **2.** (*nelle determinazioni di tempo*) closing, expiring: *mese —,* closing (*o* expiring) month.

uscière, *s.m.* **1.** (*ufficiale giudiziario*) bailiff: *mandare gli uscieri,* to put in the bailiffs **2.** (*di tribunale*) usher **3.** (*rar.*) (*portiere*) door-keeper.

úscio, *s.m.* door; (*porta di strada*) front door, main door, street door: *abitare — a — con qlcu.,* to live next door to s.o.; *aprire, chiudere, sbattere l'—,* to open, to close, to bang the door; *mettere qlcu. fuori dell'—,* to turn s.o. out (of doors) ‖ *non si trovano a ogni —,* they don't grow on trees ‖ *essere tra l'— e il muro, fig.* to be between the devil and the deep blue sea (*o* to be in dire straits) ‖ *mettere, stringere qlcu. tra l'— e il muro, fig.* to drive s.o. to the wall (*o* to put s.o. on the spot) ‖ *prendere l'—, fig.* (*svignarsela*) to make off (*o* to make for the door).

usciolàre, *v.i.* to eavesdrop.

uscíre, *v.i.* **1.** **to go out; to come out** (anche *fig.*); **to get out;** (*lasciare*) **to leave** (a place): *esce ogni sera,* he goes out every evening; *la luna uscì dalle nubi,* the moon emerged from the clouds; *non esce molto,* she does not go out much (into society, to parties); *quando uscii da quel labirinto, da quella folla,* when I got out of that maze, of that crowd; *il sangue gli usciva di bocca,* blood was streaming from his mouth; *il treno uscì dal tunnel,* the train emerged from the tunnel; *uscì a dire che non era vero,* he came out saying that it was not true; *uscite!,* (*andate fuori*) go out!; (*venite fuori*) come out!; *uscì a piedi,* he went out on foot; *uscì con osservazioni non a proposito,* he came out with remarks which were beside the point; *uscì dalla camera,* he left the room; *uscì dall'automobile,* he got out of the car; *uscendo da teatro, lo incontrai,* on leaving the theatre I met him; *uscì in un fiume di parole piene di collera,* he burst out in a flood of angry words; *usciamo insieme!,* let us go out together!; *— a cavallo,* to ride out; *— correndo,* to run out: *uscì correndo dalla stanza,* he ran out of the room; *— dal letto,* to leave one's bed (*o* to get up); (*di fiume*) to overflow; *— furtivamente, di soppiatto,* to steal out: *il ragazzo uscì di soppiatto dalla stanza,* the boy stole out of the room; *— in automobile,* to drive out; *— precipitosamente,* to rush out: *uscì precipitosamente dal negozio,* he rushed out of the shop; *far — qlcu.,* (*accompagnandolo alla porta*) to show s.o. out; (*mandandolo via*) to bid s.o. go out: *non fatelo —!,* don't let him out!; *impedire a qlcu. di —,* to keep s.o. in ‖ *esce, escono,* (*nei copioni teatrali*) exit, exeunt: *esce Amleto,* exit Hamlet; *escono tutti, eccetto Amleto,* exeunt all except Hamlet ‖ *di qui non si esce: o è uno stupido o è un ladro,* there is nothing more to it: he is either a fool or a thief ‖ *mi esce dagli occhi,* I'm fed up with it (*o* I can't stand it any longer) ‖ *gli occhi gli uscivano dalla testa,* his eyes were starting out of his head ‖ *— dai gangheri,* to lose one's temper ‖ *— dai limiti, fig.* to exceed (*o* to pass all bounds): *questo esce dai limiti dei miei diritti,* this exceeds my rights; *la sua impudenza esce* *dai limiti*, his impudence passes all bounds || — *dal seminato*, *fig.* to digress || — *di infanzia*, to emerge from childhood; — *di minorità*, to come of age || — *di moda*, to go out of fashion || — *di senno*, to go mad (*o* to become insane) || — *di sentimento*, to faint (*o* to swoon) **2.** (*di pubblicazioni*) **to come out, to be issued, to be published**: *quando uscirà il prossimo numero?*, when will the next number come out?; *questa rivista esce il martedì*, this magazine comes out (*o* appears) on Tuesdays; *questo libro è appena uscito*, this book is just out **3.** (*riuscire*) **to come**: *egli uscì primo*, he came first **4.** (*essere estratto*) **to be drawn**: *per primo uscì il numero cinque*, number five was drawn first **5.** (*sfuggire*) **to slip**: *il bicchiere mi è uscito di mano*, the glass slipped out of my hands; *questa parola mi è uscita di mente*, this word has slipped (*o* gone out of) my memory **6.** (*sboccare*) **to lead** (to sthg.), **to end** (at sthg.): *questo sentiero esce sulla strada principale*, this path ends at the high road; *la strada esce su una piazza*, the road leads to a square **7.** (*dirottare*, *deragliare*) **to go off** (sthg.): *la macchina uscì di strada*, the car went off the road; *il treno uscì dalle rotaie*, the train went off the rails; *uscì dalla retta via*, he went off the straight and narrow path (*o* he went astray) **8.** (*discendere*) **to spring**; **to issue**; **to descend**: *egli esce da una buona famiglia*, he comes of a good family; *quell'uomo esce da una delle più antiche famiglie del luogo*, that man springs (*o* descends *o* issues) from one of the oldest families in the land **9.** (*derivare*, *provenire*): *che cosa uscirà fuori da tutto ciò?*, what will be the outcome (*o* the result) of it all?; *gli ingegneri usciti dal Politecnico*, engineers who have been trained at the "Politecnico" || *da quel taglio di stoffa esce una gonna*, that cloth will do for a skirt || *questo vestito uscì dalle mani di Dior*, this dress was made by Dior **10.** (*cavarsela*) **to get out; to extricate oneself**: *con meno di ventimila lire non ne uscirai*, you won't make it with less than twenty thousand lire; *uscirne bene*, *male*, to come off well, badly; — *da un imbroglio*, *dai pasticci*, *da una situazione difficile*, to get out of a scrape, of troubles, of a difficult situation **11.** (*ritirarsi*) **to leave** (sthg.), **to retire**: *egli uscì di carica*, he retired from his position; — *dai ranghi*, (*mil.*) to leave one's place in the ranks **12.** (*a carte*) **to lead** (a card): — *a*, *di fiori*, to lead clubs **13.** (*terminare*, *di parola*) **to end** (in sthg.): *questa parola esce in « t »*, this word ends in "t".

uscíta, *s.f.* **1.** (*l'uscire*) going out, coming out; (*il lasciare*) leaving (a place): *all' — dalla scuola*, on coming out of school; *all' — dal teatro*, on leaving the theatre; *alla sua — attirò su di sè l'attenzione di tutti*, when he came out he attracted everybody's attention || *bolletta d' —*, (*comm.*) export invoice; *dazio d' —*, (*comm.*) export duty; *dichiarazione d' —*, (*comm.*) customs declaration; *permesso d' —*, (*comm.*) customs clearance; *buona —*, (*per una casa*) key-money; (*liquidazione ad un impiegato*) leaving-bonus || *oggi è il mio giorno di libera —*, to-day is my day off; *essere in libera —*, to be off duty **2.** (*passaggio per il quale si esce*) exit, way out (anche *fig.*): — *di sicurezza*, emergency exit; *all' — del teatro*, at the exit of the theatre; *dobbiamo cedere*, *non c'è via d' —*, we must give in, there is no way out of it (*o* no escape *o* no help for it); *dov'è l' —?*, where is the exit?; *ho trovato una via d' —*, I have found a way out || *mostrare il biglietto all' —*, (*della stazione*) to show one's ticket at the barrier **3.** (*sbocco*) outlet: *dov'è l' — per l'acqua?*, where is the outlet for the water? || *strada senza —*, blind-alley (*o* dead-end) **4.** (*motto di spirito*) witty remark, joke: *le sue uscite lo rendono molto simpatico*, his witty remarks make him very popular **5.** (*spesa*) expenditure, outlay, expense: *le uscite non dovrebbero mai superare le entrate*, expenses should never be higher than receipts; *questo comporta una grande — di fondi*, this entails a large expenditure (*o* outlay) **6.** (*a carte*) opening.

Uscòcchi, *s.m.pl.* (*st.*) Uskoks.

usignuòlo, *s.m.* nightingale || « *Il gufo e l'* — », (*lett.*) "The Owl and the Nightingale".

usitataménte, *av.* usually, habitually.

usitàto, *ag.* **1.** (*in uso*) used, in use: *idiotismi usitati*, idioms in use **2.** (*usuale*) usual.

úso, *ag.* used, accustomed: *non sono — a essere insultato*, I am not used to being insulted; *non sono — a queste cose*, *a fare queste cose*, I am not used (*o* accustomed) to these things, to doing these things || *s.m.* **1.** use: *l' — del carbone per riscaldare le case*, the use of coal to heat houses; — *errato di una frase*, wrong use of a phrase; *un'automobile fuori —*, a car out of use; *istruzioni per l' —*, directions (*o* instructions) for use; *logoro dall' —*, worn with use (*o* worn-out); *oggetto di — corrente*, object of everyday use; *per — esterno*, for external use; *per mio — e consumo*, for my own use; *uno strumento a più usi*, a tool with several uses; *l' — di un simile linguaggio è contro le buone maniere*, the use of such language is against good manners; *a che — serve?*, what is its use?; *c'è un extra per l' — dell'automobile*, there is an extra for the use of the car; *è diventato troppo largo con l' —*, it has become too large with use; *è necessario l' — delle forbici*, the use of a pair of scissors is necessary; *questa grammatica è ancora in —*, this grammar is still in use; *questo idiotismo è fuori —*, this idiom is out of use (*o* is not in use); *andare fuori —*, to go (*o* to fall) out of use; *avere pieno — delle proprie facoltà*, to have full use of one's faculties; *fare — di ql.co.*, to make use of sthg.: *fare buon*, *cattivo — del proprio denaro*, to make good, bad use of one's money; *migliorare con l' —*, to improve with use; *perdere l' — di un braccio*, to lose the use of an arm; *venire in —*, to come into use **2.** (*usanza*) usage, use, custom; fashion: *gli usi del nostro paese*, the usages (*o* customs *o* uses) of our country; *usi e costumi*, usages and customs; *consacrato dall' —*, sanctified by usage (*o* custom); *nell' — moderno*, in modern usage; *c'è l' — di mangiare il tacchino a Natale*, it is customary to eat turkey at Christmas || *secondo l' —*, according to use and wont: *secondo l' —*, *all' — dei Greci*, after the Greek fashion || *d' —*, usual; habitual: *complimenti d' —*, habitual compliments; *con le referenze d' —*, with the usual references; *frasi d' —*, conversational commonplaces.

usofrútto, *V.* usufrútto.

ússaro, ússero, *s.m.* (*mil.*) hussar.

Ussíti, *s.m.pl.* (*st. relig.*) Hussites.

ústa, *s.f.* scent (of a wild animal).

ustionàre, *v.t.* to scald || **ustionàrsi,** *v.r.* to scald oneself: *egli si ustionò con l'acqua bollente*, he scalded himself with boiling water.

ustióne, *s.f.* scald: *morire per le ustioni*, to be scalded to death.

ústo, *ag.* (*letter.*) burnt.

ustolàre, *v.i.* **1.** (*di cane da caccia*) to give tongue **2.** (*di persona*) to look at food greedily.

ustòrio, *ag.* burning: *specchio —*, (*fis.*) burning glass.

usuàle, *ag.* usual, customary, habitual, common, ordinary: *la sua — gentilezza*, his usual (*o* customary) kindness || *come d' —*, as usual || *lo fece meglio dell' —*, he did it better than usual.

usualménte, *av.* usually, commonly, ordinarily, habitually.

usuàrio, *s.m.* (*dir.*) user.

usucapióne, *s.f.* (*dir.*) usucap(t)ion.

usucapíre, *v.t.* (*dir.*) to usucapt, to acquire by usucap(t)ion.

usufruíre, *v.i.* to take advantage (of sthg.), to profit (by sthg.), to benefit (by, from sthg.): *egli cercò di — il più possibile di quanto gli offrivano*, he tried to benefit as much as possible by what they offered him; *perchè non dovrei — di questo sconto?*, why shouldn't I take advantage of this discount?;

— *di una buona occasione*, to take advantage of a good opportunity.

usufrútto, *s.m.* (*dir.*) usufruct: *avere in —*, to hold in usufruct.

usufruttuàrio, *ag.s.m.* (*dir.*) usufructuary: *diritto —*, usufructuary right.

usúra[1], *s.f.* usury: *imprestare a —*, to lend on usury; *praticare l'—*, to practise usury; *restituire a —*, to return with interest (*o* with usury).

usúra[2], *s.f.* (*logorio*) wear (and tear): *l'— del tempo*, the wear and tear of time; *molti incidenti ferroviari sono causati dall'— del materiale ferroviario*, many accidents are due to worn out rolling-stock; *resistere all'—*, to stand wear and tear || *guerra d'—*, war of attrition.

usuràio, *s.m.* usurer.

usuràrio, *ag.* usurious.

usureggiàre, *v.i.* to practise usury.

usurpaménto, *s.m.* usurpation.

usurpàre, *v.t.* to usurp, to encroach on (sthg.): *— il trono*, to usurp the throne.

usurpatóre, *s.m.*, **usurpatríce,** *s.f.* usurper.

usurpazióne, *s.f.* usurpation.

utensile, *s.m.* tool, implement; (*da cucina*) utensil: *— a filettare*, threading tool; *— a sfacciare*, facing tool; *— a sgrossare*, rougher (*o* roughing tool); *— a tornire*, turning tool; *— a troncare*, parting (*o* cutting -off) tool; *utensili da falegname*, carpenter's tools; *— da taglio*, cutting tool; *— da tornio*, lathe cutting tool; *— per aprire*, opener; *— per piegare*, creaser; *— per zigrinare*, knurling tool; *— portatile*, (*elettrico, meccanico, pneumatico*) power-driven hand tool; *— sagomato*, forming tool; *a utensili multipli*, multicut; *cassetta portautensili*, tool box; *macchina —*, machine -tool.

utensilería, *s.f.* **1.** *coll.* (*complesso di utensili*) tools (*pl.*); tooling **2.** (*reparto d'officina*) toolroom.

utènte, *s.c.* user, consumer: *gli utenti del telefono a Milano sono in aumento*, the telephone users in Milan are increasing; *la società del gas ha mandato un avviso a tutti gli utenti*, the gas company has sent a notice to all its consumers.

utènza, *s.f.* **1.** right of use **2.** (*l'insieme degli utenti*) users (*pl.*), consumers (*pl.*); body of users, body of consumers.

uterìno, *ag.* uterine: *fratello —*, uterine brother; *ghiandola uterina*, (*anat.*) uterine gland.

útero, *s.m.* (*anat.*) uterus (*pl.* uteri); womb.

útile, *ag.* useful; helpful; (*fam.*) handy: *avvertimenti utili*, useful warnings; *consiglio —*, helpful advice; *credo — farlo al più presto*, I think it advisable to do it as soon as possible; *questo arnese è molto —*, this gadget is very useful (*o* handy); *questo libro è molto —*, this book is very useful; *rendersi —*, to make oneself useful; *tornar —*, to come in handy || *in tempo —*, in time (*o* duly); *il tempo — per la presentazione delle domande è scaduto*, the term for sending in applications has elapsed || *s.m.* profit, benefit; (*in-*

teresse) interest: *— lordo, netto*, gross, net profit; *egli pensa solo al suo —*, he only thinks of his own interest; *non ne traggo alcun —*, I don't get any profit (*o* benefit) out of it; *dare, produrre un — del 5 %*, (*comm.*) to yield a profit of 5 %; *dividere gli utili*, (*comm.*) to allot the profits; *partecipare agli utili*, (*comm.*) to share in the profits || *unire l'— al dilettevole*, to join pleasure and profit.

utilità, *s.f.* **1.** utility; usefulness; use: *l'— di un arnese*, the usefulness of a tool; *l'— di conoscere le lingue straniere*, the usefulness of knowing foreign languages; *— marginale*, (*econ. pol.*) marginal utility; *opera di pubblica —*, work of public utility; *non è di nessuna —*, it is no use; *non ne vedo l'—*, I don't see the use of it; *qual è l'— di lavorare tanto?*, what is the use of working so much? **2.** (*vantaggio*) profit, benefit: *non ne trarrai alcuna —*, you won't get any profit (*o* benefit) out of it.

utilitària, *s.f.* (*aut.*) utility passenger car.

utilitàrio, *ag.* utilitarian: *sistema —*, utilitarian system || *s.m.* utilitarian.

utilitarísmo, *s.m.* (*st. fil.*) utilitarianism.

utilitarísta, *s.m.* (*st. fil.*) utilitarian.

utilizzàbile, *ag.* utilizable.

utilizzàre, *v.t.* to utilize, to make use of (sthg.): *avevano utilizzato la cantina come prigione*, they had utilized the cave as a prison; *egli utilizzò quel denaro per farsi ricostruire la casa*, he used that money to rebuild his house; *— bene il proprio tempo*, to make good use of one's time.

utilizzazióne, *s.f.* utilization, use.

utilménte, *av.* usefully.

utopía, *s.f.* utopia: *la felicità universale è un'—*, universal happiness is a utopia || *l'«Utopia» di Tommaso Moro*, Thomas More's "Utopia".

utopísta, *s.c.* utopian.

utopístico, *ag.* utopian: *un piano —*, a utopian plan.

úva, *s.f.* grapes (*pl.*); (*usato nei composti*) grape: *— da tavola*, table (*o* dessert) grapes; *— di Corinto*, dried currants; *— di Smirne*, sultanas; *— di volpe*, herb Paris; *— orsina*, bearberry; *— passa*, raisin; *— spina*, gooseberry; *acino d'—*, grape-stone; (*chicco*) grape; *cura dell'—*, grape-cure; *un grappolo d'—*, a bunch of grapes; *succo d'—*, grape-juice; *zucchero d'—*, grape -sugar; *dammi dell'—*, give me some grapes; *quest'— è brusca*, these grapes are sour; *pigiare l'—*, to tread grapes; *raccogliere l'—*, to gather grapes.

uvàceo, *ag.* grapy.

úvea, *s.f.* (*anat.*) uvea.

uvétta, *s.f.* raisin.

uxoricída, *s.m.* uxoricide; wife-murderer.

uxoricídio, *s.m.* uxoricide; wife-murder.

úzza, *s.f.* cool breeze.

úzzo, *s.m.* bulge (of a cask).

úzzolo, *s.m.* whim, fancy, caprice: *gli è venuto l'— del giardinaggio*, he has taken a fancy to gardening.

V

v, *s.f.m.* **1.** (*ventesima lettera dell'alfabeto italiano*) v (*pl.* vs, v's) ‖ — *come Venezia*, (*tel.*) v for Victor ‖ *fatto a V*, V-shaped: *scollatura* (*fatta*) *a V*, V-(shaped) neck **2.** *V*, (*numero romano equivalente a 5*) V (five).

vacànte, *ag.* vacant, unoccupied: *cattedra, trono* —, vacant chair, throne; *posto, carica* —, vacancy; *sede* —, vacant Papal see; *successione* —, (*dir.*) estate in abeyance.

vacànza, *s.f.* **1.** holiday, vacation: *vacanze di Natale, di Pasqua*, Christmas, Easter holidays; *vacanze estive*, summer holidays; (*di università*) long vacation; *l'inizio delle vacanze*, breaking-up day; *abbiamo passato delle bellissime vacanze*, we have had a wonderful holiday (*o* vacation); *domani è* —, to-morrow is a holiday; *le nostre vacanze iniziano il giorno 4*, we break up on the fourth; *passammo le vacanze al mare*, we spent our holidays at the seaside; *voglio prendermi un mese di* —, I want to take a month's holiday; *dare un giorno di* — *a qlcu.*, to give s.o. the day off; *essere in* —, to be on (a) holiday; *fare un giorno di* —, to take the day off **2.** (*di un Parlamento*) recess **3.** (*posto vacante*) vacancy: *ti scriverò appena ci sarà una* — *che possa interessarti*, I shall write to you as soon as there is a vacancy that may interest you.

vacàre, *v.i.* to be vacant.

vàcca, *s.f.* cow: — *da latte*, milker (*o* milch cow).

vaccàio, *s.m.* cowherd; (*arc.*) neat-herd.

vaccarèlla, *s.f.* heifer.

vaccàro, *s.m.* cowherd; (*arc.*) neat-herd.

vaccherèlla, *s.f.* heifer.

vacchería, *s.f.* **1.** (*stalla*) cowhouse, byre, cowshed **2.** (*latteria*) dairy-farm.

vacchètta, *s.f.* (*cuoio*) cowhide; neat's leather.

vaccína, *s.f.* cow.

vaccinàbile, *ag.* that can be vaccinated.

vaccinàre, *v.t.* (*med.*) to vaccinate: *farsi* —, to get (*o* to have oneself) vaccinated.

vaccinatóre, *s.m.* vaccinator.

vaccinazióne, *s.f.* (*med.*) vaccination.

vaccínico, *ag.* (*med.*) vaccinic, vaccinal; vaccine (*attributivo*).

vaccíno, *ag.* (*di vacca*) vaccine ‖ *s.m.* **1.** (*med.*) vaccine **2.** (*vet.*) vaccinia, cow-pox.

vaccinògeno, *ag.* (*med.*) vaccinogenous, vaccigenous.

vaccinoterapìa, *s.f.* (*med.*) vaccinotherapy.

vacillaménto, *s.m.* **1.** tottering, staggering; unsteadiness; (*di mobile*) wobbling; (*di barca*) bobbing up and down **2.** (*di luce, fiamma*) flickering **3.** *fig.* vacillation, shilly-shallying, wavering, hesitation.

vacillànte, *ag.* **1.** tottering, staggering; unsteady: *quel tavolo è* —, that table is unsteady (*o* wobbly); *scriveva con mano* —, he was writing with a shaky hand **2.** (*di luce, fiamma*) flickering, unsteady **3.** *fig.* vacillating, wavering, undecided; uncertain: *memoria, salute* —, uncertain memory, health **4.** (*bot.*) versatile.

vacillàre, *v.i.* **1.** to totter, to wobble, to stagger, to be unsteady: *la lampada vacillò e cadde*, the lamp wobbled and fell; *vacilla sulle gambe*, he is shaky (*o* groggy) on his legs; *entrare, uscire vacillando*, to stagger (*o* to lurch) in, to stagger (*o* to lurch) out ‖ *far* — *il tavolo*, to shake the table **2.** (*di luce, fiamma*) to flicker **3.** *fig.* to vacillate, to waver, to be undecided, to be uncertain, to shilly-shally: *vacillava fra due opinioni contrarie*, he was wavering between two opposite opinions.

vacillazióne, *V.* **vacillaménto**.

vacuità, *s.f.* vacuity, emptiness.

vàcuo, *ag.* **1.** vacuous, empty: *un'espressione vacua*, a vacuous expression; *mente vacua*, vacuous (*o* empty) mind **2.** (*vano*) vain, empty: *promesse vacue*, vain (*o* empty) promises.

vademècum, *s.m.* vade-mecum.

va-e-vièni, *s.m.* **1.** (*mec.*) to-and-fro: *teleferica a* —, to-and-fro aerial ropeway (*o* railway) **2.** *V.* **viavài**.

vagabondàggio, *s.m.* **1.** vagrancy, vagabondage **2.** (*il vagabondare*) wandering, roaming.

vagabondàre, *v.i.* to wander (a place), to rove (a place), to roam (a place): *mi piace* —, I like wandering about; — *per il mondo*, to rove (*o* to wander) (about) the world.

vagabóndo, *ag.* **1.** vagabond, vagrant; roaming, roving, wandering: *gente vagabonda*, vagabond (*o* vagrant) people; *immaginazione vagabonda*, roving imagination; *pensieri vagabondi*, vagrant thoughts; *vita vagabonda*, vagabond (*o* vagrant *o* roving) life **2.** (*ozioso*) idle ‖ *s.m.* **1.** vagabond, vagrant, tramp, rover **2.** (*fannullone*) idler.

vagaménte, *av.* **1.** vaguely, dimly, hazily: *comprendere* —, to understand vaguely; *sospettare* —, to have a vague suspicion **2.** (*graziosamente*) prettily, gracefully: — *ornato*, prettily adorned.

vagànte, *ag.* wandering, roaming, roving: — *per il mondo*, roaming about the world; *pensieri vaganti*, wandering thoughts.

vagàre, *v.i.* to wander, to roam, to rove: *la sua mente vagava di pensiero in pensiero*, his mind was wandering from thought to thought; — *nella foresta*, to wander (*o* to roam *o* to rove) in the forest.

vagèllo, *s.m.* **1.** (*caldaia*) boiler; (*dei tintori*) dyer's vat **2.** (*colorante usato in tintoria*) blue dye.

vagheggiaménto, *s.m.* **1.** (*il guardare con compiacimento*) gazing: — *di ql.co.*, gazing at (*o* upon) sthg. **2.** (*di innamorati*) ogling **3.** (*aspirazione*) longing (for sthg.), yearning (for sthg.); (*di una speranza*) cherishing.

vagheggiàre, *v.t.* **1.** (*guardare con compiacimento*) to gaze fondly at (s.o., sthg.), to gaze fondly on (s.o., sthg.), to look lovingly at (s.o., sthg.), to look lovingly on (s.o., sthg.): *l'artista vagheggiava la sua opera*, the artist was gazing fondly at (*o* on) his work **2.** (*di innamorati*) to ogle at (s.o.) **3.** (*pensare con desiderio a*) to long for (sthg.), to cherish, to yearn for (sthg.): *vagheggiava una lunga vacanza*, she was longing for a long holiday; — *una speranza*, to cherish a hope ‖ **vagheggiàrsi**, *v.r.* (*contemplarsi*) to look at oneself complacently.

vagheggiatóre, *s.m.* **1.** lover, ogler **2.** (*chi pensa con desiderio a ql.co.*) cherisher **3.** (*vagheggino*) beau (*pl.* beaux), fop, dandy, gallant.

vagheggìno, *s.m.* beau (*pl.* beaux), fop, dandy, gallant.

vaghézza, *s.f.* **1.** (*leggiadria*) charm, grace(fulness); (*bellezza*) beauty **2.** (*desiderio*) longing, yearning, desire: *gli prese* — *della pittura del trecento*, he took a fancy to fourteenth-century painting; *mi punge* — *di una fetta di torta*, I fancy a slice of cake; *sento* — *per ogni cosa che mi ricorda la mia infanzia*, I feel a longing for everything that reminds me of my childhood **3.** (*diletto*) delight: *prendere* — *in ql.co.*, to take delight in sthg. **4.** (*indeterminatezza*) vagueness.

vagína, *s.f.* **1.** (*anat.*) vagina (*pl.* vaginas, vaginae) **2.** (*rar.*) (*guaina*) sheath.

vagìnàle, *ag.* (*anat.*) vaginal.

vagíre, *v.i.* **1.** (*di neonato*) to cry, to wail **2.** (*di piccoli animali*) to whimper; (*di gattino*) to mew(l); (*di agnellino, capretto*) to bleat.

vagíto, *s.m.* **1.** (*di neonato*) cry(ing), wail(ing); (*di piccoli animali*) whimper(ing); (*di gattino*) mewl(ing); (*di agnellino, capretto*) bleat(ing) **2.** *pl. fig.* (*inizi di arte, civiltà, ecc.*) stirrings: *i primi vagiti della civiltà,* the first beginnings of civilization.

vàglia¹, *s.m.* (*valore*) worth; (*merito*) merit; (*capacità*) ability: *di gran —,* of great worth (*o* merit).

vàglia², *s.m.* (*titolo di credito*) money-order: — *bancario,* cheque (*o amer.* check); — *postale,* postal order; — *telegrafico,* telegraph money-order.

vagliàre, *v.t.* **1.** (*passare allo staccio*) to sieve, to sift: — *farina,* to sieve (*o* to sift) flour **2.** (*ind.*) to riddle **3.** (*esaminare minutamente*) to weigh, to consider thoroughly, to examine thoroughly, to sift: — *i pro e i contro,* to weigh the pros and cons; — *una questione,* to consider a question thoroughly (*o* to sift a question to the bottom).

vagliàta, *s.f.* sifting.

vagliatóre, *s.m.* siever, sifter.

vagliatríce, *s.f.* (*mec.*) sifting-machine.

vagliatúra, *s.f.* **1.** (*ind.*) riddling, screening **2.** (*lolla*) siftings (*pl.*).

vàglio, *s.m.* **1.** (*staccio*) sieve, sifter **2.** (*ind.*) screen, riddle **3.** (*esame minuzioso*) sifting.

vàgo, *ag.* **1.** (*indefinito*) vague, faint, indefinite; dim, hazy: *un colore —,* an indefinite (*o* indeterminate) colour; *una conoscenza vaga,* a hazy knowledge; *idee vaghe,* vague ideas; *un ricordo —,* a hazy recollection; *un sorriso —,* a shadowy smile (*o* a ghost of a smile); *un sospetto —,* a vague suspicion; *non ne ho la più vaga idea,* I haven't the faintest idea **2.** (*leggiadro*) graceful, pretty: *una vaga fanciulla,* a graceful girl **3.** (*letter.*) (*desideroso*) longing (for sthg.); eager (for sthg.): — *di piaceri,* eager for pleasure ‖ *s.m.* (*anat.*) vagus (*pl.* vagi).

vagolànte, *V.* **vagànte.**

vagolàre, *V.* **vagàre.**

vagóne, *s.m.* (*per passeggeri*) carriage, coach; (*per merci*) wag(g)on, truck: — *cisterna,* tank-wag(g)on; — *frigorifero,* refrigerator van; — *letto,* sleeping-car; — *merci,* goods-wagon; — *ristorante,* dining-car ‖ *franco* —, (*comm.*) free on truck.

vagonétto, *s.m.* (*miner.*) mine-car, wagon, tram, corf: — *ribaltabile Decauville,* Decauville tilting wagon.

vainíglia, *s.f.* vanilla: *gelato alla* —, vanilla ice.

vàio¹, *ag.* (*colore grigio scuro*) dark grey.

vàio², *s.m.* (*pelliccia*) vair.

vaiòlo, *s.m.* (*patol.*) smallpox, variola: — *nero,* black smallpox.

vaiolòide, *s.f.* (*patol.*) varioloid.

vaiolóso, *ag.* variolous, affected with smallpox, suffering from smallpox ‖ *s.m.* smallpox subject.

Valàcchia, *no.pr.f.* (*geog.*) Walachia, Wallachia.

Valàceo, *ag.* Wal(l)achian ‖ *s.m.* Wal(l)ach, Wal(l)achian.

Valàlla, *s.m.* (*mit. nordica*) Valhalla, Walhalla.

valànga, *s.f.* avalanche; *fig.* avalanche, shower: *una — di regali,* an avalanche (*o* a shower) of presents.

valchíria, *s.f.* (*mit. nordica*) Walkyrie, Valkyrie, Valkyr.

Valdemàro, *no.pr.m.* (*st.*) Waldemar, Valdemar.

valdése, *ag.s.c.* (*st. relig.*) Waldensian ‖ *i Valdesi,* the Waldenses.

vàle, *inter.* (*lat.*) farewell, good-bye.

vàle, *s.m.* (*lat.*) farewell, good-bye: *l'ultimo —,* the last farewell.

valènte, *ag.* **1.** skilful, capable, clever: *un operaio* —, a skilful worker; *un uomo* —, a clever man (*o* a man of worth) **2.** (*valoroso*) brave, valiant, courageous.

valenteménte, *av.* **1.** skilfully, capably, cleverly **2.** (*valorosamente*) bravely, courageously, valiantly.

valentía, *s.f.* **1.** skill, ability, capability; cleverness **2.** (*valore*) worth.

Valentiniàno, *no.pr.m.* (*st.*) Valentinian.

Valentíno, *no.pr.m.* Valentine.

valentuòmo, *s.m.* worthy man.

valènza¹, *s.f.* (*chim.*) valence, valency.

Valènza², *no.pr.f.* (*geog.*) Valencia.

valére, *v.i.* **1.** to be worth: *il dollaro vale più di 600 lire,* the dollar is worth more than 600 lire; *lo comperai per 3.000 lire, ma vale di più,* I bought it for 3,000 lire, but it is worth more; — *molto, poco,* to be worth a lot, little: *un uomo che vale molto,* a man of worth; *come attore non vale molto,* as an actor he is not up to much ‖ *vale tanto oro quanto pesa, vale un tesoro, un Perù,* it is worth its weight in gold; *non vale un fico secco, un corno,* (*fam.*) it is not worth a brass farthing (*o* twopence *o* a rap) ‖ *tanto vale,* it is just the same: *per me tanto vale che tu prenda anche questo,* it would be just the same to me if you took this too; *se lo fai così, tanto vale che tu non lo faccia,* if you do it like that, you might as well not do it at all; *tanto vale restare qui,* we may as well stay here; *tanto valeva che venisse anche lui,* he might as well have come too ‖ *l'uno vale l'altro,* one is as bad as the other ‖ — *la pena,* to be worth (while): *fu molto difficile, ma ne valeva proprio la pena,* it was very difficult, but it was well worth it; *non ne vale la pena,* it is not worth while; *non vale la pena far tanto per lui,* it isn't worth while doing so much for him; *non vale la pena di leggere questo libro,* this book is not worth reading; *varrebbe la pena di andarci,* it would be worth going ‖ *vendere ql.co. per quel che vale,* to sell sthg. for what it is worth ‖ *far* — *le proprie ragioni,* to make oneself heard; *far* — *i propri diritti,* to assert (*o* to enforce) one's rights (*o* one's claims); *far* — *il proprio danaro,* to invest one's money to good account (*o* well) ‖ *farsi* —, to make oneself appreciated (*o* to make oneself felt) **2.** (*contare, aver peso*) to count, to be of account; to weigh, to be of weight, to have weight: *la prima partita non vale,* the first game doesn't count; *quello che dici non vale niente in questo caso,* what you are saying counts for nothing (*o* is of no account) in this case; *la sua dichiarazione non valse niente per i giudici,* his declaration didn't weigh at all with the judges; *le tue considerazioni non valgono in simili circostanze,* your considerations have no weight in such circumstances ‖ *val meglio tacere,* it is better keep quiet ‖ *non vale!, (al giuoco)* that's not fair! **3.** (*servire, giovare*) to be of use, to be of avail, to count: *a che cosa ti valse tutto il tuo zelo?,* where did all your zeal get you?; *a che vale lavorare tanto?,* what is the use (*o* good) of working so much?; *l'intelligenza senza la buona volontà vale poco,* intelligence without good will counts for little; *i miei consigli non valsero a fargli cambiare condotta,* my advice did not succeed in making him change his behaviour; *questa azione gli valse la medaglia,* this act won him the decoration; *il suo entusiasmo valse solo a complicare le cose,* his enthusiasm did nothing but complicate things; *tutto quello che feci non valse a nulla,* all I did was of no use (*o* of no avail); *una vita tranquilla vale più di tante medicine,* a quiet life is better than any number of medicines ‖ *la pratica vale più della grammatica,* practice is better than theory **4.** (*essere valido*) to be valid: *questo biglietto vale per 24 ore,* this ticket is valid for 24 hours; *questo contratto non vale più,* this contract is no longer valid **5.** (*equivalere*) to be equal to (sthg.), to be worth: *uno scudo valeva 5 lire,* a crown was worth 5 lire; *una sillaba lunga vale due brevi,* a long syllable is equal to two short ones; *il suo comportamento vale un insulto,* his behaviour is nothing better than an insult ‖ *vale a dire,* (*cioè*) that is (to say); (*significa che*) that's as much as to say; (*speci-*

ficatamente) namely (*abbr. viz.*) ‖ **valérsi**, *v.r.* to avail oneself (of sthg.), to make use (of sthg.), to take advantage (of sthg.); to use (s.o., sthg.): *si valse del mio nome*, he made use of my name; *si valse di ogni opportunità, di tutti i suoi diritti*, he availed himself (*o* he took advantage) of every opportunity, of all his rights; *si valse di tutte le sue conoscenze per tacitare lo scandalo*, he availed himself of all his acquaintances to hush up the scandal; *si valse di tutto quel che trovò per spegnere il fuoco*, he used everything he could find to put out the fire.

valeriàna, *s.f.* (*bot. farm.*) valerian.

valerianàto, *s.m.* (*chim.*) valerianate.

valeriànico, *ag.* (*chim.*) valerianic.

Valeriàno, *no.pr.m.* (*st.*) Valerian, Valerianus.

Valèria, *no.pr.f.* Valeria, Valerie.

Valèrio, *no.pr.m.* Valerius.

valetudinàrio, *ag.s.m.* (*letter.*) valetudinary, valetudinarian.

valévole, *ag.* **1.** (*valido*) valid; good: *questa scusa non sarà* —, this excuse will not be valid (*o* accepted *o* taken into account); *queste obiezioni non sono valevoli in questo caso*, these objections are not valid in this case; *questo biglietto è* — *per tre giorni*, this ticket is valid (*o* good) for three days **2.** (*efficace*) efficacious.

valevolménte, *av.* **1.** validly **2.** (*efficacemente*) efficaciously.

vàlgo, *ag.* (*med.*) valgus.

valieàre, *v.t.* to cross: — *un fiume*, to cross a river; (*a guado*) to ford a river; — *un monte*, to cross over a mountain.

vàlieo, *s.m.* **1.** (mountain) pass; (*guado*) ford ‖ *il* — *del Bernina*, the Bernina Pass **2.** (*il valicare*) crossing, passage; (*il guadare*) fording.

validaménte, *av.* **1.** validly **2.** (*fondatamente*) soundly **3.** (*fortemente*) strongly **4.** (*efficacemente*) efficaciously.

validità, *s.f.* validity.

vàlido, *ag.* **1.** valid: *contratto, matrimonio* —, valid contract, marriage; *questo biglietto non è più* —, this ticket is no longer valid ‖ — *a*, fit for: — *alle armi*, fit for service **2.** (*fondato*) good, sound, well -grounded: *argomenti validi*, sound arguments; *ragioni valide*, good reasons; *scusa valida*, good excuse **3.** (*forte*) strong: *è ancora abbastanza* — *per portare cose pesanti*, he is still strong enough to carry heavy things **4.** (*efficace*) efficient; efficacious, effective: *la valida azione della penicillina*, the efficient action of penicillin; — *contributo*, substantial contribution; — *rimedio*, efficacious remedy; *mi fu di* — *aiuto*, he proved of great help to me.

valigería, *s.f.* **1.** (*negozio*) leatherware shop, leather -goods shop **2.** (*fabbrica*) trunk manufactory.

valígia, *s.f.* suit-case; travelling bag: *fare le valigie*, to pack (up): *fare le valigie non è così facile*, packing is not so easy ‖ — *diplomatica*, diplomatic bag (*o* embassy dispatch-bag).

valigiàio, *s.m.* **1.** (*chi fabbrica valigie*) trunk -maker **2.** (*chi vende valigie*) leatherware merchant.

vallàta, *s.f.* valley.

vàlle, *s.f.* **1.** valley: *la* — *del Po*, the Po Valley; *il fiume scende a* —, the river flows down; *i pastori scendono a* —, the shepherds come down to the plain **2.** (*poet.*) vale, dale: *per monti e per valli*, up-hill and down-dale (*o* over hill and dale) ‖ *in questa* — *di lacrime*, in this vale of tears (*o* of woe).

vallèa, *s.f.* (*poet.*) vale, dale.

vallétto, *s.m.* **1.** valet, man-servant (*pl.* men-servants) **2.** (*st.*) page.

valligiàno, *s.m.* inhabitant of the valley(s), valley -dweller, dalesman (*pl.* dalesmen).

vàllo, *s.m.* **1.** (*negli accampamenti romani*) vallum **2.** (*opera difensiva*) rampart, wall **3.** (*anat.*) vallum: — *ungueale*, vallum unguis.

vallombrosàno, *s.m.* (*st. eccl.*) Vallombrosan.

vallóne, *ag. s.m.* Walloon.

vallonèa, *s.f.* (*bot.*) valonia oak.

valóre, *s.m.* **1.** value, worth: *il* — *di un libro, di una casa*, the value of a book, of a house; — *intrinseco*, intrinsic value; *di grande, poco, nessun* —, of great, little, no value: *un uomo, uno studioso di grande* —, a man, a scholar of great worth; *senza* —, worthless (*o* valueless); *il dollaro ha un* — *di circa...*, the dollar has the value of about...; *ha comperato gioielli per il* — *di due milioni*, he has bought two million worth of jewels; *egli non conosce il* — *del tempo*, he doesn't know the value of time; *pochi conoscono il suo vero* —, few know his true worth; *la vostra osservazione non è senza* —, there is some truth in what you say; *avere, non avere* —, to be of value, of no value: *le sue obiezioni non hanno alcun* — *in questo caso*, his objections count for nothing (*o* have no weight *o* are of no account) in this case; *dare poco, molto* — *a ql.co.*, to set a low, a high value on sthg.: *dò molto* — *alla sua opinione*, I attach great importance to his opinion; *mettere in* —, to emphasize; *mettere in* — *un terreno*, to improve a piece of land ‖ *valori etici, umani*, ethical, human values ‖ *egli è un* —, he is a man of great worth **2.** (*comm.*) value: — *attuale*, present value; — *d'inventario*, inventory estimate; — *mercato*, market value; — *imponibile*, rateable (*o* taxable) value; — *locativo*, rental value; — *presunto*, constructive value; *al disotto, al disopra del* —, below, above its value; *aumentare, diminuire il* —, to increase, to diminish the value; *aumentare, diminuire di* —, to rise, to diminish in value ‖ *valori attivi*, assets ‖ *valori mobiliari*, stocks and shares (*o* transferable securities) ‖ *valori passivi*, liabilities ‖ *Borsa Valori*, Stock Exchange ‖ *campione senza* —, sample post **3.** (*significato, funzione*) value, meaning, import: *il* — *delle parole*, the import of words; *aggettivo con* — *di avverbio*, adjective used as an adverb **4.** (*coraggio*) bravery, courage, gallantry: *un atto di* —, an act of bravery; *combattere con* —, to fight gallantly; — *civile, militare*, civic, military valour; *medaglia al* —, medal for valour **5.** (*mus. mat. elett. chim.*) value **6.** *pl.* (*oggetti di valore*) valuables.

valorizzàre, *v.t.* to turn to account, to exploit, to use to advantage; (*accentuare*) to emphasize: *con una luce migliore questo quadro sarà meglio valorizzato*, under a better light this picture will show to better advantage; *dovresti* — *meglio le tue abilità artistiche*, you should turn your artistic abilities to better account (*o* exploit your artistic abilities better); *parlando con lui ho valorizzato tutte le tue buone qualità*, speaking to him I emphasized all your good qualities ‖ — *una terra*, to put a piece of land to its best use.

valorizzazióne, *s.f.* **1.** turning to account, exploitation, utilization, utilizing **2.** (*comm.*) valorization.

valorosaménte, *av.* bravely, valiantly, valorously, gallantly: *combattere* —, to fight gallantly.

valoróso, *ag.* brave, valiant, valorous, gallant: *un'azione valorosa*, a brave action; *un soldato* —, a brave (*o* valiant *o* valorous *o* gallant) soldier.

valpolicèlla, *s.m.* " valpolicella " (kind of Italian red wine).

valsènte, *s.m.* (*comm.*) commercial value, market value, price.

valúta, *s.f.* **1.** (*valore monetario*) (monetary) value: *la* — *del dollaro*, the (monetary) value of the dollar **2.** (*moneta*) currency; money (*solo sing.*): — *argentea, aurea, cartacea*, silver, gold, paper currency; — *corrente*, current money; — *in conto*, money on account; — *estera, nazionale*, foreign, domestic currency (*o* money); — (*a corso*) *legale*, legal tender; — *metallica*, specie (*o* coin) ‖ — *intesa*, agreed value **3.** (*scadenza*) value: — *al 31 dicembre*, value due on December 31st; — *immediata*, value this day; — *retrodata*, back-dated value ‖ — *a convenirsi*, terms of payment to be established ‖ — *1° ottobre, (decorrenza degli interessi)* interests running from October Ist.

valutàre, *v.t.* **1.** to value, to estimate; to appraise: *egli valutò questo quadro 200.000 lire*, he valued (*o* estimated) this painting at 200,000 lire; *mi valuti troppo*, you overestimate me (*o* you think too highly of me); *questa casa fu valutata più, meno del suo valore*, this house was overvalued, undervalued; — *a zero*, to set at naught; — *danni, perdite*, to value (*o* estimate) damages, losses; — *l'intelligenza di uno scolaro*, to appraise the intelligence of a pupil **2.** (*considerare, soppesare*) to consider, to weigh: *abbiamo valutato tutti i pro e i contro*, we have weighed all the pros and cons; *devi — anche gli aspetti positivi*, you must consider the positive aspects as well.

valutàrio, *ag.* (*comm.*) monetary; money (*attributivo*), currency (*attributivo*): *norme valutarie*, currency regulations.

valutatívo, *ag.* of (e)valuation: *criterio —*, principle of (e)valuation.

valutazióne, *s.f.* **1.** (e)valuation, estimate, appraisal; (*di efficienza del personale di azienda*) merit-rating **2.** (*considerazione*) careful consideration, weighing.

vàlva, *s.f.* (*bot. zool.*) valve.

valvassóre, *s.m.* (*st.*) vavasour.

vàlvola, *s.f.* **1.** (*mec.*) valve: — *a cerniera*, flap-valve (*o* flapper); — *a due vie*, two-way valve; — *a farfalla, (di motore)* throttle-valve; (*di stufa, ecc.*) butterfly-valve; — *a saracinesca*, gate-(*o* sluice-) valve; — *a sfera*, ball-valve; — *della camera d'aria*, inner-tube valve; — *di arresto*, stop-valve; (*aer.*) cut-off valve (*o* cock); — *di aspirazione*, (*di motore*) inlet-valve; (*di pompa*) intake-valve; — *di scarico*, exhaust-valve; (*di vapore*) blowing-off valve; — *di sfiato*, air-valve; — *di sicurezza*, safety-valve; — *di tiraggio, regolatrice*, damper **2.** (*rad. tv.*) valve, tube: — *chiave*, (*tv.*) keying tube; *apparecchio a sei valvole*, six-valve set **3.** (*elett.*) fuse: — *a tabacchiera*, box-fuse; — *a tappo*, plug-fuse; *è saltata una —*, a fuse has blown **4.** (*anat.*) valve: — *cardiaca*, cardiac valve.

valvolàre, *ag.* valvular.

vàlzer, *s.m.* waltz: *ballare il —*, to waltz; *fare un giro di —*, to have a waltz ‖ — *a due tempi*, quick (*o* deux-temps) waltz; — *a tre tempi*, trois-temps waltz.

vàmpa, *s.f.* **1.** blaze; flame; flash: *la — del sole*, the blaze of the sun; *la — di un cannone*, the flash of a gun ‖ — *di ritorno*, (*di arma da fuoco*) blowback **2.** (*al viso*) flush, blush: *queste parole gli fecero venire le vampe al viso*, these words brought a flush to his face (*o* made him flush).

vampàta, *s.f.* **1.** blaze, burst of flame: *una — di calore*, a burst of heat; *l'incendio esplose in una —*, the fire burst into a blaze **2.** (*folata*) blast, rush: *una — d'aria calda*, a blast of hot air **3.** (*al viso*) (hot) flush.

vampeggiàre, *v.i.* to blaze; to flame; to flash.

vampíro, *s.m.* **1.** (*zool.*) vampire (-bat) **2.** (*mit.*) vampire **3.** *fig.* (*usuraio, speculatore*) vampire, blood-sucker, extortioner.

vanàdio, *s.m.* (*chim.*) vanadium.

vanaglòria, *s.f.* vainglory, empty pride, conceit, boastfulness.

vanagloriàrsi, *v.r.* to boast, to brag: — *di ql.co.*, to brag of (*o* about) sthg.

vanagloriosaménte, *av.* vaingloriously, conceitedly; boastfully.

vanaglorióso, *ag.* vainglorious, conceited, vain; boastful.

vanaménte, *av.* **1.** (*invano*) vainly, in vain, uselessly **2.** (*vanitosamente*) vainly, conceitedly; boastfully.

vandàlico, *ag.* vandalic, vandalistic: *furia vandalica*, vandalic fury.

vandalísmo, *s.m.* vandalism.

vàndalo, *ag.* **1.** Vandal **2.** *fig.* vandal: *chi calpesta i fiori è un—*, people who trample on flowers are vandals.

Vandèa, *no.pr.f.* (*geog.*) Vendée.

vandeàno, *ag. s.m.* Vendean.

vaneggiaménto, *s.m.* raving: *i vaneggiamenti di un pazzo*, the ravings of a madman.

vaneggiàre, *v.i.* to rave: *quando aveva la febbre alta vaneggiava*, when he had that high temperature he was delirious; *stai vaneggiando?*, are you raving?; *vaneggia da tre ore*, he has been raving three hours.

vanerèllo, *ag.* (*vanitoso*) vain, conceited.

vanescènte, *ag.* fading, evanescent: *colori vanescenti*, fading colours.

vanèsio, *ag.* foppish, vain.

vanéssa, *s.f.* (*entom.*) vanessa.

vànga, *s.f.* spade.

vangàre, *v.t.* to dig: — *il terreno*, to dig the ground.

vangàta, *s.f.* **1.** (*colpo di vanga*) blow with a spade **2.** (*lavoro di vanga*) digging **3.** (*quantità di terra rivoltata dalla vanga*) spadeful.

vangatóre, *s.m.* digger.

vangatríce, *s.f.* **1.** (*chi vanga*) digger **2.** (*mec.*) navvy.

vangatúra, *s.f.* digging.

vangelísta, *s.m.* evangelist.

Vangèlo, *s.m.* Gospel: *il — secondo S. Matteo*, the Gospel according to St. Matthew; *predicare il —*, to preach the Gospel ‖ **vangèlo**, *s.m.* gospel: *quello che dice è — per me*, I take what he says as gospel truth; *prendere ql.co. come —*, to take sthg. as gospel.

vanghétto, *s.m.* (*piccola vanga*) hoe.

vaníglia, *s.f.* (*bot.*) vanilla.

vanigliàto, *ag.* vanilla (*attributivo*), vanilla-flavoured.

vanilòquio, *s.m.* empty talk, random talk, twaddle, nonsense: *sono stanco di ascoltare i suoi vaniloqui*, I am tired of listening to his empty talk (*o* his chattering).

vaníre, *v.i.* (*poet.*) to vanish, to fade.

vanità, *s.f.* **1.** (*inconsistenza, falsità*) vanity: *la — dei piaceri terreni*, the vanity of earthly pleasures; *le — di questo mondo*, the vanities of this world **2.** (*vanagloria*) vanity, conceit: *la sua — la condusse a fare questo*, her vanity drove her to do that.

vanitosaménte, *av.* vainly, conceitedly.

vanitóso, *ag.* vain, conceited.

vàno, *ag.* **1.** (*inutile*) vain, useless: *vane discussioni*, vain (*o* useless) discussions; *vani sforzi, tentativi*, vain (*o* useless) efforts, attempts **2.** (*inconsistente*) vain, empty: *vane speranze*, vain hopes **3.** (*vanitoso*) vain, conceited: *una persona vana*, a vain person **4.** (*rar.*) (*vuoto*) empty ◊ *s.m.* **1.** (*parte vuota*) space, room: *il — della finestra, porta*, the window-space, door-space; *metterò l'armadio in questo —*, I shall put the wardrobe in this space; *questo — non è sufficiente per il tuo cassettone*, this space is not big enough for your chest of drawers **2.** (*stanza*) room: *un appartamento di otto vani*, an eight-room flat.

vantaggiàre, *v.t.* (*rar.*) to outdo ‖ **vantaggiàrsi**, *v.r.* (*rar.*) to draw advantage (from sthg.), to profit (by sthg.).

vantàggio, *s.m.* **1.** (*utilità, profitto*) advantage, benefit; profit: *i vantaggi di vivere in campagna*, the advantages of living in the country; *egli pensa solo al suo —*, he thinks only of his own interests; *non ne ebbi alcun —*, I didn't get any advantage (*o* benefit) out of it; *questa alternativa ha molti vantaggi su quella proposta da lui*, this alternative has many advantages over his proposal; *questo va a tuo —*, this turns (*o* is) to your advantage; *volgere ql.co. a proprio —*, to turn sthg. to one's own advantage **2.** (*superiorità*) advantage: *hai su di me il — di una migliore educazione*, you have the advantage over me of a better education; *acquistare un — su qlcu.*, to gain an advantage over s.o. **3.** (*spor.*) odds (*pl.*); start: *gli diedi venti metri di —*, I gave him twenty metres' start; *dare del — a qlcu.*, to give s.o. odds.

vantaggiosaménte, *av.* advantageously: *vendere ql.co. —*, to sell sthg. to good advantage.

vantaggióso, *ag.* advantageous, favourable, profitable: *condizioni vantaggiose,* favourable conditions; *patti vantaggiosi,* advantageous agreements; *questo non è un affare —,* this piece of business is not profitable; *questo sarà — per tutti,* this will turn (*o* be) to everybody's advantage.

vantàre, *v.t.* **1.** (*pregiarsi di*) to boast, to boast of (s.o., sthg.): *la sua famiglia vanta molti uomini celebri,* his family can boast a great many famous men **2.** (*lodare*) to praise, to extol: *non fece che — le qualità di suo fratello,* he did nothing but praise (*o* extol) his brother's qualities **3.** (*millantare*) to boast of (sthg.), to brag of (sthg.): *— la propria ricchezza, i propri successi,* to boast of one's riches, successes **4.** *— un diritto,* to set up a claim ‖ **vantàrsi,** *v.r.* to boast, to brag, to be proud: *di che cosa ti vanti?,* what are you bragging of?; *l'ho fatto e me ne vanto,* I have done it and I am proud of it; *non vantarti troppo,* don't be too proud (*o* boastful); *si vanta di essere il migliore nuotatore della città,* he boasts of being (*o* that he is) the best swimmer in (the) town.

vantatóre, *s.m.,* **vantatríce,** *s.f.* boaster, braggart.

vanterìa, *s.f.* **1.** boast: *non posso sopportare le sue vanterie,* I cannot stand his boasts (*o* bragging *o* boasting) **2.** (*il vantarsi*) boasting, bragging.

vànto, *s.m.* boast: *egli è il — della sua famiglia,* he is the boast of his family; *il non aver mai ceduto è il mio —,* it is my boast that I have never given in; *si dà — di averlo fatto da solo,* he prides himself on having done it by himself; *si dà, mena — di essere molto bravo in matematica,* he boasts of being very good at mathematics.

vanúme, *s.m.* **1.** (*agr.*) empty ears of corn (*pl.*) **2.** *fig.* vain things (*pl.*).

vànvera, a, *l.av.: parlare a —,* (*senza fondamento*) to speak for speaking's sake; (*a casaccio*) to speak at random.

vaporànte, *ag.* evaporating.

vaporàre, *v.i.* to evaporate.

vaporatívo, *ag.* evaporative.

vaporatóre, *s.m.* evaporator.

vaporazióne, *s.f.* evaporation.

vapóre, *s.m.* **1.** vapour; (*acqueo*) steam: *— di iodio, zolfo, iodine,* sulphur vapour; *bagno a —,* vapour bath; *caldaia a —,* steam-boiler; *macchina a —,* steam-engine; *riscaldato a —,* steam-heated; *trazione a —,* steam-traction ‖ *andare a tutto —,* to go at full speed **2.** *pl.: i vapori del vino,* (*fumi*) the fumes of wine **3.** (*mar.*) (*piroscafo*) steamer, steamship: *— postale,* mail-steamer (*o* packet).

vaporétto, *s.m.* (*mar.*) steamer, steamship, steam-boat.

vaporièra, *s.f.* locomotive, steam-engine.

vaporizzàre, *v.t.i.* to vaporize.

vaporizzatóre, *s.m.* vaporizer.

vaporizzazióne, *s.f.* vaporization, evaporation.

vaporosità, *s.f.* **1.** (*di atmosfera, ecc.*) mistiness, haziness; (*umidità di vapore*) steaminess **2.** (*di idee, stile, ecc.*) haziness, vagueness **3.** (*di abito trasparente e leggero*) gauziness.

vaporóso, *ag.* **1.** (*di atmosfera, ecc.*) misty, hazy; (*umido di vapore*) steamy **2.** (*di idee, stile, ecc.*) vaporous, hazy, vague **3.** (*di abito*) gauzy, flimsy.

varaménto, *s.m.* (*rar.*) launching.

varàre, *v.t.* (*mar.*) to launch (anche *fig.*): *un'impresa,* to launch an enterprise; *— una nave,* to launch a ship ‖ *— una legge,* to pass a law.

varcàbile, *ag.* passable; (*di guado*) fordable.

varcàre, *v.t.* to cross, to pass: *— il confine,* to cross a frontier (*o* border); *— un fiume,* to cross a river; *— i limiti,* to pass (*o* to overstep *o* to exceed) the limits ‖ *ha varcato la quarantina,* he is over forty (*o* he is in his early forties).

vàrco, *s.m.* passage, opening, way: *ci aprimmo*

un — nella siepe, we forced a passage through the hedge; *aprirsi un — fra la folla,* to force one's way through the crowd ‖ *aspettare al — qlcu.,* to lie in wait for s.o.

varechína, varecchína, *s.f.* (*chim.*) chlorine: *acqua di —,* bleach.

variàbile, *ag.* variable, changeable, unsettled; (*volubile*) fickle; (*instabile*) unsteady, unstable: *clima —,* variable (*o* changeable) climate; *prezzi variabili,* unsteady prices; *quantità —,* (*mat.*) variable quantity; *tempo —,* variable (*o* unsettled) weather; *vento —,* changeable (*o* variable) wind; *il barometro è —,* the barometer is unsteady; *il suo umore è molto —,* his mood is very changeable (*o* he is very moody).

variabilità, *s.f.* variability, changeability, changeableness; (*volubilità*) fickleness; (*instabilità*) unsteadiness.

variabilménte, *av.* variably, inconstantly; unsteadily.

variaménte, *av.* variously; (*in modo diverso*) differently.

variaménto, *s.m.* varying.

variànte, *ag.* varying ‖ *s.f.* variant: *ci sono molte varianti nella grafia di questa parola,* there are many variants in the spelling of this word.

variàre, *v.t.i.* **1.** to vary; (*differenziare*) to diversify; (*cambiare*) to change: *dovresti — le tue espressioni,* you should vary your expressions; *le loro opinioni variano moltissimo,* their opinions vary a great deal; *i prezzi variano secondo la qualità,* prices vary according to quality; *il tempo non varierà per alcuni giorni,* the weather will not change for a few days; *— una dieta, una cura,* to vary a diet, a treatment ‖ *tanto per —,* just for a change **2.** (*di mercato*) to fluctuate: *i prezzi variano secondo la situazione internazionale,* prices fluctuate according to the international situation **3.** (*rad. tv.*) to fade.

variàto, *V.* **vàrio 1.**

variatóre, *s.m.* (*mec.*) variator: *— di fase,* (*elett.*) phase transformer; *— di frequenza,* (*elett.*) frequency changer (*o* converter); *— di velocità,* (*mec.*) speed variator; *— della velocità di presa,* (*cine.*) variator (*o* stop motion).

variazióne, *s.f.* variation; (*cambiamento*) change: *variazioni della bussola,* compass variations; *— di frequenza,* (*elett.*) frequency change; *— graduale,* (*rad. tv.*) fading; *— di pendenza,* (*topografia*) change of gradient; *variazioni di temperatura,* variations (*o* fluctuations) of temperature; *variazioni del tempo,* changes in the weather; *variazioni sul tema,* (*mus.*) variations on the theme; *abbiamo fatto alcune variazioni nel programma,* we have made a few changes in the programme; *riportò i fatti con alcune variazioni,* he related the facts with a few variations.

varíce, *s.f.* **1.** (*med.*) varix (*pl.* varices), varicose vein **2.** (*di conchiglia*) varix (*pl.* varices).

varicèlla, *s.f.* (*patol.*) chicken-pox, varicella.

varicocèle, *s.m.* (*med.*) varicocele.

varicóso, *ag.* varicose: *vene varicose,* varicose veins.

variegàto, *ag.* variegated: *foglia variegata,* variegated leaf.

varietà, *s.f.* **1.** variety, diversity; (*di panorama*) variedness: *— di opinioni,* diversity of opinions; *una — di pietanze eccellenti,* a variety of excellent dishes; *una grande — di reparti,* (*in uffici, negozi*) a wide range of departments; *una straordinaria — di tipi,* an extraordinary variety of types **2.** (*specie*) variety; (*genere*) kind, sort: *una rara — di cani,* a rare species of dog; *ti farò vedere più — di fiori,* I shall show you different sorts of flowers ‖ *s.m.* variety (show): *teatro di —,* variety theatre (*o* music-hall); *ieri sono andato al —,* yesterday I went to a variety show.

varifórme, *ag.* variform.

vàrio, *ag.* **1.** (*variato*) varied: *una cultura varia,* a wide culture; *un panorama —,* a varied landscape; *uno stile —,* a varied style; *uomo di — ingegno,* a versatile man; *la sua conversazione era varia e piacevole*, his conversation was varied and delightful ‖ *tempo* —, changeable wheather **2.** (*differente*) various, different: *di vari tipi*, of various kinds; *in vari modi*, in various ways; *in varie occasioni*, in various occasions; *nei vari casi*, in the various (*o* different) cases; *per varie ragioni*, for various reasons ‖ *articoli vari*, (comm.) sundry articles (*o* sundries) **3.** *pl.* (*parecchi*) various, several: *ho fatto varie cose*, I have done various (*o* several) things; *ho visto varie persone*, I have seen various people; *lo vidi varie volte*, I saw him several times ‖ *s.m.pl.* several people: *vari dicono che...*, several people say that....

variolàto, *ag.* **1.** speckled **2.** (*patol.*) variolate(d).

variòmetro, *s.m.* **1.** (*elett.*) variometer **2.** (*aer.*) rate -of-climb indicator, variometer.

variopìnto, *ag.* many-coloured, multicoloured, variegated, gaily-coloured: *una farfalla variopinta*, a gaily -coloured butterfly.

vàrmetro, *s.m.* (*elett.*) varmeter.

vàro[1], *s.m.* (*mar.*) launch, launching: *il — di una nave*, the launching of a ship.

vàro[2], *ag.* (*med.*) varius.

varoràmetro, *s.m.* (*elett.*) varhourmeter.

Varróne, *no.pr.m.* (*st.*) Varro.

Varsàvia, *no.pr.f.* (*geog.*) Warsaw.

varsaviàna, *s.f.* (*danza polacca*) varsovienne, varsoviana.

vasàio, *s.m.* potter.

vasàme, *s.m.* pottery.

vàsca, *s.f.* **1.** basin; (*tinozza*) tub: *— da bagno*, bath (tub) (*o fam.* tub); *— da giardino*, (arch.) fountain; *— da nuoto*, swimming-pool; *— da pesci*, fish-pond; *la — di una fontana*, the basin of a fountain **2.** (*cisterna*) tank, vat, reservoir: *— di sedimentazione*, settling tank; *— di sviluppo*, (foto.) developing tank; *— per il candeggio*, (ind. tessile) bleaching vat; *— sperimentale*, (mar. aer.) test-tank.

vasèllo, *s.m.* (*mar.*) vessel, ship: *— mercantile*, trading vessel (*o* merchantman) ‖ *capitano di —*, sea -captain ‖ *il Vascello Fantasma*, the Flying Dutchman.

vaschétta, *s.f.* **1.** (*piccola vasca*) small basin **2.** (*di termometro*) bulb; (*di barometro*) reservoir **3.** (*di carburatore*) float chamber.

vascolàre, *ag.* (*anat. bot.*) vascular: *fascio, tessuto —*, (bot.) vascular bundle, tissue; *sistema —*, vascular system.

vàscolo, *s.m.* vasculum (*pl.* vascula).

vascolóso, *ag.* (*anat. bot.*) vasculose, vasculous.

vaselìna, *s.f.* (*chim.*) vaseline.

vasellàme, *s.m.* **1.** (*di terracotta*) earthenware, crockery; faïence **2.** (*di porcellana*) china **3.** (*di stagno*) pewter **4.** (*di maiolica*) majolica **5.** *— d'argento, d'oro*, silver, gold plate.

vàso, *s.m.* **1.** vase: *un — di fiori*, a vase with flowers in it; *ha dei bellissimi vasi cinesi*, he has some very fine Chinese vases ‖ *portare vasi a Samo*, to carry coals to Newcastle **2.** (*generalmente rotondo*) pot: *— da fiori*, flower-pot; *— da notte*, chamber-pot **3.** (*con coperchio per conservare cibi*) jar; pot: *un — di marmellata, di salsa di pomodoro*, a jar (*o* pot) of jam, of tomato sauce; *mettere in —*, to pot: *devo ancora mettere la marmellata di ciliegie nei vasi*, I still have to pot the cherry jam **4.** (*recipiente*) vessel: *c'è un grande — per raccogliere l'acqua*, there is a large vessel to collect water ‖ *il Vaso di elezione*, (Bibbia) the Chosen Vessel **5.** (*tec.*) box, can, vessel, jar, container: *— di espansione*, (impianti riscaldamento) hydraulic air vessel; *— poroso*, (di pila elettrica, ecc.) porous pot **6.** (*anat.*) vessel: *— capillare, sanguigno*, capillary, blood-vessel.

vasomotóre, *ag.* (*anat.*) vasomotor: *nervo —*, vasomotor (nerve).

vassallàggio, *s.m.* **1.** (*st.*) vassallage **2.** (*sudditanza, soggezione*) subjection; dependence, subordination.

vassàllo, *ag.* vassal; subject; subordinate, depen-

dent: *regione vassalla di...*, region under the suzerainty of...; *regno, stato —*, vassal kingdom, state; *l'Italia non deve essere vassalla di nessuno*, Italy must not be subject to anybody ‖ *s.m.* **1.** (*st.*) vassal: *i grandi vassalli*, the great vassals **2.** (*soggetto, suddito*) subject; dependent, subordinate **3.** (*spreg.*) (*servo*) servant.

vassóio, *s.m.* **1.** tray: *— da caffè*, coffee-tray; *— da tè*, tea-tray **2.** (*per muratori*) hawk, mortarboard, hod.

vastaménte, *av.* widely, largely, extensively.

vastità, *s.f.* (*l'essere vasto*) vastness, vastitude; (*estensione*) extent, expanse, vastness: *la — dell'oceano*, the expanse of the ocean; *la — della sua cultura*, the extent of his culture.

vàsto, *ag.* wide, large, vast, immense, extensive; spacious: *una vasta clientela*, a large number of customers; *vasta conoscenza*, wide (*o* extensive) knowledge; *vasta estensione di terra*, vast expanse of land; *vasti interessi*, wide interests; *il — mondo*, the wide world; *— programma*, wide programme; *vaste ricerche*, extensive researches; *— spazio*, vast space; *— territorio*, vast territory ‖ *su vasta scala*, on a large scale.

vàte, *s.m.* **1.** (*profeta*) prophet **2.** (*poeta*) poet, bard.

Vaticàno, *no.pr.m.* Vatican: *la Città del —*, the Vatican City.

vaticinàre, *v.t.* to vaticinate, to prophesy, to foretell.

vaticinatóre, *s.m.* vaticinator, prophet.

vaticìnio, *s.m.* vaticination, prophecy, prediction.

vaudeville, *s.m.* (*teat.*) vaudeville, musical comedy.

ve[1], *av.* (*là*) there: *lo misi io*; I put it there; *— ne sono due*, there are two.

ve[2], *particella pronominale* to you; you: *— lo diedi*, I gave it to you; *— lo dissi*, I told you so.

ve[3], (*forma tronca di vedi*) look, see: *— che strano individuo*, look what a queer fellow; *bada —!*, be careful! (*o* take care! *o* look out! *o* mind!).

vècchia, *s.f.* old woman.

vecchiàia, *s.f.* old age: *il bastone della mia —*, the support of my old age; *morire di —*, to die of old age.

vecchierèlla, *ag.* oldish, rather old ‖ *s.f.* poor old woman, good old woman.

vecchierèllo, *ag.* oldish, rather old ‖ *s.m.* poor old man, good old man.

vecchiétta, *V.* **vecchierèlla.**

vecchiétto, *V.* **vecchierèllo.**

vecchiézza, *s.f.* great age: *la — di quelle piante*, the great age of those trees.

vècchio, *ag.* **1.** old: *un — amico, libro, rancore*, an old friend, book, grudge; *una vecchia casa, storia*, an old house, story; *scarpe vecchie*, old shoes; *egli è molto —*, he is very old ‖ *— come Matusalemme*, as old as Methuselah; *— decrepito*, as old as the hills **2.** (*antico*) ancient, old: *vecchia civiltà, tradizione*, old civilization, tradition ‖ *il Vecchio Testamento*, the Old Testament **3.** (*stantio*) stale: *pane —*, stale bread **4.** (*di vino*) mellow ‖ *s.m.* old man: *i vecchi*, the old (*o* old people); *vidi due vecchi*, I saw two old men ‖ *ciao, — mio!*, hallo, old man! ‖ *i nostri vecchi*, (genitori) our parents; (antenati) our ancestors.

vecchiùme, *s.m.* old things (*pl.*), old rubbish.

vèccia, *s.f.* (*bot.*) vetch, tare.

vecciàto, veccióso, *ag.* vetchy.

véce, *s.f.* **1.** stead, place: *in mia, sua —*, in my, his stead; *farò le sue veci, le veci del direttore mentre sarà via*, I shall take his place, the manager's place while he is away; *fece le veci di capostazione*, he took the station master's place; *fece le veci di padre a quel ragazzo*, he was a father to that boy **2.** (*letter.*) (*mutamento, vicenda*) change; vicissitude; (*successione*) succession: *con — assidua*, in alternate succession.

Vèda, *s.m.pl.* (*relig. indù*) Vedas.

vedére, *v.t.* **1.** to see: *il bambino vide un grosso cane*, the child saw a big dog; *ci vedi con questa luce?*, can you see with this light?; *ci vedo bene, male*, I can, cannot see well; *egli non vuole — nessuno*, he doesn't want to see anybody; *fu visto cadere*, he was seen to fall; *lo vidi cadere nell'acqua*, I saw him fall into the water; *lo vidi correre verso il fiume*, I saw him running towards the river; *lo vidi salvare da un marinaio*, I saw him saved by a sailor; *sarò molto felice quando vedrò la fine di questo lavoro*, I shall be very happy when I see the end of this job; *vedemmo arrestare il ladro*, we saw the thief arrested; *vedemmo il ladro arrestato*, we saw the arrested thief ‖ *ci vedo poco chiaro*, I think there is something fishy here ‖ *la, lo vedremo!*, I'll show you! (*o you will answer for this!*) ‖ *non ci vedeva più dalla rabbia*, he was blind with rage; *non ci vedo più dalla fame*, I am starving (to death); *quando cominciò a parlare male di te non ci vidi più*, when he began to speak ill of you I lost my temper ‖ *non posso — quell'uomo*, I cannot bear the sight of that man; *non posso — queste cose*, I cannot stand (*o* put up with) these things ‖ *si vede questa macchia?*, does this spot show? ‖ *stiamo a — cosa succede*, let's wait and see what happens ‖ *— bene, male ql.co.*, to approve, to disapprove of sthg. ‖ *— doppio*, to see double ‖ *— la luce*, (*nascere*) to see the light of day (*o* to be born) ‖ *— le stelle, fig.* to see stars ‖ *ciò non ha niente a che — con*, it has nothing to do with it ‖ *dare a —*, to give signs: *dava a — di essere molto disgustata*, she gave signs of great disgust ‖ *essere ben visto*, to be well thought of (*o* to be approved of); *essere mal visto*, not to be well thought of (*o* to be disapproved of) ‖ *farsi —*, to show oneself: *fatti — quando puoi*, come and see us (*o* look us up) when you can; *non si fa — da due settimane*, he hasn't shown up (*o* he hasn't put in an appearance) for two weeks; *non si vuol far —*, he doesn't want to show himself ‖ *far —*, to show: *fammelo —*, let me see it; *fammi — come fai*, show me how you do it ‖ *non — l'ora di fare ql.co.*, to be longing to do sthg. **2.** (*osservare, guardare*) to see: *andrò a — l'« Aida »*, I shall go and see "Aida"; *l'accompagnai a — i monumenti di Roma*, I took him round Rome sight-seeing; *non ho mai avuto modo di — la Sicilia*, I have never had the chance of seeing (*o* visiting) Sicily ‖ *vedi pag. 50*, see (*abbr.* v.) p. 50 ‖ *vediamo un po'*, now then, let's see **3.** (*visitare*) to see, to visit: *andrò questa settimana a — i nonni*, I shall go and see my grandparents this week **4.** (*esaminare*) to examine, to have a look at (*s.o.*, sthg.); to look over (sthg.): *fece — il figlio al dottore*, he got the doctor to have a look at (*o* to examine) his son; *ho passato tre ore a — la tua traduzione*, I spent three hours looking over your translation; *— i conti*, to examine (*o* to check) the accounts **5.** (*pensare, considerare*) to think; (*decidere*) to decide: *vedi tu cosa è il caso di fare*, you decide what had better be done; *vedremo in seguito*, we'll think it over later on; *vedrò cosa posso fare per lui*, I shall try and see what I can do for him ‖ *a mio modo di —*, in my opinion **6.** (*capire*) to understand, to see: *vedi, sbagliasti a dire questo*, you see, you were wrong to say that; *vedo che avete capito*, I see you have understood; *non vedi che sto male?*, can't you see I am ill?; *non vedo dove vuoi arrivare*, I can't understand what you are leading up to (*o* what you are driving at); *non vedo la ragione, il vantaggio di farlo*, I don't see the reason for, the advantage of doing it **7.** (*procurare, fare in modo*) to see, to try, to take care: *vedi che questo lavoro sia fatto prima di sera*, see (*o* to it) that this job is done before evening; *vedi di non svegliarlo*, take care not to wake him up; *vedrò di aiutarlo*, I shall try to help him ‖ **vedérsi**, *v.r.* **1.** to see oneself (doing); (*guardarsi*) to look at oneself: *non posso vedermi a fare certe cose*, I cannot see myself doing certain things; *non posso vedermi tra quella gente*, I don't feel at ease among those people ‖ *si vedeva già perduto*, he already considered himself lost **2.** (*vedersela, sbrigarsela*) to

deal with (s.o., sthg.): *veditela lu con lui*, you deal with him ‖ *v.r. reciproco* to meet: *ci vediamo spesso*, we often meet.

vedétta, *s.f.* **1.** (*posto di osservazione*) look-out, look-out post ‖ *stare alle vedette, fig.* to be on the look -out (*o* to be on the watch) **2.** (*sentinella*) watch, sentinel, vedette, look-out man **3.** (*mar. mil.*) (*nave vedetta*) vedette(-boat) **4.** (*teat.*) star, vedette.

vèdico, *ag.* (*relig. indù*) Vedic.

védova, *s.f.* widow.

vedovànza, *s.f.* widowhood.

vedovíle, *ag.* (*di vedova*) of a widow; (*di vedovo*) of a widower: *abiti vedovili*, mourning (clothes) ‖ *s.m.* **1.** (*lutto vedovile*) widow's weeds **2.** (*parte dell'eredità assegnata alla vedova*) (widow's) dower.

védovo, *ag.* **1.** *rimanere vedova*, —, to be left (*o* to remain) a widow, a widower ‖ *mi sento — e solo*, I feel lonely and forsaken **2.** *fig.* (*privo*) bereft, deprived ‖ *s.m.* widower: *è un —*, he is a widower.

vedrétta, *s.f.* (*piccolo ghiacciaio*) small steep glacier.

vedúta, *s.f.* **1.** sight, view: *— a volo d'uccello*, bird's -eye view; *comprai alcune vedute di Napoli*, I bought a few views of Naples; *di là si gode una bellissima —*, from there one can enjoy a wonderful view; *parlava delle vedute di Roma*, he was speaking of the sights of Rome **2.** (*idea, opinione*) view, idea, opinion: *mi piacerebbe conoscere le sue vedute su questo argomento*, I should like to know his views (*o* opinions) on this subject ‖ *una persona di larghe vedute*, a broad-minded person **3.** (*atto, facoltà del vedere*) sight.

veemènte, *ag.* vehement, furious; passionate; impetuous: *un desiderio —*, a vehement desire; *una passione —*, a violent passion.

veementeménte, *av.* vehemently; passionately.

veemènza, *s.f.* vehemence, fury; passion; impetuosity.

Véga, *no.pr.f.* (*astr.*) Vega.

vegetàle, *ag.* vegetable: *cibo —*, vegetable food; *olii vegetali*, vegetable oils; *il regno —*, the vegetable kingdom; *seta, lana —*, vegetable silk, wool ‖ *s.m.* vegetable: *la zucca è un —*, the pumpkin is a vegetable.

vegetàre, *v.i.* to vegetate (anche *fig.*).

vegetarianísmo, *s.m.* vegetarianism.

vegetariàno, *ag.s.m.* vegetarian.

vegetatívo, *ag.* vegetative: *sistema nervoso —* vegetative nervous system.

vegetazióne, *s.f.* vegetation: *— ricca, lussureggiante*, rich, luxuriant vegetation.

vègeto, *ag.* **1.** (*di pianta*) thriving: *un albero —*, a thriving tree **2.** (*di persona*) vigorous, strong, hale: *vivo e —, sano e —*, hale and hearty; *quel vecchietto è ancora —*, that old man is still active.

vegetomineràle, *ag.* vegeto-mineral.

veggènte, *ag.* seeing ‖ *s.m.* **1.** seer **2.** (*profeta*) prophet ‖ *s.f.* **1.** seer **2.** (*profetessa*) prophetess.

véglia, *s.f.* **1.** waking: *fra il sonno e la —*, between sleeping and waking; *ore di —*, waking-hours **2.** (*il vegliare*) watch: *nelle veglie notturne*, in the watches of the night; *dovetti fare la — tutta notte*, I had to keep watch (*o* to sit up) all night; *fare la — a un malato*, to watch at the bedside of (*o* to keep watch over *o* to sit up with) a sick person; *fare la — a un morto*, to keep vigil by the bedside of a dead person **3.** (*trattenimento serale*) (evening) party, evening gathering: *— danzante*, dance.

vegliàrda, *s.f.* (*letter.*) old woman.

vegliàrdo, *s.m.* (*letter.*) old man.

vegliàre, *v.i.* **1.** to be awake; to keep awake: *vegliai fino al loro ritorno*, I sat up for them; *vegliai tutta la notte*, I was awake all night (*o fam.* I didn't have a wink of sleep all night) **2.** (*fare la veglia*) to watch, to keep watch: *vegliai al suo capezzale tutta la notte*, I watched all night at his bedside **3.** (*vigilare*) to watch (over s.o.): *veglia su lui!*, watch over him! ‖ *v.t.* to watch by (s.o.): — *un malato*, to watch at the bedside of (*o* to keep watch over *o* to sit up with *o* to watch by) a sick person ‖ — *un morto*, to keep vigil by the bedside of a dead person.

veglióne, *s.m.* (*ballo mascherato*) masked ball.

veícolo, *s.m.* **1.** vehicle: *le strade sono affollate di veicoli*, the streets are crowded with vehicles **2.** (*mezzo, conduttore*) vehicle, medium, carrier: — *di elettricità, energia*, vehicle of electricity, energy; — *di infezione*, carrier of infection; *i giornali sono un — di informazione*, the press is a vehicle of information.

véla, *s.f.* sail: — *di gabbia*, topsail; — *di maestra*, mainsail; — *di mezzana*, mizzen-sail; — *di pappafico*, top-gallant sail; — *di parrocchetto*, fore topsail; — *di straglio*, staysail; — *di trinchetto*, foresail; — *latina*, lateen sail; — *quadra*, squaresail; *vele maggiori*, lower sails; *a vele spiegate*, under sail (*o* in full sail); *barca a* —, sailing-boat; *volo a* —, (*aer.*) sail-flying; *ammainare le vele*, to strike (*o* to lower) the sails; *far* —, to set sail (*o* to sail); *far forza di vele*, to crowd all sails; *issare una* —, to hoist a sail ‖ *tutto gli va a gonfie vele*, everything is going well with him ‖ *volgere la — secondo il vento*, *fig.* to trim one's sails according to the wind.

velaccíno, *s.m.* (*mar.*) fore top-gallant (sail).

velàme, *s.m.* **1.** (*velo*) veil (anche *fig.*) **2.** (*mar.*) sails (*pl.*).

velaménto, *s.m.* (*letter.*) veiling.

velàre[1], *v.t.* **1.** to veil (anche *fig.*); to cover with a veil: *le lacrime le velarono gli occhi*, tears veiled her eyes; — *una statua*, to veil a statue **2.** *fig.* (*offuscare*) to dim, to cloud: *l'ambizione vela il suo giudizio*, ambition clouds his judgement; *la morte velò i suoi occhi*, death glazed his eyes; *la nebbia velava la luce della luna*, the mist dimmed the moonlight **3.** *fig.* (*nascondere*) to veil, to conceal; to disguise: — *le proprie intenzioni*, to conceal one's intentions ‖ **velàrsi,** *v.r.* **1.** to veil oneself, to cover oneself: *in Arabia le donne si velano il viso*, in Arabia women veil their faces **2.** *fig.* (*annebbiarsi*) to mist: *gli occhi le si velarono di lacrime*, her eyes became misty with tears ‖ *quando ho il raffreddore mi si vela la voce*, when I have a cold my voice gets husky.

velàre[2], *ag.s.f.* (*fonet.*) velar.

velàrio, *s.m.* (*teat.*) **1.** (*st.*) velarium (*pl.* velaria) **2.** (*sipario*) curtain.

velataménte, *av.* covertly ‖ *mi ha fatto — capire che...*, he gave me to understand that....

velàto, *ag.* **1.** veiled: *occhi velati di lacrime*, eyes veiled with tears; *viso* —, veiled face **2.** *fig.* (*coperto, nascosto*) veiled, half-hidden, covert: *un — rimprovero*, a covert (*o* hinted) reproof ‖ *voce velata*, muted voice; (*per raffreddore*) husky voice.

velatúra[1], *s.f.* (*mar.*) sail; sails (*pl.*): — *di cappa*, stormsail; *una nuova* —, a new set of sails; *superficie della — utilizzata*, windage; *forzare la* —, to crowd sail; *ridurre la* —, to shorten sail.

velatúra[2], *s.f.* **1.** (*il velare*) veiling **2.** (*offuscamento*) dimming **3.** (*foto.*) fog **4.** (*pitt.*) glazing.

veleggiaménto, *s.m.* **1.** (*mar.*) sailing **2.** (*aer.*) soaring, sailplaning.

veleggiànte, *ag.* (*mar.*) sailing.

veleggiàre, *v.t.i.* **1.** (*mar.*) to sail: — *i mari*, to sail the seas; — *verso il nord*, to sail northwards **2.** (*aer.*) to soar, to sailplane.

veleggiàta, *s.f.* (*mar.*) sail.

veleggiatóre, *s.m.* **1.** (*chi veleggia*) sailer **2.** (*aliante*) glider, sailplane.

veleggiatríce, *s.f.* sailer.

veléggio, *s.m.* **1.** (*mar.*) sailing **2.** (*aer.*) soaring, sailplaning, gliding: — *orizzontale*, float.

velenífero, *ag.* poisonous; venomous.

veléno, *s.m.* poison (anche *fig.*); (*di animali*) venom (anche *fig.*): *il — di un serpente*, the venom of a snake; — *per i topi*, rat-poison; *il — dell'invidia, del sospetto*,

the poison of envy, of suspicion; *l'arsenico è un — mortale*, arsenic is a deadly poison; *le sue parole erano piene di* —, his words were full of venom ‖ *una lingua che sputa* —, a venomous tongue ‖ *mangialo, non è mica* —!, (*fam.*) eat it up, it won't poison you! ‖ *avere del — contro qlcu.*, to have a grudge against s.o.

velenosaménte, *av.* poisonously, venomously (anche *fig.*).

velenosità, *s.f.* poisonousness, venomousness (anche *fig.*).

velenóso, *ag.* **1.** poisonous, venomous: *funghi velenosi*, poisonous mushrooms; *piante, sostanze velenose*, poisonous plants, substances; *una puntura velenosa*, a venomous sting **2.** *fig.* (*pieno di livore*) venomous, malignant, virulent: *invettiva velenosa*, virulent invective; *osservazione velenosa*, malicious (*o* malignant) remark; *uno scrittore* —, a venomous writer **3.** *fig.* (*dannoso*) poisonous: *dottrina velenosa*, poisonous doctrine.

velería, *s.f.* **1.** (*luogo dove si riparano vele*) sail-loft **2.** (*insieme di vele*) sails (*pl.*).

velétta[1], *s.f.* (*di cappello da donna*) (hat-)veil.

velétta[2], *s.f.* (*mar.*) topsail.

velièro, *s.m.* sailing-ship: — *veloce*, clipper.

velína (càrta), *s.f.* tissue-paper.

vèlite, *s.m.* (*st. romana*) velite.

velívolo, *V.* **aeroplàno.**

velleità, *s.f.* **1.** (*ambizione infondata*) foolish ambition, foolish aspiration: *ha la — di diventare pittore*, he has the foolish ambition to become a painter; *tutti ridono delle sue — letterarie*, everybody laughs at his foolish literary ambitions **2.** (*capriccio*) fancy; whim: *gli è venuta la — del giardinaggio*, he has taken a fancy to gardening.

vellicaménto, *s.m.* tickling, titillation.

vellicàre, *v.t.* to tickle, to titillate.

vellicazióne, *s.f.* tickling, titillation.

vèllo, *s.m.* fleece: — *corto*, shabby fleece; — *ruvido*, rough fleece ‖ *il Vello d'Oro*, (*mit.*) the Golden Fleece.

vellosità, *s.f.* hairiness, shagginess.

vellóso, *ag.* hairy, shaggy.

vellutàto, *ag.* **1.** velvety, velvet-like; soft as velvet (*predicativo*) **2.** *fig.* (*morbido come velluto*) downy: *pelle vellutata*, downy skin.

vellutatúra, *s.f.* (*di stoffe, di voce*) velvetiness, softness; (*di animali, di pelle*) down; (*di frutti*) bloom.

vellutíno, *s.m.* **1.** (*velluto leggero*) fine velvet **2.** (*nastro di velluto*) velvet ribbon.

vellúto[1], *ag.* (*letter.*) (*velloso*) hairy, shaggy.

vellúto[2], *s.m.* velvet: — *a coste*, corduroy (*o* ribbed velvet); — *di cotone*, velveteen (*o* cotton velvet); — *di seta*, silk velvet; *morbido come* —, as soft as velvet ‖ *pugno di ferro in guanto di* —, an iron hand in a velvet glove ‖ *essere sul* —, *fig.* to be on velvet.

vélo, *s.m.* **1.** veil (anche *fig.*): *i veli della notte*, the shades of night; *un — di lacrime*, a veil of tears; *un — di nebbia*, a veil of mist; *un — di silenzio*, a veil of silence; *un — di zucchero*, a coating of sugar; *un — d'olio*, (*mec.*) a film of oil; *l'ambizione gli fa* —, ambition clouds his mind; *sotto il — della modestia egli nasconde un animo malvagio*, under the mask (*o* veil) of modesty he hides an evil mind; *si tirò il — sugli occhi*, she drew the veil over her eyes ‖ *avere un — davanti agli occhi*, *fig.* to be blind; *coprire ql.co. con un* —, to cover sthg. with a veil (*o* to veil sthg.); *stendere un — su ql.co.*, to draw a veil over sthg. ‖ *prendere il* —, to take the veil (*o* to become a nun) **2.** (*ind. tessile*) web: — *di carda*, card web **3.** (*tessuto*) voile: *un abito di* —, a dress in voile **4.** (*anat. bot.*) velum (*pl.* vela): — *palatino*, velum palatinum **5.** (*foto.*) fog, haze: *densità del* —, fog density **6.** (*radiologia*) fog.

velóce, *ag.* swift, fast, quick, rapid: — *come il pensiero*, as swift as thought; — *nel fare le cose*, quick in doing things; *andatura* —, rapid gait; *cavallo* —, fast horse; *corrente* —, rapid current; *corridore*

—, swift runner; *movimenti veloci*, swift movements; *movimento* —, swift (*o* quick) motion; *passi veloci*, quick steps; *progresso* —, rapid progress; *treno* —, fast (*o* quick) train; *sii* —*!*, be quick! || *av. V.* **veloceménte.**

veloceménte, *av.* swiftly, fast, quickly, rapidly: *fa tutto* —, he does everything quickly; *parla molto* —, he speaks very fast; *il tempo scorre* —, time goes quickly.

velocífero, *s.m.* stage coach.

velocipedàstro, *s.m.* careless cyclist, reckless cyclist; (*fam.*) scorcher.

velocípede, *s.m.* velocipede.

velocipedísta, *s.c.* velocipedist.

velocísta, *s.c.* (*spor.*) sprinter.

velocità, *s.f.* speed, velocity (anche *fis.*); rapidity, quickness, swiftness: — *aerea*, air speed; — *angolare*, (*mec.*) angular velocity; *la* — *della luce, del suono, del vento*, the velocity (*o* speed) of light, sound, wind; — *di atterraggio*, (*aer.*) landing speed; — *di decollo*, (*aer.*) take-off speed; — *di immersione*, diving speed; — *di lavoro*, working speed; — *limite*, speed limit; — *media*, average speed; *a una* — *di 40 miglia all'ora*, at a speed of 40 miles per hour; *a due* —, (*mec.*) two speed; *alla massima, a tutta* —, at full speed; *cambio di* —, (*aut.*) gearbox (*o* transmission); *a grande* —, at high speed; (*ferr.*) by fast (*o* passenger) train (*o amer.* through freight); *indicatore di* —, speedometer (*o* speed indicator); *limite di* —, speed limit; *a piccola* —, (*ferr.*) by goods (*o* slow) train (*o amer.* slow freight); *potenziale di* —, velocity potential; *prima, seconda, terza* —, (*aut.*) first (*o* low), second, third gear; *quarta* —, (*aut.*) direct (*o* top) gear; *la* — *è controllata dal radar*, the speed is checked by radar; *devi ridurre la* —, you must reduce your speed; *egli parlò della* — *di certi uccelli*, he spoke of the swiftness of certain birds; *non puoi neppure immaginare la* — *di quel treno*, you can't even imagine the fastness of that train; *la sua* — *nel rispondere mi sorprese*, his quickness in answering surprised me.

velocréspo, *s.m.* chiffon.

velòdromo, *s.m.* (*spor.*) cycle-racing track.

véltro, *s.m.* (*zool.*) greyhound.

véna, *s.f.* **1.** (*anat.*) vein; (*arteria*) artery: — *cava*, vena cava; — *porta*, portal vein; — *varicosa*, varicose vein; *tagliarsi le vene*, to sever one's veins || *non avevo più sangue nelle vene* (*per lo spavento*), my blood ran cold || *non ha sangue nelle vene*, he is rather spineless || *si sentì bollire il sangue nelle vene*, his blood boiled **2.** (*venatura*) vein, streak: *le vene del legno, del marmo*, the veins of wood, of marble **3.** (*filone*) vein, lode; (*di carbone*) seam: *questa* — *è esaurita*, this vein is worked out **4.** (*rigagnolo sotterraneo*) (underground) stream, (underground) rivulet: *scoprì una* — *d'acqua*, he discovered a spring of water **5.** *fig.* (*inclinazione*) vein; (*ispirazione*) inspiration; (*disposizione, umore*) vein, mood, disposition: — *poetica*, poetic vein; *la sua* — *musicale si è esaurita*, his musical inspiration has become exhausted || *ha una* — *di pazzia*, (*scherz.*) he has a mad streak in him || *essere in* — *di fare ql.co.*, to feel like doing sthg.: *è in* — *di generosità*, he is in a giving humour || *fare una cosa di* —, to do sthg. willingly.

venàle, *ag.* **1.** saleable: *prezzo* —, sale price; *valore* —, selling value **2.** *fig.* (*corruttibile*) venal; mercenary: *un giudice, un politicante* —, a venal judge, politician.

venalità, *s.f.* **1.** saleability **2.** (*corruttibilità*) venality.

venalménte, *av.* **1.** saleably **2.** (*corruttibilmente*) venally.

venaménto, *s.m.* veining.

venàre, *v.t.* to vein; (*legno*) to grain || **venàrsi,** *v.r.* to become veined; (*di legno*) to become grained.

venàto, *ag.* veined; (*di legno*) grained.

venatòrio, *ag.* venatorial, hunting (*attributivo*): *arte venatoria*, hunting.

venatúra, *s.f.* **1.** vein; (*di legno*) grain: *le venature di una foglia*, the veins of a leaf; *un marmo con vena-*

ture verdi, a green-veined marble **2.** (*disposizione delle vene*) veining; (*di foglie, ali d'insetti*) venation: *un marmo con una fitta* —, a marble with (a) thick veining.

Venceslào, *no.pr.m.* Wenceslaus.

vendémmia, *s.f.* **1.** vintage, grape-gathering, vine harvest **2.** (*il raccolto*) vintage **3.** (*il tempo della vendemmia*) vintage (time).

vendemmiàbile, *ag.* ripe for gathering: *uva* —, grapes ripe for gathering.

vendemmiàio, *s.m.* (*st. francese*) Vendimiaire.

vendemmiàre, *v.t.* to gather || *v.i.* to gather grapes.

vendemmiatóre, *s.m.*, **vendemmiatríce,** *s.f.* vintager, grape-gatherer, vine-harvester.

véndere, *v.t.* **1.** to sell: *abbiamo venduto tutto*, we are sold out; *gli ho venduto dei mobili*, I have sold him some furniture; *l'ho venduto per due sterline*, I have sold it for two pounds; *questo articolo si vende molto bene*, this article sells very well; *si vende a credito*, no cash down; — *a buon mercato*, to sell cheaply; — *a caro prezzo*, to sell at a high price; — *a credito*, to sell on credit; — *all'ingrosso*, to sell wholesale; — *al minuto*, to sell by retail; — *a meno dei propri concorrenti*, to undersell one's competitors; — *a metà prezzo*, to sell at half price; — *a provvigione*, to sell on commission; — *a rate*, to sell by instalments; — *in blocco*, to sell in bulk; — *a propria libertà, il proprio onore*, to sell one's freedom, honour; — *sotto costo*, to sell under cost; — *sotto mercato*, to undersell || *corsa a* —, (*ippica*) selling-race || *ha ragione da* —, he is dead right || *ho pazienza da* —, I am very patient || — *fumo*, to bluff || — *la pelle dell'orso prima che sia ucciso*, to count one's chickens before they are hatched **2.** (*dir.*) to vend: *il diritto di* — *libri e giornali*, the right to vend books and newspapers || **véndersi,** *v.r.* to sell oneself.

venderéccio, *ag.* **1.** saleable **2.** *fig.* (*corruttibile*) venal.

vendétta, *s.f.* revenge, vengeance; (*tra famiglie, tribù, ecc.*) feud, vendetta: *desiderio di* —, desire for revenge; *per* —, in revenge; *una sanguinosa* —, a bloody revenge; *un delitto che grida* —, a crime that cries out for vengeance; *voglio fare* —, I want to be revenged (*o* I want to revenge myself); *fare* — *su qlcu.*, to revenge oneself upon s.o. (*o* to take vengeance upon s.o.).

vendíbile, *ag.* saleable, marketable.

vendicàbile, *ag.* that can be avenged.

vendicàre, *v.t.* **1.** to revenge, to avenge: — *un assassinio, un torto*, to avenge a murder, a wrong; — *qlcu.*, to avenge s.o. **2.** (*rivendicare*) to vindicate || **vendicàrsi,** *v.r.* to revenge oneself (on s.o., for sthg.), to avenge oneself (on s.o., for sthg.): — *di ql.co.*, to take vengeance for sthg.

vendicativaménte, *av.* revengefully, vindictively.

vendicatívo, *ag.* revengeful, vindictive.

vendicatóre, *s.m.* **1.** revenger, avenger **2.** (*rivendicatore*) vindicator.

vendicatríce, *s.f.* **1.** revenger, avenger **2.** (*rivendicatrice*) vindicatress.

vendifròttole, *s.m.* swindler, cheat.

véndita, *s.f.* sale: — *all'asta*, (sale by) auction; — *all'ingrosso, al minuto*, wholesale, retail (sale): *esercitare la* — *all'ingrosso, al minuto*, to sell wholesale, retail; — *a rate*, sale by instalments; — *di fine anno*, winter sale; *questa casa non è in* —, this house is not for sale || *addetto, addetta alle vendite*, salesman, saleswoman; *condizioni di* —, terms of sale; *conto vendite*, sales account; *libro vendite*, sales book; *prezzo di* —, selling price; *reparto vendite*, sales department || *la* — *della sua vecchia casa lo rese triste*, the sale of his old house made him sad || *avere buona* —, to sell easily; *esporre in* —, to exhibit for sale; *essere in* —, to be on (*o* for) sale; *mettere in* —, to put up for (*o* on) sale.

venditóre, *s.m.*, **venditríce,** *s.f.* **1.** seller, vendor: — *al dettaglio*, retail dealer (*o* retailer); — *all'ingrosso*, wholesale dealer (*o* wholesaler); — *ambulante*, pedlar *(o* hawker) ‖ — *di fumo,* swindler **2.** *(commesso, commessa)* shop-assistant.

vendúto, *ag.* **1.** sold **2.** *fig. (corrotto)* corrupted.

venefício, *s.m.* poisoning.

venèfico, *ag.* poisonous (anche *fig.*), venomous (anche *fig.*): *dottrina venefica,* poisonous doctrine; *gas* —, poisonous gas; *lingua venefica,* venomous tongue; *scrittore* —, venomous writer.

veneràbile, *ag.s.m.* venerable.

venerabilità, *s.f.* venerability, venerableness.

veneràndo, *ag.* venerable.

veneràre, *v.t.* to worship, to venerate: — *la memoria di qlcu.,* to venerate s.o.'s memory; — *i propri genitori,* to worship one's parents.

veneratóre, *ag.* worshipping, venerating ‖ *s.m.,* **veneratríce,** *s.f.* worshipper, venerator.

venerazióne, *s.f.* worship, veneration.

venerdí, *s.m.* Friday ‖ *Venerdì Santo,* Good Friday ‖ *gli manca un* —, he has a screw *(o* a tile) loose.

Vènere, *no.pr.f.* **1.** *(mit.)* Venus ‖ — *di Cnido, di Milo,* Venus of Cnidus, de *(o* of) Milo **2.** *(astr.)* Venus ‖ **vènere,** *s.f. (donna bella)* Venus, beauty: *non è una* —, she is no beauty *(o* Venus).

venèreo, *ag.* venereal: *malattie veneree,* venereal diseases.

Vèneto, *no.pr.m. (geog.)* Venetia.

vèneto, *ag.s.m.* Venetian.

Venèzia, *no.pr.f. (geog.)* **1.** *(città)* Venice **2.** *(regione)* Venetia: — *Giulia,* Venetia Julia.

veneziàno, *ag.s.m.* Venetian.

vènia, *s.f. (letter.)* pardon: *chiedere* — *a qlcu.,* to beg s.o.'s pardon; *chiedere* — *per ql.co.,* to apologize for sthg.

veniàle, *ag.* venial: *peccato* —, venial sin.

venialità, *s.f.* veniality.

veniènte, *ag.* coming; *(prossimo)* next.

venire, *v.i.* **1.** to come: *vengo!,* I am coming; *venite, dunque!,* come along, then!; *viene qui ogni sorta di gente,* all sorts of people come here; *vieni a teatro con me?,* will you come to the theatre with me?; *vieni a trovarmi,* come and see me; *vieni a vedere chi c'è,* come and see who is here; *vieni da piazza della Scala?,* have you just come from piazza della Scala?; *il chiodo è venuto via,* the nail has come out; *da che paese vieni?,* where do you come from?; *devo* — *con te?,* shall I come with you?; *dico le cose come mi vengono,* I say things as they come into my head; *dopo il gennaio viene il febbraio,* after January comes February; *è venuto il tempo di dirglielo,* time has come to tell him; *mi viene un'idea,* I've got an idea; *non è ancora venuto,* he hasn't come yet; *quando verrà, diglielo,* when he comes, tell him; *quando verrà l'estate ti rivedrò,* I shall see you again when Summer comes *(o* next Summer); *quando viene l'occasione,* when opportunity offers; *se gli dovesse venire la febbre,* if he should get a temperature; *sono venuto a piedi, in automobile, per mare,* I have come on foot, by car, by sea; *sono venuto a prendere tuo fratello,* I have come for your brother ‖ *venne a dire che lui sapeva tutto su questa faccenda,* he spoke up and said he knew all about this matter ‖ *viene da una buona famiglia,* he comes of a good family ‖ *vieni dentro,* come in ‖ *bisogna prendere le cose come vengono,* we must take things as they come *(o* we must take the rough with the smooth) ‖ *egli venne fuori con delle scuse molto meschine,* he came out with some shabby excuses ‖ *lascialo* —, let him come ‖ *lasciate che i pargoli vengano a me,* *(Bibbia)* suffer little children to come unto me ‖ *quanto viene a costare?,* how much does it cost? ‖ *questo cibo mi fa* — *l'acquolina in bocca, la nausea,* this food makes my mouth water, makes me sick ‖ *se viene all'orecchio del tuo insegnante, sarai punito,* if your teacher hears about it *(o* if it comes to your teacher's ears), you will be punished ‖ — *a un accordo,* to come to an agreement; — *a capo di ql.co.,* to get to the bottom of sthg.: *non riesco a venirne*

a capo, I can't make head or tail of it; — *a una decisione,* to come to a decision; — *a patti,* to come to terms ‖ — *alla luce, (essere scoperto)* to come to light; *(nascere)* to be born ‖ — *alle mani,* to come to blows ‖ — *al mondo,* to come into the world *(o* to be born) ‖ — *a parole con qlcu.,* to have words with s.o. ‖ — *a proposito, (al momento giusto)* to come just at the right moment; *(al proprio scopo)* to suit one's purpose ‖ — *a sapere ql.co.,* to come to know *(o* to get to know) of sthg. ‖ — *al sodo,* to come to the point ‖ — *fuori,* to come out; *(essere pubblicato)* to be published: *vieni fuori!,* come out!; *il libro è già venuto fuori,* the book has already come out *(o* been published) ‖ — *giù,* to come down; *(al piano inferiore)* to come downstairs; — *su,* to come up; *(al piano superiore)* to come upstairs; *fig. (crescere)* to grow: *viene su una bellissima ragazza, (fam.)* she is growing into a very beautiful girl; *queste piante vengono su molto bene,* these plants are coming on well ‖ — *in mente,* to come into one's head: *come ti venne in mente questa idea?,* how did this idea come into your head?; *non mi viene in mente il suo nome,* I cannot call his name to mind ‖ — *in possesso,* to come into possession ‖ — *meno, (svenire)* to faint; *(mancare)* to fail; *(di cose materiali)* to run short; to be short *(costruzione pers.):* ci venne *meno la benzina,* we ran short of petrol ‖ *far* —: *devi far* — *un barile di birra,* you must order *(o* send for) a barrel of beer; *fa* — *i suoi abiti da Parigi,* she has her dresses sent from Paris; *fallo* — *in orario,* make him come in time; *fate* — *il dottore,* send for *(o* call in) the doctor ‖ *negli anni a* —, in the years to come ‖ *la confidenza viene dal sapere, prov.* confidence is born of knowledge **2.** *(riuscire)* to turn out: *il dolce non è venuto bene,* the cake has not turned out well; *non vengo bene in fotografia,* I don't photograph well *(o* I don't come out well in photographs) ‖ *tienilo, può* — *buono,* keep it, it may come in handy *(o* useful) ‖ *questo lavoro mi è venuto a noia, in odio,* I am fed up with *(o* I am sick of) this work **3.** *(derivare)* to derive: *questa parola viene dal latino,* this word derives from Latin **4.** *(sentire desiderio)* to feel like (doing) *(costruzione pers.):* mi *venne da piangere,* I felt like crying *(o* I felt moved to tears); *mi venne da ridere,* I felt like laughing ‖ *mi fa* — *da piangere, da ridere,* it makes me cry, laugh **5.** — *fatto di,* to happen *(gener. costruzione pers.):* mi *venne fatto di dirglielo,* I happened to tell him **6.** *(cominciare)* to begin: *venne a piovere,* it began to rain *(o* it came on to rain) **7.** *(usato come ausiliare del passivo in sostituzione del verbo essere)* to be: *la casa venne distrutta da una bomba,* the house was destroyed by a bomb; *il lavoro venne eseguito male,* the work was done badly **8.** *(letter.) (in unione a gerundio con significato analogo a quello di stare)* to be (doing): *vengo scrivendo,* I am writing; *mi vengo accorgendo che avevi ragione,* I am beginning to realize that you were right.

venosità, *s.f.* venosity.

venóso, *ag.* venous.

ventàglia, *s.f. (st.)* ventail.

ventagliàio, *s.m.* fan-maker.

ventàglio, *s.m.* fan ‖ *a* —, fan-shaped *(o* fan-wise): *delta a* —, *(geog.)* fan delta; *volta a* —, *(arch.)* fan vaulting; *aprirsi a* —, *(di truppe)* to fan out.

ventàre, *v.i. (letter.)* to blow.

ventaruòla, *s.f.* **1.** *(banderuola)* weathercock, vane **2.** *(ventola)* fire-fan.

ventàta, *s.f.* gust of wind, blast of wind.

ventennàle, *ag.* twenty-year *(attributivo); (che ricorre ogni 20 anni)* recurring every twenty years.

ventènne, *ag.* twenty years old *(predicativo);* twenty-year-old *(attributivo)* ‖ *s.m.* twenty-year-old man ‖ *s.f.* twenty-year-old woman.

ventènnio, *s.m.* period of twenty years.

ventèsimo, *ag.num.ord.s.m.* twentieth.

vénti, *ag.num.card.s.m.* twenty.

venticínque, *ag.num.card.s.m.* twenty-five.

venticinquènne, *ag.* twenty-five years old (*predicativo*); twenty-five-year old (*attributivo*) ‖ *s.m.* twenty-five-year old man ‖ *s.f.* twenty-five-year old woman.

venticinquèsimo, *ag.num.ord.s.m.* twenty-fifth.

ventidúe, *ag.num.card.s.m.* twenty-two.

ventiduènne, *ag.* twenty-two years old (*predicativo*); twenty-two-year old (*attributivo*) ‖ *s.m.* twenty-two-year old man ‖ *s.f.* twenty-two-year old woman.

ventiduèsimo, *ag.num.ord.s.m.* twenty-second.

ventilàbro, *s.m.* 1. (*agr.*) winnowing-fan 2. (*mus.*) organ valve.

ventilàre, *v.t.* 1. to ventilate (anche *fig.*), to air, to fan: — *una idea*, to make an idea public (o to ventilate an idea); — *una stanza*, to ventilate a room 2. (*agr.*) to winnow: — *frumento*, to winnow wheat.

ventilàto, *ag.* 1. airy; windy: *una località ventilata*, a windy spot; *una stanza ventilata*, an airy room 2. (*di grano*) winnowed.

ventilatóre, *s.m.* fan, ventilator; (*di automobile*) fan: — *elettrico*, electric fan; — *in aspirazione*, suction fan.

ventilazióne, *s.f.* 1. ventilation: — *in depressione*, (*miner.*) vacuum ventilation; — *in parallelo*, (*miner.*) split ventilation; *sottopassaggio di* —, (*miner.*) undercast 2. (*agr.*) winnowing.

ventína, *s.f.* score (*invariato al pl.*): *due ventine di bottoni*, two score of buttons ‖ *deve avere una — d'anni*, he must be about twenty; *deve aver passato la* —, he must be in his twenties.

ventíno, *s.m.* (*st.*) (*moneta italiana da 20 centesimi*) twenty-cent coin.

ventinòve, *ag.num.card.s.m.* twenty-nine.

ventinovèsimo, *ag.num.ord.s.m.* twenty-ninth.

ventiquattrèsimo, *ag.num.ord.s.m.* twenty-fourth.

ventiquàttro, *ag.num.card.s.m.* twenty-four ‖ *alle* —, at midnight (o at twelve).

ventiseènne, *ag.* twenty-six years old (*predicativo*); twenty-six-year old (*attributivo*) ‖ *s.m.* twenty-six-year old man ‖ *s.f.* twenty-six-year old woman.

ventiseèsimo, *ag.num.ord.s.m.* twenty-sixth.

ventisèi, *ag.num.card.s.m.* twenty-six.

ventisètte, *ag.num.card.s.m.* twenty-seven.

ventisettèsimo, *ag.num.ord.s.m.* twenty-seventh.

ventitré, *ag.num.card.s.m.* twenty-three ‖ *avere il cappello sulle* —, to have one's hat on askew (o crooked).

ventitreèsimo, *ag.num.ord.s.m.* twenty-third.

vènto, *s.m.* wind: — *contrario, favorevole*, contrary, fair wind; — *di tramontana*, north wind; *la furia del* —, the fury of the wind; *raffica di* —, gust (of wind); *turbine di* —, whirlwind; *il — si alza, cala*, the wind is rising, falling; *il — soffia dal nord*, the wind is blowing from the north ‖ *mulino a* —, windmill ‖ *parole gettate al* —, words thrown to the wind ‖ *qual buon — ti porta?*, what lucky chance brings you here? ‖ *avere il — in poppa*, to sail before the wind (anche *fig.*) ‖ *cercare di sapere da che parte spira il* —, *fig.* to find out how the wind blows ‖ *correre come il* —, to run like the wind ‖ *essere sotto* —, *navigare contro* —, to sail against the wind ‖ *far(si) vento*, to fan (oneself) ‖ *navigare secondo il* —, *fig.* to swim with the tide ‖ *spiegare le vele al* —, to unfurl the sails.

vèntola, *s.f.* 1. (*per il fuoco*) fire-fan 2. (*paralume*) lamp-shade 3. (*agr.*) (*ventilabro*) winnowing fan 4. *muro a* —, (*tramezzo*) partition.

ventolàre, *v.t.* 1. (*ventilare*) to fan; to ventilate 2. (*agr.*) to winnow 3. (*sventolare*) to wave: — *una bandiera*, to wave a flag.

ventósa, *s.f.* 1. (*tentacolo di mollusco*) sucker 2. (*med.*) cupping-glass: *applicare ventose a qlcu.*, to cup s.o.

ventosità, *s.f.* (*med.*) flatulence.

ventóso, *ag.* 1. windy: *luogo* —, windy place 2. (*med.*) flatulent ‖ *s.m.* (*st. francese*) Ventôse.

ventottèsimo, *ag.num.ord.s.m.* twenty-eighth.

ventòtto, *ag.num.card.s.m.* twenty-eight.

ventràia, *s.f.* (*spreg.*) big belly.

ventràle, *ag.* ventral.

vèntre, *s.m.* 1. abdomen, stomach; (*volg.*) belly; (*fam.*) tummy: *avere mal di* —, to have a stomach-ache (o tummy-ache) ‖ — *a terra*, (*di gran carriera*) at full speed 2. (*di una botte*) bilge.

ventrésca, *s.f.* (*di tonno*) undercut; (*di maiale*) bacon.

ventricolàre, *ag.* ventricular.

ventrícolo, *s.m.* (*anat.*) ventricle: — *del cervello*, ventricle of the brain; — *del midollo spinale*, ventricle of the spinal cord; — *destro, sinistro del cuore*, right, left ventricle of the heart.

ventrièra, *s.f.* (*body-*)belt.

ventríglio, *s.m.* (*stomaco degli uccelli*) gizzard.

ventrilòquio, *s.m.* ventriloquism, ventriloquy.

ventríloquo, *ag.* ventriloquous ‖ *s.m.* ventriloquist.

ventríno, *s.m.* 1. (*equitazione*) girth; (*amer.*) cinch 2. (*mar.*) bunt gasket.

ventunènne, *ag.* twenty-one years old (*predicativo*); twenty-one-year old (*attributivo*) ‖ *s.m.* twenty-one-year old man ‖ *s.f.* twenty-one-year old woman.

ventunèsimo, *ag.num.ord.s.m.* twenty-first.

ventúno, *ag.num.card.s.m.* twenty-one.

ventúra, *s.f.* 1. chance; fortune, luck: *buona, mala* —, good, ill luck; *per buona, mala* —, luckily, unluckily; *dire la — a qlcu.*, to tell s.o. his fortune; *farsi dire la buona* —, to have one's fortune told; *tentare la* —, to try one's fortune ‖ *alla* —, at a venture (o at random): *andare alla* —, to take one's chance 2. (*st.*): *capitano di* —, captain of fortune (o of mercenary troops); *compagnie di* —, mercenary troops; *soldato di* —, soldier of fortune.

venturière, *s.m.* (*soldato mercenario*) soldier of fortune, mercenary (soldier).

venturièro, *ag.* odd-job (*attributivo*) ‖ *s.m.* (*avventuriero*) adventurer.

venturímetro, *s.m.* (*fis.*) Venturi meter, Venturi tube.

ventúro, *ag.* next, coming, future: *l'anno* —, next year; *negli anni venturi*, in the coming years (o in the years to come); *nelle età venture*, in future ages; *la settimana ventura*, next week; *la stagione ventura*, the coming season.

venturosaménte, *av.* 1. (*fortunatamente*) luckily, fortunately 2. (*felicemente*) happily.

venturóso, *ag.* 1. (*fortunato*) lucky, fortunate 2. (*felice*) happy.

venustà, *s.f.* (*letter.*) beauty, loveliness; charm.

venústo, *ag.* (*letter.*) beautiful, lovely; charming.

venúta, *s.f.* coming, arrival: *alla sua — non c'era niente di pronto*, when he arrived there was nothing ready; *aspettiamo la sua* —, we are waiting for his arrival; *nessuno era soddisfatto della sua* —, nobody was happy about his coming.

venúto, *ag.* coming: *una persona venuta da lontano*, a person coming from afar ‖ *ben* —, welcome ‖ *s.m.* comer: *un nuovo* —, a new comer; *il primo* —, the first comer.

vèra, *s.f.* 1. (*di pozzo*) well-curb 2. (*dial.*) (*anello nuziale*) wedding ring.

veràce, *ag.* 1. (*veritiero*) true, veracious, truthful 2. (*vero*) true, real, genuine.

veraceménte, *av.* truthfully.

veracità, *s.f.* veracity, truth, truthfulness: *la — di un'affermazione*, the truth of a statement; *la — di un racconto*, the truth (o veracity) of a tale.

veraménte, *av.* 1. really, truly; (*davvero*) indeed: *era — brutto*, it was really ugly; *fui — felice quando lo seppi*, I was happy indeed when I was told (o when I got to know it); *sono — spiacente*, I am truly sorry; *sono — stanco*, I am really tired 2. (*a dire il vero*) to tell the truth, as a matter of fact: — *non lo sapevo*, to tell the truth, I didn't know it.

verànda, *s.f.* veranda(h); (*amer.*) porch.

veràtro, *s.m.* (*bot.*) veratrum, hellebore.

verbàle, *ag.* verbal: *desinenza, forma, nome* —, (*gram.*) verbal ending, form, noun; *errore* —, verbal error; *esame* —, oral examination; *ordine, promessa, spiegazione* —, verbal order, promise, explanation; *traduzione* —, verbal (*o* literal) translation ‖ *s.m.* minutes (*pl.*), record: *il* — *delle testimonianze,* (*dir.*) (shorthand) report of evidence; *il* — *di un'assemblea,* the minutes of a meeting; — *di collaudo,* (*mec.*) inspection report; *libro dei verbali,* minute-book; *fare un* —, to draw up a statement (*o* report); *mettere ql.co. a* —, to enter sthg. in the minutes (*o* to record sthg.).

verbalizzàre, *v.t.* to record: — *un'assemblea,* to record (the proceedings of) a meeting.

verbalménte, *av.* verbally, orally, by word of mouth.

verbàsco, *s.m.* (*bot.*) Verbascum.

verbèna, *s.f.* (*bot.*) vervain, verbena.

verbigràzia, *l.av.* (*lat.*) for instance, for example (*abbr.* e. g.).

vèrbo, *s.m.* **1.** (*gram.*) verb: — *regolare, irregolare,* regular, irregular verb **2.** (*parola*) word: *il* — *divino,* the word of God; *non disse* —, he did not say a word ‖ *il Verbo,* (*teol.*) the Word: *il Verbo s'è fatto carne,* the Word was made flesh.

verbosaménte, *av.* verbosely, wordily, prolixly, prosily.

verbosità, *s.f.* verbosity, wordiness, prolixity, prosiness.

verbóso, *ag.* verbose, wordy, prolix, prosy: *oratore* —, prosy orator.

verdàstro, *ag.* greenish.

verdazzúrro, *ag.* bluish-green, sea-green.

vérde, *ag.* **1.** green: — *chiaro, scuro,* light, dark green; — *oliva, bottiglia,* olive-green, bottle-green ‖ *fagiolini verdi,* French beans ‖ *altro che pallido, è* —!, he is not only pale, he is green! ‖ *essere* — *di invidia,* to be green with envy **2.** (*non maturo*) green, unripe: *frutta* —, green (*o* unripe) fruit ‖ *legna* —, green wood **3.** (*giovanile*) young; (*vigoroso*) vigorous: — *vecchiezza,* green old age; *nella più* — *età,* in one's earliest youth; *nei miei verdi anni,* in my youth (*o* when young) ‖ *vivo e* —, hale and hearty ‖ *s.m.* green: *i verdi di un quadro,* the different greens of a picture; *il* — *è il colore che preferisco,* green is my favourite colour; *è vestita di* —, she is dressed in green; *dipingere ql.co. di* —, to paint sthg. green ‖ *essere al* —, to be hard up (*o* penniless) ‖ *mettere le bestie al* —, to turn the cattle out to grass.

verdeggiànte, *ag.* verdant: *prato* —, verdant meadow.

verdeggiàre, *v.i.* **1.** (*essere verde*) to be verdant; (*diventare verde*) to turn green, to become green, to grow green **2.** (*tendere al colore verde*) to be greenish.

verdemàre, *s.m.* sea-green.

verderàme, *s.m.* verdigris.

verdétto, *s.m.* verdict: — *di condanna, di assoluzione,* verdict of guilty, of not guilty; *il* — *della corte fu contro di lui,* the verdict of the court was against him; *pronunciare un* — *contro, a favore di qlcu.,* to bring in (*o* to return) a verdict against, for s.o.

verdíccio, verdógnolo, *ag.* greenish.

verdóne, *ag.* dark green ‖ *s.m.* (*ornit.*) greenfinch, green linnet.

verdúra, *s.f.* **1.** (*ortaggi*) vegetables (*pl.*), greens (*pl.*): *minestra di* —, vegetable soup; *questa* — *non è cotta,* these vegetables are not cooked **2.** (*vegetazione*) verdure, greenery, green vegetation: *la* — *dei campi in primavera,* the green of the fields in spring.

verecondaménte, *av.* modestly, bashfully.

verecóndia, *s.f.* modesty, bashfulness.

verecóndo, *ag.* modest, bashful.

vérga, *s.f.* **1.** (*ramoscello*) twig ‖ *tremare come una* —, *a* — *a* —, to shake like a leaf **2.** (*bacchetta*) rod, bar, switch: — *d'oro, di ferro,* gold, iron bar (*o* rod) ‖ — *magica,* magician's wand ‖ — *pastorale,* (*eccl.*) crozier

(*o* pastoral staff) ‖ *gemere sotto la* — *dei tiranni,* to groan under the yoke of tyranny **3.** (*ind. tessile*) leash rod, lease bar **4.** (*anat.*) membrum virile.

vergàre, *v.t.* **1.** (*frustare*) to flog, to whip **2.** (*rigare*) to stripe; to rule, to draw lines on (sthg.) **3.** (*scrivere*) to write.

vergàta, *s.f.* blow with a rod: *una buona dose di vergate,* a good flogging (*o* thrashing).

vergatíno, *s.m.* (*stoffa a righe*) striped cloth, striped material.

vergàto, *ag.* **1.** striped, ruled: *carta vergata,* laid paper; *stoffa vergata,* striped cloth **2.** (*scritto*) written.

vergèlla, *s.f.* **1.** (*metal.*) (wire) rod **2.** *pl.* (*ind. cartaria*) laid wires ‖ *carta* —, laid paper.

vergènza, *s.f.* **1.** (*rar.*) (*tendenza*) tendency, propensity **2.** (*ott.*) vergency.

vèrgere, *v.i.* to turn (towards sthg.); (*tendere*) to tend (to sthg.).

verginàle, *ag.* virgin(al), maidenly: *modestia* —, maidenly (*o* virginal) modesty.

vérgine, *ag.* virgin: *cera* —, virgin wax; *foresta, terra* —, virgin forest, soil ‖ *s.f.* virgin ‖ *la Vergine,* (*la Madonna*) the Virgin: *la Beata Vergine Maria,* the Blessed Virgin Mary; *le Vergini di Raffaello,* the Virgins of Raphael ‖ *Vergine,* (*astr.*) Virgo (*o* Virgin) ‖ *le vergini folli,* the foolish virgins.

vergíneo, *ag.* virginal.

verginità, *s.f.* virginity.

vergógna, *s.f.* **1.** shame: *egli sentì* — *per aver fatto una cosa simile,* he felt shame at having done such a thing; *era pieno di* —, he was deeply ashamed; *gente che non ha, che non sente* —, people who have no (sense of) shame (*o* shameless people); *avere* —, to be ashamed: *avere* — *delle proprie azioni,* to be ashamed of one's actions; *arrossire di* —, to blush with shame ‖ —!, shame (on you)!; *che* —!, how shameful! **2.** (*disonore*) shame, disgrace, dishonour: *coprire qlcu. di* —, to cover s.o. with shame (*o* to bring shame on s.o.); *essere la* — *di qlcu.,* to be a disgrace (*o* dishonour) to s.o. **3.** (*timidezza*) shyness, bashfulness: *prendi quello che vuoi, non aver* —, take all you want, don't be shy (*o* bashful).

vergognàrsi, *v.r.* **1.** to be ashamed, to feel ashamed: *dovresti vergognarti di quello che hai fatto,* you ought to be ashamed of what you have done; *mi vergognai per lui,* I felt ashamed for him; *si vergognava di dirmi che non l'aveva ancora fatto,* he was ashamed to tell me (that) he had not done it yet; — *di se stesso,* to be ashamed of oneself ‖ *vergognatevi!,* shame on you! **2.** (*per timidezza*) to be shy, to be bashful: *non lo prese perchè si vergognava,* he did not take it because he was shy (*o* bashful).

vergognosaménte, *av.* **1.** shamefully **2.** (*timidamente*) bashfully.

vergognóso, *ag.* **1.** (*che reca vergogna*) shameful, disgraceful: *azioni vergognose,* shameful actions; *un insuccesso* —, a disgraceful failure; *in un modo* —, disgracefully (*o* shamefully); *è* — *che egli non ti aiuti,* it is a shame that he doesn't help you **2.** (*timido*) shy, bashful: *uno sguardo* —, a shy glance; *non le piacciono i ricevimenti perchè è molto vergognosa,* she doesn't like parties because she is very shy (*o* bashful) **3.** (*pieno di vergogna*) ashamed (*predicativo*): *stette in silenzio tutto* —, he kept silent, deeply ashamed.

vérgola, *s.f.* twisted silk thread.

veridicaménte, *av.* veraciously, truthfully.

veridicità, *s.f.* veracity, truthfulness: *la* — *di un racconto,* the truth of a story.

verídico, *ag.* veracious, truthful.

verífica, *s.f.* verification; inspection; examination; check, control; (*comm.*) audit: — *dei conti,* (*comm.*) audit of accounts; — *dei fatti,* verification of facts; — *di cassa,* (*comm.*) cash inspection; — *di somme,* checking of sums; *fare la* — *dei libri,* (*comm.*) to audit the books; *fare la* — *della merce,* to check the goods;

fare la — di un'addizione, to check an addition; *fare la — di una dichiarazione*, to verify a statement.

verificàbile, *ag.* verifiable.

verificàre, *v.t.* to verify; to inspect; to examine; to check, to control; (*comm.*) to audit: — *le affermazioni di qlcu.*, to verify s.o.'s statements; — *le cifre*, to verify (*o* to check) figures; — *i conti, i libri*, (*comm.*) to audit the accounts, the books; — *i fatti, una teoria*, to verify (*o* to check) facts, a theory ‖ **verificàrsi**, *v.r.* 1. (*accadere*) to happen, to take place, to come to pass: *questo si verifica troppo spesso*, this happens too often; *questo si verificò 10 anni fa*, this happened 10 years ago 2. (*avverarsi*) to come true: *si verificò quello che temevo*, what I dreaded came true.

verificatóre, *s.m.* verifier; examiner; controller: — *dei conti*, (*comm.*) auditor; — *dei pesi*, inspector of weights.

verificazióne, *V.* **verifica**.

verisimigliànte, *e derivati*, *V.* **verosimigliànte**, *e derivati*.

verísmo, *s.m.* (*art. lett.*) realism.

verista, *ag.* realistic: *uno scrittore —*, a realistic writer ‖ *s.c.* realist.

verità, *s.f.* truth, verity: *le — della scienza*, the truths of science; *le — eterne*, the eternal verities; *la — storica*, the historical truth; *cercare, negare la —*, to seek, to deny the truth; *dire la —*, to tell (*o* to speak) the truth; *dubitare della — delle affermazioni di qlcu.*, to doubt the truth (*o* veracity) of s.o.'s statements ‖ *in —*, really ‖ *quella donna è la bocca della —*, that woman is absolutely truthful (*o* is the soul of truth) ‖ *a dire la —*, to tell the truth.

veritièro, *ag.* truthful, veracious; sincere; true: *un racconto —*, a true tale; *testimonianza veritiera*, truthful evidence.

vèrme, *s.m.* worm (anche *fig.*): *il — della coscienza*, the worm of conscience; — *della terra*, earth-worm; — *solitario*, tapeworm; *quell'uomo è un —*, that man is a worm; *avere i vermi*, to have worms.

vermèna, *s.f.* (*rar.*) (*ramoscello*) shoot, twig.

vermicàio, *s.m.* wriggling mass of worms.

vermicèlli, *s.m.pl.* (*cuc.*) " vermicelli " (kind of Italian thin spaghetti).

vermicolàre, *ag.* vermicular.

vermiculìte, *s.f.* (*min.*) vermiculite.

vermifórme, *ag.* vermiform, worm-shaped.

vermífugo, *ag.s.m.* (*med. farm.*) vermifuge.

vermíglio, *ag.* vermilion, bright red, brilliant red.

vermiglióne, *s.m.* vermilion.

verminazióne, *s.f.* (*med.*) vermination.

verminóso, *ag.* verminous.

vèrmut, *s.m.* vermouth: *un — liscio*, a vermouth neat; — *secco, dolce*, dry, sweet vermouth.

vernàccia, *s.f.* " vernaccia " (white table-wine).

vernàcolo, *ag.* vernacular: *un poeta —*, a vernacular poet ‖ *s.m.* vernacular: *questa poesia è scritta in —*, this poem is written in the vernacular.

vernàre, *v.i.* (*letter.*) to winter.

vernìce, *s.f.* 1. paint; (*trasparente*) varnish: — *a fuoco*, stove enamel; — *a olio*, oil-paint; — *a smalto*, enamel-paint; — *a spirito*, spirit varnish; — *bituminosa*, bituminous paint; — *coprente*, (*foto.*) opaque retouching dye; — *fosforescente*, luminous paint; — *isolante*, insulating varnish; — *opaca*, flat varnish; — *per ritocco*, (*foto.*) dope; *mano di —*, coat of paint ‖ — *fresca*, (*sui cartelli*) wet paint 2. *fig.* (*apparenza*) varnish, gloss; (*conoscenza superficiale*) smattering: *una — di francese*, a smattering of French; *una — di rispettabilità*, a veneer of respectability 3. *fig.* (*cerimonia d'inaugurazione di una mostra*) varnishing-day 4. (*pelle verniciata*) patent leather.

verniciàre, *v.t.* 1. to paint; (*con vernice trasparente*) to varnish: — *a smalto*, to enamel; — *a spruzzo*, to spray; — *a tampone*, to pad (*o* to French-polish); — *con vernice alla nitro*, to lacquer; — *porte*, to paint

doors 2. (*lucidare*) to polish: — *mobili*, to polish furniture 3. (*metal.*) to dress.

verniciatóre, *s.m.* painter; varnisher.

verniciatúra, *s.f.* 1. painting; (*con vernice trasparente*) varnishing: — *a buratto*, rumbling; — *a centrifugazione*, whirling; — *a immersione*, dipping; — *a mano*, brush-painting; — *a rullo*, roller coating; — *a smalto*, enamelling; — *a spirito*, spirit varnishing; — *a spruzzo*, spray painting; — *a tampone*, padding; — *bicolore*, (*di automobile*) two-colour painting; — *di fondo*, undercoat 2. (*lucidatura*) polishing 3. (*metal.*) dressing.

vèrno, *s.m.* (*poet. rar.*) winter.

véro, *ag.* 1. true; (*reale, autentico*) real, genuine: *un — amico*, a true (*o* real *o* sincere) friend; *il — colpevole*, the real culprit; *un — eroe, poeta*, a real hero, poet; *un — inglese*, a real (*o* true-born) Englishman; *oro —*, real gold; *una storia vera*, a true story; *è vera seta*, it is real silk; *qual è il suo — nome?*, what is his real name? ‖ *è —?, non è —?*, (*chiedendo conferma o attenzione*): *mangia molto, non è —?*, he eats a lot, doesn't he?; *non l'hai visto, è —?*, you haven't seen him, have you?; *puoi venire, non è —?*, you can come, can't you? ‖ *tempo —*, (*astr.*) true time ‖ *non mi par — di esserci riuscito*, I can hardly believe I have succeeded ‖ *te lo dico di — cuore*, I tell you sincerely ‖ *com'è — Dio me la dovrai pagare!*, (*fam.*) I swear you'll pay for it! 2. (*fam.*) (*perfetto, completo*) thorough, perfect, regular, precious: *un — furfante*, a regular (*o* precious) rascal; *un — imbroglione*, a thorough (*o* regular) swindler; *un — stupido*, a perfect fool ‖ *s.m.* (*verità*) truth: *il — e il falso*, truth and falsehood; *c'è del — in quella diceria*, there is some truth in that rumour; *a dire il —*, to tell the truth; *far passare ql.co. per —*, to pass sthg. off as true ‖ *per —, da —*, really (*o* in earnest) ‖ *essere nel —*, to be right ‖ *dipingere dal —*, to paint from life.

veróne, *s.m.* (*letter.*) balcony.

verònica[1], *s.f.* 1. (*relig.*) (*reliquia della Passione*) veronica, vernicle 2. (*bot.*) veronica.

Verònica[2], *no.pr.f.* Veronica.

verosimigliànte, *V.* **verosìmile**.

verosimigliànza, *s.f.* likelihood; verisimilitude: *la — di ciò che disse*, the likelihood of what he said.

verosìmile, *ag.* likely, probable; verisimilar: *una conclusione —*, a probable conclusion; *ciò che disse non è molto —*, what he said is not very likely.

verosimilménte, *av.* likely, probably.

verricèllo, *s.m.* (*mec.*) windlass; winch (anche *mar.*): — *per battipalo*, (*edil.*) piling winch; — *salpareti*, (*mar.*) trawl winch.

verrína, *s.f.* (*strum.*) auger.

vèrro, *s.m.* (*zool.*) boar.

verrúca, *s.f.* wart, verruca (*pl.* verrucae).

verrucóso, *ag.* warty, verrucous.

versaménto, *s.m.* 1. (*il versare*) pouring; spilling; shedding 2. (*comm.*) (*pagamento*) payment; (*deposito*) deposit: *distinta di —*, paying-in slip; *fare un — in banca*, to make a payment into a bank.

versànte, *s.m.* side; slope; versant.

versàre, *v.t.* 1. to pour (out): *versami un po' d'acqua*, pour me out some water; *versa il caffè nelle tazze*, pour the coffee into the cups; — *da bere a qlcu.*, to pour out a drink for s.o. 2. (*rovesciare*) to spill: *il bambino ha versato il vino sulla tovaglia*, the child has spilt the wine on the table-cloth 3. (*spargere*) to shed: — *lacrime*, to shed tears; — *il proprio sangue per una causa*, to shed one's blood for a cause 4. (*comm.*) (*pagare*) to pay: *la banca versò due milioni*, the bank paid out two millions; *gli ho versato tutto quello che gli dovevo*, I have paid him off; *ho versato in banca 200.000 lire*, I have paid 200,000 lire into the bank ‖ — *in deposito*, to deposit ‖ *v.i.* 1. (*di recipienti*) (*perdere*) to leak: *la botte versa*, the hogshead is leaking 2. (*essere, trovarsi*) to be, to live: — *in cattive condizioni*, to be in a bad condition (*o* state); — *in pericolo di vita*, to be in danger of death; — *in una squallida miseria,* to live in extreme poverty ‖ **versàrsi,** *v.r.* **1.** to spill: *mi sono versato del caffè sui pantaloni,* I have spilt some coffee on my trousers **2.** (*di fiume, ecc.*) to flow **3.** *fig.* (*dedicarsi*) to devote oneself (to sthg.): — *con tutta l'anima nello studio,* to devote oneself whole-heartedly to study.

versàtile, *ag.* versatile: *intelligenza* —, versatile mind.

versatilità, *s.f.* versatility.

versàto, *ag.* **1.** poured out; (*sparso*) spilt; shed: *lacrime versate,* shed tears **2.** (*esperto*) versed; proficient; (*generalmente riferito a lavori manuali*) skilled: — *in filosofia,* versed in philosophy; — *in matematica,* proficient in mathematics **3.** (*comm.*) paid: *capitale* —, paid-up capital.

verseggiàre, *v.t.* (*mettere in versi*) to versify, to turn into verse: — *un racconto,* to versify a tale ‖ *v.i.* (*scrivere versi*) to versify, to write verse.

verseggiatóre, *s.m.,* **verseggiatríce,** *s.f.* versifier.

verseggiatúra, *s.f.* versification.

versétto, *s.m.* **1.** (*verso breve*) short line **2.** (*della Bibbia*) verse; (*dei canti liturgici*) versicle.

versièra, *s.f.* **1.** (*diavolessa*) she-devil **2.** (*donna brutta e cattiva*) hag, witch, crone.

versificàre, *v.t.* to versify, to turn into verse.

versificatóre, *s.m.,* **versificatríce,** *s.f.* versifier.

versificazióne, *s.f.* versification.

versióne, *s.f.* **1.** version, translation: *una* — *inglese della « Divina Commedia »,* an English version of "The Divine Comedy"; *devo fare una* — *dall'italiano in inglese,* I must do a translation from Italian into English ‖ *Versione Ufficiale della Bibbia,* Authorized Version of the Bible **2.** (*relazione*) version: *la sua* — *della faccenda è completamente diversa,* his version of the matter is completely different.

versipèlle, *ag.* cunning, wily, crafty, sly ‖ *s.m.* cunning person, wily person, crafty person, sly person; (*fam.*) slyboots.

vèrso[1], *prep.* **1.** (*direzione*) **towards, toward:** — *est, ovest,* towards the east (*o av.* eastward(s), *ag.* eastward), towards the west (*o av.* westward(s), *ag.* westward); *la mia camera guarda* — *le montagne,* my room looks towards the mountains; *vado* — *la stazione,* I am going towards the station; *vide un'automobile che veniva* — *di lui,* he saw a car coming towards him; *andare* — *casa,* to go towards home (*o* homewards) **2.** (*nei confronti di*) **to, towards:** *è sempre molto gentile* — *di me,* he is always very kind to (*o* towards) me; *mi sento obbligato* — *mio cugino,* I feel obliged to my cousin **3.** (*riferito a tempo*) (*circa*) **about;** (*verso, ma non oltre*) **towards, toward:** — *la fine della settimana,* towards the end of the week; — *sera,* towards evening; *era* — (*la*) *mezzanotte,* it was about midnight; it was towards midnight; *tornò* — *i primi del mese,* he came back at the beginning of the month; *venne* — *le cinque,* he came at about five o'clock **4.** (*contro*) **against:** *suscitare odio* — *il nemico,* to stir up hatred against the enemy.

vèrso[2], *s.m.* **1.** (*riga di scrittura*) line: *ti scriverò due versi,* I'll drop you a line **2.** (*poes.*) verse (*gener. sing.*); poetry (*solo sing.*); (*riga di poesia*) line: *versi d'occasione,* occasional verse; *in* — *esametro,* in hexameter verse; *in* — *sciolto,* in blank verse; *una strada di sei versi,* a six-line verse; *mi piacciono i suoi versi,* I like his poetry; *questi versi furono scritti subito dopo la morte di suo padre,* these lines were written just after his father's death; *studiate i primi venti versi,* study the first twenty lines; *comporre versi,* to write verse(s); *mettere in versi una leggenda,* to put a legend into verse; *recitare versi,* to recite lines of verse; *scrivere in versi,* to write in verse **3.** (*suono*) sound: *il* — *delle zampogne,* the sound of the bagpipes **4.** (*modo di gridare dell'animale*) sound, noise; (*di uccello*) note, call: *il* — *del cane,* the noise of the dog; *l'allegro* — *dell'allodola,* the merry note of the skylark **5.** (*grido di venditori ambulanti, ecc.*) cry: *il* — *dello spazzaca-*

mino, the cry of the chimney-sweep **6.** (*cadenza*) cadence, sound: *il* — *dei veneziani,* the cadence of Venetians **7.** (*gesto, mossa*) gesture: *fa molti versi quando parla,* he makes many gestures while speaking ‖ *rifare il* — *a qlcu.,* to mimic s.o. **8.** (*direzione*) direction, way; (*lato*) side: *prendete per questo* — *e poi voltate a sinistra,* go this way and then turn left; *il vento soffia sempre da quel* —, the wind always blows from that direction; *spazzolare una stoffa contro il suo* —, to brush a cloth against the grain ‖ *per un* — *lo approvo, per l'altro no,* I approve of him in some ways but not in others ‖ *quella persona non mi va a* —, I don't like that person ‖ *avere il* — *a fare qlc.co.,* to be accustomed to doing sthg. ‖ *esaminare la questione da tutti i versi,* to examine the matter from all sides ‖ *lasciare andare le cose per il loro* —, to let things take their course ‖ *prendere qlcu. per il suo* —, to approach s.o. from the right angle **9.** (*modo, maniera*) way: *devi trovare il* — *di vederlo,* you must find a way of seeing him; *non c'è* — *di saperlo,* there is no way of knowing; *per un* — *o per un altro egli riesce sempre,* in one way or another he is always successful; *voi dovete fare sempre a* — *suo,* you must always do what he wants ‖ *rispondere a* —, to answer to the point **10.** (*ragione*) reason: *ora per un* — *ora per un altro non riesco mai ad andare a teatro,* for one reason or another I never manage to go to the theatre; *per un* — *o per l'altro erano tutti insoddisfatti,* for one reason or another they were all dissatisfied.

verso[3], *s.m.* (*retro*) verso (*pl.* versos), reverse, back: *il* — *di una moneta, di una pagina,* the verso (*o* reverse *o* back) of a coin, of a page.

versóio, *s.m.* (*agr.*) moldboard, mouldboard.

vèrsta, *s.f.* (*misura russa equivalente a metri 1066*) verst.

vèrtebra, *s.f.* vertebra (*pl.* vertebrae).

vertebràle, *ag.* vertebral, spinal: *colonna* —, spinal column (*o* backbone *o* spine).

vertebràto, *ag.* vertebrate(d) ‖ *s.m.* vertebrate ‖ *i vertebrati,* the Vertebrata.

vertènte, *ag.* regarding (s.o., sthg.), concerning (s.o., sthg.), having relation (to s.o., sthg.): — *sui problemi dell'educazione,* regarding the problems of education.

vertènza, *s.f.* dispute, quarrel, controversy: — *giudiziaria,* judicial controversy; *definire una* —, to settle a dispute.

vèrtere, *v.i.* to be about (s.o., sthg.), to regard (s.o., sthg.), to concern (s.o., sthg.): *la discussione verte sul recente aumento dei prezzi,* the discussion is about the recent increase in prices; *la lite verte tra lui e il socio,* the dispute regards (*o* is between) him and his partner; *la questione verte su questi problemi,* the question regards these problems.

verticàle, *ag.* vertical, upright: *una linea* —, a vertical line ‖ *un pianoforte* —, an upright piano ‖ *s.f.* vertical.

verticalménte, *av.* vertically, upright.

vèrtice, *s.m.* **1.** vertex (*pl.* vertices): *il* — *di un cono,* the vertex of a cone **2.** (*sommità, culmine*) top, summit; *fig.* height: *il* — *di una montagna,* the top of a mountain; *è al* — *del suo successo,* he is at the height of his success ‖ *conferenza al* —, summit conference.

verticillàto, *ag.* (*bot.*) verticillate(d).

verticillo, *s.m.* (*bot.*) verticil.

vertígine, *s.f.* dizziness (*solo sing.*), giddiness (*solo sing.*); (*med.*) vertigo (*pl.* vertigoes, vertigines): *un attacco di vertigini,* a fit of giddiness (*o* dizziness); *fui preso da* —, I was seized by dizziness (*o* giddiness); *mi dà le vertigini,* it makes me giddy; *avere le vertigini,* to feel dizzy (*o* to be giddy *o* to have fits of giddiness); *soffrire di vertigini,* to suffer from giddiness.

vertiginosaménte, *av.* dizzily, giddily; (*vorticosamente*) vortically.

vertiginóso, *ag.* dizzy, giddy: *altezza vertiginosa,*

dizzy (o giddy) height; *velocità vertiginosa*, dizzy speed.

Verulàmio, *no.pr.f.* (*geog. st.*) Verulamium.

verúno, *ag.* no; (*in presenza di altra negazione*) **any**: *non fa male* —, it does not do any harm ‖ *pron.* **no one**, **nobody**; (*in presenza di altra negazione*) **anyone**, **anybody**: *non ho visto* —, I did not see anybody (*o* I saw nobody).

verve, *s.f.* verve: *recitare con molta* —, to act with great verve.

vèrza, *s.f.* **1.** savoy (cabbage) **2.** (*scheggia*) stick, splinter.

verzicànte, *ag.* (*verdeggiante*) verdant.

verzicàre, *v.i.* **1.** (*verdeggiare*) to be verdant **2.** (*cominciare a verdeggiare*) to grow verdant, to turn green.

verzière, *s.m.* (*arc.*) orchard.

verzíno, *s.m.* (*bot.*) Brazil-wood.

verzúra, *s.f.* **1.** verdure, greenery **2.** (*verdura*) greens (*pl.*).

véscia, *s.f.* **1.** (*bot.*) puff-ball **2.** (*chiacchiera*) chatter.

vescíca, *s.f.* **1.** (*anat.*) bladder; vesica (*pl.* vesicae): — *biliare*, gall-bladder; — *urinaria*, urinary vesica **2.** — *natatoria*, (*di pesce*) swim-bladder **3.** (*della pelle*) blister.

vescicànte, *s.m.* **1.** (*farm.*) vesicant, blistering ointment **2.** (*persona noiosa*) bore.

vescicatòrio, *ag.s.m.* vesicatory.

vescicazióne, *s.f.* vesication, blistering.

vescichétta, *s.f.* **1.** (*anat.*) small bladder, vesicle — *biliare*, gall-bladder **2.** (*della pelle*) small blister.

vescicolàre, *ag.* (*anat.*) vesicular.

vescovàdo, *s.m.* (*residenza di vescovo*) bishop's residence, bishop's palace.

vescovàto, *s.m.* **1.** (*ufficio di vescovo*) bishopric **2.** (*residenza di vescovo*) bishop's residence, bishop's palace.

vescovíle, *ag.* episcopal, bishop's: *palazzo* —, episcopal (*o* bishop's) palace.

véscovo, *s.m.* bishop.

vèspa, *s.f.* **1.** wasp ‖ *vita di* —, wasp-waist **2.** (*leggera motocicletta*) " vespa " (a kind of motor-scooter).

vespàio, *s.m.* **1.** wasps' nest, vespiary **2.** *fig.* hornets' nest: *stuzzicare il* —, to stir up a hornets' nest (*o* to bring a hornets' nest about one's ears).

Vespasiàno[1], *no.pr.m.* (*st.*) Vespasian.

vespasiàno[2], *s.m.* (public) urinal.

vesperàle, *ag.* vespertine.

Vespero, *no.pr.m.* (*astr.*) Vesper, Evening Star, Hesperus ‖ **vèspero**, *s.m.* (*poet.*) (*vespro*) vesper, evening: *la campana del* —, the vesper-bell.

vespertíno, *ag.* vespertine, crepuscular; evening (*attributivo*).

vèspro, *s.m.* **1.** (*sera*) evening: *campana del* —, vesper -bell **2.** (*eccl.*) vespers (*pl.*); evening prayer, evensong: *cantare il* —, to sing Vespers ‖ *i Vespri Siciliani*, (*st.*) the Sicilian Vespers.

vessàre, *v.t.* to vex; to oppress, to harass, to annoy: *essere vessato da qlco.*, to be vexed at sthg.

vessatóre, *ag.* vexing, vexatious, oppressive ‖ *s.m.*, **vessatríce**, *s.f.* vexer, oppressor.

vessatòrio, *ag.* vexatious, oppressive.

vessazióne, *s.f.* vexation; oppression: *le vessazioni cui è sottoposto questo popolo*, the vexations to which the people of this country are subjected.

vessillàrio, **vessillífero**, *s.m.* (*st. romana*) vexillary, standard-bearer.

vessíllo, *s.m.* (*bandiera*) flag; (*stendardo*) standard; (*st. romana*) vexillum (*pl.* vexilla).

Vèsta, *no.pr.f.* (*mit.*) Vesta.

vestàglia, *s.f.* dressing-gown.

vestàle, *s.f.* (*st. romana*) vestal (virgin).

vèste, *s.f.* **1.** dress; *pl.* clothes, garments: — *da camera*, dressing-gown; *vesti invernali*, winter clothes; *un giudice nella sua* —, a judge in his gown; *in ricche vesti*, luxuriously dressed (*o* in luxurious attire); *sotto le misere vesti egli nascondeva la sua nobile origine*, under his mean appearance he hid his noble origin;

togliersi le vesti, to throw off one's garments (*o* to take off one's clothes) **2.** (*eccl.*) vestment: *portare la* —, to wear the cassock **3.** (*qualità*) quality, capacity: *in* — *ufficiale*, in an official capacity; *nella mia* — *di avvocato*, in my capacity as a lawyer ‖ *in falsa* —, in guise (*o* in false appearance): *egli venne da me sotto la falsa* — *di consigliere*, he came to me in the guise of an adviser **4.** (*facoltà*, *diritto*) right; authority: *non ho* — *per fare ciò*, I have no authority to do it.

Vestfàlia, *no.pr.f.* (*geog.*) Westphalia.

vestiàrio, *s.m.* clothes (*pl.*); clothing: *un capo di* —, a garment (*o* a dress); *essa spende moltissimo in* —, she spends a great deal of money on clothes (*o* in dressing); *tengo tutto il mio* — *in questo guardaroba*, I keep all my clothes in this wardrobe.

vestiarísta, *s.c.* (*teat.*) costumier, costume dealer, fancy-dress dealer.

vestíbolo, *s.m.* **1.** (*di casa moderna*) hall, lobby **2.** (*archeol.*) vestibule **3.** (*anat.*) vestibule.

vestígio, *s.m.* **1.** (*orma*) footprint, footmark; trace: *seguire le vestigia di qlcu.*, to follow in s.o.'s footsteps **2.** *fig.* vestige; remains (*pl.*); trace: *le vestigia della loro antica grandezza*, the vestiges of their ancient splendour; *le vestigia di un'antica civiltà*, the traces of an ancient civilization.

vestiménto, *V.* **vèste**.

vestíre, *v.t.* **1.** to dress: *la bambina vestiva la sua bambola*, the little girl was dressing her doll; *è molto costoso* — *una famiglia numerosa*, it is very expensive to dress a big family; *ella aveva vestito i suoi bambini particolarmente bene*, she had dressed up her children **2.** (*procurare vestiti a*) to clothe: — *i poveri*, to clothe the poor **3.** (*fare vestiti a*) to make (s.o.'s) clothes **4.** *fig.* to clothe: *egli veste i suoi pensieri con uno stile molto elaborato*, he clothes his thoughts in a very elaborate style; *la primavera veste i campi d'erba*, spring clothes the fields with grass **5.** (*indossare*) to wear, to have on: *vestiva un soprabito rosso*, she was wearing (*o* she had on) a red coat ‖ — *l'abito monacale*, (*farsi monaca*) to take the veil (*o* to become a nun); (*farsi monaco*), to become a monk ‖ *v.i.* to dress, to be dressed: *ella non veste molto bene*, she doesn't dress very well; *non mi piace il suo modo di* —, I don't like the way she dresses; *veste sempre di nero*, he is always dressed in black ‖ **vestírsi**, *v.r.* **1.** to dress (oneself); (*fam.*) to get dressed: *il bambino non è capace di* —, the child cannot dress himself; *va a vestirti*, go and dress yourself (*o* go and get dressed); — *di nero, di seta*, to be dressed in black, in silk ‖ *so di che panni si veste*, I know what he is ‖ *saper* —, to dress with taste **2.** (*agghindarsi*) to dress (up): *bisogna* — *bene per entrare?*, has one to be dressed up to get in?; *in questo albergo non ci vestiamo mai per il pranzo*, at this hotel we never dress for dinner; *si era vestita a festa*, she had put on her Sunday clothes (*o* Sunday best) **3.** (*farsi fare i vestiti*) to have one's clothes made (by s.o.).

vestíto, *ag.* dressed (in sthg.); clad (in sthg.), clothed (with sthg.), robed (in sthg.): — *da festa*, in one's Sunday clothes (*o* in one's Sunday best); — *di bianco*, dressed in white; — *leggero*, lightly clad; — *poveramente*, poorly dressed (*o* in poor attire); *colline vestite di verde*, green-clad hills; *colline vestite di vigne*, vine-clad hills; *professori vestiti colle toghe*, professors (robed) in their gowns; *tutto* — *di nero*, all (dressed) in black ‖ *nascere* —, (*fortunato*) to be born with a silver spoon in one's mouth ‖ *s.m.* (*da donna*) frock, gown; dress; *pl.* clothes, garments; (*da uomo*) suit (of clothes): *vestiti da casa*, casuals; — *da cerimonia*, full-dress; — *da mezza sera*, cocktail-dress (*o* half -length dress); — *da sera*, (*da donna*) evening-dress (*o* evening-gown); (*da uomo*) evening-dress (*o* dress -suit); — *della domenica*, Sunday best; *devo farmi fare un* —, I must have a dress made; *tengo i miei vestiti in questo armadio*, I keep my clothes in this wardrobe.

vestitúra, *s.f.* dressing, clothing.

vestizióne, *s.f.* (*eccl.*) (ceremony of) taking the habit; (*di monaca*) (ceremony of) taking the veil.

Vesúvio, *no.pr.m.* (*geog.*) Vesuvius.

veteráno, *ag.* veteran ‖ *s.m.* veteran (anche *mil.*); (*mil. amer.*) ex-serviceman (*pl.* ex-servicemen).

veterinária, *s.f.* veterinary science.

veterinário, *ag.* veterinary ‖ *s.m.* veterinary (surgeon); (*fam.*) vet.

véto, *s.m.* veto (*pl.* vetoes): *diritto di —*, (right of) veto: *esercitare il diritto di —*, to exercise one's right of veto; *mettere il — a una proposta*, to put a (*o* one's) veto on a proposal (*o* to veto a proposal).

vetràio, *s.m.* 1. glazier 2. (*chi lavora il vetro*) glass -maker, glass-blower; (*chi fabbrica vetro*) glass manufacturer 3. (*chi vende articoli in vetro*) glass merchant.

vetràme, *s.m.* glassware.

vetràrio, *ag.* glass (*attributivo*): *industria vetraria*, glass manufacture.

vetràta, *s.f.* 1. (*porta a vetri*) glass door; (*parete, divisione a vetri*) glass wall, glass partition 2. (*grande finestra*) large window: *le vetrate a colori di una chiesa*, the stained glass windows of a church.

vetràto, *ag.* glazed ‖ *carta vetrata*, glass-paper (*o* sand-paper).

vetrería, *s.f.* 1. (*fabbrica di vetri*) glass-work 2. *pl.* (*articoli di vetro*) glassware (*sing.*).

vetriàta, *V.* **vetràta**.

vétrice, *s.f.* (*bot.*) osier.

vetriciàio, *s.m.* (*bot.*) osier-bed.

vetrièra, *s.f.* glass-door.

vetrifieàbile, *ag.* vitrifiable.

vetrifieàre, *v.t.i.*, **vetrifieàrsi**, *v.r.* to vitrify.

vetrifieazióne, *s.f.* vitrification, vitrifaction.

vetrígno, *ag.* vitric, glass-like.

vetrina, *s.f.* 1. shop-window: *gli articoli in —*, the articles shown in the window; *lo vidi in una —*, I saw it in a shop-window 2. (*bacheca*) glass show-case, vitrine 3. (*cristalliera*) glass cupboard 4. (*vernice vetrosa*) glaze.

vetrinísta, *s.c.* window dresser, window decorator.

vetríno, *ag.* brittle; fragile: *unghie vetrine*, brittle finger-nails ‖ *s.m.* (*per microscopio*) slide.

vetrioleggiàre, *v.t.* to vitriolize, to vitriolate.

vetri(u)òlo, *s.m.* vitriol: *— di ferro*, (*verde*) iron (*o* green) vitriol; *— di rame*, (*azzurro*) copper (*o* blue) vitriol; *— di zinco*, (*bianco*) zinc (*o* white) vitriol; *olio di —*, oil of vitriol.

vétro, *s.m.* glass; (*di finestra*) (window-)pane: *— colorato*, stained glass; *— opaco*, opaque glass; *— smerigliato*, ground glass; *— stampato*, moulded glass; *una lastra di —*, a pane of glass; *lavoro in —*, glasswork; *oggetti di —*, glassware; *devo far cambiare un —*, I must have a pane changed; *ha rotto un — con un sasso*, he has broken a (window-)pane with a stone; *mettere un —*, to put in a pane of glass; *soffiare il —*, to blow glass.

vetroceménto, *s.m.* (*edil.*) concrete and glass.

vetrocromía, *s.f.* (*pitt.*) glass-painting.

vetrofanía, *s.f.* decalcomania.

vetróso, *ag.* vitreous, glassy.

vétta, *s.f.* 1. top, summit, peak: *la — di un albero*, the top of a tree; *la — di un monte*, the top (*o* summit) of a mountain 2. (*mar.*) end.

vettóre, *s.m.* 1. (*geom. astr.*) vector: *raggio —*, radius vector 2. (*corriere*) carrier.

vettoriàle, *ag.* vectorial.

vettovàglia, *s.f.* provision, supply.

vettovagliaménto, *s.m.* provisioning, victualling.

vettovagliàre, *v.t.* to provision, to victual, to supply with provisions (*o* victuals): *— una nave*, to victual a ship (*o* to supply a ship with food).

vettovàglie, *s.f.pl.* provisions, victuals.

vettúra, *s.f.* 1. (*carrozza*) coach; (*automobile*) car: *— di piazza*, (*taxi*) taxi(-cab) (*o amer.* cab); (*carrozza*) (hackney-)cab (*o* hackney-carriage) 2. (*ferr.*) carriage, coach; (*amer.*) car; (*tranviaria*) tram: *le vetture dirette sono in testa*, the through-carriages are in front ‖ *tutti in —!*, (*amer.*) all aboard! 3. (*trasporto*) carriage: *bestie da —*, draught animals; *lettera di —*, (*ferr.*) carriage (*o* consignment) note.

vetturàle, **vetturíno**, *s.m.* driver; (*di carrozza*) cabman (*pl.* cabmen), coachman (*pl.* coachmen).

vetustà, *s.f.* antiquity; (old) age.

vetústo, *ag.* ancient, (very) old.

vezzeggiaménto, *s.m.* fondling, petting, caressing.

vezzeggiàre, *v.t.* to fondle, to pet, to caress: *— un bambino*, to fondle a child.

vezzeggiatívo, *s.m.* 1. diminutive form of a noun 2. (*nomignolo*) pet-name.

vézzo, *s.m.* 1. (*abitudine*) habit: *ha il brutto — di muovere troppo le mani quando parla,* he has a bad habit of moving his hands too much while speaking 2. (*fascino, grazia*) charm: *i suoi vezzi l'hanno conquistato*, her charm has conquered him 3. *pl.* (*moine*) mincing ways, affected ways: *smetti di fare tanti vezzi*, stop that affected way of behaving; *i suoi vezzi mi danno ai nervi*, her mincing ways get on my nerves; *fare vezzi a un bambino*, to fondle a child 4. (*collana*) necklace.

vezzosaménte, *av.* charmingly, gracefully.

vezzóso, *ag.* 1. (*grazioso*) charming, graceful: *vezzosa fanciulla*, charming (*o* graceful) girl 2. (*lezioso*) mincing, affected: *modi vezzosi*, mincing (*o* affected) ways; *non mi piace quando fa la vezzosa*, I don't like her when she puts on those mincing ways.

vi¹, *pron.* 1. *pers.* 2ª *persona pl. oggetto e obliquo* you: *— dico che avete torto*, I tell you you are wrong; *— ringrazio molto*, (I) thank you very much; *— sono molto obbligato*, I am very much obliged to you; *— sto cercando da un'ora*, I have been looking for you for an hour; *quando — posso trovare in casa?*, when can I find you at home (*o* in)?; *vorrei darvi anche questo*, I should like to give you this too 2. *pers.* 2ª *persona sing. oggetto e obliquo* (*formula di cortesia*) you; (*con verbi riflessivi*) yourself (*spesso sottinteso*): *— trovate bene con lui?*, do you feel (yourself) at home with him?; *quando Vi posso trovare a casa, dottore?*, when will I find you at home, doctor?; *scusate, Vi dispiacerebbe darmi una mano?*, excuse me, would you mind giving me a hand (*o* helping me)? 3. *r.* 2ª *persona pl.* yourselves (*spesso sottinteso*): *— siete svegliati presto stamattina*, you woke up early this morning; *lavatevi*, wash yourselves; *non — sentite bene?*, don't you feel well?; *so che non — siete divertiti molto ieri sera*, I know you didn't enjoy yourselves very much last night 4. *reciproco* each other (*tra due persone*); one another (*tra molti*): *dovreste aiutarvi di più*, you should help each other (one another) more 5. *dimostrativo* this; that; it: *io non — ho creduto*, I didn't believe it; *non ho niente a che vedervi*, I have nothing to do with that, this; *senza farvi caso*, without paying any attention to it.

vi², *av. di luogo* there: *— sarò domani*, I shall be there to-morrow; *— trovò molta gente*, he found many people there; *non — era nessuno*, there was nobody ‖ *v'è, — sono*, there is, there are.

vi³, *s.f.m.* letter V.

via¹, *s.f.* 1. street; (*strada di comunicazione*) road: *una — molto larga, molto lunga*, a very wide, a very long road; *una — romana*, a Roman road; *dall'altra parte della —*, on the other side of the road; *abitiamo nella stessa —*, we live in the same street; *abito in — Roma*, I live in via Roma; *lo incontrai per la —*, I met him on the road (*o* on the way); *prendi la prima — a destra*, take the first street on the right ‖ *la Via Appia*, the Appian Way ‖ *la Via Crucis*, the Way of the Cross ‖ *la Via Lattea*, the Milky Way 2. (*cammino*) way (anche *fig.*); path (anche *fig.*): *la — della gloria*, the path(s) of glory; *le vie del Signore*, the ways of the

Lord; *a metà* , halfway: *lo incontrai a metà* —, I met him halfway; *qual'è la* — *più corta per la stazione?*, which is the shortest way to the station?; *vieni per questa* —, come this way; *aprire la* —, to lead (*o* to pave) the way; *mettere qlcu. sulla retta* —, to put s.o. on the right track (*o* path) ‖ — *mare*, — *terra*, by sea, by land; *per* — *aerea*, by air; (*termine postale*) by air-mail ‖ — *Napoli*, via Naples ‖ *vie respiratorie*, (*anat.*) respiratory organs ‖ *foglio di* —, pass (*o* travel warrant) ‖ *in* — *di costruzione*, in course of construction 3. (*linea di condotta*) course, line: *la* — *da seguire*, the course to be followed 4. (*modo, mezzo*) way: *in* — *amichevole*, in a friendly way; *in* — *diplomatica*, through diplomatic channels; *in* — *eccezionale, provvisoria*, exceptionally, provisionally; *per vie traverse*, by underhand means; *non c'è* — *di saperlo*, there is no way of knowing; *non c'è* — *di scampo, d'uscita*, there is no way out (*o* there is no help for it); *questa è l'unica* —, this is the only way ‖ *in* — *di*, (*per mezzo di*) by means of: *in* — *di diritto*, by right ‖ *per* — *di, che*, (*a causa di*) owing to (*o* on account of).

vía[2], *av.* 1. (*in unione a voci verbali*) **away, off:** *andar* —, (*andarsene*) to go away (anche *fig.*); (*di macchie*) to come out; (*di merce*) to sell like hot cakes; (*di denaro*) to go like water; *cacciar, mandar* —, to send away; *dar* —, to give away; (*smerciare*) to sell off; *essere* —, to be away: *è* — *da casa*, he is away from home; *gettare, buttare* —, to throw away; (*sprecare*) to waste; *fuggire, correre* —, to run away; *levar, tirar* —, to take away; (*macchie*) to remove; *portar* —, to take away; (*trasportare*) to carry away; *venir* —, to come away; (*staccarsi*) to come off (*o* away); *volar* —, to fly away: *far volar* — *ql.co.*, to blow sthg. off 2. (*con valore moltiplicativo*): *tre* — *quattro*, three times four 3. (*arc.*) (*premesso ai comp. con valore di molto*) **much** ‖ *inter.*: —*!*, (*per scacciare*) shoo!; (*come segnale di partenza*) go!; —, *coraggio!*, come on, cheer up!; —, *dimmi quello che sai*, come on, tell me what you know; —, *non dire queste cose*, come now, don't say such things; —, *non è poi così difficile*, get away with you, it isn't so difficult; *non c'è male*, —, *sono contento*, well, it isn't too bad, I am satisfied; *non spaventarti*, —*!*, now then, don't be afraid! 4. (**Fraseologia**): *via via:* — — *che arrivano mandali da me*, as they arrive send them to me; — — *che lo conosco mi piace sempre di più*, the more I know him, the more I like him; *va* — — *diminuendo*, it is decreasing little by little ‖ — *come una saetta*, off like a shot ‖ — *di lì*, get away from there ‖ *e così* —, and so on (*o* and so forth *o* and so on and so forth) ‖ *e* — *dicendo, e* — *discorrendo*, and so on.

vía[2], *s.m.* start: *dare il* — , (*spor.*) to give the starting signal; *dare il* — *a una discussione*, to open a debate; *dare il* — *ai lavori*, to start work.

viabilità, *s.f.* state of the roads; road conditions (*pl.*): *la* — *di una strada*, the state (*o* condition) of a road.

viadòtto, *s.m.* viaduct.

viaggiànte, *ag.* travelling; on the way (*predicativo*): *merce* —, (*in transito*) goods in transit; *personale* —, (*ferr.*) travelling staff.

viaggiàre, *v.i.* to travel, to journey, to make a trip; (*per mare*) to voyage; (*per aereo*) to fly: *è un uomo che ha viaggiato molto*, he is a well-travelled man; *la merce viaggia a rischio del proprietario*, the goods travel at owner's risk; *sono stanco di* —, I am tired of travelling; — *in prima, seconda classe*, to travel first, second class; — *in treno, automobile, aeroplano, nave*, to travel by train, car, air, sea; — *in tutto il mondo*, to travel the whole world over (*o* all over the world); — *per affari*, to travel on business; — *per una ditta*, to travel for a firm ‖ *il treno viaggia con venti minuti di ritardo*, the train is twenty minutes late.

viaggiàre, *s.m.* travelling.

viaggiatóre, *s.m.*, **viaggiatríce**, *s.f.* 1. traveller: — *di commercio*, commercial traveller (*o* travelling salesman *o fam. amer.* drummer) 2. (*passeggero*) passenger: *tutti i viaggiatori devono presentare il loro passaporto*, all passengers must show their passports.

viàggio, *s.m.* 1. journey, trip; (*per mare*) voyage; (*per aereo*) flight: — *di affari*, business trip; — *di andata, di ritorno*, outward, return journey (*o* voyage); — *di nozze*, honeymoon (trip); — *di piacere*, pleasure trip; *un* — *di una settimana*, a week's journey (*o* voyage); — *interplanetario*, interplanetary voyage; *un* — *intorno al mondo*, a round-the-world trip; — *turistico*, tour; *abito da* —, travelling costume (*o* dress); *compagno di* —, fellow-traveller; *indennità di* —, travelling allowance (*o* indemnity); *un lungo* — *in Cina*, a long journey in China; *spese di* —, travelling expenses; *ho fatto un lungo* — *per tutta l'Europa*, I went on a long journey all over Europe; *essere in* —, to be on a journey (*o* voyage *o* trip); *fare, intraprendere un* —, to go on (*o* to take *o* to make) a journey (*o* trip); *fare buon* —, to have a nice (*o* pleasant) trip (*o* journey): (*fa'*) *buon* —*!*, have a nice journey! ‖ *l'ultimo* —, one's last journey ‖ *se non riesci, buon* —, (*non importa*) if you don't succeed it doesn't matter 2. *pl.* (*in senso collettivo*) travel(s): *agenzia di viaggi*, travel agency (*o* bureau); *libro di viaggi*, travel book; *raccontami ql.co. dei tuoi viaggi*, tell me sthg. about your travels ‖ *i Viaggi di Gulliver*, Gulliver's Travels.

viàle, *s.m.* avenue, boulevard: *un largo* —, a wide avenue.

vialétto, *s.m.* alley.

viandànte, *s.m.* 1. wayfarer: *incontrammo solo pochi viandanti per la strada*, we met only few wayfarers on the road 2. (*viaggiatore*) traveller.

viàtico, *s.m.* 1. (*eccl.*) viaticum (*pl.* viatica): *morire senza* —, to die without the Sacraments 2. (*provviste per il viaggio*) provisions for a journey (*pl.*), viaticum.

viavài, *s.m.* coming-and-going, bustle: *un* — *di gente*, people coming and going.

vibrànte, *ag.* vibrant (with sthg.), vibrating (with sthg.), quivering (with sthg.): — *di entusiasmo, passione*, quivering (*o* trembling *o* shaking) with enthusiasm, passion; *note vibranti*, vibrating notes; *suono* —, quivering sound.

vibràre, *v.t.* 1. (*agitare, scuotere*) to vibrate, to brandish: — *la spada*, to brandish the sword 2. (*colpi*) to strike, to deliver, to deal: *le vibrò una coltellata*, he delivered (*o* dealt) her a stab; — *un colpo*, to strike a blow 3. (*scagliare*) to hurl (anche *fig.*): — *una lancia*, to hurl a spear; — *maledizioni*, to hurl curses ‖ *v.i.* 1. to vibrate, to quiver: *le corde del violino vibrano*, the strings of the violin vibrate (*o* quiver) ‖ *far* — *una corda*, to make a string vibrate; *far* — *le corde dell'anima*, to move the soul 2. (*mec.*) to chatter 3. — *aeroelasticamente*, (*aer.*) to flutter.

vibratézza, *s.f.* 1. (*energia*) energy, force 2. (*concisione*) conciseness.

vibràtile, *ag.* vibratile: *ciglio* —, vibratile cilium.

vibràto, *ag.* 1. (*energico*) energetic, strong 2. (*conciso*) concise.

vibratóre, *s.m.* (*elett. fis.*) vibrator: — *a cicala*, (*elett.*) buzzer; — *ad alta frequenza*, (*med.*) high-frequency vibrator; — *asincrono*, (*elett.*) asynchronous vibrator; *bobina del* —, (*aer. mec.*) booster coil; *lamina mobile di un* —, (*elett.*) whip.

vibratòrio, *ag.* vibratory, vibrating, vibrative: *circuito* —, oscillatory circuit; *massaggio* —, vibro-massage.

vibrazióne, *s.f.* 1. vibration, quivering: *le vibrazioni delle ali di un insetto*, the quivering of an insect's wings 2. (*fis. mec.*) vibration: — *acustica*, sound vibration; — *aeroelastica*, (*aer.*) flutter: — *aeroelastica alare*, (*aer.*) wing flutter; — *sonora*, sonorous vibration; *dieci vibrazioni al secondo*, ten vibrations per second; *senza vibrazioni*, vibration-proof; *ventre di* — (*di un'onda*), (*fis.*) antinode; *allentarsi sotto l'effetto di vibrazioni*, (*mec.*) to shake loose.

vibrióne, s.m. (biol.) vibrio.
vibríssa, s.f. (zool.) vibrissa (pl. vibrissae).
vibrògrafo, s.m. vibrograph.
vibroscòpio, s.m. vibroscope.
vibrotrasportatóre, s.m. vibrating conveyor, vibratory conveyor.
vibrovàglio, s.m. (miner.) vibrating screen.
vibúrno, s.m. (bot.) viburnum.
vicaría, s.f. (ufficio del vicario) vicarship, vicariate.
vicariàle, ag. vicarial.
vicariàto, s.m. 1. (dignità, ufficio del vicario e sua durata) vicarship, vicariate 2. (giurisdizione) vicariate.
vicàrio, s.m. vicar: cardinale —, cardinal vicar ‖ — apostolico, vicar-apostolic ‖ il — di Cristo, the Vicar of Christ.
viceammiràglio, s.m. vice-admiral.
vicebibliotecàrio, s.m. assistant librarian.
vicecancellière, s.m. vice-chancellor.
vicecònsole, s.m. vice-consul.
vicedirettóre, s.m. (di azienda) vice-director, assistant-director; (di negozi, ristoranti, ecc.) assistant manager, sub-manager; (di scuola) deputy headmaster; (di giornale) assistant editor.
vicegerènte, s.m. vicegerent.
vicegovernatóre, s.m. vice-governor.
vicemàdre, s.f. foster-mother.
vicènda, s.f. 1. vicissitude, up and down: le vicende della mia vita, the vicissitudes (o ups and downs) of my life; dopo molte vicende si sistemò in un piccolo villaggio di campagna, after many vicissitudes he settled down in a small country village 2. (evento) event: vicende felici e infelici, lucky and unlucky events 3. (successione) succession, train: una — di cose buone e cattive, a succession of good and bad things ‖ a —, (fra due) each other; (fra molti) one another; (alternatamente) in turn(o by turns): lavoravano a —, they worked in turn (o by turns); si insultavano a —, they were insulting each other.
vicendévole, ag. mutual, reciprocal.
vicendevolménte, av. mutually, reciprocally; (tra due) each other; (tra molti) one another.
vicepàdre, s.m. foster-father.
viceprefètto, s.m. subprefect.
vicepresidènte, s.m. vice-president, vice-chairman (pl. vice-chairmen).
vicepresidènza, s.f. vice-presidency, vice-presidentship, vice-chairmanship.
viceré, s.m. viceroy.
vicereàle, ag. vice-regal.
vicereàme, s.m. viceroyalty.
vicereggènte, s.m. viceregent, deputy regent.
viceregina, s.f. vice-queen, vice-reine.
vicesegretariàto, s.m. vice-secretaryship.
vicesegretàrio, s.m. vice-secretary.
vicevèrsa, av. vice versa: io cercavo lui e —, I was looking for him and vice versa ‖ cong. whereas, while on the contrary: io mi preoccupai tanto, — non ce n'era ragione, I worried very much about it whereas there was no reason for doing so.
Vichíngo, s.m. (st.) Viking, Wi(c)king.
vicína, s.f. neighbour: una — di casa, a woman (o lady) next door.
vicinàle (stràda), s.f. local road; by-road.
vicinànza, s.f. 1. (l'essere vicino) closeness, nearness, proximity; vicinity; adjacency: la — della stazione è un vantaggio, proximity to the station (o the proximity of the station) is an advantage; la — delle vacanze lo rende felice, the proximity (o the approach) of the holidays makes him happy; preferisco questa casa per la — al centro, I prefer this house for its closeness to the centre; siamo in — della chiesa, we are close to (o near) the church; (ci stiamo avvicinando) we are approaching the church 2. pl. (adiacenze, dintorni) neighbourhood (sing.), vicinity (sing.): nelle vicinanze di Roma, in the neighbourhood of Rome;

ci sono due teatri in queste vicinanze, there are two theatres in this neighbourhood (o in the vicinity).
vicinàre, v.i. to be near (s.o., sthg., to s.o., sthg.).
vicinàto, s.m. 1. (dintorni) neighbourhood: tutti lo sanno in questo —, everybody knows it in this neighbourhood 2. (vicini) neighbours (pl.): rapporti di buon —, neighbourliness: siamo in rapporti di buon —, we are on good terms with our neighbours; tutto il — cercò di aiutarmi, all my neighbours tried to help me.
vicinióre, ag. (lat.) nearest.
vicinità, (rar.) per **vicinànza.**
vicíno, ag. 1. near, close; near at hand (predicativo): l'albergo più —, the nearest hotel; gli esami sono vicini, the examinations are near at hand (o are approaching); la sua casa è molto vicina, his house is very near (o close) 2. (limitrofo) neighbouring; adjoining: il villaggio —, the neighbouring village; abita nella casa vicina, he lives next door ‖ s.m. neighbour: il mio — di destra, di sinistra, my right-, left-hand neighbour; il mio — di tavola, my neighbour at table; siamo vicini di casa, we are next-door neighbours ‖ vicíno, av. near, close, near by, close by, near at hand: lontano e —, far and near; è lì —, it is close by (o near by); lavoro qui —, I work near at hand; non vede bene da —, he is long-sighted; quando la vedrai da —, ne sarai molto deluso, when you see her at close quarters (o close up), you'll be deeply disappointed; sta' —!, stay close!; vedi bene da —?, can you see well when you are near things?; vieni più —, come nearer (o closer) ‖ **vicíno** a, prep. near, close to, by; beside: la chiesa è — al ponte, the church is near the bridge; è — a Roma, it is near Rome; egli mi fu — durante la malattia di mio padre, he stood by me during my father's illness; egli venne — a me, he came near me; sedeva — a me, he was sitting by (o beside) me; stammi —, stay near me ‖ — a morire, at death's door; più volte mi sono trovato — alla morte, it has been touch and go with me more than once (o I have often had one foot in the grave).
vicissitúdine, s.f. vicissitude: le vicissitudini della sua vita, the vicissitudes (o ups and downs) of his life.
víco, s.m. 1. (vicolo) lane; alley 2. (villaggio) hamlet, small village.
vícolo, s.m. lane; alley: — cieco, blind alley.
vídeo, s.m. (tv.) video.
vidimàre, v.t. 1. (firmare) to sign 2. (autenticare) to authenticate 3. (vistare) to visé: far — un passaporto, to have a passport viséd (o visaed) 4. (legalizzare) to legalize.
vidimazióne, s.f. 1. (firma) signature 2. (autenticazione) authentication 3. (visto) visa, visé 4. (legalizzazione) legalization.
víe, av. (arc.) (premesso ai comp. con valore di molto) much.
Viènna, no.pr.f. (geog.) Vienna.
viennése, ag. Viennese ‖ s.c. Viennese (invariato al pl.).
viepiú, av. more and more.
vietàbile, ag. that can be forbidden.
vietaménto, s.m. prohibition.
vietàre, v.t. to forbid, to prohibit (from doing); to prevent (from doing); to impede: gli vietarono di parlare, they forbade him to speak (o he was forbidden to speak); gli vietarono il vino, they forbade him wine (o he was forbidden to drink wine); la legge non ti vieta di comperarlo, ma di venderlo, the law doesn't prohibit you from buying it, but from selling it; la legge vieta l'importazione di questi articoli, the law prohibits the importation of these articles; nulla ti vieta di partire, nothing prevents you from leaving.
vietàto, ag. forbidden, prohibited: piaceri vietati, forbidden pleasures ‖ vietata l'affissione, no bill-sticking (o stick no bills); — fumare, no smoking ‖ — entrare, no admittance; — ai minori di sedici anni, no admittance to under-sixteens (o adults only).

vièto, *ag.* **1.** (*antiquato*) antiquated; obsolete; old: *parole viete,* obsolete words; *procedure viete,* antiquated (*o* old) procedures **2.** (*stantio*) stale.

vigènte, *ag.* in force (*predicativo*): *legge* —, law in force.

vígere, *v.i.* to be in force, to be in use: *questa legge vige ancora,* this law is still in force; *questa usanza non vige più,* this custom is no longer in use (*o* has gone out of use).

vigèsimo, *ag. num.ord. s.m.* twentieth.

vigilànte, *ag.* vigilant, watchful, alert; on the look -out (*predicativo*), on the alert (*predicativo*).

vigilaménte, *av.* vigilantly, watchfully, alertly.

vigilànza, *s.f.* vigilance; watch; surveillance: *comitato di* —, watch committee; *esercitare* — *su qlcu.,* to watch over s.o. (*o* to keep a watch on s.o.); *evitare la* — *di qlcu.,* to avoid s.o.'s surveillance.

vigilàre, *v.t.* to watch over (s.o., sthg.), to keep a watch on (s.o., sthg.): *era vigilato da un poliziotto in borghese,* he was watched over by a plain-clothes detective; *i pastori vigilano le loro pecore,* the shepherds watch over their sheep; *vigila i bambini finchè torno,* watch (over) the children till I come back ‖ *v.i.* to be on the alert, to be on one's guard; to be on the look -out, to keep watch, to be on the watch: *c'erano tre soldati che vigilavano,* there were three soldiers on watch (*o* on guard); *vigila se vuoi che tutto vada bene,* be on the alert (*o* on the look-out *o* on the watch) if you want everything to be all right.

vigilàto, *ag.* watched.

vígile, *ag.* watchful, alert, vigilant ‖ *s.m.* **1.** (*di polizia urbana*) policeman (*pl.* policemen); (*sl.*) bobby; (*sl. amer.*) cop **2.** (*del fuoco*) fireman (*pl.* firemen): *i vigili del fuoco,* the fire-brigade **3.** (*guardia*) watch; watchman (*pl.* watchmen).

vigília, *s.f.* **1.** eve (anche *fig.*): *la* — *dei Santi,* All Hallow(s); *la* — *di Natale,* Christmas Eve; *alla* — *della battaglia,* on the eve of the battle; *è alla* — *del fallimento,* he is on the verge of bankruptcy; *si era alla* — *di grandi avvenimenti,* we were on the eve of great events **2.** (*eccl.*) (*digiuno*) fast; fasting: *giorno di* —, fast-day; *osservare la* —, to fast; *rompere la* —, to break one's fast **3.** (*st.*) watch ‖ — *d'armi,* (*st. medioevale*) vigil of arms **4.** *fig.* (*sentinella*) watch; watchman (*pl.* watchmen); sentry **5.** (*letter.*) (*veglia notturna*) watch, vigil.

vigliaccaménte, *av.* in a cowardly way, cravenly.

vigliaccheria, *s.f.* **1.** (*l'essere vigliacco*) cowardice, cowardliness **2.** (*azione da vigliacco*) cowardly action, mean action: *è una* — *bella e buona,* it's a real piece of cowardice.

vigliàcco, *ag.* cowardly, craven ‖ *s.m.* coward, craven.

vígna, *s.f.* **1.** vineyard ‖ *la* — *del Signore,* the vineyard of the Lord ‖ *non è terreno da piantar* —, *fig.* (*di persona non facilmente ingannabile*) he is not easily taken in; (*di cosa su cui non si può fare assegnamento*) you can't rely (*o* count) on that **2.** *fig.* (*cuccagna*) godsend: *questa è proprio la* — *!,* this is truly a godsend! **3.** (*st. romana*) vinea (*pl.* vineae).

vignaiuòlo, *s.m.* vine-dresser.

vignàto, *ag.* planted with vines.

vignéto, *s.m.* vineyard.

vignétta, *s.f.* cartoon, vignette, sketch.

vigógna, *s.f.* (*zool.*) vicuna ‖ *stoffa di* —, vicuna cloth).

vigóre, *s.m.* **1.** vigour; (*forza*) strength: *il* — *delle sue parole,* the vigour (*o* force) of his words; *lavorare con* —, to work with vigour (*o* to work hard); *riprendere* —, to recover strength **2.** (*dir.*): *in* —, in force: *questa legge è ancora in* —, this law is still in force; *entrare in* —, to come into force.

vigoreggiànte, *ag.* thriving; vigorous.

vigoreggiàre, *v.i.* **1.** (*prendere vigore*) to acquire strength **2.** (*essere vigoroso*) to be vigorous, to thrive.

vigoría, *s.f.* vigour, energy, vitality; (*forza*) strength.

vigorosaménte, *av.* vigorously, energetically; (*con forza*) strongly.

vigorosità, *s.f.* vigorousness, energy; (*forza*) strength.

vigoróso, *ag.* vigorous, energetic; (*forte*) strong, powerful: *un cavallo* —, a strong (*o* vigorous) horse; *un colpo* —, a powerful blow; *una pianta vigorosa,* a thriving tree; *uno stile* —, a vigorous style.

víle, *ag.* **1.** (*vigliacco*) cowardly, faint-hearted, pusillanimous: *in quell'occasione si mostrò* —, on that occasion he proved cowardly; *sarà timido ma non è* —, he may be shy but not cowardly **2.** (*meschino*) mean, vile, base: *c'è qlco. di* — *in lui,* there is sthg. base about him; *non c'è nulla di più* — *che...,* there is nothing baser than... ‖ *il vil metallo,* (*fam.*) filthy lucre **3.** (*basso*) low; humble: *di vili natali,* of humble origins (*o* of low birth); *l'ha venduto al* — *prezzo di...,* he sold it at the miserable price of... ‖ *s.c.* coward.

Vilfrèdo, *no.pr.m.* Wilfred, Wilfrid.

vilipèndere, *v.t.* to despise, to hold in contempt, to scorn.

vilipèndio, *s.m.* contempt, scorn, despite.

vilipéso, *ag.* despised, scorned.

vílla, *s.f.* " villa " (*pl.* villas); (*casa di campagna*) country-house; (*molto lussuosa*) country-seat.

villàggio, *s.m.* village; (*piccolo*) hamlet.

villàna, *s.f.* **1.** (*contadina*) country-woman (*pl.* country-women); peasant **2.** (*donna maleducata*) rude woman, ill-bred woman, boor: *è una bella* —, (*fam.*) she has no manners at all.

villanàccio, *s.m.* (*spreg.*) ill-bred fellow, boor.

villanaménte, *av.* rudely, impolitely, uncivilly, discourteously.

villanàta, *s.f.* (*atto da villano*) rude action; (*parola da villano*) rude word: *mi disse delle villanate,* he said rude things to me (*o* he spoke rudely to me *o* he insulted me).

villanèlla, *s.f.* **1.** country-girl, country-lass **2.** (*poes.*) villanelle **3.** (*musica, danza*) villanella (*pl.* villanelle).

villanèllo, *s.m.* country-boy, country-lad.

villanescaménte, *av.* boorishly, rudely.

villanésco, *ag.* boorish, rude.

villanía, *s.f.* **1.** rudeness; bad manners (*pl.*): *non posso sopportare la sua* —, I cannot stand his rudeness (*o* bad manners) **2.** (*azione da villano*) rude action; (*parola da villano*) rude word: *non fa che dire delle villanie alla gente,* he does nothing but say rude things to people (*o* he does nothing but insult people).

villàno, *ag.* rude, impolite, ill-mannered, uncivil, discourteous: *egli è molto* —, he is very rude (*o* impolite *o* uncivil); *fu molto* — *con me,* he was very rude (*o* impolite) to me; *non posso perdonare i suoi modi villani,* I cannot forgive his bad manners ‖ *s.m.* **1.** (*contadino*) countryman (*pl.* countrymen); peasant **2.** (*persona maleducata*) rude fellow, ill-bred fellow, boor ‖ *un* — *rifatto,* an upstart (*o* a parvenu).

villanzóna, *s.f.,* **villanzóne,** *s.m.* ill-bred person, rude person.

villeggiànte, *s.c.* holiday-maker, person on holiday; (*amer.*) vacationer, vacationist.

villeggiàre, *v.i.* to spend one's holidays: *dove andasti a* — *l'anno scorso?,* where did you (go and) spend your holidays last year?

villeggiatúra, *s.f.* holiday(s): *in* —, on holiday; *l'inizio, la fine della* —, the beginning, the end of the (summer) holidays; *luogo di* —, (holiday) resort; *luogo di* — *estiva, invernale,* summer, winter resort; *periodo di* —, holiday season; *feci una lunga* — *a Viareggio,* I took a long vacation at Viareggio; *sono andati a Rapallo in* —, they went to Rapallo to spend their holidays; *sono tornato dalla* — *la settimana scorsa,* I came back from my holidays last week.

villeréccio, *ag.* rustic, rural: *danza villereccia,* country dance; *usi villerecci,* rustic (*o* rural) customs.

víllico, *s.m.* villager; peasant, countryman (*pl.* countrymen), country people).

villíno, *s.m.* cottage; small villa.

víllo, *s.m.* (*anat.*) villus (*pl.* villi).

villosità, *s.f.* hairiness; shagginess.

villóso, *ag.* hairy; shaggy.

villòtta, *s.f.* (*musica, danza*) villota (*pl.* villote).

vilménte, *av.* 1. (da *vigliacco*) cowardly, faint -heartedly 2. (*meschinamente*) meanly, vilely, basely.

viltà, *s.f.* 1. (*vigliaccheria*) cowardice, faint-heartedness; (*azione da vigliacco*) cowardly action: *questa è una —,* this is a cowardly action 2. (*meschinità*) meanness, vileness; (*azione meschina*) mean action.

vilúcchio, *s.m.* (*bot.*) bearbind, bearbine.

vilúppo, *s.m.* 1. tangle; entanglement; ravel: *un — di corde, fili,* a tangle of strings, threads 2. *fig.* (*confusione*) confusion; intricacy.

vímine, *s.m.* withe, withy: *lavoro in vimini,* wicker -work; *paniere di vimini,* wicker (*o* osier) basket; *sedia di vimini,* wicker chair.

vináccia, *s.f.* dregs of pressed grapes (*pl.*).

vinacciuòlo, *s.m.* grape-stone.

vinàio, *s.m.* wine-merchant, vintner.

vinàrio, *ag.* wine (*attributivo*): *commercio —,* wine trade.

vincàstro, *s.m.* (sheperd's) crook.

vincènte, *ag.* winning: *numero —,* winning number || *s.m.* winner: *il — di una gara,* the winner of a race.

Vincènzo, *no.pr.m.* Vincent.

víncere, *v.t.* 1. to win: *gli ho vinto 2.000 lire al poker,* I won 2,000 liras from (*o* off) him at poker; *la sua gentilezza mi vinse,* I was won over by his kindness; *— una battaglia, una corsa,* to win a battle, a race; *— un concorso,* to win a competition; *— una guerra,* to win a war; *— per una lunghezza,* (*corse di cavalli*) to win by a length; *— un premio,* to win (*o* to carry off) a prize; *— una scommessa,* to win a bet 2. (*battere, sconfiggere*) to beat; to defeat: *l'ho vinto agli scacchi,* I have beaten him at chess; *— un concorrente,* to beat (*o* to outdo *o* to defeat) a competitor; *— il nemico,* to beat (*o* to defeat) the enemy 3. (*sopraffare*) to overcome: *fu vinto dall'ira,* he was overcome by anger; *fui vinto dal sonno, dalla paura,* I was overcome by sleep, by fear || *— ogni resistenza,* to overcome all resistance || *lasciarsi — dalla tentazione,* to yield to temptation (*o* to give way to temptation) 4. (*dominare*) to master: *— un cavallo,* to master a horse; *— le proprie passioni,* to master one's passions 5. (*conquistare*) to conquer, to vanquish 6. (*superare*) to outdo: *— qlcu. in gentilezza, in intelligenza,* to outdo s.o. in kindness, in intelligence || *v.i.* to win: *chi vinse?,* who won?; *il partito democratico ha vinto,* the democratic party has won || **víncersi,** *v.r.* (*dominarsi*) to control oneself: *quando è preso dalla collera non sa —,* when he is seized by anger he is unable to control himself.

vinchéto, *s.m.* osier-bed, osier-holt, osiery.

vincíbile, *ag.* conquerable, vanquishable.

víncido, *ag.* (*rar.*) (*floscio*) flabby.

vineíglio, *s.m.* 1. (*vinco*) withe, withy 2. (*vincastro*) (shepherd's) crook.

víncita, *s.f.* 1. win; winning: *dopo due vincite non volle più giocare,* after two wins he didn't want to play any more 2. (*denaro vinto*) winnings (*pl.*): *dividemmo la —,* we shared the winnings; *ho fatto una grossa — alla roulette,* I have won a good deal of money at roulette.

vincitóre, *ag.* winning, conquering, victorious: *l'esercito —,* the victorious army; *uscire — da una prova,* to undergo a test successfully || *s.m.* 1. (*al giuoco o in qualsiasi contesa*) winner, prize-winner 2. (*conquistatore*) conqueror, vanquisher, victor.

vincitríce, *s.f.* 1. (*al giuoco, ecc.*) winner, prize -winner 2. (*conquistatrice*) conqueress, victress.

vínco, *s.m.* withe, withy.

vincolàre, *v.t.* 1. to bind: *è vincolato da un contratto,* he is bound by a contract; *questa promessa li vincola,* this promise is binding on them 2. (*comm.*) to lock

up, to tie up: *— il proprio capitale,* to lock up (*o* to tie up) one's capital 3. (*mec.*) to constrain; to restrain.

víncolo, *s.m.* 1. tie, bond: *i vincoli del sangue, dell'amicizia,* the ties of blood, of friendship; *uno stretto — d'affetto,* a close bond of affection 2. (*mec. elett.*) constraint; restraint.

víndice, *ag.* (*letter.*) avenging, revenging || *s.c.* (*letter.*) avenger, revenger.

vínea, *s.f.* (*st. mil.*) vinea.

vinèllo, *s.m.* light wine.

vinícolo, *ag.* wine (*attributivo*): *industria vinicola,* wine industry; *mercato —,* wine market.

vinífero, *ag.* wine-producing, viniferous: *terreno —,* wine-producing soil.

vinificazióne, *s.f.* wine-making.

viníle, *s.m.* (*chim.*) vinyl.

víno, *s.m.* wine: *— bianco, rosso, secco, dolce, spumante,* white, red, dry, sweet, sparkling wine; *— brulè,* mulled wine; *— da bottiglia,* choice wine; *— da tavola,* table-wine; *— del Reno,* Rhine wine (*o* hock); *— di marca,* vintage wine; *— di mele,* cider; *— non spumante,* still wine; *— nostrano,* local wine; *commerciante di —,* wine-merchant (*o* vintner); *commercio di vini,* wine-trade; *far il —,* to make wine || *non sa portare il —,* he cannot carry his wine || *buon — fa buon sangue,* good wine makes people good-humoured || *il buon — non vuole frasca,* good wine needs no bush.

vinolènto, *ag.* (*letter.*) 1. (*che puzza di vino*) smelling of wine 2. (*ubriaco*) drunk (*predicativo*); drunken (*attributivo*); intoxicated, inebriate(d).

vinosità, *s.f.* vinosity.

vinóso, *ag.* vinous.

vínto, *ag.* 1. that has been won, that was won: *una battaglia vinta,* a victorious battle; *questo è il denaro —,* these are the winnings || *non gliela darò vinta,* I won't let him have it all his own way 2. (*sconfitto*) beaten, defeated: *il nemico —,* the beaten (*o* defeated) enemy || *darsi —,* to give in (*o* to surrender) 3. (*sopraffatto*) overcome: *— dal sonno,* overcome by sleep 4. (*conquistato*) conquered, vanquished || *s.m.* (*al giuoco o in qualsiasi contesa*) loser; (*in battaglia*) vanquished man || *i vinti,* the vanquished.

viòla¹, *ag. s.m.* (*colore*) violet || *s.f.* (*bot.*) violet: *— del pensiero,* pansy.

viòla², *s.f.* (*mus.*) viola.

violàbile, *ag.* violable.

violacciòca, *s.f.* (*bot.*) wallflower.

violàcee, *s.f.pl.* (*bot.*) Violaceae.

violàceo, *ag.* violaceous, violet.

violàre, *v.t.* 1. to violate, to transgress, to infringe: *— un accordo,* to violate an agreement; *— un giuramento,* to violate (*o* to infringe) an oath; *— una legge,* to violate (*o* to transgress *o* to infringe) a law; *— un segreto,* to violate a pledge of secrecy || *— il domicilio di qlcu.,* to enter s.o.'s house illegally 2. (*profanare*) to violate, to profane, to desecrate: *— un luogo sacro,* to violate (*o* to profane) a sacred place.

violatóre, *s.m.,* **violatríce,** *s.f.* 1. violator; transgressor 2. (*chi profana*) profaner, desecrator.

violazióne, *s.f.* 1. violation, transgression || *— di domicilio,* house-breaking 2. (*profanazione*) profanation.

violentàre, *v.t.* 1. to rape, to violate, to ravish: *— una donna,* to rape (*o* to violate *o* to ravish) a woman 2. *fig.* to do violence to (s.o., sthg.): *— i sentimenti di qlcu.,* to do violence to s.o.'s feelings.

violenteménte, *av.* violently.

violènto, *ag.* violent: *carattere —,* violent temper; *colpo, vento —,* violent blow, wind; *parole violente,* violent words; *ho un — mal di capo,* I have a violent headache; *morire di morte violenta,* to die a violent death || *s.m.* violent fellow.

violènza, *s.f.* violence: *la — di un colpo, di una passione,* the violence of a blow, of a passion; *la — di un temporale,* the violence of a storm; *far — a* *qlcu.*, *ai sentimenti di qlcu.*, to do violence to s.o., to s.o.'s feelings.

violétta, *s.f.* (*bot.*) sweet violet.

violétto, *ag.s.m.* violet.

violinàio, *s.m.* violin-maker.

violinísta, *s.c.* violinist, violin-player.

violíno, *s.m.* violin; (*fam.*) fiddle: *chiave di —*, violin clef; *primo, secondo —*, first, second violin; *è il primo — della Scala*, he is the first violin at La Scala; *suonare il —*, to play the violin.

violoncellísta, *s.c.* violoncellist, 'cellist.

violoncèllo, *s.m.* (*mus.*) violoncello, (*pl.* violoncellos), 'cello (*pl.* 'cellos).

violóne, *s.m.* (*mus.*) violone.

viòttola, *s.f.*, **viòttolo**, *s.m.* path; lane: *un(a) — tra i boschi*, a path through the woods.

vípera, *s.f.* **1.** (*zool.*) viper, adder **2.** *fig.* (*persona maligna*) viper: *quella donna è una —*, that woman is a viper.

viperàio, *s.m.* nest of vipers.

vipèreo, *ag.* viperine, viperous (anche *fig.*).

vipèridi, *s.m.pl.* (*zool.*) Viperidae.

viperíno, *ag.* viperine; viperous (anche *fig.*): *lingua viperina*, viperous (o venomous) tongue.

viràggio, *s.m.* **1.** (*foto.*) toning **2.** (*chim.*) colour change **3.** (*mar.*) veering; tacking.

viràgine, **viràgo**, *s.f.* (*letter.*) virago (*pl.* viragoes, viragos).

viràre, *v.t.* **1.** (*mar.*) to veer; to tack: *— di bordo*, to veer round; *fig.* to turn about **2.** (*aer.*) to turn **3.** (*foto.*) to tone **4.** (*chim.*) to change colour.

viràta, *s.f.* **1.** (*mar.*) veer; tacking **2.** (*aer.*) turn: *— ad ampio raggio*, gentle turn.

virènte, *ag.* (*poet.*) verdant.

virescènza, *s.f.* (*bot.*) virescence.

virgiliàno, *ag.* Virgilian.

Virgílio, *no.pr.m.* (*st. lett.*) Virgil.

virginàle, **virgíneo**, *V.* **verginàle**, **vergíneo**.

Virgínia[1], *no.pr.f.* Virginia ‖ (*geog.*) Virginia.

virgínia[2], *s.m.* (*tabacco*) Virginia; (*sigaro*) Virginia cigar.

Virgínio, *no.pr.m.* Virginius.

vírgola, *s.f.* **1.** (*gram.*) comma: *punto e —*, semicolon ‖ *bacillo —*, (*biol.*) comma bacillus ‖ *non ho cambiato una —, fig.* I didn't change a single word **2.** (*mat.*) point: *quattro — cinque*, four point five.

virgolàre, *v.t.* **1.** to mark with commas **2.** (*mettere le virgolette a*) to insert inverted commas in (sthg.).

virgolatúra, *s.f.* punctuation.

virgolétte, *s.f.pl.* inverted commas, quotation marks: *tra —*, in inverted commas.

virgúlto, *s.m.* (*bot.*) shoot, sucker.

viridàrio, *s.m.* (*archeol.*) viridarium (*pl.* viridaria).

viríle, *ag.* manly, virile, manlike: *coraggio —*, manlike courage; *età, forza —*, virile age, strength; *modi virili*, manly manners; *uno stile —*, a virile style; *voce —*, manly voice ‖ *età —*, manhood ‖ *porzione —*, (*dir.*) lawful share ‖ *toga —*, (*st. romana*) toga virilis.

virilità, *s.f.* **1.** manliness, virility **2.** (*età virile*) manhood.

virilménte, *av.* manfully, in a manly manner.

virtú, *s.f.* **1.** virtue: *la via della —*, the path of virtue; *esercitare la —*, to practise virtue ‖ *la — è premio a se stessa*, virtue is its own reward ‖ *fare di necessità —*, to make a virtue of necessity **2.** (*pregio, merito*) virtue: *quella donna ha la — di saper tacere*, that woman has the virtue of being able to keep silent **3.** (*facoltà, proprietà*) virtue, efficacy, power: *le — medicinali di certe piante*, the healing virtues (o properties) of some plants; *la — di certe acque di curare disturbi di fegato*, the virtue of certain waters to cure liver troubles ‖ *in — di*, by (o in) virtue of: *in — della mia esperienza*, in virtue of my own experience; *in — di quel trattato*, under that agreement **4.** (*forza, vigore*) strength, vigour **5.** (*valor militare*) valour **6.** (*teol.*)

virtue: *le — cardinali, teologiche*, the cardinal, theological (o Christian) virtues **7.** *pl.* (*quinta gerarchia degli angeli*) Virtues.

virtuàle, *ag.* virtual.

virtualità, *s.f.* virtuality.

virtualménte, *av.* virtually.

virtuosaménte, *av.* virtuously.

virtuosísmo, *s.m.* virtuosity.

virtuosità, *s.f.* **1.** virtuousness **2.** (*virtuosismo*) virtuosity.

virtuóso, *ag.* virtuous: *azione, donna virtuosa*, virtuous action, woman ‖ *s.m.* **1.** virtuous man **2.** (*art. mus.*) virtuoso (*pl.* virtuosos, virtuosi).

virulènto, *ag.* virulent (anche *fig.*): *virulent disease*; *una satira virulenta*, a virulent satire.

virulènza, *s.f.* virulence (anche *fig.*).

vírus, *s.m.* (*med.*) virus.

vis-à-vis, *av.* face to face: *eravamo seduti —*, we were sitting face to face ‖ *prep.* opposite (s.o., sthg.), facing (s.o., sthg.) ‖ *s.m.* vis-à-vis; opposite number.

visceràle, *ag.* visceral.

víscere, *s.m.*; *pl.m.* **vísceri** (*net sensi* **1.** **2.**); *pl.f.* **víscere** (*nei sensi* **3.** **4.** **5.**) **1.** vital organ, internal organ **2.** *pl.* viscera: *il cuore, i polmoni, gli intestini sono visceri*, the heart, the lungs, the intestines are viscera **3.** *pl.* (*intestini*) bowels, intestines; (*di animale*) entrails: *essere malato di —*, to have intestinal troubles **4.** *pl.* (*grembo materno*) womb (*sing.*) **5.** *pl. fig.* (*la parte più interna di ql.co.*) bowels: *le viscere della terra*, the bowels of the earth.

víschio, *s.m.* **1.** (*bot.*) mistletoe **2.** (*sostanza appiccicosa*) bird-lime **3.** *fig.* (*inganno*) snare, trap.

vischióso, *ag.* viscous, sticky, slimy.

viscidézza, viscidità, *s.f.* viscidity, stickiness.

víscido, *ag.* **1.** (*attaccaticcio*) viscid, sticky, slimy **2.** (*scivoloso*) slippery.

viscidúme, *s.m.* mass of sticky stuff.

vísciola, *s.f.* (*bot.*) wild cherry.

vísciolo, *s.m.* (*bot.*) wild-cherry tree.

vis còmica, *s.f.* vis comica, comic power.

viscontàdo, *s.m.* viscounty.

viscónte, *s.m.* viscount.

viscontéssa, *s.f.* viscountess.

viscósa, *s.f.* (*chim.*) viscose.

viscosità, *s.f.* viscosity, stickiness.

viscóso, *ag.* viscous, sticky, slimy.

visíbile, *ag.* visible; (*evidente*) clear, evident.

visíbilio, *s.m.* great number, profusion: *un — di cose*, a great number of things ‖ *andare, mandare in —*, to go, to throw into raptures.

visibilità, *s.f.* visibility.

visibilménte, *av.* visibly; *fig.* (*in modo evidente, manifesto*) clearly, evidently, openly.

visièra, *s.f.* **1.** (*di elmo*) visor, vizor, visard, vizard **2.** (*di berretto*) peak; visor **3.** (*maschera da scherma*) fencing mask.

visigòtico, *ag.* Visigothic.

Visigòto, *s.m.* Visigoth.

visionàrio, *ag.s.m.* visionary.

visióne, *s.f.* vision: *— di ricchezza, felicità*, vision of wealth, happiness; *campo di —*, field of vision; *avere una — pessimistica della vita*, to have a pessimistic vision of (o a pessimistic outlook on) life; *avere delle visioni*, to have (o to see) visions ‖ *prendere — di ql.co.*, to look over (o into) sthg. ‖ *prima —*, (*cine.*) first screening (o *amer.* first view).

visir, *s.m.* vizi(e)r: *gran —*, Grand Vizier.

vísita, *s.f.* **1.** visit; (*breve*) call: *una — a un malato*, a visit to a patient; *una — a un museo, a una chiesa*, a visit to a museum, to a church; *— di cortesia*, courtesy visit; *ore di —*, visiting hours; *ci fa una breve — tutte le sere*, he looks in (o *fam.* pops in) every evening; *ero in — da un amico*, I was on a visit to a friend of mine; *fare una — a qlcu.*, to pay s.o. a visit (o to call on s.o.); *fare una breve —, una visitina*, to make a call; *scambiarsi visite*, to exchange visits ‖ — *doganale*, customs examinations ‖ — *turistica*, sightseeing ‖ *biglietto da* —, visiting card ‖ — *della Vergine a Santa Elisabetta*, (*relig.*) Visitation of the Virgin to St. Elizabeth **2.** (*persona che visita*) visitor, caller: *ho avuto due visite ieri*, I had two visitors yesterday **3.** (*med.*) examination: — *medica*, medical examination; (*mil.*) medical inspection: *sottoporsi a* — *medica*, to undergo (*o* to have) a medical examination (*o* to be medically examined); *giro di visite*, round of visits; *il dottore è in giro per visite*, the doctor is going on his round; *quanto prende quel medico per* — *?*, what is that doctor's fee for a visit?; *subire una* — *agli occhi*, to have one's eyes tested ‖ *passar* —, (*mil.*) to go before the medical officer **4.** (*eccl.*) visitation: — *pastorale*, pastoral visitation.

visitàre, *v.t.* **1.** to visit: *ho visitato tutte le stanze della casa*, I have been into every room of the house; *il nuovo direttore ha visitato la scuola*, the new headmaster has visited the school; — *una città, un paese, un museo*, to visit a city, a country, a museum; *andare a* — *le bellezze di una città*, to go sight-seeing (*o* to go to see the sights of a city) ‖ *fecero* — *la casa agli amici*, the friends were shown over the house **2.** (*andare a trovare*) to visit, to pay a visit to (*s.o.*), to see; to call on (*s.o.*): *vado a* — *tuo padre ogni tanto*, I go and see your father now and then; *venne qui a* — *i suoi parenti*, he came here to visit his relatives; — *i poveri*, to visit the poor ‖ *la sventura ci ha visitati*, misfortune has befallen (*o* has come upon) us **3.** (*med.*) to visit, to examine: *il dottore è venuto a* — *il malato*, the doctor has come to visit the patient; *mi visitò accuratamente*, he examined me carefully.

visitatóre, *s.m.*, **visitatríce**, *s.f.* visitor: *i visitatori di uno zoo*, the visitors to a zoo.

visitazióne, *s.f.* (*relig.*) Visitation.

visìvo, *ag.* visual, of vision: *angolo* —, visual angle; *campo* —, field of vision (*o* visual field); *facoltà visiva*, faculty of vision (*o* sight); *memoria, impressione visiva*, visual memory, impression; *raggi visivi*, visual rays.

vìso, *s.m.* face: *un* — *sorridente, radioso, scuro*, a smiling, radiant, gloomy (*o* sullen) face; *non mi è un* — *nuovo*, it is not an unknown face to me; *accendersi in* —, to grow red in the face (*o* to flush); *guardare qlcu. in* —, to look s.o. in the face; *lavarsi il* —, to wash one's face ‖ — *a* —, face to face ‖ *dire ql.co. sul* —, to say sthg. to s.o.'s face ‖ *fare il* — *lungo*, to pull a long face ‖ *fare buon* — *a cattiva sorte*, to make the best of a bad bargain (*o* to take the rough with the smooth); *fare buon* — *a una cosa sgradevole*, to put a good (*o* bold) face on an unpleasant thing ‖ *ridere in* — *a qlcu.*, to laugh in s.o.'s face.

visóne, *s.m.* (*zool.*) mink: *pelliccia di* —, mink coat.

vispézza, *s.f.* liveliness, briskness, sprightliness.

vìspo, *ag.* lively, sprightly, brisk: *un* — *vecchietto*, a sprightly old man; *quel bimbo è molto* —, that child is very lively.

vissùto, *ag.* lived: — *a lungo*, long-lived; — *per breve tempo*, short-lived ‖ *racconti di vita vissuta*, stories taken from real life (*o* from personal experience) ‖ *un uomo* —, a man of the world.

vìsta, *s.f.* **1.** sight: *gli organi della* —, the organs of sight; *alla* — *del sangue ella svenne*, she fainted at the sight of blood; *avere una* — *buona, cattiva*, to have good, bad sight; *avere la* — *corta*, to have short sight (*o* to be short-sighted) (anche *fig.*); *avere la* — *lunga*, to have long sight (anche *fig.*); *fig.* to have second sight; *perdere la* —, to lose one's sight (*o* to become blind) ‖ *a prima* —, at first sight: *amore a prima* —, love at first sight; *suonare a prima* —, to play at sight ‖ *in* — *di*, considering (*o* in view of): *in* — *delle sue condizioni di salute*, considering his health ‖ *punto di* —, point of view ‖ *è una persona molto in* —, he is a very well-known person ‖ *ho in* — *ql.co. di interessante*, I have sthg. interesting in

view ‖ *conoscere qlcu. di* —, to know s.o. by sight ‖ *crescere a* — *d'occhio*, to grow under s.o.'s eyes ‖ *far* — *di non capire*, to pretend not to understand **2.** (*occhi*) eyes (*pl.*): *smetto di leggere perchè ho la* — *stanca*, I am stopping reading because my eyes are tired **3.** (*veduta*) sight, view: *le Alpi sono una delle più belle viste del mondo*, the Alps are one of the most beautiful sights in the world; *la casa ha una bella* — *sulla baia*, the house has a fine view over the bay ‖ *far bella* —, to show **4.** (*campo visivo*) view: *tieni in* — *queste carte*, keep these papers in view; *perdere di* —, to lose sight of **5.** (*comm.*) sight: *a 30 giorni* —, 30 days after sight; *cambiale a* — *sight bill*; *pagabile a* —, payable at sight.

vistàre, *v.t.* to visé, to visa: — *un passaporto*, to visé (*o* to visa) a passport.

vìsto, *ag.* seen: *non* —, unseen, unnoticed ‖ *vista la sua buona volontà gli diedero un premio*, in consideration of his good will they gave him a prize; — *che non lo vuoi lo dò a lui*, as you don't want it I shall give it to him ‖ *è ben* — *da tutti*, he is popular with everybody (*o* he is well liked by everybody); *è mal* — *da tutti*, he is disliked by everybody (*o* everybody dislikes him) ‖ *s.m.* visé, visa: *mettere il* — *a un passaporto*, to visé (*o* to visa) a passport.

Vìstola, *no.pr.f.* (*geog.*) Vistula.

vistosità, *s.f.* showiness, gaudiness.

vistóso, *ag.* **1.** showy, gaudy: *abito* —, showy dress; *colore* —, gaudy colour **2.** *fig.* (*grande*) big, considerable, large: *una somma vistosa*, a considerable sum.

visuàle, *ag.* visual: *angolo* —, visual angle ‖ *s.f.* **1.** (*vista, panorama*) sight, view **2.** (*campo visivo*) view, field of vision ‖ — *ravvicinata*, (*cine.*) close up.

vìta, *s.f.* **1.** life (*pl.* lives): — *animale, vegetale*, animal, plant life; *la* — *dell'anima*, the life of the soul; *la* — *eterna*, eternal life; — *terrena*, life on earth; *l'altra* —, *questa* —, the other life, this life; *assicurazione sulla* —, life-assurance; *lotta per la* —, struggle for life; *i piaceri della* —, the pleasures of life; *la* — *è piena di sorprese*, life is full of surprises; *è in giuoco la sua* —, his life is at stake; *è questione di* — *o di morte*, it is a question (*o* matter) of life and death; *lo giuro sulla mia* —, I swear it on my life; *dare la* — *per una causa*, to give one's life for a cause; *essere ancora in* —, to be still alive (*o* living); *essere tra la* — *e la morte*, to be between life and death; *richiamare in* — *qlcu.*, to bring s.o. back to life; *salvare la* — *a qlcu.*, to save s.o.'s life; *togliersi la* —, to take one's own life (*o* to commit suicide *o* to kill oneself); *l'aria e la luce sono la nostra* —, air and light are (*o* mean) life to us; *la pubblicità è la* — *del commercio*, publicity is indispensable to trade ‖ *essere attaccati alla* —, to love life ‖ *non dar segno di* —, not to show any sign of life (anche *fig.*) ‖ *passare a miglior* —, to pass away (*o* to breathe one's last) ‖ *vendere cara la propria* —, to sell one's life dearly ‖ *finchè c'è* —, *c'è speranza*, *prov.* while there's life there's hope **2.** (*periodo di vita*) life; (*durata di una vita*) lifetime: — *lunga*, long life; *durante la sua* —, during his lifetime; *tutta una* — *di felicità*, a lifetime of happiness; *capita solo una volta nella* —, it happens only once in a lifetime; *non l'ho mai fatto in* — *mia*, I have never done it in my life; *quel giornale ha avuto* — *breve*, that newspaper had short life; *essere menomato per la* —, to be maimed for life ‖ — *natural durante*, for one's natural life ‖ *a* — for life: *essere condannato a* —, to be given a life sentence; *pensione a* —, life pension ‖ *in* —, during one's life: *in* — *non è stato un gran che*, during his lifetime he wasn't up to much; *in* — *non ebbe molto successo*, while he lived he wasn't a great success ‖ *per la* —, for life: *sono amici per la* —, they are very close friends **3.** (*modo di vivere*) life, existence: — *di campagna, di città*, country, town life; *una* — *misera*, a miserable existence; *tenore di* —, standard of living (*o* living standard); *cam-*

biare —, to mend one's ways; *condurre una — tranquilla*, to lead a quiet life; *vivere una — disordinata, monotona*, to live (o to lead) a disorderly, dull life || *— da cani*, dog's life || *che* —!, what a life! || *come va la* —?, how's life? (o how are you getting on?) || *so* —, *morte e miracoli di quell'uomo*, I know everything about that man || *fare la — del gran signore*, to live like a lord || *poca brigata — beata, prov.* the fewer the better **4.** (*il necessario per vivere*) living, livelihood: *il costo della — sta salendo*, the cost of living is rising; *riesce a stento, a fatica a guadagnarsi la* —, he can hardly make a living (o make ends meet); *si guadagna la — insegnando*, he earns his living by teaching; *si guadagna onestamente la* —, he earns an honest living **5.** (*vitalità*) vitality, life; (*animazione*) animation: *città, strada piena di* —, town, street full of life; *commedia che manca di* —, play that lacks vitality; *musica piena di* —, music full of vitality; *senza* —, lifeless; *stile privo di* —, lifeless style; *è piena di* —, she is full of life (o bubbling over with vitality); *dar — a una festa*, to liven up a party **6.** (*essere, persona*) life (*pl.* lives): *la guerra costa molte vite*, war costs many lives; *non c'era traccia di — per le strade*, there was no sign of life in the streets; *non si lamenta alcuna perdita di vite umane*, no lives were lost (o there was no loss of life) **7.** (*parte del corpo*) waist: *— di vespa*, wasp-waist; *una — stretta, larga*, a slender, thick waist; *intorno alla* —, round the waist; *prendere qlcu. per la* —, to seize s.o. by the waist **8.** (*biografia*) life (*pl.* lives), biography: *hai letto le vite di Plutarco?*, have you read Plutarch's lives?.

vitàccia, *s.f.* wretched life, miserable life.

vitaiuòlo, *s.m.* (*chi fa bella vita*) bon viveur.

vitàlba, *s.f.* (*bot.*) traveller's joy, clematis.

vitàle, *ag.* **1.** vital (anche *fig.*): *di — importanza*, of vital importance; *forza* —, vital force; *parte* —, vital part **2.** (*di neonato*) viable.

vitalità, *s.f.* **1.** vitality **2.** (*di neonato*) viability.

vitalízio, *ag.* (lasting) for life; life (*attributivo*): *socio* —, life member; *pensione vitalizia*, pension for life || *Camera Vitalizia*, (*st.*) Senate || *s.m.* (life) annuity: *fare un* —, to take out a life annuity.

vitalménte, *av.* vitally.

vitamína, *s.f.* vitamin(e).

vitamínico, *ag.* vitaminic.

vitaminología, *s.f.* vitaminology.

víte[1], *s.f.* (*bot.*) vine: *potare le viti*, to prune vines.

víte[2], *s.f.* (*mec.*) screw: *— a legno*, woodscrew (o screw nail); *— di avanzamento*, feeding screw; *— maschio, femmina*, male, female screw; *— perpetua*, endless (o perpetual) screw; *giro di* —, turn of screw; *la — è lenta*, the screw is loose; *allentare una* —, to loosen a screw.

vitèlla, *s.f.* heifer.

vitèllo, *s.m.* **1.** calf (*pl.* calves): *questo — nacque l'anno scorso*, this calf was born last year || *— marino*, (*zool.*) sea-calf **2.** (*cuc.*) veal: *cotolette di* —, veal cutlets.

vitíccio, *s.m.* (*bot.*) vine-tendril.

vitícolo, *ag.* viticultural.

viticoltóre, *s.m.* viticulturist, viticulturer, vine-grower.

viticoltúra, *s.f.* grape-growing, viticulture.

vitífero, *ag.* vine-bearing.

vítreo, *ag.* vitreous, glassy: *uno sguardo* —, a glassy look; *umor* —, (*anat.*) vitreous humour.

vitriòlo, *e derivati*, *V.* **vetri(u)òlo**, *e derivati*.

Vitrúvio, *no.pr.m.* (*st. romana*) Vitruvius.

víttima, *s.f.* victim: *una — del dovere*, a victim of one's duty; *le vittime di un'epidemia, di un bombardamento aereo*, the victims of an epidemic, of an air-raid; *egli è — del suo ambiente*, he is a victim to his environment; *egli fu — della sua ambizione*, he was (o fell) a victim to his ambition; *sacrificare una — a un dio*, to sacrifice a victim to a god.

vittimísmo, *s.m.* victimization.

vítto, *s.m.* **1.** (*cibo*) food; provisions (*pl.*): *un — sano, malsano*, a wholesome, unwholesome food; *il — è molto caro in questo paese*, food is very expensive in this country; *ho speso 50.000 lire in* —, I have spent 50,000 lire on food (o provisions) **2.** (*pasti consumati in una pensione, albergo*) board: *quanto fate per — e alloggio?*, how much do you charge for board and lodging?; *quanto pagavi per il* —?, how much did you pay for board?.

Vittóre, *no.pr.m.* Victor.

vittòria[1], *s.f.* **1.** victory; triumph; success: *una — schiacciante*, an overwhelming victory; *la dea della* —, the goddess of victory; *conseguire una — sul nemico*, to gain (o to win) a victory over the enemy || *— di Pirro*, Pyrrhic victory || *cantar* —, to crow (over a victory): *non cantar — prima del tempo*, don't count your chickens before they are hatched **2.** (*spor.*) win.

vittòria[2], *s.f.* (*carrozza a quattro ruote*) victoria.

Vittòria[3], *no.pr.f.* Victoria.

vittoriàle, *ag.* (*letter.*) triumphal.

Vittòrio, *no.pr.m.* Victor.

vittoriosaménte, *av.* victoriously.

vittorióso, *ag.* victorious; (*rar.*) victor (*attributivo*): *l'esercito* —, the victorious army.

vituperàbile, **vituperàndo**, *V.* **vituperévole**.

vituperàre, *v.t.* to vituperate, to revile; (*disonorare*) to disgrace.

vituperatívo, *ag.* vituperative.

vituperatóre, *ag.* vituperating || *s.m.*, **vituperatríce**, *s.f.* vituperator.

vituperazióne, *s.f.* vituperation.

vituperévole, *ag.* contemptible; ignominious, shameful.

vitupèrio, *s.m.* **1.** (*insulto*) insult: *mi accolse con una serie di vituperi*, he greeted me with a shower of insults **2.** (*disonore*) shame, disgrace: *è il — della sua famiglia*, he is the shame (o disgrace) of his family.

vituperosaménte, *av.* shamefully, disgracefully, ignominiously, despicably.

vituperóso, *ag.* shameful, disgraceful, ignominious, despicable: *atti vituperosi*, shameful actions.

viúzza, *s.f.* lane; alley.

víva, *inter.* hurrah, hurray: *— l'allegria!*, let us be merry!; *— il Re, la Regina!*, long live the King, the Queen!; *— il vincitore!*, hurrah (o three cheers) for the winner!.

vivacchiàre, *v.i.* (*vivere poveramente*) to live poorly; to get a bare living; (*tirare avanti*) to get along, to rub along.

vivàce, *ag.* **1.** (*pieno di vita, brio*) lively, sprightly, vivacious; (*sl. amer.*) live (*attributivo*): *una — descrizione*, a lively description; *una — discussione*, a lively (o live) discussion; *un bambino* —, a lively (o live) child; *immaginazione, espressione* —, lively imagination, expression; *il suo modo — di raccontare le cose*, his lively way of telling things; *questo bambino è molto* —, this child is very lively (o vivacious) **2.** (*pronto, sveglio*) quick: *intelligenza* —, quick understanding **3.** (*vivo, gaio*) bright, lively: *colore* —, bright (o lively) colour.

vivaceménte, *av.* **1.** (*in modo brioso*) lively, vivaciously **2.** (*prontamente*) quickly **3.** (*vivamente, gaiamente*) brightly; gaily.

vivacità, *s.f.* **1.** liveliness, sprightliness, vivacity **2.** (*prontezza*) quickness **3.** (*gaiezza*) brightness.

vivaddío, *inter.* by God!, upon my word!.

vivàgno, *s.m.* (*cimosa*) selvage, selvedge.

vivàio, *s.m.* (*di pesci*) fish-pond; fish-preserve; (*di piante*) nursery: *— forestale*, seedling nursery.

vivaménte, *av.* **1.** (*profondamente*) deeply; keenly, acutely: *siamo — commossi*, we are deeply touched **2.** (*con interesse*) keenly: *le notizie erano — attese*, the news was keenly waited for **3.** (*caldamente*) warmly, heartily:

vi ringrazio —, I thank you heartily (*o* warmly) **4.** (*fortemente*) strongly.

vivànda, *s.f.* **1.** (*cibo*) food; victuals (*pl.*): *vivande conservate,* tinned foods; *vivande delicate,* choice viands; *vivande semplici,* plain food; *un arnese per tener calde le vivande,* a device for keeping food warm; *preparare le vivande per la tavola,* to prepare food for the table **2.** (*pietanza, piatto*) dish: *la trota bollita è un'ottima* —, boiled trout is a very good dish.

vivandièra, *s.f.* (*mil.*) sutler, vivandière.

vivandière, *s.m.* (*mil.*) sutler.

vivènte, *ag.* alive (*predicativo*), living: *un essere* —, a living being (*o* creature); *il miglior direttore d'orchestra* —, the greatest living conductor; *è ancora* —, he is still alive; *è l'immagine* — *di suo nonno,* he is the living (*o* the spitten) image of his grandfather ‖ *lingua* —, modern language ‖ *non c'era anima* —, there was not a living soul ‖ *s.m.* living being.

vívere, *v.i.* **1.** to live: *il dottore crede che non vivrà più di due giorni,* the doctor thinks he will not live longer (*o* more) than two days; *egli vive ancora,* he is still living (*o* he is still alive); *le farfalle non vivono a lungo,* butterflies are short-lived; *i pappagalli vivono a lungo,* parrots are long-lived; *cessare di* —, to die; *essere stanco di* —, to be tired of life; — *fino a tarda età,* to live to a great age (*o* to live to be very old) ‖ *viva la Regina!,* long live the Queen! ‖ *possa egli* — *a lungo!,* may he live long! ‖ *chi vivrà vedrà,* time will show **2.** (*campare, passare la vita*) to live (on, by sthg.): *non guadagno abbastanza per* —, I don't earn (*o* make) enough to live on; *riesce a stento a guadagnarsi da* —, he can hardly make a living (*o* make ends meet); — *bene,* to live in comfort (*o* to live well); — *da gran signore,* to live like a lord; — *del proprio lavoro, della propria penna,* to live by one's work, by one's pen; — *dello stretto necessario,* to live sparingly; — *di espedienti,* to live by one's wits; — *di rendita,* to live on a private income; — *di elemosina, speranze,* to live on alms, hopes; — *modestamente,* to live modestly; — *nel peccato,* to live in sin; — *onestamente,* to live honestly (*o* to live an honest life); — *secondo le proprie entrate,* to live within one's income; *aver di che* —, to have enough to live on; *insegnare a* — *a qlcu.,* to teach s.o. good (*o* better) manners; *lavorare per* —, to work for one's living; *saper* —, to know how to get on in life; (*sapersi comportare*) to know how to behave ‖ — *alla giornata,* to live from hand to mouth ‖ — *alle spalle di qlcu.,* to sponge on s.o. ‖ — *d'aria,* to live on air ‖ — *del sudore della propria fronte,* to live by the sweat of one's brow ‖ *come si vive così si muore,* prov. as we live so shall we die ‖ — *e lasciar* —, prov. to live and let live **3.** (*abitare*) to live: *vivo a Roma,* I live in Rome; *vivo qui da quasi due anni,* I have been living here (for) almost two years; — *con qlcu.,* to live (*o* to keep house) with s.o. (*o* to cohabit with s.o.) **4.** (*durare*) to live (on), to last, to endure: *opera che vivrà,* work that will live (*o* endure); *il suo nome vivrà,* his name will live (on); *tradizioni che vivono ancora,* traditions that are still alive ‖ *v.t.* to live: *le vicende che egli visse,* the events he lived through; — *una vita tranquilla,* to live a quiet life.

vívere, *s.m.* life, living; (*modo di vivere*) way of living: *il* — *degli antichi,* the way of living of the ancients ‖ *per amore del quieto* —, for the sake of a quiet life.

víveri, *s.m.pl.* victuals, provisions; supplies: *i* — *erano scarsi,* victuals were running short; *gli tagliarono i* —, they cut off (*o* stopped) his supplies; *mancavamo di* —, we were short of provisions; *provvedere una nave, un esercito di* —, to victual a ship, an army.

viveur, *s.m.* rake; man about town; man who goes the pace.

vivèrra, *s.m.* (*zool.*) civet-cat.

vivézza, *s.f.* **1.** (*vivacità*) liveliness, sprightliness: — *di conversazione,* liveliness of conversation; — *d'in-*

gegno, quick-wittedness (*o* readiness of mind) **2.** (*di colori*) brightness, liveliness, vividness.

Viviàna, *no.pr.f.* Vivian.

Viviàno, *no.pr.m.* Vivian.

vívido, *ag.* vivid: *una vivida descrizione, immaginazione,* a vivid description, imagination.

vivifieànte, *ag.* enlivening, vivifying; (*di aria*) invigorating.

vivifieàre, *v.t.* to enliven, to give life to (s.o., sthg.) (anche *fig.*): *il sole vivifica la natura,* the sun gives life to nature; — *il commercio, l'industria,* to enliven trade, industry.

vivifieatívo, *ag.* vivifying.

vivifieatóre, *ag.* vivifying ‖ *s.m.*, **vivifieatríce,** *s.f.,* vivifier.

vivifieazióne, *s.f.* enlivening, vivification.

vivífieo, *ag.* (*letter.*) vivifying.

vivíparo, *ag.* viviparous.

visezióne, *s.f.* vivisection: *fare la* — *di un animale,* to vivisect an animal.

vívo, *ag.* **1.** living; alive (*predicativo*); live (*attributivo*): *è ancora* —, he is still living; *fu sepolto* —, he was buried alive; *la pianta è ancora viva,* the plant is still living; *nascere* —, to be born alive ‖ *a viva forza,* by main (*o* sheer) force ‖ *acqua viva,* running water ‖ *anima viva,* living soul: *non c'era anima viva,* there was not a living soul ‖ *argento* —, quicksilver: *aver l'argento* —, fig. to be like an eel ‖ *calce viva,* quick-lime ‖ *le lingue vive,* the modern languages ‖ *peso* —, live weight ‖ *roccia viva,* live (*o* living) rock ‖ *siepe viva,* quickset hedge ‖ *vapore* —, live steam ‖ *l'ho sentito dalla sua viva voce,* I heard it from him in person ‖ *questo è un problema ancora* — *nel nostro paese,* this is still a live issue in our country ‖ *tieni* — *il fuoco,* keep the fire in ‖ *trovi questa espressione solo nella lingua viva,* you find this expression only in the spoken language ‖ *farsi* —, to turn up: *fatevi* — *ogni tanto,* come and see us now and then; *non si fa* — *da due mesi,* he hasn't given any news of himself for two months; *si fece* — *improvvisamente,* he suddenly turned up **2.** (*vivace*) lively, sprightly; (*animato*) animated: *una viva discussione,* a lively (*o* animated) discussion; *uno spirito* —, a sprightly wit; *uno stile* —, a sprightly style; *è un ragazzo un po'* —, he is rather a lively boy **3.** (*profondo*) deep; (*acuto*) keen, sharp: — *dolore,* deep sorrow; *una viva impressione,* a deep impression; *una viva intelligenza,* a keen intelligence; *un* — *interesse,* a keen interest; *una viva sensazione di paura,* a sharp sensation of fear; *ho un* — *desiderio di vederlo,* I have great desire to see him **4.** (*vivido*) vivid, clear: *un* — *ricordo,* a vivid memory; *quelle impressioni sono ancora vive nella mia mente,* those impressions are still clear in my mind; *tener* — *il ricordo di qlcu.,* to keep s.o.'s memory green **5.** (*di colore*) bright: *colori vivi,* bright colours ‖ *s.m.* **1.** living person: *i vivi e i morti,* the living and the dead **2.** (*parte vivente*) living part; *fig.* (*essenza*) heart: *entrare nel* — *di una questione,* to get to the heart of a matter; *toccare, pungere nel* —, to pierce to the quick (*o* to touch on the raw) **3.** *al* —, to the life: *ritrarre qlcu. al* —, to portray s.o. to the life.

vívole, *s.f.pl.* (*vet.*) vives.

vivucchiàre, *V.* vivacchiàre.

viziàre, *v.t.* **1.** to spoil; to pamper: *ella vizia troppo i suoi bambini,* she spoils (*o* indulges) her children too much **2.** (*corrompere, guastare*) to vitiate: *questo fumo vizia l'aria,* this smoke vitiates the air **3.** (*dir.*) (*render nullo*) to vitiate: *queste omissioni viziano il contratto,* these omissions vitiate the contract.

viziaménte, *av.* imperfectly, faultily.

viziàto[1]**,** *ag.* **1.** spoilt: *un bambino* —, a spoilt child **2.** (*corrotto, guasto*) vitiated: *aria viziata,* vitiated air **3.** (*dir.*) (*nullo*) vitiated: *questo contratto è* —, this contract is vitiated.

viziàto[2]**,** *s.m.* (*agr.*) cutting of a vine.

viziatúra, *s.f.* (*rar.*) vice.

vízio, *s.m.* **1.** vice: *il — della gola*, the vice of gluttony; *corrotto dal —*, corrupted by vice; *immerso nel —*, sunk in vice; *vivere nel —*, to live in vice **2.** (*cattiva abitudine*) bad habit: *ha il — del fumo, di succhiarsi il dito*, he has the bad habit of smoking, of sucking his thumb **3.** (*difetto*) vice; defect, flaw: *i vizi del sistema politico attuale*, the vices (*o* defects) of the present political system; *un — di cuore*, a heart defect || *un — di forma*, (*dir.*) a vice of form (*o* a flaw) || *per — di imballaggio*, (*comm.*) because of defective packing.

viziosaménte, *av.* viciously.

viziosità, *s.f.* viciousness: *— d'argomentazione*, viciousness of reasoning.

viziòso, *ag.* **1.** vicious, depraved: *uomo —*, vicious (*o* depraved) man; *vita viziosa*, vicious life **2.** (*difettoso*) defective, faulty: *pronuncia viziosa*, faulty pronunciation || *contratto —*, vitiated contract **3.** (*di cavallo*) tricky, restive; bad-tempered **4.** *circolo —*, vicious circle || *s.m.* vicious fellow; depraved fellow.

vízzo, *ag.* **1.** (*avvizzito*) withered; faded **2.** (*floscio*) flabby.

vocabolàrio, *s.m.* **1.** (*insieme di vocaboli propri a una disciplina, una persona*) vocabulary: *— medico, scientifico, tecnico*, medical, scientific, technical vocabulary; *il mio — è molto limitato*, my vocabulary is very limited **2.** (*dizionario*) dictionary: *ho comperato un nuovo —*, I have bought a new dictionary.

vocabolarísta, *s.c.* lexicographer, dictionary maker.

vocàbolo, *s.m.* word; vocable; (*terminé*) term: *vocaboli tecnici*, technical terms; *una lista di nuovi vocaboli*, a list of new words.

vocàle, *ag.* vocal: *corde, organi vocali*, vocal cords, organs; *musica —*, vocal music || *s.f.* (*gram.*) vowel.

vocalizzàre, *v.t.i.* to vocalize.

vocalizzazióne, *s.f.* vocalization.

vocalízzo, *s.m.* (*mus.*) vocalization; vocalism.

vocatívo, *ag.s.m.* (*gram.*) vocative: *al —*, in the vocative.

vocazióne, *s.f.* vocation, calling; inclination, bent; (*eccl.*) vocation: *l'insegnamento è la mia —*, teaching is my calling; *non ha molta — per la pittura*, he has little vocation for painting; *non sento la — al sacerdozio*, I feel no calling for (*o* no call to) the Church (*o* priesthood); *aver — per il commercio*, to have a bent (*o* head) for business; *aver — per fare il soldato*, to be cut out for a soldier.

vóce, *s.f.* **1.** voice (*anche fig.*): *una — acuta, dolce, grossa, monotona, nasale, rauca*, a shrill, gentle, thick, dull, nasal, hoarse voice; *la — dell'allodola*, the song of the sky-lark; *la — della coscienza, del cuore*, the voice of the conscience, of the heart; *la — della natura*, the call of nature; *la — del popolo*, public opinion (*o* vox populi); *— di gola, petto, testa*, throaty-, chest-, head-voice; *— di tenore, soprano*, tenor, soprano voice; *mi sta andando giù la —*, I'm losing my voice; *abbassare, alzare la —*, to lower, to raise one's voice; *parlare a — alta, bassa*, to speak in a loud, in a low voice; *parlare sotto—*, to speak under one's breath (*o* to whisper) || *— bianca*, boy's, girl's voice || *l'ho sentito dalla sua viva —*, I heard it from him in person || *tu in queste cose non hai — in capitolo*, you have no voice in these matters || *dar — alle proprie emozioni*, to give voice to one's emotions || *dare una — a qlcu.*, (*chiamarlo*) to call s.o. || *dar sulla — a qlcu.*, (*contraddirlo*) to contradict s.o. **2.** (*diceria*) rumour: *corre — che egli sia colpevole*, it is rumoured that he is guilty; *spargere una —*, to spread a rumour **3.** (*parola*) word: *è una — nuova, antiquata*, it is a new, an obsolete word **4.** (*gram.*) (*genere del verbo*) voice; (*parte del verbo*) part: *— attiva, passiva*, active, passive voice; « *siamo* » *è — del verbo* « *essere* », "siamo" is part of the verb "essere" **5.** (*articolo di elenco, documento, ecc.*) item: *ho cancellato alcune voci dalla lista*, I have crossed a few items off the list.

vociare, *v.i.* to shout, to bawl.

vociferànte, *ag.* shouting, bawling, yelling, vociferant, vociferous.

vociferàre, *v.i.* **1.** (*gridare*) to shout, to bawl, to yell, to vociferate **2.** (*spargere una voce*) to rumour; to report: *si vocifera che egli sarà mandato via*, it is rumoured that he will be sent away.

vociferatóre, *s.m.* **1.** (*chi grida*) shouter, bawler, vociferator **2.** (*propalatore di notizie*) divulger, reporter.

vociferazióne, *s.f.* **1.** (*gridío*) vociferation, shouting, bawling, yelling **2.** (*diceria*) rumour; report.

vocío, *s.m.* shouting, bawling, yelling.

vòdca, *s.f.* vodka.

vóga[1], *s.f.* **1.** (*il vogare*) rowing **2.** (*spinta data all'imbarcazione coi remi*) stroke **3.** (*energia*) energy, ardour: *lavorare con —*, to work with energy (*o* to work hard).

vóga[2], *s.f.* (*moda*) fashion, vogue: *colori in —*, fashionable colours; *il rosso torna in —*, red becomes fashionable again; *essere in —*, to be in fashion (*o* fashionable).

vogàre, *v.i.* to row: *sai —?*, can you row?.

vogàta, *s.f.* **1.** (*atto e modo di vogare*) row; rowing *fare una —*, to have a row **2.** (*spinta data all'imbarcazione coi remi*) stroke.

vogatóre, *s.m.* rower, oarsman (*pl.* oarsmen).

vòglia, *s.f.* **1.** (*desiderio*) wish, desire; longing; fancy, whim: *hai — di venire con me?*, do you fancy coming with me?; *ho — di fare due passi*, I want to go for a walk (*o* I feel like going for a walk); *ho — di un po' di birra*, I fancy some beer (*o* I feel like some beer); *ho una gran — di rivederlo*, I am longing to see him again (*o* I am looking forward very much to seeing him again); *mi fa venire — di ridere*, he makes me laugh; *mi viene — di dirglielo*, I feel like telling him; *non ho — di lavorare*, I don't feel like working (*o* I have no wish to work); *non ho — di parlare con lui*, I have no wish to speak to him (*o* I don't want to speak to him); *vuol soddisfare tutte le sue voglie*, he wants to satisfy all his desires (*o* whims) **2.** (*volontà*) will: *mi è scappata la — di farlo*, I have lost the will to do it; *la sua buona — fu ricompensata*, his good will was rewarded; *lo feci di mala —, contro —*, I did it against my will; *lavorare di buona —*, to work with a will **3.** (*macchia della pelle*) birthmark.

vogliosaménte, *av.* with pleasure; willingly.

voglióso, *ag.* (*desideroso*) desirous (*predicativo*); (*capriccioso*) fanciful; (*disposto*) willing.

vói, *pron. pers. m.f.* 2[a] *persona pl.* **1.** *sogg.* you: *— ed io andremo in treno*, you and I will go by train; *—, finitela di parlare!*, you, stop talking!; *eravate —?, was it you?*; *l'avete fatto —?*, have you done it?; *siete stati — a romperlo*, it was you who broke it; *sono più vecchio di —*, I am older than you || *— stessi; proprio —*, you yourselves, you... yourselves: *— stessi l'avete visto*, you yourselves saw him; *l'avete detto proprio —*, you said so yourselves || *beati —!*, lucky you! || *— francesi non siete come noi*, you French people are not like us || *— due, tutti sarete puniti*, you shall both, all be punished; *— eravate là tutti e due*, all two of you were there **2.** (*come pred. nominale*): *non siete, sembrate più —*, you are no longer, you no longer seem your former selves; *se io fossi —*, if I were you **3.** *obliquo e oggetto* you: *tra — e me*, between you and me; *è a — che parlo*, it's you I am talking to; *parlavamo di —*, we were speaking of you; *spero di passare due giorni con —*, I hope to spend two days with you || *a —!*, your turn! || *eccomi a —*, now I'm with you || *come si festeggia da — la Pasqua?*, how do they celebrate Easter in your country? || *l'ha dato proprio a —*, he gave it to you in person || *non dovete ingannare — stessi*, you must not deceive yourselves **4.** *sogg., oggetto e obliquo* (*formula di cortesia, riferito a persona sing.*) you: *Voi siete stata molto buona con me*, you have been very kind to me; *vorrei parlare con Voi, signore*, I should like to speak to you, Sir ‖ *dare del — a qlcu.*, to address s.o. as "voi" (using the 2nd person plural).

voiàltri, voiàltre, *pron. pers. 2ª persona pl.* **you** (others); (*spreg.*) **you lot:** — *starete qui*, you (others) will stay here.

voile, *s.m.* (*tessuto*) voile, muslin.

voivòda, *s.m.* (*st. pol.*) voivode, vaivode.

volànda, *s.f.* flour dust.

volàno, *s.m.* **1.** (*gioco*) battledore and shuttlecock, badminton **2.** (*palla con cui si gioca al volano*) shuttlecock **3.** (*mec.*) fly-wheel.

volànte, *ag.* flying: *dischi volanti*, flying saucers; *fortezza —*, (*aer.*) flying fortress ‖ *cervo —*, kite ‖ *foglio —*, loose sheet ‖ *pesce volante*, flying fish ‖ *squadra —*, flying-squad ‖ *s.m.* (*aut.*) (steering-)wheel: *stare al —*, to be at the wheel (*o* to drive) ‖ *s.f.* (*squadra di polizia*) flying-squad.

volantino, *s.m.* **1.** leaflet, pamphlet **2.** (*mec.*) hand-wheel.

volàre, *v.i.* **1.** to fly (*anche fig.*): *gli aerei volavano a bassa quota*, the planes were flying low; *le aquile volano alte*, eagles fly high; *devo — alla stazione*, I must fly to the station; *il treno volava attraverso la campagna*, the train sped (*o* flew) through the country-side; *l'uccello volò via*, the bird flew away ‖ *il mio pensiero volava a te*, my thoughts flew to you ‖ *— controvento*, (*aer.*) to fly head to wind ‖ *far —*, to blow: *il vento mi fece — via il cappello*, the wind blew my hat off **2.** (*di cose leggere, librarsi*) to blow: *le foglie volavano per il giardino*, leaves were blowing across the garden **3.** (*di tempo, passare veloce*) to fly, to pass quickly: *le nostre vacanze sono volate*, our holiday passed quickly; *il tempo vola*, time flies **4.** (*propagarsi*) to fly, to spread quickly: *la notizia volò per tutto il paese*, the news flew (*o* spread quickly) all over the town **5.** (*essere scagliato*) to fly, to be thrown about: *volavano piatti*, they were throwing plates about ‖ *cominciarono a — schiaffi*, blows began to fly.

volàta, *s.f.* **1.** flight **2.** (*corsa*) rush: *ho fatto una — a casa*, I rushed home **3.** (*spor.*) final sprint: *il corridore vinse in —*, the runner won the final sprint **4.** (*di cannone*) muzzle **5.** *— d'uccelli*, (*stormo*) flock of birds.

volàtile, *ag.* **1.** (*alato*) winged **2.** (*che evapora rapidamente*) volatile ‖ *s.m.* bird.

volatilità, *s.f.* volatility.

volatilizzàbile, *ag.* volatilizable.

volatilizzàre, *v.t.i.*, **volatilizzàrsi**, *v.r.* to volatilize.

volatilizzazióne, *s.f.* volatilization.

volatóre, *ag.* flying ‖ *s.m.*, **volatríce**, *s.f.* flyer, flier.

vol-au-vent, *s.m.* (*cuc.*) vol-au-vent.

volènte, *ag.* willing: *— o nolente*, willy-nilly: *— o nolente lo deve fare*, willy-nilly he must do it (*o* he must do it whether he likes it or not).

volenteróso, *e derivati*, *V.* **volonteróso**, *e derivati*.

volentièri, *av.* willingly; with pleasure: *lo farò —*, I will do it willingly; *«Vieni con me?»*, *«Volentieri!»*, "Will you come with me?", "With pleasure!" ‖ *spesso e —*, very often.

volére, *v.t.* **1.** (*quando esprime volontà intensa*) (*pres. indic. e congiunt.*) **will**; (*pass. indic. e congiunt.; condiz.*) **would**; (*se seguito da compl. oggetto o da che con il congiunt.*) **will have**; **would have**: *voglio riuscire!*, I will succeed! (*o* I am determined to succeed!); *vorrebbe aiutarci, ma non può*, he would help us but he cannot; *vuol fumare, benchè gli faccia male alla salute*, he will smoke though it is bad for his health; *avrebbe potuto andarci, ma non volle*, he could have gone, but he would not; *disse che voleva riuscire ad ogni costo*, he said he would succeed at all costs; *non voglio che parli così*, I won't have him speaking (*o* speak) like that; *non voglio scene qui!*, I won't have any scenes here!; *non volle far nulla per aiutarmi*, he would do nothing to help me; *ora ti dispiace che io*

l'abbia fatto, ma sei tu che l'hai voluto, now you are sorry that I did it, but you would have me do it: *potresti se volessi*, you could if you would ‖ *il chiodo non vuole entrare*, (*fam.*) the nail won't go in; *il dolore non vuol passare*, (*fam.*) the pain won't pass **2.** (*assoluto e nel significato di disporre, stabilire*) **to will:** *ciò che Dio vuole è giusto*, what God wills is right; *come Dio vuole*, as God wills; *Dio ha voluto così*, God has willed it so; *il fato ha voluto che morisse*, Fate willed that he should die; *il re vuole che...*, the king wills that...; *l'uomo è capace di intendere e —*, man has intelligence and will ‖ *non cade foglia che Dio non voglia*, prov. God watches over all things **3.** (*quando esprime desiderio*) **to want**; **to wish**; (*nel senso di piacere, gradire*) **to like** (*costruzione pers.*); (*al condiz.*) *pres.* **should like**, **would like**; *pass.* **should have liked**, **would have liked:** *voglio andare a casa*, I want to go home; *volendo, potrebbe andare*, he could go if he wanted to; *vorrei, avrei voluto che venisse con me*, I should like, I should have liked him to come with me; *vorrei del pane*, I should like some bread; *vorrei vedere delle scarpe*, I should like to see some shoes; *vuoi andare a teatro stasera?*, do you want (*o* would you like *o* do you wish) to go to the theatre tonight?; *vuoi che ti porti ql.co. dalla città?*, do you want me (*o* would you like me) to bring you anything from the town?; *vuoi venire?*, do you want (*o* would you like) to come? (*o* will you come?); *vuole che io studi di più*, he wants me to study harder; *avrei voluto venire prima*, I should have liked to come earlier; *che cosa vuoi?*, what do you want?; *fa' come vuoi*, do as you like; *non voleva vedermi*, he did not want to see me; *non volevo che tu lo facessi*, I did not want you to do it; *i passeggeri che vogliono inviare telegrammi sul continente, si rivolgano a...*, passengers who wish to send telegrams to the continent should go to...; *puoi andare se, quando vuoi*, you may go if, when you like (*o* want *o* wish); *puoi fare tutto quello che vuoi*, you may do whatever you like (*o* want *o* wish); *i suoi genitori volevano che si facesse prete*, his parents wanted him to be a priest ‖ *neanche a volerlo, even if one wanted: neanche a volerlo potresti farlo*, you could not do it, even if you wanted (to) ‖ *non volendo, senza —*, (*involontariamente*) without wishing it (*o* to) ‖ *— qlcu. per, come*, to want s.o. for (*o* as): *nessuno lo vuole per, come amico*, nobody wants him for (*o* as) a friend **4.** (*quando esprime desiderio intenso, generalmente irrealizzabile*) **to wish** (*con congiunt. se riferito al pres. o pass.; con condiz. se riferito al futuro e talvolta al pres.*): *vorrei averti ascoltato!*, I wish I had listened to you!; *vorrei che venisse*, I wish he would come; *vorrei che tu stessi fermo*, I wish you would keep still; *vorrei che vincesse la gara*, I wish he could win the competition; *vorrei essere a Parigi!*, I wish I were in Paris!; *come avrebbe voluto esserti vicino!*, how he wished he were with you! **5.** (*in formule di cortesia*) (*nelle richieste*) **will**, **can**; **would**, **would mind**; (*nelle offerte*) **will have**, **would like:** *vorresti aprire la finestra?*, would you open (*o* do you mind opening *o* would you mind opening) the window?; *vuoi passarmi quelle carte, per favore?*, will (*o* can) you pass me those papers, please? (*o* would you pass me those papers? *o* do you mind passing me those papers?); *vuoi ql.co. da mangiare?*, will (*o* would you like) sthg. to eat?; *non vorresti entrare?*, won't you come in? **6.** (*aver bisogno di, richiedere*) **to need**, **to want**, **to require**, **to take:** *piante che vogliono molta acqua*, plants that need (*o* require) a lot of water; *verbo che vuole il congiuntivo*, verb that takes (*o* needs *o* requires) the subjunctive **7.** (*cercare*) **to ask for** (s.o.), **to want:** *c'è un signore che vuole tuo padre*, there is a man asking for your father; *chi volete?*, who do you want? (*o* who are you asking for?); *la mamma ti vuole*, mother wants (*o* is asking for) you **8.** (*avere intenzione di*) **to intend**, **to mean:** *volevo andarci, ma me ne dimenticai*, I intended (*o* meant) to go there, but I forgot about it 9. (*essere disposto a*) **to be willing**: *gliel'ho già domandato, ma non vuole farlo*, I have already asked him, but he is not willing to do it 10. (*esigere*) **to want**: *quanto vuole per questo orologio?*, how much do you want for that watch? 11. (*pretendere*) **to expect**: *da me vuol troppo*, he expects too much of me; *ma che cosa vogliono da un povero diavolo come lui?*, but what do they expect of a poor fellow like him? 12. (*permettere*) **to let, to allow**: *non vuole che esca sola di sera*, he doesn't let her go out alone at night; *verrò, se vuole la mamma*, I'll come if my mother lets me 13. (*dire, comandare*) **to say**: *il galateo, la legge vuole che...*, the book of etiquette, the law says that... 14. (*con verbi imp.*) (*quando esprime imminenza*) **to be going** (to do); (*quando esprime eventualità*) **to look like** (doing): *pare che voglia rasserenarsi*, it looks like clearing up; *secondo me vuol piovere*, I think it is going to rain 15. *voler dire*, **to mean**: *che cosa vuoi dire* (*con questo*)?, what do you mean (by this)?; *che cosa vuol dire questa parola?*, what does this word mean?; *questo vuol dire che è colpa tua*, this means it is your fault; *questo non vuol dir niente*, this does not mean anything || *voglio dire*, I mean; (*cioè*) that is to say: *Giovanni, voglio dire Mario...*, Giovanni, Mario I mean... || *volevo ben dire!*, I thought as much! || *non vuol dire!*, not necessarily! 16. *si vuole, vogliono* (*con valore di* si dice, dicono): *vogliono che ci sia stato un imbroglio*, they say there has been some trickery; *si vuole che fosse conte*, they say he was a count || *v.i.* **to need, to want, to be required**; **to take** (*non usato al passivo*): *ci vogliono cinque matasse di lana per un golf*, five skeins of wool are required (o needed) for a cardigan; *ci vogliono molti denari per fare...*, it takes a lot of money to do...; *ci vogliono sette ore per andare a Roma*, it takes seven hours to go to Rome (o the journey to Rome takes seven hours); *ci vuole uno specialista per questo lavoro*, it takes a specialist to do this work; *quanto ti ci vorrà per...*, how long will it take you to...; *per questo impiego ci vuole una laurea in matematica*, a university degree in mathematics is needed (o required) for this job || *ce n'è voluto!*, it took some doing!; *ci volle del bello e del buono per farlo venire*, it was quite a job to make him come || *ci vuol altro!*, it takes more than that!; *ci vuol altro che...*, it takes more than... || (*non*) *ci vorrebbe altro!*, that would be the last straw!; *non ci vorrebbe altro adesso che egli venisse!*, all it wants now is for him to come! 17. (**Fraseologia**): *voglia o non voglia..., che tu, egli, ecc. voglia o no...*, whether you like, he likes, etc. it or not...; — *o voglia, willy-nilly* || *voglio che tu abbia ragione...*, (*ammetto che*) I admit that you are right... || *voglio che sappiate che...*, I'll have you know that... || *volete tacere?*, will you shut up! || *vorrei sbagliarmi, credetelo*, that's how it is, I am afraid || *vorrei vedere che egli fosse d'accordo!*, I can't imagine him agreeing to that! || *vuoi... che, vuoi... vuoi*, (*sia... sia*), both... and: *egli scrive bene, vuoi in prosa, vuoi in versi*, he writes well, both in prose and in poetry || *che vuoi?, che volete?, Ha fatto tutto il possibile*, what would you have him do? He has done his best; *che vuoi? Non c'è altro mezzo*, what would you have us (o me) do? There is no other way || *come Dio volle, arrivarono a casa*, somehow they managed to get home || *Dio lo voglia!*, God grant it!; *Dio non voglia!*, God forbid!; *Dio voglia che torni salvo!*, God grant he comes back safely home!; *Dio volesse che fosse ancora vivo!*, would to God he were still alive; *Dio volesse che non fossi venuto!*, would to God I had not come! || *non volevo convincermi che...*, I couldn't believe (that)... || *qui ti voglio!*, there is the rub! (o that's the problem!) || *ritornerà quando Dio vuole*, he will come back in God's good time || *se Dio vuole, ci vedremo domani!*, thank Heavens, we'll meet tomorrow at last!; *siamo arrivati se Dio vuole*, thank Heavens we've arrived at

last || — *bene*, to love; *ricordatevi di me e vogliatemi bene*, remember me and think kindly of me || — *male*, to hate; (*portare rancore*) to bear ill-will (*o* to bear a grudge); *non volermene male*, don't bear me a grudge.

volére, *s.m.* 1. wish: *il* — *è già qualcosa*, the wish is something at least; *non basta il* —, the wish isn't enough || — *è potere*, *prov.* where there is a will, there is a way 2. (*volontà*) will: *lo feci contro il* — *di mio padre*, I did it against my father's will; *sia fatto il* — *di Dio*, God's will be done; *tutto dipende dal* — *di Dio*, everything depends on the will of God; *essere tutti di un* —, to be all of the same mind || *a mio, tuo* —, as I, you like; *di mio, tuo, ecc.* —, (*spontaneamente*) of my own, your own, etc. accord || *di buon* —, readily 3. *pl.*: *concordia di voleri*, concurrence of wishes; *i divini voleri*, the Divine Will.

volgàre, *ag.* 1. vulgar, common; (*triviale*) coarse, unrefined: *aspetto* —, vulgar (*o* common) appearance; *donna* —, vulgar (*o* common) woman; *espressione, linguaggio* —, vulgarism, coarse language; *gusti volgari*, vulgar (*o* common) tastes || *cadere nel* —, to lapse into vulgarity 2. (*popolare*) vulgar, vernacular: *lingua* —, vernacular (*o* vulgar tongue); *l'opinione* —, the common (*o* general) opinion || *s.m.* (*lett.*) vulgar tongue, vernacular.

volgarísmo, *s.m.* vulgarism.

volgarità, *s.f.* vulgarity: *non posso sopportare una simile* —, I cannot bear such vulgarity.

volgarizzaménto, *s.m.* 1. translation into the vernacular 2. (*divulgazione*) popularization, vulgarization.

volgarizzàre, *v.t.* 1. to translate into the vernacular 2. (*divulgare*) to popularize; to divulge.

volgarizzatóre, *s.m.*, **volgarizzatríce**, *s.f.* 1. translator into the vulgar tongue 2. (*chi divulga*) popularizer.

volgarizzazióne, *s.f.* popularization; vulgarization: *opera di* —, popularizing work (*o* treatise).

volgarménte, *av.* vulgarly, commonly; (*trivialmente*) coarsely: *parlare* —, to speak vulgarly.

volgàta, *s.f.* (*traduzione latina della Bibbia*) Vulgate.

vòlgere, *v.t.* 1. (*indirizzare*) to turn: *volse i propri passi verso casa*, he turned his steps homewards: — *i propri pensieri, sforzi verso ql.co.*, to turn one's thoughts, efforts to sthg.; — *ql.co. a proprio vantaggio*, to turn sthg. to one's own advantage; — *il viso, lo sguardo verso ql.co.*, to turn one's face, one's eyes towards sthg. 2. (*mutare*) to turn, to put: *volgi le cose in tal modo che sembra tu abbia ragione*, you put things in such a way that you seem to be right; — *una frase in latino*, to turn (*o* to translate) a sentence into Latin; — *in ridicolo*, to turn into a joke (*o* to laugh off); — *tutto in bene, in male*, to put a good, a bad complexion upon everything 3. (*girare*) to turn (over): — *le pagine di un libro*, to turn (over) the pages (*o* the leaves) of a book; — *una ruota*, to turn a wheel || — *ql.co. nella mente*, to turn sthg. over and over in one's mind || — *le spalle a qlcu.*, to turn one's back to s.o.; *fig.* to turn one's back on s.o. (*o* to give s.o. the cold shoulder) || *v.i.* to turn: *la strada volge a sinistra*, the road turns to the left; *il tempo concesso volge al termine*, the time is nearly up (*o* the time granted has almost expired); *il tempo volge al brutto*, the weather is changing for the worse || *il sole volgeva al tramonto*, the sun was setting || **vòlgersi**, *v.r.* 1. to turn: *si volse a guardarla*, he turned (round) to look at her; *si volse indietro, da questa parte*, he turned back, this way; *si volse alla musica*, *fig.* he turned to music 2. (*mutarsi*) to turn (to sthg.), to change (to sthg.): *il suo amore si è volto in odio*, his love has turned (*o* changed) to hate.

vòlgere, *s.m.* course: *il* — *degli eventi*, the course of events; *col* — *del tempo*, in the course of time; *nel* — *di tre anni*, in the course (*o* space) of three years.

vólgo, *s.m.* common people; vulgar herd; populace.

volicchiàre, volitàre, *v.i.* to flit, to flutter.

volitívo, *ag.* **1.** volitive, volitional: *futuro —*, *(gram.)* volitive future **2.** *(di persona)* strong-willed.

volizióne, *s.f.* *(fil.)* volition, will.

vólo, *s.m.* **1.** flight (anche *fig.*): *un — dell'immaginazione, dell'ingegno*, a flight of the imagination, of genius; *il — di un uccello*, the flight of a bird; *in —*, on the wing: *sparare a un uccello in —*, to shoot at a bird on the wing; *spiccare il —*, to fly away (o off) ‖ *capire qlco. al —*, to grasp sthg. immediately ‖ *cogliere un'occasione al —*, to seize an opportunity as it presents itself (o to grasp an opportunity o to leap at an opportunity) ‖ *colpire una palla al —*, to hit a ball full toss ‖ *correre a casa di —*, to dash home ‖ *prendere il —*, *fig.* to make off (o to run away) ‖ *vedere a — di uccello*, to have a bird's eye view **2.** *(aer.)* flight; flying: *— acrobatico*, acrobatic flying; *— a impulsi successivi*, *(di missili a razzo)* skip flight; *— a punto fisso*, *(di elicottero)* hovering; *— a vela*, soaring flight (o sail-flying); *— cieco, strumentale*, blind flying, instrument flying; *— di allenamento*, practice flight; *— di collaudo*, test flight; *— in picchiata*, dive; *— isobaro*, pressure-pattern flying; *— librato, planato*, glide, volplane; *— orizzontale*, level flight; *— senza scalo*, nonstop flight; *comandi di —*, flying controls; *durata del —*, flight (o flying) time; *piano di —*, flight plan; *l'aeroplano è in —*, the airplane is in flight; *spiccare il — da una nave portaerei*, to take off from an aircraft carrier.

volontà, *s.f.* will: *— di ferro*, will of iron (o iron will); *di sua spontanea —*, of his own free-will (o spontaneously o of his own accord); *indipendentemente dalla — di qlcu.*, beyond s.o.'s control; *mancanza di —*, lack of will (o lack of will-power); *la — di riuscire aiuta molto*, the will to succeed helps a great deal; *ha molta buona —*, he is full of good will; *lo feci contro la mia —*, *contro la — di mio padre*, I did it against my will, against my father's will; *la sua buona — fu ricompensata*, his good will was rewarded; *avere una — forte, debole*, to have a strong, weak will ‖ *a —*, at will (o at pleasure): *ne puoi prendere a —*, you may take as much as you want ‖ *forza di —*, will-power ‖ *le ultime — di*, the last wishes of (o the last will and testament of) ‖ *sia fatta la Tua —*, Thy will be done.

volontariaménte, *av.* voluntarily; spontaneously; willingly.

volontariàto, *s.m.* voluntary service.

volontàrio, *ag.* voluntary: *assistente, servizio —*, voluntary assistant, service; *azione volontaria*, voluntary action: *muscolo —*, *(anat.)* voluntary muscle ‖ *s.m.* *(mil.)* volunteer.

volonterosaménte, *av.* willingly, with a good will.

volonteróso, *ag.* willing: *uno scolaro —*, a willing pupil (o a pupil full of good will); *egli è molto —*, he is very willing.

volontièri, *V.* **volentièri**.

volpacchiòtto, *s.m.* fox-cub, young fox.

volpàia, *s.f.* fox's den, fox-hole, fox-burrow.

volpàre, *v.i.* to get blighted; to get smut.

volpàto, *ag.* *(di cereali)* blighted; smutted.

vólpe, *s.f.* **1.** fox: *— argentata*, silver fox; *— femmina*, vixen (o she-fox o bitch fox); *caccia alla —*, fox-hunting **2.** *(persona astuta)* old fox, sly fox: *quell'uomo è una —*, that man is a sly fox **3.** *(malattia dei cereali)* blight; smut.

volpeggiàre, *v.i.* to be crafty.

volpíno, *ag.* **1.** foxy, vulpine; *(di colore)* fox-coloured **2.** *(astuto)* crafty, cunning, sly **3.** *(di cane)* Pomeranian ‖ *s.m.* *(cane)* Pomeranian (dog).

volpóne, *s.m.* **1.** old fox **2.** *(persona astuta)* old fox, sly fox: *è un —*, he is an old fox.

vòlsci, *s.m.pl.* *(st.)* Volsci.

vòlt, vòlta¹, *s.m.* *(elett.)* volt.

vòlta², *s.f.* **1.** time: *una —*, once; *due volte*, twice; *tre volte*, three times (o arc. thrice); *quattro volte*, four times; *una — ancora*, once more (o once again); *una*

— e mezzo, half, as much (o many) again; *una — o l'altra*, sooner or later; *una — o due*, once or twice; *due, tre volte più grande del tuo*, twice, three times as big as yours; *molte volte*, many a time (o many times); *per questa —*, for this once; *più di una —*, more than once; *la prossima —*, next time; *qualche —, a volte*, sometimes; *quante volte?*, how many times? (o how often?); *rare volte*, seldom; *tutte le volte che*, everytime (o whenever); *tutti in una —*, all at once; *l'ultima —*, last time; *uno, due per —*, one, two at a time; *5 volte 2 fa 10*, 5 times 2 makes 10 ‖ *— per —*, everytime ‖ *una — per sempre*, once and for all ‖ *una — tanto*, once in a while ‖ *c'era una —...*, once upon a time there was... ‖ *questa è la — buona*, this is the right time ‖ *te l'ho detto una dozzina di volte*, I have told you a dozen times **2.** *(turno)* turn: *a mia —*, in my turn; *questa è la tua —*, this is your turn.

vòlta³, *s.f.* turning; *(curva)* turn, bend: *le volte di una strada*, the bends (o turns) in a road; *fare una —*, to take a turn ‖ *a — di corriere*, by return (of post) ‖ *gli è dato di — il cervello*, he has gone off his head ‖ *partire alla — di un luogo*, to set out for a place.

vòlta⁴, *s.f.* *(arch.)* vault: *— a botte*, barrel (o circular) vault; *— a crociera*, cross vault; *— a cupola*, dome vault; *un soffitto a —*, a vaulted roof ‖ *la — del cielo*, the vault of heaven ‖ *chiave di —*, keystone (anche *fig.*).

voltàbile, *ag.* that can be turned.

voltafàccia, *s.m.* volte-face: *fare un —*, to make a volte-face.

voltàggio, *s.m.* *(elett.)* voltage.

voltàico, *ag.* *(elett.)* voltaic: *pila, batteria voltaica*, voltaic pile, battery.

voltàmetro, *s.m.* *(elett.)* voltameter.

voltàre, *v.t.* **1.** to turn: *volta la pagina*, turn the page; *— lo sguardo, la testa verso ql.co.*, to turn one's eyes, one's head towards sthg.; *— le spalle a qlcu.*, to turn one's back on s.o. (anche *fig.*) **2.** *(tradurre)* to translate: *— da una lingua in un'altra*, to translate from one language into another ‖ *v.i.* to turn: *— a destra, a sinistra*, to turn to the right, to the left ‖ **voltàrsi**, *v.r.* to turn: *si voltò da un lato*, he turned aside; *si voltò indietro*, he turned back; *il malato non ha fatto che — e rivoltarsi*, the patient has done nothing but toss and turn in his bed ‖ *non so da che parte voltarmi*, I don't know which way to turn ‖ *— contro qlcu.*, to turn against s.o.

voltàta, *s.f.* turning; *(curva)* bend, curve: *la prima — a sinistra*, the first turning on the left; *una strada piena di voltate*, a road full of curves (o bends); *fece una — a destra*, he turned to the right; *prese la — a tutta velocità*, he took the curve at full speed.

voltàto, *ag.* turned: *— all'insù, all'ingiù, all'infuori*, turned up, down, out; *un naso — all'insù*, a snub nose.

volteggiaménto, *s.m.* *(equitazione, ginnastica)* vaulting.

volteggiàre, *v.i.* **1.** to whirl: *i ballerini volteggiavano per la sala*, the dancers whirled round the room **2.** *(svolazzare)* to fly about: *un gabbiano volteggiava sopra di noi*, a sea-gull was flying about above us **3.** *(equitazione, ginnastica)* to vault.

voltéggio, *s.m.* *(equitazione, ginnastica)* vaulting.

volterrianísmo, *s.m.* *(st. fil.)* Voltair(ian)ism.

volterriàno, *ag.* Voltairian.

voltímetro, *s.m.* *(elett.)* voltmeter.

vòlto¹, *s.m.* **1.** *(viso)* face; visage, countenance: *un — simpatico*, a nice face; *ella è una donna dal — espressivo*, she is a woman with an expressive countenance **2.** *(aspetto)* aspect, appearance.

vòlto², *ag.* **1.** turned: *— all'insù, all'ingiù*, turned up, down; *le mie finestre sono volte a sud, verso il mare*, my windows look south, on the sea **2.** *(rivolto)* directed: *i suoi interessi sono tutti volti al lavoro*, his interests are all directed to his work ‖ *s.m.* *(arch.)* vault.

voltolàre, *v.t.* to roll: *— un pesante sasso*, to roll a heavy stone ‖ **voltolàrsi**, *v.r.* to roll about; to roll over; to wallow: — *nell'erba*, to roll about in the grass; — *nel fango, nella sabbia, nell'acqua sporca*, to wallow in mud, in sand, in dirty water.

voltolóni, *av.* by rolling, by tumbling: *venne giù —*, he rolled (*o* tumbled) down.

voltòmetro, *s.m.* (*elett.*) voltameter.

voltúra, *s.f.* (*dir.*) transfer, assignment.

volúbile, *ag.* 1. fickle, changeable, inconstant: *una persona —*, a fickle person; *tempo —*, changeable weather 2. (*di pianta*) voluble, climbing.

volubilità, *s.f.* fickleness, inconstancy.

volubilménte, *av.* inconstantly.

volúme, *s.m.* 1. (*geom. fis. chim.*) volume: *il — di un solido*, the volume of a solid; *il — di una voce*, the volume of a voice; — *molecolare*, (*chim.*) molecular volume; — *specifico*, (*fis.*) specific volume; *regolatore di —*, (*rad.*) volume control 2. (*tomo*) volume: *primo, secondo —*, first, second volume; *fu pubblicato in tre volumi*, it was published in three volumes 3. (*massa*) volume, quantity, mass, bulk: *un gran — d'acqua*, a great quantity (*o* mass) of water; — *di capelli*, mass of hair.

volumenòmetro, *s.m.* (*fis.*) volumenometer.

volumètrico, *ag.* volumetric(al).

volúmetro, *s.m.* (*fis.*) volumeter.

voluminosaménte, *av.* voluminously.

voluminosità, *s.f.* voluminosity, voluminousness.

voluminóso, *ag.* 1. (*di molti volumi*) voluminous: *una voluminosa enciclopedia*, a voluminous encyclopedia 2. (*grosso, grande*) voluminous, bulky: *un pacco —*, a bulky parcel.

volúta, *s.f.* 1. (*arch.*) volute 2. (*zool.*) volute 3. (*letter.*) (*avvolgimento*) spiral, swirl.

volutaménte, *av.* intentionally, deliberately, purposely.

voluttà, *s.f.* 1. (*piacere*) delight, pleasure: *la — di una bella nuotata*, the pleasure of a good swim 2. (*diletto dei sensi*) voluptuousness.

voluttuàrio, *ag.* 1. voluptuary 2. (*non indispensabile*) unnecessary: *spese voluttuarie*, unnecessary expenses.

voluttuosaménte, *av.* voluptuously.

voluttuóso, *ag.* voluptuous.

vòlvolo, *s.m.* (*med.*) volvulus.

vòmere, **vòmero**, *s.m.* 1. (*aratro*) ploughshare 2. (*anat.*) vomer.

vòmica, *s.f.* (*med.*) vomica.

vòmico, *ag.* emetic, vomitive, vomitory ‖ *noce vomica*, (*bot. farm.*) nux vomica.

vomitaménto, *s.m.* vomiting.

vomitàre, *v.t.* 1. to vomit, to bring up (one's food); (*fam.*) to be sick: — *sangue*, to vomit blood; *aver voglia di —*, to feel sick ‖ *fa venir voglia di —*, it is enough to make one sick (*o* it is nauseating) 2. (*di vulcano, ecc.*) to vomit, to belch forth: *il vulcano vomitava fumo*, the volcano was vomiting (*o* belching forth) smoke 3. (*insulti, bestemmie*) to vomit, to spit out.

vomitatívo, **vomitatòrio**, *ag.s.m.* (*farm.*) emetic, vomitory.

vòmito, *s.m.* vomiting: *conato di —*, retch; *una malattia caratterizzata dal —*, an illness characterized by vomiting; *mi fa venire il —*, it makes me sick (anche *fig.*); *eccitare il —*, to excite (*o* to induce) vomiting; *sentirsi venire il —*, to feel sick ‖ — *nero*, (*patol.*) black vomit.

vomitòrio, *ag.* (*farm.*) vomitory ‖ *s.m.* (*archeol.*) vomitorium (*pl.* vomitoria).

vóngola, *s.f.* (*zool.*) hen clam.

voràce, *ag.* voracious (anche *fig.*); (*ingordo*) greedy, gluttonous: *un animale —*, a voracious animal; *un — lettore*, a voracious reader.

voraceménte, *av.* voraciously (anche *fig.*); (*ingordamente*) greedily, gluttonously.

voracità, *s.f.* voracity, voraciousness (anche *fig.*); (*ingordigia*) greed(iness), gluttony.

voràgine, *s.f.* chasm, gulf, abyss (anche *fig.*).

voraginóso, *ag.* chasmy; (*poet.*) abysmal (anche *fig.*).

vòrtice, *s.m.* 1. whirl; eddy, swirl: — *d'acqua*, eddy (*o* whirlpool); — *di vento*, whirlwind; *la macchina scomparve in un — di polvere*, the motor-car disappeared in a whirl of dust 2. *fig.* whirl, vortex (*pl.* vortexes, vortices): *il — della vita moderna*, the whirl of modern life; *un — di passione*, a whirl of passion.

vorticèlla, *s.f.* (*biol.*) vorticella (*pl.* vorticellae).

vorticosaménte, *av.* vortically, in whirls.

vorticóso, *ag.* whirling, swirling, vortical, vorticose: *moto —*, whirling (*o* vortical) motion; *velocità vorticosa*, giddy speed.

Vòsgi, i, *no.pr.m.pl.* (*geog.*) the Vosges.

vossignoría, *s.f.* (*detto a un signore*) Your Lordship; (*a una signora*) Your Ladyship.

vòstro, *ag.poss.* 1. **your**; (*vostro proprio*) **your own**: *un — cugino*, one of your cousins (*o* a cousin of yours); — *figlio e vostra figlia*, your son and (your) daughter; *alcuni dei vostri amici*, some of your friends (*o* some friends of yours); *ecco i vostri libri*, here are your books; *è affar —*, that's your business (*o* affair); *quando avrete una casa vostra?*, when will you have your own house? (*o* a house of your own?) ‖ *in vece vostra*, instead of you (*o* in your place *o* in your stead) ‖ *lo faremo per amor —*, we'll do it for your sake 2. (*come pred. nominale*) **yours**: *questo dizionario è —*, this dictionary is yours (*o* belongs to you) 3. (*in espressioni ellittiche*): *alla vostra* (*salute*)!, your health! (*o* here's to you! *o* cheerio!); *anche voi avete le vostre* (*disgrazie*), you have got your own worries (*o* problems); *ne avete fatta un'altra delle vostre*, you've been up to your tricks again; *rispondiamo alla vostra* (*lettera*) *del 5 aprile*, in reply to yours (*o* your letter) of April 5th; *sono dalla vostra* (*parte*), I am on your side ‖ *pron. poss.*: **yours**: *i miei figli assomigliano ai vostri*, my children are like yours; *la nostra casa è meno grande della vostra*, our house is smaller than yours ‖ *s.m.* 1. *dovete distinguere tra il — e il nostro*, you must distinguish between what is yours and what is yours; *non sapevo che aveste perso tutto il —*, I didn't know you had lost everything 2. (*partitivo*): *qualcosa, niente di —*, something, nothing of your own 3. *pl.*: *i vostri*, your family; your relatives; (*fam.*) your folks; your people; (*partigiani, seguaci*) your supporters.

votàggine, *s.f.* emptiness, vacuity.

votànte, *ag. s.c.* voter.

votàre[1], *V.* **vuotàre**.

votàre[2], *v.i.* to vote, to give one's vote: — *a mano alzata*, to vote by show of hands; — *contro una proposta*, to vote against a proposal; — *in bianco*, to return a blank voting paper; — *per, contro qlcu.*, to vote for, against s.o. ‖ *v.t.* 1. (*approvare*) to pass, to vote through: — *una proposta di legge*, to pass a bill (*o* to vote a bill through) 2. (*offrire, consacrare*) to offer; to consecrate; to vow: — *la propria vita a Dio*, to vow one's life to God ‖ **votàrsi**, *v.r.* (*dedicarsi*) to devote oneself, to vow oneself: — *a Dio*, to devote oneself to God.

votàto, *ag.* 1. (*approvato*) passed, approved 2. (*dedicato, consacrato*) devoted, consecrated: — *al sacrificio*, vowed to sacrifice.

votatóre, *s.m.*, **votatrice**, *s.f.* voter.

votatúra, *s.f.* (*il vuotare*) emptying.

votazióne, *s.f.* voting, poll: — *politica*, political voting; — *per appello nominale*, voting by roll-call; — *segreta*, secret voting (*o* ballot); *apertura, chiusura della —*, opening, close of the poll; *con — unanime*, by a unanimous vote; *una legge in corso di —*, a bill before the House; *dichiarare il risultato delle votazioni*, to declare the poll; *prendere parte alle votazioni*, to go to the polls.

votàzza, *s.f.* (*mar.*) bailing scoop, bailer.

votívo, *ag.* votive: *lampada, offerta votiva*, votive lamp, offering.

vóto[1], *s.m.* **1.** (*promessa solenne*) vow: — *di castità, di povertà*, vow of chastity, of poverty; *voti monastici*, monastic vows; *ho fatto il — di non fumare*, I vowed to give up smoking; *fare, mantenere, osservare, rompere, sciogliere un —*, to make, to keep, to perform, to break, to fulfil a vow; *pronunziare i voti*, to pronounce (o to take) one's vows; *sciogliere qlcu. da un —*, to release s.o. from a vow **2.** (*offerta votiva*) votive offering **3.** (*augurio, desiderio*) wish: *con i migliori voti per una pronta guarigione*, with my best wishes for a quick recóvery; *faccio — che tu sia felice*, I wish you happiness; *esaudire i voti di qlcu.*, to crown s.o.'s wishes (o to grant s.o.'s prayers) **4.** (*per elezione*) vote: — *di censura, di fiducia*, vote of censure, of confidence; — *palese, segreto*, open, secret vote; *diritto di —*, right to vote; *in Italia le donne hanno il —*, in Italy women have the vote; *avere il maggior numero di voti*, to be at the head of the poll; *contare i voti*, to count (o to tell) the votes; *dare il proprio — a qlcu.*, to give one's vote to (o to vote for) s.o.; *escludere le donne dal —*, to exclude women from the poll; *mettere ai voti*, to put to the vote; *ottenere un migliaio di voti*, to poll about a thousand votes **5.** (*scolastico*) mark; (*amer.*) grade: *a pieni voti*, with full marks (o with flying colours); *prendere dei bei, brutti voti*, to get good, bad marks.

vòto[2], *V.* **vuòto.**

vulcànico, *ag.* volcanic (anche *fig.*): *eruzione vulcanica*, volcanic eruption; *temperamento —*, volcanic nature.

vulcànio, *ag.* (*di Vulcano*) Vulcanian: *armi vulcanie*, Vulcanian arms.

vulcanísmo, *s.m.* vulcanism.

vulcaníte, *s.f.* (*caucciù vulcanizzato*) vulcanite.

vulcanizzàre, *v.t.* (*ind.*) to vulcanize, to cure: — *un pneumatico*, to vulcanize a tyre.

vulcanizzazióne, *s.f.* (*ind.*) vulcanization, cure: — *rafreddo*, cold cure; — *a vapore*, steam vulcanization.

Vulcàno, *no.pr.m.* (*mit.*) Vulcan ‖ **vulcàno,** *s.m.* volcano (*pl.* volcanoes): *un — attivo, spento*, an active, extinct volcano; — *inattivo*, dormant (o sleeping) volcano ‖ *quell'uomo è un —*, that man is bursting with energy ‖ *avere la testa come un —*, to be bursting with schemes and plans (o to have a vivid imagination).

vulcanología, *s.f.* vulcanology.

vulcanòlogo, *s.m.* vulcanologist, volcanist, vulcanist.

vúlgo[1], (*letter.*) per **vólgo.**

vulgo[2], *av.* (*lat.*) (*comunemente*) commonly.

vulneràbile, *ag.* vulnerable: *trovare il punto — di qlcu.*, to find s.o.'s vulnerable spot.

vulnerabilità, *s.f.* vulnerability, vulnerableness.

vulneràre, *v.t.* **1.** (*ferire*) to wound **2.** (*offendere*) to offend against (sthg.); (*danneggiare*) to injure: — *una legge*, to offend against a law.

vulnerària, *s.f.* (*bot.*) woundwort, kidney-vetch.

vulneràrio, *ag.* vulnerary, healing.

vúlva, *s.f.* (*anat.*) vulva.

vulvària, *s.f.* (*bot.*) stinking goose-foot.

vulvàrio, *ag.* (*anat.*) vulvar, vulval.

vulvíte, *s.f.* (*patol.*) vulvitis.

vuotàggine, *s.f.* emptiness, vacuity.

vuotàre, *v.t.* to empty; (*sgomberare, ripulire*) to clear out; (*pozzo, cisterna*) to drain (off): — *il bicchiere*, to empty (o to drain) one's glass; — *un cassetto*, to clear out (o to empty out) a drawer; — *un'imbarcazione*, — *l'acqua da una imbarcazione*, to bail (o to bale) (out) a boat, to bail the water out of a boat ‖ *vuotate i bicchieri!*, drink up! ‖ — *una bottiglia insieme*, to empty a bottle together ‖ — *il sacco*, *fig.* to speak out one's mind (o to unbosom oneself) ‖ **vuotàrsi,** *v.r.* to empty, to be emptied: *la sala si vuotò in pochi minuti*, the hall emptied (o was emptied) in a few minutes.

vuòto, *ag.* **1.** empty (anche *fig.*): *un baule, cassetto —*, an empty trunk, drawer; *un'esistenza vuota*, an aimless life; *la bottiglia, la casa, la scatola è vuota*, the bottle, the house, the box is empty; *ho la testa completamente vuota*, my mind is a complete blank; *mi sento —*, (*per fame*) I feel empty; *quella ragazza ha la testa vuota*, that girl is very silly (o has an empty head); *la scena resta vuota*, the stage remains empty **2.** (*sprovvisto, mancante*) void, devoid; lacking (in sthg.): *è completamente — di senso comune*, he is completely (de)void of (o lacking in) common sense **3.** (*vacante*) vacant, unoccupied: *posto —*, vacant seat ‖ *s.m.* **1.** empty space: *dobbiamo riempire questo —*, we must fill up (o in) this empty space (o this gap) ‖ *uno spiacevole senso di —*, an unpleasant feeling of void ‖ *egli ha lasciato un grande — fra noi*, we miss him very much; *sento un grande — quando egli non è qui*, I feel lonely when he is not here; *la sua morte lascia un — nella famiglia*, his death leaves a gap (o a blank) in the family circle ‖ *fare il — intorno a qlcu.*, to isolate s.o. **2.** (*recipiente vuoto*) empty: *dovete restituire i vuoti*, you must return the empties **3.** (*vacuità, vuotaggine*) emptiness **4.** (*fis.*) vacuum: — *assoluto*, absolute vacuum; *produrre un —*, to produce (o to create) a vacuum ‖ — *d'aria*, (*aer.*) air pocket **5.** *a —*, (*invano*) in vain; (*senza effetto*) to no purpose: *funzionando a —*, (*mec.*) idling; *emettere un assegno a —*, (*comm.*) to draw an uncovered (o a dud) cheque; *girare, marciare a —*, (*mec.*) to idle; *tirare a —*, to miss the mark.

W

w, *s.f.m.* **1.** *(lettera usata soltanto in parole di origine straniera)* w *(pl.* ws, w's) ‖ — *come Washington, (tel.)* w for William **2.** *(elett.)* watt **3.** W, *sigla dell'inter.* viva.

wad, *s.m. (min.) (idrossido di manganese)* wad.

wàfer, *s.m. (cialda)* wafer.

wagneriàno, *ag.* Wagnerian.

wagnerísmo, *s.m. (mus.)* Wagnerism, Wagnerianism.

wagneríte, *s.f. (min.)* wagnerite.

wahabíta, *s.m. (appartenente ad una setta rigorista musulmana fondata nel XVIII secolo)* Wahabi.

Waldemàro, *no.pr.m.* Waldemar.

Walhàlla, *s.m. (mit. nordica)* Valhalla, Valhall.

walkíria, *s.f. (mit. nordica)* Walkyria, Valkyrie, Valkyr *(pl.* Valkyries, Valkyrs).

Wàlter, *no.pr.m.* Walter.

wàlzer, *s.m. (musica, danza)* waltz.

wapíti, *s.m. (zool.)* wapiti.

watt, *s.m. (elett.)* watt.

wattmètro, wattòmetro, *s.m. (elett.)* watt-meter.

wattóra, *s.m. (elett.)* watt-hour.

wattoràmetro, *s.m. (elett.)* watt-hour meter.

wavellíte, *s.f. (min.)* wavellite.

wealdiàno, *ag. (geol.)* Wealden.

wèber, *s.m. (elett.)* weber.

websteríte, *s.f. (min.)* websterite.

wellingtònia, *s.f. (bot.)* Wellingtonia.

wesleyàno, *ag. s.m. (st. relig.)* Wesleyan.

wolfràmio, *s.m. (chim.)* wolfram, tungsten.

wolframíte, *s.f. (min.)* wolframite.

Wòtan, *no.pr.m. (mit. nordica)* Odin, Woden.

wulfeníte, *s.f. (min.)* wulfenite.

wurmiàno, *ag. (geol.)* Würmian ‖ *s.m. (geol.)* Würm.

wyeliffísmo, *s.m. (st. relig.)* Wycliffism, Wiclifism.

wyeliffíta, *s.c. (st. relig.)* Wycliffite, Wyclifite.

X

x, *s.f.m* **1.** (*lettera usata soltanto in parole di origine straniera*) x (*pl.* xs, x's) ‖ — *come Xanthia*, (*tel.*) x for Xmas ‖ *raggi* —, X-rays ‖ *il signor X*, Mr. X **2.** (*mat.*) x, unknown quantity **3.** X, (*numero romano equivalente a dieci*) X (ten).

xanteina, *s.f.* (*chim.*) xanthein.

xàntico, *ag.* (*chim.*) xanthic: *acido* —, xanthic acid.

xantína, *s.f.* (*chim.*) xanthin.

xantofílla, *s.f.* (*bot.*) xanthophyll.

xantogenàto, *s.m.* (*chim.*) xanthate, xanthogenate.

xantòma, *s.m.* (*patol.*) xanthoma (*pl.* xanthomata, xanthomas).

xantopsía, *s.f.* (*med.*) xanthopsia.

xantorrèa, *s.f.* (*bot.*) xanthorrhoea.

xantosarcòma, *s.m.* (*patol.*) xanthosarcoma.

xantòsi, *s.f.* (*med.*) xanthosis.

xèno, *s.m.* (*chim.*) xenon.

xenodòchio, *s.m.* (*st.*) xenodochium.

xenofobía, *s.f.* xenophobia.

xenòfobo, *s.m.* xenophobe.

xènon, *s.m.* (*chim.*) xenon.

Xères, *s.m.* (*vino*) sherry.

xerodèrma, *s.m.* (*patol.*) xeroderma.

xeròfilo, *ag.* (*bot.*) xerophilous.

xifòide, *s.f.* (*anat.*) xiphoid, xiphisternum.

xifoidèo, *ag.* (*anat.*) xiphoid.

xilèma, *s.m.* (*bot.*) xylem.

xilène, *s.m.* (*chim.*) xylene.

xilidína, *s.f.* (*chim.*) xylidin.

xilobàlsamo, *s.m.* (*bot.*) xylobalsamum.

xilòfago, *ag.* xylophagous ‖ *s.m.* (*entom.*) xylophagan.

xilofonísta, *s.c.* (*mus.*) xylophonist.

xilòfono, *s.m.* (*mus.*) xylophone.

xilografía, *s.f.* **1.** (*arte di incidere su legno*) xylography **2.** (*incisione su legno*) xylograph.

xilogràfico, *ag.* xylographic(al).

xilògrafo, *s.m.* xylographer, xylographist.

xilòide, *ag.* xyloid: *lignite* —, xyloid lignite.

xilòlo, *s.m.* (*chim.*) xylol, xylene.

xilòmetro, *s.m.* xylometer.

xilopirografía, *s.f.* xylopyrography.

Y

y, *s.f.m.* **1.** (*lettera usata soltanto in parole di origine straniera*) y (*pl.* ys, y's) ‖ — *come York*, (*tel.*) y for yellow **2.** (*mat.*) y, second unknown quantity.

yacht, *s.m.* (*mar.*) yacht: — *a vapore, a vela*, steam yacht; — *da corsa*, racing yacht; *crociera su* —, yachting cruise.

yak, *s.m.* (*zool.*) yak.

yard, **yàrda**, *s.f.* yard (*misura di lunghezza* = cm. 91,4399).

yatagàn, *s.m.* (*sciabola turca*) yatag(h)an.

yen, *s.m.* (*moneta giapponese*) yen.

yòga, *s.m.* **1.** (*fil. indiana*) yoga **2.** (*chi la pratica*) yogi.

yòghurt, *s.m.* yog(h)urt.

yole, *s.f.* (*mar.*) gig.

ypríte, *s.f.* (*chim.*) mustard gas, yperite.

Z

z, _s.f.m._ (_ventunesima lettera dell'alfabeto italiano_) z (_pl._ zs, z's) ‖ — _come Zara,_ (_tel._) z for zebra ‖ _dall'a alla_ —, from beginning to end.

zabaglióne, zabaióne, _s.m._ sillabub, "zabaglione".

Zaccaría, _no.pr.m._ Zachariah, Zacharias, Zachary.

zàcchera, _s.f._ splash (of mud).

zaccheróna, _s.f._ slattern.

zaccheróne, _s.m._ sloven.

zaccheróso, _ag._ bespattered with mud.

zaffàre, _v.t._ **1.** to wad, to plug **2.** (_una botte_) to bung.

zaffàta, _s.f._ (_di cattivo odore_) stench; (_d'aria, fumo_) whiff: _una_ — _d'aria calda,_ a whiff of hot air.

zàffera, _s.f._ (_chim._) zaffre, zaffer.

zafferanàto, _ag._ **1.** (_contenente zafferano_) containing saffron (_predicativo_) **2.** (_di color zafferano_) saffron -coloured.

zafferàno, _s.m._ saffron: _giallo_ —, saffron yellow.

zaffiríno, _ag._ sapphire: _colore_ —, sapphire colour.

zaffíro, _s.m._ sapphire.

zàffo, _s.m._ **1.** (_di botte_) bung: _chiudere con lo_ —, to bung **2.** (_med._) (_tampone_) wadding.

zagàglia, _s.f._ assagai, assegai.

zàino, _s.m._ knapsack; pack: _preparare lo_ —, to pack one's knapsack.

Zambési, _no.pr.m._ (_geog._) Zambezi, Zambesi.

zàmpa, _s.f._ **1.** (_di cani, lupi, felini_) paw; (_di cavallo, capra_) hoof (_pl._ hoofs, hooves); (_di pecora, maiale_) trotter; (_di volatile_) claw; (_di insetto_) leg: _le zampe di un cane,_ the paws of a dog; _le zampe di una mosca,_ the legs of a fly; _le zampe del passero,_ the sparrow's claws ‖ _zampe di gallina,_ (_scrittura indecifrabile_) scrawl; (_rughe intorno agli occhi_) crow's feet ‖ _cavare la castagna dal fuoco con la_ — _del gatto,_ to use s.o. as a cat's paw **2.** (_scherz._) (_mano_) paw; hand; (_piede_) hoof (_pl._ hoofs, hooves), trotter: _dammi la_ —, give me your paw; _giù le zampe!,_ hands off!; _stringiamoci la_ — _e facciamo la pace,_ let's shake (hands) and make it up ‖ _leccare le zampe a uno,_ to lick s.o.'s boots **3.** (_piede di mobile_) leg: _una tavola a tre zampe,_ a three-legged table.

zampàta, _s.f._ blow with a paw.

zampettàre, _v.i._ (_spec. di bambini_) to toddle.

zampillànte, _ag._ gushing, spurting, springing, spouting.

zampillàre, _v.i._ to gush, to spurt, to spout: _zampillava acqua dal terreno,_ water was gushing (_o_ spurting _o_ spouting) from the ground.

zampillío, _s.m._ gushing, spurting, springing, spouting.

zampíllo, _s.m._ gush, spurt, spring, spout, jet: — _di sangue,_ spurt of blood.

zampíno, _s.m._ little paw ‖ _credo che ci abbia messo lo_ —, _fig._ I think he had a hand in the matter (_o_ a finger in the pie).

zampógna, _s.f._ reed-pipe; (_cornamusa_) bag-pipe.

zampognàre, _v.i._ to pipe.

zampognàro, _s.m._ piper.

zampóne, _s.m._ **1.** (_grossa zampa_) big paw **2.** (_cuc._) "zampone" (trotter stuffed with chopped seasoned meat).

zàna, _s.f._ **1.** (_cesto_) basket **2.** (_culla_) cradle **3.** (_barella_) litter **4.** (_arch._) (_nicchia_) niche, recess.

zanàio, _s.m._ (_fabbricante di cesti_) basket-maker.

zàngola, _s.f._ churn.

zànna, _s.f._ (_di elefanti, trichechi, cinghiali_) tusk; (_di cani, lupi, felini_) fang ‖ _mostrare le zanne, fig._ to show one's teeth.

zannàta, _s.f._ blow with the tusk; bite with the fangs; (_morso_) snap.

zannésco, _ag._ clownish.

zànni, _s.m._ clown, zany, buffoon.

zannúto, _ag._ (_di elefanti, trichechi, cinghiali_) tusked; (_di cani, lupi, felini_) fanged.

zanzàra, _s.f._ mosquito (_pl._ mosquitoes, mosquitos).

zanzarièra, _s.f._ mosquito-net, mosquito-curtain.

zàppa, _s.f._ hoe ‖ _darsi la_ — _sui piedi, fig._ to cut one's own throat.

zappàre, _v.t._ to hoe; to dig: — _la terra,_ to hoe (_o_ to dig) the ground.

zappàta, _s.f._ **1.** (_lo zappare_) hoeing; digging **2.** (_colpo con la zappa_) blow with a hoe.

zappatóre, _s.m._ **1.** hoer; digger **2.** (_mil._) pioneer ‖ _Genio Zappatori,_ (Corps of) pioneers.

zappatúra, _s.f._ hoeing; digging.

zappettàre, _v.t._ (_agr._) to hoe.

zaptiè, _s.m._ (_poliziotto eritreo_) saptieh.

zar, _s.m._ czar, tsar, tzar.

zarína, _s.f._ czarina, tsarina, tzarina.

zarzuèla, _s.f._ (_teat._) zarzuela.

zàttera, _s.f._ raft; (_per scaricare navi_) lighter.

zavòrra, _s.f._ **1.** ballast: _in_ —, in ballast; _gettar via_ —, to jettison ballast **2.** (_cose, persone di nessun valore_) waste; dregs (_pl._); rubbish.

zavorràre, _v.t._ to ballast.

zàzzera, _s.f._ mane, shock of hair.

zazzeróne, _s.m._ **1.** mane, shock of hair **2.** (_persona con zazzera_) shock-headed person.

zazzerúto, _ag._ long-haired (_attributivo_), wearing one's hair long (_predicativo_).

zèbra, _s.f._ (_zool._) zebra.

zebràto, _ag._ striped; stripy ‖ _passaggio_ —, (_segnaletica stradale_) zebra crossing.

zebú, _s.m._ (_zool._) zebu.

zécca¹, _s.f._ (_luogo in cui si coniano monete_) mint ‖ _nuovo di_ —, brand-new.

zécca², _s.f._ (_entom._) tick.

zecchière, _s.m._ minter.

zecchíno, _ag._: _oro_ —, first-quality gold ‖ _s.m._ (_antica moneta_) sequin.

Zèffiro, _no.pr.m._ (_mit._) Zephyrus ‖ **zèffiro¹,** _s.m._ (_vento di ponente_) zephyr; (_lieve brezza_) light breeze.

zeffíro², _s.m._ (_tessuto leggero_) zephyr.

Zelànda, _no.pr.f._ (_geog._) Zealand ‖ _Nuova_ —, New Zealand.

zelànte, _ag._ zealous: _è molto_ — _nel fare il suo dovere,_ he is very zealous in doing his duty; _un lavoratore_ —, a zealous worker.

zelanteménte, _av._ zealously.

zelantería, _s.f._ excessive zeal.

zelatóre, _s.m._, **zelatríce,** _s.f._ zealot.

zèlo, _s.m._ zeal: _eccesso di_ —, excess of zeal.

zendàdo, _s.m._ (_drappo di seta_) sendal.

zènit, _s.m._ (_astr._) zenith (_anche fig._): _era allo_ — _della sua fama,_ he was at the zenith of his fame.

zenitàle, _ag._ (_astr._) zenithal.

Zenòbia, _no.pr.f._ (_st._) Zenobia.

Zenóne, _no.pr.m._ (_st. fil._) Zeno.

zènzero, _s.m._ (_bot._) ginger.

zeolíte, *s.f.* (*min.*) zeolite.

zéppa, *s.f.* (*bietta*) wedge: *mettere una — sotto un tavolo*, to put a wedge under a table ‖ *mettere una — a ql.co.*, *fig.* (*raffazzonarla*) to patch up sthg.

zeppàre, *v.t.* (*riempire calcando*) to cram.

zéppelin, *s.m.* (*aer.*) zeppelin.

zéppo, *ag.* full, crammed; crowded: *un cassetto — di carte*, a drawer crammed with papers; *la stanza era piena zeppa di gente*, the room was crammed (o over-crowded) with people.

zerbíno[1], *s.m.* (*piccola stuoia*) door-mat.

zerbíno[2], **zerbinòtto**, *s.m.* dandy, fop: *fare lo —*, to play the dandy.

zèro, *s.m.* **1.** cipher, cypher, nought; (*spec. in scale, gradazioni*) zero (*pl.* zero, zeroes): *lo — assoluto*, zero absolute; *— virgola cinque*, nought (o zero) point five; *una fila di zeri*, a row of ciphers (o of noughts o of zeroes); *10 gradi sopra, sotto —*, 10 degrees above, below zero; *l'ago è tornato a —*, the needle has returned to zero ‖ *ora —*, zero hour **2.** (*tel.*) o: *il mio numero di telefono è 40503*, my telephone number is four, o, five, o, three **3.** *fig.* (*niente*) nought, nothing: *non me ne importa uno —*, I couldn't care less; *non vale uno —*, it is not worth a brass farthing (o it is worthless): *come medico non vale uno —*, as a doctor he is useless; *quell'uomo è uno —*, that man is a nobody; *ridurre a —*, to bring to naught; *ridursi a —*, to come to naught.

zèta, *s.f.* zed; (*amer.*) zee: *dalla a alla —*, from A to Z (o from beginning to end).

zetètico, *ag.* (*fil.*) zetetic.

zèugma, *s.m.* (*gram.*) zeugma.

Zèus, *no.pr.m.* (*mit.*) Zeus.

zía, *s.f.* aunt; (*fam.*) auntie: *la — Barbara*, Aunt Barbara.

zibaldóne, *s.m.* **1.** (*miscellanea letteraria*) miscellany **2.** (*insieme di cose diverse*) medley, miscellany.

zibellíno, *s.m.* (*zool.*) sable: *una pelliccia di —*, a sable fur.

zibétto, *s.m.* **1.** (*zool.*) civet, civet-cat: *— indiano*, zibet **2.** (*profumo*) civet.

zibíbbo, *s.m.* (*bot.*) raisin.

zigàno, *ag.* tzigane ‖ *s.m.* tzigane; Hungarian gipsy.

zígolo, *s.m.* (*zool.*) bunting.

zígomo, *s.m.* (*anat.*) cheek-bone; zygoma (*pl.* zygomata).

zigrinàto, *ag.* shagreened.

zigríno, *s.m.* shagreen.

zigzàg, *s.m.* **1.** zigzag: *linea, sentiero a —*, zigzag line, path; *andare a —*, to zigzag **2.** (*entom.*) gipsy-moth.

zigzagàre, *v.i.* to zigzag.

zimàrra, *s.f.* **1.** long coat; robe **2.** (*dei preti*) cassock.

zimàsi, *s.f.* (*chim.*) zymase.

zimbellàre, *v.t.* to decoy (anche *fig.*).

zimbèllo, *s.m.* **1.** (*uccello per richiamo*) decoy (anche *fig.*) **2.** (*pop.*) (*oggetto di scherno*) laughing-stock: *essere lo — di una compagnia*, to be the laughing-stock of a party.

zimología, *s.f.* (*scient.*) zymology.

zinàle, *s.m.* apron.

zincàre, *v.t.* (*metal.*) to zinc, to coat with zinc, to plate with zinc; to galvanize: *— a caldo*, to hot-galvanize.

zincàto, *ag.* coated with zinc, zinc plated ‖ *s.m.* (*chim.*) zincate.

zincatúra, *s.f.* (*metal.*) zinc-plating; galvanization.

zínco, *s.m.* (*min.*) zinc: *carbonato, ossido di —*, zinc carbonate, oxide; *lamiera di —*, zinc sheet.

zincografía, *s.f.* (*tip.*) zincography.

zincogràfico, *ag.* zincographic.

zincògrafo, *s.m.* zincographer.

zincotipía, *s.f.* (*tip.*) zincotype.

zíngara, *s.f.* gipsy, gypsy: *vivere come una —*, to live like a gipsy.

zingarésca, *s.f.* (*mus.*) gipsy song.

zingarésco, *ag.* gipsyish; gipsy (*attributivo*).

zíngaro, *s.m.* gipsy, gypsy.

zínnia, *s.f.* (*bot.*) zinnia.

zinzíno, *s.m.* **1.** (*pezzettino*) tiny bit, small quantity **2.** (*sorsettino*) sip: *bere a —*, to sip.

zío, *s.m.* uncle: *lo — Giovanni*, Uncle John; *— materno, paterno*, maternal, paternal uncle ‖ *— d'America*, *fig.* rich uncle.

zípolo, *s.m.* (*tappo*) spigot.

zirconàto, *s.m.* (*chim.*) zirconate.

zireóne, *s.m.* (*min.*) zircon.

zircònia, *s.f.* (*chim.*) zirconia.

zircònio, *s.m.* (*chim.*) zirconium.

zirconíte, *s.m.* (*min.*) zirconite, jargo(o)n.

zirlàre, *v.i.* (*di uccello*) to whistle, to chirp; (*di topo*) to squeak.

zírlo, *s.m.* thrush's whistle.

zíro, *s.m.* (*orcio*) jar.

zitèlla, *s.f.* **1.** (*donna nubile*) spinster, old maid: *abitudini da —*, old-maidish habits **2.** (*giovinetta*) maid.

zitellóne, *s.m.* (*chim.*) old bachelor, confirmed bachelor.

zittíre, *v.t.i.* to hiss, to hoot, to boo: *l'uditorio cominciò a —*, the audience began hissing; *— un oratore*, to hiss (o to boo o to hoot) a speaker.

zítto, *ag.* silent: *star —*, to be (o to keep) silent (o quiet): *sta' —!*, keep quiet! (o be quiet! o *fam.* shut up!).

zizzània, *s.f.* (*bot.*) zizania, darnel; *fig.* discord, dissension: *seminare —*, to sow discord (o dissension).

zízzola, *s.f.* **1.** (*bot.*) jujube **2.** (*fig. fam.*) (*colpo*) blow: *che —!*, what a blow!.

zízzolo, *s.m.* (*bot.*) jujube-tree.

zoantropía, *s.f.* (*patol.*) zoanthropy.

zoànto, *s.m.* (*zool.*) zoanthid.

zoccolàio, *s.m.* clog-maker, sabot-maker.

zoccolànte, *ag.* wearing clogs ‖ *s.m.* (*eccl.*) Franciscan friar.

zoccolàre, *v.i.* to clatter about with one's clogs.

zoccolàta, *s.f.* blow with a clog.

zòccolo, *s.m.* **1.** clog, sabot, wooden-shoe **2.** (*degli equini*) hoof (*pl.* hoofs, hooves) **3.** (*piedistallo di statua, colonna, ecc.*) plinth, base, socle **4.** (*striscia alla base di una parete*) skirting board, baseboard ‖ *— decorato*, dado **5.** (*mec.*) (*di freno*) shoe **6.** (*elett.*) base ‖ *— di valvola*, (*rad.*) tube base (o valve base).

zodiacàle, *ag.* zodiacal.

zodíaco, *s.m.* zodiac: *i segni dello —*, the signs of the zodiac.

Zòe, *no.pr.f.* Zoe.

zoèa, *s.f.* (*zool.*) zoea (*pl.* zoeae).

Zòilo, *no.pr.m.* (*st. lett.*) Zoilus ‖ **zòilo**, *s.m.* *fig.* Zoilus, ill-natured critic, petty critic, criticaster.

zoisíte, *s.f.* (*min.*) zoisite.

zolfanèllo, *s.m.* (*sulphur*) match.

zolfàra, **zolfatàra**, *s.f.* sulphur mine.

zolfàre, *v.t.* (*agr.*) to sulphurate, to sulphurize.

zólfo, *s.m.* sulphur: *— libero*, (*chim. ind.*) free sulphur; *— raffinato*, (*chim. ind.*) processed sulphur; *fiori di —*, flowers of sulphur; *miniera di —*, sulphur mine.

zòlla, *s.f.* **1.** clod, lump: *— di terra*, clod (of earth); (*con erba*) turf (o sod) **2.** (*di zucchero*) lump.

zollétta, *s.f.* lump: *— di zucchero*, lump of sugar; *zucchero in zollette*, lump sugar (o sugar in lumps o lumps of sugar).

zompàre, *v.i.* (*dial.*) to jump, to leap.

zómpo, *s.m.* (*dial.*) jump, jumping, leap, leaping.

zóna, *s.f.* zone; (*regione*) belt; (*area*) area: *— artica, temperata, torrida*, frigid, temperate, torrid zone; *— degli alisei*, trade-wind belt; *la — del cotone, grano*, the cotton, wheat zone (o belt); *— di alloggiamento*, (*mil.*) billeting (o staging) area; *— di alta pressione*, (*meteorologia*) area of high pressure; *— di atterraggio*, (*aer.*) landing area; *— di calma*, calm belt; *— di depressione*, (*meteorologia*) trough; *— di influenza*, zone of influence; *una — di libero scambio*, a zone of free trade; *— di* segnalazione, (aer.) signal area; — minata, (mil.) mined area; — pericolosa, dangerous zone (o space); — per parcheggio, parking lot; — residenziale, residential area; — sferica, (geom.) spherical zone; questa è una — ancora inesplorata, this is a zone still unexplored || — del silenzio, silent zone; (rad.) blind (o dead) spot; — morta, (mil.) dead-ground; (radar) blind spot.

zónzo, a, l.av.: andare a —, to loaf (o to loiter o to saunter); essere a —, to be loafing (o loitering o sauntering) about.

zòo, s.m. zoo.

zoochímica, s.f. zoochemistry.

zoòfago, ag. zoophagous.

zoofilía, s.f. zoophily, zoophilism, zoophilia.

zoòfilo, ag. zoophilous || s.m. zoophile; animal lover.

zoofito, s.m. zoophyte (pl. zoophyta).

zoofobía, s.f. zoophobia.

zoogeografía, s.f. zoogeography.

zoografía, s.f. zoography.

zooiàtra, s.c. veterinary surgeon.

zooiatría, s.f. veterinary science.

zoolatría, s.f. zoolatry.

zoolíto, s.m. (paleont.) zoolite.

zoología, s.f. zoology.

zoològico, ag. zoological: giardino —, zoological garden(s).

zoòlogo, s.m. zoologist.

zootecnía, s.f. zootechny.

zootècnica, s.f. zootechnics.

zootècnico, ag. zootechnic || patrimonio —, live-stock || s.m. animal expert.

zootomía, s.f. zootomy.

zootomísta, s.c. zootomist.

zoppàggine, s.f. lameness, limp.

zoppicaménto, s.m. limping; limp.

zoppicànte, ag. limping; lame (anche fig.): un ragionamento —, a lame argument; verso —, halting line.

zoppicàre, v.i. 1. to limp, to walk with a limp; (camminare come zoppo) to hobble: quell'uomo zoppica, that man is limping 2. (di seggiola, tavolo) to be shaky, to be unsteady, to be wobbly || un ragionamento che zoppica, a lame (o weak) argument.

zoppicóne, zoppicóni, av. with a limp: camminare —, to limp (o to walk with a limp); procedere —, to limp along (o to hobble along).

zòppo, ag. 1. lame; limping: essere —, to be lame (o to limp): è — dalla gamba destra, he is lame in his right leg ; essere molto —, to have a bad limp 2. (di seggiola, tavolo) shaky, rickety, wobbly, unsteady 3. fig. lame, halting || s.m. lame person.

zorílla, s.m. (zool.) zoril, zorilla.

zòstera, s.f. (bot.) grass-wrack, sea-wrack.

zoticàggine, s.f. boorishness, uncouthness.

zoticaménte, av. boorishly, uncouthly.

zotichézza, s.f. boorishness, uncouthness.

zòtico, ag. boorish, uncouth, rough; (grossolano) coarse; (goffo) clumsy: maniere zotiche, boorish (o rough) manners || s.m. boor, uncouth fellow, rough fellow.

zoticóne, s.m. boor, rough fellow, uncouth fellow.

zuàva, s.f. (giacchetta) zouave.

zuàvo, s.m. (mil.) zouave || calzoni alla zuava, plus-fours (o knickerbockers).

zúcca, s.f. 1. (bot.) pumpkin; (cucurbita) gourd: semi di —, pumpkin seeds 2. (recipiente) gourd 3. fig. (testa) pate: una — pelata, a bald pate; grattarsi la —, to scratch one's pate || non aver sale in —, to be a blockhead.

zuccàia, s.f. pumpkin bed.

zuccàta, s.f. knock on the head: diedi una — contro il muro, I knocked my head against the wall.

zuccheràre, v.t. to sugar (anche fig.), to sweeten (anche fig.): — una pillola, to sugar a pill.

zuccheràto, ag. sugared (anche fig.), sweetened (anche fig.): acqua zuccherata, sugar and water; il mio tè è troppo —, my tea is too sweet.

zuccherièra, s.f. sugar-basin.

zuccherifício, s.m. sugar-refinery.

zuccheríno, ag. sugary; (dolce) sweet || s.m. 1. (cosa dolce) sweet; (arc.) sweetmeat 2. fig. (consolazione, premio) sugar-plum.

zúcchero, s.m. sugar: — in pani, loaf-sugar; — in polvere, castor sugar; — in zollette, lump sugar; barbabietola da —, sugar-beet; canna da —, sugar-cane; pinze da —, sugar-tongs; raffineria di —, sugar-refinery || è uno —!, fig. she is a treasure (o a darling).

zuccheróso, ag. sugary.

zucchétto, s.m. skull-cap, zucchetto.

zucchíno, s.m. vegetable marrow; (amer.) Italian squash.

zucconàre, v.t. to crop s.o.'s hair.

zuccóne, s.m. (fam.) 1. (grossa testa) big head 2. fig. (persona ottusa) blockhead, dunce; (testardo) donkey.

zúffa, s.f. row, brawl, scuffle, tussle.

zufolaménto, s.m. 1. whistling 2. (agli orecchi) singing, buzz(ing).

zufolàre, v.t. to whistle: — un motivo, to whistle a tune || v.i. 1. to whistle: sa — molto bene, he can whistle very well 2. (degli orecchi) to sing, to buzz: mi zufolano gli orecchi, my ears are singing (o I have a buzzing in my ears).

zufolatóre, s.m., zufolatríce, s.f. whistler.

zufolío, s.m. 1. whistling; whistle 2. (agli orecchi) singing, buzz(ing).

zúfolo, s.m. 1. whistle 2. (strumento a fiato primitivo) flageolet, pipe.

zulú, s.m. 1. Zulu: il paese degli —, Zululand 2. fig, (persona incivile) bad-mannered fellow, uncouth fellow, boor.

zumàre, v.i. (gergo tv.) to zoom.

zúppa, s.f. 1. soup: — di pesce, fish-soup; — di verdura, vegetable soup || — inglese, (dolce) trifle || se non è — è pan bagnato, it is always the same old story 2. fig. (confusione) mess, confusion, medley; (noia) bore: che —!, what a bore!.

zuppièra, s.f. (soup-)tureen.

zúppo, ag. wet (through), soaked, drenched.

Zurìgo, no.pr.f. (geog.) Zurich.

zurlàre, v.i. to romp, to frolic.

zuzzurellóna, zuzzurullóna, s.f. skittish girl.

zuzzurellóne, zuzzurullóne, s.m. skittish boy.

APPENDIX

ABBREVIATIONS IN COMMON USE IN ITALY

a, *ara*, a, are.

A, *ampere*, A, ampere.

A., **1.** *Alpi*, Alps **2.** *Altezza*, *(titolo)* Highness **3.** *(lettera)* *assicurata*, charged letter **4.** *atto*, *(teat.)* act **5.** *autore*, auth., author.

A, *angstrom*, *(fis.)* A, Å angstrom (unit).

A.A., **1.** *Accademia Aeronautica*, Air Force Academy **2.** *Assistenza Automobilistica*, organization for assisting motorists.

ab., *abitanti*, pop., population.

abbr., **1.** *abbreviato*, abbr., abbrev., abbreviated **2.** *abbreviazione*, abbr., abbrev., abbreviation.

abl., *ablativo*, abl., ablative.

a.c., **1.** *a capo*, n.p., new paragraph **2.** *anno corrente*, current year **3.** *assegno circolare*, banker's cheque.

a.C., *avanti Cristo*, B.C., before Christ.

Ac, *attinio*, *(chim.)* Ac, actinium.

acc., **1.** *accidenti!*, d—d, damned! **2.** *accusativo*, acc., accusative.

A.C.C., *Alta Corte Costituzionale*, High Constitutional Court.

A.C.D.G., *Associazione Cristiana dei Giovani*, Y.M.C.A., Young Men's Christian Association.

A.C.I., **1.** *Automobile Club d'Italia*, Italian Automobile Association **2.** *Aviazione Civile Italiana*, Italian Civil Aircraft **3.** *Azione Cattolica Italiana*, Italian Catholic Action.

A.C.I.S., *Alto Commissariato per l'Igiene e la Sanità*, High Board for Hygiene and Health.

A.C.L.I., *Associazione Cristiana dei Lavoratori Italiani*, Italian Christian Workers' Society.

ac.to, *acconto*, *(comm.)* partial payment.

A.D., *(lat.: Anno Domini) dopo Cristo*, A.D., in the year of the Lord.

ag., **1.** *aggettivo*, a., adj., adjective **2.** *agosto*, Aug., August.

Ag, *argento*, *(chim.)* Ag, silver.

AG, *(targa aut.)* *Agrigento*.

A.G.I.P., *Azienda Generale Italiana Petroli*, National Italian Oil Company.

ago., *agosto*, Aug., August.

Ah, *amperora*, Ah, ampere-hour.

A.I., *Aeronautica Italiana*, Italian Air Force.

A.I.E., *Associazione Italiana degli Editori*, Italian Publishers' Association.

Al, *alluminio*, *(chim.)* Al, aluminium.

AL, *(targa aut.)* *Alessandria*.

alg., *algebra*, alg., algebra.

ALITALIA, *Aerolinee Italiane Internazionali*, Italian Air Lines.

all., *allegato*, encl., enclosure.

alt., **1.** *altezza*, ht., height **2.** *altitudine*, alt., altitude; ht., height.

a.m., *antimeridiano*, a.m., before midday.

Am, *americio*, *(chim.)* Am, americium.

A.M., **1.** *Accademia Militare*, Military Academy **2.** *(targa aut.)* *Aeronautica Militare*, (Italian) Air Force.

amer., *americano*, Am., Amer., American.

AMIG, *Associazione Mutilati e Invalidi di Guerra*, Association of Disabled Servicemen.

AN, *(targa aut.)* *Ancona*.

A.N.A.S., *Azienda Nazionale Autonoma della Strada*, National Road Board.

ANIC, *Azienda Nazionale Idrogenazione Carburanti*, National Corporation for the Hydrogenation of Fuels.

A.N.L., *Accademia Nazionale dei Lincei*, Lincei Academy.

A.N.P.I., *Associazione Nazionale Partigiani d'Italia*, National Association of Italian Partisans.

A.N.S.A., *Agenzia Nazionale Stampa Associata*, Italian News Agency.

ant., *antimeridiano*, a.m., before midday.

AO, *(targa aut.)* *Aosta*.

AP, *(targa aut.)* *Ascoli Piceno*.

A.P., *alta pressione*, h.p., H.P., high pressure.

apr., *aprile*, Ap., Apr., April.

AQ, *(targa aut.)* *L'Aquila*.

Ar, *argo*, *(chim.)* A, argon.

AR, *(targa aut.)* *Arezzo*.

A.R., **1.** *Altezza Reale*, R.H., Royal Highness **2.** *andata e ritorno*, *(ferr.)* return ticket.

A.R.A.R., *Azienda Rilievo e Alienazione Residuati*, Organization for the Resale of Army Surplus Stores.

Arc., *arcivescovo*, Arch., Archbp., Archbishop.

arch., *architetto*, arch., archt., architect.

A.R.S., *Assemblea Regionale Siciliana*, Sicilian Regional Assembly.

art., *articolo*, *(gram.)* art., article.

As, *arsenico*, *(chim.)* As, arsenic.

A.S., *Altezza Serenissima*, Serene Highness.

A.S.C.I., *Associazione Scoutistica Cattolica Italiana*, Catholic Boy Scouts.

at, *atmosfera (metrica)*, at, (metric) atmosphere.

At, *astato*, *(chim.)* At, astatine.

AT, *(targa aut.)* *Asti*.

A.T., **1.** *alta tensione*, H.V., high voltage **2.** *Antico Testamento*, O.T., Old Testament.

Atm, *atmosfera (fisica)*, Atm, (standard) atmosphere.

A.T.M., *Azienda Tranviaria Municipale*, Municipal Tram Company.

att., *attivo*, *(gram.)* a., act., active.

attr., *attributo*, *(gram.)* attrib., attribute.

Au, *oro*, *(chim.)* Au, gold.

av., *avverbio*, ad., adv., adverb.

AV, *(targa aut.)* *Avellino*.

A.V.I.S., *Associazione Volontari Italiani del Sangue*, Association of Voluntary Italian Blood-donors.

avv., **1.** *avverbio*, ad., adv., adverb **2.** *avvocato*, law., lawyer; Sol., solicitor; bar., barr., barrister.

B

B, *boro*, *(chim.)* B, boron.

B., *Beato*, Bl., Blessed.

Ba, *bario*, *(chim.)* Ba, barium.

BA, *(targa aut.)* *Bari*.

B.A., *Belle Arti*, Fine Arts.

bar., *Barone*, B., Baron.

Be, *berillio*, *(chim.)* Be, beryllium.

Benelux, BE.NE.LUX., *Belgio, Olanda, Lussemburgo*, Benelux, Belgium, Netherlands, Luxemburg.

BG, *(targa aut.)* *Bergamo*.

Bi, *bismuto*, *(chim.)* Bi, bismuth.

B.I., *Banca d'Italia*, Bank of Italy.

bibl., **1.** *bibliografia*, bibl., bibliography **2.** *biblioteca*, lib., library.

Bk, *berkelio*, *(chim.)* Bk, berkelium.

BL, *(targa aut.)* *Belluno*.

BN, *(targa aut.)* *Benevento*.

BO, *(targa aut.)* *Bologna*.

B.P., *bassa pressione*, l.p., low pressure.

Br, *bromo*, *(chim.)* Br, bromine.

BR, *(targa aut.)* *Brindisi*.

brev., *brevetto*, brev., brevet; pat., patent.

BS, *(targa aut.)* *Brescia*.

b.ssa, *baronessa*, baroness.

B.T., *bassa tensione*, L.V., low voltage.

B.U., *Bollettino Ufficiale*, Official Bulletin.

B.V.M., *Beata Vergine Maria*, B.V.M., Blessed Virgin Mary.

BZ, *(targa aut.)* *Bolzano*.

C

c., **1.** *capitolo*, c., cap., ch., chap., chapter **2.** *carta*, (*bibliografia*) fo., fol., folio **3.** *circa*, ca., about **4.** *codice*, (*dir.*) code **5.** *corpo*, (*tip.*) type-size.

C, **1.** *carbonio*, (*chim.*) C, carbon **2.** *Celsius*, C, Celsius **3.** *coulomb*, C, coulomb.

c.a., *corrente alternata*, a.c., A.C., alternating current.

Ca, *calcio*, (*chim.*) Ca, calcium.

CA, (*targa aut.*) *Cagliari*.

cabl., *cablogramma*, cable.

cad., *cadauno*, ea., each.

C.A.I., *Club Alpino Italiano*, Italian Alpine Club.

cal, *piccola caloria*, cal., small calorie.

Cal, *grande caloria*, Cal., large calorie.

cap., *caporale*, corp., corporal.

Cap., **1.** *capitano*, Capt., Captain **2.** *capitolo*, c., cap., ch., chap., chapter.

Capp., *capitoli*, cc., chapters.

C.A.R., *Centro Addestramento Reclute*, Recruit Training Centre.

Card., *Cardinale*, Card., Cardinal.

Cav., *Cavaliere*.

CB, (*targa aut.*) *Campobasso*.

c.c., **1.** *conto corrente*, A/C, Ca/C, current account **2.** *corrente continua*, d.c., D.C., direct current.

c c, *conto corrente*, A/C, Ca/C, current account.

C.C., **1.** *Carabinieri*, Carabinieri (Italian gendarmerie) **2.** *Carta Costituzionale*, Constitutional Charter **3.** *Codice Civile*, C.C., Code Civil **4.** *Codice di Commercio*, Commercial Code **5.** *Corpo Consolare*, Consular Corps **6.** *Corte Costituzionale*, Constitutional Court **7.** *Corte di Cassazione*, Supreme Court of Appeal.

C.C.I., *Camera di Commercio Internazionale*, International Chamber of Commerce.

c.c.p., *conto corrente postale*, current postal account.

Cd, *cadmio*, (*chim.*) Cd, cadmium.

C.D., **1.** *Consigliere Delegato*, Managing Director **2.** *Corpo Diplomatico*, C.D., Corps Diplomatique.

C. d'A., **1.** *Corpo d'Armata*, A.C., Army Corps **2.** *Corte d'Assise*, Court of Assizes.

c.d.d., *come dovevasi dimostrare*, q.e.d., which was to be demonstrated.

C.d.G., *Compagnia di Gesù*, S. J., Society of Jesus.

C.d.L., *Camera del Lavoro*, Trade Union Head Quarters.

C.d.R., *Cassa di Risparmio*, Savings Bank.

C.d.S., **1.** *Circolo della Stampa*, Press Club **2.** *Codice della Strada*, Highway Code **3.** *Consiglio di Sicurezza*, Security Council.

Ce, *cerio*, (*chim.*) Ce, cerium.

CE, (*targa aut.*) *Caserta*.

C.E., **1.** *Comitato Esecutivo*, Executive Committee **2.** *Consiglio Europeo*, CE, Council of Europe.

C.E.C.A., *Comunità Europea per il Carbone e l'Acciaio*, ECSC, European Coal and Steel Community.

C.E.D., *Comunità Europea di Difesa*, E.D.C., European Defense Community.

C.E.E.A., *Comunità Europea per l'Energia Atomica*, European Atomic Energy Community.

C.E.R.N., (*francese: Centre Européen des Recherches Nucléaires*) *Consiglio Europeo per le Ricerche Nucleari*, CERN, European Council for Nuclear Research.

Cf, *californio*, (*chim.*) Cf, californium.

cfr., *confronta*, cf., compare.

cg, *centigrammo*, cg, centigram(me).

C.G., *Console Generale*, C.G., Consul General.

C.G.I.L., *Confederazione Generale Italiana del Lavoro*, Federation of Italian Trade Unions (with extreme-left-wing political trend).

C.G.S., (*unità, sistema*) *centimetro-grammo massa-secondo*, C.G.S., centimetre-gram(me)-second(unit, system).

Ch, *coseno iperbolico*, cosh, hyperbolic cosine.

CH, (*targa aut.*) *Chieti*.

chir., *chirurgia*, surg., surgery.

C.ia, *Compagnia*, Co., Company.

c.i.f., *costo compreso il nolo e l'assicurazione*, c.i.f., cost insurance freight.

C.I.O., *Comitato Internazionale Olimpico*, International Olympic Committee.

C.I.S.L., *Confederazione Italiana Sindacati Liberi*, Federation of Italian Trade Unions (officially non-party, but with moderate Socialist-Christian Democrat trend).

C.I.S.Na.L., *Confederazione Italiana Sindacati Nazionali Liberi*, Federation of Italian Trade Unions (with right-wing tendency).

C.I.T., *Compagnia Italiana Turismo*, Italian Travel Agency.

cl, *centilitro*, cl, centilitre.

Cl, *cloro*, (*chim.*) Cl, chlorine.

CL, (*targa aut.*) *Caltanissetta*.

C.L.N., *Comitato di Liberazione Nazionale*, organizers of Resistance Movement (during World War II).

cm, *centimetro*, cm, centimetre.

c.m., *corrente mese*, inst., instant, the present month.

Cm, *curio*, (*chim.*) Cm, curium.

CN, (*targa aut.*) *Cuneo*.

Co, *cobalto*, (*chim.*) Co, cobalt.

CO, (*targa aut.*) *Como*.

cod., *codice*, cod., codex.

coeff., *coefficiente*, coeff., coefficient.

Col., *Colonnello*, Col., Colonel.

coll., *collettivo*, coll., collective.

com., *comandante*, Com., Commander.

comm., *commendatore*.

comp., *comparativo*, comp., compar., comparative.

cond., *condizionale*, (*gram.*) conditional.

cong., **1.** *congiuntivo*, subj., subjunctive **2.** *congiunzione*, conj., conjunction.

C.N.R., *Consiglio Nazionale delle Ricerche*, National Research Council.

CONFAGRICOLTURA, *Confederazione Generale dell'Agricoltura Italiana*, General Confederation of Italian Agriculture.

CONFARTIGIANATO, *Confederazione Generale dell'Artigianato Italiano*, General Confederation of Italian Crafts.

CONFCOMMERCIO, *Confederazione Generale del Commercio*, General Confederation of Commerce.

CONFEDELTERRA, *Confederazione Nazionale dei Lavoratori della Terra*, National Confederation of Workers on the Land.

CONFINDUSTRIA, *Confederazione Generale dell'Industria Italiana*, General Confederation of Italian Industry.

CONFINTESA, *Intesa fra le Confederazioni Italiane degli Industriali, Commercianti, Agricoltori e dell'Artigianato*, Agreement between the Italian Confederation of Industrialists, Businessmen, Farmers, and Craftsmen.

C.O.N.I., *Comitato Olimpico Nazionale Italiano*, Italian Olympic Games Committee.

contr., *contrazione*, contr., contraction.

cont.ssa, *contessa*, countess.

cos, *coseno*, cos, cosine.

cosec, *cosecante*, cosec, cosecant.

cost., *costante*, (*mat.*) const., constant.

c.p., *cartolina postale*, p.c., P.C., postcard.

C.P., **1.** *Casella Postale*, Post Box **2.** *Codice Penale*, Penal Code **3.** *Consiglio Provinciale*, District Council.

C.P.C., *Codice di Procedura Civile*, C.C.P., Code of Civil Procedure.

C.P.P., *Codice di Procedura Penale*, C.Cr.P., Code of Criminal Procedure.

Cr, *cromo*, (*chim.*) Cr, chromium.

CR, (*targa aut.*) *Cremona*.

C.R.A.L., *Circolo Ricreativo Assistenza Lavoratori*, Recreational Clubs organized by National Assistance Board.

C.R.I., **1.** *Croce Rossa Internazionale*, International Red Cross **2.** *Croce Rossa Italiana*, Italian Red Cross.

c.s., *come sopra,* as above.
Cs, *cesio, (chim.)* Cs, caesium.
CS, *(targa aut.) Cosenza.*
C.S., 1. *Codice della Strada,* Highway Code **2.** *Comando Supremo,* Supreme Command **3.** *Consiglio di Sicurezza,* Security Council.
C.S.C., *Centro Sperimentale di Cinematografia,* Experimental Film Studios.
C.so, *Corso,* Rd., Road.
CT, *(targa aut.) Catania.*
ctg, *cotangente,* cot, cotangent.
C.T.I., *Consociazione Turistica Italiana,* Italian Touring Club.
c.to, *conto,* ac., a/c, account.
Cu, *rame, (chim.)* Cu, copper.
CV, *cavallo vapore,* CV, cheval-vapeur.
CVh, *cavallo vapore ora.*
c.v.d., *come volevasi dimostrare,* q.e.d., which was to be demonstrated.
CZ, *(targa aut.) Catanzaro.*

D

dag, *decagrammo,* dkg, decagram(me).
dal, *decalitro,* dkl, dal, decalitre.
dam, *decametro,* dkm, decametre.
dat., *dativo,* dat., dative.
d.c., *da capo,* n.p., new paragraph.
d.C., *dopo Cristo,* A.D., Anno Domini, in the year of the Lord.
D.C., *Democrazia Cristiana, (pol.)* Christian Democrat Party.
D.D.T., *diclorodifeniltricloroetano,* DDT, dichlorodiphenyltrichloroethane.
dev., dev.mo, *devotissimo, (nelle lettere)* yours truly.
dg, *decigrammo,* dg, decigram(me).
D.G., 1. *Direttore Generale,* Managing Director **2.** *Direzione Generale,* Managing Director's Office.
dic., *dicembre,* D., Dec., December.
dl, *decilitro,* dl, decilitre.
D.L., *Decreto Legge,* law by decree.
dm, *decimetro,* dec, dm, decimetre.
dom., *domenica,* Su., Sun., Sund., Sunday.
dott., *Dottore,* Dr., Doctor.
D.P., *Decreto Presidenziale,* Decree of the President.
dr., *Dottore,* Dr., Doctor.
dr.ssa, *Dottoressa,* dr., Doctor.
d.ssa, duc.sa, *Duchessa,* D., Duchess.
Dy, *disprosio, (chim.)* Dy, dysprosium.

E

E., *Est,* E., East.
E.A., *Ente Autonomo,* Independent Committee.
E.C.A., *Ente Comunale di Assistenza,* Municipal Public Assistance Board.
ecc., *eccetera,* etc., &c., and so on.
Ecc., *Eccellenza, (per ambasciatore, ministro, ecc.)* Exc., Excellency; *(per vescovo)* Ldp., Lp., Lordship.
EE, *(targa per automobili straniere provvisoriamente immatricolate in Italia) Escursionisti Esteri.*
E.F.T.A., *Associazione europea di libero scambio,* European Free Trade Association.
Egr. Sig., *Egregio Signore, (negli indirizzi)* Mr.
E.I., 1. *Enciclopedia Italiana,* Italian Encyclopaedia **2.** *Esercito Italiano, (targa aut.)* Italian Army.
Em., *Eminenza,* Eminence.
EN, *(targa aut.) Enna.*
E.N.A.L., *Ente Nazionale Assistenza Lavoratori,* National Association for Assistance to Workers.
E.N.I., *Ente Nazionale Idrocarburi,* National Hydrocarbon Corporation.
E.N.I.C., *Ente Nazionale Industrie Cinematografiche,* National Association of Film Producers.
E.N.I.T., *Ente Nazionale Industrie Turistiche,* National Institution for the Promotion of Tourist Industry.

E.N.P.A.S., *Ente Nazionale Previdenza e Assistenza per i Dipendenti Statali,* National Insurance and Welfare Board for Civil Servants.
E.N.P.I., *Ente Nazionale Prevenzione Infortuni,* National Institution for the Prevention of Accidents.
E.P.T., *Ente Provinciale per il Turismo,* Provincial Board for Promotion of Tourist Industry.
Er, *erbio, (chim.)* Er, erbium.
E.R.P., *Programma di Ricostruzione Europea,* European Recovery Programme.
es., *esempio,* ex., example.
Eu, *europio, (chim.)* Eu, europium.
E.U.R., *Esposizione Universale Roma,* Roman Universal Exhibition.
EURATOM, *Ente europeo per l'energia atomica,* European Atomic Energy Organization.
Eurovision, *Televisione Europea,* Eurovision, European Television.
E.V., 1. *Eccellenza Vostra,* Your Excellency **2.** *Era Volgare,* A.D., Anno Domini.

F

f., *femminile,* f., fem., feminine.
F, 1. *Fahrenheit,* F, Fahrenheit **2.** *farad,* F, farad **3.** *fluoro, (chim.)* F, fluorine.
fatt., *fattura,* inv., invoice.
f.co, *franco, (comm.)* free.
Fe, *ferro, (chim.)* Fe, iron.
FE, *(targa aut.) Ferrara.*
feb., *febbraio,* Feb., February.
fem., *femminile,* f., fem., feminine.
ferr., *ferrovia,* Ry., railway.
F.E.R.T., *Fortitudo Eius Rhodum Tenuit, (motto della Casa di Savoia e dell'Ordine dell'Annunziata)* its valour saved the island of Rhodes.
FF.SS., *Ferrovie dello Stato,* (Italian) State Railways
FG, *(targa aut.) Foggia.*
FI, *(targa aut.) Firenze,* Florence.
F.I.A.P., *Federazione Italiana Atletica Pesante.*
F.I.A.T., *Fabbrica Italiana Automobili Torino,* Italian Automobile Factory Turin.
F.I.D.A.L., *Federazione Italiana di Atletica Leggera.*
F.I.E., *Fondazione Figli Italiani all'Estero,* Foundation of sons of Italy abroad.
F.I.G.C., *Federazione Italiana Giuoco Calcio,* Italian Football Association.
FINMARE, *Società Finanziaria Marittima,* Maritime Finance Company.
FINMECCANICA, *Società Finanziaria Meccanica,* Mechanical Finance Company.
FINSIDER, *Società Finanziaria Siderurgica,* Iron and Steel Finance Company.
FIOM, *Federazione Impiegati e Operai Metallurgici,* Federation of Metal Employees and Workers.
F.I.P., *Federazione Italiana Pallacanestro,* Italian Basketball Association.
F.I.S., *Federazione Italiana Scherma,* Italian Fencing Association.
F.I.S.I., *Federazione Italiana Sport Invernali,* Italian Winter Sports Association.
F.I.T., *Federazione Italiana Tennis,* Italian Lawn Tennis Association.
F.lli, *Fratelli, (comm.)* Bros., Brothers.
Fm, *fermio, (chim.)* Fm, fermium.
F.M.I., *Federazione Motociclistica Italiana,* Italian Motorcycle Federation.
FO, *(targa aut.) Forlì.*
f.o.b., *franco a bordo,* f.o.b., free on board.
fonet., *fonetica,* phon., phonet., phonetics.
foto., *fotografia,* phot., photography.
F.P.I., *Federazione Pugilistica Italiana,* Italian Boxing Association.
Fr, *francio, (chim.)* Fr, francium.
FR, *(targa aut.) Frosinone.*
Fr. b., *franco belga,* Belgian franc.

Fr.f., *franco francese,* French franc.

Fr.s., *franco svizzero,* Swiss franc.

F.S., *Ferrovie dello Stato,* Italian State Railways.

f.to, *firmato,* s., signed.

F.U.C.I., *Federazione Universitaria Cattolica Italiana,* Italian Catholic University Association.

fut., *futuro, (gram.)* fut., future.

G

g, 1. *accelerazione di gravità,* g, acceleration of gravity **2.** *grammo,* g, gram(me).

g., *giorno,* d., day.

Ga, *gallio, (chim.)* Ga, gallium.

G.A., *Giunta Amministrativa,* Municipal Council.

G.B., *Gran Bretagna,* G.B., Great Britain.

G.C., 1. *Gesù Cristo,* J.C., Jesus Christ **2.** *Gran Croce, (decorazione)* Grand Cross.

Gd, *gadolino, (chim.)* Gd, gadolinium.

G.D., *Granduca,* G.D., Grand Duke.

G.d.F., *Guardia di Finanza,* Revenue Guard.

Ge, *germanio, (chim.)* Ge, germanium.

GE, *(targa aut.)* Genova, Genoa.

G.E.I., *Giovani Esploratori Italiani,* Italian Boy Scouts.

gen., 1. *genitivo,* gen., genit., genitive **2.** *gennaio,* Jan., January.

Gen., *Generale,* Gen., General.

gener., *generalmente,* gen., generally.

ger., *gerundio,* ger., gerund.

Ge.sta.po., *(tedesco: Geheime Stattliche Polizei) Polizia segreta politica,* Gestapo (Nazi secret police).

Ghe.Pe.U., *(russo: Gossudàrstvennoie Politiceskoie Upravlènie) Polizia Segreta Russa,* Ogpu, Unified State Political Directorate (Russian secret police, 1922-34).

gio., giov., *giovedì,* Thur., Thurs., Thursday.

giri/min, *giri al minuto,* rpm, r.p.m., revolutions per minute.

giri/sec, *giri al secondo,* rps, r.p.s., revolutions per second.

giu., *giugno,* Ju., Jun., June.

GO, *(targa aut.)* Gorizia.

G.P.A., *Giunta Provinciale Amministrativa,* County Council.

GR, *(targa aut.)* Grosseto.

G.U., *Gazzetta Ufficiale,* Official Gazette.

G.V., *Grande Velocità, (ferr.)* express goods service.

H

h, *ora,* h., hr., hour.

H, 1. *henry, (elett.)* H, henry **2.** *idrogeno, (chim.)* H, hydrogen.

ha, *ettaro,* ha, hectare.

He, *elio, (chim.)* He, helium.

Hf, *afnio, (chim.)* Hf, hafnium.

H.F., *alta frequenza, (rad. tv.),* H.F., high frequency.

hg, *ettogrammo,* hg, hectogram(me).

Hg, *mercurio, (chim.)* Hg, mercury.

hl, *ettolitro,* hl, hectolitre.

hm, *ettometro,* hm, hectometre.

Ho, *olmio, (chim.)* Ho, holmium.

Hz, *hertz,* Hz, hertz.

I

I, 1. *iodio, (chim.)* I, iodine **2.** *(targa aut.)* Italia, Italy·

ibid., *(lat.: ibidem) nello stesso luogo,* ib., ibid., in the same place.

I.C.S., *Istituto Centrale di Statistica,* National Statistics Office.

id., *(lat.: idem) lo stesso,* id., the same.

I.G.E., *Imposta Generale sull'Entrata,* turnover tax.

IM, *(targa aut.)* Imperia.

imp., imper., *imperativo,* imp., imper., impv., imperative.

imperf., impf., *imperfetto,* imp., imperf., impf., imperfect.

In, *indio, (chim.)* In, indium.

I.N.A., *Istituto Nazionale Assicurazioni,* National Insurance Service.

I.N.A.D.E.L., *Istituto Nazionale per l'Assistenza ai Dipendenti degli Enti Locali,* National Institute for Welfare of Employees of Local Bodies.

I.N.A.I.L., *Istituto Nazionale per l'Assicurazione contro gli Infortuni sul Lavoro,* National Institute for Insurance against Industrial Injuries.

I.N.A.M., *Istituto Nazionale per l'Assicurazione contro le Malattie,* National Health Insurance Service.

I.N.C.I.S., *Istituto Nazionale per le Case degli Impiegati dello Stato,* Institute for providing houses for Civil Servants.

IN.COM., *Industria Cortometraggi,* Short Film Industry.

indic., *indicativo,* ind., indic., indicative.

inf., *infinito,* inf., infin., infinitive.

in-fol., *in folio,* fo., fol., folio.

ing., *ingegnere,* eng., engineer.

I.N.P.I., *Istituto Nazionale per la Prevenzione degli Infortuni,* National Institution for the Prevention of Accidents.

I.N.P.S., *Istituto Nazionale Previdenza Sociale,* National Institute of Social Insurance.

int., *interiezione,* int., interj., interjection.

I.N.T., *Istituto Nazionale Trasporti,* National Transport Institute.

inter., *interiezione,* int., interj., interjection.

INTER.POL., *Polizia Internazionale,* INTER.POL., International Police.

intr., intrans., *intransitivo,* i., int., intr., intrans., intransitive.

I.P.S., *Istituto Poligrafico dello Stato,* State printing works and stationery office.

Ir, *iridio, (chim.)* Ir, iridium.

I.R.I., *Istituto per la Ricostruzione Industriale,* Institute for the Reconstruction of Industry.

ITAL-CABLE, *Compagnia Italiana dei Cavi Telegrafici e Telefonici Sottomarini,* Italian Cable Company.

J

J, *joule,* J, joule.

K

K, 1. *Kelvin,* K, Kelvin **2.** *potassio, (chim.)* K, potassium.

kc, *chilociclo, (rad.)* kc, kc., kilocycle.

kcal, *chilocaloria,* kg-cal, kilogram-calorie.

kc/s, *chilocicli al secondo, (rad.)* kc, kc., kilocycles per second.

kg, *chilogrammo,* kg, kgm, kilogram(me).

kgm, *chilogrammetro,* kg-m, kilogram-metre.

kl, *chilolitro,* kl, kilolitre.

km, *chilometro,* km, kilometre.

km/h, *chilometri all'ora,* kmph., kilometres per hour.

kmq, *chilometro quadrato,* sq. km., square kilometre.

km/sec, *chilometri al secondo,* kmps., kilometres per second.

k.o., *fuori combattimento,* K.O., knock out.

Kr, *cripto, (chim.)* Kr, krypton.

kV, *chilovolt,* kv., kilovolt(s).

kW, *chilowatt,* kw., kilowatt.

kWh, *chilowattora,* K.W.H., kw-h, kw-hr, kilowatt-hour.

L

l, *litro,* l, litre.

l., *lunedì,* M., Mon., Monday.

La, *lantanio, (chim.)* La, lanthanum.

lat., *latitudine,* l., lat., latitude.

l.c., *luogo citato,* l., loc. cit., in the place cited.

LE, *(targa aut.)* Lecce.

lett., 1. *letterario,* lit., literary **2.** *letteratura,* lit., literature.

L.F., *low frequency, (rad. tv.)* L.F., bassa frequenza.

Li, *litio*, *(chim.)* Li, lithium.
LI, *(targa aut.)* *Livorno*, Leghorn.
Lit., *Lire italiane*, Italian lire.
LL.PP., *Lavori Pubblici*, Public Works.
lm, *lumen*, *(fis.)* lm, lumen.
l.m., *livello del mare*, s.l., sea level.
ln, *logaritmo naturale*, ln, natural logarithm.
loc.cit., *(lat.: loco citato) luogo citato*, loc. cit., l.c., in the place cited.
log, *logaritmo*, log, log., logarithm.
long., *longitudine*, lon., long., longitude.
L.st., *lira sterlina*, £, pound (sterling).
LT, *(targa aut.)* *Latina*.
lu., *luglio*, Jul., July.
Lu, *lutezio*, *(chim.)* Lu, lutetium.
LU, *(targa aut.)* *Lucca*.
lug., *luglio*, Jul., July.
lun., *lunedì*, M., Mon., Monday.
lx, *lux*, *(fis.)* lx, lux.

M

m, *metro*, m, metre.
m., **1.** *maschile*, m., masc., masculine **2.** *mese*, m., month **3.** *morto*, d., dead.
μ, *micron*, μ, micron.
M., *Monte*, Mt., Mount.
mA, *milliampere*, Ma., M.A., milliampere.
μA, *microampere*, μA, microampere.
M.A.E., *Ministero degli Affari Esteri*, Ministry of Foreign Affairs.
mag., *maggio*, May.
Magg., *Maggiore*, Maj., Major.
mar., **1.** *martedì*, T., Tu., Tues., Tuesday **2.** *marzo*, M., Mar., March.
Mar., *Maresciallo (dei Carabinieri)*.
march., *Marchese*, Marq., Marquis.
mart., *martedì*, T., Tu., Tues., Tuesday.
MAS, *motoscafo antisommergibile*, M.T.B., motor torpedo-boat.
max., *massimo*, max., maximum.
m.c., *mese corrente*, inst., the present month.
MC, *(targa aut.)* *Macerata*.
M.C.D., *massimo comun divisore*, h.c.f., highest common factor.
m.c.m., *minimo comune multiplo*, l.c.m., lowest (or least) common multiple.
ME, *(targa aut.)* *Messina*.
M.E., **1.** *Medio Evo*, Middle Ages **2.** *Movimento Europeo*, European Movement.
M.E.C., *Mercato Europeo Comune*, E.C.M., European Common Market.
mer., **merc.**, *mercoledì*, We., Wed., Wednesday.
μF, *microfarad*, μF, microfarad.
M.F., **1.** *media frequenza*, *(rad. tv.)* M.F., medium frequency **2.** *modulazione di frequenza*, *(rad.)* F.M., frequency modulation.
M.F.E., *Movimento Federalista Europeo*, European Federalist Movement.
mg, *milligrammo*, mg, milligram(me).
Mg, **1.** *magnesio*, *(chim.)* Mg, magnesium **2.** *miriagrammo*, myg., myriagram(me).
MI, *(targa aut.)* *Milano*, Milan.
min, *minuto*, m., min., minute.
min., *minimo*, min., minim(um).
mitt., *mittente*, sender.
ml, *millilitro*, ml, millilitre.
Ml, *mirialitro*, myl., myrialitre.
mm, *millimetro*, mm, millimetre.
mμ, *millimicron*, mμ, millimicron.
Mm, *miriametro*, mym., myriametre.
M.M., *Marina Militare*, Italian Navy.
m'min, *metri al minuto*, mpm., metres per minute.
Mn, *manganese*, *(chim.)* Mn, manganese.
MN, *(targa aut.)* *Mantova*, Mantua.
M/N, *motonave*, M/S, motorship.

Mo, *molibdeno*, *(chim.)* Mo, molybdenum.
Mo., *Maestro (di musica)*, Maestro.
MO, *(targa aut.)* *Modena*.
mons., *monsignore*, *(eccl.)* Mgr., Monsignor.
M.PP.TT., *Ministero delle Poste e delle Telecomunicazioni*, Post Office Board.
M.R., **1.** *Magnifico Rettore*, *(nelle università)* Vice-Chancellor **2.** *Molto Reverendo*, *(eccl.)* R.R., Right Reverend.
ms., **MS.**, *manoscritto*, ms., MS., manuscript.
MS, *(targa aut.)* *Massa Carrara*.
M.S., *Mutuo Soccorso*, Mutual Aid.
M.sa, *Marchesa*, March., Marchioness.
M.se, *Marchese*, Marq., Marquis.
m/sec, *metri al secondo*, mps., metres per second.
M.S.I., *Movimento Sociale Italiano*, neo-Fascist Party.
MT, *(targa aut.)* *Matera*.
mus., **1.** *musica*, mus., music **2.** *musicale*, mus., musical.
M.V., *Maria Vergine*, the Virgin Mary.

N

n., **1.** *nato*, b., n., born **2.** *neutro*, n., neut., neuter.
N, *azoto*, *(chim.)* N, nitrogen.
N., *Nord*, N., No., North.
Nº, *numero*, No., number.
Na, *sodio*, *(chim.)* Na, sodium.
NA, *(targa aut.)* *Napoli*, Naples.
N.A.T.O., *Organizzazione del Trattato Nord-Atlantico*, N.A.T.O., North Atlantic Treaty Organization.
naz., *nazionale*, nat., national.
Nb, *niobio*, *(chim.)* Nb, niobium.
N.B., *nota bene*, N.B., note well.
Nd, *neodimio*, *(chim.)* Nd, neodymium.
N.D., *Nobil Donna*, member of a noble family.
N. d. A., *Nota dell'Autore*, author's note.
N. d. D., *Nota della Direzione*, note by the editor (of a newspaper).
N. d. E., *Nota dell'Editore*, publisher's note.
N. d. R., *Nota della Redazione*, editor's note.
N. d. T., *Nota del Traduttore*, translator's note.
Ne, *neo*, *(chim.)* Ne, neon.
N.E., *Nord-Est*, N.E., North-East.
N.H., *(lat.: Nobilis Homo) Nobil Uomo*, member of a noble family.
Ni, *nichel*, *(chim.)* Ni, nickel.
N.N., *(lat.: Nescio Nomen) di paternità ignota*, *(sui certificati di nascita, ecc.)* name (of father) unknown.
No., *numero*, No., number.
NO, *(targa aut.)* *Novara*.
N.O., *Nord-Ovest*, N.W., North-West.
nob., *nobile*, nobleman.
nom., *nominativo*, *(gram.)* n., nom., nominative.
nov., *novembre*, Nov., November.
Np, *nettunio*, *(chim.)* Np, neptunium.
ns., *nostro*, our.
N.T., *Nuovo Testamento*, N.T., New Testament.
NU, *(targa aut.)* *Nuoro*.
N.U., **1.** *Nazioni Unite*, UN, U.N., United Nations **2.** *Nettezza Urbana*, Municipal service for collecting rubbish, cleaning streets, etc.

O

O, *ossigeno*, *(chim.)* O, oxygen.
O., *Ovest*, W., West.
Ω, *ohm*, Ω, ohm.
obb.mo, **obbl.mo**, *obbligatissimo*, your obedient servant.
O. d. G., *ordine del giorno*, *(amm.)* agenda; *(mil.)* dispatches; *(pol.)* parliamentary motion.
O.E.C.E., *Organizzazione Economica per la Cooperazione Europea*, O.E.E.C., Organization for European Economic Co-operation.
O.F.M., *Ordine dei Frati Minori*, O.F.M., Order of Friars Minor.
O.I.L., *Organizzazione Internazionale del Lavoro*, I.L.O., International Labour Organization.

O.K., *tutto bene*, O.K., all correct.

O.M.R., *Ordine (cavalleresco) al Merito della Repubblica*, Order of Merit of the Republic.

on., *onorevole*, M.P., Member of Parliament.

O.N.M.I., 1. *Opera Nazionale per il Mezzogiorno d'Italia*, National Board for the South of Italy 2. *Opera Nazionale per la Protezione della Maternità e dell'Infanzia*, National Board for Maternity and Child Welfare.

O.N.U., *Organizzazione delle Nazioni Unite*, U.N.O., United Nations Organization.

OO.PP., *Opere Pubbliche*, Public Works.

O.P., *Ordine dei Predicatori*, (*Domenicani*) Order of Preachers.

op. cit., (*lat.*: *opere citato*) *opera citata*, op. cit., in the work cited.

Os, *osmio*, (*chim.*) Os, osmium.

O.S.SS.A., *Ordine Supremo della Santissima Annunziata*, Supreme Order of the Holy Annunciation.

ott., *ottobre*, O., Oct., October.

O.V.R.A., *Opera Volontaria per la Repressione dell'Antifascismo*, Fascist Secret Police.

P

p., *pagina*, p., page.

P, 1. *fosforo*, (*chim.*) P, phosphorus 2. *Posteggio*, P, Parking.

P., *Padre*, (*eccl.*) Fr., Father.

Pa, *protoattinio*, (*chim.*) Pa, protoactinium.

PA, (*targa aut.*) Palermo.

P.A., 1. *Patto Atlantico*, Atlantic Treaty 2. *Posta Aerea*, Air Mail.

pag., *pagina*, p., page.

par., *paragrafo*, par., paragraph.

part., *participio*, p., part., participle.

partic., *particella*, (*gram.*) particle.

pass., 1. *passato*, (*gram.*) p., past 2. (*lat.*: *passim*) *passim, in diversi luoghi*, (*nelle citazioni*) pass., passim, in every part 3. *passivo*, (*gram.*) pass., passive.

Pb, *piombo*, (*chim.*) Pb, lead.

PC, (*targa aut.*) Piacenza.

p.c.c., *per copia conforme*, certified true copy.

P.C.I., *Partito Comunista Italiano*, Italian Communist Party.

Pd, *palladio*, (*chim.*) Pd, palladium.

PD, (*targa aut.*) Padova, Padua.

P.d.A., *Partito di Azione*, Action Party.

P.D.C., *Partito Democratico Cristiano*, Christian Democrat Party.

P.D.I., *Partito Democratico Italiano*, Italian Democratic Party.

p.e., *per esempio*, e.g., for instance; f.e., for example.

PE, (*targa aut.*) Pescara.

per/sec, *periodi al secondo*, c/s, cycles per second.

p.es., *per esempio*, e.g., for instance; f.e., for example.

p.f., *per favore*, please.

PG, (*targa aut.*) Perugia.

P.G., *Procuratore Generale*, A.G., Att.-Gen., Attorney General.

PI, (*targa aut.*) Pisa.

P.I., *Pubblica Istruzione*, Public Education.

pl., *plurale*, pl., plu., plural.

P.L.I., *Partito Liberale Italiano*, Italian Liberal Party.

p.m., *pomeridiano*, p.m., after midday.

Pm, *prometeo*, (*chim.*) Pm, promethium.

P.M., 1. *Polizia Militare*, M.P., Military Police 2. *Pubblico Ministero*, Public Prosecutor.

P.M.P., *Partito Monarchico Popolare*, Popular Monarchist Party.

P.N.F., *Partito Nazionale Fascista*, National Fascist Party.

P.N.M., *Partito Nazionale Monarchico*, National Monarchist Party.

Po, *polonio*, (*chim.*) Po, polonium.

pol., 1. *politica*, pol., politics 2. *politico*, pol., political.

pop., *popolazione*, pop., population.

p.p., 1. *pacco postale*, p.p., parcel post 2. *per procura*, p.p., by proxy.

PP., *porto pagato*, carriage paid.

P.P., *posa piano*, (*sui colli postali*) handle with care.

pr., 1. *preposizione*, prep., preposition 2. *pronome*, pr., pron., pronoun.

p.r., *per ringraziamento*, with thanks.

Pr, *praseodimio*, (*chim.*) Pr, praseodymium.

PR, (*targa aut.*) Parma.

pred., *predicato*, pred., predicate.

pref., 1. *prefazione*, pref., preface 2. *prefisso*, pref., prefix.

prep., *preposizione*, prep., preposition.

pres., *presente*, (*gram.*) pr., pres., present.

P.R.I., 1. *Partito Radicale Italiano*, Italian Radical Party 2. *Partito Repubblicano Italiano*, Italian Republican Party.

Prin.sa, *Principessa*, Princess.

Proc. Gen., *Procuratore Generale*, A.G., Att.-Gen., Attorney General.

prof., *professore*, Prof., Professor.

prof.sta, *professionista*, professional man.

pron., *pronome*, pr., pron., pronoun.

PS, (*targa aut.*) Pesaro.

P.S., 1. *post scriptum*, P.S., postscript 2. *Pubblica Sicurezza*, Police.

P.S.D.I., *Partito Socialista Democratico Italiano*, Italian Socialist Democratic Party.

P.S.I., *Partito Socialista Italiano*, Italian Socialist Party.

Pt, *platino*, (*chim.*) Pt, platinum.

PT, (*targa aut.*) Pistoia.

P.T., *Poste e Telegrafi*, Post and Telegraph Service.

P.T.P., *Posto Telefonico Pubblico*, public thelephone.

Pu, *plutonio*, (*chim.*), Pu, plutonium.

p.v., *prossimo venturo*, prox., next (month).

PV, (*targa aut.*) Pavia.

P.V., *Piccola Velocità*, (*ferr.*) ordinary goods service.

PZ, (*targa aut.*) Potenza.

P.za, *piazza*, sq., square.

Q

q, *quintale*, q, quintal.

q., *quadrato*, sq., square.

q.b., *quanto basta*, (*nelle ricette*) q.s., a sufficient quantity.

q.e.d., (*lat.*: *quod erat demonstrandum*) *come dovevasi dimostrare*, q.e.d., which was to be demonstrated.

Q.G., *Quartier Generale*, H.Q., headquarters.

R

r, *raggio*, (*geom.*) R, radius.

r., *recto*, (*bibliografia*) r., recto.

R., 1. *raccomandata*, registered letter 2. *Re*, R., King 3. *Regina*, R., Queen 4. *Repubblica*, Repub., Republic 5. *Reverendo*, (*eccl.*) Rev., Reverend 6. *Rifugio* (*antiaereo*), S., Shelter.

Ra, *radio*, (*chim.*) Ra, radium.

RA, (*targa aut.*) Ravenna.

racc., *raccomandata*, registered letter.

rag., *ragioniere*, certified accountant.

R.A.I., *Radio Audizioni Italiane*, Italian Broadcasting Corporation.

R.A.U., *Repubblica Araba Unita*, U.A.R., United Arab Republic.

Rb, *rubidio*, (*chim.*) Rb, rubidium.

Re., *radice cubica*, cubic root.

RC, (*targa aut.*) Reggio Calabria.

R.C., *Rotary Club*.

R.D., *Regio Decreto*, Royal Decree.

R.D.L., *Regio Decreto Legge*, Law by Royal Decree.

R.D.T., *Repubblica Democratica Tedesca,* German Democratic Republic.
Re, *renio, (chim.)* Re, rhenium.
RE, *(targa aut.) Reggio Emilia.*
Rep., *repubblica,* rep., republic.
Rev., *Reverendo, (eccl.)* Rev., Reverend.
Rev.mo, *Reverendissimo, (eccl.)* Rt. Rev., Right Reverend.
R.F.T., *Repubblica Federale Tedesca,* German Federal Republic.
RG, *(targa aut.) Ragusa.*
Rh, *rodio, (chim.)* Rh, rhodium.
RI, *(targa aut.) Rieti.*
R.I., *Repubblica Italiana,* Italian Republic.
ric., *ricevuta,* rec., receipt.
rifl., *riflessivo,* refl., reflexive.
R.M., *Ricchezza Mobile,* (tax on) income.
Rn, *rado, (chim.)* Rn, radon.
RO, *(targa aut.) Rovigo.*
ROMA, *(targa aut.) Roma,* Rome.
Rq., *radice quadrata,* square root.
RSM, *(targa aut.) Repubblica di San Marino,* Republic of San Marino.
R.S.V.P., *(francese: répondez s'il vous plaît)* si prega rispondere, R.S.V.P., reply if you please.
R.T., *radiotelegrafia,* W.T., wireless telegraphy.
Ru, *rutenio, (chim.)* Ru, ruthenium.
R.U., *Regno Unito, (Gran Bretagna e Irlanda del Nord)* U.K., United Kingdom.

S

s, *secondo,* s., sec., second.
s., 1. *sabato,* Sa., Sat., Stdy., Saturday **2.** *sostantivo,* n., noun.
S, 1. *siemens,* S, siemens **2.** *solfo, (chim.)* S, sulphur.
S., 1. *Santo,* S., St., Saint **2.** *Sud,* S., So., South.
SA, *(targa aut.) Salerno.*
S.A., 1. *Società Anonima,* (joint stock) Company **2.** *Sua Altezza,* H.H., His, Her Highness.
sab., *sabato,* Sa., Sat., Stdy., Saturday.
S.A.R., *Sua Altezza Reale,* H.R.H., His, Her Royal Highness.
Sb, *antimonio, (chim.)* Sb, antimony.
s.b.f., *salvo buon fine, (comm.)* under usual reserve.
Sc, *scandio, (chim.)* Sc, scandium.
S.C., 1. *Sede Centrale,* H.O., head office **2.** *Suprema Corte,* S.C., Supreme Court.
S.C.V., *Stato della Città del Vaticano,* Vatican City.
s.d., *senza data, (bibliografia)* n.d., no date.
s.d.l., *senza data o luogo, (bibliografia)* n.p. or d., no place or date.
S.D.N., *Società delle Nazioni,* League of Nations.
Se, *selenio, (chim.)* Se, selenium.
S.E., 1. *Sua Eccellenza,* H.E., His Excellency; *(eccl.)* His Lordship **2.** *Sud-Est,* S.E., South East.
S.E.A.T.O., *Organizzazione del Trattato relativo al Sud-Est Asiatico,* S.E.A.T.O., South-East Asia Treaty Organization.
sec, 1. *secante,* sec, secant **2.** *secondo,* s., sec., second.
sec., *secolo,* c., cent., century.
S.E.D.I., *Società Editrice Documentari Italiani,* Italian Newsreel Company.
seg., *seguente,* f., fol., following.
S.Em., *Sua Eminenza,* H.E., His Eminence.
sen, *seno, (trigonometria)* sin, sine.
sen., *senatore,* sen., senator.
S.E.O., *salvo errori ed omissioni, (comm.)* E.&O.E., errors and omissions excepted.
serg., *sergente,* sergt., sergeant.
sett., *settembre,* Sep., Sept., September.
sfr, *sotto fascia raccomandata, (servizio postale)* registered printed matter.
sfs, *sotto fascia semplice, (servizio postale)* unregistered printed matter.

S.G., 1. *secondo grandezza, (sui menù)* (price) according to size of portion **2.** *Sua Grazia,* H.G., His, Her Grace.
Sh, *seno iperbolico, (trigonometria)* sinh, hyperbolic sine.
Si, *silicio, (chim.)* Si, silicon.
SI, *(targa aut.) Siena,* Sienna, Siena.
S.I.A.E., *Società Italiana Autori ed Editori,* Italian Authors' and Publishers' Association.
Sig., *Signore,* Mr., Mister.
Sig.a, *Signora,* Mrs., Mistress.
Sigg., *Signori,* Messrs., Messieurs.
Sig.na, *Signorina,* Miss.
sing., *singolare,* s., sing., singular.
S.I.S.A.L., *Società Italiana Sistemi A Lotto,* Italian Society of State-Lottery Systems.
s.l.m., *sul livello del mare,* above sea level.
Sm, *samario, (chim.)* Sm, samarium.
S.M., 1. *Stato Maggiore,* Staff **2.** *Sua Maestà,* H.M., His, Her Majesty.
S.M.G., *Stato Maggiore Generale,* G.S., General Staff.
S.M.O.M., *Sovrano Militare Ordine di Malta,* Sovereign Military Order of Malta.
Sn, *stagno, (chim)* Sn, tin.
S.N.D.A., *Società Nazionale Dante Alighieri,* National Dante Alighieri Society.
SO, *(targa aut.) Sondrio.*
S.O., *Sud-Ovest,* S.W., South-West.
Soc., *Società,* Soc., Society.
S.O.S., *segnale internazionale di richiesta di soccorso,* S.O.S., (Save Our Souls) appeal for help or rescue.
sost., *sostantivo,* n., noun.
Sott.te, *Sottotenente,* Sub-Lieutenant.
SP, *(targa aut.) La Spezia.*
S.P., *Santo Padre,* H.H., His Holiness.
S.p.A., *Società per Azioni,* joint stock Company.
S.P.A., *Società Protettrice degli Animali,* S.P.C.A., Society for the Prevention of Cruelty to Animals.
spec., *specialmente,* esp., espec., especially.
Spett., *(comm.) Spettabile.*
S.P.M., *sue proprie mani,* personal for addressee.
S.P.Q.R., *(lat.: Senatus Populusque Romanus) Senato e Popolo Romano,* S.P.Q.R., the Senate and People of Rome.
S.Q., *Secondo Quantità, (sui menù)* (price) according to quantity consumed.
Sr, *stronzio, (chim.)* Sr, strontium.
SR, *(targa aut.) Siracusa,* Syracuse.
S.R., *Sacra Rota,* the Sacred Rota.
S.R.C., *Santa Romana Chiesa,* S.R.E., Holy Roman Church.
S.R.I., *Sacro Romano Impero,* S.R.I., Holy Roman Empire.
S.r.l., *Società a responsabilità limitata,* Ltd. (Co.), Limited (Company).
SS, *(targa aut.) Sassari.*
SS., 1. *(tedesco: Schutzstaffel) milizia di protezione nazista,* SS., Hitler bodyguard **2.** *Santi,* SS., Saints **3.** *Santissimo,* SS., Most Holy.
S.S., 1. *Santa Sede,* Holy See **2.** *Sua Santità,* H.H., His Holiness.
SS.PP., *Santi Padri,* Holy Fathers.
S.Ten., *Sottotenente,* Sub-Lieutenant.
STET, *Società Torinese Esercizio Telefoni,* Turin Telephone Company.
STIPEL, *Società Telefonica Interregionale Piemonte e Lombardia,* Company controlling telephone services in Piedmont and Lombardy.
S.U., *Stati Uniti,* U.S., United States.
S.U.A., *Stati Uniti d'America,* U.S.A., United States of America.
sup., *superlativo,* sup., superl., superlative.
SV, *(targa aut.) Savona.*
S.V.P., 1. *(tedesco: Südtiroler Volkspartei) Partito Popolare Sudtirolese,* Party of the German-speaking minority in Alto Adige **2.** *(francese: s'il vous plaît) per favore,* S.V.P., please.

T

t, *tonnellata,* t, ton(s).
Ta, *tantalio, (chim.)* Ta, tantalum.
TA, *(targa aut.) Taranto.*
Tb, *terbio, (chim.)* Tb, terbium.
tbc, TBC, *tubercolosi,* T.B., tuberculosis.
Tc, *tecnezio, (chim.)* Tc, technetium.
T.C.I., *Touring Club Italiano,* Italian Touring Club.
Te, *tellurio, (chim.)* Te, tellurium.
TE, *(targa aut.) Teramo.*
tec., 1. *tecnica,* techn., technology 2. *tecnico,* techn., technical.
tel., *telefono,* tel., telephone.
TELVE, *Società Telefoni delle Venezie,* Company controlling telephone services in the Three Venetias.
Ten., *Tenente,* Lieut., Lieutenant.
TETI, *Telefoni del Tirreno,* Company controlling telephone services along the Tyrrhenian Coast.
tg, *tangente,* tan, tangent.
Th, 1. *tangente iperbolica,* tanh, hyperbolic tangent 2. *torio, (chim.)* Th, thorium.
Ti, *titanio, (chim.)* Ti, titanium.
TIMO, *Società Telefoni Italiani Medio-Orientali,* Company controlling telephone services in Central and Eastern Italy.
Tl, *tallio, (chim.)* Tl, thalium.
Tm, *tulio, (chim.)* Tm, thulium.
TN, *(targa aut.) Trento,* Trent.
TO, *(targa aut.) Torino,* Turin.
tom., *tomo, (bibliografia)* t., tome.
TOT.IP, *Totalizzatore Ippico,* Horse-race Pools.
TOTO.CALCIO, *Totalizzatore Calcistico,* Football Pools.
TP, *(targa aut.) Trapani.*
tr., *tratta,* dft., draft.
TR, *(targa aut.) Terni.*
trag., *tragedia,* trag., tragedy.
trans., *transitivo,* t., tr., trans., transitive.
trim., *trimestre,* term.
TS, *(targa aut.) Trieste.*
T.S.F., *Telegrafo senza fili,* wireless.
T.U., *Testo Unico, (dir.)* Consolidation Act.
TV, 1. *televisione,* TV, television 2. *(targa aut.) Treviso.*

U

U, *uranio, (chim.)* U, uranium.
U.C., 1. *Ufficiale di Complemento,* Territorial Army Officer 2. *Ufficio di Collocamento,* Employment Bureau.
U.C.D.G., *Unione Cristiana delle Giovani,* Y.W.C.A., Young Women's Christian Association.
U.C.I., *Unione Ciclistica Internazionale,* International Cycling Union.
UD, *(targa aut.) Udine.*
U.D.E., *Unione Doganale Europea,* European Customs Union.
U.D.I., *Unione Donne Italiane,* Association of Italian Women (with Communist trend).
U.H.F., *frequenza ultraelevata, (rad. tv.)* U.H.F., ultrahigh frequency.
U.I.C., *Unione Italiana Ciechi,* Italian Union of the Blind.
U.I.L., 1. *Ufficio Internazionale del Lavoro,* International Labour Office 2. *Unione Italiana dei Lavoratori,* Italian Federation of Trade Unions (with moderate Socialist and Republican trend).
U.M., *Unione Militare,* Military Union.
UNESCO, *Organizzazione educativa, scientifica e culturale delle Nazioni Unite,* UNESCO, United Nations Educational, Scientific, and Cultural Organization.
U.N.R.R.A., *Soccorso per i territori europei danneggiati dalla guerra,* UNRRA, United Nations Relief and Rehabilitation Administration.
U.P.U., *Unione Postale Universale,* U.P.U., Universal Postal Union.
urg., *urgente,* urgent.

U.R.S.S., *Unione Repubbliche Socialiste Sovietiche,* RSFSR, R.S.F.S.R., Russian Soviet Federated Socialist Republic; USSR, U.S.S.R., Union of Soviet Socialist Republics.
u.s., *ultimo scorso,* ult, last (month).
U.S., 1. *Ufficio Stampa,* Press Agency 2. *Uscita di Sicurezza,* Emergency Exit.
U.S.A., *Stati Uniti d'America,* U.S.A., United States of America.
U.S.I.S., *Ufficio Informazioni per gli Stati Uniti d'America,* U.S.I.S., United States Information Service.
U.V.I., *Unione Velocipedistica Italiana,* Italian Cycling Union.

V

v., 1. *vedi,* q.v., which see 2. *venerdì,* Fr., Fri., Friday 3. *verbo,* v., vb., verb 4. *verso, (bibliografia)* v., verso 5. *verso, (poes.)* v., verse.
V, 1. *vanadio, (chim.)* V, vanadium 2. *volt,* V, v, volt.
V., *Via,* St., Street.
VA, *(targa aut.) Varese.*
val., *valuta,* cur., cy., currency.
Vat., *Vaticano,* Vat., Vatican.
vb., *verbo,* v., vb., verb.
VC, *(targa aut.) Vercelli.*
V.C., *Vice-Console,* V.C., Vice-Consul.
VE, *(targa aut.) Venezia,* Venice.
V.E., *Vostra Eccellenza,* Your Excellency; *(eccl.)* Your Grace, Your Lordship.
V.Em., *Vostra Eminenza,* Your Eminence.
ven., *venerdì,* Fr., Fri., Friday.
Ven., *Venerabile,* Ven., Venerable.
ver., *versamento,* payt., payment; rem., remittance.
vet., *veterinario,* vet., veterinary.
V.F., *(targa aut.) Vigili del Fuoco,* Fire Brigade.
V.G., *Vostra Grazia,* Your Grace.
V.H.F., *altissima frequenza, (rad. tv.)* V.H.F., very high frequency.
VI, *(targa aut.) Vicenza.*
V.le, *Viale,* Blvd., Boul., Boulevard; av., avenue.
V.L.F., *bassissima frequenza, (rad. tv.)* V.L.F., very low frequency.
V.M., *Vostra Maestà,* Your Majesty.
voc., *vocativo,* V., voc., vocative.
vol., *volume,* v, V, vol., volume.
v.r., *vedi retro,* p.t.o., please turn over.
VR, *(targa aut.) Verona.*
vs., *vostro,* yr., your; yrs., yours.
VT, *(targa aut.) Viterbo.*
V.T., *Vecchio Testamento,* O.T., Old Testament.

W

W, 1. *viva!,* long live! 2. *volframio, (chim.)* W, tungsten 3. *watt,* w., watt.
W.C., *gabinetto di decenza,* W.C., water closet.
Wh, *wattora,* wh., whr., watt-hour.
W.L., *carrozza-letto,* Sleeping-car.

X

X, *xeno, (chim.)* X, Xe, xenon.
X., *Cristo,* X., Xt., Christ.

Y

Y, *ittrio, (chim.)* Y, yttrium.
Yb, *itterbio, (chim.)* Yb, ytterbium.
Y.C.I., *Yacht Club Italia,* Italian Yacht Club.

Z

z, *numero atomico,* Z, atomic number.
Z.C.L., *Zona di Commercio Libero,* (European) Free Trade Area.
Z. d. G., *Zona di Guerra,* War Zone.
Zn, *zinco, (chim.)* Zn, zinc.
Zr, *zirconio, (chim.)* Zr, zirconium.

&

&, *(lat.: et)* e, &, and.

ENGLISH-ITALIAN

A

a [ei], *pl.* **as, a's** [eiz], *s.* **1.** (*prima lettera dell'alfabeto inglese*) a ‖ — *for Andrew,* (*tel.*) a come Ancona **2.** (*alg.*) prima quantità nota **3.** (*mus.*) la (sesta nota) ☆ *A-bomb,* bomba atomica ‖ **A1** ['ei'wʌn], sigla di nave di prima classe (nel registro marittimo del Lloyd); (*fam.*) eccellente, splendido: *I am A1,* sto benone.

a¹, an¹ [ei, æn (*forme forti*), ə, ən (*forme deboli*)], *art. indeterminativo* (*davanti a consonante e suoni consonantici* [ju, wʌ]: **a:** *a book,* un libro; *a European,* un europeo; *a ewer,* una brocca; *a union,* un'unione; *davanti a vocale o h muta:* **an:** *an apple,* una mela; *an hour,* un'ora **1.** un, uno, una, **un':** *he reads a book,* egli legge un libro; *he wrote an essay,* scrisse un saggio **2.** il, lo, la, l': *he smokes a pipe, and not cigarettes,* fuma la pipa e non sigarette; *he was not in a position to help,* non era nella condizione di aiutare; *she has a small mouth,* ella ha la bocca piccola **3.** un certo, una certa: *in a sense, way,* in un certo senso, modo; *I know a Mr. B.,* conosco un certo signor B.**4.** stesso, stessa: *two at a time,* due per volta, nello stesso tempo; *to be of a mind,* essere della stessa opinione **5.** (*talvolta non si traduce*): *what a clever book!,* che libro intelligente!; *many a time,* molte volte; *what a kind man!,* che uomo gentile!; *he is an Indian, a doctor, a Muslim,* egli è indiano, dottore, musulmano **6.** *a few,* alcuni; *a good many* (o *a great many*), parecchi: *a few books,* alcuni libri; *a good many people,* parecchia gente.

a², an² [ə, ən], *prep.* **1.** ogni, a, al, il: *once a year,* una volta (al)l'anno; *sixpence a pound,* mezzo scellino la libbra; *three times a week,* tre volte la settimana **2.** (*in unione a nomi verbali spec.* dopo *to* o *to set*): *he set the bell a-ringing,* egli fece suonare la campana; *to go a-hunting,* andare a caccia.

a³, *pron.* (*arc.*) per *he,* egli; *she,* ella; *it,* esso, essa; *they,* essi, esse.

a⁴, (*dial.* per *have*): *who would a thought it!,* chi l'avrebbe pensato!.

a⁵, *particella* (*amer. volg.* per *to;* si trova dopo il suono di *t*): *he oughta know,* egli dovrebbe saper(lo).

aardvark ['ɑ:dvɑ:k], *s.* (*zool.*) oritteropo.

aardwolf ['ɑ:dwulf], *s.* (*zool.*) protele.

Aaron ['ɛərən], *no.pr.m.* Aronne.

Aaron's beard ['ɛərənz'biəd], *s.* (*bot.*) iperico.

Aaron's rod ['ɛərənz'rɔd], *s.* (*bot.*) verga d'oro.

aback [ə'bæk], *av.* **1.** (*mar.*) a collo (di vele) **2.** dietro, di dietro, all'indietro ‖ *to be taken —, fig.* essere sorpreso, preso alla sprovvista.

abacus ['æbəkəs], *s.* **1.** pallottoliere **2.** (*arch.*) abaco.

Abaddon [ə'bædən], *s.* **1.** « il distruttore », « l'angelo dell'abisso »; il diavolo **2.** (*poet.*) l'Inferno.

abaft [ə'bɑ:ft], *av.prep.* (*mar.*) a poppa, a poppavia.

abandon [ə'bændən], *s.* abbandono; trasporto, effusione.

to abandon, *v.t.* **1.** abbandonare, lasciare: *— ship!,* abbandonate la nave!; *to — oneself to,* abbandonarsi, lasciarsi andare, darsi a **2.** desistere; rinunciare a: *they abandoned all hope,* rinunciarono ad ogni speranza.

abandoned [ə'bændənd], *ag.* depravato, dissoluto.

abandonee [ə,bændə'ni:], *s.* (*dir.*) abbandonatario (assicuratore marittimo, cessionario dei diritti sulla cosa assicurata o su quanto rimanga di essa).

abandoner [ə'bændənə*], *s.c.* chi abbandona.

abandoning [ə'bændəniŋ], *s.* **1.** abbandono **2.** cessione di beni.

abandonment [ə'bændənmənt], *s.* **1.** abbandono; rinuncia **2.** cessione (di beni) **3.** abbandono, trasporto, effusione ☆ *self- —,* abnegazione.

to abase [ə'beis], *v.t.* abbassare, umiliare, degradare: *to — oneself,* abbassarsi, umiliarsi.

abasement [ə'beismənt], *s.* umiliazione.

to abash [ə'bæʃ], *v.t.* confondere, sconcertare, mettere nell'imbarazzo.

abashment [ə'bæʃmənt], *s.* confusione; vergogna.

to abate [ə'beit], *v.t.i.* **1.** diminuire, ridurre; abbassare; mitigare, alleviare; calmare, calmarsi; indebolirsi; abbassarsi (di acque); rallentare (il passo): *the doctor gave him some medicine to — his pain,* il dottore gli diede una medicina per alleviargli il dolore; *the wind abated,* il vento si calmò **2.** por fine a, far cessare: *we must — the smoke nuisance in our big cities,* dobbiamo eliminare l'inconveniente del fumo nelle nostre città **3.** (*comm.*) ribassare (prezzi); defalcare, detrarre **4.** (*dir.*) annullare; cassare.

abatement [ə'beitmənt], *s.* **1.** diminuzione; riduzione; indebolimento; abbassamento (di acque); il placarsi, calmarsi (di vento, tempesta, ecc.) **2.** abolizione, soppressione **3.** (*comm.*) ribasso, sconto, defalco **4.** (*dir.*) annullamento; riduzione.

abatis ['æbətis], **abattis** [ə'bætis], *s.* (*mil.*) abbattuta.

abattoir ['æbətwɑ:*], *s.* mattatoio.

abb [æb], *s.* (*ind. tessile*) filo per l'ordito.

abbacy ['æbəsi], *s.* giurisdizione di abate.

abbatial [ə'beiʃəl], *ag.* abbaziale.

abbé ['æbei], *s.* abate.

abbess ['æbis], *s.* badessa.

abbey ['æbi], *s.* abbazia, badia.

abbot ['æbət], *s.* abate.

abbotship ['æbət-ʃip], *s.* ufficio o dignità di abate.

to abbreviate [ə'bri:vieit], *v.t.* abbreviare.

abbreviation [ə,bri:vi'eiʃən], *s.* abbreviazione.

ABC ['eibi:'si:], *s.* abbiccì.

abdicant ['æbdikənt], *ag.s.* abdicante.

to abdicate ['æbdikeit], *v.t.* abdicare, rinunciare a (diritti, ecc.); dimettersi da (una carica).

abdication [,æbdi'keiʃən], *s.* abdicazione, rinuncia; dimissioni.

abdomen ['æbdəmen], *s.* addome.

abdominal [æb'dɔminl], *ag.* addominale.

abdominous [æb'dɔminəs], *ag.* corpulento, panciuto.

abducent [æb'dju:sənt], *ag.* (*anat.*) abducente.

to abduct [æb'dʌkt], *v.t.* **1.** rapire **2.** (*fisiol. chir.*) abdurre.

abduction [æb'dʌkʃən], *s.* **1.** rapimento, ratto **2.** (*fisiol. chir.*) abduzione.

abductor [æb'dʌktə*], *s.* **1.** rapitore **2.** (*anat.*) abduttore.

Abe [eib], *no.pr.m. dim.* di **Abraham**.

abeam [ə'bi:m], *av.* (*mar.*) al traverso: *the lighthouse was — of us,* il faro si ergeva al traverso.

abecedarian [,eibi(:)si(:)'dɛəriən], *ag.* **1.** (in ordine) alfabetico **2.** ignorante **3.** elementare ‖ *s.* (*amer.*) chi impara l'alfabeto; principiante.

abed [ə'bed], *av.* a letto: *to be —,* essere a letto.

Abel ['eibəl], *no.pr.m.* Abele.

abele [ə'bi:l], *s.* (*bot.*) gattice.

abelmosk ['eibəlmɔsk], *s.* (*bot.*) abelmosco.

aberdevine [ˌæbədə'vain], *s.* (*ornit.*) lucherino.

Aberdonian [ˌæbə'dounjən], *ag.s.c.* (abitante) di Aberdeen.

aberrance [æ'berəns], **aberrancy** [æ'berənsi], *s.* aberrazione.

aberrant [æ'berənt], *ag.* **1.** sviato, traviato **2.** (*zool. bot.*) aberrante, anormale.

aberration [ˌæbə'reiʃən], *s.* **1.** aberrazione, sviamento, traviamento **2.** (*astr. fis. patol.*) aberrazione.

to abet [ə'bet], *pass.p.p.* **abetted** [ə'betid], *v.t.* incoraggiare, incitare, istigare; favoreggiare, avere parte in, rendersi complice di (delitto, ecc.): *to — s.o. in a crime*, incitare qlcu. ad un delitto; *to aid and —*, (*dir.*) essere complice di qlcu.

abetment [ə'betmənt], *s.* incitamento; favoreggiamento, complicità (in un delitto).

abetter, abettor [ə'betə*], *s.c.* fautore, fautrice; favoreggiatore, favoreggiatrice; complice.

abeyance [ə'beiəns], *s.* sospensione (di legge, ecc.); vacanza (di carica): *estate in —*, (*dir.*) eredità vacante; *law in —*, legge non più in vigore; *the matter is still in —*, la questione è ancora in sospeso; *to leave a decree in —*, sospendere un decreto.

to abhor [əb'hɔ:*], *pass.pp.* **abhorred** [əb'hɔ:d], *v.t.* aborrire, detestare.

abhorrence [əb'hɔrəns], *s.* aborrimento, avversione, orrore: *to hold in —*, avere in orrore.

abhorrent [əb'hɔrənt], *ag.* **1.** odioso; ripugnante, disgustoso: *to be — of* (*o from*) *sthg.*, aborrire ql.co.; *to be — to s.o.*, essere odioso a qlcu. **2.** contrario a, incompatibile con: *to be — to* (*o from*) *sthg.*, essere incompatibile con ql.co.

abidance [ə'baidəns], *s.* **1.** dimora **2.** osservanza, il conformarsi: *— by the rules of the game*, l'osservare le regole del giuoco.

to abide [ə'baid], *pass.p.p.* **abode** [ə'boud], **abided** [ə'baidid], *v.t.i.* **1.** aspettare: *I — my time*, (*rar.*) attendo l'occasione **2.** (*fam.* in frasi negative e interrogative) sopportare: *I can't — him*, non lo posso soffrire **3.** dimorare, restare; abitare **4.** *to — by* (*sthg.*), conformarsi a: *to — by a decision*, conformarsi ad una decisione; *to — by a promise*, mantenere una promessa.

abiding [ə'baidiŋ], *ag.* costante, stabile, durevole.

abidingly [ə'baidiŋli], *av.* costantemente, stabilmente, durevolmente.

Abigail ['æbigeil], *no.pr.f.* Abigaille ǁ **abigail**, *s.* servetta.

ability [ə'biliti], *s.* **1.** capacità, potere, facoltà **2.** abilità, capacità, competenza; sapere, talento: *a man of great —*, un uomo di grande talento ǁ *to the best of my —*, come meglio potrò **3.** *pl.* (*comm.*) fondi.

abintestate [ˌæbin'testit], *ag.* (*dir.*) ab intestato.

abiogenesis [ˌeibaiou'dʒenisis], *s.* (*biol.*) abiogenesi.

abiogenetic [ˌeibaioudʒi'netik], *ag.* (*biol.*) abiogenetico.

abiogeny [ˌeibai'ɔdʒini], *s.* (*biol.*) abiogenesi.

abject ['æbdʒekt], *ag.* **1.** abietto, vile, spregevole (di persone) **2.** miserabile; degradante: *to live in a — poverty*, vivere in una miseria degradante ǁ *s.* (*rar.*) reietto; disperato.

abjection [æb'dʒekʃən], *s.* **1.** abiezione, viltà **2.** degradazione; miseria.

abjectly ['æbdʒektli], *av.* in modo abietto, vile.

abjectness ['æbdʒektnis], *s.* abiettezza, viltà.

abjuration [ˌæbdʒuə'reiʃən], *s.* abiura.

to abjure [əb'dʒuə*], *v.t.* abiurare; ripudiare.

abjurer [əb'dʒuərə*], *s.* chi abiura.

ablactation [ˌæblæk'teiʃən], *s.* divezzamento.

ablation [æb'leiʃən], *s.* **1.** (*geol.*) erosione **2.** (*chir.*) asportazione.

ablative ['æblətiv], *ag.s.* (*gram.*) ablativo.

ablaze [ə'bleiz], *av.* in fiamme ǁ *ag. predicativo* in fiamme; risplendente: *her face was — with anger*, *fig.* il suo volto era rosso di collera; *the house was — with lights*, la casa risplendeva di luci.

able ['eibl], *ag.* **1.** capace, abile, esperto, competente: *a very — man*, un uomo di grandi capacità; *he was defended by an — lawyer*, fu difeso da un abile avvocato ǁ *to be —*, potere, esser in grado di **2.** (*dir.*) capace ☆ *— - bodied*, robusto, forte; (*mil.*) abile: *— - bodied seaman*, (*mar.*) marinaio scelto; *— - minded*, intelligente, di grande capacità intellettuale.

ablings, ablins ['eiblinz], *av.* (*scoz.*) forse, probabilmente.

abloom [ə'blu:m], *av.ag.predicativo* in fiore, fiorito.

ablush [ə'blʌʃ], *av.ag.predicativo* soffuso di rossore.

ablution [ə'blu:ʃən], *s.* abluzione.

ably ['eibli], *av.* abilmente, destramente.

to abnegate ['æbnigeit], *v.t.* **1.** rinunciare a **2.** rinnegare, abiurare.

abnegation [ˌæbni'geiʃən], *s.* **1.** abnegazione **2.** abiura.

abnormal [æb'nɔ:məl], *ag.* anormale, abnorme.

abnormality [ˌæbnɔ:'mæliti], *s.* anormalità; anomalia.

abnormally [æb'nɔ:məli], *av.* in modo anormale.

abnormity [æb'nɔ:miti], *s.* anormalità; anomalia.

aboard [ə'bɔ:d], *av.prep.* a bordo: *— a ship*, a bordo di una nave; *to go —*, imbarcarsi, salire a bordo; *to take —*, imbarcare.

abode [ə'boud], *pass. p.p.* di *to* **abide** ǁ *s.* soggiorno, dimora, residenza: *to take up one's —*, stabilire la propria residenza.

aboil [ə'bɔil], *av.* in bollore ǁ *ag. predicativo* bollente.

to abolish [ə'bɔliʃ], *v.t.* abolire, sopprimere.

abolisher [ə'bɔliʃə*], *s.c.* abolitore, abolitrice.

abolishment [ə'bɔliʃmənt], **abolition** [ˌæbə'liʃən], *s.* abolizione.

abolitionism [ˌæbə'liʃənizəm], *s.* abolizionismo.

abolitionist [ˌæbə'liʃənist], *s.* abolizionista.

abominable [ə'bɔminəbl], *ag.* abominevole, detestabile, odioso; (*fam.*) disgustoso: *an — dinner*, un pranzo disgustoso.

to abominate [ə'bɔmineit], *v.t.* abominare, aborrire, detestare.

abomination [əˌbɔmi'neiʃən], *s.* **1.** abominazione; odio; disgusto: *this coffee is an —*, (*fam.*) questo caffè è disgustoso; *to be held in — by s.o.* (*o to be an — to s.o.*), essere in odio a qlcu. **2.** infamia: *it is an — before the Lord!*, è un sacrilegio!.

aboriginal [ˌæbə'ridʒənl], *ag.s.* aborigeno.

aborigines [ˌæbə'ridʒini:z], *s.pl.* aborigeni.

to abort [ə'bɔ:t], *v.t.i.* **1.** abortire, fare abortire; *fig.* fallire **2.** (*biol.*) isterilirsi, avere un arresto di sviluppo.

abortifacient [əˌbɔ:ti'feiʃənt], *ag.s.* (*med.*) abortivo.

abortion [ə'bɔ:ʃən], *s.* **1.** aborto (anche *fig.*). **2.** (*biol.*) arresto di sviluppo.

abortive [ə'bɔ:tiv], *ag.* **1.** abortivo, prematuro **2.** *fig.* fallito, mancato; vano **3.** (*biol.*) non sviluppato.

abortively [ə'bɔ:tivli], *av.* prematuramente.

abortiveness [ə'bɔ:tivnis], *s.* insuccesso.

aboulia [ə'bu:liə], *s.* (*patol.*) abulia.

to abound [ə'baund], *v.i.* abbondare: *to — in*, essere ricco di; *to — with*, essere pieno di.

abounding [ə'baundiŋ], *ag.* abbondante, ricco: *country — in wheat*, paese ricco di grano.

about [ə'baut], *av.* circa, all'incirca, press'a poco; intorno, attorno, all'ingiro; vicino, presso: *— half*, circa metà; *she always leaves her things —*, lascia sempre in giro le sue cose ǁ *to be — to do sthg.*, star per fare ql.co.; *to bring sthg. —*, far accadere ql.co.; *to come —*, accadere, avvenire; (*mar.*) virare di bordo ǁ *to order —*, (*scherz.*) impartire, imporre ordini ǁ *to put a tale —*, mettere in giro una storiella ǁ *to take turns —*, fare a turno, alternarsi ǁ *prep.* circa; quasi; intorno a, attorno a; vicino a; presso di; sopra; quanto a: *the country — London*, la campagna attorno a Londra; *he never has money — him*, non ha mai denaro con sè; *he spoke — you*, parlò di voi ǁ *— that*, su ciò, a questo proposito ǁ *all —*, ovunque ǁ *a man — town*, un perdigiorno, un buontempone ‖ *much ado — nothing*, molto rumore per nulla ‖ *I went to town — my father's business*, mi recai in città per gli affari di mio padre; *send him — his business*, mandalo ad occuparsi degli affari suoi ‖ *there is something wrong — him*, c'è qualcosa in lui che non va ‖ *what — them?*, e quanto a loro?; *what — going to the cinema?*, che ne direste se andassimo al cinema? ‖ *what are you —?*, cosa stai facendo?.

to **about**, *v.t.* (*mar.*) far virare di bordo (una nave).

above [ə'bʌv], *av.* in alto, in su, lassù, lassù in alto; in cima, più in su, oltre; al di sopra, qui sopra; in cielo: *as* —, come sopra; *a voice from* —, una voce dall'alto ‖ *prep.* su, sopra, al di sopra di; al di là, oltre, più di: — *all*, soprattutto; — *ten*, più di dieci; *he flew — the clouds*, volò al di sopra delle nuvole; *he is — telling a lie*, non si abbassa a dire menzogne; *he lives — me*, abita sopra di me; *he was swimming with his head — water*, nuotava tenendo la testa a flor d'acqua; *his behaviour is — criticism*, la sua condotta è al di sopra di ogni critica ‖ *his voice cannot get — C*, (*mus.*) la sua voce non oltrepassa il do; *this is — my understanding*, ciò va oltre la mia comprensione ☆ — *-cited*, predetto; — *-mentioned*, suddetto, succitato.

above-board [ə'bʌv'bɔːd], *ag.* predicativo aperto, leale ‖ *av.* lealmente.

abracadabra [ˌæbrəkə'dæbrə], *s.* abracadabra (parola cabalistica); incantesimo, formula magica.

to **abrade** [ə'breid], *v.t.* 1. abradere; scorticare (la pelle); corrodere, logorare (anche *fig.*) 2. (*mec.*) abradere, grattare; molare.

Abraham ['eibrəhæm], *no.pr.m.* Abramo.

abranchial [ə'bræŋkiəl], **abranchiate** [ə'bræŋkiit], *ag.* abranchiato.

abrasion [ə'breiʒən], *s.* 1. abrasione; escoriazione 2. attrito; logorio.

abrasive [ə'breisiv], *ag.s.* abrasivo.

abreaction [ˌæbri'ækʃən], *s.* (*psicanalisi*) abreazione.

abreast [ə'brest], *av.* 1. di fianco: *to come — of a car*, affiancarsi a un'automobile; *to march two —*, marciare a due a due ‖ *to keep — of the thought of one's age*, *fig.* marciare con i tempi 2. (*aer.*) alla stessa quota 3. (*mar.*) al traverso; opposto; affiancato.

to **abridge** [ə'bridʒ], *v.t.* 1. accorciare, abbreviare: *abridged edition*, edizione ridotta 2. limitare, ridurre, privare di (diritti, privilegi, autorità, ecc.): *to — s.o. of a right*, privare qlcu. di un diritto.

abridgement [ə'bridʒmənt], *s.* 1. abbreviazione; sunto, sommario, compendio (di opera) 2. limitazione, privazione (di diritti, ecc.).

abridger [ə'bridʒə*], *s.c.* abbreviatore, abbreviatrice; riduttore, riduttrice.

abridgment, *V.* **abridgement**.

abroach [ə'broutʃ], *av.* in modo da lasciar uscire un liquido: *to set —*, spillare (una botte) ‖ *ag. predicativo*, aperto; sturato; spillato.

abroad [ə'brɔːd], *av.* 1. fuori, fuori di casa; all'estero: *travels —*, viaggi all'estero; *he has just come from —*, è appena arrivato dall'estero; *to go —*, andare all'estero ‖ *you are all —*, *fig.* siete tutti in errore 2. dappertutto: *bad rumours are —*, ci sono in giro brutte notizie; *there is a rumour — that...*, corre voce che....

to **abrogate** ['æbrougeit], *v.t.* abrogare.

abrogation [ˌæbrou'geiʃən], *s.* abrogazione.

abrupt [ə'brʌpt], *ag.* 1. scosceso, ripido, a picco (di terreno) 2. brusco (di modi) 3. sconnesso (di stile) 4. inaspettato, repentino: — *death*, morte repentina.

abruptly [ə'brʌptli], *av.* 1. ripidamente, a picco 2. bruscamente 3. improvvisamente.

abruptness [ə'brʌptnis], *s.* 1. ripidezza (di pendio, ecc.) 2. rudezza, asprezza; scortesia 3. sconnessione (di stile) 4. precipitazione (di partenza).

Absalom ['æbsələm], *no.pr.m.* (*Bibbia*) Assalonne.

abscess ['æbsis], *s.* (*patol.*) ascesso.

absciss(e) ['æbsis], *pl.* **abscisses** ['æbsisiːz], *s.* (*mat.*) ascissa.

abscissa [æb'sisə], *pl.* **abscissae** [æb'sisiː], **abscissas** [æb'sisəz], *s.* (*mat.*) ascissa.

abscission [æb'siʒən], *s.* (*chir.*) escissione.

to **abscond** [əb'skɔnd], *v.i.* nascondersi, fuggire, rendersi latitante.

abscondence [əb'skɔndəns], *s.* latitanza, contumacia.

absconder [əb'skɔndə*], *s.c.* fuggiasco, fuggiasca; latitante.

absence ['æbsəns], *s.* assenza; mancanza; disattenzione: — *of mind*, distrazione; — *of taste*, mancanza di gusto; *did anything happen in my —?*, è successo ql.co. durante la mia assenza?.

absent ['æbsənt], *ag.* assente; mancante; distratto: *the — one*, la persona assente; *the — ones*, gli assenti ☆ — *-minded*, distratto, con la mente assente; — *-mindedly*, distrattamente; — *-mindedness*, distrazione.

to **absent** [æb'sent], *v.t.* (*arc.*) assentare: *to — oneself from*, assentarsi da.

absentee [ˌæbsən'tiː], *s.* 1. assente 2. proprietario che abbandona spesso le sue terre.

absenteeism [ˌæbsən'tiːizəm], *s.* assenteismo.

absenter [æb'sentə*], *s.c.* chi si assenta.

absently ['æbsəntli], *av.* distrattamente.

absinth(e) ['æbsinθ], *s.* assenzio.

absolute ['æbsəluːt], *ag.* 1. assoluto; completo; autoritario: *an — government*, un governo assolutista; — *power*, potere assoluto ‖ *the —*, (*fil.*) l'assoluto 2. puro: — *alcohol*, alcool puro.

absolutely ['æbsəluːtli], *av.* assolutamente: *verb used —*, (*gram.*) verbo usato in senso assoluto; *you are — right*, hai perfettamente ragione.

absoluteness ['æbsəluːtnis], *s.* assolutezza.

absolution [ˌæbsə'luːʃən], *s.* assoluzione.

absolutism ['æbsəluːtizəm], *s.* 1. (*pol.*) assolutismo, dispotismo 2. (*relig.*) teoria della predestinazione.

absolutist ['æbsəluːtist], *s.c.* assolutista.

absolutory [əb'səluːtəri], *ag.* assolutorio.

to **absolve** [əb'zɔlv], *v.t.* assolvere.

absonant ['æbsənənt], *ag.* discordante.

to **absorb** [əb'sɔːb], *v.t.* assorbire.

absorbability [əbˌsɔːbə'biliti], *s.* assorbibilità.

absorbable [əb'sɔːbəbl], *ag.* che può essere assorbito.

absorbed [əb'sɔːbd], *ag.* assorbito; molto occupato, assorto, interessato: *he was much — in his work*, era completamente assorbito dal suo lavoro.

absorbefacient [əbˌsɔːbi'feiʃənt], *ag. s.* assorbente.

absorbent [əb'sɔːbənt], *ag.s.* assorbente.

absorber [əb'sɔːbə*], *s.* 1. (*chim. fis.*) assorbitore 2. (*mec.*) ammortizzatore ☆ *shock- —*, (*aut.*) ammortizzatore.

absorbing [əb'sɔːbiŋ], *ag.* assorbente; interessantissimo.

absorption [əb'sɔːpʃən], *s.* assorbimento.

absorptive [əb'sɔːptiv], *ag.* assorbente.

to **absquatulate** [æb'skwɔtjuleit], *v.i.* (*scherz.*) andarsene, lasciar libero il campo.

to **abstain** [əb'stein], *v.i.* astenersi.

abstainer [əb'steinə*], *s.c.* chi si astiene; astemio, astemia.

abstaining [əb'steiniŋ], *s.* astinenza.

abstemious [æb'stiːmjəs], *ag.* sobrio, frugale.

abstemiously [æb'stiːmjəsli], *av.* sobriamente.

abstemiousness [æb'stiːmjəsnis], *s.* sobrietà, temperanza; astinenza.

abstention [æb'stenʃən], *s.* astensione; astinenza.

to **absterge** [əb'stəːdʒ], *v.t.* 1. detergere 2. (*med.*) astergere.

abstergent [əb'stəːdʒənt], *ag.s.* 1. detergente 2. (*med.*) astergente.

abstersion [əb'stəːʃən], *s.* 1. detersione 2. (*med.*) astersione.

abstersive [əb'stəːsiv], *ag.s.* 1. detergente 2. (*med.*) astergente.

abstinence ['æbstinəns], **abstinency** ['æbstinənsi], *s.* astinenza; continenza; digiuno.

abstinent ['æbstinənt], *ag.* astinente, sobrio.

abstinently ['æbstinəntli], *av.* sobriamente.

abstract ['æbstrækt], *ag.* astratto ‖ *s.* **1.** astrazione; (concetto) astratto: *in the —,* in astratto **2.** estratto, sunto, compendio.

to abstract [æb'strækt], *v.t.* **1.** astrarre, fare astrazione da: distrarre **2.** sottrarre, rubare (documenti, ecc.) **3.** riassumere **4.** (*chim.*) estrarre (per distillazione).

abstracted [æb'stræktid], *ag.* **1.** astratto, distratto **2.** (*chim.*) estratto (per distillazione).

abstractedly [æb'stræktidli], *av.* **1.** astrattamente **2.** facendo astrazione **3.** distrattamente.

abstractedness [æb'stræktidnis], *s.* astrattezza, distrazione.

abstraction [æb'strækʃən], *s.* **1.** astrazione; idea astratta **2.** distrazione **3.** furto, sottrazione **4.** (*chim.*) estrazione (per distillazione).

abstractionism [æb'strækʃənizəm], *s.* (*art.*) astrattismo.

abstractionist [æb'strækʃənist], *s.* (*art.*) astrattista.

abstractly ['æbstræktli], *av.* astrattamente; distrattamente.

abstractness ['æbstræktnis], *s.* astrattezza.

abstruse [æb'stru:s], *ag.* astruso; recondito.

abstrusely [æb'stru:sli], *av.* astrusamente.

abstruseness [æb'stru:snis], *s.* astrusità.

absurd [əb'sə:d], *ag.* assurdo; sciocco, ridicolo.

absurdity [əb'sə:diti], *s.* assurdità.

absurdly [əb'sə:dli], *av.* assurdamente.

absurdness [əb'sə:dnis], *s.* assurdità.

abulia [ə'bju:liə], *s.* (*patol.*) abulia.

abundance [ə'bʌndəns], *s.* abbondanza.

abundant [ə'bʌndənt], *ag.* abbondante: *— in sthg.,* abbondante di ql.co.

abundantly [ə'bʌndəntli], *av.* abbondantemente.

abuse [ə'bju:s], *s.* **1.** abuso; cattivo uso **2.** ingiurie, insulti **3.** maldicenza.

to abuse [ə'bju:z], *v.t.* **1.** abusare **2.** ingiuriare, insultare **3.** sparlare di **4.** (*spec. al passivo*) ingannare: *you have been abused,* sei stato ingannato.

abuser [ə'bju:zə*], *s.* seduttore ‖ *s.c.* **1.** detrattore, detrattrice **2.** (*arc.*) ingannatore, ingannatrice.

abusive [ə'bju:siv], *ag.* **1.** abusivo **2.** ingiurioso.

abusively [ə'bju:sivli], *av.* **1.** abusivamente **2.** ingiuriosamente.

abusiveness [ə'bju:sivnis], *s.* ingiuria; insolenza.

to abut [ə'bʌt], *pass.p.p.* **abutted** [ə'bʌtid], *v.i.* **1.** confinare, far capo, sboccare: *his land abuts (up)on the road,* la sua terra confina con la strada **2.** (*arch.*) appoggiarsi.

abutilon [ə'bju:tilən], *s.* (*bot.*) abutilo.

abutment [ə'bʌtmənt], *s.* (*arch.*) spalla, piedritto.

abuttal [ə'bʌtl], *s.* **1.** (*arch.*) spalla, attestatura, piedritto **2.** *pl.* confini, delimitazioni (di terreno).

abutter [ə'bʌtə*], *s.* (*dir.*) confinante, proprietario di fondo limitrofo.

Aby ['eibi], *no.pr.m. dim.* di **Abraham.**

Abydos [ə'baidəs], *no.pr.* (*geog. st.*) Abido.

abysm [ə'bizm], *s.* abisso.

abysmal [ə'bizməl], *ag.* abissale, profondo, insondabile: *— ignorance,* spaventosa ignoranza.

abyss [ə'bis], *s.* abisso.

abyssal [ə'bisəl], *ag.* abissale.

Abyssinia [,æbi'sinjə], *no.pr.* (*geog.*) Abissinia.

Abyssinian [,æbi'sinjən], *ag.* abissino ‖ *s.c.* abissino, abissina ‖ *s.* lingua abissina.

acacia [ə'keiʃə], *s.* (*bot.*) acacia.

academic [,ækə'demik], *ag.s.* accademico; universitario.

academical [,ækə'demikəl], *ag.* universitario.

academically [,ækə'demikəli], *av.* accademicamente.

academicals [,ækə'demikəlz], *s.pl.* veste accademica.

academician [ə,kædə'miʃən], *s.* accademico.

academy [ə'kædəmi], **1.** *s.* accademia **2.** scuola; collegio: *— of music,* conservatorio.

Acadia [ə'keidjə], *no.pr.* (*geog.*) Acadia (Nuova Scozia).

Acadian [ə'keidjən], *ag.* dell'Acadia ‖ *s.e.* nativo, nativa dell'Acadia.

acajou ['ækəʒu:], *s.* (*bot.*) acagiù, anacardo.

acaleph ['ækəlef], *s.* (*zool.*) acalefa.

acanthus [ə'kænθəs], *s.* (*bot. arch.*) acanto.

acapsular [æ'kæpsjulə*], *ag.* (*anat. zool. bot.*) acapsulato.

acarpous [æ'kɑ:pəs], *ag.* (*bot.*) acarpo.

acarus ['ækərəs], *pl.* **acari** ['ækərai], *s.* (*entom.*) acaro.

acatalectic [æ,kætə'lektik], *ag.s.* (*poes.*) acatalettico.

acatalepsy [æ'kætəlepsi], *s.* (*fil.*) acatalessia.

acaulous [æ'kɔ:ləs], *ag.* (*bot.*) acaule.

to accede [æk'si:d], *v.i.* **1.** accedere, prendere possesso: *to — to an office,* prendere possesso di una carica; *to — to the throne,* salire al trono **2.** aderire: *to — to a party,* aderire a un partito; *to — to a request,* aderire a una richiesta.

accelerando [æk,selə'rændou], *s.* (*mus.*) accelerando.

to accelerate [æk'seləreit], *v.t.* accelerare.

accelerated [æk'seləreitid], *ag.* (*fis.*) accelerato.

accelerating [æk'seləreitiŋ], *ag.* accelerativo ‖ *s.* accelerazione.

acceleration [æk,selə'reiʃən], *s.* accelerazione.

accelerative [æk'selərətiv], *ag.* accelerativo.

accelerator [æk'seləreitə*], *s.* acceleratore.

accent ['æksənt], *s.* accento (anche *mus.*).

to accent [æk'sent], *v.t.* **1.** accentare **2.** *fig.* mettere in evidenza, accentuare.

accentor [æk'sentə*], *s.* (*ornit.*) accentorino.

accentual [æk'sentjuəl], *ag.* che riguarda l'accento: *— prosody,* prosodia accentuativa.

accentually [æk'sentjuəli], *av.* accentuatamente.

to accentuate [æk'sentjueit], *v.t.* **1.** accentare **2.** *fig.* mettere in evidenza, accentuare.

accentuation [æk,sentju'eiʃən], *s.* accentuazione; enfasi.

to accept [ək'sept], *v.t.* accettare, gradire, acconsentire a, approvare: *non accepted,* non accettato, non pagato; *to — a bill,* (*comm.*) accettare una cambiale.

acceptability [ək,septə'biliti], *s.* accettabilità, gradevolezza.

acceptable [ək'septəbl], *ag.* accettabile; gradevole.

acceptableness [ək'septəblnis], *s.* V. **acceptability.**

acceptably [ək'septəbli], *av.* accettabilmente; gradevolmente.

acceptance [ək'septəns], *s.* **1.** accoglienza favorevole; consenso, approvazione: *this proposal met with general —,* questa proposta raccolse tutti i suffragi **2.** (*comm.*) accettazione: *non —,* mancata accettazione; *— for honour,* accettazione per intervento.

acceptation [,æksep'teiʃən], *s.* **1.** accoglienza favorevole **2.** (*gram.*) accezione.

accepter, acceptor [ək'septə*], *s.*(*comm.*) accettante.

access ['ækses], *s.* **1.** accesso, adito; udienza; ammissione: *of difficult, easy —,* di accesso difficile, facile; *to have free — to...,* aver l'entrata libera in... **2.** attacco, parossismo: *she had a terrible — of anger, fever, etc.,* ebbe un terribile attacco d'ira, di febbre, ecc.

accessarily [æk'sesərili], *av.* accessoriamente.

accessary, V. **accessory.**

accessibility [æk,sesi'biliti], *s.* accessibilità.

accessible [æk'sesəbl], *ag.* accessibile.

accessibly [æk'sesəbli], *av.* accessibilmente.

accession [æk'seʃən], *s.* **1.** accessione, raggiungimento; adesione (a trattato, partito, ecc.): *— to the throne,* assunzione al trono **2.** aumento; (*dir.*) aggiunta (di proprietà, patrimonio) ☆ *— book,* registro delle accessioni (in una biblioteca).

accessorial [,ækse'sɔ:riəl], *ag.* accessorio; supplementare.

accessorily [æk'sesərili], *av.* accessoriamente.

accessoriness [æk'sesərinis], *s.* carattere accessorio.

accessory [æk'sesəri], *ag.* **1.** accessorio, complementare **2.** *predicativo* (*dir.*) partecipante, complice ‖ *s.* **1.** accessorio **2.** (*dir.*) complice (in un delitto).

acciaccatura [ɑːˌtʃɑːkkɑːˈtuːrɑː], *s.* (*mus.*) acciaccatura.

accidence [ˈæksidəns], *s.* (*gram.*) morfologia.

accident [ˈæksidənt], *s.* **1.** accidente, caso: *mere* (o *quite an*) —, un puro caso, per puro caso; *we met by* —, ci incontrammo per caso **2.** disgrazia, incidente, infortunio: *to meet with* (o *to have*) *an* —, essere vittima di un incidente **3.** irregolarità: — *of the ground*, irregolarità del terreno **4.** (*fil.*) accidente.

accidental [ˌæksiˈdentl], *ag.* accidentale, fortuito, casuale; accessorio ‖ *s.* (*mus.*) accidente.

accidentally [ˌæksiˈdentəli], *av.* accidentalmente, fortuitamente, casualmente.

acclaim [əˈkleim], *s.* acclamazione.

to acclaim, *v.t.* acclamare.

acclamation [ˌækləˈmeiʃən], *s.* acclamazione.

acclamatory [əˈklæmətəri], *ag.* laudativo.

acclimatation [əˌklaiməˈteiʃən], *s.* acclimazione.

to acclimate [əˈklaimət], *v.t.* (*amer.*) acclimare, acclimatare.

acclimation [ˌæklaiˈmeiʃən], *s.* acclimazione.

acclimatizable [əˈklaimətaizəbl], *ag.* acclimatabile.

acclimatization [əˌklaimətaiˈzeiʃən], *s.* acclimazione, acclimatazione.

to acclimatize [əˈklaimətaiz], *v.t.* acclimare, acclimatare: *to become* (o *to get*) *acclimatized*, acclimarsi, acclimatarsi.

acclivity [əˈkliviti], *s.* erta, salita.

accolade [ˈækəleid], *s.* **1.** accollata **2.** (*st.*) abbraccio **3.** (*mus.tip.*) sgraffa.

to accommodate [əˈkɔmədeit], *v.t.* **1.** adattare; conformare: *to* — *oneself to*, conformarsi a **2.** metter d'accordo; conciliare **3.** ricevere, ospitare: *this hotel can* — *500 guests*, questo albergo può ospitare 500 persone **4.** favorire, obbligare **5.** fornire, provvedere: *to* — *s.o. with sthg.*, provvedere qlcu. di ql.co.

accommodating [əˈkɔmədeitiŋ], *ag.* accomodante; servizievole, compiacente.

accommodatingly [əˈkɔmədeitiŋli], *av.* in modo accomodante, servizievole, compiacente.

accomodation [əˌkɔməˈdeiʃən], *s.* **1.** accomodamento; adattamento; aggiustamento: *to come to an* —, venire a un compromesso **2.** comodità; benessere; agio, agi: *this hotel offers the best* —, questo albergo offre ogni comodità **3.** alloggio, dimora **4.** (*comm.*) prestito, facilitazione ☆ — *bill*, cambiale di comodo, di favore; — *ladder*, (*mar.*) scala di fuori banda; — *train*, treno omnibus.

accommodative [əˈkɔmədeitiv], *ag.* accomodante, compiacente.

accomodator [əˈkɔmədeitə*], *s.c.* accomodatore, accomodatrice.

accompaniment [əˈkʌmpənimənt], *s.* accompagnamento (anche *mus.*).

accompanist [əˈkʌmpənist], *s.c.* (*mus.*) accompagnatore, accompagnatrice.

to accompany [əˈkʌmpəni], *v.t.i.* **1.** accompagnare (anche *mus.*): *he was accompanied by his secretary*, fu accompagnato dal suo segretario **2.** associare, unire: *fever accompanied by* (o *with*) *delirium*, febbre unita a delirio.

accomplice [əˈkɔmplis], *s.c.* complice.

to accomplish [əˈkɔmpliʃ], *v.t.* **1.** compiere; ultimare; realizzare; effettuare **2.** perfezionare; educare.

accomplished [əˈkɔmpliʃt], *ag.* **1.** compiuto, finito: *an* — *fact*, un fatto compiuto **2.** istruito, colto.

accomplishment [əˈkɔmpliʃmənt], *s.* **1.** compimento; adempimento; realizzazione **2.** compitezza **3.** qualità; dote; talento: *a lady with many accomplishments*, una signora dalle molte doti.

accord [əˈkɔːd], *s.* **1.** accordo; consenso: *of one's own* —, spontaneamente; *with one* —, di comune accordo **2.** (*mus. poes. art.*) armonia, accordo.

to accord, *v.t.i.* **1.** accordare, accordarsi: *to* — *with*, accordarsi con **2.** concedere: *to* — *power of procuration to s.o.*, dare procura a qlcu.

accordance [əˈkɔːdəns], *s.* **1.** accordo; conformità: *in* — *with*, in conformità con, conformemente a **2.** concessione.

accordant [əˈkɔːdənt], *ag.* concorde, conforme; in conformità.

accordantly [əˈkɔːdəntli], *av.* conformemente.

according [əˈkɔːdiŋ], *ag.* **1.** concordante, conforme **2.** (*mus.*) armonioso ‖ *av.*: — *as*, secondo che, precisamente come; — *to*, secondo, a seconda di, conformemente a.

accordingly [əˈkɔːdiŋli], *av.* **1.** in conseguenza **2.** dunque, perciò.

accordion [əˈkɔːdjən], *s.* fisarmonica.

to accost [əˈkɔst], *v.t.* **1.** indirizzarsi a, rivolgersi a; abbordare (per strada) **2.** (*arc.*) costeggiare.

accostable [əˈkɔstəbl], *ag.* accostabile, abbordabile.

accouchement [əˈkuːʃmɔŋ], *s.* parto.

accoucheur [ˌækuːˈʃəː*], *s.* ostetrico.

accoucheuse [ˌækuːˈʃəːz], *s.* ostetrica, levatrice.

account [əˈkaunt], *s.* **1.** conto, computo; lista; enumerazione; novero **2.** (*comm.*) conto, conteggio; contabilità; partita: *as per* — *rendered*, come da conto reso; *debtor's* (o *creditor's*) *accounts*, conti debitori (o creditori); *for* —, per conto: *for* — *and risk of*, per conto e rischio di; *joint* (o *mutual*) —, conto a metà; *statement of* —, estratto conto ‖ *he balanced accounts with Mr. So-and-so*, sistemò i conti col signor Tal dei Tali; *he rendered to me* (o *sent me in*) *the* —, mi inviò il conto; *sales for* — *were effected*, furono effettuate vendite su conto; *to make out an* —, compilare un conto; *to open an* — aprire un conto, una partita **3.** (*comm.*) acconto: *on* —, in acconto **4.** valore, importanza: *of no* —, senza importanza **5.** profitto: *he gave a good* — *of himself against his opponents*, egli ebbe ragione dei suoi avversari; *to put* (o *to turn*) *sthg. to* —, trarre vantaggio da ql.co.: *I turned to* — *my stay in Rome*, approfittai del mio soggiorno a Roma **6.** conto, considerazione: *he takes into* — *every little warning*, prende in considerazione ogni piccolo avvertimento **7.** resoconto, spiegazione, rapporto: *by all accounts*, a quanto si dice; *by your* —, a quanto voi dite; *to call s.o. to* —, chieder conto, spiegazione a qlcu. ‖ *he has gone to his* —, è morto; *to bring s.o. to* —, far pagare a qlcu. le proprie malefatte **8.** *on* — *of*, a causa di ‖ *on all accounts*, sotto tutti i riguardi ‖ *on no* —, per nulla al mondo ‖ *on one's own* —, per proprio conto, di propria iniziativa ‖ *on that* —, perciò ☆ — *books*, libri di conti; — *current* (o *current* —), conto corrente ‖ *bank* —, conto banca; *bills payable* —, conto effetti passivi; *bills receivable* —, conto effetti attivi; *capital* —, conto capitale; *goods* —, conto merci; *sales* —, conto vendite; *transfer* —, giro conto.

to account, *v.t.i.* **1.** considerare, riguardare, stimare: *he was accounted* (*to be*) *guilty*, fu considerato colpevole **2.** *to* — *for sthg.*, essere responsabile, render conto di, spiegare ql.co.

accountability [əˌkauntəˈbiliti], *s.* responsabilità.

accountable [əˈkauntəbl], *ag.* responsabile: *to be* — *to s.o. for sthg.*, essere responsabile verso qlcu. di ql.co.

accountableness [əˈkauntəblnis], *s.* responsabilità.

accountancy [əˈkauntənsi], *s.* ragioneria; contabilità; computisteria.

accountant [əˈkauntənt], *s.* contabile, ragioniere ☆ *chartered* —, ragioniere; *certified public* —, (*amer.*) ragioniere diplomato dallo Stato.

accountantship [əˈkauntəntʃip], *s.* impiego di contabile, ragioniere.

accounting [əˈkauntiŋ], *s.* **1.** contabilità **2.** spiegazione: *there is no* — *for it*, la cosa è inspiegabile.

to accoutre [əˈkuːtə*], *v.t.* vestire; equipaggiare; bardare.

accoutrement(s) [əˈkuːtəmənt(s)], *s.* (*mil.*) equipaggiamento; bardatura (di cavallo).

to accredit [əˈkredit], *v.t.* **1.** accreditare, registrare a credito: *to* — *sthg. to s.o.* (o *s.o. with sthg.*), mettere ql.co. sul conto di qlcu. **2.** credere a, riporre fiducia in **3.** accreditare, fornire di credenziali: *the government accredited him to the Belgian court*, il governo lo accreditò presso la corte belga.

accreditation [ə,kredi'teiʃən], *s.* accreditamento.

accredited [ə'kreditid], *ag.* accreditato; riconosciuto.

to accrete [æ'kri:t], *v.t.i.* concrescere; aggregare, aggregarsi.

accretion [æ'kri:ʃən], *s.* accrescimento, aumento.

to accrue [ə'kru:], *v.i.* **1.** derivare, provenire: *the advantages which — to society from the wireless*, i vantaggi che provengono alla società dalla radiotelegrafia **2.** accumularsi; maturarsi (di interessi): *accrued interest*, interesse maturato.

to accumulate [ə'kju:mjuleit], *v.t.i.* accumulare, accumularsi; ammucchiare, ammucchiarsi.

accumulation [ə,kju:mju'leiʃən], *s.* **1.** accumulazione: *— of capital*, aumento di capitale **2.** ammasso, mucchio.

accumulative [ə'kju:mjulətiv], *ag.* accumulativo.

accumulatively [ə'kju:mjulətivli], *av.* accumulativamente.

accumulator [ə'kju:mjuleitə*], *s.* (*elett.*) accumulatore ‖ *s.c.* accumulatore, accumulatrice.

accuracy ['ækjurəsi], *s.* esattezza, precisione.

accurate ['ækjurit], *ag.* esatto, preciso; fedele.

accurately ['ækjuritli], *av.* esattamente, con precisione; fedelmente, correttamente.

to accurse [ə'kə:s], *v.t.* (*arc.*) maledire.

accursed [ə'kə:sid], **accurst** [ə'kə:st], *ag.* **1.** maledetto **2.** (*fam.*) detestabile.

accusable [ə'kju:zəbl], *ag.* accusabile.

accusal [ə'kju:zəl], **accusation** [,ækju(:)'zeiʃən], *s.* accusa, incriminazione (anche *dir.*).

accusative [ə'kju:zətiv], *ag.s.* (*gram.*) accusativo.

accusatorial [ə,kju:zə'tɔ:riəl], *ag.* (*dir.*) accusatorio.

accusatory [ə'kju:zətəri], *ag.* accusatorio (di linguaggio, ecc.).

to accuse [ə'kju:z], *v.t.* accusare, incriminare: *to — oneself*, accusarsi; *to — s.o. of sthg., of doing...*, accusare qlcu. di ql.co., di fare....

accused [ə'kju:zd], *s.c.* accusato, accusata.

accuser [ə'kju:zə*], *s.c.* accusatore, accusatrice.

accusingly [ə'kju:ziŋli], *av.* accusativamente.

to accustom [ə'kʌstəm], *v.t.* avvezzare, abituare.

accustomed [ə'kʌstəmd], *ag.* **1.** abituale **2.** abituato: *to be — to doing sthg.*, essere abituato a fare ql.co.; *to become* (o *to get*) *— to doing sthg.*, abituarsi a fare ql.co.

ace [eis], *s.* **1.** (*carte, dadi*) asso ‖ *— up one's sleeve* (o *— in the hole*), asso nella manica **2.** asso, campione (specialmente d'aviazione): *an — salesman*, un esperto venditore **3.** *I was within an — of being run over*, (*fam.*) fui ad un pelo dall'essere investito.

acentric [ə'sentrik], *ag.* senza centro.

acephala [ə'sefələ], *s.pl.* (*zool.*) acefali.

acephalous [ə'sefələs], *ag.* acefalo (anche *zool.*).

acerb [ə'sə:b], *ag.* acerbo; acre.

acerbity [ə'sə:biti], *s.* acerbità; acredine.

acerose ['æsərous], *ag.* (*bot.*) aceroso.

acervate [ə'sə:vit], *ag.* (*bot.*) acervato.

acescence [ə'sesəns], **acescency** [ə'sesənsi], *s.* acescenza.

acescent [ə'sesənt], *ag.* acescente.

acetabulum [,æsi'tæbjuləm], *s.* (*anat. archeol. zool.*) acetabolo.

acetate ['æsiteit], *s.* (*chim.*) acetato.

acetated ['æsiteitid], *ag.* (*chim.*) trattato con acido acetico.

acetic [ə'si:tik], *ag.* (*chim.*) acetico.

acetification [ə,setifi'keiʃən], *s.* (*chim.*) acetificazione.

to acetify [ə'setifai], *v.t.* acetificare.

acetimeter [,æsi'timitə*], **acetometer** [,æsi'tɔmitə*], *s.* (*chim.*) acetometro.

acetone ['æsitoun], *s.* (*chim.*) acetone.

acetous ['æsitəs], *ag.* acetoso.

acetylene [ə'setili:n], *s.* (*chim.*) acetilene.

Achaean [ə'ki(:)ən], *ag.* acheo ‖ *s.c.* acheo, achea.

Achates [ə'keiti:z], *no.pr.m.* (*lett.*) Acate.

ache¹ [eik], *s.* dolore, male, sofferenza.

to ache¹, *v.i.* **1.** far male, dolere: *my head aches*, mi duole la testa **2.** *to — for (sthg.)*, (*fam.*) desiderare ardentemente, angosciosamente.

ache² [eitʃ], *s.* acca (la lettera h).

Acheron ['ækərɔn], *no.pr.* (*geog. mit.*) Acheronte.

achievable [ə'tʃi:vəbl], *ag.* **1.** effettuabile, fattibile **2.** raggiungibile.

to achieve [ə'tʃi:v], *v.t.* **1.** compiere, ultimare **2.** ottenere, raggiungere.

achievement [ə'tʃi:vmənt], *s.* **1.** compimento **2.** conseguimento, raggiungimento **3.** gesta, fatto illustre, azione lodevole, impresa **4.** (*arald.*) scudo.

Achilles [ə'kili:z], *no.pr.m.* (*lett.*) Achille.

achilous [ə'kailəs], *ag.* (*bot.*) senza labbri.

aching ['eikiŋ], *ag.* doloroso, dolorante; *fig.* afflitto, accorato ‖ *s.* dolore, sofferenza.

achlamydeous [,æklə'midiəs], *ag.* (*bot.*) aclamide.

achromatic [,ækrou'mætik], *ag.* acromatico.

achromatism [ə'kroumətizəm], *s.* acromatismo.

to achromatize [ə'kroumətaiz], *v.t.* rendere incolore.

acid ['æsid], *ag.s.* acido ☆ *— -proof* (o *— -resisting*), resistente agli acidi; *— -tester*, acidimetro.

acidic [ə'sidik], *ag.* (*chim.*) acido.

acidification [ə,sidifi'keiʃən], *s.* (*chim.*) acidificazione.

acidifier [ə'sidifaiə*], *s.* (*chim.*) acidificatore.

to acidify [ə'sidifai], *v.t.* (*chim.*) acidificare.

acidimeter [,æsi'dimitə*], *s.* (*chim.*) acidimetro.

acidity [ə'siditi], *s.* acidità.

to acidize ['æsidaiz], *v.t.* trattare con acido; acidificare.

acidness ['æsidnis], *s. fig.* acidità.

acidosis [,æsi'dousis], *s.* (*patol.*) acidosi.

to acidulate [ə'sidjuleit], *v.t.* (*chim.*) acidulare.

acidulent [ə'sidjulənt], **acidulous** [ə'sidjuləs], *ag.* (*chim.*) acidulo.

acinose ['æsinous], **acinous** ['æsinəs], *ag.* acinoso.

acinus ['æsinəs], *pl.* **acini** ['æsinai], *s.* acino.

ack-ack ['æk'æk], *ag.* (*sl. abbr.* di *anti-aircraft*) antiaereo (di cannone, pezzo).

to acknowledge [ək'nɔlidʒ], *v.t.* **1.** convenire, ammettere: *to — oneself beaten*, ammettere di essere stato vinto **2.** riconoscere (autorità, autenticità): *to — s.o. as one's chief*, riconoscere qlcu. come proprio capo **3.** rispondere a (lettera, cortesia, ecc.): *I — (receipt of) your letter*, accuso ricevuta della vostra (lettera).

acknowledg(e)ment [ək'nɔlidʒmənt], *s.* **1.** riconoscimento **2.** ricevuta (d'una lettera); quietanza.

aclinic [ə'klinik], *ag.* (*fis.*) isoclino ☆ *— line*, equatore magnetico.

acme ['ækmi], *s.* acme, culmine, sommo; apogeo.

acne ['ækni], *s.* (*patol.*) acne.

acock [ə'kɔk],' *av.*: *he wore his hat —*, portava il cappello sulle ventitré.

acolyte ['ækəlait], *s.* (*eccl.*) accolito; chierico.

aconite ['ækənait], *s.* (*bot.*) aconito.

aconitin [ə'kɔnitin], **aconitine** [ə'kɔnitain], *s.* (*chim.*) aconitina.

acorn ['eikɔ:n], *s.* ghianda ☆ *— -shell*, (*zool.*) balano.

acotyledon [æ,kɔti'li:dən], *s.* (*bot.*) acotiledone.

acoustic(al) [ə'ku:stik(əl)], *ag.* acustico.

acoustics [ə'ku:stiks], *s.* acustica.

to acquaint [ə'kweint], *v.t.* informare, far sapere a, annunciare a; avvisare, rendere edotto: *to — s.o. with sthg.*, informare qlcu. di ql.co. ‖ *to be acquainted with s.o., sthg.*, conoscere qlcu., essere al corrente di ql.co.; *to become acquainted with s.o., to become* (o *to make oneself*) *acquainted with sthg.*, fare la conoscenza di qlcu., prendere conoscenza di ql.co.

acquaintance [ə'kweintəns], *s.* **1.** conoscenza: *he improves upon —*, guadagna ad essere conosciuto; *to make s.o.'s —* (o *to make — with s.o.*), fare la conoscenza di qlcu. **2.** *gener. pl.* conoscenza (persona conosciuta): *friends and acquaintances*, amici e conoscenti.

acquaintanceship [ə'kweintənʃip], s. **1.** conoscenza (di persona) **2.** coll. l'insieme delle ¦conoscenze, delle relazioni: wide —, ampie relazioni.

acquest [æ'kwest], s. **1.** acquisto **2.** (dir.) proprietà non ottenuta per eredità.

to **acquiesce** [,ækwi'es], v.i. aderire, consentire; sottomettersi: to — in a request, aderire a una richiesta.

acquiescence [,ækwi'esns], s. **1.** acquiescenza, tacito consenso **2.** sommissione, docilità.

acquiescent [,ækwi'esnt], ag. acquiescente; docile.

acquirable [ə'kwaiərəbl], ag. acquistabile.

to **acquire** [ə'kwaiə*], v.t. acquistare; ottenere; acquisire: an acquired habit, un'abitudine acquisita; to — a language, imparare una lingua; to — a taste for sthg., prender gusto a ql.co.

acquirement [ə'kwaiəmənt], s. **1.** acquisizione **2.** cognizione (acquisita).

acquirer [ə'kwaiərə*], s. acquirente.

acquisition [,ækwi'ziʃən], s. **1.** acquisizione **2.** acquisto (la cosa acquistata).

acquisitive [ə'kwizitiv], ag. avido di guadagno.

acquisitiveness [ə'kwizitivnis], s. attitudine ad acquisire.

to **acquit** [ə'kwit], pass.p.p. **acquitted** [ə'kwitid], v.t. **1.** saldare, pagare (debiti) **2.** liberare, affrancare, svincolare: to — oneself of a duty, liberarsi di un dovere **3.** (dir.) assolvere, esonerare: to — s.o. of a charge, assolvere qlcu. da un'accusa **4.** to — oneself well, ill, comportarsi bene, male.

acquittal [ə'kwitl], s. **1.** saldo (di un debito) **2.** sgravio: for the — of one's conscience, a sgravio di coscienza **3.** adempimento (di un dovere) **4.** (dir.) assoluzione.

acquittance [ə'kwitəns], s. **1.** saldo, pagamento **2.** quietanza, ricevuta.

acre ['eikə*], s. **1.** (agr.) acro (misura di superficie = 40,468 are) **2.** (arc.) campo || God's —, cimitero.

acreage ['eikəridʒ], s. quantità di acri.

acrid ['ækrid], ag. acre; aspro; mordace.

acridity [æ'kriditi], **acridness** ['ækridnis], s. acredine; asprezza; mordacità.

acrimonious [,ækri'mounjəs], ag. acre; astioso.

acrimoniously [,ækri'mounjəsli], av. acremente.

acrimony ['ækriməni], s. acrimonia.

acrobat ['ækrəbæt], s. c. acrobata.

acrobatic [,ækrə'bætik], ag. acrobatico.

acrobatically [,ækrə'bætikəli], av. acrobaticamente.

acrobatics [,ækrə'bætiks], s.pl. acrobazia (anche fig.).

acrobatism ['ækrəbætizəm], s. acrobatismo.

acrocephalic[,ækrousi'fælik], **acrocephalous**[,ækrou-'sefələs], ag. (anat. patol.) acrocefalo.

acronyc(h)al [ə'krɔnikəl], ag. (astr.) acronico.

acronym ['ækrənim], s. acronimo, sigla.

acropolis [ə'krɔpolis], s. acropoli; cittadella.

across [ə'krɔs], av. attraverso, per traverso, da un capo all'altro; dall'altra parte: the distance —, la distanza trasversale, la distanza in larghezza; the lake measures six miles —, il lago misura sei miglia di larghezza; to come —, incontrare, imbattersi in; to go —, attraversare, traversare || prep. attraverso, (al) di là di: he lives — the street, abita dall'altro lato della strada; I came — him in the street, mi imbattei in lui per la strada; I saw him running — the road, lo vidi attraversare la strada correndo; they walked — the fields, camminarono attraverso (o attraversarono) i campi.

acrostic [ə'krɔstik], ag.s. (poes.) acrostico.

act [ækt], s. **1.** atto; documento; decreto, legge: — of contrition, of faith, atto di contrizione, di fede; — of justice, atto di giustizia; the Parliament passed the —, il Parlamento approvò il decreto **2.** azione: a stupid —, un'azione sciocca; your first — was to open the door, il tuo primo gesto fu di aprire la porta || Acts of the Apostles, gli Atti degli Apostoli || by — of God, (dir.) per causa di forza maggiore || in the — of, nel mo-

mento di; to catch s.o. in the (very) —, cogliere qlcu. sul fatto, in flagrante **3.** (teat.) atto **4.** tesi di laurea (discussa in pubblico): he kept the —, sostenne la sua tesi.

to **act**, v.t.i. **1.** agire, fare; comportarsi, condursi da: he acts upon my advice, agisce seguendo i miei consigli; these pills — on the heart, queste pillole agiscono sul cuore; to — for the best, agire per il meglio; to — the part of, agire da: to — the part of a judge, esercitare le funzioni di giudice; to — prudently, agire con prudenza || to — as, fungere da: he acted as secretary, faceva da segretario || to — the fool, comportarsi da sciocco || to — for, rappresentare, agire per conto di || to — up to, conformarsi a: he acted up to his principles, agì in conformità ai suoi principi **2.** (teat.) impersonare, recitare la parte di; rappresentare: he acted Romeo, impersonava Romeo; they — "Hamlet", rappresentano l'«Amleto» || to — a part, (fam.) fare la commedia, fingere **3.** funzionare: this brake is not acting well, questo freno non funziona bene.

acting ['æktin], ag. **1.** facente, avente funzione di, supplente **2.** (mec.) a effetto (semplice, doppio, ecc.) || s. **1.** azione **2.** (teat.) recitazione; rappresentazione || to go in for —, far del teatro || it is mere —, (fam.) è tutto una commedia, una finzione || — captain, (mil.) tenente facente funzione di capitano; — manager, direttore interinale; — partner, (comm.) socio gerente || double — machine, macchina a doppio effetto; single — machine, macchina ad effetto unico.

actinic [æk'tinik], ag. (chim. foto.) attinico.

actinism ['æktinizəm], s. (chim. foto.) attinicità.

actinium [æk'tiniəm], s. (chim.) attinio.

actinometer [,ækti'nɔmitə*], s. (fis.) attinometro.

actinotherapy [,æktinou'θerəpi], s. (med.) attinoterapia; radioterapia.

action ['ækʃən], s. **1.** azione; fatto, atto: a good —, una buona azione; line of —, linea di condotta; to be in —, essere in azione **2.** gesto, gesticolazione **3.** effetto, azione: the — of a drug, l'effetto di una droga **4.** (dir.) processo; causa; lite; atti (processuali): civil —, processo, causa civile; criminal —, processo penale; to bring an — against s.o., intentare un processo contro qlcu., citare qlcu. in giudizio **5.** combattimento, battaglia: killed in —, ucciso in combattimento; out of —, fuori combattimento; to go into —, andare in combattimento **6.** (teat.) azione, scena: the scene of —, la scena, il luogo della scena **7.** (mec.) funzionamento: machine in full —, macchina che funziona in pieno; the — of this spring is wrong, questa molla funziona male; to put (o to set) sthg. in —, fare agire, funzionare ql.co. ☆ — painting, (pitt.) «tachisme».

to **action**, v.t. (dir.) perseguire penalmente.

actionable ['ækʃnəbl], ag. (dir.) processabile, perseguibile.

actionless ['ækʃənlis], ag. immoto; inoperoso; (chim.) inerte.

Actium ['æktiəm], no.pr. (geog. st.) Azio.

to **activate** ['æktiveit], v.t. **1.** attivare **2.** rendere radioattivo.

active ['æktiv], ag. **1.** attivo; fattivo, laborioso; intensamente operante: — demand for iron, forte richiesta di ferro; on — service, (mil.) in servizio attivo **2.** (gram.) attivo.

actively ['æktivli], av. attivamente.

activism ['æktivizəm], s. (fil.pol.) attivismo.

activist ['æktivist], s. (fil.pol.) attivista.

activity [æk'tiviti], s. **1.** attività **2.** pl. attività, occupazioni.

actor ['æktə*], s. attore; commediante.

actress ['æktris], s. attrice; commediante.

actual ['æktjuəl], ag. reale, vero; effettivo: an — case, un caso vero; — cost, costo effettivo **2.** (rar.) presente, attuale.

actualism ['æktjuəlizəm], s. (fil.) attualismo.

actuality [ˌæktjuˈæliti], s. 1. realtà 2. pl. condizioni reali.

actualization [ˌæktjuəlaiˈzeiʃən], s. 1. realizzazione (di un'idea, una speranza) 2. rappresentazione realistica, ricostruzione (di una scena, un incidente).

to **actualize** [ˈæktjuəlaiz], v.t. 1. realizzare (un'idea, una speranza) 2. far rivivere (una scena, un incidente).

actually [ˈæktjuəli], av. realmente, effettivamente: do you — mean it?, lo dite sul serio?.

actuarial [ˌæktjuˈɛəriəl], ag. (mat.) attuariale.

actuary [ˈæktjuəri], s. (dir.) attuario.

to **actuate** [ˈæktjueit], v.t. 1. mettere in moto, in azione 2. guidare; muovere; trascinare: actuated by rage, mosso dall'ira.

actuation [ˌæktjuˈeiʃən], s. 1. (mec.) messa in moto 2. incitamento.

acuity [əˈkju(:)iti], s. acutezza.

aculeate [əˈkju(:)liit], ag. 1. (bot. zool.) aculeato 2. fig. pungente.

aculeus [əˈkju(:)liəs], pl. **aculei** [əˈkju(:)liai], s. (bot. zool.) aculeo.

acumen [əˈkju:men], s. acume.

acuminate [əˈkju:minit], ag. acuminato.

to **acuminate** [əˈkju:mineit], v.t. acuminare.

acute [əˈkju:t], ag. 1. acuto, appuntito, aguzzo; fig. acuto, perspicace; violento (di dolore); sottile (di udito); penetrante (di suono) 2. (geom. gram.) acuto.

acutely [əˈkju:tli], av. acutamente.

acuteness [əˈkju:tnis], s. acutezza (anche fig.).

ad [æd], s. (abbr. fam. di advertisement) avviso; inserzione (nei giornali); affisso, cartellone pubblicitario ☆ — -man, agente pubblicitario; — -mass, il « grosso pubblico » (dominato dalla pubblicità).

Ada [ˈeidə], no.pr.f. Ada.

adage [ˈædidʒ], s. adagio, massima.

adagio [əˈdɑ:dʒiou], s. (mus.) adagio.

Adalbert [ˈædəlbə:t], no.pr.m. Adalberto.

Adam [ˈædəm], no.pr.m. Adamo ‖ —'s apple, pomo d'Adamo.

adamant [ˈædəmənt], s. (arc.) diamante ‖ heart of —, fig. cuore di pietra.

adamantine [ˌædəˈmæntain], ag. adamantino.

Adamic [əˈdæmik], ag. adamitico.

Adamite [ˈædəmait], s. 1. discendente di Adamo 2. (st.) adamita.

to **adapt** [əˈdæpt], v.t. adattare, accomodare; modificare: to — for (a purpose), adattare per (uno scopo); to — from (the French), adattare dal (francese); to — to sthg., adattare a ql.co.

adaptability [əˌdæptəˈbiliti], s. adattabilità.

adaptable [əˈdæptəbl], ag. adattabile.

adaptation [ˌædæpˈteiʃən], s. adattamento.

adapted [əˈdæptid], ag. 1. adatto, confacente 2. ridotto, adattato: play — from the French (for children), commedia ridotta dal francese (per bambini).

adapter [əˈdæptə*], s. 1. riduttore di opere (per teatro, film) 2. (elett.) pezzo, parte, tubo di raccordo 3. (chim.) vaso di condensazione (unito al lambicco).

adaptive [əˈdæptiv], ag. adattabile, arrendevole.

adaptiveness [əˈdæptivnis], s. adattabilità, arrendevolezza.

to **add** [æd], v.t.i. 1. aggiungere; unire: this adds to my grief, questo aumenta il mio dolore; to — the interest to the capital, aggiungere l'interesse al capitale 2. (arit.) sommare, addizionare: to — four to ten, sommare quattro a dieci 3. to — in, includere 4. to — up, (arit.) fare una somma, trovare la somma di: to — up a column of figures, fare la somma di una colonna di cifre.

addax [ˈædæks], s. (zool.) orice.

addendum [əˈdendəm], pl. **addenda** [əˈdendə], s. aggiunta; appendice.

adder¹ [ˈædə*], s.c. chi addiziona ‖ s. addizionatrice.

adder², s. vipera, aspide: ☆ flying — (o —-fly), (entom.) libellula.

addict [ˈædikt], s.c. tossicomane ☆ morphia —, morfinomane: opium —, oppiomane.

to **addict** [əˈdikt], v.t. (gener. spreg.) dedicare, abituare: he addicted himself to opium, si diede all'oppio.

addiction [əˈdikʃən], s. inclinazione; dedizione: — to alcohol, dedizione all'alcool; — to science, inclinazione, dedizione alla scienza.

addition [əˈdiʃən], s. 1. (arit.) addizione, somma 2. aggiunta; aumento: in — to sthg., in più, oltre a, in aggiunta a ql.co.

additional [əˈdiʃənl], ag. supplementare; aggiunto.

additionally [əˈdiʃnəli], av. in aggiunta; inoltre.

additive [ˈæditiv], ag. aggiuntivo ‖ s. (chim.) additivo.

addle [ˈædl], ag. 1. marcio; non gallabile (uovo) 2. sterile, vuoto; scervellato ☆ — -brained, sventato, confuso.

to **addle**, v.t.i. 1. marcire, imputridire 2. confondere; istupidire.

address [əˈdres], s. 1. indirizzo, recapito: of no fixed —, senza fissa dimora 2. indirizzo, soprascritta 3. discorso; allocuzione 4. abilità; tatto; destrezza 5. pl. omaggi, corte: to pay one's addresses to, far la corte, rendere omaggio a.

to **address**, v.t.i. 1. indirizzare; rivolgere; applicare: to — oneself to sthg., dedicarsi a ql.co. 2. metter l'indirizzo su (una lettera, ecc.) 3. arringare 4. far la corte a.

addressee [ˌædreˈsi:], s.c. destinatario, destinataria.

addresser [əˈdresə*], s.c. mittente (di una lettera).

addressograph [əˈdresəgrɑ:f], s. macchina per stampare indirizzi.

to **adduce** [əˈdju:s], v.t. addurre; citare.

adduceable [əˈdju:səbl], ag. adducibile, citabile.

adducent [əˈdju:sənt], ag. (anat.) adduttore.

adducible [əˈdju:sibl], ag. adducibile; citabile.

to **adduct** [əˈdʌkt], v.t. (fisiol.) addurre.

adduction [əˈdʌkʃən], s. 1. (fisiol.) adduzione 2. citazione.

adductive [əˈdʌktiv], ag. (fisiol.) adduttore.

adductor [əˈdʌktə*], s. (anat.) (muscolo) adduttore.

Adela [ˈædilə], no.pr.f. Adele.

Adelaide [ˈædəleid], no.pr.f. Adelaide.

Adelina [ˌædiˈli:nə], **Adeline** [ˈædili:n], no.pr.f. Adelina.

Aden [ˈeidn], no.pr. (geog.) Aden.

adenoids [ˈædinɔidz], s.pl. adenoidi.

adept [ˈædept], ag.s. perito, esperto: to be — in sthg., at doing sthg., essere esperto in ql.co., nel fare ql.co.

adequacy [ˈædikwəsi], s. adeguatezza.

adequate [ˈædikwit], ag. adeguato.

adequately [ˈædikwitli], av. adeguatamente.

adespota [əˈdespətə], s.pl. scritti adespoti, anonimi.

to **adhere** [ədˈhiə*], v.i. aderire; attaccarsi; essere favorevole: the scab adheres to the wound, la crosta aderisce alla piaga; to — to a party, to a proposal, aderire a un partito, a una proposta.

adherence [ədˈhiərəns], s. aderenza, adesione.

adherent [ədˈhiərənt], ag. aderente, attaccato; incollato ‖ s. aderente, seguace, partigiano.

adhesion [ədˈhi:ʒən], s. 1. adesione 2. (patol.) aderenza.

adhesive [ədˈhi:siv], ag. adesivo; viscoso ☆ — paper, carta gommata; — plaster, cerotto adesivo.

adhesively [ədˈhi:sivli], av. adesivamente.

adhesiveness [ədˈhi:sivnis], s. aderenza; (forza di) adesione; viscosità.

to **adhibit** [ədˈhibit], v.t. applicare; somministrare (rimedi).

adhibition [ˌædhiˈbiʃən], s. applicazione; uso.

adiantum [ˌædiˈæntəm], s. (bot.) adianto; capelvenere.

adieu [əˈdju:], inter. addio! ‖ s. addio; saluto: to take (o to make) one's —, salutare, prendere congedo.

adipocere [ˌædipouˈsiə*], s. (chim.) adipocera.

adipose [ˈædipous], ag. adiposo ‖ s. grasso animale.

adiposity [ˌædiˈpositi], s. adiposità.

adit [ˈædit], *s.* **1.** accesso, entrata **2.** galleria (di miniera).

adjacency [əˈdʒeisənsi], *s.* adiacenza, vicinanza.

adjacent [əˈdʒeisənt], *ag.* adiacente, limitrofo.

adjectival [ˌædʒekˈtaivəl], *ag.* (*gram.*) aggettivale.

adjectivally [ˌædʒekˈtaivəli], *av.* (*gram.*) aggettivamente.

adjective [ˈædʒiktiv], *ag.* **1.** (*gram.*) aggettivo **2.** addizionale, accessorio; dipendente ‖ *s.* (*gram.*) aggettivo ☆ *law* —, (*dir.*) procedura.

to **adjoin** [əˈdʒoin], *v.t.* **1.** aggiungere; unire **2.** confinare con, essere contiguo a.

adjoining [əˈdʒoiniŋ], *ag.* contiguo; adiacente; vicino.

to **adjourn** [əˈdʒəːn], *v.t.i.* **1.** aggiornare, aggiornarsi; rimettere; differire, rinviare **2.** (*sl.*) trasferirsi (in altro luogo).

adjournment [əˈdʒəːnmənt], *s.* aggiornamento, rinvio.

to **adjudge** [əˈdʒʌdʒ], *v.t.* **1.** aggiudicare; accordare **2.** giudicare; sentenziare **3.** condannare.

adjudg(e)ment [əˈdʒʌdʒmənt], *s.* **1.** aggiudicazione **2.** giudizio; sentenza; decisione **3.** condanna.

to **adjudicate** [əˈdʒuːdikeit], *v.t.i.* **1.** giudicare; decidere: *to — upon a question*, pronunciare un giudizio su una questione **2.** aggiudicare.

adjudication [ə,dʒuːdiˈkeiʃən], *s.* **1.** giudizio; sentenza **2.** aggiudicazione.

adjudicative [əˈdʒuːdikeitiv], *ag.* aggiudicativo.

adjudicator [əˈdʒuːdikeitə*], *s.* arbitro, giudice; membro di giuria (in concorsi musicali, ecc.).

adjunct [ˈædʒʌŋkt], *s.* **1.** aggiunta; accessorio **2.** (*gram.*) complemento **3.** aggiunto (in uffici, servizi, ecc.) ☆ — *professor*, professore aggiunto.

adjunction [əˈdʒʌŋkʃən], *s.* aggiunzione; aggiunta.

adjunctive [əˈdʒʌŋktiv], *ag.* aggiuntivo.

adjunctively [əˈdʒʌŋktivli], *av.* aggiuntivamente.

adjuration [ˌædʒuəˈreiʃən], *s.* **1.** implorazione; supplica **2.** impegno (sotto giuramento).

to **adjure** [əˈdʒuə*], *v.t.* scongiurare; implorare; supplicare.

to **adjust** [əˈdʒʌst], *v.t.* **1.** aggiustare, accomodare; ordinare: *to — accounts*, pareggiare i conti **2.** adattare: *to — oneself to the new condition*, adattarsi alla nuova condizione **3.** regolare, mettere a punto (orologio, strumento) **4.** (*mec.*) aggiustare; calettare.

adjustable [əˈdʒʌstəbl], *ag.* aggiustabile, regolabile, spostabile: — *seat*, sedile regolabile.

adjuster [əˈdʒʌstə*], *s.c.* chi aggiusta ‖ *s.* **1.** (*comm.*) liquidatore **2.** (*mec.*) dispositivo di regolazione.

adjustment [əˈdʒʌstmənt], *s.* **1.** (*comm.*) aggiustamento, accomodamento, regolamento; liquidazione **2.** (*mec.*) regolazione, aggiustaggio, registrazione **3.** (*ott.*) rettifica.

adjutage [ˈædʒutidʒ], *s.* tubo dello zampillo.

adjutancy [ˈædʒutənsi], *s.* (*mil.*) ufficio di aiutante.

adjutant [ˈædʒutənt], *ag.* aiutante ‖ *s.* **1.** (*rar.*) assistente; (*mil.*) aiutante (ufficiale) **2.** (*ornit.*) marabù indiano, argala.

adjuvant [ˈædʒuvənt], *ag.* ausiliare; utile ‖ *s.* coadiutore, cooperatore.

to **admeasure** [ædˈmeʒə*], *v.t.* ripartire, distribuire (in giuste parti).

admeasurement [ædˈmeʒəmənt], *s.* **1.** ripartizione **2.** proporzioni, misure.

adminicle [ædˈminikl], *s.* **1.** aiuto **2.** (*dir.*) prova di conferma.

to **administer** [ədˈministə*], *v.t.i.* **1.** amministrare; governare; applicare (legge) **2.** dare, consentire; fornire, somministrare: *to — an oath*, far prestare giuramento **3.** contribuire, sovvenire: *to — to s.o.'s comfort*, contribuire al benessere di qlcu.

administrable [ədˈministrəbl], *ag.* amministrabile.

to **administrate** [ədˈministreit], *v.t.* (*amer.*) amministrare.

administration [əd,minisˈtreiʃən], *s.* **1.** amministrazione, gerenza; (*dir.*) curatela (di beni di minorenni) ‖ *Letters of Administration*, (*dir.*) autorizzazione ad amministrare il patrimonio di chi non ha fatto testamento **2.** somministrazione (di sacramenti, medicine).

administrative [ədˈministrətiv], *ag.* amministrativo.

administratively [ədˈministrətivli], *av.* amministrativamente.

administrator [ədˈministreitə*], *s.* amministratore.

administratorship [ədˈministreitəʃip], *s.* amministrazione; gerenza; (*dir.*) curatela.

administratrix [ədˈministreitriks], *pl.* **administratrices** [ədˈministreitrisiːz], *s.* amministratrice.

admirable [ˈædmərəbl], *ag.* ammirabile, mirabile.

admirably [ˈædmərəbli], *av.* mirabilmente.

admiral [ˈædmərəl], *s.* **1.** ammiraglio ‖ *Admiral of the Fleet*, comandante in capo della flotta; *Lord High Admiral*, grand'ammiraglio (in Gran Bretagna); *Rear-Admiral*, contrammiraglio; *Vice-Admiral*, vice ammiraglio **2.** — (*-ship*), nave ammiraglia.

admiralship [ˈædmərəlʃip], *s.* ammiragliato (funzione, dignità d'ammiraglio).

admiralty [ˈædmərəlti], *s.* ammiragliato; Ministero della Marina (in Gran Bretagna) ‖ *Court of Admiralty*, tribunale militare della Marina; *First Lord of the Admiralty*, Ministro della Marina.

admiration [ˌædməˈreiʃən], *s.* ammirazione; (*arc.*) stupore ‖ *note of —*, punto esclamativo.

to **admire** [ədˈmaiə*], *v.t.* **1.** ammirare; (*arc.*) meravigliarsi, stupirsi di **2.** (*sl.amer.*) desiderare, aver piacere di.

admirer [ədˈmaiərə*], *s.c.* ammiratore, ammiratrice; adoratore, adoratrice.

admiring [ədˈmaiəriŋ], *ag.* ammirativo.

admiringly [ədˈmaiəriŋli], *av.* con ammirazione.

admissibility [əd,misəˈbiliti], *s.* ammissibilità.

admissible [ədˈmisəbl], *ag.* ammissibile.

admission [ədˈmiʃən], *s.* **1.** ammissione; accesso: — *to*, accesso a; *free* —, entrata libera; *to give* —, lasciar entrare: *we were not given* —, non ci fu concesso, non ci permisero di entrare **2.** ammissione, confessione (d'una colpa): *he made full — of his faults*, fece piena confessione delle sue colpe **3.** (*mec.*) ammissione ☆ — *fee* (o — *money*), tariffa di entrata.

admissive [ədˈmisiv], *ag.* che ammette.

to **admit** [ədˈmit], *pass.p.p.* **admitted** [ədˈmitid], *v.t.i.* **1.** ammettere; lasciar entrare: *the ticket admits one*, il biglietto è valido per una persona **2.** contenere, aver posto per: *the hall admits 2,500 people*, la sala contiene 2500 persone **3.** (I) ammettere; riconoscere; confessare: *he admitted having stolen the jam*, ammise di aver rubato la marmellata; *his conduct admits of no excuse*, la sua condotta non ha giustificazioni.

admittable [ədˈmitəbl], *ag.* ammissibile.

admittance [ədˈmitəns], *s.* ammissione; entrata, accesso, ingresso ‖ *no* —, vietato l'ingresso.

admitted [ədˈmitid], *ag.* ammesso, riconosciuto.

admittedly [ədˈmitidli], *av.* per ammissione.

to **admix** [ədˈmiks], *v.t.i.* mescolare, mescolarsi.

admixture [ədˈmikstʃə*], *s.* mescolanza, miscela.

to **admonish** [ədˈmoniʃ], *v.t.* ammonire; esortare; avvertire, mettere in guardia.

admonishment [ədˈmoniʃmənt], *s.* ammonimento; esortazione; avvertimento.

admonition [ˌædməˈniʃən], *s.* ammonimento, rimprovero; avvertimento.

admonitory [ədˈmonitəri], *ag.* ammonitorio.

adnoun [ˈædnaun], *s.* (*gram.*) aggettivo (in quanto aggiunto a sostantivo); aggettivo sostantivato.

ado [əˈduː], *s.* **1.** fatica, difficoltà; stento **2.** confusione; rumore, baccano: *much — about nothing*, molto rumore per nulla.

adobe [əˈdoubi], *s.* (*edil.*) mattone cotto al sole.

adolescence [ˌædouˈlesns], **adolescency** [ˌædouˈlesnsi], *s.* adolescenza.

adolescent [,ædou'lesnt], *ag.s.c.* adolescente.

Adolf ['ædolf], **Adolphus** [ə'dolfəs], *no.pr.m.* Adolfo.

Adonis [ə'dounis], *no.pr.m. (mit.)* Adone ǁ **adonis**, *s.* **1.** *fig.* bellimbusto **2.** *(bot.)* adonide.

to **adonize** ['ædənaiz], *v.i.* azzimarsi; fare il ganimede.

to **adopt** [ə'dopt], *v.t.* adottare (una persona, un'idea); scegliere (linea di condotta, indirizzo).

adoptability [ə,doptə'biliti], *s. (dir.)* idoneità ad essere adottato.

adoptable [ə'doptəbl], *ag.* adottabile.

adopted [ə'doptid], *ag.* adottato ☆ — *son*, figlio adottivo.

adoptee [,ædop'ti:], *s.c. (dir.)* adottato, adottata.

adopter [ə'doptə*], *s.c. (dir.)* adottante.

adoption [ə'dopʃən], *s.* adozione; scelta.

adoptive [ə'doptiv], *ag.* adottivo ☆ — *father, son*, padre, figlio adottivo.

adorability [ə,do:rə'biliti], *s.* adorabilità.

adorable [ə'do:rəbl], *ag.* adorabile.

adorably [ə'do:rəbli], *av.* adorabilmente.

adoration [,ædo:'reiʃən], *s.* adorazione; venerazione.

to **adore** [ə'do:*], *v.t.* adorare; venerare: *I — your new dress*, *(fam.)* mi piace immensamente il tuo abito nuovo.

adorer [ə'do:rə*], *s.c.* adoratore, adoratrice.

to **adorn** [ə'do:n], *v.t.* adornare, abbellire.

adorning [ə'do:niŋ], **adornment** [ə'do:nmənt], *s.* ornamento, adornamento.

adown [ə'daun], *av.prep. (arc. poet.)* giù, da basso, di sotto.

adrenalin [ə'drenəlin], *s. (chim. farm.)* adrenalina.

Adrian ['eidriən], *no.pr.m.* Adriano.

Adriatic [,eidri'ætik], *ag.* adriatico ǁ *the — Sea*, il mare Adriatico ǁ *no.pr. (geog.)* l'Adriatico.

adrift [ə'drift], *av.* alla deriva (anche *fig.*).

adroit [ə'droit], *ag.* destro, abile; sagace.

adroitly [ə'droitli], *av.* destramente; sagacemente.

adroitness [ə'droitnis], *s.* destrezza, abilità; sagacia.

adry [ə'drai], *av.* a secco ǁ *ag. predicativo*, secco, assetato.

adscititious [,ædsi'tiʃəs], *ag.* ascitizio, accessorio.

to **adulate** ['ædjuleit], *v.t.* adulare.

adulation [,ædju'leiʃən], *s.* adulazione.

adulator ['ædjuleitə*], *s.c.* adulatore, adulatrice.

adulatory ['ædjuleitəri], *ag.* adulatorio.

adult ['ædʌlt], *ag.* adulto ǁ *s.c.* adulto, adulta.

adulterant [ə'dʌltərənt], *ag.s.* adulterante.

adulterate [ə'dʌltərit], *ag.* **1.** adulterato, falsificato; corrotto (di lingua, testo, ecc.) **2.** adultero.

to **adulterate** [ə'dʌltəreit], *v.t.i.* **1.** adulterare, falsificare; corrompere (lingua, testo): *adulterated milk*, latte annacquato **2.** *(arc.)* commettere adulterio.

adulteration [ə,dʌltə'reiʃən], *s.* adulterazione, falsificazione; corruzione (di lingua, testo, ecc.).

adulterator [ə'dʌltəreitə*], *s.c.* adulteratore, adulteratrice; falsificatore, falsificatrice.

adulterer [ə'dʌltərə*], *s.* adultero.

adulteress [ə'dʌltəris], *s.* adultera.

adulterine [ə'dʌltərain], *ag.* **1.** adulterino **2.** falsificato, contraffatto.

adulterous [ə'dʌltərəs], *ag.* adultero, di adulterio.

adulterously [ə'dʌltərəsli], *av.* in modo adultero.

adultery [ə'dʌltəri], *s.* adulterio.

adumbral [ə'dʌmbrəl], *ag.* ombroso.

to **adumbrate** ['ædʌmbreit], *v.t.i.* **1.** adombrare **2.** schizzare, abbozzare **3.** far presagire, lasciar intravvedere.

adumbration [,ædʌm'breiʃən], *s.* **1.** adombramento **2.** abbozzo **3.** segni precursori; presentimento.

adust [ə'dʌst], *ag.* **1.** adusto, riarso **2.** atrabiliare.

ad valorem ['ædvə'lo:rem], *ag.av.* ad valorem, secondo il valore.

advance [əd'va:ns], *s.* **1.** avanzamento, movimento in avanti; marcia, cammino; progresso: *to make advances*

(o *an* —) *to s.o.*, fare i primi passi (per riconciliazione, ecc.) verso qlcu.; *to make an — towards*, avanzare verso **2.** *(comm.)* aumento, rialzo: *an — in prices*, un aumento dei prezzi **3.** anticipo: *— against merchandise*, *(comm.)* anticipo sulla merce ǁ *in —*, anticipatamente: *to arrive in —*, arrivare in anticipo ☆ *— guard*, avanguardia; *— money*, denaro anticipato.

to **advance**, *v.t.i.* **1.** avanzare, avanzarsi; portar innanzi, portarsi innanzi; progredire, far progressi; perfezionare; salire (di grado); suggerire: *the army advanced with great difficulty*, l'esercito avanzava con grande difficoltà; *he advanced a new plan, but nobody accepted it*, suggerì un progetto nuovo, ma nessuno lo accettò; *he is far advanced in his ideas*, ha idee molto avanzate **2.** *(comm.)* aumentare, rialzare (prezzi) **3.** anticipare (denaro): *money advanced here*, qui si anticipa denaro.

advancement [əd'va:nsmənt], *s.* **1.** avanzamento; progresso **2.** *(comm.)* rialzo.

advantage [əd'va:ntidʒ], *s.* vantaggio, profitto; utilità, convenienza: *mutual —*, vantaggio reciproco; *to reciprocal —*, a vantaggio reciproco; *the army was on an — -ground*, l'esercito si trovava in posizione vantaggiosa; *to have the — over s.o.*, avere la meglio su, approfittare di qlcu.; *to sell sthg. to —*, vendere ql.co. con profitto; *to take —*, profittare, mettere a profitto, abusare di: *to take — of s.o.*, abusare della bontà (credulità) di qlcu.; *to take — of sthg.*, approfittare di ql.co., trarre profitto da ql.co.; *to turn out to s.o.'s —*, tornare a vantaggio di qlcu.; *to turn sthg. to —*, mettere ql.co. a proprio profitto, ¦trarre vantaggio da ql.co.

to **advantage**, *v.t.* avvantaggiare, favorire.

advantageous [,ædvən'teidʒəs], *ag.* vantaggioso.

advantageously [,ædvən'teidʒəsli], *av.* vantaggiosamente.

advent ['ædvənt], *s.* avvento, venuta ǁ *the Advent*, *(eccl.)* l'Avvento.

adventism ['ædvəntizəm], *s. (st. relig.)* avventismo.

Adventist ['ædvəntist], *ag.s.c. (st. relig.)* avventista.

adventitious [,ædvən'tiʃəs], *ag.* avventizio.

adventitiously [,ædvən'tiʃəsli], *av.* casualmente.

adventure [əd'ventʃə*], *s.* **1.** avventura, impresa rischiosa **2.** incidente, caso **3.** *(comm.)* speculazione.

to **adventure**, *v.t.i.* **1.** avventurare, avventurarsi **2.** rischiare, porre a repentaglio.

adventurer [əd'ventʃərə*], *s.* avventuriero.

adventuresome [əd'ventʃəsəm], *ag.* avventuroso; temerario.

adventuresomeness [əd'ventʃəsəmnis], *s.* spirito di avventura; temerarietà.

adventuress [əd'ventʃəris], *s.* avventuriera.

adventurous [əd'ventʃərəs], *ag.* avventuroso; audace.

adventurously [əd'ventʃərəsli], *av.* avventurosamente; audacemente.

adverb ['ædvə:b], *s. (gram.)* avverbio.

adverbial [əd'və:bjəl], *ag. (gram.)* avverbiale.

adverbially [əd'və:bjəli], *av. (gram.)* avverbialmente.

adversary ['ædvəsəri], *s.* avversario, antagonista.

adversative [əd'və:sətiv], *ag. (gram.)* avversativo.

adverse ['ædvə:s], *ag.* **1.** avverso, contrario: *— fortune*, fortuna avversa; *to be — to a policy*, essere avverso ad una politica **2.** di fronte, opposto.

adversely [əd'və:sli], *av.* avversamente.

adversity [əd'və:siti], *s.* avversità.

to **advert** [əd'və:t], *v.i.* volger l'attenzione; alludere: *he then adverted to another matter*, egli poi accennò ad un'altra cosa.

advertence [əd'və:təns], **advertency** [əd'və:tənsi], *s.* avvertenza.

to **advertise** ['ædvətaiz], *v.t.i.* annunziare, fare pubblicità a; fare degli annunzi; fare della pubblicità: *to — an article*, fare pubblicità a un articolo; *to — for an employment*, fare un'inserzione per trovare un impiego.

advertisement [əd'və:tismənt], *s.* avviso, avvertimento; annunzio, inserzione (nei giornali); affisso, cartellone pubblicitario.

advertiser ['mdvətaizə*], s. 1. inserzionista 2. pubblicitario.

advertising ['ædvətaiziŋ], ag. pubblicitario ‖ s. pubblicità ☆ — agency, ufficio di pubblicità; — medium, organo, mezzo di pubblicità.

advice [əd'vais], s. 1. consigli; (dir.) consulenza: — and help, consigli ed aiuti; to take medical —, consultare un medico 2. avviso, notizia (anche comm.): as per — from, secondo avviso da; without further —, senz'altro avviso 3. pl. (rar.) notizie, comunicazioni: advices from abroad, comunicazioni, informazioni dall'estero ☆ —boat, nave-avviso.

advisability [əd,vaizə'biliti], s. opportunità, agio.

advisable [əd'vaizəbl], ag. consigliabile; opportuno.

advisableness [əd'vaizəblnis], s. opportunità, agio.

advisably [əd'vaizəbli], av. opportunamente.

to advise [əd'vaiz], v.t.i. 1. (IV) consigliare; raccomandare: I strongly — you to accept, ti consiglio vivamente di accettare; to — s.o. to do sthg., consigliare a qlcu. di fare ql.co. 2. consigliarsi, consultarsi 3. (comm.) avvisare; notificare.

advised [əd'vaizd], ag. 1. deliberato, intenzionale 2. giudizioso, prudente, cauto ☆ ill- —, incauto, sconsigliato; well- —, saggio, avveduto, cauto.

advisedly [əd'vaizidli], av. 1. deliberatamente 2. con cognizione di causa.

advisedness [əd'vaizidnis], s. 1. sagacità, avvedutezza 2. opportunità, convenienza.

adviser [əd'vaizə*], s.c. consigliere, consigliera.

advisory [əd'vaizəri], ag. che consiglia; consultivo.

advocacy ['ædvəkəsi], s. 1. avvocatura 2. difesa.

advocate ['ædvəkit], s. difensore, patrocinatore; avvocato ‖ Devil's —, avvocato del diavolo ‖ Lord Advocate, Procuratore Generale (in Scozia).

to advocate ['ædvəkeit], v.t. difendere, patrocinare (una causa); sostenere.

advocation [,ædvə'keifən], s. (rar.) difesa, patrocinio (d'una causa).

advowson [əd'vauzən], s. (dir. eccl.) collazione (di beneficio); patronato.

adynamia [,ædi'neimiə], s. (patol.) adinamia.

adytum ['æditəm], pl. **adyta** ['æditə], s. (archeol.) adito, penetrale (del tempio).

adze [ædz], s. ascia (a taglio curvo); (st.) azza.

to adze, v.t. tagliare con l'ascia.

aedile ['i:dail], s. (st. romana) edile.

Aegean [i(:)'dʒi:ən], ag. egeo ‖ the — Sea, il mare Egeo ‖ no.pr. (geog.) l'Egeo.

aegis ['i:dʒis], s. 1. egida, scudo (di Giove, Minerva) 2. fig. egida, protezione.

Aegisthus [i(:)'dʒisθəs], no.pr.m. (lett.) Egisto.

aegrotat [i(:)'groutæt], s. certificato che giustifica l'assenza per malattia di un candidato da un esame universitario.

Aeneas [i(:)'ni:æs], no.pr.m. (lett.) Enea.

Aeneid ['i:niid], s. (lett.) Eneide.

Aeolian [i(:)'ouljən], **Aeolic** [i(:)'olik], ag. eolico, eolio ‖ — harp, arpa eolia; — mode, (mus.) modo eolio.

aeolipile, aeolipyle [i(:)'olipail], s. (fis.) eolipila.

aeolotropy [,i:ə'lotrəpi], s. (fis.) anisotropia.

Aeolus ['i(:)ouləs], no.pr.m. (mit.) Eolo.

aeon ['i:ən], s. 1. periodo cosmico non misurabile; eternità 2. (fil.) eone.

to aerate ['eiəreit], v.t. 1. dar aria a, aerare 2. (chim.) addizionare acido carbonico a ☆ aerated bread, pane piuma; aerated water, wine, acqua gassata, vino spumante.

aeration [,eiə'reifən], s. 1. aerazione 2. (chim.) addizione di acido carbonico.

aerial ['eəriəl], ag. aereo; etereo ‖ s. (rad.) antenna, aereo ☆ — railway (o — ropeway), teleferica ‖ receiving —, antenna ricevente; transmitting —, antenna trasmittente.

aerie ['eəri], s. 1. nido di uccelli rapaci situato in

alto 2. abitazione umana in alta montagna 3. covata (di uccelli da preda).

aeriform ['eərifɔ:m], ag. 1. aeriforme 2. irreale.

to aerify ['eərifai], v.t. cambiare in aria, in gas.

aero ['eərou], pl. **aeros** ['eərouz], s. (fam.) aeroplano.

aerobatics [,eərə'bætiks], s.pl. acrobazie aeree.

aerobe ['eəroub], s. (biol.) aerobio.

aerobomb ['eərəbom], s. bomba da aeroplano.

aerodonetics ['eəroudə'netiks], s. (aer.) tecnica del volo a vela.

aerodrome ['eərədroum], s. aerodromo.

aerodynamic ['eəroudai'næmik], ag. aerodinamico.

aerodynamics ['eəroudai'næmiks], s. (fis.) aerodinamica.

aerodyne ['eəroudain], s. (aer.) aerodina.

aeroembolism [,eərə'embəlizəm], s. (patol.) embolia da brusca diminuzione della pressione atmosferica.

aerofoil ['eərəfoil], s. (aer.) piano d'ala.

aerogram ['eərəgræm], s. aerogramma.

aerograph ['eərəgra:f], s. (tec.) aerografo.

aerolite ['eərəlait], **aerolith** ['eərəliθ], s. aerolito.

aerology [eə'rolədʒi], s. aerologia.

aerometer [eə'romitə*], s. aerometro.

aerometry [eə'romitri], s. aerometria.

aeronaut ['eərənɔ:t], s. aeronauta.

aeronautic(al) [,eərə'nɔ:tik(əl)], ag. aeronautico.

aeronautics [,eərə'nɔ:tiks], s. aeronautica ☆ technical —, aerotecnica.

aerophone ['eərəfoun], s. (tec.) aerofono.

aeroplane ['eərəplein], s. aeroplano ☆ commercial —, aeroplano da trasporto; fighting —, aeroplano da combattimento; reconnaissance —, aeroplano da ricognizione.

aerostat ['eəroustæt], s. (aer.) aerostato.

aerostatics ['eərə'stætiks], s. aerostatica.

aeruginous [iə'ru:dʒinəs], ag. color verderame.

aery ['eəri], ag. (poet.) aereo, etereo, incorporeo ‖ s. V. **aerie.**

Aeschines ['i:skini:z], no.pr.m. (st. lett.) Eschine.

Aeschylus ['i:skiləs], no.pr.m. (st. lett.) Eschilo.

Aesculapius [,i:skju'leipjəs], no.pr.m. (st. med.) Esculapio ‖ s. fig. medico.

Aesop ['i:sop], no.pr.m. (st. lett.) Esopo.

aesthete ['i:sθi:t], s. esteta.

aesthetic(al) [i:s'θetik(əl)], ag. estetico.

aesthetically [i:s'θetikəli], av. esteticamente.

aestheticism [i:s'θetisizəm], s. estetismo.

aesthetics [i:s'θetiks], s. (fil.) estetica.

aesthophysiology [,esθə,fizi'olədʒi], s. (med.) estesiologia.

aestival [i:s'taivəl], ag. estivo.

to aestivate ['i:stiveit], v.i. passare l'estate in letargo (di animali).

aestivation [,i:sti'veifən], s. 1. fioritura prematura (di piante) 2. estivazione (di animali).

aether ['i:θə*], s. etere.

Aethiopia [,i:θi'oupjə], no.pr. (geog.) Etiopia.

aetiological [,i:tiə'lodʒikəl], ag. (med.) etiologico.

aetiologically [,i:tiə'lodʒikəli], av. (med.) etiologicamente.

aetiology [,i:ti'olədʒi], s. (med.) etiologia.

Aetna ['etnə], no.pr. (geog.) Etna.

afar [ə'fa:*], av. in lontananza, lungi; da lontano: — off, lontano; from —, da lontano.

affability [,æfə'biliti], s. affabilità, cortesia.

affable ['æfəbl], ag. affabile, cortese.

affableness ['æfəblnis], s. affabilità, cortesia.

affably ['æfəbli], av. affabilmente, cortesemente.

affair [ə'fɛə*], s. 1. affare: public affairs, affari pubblici; — of honour, duello; to place one's affairs before one's creditors, (comm.) esporre la propria situazione ai creditori 2. faccenda: that is my —, è cosa che riguarda me 3. relazione amorosa.

to affect[1] [ə'fekt], v.t. 1. affettare, ostentare; darsi arie di: he affected a Spanish costume, ostentava un costume spagnuolo; he affected the freethinker, si dava arie da libero pensatore **2.** fingere, simulare (indifferenza, interesse, meraviglia).

to **affect**[2], *v.t.* **1.** intaccare (di malattia) **2.** concernere, interessare, riguardare: *this affects me personally,* ciò mi tocca personalmente **3.** commuovere, far soffrire: *his death deeply affected us all,* la sua morte fu un grave colpo per tutti noi.

affectation [,æfek'teiʃən], *s.* affettazione, ostentazione; simulazione.

affected [ə'fektid], *ag.* **1.** affettato, ricercato; sdolcinato; simulato **2.** affetto: *to be — with (a disease),* essere affetto da (una malattia) **3.** commosso **4.** disposto, incline, propenso: *well —, ill —,* ben disposto, mal disposto.

affectedly [ə'fektidli], *av.* con affettazione.

affectedness[ə'fektidnis], *s.* affettazione, ostentazione.

affecting [ə'fektiŋ], *ag.* commovente, emozionante.

affection [ə'fekʃən], *s.* **1.** affezione, affetto, amore **2.** (*patol.*) affezione **3.** impressione, emozione.

affectional [ə'fekʃənl], *ag.* affettivo.

affectionate [ə'fekʃnit], *ag.* affettuoso; affezionato; amorevole.

affectionately [ə'fekʃnitli], *av.* affettuosamente.

affectionateness [ə'fekʃnitnis], *s.* affettuosità.

affective [ə'fektiv], *ag.* affettivo.

afferent ['æfərənt], *ag.* (*fisiol.*) afferente.

affettuoso [ə,fetju'ouzou], *av.* (*mus.*) con sentimento.

affiance [ə'faiəns], *s.* (*arc.poet.*) **1.** fiducia **2.** promessa di matrimonio.

to **affiance**, *v.t.* (*letter.*) fidanzare, promettere in matrimonio: *to be affianced to s.o.,* essere fidanzato con qlcu.

affidavit [,æfi'deivit], *s.* (*dir.*) dichiarazione, deposizione scritta e giurata.

to **affiliate** [ə'filieit], *v.t.i.* **1.** (*comm.*) affiliare, affiliarsi; associare, associarsi, unirsi **2.** (*dir.*) affiliare, affiliarsi ☆ *affiliated company,* società collegata; *affiliated firm,* filiale.

affiliation [ə,fili'eiʃən], *s.* affiliazione (anche *dir.*).

affined [ə'faind], *ag.* affine, congiunto.

affinity [ə'finiti], *s.* **1.** parentela; affinità **2.** affinità (anche *chim.*); somiglianza.

to **affirm** [ə'fə:m], *v.t.i.* **1.** affermare; confermare: *to — on oath,* affermare, fare una dichiarazione sotto giuramento **2.** (*dir.*) ratificare, sanzionare (un giudizio) **3.** (*gram.*) usare una frase affermativa.

affirmable [ə'fə:məbl], *ag.* affermabile.

affirmation [,æfə:'meiʃən], *s.* **1.** affermazione; conferma; dichiarazione; (*dir.*) dichiarazione solenne **2.** (*dir.*) omologazione.

affirmative [ə'fə:mətiv], *ag.* affermativo ‖ *s.* affermativa: *to answer in the —,* rispondere affermativamente.

affirmatively [ə'fə:mətivli], *av.* affermativamente.

affirmatory [ə'fə:mətəri], *ag.* affermativo.

affix ['æfiks], *s.* aggiunta; (*gram.*) affisso.

to **affix** [ə'fiks], *v.t.* aggiungere; apporre: *he affixed his seal to the document,* appose il suo sigillo al documento.

afflatus [ə'fleitəs], *s.* afflato, ispirazione.

to **afflict** [ə'flikt], *v.t.* affliggere, tormentare.

affliction [ə'flikʃən], *s.* **1.** afflizione, dolore: *the afflictions of old age,* gli acciacchi della vecchiaia **2.** calamità.

afflictive [ə'fliktiv], *ag.* afflittivo.

affluence ['æfluəns], *s.* **1.** affluenza; abbondanza **2.** ricchezza, opulenza.

affluent ['æfluənt], *ag.* **1.** ricco, opulento: *in — circumstances,* in floride condizioni economiche ‖ *— society,* società ad alto tenore di vita **2.** abbondante ‖ *s.* (*geog.*) affluente.

affluent, *s.* (*geog.*) affluente.

affluently ['æfluəntli], *av.* abbondantemente.

afflux ['æflʌks], *s.* afflusso, affluenza (anche *fig.*).

to **afford** [ə'fɔ:d], *v.t.* **1.** offrire, dare; produrre, fornire: *this will — me a good opportunity to...,* questo mi darà una buona occasione per... **2.** (preceduto da *can, could, to be able to*) permettersi: *can you — the*

time for it?, puoi trovare il tempo per questo?; *I can, cannot — to buy that land,* posso, non posso permettermi di comperare quel terreno.

to **afforest** [æ'fɔrist], *v.t.* imboschire.

afforestation [æ,fɔris'teiʃən], *s.* imboschimento.

to **affranchise** [ə'fræntʃaiz], *v.t.* affrancare, liberare.

affray [ə'frei], *s.* rissa, tafferuglio, mischia.

affreightment [ə'freitmənt], *s.*(*comm. mar.*) noleggio.

affright [ə'frait], *s.* (*arc.*) spavento, paura.

to **affright**, *v.t.* (*arc.*) spaventare.

affront [ə'frʌnt], *s.* insulto, offesa; affronto: *to take — at sthg.,* offendersi per ql.co.

to **affront**, *v.t.* **1.** insultare, offendere; fare un affronto a **2.** affrontare.

affusion [ə'fju:ʒən], *s.* **1.** aspersione **2.** (*med.*) affusione.

Afghan ['æfgæn], *ag.* afgano ‖ *s.c.* afgano, afgana ‖ *s.* lingua afgana.

Afghanistan [æf'gænistæn], *no.pr.* (*geog.*) Afganistan.

afield [ə'fi:ld], *av.* al campo, sul campo (anche *mil.*); lontano: *to go far —,* andare lontano.

afire [ə'faiə*], *av.* in fiamme ‖ *ag.* predicativo bruciante, in fiamme (anche *fig.*): *to be — with the desire to see s.o.,* bruciare dal desiderio di vedere qlcu.

aflame [ə'fleim], *av.ag.* predicativo in fiamme (anche *fig.*): *heart — with passion,* cuore infiammato dalla passione.

afloat [ə'flout], *av.* a galla; in mare; in circolazione ‖ *ag. predicativo* **1.** galleggiante; in mare: *to get a ship —,* disincagliare una nave **2.** allagato **3.** circolante **4.** (*comm.*) in corso; instabile, fluttuante.

aflutter [ə'flʌtə*], *av.ag. predicativo* (*letter.*) palpitante, commosso.

afoam [ə'foum], *av.ag. predicativo* (*letter.*) pieno di schiuma, di bava.

afoot [ə'fut], *av.ag. predicativo* **1.** a piedi; (*mil.*) in marcia **2.** *fig.* in moto, in azione: *they knew that a plot was —,* seppero che si stava tramando un complotto.

afore [ə'fɔ:*], *prep.* (*mar.*) prima di, avanti, davanti: *— the mast,* davanti all'albero maestro, a proravia ‖ *av.* (*arc.*) precedentemente.

aforecited [ə'fɔ:,saitid], *ag.* predetto, suddetto.

aforegoing [ə'fɔ:'gouiŋ], *ag.* precedente.

aforehand [ə'fɔ:hænd], *av.* anticipatamente.

aforementioned [ə'fɔ:,menʃənd], **aforenamed** [ə'fɔ:neimd], **aforesaid** [ə'fɔ:sed], *ag.* predetto, suddetto.

aforethought [ə'fɔ:θɔ:t], *ag.* premeditato: *with malice —,* con premeditazione.

aforetime [ə'fɔ:taim], *av.* precedentemente.

afraid [ə'freid], *ag.* predicativo spaventato, impaurito; timoroso, pauroso: *to be —,* aver paura, temere: *don't be —,* non abbiate paura; *to be — of s.o., of sthg.,* aver paura di qlcu., di ql.co.; *to be — to do sthg.* (o *of doing sthg.*), aver paura di fare ql.co. ‖ *I am — I cannot tell you,* sono spiacente di non potervelo dire.

afreet ['æfri:t], *s.* (*mit. araba*) demone.

afresh [ə'freʃ], *av.* da capo, di nuovo.

Afric ['æfrik], *ag.* (*poet.*) africano.

Africa ['æfrikə], *no. pr.* (*geog.*) Africa.

African ['æfrikən], *ag.* africano ‖ *s.c.* africano, africana.

Africanism ['æfrikənizəm], *s.* africanismo (vocabolo, atteggiamento, costume di origine africana).

to **africanize** ['æfrikənaiz], *v.t.* africanizzare.

Afrikaans [,æfri'ka:ns], *s.* dialetto olandese parlato nel Sud Africa.

Afrikan(d)er [,æfri'kæn(d)ə*], *ag.* sud-africano; boero ‖ *s.c.* sud-africano, sud-africana; boero, boera.

afrit ['æfri:t], *s.* (*mit. araba*) demone.

aft [ɑ:ft], *av.* (*mar.*) a poppa, verso poppa ‖ *fore and —,* da prora a poppa ☆ *—-castle,* castello di poppa.

after ['ɑ:ftə*], *ag.* **1.** posteriore, successivo, seguente: *— years,* anni a venire **2.** (*mar.*) poppiero.

after, *prep.* dopo, dietro, in seguito a; secondo: alla maniera, alla moda di, da (un modello, ecc.),

— *all*, alla fine, dopotutto; in sostanza, per altro; — *two years*, dopo due anni; — *which*, dopo di che; *one — another*, uno dietro l'altro || *to be — s.o., sthg.*, inseguire, cercare qlcu., ql.co.: *what is he —?*, che cosa cerca?, a che scopo mira?, (*fam.*) a che sta dietro?; *to go —*, andar dietro, seguire; *to look —*, aver cura di || (*amer.*) *after* sta per l'inglese *past* per esprimere l'ora: *about half — ten*, circa le dieci e mezzo || *av.* dopo, poi, poscia, in seguito: *the day —*, il giorno dopo; *many years —*, molti anni dopo || *cong.* dopo che: *he arrived — I had left*, egli arrivò dopo che io ero partito.

after, (*nei composti*): — *-ages*, la posterità, l'avvenire, i secoli futuri; — *-cabin*, cabina di poppa; — *-clap*, avvenimento inaspettato, contraccolpo (di un avvenimento); — *-crop*, secondo raccolto (di una stagione); — *-damp*, (*miner.*) grisou combusto; — *-days*, i giorni futuri; — *-deck*, (*mar.*) ponte di poppa; — *-dinner*, dopo pranzo; — *-growth*, secondo raccolto; — *-guard*, (*mar.*) guardia di poppa; — *-hours*, le ore libere dopo il lavoro; — *-life*, la vita futura; — *-mentioned*, sottomenzionato; — *-peak*, (*mar.*) gavone di poppa; — *-reckoning*, revisione dei conti; — *-sails*, (*mar.*) vele di poppa; — *-taste*, il sapore che rimane in bocca, *fig.* strascico di un'esperienza; — *-touch*, (*spec.* in *pitt.*) ritocco; — *-treatment*, rifinitura (di prodotto); — *-war*, dopo guerra; — *-wise*, chi ha il senno di poi || *ever —*, sempre, eternamente; *never —*, mai, mai più, giammai.

afterbirth ['ɑ:ftəbə:θ], *s.* 1. (*anat.*) placenta 2. (*dir.*) figlio nato dopo la morte del padre o la compilazione del testamento 3. ultimo figlio nato.

afterburner ['ɑ:ftə,bə:nə*], *s.* postcombustore.

afterburning ['ɑ:ftə,bə:niŋ], *s.* postcombustione.

afterglow ['ɑ:ftə-glou], *s.* ultimo bagliore (del sole); (*elett.*) bagliore residuo; *fig.* gioia che perdura dopo una piacevole esperienza.

aftermath ['ɑ:ftəmæθ], *s.* 1. secondo taglio (del fieno); fieno di secondo taglio 2. *fig.* conseguenze, frutti, risultati: *the — of war*, le conseguenze della guerra.

aftermost ['ɑ:ftəmoust], *ag.* (*mar.*) più vicino alla poppa; *fig.* ultimo, in coda.

afternoon ['ɑ:ftə'nu:n], *s.* pomeriggio: *good —!*, buon giorno!; *in* (o *during*) *the —*, nel pomeriggio; *on Sunday —*, nel pomeriggio di domenica; *this —*, oggi nel pomeriggio || *the — of life*, *fig.* il meriggio della vita ☆ *— tea*, tè del pomeriggio.

afterpiece ['ɑ:ftəpi:s], *s.* (*teat.*) piccolo divertimento, farsa alla fine di una rappresentazione.

afterthought ['ɑ:ftəθɔ:t], *s.* riflessione, ripensamento.

afterward ['ɑ:ftəwəd], **afterwards** ['ɑ:ftəwədz], *av.* dopo, poi, poscia, in seguito; successivamente.

again [ə'gen], *av.* 1. ancora, ancora una volta, una seconda volta, di nuovo: *try —*, prova una seconda volta || *— and —* (o *time and —*), ripetutamente, a parecchie riprese, cento volte; *ever and —* (o *now and —*), occasionalmente, di tanto in tanto || *never —*, mai più; *once —*, una volta di più; 2. altrettanto, di più: *as big —*, più grosso del doppio; *as much —*, due volte tanto, ancora altrettanto; *as many —*, altrettanti; *half as much —*, una volta e mezzo tanto 3. d'altra parte, d'altronde, per contro.

against [ə'genst], *prep.* contro, all'incontro, contrario a; dirimpetto, in faccia; a, presso; verso: — *bad days*, per, in previsione di giorni cattivi; *— the end of*, verso la fine di; *as —*, in confronto a || *payment — documents*, pagamento contro documenti.

agama ['ægəmə], *s.* (*zool.*) iguana.

Agamemnon [,ægə'memnən], *no.pr.m.* (*mit.*) Agamennone.

agami ['ægəmi:], *s.* (*ornit.*) agami.

agamic [ə'gæmik], *ag.* (*biol.*) agamogenesi.

agamogenesis [,ægəmou'dʒenisis], *s.* (*biol.*) agamia.

agamous ['ægəməs], *ag.* (*biol.*) agamico.

agape¹ [ə'geip], *av.ag.* predicativo a bocca aperta (per meraviglia, sorpresa, ecc.).

agape² ['ægəpi:], *p.* **agape** ['ægəpi:], *s.* (*st. relig.*) agape.

agar (-agar) ['eigɑ:('eigɑ:*)], *s.* agar agar.

agaric ['ægərik], *s.* (*bot.*) agarico.

agastric [ə'gæstrik], *ag.* (*zool.*) agastrico.

agate ['ægət], *s.* (*min.*) agata.

Agatha ['ægəθə], *no.pr.f.* Agata.

agave [ə'geivi], *s.* (*bot.*) agave.

agaze [ə'geiz], *av.* con lo sguardo fisso.

age [eidʒ], *s.* 1. età: — *of discretion*, età della ragione; *full —*, maggiore età; *marriageable —*, età matrimoniale; *middle —*, mezza età; *minor —*, età minore; *old —*, vecchiaia; *retirement —*, limite di età; *tender —*, tenera età; *he is thirty years of —*, egli ha trent'anni; *it is a good old —*, è un'età veneranda; *what is your —?* (o *what — are you?*), che età avete? || *to be of —*, essere maggiorenne; *to be promoted in order of —*, essere promosso per anzianità; *to be under —*, essere minorenne; *to come of —*, diventare maggiorenne; *to look one's —*, dimostrare la propria età || *— before honesty*, i ragazzi devono la precedenza agli anziani 2. evo; periodo, tempo; generazione; secolo; epoca: *ages and ages*, secoli e secoli; *from — to —*, d'epoca in epoca; *modern —*, evo moderno; *our —*, il nostro tempo, la nostra generazione || *Middle Ages*, Medioevo || *the Victorian Age*, il periodo vittoriano || *it is ages since I went there*, (*fam.*) è un sacco di tempo che non ci vado ☆ *ice —*, (*geol.*) periodo glaciale; *stone —*, età della pietra.

to age, *v.t.i.* invecchiare.

aged ['eidʒid], *ag.* 1. vecchio, attempato || *the —*, i vecchi 2. dell'età di: — *twenty five*, dell'età di venticinque anni.

agedness ['eidʒidnis], *s.* età avanzata.

ageless ['eidʒlis], *ag.* 1. eterno 2. sempre giovane; di età indefinibile.

agelong ['eidʒlɔŋ], *ag.* eterno.

agency ['eidʒənsi], *s.* 1. causa; azione; effetto; agente: *natural agencies*, agenti naturali; *through the — of water*, per azione dell'acqua 2. intromissione, interposizione: *by the —*, per intervento di 3. (*comm.*) rappresentanza; agenzia, succursale ☆ *business —*, agenzia d'affari; *Government Agency*, organizzazione parastatale; *sole —*, rappresentanza esclusiva.

agenda [ə'dʒendə], *s.pl.* 1. ordine del giorno: *to place a question on the —*, porre una questione all'ordine del giorno 2. — (*book*), agenda, taccuino.

agent ['eidʒənt], *s.* 1. agente (anche *chim.*): *oxidizing —*, agente ossidante; *to be a free —*, agire secondo la propria volontà 2. (*comm.*) agente, rappresentante: *— of the firm...*, rappresentante della ditta...; *they are sole agents for*, hanno la rappresentanza esclusiva di 3. (*dir.*) mandatario ☆ *bank —*, direttore di succursale di banca; *business —*, funzionario esecutivo; *buying —*, agente compratore; *commission —* (o *sales —*), commissionario; *forwarding —* (o *freight —*), spedizioniere; *station —*, (*amer.*) capostazione; *ticket —* bigliettario.

agglomerate [ə'glɔmərit], *ag.* agglomerato || *s.* (*geol.* agglomerato.

to agglomerate [ə'glɔməreit], *v.t.i.* agglomerare, agglomerarsi.

agglomeration [ə,glɔmə'reiʃən], *s.* agglomerazione.

agglomerative [ə'glɔmərətiv], *ag.* agglomerante.

agglutinant [ə'glu:tinənt], *ag.s.* agglutinante.

agglutinate [ə'glu:tinit], *ag.* agglutinato; incollato.

to agglutinate [ə'glu:tineit], *v.t.i.* agglutinare, agglutinarsi; incollare.

agglutination [ə,glu:ti'neiʃən], *s.* agglutinazione.

agglutinative [ə'glu:tinətiv], *ag.* agglutinante.

to aggrandize [ə'grændaiz], *v.t.* ingrandire (potere, ricchezza di persona, Stato); esagerare.

aggrandizement [ə'grændizmənt], *s.* ingrandimento; esagerazione.

to aggravate ['ægrəveit], *v.t.* 1. aggravare, accrescere (il peso, l'offesa) 2. (*fam.*) irritare, esasperare (una persona).

aggravating ['ægrəveitiŋ], *ag.* 1. aggravante 2. (*fam.*) seccante, irritante, insopportabile.

aggravation [,ægrə'veiʃən], *s.* 1. aggravamento 2. (*fam.*) esasperazione, irritazione 3. aggravante.

aggregate ['ægrigit], *ag.* aggregato; collettivo; globale: — *output*, produzione globale ‖ *s.* aggregato; unione; complesso: *in the* —, nell'insieme, in totale.

to **aggregate** ['ægrigeit], *v.t.i.* 1. aggregare, aggregarsi; unire, unirsi 2. ammontare a: *the armies aggregated 500,000 men*, gli eserciti ammontavano a 500.000 uomini.

aggregation [,ægri'geiʃən], *s.* aggregazione; unione.

aggregative ['ægrigeitiv], *ag.* aggregativo.

to **aggress** [ə'gres], *v.i.* (*rar.*) iniziare una lite, un attacco, un'offensiva.

aggression [ə'greʃən], *s.* aggressione.

aggressive [ə'gresiv], *ag.* aggressivo, offensivo ‖ *s.* offensiva: *to assume the* —, iniziare la lite, l'offensiva.

aggressively [ə'gresivli], *av.* aggressivamente.

aggressiveness [ə'gresivnis], *s.* aggressività.

aggressor [ə'gresə*], *s.* aggressore.

to **aggrieve** [ə'gri:v], *v.t.* 1. affliggere, addolorare: *to be aggrieved by* (o *at*) *sthg.*, essere addolorato per ql.co. 2. offendere: *the aggrieved party*, (*dir.*) la parte lesa.

aghast [ə'gɑːst], *ag. predicativo* 1. atterrito 2. stupefatto.

agile ['ædʒail], *ag.* agile, pronto, svelto, destro.

agilely ['ædʒailli], *av.* agilmente, prontamente.

agility [ə'dʒiliti], *s.* agilità, prontezza, destrezza.

agio ['ædʒiou], *s.* (*comm.*) aggio, cambio.

agiotage ['ædʒotidʒ], *s.* (*comm.*) aggiotaggio.

to **agist** [ə'dʒist], *v.t.* 1. far pascolare (bestiame altrui) sulle proprie terre dietro pagamento 2. porre un gravame di carattere pubblico su (una proprietà).

to **agitate** ['ædʒiteit], *v.t.* 1. agitare, scuotere; *fig.* agitare, turbare, commuovere ‖ *to* — *for, against sthg.*, fare un'agitazione in favore di, contro ql.co. 2. dibattere, discutere.

agitated ['ædʒiteitid], *ag.* agitato ‖ *to be* —, agitarsi, turbarsi.

agitation [,ædʒi'teiʃən], *s.* 1. agitazione; *fig.* turbamento, commozione; (*pol.*) moto, tumulto 2. dibattito.

agitator ['ædʒiteitə*], *s.* 1. agitatore (specialmente politico) 2. (*strum.*) agitatore.

Aglaia [ə'glaiə], *no.pr.f.* (*mit.*) Aglaia.

agleam [ə'gli:m], *ag. predicativo* (*letter.*) brillante, scintillante: *eyes* — *with joy*, occhi brillanti di gioia.

aglet ['æglit], *s.* 1. puntale, aghetto (di stringa); lustrino, altro ornamento metallico per vestiti; puntale metallico (che scende dalla spalla di alcune uniformi militari) 2. (*bot.*) amento (di betulla, nocciuolo, ecc.).

agley [ə'gli:], *av.* (*scoz.*) obliquamente, di traverso.

aglow [ə'glou], *av.* ardentemente ‖ *ag. predicativo* ardente.

agnail ['ægneil], *s.* 1. pipita 2. patereccio.

agnate ['ægneit], *ag.* 1. (*dir.*) agnato 2. *fig.* della stessa natura ‖ *s.* (*dir.*) agnato.

agnatic [æg'nætik], *ag.* (*dir.*) agnatizio.

agnation [æg'neiʃən], *s.* (*dir.*) agnazione.

Agnes ['ægnis], *no.pr.f.* Agnese.

agnomen [æg'noumen], *s.* soprannome.

agnostic [æg'nɔstik], *ag.s.* (*fil.*) agnostico.

agnosticism [æg'nɔstisizəm], *s.* (*fil.*) agnosticismo.

ago [ə'gou], *ag. predicativo* fa, passato: *three days* —, tre giorni fa, or son tre giorni ‖ *av.* fa: *how long* —?, quanto tempo fa?; *a little while* —, poco fa: *long* —, tempo fa, già da molto tempo.

agog [ə'gɔg], *av.ag. predicativo* in orgasmo, in ansia: *we were all* — *for his return*, eravamo tutti in ansiosa attesa del suo ritorno.

agoing [ə'gouiŋ], *av.* in azione, in moto: *to set sthg., s.o.* —, mettere in moto ql.co., qlcu.

agonic [ə'gɔnik], *ag.* (*geom.*) agono; (*geog.*) agonico.

agonist ['ægənist], *s.* agonista.

agonistic(al [,ægə'nistik(əl)], *ag.* agonistico.

agonistically [,ægə'nistikəli], *av.* agonisticamente.

to **agonize** ['ægənaiz], *v.t.i.* 1. torturare; far soffrire; tormentare, tormentarsi: *to* — *after sthg.*, tormentarsi per ql.co. 2. agonizzare 3. lottare (anche *fig.*).

agonizingly ['ægənaiziŋli], *av.* angosciosamente.

agony ['ægəni], *s.* 1. agonia 2. *fig.* angoscia, dolore; parossismo, spasimo ☆ — *column*, avvisi (in giornali) per la ricerca di persone scomparse.

agora ['ægərə], *pl.* **agorae** ['ægəri:], **agoras** ['ægərəz], *s.* agora, assemblea.

agoraphobia [,ægərə'foubiə], *s.* (*patol.*) agorafobia.

agouti, agouty [ə'gu:ti], *s.* (*zool.*) aguti.

agrarian [ə'grɛəriən], *ag.* agrario ‖ *s.* (*pol.*) agrario (membro del partito agrario).

to **agree** [ə'gri:], *v.t.i.* 1. accordarsi; andar d'accordo; convenire: *we do not* — *in anything*, non andiamo d'accordo in niente; *we have agreed to help him*, ci siamo messi d'accordo per aiutarlo; *to* — *in* (o *on*) *a matter*, essere d'accordo su un argomento, una faccenda; *to* — *with what s.o. says*, convenire con ciò che qlcu. dice 2. acconsentire: *they agreed to our conditions*, accettarono le nostre condizioni; *to* — *to a proposal*, acconsentire a una proposta; *to* — *to do sthg.*, acconsentire a fare ql.co. ‖ *conditions agreed upon*, (*dir.*) condizioni concordate; *unless otherwise agreed*, salvo caso contrario 3. (*gram.*) concordare 4. (*comm.*) pareggiare (conti, partite): *to* — *an account*, far quadrare un conto 5. *to* — *with* (*s.o., sthg.*), confarsi, essere adatto a: *this food does not* — *with me*, questo cibo non mi si confà.

agreeable [ə'griəbl], *ag.* 1. gradevole, piacevole, ameno, simpatico, gioviale: *to do the* —, rendersi simpatico 2. disposto, consenziente: *to* — *sthg., to do sthg.*, (*fam.*) ben disposto a, a fare ql.co. 3. conforme: — *to*, conforme a, conveniente a, adatto a.

agreeableness [ə'griəblnis], *s.* 1. piacevolezza; gioialità 2. conformità.

agreeably [ə'griəbli], *av.* 1. gradevolmente, piacevolmente — *to* (o *with*) conformemente a.

agreement [ə'gri:mənt], *s.* 1. convenzione, patto, accordo (anche *pol.*); (*dir.*) contratto: *as per* —, come convenuto, come da contratto; *by mutual* —, di comune accordo; *gentleman's* —, accordo verbale tra due potenze; *subject to* —, previo accordo; *to come to an* —, venire ad un accordo; *to keep to an* —, attenersi ad un accordo; *to reach an* —, raggiungere un accordo 2. consenso, assenso 3. conformità 4. (*gram.*) concordanza.

agrestic [ə'grestik], *ag.* agreste; rustico; rurale.

agricultural [,ægri'kʌltʃərəl], *ag.* agricolo.

agriculture ['ægrikʌltʃə*], *s.* 1. agricoltura 2. agraria.

agriculturist [,ægri'kʌltʃərist], *s.* agricoltore.

agrimony ['ægriməni], *s.* (*bot.*) agrimonia.

agrimotor ['ægri,moutə*], *s.* trattore agricolo.

agronomic(al [,ægrə'nɔmik(əl)], *ag.* agronomico.

agronomics [,ægrə'nɔmiks], *s.* agronomia.

agronomist [ə'grɔnəmist], *s.* agronomo.

agronomy [ə'grɔnəmi], *s.* agronomia.

aground [ə'graund], *ag. predicativo* (*mar.*) incagliato, arenato ‖ *av.* (*mar.*) in secco: *running* —, incagliamento, arenamento; *to be* (o *to run*) —, incagliarsi.

ague ['eigju:], *s.* (*patol.*) febbre malarica ☆ — *-cake*, ingrossamento di fegato, milza causato da malaria; — *-drops*, (*farm.*) gocce febbrifughe.

agued ['eigju:d], *ag.* (*patol.*) colpito da febbre malarica; scosso da brividi.

aguish ['eigjuiʃ], *ag.* (*patol.*) 1. malarico 2. soggetto a febbre malarica 3. che produce febbre malarica.

ah [ɑ:], *inter.* ah!, deh!, ahimè!.

aha [ɑ(:)'hɑ:], *inter.* ah!, bene!; (*iron.*) ben gli sta!.

Ahab ['eihæb], *no.pr.m.* (*Bibbia*) Achab.

Ahasuerus [ə,hæzju'iərəs], *no.pr.m.* (*Bibbia*) Assuero.

ahead [ə'hed], *av.* avanti, in avanti; in testa: *to go* —, andare avanti; spicciarsi: *go* —!, avanti!; *things* *are going* —, le faccende procedono ‖ *to be* — *of*, essere in vantaggio, essere più avanti; *to get* — *of*, oltrepassare, superare ‖ *full, half speed* —, (*mar.*) avanti a tutta, a mezza forza; *straight* —, (*mar.*) diritto di prua.

aheap [ə'hi:p], *av.* in mucchio.

ahem [hm], *inter.* hum!, ehm!; ehi!.

ahoy [ə'hɔi], *inter.* (*mar.*) olà!.

Ahriman ['a:rimən], *no.pr.m.* (*st. relig.*) Arimane.

ahull [ə'hʌl], *av.* (*mar.*) a secco di vele, con le vele serrate.

ahungered [ə'hʌngəd], *ag. predicativo* punto dalla fame.

ai ['eiai], *s.* (*zool.*) bradipo.

aid [eid], *s.* **1.** aiuto, soccorso; *pl.* sussidi; *pl.* assistenza: *collection in* — *of*, raccolta, colletta a favore di; *to be of* —, essere d'aiuto, d'assistenza; *to call in s.o.'s* —, chiedere aiuto a qlcu. **2.** aiutante, aiuto ☆ *first-* — *post*, posto di pronto soccorso.

to **aid**, *v.t.* aiutare, soccorrere, assistere.

aide-de-camp ['eiddə'kɔn], *s.* (*mil.*) aiutante di campo.

aider ['eidə*], *s.c.* aiuto; soccorritore, soccorritrice.

aigrette ['eigret], *s.* **1.** (*ornit.*) egretta **2.** egretta; pennacchio.

aiguille ['eigwi:l], *s.* (*geol.*) guglia.

aiguillette [,eigwi'let], *V.* **aglet**.

to **ail** [eil], *v.t.i.* **1.** affliggere, addolorare, far soffrire: *what ails you?*, che cosa ti fa soffrire? **2.** essere sofferente, sentirsi male.

aileron ['eilərən], *s.* (*aer.*) alettone, alerone.

ailing ['eilin], *ag.* sofferente, malaticcio.

ailment ['eilmənt], *s.* indisposizione, disturbo.

aim [eim], *s.* **1.** mira, punto di mira **2.** *fig.* scopo, intenzione, disegno, proposito: *to take* — *at*, mirare a.

to **aim**, *v.t.i.* **1.** puntare (arma da fuoco); prendere la mira; dirigere: *to* — *a stone at*, lanciare una pietra contro **2.** *to* — *at* (*s.o., sthg.*), prendere di mira; mirare a (anche *fig.*): *he aimed at becoming a writer*, aspirava a diventare scrittore.

aimless ['eimlis], *ag.* senza scopo.

aimlessly ['eimlisli], *av.* senza scopo.

aimlessness ['eimlisnis], *s.* mancanza di scopo.

ain't [eint], (*arc. sl.*) *contr.* di *am not, is not, are not, have not, has not*.

air [ɛə*], *s.* **1.** aria, atmosfera; brezza, venticello: *breath of* —, soffio d'aria; *in the open* —, all'aria aperta; *to go out to take the* —, uscire per prendere un po' di fresco ‖ *Air Force*, aviazione militare ‖ *castles in the* —, castelli in aria; *my plans are still in the* —, i miei progetti sono ancora incerti ‖ *there are rumours in the* — *that...*, corre voce che..? ‖ *to live on* —, vivere d'aria ‖ *to walk on* —, essere pazzo di gioia ‖ *to be on the* —, (*rad.*) parlare per radio; *to put sthg. on the* —, (*rad.*) trasmettere ql.co. per radio ‖ *to send goods by* —, (*aer.*) spedire merci per via aerea **2.** aria, aspetto, sembiante, apparenza; contegno: *to give oneself airs* (o *to put on airs*), darsi delle arie, assumere un dato contegno **3.** (*mus.*) aria, melodia ☆ — *-arm*, arma aerea; — *-attack*, bombardamento aereo; — *-balloon*, palloncino di gomma, aerostato; — *-base*, base aerea; — *-beacon*, aerofaro; — *-bladder*, vescica natatoria; — *borne*, aviotrasportato; — *-brake*, freno ad aria compressa, aerofreno, freno aerodinamico; — *-chamber*, camera d'aria; — *-conditioner* (o — *-conditioning unit*), condizionatore dell'aria; — *-conditioning*, condizionamento dell'aria; — *-cooled*, raffreddato ad aria; — *crash*, incidente aereo; — *crew*, equipaggio di aereo; — *-cushion*, cuscino pneumatico; — *defences*, protezione antiaerea; — *-display*, rivista, parata aeronautica; — *-drill*, perforatrice ad aria compressa; — *-drop*, lancio con paracadute (di materiale, volantini, ecc.); — *-fleet*, flotta aerea; — *heating*, riscaldamento ad aria; — *-hostess*, «hostess», 'assistente di volo; — *inlet* (o — *intake*), presa d'aria; — *leak*, fuga d'aria; — *-lift*, ponte aereo; — *-line*, aviolinea (da trasporto), (*amer.*) linea retta, a volo

d'uccello; — *-liner*, aeroplano di linea; — *-lock*, camera di equilibrio, cassa d'aria; — *map*, carta (per la navigazione) aerea; — *-mechanic*, meccanico d'aviazione; — *-passages*, (*anat.*) vie respiratorie; — *-pilot*, pilota (di aerei); — *-pipe*, aspiratore; — *-pit*, vuoto d'aria; — *-pocket*, vuoto d'aria; — *-proof*, a tenuta d'aria, ermetico; — *-raid*, incursione aerea; — *-route*, rotta aerea; — *-screw*, elica; — *service*, servizio aereo; — *-shaft*, (*miner.*) pozzo d'aerazione; — *-sickness*, mal d'aria; — *-space*, cubatura (di sala, teatro, ecc.); (*aer.*) spazio aereo; — *-station*, scalo aereo; — *-struck*, fanatico dell'aviazione; — *survey*, fotogrammetria, rilievo aereo; — *-taxi*, tassì acreo.

to **air**, *v.t.* aerare, arieggiare; ventilare; mettere all'aria; sciorinare: *to* — *a room, linen*, aerare una stanza, sciorinare biancheria ‖ *he is always airing his knowledge*, mette sempre in mostra il suo sapere, millanta il suo sapere ‖ *the matter needs to be aired*, si deve prospettare il problema.

aircraft ['ɛə-kra:ft], *s.* (*invariato al pl.*) aeromobile, aereo: *five* — *were brought down*, cinque velivoli furono abbattuti ☆ — *-carrier*, portaerei ‖ *jet* —, aviogetto; *rocket* —, aviorazzo; *spotter* —, ricognitore.

airdrome ['ɛədroum], *s.* aerodromo.

airer ['ɛərə*], *s.* **1.** aeratore **2.** cavalletto (per biancheria).

airfield ['ɛə-fi:ld], *s.* campo d'aviazione.

airgun ['ɛəgʌn], *s.* fucile ad aria compressa.

airhole ['ɛəhoul], *s.* sfiatatoio.

airily ['ɛərili], *av.* agilmente, leggermente; *fig.* gaiamente, con disinvoltura.

airiness ['ɛərinis], *s.* **1.** aerazione, ventilazione **2.** *fig.* leggerezza; gaiezza; disinvoltura.

airing ['ɛərin], *s.* **1.** ventilazione, aerazione **2.** giro, passeggiata: *to take an* —, andare a prendere una boccata d'aria.

airless ['ɛəlis], *ag.* **1.** senz'aria **2.** senza vento, calmo.

air-mail ['ɛəmeil], *s.* posta aerea.

to **air-mail**, *v.t.* spedire per posta aerea.

airman, *pl.* **airmen** ['ɛəmən], *s.* aviatore.

airmanship ['ɛəmənʃip], *s.* arte del volo.

airplane ['ɛə-plein], *s.* (*amer.*) aeroplano.

airport ['ɛə-pɔ:t], *s.* **1.** aeroporto **2.** foro per l'aria.

airpump ['ɛə-pʌmp], *s.* pompa pneumatica.

airship ['ɛə-ʃip], *s.* (*aer.*) aeronave, dirigibile ☆ *non -rigid* —, aeronave floscia.

airtight ['ɛə-tait], *ag.* a tenuta d'aria.

airway ['ɛəwei], *s.* **1.** via aerea **2.** (*rad.*) canale **3.** (*miner.*) galleria d'aerazione.

airwoman ['ɛə,wumən], *pl.* **airwomen** ['ɛə,wimin], *s.* aviatrice.

airworthiness ['ɛə,wə:ðinis], *s.* navigabilità aerea.

airworthy ['ɛə,wə:ði], *ag.* atto alla navigazione aerea.

airy ['ɛəri], *ag.* **1.** aerato, arioso, arieggiato **2.** leggero (di tessuto, passo, ecc.) **3.** gaio, vivace, brioso, noncurante (di contegno, ecc.) **4.** (*poet.*) aereo, elevato **5.** vano, illusorio.

aisle [ail], *s.* **1.** (*arch.*) navata **2.** (*amer.*) corsia; corridoio (in carrozza ferroviaria, autobus, platea di teatro).

aisled [aild], *ag.* (*arch.*) con navate.

ait [eit], *s.* isoletta (in fiume, lago).

aitch [eitʃ], *s.* acca (la lettera *h*).

ajar[1] [ə'dʒɑ:*], *av.ag. predicativo* socchiuso.

ajar[2], *av.* in disaccordo; (*di nervi*) a pezzi.

Ajax ['eidʒæks], *no.pr.m.* (*mit.*) Aiace.

ajutage ['ædʒutidʒ], *s.* bocca di fontana artificiale.

akimbo [ə'kimbou], *av.* con le mani ai fianchi e i gomiti in fuori.

akin [ə'kin], *ag. predicativo* **1.** consanguineo **2.** simile.

alabaster ['æləbɑ:stə*], *s.* alabastro.

alabastrine [,ælə'bɑ:strin], *ag.* alabastrino.

alack [ə'læk], **alackaday** [ə'lækədei], *inter.* (*arc.*) ohimè!.

alacrity [ə'lækriti], *s.* alacrità.

alamode ['æləmoud], *ag.av.* alla moda.

Alan ['ælen], *no.pr.m.* Alano.
aland [ə'lænd], *av.* a terra, per terra ferma.
alar ['eilə*], *ag.* 1. alare 2. (*bot.*) ascellare.
Alaric ['ælərik], *no.pr.m.* (*st.*) Alarico.
alarm [ə'lɑ:m], *s.* 1. allarme; sveglia: *to raise* (o *to sound*) *the* —, dare l'allarme; *to set the* — *for five o'clock*, mettere la sveglia alle cinque 2. *fig.* agitazione: *in* —, allarmato, spaventato; *to take* (*the*) —, allarmarsi 3. (*scherma*) in guardia ☆ — *-clock*, sveglia; — *signal*, segnale d'allarme ‖ *electric* —, suoneria elettrica; *fire* —, segnalatore d'incendio.
to alarm, *v.t.* allarmare, spaventare: *to be alarmed at sthg.*, spaventarsi di ql.co.
alarming [ə'lɑ:miŋ], *ag.* allarmante.
alarmism [ə'lɑ:mizəm], *s.* allarmismo.
alarmist [ə'lɑ:mist], *s.c.* allarmista.
alas [ə'lɑ:s], *inter.* ahimè!.
alate(d) ['eileit(id)], *ag.* alato.
alb [ælb], *s.* (*eccl.*) camice (del sacerdote).
albacore ['ælbəkɔ:*], *s.* (*ittiol.*) alalonga.
Alban ['ɔ:lbən], *no.pr.m.* Albano.
Albania [æl'beinjə], *no.pr.* (*geog.*) Albania.
Albanian [æl'beinjən], *ag.s.c.* albanese.
albatross ['ælbətrɔs], *s.* (*ornit.*) albatro.
albeit [ɔ:l'bi:it], *cong.* quantunque: *a brilliant,* — *slipshod writer*, uno scrittore brillante, quantunque trascurato.
Alberic ['ælbərik], *no.pr.m.* Alberico.
Albert ['ælbət], *no.pr.m.* Alberto.
Albertine ['ælbəti:n], *no.pr.f.* Albertina.
albescent [æl'besənt], *ag.* biancheggiante.
albespine ['ælbəspain], *s.* biancospino.
Albigenses [,ælbi'dʒensi:z], *s.pl.* (*st.*) albigesi.
Albin ['ælbin], *no.pr.m.* Albino.
albiness ['ælbinis], *s.* albina.
albinism ['ælbinizəm], *s.* albinismo.
albino [æl'bi:nou], *pl.* **albinos** [æl'bi:nouz], *s.c.* albino, albina.
Albion ['ælbjən], *no.pr.* (*geog. poet.*) Albione.
albugineous [,ælbju(:)'dʒiniəs], *ag.* albuginoso.
album ['ælbəm], *s.* album.
albumen ['ælbjumin], *s.* albume.
albumin ['ælbjumin], *s.* (*chim.*) albumina.
albuminoid [æl'bju:minɔid], *ag.s.* (*chim.*) albuminoide.
albuminose [æl'bju:minous], **albuminous** [æl'bju:-minəs], *ag.* (*chim.*) albuminoso.
albuminuria [æl,bju:mi'njuəriə] *s.* (*patol.*) albuminuria.
alburn ['ælbə:n], **alburnum** [æl'bə:nəm], *s.* (*bot.*) alburno.
Alcaeus [æl'si(:)əs], *no.pr.m.* (*st. lett.*) Alceo.
alcaic [æl'keiik], *ag.* (*poes.*) alcaico.
Alcestis [æl'sestis], *no.pr.f.* (*mit.*) Alcesti.
alchemic(al) [æl'kemik(əl)], *ag.* alchimistico.
alchemist ['ælkimist], *s.* alchimista.
alchemistical [,ælki'mistikəl], *ag.* alchimistico.
to alchemize ['ælkimaiz], *v.t.* alchimizzare.
alchemy ['ælkimi], *s.* alchimia.
Alcibiades [,ælsi'baiədi:z], *no.pr.m.* (*st.*) Alcibiade.
Alcides [æl'saidi:z], *no.pr.m.* (*mit.*) Alcide.
Alcinous [æl'sinouəs], *no.pr.m.* (*mit.*) Alcinoo.
alcohol ['ælkəhɔl], *s.* alcool ☆ *absolute* —, alcool assoluto; *denaturated* —, alcool denaturato; *ethyl* —, alcool etilico; *wood* —, alcool metilico.
alcoholic [,ælkə'hɔlik], *ag.* alcoolico; ‖ *s.* alcoolizzato.
alcoholism ['ælkəhɔlizəm], *s.* alcoolismo.
to alcoholize ['ælkəhɔlaiz], *v.t.* alcoolizzare.
Alcoran [ælkɔ'rɑ:n], *s.* Corano.
alcove ['ælkouv], *s.* 1. alcova 2. nicchia 3. pergolato.
Alcuin ['ælkwin], *no.pr.m.* (*st. lett.*) Alcuino.
aldehyde ['ældihaid], *s.* (*chim.*) aldeide.
alder ['ɔ:ldə*], *s.* (*bot.*) ontano.
alderman, *pl.* **aldermen** ['ɔ:ldəmən], *s.* assessore comunale.

aldermanic [,ɔ:ldə'mænik], *ag.* assessorale.
aldermanry ['ɔ:ldəmənri], *s.* distretto affidato ad un assessore.
aldermanship ['ɔ:ldəmənʃip], *s.* assessorato.
aldern ['ɔ:ldə(:)n], *ag.* di ontano ‖ *s.* ontano.
Aldine ['ɔ:ldain], *ag.* (*tip.*) aldino.
Aldous ['ɔ:ldəs], *no.pr.m.* Aldo.
ale [eil], *s.* birra: *brown* —, birra scura; *pale* —, birra chiara ☆ — *-brewer*, birraio; — *-conner*, (*st.*) ispettore alla produzione e al commercio della birra; — *-hoof*, (*bot.*) edera terrestre; — *-house*, birreria: — *-house keeper*, birraio; — *-wife*, (*arc.*) birraia.
aleatory ['eiliətəri], *ag.* aleatorio.
Alec(k) ['ælik], *no.pr.m.dim.* di **Alexander.**
Alecto [ə'lektou], *no.pr.f.* (*mit.*) Aletto.
alee [ə'li:], *av.* (*mar.*) sottovento.
alegar ['eiligə*], *s.* aceto di malto; birra inacidita.
alembic [ə'lembik], *s.* alambicco.
alert [ə'lə:t], *ag.* 1. vigilante, all'erta 2. svelto, agile ‖ *s.* segnale d'allarme ‖ *on the* —, all'erta, sul chi vive.
alertly [ə'lə:tli], *av.* all'erta.
alertness [ə'lə:tnis], *s.* 1. vigilanza 2. vivacità.
aleuron [ə'ljuərən], **aleurone** [ə'ljuəroun], *s.* (*chim.*) aleurone.
Aleutian Islands [ə'lu:ʃjən'ailəndz], *no.pr.pl.* (*geog.*) Isole Aleutine.
Alexander [,ælig'zɑ:ndə*], *no.pr.m.* Alessandro.
Alexandra [,ælig'zɑ:ndrə], *no.pr.f.* Alessandra.
Alexandria [,ælig'zɑ:ndriə], *no.pr.* (*geog.*) Alessandria (d'Egitto).
alexandrine [,ælig'zændrain], *ag.s.* (*verso*) alessandrino.
Alexis [ə'leksis], *no.pr.m.* Alessio.
alfalfa [æl'fælfə], *s.* erba medica, trifoglio.
Alfred ['ælfrid], *no.pr.m.* Alfredo.
alfresco [æl'freskou], *ag.av.* al fresco, all'aperto.
alga ['ælgə], *pl.* **algae** [ældʒi:], *s.* (*bot.*) alga.
algazel ['ælgəzel], *s.* (*zool. arc.*) gazzella.
algebra ['ældʒibrə], *s.* algebra.
algebraic(al) [,ældʒi'breiik(əl)], *ag.* algebrico.
algebraically [,ældʒi'breiikəli], *av.* algebricamente.
algebraist [,ældʒi'breiist], **algebrist** [,ældʒi'brist], *s.* algebrista.
Algeria [æl'dʒiəriə], *no.pr.* (*geog.*) Algeria.
Algerian [æl'dʒiəriən], *ag.* algerino ‖ *s.c.* algerino, algerina.
algid ['ældʒid], *ag.* algido.
algidity [æl'dʒiditi], *s.* (*patol.*) algidità.
Algiers [æl'dʒiəz], *no.pr.* (*geog.*) Algeri.
algraphy ['ælgrəfi], *s.* (*tip.*) stampa a foglie di alluminio.
algum ['ælgəm], *s.* «algum» (albero biblico).
Ali ['ɑ:li], *no.pr.m.* Alì.
alias ['eiliæs], *s.* pseudonimo, falso nome: *to travel under an* —, viaggiare sotto un falso nome.
alias, *av.* alias, altrimenti detto.
alibi ['ælibai], *s.* alibi.
Alice ['ælis], *n.pr.f.* Alice.
Alick ['ælik], *no.pr.m.dim.* di **Alexander.**
alidad ['ælidæd], **alidade** ['ælideid], *s.* alidada.
alien ['eiljən], *ag.* 1. alieno, estraneo; straniero: — *land*, terra straniera 2. *fig.* estraneo; contrario a, che ripugna a: — *to our ideas*, contrario alle nostre idee ‖ *s.* forestiero, straniero ‖ *aliens-law* legge sugli stranieri.
to alien, (*poet.*) per to **alienate.**
alienability [,eiljənə'biliti], *s.* alienabilità.
alienable ['eiljənəbl], *ag.* alienabile.
alienage ['eiljənidʒ], *s.* condizione legale di straniero.
to alienate ['eiljəneit], *v.t.* 1. (*dir.*) alienare 2. *fig.* alienare, allontanare, estraniare.
alienation [,eiljə'neiʃən], *s.* 1. (*dir. med.*) alienazione: *mental* —, alienazione mentale 2. *fig.* alienazione, allontanamento: disaffezione.

alienator ['eiljəneitə*], *s.c.* (*dir.*) alienatore, aliena-trice.

alienee [,eiljə'ni:], *s.c.* (*dir.*) alienatario, alienataria.

alienism ['eiljənizəm], *s.* **1.** qualità, condizione di straniero **2.** studio delle forme di alienazione mentale.

alienist ['eiljənist], *s.* (*med.*) alienista.

aliform ['ælifo:m], *ag.* aliforme.

alight[1] [ə'lait], *ag. predicativo* acceso, in fiamme, infiammato; illuminato (anche *fig.*): *to set sthg.* —, dar fuoco a ql.co.

to **alight**[2], *v.i.* **1.** discendere (da un mezzo di trasporto): *do not* — *while the train is in motion*, non scendete mentre il treno è in moto; *he alighted from his horse*, smontò da cavallo **2.** posarsi; atterrare: *the bird alighted on a branch*, l'uccello si posò su di un ramo; *to* — *on land* (o *on the ground*), (*aer.*) atterrare; *to* — *on water* (o *on sea water*), (*aer.*) ammarare.

alighting [ə'laitiŋ], *s.* (*aer.*) **1.** — (*on land*), atterraggio **2.** — (*on water*), ammaraggio.

to **align** [ə'lain], *v.t.i.* allineare, allinearsi.

alignment [ə'lainmənt], *s.* allineamento.

alike [ə'laik], *ag. predicativo* simile, somigliante: *to*, simile a; *to be much* —, assomigliarsi molto ‖ *av.* del pari, similmente.

aliment ['ælimənt], *s.* **1.** alimento, cibo (anche *fig.*) **2.** (*dir.*) alimenti.

to **aliment**, *v.t.* **1.** alimentare **2.** (*dir.*) passare gli alimenti a.

alimental [,æli'mentl], *ag.* nutritivo.

alimentary [,æli'mentəri], *ag.* **1.** alimentare **2.** alimentario: — *canal*, (*anat.*) condotto alimentario ‖ — *endowment*, (*dir.*) alimenti, pensione alimentaria.

alimentation [,ælimen'teiʃən], *s.* alimentazione.

alimony ['æliməni], *s.* (*dir.*) alimonia.

to **aline** [ə'lain], *v.t.i.* allineare, allinearsi.

alinement [ə'lainmənt], *s.* allineamento.

aliphatic [,æli'fætik], *ag.* (*chim.*) alifatico.

aliquot ['ælikwɔt], *ag.s.* (*mat.*) aliquota.

alive [ə'laiv], *ag. predicativo* **1.** vivo, vivente, in vita, al mondo ‖ *any man* —, chiunque **2.** animato, vivace; attivo: *look* —*!*, (*fam.*) muoviti! ‖ *river* — *with boats*, fiume brulicante di barche **3.** *fig.* sensibile; conscio: *to be* — *to an impression*, provare una sensazione.

alizarin [ə'lizərin], *s.* (*chim.*) alizarina.

alkalescence [,ælkə'lesns], *s.* (*chim.*) alcalescenza.

alkalescent [,ælkə'lesnt], *ag.* (*chim.*) alcalescente.

alkali ['ælkəlai], *s.* (*chim.*) alcale; prodotto alcalino.

alkalifiable ['ælkəli,faiəbl], *ag.* (*chim.*) che si può alcalizzare.

to **alkalify** ['ælkəlifai], *v.t.i.* (*chim.*) alcalizzare, alcalizzarsi.

alkalimeter [,ælkə'limitə*], *s.* (*chim.*) alcalimetro.

alkalimetry [,ælkə'limitri], *s.* (*chim.*) alcalimetria.

alkaline ['ælkəlain], *ag.* (*chim.*) alcalino.

alkalinity [,ælkə'liniti], *s.* (*chim.*) alcalinità.

alkalization [,ælkəlai'zeiʃən], *s.*(*chim.*) alcalizzazione.

to **alkalize** ['ælkəlaiz], *v.t.* (*chim.*) alcalizzare.

alkaloid ['ælkələid], *s.* (*chim.*) alcaloide.

alkermes [əl'kə:miz], *s.* alchermes.

Alkoran [,ælkə'rɑ:n], *s.* Alcorano.

all [ɔ:l], *ag.* tutto; intero: — *day* (*long*), tutto il giorno; — *Italy*, tutta l'Italia; — *men*, tutti gli uomini, ognuno; — (*the*) *morning*, tutta la mattina; — *the others*, tutti gli altri; — *the time*, tutto il tempo; — *the way*, lungo tutto il cammino; fino in fondo; (*fam.*) sempre; — *that's nonsense*, sono tutte storie ‖ *for* — (o *with* —) *his faults*, malgrado tutti i suoi difetti ‖ *to go on* — *fours*, andare carponi; *to go on* — *fours with*, andare di pari passo, accordarsi con ‖ *pron.* tutto: — *of us*, noi tutti; — *three, four*, tutti e tre, quattro; — *together*, tutti insieme; — *is lost*, tutto è perduto; —*'s well*, tutto va bene; — (*of them*) *are coming*, verranno tutti (loro) ‖ — *and sundry*, tutti senza eccezione; — *in* —, di suprema importanza ‖ — *of*, (*amer.*) tutto: — *of the nations*, tutte le nazioni; — *of*

the traffic, tutto il traffico; *it will cost you* — *of a thousand dollars*, ti costerà non meno di mille dollari ‖ *at* —, affatto, punto; davvero; ammesso che; per poco che; *not at* —, nemmeno per sogno, affatto: *I am not at* — *surprised*, non sono affatto sorpreso; *nothing at* —, niente affatto ‖ *for* —, per quanto, malgrado: *for* — *I know*, per quanto io sappia ‖ *for good and* —, sempre ‖ *most of* —, soprattutto ‖ *once* (*and*) *for* —, una volta per sempre ‖ *it is* — *one to me*, per me è tutt'uno, fa lo stesso ‖ *it is* — *up*, tutto è finito, perduto, scoperto ‖ *when* — *is said and done*, in ultima analisi.

all, *av.* completamente, interamente, assolutamente: *I am* — *for liberty*, sono assolutamente per la libertà; *she is* — *alone*, è tutta sola ‖ — *at once* (o — *of a sudden*), tutto ad un tratto ‖ — *the better*, tanto mèglio ‖ — *but*, quasi: — *but certain*, quasi certo; *he* — *but fell*, è quasi caduto ‖ — *over*, ovunque ‖ — *right*, tutto bene, va bene ‖ — *the worse*, tanto peggio ‖ *he is not* — *there*, non è del tutto in sè.

all, *s.* tutto, totalità: *my* — tutto il mio (avere); *he lost his* —, perse tutto il suo; *she is his* —, essa è tutto per lui ‖ *I will do my* — *to...*, farò tutto il possibile per...

all, (*nei composti*): — -*clear* (*signal*), (segnale di) cessato allarme; — -*conquering*, che tutto conquista; — -*day*, che dura tutto il giorno; All-*father*, Odino; Giove; Dio; — -*fired*, (*sl.*) infernale; — -*hid*, rimpiattino (giuoco); — -*important*, importantissimo; — -*night* (*service*), (servizio) notturno; — -*red*, in territorio britannico (dal colore con cui si indicano generalmente sulle carte geografiche i possedimenti britannici); — -*round*, completo; — -*sufficient*, atto a tutto.

Allah ['ælə], *no.pr.m.* (*st. relig.*) Allah.

to **allay** [ə'lei], *v.t.* calmare (tempesta, ecc.); lenire (dolore, ecc.); dissipare (sospetti, ecc.).

allegation [,æle'geiʃən], *s.* allegazione; asserzione.

to **allege** [ə'ledʒ], *v.t.* allegare, produrre, addurre (prove, ragioni, pretese).

Alleghenies (the) ['æligeiniz], *no.pr.pl.* (*geog.*) Allegani, Appalachi.

allegiance [ə'li:dʒəns], *s.* fedeltà, obbedienza (al sovrano, al governo, ad un partito).

allegoric(al) [,æle'gɔrik(əl)], *ag.* allegorico.

allegorically [,æle'gɔrikəli], *av.* allegoricamente.

allegorist ['æligərist], *s.* allegorista.

to **allegorize** ['æligəraiz], *v.t.* allegorizzare.

allegory ['æligəri], *s.* **1.** allegoria **2.** (*arc.*) emblema

allegretto [,æli'gretou], *s.* (*mus.*) allegretto.

allegro [ə'leigrou], *s.* (*mus.*) allegro.

alleluia [,æli'lu:jə], *s. inter.* alleluia.

allergic [ə'lə:dʒik], *ag.* (*patol.*) allergico.

allergy ['ælədʒi], *s.* (*patol.*) allergia.

to **alleviate** [ə'li:vieit],*v.t.* alleviare, lenire; attenuare.

alleviation [ə,li:vi'eiʃən], *s.* alleviamento, lenimento; attenuazione.

alleviative [ə'li:vieitiv], *ag.* alleviante, calmante.

alleviator [ə'li:vieitə*], *ag.* alleviatorio ‖ *s.c.* consolatore, consolatrice ‖ *s.* (*farm.*) calmante.

alleviatory [ə'li:viətəri], *ag.* alleviatorio.

alley ['æli], *s.* **1.** vialetto (di giardino) **2.** vicolo ☆ *blind-* —, vicolo cieco.

All Fools' Day ['ɔ:l'fu:lzdei], *s.* il 1° aprile.

all-hail ['ɔ:l'heil], *inter.* salute!.

All-Hallows ['ɔ:l'hælouz], *s.* (*arc.* per *All Saints' Day*) Ognissanti.

alliaceous [,æli'eiʃəs], *ag.* agliaceo.

alliance [ə'laiəns], *s.* **1.** alleanza: *to enter into an* — *with*, allearsi con **2.** unione, matrimonio, parentela: *a most satisfactory* —, un'unione, un matrimonio quanto mai soddisfacente.

allied [ə'laid], *ag.* **1.** alleato, confederato ‖ *the Allied Powers*, le potenze alleate **2.** (*biol.*) della stessa famiglia, ordine, natura.

alligator ['æligeitə*], *s.* (*zool.*) alligatore.

to **alliterate** [ə'litəreit], *v.i.* (*poes.*) usare l'allitterazione.

alliteration [ə͵litə'reiʃən], s. (poes.) allitterazione.
alliterative [ə'litərətiv], ag. (poes.) allitterativo.
alliteratively [ə'litərətivli], av. (poes.) in modo alliterativo.
allocable ['æləkəbl], ag. allogabile; assegnabile.
to **allocate** ['æləkeit], v.t. allogare, collocare; assegnare; distribuire (parti, quote).
allocation [͵ælə'keiʃən], s. **1.** allogazione, assegnazione; distribuzione (di funzioni, parti); stanziamento (di somma) **2.** collocamento (di un oggetto).
allocution [͵ælou'kju:ʃən], s. allocuzione.
allodial [ə'loudjəl], ag. (st. dir.) allodiale.
allodially [ə'loudjəli], av. (st. dir.) in modo allodiale.
allodium [ə'loudjəm], s. (st. dir.) allodio.
allogamy [ə'lɔgəmi], s. (bot.) allogamia.
allonge [ə'lɔnʒ], s. (comm.) coda (di cambiale).
allopathic [͵ælou'pæθik], ag. (med.) allopatico.
allopathically [͵ælou'pæθikəli], av. (med.) allopaticamente.
allopathist [ə'lɔpəθist], s. (med.) allopatico.
allopathy [ə'lɔpəθi], s. (med.) allopatia.
to **allot** [ə'lɔt], pass.p.p. **allotted** [ə'lɔtid], v.t. distribuire, spartire; assegnare: to — sthg. to (o for) an object, destinare ql.co. ad uno scopo.
allotheism ['ælou͵θi:izəm], s. alloteismo.
allotment [ə'lɔtmənt], s. **1.** distribuzione, spartizione, ripartizione (di capitale, ecc.) **2.** porzione, parte, lotto, pezzo di terreno da coltivare.
allotropic(al) [͵ælə'trɔpik(əl)], ag. (chim.) allotropico.
allotropically [͵ælə'trɔpikəli], av. (chim.) in modo allotropico.
allotropism [ə'lɔtrəpizəm], s. (chim.) allotropismo.
allotropy [ə'lɔtrəpi], s. (chim.) allotropia.
allottee [͵ælɔ'ti:], s.c. assegnatario, assegnataria.
to **allow** [ə'lau], v.t.i. **1.** (III, IV) permettere, lasciare, concedere: — me to help you, permettetemi di aiutarvi; he is not allowed wine, non gli è permesso il vino; we shall — you time to pay, vi concederemo il tempo per pagare; to — oneself to be, lasciarsi: she does not — herself to be courted, ella non si lascia corteggiare ‖ no smoking is allowed, è proibito fumare **2.** (IV) riconoscere, ammettere (una verità): I — it to be true, ammetto che sia vero **3.** (III) assegnare, accordare; (comm.) accordare (uno sconto, una provvigione); bonificare: he allows his son 50 pounds a month, passa a suo figlio 50 sterline al mese; they — 10% discount, concedono uno sconto del 10% **4.** (sl. amer.) asserire, affermare: he allowed that he had won the race, affermò di aver vinto la corsa **5.** to — for (sthg.), tener conto di: we must — for his youth, dobbiamo tener conto della sua giovinezza.
allowable [ə'lauəbl], ag. **1.** ammissibile **2.** assegnabile, accordabile **3.** permesso, lecito.
allowableness [ə'lauəblnis], s. **1.** ammissibilità **2.** legittimità.
allowably [ə'lauəbli], ag. **1.** ammissibilmente **2.** legittimamente.
allowance [ə'lauəns], s. **1.** permesso, autorizzazione; fig. concessione; indulgenza; scusa **2.** gratifica; assegno; pensione; indennità **3.** razione (di viveri): to be put on a short (o to be reduced to a short) —, essere messo a razione ridotta **4.** riconoscimento, ammissione (di un fatto) **5.** (comm.) abbuono, sconto ‖ to make — for, tenere in debito conto ☆ entertainment —, indennità per spese di rappresentanza; family —, assegni familiari; lodging —, indennità di alloggio; mess —, indennità di mensa; the monthly —, la mesata; travelling —, indennità di viaggio.
to **allowance**, v.t. **1.** mettere a razione, razionare **2.** assegnare, fissare una pensione, una rendita a.
alloy [ə'lɔi], s. **1.** (metal.) lega: without —, senza lega, puro **2.** fig. lega.
to **alloy**, v.t. **1.** (metal.) legare, amalgamare **2.** fig. corrompere, alterare **3.** diminuire, attenuare.

All Saints' Day ['ɔ:l'seintsdei], s. Ognissanti.
All Souls' Day ['ɔ:l'soulzdei], s. Commemorazione dei Defunti, il giorno dei Morti.
allspice ['ɔ:l-spais], s. pepe di Giamaica.
to **allude** [ə'lu:d], v.i. alludere.
to **allure** [ə'ljuə*], v.t. attrarre, attirare, allettare; sedurre.
allurement [ə'ljuəmənt], s. allettamento.
allurer [ə'ljuərə*], s.c. allettatore, allettatrice; tentatore, tentatrice.
alluring [ə'ljuəriŋ], ag., allettante; seducente.
alluringly [ə'ljuəriŋli], av. in modo allettante.
allusion [ə'lu:ʒən], s. allusione.
allusive [ə'lu:siv], ag. allusivo.
allusively [ə'lu:sivli], av. allusivamente.
allusiveness [ə'lu:sivnis], s. carattere allusivo.
alluvial [ə'lu:vjəl], ag. alluvionale; (geol.) alluviale.
alluvion [ə'lu:vjən], **alluvium** [ə'lu:vjəm], pl. **alluvia** [ə'lu:vjə], s. alluvione (anche geol.).
ally ['ælai], s. alleato; associato, collegato, ausiliare: to become allies, allearsi.
to **ally** [ə'lai], v.t.i. unire, imparentare (per matrimonio); alleare, allearsi; collegare, collegarsi; confederarsi.
alma(h) ['ælmə], s. almea (danzatrice egiziana).
almadia [͵ælmə'di:ə], **almady** ['ælmədi], s. imbarcazione indiana.
almagest ['ælmədʒest], s. (st. astr.) almagesto.
Alma Mater ['ælmə'meitə*], s. alma mater (nome dato all'università da ex-studenti).
almanac ['ɔ:lmənæk], s. almanacco, calendario.
almandine ['ælməndain], s. (min.) alabandina.
almightiness [ɔ:l'maitinis], s. onnipotenza.
almighty [ɔ:l'maiti], ag. onnipotente; (sl.) grande ‖ the Almighty, l'Onnipotente (Dio) ‖ av. (sl.) estremamente.
almirah [æl'mairə], s. (ang-in.) armadio.
almoi(g)n ['ælmoin], s. elemosina; cassetta per le elemosine.
almond ['a:mənd], s. mandorla ☆ — -tree, mandorlo; — tumbler, (ornit.) piccione tomboliere; — willow, (bot.) salice bianco ‖ burnt almonds, mandorle tostate.
almoner ['a:mənə*], s. elemosiniere.
almost ['ɔ:lmoust], av. quasi, pressoché.
alms [a:mz], s. (invariato al pl.) elemosina ☆ — -bag, — -basin, borsa, piattello per l'elemosina; — -box, cassetta delle elemosine; — -fee, (eccl.) obolo di San Pietro; — -folk, questuanti; — -giving, il fare l'elemosina, la carità; — -house, ospizio di carità, ritiro per i poveri; — -man, — -woman, uomo, donna mantenuti dalla carità pubblica.
aloe ['ælou], pl. **aloes** ['ælouz], s. **1.** (bot.) aloe **2.** pl. (farm.) aloe.
aloetic(al) [͵ælou'etik(əl)], ag. (farm.) aloetico.
aloft [ə'lɔft], av. **1.** in alto; in aria; in volo **2.** (mar.) su, sopra, in alto ‖ — there!, voi lassù in coffa!.
alone [ə'loun], ag. predicativo solo: all (o quite) —, solo, soletto; to let (o to leave) —, lasciar stare, lasciar tranquillo ‖ let well —, il meglio è nemico del bene.
alone, av. solo, solamente; da solo a solo.
along [ə'lɔŋ], av. lungo; avanti: — with, in compagnia di: come — with me, vieni via con me ‖ all —, tutto il tempo: I knew that all —, l'avevo sempre saputo (dall'inizio) ‖ get — with you!, (volg.) va' là, tira via! ‖ they get — well (together), se la intendono ‖ prep. lungo; avanti: we walked — the shore, camminava lungo la spiaggia; we sailed — the coast, navigammo lungo la costa ‖ all — of, (volg.) a causa di: it's all — of him, è tutta colpa sua.
alongshore [ə'lɔŋ'ʃɔ:*], av. (mar.) lungo la costa.
alongside [ə'lɔŋ'said], av. (mar.) accanto, al fianco (della nave), accosto: — of each other, bordo a bordo; come —, (mar.) accostatevi.
aloof [ə'lu:f], av. **1.** (mar.) all'orza, al vento **2.** a distanza, lontano, lungi, alla larga: in disparte.

aloofness [ə'lu:fnis], *s.* freddezza, indifferenza, distacco.

alopecia [,ælə'pi:ʃjə], *s.* (*patol.*) alopecia, alopezia.

aloud [ə'laud], *av.* ad alta voce, forte.

alow [ə'lou], *uv.* (*mar.*) giù, sotto.

alp [ælp], *s.* monte, alpe.

alpaca [æl'pækə], *s.* alpaca (animale, stoffa).

alpenstock ['ælpinstɔk], *s.* «alpenstock», bastone da montagna.

alpestrine [æl'pestrin], *ag.* alpino; alpestre.

alpha ['ælfə], *s.* 1. alfa (prima lettera dell'alfabeto greco) 2. (*bot.*) alfa 3. (*astr.*) alfa ☆ — *ray*, (*fis.*) raggio alfa.

alphabet ['ælfəbit], *s.* alfabeto.

alphabetic(al) [,ælfə'betik(əl)], *ag.* alfabetico.

alphabetically [,ælfə'betikəli], *av.* alfabeticamente.

Alphaeus [æl'fi(:)əs], *no.pr.m.* (*mit.*) Alfeo.

Alphonso [æl'fɔnzou], *no.pr.m.* Alfonso.

alpine ['ælpain], *ag.* alpino; alpestre.

alpinism ['ælpinizəm], *s.* alpinismo.

alpinist ['ælpinist], *s.c.* alpinista.

Alps (the) [ælps], *no.pr.pl.* (*geog.*) Alpi.

already [ɔ:l'redi], *av.* già, di già.

Alsatia [æl'seiʃjə], *no.pr.* (*geog.*) Alsazia.

Alsatian [æl'seiʃjən], *ag.* alsaziano: — *dog* (o *wolf*), cane da pastore tedesco ‖ *s.c.* alsaziano, alsaziana.

also ['ɔ:lsou], *av.* inoltre, pure; anche; altresì.

alt [ælt], *s.* (*mus.*) alto.

altar ['ɔ:ltə*], *s.* altare; (*poet.*) ara ☆ — *-boy*, chierichetto; — *-cloth*, tovaglia da altare: — *-piece*, pala d'altare; — *-rail*, balaustra ‖ *high* —, altar maggiore.

to **alter** ['ɔ:ltə*], *v.t.i.* 1. alterare, cambiare, cambiarsi; mutare, mutarsi 2. correggere, ritoccare 3. (*amer. volg.*) castrare (animali).

alterability [,ɔ:ltərə'biliti], *s.* alterabilità.

alterable ['ɔ:ltərəbl], *ag.* alterabile, modificabile.

alteration [,ɔ:ltə'reiʃən], *s.* alterazione, cambiamento, variazione, modifica: *this dress needs alterations*, questo abito ha bisogno di ritocchi.

alterative ['ɔ:ltərətiv], *ag.s.* (*farm.*) alterativo.

to **altercate** ['ɔ:ltə:keit], *v.i.* altercare.

altercation [,ɔ:ltə:'keiʃən], *s.* alterco.

alternance [ɔ:l'tə:nəns], *s.* l'alternarsi; (*rad.*) alternanza.

alternant [ɔ:l'tə:nənt], *ag.* alternante.

alternate [ɔ:l'tə:nit], *ag.* alterno, alternato: — *angles*, (*geom.*) angoli alterni; — *current*, (*elett.*) corrente alternata ‖ *s.c.* (*amer.*) sostituto, sostituta.

to **alternate** [ɔ:l'tə:neit], *v.t.i.* alternare, alternarsi.

alternately [ɔ:l'tə:nitli], *av.* alternamente, alternativamente, vicendevolmente.

alternation [,ɔ:ltə:'neiʃən], *s.* alternazione, avvicendamento.

alternative [ɔ:l'tə:nətiv], *ag.* alternativo, scambievole ‖ *s.* alternativa.

alternatively [ɔ:l'tə:nətivli], *av.* alternativamente.

alternator ['ɔ:ltə:neitə*], *s.* (*elett.*) alternatore.

Althea [æl'θi:ə], *no.pr.f.* (*mit.*) Altea ‖ **althea**, *s.* (*bot.*) altea.

although [ɔ:l'ðou], *cong.* benché; sebbene, quantunque; ancorché.

altimeter ['æltimi:tə*], *s.* altimetro ☆ *radio* —, radioaltimetro, radiosonda; *sound-ranging* —, altimetro acustico.

altitude ['æltitju:d], *s.* altitudine; altezza; (*aer.*) quota: — *of a star*, altezza di un astro; *high, low* —, alta, bassa quota ☆ — *recorder*, (*aer.*) altimetro registratore; — *switch*, (*aer.*) interruttore di quota ‖ *critical* —, (*aer.*) quota critica; *cruising* —, (*aer.*) quota di navigazione; *flight* —, (*aer.*) quota di volo.

alto ['æltou], *s.* 1. (*mus.*) contralto 2. (*mus.*) alto ☆ — *clef*, (*mus.*) chiave di contralto.

altogether [,ɔ:ltə'geðə*], *s.* l'intero.

altogether, *av.* 1. interamente, affatto 2. in tutto; complessivamente; nell'insieme.

alto-relievo ['æltouri'li:vou], *s.* (*scult.*) altorilievo.

altruism ['æltruizəm], *s.* altruismo.

altruist ['æltruist], *s.c.* altruista.

altruistic [,æltru'istik], *ag.* altruistico.

altruistically [,æltru'istikəli], *av.* altruisticamente.

alum ['æləm], *s.* (*chim. min.*) allume.

to **alum**, *v.t.* allumare, trattare con allume.

alumina [ə'lju:minə], *s.* (*chim.*) allumina.

aluminium [,ælju'minjəm], *s.* (*chim.*) alluminio ☆ *hard* —, duralluminio.

aluminizing [ə'lju:minaiziŋ], *s.* alluminiatura.

aluminography [ə,lju:mi'nɔgrəfi], *V.* algraphy.

aluminose [ə'lju:minous], **aluminous** [ə'lju:minəs], *ag.* alluminoso.

aluminum [ə'lju:minəm], *s.* (*amer.*) alluminio.

alumna [ə'lʌmnə], *pl.* **alumnae** [ə'lʌmni:], *s.f.* (*amer.*) allieva; (ex)studentessa universitaria.

alumnus [ə'lʌmnəs], *pl.* **alumni** [ə'lʌmnai], *s.* (*spec. amer.*) allievo; (ex)studente universitario.

alveary ['ælviəri], *s.* alveare.

alveolar [æl'viələ*], **alveolary** [æl'viələri], *ag.* alveolare.

alveolate [æl'viəlit], *ag.* alveolato.

alveolus [æl'viələs], *pl.* **alveoli** [æl'viəlai], *s.* alveolo.

alvine ['ælvain], *ag.* (*anat.*) alvino, addominale.

alway ['ɔ:lwei], *av.* (*arc.*) sempre.

always ['ɔ:lwəz], *av.* sempre: *he* — *pays*, paga sempre; *he is* — *here*, è sempre qui.

alyssum ['ælisəm], *s.* (*bot.*) alisso.

am [æm (*forma forte*), əm, m (*forme deboli*)] 1ª persona *sing. indic. pres.* di to **be**.

amability [,æmə'biliti], *s.* amabilità.

amah ['ɑ:mə], *s.f.* (*ang.-in.*) balia.

amain [ə'mein], *av.* (*arc.*) 1. con violenza 2. precipitosamente.

amalgam [ə'mælgəm], *s.* amalgama.

to **amalgamate** [ə'mælgəmeit], *v.t.i.* amalgamare, amalgamarsi; fondersi, unirsi.

amalgamation [ə,mælgə'meiʃən], *s.* 1. amalgamazione 2. (*comm.*) fusione di due società 3. mescolanza (di razze); (*amer.*) incrocio delle razze bianca e nera.

amalgamative [ə'mælgəmeitiv], *ag.* amalgamativo.

amalgamator [ə'mælgəmeitə*], *s.c.* chi amalgama.

Amalthaea [,æməl'θi:ə], *no.pr.f.* (*mit.*) Amaltea.

amanuensis [ə,mænju'ensis], *pl.* **amanuenses** [ə,mænju'ensi:z], *s.* amanuense.

amarant ['æmərænt], **amaranth** ['æmərænθ], *s.* 1. (*bot.*) amaranto 2. (colore) amaranto.

amaranthine [,æmə'rænθain], *ag.* 1. amarantino 2. (*arc.*) imperituro.

amaryllis [,æmə'rilis], *s.* (*bot.*) amarilli.

to **amass** [ə'mæs], *v.t.* ammassare, accumulare.

amassment [ə'mæsmənt], *s.* ammasso.

amateur ['æmətə:*], *ag.s.* dilettante, amatore.

amateurish [,æmə'tə:riʃ], *ag.* dilettantesco.

amateurism ['æmətə:rizəm], *s.* dilettantismo.

amative ['æmətiv], *ag.* erotico.

amatory ['æmətəri], *ag.* amatorio, amoroso, erotico.

amaurosis [,æmɔ:'rousis], *s.* (*patol.*) amaurosi.

amaze [ə'meiz], *s.* (*poet.*) 1. stupore, sorpresa; confusione 2. sgomento.

to **amaze**, *v.t.* 1. stupire, sorprendere; confondere 2. sgomentare.

amazed [ə'meizd], *ag.* stupito, sorpreso; confuso: *to be* —, stupirsi, rimanere stupefatto (*at*, di).

amazement [ə'meizmənt], *s.* 1. sorpresa, meraviglia 2. perplessità; costernazione.

amazing [ə'meiziŋ], *ag.* 1. sorprendente; meraviglioso 2. spaventevole.

Amazon (the) ['æməzən], *no.pr.* (*geog.*) il Rio delle Amazzoni.

Amazons ['æməzɔnz], *s.pl.* (*mit.*) Amazzoni.

ambages [æm'beidʒi:z], *s.pl.* ambiguità, ambagi.

ambassador [æm'bæsədə*], *s.* ambasciatore: — *to the Court of St. James's*, ambasciatore presso la Corte d'Inghilterra ☆ — *at large*, ambasciatore a disposizione; — *extraordinary*, ambasciatore in missione speciale; — *plenipotentiary*, ambasciatore plenipotenziario.

ambassadorial [ˌæmˌbæsə'dɔːriəl], *ag.* da ambasciatore.

ambassadress [æm'bæsədris], *s.* ambasciatrice.

amber ['æmbə*], *s.* ambra.

to amber, *v.t.* ambrare.

ambergris ['æmbəgri(ː)s], *s.* ambra grigia.

ambidexter ['æmbi'dekstə*], *ag.s.* **1.** ambidestro **2.** *fig.* (individuo) ambiguo, che fa il doppio giuoco.

ambidextrous ['æmbi'dekstrəs], *ag.* **1.** ambidestro **2.** *fig.* ambiguo, dal doppio giuoco.

ambience ['æmbiəns], *s.* ambiente, atmosfera; influenze ambientali.

ambient ['æmbiənt], *ag.* ambiente ‖ *s.* ambiente, atmosfera.

ambiguity [ˌæmbi'gju(ː)iti], *s.* ambiguità.

ambiguous [æm'bigjuəs], *ag.* ambiguo.

ambiguously [æm'bigjuəsli], *av.* ambiguamente.

ambiguousness [æm'bigjuəsnis], *s.* ambiguità.

ambit ['æmbit], *s.* ambito; limiti, confini.

ambition [æm'biʃən], *s.* ambizione.

ambitionless [æm'biʃənlis], *ag.* senza ambizioni.

ambitious [æm'biʃəs], *ag.* ambizioso.

ambitiously [æm'biʃəsli], *av.* ambiziosamente.

ambitiousness [æm'biʃəsnis], *s.* **1.** ambizione **2.** carattere ambizioso, pretenzioso.

ambivalent ['æmbi'veilənt], *ag.* ambivalente.

amble ['æmbl], *s.* **1.** ambio, ambiatura **2.** passo moderato e sciolto.

to amble, *v.i.* **1.** ambiare **2.** andare lemme lemme.

ambler ['æmblə*], *s.* **1.** cavallo che va d'ambio **2.** persona che cammina lemme lemme.

amblyopia [ˌæmbli'oupiə], *s.* (*patol.*) ambliopia.

ambo ['æmbou], *s.* (*arch. eccl.*) ambone.

Ambrose ['æmbrouz], *no.pr.m.* Ambrogio.

ambrosia [æm'brouzjə], *s.* ambrosia.

ambrosial [æm'brouzjəl], *ag.* d'ambrosia, ambrosio.

Ambrosian [æm'brouzjən], *ag.* ambrosiano, di Sant'Ambrogio: — *rite*, (*eccl.*) rito ambrosiano.

ambry ['æmbri], *s.* **1.** credenza, dispensa **2.** nicchia per arredi sacri.

ambs-ace ['eimzeis], *s.* **1.** ambassi (giuoco di dadi) **2.** *fig.* inutilità; mancanza di valore **3.** sfortuna.

ambulance ['æmbjuləns], *s.* ambulanza.

ambulant ['æmbjulənt], *ag.* ambulante; ambulatorio.

to ambulate ['æmbjuleit], *v.i.* ambulare.

ambulatory ['æmbjulətəri], *ag.* ambulatorio; ambulante ‖ *s.* ambulacro.

ambuscade [ˌæmbəs'keid], **ambush** ['æmbuʃ], *s.* imboscata, agguato, tranello.

to ambuscade, to ambush, *v.t.i.* tendere un agguato, un'imboscata (a).

ameer [ə'miə*], *s.* emiro.

Amelia [ə'miːljə], *no.pr.f.* Amelia.

to ameliorate [ə'miːljəreit], *v.t.i.* migliorare, migliorarsi.

amelioration [əˌmiːljə'reiʃən], *s.* miglioramento.

ameliorative [ə'miːljərətiv], *ag.* migliorativo.

ameliorator [ə'miːljəreitə*], *s.c.* miglioratore, miglioratrice.

amen ['ɑː'men], *inter.* amen, così sia.

amenability [əˌmiːnə'biliti], *s.* **1.** responsabilità **2.** sottomissione.

amenable [ə'miːnəbl], *ag.* **1.** riferibile (a ql.co.), dipendente (da ql.co.), soggetto (a ql.co.), suscettibile (di ql.co.); responsabile (verso qlcu.) **2.** sottomesso.

amenableness [ə'miːnəblnis], *s.* **1.** responsabilità **2.** (*comm.*) trattabilità.

to amend [ə'mend], *v.t.i.* emendare; emendarsi.

amendable [ə'mendəbl], *ag.* emendabile, riparabile.

amende [ə'mɑːnd], *s.* ammenda: *to make honourable* —, far onorevole ammenda.

amender [ə'mendə*], *s.c.* riformatore, riformatrice.

amendment [ə'mendmənt], *s.* emendamento; riforma.

amends [ə'mendz], *s.* ammenda; compenso; risarcimento, indennizzo.

amenity [ə'miːniti], *s.* **1.** amenità **2.** *pl.* bellezze, attrattive (di un luogo) **3.** *pl.* gentilezze, cortesie.

ament [ə'ment], **amentum** [ə'mentəm], *pl.* **amenta** [ə'mentə], *s.* (*bot.*) amento.

to amerce [ə'məːs], *v.t.* condannare ad un'ammenda.

America [ə'merikə], *no.pr.* (*geog.*) America.

American [ə'merikən], *ag.* americano ‖ *s.c.* americano, americana ‖ *s.* lingua americana.

Americana [əˌmeri'kɑːnə], *s.pl.* documenti di americanistica.

Americanism [ə'merikənizəm], *s.* americanismo.

to Americanize [ə'merikənaiz], *v.t.i.* americanizzare, americanizzarsi.

americium [ˌæmə'risiəm], *s.* (*chim.*) americio.

amethyst ['æmiθist], *s.* (*min.*) ametista.

amiability [ˌeimjə'biliti], *s.* gradevolezza.

amiable ['eimjəbl], *ag.* amabile; gradevole.

amiableness ['eimjəblnis], *s.* amabilità; gradevolezza.

amiably ['eimjəbli], *ag.* amabilmente; gradevolmente.

amiantus [ˌæmi'æntəs], **amianthus** [ˌæmi'ænθəs], *s.* amianto.

amicability [ˌæmikə'biliti], *s.* amichevolezza.

amicable ('æmikəbl], *ag.* amichevole.

amicableness ['æmikəblnis], *s.* amichevolezza.

amicably ['æmikəbli], *av.* amichevolmente.

amice[1] ['æmis], *s.* (*eccl.*) amitto.

amice[2], *s.* (*eccl.*) mozzetta.

amid [ə'mid], *prep.* in mezzo a, entro, tra, fra.

amidships [ə'midʃips], *av.* (*mar.*) a mezza nave.

amir [ə'miə*], *s.* emiro.

amidst [ə'midst], *prep.* in mezzo a, entro, fra, tra.

amiss [ə'mis], *ag. predicativo* inopportuno; fuori posto.

amiss, *av.* male, erroneamente; a male: *to go* —, andare male, di traverso; *to take it* —, aversene a male.

amity ['æmiti], *s.* amicizia; buoni rapporti.

ammeter ['æmitə*], *s.* (*elett.*) amperometro.

Ammon ['æmən], *no.pr.m.* (*mit.*) Ammone.

ammonia [ə'mounjə], *s.* ammoniaca.

ammoniac [ə'mouniæk], **ammoniacal** [ˌæmou'naiəkəl], *ag.* ammoniacale ☆ *sal* —, cloruro di ammonio.

ammoniated [ə'mounieitid], *ag.* ammoniacato.

ammonic [ə'mounik], *ag.* ammonico.

ammonium [ə'mounjəm], *s.* (*chim.*) ammonio.

ammonite ['æmənait], *s.* (*paleont.*) ammonite.

ammunition [ˌæmju'niʃən], *s.* (*mil.*) munizioni ☆ — *-boots*, scarpe d'ordinanza; — *-bread*, pane d'ordinanza; — *-pouch*, cartuccera, giberna.

to ammunition, *v.t.* fornire di munizioni.

amnesia [æm'niːzjə], *s.* amnesia.

amnesty ['æmnesti], *s.* amnistia.

to amnesty, *v.t.* amnistiare.

amnion ['æmniən], *pl.* **amnia** ['æmniə], *s.* amnio.

amoeba [ə'miːbə], *s.* (*biol.*) ameba.

amoeboid [ə'miːboid], *ag.* (*biol.*) ameboide.

amok [ə'mɔk], *V.* **amuck**.

among [ə'mʌŋ], **amongst** [ə'mʌŋst], *prep.* **tra, fra** (più di due); **in mezzo a:** *he is one — the best*, è uno fra i migliori; *they agree, quarrel — themselves*, vanno d'accordo, litigano fra di loro; *we are — friends*, siamo fra amici; *we had but a few shillings — us*, fra tutti noi non avevamo che pochi scellini.

amontillado [əˌmɔntiˈlaːdou], *s.* «amontillado» (vino secco tipo « sherry »).

amoral [æ'mɔrəl], *ag.* amorale.

amoretto [ˌæmə'retou], *pl.* **amoretti** [ˌæmə'reti], *s.* amorino.

amorist ['æmərist], *s.* seduttore.

amorous ['æmərəs], *ag.* **1.** amoroso; affettuoso **2.** innamorato.

amorously ['æmərəsli], *av.* amorosamente; affettuosamente.

amorousness ['æmərəsnis], *s.* amorosità; affetto.
amorphism [ə'mɔ:fizəm], *s.* amorfismo.
amorphous [ə'mɔ:fəs], *ag.* amorfo.
amorphousness [ə'mɔ:fəsnis], *s.* amorfia.
amortization [ə,mɔ:ti'zeifən], *s.* (*comm.*) ammortamento.
to **amortize** [ə'mɔ:taiz], *v.t.* (*comm.*) ammortizzare.
amount [ə'maunt], *s.* **1.** ammontare, importo, totale, somma (totale): *to the — of,* fino alla concorrenza di **2.** quantità: *in small amounts,* in piccole quantità **3.** valore, importanza: *of little —,* di poca importanza.
to **amount,** *v.i.* **1.** ammontare, ascendere, salire: *the expenses — to...,* le spese ascendono a... **2.** equivalere: *his reply amounts to a refusal,* la sua risposta equivale ad un rifiuto.
amour [ə'muə*], *s.* tresca, intrigo amoroso.
amperage [æm'pɛəridʒ], *s.* (*elett.*) amperaggio.
ampere ['æmpɛə*], *s.* (*elett.*) ampère ☆ — *-meter,* (*elett.*) amperometro.
ampersand ['æmpəsænd], *s.* & (segno tipografico per *and*): *Brown & Co.,* Brown e C.
amphiarthrosis [,æmfiɑ:'θrousis], *s.* (*patol.*) anfiartrosi.
Amphibia [æm'fibiə], *s.pl.* (*zool.*) gli anfibi.
amphibian [æm'fibiən], *ag.s.* anfibio (anche *aer.*).
amphibiology [æm,fibi'olədʒi], *s.* (*zool.*) anfibiologia.
amphibious [æm'fibiəs], *ag.* anfibio.
amphibole ['æmfiboul], *s.* (*min.*) anfibolo.
amphibological [æm,fibə'lodʒikəl], *ag.* (*ret.*) anfibologico.
amphibology [,æmfi'bolədʒi], **amphiboly** [æm'fibəli], *s.* (*ret.*) anfibologia.
amphibrach ['æmfibræk], *s.* (*poes.*) anfibraco.
amphictyonie [æm,fikti'onik], *ag.* (*st.*) anfizionico.
amphictyons [æm'fiktionz], *s. pl.* (*st.*) anfizionie.
amphioxus [,æmfi'oksəs], *s.* (*zool.*) anfiosso.
amphitheatre ['æmfi,θiətə*], *s.* anfiteatro.
amphitheatrical [,æmfiθi'ætrikəl], *ag.* anfiteatrale.
Amphitrite ['æmfitraiti], *no.pr.f.* (*mit.*) Anfitrite.
Amphitryon [æm'fitriən], *no.pr.m.* (*mit.*) Anfitrione || **amphitryon** [æm'fitriən], *s.* anfitrione, ospite.
amphora ['æmfərə], *pl.* **amphorae** ['æmfəri:], **amphoras** ['æmfərəz], *s.* anfora.
ample ['æmpl], *ag.* ampio, spazioso; abbondante.
ampleness ['æmplnis], *s.* ampiezza, spaziosità.
amplification [,æmplifi'keifən], *s.* amplificazione.
amplificative ['æmplifikeitiv], *ag.* amplificativo.
amplifier ['æmplifaiə*], *s.* (*rad.*) amplificatore.
to **amplify** ['æmplifai], *v.t.i.* **1.** amplificare; ampliare **2.** diffondersi, dilungarsi **3.** esagerare.
amplitude ['æmplitju:d], *s.* **1.** ampiezza, estensione **2.** (*astr.*) amplitudine **3.** ampollosità.
amply ['æmpli], *av.* ampiamente.
ampulla [æm'pulə], *pl.* **ampullae** [æm'puli:], *s.* (*anat. eccl.*) ampolla.
to **amputate** ['æmpjuteit], *v.t.* amputare.
amputation [,æmpju'teifən], *s.* amputazione.
amtrack ['æmtræk], *s.* (*amer. contr.* di *amphibious* e *track*) veicolo anfibio per operazioni di sbarco.
amuck [ə'mʌk], *av.* (*malese*): *to run —,* correre qua e là preso da pazzia sanguinaria.
amulet ['æmjulit], *s.* amuleto.
amusable [ə'mju:zəbl], *ag.* che può divertire.
to **amuse** [ə'mju:z], *v.t.* divertire, dilettare; distrarre: *he must be amused,* deve essere distratto; *to — oneself,* divertirsi.
amused [ə'mju:zd], *ag.* divertito || *to be — at* (o *by*), essere divertito da: *I was — at him,* egli mi ha fatto ridere; *we were much — by it,* ci ha molto divertito.
amusement [ə'mju:zmənt], *s.* divertimento; passatempo; distrazione || *money for one's amusements,* denaro per i propri minuti piaceri.
amusing [ə'mju:ziŋ], *ag.* divertente; piacevole; faceto.
amusingly [ə'mju:ziŋli], *av.* piacevolmente.
amygdalic [,æmig'dælik], *ag.* (*chim.*) amigdalico.
amygdalin [ə'migdəlin], *s.* (*chim.*) amigdalina.

amygdaloid [ə'migdəloid], *ag.* (*min.*) amigdaloide.
amylaceous [,æmi'leifəs], *ag.* (*chim.*) amidaceo.
amylopsin [,æmi'lopsin], *s.* (*chim.*) amilopsina.
an[1] [æn (*forma forte*) ən (*forma debole*)], *V.* **a**[1].
an[2], *V.* **a**[2].
an[3], *cong.* (*arc.*) **1.** (*fam. abbr.* di *and*) e **2.** se; come se: — *it please you,* se non vi spiace.
anabaptism [,ænə'bæptizəm], *s.* (*st.relig.*) anabattismo.
anabaptist [,ænə'bæptist], *ag.s.* anabattista.
anabasis [ə'næbəsis], *s.* anabasi.
anabolism [ə'næbəlizəm], *s.* (*biol.*) anabolismo.
anachronie [,ænə'krɔnik], *ag.* anacronistico.
anachronism [ə'nækrənizəm], *s.* anacronismo.
anachronistie [ə,nækrə'nistik], *ag.* anacronistico.
anachronistically [ə,nækrə'nistikəli], *av.* anacronisticamente.
anaclastie [,ænə'klæstik], *ag.* (*fis.*) anaclastico.
anacoluthon [,ænəkə'lu:θon], *s.* (*gram.*) anacoluto.
anaconda [,ænə'kondə], *s.* (*zool.*) anaconda.
Anacreon [ə'nækriən], *no.pr.m.* (*st. lett.*) Anacreonte.
anacreontie [ə,nækri'ontik], *ag.* (*poes.*) anacreontico || *s.* (*poes.*) anacreontica.
anacrusis [,ænə'kru:sis], *s.* (*poes. mus.*) anacrusi.
anadromous [ə'nædrəməs], *ag.* (*ittiol.*) anadromo.
anaemia [ə'ni:mjə], *s.* (*patol.*) anemia.
anaemie [ə'ni:mik], *ag.* (*patol.*) anemico.
anaerobe [æn'eiəroub], *s.* (*biol.*) anaerobio.
anaerobic [æn,eiə'rɔbik], *ag.* (*biol.*) anaerobico.
anaesthesia [,ænis'θi:zjə], *s.* (*med.*), anestesia.
anaesthetic [,ænis'θetik], *ag.s.* (*med.*) anestetico.
anaesthetist [æ'ni:sθitist], *s.c.* (*med.*) anestesista.
anaesthetization [æ,ni:sθiti'zeifən], *s.* (*med.*) anestesia.
to **anaesthetize** [æ'ni:sθitaiz], *v.t.* (*med.*) anestetizzare.
anaglyph ['ænəglif], *s.* (*art.*) anaglifo, intaglio.
anagoge [,ænə'goudʒi], *s.* (*ret.*) anagogia.
anagogie(al) [,ænə'godʒik(əl)], *ag.* (*ret.*) anagogico.
anagogically [,ænə'godʒikəli], *av.* (*ret.*) anagogicamente.
anagram ['ænəgræm], *s.* anagramma.
anagrammatic(al) [,ænəgrə'mætik(əl)], *ag.* anagrammatico.
anagrammatically [,ænəgrə'mætikəli], *av.* anagrammaticamente.
anagrammatism [,ænə'græmətizəm], *s.* anagrammatismo.
anagrammatist [,ænə'græmətist], *s.c.* anagrammatista.
to **anagrammatize** [,ænə'græmətaiz], *v.t.* anagrammatizzare.
anal ['einəl], *ag.* anale.
analecta [,ænə'lektə], **analects** ['ænəlekts], *s.pl.* miscellanea, spigolature letterarie.
analeptic [,ænə'leptik], *ag. s.* (*med.*) analettico.
analgesia [,ænæl'dʒi:zjə], *s.* (*med.*) analgesia.
analgesic [,ænæl'dʒesik], *ag.* (*med.*) analgesico.
analogie(al) [,ænə'lodʒik(əl)], *ag.* analogico.
analogically [,ænə'lodʒikəli], *av.* analogicamente.
analogist [ə'nælədʒist], *s.* analogista.
to **analogize** [ə'nælədʒaiz], *v.t.i.* rappresentare, spiegare analogicamente; impiegare analogie.
analogous [ə'næləgəs], *ag.* analogo.
analogously [ə'næləgəsli], *av.* analogamente.
analogue ['ænəlog], *s.* parola, cosa analoga.
analogy [ə'nælədʒi], *s.* analogia.
analphabetic ['ænælfə'betik], *ag.s.c.* analfabeta.
analysable ['ænəlaizəbl], *ag.* analizzabile.
to **analyse** ['ænəlaiz], *v.t.* analizzare.
analyser ['ænəlaizə*], *s.c.* analizzatore, analizzatrice.
analysis [ə'næləsis], *pl.* **analyses** [ə'næləsi:z], *s.* analisi.
analyst ['ænəlist], *s.* analista.
analytic(al) [,ænə'litik(əl)], *ag.* analitico.
analytically [,ænə'litikəli], *av.* analiticamente.
analytics [,ænə'litiks], *s.* analitica.

anamnesis [,ænəm'niːsis], *s.* (*fil. med.*) anamnesi.
anamorphosis [,ænə'mɔːfəsis], *s.* anamorfosi.
ananas [ə'nɑːnəs], *s.* ananasso.
anandrous [ə'nændrəs], *ag.* (*bot.*) senza stami.
anapaest ['ænəpiːst], *s.* (*poes.*) anapesto.
anapaestic [,ænə'piːstik], *ag.* (*poes.*) anapestico.
anaphora [ə'næfərə], *s.* (*ret.*) anafora.
anarch ['ænɑːk], *s.* (*poet.*) capo di una rivolta.
anarchic(al) [æ'nɑːkik(əl)], *ag.* anarchico.
anarchically [æ'nɑːkikəli], *av.* anarchicamente.
anarchism ['ænəkizəm], *s.* (*rar.*) anarchia.
anarchist ['ænəkist], *s.* anarchico.
to **anarchize** ['ænəkaiz], *v.t.* ridurre allo stato d'anarchia.
anarchy ['ænəki], *s.* anarchia (anche *fig.*).
anastatic [,ænə'stætik], *ag.* anastatico.
anastigmat [ə'næstigmæt], *s.* (*ott.*) lente anastigmatica.
anastigmatic [ə,næstig'mætik], *ag.* (*ott.*) anastigmatico.
to **anastomose** [ə'næstəmouz], *v.i.* (*anat.*) anastomizzare.
anastomosis [,ænəstə'mousis], *s.* (*anat.*) anastomosi.
anastrophe [ə'næstrəfi], *s.* (*ret.*) anastrofe.
anathema [ə'næθimə], *s.* anatema.
to **anathematize** [ə'næθimətaiz], *v.t.* colpire d'anatema.
anatomic(al) [,ænə'tɔmik(əl)], *ag.* anatomico.
anatomically [,ænə'tɔmikəli], *av.* anatomicamente.
anatomist [ə'nætəmist], *s.* anatomista.
to **anatomize** [ə'nætəmaiz], *v.t.i.* anatomizzare; *fig.* analizzare.
anatomy [ə'nætəmi], *s.* **1.** anatomia (anche *fig.*) **2.** (*pop.*) scheletro; persona emaciata.
anatta [ə'nætə], *s.* (*bot.*) anatto.
Anaxagoras [,ænæk'sægərəs], *no.pr.m.* (*st. fil.*) Anassagora.
Anaximander [æ,næksi'mændə*], *no.pr.m.* (*st. fil.*) Anassimandro.
Anaximenes [,ænæk'siməniːz], *no.pr.m.* (*st.fil.*) Anassimene.
ancestor ['ænsistə*], *s.c.* antenato, antenata; avo, ava.
ancestorial [,ænsis'tɔːriəl], **ancestral** [æn'sestrəl], *ag.* avito.
ancestress ['ænsistris], *s.* antenata, ava.
ancestry ['ænsistri], *s.* schiatta, razza, stirpe.
Anchises [æn'kaisiːz], *no.pr.m.* (*lett.*) Anchise.
anchithere ['æŋkiθiə*], *s.* (*paleont.*) anchiterio.
anchor ['æŋkə*], *s.* **1.** (*mar.*) àncora: *the — drags*, l'àncora ara; *the — holds* (o *bites*), l'àncora agguanta; *the — is atrip*, l'àncora ha lasciato il fondo; *to be at —*, essere ancorato; *to cast* (o *to drop* o *to lay*) *—*, gettare l'àncora; *to come to —*, mettersi all'àncora, ancorarsi; *to let the — go*, mollare l'àncora; *to ride* (o *to lie*) *at —*, essere all'àncora, alla fonda; *to stow the —*, acceppare l'àncora; *to sweep an —*, raccogliere un'àncora perduta; *to weigh —*, levare l'àncora **2.** *fig.* appoggio, àncora di salvezza, punto di appoggio ☆ *— berth*, posto di fonda; *— buoy*, gavitello collegato all'àncora; *— clamp*, morsetto d'ancoraggio; *— dues*, (*comm.*) diritti di ancoraggio; *— -plate*, (*mec.*) piastra di fissaggio; *— -watch*, guardia, servizio di porto ‖ *bower— *, àncora di posta; *drag— *, àncora galleggiante; *ebb— *, àncora di riflusso; *foul— *, àncora inceppata, impigliata; *kedge— *, ancorotto; *mooring— *, àncora di ormeggio; *mushroom— *, àncora di attracco; *sea— *, àncora galleggiante; *sheet— *, àncora di speranza, di rispetto; *fig.* persona sulla quale si può contare completamente; *shore— *, àncora di terra; *spare— *, àncora di riserva; *stern— *, àncora di poppa.
to **anchor**, *v.t.i.* ancorare, gettar l'àncora; ancorarsi (anche *fig.*).
anchorage[1] ['æŋkəridʒ], *s.* **1.** ancoraggio **2.** *fig.* appoggio, àncora di salvezza ☆ *— dues*, diritti di ancoraggio.

anchorage[2], *s.* eremo.
anchoress ['æŋkəris], *s.* eremita (donna).
anchoret ['æŋkəret], *s.* anacoreta, eremita (uomo).
anchoretic [,æŋkə'retik], *ag.* eremitico, anacoretico.
anchorite ['æŋkərait], *s.* anacoreta, eremita (uomo).
anchovy ['æntʃəvi], *s.* acciuga ☆ *— -paste*, pasta di acciughe; *— -sauce*, salsa di acciughe.
anchusa [æŋ'kjusə], *s.* (*bot.*) anchusa.
to **anchylose** ['æŋkilouz], *v.t.i.* rendere anchilosato; diventare anchilosato.
anchylosis [,æŋkai'lousis], *s.* (*med.*) anchilosi.
ancient ['einʃənt], *ag.* antico, vecchio; (*arc.*) anziano, venerabile; (*rar.*) antiquato ‖ *s.* vecchio, anziano ‖ *the ancients*, gli antichi ‖ *the Ancient of Days*, Dio.
anciently ['einʃəntli], *av.* anticamente.
ancientness ['einʃəntnis], *s.* (*arc.*) antichità; anzianità, vecchiezza.
ancientry ['einʃəntri], *s.* **1.** antichità; tempi antichi **2.** *pl.* le antichità.
ancillary [æn'siləri], *ag.* sussidiario, ausiliario; subordinato: *— equipment*, equipaggiamento sussidiario.
ancipital [æn'sipitl], *ag.* (*bot.*) ancipite.
ancle ['æŋkl], *s.* caviglia.
ancress ['æŋkris], *s.* eremita (donna).
and [ænd (*forma forte*), ənd, ən (*forme deboli*)], *cong.* **e, ed 1.** (*tra parole*): *better — better*, sempre meglio; *by — by*, tra poco; *carriage — pair*, carrozza a due cavalli; *five — twenty*, venticinque; *milk — coffee*, latte e caffè; *now — then*, ogni tanto; *one hundred — one*, centouno; *worse — worse*, sempre peggio; *there are friends — friends*, ci sono amici e amici **2.** (*tra frasi*): *come — see me*, vieni a trovarmi; *he can read — write*, sa leggere e scrivere; *he might fall — no one notice*, egli potrebbe cadere senza che nessuno se ne accorga; *he saw her tired — would not help*, pur vedendola stanca non l'aiutava **3.** (*arc. con valore condiz.*) se, come se: *let her change her place — need be*, cambi posto se occorre.
Andalusia [,ændə'luːzjə], *no.pr.* (*geog.*) Andalusia.
Andalusian [,ændə'luːzjən], *ag.* andaluso ‖ *s.c.* andaluso, andalusa ‖ *s.* dialetto andaluso.
andante [æn'dænti], *s.* (*mus.*) andante.
andantino [,ɑːndɑː'ntiːnou], *s.* (*mus.*) andantino.
Andes (the) ['ændiːz], *no.pr.pl.* (*geog.*) Ande.
andiron ['ændaiən], *s.* alare.
Andreas ['ændriæs], **Andrew** ['ændruː], *no.pr.m.* Andrea.
androecium [æn'driːʃiəm], *s.* (*bot.*) androceo.
androgen ['ændrədʒən], *s.* ormone testicolare.
androgynous [æn'drɔdʒinəs], *ag.* androgino (anche *bot.*).
androgyny [æn'drɔdʒini], *s.* androginia (anche *bot.*).
Andromache [æn'drɔməki], *no.pr.f.* (*lett.*) Andromaca.
Andromeda [æn'drɔmidə], *no.pr.f.* (*mit.*) Andromeda ‖ *no.pr.* (*astr.*) Andromeda.
Andronicus [æn'drɔnikəs], *no.pr.m.* (*st. lett.*) Andronico.
Andy ['ændi], *no.pr.m.dim.* di **Andrew**.
anecdotage ['ænek,doutidʒ], *s.* **1.** aneddotica **2.** (*scherz.*) la garrula età dei vecchi.
anecdotal [,ænek'doutl] *ag.* aneddotico.
anecdote ['ænikdout], *s.* aneddoto.
anecdotic(al) [,ænek'dotik(əl)], *ag.* aneddotico.
anecdotist ['ænikdoutist], *s.c.* chi narra o raccoglie aneddoti.
to **anele** [ə'niːl], *v.t.* (*arc.*) **1.** ungere, consacrare **2.** amministrare l'estrema unzione a.
anelectric [,æni'lektrik], *ag.s.* (*fis.*) anelettrico.
anelectrode [,æni'lektroud], *s.* (*elett.*) anodo.
anemograph [ə'neməgrɑːf], *s.* (*fis.*) anemografo.
anemography [,æni'mɔgrəfi], *s.* anemografia.
anemometer [,æni'mɔmitə*], *s.* (*fis.*) anemometro.
anemometry [,æni'mɔmitri], *s.* anemometria.

anemone [ə'neməni], *s.* (*bot.*) anemone ☆ *sea-* —, (*zool.*) attinia.

anemoscope [ə'neməskoup], *s.* (*fis.*) anemoscopio.

anent [ɔ'nent], *prep.* (*arc. scoz.*) circa, concernente, in merito a: *he said nothing* — *this particular*, non disse nulla riguardo a questo particolare.

aneroid ['ænərɔid], *ag.s.* (*fis.*) aneroide.

aneurin ['ænjuərin], *s.* (*chim.*) aneurina, vitamina B₁.

aneurism, aneurysm ['ænjuərizəm], *s.* (*patol.*) aneurisma.

aneurismal, aneurysmal [,ænju'rizməl], *ag.* (*patol.*) aneurismatico.

anew [ə'nju:], *av.* **1.** in modo diverso **2.** di nuovo, da capo: *to begin* —, ricominciare.

anfractuosity [,ænfræktju'ɔsiti], *s.* anfrattuosità.

anfractuous [æn'fræktjuəs], *ag.* anfrattuoso.

angary ['æŋgəri], *s.* angheria (anche *dir.*).

angel ['eindʒəl], *s.* angelo: — *of death*, angelo, messaggero di morte; *evil* —, angelo cattivo; *good* —, angelo buono ☆ — *-cake*, (*amer.*) biscotto tipo savoiardo; — *-fish*, (*ittiol.*) pesce angelo; — *-like*, angelico, simile ad angelo || *guardian* —, angelo custode.

Angela ['ændʒilə], *no.pr.f.* Angela.

angelic(al) [æn'dʒelik(əl], *ag.* angelico.

Angelica¹ [æn'dʒelikə], *no.pr.f.* Angelica.

angelica², *s.* (*bot.*) angelica.

angelically [æn'dʒelikəli], *av.* angelicamente.

Angelina [,ændʒi'li:nə], *no.pr.f.* Angelina.

Angelo ['ændʒilou], *no.pr.m.* Angelo.

angelus ['ændʒiləs], *s.* (*eccl.*) angelus.

anger ['æŋgə*], *s.* collera, ira, stizza: *in a fit of* —, in un accesso d'ira; *to provoke s.o. to* —, provocare la collera di qlcu.

to anger, *v.t.* irritare, far andare in collera.

angered ['æŋgəd], *ag.* irato, furioso.

Angevin ['ændʒivin], *ag.s.* angioino.

angina [æn'dʒainə], *s.* (*patol.*) angina.

angle¹ ['æŋgl], *s.* **1.** (*geom.*) angolo: *acute, obtuse, right* —, angolo acuto, ottuso, retto; *at right angles*, perpendicolarmente **2.** *fig.* punto di vista.

to angle¹, *v.t.* (*amer.*) presentare secondo un certo punto di vista.

angle², *s.* (*arc.*) amo (da pesca) || *brother of the* —, pescatore.

to angle², *v.i.* pescare (con l'amo); *fig.* adescare: *to* — *for trout*, pescare le trote; *to* — *for compliments*, *fig.* cercare di farsi fare dei complimenti.

angled ['æŋgld], *ag.* **1.** ad angoli **2.** d'angolo.

angler ['æŋglə*], *s.* pescatore (con l'amo).

Angles ['æŋglz], *s.pl.* angli.

Anglia ['æŋgliə], *no.pr.* (*geog. st.*) Anglia.

Anglian ['æŋgliən], *ag.* **1.** anglico, degli angli **2.** inglese || *s.* **1.** anglo, uno degli angli **2.** anglico (lingua).

Anglican ['æŋglikən], *ag.s.* **1.** (*st.relig.*) anglicano **2.** (*amer.*) inglese.

Anglicanism ['æŋglikənizəm], *s.* (*st. relig.*) anglicanesimo.

Anglicism ['æŋglisizəm], *s.* anglicismo.

to anglicize ['æŋglisaiz], *v.t.* inglesizzare.

angling ['æŋgliŋ], *s.* pesca con l'amo.

Anglo-American ['æŋglouə'merikən], *ag.* anglo-americano || *s.c.* anglo-americano, anglo-americana.

Anglo-French ['æŋglou'frentʃ], *ag.* anglo-francese || *s.* anglo-francese (lingua usata in Inghilterra a corte e nei tribunali dal 1200 sino al 1400 circa).

Anglo-Indian ['æŋglou'indjən], *ag.* anglo-indiano || *s.c.* **1.** persona di discendenza anglo-indiana **2.** inglese residente in India || *s.* anglo-indiano (lingua).

Anglomania ['æŋglou'meinjə], *s.* anglomania.

Anglomaniac [,æŋglou'meinjæk], *s.c.* anglomane.

Anglo-Norman ['æŋglou'nɔ:mən], *ag.s.* anglo-normanno.

Anglophil(e) ['æŋgloufail], *ag.s.* anglofilo.

Anglophobe ['æŋgloufoub], *ag.s.* anglofobo.

Anglophobia [,æŋglou'foubjə], *s.* anglofobia.

Anglo-Saxon ['æŋglou'sæksən], *ag.* anglo-sassone || *s.c.* **1.** anglosassone **2.** persona di origine inglese || *s.* anglosassone (lingua).

Angola¹ [æŋ'goulə], *no.pr.* (*geog.*) Angola.

angola², angora [æŋ'gɔ:rə], *s.* angola, angora ☆ — *-rabbit*, coniglio d'angora.

angostura [,æŋgɔs'tjuərə], *s.* (*bot. farm.*) angostura.

angrily ['æŋgrili], *av.* irosamente; sdegnosamente.

angry ['æŋgri], *ag.* **1.** irato, arrabbiato, stizzito, in collera: *to be* — *at* (o *with*) *s.o.*, essere adirato con qlcu.; *to be* — *at* (o *about*) *sthg.*, essere in collera per qlco.; *to feel* —, irritarsi, essere irritato; *to get* (o *to grow*) —, adirarsi, andare in collera; *to make* —, far andare in collera, stizzire || — *young man*, (*neol.*) «giovane arrabbiato» (intellettuale anticonformista) **2.** collerico, iracondo.

anguine ['æŋgwin], *ag.* serpentiforme.

anguish ['æŋgwiʃ], *s.* angoscia, tormento.

to anguish, *v.t.* (*rar.*) angosciare, tormentare.

angular ['æŋgjulə*], *ag.* angolare.

angularity [,æŋgju'læriti], *s.* angolarità.

angularly ['æŋgjuləli], *av.* angolarmente.

angulate ['æŋgjuleit], *ag.* angolato.

angulation [,æŋgju'leiʃən], *s.* angolazione.

anharmonic ['ænhɑ:'mɔnik], *ag.* (*mat.*) inarmonico.

anhydride [æn'haidraid], *s.* (*chim.*) anidride.

anhydrite [æn'haidrait], *s.* (*chim.*) anidrite.

anhydrous [æn'haidrəs], *ag.* (*chim.*) anidro.

anigh [ə'nai], *av.* vicino || *prep.* vicino a.

anil ['ænil], *s.* (*bot.*) anil, anile.

anile ['einail], *ag.* senile; rimbambito.

aniline ['ænili:n], *s.* (*chim.*) anilina.

anility [æ'niliti], *s.* senilità, rimbambimento (specialmente di donna).

animadversion [,ænimæd'və:ʃən], *s.* censura, biasimo: *to make animadversions on sthg.*, criticare ql.co.

to animadvert [,ænimæd'və:t], *v.i.* censurare, criticare: *to* — (*up*)*on sthg.*, criticare ql.co.

animal ['æniməl], *ag.s.* animale.

animalcular [,æni'mælkjulə*], *ag.* microbico.

animalcule [,æni'mælkju:l], *s.* microbo.

animalism ['æniməlizəm], *s.* animalità; sensualità.

animalist ['æniməlist], *s.c.* sensualista.

animality [,æni'mæliti], *s.* animalità.

animalization ['æniməlai'zeiʃən], *s.* abbrutimento.

to animalize ['æniməlaiz], *v.t.* **1.** abbrutire **2.** (*fisiol.*) convertire in sostanza animale.

animate ['ænimit], *ag.* animato.

to animate ['ænimeit], *v.t.* animare; stimolare.

animated ['ænimeitid], *ag.* animato: *to become* —, animarsi ☆ — *cartoons* (o — *picture*), cartoni, disegni animati.

animatedly ['ænimeitidli], *av.* animatamente.

animating ['ænimeitiŋ], *ag.* vivificante.

animation [,æni'meiʃən], *s.* animazione.

animator ['ænimeitə*], *s.* animatore.

animism ['ænimizəm], *s.* (*fil.*) animismo; spiritualismo.

animosity [,æni'mɔsiti], *s.* animosità.

animus ['æniməs], *s.* **1.** animo, mente **2.** intenzione **3.** animosità.

anion ['ænaiən], *s.* (*chim.*) anione.

anise ['ænis], *s.* (*bot.*) anice, anace.

aniseed ['ænisi:d], *s.* anice, semi di anice.

anisette [,æni'zet], *s.* anisetta (liquore).

Anita [ə'ni:tə], *no.pr.f.* Anita.

ankle ['æŋkl], *s.* caviglia ☆ — *bone*, (*anat.*) astragalo; — *-deep*, che giunge sino alla caviglia; — *joint*, collo del piede; — *sock*, calzino.

anklet ['æŋklit], *s.* **1.** bracciale da caviglia **2.** cavigliera.

ankylosis [,æŋkai'lousis], *s.* (*patol.*) anchilosi.

Ann [æn], **Anna¹** ['ænə], *no.pr.f.* Anna.

anna² ['ænə], *s.* «anna» (moneta indiana).

Annabel, Annabelle ['ænəbel], *no.pr.f.* Annabella.

annalist ['ænəlist], *s.c.* annalista.

annalistic ['ænəlistik], *ag.* annalistico.
annals ['ænlz], *s.pl.* annali.
annates ['æneits], *s.pl.* (*dir. eccl.*) annualità.
Anne [æn], *no.pr.f.* Anna.
to **anneal** [ə'ni:l], *v.t.* (*ind.*) ricuocere; purificare; temperare; *fig.* temprare.
Annelida [ə'nelidə], *s.pl.* (*zool.*) gli anellidi.
annex(e) [ə'neks], *s.* **1.** allegato (ad un documento) **2.** edificio secondario; dipendenza (di albergo).
to **annex** [ə'neks], *v.t.* **1.** unire, attaccare, congiungere **2.** annettere (un paese).
annexable [ə'neksəbl], *ag.* che si può annettere.
annexation [,ænek'seiʃən], *s.* annessione.
annexationist [,ænek'seiʃənist], *s.c.* annessionista.
Annie ['æni], *no.pr.f. dim.* di **Ann.**
to **annihilate** [ə'naiəleit], *v.t.* annichilire, annientare.
annihilation [ə,naiə'leiʃən], *s.* annichilimento; annientamento.
annihilator [ə'naiəleitə*], *s.* distruttore ☆ *fire- —*, estintore.
anniversary [,æni'və:səri], *s.* anniversario.
Anno Domini ['ænou'dɔminai], *l.av.* dell'era volgare.
to **annotate** ['ænouteit], *v.t.i.* annotare; chiosare.
annotation [,ænou'teiʃən], *s.* annotazione; chiosa, postilla.
annotator ['ænouteitə*], *s.c.* annotatore, annotatrice; commentatore, commentatrice.
to **announce** [ə'nauns], *v.t.* annunziare; rivelare: *he announced his intentions to me,* egli mi rivelò le sue intenzioni.
announcement [ə'naunsmənt], *s.* annunzio; dichiarazione; proclama; affisso, avviso; bando: *— of death,* avviso mortuario.
announcer [ə'naunsə*], *s.c.* annunziatore, annunziatrice; banditore, banditrice; (*rad.*) annunciatore, annunciatrice; presentatore, presentatrice.
annoy [ə'nɔi], *s.* (*arc. poet.*) noia.
to **annoy**, *v.t.* importunare, dar noia a, infastidire, seccare: *it annoys me,* ciò mi secca.
annoyance [ə'nɔiəns], *s.* noia, fastidio, seccatura: *to give —,* dar fastidio, seccare.
annoyed [ə'nɔid], *ag.* contrariato, seccato: *to be — about* (*o at*) *sthg.,* essere contrariato per ql.co.: *to be — with s.o.,* essere seccato con qlcu.
annoyer [ə'nɔiə*], *s.c.* seccatore; seccatrice.
annoying [ə'nɔiiŋ], *ag.* noioso, fastidioso, seccante.
annual ['ænjuəl], *ag.* annuale, annuo ‖ *s.* **1.** annuario **2.** (*bot.*) pianta annuale.
annually ['ænjuəli], *av.* annualmente.
annuary ['ænjuəri], *s.* annuario.
annuitant [ə'nju(:)itənt], *s.c.* **1.** chi vive di rendita **2.** pensionato, pensionata (dello Stato, ecc.); chi usufruisce di un vitalizio.
annuity [ə'nju(:)iti], *s.* annualità; rendita (annuale) ☆ *life —,* vitalizio.
to **annul** [ə'nʌl], *pass.p.p.* **annulled** [ə'nʌld], *v.t.* annullare, abrogare, abolire.
annular ['ænjulə*], **annulary** ['ænjuləri], *ag.* anulare.
annulate ['ænjuleit], **annulated** ['ænjuleitid], *ag.* inanellato; ad anelli.
annullable [ə'nʌləbl], *ag.* annullabile.
annulment [ə'nʌlmənt], *s.* annullamento; (*dir.*) rescissione.
annulose ['ænjulous], *ag.* anelloso.
to **annunciate** [ə'nʌnʃieit], *v.t.* annunciare, proclamare.
annunciation [ə,nʌnsi'eiʃən], *s.* annuncio ‖ *the Annunciation,* (*relig.*) l'Annunciazione.
annunciator [ə'nʌnʃieitə*], *s.* **1.** annunciatore, avvisatore **2.** (*ferr.*) segnalatore (elettrico) **3.** (*elett.*) quadro di segnalazione.
anode ['ænoud], *s.* (*elett.*) anodo.
anodyne ['ænoudain], *ag.s.* (*farm.*) anodino; calmante.
to **anoint** [ə'nɔint], *v.t.* **1.** ungere (di olio, ecc.) **2.** (*eccl.*) consacrare (sacerdoti, sovrani ,ecc.).

anointing [ə'nɔintiŋ], **anointment** [ə'nɔintmənt], *s.* **1.** unzione, ungimento **2.** consacrazione (di sacerdote, ecc.); incoronazione (di sovrano, ecc.).
anomalistic [ə,nɔmə'listik], *ag.* (*astr.*) anomalistico.
anomalous [ə'nɔmələs], *ag.* anomalo.
anomaly [ə'nɔməli], *s.* anomalia.
anon [ə'nɔn], *av.* fra poco ‖ *ever and —,* ogni tanto.
anonym ['ænənim], *s.* anonimo.
anonymity [,ænə'nimiti], *s.* anonimato.
anonymous [ə'nɔniməs], *ag.* anonimo.
anonymously [ə'nɔniməsli], *av.* anonimamente.
anonymousness [ə'nɔniməsnis], *s.* anonimato.
anopheles [ə'nɔfili:z], *s.* (*entom.*) anofele.
anosmia [æ'nɔsmiə], *s.* (*patol.*) anosmia.
another [ə'nʌðə*], *ag.* **un altro** (**in più, uguale, diverso**): *— place,* un altro luogo; *— time,* un'altra volta; *— twenty years,* venti anni ancora, altri venti anni; *in quite — way,* diversamente; *he will be — Edison,* diventerà un altro Edison; *I have — friend,* ho un altro amico; *I shall stay — day,* mi fermerò un giorno ancora; *that is quite — matter,* è tutt'altra cosa ‖ *pron.* **un altro** (**in più, uguale, diverso**): *one way or —,* in un modo o nell'altro; *such —,* un altro simile ‖ *you're —!,* (*fam.*) che! non ci credo! ‖ **one another,** *pron. reciproco* **l'un l'altro** (*fra molti*): *they detest —,* si detestano l'un l'altro.
Anselm ['ænselm], *no.pr.m.* Anselmo.
anserine ['ænsərain], *ag.* **1.** d'oca ‖ *— skin,* pelle d'oca **2.** *fig.* stupido, sciocco.
answer ['ɑ:nsə*], *s.* risposta, replica; soluzione: *in — to your favour,* (*comm.*) in risposta alla vostra gradita; *an — will oblige,* (*comm.*) sarà gradita una risposta; *he made no —,* non diede risposta, non rispose; *no — is required,* non occorre risposta.
to **answer**, *v.t.i.* **1.** rispondere a: *he answered the letter,* egli rispose alla lettera; *he answered that I was right,* rispose che io avevo ragione; *I cannot — your question,* non posso rispondere alla vostra domanda; *the letter was answered,* si rispose alla lettera; *she answered the bell, the door,* essa rispose al campanello, aprì la porta; *she answered for me,* rispose al posto mio; *the ship answers the helm,* la nave risponde al timone ‖ *to — a charge,* (*dir.*) rispondere a un'accusa ‖ *to — to the name of,* rispondere al nome di, chiamarsi **2.** *fig.* rispondere; corrispondere; servire: *cotton will — (the purpose) as well as wool,* il cotone servirà quanto la lana; *he did not — (to) my expectations, hopes,* non rispose alla mia aspettativa, alle mie speranze; *that won't —,* quello non servirà allo scopo; *this answers the purpose,* questo serve allo scopo **3.** *to — for* (*s.o., sthg.*), rispondere di, rendersi garante di, esser responsabile di: *I can — for his honesty,* rispondo della sua onestà; *you have a lot to — for,* sei responsabile di molte cose **4.** *to — back,* ribattere, rimbeccare, confutare.
answerable ['ɑ:nsərəbl], *ag.* **1.** a cui si può rispondere **2.** responsabile, garante **3.** (*arc.*) corrispondente a, conforme a.
answerer ['ɑ:nsərə*], *s.c.* **1.** chi risponde **2.** corrispondente.
answering ['ɑ:nsəriŋ], *ag.* **1.** in risposta: *an — cry,* un grido di risposta **2.** corrispondente: *I saw s.o. — to your description,* vidi qualcuno che corrispondeva alla tua descrizione.
ant [ænt], *s.* formica ☆ *— -bear,* formichiere; *— -eggs,* larve di formica; *— -fly,* formica alata; *— -hill,* formicaio; *— -like,* *fig.* laborioso; *— -lion,* formicaleone ‖ *white —,* termite.
an't [ɑ:nt], *contr. fam.* di am not, are not, is not, have not, has not, had not.
antacid ['ænt'æsid], *ag.s.* antiacido.
Antaeus [æn'ti(:)əs], *no.pr.m.* (*mit.*) Anteo.
antagonism [æn'tægənizəm], *s.* antagonismo.
antagonist [æn'tægənist], *ag.s.c.* antagonista ‖ *s.* (*anat.*) (muscolo) antagonista.

antagonistic(al) [æn,tægə'nistik(əl)], *ag.* antagonistico.

antagonistically [æn,tægə'nistikəli], *av.* antagonisticamente.

to **antagonize** [æn'tægənaiz], *v.t.i.* **1.** opporsi (a), resistere (a) **2.** provocar l'ostilità di.

Antarctic [ænt'ɑ:ktik], *ag.* antartico || *the — Ocean*, l'Oceano Antartico || *no.pr.* (geog.) Antartide.

Antarctica [ænt'ɑ:ktikə], *no.pr.* (geog.) Antartide.

ante ['ænti], *s.* (poker) « buio ».

to **ante**, *v.t.* (poker) fare il « buio » di.

ante-bellum ['ænti'beləm], *ag.* anteguerra; (amer.) di prima della guerra civile.

antecedence [,ænti'si:dəns], *s.* **1.** anteriorità, precedenza **2.** (astr.) antecedenza.

antecedent [,ænti'si:dənt], *ag.* antecedente: — *to*, anteriore a, prima di || *s.* **1.** (gram. log. mat.) antecedente **2.** (mus.) tema (di una fuga) **3.** *pl.* gli antenati; il passato.

antecedently [,ænti'si:dəntli], *av.* precedentemente.

antechamber ['ænti,tʃeimbə*], *s.* anticamera.

antedate ['ænti'deit], *s.* antidata.

to **antedate**, *v.t.* antidatare; anticipare.

antediluvian ['æntidi'lu:vjən], *ag.s.* antidiluviano.

antelope ['æntiloup], *s.* antilope.

antemeridian ['æntimə'ridiən], *ag.* (rar.) (abbr. a. m.) antimeridiano.

antenatal ['ænti'neitl], *ag.* prenatale.

antenna [æn'tenə], *pl.* **antennae** [æn'teni:], *s.* antenna.

antenuptial ['ænti'nʌpʃəl], *ag.* prematrimoniale.

antepenult ['æntipi'nʌlt], **antepenultimate** ['ænti-pi'nʌltimit], *ag.s.* antipenultimo, terzultimo.

anteprandial ['ænti'prændjəl], *ag.* di prima del pranzo.

anterior [æn'tiəriə*], *ag.* anteriore, precedente.

anteriority [æn,tiəri'oriti], *s.* anteriorità.

anteriorly [æn'tiəriəli], *av.* anteriormente.

anteroom ['æntirum], *s.* anticamera.

ante-war ['ænti'wo:*], *ag.* anteguerra.

anthelion [æn'θi:ljən], *pl.* **anthelions** [æn'θi:lj-ənz], **anthelia** [æn'θi:ljə], *s.* (astr.) antelio.

anthelmintic [,ænθil'mintik], *ag.* (farm.) antelmintico.

anthem ['ænθəm], *s.* (mus.) antifona; inno, canto: *national —*, inno nazionale.

anther ['ænθə*], *s.* (bot.) antera.

anthologist [æn'θɔlədʒist], *s.* compilatore di antologie.

anthology [æn'θɔlədʒi], *s.* antologia, florilegio.

Anthony ['æntəni], *no.pr.m.* Antonio || *St. —'s fire,* (patol.) fuoco di S. Antonio, erisipela, risipola.

anthracene ['ænθrəsi:n], *s.* (chim.) antracene.

anthracite ['ænθrəsait], *s.* antracite.

anthracitic [,ænθrə'sitik], *ag.* di antracite.

anthrax ['ænθræks], *s.* (patol.) antrace.

anthropocentric [,ænθrəpə'sentrik], *ag.* (fil.) antropocentrico.

anthropoid ['ænθrəpoid], *ag.s.* (zool.) antropoide.

anthropological [,ænθrəpə'lɔdʒikəl], *ag.* antropologico.

anthropologically [,ænθrəpə'lɔdʒikəli], *av.* antropologicamente.

anthropologist [,ænθrə'pɔlədʒist], *s.* antropologo.

anthropology [,ænθrə'pɔlədʒi], *s.* antropologia.

anthropometry [,ænθrə'pɔmitri], *s.* antropometria.

anthropomorphic [,ænθrəpə'mɔ:fik], *ag.* antropomorfo.

anthropomorphism [,ænθrəpə'mɔ:fizəm], *s.* antropomorfismo.

anthropomorphist [,ænθrəpə'mɔ:fist], *s.* antropomorfista.

to **anthropomorphize** [,ænθrəpə'mɔ:faiz], *v.t.* attribuire forma, personalità umana a.

anthropomorphous [,ænθrəpə'mɔ:fəs], *ag.* antropomorfo.

anthropophagi [,ænθrə'pɔfəgai], *s.pl.* antropofagi.

anthropophagous [,ænθrə'pɔfəgəs], *ag.* antropofago.

anthropophagy [,ænθrə'pɔfədʒi], *s.* antropofagia.

anthroposophy [,ænθrə'pɔsəfi], *s.* antroposofia.

anti-abolitionist ['ænti,æbə'liʃənist], *s.* (amer.) anti-abolizionista.

antiacid ['ænti'æsid], *ag.s.* antiacido.

anti-aircraft ['ænti'ɛə-krɑ:ft], *ag.* antiaereo, controaereo ☆ *— gun,* cannone antiaereo.

antiasthmatic ['æntiæs'mætik], *ag.s.* (farm.) antiasmatico.

antibilious ['ænti'biljəs], *ag.* (farm.) antibilioso.

antibiotic ['æntibai'ɔtik], *ag.s.* (farm.) antibiotico.

antibody ['ænti,bɔdi], *s.* (fisiol.) anticorpo.

antibrachial ['ænti'breikjəl], *ag.* antibrachiale.

antic ['æntik], *ag.* (arc.) grottesco, bizzarro || *s.* **1.** (arc.) buffone **2.** *spec. pl.* buffoneria, stramberia: *he is always playing* (o *up to*) *his antics,* fa sempre buffonate.

anticardium ['ænti'kɑ:diəm], *s.* (anat.) anticardio.

anticatalyst ['ænti'kætəlist], *s.* (chim.) catalizzatore negativo.

anticatarrhal [,æntikə'tɑ:rəl], *ag.s.* (farm.) anticatarrale.

anticathode ['ænti'kæθoud], *s.* (elett.) anticatodo.

antichrist ['æntikraist], *s.* anticristo || *the Antichrist,* l'Anticristo.

antichristian ['ænti'kristjən], *ag.* anticristiano.

antichristianism ['ænti'kristjənizəm], *s.* opposizione al cristianesimo.

to **anticipate** [æn'tisipeit], *v.t.* **1.** anticipare: *he will — the money,* egli darà il denaro in anticipo **2.** prevedere; aspettarsi: *I — he will be here to-morrow,* mi aspetto che egli venga domani; *I — his ruin,* prevedo la sua rovina **3.** pregustare: *I — the pleasure of meeting you,* mi rallegro al pensiero di incontrarti **4.** accelerare.

anticipation [æn,tisi'peiʃən], *s.* **1.** anticipazione, anticipo: *thanking you in —,* ringraziandovi in anticipo **2.** previsione; aspettazione **3.** pregustazione **4.** (mus.) anticipazione (di un accordo).

anticipative [æn'tisipeitiv], *ag.* che anticipa.

anticipatively [æn'tisipeitivli], *av.* anticipatamente.

anticipator [æn'tisipeitə*], *s.c.* chi anticipa.

anticipatory [æn'tisipeitəri], *ag.* che anticipa.

anticlerical ['ænti'klerikl], *ag.* anticlericale.

anticlericalism ['ænti'klerikəlizəm], *s.* anticlericalismo.

anticlimax ['ænti'klaimæks], '*s.* (ret.) « anticlimax » (brusco passaggio da argomenti o concetti elevati ad altri banali): *the last act is an —,* l'ultimo atto cade, discende nel banale, perde d'intensità.

anticlinal ['ænti'klainl], *ag.s.* (geol.) anticlinale.

anticline ['æntiklain], *s.* (geol.) anticlinale.

anticoagulant ['æntikou'ægjulənt], *s.* anticoagulante.

anticonstitutional ['ænti,kɔnsti'tju:ʃənl], *ag.* anticostituzionale.

anticyclone ['ænti'saikloun], *s.* anticiclone.

anti-dazzle ['ænti'dæzl], *ag.* antiabbagliante, anabbagliante ☆ *— device,* (aut.) dispositivo antiabbagliante; *— headlights,* (aut.) fari anabbaglianti.

antidotal ['æntidoutl], *ag.* che serve da antidoto.

antidote ['æntidout], *s.* antidoto.

antidysenteric ['ænti,disn'terik], *ag.s.* (farm.) antidissenterico.

antiemetic ['ænti'metik], *ag.s.* (farm.) antiemetico.

anti-fading ['ænti'feidiŋ], *s.* (rad.) « anti-fading », antifluttuazione, antiaffievolimento.

antifebrile ['ænti'fi:brail], *ag.s.* (farm.) febbrifugo.

antifederal ['ænti'fedərəl], *ag.* antifederale.

antifederalist ['ænti'fedərəlist], *s.* antifederalista.

antifire ['ænti'faiə*], *s.* antincendio.

antifogging ['ænti'fɔgiŋ], *ag.s.* antiappannante; antinebbia.

anti-freeze ['ænti'fri:z], *s.* (aut.) anticongelante.

anti-freezing ['ænti'fri:ziŋ], *ag.* (aut.) anticongelante.

anti-friction ['ænti'frikʃən], *s.* (mec.) antiattrito, antifrizione.

anti-gas ['ænti'gæs], *ag.* antigas.
antigen ['æntidʒən], *s.* (*med.*) antigene.
Antigone [æn'tigəni], *no.pr.f.* (*lett.*) Antigone.
Antigonus [æn'tigənəs], *no.pr.m.* (*st.*) Antigono.
antigropelos [,ænti'gropilouz], *s.pl.* gambali impermeabili.
antihelix ['ænti'hi:liks], *pl.* **antihelixes** ['ænti'hi:liksiz], **antihelices** ['ænti'hi:lisi:z], *s.* (*anat.*) antelice.
antihistamine ['ænti'histəmi(:)n], *s.* (*farm.*) antistaminico.
antihypnotic ['æntihip'nɔtik], *ag.s.* (*farm.*) antiipnotico.
antihysteric ['æntihis'terik], *ag.s.* (*farm.*) antiisterico.
anti-icer ['ænti'aisə*], *s.* (*aer.*) dispositivo antighiaccio.
anti-imperialist ['æntiim'piəriəlist], *s.* antimperialista.
anti-Jacobin ['ænti'dʒækəbin], *ag.s.* (*st.*) antigiacobino, antirivoluzionario.
Antilles (the) [æn'tili:z], *no.pr.pl.* (*geog.*) Antille.
antilogarithm ['ænti'lɔgəriθəm], *s.* (*mat.*) antilogaritmo.
antilogy [æn'tilədʒi], *s.* antilogia, contraddizione.
antimacassar ['æntimə'kæsə*], *s.* coprischienale (di sedie, poltrone, ecc.).
anti-matter ['ænti'mætə*], *s.* (*fis.*) antimateria.
antimilitarism ['ænti'militərizəm], *s.* antimilitarismo.
antimilitarist ['ænti'militərist], *s.c.* antimilitarista.
antimonarchical ['æntimɔ'nɑ:kikəl], *ag.* antimonarchico.
antimonarchist ['ænti'mɔnəkist], *s.c.* antimonarchico, antimonarchica.
antimonial [,ænti'mounjəl], *ag.* (*chim.*) antimoniale.
antimony ['æntiməni], *s.* (*chim.*) antimonio.
antinational ['ænti'næʃənl], *ag.* antinazionale.
anti-noise ['ænti'nɔiz], *ag.* silenziatore.
antinomy [æn'tinəmi], *s.* antinomia.
Antioch ['æntiɔk], *no.pr.* (*geog. st.*) Antiochia.
Antiochus [æn'taiəkəs], *no.pr.m.* (*st.*) Antioco.
antipapal [,ænti'peipəl], *ag.* antipapale.
antipathetic(al) [æn,tipə'θetik(əl)], *ag.* avverso, contrario.
antipathetically [æn,tipə'θetikəli], *av.* in modo avverso, contrario; contrariamente.
antipathic [,ænti'pæθik], *ag.* **1.** contrario, avverso, di carattere opposto **2.** (*med.*) che ha, produce sintomi contrari.
antipathy [æn'tipəθi], *s.* antipatia, avversione; contrasto; ripugnanza: *to have an — to* (o *against*) *s.o.*, avere antipatia per qlcu.
antiphon ['æntifən], *s.* (*mus.*) antifona.
antiphonal [æn'tifənl], *ag.* (*mus.*) antifonale ‖ *s.* (*mus.*) antifonario.
antiphonary [æn'tifənəri], *s.* (*mus.*) antifonario.
antiphony [æn'tifəni], *s.* (*mus.*) antifona.
antipodal [æn'tipədl], *ag.* degli, agli antipodi (anche *fig.*).
antipode ['æntipoud], *nel senso* **2.** [æn'tipədi:z], *s.* **1.** *fig.* antipode **2.** *pl.* antipodi (anche *fig.*).
antipoison ['ænti'pɔizn], *s.* contravveleno.
antipole ['ænti'poul], *s.* polo opposto; opposto.
antipope ['æntipoup], *s.* antipapa.
antipyretic ['æntipai'retik], *ag.* (*farm.*) antipiretico.
antipyrin(e) [,ænti'paiərin], *s.* (*farm.*) antipirina.
antiquarian [,ænti'kwɛəriən], *ag.* **1.** antiquario **2.** archeologico ‖ *s.* **1.** antiquario **2.** archeologo **3.** carta da disegno in formato grande.
antiquarianism [,ænti'kwɛəriənizəm], *s.* antiquaria.
to antiquarianize [,ænti'kwɛəriənaiz], *v.i.* (*fam.*) occuparsi di antiquaria.
antiquary ['æntikwəri], *s.c.* **1.** antiquario, antiquaria **2.** archeologo, archeologa.
to antiquate ['æntikweit], *v.t.* **1.** mettere in disuso **2.** invecchiare, dare la patina d'antico a.

antiquated ['æntikweitid], *ag.* antiquato; in disuso.
antique [æn'ti:k], *ag.* antico; antiquato, all'antica ‖ *s.* **1.** antichità (resti, avanzi del passato); oggetto (d'arte) antico ‖ *the —*, l'antico (arte, stile) **2.** (*tip.*) grassetto ☆ — *dealer*, antiquario.
antiqueness [æn'ti:knis], *s.* antichità.
antiquity [æn'tikwiti], *s.* **1.** antichità, vetustà (di idee, ecc.) **2.** l'antichità (romana, greca) **3.** *pl.* ruderi, rovine **4.** *pl.* eventi, costumi, usanze dei tempi antichi.
anti-rabie ['ænti'ræbik], *ag.* (*farm.*) antirabbico.
antirrhinum [,ænti'rainəm], *s.* (*bot.*) bocca di leone.
anti-rust ['ænti'rʌst], *ag.s.* antiruggine.
antiscorbutic ['ænti-skɔ:'bju:tik], *ag.s.* (*farm.*) antiscorbutico.
antisemite ['ænti'si:mait], *ag.s.c.* antisemita.
antisemitic ['æntisi'mitik], *ag.* antisemita.
anti-Semitism ['ænti'semitizəm], *s.* antisemitismo.
antiseptic [,ænti'septik], *ag.s.* (*farm.*) antisettico.
antiskid ['ænti'skid], *ag.s.* antisdrucciolevole.
antislavery ['ænti'sleivəri], *s.* antischiavismo.
antisocial ['ænti'souʃəl], *ag.* antisociale.
antispasmodic ['æntispæz'mɔdik], *ag.s.* (*farm.*) antispasmodico.
antistrophe [æn'tistrəfi], *s.* (*poes.*) antistrofe.
anti-tank ['ænti'tæŋk], *ag.* (*mil.*) anticarro.
anti-theft ['ænti'θeft], *ag.s.* antifurto.
antithesis [æn'tiθisis], *pl.* **antitheses** [æn'tiθisi:z], *s.* antitesi (anche *fig.*).
antithetic(al) [,ænti'θetik(əl)], *ag.* antitetico.
antithetically [,ænti'θetikəli], *av.* antiteticamente.
antitoxic ['ænti'tɔksik], *ag.* (*med.*) antitossico.
antitoxin ['ænti'tɔksin], *s.* (*med.*) antitossina.
antitrade ['ænti'treid], *ag.s.* (*vento*) controaliseo.
antivenin ['ænti'venin], *s.* contravveleno, antidoto.
antler ['æntlə*], *s.* palco, ramificazione (delle corna di cervo, daino, ecc.).
antlered ['æntləd], *ag.* con corna ramificate.
Antoinette [,æntwa:'net], *no.pr.f.* Antonietta.
Antoninus [,æntə'nainəs], *no.pr.m.* (*st.*) Antonino.
Antonius [æn'tounjəs], **Antony** ['æntəni], *no.pr.m.* Antonio.
antonomasia [,æntənou'meizjə], *s.* (*ret.*) antonomasia.
antonym ['æntənim], *s.* (*ret.*) opposto: *good is the — of bad*, buono è l'opposto di cattivo.
antrum ['æntrəm], *pl.* **antrums** ['æntrəmz], **antra** ['æntrə], *s.* antro, caverna, cavità (anche *anat.*).
Antwerp ['ænt-wə:p], *no.pr.* (*geog.*) Anversa.
anurous [ə'nju:rəs], *ag.* (*zool.*) anuro.
anus ['einəs], *s.* (*anat.*) ano.
anvil ['ænvil], *s.* **1.** incudine (anche *fig.*) **2.** (*anat.*) incudine (dell'orecchio).
anxiety [æŋ'zaiəti], *s.* **1.** ansietà, inquietudine, apprensione, preoccupazione, affanno **2.** desiderio, bramosia.
anxious ['æŋkʃəs], *ag.* **1.** ansioso, inquieto, preoccupato: *don't be — about me*, non preoccupatevi per me **2.** preoccupante, angoscioso **3.** desideroso, bramoso.
anxiously ['æŋkʃəsli], *av.* ansiosamente.
any ['eni], *ag.* **1.** **qualche, alcuno, nessuno:** *without — exception*, senza nessuna eccezione; *has he not — real friends?*, non ha dei veri amici?; *he has not — real friends*, non ha dei veri amici **2.** **qualunque, qualsiasi:** *— man could do that*, qualsiasi uomo potrebbe fare ciò; *bring me — book* (*books*) *you like*, portami qualsiasi libro (numero di libri) tu voglia; *come at — time*, vieni a qualunque ora ‖ *at — rate*, in ogni modo; *in — case*, in ogni caso **3.** (*partitivo*) **una certa quantità di, del, dei, della, delle:** *have you — wine?*, hai del vino?; *I don't know whether there is — wine in the house*, non so se ci sia del vino in casa ‖ *pron.* **1.** **alcuno, nessuno:** *do you know — of these plays?*, conosci qualcuna di queste commedie? **2.** **ne:** *Have you — money?*, *I have not —*, Hai del denaro?, Non ne ho ‖ *av.* **1.** (*non sempre traducibile, rafforzativo*): *are you — better?*, stai un po' meglio?; *he could not speak —*

clearer, non potrebbe esprimersi più chiaramente ‖ *it isn't — good*, non serve a nulla **2.** (*amer.*) affatto: *he did not help us —*, non ci aiutò affatto.

anybody ['eni,bɔdi], *pron. indef.* **1. qualcuno, taluno, alcuno, nessuno**: *he does not know — here*, non conosce nessuno qui; *I cannot see —*, non vedo nessuno; *if — speaks*, se parla qualcuno; *is — coming to dinner?*, viene qualcuno a pranzo?; *was there — I know?*, c'era qualcuno là che io conosco? **2. chiunque, chicchessia**: *— can do that*, chiunque può, tutti possono farlo; *— will show you the way*, qualsiasi persona, il primo che capita vi indicherà la strada ‖ *s.* qualcuno, una personalità: *is he —?*, è qualcuno?, è una personalità?.

anyhow ['enihau], *av.cong.* **1.** in ogni caso, ad ogni modo: *it is too late now —*, in ogni caso è troppo tardi ora **2.** non importa come, in qualsiasi modo, comunque: *let me know —*, fammi sapere comunque **3.** a caso, negligentemente: *he was in such a hurry that he put his clothes on —*, aveva una tal fretta che si vestì in qualche modo, come capitava; *he works —*, lavora senza impegno.

anyone ['eniwʌn], *V.* **anybody.**

anything ['eniθiŋ], *pron. indef.* **1. qualche cosa, alcuna cosa**: *have you — to tell me?*, hai qualche cosa da dirmi?; *he does not do —*, non fa nulla **2. qualunque cosa**: *you may do — you like*, potete fare qualsiasi cosa vi piaccia ‖ *like —*, in modo eccessivo: *he ran like —*, correva come un pazzo.

anyway ['eniwei], (*amer.*) per **anyhow 1.**

anywhere ['eniwɛǝ*], *av.* dovunque, dove che sia; in qualunque luogo: *— else*, in qualsiasi altro luogo.

anywise ['eniwaiz], *av.* in qualunque modo.

Anzac ['ænzæk], *s.* **1.** soldato dell'*Australian and New Zealand Army Corps* (1914-18) **2.** *pl.* soldati australiani (in genere).

aorist ['ɛǝrist], *s.* (*gram.*) aoristo.

aorta [ei'ɔ:tǝ], *s.* (*anat.*) aorta.

apace [ǝ'peis], *av.* presto, velocemente.

apache [ǝ'pɑ:ʃ], *s.* « apache », teppista di Parigi.

Apache [ǝ'pætʃi], *s.* « apache » (membro di una tribù di pellirosse del Nord America) ‖ **apache** [ǝ'pɑ:ʃ], *s.* « apache » (teppista di Parigi).

apanage ['æpǝnidʒ], *s.* appannaggio (anche *fig.*).

apart [ǝ'pɑ:t], *av.* **1.** a parte, da parte, in disparte: *a class —*, un genere a parte; *he sat somewhat — from us*, si sedette alquanto in disparte da noi; *to live — from the world*, vivere in disparte dal mondo; *to put —*, mettere da parte **2.** separatamente, lontano: *the boys and the girls were kept —*, i ragazzi venivano tenuti separati dalle ragazze; *these lines are ten centimetres —*, queste linee sono lontane dieci centimentri una dall'altra; *they lived widely —*, abitavano molto lontano; *to get (o to take) two things —*, separare, disgiungere due cose ‖ *I cannot tell them —*, non li riconosco uno dall'altro ‖ *to take a machine —*, smontare una macchina **3.** indipendentemente, a prescindere, a parte: *— from the fact that*, a prescindere dal fatto che; *joking —*, scherzi a parte.

apartheid [ǝ'pɑ:thaid], *s.* discriminazione razziale (specialmente in Sud Africa).

apartment [ǝ'pɑ:tmǝnt], *s.* **1.** stanza, camera; (*arc.*) appartamento: *apartments to let*, si affitta un appartamento **2.** (*amer.*) appartamento.

apathetic [,æpǝ'θetik], *ag.* apatico, indifferente.

apathetically [,æpǝ'θetikǝli], *av.* apaticamente.

apathy ['æpǝθi], *s.* apatia, indifferenza; indolenza.

ape [eip], *s.* **1.** scimmia antropomorfa ‖ *the higher apes*, i primati ‖ *she will lead apes in hell*, (*sl. amer.*) morirà zitella **2.** *fig.* imitatore: *to play the —*, fare la scimmia, scimmiottare, imitare.

to ape, *v.t.* scimmiottare, imitare.

apeak [ǝ'pi:k], *av.ag. predicativo* (*mar.*) a picco.

Apelles [ǝ'peli:z], *no.pr.m.* (*st. pit.*) Apelle.

Apennines (the) ['æpinainz], *no.pr.pl.* (*geog.*) Appennini.

---

apepsy [ǝ'pepsi], *s.* (*patol.*) apepsia.

aper ['eipǝ*], *s.c.* imitatore, imitatrice.

aperçu [,æpǝ:'sju:], *s.* riassunto.

aperient [ǝ'piǝriǝnt], *ag.s.* (*farm.*) lassativo.

aperitif ['ɑ:peiri:'ti:f], *s.* aperitivo.

aperitive [ǝ'peritiv], *ag.s.* (*farm.*) lassativo.

aperture ['æpǝtjuǝ*], *s.* apertura; foro, pertugio.

apery ['eipǝri], *s.* **1.** imitazione **2.** gabbia da scimmie.

apetalous [ǝ'petǝlǝs], *ag.* (*bot.*) apetalo.

apex ['eipeks], *pl.* **apexes** ['eipeksiz], **apices** ['eipisi:z], *s.* apice, sommità; vertice (di triangolo, ecc.): *— of a career*, apogeo di una carriera; *— of the lung, of the heart*, apice del polmone, del cuore.

aphaeresis [æ'fiǝrisis], *s.* (*gram. chir.*) aferesi.

aphasia [æ'feizjǝ], *s.* (*patol.*) afasia.

aphelion [æ'fi:ljǝn], *s.* (*astr.*) afelio.

aphesis ['æfisis], *s.* (*gram.*) aferesi.

aphid ['æfid], **aphis** ['æfis], *pl.* **aphides** ['æfidi:z], *s.* (*entom.*) afide.

aphonia [æ'founjǝ], *s.* (*patol.*) afonia.

aphonic [æ'fɔnik], *ag.* afono.

aphony ['æfǝni], *s.* afonia.

aphorism ['æfǝrizǝm], *s.* aforisma.

aphoristic [,æfǝ'ristik], *ag.* aforistico.

aphoristically [,æfǝ'ristikǝli], *av.* aforisticamente.

aphrodisiac [,æfrou'diziæk], *ag.s.* afrodisiaco.

Aphrodite [,æfrǝ'daiti], *no.pr.f.* (*mit.*) Afrodite.

aphtha ['æfθǝ], *s.* (*patol.*) afta.

apiarian [,eipi'ɛǝriǝn], *ag.* di apicoltura.

apiarist ['eipjǝrist], *s.* apicoltore.

apiary ['eipjǝri], *s.* arnia, apiario, alveare.

apical ['æpikǝl], *ag.* dell'apice; all'apice.

apiculture ['eipikʌltʃǝ*], *s.* apicoltura.

apiece [ǝ'pi:s], *av.* a testa, per uno, ciascuno: *he gave us five pounds —*, ci diede cinque sterline per uno.

Apis ['ɑ:pis], *no.pr.m.* (*mit.*) Api.

apish ['eipiʃ], *ag.* **1.** scimmiesco **2.** fatuo, sciocco.

apishly ['eipiʃli], *av.* **1.** in modo scimmiesco **2.** scioccamente.

aplomb [ǝ'plɔm], *s.* **1.** perpendicolarità **2.** sicurezza, padronanza di sè.

apocalypse [ǝ'pɔkǝlips], *s.* apocalisse.

apocalyptic(al) [ǝ,pɔkǝ'liptik(ǝl)], *ag.* apocalittico.

apocope, apocopy [ǝ'pɔkǝpi], *s.* (*gram.*) apocope.

apocrypha [ǝ'pɔkrifǝ], *s.pl.* libri apocrifi.

apocryphal [ǝ'pɔkrifǝl], *ag.* apocrifo.

apod ['æpɔd], *pl.* **apodes** ['æpǝdi:z], **apoda** ['æpǝdǝ], *s.* (*zool.*) apodo.

apodeictic [,æpou'daiktik], *ag.* apodittico.

apodosis [ǝ'pɔdǝsis], *pl.* **apodoses** [ǝ'pɔdǝsi:z], *s.* (*gram.*) apodosi.

apogean [,æpou'dʒi:ǝn], *ag.* (*astr.*) all'apogeo.

apogee ['æpoudʒi:], *s.* (*astr.*) apogeo (anche *fig.*).

Apollo [ǝ'polou], *no.pr.m.* (*mit.*) Apollo.

Apollyon [ǝ'poljǝn], *no.pr.m.* Satana.

apologetic(al) [ǝ,pɔlǝ'dʒetik(ǝl)], *ag.* apologetico.

apologetically [ǝ,pɔlǝ'dʒetikǝli], *av.* apologeticamente.

apologetics [ǝ,pɔlǝ'dʒetiks], *s.* (*teol.*) apologetica.

apologia [,æpǝ'loudʒiǝ], *s.* apologia.

apologist [ǝ'pɔlǝdʒist], *s.* apologista.

to apologize [ǝ'pɔlǝdʒaiz], *v.i.* scusarsi, chiedere scusa: *he apologized for being late*, si scusò d'essere in ritardo; *to — to s.o. for stgh.*, chiedere scusa a qlcu. per ql.co.

apologue ['æpǝlɔg], *s.* apologo.

apology [ǝ'pɔlǝdʒi], *s.* **1.** scusa, giustificazione: *I offer you my apologies*, vi offro tutte le mie scuse; *to make an — to s.o.*, presentare le proprie scuse a qlcu. **2.** (*fam.*) cattivo esemplare, brutta copia: *it was an — of (o for) a dinner*, aveva solo l'apparenza di un pranzo.

apophthegm ['æpouθem], *s.* (*ret.*) apoftegma.

apoplectic [,æpǝ'plektik], *ag.s.* (*patol.*) apoplettico.

apoplexy ['æpǝpleksi], *s.* (*patol.*) apoplessia.

apostasy [ǝ'pɔstǝsi], *s.* apostasia.

apostate [ə'pɔstit], *ag.s.* apostata.

to apostatize [ə'pɔstətaiz], *v.i.* apostatare.

apostil [ə'pɔstil], *s.* postilla.

apostle [ə'pɔsl], *s.* apostolo.

apostleship [ə'pɔslʃip], **apostolate** [ə'pɔstəlit], *s.* apostolato.

apostolic(al) [,æpəs'tɔlik(əl)], *ag.* apostolico.

apostrophe[1] [ə'pɔstrəfi], *s.* (*ret.*) apostrofe.

apostrophe[2], *s.* (*gram.*) apostrofo.

to apostrophize[1] [ə'pɔstrəfaiz], *v.t.i.* (*ret.*) apostrofare.

to apostrophize[2], *v.t.* (*gram.*) apostrofàre, segnare di apostrofo.

apothecary [ə'pɔθikəri], *s.* farmacista.

apothem ['æpəθim], *s.* (*geom.*) apotema.

apotheosis [ə,pɔθi'ousis], *pl.* **apotheoses** [ə,pɔθi'ousi:z], *s.* apoteosi, deificazione, glorificazione (anche *fig.*).

to apotheosize [ə'pɔθiousaiz], *v.t.* fare l'apoteosi di, deificare, glorificare (anche *fig.*).

to appal [ə'pɔ:l], *pass.p.p.* **appalled** [ə'pɔ:ld], *v.t.i.* spaventare, spaventarsi, sgomentare; sgomentarsi; inorridire: *I was appalled at his words*, mi sgomentai alle sue parole.

Appalachians (the) [,æpə'leitʃjənz], *no.pr.pl.* (*geog.*) Appalachi.

appalling [ə'pɔ:liŋ], *ag.* spaventoso, terribile.

appallingly [ə'pɔ:liŋli], *av.* spaventosamente.

appanage ['æpənidʒ], *s.* appannaggio (anche *fig.*).

apparatus, *pl.* **apparatus** [,æpə'reitəs], **apparatuses** [,æpə'reitəsiz], *s.* 1. (*tec.*) apparecchio, congegno, dispositivo: *radiographic* —, apparecchio radiografico 2. (*anat.*) apparato ☆ — *criticus*, apparato critico (di testo) ‖ *digestive* —, apparato digerente; *lighting* —, apparecchio per illuminazione; *signalling* —, apparecchio di segnalazione; *smoke* —, (*mil.*) apparecchio fumogeno.

apparel [ə'pærəl], *s.* 1. ornamento, addobbo 2. abbigliamento, abiti: *he is simple in his* —, è semplice nel suo modo di vestire 3. (*mar. mil.*) armamento, equipaggiamento 4. (*eccl.*) paramenti.

to apparel, *pass.p.p.* **apparelled** [ə'pærəld], *v.t.* 1. ornare, addobbare 2. vestire 3. (*mar. mil.*) armare, equipaggiare.

apparent [ə'pærənt], *ag.* 1. evidente, visibile, chiaro: *from what I have said it is* — *that...*, da quanto ho detto appare evidente che... 2. (*dir.*) legittimo ☆ *heir* —, erede legittimo.

apparently [ə'pærəntli], *av.* manifestamente, evidentemente.

apparition [,æpə'riʃən], *s.* apparizione; fantasma.

apparitor [ə'pæritɔ:*], *s.* (*dir.*) apparitore, messo, usciere.

appeal [ə'pi:l], *s.* 1. (*dir.*) appello, ricorso ‖ *Court of Appeal*, Corte d'Appello 2. richiamo, attrazione: *the* — *of the sea*, l'attrazione del mare 3. preghiera, supplica, appello: *I make an* — *to your reason*, mi appello alla tua ragione.

to appeal, *v.i.* 1. appellarsi, fare appello, ricorrere: *he appealed to me for help*, chiese il mio aiuto; *to* — *to the law*, appellarsi alla legge ‖ *to* — *to the country*, sciogliere il Parlamento (dopo un voto contrario) 2. interessare, piacere: *pictures* — *to the eye*, le illustrazioni attraggono l'occhio; *your idea appeals to me*, la tua idea mi attrae.

appealable [ə'pi:ləbl], *ag.* appellabile.

appealer [ə'pi:lə*], *s.c.* 1. supplicante, richiedente 2. (*dir.*) appellante.

appealing [ə'pi:liŋ], *ag.* 1. supplichevole 2. attraente.

appealingly [ə'pi:liŋli], *av.* supplichevolmente.

to appear [ə'piə*], *v.i.* 1. apparire, presentarsi, mostrarsi: *she will* — *in "Hamlet"*, ella reciterà nell'«Amleto»; *this book appeared last month*, questo libro apparve, fu pubblicato il mese scorso; *to* — *upon the scene*, mostrarsi sulla scena 2. comparire, presentarsi in giudizio: *he appeared before the Court*, comparve davanti al Tribunale; *we must all* — *before the judge-*

ment seat, tutti dobbiamo comparire davanti al seggio della giustizia divina 3. sembrare, parere: *it appears not*, sembra di no; *it would* —, parrebbe, a quanto pare; *so it appears*, così sembra; *there appears to be a mistake*, sembra che vi sia un errore.

appearance [ə'piərəns], *s.* 1. apparenza, aspetto, sembianza; aria, cera: *of pleasing* —, di aspetto piacevole; *to all appearances*, da quanto si può vedere, a quanto sembra, all'apparenza ‖ *for the sake of appearances*, per salvare le apparenze; *to keep up appearances*, salvare le apparenze 2. apparizione, comparsa: *he put in an* —, fece atto di presenza; *she made her first* — *at the Tivoli*, fece il suo debutto al teatro Tivoli 3. (*dir.*) comparizione 4. (*comm.*) presentazione di un articolo 5. (*arc.*) fantasma; visione.

appearer [ə'piərə*], *s.c.* (*dir.*) comparente.

appearing [ə'piəriŋ], *ag.* (*amer.*) di aspetto: *a very youthful* — *man*, un uomo di aspetto molto giovanile.

appeasable [ə'pi:zəbl], *ag.* placabile; appagabile.

to appease [ə'pi:z], *v.t.* 1. placare, ammansare, pacificare, tranquillare (passione, ira, ecc.); soddisfare, calmare (appetito, fame) 2. (*pol.*) pacificare a prezzo di concessioni.

appeased [ə'pi:zd], *ag.* calmato: *to be* —, calmarsi.

appeasement [ə'pi:zmənt], *s.* 1. pacificazione, acquietamento; appagamento, soddisfazione 2. (*pol.*) pacificazione a prezzo di concessioni, sacrifici.

appeasing [ə'pi:ziŋ], *ag.* calmante, lenitivo.

appellant [ə'pelənt], *ag.s.c.* (*dir.*) appellante.

appellate [ə'pelit], *ag.* (*dir.*) di appello: — *court*, Corte d'Appello.

appellation [,æpe'leiʃən], *s.* appellazione; nome, denominazione.

appellative [ə'pelətiv], *ag.s.* appellativo.

appellatively [ə'pelətivli], *av.* a mo' di appellativo.

appellee [,æpə'li:], *s.c.* (*dir.*) appellato, appellata.

appellor [ə'pelə*], *s.c.* (*dir.*) appellante.

to append [ə'pend], *v.t.* 1. apporre, aggiungere: *to* — *a signature to a document*, apporre una firma a un documento 2. (*letter.*) appendere, sospendere.

appendage [ə'pendidʒ], *s.* 1. aggiunta; complemento; annesso 2. (*anat.*) appendice.

appendant [ə'pendənt], *ag.* 1. accessorio 2. attaccato ‖ *s.* 1. accessorio 2. dipendenza.

appendicitis [ə,pendi'saitis], *s.* (*patol.*) appendicite.

appendix [ə'pendiks], *pl.* **appendixes** [ə'pendiksiz], **appendices** [ə'pendisi:z], *s.* 1. appendice, aggiunta 2. (*anat.*) appendice.

to apperceive [,æpə(:)'si:v], *v.t.* appercepire.

apperception [,æpə(:)'sepʃən], *s.* appercezione.

to appertain [,æpə'tein], *v.i.* 1. appartenere 2. spettare, essere proprio di, riferirsi.

appetence ['æpitəns], **appetency** ['æpitənsi], *s.* 1. desiderio, brama 2. affinità; inclinazione.

appetent ['æpitənt], *ag.* bramoso, desideroso.

appetite ['æpitait], *s.* appetito; *fig.* avidità, brama.

appetitive ['æpitaitiv], *ag.* appetitivo.

to appetize ['æpitaiz], *v.t.* destare appetito in.

appetizer ['æpitaizə*], *s.* aperitivo; cibo che stimola l'appetito.

appetizing ['æpitaiziŋ], *ag.* appetitoso; allettante.

to applaud [ə'plɔ:d], *v.t.i.* applaudire; approvare.

applauder [ə'plɔ:də*], *s.c.* chi applaude; approvatore, approvatrice.

applause [ə'plɔ:z], *s.* applauso; approvazione.

applausive [ə'plɔ:siv], *ag.* plaudente.

applausively [ə'plɔ:zivli], *av.* con plauso.

apple ['æpl], *s.* mela, pomo ‖ — *of discord*, il pomo della discordia ‖ — *of the eye*, *fig.* pupilla degli occhi ‖ — *of Sodom* (*o Dead Sea* —), frutti che si riducono in cenere, azioni, fatti senza risultato ‖ *Adam's* —, il pomo di Adamo ☆ — *-blossom*, la fioritura del melo; — *-cart*, carretto a mano: *to upset s.o.'s* — *-cart*, *fig.* sconvolgere i piani di qlcu.; — *cheeked*, con le guance rosse come una mela; — *core*, torsolo di mela; — *dump-*

ling (o — *-pie* o — *tart*), (*cuc.*) torta di mele; — *-pie bed*, (*fam.*) « sacco »: *to make s.o. an* — *-pie bed*, fare il « sacco » a qlcu.; — *green*, verde mela; — *orchard*, meleto; — *-tree*, melo; — *polisher*, (*sl. amer.*) studente che adula i professori.

appliance [ə'plaiəns], *s.* **1.** applicazione **2.** strumento, congegno, apparecchio, dispositivo: *to use a mechanical* —, servirsi di un apparecchio meccanico **3.** *pl.* accessori; forniture ☆ *office appliances*, forniture per ufficio; *safety* —, dispositivo di sicurezza.

applicability [,æplikə'biliti], *s.* applicabilità.

applicable ['æplikəbl], *ag.* **1.** applicabile **2.** adatto.

applicableness ['æplikəblnis], *s.* applicabilità.

applicant ['æplikənt], *s.c.* **1.** postulante, richiedente **2.** — (*for*), (*dir.*) attore, attrice.

application [,æpli'keiʃən], *s.* **1.** applicazione: — *of ice on the forehead*, applicazione di ghiaccio sulla fronte; — *of a theory*, applicazione di una teoria ‖ *for external* —, (*farm.*) per uso esterno **2.** cura, diligenza; assiduità; *if you show* — *in your studies you will succeed*, se sarai assiduo, diligente nei tuoi studi, riuscirai **3.** domanda, richiesta; ricorso: — *for a job*, domanda di impiego ‖ *samples on* —, campioni su richiesta; *to make an* — *to*, rivolgere un'istanza a ‖ *on* — *to*, rivolgendosi a ‖ *to make* — *for shares*, sottoscrivere delle azioni.

applier [ə'plaiə*], *s.c.* **1.** richiedente **2.** chi applica.

to apply [ə'plai], *v.t.i.* **1.** applicare, applicarsi: *he applied the brake*, egli applicò il freno; *ointment was applied to the wound*, si applicò dell'unguento alla ferita; *this law applies to all cases*, questa legge si applica a tutti i casi **2.** riferirsi: *this does not* — *to you*, questo non si riferisce a voi **3.** dedicare, consacrare: *he applied his mind to the study of Latin*, egli si dedicò allo studio del latino; *to* — *oneself to one's work*, dedicarsi al proprio lavoro **4.** dirigere, dirigersi; ricorrere; rivolgere, rivolgersi; indirizzare, inoltrare (una domanda): — *within*, rivolgersi qui; *to* — *for work, a post*, chiedere lavoro, un impiego; *to* — *to s.o. for sthg.*, rivolgersi a qlcu. per ql.co.

to appoint [ə'pɔint], *v.t.* **1.** fissare, stabilire (giorno, somme, limiti): *on the day appointed*, nel giorno stabilito; *they appointed the day for the meeting*, fissarono il giorno per l'assemblea ‖ *when Heaven appoints, man must obey*, *prov.* l'uomo propone e Dio dispone **2.** nominare: *he was appointed chairman*, fu nominato presidente; *he was appointed to the office of manager*, gli fu dato l'incarico, la nomina di direttore **3.** prescrivere, ordinare; assegnare (un lavoro, ecc.): *each of the boys had his appointed task*, a ciascun ragazzo fu assegnato un compito **4.** (*dir.*) assegnare con decreto.

appointed [ə'pɔintid], *ag.* **1.** fissato, designato: *at the* — *hour*, all'ora fissata **2.** arredato, equipaggiato: *a magnificently* — *house*, una casa arredata magnificamente; *well, badly* —, bene, male equipaggiato.

appointee [əpɔin'tiː], *s.c.* persona designata ad un ufficio, chiamata a eredità, ecc.

appointive [ə'pɔintiv], *ag.* (*amer.*) da designarsi per nomina: — *offices*, cariche ottenute per nomina.

appointment [ə'pɔintmənt], *s.* **1.** appuntamento, convegno: *to make, to keep, to break an* —, fissare, mantenere, mancare a un appuntamento **2.** nomina: *his* — *as governor displeased everyone*, la sua nomina a governatore dispiacque a tutti **3.** carica, impiego: *he obtained a good* — *in a business firm*, ottenne un buon posto in una ditta **4.** prescrizione, decreto, ordine; ordinanza: *by the King's* —, per ordine del re **5.** (*dir.*) assegnazione **6.** *pl.* arredamento; equipaggiamento; arredo.

apport [ə'pɔːt], *s.* apporto (in seduta spiritica).

to apportion [ə'pɔːʃən], *v.t.* distribuire, spartire, assegnare.

apportionment [ə'pɔːʃənmənt], *s.* distribuzione, spartizione, ripartizione.

to **appose**[1] [æ'pouz], *v.t.* apporre: *to* — *one's signature to a document*, apporre la firma a un documento.

to **oppose**[2], *v.t.* (*arc.*) esaminare.

apposite ['æpəzit], *ag.* conveniente, adatto, opportuno; appropriato, giusto: *an* — *remark*, una giusta osservazione.

apposition[1] [,æpə'ziʃən], *s.* aggiunzione, apposizione; (*gram.*) apposizione.

apposition[2], *s.* (*arc.*) pubblica disputa di dotti; esame formale orale (alla St. Paul's School di Londra, ancora in uso per la festa annuale).

appositional [,æpə'ziʃənl], **appositive** [ə'pɔzitiv], *ag.* in, di apposizione.

appraisable [ə'preizəbl], *ag.* valutabile, apprezzabile.

appraisal [ə'preizəl], *s.* stima, valutazione; perizia.

to appraise [ə'preiz], *v.t.* stimare, valutare; apprezzare.

appraisement [ə'preizmənt], *V.* **appraisal**.

appraiser [ə'preizə*], *s.c.* stimatore, stimatrice ‖ *s.* (*dir.*) perito stimatore: —*'s report*, perizia.

appreciable [ə'priːʃəbl], *ag.* **1.** apprezzabile; stimabile, valutabile **2.** sensibile: *an* — *difference*, una sensibile differenza.

appreciably [ə'priːʃəbli], *av.* **1.** apprezzabilmente **2.** sensibilmente.

to appreciate [ə'priːʃieit], *v.t.i.* **1.** apprezzare; stimare, valutare giustamente: *his work has never been appreciated*, il suo lavoro non è mai stato valutato come merita; *I* — *your kindness*, apprezzo la Sua gentilezza **2.** rendersi conto di: *I* — *the fact that...* (o *amer. I* — *that...*), mi rendo conto che **3.** aumentare di valore, migliorarsi: *this land has appreciated greatly since the new railway was built*, questa terra è molto aumentata di valore da quando fu costrutta la nuova ferrovia.

appreciation [ə,priːʃi'eiʃən], *s.* **1.** apprezzamento; stima, valutazione **2.** aumento di valore, rivalutazione.

appreciative [ə'priːʃiətiv], *ag.* **1.** che apprezza **2.** elogiativo.

appreciatively [ə'priːʃiətivli], *av.* con stima.

appreciatory [ə'priːʃiətəri], *V.* **appreciative**.

to apprehend [,æpri'hend], *v.t.* **1.** prendere, arrestare **2.** (*letter.*) cogliere, afferrare, percepire **3.** (*letter.*) temere, aspettare ansiosamente.

apprehensibility ['æpri,hensi'biliti], *s.* **1.** afferrabilità **2.** percettibilità **3.** apprensione.

apprehensible [,æpri'hensəbl], *ag.* **1.** afferrabile **2.** *fig.* comprensibile, percepibile **3.** temibile.

apprehension [,æpri'henʃən], *s.* **1.** presa, arresto **2.** percezione, concezione, comprensione, intelligenza: *to be dull of* —, essere tardo di mente **3.** timore, apprensione: *he was in* — *for his life*, era in apprensione, temeva per la sua vita.

apprehensive [,æpri'hensiv], *ag.* **1.** perspicace, intelligente **2.** apprensivo, timoroso.

apprehensively [,æpri'hensivli], *av.* apprensivamente.

apprehensiveness [,æpri'hensivnis], *s.* **1.** percezione **2.** apprensione, timore.

apprentice [ə'prentis], *s.* apprendista, novizio: *to bind as* —, collocare come apprendista.

to apprentice, *v.t.* metter a mestiere, mettere a far pratica: *he was apprenticed to a tailor*, fu messo a far pratica presso un sarto.

apprenticeship [ə'prentiʃip], *s.* tirocinio, apprendistato: *to serve one's* —, fare il tirocinio.

to apprise [ə'praiz], *v.t.* informare, avvertire, dire, far sapere: *to* — *s.o. of sthg.*, avvertire qlcu. di qlco.; *to be apprised of*, essere consapevole di, sapere.

to apprize [ə'praiz], *v.t.* (*arc.*) stimare, apprezzare.

appro ['æprou], *abbr.* di **approbation 2.**

approach [ə'proutʃ], *s.* **1.** avvicinamento, accostamento: *on* — *of the enemy*, all'avvicinarsi del nemico **2.** *fig.* passo, ravvicinamento, approccio **3.** (*mat.*) approssimazione **4.** (*arc.*) accesso, viale **5.** *pl.* (*comm.*) trattative **6.** *pl.* (*mil.*) approcci; camminamento.

to **approach**, *v.t.i.* **1.** avvicinare, avvicinarsi; accostare (anche *fig.*): *the day is approaching...*, si avvicina il giorno...; *he approached me*, mi avvicinò; *he is easy to* —, è facilmente avvicinabile; *what he says approaches the truth*, ciò che dice ha quasi carattere di verità; *we are approaching Rome*, ci avviciniamo a Roma **2.** (*comm.*) iniziare delle trattative con **3.** (*mil.*) fare degli approcci con.

approachability [ə,proutʃə'biliti], *s.* accessibilità.

approachable [ə'proutʃəbl], *ag.* avvicinabile, accessibile.

approaching [ə'proutʃiŋ], *ag.* prossimo, vicino; approssimativo.

to **approbate** ['æproubeit], (*amer.*) per to approve[1].

approbation [,æprə'beiʃən], *s.* **1.** approvazione, sanzione; giudizio favorevole **2.** (*comm.*) prova: *goods on* — (o *appro*), merce in prova.

approbatory ['æproubeitəri], *ag.* approvativo.

appropriate [ə'proupriit], *ag.* appropriato, adatto.

to **appropriate** [ə'prouprieit], *v.t.* **1.** appropriare, adattare; destinare ad un certo uso; (*amer.*) stanziare (denaro) **2.** appropriarsi, far proprio.

appropriately [ə'proupriitli], *av.* appropriatamente.

appropriateness [ə'proupriitnis], *s.* appropriatezza.

appropriation [ə,proupri'eiʃən], *s.* **1.** applicazione, impiego (di denaro, ecc.); (*amer.*) stanziamento, assegnazione: *to make an* — *for a special purpose*, stanziare una somma per uno scopo determinato **2.** appropriazione.

appropriative [ə'prouprieitiv], *ag.* di appropriazione.

appropriator [ə'prouprieitə*], *s.c.* appropriatore, appropriatrice.

approvable [ə'pru:vəbl], *ag.* approvabile.

approval [ə'pru:vəl], *s.* **1.** approvazione, benestare; sanzione, ratifica: — *of sentence*, (*dir.*) ratifica di una sentenza; *your plans have my* —, i tuoi progetti hanno la mia approvazione, il mio benestare **2.** (*comm.*) prova: *goods on* — (o *on appro*), merce in prova, in esame.

to **approve**[1] [ə'pru:v], *v.t.i.* **1.** approvare; sanzionare, ratificare: *read and approved*, letto e approvato ‖ *to* — *of*, approvare, riconoscere per buono: *he does not* — *of my going to-morrow*, non approva che io vada domani **2.** provare, mostrare: *to* — *one's valour*, provare, dimostrare il proprio valore; *to* — *oneself a man of the world*, mostrarsi uomo di mondo.

to **approve**[2], *v.t.* (*dir.*) valorizzare (terre, proprietà).

approved [ə'pru:vd], *ag.* **1.** approvato; accettato; riconosciuto; stimato: *an* — *company*, (*comm.*) una società (di assicurazione) riconosciuta dallo Stato; *in* — *society*, nella buona società **2.** provato: *an* — *thief*, un ladro matricolato ☆ — *school*, riformatorio.

approvement[1] [ə'pru:vmənt], *s.* (*arc.*) il fornire le prove della colpevolezza di un imputato.

approvement[2], *s.* valorizzazione (di terre, proprietà).

approver[1] [ə'pru:və*], *s.* (*dir.*) **1.** chi approva **2.** correo che si fa testimone d'accusa.

approver[2], *s.* castaldo, amministratore.

approximate [ə'prɔksimit], *ag.* approssimativo.

to **approximate** [ə'prɔksimeit], *v.t.i.* approssimare, approssimarsi; accostare, accostarsi.

approximately [ə'prɔksimitli], *av.* approssimativamente.

approximation [ə,prɔksi'meiʃən], *s.* approssimazione.

approximative [ə'prɔksimətiv], *ag.* approssimativo.

approximatively [ə'prɔksimətivli], *av.* approssimativamente.

appurtenance [ə'pə:tinəns], *s.* **1.** (*dir.*) appartenenza **2.** appendice, aggiunta **3.** accessorio.

appurtenant [ə'pə:tinənt], *ag.* appartenente; pertinente ‖ *s.* (*dir.*) appartenenza.

apricot ['eiprikɔt], *s.* **1.** albicocca; albicocco **2.** color albicocca.

April ['eiprəl], *s.* aprile ☆ — *-fish*, pesce d'aprile; — *-fool*, vittima di un pesce d'aprile: *they made an* — *-fool of him*, gli fecero un pesce d'aprile.

April-Fools' Day ['eiprəl'fu:lzdei], *s.* il primo d'aprile.

apriority [,ei-prai'ɔriti], *s.* l'essere a priori.

apron ['eiprən], *s.* **1.** grembiale: *an* — *full of apples*, una grembialata di mele **2.** (*mec.*) riparo; parafango; piastra **3.** sporto di finestra **4.** (*teat.*) proscenio **5.** nastro trasportatore **6.** (*aer.*) area di stazionamento **7.** (*mar.*) controruota di prua **8.** graticcio (di bacino) **9.** (*artigl.*) bocchetta ☆ — *-string*, laccio di grembiule: *he is always tied to his mother's* — *-strings*, *fig.* è sempre attaccato alle gonnelle della madre.

apropos ['æprəpou], *av.* a proposito.

apse [æps], *s.* (*arch.*) abside.

apsidal ['æpsidl], *ag.* (*arch.*) absidale.

apsis ['æpsis], *pl.* **apsides** [æp'saidi:z], *s.* **1.** (*astr. arch.*) abside **2.** (*eccl.*) reliquario.

apt [æpt], *ag.* **1.** atto, adatto, idoneo; portato; propenso: *I am* — *to believe that...*, sono propenso a credere che... **2.** sveglio, intelligente: *one of my aptest pupils*, uno dei miei migliori allievi **3.** appropriato (di vocabolo); felice (di espressione) **4.** proclive, soggetto: *he is* — *to catch colds*, va soggetto a raffreddori.

apteral ['æptərəl], *ag.* (*arch. entom.*) aptero.

apteran ['æptərən], **apterous** ['æptərəs], *ag.* (*entom.*) aptero, senz'ali.

apteryx ['æptəriks], *pl.* **apteryxes** ['æptəriksiz], *s.* (*ornit.*) atterige, kivi.

aptitude ['æptitju:d], *s.* **1.** idoneità; attitudine **2.** intelligenza, perspicacia **3.** proprietà (di vocabolo).

aptitudinal [,æpti'tju:dinl], *ag.* che ha attitudine.

aptly ['æptli], *av.* a proposito; in modo adatto.

aptness ['æptnis], *V.* aptitude.

Apuleius [,æpju'li:əs], *no.pr.m.* (*st. lett.*) Apuleio.

Apulia [ə'pju:ljə], *no.pr.* (*geog. st.*) Apulia; (*geog.*) Puglia.

Apulian [ə'pju:ljən], *ag.s.c.* pugliese.

apyretic [,æpai'retik], *ag.* apiretico.

apyrexy ['æpireksi], *s.* apiressia.

aqua ['ækwə], *s.* (*chim.*) acqua ☆ — *-fortis*, acquaforte; — *-regia*, acquaregia; — *-vitae*, acquavite.

aqualung ['ækwɑ:lʌŋ], *s.* autorespiratore.

aquamarine [,ækwəmə'ri:n], *s.* (*min.*) acquamarina.

aquaplane ['ækwəplein], *s.* acquaplano.

aquarelle [,ækwə'rel], *s.* acquerello.

aquarium [ə'kwɛəriəm], *s.* acquario.

Aquarius [ə'kwɛəriəs], *no.pr.* (*astr.*) Aquario.

aquatic(al) [ə'kwætik(əl)], *ag.* acquatico.

aquatint ['ækwətint], *s.* acquatinta.

aqueduct ['ækwidʌkt], *s.* acquedotto.

aqueous ['eikwiəs], *ag.* acqueo; acquoso.

aquilegia [,ækwi'li:dʒiə], *s.* (*bot.*) aquilegia.

aquiline ['ækwilain], *ag.* aquilino.

aquosity [ə'kwɔsiti], *s.* acquosità.

Arab ['ærəb], *ag.* arabo ‖ *s.c.* arabo, araba ‖ *s.* — (*horse*), cavallo arabo ☆ *street* —, monello, birichino.

arabesque [,ærə'besk], *ag.s.* arabesco.

Arabia [ə'reibjə], *no.pr.* (*geog.*) Arabia.

Arabian [ə'reibjən], *ag.* arabo ‖ *the* — *bird*, la fenice ‖ *the* — *Gulf*, il golfo arabico ‖ *"The* — *Nights"*, « Le Mille e una Notte » ‖ *s.c.* arabo, araba ‖ *s.* cavallo arabo.

Arabic ['ærəbik], *ag.* arabico ‖ *the* — *numerals*, i numeri arabici ‖ *s.* la lingua araba.

Arabist ['ærəbist], *s.* arabista.

arable ['ærəbl], *ag.* arabile, arativo.

Araby ['ærəbi], *no.pr.* (*geog.*) Arabia.

Arachnida [ə'ræknidə], *s.pl.* aracnidi.

arachnoid [ə'ræknɔid], *s.* (*anat.*) aracnoide.

Aragon ['ærəgən], *no.pr.* (*geog.*) Aragona.

Aragonite [ə'rægənait], *s.* (*min.*) aragonite.

Aramaic [,ærə'meiik], *ag.s.* aramaico.

arapaima [,ærə'paimə], *s.* (*ittiol.*) arapaima.

araucaria [,ærɔ:'kɛəriə], *s.* (*bot.*) araucaria.

arbalest ['ɑ:bələst], *s.* balestra.

arbalester ['ɑ:bələstə*], *s.* balestriere.

arbiter ['a:bitə*], *s.* arbitro ‖ — *of taste,* arbitro dell'eleganza.

arbitrable ['a:bitrəbl], *ag.* arbitrabile.

arbitrage [,a:bi'tria:ʒ], *s.* (*comm.*) arbitraggio.

arbitral ['a:bitrəl], *ag.* arbitrale.

arbitrament [a:'bitrəmənt], *s.* **1.** (*spor.*) arbitraggio **2.** (*dir.*) arbitrato.

arbitrarily ['a:bitrərili], *av.* arbitrariamente.

arbitrariness ['a:bitrərinis], *s.* arbitrarietà.

arbitrary ['a:bitrəri], *ag.* arbitrario.

to **arbitrate** ['a:bitreit], *v.t.i.* arbitrare.

arbitration [,a:bi'treiʃən], *s.* **1.** (*comm.*) arbitraggio **2.** (*dir.*) arbitrato ‖ *by —,* arbitrariamente.

arbitrator ['a:bitreitə*], *s.* arbitro.

arbitress ['a:bitris], *s.* arbitra.

arblast ['a:bləst], *s.* balestra.

arbor[1] ['a:bə*], *s.* (*mec.*) **1.** albero **2.** mandrino **3.** armatura.

arbor[2], *s.* (*bot. chim.*) albero ‖ *Arbor Day,* (*amer.*) Festa dell'Albero ‖ *Arbor Dianae,* (*chim.*) arborescenza che si forma all'immissione di mercurio in soluzione di nitrato d'argento ‖ *Arbor Judae,* (*bot.*) Albero di Giuda ☆ — *vitae,* (*bot.*) tuia.

arboraceous [,a:bə'reiʃəs], *ag.* simile ad albero; boscoso.

arboreal [a:'bo:riəl], *ag.* arboreo.

arboreous [a:'bo:riəs], *ag.* arboreo; boschivo.

arborescence [,a:bə'resns], *s.* (*bot.*) arborescenza.

arborescent [,a:bə'resnt], *ag.* arborescente.

arboretum [,a:bə'ri:təm], *s.* giardino botanico.

arboriculture ['a:bərikʌltʃə*], *s.* arboricoltura.

arboriculturist [,a:bəri'kʌltʃərist], *s.* arboricoltore.

arborization [,a:bərai'zeiʃən], *s.* (*min. chim. anat.*) arborizzazione.

arbour ['a:bə*], *s.* pergolato, pergola; frascato.

arboured ['a:bəd], *ag.* a pergolato; a frascato.

arbutus [a:'bju:təs], *s.* (*bot.*) arbuto, corbezzolo.

arc [a:k], *s.* (*geom. elett.*) arco: *electric, voltaic —,* arco elettrico, voltaico ☆ — *lamp,* lampada ad arco.

arcade [a:'keid], *s.* **1.** galleria (con negozi) **2.** porticato, portico.

arcaded [a:'keidid], *ag.* avente arcate, ad arcate.

Arcadia [a:'keidjə], *no.pr.* **1.** (*geog. st.*) Arcadia **2.** (*fig. poet.*) Arcadia (luogo idillico, pastorale).

Arcadian [a:'keidjən], *ag.* arcadico, pastorale ‖ *s.c.* abitante dell'Arcadia, arcade.

Arcady ['a:kədi], *V.* **Arcadia.**

arcanum [a;'keinəm], *pl.* **arcana** [a:'keinə], *s.* arcano.

arch[1] [a:tʃ], *s.* **1.** arco; arcata; volta: *pointed (o segmented) —,* arco ogivale; *triumphal —,* arco trionfale ‖ *the — of the heavens, fig.* la volta celeste ‖ *Court of Arches,* (*eccl.*) Corte d'Appello ecclesiastica della provincia di Canterbury **2.** (*anat.*) arco, arcata (di sopracciglia, piedi, ecc.): — *of the aorta,* arco aortico ‖ *fallen arches,* piedi piatti ☆ — *-way,* archivolto.

to **arch**[1], *v.t.i.* **1.** congiungere con un arco; fabbricare ad arco **2.** inarcare, inarcarsi; incurvare, incurvarsi: *the cat arches its back,* il gatto incurva la schiena.

arch[2], *ag.* birichino, malizioso, furbetto: *she threw me an — look,* mi lanciò un'occhiata maliziosa.

archaeologic(al) [,a:kiə'lɔdʒik(əl)], *ag.* archeologico.

archaeologically [,a:kiə'lɔdʒikəli], *av.* archeologicamente.

archaeologist [,a:ki'ɔlədʒist], *s.* archeologo.

archaeology [,a:ki'ɔlədʒi], *s.* archeologia.

archaic(al) [a:'keiik(əl)], *ag.* arcaico.

archaism ['a:keiizəm], *s.* arcaismo.

archaistic [,a:kei'istik], *ag.* ad imitazione dell'antico.

to **archaize** ['a:keiaiz], *v.t.i.* rendere simile all'arcaico; imitare l'arcaico.

archangel ['a:k,eindʒəl], *s.* arcangelo.

archbishop ['a:tʃ'biʃəp], *s.* arcivescovo.

archbishopric [a:tʃ'biʃəprik], *s.* arcivescovado.

archdeacon ['a:tʃ'di:kən], *s.* arcidiacono.

archdeaconry [a:tʃ'di:kənri], *s.* arcidiaconato.

archdiocese ['a:tʃ'daiəsis], *s.* arcidiocesi.

archducal ['a:tʃ'dju:kəl], *ag.* arciducale.

archduchess ['a:tʃ'dʌtʃis], *s.* arciduchessa.

archduchy ['a:tʃ'dʌtʃi], *s.* arciducato (territorio).

archduke ['a:tʃ'dju:k], *s.* arciduca.

archdukedom [a:tʃ'dju:kdəm], *s.* arciducato (titolo, dignità di arciduca).

arched [a:tʃt], *ag.* ad arco; arcuato.

arch-enemy ['a:tʃ'enimi], *s.* il grande avversario, Satana.

archer ['a:tʃə*], *s.* arciere ‖ *the Archer,* (*astr.*) il Sagittario.

archery ['a:tʃəri], *s.* tiro all'arco.

archetype ['a:kitaip], *s.* archetipo.

arch-fiend ['a:tʃ'fi:nd], *s.* arcidiavolo, Satana.

Archibald ['a:tʃibəld], *no.pr.m.* Arcibaldo.

archidiaconal [,a:kidai'ækənl], *ag.* arcidiaconale.

Archie ['a:tʃi], *no.pr.m. dim.* di **Archibald** ‖ **archie,** *s.* (*sl.*) cannone antiaereo.

archiepiscopal [,a:kii'piskəpəl], *ag.* arcivescovile.

archil ['a:tʃil], *s.* (*bot.*) oricello; (*chim.*) orcina.

Archilochus [a:'kiləkəs], *no.pr.m.* (*st. lett.*) Archiloco

archimandrite [,a:ki'mændrait], *s.* archimandrita.

Archimedean [,a:ki'mi:djən], *ag.* d'Archimede ☆ — *screw,* (*mec.*) vite di Archimede, coclea.

Archimedes [,a:ki'mi:di:z], *no.pr.m.* (*st.*) Archimede.

arching ['a:tʃiŋ], *s.* arco (di volta); arcate (di edificio).

archipelago [,a:ki'peligou], *pl.* **archipelagoes** [,a:ki'peligouz], *s.* arcipelago ‖ *the Archipelago,* l'Arcipelago greco; l'Egeo.

architect ['a:kitekt], *s.* **1.** architetto **2.** *fig.* artefice, autore: *every man is the — of his own fortune,* ogni uomo è l'artefice della propria fortuna.

architectonic(al) [,a:kitek'tɔnikəl], *ag.* architettonico.

architectural [,a:ki'tektʃərəl], *ag.* architettonico.

architecture ['a:kitektʃə*], *s.* architettura.

architrave ['a:kitreiv], *s.* architrave.

archive ['a:kaiv], *s. gener. pl.* **1.** archivio **2.** documenti di archivio.

archivist ['a:kivist], *s.c.* archivista.

archivolt ['a:kivoult], *s.* (*arch.*) archivolto.

archly ['a:tʃli], *av.* maliziosamente.

archness ['a:tʃnis], *s.* malizia.

archon ['a:kən], *s.* (*st. greca*) arconte.

archpriest ['a:tʃ'pri:st], *s.* arciprete.

arch-rogue ['a:tʃ'roug], *s.* furfante matricolato.

archstone ['a:tʃ'stoun], *s.* (*arch.*) peduccio di volta, d'arco; (*amer.*) chiave di volta, d'arco; spigolo.

archwise ['a:tʃwaiz], *av.* ad arco, a volta.

Arcite ['a:sait], *no.pr.f.* (*lett.*) Arcita.

Arctic ['a:ktik], *ag.* artico ‖ *the — Circle,* il Circolo Polare Artico ‖ *the — Ocean,* l'Oceano Artico ‖ *no.pr.* (*geog.*) l'Artico.

arctics ['a:ktiks], *s.pl.* (*amer.*) soprascarpe da neve.

Arcturus [a:k'tjuərəs], *no.pr.* (*astr.*) Arturo.

arcuate ['a:kjuit], *ag.* arcuato.

ardency ['a:dənsi], *s.* ardore.

Ardennes (the) [a:'den], *no.pr.pl.* (*geog.*) Ardenne.

ardent ['a:dənt], *ag.* ardente ☆ — *spirits,* liquori.

ardently ['a:dəntli], *av.* ardentemente.

ardour ['a:də*], *s.* ardore (anche *fig.*).

arduous ['a:djuəs], *ag.* **1.** arduo, scabroso **2.** strenuo; energico.

arduously ['a:djuəsli], *av.* **1.** arduamente, scabrosamente **2.** strenuamente; energicamente.

arduousness ['a:djuəsnis], *s.* arduità, difficoltà.

are[1] [a:* (*forma forte*), ɑ*, ə* (*forme deboli*)], 2ª persona sing., 1ª, 2ª, 3ª persona pl. indic. pres. di to **be.**

are[2] [a:*], *s.* (*agr.*) ara (misura di superficie = 119.9 sq.yd.).

area ['ɛəriə], *s.* **1.** area, superficie **2.** corte, cortile, cortiletto di servizio **3.** zona: *fortified —,* (*mil.*) area fortificata; *mined —,* (*mil.*) zona minata **4.** *fig.* apertura mentale ☆ — *-bell,* campanello di servizio ‖ *landing —,* (*aer.*) zona d'atterraggio; *postal —,* distretto postale.

areca ['ærikə], *s.* (*bot.*) areca.

to arefy ['ærifai], *v.t.i.* asciugare, asciugarsi.

arena [ə'ri:nə], *s.* arena.

arenaceous ['ærineiʃəs], **arenose** [,æri'nous], *ag.* arenoso, arenaceo, sabbioso.

aren't [a:nt], *contr.* di are not.

areometer [,æri'ɔmitə*], *s.* (*fis.*) aerometro.

Areopagite [,æri'ɔpəgait], *s.* (*st. greca*) areopagita.

areopagitic [,æriopə'dʒitik], *ag.* areopagitico.

Areopagus [,æri'ɔpəgəs], *no.pr.* (*geog. st.*) Areopago ‖ *s.* areopago, alto consesso giudicante.

arête [æ'reit], *s.* cresta (di monte).

argala ['a:gələ], *s.* (*ornit.*) argala, marabù.

argali ['a:gəli], *s.* (*zool.*) argali.

argent ['a:dʒənt], *ag.* argenteo, risplendente ‖ *s.* (*arc.*) **1.** argento **2.** denaro, moneta d'argento.

argental [a:'dʒentl], *ag.* d'argento.

argentation [,a:dʒən'teiʃən], *s.* argentatura.

argentiferous [,a:dʒən'tifərəs], *ag.* argentifero.

Argentina [,a:dʒən'ti:nə], *no.pr.* (*geog.*) Argentina.

argentine[1] ['a:dʒəntain], *ag.* argentino, argenteo ‖ *s.* (*ittiol. entom.*) argentina.

Argentine[2], *ag.* argentino ‖ *s.c.* argentino, argentina.

argil ['a:dʒil], *s.* argilla.

argillaceous [,a:dʒi'leiʃəs], *ag.* argilloso, argillaceo.

to argle-bargle ['a:gl'ba:gl], *v.i.* (*scherz.*) argomentare, disputare, discutere.

argon ['a:gɔn], *s.* (*chim.*) argo.

Argonaut ['a:gənɔ:t], *s.* **1.** (*mit.*) argonauta **2.** (*amer.*) cercatore di oro; avventuriero ‖ **argonaut**, *s.* (*zool.*) nautilo.

argosy ['a:gəsi], *s.* (*arc.*) nave mercantile.

argot ['a:gou], *s.* gergo (specialmente dei bassifondi).

arguable ['a:gjuəbl], *ag.* discutibile.

to argue ['a:gju:], *v.t.i.* **1.** argomentare, discutere: *don't —!*, non discutere (tanto)! **2.** provare, dimostrare, denotare: *his action argues courage*, la sua azione dimostra coraggio **3.** ragionare: *he argued soundly*, ragionò assennatamente ‖ *to — s.o. out of, into doing sthg.*, dissuadere, persuadere a forza di ragionamenti qlcu. dal, a fare ql.co.

to arguify ['a:gjufai], *v.i.* (*dial.*) argomentare, sofisticare, cavillare.

argument ['a:gjumənt], *s.* **1.** discussione, disputa, controversia: *for —'s sake*, per il gusto di discutere; *it is beyond —*, è indiscutibile **2.** argomento: *— against, for*, argomento contro, a favore di **3.** sommario.

argumental [,a:gju'mentl], *ag.* argomentativo.

argumentation [,a:gjumen'teiʃən], *s.* argomentazione, discussione.

argumentative [,a:gju'mentətiv], *ag.* polemico.

Argus ['a:gəs], *no.pr.m.* (*mit.*) Argo.

argute [a:'gju:t], *ag.* **1.** acuto, perspicace **2.** acuto (di suono).

aria ['a:riə], *s.* (*mus.*) aria.

Ariadne [,æri'ædni], *no.pr.f.* (*mit.*) Arianna.

Arian ['ɛəriən], *ag.s.* (*st. relig.*) ariano.

Arianism ['ɛəriənizəm], *s.* (*st. relig.*) arianesimo.

to Arianize ['ɛəriənaiz], *v.t.i.* (*st. relig.*) diventare ariano; convertire all'arianesimo.

arid ['ærid], *ag.* arido (anche *fig.*).

aridity [æ'riditi], **aridness** ['æridnis], *s.* aridità.

Ariel ['ɛəriəl], *no.pr.m.* (*lett.*) Ariele.

Aries ['ɛəri:z], *no.pr.* (*astr.*) Ariete.

aright [ə'rait], *av.* bene, giustamente: *if I heard —*, se ho sentito bene.

Arion [ə'raiən], *no.pr.m.* (*mit.*) Arione.

to arise [ə'raiz], *pass.* **arose** [ə'rouz], *p.p.* **arisen** [ə'rizn], *v.i.* **1.** alzarsi, levarsi; sorgere: *along the road a new building arose*, lungo la strada sorse un nuovo palazzo; *the sun arose behind the mountains*, il sole si levò dietro le montagne ‖ *to arise from the dead*, (*arc.*) risuscitare **2.** *fig.* nascere; presentarsi; venire alla ribalta: *good opportunities do not — every day*, le buone

occasioni non si presentano ogni giorno; *new difficulties arose*, nacquero nuove difficoltà; *new thoughts arose in his mind*, nuovi pensieri gli si presentarono alla mente **3.** provenire, derivare: *his success arose from his will and intelligence*, il suo successo derivò dalla sua volontà e intelligenza ‖ *thence it arises that...*, da ciò risulta che....

arista [ə'ristə], *s.* (*bot.*) arista.

Aristarchus [,æris'ta:kəs], *no.pr.m.* (*st. lett.*) Aristarco.

aristate [ə'risteit], *ag.* (*bot.*) aristato.

Aristides [,æris'taidi:z], *no.pr.m.* (*st.*) Aristide.

aristocracy [,æris'tɔkrəsi], *s.* aristocrazia.

aristocrat ['æristəkræt], *s.* aristocratico.

aristocratic [,æristə'krætik], *ag.* aristocratico.

aristocratically [,æristə'krætikəli], *av.* aristocraticamente.

Aristophanes [,æris'tɔfəni:z], *no.pr.m.* (*st. lett.*) Aristofane.

Aristophanic [,æristou'fænik], *ag.* (*lett.*) aristofanesco.

Aristotelean, Aristotelian [,æristo'ti:ljən], *ag.s.* aristotelico.

Aristotelianism [,æristo'ti:ljənizəm], *s.* aristotelismo.

Aristotelic [,æristo'telik], *ag.* aristotelico.

Aristotle ['æristotl], *no.pr.m.* (*st. fil.*) Aristotele.

arithmetic [ə'riθmətik], *s.* aritmetica.

arithmetic(al) [,æriθ'metik(əl)], *ag.* aritmetico.

arithmetically [,æriθ'metikəli], *av.* aritmeticamente.

arithmetician [ə,riθmə'tiʃən], *s.* aritmetico.

arithmometer [,æriθ'mɔmitə*], *s.* macchina calcolatrice.

Arius ['ɛəriəs], *no.pr.m.* (*st. relig.*) Ario.

ark [a:k], *s.* arca: *the — of the Lord*, l'arca Santa, l'arca del Signore; *Noah's —*, l'arca di Noè.

arm[1] [a:m], *s.* braccio (anche *fig.*): *— of a building*, braccio di un edificio; *the — of the law*, il braccio della legge, polizia; *— of a lever, of a balance*, braccio di una leva, di una bilancia; *— of the sea*, braccio di mare; *I saw her on her husband's —*, la vidi al braccio di suo marito; *to fold one's arms*, incrociare le braccia; *to give one's — to s.o.*, dare il braccio a qlcu. ‖ *the secular —*, il braccio secolare ‖ *to keep s.o. at —'s length*, tenere qlcu. a distanza‖ *to receive s.o. with open arms*, ricevere qlcu. a braccia aperte.

arm[2], *s.* **1.** *gener. pl.* arma: *comrade in arms*, compagno d'armi; *in arms*, armato; *stand of arms*, (*arc.*) armamento di un singolo soldato; *under arms*, in assetto di guerra; *to bear arms*, essere sotto le armi ‖ *to lay down arms*, deporre le armi, cessare le ostilità; *to take up arms*, prendere le armi ‖ *to be up in arms against s.o.*, essere in rivolta contro qlcu. **2.** arma, specialità dell'esercito: *the — of artillery*, l'arma di artiglieria **3.** (*arald.*) arma: *coat of arms*, scudo araldico, stemma ☆ *the air- —* (o *the fourth —*), l'aviazione; *fire-arms*, armi da fuoco; *man-at-arms*, uomo d'arme; *side-arms*, armi bianche.

to arm[2], *v.t.i.* armare, armarsi: *armed neutrality*, neutralità armata; *armed to the teeth*, armato fino ai denti; *armed with full powers*, armato di pieni poteri; *he was armed with a rifle*, era armato di moschetto.

armada [a:'ma:də], *s.* armata (specialmente navale) ‖ *the Invincible Armada*, (*st.*) l'Invincibile Armata ☆ *air —*, flotta aerea.

armadillo [,a:mə'dilou], *s.* (*zool.*) armadillo.

armament ['a:məmənt], *s.* (*mar. mil.*) armamento.

armature ['a:mətjuə*], *s.* armatura.

armchair ['a:m'tʃɛə*], *s.* poltrona.

Armenia [a:'mi:njə], *no.pr.* (*geog.*) Armenia.

Armenian [a:'mi:njən], *ag.* armeno ‖ *s.c.* armeno, armena ‖ *s.* lingua armena.

armful ['a:mful], *s.* bracciata.

armhole ['a:mhoul], *s.* giro della manica.

Armida [a:'mi:də], *no.pr.f.* (*lett.*) Armida.

armiger ['a:midʒə*], *s.* armigero.

armillary ['ɑ:miləri], *ag.* armillare.

arm-in-arm ['ɑ:min'ɑ:m], *av.* a braccetto.

Arminian [ɑ:'minion], *ag.s.* (*st. relig.*) arminiano.

armistice ['ɑ:mistis], *s.* armistizio.

armless[1] ['ɑ:mlis], *ag.* senza braccia.

armless[2], *ag.* inerme.

armlet ['ɑ:mlit], *s.* **1.** bracciale **2.** piccolo braccio di mare.

armorer, (*amer.*) per **armourer**.

armorial [ɑ:'mɔ:riəl], *ag.* araldico: *with — bearings*, portante lo stemma, blasonato ‖ *s.* libro di araldica.

armorist ['ɑ:mərist], *s.* studioso di araldica.

armory ['ɑ:məri], *s.* araldica.

armour ['ɑ:mə*], *s.* **1.** armatura, corazza **2.** blindatura **3.** scafandro **4.** (*zool. bot.*) protezione, corazza ☆ *— bearer*, scudiero; — *-clad*, blindato, corazzato; — *-plating*, piastre di protezione.

to **armour**, *v.t.* rivestire d'armatura, corazzare, blindare ☆ *armoured-car*, autoblindo; *armoured -cruiser*, incrociatore corazzato.

armourer ['ɑ:mərə*], *s.* **1.** armaiolo **2.** (*mil.*) armiere.

armoury ['ɑ:məri], *s.* **1.** arsenale; (*amer.*) fabbrica d'armi **2.** armeria **3.** sala d'armi.

armpit ['ɑ:mpit], *s.* ascella.

army ['ɑ:mi], *s.* **1.** esercito: *to assemble* (o *to gather) an —*, raccogliere un esercito; *to be in the —*, prestare servizio militare; *to go into* (o *to join) the —*, entrare nell'esercito ‖ *Army Club*, circolo militare ‖ *Salvation Army*, Esercito della Salvezza **2.** grande moltitudine ☆ *— -corps*, corpo d'armata; *— -list*, annuario militare; *— men*, soldati, militari; *— pensioner*, militare in pensione ‖ *standing —* (o *regular —*), esercito permanente.

arnica ['ɑ:nikə], *s.* (*bot.*) arnica.

Arnold ['ɑ:nld], *no.pr.m.* Arnoldo, Arnaldo.

aroint [ə'rɔint], *inter.* (*arc.*) via!.

aroma [ə'roumə], *s.* aroma.

aromatic(al) [,ærou'mætik(əl)], *ag.* aromatico; fragrante.

to **aromatize** [ə'roumətaiz], *v.t.* aromatizzare; profumare.

arose [ə'rouz], *pass.* di to **arise**.

around [ə'raund], *av.* **1.** intorno, all'intorno: *all —*, tutt'intorno, da tutte le parti **2.** (*amer.* per *round, about*) qua e là, in giro, a caso: *to wander —*, girovagare ‖ *he is now beginning to get — again*, è di nuovo in piedi (sta meglio) ‖ *prep.* **1.** attorno a, intorno a: *with her arms — his neck*, con le braccia attorno al collo di lui; *he walked — the garden*, passeggiò per il giardino **2.** (*amer.*) circa: *— 5,000 people were present*, circa 5000 persone erano presenti.

to **arouse** [ə'rauz], *v.t.* **1.** destare, svegliare; ridestare, risvegliare **2.** eccitare, stimolare.

aroynt [ə'rɔint], *inter.* (*arc.*) via!: *— thee!*, vattene!.

arquebus ['ɑ:kwibəs], *s.* archibugio.

arquebusier [,ɑ:kwibə'siə*], *s.* archibugiere.

arrack ['ærək], *s.* «arac» (liquore orientale).

to **arraign** [ə'rein], *v.t.* **1.** accusare; chiamare in giudizio **2.** biasimare; attaccare (un'opinione).

arraignment [ə'reinmənt], *s.* **1.** accusa **2.** biasimo.

to **arrange** [ə'reindʒ], *v.t.i.* **1.** accomodare, aggiustare, ordinare, assettare: *to — one's affairs*, ordinare i propri affari **2.** preparare, combinare; predisporre; stabilire; organizzare: *I have arranged for him to come*, ho combinato che egli venga; *we shall — to go*, combineremo di andare; *to — a marriage*, combinare un matrimonio; *to — a meeting*, predisporre un incontro; *to — a treaty*, preparare un trattato **3.** prendere accordi; accordarsi, venire a un accordo **4.** (*mus.*) ridurre; arrangiare **5.** comporre (una lite).

arrangement [ə'reindʒmənt], *s.* **1.** accomodamento, ordinamento, assestamento; aggiustamento **2.** combinazione; preparazione **3.** (*mus.*) arrangiamento **4.** accomodamento, intesa: *to make an — with s.o.*, intendersi con qlcu. **5.** *pl.* preparativi, disposizioni: *arran-*

gements have been made, si sono fatti preparativi; *to make arrangements to do sthg.*, fare i preparativi per fare ql.co. **6.** (*comm.*) concordato, compromesso **7.**, dispositivo, congegno.

arranger [ə'reindʒə*], *s.* **1.** chi accom da, modifica **2.** (*mus.*) arrangiatore.

arrant ['ærənt], *ag.* famigerato, di cattiva nomea: *— knave*, briccone matricolato.

arras ['ærəs], *s.* arazzo.

array [ə'rei], *s.* **1.** apparato, mostra **2.** (*poet.*) abbigliamento; ornamento **3.** (*dir.*) lista dei giurati **4.** (*mil.*) ordine, spiegamento; schiera ☆ *battle —*, ordine di battaglia.

to **array**, *v.t.* **1.** ornare; abbigliare **2.** (*mil.*) schierare spiegare **3.** (*dir.*) far l'appello di (una giuria).

arrear [ə'riə*], *s.* **1.** *gener. pl.* arretrato, arretrati ‖ *in —*, in arretrato **2.** (*mil.*) retroguardia.

arrearage [ə'riəridʒ], *s.* **1.** ritardo (nel lavoro, ecc.) **2.** *pl.* debiti.

arrect [ə'rekt], *ag.* **1.** dritto, rizzato (di orecchio) **2.** *fig.* in guardia, vigilante.

arrest [ə'rest], *s.* **1.** arresto: *under —*, in arresto; (*mil.*) agli arresti **2.** fermata, sosta **3.** (*dir.*) sospensione (di giudizio).

to **arrest**, *v.t.* **1.** arrestare **2.** fermare, fissare (l'attenzione) **3.** (*dir.*) sospendere (un giudizio).

arrestation [,æres'teiʃən], *s.* arresto; impedimento.

arrester [ə'restə*], *s.* **1.** chi arresta **2.** (*rad.*) scaricatore a terra.

arrestive [ə'restiv], *ag.* che tende a fermare.

arrestment [ə'restmənt], *s.* arresto.

arrhythmy ['æriθmi], *s.* (*patol.*) aritmia.

to **arride** [ə'raid], *v.t.* (*arc.*) arridere a; piacere a.

'Arriet ['æriət], *no.pr.f.* (*pop.*) per **Harriet** (compagna di **'Arry**).

arris ['æris], *s.* spigolo.

arrival [ə'raivəl], *s.* arrivo, venuta.

to **arrive** [ə'raiv], *v.i.* arrivare, giungere: *he will — to-day at ten*, arriverà oggi alle dieci; *to — at*, arrivare a, raggiungere: *he arrived at Bath*, arrivò a Bath; *to — in*, arrivare in, a (paese, città grande): *he arrived in England, in Rome*, arrivò in Inghilterra, a Roma ‖ *to — at a conclusion, a decision*, giungere ad una conclusione, una decisione; *to — at the age of*, raggiungere l'età di.

arrogance ['ærəgəns], **arrogancy** ['ærəgənsi], *s.* arroganza.

arrogant ['ærəgənt], *ag.* arrogante.

arrogantly ['ærəgəntli], *av.* arrogantemente.

to **arrogate** ['ærougeit], *v.t.* **1.** arrogare: *to — sthg. to oneself*, arrogarsi ql.co. **2.** attribuire ingiustamente.

arrogation [,ærou'geiʃən], *s.* pretesa (arrogante); usurpazione.

arrow ['ærou], *s.* freccia, strale, dardo ☆ *— -head*, punta di freccia; (*bot.*) sagittaria; *— -headed*, cuneiforme (lettera, ecc.); *— -root*, fecola dell'arundinacea ‖ *broad — (head)*, punta larga di freccia (usata come contrassegno di oggetti, ecc. di proprietà dello Stato).

arrowy ['æroui], *ag.* di freccia; *fig.* acuto; rapido.

'Arry ['æri], *no.pr.m.* (*pop.*) per **Harry** («Arry», giovane di Londra, venditore ambulante, non pronuncia l'h dove dovrebbe, dice *'am and heggs* per *ham and eggs*).

arsenal ['ɑ:sinl], *s.* arsenale.

arsenate ['ɑ:sinit], **arseniate** [ɑ:'sinieit], *s.* (*chim.*) arseniato.

arsenic ['ɑ:snik], *s.* (*chim.*) arsenico.

arsenical [ɑ:'senikəl], *ag.* (*chim.*) arsenicale.

arsenious [ɑ:'si:njəs], *ag.* (*chim.*) arsenioso.

Arsenius [ɑ:'si:njəs], *no.pr.m.* Arsenio.

arsis ['ɑ:sis], *pl.* **arses** [ɑ:'si:z], *s.* (*poes.*) arsi.

arson ['ɑ:sn], *s.* incendio doloso: *to commit —*, provocare dolosamente un incendio.

art[1] [ɑ:t], *s.* **1.** arte ‖ *the fine arts*, le belle arti; *the liberal arts*, le arti liberali; *the mechanical* (o *useful*) *arts*, le arti industriali **2.** *pl.* belle lettere ‖ *Bachelor,*

Master of Arts, diplomato, laureato in lettere; *Faculty of Arts,* facoltà di lettere ☆ — *-school,* scuola di pittura (ed altre arti figurative) ‖ *black —,* magia.

art[2] [α:t (*forma forte*), ət (*forma debole*)], 2ª persona sing. pres. (*arc.*) di to **be.**

Artaxerxes [ˌα:təgˈzə:ksi:z], *no.pr.m.* (*st.*) Artaserse.

artefact [ˈα:tifækt], *s.* manufatto.

Artemis [ˈα:timis], *no.pr.f.* (*mit.*) Artemide.

arterial [α:ˈtiəriəl], *s.* arterioso, arteriale ☆ — *road,* grande via di comunicazione.

arterialization [α:ˌtiəriəlaiˈzeiʃən], *s.* (*med.*) il trasformarsi del sangue venoso in arterioso.

to **arterialize** [α:ˈtiəriəlaiz], *v.t.* (*med.*) trasformare in arterioso (il sangue venoso).

arteriosclerosis [α:ˈtiəriou-skliəˈrousis], *s.* (*patol.*) arteriosclerosi.

arteriotomy [α:ˌtiəriˈotəmi], *s.* (*chir.*) arteriotomia.

artery [ˈα:təri], *s.* arteria.

artesian [α:ˈti:zjən], *ag.* artesiano.

artful [ˈα:tful], *ag.* **1.** destro, abile; astuto **2.** artificioso **3.** (*arc.*) fatto ad arte.

artfully [ˈα:tfuli], *av.* astutamente; destramente.

artfulness [ˈα:tfulnis], *s.* astuzia, furberia; destrezza.

arthritic [α:ˈθritik], *ag.* artritico.

arthritis [α:ˈθraitis], *s.* artrite.

Arthur [ˈα:θə*], *no.pr.m.* Arturo; (*lett.*) Artù.

artichoke [ˈα:titʃouk], *s.* carciofo ☆ *Jerusalem —,* topinamburo.

article [ˈα:tikl], *s.* **1.** articolo; oggetto **2.** articolo (di giornale) **3.** (*gram.*) articolo: *definite, indefinite —,* articolo definito, indefinito **4.** clausola, condizione **5.** capoverso **6.** *gener. pl.* (*dir. comm.*) contratto; convenzioni, regolamenti; statuto: *articles of association,* statuto di società anonima; *ship's articles,* contratto di arruolamento su nave ☆ *leading —,* articolo di fondo.

to **article,** *v.t.* **1.** esporre per particolari **2.** obbligare con clausole **3.** accusare **4.** collocare come apprendista: *to — s.o. to an architect,* collocare qlcu. come apprendista presso un architetto ☆ *articled clerk,* apprendista.

articular [α:ˈtikjulə*], *ag.* articolare.

articulate [α:ˈtikjulit], *ag.* **1.** articolato **2.** distinto, chiaro ‖ *s.* animale articolato.

to **articulate** [α:ˈtikjuleit], *v.t.i.* **1.** articolare, articolarsi **2.** pronunciare, parlare distintamente.

articulately [α:ˈtikjulitli], *av.* articolatamente.

articulateness [α:ˈtikjulitnis], *s.* articolazione.

articulation [α:ˌtikjuˈleiʃən], *s.* **1.** (*anat.*) articolazione **2.** pronuncia distinta.

artifact [ˈα:tifækt], *s.* prodotto lavorato.

artifice [ˈα:tifis], *s.* **1.** artificio **2.** abilità, destrezza.

artificer [α:ˈtifisə*], *s.* **1.** fabbricante, artefice (anche *fig.*) **2.** inventore **3.** (*mil.*) artificiere.

artificial [ˌα:tiˈfiʃəl], *ag.* artificiale; finto; fittizio.

artificiality [ˌα:tifiʃiˈæliti], *s.* cosa artificiale.

to **artificialize** [ˌα:tiˈfiʃəlaiz], *v.t.* rendere artificiale, rendere artificioso, artefare.

artificially [ˌα:tiˈfiʃəli], *av.* artificialmente.

artificialness [ˌα:tiˈfiʃəlnis], *V.* **artificiality.**

artillerist [α:ˈtilərist], *s.* artigliere.

artillery [α:ˈtiləri], *s.* artiglieria ☆ *coastal —,* artiglieria costiera; *field —,* artiglieria da campagna; *fortress —,* artiglieria da fortezza; *heavy —,* artiglieria pesante; *horse —,* artiglieria a cavallo; *naval —,* artiglieria navale; *siege —,* artiglieria da assedio.

artilleryman, *pl.* **artillerymen** [α:ˈtiləримən], *s.* artigliere.

artiodactyl(e) [ˌα:tiouˈdæktil], *ag.s.* (*zool.*) artiodattilo.

artisan [ˌα:tiˈzæn], *s.* artigiano.

artist [ˈα:tist], *s.c.* artista (specialmente pittore, pittrice).

artiste [α:ˈti:st], *s.* (*teat.*) artista (donna).

artistic(al) [α:ˈtistik(əl)], *ag.* artistico.

artistically [α:ˈtistikəli], *av.* artisticamente.

artistry [ˈα:tistri], *s.* arte, abilità artistica.

artless [ˈα:tlis], *ag.* ingenuo, semplice.

artlessly [ˈα:tlisli], *av.* ingenuamente.

artlessness [ˈα:tlisnis], *s.* ingenuità.

arty [ˈα:ti], *ag.* (*fam.*) che ha pretese artistiche ☆ — *-crafty,* di pretese artistiche, ma inutile.

arum [ˈɛərəm], *s.* (*bot.*) aro.

Aryan [ˈɛəriən], *ag.* ariano (di stirpe indo-europea) ‖ *s.c.* ariano, ariana (di stirpe indo-europea) ‖ *s.* lingua ariana (indo-europea).

as[1] [æz (*forma forte*), əz (*forma debole*)], *av.* **1.** (*in frasi comparative*) così, come; tanto, quanto: *he is — young — I (am),* è giovane quanto me; *is he not — rich — you are?,* non è ricco quanto te?; *she came — soon — she could,* è venuta appena ha potuto; *you are — tall — he is,* sei alto come lui ‖ *— a man lives so shall he die,* come si vive così si muore ‖ *he is — deaf — a post,* è sordo come una campana **2.** (*con inf.*) da: *we ran so — to catch the train,* corremmo in modo da prendere il treno; *will you be so kind — to tell me...?,* vuoi essere così gentile da dirmi...? ‖ *cong.* **1.** come; nello stesso modo che; secondo, conforme a: *— above,* come sopra; *— before,* come prima; *— compared with,* in confronto a; *— an honest man,* da uomo onesto; *— a rule,* di regola; *— usual,* come al solito; *according —,* secondo; *— the case may be,* come sarà il caso; *— I was saying,* come dicevo; *— it is,* come stanno le cose; *— it were,* per così dire; *do — I do,* fai come me; *they rose — one man,* si alzarono come un sol uomo **2.** siccome, poichè, giacchè: *— I was tired, I stayed at home,* poichè ero stanco, restai a casa **3.** quando; mentre: *— he came, we were out,* quando venne, eravamo fuori; *I met him — I was coming home,* l'incontrai mentre venivo a casa **4.** quantunque, benchè: *poor — he is, he is happy,* benchè povero è felice ‖ *pron. rel.* che: *he will sell you the same goods — he sold me,* ti venderà la stessa merce che vendette a me; *I can send you such goods — will satisfy you,* posso inviarvi tali merci che vi soddisferanno; *she was a foreigner, — they perceived from her aspect,* ella era straniera, il che compresero dal suo aspetto ‖ (**Fraseologia**): *— far —,* fino a (distanza); per quanto: *— far — I am concerned,* per quanto mi riguarda ‖ *— for* (o *— regards* o *— to*), quanto a, per quanto riguarda: *— for that man,* quanto a quell'uomo ‖ *— from,* da: *the dividend is payable — from the 31st of May,* il dividendo è pagabile dal 31 maggio ‖ *— good —,* quasi: *he has — good — accepted,* ha quasi accettato ‖ *— if* (o *— though*), come se ‖ *— long —,* finchè; purchè; *so long —,* purchè ‖ *— much —,* *— many —,* tanto quanto, tanti quanti ‖ *— per,* (*comm.*) come da ‖ *— recently —,* non più tardi di: *I saw him — recently — last week,* lo vidi non più tardi della settimana scorsa ‖ *— soon —,* immediatamente; non appena: *— soon — possible,* al più presto possibile ‖ *— well,* pure, anche: *you may come — well,* voi pure potete venire ‖ *— well —,* come pure.

as[2] [æs], *s.* (*st. romana*) asse (unità di peso = 0.722 lb.).

asafoetida [ˌæsəˈfetidə], *s.* (*bot.*) assafetida.

asbestine [æzˈbestin], *ag.* incombustibile.

asbestos [æzˈbestos], *s.* (*min.*) asbesto, amianto.

Ascanius [æsˈkeinjəs], *no.pr.m.* (*lett.*) Ascanio.

to **ascend** [əˈsend], *v.t.i.* **1.** salire, ascendere, innalzarsi: *he has ascended to heaven,* è salito in cielo; *the king ascended the throne ten years ago,* il re salì al trono dieci anni fa **2.** risalire.

ascendable [əˈsendəbl], *ag.* ascendibile.

ascendancy [əˈsendənsi], *s.* ascendente, influenza.

ascendant [əˈsendənt], *ag.* ascendente (anche *astr.*); *fig.* superiore, dominante ‖ *s.* **1.** ascendente (anche *astr.*) **2.** antenato.

ascendency [əˈsendənsi], *s.* ascendente, influenza.

ascendent, *V.* **ascendant.**

ascending [əˈsendiŋ], *ag.* (*astr. mus.*) ascendente.

ascension [ə'sɛnʃən], *s.* ascensione ‖ *Ascension-day*, (*eccl.*) giorno dell'Ascensione.

ascensional [ə'sɛnʃənl], *ag.* ascensionale.

ascent [ə'sent], *s.* **1.** ascensione, ascesa **2.** salita, pendio: *easy* —, dolce pendio; *steep* —, salita ripida ☆ *a balloon* —, un'ascensione in pallone.

to ascertain [,æsə'tein], *v.t.* assicurarsi, accertarsi di; venire a sapere; constatare: *it is difficult to* — *whether...*, è difficile sapere se....

ascertainable [,æsə'teinəbl], *ag.* accertabile.

ascertainment [,æsə'teinmənt], *s.* accertamento.

ascetic [ə'setik], *ag.* ascetico ‖ *s.c.* asceta.

ascetical [ə'setikəl], *ag.* ascetico.

ascetically [ə'setikəli], *av.* asceticamente.

asceticism [ə'setisizəm], *s.* ascetismo.

ascidium [ə'sidiəm], *pl.* **ascidia** [ə'sidiə], *s.* (*zool. bot.*) ascidio.

Asclepiad[1] [æs'kli:piæd], *s.* (*poes.*) (verso) asclepiadeo.

asclepiad[2], *s.* (*bot.*) asclepiade.

Asclepiades [,æskli'pi:ədi:z], *no.pr.m.* (*st.*) Asclepiade.

ascorbic [əs'kɔ:bik], *ag.* (*chim.*) ascorbico ☆ — *acid*, vitamina C.

Ascot ['æskət], *no.pr.* (*geog.*) (città ed ippodromo di) Ascot.

ascribable [əs'kraibəbl], *ag.* ascrivibile.

to ascribe [əs'kraib], *v.t.* ascrivere; attribuire.

ascription [əs'kripʃən], *s.* attribuzione.

asdic ['æzdik], *s.* (*mar.*) ecogoniometro.

asepsis [æ'sepsis], *s.* (*med.*) asepsi.

aseptic [æ'septik], *ag.s.* (*med.*) asettico.

asexual [æ'seksjuəl], *ag.* asessuale, senza sesso.

asexuality [æ,seksju'æliti], *s.* asessualità.

ash[1] [æʃ], *s.* (*bot.*) frassino ☆ — *-tree*, frassino.

ash[2], *s. gener. pl.* cenere ‖ *Ash Wednesday*, Mercoledì delle Ceneri ‖ *to reduce to ashes*, ridurre in cenere ‖ *peace to his ashes*, pace alle sue ceneri ☆ — *-bin* (o — *-bucket*), cenerario; — *-cake*, (*amer.*) torta cotta nella cenere; — *-heap*, (*metal.*) catasta di cenere; — *-hole* (o — *-pit*), cenerario (sotto le macchine): — *-pan*, cenerario (di stufa); — *-tray*, portacenere ‖ *cigar* —, cenere del sigaro.

to ash[2], *v.t.* coprire di cenere.

ashamed [ə'ʃeimd], *ag. predicativo* vergognoso, confuso: *to be* — *of*, aver vergogna di; *to be* (o *to feel*) — *to do* (o *of doing*) *sthg.*, avere, sentire vergogna di fare ql.co.

ashen[1] ['æʃn], *ag.* di legno di frassino.

ashen[2], *ag.* di color cenerino.

ashlar ['æʃlə*], *s.* (*arch.*) concio.

ashore [ə'ʃɔ:*], *av.* a terra; sulla riva: *to get* (o *to go*) —, sbarcare, prender terra; *to run* —, incagliare, gettar sulla costa.

ashy ['æʃi], *ag.* cinereo; *fig.* pallido.

Asia ['eiʃə], *no.pr.* (*geog.*) Asia ‖ — *Minor*, Asia Minore.

Asian ['eiʃən], *ag.* asiatico ‖ *s.c.* asiatico, asiatica.

Asiatic [,eiʃi'ætik], *ag.* asiatico ‖ *s.c.* asiatico, asiatica.

aside [ə'said], *av.* a parte, da parte: *to draw* —, tirar(si) da parte; *to lay* —, *to put* —, *to set* —, mettere da parte, allontanare; (*dir.*) annullare; *to stand* —, tenersi in disparte; *to turn* —, sviare, deviare, voltarsi da parte o altrove ‖ — *from*, in disparte; (*amer.*) a parte, eccetto: — *from the fright, he was uninjured*, a parte lo spavento, egli rimase incolume.

aside, *s.* a parte, a solo (specialmente di attore).

asinine ['æsinain], *ag.* asinino, asinesco.

asininity [,æsi'niniti], *s.* asinità.

to ask[1] [ɑ:sk], *v.t.i.* **1.** (III, IV) domandare, chiedere: *how much are you asking for this article?*, quanto chiedete per questo articolo?; *to* — *s.o. sthg.*, domandare ql.co. a qlcu.: *I asked him a favour* (o *a favour of him*), gli chiesi un favore; *to* — *s.o. 's pardon*, chiedere perdono a qlcu.; *to* — *s.o. to do sthg.*, chiedere a qlcu. di fare ql.co.; *to* — *sthg. for s.o.*, chiedere ql.co. per qlcu. **2.** invitare: *to* — *s.o. to dinner*, invitare qlcu. a pranzo **3.** *to* — *about* (*s.o., sthg.*), informarsi di, su:

they asked me all about my work, si informarono minuziosamente del mio lavoro **4.** *to* — *after* (*s.o., sthg.*), informarsi di, chiedere notizie di: *to* — *after s.o.'s health*, informarsi della salute di qlcu. **5.** *to* — *for* (*s.o., sthg.*), chiedere, esigere: *to* — *for attention*, esigere attenzione; *to* — (*s.o.*) *for sthg.*, chiedere ql.co. (a qlcu.) ‖ *to* — *for trouble*, cercar fastidi.

ask[2], *s.* (*zool.*) tritone.

askance [əs'kæns], **askant** [əs'kænt], *av.* obliquamente, di traverso: *to look* —, guardare con sospetto.

askari ['æskəri], *s.* ascaro.

asker[1] ['ɑ:skə*], *s.c.* sollecitatore, sollecitatrice.

asker[2], *s.* (*arc. zool.*) tritone.

askew [əs'kju:], *av.* di traverso, obliquamente ‖ *ag. predicativo* bieco, storto, obliquo.

aslant [ə'slɑ:nt], *av.* obliquamente, da un lato, di sghembo ‖ *prep.* a, di, per traverso (di), attraverso.

asleep [ə'sli:p], *av. ag. predicativo* **1.** addormentato, che dorme: *to be* —, dormire; *to fall* —, addormentarsi **2.** intirizzito, paralizzato (dal freddo, ecc.).

aslope [ə'sloup], *av.* in pendio; di sghembo ‖ *ag. predicativo* inclinato, in pendenza, obliquo.

Asmodeus [æs'moudjəs], *no.pr.m.* (*Bibbia*) Asmodeo.

asp[1] [æsp], *s.* (*zool.*) aspide; (*poet.*) serpente velenoso.

asp[2], *s.* (*bot.*) pioppo tremulo.

asparagus [əs'pærəgəs], *s.coll.* (*bot.*) asparago, asparagi.

aspect ['æspekt], *s.* **1.** aspetto, apparenza **2.** esposizione (*p. e.* di una casa): *the house has a southern* —, la casa guarda verso sud.

aspen ['æspən], *ag.* **1.** di, simile a pioppo tremulo **2.** *fig.* tremante, timoroso ‖ *s.* (*bot.*) pioppo tremulo.

aspergillum [,æspə'dʒiləm], *s.* (*eccl.*) aspersorio.

aspergillus [,æspə'dʒiləs], *s.* (*bot.*) aspergillo.

asperity [æs'periti], *s.* **1.** asperità (di terreno, ecc.) **2.** rigore (di clima) **3.** *fig.* asprezza, rudezza.

to asperse [əs'pə:s], *v.t.* **1.** aspergere **2.** *fig.* calunniare, diffamare: *to* — *s.o. with calumnies*, diffamare qlcu. con calunnie.

asperser [əs'pə:sə*], *s.* **1.** (*eccl.*) aspersorio **2.** *fig.* calunniatore, diffamatore.

aspersion [əs'pə:ʃən], *s.* **1.** aspersione **2.** *fig.* calunnia.

aspersive [əs'pə:siv], *ag.* calunnioso, diffamatorio.

aspersorium [,æspə'sɔ:riəm], *s.* (*eccl.*) aspersorio.

asphalt ['æsfælt], *s.* asfalto.

to asphalt, *v.t.* asfaltare.

asphaltic [æs'fæltik], *ag.* asfaltico.

asphodel ['æsfədel], *s.* (*bot.*) asfodelo.

asphyxia [æs'fiksiə], *s.* asfissia.

asphyxial [æs'fiksiəl], *ag.* di asfissia.

to asphyxiate [æs'fiksieit], *v.t.* asfissiare: *asphyxiating gas*, gas asfissiante.

asphyxiation [æs,fiksi'eiʃən], *s.* soffocamento, asfissia.

aspic[1] ['æspik], *s.* (*bot.*) spigo.

aspic[2], *s.* (*cuc.*) « aspic » (piatto di carne, pesce, ecc. in gelatina).

aspic[3], *s.* (*arc. poet.*) aspide.

aspirant [əs'paiərənt], *ag.* aspirante; ambizioso ‖ *s.c.* aspirante; candidato, candidata.

aspirate ['æspərit], *ag.* aspirato ‖ *s.* consonante aspirata; il suono di h.

to aspirate ['æspəreit], *v.t.* aspirare (una consonante).

aspiration [,æspə'reiʃən], *s.* aspirazione (anche *fig.*).

aspirator ['æspəreitə*], *s.* **1.** (*mec.*) aspiratore **2.** (*agr.*) vagliatore meccanico.

to aspire [əs'paiə*], *v.i.* **1.** aspirare, agognare: *to* — *to* (o *after* o *at*) *sthg.*, aspirare a ql.co. **2.** elevarsi, salire.

aspirin ['æspərin], **aspirine** ['æspəri:n], *s.* (*farm.*) aspirina.

aspiring [əs'paiəriŋ], *ag.* aspirante; ambizioso.

asquint [ə'skwint], *ag. predicativo* strabico ‖ *av.* di traverso, obliquamente; *fig.* in modo losco: *to look* —, guardar losco.

ass [æs], *s.* asino, somaro: —*'s foal* (o —*'s colt*), asinello; —*'s milk*, latte d'asina ‖ *to make an* — *of* *oneself, fig.* rendersi ridicolo; *to make an — of s.o., fig.* rendere ridicolo qlcu.; *to play the —, fig.* fare lo sciocco, lo stupido ☆ *jack —,* asinello; *she- —,* asina; *wild —,* onagro.

assagai ['æsəgai], *s.* zagaglia.

to assail [ə'seil], *v.t.* assalire, attaccare; investire: *to — with questions,* investire di domande.

assailable [ə'seiləbl], *ag.* attaccabile; *fig.* criticabile.

assailant [ə'seilənt], *s.c.* assalitore, assalitrice.

assassin [ə'sæsin], *s.* assassino; sicario.

to assassinate [ə'sæsineit], *v.t.* assassinare.

assassination [ə,sæsi'neiʃən], *s.* assassinio.

assassinator [ə'sæsineitə*], *s.c.* assassino, assassina.

assault [ə'sɔ:lt], *s.* 1. assalto, attacco: *to take* (o *to carry*) *a town by —,* prendere una città d'assalto 2. *(dir.)* vie di fatto, atti violenti; aggressione.

to assault, *v.t.* 1. assalire, assaltare, attaccare: *he was assaulted,* fu vittima di un'aggressione 2. *(dir.)* passare a vie di fatto contro.

assaultable [ə'sɔ:ltəbl], *ag.* attaccabile.

assaulter [ə'sɔ:ltə*], *s.c.* assalitore, assalitrice; aggressore, aggreditrice.

assay [ə'sei], *s.* 1. *(metal.)* analisi, assaggio 2. *(arc.)* prova, tentativo.

to assay, *v.t.* 1. *(metal.)* assaggiare 2. *(arc.)* provare, tentare; metter alla prova.

assayable [ə'seiəbl], *ag.* *(metal.)* saggiabile.

assayer [ə'seiə*], *s.c.* *(ind.)* assaggiatore, assaggiatrice.

assegai ['æsigai], *s.* zagaglia.

assemblage [ə'semblidʒ], *s.* 1. assemblea, riunione; raduno; raccolta 2. *(mec.)* montaggio.

to assemble [ə'sembl], *v.t.i.* 1. riunire, riunirsi; adunare, adunarsi 2. *(mec.)* montare.

assembler [ə'semblə*], *s.* *(mec.)* montatore.

assembling [ə'sembliŋ], *s.* 1. riunione 2. *(mec.)* montaggio.

assembly [ə'sembli], *s.* 1. assemblea, riunione 2. *(pol.)* camera bassa (in alcuni Stati americani) 3. *(mil.)* segnale di adunata; adunata 4. *(mec.)* montaggio complessivo ☆ *— line,* catena di montaggio; — *-man,* deputato della camera bassa (di alcuni Stati americani); — *-room,* sala da ballo, da riunioni.

assent [ə'sent], *s.* consenso; sanzione.

to assent, *v.i.* assentire, acconsentire, dare l'approvazione: *to — to a proposal,* approvare una proposta.

assentation [,æsən'teiʃən], *s.* approvazione; adulazione.

assenter [ə'sentə*], *s.c.* chi assente, approva, consente.

assentient [ə'senʃənt], *ag.* assenziente, consenziente ‖ *s.c.* chi assente, consente.

assenting [ə'sentiŋ], *ag.* consenziente.

assentor [ə'sentə*], *s.c.* chi assente, approva, consente.

to assert [ə'sə:t], *v.t.* 1. asserire, affermare: *his friends asserted that he was innocent,* i suoi amici asserirono che era innocente; *to — one's good faith,* affermare la propria buona fede 2. sostenere, difendere, rivendicare (diritti): *to — one's claims to,* rivendicare i propri diritti a; *to — oneself,* farsi valere.

assertable [ə'sə:təbl], *ag.* 1. che si può asserire 2. che si può rivendicare.

assertion [ə'sə:ʃən], *s.* 1. asserzione, affermazione 2. rivendicazione, difesa.

assertive [ə'sə:tiv], *ag.* assertivo; positivo; dogmatico.

assertively [ə'sə:tivli], *av.* assertivamente; dogmaticamente.

assertor [ə'sə:tə*], *s.c.* assertore, assertrice; difensore, difenditrice.

assertory [ə'sə:təri], *ag.* assertivo; dogmatico.

to assess [ə'ses], *v.t.* 1. valutare, stimare (una proprietà) per tassare 2. tassare, multare 3. *(comm.)* ripartire: *to — the taxes,* ripartire le tasse.

assessable [ə'sesəbl], *ag.* tassabile, imponibile.

assessed [ə'sest], *ag.* tassato ☆ *— taxes,* imposte dirette.

assessment [ə'sesmənt], *s.* 1. tassa, imposta 2. valutazione, stima (anche *fig.*) 3. *(comm.)* ripartizione, distribuzione.

assessor [ə'sesə*], *s.* 1. assessore, assistente 2. agente delle tasse.

asset ['æset], *s.* 1. bene; vantaggio; risorsa: *his knowledge of foreign languages is a great — to him,* la conoscenza delle lingue straniere è un grande vantaggio per lui 2. *pl. (comm.)* disponibilità finanziaria, attività (di una ditta), attivo 3. *pl.* patrimonio (di un debitore) 4. *pl.* asse ereditario ☆ *liquid assets,* attività liquida circolante; *realizable, fixed assets,* attivo realizzabile, immobilizzato.

to assever [æ'sevə*], **to asseverate** [ə'sevəreit], *v.t.* asserire (con solennità).

asseveration [ə,sevə'reiʃən], *s.* asserzione (solenne).

to assibilate [ə'sibileit], *v.t.* rendere sibilante.

assiduity [,æsi'dju(:)iti], *s.* attenzione; *pl.* assiduità.

assiduous [ə'sidjuəs], *ag.* assiduo.

assiduously [ə'sidjuəsli], *av.* assiduamente.

assiduousness [ə'sidjuəsnis], *s.* assiduità.

assign [ə'sain], *s.* *(dir.)* cessionario.

to assign, *v.t.* 1. assegnare 2. trasferire; cedere (beni, mandati, ecc.) 3. *(dir.)* designare; delegare 4. determinare, fissare (un giorno, ecc.) 5. accampare, allegare (ragioni, ecc.).

assignable [ə'sainəbl], *ag.* 1. assegnabile 2. determinabile 3. trasferibile.

assignat [,æsin'ja:], *s.* *(st. francese)* assegnato (carta moneta).

assignation [,æsig'neiʃən], *s.* 1. assegnazione 2. *(dir.)* cessione, trasferimento (di beni): *deed of —,* atto di cessione 3. il fissare un appuntamento.

assignee [,æsi'ni:], *s.* 1. *(dir.)* procuratore; curatore (di fallimento) 2. *(comm.)* assegnatario, mandatario.

assignment [ə'sainmənt], *s.* 1. assegnazione (di denaro, ecc.); stanziamento; *(dir.)* cessione, trasferimento: *deed of —,* atto di cessione 2. *(amer.)* incarico; nomina.

assignor [,æsi'no:*], *s.* *(dir.)* cedente.

assimilable [ə'similəbl], *ag.* assimilabile.

to assimilate [ə'simileit], *v.t.i.* 1. assimilare, assimilarsi (anche *fig.*) 2. rendere simile 3. confrontare: *to — to* (o *with*), confrontare con.

assimilation [ə,simi'leiʃən], *s.* 1. assimilazione (anche *fig.*) 2. confronto 3. somiglianza.

assimilative [ə'similətiv], *ag.* assimilativo.

to assist [ə'sist], *v.t.i.* 1. assistere, aiutare 2. assistere, presenziare: *to — at a ceremony,* esser presente ad una cerimonia.

assistance [ə'sistəns], *s.* assistenza, aiuto.

assistant [ə'sistənt], *ag.* 1. assistente 2. aggiunto ‖ *s.* 1. assistente, aiuto 2. aggiunto ☆ *— -director,* *(comm.)* vice-direttore; *(cine.)* aiuto regista; — *-professor,* *(amer.)* professore aggiunto ‖ *shop —,* commesso di negozio.

assize [ə'saiz], *s.* 1. *(arc.)* calmiere: *— of bread,* calmiere del pane 2. *(dir.)* seduta 3. *pl. (dir.)* Assise, Corte d'Assise; sessione d'Assise.

to assize, *v.t.* *(arc.)* calmierare (derrate alimentari).

associability [ə,souʃiə'biliti], *s.* associabilità.

associable [ə'souʃjəbl], *ag.* associabile.

associably [ə'souʃjəbli], *av.* associabilmente.

associate [ə'souʃiit], *v.t.i.* *ag.* associato, aggiunto: — *editor* *(amer.)* condirettore (di giornale, rivista); — *judge,* giudice assessore ‖ *s.* socio; collega; alleato.

to associate [ə'souʃieit], *v.t.i.* associare, associarsi; far parte di: *to — with s.o. in sthg.,* associarsi a qlcu. in ql.co. ‖ *to — with s.o.,* frequentare qlcu.

associated [ə'souʃieitid], *ag.* associato; alleato ☆ — *company,* società consociata.

association [ə,sousi'eiʃən], *s.* 1. associazione — *o ideas,* associazione di idee 2. società: *deeds of —,* *(comm.)* statuto di una società ☆ — *football (abbr. soccer),* giuoco del calcio.

associative [ə'souʃjətiv], *ag.* associativo.

to **assoil** [ə'sɔil], *v.t.* (*arc.*) **1.** assolvere da un peccato **2.** espiare (una colpa).

assonance ['æsənəns], *s.* assonanza.

assonant ['æsənənt], *ag.* assonante.

to **assonate** ['æsouneit], *v.i.* assonare.

to **assort** [ə'sɔːt], *v.t.i.* **1.** assortire; armonizzare, armonizzarsi: *an ill-assorted couple*, una coppia male assortita **2.** classificare **3.** rifornire con assortimento (negozi, ecc.) **4.** *to — with* (*s.o.*), frequentare: *he assorts with artists*, frequenta gli artisti.

assortment [ə'sɔːtmənt], *s.* assortimento.

to **assuage** [ə'sweidʒ], *v.t.i.* calmare, calmarsi; lenire, mitigare; diminuire.

assuagement [ə'sweidʒmənt], *s.* alleviamento; sollievo.

to **assume** [ə'sjuːm], *v.t.* **1.** assumere; appropriarsi: *he assumed the direction of affairs*, egli assunse la direzione degli affari **2.** affettare, fingere: *an assumed name*, un nome falso, uno pseudonimo; *assumed virtues*, false virtù; *she assumed an appearance of indifference*, assunse, finse un'aria indifferente **3.** presumere, supporre; ammettere: *he was assumed to be wealthy*, si presumeva fosse ricco **4.** essere arrogante, presuntuoso.

assuming [ə'sjuːmiŋ], *ag.* presuntuoso; arrogante.

assumingly [ə'sjuːmiŋli], *av.* presuntuosamente; arrogantemente.

assumption [ə'sʌmpʃən], *s.* **1.** impegno, incarico **2.** *Assumption of the Virgin*, Assunzione della Vergine **3.** finzione **4.** supposizione **5.** presunzione; arroganza.

assumptive [ə'sʌmptiv], *ag.* **1.** presunto, supposto **2.** arrogante.

assurance [ə'ʃuərəns], *s.* **1.** assicurazione, affermazione, promessa formale: *I have his — that*, ho la sua promessa formale che **2.** (*dir.*) assicurazione **3.** confidenza, fiducia; certezza, sicurezza **4.** arditezza, sicurezza; presunzione: *to answer with —*, rispondere con sicurezza, dare una risposta ardita ☆ *life-* —, assicurazione sulla vita; *self-* —, fiducia in sè.

to **assure** [ə'ʃuə*], *v.t.* **1.** assicurare **2.** rassicurare; incoraggiare ‖ *I can — you*, ne rispondo io.

assured [ə'ʃuəd], *ag.* certo, sicuro, assicurato: *an — success*, un successo sicuro; *rest —*, sia certo ‖ *s.* (l')assicurato (sulla vita).

assuredly [ə'ʃuəridli], *av.* certamente, sicuramente.

assuredness [ə'ʃuədnis], *s.* certezza; sicurezza.

assurer [ə'ʃuərə*], *s.c.* assicuratore, assicuratrice.

assurgent [ə'sɔːdʒənt], *ag.* (*bot.*) assurgente.

Assyria [ə'siriə], *no.pr.* (*geog. st.*) Assiria.

Assyrian [ə'siriən], *ag.* assiro ‖ *s.c.* assiro, assira.

Assyriologist [ə,siri'ɔlədʒist], *s.* assiriologo.

Assyriology [ə,siri'ɔlədʒi], *s.* assiriologia.

astatic [ə'stætik], *ag.* (*elett.*) astatico.

aster ['æstə*], *s.* (*bot.*) astro.

asterisk ['æstərisk], *s.* asterisco.

to **asterisk**, *v.t.* segnare con asterisco.

asterism ['æstərizəm], *s.* **1.** (*astr. min.*) asterismo **2.** gruppo di tre asterischi.

astern [əs'təːn], *av.* (*mar.*) a poppa; indietro: *full speed —*, indietro a tutta velocità; *to have the wind —*, avere il vento in poppa.

asteroid ['æstərɔid], *ag.* a forma di stella ‖ *s.* (*astr.*) asteroide.

asteroidal [,æstə'rɔidl], *ag.* asteroidale.

asthenia [æs'θiːnjə], *s.* astenia, debolezza.

asthenic [æs'θenik], *ag.* astenico ‖ *s.c.* astenico, astenica.

asthma ['æsmə], *s.* (*patol.*) asma.

asthmatic [æs'mætik], *ag.* asmatico ‖ *s.c.* asmatico, asmatica.

astigmatic [,æstig'mætik], *ag.* (*patol.*) astigmatico.

astigmatism [æs'tigmətizəm], *s.* (*patol.*) astigmatismo.

astir [ə'stə:*], *av.ag. predicativo* **1.** in moto, in agitazione (anche *fig.*): *the whole town was —*, l'intera città

era in agitazione; *to set —*, mettere in moto **2.** fuori dal letto, in piedi: *to be — early*, essere alzato per tempo.

to **astonish** [əs'tɔniʃ], *v.t.* stupire, meravigliare; sorprendere: *I am astonished at nothing*, nulla mi sorprende; *I was astonished at seeing* (o *to see*) *him there*, fui stupito di vederlo là.

astonishing [əs'tɔniʃiŋ], *ag.* sorprendente, straordinario.

astonishingly [əs'tɔniʃiŋli], *av.* sorprendentemente, straordinariamente.

astonishment [əs'tɔniʃmənt], *s.* sorpresa, stupore, meraviglia: *he stood in open-mouthed —*, rimase a bocca aperta per la sorpresa.

to **astound** [əs'taund], *v.t.* stupire, sbalordire; stordire; sgomentare.

astounding [əs'taundiŋ], *ag.* stupefacente, sbalorditivo.

astraddle [əs'trædl], *av.ag. predicativo* a cavalcioni.

Astraea [æs'triːə], *no.pr.f.* (*mit.*) Astrea ‖ *no.pr.* (*astr.*) Astrea.

astragal ['æstrəgəl], *s.* (*arch.*) astragalo.

astragalus [æs'trægələs], *s.* (*anat. bot.*) astragalo.

astrakhan [,æstrə'kæn], *s.* astracan.

astral ['æstrəl], *ag.* astrale: *— body*, corpo astrale; *— hatch*, (*aer.*) finestra a cupola per osservazioni astronomiche.

astray [ə'strei], *av.ag. predicativo* fuori strada (anche *fig.*): *to go —*, smarrirsi, fuorviarsi; *to lead —*, sviare, fuorviare, traviare.

astriction [əs'trikʃən], *s.* **1.** costrizione, restrizione **2.** stitichezza.

astrictive [əs'triktiv], *ag.* astringente.

astride [ə'straid], *av.ag. predicativo* a cavalcioni: *to get —*, mettersi a cavalcioni; *to stand —*, stare ritto a gambe larghe ‖ *prep.* a cavalcioni di: *— (of) the chair*, a cavalcioni della sedia.

astringency [əs'trindʒənsi], *s.* **1.** astringenza **2.** *fig.* durezza, severità.

astringent [əs'trindʒənt], *ag.* **1.** astringente **2.** *fig.* severo ‖ *s.* astringente.

astrolabe ['æstrouleib], *s.* (*astr.*) astrolabio.

astrologer [əs'trɔlədʒə*], *s.* astrologo.

astrologic(al) [,æstrə'lɔdʒik(əl)], *ag.* astrologico.

astrologically [,æstrə'lɔdʒikəli], *av.* astrologicamente.

astrology [əs'trɔlədʒi], *s.* astrologia.

astrometer [æs'trɔmitə*], *s.* (*astr.*) astrometro.

astronaut ['æstrənɔːt], *s.* astronauta.

astronautics [,æstrə'nɔːtiks], *s.* astronautica.

astronomer [əs'trɔnəmə*], *s.* astronomo.

astronomic(al) [,æstrə'nɔmik(əl)], *ag.* astronomico.

astronomically [,æstrə'nɔmikəli], *av.* astronomicamente.

astronomy [əs'trɔnəmi], *s.* astronomia.

astrophysics ['æstrou'fiziks], *s.* astrofisica.

astute [əs'tjuːt], *ag.* astuto, scaltro, sagace.

astutely [əs'tjuːtli], *av.* astutamente, sagacemente.

astuteness [əs'tjuːtnis], *s.* astuzia, scaltrezza, sagacia.

Astyanax [əs'taiənæks], *no.pr.m.* (*lett.*) Astianatte.

asunder [ə'sʌndə*], *av.* **1.** separatamente: *to come —*, disgiungersi, disunirsi in pezzi: *to fall —*, rompersi; *to tear —*, fare a pezzi.

asylum [ə'sailəm], *s.* **1.** asilo, rifugio: *to afford — to s.o.*, dare asilo, offrire ricovero a qlcu. **2.** casa di ricovero; istituto: *— for the blind*, istituto dei ciechi ☆ *lunatic —*, manicomio; *orphan- —*, (*arc.*) orfanotrofio.

asymmetric(al) [,æsi'metrik(əl)], *ag.* asimmetrico.

asymmetry [æ'simitri], *s.* asimmetria.

asymptote ['æsimptout], *s.* (*geom.*) asintote.

asynchronism [æ'siŋkrənizəm], *s.* (*mec.*) asincronismo.

asyndeton [æ'sinditən], *s.* (*ret.*) asindeto.

at[1] [æt (*forma forte*), ət (*forma debole*)], *prep.* **a, ad, da, in**: **1.** (*luogo*) *he is — Monza, — the hotel, — the* *window*, — *home*, — *church*, — *school*, — *Mr. Smith's*, è a Monza, all'albergo, alla finestra, a casa, in chiesa, a scuola, dal sig. Smith **2.** (*tempo*): — *the same time*, nello stesso tempo; — *that time, moment*, in quel tempo, momento; — *two o'clock, noon, night*, alle due, a mezzogiorno, di notte **3.** (*occupazione*): — *work, dinner, etc.*, al lavoro, a pranzo, ecc.; *what is he* —?, che cosa cerca di fare? **4.** (*maniera*): — *sight*, a vista; — *will*, a volontà **5.** (*moto, direzione*): *to aim* — *s.o., sthg.*, mirare a qlcu., ql.co.; *to arrive* — *a place*, arrivare in un luogo; *to get* —, arrivare: *I cannot get* — *the meaning of it*, non riesco a capirlo; *to look, to point* —, guardare, indicare; *to fire sthg.* — *s.o., sthg.*, gettare, sparare ql.co. a qlcu., a ql.co. **6.** (*unita a verbo spesso ne modifica il significato*): *to call* —, passare da; fare scalo; *to laugh* —, ridere di, irridere **7.** (**Fraseologia**): — *all*, affatto, punto: *I don't know him* — *all*, non lo conosco affatto ‖ — *all events*, in tutti i casi; — *any rate*, ad ogni modo ‖ — *arm's length*, alla distanza di un braccio ‖ — *a time*, alla volta: *two* — *a time*, due alla volta ‖ — *first*, al principio; — *last*, finalmente, infine ‖ — *hand*, a portata di mano, vicino; — *near* — *hand*, vicinissimo ‖ — *a high, low price*, a un prezzo alto, basso ‖ — *least, most*, almeno, al massimo ‖ — *once*, subito ‖ — *s.o.'s orders*, agli ordini di qlcu. ‖ — *present*, al presente, ora ‖ — *them!*, (*fam.*) addosso!, prendi! ‖ *to be* — *a loss*, non riuscire a ‖ *to be clever, slow* —, essere bravo, tardo in; *to be surprised, pleased* —, essere sorpreso, contento di ‖ *to work, to play* —, lavorare, giocare a: *they played* — (*being*) *robbers*, giocarono ai ladri.

At² [æt], *s.f.* donna addetta al servizio territoriale (1941-49).

ataraxia [ˌætəˈræksiə], **ataraxy** [ˈætəræksi], *s.* (*fil.*) atarassia.

ataunto [əˈtɔːntou], *av.* (*mar.*) a vele spiegate.

atavie [əˈtævik], *ag.* atavico.

atavism [ˈætəvizəm], *s.* atavismo.

atavistic [ˌætəˈvistik], *ag.* atavistico.

ataxy [əˈtæksi], *s.* (*patol.*) atassia.

ate [et], *pass.* di **to eat**.

Athaliah [ˌæθəˈlaiə], *no.pr.f.* (*Bibbia*) Atalia.

Athanasius [ˌæθəˈneijəs], *no.pr.m.* (*st. relig.*) Atanasio.

atheism [ˈeiθiizəm], *s.* ateismo.

atheist [ˈeiθiist], *s.* ateo.

atheistic(al) [ˌeiθiˈistik(əl)], *ag.* ateistico.

atheling [ˈæθəliŋ], *s.* **1.** (*st.*) nobile anglosassone **2.** erede legittimo al trono.

Athena [əˈθiːnə], *no.pr.f.* (*mit.*) Atena.

athenaeum [ˌæθiˈni(ː)əm], *s.* circolo letterario o scientifico; ateneo; sala di lettura; biblioteca.

Athenian [əˈθiːnjən], *ag.s.c.* ateniese.

Athens [ˈæθinz], *no.pr.* (*geog.*) Atene.

athirst [əˈθəːst], *ag. predicativo* **1.** assetato **2.** *fig.* bramoso, desideroso.

athlete [ˈæθliːt], *s.c.* atleta.

athletic [æθˈletik], *ag.* atletico.

athletically [æθˈletikəli], *av.* atleticamente.

athleticism [æθˈletisizəm], *s.* atletismo.

athletics [æθˈletiks], *s.* atletica.

at-home [ətˈhoum], *s.* ricevimento (in casa): *her at-homes are very pleasant*, i suoi ricevimenti sono molto accoglienti.

athwart [əˈθwɔːt], *av.prep.* **1.** a, di, per traverso; da parte a parte; obliquamente; trasversalmente **2.** in opposizione a **3.** (*mar.*) per il traverso di, per madiere.

atilt [əˈtilt], *av.* **1.** inclinato: *with hat* —, col cappello sulle ventitrè **2.** *spec. fig.* con la lancia in resta: *to run* —, giostrare; *to run* — *against s.o., fig.* venire in urto con qlcu.

atlantean [ˌætlænˈtiːən], *ag.* **1.** fortissimo **2.** relativo all'Atlantide.

Atlantic [ətˈlæntik], *ag.* atlantico ‖ — *Charter*, (*pol.*) Carta atlantica ‖ *North* — *Treaty* (o *Pact*), (*pol.*) Patto atlantico ‖ *no.pr.* (*geog.*) Atlantico.

Atlantis [ətˈlæntis], *no.pr.* (*geog. mit.*) Atlantide.

Atlas [ˈætləs], *no.pr.m.* (*geog. mit.*) Atlante ‖ **atlas**, *pl.* **atlases** [ˈætləsiz], *s.* atlante (anche *anat.*).

atmosphere [ˈætməsfiə*], *s.* atmosfera (anche *fig.*).

atmospheric(al) [ˌætməsˈferik(əl)], *ag.* atmosferico.

atmospherics [ˌætməsˈferiks], *s.* (*rad.*) scariche.

atoll [ˈætɔl], *s.* atollo.

atom [ˈætəm], *s.* **1.** (*fis. chim.*) atomo **2.** cosa infinitamente piccola: *to crush to atoms*, sbriciolare ☆ — *bomb*, bomba atomica.

atomic(al) [əˈtɔmik(əl)], *ag.* atomico ☆ — *bomb*, bomba atomica; — *energy*, energia atomica; — *model*, modello di atomo; — *number*, numero atomico; — *pile*, pila atomica; — *weight*, peso atomico.

atomicity [ˌætəˈmisiti], *s.* (*chim.*) valenza; (*fis.*) atomicità.

atomism [ˈætəmizəm], *s.* (*st. fil.*) atomismo.

atomist [ˈætəmist], *s.* (*st. fil.*) atomista.

atomistic [ˌætəˈmistik], *ag.* atomistico.

atomization [ˌætəmaiˈzeiʃən], *s.* (*fis.*) atomizzazione; polverizzazione, nebulizzazione.

to **atomize** [ˈætəmaiz], *v.t.* (*fis.*) atomizzare; nebulizzare.

atomizer [ˈætəmaizə*], *s.* (*med.*) polverizzatore; spruzzatore; nebulizzatore.

atomy¹ [ˈætəmi], *s.* scheletro; corpo scheletrico.

atomy², *s.* atomo; essere piccolissimo.

atonable [əˈtounəbl], *ag.* espiabile, riparabile.

atonal [æˈtounl], *ag.* (*mus.*) atonale.

to **atone** [əˈtoun], *v.t.i.* **1.** espiare: *to* — *for a fault*, espiare un fallo **2.** (*arc.*) riconciliare (nemici); comporre (una lite).

atonement [əˈtounmənt], *s.* **1.** espiazione, riparazione **2.** conciliazione.

atonic [æˈtɔnik], *ag.* **1.** (*gram.*) atono **2.** (*patol.*) atonico ‖ *s.* parola atona.

atony [ˈætəni], *s.* atonia.

atop [əˈtɔp], *av.* in cima: — *of the hill*, in cima alla collina.

atrabilious [ˌætrəˈbiljəs], *ag.* atrabiliare.

Atreus [ˈeitriuːs], *no.pr.m.* (*mit.*) Atreo.

atrip [əˈtrip], *ag. predicativo* (*mar.*) spedata, che ha lasciato il fondo (di àncora).

atrium [ˈɑːtriəm], *pl.* **atria** [ˈɑːtriə], **atriums** [ˈɑːtriəmz], *s.* (*anat. arch.*) atrio.

atrocious [əˈtrouʃəs], *ag.* atroce: *her hat was simply* —, (*fam.*) il suo cappello era proprio un orrore.

atrociously [əˈtrouʃəsli], *av.* atrocemente.

atrociousness [əˈtrouʃəsnis], *s.* atrocità.

atrocity [əˈtrɔsiti], *s.* atrocità.

atrophic [æˈtrɔfik], *ag.* atrofico.

atrophy [ˈætrəfi], *s.* atrofia.

to **atrophy**, *v.t.i.* atrofizzare, atrofizzarsi.

atropine [ˈætrəpin], *s.* (*chim.*) atropina.

Atropos [ˈætrəpɔs], *no.pr.f.* (*mit.*) Atropo.

attaboy [ˈætəbɔi], *inter.* (*amer.*) bene!, bravo!, avanti!.

to **attach** [əˈtætʃ], *v.t.i.* **1.** attaccare, attaccarsi, unire, unirsi, fissare; aderire **2.** affezionare; attrarre, avvincere: *he has the gift of attaching people to him*, ha il dono di attrarre la gente **3.** attribuire, annettere; imputare: *I* — *no importance to the matter*, non attribuisco nessuna importanza alla cosa **4.** (*dir.*) sequestrare (beni, persone, ecc.).

attachable [əˈtætʃəbl], *ag.* **1.** attaccabile **2.** che si affeziona **3.** sequestrabile.

attaché [əˈtæʃei], *s.* addetto (diplomatico o militare) ☆ — *case*, valigetta per documenti.

attached [əˈtætʃt], *ag.* **1.** addetto, assegnato (a ufficio, posto): *officer* — *to the staff*, ufficiale assegnato allo stato maggiore **2.** affezionato, devoto.

attachment [əˈtætʃmənt], *s.* **1.** attaccamento, unione **2.** affezione, affetto: *to entertain an* — *for s.o.*, nutrire dell'affetto per qlcu. **3.** (*dir.*) sequestro **4.** (*mec.*) accessorio, strumento di corredo ☆ *foreign-* —, sequestro di beni di stranieri.

attack [ə'tæk], *s.* **1.** attacco, assalto, offensiva: *to make an — on*, fare un attacco su; *to return to the* —, ritornare all'attacco (anche *fig.*) **2.** attacco, accesso (di malattia): *— of gout*, attacco di gotta.

to **attack**, *v.t.* **1.** attaccare, assalire (anche *fig.*): *to — a task*, mettersi di lena a fare un compito **2.** (*chim.*) attaccare: *not attacked by acids*, inattaccabile dagli acidi.

attackable [ə'tækəbl], *ag.* attaccabile, assalibile.

attacker [ə'tækə*], *s.c.* assalitore, assalitrice; aggressore, aggreditrice.

to **attain** [ə'tein], *v.t.i.* ottenere, conseguire, raggiungere; arrivare; giungere a: *he attained the age of ninety*, giunse ai novanta anni di età; *to — one's end*, raggiungere lo scopo prefisso; *to — to perfection*, raggiungere la perfezione.

attainability [ə,teinə'biliti], *s.* possibilità di ottenere, di conseguire, di raggiungere; accessibilità.

attainable [ə'teinəbl], *ag.* ottenibile, conseguibile, raggiungibile, accessibile.

attainder [ə'teində*], *s.* (*dir. arc.*) confisca dei beni; estinzione dei diritti civili (come conseguenza di proscrizione).

attainment [ə'teinmənt], *s.* **1.** raggiungimento, realizzazione, conseguimento **2.** *spec. pl.* cognizioni; cultura, sapere: *man of small attainments*, uomo poco istruito.

attaint [ə'teint], *ag.* **1.** corrotto, infetto **2.** macchiato, disonorato ‖ *s.* **1.** macchia, disonore **2.** (*dir. arc.*) confisca dei beni; estinzione dei diritti civili **3.** stoccata.

to **attaint**, *v.t.* **1.** corrompere, infettare **2.** ledere, disonorare **3.** (*dir. arc.*) confiscare i beni a; privare dei diritti civili.

Attalus ['ætələs], *no.pr.m.* (*st.*) Attalo.

attar ['ætə*], *s.* essenza: *— of roses*, essenza di rose.

to **attemper** [ə'tempə*], *v.t.* **1.** temperare, mitigare, moderare **2.** (*metal.*) temprare **3.** adattare, appropriare.

attemperment [ə'tempəmənt], *s.* **1.** moderazione **2.** proporzione; giusta mescolanza.

attempt [ə'tempt], *s.* **1.** tentativo, prova; sforzo: *at escaping* (o *to escape*), tentativo d'evasione; *to make an — at doing* (o *to do*) *sthg.*, sforzarsi di fare ql.co. **2.** attentato: *to make an — on the State, on s.o.'s life*, attentare allo Stato, alla vita di qlcu.

to **attempt**, *v.t.* **1.** tentare, provare, provarsi, cercare: *to — the impossible* (o *to — impossibilities*), tentare l'impossibile **2.** attentare a: *he attempted my life*, egli attentò alla mia vita **3.** (*arc.*) tentare (al male).

attemptable [ə'temptəbl], *ag.* tentabile.

attempter [ə'temptə*], *s.c.* **1.** chi tenta **2.** attentatore, attentatrice.

to **attend** [ə'tend], *v.t.i.* **1.** badare, prestare attenzione: *— to my words*, badate alle mie parole **2.** occuparsi, accudire: *I have my business to — to*, ho i miei affari di cui occuparmi; *will you — to the matter?*, volete occuparvi della faccenda? **3.** assistere, curare (un malato, ecc.): *that doctor attends the poor free*, quel dottore assiste i poveri gratis **4.** obbedire: *— to my orders*, eseguite i miei ordini **5.** assistere, presenziare, intervenire a (riunioni, ecc.); seguire (lezioni); frequentare (scuola, chiesa): *we attended the meeting*, presenziammo alla riunione **6.** accompagnare, seguire: *may happiness always — you!*, possa la felicità accompagnarti sempre! **7.** servire, essere al servizio di: *he attends (upon* o *on) the King*, è al servizio del Re **8.** (*arc.*) aspettare.

attendance [ə'tendəns], *s.* **1.** servizio: *to be in — on*, essere al servizio di ‖ *— included*, servizio incluso **2.** assistenza, cure, prestazioni (di un medico, ecc.) ‖ *lady in —*, dama di compagnia **3.** frequenza, presenza; complesso delle persone presenti **4.** *— to*, attenzione a ☆ *— -register*, registro delle presenze.

attendant [ə'tendənt], *ag.* **1.** che accompagna **2.** dipendente, al servizio di **3.** presente: *the — crowd*, la

folla presente ‖ *s.* **1.** servo, servitore, inserviente; guardiano, sorvegliante **2.** assistente; assiduo frequentatore **3.** *pl.* servitù; satelliti (di re, ecc.); personale (di negozio, ecc.).

attention [ə'tenʃən], *s.* **1.** attenzione: *to attract* (o *to call* o *to draw*) —, richiamare, attrarre l'attenzione; *to give* (o *to pay*) *one's* —, fare attenzione; *to turn one's — to sthg.*, rivolgere l'attenzione a ql.co. ‖ *—!*, attenzione!; (*mil.*) attenti! ‖ *to be all* —, (*fam.*) essere tutt'orecchi **2.** interessamento; cura: *to be full of attentions for s.o.* (o *to be all* — o *attentions to s.o.*), essere pieno di riguardi per qlcu. ‖ *to pay* — (o *one's attentions*) *to a lady*, (*fam.*) fare la corte a una signora.

attentive [ə'tentiv], *ag.* **1.** attento **2.** assiduo; sollecito; riguardoso.

attentively [ə'tentivli], *av.* **1.** attentamente; con cura **2.** assiduamente.

attentiveness [ə'tentivnis], *s.* attenzione; cura.

attenuant [ə'tenjuənt], *ag.s.* attenuante, diluente.

attenuate [ə'tenjuit], *ag.* **1.** assottigliato; dimagrato **2.** attenuato; tenue.

to **attenuate** [ə'tenjueit], *v.t.i.* **1.** assottigliare; dimagrire, far dimagrire **2.** attenuare.

attenuation [ə,tenju'eiʃən], *s.* **1.** assottigliamento **2.** attenuazione.

to **attest** [ə'test], *v.t.i.* **1.** attestare, testimoniare, certificare; affermare (con giuramento); far giurare: *attested copy*, copia vidimata; *to — a signature*, legalizzare una firma **2.** (*mil.*) arruolarsi.

attestant [ə'testənt], *ag.* attestante ‖ *s.* (*dir.*) teste, testimonio.

attestation [,ætes'teiʃən], *s.* **1.** attestazione, testimonianza; prova **2.** legalizzazione (di una firma, ecc.).

attestor [ə'testə*], *s.c.* (*dir.*) testimone.

Attic[1] ['ætik], *ag.* attico, ateniese, (*arc.*) greco: *— salts* (o *wit*), arguzia, spirito attico ‖ *s.* dialetto attico.

attic[2], *s.* **1.** (*arch.*) attico **2.** soffitta, sottotetto.

atticism ['ætisizəm], *s.* atticismo.

to **atticize** ['ætisaiz], *v.t.i.* atticizzare.

Atticus ['ætikəs], *no.pr.m.* (*st.*) Attico.

attire [ə'taiə*], *s.* **1.** abbigliamento; vestiti, abiti; ornamenti; acconciatura **2.** (*arald.*) palchi (del cervo).

to **attire**, *v.t.* abbigliare; ornare; acconciare.

attitude ['ætitjuːd], *s.* posa; atteggiamento: *— of mind*, modo di pensare.

attitudinarian [,ætitjuːdi'nɛəriən], *s.c.* posatore, posatrice.

to **attitudinize** [,æti'tjuːdinaiz], *v.i.* atteggiarsi, posare; assumere un atteggiamento.

to **attorn** [ə'təːn], *v.t.i.* (*dir.*) **1.** trasferire (la proprietà) **2.** riconoscere l'autorità del nuovo padrone.

attorney[1] [ə'təːni], *s.* (*dir.*) **1.** procuratore **2.** — (*-at -law*), procuratore legale, avvocato (con facoltà di discutere cause presso le corti di grado inferiore, dal 1873, in Inghilterra, gli compete il titolo di *solicitor*) ‖ *Attorney-General*, Procuratore Generale; (*negli Stati Uniti*) Ministro della Giustizia.

attorney[2], *s.* procura: *letter* (o *power* o *warrant*) *of* —, procura.

attorneyship [ə'təːniʃip], *s.* ufficio, carica di procuratore.

to **attract** [ə'trækt], *v.t.* attrarre, attirare (anche *fig.*): *magnet attracts iron*, la calamita attira il ferro; *the plan does not — him*, il progetto non lo attira.

attractable [ə'træktəbl], *ag.* che può essere attratto.

attraction [ə'trækʃən], *s.* **1.** (*astr. fis.*) attrazione **2.** attrattiva; vezzo; seduzione.

attractive [ə'træktiv], *ag.* **1.** (*fis.*) attrattivo **2.** attraente.

attractively [ə'træktivli], *av.* **1.** attrattivamente **2.** attraentemente.

attractiveness [ə'træktivnis], *s.* **1.** attrazione **2.** attrattiva.

attributable [ə'tribjutəbl], *ag.* attribuibile.

attribute ['ætribjuːt], *s.* attributo (anche *gram.*).

to **attribute** [ə'tribju(ː)t], *v.t.* attribuire; ascrivere.

attribution [ˌætriˈbjuːʃən], s. attribuzione.

attributive [əˈtribjutiv], ag. attributivo (anche gram.) ǁ s. attributo.

attributively [əˈtribjutivli], av. attributivamente.

attrited [əˈtraitid], ag. logoro (per sfregamento, attrito).

attrition [əˈtriʃən], s. **1.** attrito; logorio **2.** (teol.) attrizione.

to **attune** [əˈtjuːn], v.t. accordare, intonare, armonizzare: tastes attuned to mine, gusti all'unisono coi miei.

atypical [əˈtipikəl], ag. atipico.

aubade [ouˈbaːd], s. lirica, canzone, musica cantata al mattino o che lo richiami.

auberge [ouˈbɛəʒ], s. locanda.

aubergine [ˈoubəʒiːn], s. melanzana (pianta, frutto).

Aubrey [ˈoːbri], no.pr.m. Alberico.

auburn [ˈoːbən], ag. castano chiaro con riflessi ramati.

auction [ˈoːkʃən], s. incanto, asta: by —, all'incanto; to put up to (o for o amer. at) —, vendere all'incanto ☆ — room, sala di vendite pubbliche; — sale, vendita all'asta.

to **auction**, v.t. vendere all'asta, all'incanto.

auctioneer [ˌoːkʃəˈniə*], s. banditore, venditore all'incanto.

to **auctioneer**, v.t. vendere all'asta, all'incanto.

audacious [oːˈdeiʃəs], ag. audace, intrepido.

audaciously [oːˈdeiʃəsli], av. audacemente.

audaciousness [oːˈdeiʃəsnis], **audacity** [oːˈdæsiti], s. audacia.

audibility [ˌoːdiˈbiliti], s. udibilità.

audible [ˈoːdəbl], ag. udibile, intelligibile.

audibleness [ˈoːdəblnis], s. udibilità.

audibly [ˈoːdəbli], av. ad alta voce, distintamente.

audience [ˈoːdjəns], s. **1.** udienza: to give — to s.o., dare udienza a qlcu. **2.** uditorio, pubblico ☆ — chamber, sala d'udienza; — court, tribunale ecclesiastico.

audiometer [ˌoːdiˈomitə*], s. (fis.) audiometro.

audiphone [ˈoːdifoun], s. (med.) audifono.

audit [ˈoːdit], s. verifica, revisione (di conti); resa dei conti (anche fig.).

to **audit**, v.t. verificare, rivedere (conti).

audition [oːˈdiʃən], s. **1.** udito, facoltà di udire **2.** audizione.

auditive [ˈoːditiv], ag. auditivo.

auditor [ˈoːditə*], s. **1.** uditore **2.** revisore (di conti); (comm.) sindaco (di società) ☆ standing, substitute —, sindaco effettivo, supplente.

auditorium [ˌoːdiˈtoːriəm], s. **1.** sala (di concerti, conferenze), auditorio **2.** parlatorio (di un convento).

auditorship [ˈoːditəʃip], s. carica di revisore (dei conti), di sindaco (di società).

auditory [ˈoːditəri], ag. (anat.) uditorio ǁ s. uditorio.

auger [ˈoːgə*], s. (strum. artig.) trivella; succhiello.

aught¹ [oːt], s. (scoz.) proprietà, possesso.

aught², s. ogni cosa: for — I know, per quanto mi risulta ǁ av. (arc.) assolutamente, in ogni modo.

augment [ˈoːgmənt], s. (gram.) aumento.

to **augment** [oːgˈment], v.t.i. aumentare, aumentarsi.

augmentable [oːgˈmentəbl], ag. aumentabile.

augmentation [ˌoːgmenˈteiʃən], s. aumento.

augmentative [oːgˈmentətiv], ag.s. (gram.) accrescitivo.

augmenter [oːgˈmentə*], s.c. chi aumenta.

augur [ˈoːgə*], s. (st.) augure.

to **augur**, v.t.i. predire, pronosticare: it augurs well, ill, no good, promette bene, male, nulla di buono.

augural [ˈoːgjurəl], ag. augurale.

augury [ˈoːgjuri], s. pronostico; presagio.

august¹ [oːˈgʌst], ag. augusto, maestoso.

August² [ˈoːgəst], s. agosto ǁ — Bank Holiday, Ferragosto inglese (primo lunedì di agosto).

Augusta [oːˈgʌstə], no.pr.f. Augusta.

Augustan [oːˈgʌstən], ag. di Augusto, augusteo ǁ the — Age, il secolo di Augusto; (lett. inglese) l'età di Dryden e Pope (1660-1744).

Augustin(e) [oːˈgʌstin], no.pr.m. Agostino.

Augustinian [ˌoːgəsˈtiniən], ag. agostiniano ǁ s.c. agostiniano, agostiniana.

augustly [oːˈgʌstli], av. maestosamente.

augustness [oːˈgʌstnis], s. maestosità.

Augustus [oːˈgʌstəs], no.pr.m. Augusto.

auk [oːk], s. (ornit.) alca.

auld [oːld], ag. (scoz.) vecchio: — lang syne, nei bei tempi del passato.

aulic [ˈoːlik], ag. aulico.

aunt [aːnt], s. zia ☆ great- —, prozia.

auntie, aunty [ˈaːnti], s. zietta.

aura [ˈoːrə], s. **1.** esalazione, emanazione **2.** fig. atmosfera **3.** (patol.) aura.

aural¹ [ˈoːrəl], ag. auricolare ☆ — witness, testimone auricolare.

aural², ag. dell'aura.

aureate [ˈoːriit], ag. (letter.) aureo.

Aurelia [oːˈriːljə], no.pr.f. Aurelia.

Aurelian [oːˈriːljən], no.pr.m. (st.) Aureliano.

Aurelius [oːˈriːljəs], no.pr.m. (st.) Aurelio.

aureola [oːˈriələ], **aureole** [ˈoːrioul], s. aureola.

aureomycin [ˌoːriouˈmaisin], s. (farm.) aureomicina.

auric [ˈoːrik], ag. **1.** d'oro **2.** (chim.) derivante dall'oro.

auricle [ˈoːrikl], s. (anat.) **1.** padiglione auricolare **2.** orecchietta (del cuore).

auricled [ˈoːrikld], ag. auricolato.

auricula [əˈrikjulə], pl. **auriculae** [əˈrikjuliː], s. **1.** (anat.) padiglione auricolare **2.** (bot.) auricula; (pop.) orecchio d'orso **3.** (zool.) specie di mollusco.

auricular [oːˈrikjulə*], ag. auricolare.

auriculate [oːˈrikjulit], ag. auricolato.

auriferous [oːˈrifərəs], ag. aurifero.

auriform [ˈoːrifoːm], ag. auriforme.

aurist [ˈoːrist], s. (med.) otoiatra.

aurochs [ˈoːroks], s. (zool.) uro.

Aurora [oːˈroːrə], no.pr.f. (mit.) Aurora ǁ **aurora**, s. aurora ☆ — borealis, aurora boreale.

auroral [oːˈroːrəl], ag. aurorale.

to **auscultate** [ˈoːskəlteit], v.t. (med.) auscultare.

auscultation [ˌoːskəlˈteiʃən], s. (med.) auscultazione.

auscultator [ˈoːskəlteitə*], s. (med.) chi ausculta.

to **auspicate** [ˈoːspikeit], v.t.i. **1.** iniziare sotto buoni auspici; inaugurare **2.** prendere auspici.

auspices [ˈoːspisiz], s.pl. **1.** auspicio **2.** patronato, protezione: under the — of, sotto gli auspici di.

auspicious [oːsˈpiʃəs], ag. auspicale; propizio, fausto.

auspiciously [oːsˈpiʃəsli], av. sotto felici auspici.

auspiciousness [oːsˈpiʃəsnis], s. felici auspici.

Aussie [ˈoːsi], s.c. (fam.) australiano, australiana.

austere [əsˈtiə*], ag. austero.

austerely [əsˈtiəli], av. austeramente.

austereness [əsˈtiənis], **austerity** [əsˈteriti], s. **1.** austerità **2.** stretta economia.

austral [ˈoːstrəl], ag. (geog.) australe, meridionale.

Australasia [ˌoːstrəˈleiʒə], no.pr. (geog.) Australasia.

Australasian [ˌoːstrəˈleiʒən], ag. australasiano ǁ s.c. australasiano, australasiana.

Australia [əsˈtreiljə], no.pr. (geog.) Australia.

Australian [əsˈtreiljən], ag. australiano ǁ s.c. australiano, australiana.

Austria [ˈoːstriə], no.pr. (geog.) Austria.

Austrian [ˈoːstriən], ag. austriaco ǁ s.c. austriaco, austriaca.

Austro-Hungarian [ˈoːstrou-hʌŋˈgɛəriən], ag.s. (st.) austro-ungarico.

autarchy [ˈoːtəki], s. dispotismo.

autarky [ˈoːtəki], s. autarchia.

authentic(al) [oːˈθentik(əl)], ag. autentico.

authentically [oːˈθentikəli], av. autenticamente.

to **authenticate** [oːˈθentikeit], v.t. **1.** autenticare, legalizzare **2.** stabilire la validità di; verificare.

authentication [oːˌθentiˈkeiʃən], s. **1.** autenticazione **2.** scoperta, verifica della autenticità (di un documento).

authenticity [,ɔ:θen'tisiti], *s.* autenticità.
author ['ɔ:θə*], *s.c.* autore, autrice.
authoress ['ɔ:θəris], *s.* autrice.
authorial [ɔ:'θɔ:riəl], *ag.* di, da autore.
authoritarian [ɔ:θɔrl'tɛəriən], *ag.s.* assolutista.
authoritative [ɔ:'θɔritətiv], *ag.* 1. autoritario 2. autorevole: *to know sthg. from an — source*, sapere ql.co. da fonte autorevole.
authoritatively [ɔ:'θɔritətivli], *av.* 1. autoritariamente 2. autorevolmente.
authoritativeness [ɔ:'θɔritətivnis], *s.* 1. autorevolezza 2. tono autoritario, perentorio.
authority [ɔ:'θɔriti], *s.* 1. autorità: *to have — over s.o.*, avere autorità su qlcu. || *— of father*, patria potestà 2. influenza, ascendente 3. competente, erudito, specialista 4. *fig.* fonte (di informazioni): *to quote one's authorities*, citare le fonti 5. autorizzazione: *he has my — to do it*, ha la mia autorizzazione a fare ciò 6. *pl.* le autorità.
authorizable ['ɔ:θəraizəbl], *ag.* autorizzabile.
authorization [,ɔ:θərai'zeiʃən], *s.* autorizzazione: *— in writing*, autorizzazione scritta.
to **authorize** ['ɔ:θəraiz], *v.t.* autorizzare.
authorized ['ɔ:θəraizd], *ag.* 1. autorizzato || *Authorized Version (of the Bible)*, Versione autorizzata (traduzione ufficiale, Anglicana della Bibbia, 1611) 2. competente.
authorless ['ɔ:θəlis], *ag.* anonimo.
authorship ['ɔ:θəʃip], *s.* 1. professione di scrittore 2. paternità (di un libro).
auto ['ɔ:tou], *s.* (*amer.*) automobile.
autobiographer [,ɔ:toubai'ɔgrəfə*], *s.* autobiografo.
autobiographic(al) ['ɔ:tou,baiou'græfik(əl)], *ag.* autobiografico.
autobiography [,ɔ:toubai'ɔgrəfi], *s.* autobiografia.
autobus ['ɔ:təbʌs], *s.* (*amer.*) autobus.
autocamp ['ɔ:təkæmp], *s.* (*amer.*) accampamento per automobilisti.
autocar ['ɔ:touka:*], *s.* automobile.
autochthon [ɔ:'tɔkθən], *pl.* **autochthons** [ɔ:'tɔkθənz], **autochthones** [ɔ:'tɔkθəni:z], *s.* autoctono.
autoclave ['ɔ:toukleiv], *s.* autoclave.
autocracy [ɔ:'tɔkrəsi], *s.* (*pol.*) autocrazia.
autocrat ['ɔ:təkræt], *s.* autocrata, autocrate.
autocratic(al) [,ɔ:tə'krætik(əl)], *ag.* autocratico.
autocratically [,ɔ:tə'krætikəll], *av.* autocraticamente.
autodidact ['ɔ:toudidækt], *s.c.* autodidatta.
autodrome ['ɔ:toudroum], *s.* autodromo.
autogiro ['ɔ:tou'dʒaiərou], *s.* (*aer.*) autogiro.
autograph ['ɔ:təgra:f], *s.* 1. autografo 2. firma 3. (*tip.*) riproduzione autografica.
to **autograph**, *v.t.* 1. scrivere di proprio pugno 2. firmare 3. (*tip.*) autografare.
autographic(al) [,ɔ:tə'græfik(əl)], *ag.* autografico (anche *tip.*).
autography [ɔ:'tɔgrəfi], *s.* autografia (anche *tip.*).
autogyro [ɔ:tou'dʒaiərou], *s.* (*aer.*) autogiro.
autolysis [ɔ:'tɔlisis], *s.* autolisi.
automat ['ɔ:təmæt], *s.* (*amer.*) ristorante con distribuzione automatica delle vivande.
automatic [,ɔ:tə'mætik], *ag.* automatico || *s.* pistola automatica ☆ *— control*, (*elett.*) comando automatico; *— machine*, distributore automatico.
automatically [,ɔ:tə'mætikəli], *av.* automaticamente.
automation [,ɔ:tə'meiʃən], *s.* (*neol.*) automazione.
automatism [ɔ:'tɔmətizəm], *s.* (*fil.*) automatismo.
automaton [ɔ:'tɔmətən], *pl.* **automatons** [ɔ:'tɔmətənz], **automata** [ɔ:'tɔmətə], *s.* automa.
Automedon [ɔ:'tɔmidən], *no.pr.m.* (*lett.*) Automedonte.
automobile ['ɔ:təməbi:l], *s.* (*amer.*) automobile.
to **automobile**, *v.i.* (*amer.*) andare in automobile.
automobilist [,ɔ:təmə'bi:list], *s.c.* automobilista.
autonomic [,ɔ:tou'nɔmik], **autonomous** [ɔ:'tɔnəməs], *ag.* autonomo.

autonomy [ɔ:'tɔnəmi], *s.* autonomia.
autoplasty ['ɔ:tə,plæsti], *s.* (*chir.*) autoplastica.
autopsy ['ɔ:təpsi], *s.* autopsia.
auto-suggestion ['ɔ:tousə'dʒestʃən], *s.* autosuggestione.
autotype ['ɔ:tətaip], *s.* (*tip.*) facsimile; autotipia.
autovac ['ɔ:təvæk], *s.* (*aut.*) pompa di aspirazione.
autumn ['ɔ:təm], *s.* autunno.
autumnal [ɔ:'tʌmnəl], *ag.* autunnale.
auxiliary [ɔ:g'ziljəri], *ag.* ausiliare (anche *gram.*) || *s.* 1. ausiliare (anche *gram.*) 2. *pl.* milizie ausiliarie.
avail [ə'veil], *s.* 1. profitto, utilità, vantaggio: *of what — is it to hope?*, a che serve sperare?; *to be of no —*, non servir a nulla, essere inutile 2. *pl.* (*amer.*) frutto (di una vendita); reddito (di una terra, ecc.).
to **avail**, *v.t.i.* servire (a), giovare (a), essere utile (a), aiutare, favorire: *his help availed (me) in that matter*, il suo aiuto (mi) giovò in quell'affare || *to — oneself of*, approfittare di, servirsi di, utilizzare: *I — myself of the opportunity*, approfitto dell'occasione.
availability [ə,veilə'biliti], *s.* 1. disponibilità (di materiale, uomini) 2. validità (di biglietto ferroviario).
available [ə'veiləbl], *ag.* 1. disponibile, libero 2. accessibile 3. utilizzabile 4. valevole (di biglietto ferroviario): *period for which a ticket is —*, validità di un biglietto.
availableness [ə'veiləblnis], *V.* **availability**.
avalanche ['ævəla:nʃ], *s.* valanga.
avarice ['ævəris], *s.* 1. avarizia 2. cupidigia, brama di ricchezza.
avaricious [,ævə'riʃəs], *ag.* 1. avaro 2. cupido.
avariciously [,ævə'riʃəsli], *av.* 1. avaramente 2. avidamente.
avast [ə'va:st], *inter.* (*mar.*) ferma!; basta!.
avatar [,ævə'ta:*], *s.* (*mit. indiana*) 1. incarnazione 2. manifestazione.
avaunt [ə'vɔ:nt], *inter.* (*arc.*) via!, indietro!, vattene!.
ave ['a:vi], *s.* avemaria.
ave, *inter.* salute, addio, salve.
ave-bell ['a:vibel], *s.* campana dell'Angelus.
to **avenge** [ə'vendʒ], *v.t.* vendicare: *to — oneself (on)*, vendicarsi (su); *to — a wrong*, vendicare un torto.
avengement [ə'vendʒmənt], *s.* (*arc.*) vendetta.
avenger [ə'vendʒə*], *s.c.* vendicatore, vendicatrice.
avenging [ə'vendʒiŋ], *ag.* vendicatore.
Aventine ['ævəntain], *no.pr.* (*geog.*) Aventino.
aventurine [ə'ventjurin], *s.* (*min.*) avventurina.
avenue ['ævinju:], *s.* 1. viale alberato 2. (*amer.*) strada (molto larga) 3. accesso.
to **aver** [ə'və:*], *pass.p.p.* **averred** [ə'və:d], *v.t.* 1. affermare, dichiarare 2. (*dir.*) provare; giustificare.
average ['ævəridʒ], *ag.* medio, normale, ordinario: *the — Italian*, l'italiano medio || *s.* 1. media: *on an —*, in media 2. (*comm. mar.*) avaria: *general, particular —*, avaria generale, particolare ☆ *— adjuster*, liquidatore d'avaria; *— bond*, obbligazione d'avaria.
to **average**, *v.t.* 1. fare, prendere, raggiungere la media di; avere in media 2. lavorare una media di.
averment [ə'və:mənt], *s.* 1. affermazione; asserzione 2. (*dir.*) testimonianza, prova.
Avernus [ə'və:nəs], *no.pr.* (*geog. mit.*) Averno.
to **averruncate** [,ævə'rʌŋkeit], *v.t.* (*arc.*) sradicare.
averruncator [,ævə'rʌŋkeitə*], *s.* (*strum.*) pennato.
averse [ə'və:s], *ag.* avverso, contrario, riluttante: *to be — to (o from) sthg.*, essere avverso a ql.co.
aversely [ə'və:sli], *av.* avversamente.
averseness [ə'və:snis], **aversion** [ə'və:ʃən], *s.* avversione, antipatia.
to **avert** [ə'və:t], *v.t.i.* sviare, sviarsi; allontanare; allontanarsi; distogliere, distogliersi.
avertable, **avertible** [ə'və:təbl], *ag.* allontanabile; sviabile.
aviary ['eivjəri], *s.* uccelliera.
to **aviate** ['eivieit], *v.i.* volare in aereo.
aviation [,eivi'eiʃən], *s.* aviazione.

aviator ['eivieitə*], *s.c.* aviatore, aviatrice.

aviculture ['eivikʌltʃə*], *s.* avicoltura.

avid ['ævid], *ag.* avido.

avidity [ə'viditi], *s.* avidità.

avifauna ['eivi,fɔ:nə], *s.* avifauna.

aviso [ə'vaizou], *s.* (*mar.*) avviso.

to avocate ['ævoukeit], *v.t.* (*dir.*) avocare.

avocation [,ævou'keiʃən], *s.* **1.** occupazione **2.** (*dir.*) avocazione.

avocet ['ævouset], *s.* (*ornit.*) avosetta.

to avoid [ə'vɔid], *v.t.* **1.** (I) evitare; scansare, schivare: *to — doing sthg.*, evitare di fare ql.co. **2.** (*dir.*) annullare, invalidare.

avoidable [ə'vɔidəbl], *ag.* **1.** evitabile **2.** (*dir.*) annullabile.

avoidance [ə'vɔidəns], *s.* **1.** fuga, scampo; l'evitare **2.** (*dir.*) risoluzione, annullamento.

avoidless [ə'vɔidlis], *ag.* inevitabile.

avoirdupois [,ævədə'pɔiz], *s.* — (*weight*), « avoirdupois » (sistema di pesi usato in Gran Bretagna e negli Stati Uniti per ogni tipo di merce eccetto pietre e metalli preziosi, medicinali): *— dram*, dramma avoirdupois (= gr. 1,772); *— ounce*, oncia avoirdupois (= gr. 28,349); *— pound*, libbra avoirdupois (= gr. 453,592).

to avouch [ə'vautʃ], *v.t.i.* affermare, dichiarare; garantire: *to — (for) sthg.*, rendersi garante per ql.co.

avouchable [ə'vautʃəbl], *ag.* affermabile; garantibile.

avouchment [ə'vautʃmənt], *s.* dichiarazione; affermazione; garanzia.

to avow [ə'vau], *v.t.* ammettere, confessare; dichiarare apertamente; affermare: *he avowed himself the author*, egli ammise di essere l'autore.

avowable [ə'vauəbl], *ag.* ammissibile; confessabile; affermabile.

avowal [ə'vau-əl], *s.* ammissione; confessione; dichiarazione; affermazione.

avowed [ə'vaud], *ag.* confessato; manifesto; aperto, *an — enemy*, un nemico dichiarato; *with the — purpose*, con lo scopo manifesto.

avowedly [ə'vauidli], *av.* apertamente.

avulsion [ə'vʌlʃən], *s.* separazione forzata.

avuncular [ə'vʌnkjulə*], *ag.* **1.** di zio **2.** (*iron.*) di usuraio.

to await [ə'weit], *v.t.* attendere, aspettare: *awaiting your orders, delivery, kind reply*, in attesa dei vostri ordini, della consegna, della vostra cortese risposta; *we — your reply*, attendiamo la vostra risposta.

awake [ə'weik], *ag. predicativo* **1.** sveglio, desto: *wide —*, ben sveglio **2.** sensibile, conscio: *to be — to a danger*, essere conscio di un pericolo.

to awake, *pass.* **awoke** [ə'wouk], *p.p.* **awaked** [ə'weikt], **awoke**, *v.t.i.* **1.** svegliare, svegliarsi, risvegliarsi: *Byron awoke to find himself famous*, Byron si svegliò e si trovò famoso **2.** *to — to (sthg.)*, diventare conscio di: *he awoke to the danger he was in*, si rese conto del pericolo in cui si trovava.

to awaken [ə'weikən], *v.t.i. fig.* risvegliare, risvegliarsi; far aprire gli occhi: *I awakened him to a sense of his danger*, gli aprii gli occhi al pericolo che correva.

awakener [ə'weikənə*], *s.* chi, che risveglia (l'intelligenza, ecc.).

awakening [ə'weikniŋ], *s.* risveglio (anche *fig.*): a *rude —*, un amaro risveglio.

award [ə'wɔ:d], *s.* **1.** sentenza, giudizio arbitrale; arbitrato **2.** ricompensa: *— for valour*, ricompensa al valore.

to award, *v.t.* **1.** aggiudicare; accordare; assegnare: *to — damages*, risarcire i danni **2.** giudicare, decretare.

awarder [ə'wɔ:də*], *s.* arbitro.

aware [ə'wɛə*], *ag. predicativo* informato, prevenuto, conscio, consapevole: *to be — of sthg.*, conoscere, ac-

corgersi di ql.co.; *to make s.o. — that*, informare qlcu. che.

awareness [ə'wɛənis], *s.* **1.** prontezza di spirito **2.** consapevolezza.

awash [ə'wɔʃ], *ag. predicativo* **1.** a galla; a flor d'acqua **2.** inondato: *the street was —*, la strada era inondata.

away [ə'wei], *av.* **1.** (*distanza, allontanamento*) via; **lontano, lungi**: *— from*, via, assente da; *to be —*, essere assente; *to go —*, andarsene; *to live far —*, vivere, abitare lontano; *to look —*, volgere lo sguardo altrove; *to stay —*, assentarsi, rimanere assente; *to take —*, togliere, portar via ‖ *he passed — quietly*, si spense in pace ‖ *to do — with*, distruggere; fare a meno di ‖ *to fool —*, sprecare, sperperare ‖ *to give —*, donare; distribuire; dare (in sposa); tradire (persona, segreto) ‖ *to make — with*, distruggere; far scomparire; dissipare (beni) **2.** (*uso esclamativo ed ellittico*): *—!*, su!, via!, partiamo!, partite!; *— with fear!*, basta con la paura!; *— with him!*, conducetelo, portatelo via!; *eat —!*, su via, mangia!; *one, two, three and —!*, uno, due, tre, via!; *we must — at once*, dobbiamo andarcene subito **3.** (**tempo**): *— back*, sin dal tempo di: *I knew him — back in our schooldays*, lo conoscevo sin dai giorni di scuola; *— behind*, molto addietro **4.** (**continuità di azione**): *to laugh —*, continuare a ridere.

awe¹ [ɔ:], *s.* timore, paura; meraviglia; timore reverenziale: *to keep in —*, tenere in soggezione; *to strike s.o. with —*, ispirare a qualcuno timore reverenziale ☆ *— -inspiring*, maestoso, imponente; *— -stricken* (o *-struck*), in preda a timore reverenziale.

to awe¹, *v.t.* incutere rispetto, timore; far tremare.

awe², *s.* (*tec.*) galleggiante di ruota (sotto una turbina idraulica).

aweary [ə'wieri], *ag. predicativo* stanco.

aweather [ə'weðə*], *av.* (*mar.*) al vento; sopravvento.

aweigh [ə'wei], *av.* (*mar.*) pendente: *with anchor —*, con l'ancora staccata dal fondo.

aweless ['ɔ:lis], *ag.* intrepido, senza timore; senza rispetto.

awesome ['ɔ:səm], *ag.* che incute timore, terrificante; imponente, grandioso.

awful ['ɔ:ful], *nel senso* **3.** ['ɔ:fl], *ag.* **1.** terribile, spaventevole **2.** imponente, maestoso **3.** (*fam. usato come rafforzativo*): *an — bore*, un terribile seccatore, una grande seccatura; *you're an — fool!*, sei un gran cretino!.

awfully ['ɔ:fuli], *nel senso* **2.** ['ɔ:fli], *av.* **1.** terribilmente, spaventevolmente **2.** (*fam.*) molto: *I am — glad, sorry*, sono molto contento, spiacente; *thanks —*, grazie mille.

awfulness ['ɔ:fulnis], *s.* **1.** importanza, maestosità **2.** cattiva condotta.

awhile [ə'wail], *av.* un momento, per un istante; qualche tempo: *wait —*, aspettate un po'.

awkward ['ɔ:kwəd], *ag.* **1.** goffo; malaccorto; inelegante **2.** scomodo, poco maneggevole: *an — tool*, un arnese scomodo **3.** *fig.* imbarazzante; inopportuno: *an — remark*, un'osservazione inopportuna **4.** delicato, difficilmente risolvibile: *the situation was —*, la situazione era delicata **5.** imbarazzato: *at our first meeting I felt very —*, al nostro primo incontro mi sentii molto imbarazzato.

awkwardish ['ɔ:kwədiʃ], *ag.* sgraziato.

awkwardly ['ɔ:kwədli], *av.* **1.** goffamente; in modo malaccorto **2.** in modo imbarazzante, imbarazzato.

awkwardness ['ɔ:kwədnis], *s.* **1.** goffaggine, mancanza di grazia, di tatto **2.** difficoltà; imbarazzo.

awl [ɔ:l], *s.* (*strum. artig.*) lesina, punteruolo.

awn [ɔ:n], *s.* barba (del grano, avena, ecc.).

awning ['ɔ:niŋ], *s.* tenda di riparo (anche su nave); riparo.

awoke [ə'wouk], *pass.p.p.* di *to awake*.

awry [ə'rai], *ag. predicativo* storto; bieco, perverso; errato ‖ *av.* per traverso, erratamente; perversamente.

ax(e) [æks], *s.* scure; accetta; ascia: *executioner's* —, mannaia ☆ *pick-* —, piccone.

axial ['æksiəl], *ag.* assiale.

axil ['æksil], *s.* (*bot.*) ascella.

axile ['æksail], *ag.* (*bot.*) assile.

axilla [æk'silə], *pl.* **axillae** [æk'sili:], *s.* **1.** (*anat.*) ascella; spalla **2.** (*bot.*) ascella.

axillary [æk'siləri], *ag.* (*bot.*) ascellare.

axiom ['æksiəm], *s.* assioma.

axiomatic(al) [,æksiə'mætik(əl)], *ag.* assiomatico.

axiomatically [,æksiə'mætikəli], *av.* assiomaticamente, in modo assiomatico.

axis ['æksis], *pl.* **axes** ['æksi:z], *s.* **1.** asse (di sfera, cristallo, ecc.): — *of revolution*, asse di rotazione **2.** (*pol.*) asse, alleanza fra potenze.

axle ['æksl], *s.* (*mec.*) asse, assale ☆ — *-box*, (*ferr.*) boccola; — *-tree*, asse della ruota ‖ *coupled* —, (*ferr.*) asse accoppiato; *driving* —, asse motore; *sliding* —, asse mobile.

axolotl [,æksə'lotl], *s.* (*zool.*) axolotl.

ay[1], **aye**[1] [ei], *av.* (*poet.*) sempre ‖ *for* —, per sempre.

ay[2], **aye**[2], *inter.* ah!: — *me!*, ahimè!.

ay[3], **aye**[3] [ai], *s.* voto di assenso: *the ayes have it*, la maggioranza dei voti è favorevole ‖ *inter. av.* sì, certo; già, già.

ayah ['aiə], *s.* (*ang.-in.*) bambinaia, cameriera indiana.

aye-aye ['aiai], *s.* (*zool.*) aye-aye.

azalea [ə'zeiljə], *s.* (*bot.*) azalea.

azarole ['æzəroul], *s.* (*bot.*) azzeruola ☆ — *-tree*, azzeruolo.

azimuth ['æziməθ], *s.* (*astr.*) azimut ☆ — *angle*, angolo azimutale; — *circle*, arco azimut, cerchio azimutale; — *compass*, bussola azimutale, ecclimetro; — *difference*, (*ott.*) parallasse.

azimuthal ['æzimju:θəl], *ag.* (*astr.*) azimutale.

azoic [ə'zouik], *ag.* (*geol.*) azoico.

Azores (the) [ə'zɔ:z], *no.pr.pl.* (*geog.*) Azzorre.

azote [ə'zout], *s.* (*chim.*) azoto.

azotic [ə'zɔtik], *ag.* (*chim.*) azotico.

to azotize ['æzətaiz], *v.t.* (*chim.*) azotare, impregnare di azoto.

azotized ['æzətaizd], *ag.* (*chim.*) azotato.

Aztec ['æztek], *ag.* azteco ‖ *s.c.* azteco, azteca.

azure ['æʒə*, 'eiʒə*], *ag.* azzurro ‖ *s.* **1.** azzurro, cielo **2.** (*min.*) lapislazzuli.

to azure, *v.t.* azzurrare, tingere in azzurro.

azurin(e) ['æʒurin], *ag.* azzurrino.

azurite ['æʒurait], *s.* (*min.*) azzurrite.

azury ['æʒəri], *ag.* azzurrastro.

azygous ['æzigəs], *ag.* (*fisiol.*) singolo, che non si trova mai appaiato ‖ *s.* parte organica singola.

azyme ['æzim], *s.* pane azzimo.

azymous ['æziməs], *ag.* azzimo, non lievitato.

B

b [bi:], *pl.* **bs, b's** [bi:z], *s.* **1.** (*seconda lettera dell'alfabeto inglese*) b ‖ — *for Benjamin*, (*tel.*) b come Bologna **2.** *B*, (*mus.*) si: *B flat*, *B natural*, si bemolle, si bequadro **3.** (*scherz.*) cimice **4.** *b.* (*abbr.* di *born*), nato: *b. 1933*, nato nel 1933.

baa [bɑː], *s.* belato ☆ — *-lamb*, (*scherz.*) agnellino.

to baa, *v.i.* belare.

baaing [ˈbɑːiŋ], *s.* belato.

Baal [ˈbeiəl], *pl.* **Baalim** [ˈbeiəlim], *no.pr.m.* Baal (dio fenicio) ‖ **baal**, *s.* idolo.

baas [bɑːs], *s.* (*Sud-Africa*) padrone.

babbie [ˈbæbi], (*dial.*) per **baby**.

Babbitt [ˈbæbit], *s.* « Babbit » (personificazione dell'uomo d'affari nordamericano, ignorante e convenzionale).

Babbitt metal [ˈbæbit,metl], *s.* metallo antifrizione.

babble [ˈbæbl], *s.* balbettamento; ciarla, chiacchiera; mormorio (di ruscello, ecc.).

to babble, *v.t.i.* balbettare; ciarlare, chiacchierare; mormorare (di ruscello, ecc.).

babblement [ˈbæblmənt], *V.* **babble**.

babbling [ˈbæbliŋ], *ag.* ciarliero; mormorante ‖ *s.* chiacchierio; mormorio.

babby [ˈbæbi], (*dial.*) per **baby**.

babe [beib], *s.c.* (*poet.*) bambino, bambina.

Babel [ˈbeibəl], *no.pr.* (*geog. st.*) Babele ‖ **babel**, *s.* confusione, frastuono.

babiroussa, babirussa [ˌbɑːbiˈruːsə], *s.* (*zool.*) babirussa.

baboo [ˈbɑːbuː], *s.* (*ang.-in.*) signore; impiegato anglo-indiano; (*spreg.*) indiano anglicizzato.

baboon [bəˈbuːn], *s.* (*zool.*) babbuino.

babu, *V.* **baboo**.

babushka [bəˈbuʃkə], *s.* (*amer.*) fazzoletto per la testa.

baby [ˈbeibi], *s.c.* neonato, neonata; bimbo, bimba ☆ — *-boy*, — *-girl*, bambino, bambina; — *buggy* (o — *carriage*), (*amer.*) carrozzina per bambini; — *-car*, piccola automobile utilitaria; — *-farm*, (*spreg.*) nido d'infanzia; — *-farmer*, donna che tiene a balia un bambino; — *-grand*, pianoforte a mezza-coda; — *-pin*, spillo da balia; — *-sitter*, « baby-sitter » (chi custodisce i bambini durante l'assenza dei genitori).

babyhood [ˈbeibihud], *s.* prima infanzia.

babyish [ˈbeibiiʃ], *ag.* bambinesco, infantile.

Babylon [ˈbæbilən], *no.pr.* (*geog. st.*) Babilonia.

Babylonian [ˌbæbiˈlounjən], *ag.s.* babilonese.

Babylonish [ˌbæbiˈlouniʃ], *ag.* babelico.

baccalaureate [ˌbækəˈlɔːriit], *s.* baccalaureato.

Bacchanal [ˈbækənl], *ag.* **1.** bacchico **2.** ubriaco ‖ *s.c.* **1.** baccante; sacerdote, sacerdotessa di Bacco **2.** ubriacone, ubriacona ‖ *s.* **1.** baccanale **2.** orgia.

Bacchanalia [ˌbækəˈneiljə], *s.pl.* **1.** baccanale **2.** orgia.

Bacchanalian [ˌbækəˈneiljən], *ag.* **1.** di, da baccanale **2.** di, da ubriaco ‖ *s.c.* ubriacone, ubriacona.

Bacchant [ˈbækənt], *s.c.* **1.** sacerdote, sacerdotessa di Bacco; baccante **2.** ubriaco, ubriaca.

Bacchante [bəˈkænti], *s.* **1.** baccante, sacerdotessa di Bacco **2.** ubriaca.

Bacchantic [bəˈkæntik], *ag.* di, da baccante.

Bacchic [ˈbækik], *ag.* bacchico.

Bacchus [ˈbækəs], *no.pr.m.* (*mit.*) Bacco.

Bacchylides [bæˈkilidiːz], *no.pr.m.* (*st. lett.*) Bacchilide.

baccy [ˈbæki], (*pop.*) per **tobacco**.

to bach [bætʃ], *v.i.* (*sl. amer.*) vivere da scapolo.

bachelor [ˈbætʃələ*], *s.m.* **1.** baccelliere ‖ *Bachelor of Arts*, laureato in lettere; *Bachelor of Science*, laureato in scienze **2.** scapolo, celibe: *old* —, vecchio scapolo ☆ — *flat*, appartamento da scapolo; — *-girl*, ragazza indipendente che vive sola.

bachelorhood [ˈbætʃələhud], *s.* celibato.

bacillar [bəˈsilə*], **bacillary** [bəˈsiləri], *ag.* bacillare.

bacilliform [bəˈsilifɔːm], *ag.* bacilliforme.

bacillus [bəˈsiləs], *pl.* **bacilli** [bəˈsilai], *s.* bacillo.

back [bæk], *ag.* posteriore, di dietro.

back, *s.* **1.** dorso, schiena; spalle (anche *fig.*); reni; didietro, lombo (di coniglio, lepre): *at the* —, sul didietro; *behind my* —, dietro di me, alle mie spalle; *excuse my* —, scusa se ti volto le spalle; *he does not bow his* — *to anyone*, non si piega davanti ad alcuno; *he has all his family on his* —, ha tutta la famiglia sulle spalle; *he has a big bank at his* —, lo sostiene una banca importante; *he is at the* — *of it all*, dietro a tutto questo c'è lui; *he turned his* — *on a very good position*, volse le spalle a un'ottima posizione; *his* — *is not equal to the burden*, è un peso sproporzionato alle sue forze; *they put him with his* — *to the wall*, lo misero con le spalle al muro ‖ *he gets his* — *up for nothing*, si arrabbia per un nonnulla; *this got his* — *up*, questo lo irritò **2.** dorso (della mano, di un libro); schienale (di sedile); rovescio (di stoffa, di medaglia); retro (di una casa, ecc.) **3.** fondo, sfondo; resto: — *of the stage*, sfondo del palcoscenico ‖ *on the* — *of everything he fell ill*, oltre a tutto il resto si ammalò **4.** (*mil.*) retroguardia.

back, *av.* **1.** dietro, di dietro; indietro; di ritorno: *money* — *if not satisfied*, (*comm.*) il denaro sarà rifuso se il cliente non sarà soddisfatto; *call him* — *at once*, richiamalo subito; *he went* — *on his word*, si rimangiò la parola; *he won* — *her affection*, riconquistò il suo affetto; *they made their way* — *to the village*, rifecero il cammino verso il villaggio; *they paid me* — *all the money*, mi restituirono tutto il denaro ‖ *to answer* —, ribattere; *to be* —, essere di ritorno; *to come* —, ritornare, tornare indietro: *they came* — *home yesterday*, ritornarono a casa ieri; *to get* —, ritornare; *to keep* —, trattenere; *to walk* —, tornare a piedi **2.** fa; addietro; prima: *a few days* —, alcuni giorni fa; *they had seen her a week* —, l'avevano veduta una settimana prima ‖ — *and forth*, innanzi e indietro; — *of*, (*amer.*) dietro a.

back, *inter.* indietro!

back, (*nei composti*): — *-bencher*, (*pol.*) parlamentare inglese di secondo piano; — *-blocks*, (*fam.*) regioni nell'interno dell'Australia; — *-bone*, spina dorsale; *fig.* fermezza, carattere; fondamento; — *-breaking* (*work*), lavoro molto duro; — *-chat*, (*sl.*) rimbecco; — *-comb*, pettine da crocchia; — *-dated*, (*comm.*) retrodatato; — *-district*, zona di campagna; — *-door*, porta di servizio; *fig.* mezzo segreto di approccio; — *-fall*, caduta all'indietro (nella lotta); — *-garden*, giardino interno; — *-hand* (o — *-stroke*), rovescio (al tennis); — *-handed*, come un manrovescio; inatteso; sleale; inclinato verso sinistra (di scrittura); — *-log*, grosso ceppo posto contro la parete del camino; — *-number*, numero arretrato (di periodico, ecc.); *fig.* persona antiquata; (*fam.*) persona di nessun conto; — *-room*, stanza di servizio; — *-slang*, gergo in cui ogni parola è scritta o pronunciata a ritroso; — *-stitch*, punto indietro, impuntura ‖ *full-* —, (*spor.*) terzino; *half-* —, (*spor.*) mediano.

to **back**, *v.t.i.* 1. rinforzare; sostenere, secondare, spalleggiare: *to* — (*up*) *s.o.*, sostenere qlcu. 2. trarre indietro; indietreggiare; fare indietreggiare, far rincular: *to* — (*a car*), (*aut.*) far marcia indietro ‖ *to* — *water*, (*mar.*) sciare 3. scrivere sul retro di; apporre la firma a; controfirmare (un documento): *to* — *a bill*, avallare una cambiale 4. montare su (un cavallo) 5. servire da sfondo a; addossarsi a: *the mountains that* — *the town*, le montagne che si elevano dietro la città 6. (*mar.*) mascherare; mettere (le vele) a collo; appennellare (l'àncora) 7. scommettere su (un cavallo) ‖ *he has backed a winner*, *fig.* ha avuto un colpo di fortuna 8. *to* — *down*, abbandonare un reclamo, una pretesa; ritirarsi dalla lotta 9. *to* — *out*, ritirarsi indietreggiando, ritirarsi da una impresa.

to **backbite** ['bækbait], *pass.* **backbit** ['bækbit], *p.p.* **backbit**, **backbitten** ['bæk,bitn], *v.t.i.* sparlare (di), calunniare.

backbiter ['bæk,baitə*], *s.c.* calunniatore, calunniatrice, maldicente.

backbiting ['bæk,baitiŋ], *ag.* maldicente ‖ *s.* maldicenza, calunnia.

backcourt ['bæk'kɔ:t], *s.* retrocorte.

backed [bækt], *ag.* 1. dal dorso, dalla schiena 2. *fig.* orgoglioso ☆ *broad-* —, dalle spalle larghe; *stiff-* —, dalla schiena rigida.

backer ['bækə*], *s.* 1. scommettitore 2. sostenitore ☆ *theatrical* —, finanziatore teatrale.

backfire ['bæk'faiə*], *s.* (*mec.*) ritorno di fiamma.

backgammon [bæk'gæmən], *s.* (*giuoco*) tavola reale.

background ['bækgraund], *s.* 1. sfondo (di quadro, di scena) 2. ambiente.

backing ['bækiŋ], *s.* 1. marcia indietro 2. sostegno; gruppo di sostenitori.

backless ['bæklis], *ag.* senza dorso.

backmost ['bækmoust], *ag.* il più indietro possibile.

backsheesh ['bækʃi:ʃ], *s.* mancia; gratificazione.

backside ['bæk'said], *s.* deretano.

to **backslide** ['bæk'slaid], *pass. p.p.* **backslid** ['bæk'slid], *v.i.* apostatare; ricadere nell'errore.

backslider ['bæk'slaidə*], *s.* apostata.

backsliding ['bæk'slaidiŋ], *s.* apostasia.

backstage ['bæk'steidʒ], *ag.av.* dietro le scene; nel retroscena.

backstair ['bæk'stɛə*], **backstairs** ['bæk'stɛəz], *s.* scala di servizio ☆ — *influence*, *fig.* influenza segreta, appoggio nascosto.

backstay ['bæk-stei], *s.* 1. (*mar.*) paterasso, paterazzo 2. reggischiena.

backward ['bækwəd], *ag.* lento; tardivo (di frutto, ecc.); tardo (di ingegno, ecc.); ultimo: in ritardo (nel lavoro, studio, ecc.): *a* — *child*, un bimbo tardivo; *to be* — *in doing sthg.*, esitare a fare ql.co.

backward(s) ['bækwəd(z)], *av.* indietro, addietro, all'indietro; verso il retro; sul retro; in senso inverso, a ritroso: *to look* —, guardare indietro; *to stroke the cat* —, carezzare il gatto contropelo ‖ *backwards and forwards*, avanti e indietro ‖ *to fall over backwards to*, (*fam.*) fare l'impossibile per.

backwardation [,bækwə'deiʃən], *s.* (*comm.*) deporto.

backwardly ['bækwədli], *av.* 1. all'indietro 2. lentamente; con riluttanza.

backwardness ['bækwədnis], *s.* lentezza (dell'intelligenza); tardività (di frutti); ritardo (di stagione).

backwash ['bækwɔʃ], *s.* risucchio; risacca.

backwater ['bæk,wɔ:tə*], *s.* acqua stagnante; seno comunicante col mare; acqua di rifiuto delle navi; *fig.* condizione, situazione stagnante.

backwoods ['bækwudz], *s.pl.* foreste (nell'interno di un continente, specialmente dell'America del Nord).

bacon ['beikən], *s.* lardo affumicato; prosciutto grasso; pancetta ‖ *to bring home the* —, (*sl. amer.*)

riuscire in un'impresa ‖ *to save one's* —, salvare la pelle.

Bacon, *no.pr.* (*st. fil.*) Bacone.

Baconian [bei'kounjən], *ag.* (*fil.*) baconiano, di Bacone ‖ *s.* (*fil.*) seguace di Bacone.

bacony ['beikəni], *ag.* lardaceo ‖ — *degeneration* (o — *infiltration*), (*patol.*) degenerazione amiloide; — *spleen*, (*patol.*) milza lardacea, in degenerazione amiloide.

bacterial [bæk'tiəriəl], *ag.* batterico.

bacteriological [bæk,tiəriə'lɔdʒikəl], *ag.* batteriologico.

bacteriologist [bæk,tiəri'ɔlədʒist], *s.* batteriologo.

bacteriology [bæk,tiəri'ɔlədʒi], *s.* batteriologia.

bacterium [bæk'tiəriəm], *pl.* **bacteria** [bæk'tiəriə] *s.* batterio.

baculine ['bækjulain], *ag.* di verga, di staffile.

bad [bæd], *comp.* **worse** [wə:s], *superl.* **worst** [wə:st], *ag.* cattivo, malvagio; tristo; brutto; vizioso; malsano; nocivo; forte (di mal di testa, raffreddore, ecc.); ammalato; marcio: — *air*, aria malsana, — *blood*, malanimo; — *coin*, moneta falsa; — *cold*, forte raffreddore; — *crop*, cattivo raccolto; — *debt*, debito insolvibile; — *form*, cattiva educazione; — *language*, linguaggio grossolano; bestemmie; *to feel* —, sentirsi male; *to get* —, marcire; corrompersi; peggiorare; *to go* —, andare a male, corrompersi; *to have a* — *finger*, *foot*, aver male a un dito, un piede ‖ *a* — *lot* (o — *egg*), (*fam.*) un cattivo soggetto ‖ *too* — *of him*, troppo scortese da parte sua ‖ *is it as* — *as all that?*, si è giunti a tal punto? ‖ *that's too* —!, è un po' troppo!, che peccato!; *that's not (so)* —!, non c'è male! ‖ *to be* — *at sthg.*, non aver attitudini per ql.co., non essere bravo in ql.co. ‖ *av.* (*fam.*) per **badly** ☆ — *egg*, (*sl.*) tipaccio; — *-hearted*, malvagio di cuore; — *-looking*, di aspetto brutto, triste; — *-tempered*, di carattere irascibile.

bad, *s.* male, rovina: *to take the* — *with the good*, accettare il male e il bene, la cattiva come la buona sorte ‖ £ *300 to the* —, (*comm.*) 300 sterline a conto perdita ‖ *to go to the* —, andare in rovina.

baddish ['bædiʃ], *ag.* piuttosto, alquanto cattivo.

bade [beid], *pass.* di to **bid**.

badge [bædʒ], *s.* insegna; simbolo; distintivo; segno (d'ufficio, ecc.); (*mil.*) gallone.

badger[1] ['bædʒə*], *s.* (*zool.*) tasso ☆ — *-dog*, cane bassotto; — *-legged*, con le gambe di lunghezza disuguale.

to **badger**[1], *v.t.* tormentare; molestare.

badger[2], *s.* (*dial.*) venditore ambulante.

badinage ['bædina:ʒ], *s.* scherzo, burla.

badly ['bædli], *av.* male, malamente ‖ — *off*, povero, spiantato; *fig.* disgraziato.

badmash [bʌd'ma:ʃ], *s.* (*ang.-in.*) mascalzone.

badminton ['bædmintən], *s.* 1. « badminton » (bevanda fatta di vino rosso, zucchero, seltz) 2. (*giuoco*) volano.

badness ['bædnis], *s.* 1. cattiveria, malvagità 2. cattiva qualità; cattivo stato: *the* — *of the food*, la cattiva qualità del cibo; *the* — *of the roads*, il cattivo stato delle strade 3. inclemenza, rigore (di clima).

baffle ['bæfl], *s.* 1. inganno; impedimento; confusione 2. (*mec.*) deflettore, diaframma, schermo 3. (*rad.*) schermo acustico.

to **baffle**, *v.t.* eludere; confondere; frustrare; impedire: *to* — *the imagination*, confondere l'immaginazione.

baffling ['bæfliŋ], *ag.* sconcertante; che impedisce, confonde ☆ — *wind*, (*mar.*) vento incostante, variabile.

bag[1] [bæg], *s.* 1. sacco: — *of money*, sacco di denaro ‖ — *of bones*, sacco d'ossa, persona magrissima ‖ *to let the cat out of the* —, lasciarsi sfuggire un segreto ‖ *to set one's* — *for an office*, (*amer.*) farsi avanti per ottenere un incarico 2. borsa: — *and baggage*, armi e bagagli 3. carniere: *a good* —, un carniere ben fornito 4. *pl.* (*sl.*) pantaloni ☆ *brief-* —, borsa da avvocato; *ice-* —, borsa per il ghiaccio; *mail-* —, sacco della posta; *sleeping-* —, sacco a pelo; *travelling-* —, sacca da viaggio; *vanity-* —, borsetta (da teatro, sera, ecc.).

to **bag**[1], *pass.p.p.* **bagged** [bægd], *v.t.i.* 1. gonfiare, gonfiarsi 2. impadronirsi di; catturare (selvaggina); rubare, far sparire ‖ bags I !, (sl. scolastico) me lo prendo io! 3. insaccare 4. (mar.) far sacco (di vela) 5. (mar.) uscire dalla giusta rotta.

to bag², v.t. falciare.

bagasse [bə'gæs], s. (ind. saccarifera) bagasse.

bagatelle [,bægə'tel], s. bagatella, inezia.

bagful ['bægful], s. carniere pieno.

baggage ['bægidʒ], s. 1. (solo sing.) (amer.) bagaglio, bagagli; (mil.) salmeria, bagaglio 2. (fam.) prostituta; ragazza sfrontata ☆ — -check (amer.), scontrino per il bagaglio; — -waggon, bagagliaio (di treno).

bagging ['bægiŋ], s. tela da sacco.

baggy ['bægi], ag. rigonfio; che ha perso ogni forma.

bagman, pl. **bagmen** ['bægmən], s. (fam.) commesso viaggiatore.

bagpipe ['bægpaip], s. cornamusa.

bagpiper ['bæg,paipə*], s. suonatore di cornamusa.

bah [bɑ(:)], inter. ohibò!.

Bahamas (the) [bə'hɑ:məz], no.pr.pl. (geog.) isole Bahama.

baignoire ['beinwɑ:*], s. (teat.) barcaccia.

bail¹ [beil], s. (dir.) 1. cauzione; garanzia: to grant —, concedere la libertà provvisoria su cauzione; to refuse —, rifiutare la domanda di libertà provvisoria 2. garante: to go — for s.o., rendersi garante di qlcu. (per ottenerne la libertà provvisoria) 3. cauzione, somma fornita come garanzia.

to bail¹, v.t. (dir.) dar garanzia per: to — s.o. (out), ottenere per qlcu. la libertà provvisoria versando una cauzione 2. affidare: to — goods to s.o., affidare a qlcu. merce in consegna.

bail², s. 1. cerchio (per sorreggere la copertura di un carro, di una barca, ecc.) 2. manico della teiera.

bail³, s. 1. (arch. mil.) palizzata, bastione 2. recinto esterno di un castello feudale 3. tramezzo di stalla.

to bail³, v.t.i. 1. (rar.) confinare 2. to — up, (austral.) assicurare (una mucca) ad un tramezzo durante la mungitura; disarmare per derubare (di brigante); alzare le mani (in segno di resa).

bail⁴, s. (cricket) una delle sbarrette (che riuniscono i picchetti).

bail⁵, s. (mar.) sessola, gottazza.

to bail⁵, v.t.i. 1. sgottare, aggottare (una barca) 2. to — out, (aer.) lanciarsi col paracadute.

bailable ['beiləbl], ag.: — offence, (dir.) reato che consente la libertà provvisoria dietro cauzione.

bailee [bei'li:], s. (dir. comm.) depositario; consegnatario.

bailer¹ ['beilə*], s. (dir. comm.) depositante; garante.

bailer², s. (cricket) palla che colpisce una delle sbarrette (che riuniscono i picchetti).

bailer³, s. (mar.) sessola, gottazza.

bailey ['beili], s. muro esterno; corte di castello ‖ the Old Bailey, l'«Old Bailey» (tribunale penale di Londra).

bailie ['beili], s. (amm. scoz.) assessore comunale.

bailiff ['beilif], s. 1. (dir.) magistrato inquirente 2. (amm.) ufficiale fiscale 3. king's —, (st.) balivo 4. fattore, amministratore di una tenuta.

bailiwick ['beiliwik], s. (dir.) ufficio, giurisdizione di giudice.

bailment ['beilmənt], s. 1. (comm.) consegna di merci (da custodire) 2. (dir.) libertà provvisoria dietro cauzione; cauzione.

bailor ['beilə*], s. (dir. comm.) depositante; garante.

bailsman, pl. **bailsmen** ['beilzmən], s. (dir.) garante, mallevadore.

bain-marie [,bæn,mɑ:'ri:], s. (cuc.) bagnomaria.

Bairam ['baira:m], s. (relig.) Bairam.

bairn [bɛən], s.c. (scoz.) bambino, bambina.

bait [beit], s. 1. esca; fig. lusinga 2. sosta (per ristoro); posta (dei cavalli) 3. il lanciare cani contro animali incatenati 4. (mec.) fulcro.

to bait, v.t.i. 1. adescare; fig. lusingare 2. fornire d'esca (amo, ecc.) 3. fermarsi per prendere ristoro; nutrire (un cavallo) durante una sosta 4. tormentare (un animale); fig. stuzzicare, tormentare: to — a bull with dogs, far combattere, lanciare dei cani contro un toro.

baiting ['beitiŋ], s. il tormentare animali incatenati aizzando contro loro dei cani; fig. lo schernire (persone) ☆ bear- —, combattimento di cani contro orsi; bull- —, combattimento di cani contro tori.

baize [beiz], s. panno di lana pesante (per porte, mobili): green —, panno verde, tappeto verde.

to bake [beik], v.t.i. cuocere al forno; indurire (per effetto di calore), indurirsi; abbronzare; far maturare col calore.

bakehouse ['beikhaus], s. forno, panificio.

bakelite ['beikəlait], s. bachelite.

baker ['beikə*], s. fornaio, panettiere: — s' (shop), panetteria ‖ —'s dozen, il numero tredici; peso abbondante ☆ — -legged, con le gambe a x.

bakery ['beikəri], s. forno, panificio.

baking ['beikiŋ], s. cottura al forno; infornata (di pane); cotta (di mattoni) ☆ — -hot, torrido; — -powder, lievito in polvere; — -soda, (chim.) bicarbonato di sodio; — -tin, teglia.

baksheesh, bakshish ['bækʃi:ʃ], s. mancia.

Balaam ['beiləm], s. 1. cattivo profeta 2. (giornalismo) articoli usati come riempitivo.

Balaclava [,bælə'klɑ:və], no.pr. (geog.) Balaclava ☆ — helmet, passamontagna.

balalaika [,bælə'laikə], s. (mus.) balalaica.

balance ['bæləns], s. 1. bilancia: to cast the (o to turn the) —, dare il tracollo alla bilancia; to throw into the —, gettare sulla bilancia ‖ Balance, (astr.) Bilancia ‖ on —, tutto sommato 2. bilanciere (d'orologio) 3. equilibrio; contrappeso: — of power, equilibrio (di forze politiche); want of —, mancanza d'equilibrio; to lose one's —, perdere l'equilibrio, avere la mente sconvolta 4. (comm.) bilancio; pareggio; conguaglio; saldo: — in hand, saldo a credito; — of payments, bilancia dei pagamenti; — of trade, bilancio (esportazioni-importazioni); to strike a —, fare un bilancio ☆ — beam, braccio della bilancia; — maker, bilanciaio; — -sheet, bilancio di esercizio; — spring, molla per bilanciere; — weight, contrappeso; — -wheel, bilanciere ‖ credit, debit —, saldo a credito, a debito; closing —, bilancio di chiusura; final —, bilancio consuntivo; opening —, bilancio di apertura; trial- —, bilancio di verifica.

to balance, v.t.i. 1. pesare (anche fig.) 2. bilanciare, bilanciarsi; bilibrare; mantenere l'equilibrio; contrappesare 3. oscillare 4. (comm.) saldare; pareggiare; fare il bilancio.

balaneer ['bælənsə*], s. 1. bilanciere 2. equilibrista.

balas ['bæləs], s. (min.) balascio.

balconied ['bælkənid], ag. fornito di balcone.

balcony ['bælkəni], s. 1. balcone; terrazzino 2. (teat.) balconata 3. (mar.) galleria di poppa.

bald [bɔ:ld], ag. 1. calvo, pelato; spelacchiato; senza penne; senza alberi; senza foglie 2. macchiato di bianco (di cavallo) 3. povero, nudo, disadorno, monotono (di stile) ☆ — -head, calvo; testa calva.

baldachin ['bɔ:ldəkin], s. baldacchino.

bald-coot ['bɔ:ldku:t], s. 1. (ornit.) folaga 2. calvo.

balderdash ['bɔ:ldədæʃ], s. guazzabuglio (di parole); ciance; sciocchezze.

baldly ['bɔ:ldli], av. nudamente; poveramente ‖ to put it —, per dirla in parole povere.

baldness ['bɔ:ldnis], s. 1. calvizie 2. fig. nudità.

baldpate ['bɔ:ldpeit], s. 1. testa calva; (fam.) zucca pelata; pelata, boccia 2. anitra selvatica.

baldpated ['bɔ:ld,peitid], ag. calvo.

baldric(k) ['bɔ:ldrik], s. balteo.

Baldwin ['bɔ:ldwin], no.pr.m. Baldovino.

bale¹ [beil], s. (arc. poet.) disgrazia; tristezza; dolore.

bale², s. 1. (arc.) pira 2. segnale luminoso.

bale³, s. (comm.) balla (di merce).

to **bale³**, v.t. (comm.) imballare.

to **bale⁴**, V. to **bail⁵**.

Bâle [ba:l], no.pr. (geog.) Basilea.

baleen [bə'li:n], s. fanone.

balefire ['beilfaiə*], s. (arc.) falò; rogo funerario.

baleful ['beilful], ag. (letter.) 1. funesto; pericoloso 2. accorato.

balefully ['beilfuli], av. (letter.) 1. biecamente 2. accoratamente.

balefulness ['beilfulnis], s. (letter.) 1. ostilità 2. accoratezza.

baler ['beilə*], s. 1. imballatore 2. pressaballe; pressaforaggio.

balk [bɔ:lk], s. 1. (agr.) dorso; porca 2. fig. ostacolo; impedimento 3. (arch.) catena 4. funicella (delle reti da pesca).

to **balk**, v.t. 1. (arc.) arare (la terra) 2. evitare; omettere; ostacolare; sventare; impedire.

Balkan ['bɔ:lkən], ag. balcanico.

Balkans (the) ['bɔ:lkənz], no.pr. pl. (geog.) Balcani.

ball¹ [bɔ:l], s. palla (di cannone, fucile, biliardo, per votare, ecc.); pallone; gomitolo; pallottola; (poet.) la terra: — the eye, globo oculare; — of the foot, avampiede; — of the thumb, polpastrello del pollice ‖ three balls, insegna di un banco di pegni ‖ to keep the — rolling, (fam.) continuare senza interruzione: we kept the — running, mantenemmo viva la conversazione; while we were away, John kept the — running, durante la nostra assenza, John mandò avanti la baracca ☆ — -bearing, cuscinetto a sfere; — -cartridge, cartuccia a palla; — -cock (o — -tap), galleggiante (di chiusura automatica di cisterna); — -point (pen), penna a sfera; — -proof, a prova di proiettile ‖ meat- —, polpetta.

to **ball¹**, v.t.i. appallottolare, appallottolarsi; aggomitolare ‖ to be balled up, (amer.) essere confuso ‖ to be black-balled, ricevere voto sfavorevole.

ball², s. ballo; festa da ballo: to attend a —, presenziare a un ballo ☆ — -room, sala da ballo ‖ fancy-dress —, ballo in costume; masked- —, ballo in maschera.

ballad ['bæləd], s. ballata (componimento poetico di carattere popolare).

ballade [bæ'la:d], s. ballata (componimento poetico, in origine musicato e destinato ad accompagnare danze; componimento musicale).

ballast ['bæləst], s. 1. zavorra 2. fig. equilibrio 3. ballastro, massicciata (di ferrovia, strada, ecc.).

to **ballast**, v.t. 1. (mar.) zavorrare 2. fig. consolidare 3. massicciare.

ballerina [,bælə'ri:nə], s. ballerina.

ballet ['bælei], s. 1. balletto 2. (teat.) corpo di ballo ☆ — -dancer, danzatore classico, danzatrice classica; — -girl, danzatrice classica; — -skirt, tutù.

bal(l)ista [bə'listə], pl. **bal(l)istae** [bə'listi:], s. (st. mil.) balista.

ballistic [bə'listik], ag. (mil.) balistico, di balistica.

ballistics [bə'listiks], s. (mil.) balistica.

ballistite ['bælistait], s. (chim.) ballistite.

balloon [bə'lu:n], s. 1. pallone; pallone aerostatico 2. (arch.) globo, sfera 3. (chim.) lambicco 4. fumetto (nei giornaletti) ☆ — -park, (aer.) parco aerostatico ‖ barrage —, pallone di sbarramento; captive —, pallone frenato; pilot —, pallone pilota; sounding —, pallone sonda.

to **balloon**, v.t.i. 1. (aer.) andare in pallone 2. gonfiare, gonfiarsi come un pallone.

balloonist [bə'lu:nist], s. (aer.) aeronauta.

ballot¹ ['bælət], s. 1. palla, pallina (per votare) 2. scheda (di votazione); scrutinio; voto (atto del votare): by —, allo scrutinio ‖ second —, ballottaggio ☆ — -box, urna.

to **ballot¹**, v.i. votare a scrutinio segreto.

ballot², s. (comm.) piccola balla.

ballotage ['bælətidʒ], s. ballottaggio.

bally ['bæli], ag. (sl.) maledetto.

ballyhoo ['bælihu:], s. strombazzata pubblicitaria.

to **ballyhoo**, v.t. fare pubblicità in modo sensazionale a.

to **ballyrag** ['bæliræg], pass. p.p. **ballyragged** ['bælirægd], v.t.i. (sl.) 1. tormentare con scherzi grossolani 2. scherzare grossolanamente.

balm [ba:m], s. balsamo.

to **balm**, v.t. (arc.) 1. ungere; spalmare di balsamo 2. calmare; alleviare.

balm-cricket [ba:m,krikit], s. (entom.) cicala.

balminess ['ba:minis], s. soffio balsamico; fragranza.

Balmoral [bæl'mɔrəl], no.pr. (geog.) Balmoral ‖ — Castle, Castello di Balmoral (residenza scozzese dei reali inglesi).

balmy ['ba:mi], ag. 1. balsamico; calmante; fig. dolce; fragrante 2. (sl.) sventato.

balsam ['bɔ:lsəm], s. 1. balsamo 2. (bot.) balsamina.

balsamic(al) [bɔ:l'sæmik(ə)l], ag. balsamico.

balsamine ['bɔ:lsəmin], s. (bot.) balsamina.

balsamous ['bɔ:lsəməs], ag. balsamico.

Balthazar [bæl'θæzə*], no.pr.m. Baldassarre.

Baltic ['bɔ:ltik], ag. Baltico ‖ the — Sea, il mare Baltico ‖ s. il Baltico.

Baltimore ['bɔ:ltimɔ:*], no.pr. (geog.) Baltimora.

Baluchistan [bə'lu:tʃista:n], no.pr. (geog.) Belucistan.

baluster ['bæləstə*], s. balaustro; balaustrino.

balustered ['bæləstəd], ag. balaustrato.

balustrade [,bæləs'treid], s. balaustrata.

balustraded [,bæləs'treidid], ag. balaustrato.

bam [bæm], s. (sl. arc.) inganno.

bambino [ba:m'bi:nou], pl. **bambini** [ba:m'bi:ni], s. immagine del Bambino Gesù.

bamboo [bæm'bu:], s. (bot.) bambù.

to **bamboozle** [bæm'bu:zl], v.t. (sl.) turlupinare; ingannare.

bamboozlement [bæm'bu:zlmənt], s. (sl.) turlupinatura; inganno.

bamboozler [bæm'bu:zlə*], s.c. (sl.) turlupinatore, turlupinatrice; ingannatore, ingannatrice.

ban [bæn], s. 1. bando (annunzio pubblico): to publish the bans, fare le pubblicazioni matrimoniali 2. bando; interdizione; scomunica.

to **ban**, pass.p.p. **banned** [bænd], v.t. proibire; interdire; mettere all'indice.

banal [bə'na:l], ag. banale, comune.

banality [bə'næliti], s. banalità, luogo comune.

banana [bə'na:nə], s. 1. banana 2. —(-tree), banano ☆ — oil, (chim.) acetato di anile.

bane [bæŋk], **banco** ['bæŋkou], s. banco, seggio ‖ in —, in seduta plenaria.

band¹ [bænd], s. vincolo, legame.

to **band¹**, v.t. legare con legami.

band², s. 1. benda; striscia, lista; fascia; nastro; cerchio (di botte) 2. (eccl.) fasciola 3. pl. baverina di collare (di prete, magistrato, ecc.) ☆ — -saw, sega a nastro; — -wheel, puleggia a fascia piana ‖ elastic —, fascia elastica.

to **band²**, v.t. segnare con striscie.

band³, s. 1. (mus.) banda; orchestrina 2. banda; comitiva, compagnia organizzata: — of robbers, banda di ladri ☆ — -stand, palco dell'orchestra; — -wagon, (amer.) carro della banda musicale (che precede una parata, specialmente durante le elezioni): on the — -wagon, con il favore popolare, dalla parte del vincente ‖ brass —, fanfara.

to **band³**, v.t.i. riunire, riunirsi; associare, associarsi.

bandage ['bændidʒ], s. benda, fascia; fasciatura.

to **bandage**, v.t. bendare, fasciare.

bandana [bæn'da:nə], **bandanna** [bæn'dænə], s. fazzoletto di seta, cotone a colori vivaci.

bandbox ['bændbɔks], s. cappelliera.

bandeau ['bændou], pl. **bandeaux** ['bændouz], s. « bandeau » (striscia, benda che cinge i capelli).

banderol(e) ['bændəroul], *s.* banderuola, pennone.
bandit ['bændit], *pl.* **bandits** ['bændits], **banditti** [bæn'diti(:)], *s.* bandito, brigante.
bandlet ['bændlit], *s.* (*arch.*) listello.
bandmaster ['bænd,mɑ:stə*], *s.* capobanda.
bandog ['bændɔg], *s.* cane da guardia; mastino.
bandoleer [,bændə'liə*], *s.* bandoliera.
bandolero [,bɑ:ndə'leirou], *s.* brigante.
bandolier [,bændə'liə*], *s.* bandoliera.
bandoline ['bændəli:n], *s.* fissatore per capelli.
bandsman, *pl.* **bandsmen** ['bændzmən], *s.* (*mus.*) bandista; musicante.
bandy ['bændi], *ag.* curvo, storto (di gambe) ☆ — -legged, dalle gambe storte, arcuate.
bandy, *s.* 1. palla al maglio (oggi hockey) 2. mazza usata in questo giuoco.
to bandy, *v.t.* 1. palleggiare 2. scambiare (parole, accuse, ecc.); discutere; criticare.
bane [bein], *s.* (*arc.*) 1. veleno 2. sventura; flagello, rovina.
to bane, *v.t.* (*arc.*) 1. avvelenare 2. danneggiare.
baneful ['beinful], *ag.* 1. velenoso 2. pernicioso.
banefully ['beinfuli], *av.* dannosamente.
banefulness ['beinfulnis], *s.* perniciosità.
bang[1] [bæŋ], *s.* botta; colpo (di fucile, ecc.); rumore improvviso, violento (come di porta che sbatte).
to bang[1], *v.t.i.* 1. battere rumorosamente, violentemente: *to — at* (*o on*) *the door*, battere rumorosamente alla porta 2. sbattere violentemente: *the door banged shut*, la porta si chiuse violentemente; *to — a mat against the wall*, sbattere uno zerbino contro il muro.
bang[1], *av.* improvvisamente, subitamente ‖ *the whole — lot*, (*sl.*) tutto quanto, tutti quanti ‖ — *went all my money*, (*sl.*) ho perduto di colpo tutto il mio denaro ‖ *to go* —, (*fam.*) esplodere.
bang[1], *inter.* pum!, pam! (come un colpo di fucile).
bang[2], *s.* frangia (di capelli) ☆ — -tail, cavallo con la coda mozza.
to bang[2], *v.t.* tagliare (i capelli) a frangia ‖ *to — a horse's tail*, mozzare la coda di un cavallo.
banging ['bæŋiŋ], *s.* colpi violenti; detonazioni.
bangle ['bæŋgl], *s.* braccialetto (da polso, caviglia).
banian ['bæniən], *s.* 1. commerciante indù 2. giacchetta, camiciotto sciolto di lana 3. (*bot.*) fico d'India ☆ — *day*, (*mar. fig.*) giorno di magro.
to banish ['bæniʃ], *v.t.* bandire; esiliare; cacciare.
banishment ['bæniʃmənt], *s.* bando; esilio.
banister ['bænistə*], *s. gener. pl.* ringhiera (di scala).
banjo ['bændʒou], *s.* (*mus.*) banjo.
banjoist ['bændʒouist], *s.* suonatore di banjo.
bank[1] [bæŋk], *s.* 1. altura, tumulo; banco (anche di nubi, neve); terrapieno; massicciata; (*mar.*) secca; banco (di ghiaccio, di pesci) 2. argine, riva (di fiume); orlo; bordo (di precipizio, di pozzo di miniera).
to bank[1], *v.t.i.* 1. arginare 2. sopraelevare (la curva di una strada) 3. urtare contro un argine 3. (*aer.*) inclinarsi in virata 5. *to — up*, accatastare, accatastarsi.
bank[2], *s.* 1. banca: — *of issue*, banca di emissione; *people's* —, banca popolare ‖ *Bank Holiday*, festività legali (in Inghilterra, il Venerdì Santo, il lunedì di Pasqua, Pentecoste, il primo lunedì d'Agosto, Natale e S. Stefano) 2. banco (di giuoco): *to break the* —, far saltare il banco ☆ — *account*, conto in banca; — -*bill*, tratta bancaria; (*amer.*) banconota; — -*book*, libretto di deposito; — *clerk*, impiegato di banca; -*credit*, credito bancario; — -*note*, banconota, assegno circolare; — *overdraft*, scoperto bancario; — *paper*, biglietti di banca, carta simile alla cartamoneta; — *rate*, tasso bancario ‖ *blood*- —, banca del sangue; *branch* —, filiale di banca; *credit* —, banco di credito; *deposit* —, banca di deposito; *discount* —, banco di sconto; *eye* —, banca degli occhi; *joint-stock* —, banca per azioni; *savings* —, cassa di risparmio.
to bank[2], *v.t.i.* 1. gestire una banca 2. depositare in

una banca ‖ *to — with*, depositare denaro presso, aver per banchiere: *whom do you — with?*, in quale banca depositi i tuoi denari? 3. tenere il banco (nei giuochi) 4. *to — (up)on* (*s.o.*, *sthg.*), contare su.
bank[3], *s.* 1. fila di remi (in una galera); banco dei rematori; sedile 2. (*mus.*) tastiera (di organo).
bankable ['bæŋkəbl], *ag.* (*comm.*) scontabile.
banker[1] ['bæŋkə*], *s.* 1. banchiere 2. banchiere, chi tiene il banco (in alcuni giuochi) 3. giuoco d'azzardo.
banker[2], *s.* 1. imbarcazione adibita alla pesca del merluzzo (in Terranova) 2. sterratore 3. (*caccia*) cavallo che salta ostacoli.
banker[3], *s.* banco (su cui si riducono alla giusta misura mattoni o pietre).
banket ['bæŋkit], *s.* (*min.*) conglomerato aurifero.
banking[1] ['bæŋkiŋ], *s.* arginatura.
banking[2], *ag.* di banca, bancario ‖ *s.* tecnica bancaria; professione di banchiere ☆ — *account*, conto di banca; — *hours*, orario di banca.
bankrupt ['bæŋkrəpt], *ag.* fallito; carico di debiti; fraudolento; doloso ‖ *s.* fallito; (*iron.*) bancarottiere: *discharged* —, fallito riabilitato; *to go, to become* —, fallire, far fallimento.
to bankrupt, *v.t.* far fallire; (*fam.*) rovinare.
bankruptcy ['bæŋkrəptsi], *s.* (*comm.*) fallimento; bancarotta: *fraudulent* —, bancarotta fraudolenta.
banksman, *pl.* **banksmen** ['bæŋksmən], *s.* sorvegliante esterno di miniera di carbone.
banner ['bænə*], *ag.* (*amer.*) eccellente; eccezionale ‖ *s.* 1. vessillo; stendardo; bandiera ‖ *to join s.o.'s* —, (*fam.*) mettersi al seguito di qlcu. 2. titolo a caratteri cubitali.
bannered ['bænəd], *ag.* (*mar.*) imbandierato.
banneret ['bænərit], *s.* (*st.*) banderese.
bannerman, *pl.* **bannermen** ['bænəmən], *s.* porta bandiera.
bannerol ['bænəroul], *s.* banderuola.
bannock ['bænək], *s.* (*scoz.*) focaccia d'avena.
Bannockburn ['bænəkbə:n], *no.pr.* (*geog.*) Bannockburn (teatro della battaglia in cui gli scozzesi sconfissero gli inglesi conquistando l'indipendenza, 1314).
banns [bænz], *s.pl.* pubblicazioni matrimoniali: *to put up* (*o to publish*) *the* —, fare le pubblicazioni matrimoniali.
banquet ['bæŋkwit], *s.* banchetto.
to banquet, *v.t.i.* offrire un banchetto a; convitare; banchettare; festeggiare.
banqueter ['bæŋkwitə*], *s.* banchettante; commensale; convitato.
banqueting ['bæŋkwitiŋ], *s.* il banchettare ☆ — -*hall* (*o* -*room*), sala dei banchetti.
banquette [bæŋ'ket], *s.* banchina di tiro.
Banquo ['bæŋkwou], *no.pr.m.* (*lett.*) Banco.
banshee [bæn'ʃi], *s.* (*irl. scoz.*) spirito (di donna) preannunciante morte.
to bant [bænt], *v.i.* (*scherz.*) stare a dieta dimagrante, non farinacea.
bantam ['bæntəm], *s.* gallo piccolissimo ma forte e battagliero ☆ — -*weight*, peso gallo (di pugile).
banter ['bæntə*], *s.* beffa; canzonatura.
to banter, *v.t.i.* beffare; canzonare; fare dell'ironia (su).
banterer ['bæntərə*], *s.c.* burlone, burlona.
bantering ['bæntəriŋ], *s.* beffa; canzonatura.
bantling ['bæntliŋ], *s.* marmocchio; bamboccio.
Bantu ['bæn'tu:], *ag.s.c.* bantù.
banyian, *V.* **banian**.
baobab ['beiəbæb], *s.* (*bot.*) baobab.
baptism ['bæptizm], *s.* battesimo.
baptismal [bæp'tizməl], *ag.* battesimale.
baptist ['bæptist], *s.* 1. chi battezza ‖ *John the Baptist*, (*relig.*) Giovanni Battista 2. (*st. relig.*) anabattista.
baptist(e)ry ['bæptist(ə)ri], *s.* battistero.
to baptize [bæp'taiz], *v.t.* battezzare.

bar¹ [ba:*], *prep.* (*fam.*) eccetto, tranne, a parte: *all — him*, tutti tranne lui.

bar², *s.* **1.** sbarra, stanga, spranga (di metallo, legno); stecca (di cioccolata): *gold in bars*, oro in lingotti **2.** striscia; riga: *a — of light*, una striscia di luce **3.** (*arald.*) sbarra, banda (su scudo) **4.** diga; chiusa **5.** impedimento; ostacolo: *a — to success*, un ostacolo al successo **6.** (*dir.*) barra (divisorio che separa i giudici dagli accusati); *fig.* tribunale: *the prisoner at the —*, l'accusato; *to appear at the —*, apparire in giudizio; *to be called to the —*, essere iscritto all'albo degli avvocati ‖ *the Bar*, l'Ordine degli avvocati **7.** bar (locale, banco) **8.** (*mus.*) sbarretta; battuta: *three bars' rest*, tre battute d'arresto ☆ *— -keeper* (o *fam. — -keep*), proprietario di bar; *— -tender*, barista ‖ *door —*, catenaccio; *harbour, river —*, banco, sbarramento del porto, del fiume; *horizontal —*, (*ginnastica*) sbarra orizzontale; *parallel bars*, (*ginnastica*) parallele.

to bar², *pass.p.p.* **barred** [ba:d], *v.t.* **1.** sprangare; sbarrare **2.** rigare, listare **3.** ostruire; *fig.* ostacolare: *to — s.o. from doing sthg.*, impedire a qlcu. di fare ql.co.; *to — the way to progress*, ostacolare il progresso **4.** escludere; interdire, proibire; (*sl.*) disapprovare: *she barred smoking in the dining-room*, non permetteva che si fumasse in sala da pranzo **5.** *to — in*, chiudere dentro: *to — oneself in*, barricarsi **6.** *to — out*, chiudere fuori: *to — s.o. out*, sbarrare la porta a qlcu.

Barabbas [bə'ræbəs], *no.pr.m.* (*Bibbia*) Barabba.

barathrum ['bærəθram], *s.* baratro, abisso.

barb¹ [ba:b], *s.* **1.** punta (d'amo, di freccia, ecc.) **2.** cirro (di alcuni pesci); barba di una piuma **3.** pungiglione **4.** soggolo.

to barb¹, *v.t.* munire di punta; armare (una freccia).

barb², *s.* **1.** cavallo di Barberia **2.** piccione di Barberia.

Barbado(e)s [ba:'beidouz], *no.pr.* (*geog.*) Barbados.

Barbara ['ba:bərə], *no.pr.f.* Barbara.

barbaresque [,ba:bə'resk], *ag.* barbaresco.

barbarian [ba:'bɛəriən], *ag.s.* barbaro; straniero; selvaggio.

barbaric [ba:'bærik], *ag.* barbarico; primitivo.

barbarically [ba:'bærikəli], *av.* barbaramente.

barbarism ['ba:bərizəm], *s.* **1.** barbarie **2.** barbarismo (nel linguaggio).

barbarity [ba:'bæriti], *s.* barbarie.

to barbarize ['ba:bəraiz], *v.t.i.* **1.** rendere, diventare barbaro **2.** barbarizzare (il linguaggio).

barbarous ['ba:bərəs], *ag.* barbaro.

barbarously ['ba:bərəsli], *av.* barbaramente.

barbarousness ['ba:bərəsnis], *s.* barbarie.

Barbary ['ba:bəri], *no.pr.* (*geog. st.*) Barberia ☆ *— corsairs*, corsari di Barberia; *— horse*, cavallo barbero.

barbate ['ba:beit], *ag.* (*zool. bot.*) barbato, barbuto.

barbecue [ba:bikju:], *s.* **1.** animale arrostito intero **2.** graticola **3.** (*amer.*) festa campestre.

to barbecue, *v.t.* far arrostire (un animale) tutto intero.

barbed [ba:bd], *ag.* **1.** dentato, dentellato; uncinato (come l'amo) **2.** (*bot.*) barbato **3.** *fig.* acuto; pungente ☆ *— arrow*, freccia dentata; *— -wire*, filo di ferro spinato.

barbel ['ba:bəl], *s.* **1.** (*ittiol.*) barbio **2.** *pl.* filamenti; cirri (pendenti dalla bocca di pesci).

barber ['ba:bə*], *s.* barbiere ☆ *—'s basin*, catino per la barba; *—'s block*, porta parrucca.

barberry ['ba:bəri], *s.* (*bot.*) crespino.

barbette [ba:'bet], *s.* (*mar. mil.*) barbetta.

barbican ['ba:bikən], *s.* (*arch. mil.*) barbacane.

barbiturate [,ba:bi'tjuərit], *s.* (*farm.*) barbiturico.

barbituric [,ba:bi'tjuərik], *ag.* (*farm.*) barbiturico.

barcarol(l)e ['ba:kəroul], *s.* (*mus.*) barcarola.

bard¹ [ba:d], *s.* (*st.*) bardo.

bard², *s.* (*st.*) barda.

to bard², *v.t.* bardare.

barded [ba:did], *ag.* bardato (di cavallo).

bardic [ba:dik], *ag.* (*st.*) da bardo.

bardism ['ba:dizəm], *s.* (*st.*) l'arte dei bardi.

bare [bɛə*], *ag.* **1.** nudo, spoglio; scoperto: *— of clothes*, senz'abiti; *— of money*, al verde ‖ *to lay —*, mettere a nudo, rivelare: *all his faults were laid —*, tutti i suoi difetti furono messi a nudo, rivelati **2.** logoro, usato (di vestito) **3.** vuoto: *a room — of furniture*, una stanza vuota, priva di mobili **4.** semplice: *the — idea* (o *fact*), la sola idea; *the — truth*, la semplice verità, *to earn a — living*, guadagnarsi appena da vivere.

to bare, *v.t.* **1.** denudare, mettere a nudo **2.** smascherare, scoprire, rivelare **3.** sfoderare, sguainare.

barebacked ['bɛəbækt], *ag.* senza sella (di cavallo).

barebone ['bɛəboun], *s.* persona scarna, scheletrita.

barefaced ['bɛəfeist], *ag.* **1.** imberbe **2.** a viso scoperto; senza maschera **3.** aperto; chiaro **4.** sfacciato, spudorato.

barefacedly ['bɛəfeistli], *av.* sfacciatamente.

barefacedness ['bɛəfeistnis], *s.* sfacciataggine.

barefoot ['bɛəfut], **barefooted** ['bɛə'futid], *ag.* scalzo ‖ *av.* a piedi scalzi.

barehanded ['bɛə'hændid], *ag.av.* a mano nuda; senza armi.

bareheaded ['bɛə'hedid], *ag.av.* a capo scoperto, senza cappello.

barelegged ['bɛə'legd], *ag.av.* con le gambe nude.

barely ['bɛəli], *av.* **1.** apertamente; nudamente; esplicitamente **2.** semplicemente; appena: *I — know him*, lo conosco appena.

bareness ['bɛənis], *s.* **1.** nudità **2.** scarsezza; povertà.

baresark ['bɛəsa:k], *V.* **berserker**.

bargain ['ba:gin], *s.* **1.** contratto; patto; mercato; affare: *a bad —*, un cattivo affare; *a capital —*, un affarone; *a good —*, un buon affare ‖ *into the —*, per giunta, in più (di quanto stabilito) ‖ *to make the best of a bad —*, trarre il meglio da un cattivo affare ‖ *to strike a — with s.o.*, concludere un affare con qualcuno **2.** occasione, buon affare: *it's a —*, è un'occasione, un affare vantaggioso ☆ *— sale*, vendita a stralcio.

to bargain, *v.t.i.* **1.** contrattare, pattuire, negoziare **2.** *to — for (sthg.)*, attendersi, aspettarsi: *I didn't — for that*, questo non me l'aspettavo.

bargainee [,ba:gi'ni:], *s.* (*dir.*) acquirente.

bargainer ['ba:ginə*], *s.* (*dir.*) venditore; mercante.

bargaining ['ba:giniŋ], *s.* contrattazione, mercanteggiamento: *collective —*, (*sindacalismo*) contrattazione collettiva.

barge [ba:dʒ], *s.* (*mar.*) **1.** chiatta, bettolina, maona **2.** scialuppa; lancia di parata ☆ *admiral's —*, lancia dell'ammiraglio; *unloading —*, chiatta da sbarco.

to barge, *v.t.i.* **1.** trasportare su chiatta **2.** *to — against, into (s.o., sthg.)*, (*sl.*) urtare pesantemente contro **3.** *to — about*, (*sl.*) avanzare traballando **4.** *to — in*, (*sl.*) intervenire a sproposito.

bargee [ba:'dʒi:], **bargeman**, *pl.* **bargemen** ['ba:dʒmən], *s.* barcaiolo; battelliere.

barie ['bærik], *ag.* (*chim.*) di bario, barico.

baritone ['bæritoun], *s.* (*mus.*) baritono.

barium ['bɛəriəm], *s.* (*chim.*) bario.

bark¹ [ba:k], *s.* scorza, corteccia.

to bark¹, *v.t.* scortecciare ‖ *to — one's knuckles*, sbucciarsi le nocche.

bark², *s.* **1.** latrato ‖ *his — is worse than his bite*, can che abbaia non morde **2.** (*sl.*) tosse.

to bark², *v.i.* **1.** latrare, abbaiare ‖ *to — at the moon*, abbaiare alla luna ‖ *to — up the wrong tree*, prendersela con chi non c'entra **2.** parlare rabbiosamente **3.** (*sl.*) tossire.

bark³, *s.* (*mar.*) brigantino a palo; (*poet.*) naviglio.

to barken ['ba:kən], *v.t.i.* disseccare; seccarsi formando crosta.

barkentine ['ba:kənti:n], *s.* nave goletta.

barker ['ba:kə*], *s.c.* chi abbaia; (*amer.*) strillone, strillona; imbonitore, imbonitrice ‖ *s.* (*sl.*) pistola.

barking¹ ['ba:kiŋ], *s.* scortecciamento.

barking², *s.* **1.** abbaiamento **2.** *fig.* grido rabbioso **3.** (*sl.*) tosse.

barley ['bɑ:li], s. orzo ☆ — -*broth*, birra forte; — -*meal*, farina d'orzo; — -*sugar*, zucchero d'orzo; — -*water*, decotto, acqua d'orzo ‖ *great* —, spelta, farro; *hulled* —, orzo mondato; *malted* —, orzo tallito, malto; *pearl*- —, orzo perlato.

barleycorn ['bɑ:likɔ:n], s. grano d'orzo ‖ *John Barleycorn*, (*fam.*) personificazione dello whisky, della birra.

barm [bɑ:m], s. lievito di birra.

barmaid ['bɑ:meid], s. cameriera al banco.

barman, pl. **barmen** ['bɑ:mən], s. barista.

barmy ['bɑ:mi], ag. 1. che contiene lievito; schiumoso; in fermentazione 2. balordo.

barn [bɑ:n], s. 1. granaio; (*spreg.*) baracca 2. (*amer.*) stalla 3. (*amer.*) rimessa tramviaria ☆ — -*dance*, danza campestre; — -*door*, porta di granaio: *he could not hit a* — -*door*, (*fam.*) non sapeva colpire nemmeno in più grosso bersaglio; — -*floor*, aia; — -*owl*, civetta; — -*stormer*, attore girovago.

Barnabas ['bɑ:nəbəs], no.pr.m. Barnaba.

Barnabite ['bɑ:nəbait], s. (*eccl.*) barnabita.

Barnaby ['bɑ:nəbi], no.pr.m. Barnaba.

barnacle[1] ['bɑ:nəkl], s. 1. (*zool.*) cirripede 2. (*sl.*) persona attaccaticcia 3. — (-*goose*), (*ornit.*) bernacla.

barnacle[2], s. gener. pl. 1. morso da cavalli (usato dal maniscalco) 2. (*sl.*) occhiali.

barnyard ['bɑ:njɑ:d], s. cortile ☆ — *fowls*, animali da cortile.

barograph ['bærougrɑ:f], s. barografo.

barology [bə'rɔlədʒi], s. barologia.

barometer [bə'rɔmitə*], s. barometro ☆ *aneroid* —, barometro aneroide; *siphon* —, barometro a sifone; *wheel* —, barometro a ruota.

barometric(al) [,bærə'metrik(əl)], ag. barometrico.

barometrically [,bærə'metrikəli], av. per mezzo di un barometro.

barometry [bə'rɔmitri], s. barometria.

baron ['bærən], s. 1. (*arald. st.*) barone 2. (*amer.*) grande industriale ☆ *beer* —, il re della birra.

baronage ['bærənidʒ], s. 1. baronia; i baroni; (*st.*) i grandi vassalli della corona 2. lista dei baroni; annuario della nobiltà.

baroness ['bærənis], s. baronessa.

baronet ['bærənit], s. baronetto.

to baronet, v.t. elevare al rango di baronetto, creare baronetto.

baronetage ['bærənitidʒ], s. 1. la classe dei baronetti 2. lista dei baronetti.

baronetcy ['bærənitsi], s. dignità di baronetto.

baronial [bə'rounjəl], ag. baronale.

barony ['bærəni], s. 1. baronia 2. suddivisione di una contea (in Irlanda) 3. proprietà terriera (in Scozia).

baroque [bə'rouk], ag.s. barocco (anche *fig.*).

barouche [bə'ru:ʃ], s. baroccio; calesse.

barque [bɑ:k], s. (*mar.*) brigantino a palo; (*poet.*) naviglio.

barquentine ['bɑ:kənti:n], s. nave goletta.

barracan ['bærəkæn], s. barracano.

barrack[1] ['bærək], s. gener.pl. caserma; baracca.

to barrack[1], v.t.i. accasermare; vivere in baracche.

to barrack[2], v.t. schernire, fischiare (giocatori).

barracoon [,bærə'ku:n], s. recinto per schiavi negri o forzati (nell'Africa Francese).

barracuda [,bærə'ku:də], s. (*ittiol.*) barracuda.

barrage ['bærɑ:ʒ], s. sbarramento, diga; (*mil.*) sbarramento ☆ — -*balloon*, (*mil.*) pallone di sbarramento; — -*fire*, tiro di sbarramento ‖ *anti-aircraft* —, (*mil.*) sbarramento antiaereo; *supersonic* —, (*mar.*) sbarramento ultrasonico.

barrator ['bærətə*], s. 1. (*dir.*) attaccabrighe 2. barattiere.

barratry ['bærətri], s. 1. (*dir.*) incitamento alle liti; discordia 2. (*mar. arc.*) baratteria.

barred [bɑ:d], ag. barrato; sbarrato.

barrel ['bærəl], s. 1. barile, botte, fusto 2. tamburo (d'orologio, di rivoltella, ecc.); cassa (di tamburo);

(*mar.*) tamburo, campana 3. cilindro; serbatoio (di penna stilografica); cannuccia (di pipa); cannello (di penna); canna (d'arma da fuoco); cilindro (d'organo) 4. « barrel » (misura di capacità = 1. 163,65) ☆ — -*organ*, organetto a cilindro; — -*vault*, (*arch.*) volta a botte.

to barrel, pass.p.p. **barrelled** ['bærəld], v.t. imbarilare; imbottare.

barrelled ['bærəld], ag. messo in barili, in botti; a forma di barile ☆ *single*- —, *double*- — *gun*, fucile a una canna, a due canne.

barren ['bærən], ag. sterile; arido; povero; poco proficuo: — *of*, totalmente mancante di: *mind* — *of ideas*, spirito sprovvisto di idee ‖ s. landa.

barrenly ['bærənli], av. sterilmente.

barrenness ['bærənnis], s. sterilità; aridità.

barret ['bærit], s. berretta.

barricade [,bæri'keid], s. barricata; steccato; barriera (anche *fig.*).

to barricade, v.t. barricare; asserragliare; ostruire.

barrier ['bæriə*], s. barriera; barricata; palizzata; cancello; spalto; limite ‖ *the Great Ice Barrier*, la Banchisa ☆ — *cream*, crema antivampa ‖ *transonic* — (-*o sound* —), (*fis.*) muro del suono.

to barrier, v.t. chiudere con una barriera.

barring ['bɑ:riŋ], V. **bar**[1].

barrister ['bæristə*], s. avvocato (con facoltà di discutere cause presso le corti di grado superiore) ‖ *revising* —, (*dir.*) controllore delle liste elettorali ‖ *to appear on the roll of barristers*, essere iscritto all'albo degli avvocati.

barristerial [,bæris'tiəriəl], ag. da, di avvocato.

barristership ['bæristəʃip], s. avvocatura (di grado superiore).

barrow[1] ['bærou], s. 1. (*hand*-) —, barella 2. (*wheel*-) —, carriuola ☆ *coster's* —, carretta a due ruote di venditore ambulante.

barrow[2], s. 1. collina, altura (nei nomi di località) 2. (*arc.*) tumulo.

barrow[3], s. cinghiale castrato.

barse [bɑ:s], s. (*dial.*) pesce persico.

barter ['bɑ:tə*], s. 1. baratto, scambio 2. (*arit.*) equivalenza.

to barter, v.t.i. 1. barattare, scambiare; praticare il baratto 2. *to* — **away**, (*spreg.*) vendere: *to* — *away one's liberty*, vendere la propria libertà.

barterer ['bɑ:tərə*], s.c. barattatore, barattatrice.

Bartholomew [bɑ:'θɔləmju:], no.pr.m. Bartolomeo.

bartizan ['bɑ:tizæn], s. (*arch.*) bertesca.

barton ['bɑ:tn], s. 1. cortile di fattoria 2. (*arc.*) rustici di proprietà signorile.

barycentric [,bæri'sentrik], ag. baricentrico.

barysphere ['bærisfiə*], s. (*geol.*) barisfera.

baryta [bə'raitə], s. (*chim.*) barite.

barytes [bə'raiti:z], s. (*chim.*) baritina.

barytic [bə'ritik], ag. (*chim.*) barico.

barytone ['bæritoun], s. (*mus.*) baritono.

basal ['beisl], ag. fondamentale, basilare.

basalt ['bæsɔ:lt], s. (*min.*) basalto.

basaltic [bə'sɔ:ltik], ag. (*min.*) basaltico.

basan ['bæzən], s. bazzana.

baseule ['bæskju:l], s. bascula, pesa ☆ — *bridge*, ponte levatoio.

base[1] [beis], ag. basso; vile, indegno ☆ — -*born*, di umili natali; — -*load*, (*elett.*) carica minima; — *metals*, metalli vili; — -*minded*, di animo basso.

base[2], s. 1. base (di triangolo, ecc.); fondamento; basamento; zoccolo; piedistallo 2. (*chim.*) base 3. (*mil. spor.*) base ☆ — -*line*, base di approvvigionamento ‖ *advanced* —, (*mil.*) base avanzata; *air*- —, base aerea.

to base[2], v.t. basare, fondare.

baseball ['beisbɔ:l], s. (*amer.*) « base-ball », palla a basi.

basecourt ['beiskɔ:t], s. cortile esterno di castello; cortile posteriore di fattoria.

Basel ['ba:zəl], *no.pr.* (*geog.*) Basilea.
baseless ['beislis], *ag.* senza base; infondato.
baselessness ['beislisnis], *s.* infondatezza.
basely ['beisli], *av.* bassamente, indegnamente.
basement ['beismənt], *s.* **1.** fondamento **2.** seminterrato ☆ — *flat*, appartamento al seminterrato.
baseness ['beisnis], *s.* bassezza; illegittimità (di nascita).
bash [bæʃ], *s.* (*sl.*) colpo forte.
to bash, *v.t.* (*sl.*) fracassare; colpire violentemente.
basher ['bæʃə*], *s.* (*sl.*) fracassone; pugilatore.
bashful ['bæʃful], *ag.* vergognoso, timido; modesto.
bashfully ['bæʃfuli], *av.* timidamente; con modestia.
bashfulness ['bæʃfulnis], *s.* timidezza; modestia.
basic ['beisik], *ag.* **1.** fondamentale || *Basic English*, inglese essenziale (per uso internazionale) **2.** (*chim.*) di base, basico.
basicity [bə'sisiti], *s.* (*chim.*) basicità.
to basify ['beisifai], *v.t.* (*chim.*) basificare.
Basil ['bæzl], *no.pr.m.* Basilio.
basil, *s.* basilico.
basilar ['bæsilə*], **basilary** ['bæsiləri], *ag.* basilare.
basilica [bə'zilikə], *s.* basilica.
basilican [bə'zilikən], *ag.* basilicale.
basilicon [bə'zilikən], *s.* (*arc.*) unguento sovrano.
basilisk ['bæzilisk], *s.* (*mit.*) basilisco.
basin ['beisn], *s.* **1.** bacino, bacile; catino, bacinella; scodella; lavabo **2.** (*mar.*) bacino, darsena **3.** (*geog. geol.*) bacino ☆ *sugar* —, zuccheriera.
basinful ['beisnful], *s.* il contenuto di un catino.
basin-stand ['beisn'stænd], *s.* portacatino.
basis ['beisis], *pl.* **bases** ['beisi:z], *s.* base; fondamento.
to bask [ba:sk], *v.i.* scaldarsi, esporsi, sdraiarsi (al sole, davanti al fuoco): *to — in the sun*, prendere il sole.
basket ['ba:skit], *s.* canestro, cesto; sporta; gerla; zana || *the pick of the* —, la persona, l'oggetto migliore fra tutti ☆ — *-ball*, pallacanestro; pallone per pallacanestro; — *-chair*, sedia di vimini; — *-lunch*, (*amer.*) colazione al sacco; — *-maker*, panieraio; — *-work*, arte del panieraio; merce del panieraio || *hand-* —, cestino a mano; *waste-paper* —, cestino per la carta straccia; *work-* —, cestino da lavoro.
to basket, *v.t.* cestinare; gettare nel cestino.
basketful ['ba:skitful], *s.* panierata.
basketry ['ba:skitri], *s.* l'arte del panieraio.
Basque [ba:sk], *ag.* basco || *s.c.* basco, basca || *s.* lingua basca.
bass[1] [beis], *ag.s.* (*mus.*) basso ☆ — *-viol*, viola da gamba || *deep* —, basso profondo; *first* —, primo basso assoluto.
bass[2] [bæs], *s.* **1.** tiglio americano **2.** stuoia (di tiglio americano).
bass[3], *s.* pesce persico; branzino.
basset[1] ['bæsit], *s.* cane bassotto.
basset[2], *s.* bassetta (giuoco a carte).
basset[3], *s.* (*geol.*) affioramento di un filone.
basset-horn ['bæsitho:n], *s.* (*mus.*) corno di bassetto.
bassinet [,bæsi'net], *s.* culla di vimini.
basso ['bæsou], *s.* (*mus.*) basso (voce, cantante).
bassoon [bə'su:n], *s.* (*mus.*) fagotto.
bassoonist [bə'su:nist], *s.* suonatore di fagotto.
bass-relief ['bæsri,li:f], *s.* bassorilievo.
basswood ['bæswud], *s.* (legno di) tiglio.
bast [bæst], *s.* fibra di tiglio.
bastard ['bæstəd], *ag.* bastardo, illegittimo, spurio || *s.c.* bastardo, bastarda.
to bastardize ['bæstədaiz], *v.t.* **1.** imbastardire **2.** dichiarar bastardo.
bastardy ['bæstədi], *s.* bastardaggine; bastardume.
to baste[1] [beist], *v.t.* imbastire.
to baste[2], *v.t.* **1.** spruzzare (l'arrosto) con burro, grasso **2.** versare cera fusa su (lucignoli) (nella fabbricazione delle candele).
to baste[3], *v.t.* battere, bastonare.

bastille [hæs'ti:l], *s.* fortezza, prigione || *the Bastille*, (*st.*) la Bastiglia.
bastinado [,bæsti'neidou], *s.* (*st.*) bastonatura della pianta dei piedi.
to bastinado, *v.t.* (*st.*) punire bastonando la pianta dei piedi.
basting[1] ['beistiŋ], *s.* imbastitura.
basting[2], *s.* (*fam.*) bastonatura.
bastion ['bæstiən], *s.* bastione.
Basutoland [bə'su:toulænd], *no.pr.* (*geog.*) Basutoland.
bat[1] [bæt], *s.* pipistrello || *he is as blind as a* —, è cieco come una talpa || *to have bats in the belfry*, essere un po' strambo, tocco.
bat[2], *s.* **1.** mazza (da cricket, da baseball); racchetta da ping pong || *a good* —, un buon giocatore di cricket **2.** velocità (del passo, del colpo nel cricket) || *he went off at a rare* —, partì a passo di marcia **3.** (*sl. amer.*) bevuta collettiva.
to bat[2], *pass.p.p.* **batted** ['bætid], *v.t.i.* maneggiare la mazza (al cricket, al baseball); battere (la palla) con la mazza.
to bat[3], *pass.p.p.* **batted**, *v.t.* (*amer.*) battere (le palpebre): *he did not — an eye*, non battè ciglio.
Batavian [bə'teivjən], *ag.s.* batavo; olandese.
batch [bætʃ], *s.* infornata (di pane); lotto (di merci); gruppo (di persone).
bate[1] [beit], *s.* (*chim.*) soluzione alcalina per la concia delle pelli.
to bate[1], *v.t.* macerare (pelli) in soluzione alcalina.
to bate[2], *v.t.* (*arc.*) ridurre; (*comm.*) defalcare || *to speak with bated breath*, parlare con un fil di voce.
bath [ba:θ], *pl.* **baths** [ba:ðz], *s.* bagno; stanza da bagno: *hot, cold* —, bagno caldo, freddo; *to take a* —, fare un bagno || *Order of the Bath*, ordine cavalleresco (inglese) del Bagno ☆ — *-heater*, scaldabagno; — *-mat*, stuoia da bagno; — *-robe*, accappatoio; — *-salts*, sali per bagno; — *-towel*, asciugamano da bagno; — *-tub*, tinozza; — *-wrap*, accappatoio || *foot-* —, pediluvio; *mud-* —, bagno di fango; *sun-* —, bagno di sole.
to bath, *v.t.* bagnare; fare il bagno a.
Bath, *no.pr.* (*geog.*) Bath ☆ — *-brick*, mattoncino usato per la pulitura dei metalli; — *-bun*, dolce (tipo di veneziana, specialità di Bath); — *-chair*, poltrona a rotelle per invalidi.
bathe [beið], *s.* bagno (in fiume, mare, piscina): *to go for a* —, andare a fare il bagno.
to bathe, *v.t.i.* bagnare, bagnarsi; fare il bagno.
bather ['beiðə*], *s.c.* bagnante.
bathhouse ['ba:θhaus], *s.* **1.** stabilimento balneare **2.** cabina balneare.
bathing ['beiðiŋ], *s.* il bagnarsi; i bagni ☆ — *-hut* (o — *-cabin* o — *-box*), cabina da bagno; — *-cap*, cuffia da bagno; — *-costume* (o — *-suit*), costume da bagno; — *-drawers* (o — *-trunks*), mutandine da bagno; — *-establishment*, stabilimento di bagni, bagni pubblici; — *-machine*, cabina da bagno a ruote; — *-place*, luogo dove si fa il bagno; — *-resort*, stazione balneare.
bathometer [bə'θɔmitə*], *s.* batometro.
bathorse ['bæθɔ:s], *s.* cavallo da soma.
bathos ['beiθɔs], *s.* goffa discesa dal sublime al ridicolo; rappresentazione molto al di sotto dell'attesa.
bathroom ['ba:θrum], *s.* stanza da bagno.
Bathsheba ['bæθʃibə], *no.pr.f.* (*Bibbia*) Betsabea.
bathymetry [bə'θimitri], *s.* batimetria.
bathyscaphe ['bæθiskeif], *s.* batiscafo.
bathysphere ['bæθisfiə*], *s.* batisfera.
batick, *V.* **battick**.
batiste [bæ'ti:st], *s.* batista (tela).
batman, *pl.* **batmen** ['bætmən], *s.* (*mil.*) ordinanza, attendente (generalmente di ufficiale di cavalleria).
baton ['bætən], *s.* **1.** bastone (di maresciallo, di poliziotto) **2.** bacchetta (di direttore d'orchestra).
to baton, *v.t.* bastonare.
batsman, *pl.* **batsmen** ['bætsmən], *s.* battitore (al cricket, baseball).

batrachian [bə'treikjən], *ag.s.* (*zool.*) (di) batrace.
batta ['bætə], *s.* (*sl. ang.-in.*) indennità (per militari).
battalion [bə'tæljən], *s.* (*mil.*) battaglione.
battels ['bætlz], *s. pl.* retta di collegio (ad Oxford).
batten[1] ['bætn], *s.* assicella (per pavimenti); piccola traversa; tavoletta; tassello; (*mar.*) bietta.
to **batten**[1], *v.t.* **1.** chiudere con assicelle **2.** *to* — **down**, (*mar.*) chiudere (i boccaporti) con rinforzi di legno.
batten[2], *s.* (*ind. tessile*) battente.
to **batten**[3], *v.i.* **1.** ingozzarsi: *to* — *on sthg.*, ingozzarsi di ql.co. **2.** ingrassare.
batter[1] ['bætə*], *s.* **1.** (*cuc.*) pastella **2.** (*tip.*) carattere avariato.
to **batter**[1], *v.t.i.* **1.** colpire, battere: *to* — *at the door*, battere ripetutamente alla porta ‖ *to* — *eggs*, sbattere uova **2.** (*artigl.*) battere; battere in breccia; atterrare **3.** *to* — **down**, rompere, rovinare; logorare; demolire; abbattere **4.** *to* — **in**, sfondare (una porta, ecc.) a furia di colpi.
batter[2], *s.* pendenza (di muro).
to **batter**[2], *v.i.* essere in pendenza (di muro).
batter[3], *V.* **batsman.**
battering ['bætəriŋ], *s.* il battere; (*artigl.*) il cannoneggiare; il battere in breccia ☆ — *-charge*, carica completa da cannone; — *-piece*, cannone di grosso calibro; — *-ram*, ariete.
battery ['bætəri], *s.* **1.** (*artigl. elett.*) batteria: *to charge a* —, caricare una batteria **2.** (*dir.*) assalto, aggressione ‖ (*assault and*) —, vie di fatto **3.** batteria (di cucina) ☆ — *-chicken*, pollo d'allevamento ‖ *anti-aircraft* —, batteria contraerea; *coast* —, batteria costiera; *dry* —, (*elett.*) batteria a secco; *horse* —, (*mil.*) batteria a cavallo; *storage* —, (*elett.*) accumulatore; *trench-mortar* —, batteria da mortaio.
battik ['bætik], *s.* (*artig.*) «battik» (metodo di colorazione per tessuti).
batting ['bætiŋ], *s.* fibra di cotone per coperte imbottite.
battle ['bætl], *s.* battaglia, combattimento: *to fight a* —, dare, fare battaglia; *to join* — *with s.o.*, entrare in lotta con qlcu. ☆ — *-axe*, (*st.*) azza; (*fam.*) donna bisbetica; — *-cruiser*, incrociatore da battaglia; — *-cry*, grido di battaglia; — *-dress*, uniforme da campo; — *-field* (o — *-ground*), campo di battaglia; — *-fleet*, flotta da battaglia; — *-horse*, cavallo da battaglia; — *-plane*, aeroplano da combattimento; — *royal*, mischia; — *song*, canto di battaglia ‖ *air* —, combattimento aereo; *pitched* —, battaglia campale; *sham* —, finta battaglia.
to **battle**, *v.t.i.* combattere, battersi, battagliare: *to* — *for*, *against*, combattere per, contro.
battledore ['bætldɔ:*], *s.* piccola pala di legno; racchetta (del volano) ‖ — *and shuttlecock*, il volano.
battlement ['bætlmənt], *s.* (*arch.*) merlo; bastione.
battlemented ['bætlmentid], *ag.* (*arch.*) merlato.
battleship ['bætlʃip], *s.* nave da guerra.
battue [bæ'tu:], *s.* **1.** battuta (di caccia) **2.** massacro.
batty ['bæti], *ag.* (*sl.*) pazzo; strambo.
bauble ['bɔ:bl], *s.* **1.** bagattella, bazzecola; giocattolo **2.** bastone dei giullari.
Baucis ['bɔ:sis], *no. pr. f.* (*mit.*) Bauci.
(to) **baulk**, *V.* (to) **balk.**
bauxite ['bɔ:ksait], *s.* (*min.*) bauxite.
Bavaria [bə'vɛəriə], *no.pr.* (*geog.*) Baviera.
Bavarian [bə'vɛəriən], *ag.s.c.* bavarese.
bavin ['bævin], *s.* **1.** fascina, fastello **2.** calcare impuro.
bawd [bɔ:d], *s.* **1.** mezzana **2.** discorso osceno.
bawdiness ['bɔ:dinis], *s.* oscenità.
bawdry ['bɔ:dri], *s.* oscenità; linguaggio osceno.
bawdy ['bɔ:di], *ag.* osceno ☆ — *house*, bordello.
bawl [bɔ:l], *s.* vocìo, schiamazzo.
to **bawl**, *v.t.i.* proclamare ad alta voce; vociare.
bawler ['bɔ:lə*], *s.c.* strillone, strillona.
bawling ['bɔ:liŋ], *s.* gridìo; schiamazzo; clamore.
bawn [bɔ:n], *s.* cortile di castello.
bay[1] [bei], *s.* **1.** baia, insenatura del mare ‖ *Hudson*

Bay, la baia di Hudson **2.** incavatura; recesso (nelle montagne) **3.** (*amer.*) prato circondato da foreste ☆ — *-salt*, sale da cucina, non raffinato.
bay[2], *s.* — (*-tree*), albero di lauro ‖ *to carry off the bays*, riportare la vittoria, gli allori ☆ — *-berry*, bacca d'alloro; — *-rum*, profumo, lozione distillata dalle foglie d'alloro; — *wreath*, corona d'alloro.
bay[3], *s.* (*arch.*) **1.** spazio fra trave e trave, fra colonna e colonna **2.** apertura nel muro per una finestra o porta; recesso ☆ — *-window*, bovindo.
bay[4], *s.* latrato (di cane da caccia); abbaiamento ‖ *to be* (o *to stand*) *at* —, essere, trovarsi in scacco; *to bring a deer to* —, ridurre agli estremi un cervo.
to **bay**[4], *v.t.i.* abbaiare, latrare (di cane grosso, da caccia) ‖ *to* — (*at*) *the moon*, abbaiare alla luna.
bay[5], *ag.s.* baio: *dapple*, *dark*, *light* —, baio pomellato, scuro, chiaro.
bay[6], *s.* argine, diga.
to **bay**[6], *v.t.* arginare.
bayadere [ˌbɑ:jə'diə*], *s.* baiadera.
Bayard ['beiɑ:d], *no.pr.m.* Baiardo ‖ **bayard**, *s.* cavallo baio.
bayonet ['beiənit], *s.* **1.** baionetta: *with fixed* —, con la baionetta inastata **2.** *pl.* soldati armati di baionetta ☆ — *thrust*, baionettata ‖ *sword* —, sciabola.
to **bayonet**, *v.t.* colpire con la baionetta.
baza(a)r [bə'zɑ:*], *s.* **1.** bazar **2.** vendita di beneficenza.
bazooka [bə'zu:kə], *s.* (*mil.*) bazooka.
bdellium ['deliəm], *s.* (*bot.*) bdellio.
to **be** [bi: (*forma forte*), bi (*forma debole*)], *pass.* **was** [wɔz (*forma forte*), wəz, wz (*forme deboli*)], *p.p.* **been** [bi:n (*forma forte*), bin (*forma debole*)], *v.i.*; (*indic.pres. sing.* **am** [æm (*forma forte*), əm, m (*forme deboli*)]; **are** [ɑ:* (*forma forte*), ɑ*, ə* (*forme deboli*)], (*arc.*) **art** [ɑ:t]; **is** [iz (*forma forte*), z, s (*forme deboli*)]; *pl.* **are**) *indic.pass.sing.* **was**; **were** [wə:* (*forma forte*), wə* (*forma debole*)], (*arc.*) **wast** [wɔst (*forma forte*), wəst (*forma debole*)]; **was**; *pl.* **were** ‖ *congiunt. pres.* **be** ‖ *congiunt.pass.* **were**; 2ª *persona sing.* (*arc.*) **wert** [wə:t (*forma forte*), wət (*forma debole*)]) **1.** *essere*: *he has been kind to me*, è stato gentile con me ‖ *Thy will* — *done*, sia fatta la Tua volontà **2.** *esistere*: *God alone is*, solo Dio esiste; *I am*, sono, vivo, esisto ‖ *to* — *or not to* —, essere o non essere **3.** *stare*, *trovarsi*; *andare*; *venire*: *has anyone been?*, (*fam.*) è venuto qlcu.?; *have you been to see him?*, sei stato, andato a trovarlo?; *he is from India*, viene dall'India; *he is in London now*, ora egli è, si trova a Londra; *I have been to Rome*, sono stato, andato a Roma **4.** *stare* (*di salute*): *how are you?*, come stai?; *I am well*, *ill*, sto bene, male **5.** *avvenire*, *accadere*; *aver luogo*: *how can such things be?*, come possono accadere simili cose?; *when is the concert?*, quando avrà luogo il concerto?; *when is the wedding to* —?, quando avrà luogo il matrimonio?; *when is your birthday?*, quando è il tuo compleanno? **6.** *costare*: *how much is that?*, quanto costa? **7.** (*ausiliare: nelle forme progressive e passive, e con alcuni verbi nello stile elevato*) *stare*, *essere*, *venire*: *he is reading*, sta leggendo, legge; *the house is being built* o (*forma attiva con senso passivo*) *the house is building*, la casa è in costruzione; *she is loved*, essa è amata ‖ *he is fallen low*, è caduto in basso ‖ *he is gone*, è andato, spirato ‖ *the sun is set*, il sole è tramontato **8.** *dovere* (*per predestinazione*, *previsione*, *accordo precedente*): *he is to* — *helped*, deve essere aiutato, lo si deve aiutare; *he was to have become her husband*, doveva, avrebbe dovuto diventare suo marito; *what am I to do?*, che cosa devo fare? **9.** (*usato impersonalmente*) *essere*; *fare*: *it is five o'clock*, sono le cinque; *it is late*, è tardi; *it was a year since I had seen him*, non lo vedevo da un anno, era un anno che non lo vedevo; *there it is!*, eccolo!; è così!; *what is it?*, che cosa è?; *che cosa è avvenuto?*; *who is it?*, chi è?; *it is I* (o *me*), sono io; *it is we* (o *us*), sono io, siamo noi ‖ *it is cold*, *warm to-day*, oggi fa freddo, caldo **10.** *avere* (*in certe espressioni*):

to — *right, wrong, hungry, thirsty, sleepy, etc.*, aver ragione, torto, fame, sete, sonno, ecc. ‖ *my hands are cold*, ho freddo alle mani **11**. (**Fraseologia**): *as it were*, per così dire: *he is divided, as it were, between hatred and pity*, egli è diviso, per così dire, fra l'odio e la pietà ‖ — *it said in confidence*, sia detto in confidenza ‖ *for the time being*, per il momento, per ora, temporaneamente ‖ *he is like his mother*, assomiglia a sua madre ‖ *he was a long time going there*, ci mise molto tempo per andarvi ‖ *here he is*, eccolo (qui); *there they are*, eccoli (là) ‖ *how far is the river?*, quanto dista il fiume? ‖ *I am for Tariff Reform*, sono, parteggio per la riforma doganale ‖ *"What's yours?", " Mine's a beer "*, « Che cosa prendi? », « Una birra » ‖ *it may* —, può essere; — *that as it may*, sia come sia ‖ *let it* —, così sia, rimanga così, lasciate stare; *and so* — *it*, e così sia; *well,* — *it so!*, ebbene, sia! ‖ *let there* — *light!*, sia fatta la luce! ‖ *there] is no pleasing him*, non c'è verso di accontentarlo ‖ *three and two are five*, tre e due fanno cinque; *twice three is six*, due volte tre fa sei ‖ *what is that to me?*, che cosa me ne importa? ‖ *to* — *born*, nascere: *when were you born?*, quando sei nato? **12**. **in funzione di ag.** o s.: *the* — *-all and end-all*, l'intera essenza; lo scopo supremo ‖ *the to-* —, il futuro; *the bride to-* —, la futura sposa ‖ *a has-been*, un vecchio rammollito; un uomo finito; una bellezza sfiorita ‖ *might-have-been*, quello che avrebbe potuto essere, le possibilità perdute; una persona che avrebbe potuto diventare importante ‖ *a would-* — *poet*, un sedicente poeta **13**. **uso enfatico** (*in tal caso si pronuncia con enfasi, si scrive sottolineandolo, si stampa in corsivo e gener. si traduce con il v. e un av. rafforzativo*): *he is doing his best*, fa proprio del suo meglio; *I am glad to see you!*, son ben contento di vederti! **14**. *to* — **about**, stare per: — *to* — *about to do sthg.*, stare per fare ql.co. **15**. *to* — **in**, essere in casa; (*fam.*) essere di moda **16**. *to* — **long**, tardare **17**. *to* — **off**, (*fam.*) andarsene; essere sospeso, cancellato: — *off!*, via!; *I'am off home because the concert is off*, me ne vado a casa perchè il concerto è sospeso **18**. *to* — **out**, essere fuori; (*fam.*) non essere più di moda **19**. *to* — **through**, (*fam.*) avere finito, aver terminato: *to* — *through with a person, a thing*, aver finito con una persona, aver terminato una cosa.

beach [bi:tʃ], *s.* **1**. spiaggia; riva; lido **2**. ghiaia marina ☆ — *-master*, ufficiale che sorveglia lo sbarco di truppe; — *-rescue*, bagnino di salvataggio; — *umbrella*, ombrellone.

to **beach**, *v.t.* tirare a spiaggia (un'imbarcazione).

beachcomber ['bi:tʃ,koumə*], *s.* uomo che vive di ciò che il mare rigetta sulla spiaggia (in Polinesia).

beached [bi:tʃt], *ag.* **1**. dotato di spiaggia **2**. (*mar.*) tirato a secco.

beachhead ['bi:tʃhed], *s.* (*mil.*) testa di sbarco.

beachy ['bi:tʃi], *ag.* sassoso; ghiaioso.

beacon ['bi:kən], *s.* **1**. segnale **2**. (*mar.*) faro ☆ *radio* —, (*aer.*) radiofaro.

to **beacon**, *v.t.i.* **1**. illuminare **2**. risplendere (come un faro) **3**. dotare di fari.

bead [bi:d], *s.* **1**. grano (di rosario, di collana, ecc.); perlina di vetro **2**. goccia (di rugiada, di sudore); bolla **3**. *pl.* vezzo di perline; rosario: *to tell one's beads*, dire il rosario **4**. mirino (di fucile): *to draw a* — *on s.o.*, puntare su, prender di mira qlcu. **5**. (*arch.*) modanatura **6**. (*mec.*) nervatura.

to **bead**, *v.t.i.* **1**. imperlare, imperlarsi **2**. infilare perline.

beadhouse ['bi:dhaus], *s.* pio ricovero.

beadle ['bi:dl], *s.* **1**. scaccino, sagrestano **2**. mazziere.

beadledom ['bi:dldəm], *s.* stupido formalismo.

beadsman, *pl.* **beadsmen** ['bi:dzmən], *s.* **1**. uomo pagato per pregare per altri **2**. (*scoz.*) mendicante.

beadwoman ['bi:d,wumən], *pl.* **beadwomen** ['bi:d,wimin], *s.* **1**. donna pagata per pregare per altri **2**. (*scoz.*) mendicante.

beadwork ['bi:dwə:k], *s.* guarnizione con perline, corallini.

beady ['bi:di], *ag.* **1**. piccolo e lucente **2**. imperlato.

beagle ['bi:gl], *s.* **1**. cane usato per la caccia alla lepre **2**. *fig.* spia (della polizia).

beak[1] [bi:k], *s.* **1**. becco; rostro **2**. naso aquilino **3**. (*mar.*) sperone, rostro **4**. corno di incudine **5**. beccuccio (di teiera, ecc.).

to **beak**,[1] *v.t.* beccare.

beak[2], *s.* (*sl.*) **1**. magistrato **2**. maestro di scuola.

beaked [bi:kt], *ag.* **1**. munito di becco **2**. rostrato.

beaker ['bi:kə*], *s.* **1**. (*letter.*) coppa **2**. lambicco.

beakful ['bi:kful], *s.* imbeccata.

beam [bi:m], *s.* **1**. trave **2**. raggio (di luce, di sole); splendore; sorriso **3**. treno d'aratro **4**. giogo (di bilancia); bilancia ‖ *to kick the* —, (*fam.*) essere scalzato, battuto **5**. (*mar.*) fusto d'ancora; fianco di nave **6**. corna (di cervo) **7**. timone (di carrozza) **8**. (*artig.*) subbio **9**. (*rad.*) fascio, portata, raggio d'azione; segnale unidirezionale ☆ — *-compass*, compasso a regolo; — *-ends*, (*mar.*) fianco: *on her* — *-ends*, sul fianco, quasi capovolta (di nave); *to be on one's* — *-ends*, *fig.* essere in difficoltà finanziarie.

to **beam**, *v.t.i.* **1**. irradiare; brillare; sfavillare: *his eyes were beaming with joy*, gli sfavillavano gli occhi di gioia **2**. sorridere radiosamente **3**. (*rad.*) orientare; individuare a mezzo radar; irradiare: *to* — *a message*, trasmettere un messaggio per onde comandate.

beaming ['bi:miŋ], *ag.* raggiante ‖ *s.* irraggiamento.

beamless ['bi:mlis], *ag.* senza raggi.

beamy ['bi:mi], *ag.* **1**. fulgido, radioso **2**. massiccio: vasto **3**. ramoso (di corna di cervo).

bean [bi:n], *s.* fava; fagiolo ‖ *to know how many beans make five*, essere intelligente ‖ *he hasn't a* —, non ha un soldo **2**. (*amer.*) testa; cocuzzolo ‖ *old* —, caro amico, mio caro ‖ *to be full of beans*, essere pieno di energia, essere veramente allegro ‖ *to give s.o. beans*, dare a qlcu. una lavata di capo; battere, maltrattare qlcu. ☆ — *pod* (o — *shell*), baccello ‖ *coffee* —, grano di caffè; *French beans*, fagiolini; *haricot* - (o *kidney*- —), fagiolo; *horse-* —, fava cavallina.

beanfeast ['bi:nfi:st], *s.* (*fam.*) pranzo annuale offerto dal principale ai dipendenti; festa.

beanstalk ['bi:nsto:k], *s.* gambo di pianta di fagiolo.

bear[1] [bɛə*], *s.* **1**. orso ‖ *the Great, Little Bear*, (*astr.*) l'Orsa Maggiore, Minore ‖ *what a* —*!*, che orso! ‖ *to be like a* — *with a sore head*, essere di umore nero, essere immusonito **2**. (*Borsa*) speculatore al ribasso **3**. — *'s breech*, (*bot.*) acanto ☆ — *-baiting*, combattimento di cani contro un orso; — *-garden*, recinto degli orsi; *fig.* confusione, tumulto; — *-pit*, fossa degli orsi ‖ *polar* —, orso polare; *she-* —, orsa.

to **bear**[1], *v.t.i.* (*Borsa*) speculare al ribasso; provocare un ribasso dei prezzi di: *he has beared the market too often*, ha provocato un ribasso dei titoli troppo spesso.

to **bear**[2], *pass.* **bore** [bo:*], (*arc.*) **bare** [bɛə*], *p.p.* **borne** [bo:n], *nel senso* 3. *passivo* **born** [bo:n], *v.t.i.* **1**. portare (anche *fig.*); sorreggere: *he was bearing a large parcel*, portava un grosso pacco; *to* — *arms*, portare le armi: *to* — *a grudge*, portare rancore; *to* — *in mind*, tenere a mente; *to* — *love*, portare affetto; *to* — *a part in*, sostenere una parte in; *to* — *reference to*, riferirsi a; *to* — *s.o. company*, far compagnia a qlcu.; *to* — *s.o. a hand*, aiutare, dare una mano a qlcu.; *to* — *witness*, far testimonianza; *to* — *comparison with*, reggere il paragone con **2**. sopportare, tollerare: *the grief was too great to* — (o *to be borne*), il dolore era troppo grave perchè lo si sopportasse; *he bore the pain bravely*, sopportò il dolore con coraggio; *I cannot* — *him*, non lo posso soffrire; *I cannot* — *him to speak to me*, non sopporto che egli mi parli; *I cannot* — *to look at such things*, non sopporto tali spettacoli; *some people cannot* — *listening to jazz music*, alcuni non sopportano di ascoltare la musica jazz ‖ *to* — *hard*, sopportare a malincuore **3**. generare, produrre, partorire: *she bore three sons*, ha avuto tre figli; *that son borne by her*, quel figlio generato da lei; *this tree bears no fruit*, quest'albero non dà frutti ‖ *he was born in 1911* 4. spingere, forzare; premere ‖ *to — through*, far attraversare ‖ *to bring to —*, far pesare: *he brought all his influence to — on the minister*, fece pesare tutta la sua autorità sul ministro 5. girare, voltare: — *(to the) right at the corner*, all'angolo gira a destra; *the cape bears south*, il capo è in direzione sud 6. riferirsi: *the fact does not — on the matter*, il fatto non ha alcun riferimento con la questione 7. *to — oneself*, comportarsi 8. *to — with* (s.o., *sthg.*), avere pazienza con 9. *to — away*, portar via; (*mar.*) deviare dalla rotta ‖ *to — away (for a point)*, (*mar.*) lasciarsi portare (su un punto) 10. *to — down*, schiacciare, vincere ‖ *to — down on the enemy*, piombare sul nemico 11. *to — in*, imprimersi (nella mente): *it has borne in upon me that...*, mi sono gradualmente convinto che... 12. *to — up*, sostenere; sostenere il morale di; (*mar.*) poggiare ‖ *to — up against pain*, resistere al dolore.

bearable ['bɛərəbl], *ag.* sopportabile.

bearably ['bɛərəbli], *av.* sopportabilmente.

bearberry ['bɛəbəri], *s.* (*bot.*) corbezzolo.

bearbind ['bɛəbaind], **bearbine** ['bɛəbain], *s.* (*bot.*) convolvolo.

beard [biəd], *s.* 1. barba: *thin —*, barba rada; *to grow a —*, lasciarsi crescere la barba; *to wear a —*, portare la barba 2. chioma (di cometa) 3. (*bot.*) resta.

to **beard**, *v.t.* sfidare: *to — the lion in his den*, sfidare il leone nel suo covo; *fig.* affrontare l'ira di qlcu.

bearded ['biədid], *ag.* barbuto: — *comet*, (*astr.*) cometa chiomata ☆ *black- — man*, uomo con la barba nera.

beardless ['biədlis], *ag.* senza barba.

bearer ['bɛərə*], *s.* 1. portatore, latore: — *of good news*, latore di buone notizie; *payable to —*, (*comm.*) pagabile al portatore 2. becchino 3. (*arch.*) sostegno, supporto 4. albero fruttifero ☆ — *-cheque*, (*comm.*) assegno al portatore; — *-bond*, (*comm.*) titolo, obbligazione al portatore ‖ *standard- —*, porta stendardo.

bearing ['bɛəriŋ], *s.* 1. il portare 2. il sopportare, tolleranza: *beyond* (o *past*) —, insopportabile 3. patimento; angoscia 4. rapporto, relazione: *what is the — of this on our problem?*, che rapporto c'è tra questo e il nostro problema? 5. condotta, contegno 6. portamento; andatura 7. *pl.* aspetto: *consider it in all its bearings*, consideratelo sotto tutti i suoi aspetti 8. (*agr.*) raccolto; frutto: *in full —*, in pieno frutto 9. (*arald.*) arme 10. (*arch.*) sostegno; sporto 11. (*geol.*) giacimento 12. (*mar.*) rilevamento: *to take the bearings of a coast*, rilevare una costa ‖ *to lose one's bearings*, perdere l'orientamento; *to take one's bearings*, orientarsi 13. (*mat.*) direzione 14. (*mec.*) supporto; cuscinetto ☆ *ball-bearings*, cuscinetti a sfere; *compass —*, rilevamento con la bussola.

bearish ['bɛəriʃ], **bearlike** ['bɛəlaik], *ag.* da orso, di orso; poco socievole; grossolano, rozzo.

bearskin ['bɛə-skin], *s.* 1. pelle d'orso 2. colbacco (di pelo d'orso).

beast [bi:st], *s.* 1. bestia, animale: — *of burden*, bestia da soma; *wild —*, bestia feroce 2. natura animalesca dell'uomo; bruto ‖ *the Beast*, l'Anticristo ‖ *to make a — of oneself*, *fig.* ridursi come una bestia, abbrutirsi 3. *pl.* il bestiame ☆ *horned- —*, bestia cornuta; *riding- —*, cavalcatura.

beastie ['bi:sti], *s.* bestiola.

beastlike ['bi:stlaik], *ag.* bestiale; da bestia.

beastliness ['bi:stlinis], *s.* 1. bestialità, brutalità 2. oscenità, turpitudine.

beastly ['bi:stli], *ag.* 1. bestiale, brutale 2. sporco, lurido, schifoso: *this place is in a — condition*, questo posto è in uno stato schifoso; *what — weather!*, che tempo orribile! ‖ *av.* terribilmente: *he was — drunk*, era ubriaco fradicio.

beat [bi:t], *s.* 1. il battere; colpo (di tamburo); battito (del polso, ecc.); (*mus.*) battuta 2. zona di sorveglianza (di sentinella, di agente di polizia); ronda 3. (*sl. amer.*) truffatore; vagabondo 4. esponente della « beat generation » 5. (*fis. elett.*) battimento.

to **beat**, *pass.* **beat**, *p.p.* **beaten** ['bi:tn], **beat**, *v.t.i.* 1. battere; bastonare, percuotere: *to — one's breast*, battersi il petto; *to — the record*, battere il primato; *to — time*, (*mus.*) battere il tempo; *to — to death*, colpire a morte ‖ *to — the air*, fare cosa inutile ‖ *to — black and blue*, conciare per le feste ‖ *to — a retreat*, battere in ritirata ‖ *to — to arms*, (*mil.*) suonare a raccolta 2. *fig.* tormentarsi: *to — one's brain*, lambiccarsi il cervello 3. perlustrare: *to — the countryside for the fugitive*, battere una zona per trovare il fuggiasco ‖ *to — about the bush*, menare il can per l'aia 4. foggiare 5. pestare, stritolare 6. sorpassare in velocità 7. sbattere (delle ali) 8. (*amer.*) aprirsi (una via): *to — one's way*, farsi strada ‖ *to — it*, (*sl.*) darsela a gambe 9. palpitare 10. (*fam.*) vincere: *that beats everything!* (o *that beats the band!*), questo supera tutto!; *that beats me!*, ciò mi lascia perplesso! 11. (*fam.*) gabbare, ingannare; (*fam. amer.*) defraudare: *to be beaten*, essere gabbato 12. *to — about*, (*mar.*) bordeggiare 13. *to — back*, cacciare, respingere 14. *to — down*, abbattere; (*fam.*) far ribassare (i prezzi) 15. *to — in*, sfondare; far entrare 16. *to — off*, respingere 17. *to — out*, far uscire con forza: *to — s.o.'s brains out*, accoppare qlcu. 18. *to — up*, sbattere; (*mar.*) bordeggiare: *to — up eggs*, sbattere le uova.

beaten ['bi:tn], *ag.* 1. battuto: *the — track*, la via seguita da tutti: *that's off the — track*, (*fam.*) è una cosa insolita 2. *fig.* abbattuto, prostrato.

beater ['bi:tə*], *s.* 1. battitore 2. (*ind. della carta*) olandese.

beat generation ['bi:t,dʒenə'reiʃən], *s.* gioventù bruciata; negli Stati Uniti una corrente intellettuale anticonformista.

beatific(al) [,bi:ə'tifik(əl)], *ag.* beatifico.

beatifically [,bi:ə'tifikəli], *av.* beatificamente.

beatification [bi(:),ætifi'keiʃən], *s.* (*eccl.*) beatificazione.

to **beatify** [bi(:)'ætifai], *v.t.* 1. (*eccl.*) beatificare 2. rendere felice.

beating ['bi:tiŋ], *s.* 1. bastonata; *fig.* punizione: *to get a —*, essere bastonato, punito; *to give a —*, bastonare, punire 2. battito (di cuore, d'ali, ecc.) 3. sconfitta.

beatitude [bi(:)'ætitju:d], *s.* beatitudine.

beatnik ['bi:tnik], *s.* esponente della « beat generation ».

Beatrice ['biətris], **Beatrix** ['biətriks], *no.pr.f.* Beatrice.

beau [bou], *pl.* **beaux** [bouz], *s.* 1. damerino, zerbinotto 2. cicisbeo, vagheggino.

beauteous ['bju:tjəs], *ag.* (*poet.*) bello; vago.

beautician [bju:'tiʃən], *s.c.* estetista.

beautifier ['bju:tifaiə*] *s.c.* persona che abbellisce.

beautiful ['bju:təful], *ag.* bello, vago, leggiadro; stupendo, magnifico ‖ *the —*, il bello; la bellezza.

beautifully ['bju:təfli], *av.* in modo bello, leggiadro; perfettamente, in modo mirabile.

to **beautify** ['bju:tifai], *v.t.* abbellire; ornare.

beauty ['bju:ti], *s.* 1. bellezza, leggiadria; vaghezza; perfezione di lineamenti 2. donna bella ‖ *the Sleeping Beauty*, la Bella Addormentata ☆ — *-parlour*, istituto di bellezza; — *-sleep*, primo sonno; — *-spot*, neo; luogo pittoresco.

beaver[1] ['bi:və*], *s.* 1. (*zool.*) castoro 2. pelliccia, cappello di castoro 3. (*sl.*) barba; uomo con barba ☆ — *-rat*, topo muschiato; — *-tree*, (*bot.*) magnolia glauca.

beaver[2], *s.* parte inferiore della visiera di un elmo.

bebop ['bi:bɔp], *s.* « bebop » (tipo di musica jazz).

to **becall** [bi'kɔ:l], *v.t.* soprannomináre.

to **becalm** [bi'kɑːm], *v.t.* abbonacciare (anche *fig.*).
became [bi'keim], *pass.* di to **become**.

because [bi'kɔz], *cong.* perchè (*esplicativo*), perciocchè, poichè: *they can't come — they are busy*, non possono venire perchè sono occupati; *Why are you crying?, — I'm sad*, Perchè piangi?, Perchè sono triste ‖ *— of*, a causa di: *— of his illness he cannot work*, a causa della malattia non può lavorare.

bechamel ['beiʃəmel], *s.* (*cuc.*) balsamella.

to **bechance** [bi'tʃɑːns], *v.i.* accadere (per caso).

Bechuanaland [ˌbetʃu'ɑːnəlænd], *no.pr.* (*geog.*) Beciuania.

beck[1] [bek], *s.* cenno, segno (col capo, col dito) ‖ *to be at s.o.'s — and call*, esser sempre agli ordini di qlcu.

to **beck**[1], (*poet.*) per to **beckon**.

beck[2], *s.* ruscello (di montagna).

becket ['bekit], *s.* (*mar.*) gancio, uncino, anello di fissaggio, manetta.

to **beckon** ['bekən], *v.t.i.* chiamare con un cenno; far segnali.

Becky ['beki], *no.pr.f.* dim. di **Rebecca**.

to **becloud** [bi'klaud], *v.t.* annuvolare; oscurare.

to **become** [bi'kʌm], *pass.* **became** [bi'keim], *p.p.* **become** [bi'kʌm], *v.t.i.* **1.** diventare, divenire: *he became very thin*, diventò molto magro; *the sky became darker and darker*, il cielo divenne sempre più scuro; *to — acquainted with*, fare la conoscenza di **2.** accadere; avvenire: *what has — of him?*, che ne è di lui? **3.** addirsi a; stare bene a; essere conveniente, adatto a: *how that hat becomes you!*, come ti sta bene quel cappello!; *it ill becomes you to complain*, non è da te lamentarti.

becoming [bi'kʌmiŋ], *ag.* adatto, conveniente, appropriato; che si addice, che dona: *with — words*, con parole appropriate; *what a — hat!*, come ti dona quel cappello!.

becomingly [bi'kʌmiŋli], *av.* convenientemente.

becomingness [bi'kʌmiŋnis], *s.* convenienza.

bed [bed], *s.* **1.** letto; *fig.* matrimonio: *the head of the —*, il capezzale; *single, double, spare —*, letto semplice, matrimoniale, disponibile; *to get into, out of —*, entrare nel letto, uscire dal letto; *to go to —*, andare a letto; *to lie in —*, giacere a letto; *to make a —*, rifare un letto ‖ *you have made your —, now you must lie on it*, *fig.* ti sei messo nei guai, ora arrangiati ‖ *to be brought to —*, partorire ‖ *to keep to one's —*, essere ammalato ‖ *to lie on a — of roses*, *fig.* giacere su un letto di rose **2.** lettiera **3.** basamento (di motore, ecc.) **4.** (*flower-*) *—*, aiuola **5.** fondo (di mare); alveo **6.** (*geol.*) strato, giacimento **7.** fondo: *fondo stradale* ☆ *— -cover*, copriletto; *— -fast* (o *— -ridden*), costretto a letto; *— -maker*, chi riassetta gli alloggi degli studenti (a Oxford, Cambridge, ecc.); *— -pan*, padella per ammalati; *— -posts*, colonne del letto; *— -sore*, piaga da decubito ‖ *box- —* (o *camp- —* o *field- —*), letto da campo; *death- —*, letto di morte; *folding- —*, letto pieghevole, branda; *sick- —*, letto di dolore; *spring- —*, letto elastico; *twin beds*, letti gemelli.

to **bed**, *pass.p.p.* **bedded** ['bedid], *v.t.* **1.** portare a letto, mettere a letto **2.** fissare; (*mec.*) assestare **3.** piantare in un'aiuola **4.** sistemare in strati.

to **bedabble** [bi'dæbl], *v.t.* spruzzare, inzaccherare.

bedad [bi'dæd], *inter.* (*irl.*) per Bacco!.

to **bedaub** [bi'dɔːb], *v.t.* **1.** imbrattare di colore; *fig.* dipingere male **2.** vestire in modo sgargiante.

to **bedazzle** [bi'dæzl], *v.t.* abbagliare.

bedbug ['bedbʌg], *s.* (*entom.*) cimice.

bedchamber ['bed,tʃeimbə*], *s.* (*arc.*) camera da letto ‖ *Gentleman of the Bedchamber*, gentiluomo di camera.

bedclothes ['bedklouðz], *s.pl.* coperte da letto.

bedded ['bedid], *ag.* coricato.

bedder ['bedə*], *s.* **1.** chi fa i letti (specialmente per gli studenti dei college) **2.** (*bot.*) pianta per aiuole.

bedding ['bediŋ], *s.* **1.** quanto serve per un letto (coperte, materasso, ecc.) **2.** lettiera **3.** fondo (di strada, ecc.) **4.** (*geol.*) stratificazione.

Bede [biːd], *no.pr.m.* (*sl. lett.*) Beda.

to **bedeck** [bi'dek], *v.t.* ornare, abbellire; decorare.

to **bedevil** [bi'devl], *v.t.* **1.** maltrattare **2.** rendere ndemoniato.

bedevilment [bi'devlmənt], *s.* **1.** confusione **2.** l'essere indemoniato.

to **bedew** [bi'djuː], *v.t.* (*poet.*) irrorare.

bedfellow ['bed,felou], *s.* compagno di letto.

bedight [bi'dait], *ag.* (*poet.*) ornato.

to **bedim** [bi'dim], *pass.p.p.* **bedimmed** [bi'dimd], *v.t.* oscurare, offuscare.

to **bedizen** [bi'daizn], *v.t.* vestire in modo sgargiante.

bedlam [ˈbedləm], *s.* **1.** manicomio **2.** *fig.* tumulto.

bedlamite ['bedləmait], *s.* matto, pazzo.

bedlinen ['bed'linin], *s.* biancheria da letto.

bedouin ['beduin], *ag.* beduino ‖ *s.c.* beduino, beduina.

bedplate ['bedpleit], *s.* (*ind.*) basamento di macchina; platea di fondo.

to **bedraggle** [bi'drægl], *v.t.* inzaccherare, impillaccherare.

bedroom ['bedrum], *s.* camera da letto.

bedside ['bedsaid], *s.* fianco del letto; capezzale ☆ *— manner*, ⸢modi rassicuranti⸥ (specialmente di medico).

bedspread ['bedspred], *s.* copriletto.

bedstead ['bedsted], *s.* telaio del letto.

bedtime ['bedtaim], *s.* l'ora di andare a letto.

bee[1] [biː], *s.* **1.** (*entom.*) ape, pecchia; *fig.* lavoratore indefesso ‖ *to have a — in one's bonnet*, avere un'idea fissa, una mania **2.** (*amer.*) incontro, riunione, gara amichevole: ☆ *— -bread*, miscela di miele e di polline; *— -eater*, (*ornit.*) gruccione; *— -line*, linea d'aria, linea retta: *to make a — -line for s.o., sthg.*, dirigersi con decisione verso qlcu., ql.co.; *— -keeper* (o *— -master*), apicoltore ‖ *busy- —*, persona indaffarata; *bumble- —*, calabrone; *hive- —*, ape domestica; *queen- —*, ape regina; *fig.* persona che si dà molta importanza; *working — —*, ape operaia.

bee[2], *s.* (*arc.*) anello di metallo.

beech [biːtʃ], *s.* (*bot.*) faggio ☆ *— -marten*, (*zool.*) faina; *— -mast* (o *— -nut*), (*bot.*) faggiuola, faggina; *— -oil*, olio di faggiuola.

beechen ['biːtʃən], *ag.* (*bot.*) di faggio.

beef [biːf], *s.* **1.** manzo; carne di manzo **2.** bue da macello **3.** (*fam.*) muscolo **4.** *pl.* (*rar.*) carcassa di bue ☆ *boiled —*, manzo lesso; *roast- —*, arrosto di manzo; *salt- —*, manzo salato; *tinned —* (o *amer. canned —*), manzo in scatola.

beefeater ['biːf,iːtə*], *s.* **1.** mangione **2.** guardia della Torre di Londra.

beefsteak ['biːf'steik], *s.* bistecca.

beeftea ['biːf'tiː], *s.* brodo ristretto.

beefy ['biːfi], *ag.* muscoloso; solido.

beehive ['biːhaiv], *s.* alveare, arnia.

Beelzebub [bi(ː)'elzibʌb], *no.pr.m.* Belzebù.

been [biːn], *p.p.* di to **be**.

beer [biə*], *s.* birra: *small —*, birra leggera; *strong —*, birra forte ‖ *to think no small — of oneself*, avere un'alta opinione di sè ☆ *— -barrel*, barile da birra; *— -engine*, macchina per pompare la birra; *— -garden*, birreria, caffè all'aperto; *— -house* (o *— -shop*), birreria; *— -money*, mancia ‖ *draught —*, birra alla spina.

beery ['biəri], *ag.* **1.** di birra **2.** ubriaco di birra.

beestings ['biːstiŋz], *s. pl.* colostro (di vacca).

beeswax ['biːzwæks], *s.* cera vergine.

beeswing ['biːzwiŋ], *s.* **1.** vino vecchio **2.** pellicola del vino.

beet [biːt], *s.* barbabietola; rapa ☆ *— -sugar*, zucchero di barbabietola.

beetle[1] ['biːtl], *s.* coleottero; scarabeo ☆ *— -crusher*, (*sl.*) scarpone, stivalone; poliziotto ‖ *black —*, scarafaggio.

beetle[2], *s.* (*strum. artig.*) mazzuolo.

to **beetle**[2], *v.t.* battere col mazzuolo.

beetle[3], *ag.* prominente; irsuto ☆ — *-browed*, dalle sopracciglia folte, cespugliose; *fig.* accigliato.

to **beetle**[3], *v.i.* sporgere (di sopracciglia); strapiombare (di roccia); sovrastare (del destino).

beetroot ['bi:tru:t], *s.* barbabietola.

beezer ['bi:zə*], *s.* (*sl.*) naso.

to **befall** [bi'fɔ:l], *pass.* **befell** [bi'fel], *p.p.* **befallen** [bi'fɔ:lən], *v.t.i.* accadere, avvenire: *what befell you there?*, che vi accadde là?; *whatever may — him*, qualunque cosa gli possa succedere.

to **befit** [bi'fit], *pass.p.p.* **befitted** [bi'fitid], *v.t.* convenire a; addirsi a: *it does not — you to...*, non si addice a te di....

befitting [bi'fitiŋ], *ag.* conveniente, adatto.

to **befog** [bi'fɔg], *pass.p.p.* **befogged** [bi'fɔgd], *v.t.* annebbiare, confondere; offuscare; ottenebrare: *wine befogs the senses*, il vino ottenebra i sensi.

to **befool** [bi'fu:l], *v.t.* trattare da sciocco; mettere in ridicolo ‖ *to — oneself*, farsi illusioni.

before [bi'fɔ:*], *av.* prima, precedentemente, già, **avanti, innanzi:** *I have seen you —*, vi ho già visto; *I told you —*, te l'ho già detto; *to go on —*, andare avanti; *to go on as —*, andare avanti come prima ‖ *prep.* prima (di); **davanti a:** *he stopped — the palace*, si fermò dinanzi al palazzo; *think — speaking*, pensa prima di parlare; *you are — your time*, precorri i tempi; *you spoke — me*, parlasti prima di me ‖ *Before Christ (abbr. B. C.)*, avanti Cristo ‖ *— God and man*, davanti a Dio ed agli uomini ‖ *— long*, fra non molto ‖ *the night — last*, l'altra notte ‖ *cong.* **prima che; piuttosto che:** *come and see me — you leave*, venite a trovarmi prima di partire; *I would die — I told him*, morirei piuttosto che dirglielo* ☆ *— -cited*, *— - mentioned*, già citato, menzionato.

beforehand [bi'fɔ:hænd], *av.* anticipatamente ‖ *to be — with s.o.*, precedere, superare qlcu. ‖ *to be — with the world*, (*fam.*) essere nell'agiatezza.

beforetime [bi'fɔ:-taim], *av.* tempo fa; precedentemente; anticamente; altre volte.

to **befoul** [bi'faul], *v.t.* insudiciare.

to **befriend** [bi'frend], *v.t.* aiutare, favorire; essere, mostrarsi amico di.

to **beg** [beg], *pass.p.p.* **begged** [begd], *v.t.i.* **1.** (III, IV) domandare, chiedere: *to — a favour of s.o.*, chiedere un favore a qlcu.; *to — (for) sthg.*, chiedere ql.co.; *to — for sthg. to be done*, chiedere che ql.co. sia fatto; *to — a person's pardon*, chiedere scusa a una persona; *to — s.o. to do sthg.*, pregare uno di far una cosa: *I begged him to go away*, gli chiesi di andarsene; *to — sthg. of s.o.*, chiedere ql.co. a qlcu. ‖ *to — the question*, prendere la cosa per certa **2.** (III, IV) domandare insistentemente, pregare, supplicare: *to — leave to do sthg.*, chiedere il permesso per fare ql.co. ‖ *I — your pardon*, mi scusi, vuol ripetere per favore **3.** chiedere l'elemosina **4.** (*comm.*) pregiarsi: *I — to state*, mi pregio comunicarvi ‖ *we — to acknowledge receipt of your favour*, accusiamo ricevuta della pregiata vostra **5.** *to — off*, chiedere grazia per; chiedere il permesso di assentarsi.

begad [bi'gæd], *inter.* perdinci!.

began [bi'gæn], *pass.* di to **begin**.

to **beget** [bi'get], *pass.* **begot** [bi'gɔt], *p.p.* **begot, begotten** [bi'gɔtn], *v.t.* **1.** generare, procreare; far nascere: *discord begets crime*, la discordia genera il delitto ‖ *the only Begotten of the Father*, (*teol.*) il Figlio unigenito del Padre **2.** causare, cagionare; suscitare.

begetter [bi'getə*], *s.* generatore, padre; *fig.* autore.

beggar ['begə*], *s.* accattone, accattona; povero, povera; mendicante, pezzente ‖ *poor little — !*, poveraccio!; *you insolent —*, villano insolente ‖ *beggars can't be choosers*, *prov.* o mangiar questa minestra o saltar quella finestra ☆ *—'s lice*, (*bot.*) lappola ‖ *— -my-neighbour*, rubamazzetto (a carte).

to **beggar**, *v.t.* ridurre alla mendicità, in miseria; impoverire ‖ *to — description*, essere indescrivibile: *it's too beautiful, it beggars description*, è troppo bello, è al di là di ogni descrizione.

beggarly ['begəli], *ag.* mendico, misero, povero; sordido; meschino, gretto: *— action*, azione meschina, vile; *— clothes*, abiti a brandelli ‖ *av.* miserabilmente. miseramente.

beggary ['begəri], *s.* **1.** mendicità; indigenza; *fig.* miseria: *to be reduced to —*, essere ridotti alla mendicità **2.** *coll.* gli indigenti.

begging ['begiŋ], *ag.* mendicante ‖ *s.* mendicità, accattonaggio ‖ *to go (a-) —*, non essere accettato ☆ *— -friar*, frate questuante.

to **begin** [bi'gin], *pass.* **began** [bi'gæn], *p.p.* **begun** [bi'gʌn], *v.t.i.* (II) cominciare, incominciare; esordire: *he began reading (o to read) the letter*, cominciò a leggere la lettera; *how did this —?*, com'è cominciato?; *I — to see*, comincio a capire; *to — again*, ricominciare; *to — at the beginning*, per cominciare dal principio; *to — business*, esordire negli affari; intraprendere ql.co.; *to — by doing sthg.*, cominciare col fare ql.co. ‖ *to — with*, in primo luogo, per cominciare ‖ *well begun is half done*, *prov.* chi ben comincia è a metà dell'opera.

beginner [bi'ginə*], *s.c.* principiante, esordiente; iniziatore, iniziatrice; novizio, novizia.

beginning [bi'giniŋ], *s.* principio, inizio, esordio.

to **begird** [bi'gə:d], *pass.* **begirded** [bi'gə:did], *p.p.* **begirt** [bi'gə:t], *v.t.* cingere, circondare; accerchiare.

begone [bi'gɔn], *inter.* andate via!.

begonia [bi'gounjə], *s.* (*bot.*) begonia.

begot [bi'gɔt], *pass. p.p.* di to **beget**.

begotten [bi'gɔtn], *p.p.* di to **beget**.

to **begrime** [bi'graim], *v.t.* annerire; sporcare.

to **begrudge** [bi'grʌdʒ], *v.t.* **1.** invidiare **2.** lesinare; dare malvolentieri.

to **beguile** [bi'gail], *v.t.* **1.** illudere; ingannare; imbrogliare ‖ *to — the time*, ingannare, far passare il tempo **2.** incantare, sedurre.

beguilement [bi'gailmənt], *s.* **1.** inganno **2.** seduzione, allettamento.

beguiler [bi'gailə*], *s.c.* seduttore, seduttrice.

beguinage ['beginidʒ], *s.* (*st.*) beghinaggio.

beguine[1] ['begin], *s.* (*st.*) beghina.

beguine[2] [bə'gi:n], *s.* « beguine » (musica e danza originaria della Martinica).

begum ['beigəm], *s.* regina, principessa indiana.

begun [bi'gʌn], *p.p.* di to **begin**.

behalf [bi'hɑ:f], *s.* profitto, vantaggio, interesse, favore, pro; parte: *in (o on) — of*, nell'interesse di, a favore di; *on my —*, per conto mio, a nome mio.

to **behave** [bi'heiv], *v.i.* agire, portarsi, comportarsi bene: *— yourself!*, comportati bene!, sta buono!; *he behaved like a hero*, si comportò da eroe **2.** funzionare (di macchina) ☆ *ill-behaved*, maleducato; *well -behaved*, beneducato.

behaviour [bi'heivjə*], *s.* **1.** comportamento, condotta, contegno: *his — towards me shows that he doesn't like me*, il suo comportamento verso di me mostra che non gli piaccio ‖ *good — certificate*, certificato di buona condotta ‖ *to be on one's best —*, fare del proprio meglio **2.** (*mec.*) funzionamento.

to **behead** [bi'hed], *v.t.* decapitare.

beheading [bi'hediŋ], *s.* decapitazione.

beheld [bi'held], *pass. p.p.* di to **behold**.

behemoth [bi'hi:mɔθ], *s.* (*Bibbia*) animale enorme.

behest [bi'hest], *s.* (*poet.*) comando, ordine.

behind [bi'haind], *av.* **dietro, di dietro, indietro, all'indietro, posteriormente, in arretrato, in ritardo:** *to be — in (o with) one's work*, essere in arretrato, in ritardo col lavoro; *to come —*, seguire; *to leave —*, dimenticare: *he left his umbrella —*, (si) dimenticò l'ombrello; *to stay —*, restare indietro ‖ *prep.* **dietro (a), di dietro (a):** *— the scenes*, dietro le quinte (anche *fig.*); *— the times*, in arretrato coi tempi; *— s.o.'s back*, all'insaputa di qlcu.; *he left three children — him*, alla sua morte lasciò tre bimbi; *there is sthg. — this*, *fig.* c'è sotto ql.co. ‖ *those — us*, i nostri posteri.

behind, *s.* parte posteriore di persona, abito: *he kicked the boy's* —, prese a calci il ragazzo.

behindhand [bi'haindhænd], *av.ag.* predicativo in arretrato, in ritardo: *I am* — *with my work,* sono in ritardo con il mio lavoro.

to behold [bi'hould], *pass.p.p.* **beheld** [bi'held], *v.t.* guardare, vedere, scorgere; osservare, contemplare.

beholden [bi'houldən], *ag.* obbligato, grato.

beholder [bi'houldə*], *s.c.* spettatore, spettatrice; osservatore, osservatrice.

behoof [bi'hu:f], *s.* vantaggio, profitto, interesse.

to behoove [bi'hu:v], (amer.) per *to* **behove.**

to behove [bi'houv], *v.t. imp.* essere necessario, doveroso, giusto; convenire: *it behoves him to do so,* conviene che egli faccia così.

being ['bi:iŋ], *ag.* presente, attuale: *for the time* —, per il momento, per ora ‖ *s.* **1.** essere vivente, creatura: *human beings,* esseri umani ‖ *the Supreme Being,* Dio, l'Ente Supremo **2.** l'essere, esistenza: *in* —, esistente, in vita; vigente, in vigore; *to call into* —, chiamare alla vita, dar vita a.

to bejewel [bi'dʒu:əl], *pass.p.p.* **bejewelled** [bi'dʒu:əld], *v.t.* ornare con gioielli.

to belabour [bi'leibə*], *v.t.* **1.** battere, bastonare, picchiare **2.** *fig.* attaccare, assalire con parole.

belated [bi'leitid], *ag.* **1.** sorpreso dall'oscurità **2.** tardo; tardivo.

to belaud [bi'lɔ:d], *v.t.* lodare soverchiamente.

to belay [bi'lei], *v.t.* **1.** (mar.) attaccare, legare, assicurare (una gomena) ‖ — *there!,* (sl. mar.) ferma!, fermatevi!, basta! **2.** (alpinismo) assicurare (una corda) ☆ *belaying-pin,* (mar.) caviglia.

belch [beltʃ], *s.* **1.** rutto; eruzione (di vulcano); scoppio (di fiamme, cannone, ecc.) **2.** (spreg.) birra cattiva.

to belch, *v.t.i.* ruttare; vomitare (anche *fig.*); eruttare: *to* — *forth flames,* eruttare fiamme.

belcher ['beltʃə*], *s.* fazzoletto da collo colorato.

beldam(e) ['beldəm], *s.* megera; virago.

to beleaguer [bi'li:gə*], *v.t.* assediare (anche *fig.*).

belemnite ['beləmnait], *s.* belemnite (fossile).

belfry ['belfri], *s.* campanile; cella campanaria.

Belgian ['beldʒən], *ag.s.c.* belga.

Belgic ['beldʒik], *ag.* belga.

Belgium ['beldʒəm], *no.pr.* (geog.) Belgio.

Belgrade [bel'greid], *no.pr.* (geog.) Belgrado.

Belgravia [bel'greivjə], *no.pr.* Belgravia (quartiere elegante nel centro di Londra).

Belial ['bi:ljəl], *no.pr.m.* Satana, il Maligno.

to belie [bi'lai], *v.t.* **1.** smentire **2.** contraffare **3.** mancare a (una promessa); deludere (una speranza).

belief [bi'li:f], *s.* credenza, fede, credo ‖ *beyond* (o *past all*) —, incredibile ‖ *to the best of my* —, per quanto io ne sappia.

believable [bi'li:vəbl], *ag.* credibile.

to believe [bi'li:v], *v.t.i.* **1.** credere, aver fiducia, prestar fede: *I don't* — *much in this machine,* questa macchina non mi dà un grande affidamento; *I don't* — *you,* non ti credo; *I should* — *so!,* lo credo bene!; *we* — *in God,* crediamo in Dio; *you can't make me* — *that,* non potete farmi credere questo **2.** (IV) ritenere, reputare ‖ *to make* —, far finta, fingere.

believer [bi'li:və*], *s.c.* credente.

believing [bi'li:viŋ], *ag.* fiducioso, credente.

believingly [bi'li:viŋli], *av.* fiduciosamente.

belike [bi'laik], *av.* (arc.) forse, probabilmente.

Belinda [bi'lində], *no.pr.f.* Belinda.

to belittle [bi'litl], *v.t.* rimpicciolire, sminuire; *fig.* deprezzare.

bell[1] [bel], *s.* **1.** campana, campanello: *chime of bells,* carillon di campane ‖ —, *book and candle,* (eccl.) esorcismo ‖ *as sound as a* —, *fig.* sano come un pesce **2.** (mar.) turno di mezz'ora di guardia: *three bells,* tre mezze ore; *to strike eight bells,* battere il mezzogiorno **3.** (bot.) campanula; corolla a forma di campana ☆ — *-boy* (o — *-hop*), (sl. amer.) fattorino d'albergo; — *-buoy,* (mar.)

boa con campana; — *-clapper,* batacchio; — *-clock,* sveglia; — *-cord,* cordone del campanello; — *-founder,* fonditore di campane; — *-flower,* (bot.) campanella; — *-metal,* bronzo di campane; — *-pull,* cordone del campanello; — *-push,* pulsante del campanello; — *-ringer,* campanaro; — *-ringing,* l'arte del campanaro; — *-rope,* fune di campana; — *-shaped,* a forma di campana, scampanato; — *-tent,* tenda conica; — *-tower,* campanile; — *-wether,* pecora guida; (spreg.) capo di folla turbolenta ‖ *diving-* —, campana per palombaro; *door-* —, campanello della porta; *dumb-bells,* (ginnastica) manubri; *hand-* —, campanello a mano.

to bell[1], *v.t.* fornire di campanello.

bell[2], *s.* bramito (di cervo in amore).

to bell[2], *v.i.* bramire (di cervo in amore).

belladonna [,belə'dɔnə], *s.* (bot. farm.) belladonna.

belle [bel], *s.* bella, bella donna: *the* — *of the ball,* la reginetta del ballo.

bellicose ['belikous], *ag.* bellicoso; guerresco.

bellicosity [,beli'kɔsiti], *s.* bellicosità.

bellied ['belid], *ag.* obeso; panciuto; corpulento.

belligerency [bi'lidʒərənsi], *s.* belligeranza.

belligerent [bi'lidʒərənt], *ag.s.* belligerante.

bellman, *pl.* **bellmen** ['belmən], *s.* (arc.) banditore.

bellow ['belou], *s.* muggito.

to bellow, *v.t.i.* mugghiare, muggire; rombare; rumoreggiare; urlare rabbiosamente.

bellowing ['belouiŋ], *s.* muggito.

bellows ['belouz], *s.pl.* soffietto; mantice: *a pair of* —, mantici.

belly ['beli], *s.* **1.** ventre, addome, pancia **2.** oggetto, vaso panciuto **3.** *fig.* golosità, fame ☆ — *-ache,* mal di ventre; — *-band,* sottopancia dei cavalli; — *-belt,* ventriera; — *-landing,* (aer.) atterraggio sulla pancia; — *-laugh,* risata grassa; — *-worm,* verme intestinale.

to belly, *v.t.i.* gonfiare, gonfiarsi (di vela).

bellyful ['beliful], *s.* scorpacciata.

to belong [bi'lɔŋ], *v.i.* **1.** appartenere: *now you* — *to our society,* ora appartieni alla nostra società; *this belongs to me,* questo mi appartiene **2.** concernere, spettare **3.** essere originario (di un posto), abitare: *they* — *to London,* sono di Londra **4.** star di posto, essere riposto: *the cups* — *on the shelf,* le tazze stanno sulla mensola.

belongings [bi'lɔŋiŋz], *s.pl.* **1.** proprietà, roba: *personal* —, effetti personali **2.** parenti.

beloved [bi'lʌvd], *ag.s.* amato, caro, diletto: — *of the gods,* amato dagli dei; *my* —, amato mio.

below [bi'lou], *av.* al di sotto, giù, in giù, quaggiù: *the blue sea* —, il mare azzurro sottostante; *here* —, quaggiù ‖ *prep.* sotto, al di sotto di; qua sotto; più innanzi a: — *sea level,* sotto il livello del mare; — *zero,* sotto zero; *a sum* — *five pounds,* una somma inferiore a cinque sterline; *the sun is sinking* — *the horizon,* il sole cala sull'orizzonte ‖ — *ground,* morto e seppellito ‖ — *par,* (comm.) sotto la pari; — *sample,* inferiore al campione; *it fell* — *my estimate,* si rivelò inferiore alla mia valutazione ‖ *he is feared by all* — *him,* è temuto da tutti i suoi dipendenti.

Belshazzar [bel'ʃæzə*], *no.pr.m.* (Bibbia) Baldassarre.

belt [belt], *s.* **1.** cintura; cinghia (anche mec.) **2.** zona, regione: *the wheat* —, la zona, la regione granifera; *to hit below the* —, *fig.* dare un colpo basso ☆ — *line,* (amer.) linea di circonvallazione di tram; *life-* —, *safety-* —, cintura di salvataggio.

to belt, *v.t.* **1.** cingere con una cintura **2.** battere con una cinghia **3.** tosare.

belted ['beltid], *ag.* cinto ☆ — *earl,* signore di alto lignaggio.

belting ['beltiŋ], *s.* **1.** (ind.) cinghie **2.** (sl. amer.) staffilata.

Beluchistan [bə'lu:tʃistɑ:n], *no.pr.* (geog.) Belucistan.

belvedere ['belvidiə*], *s.* belvedere.

bema ['bi:mə], *pl.* **bemata** ['bi:mətə], *s.* **1.** tribuna di assemblea ateniese **2.** presbiterio.

to **bemire** [bi'maiə*] *v.t.* infangare.

to **bemoan** [bi'moun], *v.t.i.* **1.** lamentare, lamentarsi **2.** compiangere.

to **bemuse** [bi'mju:z], *v.t.* confondere, stupefare.

ben¹ [ben], *ag.* (*scoz.*) interno ‖ *s.* (*scoz.*) stanza interna ‖ *but and* —, la stanza interna e quella esterna.

ben¹, *av.prep.* (*scoz.*) all'interno.

ben², *s.* (*scoz.*) picco, montagna ‖ *Ben Nevis*, Ben Nevis (la più alta montagna della Scozia).

bench [bentʃ], *s.* **1.** panca; banco (di barca) **2.** banco di lavoro **3.** seggio, scanno, sedile: *the episcopal* —, il seggio dei vescovi (alla Camera dei Lord); *the judge's* —, il seggio del giudice ‖ *the Treasury Bench*, il seggio ministeriale (alla Camera dei Comuni) ‖ *the King's Bench*, regia corte (tribunale inglese) ‖ *to be on the* —, essere magistrato ‖ *to be raised to the* —, essere nominato giudice, vescovo ☆ *testing* —, banco di prova.

bencher ['bentʃə*], *s.* avvocato anziano; membro del Collegio degli avvocati.

bend¹ [bend], *s.* **1.** curvatura, piegatura, flessione; declivio; inclinazione; curva, gomito (di fiume, ecc.) ‖ *round the* —, (*fam.*) pazzo **2.** *pl.* (*fam. patol.*) malattia dei cassoni.

to **bend**¹, *pass.p.p.* **bent** [bent], *v.t.i.* **1.** curvare, curvarsi; piegare, piegarsi; chinare, chinarsi: *he bent down and saw it*, si chinò e lo vide; *she bent her head and was silent*, abbassò la testa e tacque **2.** tendere (una rete, un arco) **3.** inarcare (le sopracciglia); voltare, volgere (gli occhi) **4.** *fig.* sottomettere, assoggettare: *to* — *s.o. to one's will*, piegare qlcu. ai propri voleri.

bend², *s.* (*mar.*) nodo (di vari generi).

to **bend**², *v.t.* (*mar.*) legare, assicurare con nodo.

bend³, *s.* (*arald.*) banda: — *sinister*, banda di bastardigia.

bender ['bendə*], *s.* **1.** curvatore **2.** macchina curvatrice.

beneaped [bi'ni:pt], *ag.* rimasto a secco per ritiro della marea.

beneath [bi'ni:θ], *av.* giù, abbasso, di sotto ‖ *prep.* sotto, al di sotto, più in basso di: *to marry* — *oneself*, sposare persona di classe inferiore ‖ — *contempt*, indegno, ignobile ‖ *this is* — *you*, ciò non è degno di te.

Benedict ['benidikt], *no.pr.m.* Benedetto.

Benedictine [,beni'diktin], *ag.s.* (*eccl.*) benedettino.

benediction [,beni'dikʃən], *s.* benedizione.

benedictory [,beni'diktəri], *ag.* benedicente.

benefaction [,beni'fækʃən], *s.* beneficenza.

benefactor ['benifæktə*], *s.* benefattore.

benefactress ['benifæktris], *s.* benefattrice.

benefic [bi'nefik], *ag.* propizio.

benefice ['benifis], *s.* (*eccl.*) beneficio; prebenda.

beneficed ['benifist], *ag.* (*eccl.*) beneficiato.

beneficence [bi'nefisəns], *s.* beneficenza.

beneficent [bi'nefisənt], *ag.* benefico; generoso.

beneficently [bi'nefisəntli], *av.* beneficamente; generosamente.

beneficial [,beni'fiʃəl], *ag.* **1.** utile, vantaggioso **2.** (*dir.*) che gode di usufrutto **3.** (*eccl.*) beneficiale.

beneficially [,beni'fiʃəli], *av.* utilmente.

beneficialness [,beni'fiʃəlnis], *s.* utilità; vantaggio.

beneficiary [,beni'fiʃəri], *ag.s.* **1.** feudatario **2.** (*eccl. dir. comm.*) beneficiario.

benefit ['benifit], *s.* **1.** vantaggio; profitto; utilità: *the public* —, il bene pubblico; *he derived no* — *from it*, non gliene venne nessun vantaggio; *to be of great* —, essere di grande vantaggio ‖ *for the* — *of*, a vantaggio di **2.** — (*night* o *performance*), (*teat.*) recita di beneficenza, beneficiata **3.** indennità, risarcimento **4.** (*dir.*) beneficio: — *of the doubt*, beneficio di dubbio ☆ *medical* —, assistenza medica; *unemployment* —, indennità di disoccupazione.

to **benefit**, *v.t.i.* **1.** giovare a, far del bene a, beneficare: *a steady change benefits trade*, un cambio stabile giova al commercio **2.** profittare, avvantaggiarsi: *to* — *by sthg.*, approfittare di ql.co.

benevolence [bi'nevələns], *s.* **1.** benevolenza; carità **2.** (*st.*) prestito forzoso.

benevolent [bi'nevələnt], *ag.* benevolo; caritatevole.

benevolently [bi'nevələntli], *av.* benevolmente; caritatevolmente.

Bengal [beŋ'gɔ:l], *no. pr.* (*geog.*) Bengala: *the Bay of* —, il golfo del Bengala ☆ — *light*, bengala.

benighted [bi'naitid], *ag.* **1.** sorpreso dalla notte **2.** ottenebrato (mentalmente).

benign [bi'nain], *ag.* **1.** benevolo, favorevole **2.** (*med.*) benigno.

benignancy [bi'nignənsi], *s.* benignità, benevolenza.

benignant [bi'nignənt], *ag.* benignità, benevolenza.

benignantly [bi'nignəntli], *av.* benignamente.

benignity [bi'nigniti], *s.* benignità, benevolenza.

benison ['benizn], *s.* (*arc.*) benedizione.

Benjamin ['bendʒəmin], *no.pr.m.* Beniamino.

Bennet ['benit], *no.pr.m.* Benito.

bent¹ [bent], *pass.p.p.* di to **bend** ‖ *ag.* **1.** curvato, piegato **2.** *fig.* risoluto, deciso: — *on doing sthg.*, risoluto a fare ql.co.

bent¹, *s.* tendenza, disposizione, inclinazione: *he determined to follow his own* —, decise di seguire la sua inclinazione; *to have a natural* — *for music*, avere disposizione per la musica.

bent², *s.* **1.** (*bot.*) agrostide **2.** pascolo, prateria.

to **benumb** [bi'nʌm], *v.t.* intorpidire; *fig.* paralizzare.

benumbment [bi'nʌmmənt], *s.* torpore, intorpidimento.

benzene ['benzi:n], *s.* (*chim.*) **1.** benzene, benzolo **2.** benzina.

benzine ['benzi:n], *s.* (*chim.*) benzina.

benzoate ['benzoueit], *s.* (*chim.*) benzoato.

benzoic [ben'zouik], *ag.* (*chim.*) benzoico.

benzoin ['benzouin], *s.* (*chim.*) benzoino.

benzol ['benzɔl], *s.* (*chim.*) benzolo.

benzoline ['benzɔli:n], *s.* (*chim.*) benzina.

benzpyrene [benz'pairi:n], *s.* (*chim.*) benzipirene.

to **bequeath** [bi'kwi:ð], *v.t.* legare per testamento; *fig.* trasmettere: *he bequeathed his talent to his son*, trasmise al figlio il suo talento.

bequeather [bi'kwi:ðə*], *s.c.* testatore, testatrice.

bequest [bi'kwest], *s.* lascito; eredità.

to **berate** [bi'reit], *v.t.* (*amer.*) rimproverare.

Berber ['bə:bə*], *ag.* berbero ‖ *s.c.* berbero, berbera ‖ *s.* lingua berbera.

to **bereave** [bi'ri:v], *pass.p.p.* **bereaved** [bi'ri:vd], **bereft** [bi'reft], *v.t.* privare, spogliare; orbare: *an accident bereaved him of his son*, perdette il figlio in un incidente; *bereft of sight*, privo della vista ‖ *the bereaved*, i familiari del defunto.

bereavement [bi'ri:vmənt], *s.* lutto: *owing to a recent* —, a causa di un recente lutto.

bereft [bi'reft], *pass.p.p.* di to **bereave**.

Berenice [,beri'naisi(:)], *no.pr.f.* Berenice.

beret ['berei], *s.* berretto; basco.

berg [bə:g], *s.* **1.** (*abbr.* di *iceberg*) iceberg, massa di ghiaccio galleggiante **2.** (*Sud Africa*) montagna.

bergamot ['bə:gəmɔt], *s.* (*bot.*) bergamotto; essenza di bergamotto.

to **berhyme** [bi'raim], *v.t.* verseggiare.

beriberi ['beri'beri], *s.* (*patol.*) beriberi.

Berlin [bə:'lin], *no. pr.* (*geog.*) Berlino.

berlin(e) [bə:'lin], *s.* berlina (vettura).

Berliner [bə:'linə*], *s.c.* berlinese.

Berlinese [,bə:li'ni:z], *ag.* berlinese.

Bermudas (the) [bə(:)'mju:dəz], *no. pr.* (*geog.*) Bermude.

bernacle ['bə:nəkl], *V.* **barnacle**¹ **1.**

Bernard ['bə:nəd], *no.pr.m.* Bernardo.

Bernardine ['bə:nədin], *ag.s.* (*eccl.*) cistercense ‖ *no.pr.f.* Bernardina.

berried ['berid], *ag.* che ha bacche.

berry ['beri], *s.* **1.** bacca, coccola; chicco ‖ *as brown as a* —, nero come un tizzo **2.** uovo di pesce.

to **berry**, *v.i.* **1.** diventare bacca **2.** raccogliere bacche.

berserk(er) ['bɔːsɔːk(ə*)], *s.* guerriero leggendario norvegese (che combatteva con cieca ira).

Bert [bəːt], *no.pr.m. dim.* di **Albert**.

berth [bəːθ], *s.* **1.** (*mar.*) ancoraggio, posto di fonda, d'ormeggio **2.** (*mar. ferr.*) cuccetta **3.** *fig.* posto: *to be in a good* —, avere un buon posto, impiego ‖ *to give a wide* — *to*, evitare, scansare ☆ *loading-* —, posto di caricamento.

to **berth**, *v.t.i.* **1.** (*mar.*) ancorare; amarrare **2.** avere un posto per dormire; dare un posto per dormire a.

Bertha ['bəːθə], *no.pr.f.* Berta.

Bertram ['bəːtrəm], *no.pr.m.* Bertrando.

beryl ['bɛril], *s.* (*min.*) berillo.

beryllium [be'riljəm], *s.* (*chim.*) berillio, glucinio.

to **beseech** [bi'siːtʃ], *pass.p.p.* **besought** [bi'sɔːt], *v.t.* supplicare; scongiurare; implorare: *I — you!*, vi prego!.

beseecher [bi'siːtʃə*], *s. c.* supplicante; implorante.

beseeching [bi'siːtʃiŋ], *ag.* supplicante ‖ *s.* supplica.

to **beseem** [bi'siːm], *v.t.* convenire (a), addirsi (a): *it ill beseems you to say so*, non sta bene che tu dica così.

beseeming [bi'siːmiŋ], *ag.* adatto, conveniente.

beseemingly [bi'siːmiŋli], *av.* convenientemente.

to **beset** [bi'set], *pass.p.p.* **beset**, *v.t.* **1.** circondare; ridurre alle strette **2.** *fig.* assediare; assalire: *to be — by doubts*, essere assalito da dubbi.

besetment [bi'setmənt], *s.* **1.** assedio; aggiramento **2.** punto debole.

besetting [bi'setiŋ], *ag.* incombente; assillante ‖ *his — sin*, il suo vizio inveterato.

to **beshrew** [bi'ʃruː], *v.t.* (*arc.*) maledire: — *the day!*, maledetto sia il giorno!; — *me if*, che il diavolo mi porti se.

beside [bi'said], *prep.* **accanto, presso, vicino a; fuori di:** *sit — me*, siediti accanto a me; *to be — oneself with grief*, esser fuori di sè per il dolore ‖ *that's — the point*, questo esula dalla questione.

besides [bi'saidz], *av.* **inoltre, per di più, d'altronde, altrimenti, diversamente:** — *I have no money*, oltre al resto non ho denaro; *many others* —, molti altri ancora ‖ *prep.* **oltre a:** *I have no friend — him*, non ho altro amico che lui.

to **besiege** [bi'siːdʒ], *v.t.* assediare, accerchiare, assalire (anche *fig.*).

besieger [bi'siːdʒə*], *s.* assediante.

to **beslaver** [bi'slævə*], *v.t.* **1.** coprire di bava **2.** *fig.* adulare.

to **beslobber** [bi'slɔbə*], *v.t.* **1.** coprire di bava **2.** *fig.* adulare **3.** baciare con eccessivo trasporto.

to **besmear** [bi'smiə*], *v.t.* imbrattare, sporcare.

to **besmirch** [bi'sməːtʃ], *v.t.* sporcare; scolorire; oscurare (fama, nome).

besom ['biːzəm], *s.* granata, scopa.

to **besom**, *v.t.* scopare.

to **besot** [bi'sɔt], *pass.p.p.* **besotted** [bi'sɔtid], *v.t.* istupidire: *to — oneself*, abbrutirsi.

besought [bi'sɔːt], *pass.p.p.* di to **beseech**.

to **bespangle** [bi'spæŋgl], *v.t.* adornare, cospargere di lustrini.

to **bespatter** [bi'spætə*], *v.t.* **1.** inzaccherare **2.** *fig.* coprire (di insulti).

to **bespeak** [bi'spiːk], *pass.* **bespoke** [bi'spouk], *p.p.* **bespoken** [bi'spoukən], *v.t.* **1.** ordinare; prenotare **2.** rivelare: *his language bespeaks him a scholar*, dal suo modo di parlare si rivela uno studioso **3.** (*arc.*) chiedere (un favore).

bespoke [bi'spouk], *ag.* ordinato in anticipo ☆ — *garments*, abiti su misura.

to **besprinkle** [bi'spriŋkl], *v.t.* spruzzare; cospargere.

Bess [bes], *no.pr.f. dim.* di **Elizabeth**.

Bessemer-process ['besimə'prouses], *s.* (*metal.*) processo Bessemer.

Bessie ['besi], *no.pr.f. dim.* di **Elizabeth**.

best [best], *ag.* (*superl.* di *good*) **il migliore:** *the — book in the library*, il miglior libro della biblio-

teca; *the — days of my life*, i migliori giorni della mia vita; *the — part of the year*, la maggior parte dell'anno ☆ — *man*, testimone dello sposo; — *-seller*, libro che si vende in quantità, di gran successo.

best, *s.* **il meglio, il migliore:** *the — of it is that...*, la cosa più bella, strana, comica (della faccenda) è che...; *dressed in his* —, vestito dei suoi abiti migliori; *to the — of my ability*, con tutta la mia abilità, come meglio mi è possibile; *I am in the — of health*, godo della migliore salute ‖ *to do one's* — (o *the — in one's power*), fare del proprio meglio; *to have* (o *to get*) *the — of it*, (*fam.*) aver la meglio; *to look one's* —, essere nelle migliori condizioni, in gran forma; *to make the — of sthg.*, cavarsela alla meno peggio; *to sing one's* —, cantare il meglio possibile.

best, *av.* (*superl.* di *well*) **1. nel modo migliore; meglio:** *he does it (the)* —, egli lo fa meglio di tutti; *he works — in the early morning*, egli lavora meglio al mattino presto; *I helped her as — I could*, l'aiutai come meglio potei; *you know — what to do*, tu sai meglio di tutti che cosa fare **2. di più; maggiormente:** *Mr. Brown is the — loved teacher in the school*, il Prof. Brown è l'insegnante più amato della scuola ‖ *to like* —, preferire (fra più di due).

to **best**, *v.t.* (*fam.*) vincere, superare.

to **bestead** [bi'sted], *v.t.i.* aiutare; profittare.

bestial ['bestjəl], *ag.* bestiale, brutale; sensuale.

bestiality [,besti'æliti], *s.* bestialità; brutalità.

to **bestialize** ['bestjəlaiz], *v.t.* abbrutire.

bestially ['bestjəli], *av.* bestialmente.

bestiary ['bestiəri], *s.* bestiario.

to **bestir** [bi'stəː*], *pass.p.p.* **bestirred** [bi'stəːd], *v.t.* agitare, muovere: *to — oneself*, muoversi, mettersi in moto; brigare.

to **bestow** [bi'stou], *v.t.* **1.** accordare, concedere, donare: *to — a favour on s.o.*, concedere un favore a qlcu. **2.** mettere, depositare.

bestowal [bi'stouəl], *s.* conferimento, donazione; concessione (di un privilegio, ecc.).

to **bestrew** [bi'struː], *pass.* **bestrewed** [bi'struːd], *p.p.* **bestrewed, bestrewn** [bi'struːn], *v.t.* disseminare, cospargere.

to **bestride** [bi'straid], *pass.* **bestrode** [bi'stroud], *p.p.* **bestridden** [bi'stridn], *v.t.* **1.** cavalcare; montare, stare a cavallo di **2.** coprire, far scudo a.

bestudded [bi'stʌdid], *ag.* tempestato, cosparso: *the sky was — with stars*, il cielo era tempestato di stelle.

bet [bet], *s.* scommessa: *to make* (o *to lay*) *a* —, fare una scommessa.

to **bet**, *pass.p.p.* **bet**, *v.t.i.* scommettere ‖ *you can — your boots* (o *bottom dollar*) *that...*, puoi essere sicuro che....

beta ['biːtə], *s.* beta (seconda lettera dell'alfabeto greco).

to **betake** [bi'teik], *pass.* **betook** [bi'tuk], *p.p.* **betaken** [bi'teikən], *v.r.*: *to — oneself to a place*, dirigersi verso un luogo; *to — oneself to drink*, darsi al bere.

betatron ['biːtətrɔn], *s.* (*fis.*) betatrone.

betel ['biːtəl], *s.* (*bot.*) betel ☆ — *nut*, noce di betel.

bethel ['beθəl], *s.* luogo sacro.

to **bethink** [bi'θiŋk], *pass.p.p.* **bethought** [bi'θɔːt], *v.r.*: *to — oneself*, considerare, riflettere; ricordarsi.

Bethlehem ['beθlihem], *no.pr.* (*geog.*) Betlemme.

to **betide** [bi'taid], *v.t.i.* (solo alla 3ª *persona sing. pres. congiunt.*) accadere, avvenire: *whatever* —, qualunque cosa accada; *woe — him who...*, male incolga colui che....

betimes [bi'taimz], *av.* per tempo; presto.

to **betoken** [bi'toukən], *v.t.* presagire; indicare, suggerire.

beton ['betən], *s.* calcestruzzo, cemento idraulico.

betony ['betəni], *s.* (*bot.*) betonica.

betook [bi'tuk], *pass.p.p.* di to **betake**.

to **betray** [bi'trei], *v.t.* **1.** tradire; denunciare; palesare: *to — oneself*, tradirsi **2.** *fig.* far cadere (in errore).

betrayal [bi'treiəl], *s.* tradimento.
betrayer [bi'treiə*], *s.c.* traditore, traditrice; delatore, delatrice.
to **betroth** [bi'trouð], *v.t.* fidanzare, promettere in matrimonio.
betrothal [bi'trouðəl], *s.* fidanzamento.
betrothed [bi'trouðd], *ag.* fidanzato: *the* —, i promessi sposi ‖ *s.c.* fidanzato, fidanzata.
betrothment [bi'trouðmənt], *s.* fidanzamento.
Betsy ['betsi], *no.pr.f. dim.* di **Elizabeth**.
better[1] ['betə*], *ag.* (*comp.* di *good*) migliore, meglio: *she is* — *than he is*, ella è migliore di lui; *to be* —, esser meglio, star meglio, valer meglio; esser migliore, superiore: *he was* — *than his word*, fece meglio di quanto aveva promesso; *to grow* —, farsi migliore; *to look* —, aver miglior cera ‖ *all the* —, tanto meglio ‖ *for* — *or* (*for*) *worse*, nella buona e nell'avversa fortuna ‖ *my* — *half*, mia moglie ‖ *the sooner the* —, più presto è, meglio è ‖ *he is no* — *than a fool*, non è altro che uno sciocco ‖ *he is* — *off than I am*, è più ricco di me.
better[1], *av.* (*comp.* di *well*) **1.** meglio, in modo migliore: — *and* —, di bene in meglio; — *late than never*, meglio tardi che mai; *so much the* —, tanto meglio ‖ *to like* —, preferire (fra due) ‖ *had* —, (V) sarebbe bene che: *you had* — *go*, sarebbe bene che andaste, fareste bene ad andarvene **2.** (*fam.*) di più: *I'll like it* — *when I understand it more*, mi piacerà di più quando lo capirò meglio.
better[1], *s.* **1.** il meglio: *all for the* —, tutto per il meglio; *to get the* — *of*, superare, sorpassare **2.** superiore: *your betters*, i vostri superiori.
to **better**[1], *v.t.i.* migliorare: *to* — *oneself*, migliorare le proprie condizioni, la propria situazione economica.
better[2], *s.* scommettitore.
betterment ['betəmənt], *s.* **1.** miglioramento, miglioria **2.** (*comm.*) plus-valore.
betting ['betiŋ], *s.* lo scommettere.
bettor ['betə*], *s.* scommettitore.
Betty ['beti], *no.pr.f. dim.* di **Elizabeth**.
between [bi'twi:n], *av.* in mezzo: *his visits are few and far* —, le sue visite sono molto intervallate; *to squeeze in* —, cacciarsi, introdursi in mezzo ‖ *prep.* tra, fra, in mezzo a, a certi intervalli (fra due): — *you and me*, fra te e me; *she sat* — *her parents*, stava seduta fra i suoi genitori; *we bought it* — *us*, l'abbiamo comperato in società ‖ — *the devil and the deep* (*blue*) *sea*, tra l'incudine e il martello.
between-whiles [bi'twi:n-wailz], *av.* negli intervalli.
betwixt [bi'twikst], *av. prep.* (*arc. poet.*) tra, fra.
bevatron ['bevətrən], *s.* (*fis.*) bevatrone.
bevel ['bevəl], *s.* **1.** angolo obliquo; sghembo; ugnatura **2.** (*mec.*) bisello; smusso ☆ — -*gear*, ingranaggio conico; — -*wheel*, ruota dentata conica.
to **bevel**, *pass.p.p.* **bevelled** ['bevəld], *v.t.* smussare: *to* — *a glass*, molare un vetro a smusso.
bevelling ['bevəliŋ], *s.* inclinazione.
beverage ['bevəridʒ], *s.* bevanda.
bevy ['bevi], *s.* gruppo, frotta; stormo (di uccelli).
to **bewail** [bi'weil], *v.t.i.* lamentare, lamentarsi; deplorare: *to* — *one's lot*, lamentarsi della propria sorte.
bewailer [bi'weilə*], *s.c.* piagnucolone, piagnucolona.
to **beware** [bi'weə*], *v.t.i.* guardarsi, stare attento: — *of the dog!*, attenti al cane!; — *of pick-pockets!*, attenti ai borsaiuoli!.
to **bewilder** [bi'wildə*], *v.t.* rendere perplesso; disorientare; sconcertare; confondere.
bewildering [bi'wildəriŋ], *ag.* sbalorditivo; sconcertante; stupefacente.
bewilderingly [bi'wildəriŋli], *av.* in modo sbalorditivo, sconcertante, stupefacente.
bewilderment [bi'wildəmənt], *s.* confusione, smarrimento.
to **bewitch** [bi'witʃ], *v.t.* incantare, stregare; am-

maliare: *she danced so well that she bewitched everybody* danzò così bene che ammaliò tutti.
bewitcher [bi'witʃə*], *s.c.* stregone, strega; incantatore, incantatrice; ammaliatore, ammaliatrice.
bewitchery [bi'witʃəri], *s.* stregoneria, incanto.
bewitching [bi'witʃiŋ], *ag.* affascinante, seducente.
bewitchingly [bi'witʃiŋli], *av.* con incanto, con malia; in modo affascinante.
bewitchment [bi'witʃmənt], *s.* malia, stregoneria; incanto, fascino.
to **bewray** [bi'rei], *v.t.* (*arc.*) rivelare involontariamente.
bey [bei], *s.* bei.
beyond [bi'jond], *av.* inoltre, più in là: *the lands* —, le terre lontane ‖ *prep.* di là di, oltre, più in là di, sopra: — *belief*, incredibile; — *endurance*, insopportabile; — *the seas*, al di là dei mari; *the garden* — *the gate*, il giardino al di là del cancello; *this is* — *him*, non è in grado di capire questo ‖ *s.* l'aldilà, la vita futura: *she heard voices from the* —, sentiva delle voci dall'aldilà ‖ *the back of* —, il più remoto angolo del mondo.
bezel ['bezl], *s.* **1.** sfaccettatura (di gemma) **2.** castone (di anello).
bezique [bi'zi:k], *s.* bazzica (giuoco di carte).
bezonian [bi'zouniən], *s.* (*arc.*) mendicante.
bhang [bæŋ], *s.* «bang» (canapa indiana usata come narcotico).
bheesty ['bi:sti], *s.* (*ang.-in.*) portatore d'acqua.
bias ['baiəs], *s.* **1.** materia, peso eccedente di una boccia; inclinazione di una boccia causata da peso eccedente **2.** predisposizione; pregiudizio: *free from* —, senza pregiudizi; *without* —, senza preconcetti; *to have a* — *against s.o.*, avere una prevenzione contro qlcu.; *to have a* — *towards s.o.*, propendere per qlcu. **3.** (*sartoria*) cucitura diagonale; sbieco: *to cut on the* —, tagliare sbieco.
to **bias**, *pass.p.p.* **bias(s)ed** ['baiəst], *v.t.* **1.** fare inclinare **2.** influenzare (specialmente in modo negativo): *you are biased*, siete prevenuto.
biaxial [bai'æksiəl], *ag.* (*fis.*) biassiale.
bib [bib], *s.* bavaglino; pettorina.
to **bib**, *pass.p.p.* **bibbed** [bibd], *v.i.* bere assai, trincare.
bibasie [bai'beisik], *ag.* (*chim.*) bibasico.
bibber ['bibə*], *s.* bevitore.
bibcock ['bibkɔk], *s.* rubinetto.
Bible ['baibl], *s.* Bibbia ‖ **bible**, *s.* **1.** qualsiasi libro che abbia autorità **2.** libro, omaso (di ruminante) ☆ — -*clerk*, studente di Oxford che legge i testi sacri nella cappella; — -*oath*, giuramento sulla Bibbia.
biblical ['biblikəl], *ag.* biblico.
biblically ['biblikəli], *av.* biblicamente.
biblicist ['biblisist], *s.* studioso della Bibbia.
bibliographer [,bibli'ɔgrəfə*], *s.* bibliografo.
bibliographic(al) [,bibliə'græfik(əl)], *ag.* bibliografico.
bibliography [,bibli'ɔgrəfi], *s.* bibliografia.
bibliolatry [,bibli'ɔlətri], *s.* bibliolatria.
bibliomania [,bibliou'meinjə], *s.* bibliomania.
bibliomaniac [,bibliou'meiniæk], *s.* bibliomane.
bibliophil(e) [biblioufail], *s.* bibliofilo.
biblist ['biblist], *s.* studioso della Bibbia.
bibulous ['bibjuləs], *ag.* bibulo, assorbente.
bicameral [bai'kæmərəl], *ag.* (*dir.*) bicamerale.
bicarbonate [bai'kɑ:bənit], *s.* (*chim.*) bicarbonato.
bice [bais], *s.* colore blu, verde pallido.
bicentenary [,baisen'ti:nəri], *ag.s.* bicentenario.
bicentennial [,baisen'tenjəl], *ag.* bicentennale.
bicephalous [bai'sefələs], *ag.* bicefalo.
biceps ['baiseps], *s.* (*anat.*) bicipite.
bicker[1] ['bikə*], *s.* **1.** lite; zuffa **2.** gorgoglio (di fiume); frastuono.
to **bicker**[1], *v.i.* **1.** altercare, disputare, litigare **2.** risplendere (di fiamma) **3.** gorgogliare (di fiume).
bicker[2], *s.* (*scoz.*) coppa.
bickerer ['bikərə*], *s.c.* chi litiga, chi disputa.
biconcave [bai'kɔnkeiv], *ag.* biconcavo.

biconvex [bai'kɔnveks], *ag.* biconvesso.
bicuspid [bai'kʌspid], *ag.* bicuspide ‖ *s.* premolare.
bicycle ['baisikl], *s.* bicicletta.
to **bicycle**, *v.i.* andare in bicicletta.
bicycling ['baisiklin], *s.* ciclismo.
bicyclist ['baisiklist], *s.c.* ciclista.
to **bid**[1] [bid], *pass.* **bade** [bæd], **bad** [bæd], *p.p.* **bidden** ['bidn], *v.t.i.* **1.** (V) comandare, ordinare: — *him go*, ordinagli di andare; *do as you are bidden*, fai come ti comandano **2.** dire: *to* — *good-bye*, accomiatarsi; salutare; *to* — *good-morning*, augurare il buon giorno; *to* — *farewell*, dire addio **3.** promettere: *to* — *fair*, promettere bene: *the weather bids fair to improve*, il tempo promette di migliorare **4.** pregare **5.** (*arc.*) invitare.
bid[2], *s.* **1.** offerta (ad un'asta): *to make a* — *for sthg.*, *fig.* fare un tentativo per ottenere, raggiungere ql.co. **2.** appalto: *advertisement for bids*, bando di appalto; *to make a* —, fare offerta di appalto.
to **bid**[2], *pass.* **bid**, *p.p.* **bid**, *v.t.i.* **1.** offrire (ad un'asta); fare offerta di appalto: *to* — (*money*) *for a thing*, offrire denaro per una cosa **2.** (*carte*) dichiarare **3.** *to* — *in*, aumentare l'offerta **4.** *to* — *up*, far salire l'offerta.
biddable ['bidəbl], *ag.* obbediente, docile.
bidden ['bidn], *p.p.* di **to bid**[1].
bidder ['bidə*], *s.* offerente ad un'asta; appaltatore: *to the highest* —, al miglior offerente.
bidding[1] ['bidin], *s.* **1.** ordine; comando **2.** invito.
bidding[2], *s.* **1.** offerta ad un'asta **2.** (*carte*) dichiarazione.
to **bide** [baid], *pass.* **bode** [boud], *p.p.* **bided** ['baidid], *v.t.i.* (*arc. poet.*) aspettare: *to* — *one's time*, aspettare un'occasione migliore.
biennial [bai'eniəl], *ag.s.* (pianta) biennale.
biennially [bai'eniəli], *av.* ogni due anni.
biennium [bai'eniəm], *s.* biennio.
bier [biə*], *s.* bara, feretro, cataletto; *fig.* tomba.
biff [bif], *s.* (*sl.*) scapaccione.
to **biff**, *v.t.* (*sl.*) dare uno scapaccione a.
biffin ['bifin], *s.* mela da cuocere.
bifid ['baifid], *ag.* bifido.
bifocal ['bai'foukəl], *ag.* (*ott.*) bifocale.
bifold ['baifould], *ag.* doppio.
bifoliate [bai'fouliit], *ag.* (*bot.*) che ha due foglie.
to **bifurcate**, *v.t.i.* biforcare, biforcarsi.
bifurcation [ˌbaifə:'keiʃən], *s.* biforcazione.
big [big], *comp.* **bigger** ['bigə*], *superl.* **biggest** ['bigist], *ag.* **1.** grosso, grande; notevole, importante: — *drop in prices*, (*comm.*) forte ribasso nei prezzi; — *words*, parole grosse; *he had* — *ideas*, aveva delle idee grandiose; *he is* — *enough to defend himself*, è abbastanza grande per difendersi; *to grow* — (o *bigger*), ingrassare; crescere ‖ *Big Ben*, « Big Ben » (orologio della torre di Westminster) ‖ *the Big Four*, i quattro Grandi (Stati Uniti, Unione Sovietica, Gran Bretagna, Francia) ‖ *he earns* — *money*, guadagna molto ‖ *to be too* — *for one's shoes* (o *boots*), darsi delle arie; *to look* —, pavoneggiarsi **2.** attivo: — *trade*, commercio attivo **3.** pieno; gonfio; gravido, pregno: — *with danger*, pieno di pericoli; — *with news*, ricco di notizie ‖ — *with child*, incinta; — *with young*, gravido (di animale) ‖ *av.*: *to talk* —, dire smargiassate ☆ — -*bug*, (*fam.*) pezzo grosso; — *end*, (*mec.*) testa; — *game*, caccia grossa; — -*headed*, presuntuoso; — *name*, personaggio, personalità; — *toe*, alluce.
bigamist ['bigəmist], *s.c.* bigamo, bigama.
bigamous ['bigəməs], *ag.* bigamo.
bigamy ['bigəmi], *s.* bigamia.
bigaroon [ˌbigə'ruːn], **bigarreau** ['bigərou], *s.* ciliegia corniola, duracina.
bigeminal [bai'dʒeminl], *ag.* (*bot.*) bigeminato.
biggish ['bigiʃ], *ag.* piuttosto grosso, grande.
bight [bait], *s.* **1.** ansa (di fiume); golfo, baia **2.** (*mar.*) doppino.

bigness ['bignis], *s.* grossezza, grandezza.
bigot ['bigət], *s.c.* **1.** bigotto, bigotta **2.** fanatico, fanatica; settario, settaria.
bigoted ['bigətid], *ag.* **1.** bigotto **2.** fanatico, settario.
bigotry ['bigətri], *s.* **1.** bigottismo **2.** fanatismo, settarismo.
bigwig ['bigwig], *s.* (*fam.*) persona importante.
bijouterie [biˈʒuːtəriː], *s.* bigiotteria, minuteria.
bike [baik], *s.* (*fam.*) bicicletta, bici.
to **bike**, *v.i.* (*fam.*) andare in bicicletta, in bici.
bikini [bi'kiːni], *s.* bikini.
bilabial [bai'leibjəl], *ag.* **1.** (*bot.*) bilabiato **2.** (*fonet.*) bilabiale ‖ *s.* consonante bilabiale.
bilateral [bai'lætərəl], *ag.* bilaterale.
bilberry ['bilbəri], *s.* (*bot.*) mirtillo.
bilbo ['bilbou], *pl.* **bilbos** ['bilbouz], *s.* spada.
bile [bail], *s.* **1.** (*fisiol.*) bile **2.** *fig.* rabbia, ira ☆ — -*stone*, (*patol.*) calcolo biliare.
bilge [bildʒ], *s.* **1.** (*mar.*) sentina; curvatura della carena **2.** (*sl.*) sciocchezze; parolacce: *don't talk* —!, non dire scemenze! ☆ — *block*, (*mar.*) puntello di bacino; — -*keel*, aletta, chiglia di rollio; — -*pump*, pompa di sentina; — -*water*, acqua di sentina; — *ways*, invasatura, taccate.
to **bilge**, *v.t.i.* **1.** (*mar.*) far acqua; aprire una falla nella sentina **2.** (*sl. amer.*) essere bocciato e costretto a dimettersi.
bilgy ['bildʒi], *ag.* fetido.
biliary ['biljəri], *ag.* biliare.
bilingual [bai'lingwəl], *ag.* bilingue.
bilious ['biljəs], *ag.* biliare; *fig.* collerico, irritabile, stizzoso ☆ — *attack*, travaso di bile.
biliousness ['biljəsnis], *s.* stato bilioso; attacco di bile; crisi epatica.
biliteral [bai'litərəl], *ag.* di due lettere ‖ *s.* parola, sillaba, radice di due lettere.
to **bilk** [bilk], *v.t.* ingannare: *to* — *a creditor*, ingannare, evitare di pagare un creditore.
Bill, *no.pr.m. dim.* di **William**.
bill[1] [bil], *s.* **1.** progetto di legge (presentato al Parlamento): *private* —, progetto di legge di interesse locale ‖ *Bill of Rights*, (*st.*) legge del 1689 sui diritti del cittadino inglese; (*negli Stati Uniti*) emendamenti del 1791 alla costituzione del 1787 **2.** certificato; patente; polizza; bolletta: — *of entry*, bolletta di entrata; — *of health*, certificato sanitario; — *of lading*, polizza di carico **3.** (*comm.*) effetto, lettera di cambio: — *of exchange*, cambiale; *bills payable*, *receivable*, effetti da pagare, da esigere; *to endorse a* —, girare una cambiale **4.** (*amer.*) biglietto di banca **5.** conto, nota, fattura **6.** lista: — *of fare*, lista delle vivande, menù: — *of quantities*, preventivo di costruzione **7.** affisso, annunzio; programma di spettacolo, locandina teatrale **8.** (*dir.*) atto: — *of sale*, atto di vendita ☆ — -*board*, pannello, spazio per la pubblicità; — -*poster*, attacchino; avviso; pannello per avvisi; — -*sticker*, attacchino; *bank-* —, (*amer.*) banconota; *transit-* —, bolletta di transito (in dogana).
to **bill**[1], *v.t.* **1.** fatturare **2.** affiggere **3.** (*teat.*) mettere in programma.
bill[2], *s.* **1.** alabarda **2.** falcetto ☆ *hedging* —, roncola.
bill[3], *s.* **1.** becco; rostro **2.** arpione **3.** promontorio.
to **bill**[3], *v.i.* beccuzzarsi (di uccelli) ‖ *to* — *and coo*, (*fam.*) tubare.
billabong ['biləbɔn], *s.* ramo di un fiume che forma un canale cieco o una palude (in Australia).
billet[1] ['bilit], *s.* (*mil.*) alloggio, accantonamento; buono d'alloggio ‖ *every bullet has its* —, (*fam.*) ogni colpo giunge a segno; non si lotta contro il destino.
to **billet**[1], *pass.p.p.* **billeted** ['bilitid], *v.t.* (*mil.*) alloggiare (soldati): *to* — *troops on s.o.*, *in a town*, alloggiare truppe presso qlcu., accantonare truppe in una città.
billet[2], *s.* **1.** ceppo (da ardere) **2.** (*metal.*) billetta **3.** (*arch.*) modanatura.

billet[3], *s.* (*scherz.*) biglietto, lettera ☆ — *-doux*, lettera amorosa.

billfold ['bilfould], *s.* (*amer.*) portafogli.

billful ['bilful], *s.* beccata (cibo preso in una volta).

billiard ['biljəd], *ag.* di, da biliardo ☆ — *-ball*, — *-cue*, palla, stecca da biliardo; — *-marker*, marcatore; — *-room*, sala da biliardo; — *-table*, tavolo da biliardo.

billiards ['biljədz], *s.pl.* biliardo (giuoco).

Billingsgate ['biliŋzgit], *no.pr.* « Billingsgate » (mercato del pesce a Londra) ‖ **billingsgate**, *s.* (*fam.*) linguaggio (volgare) da pescivendoli.

billion ['biljən], *s.* bilione; (*amer.*) miliardo.

billow ['bilou], *s.* 1. onda, flutto, maroso 2. (*poet.*) il mare.

to billow, *v.i.* ondeggiare; fluttuare.

billowy ['biloui], *ag.* ondoso; fluttuante.

Billy, *no.pr.m. dim.* di **William**.

billy ['bili], *s.* 1. (*amer.*) manganello (dei poliziotti) 2. (*Australia*) pentolino, gavetta (per il tè).

billycock ['bilikɔk], *s.* (*sl.*) bombetta.

billygoat ['biligout], *s.* capro, becco.

bilobate [bai'loubeit], *ag.* bilobato.

biltong ['biltɔŋ], *s.* carne seccata al sole.

bimane ['baimein], *pl.* **bimanes** ['baimeinz], **bimana** ['bimənə], *s.* bimane.

bimeby ['baimbai], *av.* (*fam. amer.* per *by and by*) fra breve.

bimestrial [bai'mestriəl], *ag.* bimestrale.

bimetallic [,baimi'tælik], *ag.* (*econ.*) bimetallico.

bimetallism [bai'metəlizəm], *s.* (*econ.*) bimetallismo.

bimetallist [bai'metəlist], *s.* (*econ.*) bimetallista.

bimonthly ['bai'mʌnθli], *ag.* bimensile ‖ *s.* pubblicazione bimensile.

bimonthly, *av.* 1. ogni due mesi 2. due volte al mese.

bin [bin], *s.* 1. recipiente (per grano, carbone, pane, ecc.) 2. cartellino (distintivo dei materiali) ☆ *dust-* —, bidone della spazzatura; *ore-* —, silo per minerale; *wine* - —, ripostiglio per vino in bottiglia.

binary ['bainəri], *ag.* binario.

binate ['baineit], *ag.* binato.

binaural [bin'ɔːrəl], *ag.* biaurale, che appartiene alle due orecchie ☆ — *arch*, linea che unisce i due punti auricolari passando per il vertice del capo; — *stethoscope*, stetoscopio biauricolare.

bind [baind], *s.* 1. legame; fascia 2. (*mus.*) legatura 3. (*mec.*) incastratura 4. (*geol.*) terra indurita chiusa fra due strati di carbone.

to bind, *pass.p.p.* **bound** [baund], *v.t.i.* 1. legare; allacciare; attaccare; far aderire; incatenare; fasciare; bendare; bordare: *to* — *grain in bundles*, legare grano in covoni; *to* — (*up*) *a wound*, fasciare una ferita ‖ *to* — *s.o. hand and foot*, legare qlcu. mani e piedi 2. rilegare: *I'll have my books bound in leather*, mi farò rilegare i libri in pelle 3. obbligare, costringere, impegnare, legare, vincolare: *to* — *oneself*, obbligarsi; *he has bound himself to do it*, egli si è impegnato a farlo; *to* — *s.o.* (*down*) *to do sthg.*, obbligare qlcu. a fare ql.co. ‖ *I'll be bound*, scommetto ‖ *it was bound to happen*, doveva accadere ‖ *to* — *apprentice*, allogare come apprendista: *he is bound apprentice to a printer*, è apprendista tipografo ‖ *to be bound by affection*, sentirsi legato da affetto 4. stringere, indurire; (*mec.*) indurirsi, gripparsi 5. (*chim.*) legare 6. *to* — **over**, (*dir.*) obbligare (sotto pena di multa).

binder ['baində*], *s.* 1. rilegatore 2. rilegatura mobile (per giornali, ecc.) 3. macchina per legare i covoni 4. (*mec.*) legatrice 5. (*chim.*) legante 6. (*arch.*) tirante.

bindery ['baindəri], *s.* (*amer.*) legatoria.

binding ['baindiŋ], *ag.* obbligatorio; impegnativo: — *offer*, offerta impegnativa ‖ *s.* 1. legatura; legame; fasciatura; nastro, bordura 2. rilegatura; copertina 3. (*mec.*) inceppamento, grippaggio.

bindweed ['baindwiːd], *s.* convolvolo; rampicante.

bine [bain], *s.* gambo sottile di rampicante; germoglio flessibile.

binge [bindʒ], *s.* (*sl.*) baldoria, festa rumorosa.

binnacle ['binəkl], *s.* (*mar.*) chiesuola, abitacolo.

binocle ['binɔkl], *s.* binocolo.

binocular [bai'nɔkjulə*], *ag.* binoculare ‖ *s. gener. pl.* binocolo.

binomial [bai'noumjəl], *ag.* (*alg.*) appartenente a un binomio ‖ *s.* (*alg.*) binomio.

binominal [bai'nɔminl], *ag.* che ha due nomi.

biochemical ['baiou'kemikəl], *ag.* biochimico.

biochemist ['baiou'kemist], *s.* biochimico.

biochemistry ['baiou'kemistri], *s.* biochimica.

biogenesis [baiou'dʒenisis], *s.* biogenesi.

biograph ['baiougrɑːf], *s.* riproduzione fotografica di un'azione continuata (il cinematografo primitivo).

biographer [bai'ɔgrəfə*], *s.* biografo.

biographic(al) [,baiou'græfik(əl)], *ag.* biografico.

biographically [,baiou'graefikəli], *av.* biograficamente.

biography [bai'ɔgrəfi], *s.* biografia.

biological [,baiə'lɔdʒikəl], *ag.* biologico.

biologically [,baiə'lɔdʒikəli], *av.* biologicamente.

biologist [bai'ɔlədʒist], *s.* biologo.

biology [bai'ɔlədʒi], *s.* biologia.

biometry [bai'ɔmitri], *s.* biometria.

bionomics ['baiou'nɔmiks], *s.* bionomia.

biophysics ['baiou'fiziks], *s.* biofisica.

bioplasm ['baiəplæzəm], *s.* bioplasma.

bioplast ['baiəplæst], *s.* protoplasma.

bioscope ['baiəskoup], *V.* **biograph**.

bipartite [bai'pɑːtait], *ag.* (*bot. dir.*) bipartito.

biped ['baiped], *ag.s.* bipede.

bipedal ['bai,pedl], *ag.* bipede.

biplane ['bai-plein], *s.* (*aer.*) biplano.

bipolar [bai'poulə*], *ag.* (*elett.*) bipolare.

biquadrate [bai'kwɔdrit], *s.* (*alg.*) biquadrato, quarta potenza.

to biquadrate [bai'kwɔdreit], *v.t.* (*alg.*) elevare alla quarta potenza.

biquadratic [,baikwɔ'drætik], *ag.* (*alg.*) biquadratico, alla quarta potenza: — *equation*, equazione biquadratica ‖ *s.* biquadrato, quarta potenza; equazione biquadratica.

birch [bəːtʃ], *s.* 1. betulla 2. verga, sferza: *to flog with a* —, sferzare ☆ — *-rod*, verga.

to birch, *v.t.* sferzare.

birchen ['bəːtʃən], *ag.* di betulla.

bird [bəːd], *s.* 1. uccello: — *of passage*, uccello migratore (anche *fig.*); — *of prey*, uccello rapace ‖ — *in hand*, cosa sicura ‖ — *of Jove*, aquila; — *of Juno*, pavone; *muses' birds*, api ‖ *a* — *in the hand is worth two in the bush*, *prov.* meglio un uovo oggi che una gallina domani ‖ *the early* — *catches the worm*, *prov.* le ore del mattino hanno l'oro in bocca ‖ *to kill two birds with one stone*, *prov.* prendere due piccioni con una fava 2. (*sl.*) tipo, individuo: *who's that old* —?, chi è quel tipo là?; *he is a queer* —, è un tipo strano ‖ *the* — *is flown*, il prigioniero è fuggito ‖ *birds of a feather*, gente dello stesso stampo: *birds of a feather flock together*, *prov.* ogni simile ama il suo simile ☆ — *-cage*, gabbia per uccelli, uccelliera; — *-catcher*, uccellatore; — *-catching*, uccellagione; — *-fancier*, amatore, allevatore, commerciante di uccelli; — *-lime*, vischio, pania; — *-of-paradise*, uccello del paradiso; —*'s-eye*, (*bot.*) veronica; tabacco intrecciato a corda e trinciato; —*'s-eye view*, vista a volo d'uccello; —*'s-nest*, nido di uccello; —*'s-nesting*, caccia ai nidi; — *-seed*, miglio, panico; — *-stuffer*, impagliatore d'uccelli ‖ *hen* —, femmina di uccello.

to bird, *v.i.* uccellare, andare a caccia di uccelli.

birdcall ['bəːdkɔːl], *s.* richiamo, fischio per uccelli.

birdie ['bəːdi], *s.* 1. (*spor.*) « birdie » (colpo al golf) 2. (*fam.*) uccellino, passerotto.

birdlike ['bəːdlaik], *ag.* da, simile ad uccello.

bireme ['bairiːm], *s.* (*st.*) bireme.

biretta [bi'retə], *s.* berretta da prete.

birth [bə:θ], *s.* **1.** nascita: *French by* —, francese di nascita; *to give* — *to*, partorire, dare alla luce **2.** discendenza, stirpe, parentado: *of good* —, di buona razza; *of high* —, di alto lignaggio **3.** *fig.* origine, principio: *the* — *of an idea*, la genesi di un'idea ☆ — *-control*, limitazione delle nascite; — *-mark*, voglia; — *-rate*, natalità: *fall in the* — *-rate*, denatalità ‖ *new-* —, rigenerazione.

birthday [ˈbə:θdei], *s.* giorno natalizio, compleanno ☆ — *present*, regalo di compleanno; — *-suit*, (*scherz.*) la propria pelle.

birthplace [ˈbə:θpleis], *s.* luogo di nascita.

birthright [ˈbə:θ-rait], *s.* diritto di primogenitura.

bis [bis], *av.* bis.

Biscay [ˈbiskei], *no.pr.* (*geog.*) Biscaglia: *the Bay of* —, il golfo di Biscaglia.

biscuit [ˈbiskit], *ag.* (color) marrone chiaro ‖ *s.* **1.** biscotto: *military* —, galletta (per militari); *ship's* —, galletta (per marinai) **2.** biscuit (porcellana bianca non verniciata) ☆ *ship('s)* — (o *sea-* —), galletta.

to bisect [baiˈsekt], *v.t.i.* dividere in due parti; biforcarsi; (*geom.*) bisecare.

bisection [baiˈsekʃən], *s.* (*geom.*) bisezione.

bisector [baiˈsektə*], *s.* (*geom.*) bisettrice, bisecante.

bisexual [ˈbaiˈseksjuəl], *ag.* bisessuale.

bishop[1] [ˈbiʃəp], *s.* **1.** vescovo **2.** alfiere (agli scacchi) **3.** bevanda di vino caldo aromatizzato, «vin brulé».

to bishop[1], *v.t.* **1.** far vescovo **2.** (*arc.*) cresimare.

to bishop[2], *v.t.* **1.** limare i denti a (un cavallo, per farlo sembrare più giovane) **2.** far annegare.

bishopric [ˈbiʃəprik], *s.* vescovato.

bismuth [ˈbizməθ], *s.* (*chim.*) bismuto.

bison [ˈhaisn], *s.* (*zool.*) bisonte.

bisque[1] [bisk], *s.* (*spor.*) concessione di un vantaggio a un giocatore più debole.

bisque[2], *s.* biscuit (porcellana bianca non verniciata).

bisque[3], *s.* zuppa (con brodo di uccelli, di pesci).

bissextile [biˈsekstail], *ag.s.* (anno) bisestile.

bister [ˈbistə*], *ag.s.* (color) bistro.

bistort [ˈbistɔ:t], *s.* (*bot.*) bistorta, serpentina.

bistoury [ˈbisturi], *s.* (*chir.*) bisturi.

bistre [ˈbistə*], *ag.s.* (color) bistro.

bit[1] [bit], *s.* **1.** qualche cosa da mangiare **2.** (*mec.*) parte tagliente di un utensile; punta (di trapano); scalpello; morsa (di tenaglia, ecc.); ingegno (nella chiave) **3.** morso (del cavallo) ‖ *to champ the* —, mordere il freno (anche *fig.*); *to take the* — *between one's teeth*, *fig.* essere ribelle, indomabile.

to bit[1], *v.t.* imbrigliare, mettere il morso a.

bit[2], *s.* pezzettino; bocconcino; un poco: *a dainty* —, un bocconcino prelibato; *wait a* —, aspetta un poco ‖ — *by* —, a poco a poco ‖ *a* — *of a coward*, alquanto vile ‖ *a threepenny* —, una monetina da tre penny ‖ *to do one's* —, fare la propria parte ‖ *to give a* — *of one's mind*, parlare con franchezza.

bit[3], *pass.p.p.* di to **bite**.

bitch [bitʃ], *s.* **1.** cagna; lupa; volpe femmina **2.** (*fig. spreg.*) cagna, donna scostumata.

bite [bait], *s.* **1.** morso, morsicatura ‖ *his bark is worse than his* —, *prov.* can che abbaia non morde **2.** boccone **3.** l'abboccare (di pesci) **4.** dolore acuto (fisico, morale) **5.** presa, stretta.

to bite, *pass.* **bit** [bit], *p.p.* **bit**, **bitten** [ˈbitn], *v.t.i.* **1.** mordere, morsicare, addentare: *to* — *at sthg.*, mordere ql.co. (specialmente di cani); *to* — *one's lips*, *nails*, mordersi le labbra, le unghie ‖ *bitten with*, affetto da: *to be bitten with a desire to do sthg.*, ardere dal desiderio di fare ql.co. ‖ *to* — *the dust*, *fig.* mordere la polvere **2.** abboccare: *the fish bites*, il pesce abbocca **3.** far presa; (*mar.*) mordere, tenere (di ancora) **4.** ferire (di spada) **5.** corrodere: *acid bites into metal*, l'acido corrode il metallo **6.** ingannare: *to get bitten*, farsi imbrogliare **7.** to — **off**, portar via con un morso ‖ *to* — *off more than one can chew*, *prov.* fare il passo più lungo della gamba.

biter [ˈbaitə*], *s.c.* **1.** chi morde **2.** *fig.* ingannatore; ingannatrice; imbroglione, imbrogliona: *the* — *bit*, il truffatore truffato.

Bithynia [biˈθiniə], *no.pr.* (*geog. st.*) Bitinia.

Bithynian [biˈθiniən], *ag.s.* bitinico.

biting [ˈbaitiŋ], *ag.* **1.** mordente, pungente, tagliente **2.** acre; piccante **3.** mordace, sarcastico, caustico.

bitingly [ˈbaitiŋli], *av.* pungentemente.

bitless [ˈbitlis], *ag.* senza mordente.

bitt [bit], *s. gener. pl.* (*mar.*) bitta.

to bitt, *v.t.* (*mar.*) abbittare, dar volta alla bitta.

bitten [ˈbitn], *p.p.* di to **bite**.

bitter[1] [ˈbitə*], *ag.* **1.** amaro (anche *fig.*): — *beer*, birra amara; — *experience*, esperienza penosa; — *reproach*, rimprovero amaro; — *tears*, lacrime amare **2.** pungente, rigido (di clima) **3.** acre, aspro (di tono) **4.** accanito: — *enemies*, nemici mortali; — *hatred*, odio accanito ‖ *s.* birra amara; liquore amaro ‖ *we must take the* — *with the sweet*, *prov.* non c'è rosa senza spine ☆ — *-sweet*, agrodolce; (*bot.*) dulcamara.

to bitter[1], *v.t.* rendere amaro; *fig.* amareggiare.

bitter[2], *s.* (*mar.*) volta di bitta.

bitter-end [ˈbitərend], *s.* (*mar.*) parte terminale entro bordo di una cima, catena, cavo ‖ *to the* —, a oltranza: *to go on* (o *to resist*), *to fight to the* —, resistere, combattere a oltranza.

bitterish [ˈbitəriʃ], *ag.* amarognolo.

bitterly [ˈbitəli], *av.* **1.** amaramente; aspramente: — *disappointed*, amaramente deluso **2.** rigidamente (di clima): *it's* — *cold*, fa un freddo birbone.

bittern [ˈbitə(:)n], *s.* (*ornit.*) tarabuso.

bitterness [ˈbitənis], *s.* **1.** amarezza (di dolore); gusto amaro **2.** rancore **3.** rigidità (di clima).

bitters [ˈbitəz], *s.pl.* amaro (liquore ricavato da erbe e usato come stomatico).

bittock [ˈbitək], *s.* (*fam.*) pezzetto.

bitumen [ˈbitjumin], *s.* bitume.

to bituminize [biˈtju:minaiz], *v.t.* bituminare.

bituminous [biˈtju:minəs], *ag.* bituminoso.

bivalence [ˈbai,veiləns], *s.* (*chim.*) bivalenza.

bivalent [ˈbai,veilənt], *ag.* (*chim.*) bivalente.

bivalve [ˈbaivælv], *ag.s.* bivalve.

bivalved [ˈbaivælvd], **bivalvular** [baiˈvælvjulə*], *ag.* bivalve.

bivouac [ˈbivuæk], *s.* (*mil.*) bivacco.

to bivouac, *pass.p.p.* **bivouacked** [ˈbivuækt], *v.i.* bivaccare.

bi-weekly [ˈbaiˈwi:kli], *ag.* bisettimanale ‖ *s.* pubblicazione bisettimanale ‖ *av.* due volte la settimana.

biz [biz], *s.* (*sl. abbr.*) di **business**.

bizarre [biˈzɑ:*], *ag.* bizzarro, strano, eccentrico, grottesco.

bizarrerie [biˈzɑ:rəri], *s.* bizzarria, eccentricità.

blab [blæb], *s.c.* (*fam.*) ciarlone, ciarlona.

to blab, *pass.p.p.* **blabbed** [blæbd], *v.t.i.* cianciare, chiacchierare; palesare, rivelare; spifferare, spiattellare: *he bladded it all out*, spiattellò tutto.

blabber [ˈblæbə*], *s.c.* (*fam.*) ciarlone, ciarlona.

black [blæk], *ag.* **1.** nero, negro; oscuro, buio; annerito; sporco: — *with age*, annerito dal tempo; *his hands were* —, aveva le mani sporche ‖ *Black Country*, distretti minerario-siderurgici del centro Inghilterra ‖ — *in the face*, congestionato ‖ *Black Rod*, usciere dell'ufficio del Lord Ciambellano, della Camera dei Lord, dell'Ordine della Giarrettiera ‖ *Black Sea*, (*geog.*) Mar Nero ‖ *Black Watch*, il secondo reggimento Highlanders ‖ *as* — *as a raven's wing*, corvino: *hair as* — *as raven's wing*, capelli corvini **2.** *fig.* malvagio, sinistro; mostruoso; lugubre, triste; funesto; minaccioso, irato, astioso; disastroso: *things look* —, le cose vanno male, le cose prendono una brutta piega; *to give s.o. a* — *look*, lanciare un'occhiataccia a qlcu.; *to look* —, guardare bieco ‖ *to look as* — *as thunder*, essere nero nero, avere l'aria furiosa ‖ *s.* **1.** color nero: *I like to wear* —, mi piace vestirmi di nero **2.** vernice, tintura nera; macchia nera **3.** abito nero, lutto: *to put on* —, mettere il lutto **4.** fuliggine **5.** fungo nero (che attacca il frumento) **6.** negro **7.** cavallo nero ☆ — *and blue*, pieno di lividi; — *-and-white*, per iscritto: *to set sthg. down in* — *-and-white*, mettere ql.co. per iscritto; — *art*, magia nera, negromanzia; — *-beetle*, (*entom.*) scarafaggio, piattola; — *belt*, (*fam.*) zona siderurgica del centro Inghilterra; (*amer.*) zona abitata provalentemente da negri; — *book*, libro nero: *to be on s.o.'s* — *books*, essere in disgrazia presso qlcu.; — *-currant*, (*bot.*) ribes europeo; — *-death*, peste; — *dog*, *fig.* malumore, depressione; — *-draught*, (*farm.*) infuso di senna; — *eye*, occhio nero, pesto; — *-faced*, *fig.* dalla faccia scura; — *-flag*, bandiera di nave pirata; bandiera issata dopo l'esecuzione di una sentenza di morte; — *-friar*, frate domenicano; — *-hole*, cella, camera di sicurezza; — *-lead*, grafite; — *-letter*, (*tip.*) carattere gotico; — *-list*, lista nera; — *man*, negro; — *Maria*, furgone cellulare; — *mark*, marchio; — *market*, mercato nero, borsa nera; — *marketeer*, borsanerista; — *Monday*, lunedì di Pasqua; (*sl.*) primo giorno di scuola dopo le vacanze; — *monk*, monaco benedettino; — *-pudding*, sanguinaccio; — *sheep*, pecora nera; — *swan*, mosca bianca; — *-thorn*, (*bot.*) prugnolo; — *tie*, cravatta nera a farfalla; — *troops*, truppe indigene; — *widow*, (*entom.*) vedova nera; — *woman*, negra.

to **black**, *v.t.* **1.** annerire, tingere di nero; lucidare, verniciare di nero; imbrattare, insudiciare; *fig.* diffamare **2.** *to* — *out*, cancellare (con un tratto nero) **3.** V. to **blackout**.

blackamoor ['blækəmuə*], *s.c.* negro, negra; moro, mora.

black-ball ['blækbɔ:l], *s.* palla nera (indicante voto contrario); (*amer.*) voto contrario, voto segreto.

to **black-ball**, *v.t.* **1.** votare contro, bocciare **2.** bandire; interdire.

blackberry ['blækbəri], *s.* (*bot.*) mora selvatica ☆ — *bush*, rovo.

blackberrying ['blæk,beriiŋ], *s.* raccolta delle more.

blackbird ['blækbə:d], *s.* merlo.

blackboard ['blækbɔ:d], *s.* lavagna: *to write on the* —, scrivere alla lavagna.

blackcap ['blækkæp], *s.* **1.** berretto nero (calzato dal giudice quando pronuncia la sentenza di morte) **2.** (*ornit.*) capinera.

to **blacken** ['blækən], *v.t.i.* **1.** annerire, diventare nero; affumicare; oscurare; oscurarsi; lucidare di nero: *the sky blackened*, il cielo si oscurò **2.** *fig.* calunniare, diffamare.

Blackfeet ['blækfi:t], *s.pl.* « Piedi neri » (tribù pellerossa).

blackfellow ['blæk,felou], *s.* aborigeno australiano.

blackguard ['blægɑ:d], *ag.* disonesto, malvagio ‖ *s.* birbone, furfante, mascalzone.

to **blackguard**, *v.t.i.* **1.** insultare, ingiuriare **2.** agire da furfante, da mascalzone.

blackguardism ['blæ,gɑ:dizəm], *s.* furfanteria, condotta da furfante.

blackguardly ['blægɑ:dli], *av.* da furfante.

blackhead ['blækhed], *s.* comedone.

blacking ['blækiŋ], *s.* lucido nero (per scarpe).

blackish ['blækiʃ], *ag.* nerastro.

blackjack ['blækdʒæk], *s.* **1.** boccale di cuoio catramato **2.** (*min.*) blenda **3.** (*amer.*) quercia **4.** (*amer.*) bandiera nera (di nave pirata) **5.** (*amer.*) sfollagente **6.** (*amer.*) « blackjack » (giuoco di carte).

to **blackjack**, *v.t.* (*amer.*) **1.** colpire con uno sfollagente **2.** *fig.* indurre con minacce a fare ql.co.

blackleg ['blækleg], *s.* **1.** truffatore (specialmente alle corse) **2.** crumiro **3.** malattia infettiva di bestiame, piante.

blackly ['blækli], *av.* tristemente, tetramente; minacciosamente; sinistramente.

blackmail ['blækmeil], *s.* **1.** ricatto; estorsione **2.** (*st.*)

tributo (pagato a pirati, briganti per averne l'immunità).

to **blackmail**, *v.t.* ricattare.

blackmailer ['blæk,meilə*], *s.c.* ricattatore, ricattatrice.

blackness ['blæknis], *s.* nerezza; oscurità.

blackout ['blækaut], *s.* **1.** oscuramento, schermatura (in tempo di guerra) **2.** annebbiamento della vista; perdita temporanea di coscienza **3.** (*tv.*) mascheramento, soppressione.

to **blackout**, *v.t.i.* **1.** oscurare, schermare, mascherare, obliterare **2.** perdere temporaneamente coscienza.

Blackshirt ['blækʃə:t], *s.* fascista, camicia nera.

blacksmith ['blæksmiθ], *s.* fabbro ferraio; maniscalco; magnano: —*'s* (*shop*) (o *smithy*), fucina.

blacky ['blæki], *s.* (*fam.*) negro, negretto.

bladder ['blædə*], *s.* **1.** (*anat.*) vescica urinaria; vescica **2.** (*bot.*) pericarpio turgido; vescica d'aria (in alghe, ecc.) **3.** *fig.* testa vuota, pallone gonfiato ☆ *foot-ball* —, camera d'aria di un pallone.

to **bladder**, *v.t.* mettere (strutto) in vesciche.

bladdered ['blædəd], *ag.* gonfio; enfiato.

bladdery ['blædəri], *ag.* gonfio come una vescica; pieno di vesciche.

blade [bleid], *s.* **1.** filo, stelo (d'erba); gambo, lamina (di foglia): *corn in the* —, grano verde, ancora senza spiga **2.** lama; spada **3.** *fig.* spadaccino; attaccabrighe: *a cunning* —, un tipo scaltro **4.** — (*-bone*), (*anat. zool.*) osso piatto **5.** (*ferr.*) ago **6.** (*foto.*) lamella **7.** (*mar.*) palma di remo **8.** (*mec.*) pala, paletta, ☆ *razor* —, lama di rasoio; *shoulder* —, (*anat.*) scapola.

bladed ['bleidid], *ag.* **1.** munito di stelo **2.** munito di lama **3.** che comincia a spuntare (di grano).

blain [blein], *s.* vescicola cutanea.

blamable ['bleiməbl], *ag.* biasimevole.

blame [bleim], *s.* biasimo; rimprovero; accusa; colpa; responsabilità: *to bear the* —, accollarsi il biasimo; *to lay the* — *upon* (o *to throw the* — *on*) s.o., incolpare qlcu.

to **blame**, *v.t.* biasimare; rimproverare; accusare; incolpare: *to* — *oneself for sthg.*, rimproverarsi ql.co.; *to* — *sthg. on s.o.*, addossare a qlcu. la colpa di ql.co.; *to be to* —, essere colpevole.

blameful ['bleimful], *ag.* biasimevole.

blamefully ['bleimfuli], *av.* biasimevolmente.

blameless ['bleimlis], *ag.* irreprensibile, incensurabile.

blamelessly ['bleimlisli], *av.* irreprensibilmente, in modo incensurabile.

blamelessness ['bleimlisnis], *s.* irreprensibilità.

blameworthy ['bleim,wə:ði], *ag.* biasimevole, riprovevole.

to **blanch** [blɑ:ntʃ], *v.t.i.* **1.** impallidire, far impallidire **2.** imbiancare, sbiancare (metallo, ecc.) **3.** mondare (mandorle, ecc.) **4.** *to* — *over*, attenuare, mitigare.

Blanche [blɑ:ntʃ], *no.pr.f.* Bianca.

blancmange [blə'mɔnʒ], *s.* (*cuc.*) biancomangiare.

bland [blænd], *ag.* **1.** blando, dolce, mite, soave, carezzevole **2.** ironico.

to **blandish** ['blændiʃ], *v.t.* blandire, lusingare.

blandisher ['blændiʃə*], *s.c.* chi blandisce, lusinga.

blandishment ['blændiʃmənt], *s. gener. pl.* blandizia, lusinga: *with female blandishments*, con blandizie, lusinghe femminili.

blandly ['blændli], *av.* **1.** blandamente, dolcemente, soavemente **2.** ironicamente.

blandness ['blændnis], *s.* dolcezza, mitezza, soavità.

blank [blæŋk], *ag.* **1.** in bianco: — *cheque*, assegno in bianco **2.** vuoto; *fig.* vacuo: *a* — *look*, uno sguardo vacuo; — *space*, spazio vuoto **3.** (*poes.*) sciolto: — *verse*, versi sciolti ☆ — *cartridge*, cartuccia a salve.

blank, *s.* **1.** spazio vuoto, in bianco: *she left many blanks in her translation*, ella lasciò molte parti in bianco nella traduzione **2.** vuoto; lacuna; cosa priva di significato: *his death left a* —, la sua morte lasciò un gran vuoto; *my mind is a* —, ho la testa completamente vuota **3**. mira, centro (di bersaglio) **4**. biglietto di lotteria non vincente: *to draw a* —, sortire un biglietto non vincente; (*sl.*) far fiasco **5**. (*amer.*) modulo **6**. disco metallico per conio; (*mec.*) pezzo greggio **7**. (*tip.*) lineetta (usata in luogo di parola volgare, ingiuriosa) ☆ *point-* —, di punto in bianco.

to **blank**, *v.t.* **1**. coprire, nascondere, velare **2**. (*tip.*) indicare con lineetta **3**. (*spor. amer.*) impedire di segnare punti a (un avversario) **4**. (*mec.*) tranciare.

blanket ['blæŋkit], *s.* coperta di lana; copertura (anche *fig.*): — *of snow*, coltre di neve || *born on the wrong side of the* —, illegittimo ☆ *wet* —, guastafeste.

to **blanket**, *v.t.* **1**. coprire con una coperta **2**. (*fam.*) soffocare (uno scandalo) **3**. (*rad.*) disturbare (volutamente) la ricezione di (apparecchi riceventi) **4**. (*mar.*) rubare il vento a.

blankly ['blæŋkli], *av.* **1**. senza espressione: *she looked at me* —, mi guardò senza espressione **2**. decisamente, recisamente, assolutamente: *to deny* —, negare assolutamente.

blankness ['blæŋknis], *s.* **1**. espressione vacua **2**. mancanza di avvenimenti, idee, interesse.

blare [blɛə*], *s.* squillo (di tromba).

to **blare**, *v.t.i.* suonare (tromba); squillare (di tromba); annunciare a suon di tromba, a gran voce: *to* — (*forth*) *the news*, proclamare la notizia a gran voce.

blarney ['blɑːni], *s.* (*fam.*) lusinga, adulazione, blandizie, moine.

to **blarney**, *v.t.i.* (*fam.*) lusingare, adulare, blandire, incensare; servirsi dell'adulazione.

to **blaspheme** [blæs'fiːm], *v.t.i.* bestemmiare; ingiuriare.

blasphemer [blæs'fiːmə*], *s.c.* bestemmiatore, bestemmiatrice; blasfemo, blasfema.

blasphemous ['blæsfiməs], *ag.* blasfemo; empio; profano; irriverente.

blasphemously ['blæsfiməsli], *av.* empiamente.

blasphemy ['blæsfimi], *s.* bestemmia; empietà.

blast [blɑːst], *s.* **1**. raffica, colpo di vento; bufera; getto; soffio; corrente d'aria: — *of steam*, getto di vapore; *cold* —, vento gelido || *in full* —, a tutta velocità **2**. suono di strumento a fiato; squillo **3**. esplosione, scoppio; carica di esplosivo **4**. influenza perniciosa; flagello: *a* — *on the population*, un flagello per la popolazione ☆ —*burner*, bruciatore di soffieria; —-*furnace*, (*metal.*) altoforno; —-*hole*, fornello di mina; — *inlet*, (*metal.*) entrata dell'aria; —-*pipe*, (*ferr.*) scappamento, zampillo soffiante; —-*powder*, polvere per mine || *atomic* —, esplosione atomica.

to **blast**, *v.t.* **1**. fare esplodere, far brillare, far saltare (con esplosivi) **2**. rovinare, distruggere; disseccare; far inaridire, far appassire **3**. (*sl.*) maledire, bestemmiare: — *that fellow!*, al diavolo quel tale!.

blasted ['blɑːstid], *ag.* **1**. disseccato **2**. (*sl.*) maledetto.

blat [blæt], *s.* (*amer.*) belato.

to **blat**, *pass.p.p.* **blatted** ['blætid], *v.t.i.* (*amer.*) **1**. belare **2**. chiacchierare; rivelare.

blatancy ['bleitənsi], *s.* **1**. schiamazzo, strepito, clamore **2**. appariscenza; sfoggio, ostentazione.

blatant ['bleitənt], *ag.* **1**. assordante, fragoroso, chiassoso **2**. appariscente, vistoso.

blather ['blæðə*], *s.* chiacchiere sciocche.

to **blather**, *V.* to **blether**.

blatherskite ['blæðəskait], *s.* (*fam.*) ciarlone.

blatter ['blætə*], *s.* **1**. chiacchiere; fiume di parole **2**. crepitio (di grandine, ecc.).

to **blatter**, *v.i.* **1**. cianciare, ciarlare **2**. crepitare (di grandine, ecc.).

blaze¹ [bleiz], *s.* **1**. fiamma, vampa, fiammata: *all Europe was in a* —, tutta Europa era in fiamme || *go to blazes!*, (*sl.*) va' all'inferno! **2**. scoppio violento (di passione, collera) || *like blazes*, come una furia **3**. splendore (di colore, bellezza).

to **blaze**¹, *v.i.* ardere, avvampare, divampare; fiammeggiare; sfavillare, risplendere (anche *fig.*).

blaze², *s.* **1**. macchia bianca sulla fronte d'un cavallo, d'un bue **2**. segnavia (inciso su un albero).

to **blaze**², *v.t.* indicare (un sentiero) con incisioni su alberi || *to* — *a trail*, tracciare una via (anche *fig.*).

to **blaze**³, *v.t.* divulgare, diffondere: *to* — *the news abroad*, diffondere notizie.

blazer ['bleizə*], *s.c.* chi diffonde notizie || *s.* giacca sportiva.

blazon ['bleizn], *s.* **1**. (*arald.*) blasone, stemma **2**. proclamazione, divulgazione **3**. relazione, descrizione (specialmente di virtù).

to **blazon**, *v.t.* **1**. proclamare, divulgare: *to* — *forth*, divulgare **2**. esaltare, celebrare; dar lustro a: *to* — *his own worthless name*, per dar lustro al suo nome insignificante.

blazoner ['bleiz‌nə*], *s.* blasonista.

blazonry ['bleiznri], *s.* araldica.

bleach [bliːtʃ], *s.* **1**. imbianchimento, candeggio; scolorimento **2**. (*chim.*) decolorante.

to **bleach**, *v.t.i.* imbiancare, imbiancarsi; candeggiare; scolorire, scolorirsi.

bleacher ['bliːtʃə*], *s.c.* chi imbianca || *s.* **1**. recipiente per candeggio **2**. *gener. pl.* (*amer.*) posto allo scoperto (di stadio).

bleaching ['bliːtʃiŋ], *s.* (*chim.*) imbianchimento, candeggio ☆ —-*powder*, cloruro di calcio.

bleak¹ [bliːk], *ag.* **1**. esposto al vento, al freddo **2**. squallido, deserto, brullo, nudo: *a* — *moor*, una squallida landa **3**. pallido, incolore: *a* — *smile*, un pallido sorriso **4**. desolato, triste, deprimente, lugubre.

bleak², *s.* (*ittiol.*) leucisco.

bleakly ['bliːkli], *av.* **1**. freddamente **2**. squallidamente **3**. pallidamente **4**. tristemente.

bleakness ['bliːknis], *s.* **1**. freddezza **2**. squallore **3**. pallore **4**. desolazione.

blear [bliə*], *ag.* cisposo, velato (di occhi); ottuso (di mente); oscuro, indistinto, confuso ☆ —-*eyed*, dagli occhi cisposi; dalla mente ottusa; —-*witted*, dalla mente ottusa.

to **blear**, *v.t.* rendere (gli occhi) cisposi; offuscare, annebbiare, velare (la vista); ottenebrare (la mente); rendere indistinto (contorni, ecc.).

bleat [bliːt], *s.* belato; *fig.* piagnucolio.

to **bleat**, *v.t.i.* belare; *fig.* piagnucolare; dire con voce piagnucolosa.

bleating ['bliːtiŋ], *ag.* belante; *fig.* piagnucoloso || *s.* belio, belato continuo; *fig.* piagnucolio.

bleb [bleb], *s.* vescichetta, bolla; bolla d'aria.

to **bleed** [bliːd], *pass.p.p.* **bled** [bled], *v.t.i.* **1**. sanguinare (anche *fig.*); morire di ferite: *his heart bled*, gli sanguinava il cuore; *his nose is bleeding* (o *he is bleeding at the nose*), perde sangue dal naso; *to* — *to death*, morire dissanguato **2**. (*bot.*) emettere linfa **3**. (*med.*) salassare **4**. estorcere denaro a; subire una estorsione; perdere denaro: *he was bled by a foreigner*, gli fu estorto del denaro da uno straniero.

bleeder ['bliːdə*], *s.* **1**. chi sanguina facilmente **2**. (*med.*) salassatore.

bleeding ['bliːdiŋ], *s.* **1**. (*med.*) salasso; emorragia **2**. fuga (d'acqua, di gas) **3**. (*foto.*) frangia.

blemish ['blemiʃ], *s.* difetto (fisico, morale); imperfezione, macchia.

to **blemish**, *v.t.* sfigurare, deformare; offuscare, macchiare (reputazione).

to **blench** [blentʃ], *v.t.i.* **1**. ritrarsi, indietreggiare; evitare **2**. *fig.* chiudere gli occhi su.

blend [blend], *s.* miscela, mistura (di tè, tabacchi, liquori, ecc.).

to **blend**, *pass.p.p.* **blended** ['blendid], (*letter.*) **blent** [blent], *v.t.i.* mescolare, mescolarsi; mischiare, mischiarsi (di tè, tabacchi, liquori, ecc.); fondere, fondersi (di colori, gusti, ecc.); armonizzare.

blende [blend], *s.* (*min.*) blenda.

blender ['blendə*], *s.c.* mescolatore, mescolatrice.

blent [blent], *pass.p.p.* (*letter.*) di to **blend**.

to bless [bles], *pass.p.p.* **blessed** [blest], (*poet.*) **blest** [blest], *v.t.* benedire; consacrare; beatificare; santificare; invocare il favore divino su; render felice ‖ — *me!*; — *my heart!*; — *my soul!*; *God* — *me!*, (esclamazioni di meraviglia, indignazione) Dio mio!; misericordia!; ecc.; *God* — *you!*, Dio vi benedica!.

blessed ['blesid], *ag.* benedetto; consacrato; beato; santo; felice ‖ *the* —, i Beati; *the Blessed Sacrament*, il Santissimo Sacramento; *the Blessed Virgin*, la Vergine Santissima ‖ *every* — *day*, ogni santo giorno ‖ *to be* — *with sthg.*, avere la fortuna di possedere ql.co.

blessedly ['blesidli], *av.* felicemente, fortunatamente.

blessedness ['blesidnis], *s.* beatitudine; felicità ‖ *single* —, (*iron.*) celibato.

blessing ['blesiŋ], *s.* **1.** benedizione; fortuna; felicità: *he gave us his* —, ci diede la sua benedizione **2.** (*eccl.*) benedicite: *to ask* (o *to say*) *a* —, dire il benedicite ‖ *a* — *in disguise*, un beneficio inaspettato.

blest [blest], *pass.p.p.* (*poet.*) di to **bless** ‖ *ag.* (*poet.*) per **blessed**.

blether ['bleðə*], *s.* chiacchiere sciocche.

to blether, *v.i.* chiacchierare scioccamente, blaterare ‖ *blethering idiot*, (*fam.*) perfetto idiota.

bletherskate ['bleðəskeit], *s.* (*fam.*) ciarlone.

blew [blu:], *pass.* di to **blow**[1], to **blow**[2].

blight [blait], *s.* **1.** (*agr.*) golpe, carbonchio, nebbia **2.** *fig.* influenza maligna: *that accident was a* — *up on his youth*, quell'incidente gli avvelenò la giovinezza.

to blight, *v.t.* **1.** fare appassire, far sfiorire (per golpe) **2.** *fig.* rovinare.

blighter ['blaitə*], *s.* (*sl.*) buono a nulla.

Blighty ['blaiti], *s.* (*sl. mil.*) l'Inghilterra: — *wound*, ferita che assicura il ritorno in patria.

blim(e)y ['blaimi], *inter.* (*pop.*) accidenti!, al diavolo!.

blind [blaind], *ag.* cieco: *a* — *man*, un cieco; — *in one eye*, orbo, guercio ‖ *the* —, i ciechi ‖ *as* — *as a mole* (o *bat* o *beetle*), cieco come una talpa‖*to drink oneself* —, bere fino a non capire più nulla ‖ *to fly* —, (*aer.*) volare alla cieca ☆ — *-alley*, vicolo cieco (anche *fig.*); — *-coal*, antracite; — *-door*, porta murata; — *-drunk*, ubriaco fradicio; — *-flight*, (*aer.*) volo cieco; — *-shell*, obice inesploso; — *-side*, lato, punto debole, non protetto (anche *fig.*); — *-spot*, zona senza echi (*rad.*) zona di silenzio; — *-track*, binario morto ‖ *stone-* —, completamente cieco.

blind, *s.* **1.** tendina, cortina **2.** paraocchi **3.** *fig.* pretesto, finzione: *her piety is only a* —, la sua pietà è solo una finzione ☆ *shutter-* —, persiana; *Venetian* —, persiana alla veneziana.

to blind, *v.t.i.* **1.** accecare; abbagliare **2.** ingannare **3.** (*mil.*) blindare, corazzare **4.** (*rad.*) schermare **5.** (*sl.*) procedere alla cieca (di automobilisti incoscienti).

blindage ['blaindidʒ], *s.* **1.** (*mil.*) blindaggio **2.** (*rad.*) schermaggio.

blinder ['blaində*], *s.c.* accecatore, accecatrice ‖ **blinders**, *s.pl.* (*amer.*) paraocchi.

blindfold ['blaindfould], *ag.* con gli occhi bendati; con gli occhi chiusi; *fig.* irriflessivo ‖ *av.* ad occhi bendati; ad occhi chiusi; *fig.* senza riflettere.

to blindfold, *v.t.* bendare gli occhi a (anche *fig.*).

blindless ['blaindlis], *ag.* senza persiana.

blindly ['blaindli], *av.* ciecamente.

blindness ['blaindnis], *s.* **1.** cecità: *struck with* —, colpito da cecità **2.** *fig.* ignoranza.

blindworm ['blaindwə:m], *s.* (*zool.*) cecilia.

blink [bliŋk], *s.* **1.** rapido sguardo, occhiata **2.** guizzo, lampo (di luce) ☆ *ice-* —, riverbero (di ghiaccio).

to blink, *v.t.i.* **1.** batter le palpebre, ammiccare; *fig.* eludere, schivare, evitare: *to* — *the facts*, chiudere gli occhi ai fatti, alla verità **2.** vacillare, lampeggiare (di luce) **3.** inacidire (di latte, birra).

blinker ['bliŋkə*], *s.* **1.** (*aut.*) lampeggiatore **2.** *pl.* occhiali ortottici **3.** *pl.* paraocchi **4.** *pl.* (*sl.*) occhi.

blinking ['bliŋkiŋ], *ag.* **1.** ammiccante **2.** scintillante, luccicante **3.** (*sl.*) maledetto, dannato: *you* — *fellow*, tu, maledetto individuo ‖ *s.* **1.** ammicco **2.** inacidimento (di birra, latte).

bliss [blis], *s.* beatitudine; felicità.

blissful ['blisful], *ag.* **1.** beato; felice **2.** delizioso: *it was a* — *day*, fu una giornata deliziosa; *what a* — *dress!*, (*fam.*) che abito delizioso!.

blissfully ['blisfuli], *av.* **1.** beatamente; felicemente **2.** deliziosamente.

blissfulness ['blisfulnis] *s.* beatitudine; felicità.

blister ['blistə*], *s.* **1.** pustola, gonfiore, vescichetta, bolla **2.** bolla (su superficie di metallo, legno, ecc.) **3.** (*farm.*) vescicante.

to blister, *v.t.i.* **1.** produrre vesciche, coprirsi di vesciche: *it was blistered*, era coperto di vesciche **2.** (*med.*) applicare un vescicante a **3.** (*sl.*) annoiare ☆ — *-beetle* (o — *-fly*), (*entom.*) cantaride.

blithe [blaið], *ag.* gaio, gioioso, allegro.

blithely ['blaiðli], *av.* gaiamente, allegramente.

blitheness ['blaiðnis], *s.* allegria.

blithesome ['blaiðsəm], *ag.* gaio, gioioso, allegro.

to blither ['bliðə*], *V.* to **blether**.

blithesomeness ['blaiðsəmnis], *s.* allegria.

blitz [blits], *s.* (*mil.*) attacco improvviso; guerra lampo ‖ *the* —, (*fam.*) gli attacchi aerei del 1940-41.

to blitz, *v.t.* distruggere (specialmente con attacco aereo).

blitzkrieg ['blitskri:g], *s.* (*mil.*) « Blitzkrieg », guerra lampo.

blizzard ['blizəd], *s.* **1.** bufera di neve, tormenta **2.** colpo violento.

to bloat[1] [blout], *v.t.* affumicare (le aringhe).

to bloat[2], *v.t.i.* gonfiare, gonfiarsi.

bloated[1] ['bloutid], *ag.* affumicato (di aringa).

bloated[2], *ag.* gonfio; tronfio; sovrabbondante: — *aristocrat*, nobiluomo tronfio; — *armaments*, armamenti eccessivi.

bloater ['bloutə*], *s.* aringa affumicata (di aringa).

blob [blob], *s.* **1.** bolla d'aria; gonfiore **2.** goccia **3.** macchia, chiazza.

blobber ['blobə*], *ag.* tumido.

bloc [blok], *s.* (*pol.*) blocco (di partiti, nazioni).

block [blok], *s.* **1.** ceppo; forma di legno (per calzature, cappelli, ecc.) ‖ *a chip of the old* —, un figlio che somiglia al padre **2.** (*mec.*) carrucola; (*mar.*) bozzello **3.** (*tip.*) zincotipia montata su legno, « cliché » **4.** masso; cubo (giocattolo); blocco (per edilizia) **5.** isolato (di case) **6.** ostacolo, ingombro; nota (per respingere un progetto di legge) **7.** *fig.* persona stupida, ottusa ☆ — *letters*, (*tip.*) stampatello; — *post*, (*ferr.*) posto di blocco; — *-signal*, (*ferr.*) segnale di blocco; — *-system*, (*ferr.*) sistema di blocco; — *-tin*, (*metal.*) stagno in pani ‖ *brake-* —, (*mec. ferr.*) ceppo del freno; *breech* —, (*mec.*) otturatore (di fucile); *cylinder-* —, (*mec.*) blocco cilindrico, monoblocco; *link* — (o *sliding* —), (*mec.*) pattino; *telephone* — *-system*, (*ferr.*) blocco telefonico.

to block, *v.t.* **1.** chiudere, bloccare, ostacolare: *the policeman blocked the traffic*, il vigile arrestò il traffico; *to* — *a bill*, (*pol.*) opporsi ad un progetto di legge; *to* — *s.o.'s way*, ostruire il passaggio a qlcu. ‖ *road blocked*, strada sbarrata **2.** *to* — *in*, schizzare; progettare **3.** *to* — *out*, schizzare; sbozzare (statua); progettare **4.** *to* — *up*, ostruire (strada, ecc.); murare (porta).

blockade [blo'keid], *s.* (*mil.*) blocco, assedio: *to raise the* —, togliere il blocco; *to run the* —, forzare il blocco ☆ — *-runner*, persona, nave che forza il blocco.

to blockade, *v.t.* bloccare, assediare; ostruire.

blockader [blo'keidə*], *s.* **1.** chi assedia o blocca **2.** (*pol.*) chi si oppone ad un progetto di legge.

blockhead ['blokhed], *s.c.* stupido, stupida; sciocco, sciocca.

blockhouse ['blɔkhaus], s. (mil.) fortino, casamatta.

blockish ['blɔkiʃ], ag. stupido, ottuso, tardo.

bloke [blouk], s. (sl.) 1. tipo; individuo 2. stupido; zoticone.

blond [blɔnd], ag. biondo ‖ s. biondo; (fam.) biondino.

blonde [blɔnd], ag. biondo (di donna) ‖ s. 1. bionda; (fam.) biondina 2. blonda (pizzo di seta).

blood [blʌd], s. 1. sangue: to draw —, far sanguinare; to shed (o to spill) —, versare sangue ‖ in cold —, a sangue freddo ‖ he is out for —, è trasportato dall'ira; his — is up, è in collera; it makes my — boil, mi fa ribollire il sangue ‖ there is bad — between them, c'è cattivo sangue tra di loro ‖ — is thicker than water, il sangue non è acqua 2. stirpe; prole, discendenza; parentela ‖ blue —, sangue blu; a Prince of the —, un principe del sangue (o reale) ‖ one's flesh and —, i propri figli 3. zerbinotto, elegantone: the bloods, i giovani eleganti ☆ — -and-thunder, violento, drammatico; — -brother, fratello carnale; — -curdling, raccapricciante, a forti tinte; — -feud, faida; — -giver, donatore di sangue; — -group, gruppo sanguigno; — -heat, temperatura normale del sangue; — -horse, purosangue; — -money, prezzo del sangue; — -orange, arancia sanguigna; — -poisoning, (patol.) setticemia; — -red, rosso sangue; — -relation, consanguineo; — -royal, stirpe regale; — -vessel, vaso sanguigno.

to **blood**, v.t. 1. (med.) salassare 2. (caccia) far vedere, odorare il sangue a (un cane); fig. incitare, esasperare.

bloodhound ['blʌdhaund], s. segugio; fig. poliziotto, « detective ».

bloodily ['blʌdili], av. sanguinosamente.

bloodiness ['blʌdinis], s. istinto sanguinario.

bloodless ['blʌdlis], ag. 1. esangue, pallido, anemico; fig. insensibile, freddo 2. incruento.

bloodlessly ['blʌdlisli], av. in modo incruento.

bloodletting ['blʌd,letiŋ], s. (med.) salasso.

bloodshed ['blʌdʃed], s. spargimento di sangue; ecatombe.

bloodshedder ['blʌd,ʃedə*], s.c. assassino, assassina.

bloodshedding ['blʌd,ʃediŋ], V. bloodshed.

bloodshot ['blʌdʃɔt], ag. iniettato di sangue: — eyed, occhi arrossati, infiammati.

bloodstain ['blʌdstein], s. macchia di sangue.

bloodstained ['blʌdsteind], ag. 1. macchiato di sangue 2. colpevole di omicidio.

bloodstone ['blʌdstoun], s. (min. bot.) eliotropia.

bloodsucker ['blʌd,sʌkə*], s. sanguisuga, mignatta; fig. usuraio; vampiro.

bloodthirsty ['blʌd,θə:sti], ag. assetato di sangue.

bloody ['blʌdi], ag. 1. sanguinante 2. cruento, sanguinoso: — fight, conflitto sanguinoso 3. sanguinario ‖ Bloody Mary, Maria la Sanguinaria (Maria Tudor) 4. (volg.) maledetto: — fool, maledetto idiota ☆ — -minded, (volg.) sanguinario, crudele.

bloody, av. (volg.) molto: — fine, maledettamente bello, bellissimo.

to **bloody**, v.t. macchiare di sangue, insanguinare.

bloom[1] [blu:m], s. 1. fiore; fioritura; fig. freschezza: in the — of youth, nel fiore della giovinezza; in full —, in piena fioritura 2. lanugine (di frutta, gemme); pruina 3. rossore (delle gote) 4. efflorescenza (su muro, di vino, ecc.) 5. (tv.) bagliore, sopraluminosità.

to **bloom**[1], v.i. 1. (far) fiorire, essere in fiore; sbocciare (di bellezza) 2. arrossire, risplendere 3. to — into (sthg.), fig. diventare.

bloom[2], s. 1. sbarra, lingotto di ferro 2. massa di vetro fuso.

to **bloom**[2], v.t. massellare (massa di ferro greggio).

bloomer[1] ['blu:mə*], s. 1. (tip.) lettera ornata 2. (sl.) sbaglio, errore.

bloomer[2], s. 1. gener. pl. (st.) « bloomer » (costume femminile consistente in pantaloni stretti alle caviglie e gonnellino) 2. pl. calzoni (femminili) da sport.

bloomery ['blu:məri], s. ferriera.

blooming ['blu:miŋ], ag. florente, in fiore ‖ you're a — fool, (sl.) sei un perfetto imbecille.

bloomy ['blu:mi], ag. 1. fiorito 2. lucente 3. vellutato.

blossom ['blɔsəm], s. fiore d'albero (fruttifero): in full —, in piena fioritura.

to **blossom**, v.i. 1. fiorire; sbocciare 2. to — into (sthg.), fig. svilupparsi, diventare.

blossomless ['blɔsəmlis], ag. senza fiori.

blot[1] [blɔt], s. 1. macchia (di inchiostro, ecc.); cancellatura; sgorbio 2. fig. difetto (morale); colpa.

to **blot**[1], pass.p.p. **blotted** ['blɔtid], v.t.i. 1. macchiare, macchiarsi; sgorbiare; fig. infamare: he has blotted his copy-book, (fam. fig.) si è rovinato la reputazione 2. asciugare (con carta assorbente) 3. to — out, cancellare.

blot[2], s. 1. pedina scoperta (al trictrac) 2. (mil.) punto debole in strategia.

blotch [blɔtʃ], s. 1. macchia, chiazza; sgorbio 2. pustola, enfiatura.

to **blotch**, v.t.i. 1. coprire di macchie 2. coprirsi di pustole.

blotched [blɔtʃt], **blotchy** ['blɔtʃi], ag. 1. macchiato 2. bitorzoluto.

blotter ['blɔtə*], s. 1. tampone di carta assorbente 2. (comm.) brogliaccio.

blotting ['blɔtiŋ], s. 1. il macchiare, lo sporcare 2. l'asciugare ☆ — -pad, blocco di carta assorbente; sottomano; — -paper, carta assorbente.

blotto ['blɔtou], ag. (sl.) ubriaco fradicio.

blouse [blauz], s. blusa, camicetta; camiciotto.

blow[1] [blou], s. soffio; raffica, colpo di vento; soffiata (di naso); soffiata (in strumento a fiato) ☆ — -hole, sfiatatoio; — -out, scoppio di pneumatico; (elett.) fusione; (sl.) pasto abbondante.

to **blow**[1], pass. **blew** [blu:], p.p. **blown** [bloun], v.t.i. 1. soffiare (di vento, aria): a gale was blowing, soffiava vento di tempesta; my cap was blown off by the wind, il berretto mi fu portato via dal vento; the wind blew the door open, una ventata spalancò la porta; the wind was blowing the snow against our faces, il vento ci sbatteva la neve in faccia ‖ what good wind blows you here?, (fam.) qual buon vento ti mena? ‖ 'tis an ill wind that blows nobody any good, prov. non tutto il male viene per nuocere 2. soffiare (con la bocca, con mantici, ecc.); gettar fuori acqua dallo sfiatatoio (di cetaceo): she blew him a kiss, gli lanciò un bacio; to — glass, soffiare il vetro; to — one's fingers, soffiarsi sulle dita; to — one's nose, soffiarsi il naso ‖ to — upon s.o.'s reputation, screditare qlcu. 3. ansare, ansimare 4. suonare (strumenti a fiato): to — a trumpet, suonare la tromba ‖ to — one's own trumpet, fig. cantare le proprie lodi 5. (elett.) saltare (di valvola), far saltare (valvola) 6. to — about, (far) volare di qua e di là 7. to — in, (fam.) entrare come un ciclone 8. to — off, diminuire la pressione (di vapore, ecc.): to — off steam, liberare vapore, (fig. fam.) sfogarsi 9. to — out, spegnere: he blew out the candle, spense la candela ‖ to — out one's brains, farsi saltare le cervella 10. to — over, ridursi a nulla, svanire 11. to — up, (far) saltare per aria.

blow[2], s. fioritura.

to **blow**[2], pass. **blew**, p.p. **blown**, v.i. aprirsi, sbocciare, fiorire, germogliare.

blow[3], s. colpo; fig. disgrazia: his death was a — for all of us, la sua morte fu un colpo per noi tutti; they came to blows, vennero alle mani ‖ at a —, in un colpo solo ‖ without striking a —, senza colpo ferire ‖ to strike a — for, against s.o., intervenire a favore di, contro qlcu.

blower ['blouə*], s.c. soffiatore, soffiatrice ‖ s. (mec.) sfiatatoio.

blowfly ['blou-flai], s. (entom.) tafano.

blown [bloun], p.p. di to blow[1], to blow[2].

blowpipe ['blou-paip], s. 1. (strum. artig.) cannello per soffiare; ferruminatore 2. cerbottana.

blowy ['bloui], ag. ventoso.

blowzy ['blauzi], *ag.* **1.** rosso in viso **2.** trasandato.

to **blub** [blʌb], *pass.p.p.* **blubbed** [blʌbd], *V.* to **blubber**[1].

blubber[1] ['blʌbə*], *ag.* tumido, gonfio (di labbra) || *s.c.* chi piange a dirotto.

to **blubber**[1], *v.t.i.* **1.** singhiozzare, piangere a dirotto **2.** gonfiare (il viso) piangendo.

blubber[2], *s.* **1.** grasso di balena **2.** (*zool. pop.*) medusa.

bluchers ['bluːtʃəz], *s.pl.* (*fam.*) stivaletti.

bludgeon ['blʌdʒən], *s.* randello.

to **bludgeon**, *v.t.* colpire con un randello.

blue [bluː], *ag.* **1.** azzurro, celeste, blu: *her new dress is* —, il suo nuovo abito è azzurro || — *blood*, sangue blu || — *funk*, (*sl.*) paura tremenda || — *John*, (*min.*) fluorite || *Blue Peter*, (*mar.*) segnale di partenza || — *ribbon*, nastro dell'ordine della Giarrettiera || *the* — *ribbon* (*of the Atlantic*), nastro azzurro (ottenuto dalle navi che attraversano l'Atlantico nel minor tempo) || *once in a* — *moon*, molto raramente || *to burn* —, bruciare con fiamma azzurra **2.** livido **3.** triste, nervoso, depresso: *to feel* (o *to look*) —, sentirsi depresso, aver l'aria stanca e depressa || — *devils*, apparizioni durante il delirio, depressione di spirito **4.** funesto, calamitoso || *things look* —, la situazione sembra disperata **5.** puritano, rigoroso: — *laws*, (*amer.*) leggi ispirate al puritanesimo **6.** (*fam.*) indecente, osceno.

blue, *s.* **1.** azzurro, celeste, blu: *dark, light* —, azzurro scuro, chiaro (colori di Oxford e Cambridge) **2.** mare; cielo || *bolt from the* —, fulmine a ciel sereno **3.** *pl.* (*amer.*) tristezza, depressione: *to have the blues*, essere depresso **4.** « blues » (canzoni negroamericane di tono melanconico).

to **blue**, *v.t.* **1.** tingere in blu **2.** (*sl.*) spendere pazzamente, scialacquare.

blue (*nei composti*): — *-black*, blu nero; — *-bonnet*, (*bot.*) centaurea; — *-eyed*, dagli occhi azzurri; — *-gum*, (*bot.*) eucalyptus; — *-mould*, muffa (di formaggio, pane); — *-pills*, pillole lassative.

Bluebeard ['bluːbiəd], *no.pr.m.* Barbablù.

bluebell ['bluːbel], *s.* campanula; giacinto di bosco.

blueberry ['bluːˌberi], *s.* (*amer.*) mirtillo.

bluebird ['bluːbəːd], *s.* (*ornit.*) cutrettola.

bluebottle ['bluːˌbɔtl], *s.* **1.** (*bot.*) fiordaliso **2.** (*entom.*) tafano **3.** (*sl.*) poliziotto.

bluecoat ['bluːˌkout], *s.* soldato, marinaio, poliziotto dall'abito blu.

blueness ['bluːˌnis], *s.* **1.** azzurrità **2.** livido.

to **blue-pencil** ['bluːˈpensl], *pass.p.p.* **blue-pencilled** ['bluːˈpensld], *v.t.* correggere, fare tagli in (un testo).

blueprint ['bluːˈprint], *s.* **1.** cianografia **2.** progetto; programma.

bluestocking ['bluːˌstɔkiŋ], *s.* « bas-bleu » (donna intellettuale; donna saccente).

bluff[1] [blʌf], *ag.* **1.** ripido (di scogli, ecc.) **2.** franco, cordiale **3.** brusco, sgarbato || *s.* **1.** ampia, ripida scogliera **2.** (*mar.*) grossa prua.

bluff[2], *s.* bluff (al poker); inganno, millanteria.

to **bluff**[2], *v.t.i.* bluffare (al poker); ingannare; vantarsi; fare lo smargiasso.

bluffer ['blʌfə*], *s.c.* ingannatore, ingannatrice; millantatore, millantatrice.

bluffness ['blʌfnis], *s.* franchezza.

bluish ['bluː(ː)iʃ], *ag.* bluastro.

blunder ['blʌndə*], *s.* errore grossolano; fallo; sbaglio; equivoco: *to make a* —, prendere un granchio.

to **blunder**, *v.t.i.* **1.** muoversi goffamente; inciampare: *to* — *into sthg.*, inciampare in ql.co. **2.** commettere un errore grossolano; agire stupidamente **3.** *to* — *through* (*sthg.*), cavarsela in **4.** *to* — *upon* (*s.o., sthg.*), trovare per caso **5.** *to* — *out*, dire storditamente.

blunderbuss ['blʌndəbʌs], *s.* (*st.*) trombone (schioppo).

blunderer ['blʌndərə*], *s.c.* confusionario, confusionaria.

blunderhead ['blʌndəhed], *s.c.* stordito, stordita; sciocco, sciocca.

to **blunge** [blʌndʒ], *v.t.* mescolare con acqua (nella fabbricazione di terrecotte).

blunt [blʌnt], *ag.* **1.** smussato, spuntato; senza spigoli: — *pencil*, matita senza punta; *this knife is* —, questo coltello non taglia **2.** ottuso **3.** schietto, brusco: *a* — *answer*, una risposta schietta || *s.* **1.** ago passanastro **2.** (*sl.*) denaro spicciolo ☆ — *instrument*, corpo contundente; — *-witted*, d'intelligenza ottusa.

to **blunt**, *v.t.* smussare; attutire; ottundere.

bluntish ['blʌntiʃ], *ag.* ottuso; insensibile.

bluntly ['blʌntli], *av.* seccamente; schiettamente.

bluntness ['blʌntnis], *s.* **1.** schiettezza **2.** ottusità.

blur [bləː*], *s.* macchia (d'inchiostro, ecc.); *fig.* infamia, macchia **2.** offuscamento, apparenza confusa.

to **blur**, *pass.p.p.* **blurred** [bləːd], *v.t.* **1.** macchiare (d'inchiostro, ecc.), insudiciare **2.** rendere confuso, indistinto; oscurare.

blurb [bləːb], *s.* soffietto editoriale.

to **blurt** [bləːt], *v.t.* dire inconsideratamente: *to* — (*out*) *a secret*, svelare un segreto improvvisamente.

blush [blʌʃ], *s.* **1.** rossore: *to put to the* —, far arrossire **2.** color roseo **3.** occhiata: *at the first* —, a prima vista.

to **blush**, *v.i.* arrossire: *to* — *for shame*, vergognarsi.

blushingly ['blʌʃiŋli], *av.* con rossore.

bluster ['blʌstə*], *s.* **1.** temporale; raffica **2.** baccano, turbolenza; scoppio d'ira.

to **bluster**, *v.t.i.* **1.** infuriare, rumoreggiare (di acque, vento); parlare violentemente: *to* — *at a person*, gridare contro qlcu. **2.** *to* — *out*, urlare, dire in modo violento.

blusterer ['blʌstərə*], *s.c.* chiassone, chiassona; fanfarone, fanfarona.

blustering ['blʌstəriŋ], *ag.* chiassoso, spaccone.

blusterous ['blʌstərəs], **blustery** ['blʌstəri], *ag.* rumoroso; borioso; tempestoso.

bo[1] [bou], *inter.* bù (per spaventare, usata specialmente coi bambini) || *he can't say* — *to a goose*, ha paura anche di una mosca.

bo[2], *s.* (*sl. amer.*) tizio, individuo: *say,* —, *can you come with me?*, ehi, tu, puoi venire con me?.

boa ['bouə], *s.* boa (serpente e stola di pelliccia) ☆ — *constrictor*, (*zool.*) pitone, boa.

boar [bɔː*], *s.* (*zool.*) verro ☆ *wild* —, cinghiale.

board [bɔːd], *s.* **1.** asse; assito; pancone; tavola || *above* —, con le carte in tavola, sinceramente **2.** *pl.* (*teat.*) palcoscenico: *to tread the boards*, calcare le scene **3.** desco, mensa; vitto; pensione: — *and lodging*, vitto e alloggio; *full* —, pensione completa; *to put s.o. to* —, mettere qlcu. a pensione || *bed and* —, pensione completa, vitto e alloggio; rapporti coniugali **4.** tavolo di consiglio; ministero: — *of directors*, consiglio d'amministrazione; — *of examiners*, commissione d'esami; *Board of Trade*, Ministero del Commercio || *to serve on the* —, far parte del consiglio **5.** (*mar.*) bordo, ponte: *on* —, a bordo: *to go on* —, imbarcarsi, andare a bordo || *to go by the* —, andare perduto (albero, vela, ecc.) ☆ — *-room*, sala del consiglio; — *wages*, lavoro compensato con cibo e alloggio || *wash-* —, asse per lavare.

to **board**, *v.t.i.* **1.** fornire di assi; intavolare **2.** essere, prendere a pensione **3.** (*mar.*) abbordare; attaccare; imbarcarsi **4.** *to* — *out*, mettere a pensione **5.** *to* — *up*, chiudere con assi.

boarder ['bɔːdə*], *s.c.* pensionante; convittore; educanda: *to take in boarders*, tenere dei pensionanti || *s.* (*mar.*) chi va all'abbordaggio ☆ *day-* —, esterno (di collegio, di convitto).

boarding ['bɔːdiŋ], *s.* **1.** assito, tavolato **2.** pensione **3.** (*mar.*) abbordaggio ☆ — *-house*, pensione; — *-school*, collegio, convitto.

boarhound ['bɔːhaund], *s.* cane danese (usato nella caccia al cinghiale).

boarish ['bɔːriʃ], *ag.* maialesco (anche *fig.*).

boart [bɔ:t], *s.* diamante greggio.

boast[1] [boust], *s.* vanto, vanteria.

to boast[1], *v.t.i.* esaltare; gloriarsi; vantare, vantarsi: *the school boasts a fine library*, la scuola vanta una bella biblioteca ‖ *that's nothing to — of*, non c'è niente di cui vantarsi.

to boast[2], *v.t.* (*scult.*) sbozzare.

boaster[1] ['boustə*], *s.c.* spaccone, spaccona; fanfarone, fanfarona.

boaster[2], *s.* (*scult.*) scalpello da sbozzo.

boastful ['boustful], *ag.* vanaglorioso.

boastfully ['boustfuli], *av.* vanagloriosamente.

boastfulness ['boustfulnis], *s.* millanteria; vanagloria, iattanza.

boasting ['boustiŋ], *ag.* vanaglorioso.

boastingly ['boustiŋli], *V.* **boastfully**.

boat [bout], *s.* barca; battello; scafo; piccola nave; lancia; imbarcazione ‖ *to be in the same —*, (*fam.*) trovarsi nelle medesime condizioni ‖ *to burn one's boats*, (*fam.*) tagliarsi i ponti alle spalle ☆ *— -hook*, (*mar.*) gaffa; *— -train*, treno in coincidenza con navi in partenza o arrivo ‖ *ferry- —*, traghetto; *fishing- —*, peschereccio; *flying- —*, idrovolante; *sauce- —*, salsiera.

to boat, *v.t.i.* andare in barca; trasportare in barca.

boater ['boutə*], *s.* canottiera, paglietta.

boatful ['boutful], *s.* il contenuto di una barca.

boathouse ['bouthaus], *s.* riparo coperto per barche.

boating ['boutiŋ], *s.* canottaggio: *to go —*, andare in barca, fare del canottaggio.

boatload ['boutloud], *s.* il contenuto di una barca.

boatman, *pl.* **boatmen** ['boutmən], *s.* barcaiolo.

boatrace ['bout-reis], *s.* gara di canottaggio.

boatswain ['bousn], *s.* (*mar.*) nostromo.

Bob, *no.pr.m.dim.* di **Robert** ‖ *—'s your uncle!*, (*sl.*) tutto va bene! ☆ *dry-bob*, giocatore di cricket (a Eton); *light-bob*, (*mil.*) soldato di fanteria leggera; *wet-bob*, canottiere (a Eton).

bob[1] [bɔb], *s.* **1.** pendolo; bilanciere **2.** ciondolo; orecchino **3.** ciocca, ricciolo **4.** coda di cavallo monca **5.** (*poes.*) refrain di una canzone ☆ *— -wig*, parrucca a ricciolini.

to bob[1], *pass.p.p.* **bobbed** [bɔbd], *v.t.* **1.** tagliare (capelli) a zazzera **2.** moncare (coda di cavallo) ☆ *bobbed hair*, capelli corti a zazzera.

bob[2], *s.* colpetto, piccola scossa.

to bob[2], *v.t.* **1.** colpire con uno strumento nodoso **2.** dare un colpetto leggero a.

bob[3], *s.* **1.** movimento in avanti e indietro **2.** inchino.

to bob[3], *v.t.i.* **1.** muoversi in avanti e indietro **2.** inchinarsi, fare (un inchino) **3.** *to — for* (*sthg.*), cercare di afferrare con i denti (un frutto appeso) **4.** *to — in*, fare una capatina **5.** *to — up*, venire improvvisamente a galla (anche *fig.*).

bob[4], *s.* scampanio, variazione nello scampanio.

bob[5], *s.* (*artig.*) strumento per lucidare superfici di metallo brunito.

bob[6], *s.* (*invariato al pl.*) (*sl.*) scellino: *two —*, due scellini.

bob[7], *s.* (*spor.*) bob, guidoslitta.

bobbery ['bɔbəri], *s.* rumore; baccano; baldoria.

bobbin ['bɔbin], *s.* bobina, rocchetto; spola.

bobbinet ['bɔbinet], *s.* pizzo a macchina uso tombolo.

bobbish ['bɔbiʃ], *ag.* (*sl.*) vivace, spigliato; abile.

Bobby ['bɔbi], *no.pr.m.dim.* di **Robert** ‖ **bobby**, *s.* (*sl.*) poliziotto.

bobbysocks ['bɔbisɔks], *s.pl.* (*sl. amer.*) calzini.

bobbysoxer ['bɔbi‚sɔksə*], *s.* (*sl. amer.*) ragazzina dalle calze corte (fanatica per i divi del cinema, ecc.).

bobolink ['bɔbəliŋk], *s.* (*ornit.*) doliconice.

bobsled ['bɔbsled], **bobsleigh** ['bɔbslei], *V.* **bob**[7].

bobstay ['bɔbstei], *s.* (*mar.*) briglia di bompresso.

bobtail ['bɔbteil], **bobtailed** ['bɔbteild], *ag.s.* (cavallo, cane) con la coda mozza.

bock [bɔk], *s.* birra tedesca (forte e scura); bicchiere di birra.

to bode [boud], *v.t.i.* presagire: *to — well, ill*, essere di buono, di cattivo augurio.

bode [boud], *pass.* di **to bide**.

bodeful ['boudful], *ag.* di buono, cattivo augurio.

bodega [bou'di:gə], *s.* osteria, cantina.

bodice ['bɔdis], *s.* corsetto; busto ☆ *under- —*, copribusto.

bodied ['bɔdid], *ag.* fornito di corpo; dal corpo ☆ *thin- —*, dal corpo gracile, sottile.

bodiless ['bɔdilis], *ag.* incorporeo.

bodily ['bɔdili], *ag.* corporeo; corporale.

bodily, *av.* **1.** corporalmente; di persona **2.** in massa; tutt'insieme; interamente.

boding ['boudiŋ], *ag.* presago ‖ *s.* presagio.

bodkin ['bɔdkin], *s.* **1.** punteruolo; spillone; passanastro **2.** (*arc.*) stiletto **3.** (*tip.*) pinzette per comporre i caratteri **4.** *to sit —*, sedere stretto fra due persone.

Bodleian [bɔd'li(:)ən], *ag.* bodleiano ‖ *the —* (*Library*), la biblioteca bodleiana (a Oxford).

body ['bɔdi], *s.* **1.** corpo, struttura fisica (di uomo, di animale) **2.** tronco, torso **3.** cadavere; carogna **4.** parte essenziale (di ql.co.); (*arch.*) navata centrale; fusto di colonna; (*mar.*) scafo; (*aer.*) fusoliera; (*mec.*) gambo; (*aut.*) carrozzeria; cassone (di autocarro): *streamlined —*, carrozzeria aerodinamica **5.** gruppo di persone; sodalizio; corporazione; società: *a public —*, un ente pubblico; *the public —*, lo Stato; *they came in a —*, vennero in massa **6.** massa, quantità: *the sea is a — of water*, il mare è una massa di acqua **7.** sostanza; consistenza: *a wine of good —*, un vino generoso **8.** (*geom.*) solido **9.** (*min.*) giacimento **10.** corpetto, corsetto **11.** (*astr.*) corpo: *the heavenly bodies*, i corpi celesti **12.** persona: *a decent —*, una persona per bene ☆ *—belt*, panciera; *— -linen*, biancheria intima; *— -servant*, valletto; *— -snatcher*, (*arc.*) chi disseppelliva cadaveri per venderli ai laboratori.

to body, *v.t.* dar corpo a, dar forma a, plasmare.

bodyguard ['bɔdiga:d], *s.* guardia del corpo.

Boeotia [bi'ouʃə], *no. pr.* (*geog. st.*) Beozia.

Boeotian [bi'ouʃən], *ag.s.c.* beota (anche *fig.*).

Boer ['bouə*], *ag.* boero ‖ *s.c.* boero, boera.

Boethius [bou'i:θjəs], *no.pr.m.* (*st. fil.*) Boezio.

boffin ['bɔfin], *s.* (*sl.*) ricercatore; scienziato.

bog[1] [bɔg], *s.* **1.** palude; pantano; acquitrino ☆ *— -oak*, legno di quercia conservato in terreno paludoso.

to bog[1], *pass.p.p.* **bogged** [bɔgd], *v.t.i.* affondare in un pantano; impantanare, impantanarsi.

bog[2], *s.* (*volg.*) cesso, latrina.

bogey[1] ['bougi], *s.* (*golf*) norma.

bogey[2], *V.* **bogy**.

bogginess ['bɔginis], *s.* l'essere paludoso.

to boggle ['bɔgl], *v.i.* **1.** trasalire **2.** esitare: *to — at* (o *about*) *doing sthg.*, esitare a far ql.co. **3.** eludere la verità con parole ambigue.

boggler ['bɔglə*], *s.* individuo dubbioso.

boggy ['bɔgi], *ag.* paludoso.

bogie ['bougi], *s.* (*ferr.*) carrello.

bogle ['bougl], *s.* (*scoz.*) spirito; spaventapasseri.

bogus ['bougəs], *ag.* falso, finto; simulato: *— company*, (*comm.*) società inesistente, simulata.

bogy ['bougi], *s.* spettro; spauracchio; babau ☆ *— -man*, orco (dei bambini).

Bohemia [bou'hi:mjə], *no. pr.* (*geog.*) Boemia.

Bohemian [bou'hi:mjən], *ag.* **1.** boemo **2.** di, da zingaro **3.** «bohémien», di, da artista ‖ *s.c.* **1.** boemo, boema **2.** zingaro, zingara **3.** «bohémien», «bohémienne»; artista.

bohemianism [bou'hi:mjənizəm], *s.* «bohème», vita irregolare, da artista.

boil[1] [bɔil], *s.* punto d'ebollizione, bollitura: *the water is on the —*, l'acqua sta in ebollizione.

to boil[1], *v.t.i.* **1.** bollire, far bollire; cuocere, lessare; *fig.* ribollire: *to — with rage*, ribollire di rabbia ‖ *to keep the pot boiling*, (*fam.*) far andare avanti la baracca; guadagnarsi la vita; non interrompere l'evol-

versi, la continuità di una serie di azioni, eventi **2.** *to —
away*, consumarsi, evaporare **3.** to — **down**, condensare, condensarsi **4.** *to —* **over**, traboccare bollendo.

boil², *s.* foruncolo; vescichetta.

boiled [boild], *ag.* bollito: *a* — *egg*, un uovo alla coque; — *meat*, — *beef*, bollito, lesso; — *potatoes*, patate lesse ☆ — *shirt*, (*sl. amer.*) camicia inamidata ‖ *hard* — *egg*, uovo sodo.

boiler ['boilǝ*], *s.* caldaia; bollitore ☆ — *-suit*, tuta; — *works*, fabbrica di caldaie ‖ *gas-fired* —, caldaia a gas; *oil-fired* —, caldaia a nafta; *steam-* —, caldaia a vapore.

boiling ['boiliŋ], *ag.* bollente ‖ *s.* ebollizione; bollitura ☆ — *off*, cottura; — *plate*, fornello elettrico a piastra radiante; — *-point*, (*fis.*) punto di ebollizione; — *ring*, fornello elettrico a resistenza scoperta.

boisterous ['boistǝrǝs], *ag.* **1.** chiassoso, rumoroso **2.** tempestoso; violento.

boisterously ['boistǝrǝsli], *av.* rumorosamente.

boisterousness ['boistǝrǝsnis], *s.* fracasso, tumulto.

boko ['boukou], *s.* (*sl.*) naso.

bold [bould], *ag.* **1.** audace, coraggioso **2.** sfacciato, sfrontato: *to be* — *with s.o.*, prendersi delle libertà con qlcu.; *to make* —, prender la libertà di **3.** vigoroso; chiaro; ben delineato: — *handwriting*, calligrafia chiara ☆ — *-face*, (*tip.*) neretto; — *-faced*, sfacciato.

boldly ['bouldli], *av.* **1.** arditamente, coraggiosamente **2.** sfacciatamente.

boldness ['bouldnis], *s.* **1.** audacia, coraggio **2.** sfacciataggine, impudenza.

bole¹ [boul], *s.* tronco d'albero.

bole², *s.* (*min.*) bolo ☆ — *armeniac*, bolo armeno.

bole³, *s.* nicchia quadrata per oggetti.

bole⁴, *s.* crogiuolo.

bolero [bǝ'lɛǝrou], *nel senso* **2.** ['bolǝrou], *s.* **1.** bolero (danza) **2.** bolero (indumento per signora).

Boleyn ['bulin], *no.pr.* (*st.*) Boleyn: *Anne* —, Anna Bolena.

bolide ['bolaid], *s.* (*astr.*) bolide; meteora.

Bolivia [bǝ'liviǝ], *no.pr.* (*geog.*) Bolivia.

boll¹ [boul], *s.* capsula globosa (di lino, cotone).

boll², *s.* (*st.*) «boll» (antica misura di capacità variabile per cereali).

bollard ['bolǝd], *s.* (*mar.*) bitta, palo d'ormeggio.

Bologna [bǝ'lounjǝ], *no.pr.* (*geog.*) Bologna ‖ *s.* — (*sausage*), mortadella.

bolometer [bou'lomitǝ*], *s.* (*fis.*) bolometro.

boloney [bǝ'louni], *s.* (*sl.*) frottola; sciocchezze.

bolshevik ['bolʃivik], *ag.s.* (*pol.*) bolscevico.

bolshevism ['bolʃivizǝm], *s.* (*pol.*) bolscevismo.

bolshevist ['bolʃivist], *ag.s.* (*pol.*) bolscevico.

bolshie, bolshy ['bolʃi], (*abbr. fam.*) di **bolshevik**.

bolster ['boulstǝ*], *s.* **1.** capezzale **2.** (*mec.*) cuscino, cuscinetto; supporto.

to **bolster**, *v.t.i.* **1.** sostenere (anche *fig.*): *to —* *s.o.* (*up*), sostenere qlcu. con un cuscino **2.** far la lotta con i cuscini.

bolstering ['boulstǝriŋ], *s.* sostegno, appoggio.

bolt¹ [boult], *s.* **1.** catenaccio; chiavistello; stanga; spranga **2.** bullone: *bolts and nuts*, bulloneria **3.** otturatore (di armi da fuoco) **4.** ferri (ai piedi) **5.** freccia, dardo **6.** fulmine, saetta ‖ *a* — *from the blue*, un fulmine a ciel sereno **7.** salto, balzo **8.** l'inghiottire senza masticare **9.** (*amer.*) diserzione (politica) ☆ — *-handle*, manubrio (di arma da fuoco); — *-head*, (*mec.*) testa del bullone; — *-rope*, (*mar.*) gratile, ralinga ‖ *stay-* —, (*mec.*) tirante; *stud-* —, (*mec.*) prigioniero, vite prigioniera.

to **bolt¹**, *v.t.i.* **1.** chiudere con catenaccio, sprangare **2.** imbullonare **3.** inghiottire senza masticare **4.** svignarsela, scappar via; (*amer.*) disertare (un partito) **5.** *to —* **in**, rinchiudere a catenaccio **6.** *to —* **out**, chiuder fuori (a catenaccio).

bolt¹, *av.* come una freccia ☆ — *-upright*, diritto come un fuso.

bolt², *s.* setaccio, buratto.

to **bolt²**, *v.t.* setacciare, abburattare.

bolter¹ ['boultǝ*], *s.* **1.** cavallo in fuga **2.** chi fugge; (*amer.*) chi abbandona il proprio partito.

bolter², *s.* setaccio, buratto.

bolting¹ ['boultiŋ], *s.* **1.** il chiudere a catenaccio **2.** l'azione di svignarsela.

bolting², *s.* abburattatura ☆ — *-cloth*, stamigna; — *-hutch*, frullone; — *-machine*, staccio a macchina.

bolus ['boulǝs], *s.* (*farm.*) pillola.

bomb [bom], *s.* bomba ☆ — *-bay*, (*aer.*) vano bombe; — *-calorimeter*, calorimetro con bomba calorimetrica; — *-carrier*, aeroplano da bombardamento; — *-sight*, (*aer.*) dispositivo di puntamento; — *-thrower*, lanciabombe; addetto al lanciabombe ‖ *armour-piercing* —, bomba perforante; *atomic* — (o *atom* —), bomba atomica; *azon-* —, bomba (a direzione) radioguidata; *C-* —, bomba al cobalto; *chemical* —, bomba a gas; *H-* —, bomba all'idrogeno; *fire* —, bomba incendiaria; *smoke-* —, bomba fumogena; *submarine* —, bomba sottomarina.

to **bomb**, *v.t.* **1.** bombardare (dall'aria) **2.** *to —* **out**, costringere ad abbandonare luogo, casa, ecc. con bombardamento aereo **3.** *to —* **up**, (*aer.*) fare il carico di bombe.

bombard ['bomba:d], *s.* **1.** bombarda **2.** (*mus.*) fagotto.

to **bombard** [bom'ba:d], *v.t.* bombardare (anche *fis.*).

bombardier [,bombǝ'diǝ*], *s.* bombardiere.

bombardment [bom'ba:dmǝnt], *s.* bombardamento.

bombardon [bom'ba:dn], *s.* (*mus.*) bombardone.

bombasine ['bombǝsi:n], *s.* tessuto di seta, cotone misto a lana (molto usato per abiti da lutto).

bombast ['bombæst], *s.* magniloquenza; ampollosità; enfasi.

bombastic [bom'bæstik], *s.* ampolloso; enfatico.

bombed-out ['bomd'aut], *ag.* sinistrato.

bomber ['bomǝ*], *s.* (*artigl. aer.*) bombardiere ‖ *dive* - —, bombardiere in picchiata ☆ *heavy, light* —, aeroplano da bombardamento pesante, leggero.

bombing ['bomiŋ], *s.* bombardamento ☆ — *aviation*, aviazione da bombardamento; — *plane*, aeroplano da bombardamento ‖ *dive* —, bombardamento in picchiata.

bombproof ['bom-pru:f], *ag.* a prova di bomba.

bombshell ['bom-ʃel], *s.* **1.** obice; granata **2.** notizia, evento sconvolgente, sorprendente.

bona fide ['bounǝ'faidi], *ag.* sincero, genuino ‖ *av.* in buona fede; sinceramente.

bonanza [bou'nænzǝ], *s.* **1.** (*geol. miner.*) filone d'oro, d'argento **2.** *fig.* fonte di prosperità, ricchezza.

bon-bon ['bonbon], *s.* chicca, zuccherino.

bond¹ [bond], *ag.* (*arc.*) schiavo.

bond², *s.* **1.** vincolo, legame (anche *fig.*): *the* — *of wedlock*, il legame matrimoniale **2.** *pl.* prigionia: *to be in bonds*, essere in prigionia: *to break one's bonds asunder*, spezzare le catene **3.** legaccio di giunco per fascine **4.** patto, impegno: *to enter into a* —, impegnarsi **5.** (*Borsa*) obbligazione, polizza, buono; titolo: — *to bearer*, obbligazione al portatore **6.** (*comm.*) «bond», (condizione delle merci in processo di acquisto): *goods in* —, merci in attesa di sdoganamento **7.** cauzione **8.** (*chim.*) legame **9.** (*elett.*) collegamento **10.** (*ind.*) sostanza agglutinante, cemento **11.** (*edil.*) apparecchio ☆ — *-creditor*, creditore garantito da cauzione; — *energy*, (*fis. chim.*) energia di legame; — *-holder*, portatore di obbligazioni; — *strength*, (*fis.*) coesione ‖ *arbitration* —, patto arbitrale; *income* —, obbligazione semplice, non garantita; *mortgage* —, obbligazione ipotecaria; *state* —, titolo di stato; *treasury* —, buono del tesoro; *warehouse* —, buono di carico (di magazzino).

to **bond²**, *v.t.* **1.** (*comm.*) mettere in deposito doganale in punto franco **2.** mettere insieme, allineare (mattoni, pietre); costruire (un muro).

bond³, *s.* lega, confederazione (detto della Confederazione Sud-Africana).

bondage ['bondidʒ], *s.* schiavitù; servitù.

bonded ['bɔndid], *ag.* legato; (*comm.*) vincolato ☆ — *warehouse*, magazzino doganale, deposito franco.

bondmaid ['bɔndmeid], **bondmaiden** ['bɔnd‚meidn], *s.* (*arc.*) giovane schiava.

bondman, *pl.* **bondmen** ['bɔndmən], *V.* **bondsman.**

bondslave ['bɔndsleiv], *s.c.* schiavo, schiava.

bondsman, *pl.* **bondsmen** ['bɔndzmən], *s.* **1.** schiavo **2.** *to be* — *for s.o.*, (*comm.*) rendersi garante per qlcu.

bondswoman ['bɔndz‚wumən], *pl.* **bondswomen** ['bɔndz‚wimin], **bondwoman** ['bɔnd‚wumən], *pl.* **bondwomen** ['bɔnd‚wimin], *s.* schiava.

bone[1] [boun], *s.* **1.** osso: *skin and* —, pelle ed ossa; *to pick a* —, rosicchiare un osso ‖ — *of contention*, pomo della discordia ‖ *he is (nothing but) a bag of bones*, (non) è (che) un sacco d'ossa ‖ *he was chilled to the* —, era gelato fino alle ossa ‖ *I feel it in my bones*, *fig.* me lo sento nelle ossa, ho il presentimento ‖ *to have a* — *to pick with s.o.*, *fig.* aver motivo di litigare con qlcu. **2.** stecca di busto **3.** *pl. fig.* resti mortali **4.** *pl.* pedine, dadi (d'osso, di avorio) ‖ *to make no bones about doing sthg.*, non esitare, non farsi scrupolo di fare ql.co. ☆ — *-dust*, polvere, cenere d'ossa (per concimare); — *-dry*, secco come un chiodo; — *idle*, pigrone; — *-setter*, conciaossa ‖ *back-* —, spina dorsale; *cheek-* —, zigomo; *fish-* —, lisca di pesce.

to bone[1], *v.t.* **1.** disossare **2.** mettere le stecche a (un busto) **3.** (*sl.*) rubare.

to bone[2], *v.t.* misurare il livello di.

boned [bound], *ag.* **1.** ossuto **2.** disossato **3.** fornito di stecche ☆ *small-* —, dalle ossa piccole.

boneless ['bounlis], *ag.* senz'ossa; disossato.

boneshaker ['boun‚ʃeikə*], *s.* veicolo traballante.

bonfire ['bɔn‚faiə*], *s.* falò.

bonhom(m)ie ['bɔnɔmi:], *s.* bonomia.

Boniface ['bɔnifeis], *no.pr.m.* Bonifazio ‖ **boniface**, *s.* oste.

bon mot [‚bɔ:n'mou], *s.* spiritosaggine.

bonne [bɔ:n], *s.* domestica, cameriera; bambinaia.

bonnet ['bɔnit], *s.* **1.** berretto scozzese da uomo; cuffia da donna ‖ *to have a bee in one's* —, essere fissato **2.** *fig.* complice (in asta, giuoco) **3.** (*mar.*) vela di riserva, bonetta **4.** copertura di protezione (di macchina, motore); (*aut.*) cofano.

to bonnet, *v.t.* mettere il cappello in testa a; calcare il cappello sugli occhi di.

bonneted ['bɔnitid], *ag.* che porta il berretto.

bonnily ['bɔnili], *av.* (*scoz.*) graziosamente.

bonny ['bɔni], *ag.* (*scoz.*) grazioso; (*fam.*) paffuto.

bon ton [‚bɔ:n'tɔ:n], *s.* buone maniere, signorilità.

bonus ['bounəs], *s.* compenso, premio; indennità; gratifica; extradividendo, riparto straordinario di utili ☆ — *shares*, azioni di godimento ‖ *cost of living* —, carovita; *long service* —, premio di anzianità.

bon vivant [‚bɔ:n‚vi:'vɑ:n], *s.* gaudente.

bony ['bouni], *ag.* **1.** osseo **2.** ossuto, scarno.

bonze [bɔnz], *s.* bonzo (sacerdote buddista).

bonzer ['bɔnzə*], *ag.* (*austral.*) eccellente.

to boo [bu:], *v.t.i.* fischiare (attori, ecc.).

boo, *inter.* oibò!

boob [bu:b], *s.* (*sl. amer.*) per **booby.**

booby ['bu:bi], *s.* sciocco, stupido ☆ — *prize*, premio scherzoso dato al peggiore dei concorrenti; — *trap*, scherzo per cui ql.co. cade in testa a chi entra da una porta; (*mil.*) ordigno esplosivo dall'apparenza innocua.

boobyish ['bu:biiʃ], *ag.* goffo, sciocco.

boodle ['bu:dl], *s.* (*sl.*) **1.** quattrini **2.** (*amer.*) fondi segreti (per elezioni) **3.** «boodle» (giuoco di carte) **4.** gruppo, massa: *the whole* —, tutto quanto.

boogie, boogy ['bu:gi], *s.* (*amer.*) negro ☆ — *-woogie*, boogie woogie (danza).

boohoo [‚bu:'hu:], *s.* pianto; rumore di pianto.

to boohoo, *v.i.* (*fam.*) piangere a dirotto.

book [buk], *s.* **1.** libro: — *of reference*, libro di consultazione; *ship's books*, (*mar.*) libro di bordo ‖ *to be in s.o.'s good, bad books*, (*fam.*) essere, non essere nelle

grazie di qlcu. ‖ *to speak by the* —, parlare con cognizione di causa ‖ *to take a leaf out of s.o.'s* —, (*fam.*) imitare l'esempio di qlcu. ‖ *to talk like a* —, (*fam.*) parlare come un libro stampato **2.** (*comm.*) registro: *to keep the books of a firm*, tenere la contabilità di una ditta **3.** *Book*, Bibbia: *to swear on the Book*, giurare sulla Bibbia **4.** libretto d'opera ☆ — *-binder*, legatore di libri; — *-club*, club del libro; — *-designer*, impaginatore; — *-keeping*, contabilità, computisteria; — *-learning*, sapere libresco; — *-man*, dotto, erudito; — *-mark*, segnalibro; — *-muslin*, mussolina (usata per rilegare libri); — *-plate*, exlibris; — *-post*, tariffa postale libraria; — *-rest*, leggio; — *-seller*, libraio; — *-stand*, edicola (per la vendita di libri); leggio; — *trade*, commercio librario; — *-value*, valore d'inventario; — *-work*, (*tip.*) opera curata, di mole; studio dei testi ‖ *account* —, libro dei conti; *bank* —, libretto degli assegni; *cash* —, libro cassa; *copy* —, quaderno; copialettere; *day* —, diario; *exercise* —, quaderno dei compiti; *invoice* —, libro fatture; *letter* —, copialettere; *log* —, (*mar.*) giornale di bordo; (*aut.*) libretto di circolazione; *minute* —, libro dei verbali; registro; *note* —, taccuino; *pocket-size* —, libro tascabile; *reading* —, libro di lettura; *signals* —, codice dei segnali; *telephone* —, guida telefonica; *warehouse* —, registro di magazzino; *waste* —, brogliaccio.

to book, *v.t.* **1.** scrivere (in un libro); prendere nota di; registrare (un'ordinazione, un ospite in albergo, ecc.): *we are heavily booked*, abbiamo molti ordini da eseguire **2.** prenotare, fissare (posti a teatro, albergo, treno, ecc.): *I'm booked up for the whole day*, (*fam.*) sono impegnato per l'intera giornata **3.** prendere un biglietto (di viaggio): *we booked to Rome*, abbiamo un biglietto per Roma.

bookbinding ['buk‚baindiŋ], *s.* rilegatura di libri.

bookcase ['bukkeis], *s.* libreria, scaffale (per libri).

bookie ['buki], *s.* (*fam.*) allibratore.

booking ['bukiŋ], *s.* registrazione; iscrizione; prenotazione ☆ — *-clerk*, impiegato della biglietteria; — *-office*, biglietteria, ufficio prenotazioni.

bookish ['bukiʃ], *ag.* **1.** studioso **2.** libresco, pedante.

bookishness ['bukiʃnis], *s.* **1.** passione per i libri **2.** pedanteria.

bookkeeper ['buk‚ki:pə*], *s.* contabile.

booklet ['buklit], *s.* libretto, opuscolo.

booklouse ['buklaus], *pl.* **booklice** ['buklais], *s.* tarlo.

booklover ['buk‚lʌvə*], *s.* bibliofilo.

bookmaker ['buk‚meikə*], *s.* **1.** allibratore **2.** scrittore di poco valore.

bookmaking ['buk‚meikiŋ], *s.* **1.** professione dell'allibratore **2.** industria del libro.

bookshelf ['bukʃelf], *pl.* **bookshelves** ['bukʃelvz], *s.* scaffale (per libri).

bookshop ['bukʃɔp], *s.* libreria (negozio).

bookstall ['bukstɔ:l], *s.* edicola, chiosco; bancarella (per vendita di libri).

bookworm ['bukwə:m], *s.* **1.** (*entom.*) tignuola **2.** *fig.* topo di biblioteca.

booky ['buki], (*fam.*) per **bookish.**

boom[1] [bu:m], *s.* **1.** (*mar.*) boma; asta; palo; bastone di coltellaccio **2.** barriera galleggiante di tronchi attraverso un fiume, una baia.

to boom[1], *v.t.* **1.** *to* — *(out) the sails*, (*mar.*) mettere le vele a coltellaccio **2.** *to* — *(off) part of a river*, dividere parte di un fiume con una barriera galleggiante.

boom[2], *s.* rombo, rimbombo; tuono.

to boom[2], *v.i.* **1.** rimbombare; tuonare **2.** (*mar.*) viaggiare a vele spiegate.

boom[3], *s.* (*econ.*) aumento improvviso di attività, di sviluppo; rapido fiorire (di un'industria, di un'impresa); improvvisa popolarità (di un'invenzione, di un prodotto) raggiunta con mezzi reclamistici ☆ — *-town*, città diventata prosperosa improvvisamente.

to boom[3], *v.t.i.* **1.** (*econ.*) essere in periodo di attività, di voga, di sviluppo: *his books are booming,* i suoi libri sono in gran voga 2. (*comm.*) fare il lancio pubblicitario di.

boomer ['bu:mə*], *s.* grosso canguro maschio.

boomerang ['bu:məræŋ], *s.* **1.** boomerang **2.** (*amer. fam.*) argomento, accusa che ricade su chi l'ha lanciata.

boon [bu:n], *ag.* **1.** (*poet.*) generoso, benigno **2.** allegro: *a — companion*, compagno di bagordi ‖ *s.* **1.** richiesta, domanda (di un favore) **2.** favore; dono; grazia: *to ask a — of s.o.*, chiedere una grazia a qlcu.

boor [buə*], *s.* persona rozza, zotica, villana.

boorish ['buəriʃ], *ag.* rustico; maleducato.

boorishly ['buəriʃli], *av.* rozzamente, zoticamente.

boorishness ['buəriʃnis], *s.* rozzezza, zoticaggine.

boost [bu:st], *s.* **1.** (*sl. amer.*) lancio pubblicitario eccezionale **2.** (*elett.*) aumento della tensione; (*fis.*) spinta; pressione; (*mec.*) sovralimentazione.

to boost, *v.t.* **1.** (*sl. amer.*) lanciare (un prodotto, un'attrice, ecc.) con pubblicità eccezionale **2.** (*elett.*) elevare la tensione di; (*fis.*) spingere; (*mec.*) sovralimentare.

booster ['bu:stə*], *s.* **1.** (*sl. amer.*) chi pratica pubblicità sensazionale **2.** (*tec.*) elevatore; (*tv.*) preamplificatore.

boot[1] [bu:t], *s.* **1.** stivale, calzatura, scarpa: *to put on, to take off one's boots*, mettersi, togliersi gli stivali ‖ *the — is on the other pot*, *fig.* ora le cose sono completamente diverse, la situazione è il contrario di quello che era ‖ *you are not fit to black his boots*, *fig.* non sei degno di lustrargli le scarpe **2.** (*st.*) strumento di tortura **3.** (*aut.*) portabagagli ☆ *— -hook*, allacciascarpe; *— -jack*, cavastivali; *— -lace*, stringa; *— -last* (o *— -tree*), forma di legno per scarpe; *— -maker*, calzolaio.

to boot[1], *v.t.* **1.** calzare stivali: *to — s.o.*, mettere gli stivali a qlcu. **2.** calciare; mandare via a pedate.

boot[2], *s.* (*arc.*) bene, vantaggio: *to —*, in più, in aggiunta: *she is beautiful, and rich to —*, essa è bella e per di più ricca.

to boot[2], *v.t.imp.* (*arc.*) essere di vantaggio: *what boots it to weep?*, a che serve piangere?.

bootblack ['bu:tblæk], *s.* lustrascarpe.

bootee ['bu:ti:], *s.* stivaletto per donna; scarpetta di lana per bambini.

booted ['bu:tid], *ag.* che calza stivali.

Boötes [bou'outi:z], *no.pr.* (*astr.*) Boote.

booth [bu:ð], *s.* baracca; capanna ☆ *telephone —*, cabina telefonica.

to bootleg ['bu:tleg], *v.i.* (*amer.*) fare il contrabbando di bevande alcooliche.

bootlegger ['bu:t,legə*], *s.* (*amer.*) contrabbandiere di bevande alcooliche.

bootless ['bu:tlis], *ag.* (*poet.*) vano.

bootlessly ['bu:tlisli], *av.* (*poet.*) vanamente.

boots [bu:ts], *s.* lustrascarpe, facchino (d'albergo).

booty ['bu:ti], *s.* preda; bottino.

booze [bu:z], *s.* (*fam.*) **1.** sbornia **2.** bevanda alcoolica.

to booze, *v.i.* (*fam.*) ubriacarsi.

boozer ['bu:zə*], *s.* (*fam.*) **1.** beone **2.** taverna; bar.

boozy ['bu:zi], *ag.* (*fam.*) ubriaco.

bopeep [bou'pi:p], *s.* (*fam.*) cucù (giuoco infantile).

boracic [bə'ræsik], *ag.* (*chim.*) boracico.

boracite ['bo:rəsait], *s.* (*min.*) boracite.

borage ['bɔridʒ], *s.* (*bot.*) borraggine.

borate ['bo:reit], *s.* (*chim.*) borato.

borax ['bo:ræks], *s.* (*chim.*) borace.

border ['bo:də*], *s.* **1.** orlo; bordo; limite **2.** frontiera ‖ *the Border*, zona di confine fra Scozia e Inghilterra ☆ *— -line*, linea di demarcazione.

to border, *v.t.i.* **1.** orlare **2.** *to — up(on)* (*sthg.*), confinare con (anche *fig.*); esser situato sul confine di.

borderer ['bo:dərə*], *s.c.* abitante di confine (specialmente fra Scozia e Inghilterra).

borderland ['bo:dəlænd], *s.* terra di confine; confine.

bordure ['bo:djuə*], *s.* (*arald.*) bordura.

bore[1] [bo:*], *s.* **1.** buco, foro **2.** calibro (di arma da fuoco) **3.** scandaglio **4.** (*artig.*) trivello, foratoio ☆ *arte-*

sian —, pozzo artesiano; *heavy —*, di grosso calibro.

to bore[1], *v.t.i.* **1.** forare, bucare, perforare; trapanare: *to — through sthg.*, perforare ql.co. da lato a lato **2.** (*mec.*) fresare **3.** scandagliare, sondare **4.** spingere la testa in avanti (di cavallo).

bore[2], *s.* seccatura, noia ‖ *s.c.* seccatore, seccatrice.

to bore[2], *v.t.* annoiare, infastidire; (*fam.*) seccare: *did he — you with his words?*, ti annoiò con le sue parole?; *I was bored to death*, mi sono seccato a morte.

bore[3], *s.* cavallone; maroso.

bore[4], *pass.* di to bear[2].

boreal ['bo:riəl], *ag.* boreale.

Boreas ['bo:riæs], *no.pr.m.* **1.** (*mit.*) Borea (dio dei venti) **2.** il vento del Nord.

boredom ['bo:dəm], *s.* noia, fastidio.

borer ['bo:rə*], *s.* **1.** (*miner.*) trivella **2.** operaio scavapozzi.

boric ['bo:rik], *ag.* (*chim.*) borico.

boring[1] ['bo:riŋ], *ag.* noioso.

boring[2], *s.* (*mec.*) alesatura ☆ *— test*, sondaggio.

born [bo:n], *p.p.* di to bear[2] ‖ *ag.* nato, generato: *— of*, nato, generato da; *he is a — poet*, è un poeta nato; *a Londoner, — and bred*, un londinese nato e cresciuto; *they were — and bred conservatives*, erano conservatori già in culla ‖ *in all my — days*, da quando solo al mondo ☆ *— -blind*, nato cieco; *— fool*, (*sl.*) perfetto idiota ‖ *base-*, bastardo; *first- —*, figlio primogenito; *high- —*, di alta nascita; *London —*, nativo di Londra; *low- —*, di umili natali.

borne [bo:n], *p.p.* di to bear[2].

Borneo ['bo:niou], *no.pr.* (*geog.*) Borneo.

boron ['bo:ron], *s.* (*min.*) boro.

borough ['bʌrə], *s.* borgo; cittadina; municipio; circoscrizione elettorale, amministrativa; mandamento ‖ *rotten boroughs*, (*st. inglese*) sezioni elettorali con pochissimi votanti (abolite nel 1832).

to borrow ['borou], *v.t.* **1.** prendere a prestito; farsi prestare: *the book I borrowed last week*, il libro che mi prestarono la settimana scorsa; *they will — money from* (o *of*) *him*, si faranno prestare del denaro da lui ‖ *borrowed plumes*, *fig.* penne di pavone **2.** adottare; derivare.

borrower ['borouə*], *s.c.* chi prende a prestito.

borrowing ['borouiŋ], *s.* **1.** il prendere a prestito **2.** adozione.

bort [bo:t], *s.* diamante industriale.

boscage ['boskidʒ], *s.* (*poet.*) boschetto.

bosh[1] [boʃ], *s.* (*sl.*) chiacchiera; sciocchezza; follia.

to bosh[1], *v.t.i.* **1.** (*sl. scolastico*) canzonare, punzecchiare **2.** chiacchierare, dire sciocchezze.

bosh[1], *inter.* (*sl.*) sciocchezze!, stupidaggini!.

bosh[2], *s.* (*metal.*) sacca (parte inferiore dell'altoforno).

bosk [bosk], **boskage** ['boskidʒ], *s.* boschetto.

boskage ['boskidʒ], *s.* (*poet.*) boschetto.

bosker ['boskə*], *ag.* (*sl. austral.*) eccellente.

bosket ['boskit], *s.* boschetto.

bosky ['boski], *ag.* **1.** boscoso **2.** (*sl.*) ubriaco.

bo's'n, bos'n ['bousn], *contr.* di **boatswain**.

bosom ['buzəm], *s.* **1.** petto, seno (anche *fig.*): *in the — of one's family*, in seno alla famiglia; *to keep in one's —*, tenere segreto ‖ *to nurse a viper in one's —*, scaldar la serpe in seno **2.** *fig.* affetto; cuore; desiderio ‖ *my — friend*, il mio più intimo amico **3.** (*amer.*) superficie di lago, fiume **4.** (*amer.*) il davanti di una camicia.

Bosphorus ['bosfərəs], *no.pr.* (*geog.*) Bosforo.

boss[1] [bos], *s.* (*sl.*) capo, direttore, padrone; (*amer.*) capo di partito politico.

to boss[1], *v.t.* (*sl.*) spadroneggiare; comandare.

boss[2], *s.* **1.** protuberanza **2.** (*arch.*) bugna; borchia, risalto, aggetto **3.** (*mec.*) mozzo; punzone.

to boss[2], *v.t.* **1.** lavorare a borchie **2.** costruire a bugnato **3.** (*mec.*) punzonare.

bossage ['bosidʒ], *s.* (*arch.*) bugnato.

bossy[1] ['bosi], *ag.* (*sl.*) prepotente; autoritario.

bossy[2], *ag.* protuberante; (*arch.*) a bugnato.

Boston ['bostən], *no.pr.* (*geog.*) Boston || **boston**, *s.* **1.** «boston» (valzer lento e strisciato) **2.** «boston» (giuoco a carte).

botanic(al) [bə'tænik(əl)], *ag.* botanico.

botanically [bə'tænikəli], *av.* botanicamente.

botanist ['botənist], *s.* botanico.

to **botanize** ['botənaiz], *v.i.* erborare, erborizzare.

botanizer ['botənaizə*], *s.c.* erborista.

botanizing ['botənaiziŋ], *s.* erborizzazione.

botany ['botəni], *s.* botanica.

Botany, *s.* — (*wool*), lana australiana.

botargo [bou'ta:gou], *s.* bottarga (tipo di caviale).

botch [botʃ], *s.* **1.** bitorzolo **2.** lavoro male eseguito; rattoppo mal fatto.

to **botch,** *v.t.i.* abborracciare, rappezzare, rattoppare malamente: *to* — (*up*) *a comedy,* raffazzonare una commedia.

botcher ['botʃə*], *s.c.* pasticcione, pasticciona; rappezzatore, rappezzatrice.

botchy ['botʃi], *ag.* **1.** pieno di bitorzoli **2.** rappezzato; fatto malamente.

both [bouθ], *ag.* ambedue, entrambi, tutti e due: *on* — *sides,* d'ambo le parti; *she kissed him on* — *cheeks,* lo baciò su entrambe le guance || *pron.* **ambedue, entrambi, tutti e due:** — *are poets,* sono entrambi poeti; — *of them saw you,* ti videro tutti e due; *they are* — *alike,* sono tutti e due uguali || *av.* **nel medesimo tempo, ad un tempo, insieme:** — ... *and,* sia... sia, tanto... quanto: *he is* — *a poet and a painter,* egli è ad un tempo poeta e pittore; *she is* — *beautiful and clever,* essa è tanto bella quanto intelligente; *he* — *sings and acts well,* egli è valente sia come cantante che come attore.

bother ['boðə*], *s.* seccatura, noia: *what a* —!, che seccatura!.

to **bother,** *v.t.i.* **1.** infastidire; seccare: — *it!,* all'inferno!; *don't* — *me!,* lasciami stare! **2.** preoccuparsi: *don't* — *about me,* non disturbatevi per me.

botheration [,boðə'reiʃən], *s.* seccatura.

botheration, *inter.* all'inferno!.

bothersome ['boðəsəm], *ag.* seccante, noioso.

bottle[1] ['botl], *s.* bottiglia; fiasco; boccetta: *to cork a* —, turare una bottiglia; *to crack* (o *to uncork*) *a* —, sturare una bottiglia; *to stand a* —, offrire una bottiglia || *the* —, il bere || *child brought up on the* —, bambino allevato artificialmente || *over a* —, mentre si beve ☆ — *-companion,* compagno di bagordi; — *-fed,* allevato artificialmente; — *-feeding,* allattamento artificiale; — *-green,* verde bottiglia; — *-neck,* collo di bottiglia; *fig.* ingorgo; — *nose,* (*zool. pop.*) cetaceo della famiglia dei delfini; *fig.* naso grosso e rosso; — *-party,* ricevimento in cui gli ospiti portano bottiglie da bere; — *-shouldered,* dalle spalle spioventi; — *-washer,* factotum || *feeding-* — (o *child's* —), poppatoio; *wine* — -, bottiglia da vino.

to **bottle**[1], *v.t.* **1.** imbottigliare, infiascare: *bottled wine,* vino in bottiglia **2.** *to* — **up,** imbottigliare (traffico, ecc.); *fig.* reprimere (sentimenti).

bottle[2], *s.* fascio di fieno, di paglia || *to look for a needle in a* — *of hay,* cercare un ago in un pagliaio.

bottom ['botəm], *ag.* **1.** inferiore; ultimo: — *dollar,* l'ultimo dollaro **2.** basilare, fondamentale, essenziale || *s.* **1.** fondo; estremità; letto di fiume: *from top to* —, dall'alto al basso; *to go* (o *to sink*) *to the* —, colare a picco; *to send a ship to the* —, affondare una nave; *to touch* —, toccare il fondo (anche *fig.*) || *from the* — *of one's heart,* sinceramente **2.** *fig.* fondamento; essenza; causa, origine || *at* —. in fondo; *to be at the* — *of* (*an affair*), avere la parte principale in (una faccenda) || *to get to the* — *of sthg.,* andare a fondo in una cosa **3.** sedere, deretano **4.** fondamenta; piedistallo **5.** (*mar.*) chiglia, carena; barca **6.** resistenza, (capacità di) sopportazione ☆ — *lands,* (*amer.*) terre alluvionali; — *prices,* (*comm.*) prezzi minimi.

to **bottom,** *v.t.i.* **1.** mettere il fondo a; impagliare (sedie); lastricare (una strada); toccare il fondo del mare (di nave) **2.** *fig.* arrivare al significato, all'essenza di; capire **3.** *fig.* basare: *to* — (*an argument*) *upon sthg.,* basare (un argomento) su ql.co.

bottomless ['botəmlis], *ag.* senza fondo; *fig.* senza fine || *the* — *pit,* l'inferno.

bottommost ['botəmmoust], *ag.superl.* il più basso.

bottomry ['botəmri], *s.* (*comm.*) cambio marittimo.

botulism ['botjulizəm], *s.* (*med.*) botulismo.

boudoir ['bu:dwa:*], *s.* boudoir, salottino.

bouffe [bu:f], *ag.* (*mus.*) buffo.

bougainvillea [,bu:gən'viliə], *s.* (*bot.*) buganvillea.

bough [bau], *s.* ramo (d'albero).

bought [bo:t], *pass. p.p.* di to **buy.**

bougie ['bu:ʒi:], *s.* **1.** candela **2.** (*chir.*) catetere.

boulder ['bouldə*], *s.* ciottolo; macigno; (*geol.*) masso erratico.

boulevard ['bu:lva:*], *s.* (*amer.*) viale; corso.

bounce [bauns], *s.* **1.** balzo; rimbalzo: *to take* (o *to catch*) *the ball on the* —, *fig.* cogliere la palla al balzo || *to get the* —, (*sl. amer.*) essere licenziato **2.** *fig.* esagerazione; vanagloria.

to **bounce,** *v.t.i.* **1.** rimbalzare; far rimbalzare || *to* — *into, out of a room,* irrompere in, balzar fuori da una stanza **2.** vantarsi, gloriarsi; bluffare **3.** raggirare: *to* — *s.o. into doing sthg.,* costringere con lusinghe qlcu. a fare ql.co. **4.** (*sl. amer.*) licenziare.

bounce, *av.* **1.** improvvisamente: *to come* —, giungere all'improvviso **2.** rumorosamente.

bouncer ['baunsə*], *s.c.* fanfarone, fanfarona || *s.* **1.** (*sl.*) grossa bugia **2.** (*amer. teat.*) buttafuori.

bouncing ['baunsiŋ], *ag.* vigoroso; vivace: *a* — *lass,* una ragazza piena di salute.

bound[1] [baund], *s. gener. pl.* confine, limite; restrizione: *to go beyond the bounds of reason,* uscire dai limiti della ragione; *to go out of bounds,* passare il limite; *to keep within bounds,* non uscire dai limiti.

to **bound**[1], *v.t.* confinare; porre limiti a; restringere.

bound[2], *s.* salto; balzo; rimbalzo: *at a* —, con un balzo || *to advance by leaps and bounds,* *fig.* far passi da gigante.

to **bound**[2], *v.i.* balzare; rimbalzare; saltare.

bound[3], *ag.* diretto, incamminato; (*mar.*) in partenza per, con destinazione: *to be* — *for,* essere diretto a: *where are you* — *for?,* dove siete diretto? ☆ *homeward-* —, diretto verso casa, verso la patria.

bound[4], *pass.p.p.* di to **bind** || *ag.* **1.** legato; unito a; connesso con: *his welfare was* — *up with the welfare of his family,* il suo benessere era legato a quello della sua famiglia **2.** rilegato **3.** obbligato, costretto **4.** certo; destinato: *the best horse is* — *to win,* vincerà certamente il cavallo migliore; *he is* — *to come,* è certo che verrà ☆ *half-* —, rilegato in mezza pelle.

boundary ['baundəri], *s.* limite, termine; frontiera ☆ — *-line,* linea di confine, linea di demarcazione.

bounden ['baundən], *p.p.* (*arc.*) di to **bind** || *ag.*: — *duty,* sacro dovere.

bounder[1] ['baundə*], *s.* chi limita.

bounder[2], *s.* (*sl.*) fracassone; maleducato; mascalzone.

boundless ['baundlis], *ag.* illimitato; sconfinato.

boundlessness ['baundlisnis], *s.* infinità, vastità.

bounteous ['bauntiəs], **bountiful** ['bauntiful], *ag.* (*poet. ret.*) liberale, generoso; benefico.

bounty ['baunti], *s.* **1.** generosità **2.** dono; (*mil.mar.*) premio di arruolamento; (*comm.*) premio.

bouquet ['bukei], *s.* **1.** mazzolino, mazzo (di fiori) **2.** profumo, aroma (di vino).

bouquetin ['bu:kətin], *s.* (*zool.*) stambecco.

Bourbon ['buəbən], *no.pr.* (*st.*) Borbone.

bourgeois ['buəʒwa:], *ag.s.* borghese.

bourgeoisie [,buəʒwa:'zi:], *s.* borghesia.

bourn [buən], *s.* ruscello.

bourn(e) [buən], *s.* **1.** (*poet.*) meta; scopo **2.** confine.

bourse [buəs], *s.* (*comm.*) borsa valori.

bouse[1] [bu:z], *s.* **1.** bevanda, liquore **2.** gozzoviglia.

to **bouse**[1], *v.t.i.* (*fam.*) bere; ubriacarsi.

to **bouse**[2] [bauz], *v.t.* (*mar.*) tirare con un paranco.

bouse[3], *s.* minerale di piombo allo stato grezzo.

boustrophedon [ˌbaustrə'fi:dən], *ag.* (*archeol.*) bustrofedo.

bout [baut], *s.* **1.** prova **2.** periodo di attività **3.** attacco (di malattia) **4.** lotta **5.** (*spor.*) turno; ripresa.

bovine ['bouvain], *ag.* **1.** bovino **2.** *fig.* ottuso.

bovril ['bovril], *s.* estratto di carne di bue.

bow[1] [bou], *s.* **1.** arco **2.** archetto (di violino, ecc.) **3.** (*saddle-*) —, arcione **4.** nodo; fiocco ☆ — *-legged*, dalle gambe arcuate; — *-saw*, sega ad archetto, a tensione; — *-tie*, cravatta a farfalla; — *-window*, (*arch.*) bovindo, finestra ad arco ‖ *rain-* —, arcobaleno.

to **bow**[1], *v.t.* suonare (uno strumento) con l'archetto.

bow[2] [bau], *s.* saluto, inchino: *to make one's* —, salutare.

to **bow**[2], *v.t.i.* **1.** piegare, piegarsi; curvare, curvarsi; chinarsi; inchinarsi; *to* — *low*, inchinarsi profondamente; *to* — *one's head*, chinare il capo, salutare chinando il capo **2.** sottomettersi **3.** *to* — **down**, inginocchiarsi, piegarsi **4.** *to* — **in**, introdurre **5.** *to* — **out**, accompagnare fuori: *to* — *oneself out*, prender congedo.

bow[3], *s.* (*mar.*) prua, prora.

Bow bells ['bou'belz], *s.* le campane di St.-Mary-le-Bow (chiesa della City a Londra) ‖ *within the sound of* —, nel cuore di Londra.

bowdlerization [ˌbaudlərai'zeiʃən], *s.* espurgazione (di un libro).

to **bowdlerize** ['baudləraiz], *v.t.* espurgare (un libro).

bowel ['bauəl], *s. gener. pl.* **1.** (*anat.*) viscere (anche *fig.*); budella: *the bowels of the earth*, le viscere della terra **2.** *fig.* sentimenti di compassione ☆ — *complaint*, disturbo intestinale.

bower[1] ['bauə*], *s.* **1.** pergolato, luogo ombreggiato **2.** (*poet.*) capanna; dimora, ritiro campestre **3.** (*arc.*) camera, appartamento femminile.

to **bower**[1], *v.t.* circondare con un pergolato.

bower[2], *s.* (*mar.*) àncora di posta.

bower[3], *s.* (*mus.*) suonatore di strumenti ad arco.

bowery[1] ['bauəri], *ag.* ombreggiato.

bowery[2], *s.* (*amer.*) piantagione dei primi coloni olandesi a New York ‖ *the Bowery*, quartiere popolare di New York.

bowie-knife ['bouinaif], *s.* (*amer.*) coltello da caccia; coltello usato come pugnale.

bowl[1] [boul], *s.* **1.** scodella, tazza, ciotola; vaso; bacino **2.** cavità (della pipa, del cucchiaio, ecc.).

bowl[2], *s.* boccia: *game of bowls*, giuoco delle bocce.

to **bowl**[2], *v.t.i.* **1.** rotolare, far rotolare **2.** giocare a bocce **3.** (*cricket*) servire **4.** *to* — **along**, andare rapidamente (di carrozza, barca, ecc.).

bowler[1] ['boulə*], *s.* bombetta, cappello duro.

bowler[2], *s.* (*spor.*) **1.** giocatore di bocce **2.** (*cricket*) giocatore che serve la palla.

bowlful ['boulful], *s.* scodellata.

bowline ['boulin], *s.* (*mar.*) bolina.

bowling ['boulin], *s.* giuoco delle bocce ☆ — *-green* (o — *-ground*), campo di bocce.

bowman[1], *pl.* **bowmen** ['boumən], *s.* arciere.

bowman[2], *pl.* **bowmen** ['baumən], *s.* rematore di prora.

bowshot ['bou-ʃot], *s.* tiro d'arco.

bowsprit ['bou-sprit], *s.* (*mar.*) bompresso.

bowstring ['bou-striŋ], *s.* corda d'arco; laccio.

to **bowstring**, *v.t.* strangolare con un laccio.

bow wow ['bau'wau], *inter. s.* **1.** bau bau (imitazione dell'abbaiare di un cane) **2.** bau-bau, il cane (nel linguaggio infantile) ☆ — *style*, modo di parlare, di scrivere enfatico.

box[1] [boks], *ag.* di bosso ‖ *s.* bosso (albero, legno).

box[2], *s.* **1.** scatola, cassa, cassetta **2.** cabina **3.** (*teat.*) palco **4.** stalla (per cavalli da corsa) **5.** stanzetta; cubicolo; scompartimento **6.** bossolo **7.** (*dir.*) banco, sbarra **8.** (*elett.*) vaso ☆ — *-bed*, letto ad ar-

madio; — *-car*, (*amer.*) vagone merci chiuso; — *-coat*, pastrano pesante dei barocciai; — *-number*, casella postale; — *-office*, botteghino di teatro ‖ *call-* — (o *telephone-* —), cabina telefonica; *Christmas* —, strenna, gratifica natalizia; *dice-* —, bossolo per dadi; *jury-* —, banco dei giudici; *letter* —, casella per le lettere; *money* - —, salvadanaio; *post-office* —, casella postale; *strong* - —, cassaforte; *witness* —, banco dei testimoni.

to **box**[2], *v.t.* porre in scatola, incassare.

box[3], *s.* pugno; schiaffo, ceffone.

to **box**[3], *v.t.i.* lottare a pugni, fare del pugilato; schiaffeggiare ‖ *to* — *s.o.'s ears*, schiaffeggiare qlcu.

box-calf ['boksku:f], *s.* cuoio di vitello cromato.

boxer ['boksə*], *s.* pugile ‖ *Boxer*, (*st.*) membro di una società segreta cinese contro gli stranieri.

boxing[1] ['boksiŋ], *s.* l'inscatolare.

boxing[2], *s.* pugilato ☆ — *-match*, gara di pugilato.

Boxing-day ['boksiŋdei], *s.* S. Stefano (giorno delle strenne ai fornitori, ecc.).

boxseat ['boks,si:t], *s.* posto a cassetta (in una diligenza).

boxwood ['bokswud], *s.* bosso (legno, pianta).

boy [boi], *s.* **1.** ragazzo, fanciullo; adolescente: *little* —, bambino ‖ *my dear* —, mio caro; *old* — *!*, vecchio mio! **2.** garzone, fattorino; servo indigeno ☆ *Boy Scout*, giovane esploratore ‖ *cabin-* —, (*mar.*) mozzo.

boycott ['boikɔt], *s.* boicottaggio.

to **boycott**, *v.t.* boicottare.

boycotter ['boikɔtə*], *s.c.* chi boicotta.

boyfriend ['boifrend], *s.* ragazzo, compagno preferito (di una ragazza).

boyhood ['boihud], *s.* fanciullezza.

boyish ['boiiʃ], *ag.* fanciullesco.

boyishly ['boiiʃli], *ag.* fanciullescamente.

boyishness ['boiiʃnis], *s.* fanciullaggine.

boylike ['boilaik], *ag.* fanciullesco.

bra [brɑ:], *s.* (*abbr. di brassière*) reggipetto.

brabble ['bræbl], *s.* (*arc. dial.*) lite rumorosa.

to **brabble**, *v.i.* (*arc. dial.*) litigare schiamazzando.

brace [breis], *s.* **1.** qualunque cosa che tiene unito, fermo **2.** *pl.* bretelle **3.** tirante (del tamburo) **4.** (*mar.*) braccio **5.** (*mec.*) sostegno; collegamento **6.** (*falegnameria*) trapano: — *and bit*, trapano a manubrio **7.** (*tip.*) graffa **8.** (*mus.*) legatura **9.** (*invariato al pl.*) paio: *three* — *of partridges*, tre coppie di pernici **10.** (*edil.*) putrella.

to **brace**, *v.t.* **1.** fasciare, cingere; legare; stringere **2.** fortificare; *fig.* rinvigorire: *the sea air will* — *your nerves*, l'aria di mare ti rinvigorirà **3.** (*mar.*) bracciare **4.** accoppiare.

bracelet ['breislit], *s.* braccialetto ☆ — *-watch*, orologio da polso.

brachial ['breikjəl], *ag.* (*anat.*) brachiale.

brachycephalic [ˌbræki'kefælik], **brachycephalous** [ˌbræki'kefələs], *ag.* (*anat.*) brachicefalo.

brachycephaly [ˌbræki'kefəli], *s.* (*anat.*) brachicefalia.

brachylogy [brə'kilədʒi], *s.* brachilogia.

bracing ['breisiŋ], *ag.* fortificante; tonificante.

bracken ['brækən], *s.* (*bot.*) felce; grande quantità di felci.

bracket ['brækit], *s.* **1.** mensola **2.** braccio portalampada **3.** (*mec.*) tassello di sostegno **4.** parentesi: *between brackets*, fra parentesi **5.** (*artigl.*) forcella di cannone.

to **bracket**, *v.t.i.* **1.** mettere fra parentesi **2.** (*mil.*) fare forcella.

brackish ['brækiʃ], *ag.* salmastro, salato.

brackishness ['brækiʃnis], *s.* salsedine; sapore salmastro.

bract [brækt], *s.* (*bot.*) brattea.

brad [bræd], *s.* chiodo con testa piccola.

bradawl ['brædɔ:l], *s.* punteruolo.

Bradshaw ['brædʃɔ:], *s.* (*fam.*) orario ferroviario.

brae [brei], *s.* (*scoz.*) fianco di collina; argine ripido.

brag [bræg], *s.* vanto, millanteria; fanfaronata.

to **brag**, _pass.p.p._ **bragged** [brægd], _v.t.i._ vantare, vantarsi.

braggadocio [ˌbrægə'doutʃiou], _s._ millanteria.

braggart ['brægət], _ag.s._ spaccone; millantatore.

Brahma ['brɑːmə], _no.pr.m._ (_relig. indù_) Brahma.

Brahman ['brɑːmən], _s._ **1.** bramino **2.** (_sl. amer._) intellettuale.

Brahmanic(al) [brɑː'mænik(əl)], _ag._ bramanico.

Brahmanism ['brɑːmənizəm], _s._ bramanesimo.

Brahmaputra [ˌbrɑːmə'puːtrə], _no.pr._ (_geog._) Bramaputra.

Brahmin ['brɑːmin], _V._ **Brahman**.

Brahminee ['brɑːminiː], _s._ bramina.

Brahminic(al) [brɑː'minik(əl)], _ag._ bramanico.

Brahminism ['brɑːminizəm], _s._ bramanesimo.

braid [breid], _s._ **1.** treccia (di capelli) **2.** gallone; spighetta.

to **braid**, _v.t._ **1.** intrecciare (capelli, nastri) **2.** guarnire (di spighetta, gallone, ecc.).

braille [breil], _s._ « braille » (metodo di scrittura a rilievo per i ciechi).

brain [brein], _s._ (_anat._) cervello; _fig. gener. pl._ intelligenza, senno, capacità intellettiva: _he has no brains at all_, è senza cervello; _to cudgel one's brains_ (o _to rack one's brains_), _fig._ torturarsi il cervello, stillarsi il cervello ☆ — _-fag_, esaurimento cerebrale; — _-fever_, infiammazione cerebrale; — _-pan_, cranio; — _-power_, intelligenza; — _-storm_, attacco di pazzia; _brains trust_, convegno radiofonico, ecc. nel quale si espongono opinioni su vari argomenti; — _washing_, lavaggio del cervello; — _-wave_, onda telepatica, (_fam._) idea luminosa; — _-work_, lavoro di testa; — _-worker_, lavoratore intellettuale.

to **brain**, _v.t._ far saltar le cervella a, romper la testa a.

brained [breind], _ag._ dotato di cervello; giudizioso ☆ _hare-_ — (o _scatter-_ —), scervellato.

brainless ['breinlis], _ag.fig._ senza cervello; senza testa.

brain-sick ['brein-sik], _ag._ pazzo.

brainy ['breini], _ag._ intelligente, abile: _how — of you!_, che eccellente idea!.

braird [brɛəd], _s._ (_spec. scoz._) primi germogli.

to **braird**, _v.i._ (_spec. scoz._) germogliare.

to **braise** [breiz], _v.t._ brasare, cuocere a stufato.

brake[1] [breik], _s._ felce.

brake[2], _s._ boschetto, cespuglio.

brake[3], _s._ gramola, maciulla.

to **brake**[3], _v.t._ gramolare, maciullare.

brake[4], _s._ freno (di treno, vettura, bicicletta, ecc.): _to clap on the_ —, dare un colpo di freno; _to put on the_ —, tirare il freno ‖ _to act as a_ — _on s.o.'s activities_, _fig._ agire da freno alle attività di qlcu. ☆ — _drum_, tamburo di freno; — _horsepower_, potenza del freno ‖ _air_ —, (_mec._) freno ad aria compressa; _band_ —, (_mec._) freno a nastro; _emergency_ —, (_ferr._) segnale di allarme, freno di sicurezza; _foot_ —, (_aut._) freno a pedale; _four-wheel_ —, freno sulle quattro ruote; _hand_ —, freno a mano; _parking_ —, (_aut._) freno di blocco, freno a mano; _self-acting_ —, (_mec._) freno automatico.

to **brake**[4], _v.t.i._ **1.** frenare **2.** _to_ — **up**, rallentare.

brake[5], _pass._ (_arc._) di to **break**[1].

brakeless ['breiklis], _ag._ senza freni.

brakesman, _pl._ **brakesmen** ['breiksmən], _s._ frenatore.

bramble ['bræmbl], _s._ rovo, pruno ☆ — _-berry_, (_bot._) mora; — _-bush_, roveto; — _-rose_, rosa canina.

brambling ['bræmbliŋ], _s._ fringuello dei monti.

brambly ['bræmbli], _ag._ pieno di rovi.

bran [bræn], _s._ crusca ☆ — _-mash_, pastone.

brancard ['bræŋkəd], _s._ lettiera di cavallo.

branch [brɑːntʃ], _s._ **1.** ramo (di albero) **2.** ramificazione (di catena di montagne); ramo, braccio (di fiume); (_amer._) ruscello; diramazione (di strada, ferrovia) **3.** ramo (di famiglia, commercio, industria) **4.** succursale, filiale (di società, banca, ecc.) **5.** (_tec._) diramazione di tubatura **6.** (_arch._) nervatura di volta gotica **7.** (_geom._) ramo (di iperbole) ☆ — _circuit_, (_elett._) circuito derivato; — _house_, succursale; — _line_, ferrovia di dira-

mazione; — _office_, agenzia filiale ‖ _provincial_ —, succursale (fuori Londra).

to **branch**, _v.i._ **1.** metter rami; ramificarsi **2.** _to_ — _off_, biforcarsi, diramarsi **3.** _to_ — **out**, estendersi.

branched [brɑːntʃt], _ag._ ramoso.

branchia ['bræŋkiə], _pl._ **branchiae** ['bræŋkiiː], _s._ (_zool._) branchia.

branchial ['bræŋkiəl], _ag._ (_zool._) branchiale.

branchiate['bræŋkieit], _ag._(_zool._)munito di branchie.

branchless ['brɑːntʃlis], _ag._ senza rami.

branchy ['brɑːntʃi], _ag._ ramoso.

brand [brænd], _s._ **1.** tizzone **2.** marchio a fuoco; stampo in ferro per marchio a fuoco **3.** marchio d'infamia, stigma: — _of Cain_, marchio di Caino **4.** marchio di fabbrica; marca, qualità (di merce): _a famous_ —, una marca famosa **5.** (_poet._) spada, brando ☆ — _-new_, nuovo fiammante.

to **brand**, _v.t._ **1.** marchiare (con ferro rovente, ecc.) **2.** _fig._ stigmatizzare **3.** imprimere: _to_ — _on one's memory_, imprimere indelebilmente nella memoria ☆ _branding-iron_, ferro da marchio.

to **brandish** ['brændiʃ], _v.t._ brandire.

brandy ['brændi], _s._ acquavite ☆ — _-ball_, cioccolatino al liquore; — _pawnee_, acquavite annacquata; — _-snap_, panpepato ‖ _cherry-_ —, cherry-brandy.

brank-ursine [ˌbræŋk'əːsin], _s._ (_bot._) acanto.

brash[1] [bræʃ], _ag._ fragile (generalmente di legno).

brash[3], _s._ **1.** scroscio di pioggia improvviso **2.** disturbo, indisposizione ☆ _teeth-_ —, disturbi della dentizione; _water-_ —, pirosi; _weaning-_ —, disturbi dello svezzamento.

brash[4], _s._ **1.** frammenti (di roccia, ghiaccio) **2.** tralci, rami potati ☆ — _-ice_, ghiaccio in disgelo.

brass [brɑːs], _ag._ **1.** di ottone ‖ _I don't care a_ — _farthing_, (_sl._) non me ne importa un bel niente ‖ _let's get down to_ — _tacks_, (_sl._) veniamo al sodo **2.** _fig._ sfacciato — _s._ **1.** ottone **2.** (_mec._) bronzina **3.** _pl._ (_mus._) ottoni **4.** _pl._ articoli di ottone **5.** _fig._ sfacciataggine, sfrontatezza, impudenza **6.** (_sl._) moneta, denaro **7.** (_sl._) galloni (di graduato) ☆ — _band_, fanfara; — _hat_, (_sl._) ufficiale superiore; — _plate_, targa d'ottone; — _sheet_, lamiera, tubo d'ottone; — _wire_, filo d'ottone.

brassage ['bræsidʒ], _s._ diritto di conio.

brassard ['bræsɑːd], _s._ bracciale.

brassie ['brɑːsi], _s._ (_golf_) mazza con paletta d'ottone.

brassière ['bræsiɛə*], _s._ reggipetto.

brassiness ['brɑːsinis], _s._ sfrontatezza.

brassware ['brɑːswɛə*], _s._ ottoname.

brassy ['brɑːsi], _ag._ **1.** d'ottone **2.** _fig._ sfacciato ‖ _s._ (_golf_) mazza con paletta d'ottone.

brat [bræt], _s.c._ (_spreg._) marmocchio, marmocchia; monello, monella.

bravado [brə'vɑːdou], _s._ bravata, smargiassata.

brave [breiv], _ag._ **1.** prode, audace, coraggioso **2.** (_arc. letter._) elegante, ben vestito; vistoso ‖ _s._ **1.** prode **2.** guerriero pellirossa **3.** (_arc._) bravo.

to **brave**, _v.t._ sfidare, affrontare (pericoli).

bravely ['breivli], _av._ **1.** coraggiosamente, audacemente **2.** (_arc. letter._) elegantemente; splendidamente.

bravery ['breivəri], _s._ **1.** coraggio; audacia **2.** splendore, magnificenza; eleganza.

bravo[1] ['brɑː'vou], _pl._ **bravos, bravoes** ['brɑː'vouz], _s._ bravo; sicario.

bravo[2], _inter._ bravo!; bene!.

bravura [brə'vuərə], _s._ (_mus._) aria, pezzo di bravura.

brawl [brɔːl], _s._ rissa; schiamazzo.

to **brawl**, _v.i._ **1.** rissare, azzuffarsi, schiamazzare **2.** rumoreggiare (di torrente, acqua).

brawler ['brɔːlə*], _s.c._ chi litiga, fa fracasso.

brawling ['brɔːliŋ], _s._ **1.** rissa, schiamazzo **2.** il rumoreggiare (di torrente, acqua).

brawn [brɔːn], _s._ **1.** muscolo; forza muscolare **2.** (_cuc._) carne di maiale; soprassata.

brawniness ['brɔːninis], *s.* muscolosità; robustezza.

brawny ['brɔːni], *ag.* muscoloso; robusto.

braxy ['bræksi], *s.* (*vet.*) carbonchio.

bray[1] [brei], *s.* **1.** squillo (di tromba) **2.** raglio.

to bray[1], *v.i.* **1.** echeggiare **2.** ragliare.

to bray[2], *v.t.* pestare, macinare (colori, ecc.).

to braze[1] [breiz], *v.t.* **1.** ottonare **2.** *fig.* indurire.

to braze[2], *v.t.* saldare (con una lega di ottone e zinco).

brazen ['breizn], *ag.* **1.** di ottone **2.** come ottone **3.** sfacciato ☆ — *face*, faccia di bronzo.

to brazen, *v.t.i.* **1.** rendere sfacciato **2.** *to — out*, fare sfacciatamente ‖ *to — it out*, comportarsi con sfacciataggine.

brazenly ['breizuli], *av.* sfacciatamente.

brazenness ['breiznnis], *s.* sfacciataggine.

brazier[1] ['breizjə*], *s.* ottonaio; calderaio.

brazier[2], *s.* braciere.

Brazil [brə'zil], *no.pr.* (*geog.*) Brasile ☆ — *-nut*, noce del Brasile.

Brazilia [brə'ziljə], *no.pr.* (*geog.*) Brasilia.

Brazilian [brə'ziljən], *ag.* brasiliano ‖ *s.c.* brasiliano, brasiliana.

breach [briːtʃ], *s.* **1.** frattura; (*mar.*) rottura; (*mil.*) breccia: *to stand in the* —, sostenere l'assalto, *fig.* stare sulla breccia **2.** *fig.* violazione; infrazione; rottura; abuso: — *of contract*, rottura di contratto; — *of duty*, infrazione al dovere; — *of law*, violazione della legge; — *of the peace*, violazione dell'ordine pubblico; — *of promise*, rottura di promessa di matrimonio; — *of trust*, abuso di fiducia **3.** salto di balena.

to breach, *v.t.i.* **1.** aprire una breccia, una falla in (muro, diga); fendersi **2.** emergere (di balena).

bread [bred], *s.* **1.** pane: *a loaf of* —, una pagnotta; *new* —, pane fresco; *a roll of* —, un panino; *stale* —, pane raffermo; *unleavened* —, pane azzimo ‖ *his — is buttered on both sides*, *fig.* la vita per lui è facile ‖ *to be on — and water*, essere a pane e acqua ‖ *to break* —, rompere il digiuno; somministrare, prendere la comunione ‖ *to know on which side one's — is buttered*, *fig.* saper quale sia il proprio vantaggio ‖ *to live on — and cheese*, vivere frugalmente **2.** vitto, sostentamento, cibo: *to earn one's daily* —, guadagnarsi il cibo quotidiano ☆ — *-and-butter*, *fig.* cibo necessario: *to earn one's — -and-butter*, guadagnarsi il necessario; — *-basket*, cestino per il pane; (*sl.*) stomaco; — *-card*, — *-coupon*, tessera, tagliando per il pane; — *-tree*, albero del pane ‖ *brown* —, pane scuro.

bread-crumb ['bredkrʌm], *s.* **1.** mollica **2.** *pl.* briciole; pan grattato.

to bread-crumb, *v.t.* impanare.

breadfruit ['bredfruːt], *s.* frutto dell'albero del pane.

breadth [bredθ], *s.* **1.** larghezza, ampiezza; altezza (di stoffa): *a carpet ten feet in* —, un tappeto largo 10 piedi ‖ — *of wings*, (*aer.*) apertura d'ali ‖ *to a hair's* —, esattamente **2.** *fig.* liberalità; larghezza di vedute.

breadthways ['bredθweiz], **breadthwise** ['bredθwaiz], *av.* in larghezza, secondo la larghezza.

breadwinner ['bred,winə*], *s.c.* chi guadagna il pane per tutta la famiglia.

break[1] [breik], *s.* **1.** rottura, frattura; (*mec.*) rottura; (*elett.*) interruzione; (*geol.*) faglia: *a — in the voice*, un'incrinatura nella voce (per l'emozione) ‖ — *of day*, lo spuntar del giorno **2.** interruzione; intervallo; pausa: *the — is over*, l'intervallo è finito **3.** infrazione, violazione, irregolarità **4.** (*cricket*) deviazione di una palla **5.** possibilità; opportunità, occasione: *to give s.o. a* —, dare a qlcu. una possibilità **6.** (*mus.*) mutamento di registro **7.** (*tip.*) ultima riga ☆ — *-up*, (*patol.*) collasso; smembramento (di impero, ecc.); distruzione (di nave); fine (dell'anno scolastico); disgelo.

to break[1], *pass.* **broke** [brouk], (*arc.*) **brake** [breik], *p.p.* **broken** ['broukən], (*arc.*) **broke**, *v.t.i.* **1.** rompere, rompersi; spezzare, spezzarsi; infrangere, infrangersi; frantumare, frantumarsi: *the cup broke into pieces*, la tazza andò in frantumi; *this breaks my heart*,

questo mi spezza il cuore; *the waves — against the rocks*, le onde si infrangono contro gli scogli; *to — the ice*, rompere il ghiaccio (anche *fig.*); *to — one's neck*, rompersi l'osso del collo; *to — new* (o *fresh*) *ground*, dissodare il terreno, *fig.* eseguire un lavoro originale, da pioniere; *to — a spell*, spezzare un incantesimo ‖ *to — bulk*, cominciare a scaricare ‖ *to — loose*, spezzare i legami, liberarsi ‖ *to — the news*, comunicare per primo la notizia ‖ *to — open*, aprire con violenza, scassinare ‖ *to — a record*, battere un primato ‖ *to — a strike*, far fallire uno sciopero ‖ *to — wind*, ruttare **2.** interrompere: *to — a journey*, interrompere un viaggio **3.** soggiogare, domare **4.** spezzarsi (di voce: per emozione o nella pubertà) **5.** indebolire; declinare, venir meno (di forze) **6.** rovinare (finanziariamente); far bancarotta ‖ *to — the bank*, (*giuoco*) far saltare il banco **7.** venir meno, trasgredire, violare: *he broke his word*, venne meno alla sua promessa; *to — faith* (*with s.o.*), venir meno alla parola data (a qlcu.) **8.** *to — into* (*sthg.*), irrompere (in una casa, ecc.); forzare; scoppiare (in pianto, riso): *the burglars broke into the house*, i ladri irruppero nella casa (con scasso); *he broke into laughter*, scoppiò in una risata **9.** *to — upon* (*s.o.*, *sthg.*), scagliarsi su **10.** *to — away*, distaccare, distaccarsi; fuggire **11.** *to — down*, demolire, abbattere; (*mec. aut.*) restare in panna, guastarsi; (*mar.*) fare avaria; (*chim.*) decomporre; (*comm.*) analizzare (costi, ecc.); deprimersi; rovinarsi (della salute): *after working too hard he broke down*, si esaurì per il troppo lavoro **12.** *to — forth*, irrompere; scaturire; espandersi (di luce) **13.** *to — in*, irrompere; interrompere; domare, ammaestrare **14.** *to — off*, interrompere, cessare bruscamente; litigare: *the match was broken off*, il matrimonio andò a monte; *to — off an appointment*, *a contract*, mandare a monte un appuntamento, un contratto; *to — off with s.o.*, litigare con qlcu. **15.** *to — out*, scoppiare (di malattia, guerra, incendio); fuggire; zampillare **16.** *to — through*, aprirsi un varco a forza **17.** *to — up*, rompere, fare in pezzi; disperdere (folla, ecc.); sciogliersi (di assemblea, ecc.); iniziare le vacanze (di scuola).

break[2], *s.* « break » (carrozza a quattro ruote con due sedili di fronte, disposti in senso verticale al sedile del cocchiere).

(to) **break**[3], *V.* (to) **brake**[4].

breakable ['breikəbl], *ag.* fragile.

breakage ['breikidʒ], *s.* rottura, spaccatura, frattura: *you must pay for the* —, dovete pagare i danni.

breakaway ['breikəwei], *s.* **1.** separazione; defezione, fuga; (*spor.*) separazione (di due pugilatori) **2.** (*ferr.*) sbandamento (di vagoni) **3.** (*austral.*) sbandamento (di greggo) **4.** (*cine.*) scenario destinato a crollare.

breakdown ['breikdaun], *s.* **1.** collasso **2.** insuccesso, rottura (di negoziati) **3.** dissesto, sfacelo (di ditta, di governo): *the — of the Roman Empire*, il crollo dell'impero romano **4.** sospensione (di servizio) **5.** (*aut. mec.*) panna, guasto, danno; (*mar.*) avaria **6.** (*comm.*) analisi, classificazione **7.** « breakdown » (danza negra) ☆ — *repairs*, riparazioni di fortuna; — *service*, servizio riparazioni; — *train*, convoglio di soccorso; — *van*, carro attrezzi ‖ *nervous* —, esaurimento nervoso.

breaker[1] ['breikə*], *s.c.* **1.** rompitore, rompitrice **2.** violatore, violatrice **3.** domatore, domatrice; ammaestratore, ammaestratrice ‖ *s.* **1.** (*mec.*) macchina rompitrice **2.** (*mar.*) frangente **3.** (*elett.*) interruttore ☆ *circuit-* —, (*elett.*) interruttore; *record-* —, (*spor.*) primatista; *stone-* —, spaccapietre.

breaker[2], *s.* (*mar.*) bariletto.

breakfast ['brekfəst], *s.* prima colazione.

to breakfast, *v.i.* far la prima colazione: *to — on boiled eggs*, far colazione con uova alla coque.

breakfastless ['brekfəstlis], *ag.* a digiuno.

breaking ['breikiŋ], *s.* **1.** rottura, spaccatura; frattura; sfracellamento **2.** infrazione, violazione ☆ — *down*, demolizione (di muro, ecc.); (*mec.*) panna, guasto;

(*chim.*) decomposizione; — *in*, irruzione; domatura, addestramento; (*aut.*) rodaggio; — *off*, rottura (di negoziati, matrimonio, ecc.); interruzione (di lavoro); pausa (in un discorso); — *open*, il forzare (porta, ecc.); — *out*, (*patol.*) eruzione, sfogo; — *point*, limite di rottura, di resistenza; — *up*, demolizione; scioglimento (di assemblea, ecc.); dispersione (di folla); smembramento (di impero, ecc.); inizio delle vacanze scolastiche; disgelo; (*chim.*) decomposizione.

breakneck ['breiknek], *ag.* pericoloso: *to go at — speed*, andare a rotta di collo.

breakthrough ['breik'θru:], *s.* 1. (*geol.*) affioramento 2. (*mil.*) penetrazione (nelle linee nemiche) 3. (*miner.*) passaggio di comunicazione.

breakwater ['breik,wo:tə*], *s.* frangiflutti; argine; diga.

bream¹ [bri:m], *s.* (*ittiol.*) abramide ☆ *sea- —*, pagello.

to bream², *v.t.* bruscare (la carena di una barca).

breast [brest], *s.* 1. petto, mammella, poppa (anche di animale); *fig.* sorgente di nutrimento 2. *fig.* cuore; coscienza; *fig.* affetto ‖ *to make a clean — of sthg.*, fare una completa confessione 3. davanti (di abito) 4. fianco (di bastimento) 5. (*arch.*) parapetto 6. (*miner.*) fronte d'avanzamento ☆ *— -bone*, (*anat.*) sterno; *— -deep*, che giunge fino al petto; *— -pin*, spilla da cravatta; spilla (per donna); *— -pocket*, taschino all'altezza del petto; *inside — -pocket*, tasca interna; *— -stroke*, nuoto a rana.

to breast, *v.t.* affrontare; resistere a.

breasted ['brestid], *ag.* dal petto ☆ *broad- —*, dal petto ampio; *double- —*, a doppio petto: *a double- coat*, un cappotto a doppio petto; *single- —*, a un petto solo.

breastplate ['brestpleit], *s.* 1. corazza 2. pettorale (di cavallo).

breastsummer ['bresəmə*], *s.* (*arch.*) architrave.

breastwork ['brest-wə:k], *s.* (*arch. mil.*) parapetto, muro basso di difesa.

breath [breθ], *s.* 1. respiro, alito, fiato; soffio (anche *fig.*): *the — of life*, il soffio della vita; *bad —*, alito cattivo; *last —*, l'ultimo respiro; *out of —*, senza fiato; *shortness of —*, (*patol.*) asma; *to be short of —*, avere il respiro corto; *to draw —*, respirare, vivere; *to hold (o to catch) one's —*, trattenere il respiro; *to recover —*, riprendere fiato; *to take —*, riposare; *to take s.o.'s — away*, togliere il fiato a qlcu.; *to waste one's —*, sprecare il fiato ‖ *below (o under) one's —*, sottovoce ‖ *in one —*, in un lampo 2. venticello, brezza: *a — of wind, of air*, un soffio di vento, d'aria 3. mormorio, sussurro ☆ *— -taking*, sorprendente.

breathable ['bri:ðəbl], *ag.* respirabile.

to breathe [bri:ð], *v.t.i.* 1. respirare, prender fiato; soffiare: *the fat man was breathing short*, il grassone ansimava; *he was breathing hard when he finished the race*, respirava a fatica, quando smise di correre; *to — new life into s.o., into a conversation*, rianimare qlcu., una conversazione: *they breathed new life into him*, gli infusero nuova vita ‖ *to — one's last (breath)*, spirare, esalare l'ultimo respiro ‖ *to — a sigh*, sospirare ‖ *to — a vein*, (*chir.*) fare un salasso 2. sussurrare: *don't — word of it to him*, non farne parola con lui; *he breathed sthg. to me*, mi sussurrò ql.co.; *to — a prayer*, mormorare una preghiera 3. (*fonet.*) aspirare 4. *to — forth*, esalare: *to — forth perfume*, esalare profumo 5. *to — in*, inspirare (aria) 6. *to — out*, espirare (aria).

breather ['bri:ðə*], *s.* 1. chi respira; essere vivente 2. pausa (per riprendere fiato) 3. sfiatatoio.

breathing ['bri:ðiŋ], *ag.* respirante, vivente; esalante ‖ *s.* 1. respiro, respirazione 2. soffio di vento, brezza 3. (*fonet.*) aspirazione, spirito (in greco) ☆ *— -hole*, spiraglio; *— -place*, (*mus.*) respiro; *— -space (o — -spell o — -time)*, intervallo di riposo; tempo per respirare ‖ *rough —*, (*fonet.*) spirito aspro; *smooth —*, (*fonet.*) spirito dolce.

breathless ['breθlis], *ag.* 1. ansante, senza respiro ‖

to wait in — suspense, *fig.* aspettare con vivissima attesa 2. esanime, senza vita.

breathlessly ['breθlisli], *av.* con il fiato sospeso; con viva attesa.

breathlessness ['breθlisnis], *s.* mancanza di respiro, oppressione, affanno.

breathy ['breθi], *ag.* 1. relativo al respiro 2. (*fonet.*) accompagnato da emissione di respiro.

breccia ['bretʃiə], *s.* (*geol.*) breccia.

bred [bred], *pass.p.p.* di **to breed** ‖ *ag.* allevato ☆ *ill- —*, maleducato; *well- —*, ben educato, gentile.

breech [bri:tʃ], *s.* la parte posteriore di ql.co.; culatta (di fucile, ecc.); deretano ☆ *— -loader*, fucile, arma a retrocarica.

to breech, *v.t.* mettere in calzoncini (un bimbo, per la prima volta).

breeches ['britʃiz], *s.pl.* calzoni; brache ☆ *knee- —*, calzoni alla zuava; *riding- —*, calzoni da cavallerizzo.

breeching ['britʃiŋ], *s.* 1. imbraca 2. imbracatura (di cannone).

breechless ['britʃlis], *ag.* senza calzoni.

breed [bri:d], *s.* razza; famiglia, stirpe, progenie ‖ *— will tell*, buon sangue non mente.

to breed, *pass.p.p.* **bred** [bred], *v.t.i.* 1. generare, procreare: *birds — in spring*, gli uccelli procreano in primavera 2. nascere, originarsi: *crime often breeds in slums*, la criminalità ha spesso origine nei quartieri più poveri 3. *fig.* produrre, causare: *to — ill blood*, far cattivo sangue; *to — quarrels*, causare dispute 4. allevare; educare: *he was bred (up) to the law*, fu avviato alla carriera giuridica; *to — cattle*, allevare bestiame.

breeder ['bri:də*], *s.* 1. chi genera (anche *fig.*); animale, pianta di riproduzione 2. allevatore.

breeding ['bri:diŋ], *s.* 1. generazione, procreazione ‖ *— in*, accoppiamento tra consanguinei 2. allevamento 3. educazione, buone maniere, finezza.

breeze¹ [bri:z], *s.* 1. brezza, venticello, soffio d'aria ‖ *to go like a —*, camminare a cuor leggero 2. (*fam.*) eccitamento, litigio 3. voce, diceria ☆ *land- —*, vento di terra; *sea- —*, vento di mare.

to breeze¹, *v.i.* (*rar.*) 1. alitare (di vento) 2. (*sl.*) vantarsi, fare il furbo 3. *to — up*, rinfrescarsi (di vento).

breeze², *s.* (*entom.*) tafano.

breeze³, *s.* scorie di fornace.

breezily ['bri:zili], *av.* 1. con vento, brezza 2. (*fam.*) cordialmente, con giovialità, con disinvoltura.

breeziness ['bri:zinis], *s.* cordialità, giovialità; disinvoltura; brio (di persona, stile, discorso).

breezy ['bri:zi], *ag.* 1. ventoso, ventilato; arieggiato 2. gioviale; allegro, brioso.

brehon ['bri:hən], *s.* (*st.*) giudice irlandese.

brekker ['brekə*], *s.* (*sl. universitario*) prima colazione.

Bren [bren], *s.* *— (gun)*, «bren» (fucile mitragliatore).

brent [brent], *s.* *— (-goose)*, oca, colombaccio.

bressummer ['bresəmə*], *s.* (*arch.*) architrave.

brer [brə:*], (*sl. amer. abbr.*) di **brother**.

brethren ['breðrin], *pl.* di **brother** 3.

Breton ['bretən], *ag.s.* bretone.

breve [bri:v], *s.* 1. (*mus.*) breve 2. (*tip.*) segno per distinguere una vocale breve 3. breve (lettera papale).

brevet ['brevit], *s.* (*mil.*) 1. brevetto, nomina, promozione 2. posizione onorifica, nominale.

to brevet, *v.t.* (*mil.*) 1. consegnare il brevetto a 2. conferire la promozione onoraria a (un ufficiale).

breviary ['bri:vjəri], *s.* (*eccl.*) breviario.

brevier [brə'viə*], *s.* (*tip.*) corpo 8.

brevity ['breviti], *s.* brevità, concisione.

brew [bru:], *s.* 1. mescolanza, mistura (di liquidi); infuso, tisana 2. fermentazione (della birra) ‖ *a good — of beer*, una buona qualità di birra.

to brew, *v.t.i.* 1. mescolare (liquidi); essere in infusione, in fermentazione 2. fare (la birra) 3. *fig.* macchinare, preparare, prepararsi; tramare: *I should like to know what is brewing*, mi piacerebbe sapere cosa bolle in pentola; *there is sthg. brewing*, c'è ql.co. in aria; *there is a storm brewing*, (*fam.*) si prepara un temporale; *to — mischief*, tramare una malefatta.

brewage ['bru:idʒ], *V.* **brew.**

brewer ['bru:ə*], *s.c.* birraio, birraia.

brewery ['bruəri], *s.* fabbrica di birra.

brewing ['bru:iŋ], *s.* **1.** fabbricazione della birra **2.** quantità di birra fatta in una volta.

brewis ['bru:is], *s.* (*arc. dial.*) brodo.

briar, *V.* **brier**[1].

Briareus [brai'ɛəriəs], *no.pr.m.* (*mit.*) Briareo.

bribability [,braibə'biliti], *s.* corruttibilità.

bribable ['braibəbl], *ag.* corruttibile.

bribe [braib], *s.* dono offerto a scopo di corruzione; esca; allettamento.

to **bribe**, *v.t.* corrompere; sedurre: *to — s.o. to silence*, comprare il silenzio di qlcu.

bribee [brai'bi:], *s.c.* chi si lascia corrompere.

briber ['braibə*], *s.c.* corruttore, corruttrice.

bribery ['braibəri], *s.* corruzione: *open to —*, corruttibile.

bric-a-brac ['brikəbræk], *s.* « bric-a-brac », anticaglie, cianfrusaglie.

brick [brik], *s.* **1.** mattone, laterizio ‖ *to drop a —*, fare una gaffe **2.** pane (di sapone, ecc.) **3.** *pl.* costruzioni (giuoco infantile) **4.** (*fam.*) persona buona e fidata: *he was a real — to me*, fu un vero amico per me, mi fu di grande aiuto ☆ *— -clay* (o *— -earth*), argilla per mattoni; *— -dust*, polvere di mattone; *— -flooring*, ammattonato; *— -kiln*, fornace per mattoni; *— -red*, rosso mattone; *— -wall*, muro di mattoni ‖ *flue- —* (o *hollow- —*), mattone forato; *light- —*, mattone leggero.

to **brick**, *v.t.* murare; costruire in mattoni.

brickbat ['brikbæt], *s.* **1.** pezzo di mattone (generalmente usato come proiettile): *to throw brickbats at*, lanciar sassi, prendere a sassate **2.** *fig.* insulti, frecciate: *they were very angry and shied brickbats at one another*, erano molto in collera e si scambiavano insulti.

brickfield ['brikfi:ld], *s.* mattonaia.

bricklayer ['brik,leiə*], *s.* muratore.

brickle ['brikl], *ag.* debole; fragile (anche *fig.*).

brickmaker ['brik,meikə*], *s.* mattonaio.

brickmaking ['brik,meikiŋ], *s.* fabbricazione dei mattoni.

brickwork ['brikwə:k], *s.* muratura in mattoni.

bricky ['briki], *ag.* **1.** di mattoni **2.** color mattone.

brickyard ['brikja:d], *s.* mattonaia.

bricole ['brikəl], *s.* (*mil.*) **1.** briccola **2.** sopraspalla.

bridal ['braidl], *ag.* nuziale ‖ *s.* sposalizio.

bride[1] [braid], *s.* sposa, sposa novella: *to become a —*, maritarsi ‖ *the — and bridegroom*, gli sposi ☆ *— -cake*, torta nuziale.

bride[2], *s.* (*ricamo*) punto tulle.

bridegroom ['braidgrum], *s.* sposo.

bridesmaid ['braidzmeid], *s.* damigella d'onore di una sposa.

bridesman, *pl.* **bridesmen** ['braidzmən], *s.* testimone dello sposo.

bridewell ['braidwəl], *s.* casa di correzione; prigione.

bridge[1] [bridʒ], *s.* **1.** ponte: *— of boats*, ponte di barche; *to throw a — over* (o *across*) *a river*, gettare un ponte su un fiume **2.** (*mar.*) ponte di comando, plancia **3.** (*mec. med.*) ponte **4.** (*mus.*) ponticello (di strumento ad arco) **5.** (*anat.*) dorso (del naso) ☆ *— -head*, (*mil.*) testa di ponte; *— -train*, (*mil.*) compagnia di genieri con materiale per la posa di un ponte ‖ *arch — —*, ponte ad arco; *bascule- —* (o *draw- —*), ponte levatoio; *flying- —*, ponte sospeso; *fore-and-aft- —*, (*mar.*) passerella; *jury- —*, ponte di fortuna; *pontoon- —*, ponte di barche; *suspension- —* (o *swing- —* o *revolving- —*), ponte girevole; *toll- —*, ponte a pedaggio.

to **bridge**[1], *v.t.* **1.** costruire un ponte sopra; attraversare come un ponte: *the road was bridged by the*

fallen tree, l'albero caduto faceva come un ponte sopra la strada ‖ *to — a gap*, *fig.* colmare una lacuna **2.** (*elett.*) collegare.

bridge[2], *s.* (*giuoco*) « bridge », ponte ‖ *— -fiend*, giocatore fanatico di « bridge »; *— -marker*, blocchetto per segnare i punti al « bridge ».

bridged [bridʒd], *ag.* provvisto di ponte ☆ *high — nose*, naso pronunciato.

bridgeless ['bridʒlis], *ag.* senza ponte (di fiume); *fig.* insormontabile, insuperabile (di abisso, malinteso, ecc.) ‖ *an almost — nose*, un naso piatto.

Bridget ['bridʒit], *no.pr.f.* Brigida.

bridging ['bridʒiŋ], *ag.* **1.** che attraversa **2.** che sostituisce; provvisorio: *— title*, titolo provvisorio (di film, ecc.).

bridle ['braidl], *s.* **1.** briglia: *to give the horse the —*, allentare le briglie **2.** ostacolo; ritegno; freno: *to put a — on one's passions*, porre un freno alle proprie passioni **3.** (*mar.*) gomena **4.** (*anat.*) frenulo; briglia ☆ *— -bit*, morso; *— -hand*, mano sinistra; *— -path* (o *— -road* o *— -way*), strada percorribile a cavallo.

to **bridle**, *v.t.i.* **1.** imbrigliare (anche *fig.*) **2.** frenare (anche *fig.*) **3.** alzare il capo in atteggiamento sdegnoso, fare l'offeso, risentirsi, stizzirsi.

bridoon [bri'du:n], *s.* (*mil.*) bridone.

Brie [bri:], *s.* « Brie » (formaggio dolce).

brief [bri:f], *ag.* breve; conciso: *to be —*, essere breve (nel discorso) ‖ *in —*, a farla breve, in sunto.

brief, *s.* **1.** riassunto **2.** (*aer.*) istruzioni sommarie **3.** (*dir.*) fascicolo ‖ *to hold a —*, *no — for*, essere non essere incaricato della difesa of **4.** breve, lettera papale ☆ *— -case* (o *— -bag*), borsa da avvocato.

to **brief**, *v.t.* **1.** (*dir.*) riassumere per sommi capi: *to — a case*, fare il riassunto di una causa ‖ *to — a lawyer*, affidare una causa ad un avvocato **2.** impartire istruzioni a (equipaggio di un aereo).

briefless ['bri:flis], *ag.* senza cause (di avvocato).

briefly ['bri:fli], *av.* brevemente.

briefness ['bri:fnis], *s.* brevità; concisione.

brier[1] ['braiə*], *s.* (*bot.*) rovo; rosa selvatica: *sweet —*, rosa selvatica profumata ☆ *— rose*, rosa canina.

brier[2], *s.* **1.** (*bot.*) erica bianca **2.** pipa di erica bianca.

brig[1] [brig], *s.* (*mar.*) brigantino.

brig[2], *s.* (*scoz.*) ponte.

brigade [bri'geid], *s.* **1.** (*mil.*) brigata ‖ *one of the old —*, uno della vecchia guardia **2.** associazione, corpo organizzato di persone a scopo pubblico ☆ *Church- —*, associazione parrocchiale di giovani e ragazzi; *fire- —*, (corpo dei) pompieri.

to **brigade**, *v.t.* (*mil.*) unire in brigate.

brigadier-general ['brigədiə'dʒenərəl], *s.* comandante di brigata.

brigand ['brigənd], *s.* brigante.

brigandage ['brigəndidʒ], *s.* brigantaggio.

brigandish ['brigəndiʃ], *ag.* brigantesco.

brigandism ['brigəndizəm], *s.* brigantaggio.

brigantine ['brigəntain], *s.* (*mar.*) brigantino.

bright [brait], *ag.* **1.** lucido, risplendente; vivido: *a — complexion*, una carnagione chiara; *— red*, rosso vivo; *— steel*, acciaio lucido, bianco; *— weather*, tempo bello, limpido; *to make —*, rendere brillante ‖ *— and early*, di prima mattina **2.** gioioso; vivace; intelligente: *a — girl*, una ragazza sveglia ‖ *the — side of things*, il lato buono delle cose; *to look on the — side*, vedere tutto rosa, essere ottimista ‖ *— young people* (o *things*), i figli di papà **3.** illustre ☆ *— -hued*, dal colore brillante.

bright, *av.* **1.** luminosamente **2.** allegramente.

to **brighten** ['braitn], *v.t.i.* **1.** brillare; far brillare; ravvivare (anche *fig.*) **2.** *fig.* animare, animarsi, rallegrare, rallegrarsi: *his face brightened*, il suo volto si animò ‖ *things are brightening up*, le prospettive migliorano, l'avvenire si annuncia più sereno.

brightly ['braitli], *av.* **1.** luminosamente **2.** allegramente; vivacemente.

brightness ['braitnis], s. 1. splendore, luminosità 2. gaiezza; vivacità.

Brigid ['bridʒid], no.pr.f. Brigida.

brill [bril], s. (ittiol.) rombo.

brilliance ['briljəns], **brilliancy** ['briljənsi], s. 1. lucentezza, brillantezza; splendore (anche fig.) 2. vivezza d'ingegno 3. (ott.) luminosità.

brilliant ['briljənt], ag. 1. brillante, lucente 2. vivace; pieno di talento: he was a — musician, era un musicista di talento || s. 1. brillante (diamante sfaccettato) 2. taglio a brillante.

brilliantine [,briljən'ti:n], s. brillantina.

brilliantly ['briljəntli], av. 1. brillantemente, con lucentezza 2. vivacemente; con talento.

brim [brim], s. 1. orlo; bordo, margine; sponda: full to the —, pieno fino all'orlo, colmo 2. tesa, ala (di cappello).

to **brim**, pass.p.p. **brimmed** [brimd], v.t.i. 1. colmare, essere pieno fino all'orlo (anche fig.) 2. to — over, traboccare: brimming over with life, traboccante di vita; eyes brimming over with tears, occhi pieni di lacrime.

brimful ['brim'ful], ag. ricolmo, colmo; fig. pieno; colmo: prose — with adjectives, prosa gonfia, traboccante di aggettivi.

brimless ['brimlis], ag. 1. senza orlo 2. senza tesa.

brimmed [brimd], ag. 1. colmo sino all'orlo 2. con orlo, bordo, ala, tesa ☆ broad- — hat, cappello a larga tesa.

brimmer ['brimə*], s. 1. bicchiere pieno, raso 2. cappello a tesa.

brimstone ['brimstən], s. 1. (arc.) zolfo 2. fig. zolfo infernale: there was an air of — about that man, quell'uomo puzzava d'inferno, c'era qualcosa di diabolico in quell'uomo ☆ — yellow, giallo zolfo.

brimstony ['brimstəni], ag. (arc.) sulfureo.

brindle(d) ['brindl(d)], ag. macchiato, chiazzato; pezzato — cows, mucche dal mantello pezzato.

brine [brain], s. 1. acqua salmastra 2. acqua salata per salamoia 3. (poet.) mare 4. (poet.) lacrime ☆ —-pit, salina; — spring, sorgente salata.

to **brine**, v.t. mettere in salamoia.

to **bring** [briŋ], pass.p.p. **brought** [bro:t], v.t. 1. portare; condurre; recare: — him to me, conducilo da me; can you — me some water, please?, puoi portarmi dell'acqua, per favore?; I brought him the reply, gli portai la risposta; to — word to s.o., portare notizie a qlcu. || to — into question, fare entrare in discussione || to — tears (in)to s.o.'s eyes, fare venire la lacrime agli occhi di qlcu. || to — to pass, causare, far succedere || to — sthg. home to s.o., aprire gli occhi a qlcu.: his death brought home to me the value of his friendship, la sua morte mi ha fatto capire il valore della sua amicizia || to — (influence, pressure) to bear on, esercitare (influenza, pressione) su: you must — more pressure to bear on him, devi esercitare maggiore pressione su di lui; we brought out big guns to bear on the enemy, usammo i nostri potenti cannoni contro il nemico 2. indurre, persuadere: I cannot — myself to believe, non posso persuadermi a credere 3. fig. procurare: you have brought it on yourself, te lo sei tirato addosso da solo 4. addurre: I brought a new argument, addussi un nuovo motivo 5. (dir.) presentare: to — an action against s.o., intentare un processo contro qlcu.; to — a charge against s.o., presentare un'accusa contro qlcu. 6. to — about, causare, far accadere; ottenere; effettuare; conseguire: to — about a change, operare un cambiamento; to — about s.o.'s ruin, causare la rovina di qlcu.; to — about a war, provocare una guerra 7. to — along, portare, condurre con sè: may I — my child along?, posso condurre mio figlio con me? 8. to — away, portar via 9. to — back, restituire; riportare; richiamare alla memoria: her letter brings back many memories, la sua lettera mi richiama alla memoria molti ricordi 10. to — down, far scendere (prezzo, ecc.); abbattere (un albero, un aeroplano);

smorzare (l'orgoglio di qlcu.); atterrare (un avversario) || to — down the house, far crollare il teatro dagli applausi 11. to — forth, dare alla luce; causare, produrre; esibire 12. to — forward, portare avanti; produrre (un testimonio), produrre (una prova); (mat.) riportare 13. to — in, introdurre, far entrare; presentare (un progetto di legge); emettere (verdetto): to — in s.o. guilty, (dir.) dichiarare qlcu. colpevole (da parte dei giurati); to — in a verdict, emettere un verdetto 14. to — off, portar via, liberare, salvare; portare felicemente a compimento 15. to — on, produrre; cagionare (malattia); far fare dei progressi; (teat.) portare in scena: to — on a subject for discussion, introdurre un argomento di discussione; to — s.o. on for an examination, assistere qlcu. per un esame 16. to — out, portar fuori, far uscire; mettere in evidenza, dar valore a; pubblicare; esporre; lanciare (un'attrice, un brevetto); presentare (una ragazza) in società 17. to — over, trasportare; persuadere, convincere: these cloths are brought over from England, queste stoffe sono importate dall'Inghilterra; to — s.o. over to a cause, convertire qlcu. ad una causa 18. to — round, portare; persuadere; (fam.) far rinvenire 19. to — through, far passare, far attraversare; salvare (un ammalato) 20. to — to, (mar.) fermarsi (di nave); (fam.) fermare, ostacolare || to — s.o. to, far rinvenire qlcu. 21. to — together, riunire; mettere in contatto: I brought them together again, li feci riconciliare 22. to — under, sottomettere 23. to — up, far salire; vomitare; avvicinare; allevare, educare (bimbi, animali); richiamare l'attenzione su; introdurre (argomento nella conversazione); fermare, fermarsi || to — s.o. up before a court, (dir.) chiamare, citare qlcu. in tribunale.

bringer ['briŋə*], s. (arc.) portatore, latore (di notizie, ecc.).

brinish ['brainiʃ], ag. salmastro.

brinjal ['brindʒo:l], s. (ang.-in.) melanzana (pianta, frutto).

brink [briŋk], s. orlo, bordo, margine: on the — of despair, sull'orlo della disperazione; he was on the — of doing sthg. foolish, era sul punto di fare una sciocchezza.

brinkmanship ['briŋkmənʃip], s. (neol.) lo spingersi, nell'azione politica, sino all'estremo rischio di guerra.

briny ['braini], ag. salato; marino || the —, (sl.) il mare || the — deep, (poet.) il mare.

brio ['bri(:)ou], s. (mus.) brio.

brioche ['bri(:)ouʃ], s. « brioche ».

briony ['braiəni], s. (bot.) brionia; (pop.) vite bianca.

briquet ['brikit], **briquette** [bri'ket], s. mattonella, formella di carbone.

brise-bise ['bri:z'bi:z], s. « brise-bise » (tenda che ricopre la parte inferiore di una finestra).

brisk [brisk], ag. 1. vivace, vispo; svelto: — manners, modi spicci; — market, (comm.) mercato attivo; at a — pace, a passo svelto 2. frizzante: — air, aria fresca, frizzante.

to **brisk**, v.t.i. animare, animarsi; rianimare, rianimarsi: I brisked (up), mi rianimai: to — s.o. (up), rianimare, pungolare qlcu.

brisket ['briskit], s. (cuc.) punta (di petto).

briskly ['briskli], av. vivacemente; attivamente; in modo spicciativo.

briskness ['brisknis], s. vivacità; sveltezza.

brisling ['brisliŋ], s. (ittiol.) spratto.

bristle ['brisl], s. setola; pelo ruvido, duro || to set up one's bristles, cacciar fuori le unghie; andare in collera.

to **bristle**, v.t.i. 1. rizzare (peli, capelli), rizzarsi (di peli, capelli); fig. andare in collera 2. essere irto di, spinoso: his style is bristling with learned words, il suo stile è pieno, irto di parole dotte.

bristled ['brisld], ag. setoloso.

bristly ['brisli], ag. setoloso; ruvido (anche fig.).

Bristol ['bristl], no.pr. (geog.) Bristol || — board, cartoncino bristol.

Britain ['britn], *no.pr.* (*geog. st.*) Britannia ‖ (*Great*) —, Gran Bretagna.

Britannia [bri'tænjə], *no.pr.* Britannia (nome antico o simbolico della Gran Bretagna) ‖ — *metal*, lega metallica di stagno, antimonio e rame.

Britannic [bri'tænik], *ag.* britannico: *His* — *Majesty*, Sua Maestà britannica.

Briticism ['britisizəm], *s.* (*amer.*) anglicismo.

British ['britiʃ], *ag.* britannico; inglese: — *Academy*, Accademia britannica (delle scienze morali e politiche); — *Association*, Accademia britannica (delle scienze); *the* — *Empire*, l'Impero britannico; *the* — *Isles*, le Isole britanniche ‖ *the* —, gli inglesi ‖ *the* — *Channel*, la Manica.

Britisher ['britiʃə*], *s.c.* (*amer.*) persona di discendenza inglese.

Britishism ['britiʃizəm], *s.* (*amer.*) anglicismo,

Briton ['britn], *s.* (*st.*) britanno.

Brittany ['britəni], *no. pr.* (*geog.*) Bretagna.

brittle ['britl], *ag.* fragile; friabile.

brittleness ['britlnis], *s.* fragilità; friabilità.

broach[1] [broutʃ], *s.* 1. spiedo 2. (*arch.*) guglia 3. punteruolo, spina.

to broach[1], *v.t.* 1. spillare (vino, ecc.) 2. intavolare, avviare un discorso su: *I broached the subject to him*, gli accennai la cosa 3. (*mec.*) brocciare.

to broach[2], *v.t.i.* (*mar.*) straorzare.

broad [broːd], *ag.* 1. largo, ampio, esteso: *a* — *grin*, un ampio sorriso; *a* — *outlook*, ampie vedute; *in* — *daylight*, in pieno giorno; *a road thirty feet* —, una strada larga trenta piedi ‖ *it is as* — *as it is long*, è la stessa cosa ‖ *to grow* —, allargarsi ‖ *to have a* — *back*, avere le spalle robuste (anche *fig.*) 2. chiaro; ovvio: *the* — *facts*, i fatti puri e semplici; *a* — *purpose*, un'ovvia intenzione 3. marcato; rustico; volgare: — *accent*, accento marcato; — *speech*, linguaggio volgare; *a* — *story*, un racconto volgare, salace 4. tollerante, liberale ‖ *Broad Church*, chiesa liberale, latitudinaria 5. generale; principale; essenziale: *in* — *outline*, a grandi linee; *in a* — *sense that's true*, in generale ciò è vero ‖ *s.* larghezza, ampiezza: *the* — *of the back*, tutta la larghezza delle spalle.

broad, *av.* ampiamente; completamente: — *awake*, completamente sveglio.

broad, (*nei composti*): — *-arrow*, marchio che denota le proprietà dello Stato; — *-backed*, dal dorso largo; — *-brim(med)*, (cappello) dalle tese larghe; — *-faced*, dalla faccia larga; — *-lighting*, (*cine.*) illuminazione frontale; — *-minded*, di larghe vedute; — *-mindedness*, larghezza di vedute, tolleranza; — *-shouldered*, dalle spalle larghe; — *-walk*, lungomare.

broadcast ['broːdkaːst], *ag.* 1. (*agr.*) seminato; sparso (anche *fig.*) 2. radiodiffuso ‖ *s.* 1. (*agr.*) semina (per spargimento) 2. (*rad.*) radiodiffusione; radiocomunicazione; programma, audizione radiofonica ☆ — *account*, radiocronaca; — *announcement*, comunicazione radiofonica.

to broadcast, *pass. p.p.* **broadcast**, *nel senso* 2.

broadcasted ['broːd,kaːstid], *v.t.* 1. seminare (spargendo le sementi); *fig.* disseminare, divulgare 2. radiodiffondere, trasmettere per radio.

broadcast, *av.* in modo sparso; largamente.

broadcaster ['broːd,kaːstə*], *s.* (*rad.*) apparecchio trasmittente, trasmettitore ‖ *s.c.* chi parla alla radio.

broadcasting ['broːd,kaːstiŋ], *s.* 1. (*agr.*) seminagione (per spargimento) 2. (*rad.*) radiodiffusione ‖ *British Broadcasting Corporation* (*abbr. B.B.C.*), Ente Radiofonico Britannico ☆ — *station*, stazione radiotrasmittente.

broadcloth ['broːdkloθ], *s.* fine panno nero (generalmente per uomo).

to broaden ['broːdn], *v.t.i.* allargare, allargarsi; spandere. spandersi.

broadly ['broːdli], *av.* largamente; ampiamente; — *speaking*, parlando in generale.

broadness ['broːdnis], *s.* 1. larghezza 2. grossolanità, volgarità.

broadsheet ['broːdʃiːt], *s.* manifesto.

broadside ['broːdsaid], *s.* (*mar.*) bordata; murata.

broadsword ['broːdsoːd], *s.* sciabola.

Broadway ['broːdwei], *no. pr.* Broadway (strada di New York famosa per i teatri, i locali notturni, ecc.).

broadways ['broːdweiz], **broadwise** ['broːdwaiz], *av.* nel senso della larghezza.

Brobdingnag ['brobdiŋnæg], *no.pr.* (*lett.*) Brobdingnag.

brocade [brə'keid], *s.* broccato.

to brocade, *v.t.* (*arc.*) broccare.

brocaded [brə'keidid], *ag.* di broccato.

brochure ['brouʃjuə*], *s.* opuscolo.

brock [brok], *s.* (*zool.*) tasso; *fig.* puzzone.

brocket ['brokit], *s.* cerbiatto dalle corna dritte (nel secondo anno di vita).

bro(c)coli ['brokəli], *s.* broccolo.

brogue[1] [broug], *s.* 1. rozza scarpa di cuoio grezzo (usata dai contadini irlandesi e dai montanari scozzesi) 2. scarpa chiodata per il golf ☆ *fishing brogues*, stivaloni impermeabili per la pesca.

brogue[2], *s.* (*spec. irl.*) cadenza dialettale.

to broider ['broidə*], (*arc. poet.*) per **to embroider**.

broidery ['broidəri], (*arc. poet.*) per **embroidery**.

broil[1] [broil], *s.* rissa; tumulto.

to broil[1], *v.t.i.* coinvolgere in risse o tumulti, essere coinvolto in una rissa.

broil[2], *s.* carne arrostita alla griglia o allo spiedo

to broil[2], *v.t.i.* 1. cuocere carne alla griglia o allo spiedo 2. essere esposto a grande calore.

broiler[1] ['broilə*], *s.* fomentatore di risse.

broiler[2], *s.* 1. graticola 2. pollastro da arrostire.

brokage ['broukidʒ], *s.* mediazione, senseria.

broke [brouk], *pass.* (*arc.*) *p.p.* di **to break** ‖ *ag.* (*sl.*) squattrinato; rovinato ‖ *to go* —, fallire; far bancarotta.

broken ['broukən], *p.p.* di **break** ‖ *ag.* 1. rotto, spezzato, interrotto (anche *fig.*): *a* — *promise*, una promessa mancata; *I fear his leg is* —, temo si sia rotto la gamba; *she wept and told her story in* — *tones*, pianse e raccontò la sua storia con voce rotta ‖ *a* — *sleep*, un sonno agitato 2. incerto, variabile (di tempo); ineguale, accidentato (di terreno); increspato (di acque) 3. indebolito, deperito: — *health*, salute debole, malferma 4. accorato, avvilito, scoraggiato: *a* — *man*, un uomo finito 5. scorretto: — *English*, inglese scorretto ☆ — *-backed*, dalla schiena rotta; — *-down*, avvilito; finito, rovinato; — *-hearted*, dal cuore spezzato; — *meats*, avanzi (di pranzo, ecc.); — *money*, moneta spicciola; — *numbers*, frazioni; — *-week*, settimana interrotta da una festa; — *-winded*, ansante; bolso (di cavallo).

brokenly ['broukənli], *av.* a scatti; interrottamente; ad intervalli; irregolarmente.

broker ['broukə*], *s.* (*comm.*) 1. sensale, mediatore 2. agente, commissionario ☆ *ship-* —, mediatore di noleggi marittimi; *stock-* — agente di cambio.

brokerage ['broukəridʒ], *s.* senseria, mediazione.

broking ['broukiŋ], *s.* commercio di mediatore.

brolly ['broli], *s.* (*sl.*) ombrello.

bromate ['broumeit], *s.* (*chim.*) bromato.

bromic ['broumik], *ag.* (*chim.*) bromico.

bromide ['broumaid], *s.* 1. (*chim.*) bromuro 2. (*sl. amer.*) persona noiosa; banalità; convenzionalismo.

bromine ['broumiːn], *s.* (*chim.*) bromo.

bromism ['broumizəm], *s.* (*patol.*) bromismo.

to bromize ['broumaiz], *v.t.* (*chim.*) trattare con bromo.

bronchi ['broŋkai], **bronchia** ['broŋkiə], *s.pl.* (*anat.*) bronchi.

bronchial ['broŋkjəl], *ag.* bronchiale.

bronchitic [broŋ'kitik], *ag.* di bronchite; affetto da bronchite.

bronchitis [broŋ'kaitis], *s.* (*patol.*) bronchite.

bronchocele ['brɔŋkəsi:l], *s.* (*patol.*) gozzo.

broncho-pneumonia ['brɔŋkounju(:)'mounjə], *s.* (*patol.*) broncopolmonite.

bronchotomist [brɔŋ'kɔtəmist], *s.* (*chir.*) colui che pratica la broncotomia.

bronchotomy [brɔŋ'kɔtəmi], *s.* (*chir.*) broncotomia.

bronco ['brɔŋkou], *s.* (*amer.*) cavallo selvaggio.

brontosaurus [,brɔntə'sɔ:rəs], *s.* (*paleont.*) brontosauro.

Bronx [brɔŋks], *no.pr.* Bronx (quartiere di New York) || *s.* «Bronx» (cocktail di gin, vermut e succo d'arancia).

bronze [brɔnz], *s.* **1.** bronzo; oggetto, opera in bronzo || *the — age*, l'età del bronzo **2.** color bronzo **3.** *fig.* sfacciataggine, impudenza; faccia di bronzo.

to **bronze**, *v.t.i.* **1.** bronzare; brunire; abbronzare, abbronzarsi **2.** (*foto.*) metallizzare.

bronzing ['brɔnziŋ], *s.* abbronzatura.

bronzy ['brɔnzi], *ag.* bronzeo.

brooch [broutʃ], *s.* fermaglio, spilla.

brood [bru:d], *s.* **1.** covata, nidiata; (*scherz.*) prole, figliolanza **2.** sciame; turba **3.** (*ittiol.*) razza ☆ *— -hen*, chioccia; *— -mare*, cavalla di razza.

to **brood**, *v.t.i.* **1.** covare **2.** *fig.* rimuginare, meditare: *you must not — over your sorrows*, non devi rimuginare troppo sui tuoi dolori || *there is sthg. brooding*, gatta ci cova.

brooder ['bru:də*], *s.* **1.** chioccia **2.** (*amer.*) incubatrice || *s.c.* chi medita.

broodiness ['bru:dinis], *s.* tendenza a covare.

broody ['bru:di], *ag.* **1.** che vuole covare (di gallina) **2.** *fig.* meditabondo, che rimugina.

brook¹ [bruk], *s.* ruscello.

to **brook²**, *v.t.* tollerare, soffrire, sopportare: *the matter brooks no delay*, la faccenda non ammette ritardo alcuno.

brooklet ['bruklit], *s.* ruscelletto.

Brooklyn ['bruklin], *s.* Brooklyn (quartiere popolare di New York).

broom [bru:m], *s.* **1.** (*bot.*) ginestra **2.** scopa || *a new — sweeps clean*, *prov.* scopa nuova scopa bene ☆ *— -land*, brughiera; *— stick*, manico di scopa || *butcher's —*, (*bot.*) pungitopo; *dyer's —*, (*bot.*) ginestra dei tintori; *prickly —*, (*bot.*) ginestrone.

to **broom**, *v.t.* scopare.

broth [brɔθ], *s.* brodo: *thin —*, brodo leggero || *a — of a girl*, (*irl.*) una perla di ragazza.

brothel ['brɔθl], *s.* casa di malaffare, bordello.

brother ['brʌðə*], *pl. nel senso* **3.** **brethren** ['breðrin], *s.* **1.** fratello: *elder —*, fratello maggiore; *younger —*, fratello minore **2.** collega; camerata **3.** confratello: *my dearly beloved brethren*, (*eccl.*) miei benamati confratelli ☆ *— -german*, fratello germano; *— -in-arms*, commilitone, compagno d'armi; *— -in-law*, cognato || *foster —*, fratello di latte; *half —*, fratellastro; *lay —*, frate laico, converso.

brotherhood ['brʌðəhud], *s.* **1.** fratellanza; cameratismo; amor fraterno **2.** confraternita.

brotherless ['brʌðəlis], *ag.* senza fratelli.

brotherlike ['brʌðəlaik], *ag.* fraterno.

brotherliness ['brʌðəlinis], *s.* fratellanza.

brotherly ['brʌðəli], *ag.* fraterno.

brotherly, *av.* fraternamente.

brougham ['bru(:)əm], *s.* **1.** «brum» (carrozza chiusa) **2.** limousine (automobile con guida esterna).

brought [brɔ:t], *pass.p.p.* di to **bring**.

brow¹ [brau], *s.* **1.** fronte **2.** *pl.* sopracciglia: *to pucker* (o *to knit*) *one's brows*, aggrottare le sopracciglia **3.** orlo (di precipizio, di scarpata, ecc.) **4.** cima, sommità di rampa stradale ☆ *high- —*, (*fam.*) intellettuale; *low - —*, (*fam.*) persona di scarsi interessi intellettuali.

brow², *s.* (*mar.*) passerella.

to **browbeat** ['braubi:t], *pass.* **browbeat**, *p.p.* **browbeaten** ['braubi:tn], *v.t.* guardare con cipiglio; intimidire (con parole, sguardi).

browed [braud], *ag.* munito di sopracciglia ☆ *heavy - —*, con sopracciglia folte; *high- —*, dalla fronte alta.

browless ['braulis], *ag.* senza sopracciglia.

brown [braun], *ag.* **1.** bruno; marrone; castano: *— bear*, orso bruno; *— eyes*, occhi castani; *— shoes*, scarpe gialle || *Brown Bess*, (*sl.*) «Brown Bess» (vecchio tipo di moschetto) || *— study*, meditazione, fantasticheria: *to be in a — study*, essere assorto nei propri pensieri || *to do —*, rosolare **2.** scuro; abbronzato ☆ *— bread*, pane integrale; *— coal*, lignite; *— paper*, carta d'imballaggio; *— sugar*, zucchero grezzo; *— ware*, terracotta.

brown, *s.* **1.** color bruno, marrone **2.** (*sl.*) moneta di rame.

to **brown**, *v.t.i.* render bruno, diventare bruno; abbronzare, abbronzarsi; rosolare ☆ *browned off*, (*sl.*) annoiato, scocciato.

brownie ['brauni], *s.* **1.** folletto **2.** giovane esploratrice **3.** «brownie» (tipo di macchina fotografica).

Browning ['brauniŋ], *s.* «Browning» (rivoltella automatica).

brownish ['brauniʃ], *ag.* brunastro.

Brownists ['braunists], *s.* (*st. relig.*) seguaci di Robert Brown (che fondò una setta nel 1580).

brownness ['braunnis], *s.* color bruno, marrone.

brownstone ['braun,stoun], *s.* (*edil.*) tipo di arenaria di colore rossastro per costruzioni.

browse [brauz], *s.* **1.** (*bot.*) pollone; tenero germoglio **2.** brucatura.

to **browse**, *v.t.i.* **1.** pascersi di polloni; brucare **2.** *fig.* scorrere libri, leggere per diletto: *to — among books*, curiosare fra i libri.

browsing ['brauziŋ], *ag.* pascolante || *s.* **1.** il brucare **2.** *fig.* il leggere a spizzico.

bruise [bru:z], *s.* ammaccatura; contusione.

to **bruise**, *v.t.i.* **1.** ammaccare, ammaccarsi; schiacciare, stritolare, frantumare, tritare; battere (un metallo) **2.** (*caccia*) cavalcare a rotta di collo.

bruised [bru:zd], *ag.* ammaccato; contuso: *— all over*, tutto ammaccato.

bruiser ['bru:zə*], *s.* **1.** pugile (combattente senza guanti); *fig.* persona prepotente; uomo combattivo **2.** macinatrice; frantoio, frantumatrice.

bruising ['bru:ziŋ], *s.* ammaccatura; contusione.

bruit [bru:t], *s.* **1.** (*arc.*) rumore, diceria **2.** (*med.*) rumori anormali percepiti all'auscultazione.

to **bruit**, *v.t.* (*arc.*) spargere, divulgare (rumore, diceria): *it was bruised that...*, correva voce che....

Brumaire [,brju:'mɛə*], *s.* (*st. francese*) brumaio.

brumby ['brʌmbi], *s.* (*austral.*) cavallo non domato.

Brummagem ['brʌmədʒəm], *ag.s.* (*dial. spreg.*) (articolo) vistoso e da poco prezzo (bigiotteria, ecc.).

brumous ['bru:məs], *ag.* brumale; invernale; brumoso.

brunch [brʌntʃ], *s.* (*sl. contr.* di *breakfast* e *lunch*) pasto che sostituisce la prima e la seconda colazione.

Brunei [bru:'nai], *no.pr.* (*geog.*) Brunei.

brunette [bru:'net], *ag.s.* bruna, brunetta.

Brunhild ['bru:nhilt], *no.pr.f.* (*lett.*) Brunilde.

Bruno ['bru:nou], *no.pr.m.* Bruno.

brunt [brʌnt], *s.* urto, scontro.

brush [brʌʃ], *s.* **1.** spazzola; spazzolino **2.** spazzolata, colpo di spazzola **3.** pennello; *fig.* pittura: *from the same — *, dello stesso pennello **4.** (*elett.*) spazzola, scarico a fiocco; (*fis.*) fascio di raggi luce **5.** *fig.* rissa, scontro, schermaglia: *a — with the enemy*, uno scontro con il nemico **6.** coda folta (specialmente di volpe) **7.** (*arc. amer. austral.*) boscaglia, sottobosco, sterpaglia ☆ *— -down*, spazzolata (in giù, degli abiti), strigliatura; *— -up*, spazzolata (in su, ai capelli, ecc.), ripasso (di studio, di lingua) || *clothes- —*, spazzola per abiti; *hair- —*, spazzola per capelli; *point- —*, pennello per dipingere; *shaving- —*, pennello da barba.

to **brush**, *v.t.i.* **1.** spazzolare: *to — one's hair*, spazzolarsi i capelli **2.** *to — against* (o *by* o *past*) (*s.o.*, *sthg.*), rasentare, sfiorare **3.** *to — aside*, scostare; *fig.* passar sopra a, ignorare **4.** *to* — **away**, spazzar via; asciugarsi (una lacrima) **5.** *to* — **over**, dipingere con leggeri tocchi di pennello **6.** *to* — **up**, spazzolare accuratamente; *fig.* rinfrescare (la memoria), rivedere, rileggere, ripassare: — *up your English*, rinfresca, ripassa il tuo inglese.

brushwood ['brʌʃwud], *s.* macchia; sottobosco.

brushy ['brʌʃi], *ag.* **1.** setoloso; ispido **2.** fitto, folto (di boscaglia).

brusque [brusk], *ag.* brusco; rude.

brusquely ['bruskli], *av.* bruscamente, rudemente.

brusqueness ['brusknis], **brusquerie** [ˌbru:skə'ri:], *s.* rudezza; asprezza.

Brussels ['brʌslz], *no.pr.* (*geog.*) Bruxelles ☆ — *carpet*, tappeto di Bruxelles; — *lace*, pizzo di Bruxelles; — *sprouts*, cavolini di Bruxelles.

brutal ['bru:tl], *ag.* brutale.

brutalism ['bru:təlizəm], *s.* brutalità.

brutality [bru:'tæliti], *s.* brutalità.

brutalization [ˌbru:təlai'zeiʃən], *s.* abbrutimento.

to **brutalize** ['bru:təlaiz], *v.t.i.* **1.** imbestialire, imbestialirsi; abbrutire, abbrutirsi **2.** brutalizzare.

brutally ['bru:təli], *av.* brutalmente.

brute [bru:t], *ag.* brutale, selvaggio, animale ‖ *s.* bruto.

brutification [ˌbru:tifi'keiʃən], *s.* abbrutimento.

to **brutify** ['bru:tifai], *v.t.i.* abbrutire, abbrutirsi.

brutish ['bru:tiʃ], *ag.* **1.** brutale, bestiale; abbrutito **2.** rozzo; ignorante.

brutishly ['bru:tiʃli], *av.* brutalmente; bestialmente.

brutishness ['bru:tiʃnis], *s.* **1.** abbrutimento **2.** brutalità.

Brutus ['bru:təs], *no.pr.m.* (*st.*) Bruto.

bryologist [brai'ɔlədʒist], *s.* studioso di briologia.

bryology [brai'ɔlədʒi], *s.* briologia.

bryony ['braiəni], *s.* (*bot.*) brionia; (*pop.*) vite bianca.

bubal ['bju:bəl], *s.* (*zool.*) bubalo.

bubble ['bʌbl], *s.* **1.** bolla (d'aria, di sapone, ecc.); cavità visibile (nel vetro, nell'ambra, ecc.) **2.** gorgoglio (di liquido in ebollizione) **3.** *fig.* sogno; chimera **4.** impostura, frode ☆ — *car*, piccola automobile utilitaria.

to **bubble**, *v.t.i.* **1.** (far) gorgogliare; ribollire; spumeggiare **2.** ingannare (con progetti inconsistenti) **3.** *to* — **over**, traboccare ‖ *to* — *over with laughter*, scoppiare dal ridere **4.** *to* — **up**, gorgogliare; scaturire (di sorgente).

bubbling ['bʌbliŋ], *s.* gorgogliamento; ribollimento.

bubbly ['bʌbli], *ag.* pieno di bolle; che emette bolle ‖ *s.* (*fam.*) champagne ☆ — *jock*, (*scoz.*) tacchino.

bubo ['bju:bou], *s.* bubbone.

bubonic [bju(:)'bɔnik], *ag.* bubbonico ☆ — *plague*, peste bubbonica.

bubonocele [bju(:)'bɔnəsi:l], *s.* ernia inguinale.

buccal ['bʌkəl], *ag.* delle guance, della bocca.

buccaneer [ˌbʌkə'niə*], *s.* bucaniere, filibustiere.

to **buccaneer**, *v.i.* pirateggiare.

buccaneering [ˌbʌkə'niəriŋ], *s.* pirateria.

buccaneerish [ˌbʌkə'niəriʃ], *ag.* piratesco.

buccinator ['bʌksineitə*], *s.* (*anat.*) buccinatorio.

Bucephalus [bju(:)'sefələs], *no.pr.m.* (*mit.*) Bucefalo ‖ *s.* (*iron.*) cavallo.

Bucharest ['bjukərest], *no.pr.* (*geog.*) Bucarest.

buck[1] [bʌk], *s.* **1.** daino; cervo; caprone; maschio di antilope, renna, coniglio, lepre **2.** *fig.* zerbinotto **3.** (*sl. amer.*) maschio **4.** (*sl. amer.*) pellerossa; negro ☆ — *nigger*, (*amer.*) negro; — *private*, (*amer.*) soldato semplice; — *-shot*, pallini per cartucce da caccia; — *-teeth*, denti sporgenti.

to **buck**[1], *v.t.* accoppiarsi con (detto di caprone, maschio di daino, cervo, antilope, renna, coniglio, lepre).

to **buck**[2], *v.t.i.* **1.** saltare col dorso arcuato, impennarsi (di cavallo) **2.** (*sl. aer.*) cabrare **3.** *to* — **off**, gettare di sella, disarcionare.

buck[3], *s.* cestone per pescare le anguille.

buck[4], *s.* carrozzeria (di una carrozza) ☆ — *cart*, carrozza lunga, piatta.

buck[5], *s.* intelaiatura a croce ☆ — *-saw*, sega da falegname.

buck[6], *s.* (*sl. poker*) gettone ‖ *to pass the* — *to s.o.*, scaricare su di un altro la propria responsabilità.

buck[7], *s.* (*sl. amer.*) dollaro.

to **buck**[8], *v.t.i.* (*sl.*) **1.** affrettarsi: — *up!*, sbrigati! **2.** rincuorare, rincuorarsi; rallegrare, rallegrarsi; rinvigorire, rinvigorirsi.

to **buck**[9], *v.i.* chiacchierare, vantarsi.

to **buck**[10], *v.t.* frantumare (minerale).

buckbean ['bʌkbi:n], *s.* (*bot.*)trifoglio acquatico.

buckboard ['bʌkbɔ:d], *s.* carro a quattro ruote.

bucker[1] ['bʌkə*], *s.* cavallo che si impenna, riottoso.

bucker[2], *s.* martello per rompere un minerale.

bucket ['bʌkit], *s.* **1.** secchio, secchia ‖ *to give the* —, (*sl.*) licenziare ‖ *to kick the* —, (*sl.*) crepare **2.** (*mec.*) tazza; benna; pistone valvolato; paletta mobile; cucchiaia (di draga) **3.** (*mar.*) bugliolo ☆ — *-seat*, sedile con schienale (di auto, aereo); — *-shop*, (*comm.*) agenzia di cambio clandestina.

to **bucket**, *v.t.i.* **1.** portare (acqua) in secchi **2.** cavalcare sfrenatamente; forzare (il cavallo) **3.** remare con ritmo affrettato; (*fam.*) affrettarsi **4.** (*comm.*) fare affari (di borsa) clandestinamente **5.** (*sl.*) ingannare.

bucketful ['bʌkitful], *s.* secchiata.

buckhorn ['bʌkhɔ:n], *s.* corno di daino (per manichi).

Buckingham Palace ['bʌkiŋəm'pælis], *s.* «Buckingham Palace» (residenza londinese dei re d'Inghilterra).

buckish ['bʌkiʃ], *ag.* **1.** caprino **2.** vanitoso.

buckle ['bʌkl], *s.* fibbia; fermaglio.

to **buckle**, *v.t.i.* **1.** affibbiare, affibbiarsi; allacciare con fibbia, allacciarsi **2.** indossare (l'armatura); affibbiare (la spada): *to* — (*on*) *one's sword*, cingere la spada **3.** curvare, curvarsi; piegarsi; deformarsi (di metalli per calore): *buckled with the heat of the fire*, piegato per il calore del fuoco **4.** *to* — **down**, accingersi, disporsi: *to* — *down to work*, mettersi al lavoro.

buckler ['bʌklə*], *s.* scudo; *fig.* protezione.

to **buckler**, *v.t.* fare scudo a; *fig.* proteggere.

buckram ['bʌkrəm], *s.* **1.** tela da fusto; garza rigida (per forme di capelli, per rilegare i libri, ecc.) **2.** durezza, rigidezza di maniere **3.** parvenza di forza.

to **buckram**, *v.t.* rinforzare con tela da fusto.

buckshee ['bʌkʃi:], *av.* (*sl.*) gratuitamente ‖ *s.* (*sl. mil.*) razione supplementare; paga supplementare.

buckskin ['bʌkskin], *s.* pelle di daino, antilope, renna.

buckwheat ['bʌkwi:t], *s.* grano saraceno.

bucolic [bju(:)'kɔlik], *ag.* bucolico, agreste, pastorale ‖ *s.* **1.** (*poes.*) bucolica ‖ *the Bucolics*, le Bucoliche **2.** poeta pastorale **3.** (*iron.*) contadino.

bucolically [bju(:)'kɔlikəli], *av.* alla maniera bucolica.

bud [bʌd], *s.* **1.** gemma; germoglio;bottone, boccio, bocciuolo: *in the* —, in boccio: *poets in the* —, poeti in erba ‖ *a young Mayfair* —, una debuttante di Mayfair ‖ *to nip sthg. in the* —, troncare ql.co. sul nascere **2.** (*bot. zool.*) germe; cellula **3.** (*sl. amer.*) ragazza.

to **bud**, *pass.p.p.* **budded** ['bʌdid], *v.t.i.* **1.** germogliare, spuntare (di gemme); sbocciare **2.** *fig.* nascere, svilupparsi: *a budding lawyer*, un avvocato in erba **3.** innestare (piante, fiori); fare innesti.

Buddha ['budə], *no.pr.m.* (*st. relig.*) Budda.

Buddhism ['budizəm], *s.* buddismo.

Buddhist ['budist], *ag.* buddistico ‖ *s.* buddista.

Buddhistic(al) [bu'distik(əl)], *ag.* buddistico.

budding ['bʌdiŋ], *s.* riproduzione per innesto.

buddy ['bʌdi], *s.* (*sl. amer.*) camerata; fratello.

to **budge** [bʌdʒ], *v.t.i.* **1.** scostarsi: *he refused to* —, si rifiutò di muoversi; *won't* — *an inch*, non indietreggerò di un centimetro **2.** smuovere, scostare: *she can't* — *the heavy door*, non riesce a smuovere la pesante porta; *I can't* — *him*, non riesco a smuoverlo.

budget ['bʌdʒit], *s.* **1.** *gener. fig.* fascio, sacco: *a* — *of news*, un sacco di notizie **2.** raccolta (di documenti) **3.** (*pol. comm.*) bilancio preventivo ‖ *the* (*State*) —, il bilancio (dello Stato); *to introduce the* —, presentare il bilancio **4.** preventivo di cassa ☆ *household* —, (*fam.*) entrate ed uscite, contabilità di casa.

to **budget**, *v.i.* fare un bilancio preventivo: *to* — *for an expenditure*, stanziare una spesa nel bilancio.

budless ['bʌdlis], *ag.* senza gemme; senza bocciuoli.

budlet ['bʌdlit], *s.* piccola gemma; bocciuolo.

buff¹ [bʌf], *ag.* **1.** scamosciato **2.** marrone ‖ *s.* **1.** pelle scamosciata di bufalo, di bovino **2.** color camoscio ‖ *the Buffs*, reggimento del Kent orientale (dal colore dei risvolti della giacca) **3.** la nuda pelle: *in* —, nudo; *stripped to the* —, denudato ☆ — -*jerkin*, farsetto di cuoio.

to **buff¹**, *v.t.* **1.** lucidare (un metallo) con pelle scamosciata; (*mec.*) brillantare **2.** scamosciare.

buff², *s.* (*rar.*) buffetto, colpetto ☆ *blind-man's* —, mosca cieca.

buffalo ['bʌfəlou], *s.* **1.** bufalo **2.** (*mar. mil.*) mezzo corazzato anfibio.

buffer¹ ['bʌfə*], *s.* (*tec.*) pulitrice.

buffer², *s.* (*mec. ferr.*) respingente, paracolpi ‖ — *State*, Stato cuscinetto.

buffer³, *s.* (*sl. spreg.*) individuo inetto, imbecille: *old* —, vecchio imbecille.

buffet¹ ['bʌfit], *s.* schiaffo; *fig.* colpo avverso.

to **buffet¹**, *v.t.i.* **1.** schiaffeggiare **2.** lottare, lottare contro: *to* — (*with*) *the waves*, lottare con le onde.

buffet², *nel senso* **2.** ['bufei], *s.* **1.** credenza **2.** « buffet », tavola di rinfreschi ☆ *cold* —, cibi freddi.

buffo ['bufou], *ag.* comico ‖ *s.* buffo (cantante comico di opera lirica).

buffoon [bʌ'fu:n], *s.* buffone.

to **buffoon**, *v.i.* fare il buffone.

buffoonery [bʌ'fu:nəri], *s.* buffoneria, buffonata.

bug [bʌg], *s.* cimice; (*amer.*) piccolo insetto ‖ *a big* —, (*sl.*) una persona importante ☆ — -*hunter*, entomologo.

bugaboo ['bʌgəbu:[, **bugbear** ['bʌgbɛə*], *s.* spauracchio, babau.

bugger ['bʌgə*], *s.* **1.** sodomita **2.** (*volg.*) individuo; mendicante.

to **bugger**, *v.t.i.* sodomitare (con).

buggery ['bʌgəri], *s.* sodomia.

buggy¹ ['bʌgi], *ag.* pieno di cimici.

buggy², *s.* **1.** carrozzino (scoperto) **2.** carretto.

bugle¹ ['bju:gl], *s.* tromba.

to **bugle¹**, *v.t.i.* suonare la tromba; chiamare a raccolta a suon di tromba.

bugle², *s.* (*bot.*) bugola.

bugle³, *s.* perlina (di vetro).

bugler ['bju:glə*], *s.* trombettiere.

buglet ['bju:glit], *s.* cornetta (da bicicletta).

bugloss ['bju:glos], *s.* (*bot.*) buglossa.

buhl [bu:l], *ag.* intarsiato in oro, ottone, tartaruga ‖ *s.* tessera in oro, ottone, tartaruga (per intarsio).

build [bild], *s.* **1.** costruzione, stile di un edificio **2.** corporatura: *a man of my* —, un uomo della mia corporatura ☆ — -*up*, l'attribuire una buona reputazione (spesso non meritata); (*sl.*) campagna pubblicitaria.

to **build**, *pass.p.p.* **built** [bilt], *v.t.i.* **1.** costruire (anche *fig.*); fabbricare, edificare; nidificare: *the house is being built*, la casa si è in costruzione; *to* — *castles in the air*, fare castelli in aria; *to* — *a theory on facts*, fondare una teoria sui fatti ‖ *he's built that way*, (*fam.*) è fatto così **2.** *to* — *in*, incorporare, incassare, murare **3.** *to* — *up*, murare; costruire (anche *fig.*).

builder ['bildə*], *s.* costruttore (anche *fig.*); capomastro.

building ['bildiŋ], *ag.* edile; edilizio ‖ *s.* **1.** edificio, costruzione, fabbricato **2.** il costruire, il fabbricare ☆ — -*lot*, area fabbricabile; — -*materials*, materiali da costruzione; — *society*, credito edilizio ‖ *cheap* —, casa popolare.

built [bilt], *pass.p.p.* di to **build** ‖ *ag.* formato ☆ — -*up area*, agglomerato urbano ‖ *well-* —, ben disposto, ben piantato.

bulb [bʌlb], *s.* **1.** (*bot. anat.*) bulbo **2.** lampadina elettrica ☆ — *socket*, portalampada ‖ *hair-* —, bulbo dei capelli; *rubber* —, pera di gomma; *sixty candle -power* —, lampadina di sessanta candele.

to **bulb**, *v.i.* gonfiarsi in forma di bulbo; produrre bulbi.

bulbiferous [bʌl'bifərəs], *ag.* che produce bulbi.

bulbiform ['bʌlbifo:m], *ag.* bulbiforme.

bulbous ['bʌlbəs], *ag.* bulboso.

bulbul ['bulbul], *s.* usignolo dell'Oriente; *fig.* cantore, poeta.

Bulgaria [bʌl'gɛəriə], *no.pr.* (*geog.*) Bulgaria.

bulge [bʌldʒ], *s.* **1.** convessità; gonfiore; protuberanza **2.** (*sl.*) vantaggio: *to have* (o *to get*) *the* — *on*, avere un vantaggio su.

to **bulge**, *v.t.i.* gonfiare, gonfiarsi: *to* — (*out*), sporgere.

bulger ['bʌldʒə*], *s.* « bulger » (mazza da golf).

bulginess ['bʌldʒinis], *s.* gonfiore; protuberanza.

bulging ['buldʒiŋ], *ag.* gonfio; protuberante, sporgente: — *eyes*, occhi sporgenti.

bulgy ['bʌldʒi], *ag.* rigonfio; protuberante.

bulimia [bju'limiə], **bulimy** ['bju:limi], *s.* (*patol.*) bulimia (anche *fig.*).

bulk [bʌlk], *s.* **1.** (*mar.*) carico: *to load* (*a ship*) *in* —, caricare una nave con merce sciolta **2.** grande massa, volume: *of vast* —, di notevole grossezza; *to buy, to sell in* —, comprare, vendere all'ingrosso **3.** la maggior parte: *the* — *of the army*, il grosso dell'esercito; *the* — *of mankind*, la maggior parte dell'umanità; *to leave the* — *of one's fortune to s.o.*, lasciare a qlcu. la maggior parte delle proprie ricchezze.

to **bulk**, *v.t.i.* **1.** essere grande, importante ‖ *to* — *large*, occupare un posto importante **2.** ammassare **3.** verificare il peso del contenuto di (una cassa, alla dogana) **4.** *to* — *up*, ammontare.

bulkhead ['bʌlkhed], *s.* (*mar.*) paratia, compartimento ☆ *collision* —, paratia di collisione; *watertight* —, paratia stagna.

bulkily ['bʌlkili], *av.* voluminosamente.

bulkiness ['bʌlkinis], *s.* voluminosità; l'essere ingombrante.

bulky ['bʌlki], *ag.* massiccio, voluminoso.

bull¹ [bul], *s.* **1.** toro; maschio (di alcuni mammiferi) ‖ *a* — *in a china shop*, chi agisce goffamente in faccende delicate ‖ *to take the* — *by the horns*, prendere il toro per le corna, affrontare una situazione con decisione ‖ *the Bull*, (*astr.*) il Toro **2.** (*Borsa*) rialzista ☆ — -*calf*, torello; — -*finch*, (*ornit.*) ciuffolotto; — -*headed*, ostinato; — -*ring*, arena; — -*'s-eye*, oblò; centro di bersaglio; lente sporgente; lanterna a lente sporgente; — -*terrier*, incrocio fra il mastino e il terrier; — -*trout*, (*ittiol.*) trota marina.

to **bull¹**, *v.t.i.* (*Borsa*) speculare al rialzo; cercare di fare rialzare il prezzo di (titoli).

bull², *s.* (*eccl.*) bolla pontificia.

bull³, *s.* discorso inconsistente, contraddittorio; il saltare di palo in frasca; freddura.

bull⁴, *s.* bevanda fatta con acqua aromatizzata in un barile da liquori.

bullace ['bulis], *s.* (*bot.*) **1.** susina selvatica **2.** susino selvatico.

bullate ['buleit] *ag.* **1.** (*bot.*) gonfio **2.** (*fisiol.*) coperto di vescichette.

bulldog ['buldog], *s.* **1.** bulldog, mastino **2.** censore (a Oxford, Cambridge) **3.** grossa rivoltella.

bulldozer ['bul,douzə*], *s.* **1.** (*mec.*) fucinatrice **2.** apripista.

bullet ['bulit], *s.* pallottola ☆ — -*proof*, blindato ‖ *explosive* —, pallottola esplosiva.

bulletin ['bulitin], *s.* bollettino, comunicato ☆ *news* —, (*rad.*) giornale radio; *war* —, comunicato di guerra.

bullfight ['bul-fait], *s.* corrida.

bullfighter ['bul-faitə*], *s.* torero.

bullfighting ['bul-faitiŋ], *s.* tauromachia.

bullfrog ['bul-frog], *s.* rana gigante.

bullion[1] ['buljən], *s.* oro, argento in verghe.
bullion[2], *s.* frangia d'oro, d'argento.
bullock ['buløk], *s.* manzo.
bully[1] ['buli], *ag.* 1. borioso 2. (*sl. amer.*) magnifico, splendido ‖ — *for you!*, bravo te! ‖ *s.* spaccone, bravaccio, bullo ‖ *s.c.* persona prepotente e crudele.
to bully[1], *v.t.i.* 1. fare lo spaccone, il bullo 2. comandare, tiranneggiare: *to — s.o. into doing sthg.*, costringere qlcu. a fare ql.co.
bully[2], *s.* manzo lesso in scatola.
to bullyrag ['buliræg], *pass.p.p.* **bullyragged** ['bulirægd], *V.* to **ballyrag**.
bulrush ['bulrʌʃ], *s.* giunco (di palude, ecc.).
bulwark ['bulwøk], *s.* 1. bastione, spalto; baluardo (anche *fig.*) 2. (*mar.*) parapetto.
bum[1] [bʌm], *s.* (*volg.*) deretano.
bum[2], *ag.* (*amer.*) di cattiva qualità ‖ *s.* 1. ozioso, disutile, mangiapane a ufo; vagabondo: *to go on the —*, vivere alle spalle della comunità 2. (*sl.*) individuo dissoluto.
to bum[2], *pass.p.p.* **bummed** [bʌmd], *v.t.i.* 1. (*amer.*) vivere alle spalle della comunità; oziare 2. (*sl.*) scroccare.
bumble[1] ['bʌmbl], *s.* 1. bidello 2. (*spreg.*) piccolo funzionario borioso.
to bumble[2], *v.i.* (*arc.*) ronzare.
bumble-bee ['bʌmblbi:], *s.* calabrone.
bumble-puppy ['bʌmbl͵pʌpi], *s.* tennis, «whist» giocati senza seguirne le regole.
bumbo ['bʌmbou], *s.* ponce al rum freddo.
bumboat ['bʌmbout], *s.* barca dei viveri.
bumkin ['bʌmkin], *s.* (*mar.*) buttafuori.
bummaree [͵bumə'ri:], *s.* facchino del mercato di Smithfield, Londra.
bump[1] [bʌmp], *s.* 1. urto, colpo 2. enfiagione, protuberanza; bernoccolo (anche *fig.*): *the — of mathematics*, il bernoccolo della matematica.
to bump[1], *v.t.i.* 1. urtare; collidere; battere, colpire: *to — against* (o *on*), urtare, andare a sbattere contro 2. *to — along*, avanzare sobbalzando (di veicolo) 3. *to — down*, abbattere con un urto 4. *to — off*, (*sl. amer.*) assassinare.
bump[1], *av.* improvvisamente; violentemente.
bump[2], *s.* grido (del tarabuso).
to bump[2], *v.i.* gridare (del tarabuso).
bumper ['bʌmpə*], *s.* 1. bicchiere pieno, colmo 2. (*aut.*) paraurti; (*ferr.*) respingente ☆ — *crop*, (*sl.*) raccolto abbondante; — *house*, (*teat.*) grande teatro.
bumpety-bump ['bʌmpiti'bʌmp], *av.* (*fam.*) a sbalzi: *that made my heart go —*, (*fam.*) ciò mi fece venire il batticuore.
bumpiness ['bʌmpinis], *s.* irregolarità (di strada, terreno).
bumpkin[1] ['bʌmpkin], *s.* zoticone.
bumpkin[2], *s.* (*mar.*) buttafuori.
bumptious ['bʌmpʃəs], *ag.* presuntuoso.
bumptiously ['bʌmpʃəsli], *av.* presuntuosamente.
bumptiousness ['bʌmpʃəsnis], *s.* presunzione.
bumpy ['bʌmpi], *ag.* 1. sassoso, ineguale (di strada, ecc.) 2. con protuberanze.
bun[1] [bʌn], *s.* 1. focaccia, ciambella dolce 2. « chignon », crocchia.
bun[2], *s.* personificazione dello scoiattolo, del coniglio.
bunch [bʌntʃ], *s.* 1. fascio, mazzo; grappolo: *a — of flowers, of keys*, un mazzo di fiori, di chiavi; *a — of grapes*, un grappolo d'uva ‖ *— of fives*, (*sl.*) pugno chiuso, mano 2. (*fam.*) gruppo (di persone): *the best of the —*, il migliore tra tutti 3. (*amer.*) branco (di bestiame).
to bunch, *v.t.i.* 1. riunire in fascio, mazzo 2. *to — (together)*, serrarsi, ammucchiarsi, raggrupparsi.
bunchy ['bʌntʃi], *ag.* a grappoli, a mazzi.
(to) bunco, *V.* (to) **bunko**.
buncombe ['bʌŋkəm], *V.* **bunkum**.
bund [bʌnd], *s.* (*ang.-in.*) molo, banchina; argine.

bunder ['bʌndə*], *s.* molo, banchina.
bundle ['bʌndl], *s.* 1. fagotto, involto; rotolo; fascina (di legna) 2. fascio (di nervi): *he is a — of nerves*, (*fam.*) è tutto nervi.
to bundle, *v.t.i.* 1. legare a fasci, riunire in mazzo, affastellare; impacchettare; fare un involto; fare i bagagli 2. *to — away, off*, andarsene senza tanti complimenti, sbarazzarsi senza tanti complimenti di 3. *to — in*, entrare in fretta 4. *to — out*, uscire in fretta.
bundook ['bʌnduk], *s.* (*ang.-in.*) fucile, moschetto.
bung [bʌŋ], *s.* 1. tappo, turacciolo; zipolo 2. (*sl.*) bugia ☆ — *-hole*, cocchiume.
to bung, *v.t.* tappare ‖ *eyes, nose bunged up*, (*fam.*) occhi gonfi, naso chiuso.
bungalow ['bʌŋgəlou], *s.* «bungalow» (casa ad un piano generalmente con verande).
bungle ['bʌŋgl], *s.* lavoro mal fatto, pasticcio, abborracciatura.
to bungle, *v.t.i.* 1. abborracciare, lavorare alla peggio, tirar via 2. guastare, sciupare: *she bungled her life*, ella ha sciupato la sua vita.
bungler ['bʌŋglə*], *s.c.* confusionario, confusionaria; guastamestieri.
bungling ['bʌŋgliŋ], *ag.* 1. mal fatto; sciupato 2. mallaccorto, goffo, balordo ‖ *s.* goffaggine, balordaggine.
bunion ['bʌnjən], *s.* callo, infiammazione (ai piedi).
bunk[1] [bʌŋk], *s.* (*mar. ferr.*) cuccetta.
to bunk[1], *v.i.* dormire (in cuccetta): *the crew — forward*, l'equipaggio ha le cuccette a prua.
bunk[2], *s.* (*sl.*) fuga.
to bunk[2], *v.i.* (*sl.*) darsela a gambe, fuggire.
bunk[3], *s. abbr.* di **bunkum**.
bunker ['bʌŋkə*], *s.* 1. carbonile, deposito di combustibile (generalmente di nave) 2. (*mil.*) «bunker», fortino 3. (*golf*) ostacolo.
to bunker, *v.t.* 1. fornire di carbone 2. mettere in difficoltà: *to be bunkered*, trovarsi in. difficoltà.
bunko ['bʌŋkou], *s.* (*sl. amer.*) truffa; imbroglio (specialmente nel giuoco delle carte).
to bunko, *v.t.* (*sl. amer.*) truffare; imbrogliare (specialmente nel giuoco delle carte).
bunkum ['bʌŋkəm], *s.* (*fam.*) chiacchiere, parole vuote: *that's all —!*, sono tutte sciocchezze!.
bunnia ['bʌniə], *s.* (*ang.-in.*) commerciante, negoziante.
bunny ['bʌni], *s.* coniglietto ☆ — *-hug*, danza americana.
bunt[1] [bʌnt], *s.* (*mar.*) 1. fondo di rete da pesca 2. parte mediana di vela.
to bunt[1], *v.i.* (*mar.*) gonfiare, gonfiarsi (di vele).
bunt[2], *s.* ruggine del frumento.
bunt[3], *s.* 1. (*baseball*) colpo 2. (*aer.*) virata imperiale.
to bunt[3], *v.t.i.* 1. (*baseball*) fermare (la palla) con la mazza 2. (*aer.*) fare una virata imperiale.
bunting[1] ['bʌntiŋ], *s.* 1. (*ornit.*) zigolo 2. (*zool.*) tipo di gamberetto di mare 3. persona piccola, paffutella.
bunting[2], *s.* 1. stamigna (tessuto per far bandiere) 2. bandiere; pavese.
buoy [bɔi], *s.* (*mar.*) gavitello, boa ☆ *life- —*, salvagente; *marker- —*, boa di posizione; *mooring —*, boa d'ormeggio.
to buoy, *v.t.i.* 1. far galleggiare; tenere a galla; riportare a galla; *fig.* sostenere, appoggiare: *buoyed (up) with new hope*, animato, sostenuto da una nuova speranza 2. segnare con boe; disporre le boe.
buoyage ['bɔiidʒ], *s.* (*mar.*) collocamento, sistema di boe, di gavitelli.
buoyancy ['bɔiənsi], *s.* 1. galleggiabilità; (*mar.*) spinta di galleggiamento; (*aer.*) spinta statica, forza ascensionale 2. *fig.* elasticità (di mente); ottimismo: *man full-of —*, uomo pieno di risorse, che non si lascia scoraggiare 3. (*comm.*) tendenza al rialzo dei prezzi.
buoyant ['bɔiənt], *ag.* 1. galleggiante; galleggiabile: *salt water is more — than fresh*, l'acqua salata sostiene

meglio dell'acqua dolce 2. *fig.* ottimista, allegro; pieno di risorse: *to be of a — disposition*, tendere all'ottimismo 3. *the market is —*, (*comm.*) il mercato è alto.

buoyantly ['bɔiəntli], *av.* allegramente; con ottimismo.

bur [bə:*], *s.* 1. (*bot.*) lappola, bardana 2. persona appiccicaticcia 3. riccio (di castagna) 4. nodo (di pianta).

Burberry ['bə:bəri], *s.* (stoffa) impermeabile di marca Burberry.

to **burble** ['bə:bl], *v.i.* gorgogliare; parlottare.

burbot ['bə:bət], *s.* (*ittiol.*) barbio.

burden ['bə:dn], *s.* 1. peso, fardello, carico (anche *fig.*): *the — of (the) years*, il peso degli anni; *beast of —*, bestia da soma; *ship of —*, nave mercantile; *his family is a — to him*, ha famiglia a carico; *to make s.o.'s life a —*, rendere la vita impossibile a qlcu. || *the white man's —*, la responsabilità dell'uomo bianco verso le razze di colore 2. (*mar.*) tonnellaggio, stazzatura, portata (di nave): *ship of ten thousand tons —*, nave da diecimila tonnellate 3. — *of proof*, (*dir.*) obbligo di fornire le prove (da parte dell'accusatore) 4. ritornello di canzone; tema (di discorso, poesia, ecc.).

to **burden**, *v.t.* caricare, gravare; *fig.* opprimere: *to — the people with taxes*, gravare la popolazione di tasse.

burdensome ['bə:dnsəm], *ag.* gravoso, pesante.

burdock ['bə:dɔk], *s.* (*bot.*) lappa, bardana.

bureau [bjuə'rou], *pl.* **bureaux** [bjuə'rouz], *s.* 1. scrittoio (con cassetti) 2. studio, ufficio; ufficio statale.

bureaucracy [bjuə'rɔkrəsi], *s.* burocrazia.

bureaucrat ['bjuəroukræt], *s.* burocrate.

bureaucratic [,bjuərou'krætik], *ag.* burocratico.

bureaucratically [,bjuərou'krætikəli], *av.* burocraticamente.

bureaucratism [bjuə'rɔkrətizəm], *s.* burocrazia.

bureaucratist [bjuə'rɔkrətist], *s.* burocrate.

burette [bjuə'ret], *s.* (*chim.*) buretta.

burg [bə:g], *s.* 1. (*st.*) fortezza; città fortificata 2. (*fam.*) città.

burgage ['bə:gidʒ], *s.* antico possedimento terriero.

burgee ['bə:dʒi:], *s.* (*mar.*) pennello (per yachts, ecc.).

burgeon ['bə:dʒən], *s.* (*poet.*) germoglio, gemma.

to **burgeon**, *v.i.* (*poet.*) germogliare (anche *fig.*).

burgess ['bə:dʒis], *s.* 1. cittadino; elettore: *the burgesses*, i cittadini 2. (*st.*) deputato al Parlamento inglese (rappresentante di borgo, università).

burgh ['bʌrə], *s.* (*scoz.*) borgo, borgata, municipio: *Parliamentary —*, città rappresentata direttamente (o indirettamente) nel Parlamento inglese.

burgher ['bə:gə*], *s.* (*st.*) cittadino.

burglar ['bə:glə*], *s.* scassinatore (notturno); svaligiatore ☆ — *alarm*, campanello antifurto.

burglarious [bə'glɛəriəs], *ag.* ladresco, brigantesco.

burglariously [bə'glɛəriəsli], *av.* con scasso; brigantescamente.

burglary ['bə:gləri], *s.* furto (notturno) con scasso.

to **burgle** ['bə:gl], *v.t.i.* svaligiare (una casa); commettere un furto con scasso.

burgling ['bə:gliŋ], *s.* furto con scasso, svaligiamento.

burgomaster ['bə:gə,mɑ:stə*], *s.* borgomastro.

burgonet ['bə:gənet], *s.* (*st.*) elmetto con visiera.

burgoo [bə:'gu:], *s.* 1. (*sl. mar.*) pappa di farina d'avena 2. (*amer.*) sorta di minestra (a base di carne e verdura).

Burgundian [bə:'gʌndiən], *ag.* borgognone || *s.c.* borgognone, borgognona.

Burgundy ['bə:gəndi], *no.pr.* (*geog.*) Borgogna || **burgundy**, *s.* borgogna (vino).

burial ['beriəl], *s.* seppellimento, sepoltura; esequie; inumazione ☆ — *-ground*, cimitero; — *-place*, luogo di sepoltura; — *-service*, ufficio funebre.

burin ['bjuərin], *s.* (*strum. artig.*) bulino.

burinist ['bjuərinist], *s.* bulinista, incisore.

to **burke** [bə:k], *v.t.* soffocare (uno scandalo); mettere sotto silenzio.

burl [bə:l], *s.* (*ind. tessile*) nodo.

to **burl**, *v.t.* (*ind. tessile*) liberare dai nodi.

burlap ['bə:læp], *s.* tela da imballaggio.

burlesque [bə:'lesk], *ag.* burlesco || *s.* 1. farsa; parodia; poema eroicomico 2. (*teat. amer.*) « burlesque » (specie di spettacolo di varietà).

to **burlesque**, *v.t.* mettere in ridicolo, parodiare.

burliness ['bə:linis], *s.* corpulenza.

burly ['bə:li], *ag.* grande e grosso; corpulento.

Burma ['bə:mə], *no.pr.* (*geog.*) Birmania.

Burmese [bə:'mi:z], *ag.* birmano || *s.c.* birmano, birmana.

burn[1] [bə:n], *s.* ustione, scottatura.

to **burn**[1], *pass.p.p.* **burnt** [bə:nt], (*rar.*) **burned** [bə:nd], *v.t.i.* 1. bruciare, ardere: *to — low*, bruciare a fiamma bassa; *to be burnt alive*, essere bruciato vivo || *to — to ashes*, incenerire, incenerirsi || *to — the candle at both ends*, *fig.* affaticarsi eccessivamente con troppe attività || *to — the earth* (o *the wind*), (*amer.*) bruciare le tappe || *to — the midnight oil*, lavorare fino a notte alta || *to — one's boats*, *fig.* precludersi ogni via di ritirata || *to — one's fingers*, *fig.* rimanere scottato || *to be burnt to death*, morire carbonizzato || *burnt child fears the fire*, *prov.* il cane scottato dall'acqua calda ha paura della fredda 2. *fig.* ardere, scottare: *to — with desire*, ardere di desiderio; *to — with fever*, scottare per la febbre 3. illuminare, divampare; mandar luce, risplendere: *the lamp burns clear*, la lampada fa bella luce; *to — dim*, far poca luce 4. (*ind.*) cuocere, calcinare 5. (*chim.*) combinare con ossigeno 6. (*med.*) cauterizzare 7. *to — away*, consumare, consumarsi 8. *to — down*, distruggere col fuoco, radere al suolo con un incendio: *the house was burnt down*, la casa fu distrutta dal fuoco 9. *to — in*, incidere col fuoco, con acidi; *fig.* imprimere indelebilmente 10. *to — out*, bruciare fino in fondo estinguendosi, bruciarsi (di lampadina); provocare un corto circuito || *to — oneself out*, (*amer.*) rovinarsi la salute 11. *to — up*, bruciare interamente, consumare; (*sl.*) adirarsi; sgridare aspramente.

burn[2], *s.* 1. (*arc.*) sorgente, fonte; corso d'acqua 2. (*scoz. poet.*) ruscello.

burner ['bə:nə*], *s.* 1. chi, che brucia, incendia 2. becco a gas 3. bruciatore ☆ *Bunsen —*, becco Bunsen.

burnet ['bə:nit], *s.* (*bot.*) pimpinella.

burning ['bə:niŋ], *ag.* bruciante, ardente; scottante, cocente (anche *fig.*): — *coals*, brace; — *question*, problema scottante; — *shame*, cocente vergogna || *s.* 1. incendio; combustione; bruciatura; bruciore; *fig.* fuoco || *a smell of —*, un odore di bruciato 2. (*ind.*) cottura 3. (*metal.*) fusione ☆ — *-glass*, specchio ustorio; — *-hot*, rovente.

burnish ['bə:niʃ], *s.* brunitura.

to **burnish**, *v.t.* lustrare, brunire.

burnisher ['bə:niʃə*], *s.* 1. brunitore 2. (*metal.*) brunitoio.

burnishing ['bə:niʃiŋ], *s.* brunitura.

burnouse [bə:'nu:z], *s.* « burnus » (mantello con cappuccio degli arabi).

burnt [bə:nt], *pass. p.p.* di to **burn** || *ag.* bruciato; tostato ☆ — *-offering*, olocausto.

burr[1] [bə:*], *s.* 1. cerchio; alone luminoso (intorno alla luna, astro, ecc.) 2. (*mec.*) riparella, rosetta.

burr[2], *s.* (*mec.*) bavatura, ricciolo.

burr[3], *s.* (*min.*) pietra silicea per frese.

burr[4], *s.* pronunzia arrotata della lettera *r* in gola (*r* francese).

to **burr**[4], *v.t.i.* 1. arrotare (la *r*) alla francese: *to — one's r's*, arrotare la *r* 2. parlare non chiaramente.

burro ['burou], *s.* (*sl. amer.*) asinello.

burrow ['bʌrou], *s.* tana, covo (di coniglio, volpe, ecc.) (anche *fig.*): *never to leave one's —*, (*fam.*) non uscir mai dal proprio guscio.

to **burrow**, *v.t.i.* 1. fare, farsi una tana; vivere in una tana; scavare; traforare 2. rintanarsi; nascondersi **3.** far ricerche, investigare: *to — into the archives*, fare delle ricerche negli archivi.

bursar [ˈbəːsə*], *s.* **1.** economo (di un collegio, ecc.) **2.** (*scoz.*) borsista (studente che usufruisce di una borsa di studio).

bursarship [ˈbəːsəʃip], *s.* **1.** economato **2.** (*scoz.*) borsa di studio.

bursary [ˈbəːsəri], *s.* **1.** ufficio dell'economato **2.** borsa di studio.

burst [bəːst], *s.* **1.** scoppio, esplosione (anche *fig.*); scroscio (di risa, tuono, ecc.): *— of gunfire*, raffica di fucileria **2.** squarcio, fenditura **3.** (*spor.*) volata finale.

to **burst**, *pass.p.p.* burst, *v.t.i.* **1.** scoppiare, prorompere; esplodere, fare esplodere (anche *fig.*): *to — into laughter, tears*, scoppiare a ridere, a piangere ‖ *to — one's sides with laughing*, scoppiare dalle risa ‖ *to — upon*, comparire improvvisamente: *the truth — upon me*, improvvisamente mi apparve la verità ‖ *to — with envy*, crepare di invidia **2.** irrompere; spalancare; forzare, sfondare: *the river — its banks*, il fiume ruppe gli argini; *to burst into a room, out of a room*, precipitarsi in una stanza, fuori da una stanza ‖ *to — open*, aprire violentemente **3.** apparire improvvisamente **4.** *to — forth*, sorgere improvvisamente (del sole); scoppiare (di temporale); zampillare, sgorgare (di lacrime, sangue) **5.** *to — in*, entrare con violenza **6.** *to — out*, mostrarsi improvvisamente (del sole dietro le nubi); esclamare, scoppiare: *to — out laughing, crying*, scoppiare a ridere, a piangere.

bursting [ˈbəːstiŋ], *ag.* che scoppia: *— heart*, cuore gonfio, che sta per scoppiare; *— with importance, impatience*, gonfio d'importanza, che scoppia d'impazienza ‖ *s.* esplosione (di bomba), scoppio (di temporale, penumatico, ecc.) ☆ *— bomb*, bomba dirompente.

burthen [ˈbəːðən], *V.* **burden**.

burton [ˈbəːtn], *s.* piccola carrucola a mano.

to **bury** [ˈberi], *v.t.* **1.** seppellire (anche *fig.*); sotterrare, interrare: *they buried two sons*, perdettero due figli; *to — oneself in the country, fig.* seppellirsi in campagna ‖ *to — the hatchet*, fare la pace **2.** immergere, affondare: *to — one's head in one's hands*, nasconder la testa tra le mani.

burying [ˈberiiŋ], *V.* **burial**.

bus [bʌs], *pl.* **buses** [ˈbʌsiz], *s.* **1.** autobus: *to miss the —*, perdere l'autobus; (*fam.*) lasciarsi sfuggire l'occasione **2.** (*sl.*) aeroplano; automobile; motocicletta ☆ *double-deck —*, autobus a due piani; *trolley —*, filobus.

to **bus**, *pass.p.p.* bussed [bʌst], *v.i.* andare in autobus: *we bussed it from*, siamo venuti in autobus da.

busby [ˈbʌzbi], *s.* (*mil.*) colbac, colbacco.

bush¹ [buʃ], *s.* **1.** cespuglio, macchia, fratta ‖ *to beat about the —*, *fig.* menare il can per l'aia ‖ *to take to the —*, *fig.* darsi alla macchia **2.** frasca (di osteria): *good wine needs no —*, il buon vino non ha bisogno d'insegna **3.** *V.* **scrub**¹ **3.** ☆ *— -fighting*, guerriglia ‖ *rose —*, rosaio.

to **bush**¹, *v.t.i.* **1.** infittirsi (come un cespuglio) **2.** recingere, decorare (con cespugli).

bush², *s.* **1.** (*mec.*) boccola, bussola **2.** (*elett.*) rivestimento, guaina isolante.

to **bush**², *v.t.* **1.** (*mec.*) imboccolare, imbussolare **2.** (*elett.*) coprire con rivestimento, guaina isolante.

bushel [ˈbuʃl], *s.* staio (misura di capacità per cereali = 1. 36,35) ‖ *bushels of sthg.*, (*fam.*) grande quantità di ql.co.

bushelful [ˈbuʃlful], *s.* staiata.

Bushman, *pl.* **Bushmen** [ˈbuʃmən], *s.* boscimane ‖ **bushman**, *s.* colonizzatore d'Australia.

Bushido [ˈbuːʃiˌdou], *s.* Bushido (codice d'onore dei Samurai).

bushiness [ˈbuʃinis], *s.* cespugliosità.

bushy [ˈbuʃi], *ag.* folto, spesso; cespuglioso: *— eyebrows*, sopracciglia folte.

busily [ˈbizili], *av.* attivamente; alacremente.

business [ˈbiznis], *s. gener. sing.* **1.** affare, lavoro, occupazione, mestiere: *are you in London on pleasure or on —?*, sei a Londra per diporto o per lavoro?; *to go to —*, andare al lavoro ‖ *he means —*, intende fare le cose sul serio ‖ *it is none of my —*, non è affar mio; *it is not my —*, non mi riguarda ‖ *mind your own —*, bada ai fatti tuoi ‖ *send him about his —*, (*fam.*) mandalo per i fatti suoi ‖ *you had no — to do so*, non toccava a te farlo **2.** affari, commercio: *to be in —*, essere nel commercio; *to do —*, fare affari; *to give up —*, ritirarsi dagli affari; *to go into —*, mettersi nel commercio; *to have — with s.o.*, avere rapporti di affari con qlcu. ‖ *to talk —*, parlare d'affari ‖ *man of —*, agente legale (di famiglia, personale) **3.** (anche *pl.*) ditta, azienda, casa di commercio: *a well-known —*, una ditta famosa **4.** scopo; dovere: *the — of the meeting*, lo scopo dell'assemblea ‖ *on what — did he come?*, a che scopo è venuto? ‖ *to make it one's — to do sthg.*, farsi un dovere di fare ql.co. **5.** (*teat.*) pantomima, recitazione; parte ☆ *— agent*, agente commerciale; *— hours*, orario d'ufficio; *— -like*, metodico, sistematico; *— -man*, uomo d'affari; *— suit*, (*amer.*) abito da passeggio.

busk¹ [bʌsk], *s.* stecca (da busto).

to **busk**², *v.t.i.* **1.** preparare, attrezzare; mettere in ordine **2.** (*arc.*) vestire, vestirsi.

busker [ˈbʌskə*], *s.* (*sl.*) attore, suonatore girovago.

buskin [ˈbʌskin], *s.* **1.** stivaletto; (*teat.*) coturno **2.** *fig.* tragedia; vena tragica.

buskined [ˈbʌskind], *ag.* calzato di stivaletti; (*teat.*) calzato di coturni.

busman, *pl.* **busmen** [ˈbʌsmən], *s.* conducente di autobus ‖ *—'s holiday*, vacanza passata facendo un lavoro simile a quello abituale.

buss¹ [bʌs], *s.* battello per la pesca delle aringhe.

buss², *s.* (*arc.*) bacio.

to **buss**², *v.t.* (*arc.*) baciare.

bust [bʌst], *s.* **1.** (*scult.*) busto **2.** busto, petto, seno.

bustard [ˈbʌstəd], *s.* (*ornit.*) ottarda.

buster [ˈbʌstə*], *s.* (*sl. amer.*) **1.** ql.co. che toglie il respiro **2.** baldoria.

bustle¹ [ˈbʌsl], *s.* trambusto, scompiglio, agitazione.

to **bustle**¹, *v.t.i.* **1.** muoversi, agitarsi, essere in agitazione: *the room bustled with people*, la stanza era piena di gente che si agitava; *we must —*, dobbiamo muoverci ‖ *to — in and out*, entrare e uscire con aria affaccendata **2.** sollecitare, incalzare **3.** *to — about*, darsi da fare, sfaccendare, affaccendarsi.

bustle², *s.* crinolina.

bustler [ˈbʌslə*], *s.c.* persona attiva.

bustling [ˈbʌsliŋ], *ag.* affaccendato.

busy [ˈbizi], *ag.* affaccendato, occupato: attivo: *to be — at* (o *with* o *over*) *sthg.*, esser occupato a fare ql.co. ‖ *get —!*, (*fam.*) sbrigati! muoviti!.

to **busy**, *v.t.* occupare, affaccendare: *to — oneself with* (o *in* o *about*) *sthg.*, occuparsi di ql.co.

busybody [ˈbiziˌbodi], *s.c.* ficcanaso, intrigante.

busyness [ˈbizinis], *s.* attività, l'essere affaccendato.

but [bʌt (*forma forte*), bət (*forma debole*)], *cong.* **ma:** *poor — honest*, povero ma onesto ‖ *av.* solo, soltanto, **non ... che:** *had I — known it!*, se solo l'avessi saputo!; *he can — refuse*, può solo rifiutare; *I have — two friends*, non ho che due amici ‖ *prep.* **eccetto, tranne, fuorchè:** *they all went —*, andarono tutti tranne me ‖ *the last — one*, il penultimo ‖ *pron.rel.negativo* **che non, se non, a meno che, senza:** *I never see him — he is smoking*, non lo vedo mai che non stia fumando ‖ *s.* **ma**, obiezione: *there is a —*, c'è un ma ‖ (**Fraseologia**): *— a little*, soltanto un poco ‖ *— for*, se non fosse per, senza: *— for him, I should be away*, se non fosse per lui, sarei partito ‖ *— that*, se non: *— that he swore it*, se non l'avesse giurato ‖ *— then*, ma d'altra parte ‖ *nothing —*, null'altro che: *I swear to tell the* *truth and nothing — the truth*, giuro di dire la verità e null'altro che la verità ‖ *he is anything — intelligent*, è tutt'altro che intelligente ‖ *can —*, potere soltanto, non restare che: *we can — pay him*, non ci resta che pagarlo ‖ *cannot —*, non poter fare a meno di, essere costretto a: *I cannot — admit you are right*, non posso fare a meno di ammettere che avete ragione ‖ *to do anything —*, far qualunque cosa fuorchè: *I would do anything — beg*, farei qualsiasi cosa tranne che chiedere l'elemosina ‖ *to do nothing —*, non far altro che: *he does nothing — read*, non fa altro che leggere.

to **but** [bʌt], *v.t.* (*arc. scherz.*): *— me no buts*, non dirmi dei «ma», non sollevare obiezioni.

butane ['bju:tein], *s.* (*chim.*) butano.

butcher ['butʃə*], *s.* macellaio: *— 's shop*, macelleria ☆ — *'s meat*, carne macellata (ovina, bovina, suina); *— 's-broom*, (*bot.*) pungitopo.

to **butcher**, *v.t.* 1. macellare; massacrare (anche *fig.*) 2. stroncare con aspra critica.

butcherly ['butʃəli], *ag.* da macellaio; brutale, sanguinario.

butchery ['butʃəri], *s.* 1. macelleria; macello 2. commercio di carni macellate 3. *fig.* macello, strage.

butler ['bʌtlə*], *s.* 1. maggiordomo 2. cantiniere, cameriere addetto all'argenteria, ai vini.

butlery ['bʌtləri], *s.* dispensa ☆ — *-hatch*, passavivande.

butt[1] [bʌt], *s.* botte (di circa 600 litri), barile.

butt[2], *s.* (*ittiol.*) ippofago.

butt[3], *s.* 1. calcio (di arma da fuoco); impugnatura (di utensile) 2. ceppo (di albero) 3. (*conceria*) scagnello 4. mozzicone (di sigaretta, ecc.) 5. matrice di assegno 6. (*mec.*) cerniera.

butt[4], *s.* 1. monticello di terra dietro al bersaglio 2. riparo per la caccia alla starna 3. *pl.* poligono di tiro 4. mira, scopo 5. zimbello.

butt[5], *s.* cozzo; cornata.

to **butt**[5], *v.t.i.* 1. urtare con la testa, con le corna; cozzare: *to — against*, cozzare contro ‖ *to — into a discussion*, gettarsi a capofitto in una discussione 2. *to — in*, inframmettersi; capitare d'improvviso: *let me — in*, lasciatemi dire la mia.

butter ['bʌtə*], *s.* burro: *melted —*, burro fuso ‖ *— fingers*, persona dalle mani di pasta frolla ‖ *she looks as though — wouldn't melt in her mouth*, fa la santerellina ‖ *to lay — on*, *fig.* ungere, lusingare ☆ — *-bean*, qualità di fagiuolo; — *-boat*, salsiera per burro fuso; — *-dairy*, cascina, fabbrica di burro; — *-dish*, piattino del burro; — *-knife*, coltellino da burro; — *-milk*, siero di latte; — *-pat*, pallina di burro; — *-scotch*, qualità di caramelle; — *-stamp*, stampo per burro.

to **butter**, *v.t.* 1. imburrare; cuocerè con burro: *buttered bread*, pane imburrato ‖ *his bread is buttered on both sides*, ha la vita facile, vive nell'abbondanza 2. *to — up*, *fig.* adulare, lusingare.

butterbump ['bʌtəbʌmp], *s.* (*ornit.*) tarabuso.

butterbur ['bʌtəbə:*], *s.* (*bot.*) tignamica.

buttercup ['bʌtəkʌp], *s.* (*bot.*) botton d'oro, ranuncolo.

butterfly ['bʌtəflai], *s.* farfalla; *fig.* persona frivola ☆ — *-nut*, (*mec.*) dado ad alette, galletto; — *-stroke*, nuoto a farfalla.

butternut ['bʌtənʌt], *s.* pezzetto, noce di burro.

butterwort ['bʌtəwə:t], *s.* (*bot.*) pinguicola.

buttery ['bʌtəri], *ag.* burroso ‖ *s.* dispensa.

buttock ['bʌtək], *s.* 1. natica 2. mossa nella lotta libera.

to **buttock**, *v.t.* scaraventare a terra (nella lotta libera).

button ['bʌtn], *s.* 1. bottone: *to sew a — on*, attaccare un bottone ‖ *I don't care a —*, (*fam.*) non me ne importa un fico ‖ *to be a — short*, (*fam.*) essere un po' corto (di intelletto) ‖ *to take by the —*, *fig.* attaccare un bottone 2. (*amer.*) bottoncino per colletto; gemello

da polsino; bottone, distintivo (da occhiello) 3. (*bot.*) bocciuolo 4. pulsante ☆ — *-boot*, polacca; — *-hook*, allacciaguanti; allacciascarpe; — *-maker*, fabbricante di bottoni; — *-wood*, (*bot.*) platano d'America.

to **button**, *v.t.i.* 1. abbottonare, abbottonarsi (anche *fig.*); fornire di bottoni: *he buttoned (up) his coat*, si abbottonò il cappotto 2. (*comm.*) evadere 3. gemmare, germogliare (di fiore, pianta) 4. (*scherma*) toccare.

buttoned ['bʌtnd], *ag.* abbottonato; adorno di bottoni ☆ *close —*, *fig.* abbottonato, di poche parole.

button-hole ['bʌtnhoul], *s.* occhiello, asola; fiore da mettere all'occhiello.

to **button-hole**, *v.t.* 1. far occhielli, asole 2. *fig.* attaccar bottone: *he button-holed me*, mi attaccò un bottone.

button-holer ['bʌtn,houlə*], *s.c.* attaccabottoni.

buttonless ['bʌtnlis], *ag.* senza bottoni.

buttons ['bʌtnz], *s.* ragazzo in livrea.

buttony ['bʌtni], *ag.* con molti bottoni.

buttress ['bʌtris], *s.* sostegno, appoggio; contrafforte, sperone.

to **buttress**, *v.t.* sostenere (con pilastro, sperone, ecc.).

butty ['bʌti], *s.* 1. (*fam.*) compagno, camerata 2. chi fa da intermediario fra il proprietario di una miniera e i minatori.

butyric [bju:'tirik], *ag.* (*chim.*) butirrico.

butyrin(e) ['bju:tərin], *s.* (*chim.*) butirrina, butirina.

butyrous ['bju:tərəs], *ag.* butirroso, burroso.

buxom ['bʌksəm], *ag.* paffuto, grassoccio; formoso, avvenente (di donna).

buxomness ['bʌksəmnis], *s.* avvenenza, formosità.

buy [bai], *s.* (*fam.*) acquisto, compera.

to **buy**, *pass.p.p.* **bought** [bo:t], *v.t.* 1. comprare, acquistare: *to — for cash*, comprare a contanti; *to — sthg. from* (o *of*) *s.o.*, comprare ql.co. da qlcu.: *I bought this book from him*, comprai questo libro da lui; *to — s.o. sthg.*, comprare ql.co. per qlcu.: *I bought him a book*, gli comprai un libro; *to — sthg. for s.o.*, comprare ql.co. per qlcu.: *I bought a book for him, not for her*, comprai un libro per lui, non per lei 2. *to — back*, ricomprare; riscattare 3. *to — in*, comprare (in quantità); comprare all'asta 4. *to — out*, indennizzare affinchè uno abbandoni un posto, una proprietà: *he was bought out for £ 5000*, la sua parte, la sua quota, il suo interesse (nella ditta, nell'affare, ecc.) fu rilevato per Lst. 5000 5. *to — over*, corrompere, comprare 6. *to — up*, comprare in quantità, accaparrare.

buyable ['bai-əbl], *ag.* acquistabile.

buyer ['bai-ə*], *s.c.* compratore, compratrice; acquirente; addetto, addetta all'ufficio acquisti ☆ — *-up*, accaparratore.

buying ['baiiŋ], *s.* compra, acquisto.

buzz[1] [bʌz], *s.* 1. ronzio (di api, ecc.) 2. mormorio, brusio (di persone, ecc.) ☆ — *bomb*, (*fam.*) bomba volante, V.1.

to **buzz**[1], *v.t.i.* 1. ronzare (anche *fig.*): *the bees were buzzing busily*, le api ronzavano affaccendate 2. mormorare, bisbigliare 3. *to — about, around*, affannarsi: *what are you buzzing about for?*, ma perchè ti affanni? 4. *to — away, off*, (*sl.*) tagliare la corda.

buzz[2], *s.* (*entom.*) rizotrogo solstiziale.

to **buzz**[3], *v.t.* scolare (una bottiglia).

buzzard ['bʌzəd], *s.* (*ornit.*) poiana.

buzzer ['bʌzə*], *s.* 1. insetto che ronza 2. persona che bisbiglia 3. segnale acustico; cicala; sirena; (*aut.*) clacson; (*amer. mil.*) segnalatore ☆ *desk- —*, cicala; campanello da tavolo.

buzzing ['bʌziŋ], *ag.* ronzante ‖ *s.* ronzio; brusio: *a — in the ears*, un ronzio negli orecchi.

by [bai], *av.* 1. vicino: *close* (o *hard*) —, molto vicino: *he lives hard —*, abita molto vicino; *when no one was —*, quando non c'era nessuno vicino, presente 2. accanto: *to go —*, passare; *to hurry —*, passare in fretta; *to run* —, passare correndo **3. da parte, in disparte:** *to keep sthg.* —, tener ql.co. da parte; *to put (to lay, to set) sthg.* —, mettere da parte, tenere in riserva ql.co.; *to stand* —, stare in attesa; tenersi in disparte; appoggiare, sostenere, aiutare; (*mil.*) tenersi pronto per un'azione: *stand* —, (*rad.*) mantenetevi in ascolto **4. (Fraseologia):** — *and* —, fra breve; — *and large*, (*amer.*) generalmente parlando, di gran lunga; — *the by(e)*, a proposito.

by, *prep.* **1.** (*indicante agente, mezzo, ecc.*) **per, da, con, a, di:** — *paying*, mediante pagamento; *a book (written)* — *Hardy*, un libro di (scritto da) Hardy; *he lives* — *writing novels*, vive scrivendo romanzi; *I took her* — *the hand*, la presi per mano; *it was done* — *him*, fu fatto da lui; *the letter came* — *post*, la lettera arrivò per posta; *they are cousins* — *blood*, sono cugini di sangue; *they make things* — *machinery*, essi lavorano a macchina; *we shall lose nothing* — *waiting*, non perderemo nulla aspettando ‖ *to be known* — *the name of*, essere conosciuto sotto, con il nome di; *to begin* —, cominciare con; *to come, to go* — *tram*, (*motor-*) *car, etc.*, venire, andare con il tram, l'automobile, ecc.; *to end* —, finire con: *she ended* — *marrying him*, essa finì con lo sposarlo; *to learn* — *heart*, imparare a memoria; *to multiply, to divide 300* — *5*, moltiplicare, dividere 300 per 5; *to travel* — *rail(way)*, *land, air, sea*, viaggiare per ferrovia, terra, aria, mare; *to swear* — *God*, giurare nel nome di Dio ‖ — *chance*, per caso; — *mistake*, per sbaglio; — *oneself*, da solo; — *sight*, di vista; — *your leave*, con il vostro permesso **2.** (*tempo*) **durante, di, entro, per:** — *day, night, daylight, moonlight*, di giorno, notte, alla luce del giorno, della luna; *day* — *day*, di giorno in giorno; *he ought to be here* — *now* (o— *this time*), a quest'ora dovrebbe già essere qui; *the work will be finished* — *to-morrow*, il lavoro sarà finito per domani **3.** (*luogo*) **vicino a, al lato di, presso (di, a), davanti, via, attraverso:** — *the side of*, a lato di; *a house* — *the sea*, una casa sul mare; *side* — *side*, lato a lato; *he went to London* — *Paris*, è andato a Londra via Parigi; *I have no money* — *me*, non ho denaro con me; *I pass* — *your house every day*, passo davanti alla vostra casa tutti i giorni; *I shall do my duty* — *you*, farò il mio dovere verso di te **4.** (*misura, peso, proporzione, ecc.*) **per, a, di:** — *degrees*, per gradi; — *hundreds*, a centinaia; *a carpet four feet* — *six (feet)*, un tappeto di quattro piedi per sei; *little* — *little*, poco a poco; *longer* — *three feet*, più lungo di tre piedi; *older, younger* — *ten years*, più vecchio, più giovane di dieci anni; *one* — *one*, ad uno ad uno; *taller* — *three inches*, più alto di tre pollici; *he is* — *far the best*, egli è di gran lunga il migliore; *he won the race* — *two meters*, vinse la corsa per due metri; *to sell* — *the pound*, vendere a libbre **5.** (*mezzo, ragione di giudizio*) **da, secondo:** *one must not judge a person* — *appearances*: non si deve giudicare una persona dalle apparenze ‖ — *all means*, certamente, senz'altro ‖ — *the way*, cammin facendo, incidentalmente: *be it said* — *the way*, sia detto incidentalmente, tra parentesi; *he has many paintings* (*none of value,*

— *the way*) *and statues...*, egli ha molti dipinti (però, nessuno di valore) e statue... ‖ *this is* — *no means true*, questo non è affatto vero.

by, *ag.* attributivo secondario, indiretto: — *effect*, effetto secondario; — *consideration*, considerazione secondaria.

by, (*nei composti*): — *-blow*, colpo traverso; — *-business*, attività collaterale; — *-dweller*, vicino di casa; — *-election*, (*pol.*) elezione straordinaria (per sostituire un membro del Parlamento); — *-end*, secondo fine; — *-incident*, incidente secondario; — *-issue*, questione d'interesse secondario; — (o *bye*)-*law*, legge locale, statuto (municipale, amministrativo), regolamento, norma, prescrizione; — *-name*, soprannome, nomignolo; — *-passer* (o *passer-* —), passante; — *-play*, (*teat.*) controscena, azione secondaria; — *-plot*, (*teat.*) intreccio secondario; — *-product*, sottoprodotto, prodotto secondario; — *-stander*, astante, spettatore; — *-step*, passo laterale; — *-street*, via appartata, fuori mano, viuzza.

bye [bai], *ag.* attributivo secondario, indiretto.

bye, *s.* (*cricket*) punto per palla passata.

bye-bye ['bai'bai], *inter.* (*abbr. di good-bye*) addio, arrivederci.

bye-bye ['baibai], *s.* (*fam.*) nanna: *to go to* —, andare a nanna.

bygone ['baigɔn], *ag.* passato, del passato: *in* — *days*, nei tempi che furono, una volta.

bygones ['baigɔnz], *s.pl.* passato: *let* — *be* —, dimentica il passato, metti una pietra sul passato: acqua passata non macina più.

by-pass ['bai-pɑːs], *s.* **1.** (*mec.*) bipasso, tubo di derivazione, ausiliare **2.** circonvallazione **3.** (*elett.*) « shunt », derivazione.

to by-pass, *v.t.* **1.** girare intorno a, evitare (città, traffico, ecc.) **2.** fornire (una città) di circonvallazione.

bypath ['bai-pɑːθ], *s.* sentiero appartato.

byre ['baiə*], *s.* vaccheria.

byroad ['bairoud], *s.* strada secondaria.

Byronic [bai'rɔnik], **1.** *ag.* byroniano **2.** *fig.* vulcanico; melanconico.

byssaceous [bi'seiʃəs], *ag.* (*bot.*) bissaceo.

byssal ['bisəl], *ag.* bissale.

byssiferous [bi'sifərəs], *ag.* (*zool.*) bissifero.

byssine ['bisin], *ag.* bissino (di tessuto).

byssoid ['bisɔid], *ag.* (*bot.*) bissaceo.

byssus ['bisəs], *s.* **1.** bisso (di mollusco) **2.** (*tessuto*) bisso.

byway ['baiwei], *s.* scorciatoia; strada poco frequentata; via traversa (anche *fig.*): *the byways of history*, i meandri della storia.

byword ['baiwəːd], *s.* **1.** proverbio, detto **2.** (*spreg.*) zimbello: *he is the* — *of the village*, egli è la favola del villaggio.

bywork ['baiwəːk], *s.* lavoro secondario (da fare nei momenti d'ozio).

Byzantian [bi'zæntiən], **Byzantine** [bi'zæntain], *ag.* bizantino (anche *fig.*) ‖ *s.c.* bizantino, bizantina.

Byzantinism [bi'zæntinizəm], *s.* bizantinismo (anche *fig.*).

Byzantium [bi'zæntiəm], *no.pr.* (*geog. st.*) Bisanzio.

C

c [si:], *pl.* cs, c's [si:z], *s.* 1. (*terza lettera dell'alfabeto inglese*) c ‖ — *for Charlie*, (*tel.*) c come Como 2. C, (*mus.*) do; chiave di do 3. C (*cifra romana*), 100.

Caaba ['kɑ:əbə], *s.* Ca(a)ba.

cab[1] [kæb], *s.* 1. vettura di piazza; tassì 2. cabina ☆ — -*rank* (o — -*stand*), posteggio di tassì ‖ *taxi*- —, tassì.

to cab[1], *pass.p.p.* **cabbed** [kæbd], *v.i.* (*fam.*) andare in vettura, in tassì; prendere una vettura, un tassì: *we cabbed it to...*, siamo andati in tassì a....

cab[2], *s.* (*sl.*) bigino.

to cab[2], *pass.p.p.* **cabbed**, *v.i.* (*sl.*) usare un bigino (nel preparare le lezioni).

cabal [kə'bæl], *s.* 1. congiura; intrigo 2. *the Cabal*, (*st. inglese*) comitato degli affari esteri di Carlo II.

to cabal, *pass.p.p.* **caballed** [kə'bæld], *v.i.* intrigare; complottare, congiurare.

caballer [kə'bælə*], *s.c.* imbroglione, imbrogliona; intrigante.

cabana [kə'bɑ:nə], *s.* «cabana» (tipo di sigaro).

cabaret ['kæbərei], *s.* «cabaret», caffè concerto.

cabbage ['kæbidʒ], *s.* cavolo ☆ — -*butterfly*, (*entom.*) cavolaia; — -*lettuce*, cespo di lattuga; — -*patch*, orto di cavoli; — -*rose*, rosa centifoglie; — -*stump*, torso di cavolo.

cab(b)ala [kə'bɑ:lə], *s.* cabala.

cab(b)alism ['kæbəlizəm], *s.* cabalismo.

cab(b)alist ['kæbəlist], *s.* cabalista.

cab(b)alistic [,kæbə'listik], *ag.* cabalistico.

cab(b)alistically [,kæbə'listikəli], *av.* cabalisticamente.

cabby ['kæbi], *s.* (*fam.*) cocchiere, vetturino; tassista.

caber ['keibə*], *s.* (*scoz.*) «caber» (tronco di pino senza rami usato nella gara di lancio detta «tossing the caber»).

cabin ['kæbin], *s.* 1. capanna; casa piccola e rozza 2. (*aer. ferr. mar.*) cabina ☆ — -*boy*, mozzo, addetto ai servizi di cabina; — -*ship*, nave a classe unica; — -*trunk*, baule da cabina.

to cabin, *v.t.i.* 1. rinchiudere in una cabina, in piccolo spazio 2. abitare in una cabina.

cabinet ['kæbinit], *s.* 1. gabinetto; stanzino 2. stipo, scrigno, armadietto 3. *Cabinet*, (*pol.*) gabinetto; consiglio dei ministri ‖ *Cabinet-Council*, consiglio di gabinetto ☆ — -*maker*, ebanista; — -*making*, ebanisteria; — -*minister*, membro del gabinetto; — -*photograph*, fotografia formato album.

cable ['keibl], *s.* 1. cavo (elettrico, telegrafico, sottomarino): *by* —, per cavo 2. cablogramma ☆ — -*address*, indirizzo telegrafico; — -*car* (o — -*railway* o — -*tram*), funicolare, funivia, teleferica; — -*laid rope*, cavo formato da tre funi; — -*ship*,.nave per la posa dei cavi; — -*way*, cavo aereo; teleferica.

to cable, *v.t.i.* 1. fornire di cavo; legare con un cavo 2. trasmettere per cablogramma: *to* — (*to*) *s.o.*, mandare un cablogramma a qlcu.

cablegram ['keiblgræm], *s.* cablogramma.

cablet ['keiblit], *s.* piccolo cavo.

cabman, *pl.* **cabmen** ['kæbmen], *s.* vetturino; tassista.

cabochon [,kɑ:bə'ʃɔ:ŋ], *s.* pietra preziosa lavorata, ma non sfaccettata.

caboodle [kə'bu:dl], *s.* (*sl.*) folla ‖ *the whole* —, tutto quanto.

caboose [kə'bu:s], *s.* 1. (*mar.*) cucina, cambusa 2. (*amer. ferr.*) furgone, carro di servizio.

cabotage ['kæbətɑ:ʒ], *s.* (*mar.*) cabotaggio.

cabriolet [,kɑ:briou'lei], *s.* 1. calessino 2. (*aut.*) «cabriolet», vettura da turismo.

cacao [kə'kɑ:ou], *s.* (*bot.*) cacao (seme, albero) ☆ — -*bean*, seme di cacao; — -*butter*, burro di cacao; — -*nibs*, mandorle di cacao sbucciate e tostate.

cachalot ['kæʃəlɔt], *s.* (*zool.*) capidoglio.

cache [kæʃ], *s.* 1. nascondiglio (per tesoro, munizioni, provviste) 2. provviste nascoste.

to cache, *v.t.* nascondere (tesoro, munizioni, provviste).

cachet ['kæʃei], *s.* 1. sigillo 2. segno d'autenticità, marca 3. (*farm.*) capsula d'ostia.

cachectic [kə'kektik], *ag.* (*patol.*) cachettico.

cachexy [kə'keksi], *s.* (*patol.*) cachessia.

to cachinnate ['kækineit], *v.i.* ridere smoderatamente.

cachinnation [,kæki'neiʃən], *s.* riso smodato.

cachinnatory [kə'kinətəri], *ag.* di riso smodato.

cacholong ['kæʃəlɔŋ], *s.* (*min.*) cacciolongo.

cachou [kə'ʃu:], *s.* pasticca aromatica.

cacique [kæ'si:k], *s.c.* cacicco (capo indiano d'America).

cackle ['kækl], *s.* 1. schiamazzo (di oca, gallina) 2. *fig.* chiacchierio; risolino soffocato.

to cackle, *v.i.* 1. schiamazzare (di oca, gallina) 2. *fig.* chiacchierare; ridacchiare.

cackler ['kæklə*], *s.* 1. gallina che chioccia 2. *fig.* chiacchierone.

cacodemon [,kækə'di:mən], *s.* cacodemone, spirito maligno.

cacoethes [,kækə'i:θi:z], *s.* cattiva abitudine.

cacography [kæ'kɔgrəfi], *s.* cacografia.

cacophonous [kæ'kɔfənəs], *ag.* cacofonico.

cacophony [kæ'kɔfəni], *s.* cacofonia.

cactaceous [kæk'teiʃəs], *ag.* (*bot.*) di cacto.

cactus ['kæktəs], *pl.* **cactuses** ['kæktəsiz], **cacti** ['kæktai], *s.* (*bot.*) cacto, cactus.

Cacus ['keikəs], *no.pr.m.* (*mit.*) Caco.

cad [kæd], *s.* maleducato; mascalzone.

cadastral [kə'dɑ:strəl], *ag.* catastale.

cadastre [kə'dɑ:stə*], *s.* catasto.

cadaveric [kə'dævərik], *ag.* cadaverico.

cadaverous [kə'dævərəs], *ag.* cadaverico; esangue, pallidissimo.

caddice ['kædis], *s.* (*entom.*) friganea.

caddie ['kædi], *s.* (*golf*) «caddie» (chi porta le mazze).

caddis ['kædis], *s.* (*entom.*) friganea.

caddish ['kædiʃ], *ag.* (*fam.*) maleducato; volgare; villano.

caddishness ['kædiʃnis], *s.* (*fam.*) villania.

caddy[1] ['kædi], *s.* (*tea-*) —, scatoletta da tè.

caddy[2], *s.* babau.

caddy[3], *s.* (*golf*) «caddie» (chi porta le mazze).

cadence ['keidəns], *s.* 1. cadenza, ritmo 2. intonazione, modulazione (di voce) 3. (*mus.*) fine di frase musicale.

cadenced ['keidənst], *ag.* cadenzato.

cadency ['keidənsi], *s.* discendenza di un ramo cadetto.

cadenza [kə'denzə], *s.* (*mus.*) cadenza.

cadet [kə'det], *s.* 1. cadetto 2. cadetto; allievo (di scuola militare).

cadge[1] [kædʒ], *s.* **1.** accattonaggio **2.** estorsione; scrocco.

to cadge[1], *v.t.i.* **1.** accattare, mendicare **2.** estorcere; scroccare.

cadge[2], *s.* **1.** (*st.*) gabbia per falconi **2.** bisaccia.

cadger ['kædʒə*], *s.* **1.** mendicante **2.** scroccatore **3.** venditore ambulante.

cadi ['kɑ:di], *s.* cadì (magistrato musulmano).

Cadiz [kə'diz], *no.pr.* (*geog.*) Cadice.

Cadmean [kæd'mi(:)ən], *ag.* di Cadmo ‖ — *victory*, *fig.* vittoria di Pirro.

cadmic ['kædmik], *ag.* (*chim.*) cadmico.

cadmium ['kædmiəm], *s.* (*chim.*) cadmio.

Cadmus ['kædməs], *no.pr.m.* (*mit.*) Cadmo.

cadre ['kɑ:də*], *s.* **1.** canovaccio (di opera, lavoro teatrale) **2.** (*mil.*) quadro (di ufficiali).

caduceus [kə'dju:sjəs], *pl.* **caducei** [kə'dju:sjai], *s.* (*mit.*) caduceo.

caducity [kə'dju:siti], *s.* caducità; fugacità.

caducous [kə'dju:kəs], *ag.* caduco; fugace.

caecal ['si:kəl], *ag.* (*anat.*) cecale.

caecitis [si'saitis], *s.* (*patol.*) tiflite.

caecum ['si:kəm], *pl.* **caeca** ['si:kə], *s.* (*anat.*) cieco.

Caesar ['si:zə*], *no.pr.m.* Cesare ‖ *s.* **1.** cesare; imperatore ‖ —*'s wife*, *fig.* persona al di sopra di ogni sospetto ‖ *to appeal to* —, appellarsi alle autorità superiori **2.** autocrate.

Caesarean, Caesarian [si(:)'zɛəriən], *ag.* cesareo, di Cesare; imperiale ‖ *s.* seguace di Cesare; sostenitore di un'autocrazia ☆ — *operation* (o — *section*), (*chir.*) parto cesareo.

Caesarism ['si:zərizm], *s.* cesarismo, governo assoluto.

Caesarist ['si:zərist], *s.* sostenitore di un governo assoluto.

caesium ['si:zjəm], *s.* (*min.*) cesio.

caesura [si(:)'zjuərə], *s.* (*poes.*) cesura.

café ['kæfei], *s.* caffè; ristorante.

cafeteria [,kæfi'tiəriə], *s.* ristorante ove i clienti si servono da soli.

caffeine ['kæfii:n], *s.* caffeina.

Caffre, *V.* **Kaffir**.

caftan ['kæftən], *s.* caffetano.

cage [keidʒ], *s.* **1.** gabbia **2.** prigione **3.** (*edil.*) palizzata; impalcatura; armatura **4.** (*elett. mec.*) gabbia ☆ *lift* —, gabbia d'ascensore; montacarichi.

to cage, *v.t.* **1.** mettere, tenere in gabbia **2.** imprigionare.

cagebird ['keidʒbə:d], *s.* uccello da gabbia.

cahoots [kə'hu:ts], *s. pl.* (*amer.*) società, lega.

caiman ['keimən], *s.* (*zool.*) caimano.

Cain [kein], *no.pr.m.* Caino ‖ *to raise* —, fare una sfuriata ‖ *s.* fratricida.

caique [kai'i:k], *s.* (*mar.*) caìcco, scialuppa.

cairn [kɛən], *s.* tumulo.

cairngorm ['kɛən'gɔ:m], *s.* (*min.*) quarzo giallo, bruno.

caisson [kə'su:n], *s.* **1.** (*arch.*) cassettone (di soffitto) **2.** (*mar.*) cassone pneumatico, cassone di immersione; barca porta cassone **3.** (*mil.*) cassonetto.

caitiff ['keitif], *ag.s.* (*arc. poet.*) vile; codardo.

Caius ['kaiəs], *no.pr.m.* (*st.*) Caio.

to cajole [kə'dʒoul], *v.t.* blandire, lusingare, adulare.

cajolement [kə'dʒoulmənt], *V.* **cajolery**.

cajoler [kə'dʒoulə*], *s.c.* adulatore, adulatrice.

cajolery [kə'dʒouləri], *s.* lusinga, adulazione, allettamento.

cajolingly [kə'dʒoulinli], *av.* con lusinghe, con allettamenti.

cake [keik], *s.* **1.** torta; focaccia; pagnottina dolce; pasticcio al forno ‖ *cakes and ale*, le buone cose della vita ‖ *a piece of* —, (*sl.*) ql.co. di facile e gradito ‖ *to take the* —, *fig.* riportare la palma ‖ *you cannot eat your* — *and have it too*, *prov.* non si può avere la botte piena e la moglie ubriaca **2.** *pl.* (*amer.*) frittelle **3.** tavoletta (di sostanza compressa); saponetta: *a* — *of chocola-*

te, una tavoletta di cioccolato **4.** grumo, crosta (di sangue, ecc.) ☆ — *-shop*, pasticceria; — *-walk*, danza negra ‖ *wedding-* —, torta nuziale.

to cake, *v.t.i.* incrostare, incrostarsi; indurire, indurirsi; coagularsi, agglutinarsi: *caked with blood, mud*, incrostato di sangue, fango.

caky ['keiki], *ag.* **1.** simile a focaccia **2.** agglutinante, che si rapprende.

calabar ['kæləbɑ:*], *s.* vaio.

calabar-bean ['kæləbə:'bi:n], *s.* (*bot.*) fava del Calabar.

calabash ['kæləbæʃ], *s.* caravazza (tipo di zucca e recipiente da essa ricavato) ☆ — *-gourd*, caravazza; — *-pipe*, pipa di caravazza, a forma di caravazza.

calaboose [,kælə'bu:z], *s.* (*fam. amer.*) prigione.

Calabrian [kə'læbriən], *ag.s.c.* calabrese.

calamander [,kælə'mændə*], *s.* calamandra.

calamary ['kæləməri], *s.* (*zool.*) calamaro.

calamine ['kæləmain], *s.* (*min.*) calamina.

calamint ['kæləmint], *s.* (*bot.*) calaminta.

calamite ['kæləmait], *s.* (*paleont.*) vegetale fossile.

calamitous [kə'læmitəs], *ag.* calamitoso, disastroso.

calamitously [kə'læmitəsli], *av.* disastrosamente.

calamity [kə'læmiti], *s.* calamità, disastro, sinistro ☆ — *howler*, (*sl. amer.*) pessimista.

calamus ['kæləməs], *s.* (*bot.*) calamo.

calando [kɑ:'lɑ:ndou], *s.* (*mus.*) calando.

calash [kə'læʃ], *s.* **1.** calesse **2.** mantice mobile di calesse **3.** (*st.*) specie di cappuccio da donna.

calcar[1] ['kælkɑ:*], *s.* **1.** (*vetreria*) calcara **2.** (*metal.*) forno di ricottura.

calcar[2], *s.* (*bot.*) sperone.

calcareous [kæl'kɛəriəs], *ag.* calcareo.

calceolaria [,kælsiə'lɛəriə], *s.* (*bot.*) calceolaria.

calceolate ['kælsiəleit], *ag.* (*bot.*) calceolato.

calcic ['kælsik], *ag.* (*chim.*) calcico.

calciferous [kæl'sifərəs], *ag.* (*min.*) calcifero.

calcific [kæl'sifik], *ag.* (*chim.*) calcificante; calcificato.

calcification [,kælsifi'keiʃən], *s.* calcificazione.

to calcify ['kælsifai], *v.t.i.* calcificare, calcificarsi.

calcinable [kæl'sainəbl], *ag.* calcinabile.

calcination [,kælsi'neiʃən], *s.* calcinazione.

to calcine ['kælsain], *v.t.i.* calcinare, calcinarsi.

calcite ['kælsait], *s.* (*min.*) calcite.

calcium ['kælsiəm], *s.* (*chim.*) calcio ☆ — *carbide*, carburo di calcio; — *carbonate*, carbonato di calcio; — *chloride*, cloruro di calcio; — *cyanamide*, calciocianamide; — *nitrate*, nitrato di calcio.

calculable ['kælkjuləbl], *ag.* calcolabile.

to calculate ['kælkjuleit], *v.t.i.* **1.** calcolare **2.** fare affidamento, contare: *to* — *on sthg.*, contare su ql.co.: *to* — *on sthg. happening*, contare che avvenga ql.co.; *to* — *to sthg.*, (*amer.*) contare di fare ql.co. **3.** (*amer.*) supporre, credere.

calculated ['kælkjuleitid], *ag.* **1.** calcolato **2.** deliberato, premeditato: — *insolence*, insolenza deliberata **3.** *fig.* adatto, idoneo: *news* — *to surprise the world*, notizie tali da sorprendere il mondo.

calculating ['kælkjuleitiŋ], *ag.* calcolatore: *a cool man*, un uomo freddo e calcolatore ☆ — *machine*, macchina calcolatrice.

calculation [,kælkju'leiʃən], *s.* **1.** calcolo **2.** opinione; previsione.

calculator ['kælkjuleitə*], *s.c.* calcolatore, calcolatrice ‖ *s.* macchina calcolatrice.

calculous ['kælkjuləs], *ag.* (*patol.*) calcoloso.

calculus ['kælkjuləs], *pl.* **calculi** ['kælkjulai], *s.* **1.** (*patol.*) calcolo **2.** (*mat.*) calcolo.

caldron ['kɔ:ldrən], *s.* caldaia, calderone.

Caledonia [,kæli'dounjə], *no.pr.* (*geog.*) Caledonia, Scozia.

Caledonian [,kæli'dounjən], *ag.s.c.* (*st.*) caledone, scozzese.

calefacient [,kæli'feiʃənt], *ag.s.* (*med.*) calefaciente.

calefactory [,kæli'fæktəri], *ag.* calefattivo ‖ *s.* calefattore.

calendar ['kælində*], s. 1. calendario, almanacco; annuario (d'università) 2. lista, elenco ☆ — -pad, blocco del calendario.

to **calendar**, v.t. 1. inscrivere (in un calendario, in una lista) 2. classificare; elencare; schedare (documenti, ecc.).

calender[1] ['kælində*], s. (mec.) calandra, mangano.

to **calender**[1], v.t. calandrare (tessuti, carta, ecc.).

calender[2], s. derviscio nomade.

calends ['kælindz], s.pl. calende || on (o at) the Greek —, alle calende greche.

calenture ['kæləntjuə*], s. (patol.) calentura.

calf[1] [ka:f], pl. **calves** [ka:vz], s. 1. vitello, vitellino: cow in (o with) —, mucca gravida || the golden —, il vitello d'oro; fig. la ricchezza 2. il piccolo di alcuni grossi mammiferi 3. giovincello, bamboccio 4. stupido, ignorante ☆ — -bound, rilegato in pelle di vitello; — -love, amore fra adolescenti || — -time, giovinezza.

calf[2], pl. **calves**, s. polpaccio.

calfskin ['ka:fskin], s. pelle di vitello.

Caliban ['kælibæn], no.pr.m. (lett.) Calibano || s. uomo di natura bestiale.

caliber, V. **calibre**.

to **calibrate** ['kælibreit], v.t. 1. calibrare, misurare il calibro di 2. graduare 3. (mec.) tarare.

calibration [,kæli'breiʃən], s. (mec.) calibratura, taratura.

calibre ['kælibə*], s. 1. calibro (di cannone, ecc.) 2. fig. importanza.

calibred ['kælibəd], ag. calibrato.

calicle ['kælikl], s. (biol.) caliculo.

calico ['kælikou], ag. di calicò || s. calicò (tela di cotone); (amer.) tela di cotone stampata.

calicular [kə'likjulə*], ag. (biol.) caliculare.

calif ['kælif], s. califfo.

caliginosity [kə,lidʒi'nositi], s. caliginosità.

caliginous [kə'lidʒinəs], ag. caliginoso.

Caligula [kə'ligjulə], no.pr.m. (st.) Caligola.

calipash ['kælipæʃ], **calipee** ['kælipi:], s. (cuc.) grasso gelatinoso di tartaruga.

caliper ['kælipə*], s. (gener. pl.) compasso; calibro.

caliph ['kælif], s. califfo.

caliphate ['kælifeit], s. califfato.

calix, V. **calyx**.

calk[1] [ko:k], s. rampone.

to **calk**[1], v.t. fornire (scarpe) di ramponi; ferrare (cavalli) a ghiaccio.

to **calk**[2], v.t. decalcare (un disegno, ecc.).

to **calk**[3], V. to **caulk**.

calker, V. **caulker**.

calkin ['kælkin, 'ko:kin], s. rampone (da cavallo o per scarpe).

calking ['ko:kiŋ], s. ricalco.

call [ko:l], s. 1. chiamata, appello, richiamo (anche fig.): — of the wild, richiamo della foresta; duty's —, l'appello del dovere; to come at (o to answer) s.o.'s —, rispondere all'appello di qlcu. || to be within —, essere a portata di mano || to have a close —, (fam.) scamparla bella, per miracolo 2. breve visita: to pay s.o. a —, fare una visita breve a qlcu. 3. (dir.) appello; citazione: — of the House, appello nominale (alla Camera inglese) 4. grido: a — for help, un grido d'aiuto 5. fischio, richiamo (di uccello); segnale; suono (di cornetta) 6. (mil.) adunata 7. diritto, titolo, autorità: what — has she to say that?, che diritto ha di dire ciò? 8. vocazione; ispirazione: he felt a —, sentì la vocazione 9. (comm.) richiesta (di denaro): — of capital, richiesta di versamento di quote (sul capitale); — on shares, richiesta di versamento di quote o decimi (su azioni) || buying on —, compere a richiesta; deposit at —, deposito a vista; payable at —, pagabile a vista 10. (mar.) scalo: port of —, porto di scalo 11. (eccl.) nomina ☆ — -bell, campanello; — -bird, uccello da richiamo; — -box, cabina telefonica; — -boy, (teat.) buttafuori; — -girl, (neol.) ragazza squillo; — -loan, (o — -money), prestiti giornalieri, proroghe; — -office,

ufficio telefonico; — -sign, (rad. tel.) segnale di chiamata; — -station, centrale telefonica; — -up, chiamata alle armi || bugle- —, squillo di cornetta; international trunk- —, telefonata internazionale; local —, telefonata locale; roll- —, appello con il rolino; telephone —, telefonata; trunk- — (o long-distance —), telefonata intercomunale.

to **call**, v.t.i. 1. chiamare, chiamarsi; richiamare; nominare: my baby is called after his grandfather, il mio piccino porta il nome di suo nonno; to — the roll, fare l'appello con il rolino; to — s.o.'s attention on sthg., richiamare l'attenzione di qlcu. su ql.co.; to — s.o. to order, richiamare qlcu. all'ordine; to — to arms, chiamare alle armi; to — s.o. to the bar, nominare qlcu. avvocato; to — to mind, richiamare alla mente || this is London calling, (rad.) qui parla Londra || to — aside, chiamare in disparte || to — the banns, fare le pubblicazioni matrimoniali || to — into being, creare, far nascere || to — s.o. names, ingiuriare qlcu. || to — s.o. to account, chiamare qlcu. alla resa dei conti 2. invitare, esortare; ordinare: to — a halt, intimare di fermarsi; to — a strike, ordinare, proclamare uno sciopero 3. riunire, convocare 4. citare, prendere a testimonio 5. gridare: to — aloud, chiamare a gran voce; to — to s.o. to do sthg., gridare a qlcu. di fare ql.co. 6. fare una breve visita: to — at, passare da (un luogo); to — on, visitare, andare a trovare (una persona) || to — at a port, far scalo ad un porto 7. richiamare (uccelli, ecc.) 8. to — for (s.o., sthg.), chiedere, richiedere, esigere; passare a prendere: — for me this evening, passa a prendermi stasera || letter to be kept till called for, lettera che si prega trattenere fino al ritiro || this letter calls for no answer, questa lettera non richiede risposta 9. to — (up)on (s.o.), implorare, invocare; invitare: they called upon Mr. A. for a speech, invitarono il Sig. A. a fare un discorso || I feel called upon to inform you that..., mi sento in dovere di informarvi che... 10. to — back, richiamare; revocare, ritrattare 11. to — down, far scendere, chiamare giù; (sl. amer.) ingiuriare, rimproverare 12. to — forth, causare, far nascere; suscitare, evocare 13. to — in, invitare a entrare, far entrare; farsi restituire (denaro); ricorrere a 14. to — off, rompere, venir meno a (un impegno) 15. to — out, invitare a uscire, far uscire; chiamare ad alta voce; esclamare; sfidare a duello; chiamare (truppe) in aiuto 16. to — over, chiamare facendo l'appello 17. to — up, (mil.) richiamare; chiamare al telefono; (far) ricordare, rievocare.

caller ['ko:lə*], s.c. visitatore, visitatrice.

calligrapher [kə'ligrəfə*], s. calligrafo.

calligraphic [,kæli'græfik], ag. calligrafico.

calligraphy [kə'ligrəfi], s. calligrafia.

Callimachus [kə'liməkəs], no.pr.m. (st. lett.) Callimaco.

calling ['ko:liŋ], s. 1. appello, chiamata 2. mestiere, occupazione, professione 3. vocazione 4. visita ☆ — hours, ore di visita.

Calliope [kə'laiəpi], no.pr.f. (mit.) Calliope.

calliper ['kælipə*], s. (gener. pl.) compasso; calibro.

to **calliper**, v.t. calibrare.

callisthenics [,kælis'θeniks], s. ginnastica ritmica.

callosity [kæ'lositi], s. 1. callosità 2. fig. insensibilità: — of heart, durezza di cuore.

callous ['kæləs], ag. 1. calloso 2. fig. insensibile, incallito, senza cuore.

callously ['kæləsli], av. senza pietà.

callousness ['kæləsnis], s. 1. callosità, durezza 2. fig. insensibilità, mancanza di cuore.

callow ['kælou], ag. implume; fig. inesperto, imberbe: a — youth, (fam.) un giovane imberbe.

callus ['kæləs], s. callo, callosità.

calm[1] [ka:m], ag. calmo, tranquillo: to fall —, (mar.) calmarsi (del vento); to grow —, calmarsi; to keep —, mantenersi calmo, non eccitarsi || s. calma; tranquillità (d'animo): a —, un periodo senza vento; — before the storm, bonaccia prima della tempesta; dead —, calma perfetta (del mare) ‖ *the calms of the tropics*, le zone calme dei tropici.

to **calm**[1], *v.t.i.* **1.** calmare, sedare (tempesta, ira): *to — s.o.* (*down*), rappacificare, calmare, tranquillizzare qlcu. **2.** *to —* **down**, calmarsi (di tempesta, dolore).

calm[2], *s.* **1.** (*metal.*) stampo da fonderia **2.** (*ind. tessile*) liccio di telaio.

calmative ['kælmətiv], *ag.s.* (*farm.*) calmante.

calming ['kɑ:miŋ], *ag.* calmante.

calmly ['kɑ:mli], *av.* con calma, tranquillamente.

calmness ['kɑ:mnis], *s.* calma, tranquillità.

calomel ['kæləmel], *s.* (*farm.*) calomelano.

caloric [kə'lɔrik], *s.* calore ☆ *— -engine*, motore ad aria calda.

calorie ['kæləri], *s.* caloria.

calorifacient [kə,lɔri'feiʃənt], *ag.* (*fis.*) calorifico.

calorific [,kælə'rifik], *ag.* (*fis.*) calorifico.

calorification [kə,lɔrifi'keiʃən], *s.*(*fis.*) calorificazione.

calorimeter [,kælə'rimitə*], *s.* (*fis.*) calorimetro.

calorimetrical [,kæləri'metrikəl], *ag.* (*fis.*) calorimetrico.

calorimetry [,kælə'rimitri], *s.* (*fis.*) calorimetria.

calory ['kæləri], *s.* caloria.

calotte [kə'lɔt], *s.* **1.** calotta, zucchetto (di ecclesiastico) **2.** (*geol.*) calotta glaciale.

calumet ['kæljumet], *s.* «calumet» (pipa degli Indiani del Nord America) ‖ *to smoke the — of peace with s.o.*, fare la pace con qlcu.

to **calumniate** [kə'lʌmnieit], *v.t.* calunniare.

calumniation [kə,lʌmni'eiʃən], *s.* calunnia.

calumniator [kə'lʌmnieitə*], *s.c.* calunniatore, calunniatrice.

calumnious [kə'lʌmniəs], *ag.* calunnioso.

calumniously [kə'lʌmniəsli], *av.* calunniosamente.

calumny ['kæləmni], *s.* calunnia.

Calvary ['kælvəri], *no.pr.* (*geog.*) Calvario, Golgota ‖ **calvary**, *s.* calvario, Via Crucis.

to **calve** [kɑ:v], *v.t.i.* **1.** figliare, partorire (di vacca) **2.** lasciar cadere blocchi di ghiaccio (di iceberg, ghiacciaio).

calves [kɑ:vz], *pl.* di **calf**[1], **calf**[2].

Calvinism ['kælvinizəm], *s.* (*st. relig.*) calvinismo.

Calvinist ['kælvinist], *s.c.* (*st. relig.*) calvinista.

Calvinistic(al) [,kælvi'nistik(əl)], *ag.* calvinistico.

to **Calvinize** ['kælvinaiz], *v.t.i.* convertire, convertirsi al calvinismo.

calx [kælks], *pl.* **calces** ['kælsi:z], *s.* (*metal.*) residuo di minerale o metallo bruciato.

calycanthus [,kæli'kænθəs], *s.* (*bot.*) calicanto.

calyciform [kə'lisifɔ:m], *ag.* (*bot.*) a forma di calice.

Calypso [kə'lipsou], *no.pr.f.* (*mit.*) Calipso.

calypso, *s.* calipso (danza, canto originario di Trinidad).

calyx ['keiliks], *pl.* **calyxes** ['keiliksiz], **calyces** ['keilisi:z], *s.* (*bot.*) calice.

cam[1] [kæm], *s.* (*mec.*) camma.

cam[2], *s.* cresta, monticello di terra.

camaron [,kɑ:mɑ:'roun], *s.* (*zool.*) granchio d'acqua dolce.

Camberwell Beauty ['kæmbəwəl 'bju:ti], *s.* (*entom.*) vanessa antiopa.

cambist ['kæmbist], *s.* cambista, cambiavalute.

Cambodia [kæm'boudjə], *no.pr.* (*geog.*) Cambogia.

Cambrian ['kæmbriən], *ag.* **1.** gallese **2.** (*geol.*) cambriano ‖ *s.c.* antico abitatore, abitatrice del Galles ‖ *s.* (*geol.*) periodo, sistema cambriano.

cambric ['keimbrik], *s.* cambrì, percalle.

Cambridge ['keimbridʒ], *no.pr.* (*geog.*) Cambridge (famoso centro universitario inglese).

came [keim], *pass.* di to **come**.

camel ['kæməl], *s.* **1.** (*zool.*) cammello **2.** cassone pneumatico ☆ *— -corps*, (*mil.*) corpo di meharisti; *— -driver*, cammelliere ‖ *Arabian —* (o *one-humped —*), dromedario; *Bactrian —* (o *two-humped —*), cammello a due gobbe.

cameleer [,kæmi'liə*], *s.* cammelliere.

cameline ['kæməlin], *s.* tessuto di pelo di cammello.

camellia [kə'mi:ljə], *s.* (*bot.*) camelia.

camelopard ['kæmiləpɑ:d], *s.* (*zool.*) giraffa.

Camelot ['kæmilɔt], *no.pr.* (*geog. lett.*) Camelot (leggendaria sede della corte di re Artù).

camelry ['kæməlri], *s.* (*mil.*) compagnia di meharisti.

cameo ['kæmiou], *s.* cammeo.

camera ['kæmərə], *s.* **1.** (*foto.*) macchina fotografica; (*tv.*) telecamera **2.** (*dir.*) Camera di Consiglio; gabinetto del giudice ‖ *in —*, a porte chiuse ☆ *— -man*, giornalista fotografo; operatore cinematografico, televisivo; *— obscura*, (*ott.*) camera oscura.

camerlingo [,kæmə'lingou], *s.* (*eccl.*) camerlengo.

Cameroons ['kæməru:nz], *no.pr.* (*geog.*) Camerun (inglese).

Cameroun [kæm'ru:n], *no.pr.* (*geog.*) Camerun (francese).

cami-knickers ['kæmi'nikəz], *s.pl.* pagliaccetto.

Camilla [kə'milə], *no.pr.f.* Camilla.

Camillus [kə'miləs], *no.pr.m.* (*st.*) Camillo.

camion [,kɑ:'miɔːŋ], *s.* (*rar.*) camion, autocarro.

cami-petticoat ['kæmi'petikout], *s.* combinazione, pagliaccetto a tre pezzi.

camisole ['kæmisoul], *s.* corpetto; camiciola; copribusto.

camlet ['kæmlit], *s.* (tessuto di pelo di) cammello.

camomile ['kæməmail], *s.* camomilla ☆ *— -tea*, tisana di camomilla.

Camorra [kə'mɔrə], *s.* (*st. napoletana*) camorra.

camorrism [kə'mɔrizəm], *s.* camorrismo, anarchia.

camouflage ['kæmuflɑ:ʒ], *s.* **1.** mascheramento **2.** (*mil.*) mimetizzazione.

to **camouflage**, *v.t.* **1.** mascherare **2.** (*mil.*) mimetizzare.

camp [kæmp], *s.* (*mil.*) campo; accampamento; campeggio: *to be in —*, essere accampato; *to go to —*, andare al campo; *to pitch a —*, impiantare un accampamento ☆ *— -bed*, letto da campo, brandina; *— -chair*, sedia pieghevole; *— -fever*, tifo, febbre tifoidea; *— -followers*, civili al seguito di un esercito; *— -kettle*, (*mil.*) marmitta; *— stool*, seggiolino pieghevole.

to **camp**, *v.t.i.* accampare (truppe), accamparsi; attendarsi; dormire all'addiaccio.

campaign [kæm'pein], *s.* campagna (militare, ecc.) ☆ *anti-waste —*, campagna contro lo spreco; *electoral —*, (*fam.*) campagna elettorale.

to **campaign**, *v.i.* fare una campagna (militare, ecc.).

campaigner [kæm'peinə*], *s.* militare in campagna ☆ *old —*, reduce; veterano; *fig.* vecchia volpe.

campaigning [kæm'peiniŋ], *s.* vita di campagna (militare), di soldato.

campaniform [kəm'pænifɔ:m], *ag.* campaniforme.

campanile [,kæmpə'ni:li], *s.* campanile.

campanist ['kæmpənist], *s.* esperto in campane.

campanology [,kæmpə'nɔlədʒi], *s.* campanologia.

campanula [kəm'pænjulə], *s.* (*bot.*) campanula.

campanulate [kæm'pænjulit], *ag.*(*bot.*) campanulato.

camper ['kæmpə*], **camper-out** ['kæmpəraut], *s.c.* campeggiatore, campeggiatrice.

campestral [kæm'pestrəl], *ag.* (*rar.*) campestre.

camphor ['kæmfə*], *s.* (*chim.*) canfora.

camphorate ['kæmfərit], *s.* (*chim.*) canforato.

to **camphorate** ['kæmfəreit], *v.t.* (*chim.*) canforare ☆ *camphorated oil*, olio canforato.

camphoric [kæm'fɔrik], *ag.* (*chim.*) canforico.

camping ['kæmpiŋ], *s.* **1.** (*mil.*) accampamento **2.** campeggio ☆ *— -ground*, luogo per campeggio.

campus ['kæmpəs], *s.* (*amer.*) **1.** l'insieme dei terreni, campi di giuoco, edifici su cui sorge una scuola, un istituto universitario **2.** *fig.* mondo universitario.

can[1] [kæn], *s.* **1.** recipiente di latta, di rame; bidone; (*amer.*) barattolo, scatola di latta per cibi conservati **2.** (*sl. amer.*) aeroplano; automobile: *an old tin —*, un vecchio macinino ☆ *— -opener*, apriscatole ‖ *milk —*, bidone per il latte.

to **can**[1], *pass.p.p.* **canned** [kænd], *v.t.* (*amer.*) mettere, conservare in scatola (carne, cibi).

can[2] [kæn (*forma forte*), kən, kn (*forme deboli*)], *v. difettivo* (V); (*indic. congiunt. pres.* **can**; *indic. congiunt. pass. e condiz.* **could** [kud (*forma forte*), kəd (*forma debole*)]; 2ª *persona sing. pres. indic.* (*poet.*) **canst** [kænst (*forma forte*), kənst (*forma debole*)]; *forme negative:* **cannot** ['kænɔt], **cannot** [kæn nɔt], **could not** [kudnɔt]; *forme contratte:* **can't** [ka:nt], **couldn't** ['kudnt]) **1. potere, essere capace di, essere in grado di; sapere;** (*fam.*) essere lecito, permesso, possibile: — *you play the piano?*, sapete suonare il piano?; *can't you help me?*, non potete aiutarmi?; *he* — *lift thirty kilograms with one hand*, può sollevare trenta chilogrammi con una mano; *he* — *speak five languages*, può, sa parlare cinque lingue; *I cannot tell you his name*, non posso dirvi il suo nome; *it cannot be done*, non è possibile fare ciò; *that cannot be*, ciò non può essere ‖ *could you go for me?*, potresti andare tu per me?; *he could have written*, avrebbe potuto scrivere; *I would help you if I could*, vi aiuterei se potessi; *she could not go*, ella non potè andare; *she could not have been kinder*, ella non avrebbe potuto essere più gentile **2.** (*can, could* spesso non si traducono): — *you see with this light?*, vedi con questa luce?; *I* — *smell sthg. burning*, sento bruciare ql.co.; *we could see them among the trees*, li vedevamo fra gli alberi; *you never* — *tell*, non si sa mai **3.** (**Fraseologia**): *as soon as* — *be*, appena possibile ‖ *as sure as* — *be*, indubbiamente ‖ *cannot help*, (I) non poter fare a meno: *I cannot help thinking that...*, non posso fare a meno di pensare che...; *it can't be helped*, (ciò) è inevitabile ‖ — *but*, poter soltanto, non restare che: *we* — *but pay him*, non ci resta che pagarlo ‖ *cannot but*, non poter far a meno, essere costretto a: *I cannot but admit you are right*, devo ammettere che avete ragione ‖ *I can't very well accept*, (*fam.*) mi è difficile accettare.

Canaan ['keinən], *no.pr.* (*geog. st.*) Canaan.

Canada ['kænədə], *no.pr.* (*geog.*) Canada.

Canadian [kə'neidjən], *ag. s.c.* canadese.

canal [kə'næl], *s.* **1.** canale ‖ *the Grand Canal*, il Canal Grande (a Venezia) ‖ *the Panama Canal*, il Canale di Panama **2.** (*anat. zool.*) canale, tubo ☆ — *rays*, (*fis.*) raggi positivi ‖ *branch* —, canale derivato.

canalization [,kænəlai'zeiʃən], *s.* canalizzazione.

to **canalize** ['kænəlaiz], *v.t.* **1.** canalizzare; fornire di canali **2.** *fig.* convogliare.

canard [kæ'na:d], *s.* **1.** fandonia, frottola, panzana (dei giornali) **2.** (*aer.*) canard.

Canary [kə'nɛəri], *no.pr.* (*geog.*) la Gran Canaria ‖ *the* — *Islands* (o *the Canaries*), le (Isole) Canarie.

canary, *ag.* giallo canarino ‖ *s.* **1.** — (*-bird*), (*ornit.*) canarino **2.** « canary » (antica danza spagnola) **3.** color giallo canarino ☆ — *grass*, (*bot.*) canaria; — *seed*, (*bot.*) scagliuola ‖ *hen-* —, (*ornit.*) canarina.

canasta [kə'næstə], *s.* canasta (giuoco di carte).

canaster [kə'næstə*], *s.* **1.** canestro (per imballare il tabacco) **2.** tabacco seccato e tagliuzzato.

cancel ['kænsəl], *s.* **1.** contrordine **2.** (*tip.*) soppressione (di pagine stampate); la pagina stampata soppressa o quella che la sostituisce **3.** *pl.* (*pair of*) *cancels*, (*ferr.*, ecc.) pinza per forare i biglietti.

to **cancel**, *pass.p.p.* **cancelled** ['kænsəld], *v.t.i.* **1.** cancellare; annullare (assegno, francobollo, ordine, debito, ecc.); sopprimere: *he cancelled his booking for that journey*, egli ha annullato la sua prenotazione per quel viaggio **2.** revocare (testamento); rescindere (contratto, ecc.) **3.** (*mat.*) elidere (fattori comuni) **4.** *to* — **out**, annullarsi, eliminarsi (anche *mat.*).

cancellable ['kænsələbl], *ag.* cancellabile, annullabile.

cancellate(d) ['kænsəleit(id)], *ag.* (*bot. zool.*) reticolato.

cancellation [,kænse'leiʃən], *s.* cancellatura; cassatura; annullamento; soppressione.

cancellous ['kænsələs], *ag.* (*anat.*) **1.** cellulare **2.** spongioso.

Cancer ['kænsə*], *no.pr.* (*astr.*) Cancro ‖ *The Tropic of* —, il Tropico del Cancro ‖ **cancer**, *s.* (*patol.*) cancro, carcinoma ☆ — *patient*, ammalato di cancro, canceroso.

cancered ['kænsəd], **cancerous** ['kænsərəs], *ag.* (*patol.*) canceroso.

cancroid ['kænkrɔid], *ag.* **1.** (*patol.*) cancroide **2.** (*zool.*) cancriforme, a forma di granchio ‖ *s.* **1.** (*patol.*) cancroide **2.** (*zool.*) crostaceo simile a granchio.

candelabrum [,kændi'la:brəm], *pl.* **candelabra** [,kændi'la:brə], *s.* candelabro; lampadario.

candescence [kən'desəns], *s.* candescenza.

candescent [kən'desənt], *ag.* candescente.

Candia ['kændiə], *no.pr.* (*geog.*) Candia.

candid ['kændid], *ag.* **1.** franco, sincero, schietto; candido **2.** imparziale; senza pregiudizi: *give me a* — *hearing*, ascoltami senza pregiudizi.

Candida ['kændidə], *no.pr.f.* Candida.

candidacy ['kændidəsi], *s.* candidatura.

candidate ['kændidit], *s.* candidato.

candidature ['kændiditʃə*], *s.* candidatura.

candidly ['kændidli], *av.* **1.** sinceramente, francamente; candidamente **2.** imparzialmente.

candidness ['kændidnis], *s.* **1.** sincerità, buona fede **2.** imparzialità.

candied ['kændid], *ag.* **1.** candito **2.** *fig.* mellifluo ☆ — *fruit*, frutta candita.

candle ['kændl], *s.* candela ‖ *the game is not worth the* —, il giuoco non vale la candela ‖ *to burn the* — *at both ends*, (*fam.*) lavorare eccessivamente, esaurirsi ☆ — *end*, moccolo; — *holder*, candelabro; — *light*, lume di candela; *by* — *light*, al lume di candela; — *power*, (*fis.*) intensità luminosa (in candele): *100* — *power*, da 100 candele; — *snuffer*, smoccolatoio; — *waster*, chi studia a notte tarda, chi fa della notte giorno; — *wick*, stoppino, lucignolo ‖ *church* —, cero; *Roman* —, candela romana, bengala; *stearine, tallow, wax* —, candela di stearina, sego, cera.

Candlemas ['kændlməs], *s.* (*eccl.*) Candelora.

candlestick ['kændlstik], *s.* candeliere.

candour ['kændə*], *s.* **1.** franchezza, sincerità; candore **2.** imparzialità.

candy ['kændi], *s.* **1.** (*sugar-*) —, candito **2.** (*amer.*) dolciume: *a box of candies*, una scatola di dolciumi ☆ — *floss*, zucchero filato.

to **candy**, *v.t.i.* **1.** candire **2.** cristallizzarsi (di zucchero).

candytuft ['kænditʌft], *s.* (*bot.*) iberide.

cane [kein], *s.* **1.** canna; giunco **2.** bastone da passeggio; bastoncino flessibile (usato per punire gli scolari discoli) ☆ — *bottomed chair*, sedia con sedile di canna; — *sugar*, zucchero di canna ‖ *Malacca-* —, bastone di Malacca; *sugar-* —, canna da zucchero.

to **cane**, *v.t.* **1.** bastonare (con una canna) ‖ *he caned Latin into me*, mi insegnò il latino a furia di botte **2.** inserire cannucce in (una sedia, ecc.).

canescent [kə'nesənt], *ag.* bianchiccio.

canful ['kænful], *s.* bidone pieno.

canicular [kə'nikjulə*], *ag.* canicolare.

canine ['keinain], *come s.* ['kænain], *ag.* canino, di cane ‖ *s.* (dente) canino.

caning ['keiniŋ], *s.* bastonatura: *a good* (o *a sound*) —, una buona bastonatura.

canister ['kænistə*], *s.* scatola di metallo bianco ☆ — *shot*, proietto a mitraglia ‖ *tea* —, scatola da tè.

canker ['kæŋkə*], *s.* **1.** (*patol.*) stomatite aftosa; noma **2.** *fig.* influenza corruttrice, nefasta **3.** (*arc.*) rosa canina **4.** (*bot.*) malattia degli alberi da frutta **5.** (*vet.*) malattia al piede del cavallo.

to **canker**, *v.t.i.* ulcerarsi, andare in cancrena; corrodere, rodere (albero, fiore, ecc.); *fig.* corrompere (un'anima, una società).

cankered ['kæŋkəd], *ag.* affetto da ulcerazione; infetto; corroso: — *rose*, rosa corrosa (dai bruchi).

cankerous ['kæŋkərəs], *ag.* (*patol.*) cancrenoso.

canna ['kænə], *s.* (*bot.*) canna.

canned [kænd], *ag.* conservato in scatola ☆ — *meat*,

carne in scatola; — *music*, (*scherz.*) musica riprodotta, incisa.

cannel ['kænl], *s.* carbone bituminoso ☆ — *-coal*, carbone a lunga fiamma.

canner ['kænə*], *s.* (*amer.*) chi mette in scatola cibi per conservarli.

cannery ['kænəri], *s.* (*amer.*) fabbrica di conserve alimentari.

cannibal ['kænibəl], *s.c.* cannibale.

cannibalism ['kænibəlizəm], *s.* cannibalismo.

cannibalistic [,kænibə'listik], *ag.* cannibalesco.

to **cannibalize** ['kænibəlaiz], *v.t.* « cannibalizzare », smontare (motori) per utilizzarne i pezzi.

cannikin ['kænikin], *s.* piccola scatola di latta.

cannily ['kænili], *av.* (*scoz.*) astutamente; prudentemente.

canniness ['kæninis], *s.* (*scoz.*) circospezione; cortesia.

cannon[1] ['kænən], *s.* **1.** (*gener. invariato al pl.*) cannone **2.** (*biliardo*) carambola ☆ — *-ball*, palla da cannone; — *-shot*, colpo di cannone.

to **cannon**[1], *v.t.i.* **1.** cannoneggiare **2.** (*biliardo*) far carambola; *fig.* scontrarsi: *to — into* (o *against*) *s.o.*, *sthg.*, urtare violentemente qlcu., ql.co.

cannon[2], *s.* ricciolone, boccolotto.

cannonade [,kænə'neid], *s.* cannoneggiamento; bombardamento.

to **cannonade**, *v.t.i* cannoneggiare; bombardare.

cannoneer [,kænə'niə*], *s.* cannoniere.

cannot ['kænət], *V.* **can.**

canny ['kæni], *ag.* circospetto; astuto; prudente; abile ‖ *ca'* —, (*scoz.*) va prudente, guardingo.

canoe [kə'nu:], *s.* canoa ‖ *to paddle one's own* —, (*fam.*) occuparsi dei fatti propri.

to **canoe**, *v.i.* andare in canoa.

canoeist [kə'nu:ist], *s.* rematore di canoa.

canon[1] ['kænən], *s.* **1.** (*eccl. dir. mus.*) canone **2.** regola, disciplina ☆ — *-law*, diritto canonico.

canon[2], *s.* (*eccl.*) canonico.

cañon, *V.* **canyon.**

canoness ['kænənis], *s.* (*eccl.*) canonichessa.

canonical [kə'nɔnikəl], *ag.s.* (*eccl.*) canonico ☆ — *hour*, ora canonica.

canonically [kə'nɔnikəli], *av.* (*eccl.*) canonicamente.

canonicals [kə'nɔnikəlz], *s.pl.* abiti sacerdotali.

canonicate [kə'nɔnikeit], *s.* (*eccl.*) canonicato.

canonist ['kænənist], *s.* canonista.

canonizable ['kænənaizəbl], *ag.* (*eccl.*) canonizzabile.

canonization [,kænənai'zeiʃən], *s.* (*eccl.*) canonizzazione.

to **canonize** ['kænənaiz], *v.t.* (*eccl.*) canonizzare.

canonry ['kænənri], *s.* (*eccl.*) canonicato.

canopy ['kænəpi], *s.* **1.** baldacchino **2.** volta (del cielo): *the — of heaven*, la volta del cielo ‖ *no one under God's* —, (*amer. fam.*) nessuno al mondo **3.** (*arch.*) sporgenza ornamentale a guisa di tetto **4.** (*aer.*) calotta, tettuccio.

to **canopy**, *v.t.* coprire con baldacchino, fornire di baldacchino.

canorous [kə'nɔ:rəs], *ag.* canoro; armonioso; sonoro.

canst [kænst (*forma forte*), kənst (*forma debole*)], 2ª *persona sing. pres. indic.* (*arc.*) di **can.**

cant[1] [kænt], *s.* **1.** (*arch.*) angolo esterno; angolo tronco; angolo di muro smussato **2.** (*ferr.*) sopraelevazione: — *of a track*, sopraelevazione di una rotaia **3.** (*mar.*) ordinata deviata, costa deviata **4.** inclinazione, curvatura **5.** spinta, urto (che fa inclinare ql.co.).

to **cant**[1], *v.t.i.* **1.** (*arch.*) smussare **2.** inclinare, curvare (una trave), curvarsi; pendere **3.** spingere; urtare.

cant[2], *ag.* **1.** di gergo **2.** trito, banale, comune **3.** falso ‖ *s.* **1.** gergo (di determinati ambienti, tempi): *in the — of the day*, nel linguaggio di quel tempo **2.** frase fatta, luogo comune **3.** parlata piena d'unzione; ipocrisia **4.** chiacchiere false: *that's all* —, sono tutte chiacchiere.

to **cant**[2], *v.i.* **1.** piagnucolare (come un mendicante) **2.** parlare in gergo **3.** parlare con affettazione, con ipocrisia **4.** fare l'ipocrita, il bacchettone.

can't [kɑ:nt], (*contr.*) di *can not.*

Cantab ['kæntæb], *s.* (*sl.*) membro dell'università di Cambridge.

Cantabrigian [,kæntə'bridʒiən], *ag.s.* (membro) dell'università di Cambridge.

cantaloup ['kæntəlu:p], *s.* (*bot.*) melone.

cantankerous [kən'tæŋkərəs], *ag.* (*fam.*) stizzoso; litigioso: *to be* —, avere un cattivo carattere.

cantankerously [kən'tæŋkərəsli], *av.* stizzosamente.

cantakerousness [kən'tæŋkərəsnis], *s.* carattere bisbetico, scontroso.

cantata [kæn'tɑːtə], *s.* (*mus.*) cantata.

canteen [kæn'tiːn], *s.* **1.** (*mil.*) cantina, dispensa **2.** (*mil.*) mensa aziendale **4.** cestino per le posate ☆ — *-keeper*, cantiniere ‖ *dry* —, cantina per provvigioni; *wet* —, cantina per liquori.

canter[1] [kæntə*], *s.* **1.** chi usa un gergo **2.** ipocrita; chi parla con unzione.

canter[2], *s.* piccolo galoppo.

to **canter**[2], *v.t.i.* andare a piccolo galoppo; fare andare (un cavallo) a piccolo galoppo.

Canterbury ['kæntəbəri], *no.pr.* (*geog.*) Canterbury ‖ **canterbury**, *s.* scaffale per musica ☆ — *bell*, (*bot.*) specie di campanula.

cantharides [kæn'θæridi:z], *s.pl.* (*farm.*) cantaridi.

canticle ['kæntikl], *s.* cantico ‖ *"The Canticles"*, (*Bibbia*) « Il Cantico dei Cantici ».

cantilever ['kæntiliːvə*], *s.* (*arch.*) trave a sbalzo ☆ — *bridge*, ponte a mensola.

cantle ['kæntl], *s.* **1.** pezzetto (di pane, formaggio); frammento **2.** arcione posteriore (di sella).

canto ['kæntou], *pl.* **cantos** ['kæntouz], *s.* (*mus. poes.*) canto.

canton ['kæntən], *s.* (*geog.*) cantone.

to **canton** [kæn'ton], *nel senso 2.* [kən'tu:n], *v.t.* **1.** dividere in cantoni **2.** (*mil.*) accantonare (truppe).

cantonment [kən'tu:nmənt], *s.* (*mil.*) accantonamento, acquartieramento.

cantor ['kæntɔ:*], *s.* (*eccl.*) cantore.

cantorial [kæn'tɔ:riəl], *ag.* (*eccl.*) di, da cantore.

cantrip ['kæntrip], *s.* (*scoz.*) **1.** incantesimo **2.** burla, scherzo.

canty ['kænti], *ag.* (*scoz.*) allegro.

Canuck [kə'nʌk], *s.* **1.** (*amer.*) canadese; (*sl.*) franco-canadese **2.** cavallo canadese.

Canute [kə'nju:t], *no.pr.m.* (*st.*) Canuto.

canvas ['kænvəs], *s.* **1.** canovaccio, grossa tela di canapa ‖ *under* —, (*mil.*) sotto la tenda **2.** (*mar.*) velatura, vele: *under* —, a vele spiegate; *with all her — spread* (o *with every stitch of — set*), con tutte le vele distese, spiegate **3.** tela, quadro ☆ — *town*, tendopoli, grande campeggio.

canvass ['kænvəs], *s.* **1.** esame **2.** (*pol. comm.*) sollecitazione (di voti, ordini, azioni).

to **canvass**, *v.t.i.* **1.** passare al vaglio, discutere **2.** (*pol.*) sollecitare (voti), fare un giro elettorale; (*comm.*) sollecitare (ordinazioni).

canvasser ['kænvəsə*], *s.c.* **1.** (*pol.*) agente elettorale; sollecitatore, sollecitatrice di voti degli elettori **2.** (*comm.*) piazzista.

canvassing ['kænvəsiŋ], *V.* **canvass.**

canyon ['kænjən], *s.* (*geol. geog.*) « canyon », profondo burrone, vallone.

canzone [kæn'tsouni], *s.* (*poes.*) canzone.

canzonet [,kænzə'net], *s.* (*poes.*) canzonetta.

caoutchouc ['kautʃuk], *ag.* di cauccìù ‖ *s.* cauccìù.

cap[1] [kæp], *s.* **1.** berretto, copricapo; berretta (da cardinale); berretto da militare, da marinaio; cuffia, cuffietta: *housemaid's* —, cuffietta, cresta di cameriera ‖ — *and bells*, berretto a sonagli (del buffone, giullare) ‖ *the — fits*, *fig.* l'osservazione è giusta ‖ — *in hand*, umilmente, ‖ — *of liberty*, berretto frigio ‖ *a feather* *in one's* —, *fig.* una ragione di onore, un segno di distinzione ‖ *in* — *and gown*, in tocco e toga, in costume accademico ‖ *to set one's* — *at*, cercare di cattivarsi le simpatie 2. (*arch.*) capitello, coronamento 3. (*chim. mec. elett.*) cappuccio, cappello, coperchio, tappo, capsula, calotta, cappa, puntalino 4. (*mar.*) testa di moro (di albero) 5. cappello di fungo 6. cappuccio di uccello ☆ — -*paper*, carta da pacchi, carta da scrivere; — *screw*, vite mordente; — -*stone*, cresta, tettuccio (di muro) ‖ *bathing*- —, cuffia da bagno; *black* - —, berretto nero indossato dal giudice quando pronuncia una sentenza di morte; *cartridge*- — (o *percussion*- —), capsula, cappellotto (di cartuccia); *skull* - —, calotta, papalina, zucchetto; *steel* —, elmetto.

to **cap**[1], *pass.p.p.* **capped** [kæpt], *v.t.i.* 1. coprire (il capo) con berretto, cuffia; conferire una laurea a (in università scozzesi); incoronare ‖ *that caps all!*, è il colmo! 2. coprire con coperchio, capsula; tappare 3. ricostruire (un pneumatico), applicare un nuovo battistrada a 4. (*spor.*) scegliere (membro di squadra sportiva) 5. (*fam.*) salutare, levarsi il cappello di fronte a 6. sorpassare: *to* — *an anecdote*, fare seguito ad un aneddoto con un altro non meno interessante o anche migliore.

cap[2], *s.* (*sl. abbr.* di *captain*) capitano.
capability [ˌkeipəˈbiliti], *s.* 1. capacità, idoneità, abilità 2. possibilità: *the plan has capabilities*, il piano ha delle possibilità ‖ — *to do sthg.*, facoltà di fare ql.co.
capable [ˈkeipəbl], *ag.* 1. capace, abile, competente, esperto: — *of* (*doing*) *sthg.*, capace di (fare) ql.co.; *very* — *doctor*, medico molto competente 2. suscettibile (di miglioramento, ecc.).
capacious [kəˈpeiʃəs], *ag.* vasto, spazioso, capace.
capaciousness [kəˈpeiʃəsnis], *s.* vastità, capacità, spaziosità.
to **capacitate** [kəˈpæsiteit], *v.t.* rendere, fare capace, qualificare: *to* — *s.o. to act*, (*dir.*) dare a qlcu. il potere, la capacità legale di agire.
capacitor [kəˈpæsitə*], *s.* (*elett.*) condensatore.
capacity [kəˈpæsiti], *s.* 1. capacità, abilità: *a person of* —, una persona capace 2. (*dir.*) capacità, competenza legale: *to act in one's official* —, agire nell'esercizio delle proprie funzioni; *to have* — *to act*, avere la capacità (legale) di agire 3. capacità, capienza 4. (*elett.*) potenza (di motore) ☆ *business* —, abilità negli affari; *carrying* —, carico massimo (di carro, ecc.); *productive* —, (*ind.*) capacità produttiva; *seating* —, numero di posti a sedere (in teatro, ecc.).
cap-à-pie [ˌkæpəˈpiː], *av.* da capo a piedi.
caparison [kəˈpærisn], *s.* 1. gualdrappa, bardatura (di cavallo) 2. abbigliamento sontuoso.
to **caparison**, *v.t.* bardare (un cavallo).
cape[1] [keip], *s.* capo, promontorio ‖ *the Cape (of Good Hope)*, il Capo di Buona Speranza ‖ *Cape boy*, ragazzo sudafricano di sangue misto; *Cape colony* (o *fam. the Cape*), Colonia del Capo; *Cape Dutch*, gli olandesi della Colonia del Capo; la lingua parlata dagli Afrikander ‖ *to go round* (o *to round*) *Cape Horn*, doppiare il Capo Horn.
cape[2], *s.* cappa, mantellina ‖ — *and sword novel*, romanzo di cappa e spada.
caper[1] [ˈkeipə*], *s.* (*bot.*) cappero ☆ — -*bush* (o — -*plant*), (pianta del) cappero; — -*sauce*, salsa di capperi.
caper[2], *s.* capriola, salto; *fig.* stramberia: *to cut capers*, far capriole; *fig.* far stramberie.
to **caper**[2], *v.i.* far capriole, salti ‖ *to* — *about*, saltellare qua e là.
caper[3], *s.* (*st.*) pirata; capitano di nave corsara.
capercaillie[ˌkæpəˈkeilji], **capercailzie**[ˌkæpəˈkeilzi], (*ornit.*) gallo cedrone.
caperer [ˈkeipərə*], *s.c.* chi fa capriole.
Capernaum [kəˈpəːnjəm], *no.pr.* (*geog.*) Cafarnao.
Capetown [ˈkeiptaun], *no.pr.* (*geog.*) Città del Capo.
capful [ˈkæpful], *s.* il contenuto di un berretto, cappellata ‖ *a* — *of wind*, una folata di vento.

capias [ˈkeipiæs], *s.* (*dir.*) mandato di cattura.
capillarity [ˌkæpiˈlæriti], *s.* (*fis.*) capillarità.
capillary [kəˈpiləri], *ag.* capillare ‖ *s.* (*anat.*) vaso capillare ☆ — *attraction, repulsion*, (*fis.*) attrazione, repulsione capillare.
capital[1] [ˈkæpitl], *ag.* 1. capitale: *of* — *importance*, di importanza capitale 2. magnifico, eccellente (specialmente nelle esclamazioni) ‖ *s.* 1. — (*city*), capitale (di uno Stato) 2. (*letter.*) lettera maiuscola 3. (*comm.*) capitale: *paid in* (o *paid-up*) —, capitale versato, effettivo ‖ *to make* — *out of sthg.*, trarre vantaggio da ql.co. ☆ — *account*, conto capitale; — *crime*, (*dir.*) delitto capitale; — -*levy*, imposta sul capitale; — *punishment*, pena di morte ‖ *company's* —, capitale sociale; *registered* —, capitale sociale nominale; *working* —, capitale circolante.
capital[2], *s.* (*arch.*) capitello.
capitalism [ˈkæpitəlizm], *s.* capitalismo.
capitalist [ˈkæpitəlist], *s.* capitalista.
capitalistic [ˌkæpitəˈlistik], *ag.* capitalistico.
capitalizable [ˈkæpitəˌlaizəbl], *ag.* che si può capitalizzare.
capitalization [kəˌpitəlaiˈzeiʃən], *s.* 1. capitalizzazione 2. uso delle lettere maiuscole.
to **capitalize** [kəˈpitəlaiz], *v.t.* 1. capitalizzare 2. scrivere (una parola) con lettera iniziale maiuscola.
capitally [ˈkæpitli], *av.* 1. a meraviglia, in modo eccellente 2. con pena capitale.
capitation [ˌkæpiˈteiʃən], *s.* (*dir.*) testatico.
Capitol (the) [ˈkæpitl], *s.* Campidoglio (a Roma, a Washington).
Capitoline [kəˈpitəlain], *ag.* capitolino.
capitular [kəˈpitjulə*], *ag.* (*eccl.*) capitolare.
capitulary [kəˈpitjuləri], *s.* (*st.*) capitolare: *the capitularies of Charlemagne*, i capitolari di Carlo Magno.
to **capitulate** [kəˈpitjuleit], *v.i.* (*mil.*) capitolare, arrendersi.
capitulation [kəˌpitjuˈleiʃən], *s.* 1. capitolazione, resa 2. *pl.* patti della resa.
capless [ˈkæplis], *ag.* senza berretto, cappello.
capon [ˈkeipən], *s.* cappone.
caponier [ˌkæpəˈniə*], *s.* (*mil. aer.*) capponiera.
to **caponize** [ˈkeipənaiz], *v.t.* capponare.
caporal [ˌkæpəˈrɑːl], *s.* «caporal» (tipo di tabacco francese).
capot [kəˈpɔt], *s.* cappotto (al giuoco).
to **capot**, *pass.p.p.* **capotted** [kəˈpɔtid], *v.t.* dar cappotto a (giocando a carte).
capote [kəˈpout], *s.* mantello con cappuccio (da militare, da viaggio).
capric [ˈkæprik], *ag.* (*chim.*) caprico.
capriccio [kəˈpritʃiou], *s.* (*mus.*) capriccio.
caprice [kəˈpriːs], *s.* capriccio, fantasia.
capricious [kəˈpriʃəs], *ag.* capriccioso; incostante.
capriciously [kəˈpriʃəsli], *av.* capricciosamente.
capriciousness [kəˈpriʃəsnis], *s.* capricciosità.
Capricorn [ˈkæprikɔːn], *no.pr.* (*astr.*) Capricorno ‖ *the Tropic of* —, il Tropico del Capricorno.
caprification [ˌkæprifiˈkeiʃən], *s.* caprificazione.
caprine [ˈkæprain], *ag.* (*zool.*) caprino.
capriole [ˈkæprioul], *s.* l'impennarsi, lo sgroppare (di cavallo).
to **capriole**, *v.i.* impennarsi, sgroppare (di cavallo).
caproic [kəˈprouik], *ag.* (*chim.*) caproico.
capsicum [ˈkæpsikəm], *s.* (*bot.*) capsico; pimento.
capsizable [kæpˈsaizəbl], *ag.* rovesciabile, ribaltabile.
capsizal [kæpˈsaizl], *s.* capovolgimento.
to **capsize** [kæpˈsaiz], *v.t.i.* rovesciare, rovesciarsi, capovolgere, capovolgersi (di barca, nave); ribaltare.
capstan [ˈkæpstən], *s.* (*mar.*) argano, cabestano.
capsular [ˈkæpsjulə*], *ag.* di capsula.
capsule [ˈkæpsjuːl], *s.* 1. capsula (di bottiglia, ecc.) 2. (*bot.*) pericarpo 3. (*farm.*) capsula; pillola; (*chim.*) capsula 4. (*fisiol.*) capsula 5. (*amer.*) riassunto, schema.
to **capsule**, *v.t.* 1. incapsulare 2. (*amer.*) schematizzare.

capsuliform ['kæpsjulifɔ:m], *ag.* a forma di capsula.

captain ['kæptin], *s.* **1.** (*mil. mar. spor., ecc.*) capitano, comandante; (*amer.*) comandante di polizia **2.** capo: *the great captains of industry*, i magnati dell'industria **3.** capoclasse **4.** capitano (titolo onorifico).

to **captain**, *v.t.* capitanare, comandare.

captaincy ['kæptinsi], *s.* grado di capitano.

captainship ['kæptinʃip], *s.* **1.** grado di capitano **2.** l'arte di comandare.

caption ['kæpʃən], *s.* **1.** arresto; cattura **2.** (*dir.*) allegato **3.** (*amer.*) intestazione, titolo (di libro, giornale, ecc.) **4.** (*cine.*) sottotitolo, didascalia.

captious ['kæpʃəs], *ag.* capzioso, insidioso; sofistico.

captiously ['kæpʃəsli], *av.* capziosamente; sofisticamente.

captiousnèss ['kæpʃəsnis], *s.* carattere capzioso, insidioso.

to **captivate** ['kæptiveit], *v.t.* cattivare, cattivarsi; affascinare, ammaliare, incantare, sedurre.

captivating ['kæptiveitiŋ], *ag.* cattivante; seducente, affascinante.

captivation [,kæpti'veiʃən], *s.* seduzione, fascino, incanto.

captive ['kæptiv], *ag.s.* prigioniero, schiavo: *to hold* —, tenere prigioniero; *to take* —, far prigioniero ☆ — *balloon*, (*aer.*) pallone frenato.

captivity [kæp'tiviti], *s.* cattività, prigionia.

captor ['kæptə*], *s.* chi fa prigioniero, chi cattura; catturatore.

captress ['kæptris], *s.* catturatrice.

capture ['kæptʃə*], *s.* **1.** cattura: — *at sea*, cattura di nave **2.** preda, bottino.

to **capture**, *v.t.* prendere (città, ecc.); far prigioniero (anche *fig.*): *he was captured*, fu fatto prigioniero; *to — the market*, (*comm.*) accaparrare il mercato.

capturer ['kæptʃərə*], *V.* **captor.**

capturing ['kæptʃəriŋ], *s.* cattura (di nave, malfattore, ecc.); presa (di città, ecc.).

Capuchin ['kæpjuʃin], *s.* **1.** (*eccl.*) Cappuccino **2.** cappotto da donna con cappuccio **3.** (*zool.*) cebo (scimmia dell'America centrale e meridionale) **4.** — (*-pigeon*), (*ornit.*) piccione con cappuccio.

Capulet ['kæpjulet], *no.pr.* (*st.*) Capuleto.

capybara [,kæpi'bɑ:rə], *s.* (*zool.*) capibara.

car [kɑ:*], *s.* **1.** carro, carretta (anche *poet.*): *the — of the sun*, il carro del sole **2.** (*aut. fam.* per *motor-car*), automobile, autovettura: *I went by* —, andai in macchina **3.** (*ferr. amer.*) vagone, carrozza **4.** cabina di ascensore **5.** (*aer.*) navicella di dirigibile **6.** (*miner.*) vagonetto ☆ — *-licence*, permesso di circolazione; — *-load*, carico di una vettura ‖ *armoured-* —, (*mil. amer.*) autoblinda; *baggage-* —, (*amer.*) bagagliaio; *cable-* —, funicolare; *dining-* —, vagone ristorante; *four-seater* —, auto a quattro posti; *freight-* —, carro merci; *mail-* —, (*amer.*) vagone postale; *pullman-* —, vettura salone; *sleeping-* —, vagone letto; *street-* —, (*amer.*) vettura tranviaria; *tank-* —, (*amer.*) vagone cisterna; *touring-* —, torpedone; *tram-* —, vettura tranviaria; *tram triumphal* —, carro trionfale; *trolley-* —, (*amer.*) vettura tranviaria.

carabin ['kærəbin], **carabine** ['kærəbain], *s.* carabina.

carabineer [,kærəbi'niə*], *s.* carabiniere.

caracal ['kærəkæl], *s.* (*zool.*) «caracal» (lince delle steppe).

caracole ['kærəkoul], *s.* caracollo.

to **caracole**, *v.i.* caracollare.

caracul ['kærəku:l], *s.* «caracul» (agnellino di Persia).

carafe [kə'rɑ:f] *s.* caraffa.

caramel ['kærəmel], *s.* **1.** caramello, zucchero bruciato **2.** caramella **3.** color caramello.

carapace ['kærəpeis], *s.* carapace.

carat ['kærət], *s.* **1.** carato (misura di peso per pietre preziose = mg. 200) **2.** carato (misura di purezza dell'oro).

caravan [,kærə'væn], *s.* **1.** carovana: *to travel in* —,

viaggiare in carovana, in comitiva **2.** carro (di saltimbanchi, zingari, ecc.); (*aut.*) «roulotte».

to **caravan**, *v.i.* viaggiare in «roulotte».

caravaneer [,kærəvə'niə*], *s.* carovaniere.

caravanserai [,kærə'vænsərai], *s.* caravanserraglio.

caravel ['kærəvel], *s.* (*st. mar.*) caravella.

caraway ['kærəwei], *s.* (*bot.*) comino ☆ — *seeds*, semi di comino.

carbide ['kɑ:baid], *s.* (*chim.*) carburo ☆ — *lamp*, lampada a carburo.

carbine ['kɑ:bain], *s.* carabina.

carbineer [,kɑ:bi'niə*], *s.* carabiniere.

carbohydrate ['kɑ:bou'haidreit], *s.* (*chim.*) carboidrato.

carbolic [kɑ:'bolik], *ag.* (*chim.*) fenico ☆ — *acid*, acido fenico, fenolo.

carbon ['kɑ:bən], *s.* **1.** (*chim.*) carbonio **2.** (*elett.*) carbone ☆ — *black*, nerofumo; — *copy*, copia (fatta con carta carbone); — *paper*, carta carbone, carta copiativa; — *process*, (*foto.*) processo al carbone.

carbonaceous [,kɑ:bə'neiʃəs], *ag.* di carbone; carbonoso.

carbonate ['kɑ:bənit], *s.* (*chim.*) carbonato.

to **carbonate**, *v.t.* **1.** (*chim.*) trasformare in carbonato **2.** impregnare con anidride carbonica **3.** carbonizzare.

carbonic [kɑ:'bonik], *ag.* (*chim.*) carbonico ☆ — *acid*, acido carbonico; — *acid gas*, anidride carbonica.

carboniferous [,kɑ:bə'nifərəs], *ag.* (*geol.*) carbonifero.

carbonization [,kɑ:bənai'zeiʃən], *s.* carbonizzazione.

to **carbonize** ['kɑ:bənaiz], *v.t.* carbonizzare.

carborundum [,kɑ:bə'rʌndəm], *s.* (*chim.*) carborundo.

carboy ['kɑ:boi], *s.* damigiana per liquidi corrosivi.

carbuncle ['kɑ:bʌŋkl], *s.* **1.** (*min.*) carbonchio (rubino rosso acceso) **2.** (*patol.*) carbonchio, pustola, foruncolo maligno.

carbuncled ['kɑ:bʌŋkld], *ag.* **1.** ornato di carbonchi **2.** (*patol.*) coperto di pustole, di bitorzoli.

carbuncular [kɑ:'bʌŋkjulə*], *ag.* (*patol.*) carbonchioso.

carburant ['kɑ:bjurənt], *s.* carburante.

to **carburate** ['kɑ:bjureit], *v.t.* carburare.

carburation [,kɑ:bju'reiʃən], *s.* carburazione.

carburet ['kɑ:bjuret], *s.* (*chim.*) carburo

to **carburet**, *pass.p.p.* **carburetted** ['kɑ:bjuretid], *v.t.* carburare.

carburetion [,kɑ:bju'reiʃən], *s.* (*mec.*) carburazione.

carburetter, carburetter, carburettor ['kɑ:bjuretə*], *s.* (*mec.*) carburatore.

to **carburize** ['kɑ:bjuraiz], *v.t.* carburare; (*metal.*) carburare, cementare (acciaio, ecc.).

carcanet ['kɑ:kənet], *s.* (*arc.*) monile.

carcase, carcass ['kɑ:kəs], *s.* **1.** carcassa, cadavere di animale **2.** (*spreg.*) cadavere umano **3.** armatura (di casa); ossatura (di nave); carcassa (di pneumatico).

carcinoma [,kɑ:si'noumə], *pl.* **carcinomata** [,kɑ:si'noumətə], *s.* (*patol.*) carcinoma.

card[1] [kɑ:d], *s.* **1.** cartoncino; cartolina; biglietto ‖ *to speak by the* —, parlare con precisione **2.** carta da giuoco: *game of cards*, partita a carte; *pack of cards*, mazzo di carte; *to play (at) cards*, giocare a carte ‖ *he is a queer* —, (*sl.*) è uno strano tipo ‖ *he's a knowing* —, è uno che la sa lunga ‖ *it is on the cards*, è una cosa probabile, possibile; *it is a sure* —, (*sl.*) è una cosa certa ‖ *to have a* — *up one's sleeve*, *fig.* avere un asso nella manica **3.** tessera **4.** (*mar. arc.*) quadrante ☆ — *-case*, portabiglietti da visita; — *-index*, schedario; — *-playing*, il giocare a carte; — *-sharper*, baro ‖ *admission-* —, biglietto d'entrata; *bread-* —, tessera per il pane; *business-* —, biglietto da visita di una ditta; *Christmas-* —, biglietto natalizio; *marine's* —, quadrante della bussola; *visiting* —, biglietto da visita.

to **card**[1], *v.t.* **1.** schedare, annotare su cartoncini **2.** iscrivere.

card², s. (*tessitura*) cardo, scardasso ☆ — -*thistle*, (*bot.*) cardo (usato per cardare).

to card², v.t. (*tessitura*) cardare.

cardamom ['kɑ:dəməm], s. (*bot.*) cardamomo, cardamone.

cardan ['kɑ:dən], s. (*mec.*) cardano ☆ — *joint*, giunto cardanico.

cardboard ['kɑ:dbɔ:d], s. cartone ☆ *fine* —, cartoncino.

carder ['kɑ:də*], s.c. (*tessitura*) cardatore, cardatrice ‖ s. cardatrice (macchina).

cardiac ['kɑ:diæk], ag. cardiaco ‖ s. (*farm.*) cordiale, stimolante (per il cuore).

cardigan ['kɑ:digən], s. giacca di lana lavorata a maglia.

cardinal ['kɑ:dinl], ag. cardinale ‖ s. (*eccl.*) cardinale ☆ — *altar*, altare maggiore; — -*bird*, (*ornit.*) cardinale; *the* — *numbers*, i numeri cardinali; *the* — *points*, i punti cardinali; *the* — *virtues*, le virtù cardinali.

cardinalate ['kɑ:dinəleit], s. cardinalato.

cardinally ['kɑ:dinəli], av. fondamentalmente.

cardinalship ['kɑ:dinlʃip], s. cardinalato.

carding ['kɑ:diŋ], s. (*tessitura*) cardatura ☆ — -*machine*, cardatrice.

cardiogram ['kɑ:diougræm], s. (*med.*) cardiogramma.

cardiograph ['kɑ:diougrɑ:f], s. (*med.*) cardiografo.

cardiography [,kɑ:di'ogrəfi], s. (*med.*) cardiografia.

cardiology [,kɑ:di'olədʒi], s. cardiologia.

carditis [kɑ:'daitis], s. (*patol.*) cardite.

cardoon [kɑ:'du:n], s. (*bot.*) cardone, cardo.

care [kɛə*], s. **1.** cura, diligenza, attenzione; sollecitudine; protezione; vigilanza: *in* (o *under*) *the* — *of*, sotto la vigilanza, la cura di; *want of* —, incuria, negligenza; *take* (o *have a*) —*!*, attenzione!; *to show* — *in doing sthg.*, aver cura nel fare ql.co.; *to take* (o *to have a*) —, aver cura, badare: *take* — (*that*) *you don't break it*, badate di non romperlo; *to take* — *of*, aver cura di, vigilare, curare **2.** preoccupazione, affanno, pena, inquietudine; responsabilità: *cares of State*, responsabilità di Stato; *free from* —, senza pensieri ‖ — *of* (o *amer. in* — *of*), presso (per indirizzi): *write to me* — *of Mr. X*, scrivetemi presso il sig. X ‖ *with* —*!*, attenzione!, fragile! ‖ — *killed the cat*, prov. le preoccupazioni conducono alla tomba ☆ — -*committee*, comitato di beneficenza; — -*free*, senza pensieri; — -*laden* (o — -*worn*), pieno di pensieri, di preoccupazioni.

to care, v.i. **1.** curarsi, preoccuparsi, importare, interessarsi: *as if I cared*, per me è lo stesso; *he can go to hell, for all I* —, per quanto mi riguarda può andare all'inferno; *I don't* —, non me ne importa; *who cares?*, a chi importa?, chi ci bada? ‖ *I don't* — *a bean* (o *a damn* o *a button* o *a pin* o *a farthing* o *a fig.*), (*sl.*) non me ne importa un bel niente, un fico secco **2.** *to* — *for* (*s.o.*, *sthg.*), provar piacere, interesse in; voler bene a; curare, provvedere a: *children well cared for*, bambini ben curati; *do you* — *for fishing?*, ti piace la pesca?; *do you* — *for this music?*, ti piace questa musica?; *he cares for nothing*, non si interessa di nulla; *I don't* — *for reading*, non mi piace leggere; *I don't* — *for you to speak to him*, non mi piace che tu gli parli; *she cares for me*, ella mi vuol bene; *to* — *for invalids*, curare gli invalidi.

to careen [kə'ri:n], v.t.i. (*mar.*) **1.** carenare **2.** sbandare.

careenage [kə'ri:nidʒ], s. (*mar.*) carenaggio.

careening [kə'ri:niŋ], s. (*mar.*) **1.** carenaggio **2.** sbandamento ☆ — -*basin*, bacino di carenaggio.

career [kə'riə*], s. **1.** carriera: *to take up a* —, abbracciare una carriera, una professione **2.** corsa, andatura veloce: *to be off in full* —, partire a tutta velocità ☆ — -*girl* (o — -*woman*), donna che si interessa soprattutto di fare carriera; — *man*, (*amer.*) diplomatico di carriera.

to career, v.i. **1.** andare a gran velocità: *to* — *about* (o *over*) *a place*, attraversare un posto a gran velo-

cità **2.** *to* — *along*, andare avanti a tutta velocità.

careerist [kə'riərist], s. arrivista.

careful ['kɛəful], ag. **1.** accurato, curato: *a* — *reading*, una lettura accurata **2.** attento, prudente, sollecito, guardingo: *be* —*!*, stai attento!.

carefully ['kɛəfli], av. **1.** accuratamente **2.** attentamente, sollecitamente.

carefulness ['kɛəfulnis], s. **1.** accuratezza **2.** attenzione, sollecitudine.

careless ['kɛəlis], ag. **1.** noncurante, trascurato: *he is* — *of his health*, è incurante della propria salute **2.** spensierato.

carelessly ['kɛəlisli], av. **1.** trascuratamente, negligentemente **2.** spensieratamente.

carelessness ['kɛəlisnis], s. **1.** trascuratezza, negligenza **2.** spensieratezza.

caress [kə'res], s. carezza.

to caress, v.t. accarezzare, carezzare; vezzeggiare.

caressing [kə'resiŋ], ag. carezzevole.

caressingly [kə'resiŋli], av. carezzevolmente.

caret ['kærət], s. (*tip.*) segno di omissione.

caretaker ['kɛə,teikə*], s. custode, guardiano ☆ — *government*, (*pol.*) ministero scaduto che si limita all'espletamento degli affari correnti.

cargo ['kɑ:gou], pl. **cargoes** ['kɑ:gouz], s. carico (di nave), merce imbarcata ☆ — -*boat*, nave da carico.

to cargo, v.t. caricare (una nave): *ship cargoed with wheat*, nave carica di grano.

Carib ['kærib], ag. caraibico ‖ s. caraibo.

Caribbean [,kæri'bi(:)ən], ag. caraibico: *the* — *Sea*, il Mar dei Caraibi.

caribou ['kæribu:], s. (*zool.*) caribù.

caricaturable [,kærikə'tjuərəbl], ag. che si presta alla caricatura.

caricature [,kærikə'tjuə*], s. caricatura.

to caricature, v.t. mettere in caricatura; fare la caricatura di.

caricaturist [,kærikə'tjuərist], s. caricaturista.

caries ['kɛərii:z], s. (*patol.*) carie.

carillon [kə'riljən], s. (*mus.*) «carillon».

Carinthia [kə'rinθiə], no.pr. (*geog.*) Carinzia.

carious ['kɛəriəs], ag. (*patol.*) cariato.

carking ['kɑ:kiŋ], ag.: — *care*, preoccupazioni gravose.

carline ['kɑ:lin], s. (*bot.*) carlina.

Carlism ['kɑ:lizəm], s. (*st.*) Carlismo.

Carlist ['kɑ:list], s. (*st.*) carlista.

Carlovingian [,kɑ:lou'vindʒiən], ag. (*st.*) carolingio.

carman, pl. **carmen** ['kɑ:mən], s. carrettiere.

Carmelite ['kɑ:milait], ag. (*eccl.*) carmelitano: — *nun*, Carmelitana ‖ s.c. (*eccl.*) carmelitano, carmelitana ‖ s. lana di vigogna.

carminative [kɑ:'minətiv], ag.s. (*med.*) carminativo.

carmine ['kɑ:main], ag.s. carminio.

to carmine, v.t. tingere di carminio.

carnage ['kɑ:nidʒ], s. carneficina, macello, strage.

carnal ['kɑ:nl], ag. carnale, sensuale: — *sins*, peccati carnali ☆ — -*minded*, sensuale.

carnality [kɑ:'næliti], s. carnalità, sensualità.

carnation¹ [kɑ:'neiʃən], ag. carnicino, color rosa.

carnation², s. (*bot.*) garofano.

carnelian [kə'ni:ljən], s. (*min.*) cornalina.

carnification [,kɑ:nifi'keiʃən], s. (*patol.*) carnificazione.

to carnify ['kɑ:nifai], v.t.i. (*patol.*) carnificare, carnificarsi.

carnival ['kɑ:nivəl], s. carnevale.

Carnivora [kɑ:'nivərə], s.pl. (*zool.*) i carnivori.

carnivore ['kɑ:nivo:*], s. (*zool. bot.*) carnivoro.

carnivorous [kɑ:'nivərəs], ag. carnivoro.

to carny ['kɑ:ni], v.t. (*fam.*) blandire, persuadere con moine.

carob ['kærəb], s. (*bot.*): — (-*bean*), carruba; — (-*tree*), carrubo.

carol ['kærəl], *s.* canzone di gioia, canto, inno; carola ☆ *Christmas* —, canto, inno di Natale.

to carol, *pass.p.p.* **carolled** ['kærəld], *v.t.i.* cantare con gioia; inneggiare a.

caroler ['kærələ*], *s.c.* cantatore, cantatrice (di inni di Natale).

Carolina [,kærə'lainə], *no.pr.f.* Carolina.

Caroline ['kærəlain], *ag.* del tempo di Carlomagno, Carlo I, Carlo II d'Inghilterra.

Caroline, *no.pr.f.* Carolina.

Carolingian [,kærə'lindʒiən], *ag.s.* (*st.*) carolingio.

caroller, *V.* **caroler.**

carom ['kærəm], *s.* (*amer.*) carambola (al biliardo).

to carom, *v.i.* (*amer.*) fare carambola (al biliardo).

carotid [kə'rɔtid], *ag.* (*anat.*) carotico, carotideo ‖ *s.* (*anat.*) carotide ☆ — *plexus*, plesso carotico; — *sinus*, seno carotideo.

carousal [kə'rauzəl], **carouse** [kə'rauz], *s.* gozzoviglia.

to carouse [kə'rauz], *v.i.* gozzovigliare.

carousel [,kɑ:ru:'zel], *s.* carosello.

carouser [kə'rauzə*], *s.c.* chi gozzoviglia.

carp[1] [kɑ:p], *s.* (*ittiol.*) carpa.

to carp[2], *v.i.* **1.** ciarlare **2.** cavillare; fare obiezioni ingiustificate; trovare da ridire: *to* — *at s.o.*, *sthg.*, censurare qlcu., trovar da ridire su ql.co.

carpal ['kɑ:pəl], *ag.* (*anat.*) carpale, carpico ☆ — *articulation*, articolazione radiocarpica.

Carpathians (the) [kɑ:'peiθjənz], *no.pr.pl.* (*geog.*) Carpazi.

carpel ['kɑ:pel], *s.* (*bot.*) carpello.

carpenter ['kɑ:pintə*], *s.* carpentiere, falegname ‖ *the* —*'s son*, Gesù Cristo ☆ — *bee*, (*entom.*) ape legnaiola ‖ *ship's* —, (*mar.*) carpentiere di bordo; *stage* —, (*teat.*) macchinista.

to carpenter, *v.i.* fare il carpentiere, il falegname.

carpentry ['kɑ:pintri], *s.* carpenteria.

carper ['kɑ:pə*], *s.* critico malevolo.

carpet ['kɑ:pit], *s.* tappeto ‖ *on the* —, in discussione ☆ — *-bag*, sacco da viaggio; — *-bagger*, avventuriero politico; candidato al Parlamento residente fuori della circoscrizione; — *-bed*, aiuola con fiori a disegno; — *dance*, ballo in famiglia; — *-knight*, eroe da salotto; — *-slippers*, pantofole in tessuto da tap, peto; — *-snake*, pitone variegato australiano; — *-sweeper*, spazzola (elettrica) per tappeti ‖ *bedside* —, scendiletto; *pile-* —, tappeto vellutato.

to carpet, *v.t.* **1.** coprire con tappeto; tappezzare **2.** (*fam.*) sgridare (un servo).

carpeted ['kɑ:pitid], *ag.* coperto con tappeto: — *with flowers*, tappezzato di fiori.

carping ['kɑ:piŋ], *ag.* cavilloso: *an envious* — *tongue*, una mala lingua.

carpology [kɑ:'pɔlədʒi], *s.* (*agr.*) carpologia.

carpus ['kɑ:pəs], *s.* (*anat.*) carpo.

carrageen ['kærəgi:n], *s.* (*bot.*) crondo crispo.

carriage ['kæridʒ], *s.* **1.** (*comm.*) trasporto; spesa di trasporto, porto **2.** carrozza, vettura; (*mil.*) treno, carriaggio; (*mec.*) carrello ‖ — *and pair*, — *and four*, tiro a due, a quattro **3.** portamento, andatura; contegno ☆ — *-builder*, fabbricante di carrozze; — *-drive*, viale per carrozze; — *-entrance* (o — *-gate*), porta carraia; — *-forward*, (*comm.*) porto assegnato; — *-free*, (*comm.*) franco di porto; — *-included*, porto compreso; — *-paid*, porto affrancato; — *-road* (o — *-way*), strada rotabile ‖ *baby* —, carrozzina per bambini; *gun* —, (*artigl.*) affusto (di cannone); *railway* —, vettura, carrozza ferroviaria.

carriageable ['kæridʒəbl], *ag.* **1.** trasportabile **2.** carrozzabile.

carriageful ['kæridʒful], *s.* carrozzata.

carrickbend ['kærik'bend], *s.* (*mar.*) nodo vaccaio.

Carrie ['kæri], *no.pr.f. dim.* di **Caroline.**

carrier ['kæriə*], *s.* **1.** portatore; corriere, spedizioniere; (*amer.*) postino **2.** (*air craft-*) —, (*mar.*) por-

taerei **3.** (*mec.*) trasportatore; piastra portante **4.** portapacchi (per bicicletta) **5.** supporto; cavalletto (per macchina fotografica) ☆ — *-bag*, sacchetto di carta per contenere gli acquisti; — *frequency*, (*rad.*) frequenza portante; — *-pigeon*, piccione viaggiatore; — *wave*, (*rad.*) onda portante ‖ *belt* —, (*mec.*) trasportatore a nastro; *cable-* —, (*elett.*) portafili; *common* —, (*dir.*) vettore; *escort* —, portaerei di scorta; *germ-* —, veicolo portatore di microbi; *luggage* —, portabagagli; *troop* —, aeroplano per trasporto truppe.

carriole ['kærioul], *s.* **1.** biroccino **2.** slitta canadese.

carrion ['kæriən], *ag.* putrido; sporco ‖ *s.* carogna, carne putrefatta ☆ — *crow*, corvo nero; avvoltoio.

carronade [,kærə'neid], *s.* (*mar. mil. st.*) caronata.

carrot ['kærət], *s.* **1.** carota **2.** *pl.* (*fam.*) capelli rossi; persona dai capelli rossi.

carroty ['kærəti], *ag.* (*fam.*) di colore carota; dai capelli rossi.

carry ['kæri], *s.* **1.** portata (di fucile, ecc.) **2.** (*golf*) traiettoria di una palla **3.** trasporto ‖ *cash and* —, (*comm.*) pagamento in contanti ☆ — *-cot*, lettino, culla portatile.

to carry, *pass.p.p.* **carried** ['kærid], *v.t.i.* **1.** portare (un peso, un pacco, ecc.); trasportare, portare (di nave, automobile, ecc.): *I cannot* — *this weight*, non posso portare questo peso; *our ship was carrying livestock*, la nostra nave trasportava bestiame; *to* — *a burden*, portare un peso, un fardello (anche *fig.*) ‖ *he was carried shoulder high*, fu portato in trionfo ‖ *to* — *a child*, essere incinta (di donna) **2.** (*arch.*) portare, sostenere: *those columns* — *the weight of the whole roof*, quelle colonne sostengono il peso di tutto il tetto **3.** trasmettere (suoni): *the air carries sounds*, l'aria trasmette i suoni **4.** recare, condurre: *modesty will not* — *you far*, la modestia non ti condurrà lontano; *to* — *destruction everywhere*, portare ovunque la distruzione; *to* — *the war into the enemy's country*, portare la guerra nel paese del nemico; *fig.* attaccare per difendersi **5.** espugnare, prendere d'assalto; vincere, conquistare (anche *fig.*) ‖ *to* — *all before one*, essere irresistibile, aver successo; *to* — *one's hearers with one*, trascinare il proprio uditorio; *to* — *one's points*, imporre il proprio modo di vedere, averla vinta ‖ *to* — *the day*, riportar vittoria, vincere ‖ *to* — *the house*, (*teat.*) conquistare l'uditorio **6.** far accogliere, far approvare: *the bill was carried*, il progetto fu approvato; *to* — *a resolution*, *a proposal*, far approvare una deliberazione, una proposta **7.** (*mat.*) riportare **8.** raggiungere (di voce, di pallottola, di suono): *the bullet carries 200 yards*, la pallottola raggiunge 200 iarde; *her voice carries a long way*, la sua voce è chiara anche da lontano **9.** avere: *to* — *authority*, *weight*, avere autorità, peso **10.** portare, tenere: *he carried himself proudly*, aveva un aspetto orgoglioso; *he carried his arm in a sling*, portava il braccio al collo; *you can* — *your head high*, puoi andare a testa alta **11.** implicare: *his statement carries conviction*, il suo giudizio implica convinzione **12.** (*amer.*) tenere (in negozio per vendere) **13.** (*amer.*) portare, includere (di giornale): *the Tribune carries an important editorial*, la Tribuna porta un importante articolo di fondo **14.** (*comm.*) accordare un credito a (un cliente) **15.** *to* — *about*, portare in giro, portare addosso (denari, ecc.) **16.** *to* — *across*, trasportare (dall'altra parte, all'altra riva) **17.** *to* — *away*, portar via, trasportare, portare altrove: *to be carried away*, essere trasportato (da un discorso, dalla musica, ecc.); soccombere (a una malattia, ecc.) **18.** *to* — *back*, riportare; ricordare (i vecchi tempi): *this carries me back to my youth*, questo mi riporta alla mia giovinezza **19.** *to* — *down*, portar giù dall'alto, far discendere; avallare, far accettare **20.** *to* — *forward*, (*contabilità*) riportare **21.** *to* — *off*, portare via a forza; far morire; vincere (un premio): *he carried off the first prize*, egli riportò il primo premio ‖ *to* — *it off*, (*fam.*) riuscire nel colpo, riuscire nell'intento 22. *to* — **on**, proseguire, continuare, persistere in (lavoro, compito): — *on!*, sempre avanti!; — *on the work during my absence*, continuate il lavoro durante la mia assenza; *to* — *on a business*, gestire un'azienda ‖ *please don't* — *on like that!*, (*fam.*) ti prego di non fare scene! ‖ *those two are carrying on*, quei due se la intendono 23. *to* — **out**, portar fuori; eseguire, effettuare (progetti, ordini, istruzioni); mettere in pratica, realizzare, compiere; mantenere (una promessa) 24. *to* — **over**, trasportare (dall'altra parte); (*contabilità*) riportare (una somma); (*Borsa*) fare un riporto 25. *to* — **through**, trasportare attraverso; *fig.* eseguire completamente, portare (un'impresa) a buon fine: *his courage will* — *him through*, il suo coraggio gli farà superare ogni ostacolo.

carry-all [ˈkæriɔːl], *s.* grossa borsa floscia (per portare pacchetti, ecc.).

carrying [ˈkæriiŋ], *s.* 1. trasporto, l'azione di trasportare 2. espugnazione (di fortezza) 3. approvazione di progetto ☆ — *company*, società di trasporti; — *money*, spesa viva (di trasporto marittimo); — *trade*, trasporto merci (specialmente per mare).

cart [kɑːt], *s.* carro (pesante a due ruote); carro da trasporto ‖ *in the* —, (*sl.*) in difficoltà, nei guai ‖ *to put the* — *before the horse*, (*fam.*) mettere il carro innanzi ai buoi ☆ — *-horse*, cavallo da traino; — *-house* (o — *-shed*), rimessa per carri; — *-load*, carrettata; — *-prop*, puntello (del carro); — *-road*, strada non carrozzabile; — *-rut*, carreggiata; — *-wheel*, ruota da carro; (*sl.*) grossa moneta (d'argento); (*ginnastica*) ruota: *to turn* — *-wheel*, far la ruota ‖ *apple-* —, proposito, piano: *to upset a person's apple-* —, rovinare i piani di una persona.

to cart, *v.t.* trasportare (con carro).

cartage [ˈkɑːtidʒ], *s.* trasporto con carri.

carte[1] [kɑːt], *s.* 1. lista ‖ *à la* —, alla carta: *à la* — *dinner*, pranzo alla carta 2. carta da giuoco.

carte[2], *s.* quarta (posizione nella scherma).

cartel [kɑːˈtel], *s.* 1. cartello di sfida (per un duello) 2. accordo per lo scambio di prigionieri 3. (*comm.*) consorzio di industriali, cartello 4. (*pol.*) blocco.

carter [ˈkɑːtə*], *s.* carrettiere.

Cartesian [kɑːˈtiːzjən], *ag.s.* (*fil.*) cartesiano.

Cartesianism [kɑːˈtiːzjənizm], *s.* (*fil.*) cartesianismo.

cartful [ˈkɑːtful], *s.* carrettata.

Carthage [ˈkɑːθidʒ], *no.pr.* (*geog. st.*) Cartagine.

Carthaginian [ˌkɑːθəˈdʒiniən], *ag.s.c.* cartaginese.

cartilage [ˈkɑːtilidʒ], *s.* (*anat.*) cartilagine.

Carthusian [kɑːˈθjuːzjən], *ag.s.* 1. (*eccl.*) certosino 2. (allievo) della scuola di « Charterhouse ».

cartilaginoid [ˌkɑːtiˈlædʒinoid], *ag.* cartilagineo.

cartilaginous [ˌkɑːtiˈlædʒinəs], *ag.* cartilaginoso.

cartographer [kɑːˈtɔgrəfə*], *s.* cartografo.

cartographic(al) [ˌkɑːtəˈgræfik (əl)], *ag.* cartografico.

cartography [kɑːˈtɔgrəfi], *s.* cartografia.

cartomancy [ˈkɑːtoumænsi], *s.* cartomanzia.

carton [ˈkɑːtən], *s.* 1. cartone; scatola di cartone 2. centro bianco (di bersaglio).

cartoon [kɑːˈtuːn], *s.* 1. cartone (disegno per affresco, mosaico, ecc.) 2. vignetta (generalmente a carattere politico) 3. (*cine.*) cartone, disegno animato.

to cartoon, *v.t.i.* 1. disegnare un cartone (per affresco, mosaico, ecc.) 2. fare una caricatura di; fare una vignetta (generalmente a carattere politico) 3. (*cine.*) disegnare cartoni animati.

cartoonist [kɑːˈtuːnist], *s.* 1. caricaturista; vignettista 2. disegnatore (di cartoni animati).

cartouche [kɑːˈtuːʃ], *s.* 1. (*arch.*) cartoccio, cartiglio 2. cartuccia.

cartridge [ˈkɑːtridʒ], *s.* 1. cartuccia 2. (*foto.*) rotolo ☆ — *-belt*, cartuccera, caricatore a nastro; — *-paper*, carta grossa (anche da disegno); — *-pouch*, giberna ‖ *blank* —, cartuccia a salve: *to fire* (*with*) *blank* —, sparare a salve; *rocket-* —, cartuccia tracciante.

cartulary [ˈkɑːtjuləri], *s.* cartolare.

caruncle [ˈkærəŋkl] *s.* 1. (*patol.*) caruncola 2. (*bot.*) piccola protuberanza.

to carve [kɑːv], *pass.* **carved** [kɑːvd], *p.p.* **carved**, (*arc.*) **carven** [ˈkɑːvən], *v.t.i.* 1. scolpire; incidere; cesellare; intagliare ‖ *to* — *one's way through*, *fig.* farsi strada con sforzo 2. trinciare, tagliare (carne, ecc.).

carvel [ˈkɑːvil], *s.* (*mar. st.*) caravella.

carver [ˈkɑːvə*], *s.* 1. intagliatore, scultore (in legno, avorio) 2. chi taglia la carne, ecc. a tavola 3. trinciante (coltello).

carving [ˈkɑːviŋ], *s.* 1. scultura, intaglio (in legno, avorio) 2. l'atto di trinciare carne, ecc. ☆ — *-knife*, trinciante; — *-wood*, legno da intaglio.

caryatid [ˌkæriˈætid], *pl.* **caryatides** [ˌkæriˈætidiːz], **caryatids** [ˌkæriˈætidz], *s.* cariatide.

cascade [kæsˈkeid], *s.* 1. cascata 2. drappeggio.

to cascade, *v.i.* scendere come una cascata.

case[1] [keis], *s.* 1. caso, avvenimento, fatto; incidente: *in any* —, ad ogni modo, in qualsiasi caso; *in* —, qualora: *in* — *of need apply to*, (*comm.*) al bisogno rivolgersi a; *in such a* —, in tal caso; *such being the* —, stando così le cose; *that alters the* —, (*fam.*) questo è un altro affare, questo è un altro paio di maniche; *to make out one's* —, (*fam.*) esporre il proprio caso, provare le proprie ragioni; *to state the* —, esporre i fatti 2. (*dir.*) processo, causa: *to win a* —, vincere una causa 3. (*med.*) caso 4. (*fam.*) individuo, tipo, carattere 5. (*gram.*) caso ☆ — *-book*, raccolta di dati giuridici; — *-history*, (*med.*) cartella clinica; *fig.* curriculum di una persona; — *-law*, giurisprudenza ‖ *doctor's* — *-book*, registro del medico; *the genitive* —, il caso genitivo.

case[2], *s.* 1. cassa, cassetta, scatola; (*tip.*) cassa tipografica 2. custodia, astuccio, fodero; copertina; pelle (di salumi, ecc.) ☆ — *-binding*, rilegatura di libri in cartone ‖ *bill-* —, portafoglio; *cigar-* —, portasigari; *glass-* —, vetrinetta, campana di vetro; *lower* —, *upper* —, (*tip.*) cassa per lettere minuscole, maiuscole; *powder-* —, (*artigl.*) bossolo; *pistol-* —, fodero di rivoltella; *show-* —, vetrina; *tin-lined* —, cassa foderata di latta.

to case[2], *v.t.* 1. mettere in casse, imballare: *to* — *goods* (*up*), rinchiudere merci in casse 2. rivestire, ricoprire; foderare: *cased in steel*, rivestito di acciaio.

to case-harden [ˈkeisˌhɑːdn], *v.t.* (*metal.*) cementare.

casein [ˈkeisiin], *s.* (*chim.*) caseina.

casemate [ˈkeis-meit], *s.* (*mil.*) casamatta.

casement [ˈkeismənt], *s.* 1. telaio di finestra a due battenti 2. (*-window*), finestra a due battenti.

caseous [ˈkeisiəs], *ag.* caseoso.

cash[1] [kæʃ], *s.* (*solo sing.*) cassa; denaro; contanti ‖ — *against documents*, pagamento contro documenti; — *before delivery* (*C.B.D.*), pagamento prima della consegna; — *and carry*, pagamento in contanti; — *on delivery* (*C.O.D.*), pagamento alla consegna; — *on hand*, fondo di cassa ‖ *by* (*ready*) —, *for* —, per, in contanti ‖ *to be in* —, avere fondi; *to be out of* —, essere senza fondi ‖ *to pay* (*in*) —, pagare in contanti ☆ — *-account*, conto cassa; — *-book*, libro cassa; — *-box*, cassetta dei contanti; — *-clerk*, cassiere; — *-desk*, cassa; — *down*, a pronta cassa; — *-payment*, pagamento in contanti; — *-price*, prezzo per contanti; — *-register*, registratore di cassa; — *-sale*, vendita per contanti; — *-store*, negozio dove si vende solo a contanti; — *terms*, condizioni per pagamento in contanti ‖ *hard* —, (*fam.*) denaro sonante; *net* —, netto cassa.

to cash[1], *v.t.* 1. incassare, riscuotere; convertire in denaro 2. *to* — *in*, incassare; (*sl. amer.*) tirare le cuoia: *to* — *in on sthg.*, trar profitto da ql.co.

cash[2], *pl.* **cash**, *s.* monetina cinese perforata.

cashew [kæˈʃuː], *s.* (*bot.*) acagiù, mogano.

cashier[1] [kæˈʃiə*], *s.* cassiere: — *'s desk*, cassa; — *'s office*, ufficio cassa.

to cashier[2] [kəˈʃiə*], *v.t.* (*mil.*) destituire.

Cashmere [kæʃ'miə*], *no.pr.* (*geog.*) Cachemire ‖ **cashmere**, *s.* cachemire (stoffa di lana).

casino [kə'si:nou], *pl.* **casinos** [kə'si:nouz], *s.* casinò.

cask [kɑ:sk], *s.* barile, botte.

to **cask**, *v.t.* imbarilare.

casket ['kɑ:skit], *s.* **1.** scrigno, cofanetto **2.** (*amer.*) cassa da morto; urna per ceneri.

Caspar ['kæspə*], *no.pr.m.* Gasparc.

Caspian ['kæspiən], *ag.* (*geog.*) caspico: *the — Sea,* il Mar Caspio.

casque [kæsk], *s.* (*st.*) casco, elmo.

Cassandra [kə'sændrə], *no.pr.f.* (*lett.*) Cassandra (anche *fig.*).

cassation [kæ'seiʃən], *s.* (*dir.*) cassazione, annullamento: *Court of Cassation,* Corte di cassazione.

cassava [kə'sɑ:və], *s.* cassava (anche *bot.*).

casserole ['kæsəroul], *s.* casseruola.

cassia ['kæsiə], *s.* (*bot.*) cassia.

Cassiodorus [,kæsiə'dourəs], *no.pr.m.* (*st.*) Cassiodoro.

Cassiope [kə'saiəpi:], **Cassiopei(a)** [,kæsiə'pi(:)ə], *no.pr.f.* (*mit.*) Cassiopea.

Cassius ['kæsiəs], *no.pr.m.* (*st.*) Cassio.

cassock ['kæsək], *s.* tunica del clero anglicano.

cassolette [,kæsou'let], *s.* incensiere; scatoletta (con il coperchio perforato) per profumi.

cassowary ['kæsəwɛəri], *s.* (*ornit.*) casuario.

cast [kɑ:st], *s.* **1.** getto; colpo; tiro, lancio (di dadi, missili, reti da pesca, ecc.): *to stake all on a single —,* impegnare tutto su un solo colpo di dadi ‖ *at a single —,* di getto **2.** abbozzo (di qualsiasi tipo di lavoro) **3.** (*metal.*) getto, gettata; stampo **4.** tendenza; caratteristica: *— of mind,* forma mentis; *a man of his —,* un uomo della sua tempra ‖ *he has a — in his eye,* egli è leggermente strabico **5.** congettura, pronostico **6.** (*teat.*) complesso (di attori); distribuzione delle diverse parti (agli attori) **7.** rapido movimento (di una parte del corpo) **8.** sguardo, occhiata **9.** tinta, sfumatura **10.** (*mat.*) calcolo; addizione **11.** escrementi (di insetti); rifiuti (di falchi, gufi, ecc.).

to **cast**, *pass.p.p.* **cast**, *v.t.i.* **1.** gettare, lanciare (anche *fig.*): *to — anchor,* gettare l'ancora; *to — the blame on s.o.,* dare la colpa a qlcu.; *to — for fish,* pescare con canna da lancio; *to — a glance at s.o.,* gettare uno sguardo a qlcu; *to — the lead,* (*mar.*) gettare lo scandaglio; *to — light on sthg.,* mettere ql.co. in luce; *to — a line,* lanciare una lenza; *to — oneself on s.o.'s feet,* gettarsi ai piedi di qlcu.; *to — s.o. into prison,* gettare qlcu. in prigione ‖ *the die is —,* il dato è tratto ‖ *to — sthg. in s.o.'s teeth,* rinfacciare ql.co. a qlcu. **2.** proiettare; gettare: *coming events — their shadows before,* avvenimenti futuri proiettano innanzi le loro ombre **3.** mutare, cambiare (penne, pelo, pelle); perdere (i denti) **4.** riformare (soldati, cavalli) **5.** calcolare; dedurre; trarre: *to — a horoscope,* trarre un oroscopo **6.** (*teat.*) distribuire (le parti agli attori): *he is — for Romeo,* ha la parte di Romeo; *Romeo is — to him,* gli è stata assegnata la parte di Romeo **7.** (*metal.*) fondere (in stampo) **8.** rimettere, rigettare (di falchi, gufi) **9.** partorire innanzi tempo (di animali) **10.** *to — about,* cercare qua e là; girare (lo sguardo); escogitare mezzi **11.** *to — aside,* gettare da parte; disfarsi di **12.** *to — away,* gettar via: *to be — away,* naufragare **13.** *to — back,* gettare indietro; *fig.* ritornare, rivolgersi: *to — one's thoughts back on the past,* ritornare col pensiero al passato **14.** *to — down,* gettar giù (armi, ecc.); abbassare (gli occhi): *to be — down,* essere abbattuto, depresso **15.** *to — in: to — in one's lot with s.o.,* dividere la propria sorte con qlcu. **16.** *to — off,* respingere; radiare; spogliarsi di; scuotere (il giogo); liberare (cani da caccia); buttare giù i punti (di lavoro a maglia) **17.** *to — on,* mettere su i punti (di lavoro a maglia) **18.** *to — out,* scacciare (demoni); mettere fuori, alla porta **19.** *to — up,* alzare (gli occhi); contare, calcolare; vomitare.

cast, (*nei composti*): *— -iron,* ferro fuso, ghisa: *—*

-iron constitution, salute di ferro; *— -iron discipline,* disciplina di ferro; *— -iron stove,* cucina (economica) di ghisa; *— -steel,* acciaio fuso ‖ *plaster —,* stampo in gesso.

Castalia [kæs'teiljə], *no.pr.* (*geog. mit.*) Castalia.

Castalian [kæs'teiljən], *ag.* (*mit.*) castalio.

castanet [,kæstə'net], *s.* **1.** (*zool.*) crotalo; serpente a sonagli **2.** *pl.* (*mus.*) (*a pair of*) castanets, castagnette.

castaway ['kɑ:stəwei], *ag.* arenato; rigettato, respinto, inutile ‖ *s.* **1.** naufrago **2.** reprobo ☆ *— crew,* naufraghi di una equipaggio.

caste [kɑ:st], *s.* casta ‖ *to lose —,* scendere di grado nella classe sociale ☆ *high- —, low- — Indian,* Indiano di casta alta, di casta bassa.

castellan ['kɑ:stələn], *s.* castellano.

castellated ['kæstəleitid], *ag.* turrito; (luogo) ricco di castelli fortificati.

caster ['kɑ:stə*], *s.* **1.** lanciatore **2.** (*metal.*) fonditore, modellatore **3.** calcolatore; computista: *— of horoscopes,* chi trae gli oroscopi **4.** *V.* castor[1] **1. 5.** (*mec.*) ruota orientabile; girella, rotella da mobili **6.** cappello di pelo di castoro.

to **castigate** ['kæstigeit], *v.t.* castigare, punire.

castigation [,kæsti'geiʃən], *s.* castigo, punizione.

castigator ['kæstigeitə*], *s.c.* castigatore, castigatrice.

castigatory ['kæstigeitəri], *ag.* punitivo.

Castile [kæs'ti:l], *no.pr.* (*geog.*) Castiglia.

Castilian [kæs'tiliən], *ag.* castigliano ‖ *s.c.* castigliano, castigliana.

casting ['kɑ:stiŋ], *s.* **1.** il gettare **2.** (*metal.*) getto, colata, colatura **3.** muta (di penne, pelo, pelle) **4.** pesca con lancio della lenza **5.** distribuzione (delle parti agli attori) ☆ *— -net,* (*mar.*) ritrecine; *— -vote,* voto decisivo; *— weight,* peso decisivo.

castle ['kɑ:sl], *s.* **1.** castello ‖ *to build castles in the air* (o *in Spain*), *fig.* fare castelli in aria **2.** (*scacchi*) torre ☆ *— -builder,* sognatore.

to **castle,** *v.t.i.* fortificare con un castello ‖ *to — (the King),* (*scacchi*) arroccare (il Re).

Castor, *no.pr.m.* (*mit.*) Castore ‖ *no.pr.* (*astr.*) Castore.

castor[1] ['kɑ:stə*], *s.* **1.** pepaiuolo; saliera; spargizucchero; ampolla: *a set of castors,* ampolliera **2.** girella, rotella da mobili ☆ *— sugar,* zucchero raffinato.

castor[2], *s.* **1.** (*arc.*) castoro **2.** (*farm.*) castoreo.

castor[3], *s.* castagna (callosità sugli arti degli equini).

castoreum [kæs'to:riəm], *s.* (*farm.*) castoreo.

castor-oil ['kɑ:stər'oil], *s.* (*farm.*) olio di ricino ☆ *— bean,* seme del ricino; *— plant,* ricino.

castrametation [,kæstrəme'teiʃən], *s.* (*archeol. mil.*) castrametazione.

to **castrate** [kæs'treit], *v.t.* **1.** castrare **2.** *fig.* espurgare (libri).

castration [kæs'treiʃən], *s.* **1.** castrazione **2.** *fig.* espurgazione (di libri).

casual ['kæʒjuəl], *ag.* casuale, accidentale; fortuito, occasionale: *a — meeting,* un incontro fortuito ‖ *he is really too —,* egli fa veramente troppo il suo comodo ‖ *s.* **1.** avventizio **2.** *pl.* (*neol.*) indumenti (specialmente scarpe) trasandati, per casa (anche per sport) ☆ *— labourer,* lavoratore avventizio; *— ward,* ospizio dei poveri.

casualism ['kæʒjuəlizəm], *s.* (*fil.*) casualismo.

casualist ['kæʒjuəlist], *s.* (*fil.*) casualista.

casually ['kæʒjuəli], *av.* per caso, accidentalmente.

casualness ['kæʒjuəlnis], *s.* irregolarità; mancanza di metodo; noncuranza.

casualty ['kæʒjuəlti], *s.* **1.** infortunio, incidente; disgrazia, disastro **2.** infortunato **3.** (*mil.*) morto; ferito **4.** *pl.* vittime, perdite (di uomini): *the list of casualties,* la lista delle vittime ☆ *— ward,* pronto soccorso.

casuarina [,kæʒjuə'rainə], *s.* (*bot.*) equiseto australiano, coda di cavallo.

casuist ['kæʒjuist], *s.* (*teol.*) casista.

casuistic(al) [,kæʒju'istik(əl)], *ag.* (*teol.*) casistico.

casuistically [,kæʒju'istikəli], *av.* (*teol.*) casisticamente.

casuistry ['kæzjuistri], *s.* (*teol.*) casistica.

cat [kæt], *s.* **1.** gatto, gatta; felino; (*fam.*) donna dispettosa ‖ *a — may look at a king*, anche il più umile ha dei diritti ‖ *it would make a — laugh*, (*fam.*) farebbe ridere i polli ‖ *to be like a — on hot bricks*, (*fam.*) star sui carboni ardenti ‖ *to fight like kilkenny cats*, combattere come cane e gatto ‖ *to let the — out of the bag*, svelare un segreto ‖ *to rain cats and dogs*, piovere a catinelle ‖ *to see which way the — jumps*, vedere da che parte tira il vento ‖ *care killed the —*, *prov.* le troppe preoccupazioni uccidono anche i forti ‖ *when the —'s away the mice will play*, *prov.* via la gatta i topi ballano **2.** (*mar.*) capone ☆ *— -and-dog life*, vita da cani e gatti; *— -block*, (*mar.*) paranco di capone; *— -burglar*, ladro acrobata; *— -call*, fischio; fischietto (usato a teatro); *—'s-eye*, (*min.*) occhio di gatto; *catarifrangente*; *— -eyed*, dagli occhi di gatto; *— -fish*, gatto marino; *— ('s)-lick*, leccata del gatto: *to have a —'s-lick*, (*fam.*) lavarsi come i gatti; *— -nap*, sonnellino; *— -o' nine-tails*, gatto a nove code; *—'s-paw*, (*mar.*) brezza; *— ('s)-whisker*, (*rad.*) spirale metallica del rivelatore ‖ *Tom- —*, gatto (maschio); *Tabby- —*, gatta.

to cat, *pass.p.p.* **catted** ['kætid], *v.t.i.* **1.** (*mar.*) caponare (l'ancora) **2.** (*fam.*) vomitare.

catabolism [kə'tæbəlizəm], *s.* (*biol.*) catabolismo.

catachresis [,kætə'kri:sis], *s.* (*ret.*) catacresi.

cataclysm ['kætəklizəm], *s.* cataclisma, disastro, catastrofe.

cataclysmic(al) [,kætə'klizmik(əl)], *ag.* di cataclisma.

catacomb ['kætəkoum], *s.* catacomba.

catacoustics [,kætə'ku:stiks], *s.* (*fis.*) catacustica.

catafalque ['kætəfælk], *s.* catafalco.

Catalan ['kætələn], *ag.* catalano ‖ *s.c.* catalano, catalana.

catalectic [,kætə'lektik], *ag.* (*poes.*) catalettico.

catalepsy ['kætəlepsi], *s.* catalessi.

cataleptic [,kætə'leptik], *ag.s.* catalettico.

catalog ['kætələg], *s.* (*amer.*) annuario (di università).

catalogue ['kætələg], *s.* catalogo.

to catalogue, *v.t.* catalogare.

cataloguer ['kætə,logə*], *s.c.* chi cataloga.

Catalonia [,kætə'louniə], *no.pr.* (*geog.*) Catalogna.

catalpa [kə'tælpə], *s.* (*bot.*) catalpa.

catalysis [kə'tælisis], *s.* (*chim.*) catalisi.

catalyst ['kætəlist], *s.* (*chim.*) catalizzatore.

catalytic [,kætə'litik], *ag.* (*chim.*) catalitico.

catalyzer ['kætəlaizə*], *s.* (*chim.*) catalizzatore.

catamaran [,kætəmə'ræn], *s.* **1.** « catamaran » (zattera a tre alberi) **2.** (*sl.*) donna litigiosa.

catamountain [,kætə'mauntin], *ag.* feroce; selvaggio ‖ *s.* **1.** (*zool.*) leopardo; pantera **2.** persona litigiosa.

cataplasm ['kætəplæzəm], *s.* (*med.*) cataplasma.

catapult ['kætəpʌlt], *s.* **1.** (*mil. aer.*) catapulta **2.** fionda (a forcella).

to catapult, *v.t.* catapultare.

cataract ['kætərækt], *s.* **1.** cateratta, cascata **2.** (*patol.*) cateratta.

catarrh [kə'ta:*], *s.* catarro.

catarrhal [kə'ta:rəl], *ag.* catarrale.

catar(r)hine ['kætərain], *s.* (*zool.*) catarrina.

catarrhous [kə'ta:rəs], *ag.* catarroso.

catastrophe [kə'tæstrəfi], *s.* catastrofe, disastro, calamità.

catastrophic(al) [,kætə'strofik(əl)], *ag.* catastrofico.

catastrophism [kə'tæstrəfizm], *s.* catastrofismo.

catastrophist [kə'tæstrəfist], *s.* catastrofista.

catboat ['kætbout], *s.* «catboat» (battello ad una sola vela con albero prodiero).

catch [kætʃ], *s.* **1.** presa, cattura; preda ‖ *no —*, (*fam.*) cattivo affare ‖ *he is a good —*, (*cricket*) è bravo a prendere la palla ‖ *she is no great —*, non è un buon partito **2.** pesca **3.** trappola, agguato; inganno **4.** giuoco di parole **5.** (*mus.*) ritornello **6.** intervallo; frammento,

brano: *catches of conversation*, brani di conversazione ‖ *— of the breath*, sussulto (del respiro, della voce) **7.** saliscendi, paletto (di porta, finestra, ecc.) ☆ *— -phrase*, slogan.

to catch, *pass.p.p.* **caught** [ko:t], *v.t.i.* **1.** afferrare, acchiappare, prendere, cogliere (anche *fig.*): *the ball caught him in the eye*, la palla lo colpì in un occhio; *did you — the humour of his remark?*, hai colto la comicità della sua osservazione?; *he caught her eye*, egli incontrò il suo sguardo; *to — a cold*, prendere un raffreddore; *to — fire*, prendere fuoco; *to — a train*, prendere un treno ‖ *at noon we shall — sight of Liverpool*, saremo in vista di Liverpool a mezzogiorno ‖ *he caught his foot*, inciampò ‖ *he caught it*, (*sl.*) si prese una bella sgridata ‖ *to — a tartar*, (*sl.*) avere a che fare con un osso duro **2.** pescare **3.** sorprendere: *I caught him at it*, lo sorpresi nell'atto di fare ciò ‖ *— me!*, (*sl.*) non credere che io abbocchi! **4.** attrarre (attenzione, ecc.): *to — s.o.'s eye*, attrarre l'attenzione di qlcu. **5.** *to — at* (*sthg.*), cercare di afferrare; ottenere a fatica: *to — at a straw*, *fig.* attaccarsi a un filo **6.** *to — on*, comprendere; incontrare il gusto delle masse; diventare popolare (di canzone, ecc.) **7.** *to — out*, (*cricket*) mettere fuori combattimento (anche *fig.*) **8.** *to — up*, riuscire a raggiungere; afferrare in fretta, sorpassare; riguadagnare il tempo perduto; interrompere (chi parla); annodare, far nodi: *I can't — up tunes easily*, non imparo facilmente le melodie.

catchable ['kætʃəbl], *ag.* afferrabile, prendibile, raggiungibile.

catch-as-catch-can ['kætʃəz'kætʃ'kæn], *s.* (*spor.*) lotta libera.

catcher ['kætʃə*], *s.* **1.** chi afferra, chi prende **2.** (*mec.*) arresto (di serratura) **3.** (*ind.*) separatore ☆ *dog —*, accalappiacani.

catching ['kætʃiŋ], *ag.* **1.** attraente **2.** orecchiabile (di melodia) **3.** contagioso, infettivo.

catchment ['kætʃmənt], *s.* presa d'acqua, captazione d'acqua.

catchpenny ['kætʃ,peni], *s.* pubblicazione di nessun valore, diffusa a scopo di lucro.

catchpole, catchpoll ['kætʃpoul], *s.* ufficiale giudiziario.

catchword ['kætʃwə:d], *s.* **1.** (*tip.*) esponente (in testa di pagina in un dizionario, ecc.) **2.** (*teat.*) ultima parola di una battuta **3.** slogan.

catchy ['kætʃi], *ag.* **1.** attraente **2.** orecchiabile (di melodia) **3.** insidioso: *— question*, domanda insidiosa.

catechesis [,kæti'ki:sis], *s.* (*eccl.*) catechesi.

catechetic(al) [,kæti'ketik(əl)], *ag.* catechistico.

catechetically [,kæti'ketikəli], *av.* catechisticamente.

catechism ['kætikizəm], *s.* catechismo.

catechist ['kætikist], *s.* catechista.

to catechize ['kætikaiz], *v.t.* catechizzare; interrogare, porre domande a.

catechizer ['kætikaizə*], *s.c.* catechista; chi interroga.

catechu ['kætitʃu:], *s.* (*farm.*) catecù, cacciù.

catechumen [,kæti'kju:men], *s.* catecumeno.

categoric(al) [,kæti'gorik(əl)], *ag.* categorico.

categorically [,kæti'gorikəli], *av.* categoricamente.

category ['kætigəri], *s.* categoria.

catenary [kə'ti:nəri], **catenarian** [,kæti'nɛəriən], *ag.* (*geom.*) a guisa di catenaria ‖ *s.* (*geom.*) catenaria ☆ *— (suspension) bridge*, ponte a sospensione.

to catenate ['kætineit], *v.t.* concatenare.

catenation [,kæti'neiʃən], *s.* concatenamento.

cater¹ ['keitə*], *s.* (*arc.*) il quattro (di carte da giuoco, di dadi).

to cater², *v.i.* provvedere cibo; procacciare divertimento: *to — for* (o *to*) *all tastes*, provvedere a soddisfare tutti i gusti; *to — for s.o.*, provvedere al nutrimento di qlcu.

caterer ['keitərə*], *s.c.* procacciatore, procacciatrice di cibo, di divertimenti.

cater-cousin ['keitə,kʌzn], *s.* amico intimo.

caterpillar ['kætəpilə*], *s.* **1.** (*entom.*) bruco **2.** persona rapace **3.** (*mec.*) cingolo; « caterpiller » (mezzo cingolato) ☆ — -*chain* (o — -*track*), catena a cingoli; — *motor-lorry*, autocarro a cingoli; — -*tractor*, trattore a cingoli.

caterwaul ['kætəwɔ:l], *s.* miagolio (di gatto in calore).

to caterwaul, *v.i.* miagolare (di gatto in calore).

catgut ['kætgʌt], *s.* minugia (budello animale variamente usato).

Catharine ['kæθərin], *no.pr.f.* Caterina.

catharsis [kə'θɑ:sis], *s.* **1.** catarsi **2.** (*med.*) evacuazione.

cathartic [kə'θɑ:tik], *ag.* (*farm.*) catartico, purgativo ‖ *s.* purgante.

Cathay [kæ'θei], *no.pr.* (*geog. st.*) Catai.

cathedral [kə'θi:drəl], *s.* cattedrale ☆ — *glass*, vetro cattedrale; — *town*, città sede episcopale.

Catherine ['kæθərin], *no.pr.f.* Caterina ☆ — -*wheel*, (*arch.*) rosone; (*pirotecnica*) girandola, fuoco d'artificio.

catheter ['kæθitə*], *s.* (*med.*) catetere.

cathode ['kæθoud], *s.* (*elett.*) catodo.

catholic ['kæθəlik], *ag.* **1.** universale; eclettico: — *mind*, mente aperta **2.** cattolico ‖ *the Catholic Church*, la Chiesa Cattolica ‖ *His Catholic Majesty*, Sua Maestà Cattolica ‖ *s.c.* cattolico, cattolica ‖ *Anglo-Catholic*, sostenitore della cattolicità della Chiesa Anglicana; *Roman Catholic*, cattolico.

Catholicism [kə'θɔlisizəm], *s.* cattolicesimo.

catholicity [,kæθə'lisiti], *s.* **1.** universalità; tolleranza; eclettismo **2.** cattolicità.

to catholicize [kə'θɔlisaiz], *v.t.* cattolicizzare.

catholically [kə'θɔlikəli], **catholicly** ['kæθəlikli], *av.* **1.** cattolicamente **2.** senza pregiudizi.

catholicon [kə'θɔlikən], *s.* panacea.

Catiline ['kætilain], *no.pr.m.* (*st.*) Catilina.

cation ['kætaiən], *s.* (*fis.*) catione.

catlike ['kætlaik], *ag.* felino.

catling ['kætliŋ], *s.* **1.** gattino **2.** minugia sottile **3.** (*chir.*) amputante.

catmint ['kætmint], *s.* (*bot.*) gattaria, erba gatta.

Cato ['keitou], *no.pr.m.* (*st.*) Catone: — *the Elder*, Catone il Censore.

cat o' mountain, *V.* **catamountain.**

catoptric [kæ'tɔptrik], *ag.* (*ott.*) catottrico.

catoptrics [kæ'tɔptriks], *s.* (*ott.*) catottrica.

catsup ['kætsəp], *V.* **ketchup.**

cattish ['kætiʃ], *ag.* **1.** felino **2.** (*fam.*) dispettoso; sornione (generalmente di donna).

cattle ['kætl], *s.pl.* bestiame, armenti; (*sl.*) cavalli ☆ — *breeder*, allevatore di bestiame; — *dealer*, negoziante di bestiame; — -*drover*, bovaro; — -*leader*, nasiera; — -*lifter*, ladro di bestiame; — *lifting*, furti di bestiame; — -*man*, (*amer.*) allevatore di bestiame; — -*plague*, peste bovina; — -*run*, pastura; — -*shed*, stalla per i buoi ‖ *black*—, buoi di razza scozzese, gallese.

catty ['kæti], *V.* **cattish.**

Catullus [kə'tʌləs], *no.pr.m.* (*st. lett.*) Catullo.

Caucasian [kɔ:'keizjən], *ag. s.* caucasico; indo-europeo; (*persona*) di razza bianca.

Caucasic [kɔ:'kæsik], *ag.* caucasico.

Caucasus ['kɔ:kəsəs], *no.pr.* (*geog.*) Caucaso.

caucus ['kɔ:kəs], *s.* comitato; cricca politica; (*amer.*) comizio (elettorale).

caudal ['kɔ:dl], *ag.* caudale.

caudate ['kɔ:deit], *ag.* (*anat. bot.*) caudato.

caught [kɔ:t], *pass.p.p.* di **to catch.**

caul [kɔ:l], *s.* **1.** reticella per capelli; cuffia **2.** (*anat.*) amnio ‖ *to be born with a* —, *fig.* nascere con la camicia.

cauldron ['kɔ:ldrən], *s.* caldaia, calderone.

caulescent [kɔ:'lesənt], *ag.* (*bot.*) caulescente.

cauliflower ['kɔliflauə*], *s.* cavolfiore.

cauline ['kɔ:lain], *ag.* (*bot.*) caulinare.

to caulk [kɔ:k], *v.t.* **1.** (*mar.*) calafatare **2.** (*mec.*) cianfrinare, presellare.

caulker ['kɔ:kə*], *s.* **1.** (*mar.*) calafato **2.** (*mec.*) presello, cianfrino.

caulking ['kɔ:kiŋ], *s.* **1.** (*mar.*) calafataggio **2.** (*mec.*) presellatura, cianfrinatura.

causal ['kɔ:zəl], *ag.* causale.

causality [kɔ:'zæliti], *s.* causalità; rapporto fra causa ed effetto.

causally ['kɔ:zəli], *av.* causalmente.

causation [kɔ:'zeifən], *s.* il causare; causalità; rapporto fra causa ed effetto.

causationism [kɔ:'zeifənizəm], *s.* (*fil.*) causalismo.

causative ['kɔ:zətiv], *ag.* causativo.

causatively ['kɔ:zətivli], *av.* (*fil.*) causativamente.

cause [kɔ:z], *s.* **1.** causa: — *and effect*, causa ed effetto **2.** ragione, motivo: *to complain without a* (o *any*) —, lamentarsi senza motivo: *to give serious* — *for complaint*, dare un serio motivo di lamentela; *to have good* — *for doing sthg.*, avere buone ragioni per far ql.co. **3.** causa; processo (anche *dir.*): *to make common* — *with s.o.*, fare causa comune con qlcu.; *to plead s.o.'s* —, perorare la causa di qlcu. ‖ *the First Cause*, (*teol.*) la Causa prima ☆ *final* —, scopo, fine.

to cause, *v.t.* (III, IV) causare, cagionare, provocare; far nascere (una questione); indurre a, far sì che: *he caused me to miss my train*, mi fece perdere il treno; *what caused the accident?*, che cosa provocò l'incidente?; *what caused him to change his mind?*, che cosa gli fece cambiare idea?; *to* — *s.o. to do sthg.*, far fare ql.co. a qlcu.

causeless ['kɔ:zlis], *ag.* **1.** casuale, fortuito **2.** ingiustificato, infondato.

causelessly ['kɔ:zlisli], *av.* senza motivo, senza ragione, ingiustificabilmente.

causer ['kɔ:zə*], *s.c.* causatore, causatrice.

causerie ['kouzəri(:)], *s.* conversazione, articolo leggero (specialmente di argomento letterario).

causeway ['kɔ:zwei], **causey** ['kɔ:zei], *s.* strada rialzata (specialmente su terreno acquitrinoso); marciapiede; strada selciata.

to causeway, **to causey,** *v.t.* provvedere di strada rialzata, marciapiede; selciare.

caustic ['kɔ:stik], *ag.* caustico; corrosivo; *fig.* mordace, pungente, sarcastico ‖ *s.* (*chim.*) caustico.

caustically ['kɔ:stikəli], *av.* causticamente; *fig.* mordacemente.

causticity [kɔ:s'tisiti], *s.* causticità; *fig.* mordacità.

cauterization [,kɔ:tərai'zeifən], *s.* (*chir.*) cauterizzazione.

to cauterize ['kɔ:təraiz], *v.t.* (*chir.*) cauterizzare.

cautery ['kɔ:təri], *s.* (*chir.*) cauterio ☆ — -*knife*, termocauterio.

caution ['kɔ:ʃən], *s.* **1.** prudenza, circospezione, cautela; previdenza, accortezza: *with due* —, con la dovuta precauzione **2.** cauzione, garanzia **3.** avviso, avvertimento; rimprovero: —!, attenzione! ‖ *he was let off with a* —, (*dir.*) fu assolto con diffida **4.** (*sl. amer.*) persona, cosa originale; avvenimento singolare ☆ — -*money*, cauzione, pegno, garanzia.

to caution, *v.t.* **1.** premunire, mettere in guardia: *to* — *s.o. against sthg.*, *s.o.*, mettere in guardia qlcu. contro ql.co., qlcu. **2.** raccomandare a **3.** rimproverare; minacciare; diffidare.

cautionary ['kɔ:ʃnəri], *ag.* di precauzione, avvertimento ☆ — *signal*, segnale d'avviso.

cautious ['kɔ:ʃəs], *ag.* cauto, prudente: *to be* — *in doing sthg.*, andar coi piedi di piombo nel fare ql.co.

cautiously ['kɔ:ʃəsli], *av.* cautamente, prudentemente, con circospezione.

cautiousness ['kɔ:ʃəsnis], *s.* cautela, prudenza.

cavalcade [,kævəl'keid], *s.* cavalcata.

cavalier [,kævə'liə*], *ag.* **1.** (*st.*) realista; seguace di Carlo I **2.** superbo, altezzoso, sdegnoso **3.** disinvolto ‖ *s.* **1.** uomo a cavallo, cavaliere **2.** cavalier servente (di una dama) **3.** (*st.*) realista; seguace di Carlo I.

to cavalier, *v.t.* fare da cavaliere a (una signora).

cavalierly [ˌkævəˈliəli], *av.* **1.** alteramente **2.** disinvoltamente; alla buona, senza cerimonie.

cavalry [ˈkævəlri], *s.* (*mil.*) cavalleria.

cavalryman, *pl.* **cavalrymen** [ˈkævəlrimən], *s.* soldato di cavalleria.

cavatina [ˌkævəˈtiːnə], *s.* (*mus.*) cavatina.

cave[1] [keiv], *s.* **1.** cava; spelonca, caverna; sotterraneo **2.** (*pol.*) secessione: *the* —, i dissidenti ☆ — *-dweller*, troglodita; — *-man*, troglodita; (*sl.*) uomo rude, violento.

to cave[1], *v.t.i.* **1.** incavare; scavare **2.** vivere in caverne **3.** (*pol.*) fare una secessione.

to cave[2], *v.i.*: *to* — *in*, cedere, franare (di suolo, muro, ecc.); schiacciare, sformare (testa, cappello, ecc.); *fig.* cedere, sottomettersi.

cave[3] [ˈkeivi], *inter.* (*sl. scolastico*) attenzione!.

caveat [ˈkeiviæt], *s.* **1.** (*dir.*) opposizione; procedimento per ottenere una sospensiva: *to enter a* —, chiedere una sospensiva **2.** avviso di opposizione al rinnovo di un brevetto **3.** ammonimento; diffida **4.** (*amer.*) domanda di brevetto provvisorio.

cavendish [ˈkævəndiʃ], *s.* tabacco ammorbidito e compresso in tavolette.

cavern [ˈkævən], *s.* caverna, grotta.

caverned [ˈkævənd], *ag.* **1.** pieno di caverne, cavernoso **2.** chiuso in una caverna.

cavernous [ˈkævənəs], *ag.* cavernoso (anche *fig.*).

caves(s)on [ˈkævisən], *s.* cavezzone.

caviar(e) [ˈkævɪɑː*], *s.* caviale ‖ *it is — to the general*, *fig.* sono perle per i maiali.

cavil [ˈkævil], *s.* cavillo.

to cavil, *pass.p.p.* **cavilled** [ˈkævild], *v.i.* cavillare: *to* — *about* (o *at*) *sthg.*, cavillare su ql.co.

cavillation [ˌkævilˈeiʃən], *s.* (*rar.*) cavillazione.

caviller [ˈkævilə*], *s.c.* cavillatore, cavillatrice.

cavilling [ˈkæviliŋ], *ag.* cavilloso ‖ *s.* il cavillare.

cavillous [ˈkæviləs], *ag.* cavilloso.

cavitation [ˌkæviˈteiʃən], *s.* (*mar. aer. mec.*) cavitazione.

cavity [ˈkæviti], *s.* **1.** cavità **2.** (*mec.*) intercapedine.

to cavort [kəˈvɔːt], *v.i.* (*sl. amer.*) **1.** impennarsi (di cavallo) **2.** salterellare.

cavy [ˈkeivi], *s.* (*zool.*) cavia.

caw [kɔː], *s.* gracchiamento (di corvo, cornacchia, ecc.)

to caw, *v.t.i.* **1.** gracchiare (di corvo, cornacchia, ecc.) **2.** *to* — *out*, gracchiare (lugubri profezie).

cay [kei], *s.* banco di corallo, di sabbia, ecc.

Cayenne [keiˈen], *no.pr.* (*geog.*) Caienna ☆ — *-pepper*, pepe di Caienna, pepe rosso.

cayman [ˈkeimən], *s.* (*zool.*) caimano.

cease [siːs], *s.*: *without* —, senza pausa, incessantemente.

to cease, *v.t.i.* (I) cessare, finire; desistere; fermarsi: *he ceased reading*, ha cessato di leggere; *he has ceased to see anybody*, non vede più nessuno; *to — from work*, *from doing sthg.*, smettere di lavorare, di fare ql.co. ‖ *to — fire*, (*mil.*) cessare il fuoco.

ceaseless [ˈsiːslis], *ag.* incessante, continuo.

ceaselessly [ˈsiːslisli], *av.* incessantemente, continuamente.

ceaselessness [ˈsiːslisnis], *s.* continuità, persistenza.

ceasing [ˈsiːsiŋ], *s.* cessazione, fine.

Cecil [ˈsesl], *no.pr.m.* Cecilio ‖ *no.pr.f.* Cecilia.

Cecilia [siˈsiljə], **Cecily** [ˈsisili], *no.pr.f.* Cecilia.

cecity [ˈsisiti], *s.* (*rar. gener. fig.*) cecità.

cedar [ˈsiːdə*], *s.* cedro; legno di cedro: — *of Lebanon*, cedro del Libano.

cedarn [ˈsiːdən], *ag.* (*poet.*) di cedro.

to cede [siːd], *v.t.* (*dir.*) cedere (territorio, beni immobili, ecc.); rinunciare a (diritti, ecc.).

cedilla [siˈdilə], *s.* cediglia.

cee [siː], *s.* la lettera c ☆ — *spring*, molla a forma di c.

to ceil [siːl], *v.t.i.* **1.** soffittare, ornare con rilievi il soffitto di (una stanza) **2.** (*aer.*) volare alla quota di tangenza.

ceiling [ˈsiːliŋ], *s.* **1.** soffitto **2.** (*aer.*) quota di tangenza **3.** (*mar.*) fasciame interno (di nave) **4.** limite massimo (di prezzi, ecc.).

celadon [ˈselədən], *ag.s.* verde pallido.

celandine [ˈseləndain], *s.* (*bot.*) celidonia ☆ *greater* —, celidonia maggiore; *lesser* —, celidonia minore.

celanese [ˌseləˈniːz], *s.* celanese.

celebrant [ˈselibrənt], *s.* (*eccl.*) celebrante.

to celebrate [ˈselibreit], *v.t.i.* **1.** celebrare; solennizzare; commemorare; onorare **2.** (*eccl.*) celebrare (la S. Messa, un matrimonio, una festa) **3.** festeggiare, far festa.

celebrated [ˈselibreitid], *ag.* famoso, illustre.

celebration [ˌseliˈbreiʃən], *s.* celebrazione.

celebrator [ˈselibreitə*], *s.* celebratore.

celebrity [siˈlebriti], *s.* **1.** celebrità **2.** persona famosa.

celerity [siˈleriti], *s.* celerità, velocità.

celery [ˈseləri], *s.* (*bot.*) sedano.

celesta [siˈlestə], *s.* (*mus.*) celesta.

celeste [siˈlest], *ag.* azzurro cielo ‖ *s.* azzurro cielo ‖ **Celeste**, *no.pr.f.* Celeste.

celestial [siˈlestjəl], *ag.* **1.** celeste, azzurro **2.** celestiale, paradisiaco **3.** *Celestial*, cinese: *the Celestial Empire*, il Celeste Impero ‖ *s.* abitante del cielo ‖ *Celestial*, cinese.

Celestine[1] [ˈselistain], *no.pr.m.* Celestino ‖ *no.pr.f.* Celestina ‖ **celestine**, *s.* (*min.*) celestite.

Celestine[2], *s.* (*eccl.*) celestino.

Celia [ˈsiːljə], *no.pr.f.* Celia.

celibacy [ˈselibəsi], *s.* celibato.

celibatarian [ˌselibəˈtɛəriən], *ag.s.* celibatario.

celibate [ˈselibit], *ag.s.c.* celibe, nubile.

cell [sel], *s.* **1.** cella (di monastero, prigione, alveare) **2.** (*poet.*) capanna **3.** (*poet.*) tomba **4.** (*anat. biol.*) cellula: *the cells of the brain*, le cellule del cervello **5.** (*mil.*) nucleo di combattimento; (*pol.*) cellula **6.** (*elett.*) accumulatore, elemento, pila, cellula, cella ☆ — *-body*, protoplasma.

cellar [ˈselə*], *s.* cantina; scantinato, sottosuolo, sotterraneo ☆ — *-flap*, ribalta della botola; — *-kitchen*, cucina sotterranea.

to cellar, *v.t.* mettere in cantina.

cellarage [ˈseləridʒ], *s. coll.* **1.** cantine, scantinati **2.** spese di magazzinaggio.

cellarer [ˈselərə*], *s.* cantiniere; dispensiere (anche *eccl.*).

cellaret [ˌseləˈret], *s.* mobile-bar.

cellarist [ˈselərist], *s.* cantiniere; dispensiere (anche *eccl.*).

cellarman, *pl.* **cellarmen** [ˈseləmən], *s.* cantiniere.

cellated [ˈseleitid], **celled** [seld], *ag.* **1.** (*biol.*) cellulato **2.** (*elett.*) a pile ☆ *two- — battery*, batteria a due pile.

celliform [ˈselifɔːm], *ag.* celliforme.

'cellist [ˈtʃelist], *abbr.* di **violoncellist**.

'cello [ˈtʃelou], *abbr.* di **violoncello**.

cellophane [ˈseləfein], *s.* cellofane.

cellular [ˈseljulə*], *ag.* cellulare; alveolare ☆ — *linen*, tessuto a nido d'ape; — *radiator*, (*mec.*) radiatore a nido d'ape.

cellulation [ˌseljuˈleiʃən], *s.* cellulazione, sviluppo di cellule.

cellule [ˈseljuːl], *s.* (*anat. biol.*) cellula.

celluliferous [ˌseljuˈlifərəs], *ag.* cellulifero.

cellulitis [ˌseljuˈlaitis], *s.* (*patol.*) cellulite.

celluloid [ˈseljuloid], *ag.s.* (di) celluloide.

cellulose [ˈseljulous], *ag.s.* celluloso ‖ *s.* (*chim.*) cellulosa: ☆ — *acetate*, (*chim.*) acetato di cellulosa ‖ *pure* —, (*chim.*) cellulosio.

cellulosity [ˌseljuˈlositi], *s.* cellulosità.

Celt[1] [kelt], *s.c.* (*st.*) celta.

celt[2] [selt], *s.* (*archeol.*) strumento tagliente di pietra, di bronzo dell'epoca preistorica.

Celtic [ˈkeltik], *ag.* celtico ‖ *s.* celtico, lingua celtica.

celtically [ˈkeltikəli], *av.* celticamente.

celticism [ˈkeltisizəm], *s.* costumi ed usi dei celti.

to celticize [ˈkeltisaiz], *v.t.i.* rendere, diventare celtico.

cement [si'ment], *s.* **1.** cemento **2.** mastice, stucco; cemento dentario ☆ — *-mixer*, betoniera; — *plastering*, intonaco di cemento ‖ *hydraulic* —, cemento idraulico.

to cement, *v.t.* cementare (anche *fig.*).

cemetery ['semitri], *s.* cimitero, camposanto.

cenobite ['si:noubait], *s.* cenobita.

cenotaph ['śenɑtɑ:f], *s.* cenotafio.

to cense [sens], *v.t.* incensare.

censer ['sensə*], *s.* incensiere, turibolo ☆ — *-bearer*, (*eccl.*) turiferario.

censor ['sensə*], *s.* **1.** (*st. romana*) censore **2.** censura **3.** *fig.* censore, persona ipercritica.

to censor, *v.t.* censurare.

censorial [sen'so:riəl], *ag.* **1.** censorio **2.** (*psicoanalisi*) censorio.

censorious [sen'so:riəs], *ag.* ipercritico.

censoriously [sen'so:riəsli], *av.* in modo ipercritico.

censoriousness [sen'so:riəsnis], *s.* atteggiamento ipercritico, di biasimo, di censura.

censorship ['sensəſip], *s.* **1.** censura; censorato: — *of the Press*, censura sulla stampa **2.** (*psicoanalisi*) censura.

censurable ['senſərəbl], *ag.* censurabile.

censure ['senſə*], *s.* censura, biasimo: *vote of* —, voto di biasimo; *to incur general* —, incorrere nel biasimo generale; *to pass* — *on the Government*, censurare il governo.

to censure, *v.t.* censurare; criticare.

censurer ['senſərə*], *s.* censore, critico.

census ['sensəs], *s.* censo, censimento: *to take a* — *of the population*, fare il censimento della popolazione ☆ — *-paper*, scheda di censimento.

cent [sent], *s.* (*amer.*) centesimo di dollaro; (*fam.*) soldo, monetina ‖ *per* —, (*comm.*) per cento: *he has a 10 % commission on all orders*, ha una provvigione del 10 % su tutte le ordinazioni ☆ *red* —, monetina di rame: *he hasn't a red* —, non ha il becco di un quattrino.

cental ['sentl], *s.* cento libbre (misura di peso = kg. 45,36).

centaur ['sento:*], *s.* (*mit.*) centauro.

centaury ['sento:ri], *s.* (*bot.*) centaurea.

centenarian [,senti'nɛəriən], *ag.s.* centenario (di persona).

centenary [sen'ti:nəri], *ag.s.* centenario.

centennial [sen'tenjəl], *ag.* centennale ‖ *s.* centenario, **center**, (*amer.*) per **centre**.

centesimal [sen'tesiməl], *ag.* centesimale.

centigrade ['sentigreid], *ag.* centigrado.

centigramme ['sentigræm], *s.* centigrammo (misura di peso = 0.154 gr.).

centilitre ['senti,li:tə*], *s.* centilitro (misura di capacità = 0.352 fluid oz.).

centimetre ['senti,mi:tə*], *s.* centimetro (misura di lunghezza = 0.393 in.).

centipede ['sentipi:d], *s.* (*entom.*) millepiedi.

cento ['sentou], *s.* (*lett. mus.*) centone.

central ['sentrəl], *ag.* **1.** centrale ‖ *the Central Powers*, (*st.*) le Potenze centrali (Germania, Austria, Ungheria) **2.** principale, fondamentale ‖ *s.* (*amer.*) centrale telefonica ☆ — *government*, governo centrale; — *heating*, riscaldamento centrale.

centralism ['sentrəlizəm], *s.* (*pol.*) accentramento.

centralist ['sentrəlist], *s.* (*pol.*) accentratore di poteri.

centrality [sen'træliti], *s.* centralità.

centralization [,sentrəlai'zeiſən], *s.* accentramento, concentrazione di poteri.

to centralize ['sentrəlaiz], *v.t.i.* accentrare, accentrarsi; concentrare, concentrarsi.

centrally ['sentrəli], *av.* centralmente.

centre ['sentə*], *s.* **1.** centro; punto centrale, parte centrale; interno: — *of attraction*, centro d'attrazione; *fig.* chi attira l'attenzione, l'ammirazione; — *of gravity*, centro di gravità; — *of learning*, centro culturale; *in the* —, nel centro **2.** (*biol.*) nucleo **3.** perno, asse; (*mec.*) punta **4.** (*arch.*) centina ☆ — *-bit*, trivella a centro, a tre punte; — *-board*, (*mar.*) centrochiglia; — *-forward*,

(*spor.*) centro avanti, centro attacco; — *-half* (o —*-back*), (*spor.*) centro mediano; — *party*, (*pol.*) partito di centro, partito moderato; — *-piece*, centro tavola (di fiori, ecc.); — *-rail*, (*ferr.*) cremagliera ‖ *health* —, centro sanitario.

to centre, *v.t.i.* **1.** concentrare, concentrarsi; accentrare: *he centred his affections on his daughter*, concentrò tutto il suo affetto sulla figlia; *to* — *in*, *on* (o *round* o *about*) *s.o.*, *sthg.*, concentrarsi in, su qlcu., ql.co. **2.** (*spor.*) centrare.

centric(al) ['sentrik(əl)], *ag.* centrale.

centricity [sen'trisiti], *s.* centralità.

centrifugal [sen'trifjugəl], *ag.* (*fis.*) centrifugo

centripetal [sen'tripitl], *ag.* (*fis.*) centripeto.

centrist ['sentrist], *s.* (*pol.*) centrista.

centuple ['sentjupl], *ag.s.* centuplo.

to centuple, *v.t.* centuplicare.

centuplicate [sen'tju:plikit], *ag.s.* centuplicato.

to centuplicate [sen'tju:plikeit], *v.t.* centuplicare.

centurion [sen'tjuəriən], *s.* (*st. romana*) centurione.

century ['sentjuri], *s.* **1.** secolo: *in the twentieth* —, nel ventesimo secolo **2.** (*st. romana*) centuria **3.** centinaio **4.** (*sl. amer.*) cento dollari.

cephalalgy ['sefəlældʒi], *s.* (*patol.*) cefalea.

cephalic [ke'fælik], *ag.* cefalico.

cephalopod ['sefəloupɔd], *s.* (*zool.*) cefalopodo.

Cephalopoda [,sefə'lopədə], *s.pl.* (*zool.*) cefalopodi.

ceramic [si'ræmik], *ag.* della ceramica.

ceramics [si'ræmiks], *s.* (*arte della*) ceramica.

ceramist ['serəmist], *s.* ceramista.

cerastes [si'ræsti:z], *s.* (*zool.*) cerasta.

cerastium [si'ræstiəm], *s.* (*bot.*) centonchio.

Cerberus ['sə:bərəs], *no.pr.m.* (*mit.*) Cerbero.

cere [siə*], *s.* cera (del becco degli uccelli).

cereal ['siəriəl], *ag.* cereale ‖ *s.* **1.** cereale **2.** *pl.* (*amer.*) fiocchi d'avena, di frumento, ecc.

cerebellum [,seri'beləm], *s.* (*anat.*) cervelletto.

cerebral ['seribrəl], *ag.* (*anat.*) cerebrale.

cerebralism ['seribrəlizəm], *s.* cerebralismo.

cerebration [,seri'breiſən], *s.* lavorio, attività mentale.

cerebro-spinal [,seribrou'spainl], *ag.* (*anat.*) cerebro-spinale.

cerebrum ['seribrəm], *s.* (*anat.*) cervello.

cerecloth ['siəklɔθ], *s.* tela incerata.

cerement(s) ['siəmənt(s)], *s.* sudario.

ceremonial [,seri'mounjəl], *ag.* da cerimonia ‖ *s.* **1.** cerimoniale, etichetta **2.** (*eccl.*) rituale ☆ *Court* —, etichetta di corte.

ceremonially [,seri'mounjəli], *av.* **1.** con grande cerimonia **2.** secondo il cerimoniale.

ceremonialism [,seri'mounjəlizəm], *s.* (*eccl.*) ritualismo.

ceremonialist [,seri'mounjəlist], *s.* (*eccl.*) ritualista.

ceremonious [,seri'mounjəs], *ag.* cerimonioso.

ceremoniously [,seri'mounjəsli], *av.* cerimoniosamente.

ceremoniousness [,seri'mounjəsnis], *s.* modi cerimoniosi.

ceremony ['seriməni], *s.* cerimonia: *with* —, solennemente; *without* —, senza cerimonie ‖ *Master of Ceremonies*, Maestro delle cerimonie ‖ *to stand on* (o *upon*) —, far complimenti.

Ceres ['siəri:z], *no.pr.f.* (*mit.*) Cerere.

cerise [sə'ri:z], *ag.s.* (*colore*) rosso ciliegia.

cerium ['siəriəm], *s.* (*chim.*) cerio.

ceroplastic ['siərou'plæstik], *ag.* (*art.*) ceroplastico.

ceroplastics ['siərou'plæstiks], *s.* (*art.*) ceroplastica.

cert [sə:t], *s.* **1.** (*sl.*) certezza: *it's a* (*dead*) —, è una certezza (assoluta) **2.** (*comm. abbr.* di *certificate*) certificato.

certain ['sə:tn], *ag.* **1.** certo, sicuro, infallibile; inconfutabile: *for* —, di sicuro, sicuramente, certamente; *he is* — *to come*, è certo che verrà; *it is quite* —, è del tutto certo; *I know it for* —, lo so di sicuro; *to make* — *of a seat*, assicurarsi un posto a sedere; *to make* — *of sthg.*, assicurarsi di ql.co., constatare ql.co. **2.** indeterminato, certo: *a — day*, un certo giorno; *a — Mr. A.*, un certo signor A.

certainly ['sə:tnli], *av.* certamente, senza fallo.

certainty ['sə:tnti], *s.* **1.** certezza; cosa certa ‖ *for a —*, senza alcun dubbio, per certo: *I know it for a —*, lo so per certo; *of a —*, a colpo sicuro **2.** certezza morale; convinzione.

certes ['sə:tiz], *av.* (*arc.*) certamente, in verità.

certifiable ['sə:tifaiəbl], *ag.* **1.** attestabile **2.** che dovrebbe essere classificato come pazzo.

certificate [sə'tifikit], *s.* **1.** certificato, attestato, atto; diploma: *— of clearance inwards*, (*mar.*) per lo scarico di una nave; *— of clearance outwards*, (*mar.*) nullaosta per la partenza di una nave; *— of good character*, certificato di buona condotta; *— of health*, certificato di sana costituzione; *— of registry*, (*mar.*) atto di nazionalità; certificato di classificazione **2.** (*amer.*) certificato, documento di ammissione (a scuola, ecc.) **3.** (*comm.*) titolo, documento di credito ☆ *birth, marriage, death —*, certificato, atto di nascita, matrimonio, morte; *consols —*, titolo del debito consolidato; *doctor's —*, certificato medico; *higher school —*, diploma di scuola media superiore; *master's —*, (*mar.*) brevetto di capitano marittimo; *registration —*, (*aer. dir.*) certificato di immatricolazione.

to **certificate** [sə'tifikeit], *v.t.* consegnare un certificato, diploma, brevetto a; riconoscere per mezzo di certificato, diploma, brevetto: *certificated teacher*, insegnante diplomato, abilitato.

certification [‚sə:tifi'keiʃən], *s.* certificazione.

certified ['sə:tifaid], *ag.* (*dir.*) legalizzato, autenticato ☆ *— transfer*, (*comm.*) cessione documentata.

certifier ['sə:tifaiə*], *s.c.* chi certifica, chi attesta.

to **certify** ['sə:tifai], *v.t.i.* **1.** certificare, attestare, dichiarare: *I — this (to be) a true copy*, per copia conforme; *to — a death*, constatare una morte; *to — to sthg.*, attestare ql.co. **2.** classificare come pazzo **3.** (*dir.*) autenticare, legalizzare: *certified copy*, copia autenticata.

certitude ['sə:titju:d], *s.* certezza, sicurezza.

cerulean [si'ru:ljən], *ag.* ceruleo.

cerumen [si'ru:men], *s.* cerume.

ceruminous [si'ru:minəs], *ag.* ceruminoso.

ceruse ['siəru:s], *s.* (*chim.*) cerussa, biacca di piombo.

cervical ['sə:vikəl], *ag.* (*anat.*) cervicale ‖ *s.* (*anatomia*) **1.** vertebra cervicale **2.** *pl.* nervi cervicali.

cervine ['sə:vain], *ag.* cervino.

cess[1] [ses], *s.* (*arc. irl.*) tassa, tributo, imposta.

cess[2], *s.*: *bad — to him!*, (*irl.*) che vada al diavolo!.

cessation [se'seiʃən], *s.* cessazione, sospensione, pausa: *— from work*, sospensione, interruzione del lavoro; *— of hostilities*, cessazione delle ostilità.

cesser ['sesə*], *s.* (*dir.*) cessazione, fine (di impegni, ecc.).

cession ['seʃən], *s.* (*dir.*) cessione, rinuncia (di beni, diritti, ecc.).

cessionary ['seʃənəri], *s.* (*dir.*) cessionario.

cesspit ['sespit], **cesspool** ['sespu:l], *s.* pozzo nero.

cestoid ['sestɔid], *s.* (*zool.*) cestoide.

cestus[1] ['sestəs], *s.* (*invariato al pl.*) cesto (guanto da pugile presso i Romani).

cestus[2], *pl.* **cesti** ['sestai], *s.* cesto (cinto di Venere).

cetacean [si'teiʃjən], *ag. s.* cetaceo.

cetaceous [si'teiʃjəs], *ag.* di cetaceo.

ceteosaur ['si:tiousɔ:*], **ceteosaurus** [‚si:tiou'sɔ:rəs], *s.* (*paleont.*) cetosauro.

ceterach ['setəræk], *s.* (*bot.*) asplenio.

Cevennes (the) [si'ven], *no.pr. pl.* (*geog.*) Cevenne.

Ceylon [si'lon], *no.pr.* (*geog.*) Ceylon.

Ceylonese [‚silə'ni:z], *ag.s.c.* cingalese.

Chablis ['ʃæbli(:)], *s.* vino bianco di Chablis.

chafe [tʃeif], *s.* **1.** frizione, massaggio; (*mec.*) sfregamento; riscaldamento **2.** irritazione (di pelle) **3.** *fig.* malumore; collera, stizza: *in a —*, di cattivo umore.

to **chafe**, *v.t.i.* **1.** fregare, fregarsi; stropicciare; riscaldare (per sfregamento, per attrito); irritare; mas-

saggiare, massaggiarsi: *the alpinist had his feet chafed*, l'alpinista si fece fare delle frizioni ai piedi **2.** consumare, consumarsi **3.** *fig.* irritare, irritarsi; andare in collera: *don't — her, she is not well*, non irritarla, non sta bene; *to — at (o under) sthg.*, irritarsi per ql.co.

chafer ['tʃeifə*], *s.* (*entom.*) scarabeo.

chaff[1] [tʃɑ:f], *s.* **1.** pula, loppa; paglia trinciata, fieno trinciato ‖ *to scatter like —*, spargere al vento **2.** *coll.* oggetti di nessun valore ☆ *— -cutter* (o *— -chopper*), trinciapaglia.

to **chaff**[1], *v.t.* trinciare (paglia, ecc.).

chaff[2], *s.* (*fam.*) ironia, sarcasmo; beffa, burla.

to **chaff**[2], *v.t.* (*fam.*) beffeggiare, schernire, prendersi giuoco di: *he's only chaffing you*, ti prende soltanto in giro, parla solo per scherzo.

chaffer[1] ['tʃɑ:fə*], *s.* (*fam.*) burlone; schernitore.

chaffer[2] ['tʃæfə*], *s.* il mercanteggiare, il contrattare.

to **chaffer**[2], *v.i.* mercanteggiare, tirare sul prezzo: *to — with s.o. for sthg.*, mercanteggiare ql.co. con qlcu.

chaffinch ['tʃæfintʃ], *s.* (*ornit.*) fringuello.

chaffy ['tʃɑ:fi], *ag.* **1.** coperto di pula; simile a pula **2.** *fig.* arido, sterile **3.** senza valore.

chafing ['tʃeifiŋ], *s.* **1.** frizione, massaggio; (*mec.*) sfregamento **2.** irritazione (di pelle) **3.** *fig.* collera, stizza ☆ *— -dish* (o *— -pan*), scaldavivande.

chagrin ['ʃægrin], *s.* dispiacere; contrarietà; dispetto.

to **chagrin**, *v.t.* affliggere; contrariare; indispettire.

chain [tʃein], *s.* **1.** catena; ornamento a catena; *pl.* catene, ceppi; *fig.* prigionia: *to burst one's chains*, *fig.* spezzare le proprie catene; *to put a dog on the —*, mettere un cane alla catena ‖ *a — is as strong as its weakest link*, *prov.* una catena è forte quanto il suo anello più debole **2.** concatenazione, serie: *— of events*, serie di avvenimenti; *— of ideas*, concatenamento di idee **3.** (*chim.*) catena **4.** « chain » (misura di lunghezza = m. 20,16) ☆ *— -armour*, corazza, lorica a maglia; *— -cable*, (*mar.*) catena dell'àncora; *— -drive*, (*mec.*) trasmissione a catena; *— measure*, catena metrica; *— -plate*, (*mar.*) landa, landra; *— -reaction*, (*chim.*) reazione a catena; *— -shot*, (*artigl.*) palle ramate, palle incatenate; *— -stitch*, punto catenella; *— -store*, negozio a catena; *— -track*, (*mec.*) cingolo a catena; *— -wheel*, (*mec.*) puleggia per catena; *— -wale*, (*mar.*) parasartia ‖ *block- —*, (*mec.*) catena di trasmissioni; *lashing- —* (o *mooring- —*), (*mar.*) catena di ormeggio; *mountain- —*, (*geog.*) catena di montagne; *skid- —* (o *tire- —*), (*aut.*) catena antineve.

to **chain**, *v.t.* incatenare; assicurare, fermare con una catena (porta, ecc.); mettere alla catena (cane, ecc.); *fig.* mettere in ceppi: *to — s.o., sthg. to sthg.*, incatenare qlcu., ql.co. a ql.co.

chainless ['tʃeinlis], *ag.* senza catena, catene ☆ *— bicycle*, bicicletta senza catena.

chainlet ['tʃeinlit], *s.* catenina, catenella.

to **chain-smoke** ['tʃein 'smouk], *v.i.* fumare accanitamente.

chair [tʃɛə*], *s.* **1.** sedia: *to take a —*, sedersi **2.** seggio (di autorità); cattedra (universitaria) ‖ *the —*, la presidenza: *to address the —*, rivolgersi al presidente; *to be in* (o *to occupy*) *the —*, occupare il seggio presidenziale, presiedere l'assemblea del consiglio (di una società); *to leave* (o *to vacate*) *the —*, togliere la seduta; *to take the —*, assumere la presidenza ‖ « *—! — !* », invito alla calma in un'assemblea **3.** (*amer.*) banco dei testimoni **4.** (*amer.*) sedia elettrica **5.** (*amer.*) portantina **6.** (*ferr.*) ganascia, supporto laterale di rotaia **7.** (*mec.*) mozzo di ruota ☆ *— -back*, schienale; *— -lift*, seggiovia; *— -maker*, seggiolaio ‖ *Bath- —*, poltrona a rotelle per invalidi; *dentist's —*, poltrona odontoiatrica; *curule- —*, (*st. romana*) sedia curule; *deck- —*, sedia a sdraio; *easy- —* (o *elbow- —*), poltrona.

to **chair**, *v.t.* **1.** insediare, portare alla presidenza **2.** portare in trionfo (vincitore di gare sportive).

chairman, *pl.* **chairmen** ['tʃɛəmən], *s.c.* **1.** presidente, presidentessa (di consiglio, assemblea): *Mr.*

Chairman, Madam Chairman, Signor Presidente, Signora Presidentessa; *to act as* —, presiedere (un'assemblea, ecc.) **2.** chi conduce la carrozzella d'un ammalato ‖ *s.* portatore di portantina.

chairmanship ['tʃəⱳmənʃip], *s.* presidenza: *under the* — *of*, sotto la presidenza di.

chaise [ʃeiz], *s.* calesse, biroccino; carrozza da nolo.

chalcedony [kæl'sedəni], *s.* (*min.*) calcedonia.

chalcography [kæl'kɔgrəfi], *s.* calcografia.

chalcopyrite [ˌkælkouˈpairait], *s.* (*min.*) calcopirite.

Chaldaic [kæl'deiik], *ag.* caldeo ‖ *s.* lingua caldea.

Chaldea [kæl'di(:)ə], *no.pr.* (*geog. st.*) Caldea.

Chaldean [kæl'di(:)ən], **Chaldee** [kæl'di:], *ag.* caldeo ‖ *s.c.* caldeo, caldea.

chalet ['ʃælei], *s.* « chalet ».

chalice ['tʃælis], *s.* calice, coppa; (*eccl.*) calice.

chalk [tʃɔ:k], *s.* **1.** gesso; pastello ‖ *not by a long* —, (*sl.*) per nulla, affatto ‖ *he doesn't know* — *from cheese*, (*fam.*) non capisce niente, non sa niente di niente, prende lucciole per lanterne ‖ *to be as different as* — *and cheese*, essere del tutto dissimili; *to be as like as* — *and cheese*, (*scherz.*) assomigliarsi come il giorno e la notte **2.** (*min.*) calcare ☆ — *-drawing*, disegno a pastello; — *-mixture*, (*farm.*) preparato di gesso; — *-pit*, cava di calcare; — *-stone*, (*patol.*) calcolo.

to chalk, *v.t.* **1.** segnare, scrivere con gesso ‖ *to* — (*up*) *the drinks*, scrivere col gesso (su una lavagna) le consumazioni **2.** *to* — *out*, *fig.* progettare, abbozzare (un piano, un progetto).

chalkiness ['tʃɔ:kinis], *s.* **1.** natura gessosa (di terreno) **2.** estremo pallore.

chalky ['tʃɔ:ki], *ag.* **1.** gessoso; calcareo **2.** pallido, terreo (di colorito).

challenge ['tʃælindʒ], *s.* **1.** sfida; provocazione: *to issue a* —, lanciare una sfida; *to send s.o. a* —, mandare a qlcu. i padrini **2.** (*mil.*) intimazione, il chi va là (della sentinella) **3.** (*dir.*) rigetto, ricusazione (di giurato); opposizione (a giurato) ☆ — *-cup*, (*spor.*) coppa, trofeo.

to challenge, *v.t.* **1.** (IV) sfidare (a duello, a gara sportiva, ecc.); provocare: *to* — *s.o. to fight*, sfidare qlcu. a combattere **2.** (*mil.*) intimare (di sentinella) **3.** (*dir.*) rifiutare, ricusare, opporsi a (un giurato); mettere in dubbio (onore, parola, ecc.) **4.** *fig.* provocare, eccitare (ammirazione, critica, ecc.).

challengeable ['tʃælindʒəbl], *ag.* **1.** che si può sfidare **2.** criticabile **3.** (*dir.*) ricusabile.

challenger ['tʃælindʒə*], *s.c.* **1.** sfidatore, sfidatrice; provocatore, provocatrice; (*spor.*) sfidante: *the challengers*, gli sfidanti; *the holder and the* —, il detentore (di primato, coppa, ecc.) e lo sfidante **2.** (*dir.*) chi ricusa (un giurato).

challenging ['tʃælindʒiŋ], *ag.* sfidante; provocatore.

chalybeate [kə'libiit], *ag.* ferruginoso.

cham [kæm], *s.* (*arc.*) **1.** can (dignità orientale) **2.** *fig.* autocrate ‖ *Great Cham*, (*fam.*) personalità, personaggio.

chamber ['tʃeimbə*], *s.* **1.** sala, aula; (*arc. poet.*) camera, camera da letto ‖ *Chamber of Commerce*, Camera di commercio ‖ *Lower Chamber, Upper Chamber*, Camera alta (dei Lord), Camera bassa (dei Comuni) nel Parlamento inglese **2.** cavità (di corpo, pianta, ecc.) **3.** camera di scoppio, di caricamento (in arma da fuoco); (*tec.*) camera **4.** (*ing.*) conca idraulica **5.** *pl.* ufficio d'avvocato; gabinetto di giudice **6.** *pl.* appartamento (generalmente da scapolo) ☆ — *concert*, concerto di musica da camera; — *-council*, consiglio segreto; — *-counsel*, avvocato consulente; — *-maid*, cameriera (specialmente d'albergo); — *-music*, musica da camera; — *-pot*, vaso da notte ‖ *audience* —, sala delle udienze; *council* —, sala del consiglio; *escape* —, (*mar.*) camera di salvataggio.

to chamber, *v.t.* (*ing. mec.*) traforare, forare.

chambered ['tʃeimbəd], *ag.* provvisto di camere, diviso in compartimenti ☆ *six-* — *revolver*, rivoltella a sei colpi.

chamberlain ['tʃeimbəlin], *s.* **1.** ciambellano **2.** camerlengo; tesoriere.

chameleon [kə'mi:ljən], *s.* (*zool.*) camaleonte; *fig.* persona incostante.

chameleonic [kəˌmi:li'ɔnik], *ag.* camaleontico; *fig.* incostante.

chamfer ['tʃæmfə*], *s.* (*arch.*) smussatura, modanatura; (*mec.*) bisello, taglio a sbieco.

to chamfer, *v.t.* (*arch. mec.*) smussare, bisellare; scanalare.

chamois ['ʃæmwa:], *s.* (*zool.*) camoscio.

chamomile, *V.* **camomile**.

champ[1] [tʃæmp], *s.* masticazione rumorosa.

to champ[1], *v.t.* masticare rumorosamente; mordere ‖ *to* — *the bit*, mordere il freno (anche *fig.*).

champ[2], *s.* (*sl. amer. abbr. di champion*) campione.

champac ['tʃæmpək], *s.* magnolia dai fiori gialli odorosissimi (« Michelia Champaca »).

champagne [ʃæmˈpein], *s.* sciampagna.

champaign ['tʃæmpein], *s.* campagna aperta; pianura.

champignon [tʃæmˈpinjən], *s.* fungo commestibile.

champion ['tʃæmpjən], *ag.* campione; vincitore **2.** (*fam.*) magnifico ‖ *that's* —!, benone!, bravo! ‖ *s.* **1.** campione **2.** difensore, protettore: *a* — *of the oppressed*, un difensore degli oppressi ☆| — *tennis-player*, campione di tennis ‖ *world* —, campione mondiale.

to champion, *v.t.* difendere, sostenere (una causa).

championship ['tʃæmpjənʃip], *s.* campionato.

chance [tʃɑ:ns], *ag.* fortuito, casuale, accidentale: *a* — *acquaintance*, una conoscenza casuale ‖ *s.* **1.** caso, avvenimento fortuito, sorte, fortuna; probabilità: *by (mere)* —, per (puro) caso; *by a lucky* —, per un caso fortunato; *on the off* —, nell'eventualità; *the chances are...*, le probabilità sono...; *he hasn't the least* (*o the ghost of a*) — *of succeeding*, non ha la minima probabilità di riuscita; *will you be there by any* —?, vi troverete là, per caso?; *to have an even* —, avere uguali possibilità di riuscire o di fallire; *to leave sthg. to* —, lasciare ql.co. al caso; *to stand a good* —, avere buone probabilità **2.** azzardo; (*amer.*) rischio: *game of* —, giuoco d'azzardo; *to take a* —, correre un rischio **3.** occasione, opportunità: *it is your last* —, è l'ultima occasione che ti si presenta ☆ — *meeting*, incontro casuale; — *met*, incontrato per caso.

to chance, *v.t.i.* **1.** (*gener.* costruzione *pers.*) accadere: *I chanced to meet him*, lo incontrai per caso; *it chanced that I...*, accadde che io... **2.** (*fam.*) arrischiare: *I'll* — *it*, lo tento; *let's* — *it*, arrischiamolo; *to* — *the consequences*, arrischiare le conseguenze **3.** *to* — *upon* (*s.o., sthg.*), incontrare, trovare per caso.

chancel ['tʃɑ:nsəl], *s.* (*arch. eccl.*) presbiterio, coro.

chancellery ['tʃɑ:nsələri], *s.* cancelleria.

chancellor ['tʃɑ:nsələ*], *s.* **1.** cancelliere ‖ *the Lord (High) Chancellor* (o *the Chancellor of England*), il Gran Cancelliere; *the Chancellor of the Exchequer*, Cancelliere dello Scacchiere (Ministro delle Finanze, del Tesoro) **2.** capo titolare in alcune università.

chancellorship ['tʃɑ:nsələʃip], *s.* cancellierato.

chancellory ['tʃɑ:nsələri], *s.* cancelleria.

chance-medley [ˌtʃɑ:ns'medli], *s.* **1.** azione (specialmente omicidio) preterintenzionale **2.** inavvertenza.

chancery ['tʃɑ:nsəri], *s.* cancelleria (sezione dell'Alta Corte di Giustizia) ‖ *in* —, in difficoltà; (*dir.*) in contestazione, in lite ‖ *a ward in* —, un minorenne sotto tutela legale **2.** cancelleria; archivio.

chancy ['tʃɑ:nsi], *ag.* incerto, rischioso, arrischiato.

chandelier [ˌʃændi'liə*], *s.* candeliere; lampadario.

chandler ['tʃɑ:ndlə*], *s.* droghiere; fornitore ☆ *corn* - —, rivenditore di grano; *ship* —, fornitore navale.

chandlery ['tʃɑ:ndləri], *s.* **1.** piccola spezieria, drogheria **2.** *pl.* articoli di spezieria.

change [tʃeindʒ], *s.* **1.** cambio, mutamento; alterazione; variazione; sostituzione: — *for the better, for the worse*, cambiamento in meglio, in peggio; — *of* *abode*, cambiamento di domicilio; — *of clothes, of linen*, cambio di abiti, di biancheria; — *in the moon*, luna nuova; *you need a* — *of air*, hai bisogno di un cambiamento d'aria; *to effect a* —, effettuare un cambiamento; *to undergo a* —, subire un cambiamento || — *of life*, (*fisiol.*) menopausa || *for a* —, tanto per cambiare || *to ring the changes*, scampanare con variazioni: *to ring the changes on a subject*, (*fam.*) cantarla in tutti i toni 2. cambio, moneta spicciola; resto: *small* —, spiccioli: *you'll get sixpence* —, devi avere sei penny di resto 3. *Change* (*comm. abbr.* di *Exchange*), Borsa: *on* —, in Borsa 4. vicenda, vicissitudine: *the changes of life*, le vicissitudini della vita ☆ — *-over*, cambiamento (di sistema); cambiamento radicale (politico); cambio di funzionari; (*elett.*) commutazione || *gear-* —, (*mec.*) cambio di velocità.

to **change**, *v.t.i.* **1.** cambiare, cambiarsi; mutare, mutarsi; modificare, modificarsi; sostituire; variare: *at Milan we must* — (*trains*) *for Venice*, a Milano dobbiamo cambiare (treno) per Venezia; *can you* — *this pound note for me?*, potete cambiarmi questo biglietto da una sterlina?; *this house has changed hands many times*, questa casa ha cambiato spesso di proprietario; *to* — (*one's clothes*), cambiarsi d'abito; *to* — *colour*, cambiar colore (arrossire, impallidire); (*chim.*) virare; *to* — *one's mind*, cambiare idea; *to* — *places with s.o.*, cambiare di posto con qlcu.; *to* — *the subject*, cambiare argomento, parlare d'altro || — *foot!* (o *step!*), cambiar passo! || *to* — *one's condition*, sposarsi || *to* — *one's feet*, (*fam.*) cambiarsi di scarpe || *to* — *one's tune*, (*sl.*) cambiare tono, umore **2.** (*mec.*) sostituire **3.** *to* — *about*, parlare voltafaccia, cambiare continuamente opinione **4.** *to* — *down*, (*aut.*) passare a una velocità inferiore **5.** *to* — *over*, fare un cambiamento; darsi il cambio (di sentinelle, ecc.); (*elett.*) commutare: *to* — *over from one system to another*, passare da un sistema a un altro **6.** *to* — *up*, (*aut.*) passare a una velocità superiore.

changeability [ˌtʃeindʒəˈbiliti], *s.* mutabilità, incostanza; variabilità.

changeable [ˈtʃeindʒəbl], *ag.* mutabile; variabile; mutevole; incostante.

changeableness [ˈtʃeindʒəblnis], *s.* mutevolezza; volubilità; variabilità.

changeful [ˈtʃeindʒful], *ag.* (*poet.*) incostante, capriccioso, mutevole.

changeless [ˈtʃeindʒlis], *ag.* costante; inalterabile.

changeling [ˈtʃeindʒliŋ], *s.* (*poet.*) bimbo sostituito, rapito (specialmente in racconti di fate).

changer [ˈtʃeindʒə*], *s.* **1.** cambiavalute **2.** (*elett.*) commutatore ☆ *frequency* —, (*elett.*) variatore di frequenza; *money-* —, cambiavalute.

changing [ˈtʃeindʒiŋ], *ag.* cangiante; mutevole, incostante, volubile || *s.* cambio: *the* — *of the guard*, il cambio della guardia.

channel[1] [ˈtʃænl], *s.* **1.** canale; stretto || *the* (*English*) *Channel*, la Manica; *St. George's Channel*, il Canale di S. Giorgio **2.** letto (di fiume) **3.** canale, condotto (di liquidi, metalli fusi, ecc.) **4.** (*arch.*) scanalatura (di colonna) **5.** *pl.* mezzi, vie di comunicazione; fonti (di notizie, ecc.): *the channels of communication of a country*, le grandi vie di comunicazione di un paese; *the channels of diplomacy*, le vie diplomatiche; *to go through official channels*, seguire la trafila burocratica **6.** *pl.* sbocco: *to open up new channels for trade*, aprire nuovi sbocchi commerciali **7.** (*tv. aer.*) canale.

to **channel**[1], *pass.p.p.* **channelled** [ˈtʃænld], *v.t.* **1.** fare canali, solchi in **2.** incanalare **3.** (*arch.*) scanalare.

channel[2], *s.* (*mar.*) parasartia.

chant [tʃɑːnt], *s.* (*mus.*) canto (monotono), melologo, salmodia ☆ *Gregorian* —, canto gregoriano.

to **chant**, *v.t.* **1.** (*eccl.*) salmodiare **2.** (*arc. poet.*) cantare || *to* — *s.o.'s praises*, cantare le lodi di qlcu. **3.**(*sl.*) vendere (cavalli) di frodo.

chantage [ˈtʃɑːntidʒ], *s.* ricatto.

chanter [ˈtʃɑːntə*], *s.* **1.** (*eccl.*) cantore **2.** (*sl.*) venditore fraudolento di cavalli.

chantey [ˈtʃɑːnti], *s.* coro di marinai al lavoro.

chanticleer [ˌtʃæntiˈkliə*], *s.* (*lett. scherz.*) gallo.

chantry [ˈtʃɑːntri], *s.* **1.** dotazione per messe di suffragio **2.** cappella dove si celebrano messe di suffragio.

chanty [ˈtʃɑːnti], *s.* coro di marinai al lavoro.

chaos [ˈkeiɔs], *s.* caos.

chaotic [keiˈɔtik], *ag.* caotico.

chaotically [keiˈɔtikəli], *av.* caoticamente.

chap[1] [tʃæp], *s.* **1.** screpolatura (della pelle) **2.** fessura.

to **chap**[1], *pass.p.p.* **chapped** [tʃæpt], *v.t.i.* screpolare, screpolarsi (della pelle): *chapped hands*, mani screpolate.

chap[2], *s. gener. pl.* mandibola (specialmente di maiale); (*scherz.*) ganascia, mascella umana.

chap[3], *s.* **1.** (*arc.*) cliente, compratore **2.** (*fam.*) ragazzo, individuo: *a nice young* —, un simpatico ragazzo || *old* —, vecchio mio.

chapel [ˈtʃæpəl], *s.* **1.** cappella; funzione religiosa: — *of ease*, cappella sussidiaria **2.** tempio (di dissidenti) || *is he Church or Chapel?*, è anglicano o dissidente? **3.** laboratorio tipografico; associazione, adunata di tipografi ☆ — *royal*, cappella del palazzo reale || *Lady* —, cappella della Madonna.

chaperon [ˈʃæpəroun], *s.* «chaperon» (accompagnatrice di signorine in società).

to **chaperon**, *v.t.* fare da «chaperon» a.

chaperonage [ˈʃæpərounidʒ], *s.* sorveglianza, tutela, guida (di una signorina).

chapiter [ˈtʃæpitə*], *s.* (*arch.*) capitello.

chaplain [ˈtʃæplin], *s.* cappellano ☆ *army* —, cappellano militare.

chaplaincy [ˈtʃæplinsi], **chaplainship** [ˈtʃæplinʃip], *s.* ufficio di cappellano.

chaplet [ˈtʃæplit], *s.* **1.** ghirlanda; corona di fiori **2.** (*eccl.*) corona, rosario **3.** (*arch.*) modanatura a forma di grani, perline.

chapman, *pl.* **chapmen** [ˈtʃæpmən], *s.* venditore ambulante.

chappie, **chappy**[1] [ˈtʃæpi], *s.* (*fam.*) ragazzo, individuo.

chappy[2], *ag.* screpolato; arido, riarso.

chapter [ˈtʃæptə*], *s.* **1.** capitolo (di libro, ecc.) || *a* — *of accidents*, (*fam.*) un susseguirsi di guai || *to give* — *and verse*, citare capitolo e verso, citare le autorità **2.** (*eccl.*) capitolo.

char[1] [tʃɑː*], *s.* sostanza carbonizzata; nero animale.

to **char**[1], *v.t.i.* carbonizzare, carbonizzarsi.

char[2], *s.* **1.** lavoro a giornata (generalmente in casa) **2.** (*abbr.* di *charwoman*) domestica a ore.

to **char**[2], *pass.p.p.* **charred** [tʃɑːd], *v.i.* lavorare a giornata (o *to go out charring*, andare a lavorare a giornata (di domestica).

char-à-banc, **charabane** [ˈʃærəbæŋ], *s.* carrozza od automobile con sedili trasversali; torpedone.

charabancer [ˈʃærəˌbæŋkə*], *s.c.* escursionista (in torpedone).

character [ˈkæriktə*], *s.* **1.** carattere (fisico, morale); indole; caratteristica, qualità **2.** reputazione: *of bad* —, di cattiva fama **3.** scrittura; (*tip.*) carattere: *printed in Roman characters*, stampato in caratteri romani **4.** stile, personalità: *work lacking* —, opera che manca di personalità **5.** benservito; certificato di buona condotta || *to give s.o. a good* —, (*fam.*) parlare bene di qlcu. **6.** (*lett. teat.*) personaggio, parte; *pl.* elenco dei personaggi **7.** tipo: *a bad* —, un cattivo soggetto; *a strange* —, un tipo strano ☆ — *actor*, caratterista; — *-drawing*, caratterizzazione dei personaggi.

characteristic [ˌkæriktəˈristik], *ag.* caratteristico || *s.* caratteristica.

characteristically [ˌkæriktəˈristikəli], *av.* caratteristicamente; tipicamente.

characterization [ˌkæriktəraiˈzeiʃən], *s.* (*lett. teat.*) caratterizzazione.

to **characterize** ['kæriktəraiz], *v.t.* **1.** caratterizzare; essere caratteristico di **2.** definire: *I should — him as being perfectly honest*, lo potrei definire uomo di specchiata onestà.

characterless ['kæriktəlis], *ag.* senza carattere.

charade [ʃə'ra:d], *s.* sciarada.

charcoal ['tʃa:koul], *s.* **1.** carbone di legna, carbonella **2.** carboncino (da disegno) ☆ — *-burner*, carbonaio; — *drawing*, disegno a carboncino; — *-pan*, braciere. (to) **chare** [tʃɛə*], *V.* (to) char[2].

charge [tʃa:dʒ], *s.* **1.** spesa, prezzo (richiesto), costo: — *for admittance*, prezzo di ingresso; *free of —*, esente da spese; franco di porto; *sundry charges*, spese varie; *all is at his own —*, tutto è a carico suo; *no — is made for packing*, imballo compreso; *what is the — for a room?*, qual è il costo di una camera?; *to make a — for sthg.*, far pagare, conteggiare ql.co. **2.** incarico, carica; sorveglianza, cura, guardia: *a child in — of a nurse*, un bambino sotto la sorveglianza di una bambinaia; *official in —*, (*amm.*) funzionario incaricato; *person in —*, incaricato, addetto; *to be in — of*, avere la sorveglianza di, dirigere; *to give s.o. a —*, dare un incarico a qlcu.; *to give s.o. in —*, fare arrestare qlcu.; *to take — of*, assumere la sorveglianza, la direzione di; *to take s.o. in —*, arrestare qlcu. ‖ *a nurse with her young charges*, una balia con i bambini a lei affidati ‖ *the priest and his —*, il sacerdote e i suoi parrocchiani **3.** (*dir.*) accusa: *what is the — against the prisoner?*, quale è l'accusa contro il prigioniero?; *to bring* (o *to lay*) *a — against s.o.*, portare una accusa contro qlcu. **4.** esortazione, allocuzione (di giudice alla giuria, di vescovo) **5.** (*mil.*) carica, attacco: *to return to the —*, tornare alla carica **6.** carica (d'arma da fuoco) ☆ — *-account*, (*amer.*) conto corrente; *charges forward*, (*comm.*) spese a carico del destinatario ‖ *bursting —*, carica di scoppio.

to **charge**, *v.t.i.* **1.** far pagare; addebitare; conteggiare: — *it to my account*, addebitatelo al mio conto; *cases are charged extra*, le casse sono conteggiate in più; *to — an account with the expenses*, addebitare le spese ad un conto; *to — for*, far pagare, addebitare per: *he charged me three shillings for taking my bag to the station*, mi fece pagare tre scellini per avermi portato la valigia alla stazione; *calls are charged for*, le chiamate (telefoniche) vengono addebitate **2.** incaricare: *he was charged with the task of watching...*, gli fu affidato il compito di sorvegliare...; *to — oneself with*, assumersi l'incarico di; *to — s.o. with a commission*, incaricare qlcu. di una commissione **3.** (*dir.*) accusare: *to — s.o. with a crime* (o *to — a crime on s.o.*), accusare qlcu. di un delitto; *to be charged with* (*stealing*), essere accusato di (furto) **4.** *to — the jury*, (*dir.*) fare l'allocuzione alla giuria **5.** caricare (arma da fuoco, accumulatore elettrico, ecc.); riempire; saturare: *air is charged with vapour*, l'aria è satura di vapore **6.** (*mil.*) caricare, andare alla carica ‖ *to — into sthg.*, (*sl.*) battere la testa contro ql.co.

chargeability [ˌtʃa:dʒə'biliti], *s.* imputabilità.

chargeable ['tʃa:dʒəbl], *ag.* **1.** a carico di, da addebitarsi a; imponibile: *poor — to the parish*, i poveri a carico della parrocchia; *repairs — on the owner*, riparazioni a carico del proprietario **2.** accusabile, imputabile.

chargee [tʃa:'dʒi:], *s.* (*dir.*) creditore privilegiato.

charger[1] ['tʃa:dʒə*], *s.* (*arc.*) piatto da portata.

charger[2], *s.* **1.** destriero **2.** caricatore (di arma da fuoco), calcatoio **3.** accumulatore elettrico.

charily ['tʃɛərili], *av.* **1.** cautamente, prudentemente **2.** frugalmente; parcamente; economicamente.

chariness ['tʃɛərinis], *s.* **1.** cautela, prudenza **2.** frugalità; parsimonia; economicità.

chariot ['tʃæriət], *s.* cocchio; carro (trionfale, ecc.); biga ☆ *war —*, biga da combattimento.

charioteer [ˌtʃæriə'tiə*], *s.* auriga.

charitable ['tʃæritəbl], *ag.* caritatevole.

charitableness ['tʃæritəblnis], *s.* l'essere caritatevole.

charitably ['tʃæritəbli], *av.* caritatevolmente.

charity ['tʃæriti], *s.* **1.** elemosina: *to ask for —*, chiedere l'elemosina; *to live on —*, vivere di carità ‖ *for —'s sake* (o *out of —*), per carità **2.** istituzione benefica: *she will leave all her money to charities*, lascerà tutto il suo denaro ad istituti di carità **3.** carità, pietà, benevolenza, equità ‖ *Sister of Charity*, suora di carità ‖ *— begins at home*, *prov.* la carità comincia in casa propria ☆ — *ball*, ballo di beneficenza; — *boy*, — *girl*, ragazzo, ragazza di un istituto di beneficenza pubblica; — *-school*, scuola gratuita.

charivari ['ʃa:ri'va:ri], *s.* chiassata; serenata burlesca.

charlady ['tʃa:ˌleidi], *s.f.* (*scherz.*) domestica ad ore, a giornata.

charlatan ['ʃa:lətən], *s.* ciarlatano, imbroglione.

charlatanish ['ʃa:lətəniʃ], *ag.* ciarlatanesco.

charlatanism ['ʃa:lətənizəm], **charlatanry** ['ʃa:lətənri], *s.* ciarlataneria.

Charlemagne ['ʃa:lə'main], *no.pr.m.* (*st.*) Carlomagno.

Charles [tʃa:lz], *no.pr.m.* Carlo ‖ *— the Bold*, (*st.*) Carlo il Temerario; — *the Fair*, (*st.*) Carlo il Bello; — *the Fat*, (*st.*) Carlo il Grosso.

charleston ['tʃa:lstən], *s.* «charleston» (danza vivace). to **charleston**, *v.i.* danzare il «charleston».

Charley, Charlie [tʃa:li], *no.pr.m.* dim. di **Charles** ‖ *s.* (*arc. fam.*) guardiano notturno.

charlock ['tʃa:lɔk], *s.* (*bot.*) senape dei campi.

charlotte[1] ['ʃa:lət], *s.* (*cuc.*) «charlotte» (torta di frutta).

Charlotte[2], *no.pr.f.* Carlotta.

charm[1] [tʃa:m], *s.* **1.** fascino, incanto, attrattiva: *the — of youth*, il fascino della giovinezza; *she has —*, ha del fascino **2.** incantesimo, malia **3.** amuleto; ciondolo: *a — against bad luck*, un amuleto contro il malocchio.

to **charm**[1], *v.t.i.* **1.** affascinare; incantare; deliziare: *charmed to see you!*, felicissimo di vedervi!; *I was charmed by their kindness*, fui incantato dalla loro gentilezza **2.** render fatato; sottoporre a magia; praticare la magia ‖ *they charmed the secret out of him*, gli strapparono il segreto come per magia.

charm[2], *s.* chiacchierio, cinguettio (di scolaretti, uccelli, ecc.).

charmer ['tʃa:mə*], *s.c.* incantatore, incantatrice ☆ *snake-* —, incantatore di serpenti.

charmeuse ['ʃa:mə:z], *s.* raso morbido e opaco.

charming ['tʃa:miŋ], *ag.* incantevole, affascinante ‖ *Prince Charming*, il Principe Azzurro.

charmingly ['tʃa:miŋli], *av.* in modo incantevole, con fascino.

charmless ['tʃa:mlis], *ag.* privo di fascino, attrattiva.

charnel (-house) ['tʃa:n](haus)], *s.* ossario.

Charon ['kɛərən], *no.pr.m.* (*mit.*) Caronte.

charpoy ['tʃa:pɔi], *s.* (*ang.-in.*) letto indiano.

chart [tʃa:t], *s.* **1.** (*mar.*) carta marina, carta idrografica **2.** grafico, diagramma (statistico) ☆ *night flying —*, (*aer.*) carta per volo notturno; *pilot —*, (*mar.*) carta nautica; *wind-* —, carta dei venti.

to **chart**, *v.t.* **1.** fare la carta idrografica di **2.** fare il grafico, il diagramma di (temperatura, ecc.).

charter ['tʃa:tə*], *s.* **1.** (*st. dir.*) carta, documento costitutivo (di città, ecc.) ‖ *the Atlantic Charter*, (*pol.*) la Dichiarazione Atlantica ‖ *the Great Charter*, (*st.*) la Magna Charta **2.** (*dir.*) patente **3.** (*comm.*) statuto, contratto ☆ — *-member*, (*amer.*) socio fondatore.

to **charter**, *v.t.* **1.** (*comm.*) concedere statuto, privilegio a (società, ecc.); istituire (società) per mezzo di documento ufficiale **2.** noleggiare (nave); (*fam.*) noleggiare (automobile, ecc.) ☆ *chartered accountant*, ragioniere diplomato; *chartered company*, società, compagnia privilegiata, riconosciuta.

Charterhouse ['tʃa:təhaus], *s.* **1.** certosa **2.** Charterhouse (antico monastero di Certosini in Londra, adibito in seguito a scuola e ospedale).

charterparty ['tʃɑ:tə,pɑ:ti], *s.* (*mar.*) contratto di noleggio.

charthouse ['tʃɑ:thaus], *s.* (*mar.*) sala nautica.

Chartism ['tʃɑ:tizm], *s.* (*st. inglese*) cartismo.

Chartist ['tʃɑ:tist], *s.* (*st. inglese*) seguace del cartismo.

chartless ['tʃɑ:tlis], *ag.* **1.** senza statuto, senza privilegio **2.** (*mar.*) non segnato sulla carta idrografica; senza carte di navigazione (di nave).

chartographer [kɑ:'tɔgrəfə*], *s.* cartografo.

chartographical [,kɑ:tə'græfikəl], *ag.* cartografico.

chartography [kɑ:'tɔgrəfi], *s.* cartografia.

chartreuse [ʃɑ:'trə:z], *s.* **1.** certosa **2.** « chartreuse » (liquore dei certosini) **3.** color verde pallido.

chartroom ['tʃɑ:tru:m], *s.* (*mar.*) sala nautica.

charwoman ['tʃɑ:,wumən], *pl.* **charwomen** ['tʃɑ:,wimin], *s.f.* domestica ad ore, a giornata.

charwork ['tʃɑ:wə:k], *s.* lavoro di domestica ad ore.

chary ['tʃɛəri], *ag.* **1.** cauto, prudente: *to be — of doing sthg.*, esitare a fare ql.co. **2.** parco; parsimonioso: *— of praises*, avaro di lodi; *— of words*, parco di parole.

Charybdis [kə'ribdis], *no.pr.f.* (*mit.*) Cariddi ‖ *no.pr.* (*geog.*) Cariddi ‖ *to be between Scylla and —*, essere tra Scilla e Cariddi.

chase[1] [tʃeis], *s.* **1.** caccia; inseguimento: *to give — to*, dare la caccia a ‖ *a wild goose —*, (*fam.*) inseguimento vano, un'impresa sbagliata **2.** diritto di caccia **3.** riserva di caccia **4.** cacciagione **5.** *coll.* cacciatori **6.** — (*gun*), (*mar.*) i cannoni da caccia di una nave ☆ *paper- —*, giuoco a rimpiattino con una traccia di pezzetti di carta.

to **chase**[1], *v.t.* **1.** cacciare; inseguire: *to — the enemy*, inseguire il nemico **2.** rincorrere (per giuoco): *the boys chased each other round the room*, i ragazzi si rincorrevano intorno alla stanza **3.** *to — away*, scacciare, far scappar via **4.** *to — off*: *to — off after sthg.*, partire all'inseguimento di ql.co. **5.** *to — out*, cacciar fuori.

chase[2], *s.* castone (di una gemma).

to **chase**[2], *v.t.* (*artig.*) cesellare, incidere; intagliare; sbalzare (metalli); incastonare (una gemma).

chase[3], *s.1.* (*artigl.*) volata (di arma da fuoco) **2.** (*edil.*) traccia, incassatura.

to **chase**[3], *v.t.* (*mec.*) filettare, scanalare.

chase[4], *s.* (*tip.*) telaio (per l'impaginazione).

chaser[1] ['tʃeisə*], *s.* **1.** cacciatore; inseguitore **2.** (*mar.*) caccia, cacciatorpediniere; (*aer.*) caccia, aeroplano da caccia **3.** (*fam.*) bibita presa subito dopo il caffè o dopo liquori ☆ *bow- —*, cannone di prua; *stern- —*, cannone di poppa; *submarine —*, cacciasommergibili.

chaser[2], *s.* (*artig.*) cesellatore, incisore.

chasing ['tʃeisiŋ], *s.* **1.** (*artig.*) cesellatura **2.** (*mec.*) filettatura di una vite **3.** incastonatura ☆ *— tool*, (*falegnameria*) bedano, unghietta.

chasm ['kæzəm], *s.* **1.** baratro, abisso (anche *fig.*) **2.** *fig.* lacuna, vuoto.

chasmogamous [kæz'mɔgəməs], *ag.* (*bot.*) casmogamo.

chasmy ['kæzmi], *ag.* pieno di burroni, spaccature, abissi (di terreno).

chassis ['ʃæsi], *pl.* **chassis** ['ʃæsiz], *s.* **1.** « chassis », telaio, intelaiatura **2.** (*fam.*) rotabili, veicoli (di impresa di trasporti).

chaste [tʃeist], *ag.* **1.** casto, virtuoso, puro (di persona) **2.** decente, conveniente (di discorso) **3.** severo, semplice, puro (di stile, gusto).

chastely ['tʃeistli], *av.* **1.** castamente, virtuosamente **2.** decentemente, convenientemente **3.** severamente.

to **chasten** ['tʃeisn], *v.t.* **1.** castigare; correggere castigando **2.** raffinare, purificare, castigare (stile, lingua).

chastened ['tʃeisnd], *ag.* provato, abbattuto, avvilito.

chastener ['tʃeisnə*], *s.* castigatore.

chasteness ['tʃeistnis], *s.* **1.** castità, purezza **2.** castigatezza, purezza, semplicità (di stile).

chastening ['tʃeisniŋ], *s.* mortificazione (di passioni).

to **chastise** [tʃæs'taiz], *v.t.* castigare, punire; correggere.

chastisement ['tʃæstizmənt], *s.* castigo, punizione; correzione.

chastiser [tʃæs'taizə*], *s.c.* punitore, punitrice.

chastity ['tʃæstiti], *s.* **1.** castità, verginità **2.** castigatezza, semplicità (di stile, gusto).

chasuble ['tʃæzjubl], *s.* (*eccl.*) casula, pianeta.

chat [tʃæt], *s.* ciarla, chiacchiera; cicaleccio; *a little —*, una chiacchieratina; *a long —*, una lunga chiacchierata.

to **chat**, *pass.p.p.* **chatted** ['tʃætid], *v.i.* chiacchierare, ciarlare: *to — with s.o. about sthg.*, chiacchierare con ql.cu. di ql.co.

chatelaine ['ʃætəlein], *s.* **1.** castellana; padrona di casa **2.** catenella (per chiavi, ecc. portata alla cintura).

chattel ['tʃætl], *s. gener. pl.* (*dir.*) bene mobile, beni mobili ‖ *goods and chattels*, (*fam.*) beni ed effetti, tutto quello che uno possiede ☆ *— mortgage*, ipoteca su beni mobili ‖ *real chattels*, beni immobili.

chatter ['tʃætə*], *s.* **1.** chiacchiera; ciancia; chiacchierio; cinguettio (di uccelli); cicaleccio (di scimmie) **2.** il battere (dei denti) **3.** (*rad.*) bisbiglio; (*mec.*) rumore (dovuto a vibrazione).

to **chatter**, *v.i.* **1.** chiacchierare, ciarlare; cinguettare (di uccelli); cicalare (di scimmie) **2.** battere (di denti) **3.** (*mec.*) vibrare, battere, far rumore.

chatterbox ['tʃætəbɔks], **chatterer** ['tʃætərə*], *s.c.* chiacchierone, chiacchierona.

chattering ['tʃætəriŋ], *s.* **1.** chiacchierio **2.** il battere (dei denti) **3.** crepitio.

chattily ['tʃætili], *av.* **1.** da chiacchierone; loquacemente **2.** familiarmente.

chattiness ['tʃætinis], *s.* loquacità.

chatty ['tʃæti], *ag.* chiacchierone, ciarliero: *she's a — old lady*, è una vecchia signora chiacchierona.

Chaucerian [tʃɔ:'siərion], *ag.* (*lett.*) di Chaucer ‖ *s.* studioso, ammiratore di Chaucer.

chauffer ['tʃɔ:fə*], *s.* caldano, scaldino.

chauffeur ['ʃoufə*], *s.* autista.

chauvinism ['ʃouvinizəm], *s.* sciovinismo.

chauvinist ['ʃouvinist], *ag.s.* sciovinista.

chauvinistic [,ʃouvi'nistik], *ag.* sciovinista.

chaw [tʃɔ:], *s.* (*volg.*) cicca (tabacco da masticare) ☆ *— -bacon*, campagnolo; (*sl.*) villanzone.

to **chaw**, *v.t.* **1.** (*volg.*) ciccare, masticare tabacco **2.** (*arc.*) borbottare **3.** *to — up*, (*sl. amer.*) distruggere, demolire; annientare.

chawl [tʃɔ:l], *s.* baracca per indigeni (nelle Indie).

cheap [tʃi:p], *ag.* a buon mercato, a basso prezzo, economico; di poco valore: *to buy sthg. —*, comprare ql.co. a buon mercato ‖ *— and nasty*, di poco prezzo, di cattiva qualità ‖ *Cheap Jack*, venditore ambulante ‖ *dirt* (o *dog*) *—*, a bassissimo prezzo; *to do sthg. on the —*, fare ql.co. con poca spesa ‖ *to feel —*, (*fam.*) sentirsi poco considerato, depresso ‖ *to get off —*, (*fam.*) cavarsela a buon mercato ‖ *to hold s.o., sthg. —*, tenere in poco conto qlcu., ql.co. ‖ *to make oneself —*, mancare alla propria dignità ☆ *— currency*, valuta deprezzata; *— trip*, gita economica; *cheapest port*, (*comm.*) porto dove il nolo è meno caro.

to **cheapen** ['tʃi:pən], *v.t.i.* **1.** ridurre, calare il prezzo di; ridursi, calare di prezzo; diminuire di valore **2.** *fig.* screditare; deprezzare: *you mustn't — yourself*, non devi sottovalutarti.

cheapish ['tʃi:piʃ], *ag.* (abbastanza) a buon mercato.

cheaply ['tʃi:pli], *av.* a buon prezzo, economicamente.

cheapness ['tʃi:pnis], *s.* buon mercato, prezzo basso **2.** scarso valore, mediocrità (di ql.co.).

cheat [tʃi:t], *s.c.* imbroglione, imbrogliona; truffatore, truffatrice; chi bara ‖ *s.* frode, inganno; trucco ‖ *to put a — upon*, ingannare.

to **cheat**, *v.t.i.* ingannare; imbrogliare, truffare; barare: *to — the customs*, frodare la dogana; *to — s.o. into doing sthg.*, usare degli inganni per far fare ql.co. a qlcu.; *to — s.o. out of sthg.*, privare con inganno qlcu.

di ql.co. ‖ to — the gallows, sfuggire alla forca ‖ to — tedium, ingannare la noia.

cheater ['tʃi:tə*], s. truffatore, imbroglione; baro.

cheating ['tʃi:tiŋ], s. inganno; truffa; imbroglio.

check[1] [tʃek], s. **1.** (scacchi) scacco: to give — to the king, dare scacco al re **2.** arresto; ripulsa; lieve sconfitta **3.** pausa; fermata; impedimento; freno; ostacolo: to keep the enemy in —, tenere il nemico in scacco; to meet with a —, incontrare un ostacolo, subire uno scacco; to put a — on sthg., s.o., metter freno a ql.co., a qlcu. **4.** controllo, verifica, visto **5.** tagliando; scontrino; contromarca **6.** (amer.) conto (al ristorante, ecc.) **7.** (amer.) gettone, « fiche » ☆ — -clerk, (comm.) impiegato addetto alla verifica; — -list, (amer.) lista di controllo; — -rein, redine che unisce i cavalli di una pariglia; — ,room, (amer.) deposito bagagli; — sample, campione di controllo; — -taker, controllore dei biglietti; — -up, (amer.) verifica dei conti: — -up committee, comitato di controllo, collegio dei sindaci ‖ final —, collaudo.

to **check**[1], v.t.i. **1.** (scacchi) dare scacco a **2.** far fermare, arrestare (movimento); frenare, impedire, ostacolare; contenere (il nemico): to — oneself, contenersi **3.** controllare, verificare: to — accounts, the books, (comm.) controllare i conti, verificare la contabilità **4.** (amer.) combaciare, concordare: these figures —, queste cifre concordano **5.** depositare: to — luggage, depositare bagaglio (alla ferrovia) **6.** emettere un assegno **7.** to — in, registrare (merce) all'arrivo **8.** to — off, spuntare, verificare: to — off names on a list, spuntare un elenco di nomi **9.** to — out, (amer.) pagare il conto e lasciare l'albergo; (sl.) morire **10.** to — up, verificare, controllare; fare una verifica.

check[2], s. scacco, quadrettino; tessuto, disegno a scacchi, a quadretti.

to **check**[3], V. to **cheque.**

checked [tʃekt], ag. quadrettato ☆ — material, stoffa a quadretti.

checker[1] ['tʃekə*], s. **1.** cronometrista, tempista, rilevatore di tempo **2.** (metal.) camera di recupero, di rigenerazione **3.** (ott.) cercatore (di telescopio).

(to) **checker**[2], V. (to) **chequer.**

checking ['tʃekiŋ], s. **1.** repressione **2.** controllo, verifica **3.** registrazione bagagli ☆ — account, (amer.) conto in banca; — -room, deposito bagagli.

checkmate ['tʃek'meit], s. scacco matto.

to **checkmate**, v.t. dar scacco matto a (anche fig.).

Cheddar ['tʃedə*], s. varietà di formaggio dolce.

cheddite ['tʃedait], s. (esplosivo) cheddite.

cheek [tʃi:k], s. **1.** guancia, gota ‖ — by jowl with s.o., fig. molto vicino a qlcu., intimo di qlcu. ‖ — to —, guancia a guancia ‖ tongue in —, scherzosamente **2.** (fam.) sfacciataggine, sfrontatezza: what —!, che sfacciataggine!, che faccia tosta!; to have the — to, avere la sfrontatezza di **3.** (arch.) lato di una apertura **4.** (mec.) ganascia ☆ — -bone, zigomo; — -tooth, dente molare.

to **cheek**, v.t. (fam.) fare l'insolente on; parlare in modo insolente a.

cheekily ['tʃi:kili], av. (fam.) sfacciatamente, sfrontatamente.

cheekiness ['tʃi:kinis], s. (fam.) sfacciataggine, sfrontatezza.

cheeky ['tʃi:ki], ag. sfacciato, sfrontato.

cheep [tʃi:p], s. pigolio.

to **cheep**, v.i. pigolare.

cheer [tʃiə*], s. **1.** disposizione di spirito; buon umore, buona disposizione di spirito ‖ what —?, come va?, come vanno le cose? **2.** incoraggiamento, conforto; applauso, evviva: three cheers for..., tre urrà per...; words of —, parole di incoraggiamento; be of good —!, su, coraggio! **3.** cibo, vivande ‖ to make good —, banchettare ☆ — -leader, (amer.) chi dirige la « claque ».

to **cheer**, v.t.i. **1.** rallegrare **2.** confortare **3.** applaudire **4.** to — on, incitare: to — s.o. on to do sthg.,

incoraggiare qlcu. a continuare a fare ql.co. **5.** to — up, rallegrare, rallegrarsi; incoraggiare, prendere coraggio ‖ — up!, su allegro!.

cheerer ['tʃiərə*], s.c. **1.** chi infonde buon umore **2.** animatore, animatrice; chi applaude.

cheerful ['tʃiəful], ag. di buon umore, allegro; sereno, ridente; vivace, animato: he always keeps —, è sempre di buon umore; to look —, aver l'aria allegra.

cheerfully ['tʃiəfuli], av. allegramente, di buon umore; vivacemente.

cheerfulness ['tʃiəfulnis], s. buon umore, allegria.

cheerily ['tʃiərili], av. allegramente, gaiamente.

cheeriness ['tʃiərinis], s. carattere allegro; buon umore; espansività.

cheering ['tʃiəriŋ], ag. incoraggiante ‖ s. acclamazioni, evviva.

cheerio ['tʃiəri'ou], inter. (sl.) **1.** ciao, arrivederci! **2.** evviva! (nei brindisi).

cheerless ['tʃiəlis], ag. triste, tetro.

cheerlessly ['tʃiəlisli], av. tristemente.

cheerlessness ['tʃiəlisnis], s. tristezza.

cheerly ['tʃiəli], av. spontaneamente, con trasporto.

cheero ['tʃiərou], V. **cheerio.**

cheery ['tʃiəri], ag. allegro, di buon umore.

cheese[1] [tʃi:z], s. formaggio: a —, una forma di formaggio ‖ big —, (sl.) personaggio importante, pezzo grosso ‖ to believe the moon is made of green —, prendere lucciole per lanterne ☆ — -biscuit, salatino; — -cake, torta di formaggio; (sl.) ragazza piccante; — -cloth, garza, stamigna (per formaggi) — -finger, biscottino al formaggio; — -hopper, verme del formaggio; — -parer, (fam.) avaro; — -paring, il levare con cura la crosta al formaggio; fig. lesineria, avarizia: — -paring economy, risparmio di cose inutili; — -rennet, caglio; (bot.) erba zolfina; — -straws, bastoncini al formaggio ‖ Dutch —, formaggio olandese; green —, formaggio fresco; toasted —, « toast », tosto al formaggio.

cheese[2], s. (sl.) la cosa corretta, giusta: that's the —, è la cosa corretta, adatta, va benissimo! ‖ he thinks he is quite the —, (sl.) si crede elegantissimo.

to **cheese**[3], v.t.: — it!, (sl.) smettila!, piantala!.

cheesemonger ['tʃi:z,mʌŋə*], s. formaggiaio.

cheesy[1] ['tʃi:zi], ag. con formaggio; simile a, che sa di formaggio.

cheesy[2], ag. (sl.) elegante.

cheetah ['tʃi:tə], s. (zool.) ghepardo.

chef [ʃef], s. capocuoco.

chef-d'oeuvre [ʃei'də:vr], s. capolavoro.

cheiromancer ['kaiərəmænsi], s. chiromanzia.

cheiropteran [kai'rɔptərən], s. (zool.) chirottero.

cheiropterous [kai'rɔptərəs], ag. (zool.) chirottero.

chela[1] ['tʃeilə], s. novizio (nella religione buddista).

chela[2] ['ki:lə], pl. **chelae** ['ki:li:], s. (zool.) chela.

Chelonia [ki'lounjə], s.pl. (zool.) cheloni.

Chelsea ['tʃelsi], no.pr. Chelsea (quartiere degli artisti a Londra) ‖ — pensioner, ospite del « Royal Hospital »; — Royal Hospital, ospizio per veterani ed invalidi di guerra ☆ — ware, terraglia fabbricata a Chelsea nel XVIII sec.

chemical ['kemikəl], ag. chimico ☆ — action, azione chimica; — analysis, analisi chimica; — engineering, (neol.) ingegneria chimica; — plant, stabilimento chimico; — warfare, (mil.) guerra chimica.

chemicals ['kemikəlz], s. pl. prodotti chimici.

chemically ['kemikəli], av. chimicamente.

chemise [ʃi'mi:z], s. camicia (da donna).

chemisette [,ʃemi(:)'zet], s. **1.** camicetta **2.** davantino di pizzo (per donna).

chemism ['kemizm], s. (biol.) chimismo.

chemist ['kemist], s. **1.** chimico **2.** farmacista: —'s (shop), farmacia ☆ analytical —, chimico analitico; dispensing —, farmacista diplomato.

chemistry ['kemistri], s. chimica ☆ inorganic, organic, applied —, chimica inorganica, organica, applicata; nuclear —, chimica nucleare.

chemotaxis [ˌkeməˈtæksis], *s.* (*biol.*) chemiotassi.

chemurgy [ˈkeməːdʒi], *s.* chimica organica industriale per l'utilizzazione dei prodotti agricoli.

chenille [ʃəˈniːl], *s.* ciniglia.

Cheops [ˈkiːɔps], *no.pr.m.* (*st. egiziana*) Cheope.

cheque [tʃek], *s.* (*comm.*) assegno bancario: — *to bearer*, assegno al portatore, all'ordine; — *to order*, assegno all'ordine; *to cash a* —, cambiare un assegno; *to effect payment by* —, effettuare un pagamento mediante assegno ☆ — *book*, libretto d'assegni ‖ *blank* —, assegno in bianco; *crossed* —, assegno sbarrato; *open* —, assegno non sbarrato.

chequer [ˈtʃekə*], *s.* 1. scacchiera 2. *gener. pl.* tessuto a quadretti, a scacchi 3. *pl.* (*amer. giuoco*) dama 4. *pl.* (*arch.*) pietre disposte a scacchiera ☆ — *-board*, scacchiera; — *-work*, modello, disegno a quadretti, a scacchi.

to chequer, *v.t.* 1. quadrettare (stoffa, ecc.); marcare con disegno a scacchi 2. striare; screziare; variegare 3. variare; *chequered career*, carriera movimentata.

Chequers [ˈtʃekəz], *s.* Chequers (residenza di campagna del primo ministro inglese).

to cherish [ˈtʃeriʃ], *v.t.* 1. nutrire, serbare (in cuore): *to* — *hopes*, nutrire speranze; *to* — *the memory of s.o.*, *sthg.*, conservare il ricordo di qlcu., ql.co.; *to* — *resentment*, nutrire risentimento 2. amare, curare teneramente: *to* — *one's children*, coccolare i propri bambini.

cheroot [ʃəˈruːt], *s.* sigaro spuntato (specialmente sigaro di Manila).

cherry [ˈtʃeri], *s.* ciliegia ☆ — *-bay*, (*bot.*) lauro ceraso; — *-bob*, grappolo di ciliegie; — *-brandy*, cerasella; — *-pie*, torta di ciliegie; (*bot.*) eliotropio; — *-red*, rosso ciliegia; — *-stone*, nocciolo di ciliegia; — *-tree*, ciliegio; — *-wood*, (legno di) ciliegio ‖ *brandied cherries*, ciliegie sotto spirito.

chersonese [ˈkəːsəniːs], *s.* (*poet.*) penisola ‖ **Chersonese**, *no.pr.* (*geog.*) Chersoneso.

chert [tʃəːt], *s.* (*min.*) selce nera; calcedonia.

cherub [ˈtʃerəb], *pl.* **cherubim** [ˈtʃerəbim], *nel senso* 2. **cherubs** [ˈtʃerəbz], *s.* 1. (*relig.*) cherubino 2. angioletto (anche *fam.*).

cherubic [tʃeˈruːbik], *ag.* di, da cherubino.

chervil [ˈtʃəːvil], *s.* (*bot.*) cerfoglio.

Cheshire [ˈtʃeʃə*], *no.pr.* (*geog.*) Cheshire (contea in Inghilterra) ‖ *to grin like a* — *cat*, sorridere follemente, fare un largo sorriso ☆ — *cheese*, formaggio del Cheshire.

chess[1] [tʃes], *s.* (giuoco degli) scacchi: *a game of* —, una partita a scacchi; *to play* —, giocare a scacchi ☆ — *-board*, scacchiera; — *-men*, pezzi degli scacchi.

chess[2], *s.* (*mil. mar.*) asse (di ponte di barche).

chess[3], *s.* (*bot.*) zizzania.

chessel [ˈtʃesəl], *s.* stampo per formaggio.

chesstree [ˈtʃestriː], *s.* (*mar.*) bozzello fissato all'opera morta.

chest [tʃest], *s.* 1. cassa; cassetta; scrigno; cassapanca; *fig.* tesoro 2. scatola, recipiente (specialmente per il tè): — *of drawers*, cassettone 3. (*anat.*) petto, torace ‖ *to get it off one's* —, (*fam.*) sfogarsi ‖ *to throw out one's* —, camminare impettito ☆ — *cold*, raffreddore di petto; — *-note*, (*mus.*) nota di petto; — *troubles*, malattie di petto; — *-voice*, (*mus.*) voce di petto ‖ *ice* — -, ghiacciaia.

chesterfield [ˈtʃestəfiːld], *s.* 1. divano imbottito 2. soprabito lungo a un petto solo.

chestnut [ˈtʃesnʌt], *ag.* (di colore) castano; di castagno; sauro (di cavallo) ‖ *s.* 1. castagno; castagna 2. aneddoto vecchio e risaputo 3. castagna (callosità negli arti degli equini) ☆ — *-grove*, castagneto ‖ *horse-* —, ippocastano.

chesty [ˈtʃesti], *ag.* 1. (*sl. amer.*) con ampio torace 2. vanitoso 3. delicato di bronchi.

cheval-glass [ʃəˈvælglaːs], *s.* psiche (grande specchio).

chevalier [ˌʃevəˈliə*], *s.* (*arc.*) cavaliere; membro di ordini cavallereschi.

chevet [ʃəˈve], *s.* (*arch.*) abside (di chiesa).

cheviot [ˈtʃeviət], *s.* «cheviot» (stoffa di lana).

chevron [ˈʃevrən], *s.* 1. (*mil.*) gallone indicante il grado di sottufficiale 2. (*arch.*) puntone (del tetto) ☆ — *moulding*, modanatura a zigzag.

chevy [ˈtʃevi], *s.* caccia, inseguimento.

to chevy, *v.t.i.* 1. cacciare, inseguire 2. correre.

chew [tʃuː], *s.* 1. masticazione 2. ciò che si è masticato: *cicca* (di tabacco).

to chew, *v.t.i.* masticare (tabacco), ciccare ‖ *to* — *the cud*, ruminare; *fig.* rimuginare ‖ *to* — *over* (o *upon*) *sthg.*, *fig.* meditare, riflettere su ql.co. ☆ *chewing -gum*, «chewing-gum», gomma da masticare.

chewer [ˈtʃuːə*], *s.* masticatore (di tabacco).

chianti [kiˈænti], *s.* chianti (vino toscano).

chiaroscuro [kiˌɑːrəsˈkuərou], *ag.s.* (*pitt.*) chiaroscuro.

chiasmus [kaiˈæzməs], *s.* (*ret.*) chiasma.

chiastic [kaiˈæstik], *ag.* (*ret.*) chiastico.

chibol [ˈtʃibəl], *s.* (*dial.*) cipolla.

chic [ʃiːk], *ag.* elegante, alla moda ‖ *s.* stile, eleganza.

Chicagoan [ʃiˈkɑːgouən], *ag.s.* (nativo) di Chicago.

chicane [ʃiˈkein], *s.* sotterfugio; stratagemma; artificio; cavillo.

to chicane, *v.t.i.* usare sotterfugi, inganni, cavilli; ingannare: *to* — *s.o. into*, *out of doing sthg.*, indurre qlcu. con inganno a fare ql.co., dissuadere qlcu. con l'inganno dal fare ql.co.

chicanery [ʃiˈkeinəri], *s.* cavillo legale; rigiro; sofisma.

chick[1] [tʃik], *s.* pulcino; uccellino; *fig.* bambino ‖ *to have neither* — *nor child*, (*fam. scherz.*) non avere figli ☆ — *-pea*, (*bot.*) cece.

chick[2], *s.* stuoia, stoino.

chick[3], *s.* (*scoz.*) battito (di orologio, ecc.).

chickabiddy [ˈtʃikəˌbidi], *s.* (*fam.*) coccolo.

chicken [ˈtʃikin], *s.* 1. pulcino; pollastro; gallinella; gallinaceo giovane; pollo ‖ *she's no* —, (*fam.*) non è più tanto giovane ‖ *don't count your chickens before they are hatched*, *prov.* non dire quattro finché non l'hai nel sacco 2. (*fig. fam.*) persona poco coraggiosa ☆ — *-breasted*, (*patol.*) che ha lo sterno carenato, rachitico; — *-farming*, (*amer.*) allevamento di polli; — *-feed*, (*fam.*) piccola somma di denaro; — *-hearted*, timido, pauroso; — *-pox*, (*patol.*) varicella; — *-run*, recinto per i polli ‖ *Mother Cary's* —, (*ornit. pop.*) procellaria; *roast-* —, pollo arrosto; *spring* —, pollo novello.

chickling[1] [ˈtʃikliŋ], *s.* pulcino.

chickling[2], *s.* (*bot.*) latiro.

chickweed [ˈtʃikwiːd], *s.* (*bot.*) centonchio, centocchio (bianco), mordigallina.

chicory [ˈtʃikəri], *s.* (*bot.*) cicoria.

to chide [tʃaid], *pass.* **chid** [tʃid], **chided** [ˈtʃaidid], *p.p.* **chidden** [ˈtʃidn], **chid**, **chided**, *v.t.i.* 1. (*arc. letter.*) rimproverare, sgridare; borbottare; rampognare: *to* — *against fortune*, mormorare contro la fortuna 2. mugghiare (di vento, mare); mugolare.

chief [tʃiːf], *ag.* principale, primo, il più importante: *the chief(est) good*, (*arc.*) il bene supremo ‖ *s.* 1. capo, comandante; (*ret.*) condottiero ‖ — *of staff*, (*mil.*) capo di stato maggiore 2. (*arald.*) la sommità dello scudo ☆ — *clerk*, capo-ufficio; — *engineer*, ingegnere capo; — *surgeon*, primario chirurgo; — *town*, capoluogo ‖ *commander-in-* —, comandante in capo.

chiefdom [ˈtʃiːfdəm], *s.* dignità, rango di capo.

chiefly [ˈtʃiːfli], *ag.* di, da capo.

chiefly, *av.* soprattutto, principalmente.

chiefship [ˈtʃiːfʃip], *s.* dignità di capo; autorità.

chieftain [ˈtʃiːftən], *s.* capo (di tribù, «clan», ecc.); (*poet.*) condottiero.

chieftainship [ˈtʃiːftənʃip], *s.* dignità, rango, autorità di capo (di tribù, «clan», ecc.).

chield [tʃiːld], *s.* (*scoz.*) uomo; ragazzo.

chiff-chaff [ˈtʃif-tʃæf], *s.* (*ornit.*) luì.

chiffon [ˈʃifon], *s.* «chiffon», velocrespo.

chiffonier [ˌʃifəˈniə*], *s.* «chiffonnière», stipo a cassettini.

chignon ['ʃiːnjɔːŋ], s. « chignon », crocchia.
chigoe ['tʃigou], s. pulce penetrante.
chilblain ['tʃilblein], s. (patol.) gelone.
child [tʃaild], pl. **children** ['tʃildrən], s.c. **1.** bambino, bambina; ragazzo, ragazza; figlio, figlia; discendente: *he has been delicate since he was a* —, egli è sempre stato delicato fin da bambino; *we have four children, two sons and two daughters*, abbiamo quattro figli, due maschi e due femmine ‖ *a* — *of love*, un figlio illegittimo ‖ *to be with* —, essere incinta **2.** *V.* **childe** ☆ — *-bearing*, gravidanza; — *-life*, infanzia; — *-murder*, infanticidio; — *'s play*, *fig.* lavoro facilissimo; — *-wife*, moglie bambola, bambina ‖ *boy* —, *girl* —, ragazzetto, ragazzetta; *foster-* —, figlio di latte; *only* —, figlio unico; *still-born* —, bimbo nato morto.
childbed ['tʃaildbed], **childbirth** ['tʃaildbəːθ], s. parto.
childe [tʃaild], s. (arc. letter.) titolo dato ai figli di famiglia nobile ‖ *" Childe Harold's Pilgrimage "*, « Il pellegrinaggio del giovane Aroldo ».
Childermas-day ['tʃildəmæs-dei], **Childermas-tide** ['tʃildəmæs-taid], s. (eccl.) festa degli Innocenti (28 dicembre).
childhood ['tʃaildhud], s. infanzia, età puerile ☆ *second* —, seconda infanzia, senilità.
childish ['tʃaildiʃ], ag. puerile, infantile.
childishly ['tʃaildiʃli], av. puerilmente, infantilmente; ingenuamente.
childishness ['tʃaildiʃnis], s. puerilità, fanciullaggine.
childless ['tʃaildlis], ag. senza bambini, senza figli.
childlessness ['tʃaildlisnis], s. il non aver bambini, sterilità.
childlike ['tʃaildlaik], ag. infantile, da bambino: — *simplicity*, semplicità infantile.
childly ['tʃaildli], ag. fanciullesco, puerile.
childly, av. fanciullescamente, puerilmente.
children ['tʃildrən], pl. di **child**.
Chile ['tʃili], no.pr. (geog.) Cile.
Chilean ['tʃilian], ag. cileno ‖ s.c. cileno, cilena.
chiliad ['kiliæd], s. mille (anni).
•**Chilian**, (arc.) per **Chilean**.
chiliasm ['kiliæzm], s. (st. relig.) chiliasmo.
chiliast ['kiliæst], s. (st. relig.) chiliasta.
chill [tʃil], ag. freddo (anche fig.) ‖ s. **1.** colpo di freddo; (sensazione di) freddo (anche fig.): *a* — *came over me*, mi sono sentito rabbrividire; *to catch a* —, prendere freddo; *to take the* — *off sthg.*, intiepidire (acqua, ecc.) **2.** (fonderia) conchiglia; raffreddatore; raffreddamento rapido ☆ — *-cast*, fuso in conchiglia; — *-casting*, (metal.) fusione in conchiglia.
to chill, v.t.i. **1.** raffreddare, raffreddarsi; gelare, agghiacciare (anche fig.); congelare; refrigerare: *he was chilled with fear at the news*, la notizia gli agghiacciò il sangue per la paura ‖ *he was chilled to the marrow* (of his bones), era gelato fino alle midolla (delle ossa) **2.** fig. deprimere **3.** (metal.) fondere in conchiglia; temprare, temprarsi.
chilled [tʃild], ag. **1.** congelato; refrigerato **2.** (metal.) fuso in conchiglia, temperato ☆ — *meat*, carne congelata.
chilli ['tʃili], s. (cuc.) pepe di Caienna.
chilliness ['tʃilinis], s. **1.** freddo **2.** fig. freddezza.
chilling ['tʃiliŋ], ag. **1.** glaciale; agghiacciante **2.** (metal.) raffreddante; temprante ‖ s. **1.** refrigerazione; congelamento **2.** (metal.) tempra.
chilly ['tʃili], ag. **1.** freddoloso (di persona); fresco (di tempo, ecc.): *to feel* —, aver freddo **2.** fig. freddo, senza cordialità: *a* — *reception*, un'accoglienza fredda.
Chiltern Hundreds ['tʃiltə(ː)n'hʌndrədz], no.pr.pl. (geog.) Chiltern Hundreds (distretto nel Buckinghamshire, Inghilterra, che appartiene alla Corona e il cui amministratore non può essere deputato al Parlamento) ‖ *to apply for* (o *to accept*) *the* —, dare le dimissioni da deputato al Parlamento.
chime¹ [tʃaim], s. **1.** concerto di campane, scampanio:

to ring the chimes, scampanare, suonare a festa **2.** melodia, ritmo; fig. accordo.
to chime¹, v.t.i. **1.** scampanare, suonare a festa (di campane); suonare (della soneria di un orologio): *to* — *the bells*, suonare le campane a festa; *to* — *the hour*, suonare le ore, rintoccare (di orologio, campana) **2.** ripetere meccanicamente **3.** *to* — *in*, (fam.) intervenire nella conversazione; associarsi ‖ *to* — *in with*, accordarsi con, associarsi a **4.** *to* — *together*, (fam.) essere d'accordo.
chime², s. caruggine (di botte).
to chime², v.t. carugginare (botte).
chimer(e) [tʃi'miə*], s. abito vescovile.
chimera [kai'miərə], s. **1.** (mit.) chimera **2.** illusione.
chimerical [kai'merikəl], ag. chimerico; impossibile.
chimerically [kai'merikəli], av. chimericamente.
chiming ['tʃaimiŋ], s. scampanio, lo scampanare ☆ — *clock*, pendola a carillon.
chimney ['tʃimni], s. **1.** camino, focolare **2.** comignolo, fumaiolo, ciminiera **3.** (geol.) camino di vulcano **4.** (alpinismo) camino ☆ — *boy*, (arc.) spazzacamino; — *cap*, cappa del camino; — *-corner*, angolo del focolare; — *-flue*, gola, condotto del fumo; — *-glass*, tubo di vetro per lampada; — *-piece*, mensola del camino; — *-pot*, comignolo di terracotta; — *-shaft*, comignolo; — *-stack*, gruppo di camini; — *-stalk*, torretta, fumaiolo; — *-sweep(er)*, spazzacamino.
chimpanzee [ˌtʃimpən'ziː], s. (zool.) scimpanzè.
chin [tʃin], s. mento ‖ *to be up to the* — (o *to be* — *-deep*) *in water*, trovarsi con l'acqua alla gola ☆ — *-bandage*, (chir.) mentiera; — *-rest*, mentiera (di violino); — *-strap*, sottogola (di elmo, berretto, ecc.) ‖ *double* —, doppio mento.
to chin, pass.p.p. **chinned** [tʃind], v.t. **1.** *to* — *the bar*, (ginnastica) toccare la sbarra con il mento **2.** (sl. amer.) chiacchierare.
China ['tʃainə], no.pr. (geog.) Cina ‖ **china**, s. — (-ware), porcellana fine; (fam.) stoviglie di porcellana, ceramica ☆ — *-clay*, caolino; — *-ink*, inchiostro di China; — *-root*, (bot.) china dolce (radice).
china-bark ['tʃainəbaːk], s. (farm.) corteccia di china, cincona.
Chinaman, pl. **Chinamen** ['tʃainəmən], s. **1.** (fam.) cinese **2.** commerciante in cineserie.
Chinatown ['tʃainətaun], s. Chinatown (quartiere cinese di Londra); quartiere cinese (in città occidentale).
chinch [tʃintʃ], s. (amer.) cimice.
chinchilla [tʃin'tʃilə], s. (zool.) cincillà.
chin-chin ['tʃin'tʃin], **1.** saluto cortese **2.** conversazione cerimoniosa.
chine¹ [tʃain], s. burrone, (geol.) calanco, botro.
to chine¹, v.i. (arc.) spaccarsi; fendersi.
chine², s. **1.** (anat.) spina dorsale **2.** (cuc.) lombata **3.** cresta (di montagna).
to chine², v.t. spezzare la spina dorsale a; tagliare lungo la spina dorsale (maiale, pesce, ecc.).
Chinee [tʃai'niː], s.c. (sl.) cinese.
Chinese ['tʃai'niːz], ag.s.c. cinese ‖ s. lingua cinese.
chink¹ [tʃiŋk], s. attacco convulso di tosse, di riso.
to chink¹, v.i. boccheggiare per un attacco di tosse, di riso.
chink², s. interstizio; fessura; crepaccio; crepa.
to chink², v.t.i. **1.** fendersi; screpolare, screpolarsi; spaccare, spaccarsi **2.** *to* — *up*, riempire (una crepa, una fessura): *to* — *up a crack*, chiudere un interstizio.
chink³, s. **1.** tintinnio **2.** (sl.) denaro in contanti
to chink³, v.t.i. tintinnare; far tintinnare.
Chink⁴, s.c. (sl.) cinese.
chinless ['tʃinlis], ag. dal mento sfuggente.
Chinook [tʃi'nuk], s. **1.** « Chinook » (indiano del Nord Ovest degli Stati Uniti) **2.** gergo ibrido di parole francesi, inglesi e locali di taluni indiani ☆ — *wind*, vento umido e caldo che soffia sulle coste del Pacifico.

chintz [tʃints], *s.* «chintz» (stoffa lucida di cotone, stampata a colori).

chip¹ [tʃip], *s.* **1.** scheggia; truciolo; frammento; scaglia (di materiale duro) ‖ *a — of the old block*, un figlio che somiglia al padre **2.** (*cuc.*) patatina fritta: *fish and chips*, pesce fritto con patatine **3.** gettone (nei giuochi d'azzardo); (*sl.*) sovrana (moneta); *pl.* (*sl.*) quattrini **4.** scheggiatura (negli oggetti di ceramica) **5.** *pl.* sterco bovino usato per combustibile ☆ — *-axe*, ascia; — *carving*, intaglio.

to **chip¹**, *pass.p.p.* **chipped** [tʃipt], *v.t.i.* **1.** scheggiare, scheggiarsi **2.** rompere: *to — an egg*, rompere un (guscio d')uovo (specialmente di pulcini) **3.** tagliare a fettine **4.** *to — in*, intervenire (nella conversazione, in un giuoco di carte) **5.** *to — off*, scheggiarsi (di smalto) ☆ *chipped potatoes*, patatine fritte.

chip², *s.* sgambetto, trucco per atterrare l'avversario (nella lotta).

to **chip²**, *v.t.* fare lo sgambetto a (nella lotta).

chipboard [tʃipbo:d], *s.* (*neol.*) legno ricostituito.

chipmunk [tʃipmʌŋk], *s.* (*zool.*) tamia orientale.

Chippendale [tʃipəndeil], *ag.* «Chippendale» (di stile di mobilio).

chipping [tʃipiŋ], *s.* **1.** il tagliare (a schegge, ecc.) **2.** *pl.* trucioli; schegge (di pietra, marmo).

chippy [tʃipi], *ag.* (*sl.*) **1.** scipito, insipido **2.** indisposto: *to feel —*, non sentirsi bene, essere indisposto.

chirograph [kaiərəgra:f], *s.* (*dir.*) chirografo.

chirographary [ˌkaiərogrəfəri], *ag.* (*dir.*) chirografario.

chiromancer [kaiərəmænsə*], *s.c.* chiromante.

chiromancy [kaiərəmænsi], *s.* chiromanzia.

Chiron [kaiərən], *no.pr.m.* (*mit.*) Chirone.

chiropodist [ki'ropədist], *s.* pedicure, callista.

chiropody [ki'ropədi], *s.* l'arte del pedicure.

chirp [tʃə:p], *s.* cinguettio, pigolio, canto (di uccello); canto, stridio (di grillo, cavalletta, cicala, ecc.).

to **chirp**, *v.i.* cinguettare, pigolare, cantare (di uccello); frinire, stridere (di grillo, cicala, cavalletta, ecc.).

chirpiness [tʃə:pinis], *s.* umore gaio.

chirpy [tʃə:pi], *ag.* d'umore gaio, allegro.

chirr [tʃə:*], *s.* canto, stridio (di cavalletta, grillo, cicala, ecc.).

to **chirr**, *v.i.* stridere (di cavalletta, grillo, cicala).

chirrup [tʃirəp], *s.* **1.** *V.* **chirp 2.** (*sl. teat.*) applausi (di claque).

to **chirrup**, *v.i.* **1.** *V.* to **chirp 2.** (*sl. teat.*) applaudire per incitare, fare la claque.

chisel¹ [tʃizl], *s.* **1.** (*strum. artig.*) cesello; scalpello; bulino ‖ *the —*, l'arte dello scultore **2.** (*sl.*) inganno.

to **chisel¹**, *pass.p.p.* **chiselled** [tʃizld], *v.t.* **1.** cesellare; scalpellare; bulinare ‖ *chiselled features*, lineamenti finemente cesellati **2.** (*sl.*) ingannare.

chisel², **chissel** [tʃizl], *s.* crusca.

chit¹ [tʃit], *s.c.* (*fam.*) marmocchio; bimbo, bimba ‖ *s.* (*spreg.*) donnetta: *a — of a girl*, una donnetta.

chit², *abbr.* di **chitty**.

chitchat [tʃittʃæt], *s.* (*fam.*) chiacchiera; cicaleccio.

chitin [kaitin], *s.* (*zool.*) chitina.

chiton [kaiton], *s.* chitone.

to **chitter** [tʃitə*], *v.i.* **1.** pigolare (di uccello) **2.** (*dial.*) rabbrividire (di freddo).

chitty [tʃiti], *s.* (*ang.-in.*) **1.** (*fam.*) lettera; biglietto **2.** autorizzazione scritta, lasciapassare; benservito.

chivalric [ʃivəlrik], **chivalrous** [ʃivəlrəs], *ag.* (*poet.*) cavalleresco.

chivalrously [ʃivəlrəsli], *av.* cavallerescamente.

chivalrousness [ʃivəlrəsnis], *s.* condotta cavalleresca; cortesia.

chivalry [ʃivəlri], *s.* **1.** (*st. mil.*) cavalleria: *the flower of —*, il fior fiore dei cavalieri **2.** condotta cavalleresca; cortesia.

chive [tʃaiv], *s.* (*bot.*) **1.** aglio di serpe **2.** piccolo bulbo.

chiv(v)y [tʃivi], *s.* caccia, inseguimento.

to **chiv(v)y**, *v.t.i.* **1.** cacciare, inseguire **2.** correre.

chlamys [klæmis], *s.* clamide.

Chloe [kloui], *no.pr.f.* Cloe.

chloral [klo:rəl], *s.* (*chim.*) cloralio.

to **chloralize** [klo:rəlaiz], *v.t.* (*chim.*) trattare col cloralio.

chlorate [klo:rit], *s.* (*chim.*) clorato.

chlorhydrate [klo:'haidreit], *s.* (*chim.*) cloridrato.

chloric [klo:rik], *ag.* (*chim.*) clorico.

chloride [klo:raid], *s.* (*chim.*) cloruro: — *of lime*, cloruro di calce ☆ *calcium —*, (*chim.*) cloruro di calcio.

chlorination [ˌklo:ri'neiʃən], *s.* (*chim.*) clorurazione.

chlorine [klo:ri:n], *s.* (*chim.*) cloro.

chlorite¹ [klo:rait], *s.* (*chim.*) clorito.

chlorite², *s.* (*min.*) clorite.

chlorodyne [klo:rədain], *s.* (*chim.*) clorodina.

chloroform [klo:rəfo:m], *s.* (*chim.*) cloroformio.

to **chloroform**, *v.t.* (*med.*) cloroformizzare.

chloroformic [ˌklo:rə'fo:mik], *ag.* (*chim.*) cloroformico.

chloroformist [klo:rəfo:mist], *s.* cloroformizzatore.

chloromycetin [ˌklo:roumai'si:tin], *s.* (*chim. farm.*) cloromicetina.

chlorophyl(l) [klo:rəfil], *s.* (*bot.*) clorofilla.

chlorosis [klə'rousis], *s.* (*patol.*) clorosi.

chlorotic [klə'rotik], *ag.* clorotico.

chock [tʃok], *s.* **1.** cuneo, zeppa; tassello di legno **2.** (*mar.*) bocca di rancio, passacavi ☆ — *-full*, (*fam.*) pieno zeppo.

to **chock**, *v.t.* tenere fermo con tasselli (barca, botte, ecc.); calzare (con biette): *to — (up) a wheel*, bloccare una ruota ‖ *chocked (up) with*, (*fam.*) ingombro di.

chocolate [tʃokəlit], *ag.* **1.** di cioccolato **2.** colore cioccolata ‖ *s.* **1.** cioccolato; cioccolata: *cake of —*, tavoletta di cioccolato **2.** il color cioccolata ☆ — *cream*, cioccolatino farcito; — *-maker*, cioccolatiere; — *-nut*, frutto di cacao; — *-pot*, cioccolatiera.

choice [tʃois], *ag.* scelto; di prima qualità, squisito: — *wine*, vino scelto ‖ *s.* **1.** scelta; alternativa; preferenza: *at —*, a volontà; *the country of my —*, la mia patria d'elezione; *for —*, di preferenza; *to make* (o *to take*) *one's —*, fare la propria scelta **2.** la cosa scelta, preferita **3.** scelta, assortimento: *wide — of*, (*comm.*) largo assortimento di **4.** fior fiore, élite.

choicely [tʃoislii], *av.* con cura, con gusto.

choiceness [tʃoisnis], *s.* finezza; squisitezza; eccellenza: *the — of his language*, il suo linguaggio scelto.

choir [kwaiə*], *s.* **1.** (*arch.*) coro (di chiesa) **2.** coro (di cantori, angeli) ☆ — *-boy*, ragazzo cantore; — *-master*, maestro di cappella; — *-screen*, chiudenda (del coro).

to **choir**, *v.t.i.* (*poet.*) cantare in coro.

choirman, *pl.* **choirmen** [kwaiəmən], *s.* cantore; corista.

chokage [tʃoukidʒ], *s.* ingorgo; ostruzione.

choke¹ [tʃouk], *s.* **1.** soffocamento, accesso di soffocazione (di respiro, voce): *he answered with a — in his voice*, rispose con voce soffocata **2.** strozzamento, ingorgo (di tubo); diffusore; valvola dell'aria **3.** cuore del carciofo.

to **choke¹**, *v.t.i.* **1.** togliere il respiro a, soffocare (anche *fig.*), soffocarsi; asfissiare; strozzare, strozzarsi: *choked with rage*, soffocato dalla rabbia **2.** ostruire; ingorgare, ingorgarsi **3.** *to — back*, trattenere (parole) **4.** *to — down*, ingoiare (cibo); soffocare (singhiozzi) **5.** *to — off*, (*sl.*) allontanare, impedire la curiosità, le attenzioni di **6.** *to — up*, *in*, ostruire completamente; (*fam. amer.*) tacere, frenarsi nel parlare.

choke², *s.* (*dial.*) mandibole.

chokedamp [tʃoukdæmp], *s.* (*chim.*) anidride carbonica; gas mefitico (di miniera).

choker [tʃoukə*], *s.* **1.** soffocatore; strozzatore; (*rad.*) bobina d'arresto; (*elett.*) reattanza; valvola dell'aria **2.** (*sl.*) argomento inoppugnabile: *that's a —*, ciò riduce al silenzio ☆ *fur —*, cravatta di pelliccia; *white —*, (*sl.*) colletto bianco inamidato; (*eccl.*) collarino.

chokra ['tʃoukrə], *s.* (*ang.-in.*) ragazzo (specialmente servitore).

choky ['tʃouki], *ag.* **1.** soffocante **2.** soffocato: *in a — voice*, (*fam.*) con voce soffocata.

choler ['kolə*], *s.* **1.** (*med. arc.*) bile **2.** (*poet.*) collera, irascibilità.

cholera ['kolərə], *s.* (*patol.*) colera.

choleraic [,kolə'reiik], *ag.* (*patol.*) coleroso.

choleric ['kolərik], *ag.* collerico, irascibile.

cholerine ['kolərain], *s.* (*patol.*) colerina.

choliamb ['kouliæmb], *s.* (*poes.*) coliambo.

choliambic [,kouli'æmbik], *ag.* (*poes.*) coliambico.

to choose [tʃu:z], *pass.* **chose** [tʃouz], *p.p.* **chosen** ['tʃouzn], *v.t.i.* **1.** scegliere, fare la scelta di; optare per: *— for yourself*, lascio a voi la scelta; *he has chosen a fine present for himself*, si è scelto un bel regalo; *he was chosen king*, fu scelto re; *he was chosen out of ten*, fu scelto fra dieci; *I cannot — but obey*, non ho altra scelta che ubbidire; *I cannot but — to do so*, non ho altra alternativa; *there isn't much to — from*, c'è poco da scegliere; *there is nothing to — between them*, non c'è scelta fra di loro, l'uno vale l'altro; *you have many friends to — from*, hai molti amici fra cui scegliere ǁ *many are called but few are chosen*, molti sono i chiamati, ma pochi gli eletti ǁ *to pick and —*, (*fam.*) scegliere meticolosamente **2.** volere; gradire; preferire: *as you —*, come volete; *I didn't —* (o *I chose not*) *to go*, non ho voluto andare, ho preferito non andare; *if I chose I could live without working*, se volessi potrei vivere senza lavorare; *if you —*, se vi garba.

chooser ['tʃu:zə*], *s.c.* chi sceglie.

choos(e)y ['tʃu:zi], *ag.* (*sl.*) pignolo.

choosing ['tʃu:ziŋ], *s.* scelta, l'atto di scegliere: *the — of a present*, la scelta di un regalo; *the difficulty of —*, l'imbarazzo della scelta.

chop[1] [tʃop], *s.* **1.** colpo (di scure, d'ascia, ecc.) **2.** (*cuc.*) braciola **3.** maretta **4.** (*tennis*) taglio ☆ *—-feed*, fieno triturato; *—-house*, trattoria ǁ *lamb—, mutton—, pork—*, braciola di agnello, di montone, di maiale.

to chop[1], *pass.p.p.* **chopped** [tʃopt], *v.t.i.* **1.** tagliare, fendere, spaccare (legna, ecc.): *chopped wood*, legna spaccata; *to — sthg. to pieces*, fare a pezzi ql.co. **2.** tritare (carne, verdura, ecc.): *a finely chopped onion*, una cipolla ben tritata **3.** spiccar bene le sillabe di (una parola) **4.** *to — away*, tagliar via, troncare **5.** *to — down*, abbattere (alberi, ecc.) **6.** *to — in*, intervenire, interporsi **7.** *to — off*, tagliar via, recidere: *— his head off!*, tagliategli la testa! **8.** *to — up*, sminuzzare.

chop[2], *s.* mascella, mandibola ǁ *to lick one's chops*, (*fam.*) leccarsi le labbra, i baffi ☆ *—-fallen*, avvilito, abbattuto.

chop[3], *s.* (*arc.*) baratto, scambio ǁ *chops and changes*, (*fam.*) mutamenti, vicissitudini.

to chop[3], *v.t.i.* **1.** (*arc.*) barattare, scambiare ǁ *to — and change*, (*fam.*) vacillare, essere incostante ǁ *to — logic*, (*fam.*) cavillare, sofisticare **2.** (*mar.*) mutare direzione (del vento).

chop[4], *s.* **1.** sigillo ufficiale (in India, Cina) **2.** licenza, permesso autenticato (in India, Cina) **3.** (*comm.*) marca di fabbrica (in India, Cina) **4.** (*sl.*) qualità ☆ *first, second —*, prima, seconda qualità; *no —*, cattiva qualità.

chopper[1] ['tʃopə*], *s.* **1.** tagliatrice (macchina) **2.** ascia, mannaia (del macellaio) **3.** (*amer.*) controllore (di biglietti teatrali, tranviari, ferroviari) ǁ *s.c.* chi taglia con l'ascia.

chopper[2], *s.* (*arc.*) trafficante (specialmente di benefizi ecclesiastici).

chopper[3], *s.* (*ang.-in.*) tetto di paglia.

chopping ['tʃopiŋ], *ag.* V. **choppy**[1] ǁ *s.* il tagliare, l'abbattere ☆ *—-block*, ceppo, tagliere; *—-knife*, coltello per tritare.

choppiness ['tʃopinis], *s.* (*mar.*) maretta.

choppy[1] ['tʃopi], *ag.* increspato (del mare): *— sea*, mare increspato.

choppy[2], *ag.* instabile, variabile.

chopsticks ['tʃopstiks], *s.pl.* bastoncini d'avorio (usati come posate dai Cinesi).

choral ['ko:rəl], *ag.* (*mus.*) corale ☆ *— society*, società corale.

choral(e) [ko'ra:l], *s.* (*mus.*) corale.

choralist ['ko:rəlist], *s.* (*mus.*) corista.

chorally ['ko:rəli], *av.* in coro.

chord[1] [ko:d], *s.* **1.** corda (di strumento musicale) ǁ *to touch the right —*, (*fam.*) toccare il tasto giusto **2.** (*anat.*) corda **3.** (*geom.*) corda (di un arco).

chord[2], *s.* (*mus.*) accordo: *to strike a —*, suonare un accordo ☆ *common —*, accordo perfetto.

chore [tʃo:*], V. **char**[2] **1.**

to chore, V. to **char**[2].

chorea [ko'riə], *s.* (*patol.*) corea, ballo di San Vito.

choree [ko'ri:], *s.* (*poes.*) coreo, trocheo.

choreograph(er) [,kori'ogrəfə*], *s.* coreografo.

choreographic [,koriə'græfik], *ag.* coreografico.

choreography [,kori'ogrəfi], *s.* coreografia.

choriamb ['koriæmb], *s.* (*poes.*) coriambo.

choriambic [,kori'æmbik], *ag.* (*poes.*) coriambico.

choriambus [,kori'æmbəs], *s.* (*poes.*) coriambo.

choric ['korik], *ag.* del coro.

chorion ['ko:rion], *s.* (*anat.*) corio.

chorister ['koristə*], *s.* **1.** corista **2.** (*amer.*) direttore del coro (in chiesa).

chorographer [kə'rogrəfə*], *s.* corografo, autore di mappe.

chorographic(al) [,kourə'græfik(əl)], *ag.* corografico.

chorographically [,kourə'græfikəli], *av.* corografiticamente.

chorography [kə'rogrəfi], *s.* corografia.

choroid ['ko:roid], *ag.s.* (*anat.*) coroide.

chorology [kə'rolədʒi], *s.* (*biol.*) corologia.

chortle ['tʃo:tl], *s.* riso represso.

to chortle, *v.i.* ridacchiare.

chorus ['ko:rəs], *s.* **1.** coro: *to sing in —*, cantare in coro **2.** ritornello: *to join in the —*, cantare il ritornello in coro ☆ *—-girl*, ballerina di fila (in un varietà); *—-singer*, corista (in un'opera).

to chorus, *v.t.i.* fare coro; cantare in coro: *to — sthg.*, ripetere ql.co. in coro.

chose [tʃouz], *pass.* di to **choose**.

chosen ['tʃouzn], *p.p.* di to **choose** ǁ *ag.* scelto ǁ *the —*, gli eletti; *the — people*, il popolo eletto; *to speak to a — few*, parlare a un pubblico eletto.

chou [ʃu:], *s.* rosetta ornamentale di nastro.

chough [tʃʌf], *s.* (*ornit.*) gracchia.

chouse [tʃaus] *s.* (*fam.*) inganno, truffa.

to chouse, *v.t.* (*fam.*) ingannare, truffare.

Chow [tʃau], *ag.* (*sl. austral.*) cinese ǁ *s.* **1.** (*sl. austral.* cinese **2.** *abbr.* di **chow-chow**.

chow-chow ['tʃau'tʃau], *s.* **1.** conserva cinese di zenzero, scorza d'arancia, ecc. **2.** «chow-chow» (cane cinese).

chowder ['tʃaudə*], *s.* zuppa di pesce.

chrematistic [,kri:mə'tistik], *ag.* economico; cremaltologico.

chrestomathy [kres'toməθi], *s.* crestomazia.

chrism ['krizəm], *s.* (*eccl.*) crisma.

chrisom ['krizəm], *s.* candida veste apposta al bambino durante il battesimo ☆ *—-child*, bimbo che ha meno di un mese.

Christ [kraist], *no.pr.m.* Cristo: *Jesus —*, Gesù Cristo ☆ *—-Child*, Gesù Bambino; *—'s- thorn*, (*bot.*) spina Christi.

Christabel ['kristəbel], *no.pr.f.* (*lett.*) Cristabella.

to christen ['krisn], *v.t.* **1.** (*relig.*) battezzare **2.** dare un nome a: *to — a child after s.o.*, dare ad un bambino il nome di qlcu.

Christendom ['krisndəm], *s.* cristianità.

christening ['krisniŋ], *s.* (*relig.*) battesimo.

Christian[1] ['kristjən], *ag.* cristiano ‖ *s.c.* cristiano, cristiana: *to become a* —, farsi cristiano; *to behave like a* —, comportarsi da cristiano, da uomo civile ☆ — *era*, era cristiana; — *name*, nomo di battesimo.

Christian[2], *no.pr.m.* Cristiano.

Christiana [‚kristi'a:nə], *no.pr.f.* Cristiana.

Christiania [‚kristi'a:njə], *no.pr.* (*geog.*) Cristiania (antico nome di Oslo) ‖ *s.* (*spor.*) cristiania.

Christianity [‚kristi'æniti], *s.* cristianesimo.

to **christianize** ['kristjənaiz], *v.t.i.* convertire, convertirsi al cristianesimo.

christianlike ['kristjənlaik], *ag.* (da) cristiano.

christianly ['kristjənli], *ag.* cristiano ‖ *av.* cristianamente.

Christina [kris'ti:nə], *no.pr.f.* Cristina.

Christlike ['kraistlaik], *ag.* rassomigliante a Cristo ‖ — *patience*, pazienza evangelica.

Christmas ['krisməs], *s.* Natale: *a merry* —*!*, buon Natale!; *at* —, a Natale ☆ — *box*, cartoncino natalizio; — *carol*, canto di Natale; — *-day*, (giorno di) Natale: *on* — *-day*, nel giorno di Natale; — *-eve*, vigilia di Natale; — *-gift*, regalo di Natale, strenna; — *-pudding*, budino natalizio; — *rose* (o — *flower*), (*bot.*) elleboro, rosa di Natale; — *-stocking*, calza di Natale; — *-tide* (o — *-time*), tempo natalizio; — *-tree*, albero di Natale ‖ *Father* —, Babbo Natale.

Christmas(s)y ['krisməsi], *ag.* (*fam.*) natalizio; festoso.

Christolatry [kris'tolətri], *s.* cristolatria.

Christologist [kris'tolədʒist], *s.* cristologo.

Christology [kris'tolədʒi], *s.* cristologia.

Christopher ['kristəfə*], *no.pr.m.* Cristoforo ‖ — *Columbus*, Cristoforo Colombo.

Christy minstrels ['kristi'minstrəlz], *s.* gruppo di cantori e comici truccati da negri.

chromate ['kroumit], *s.* (*chim.*) cromato ☆ — *treatment*, (*metal.*) cromatura.

chromatic [krə'mætik], *ag.* cromatico ☆ — *printing*, (*tip.*) stampa a colori; — *scale*, (*mus.*) scala cromatica.

chromatically [krə'mætikəli], *av.* cromaticamente.

chromatics [krə'mætiks], *s.* cromatologia.

chromatism ['kroumətizəm], *s.* cromatismo.

chromatography [‚kroumə'togrəfi], *s.* cromatografia.

chrome [kroum], *s.* (*chim.*) cromo ☆ — *-leather*, cuoio al cromo; — *-steel*, acciaio al cromo; — *-yellow*, crocoisite; giallo di cromo.

to **chrome**, *v.t.* (*chim.*) cromare.

chromic ['kroumik], *ag.* (*chim.*) cromico ☆ — *iron*, sidercromo, ferrocromato.

chromite ['kroumait], *s.* (*min.*) cromite.

chromium ['kroumjəm], *s.* (*chim.*) cromo ☆ — *-plated*, cromato; — *-plating*, cromatura; — *-steel*, acciaio al cromo.

chromo ['kroumou], *s.* (*fam. tip.*) cromolitografia.

chromolithograph ['kroumou'liθəgra:f], *s.* (*tip.*) cromolitografia.

chromolithographic ['kroumou‚liθə'græfik], *ag.* (*tip.*) cromolitografico.

chromolithography ['kroumouli'θəgrəfi], *s.* (*tip.*) cromolitografia (il processo).

chromosome ['krouməsoum], *s.* (*biol.*) cromosoma.

chromotypography ['kroumoutai'pogrəfi], *s.* (*tip.*) cromotipografia.

chronic ['kronik], *ag.* **1.** cronico (anche *fig.*) **2.** (*sl.*) insopportabile, terribile: *a* — *headache*, un terribile mal di testa.

chronically ['kronikəli], *av.* cronicamente.

chronicity [kro'nisiti], *s.* cronicità.

chronicle ['kronikl], *s.* cronaca ‖ *" The Chronicles "*, (*Bibbia*) « I Paralipomeni » ‖ *" The Anglo-Saxon Chronicle "*, (*lett.*) « La Cronaca Anglosassone ».

to **chronicle**, *v.t.* fare la cronaca di; mettere negli annali.

chronicler ['kroniklə*], *s.* cronista.

chronogram ['kronəgræm], *s.* cronogramma.

chronogrammatic [‚kronəgrə'mætik], *ag.* cronogrammatico.

chronograph ['kronəgra:f], *s.* (*fis. mec.*) cronografo.

chronological [‚kronə'lodʒikəl], *ag.* cronologico.

chronologically [‚kronə'lodʒikəli], *av.* cronologicamente.

chronologist [krə'nolədʒist], *s.* cronologista.

to **chronologize** [krə'nolədʒaiz], *v.t.* fare la cronologia di; sistemare cronologicamente.

chronology [krə'nolədʒi], *s.* cronologia.

chronometer [krə'nomitə*], *s.* cronometro ☆ *box* — (o *marine* —), cronometro marino.

chronometric(al) [‚kronə'metrik(əl)], *ag.* cronometrico.

chronometrically [‚kronə'metrikəli], *av.* cronometricamente.

chronometry [krə'nomitri], *s.* cronometria.

chronoscope ['kronouskoup], *s.* cronoscopio.

chrysalid ['krisəlid], *pl.* **chrysalids** ['krisəlidz], **chrysalides** [kri'sælidi:z]; **chrysalis** ['krisəlis], *pl.* **chrysalises** ['krisəlisiz], *s.* crisalide.

chrysanthemum [kri'sænθəməm], *s.* (*bot.*) crisantemo.

Chryseis [krai'si:is], *no.pr.f.* (*mit.*) Criseide.

chryselephantine [‚kriseli'fæntin], *ag.* (*scult. greca*) criselefantino.

chrysoberyl ['krisou‚beril], *s.* (*min.*) crisoberillo.

chrysolite ['krisəlait], *s.* (*min.*) crisolito.

chrysoprase ['krisəpreiz], *s.* (*min.*) crisoprazio.

chrysotile ['krisətil], *s.* (*min.*) crisotile.

chub [tʃʌb], *s.* (*ittiol.*) ghiozzo.

chubb [tʃʌb], *s.* — (-*lock*), serratura di sicurezza.

chubbiness ['tʃʌbinis], *s.* aspetto paffuto (delle guance, ecc.).

chubby ['tʃʌbi], *ag.* paffuto, pienotto, rotondo (di guance, ecc.) ☆ — *-cheeked*, dalle guance paffute.

chuck[1] [tʃʌk], *s.* il chiocciare (di gallina).

to **chuck**[1], *v.i.* **1.** chiocciare (di gallina) **2.** (*fam.*) schioccare (di lingua).

chuck[2], *s.* **1.** buffetto (sotto il mento) **2.** (*fam.*) lancio ‖ *to get the* —, (*fam.*) essere licenziato; *to give s.o. the* —, (*fam.*) congedare, licenziare **3.** (*sl. amer.*) cibo.

to **chuck**[2], *v.t.* **1.** dare un buffetto a: *to* — *s.o. under the chin*, dare un buffetto sotto il mento a qlcu. **2.** (*fam.*) gettare, tirare: *he chucked a stone at me*, mi ha tirato un sasso: *to* — *sthg. on the floor*, gettare ql.co. a terra ‖ — *it!*, (*sl.*) piantala!, finiscila! ‖ *to be chucked at an examination*, (*fam.*) essere fregato a un esame **3.** *to* — *about*, (*fam.*) sperperare (denaro, ecc.) **4.** *to* — **away**, buttar via; sperperare **5.** *to* — **in**: *to* — *one's hand in*, (*sl.*) gettare le carte sulla tavola; darsi per vinto **6.** *to* — **out**, (*fam.*) sbatter fuori, buttar fuori, mettere alla porta, espellere **7.** *to* — **up**, rinunciare a, abbandonare (lavoro, posto); lanciare in aria ☆ *chucking-out time*, (*sl.*) ora di chiusura (delle mescite pubbliche).

chuck[3], *s.* **1.** (*cuc.*) spalla **2.** (*mec.*) mandrino **3.** (*mec.*) autocentrante.

to **chuck**[3], *v.t.* (*mec.*) bloccare nel mandrino; mettere nel mandrino.

chuck[4], *s.* (*spec. dial.*) pulcino (appellativo affettuoso).

chucker ['tʃʌkə*], *s.* lanciatore (di un sasso, ecc.) ☆ — *-out*, (*fam.*) chi mantiene l'ordine allontanando gli intrusi (ad un'adunanza, in un locale pubblico).

chuckle[1] ['tʃʌkl], *s.* **1.** riso basso, soffocato **2.** il chiocciare (della gallina).

to **chuckle**[1], *v.i.* **1.** ridere basso, soffocato **2.** chiocciare (della gallina).

chuckle[2], *ag.s.* stupido, sciocco ☆ — *-head(ed)*, stupido, sciocco.

chug [tʃʌg], *s.* (*aut.*) scoppiettio; (*ferr.*) sbuffo.

to **chug**, *pass.p.p.* **chugged** [tʃʌgd], *v.i.* **1.** scoppiettare (di automobile), sbuffare (di locomotiva) **2.** *to* — *off*, allontanarsi scoppiettando (di automobile).

chum [tʃʌm], *s.* compagno di camera; camerata; amico intimo ☆ *new* —, (*austral.*) nuovo arrivato, emigrante.

to **chum**, *pass.p.p.* **chummed** [tʃʌmd], *v.i.* (*fam.*) occupare la stessa camera; essere amici ‖ *to* — (*up*) *with s.o.*, fare amicizia con qlcu.

chummy¹ ['tʃʌmi], *ag.s.* (*fam.*) (amico) intimo.

chummy², *s.* (*sl.*) garzone di spazzacamino.

chump [tʃʌmp], *s.* **1.** ceppo, ciocco **2.** (*fam.*) sciocco, stupido, testa di legno **3.** (*sl.*) testa: *to be off one's* —, aver perso la testa ☆ — *-chop*, braciola di montone.

chunk [tʃʌnk], *s.* (*fam.*) grosso pezzo (di legno, pane, formaggio, ecc.).

church [tʃəːtʃ], *s.* **1.** chiesa: *to go to* —, andare in chiesa ‖ *to be late for* —, essere in ritardo per la funzione religiosa; *to be as poor as a* — *mouse*, essere povero in canna **2.** comunità dei fedeli; clero ‖ *the Church of England* (o *the Anglican* o *English Church*), la chiesa anglicana; *the Church of Scotland*, la chiesa presbiteriana scozzese ‖ *Church militant*, Chiesa militante; *Church triumphant*, Chiesa trionfante ‖ *Established Church*, Chiesa di stato; religione ufficiale; *Roman Catholic Church*, Chiesa Cattolica Romana ‖ *to be received into the Church*, prendere il velo; diventare cristiano col battesimo; fare la prima Comunione ‖ *to go into the Church*, prendere gli ordini sacri ☆ — *-burial*, sepoltura religiosa; — *-goer*, praticante (di cattolico); assiduo ai servizi religiosi (di protestante); — *-going*, pratica religiosa (di cattolico); assiduità ai servizi religiosi (di protestante); — *-lands*, terre, beni della Chiesa; — *-living*, beneficio ecclesiastico; — *-party*, partito clericale; — *-service*, funzione religiosa; — *-text*, (*tip.*) carattere nero gotico; — *warden*, fabbriciere; pipa di argilla; — *-work*, lavoro relativo alla chiesa; — *-worker*, chi partecipa attivamente al lavoro connesso con la chiesa.

to **church**, *v.t.* condurre in chiesa (specialmente una puerpera, una coppia di sposi) per ricevere benedizione e rendere grazie.

churchless ['tʃəːtʃlis], *ag.* senza chiesa.

churchman, *pl.* **churchmen** ['tʃəːtʃmən], *s.* **1.** uomo di chiesa, ecclesiastico **2.** membro della Chiesa anglicana.

churchwoman ['tʃəːtʃˌwumən], *pl.* **churchwomen** ['tʃəːtʃˌwimin], *s.* donna appartenente alla Chiesa anglicana.

churchy ['tʃəːtʃi], *ag.* bigotto.

churchyard ['tʃəːtʃˌjaːd], *s.* cimitero (presso una chiesa).

churl [tʃəːl], *s.* **1.** contadino; villano; zotico **2.** spilorcio.

churlish ['tʃəːliʃ], *ag.* **1.** contadinesco; zotico **2.** avaro.

churlishly ['tʃəːliʃli], *av.* **1.** rozzamente **2.** villanamente.

churlishness ['tʃəːliʃnis], *s.* **1.** rozzezza **2.** spilorceria.

churn [tʃəːn], *s.* zangola ☆ — *-dasher* (o — *-staff*), paletta della zangola; — *-milk*, latte scremato; siero.

to **churn**, *v.t.i.* **1.** fare (il burro) nella zangola **2.** agitare, agitarsi; ribollire (di acqua, mare, ecc.).

churning ['tʃəːniŋ], *s.* **1.** il fare il burro **2.** quantità di burro fatta in una volta.

churr [tʃəː*], *s.* il vibrare di ali.

to **churr**, *v.i.* far vibrare l'aria (con le ali).

chut [tʃʌt], *inter.* basta!.

chute [ʃuːt], *s.* **1.** cascata d'acqua **2.** (*mec.*) scivolo a canale; tubo, canale di scarico; tramoggia; (*geol.*) canale di scolo **3.** (*spor.*) pista inclinata **4.** tela a scivolo (dei pompieri) **5.** (*miner.*) fornello di gettito.

chutney ['tʃʌtni], *s.* (*ang.-in. cuc.*) «chutney» (condimento a base di droghe).

chyle [kail], *s.* (*fisiol.*) chilo.

chyliferous [kai'lifərəs], *ag.* (*fisiol.*) chilifero.

chylification [ˌkailifi'keiʃən], *s.* (*fisiol.*) chilificazione, formazione di chilo.

to **chylify** ['kailifai], *v.t.* (*fisiol.*) chilificare.

chyme [kaim], *s.* (*fisiol.*) chimo.

chymification [ˌkaimifi'keiʃən], *s.* (*fisiol.*) chimificazione, formazione del chimo.

to **chymify** ['kaimifai], *v.t.* (*fisiol.*) chimificare.

chymistry ['kimistri], *V.* **chemistry**.

ciborium [si'boːriəm], *s.* (*eccl.*) ciborio.

cicada [si'kaːdə], **cieala** [si'kaːlə], *s.* cicala.

cicatrice ['sikətris], *V.* **cicatrix**.

cicatrice(u)le [si'kætrik(juː)l], *s.* **1.** (*biol.*) cicatricula **2.** (*bot.*) ilo **3.** piccola cicatrice.

cicatrix ['sikətriks], *pl.* **cicatrices** [ˌsikə'traisiːz], *s.* **1.** cicatrice **2.** (*bot.*) ilo **3.** (*biol.*) cicatricula.

cicatrization [ˌsikətrai'zeiʃən], *s.* cicatrizzazione.

to **cicatrize** ['sikətraiz], *v.t.i.* cicatrizzare, cicatrizzarsi.

cicely ['sisili], *s.* (*bot.*) cerfoglio ☆ *sweet* —, mirride odorosa; (*pop.*) finocchiella.

Cicero ['sisərou], *no.pr.m.* (*st. lett.*) Cicerone.

cicerone [ˌtʃitʃə'rouni], *s.* cicerone, guida.

Ciceronian [ˌsisə'rounjən], *ag.* ciceroniano, eloquente, classico ‖ *s.* studioso di Cicerone.

cicisbeism [ˌtʃitʃiz'beiizəm], *s.* cicisbeismo.

cicisbeo [ˌtʃitʃiz'beiou], *pl.* **cicisbei** [ˌtʃitʃiz'beii], *s.* cicisbeo.

cicuta [si'kjuːtə], *s.* (*bot.*) cicuta.

cider ['saidə*], *s.* sidro ☆ — *-cup*, «cider-cup» (bevanda di sidro ghiacciata); — *-press*, torchio da sidro.

cig [sig], (*sl.*) per **cigarette**.

cigala [si'gaːlə], *s.* cicala.

cigar [si'gaː*], *s.* sigaro ☆ — *-case*, portasigari; — *-cutter*, tagliasigari; — *-end*, mozzicone di sigaro; — *-holder*, bocchino per sigaro; — *-lighter*, accendisigari; — *-maker*, sigaraio; — *-shaped*, a forma di sigaro.

cigarette [ˌsigə'ret], *s.* sigaretta: *a packet of cigarettes*, un pacchetto di sigarette ☆ — *-case*, portasigarette; — *-end*, mozzicone di sigaretta; — *-holder*, bocchino per sigaretta; — *-lighter*, accendisigari; — *-paper*, cartina per sigarette ‖ *gold-tipped* —, sigaretta col bocchino dorato.

cilia ['siliə], *s. pl.* ciglia; (*biol. zool.*) ciglia vibratili.

ciliary ['siliəri], *ag.* ciliare.

ciliate ['siliit], **ciliated** ['silieitid], *ag.s.* (*biol. zool.*) ciliato.

cilice ['silis], *s.* cilicio.

ciliform ['silifoːm], *ag.* (*biol. zool.*) a forma di ciglia.

Cimbri ['simbrai], *s.pl.* (*st.*) cimbri.

Cimbrian ['simbriən], *ag.* (*st.*) cimbrico ‖ *s.c.* (*st.*) cimbro, cimbra ‖ *s.* lingua dei cimbri.

Cimmerian [si'miəriən], *ag.* cimmerio; tenebroso, oscuro.

Cimon ['saimən], *no.pr.m.* (*st.*) Cimone.

cinch [sintʃ], *s.* **1.** (*amer.*) straccale (di sella) ‖ *to have a* — *on s.o.*, *fig.* aver presa su qlcu. **2.** (*sl. amer.*) cosa facile: *cosa sicura*: *it's a* —, è una cosa sicura.

to **cinch**, *v.t.* (*amer.*) **1.** fissare lo straccale di (una sella) **2.** (*sl.*) dominare **3.** (*sl.*) accertarsi, assicurarsi di.

cinchona [siŋ'kounə], *s.* **1.** (*bot.*) china **2.** (*farm.*) corteccia di china, cincona.

cinchonaceous [ˌsiŋkə'neiʃəs], *ag.* (*farm.*) chinato.

cinchonine ['siŋkəniːn], *s.* (*chim.*) cinconina.

cinchonism ['siŋkənizəm], *s.* (*patol.*) cinconismo.

Cincinnatus [ˌsinsi'neitəs], *no.pr.m.* (*st.*) Cincinnato.

cincture ['siŋktʃə*], *s.* **1.** (*poet.*) cintura **2.** cinta (di città) **3.** (*arch.*) listello, filetto.

to **cincture**, *v.t.* cingere; attorniare.

cinder ['sində*], *s.* brace, residuo di un fuoco; (*metal.*) scoria; *pl.* cenere ☆ — *track*, (*spor.*) pista di cenere.

to **cinder**, *v.t.* incenerire.

Cinderella [ˌsində'relə], *no.pr.f.* Cenerentola.

cine-camera ['siniˌkæmərə], *s.* (*cine.*) macchina da presa.

cinema ['sinimə], *s.* **1.** cinematografo, cinema (industria, arte del cinematografo) **2.** cinematografo, cinema (sala cinematografica) ☆ — *fan*, appassionato del cinematografo; — *star*, stella del cinema.

cinemascope ['siniməskoup], *s.* (*neol. cine.*) cinemascope.

cinematograph [ˌsini'mætəgrɑːf], *s.* (*cine.*) **1.** proiettore cinematografico, apparecchio di proiezione **2.** (*amer.*) macchina da presa **3.** cinematografo.

to **cinematograph**, *v.t.i.* **1.** filmare (una scena) **2.** proiettare una pellicola.

cinematographer [ˌsinimə'togrəfə*], *s.* **1.** operatore cinematografico **2.** cineasta.

cinematographic [ˌsiniˌmætə'græfik], *ag.* cinematografico.

cinematographically [ˌsiniˌmætə'græfikəli], *av.* cinematograficamente.

cinematography [ˌsinimə'togrəfi], *s.* cinematografia.

cine-projector ['siniprə'dʒektə*], *s.* (*cine.*) apparecchio di proiezione.

cinerama [ˌsini'rɑːmə], *s.* (*neol. cine.*) cinerama.

cineraria [ˌsinə'rɛəriə], *s.* (*bot.*) cineraria.

cinerarium [ˌsinə'rɛəriəm], *s.* colombario.

cinerary ['sinərəri], *ag.* cinerario.

cineration [ˌsinə'reifən], *s.* incenerimento.

cinereous [si'niəriəs], *ag.* cinereo.

Cingalese [ˌsiŋgə'liːz], *ag.s.c.* singalese.

cinnabar ['sinəbɑ*], *s.* **1.** (*chim.*) cinabro **2.** (*pitt.*) cinabrese; vermiglione.

cinnamon ['sinəmən], *ag.* di color cinnamomo, cannella ‖ *s.* **1.** (*bot.*) cinnamomo, cannella: *a roll of* —, un bastoncino di cannella **2.** color cinnamomo, cannella ☆ — *-bark*, cannella, (scorza del) cinnamomo; — *bear*, orso bruno.

cinque [siŋk], *s.* cinque (a carte, dadi).

cinquecentist [ˌtʃiŋkwi'tʃentist], *s.* cinquecentista.

cinquecento [ˌtʃiŋkwi'tʃentou], *s.* (*art. lett. italiɪna*) cinquecento.

cinq(ue)foil ['siŋkfɔil], *s.* **1.** (*bot.*) cinquefoglie **2.** (*arch.*) pentalobo.

Cinque Ports ['siŋk'pɔːts], *s.pl.* (*st.*) I Cinque Porti (Dover, Hastings, Hythe, Romney e Sandwich).

cipher ['saifə*], *s.* **1.** (*arit.*) zero **2.** *fig.* nulla, nullità: *he's a mere* —, è una nullità **3.** cifrario, messaggio cifrato; scrittura convenzionale: *to write in* —, scrivere in cifra **4.** monogramma, cifra **5.** cifra (araba) ☆ — *-key*, chiave di un cifrario.

to **cipher**, *v.t.i.* **1.** conteggiare, fare calcoli **2.** cifrare (un messaggio, ecc.), trasmettere in cifra **3.** calcolare: *to* — (*out*) *a sum*, calcolare una somma **4.** *to* — *out*, (*amer.*) decifrare ‖ *to* — *out a question*, approfondire una questione.

cipolin ['sipəlin], *s.* marmo cipollino.

Circassia [səː'kæsiə], *no.pr.* (*geog. st.*) Circassia.

Circassian [səː'kæsiən], *ag.* circasso ‖ *s.c.* circasso, circassa.

Circe ['səːsi], *no.pr.f.* (*mit.*) Circe.

Circean [səː'siːən], *ag.* **1.** (*mit.*) di Circe **2.** incantatore.

circinate ['səːsinit], *ag.* (*bot.*) circinale, circinato.

circle ['səːkl], *s.* **1.** cerchio; circolo (anche *fig.*); circonferenza; anello; alone: *vicious* —, circolo vizioso; *to argue in a* —, discutere senza concludere; *to come the full* —, ritornare al punto di partenza; *to draw a* —, tracciare un cerchio **2.** orbita (di pianeta) **3.** cerchia, circolo (di persone) **4.** (*teat.*) galleria **5.** periodo, ciclo: *the* — *of the seasons*, il ciclo delle stagioni **6.** *fig.* sfera, area (d'influenza, ecc.): *the guests were drawn from every political* —, gli invitati rappresentavano i diversi ambienti politici **7.** (*geog.*) meridiano, parallelo ☆ *family* —, ambito familiare; (*teat.*) seconda galleria; *upper* —, (*teat.*) prima galleria; *upper* (o *high*) *circles*, ambienti aristocratici.

to **circle**, *v.t.i.* **1.** (*poet.*) circondare, cingere, accerchiare **2.** girare intorno a: *the moon circles the earth*, la luna gira intorno alla terra **3.** volteggiare (anche *spor.*): *the aeroplane circled above us*, l'aeroplano volteggiò sopra di noi.

circlet ['səːklit], *s.* cerchietto; anello.

circs [səːks], *s.pl.* (*fam. abbr.* di *circumstances*) circostanze: *under the* —, nelle presenti circostanze.

circuit ['səːkit], *s.* **1.** circonferenza, cinta; circonvallazione; circondario **2.** rivoluzione, rotazione, giro (del sole, ecc.) **3.** circoscrizione (di giudice, ecc.): *to go on* —, spostarsi di città in città per amministrarvi la giustizia **4.** giro, viaggio intorno (a regione, ecc.) **5.** catena di cinema, teatri, ecc. sotto un'unica amministrazione **6.** (*elett. spor.*) circuito **7.** *fig.* rigiro, ambage ☆ — *-breaker*, interruttore ‖ *short-* —, corto circuito.

to **circuit**, *v.t.i.* girar attorno a, fare il giro di; muoversi in circolo.

circuitous [səː(ː)'kju(ː)itəs], *ag.* indiretto; sinuoso.

circuitously [səː(ː)'kju(ː)itəsli], *av.* indirettamente.

circular ['səːkjulə*], *ag.* circolare: — *motion*, movimento circolare ‖ *s.* —, (*letter.*) lettera circolare ☆ — *note*, (*comm.*) lettera circolare di credito; — *run*, (*spor.*) circuito; — *saw*, (*mec.*) sega circolare; — *ticket*, (*ferr.*) biglietto circolare; — *tour*, viaggio circolare ‖ *the Court* —, l'effemeride di Corte.

circularity [ˌsəːkju'læriti], *s.* forma circolare.

to **circularize** ['səːkjuləraiz], *v.t.* (*comm.*) inviare circolari a (clienti, ecc.).

circularly ['səːkjuləli], *av.* circolarmente.

to **circulate** ['səːkjuleit], *v.t.i.* **1.** circolare, far circolare; mettere in circolazione; diffondere; circolare (*amer.*) inviare circolari **2.** (*mat.*) ricorrere periodicamente (di decimali).

circulating ['səːkjuleitiŋ], *ag.* circolante ☆ — *capital*, (*comm.*) capitale circolante; — *library*, biblioteca circolante: — *medium*, mezzo circolante (moneta, ecc.).

circulation [ˌsəːkju'leiʃən], *s.* **1.** circolazione (di sangue, acqua, denaro, ecc.) **2.** trasmissione, diffusione (di libri, notizie, ecc.): *a wide* —, una larga diffusione **3.** tiratura (di giornale) **4.** (*aer.*) circuitazione ☆ *monetary* —, circolazione monetaria; *road* —, circolazione stradale.

circulative ['səːkjulcitiv], *ag.* che favorisce la circolazione; che è incline a circolare.

circulator ['səːkjuleitə*], *s.* **1.** propagatore di notizie; maldicente **2.** (*mat.*) numero periodico.

circulatory ['səːkjulətəri], *ag.* circolatorio.

circumambiency [ˌsəːkəm'æmbiənsi], *s.* (*rar.*) ambiente (*p.e.* aria, ecc.).

circumambient [ˌsəːkəm'æmbiənt], *ag.* ambiente.

to **circumambulate** [ˌsəːkəm'æmbjuleit], *v.t.i.* (*letter. scherz.*) girare intorno a, andare in giro; (*fig. fam.*) menare il can per l'aia.

to **circumcise** ['səːkəmsaiz], *v.t.* **1.** circoncidere **2.** *fig.* purificare (le passioni, il cuore).

circumcision [ˌsəːkəm'siʒən], *s.* **1.** circoncisione **2.** *fig.* purificazione.

circumference [səː'kʌmfərəns], *s.* circonferenza.

circumferential [səˌkʌmfə'renʃəl], *ag.* relativo a circonferenza, circolare.

to **circumflect** [ˌsəːkəm'flekt], *V.* to **circumflex**.

circumflex ['səːkəmfleks], *ag.s.* — (*accent*), (accento) circonflesso ☆ — *nerve*, (*anat.*) nervo circonflesso, ascellare.

to **circumflex**, *v.t.* porre l'accento circonflesso su.

circumfluence [səː'kʌmfluəns], *s.* circonfluenza.

circumfluent [səː'kʌmfluənt], *ag.* circonfluente.

circumfluous [səː'kʌmfluəs], *ag.* circonfluente; circondato dalle acque.

to **circumfuse** [ˌsəːkəm'fjuːz], *v.t.* circonfondere, circondare: *circumfused with light*, circonfuso di luce; *circumfused with air, water*, circondato da aria, acqua.

to **circumgyrate** [ˌsəːkəm'dʒaireit], *v.i.* girare, viaggiare intorno.

circumjacent [ˌsəːkəm'dʒeisənt], *ag.* circonvicino.

circumlocution [ˌsəːkəmlə'kjuːʃən], *s.* circonlocuzione, perifrasi.

circumlocutional [ˌsəːkəmlə'kjuːʃənl], *ag.* (linguaggio) pieno di circonlocuzioni.

circumlocutory [ˌsəːkəmˈlɔkjutəri], *ag.* perifrastico; involuto, pieno di circonlocuzioni.

to **circumnavigate** [ˌsəːkəmˈnævigeit], *v.t.* circumnavigare.

circumnavigation [ˈsəːkəmˌnæviˈgeiʃən], *s.* circumnavigazione.

circumnavigator [ˌsəːkəmˈnævigeitə*], *s.* circumnavigatore.

circumpolar [ˈsəːkəmˈpoulə*], *ag.* circumpolare ‖ *s.* — (*star*), stella circumpolare.

to **circumscribe** [ˈsəːkəmskraib], *v.t.* **1.** circoscrivere: *to — a polygon about a circle,* circoscrivere un poligono a un cerchio **2.** limitare (anche *fig.*): *circumscribed intellect,* intelligenza limitata.

circumscriber [ˌsəːkəmˈskraibə*], *s.* chi firma una petizione.

circumscription [ˌsəːkəmˈskripʃən], *s.* **1.** circoscrizione (anche *geom.*) **2.** limitazione (anche *fig.*).

circumsolar [ˌsəːkəmˈsoulə*], *ag.* circumsolare.

circumspect [ˈsəːkəmspekt], *ag.* circospetto, cauto, guardingo.

circumspection [ˌsəːkəmˈspekʃən], *s.* circospezione.

circumspective [ˌsəːkəmˈspektiv], *ag.* circospetto.

circumspectly [ˈsəːkəmspektli], *av.* con circospezione.

circumspectness [ˈsəːkəmspektnis], *s.* circospezione.

circumstance [ˈsəːkəmstəns], *s.* **1.** *gener. pl.* circostanza: *extenuating circumstances,* circostanze attenuanti; *in* (o *under*) *the circumstances,* in queste circostanze, in questo caso; *in* (o *under*) *no circumstances,* in nessun caso, a nessuna condizione; checchè accada; *it depends on circumstances,* dipende dalle circostanze **2.** *gener. sing.* dettaglio, ragguaglio, particolare: *with much —,* con molti particolari; *don't omit a single —,* non omettere un solo dettaglio **3.** fatto, avvenimento, circostanza: *I was ignorant of one important —,* ero all'oscuro di un fatto importante **4.** cerimonia: *with pomp and —,* con gran pompa e cerimonia; *without —,* senza cerimonie **5.** *pl.* condizioni finanziarie: *in good, bad circumstances,* in buone, cattive condizioni finanziarie; *in humble circumstances,* di condizioni modeste.

circumstanced [ˈsəːkəmstənst], *ag.* **1.** in determinate condizioni, circostanze: *as I was —,* nelle condizioni in cui mi trovavo **2.** circostanziato.

circumstantial [ˌsəːkəmˈstænʃəl], *ag.* **1.** che deriva dalle circostanze; accidentale: *— evidence,* prove indiziarie indirette **2.** circostanziato: *a — account,* un ragguaglio circostanziato.

circumstantiality [ˈsəːkəmˌstænʃiˈæliti], *s.* abbondanza di particolari.

circumstantially [ˌsəːkəmˈstænʃəli], *av.* **1.** accidentalmente **2.** con particolari, circostanziatamente.

to **circumvallate** [ˌsəːkəmˈvæleit], *v.t.* circonvallare.

circumvallation [ˌsəːkəmvəˈleiʃən], *s.* circonvallazione (anche *mil.*)

to **circumvent** [ˌsəːkəmˈvent], *v.t.* circuire, ingannare: *to — the enemy,* circuire il nemico; *to — the law,* ingannare la legge.

circumvention [ˌsəːkəmˈvenʃən], *s.* insidia, raggiro.

circumvolution [ˌsəːkəmvəˈljuːʃən], *s.* circonvoluzione.

circus [ˈsəːkəs], *pl.* **circuses** [ˈsəːkəsiz], *s.* **1.** circo, arena; circo (equestre) ‖ *to make a — of oneself,* (*sl.*) dare spettacolo di sè **2.** crocicchio che forma una piazza rotonda, ellittica **3.** anfiteatro di colline **4.** (*sl. aer.*) carosello di aeroplani.

cirque [səːk], *s.* (*poet.*) circo, arena; anfiteatro.

cirrhosis [siˈrousis], *s.* (*patol.*) cirrosi.

cirriferous [siˈrifərəs], *ag.* (*bot. zool.*) cirrifero.

cirriped [ˈsiriped], *s.* (*zool.*) cirripede.

cirrose [siˈrous], **cirrous** [ˈsirəs], *ag.* di cirro; filamentoso.

cirrus [ˈsirəs], *pl.* **cirri** [ˈsirai], *s.* **1.** (*bot.*) viticcio **2.** (*meteorologia*) cirro **3.** (*zool.*) filamento.

cisalpine [sisˈælpain], *ag.* cisalpino.

cismontane [sisˈmontein], *ag.* cismontano.

cispadane [ˈsispədein], *ag.* cispadano.

cispontine [sisˈpontain], *ag.* sulla riva sinistra (specialmente del Tamigi, riferendosi ai quartieri nord di Londra).

cissoid [ˈsisoid], *s.* (*geom.*) cissoide.

cissy [ˈsisi], *s.* (*sl. amer.*) persona effeminata.

cist [sist], *s.* (*archeol.*) **1.** cista **2.** pietra tombale preistorica.

Cistercian [sisˈtəːʃiən], *ag.s.* (monaco) cistercense.

cistern [ˈsistən], *s.* **1.** cisterna, serbatoio **2.** vaschetta (di barometro, ecc.).

cistus [ˈsistəs], *s.* (*bot.*) cisto.

cit [sit], *s.* (*arc. gener. spreg. abbr.* di *citizen*) cittadino; borghese; nuovo ricco.

citable [ˈsaitəbl], *ag.* citabile.

citadel [ˈsitədl], *s.* cittadella, fortezza, rocca.

citation [saiˈteiʃən], *s.* **1.** (*dir.*) citazione; (*amer. mil.*) citazione (all'ordine del giorno) **2.** citazione; enumerazione.

to **cite** [sait], *v.t.* **1.** (*dir.*) citare: *to — s.o. before a court,* citare qlcu. in tribunale; *to — a witness,* citare un testimone **2.** citare (autore, fatti, ecc.); addurre: *to — an instance,* addurre un esempio.

either [ˈsiθə], **cithern** [ˈsiθən], *s.* (*mus.*) cetra.

citizen [ˈsitizn], *s.* **1.** cittadino: *— of the world,* cosmopolita; cittadino del mondo ‖ *the citizens,* la cittadinanza **2.** (*amer.*) borghese, civile ☆ *fellow —,* concittadino; compatriota.

citizeness [ˈsitiznis], *s.* cittadina.

citizenhood [ˈsitiznhud], *s.* cittadinanza: *all the — of the town,* la cittadinanza.

citizenship [ˈsitiznʃip], *s.* (diritti di) cittadinanza ‖ *good —,* civismo.

citrate [ˈsitrit], *s.* (*chim.*) citrato.

citric [ˈsitrik], *ag.* (*chim.*) citrico.

citrine [siˈtriːn], *ag.* citrino.

citron [ˈsitrən], *s.* **1.** cedro **2.** color limone.

citrus [ˈsitrəs], *s.* agrume, agrumi.

cittern [ˈsitəːn], *s.* (*mus.*) cetra.

city [ˈsiti], *s.* **1.** (grande) città: *the — of London,* la città di Londra ‖ *the City,* il centro degli affari di Londra ‖ *Celestial City* (o *Heavenly City* o *City of God*), Paradiso; *the Eternal City* (o *City of the Seven Hills*), Roma; *the Holy City,* Gerusalemme; *New York City,* la città di Nuova York; *Vatican City,* la città del Vaticano **2.** centro degli affari, nucleo originario di una città ☆ *— article,* bollettino finanziario della City; *— editor,* redattore finanziario; *— man,* uomo d'affari nella City; *— -plan,* piano regolatore; *— -planning,* urbanistica.

cityward(s) [ˈsitiwəd(z)], *av.* verso la città.

civet [ˈsivit], *s.* zibetto (animale, profumo).

civic [ˈsivik], *ag.* civico ☆ *the — authorities,* le autorità municipali; *— guard,* guardia civica.

civically [ˈsivikəli], *av.* in modo, senso civico.

civics [ˈsiviks], *s.* educazione civica.

civies [ˈsiviz], *s.pl.* (*sl.*) abito civile: *in —,* in borghese.

civil [ˈsivl], *ag.* **1.** civile: *to contract a — marriage,* sposarsi civilmente ‖ *Civil Service,* amministrazione statale **2.** civile, cortese, gentile: *he was very — to me,* fu molto gentile, educato con me ‖ *keep a — tongue in your head,* parla come si deve ☆ *— code,* codice civile; *— death,* (*dir.*) morte civile; *— engineering,* ingegneria civile; *— law,* diritto romano e civile; *— life,* vita civile; *— list,* lista civile (del sovrano); *— rights,* diritti civili; *— servant,* funzionario statale; *— -spoken,* cortese nel modo di parlare; *— war,* guerra civile; *— year,* anno civile.

civilian [siˈviljən], *ag.s.* civile, borghese.

civility [siˈviliti], *s.* civiltà, cortesia, educazione.

civilizable [ˈsivilaizəbl], *ag.* civilizzabile.

civilization [ˌsivilaiˈzeiʃən], *s.* civiltà, civilizzazione.

to **civilize** [ˈsivilaiz], *v.t.* **1.** incivilire, civilizzare **2.** to *— away,* liberarsi di (istinto, barbarie).

civilized ['sivilaizd], *ag.* civilizzato: *to become* —, incivilirsi.

civilizer ['sivilaizə*], *s.c.* civilizzatore, civilizzatrice.

civilly ['sivili], *av.* **1.** secondo la legge civile **2.** civilmente; educatamente.

civism ['sivizəm], *s.* civismo.

civvies, *V.* **civies**.

civ(v)y ['sivi], *s.* (*fam. abbr.* di *civilian*) civile.

Civ(v)y Street ['sivistri:t], *s.* (*sl.*) vita (da) civile.

clack [klæk], *s.* **1.** suono secco, improvviso; schiocco di lingua **2.** (*fam.*) ciarla, chiacchierio ☆ — *-valve*, (*tec.*) valvola a cerniera.

to clack, *v.i.* **1.** fare un suono improvviso e secco; fare schioccare la lingua **2.** (*fam.*) ciarlare, chiacchierare.

clad [klæd], *p.p.* (*arc. letter.*) di to **clothe**.

claim [kleim], *s.* **1.** richiesta; (*comm.*) reclamo; (*dir.*) rivendicazione; diritto: *to have a — on s.o.*, avere dei diritti da esigere da qlcu.; *to have a — to sthg.*, aver diritto a ql.co.; *to lodge a —*, inoltrare un reclamo; *to set up a —*, fare un reclamo **2.** asserzione; pretesa **3.** (*amer.*) concessione mineraria ☆ — *-holder*, concessionario di miniere.

to claim, *v.t.i.* **1.** chiedere, esigere; (*comm.*) reclamare; (*dir.*) rivendicare: *to — acquaintance with s.o.*, pretendere di conoscere qlcu.; *to — damages*, reclamare i danni; *to — one's due*, rivendicare i propri diritti; *to — a privilege*, pretendere un privilegio; *to — sthg. back from s.o.*, chiedere a qlcu. la restituzione di ql.co. **2.** asserire, affermare **3.** presentare una protesta.

claimable ['kleiməbl], *ag.* rivendicabile; esigibile.

claimant ['kleimənt], **claimer** ['kleimə*], *s.c.* rivendicatore, rivendicatrice; richiedente ☆ *rightful* —, l'avente diritto.

clairvoyance [klɛə'voiəns], *s.* chiaroveggenza.

clairvoyant [klɛə'voiənt], *ag.s.c.* chiaroveggente.

clam[1] [klæm], *s.* qualsiasi oggetto per tenere unite, ferme varie cose (morsa, pinza, ecc.).

clam[2] [klæm], *s.* nome comune a vari tipi di molluschi bivalvi commestibili.

clam[3], *ag.* (*dial.*) viscido; umido ‖ *s.* viscosità.

to clam[3], *pass.p.p.* **clammed** [klæmd], *v.t.i.* impiastricciare, rendere appiccicoso; essere appiccicoso.

clamancy ['kleimənsi], *s.* pressione, insistenza.

clamant ['kleimənt], *ag.* **1.** pressante, insistente **2.** rumoroso.

clamber ['klæmbə*], *s.* arrampicata, scalata.

to clamber, *v.i.* arrampicarsi (con mani e piedi): *to — over a wall*, scavalcare un muro; *to — up a ladder*, arrampicarsi su una scala.

clammily ['klæmili], *av.* con umidore attaccaticcio, viscoso.

clamminess ['klæminis], *s.* viscosità; umidità fredda.

clammy ['klæmi], *ag.* viscoso, viscido; freddo umido (di mani, pelle, aria, ecc.).

clamorous ['klæmərəs], *ag.* clamoroso, rumoroso.

clamorously ['klæmərəsli], *av.* clamorosamente, rumorosamente.

clamour[1] ['klæmə*], *s.* clamore, schiamazzo; vocio.

to clamour[1], *v.t.i.* **1.** gridare a gran voce, vociferare; domandare a gran voce: *they clamoured for bread*, chiesero a gran voce del pane **2.** *to — down*, far tacere gridando a gran voce.

to clamour[1], *v.t.* **1.** far tacere (le campane) dopo un ritmo accelerato finale **2.** far tacere.

clamp[1] [klæmp], *s.* **1.** morsa; pinza; tenaglia; morsetto; fibbia; ganascia: *skate with clamps*, pattino a ganasce **2.** (*mar.*) sotto-dormiente, serretta di baglio.

to clamp[1], *v.t.* stringere; chiudere; incastrare; rinforzare con morsetti; legare; fissare.

clamp[2], *s.* cumulo (di patate sotto paglia, terra; di mattoni da cuocere, ecc.).

to clamp[2], *v.t.* accumulare (patate, mattoni, ecc.).

clamp[3], *s.* (*spec. dial.*) passo pesante.

to clamp[3], *v.i.* (*spec. dial.*) camminare con passo pesante.

clan [klæn], *s.* **1.** (*scoz.*) « clan », tribù **2.** (*fam.*) cricca.

to clan, *v.i.*: *to — together*, sostenersi a vicenda.

clandestine [klæn'destin], *ag.* clandestino.

clandestinely [klæn'destinli], *av.* clandestinamente.

clandestineness [klæn'destinnis], *s.* clandestinità.

clang [klæŋ], *s.* suono metallico; clangore, fragore (di campane, di armi).

to clang, *v.t.i.* far risuonare con fragore; produrre un suono metallico.

clangorous ['klæŋgərəs], *ag.* fragoroso.

clangorously ['klæŋgərəsli], *av.* fragorosamente.

clangour ['klæŋgə*], *s.* clangore, fragore.

clank [klæŋk], *s.* rumore secco, metallico (di catene, di ferri).

to clank, *v.t.i.* produrre un rumore secco, metallico; far risuonare: *the prisoners — their chains*, i prigionieri fanno risonare le loro catene.

clannish ['klæniʃ], *ag.* **1.** relativo a, proprio di un « clan », di una tribù **2.** imbevuto di spirito di parte.

clannishness ['klæniʃnis], *s.* spirito di corpo, di parte.

clanship ['klæn-ʃip], *s.* sistema del « clan ».

clansman, *pl.* **clansmen** ['klænzmən], *s.* membro di un « clan ».

clap[1] [klæp], *s.* **1.** battimano, applauso **2.** colpo, colpetto (con la mano); sculacciata: *he gave me a —*, mi diede un colpetto **3.** colpo, rumore improvviso: *a — of thunder*, un colpo di tuono ☆ *thunder-* —, tuono.

to clap[1], *pass.p.p.* **clapped** [klæpt], *v.t.i.* **1.** applaudire: *he was greatly clapped*, fu molto applaudito **2.** battere: *to — one's hands*, battere le mani; *to — s.o. on the back*, dare una manata sulle spalle a qlcu. ‖ *to — eyes on s.o.*, (*fam.*) scorgere d'improvviso qlcu. **3.** mettere, cacciare in fretta, con violenza: *to — hold of (s.o., sthg.)*, afferrare con violenza (qlcu., ql.co.); *to — s.o. in prison*, sbattere qlcu. in prigione ‖ *to — on one's hat*, ficcarsi in testa il cappello con una manata **4.** battere (dello ali): *the cock clapped its wings*, il gallo battè le ali **5.** *to — to*, chiudere, chiudersi con violenza: *he clapped the door to*, sbattè la porta; *the door clapped to*, la porta si chiuse con violenza.

clap[2], *s.* (*volg. patol.*) blenorragia.

clapboard ['klæpbɔ:d], *s.* **1.** doga **2.** (*amer.*) assicella per rivestimento esterno (di edifici).

clapnet ['klæpnet], *s.* rete (per uccellare).

clapper ['klæpə*], *s.* **1.** battente (di porta) **2.** battaglio (di campana) **3.** raganella **4.** *fig.* lingua **5.** (*teat.*) applauditore, membro della claque.

to clapperclaw ['klæpəklɔ:], *v.t.* **1.** (*arc.*) graffiare **2.** *fig.* criticare aspramente.

claptrap ['klæp-træp], *s.* **1.** imbonimento **2.** sproloquio.

claque [klæk], *s.* (*teat.*) « claque ».

Clara ['klɛərə], **Clare** [klɛə*], *no.pr.f.* Clara, Chiara ‖ *the Poor Clares*, (*eccl.*) le Clarisse.

clarence ['klɛərəns], *s.* « clarence » (carrozza chiusa a quattro posti).

clarendon ['klærəndən], *s.* (*tip.*) neretto.

clare-obscure [klɛərəb'skjuə*], *s.* chiaroscuro.

claret ['klærət], *ag.* di colore rosso-violetto ‖ *s.* **1.** colore rosso-violetto **2.** chiaretto (vino rosso leggero della regione di Bordeaux) **3.** (*sl.*) sangue ☆ — *-cup*, « claret -cup » (bevanda ghiacciata a base di vino rosso, succo di limone e zucchero).

Claribel ['klæribel], *no.pr.f.* Clarabella.

Clarice ['klæris], *no.pr.f.* Clarice.

clarification [,klærifi'keiʃən], *s.* chiarificazione.

clarifier ['klærifaiə*], *s.* chiarificatore.

to clarify ['klærifai], *v.t.i.* **1.** chiarificare, chiarificarsi **2.** togliere le impurità a, raffinare (liquido, ecc.).

clarinet [,klæri'net], *s.* (*mus.*) clarinetto.

clarinettist [,klæri'netist], *s.* (*mus.*) clarinettista.

clarion ['klæriən], *s.* (*mus.*) chiarina ☆ — *-voiced*, dalla voce forte e metallica.

to clarion, *v.t.* proclamare a suon di tromba.

Clarissa [klə′risə], *no.pr.f.* Clarissa.

clarity [′klæriti], *s.* chiarità.

clary [′klɛəri], *s.* (*bot.*) schiarea, scarleggia.

clash [klæʃ], *s.* **1.** cozzo; urto; collisione; rumore, strepito **2.** *fig.* scontro, contrasto, conflitto.

to **clash**, *v.t.i.* **1.** cozzare; produrre strepito; far risuonare: *to — the door*, chiudere la porta con fracasso **2.** *fig.* scontrarsi, urtarsi (di opinioni, ecc.): *our interests —*, i nostri interessi sono contrastanti: *to — with* (*s.o.*), essere in conflitto con (qlcu.).

clashing [′klæʃiŋ], *ag.* contrario, opposto; stridente, contrastante: — *opinions*, opinioni opposte.

clasp [klɑːsp], *s.* **1.** fermaglio; fibbia; gancio **2.** abbraccio; stretta (di mano) ☆ — *-knife,* coltello a serramanico.

to **clasp**, *v.t.i.* **1.** affibbiare; agganciare; chiudersi: *this bracelet won't —*, questo braccialetto non si chiude **2.** afferrare; abbracciare; stringere || *with clasped hands*, a mani giunte.

clasper [′klɑːspə*], *s.* **1.** che stringe, afferra, tiene fermo **2.** (*bot.*) viticcio.

class [klɑːs], *s.* **1.** classe, categoria, ceto || *the classes*, (*fam.*) la gente di mondo **2.** classe, corso, lezione; (*amer.*) gli studenti di un anno accademico || *to take a —*, laurearsi con lode (a Oxford) **3.** (*ferr. mar., ecc.*) classe, categoria **4.** (*mil.*) classe, soldati di una leva **5.** (*st. naturale*) classe **6.** *fig.* qualità, distinzione: *she was no —*, essa era piuttosto volgare ☆ — *-book*, testo scolastico; — *-consciousness*, coscienza di classe; — *-fellow*, compagno di classe; — *-room*, aula; — *-war*, lotta di classe || *evening —*, corso serale; *the lower* (o *working*) *classes*, le classi lavoratrici; *the middle —*, il ceto medio; *second- —*, (*ferr.*) seconda classe: *to travel second —*, viaggiare in seconda classe.

to **class**, *v.t.* classificare || *not classed*, non classificato; fuori concorso (alle esposizioni).

classable [′klɑːsəbl], *ag.* classificabile.

classic [′klæsik], *ag.* classico || *s.* **1.** classico **2.** *pl.* studi classici, studi di umanità.

classical [′klæsikəl], *ag.* classico.

classically [′klæsikəli], *av.* classicamente.

classicism [′klæsisizəm], *s.* classicismo.

classicist [′klæsisist], *s.* classicista.

to **classicize** [′klæsisaiz], *v.t.i.* **1.** render classico **2.** imitare lo stile classico.

classifiable [′klæsifaiəbl], *ag.* classificabile.

classification [,klæsifi′keiʃən], *s.* classificazione.

classifier [′klæsifaiə*], *s.* classificatore.

to **classify** [′klæsifai], *v.t.* classificare || *the classified service*, (*amer.*) i funzionari, gli impiegati dello Stato (divisi in classi).

classman, *pl.* **classmen** [′klɑːsmən], *s.* studente di Oxford che si laurea con voti superiori al minimo o eccellenti.

classy [′klɑːsi], *ag.* (*fam.*) di buon gusto; di classe.

clastic [′klæstik], *ag.* (*geol.*) clastico ☆ — *rocks*, rocce clastiche.

clatter [′klætə*], *s.* **1.** acciottolio; fracasso **2.** (*fam.*) discorso animato, assordante.

to **clatter**, *v.t.i.* **1.** far fracasso; acciottolare (di stoviglie); far risuonare **2.** fare discorsi animati ma vuoti **3.** *to — about*, camminare facendo rumore.

clattering [′klætəriŋ], *ag.* strepitoso, rumoroso || *s.* V. **clatter**.

Claude [klɔːd], *no.pr.m.* Claudio.

Claudia [′klɔːdjə], *no.pr.f.* Claudia.

Claudius [′klɔːdjəs], *no.pr.m.* (*st.*) Claudio.

clause [klɔːz], *s.* **1.** clausola, articolo (di trattato, contratto, ecc.): — *of a law*, disposizione di legge **2.** (*gram.*) clausola, proposizione incidentale.

claustral [′klɔːstrəl], *ag.* claustrale.

claustrophobia [,klɔːstrə′foubjə], *s.* (*patol.*) claustrofobia.

clavate [′kleiveit], *ag.* (*bot.*) claviforme.

clave [kleiv], *pass.* di to **cleave**[2].

clavichord [′klævikɔːd], *s.* (*mus.*) clavicordio.

claviele [′klævikl], *s.* (*anat.*) clavicola.

clavicular [klə′vikjulə*], *ag.* (*anat.*) clavicolare.

claviform [′klævifɔːm], *ag.* claviforme.

claw [klɔː], *s.* **1.** artiglio, unghia: *to clip s.o.'s claws*, tagliare gli artigli a qlcu.; *fig.* ridurre qlcu. a miti consigli **2.** zampa (con artigli) **3.** chela, branca (di gambero, ecc.) **4.** uncino, raffio, griffa **5.** (*spreg.*) grinfia; sgrinfia, mano.

to **claw**, *v.t.i.* **1.** artigliare, dilaniare (con gli artigli); graffiare; (*arc.*) grattare **2.** *to — at* (*sthg.*), cercare di agguantare, di aggrapparsi a **3.** *to — off*, (*mar.*) prendere il largo.

clawed [klɔːd], *ag.* armato di artigli ☆ *sharp —*, dagli artigli affilati.

clay [klei], *s.* **1.** argilla; creta **2.** *fig.* il corpo umano ☆ — *-land*, terra argillosa; — *-pipe*, pipa di terracotta; — *-pit*, cava di argilla || *baked —*, terracotta; *fire- —*, argilla refrattaria; *potter's —*, argilla da stoviglie.

clayey [′kleii], *ag.* argilloso.

claymore [′kleimɔː*], *s.* (*scoz.*) spadone.

clean [kliːn], *ag.* **1.** pulito, nitido: — *linen*, biancheria di bucato || *as — as a new pin*, (*fam.*) pulito come uno specchio **2.** liscio; netto; deciso: — *outlines*, contorni netti **3.** ben fatto, ben proporzionato **4.** *fig.* puro, schietto; innocente; immune: — *and unclean animals*, animali mondi e immondi; *a — man*, un uomo leale; — *player*, giocatore impeccabile; — *tongue*, *fig.* linguaggio pulito || *to make a — sweep of sthg.*, far piazza pulita di ql.co. || *to make a — breast of sthg.*, fare una completa confessione di ql.co. || *to show a — pair of heels*, darsela a gambe || *s.* pulitura: *please, give my boots a —*, favorite dare una pulita alle mie scarpe.

to **clean**, *v.t.* **1.** pulire, nettare; mondare: *to — one's plate*, (*fam.*) pulire il piatto, vuotare il piatto **2.** *to — out*, vuotare e pulire (*p.e.* un armadio): *to — s.o. out*, (*fam.*) vuotare le tasche a qlcu. **3.** *to — up*, pulire ed assestare, fare pulizia; (*ind.*) rifinire: *to — oneself up*, (*fam.*) pulirsi.

clean. *av.* assolutamente; affatto; interamente, completamente: *I — forgot*, mi sono completamente dimenticato; *to cut — through*, tagliare da parte a parte.

clean, (*nei composti*): — *-bred*, di razza pura; — *-cut*, ben delineato (specialmente di lineamenti); — *-fingered*, agile di mani; *fig.* incorruttibile; — *-handed*, con le mani pulite (anche *fig.*); — *-handedness*, onestà, integrità; — *-minded*, puro d'animo; — *-mindedness*, purezza d'animo; — *-shaven*, completamente sbarbato; — *-up*, pulizia a fondo.

cleanable [′kliːnəbl], *ag.* che si può pulire.

cleaner [′kliːnə*], *s.c.* pulitore, pulitrice || *s.* (*ind.*) depuratore ☆ *dry- —*, smacchiatore a secco.

cleaning [′kliːniŋ], *s.* pulitura, pulizia ☆ — *-machine*, macchina pulitrice; — *-rod*, bacchetta (per pulire il fucile) || *dry- —*, lavaggio a secco; *spring- —*, pulizia di Pasqua.

cleanlily [′klenlili], *av.* in modo lindo, pulito.

cleanliness [′klenlinis], *s.* pulizia; lindura: — *of habit*, pulizia abituale.

cleanly [′klenli], *ag.* pulito, lindo (per abitudine); amante della pulizia.

cleanly [′kliːnli], *av.* in modo pulito, lindo.

cleanness [′kliːnnis], *s.* pulizia (anche *fig.*); nitidezza (di linee); purezza (dell'acqua).

to **cleanse** [klenz], *v.t.* **1.** pulire **2.** purificare (dal peccato, colpa, ecc.) **3.** (*med.*) depurare (sangue, ecc.); sanare (piaghe, ecc.); purgare **4.** (*pol.*) epurare.

cleanser [′klenzə*], *s.c.* pulitore, pulitrice || *s.* **1.** detersivo **2.** (*mec.*) pulitore; purificatore **3.** (*farm.*) depurativo, purgante.

cleansing [′klenziŋ], *ag.* purificante; risanante || *s.* **1.** purificazione (dell'anima); depurazione (del sangue) **2.** detersione ☆ — *-cream*, crema detergente (per la pelle); — *up*, (*pol.*) epurazione.

clear [klɪə*], *ag.* **1.** chiaro, limpido, trasparente; luminoso, brillante: *a — conscience*, una coscienza limpida; *a — day*, una giornata limpida, senza nuvole **2.** chiaro, distinto, evidente, manifesto: *— indication*, segno evidente; *it is — that*, è evidente, è chiaro che; *the meaning is —*, il significato è chiaro ‖ *as — as daylight*, (*fam.*) chiaro come il sole **3.** sicuro, certo: *to be — about sthg.*, essere sicuro di ql.co. **4.** assoluto, netto: *— majority*, netta maggioranza; *— profit*, guadagno netto **5.** libero; senza ostacoli; sgombro: *a — view of the sea*, vista aperta sul mare; *the town is — of the enemy*, la città è libera dal nemico ‖ *the coast is —*, (*fam.*) il campo è libero; non c'è pericolo ‖ *it's all — sailing*, (*fam.*) non ci sono ostacoli, difficoltà.

to **clear**, *v.t.i.* **1.** chiarire, chiarificare, chiarificarsi; schiarire, schiarirsi: *to — the air*, rinfrescare l'aria (di temporale); (*fam.*) mettere a punto (una questione); *to — a doubt*, chiarire un dubbio; *to — one's throat*, schiarirsi la gola **2.** dichiarare innocente; discolpare: *to — oneself*, discolparsi; *to — s.o. for secret defense work*, (*amer. pol.*) dichiarare qlcu. idoneo a lavoro segreto connesso con la difesa dello Stato; *to — s.o. of a charge*, dichiarare innocente un accusato **3.** sgomberare, liberare; vuotare: *to — the court*, (*dir.*) fare sgomberare l'aula; *to — the decks for action*, (*mar.*) preparare il ponte al combattimento; *fig.* prepararsi alla lotta; *to — the ground*, sgomberare il terreno (anche *fig.*); *to — the land*, disboscare un terreno; *to — a letter-box*, fare una levata (di posta); *to — one's plate*, vuotare il piatto; *to — a port*, (*mar.*) lasciare un porto; *to — the table*, sparecchiare la tavola; *to — the way for s.o.*, aprire la strada a qlcu. ‖ *coffee clears the head*, il caffè rischiara le idee **4.** superare (un ostacolo): *he cleared the fence*, egli superò lo steccato con un salto **5.** (*comm.*) liquidare (merci, debiti) **6.** (*comm.*) svincolare, sdoganare: *to — through the customs*, sdoganare **7.** (*comm.*) guadagnare al netto: *to — a thousand pounds*, fare un guadagno netto di mille sterline **8.** *to — away*, portare via; sparecchiare; dissiparsi (di nebbia) **9.** *to — off*, andarsene; liberarsi (da debiti) **10.** *to — out*, pulire (una stanza); vuotare (un armadio, ecc.); (*fam.*) scappare **11.** *to — up*, rassettare (una stanza); chiarire, spiegare (un malinteso, un mistero): *to — up a matter*, mettere in chiaro una faccenda.

clear, *av.* **1.** chiaramente, chiaro: *the sun is shining —*, il sole splende; *to speak —*, parlare chiaro **2.** completamente: *we went — round the globe*, abbiamo fatto il giro del mondo **3.** discosto; al di sopra: *to be — from suspicion*, essere al di sopra di ogni sospetto; *to get —*, togliersi da un impiccio; *to get — of*, allontanarsi da, liberarsi di; *to jump — of a hedge*, saltare al di sopra di una siepe; *to keep — of*, tenersi lontano da; *to stand —*, stare lontano (da pericoli, ecc.).

clear, (nei composti): *— -cut*, stagliato nettamente; *— -eyed*, dagli occhi luminosi; dalla vista buona; *fig.* perspicace; *— -sighted*, dalla vista buona; *fig.* perspicace ‖ *all— —*, (segnale di) cessato allarme.

clearance [ˈklɪərəns], *s.* **1.** chiarificazione **2.** sgombro (di sala, ecc.) **3.** (*comm.*) sdoganamento **4.** *— (sale)*, liquidazione di merce **5.** (*mec.*) giuoco ☆ *— inwards*, (*mar.*) permesso d'entrata; *— outwards*, (*mar.*) permesso di uscita ‖ *customs —*, sdoganamento: *to effect customs —*, sbrigare le pratiche doganali.

clearer [ˈklɪərə*], *s.* chi rende chiaro, purifica.

clearing [ˈklɪərɪŋ], *s.* **1.** schiarimento **2.** terreno disboscato, dissodato **3.** rimozione; sgombro; levata (di posta) **4.** (*comm.*) compensazione ☆ *— hospital*, (*mil.*) ospedale da campo; *— -house*, (*comm.*) stanza di compensazione.

clearly [ˈklɪəli], *av.* chiaramente; distintamente.

clearness [ˈklɪənis], *s.* chiarezza; trasparenza; purezza; limpidezza (di stile, idee, ecc.).

cleat [kli:t], *s.* **1.** bietta, cuneo **2.** (*mec.*) gancio; costola di aggrappamento **3.** (*mar.*) galloccia, castagnola, tacchetto.

cleavability [ˌkli:vəˈbiliti], *s.* fissilità.

cleavable [ˈkli:vəbl], *ag.* fissile.

cleavage [ˈkli:vidʒ], *s.* fessura, spaccatura; (*miner.*) clivaggio, sfaldatura.

to **cleave**[1] [kli:v], *pass.* **cleaved** [kli:vd], **cleft** [kleft], (*letter.*) **clove** [klouv], (*arc.*) **clave** [kleiv], *p.p.* **cleaved**, **cleft**, (*letter.*) **cloven** [ˈklouvn], **clove**, *v.t.i.* fendere, fendersi; spaccare, spaccarsi: *to — a tree in two*, fendere un albero in due ☆ *cleft palate*, (*patol.*) gola lupina; *cloven hoof*, piede fesso (di ruminanti, ecc.).

to **cleave**[2], *pass.* **cleaved**, (*letter.*) **clave**, *p.p.* **cleaved**, *v.i.* aderire; attaccarsi: *to — to s.o.*, attaccarsi a qlcu., essere fedele a qlcu.; *to — to sthg.*, attaccarsi a ql.co.

cleaver [ˈkli:və*], *s.* **1.** chi fende, spacca **2.** mannaia (del macellaio).

cleavers [ˈkli:vəz], *s.* (*bot.*) caglio; lappa, lappola.

cleaving [ˈkli:viŋ], *s.* **1.** il fendere; lo spaccare **2.** spaccatura del legno secondo le fibre.

cleek [kli:k], *s.* **1.** bastone da golf con pomo di ferro **2.** grosso uncino.

clef [klef], *s.* (*mus.*) chiave ‖ *the Clef*, la chiave di do ☆ *bass- —*, chiave di basso, di fa; *treble —*, chiave di violino, di sol.

cleft [kleft], *s.* fenditura; spaccatura; fessura.

cleft, *pass.p.p.* di to **cleave**[1].

cleg [kleg], *s.* (*entom.*) tafano.

cleistogamic [ˌklaistouˈgæmik], *ag.* (*bot.*) cleistogamo.

to **clem** [klem], *v.t.i.* (far) morire di fame, di sete.

clematis [ˈklemətis], *s.* (*bot.*) clematide.

Clemence [ˈkleməns], *no.pr.f.* Clemenza.

clemency [ˈklemənsi], *s.* **1.** clemenza **2.** dolcezza (di carattere) **3.** mitezza (di clima).

clement[1] [ˈklemənt], *ag.* **1.** clemente **2.** dolce, gentile (di carattere) **3.** mite (di tempo).

Clement[2], *no.pr.m.* Clemente.

Clementina [ˌklemənˈti:nə], **Clementine** [ˈkleməntain], *no.pr.f.* Clementina.

clench [klentʃ], *s.* **1.** ribaditura; chiodo ribadito **2.** (*mar.*) ormeggio **3.** argomento decisivo **4.** (*boxe*) lotta a corpo a corpo.

to **clench**, *v.t.i.* **1.** stringere (mani, denti, ecc.), stringersi, serrarsi: *he clenched his fists*, chiuse rabbiosamente i pugni **2.** (*mar.*) assicurare (cavo) **3.** (*mec.*), ribadire: *to — a rivet*, ribadire un chiodo **4.** *fig.* confermare: *to — an argument*, confermare un argomento.

elencher [ˈklentʃə*], *s.* **1.** chi ribadisce **2.** (*mec.*) graffatrice **3.** *fig.* argomento decisivo.

Cleopatra [ˌkliəˈpɑ:trə], *no.pr.f.* (*st.*) Cleopatra.

clepsydra [ˈklepsidrə], *s.* clessidra.

clerestory [ˈkliəstəri], *s.* (*arch.*) parete di chiesa munita di finestre che danno sul tetto delle navate laterali.

clergy [ˈklə:dʒi], *s.* clero; gli ecclesiastici: *two hundred — were present*, duecento membri del clero erano presenti ‖ *benefit of —*, (*st.*) privilegio ecclesiastico.

clergyman, *pl.* **clergymen** [ˈklə:dʒimən], *s.* ecclesiastico; prete (cattolico, anglicano); pastore (protestante).

clergywoman [ˈklə:dʒi,wumən], *pl.* **clergywomen** [ˈklə:dʒi,wimin], *s.* (*scherz.*) moglie, figlia di pastore protestante.

cleric [ˈklerik], *ag.* (*arc.*) clericale ‖ *s.* ecclesiastico.

clerical [ˈklerikəl], *ag.* **1.** clericale, del clero **2.** di impiegato, di scrivano ‖ *s.* (*pol.*) clericale ☆ *— error*, errore di trascrizione; *— work*, lavoro d'ufficio.

clericalism [ˈklerikəlizəm], *s.* (*pol.*) clericalismo.

clericalist [ˈklerikəlist], *s.* (*pol.*) clericale.

to **clericalize** [ˈklerikəlaiz], *v.t.* clericalizzare; sottoporre all'influenza del clero.

clerically [ˈklerikəli], *av.* clericalmente.

clerk [klɑ:k], *s.* **1.** impiegato d'ufficio; commesso di studio: *— of the course*, (*spor.*) commissario di pista; — of the court, (dir.) cancelliere del tribunale; — of the works, ispettore di lavori eseguiti da un appaltatore **2.** (amer.) commesso di negozio **3.** chierico, ecclesiastico **4.** (arc.) erudito, letterato ☆ bank —, impiegato di banca; booking- —, bigliettaio; chief — (o head — o senior —), capo ufficio; invoice —, fatturista; junior —, giovane impiegato; town- —, segretario municipale.

to **clerk,** v.i. **1.** fare il commesso, l'impiegato: I clerked it for ten years, feci l'impiegato per dieci anni **2.** fungere da segretario.

clerkdom ['klɑːkdəm], s. **1.** lavoro di impiegato, di commesso **2.** ceto impiegatizio.

clerkless ['klɑːklis], ag. ignorante.

clerkly ['klɑːkli], ag. **1.** d'impiegato **2.** (arc.) istruito, sapiente.

clerkship ['klɑːkʃip], s. **1.** ufficio, posto di impiegato; ufficio di cancelliere (di tribunale) **2.** (arc.) sapere.

clever ['klevə*], ag. **1.** intelligente; abile, capace, esperto; ingegnoso: — at mathematics, forte in matematica; — at a trade, abile in un mestiere; a — child, un ragazzo sveglio; a — device, un dispositivo ingegnoso; a — painter, un pittore valente ‖ he was too — for me, (fam.) me l'ha fatta **2.** eseguito con abilità, intelligenza: a — book, un libro scritto con intelligenza **3.** disinvolto **4.** (amer.) amabile, cortese, gentile.

cleverish ['klevəriʃ], ag. abbastanza intelligente; abbastanza abile.

cleverly ['klevəli], av. intelligentemente; abilmente; ingegnosamente.

cleverness ['klevənis], s. intelligenza; abilità, capacità, maestria, destrezza; ingegnosità.

clevis ['klevis], s. uncino a forma di U.

clew [kluː], s. **1.** gomitolo di filo **2.** (mit.) filo conduttore: Ariadne's —, il filo di Arianna **3.** (mar.) anello e radancie; angolo di vela; corde di amaca.

to **clew,** v.t. (mar.) **1.** to — down (a sail), imbrogliare (una vela) **2.** to — up (a sail), alare, tirar su (una vela).

cliché ['kliːʃei], s. **1.** (tip.) « cliché », zincotipia **2.** fig. « cliché », frase stereotipata.

click[1] [klik], s. **1.** suono secco, metallico; scatto (di rivoltella, di ruota dentata, ecc.); tintinnio (di armi, ecc.); schiocco (di lingua) **2.** paletto (di porta) **3.** (mec.) dente di arresto ☆ — -clack, click clack (suono onomatopeico).

to **click**[1], v.t.i. (fare) produrre un suono secco; (fare) tintinnare, (fare) suonare: to — one's heels, (mil.) battere i tacchi (nel salutare); to — one's tongue, fare schioccare la lingua.

to **click**[2], v.i. (sl.) **1.** aver fortuna, raggiungere lo scopo **2.** andare d'accordo; innamorarsi ‖ at the end of the play they — off, of course, alla fine della commedia, com'era ovvio, si sposano.

clickety-click ['klikəti'klik], s.av. clic clac.

client ['klaiənt], s. **1.** cliente (di professionista, commerciante) **2.** (st. romana) cliente (di un patrizio).

clientage ['klaiəntidʒ], **clientele** [ˌklaiən'tel], s. clientela.

clientless ['klaiəntlis], ag. senza clientela.

cliff [klif], s. scogliera; falesia; dirupo.

cliffed [klift], ag. dirupato, scosceso, a picco.

cliffsman, pl. **cliffsmen** ['klifsmən], s. rocciatore.

cliffy ['klifi], ag. dirupato, scosceso, a picco.

climacteric [klai'mæktərik], ag. climaterico ‖ s. climaterio, età critica ☆ the — year, l'anno climaterico.

climactic [klai'mæktik], ag. **1.** (ret.) per gradazione ascendente (di uno scritto) **2.** arrivato al suo apogeo.

climate ['klaimit], s. clima.

climatic [klai'mætik], ag. climatico.

climatically [klai'mætikəli], av. climaticamente.

climatological [ˌklaimətə'lɔdʒikəl], ag. climatologico.

climatologist [ˌklaimə'tɔlədʒist], s. climatologo.

climatology [ˌklaimə'tɔlədʒi], s. climatologia.

climax ['klaimæks], s. **1.** (ret.) « climax » (idee, espressioni disposte in gradazione ascendente): to work up to a —, procedere per gradazione ascendente; (teat.) portare l'azione al culmine dell'intensità **2.** apice, culmine, colmo, acme (di discorso, scena, ecc.): their passion had reached a —, la loro passione era al colmo ‖ this brings matters to a —, (fam.) questo è il colmo.

climb [klaim], s. **1.** rampa, erta, salita **2.** ascesa, ascensione: — of 1200 feet in the first minute, (aer.) ascensione di 1200 piedi nel primo minuto ☆ — -down, discesa; fig. (fam.) disfatta, rinunzia; — indicator, (aer.) variometro, indicatore della velocità ascensionale.

to **climb,** pass.p.p. **climbed** [klaimd], (arc. dial.) **clomb** [kloum], v.t.i. **1.** arrampicare, arrampicarsi, salire (con sforzo) (anche fig.), ascendere; scalare; valicare: the road climbs, la strada sale; to — a mountain, scalare una montagna; to — a tree, arrampicarsi su un albero ‖ to — out of (a hole), uscire arrampicandosi da (un buco); to — over (a wall, etc.), scalare, scavalcare (un muro, ecc.); to — through, arrampicarsi attraverso; to — to power, salire al potere; to — up to the top of, arrampicarsi in cima a **2.** (aer.) prender quota **3.** to — down, scendere; fig. (fam.) abbandonare (pretese); tirarsi indietro; abbassar bandiera.

climbable ['klaiməbl], ag. scalabile.

climber ['klaimə*], s. **1.** scalatore **2.** (bot.) pianta rampicante **3.** uccello rampicante **4.** arrivista **5.** pl. ramponi (per scarponi) ☆ social —, arrampicatore sociale.

climbing ['klaimiŋ], ag. rampicante ‖ s. **1.** salita; scalata **2.** arrivismo ☆ — bird, plant, uccello, pianta rampicante; — flight, (aer.) volo ascendente; — power, (ferr. aer. aut.) potenza di salita; — speed, (aut. aer., ecc.) velocità di ascensione ‖ alpine —, alpinismo.

clime [klaim], s. (poet.) clima; regione.

(to) **clinch** [klintʃ], V. (to) **clench**.

clincher ['klintʃə*], V. **clencher**.

to **cling** [kliŋ], pass.p.p. **clung** [klʌŋ], v.i. aderire strettamente; stringersi; attaccarsi; aggrapparsi; avvinghiarsi: a dress which clings to the figure, un abito aderente; she clung to him, si strinse a lui; to — to a hope, fig. aggrapparsi a una speranza; to — to an opinion, fig. rimanere radicato in un'opinione; to — together, stringersi l'uno all'altro.

clinginess ['kliŋinis], s. adesione; aderenza (di abito).

clingstone ['kliŋstoun], ag. (bot.) duracino ‖ s. — (peach), (bot.) pesca duracina.

clinic[1] ['klinik], ag. clinico ‖ s. **1.** degente **2.** (st.) chi si fa battezzare solo in punto di morte.

clinic[2], s. (med.) **1.** istruzione clinica; clinica universitaria **2.** clinica (privata).

clinical ['klinikəl], ag. clinico ☆ — medicine, clinica medica.

clinically ['klinikəli], av. clinicamente.

clinician [kli'niʃən], s. clinico.

clink[1] [kliŋk], s. tintinnio (di bicchieri, spade, ecc.).

to **clink**[1], v.t.i. tintinnare; far tintinnare: to — glasses, far tintinnare i bicchieri.

clink[2], s. (sl.) prigione, gattabuia.

to **clink**[3], v.t. (dial.) ribadire.

clinker[1] ['kliŋkə*], s. **1.** mattone durissimo (olandese); mattone vetrificato **2.** massa di lava indurita; scoria ☆ basic —, scoria basica; vitreous —, scoria vitrea.

clinker[2], s. **1.** chi tintinna **2.** pl. (sl.) ceppi, catene.

clinker[3], s.c. chi ribadisce ‖ s. fig. argomento inconfutabile ☆ — -built, a fasciame cucito, a fasciame sovrapposto (di barca, battello, ecc.).

clinking ['kliŋkiŋ], ag. **1.** tintinnante **2.** (fam.) ottimo, straordinario: — good, ottimo, d'oro; — race, ottima razza ‖ s. tintinnio.

clinometer [klai'nomitə*], s. clinometro.

clinquant ['kliŋkənt], ag. scintillante.

Clio ['klaiou], no.pr.f. (mit.) Clio.

clip[1] [klip], *s.* **1.** molletta; fermaglio (a molla, per tenere insieme carte) **2.** (*med.*) graffa (per ferite); pinza per graffe **3.** ‹ clip ›, spilla **4.** (*tec.*) morsetto; anello d'attacco (per tubi); chiodo a gancio **5.** (*mil.*) nastro (per armi a ripetizione) ☆ *hair* —, forcina per capelli.

to clip[1], *pass.p.p.* **clipped** [klipt], *v.t.* **1.** unire, tenere insieme con un fermaglio **2.** (*neol.*) bucare (biglietto ferroviario, tranviario, ecc.) **3.** (*arc. dial.*) abbracciare.

clip[2], *s.* **1.** tosatura (di pecore); taglio (di capelli) **2.** ritaglio **3.** (*sl.*) scappellotto **4.** *pl.* tosatrice (macchinetta per tosare).

to clip[2], *pass.p.p.* **clipped,** *v.t.* **1.** tosare (pecore, cavalli, cani); tagliare (una siepe); ritagliare, tosare (una moneta per falsarne il peso) ‖ *to — one's words,* (*fam.*) biascicare, mangiare le parole ‖ *to — s.o.'s claws, wings,* tagliare le unghie, tarpare le ali a qlcu. **2.** dare uno scappellotto a: *to — s.o.'s ear,* (*sl.*) dare uno scappellotto a qlcu.

clippable ['klipəbl], *ag.* che si può tosare.

clipper ['klipə*], *s.* **1.** tosatore **2.** (*arc. mar.*) goletta **3.** (*fam.*) cavallo veloce **4.** (*neol. aer.*) grande velivolo per trasporto passeggeri, aeroplano transatlantico **5.** *pl.* macchinetta, forbici per tosare, tosatrice **6.** (*sl*) persona, cosa che desta ammirazione ☆ — -built, (*mar.*) con prua lunga e aguzza.

clipping ['klipiŋ], *ag.* **1.** tagliente **2.** agile **3.** (*sl.*) ottimo, eccellente ‖ *s.* **1.** tosatura (di pecore) **2.** (*metal.*) sbavatura **3.** ritaglio (di un giornale).

clique [kli:k], *s.* cricca; combriccola.

cliquish ['kli:kiʃ], *ag.* di cricca.

cliquishness ['kli:kiʃnis], *s.* cameratismo; spirito di parte.

cliqu(e)y ['kli:ki], *V.* **cliquish.**

clitoris ['klaitəris], *s.* (*anat.*) clitoride.

clitter-clatter ['klitə′klætə*], *s.* chiacchiere, discorso inutile.

clo' [klou], *s.pl.* (*abbr.* di *clothes*) abiti ‖ *old —!,* (*fam.*) (si vendono) abiti vecchi, usati!.

cloaca [klou′eikə], *pl.* **cloaceae** [klou′eiki:], *s.* cloaca.

cloak [klouk], *s.* **1.** mantello; *fig.* manto, velo: — *of snow,* manto di neve; *under the — of night,* sotto il velo della notte **2.** pretesto, scusa: *under the — of,* sotto il pretesto di ☆ — -and-dagger (o — -and-sword) *story,* (*neol.*) romanzo di cappa e spada; — -room, guardaroba; (*ferr.*) deposito bagagli.

to cloak, *v.t.i.* **1.** coprire, coprirsi con un mantello **2.** *fig.* dissimulare, mascherare, nascondere (pensieri, progetti, ecc.).

clock[1] [klok], *s.* orologio (da muro); pendola ‖ *what o' — is it?, it is one, two o' —,* che ora è?, è l'una, sono le due ‖ *to sleep the — round,* dormire per dodici ore filate ‖ *to work the — round,* lavorare per dodici ore di seguito ‖ *alarm-* — (o *alarum-*—), sveglia; *eight-day —,* orologio con otto giorni di carica; *grandfather('s) —,* grande orologio a pendolo; *time —,* orologio di controllo (in uffici, fabbriche, ecc.); *tower —,* orologio da torre, da campanile; *water —,* clessidra idrica.

to clock[1], *v.t.i.* **1.** (*neol.*) cronometrare **2.** *to — in, to — out,* far scattare l'orologio di controllo (all'entrata, all'uscita da uffici, fabbriche, ecc.).

to clock[2], *v.t.i.* (*dial.*) covare (le uova).

clock[3], *pl.* **clocks, clox** [kloks], *s.* freccia, baghetta (sottile ricamo di seta su una calza o calzino).

clocklike ['kloklaik], *ag.* di, simile ad orologio.

clockmaker ['klok‚meikə*], *s.* orologiaio.

clockwise ['klokwaiz], *ag.* in senso orario (delle lancette dell'orologio, da sinistra a destra) ☆ *counter-* —, in senso antiorario (contrario a quello delle lancette dell'orologio, da destra a sinistra).

clockwork ['klokwə:k], *s.* orologeria (meccanismo e movimento): *everything is going like* —, tutto procede con la regolarità di un orologio.

clod [klod], *s.* **1.** zolla; terra, suolo, argilla: *to break*

(*up*) *the clods,* rompere le zolle **2.** (*letter.*) corpo umano **3.** rustico, zoticone **4.** forcella (parte bassa del collo nel bue macellato) ☆ — -hopper, contadinaccio, zoticone.

to clod, *pass.p.p.* **clodded** ['klodid], *v.t.i.* lanciare zolle; colpire con zolle.

cloddish ['klodiʃ], *ag.* **1.** zolloso, terroso **2.** zotico, rozzo; villano.

cloddishness ['klodiʃnis], *s.* rozzezza; villania.

cloddy ['klodi], *s.* zolloso, terroso.

clog [klog], *s.* **1.** ceppo, pastoia; impedimento, intoppo, impaccio (anche *fig.*) **2.** intasamento **3.** zoccolo ☆ — -dance, danza con gli zoccoli.

to clog, *pass.p.p.* **clogged** [klogd], *v.t.i.* **1.** legare (un animale) con ceppo, pastoia; ingombrare, inceppare, impedire (anche *fig.*): *the cart could not advance for it was clogged with mud,* il carro non poteva avanzare perchè impedito dal fango; *my memory is clogged,* la mia memoria fa cilecca **2.** ostruire, ostruirsi; intasare, intasarsi: *the pipe was clogged with dirt,* il tubo era intasato.

clogging ['klogiŋ], *s.* inceppamento, ingombro, impedimento.

cloggy ['klogi], *ag.* **1.** nodoso **2.** viscoso, adesivo, appiccicaticcio.

cloister ['kloistə*], *s.* **1.** chiostro; convento; monastero **2.** chiostro (loggiato nel cortile di una chiesa o d'un convento).

to cloister, *v.t.* rinchiudere in un chiostro.

cloistered ['kloistəd], *ag.* **1.** rinchiuso in un chiostro **2.** munito di chiostro ☆ — nun, suora di clausura.

cloisterer ['kloistərə*], *s.c.* chi vive in un chiostro.

cloistral ['kloistrəl], *ag.* claustrale.

clomb [kloum], *pass.p.p.* (*arc. dial.*) di to **climb.**

clonic ['klonik], *ag.* (*patol.*) clonico ☆ — spasms, spasmi clonici.

clonus ['klounəs], *s.* (*patol.*) clono, spasmo clonico.

cloop [klu:p], *s.* rumore di turacciolo estratto.

to cloop, *v.i.* fare il rumore di turacciolo che viene estratto.

close[1] [klous], *ag.* **1.** chiuso: — *character,* carattere chiuso; — *corporation,* corporazione chiusa, limitata ad un determinato ceto di persone; — *vowel,* vocale chiusa **2.** serrato: — *combat,* combattimento a corpo a corpo; — *contest,* lotta serrata (nelle elezioni politiche); — *finish,* (*spor.*) arrivo serrato (in una corsa); *in — order,* (*mil.*) in file serrate; — *reasoning,* ragionamento serrato ‖ *to come to — quarters,* (*fam.*) venire alle mani **3.** rinchiuso; viziato (di aria); afoso: — *smell,* odore di stantio; — *weather,* tempo afoso, soffocante **4.** compatto, solido, denso, conciso (di stile): — *texture,* tessuto fitto, compatto **5.** nascosto, segreto: — *secret,* segreto impenetrabile; *to keep* (o *to lie*) —, tenersi nascosto **6.** stretto, intimo: — *friend,* amico intimo; — *resemblance,* stretta somiglianza; *in — touch with s.o.,* in intimo contatto con qlcu. **7.** vicino: *his house is quite* —, la sua casa è proprio vicina **8.** attento, accurato: — *analysis,* analisi accurata; — *shave,* rasatura accurata; (*fig. fam.*) scampato pericolo; — *translation,* traduzione precisa, fedele; *you must give me your — attention,* dovete ascoltarmi attentamente **9.** avaro, parsimonioso **10.** riservato, discreto: *to be — about sthg.,* non dire niente in merito a ql.co.

close[1], *s.* spazio cintato; recinto; chiuso; area circostante una cattedrale; campo da giuoco (di scuole, ecc.).

close[1], *av.* vicino, da vicino, presso: *the closer we look into the question...,* più a fondo esaminiamo la questione...; *keep — the wall,* tenetevi vicino al muro; *stay — by me,* state vicino a me; *to be — behind s.o.,* seguire qlcu. da presso; *to cut prices* —, (*comm.*) calcolare i prezzi al minimo; *to sit, to stand* —, tenersi vicino a; *to sit closer* (*together*), sedersi più vicino; *to stand — in to the land*, (*mar.*) tenersi vicino alla costa.

close[1], (*nei composti*): — *call*, (*fam.*) scampato pericolo; — -*cropped* (o — -*cut*), tagliato raso (di capelli, erba, ecc.); — -*fisted*, spilorcio; — -*fitting*, aderente (di vestito); — -*hauled*, (*mar.*) stretto di bolina; — -*lipped* (o — -*mouthed* o — -*tongued*), parco di parole, riservato; — -*meshed*, a piccole maglie (di rete); — *season* (o — *time*), stagione, tempo in cui è vietata la caccia, la pesca; — -*set*, molto accostati (di occhi, denti); — -*shaven*, rasato con cura; — -*up*, (*cine.*) primo piano; — -*woven*, tessuto fitto (di stoffa).

close[2] [klouz], *s.* **1.** fine, termine: *at — of day*, al termine del giorno **2.** corpo a corpo: *to come to a —*, venire a un corpo a corpo **3.** (*mus.*) cadenza.

to **close**[2], *v.t.i.* **1.** chiudere, chiudersi: *the door closed*, la porta si chiuse; *he closed the door*, egli chiuse la porta; *to — the books*, (*comm.*) bilanciare i conti, chiudere i libri; *to — a circuit*, (*elett.*) chiudere un circuito; *to — the wind*, (*mar.*) serrare il vento **2.** terminare, concludere, finire, porre fine a: *the meeting closed at eight o' clock*, la riunione terminò alle otto; *to — a discussion, a speech*, por fine a una discussione, a un discorso; *to — one's days*, finire i propri giorni, morire **3.** (*mar. mil.*) avvicinarsi, riavvicinarsi: *to — ranks*, serrare le file **4.** *to — about* (*s.o.*, *sthg.*), avvicinarsi; avvolgere; circondare, accerchiare: *darkness closed about us*, l'oscurità ci avvolse; *io — about an army*, accerchiare un esercito **5.** *to — with* (*s.o.*, *sthg.*), venire ad un accordo con; venire a corpo a corpo con: *to — with an offer*, (*comm.*) accettare un'offerta **6.** *to — down*, (*amer.*) chiudere (fabbrica, stabilimento) **7.** *to — in*, avvicinarsi, circondare; accorciarsi (di giorni, ecc.): *the enemy closed in upon us*, il nemico ci circondò **8.** *to — up*, turare; otturare, otturarsi; sbarrare (strada); serrare: — *up!*, (*mil.*) serrate le file! ☆ — -*down*, (*amer.*) chiusura (di fabbrica, stabilimento); — -*out*, (*amer. comm.*) saldo per liquidazione.

closed [klouzd], *ag.* chiuso ☆ — *chain*, (*chim.*) a catena chiusa; — *circuit*, (*elett.*) circuito chiuso; — *course*, (*spor.*) circuito chiuso; — *economy*, (*econ. pol.*) economia chiusa; — *professions*, professioni chiuse; — *road*, strada chiusa (al traffico); — *season*, (*amer.*) stagione in cui è vietata la caccia o la pesca; — *shop*, azienda che assume unicamente personale iscritto alle Trade Unions.

closely ['klousli], *av.* **1.** strettamente, da vicino: — *contested*, vivamente contestato; — *related*, strettamente affine; parente **2.** attentamente: — *guarded*, guardato, custodito attentamente.

closeness ['klousnis], *s.* **1.** mancanza d'aria, aria viziata (di stanza, ecc.); afa **2.** compattezza; densità; concisione (di stile) **3.** segretezza **4.** intimità (di contatto, amicizia, ecc.); vincolo (di affetto, interesse) **5.** prossimità, vicinanza **6.** accuratezza, precisione, esattezza (di descrizione, ecc.) **7.** avarizia, parsimonia **8.** riservatezza, discrezione.

closer ['klouzə*], *s.* chi chiude; chi conclude, termina.

closet ['klozit], *s.* **1.** gabinetto; salotto privato, studio **2.** armadio a muro; (*spec. amer.*) credenza ☆ — -*play*, lavoro drammatico destinato solo alla lettura; — -*strategist*, stratega da tavolino ‖ *water*- — (*abbr. W. C.*), gabinetto di decenza.

to **closet**, *v.t.* chiudere in una stanza ‖ *to be closeted with s.o.*, tenere un colloquio privato con qlcu.

closing ['klouziŋ], *ag.* di chiusura, ultimo: *the days of March*, gli ultimi giorni di marzo ‖ *s.* chiusura (di fabbrica, teatro, seduta, ecc.) ☆ — *price*, (*Borsa*) prezzo di chiusura; — *speech*, discorso di chiusura; — *time*, ora di chiusura; — *time!*, si chiude! ‖ *early — day*, (*comm.*) giorno di chiusura pomeridiana (di negozi); *Sunday —*, (*comm.*) chiusura domenicale.

closure ['klouзə*], *s.* chiusura, fine; termine (di

una seduta, di un dibattito parlamentare, ecc.): *to move the —*, votare la mozione di chiusura.

clot [klɔt], *s.* grumo: — *on the brain*, (*patol.*) embolo cerebrale; coagulo.

to **clot**, *pass.p.p.* **clotted** ['klɔtid], *v.t.i.* raggrumare, raggrumarsi; coagulare, coagularsi: *clotted cream*, (*cuc.*) panna rappresa (di latte in ebollizione); *clotted hair*, capelli appicciati.

cloth [klɔθ], *pl.* **cloths** [klɔθs], *s.* **1.** panno, tessuto, stoffa, tela: — *in the piece*, stoffa in pezza; *coarse —*, tela ordinaria; *map mounted on —*, carta geografica montata su tela; *a piece of —*, un pezzo di stoffa ‖ *cut your coat according to the —*, prov. non fare il passo più lungo della gamba **2.** tessuto di lana **3.** (*mar.*) ferzo **4.** cencio per spolverare **5.** (*table-*) —, tovaglia: *to lay, to remove the —*, apparecchiare, sparecchiare la tavola **6.** abito (religioso): *respect to the —*, il rispetto dovuto all'abito **7.** *fig.* il clero ☆ — -*binding*, rilegatura in tela; — -*bound*, rilegato in tela; — -*hall*, (*arc.*) mercato delle stoffe; — -*maker*, fabbricante di stoffe ‖ *brown —*, tela greggia; *cotton —*, tela di cotone; *dish* - —, strofinaccio (da cucina); *duck —*, (*mar.*) tela da vele; *fancy —*, stoffa fantasia; *linen —*, tela di lino; *packing —*, tela da imballaggio; *tea-* —, tovaglia da tè; *tracing —*, tela da lucido, da disegno; *vicuña —*, vigogna; *water-proof —*, stoffa impermeabile; *wire —*, rete metallica.

to **clothe** [klouð], *pass.p.p.* **clothed** [klouðd], (*arc. letter.*) **clad** [klæd], *v.t.* vestire, abbigliare, rivestire (anche *fig.*): *clad in armour*, rivestito di armatura; *clothed in glory*, rivestito di gloria; *she was clothed in white*, era vestita di bianco; *to — the naked*, vestire gli ignudi; *to — oneself in wool*, vestirsi, coprirsi di lana; *to — thoughts in verse*, mettere in versi i pensieri; *to — with leaves*, coprire di foglie; *to — with power*, investire di un potere.

clothes [klouðz], *s.pl.* **1** abiti, vestiti, indumenti: *cast-off —*, abiti smessi; *old —*, abiti vecchi; *suit of —*, completo, abito intero; *to put one's — on*, vestirsi; *to sleep in one's —*, dormire vestito; *to take one's — off*, svestirsi **2.** biancheria da letto: *soiled —*, biancheria sporca ☆ — -*basket*, cesta per la biancheria; — -*brush*, spazzola per vestiti; — -*hook*, attaccapanni; — -*horse*, cavalletto per stendere il bucato; — -*line*, corda per stendere il bucato; — -*moth*, (*entom.*) tignola; — -*peg* (o — -*pin*), molletta ferma-bucato; — -*press*, guardaroba; — -*prop* (o *amer.* — -*pole*), palo di sostegno della corda ove è steso il bucato; — -*wringer*, macchina per torcere il bucato ‖ *old — man*, venditore di abiti usati; *Sunday go-to meeting —*, vestito della festa.

clothier ['klouðiə*], *s.* **1.** fabbricante di tessuti, di stoffe **2.** commerciante in stoffe, abiti **3.** sarto.

Clothilda [klou'tildə], *no.pr.f.* Clotilde.

clothing ['klouðiŋ], *s.* **1.** vestiario, abiti, indumenti: *articles of —*, capi di vestiario, abiti; biancheria; *soiled —*, biancheria sporca **2.** coperta, copertura ☆ *the — trade*, l'industria dell'abbigliamento.

Clotho [klouθou], *no.pr.f.* (*mit.*) Cloto.

clotting ['klɔtiŋ], *s.* coagulazione.

clotty ['klɔti], *ag.* grumoso.

cloud [klaud], *s.* **1.** nube; nuvola ‖ *in the clouds*, *fig.* nelle nuvole: *to be in the clouds*, avere il capo tra le nuvole ‖ *under a —*, in discredito, in sospetto: *to be under a —*, essere in discredito, in sospetto ‖ *wait till the clouds roll by*, aspetta circostanze più favorevoli ‖ *to drop from the clouds*, cadere dal cielo, capitare all'improvviso ‖ *every — has a silver lining*, prov. dopo il brutto viene il bello **2.** nugolo (di insetti); nuvola (di polvere, fumo) **3.** (*chim.*) intorbidamento **4.** macchia, chiazza (su marmo, pietre preziose) **5.** scialle di lana **6.** *fig.* scontento, malumore: *a — was over his face*, aveva la faccia scura ☆ — -*amount*, nuvolosità; — -*burst*, raffica di pioggia; — -*capped*, ammantato di nuvole; — -*castle*, fantasticherie; —

-ceiling, cappa; — *-cuckoo-town*, cuccagna; — *-drift*, nuvole fluttuanti, vapore fluttuante; — *-fenced*, circondato di nuvole; — *-kissing*, che tocca le nuvole, il cielo (di monte, edificio); — *-land*, regno delle nuvole, dei sogni; — *-like*, simile alle nuvole; — *-rack*, nembo.

to **cloud**, *v.t.i.* **1.** annuvolare, annuvolarsi; oscurare; offuscare, appannare || *to — the issue*, ingarbugliare la questione || *to —* (*up*, *over*), coprirsi di nubi, annuvolarsi; oscurarsi **2.** macchiare; screziare; intorbidare **3.** *fig.* rattristare, rattristarsi; rendere, diventare di cattivo umore **4.** *fig.* macchiare (reputazione), disonorare.

clouded ['klaudid], *ag.* **1.** annuvolato, coperto: — *sky*, cielo coperto **2.** torbido; screziato: — *gem*, pietra screziata; — *liquid*, liquido torbido; — *mind*, mente offuscata.

cloudily ['klaudili], *av.* nebulosamente; in modo incerto.

cloudiness ['klaudinis], *s.* **1.** nuvolosità, nebulosità; oscurità **2.** torbidezza (di liquidi) **3.** venatura, striatura, screziatura (di marmi, pietre preziose) **4.** *fig.* tristezza; cattivo umore.

cloudless ['klaudlis], *ag.* senza nubi, sereno.

cloudlessly ['klaudlisli], *av.* senza nubi.

cloudlet ['klaudlit], *s.* nuvoletta.

cloudy ['klaudi], *ag.* **1.** nuvoloso; oscuro **2.** opaco, torbido (di liquidi) **3.** venato, striato, screziato (di marmi, pietre preziose) **4.** *fig.* triste; di cattivo umore.

clough [klʌf], *s.* burrone, voragine.

clout[1] [klaut], *s.* (*arc. dial.*) **1.** rattoppo, toppa **2.** straccio, cencio **3.** placca di metallo (per scarpe, per proteggere l'asse di una ruota) **4.** colpo secco; schiaffo **5.** indumento, maglia, sottoveste || *never cast a — till May is out*, *prov.* aprile non ti scoprire, maggio va adagio **6.** (*st.*) bersaglio (nel tiro dell'arco).

to **clout**[1], *v.t.* (*arc. dial.*) **1.** rattoppare, rappezzare (anche *fig.*) **2.** proteggere (con placca, chiodi di metallo) **3.** dare un forte schiaffo.

clout[2], *s.* (*arc. dial.*) zolla di terra.

clove[1] [klouv], *s.* (*bot.*) spicchio (d'aglio, ecc.).

clove[2], *s.* **1.** (*cuc.*) chiodo di garofano **2.** (*bot.*) garofano **3.** (*fam.*) essenza di garofano.

to **clove**[2], *v.t.* (*cuc.*) aromatizzare con chiodi di garofano.

clove[3], *s.* fenditura; crepaccio.

clove[4], *abbr.* di **cloven** || *ag.* (*poet.*) diviso, spaccato in due ☆ — *-hitch*, (*mar.*) doppio collo, (nodo) parlato.

clove[4], *pass.* di to **cleave**[1].

cloven ['klouvn], *p.p.* di to **cleave**[1].

clover ['klouvə*], *s.* (*bot.*) trifoglio || *to be* (o *to live) in —*, *fig.* vivere comodamente, nell'abbondanza ☆ — *leaf*, (*amer.*) incrocio a quadrifoglio (di strade) || *sweet —*, meliloto, trifoglio odoroso.

clown [klaun], *s.* **1.** villano, zoticone; rustico **2.** clown, pagliaccio, buffone (specialmente di circo).

to **clown**, *v.i.* fare il pagliaccio.

clownery ['klaunəri], *s.* buffoneria, pagliacciata.

clownish ['klauniʃ], *ag.* **1.** zotico, rozzo; grossolano **2.** pagliaccesco, buffonesco.

clownishly ['klauniʃli], *av.* **1.** rozzamente, grossolanamente **2.** da pagliaccio.

clownishness ['klauniʃnis], *s.* **1.** rozzezza; grossolanità **2.** pagliacciata.

to **cloy** [klɔi], *v.t.* saziare, satollare, rimpinzare; nauseare: *cloyed with chocolates*, rimpinzato di cioccolatini; *cloyed with pleasure*, nauseato dai piaceri; *to — the appetite*, saziare l'appetito; *to — the reader*, stancare il lettore.

club [klʌb], *s.* **1.** randello, mazza, clava; bastone **2.** « club », circolo, gruppo, associazione, società: *a — of wits*, un circolo di buontemponi **3.** (*carte*) fiori; bastoni: *ace of clubs*, asso di fiori **4.** (*aer.*) mulinello, elica di prova ☆ — *-foot*, piede deforme, equino — *-footed*, dal piede deforme; — *-house*, circolo, luogo di ritrovo (riservato ai soci); — *-land*, rione dei circoli

a Londra (St. James e Piccadilly); — *-law*, la legge del bastone, del più forte; — *-man*, frequentatore di circoli; (*amer.*) uomo di mondo; — *-moss*, (*bot.*) licopodio clavato; — *-room*, sala delle adunanze (in circoli); — *-root*, (*bot.*) malattia delle rape; — *sandwich*, (*amer.*) grosso panino imbottito || *country —*, circolo di campagna; *Indian clubs*, (*ginnastica*) clave; *social —*, circolo familiare.

to **club**, *pass.p.p.* **clubbed** [klʌbd], *v.t.i.* **1.** colpire con una mazza; bastonare; picchiare con il calcio del fucile: *to — s.o. to death*, uccidere qlcu. a colpi di bastone **2.** riunirsi in società, formare un circolo; riunirsi (specialmente per sottoscrizioni): *to — with others for sthg.*, *to do sthg.*, associarsi ad altri per ql.co., per fare ql.co. **3.** pagare il proprio tributo (denaro, idee, ecc.) **4.** (*mar.*) scarrocciare con l'ancora.

clubbable ['klʌbəbl], *ag.* socievole.

clubbed [klʌbd], *ag.* **1.** claviforme **2.** usato come una mazza.

clubby ['klʌbi], *ag.* socievole.

to **clubhaul** ['klʌb'hɔ:l], *v.t.* (*mar.*) far virare di bordo (una nave) gettando l'ancora sottovento.

cluck [klʌk], *s.* il chiocciare (della gallina).

to **cluck**, *v.i.* chiocciare (della gallina).

clucky ['klʌki], *ag.* che chioccia ☆ — *hen*, chioccia.

clue [klu:], *s.* **1.** indizio, indicazione, traccia: *to get* (o *to find) the —* *to sthg.*, trovare, scoprire la chiave, il bandolo di ql.co.; *to have the —*, avere un indizio: *the police have got the —*, la polizia è sulla pista **2.** filo di un racconto **3.** (*rar.*) *V.* **clew 3.**

clueless ['klu:lis], *ag.* senza tracce; senza indicazioni.

clumber ['klʌmbə*], *s.* (cane) dalmata.

clump [klʌmp], *s.* **1.** blocco; massa; pezzo (di legno, ecc.) || *to give s.o. a — on the head*, (*sl.*) dare una botta in testa a qlcu. **2.** gruppo (di alberi, arbusti) **3.** grossa suola di rinforzo **4.** passo pesante **5.** (*med.*) agglutinazione **6.** (*tip.*) lingotto.

to **clump**, *v.t.i.* **1.** ammucchiare; raggruppare, raggrupparsi in massa compatta; (*med.*) aggregarsi, agglutinarsi **2.** piantare (alberi) in gruppi **3.** mettere una suola di rinforzo a (scarpe) **4.** camminare pesantemente || *to — s.o.'s head*, (*sl.*) dare una botta in testa a qlcu.

clumsily ['klʌmzili], *av.* goffamente, rozzamente; senza grazia.

clumsiness ['klʌmzinis], *s.* goffaggine, rozzezza; mancanza di tatto.

clumsy ['klʌmzi], *ag.* goffo, rozzo; senza grazia; senza tatto: — *apology*, scusa goffa; — *person*, persona goffa; — *verse*, poesia senza grazia.

clung [klʌŋ], *pass.p.p.* di to **cling**.

cluster ['klʌstə*], *s.* grappolo (d'uva, ecc.); mazzo (di fiori); gruppo (d'alberi); ammasso (di stelle); mucchio, cumulo; capannello, folla; sciame: *a — of bees*, uno sciame di api; *a — of roses*, un mazzo di rose: *to come in a —*, venire in folla || *hair in thick clusters*, capelli a grossi ricci ☆ — *-candlestick*, candelabro; — *-pine*, (*bot.*) pinastro.

to **cluster**, *v.t.i.* crescere a grappoli, a mazzi; riunire, riunirsi; ammucchiare; raggruppare, raggrupparsi; agglomerarsi, conglomerarsi: *to — round s.o.*, *sthg.*, raccogliersi intorno a qlcu., a ql.co. ☆ *clustered column*, (*arch.*) colonna polistile, pilastro a fascio.

clutch[1] [klʌtʃ], *s.* **1.** stretta, presa; artiglio, grinfia: *to be in s.o.'s clutches*, essere nelle grinfie di qlcu.; *to fall into s.o.'s clutches*, cadere nelle grinfie di qlcu.; *to make a — at sthg.*, cercare di afferrare ql.co. **2.** (*mec.*) innesto ☆ — *-pedal*, pedale d'innesto || *cone- —*, innesto a cono; *friction —*, innesto a frizione; *hydraulic —*, frizione idraulica; *single-plate —*, frizione monodisco; *starting - —*, frizione di avviamento.

to **clutch**[1], *v.t.i.* afferrare, afferrarsi; aguantare; stringere convulsamente: *to — sthg. with both hands*, afferrare ql.co. con entrambe le mani || *to — at sthg.* (o *to — hold of sthg.*), aggrapparsi, attaccarsi a ql.co.

clutch², s. covata; (spreg.) famiglia.

to clutch², v.t. covare.

clutter ['klʌtə*], s. **1.** rumore; schiamazzo **2.** confusione, disordine **3.** ingombro.

to clutter, v.t.i. **1.** far confusione, baccano **2.** muoversi disordinatamente **3.** to — up, ingombrare: the room is cluttered up with furniture, la stanza è piena zeppa di mobili.

Clyde [klaid], no.pr. (geog.) Clyde ☆ — -bank, il bacino industriale di Glasgow.

clypeate ['klipieit], ag. clipeato.

clypeiform ['klipiifo:m], ag. clipeiforme.

clypeus ['klipiəs], pl. **clypei** ['klipiai], s. (entom.) clipeo.

clyster ['klistə*], s. (arc.) clistere.

Clytemnestra [,klaitim'nestrə], no.pr.f. (lett.) Clitennestra.

coach [koutʃ], s. **1.** carrozza, cocchio; pullman, torpedone; (ferr.) carrozza, vettura: they went to Florence by —, sono andati a Firenze in pullman **2.** insegnante privato, ripetitore **3.** allenatore (di atleti) ☆ — and four, tiro a quattro; — and six, tiro a sei: to drive — and six through an act of Parliament, (fam.) abrogare una legge del Parlamento; — -box, cassetta (del cocchiere); — -horse, cavallo da traino; — -house, rimessa; — -stand, posteggio di vetture da nolo ‖ hackney - —, carrozza da nolo; mail- —, diligenza, vettura postale; motor- —, torpedone; mourning- —, carro funebre; royal —, carrozza di corte; stage- —, diligenza, corriera; stale- —, carrozza di gala.

to coach, v.t.i. **1.** andare in carrozza, in diligenza: to — to..., andare in diligenza a... **2.** dare, prendere delle lezioni private **3.** allenare (atleti).

coachbuilder ['koutʃ,bildə*], s. carrozziere.

coachbuilding ['koutʃ,bildiŋ], s. fabbricazione di carrozze.

coachful ['koutʃful], s. carrozzata.

coaching ['koutʃiŋ], s. **1.** l'andare in carrozza, in diligenza ‖ in the old — days, al tempo delle diligenze **2.** ripetizioni, lezioni: to give private —, dare ripetizioni, lezioni private **3.** allenamento (di atleti).

coachman, pl. **coachmen** ['koutʃmən], s. cocchiere.

coachwork ['koutʃwə:k], s. carrozzeria; lavoro di carrozzeria.

to coact [kou'ækt], v.i. agire insieme.

coadjacent [,kouə'dʒeisnt], ag. contiguo.

coadjutor [kou'ædʒutə*], s. **1.** collaboratore **2.** (eccl.) coadiutore.

coadjutrix [kou'ædʒutriks], s. collaboratrice.

coadunate [kou'ædjunit], ag. (bot. fisiol.) unito congenitamente.

coagulability [kou,ægjulə'biliti], s. coagulabilità.

coagulable [kou'ægjuləbl], ag. coagulabile.

coagulant [kou'ægjulənt], s. sostanza coagulante.

to coagulate [kou'ægjuleit], v.t.i. coagulare, coagularsi.

coagulation [kou,ægju'leiʃən], s. coagulazione.

coagulator [kou'ægjuleitə*], s. coagulante.

coagulum [kou'ægjuləm], s. coagulo.

coal [koul], s. carbone ‖ to blow (o to fan) the coals, fig. soffiare sul fuoco, eccitare le passioni ‖ to carry coals to Newcastle, portar acqua al mare ‖ to haul (o to call) s.o. over the coals, (fam.) dare una lavata di capo a qlcu. ‖ to heap coals of fire on s.o.'s head, suscitar rimorso restituendo bene per male ☆ — -bag, sacco del carbone; — -bearing, carbonifero; — -bed, bacino carbonifero; — -black, nero come il carbone; — -box, secchio per il carbone; — -bunker, carbonile, carbonaia; — -cellar, deposito sotterraneo di carbone; — -fed, (mec.) alimentato a carbone; — -firing, (mec.) riscaldamento a carbone; — -gas, gas illuminante; — -heaver (o — -lumper), scaricatore di carbone; — -master (o — -owner), proprietario di miniera di carbone; — -mine (o — -pit), miniera di carbone; — -scuttle, secchio per il carbone; — -shovel (o — -scoop), pala per il carbone; — -tar, catrame minerale; — -whip-

per, (mec.) scaricatrice di carbone ‖ bituminous —, carbone bituminoso; brown —, lignite; cannel —, carbone a lunga fiamma; hard —, (amer.) antracite; living —, brace, carbone ardente; white —, (elett.) carbone bianco.

to coal, v.t.i. far carbone; fornire, fornirsi di carbone: we coaled at Aden, ci rifornimmo di carbone ad Aden.

coaler ['koulə*], s. (mar.) carboniera (nave che trasporta carbone).

to coalesce [,kouə'les], v.i. unirsi, fondersi; formare una coalizione.

coalescence [,kouə'lesns], s. **1.** unione, fusione; coalizione **2.** (chim.) combinazione **3.** (anat.) coalescenza.

coalescing [,kouə'lesiŋ], s. (pol.) unione, fusione.

coalfield ['koul-fi:ld], s. bacino carbonifero.

coaling ['kouliŋ], s. (mar.) rifornimento di carbone ☆ — station (o — port), porto dove si carica il carbone.

coalite ['koulait], s. (chim.) semi-coke.

coalition [,kouə'liʃən], s. coalizione ☆ the left wing —, (pol.) la coalizione delle sinistre.

coalitionist [,kouə'liʃənist], s. fautore di coalizione.

coalless ['koullis], ag. senza carbone.

coalman ['koulmæn], pl. **coalmen** ['koulmen], s. carbonaio.

coaly ['kouli], ag. **1.** ricco di carbone **2.** color carbone.

coaming ['koumiŋ], s. **1.** (mar.) mastra (di boccaporto) **2.** (arch.) bordo rialzato.

coarctate [kou'a:kteit], ag. coartato, costretto.

coarctation [,kouа:k'teiʃən], s. coartazione, costrizione.

coarse [kɔ:s], ag. **1.** grossolano, ordinario, rozzo; volgare **2.** grosso, ruvido (di materiale): — cloth, stoffa ruvida; — fibre, fibra grossa; — grain, grana grossa (di marmo, legno) ☆ — -cut, trinciato grosso; — -featured, dalle fattezze grossolane; — -fibred (o — -grained), di grana, fibra grossa (di legno, marmo, ecc.); fig. inelegante; senza delicatezza; — -minded, poco raffinato.

coarsely ['kɔ:sli], av. grossolanamente, volgarmente.

to coarsen ['kɔ:sn], v.t.i. rendere, diventare grossolano, ruvido.

coarseness ['kɔ:snis], s. **1.** grossolanità, volgarità, indelicatezza (di modi, linguaggio, ecc.) **2.** ruvidezza (di pelle, stoffa, ecc.); grana grossa (di marmo, legno, ecc.).

coarsish ['kɔ:siʃ], ag. piuttosto volgare, grossolano.

coast [koust], s. **1.** costa, riviera, litorale ‖ the — is clear, non c'è pericolo **2.** (amer.) pista (per toboga, bicicletta, ecc.) ☆ — -defence, difesa costiera; — -guard, polizia costiera; — -line, linea costiera; — -waiter, doganiere (per sorveglianza delle coste); — -watcher, guardacoste; — watching, sorveglianza delle coste.

to coast, v.i. **1.** costeggiare, navigare lungo le coste; esercitare il commercio costiero: to — along a shore, navigare rasentando la costa **2.** discendere (da una collina) in toboga; (ciclismo) scendere senza pedalare, a ruota libera; (aut.) discendere in folle.

coastal ['koustəl], ag. costiero ☆ — navigation, navigazione costiera.

coaster ['koustə*], s. **1.** nave cabotiera **2.** sottobicchiere, sottobottiglia **3.** posapiedi (per percorrere discese senza pedali in bicicletta priva di ruota libera) **4.** trenino elettrico.

coasting ['koustiŋ], ag. cabotiero ‖ s. **1.** navigazione costiera, cabotaggio **2.** (geog.) linea costiera **3.** discesa (in bicicletta) a ruota libera; (aut.) discesa in folle **4.** (fis.) moto dovuto a gravità, inerzia **5.** (ferr.) movimento per inerzia **6.** (fam.) corteggiamento ☆ — trade, commercio cabotiero; — vessel, nave cabotiera.

coastward(s) ['koustwəd(z)], av. verso la costa.

coastwise ['koust-waiz], ag. av. lungo la costa.

coat [kout], s. **1.** giacca; soprabito; cappotto: — and skirt, ⸙ tailleur ‖ to turn one's —, (fam.) cambiar partito, voltar bandiera ‖ to wear the king's —, essere soldato ‖ it is not the — that makes the man, *prov.* l'abito non fa il monaco ‖ *to cut one's — according to one's cloth, prov.* non fare il passo più lungo della gamba **2.** manto, pelo, pelliccia (di animale) **3.** manto (di neve, ecc.) **4.** rivestimento; intonaco; strato: *a — of paint,* una mano di vernice **5.** (*anat.*) parete (di organi) ☆ *— -armour,* stemma, blasone; *— -card,* figura (nelle carte di giuoco); *— frock-,* mantello; *— of arms,* (*arald.*) arme, blasone ricamato sulla cotta; *— of mail,* (*mil.*) giaco ‖ *frock- —,* redingote.

  to coat, *v.t.* spalmare, rivestire, coprire: *he coated the door with paint,* egli verniciò la porta; *to — a pill,* (*farm.*) zuccherare una pillola.

  coated ['koutid], *ag.* **1.** ricoperto, rivestito **2.** che indossa giacca, abito ☆ *a black- — man,* un uomo dall'abito nero; impiegato.

  coatee ['kouti:], *s.* **1.** tunica; giacchetta corta **2.** giubbetto da bambino.

  coati [kou'a:ti], *s.* (*zool.*) coati, orsetto d'America.

  coating ['koutiŋ], *s.* **1.** rivestimento, mano (di pittura, vernice, ecc.) **2.** stoffa per abiti.

  to coax [kouks], *v.t.i.* persuadere con adulazione, blandire; usare blandizie: *I will — it out of him,* riuscirò a farmelo dare; *she coaxed her child to sleep,* fece addormentare il suo bimbo; *she coaxed him into buying a fur for her,* la persuase con moine ad acquistare una pelliccia.

  coaxer ['kouksə*], *s.c.* adulatore, adulatrice.

  coaxial [kou'æksiəl], *ag.* (*mat. mec.*) coassiale ☆ *— cable,* (*neol.*) cavo coassiale.

  coaxing ['kouksiŋ], *ag.* persuasivo, adulatorio: *— manner,* modi persuasivi ‖ *s.* moine, lusinghe.

  coaxingly ['kouksiŋli], *av.* in modo persuasivo, carezzevole.

  cob¹ [kɔb], *s.* **1.** cigno maschio **2.** cavallo piccolo e robusto ‖ *corn off the —,* granturco da mangiarsi in grani **4.** grossa nocciola **5.** ovulo di carbon fossile.

  cob², *s.* (*edil.*) mistura di argilla, sassi e paglia per costruzioni; mattone crudo.

  cob³, *s.* (*ornit.*) mugnaiaccio.

  cobalt [kə'bɔ:lt], *s.* (*min.*) cobalto ☆ *— blue,* azzurro carico, azzurro cobalto.

  cobaltic [kə'bɔ:ltik], *ag.* (*chim.*) cobaltico.

  cobaltite ['koubɔ:ltait], *s.* (*min.*) cobaltite.

  cobble¹ ['kɔbl], *s.* **1.** ciottolo **2.** *pl.* carbone in pezzatura media ☆ *— -stone,* ciottolo.

  to cobble¹, *v.t.* pavimentare con ciottoli.

  cobble², *s.* rattoppo.

  to cobble², *v.t.* rattoppare; rappezzare (scarpe, ecc.).

  cobbler ['kɔblə*], *s.* **1.** ciabattino **2.** (*amer.*) bevanda ghiacciata (di vino, zucchero e limone) ☆ *—'s wax,* pece da calzolaio.

  Cobdenism ['kɔbdənizəm], *s.* (*econ. pol.*) teoria propugnata da Richard Cobden (1804-1865).

  coble ['koubl], *s.* barca da pesca a fondo piatto.

  cobra ['koubrə], *s.* (*zool.*) cobra.

  Coburg ['koubə:g], *no.pr.* (*geog.*) Coburgo.

  cobweb ['kɔbweb], *s.* ragnatela; filo di ragnatela; *fig.* trappola, rete‖ *to blow away the cobwebs,* (*fam.*) prendere una boccata d'aria, *fig.* rinfrescarsi le idee.

  cobwebby ['kɔb,webi], *ag.* coperto di ragnatele.

  coca ['koukə], *s.* (*bot.*) coca; foglie di coca.

  cocaine [kə'kein], *s.* cocaina ☆ *— -addict,* cocainomane; *— -habit,* cocainomania.

  cocainism [kə'keinizəm], *s.* cocainismo.

  cocainist [kə'keinist], *s.c.* cocainomane.

  cocainization [kə,keini'zeifən], *s.* (*med.*) anestesia prodotta da cocaina.

  to cocainize [kə'keinaiz], *v.t.* **1.** somministrare cocaina a **2.** curare, anestetizzare con cocaina.

  cocciferous [kɔk'sifərəs], *ag.* che porta bacche.

  coccinella [,kɔksi'nelə], *s.* (*entom.*) coccinella.

  coccyx ['kɔksiks], *s.* (*anat.*) coccige.

  Cochin-china ['kɔtʃin'tʃainə], *no.pr.* (*geog.*) Cocincina ‖ **cochin-china,** *s.* razza di polli della Cocincina.

  cochineal ['kɔtʃini:l], *s.* (*entom.*) cocciniglia.

  cochlea ['kɔkliə], *s.* (*anat.*) coclea, chiocciola.

  cock¹ [kɔk], *s.* **1.** gallo; maschio di uccelli: *— of the north,* fringuello ‖ *a — and bull story, fig.* una panzana ‖ *the — of the walk, fig.* il gallo della Checca ‖ *old —!,* (*fam.*) vecchio amico! ‖ *to live like a fighting —, fig.* vivere nel lusso **2.** capo; (*spor.*) capitano **3.** (*mec.*) rubinetto; valvola **4.** cane di fucile: *a gun at full —,* un fucile armato **5.** ago (di bilancia); gnomone (di meridiana) ☆ *— -a doodle* (o *— -doo*), chicchirichì; *— a-hoop,* esultante; *— -crow,* canto del gallo: *to rise at — -crow,* alzarsi al canto del gallo; *— -eye,* (*fam.*) occhio strabico; *— -fight,* combattimento di galli; *— -fighting,* il combattere dei galli; *— -loft,* granaio; *— -shot,* colpo al bersaglio; *— -shy,* tiro al bersaglio ‖ *sea —,* (*mar.*) valvola (di presa dell'acqua) a mare.

  to cock¹, *v.t.i.* **1.** addestrare, usare galli da combattimento **2.** *fig.* fare il gallo, il galletto **3.** drizzare, drizzarsi (anche *fig.*): *to — one's ears,* drizzare le orecchie: *the horse cocked his ears up,* il cavallo drizzò le orecchie ‖ *to — one's eyes at s.o., fig.* lanciare un'occhiata a qlcu. ‖ *to — one's hat,* mettersi il cappello sulle ventitrè ‖ *to — one's nose at s.o., fig.* guardare qlcu. dall'alto in basso **4.** alzare il cane del fucile: *to — a gun,* armare un fucile.

  cock², *s.* **1.** piega (all'insù della falda di un cappello); falda: *he gave his hat a —,* si mise il cappello sulle ventitrè **2.** strizzatina d'occhio **3.** posizione eretta del cane del fucile.

  cock³, *s.* piccolo mucchio di fieno, covone.

  to cock³, *v.t.* ammucchiare (fieno), fare (covoni).

  cockade [kɔ'keid], *s.* coccarda.

  cockaded [kɔ'keidid], *ag.:* *— hat,* cappello con coccarda.

  Cockaigne [kɔ'kein], *s.* (il paese della) cuccagna.

  cockalorum [,kɔkəl'lɔ:rəm], *s.* (*fam.*) piccolo sciocco presuntuoso.

  cockatoo [,kɔkə'tu:], *s.* (*ornit.*) cacatoa, cacatua.

  cockatrice ['kɔkətrais], *s.* (*zool.*) basilisco.

  Cockayne [kɔ'kein], *s.* (il paese della) cuccagna.

  cockboat ['kɔkbout], *s.* (*mar.*) piccola imbarcazione.

  cockchafer ['kɔk,tʃeifə*], *s.* (*entom.*) maggiolino.

  cocked [kɔkt], *ag.* eretto, drizzato ☆ *— hat,* bicorno, tricorno: *to knock s.o. into a — hat,* (*fam.*) demolire gli argomenti di qlcu., polverizzare qlcu.

  cocker¹ ['kɔkə*], *s.* **1.** chi alleva galli da combattimento **2.** (*zool.*) cocker.

  cocker², *s.* chi ammucchia il fieno; chi fa il raccolto (di fieno, ecc.).

  cocker³, *s.* gambale.

  to cocker⁴, *v.t.:* *to — (up),* vezzeggiare, viziare, coccolare.

  Cocker, *no.pr.* Cocker (matematico del sec. XVII) ‖ *according to —,* esattamente, precisamente.

  cockerel ['kɔkərəl], *s.* galletto.

  cock-eyed ['kɔkaid], *ag.* **1.** strabico **2.** deforme; disonesto **3.** (*sl.*) assurdo.

  cock-horse ['kɔk'hɔ:s], *s.* cavallo a dondolo ‖ *av.* a cavalcioni.

  cockiness ['kɔkinis], *s.* (*fam.*) sfrontatezza, impudenza.

  cockish ['kɔkiʃ], *ag.* sfrontato, impudente.

  cockle¹ ['kɔkl], *s.* **1.** (*bot.*) loglio **2.** golpe (malattia del frumento).

  cockle², *s.* (*zool.*) cardio ‖ *cockles of the heart,* i sentimenti, il cuore: *it warms the cockles of your heart,* infonde calore al vostro cuore ☆ *— -boat,* piccola barca, guscio di noce; *— -shell,* conchiglia, nicchia.

  cockle³, *s.* grinza, increspatura (nella carta, in un tessuto, ecc.).

  to cockle³, *v.t.i.* increspare, incresparsi; raggrinzare, raggrinzarsi; accartocciarsi (di carta, tessuto, ecc.).

  cockle⁴, *s.* **1.** focolaio (di fornace da malto) **2.** *— (-stove),* stufa ad aria calda **3.** (*ind. ceramica*) forno di essiccazione.

cockney ['kɔkni], *ag.* caratteristico del « cockney » ‖ *s.* « cockney » (dialetto volgare londinese) ‖ *s.c.* (*spreg.*) nativo di Londra.

cockneydom ['kɔknidəm], *s.* (*scherz.*) Londra.

cockneyese [,kɔkni'i:z], *s.* (*scherz.*) parlata londinese.

to **cockneyfy** ['kɔknifai], *v.t.* rendere londinese, trasformare in londinese: *cockneyfied manners*, modi che riflettono quelli dei londinesi.

cockneyism ['kɔkniizəm], *s.* 1. locuzione, particolare pronunzia nel dialetto londinese 2. maniere di un londinese.

cockpit ['kɔkpit], *s.* 1. arena per combattimento di galli; *fig.* arena da combattimento 2. (*aer.*) carlinga; abitacolo 3. (*mar.*) infermeria di bordo; parte della nave verso poppa occupata dagli ufficiali inferiori; corridoio d'accesso alla cabina.

cockroach ['kɔkroutʃ], *s.* (*entom.*) scarafaggio.

cockscomb ['kɔkskoum], *s.* 1. cresta di gallo 2. (*bot.*) amaranto, cresta di gallo 3. *fig.* zerbinotto.

cocksfoot, cock's foot ['kɔksfut], *s.* — (*grass*), (*bot.*) erba mazzolina, erba pannocchia.

cockshead, cock's head ['kɔkshed], *s.* (*bot.*) lupinella.

cockspur ['kɔkspə:*], *s.* 1. sperone del gallo 2. — (*-burner*), becco (del gas) a tre fori.

cocksure ['kɔk'ʃuə*], *ag.* 1. sicurissimo: *to be — about sthg.*, non avere alcun dubbio in merito a ql. co. 2. sicuro di sè, presuntuoso.

cocksureness ['kɔk'ʃuənis], *s.* fiducia in se stesso; presunzione.

cocksy ['kɔksi], *ag.* vanitoso; impertinente.

cocktail ['kɔkteil], *s.* 1. cavallo con coda mozzata 2. (*entom.*) stafilino 3. « cocktail » 4. « parvenu » ☆ — *-cabinet*, mobile bar; — *-mixer*, barista che si prepara « cocktails »; — *-party*, ricevimento in cui si servono « cocktails »; — *-shaker*, « shaker »; — *snacks*, salatini.

cocktailed ['kɔkteild], *ag.* con la coda mozza (di cavallo).

cocky ['kɔki], *ag.* vanitoso, impertinente.

cockyolly bird [,kɔki'ɔli'bə:d], *s.* uccellino (nel linguaggio infantile).

coco, cocoa[1] ['koukou], *s.* (*bot.*) cocco, albero di cocco.

cocoa[2], *s.* (*bot.*) cacao (albero e frutto) ☆ — *-bean*, semi di cacao; — *-butter*, burro di cacao; — *-tree*, albero del cacao.

coconut ['koukənʌt], *s.* 1. (*bot.*) noce di cocco ‖ *that accounts for the milk in the* —, (*scherz.*) ora tutto è chiaro 2. (*volg.*) testa, capoccia ☆ — *-butter*, crema di cocco; — *-matting*, stuoia di fibra di noce di cocco; — *-milk*, latte di cocco; — *-oil*, olio di cocco; — *-tree* (o — *-palm*), (albero di) cocco.

cocoon [kə'ku:n], *s.* bozzolo (specialmente di baco da seta).

to **cocoon**, *v.t.i.* filare il bozzolo; avvolgere, avvolgersi nel bozzolo.

cocoonery [kə'ku:nəri], *s.* 1. bachicoltura 2. bigattiera.

Cocytus [kou'saitəs], *no.pr.* (*geog. mit.*) Cocito.

cod[1] [kɔd], *s.* 1. guscio; buccia; baccello 2. (*anat.*) scroto; (*volg.*) testicoli.

to **cod**[1], *pass.p.p.* **codded** ['kɔdid], *v.t.i.* produrre baccelli; raccogliere baccelli di (piselli).

cod[2], *s.* cuscino.

cod[3], *s.* (*invariato al pl.*) merluzzo ☆ — *-liver oil*, (*farm.*) olio di fegato di merluzzo ‖ *dried* —, stoccafisso; *salted* —, baccalà.

to **cod**[3], *v.i.* andar a pesca di merluzzi.

cod[4], *s.* (*sl.*) stupidone.

to **cod**[4], *v.t.* (*sl.*) ingannare; gabbare.

coda ['koudə], *s.* (*mus.*) coda.

to **coddle**[1] ['kɔdl], *v.t.* 1. far bollire, cuocere lentamente 2. *fig.* coccolare.

to **coddle**[2], *v.t.* curare teneramente; vezzeggiare, coccolare.

to **coddle**[3], *v.t.i.* 1. accarezzare, abbracciare teneramente 2. rannicchiarsi, accoccolarsi.

code [koud], *s.* 1. codice; regole; statuto: — *of criminal procedure*, (*dir.*) codice di procedura penale; *the — of honour*, il codice d'onore 2. cifrario ‖ *to read a* —, decifrare un cifrario; *to write a dispatch in* —, cifrare un dispaccio ☆ — *-book*, dizionario delle parole cifrate; — *word*, parola cifrata.

to **code**, *v.t.* 1. codificare (leggi) 2. cifrare (un dispaccio).

codeclination [,koudekli'neiʃən], *s.* (*astr.*) complemento della declinazione.

codeine ['koudi:n], *s.* (*farm.*) codeina.

codex ['koudeks], *pl.* **codices** ['koudisi:z], *s.* 1. codice, manoscritto antico 2. (*farm.*) ricettario; farmacopea.

codfish ['kɔdfiʃ], *s.* (*invariato al pl.*) merluzzo.

codger ['kɔdʒə*], *s.* (*sl.*) tipo, vecchio strambo.

codicil ['kɔdisil], *s.* 1. (*dir.*) codicillo 2. poscritto.

codicillary [,kɔdi'siləri], *ag.* codicillare.

codification [,kɔdifi'keiʃən], *s.* codificazione.

codifier ['kɔdifaiə*], *s.* 1. codificatore 2. compilatore di codici.

to **codify** ['kɔdifai], *v.t.* 1. codificare (leggi) 2. cifrare (un dispaccio).

coding ['koudiŋ], *s.* 1. codificazione 2. il cifrare.

co-director [,koudi'rektə*], *s.* condirettore.

codling[1] ['kɔdliŋ], *s.* piccolo merluzzo.

codling[2], *s.* mela di forma allungata da mangiar cotta.

co-ed, coed ['kou'ed], *s.* (*amer. fam.*) studentessa di scuola, di università mista.

to **co-educate** [kou'edju(:)keit], *v.t.* istruire in scuola mista.

co-education ['kou,edju(:)'keiʃən], *s.* istruzione in scuola mista.

co-educational ['kou,edju(:)'keiʃənl], *ag.* con istruzione mista ☆ — *school*, scuola mista.

coefficiency [,koui'fiʃənsi], *s.* coefficienza.

coefficient [,koui'fiʃənt], *ag.s.* (*mat. fis., ecc.*) coefficiente.

coemption [kou'empʃən], *s.* 1. (*dir.*) accaparramento 2. (*dir. romano*) coenzione.

coenobite ['si:nəbait], *s.* cenobita.

coenobitic(al) [,si:nə'bitik(əl)], *ag.* cenobitico.

coequal [kou'i:kwəl], *ag.s.* coeguale, eguale.

coequality [,koui(:)'kwɔliti], *s.* coeguaglianza, eguaglianza.

coequally [kou'i:kwəli] *av.* coegualmente, egualmente.

to **coerce** [kou'ə:s], *v.t.* 1. forzare, costringere: *to — s.o. into doing sthg.*, costringere qlcu. a fare ql.co. 2. coartare; reprimere.

coercibility ['kou,ə:si'biliti], *s.* coercibilità.

coercible [kou'ə:sibl], *ag.* coercibile.

coercion [kou'ə:ʃən], *s.* coercizione: *to employ means of* —, usare mezzi di coercizione ‖ *Coercion Act*, legge che sospende i diritti civili.

coercive [kou'ə:siv], *ag.* 1. coercitivo 2. coatto.

coercively [kou'ə:sivli], *av.* forzatamente, obbligatamente.

coerciveness [kou'ə:sivnis], *s.* coercizione.

coessential [,koui'senʃəl], *ag.* coessenziale.

coetaneous [,koui(:)'teiniəs], *V.* coeval.

coeternal [,koui(:)'tə:nl], *ag.* coeterno.

coeternally [,koui(:)'tə:nəli], *av.* in modo coeterno.

coeval [kou'i:vəl], *ag.* coevo, contemporaneo.

coexecutor [,kouig'zekjutə*], *s.* coesecutore.

coexecutrix ['kouig'zekjutriks], *s.* coesecutrice.

to **coexist** ['kouig'zist], *v.i.* coesistere.

coexistence ['kouig'zistəns], *s.* coesistenza.

coexistent ['kouig'zistənt], *ag.* coesistente.

coffee ['kɔfi], *s.* caffè ☆ — *-bean*, chicco, grano di caffè; — *-berry*, frutto del caffè; grano di caffè; — *-cup*, tazza da caffè; — *-grounds*, fondi di caffè; — *-house*, caffè; — *-pot*, caffettiera; — *-set*, servizio da caffè; — *-shop*, trattoria, bettola; — *-shrub*, pianta del caffè ‖ *black* —, caffè nero; *roasted* —, *ground* —, caffè tostato, macinato; *white* — (o — *and milk*), caffelatte.

coffer ['kɔfə*], s. **1.** cassa; cofano; forziere: *the coffers of State*, le casse dello Stato, i fondi pubblici **2.** — (-*dam*) (*arch.*) cassone (per fondamenta idrauliche, ecc.) **3.** (*arch.*) cassettone (di soffitto).

to **coffer**, *v.t.* **1.** (*miner.*) rivestire (un pozzo) **2.** (*arch.*) dividere (un soffitto) in cassettoni.

cofferdam ['kɔfədæm], s. cassone pneumatico; compartimento stagno.

coffin ['kɔfin], s. **1.** cassa da morto, bara ǁ *to drive a nail in one's* —, *fig.* affrettare la morte abusando della propria salute **2.** cavità dello zoccolo del cavallo ☆ — *nail*, (*sl. amer.*) sigaretta di infima qualità.

to **coffin**, *v.t.* **1.** deporre nella bara **2.** *fig.* deporre in luogo inaccessibile.

coffle ['kɔfl], s. convoglio (di schiavi, di animali legati uno all'altro).

cog[1] [kɔg], s. dente (di ruota) ☆ — -*rail*, (*ferr.*) dentiera, cremagliera; — -*railway* (o — -*way*), ferrovia a cremagliera; — -*wheel*, ruota dentata.

to **cog**[1], *pass.p.p.* **cogged** [kɔgd], *v.t.i.* dentellare (una ruota); ingranarsi (di ruote dentate) ☆ *cogged wheel*, ruota dentata.

cog[2], s. (*st.*) antico tipo di barca.

cog[3], s. (*mec.*) tenone; incastro a tenone, a dente.

to **cog**[3], *v.t.* congiungere mediante incastro; (*metal.*) sbozzare al laminatoio.

to **cog**[4], *v.t.i.* barare coi dadi, gettare (i dadi) in modo scorretto; truffare.

cogency ['koudʒənsi], s. **1.** forza di persuasione (di un argomento) **2.** urgenza (di una situazione).

cogent ['koudʒənt], *ag.* persuasivo, convincente, potente (di argomento, ragione).

cogently ['koudʒəntli], *av.* in modo convincente.

cogitable ['kɔdʒitəbl], *ag.* concepibile; pensabile.

to **cogitate** ['kɔdʒiteit], *v.t.i.* **1.** escogitare, concepire **2.** riflettere, ponderare, meditare.

cogitation [,kɔdʒi'teiʃən], s. riflessione, meditazione.

cogitative ['kɔdʒitətiv], *ag.* meditabondo.

cogitatively ['kɔdʒitətivli], *av.* in modo cogitabondo.

cognac ['kounjæk], s. cognac.

cognate ['kɔgneit], *ag.* **1.** consanguineo **2.** (*filologia*) appartenente alla stessa famiglia linguistica: — *words*, parole affini per origine ǁ s. **1.** consanguineo, congiunto **2.** parola, cosa, ecc. che ha la stessa origine o natura.

cognation [kɔg'neiʃən], s. **1.** consanguineità, parentela; (*dir.*) cognazione **2.** (*filologia*) discendenza dalla stessa origine.

cognition [kɔg'niʃən], s. **1.** (*fil.*) cognizione, conoscenza **2.** percezione, sensazione; intenzione.

cognitive ['kɔgnitiv], *ag.* (*fil.*) avente conoscenza ☆ — *faculty*, facoltà conoscitiva.

cognizable ['kɔgnizəbl], *ag.* **1.** (*fil.*) conoscibile; percepibile; riconoscibile **2.** (*dir.*) entro la giurisdizione di una corte: — *by a court*, di competenza di un tribunale ☆ — *offence*, delitto perseguibile dalla legge.

cognizably ['kɔgnizəbli], *av.* comprensibilmente; in modo riconoscibile.

cognizance ['kɔgnizəns], *nel senso* **2.** ['kɔnizəns], s. **1.** (*fil.*) conoscenza, percezione: *to take* — *of sthg.*, prendere conoscenza, atto di ql.co. **2.** (*dir.*) competenza: *within* (o *under*) *the* — *of a court*, di competenza di un tribunale **3.** (*arald.*) pezza distintiva (di una famiglia).

cognizant ['kɔgnizənt] *nel senso* **2.** ['kɔnizənt], *ag.* **1.** avente conoscenza: *to be* — *of a fact*, essere informato di un fatto **2.** (*dir.*) competente: *court* — *of an offence*, tribunale competente per giudicare un delitto.

to **cognize** [kɔg'naiz], *v.t.* (*fil.*) avere, prendere cognizione di.

cognomen [kɔg'noumen], s. **1.** (*st. romana*) cognome **2.** soprannome.

cognoscible [kɔg'nɔsibl], *ag.* (*fil.*) conoscibile.

cognovit [kɔg'nouvit], s. (*dir.*) riconoscimento da parte del convenuto che le ragioni dell'attore sono giuste.

to **cohabit** [kou'hæbit], *v.i.* coabitare.

cohabitation [,kouhæbi'teiʃən], s. coabitazione.

coheir ['kou'ɛə*], s. (uomo) coerede.

coheiress ['kou'ɛəris], s. (donna) coerede.

to **cohere** [kou'hiə*], *v.i.* **1.** aderire **2.** essere coerente, logico (di stile, idee, ecc.).

coherence [kou'hiərəns], **coherency** [kou'hiərənsi], s. **1.** coesione; aderenza **2.** coerenza (di stile, idee, ecc.).

coherent [kou'hiərənt], *ag.* **1.** aderente **2.** coerente.

coherently [kou'hiərəntli], *av.* coerentemente.

coherer [kou'hiərə*], s. (*fis. rad.*) rivelatore, coesore.

cohesion [kou'hi:ʒən], s. **1.** coesione; aderenza.

cohesive [kou'hi:siv], *ag.* coesivo; aderente.

cohesively [kou'hi:sivli], *av.* in modo aderente.

cohesiveness [kou'hi:sivnis], s. coesione.

cohibition [,kouhi'biʃən], s. (*fis.*) coibenza.

cohort ['kouhɔ:t], s. **1.** (*st. romana*) coorte **2.** gruppo (di persone); schiera (di soldati).

coif [kɔif], s. (*st.*) cappuccio aderente.

coiffure [kwɑ:'fjuə*], s. pettinatura, acconciatura.

coign [kɔin], s. (*arc.*) canto, angolo: — *of vantage*, posizione vantaggiosa (per osservazione, azione).

coil[1] [kɔil], s. (*arc.*) tumulto, confusione: *to shuffle off this mortal* —, (*letter.*) fuggire a questa vita di tumulto.

coil[2], s. **1.** rotolo; spira, spirale **2.** (*mec.*) serpentina: — *of piping*, tubazione a serpentina **3.** (*elett. mec.*) bobina **4.** crocchia (di capelli) ☆ — -*clutch*, innesto a spirale; — -*spring*, molla a spirale piana; — -*winding*, solenoide ǁ *induction-* —, bobina d'induzione.

to **coil**[2], *v.t.i.* **1.** *to* — (*up*), avvolgere, avvolgersi (a spirale); attorcigliare, attorcigliarsi: *she coiled* (*herself*) *up in an armchair*, si rannicchiò in una poltrona **2.** serpeggiare **3.** (*mar.*) adugliare, cogliere a ruota.

coil[3], s. mucchio di fieno.

coiled [kɔild], *ag.* avvolto, attorcigliato.

coiling ['kɔiliŋ], s. avvolgimento.

coin [kɔin], s. **1.** moneta: *a false* —, una moneta falsa; *a gold* —, una moneta d'oro **2.** denaro, contanti, quattrini: *small* —, moneta spicciola ǁ *to pay in* — *of the realm*, pagare in moneta sonante ǁ *to pay s.o. in his own* —, *fig.* rendere pan per focaccia **3.** (*arch.*) pietra d'angolo.

to **coin**, *v.t.* **1.** coniare ǁ *he is coining money*, (*fam.*) fa denari a palate **2.** inventare, creare (una parola, una bugia, ecc.): *a coined word*, una parola inventata **3.** (*ind.*) punzonare, siglare **4.** (*rar.*) fornire di pietre d'angolo.

coinage ['kɔinidʒ], s. **1.** coniatura, conio: *right of* —, diritto di coniatura **2.** valuta, denaro contante **3.** sistema monetario **4.** invenzione, creazione (di parola, ecc.); parola coniata: *the* — *of fancy*, parto della fantasia; "*radar*" *is a recent* —, « radar » è una parola di recente creazione ☆ *decimal* —, sistema monetario decimale.

to **coincide** [,kouin'said], *v.i.* coincidere; *to* —*in an opinion*, avere la stessa opinione.

coincidence [kou'insidəns], s. coincidenza: *what a* —!, che coincidenza!.

coincident [kou'insidənt], *ag.* coincidente.

coincidental [kou,insi'dentl], *ag.* coincidente: *entirely* — *occurrences*, fatti di pura coincidenza.

coincidently [kou'insidəntli], *av.* per coincidenza.

coiner ['kɔinə*], s. **1.** falsario **2.** coniatore **3.** (*fam.*) inventore, creatore (di parole, bugie, ecc.).

coinstantaneous [kou,instən'teinjəs], *ag.* simultaneo.

coir ['kɔiə*], s. fibra (della noce) di cocco ☆ — *matting*, *rope*, stuoia, fune di fibra di cocco.

coition [kou'iʃən], s. coito.

coke [kouk], s. **1.** « coke » (carbon fossile distillato) **2.** (*sl. amer.*) bibita.

to **coke**, *v.t.i.* convertire (carbon fossile) in « coke »; convertirsi in « coke ».

coker ['koukə*], **cokernut** ['koukənʌt], V. **coco**.

coky ['kouki], *ag.* simile a « coke ».

col [kɔl], s. sella, passo (fra monti).

cola ['koulə], *s.* (*bot.*) cola.

colander ['kʌləndə*], *s.* colabrodo; colatoio.

to colander, *v.t.* passare al colabrodo.

colatitude [kou'lætitjuːd], *s.* (*astr.*) complemento di latitudine.

colchicum ['kɔltʃikəm], *s.* (*bot. farm.*) colchico, zafferanone.

colcothar ['kɔlkouθə*], *s.* (*chim.*) colcotar.

cold [kould], *ag.* **1.** freddo: — *drink*, bevanda fredda; — *weather*, tempo freddo; *my hands are* —, ho le mani fredde; *to be* —, aver freddo; far freddo: *I am* —, ho freddo; *it is* — *today*, oggi fa freddo; *to feel* —, avere, sentire freddo; *to get* (o *to grow*) —, raffreddarsi; diventar freddo ‖ — *hand, warm heart*, mani fredde, cuore caldo ‖ *to be in* — *storage*, (*sl.*) essere al fresco, in gattabuia ‖ *to have* — *feet*, (*fam.*) essere timido ‖ *to throw* — *water on*, gettare acqua sul fuoco, spegnere l'entusiasmo **2.** freddo, indifferente, apatico; riservato: — *reception*, accoglienza fredda; *that leaves me* —, (*fam.*) non mi fa nè caldo nè freddo ‖ *to give s.o. the* — *shoulder*, (*fam.*) trattar qlcu. freddamente; evitare qlcu. per antipatia ‖ *to kill s.o. in* — *blood*, uccidere qlcu. a sangue freddo (di colore): *blue is a* — *colour*, il blu è un colore freddo.

cold, *s.* **1.** freddo: *in the* —, al freddo; *I suffer from the* —, soffro per il freddo; *you will catch your death of* —, (*fam.*) morirai di freddo ‖ *to leave s.o. out in the* —, (*fam.*) lasciare qlcu. in disparte **2.** raffreddore, infreddatura; raffreddamento: *to catch a* —, prendere un raffreddore; *to catch a* — *in the eye*, prendere un colpo d'aria agli occhi; *to have a* — *in the head, on the chest*, avere un raffreddore di testa, di petto; *to have a bad* —, avere un forte raffreddore.

cold, (*nei composti*): — *-blooded*, a sangue freddo (di animale); *fig.* freddo, insensibile (di persona); premeditato, a sangue freddo (di azione); — *-cream*, crema emolliente; — *-hearted*, insensibile; — *performance*, (*teat. fam.*) rappresentazione senza musica; — *-short*, (*metal.*) fragile a bassa temperatura; — *steel*, arma bianca; — *riveting*, (*mec.*) chiodatura a freddo; — *room*, cella frigorifera; — *storage*, magazzinaggio refrigerato; — *war*, guerra fredda; — *wave*, ondata di freddo; permanente a freddo ‖ *ice-* —, gelido.

coldish ['kouldiʃ], *ag.* (*fam.*) abbastanza freddo.

coldly ['kouldli], *av.* freddamente.

coldness ['kouldnis], *s.* freddezza (anche *fig.*).

cole[1] [koul], *s.* (*arc.*) brassica ☆ — *-seed*, (*bot.*) colza.

cole[2], *s.* (*sl.*) denaro.

coleopter [ˌkɔli'ɔptə*], *s.* (*entom.*) coleottero.

Coleoptera [ˌkɔli'ɔptərə], *s.pl.* (*entom.*) i coleotteri.

colerape ['koulreip], *s.* rapa.

colibri ['kɔlibri], *s.* (*ornit.*) colibrì.

colic ['kɔlik], *ag.* (*patol.*) colico ‖ *s.* (*patol.*) colica.

colicky ['kɔliki], *ag.* soggetto a coliche.

Coliseum [ˌkɔli'siəm], *s.* (*archeol.*) Colosseo.

colitis [kɔ'laitis], *s.* (*patol.*) colite.

to collaborate [kə'læbəreit], *v.i.* collaborare, cooperare.

collaboration [kəˌlæbə'reiʃən], *s.* collaborazione, cooperazione; (*pol.*) collaborazionismo.

collaborationist [kəˌlæbə'reiʃənist], *s.* (*pol.*) collaborazionista.

collaborator [kə'læbəreitə*], *s.* collaboratore.

collapsable, *V.* **collapsible**.

collapse [kə'læps], *s.* **1.** crollo (di edificio, impero, speranze, ecc.); rovina (di azienda); caduta (di prezzi, ministero); sprofondamento **2.** sgonfiamento (di pallone, ecc.) **3.** (*patol.*) collasso.

to collapse, *v.i.* **1.** crollare; cadere; rovinare; sprofondarsi: *he collapsed into an armchair*, si sprofondò, si abbandonò in una poltrona **2.** afflosciarsi; sgonfiarsi **3.** accasciarsi (improvvisamente).

collapsible [kə'læpsəbl], *ag.* pieghevole, smontabile ☆ — *boat*, canotto pneumatico; — *chair*, sedia pieghevole; — *hood*, (*aut.*) soffietto.

collar ['kɔlə*], *s.* **1.** colletto, bavero **2.** collare (per cani, ecc.) **3.** collare (distintivo di ordini equestri) **4.** (*mec.*) collare, anello, fascetta **5.** rotolo (di carne, pesce, ecc.) ☆ — *-bone*, (*anat.*) clavicola; — *-stud*, bottone del colletto.

to collar, *v.t.* **1.** afferrare per il colletto **2.** mettere un collare a (un cane, ecc.) **3.** (*spor.*) marcare **4.** (*sl.*) afferrare; appropriarsi di; (*amer.*) attaccare un bottone con **5.** (*cuc.*) arrotolare (carne, ecc.).

collared ['kɔləd], *ag.* **1.** con colletto **2.** con collare.

collarette [ˌkɔlə'ret], *s.* collettino (di pelo, pizzo, ecc.).

to collate [kɔ'leit], *v.t.* **1.** collazionare (testi) **2.** (*tip.*) controllare che ci siano tutte le segnature in (un libro) **3.** (*eccl.*) conferire un beneficio a.

collateral [kɔ'lætərəl], *ag.* **1.** collaterale, parallelo **2.** collaterale (di parentela) **3.** secondario; sussidiario, accessorio ‖ *s.* **1.** collaterale **2.** (*comm. dir.*) garanzia accessoria ☆ — *security*, (*comm. dir.*) garanzia addizionale.

collaterally [kɔ'lætərəli], *av.* **1.** parallelamente **2.** (*dir.*) collateralmente.

collation [kɔ'leiʃən], *s.* **1.** collazione (di testi) **2.** (*eccl.*) collazione **3.** pasto leggero in giorno di digiuno; (*fam.*) merenda.

collator [kɔ'leitə*], *s.* **1.** chi collaziona (testi) **2.** (*tip.*) chi controlla che ci siano tutte le segnature (in un libro) **3.** (*eccl.*) collatore.

colleague ['kɔliːg], *s.c.* collega.

to colleague, *v.i.* unirsi; cospirare, tramare.

collect ['kɔlekt], *s.* (*eccl.*) colletta, orazione.

to collect [kə'lekt], *v.t.i.* **1.** riunire, riunirsi; raccogliere, raccogliersi; mettere insieme, accumulare, accumularsi, ammassarsi; radunare, radunarsi: *to* — *the letters*, raccogliere le lettere (dalle cassette postali); *to* — *the luggage*, prendere in consegna i bagagli a domicilio ‖ *to* — *one's courage*, farsi coraggio; *to* — *one's thoughts*, concentrarsi **2.** riscuotere, incassare, esigere (tasse, ecc.): *to* — *a cheque*, incassare un assegno; *to* — *a debt*, ricuperare un debito; *to* — *for the poor*, fare una colletta per i poveri; *to* — *on delivery*, (*amer.*) riscuotere contro assegno **3.** fare una collezione, una raccolta **4.** *to* — *oneself*, riprendersi.

collectable [kə'lektəbl], *ag.* riscotibile; ricuperabile.

collectanea [ˌkɔlek'taːnjə], *s. pl.* (*lett.*) raccolta di brani, miscellanea.

collected [kə'lektid], *ag.* **1.** raccolto, riunito **2.** calmo, padrone di sè.

collectedly [kə'lektidli], *av.* con calma, con padronanza di sè.

collectedness [kə'lektidnis], *s.* calma, padronanza di sè.

collectible [kə'lektibl], *ag.* riscotibile; ricuperabile.

collecting [kə'lektiŋ], *s.* il raccogliere ☆ — *-box*, cassetta delle elemosine; — *clerk*, esattore; — *-station*, (*mil.*) centro di raccolta dei feriti ‖ *stamp* —, il raccogliere francobolli.

collection [kə'lekʃən], *s.* **1.** riunione, raccolta (di persone); ammassamento; levata (delle lettere) **2.** colletta, questua: *to take up a* —, fare una colletta (in chiesa) **3.** (*comm.*) riscossione, esazione; *pl.* effetti da incassare: — *of accounts*, riscossione **4.** collezione, raccolta: *to make a* — *of coins*, fare una raccolta di monete **5.** *pl.* esami trimestrali (ad Oxford, ecc.) ☆ — *-box*, cassetta delle elemosine.

collective [kə'lektiv], *ag.* collettivo ☆ — *farm*, fattoria collettiva; — *note*, (*diplomazia*) nota collettiva; — *noun*, (*gram.*) nome collettivo; — *ownership*, (*dir.*) proprietà collettiva; — *security*, (*pol.*) sicurezza collettiva.

collectively [kə'lektivli], *av.* collettivamente.

collectivism [kə'lektivizəm], *s.* (*pol.*) collettivismo.

collectivist [kə'lektivist], *s.* (*pol.*) collettivista.

collectivity [ˌkɔlek'tiviti], *s.* **1.** collettività **2.** comunità sociale; stato; nazione **3.** proprietà in comune.

collector [kə'lektə*], s. 1. raccoglitore; collezionista 2. esattore; (amer.) esattore doganale; (in India) funzionario amministrativo distrettuale 3. (fis.) collettore ☆ house-to-house —, esattore a domicilio; stamp- —, collezionista di francobolli; ticket- —, (ferr.) bigliettario.

collectorship [kə'lektəʃip], s. ufficio, funzioni dell'esattore; (in India) carica di funzionario amministrativo.

colleen ['kɔliːn], s. (irl.) ragazza.

college ['kɔlidʒ], s. 1. scuola secondaria con internato 2. istituto superiore annesso all'università (ad Oxford, Cambridge, ecc.); (scoz. amer.) università: he has been to —, ha studiato all'università 3. collegio (edificio); (sl.) prigione 4. (eccl.) collegio ‖ the Sacred College of Cardinals, il Collegio dei Cardinali ☆ — -cap, berretto goliardico; — man, studente universitario; — pudding, piccolo budino con uvetta ‖ Eton —, scuola di Eton; military —, naval —, scuola militare, navale; missionary —, seminario missionario.

colleger ['kɔlidʒə*], s. borsista (ad Eton).

collegial [kə'liːdʒjəl], ag. collegiale, di collegio.

collegian [kə'liːdʒjən], s. 1. membro di un collegio universitario 2. borsista 3. (sl.) carcerato.

collegiate [kə'liːdʒiit], ag. di collegio.

collegiately [kə'liːdʒiitli], av. collegialmente.

collet ['kɔlit], s. 1. (mec.) anello, colletto; mandrino 2. castone (di gemme).

to **collet**, v.t. incastonare (gemme).

to **collide** [kə'laid], v.i. scontrarsi, urtarsi, cozzare: I collided with him, ho urtato contro di lui; the trains collided, i treni si scontrarono.

collie ['kɔli], s. « collie » (cane da pastore scozzese).

collier ['kɔliə*], s. 1. minatore (di carbone) 2. (nave) carboniera.

colliery ['kɔljəri], s. miniera di carbon fossile.

to **colligate** ['kɔligeit], v.t. collegare.

colligation [,kɔli'geiʃən], s. collegamento.

to **collimate** ['kɔlimeit], v.t. (ott.) far collimare.

collimation ['kɔli'meiʃən], s. (ott.) collimazione.

collimator ['kɔlimeitə*], s. (ott.) collimatore.

collinear [kɔ'linjə*], ag. (geom.) sulla medesima retta.

collision [kə'liʒən], s. 1. collisione, scontro, urto: the ships had a —, le navi ebbero una collisione; to come into — with, scontrarsi con 2. conflitto (d'interessi), urto: to come into — with s.o.'s interests, venire a conflitto con gli interessi di qlcu.

to **collocate** ['kɔləkeit], v.t. collocare, sistemare.

collocation [,kɔlə'keiʃən], s. collocazione.

collocutor [kə'lɔkjutə*], s. c. interlocutore, interlocutrice.

collodion [kə'loudjən], s. (chim.) collodio.

to **collogue** [kə'loug], v.i. (fam.) confabulare; (dial.) tramare, cospirare.

colloid ['kɔlɔid], ag.s. (chim.) colloide.

colloidal [kə'lɔidəl], ag. (chim.) colloidale.

collop ['kɔləp], s. (arc.) fetta di carne.

colloquial [kə'loukwiəl], ag. familiare, d'uso corrente (di parole, frase, stile).

colloquialism [kə'loukwiəlizəm], s. espressione familiare.

colloquially [kə'loukwiəli], av. nella lingua familiare, parlata; con espressioni familiari.

colloquist ['kɔləkwist], s.c. interlocutore, interlocutrice.

colloquium [kə'loukwiəm], s. (rar.) colloquio (piccola riunione per discussioni).

colloquy ['kɔləkwi], s. 1. colloquio, conversazione: to engage in — with, entrare in colloquio con 2. (lett.) dialogo ‖ the Colloquies of Erasmus, i Dialoghi di Erasmo.

collotype ['kɔləutaip], s. (foto.) collotipia.

to **collude** [kə'luːd], v.i. (arc.) colludere.

collusion [kə'luːʒən], s. (dir.) collusione: to act in — with s.o., agire in collusione con qlcu; to enter into — with s.o., mettersi in collusione con qlcu.

collusive [kə'luːsiv], ag. (dir.) collusivo.

collusively [kə'luːsivli], av. (dir.) in modo collusivo.

collyrium [kə'liriəm], s. (farm.) collirio.

collywobbles ['kɔli,wɔblz], s.pl. (fam.) brontolio (dell'intestino).

colocynth ['kɔləsinθ], s. (bot.) colloquinta.

Colombia [kə'lɔmbiə], no.pr. (geog.) Columbia.

colon[1] ['koulən], s. (anat.) colon.

colon[2], s. (gram.) due punti ☆ semi- —, punto e virgola.

colon[3], s. (rar.) colono.

colonate [kə'louneit], s. (st. romana) colonato, servitù della gleba.

colonel ['kəːnl], s. 1. (mil.) colonnello 2. (amer.) « colonel » (titolo onorifico) ☆ lieutenant- —, tenente colonnello.

coloneley ['kəːnlsi], **colonelship** ['kəːnlʃip], s. grado di colonnello.

colonial [kə'lounjəl], ag. coloniale ‖ the Colonial Office, Ministero delle Colonie ‖ s. V. **colonist** ☆ — merchant, commerciante in prodotti coloniali.

colonialism [kə'lounjəlizəm], s. 1. vita coloniale 2. espressione linguistica coloniale 3. sistema coloniale, colonialismo.

colonialist [kə'lounjəlist], s. colonialista.

colonist ['kɔlənist], s. 1. colono, abitante di colonia 2. colonizzatore.

colonization [,kɔlənai'zeiʃən], s. colonizzazione.

colonizationist [,kɔlənai'zeiʃənist], s. (pol.) colonialista.

to **colonize** ['kɔlənaiz], v.t.i. 1. colonizzare 2. stabilirsi in una colonia, fondare una colonia.

colonizer ['kɔlənaizə*], s.c. colonizzatore, colonizzatrice.

colonnade [,kɔlə'neid], s. colonnato.

colonnaded [,kɔlə'neidid], ag. munito di colonne.

colony ['kɔləni], s. colonia: a — of ants, una colonia di formiche; the English — in Florence, la colonia, la comunità inglese di Firenze.

colophon ['kɔləfən], s. (tip.) colofone ‖ from title -page to —, dalla prima all'ultima pagina.

colophony [kə'lɔfəni], s. colofonia, pece greca.

(to) **color**, (amer.) per (to) **colour**.

Colorado [,kɔlə'rɑːdou], no.pr. (geog.) Colorado ☆ — beetle, (entom.) dorifora.

coloration [,kʌlə'reiʃən], s. (amer.) colorazione.

coloreast ['kʌləkɑːst], s. (tv.) trasmissione a colori.

to **coloreast**, v.t. (tv.) trasmettere a colori.

colorific [,kɔlə'rifik], ag. 1. colorante 2. fortemente colorito.

colorimeter [,kʌlə'rimitə*], s. colorimetro.

colorization [,kʌləri'zeiʃən], s. (amer.) colorazione.

colossal [kə'lɔsl], ag. colossale.

colossally [kə'lɔsli], av. in modo colossale.

Colosseum [,kɔlə'siəm], s. (archeol.) Colosseo.

colossus [kə'lɔsəs], pl. **colossi** [kə'lɔsai], **colossuses** [kə'lɔsəsiz], s. colosso ‖ the Colossus of Rhodes, (archeol.) il colosso di Rodi.

colostrum [kə'lɔstrəm], s. (fisiol.) colostro.

colour ['kʌlə*], s. 1. colore: fundamental (o primary o simple) colours, colori fondamentali; man, woman of —, uomo, donna di colore 2. colore, materia colorante 3. colorito, carnagione: a good —, un bel colorito; to change —, mutar colore; to lose, to gain —, diventare pallido, arrossire ‖ to be off —, (fam.) non sentirsi bene, essere depresso 4. aspetto, apparenza: verosimiglianza: the political — of a newspaper, il colore, l'aspetto politico di un giornale; under — of law, sotto l'apparenza della legalità; to lend — to a story, rendere verosimile un racconto; to put a false — on things, presentare le cose sotto una falsa luce; to see sthg. in its true colours, vedere le cose nel loro vero aspetto; to show one's true colours, rivelare il proprio vero carattere ‖ under — of, sotto pretesto di 5. pl. colori, bandiera ‖ with the colours, sotto le armi; to call s.o. to the colours, chiamare qlcu. sotto le armi ‖ to come *off with flying colours*, riuscire vittorioso || *to desert one's colours*, (*fig. fam.*) abbandonare i propri principi, il proprio posto, il proprio dovere; *to nail one's colours to the mast*, (*fig. fam.*) prendere apertamente una decisione e persistere in essa || *to sail under false colours*, navigare sotto falsa bandiera; (*fam.*) farsi passare per quello che non si è || *to stick to one's colours*, (*fig. fam.*) essere fedele ai propri principi || *to win one's colours*, (*spor.*) essere scelto come membro della squadra più importante ☆ — *-bearer*, (*mil.*) portabandiera; — *-blind*, daltonico; (*amer.*) antirazzista; — *blindness*, daltonismo; — *-line*, barriera fra bianchi e uomini di colore; — *-print*, incisione, stampa a colori; — *-printing*, (*tip.*) cromotipia; — *-sergeant*, sergente portabandiera; — *-wash*, tinteggiatura a colla || *the national colours*, i colori nazionali; *regimental colours*, bandiera del reggimento; *water-* —, colore all'acquerello, acquerello.

to **colour**, *v.t.i.* 1. colorare, colorire, colorirsi; tingere dipingere; macchiare: *he coloured the drawing blue*, egli colorò il disegno di azzurro; *motives* — *acts*, *fig.* il movente dà valore all'azione 2. *fig.* colorire, esagerare 3. arrossire.

colourable [ˈkʌlərəbl], *ag.* 1. plausibile, verosimile: — *imitation*, imitazione verosimile 2. ingannevole; specioso.

colourably [ˈkʌlərəbli], *av.* 1. plausibilmente 2. ingannevolmente; speciosamente.

colouration [ˌkʌləˈreiʃən], *s.* colorazione.

coloured [ˈkʌləd], *ag.* colorato, colorito (anche *fig.*); di colore: — *narrative*, *fig.* racconto colorito; — *shirt*, camicia colorata; *highly* —, a tinte vivaci || *s.c.* persona di colore ☆ *hand-* —, colorato a mano; *light-* —, di colore chiaro; — *person*, persona di colore.

colourer [ˈkʌlərə*], *s.* coloritore.

colourful [ˈkʌləful], *ag.* pieno di colore; pittoresco; vivido: — *style*, stile colorito.

colouring [ˈkʌləriŋ], *s.* 1. colorante 2. coloramento; stile, arte di applicare i colori 3. colorito; arrossimento: *the sudden* — *of her face*, l'improvviso rossore del suo viso 4. (*fam.*) apparenza: *false* —, falsa apparenza.

colourist [ˈkʌlərist], *s.* colorista.

colourless [ˈkʌləlis], *ag.* 1. senza colore, incolore; pallido 2. insipido, senza vivacità, senza carattere, molle: — *story*, *person*, storia, persona insipida, senza vivacità.

colourlessly [ˈkʌləlisli], *av.* senza espressione; in modo incolore.

colourlessness [ˈkʌləlisnis], *s.* 1. assenza di colore 2. insipidezza (di stile, di esistenza).

colourman, *pl.* **colourmen** [ˈkʌləmən], *s.* negoziante di colori.

coloury [ˈkʌləri], *ag.* di giusto colore (di caffè, ecc.).

colporteur [ˈkɔl,pɔːtə*], *s.* chi distribuisce libri religiosi per conto di una società.

colt[1] [koult], *s.* 1. puledro 2. (*fam.*) persona inesperta, principiante; (*spor.*) professionista alle prime armi (specialmente nel cricket) 3. (*mar.*) corda a nodi.

to **colt**[1], *v.t.* sferzare (con corda a nodi).

Colt[2], *s.* « Colt » (pistola a ripetizione, revolver).

colter [ˈkoultə*], *s.* (*amer.*) coltro, vomere.

coltish [ˈkoultiʃ], *ag.* 1. di puledro 2. vivace; saltellante.

coltsfoot [ˈkoultsfut], *s.* (*bot.*) tussilaggine.

colubrine [ˈkɔljubrain], *ag.* serpentino.

Columba [kəˈlʌmbə], *no.pr.* Colombano.

columbarium [ˌkɔləmˈbɛəriəm], *pl.* **columbaria** [ˌkɔləmˈbɛəriə], *s.* (*arch.*) colombario.

Columbia [kəˈlʌmbiə], *no.pr.* (*geog.*) 1. Columbia: *British* —, Columbia Britannica 2. (*poet.*) America.

Columbian [kəˈlʌmbiən], *ag.* 1. della Columbia 2. di Cristoforo Colombo.

columbine[1] [ˈkɔləmbain], *ag.* di colomba; simile a colomba || — *simplicity*, semplicità di colomba.

columbine[2], *s.* (*bot.*) aquilegia.

Columbine[3], *no.pr.f.* (*teat.*) Colombina.

column [ˈkɔləm], *s.* 1. colonna (anche *fig.*): — *of figures*, *mercury*, *smoke*, colonna di numeri, mercurio, fumo 2. (*arch.*) colonna: *Doric* —, colonna dorica 3. cronaca di giornale; rubrica; colonna 4. (*mil.*) colonna: *to march*, *move in two columns*, marciare, muoversi su due colonne ☆ *advertisement columns*, annunci economici; *aeroplane control* —, (*aer.*) barra di comando; *fifth* —, quinta colonna; *spinal* —, (*anat.*) colonna vertebrale; *sports* —, rubrica sportiva: *he writes the sports* —, tiene la rubrica sportiva.

columnar [kəˈlʌmnə*], *ag.* di colonna; a forma di colonna.

columned [ˈkɔləmd], *ag.* (*arch.*) a colonne; con colonne.

columniform [kəˈlʌmnifɔːm], *ag.* a forma di colonna.

columnist [ˈkɔləmnist], *s.* (*amer.*) giornalista che cura una rubrica; cronista mondano.

colure [ˈkouljuə*], *s.* (*astr.*) coluro.

colza [ˈkɔlzə], *s.* (*bot.*) colza.

coma[1] [ˈkoumə], *s.* (*patol.*) coma.

coma[2], *pl.* **comae** [ˈkoumiː], *s.* (*astr. bot.*) chioma.

Comanches [kəˈmæntʃiz], *no.pr.pl.* Comanci (tribù pellerossa).

comate[1] [ˈkoumeit], *ag.* (*bot.*) chiomato.

comate[2] [kouˈmeit], *s.* compagno; camerata.

comatose [ˈkoumətous], *ag.* (*patol.*) comatoso.

comb [koum], *s.* 1. pettine || *to give one's hair a* —, (*fam.*) darsi una pettinata 2. (*ind. tessile*) pettine; cardo 3. cresta (di gallo, collina, onda, ecc.) 4. favo ☆ — *-out*, rastrellamento || *curry-* —, striglia; *hair* —, pettine per capelli; *tooth-* —, pettine fitto.

to **comb**, *v.t.i.* 1. pettinare; strigliare: *to* — (*down*) *a horse*, strigliare un cavallo; *to* — *one's hair*, pettinarsi 2. (*ind. tessile*) pettinare, cardare 3. *fig.* perlustrare; rastrellare; setacciare: *we have combed the house for that book*, abbiamo perlustrato la casa in cerca di quel libro 4. frangersi (di onde) 5. *to* — *out*, fare una retata; eliminare (persone sospette, ecc.); chiamare le leve di riserva: *the police combed out the city for the murderer*, la polizia rastrellò la città in cerca dell'assassino.

combat [ˈkɔmbət], *s.* combattimento; battaglia; lotta, conflitto ☆ *single* —, duello,

to **combat**, *v.t.i.* 1. combattere 2. *fig.* lottare (contro malattia, pregiudizio, ecc.).

combatable [ˈkɔmbətəbl], *ag.* combattibile.

combatant [ˈkɔmbətənt], *ag.s.* combattente.

combative [ˈkɔmbətiv], *ag.* combattivo, battagliero.

combatively [ˈkɔmbətivli], *av.* in modo battagliero, aggressivo.

combativeness [ˈkɔmbətivnis], **combativity** [ˌkɔmbəˈtiviti], *s.* combattività; aggressività.

combe [kuːm], *s.* valletta, vallone.

comber [ˈkoumə*], *s.c.* (*ind. tessile*) pettinatore, pettinatrice; cardatore, cardatrice || *s.* 1. (*macchina*) cardatrice, pettinatrice 2. frangente (onda lunga).

combies [ˈkɔmbiz], *s.pl.* (*fam.*) combinazione (capo di biancheria femminile).

combination [ˌkɔmbiˈneiʃən], *s.* 1. combinazione (anche *chim. fis. mat.*): — *of sounds*, *atoms*, *circumstances*, combinazione di suoni, atomi, situazioni 2. associazione, federazione, lega: *right of* —, diritto di associazione 3. (*a pair of*) *combinations*, combinazione (capo di biancheria femminile) 4. (*aut.*) « sidecar » ☆ — *lock*, serratura con segreto; — *room*, sala di ritrovo (nei college a Cambridge).

combinative [ˈkɔmbinətiv], **combinatory** [kəmˈbainətəri], *ag.* combinabile.

combine [ˈkɔmbain], *s.* 1. (*comm. pol.*) associazione di persone; cartello; sindacato 2. (*agr. mec.*) mietitrebbia.

to **combine** [kəmˈbain], *v.t.i.* 1. unire, unirsi; congiungere, congiungersi: *to* — *one's effort*, unire le proprie forze || *to* — *the useful with the agreeable*, unire l'utile al dilettevole 2. contribuire: *everything combined to*

give me this impression, tutto contribuiva a darmi
questa impressione **3.** (*chim.*) combinare, combinarsi:
these elements — well, questi elementi si combinano
bene.

combined [kəm'baind], *ag.* **1.** combinato, unito, congiunto: *— efforts*, sforzi combinati; *— fleets*, flotte
unite; *— operations*, (*mil. mar.*) operazioni combinate;
— rail and road ticket, (*ferr.*) biglietto misto (ferrovia
e auto) **2.** (*chim.*) combinato ☆ *— carbon*, carbonio
combinato.

combing ['koumiŋ], *s.* **1.** pettinata; pettinatura **2.** *pl.*
capelli strappati dal pettine; (*ind. tessile*) fili strappati
dalla cardatrice☆ *— machine*, (*ind. tessile*) (macchina)
cardatrice; *— out*, retata; *— waste*, (*ind. tessile*) cascami
di pettinatura || *back —*, (*neol.*) accotonatura (di capelli).

to combust [kəm'bʌst], *v.i.* (*tec.*) entrare in combustione; bruciare.

combustibility [kəm,bʌstə'biliti], *s.* combustibilità.

combustible [kəm'bʌstəbl], *ag.* **1.** combustibile; in-
fiammabile **2.** *fig.* irascibile || *s.* combustibile.

combustion [kəm'bʌstʃən], *s.* combustione ☆ *—
chamber*, camera di combustione || *internal — engine*,
motore a combustione interna, a carburazione; *spontaneous —*, autocombustione.

combustive [kəm'bʌstiv], *ag.* (*chim.*) comburente.

come [kʌm], *s.* (*arc.*) venuta.

to come, *pass.* **came** [keim], *p.p.* **come**, *v.i.* **1.** venire, arrivare, giungere; *fig.* giungere, raggiungere (condizione, stato): *— here*, vieni qui; *has it — to this?*,
siamo giunti a questo?; *he came and saw me on Tuesday*,
è venuto a trovarmi martedì; *he came riding, running*,
giunse a cavallo, di corsa; *I have — to believe that...*,
sono giunto a credere che...; *now that I — to think
of it*, ora che ci penso; *what are things coming to?*, dove
andiamo a finire? || *—!* (o *— now!*), andiamo!, basta! ||
— Summer and I shall see you again, quando verrà
l'estate ti rivedrò || *for three months to —*, ancora
per tre mesi: *the life to —*, la vita futura; *orders to —*,
ulteriori ordini || *I saw him a week — Tuesday*, martedì
saranno otto giorni che l'ho visto || *she is coming
fifteen*, va per i quindici anni || *when it comes to*, (*l.
imp.*) quanto a, quando si tratta di || *to — to blows*,
venire alle mani || *to — to grief*, finir male || *to — to
hand*, (*comm.*) pervenire (di lettera, ecc.) || *to — to light*,
rivelarsi || *to — to oneself*, riprendere conoscenza; rin-
savire || *to — to pieces*, andare in pezzi **2.** essere, di-
venire: *he came to be a famous man*, divenne un uomo
famoso; *that comes natural to him*, ciò gli viene spon-
taneo || *to — choap*, essere in vendita a buon mercato ||
to — easy, riuscir facile || *to — right*, aggiustarsi, andare
a posto || *to — true*, avverarsi || *to — untied, unstitched*,
slegarsi, scucirsi **3.** avvenire, accadere: *what may
(o will)...*, qualunque cosa avvenga...; *how did you —
to know that?*, come hai fatto a saperlo?; *how does it
— that there is no money left?*, come mai non ci sono
più soldi? **4.** provenire, derivare: *he comes of a good
family*, viene da una buona famiglia; *it comes from
his being so ambitious*, ciò deriva dal fatto che egli è
tanto ambizioso **5.** ammontare: *how much does it —
to?*, a quanto ammonta?; *what he knows does not — to
much*, quello che egli sa non è gran cosa **6.** trovarsi,
figurare: *it comes under another heading*, figura sotto
un'altra intestazione; *on what page does it —?*, a qua-
le pagina si trova? || **Seguito da prep. 7.** *to — across*,
attraversare; incontrare per caso, trovare per caso:
the thought came across my mind that..., mi attraversò la
mente il pensiero che... **8.** *to — after*, succedere a **9.** *to —
at*, attaccare, gettarsi contro; pervenire, giungere a:
if I could only — at the truth, se solo potessi scoprire
la verità **10.** *to — before*, precedere; comparire davanti a (tribunale, ecc.); essere presentato a (Parlamento, ecc.) **11.** *to — between*, interporre, interporsi
fra **12.** *to — by*, ottenere: *this book is difficult to — by*,
è difficile riuscire ad avere questo libro **13.** *to — down*,
scendere, discendere **14.** *to — into*, entrare in (stanza,

ecc.); entrare in possesso di || *would you like to — into
it?*, (*fam.*) volete partecipare a questo affare? || *to —
into force*, entrare in vigore (di legge, ecc.) || *to —
into sight of*, giungere in vista di **15.** *to — off*, scendere
da: *to — off one's horse*, cadere da cavallo; *to — off a
ship*, sbarcare || *— off it!*, (*sl.*) piantala!, finiscila! **16.** *to
— over*, attraversare; succedere, accadere: *a change
has — over him*, un cambiamento si è prodotto in lui ||
what has — over you?, che cosa ti è preso? **17.** *to —
round*, circuire **18.** *to — through*, passare attraverso:
we came through the wood, passammo attraverso il
bosco **19.** *to — to*, ereditare **20.** *to — under*, essere
soggetto a (influsso, potenza); essere catalogato **21.** *to
— up*, salire **22.** *to — upon*, attaccare di sorpresa;
fig. colpire; venire in mente a; avere l'impressione;
reclamare (denaro, ecc.); incontrare per caso, trovare
per caso: *fear came upon him*, il timore si impadronì di
lui; *it came upon me that I had seen that man before*,
mi accorsi di aver già visto quell'uomo **23.** *to — within*, rientrare in; essere di competenza di: *that doesn't
— within my duties*, ciò non rientra nei miei doveri ||
Seguito da av. 24. *to — about*, avvenire, accadere;
(*mar.*) virare di bordo; mutare direzione (di vento) **25.** *to
— along*, venire; (*fam.*) capitare: *the things that —
along*, le cose che capitano **26.** *to — away*, venir via,
distaccarsi: *the handle came away*, il manico gli rimase
in mano **27.** *to — back*, ritornare; (*sl. amer.*) replicare: *it's
all coming back to me*, mi ritorna tutto alla mente **28.** *to
— by*, passare vicino: *I saw him — by two hours ago*,
l'ho visto passare due ore fa **29.** *to — down*, scendere,
abbassarsi; cadere; essere tramandato; ridursi (di problema, ecc.): *prices are coming down*, i prezzi calano;
these houses are coming down soon, queste case verranno
presto demolite || *to — down a peg*, abbassare la cresta ||
to — down upon s.o., riprendere severamente qlcu. ||
to — down with, sborsare (denaro) **30.** *to — forward*,
presentarsi: *to — forward as a candidate*, presentarsi
come candidato **31.** *to — in*, entrare; salire (di marea);
cominciare (di stagione, anno, moda); arrivare; servire; (*pol.*) essere eletto; (*elett.*) chiudersi, entrare in
funzione (di interruttore): *— in!*, entra!; *that's where I
— in*, ecco dove entro in ballo io; *this fashion came in
last year*, questa moda fu lanciata l'anno scorso; *to —
in first*, arrivare per primo; *to — in useful to s.o.*, *for
(doing) sthg.*, servire a qlcu., a (fare) ql.co. || *to — in for*,
avere parte in; ricevere (elogio, sgridata) **32.** *to —
near*, avvicinarsi; mancare poco; correre il rischio di:
he came near killing himself, corse il rischio di uccidersi **33.** *to — off*, distaccarsi; avere luogo; riuscire;
cavarsela: *the concert did not — off*, il concerto non ebbe
luogo; *to — off badly, cheap, with flying colours*, cavarsela malamente, a buon mercato, brillantemente **34.** *to — on*, venire avanti, avanzare; sopraggiungere (di pioggia, malattia, stagione, ecc.); entrare in
scena (di attore); far progressi: *— on!*, andiamo!,
suvvia!; *the harvest is coming on nicely*, il raccolto si
preannuncia buono || *to — on for discussion*, venire
in discussione || *to — on for trial*, (*dir.*) comparire
davanti alla Corte **35.** *to — out*, uscire; recarsi; apparire; sbocciare; essere pubblicato; debuttare; risultare, rivelarsi; stingere, scolorire; scioperare; (*elett.*)
chiudersi, aprirsi (di interruttore): *at last the truth
is coming out*, alla fine la verità viene a galla; *he always
comes out well*, è fotogenico; *he came out third*, risultò
terzo; *he has — out an excellent captain*, si è rivelato
un eccellente capitano; *when will you — out to Australia?*,
quando verrai (a trovarci) in Australia? **36.** *to —
over*, venire; cambiare (partito, opinione): *he came
over to our side*, è passato dalla nostra parte; *to —
over from, to a place*, venire da, andare in un luogo **37.** *to
— round*, fare il giro; passare da; riprendere i sensi,
riaversi; acconsentire; incontrare il vento (di nave);
mutare (di vento): *— round and see me when you can*,
venite a trovarmi appena vi è possibile; *the story has
— round to him*, la storia gli è giunta all'orecchio;

to — round to s.o.'s way of thinking, aderire al modo di pensare di qlcu. **38.** *to* — **through**, attraversare; superare: *he came through without a scratch*, ne è uscito indenne **39.** *to* — **to**, riprendere i sensi; (*mar.*) venire sul bábordo, tribordo **40.** *to* — **together**, riunirsi; incontrarsi **41.** *to* — **up**, salire; spuntare, nascere (di pianta, ecc.); comparire; diventare di moda; eguagliare; iniziare gli studi universitari: *as a violinist he does not* — *up to* X, come violinista non vale quanto X; *the tide is coming up*, la marea sale; *to* — *up after a dive*, riemergere dopo un tuffo ‖ *to* — *up against sthg.*, cozzare contro, urtare in ql.co. ‖ *to* — *up to s.o.*, avvicinarsi a qlcu. (per parlargli); *to* — *up to s.o.'s expectations*, corrispondere all'aspettativa di qlcu.; *to* — *up to town*, venire in città.

come, (*nei composti*): — *-again*, (*amm.*) rinvio, proroga; — *-and-go*, l'andare e venire; — *-at-able*, accessibile; — *-back*, ritorno (di moda, ecc.); (*pol.*) ritorno al potere; (*ind.*) lana di mezzo merino; (*amer. sl.*) ricorso; (*amer. sl.*) risposta arguta; — *-off*, conclusione; evasione (dal dovere); — *-on*, (*amer. sl.*) truffatore; (*amer. sl.*) lusinga; — *-outer*, (*amer. fam.*) secessionista, dimissionario (da partito, ecc.).

comedian [kə'mi:djən], *s.* (*teat.*) autore, attore di commedie; comico (di rivista).

comedienne [kə,medi'en], *s.* (*teat.*) attrice di commedia; attrice comica.

comedietta [kə,mi:di'etə], *s.* breve commedia di intreccio semplice.

comedown ['kʌmdaun], *s.* crollo, rovescio finanziario, rovina: *what a* —!, che rovina!, che sfacelo!.

comedy ['kɔmidi], *s.* commedia: — *of manners*, commedia di costume ‖ " *The Divine Comedy* ", « La Divina Commedia » ‖ *the human* —, la commedia umana ☆ *musical* —, commedia musicale.

comeliness ['kʌmlinis], *s.* **1.** avvenenza, grazia **2.** (*rar.*) decenza, convenienza.

comely ['kʌmli], *ag.* **1.** avvenente, grazioso (di persona) **2.** decoroso, conveniente (di comportamento).

comer ['kʌmə*], *s.c.* **1.** chi viene ‖ *open to all comers*, (gara) aperta a tutti **2.** (*sl. amer.*) persona promettente ☆ *late-* —, ritardatario; *new-* —, nuovo arrivato.

comestible [kə'mestibl], *s. gener. pl.* commestibili.

comet ['kɔmit], *s.* cometa.

cometary ['kɔmitəri], *ag.* di cometa, simile a cometa.

comether [kə'meðə*], *s.* (*irl.*) **1.** affare; circostanza **2.** amicizia; relazione amichevole.

cometic [kə'metik], *ag.* di cometa, simile a cometa.

comeuppance [kʌm'ʌpəns], *s.* (*sl. amer.*) punizione meritata.

comfit ['kʌmfit], *s.* candito; confetto ☆ — *-box*, bomboniera.

comfort ['kʌmfət], *s.* **1.** conforto, consolazione: *that's at least one* —, questa almeno è una consolazione; *to be a great* — *to s.o.*, essere di grande conforto per qlcu. ‖ *that is cold* —, è una magra consolazione; *be of good* — !, fatevi coraggio! **2.** agio, comodità, benessere, agiatezza: *to live in* —, vivere nell'agiatezza **3.** ristoro **4.** (*amer.*) trapunta ☆ *creature comforts*, buon cibo, abiti, ecc.; *public* — *station*, (*amer.*) gabinetto di decenza.

to comfort, *v.t.* **1.** confortare, consolare; ridare coraggio, speranza a: *to* — *s.o. for a loss*, consolare qlcu. per una perdita **2.** ristorare, ricreare (di bevande, ecc.).

comfortable ['kʌmfətəbl], *ag.* **1.** comodo, confortevole: *it is so* — *here*, si sta tanto bene qui; *this is a* — *house*, questa è una casa comoda; *to be* (o *to feel*) —, sentirsi a proprio agio; *to make oneself* —, mettersi a proprio agio **2.** sufficiente, adeguato: *a* — *salary*, uno stipendio sufficiente **3.** tranquillo, rassicurato: *make yourself* — *about that*, tranquillizzatevi su quel punto ‖ *s.* (*amer.*) trapunta.

comfortably ['kʌmfətəbli], *av.* comodamente, confortevolmente ‖ *to be* — *off*, essere in buone condizioni finanziarie.

comforter ['kʌmfətə*], *s.c.* consolatore, consolatrice;

confortatore, confortatrice ‖ *the Comforter*, lo Spirito Santo ‖ *s.* **1.** lunga sciarpa di lana **2.** (*amer.*) trapunta **3.** tettarella.

comforting ['kʌmfətiŋ], *ag.* confortante, consolante: — *words*, parole confortanti.

comfortless ['kʌmfətlis], *ag.* **1.** scomodo: *a* — *room*, una stanza poco accogliente, disadorna **2.** sconsolato.

comfrey ['kʌmfri], *s.* (*bot.*) consolida.

comfy ['kʌmfi], *ag. abbr.* di **comfortable**.

comic ['kɔmik], *ag.* comico; appartenente a commedia; umoristico; buffo: — *scene*, scena comica; *to see the* — *side of sthg.*, vedere il lato comico di ql.co. ‖ *s.* **1.** il ridicolo, il comico **2.** attore comico (specialmente di music-hall) **3.** *pl.* (*fam.*) racconto comico o d'avventure (a fumetti) ☆ — *opera*, (*mus.*) opera buffa; — *paper*, giornale per ragazzi; — *strip*, racconto umoristico a fumetti.

comical ['kɔmikəl], *ag.* comico, ridicolo; buffo: — *dress*, vestito ridicolo; — *expression*, espressione buffa.

comicality [,kɔmi'kæliti], *s.* comicità.

comically ['kɔmikəli], *av.* comicamente.

Cominform ['kɔminfɔ:m], *s.* (*pol.*) Cominform.

coming ['kʌmiŋ], *ag.* **1.** prossimo, futuro: *the* — *storm*, la tempesta imminente; *the* — *year*, l'anno prossimo **2.** promettente: *he is a* — *man*, è un uomo promettente ‖ *s.* venuta; arrivo: *the* — *to the throne*, l'ascesa al trono; *I remember his* — *home*, mi ricordo del suo arrivo a casa ‖ — *and going*, andirivieni: *what do these comings and goings mean?*, che cosa significa questo andare e venire? ‖ — *of age*, il diventar maggiorenne: — *of age party*, festa per celebrare il raggiungimento della maggiore età ☆ — **away**, partenza; — **back**, ritorno; — **between**, interposizione, intervento, interferenza; — **down**, discesa; ribasso (di prezzi); — **forth**, uscita; — **in**, entrata (in stanza; di fondi); introduzione (di moda, usanza); inizio (di stagione); — **on**, inizio (di malattia, tempesta, ecc.); il cadere (della notte); (*teat.*) entrata in scena; — **out**, uscita (da scuola, di pubblico dopo uno spettacolo); apparizione (di sole, ecc.); lo schiudersi (dei fiori); eruzione cutanea; caduta (dei capelli); debutto (in società, in teatro); — **together**, riunione; incontro; — **up**, avvicinamento; ascensione; arrivo ‖ *home-* —, ritorno in patria, a casa.

Comintern ['kɔmintə:n], *s.* (*pol.*) Comintern.

comitia [kə'miʃiə], *s.pl.* (*st. romana*) comizi.

comity ['kɔmiti], *s.* cortesia, gentilezza: *his* — *of manner*, il suo modo gentile ‖ — *of nations*, rispetto reciproco di leggi e costumi; (*fam.*) le nazioni amiche.

comma ['kɔmə], *s.* **1.** virgola **2.** (*mus.*) comma ☆ — *bacillus*, (*med.*) bacillo virgola ‖ *inverted commas*, virgolette: *in* (o *between*) *inverted commas*, tra virgolette.

command [kə'mɑ:nd], *s.* **1.** comando, ordine: *by royal* —, per invito reale; *to be at s.o.'s* —, essere agli ordini di qlcu.; *to do sthg. at* (o *by*) *s.o.'s* —, fare ql.co. per ordine di qlcu.; *at* —, disponibile, a disposizione **2.** (*mil.*) comando: *under* (*the*) — *of*, sotto il comando di; *to be in* — *of an army*, avere il comando di un esercito; *to get a* —, essere nominato ad un comando ‖ *Command-in-chief*, alto comando; *the Higher Command*, il Comando Supremo **3.** truppe; zona militare al comando di un capo: *he was loved by his* —, era amato dalle sue truppe **4.** padronanza, dominio (anche *fig.*): — *of language*, facilità d'espressione; — *of the seas*, dominio dei mari; — *of the world markets*, dominio dei mercati mondiali; — *over oneself*, padronanza di sè.

to command, *v.t.i.* **1.** (IV) comandare, ordinare; esercitare un potere, una autorità: *to* — *s.o. to do sthg.*, ordinare a qlcu. di fare ql.co.: *I commanded him to go*, gli ordinai di andare ‖ *yours to* —, ai vostri servigi **2.** (*mil.*) comandare (un reggimento, una nave, ecc.) **3.** *fig.* dominare, controllare: *castle that commands a view over the valley*, castello che domina la vallata; *to* — *one's passions, oneself*, dominare le

proprie passioni, se stesso **4.** ispirare, cattivarsi: *to —
sympathy, admiration, respect, etc.*, ispirare simpatia,
ammirazione, rispetto, ecc. **5.** avere (ql.co.) a propria
disposizione: *he commands as much money as he wants,*
ha a sua disposizione quanto denaro vuole.

commandant [,kɔmən'dænt], *s.* comandante (specialmente di fortezza).

commandantship [,kɔmən'dænt-ʃip], *s.* funzioni, ufficio di comandante.

to **commandeer** [,kɔmən'diə*], *v.t.* (*mil.*) **1.** requisire **2.** arruolare forzatamente.

commandeering [,kɔmən'diəriŋ], *s.* (*mil.*) **1.** requisizione **2.** reclutamento forzato.

commander [kə'mɑ:ndə*], *s.* (*mil.*) comandante;
(*mar.*) capitano di fregata; comandante (di ordine
equestre) ‖ *Commander-in-chief*, comandante in capo
☆ *wing- —*, (*aer.*) tenente colonnello, comandante
d'uno stormo.

commandership [kə'mɑ:ndəʃip], *s.* funzioni, ufficio
di comandante.

commanding [kə'mɑ:ndiŋ], *ag.* **1.** che comanda **2.** imponente, maestoso; dominante; prominente: *— beauty,*
bellezza maestosa; *— position*, posizione dominante;
— presence, aspetto imponente; *— spot*, luogo prominente; *— view,* vista imponente ☆ *— officer,* ufficiale comandante.

commandment [kə'mɑ:ndmənt], *s.* (*teol.*) comanda-
mento ‖ *the Ten Commandments*, i dieci Comandamenti;
to break, to keep the Commandments, violare, osservare
i Comandamenti.

commando [kə'mɑ:ndou], *s.* «commando», reparto
di truppe d'assalto, da sbarco, ecc. ☆ *— man*, soldato
appartenente ad un «commando».

to **commemorate** [kə'meməreit], *v.t.* commemorare;
onorare; ricordare: *prize intended to — s.o.*, premio
destinato ad onorare la memoria di qlcu.

commemoration [kə,memə'reiʃən], *s.* commemorazione.

commemorative [kə'memərətiv], *ag.* commemorativo.

to **commence** [kə'mens], *v.t.i.* **1.** (II) cominciare, incominciare, iniziare: *to — to do sthg.* (*o doing sthg.*),
cominciare a fare ql.co.; *to — work*, cominciare il
lavoro ‖ *— work!*, al lavoro! ‖ *to — M.A.*, (*arc.*)
laurearsi in lettere **2.** (*dir.*) intentare: *to — an action
against s.o.*, intentare un processo contro qlcu.

commencement [kə'mensmənt], *s.* **1.** principio,
inizio **2.** cerimonia annuale per il conferimento delle
lauree (Cambridge, Dublino, Stati Uniti).

to **commend** [kə'mend], *v.t.* **1.** lodare; encomiare: *he
was commended for his bravery,* si lodò il suo coraggio;
to — s.o. for doing sthg., lodare qlcu. per aver fatto
ql.co. **2.** (*arc.*) affidare; raccomandare: *to — one's
soul to God*, raccomandare l'anima a Dio; *to — sthg.
to s.o.'s care,* affidare ql.co. alla cura di qlcu. **3.** ottenere, riscuotere l'approvazione di: *this action commended
itself to the public,* questa azione riscosse l'approvazione del pubblico **4.** *— me to him*, (*arc.*) salutatelo da
parte mia.

commendable [kə'mendəbl], *ag.* lodevole.

commendableness [kə'mendəblnis], *s.* lodabilità.

commendably [kə'mendəbli], *av.* lodevolmente.

commendam [kə'mendæm], *s.* (*eccl.arc.*) commenda.

commendation [,kɔmen'deiʃən], *s.* **1.** lode, elogio **2.** raccomandazione ‖ *letters of —*, commendatizie.

commendatory [kɔ'mendətəri], *ag.* **1.** laudativo **2.** (*abate*) commendatario.

commensal [kə'mensəl], *ag.* **1.** (di) commensale **2.** (*bot. zool.*) commensale ‖ *s.* commensale.

commensurability [kə,menʃərə'biliti], *s.* **1.** commensurabilità **2.** proporzionalità.

commensurable [kə'menʃərəbl], *ag.* **1.** commensura-
bile **2.** proporzionale.

commensurableness [kə'menʃərəblnis], *V.* **commensurability.**

commensurate [kə'menʃərit], *ag.* proporzionato, com-
misurato: *— to* (*o with*), della stessa misura di.

commensurately [kə'menʃəritli], *av.* proporzionalmente, commisuratamente.

commensurateness [kə'menʃəritnis], *s.* commensurabilità.

commensuration [kə,menʃə'reiʃən], *s.* proporzionalità, commisurazione.

comment [*'*koment], *s.* **1.** commento, chiosa: *— on
text*, commento su un testo **2.** critica, osservazione,
commento: *to call for —*, richiedere, provocare commenti; *to make (o to pass) a — on sthg.*, fare un commento su ql.co. ‖ *the judge's —*, (*dir.*) l'apprezzamento,
i rilievi del giudice ‖ *no —*, niente da dire.

to **comment**, *v.i.* **1.** commentare: *to — on a text*, commentare un testo **2.** commentare, criticare: *to — on
s.o.'s behaviour,* criticare la condotta di qlcu.

commentary [*'*komentəri], *s.* **1.** (*lett.*) commentario
" Caesar's Commentaries", «I Commentari» di Cesare **2.** commento: *running —*, commento fedele e
particolareggiato; (*rad.*) radiocronaca.

commentation [,komen'teiʃən], *s.* annotazione, commento.

commentator [*'*komenteitə*], *s.* **1.** commentatore;
chiosatore **2.** radiocronista.

commerce [*'*komə(ː)s], *s.* **1.** commercio (specie in
grande scala); traffico; affari: *— and industry,* il commercio e l'industria ‖ *Chamber of Commerce*, Camera
di Commercio **2.** scambio; relazione; contatto (culturale, spirituale) **3.** rapporti sessuali **4.** partita a carte
☆ *— destroyer,* nave corsara.

commercial [kə'məːʃəl], *ag.* commerciale ‖ *s.* (*neol.
rad. tv.*) pubblicità commerciale ☆ *— artist*, cartello-
nista; *— car*, (*aut.*) vettura utilitaria; *— school, bank,
law, value*, scuola, banca, diritto, valore commerciale;
— traveller, viaggiatore di commercio; *— treaty*, trattato di commercio.

commercialism [kə'məːʃəlizəm], *s.* spirito commerciale; mercantilismo.

commercialist [kə'məːʃəlist], *s.* commercialista.

commerciality [kə,məːʃi'æliti], *s.* commercialità.

to **commercialize** [kə'məːʃəlaiz], *v.t.* rendere commerciabile.

commercially [kə'məːʃəli], *av.* commercialmente.

Commie [*'*komi], *s.c.* (*sl.*) comunista.

commination [,komi'neiʃən], *s.* **1.** (*dir.*) commina-
zione **2.** minacce.

comminatory [*'*kominətəri], *ag.* (*dir.*) comminatorio.

to **commingle** [ko'miŋgl], *v.t.i.* mescolare insieme; mescolarsi insieme.

to **comminute** [*'*kominjuːt], *v.t.* **1.** polverizzare, triturare, ridurre in frammenti **2.** (*chir.*) comminui-
re ☆ *comminuted fracture,* frattura comminuta.

comminution [,komi'njuːʃən], *s.* **1.** polverizzazione;
triturazione **2.** (*chir.*) comminuzione.

commiserable [kə'mizərəbl], *ag.* commiserabile.

to **commiserate** [kə'mizəreit], *v.t.i.* commiserare; dolersi: *he commiserated with me for my mother's death,*
si dolse con me per la morte di mia madre.

commiseration [kə,mizə'reiʃən], *s.* commiserazione;
compassione (*with*, per).

commiserative [kə'mizərətiv], *ag.* compassionevole.

commiseratively [kə'mizərətivli], *av.* compassionevolmente.

commissar [,komi'sɑ:*], *s.* (*amm. russa*) commissario
(del popolo).

commissarial [,komi'sɛəriəl], *ag.* di commissario,
di delegato; di vicario.

commissariat [,komi'sɛəriət], *s.* **1.** (*mil.*) commissariato, intendenza **2.** (*amm. russa*) ministero ☆ *—
department*, (*mil.*) ufficio di commissariato.

commissary [*'*komisəri], *s.* **1.** commissario; delegato ‖
Commissary for Foreign Affairs, commissario per gli affari esteri **2.** (*mil.*) ufficiale del commissariato, dell'intendenza **3.** (*amer.*) deposito di viveri; viveri **4.** (*eccl.*)

vicario (delegato dal vescovo) **5.** commissario di polizia (per Francia, Italia, ecc.).

commissaryship ['kɔmisəriʃip]. *s.* **1.** funzioni e carica di commissario **2.** (*eccl.*) vicariato **3.** (*mil.*) commissariato.

commission [kə'miʃən], *s.* **1.** commissione; comitato; delegazione: *parliamentary* —, commissione parlamentare **2.** (*mil.*) brevetto da ufficiale: *to get one's* —, essere nominato ufficiale; *to resign* (o *throw up*) *one's* —, dare le dimissioni da ufficiale **3.** commissione; incarico; mandato; missione: *work done on* —, lavoro fatto su commissione; *to carry out a* —, eseguire una commissione; *to have a roving* —, (*mar.*) aver libertà di manovra **4.** (*mar.*) l'armare (una nave da guerra): *ship in* —, nave armata, pronta per salpare **5.** (*comm.*) commissione; provvigione: *to buy, to sell on* —, comprare, vendere a provvigione; *to charge 5%* (*five per cent*) —, assegnare il 5% di provvigione **6.** (*dir.*) perpetrazione (di un crimine) ☆ — *account*, (*comm.*) conto provvigioni; — *agent* (o *merchant*), commissionario; — *house*, casa commissionaria; — *rank*, (*mil.*) grado di ufficiale.

to **commission**, *v.t.* **1.** (IV) incaricare: *to* — *s.o. to do sthg.*, incaricare qlcu. di fare ql.co.; *to be commissioned to do sthg.*, essere incaricato di fare ql.co. **2.** ordinare, commissionare (a un artista): *work commissioned by the publisher*, opera commissionata dall'editore **3.** delegare a una funzione, investire di una autorità **4.** (*mar.*) nominare comandante di una nave; assumere il comando (di una nave, da parte di ufficiale) **5.** (*mar.*) armare (una nave da guerra).

commissionaire [kə,miʃə'nɛə*], *s.* « chasseur » (d'albergo), fattorino.

commissioned [kə'miʃənd], *ag.* **1.** munito di autorità, delegato **2.** (nave) armata e equipaggiata ☆ — *officer*, (*mil.*) ufficiale; *non-* — *officer* (abbr. N.C.O.), sottufficiale.

commissioner [kə'miʃnə*], *s.* commissario, membro di commissione: — *for oaths*, commissario di dichiarazioni sotto giuramento; — *of police*, questore || *the Civil Service Commissioners*, il corpo incaricato della nomina dei funzionari dello Stato || *Lord High Commissioner*, Delegato della Corona all'Assemblea generale della Chiesa di Scozia.

commissionership [kə'miʃnəʃip], *s.* funzione, ufficio di commissario.

commissural [kə'misjurəl], *ag.* **1.** (*artig.*) di commettitura **2.** (*anat.*) commessurale.

commissure ['kɔmisjuə*], *s.* **1.** (*artig.*) commettitura **2.** (*anat.*) commessura.

to **commit** [kə'mit], *pass.p.p.* **committed** [kə'mitid], *v.t.* **1.** affidare; rimettere; mandare: *to* — *a bill*, (*pol.*) rimettere un progetto di legge ad una commissione per esame: *to* — *one's soul to God*, rimettere la propria anima a Dio; *to* — *s.o. for trial*, (*dir.*) rinviare qlcu. a giudizio; *to* — *s.o. to prison*, mandare qlcu. in prigione; *to* — *s.o., sthg., to s.o.'s care*, affidare qlcu., ql.co., alla custodia di qlcu.; *to* — *sthg. to memory*, imparare ql.co. a memoria; *to* — *sthg. to writing* (o *to paper*), mettere ql.co. per iscritto || *to* — *a body to the earth, to the waves*, seppellire un cadavere nella terra, in mare **2.** commettere; perpetrare: *to* — *a crime, a blunder*, commettere un errore, un errore **3.** impegnare (parola d'onore, ecc.): *to* — *oneself*, impegnarsi; compromettersi.

commitment [kə'mitmənt], *V.* **committal.**

committable [kə'mitəbl], *ag.* **1.** che si può affidare, rimettere **2.** che si può rinviare a giudizio (di imputato) **3.** che si può commettere (di errore, delitto).

committal [kə'mitl], *s.* **1.** mandato, incarico **2.** rinvio (di un progetto di legge ad una commissione) **3.** incarcerazione: — *for trial*, detenzione preventiva **4.** perpetrazione (di delitto, ecc.) **5.** impegno (su parola).

committed [kə'mitid], *pass.p.p.* di to **commit** || *ag. neol. lett.*) impegnato.

committee [kə'miti], *s.* comitato; commissione; con-

siglio: *the House resolves itself into a* (o *goes into*) —, la Camera si costituisce in commissione; *to appoint a* —, nominare una commissione; *to be on a* —, far parte di un comitato ☆ — *-man*, membro di comitato; — *meeting*, seduta, riunione di comitato || *executive* —, comitato esecutivo; *joint* —, commissione mista; *standing* —, commissione permanente.

to **commix** [kɔ'miks], *V.* to **commingle.**

commixture [kɔ'mikstʃə*], *s.* mescolanza, miscuglio.

commode [kə'moud], *s.* cassettone, canterano ☆ *night* —, seggetta.

commodious [kə'moudjəs], *ag.* **1.** ampio, spazioso **2.** (*arc.*) utile, comodo.

commodiously [kə'moudjəsli], *av.* spaziosamente.

commodiousness [kə'moudjəsnis], *s.* ampiezza, spaziosità.

commodity [kə'mɔditi], *s.* **1.** merce; derrata; prodotto: *free commodities*, (*comm.*) merci esenti da dogana; *staple, primary, basic* —, prodotto base **2.** oggetto di prima necessità, d'uso giornaliero ☆ — *credits*, (*comm.*) crediti commerciali.

commodore ['kɔmədɔ:*], *s.* **1.** (*mar.*) commodoro **2.** presidente di uno « yacht-club » **3.** nave del commodoro ☆ *air* —, (*aer. mil.*) generale di brigata.

Commodus ['kɔmədəs], *no.pr.m.* (*st.*) Commodo.

common ['kɔmən], *ag.* **1.** comune: *a* — *friend*, un amico comune; *the* — *good*, il bene comune; — *noun, gender*, (*gram.*) nome, genere comune; — *property*, proprietà comune; *our* — *humanity*, la nostra comune umanità; *it is a* — *opinion*, è opinione comune; *to make* — *cause with*, far causa comune con **2.** comune, solito, abituale: — *occurrence*, fatto comune, frequente; *in* — *use*, d'uso corrente; *it is* — *talk that*, è voce diffusa che || — *or garden*, (*fam.*) comune, solito: *a* — *or garden film*, un film banale || *they are as* — *as dirt*, (*fam.*) si trovano dappertutto **3.** comune, ordinario, di poco valore: — *accent*, accento, pronuncia dialettale; — *cloth*, stoffa ordinaria; — *manners*, modi grossolani || — *s.* terreno, pascolo demaniale; — *of pasture*, (*dir.*) diritto di pascolo || *out of the* —, fuori del comune, insolito; *he is a man out of the* —, è un uomo straordinario || *right of* — (o — *right*), (*dir.*) diritto di servitù attiva || *to have sthg. in* — *with s.o.*, avere ql.co. in comune con qlcu. ☆ — *divisor*, (*mat.*) comune divisore; — *law*, diritto consuetudinario; — *market*, (*neol. econ.*) mercato comune; — *people*, massa, popolo; *Common Prayer*, (*eccl.*) la liturgia anglicana; — *-room*, sala di riunione nei « college » universitari; — *-sense*, senso comune, buon senso; — *stock*, (*comm.*) titoli ordinari; — *time* (o *measure*), (*mus.*) misura in quattro battute || *the village* —, il pascolo del villaggio.

commonable ['kɔmənəbl], *ag.* **1.** che usano i pascoli comunali (di animali) **2.** di proprietà comune (di terre).

commonage ['kɔmənidʒ], *s.* **1.** diritto di pascolo **2.** comunanza (di terreni).

commonalty ['kɔmənlti], *s.* **1.** popolo; volgo; comunità **2.** corporazione.

commoner ['kɔmənə*], *s.* **1.** cittadino (non nobile) **2.** (*rar.*) membro della Camera dei Comuni **3.** studente che paga per il suo mantenimento (a Oxford) ☆ *the First Commoner*, lo « Speaker » (Presidente della Camera).

commonly ['kɔmənli], *av.* comunemente.

commonness ['kɔmənnis], *s.* **1.** banalità **2.** frequenza (di avvenimento) **3.** mediocrità (di stile); volgarità (di persona).

commonplace ['kɔmənpleis], *ag.* banale, trito, privo di originalità: *he is a very* — *kind of man*, è proprio un uomo qualunque || *s.* banalità, luogo comune ☆ — *-book*, antologia, raccolta di frasi, osservazioni, passi scelti propri o di altri || *conversational commonplaces*, frasi d'uso.

to **commonplace**, *v.t.i.* **1.** estrarre passi scelti da; raccogliere passi scelti **2.** usare, ripetere luoghi comuni.

commonplaceness [,kɔmən'pleisnis], *s.* banalità.

commons ['kɔmənz], *s.pl.* **1.** il popolo; il Terzo Stato‖ *the House of Commons,* la Camera dei Comuni: *to sit in the Commons,* appartenere alla Camera dei Comuni **2. mensa comune** (di scuola); razioni fisse (alle mense universitarie) ‖ *to be on short* —, fare un pasto magro, essere razionato.

commonweal ['kɔmənwi:l], **commonwealth** ['kɔmənwelθ], *s.* **1.** confederazione, comunità indipendente‖ *the Commonwealth of Australia,* la Federazione Australiana; *the British Commonwealth of Nations,* il « Commonwealth » Britannico **2.** repubblica (anche *fig.*): *the* — *of England,* (*st.*) la repubblica inglese (1649-60); *the* — *of learning,* la repubblica delle lettere **3.** (*amer.*) uno degli Stati Uniti **4.** (*arc.*) benessere pubblico.

commotion [kə'mouʃən], *s.* **1.** confusione: agitazione; scompiglio: *in a state of* —, in uno stato di agitazione, di confusione **2.** tumulto; insurrezione; agitazione popolare: *the* — *in the streets,* il tumulto per le strade.

to commove [kə'mu:v], *v.t.* agitare; eccitare (anche *fig.*).

communal ['kɔmjunl], *ag.* **1.** della comunità; (*amm.*) comunale **2.** (*st.*) comunardo.

communalism ['kɔmjunəlizəm], *s.* sistema di decentramento amministrativo.

communalist ['kɔmjunəlist], *s.* **1.** fautore del decentramento amministrativo **2.** (*st.*) comunardo.

commune ['kɔmju:n], *s.* (*amm.*) comune.

to commune [kə'mju:n], *v.i.* **1.** (*letter. poet.*) avere stretti rapporti spirituali **2.** (*eccl. amer.*) comunicarsi.

communicability [kə,mju:nikə'biliti], *s.* comunicabilità.

communicable [kə'mju:nikəbl], *ag.* **1.** comunicabile **2.** (*med.*) contagioso.

communicableness [kə'mju:nikəblnis], *s.* comunicabilità.

communicant [kə'mju:nikənt], *s.* **1.** (*eccl.*) comunicando **2.** informatore.

to communicate [kə'mju:nikeit], *v.t.i.* **1.** comunicare, trasmettere (movimento, calore, malattia, ecc.); far conoscere: *to* — *a discovery to s.o.,* far conoscere una scoperta a qlcu. **2.** essere, mettersi in comunicazione: *rooms that* — *with one another,* stanze comunicanti **3.** (*eccl.*) comunicare, comunicarsi.

communicating [kə'mju:nikeitiŋ], *ag.* comunicante: — *rooms,* stanze comunicanti; — *vessels,* (*fis.*) vasi comunicanti.

communication [kə,mju:ni'keiʃən], *s.* **1.** comunicazione; informazione; (*amm.*) comunicato: *he received a confidential* —, ricevette una informazione segreta **2.** relazione, rapporto; contatto: *to break off all communications with s.o.,* rompere ogni rapporto con qlcu.; *to get into* — *with s.o.,* mettersi in relazione con qlcu. **3.** mezzo, mezzi di comunicazione, di accesso: *lines of* —, linee di comunicazione; *means of* —, mezzi di comunicazione ☆ — *cord,* (*ferr.*) segnale d'allarme ‖ *long -distance* —, comunicazione interurbana.

communicative [kə'mju:nikətiv], *ag.* comunicativo, affabile, espansivo.

communicatively [kə'mju:nikətivli], *av.* in modo comunicativo.

communicativeness [kə'mju:nikətivnis], *s.* comunicativa.

communicator [kə'mju:nikeitə*], *s.c.* comunicatore, comunicatrice ‖ *s.* (*mec.*) comunicatore (di movimento).

communion [kə'mju:njən], *s.* **1.** comunione, comunanza; rapporti stretti; intima relazione spirituale: *to hold* — *with s.o.,* comunicare spiritualmente con qlcu. **2.** (*eccl.*) comunità: *the Christian* —, la società cristiana ☆ *Holy Communion,* (*relig.*) Eucarestia: *to administer, to take Holy Communion,* amministrare, ricevere la Santa Comunione; *self-* —, raccoglimento.

communiqué [kə'mju:nikei], *s.* comunicato ufficiale.

communism ['kɔmjunizəm], *s.* (*pol.*) comunismo.

communist ['kɔmjunist], *s.c.* (*pol.*) comunista.

communistic [,kɔmju'nistik], *ag.* (*pol.*) comunista.

community [kə'mju:niti], *s.* **1.** comunanza (di beni, interessi, ecc.) **2.** (*eccl.*) comunità, ordine **3.** società; collettività; organizzazione sociale: *the* —, la comunità, il pubblico; *harmful to all classes of the* —, nocivo a tutte le classi sociali; *the Jewish* —, la comunità ebraica; *the mercantile* —, la collettività commerciale ☆ — *center,* (*neol.*) sala di ricreazione (generalmente in centro rurale); — *chest,* (*amer.*) fondo di beneficenza; — *church,* (*amer.*) chiesa comunitaria (generalmente in centro rurale, frequentata da membri di diversi culti); — *singing,* canto a cui partecipano tutti i presenti.

to communize ['kɔmjunaiz], *v.t.* rendere, far diventare di proprietà comune.

commutability [kə,mju:tə'biliti], *s.* permutabilità; (*dir.*) commutabilità (di pena).

commutable [kə'mju:təbl], *ag.* permutabile; (*dir.*) commutabile (di pena).

to commutate ['kɔmjuteit], *v.t.* (*elett.*) commutare.

commutation [,kɔmju(:)'teiʃən], *s.* commutazione ☆ — *passenger,* (*amer. ferr.*) abbonato; — *ticket,* (*amer. ferr.*) biglietto di abbonamento.

commutative [kə'mju:tətiv], *ag.* commutativo.

commutator ['kɔmju(:)teitə*], *s.* (*elett.*) commutatore.

to commute [kə'mju:t], *v.t.* **1.** commutare (anche *elett.*) **2.** (*amer. ferr.*) viaggiare con abbonamento.

commuter [kə'mju:tə*], *s.c.* (*amer. ferr.*) abbonato, abbonata.

compact[1] ['kɔmpækt], *s.* patto, convenzione; contratto: *by general* —, di comune accordo ☆ *social* —, (*fil. pol.*) contratto sociale.

compact[2] [kəm'pækt], *ag.* **1.** compatto; unito; spesso **2.** serrato, conciso (di stile) ‖ *s.* **1.** cipria compatta **2.** portacipria.

to compact[2], *v.t.* **1.** rendere compatto, consolidare **2.** comporre: *to be compacted of,* essere composto di.

compactly [kəm'pæktli], *av.* in modo compatto.

compactness [kəm'pæktnis], *s.* **1.** compattezza (di massa, ecc.) **2.** concisione (di stile).

compages [kɔm'peidʒiz], *s.* compagine.

to compaginate [kɔm'pædʒineit], *v.t.* compaginare.

compagination[1] [kɔm,pædʒi'neiʃən], *s.* compaginazione.

companion[1] [kəm'pænjən], *s.c.* compagno, compagna; socio, socia ‖ *s.* **1.** vademecum; manuale: *a Latin student's* —, vademecum dello studente di latino **2.** « pendant », riscontro ☆ — *-in-arms,* commilitone ‖ *boon* —, compagno di svaghi; *lady-* —, dama di compagnia; *life* —, compagno, compagna di tutta la vita; *travelling* —, compagno, compagna di viaggio.

to companion[1], *v.t.i.* accompagnare, accompagnarsi: *to* — *with s.o.,* frequentare, tenere compagnia a qlcu.

companion[2], *s.* (*mar.*) boccaporto; cappa di boccaporto ☆ — *-way,* scaletta di boccaporto‖ *hatchway* —, cofano, cappa di boccaporto.

companionable [kəm'pænjənəbl], *ag.* socievole.

companionableness [kəm'pænjənəblnis], *s.* socievolezza.

companionably [kəm'pænjənəbli], *av.* socievolmente.

companionship [kəm'pænjənʃip], *s.* **1.** amicizia; cameratismo **2.** (*tip.*) gruppo di compositori che lavorano insieme.

company ['kʌmpəni], *s.* **1.** compagnia: *to be good, bad* —, essere di buona, cattiva compagnia; *to bear* (*o to keep*) *s.o.* —, tener compagnia a qlcu.; *to go with s.o. for* (*the sake of*) —, andar con qlcu. per il piacere della sua compagnia; *to keep one's own* —, starsene da solo, essere un po' orso; *to part* — *with s.o.,* separarsi da qlcu.; non andar più d'accordo con qlcu. ‖ *to keep* — *with s.o.,* (*fam.*) corteggiare qlcu.; lasciarsi corteggiare da qlcu. ‖ *two's* —, *three's none, prov.* poca brigata, vita beata **2.** comitiva, riunione di persone, brigata; ospiti, visitatori: *select* —, compagnia scelta; *to expect* — *to dinner*, aspettare ospiti a pranzo; *to keep low* —, frequentare cattive compagnie ‖ *present* — *excepted*, esclusi i presenti ‖ *to put on one's* — *manners*, (fam.) fare attenzione a come ci si comporta (con ospiti, estranei) ‖ *a man is known by his* —, prov. dimmi con chi vai e ti dirò chi sei 3. (comm.) società: — *limited by shares*, società anonima per azioni ‖ *Brown and Company*, Brown e Compagni 4. (teat.) compagnia 5. (mil.) compagnia 6. (mar.) equipaggio, ciurma: *ship's* —, equipaggio di una nave ☆ — *officer*, (mil.) comandante di compagnia ‖ *city* —, corporazione della città di Londra; *half-* —, (mil.) plotone; *holding* —, società finanziaria di controllo; *joint-stock* —, società per azioni; *limited* — (o *liability* —), società a responsabilità limitata; *navigation* —, *railway* —, compagnia di navigazione, ferroviaria; *touring* —, compagnia ambulante; compagnia in tournée.

to **company**, *v.t.i.* 1. associarsi; tener compagnia 2. (arc.) accompagnare.

comparable ['kɔmpərəbl], *ag.* paragonabile, comparabile.

comparably ['kɔmpərəbli], *av.* comparabilmente.

comparative [kəm'pærətiv], *ag.* 1. comparativo: — *adverb*, avverbio comparativo; — *method*, metodo comparativo 2. comparato: — *grammar, anatomy, philology*, grammatica, anatomia, filologia comparata 3. relativo: — *advantages*, vantaggi relativi; *in* — *comfort*, in relativo benessere ‖ *s.* (gram.) comparativo: *adjective in the* —, aggettivo al comparativo.

comparatively [kəm'pærətivli], *av.* 1. comparativamente 2. relativamente: — *speaking*, relativamente parlando.

compare [kəm'pɛə*], *s.* paragone, confronto: *beyond* (o *without* o *past*) —, senza paragone.

to **compare**, *v.t.i.* 1. paragonare; sostenere il confronto, confrontare; collazionare: (*as*) *compared with* (o *to*), in confronto a; *no one can* — *with you*, nessuno è paragonabile a te; *not to be compared to*, non paragonabile a; *to* — *s.o. with s.o.*, paragonare qlcu. a qlcu.; *to* — *sthg. to* (o *with*) *sthg.*, confrontare ql.co. a ql.co. ‖ *to* — *notes* (*with s.o.*), scambiare impressioni, opinioni, idee (con qlcu.) 2. (gram.) formare il comparativo di: *to* — *an adjective, an adverb*, formare i gradi di comparazione di un aggettivo, di un avverbio.

comparison [kəm'pærisn], *s.* 1. paragone, confronto: *in, by* — *with*, in, a confronto di; *without* (o *beyond all*) —, senza paragone, confronto; *to make a* — *between sthg. and sthg.*, paragonare ql.co. con ql.co. 2. (gram.) comparazione: *degrees of* —, gradi di comparazione.

to **compart** [kəm'pɑːt], *v.t.* dividere in compartimenti; ripartire.

compartment [kəm'pɑːtmənt], *s.* compartimento, scompartimento; suddivisione ☆ — *car*, (ferr.) vagone letto ‖ *smoking* —, (ferr.) compartimento per fumatori; *watertight* —, (mar.) paratia stagna, compartimento stagno.

compass ['kʌmpəs], *s.* 1. circonferenza; cerchio; estensione; spazio; portata (anche fig.): *beyond the* — *of the human mind*, oltre il limite della mente umana; *in narrow, small* —, in volume, spazio ristretto, piccolo; *knowledge within, beyond my* —, sapere entro, oltre la mia portata; *voice of great* —, voce di ampio registro; *within the* — *of a day*, nello spazio di un giorno 2. (*pair of*) *compasses*, compasso 3. bussola: *the points of the* —, i rombi, le quarte della bussola ‖ *to take a* — *bearing*, fare un rilevamento con la bussola ☆ — *-card*, rosa dei venti; — *-needle*, ago della bussola; — *-saw*, (strum. artig.) gattuccio; — *-window*, finestra sporgente, semicircolare ‖ *gyro-* —, (aer. mar.) bussola giroscopica; *mariner's* —, bussola nautica.

to **compass**, *v.t.* 1. girare attorno a 2. circondare, cingere; accerchiare: *compassed* (*about*) *by* (o *with*) *enemies*, accerchiato dai nemici; *to* — *sthg. about* (o *round*) *with sthg.*, circondare ql.co. con ql.co. 3. com-

prendere 4. (dir.) complottare, tramare: *to* — *s.o.'s death*, tramare la morte di qlcu. 5. raggiungere (uno scopo).

compassable ['kʌmpəsəbl], *ag.* 1. circondabile 2. raggiungibile: *within* — *distance of the sea*, relativamente vicino al mare.

compassion [kəm'pæʃən], *s.* compassione: *out of* —, per compassione; *to have* — *on*, aver compassione di.

compassionate [kəm'pæʃənit], *ag.* compassionevole; pietoso ☆ — *leave*, (mil.) congedo straordinario (per gravi motivi familiari).

to **compassionate** [kəm'pæʃəneit], *v.t.* compassionare, compatire.

compassionately [kəm'pæʃənitli], *av.* con compassione; pietosamente.

compatibility [kəm,pætə'biliti], *s.* compatibilità.

compatible [kəm'pætəbl], *ag.* compatibile.

compatibly [kəm'pætəbli], *av.* compatibilmente.

compatriot [kəm'pætriət], *s.c.* compatriota.

compatriotic [kəm,pætri'ɔtik], *ag.* di compatriota.

compeer [kəm'piə*], *s.* (letter.) 1. eguale, pari: *with their compeers*, con i loro pari 2. compagno, socio.

to **compel** [kəm'pel], *pass. p.p.* **compelled** [kəm'peld], *v.t.* (IV) costringere, obbligare, forzare: *I compelled him to pay*, lo costrinsi a pagare; *to* — *respect, attention, submission, admiration, etc. from s.o.*, esigere da qlcu. rispetto, attenzione, sottomissione, ammirazione, ecc.; farsi rispettare, ammirare, ecc. da qlcu.; *to* — *s.o. to obedience*, costringere qlcu. all'ubbidienza; *to be compelled to do sthg.*, essere obbligato a fare ql.co.

compellable [kəm'peləbl], *ag.* coercibile.

compelling [kəm'peliŋ], *ag.* irresistibile: — *words, eyes*, parole, occhi irresistibili.

compendious [kəm'pendiəs], *ag.* compendioso, succinto, conciso.

compendiously [kəm'pendiəsli], *av.* compendiosamente, succintamente.

compendiousness [kəm'pendiəsnis], *s.* compendiosità; concisione.

compendium [kəm'pendiəm], *pl.* **compendiums** [kəm'pendiəmz], **compendia** [kəm'pendiə], *s.* compendio, sunto.

to **compensate** ['kɔmpenseit], *v.t.i.* 1. ricompensare; indennizzare; fare ammenda; risarcire; (amer.) pagare, rimunerare: *you will be compensated by* (o *with*) *happiness*, sarai ricompensato con la felicità; *you will be compensated for what you have* (o *for having*) *suffered*, sarai ricompensato per quel che hai (o per avere) sofferto; *to* — *s.o. for sthg.*, compensare, indennizzare qlcu. per ql.co. 2. sostituire; ricomprare 3. (mec.) compensare 4. *to* — *for*, supplire.

compensating ['kɔmpenseitiŋ], *ag.* 1. che compensa: — *errors*, errori che si compensano 2. (mec.) compensatore ☆ — *gear*, (mec.) ingranaggio differenziale.

compensation [,kɔmpen'seiʃən], *s.* 1. compenso, indennità; (amer.) salario: *by way of* —, per compenso (di danni, ecc.) 2. (mec.) compensazione.

compensative [kəm'pensətiv], *ag.* compensativo.

compensator ['kɔmpenseitə*], *s.c.* compensatore, compensatrice ‖ *s.* (mec. elett.) compensatore.

compensatory [kəm'pensətəri], *ag.* compensativo.

compère ['kɔmpɛə*], *s.* (teat.) presentatore.

to **compete** [kəm'piːt], *v.i.* competere, gareggiare; concorrere: *to* — *against s.o. in sthg.*, competere con qlcu. in ql.co.; *to* — *with s.o. for sthg.*, concorrere con qlcu. a ql.co. ☆ *non-competing*, fuori gara.

competence ['kɔmpitəns], **competency** ['kɔmpitənsi], *s.* 1. mezzi sufficienti per vivere: *he has a bare* —, appena di che vivere 2. competenza; abilità, capacità: — *for sthg., to do sthg.*, competenza in ql.co., nel fare ql.co. 3. (dir.) competenza, pertinenza.

competent ['kɔmpitənt], *ag.* 1. competente; abile, capace: *a* — *manager*, un direttore capace ‖ *it is* —

to him to accept or to refuse, sta in lui accettare o rifiutare **2**. (*dir.*) competente; idoneo: — *court*, tribunale competente; — *to inherit*, idoneo ad ereditare **3**. adeguato, sufficiente: *a* — *knowledge of English*, una buona conoscenza dell'inglese.

competently ['kɔmpitəntli], *av.* con competenza; abilmente.

competition [ˌkɔmpi'tiʃən], *s.* **1**. competizione; gara: *open* (o *public*) —, concorso pubblico; *to enter into* — *with s.o.*, mettersi in gara con qlcu.; *to go in for a* —, concorrere ‖ *not for* —, fuori concorso **2**. rivalità; (*comm.*) concorrenza: *unfair* —, concorrenza sleale; *to cope with the* —, far fronte alla concorrenza.

competitive [kəm'petitiv], *ag.* **1**. di competizione, di gara, di concorso: — *spirit*, spirito agonistico **2**. di rivalità; (*comm.*) di concorrenza: — *prices*, prezzi di concorrenza ☆ — *examination*, esame di concorso.

competitively [kəm'petitivli], *av.* per mezzo di concorso: *place obtained* —, posto vinto per concorso.

competitor [kəm'petitə*], *s.* competitore; concorrente; emulo, rivale.

competitress [kəm'petitris], *s.* competitrice; concorrente; emula, rivale.

compilation [ˌkɔmpi'leiʃən], *s.* compilazione.

to **compile** [kəm'pail], *v.t.* **1**. compilare **2**. (*cricket*) segnare, marcare (punti).

compiler [kəm'pailə*], *s.* compilatore.

complacency [kəm'pleisnsi], *s.* **1**. soddisfazione, contentezza **2**. compiacenza di sè.

complacent [kəm'pleisnt], *ag.* **1**. soddisfatto di sè, contento di sè: — *air*, aria compiaciuta **2**. compiacente, cortese.

complacently [kəm'pleisntli], *av.* compiacentemente.

to **complain** [kəm'plein], *v.i.* **1**. dolersi, lagnarsi, lamentarsi: *he is always complaining*, si lamenta sempre; *she complained of a headache*, accusò mal di capo; *what has he to* — *of?*, di che cosa si lamenta?; *to* — *to s.o. about* (o *against* o *of*) *s.o., sthg.*, lamentarsi con qlcu. di qlcu., ql.co.: *I shall* — *to the manager about the bad service*, farò le mie rimostranze al direttore per il cattivo servizio **2**. (*poet.*) gemere.

complainant [kəm'pleinənt], *s.* (*dir.*) querelante.

complainer [kəm'pleinə*], *s. c.* chi si lamenta; chi fa reclami, rimostranze.

complaint [kəm'pleint], *s.* **1**. lamento; lagnanza: *I have no cause of* —, non ho alcuna ragione di cui lamentarmi; *that was the general* —, se ne lagnavano tutti; *to make* —, lamentarsi **2**. reclamo; (*dir. amer.*) querela: *to lodge a* — *against s.o.*, formulare un reclamo contro qlcu. **3**. disturbo, malattia ☆ *liver* —, disturbo epatico.

complaisance [kəm'pleizəns], *s.* compiacenza, condiscendenza; cortesia, deferenza.

complaisant [kəm'pleizənt], *ag.* compiacente, cortese.

complaisantly [kəm'pleizəntli], *av.* compiacentemente.

complement ['kɔmplimənt], *s.* **1**. complemento; il necessario per completare: *tram with its full* — *of passengers*, tram al completo di passeggeri **2**. (*gram.*) complemento predicativo: *in "he seems good", "good" is the* —, in «sembra buono», «buono» è il complemento predicativo **3**. (*mat.*) complemento (di angolo, logaritmo) **4**. (*mil. mar.*) effettivo, effettivi.

to **complement** ['kɔmpliment], *v.t.* completare; essere, fare da complemento a.

complemental [ˌkɔmpli'mentl], *ag.* complementare.

complementary [ˌkɔmpli'mentəri], *ag.* complementare: — *angles, colours*, angoli, colori complementari.

complete [kəm'pli:t], *ag.* **1**. completo, intero, totale: — *knowledge, success*, conoscenza assoluta, successo completo; *the staff is* —, il personale è al completo; *to give a* — *account*, dare un ragguaglio completo **2**. compilato, finito **3**. perfetto: *a* — *scoundrel*, un perfetto furfante **4**. (*arc.*) compito; colto, istruito.

to **complete**, *v.t.* **1**. completare; finire, terminare;

perfezionare: *to* — *some work*, terminare del lavoro; *to* — *a tea set*, completare un servizio da tè ‖ *to* — *the misfortune*, per colmo di sfortuna **2**. riempire: *to* — *a form, a questionnaire*, riempire un modulo, rispondere ad un questionario.

completely [kəm'pli:tli], *av.* completamente, totalmente.

completeness [kəm'pli:tnis], *s.* completezza, totalità, pienezza.

completion [kəm'pli:ʃən], *s.* compimento; adempimento; completamento.

completive [kəm'pli:tiv], *ag.* atto a rendere completo.

complex ['kɔmpleks], *ag.* **1**. complicato, intricato; involuto **2**. (*gram. mat.*) complesso; composto ‖ *s.* **1**. complesso, l'insieme di più parti **2**. (*psicanalisi*) complesso ☆ *inferiority* —, complesso d'inferiorità.

complexion [kəm'plekʃən], *s.* **1**. carnagione, colorito: *to have a fine* —, avere un bel colorito **2**. *fig.* aspetto, carattere: *to put a good* — *on a fact*, presentare un fatto sotto un aspetto favorevole.

complexioned [kəm'plekʃənd], *ag.* di carnagione ☆ *dark*- —, di carnagione scura; *fair*- —, di carnagione chiara.

complexity [kəm'pleksiti], *s.* complessità.

complexly [kəm'pleksli], *av.* in modo complicato, complesso.

compliance [kəm'plaiəns], *s.* **1**. condiscendenza; acquiescenza: *in* — *with your wishes*, in conformità ai vostri desideri; *to refuse* — *with an order*, rifiutare di ubbidire ad un ordine **2**. servilismo.

compliant [kəm'plaiənt], *ag.* compiacente, condiscendente **2**. servile.

compliantly [kəm'plaiəntli], *av.* con condiscendenza.

complicacy ['kɔmplikəsi], *s.* complessità.

to **complicate** ['kɔmplikeit], *v.t.* complicare: *that complicates matters*, ciò complica la faccenda.

complicated ['kɔmplikeitid], *ag.* complicato: *a* — *business*, un affare complicato; *to become* —, complicarsi, diventare complicato.

complication [ˌkɔmpli'keiʃən], *s.* complicazione.

complicity [kəm'plisiti], *s.* complicità.

compliment ['kɔmplimənt], *s.* **1**. complimento: *to pay* (o *to make*) *s.o. a* —, fare un complimento a qlcu. **2**. onore, cortesia: *do me the* — *of listening to me*, fammi (mi faccia) la cortesia di ascoltarmi ‖ *to pay compliments*, (*mil. mar.*) rendere gli onori ‖ *to pay one's compliments to s.o.*, fare una visita di cortesia a qlcu. **3**. ossequi: *with the author's, publisher's compliments*, con gli ossequi dell'autore, dell'editore; *I present* (o *send*) *my compliments to you*, vi presento i miei ossequi (a chiusa di lettera).

to **compliment** ['kɔmpliment], *v.t.* complimentare; congratularsi con: *I* — *you on your success, on having won the prize*, mi congratulo con te per il tuo successo, per aver vinto il premio.

complimentary [ˌkɔmpli'mentəri], *ag.* **1**. complimentoso **2**. di omaggio, di favore: — *tickets*, biglietti di omaggio, di favore ☆ — *close*, chiusa (di lettera).

complin(e) ['kɔmplin], *s.* (*eccl.*) compieta.

to **comply** [kəm'plai], *v.i.* accondiscendere; conformarsi; prestare osservanza: *we have complied with your request*, abbiamo soddisfatto la vostra richiesta; *to* — *with the law*, osservare la legge; *to* — *with the public taste*, conformarsi al gusto del pubblico, della maggioranza; *to* — *with s.o.'s wishes*, adattarsi ai desideri di qlcu.

component [kəm'pounənt], *ag.s.* componente.

to **comport** [kəm'pɔ:t], *v.i.* **1**. comportarsi, condursi: *to* — *oneself with dignity*, comportarsi con dignità **2**. addirsi; accordarsi.

comportment [kəm'pɔ:tmənt], *s.* (*arc.*) comportamento, condotta.

to **compose** [kəm'pouz], *v.t.* **1**. comporre, costituire: *the parts that* — *the whole*, le parti che compon-

gono l'insieme **2.** (*mus. poes. pitt. tip.*) comporre: *to —
the figures in a picture*, disporre le figure di un quadro **3.** comporre (vertenze) **4.** atteggiare; comporre: *to — one's countenance*, ricomporre il viso; *to — one's
thoughts*, raccogliere i propri pensieri; *to — oneself
to write*, raccogliersi per scrivere **5.** calmare (lo spirito, le passioni): *— yourself!*, calmati!.

composed [kəm'pouzd], *ag.* **1.** composto: *to be —
of*, comporsi di, essere composto di **2.** composto,
calmo, tranquillo: *— countenance*, viso composto.

composedly [kəm'pouzidli], *av.* compostamente, tranquillamente.

composedness [kəm'pouzidnis], *s.* compostezza; calma.

composer [kəm'pouzə*], *s.* compositore: *he was a
— of great tragedies*, fu l'autore di grandi tragedie.

composing [kəm'pouziŋ], *ag.* calmante: *— draught*,
pozione calmante ‖ *s.* **1.** l'atto del comporre **2.** (*tip.*)
composizione ☆ *— -frame*, cassa dei caratteri; *— -machine*, compositrice; *— -stick*, compositoio.

composite ['kompəzit], *ag.* composto, composito, a
struttura mista: *— ship*, nave a struttura mista; *—
style*, (*arch.*) stile composito ‖ *s.* **1.** composto, corpo
composto **2.** (*bot.*) pianta delle composite ☆ *— coach*,
(*ferr.*) vettura mista; *— print*, (*cine.*) copia sonora.

composition [,kompə'ziʃən], *s.* **1.** composizione: *the
— of the human body*, la composizione del corpo umano **2.** (*mus. lett. tip.*) composizione: *a musical —*, una
composizione musicale; *he did an English —*, fece un
tema in inglese; *he read a poem of his —*, lesse una
poesia di sua composizione; *he studies —*, (*mus.*) studia
composizione **3.** costituzione mentale: *there is a touch of
madness in his —*, c'è un pizzico di pazzia nella sua
costituzione mentale **4.** composto; mescolanza **5.** concordato, intesa; (*comm.*) concordato, transazione: *— of
ten shillings in the pound*, concordato del cinquanta
per cento; *to come to a — with s.o. over sthg.*, venire
ad un'intesa con qlcu. su ql.co.; *to make a — with
one's creditors*, fare un concordato con i propri creditori ☆ *— book*, (*amer.*) quaderno dei compiti ‖ *hand
—*, (*tip.*) composizione a mano.

compositive [kəm'pozitiv], *ag.* compositivo.

compositor [kəm'pozitə*], *s.* (*tip.*) compositore.

compos (mentis) ['kompos ('mentis)], *ag.* (*dir.*) sano
di mente: *non —*, non sano di mente, alienato.

compossible [kəm'posibl], *ag.* che può coesistere.

compost ['kompost], *s.* **1.** composto **2.** concime.

to compost, *v.t.* concimare.

composure [kəm'pouzə*], *s.* calma, posatezza, sangue freddo.

compotation [,kompou'teiʃən], *s.* **1.** bevuta in compagnia **2.** abitudine al bere.

compotator ['kompouteitə*], *s.* compagno di bevute.

compote ['kompout], *s.* composta, conserva di
frutta.

compound[1] ['kompaund], *ag.* composto, composito ‖
s. **1.** miscela, mescolanza **2.** (*chim.*) composto **3.** (*gram.*)
parola composta ☆ *— engine*, (*aer.*) motore composito; *— fracture*, (*chir.*) frattura composta; *— interest*,
(*comm.*) interesse composto; *— number*, (*arit.*) numero
composto; *— order*, (*arch.*) ordine composito; *— word*,
(*gram.*) parola composta.

to compound[1] [kəm'paund], *v.t.i.* **1.** comporre, mescolare, combinare (elementi, ingredienti); preparare
(medicine, ecc.) **2.** accordarsi; comporre (una vertenza); (*comm.*) transigere, venire a transazione **3.** regolare (un debito).

compound[2] ['kompaund], *s.* **1.** cinta attorno a case,
stabilimenti (in India, Cina) **2.** recinto dove sono confinate le abitazioni dei negri (in Sud-Africa).

compoundable [kəm'paundəbl], *ag.* conciliabile.

compounder [kəm'paundə*], *s.* **1.** conciliatore,
paciere **2.** chi prepara miscele, composti.

comprador [,komprə'do:*], *s.* mediatore indigeno di
ditte europee in Cina.

to comprehend [,kompri'hend], *v.t.* **1.** comprendere,
capire **2.** contenere; includere.

comprehensibility ['kompri,hensə'biliti], *s.* comprensibilità, intelligibilità.

comprehensible [,kompri'hensəbl], *ag.* **1.** comprensibile, intelligibile **2.** che può essere contenuto, delimitato.

comprehensibly [,kompri'hensəbli], *av.* comprensibilmente, intelligibilmente.

comprehension [,kompri'henʃən], *s.* **1.** comprensione:
it passes my —, supera la mia comprensione **2.** portata,
estensione: *a term of wide —*, una parola pregnante.

comprehensive [,kompri'hensiv], *ag.* **1.** comprensivo **2.** di vasta portata; pregnante.

comprehensively [,kompri'hensivli], *av.* comprensivamente.

comprehensiveness [,kompri'hensivnis], *s.* comprensiva, facoltà di comprendere; intelligenza.

compress ['kompres], *s.* (*med.*) compressa (di garza).

to compress [kəm'pres], *v.t.* **1.** comprimere (aria,
gas, ecc.) **2.** *fig.* condensare (idee, discorso, ecc.).

compressed [kəm'prest], *ag.* compresso; premuto;
stretto: *with — lips*, con le labbra serrate.

compressibility [kəm,presi'biliti], *s.* compressibilità.

compressible [kəm'presəbl], *ag.* compressibile.

compression [kəm'preʃən], *s.* **1.** compressione (di aria,
gas, ecc.) **2.** *fig.* concentrazione (di pensieri, stile, ecc.).

compressive [kəm'presiv], *ag.* compressivo.

compressor [kəm'presə*], *s.* compressore.

comprisable [kəm'praizəbl], *ag.* che si può comprendere, includere, raggruppare.

to comprise [kəm'praiz], *v.t.* comprendere, contenere,
includere: *the house comprises ten rooms*, la casa comprende dieci stanze.

compromise ['komprəmaiz], *s.* compromesso, transazione, accomodamento: *— with one's conscience*,
compromesso con la propria coscienza ‖ *policy of —*,
politica del compromesso ‖ *policy of no —*, politica
intransigente ‖ *to arrive at a — with s.o.*, venire ad
un compromesso con qlcu.

to compromise, *v.t.i.* **1.** venire a un compromesso;
transigere **2.** compromettere: *to — one's own or another's
reputation*, compromettere la propria o l'altrui reputazione.

compromising ['komprəmaiziŋ], *ag.* compromettente ‖ *s.* **1.** accomodamento; compromesso **2.** il compromettere.

comptometer [komp'tomitə*], *s.* macchina calcolatrice.

comptroller, *V.* **controller**.

compulsion [kəm'pʌlʃən], *s.* costrizione, obbligo:
under (o *on*) *—*, per costrizione.

compulsive [kəm'pʌlsiv], *ag.* coercitivo.

compulsively [kəm'pʌlsivli], *av.* coercitivamente.

compulsorily [kəm'pʌlsərili], *av.* obbligatoriamente.

compulsoriness [kəm'pʌlsərinis], *s.* obbligatorietà.

compulsory [kəm'pʌlsəri], *ag.* obbligatorio, forzato
☆ *— loan*, prestito pubblico obbligatorio; *— service*,
servizio obbligatorio; *— settlement*, (*comm.*) liquidazione forzosa.

compunction [kəm'pʌŋkʃən], *s.* pentimento, rimorso;
compunzione: *without —*, senza rimorsi.

compunctious [kəm'pʌŋkʃəs], *ag.* compunto; pentito.

compunctiously [kəm'pʌŋkʃəsli], *av.* con pentimento.

compurgation [,kompə:'geiʃən], *s.* (*dir. arc.*) testimonianza a discarico.

compurgator ['kompə:geitə*], *s.* (*dir. arc.*) testimone a discarico.

computable [kəm'pju:təbl], *ag.* computabile, calcolabile.

computation [,kompju(:)'teiʃən], *s.* computo, calcolo,
stima: *beyond —*, incalcolabile.

computative [kəm'pju:tətiv], *ag.* di computo; di
stima.

to compute [kəm'pju:t], *v.t.* computare, calcolare;
stimare, valutare.

computer [kəm'pju:tə*], *s.* **1.** calcolatore **2.** (macchina) calcolatrice.

comrade ['komrid], *s.* camerata; compagno: — *in arms*, commilitone.

comradeship ['komridʃip], *s.* cameratismo.

con[1] [kon], *s.* (*mar.*) governo (di nave).

to **con**[1], *pass.p.p.* **conned** [kond], *v.t.* (*mar.*) governare (una nave) ☆ *conning-tower*, torretta di comando, plancia protetta.

con[2], *s.* colpo, bussata.

to **con**[3], *pass.p.p.* **conned**, *v.t.* studiare a memoria (lezione, parte d'attore) ‖ *to — over*, ripassare, ripetere (la lezione).

con[4], *s.* (*abbr.* di *contra*) argomento contrario: *pros and cons*, i pro e i contro ‖ *av.* contro: *pro and —*, pro e contro.

conacre ['koneikə*], *s.* (*st.*) usanza irlandese di affittare piccoli appezzamenti di terreno per la durata di un solo raccolto.

conation [kou'neiʃən], *s.* (*fil.*) volizione.

conative ['kounətiv], *ag.* (*fil.*) volitivo.

to **concatenate** [kon'kætineit], *v.t. fig.* concatenare.

concatenation [kon,kæti'neiʃən], *s.* concatenazione.

concave ['kon'keiv], *ag.* concavo, incavato ‖ *s.* superficie concava: *the — of heaven*, la volta del cielo.

concavely ['kon'keivli], *av.* in modo concavo.

concavity [kon'kæviti], *s.* concavità.

to **conceal** [kən'si:l], *v.t.* **1.** nascondere, dissimulare, tener segreto: *to — sthg. from s.o.*, nascondere ql.co. a qlcu. **2.** (*dir.*) ricettare.

concealable [kən'si:ləbl], *ag.* che si può nascondere; dissimulabile.

concealment [kən'si:lmənt], *s.* **1.** occultamento; dissimulazione: *to keep s.o. in —*, tenere qlcu. nascosto **2.** nascondiglio **3.** (*dir.*) ricettazione.

to **concede** [kon'si:d], *v.t.i.* **1.** ammettere, fare una concessione: *I — that I am wrong*, ammetto di aver torto **2.** concedere (privilegi, possessi) **3.** (*sl. spor.*) perdere.

conceit [kən'si:t], *s.* **1.** vanità, presunzione **2.** (*letter.*) ricercatezza (di stile); concettismo; immagine ricercata ☆ *self- —*, presunzione.

to **conceit**, *v.t.* (*arc.*) immaginare; concepire, pensare.

conceited [kən'si:tid], *ag.* **1.** vanitoso; presuntuoso; affettato **2.** (*arc.*) concettoso, immaginoso.

conceitedly [kən'si:tidli], *av.* vanitosamente; presuntuosamente; affettatamente.

conceitedness [kən'si:tidnis], *s.* vanità; presunzione; affettazione.

conceivability [kən,si:və'biliti], *s.* concepibilità.

conceivable [kən'si:vəbl], *ag.* concepibile, immaginabile.

conceivableness [kən'si:vəblnis], *s.* concepibilità.

conceivably [kən'si:vəbli], *av.* in modo concepibile.

to **conceive** [kən'si:v], *v.t.i.* **1.** concepire, generare **2.** *fig.* concepire, ideare, immaginare; farsi un'opinione: *document conceived as follows*, documento steso, redatto come segue; *to — a great friendship, dislike for s.o.*, concepire grande amicizia, avversione per qlcu.; *to — of sthg.*, farsi un'opinione di ql.co., capire ql.co.

concent [kən'sent], *s.* (*arc.*) concento.

concentrate ['konsentreit], *s.* concentrato.

to **concentrate**, *v.t.i.* **1.** convergere: *concentrated fire*, (*mil.*) fuoco convergente; *to — the fire of a battery*, (*mil.*) far convergere il fuoco di una batteria **2.** *fig.* concentrare, concentrarsi: *to concentrate one's attention on sthg.*, concentrare la propria attenzione su ql.co. **3.** (*chim.*) condensare: *concentrated milk*, latte condensato.

concentration [,konsen'treiʃən], *s.* **1.** concentrazione **2.** ammassamento, concentramento ☆ *— camp*, campo di concentramento.

concentrative ['konsentreitiv], *ag.* concentrativo, tendente a concentrarsi.

concentrativeness ['konsentreitivnis], *s.* concentrazione.

concentrator ['konsentreitə*], *s.* (*ind.*) concentratore.

to **concentre** [kon'sentə*], *v.t.i.* **1.** concentrare, concentrarsi; convergere **2.** far convergere; mettere a fuoco.

concentric [kon'sentrik], *ag.* concentrico ‖ *— fire*, (*mil.*) fuoco concentrato in un solo punto.

concentrically [kon'sentrikəli], *av.* concentricamente.

concentricity [,konsen'trisiti], *s.* l'essere concentrico.

concept ['konsept], *s.* (*fil.*) concetto.

conceptacle [kən'septəkl], *s.* (*bot.*) ricettacolo.

conception [kən'sepʃən], *s.* **1.** concezione, concepimento ‖ *the Immaculate Conception*, (*teol.*) l'Immacolata Concezione **2.** *fig.* concetto, idea: *I haven't the remotest —*, non ne ho la minima idea.

conceptional [kən'sepʃənl], *ag.* concezionale.

conceptive [kən'septiv], *ag.* concettivo.

conceptual [kən'septjuəl], *ag.* (*fil.*) concettuale.

conceptualism [kən'septjuəlizəm], *s.* (*fil.*) concettualismo.

conceptualist [kən'septjuəlist], *s.* (*fil.*) concettualista.

conceptualistic [kən,septjuə'listik], *ag.* (*fil.*) concettualistico.

to **conceptualize** [kən'septjuəlaiz], *v.t.* (*fil.*) concettualizzare, interpretare secondo concetti.

concern [kən'sə:n], *s.* **1.** interesse, rapporto, relazione: *he has a large — in the company*, egli ha dei forti interessi nella ditta; *to have no — with sthg.*, non aver nulla a che fare con ql.co., non aver interesse in ql.co. **2.** affare, faccenda: *I'm sick of the whole —*, (*fam.*) sono disgustato da tutta la faccenda; *it is no — of mine*, questo non mi riguarda, questo non è affar mio; *mind your own concerns*, occupati dei fatti tuoi **3.** premura, ansietà, sollecitudine: *he showed his — about you*, mostrò la sua inquietudine per te **4.** (*comm.*) ditta, azienda **5.** (*fam.*) arnese, congegno, cosa: *what's that — for?*, a che serve quell'arnese? ☆ *shipping —*, società di navigazione.

to **concern**, *v.t.* concernere, riguardare, toccare, interessare: *it concerns me to know*, m'interessa sapere: *that does not — me*, ciò non mi riguarda; *to whomsoever it may —*, a chiunque possa interessare, chiunque riguardi ‖ *as far as I am concerned*, per quanto mi riguarda, quanto a me ‖ *to be concerned about*, essere preoccupato per: *I am much concerned about his health*, sono molto preoccupato per la sua salute ‖ *to be concerned with* (o *in*) *sthg.*, interessarsi di ql.co., occuparsi di ql.co., partecipare a ql.co.: *I am not concerned with his ideas*, le sue idee non mi interessano.

concerned [kən'sə:nd], *ag.* **1.** interessato; implicato: *the bank —*, la banca in questione; *the parties* (o *persons*) *—*, le parti interessate, gli interessati ‖ *the —*, gli interessati **2.** ansioso, preoccupato: *he has a very — look*, ha un'aria molto preoccupata.

concerning [kən'sə:niŋ], *prep.* circa, riguardo a, in merito a.

concernment [kən'sə:nmənt], *s.* **1.** affare, faccenda **2.** importanza: *of vital —*, d'importanza vitale, capitale **3.** interesse; preoccupazione, sollecitudine.

concert ['konsət], *s.* **1.** concerto, accordo: *to act in —*, agire di comune accordo, di concerto **2.** (*mus.*) concerto ☆ *— -grand*, pianoforte a coda, da concerto; *— -hall*, sala da concerti; *— performer*, concertista; *— -pitch*, diapason da concerto: *to keep up to — -pitch*, *fig.* mantenersi in forma ‖ *Mozart —*, concerto di musica di Mozart; *piano —*, concerto per pianoforte.

to **concert** [kən'sə:t], *v.t.i.* concertare, concertarsi.

concerted [kən'sə:tid], *ag.* **1.** concertato, convenuto: *— plan*, progetto convenuto **2.** (*mus.*) concertato: *— piece*, pezzo concertato, d'insieme.

concertina [,konsə'ti:nə], *s.* piccola fisarmonica esagonale ☆ *— vestibule*, (*ferr.*) passaggio a soffietto (per unire carrozze).

concerto [kən'tʃə:tou], *s.* (*mus.*) concerto ☆ *piano —*, concerto per pianoforte.

concessible [kən'sesibl], *ag.* concedibile.

concession [kən'seʃən], *s.* concessione (anche *dir.*).

concessionaire [kən,seʃə'nɛə*], *s.* concessionario.

concessionary [kən'seʃnəri], *ag.* concessionario ☆ — *company*, società concessionaria.

concessionnaire [kən,seʃə'nɛə*], *s.* concessionario.

concessive [kən'sesiv], *ag.* concessivo: — *clause*, (*gram.*) proposizione concessiva.

concettism [kən'tʃetizəm], *s.* (*lett.*) concettismo; preziosità.

conch [kɔŋk], *s.* **1.** (*zool.*) mollusco, crostaceo **2.** conchiglia ‖ *Triton's* —, (*mit.*) tromba di Tritone **3.** (*arch.*) conca, catino; abside **4.** (*anat.*) padiglione auricolare **5.** (*sl. mar.*) indigeno delle Bahamas.

concha ['kɔŋkə], *s.* (*anat.*) padiglione auricolare.

conchiferous [kɔŋ'kifərəs], *ag.*(*zool. geol.*) conchifero.

conchoid ['kɔŋkɔid], *s.* (*geom.*) concoide.

conchoidal [kɔŋ'kɔidl], *ag.* (*geom.*) concoidale.

conchology [kɔŋ'kɔlədʒi], *s.* conchiliologia.

conchy ['kɔnʃi], *s.* (*fam. abbr.* di *conscientious objector*) obiettore di coscienza.

concierge [,kɔ:nsi'ɛəʒ], *s.c.* portinaio, portinaia.

conciliar [kən'siliə*], **conciliary** [kən'siliəri], *ag.* conciliare: — *records*, (*eccl.*) atti conciliari.

to conciliate [kən'silieit], *v.t.* **1.** guadagnarsi, accattivarsi (stima, simpatia, ecc.): *to* — *s.o.'s goodwill*, cattivarsi la stima di qlcu.; *to* — *s.o. to one's side*, attirare qlcu. dalla propria parte **2.** conciliare (opinioni, teorie, ecc.).

conciliation [kən,sili'eiʃən], *s.* conciliazion ‖ *Court, of Conciliation*, (*dir.*) corte di conciliazione.

conciliative [kən'siliətiv], *ag.* conciliativo.

conciliator [kən'silieitə*], *s.c.* conciliatore, conciliatrice.

conciliatorily [kən'siliətərili], *av.* in modo conciliante.

conciliatory [kən'siliətəri[, *ag.* conciliante.

concinnity [kən'siniti], *s.* concinnità.

concise [kən'sais], *ag.* conciso, breve.

concisely [kən'saisli], *av.* concisamente brevemente.

conciseness [kən'saisnis], *s.* concisio,ne, brevità.

concision [kən'siʒən], *s.* **1.** concisione, brevità **2.** mutilazione **3.** (*amer.*) divisione, scisma; fazione.

conclave ['kɔnkleiv], *s.* (*eccl.*) conclave; (*fam.*) riunione segreta ‖ *to be in* — *with s.o.*, consigliarsi a quattr'occhi con qlcu.

to conclude [kən'klu:d], *v.t.i.* **1.** terminare, finire; giungere ad una conclusione, ad un accordo: *to be concluded in our next number*, la fine al prossimo numero **2.** concludere (pace, trattato, affare, ecc.) **3.** dedurre **4.** decidere: *to* — *in favour of*, decidere a favore di; *to* — *to do sthg.*, decidere di fare ql.co.

concluding [kən'klu:diŋ], *ag.* finale, ultimo ☆ — *hapter*, ultimo capitolo.

conclusion [kən'klu:ʒən], *s.* **1.** conclusione (anche *fil.*); fine: *in* —, in fine, in sostanza; *to come to a* —, venire ad una conclusione; *to draw conclusions*, tirare le conclusioni ‖ *to try conclusions with s.o.*, misurarsi con qlcu., fare a gara con qlcu. **2.** risultato finale.

conclusive [kən'klu:siv], *ag.* conclusivo; decisivo.

conclusively kən'klu:sivli], *av.* conclusivamente; in modo decisivo.

conclusiveness [kən'klu:sivnis], *s.* carattere conclusivo; prova decisiva.

to concoct [kən'kɔkt], *v.t.* **1.** mescolare (ingredienti per bibita, minestra, ecc.) **2.** inventare, architettare (una storia, ecc.); tramare (un piano, un inganno, ecc.).

concocter [kən'kɔktə*], *s.* **1.** chi prepara misture, intrugli **2.** chi elabora (piani, inganni).

concoction [kən'kɔkʃən], *s.* **1.** mistura; preparato; intruglio **2.** macchinazione (di complotto); elaborazione (di piano): *a* — *of lies*, un tessuto di menzogne.

concoctor, *V.* **concocter**.

concomitance [kən'kɔmitəns], **concomitancy** [kən-'kɔmitənsi], *s.* concomitanza.

concomitant [kən'kɔmitənt], *ag.* concomitante ‖ *s.* causa, fatto concomitante.

concomitantly [kən'kɔmitəntli], *av.* in modo concomitante, simultaneamente.

concord ['kɔŋkɔ:d], *s.* **1.** concordia, armonia **2.** (*mus.*) accordo **3.** (*gram.*) concordanza.

to concord [kən'kɔ:d], *v.i.* concordare, essere d'accordo.

concordance [kən'kɔ:dəns], *s.* **1.** accordo; armonia **2.** indice analitico (specialmente della Bibbia).

concordant [kən'kɔ:dənt], *ag.* **1.** concorde, concordante **2.** (*mus.*) armonioso.

concordantly [kən'kɔ:dəntli], *av.* concordemente.

concordat [kɔn'kɔ:dæt], *s.* (*st.*) concordato.

concourse ['kɔŋkɔ:s], *s.* **1.** concorso, affluenza (di persone, di cose) **2.** (*amer. ferr.*) sala, atrio **3.** crocicchio **4.** ampio viale.

concrescence [kən'kresns], *s.* (*biol.*) concrescenza.

concrete ['kɔnkri:t], *ag.* (*gram. fil.*) concreto: — *case*, caso concreto ‖ *in the* —, nella realtà, all'atto pratico ‖ *s.* (*edil.*) calcestruzzo, conglomerato ☆ *armoured* — (o *reinforced* —), cemento armato.

to concrete [kən'kri:t], *nel senso* **3.** ['kɔnkri:t], *v.t.i.* **1.** concretare (un sogno, un'idea) **2.** solidificarsi **3.** (*edil.*) costruire in (calcestruzzo).

concretely ['kɔnkri:tli], *av.* concretamente.

concreteness ['kɔnkri:tnis], *s.* concretezza.

concretion [kən'kri:ʃən], *s.* (*geol.*) concrezione.

concretionary [kən'kri:ʃənəri], *ag.* (*geol.*) concrezionale.

concubinage [kən'kju:binidʒ], *s.* concubinato.

concubinary [kən'kju:binəri], *ag.* che vive in concubinato ‖ *s.* concubino.

concubine ['kɔŋkjubain], *s.* concubina.

concupiscence [kən'kju:pisəns], *s.* concupiscenza.

concupiscent [kən'kju:pisənt], *ag.* concupiscente.

concupiscible [kən'kju:pisibl], *ag.* concupiscibile.

to concur [kən'kə:*], *pass.p.p.* **concurred** [kən'kə:d], *v.i.* **1.** concorrere; contribuire; coincidere (di cause, avvenimenti): *causes that* — *to an effect*, cause che concorrono a un effetto; *events that* — *in a result*, avvenimenti che concorrono ad un risultato **2.** accordarsi (su un'opinione): *I* — *with you*, sono della vostra opinione; *to* — *with a person in an opinion*, condividere l'opinione di una persona **3.** (*dir.*) essere in conflitto.

concurrence [kən'kʌrəns], *s.* **1.** concorso, incontro (di circostanze); cooperazione (di persone); (*geom.*) convergenza; simultaneità **2.** accordo, consenso **3.** (*dir.*) conflitto (di diritti).

concurrent [kən'kʌrənt], *ag.* **1.** concorrente; simultaneo; coesistente; convergente: — *cause*, (*dir.*) causa concorrente, cooperante: — *lines*, (*geom.*) linee convergenti **2.** concordante, concorde, unanime **3.** (*dir.*) in conflitto: — *rights*, diritti opposti, in conflitto ‖ *s.* **1.** causa, circostanza cooperante **2.** (*rar.*) concorrente.

concurrently [kən'kʌrəntli], *av.* **1.** simultaneamente **2.** (*dir.*) in collisione.

to concuss [kən'kʌs], *v.t.* **1.** urtare, scuotere con violenza **2.** (*dir.*) intimidire: *to* — *s.o. into doing sthg.*, obbligare qlcu. a fare ql.co.

concussion [kən'kʌʃən], *s.* **1.** scossa, urto (anche *fig.*) **2.** commozione cerebrale ☆ — *fuse*, (*artigl.*) spoletta a percussione.

to condemn [kən'dem], *v.t.* **1.** condannare (imporre una pena, ecc.): *he was condemned to death, to pay a fine*, fu condannato a morte, a pagare una multa **2.** condannare (dichiarare colpevole) **3.** censurare, biasimare **4.** dichiarare inutile **5.** confiscare ☆ *condemned cell*, cella dei condannati a morte.

condemnable [kən'demnəbl], *ag.* **1.** condannabile **2.** colpevole **3.** censurabile.

condemnation [,kɔndem'neiʃən], *s.* **1.** condanna **2.** censura; biasimo **3.** (*rar.*) sentenza di fallimento, confisca.

condemnatory [kən'demnətəri], *ag.* condannatorio.
condensability [kən,densə'biliti], *s.* condensabilità.
condensable [kən'densəbl], *ag.* condensabile.
condensate [kən'densit], *s.* (*fis. chim.*) condensato.
to **condensate** [kən'donseit], *v.t.i.* (*rar.*) condensare; condensarsi.
condensation [,kɔnden'seiʃən], *s.* 1. condensazione 2. liquido condensato.
to **condense** [kən'dens], *v.t.i.* 1. condensare, condensarsi 2. concentrare (raggi di luce) 3. *fig.* abbreviare, compendiare ☆ *condensed milk*, latte condensato.
condenser [kən'densə*], *s.* condensatore; (*chim.*) refrigerante, condensatore.
condensing [kən'densiŋ], *ag.* che condensa ‖ *s.* condensazione ☆ — *machine*, macchina condensatrice; — *unit*, complesso frigorifero.
to **condescend** [,kɔndi'send], *v.i.* accondiscendere, condiscendere; mostrarsi condiscendente: — *to sthg.*, *to do sthg.*, accondiscendere a ql.co., a fare ql.co.
condescendence [,kɔndi'sendəns], *s.* condiscendenza.
condescending [,kɔndi'sendiŋ], *ag.* condiscendente.
condescendingly [,kɔndi'sendiŋli], *av.* con condiscendenza: *to treat s.o.* —, trattare qlcu. dall'alto in basso.
condescension [,kɔndi'senʃən], *s.* 1. condiscendenza, compiacenza 2. affabilità, cortesia ‖ *out of* — *to s.o.*, per degnazione verso qlcu.
condign [kən'dain], *ag.* meritato, adeguato; esemplare: — *punishment*, punizione giusta.
condiment ['kɔndimənt], *s.* condimento.
condition [kən'diʃən], *s.* 1. condizione; clausola: *conditions of a contract*, clausole di un contratto; *conditions to be arranged*, clausole da convenirsi; *to agree to a* (o *to accept a*) —, accettare una condizione; *to impose conditions on s.o.* (o *to lay down conditions to s.o.*), imporre condizioni a qlcu.; *to make a* —, porre una condizione ‖ *on* — *that*, a condizione che ‖ *terms and conditions*, condizioni, modalità (di vendita, emissioni) 2. condizione, stato: *the* — *of the workers*, le condizioni dei lavoratori; *goods in* (*good*) —, merci in buone condizioni; *goods out of* —, merci in cattive condizioni; *of humble* —, di umili condizioni ‖ *to be in an interesting* —, essere in stato interessante ‖ *to keep oneself in* —, (*spor.*) mantenersi in forma 3. *pl.* condizioni, situazioni: *under existing conditions*, nelle presenti condizioni 4. *pl.* (*amer.*) obbligo per uno studente di colmare le sue lacune in una data materia 5. (*gram.*) periodo ipotetico ☆ *weather conditions*, condizioni metereologiche; *working conditions* (*of a machine*), funzionamento (di una macchina).
to **condition**, *v.t.i.* 1. pattuire, stipulare, negoziare: *to* — *to do sthg.*, pattuire di fare ql.co. 2. condizionare; imporre condizioni 3. condizionare (seta, lana, ecc.); verificare (l'umidità) 4. condizionare l'aria 5. (*amer.*) richiedere che uno studente colmi le sue lacune in una materia.
conditional [kən'diʃənl], *ag.* condizionale ‖ *s.* (*gram.*) condizionale.
conditionality [kən,diʃə'næliti], *s.* stato, carattere condizionale.
conditionally [kən'diʃnəli], *av.* condizionatamente.
conditioned [kən'diʃənd], *ag.* condizionato: *if I were so* —, se fossi in tale posizione ☆ — *air*, aria condizionata; — *reflex*, riflesso condizionato ‖ *well-* —, *ill* - —, in buone, cattive condizioni.
conditioner [kən'diʃənə*], *s.* verificatore (di tessili); condizionatore (di minerali); apparecchio per il condizionamento dell'aria.
conditioning [kən'diʃniŋ], *s.* condizionatura (di tessili); condizionamento (dell'aria).
condolatory [kən'doulətəri], *ag.* di condoglianza: — *letter*, lettera di condoglianza.
to **condole** [kən'doul], *v.i.* condolersi: *to* — *with s.o. upon sthg.*, condolersi con qlcu. di ql.co.

condolence [kən'douləns], *s.* condoglianza: *to offer s.o. one's condolences*, fare a qlcu. le proprie condoglianze.
condominium ['kɔndə'miniəm], *s.* (*pol.*) condominio.
condonable [kən'dounəbl], *ag.* condonabile.
condonation [,kɔndou'neiʃən], *s.* condono.
to **condone** [kən'doun], *v.t.* condonare; perdonare, passar sopra: *to* — *an offence*, passar sopra a una offesa.
condoning [kən'douniŋ], *ag.* indulgente ‖ *s.* condono.
condor ['kɔndɔ:*], *s.* (*ornit.*) condor.
condottiere [,kɔndə'tʃɛəre], *pl.* **condottieri** [,kɔndə'tʃɛəri], *s.* condottiero (di truppe mercenarie).
to **conduce** [kən'dju:s], *v.i.* contribuire, tendere (generalmente di avvenimenti); condurre (a un risultato).
conducive [kən'dju:siv], *ag.* contribuente, tendente.
conduct[1] ['kɔndəkt], *s.* 1. condotta, comportamento: *good, bad* —, buona, cattiva condotta; *to lay down a line of* — *to s.o.*, tracciare una linea di condotta a qlcu. 2. condotta, metodo; redazione, direzione (di un giornale): — *of affairs*, condotta degli affari 3. costruzione, struttura: — *of a poem*, struttura di un componimento poetico 4. il condurre, guida ☆ — *-money*, (*dir.*) indennità di viaggio pagata ad un testimone ‖ *safe-* —, salvacondotto.
to **conduct**[1] [kən'dʌkt], *v.t.i.* 1. condurre, guidare 2. dirigere: *to* — *an orchestra*, (*mus.*) dirigere un'orchestra; *to* — *the operations*, dirigere le operazioni 3. (*fis.*) condurre, trasmettere (calore, elettricità, ecc.) 4. comportarsi: *to* — *oneself well, badly*, comportarsi bene, male 5. fare, agire da capo ☆ *conducted tours*, visite turistiche con guida.
conduct[2] ['kɔndəkt], *s.* cappellano del collegio di Eton.
conductance [kən'dʌktəns], *s.* (*elett.*) conduttanza.
conductibility [kən,dʌkti'biliti], *s.* (*fis.*) conducibilità.
conductible [kən'dʌktəbl], *ag.* (*fis.*) conducibile.
conduction [kən'dʌkʃən], *s.* 1. (*fis.*) conduzione 2. convogliamento (di liquido in un condotto).
conductive [kən'dʌktiv], *ag.* conduttivo.
conductivity [,kɔndʌk'tiviti], *s.* (*fis.*) conducibilità, conduttività.
conductor [kən'dʌktə*], *s.* 1. guida (di persone); accompagnatore (di turisti) 2. direttore (di un'impresa) 3. (*mus.*) direttore (d'orchestra, coro, ecc.) 4. bigliettaio (di tram, autobus); (*amer.*) capotreno, controllore 5. (*fis.*) conduttore ☆ *lightning* —, (*elett.*) parafulmine.
conductorship [kən'dʌktəʃip], *s.* direzione (di orchestra).
conductress [kən'dʌktris], *s.* bigliettaria (di tram, autobus).
conduit ['kɔndit], *s.* 1. condotto, conduttura, canale sotterraneo 2. passaggio segreto 3. (*arc.*) fontana (con getto) ☆ *water* —, acquedotto.
condyle ['kɔndil], *s.* (*anat.*) condilo.
cone [koun], *s.* 1. oggetto conico; (*geom.*) cono 2. pigna 3. (*zool.*) cono ☆ *ice* (*-cream*) —, cono gelato.
to **cone**, *v.t.i.* 1. dare forma di cono 2. produrre pigne 3. avvolgere su bobina (seta, ecc.) 4. *to be coned*, (*aer.*) essere investito dalla luce di riflettori (nemici).
coney, *V.* **cony**.
confab ['kɔnfæb], *s.* (*fam. abbr.* di *confabulation*) confabulazione, conversazione familiare.
to **confabulate** [kən'fæbjuleit], *v.i.* confabulare, discorrere.
confabulation [kən,fæbju'leiʃən], *s.* confabulazione, conversazione familiare.
confabulatory [kən'fæbjulətəri], *ag.* confabulatorio.
confection [kən'fekʃən], *s.* 1. composizione (di ingredienti, ecc.) 2. (*farm.*) confezione 3. (*arc.*) dolce, confettura 4. indumento già confezionato (generalmente per donna).
to **confection**, *v.t.* 1. preparare (confetture, dolci, ecc.) 2. confezionare (abiti).

confectionary [kən'fekʃnəri], *ag.* di pasticceria; dolce.

confectioner [kən'fekʃnə*], *s.* confettiere, pasticciere.

confectionery [kən'fekʃnəri], *s.* **1.** dolci, confetture **2.** pasticceria.

confederacy [kən'fedərəsi], *s.* **1.** confederazione, lega **2.** cospirazione; complotto.

confederate [kən'fedərit], *ag.* confederato, alleato ‖ *s.* **1.** confederato **2.** complice; (*fam.*) compare.

to **confederate** [kən'fedəreit], *v.t.i.* **1.** confederare, confederarsi: *to — oneself with s.o.*, allearsi, formare una lega con qlcu. **2.** cospirare.

confederation [kən,fedə'reiʃən], *s.* confederazione ‖ *Swiss Confederation*, Confederazione Elvetica.

to **confer** [kən'fə:*], *pass.p.p.* **conferred** [kən'fə:d], *v.t.i.* **1.** conferire, dare, accordare: *to — a favour, a title, etc. on s.o.*, conferire un favore, un titolo, ecc. a qlcu. **2.** conferire, consultarsi: *to — with s.o. on sthg.*, consultarsi con qlcu. su ql.co.

conference ['konfərəns], *s.* **1.** conferenza; consultazione; abboccamento: *— of doctors*, consulto medico; *European —*, conferenza europea; *to be in — with s.o.*, avere un colloquio con qlcu., conferire con qlcu. ‖ *he is in —*, (*amer.*) è occupato **2.** congresso: *industrial —*, congresso industriale ☆ *press —*, conferenza stampa.

conferential [,konfə'renʃəl], *ag.* di conferenza.

conferment [kən'fə:mənt], *s.* conferimento (di titolo, ecc.).

conferrable [kən'fə:rəbl], *ag.* conferibile.

to **confess** [kən'fes], *v.t.i.* **1.** confessare, ammettere: *he confessed his crime*, confessò il suo delitto; *I — (that) I am guilty* (o *I — myself to be guilty*), confesso di essere colpevole ‖ *a fault confessed is half redressed*, *prov.* peccato confessato è mezzo perdonato **2.** (*eccl.*) confessare; confessarsi: *the priest confessed ten persons*, il prete confessò dieci persone; *to — one's sins*, confessare i propri peccati; *to — (oneself) to a priest*, confessarsi ad un prete **3.** professare: *to — the Christian faith*, professar la fede cristiana **4.** *to — to*, ammettere: *he confessed to the crime*, egli ammise il delitto; *I — to admiring her*, devo ammettere che la ammiro.

confessant [kən'fesənt], *s.c.* (*eccl.*) chi si confessa, penitente.

confessedly [kən'fesidli], *av.* per ammissione di tutti; per confessione propria; apertamente.

confession [kən'feʃən], *s.* **1.** confessione (anche *eccl.*): *the seal of —*, il segreto della confessione; *to make a full —*, fare completa confessione **2.** professione: *— of faith*, (*eccl.*) professione di fede ‖ *by general —*, per professione di tutti.

confessional [kən'feʃən], *ag.* confessionale ‖ *s.* (*eccl.*) confessionale.

confessionary [kən'feʃənəri], *ag.* confessionale.

confessionist [kən'feʃənist], *s.* (*st. relig.*) luterano confessionista.

confessor [kən'fesə*], *s.* **1.** confessore **2.** chi si confessa; chi confessa (un delitto) **3.** chi professa (una fede) ‖ *Edward the Confessor*, (*st.*) Edoardo il Confessore.

confessorship [kən'fesəʃip], *s.* (*eccl.*) confessorato.

confetti [kən'feti(:)], *s.pl.* confetti; coriandoli.

to **confide** [kən'faid], *v.t.i.* **1.** confidare, affidare: *to — a secret to s.o.*, confidare un segreto a qlcu.; *to — sthg. to s.o.'s care*, affidare ql.co. alla cura di qlcu. **2.** confidare, confidarsi: *I — in God*, confido in Dio; *to — in s.o. about sthg.*, confidarsi con qlcu. circa ql.co.

confidence ['konfidəns], *s.* **1.** fiducia: *to have — in s.o.*, aver fiducia in qlcu.; *to place — in the people*, porre fiducia nel popolo ‖ *motion of no —*, mozione di sfiducia; *vote of —*, voto di fiducia **2.** confidenza: *to be in s.o.'s —*, partecipare ai segreti di qlcu.; *to make a — to s.o.*, fare una confidenza a qlcu.; *to take s.o. into one's —*, confidarsi con qlcu.; *to tell s.o. sthg. in —*, dire ql.co. a qlcu. in confidenza ‖ *in strict —*,

con la massima riservatezza **3.** sicurezza, fiducia in se stesso ☆ *— crook* (o *— man*), truffatore; *— trick* (o *— game*), (*amer.*) truffa all'americana.

confident ['konfidənt], *ag.* **1.** fiducioso: *to be — of the future*, avere fiducia nell'avvenire; *to be — that*, essere fiducioso che; *to feel — that*, sentirsi sicuro che **2.** sicuro di sè, presuntuoso ‖ *s.c.* confidente.

confidential [,konfi'denʃəl], *ag.* confidenziale, riservato, segreto: *a — letter*, una lettera riservata; *to be — with s.o.*, fare delle confidenze a qlcu. ☆ *— secretary*, segretario particolare.

confidentiality [,konfi,denʃi'æliti], *s.* carattere confidenziale, riservato, segreto (di ql.co.).

confidentially [,konfi'denʃəli], *av.* confidenzialmente; in modo riservato, segreto.

confidentialness [,konfi'denʃəlnis], *s.* carattere confidenziale, riservato, segreto (di ql.co.).

confidently ['konfidəntli], *av.* con fiducia, sicurezza.

confider [kən'faidə*], *s.c.* chi confida; chi affida.

confiding [kən'faidiŋ], *ag.* confidente; senza sospetti: *to be of a — nature*, non essere diffidente, sospettoso per carattere.

confidingly [kən'faidiŋli], *av.* con fiducia; senza diffidenza.

configuration [kən,figju'reiʃən], *s.* **1.** configurazione, conformazione; profilo **2.** (*astr.*) configurazione.

to **configure** [kən'figə*], *v.t. spec. fig.* configurare.

confinable [kən'fainəbl], *ag.* che si può confinare.

confine ['konfain], *s. gener. pl.* confine; limite; frontiera: *at the extreme confines of the earth*, agli estremi confini della terra; *within the — of Judaea*, entro i confini della Giudea.

to **confine** [kən'fain], *v.t.i.* **1.** relegare, tenere entro certi limiti; imprigionare: *to be confined to bed, to one's room, to the house*, essere costretto a letto, a rimanere nella propria camera, in casa **2.** limitare; limitarsi: *— yourself to facts*, tenetevi ai fatti; *to — oneself to sthg.*, *to doing sthg.*, limitarsi a ql.co., a fare ql.co.; *to — the use of a word*, limitare l'uso di una parola **3.** *to be confined*, partorire (di donna) **4.** (*rar.*) essere limitrofo, confinare: *to — with a country*, confinare con un paese.

confineless [kən'fainlis], *ag.* illimitato; sconfinato.

confinement [kən'fainmənt], *s.* **1.** imprigionamento, reclusione **2.** limitazione, restrizione **3.** puerperio; parto: *her — was expected from day to day*, di giorno in giorno si aspettava che partorisse ☆ *solitary —*, segregazione cellulare.

to **confirm** [kən'fə:m], *v.t.* **1.** confermare: *to — a letter, an order, a statement*, confermare una lettera, un'ordinazione, una dichiarazione **2.** ratificare (trattato, ecc.) **3.** (*dir.*) confermare, omologare (sentenza, ecc.) **4.** corroborare (notizia, ecc.) **5.** (*eccl.*) cresimare.

confirmation [,konfə'meiʃən], *s.* **1.** conferma **2.** ratificazione, conferma (di trattato, ecc.) **3.** (*dir.*) omologazione **4.** corroborazione (di notizia, ecc.) **5.** (*eccl.*) cresima.

confirmative [kən'fə:mətiv], *ag.* confermativo; affermativo.

confirmatively [kən'fə:mətivli], *av.* in modo confermativo; affermativamente.

confirmatory [kən'fə:mətəri], *ag.* confermativo.

confirmed [kən'fə:md], *ag.* **1.** inveterato; impenitente; cronico; convinto: *— bachelor, drunkard*, scapolo impenitente, ubriacone inveterato **2.** (*eccl.*) cresimato.

confirmee [,konfə'mi:], *s.* (*eccl.*) cresimato.

confirmer [kən'fə:mə*], *s.* chi, che conferma.

confiscable [kən'fiskəbl], *ag.* confiscabile.

to **confiscate** ['konfiskeit], *v.t.* confiscare: *to — sthg. from s.o.*, confiscare ql.co. a qlcu.; *to — sthg. to s.o.*, confiscare ql.co. a beneficio di qlcu.

confiscation [,konfis'keiʃən], *s.* confisca.

confiscator ['konfiskeitə*], *s.c.* confiscatore, confiscatrice.

confiscatory [kən'fiskətəri], *ag.* di confisca: *— measures*, misure di confisca.

confiteor [kɔn'fitiɔ:*], *s.* (*eccl.*) confiteor.

conflagration [,kɔnfləˈgreiʃən], *s.* conflagrazione (anche *fig.*).

conflation [kənˈfleiʃən], *s. spec. fig.* fusione.

conflict [ˈkɔnflikt], *s. spec. fig.* conflitto; lotta; contrasto; antagonismo: *to be in — with*, essere, trovarsi in conflitto con; *to come into — with*, venire a conflitto con.

to **conflict** [kənˈflikt], *v.i.* **1.** essere in conflitto, in disaccordo: *interests that —*, interessi contrastanti **2.** *spec. fig.* contendere, lottare.

conflicting [kənˈfliktiŋ], *ag.* opposto; in conflitto; contraddittorio: *— evidence*, prove contraddittorie.

confliction [kənˈflikʃən], *s.* antagonismo, urto.

confluence [ˈkɔnfluəns], *s.* **1.** confluenza (di fiumi, ecc.); incrocio (di strade, ecc.) **2.** (*arc. letter.*) affluenza (di persone).

confluent [ˈkɔnfluənt], *ag.s.* confluente.

conflux [ˈkɔnflʌks], *s.* (*letter.*) confluenza, affluenza.

to **conform** [kənˈfɔ:m], *v.t.i.* conformare, conformarsi; uniformare, uniformarsi, obbedire: *I — to the law*, mi conformo alla legge; *to — to fashion*, seguire la moda **2.** (*relig. st.*) fare atto di sottomissione.

conformability [kənˌfɔ:məˈbiliti], *s.* conformità.

conformable [kənˈfɔ:məbl], *ag.* **1.** conforme, compatibile **2.** compiacente, docile, accomodante (di persona) **3.** (*relig. inglese*) conformista.

conformably [kənˈfɔ:məbli], *av.* conformemente: *— to your desires*, in conformità ai vostri desideri.

conformance [kənˈfɔ:məns], *s.* conformità; sottomissione.

conformation [,kɔnfɔ:ˈmeiʃən], *s.* **1.** conformazione; struttura; forma; configurazione; profilo **2.** adattamento: *the — of our lives to the duties of morality*, l'adattamento della nostra vita ai doveri della morale.

conformist [kənˈfɔ:mist], *s.* (*relig. inglese*) conformista.

conformity [kənˈfɔ:miti], *s.* **1.** conformità; somiglianza: *in — with*, in conformità a, conformemente a **2.** (*relig. inglese*) conformismo; ortodossia.

to **confound** [kənˈfaund], *v.t.* **1.** confondere; sconcertare; disorientare; turbare: *to be confounded*, essere confuso **2.** mettere in disordine; mescolare **3.** sconvolgere (piani, idee, ecc.) **4.** (*fam.*) mandare al diavolo: *— it!*, al diavolo! *— you!*, va' al diavolo! || *— me for a fool!*, che imbecille che sono!.

confounded [kənˈfaundid], *ag.* **1.** confuso, attonito: *to be — by the sight of*, confondersi, essere sorpreso, alla vista di **2.** (*fam.*) insopportabile: *a — bore*, un seccatore insopportabile; *what a — nuisance, business!*, che noia maledetta, che maledetto affare!.

confoundedly [kənˈfaundidli], *av.* (*fam.*) maledettamente; terribilmente.

confraternity [,kɔnfrəˈtə:niti], *s.* confraternita || *treaty of —*, trattato di fratellanza.

confrère [ˈkɔnfrɛə*], *s.* confratello, collega.

to **confront** [kənˈfrʌnt], *v.t.* **1.** affrontare (persone, difficoltà, ecc.) **2.** incontrarsi, trovarsi di fronte a: *the confronting armies*, gli opposti eserciti **3.** mettere a confronto: *to — s.o. with his accusers*, (*dir.*) mettere qlcu. a confronto con i suoi accusatori **4.** collazionare.

confrontation [,kɔnfrʌnˈteiʃən], *s.* confronto (di testimoni, ecc.).

Confucian [kənˈfju:ʃən], *ag.* (*relig.*) di Confucio || *s.c.* (*relig.*) seguace di Confucio.

Confucianism [kənˈfju:ʃənizəm], *s.* (*relig.*) confucianismo.

Confucianist [kənˈfju:ʃənist], *s.c.* (*relig.*) seguace del confucianismo.

Confucius [kənˈfju:ʃəs], *no.pr.m.* (*st. relig.*) Confucio.

to **confuse** [kənˈfju:z], *v.t.* **1.** disorientare, sconcertare; turbare: *to get confused*, confondersi **2.** confondere; mescolare; mettere in disordine: *to — s.o., sthg. with s.o., sthg.*, confondere qlcu., ql.co. con qlcu., ql.co.:

I confused him with his brother, lo presi per suo fratello.

confused [kənˈfju:zd], *ag.* confuso; disorientato; ingarbugliato: *— mind*, mente turbata; *— sea*, (*mar.*) mare agitato; *— voices*, voci confuse.

confusedly [kənˈfju:zidli], *av.* confusamente; con aria confusa: *to look at s.o. —*, guardare qlcu. con aria confusa.

confusedness [kənˈfju:zidnis], *s.* disordine, confusione.

confusion [kənˈfju:ʒən], *s.* **1.** confusione, disordine: *the — of languages*, la confusione delle lingue; *the enemy was thrown into —*, il nemico fu sbaragliato **2.** turbamento, vergogna: *to put s.o. to —*, confondere, turbare qlcu. **3.** (*arc.*) sconfitta: *to drink to the — of one's enemies*, bere alla sconfitta dei propri nemici.

confutable [kənˈfju:təbl], *ag.* confutabile.

confutation [,kɔnfju:ˈteiʃən], *s.* confutazione.

confutative [kənˈfju:tətiv], *ag.* confutativo.

to **confute** [kənˈfju:t], *v.t.* **1.** confutare (opinione, ecc.) **2.** dimostrare, provare l'errore di.

confutement [kənˈfju:tmənt], *s.* confutazione.

conga [ˈkɔŋgə], *s.* « conga » (musica, danza cubana).

congé [ˈkɔ:nʒei], *s.* **1.** congedo, licenziamento: *to give s.o. his —*, congedare qlcu. **2.** (*arc.*) inchino (di commiato).

to **congé**, *v.t.i.* **1.** congedare, congedarsi **2.** (*arc.*) fare un inchino (di commiato).

to **congeal** [kənˈdʒi:l], *v.t.i.* **1.** congelare, congelarsi **2.** coagulare, coagularsi; cagliare, cagliarsi.

congealable [kənˈdʒi:ləbl], *ag.* coagulabile; congelabile.

congealableness [kənˈdʒi:ləblnis], *s.* congelabilità; coagulabilità.

congealment [kənˈdʒi:lmənt], *s.* congelamento.

(to) **congee** [ˈkɔndʒi:], *V.* (to) **congé.**

congelation [,kɔndʒiˈleiʃən], *s.* congelamento.

congener [ˈkɔndʒinə*], *ag.* consimile || *s.* individuo, oggetto consimile.

congeneric [,kɔndʒiˈnerik], **congenerous** [kənˈdʒenərəs], *ag.* congenere.

congenial [kənˈdʒi:njəl], *ag.* **1.** analogo, affine; congeniale: *— tastes*, gusti affini; *— with sthg.*, affine a ql.co. **2.** simpatico, amabile: *— spirit*, persona di carattere amabile; *— surroundings*, ambiente simpatico **3.** adatto, conveniente: *employment — to me*, impiego adatto a me.

congeniality [kən,dʒi:niˈæliti], *s.* **1.** accordo, affinità (di gusti, d'indole, ecc.) **2.** carattere simpatico, gradevole.

congenially [kənˈdʒi:njəli], *av.* amabilmente, simpaticamente.

congenital [kənˈdʒenitl], *ag.* congenito.

conger[1] [ˈkɔŋgə*], *s.* (*-eel*), (*ittiol.*) gongro.

conger[2], *s.* associazione cooperativa di librai nel Settecento.

congeries [kɔnˈdʒiəri:z], *s.* (*invariato al pl.*) congerie.

to **congest** [kənˈdʒest], *v.t.i.* **1.** congestionare; ingorgare (traffico, ecc.) **2.** (*patol.*) congestionare, congestionarsi.

congested [kənˈdʒestid], *ag.* **1.** congestionato; sovrappopolato: *— traffic*, traffico congestionato; *— area*, zona sovrappopolata **2.** (*patol.*) congestionato.

congestion [kənˈdʒestʃən], *s.* congestione (anche *fig.*).

congestive [kənˈdʒestiv], *ag.* (*patol.*) congestivo.

conglobate [ˈkɔngloubeit], *ag.* conglobato.

to **conglobate**, *v.t.i.* conglobare, conglobarsi.

conglobation [,kɔnglouˈbeiʃən], *s.* conglobazione.

to **conglobe** [kənˈgloub], *v.t.i.* conglobare, conglobarsi.

conglomerate [kənˈglɔmərit], *ag.s.* (*geol.*) conglomerato.

to **conglomerate** [kənˈglɔməreit], *v.t.i.* conglomerare, conglomerarsi.

conglomeration [kən,glɔməˈreiʃən], *s.* conglomerazione.

conglutinate [kən'glu:tineit], *ag.* agglutinato.
to **conglutinate**, *v.t.i.* aggutinare, agglutinarsi.
conglutination [kən,glu:ti'neiʃən], *s.* agglutinazione.
conglutinative [kən'glu:tinətiv], *ag.* agglutinativo.
conglutinator [kən'glu:tineitə*], *s.* (*med.*) conglutinante.
Congo ['kɔŋgou], *no.pr.* (*geog.*) Congo.
congou ['kɔŋgu:], *s.* tè cinese scuro.
congrats [kən'græts], *s.pl.* (*fam.*) congratulazioni.
congratulant [kən'grætjulənt], *ag.* congratulante.
to **congratulate** [kən'grætjuleit], *v.t.* rallegrarsi con, congratularsi con: *I — you*, mi congratulo con te, ti faccio i miei complimenti; *to — oneself on sthg.*, felicitarsi con se stesso per ql.co.; *to — s.o. on sthg.*, *on having done sthg.*, congratularsi con qlcu. per ql.co., per aver fatto ql.co.
congratulation [kən,grætju'leiʃən], *s.* congratulazione, felicitazione: *to offer s.o. one's congratulations on sthg.*, congratularsi con qlcu. per ql.co.
congratulative [kən'grætjulətiv], *ag.* congratulatorio.
congratulator [kən'grætjuleitə*], *s.c.* congratulatore, congratulatrice.
congratulatory [kən'grætjulətəri], *ag.* gratulatorio: *— letter*, lettera gratulatoria, di felicitazione.
to **congregate** ['kɔŋgrigeit], *v.t.i.* raccogliere, raccogliersi; adunare, adunarsi.
congregation [,kɔŋgri'geiʃən], *s.* **1.** unione, riunione (di cose, persone); adunata, raduno; assemblea (di appartenenti ad un'università) **2.** (*eccl.*) congregazione; l'insieme dei fedeli (di una chiesa, diocesi, parrocchia) ‖ *— of Israel*, congregazione degli Israeliti ‖ *Concistorial Congregation*, Congregazione concistoriale, Concistoro.
congregational [,kɔŋgri'geiʃənl], *ag.* (*eccl.*) della congregazione: *— worship*, culto pubblico ‖ *the Congregational Church*, la Chiesa congregazionalista.
Congregationalism [,kɔŋgri'geiʃnəlizəm], *s.* (*relig.*) congregazionalismo.
Congregationalist [,kɔŋgri'geiʃnəlist], *s.* (*relig.*) congregazionalista.
congress ['kɔŋgres], *s.* congresso, riunione: *to hold a —*, tenere un congresso ‖ *Congress*, Congresso (il Parlamento negli Stati Uniti).
congressional [kɔŋ'greʃənl], *ag.* di congresso.
Congressman, *pl.* **Congressmen** ['kɔŋgresmən], *s.* (*negli Stati Uniti*) membro del Congresso.
congruence ['kɔŋgruəns], **congruency** ['kɔŋgruənsi], *s.* **1.** congruenza, conformità **2.** (*mat.*) congruenza.
congruent ['kɔŋgruənt], *ag.* **1.** congruente, conforme: *— with*, conforme a **2.** (*mat.*) congruente.
congruity [kɔŋ'gru(:)iti], *s.* conformità.
congruous ['kɔŋgruəs], *ag.* congruente, conforme.
congruously ['kɔŋgruəsli], *av.* congruamente, conformemente: *— to* (o *with*), conformemente a.
conic(al) ['kɔnik(əl)], *ag.* conico.
conically ['kɔnikəli], *av.* a forma di cono.
conicalness ['kɔnikəlnis], **conicity** [kə'nisiti], *s.* conicità.
conics ['kɔniks], *s.* (*mat.*) teoria delle coniche, geometria analitica.
conifer ['kounifə*], *s.* (*bot.*) conifera.
coniferous [kou'nifərəs], *ag.* (*bot.*) conifero.
coniform ['kounifɔ:m], *ag.* coniforme.
coni(i)ne ['koun(i)ain], *s.* (*chim.*) conina.
coniroster [,kouni'rɔstə*], *s.* (*ornit.*) conirostro.
conirostral [,kouni'rɔstrəl], *ag.* (*ornit.*) conirostro.
conjecturable [kən'dʒektʃərəbl], *ag.* congetturabile.
conjectural [kən'dʒektʃərəl], *ag.* congetturale.
conjecturally [kən'dʒektʃərəli], *av.* congetturalmente.
conjecture [kən'dʒektʃə*] *s.* congettura, supposizione.
to **conjecture**, *v.t.* congetturare, fare una congettura.
to **conjoin** [kən'dʒɔin], *v.t.i.* congiungere, congiungersi; combinare, combinarsi.
conjoint ['kɔndʒɔint], *ag.* congiunto, unito.

conjointly ['kɔndʒɔintli], *av.* congiuntamente, unitamente.
conjugal ['kɔndʒugəl], *ag.* coniugale: *— rights*, diritti coniugali.
conjugality [,kɔndʒu'gæliti], *s.* stato coniugale.
conjugally ['kɔndʒugəli], *av.* coniugalmente.
conjugate ['kɔndʒugit], *ag.* **1.** congiunto, unito **2.** (*gram.*) derivato dalla stessa radice **3.** (*mat.*) coniugato **4.** (*biol.*) fuso ‖ *s.* **1.** (*gram.*) parola derivata dalla stessa radice di un'altra **2.** (*mat.*) coniugato **3.** (*biol.*) fusione ☆ *— points*, (*geom.*) punti coniugati; *— system*, (*chim.*) sistema coniugato.
to **conjugate** ['kɔndʒugeit], *v.t.i.* coniugare, coniugarsi.
conjugation [,kɔndʒu'geiʃən], *s.* coniugazione.
conjugational [,kɔndʒu'geiʃənl] *ag.* di coniugazione.
conjunct [kən'dʒʌŋkt], *ag.* congiunto, associato, unito ‖ *s.* socio.
conjunction [kən'dʒʌŋkʃən], *s.* **1.** congiunzione, unione: *in — with s.o.*, d'accordo con, insieme con qlcu. **2.** (*gram. astr.*) congiunzione.
conjunctional [kən'dʒʌŋkʃənl], *ag.* di congiunzione.
conjunctionally [kən'dʒʌŋkʃənəli], *av.* per mezzo di congiunzione.
conjunctiva [,kɔndʒʌŋk'taivə], *s.* (*anat.*) congiuntiva.
conjunctive [kən'dʒʌŋktiv], *ag.* **1.** (*biol.*) connettivo **2.** (*gram.*) congiuntivo ‖ *s.* (*gram.*) **1.** congiuntivo **2.** congiunzione.
conjunctively [kən'dʒʌŋktivli] *av.* unitamente, insieme ‖ *words used —*, (*gram.*) locuzione congiuntiva.
conjunctivitis [kən,dʒʌŋkti'vaitis], *s.* (*patol.*) congiuntivite.
conjunctly [kən'dʒʌŋktli], *av.* unitamente, insieme.
conjuncture [kən'dʒʌŋktʃə*], *s.* congiuntura, occasione, circostanza: *in this —*, in questa circostanza.
conjuration [,kɔndʒuə'reiʃən], *s.* **1.** evocazione solenne **2.** incantesimo **3.** congiura **4.** (*arc.*) supplica, preghiera.
to **conjure** [kən'dʒuə*], *nel senso* **2.** ['kʌndʒə*], *v.t.i.* **1.** scongiurare: *to — s.o. to do sthg.*, scongiurare qlcu. di fare ql.co. **2.** fare giuochi di prestigio ‖ *a name to — with*, (*fam.*) un nome di gran prestigio **3.** *to — away*, fare scomparire (per incanto) **4.** *to — up*, evocare, fare apparire (per incanto); rievocare (memorie, idee, ecc.): *spot that conjures up old memories*, luogo che richiama antichi ricordi.
conjurer ['kʌndʒərə*], *s.* **1.** prestigiatore **2.** (*arc.*) evocatore (di spiriti).
conjuring ['kʌndʒəriŋ], *s.* **1.** prestidigitazione **2.** (*arc.*) evocazione (di spiriti).
conjuror ['kʌndʒərə*], *s.* **1.** prestigiatore **2.** (*arc.*) evocatore (di spiriti).
conk [kɔŋk], *s.* (*sl.*) **1.** naso **2.** (*amer.*) testa; colpo in testa.
to **conk**, *v.i.* **1.** (*sl. amer.*) dare un colpo in testa **2.** *to — out*, (*sl. mec.*) avariarsi, incepparsi, bloccarsi (di motore).
conkers ['kɔŋkəz], *s.pl.* «conkers» (gioco di bambini).
conky ['kɔŋki], *ag.* (*sl.*) nasuto ‖ *s.* (*sl.*) nasone.
connate ['kɔneit], *ag.* **1.** innato **2.** (*bot. zool.*) unito congenitamente.
connatural [kə'nætʃrəl], *ag.* connaturale.
to **connect** [kə'nekt], *v.t.i.* **1.** connettere, connettersi; unire, unirsi; collegare: *a railway connects this town with Milan*, una ferrovia unisce questa città a Milano; *we are connected by telephone*, siamo collegati con il telefono **2.** (*ferr.*) far coincidenza: *the two trains — at Milan*, i due treni fanno coincidenza a Milano **3.** associare (mentalmente): *doctors — crime with insanity*, i dottori associano il delitto alla pazzia; *we — orange blossoms with weddings*, noi associamo i fiori d'arancio al matrimonio **4.** (*gener. passivo*) avere relazione, aver rapporti; essere imparentato, imparentarsi; (*comm.*) fare parte di (una ditta): *he is well connected*, ha delle conoscenze importanti; *to be con-*

nected with a family, essere imparentato con una famiglia.

connected [kə'nektid], *ag.* **1.** connesso, coerente, logico: — *speech*, discorso coerente **2.** collegato, unito; imparentato: *a well — person*, una persona bene imparentata.

connectedly [kə'nektidli], *av.* coerentemente, logicamente: *to think* —, pensare logicamente.

connectedness [kə'nektidnis], *s.* concatenazione, associazione (di idee).

connecter [kə'nektə*], *s.* **1.** (*mec.*) raccordo **2.** (*elett.*) morsetto serrafili.

connectible [kə'nektəbl], *ag.* che si può connettere, unire, collegare.

connecting [kə'nektiŋ], *ag.* che connette; che unisce ‖ *s.* (*elett.*) associazione (di pile, ecc.); collegamento ☆ — *pipe*, tubo di comunicazione; — *rod*, (*mec.*) biella, tirante; — *wire*, filo di collegamento.

connection [kə'nekʃən], *s.* **1.** connessione, collegamento, comunicazione: *the concert was held in — with the opening of the Fair*, il concerto fu tenuto in occasione dell'apertura della Fiera; *what is the — between the two ideas?*, che relazione c'è fra le due idee? ‖ *in — with*, a proposito di; *in this* —, a questo proposito **2.** relazione, rapporto personale: *to break off, to form, to have a — with s.o.*, rompere, stabilire, avere rapporti con qlcu. **3.** parentela, parente: *he is no — of mine*, non è mio parente; *the whole* —, tutta la famiglia **4.** coincidenza (di treni, ecc.): *I missed my — at Milan*, ho perduto la coincidenza a Milano; *this train runs in — with the boat*, questo treno fa coincidenza con il battello **5.** (*comm.*) clientela: *that dressmaker has a good — among the wealthy women of the town*, quella sarta ha un'ottima clientela tra le ricche signore della città **6.** (*mec.*) accoppiamento, collegamento; (*elett.*) connessione, contatto **7.** setta religiosa.

connective [kə'nektiv], *ag.* (*fisiol.*) connettivo: — *tissue*, (*fisiol.*) tessuto connettivo ‖ *s.* **1.** (*fisiol.*) connettivo **2.** (*gram.*) congiunzione.

connector, *V.* **connecter**.

connexion, *V.* **connection**.

conning-tower ['koniŋ,tauə*], *V.* to **con**[1].

conniption [kə'nipʃən], *s.* (*sl. amer.*) accesso di rabbia, attacco isterico.

connivance [kə'naivəns], *s.* connivenza: — *at* (o *in*) *a crime*, complicità in un delitto.

to **connive** [kə'naiv], *v.i.* essere connivente: *to — at an abuse*, tollerare un abuso; *to — at a crime*, essere complice in un delitto.

connivent [kə'naivənt], *ag.* convergente.

connoisseur [,koni'sə:*], *s.* conoscitore, intenditore.

to **connotate** ['konouteit], *V.* to **connote**.

connotation [,konou'teiʃən], *s.* **1.** (*log.*) contenuto di un concetto **2.** significato secondario, implicito (di un termine).

connotative ['konouteitiv], *ag.* (*log.*) conseguente, implicito: — *meaning*, significato implicito.

to **connote** [ko'nout], *v.t.* **1.** (*log.*) denotare (i propri attributi, di parole) **2.** significare, dire implicitamente.

connubial [kə'nju:bjəl], *ag.* coniugale, matrimoniale.

connubially [kə'nju:bjəli], *av.* coniugalmente.

conoid ['kounoid], *ag.* (*geom.*) conoidale ‖ *s.* (*geom.*) conoide.

conoidal [kou'noidl], *ag.* (*geom.*) conoidale.

to **conquer** ['koŋkə*], *v.t.i.* **1.** conquistare, essere vincitore: *she conquered all hearts*, conquistò tutti i cuori; *to — a country*, conquistare un paese **2.** soggiogare, vincere (nemico, passioni, ecc.); sormontare (ostacoli, difficoltà).

conquerable ['koŋkərəbl], *ag.* **1.** conquistabile **2.** domabile; vincibile.

conquering ['koŋkəriŋ], *ag.* vincente; vittorioso.

conqueror ['koŋkərə*], *s.* **1.** conquistatore (anche *fig.*) ‖ *William the Conqueror*, (*st. inglese*) Guglielmo il Conquistatore **2.** *to play the* —, fare la bella (a carte).

conquest ['koŋkwest], *s.* conquista (anche *fig.*) ‖ *the* (*Norman*) *Conquest*, (*st.*) la conquista dell'Inghilterra da parte dei Normanni (1066).

Conrad ['konræd], *no.pr.m.* Corrado.

consanguine [kon'sæŋgwin], **consanguineous** [,konsæŋ'gwiniəs], *ag.* consanguineo.

consanguinity [,konsæŋ'gwiniti], *s.* consanguineità.

conscience ['konʃəns], *s.* coscienza: *in all* (o *on* o *upon one's*) —, in coscienza; *point of* —, caso di coscienza; *I would not have the — to do it*, la mia coscienza non mi permetterebbe di farlo; *it is a matter of* —, è una questione di coscienza; *to have a clean* (o *an easy* o *a good*) —. avere la coscienza pulita; *to have a guilty* (o *bad*) —, avere la coscienza sporca; *to have sthg. on one's* —, avere ql.co. sulla coscienza; *to make it a matter of* —, farne un caso di coscienza ‖ — *for' sake*, per scrupolo di coscienza ☆ — *-clause*, (*dir.*) clausola di riserva morale (in un atto); — *-money*, restituzione (anonima) di somma dovuta al fisco; — *-stricken*, preso dal rimorso: *to be — -stricken*, sentirsi rimordere la coscienza.

conscienceless ['konʃənslis], *ag.* senza coscienza; senza scrupoli.

conscientious [,konʃi'enʃəs], *ag.* coscienzioso, scrupoloso ☆ — *objector*, obiettore di coscienza; — *scruple*, scrupolo di coscienza.

conscientiously [,konʃi'enʃəsli], *av.* coscienziosamente; scrupolosamente.

conscientiousness [,konʃi'enʃəsnis], *s.* coscienziosità: *his — in his work*, la sua coscienziosità nel lavoro.

conscious ['konʃəs], *ag.* **1.** consapevole, conscio: *he spoke with — superiority*, parlava consapevole della sua superiorità; *I was — of s.o.* (o *that s.o. was*) *looking at me*, sentivo che qlcu. mi guardava; *to become — of sthg.*, accorgersi di ql.co. **2.** cosciente: — *movement*, movimento cosciente; *the old man was — to the last*, il vecchio fu cosciente fino all'ultimo; *to become* —, tornare in sè, riprendere conoscenza.

consciously ['konʃəsli], *av.* consapevolmente, coscientemente.

consciousness ['konʃəsnis], *s.* **1.** coscienza, consapevolezza: *stream of* —, (*lett. psicologia*) flusso di coscienza **2.** conoscenza: *to lose, to regain* —, perdere, riprendere conoscenza ☆ *moral* —, coscienza morale.

to **conscribe** [kon'skraib], *V.* to **conscript**.

conscript ['konskript], *ag.s.* coscritto ☆ — *fathers*, (*st. romana*) padri coscritti.

to **conscript** [kən'skript], *v.t.* coscrivere, chiamare sotto le armi.

conscription [kən'skripʃən], *s.* coscrizione ‖ — *of wealth*, tassazione straordinaria (in tempo di guerra).

consecrate ['konsikrit], *ag.* consacrato.

to **consecrate** ['konsikreit], *v.t.* **1.** (*eccl.*) consacrare; benedire: *he was consecrated archbishop of Milan*, fu consacrato arcivescovo di Milano **2.** *fig.* consacrare, dedicare: *to — one's life to a work*, consacrare, dedicare la propria vita ad un'opera.

consecrated ['konsikreitid], *ag.* (*eccl.*) consacrato, benedetto: — *ground*, terra consacrata.

consecration [,konsi'kreiʃən], *s.* **1.** consacrazione; benedizione **2.** dedizione.

consecrator ['konsikreitə*], *s.* consacratore, consacrante.

consectary [kən'sektəri], *s.* deduzione, corollario.

consecution [,konsi'kju:ʃən], *s.* **1.** successione, illazione, conclusione **2.** (*gram.*) consecuzione.

consecutive [kən'sekjutiv], *ag.* consecutivo.

consecutively [kən'sekjutivli], *av.* consecutivamente.

consecutiveness [kən'sekjutivnis], *s.* successione, seguito.

consenescence [,konsi'nesns], *s.* senescenza.

consensual [kən'senʃjuəl], *ag.* (*dir.*) consensuale.

consensus [kən'sensəs], *s.* consenso unanime; accordo.

consent [kən'sent], *s.* consenso; accordo: *by com-*

mon —, per comune consenso; *by mutual* —, amichevolmente; *with one* —, di comune accordo.

to **consent**, *v.i.* acconsentire: *to* — *to do sthg.*, acconsentire a fare ql.co.; *to* — *to sthg. being done*, acconsentire che ql.co. sia fatta.

consentaneity [kən,sentə'ni:iti], *s.* consentaneità.

consentaneous [,kɔnsen'teiniəs], *ag.* consentaneo.

consentaneously [,kɔnsen'teiniəsli], *av.* consentaneamente.

consentient [kən'senʃənt], *ag.* consenziente, d'accordo.

consequence ['kɔnsikwəns], *s.* **1.** conseguenza, effetto: *in* —, per conseguenza; *in* — *of*, a causa di; *to take the consequences*, sopportare le conseguenze ‖ *as a* — *of above*, (comm.) in seguito a quanto sopra **2.** importanza, rilievo: *he is of no* —, egli non conta nulla; *he is a person of* —, è una persona importante; *it is of no* —, non ha importanza alcuna.

consequent ['kɔnsikwənt], *ag.* **1.** conseguente, risultante **2.** (*log.*) conseguente ‖ *s.* **1.** conseguenza **2.** (*log.*) conclusione **3.** (*mat.*) conseguente.

consequential [,kɔnsi'kwenʃəl], *ag.* **1.** consequenziale **2.** importante, pieno di sè.

consequentiality [,kɔnsi,kwenʃi'æliti], *s.* **1.** logica (di ragionamento) **2.** presunzione, boria.

consequentially [,kɔnsi'kwenʃəli], *av.* **1.** indirettamente, secondariamente **2.** con importanza; presuntuosamente.

consequently ['kɔnsikwəntli], *av.* logicamente; di conseguenza ‖ *cong.* di conseguenza; dunque.

conservable [kən'sə:vəbl], *ag.* conservabile.

conservancy [kən'sə:vənsi], *s.* **1.** commissione di controllo (di porto, fiume, ecc.) ‖ *Thames Conservancy*, commissione di controllo del Tamigi **2.** conservazione, protezione (di foreste, ecc.).

conservation [,kɔnsə(:)'veiʃən], *s.* conservazione.

conservatism [kən'sə:vətizəm], *s.* (*pol.*) conservatorismo.

conservative [kən'sə:vətiv], *ag.* **1.** conservativo; conservatore; *on* — *lines*, secondo il metodo tradizionale **2.** prudente, cauto: — *estimate*, stima, valutazione prudente **3.** (*pol.*) conservatore ‖ **Conservative**, *s.* (*pol.*) conservatore ‖ *Conservative Party*, (*pol.*) partito conservatore.

conservatoire [kən'sə:vətwa:*], *s.* (*mus.*) conservatorio.

conservator ['kɔnsə(:)veitə*], *come s.* [kən'sə:vətə*], *s.c.* conservatore, conservatrice ‖ *s.* sovrintendente (di museo, ecc.).

conservatorium [kən,sə:və'tɔ:riəm], *s.* (*mus.*) conservatorium.

conservatory [kən'sə:vətri], *ag.* conservatore; conservativo ‖ *s.* **1.** serra **2.** (*amer.*) conservatorio ☆ — *principle*, principio di conservazione.

conserve [kən'sə:v], *s.* **1.** (*farm.*) confezione **2.** *pl.* (*cuc.*) conserva di frutta.

to **conserve**, *v.t.* conservare, preservare (monumenti, ecc.).

to **consider** [kən'sidə*], *v.t.i.* **1.** (I) considerare, riflettere, pensare, esaminare: *considered opinion*, opinione ben ponderata; *to* — *doing sthg.*, pensare di fare ql.co.; *to* — *what to do, where to go, how to act*, riflettere sul da farsi, dove andare, come agire ‖ *all things considered*, tutto considerato **2.** considerare, giudicare, stimare: — *it as done*, consideralo bello e fatto; *I* — *him* (*to be*) *a great painter*, lo reputo un gran pittore; *I* — *him* (*to be*) *sincere*, lo giudico sincero; *I* — *it* (*to be*) *my duty to inform you*, ritengo mio dovere informarti **3.** aver riguardo per: — *your health*, abbi riguardo della tua salute **4.** (*arc.*) guardare, contemplare: *she considered him a moment*, ella lo guardò un momento.

considerable [kən'sidərəbl], *ag.* considerevole, notevole; importante: *a* — *section of the country*, una

buona parte del paese; *I have given* — *thought to the matter*, ho pensato molto alla questione.

considerably [kən'sidərəbli], *av.* considerevolmente, notevolmente: *that* — *added to our difficulties*, ciò aumentò notevolmente le nostre difficoltà.

considerate [kən'sidərit], *ag.* **1.** rispettoso dei sentimenti altrui **2.** (*arc.*) prudente.

considerately [kən'sidəritli], *av.* **1.** premurosamente **2.** (*arc.*) prudentemente.

considerateness [kən'sidəritnis], *s.* **1.** riguardo, delicatezza **2.** (*arc.*) consideratezza, prudenza.

consideration [kən,sidə'reiʃən], *s.* **1.** considerazione, meditazione, esame: *after due, much* —, dopo dovuta, profonda riflessione; *in* — *of*, in considerazione di: *he was let off in* — *of his youth*, gli si fece grazia in considerazione della sua giovinezza; *on no* —, per nulla al mondo; *under* —, in esame: *question under* —, questione in esame; *these are my considerations*, queste sono le mie considerazioni; *to take sthg. into* —, prendere ql.co. in considerazione **2.** ricompensa, rimunerazione: *to do sthg. for a* —, fare ql.co. dietro compenso **3.** (*comm.*) interesse; provvigione: — *given for a bill of exchange*, interesse dato per una cambiale **4.** riguardo, premura, rispetto: *out of* — *for s.o.*, per riguardo verso qlcu. **5.** (*rar.*) importanza: *of great, no* —, di grande, nessuna importanza; *money is no* — *with him*, per lui il denaro non conta.

considering [kən'sidəriŋ], *prep.* tenuto conto di, visto, considerando: — *the circumstances*, viste le circostanze; — *his age*, tenuto conto della sua età; — *that*, visto che: — *that he is so young*, visto che è così giovane.

to **consign** [kən'sain], *v.t.* **1.** (*comm.*) consegnare, inviare, spedire **2.** affidare, rimettere: *to* — *sthg. to a person's care*, affidare ql.co. alle cure di una persona **3.** depositare (denari in banca).

consignation [,kɔnsai'neiʃən], *s.* (*comm.*) **1.** pagamento a persona incaricata della riscossione **2.** consegna (di merce): *to ship goods to the* — *of s.o.*, spedire merce all'indirizzo di qlcu. **3.** (*rar.*) deposito in banca.

consignee [,kɔnsai'ni:], *s.* consegnatario; destinatario.

consigner [kən'sainə*], *s.* (*comm.*) mittente.

consignment [kən'sainmənt], *s.* (*comm.*) **1.** invio, spedizione: *I am expecting a heavy* — *of...*, attendo un forte invio di...; *to send a* —, fare una spedizione **2.** deposito, consegna: *goods on* —, merce in deposito **3.** partita di merce ☆ — *note*, nota di spedizione.

consignor [kən'sainə*], *s.* (*comm.*) mittente.

consilient [kən'silient], *ag.* concordante.

to **consist** [kən'sist], *v.i.* **1.** consistere, essere composto: *his fortune consisted of several houses*, il suo patrimonio consisteva in diverse case; *what does virtue* — *in? it consists in acting...*, in che consiste la virtù? consiste nell'agire... **2.** essere in accordo, in armonia.

consistence [kən'sistəns], **consistency** [kən'sistənsi], *s.* consistenza, densità, compattezza; *fig.* costanza, risolutezza, coerenza.

consistent [kən'sistənt], *ag.* coerente, logico; conforme: *action not* — *with the law*, azione non conforme alla legge; *to be* — *with*, essere d'accordo con.

consistently [kən'sistəntli], *av.* coerentemente, uniformemente; conformemente: — *with my principles*, conformemente ai miei principi.

consistorial [,kɔnsis'tɔ:riəl], *ag.* (*eccl.*) concistoriale.

consistory [kən'sistəri], *s.* (*eccl.*) concistoro.

consociate [kən'souʃiit], *ag.* associato, consociato ‖ *s.* consocio.

to **consociate** [kən'souʃieit], *v.t.i.* associare, associarsi; consociare, consociarsi.

consociation [kən,souʃi'eiʃən], *s.* associazione, consociazione.

consolable [kən'souləbl], *ag.* consolabile.

consolation [,kɔnsə'leiʃən], *s.* consolazione: *words of*

—, parole consolatrici ☆ — *prize*, (*spor.*) premio di consolazione.

consolatory [kən'sɔlətəri], *ag.* consolante.

console[1] ['kɔnsoul], *s.* (*arch.*) mensola ☆ — *-table*, « consolle », mensola.

to **console**[2] [kən'soul], *v.t.* consolare: *to — s.o. for a loss*, consolare qlcu. di una perdita.

consoler [kən'soulə*], *s.c.* consolatore, consolatrice ☆ *baby's* —, tettarella.

to **consolidate** [kən'sɔlideit], *v.t.i.* 1. consolidare, consolidarsi: *to — a position*, (*mil.*) consolidare una posizione 2. unire (proprietà, imprese); consolidare, unificare (un debito pubblico) 3. (*fis.*) solidificare, solidificarsi; comprimere in una massa compatta ☆ *consolidated annuities*, (*econ.*) consolidato.

consolidation [kən,sɔli'deiʃən], *s.* consolidazione, consolidamento; (*amer. comm.*) fusione di società.

consolidator [kən'sɔlideitə*], *s.* consolidatore; unificatore.

consolidatory [kən'sɔlidətəri], *ag.* consolidante.

consoling [kən'souliŋ], *ag.* consolante.

consols [kən'sɔlz], *s.pl.* (*econ.*) (*abbr.* di *consolidated annuities*) consolidato.

consonance ['kɔnsənəns], *s.* 1. consonanza, armonia; (*mus.*) accordo 2. accordo, conformità (di sentimenti, ecc.): *this action is not in — with his character*, questa azione non s'accorda col suo carattere.

consonant ['kɔnsənənt], *ag.* 1. consono, conforme 2. (*mus.*) armonioso || *s.* consonante.

consonantal [,kɔnsə'næntl], *ag.* (*gram.*) di consonante.

consonantly ['kɔnsənəntli], *av.* d'accordo, in conformità.

consort[1] ['kɔnsɔ:t], *s.c.* 1. consorte 2. compagno, compagna; socio, socia; collega || *to act in — with s.o.*, agire di concerto con qlcu. || *s.* (*mar.*) nave che viaggia di conserva con altra: *to sail in —*, navigare di conserva ☆ *prince- —*, principe consorte.

to **consort**[2] [kən'sɔ:t], *v.t.i.* 1. associarsi, unirsi: *to — with s.o.*, frequentare qlcu. 2. accordarsi (di cose).

consortium [kən'sɔ:tjəm], *s.* consorzio, associazione.

conspecific [,kɔnspi'sifik], *ag.* della stessa specie.

conspectus [kən'spektəs], *s.* 1. visione d'insieme 2. compendio, prospetto; tabella sinottica.

conspicuity [,kɔnspi'kju:iti], *V.* **conspicuousness**.

conspicuous [kən'spikjuəs], *ag.* 1. cospicuo, notevole, eminente: *to play a — part*, recitare una parte importante 2. manifesto, visibile, in vista: *to make oneself —*, farsi notare, mettersi in vista || *to be — by one's absence*, (*fam.*) brillare per la propria assenza.

conspicuously [kən'spikjuəsli], *av.* cospicuamente; con evidenza.

conspicuousness [kən'spikjuəsnis], *s.* cospicuità; evidenza, vistosità.

conspiracy [kən'spirəsi], *s.* 1. cospirazione, congiura, complotto 2. intesa.

conspirator [kən'spirətə*], *s.* cospiratore.

conspiratress [kən'spirətris], *s.* cospiratrice.

to **conspire** [kən'spaiə*], *v.t.i.* 1. cospirare, congiurare (anche *fig.*): *to — to do sthg.*, complottare di fare ql.co.; *to — together*, cospirare insieme 2. contribuire, concorrere: *everything conspired to ruin him*, tutto contribuì alla sua rovina 3. (*rar.*) meditare, tramare (la rovina di qlcu.).

to **conspue** [kən'spju:], *v.t.* (*rar.*) esprimere dissenso e chiedere l'abbandono di (una politica), l'abolizione di (una legge).

constable ['kʌnstəbl], *s.* 1. (*st.*) conestabile; governatore; alto dignitario di corte || *Constable of England* (o *Lord High Constable*), Gran Conestabile d'Inghilterra; *Constable of France*, Conestabile di Francia; *Constable of the Tower of London*, Governatore della Torre di Londra 2. poliziotto, agente di polizia || *to outrun the —*, (*fam.*) spendere oltre i propri mezzi ☆ *Chief Constable*, capo della polizia di una contea, commissario

centrale; *police —*, poliziotto; *rural —*, guardia campestre; *special —*, cittadino giurato facente funzione di poliziotto.

constabulary [kən'stæbjuləri], *ag.* che riguarda la polizia || *s. coll.* la polizia ☆ *the mounted —*, la polizia a cavallo.

Constance ['kɔnstəns], *no.pr.f.* Costanza.

constancy ['kɔnstənsi], *s.* 1. costanza, fedeltà; perseveranza 2. costanza, regolarità (di temperatura, vento, ecc.)

constant ['kɔnstənt], *ag.* 1. costante, fedele, perseverante 2. invariabile || *s.* (*mat. fis.*) costante ☆ *time —*, costante di tempo.

Constantine ['kɔnstəntain], *no.pr.m.* Costantino.

Constantinople [,kɔnstænti'noupl], *no.pr.* (*geog.*) Costantinopoli.

constantly ['kɔnstəntli], *ag.* costantemente.

to **constellate** ['kɔnstəleit], *v.t.i.* 1. costellare: *to — with*, costellare di 2. formare una costellazione.

constellation [,kɔnstə'leiʃən], *s.* costellazione (anche *fig.*).

to **consternate** ['kɔnstə(:)neit], *v.t.* costernare, affliggere.

consternation [,kɔnstə(:)'neiʃən], *s.* costernazione; terrore: *look of —*, aria costernata; *they looked at each other in —*, si guardarono atterriti.

to **constipate** ['kɔnstipeit], *v.t.* rendere stitico.

constipation [,kɔnsti'peiʃən], *s.* stitichezza.

constituency [kən'stitjuənsi], *s.* (*pol.*) 1. gli elettori: *the representative member and his —*, il deputato ed i suoi elettori 2. circoscrizione elettorale.

constituent [kən'stitjuənt], *ag.* costituente, componente: *the — elements of air*, gli elementi costituenti dell'aria || *s.* 1. elemento costitutivo, costituente 2. (*pol.*) elettore, membro di un collegio elettorale ☆ *the — assembly*, (*pol.*) la costituente.

to **constitute** ['kɔnstitju:t], *v.t.* 1. costituire, fondare; formare: *she constitutes his happiness*, ella è la sua felicità || *he is strongly constituted*, ha una salute di ferro 2. nominare, eleggere ☆ *constituted authority*, l'autorità costituita.

constitution [,kɔnsti'tju:ʃən], *s.* 1. costituzione, statuto: *monarchic —*, costituzione monarchica || *Clementine Constitutions*, le costituzioni clementine 2. costituzione, composizione (dell'aria, del corpo, ecc.) || *to have an iron —*, avere una salute di ferro ☆ *the written —*, la costituzione scritta.

constitutional [,kɔnsti'tju:ʃənl], *ag.* (*pol. fisiol.*) costituzionale || *s.* passeggiata igienica: *to take one's —*, fare la propria passeggiatina igienica.

constitutionalism [,kɔnsti'tju:ʃnəlizəm], *s.* 1. costituzionalismo 2. governo costituzionale.

constitutionalist [,kɔnsti'tju:ʃnəlist], *s.* 1. costituzionalista 2. (*st. inglese*) conservatore.

constitutionality [,kɔnsti,tju:ʃə'næliti], *s.* costituzionalità; legittimità (di decreto, ecc.).

to **constitutionalize** [,kɔnsti'tju:ʃnəlaiz], *v.t.i.* 1. rendere costituzionale, legittimo (un decreto, ecc.) 2. fare una passeggiata igienica.

constitutionally [,kɔnsti'tju:ʃnəli], *av.* costituzionalmente.

constitutive ['kɔnstitju:tiv], *ag.* costitutivo; essenziale.

constitutor ['kɔnstitju:tə*], *s.* costitutore; fondatore.

to **constrain** [kən'strein], *v.t.* 1. costringere, forzare: *I find myself constrained to do...*, mi vedo costretto a fare... 2. stringere, comprimere 3. (*arc.*) confinare; imprigionare (anche *fig.*).

constrainable [kən'streinəbl], *ag.* costringibile, forzabile; vincolabile.

constrained [kən'streind], *ag.* costretto, forzato; vincolato.

constrainedly [kən'streinidli], *av.* con aria forzata: *to smile —*, sorridere con aria forzata, imbarazzata.

constraint [kən'streint], *s.* 1. costrizione; coazione;

confino: *to put s.o. under* —, mettere qlcu. in stato di coazione, internare qlcu. **2.** soggezione; imbarazzo.

to **constrict** [kən'strikt], *v.t.* **1.** costringere; restringere; comprimere: *collar that constricts the neck*, colletto che stringe il collo **2.** *(fisiol.)* contrarre (tessuti).

constriction [kən'strikʃən], *s.* **1.** costrizione; restringimento **2.** *(patol.)* contrazione (del cuore, ecc.).

constrictive [kən'striktiv], *ag.* costrittivo; restrittivo.

constrictor [kən'striktə*], *s.* **1.** *(anat.)* costrittore (muscolo) **2.** *(chir.)* compressore.

to **constringe** [kən'strindʒ], *v.t.i.* *(fisiol.)* costringere, costringersi; comprimere, comprimersi; contrarre, contrarsi.

constringent [kən'strindʒənt], *ag.* **1.** costringente, costrittore **2.** *(farm.)* astringente.

to **construct** [kən'strʌkt], *v.t.* costruire (anche *fig.*): *badly constructed sentences*, frasi mal costruite; *well constructed play*, commedia ben costruita; *to* — *a dam*, costruire una diga.

constructible [kən'strʌktəbl], *ag.* costruibile, componibile.

construction [kən'strʌkʃən], *s.* **1.** costruzione (anche *gram.*): *director of naval* —, direttore del genio navale; *in course of* (o *under*) —, in via di costruzione **2.** interpretazione: *you put a wrong* — *on my silence*, interpretate male il mio silenzio; *to put a good, bad* — *on s.o.'s words*, interpretare in bene, in male le parole di qlcu. ☆ — *labourer*, *(ferr. amer.)* sterratore ‖ *all-steel* —, costruzione interamente in acciaio.

constructional [kən'strʌkʃənl], *ag.* di costruzione: — *engineering*, costruzione meccanica.

constructive [kən'strʌktiv], *ag.* costruttivo: — *criticism*, critica costruttiva; *design based upon* — *exigencies*, progetto basato su esigenze costruttive **2.** dedotto; implicito.

constructively [kən'strʌktivli], *av.* **1.** costruttivamente **2.** per interpretazione; implicitamente.

constructor [kən'strʌktə*], *s.* costruttore ☆ *naval* —, ingegnere navale.

construe [kən'stru:], *s.* **1.** *(gram.)* analisi di una proposizione **2.** traduzione letterale.

to **construe**, *v.t.* **1.** costruire grammaticalmente **2.** fare l'analisi grammaticale di (una proposizione) **3.** interpretare, spiegare; tradurre letteralmente.

construing [kən'stru:iŋ], *V.* **construe**.

consubstantial [,kɔnsəb'stænʃəl], *ag.* *(teol.)* consustanziale: *the Son is* — *with the Father*, il Figlio è consustanziale al Padre.

consubstantiality ['kɔnsəb,stænʃi'æliti], *s.* *(teol.)* consustanzialità.

to **consubstantiate** [,kɔnsəb'stænʃieit], *v.t.i.* *(teol.)* unire, unirsi in una sola stessa sostanza.

consubstantiation ['kɔnsəb,stænʃi'eiʃən], *s.* *(teol.)* consustanziazione.

consuetude ['kɔnswitju:d], *s.* consuetudine.

consuetudinary [,kɔnswi'tju:dinəri], *ag.* consuetudinario ‖ *s.* manuale del regolamento interno (di un convento, ecc.) ☆ — *law*, diritto consuetudinario.

consul ['kɔnsəl], *s.* console ☆ — *-general*, console generale.

consulage ['kɔnsəlidʒ], *s.* diritti consolari.

consular ['kɔnsjulə*], *ag.* consolare ☆ — *certificate*, certificato consolare.

consulate ['kɔnsjulit], **consulship** ['kɔnsəlʃip], *s.* consolato.

consult [kən'sʌlt], *s.* consultazione.

to **consult**, *v.t.i.* consultare, consultarsi: *I consulted with my friends*, mi consultai con gli amici; *they consulted together*, si consultarono; *to* — *a dictionary, history*, consultare un dizionario, la storia; *to* — *s.o. on* (o *about*) *sthg.*, consultare qlcu. in merito a ql.co. ‖ *to* — *one's interests*, tener conto dei propri interessi ‖ *to* — *one's pillow*, riflettere durante la notte ‖ *to* — *s.o.'s feelings*, rispettare i sentimenti di qlcu.

consultant [kən'sʌltənt], *s.* **1.** chi consulta (un oracolo, ecc.) **2.** consulente; esperto.

consultation [,kɔnsəl'teiʃən], *s.* **1.** consultazione **2.** consulto: *to hold a* —, tenere un consulto.

consultative [kən'sʌltətiv], *ag.* consultativo.

consultee [,kɔnsʌl'ti:], *s.* consulente.

consulter [kən'sʌltə*], *s.* consultatore.

consulting [kən'sʌltiŋ], *ag.* consulente ☆ — *-hours*, orario di visita; — *-room*, ambulatorio.

consumable [kən'sju:məbl], *ag.* consumabile ‖ *s. gener. pl.* derrate alimentari, commestibili.

to **consume** [kən'sju:m], *v.t.i.* **1.** consumare, distruggere: *consumed by fire*, consumato dal fuoco **2.** sprecare **3.** *fig.* rodere, corrodere, consumarsi, struggersi: *to be consumed with desire, envy, thirst*, essere consumato dal desiderio, dall'invidia, dalla sete.

consumedly [kən'sju:midli], *av.* eccessivamente, enormemente: *to laugh* —, ridere smoderatamente.

consumer [kən'sju:mə*], *s.c.* utente; consumatore, consumatrice (di derrate, ecc.): *producers and consumers*, *(econ.)* produttori e consumatori ☆ — *('s) goods*, generi di consumo, di prima necessità.

consummate [kən'sʌmit], *ag.* consumato; perfetto; completo: — *artist*, artista consumato; — *ass*, perfetto asino; — *liar*, mentitore perfetto.

to **consummate** ['kɔnsʌmeit], *v.t.* consumare (matrimonio, sacrificio, delitto, ecc.).

consummately [kən'sʌmitli], *av.* perfettamente, completamente, con maestria consumata.

consummation [,kɔnsʌ'meiʃən], *s.* **1.** consumazione (di matrimonio, ecc.) **2.** compimento; conclusione, fine: *the* — *of the world* (o *the final* —), la fine del mondo.

consummative ['kɔnsʌmeitiv], *ag.* che compie, che esegusce.

consummator ['kɔnsʌmeitə*], *s.* consumatore; esecutore.

consumption [kən'sʌmpʃən], *s.* **1.** consumo (di derrate, ecc.) **2.** sciupio, perdita (di tempo, calore) **3.** distruzione, fine: *till the* — *of the world*, sino alla fine del mondo **4.** *(patol.)* consunzione: *to go into* —, diventar tisico ☆ *home* —, *(econ.)* consumo interno; *pulmonary* —, tubercolosi polmonare, tisi.

consumptive [kən'sʌmptiv], *ag.* **1.** che consuma, che sciupa; che distrugge **2.** tisico, tubercolotico ‖ *s.* tisico, tubercolotico: *hospital for consumptives*, sanatorio.

consumptively [kən'sʌmptivli], *av.* da tisico: — *inclined*, predisposto alla tisi.

consumptiveness [kən'sʌmptivnis], *s.* predisposizione alla tisi.

contact ['kɔntækt], *s.* **1.** contatto; relazione: *point of* —, punto di contatto; *to be in* — *with s.o.*, essere in contatto con qlcu.; *to come into* — *with s.o.*, mettersi in contatto con qlcu.; *to establish, to lose* — *with the enemy*, *(mil.)* prendere, perdere contatto col nemico **2.** *pl.* *(amer.)* relazioni, contatti, amicizie **3.** *(elett. fis.)* contatto: — *to earth*, contatto terra; *to make, to break* —, stabilire, interrompere il contatto ☆ — *breaker*, interruttore di corrente; — *flying*, *(neol. aer.)* volo a vista; — *-lens*, lente a contatto; — *screw*, morsetto di connessione.

to **contact** [kən'tækt], *v.t.i.* mettere, mettersi in contatto, in relazione con; essere in contatto.

contactor [kən'tæktə*], *s.* *(elett.)* contattore.

contagion [kən'teidʒən], *s.* **1.** contagio; malattia contagiosa **2.** corruzione morale.

contagious [kən'teidʒəs], *ag.* contagioso.

contagiously [kən'teidʒəsli], *av.* contagiosamente.

contagiousness [kən'teidʒəsnis], *s.* contagiosità.

to **contain** [kən'tein], *v.t.* **1.** contenere (anche *fig.*); includere; comprendere: *that atlas contains fifty maps*, quell'atlante contiene cinquanta carte; *this book contains many truths*, questo libro contiene molte verità; *this box contains books*, questa cassa contiene libri **2.** contenere, reprimere, frenare (sentimenti): *to* — *oneself*, contenersi, controllarsi **3.** *(mil.)* contenere, trattenere (il nemico) **4.** (*mat.*) essere divisibile per: *ten contains two and five*, dieci è divisibile per due e per cinque.

containable [kən'teinəbl], *ag.* che si può contenere, trattenere, frenare.

contained [kən'teind], *ag.* frenato, trattenuto (di sentimento).

container [kən'teinə*], *s.* recipiente; scatola.

containment [kən'teinmənt], *s.* **1.** ritenutezza, riserbo, ritegno **2.** (*neol. pol.*) tattica di arginamento.

contaminable [kən'tæminəbl], *ag.* contaminabile.

to **contaminate** [kən'tæmineit], *v.t.* contaminare; infettare; corrompere.

contamination [kən,tæmi'neifən], *s.* contaminazione (anche *letter.*).

contango [kən'tæŋgou], *pl.* **contangoes** [kən-'tæŋgouz], *s.* (*Borsa*) interesse di riporto ☆ — *-day*, giorno dei riporti; — *-rate*, prezzo del riporto.

to **contango**, *v.t.i.* (*Borsa*) riportare.

to **contemn** [kən'tem], *v.t.* (*arc. letter.*) sprezzare.

contemner [kən'temnə*], *s.c.* (*arc. letter.*) sprezzatore, sprezzatrice.

to **contemplate** ['kontempleit], *v.t.i.* **1.** contemplare; meditare, raccogliersi **2.** (I) progettare, proporsi: *he contemplates going away soon*, si propone di andar via fra breve; *to — suicide*, meditare il suicidio.

contemplation [,kontem'pleifən], *s.* **1.** contemplazione; meditazione, raccoglimento: *in — before*, in contemplazione davanti a **2.** progetto, previsione: *in — of*, in previsione, in attesa di; *to have sthg. in —*, avere in progetto, proporsi di fare ql.co.

contemplative ['kontempleitiv], *nel senso* **2.** [kən-'templətiv], *ag.* **1.** contemplativo; meditativo; pensieroso **2.** (*relig.*) contemplativo.

contemplatively ['kontempleitivli], *av.* contemplativamente; meditativamente; pensierosamente.

contemplativeness ['kontempleitivnis], *s.* contemplazione; meditazione.

contemplator ['kontempleitə*], *s.c.* contemplatore, contemplatrice.

contemporaneity [kən,tempərə'ni:iti], *s.* contemporaneità.

contemporaneous [kən,tempə'reinjəs], *ag.* contemporaneo.

contemporaneously [kən,tempə'reinjəsli], *av.* contemporaneamente.

contemporary [kən'tempərəri], *ag.* contemporaneo; coetaneo: — *events*, avvenimenti attuali ‖ *s.* contemporaneo; coetaneo: *our contemporaries*, i nostri contemporanei.

to **contemporize** [kən'tempəraiz], *v.t.i.* far accadere, accadere, esistere contemporaneamente.

contempt [kən'tempt], *s.* **1.** disprezzo: *in — of*, a dispetto di; *to fall into —*, cadere in disprezzo; *to hold s.o. in —*, provar disprezzo per qlcu. **2.** (*dir.*) disobbedienza alla legge: — *of Court*, vilipendio alla Corte.

contemptibility [kən,temptə'biliti], *s.* spregevolezza.

contemptible [kən'temptəbl], *ag.* spregevole, disprezzabile.

contemptibleness [kən'temptəblnis], *s.* l'essere spregevole.

contemptibly [kən'temptəbli], *av.* spregevolmente.

contemptuous [kən'temptjuəs], *ag.* sprezzante; insolente.

contemptuously [kən'temptjuəsli], *av.* sprezzantemente; insolentemente.

contemptuousness [kən'temptjuəsnis], *s.* disprezzo, spregio; insolenza.

to **contend** [kən'tend], *v.t.i.* **1.** contendere, combattere; contrastare: *to — with s.o. for sthg.*, lottare con qlcu. per ql.co. **2.** sostenere, affermare: *I — that poverty does not imply unhappiness*, sostengo che la povertà non implica infelicità.

contender [kən'tendə*], *s.* contendente, concorrente.

contending [kən'tendiŋ], *ag.* contendente, contrastante, rivale: *the — parties*, le parti in lotta.

content¹ ['kontent], *s.* **1.** volume (di solido); capacità (di vaso, ecc.) **2.** (solo *sing.*) contenuto, concetto **3.** (*chim. min.*) contenuto; titolo; dose **4.** *pl.* contenuto (di vaso, libro, ecc.) ‖ (*table of*) *contents*, indice (di libro).

content² [kən'tent], *ag.* contento, soddisfatto: *not — with winning one race, he tried his luck again*, non soddisfatto d'aver vinto una corsa, ritentò la sorte; *to be — to do sthg.*, essere soddisfatto di, acconsentire a fare ql.co. ‖ —, *not —*, per, contro (una mozione alla Camera dei Lords) ‖ *s.* contentezza, soddisfazione: *to one's heart's —*, fino a completa soddisfazione.

to **content²**, *v.t.* contentare, soddisfare: *to — oneself with sthg., with doing sthg.*, accontentarsi di ql.co., di fare ql.co.

contented [kən'tentid], *ag.* contento; pago: *he seems — with his life*, sembra soddisfatto della sua vita.

contentedly [kən'tentidli], *av.* con soddisfazione.

contentedness [kən'tentidnis], *s.* contentezza.

contention [kən'tenfən], *s.* **1.** contesa; disputa; rivalità ‖ *the bone of —*, il pomo della discordia **2.** emulazione **3.** opinione: *my — is that...*, io sostengo che...

contentious [kən'tenfəs], *ag.* litigioso; controverso; (*dir.*) contenzioso.

contentiously [kən'tenfəsli], *av.* contenziosamente.

contentiousness [kən'tenfəsnis], *s.* umore litigioso; litigiosità.

contentment [kən'tentmənt], *s.* il contentarsi, l'essere pago ‖ — *is better than riches*, *prov.* chi s'accontenta gode.

conterminal [kon'tə:minl], **conterminous** [kon'tə:-minəs], *ag.* contiguo, limitrofo.

contest ['kontest], *s.* contestazione; contesa; competizione, gara.

to **contest** [kən'test], *v.t.i.* contestare; contrastare; contendere, disputare; lottare: *contested election*, elezione contestata (per la validità), contesa (fra vari candidati); *to — a seat in Parliament*, disputarsi un seggio in Parlamento.

contestable [kən'testəbl], *ag.* contestabile.

contestant [kən'testənt], *s.c.* competitore, competitrice; concorrente.

contestation [,kontes'teifən], *s.* **1.** contestazione; contrasto; disputa **2.** asserzione; pretesa.

context ['kontekst], *s.* contesto.

contextual [kon'tekstjuəl], *ag.* contestuale.

contexture [kon'tekstfə*], *s.* struttura (delle ossa, ecc.); costituzione (di un organismo); trama (di un tessuto); struttura, costruzione (di poema, discorso, ecc.).

contiguity [,konti'gju(:)iti], *s.* contiguità; vicinanza.

contiguous [kən'tigjuəs], *ag.* contiguo.

contiguously [kən'tigjuəsli], *av.* contiguamente.

continence ['kontinəns], *s.* continenza; castità.

continent ['kontinənt], *ag.* continente; casto.

continent, *s.* (*geog.*) continente: *the five continents*, i cinque continenti ‖ *the Continent*, il Continente, l'Europa continentale.

continental [,konti'nentl], *ag.* continentale ‖ *s.* **1.** continentale **2.** (*fam. amer.*) moneta di poco valore.

continentalism [,konti'nentəlizəm], *s.* quanto è proprio del Continente.

to **continentalize** [,konti'nentəlaiz], *v.t.* rendere continentale (idee, carattere, ecc.).

continentally [,konti'nentəli], *av.* in maniera continentale.

continently ['kontinəntli], *av.* moderatamente; castamente.

contingence [kən'tindʒəns], *s.* contingenza; eventualità; (*geom.*) tangenza.

contingency [kən'tindʒənsi], *s.* **1.** contingenza; eventualità; caso: *prepared for all contingencies*, preparato ad ogni eventualità; *should a — arise* (o *in case of a —*), in un caso imprevisto **2.** (*fil.*) contingenza ☆ — *fund*, (*comm.*) riserva speciale.

contingent [kən'tindʒənt], *ag.* **1.** eventuale; accidentale; imprevisto: — *expenses*, spese impreviste; — *profit*, profitto accidentale || *to be — on sthg.*, dipendere da ql.co. (di avvenimento) **2.** (*fil.*) contingente || *s.* **1.** contingenza, caso fortuito **2.** (*mil.*) contingente (di soldati).

contingently [kən'tindʒəntli], *av.* contingentemente.

continuable [kən'tinjuəbl], *ag.* **1.** continuabile **2.** (*Borsa*) riportabile.

continual [kən'tinjuəl], *ag.* continuo; ininterrotto: — *complaints*, lamenti continui.

continually [kən'tinjuəli], *av.* continuamente; ininterrottamente.

continuance [kən'tinjuəns], *s.* **1.** continuità; durata: *of short, long —*, di breve, lunga durata **2.** (*dir.*) rinvio, proroga.

continuation [kən,tinju'eiʃən], *s.* **1.** continuazione, seguito; prolungamento (di muro) **2.** (*Borsa*) riporto ☆ *-rate*, prezzo di riporto; — *school*, corso serale di perfezionamento.

continuative [kən'tinjuətiv], *ag.* continuativo.

continuator [kən'tinjueitə*], *s.c.* continuatore, continuatrice.

to **continue** [kən'tinju(:)], *v.t.i.* **1.** (II) continuare; seguitare; proseguire: *he continued to work* (o *working*) *as if nothing had happened*, continuò a lavorare come se nulla fosse accaduto; *to — (on) one's way*, proseguire il (nel) proprio cammino || *to be continued in our next number*, continua al prossimo numero **2.** far continuare, mantenere: *to — s.o. in office*, mantenere qlcu. in carica **3.** permanere; restare: *to — in* (o *at*) *a place*, continuare a soggiornare in un luogo **4.** (*dir.*) aggiornare, prorogare **5.** (*Borsa*) mettere a riporto.

continued [kən'tinju(:)d], *ag.* ininterrotto, continuo.

continuity [,kɔnti'nju(:)iti], *s.* **1.** continuità: *solution of —*, soluzione di continuità **2.** (*cine.*) sceneggiatura; (*rad.*) copione ☆ — *-writer*, sceneggiatore.

continuous [kən'tinjuəs], *ag.* continuo, ininterrotto.

continuously [kən'tinjuəsli], *av.* continuamente, ininterrottamente.

contorniate [kən'tɔ:niit], *ag.* contornato || *s.* medaglia con incavo all'orlo.

to **contort** [kən'tɔ:t], *v.t.* contorcere: *face contorted with pain*, faccia stravolta dal dolore.

contortion [kən'tɔ:ʃən], *s.* contorsione.

contortionist [kən'tɔ:ʃnist], *s.c.* contorsionista; acrobata.

contour ['kɔntuə*], *s.* contorno, profilo ☆ — *-lines*, (*geog.*) linee ipsometriche.

to **contour**, *v.t.* **1.** rilevare; segnare con linee ipsometriche (carta geografica) **2.** costruire (strade) lungo una costa, una collina.

contra ['kɔntrə], *prep.* contro: *pro and —*, pro e contro || *s.* contro: *per —*, (*contabilità*) in contropartita.

contraband ['kɔntrəbænd], *ag.* proibito, illecito || *s.* **1.** contrabbando: — *of war*, contrabbando di guerra **2.** (*amer.*) schiavo rifugiato ☆ — *goods*, merci di contrabbando.

contrabandist ['kɔntrəbændist], *s.* contrabbandiere.

contrabass ['kɔntrə'beis], *s.* (*mus.*) contrabbasso ☆ — *tuba*, bombardone.

contra-bassoon ['kɔntrəbə'su:n], *s.* (*mus.*) controfagotto.

contract ['kɔntrækt], *s.* **1.** contratto, patto; convenzione; appalto: *break of —*, rottura di contratto; *by private —*, in via amichevole; *work on —* (o — *work*), lavoro in appalto; *to enter into a — with*, fare un contratto con; *to secure a —*, ottenere un appalto; *to tender for a —*, fare offerta per ottenere un appalto **2.** (*amer. ferr.*) tessera d'abbonamento **3.** (*giuoco del bridge*) giuoco; impegno ☆ *marriage- —*, contratto di matrimonio.

to **contract** [kən'trækt], *v.t.i.* **1.** contrarre, contrarsi; restringere, restringersi: *the pupil contracts in the sunlight*, la pupilla si contrae alla luce del sole; *to — the brow*, corrugare la fronte **2.** (*gram.*) contrarre: *to*

— *"do not" into "don't"*, contrarre « do not » in « don't » **3.** contrarre (obbligazione, matrimonio, malattia, ecc.): *to — a friendship with s.o.*, contrarre amicizia con qlcu. **4.** (*comm.*) contrattare, impegnarsi: *to — to do sthg.*, impegnarsi a fare ql.co. || *to — out of an obligation*, liberarsi per mezzo di contratto da obbligazioni precedentemente assunte **5.** appaltare, prendere in appalto: *to — for a supply of sthg.*, prendere in appalto il rifornimento di ql.co.

contractable [kən'træktəbl], *ag.* contrattabile.

contracted [kən'træktid], *ag.* **1.** contrattato **2.** limitato (di idee); meschino; conciso (di stile).

contractibility [kən,træktə'biliti], *s.* contrattilità.

contractible [kən'træktəbl], **contractile** [kən'træktail], *ag.* contrattile.

contractility [,kɔntræk'tiliti], *s.* contrattilità.

contracting [kən'træktin], *ag.* contraente, che contrae ☆ *the high — parties*, le alte parti contraenti.

contraction [kən'trækʃən], *s.* accorciamento, abbreviazione; contrazione (anche *gram.*).

contractive [kən'træktiv], *ag.* che tende a contrarsi.

contractor [kən'træktə*], *s.* **1.** contraente; appaltatore; imprenditore; impresario; fornitore: — *to the government*, fornitore del governo **2.** (*anat.*) muscolo contrattile ☆ *army —*, fornitore dell'esercito; *building —*, imprenditore edile.

contractual [kən'træktjuəl], *ag.* contrattuale.

contracture [kən'træktjuə*], *s.* (*fisiol.*) contrattura.

to **contradict** [,kɔntrə'dikt], *v.t.* contraddire: *to — each other*, contraddirsi (reciprocamente); *to — oneself*, contraddirsi; *to — a statement*, contraddire una dichiarazione.

contradictable [,kɔntrə'diktəbl], *ag.* che si può contraddire.

contradiction [,kɔntrə'dikʃən], *s.* contraddizione; smentita: — *in terms*, contraddizione in termini; *to give a flat —*, smentire formalmente.

contradictious [,kɔntrə'dikʃəs], *s.* contraddittorio; — *spirit*, spirito di contraddizione.

contradictor [,kɔntrə'diktə*], *s.* contraddittore.

contradictory [,kɔntrə'diktəri], *ag.* contraddittorio.

contradictorily [,kɔntrə'diktərili], *av.* contraddittoriamente.

contradistinction [,kɔntrədis'tiŋkʃən], *s.* distinzione per contrasto.

to **contradistinguish** [,kɔntrədis'tiŋgwiʃ], *v.t.* contraddistinguere.

contrail ['kɔntreil], *s.* (*neol. aer.*) scia di condensazione.

to **contra-indicate** [,kɔntrə'indikeit], *v.t.* (*med.*) controindicare.

contra-indication [,kɔntrə,indi'keiʃən], *s.* (*med.*) controindicazione.

contralto [kən'træltou], *s.* (*mus.*) contralto.

contraposition [,kɔntrəpə'ziʃən], *s.* opposizione; contrasto; antitesi.

contrapositive [,kɔntrə'pozətiv], *ag.* inverso.

contraption [kən'træpʃən], *s.* (*fam.*) dispositivo; congegno strano; invenzione bizzarra.

contrapuntal [,kɔntrə'pʌntl], *ag.* (*mus.*) contrappuntistico.

contrapuntist ['kɔntrəpʌntist], *s.* (*mus.*) contrappuntista.

contrariety [,kɔntrə'raiəti], *s.* **1.** opposizione, antagonismo **2.** discrepanza, discordanza.

contrarily ['kɔntrərili], *av.* contrariamente; viceversa.

contrariness ['kɔntrərinis], *s.* (*fam.*) spirito di contraddizione.

contrarious [kən'trɛəriəs], *ag.* **1.** (*arc.*) avverso, contrario **2.** perverso; indocile.

contrariwise ['kɔntrəriwaiz], *av.* **1.** al contrario, da un altro punto di vista; in senso contrario, opposto **2.** perversamente.

contrary ['kɔntrəri], *ag.* **1.** contrario, opposto: — *to one's principles*, contrario ai propri principi; —

winds, venti contrari; *in a — direction to*, in direzione contraria a; *to look the — way*, guardare dalla parte sbagliata **2.** *(fam.)* cattivo, perverso: *— child*, bambino cattivo ‖ *s.* (ii) contrario: *on the —*, al contrario; *quite the —*, proprio il contrario: *I have nothing to say to the —*, non ho nulla da dire in contrario ‖ *unless we hear to the —*, salvo contrordini ‖ *to proceed by contraries*, procedere per contrari ☆ *— propositions*, *(log.)* proposizioni contrarie.

to contrary, *v.t.* *(amer.)* contrariare; contrastare.

contrary, *av.* contrariamente, al contrario: *— to accepted opinions*, in contrasto con opinioni riconosciute; *— to what I thought*, all'opposto di quanto pensavo; *to act — to orders*, agire contrariamente agli ordini.

contrast ['kɔntræst], *s.* contrasto, opposizione; riscontro: *the — between light and shade*, il contrasto fra luce ed ombra; *in — with*, in antitesi con; *to form a — to*, formare un contrasto con.

to contrast [kən'træst], *v.t.i.* mettere in contrasto; far contrasto: *his vices — with his virtues*, i suoi vizi fanno contrasto con le sue virtù.

contrasty [kən'træsti], *ag.* *(spec. foto.)* contrastante.

contravallation [,kɔntrəvə'leiʃən], *s.* *(ing. mil.)* contravvallazione.

to contravene [,kɔntrə'vi:n], *v.t.* **1.** contravvenire a: *to — the law, the regulations*, contravvenire alla legge, ai regolamenti **2.** contraddire, opporsi a.

contravener [,kɔntrə'vi:nə*], *s.* contravventore.

contravention [,kɔntrə'venʃən], *s.* contravvenzione, infrazione, trasgressione: *to act in — of a regulation*, trasgredire un regolamento.

to contribute [kən'tribju(:)t], *v.t.i.* contribuire (con); fornire: *he has contributed several articles to our review*, egli ha scritto parecchi articoli per la nostra rivista; *to — money*, contribuire con denaro; *to — to the success of*, contribuire al successo di; *to — to a work of charity*, contribuire ad un'opera di carità.

contribution [,kɔntri'bju:ʃən], *s.* **1.** contributo: *— of capital*, *(comm.)* apporto di capitale; *all contributions thankfully received*, qualsiasi contributo è ben accetto; *forced —*, imposta forzata; *to pay one's —*, pagare la propria quota, il proprio contributo **2.** collaborazione (ad un giornale): *to — to a review*, articolo scritto per una rivista ☆ *war —*, contributo di guerra.

contributor [kən'tribjutə*], *s.* **1.** contributore: *— of capital*, *(comm.)* apportatore di capitale **2.** collaboratore (di giornale, ecc.).

contributory [kən'tribjutəri], *ag.* contribuente: *a cause — to the disaster*, una causa che ha contribuito al disastro.

contrite ['kɔntrait], *ag.* contrito; pentito.

contritely ['kɔntraitli], *av.* con contrizione.

contrition [kən'triʃən], *s.* contrizione, pentimento.

contrivable [kən'traivəbl], *ag.* **1.** escogitabile, che si può inventare **2.** fattibile, realizzabile.

contrivance [kən'traivəns], *s.* **1.** invenzione; progetto ‖ *beyond human —*, che supera le possibilità inventive dell'uomo **2.** espediente; ritrovato; artifizio: *the — by which orchids are fertilized*, il ritrovato adottato per la fertilizzazione delle orchidee **3.** apparato, congegno: *he had fixed up a — to open the door from his bed*, aveva inventato un congegno per aprire la porta dal letto.

to contrive [kən'traiv], *v.t.* **1.** progettare; inventare, escogitare **2.** fare in modo di, riuscire a: *can't you — to get here earlier?*, non puoi fare in modo di arrivare prima?; *he contrived to get himself into trouble* (o *into hot water*), tanto fece che si cacciò nei guai; *he contrived to persuade me*, riuscì a persuadermi; *how did you — it?*, come ci sei riuscito?; *I contrived to warn him in time*, sono riuscito ad avvisarlo in tempo **3.** macchinare, ordire **4.** cavarsela: *can you — without it?*, te la cavi, ce la fai senza?.

contriver [kən'traivə*], *s.c.* **1.** chi fa piani, progetti **2.** chi sa trarsi d'impiccio, cavarsela.

control [kən'troul], *s.* **1.** autorità; direzione; influenza: *under military —*, sotto autorità militare; *he had many employees under his —*, aveva sotto di sè molti impiegati; *he has — over a whole province*, amministra una intera provincia; *she has no — over the children*, non ha nessuna autorità sui bambini; *to have — of a firm*, essere a capo di una ditta; *to have — of an undertaking*, dirigere un'impresa **2.** padronanza, dominio: *the — of the seas*, il dominio dei mari; *circumstances beyond our —*, circostanze che non dipendono da noi; *to get under —*, riuscire a dominare; *to have absolute — over s.o.*, dominare completamente qlcu., avere un enorme ascendente sopra qlcu.; *to have, to lose, to regain — of* (o *over*) *oneself*, avere, perdere, riacquistare il dominio di sè; *to keep under —*, dominare, tenere sotto il proprio dominio **3.** controllo, regolazione; sorveglianza: *— of exchanges*, *(comm.)* controllo degli scambi **4.** *pl.* *(mec.)* comandi ☆ *— area*, *(aer.)* area di controllo; *— car*, *(aer.)* navicella di comando; *— column* (o *stick*), *(aer.)* « cloche », barra di comando; *— commission*, commissione di controllo; *— device*, *(mec.)* dispositivo di comando; *— point*, punto di controllo; *— room*, camera di manovra; *— station*, *(spor.)* posto di controllo; *— tower*, *(aer.)* torre di controllo ‖ *area —*, *(neol. aer.)* controllo d'area; *birth- —*, limitazione delle nascite; *brilliance —*, *(tv.)* regolatore di luminosità; *contrast —*, *(tv.)* regolatore di contrasto; *distant —* (o *remote —*), *(mec.)* telecomando; *intermediate —*, *(mec.)* rimando, rinvio; *quality —*, *(mec.)* collaudo di qualità; *selectivity —*, *(rad.)* regolatore di tono; *self- —*, autocontrollo, padronanza di sè; *traffic —*, regolazione del traffico; *wireless —*, radiocomando.

to control, *pass.p.p.* **controlled** [kən'trould], *v.t.* **1.** regolare, dirigere: *to — the fire*, *(mil.)* dirigere il fuoco; *to — the traffic*, dirigere il traffico; *to — an undertaking*, dirigere un'impresa **2.** esercitare autorità su, dominare: *he cannot — his pupils*, non sa dominare i suoi allievi; *to — one's fate*, dominare il proprio destino; *to — the seas*, dominare i mari **3.** controllare, regolare; verificare (conti): *controlled prices*, prezzi controllati **4.** padroneggiare; frenare, reprimere, contenere: *I can't — this horse*, non riesco a trattenere questo cavallo; *to — one's rage, one's tears*, contenere l'ira, trattenere le lacrime; *to — oneself*, frenarsi: *try to — yourself*, cerca di frenarti, di dominarti; *to — the rise in the cost of living*, frenare il rialzo dei prezzi **5.** *(aer. mar.)* pilotare, governare ☆ *controlled finance*, economia controllata, dirigismo; *American-controlled area*, zona sotto il controllo americano.

controllability [kən,troulə'biliti], *s.* manovrabilità; docilità (di cavallo, ecc.).

controllable [kən'trouləbl], *ag.* dominabile; frenabile; maneggiabile; manovrabile.

controller [kən'troulə*], *s.* **1.** controllore; verificatore; sovrintendente **2.** *(elett.)* combinatore.

controlling [kən'troulin], *ag.* che dirige, domina ‖ *s.* direzione (di affari); regolamento (di traffico); comando (di macchina); *fig.* padronanza, controllo ☆ *— gauge*, *(mec.)* manometro di controllo.

controversial [,kɔntrə'və:ʃəl], *ag.* controverso; polemico.

controversialist [,kɔntrə'və:ʃəlist], *s.* persona abile nel discutere, che ama la discussione.

controversially [,kɔntrə'və:ʃəli], *av.* polemicamente.

controversy ['kɔntrəvə:si], *s.* controversia; polemica: *the question is beyond —*, has given rise to much —, la questione è fuori discussione, ha suscitato molte controversie; *to hold* (o *to carry on*) *a — with* (o *against*) *s.o. on sthg.*, sostenere una polemica contro qlcu. su qlco.

to controvert ['kɔntrəvə:t], *v.t.* disputare su.

controvertible ['kɔntrəvə:təbl], *ag.* controvertibile.

contumacious [ˌkɔntju(:)ˈmeiʃəs], *ag.* **1.** ostinatamente ribelle, indocile, insubordinato **2.** (*dir.*) contumace.

contumaciously [ˌkɔntju(:)ˈmeiʃəsli], *av.* **1.** con ostinata insubordinazione **2.** (*dir.*) in contumacia.

contumaciousness [ˌkɔntju(:)ˈmeiʃəsnis], **contumacy** [ˈkɔntjuməsi], *s.* **1.** ribellione, indocilità, insubordinazione ostinata **2.** (*dir.*) contumacia.

contumelious [ˌkɔntju(:)ˈmi:ljəs], *ag.* ingiurioso; insolente.

contumeliously [ˌkɔntju(:)ˈmi:ljəsli], *av.* ingiuriosamente, insolentemente.

contumely [ˈkɔntju(:)mli], *s.* **1.** contumelia, ingiuria; insolenza **2.** onta: *to cast — on s.o.*, coprire qlcu. d'onta.

to contuse [kənˈtju:z], *v.t.* ammaccare; contundere.

contusion [kənˈtju:ʒən], *s.* contusione.

contusive [kənˈtju:siv], *ag.* contundente.

conundrum [kəˈnʌndrəm], *s.* enigma; indovinello: *to speak in conundrums*, parlare per enigmi.

conurbation [ˌkɔnə:ˈbeiʃən], *s.* agglomerazione di centri urbani.

to convalesce [ˌkɔnvəˈles], *v.i.* entrare in convalescenza; rimettersi in salute.

convalescence [ˌkɔnvəˈlesns], *s.* convalescenza.

convalescent [ˌkɔnvəˈlesnt], *ag.s.c.* convalescente ☆ *— home* (o *— hospital*), convalescenziario.

convection [kənˈvekʃən], *s.* (*fis.*) convezione.

convector [kənˈvektə*], *s.* (*fis.*) convettore, termoconvettore.

convenable [kənˈvi:nəbl], *ag.* convocabile; (*dir.*) citabile.

to convene [kənˈvi:n], *v.t.i.* **1.** convocare, adunare, riunire (assemblea, conferenza) **2.** radunarsi, convenire; incontrarsi: *the two gentlemen convened in London*, i due signori s'incontrarono a Londra **3.** (*dir.*) citare, convenire: *to — s.o. before a court*, citare, convenire qlcu. in giudizio **4.** (*arc.*) accordarsi.

convener [kənˈvi:nə*], *s.* convocatore (di adunanza, ecc.).

convenience [kənˈvi:njəns], *s.* **1.** comodo; convenienza, vantaggio: *a marriage of —*, un matrimonio di convenienza; *at your —*, con vostro comodo; *does that meet your —?*, vi fa comodo?; *for the sake of —*, per comodità, per vantaggio; *it is a great — to be able to phone*, è una grande comodità poter telefonare; *it will be a great — to me*, mi sarà di gran vantaggio, mi farà molto comodo ‖ *at your earliest —*, alla prima occasione, il più presto possibile ‖ *to make a — of s.o.*, abusare della bontà di qlcu. **2.** (*public*) —, gabinetto pubblico **3.** *pl.* comodità: *house fitted with modern conveniences*, casa fornita di comodità moderne.

convenient [kənˈvi:njənt], *ag.* conveniente; comodo; opportuno; adatto: *is it — for you to come to-day?*, ti fa comodo venire oggi?; *this is a very — tool for opening cans*, questo è un arnese fatto apposta per aprire le scatole di latta; *to be — to s.o. to do sthg.*, convenire a qlcu. di fare ql.co.; *to find a — opportunity to do sthg.*, trovare una conveniente occasione di fare ql.co. ‖ *— to the hand*, (*fam.*) a portata di mano.

conveniently [kənˈvi:njəntli], *av.* convenientemente.

convent [ˈkɔnvənt], *s.* convento: *to enter a —*, entrare in convento.

conventicle [kənˈventikl], *s.* conventicola.

convention [kənˈvenʃən], *s.* **1.** patto, accordo, convenzione **2.** assemblea; convenzione ‖ *the Convention*, (*st.*) la Convenzione **3.** *gener. pl.* consuetudine; convenzione (sociale): *Victorians were slaves to conventions*, i vittoriani erano schiavi delle convenzioni **4.** *pl.* regole (di giuoco): *the conventions of bridge*, le regole del «bridge».

conventional [kənˈvenʃənl], *ag.* **1.** tradizionale; convenzionale: *— art*, arte convenzionale; *"good morning" and "good evening" are — greetings*, «buon giorno» e «buona sera» sono saluti convenzionali **2.** corrente, comune, ordinario.

conventionalism [kənˈvenʃnəlizəm], *s.* convenzionalismo; formalismo.

conventionalist [kənˈvenʃnəlist], *s.* **1.** formalista **2.** membro di convenzione.

conventionality [kənˌvenʃəˈnæliti], *s.* **1.** convenzionalismo **2.** convenzionalità.

to conventionalize [kənˈvenʃnəlaiz], *v.t.* **1.** rendere convenzionale **2.** (*art.*) stilizzare.

conventionally [kənˈvenʃnəli], *av.* convenzionalmente.

conventual [kənˈventjuəl], *ag.* conventuale ‖ *s.* membro di convento.

to converge [kənˈvə:dʒ], *v.t.i.* convergere; far convergere (raggi luminosi, ecc.): *three armies were converging on Paris*, tre armate convergevano su Parigi.

convergence [kənˈvə:dʒəns], **convergency** [kənˈvə:dʒənsi], *s.* convergenza.

convergent [kənˈvə:dʒənt], *ag.* convergente.

conversable [kənˈvə:səbl], *ag.* socievole; di piacevole conversazione.

conversance [kənˈvə:səns], **conversancy** [kənˈvə:sənsi], *s.* familiarità; conoscenza.

conversant [kənˈvə:sənt], *ag.* versato, pratico; familiare, intimo: *— with finance*, competente in materia di finanza; *— with s.o.*, intimo di qlcu.; *— with sthg.*, pratico di ql.co.; *science — in* (o *with* o *about*) *a subject*, scienza che tratta, si occupa d'un argomento.

conversation [ˌkɔnvəˈseiʃən], *s.* **1.** conversazione, discorso: *private —*, discorso a quattr'occhi; *to carry on the —*, continuare la conversazione; *to change the —*, cambiare argomento, discorso; *to enter* (o *to fall*) *into — with s.o.*, entrare in conversazione con qlcu.; *to feed the* (o *to make*) *—*, alimentare la conversazione; *to hold a — with s.o.*, tenere una conversazione con qlcu. **2.** (*arc.*) tresca **3.** rapporti sessuali ☆ *— piece*, (*art.*) gruppo ‖ *criminal —*, (*dir.*) adulterio.

conversational [ˌkɔnvəˈseiʃənl], *ag.* di conversazione; amante della conversazione; abile nel conversare; loquace.

conversation(al)ist [ˌkɔnvəˈseiʃn(əl)ist], *s.* abile parlatore.

conversazione [ˈkɔnvəˌsætsiˈouni], *pl.* **conversaziones** [ˈkɔnvəˌsætsiˈouniz], **conversazioni** [ˈkɔnvəˌsætsiˈouni], *s.* riunione letteraria, artistica.

converse[1] [ˈkɔnvə:s], *s.* (*letter.*) **1.** conversazione **2.** comunione intellettuale, spirituale.

to converse[1] [kənˈvə:s], *v.i.* (*letter.*) conversare: *— with s.o. on* (o *about*) *sthg.*, parlare con qlcu. di ql.co.

converse[2] [ˈkɔnvə:s], *ag.* inverso; contrario ‖ *s.* (*mat. fil.*) proposizione inversa.

conversely [ˈkɔnvə:sli], *av.* viceversa.

conversion [kənˈvə:ʃən], *s.* conversione; trasformazione: *— of 4% stock into 3%*, conversione della rendita al 4% in 3%; *— of iron into steel*, trasformazione del ferro in acciaio; *— of Jews to Christianity*, conversione degli ebrei al Cristianesimo.

convert [ˈkɔnvə:t], *s.c.* convertito, convertita; converso, conversa: *to become a — to sthg.*, convertirsi a ql.co.; *to make a — of s.o.*, convertire qlcu.

to convert [kənˈvə:t], *v.t.* **1.** convertire; trasformare, cambiare: *he became converted*, si convertì; *he was converted to Christianity*, fu convertito al Cristianesimo: *— rags into paper*, trasformare stracci in carta **2.** (*metal.*) affinare.

converter [kənˈvə:tə*], *s.* **1.** convertitore, chi converte **2.** (*elett. metal.*) convertitore, convertitrice; commutatore, trasformatore.

convertibility [kənˌvə:təˈbiliti], *s.* convertibilità.

convertible [kənˈvə:təbl], *ag.* convertibile ☆ *— bonds*, buoni convertibili; *— car*, automobile decappottabile; *— husbandry*, (*agr.*) coltura a rotazione; *— terms*, termini sinonimi.

convertibly [kənˈvə:təbli], *av.* convertibilmente.

convertor, *V.* **converter**.

convex [ˈkɔnˈveks], *ag.* convesso.

convexity [kɔnˈveksiti], *s.* convessità.

convexly [kɔnˈveksli], *av.* con forma convessa.

to **convey** [kənˈvei], *v.t.* **1.** trasportare, portare, convogliare: *a pipe-line conveys the oil to the port*, un oleodotto convoglia il petrolio al porto; *some trains — both passengers and goods*, alcuni treni trasportano sia passeggeri che merci; *they were conveyed to the station in a bus*, un autobus li portò alla stazione **2.** trasmettere (suono, odore, malattia): *to — a disease to s.o.*, contagiare qlcu. **3.** rendere noto, comunicare; dare l'idea di: *does this — anything to you?*, questo non ti suggerisce nulla?; *the name conveys nothing to me*, quel nome non mi dice niente; *please — this information, my congratulations to him*, ti prego, comunicagli questa notizia, le mie congratulazioni; *these words — nothing to me*, queste parole non hanno alcun senso per me **4.** (*dir.*) trasferire, fare il trapasso di (proprietà).

conveyable [kənˈveiəbl], *ag.* trasportabile; portabile; trasmissibile.

conveyance [kənˈveiəns], *s.* **1.** trasporto, mezzo di trasporto: *public —*, mezzo di trasporto pubblico; *we have no means of —*, non disponiamo di alcun mezzo di trasporto **2.** trasmissione; comunicazione; (*ind.*) convogliamento: *— of heat, — of sound*, (*fis.*) trasmissione di calore, di suono **3.** (*dir.*) trasferimento, cessione (di proprietà); atto di cessione.

conveyancer [kənˈveiənsə*], *s.* notaio.

conveyer [kənˈveiə*], *s.c.* portatore, portatrice; latore, latrice; trasmettitore, trasmettitrice || *s.* (*ind.*) convogliatore, trasportatore ☆ *-belt*, trasportatore a cinghia; *— -chain*, catena di convogliamento; *— -truck*, carrello convogliatore || *belt- —*, trasportatore a nastro; *chain- —*, trasportatore a catena.

conveying [kənˈveiiŋ], *s.* (*ind.*) trasporto ☆ *— plant*, impianto di trasporto.

conveyor, *V.* **conveyer**.

convict [ˈkɔnvikt], *s.* forzato, condannato ☆ *— colony*, colonia penale.

to **convict** [kənˈvikt], *v.t.* dichiarare colpevole, condannare; convincere (di delitto): *he was convicted*, fu dichiarato colpevole; fu condannato; *you stand convicted by your own words*, le tue stesse parole ti condannano; *to — s.o. of a crime*, dichiarare qlcu. colpevole di un delitto; convincere qlcu. di un delitto.

conviction [kənˈvikʃən], *s.* **1.** (*dir.*) dichiarazione, verdetto di colpevolezza; condanna: *a previous —*, una condanna precedente **2.** persuasione; convinzione: *it is my — that he is innocent*, sono convinto che è innocente; *to be open to —*, essere pronto a ricredersi, a lasciarsi convincere; *to carry —*, essere convincente.

convictive [kənˈviktiv], *ag.* convincente.

to **convince** [kənˈvins], *v.t.* convincere, persuadere: *I am convinced that*, sono convinto che; *to allow oneself to be convinced*, lasciarsi convincere.

convincement [kənˈvinsmənt], *s.* convinzione.

convincible [kənˈvinsəbl], *ag.* convincibile.

convincing [kənˈvinsiŋ], *ag.* convincente, persuasivo.

convincingly [kənˈvinsiŋli], *av.* in modo convincente.

convivial [kənˈviviəl], *ag.* conviviale; gioviale, festevole, allegro: *— evening*, serata allegra con un buon pranzo; *— songs*, canti conviviali; *— verses*, versi conviviali.

convivialist [kənˈviviəlist], *s.* persona gioviale, allegra, socievole.

conviviality [kənˌviviˈæliti], *s.* giovialità; socievolezza.

convivially [kənˈviviəli] *av.* convivialmente; giovialmente, allegramente.

to **convocate** [ˈkɔnvəkeit], *v.t.* (*arc.*) convocare.

convocation [ˌkɔnvəˈkeiʃən], *s.* **1.** convocazione (di assemblea, concilio ecclesiastico, ecc.) **2.** (*Chiesa Anglicana*) sinodo **3.** assemblea (di alcune università).

convocational [ˌkɔnvəˈkeiʃən]], *ag.* di convocazione.

convocator [ˈkɔnvəkeitə*], *s.c.* convocatore, convocatrice.

to **convoke** [kənˈvouk], *v.t.* convocare.

convolute [ˈkɔnvəluːt], *ag.* (*bot.*) convoluto.

convolution [ˌkɔnvəˈluːʃən], *s.* circonvoluzione; sinuosità; spira: *the convolutions of a coiled rope*, le spire di una fune addugliata ☆ *cerebral convolutions*, (*anat.*) circonvoluzioni della corteccia cerebrale.

to **convolve** [kənˈvɔlv], *v.t.i.* arrotolare, arrotolarsi; avvolgere, avvolgersi; attorcigliare, attorcigliarsi.

convolvulus [kənˈvɔlvjuləs], *pl.* **convolvuluses** [kənˈvɔlvjuləsiz], *s.* (*bot.*) convolvolo.

convoy [ˈkɔnvɔi], *s.* **1.** (*mar. mil.*) convoglio **2.** scorta.

to **convoy**, *v.t.* **1.** (*mar. mil.*) convogliare **2.** scortare.

to **convulse** [kənˈvʌls], *v.t.* **1.** sconvolgere: *convulsed by an earthquake*, scosso da un terremoto **2.** dare le convulsioni a: *to be convulsed with pain, laughter, anger*, contorcersi dal dolore, dalle risa, dall'ira.

convulsion [kənˈvʌlʃən], *s.* **1.** *gener. pl.* (*patol.*) convulsione, spasimo **2.** *pl.* accesso di risa **3.** agitazione (sociale, politica).

convulsive [kənˈvʌlsiv], *ag.* convulso, convulsivo (anche *patol.*): *— pulse*, (*patol.*) polso irregolare.

cony [ˈkouni], *pl.* **conies** [ˈkouniz], *s.* (*arc.*) coniglio; pelle di coniglio.

coo [kuː], *s.* il tubare.

to **coo**, *v.i.* tubare (anche *fig.*) || *to bill and —*, (*fam.*) tubare.

cook [kuk], *s.c.* cuoco, cuoca || *too many cooks spoil the broth*, *prov.* troppi cuochi rovinano il brodo ☆ *head —*, capocuoco; *— -house*, cucina all'aperto; (*mil.*) cucina da campo; *— -room*, cucina; (*mar.*) cucina di bordo; *— -shop*, ristorante || *man- —*, *woman- —*, cuoco, cuoca.

to **cook**, *v.t.i.* **1.** cuocere, cuocersi; cucinare; far cuocere: *every woman should learn to —*, ogni donna dovrebbe imparare a cucinare; *this meat cooks well*, questa carne si cuoce bene; *to — meat, vegetables, etc.*, cucinare, far cuocere carne, verdure, ecc. || *to — s.o.'s goose*, (*fam.*) spacciare qlcu., dare il colpo di grazia a qlcu. **2.** (*fam.*) falsificare: *to — accounts*, falsificare, fare quadrare a tutti i costi i conti || *what is cooking?*, che cosa bolle in pentola?, che c'è di nuovo? **3.** *to — up*, inventare (scuse, storie, frottole, ecc.).

cookbook [ˈkukbuk], *s.* (*amer.*) libro di cucina.

cooker [ˈkukə*], *s.* **1.** fornello; cucina economica **2.** frutta da cuocere: *these apples are good cookers*, queste mele sono buone da cuocere **3.** tegame, pentola || *s.c.* falsificatore, falsificatrice ☆ *electric —*, fornello, cucina elettrica.

cookery [ˈkukəri], *s.* arte culinaria; cucina ☆ *— -book*, libro di cucina.

cookie [ˈkuki], *s.* (*amer.*) galletta; (*scoz.*) focaccina.

cooking [ˈkukiŋ], *s.* **1.** cottura **2.** arte culinaria; cucina: *to do the —*, fare la cucina **3.** falsificazione (di conti, ecc.) ☆ *plain- —*, cucina casalinga.

cooky [ˈkuki], *s.* (*fam.*) cuoca.

cool[1] [kuːl], *a.* fresco: *a — evening after a hot day*, una serata fresca dopo una giornata calda; *it is difficult to keep — on a hot summer day*, è difficile mantenersi freschi in una calda giornata d'estate; *let's sit in the shade and get —*, sediamo all'ombra per rinfrescarci **2.** fresco, leggero (di vestito): *she was wearing a — dress*, indossava un abito leggero **3.** calmo, tranquillo: *keep —*, conserva la calma; *he has a very — head*, ha molto sangue freddo || *as — as a cucumber*, (*fam.*) con sangue freddo; fresco come una rosa **4.** freddo, senza entusiasmo: *his manner was very —*, il suo modo di fare era molto freddo; *they gave him a — reception*, lo accolsero molto freddamente **5.** disinvolto; impudente, sfacciato || *a — hand*, una persona disinvolta || *what — cheek!*, (*fam.*) che sfacciataggine! || *my new car cost a — thousand*, la mia nuova automobile mi è costata la bellezza di mille sterline || *s.* fresco, frescura; freschezza: *in the ̄ — of the evening*, nella frescura della sera; *to keep food in the —*, tenere il cibo in fresco ☆ *— -headed*, calmo, imperturbabile; *— -headedness*, sangue freddo, imperturbabilità.

to **cool**[1], *v.t.i.* **1.** rinfrescare, rinfrescarsi; raffreddare, raffreddarsi (anche *fig.*): *blow on it, that will soon — it*, soffiaci sopra, si raffredderà subito; *rain cools the air*, la pioggia rinfresca l'aria; *the weather has cooled*, il tempo si è rinfrescato; *what can we do to — his enthusiasm?*, cosa possiamo fare per raffreddare il suo entusiasmo? ‖ *to — one's heels*, essere obbligato ad aspettare **2.** (*fam.*) calmare, fare una doccia fredda a **3.** *to — down, off*, rinfrescarsi; *fig.* calmarsi: *his anger has cooled down*, la sua ira è sbollita; *we stopped to let our horses — down*, ci fermammo per lasciar riposare i cavalli.

cool[2], *s.* cassetta di burro di circa 28 libbre.

coolant ['ku:lənt], *s.* (*chim.*) (liquido) refrigerante.

cooler ['ku:lə*], *s.* **1.** (*chim. ind.*) refrigeratore **2.** bibita **3.** (*sl.*) gattabuia ☆ *air -—*, (*amer.*) refrigerante per l'aria, condizionatore dell'aria; *oil —*, (*aer.*) radiatore dell'olio.

coolie ['ku:li], *s.* « coolìe », facchino, portatore, servo (in India ed Estremo Oriente).

cooling ['ku:liŋ], *ag.* rinfrescante; (*ind.*) refrigerante, raffreddante ‖ *s.* abbassamento (di temperatura); (*fis.*) raffreddamento ☆ *— -off period*, fase di raffreddamento; *— tower*, (*ind.*) torre di raffreddamento ‖ *air -—*, raffreddamento ad aria.

coolish ['ku:liʃ], *ag.* fresco.

coolly ['ku:lli], *av.* **1.** freddamente **2.** con calma, a sangue freddo **3.** con disinvoltura.

coolness ['ku:lnis], *s.* **1.** fresco, frescura **2.** sangue freddo, calma; freddezza **3.** disinvoltura.

coolth [ku:lθ], *s.* (*fam. scherz.*) freddezza; calma.

cooly, *V.* **coolie.**

coom [ku:m], *s.* morchia; sudiciume; polvere di carbone.

coomb(e) [ku:m], *s.* valletta; vallone.

coon [ku:n], *s.* (*fam. amer.*) **1.** (*zool.*) procione, tasso americano **2.** tizio, individuo: *he's a gone —*, è un individuo spacciato, finito **3.** (*spreg.*) negro ☆ *— -song*, canto dei negri.

coop[1] [ku:p], *s.* **1.** stia **2.** nassa.

to **coop**[1], *v.t.* **1.** mettere nella stia (polli) **2.** rinchiudere, confinare in uno spazio limitato (persone): *one feels cooped (up) in a ship's cabin*, nella cabina di una nave uno si sente imprigionato; *we are cooped (up o in) all day*, siamo rinchiusi tutto il giorno.

coop[2], *s.* mucchietto (di letame, ecc.).

coop[3], *s.* carro per letame.

coop[4], *s.* (*cine.*) lampada a mercurio.

co-op [kou'ɔp], *s.* (*abbr. fam.* di *co-operative*) cooperativa.

cooper[1] ['ku:pə*], *s.* **1.** bottaio **2.** assaggiatore di vini **3.** mistura di birre ☆ *dry —, wet —*, fabbricante di barili, botti, ecc. per solidi, per liquidi.

to **cooper**[1], *v.t.i.* **1.** riparare (botti, barili) **2.** imbottare, imbarilare **3.** fare il bottaio.

cooper[2], *V.* **coper.**

cooperage ['ku:pəridʒ], *s.* mestiere, negozio del bottaio.

co-operant [kou'ɔpərənt], *ag.* cooperante.

to **co-operate** [kou'ɔpəreit], *v.i.* cooperare: *to — with s.o. in sthg.*, cooperare con qlcu. in ql.co.; *to — to the success of sthg.*, cooperare al successo di ql.co.

co-operation [kou,ɔpə'reiʃən], *s.* cooperazione.

co-operative [kou'ɔpərətiv], *ag.* cooperativo.

co-operatively [kou'ɔpərətivli], *av.* in cooperazione.

co-operator [kou'ɔpəreitə*], *s.c.* cooperatore, cooperatrice.

coopery ['ku:pəri], *s.* mestiere, negozio del bottaio.

to **co-opt** [kou'ɔpt], *v.t.* eleggere a membro di un comitato (con voti di membri già eletti).

co-optation [,kouɔp'teiʃən], **co-option** [kou'ɔpʃən], *s.* elezione di un membro di un comitato (da parte dei membri eletti).

co-ordinate [kou'ɔ:dnit], *ag.* **1.** uguale, dello stesso rango **2.** (*gram.*) coordinato: *— clauses*, proposizioni coordinate ‖ *s.* **1.** (*st.*) uguale, pari (per rango, importanza) **2.** (*mat. gram.*) coordinata.

to **co-ordinate** [kou'ɔ:dineit], *v.t.* coordinare.

co-ordinately [kou'ɔ:dinitli], *av.* di pari rango, posizione.

co-ordination [kou,ɔ:di'neiʃən], *s.* coordinazione.

co-ordinative [kou'ɔ:dinətiv], *ag.* coordinativo.

coot [ku:t], *s.* **1.** (*ornit.*) folaga ‖ *to be as bald as a —*, essere stempiato **2.** (*fam.*) persona sciocca.

cootie, cooty ['ku:ti], *s.* (*sl. mil.*) pidocchio.

co-owner [kou'ounə*], *s.c.* comproprietario, comproprietaria.

co-ownership [kou'ounəʃip], *s.* comproprietà.

cop[1] [kɔp], *s.* **1.** cima (di collina, ecc.) **2.** (*ind. tessile*) bobina, spola.

to **cop**[1], *pass.p.p.* **copped** [kɔpt], *v.t.* (*ind. tessile*) incannare.

cop[2], *s.* (*sl.*) poliziotto.

to **cop**[2], *pass.p.p.* **copped**, *v.t.* (*sl.*) acchiappare ‖ *to — it*, (*sl.*) prenderle, essere punito.

copaiba [kə'paibə], **copaiva** [kə'paivə], *s.* (*farm.*) copaive ☆ *— balsam*, balsamo copaive.

copal ['koupəl], *s.* cop(p)ale (vernice).

copartner ['kou'pɑ:tnə*], *s.* (*comm.*) consocio.

copartnership ['kou'pɑ:tnəʃip], **copartnery** ['kou'pɑ:tnəri], *s.* associazione; società; società in nome collettivo ☆ *industrial —*, (*comm.*) società nella quale gli operai partecipano agli utili.

cope[1] [koup], *s.* **1.** (*eccl.*) cappa; piviale **2.** *fig.* cappa, volta (del cielo) **3.** cappa, copertura esterna **4.** (*arch.*) cimasa **5.** (*metal.*) staffa superiore ☆ *— -stone*, pietra per cimasa; *fig.* coronamento, colmo, tocco finale.

to **cope**[1], *v.t.* **1.** imporre la cappa (a un vescovo) **2.** coprire con cappa **3.** (*arch.*) fornire di cimasa.

to **cope**[2], *v.i.* far fronte, tener testa; lottare con successo: *I can't — with everything*, non posso arrivare a far tutto.

to **cope**[3], *v.t.* (*sl.*) barattare.

copeck ['koupek], *s.* copeco (moneta russa).

Copenhagen [,koupn'heigən], *no.pr.* (*geog.*) Copenhaghen.

coper ['koupə*], *s.* nave che fornisce bevande alcooliche ai pescatori del mare del Nord.

Copernican [kou'pə:nikən], *ag.* copernicano: *— system, theory*, sistema, teoria copernicana.

Copernicus [kou'pə:nikəs], *no.pr.m.* (*st. astr.*) Copernico.

copier ['kɔpiə*], *s.* **1.** copista, trascrittore **2.** imitatore.

co-pilot [kou'pailət], *s.* (*aer.*) secondo pilota.

coping ['koupiŋ], *s.* (*arch.*) cimasa, sporgenza protettiva di muro ☆ *— -stone*, pietra per cimasa.

copious ['koupjəs], *ag.* copioso, abbondante: *— style*, stile ampolloso.

copiously ['koupjəsli], *av.* copiosamente.

copiousness ['koupjəsnis], *s.* abbondanza, profusione.

copper[1] ['kɔpə*], *ag.* di rame; color rame ‖ *s.* **1.** rame **2.** moneta di rame ‖ *coppers*, (*fam.*) spiccioli **3.** caldaia, paiolo (di rame) ‖ *to have hot coppers*, (*sl.*) aver la gola riarsa (di bevitore) ☆ *— beech*, (*bot.*) faggio rosso; *— -captain*, (*fam.*) sedicente capitano; *— -coloured*, color rame; *— mill*, fucina per rame; *— mine*, miniera di rame; *— smith*, ramaio; calderaio; *— -top*, (*fam.*) capelli rossi ‖ *pig —*, (*metal.*) rame in salmoni.

to **copper**[1], *v.t.* ricoprire, rivestire di rame.

copper[2], *s.* (*sl.*) poliziotto.

copperas ['kɔpərəs], *s.* (*chim.*) solfato ferroso; copparosa verde.

copperhead ['kɔpə-hed], *s.* (*zool.*) trigonocefalo.

coppering ['kɔpəriŋ], *s.* rivestimento in rame del fondo di una nave.

copperplate ['kɔpə-pleit], *s.* **1.** lastra di rame (per incisione) **2.** incisione in rame ☆ *— engraving*, calcografia (incisione su rame).

coppery ['kɔpəri], *ag.* color rame; contenente rame.

coppice ['kɔpis], *s.* boschetto, bosco ceduo ☆ — -*wood*, sottobosco.

copra ['kɔprə], *s.* copra (polpa di noce di cocco essiccata).

copse [kɔps], *s.* boschetto, bosco ceduo.

to **copse**, *v.t.* piantare a bosco ceduo.

copsewood ['kɔps-wud], *s.* sottobosco.

Copt [kɔpt], *s.c.* (*relig.*) copto, copta.

Coptic ['kɔptik], *ag.* (*relig.*) copto ‖ *s.* lingua copta.

copula ['kɔpjulə], *pl.* **copulas** ['kɔpjuləz], **copulae** ['kɔpjuli:], *s.* (*gram.*) copula.

to **copulate** ['kɔpjuleit], *v.i.* accoppiarsi.

copulation [,kɔpju'leiʃən], *s.* accoppiamento, copulazione.

copulative ['kɔpjulətiv], *ag.* copulativo.

copy ['kɔpi], *s.* 1. copia, trascrizione: *typewritten* —, copia a macchina; *to make a — of a deed,* (*dir.*) fare copia autentica di un documento 2. copia, riproduzione: *a — from Raphael,* una copia da Raffaello 3. modello, esempio 4. copia, esemplare: *I have two copies of the same book,* ho due copie dello stesso libro 5. (*tip. giornalismo*) materiale: *the printers want more* —, i tipografi hanno bisogno di altro materiale; *this revolution will make good* —, questa rivoluzione sarà sfruttata dalla stampa ☆ — -*book,* quaderno; libro di esercizi di calligrafia; — *desk,* scrivania del redattore; — -*holder,* registratore (da ufficio); — -*reader,* revisore di stampa; — -*writer,* « copy-writer », redattore pubblicitario ‖ *certified* —, copia autenticata; *certified true* —, per copia conforme; *duplicate* —, duplicato; *fair* —, bella copia; *rough* —, minuta, brutta copia.

to **copy**, *v.t.* 1. copiare: *to* — (*out*) *a letter,* trascrivere una lettera 2. imitare; seguire l'esempio di.

copyhold ['kɔpihould], *s.* 1. proprietà di terre soggette a speciali diritti 2. terre soggette a tali diritti.

copyholder ['kɔpi,houldə*], *s.* proprietario di terre soggette a speciali diritti.

copyist ['kɔpiist], *s.* copista.

copyright ['kɔpirait], *ag.* protetto dai diritti d'autore ‖ *s.* « copyright », riproduzione vietata.

to **copyright**, *v.t.* proteggere con i diritti d'autore.

coquetry ['koukitri], *s.* civetteria.

coquette [kou'ket], *s.* (*donna*) civetta.

to **coquet(te)**, *v.i.* civettare, fare la civetta.

coquettish [kou'ketiʃ], *ag.* civettuolo.

coquettishly [kou'ketiʃli], *av.* in modo civettuolo.

coracle ['kɔrəkl], *s.* imbarcazione di vimini coperta di materiale impermeabile.

coral ['kɔrəl], *ag.s.* (di) corallo: — *lips,* (*fam.*) labbra coralline ‖ *the Coral Sea,* il mar dei Coralli ☆ — *fisher,* pescatore di coralli; — - *island,* isola corallina; — -*reef,* scogliera corallina.

coralliferous [,kɔrə'lifərəs], *ag.* corallifero.

coralliform [kə'ræilifɔ:m], *ag.* coralliforme.

coralline ['kɔrəlain], *ag.* corallino ‖ *s.* corallina.

coralloid ['kɔrələoid], *ag.* simile a corallo.

corbel ['kɔ:bəl], *s.* (*arch.*) mensola, modiglione.

corbelled ['kɔ:bəld], *ag.* a mensola, a modiglione.

corbie ['kɔ:bi], *s.* (*scoz.*) corvo ☆ — -*step,* (*arch.*) ornamento a scalini (di frontone).

Corcyra [kɔ:'saiərə], *no.pr.* (*geog. st.*) Corcira.

cord [kɔ:d], *s.* 1. corda, spago; piccola fune 2. (*elett.*) filo con spina 3. *fig.* legame: *the cords of discipline,* i legami della disciplina 4. *pl.* pantaloni di velluto a coste 5. catasta di legna (misura di volume = m³ 3,625) ☆ *spinal* —, (*anat.*) midollo spinale; *umbilical* —, (*anat.*) cordone ombelicale; *vocal cords,* (*anat.*) corde vocali.

to **cord**, *v.t.* legare con corde.

cordage ['kɔ:didʒ], *s.* cordame; (*mar.*) sartiame.

cordate ['kɔ:deit], *ag.* (*bot.*) cordato.

corded ['kɔ:did], *ag.* 1. munito di corde 2. a coste (di tessuti).

Cordelia [kɔ:'di:ljə], *no.pr.f.* (*lett.*) Cordelia.

cordelier [,kɔ:di'liə*], *s.* frate francescano.

cordial ['kɔ:djəl], *ag.* cordiale ‖ *s.* (*bevanda*) cordiale.

cordiality [,kɔ:di'æliti], *s.* cordialità.

cordially ['kɔ:djəli], *av.* cordialmente.

cordite ['kɔ:dait], *s.* (*esplosivo*) cordite.

cordon ['kɔ:dn], *s.* cordone.

cordovan ['kɔ:dəvən], *ag.* di cordovano, di pelle di capra ‖ *s.* cordovano, pelle di capra.

corduroy ['kɔ:dərɔi], *s.* 1. velluto a coste 2. *pl.* calzoni di velluto a coste.

cordwain ['kɔ:dwein], *s.* (*arc.*) cordovano.

cordwainer ['kɔ:d,weinə*], *s.* (*arc.*) chi lavora il cuoio; calzolaio.

core¹ [kɔ:*], *s.* 1. torsolo (di frutto) 2. centro, anima, nucleo; cuore (anche *fig.*): *in my heart's* —, nel profondo del mio cuore; *he is English to the* —, è inglese fino in fondo all'anima.

to **core**¹, *v.t.* 1. estrarre il torsolo da (un frutto) 2. estrarre la parte centrale da.

core², *s.* 1. gruppo, compagnia (di persone) 2. (*miner.*) squadra di minatori.

corelation ['kouri'leiʃən], *s.* correlazione.

co-religionist ['kouri'lidʒənist], *s.* correligionario.

co-respondent ['kouris,pɔndənt], *s.* (*dir.*) correo (in adulterio).

corf [kɔ:f], *s.* 1. (*miner.*) carrello 2. cesto per conservare il pesce vivo nell'acqua.

coriaceous [,kɔri'eiʃəs], *ag.* coriaceo.

coriander [,kɔri'ændə*], *s.* (*bot.*) coriandolo.

Corinne [kə'rin], *no.pr.f.* Corinna.

Corinth ['kɔrinθ], *no.pr* (*geog.*) Corinto: *Isthmus of* —, istmo di Corinto.

Corinthian [kə'rinθiən], *ag.* di Corinto, corinzio: — *temple,* tempio corinzio ‖ *s.c.* corinzio, corinzia ‖ *s.* (*arc.*) uomo dissoluto ☆ — *order,* ordine corinzio.

Coriolanus [,kɔriə'leinəs], *no.pr.m.* (*st.*) Coriolano.

cork [kɔ:k], *s.* 1. sughero; pezzo di sughero 2. tappo, turacciolo: *to draw the* — *of a bottle,* levare il tappo a una bottiglia ☆ — *jacket,* cintura di salvataggio; — -*leg,* (*fam.*) gamba di legno; — -*tipped,* con bocchino di sughero (di sigaretta); — -*tree,* quercia da sughero.

to **cork**, *v.t.* 1. turare: *to* — (*up*) *a bottle,* turare una bottiglia 2. munire di sughero (galleggianti, ecc.) 3. annerire con un turacciolo bruciato.

corkage ['kɔ:kidʒ], *s.* 1. il turare; lo sturare 2. compenso dovuto a un ristorante per sturare bottiglie acquistate altrove.

corked [kɔ:kt], *ag.* 1. tappato 2. munito di sughero 3. annerito con turacciolo bruciato 4. che sa di turacciolo: — *wine,* vino che sa di turacciolo.

corker ['kɔ:kə*], *s.* (*sl.*) 1. menzogna; vanto ‖ *that's a* —!, è un po' troppo! 2. (*amer.*) cosa, persona meravigliosa, strabiliante: *he's a* —, è un tipo strabiliante; *it's a* —, è una cosa meravigliosa.

corking ['kɔ:kiŋ], *s.* 1. turamento 2. sapore di turacciolo ☆ *bottle-* — *machine,* macchina per turare bottiglie.

corkscrew ['kɔ:kskru:], *s.* cavatturaccioli ☆ — *dive,* (*aer.*) picchiata in spirale; — *staircase,* scala a chiocciola.

to **corkscrew**, *v.t.i.* 1. tracciare (una linea) a spirale 2. procedere a spirale; (*aer.*) avvitare 3. *to* — *away at s.o.,* (*sl.*) cavare parole di bocca a qlcu.

corky ['kɔ:ki], *ag.* 1. sugheroso 2. frivolo; vivace.

corm [kɔ:m], *s.* (*bot.*) bulbo.

cormorant ['kɔ:mərənt], *s.* (*ornit.*) cormorano.

corn¹ [kɔ:n], *s.* 1. grano, granello, chicco (di cereali; pepe, ecc.) 2. cereali; piante cereali; (*in Inghilterra*) frumento, orzo, avena; granturco; (*in Scozia*) avena; (*negli Stati Uniti*) granturco: *an ear of* —, una spiga di grano; *a field of* —, un campo di grano; *a sheaf of* —, un covone ‖ *Corn Belt,* (*geog.*) zona cerealicola al centro degli Stati Uniti ☆ — -*bread,* (*amer.*) focaccia di granturco; — -*chandler,* mercante di grano; — -*cob,* pannocchia; pipa fatta con pannocchia; — -*exchange,* mercato, borsa dei cereali; — -*flakes,* (*cuc.*) fiocchi di granturco; — -*flour,* farina finissima di granturco; —

-flower, fiordaliso; — *-laws*, (*st.*) leggi sulla importazione del grano; — *-meal*, farina; (*scoz.*) farina d'avena, (*amer.*) farina di granturco; — *-merchant* (o — *-dealer*), grossista in granaglie; — *-poppy*, papavero selvatico; — *-whisky*, whisky di mais.

to **corn**[1], *v.t.* **1.** salare (carne), conservare (carne) sotto sale **2.** (*scoz.*) nutrire (cavalli) con avena **3.** coltivare (un terreno) a grano ☆ *corned beef*, manzo conservato sotto sale.

corn[2], *s.* callo; durone ‖ *to tread on s.o.'s corns*, (*fam.*) pestare i calli a qlcu. ☆ — *-plaster*, (cerotto) callifugo ‖ *soft* —, occhio di pernice.

cornea ['kɔ:niə], *s.* (*anat.*) cornea.

cornel ['kɔ:nl], *s.* (*bot.*) corniola; corniolo.

Cornelia [kɔ:'ni:ljə], *no.pr.f.* Cornelia.

cornelian [kɔ:'ni:ljən], *s.* (*min.*) corniola.

Cornelius [kɔ:'ni:ljəs], *no.pr.m.* Cornelio.

corneous ['kɔ:ni(:)əs], *ag.* corneo.

corner ['kɔ:nə*], *s.* **1.** angolo: *in every* — *of the earth*, in tutti gli angoli del mondo; *odd* —, angolo fuori mano; *to cut off a* —, prendere una scorciatoia; *to turn the* —, voltare l'angolo; *fig.* superare una crisi (di malattia) ‖ *done in a* —, fatto di nascosto ‖ *a tight* —, una situazione difficile, pericolosa ‖ *to drive* (o *put*) *s.o. into a* —, mettere qlcu. con le spalle al muro **2.** (*comm.*) accaparramento (di merce al mercato); monopolio: *to make a* — *in wheat*, effettuare l'accaparramento del frumento ☆ — *-boy*, (*neol.*) monello; — *house*, casa d'angolo (generalmente ristorante); — *radius*, (*mec.*) raggio d'angolo; — *seat*, posto d'angolo; — *-stone*, pietra angolare.

to **corner**, *v.t.i.* **1.** mettere, spingere in un angolo; *fig.* mettere con le spalle al muro, mettere alle strette: *that question cornered him*, gli fu difficile rispondere a quella domanda **2.** fare angolo **3.** accaparrare (merce sul mercato).

cornet[1] ['kɔ:nit], *s.* **1.** (*mus.*) cornetta **2.** cartoccio conico; cono (*p.e.* per gelati).

cornet[2], *s.* **1.** cornetta (cuffia delle Suore di Carità) **2.** (*arc. mil.*) cornetta, alfiere.

cornice ['kɔ:nis], *s.* (*arch.*) cornicione; cornice.

Cornish ['kɔ:niʃ], *ag.s.* (dialetto, abitante) della Cornovaglia.

cornucopia [,kɔ:nju'koupjə], *s.* cornucopia; *fig.* abbondanza.

Cornwall ['kɔ:nwəl], *no.pr.* (*geog.*) Cornovaglia.

corny[1] ['kɔ:ni], *ag.* **1.** calloso **2.** (*sl. amer.*) vecchio; ingenuo; sdolcinato; lamentoso; rustico; semplice.

corny[2], *ag.* **1.** di grano; che abbonda di grano **2.** (*sl.*) brillo.

corolla [kə'rɔlə], *pl.* **corollas** [kə'rɔləz], *s.* (*bot.*) corolla.

corollaceous [,kɔrə'leiʃəs], *ag.* con corolla; simile a corolla.

corollary [kə'rɔləri], *s.* corollario; conseguenza.

corona [kə'rounə], *pl.* **coronae** [kə'rouni:], *s.* **1.** (*anat. astr. arch.*) corona **2.** tipo di sigaro americano.

coronach ['kɔrənək], *s.* (*irl. scoz.*) canto funebre; nenia.

coronal[1] [kə'rounl], *ag.* coronale ☆ — *bone, suture*, (*anat.*) osso, sutura coronale.

coronal[2] ['kɔrənl], *s.* (*arc.*) piccola corona; ghirlanda.

coronary ['kɔrənəri], *ag.* (*anat.*) coronario ☆ — *thrombosis*, (*patol.*) trombosi delle coronarie.

coronate ['kɔrənit], *ag.* (*bot.*) coronato.

coronated ['kɔrəneitid], *ag.* (*bot.*) coronato.

coronation [,kɔrə'neiʃən], *s.* incoronazione.

coroner ['kɔrənə*], *s.* «coroner» (ufficiale inglese della Corona incaricato dell'inchiesta nei casi di morte violenta sospetta).

coronet ['kɔrənit], *s.* corona (gentilizia); diadema.

coroneted ['kɔrənetid], *ag.* chi porta corona nobiliare.

corozo [kə'rousou], *pl.* **corozos** [kə'rousouz], *s.* (*bot.*) corozo, avorio vegetale.

corporal[1] ['kɔ:pərəl], *ag.* corporale, corporeo ☆ — *punishment*, pena corporale.

corporal[2], *s.* (*mil.*) caporale ‖ *the little* —, (*fam.*) Napoleone.

corporal[3], *s.* (*eccl.*) corporale.

corporality [,kɔ:pə'ræliti], *s.* **1.** corporalità **2.** *pl.* bisogni materiali.

corporate ['kɔ:pərit], *ag.* corporativo: — *action, responsibility*, azione, responsabilità di ciascun membro di un ente corporativo; — *property*, proprietà corporativa ☆ — *body*, ente morale; — *town*, municipio.

corporately ['kɔ:pəritli], *av.* corporativamente.

corporation [,kɔ:pə'reiʃən], *s.* **1.** corporazione; ente morale **2.** (*amer. comm.*) società a responsabilità limitata **3.** azienda municipale **4.** (*scherz.*) pancione ☆ — *tramways*, tranvie municipali.

corporative ['kɔ:pərətiv], *ag.* corporativo.

corporeal [kɔ:'pɔ:riəl], *ag.* corporeo.

corporeality [kɔ:,pɔ:ri(:)'æliti], *s.* (*fil.*) materialismo.

corporeity [kɔ:pə'ri:iti], *s.* corporeità.

corposant ['kɔ:pəzænt], *s.* (*mar.*) fuoco di S. Elmo.

corps [kɔ:*], *pl.* **corps** [kɔ:z], **1.** (*mil.*) corpo; corpo d'armata; reparto **2.** gruppo (di persone): — *de ballet*, corpo di ballo; *esprit de* —, spirito di parte, di corpo ☆ *army medical* —, corpo sanitario dell'esercito; *diplomatic* —, corpo diplomatico.

corpse [kɔ:ps], *s.* salma, cadavere.

corpsman, *pl.* **corpsmen** ['kɔ:mən], *s.* (*neol. mil. amer.*) soldato di sanità; portaferiti.

corpulence ['kɔ:pjuləns], **corpulency** ['kɔ:pjulənsi], *s.* corpulenza, obesità.

corpulent ['kɔ:pjulənt], *ag.* corpulento, obeso.

corpus ['kɔ:pəs], *s.* **1.** corpo, cadavere ‖ *Corpus Christi*, (*eccl.*) Corpusdomini **2.** corpus, corpo del reato **2.** corpus, raccolta di leggi o scritti ‖ — *juris*, corpus juris **3.** (*anat.*) corpo: — *callosum, striatum*, corpo calloso, striato.

corpuscle ['kɔ:pʌsl], *s.* corpuscolo ☆ *blood* —, globulo sanguigno.

corpuscular [kɔ:'pʌskjulə*], *ag.* corpuscolare.

corral [kɔ'rɑ:l], *s.* recinto (per bestiame); cerchio di carri (per proteggere un accampamento).

to **corral**, *v.t.i.* **1.** chiudere (bestiame) in un recinto **2.** disporre (i carri) in cerchio (per difesa) **3.** (*sl. amer.*) impadronirsi di.

correct [kə'rekt], *ag.* **1.** corretto; giusto; esatto, preciso: — *answer*, risposta esatta; — *behaviour*, contegno corretto: — *calculation*, calcolo preciso; — *time*, ora esatta **2.** adatto, opportuno: *is this the* — *dress for a dinner?*, è questo il vestito adatto per un pranzo?; *to do, to say the* — *thing*, fare, dire ciò che è opportuno.

to **correct**, *v.t.* correggere; regolare; aggiustare: — *your pronunciation*, correggi la tua pronuncia; — *your watch by the radio*, regola l'orologio con la radio; *to* — *a child*, correggere, rimproverare un bambino.

correction [kə'rekʃən], *s.* correzione; rettifica: *house of* —, casa di correzione; (*arc.*) prigione ‖ *under* —, salvo errore.

correctitude [kə'rektitju:d], *s.* correttezza.

corrective [kə'rektiv], *ag.s.* correttivo.

correctly [kə'rektli], *av.* **1.** correttamente, esattamente **2.** in modo adatto, opportunamente.

correctness [kə'rektnis], *s.* correttezza; giustezza; precisione.

corrector [kə'rektə*], *s.c.* correttore, correttrice: — *of the press*, (*tip.*) correttore di bozze.

correlate ['kɔrileit], *s.* termine di correlazione.

to **correlate**, *v.t.i.* essere, mettere in correlazione.

correlation [,kɔri'leiʃən], *s.* correlazione.

correlative [kɔ'relətiv], *ag.* correlativo ‖ *s.* chi, che è in correlazione.

correlatively [kɔ'relətivli], *av.* correlativamente.

to **correspond** [,kɔris'pɔnd], *v.i.* **1.** corrispondere, essere in relazione epistolare: *I should like to* — *with an English boy*, mi piacerebbe mettermi in corrispondenza con un ragazzo inglese; *we have corresponded for many years*, siamo in corrispondenza da molti anni **2.** rispondere, accordarsi, essere in accordo: *this road does not — to the needs of modern traffic*, questa strada non risponde all'esigenza del traffico moderno; *what he says corresponds with what I think*, ciò che egli dice corrisponde a ciò che io penso **3.** corrispondere, equivalere, essere simile: *the American Congress corresponds to the British Parliament*, il Congresso americano corrisponde al Parlamento inglese.

correspondence [ˌkorisˈpondəns], *s.* **1.** corrispondenza, carteggio; epistolario: *all — to be addressed to the manager*, tutta la corrispondenza deve essere indirizzata al direttore; *have you looked through all your —?*, avete esaminato tutta la vostra corrispondenza?; *to clear off —*, sbrigare la corrispondenza **2.** accordo, armonia, rispondenza: *there is much — between poetry and music*, c'è molta rispondenza fra la poesia e la musica ☆ *business —*, corrispondenza d'affari; *foreign —*, corrispondenza con, per, dall'estero.

correspondent [ˌkorisˈpondənt], *ag.* corrispondente ‖ *s.* corrispondente: *Barclays Bank is our — in London*, la Barclays è la nostra banca corrispondente a Londra ‖ *s.c.* corrispondente: *— for Italian*, corrispondente d'italiano; *she is a bad —*, è una cattiva corrispondente ☆ *political —*, redattore politico; *special —*, inviato speciale.

correspondently [ˌkorisˈpondəntli], *av.* corrispondentemente.

corresponding [ˌkorisˈpondiŋ], *ag.* corrispondente: *— angles*, (*geom.*) angoli corrispondenti ☆ *— clerk*, (impiegato) corrispondente; *— member*, socio corrispondente.

correspondingly [ˌkorisˈpondiŋli], *av.* corrispondentemente.

corridor [ˈkorido:*], *s.* corridoio (anche *geog.*): *the Polish —*, il corridoio di Danzica ☆ *— -train*, treno con vetture intercomunicanti.

corrie [ˈkori], *s.* (*scoz.*) cavità circolare sul fianco della montagna.

corrigendum [ˌkoriˈdʒendəm], *pl.* **corrigenda** [ˌkoriˈdʒendə], *s.* cosa che deve essere corretta (specialmente errore di stampa).

corrigible [ˈkoridʒəbl], *ag.* correggibile.

corrival [kəˈraivəl], *ag.* emulo ‖ *s.c.* rivale.

corroborant [kəˈrobərənt], *ag.* corroborante ‖ *s.* (*farm.*) corroborante.

to **corroborate** [kəˈrobəreit], *v.t.* corroborare: *the evidence corroborates his statement*, l'evidenza conferma la sua dichiarazione.

corroboration [kəˌrobəˈreiʃən], *s.* avvaloramento.

corroborative [kəˈrobərotiv], *ag.* corroborante.

corroborator [kəˈrobəreitə*], *ag.* corroborante ‖ *s.c.* corroboratore, corroboratrice.

corroboratory [kəˈrobərətəri], *ag.* corroborativo.

corroboree [kəˈrobəri], *s.* « corroboree » (danza degli aborigeni australiani).

to **corrode** [kəˈroud], *v.t.i.* corrodere, corrodersi; *fig.* rodere, rodersi: *a corroding hate*, un odio che rode.

corrosion [kəˈrouʒən], *s.* corrosione.

corrosive [kəˈrousiv], *ag.s.* corrosivo.

corrosively [kəˈrousivli], *av.* in modo corrosivo.

corrosiveness [kəˈrousivnis], *s.* corrosività, causticità.

to **corrugate** [ˈkorugeit], *v.t.i.* corrugare, corrugarsi; increspare, incresparsi: *to — one's forehead*, corrugare la fronte ☆ *corrugated iron*, lamiera di ferro ondulato; *corrugated paper, cardboard*, carta, cartone increspati.

corrugation [ˌkoruˈgeiʃən], *s.* corrugamento.

corrugator [ˈkorugeitə*], *s.* (*anat.*) muscolo corrugatore.

corrupt [kəˈrʌpt], *ag.* **1.** corrotto, guasto **2.** alterato; non attendibile (di testo, ecc.) **3.** corrotto; depravato; disonesto: *— practices*, metodi corruttivi (specialmente alle elezioni).

to **corrupt**, *v.t.i.* **1.** corrompere, corrompersi; gua-

stare, guastarsi **2.** alterare (testi, ecc.) **3.** depravare.

corrupter [kəˈrʌptə*], *s.c.* corruttore, corruttrice.

corruptibility [kəˌrʌptəˈbiliti], *s.* corruttibilità.

corruptible [kəˈrʌptəbl], *ag.* corruttibile.

corruption [kəˈrʌpʃən], *s.* corruzione.

corruptive [kəˈrʌptiv], *ag.* corruttivo.

corruptly [kəˈrʌptli], *av.* corrottamente.

corruptness [kəˈrʌptnis], *s.* corruzione.

corruptor [kəˈrʌptə*], *s.c.* corruttore, corruttrice.

corsage [ko:ˈsɑ:ʒ], *s.* **1.** corpetto (di abito da donna) **2.** (*amer.*) mazzolino di fiori da portare sul corpetto.

corsair [ˈko:sɛə*], *s.* **1.** corsaro **2.** nave corsara.

corse [ko:s], *s.* (*poet.*) cadavere.

corselet [ˈko:slit], *s.* **1.** corsaletto (leggera corazza) **2.** corsetto **3.** busto intero (da donna).

corset [ˈko:sit], *s.* corsetto.

Corsica [ˈko:sikə], *no.pr.* (*geog.*) Corsica.

Corsican [ˈko:sikən], *ag.* corso ‖ *s.c.* corso, corsa.

corslet, *V.* corselet.

cortège [ko:ˈteiʒ], *s.* corteggio.

cortex [ˈko:teks], *pl.* **cortices** [ˈko:tisi:z], *s.* **1.** (*bot.*) cortice, corteccia **2.** (*anat.*) corteccia cerebrale.

cortical [ˈko:tikəl], *ag.* (*anat. bot.*) corticale.

corticate [ˈko:tikit], **corticated** [ˈko:tikeitid], *ag.* che ha la corteccia; simile a corteccia.

cortisone [ˈko:tisoun], *s.* (*farm.*) cortisone.

corundum [kəˈrʌndəm], *s.* (*min.*) corindone.

coruscant [kəˈrʌskənt], *ag.* corruscante, scintillante.

to **coruscate** [ˈkorəskeit], *v.i.* corruscare, scintillare, lampeggiare (anche *fig.*).

coruscation [ˌkorəsˈkeiʃən], *s.* corruscazione, scintillio, balenio (anche *fig.*).

corvée [ˈko:vei], *s.* **1.** (*dir. feudale*) corvée **2.** corvée, sfacchinata.

corvette [ko:ˈvet], *s.* (*mar.*) corvetta.

corvine [ˈko:vain], *ag.* corvino.

Corybant [ˈkoribænt], *pl.* **Corybants** [ˈkoribænts], **Corybantes** [ˌkoriˈbænti:z], *s.* coribante.

Corybantian [ˌkoriˈbænʃən], **Corybantic** [ˌkoriˈbæntik], **Corybantine** [ˌkoriˈbæntain], *ag.* coribantico.

Corydon [ˈkoridən], *no.pr.m.* (*lett.*) Coridone ‖ *s.* (*lett. pastorale*) pastore.

corymb [ˈkorimb], *s.* (*bot.*) corimbo.

corymbiferous [ˌkorimˈbifərəs], *ag.* (*bot.*) corimbifero.

coryphaeus [ˌkoriˈfi:əs], *pl.* **coryphaei** [ˌkoriˈfi:ai], *s.* **1.** (*teat. gr.*) corifeo, capo del coro **2.** *fig.* corifeo, capo (di un partito, di un movimento, ecc.).

coryphée [ˌko:riˈfei], *s.* (*teat.*) prima ballerina.

coryza [kəˈraizə], *s.* (*patol.*) corizza, rinite acuta.

cos[1] [kos], *s.* (*bot.*) lattuga a lunghe foglie.

cos[2], *abbr.* di cosine.

to **cose** [kouz], *v.i.* (*fam.*) mettersi a proprio agio.

cosecant [kouˈsi:kənt], *s.* (*geom.*) cosecante.

coseismal [kouˈsaizməl], *ag.* che subisce una scossa sismica simultanea ‖ *s.* linea, curva che unisce i punti soggetti alla stessa scossa sismica.

cosh [koʃ], *s.* (*sl.*) manganello, randello.

to **cosh**, *v.t.* (*sl.*) randellare.

to **cosher**[1] [ˈkoʃə*], *v.t.i.* (*irl.*) **1.** nutrire con buoni bocconi **2.** banchettare **3.** vivere a carico di parenti.

to **cosher**[2], *v.t.* (*fam.*) coccolare, vezzeggiare.

to **cosher**[3], *v.i.* (*fam.*) chiacchierare.

cosily [ˈkouzili], *av.* comodamente, agiatamente.

cosine [ˈkousain], *s.* (*geom.*) coseno.

cosiness [ˈkouzinis], *s.* agio; tepore confortevole.

to **coslettize** [ˈkozlitaiz], *v.t.* (*metal.*) coslettizzare.

cosmetic [kozˈmetik], *ag.s.* cosmetico ☆ *— surgery*, chirurgia plastica.

cosmetician [ˌkozmiˈtiʃən], *s.c.* truccatore, truccatrice.

cosmic [ˈkozmik], *ag.* cosmico: *— rays*, raggi cosmici.

cosmically [ˈkozmikəli], *av.* cosmicamente.

cosmodrome [ˈkozmədroum], *s.* (*missilistica*) cosmodromo.

cosmogonic(al) [,kozmou'gonik(əl)], *ag.* cosmogonico.
cosmogony [koz'mogəni], *s.* cosmogonia.
cosmographer [koz'mogrəfə*], *s.* cosmografo.
cosmographic(al) [,kozmou'græfik(əl)], *ag.* cosmografico.
cosmography [koz'mogrəfi], *s.* cosmografia.
cosmological [,kozmə'lodʒikəl], *ag.* (*fil.*) cosmologico.
cosmologist [koz'molədʒist], *s.* (*fil.*) cosmologo.
cosmology [koz'molədʒi], *s.* (*fil.*) cosmologia.
cosmonaut ['kozmənɔːt], *s.* (*neol.*) cosmonauta.
cosmopolis [koz'mopəlis], *s.* città cosmopolita.
cosmopolitan [,kozmə'politən], *ag.s.c.* cosmopolita.
cosmopolitanism [,kozmə'politənizəm], *s.* cosmopolitismo.
cosmopolite [koz'mopəlait], *ag. s.c.* cosmopolita.
cosmopolitical [,kozməpə'litikəl], *ag.* cosmopolitico.
cosmopolitism [koz'mopəlaitizəm], *s.* cosmopolitismo.
cosmorama [,kozmə'rɑːmə], *s.* cosmorama.
cosmos ['kozmos], *s.* **1.** cosmo **2.** (*bot.*) cosmos.
cosmotron ['kozmətron], *s.* (*neol. fis.*) cosmotrone.
Cossack ['kosæk], *s.* cosacco.
cosset ['kosit], *s.* agnellino allevato in casa.
to **cosset,** *v.t.* (*fam.*) vezzeggiare.
cost [kost], *s.* **1.** costo, prezzo; spesa ‖ — *and freight* (*c.a.f.*), costo e nolo; —, *insurance, freight* (*c.i.f.*), costo, assicurazione e nolo; — *of living*, carovita; — *of living bonus*, caroviveri ‖ *at all costs* (o *at any cost*), a qualsiasi prezzo; *fig.* a tutti i costi; *at great* —, a caro prezzo ‖ *to one's* —, *fig.* a proprie spese: *I learnt, know it to my* —, l'ho imparato, lo so a mie spese ‖ *to count the* —, calcolare il rischio **2.** *pl.* (*dir.*) spese processuali ☆ — *price*, prezzo di costo ‖ *extra* —, spesa supplementare; *first* — (o *prime* —), costo di produzione.
to **cost,** *pass.p.p.* **cost,** *v.t.i.* costare; valutare, stabilire i prezzi di: — *what it may*, costi quel che costi; *his folly* — *him his life*, la sua follia gli costò la vita; *how much does it* —?, quanto costa?; *it* — *him dearly*, gli costò caro; *this costs ten pounds*, questo costa dieci sterline; *to* — *an article*, stabilire il prezzo di un articolo.
costal ['kostl], *ag.* (*anat.*) costale.
costard ['kʌstəd], *s.* **1.** grossa mela **2.** (*arc. spreg.*) testa ☆ — *-monger*, venditore ambulante di frutta.
to **costean,** o **costeen** [kos'tiːn], *v.i.* (*miner.*) scavare pozzi alla ricerca di un filone.
coster ['kostə*], *s.* venditore ambulante (di frutta, pesce, ecc.): —*'s cart*, carretta del venditore ambulante.
costerdom ['kostədəm], *s.* (*fam.*) commercio dei venditori ambulanti.
costermonger ['kostə,mʌngə*], *s.* venditore ambulante di frutta.
costing ['kostiŋ], *s.* **1.** valutazione (dei costi di produzione) **2.** *pl.* costi di produzione ☆ — *department*, reparto costi.
costive ['kostiv], *ag.* **1.** stitico **2.** taccagno.
costiveness ['kostivnis], *s.* **1.** stitichezza **2.** taccagneria.
costless ['kostlis], *ag.* senza spesa, gratis.
costliness ['kostlinis], *s.* **1.** prezzo eccessivo **2.** ricchezza, sontuosità (di mobili, arredamento).
costly ['kostli], *ag.* **1.** costoso, caro **2.** ricco, sontuoso.
costmary ['kostmɛəri], *s.* (*bot.*) costo.
costume ['kostjuːm], *s.* **1.** costume, foggia (di abiti) **2.** abito, vestito ☆ — *ball*, ballo in costume; — *-play* (o — *piece*), commedia (storica) in costume; — *-suit*, abito a giacca ‖ *bathing*- —, costume da bagno.
to **costume,** *v.t.* vestire in costume; provvedere di costumi.
costum(i)er [kos'tjuːm(i)ə*], *s.* venditore, fabbricante, noleggiatore di costumi ☆ *theatrical* —, fornitore di costumi teatrali.
cosy ['kouzi], *ag.* comodo, gradevole, intimo (di luogo, cosa): — *corner*, angolo intimo (di una stanza);

it is — *here!*, come è piacevole qui! ‖ *s.* copriteiera.
cot¹ [kot], *s.* **1.** (*poet.*) casetta **2.** capanna, riparo (per pecore).
to **cot¹,** *pass.p.p.* **cotted** ['kotid], *v.t.* mettere (le pecore) in una capanna.
cot², *s.* **1.** aggrovigliamento (di lana) **2.** garbuglio.
cot³, *s.* (*irl.*) piccola barca primitiva (specie di piroga).
cot⁴, *s.* **1.** (*mar.*) amaca, cuccetta **2.** lettino per bambini; culla.
cot⁵, *abbr.* di **cotangent.**
cotangent ['kou'tændʒənt], *s.* (*mat.*) cotangente.
cote [kout], *s.* capannuccia, riparo (specialmente per animali) ☆ *dove-* —, colombaia; *hen-* —, pollaio; *sheep* - —, chiuso per le pecore.
cotemporary [kə'tempərəri], *ag.s.* contemporaneo.
co-tenant ['kou'tenənt], *s.* coaffittuario.
coterie ['koutəri], *s.* « coterie », cricca, brigata, congrega ☆ *literary* —, cenacolo letterario.
cothurnus [kou'θəːnəs], *pl.* **cothurni** [kou'θəːnai], *s.* **1.** coturno **2.** *fig.* tragedia; stile tragico.
cotidal [kou'taidl], *ag.* (*geog.*) cotidale ☆ — *line*, linea cotidale.
cotill(i)on [kə'tiljən], *s.* **1.** « cotillon » (danza figurata con doni, sorprese); quadriglia **2.** musica per « cotillon ».
cotta ['kotə], *s.* (*eccl.*) cotta.
cottage ['kotidʒ], *s.* « cottage », villino; casetta di campagna ☆ — *cheese*, (*amer.*) specie di giuncata; — *hospital*, piccolo ospedale senza personale medico interno; — *loaf*, grossa pagnotta casalinga; — *piano*, piccolo pianoforte verticale ‖ *Swiss* —, « châlet » svizzero.
cottager ['kotidʒə*], *s.* abitante di « cottage »; contadino.
cottar, cotter¹ ['kotə*], *s.* (*scoz.*) contadino; bracciante.
cotter², *s.* (*mec.*) chiavetta, bietta trasversale ☆ — *-pin*, (*mec.*) coppiglia.
Cottian Alps (the) ['kotiən'ælps], *no.pr. pl.* (*geog.*) Alpi Cozie.
cottier ['kotiə*], *s.* abitante di «cottage»; contadino.
cotton ['kotn], *s.* cotone ☆ — *batting*, (*amer.*) cotone idrofilo; *Cotton Belt*, zona di coltivazione del cotone nel sud degli Stati Uniti; — *-cake*, semi di cotone compressi (per foraggio); — *-cloth*, (tela di) cotone; — *-gin*, (*ind. tessile*) sgranatrice; — *-grass*, (*bot.*) erioforo; — *-mill*, filatura; cotonificio; — *-plant*, pianta del cotone; — *-press*, (*ind. tessile*) pressatrice; — *-seed-oil*, olio di semi di cotone; — *-spinner*, padrone, operaio di filatura; — *-tail*, (*amer.*) coniglio; — *-waste*, cascame di cotone; — *-wool*, cotone grezzo; ovatta, cotone idrofilo; — *-yarn*, filato di cotone; — *-yarn hank*, matassa di filato di cotone di 840 yarde (m. 765 circa) ‖ *gun* - —, (*esplosivo*) fulmicotone; *sewing-* —, filo da cucire.
to **cotton,** *v.i.* **1.** fraternizzare: *to* — *together*, andare d'accordo, accordarsi ‖ *to* — (*on*) *to s.o.*, sentirsi attratto da qlcu. **2.** *to* — *up*, fare degli approcci.
cottonocracy [,kotn'okrəsi], *s.* (*fam.*) plutocrazia del cotone.
cottony ['kotni], *ag.* di cotone.
cotyledon [,koti'liːdən], *s.* (*bot.*) cotiledone.
cotyledonous [,koti'liːdənəs], *ag.* (*bot.*) cotiledoneo.
cotyloid ['kotiloid], *ag.* a forma di coppa.
couch¹ [kautʃ], *s.* **1.** divano, canapè **2.** (*poet.*) letto, giaciglio **3.** (*rar.*) giaciglio, tana di animali **4.** (*pitt.*) fondo **5.** (*ind. birra*) strato di orzo in germinazione.
to **couch¹,** *v.t.i.* **1.** esprimere, stendere per iscritto; esprimere velatamente (il proprio pensiero): *his communication was couched in these terms*, la sua comunicazione si esprimeva in questi termini; *to* — *one's meaning under a metaphor*, esprimere il proprio pensiero con una metafora **2.** adagiare, essere adagiato: *to be couched on the ground*, essere steso a terra ‖ *couched in gold*, a

fondo oro (di ricamo) ‖ *couched in slumber, fig.* immerso nel sonno **3.** appiattirsi; abbassarsi **4.** nascondersi, imboscarsi (di persone); accucciarsi, rintanarsi (di animali) **5.** mettere (la lancia) in resta **6.** (*chir.*) togliere, abbassare (cataratta) **7.** (*ind. birra*) stendere (orzo) a germinare **8.** (*ind. carta*) posare (fogli) sui feltri.

couch[2], *s.*: — (*grass*), (*bot.*) gramigna officinale.

couchant ['kautʃənt], *ag.* **1.** giacente (di animale) **2.** (*arald.*) coricato.

cougar ['ku:gə*], *s.* (*zool.*) puma, coguaro.

cough [kɔf], *s.* tosse: *the coughs of the people present made it impossible to hear the speaker*, i presenti, col loro tossire, non permisero di udire l'oratore; *to give a* (*slight*) —, tossire leggermente (per avvertire qlcu.); *to have a bad* —, avere una forte tosse ☆ — *-drop* (*o* — *-lozenge*), pastiglia per la tosse ‖ (*w*)*hooping-* —, pertosse.

to **cough**, *v.t.i.* **1.** tossire **2.** *to* — *down*, ridurre al silenzio tossendo **3.** *to* — *out, up*, espettorare tossendo: *to* — *out blood*, sputare sangue ‖ *to* — *up*, (*sl.*) sputare (denari, confessione).

could [kud (*forma forte*), kəd (*forma debole*)], *pass.* di **can**.

couldn't ['kudnt], (*contr.*) di **could not**.

coulisse [ku:'li:s], *s.* « coulisse »; (*teat.*) quinta.

couloir ['ku:lwa:*], *s.* (*geol.*) canalone (di montagna).

coulomb ['ku:lɔm], *s.* (*elett.*) coulomb ☆ — *meter*, voltametro.

coulter ['koultə*], *s.* coltro.

coumarin ['ku:mərin], *s.* (*chim.*) cumarina.

council ['kaunsl], *s.* **1.** consiglio (adunanza di persone): *Council of State*, Consiglio di Stato; *Council of War*, Consiglio di Guerra **2.** (*eccl.*) concilio: *the Council of Trent*, (*st.*) il concilio di Trento ☆ — *-board*, tavola del consiglio, il consiglio stesso radunato per deliberare; — *-house* (*o* — *-chamber*), sala del consiglio ‖ *Cabinet* —, consiglio dei ministri; *city* (*o municipal* —), consiglio comunale; *Privy Council*, Consiglio privato della Corona (inglese).

councillor ['kaunsilə*], *s.* consigliere.

councilman, *pl.* **councilmen** ['kaunsilmən], *s.* (*amer.*) consigliere municipale.

counsel ['kaunsəl], *s.* **1.** deliberazione; consultazione: *to take* — (*together*), consigliarsi, deliberare (insieme); *to take* — *with s.o.*, consultarsi con qlcu. **2.** consiglio, avvertimento: *to give good* —, consigliare bene ‖ — *of perfection*, (*teol.*) consigli evangelici; (*fam.*) consiglio difficile da seguire **3.** intenzione; opinione: *to keep one's own* —, serbare, non rivelare le proprie opinioni **4.** (*dir.*) avvocato: *to hear* — *on both sides*, sentire gli avvocati delle due parti ‖ *King's Counsel, Queen's Counsel*, titolo onorifico concesso dal sovrano ad alcuni « barrister »; collegio (di avvocati): *the King's Counsel, the Queen's Counsel*, il Consiglio della Corona.

to **counsel**, *pass.p.p.* **counselled** ['kaunsəld], *v.t.i.* **1.** (IV) raccomandare, consigliare: *to* — *s.o. to do sthg.*, consigliare a qlcu. di fare ql.co. **2.** discutere, deliberare.

counsellor ['kaunslə*], *s.* **1.** consigliere **2.** (*amer.*) avvocato.

count[1] [kaunt], *s.* conto, calcolo, conteggio: *to keep, to lose* —, tenere, perdere il conto: *he cannot keep* — *of his numerous friends*, non riesce nemmeno a sapere quanti siano i suoi numerosi amici ‖ *to take the* —, (*boxe*) essere sconfitto per k.o. **2.** (*pol.*) scrutinio: *to ask for a* —, chiedere lo scrutinio **3.** considerazione: *I take no* — *of what he says*, non tengo in nessuna considerazione quanto egli dice **4.** (*dir.*) capo d'accusa **5.** (*ind. tessile*) titolo **6.** — *out*, aggiornamento (alla Camera dei Comuni).

to **count**[1], *v.t.i.* **1.** contare; calcolare; numerare: *to* — *the cost*, calcolare il costo; *counting from tomorrow*, a cominciare da domani; *without counting*, senza contare ‖ *to* — *up to ten*, contare fino a dieci **2.** contare; considerare; annoverare: *I* — *him among my friends*, lo annovero fra i miei amici; *I* — *it a folly to accept*,

considero una follia accettare **3.** contare; aver importanza: *that doesn't* —, questo non conta **4.** *to* — (*up*)*on* (*s.o., sthg.*), contare su, fare assegnamento su: *don't* — *on his help*, non fare assegnamento sul suo aiuto **5.** *to* — *in*, includere: *don't* — *me in*, non mi includere, lasciami fuori **6.** *to* — *out*, contare fino ad esaurimento ‖ *to* — *out the House*, (*pol.*) aggiornare la Camera (per insufficienza di presenze) ‖ *to be counted out*, (*boxe*) essere sconfitto **7.** *to* — *up*, sommare, addizionare.

count[2], *s.* (*arald.*) conte ‖ *the Counts Palatine*, (*st.*) i Conti palatini ☆ — *-bishop*, (*st.*) vescovo conte.

countable ['kauntəbl], *ag.* numerabile.

countenance ['kauntinəns], *s.* **1.** espressione del volto; aria: *to change* —, cambiare volto, espressione; *to keep* (*one's*) —, mantenersi calmo, non mutare espressione; *to lose* —, perdere il controllo, mostrare i propri sentimenti; *to put out of* —, sconcertare; *to stare s.o. out of* —, fissare qlcu. fino a confonderlo **2.** appoggio, incoraggiamento, favore: *to find* — *in s.o.*, essere incoraggiato da qlcu.; *to give* (*o to lend*) — *to s.o., to sthg.*, prestare il proprio appoggio a qlcu., a ql.co.

to **countenance**, *v.t.* **1.** autorizzare, approvare, sanzionare **2.** incoraggiare, favorire.

counter[1] ['kauntə*], *s.c.* chi conta, calcola ‖ *s.* contatore; calcolatore; misuratore; numeratore ☆ *revolution* —, contagiri.

counter[2], *s.* **1.** (*giuochi*) gettone, « fiche » **2.** sportello; cassa (di banca, ecc.); banco, cassa (di negozio): *payable at the* —, pagabile alla cassa ‖ *I bought it under the* —, lo comprai sottobanco ☆ — *-hand*, commesso, commessa; — *-jumper*, (*spreg.*) commesso.

counter[3], *s.* (*scherma*) parata di contro.

counter[4], *s.* contrafforte, sperone (di scarpa).

counter[5], *ag.* contrario; opposto; avverso: *the opinion* — *to mine*, l'opinione opposta alla mia ‖ *s.* **1.** l'opposto, il contrario **2.** (*mar.*) volta di poppa **3.** petto di cavallo **4.** *abbr.* di *counterlode*, (*miner.*) filone trasversale **5.** *abbr.* di *countershaft*, (*mec.*) contralbero ☆ — *-agent*, tendenza opposta; azione contraria; — *-approaches*, contrapprocci; — *-attraction*, attrazione opposta; attrazione in concorrenza; — *-battery*, controbatteria; — *-clockwise*, di senso antiorario; in senso antiorario; — *-espionage*, controspionaggio; — *-evidence*, controprova, controtestimonianza; — *-irritant*, (medicamento) revulsivo; — *-plot*, anticomplotto, controcongiura; — *-poison*, contravveleno, antidoto; — *-reformation*, (*st.*) controriforma; — *-revolution*, controrivoluzione; — *-statement*, dichiarazione contraria; — *-tenor*, (*mus.*) controtenore; — *-tide*, contromarea; — *-weight*, contrappeso.

counter[5], *av.* in senso inverso; contrariamente: *to act* — *to s.o.'s wishes*, agire contro i desideri di qlcu.; *to run* — *to s.o.*, opporsi a, andare contro qlcu.

to **counter**[5], *v.t.i.* **1.** agire, parlare, muoversi contro, contraddire; opporsi, contrapporsi a **2.** controbattere, parare (un colpo) **3.** (*mec.*) invertire (movimento).

to **counteract** [,kauntə'rækt], *v.t.* **1.** agire contro; contrapporsi a **2.** mandare a vuoto; neutralizzare.

counteraction [,kauntə'rækʃən], *s.* **1.** azione contraria, opposizione; antagonismo **2.** neutralizzazione.

counteractive [,kauntə'ræktiv], *ag.* opposto; antagonistico; che agisce in opposizione; neutralizzante ‖ *s.* azione contraria.

counter-attack ['kauntərə,tæk], *s.* (*mil.*) contrattacco.

to **counter-attack** [,kauntərə'tæk], *v.t.i.* (*mil.*) contrattaccare.

counterbalance ['kauntə,bæləns], *s.* **1.** contrappeso **2.** (*mec.*) controbilanciere.

to **counterbalance** [,kauntə'bæləns], *v.t.* **1.** fare da contrappeso a **2.** (*mec.*) controbilanciare.

counterblast ['kauntə-bla:st], *s.* risposta energica.

counterbond ['kauntə-bɔnd], *s.* controgaranzia.

to **counterbore** [,kauntə'bɔ:*], *v.t.* (*mec.*) accecare, allargare l'estremità di (un foro).

to **counterchange** [ˌkauntəˈtʃeindʒ], v.t.i. scambiare, scambiarsi; scambiarsi le parti.

countercharge [ˈkauntə-tʃɑ:dʒ], s. (dir.) contro-accusa.

countercharm [ˈkauntə.tʃɑ:m], s. contro-incantesimo.

to **countercharm** [ˌkaunəˈtʃɑ:m], v.t. disincantare.

countercheck [ˈkauntə.tʃek], s. forza d'arresto in senso contrario.

to **countercheck** [ˌkauntəˈtʃek], v.t. frenare con azione in senso contrario.

counter-claim [ˈkauntə-kleim], s. controreclamo; (dir.) controquerela.

to **counter-claim**, v.t.i. fare un controreclamo; (dir.) sporgere una controquerela.

counterfeit [ˈkauntəfit], ag. 1. contraffatto; falsificato: — money, denaro falso 2. simulato: — emotions, emozioni simulate ‖ s. 1. contraffazione; falsificazione 2. simulazione.

to **counterfeit**, v.t. 1. contraffare; falsificare: to — money, falsificare denaro 2. simulare: to — grief, simulare dolore.

counterfeiter [ˈkauntə.fitə*], s. falsario ‖ s.c. simulatore, simulatrice.

counterfeiting [ˈkauntə.fitiŋ], s. 1. contraffazione; falsificazione 2. simulazione.

counterfoil [ˈkauntəfoil], s. (comm.) matrice.

counterfort [ˈkauntəfo:t], s. (arch.) contrafforte.

countermand [ˌkauntəˈmɑ:nd], s. revoca, contrordine.

to **countermand**, v.t. revocare; annullare (un ordine, ecc.).

countermarch [ˈkauntə.mɑ:tʃ], s. contromarcia.

to **countermarch**, v.t.i. (far) fare marcia indietro.

countermark [ˈkauntəmɑ:k], s. (comm.) contrassegno; contromarca.

to **countermark** [ˌkauntəˈmɑ:k], v.t. contrassegnare; contromarcare.

countermine [ˈkauntə.main], s. contromina; fig. stratagemma per sventarne un altro.

to **countermine** [ˌkauntəˈmain], v.t. controminare (anche fig.).

to **countermure** [ˌkauntəˈmjuə*], v.t. rafforzare (un muro) con un altro muro.

counterpane [ˈkauntəpein], s. copriletto.

counterpart [ˈkauntəpɑ:t], s. 1. sostituto; (fam.) sosia 2. complemento: woman is the — of man, la donna è il complemento dell'uomo 3. duplicato, copia: to be the — of, essere la copia di.

counter-plot [ˈkauntə-plɔt], s. complotto, stratagemma che ne neutralizza un altro.

counterpoint [ˈkauntəpoint], s. (mus.) contrappunto.

counterpoise [ˈkauntəpoiz], s. contrappeso.

to **counterpoise**, v.t. controbilanciare; bilanciare.

counterscarp [ˈkauntə-skɑ:p], s. (mil.) controscarpa.

countershaft [ˈkauntəʃɑ:ft], s. (mec.) contralbero.

countersign [ˈkauntəsain], s. 1. contrassegno; controfirma 2. (mil.) parola d'ordine.

to **countersign**, v.t. contrassegnare; controfirmare; ratificare (un ordine).

countersink [ˈkauntəsiŋk], s. (mec.) fresa, accecatoio ☆ — -bit, fresa.

counterstroke [ˈkauntə-strouk], s. contraccolpo.

to **countervail** [ˈkauntəveil], v.t.i. 1. controbilanciare 2. prevalere.

to **counterweigh** [ˌkauntəˈwei], v.t. contrappesare.

to **counterwork** [ˌkauntəˈwə:k], v.t.i. lavorare in opposizione (a).

countess [ˈkauntis], s. contessa.

counting [ˈkauntiŋ], s. il contare, il calcolare ☆ — house (o — room), ufficio contabile; amministrazione.

countless [ˈkauntlis], ag. innumerevole.

countrified [ˈkʌntrifaid], ag. campagnuolo; rurale.

country [ˈkʌntri], s. 1. paese, regione: a fertile —, un paese fertile 2. paese, nazione: the European countries, i paesi europei; does the — want war?, il paese vuole la guerra? ‖ to appeal to the —, (pol.) consultare il paese, il corpo elettorale ‖ God's (own) —, Paradiso terrestre; (amer.) gli Stati Uniti 3. patria: — of origin, paese d'origine; Italy is my —, l'Italia è la mia patria; to return to one's —, ritornare al proprio paese 4. campagna: to go into the —, andare in campagna; to live in a town or in the —, vivere in una città o in campagna ☆ — bank, banca di provincia; — -box, casetta in campagna; — club, (amer.) circolo sportivo alla periferia di una città; — cousin, persona di campagna (aliena dalla vita cittadina), parente che abita in campagna; — dance, danza folcloristica, contraddanza; — folk, gente di campagna; — gentleman, proprietario terriero, signorotto di campagna; — -house, villa di campagna; — life, vita di provincia o di campagna; — rock, (geol.) roccia incassante; — party, (pol.) partito agrario; — people, villici; — -seat, residenza di campagna; — town, cittadina di provincia.

countryfied, V. **countrified**.

countryman, pl. **countrymen** [ˈkʌntrimən], s. 1. compaesano; compatriota 2. contadino.

countryside [ˈkʌntriˈsaid], s. campagna, regione rurale.

countrywoman [ˈkʌntri.wumən], pl. **countrywomen** [ˈkʌntri.wimin], s. 1. compaesana, compatriota 2. contadina.

county [ˈkaunti], s. 1. contea; provincia ‖ the Counties Palatine, le Contee Palatine (Cheshire, Lancashire); Home Counties, le sei contee intorno a Londra 2. gli abitanti di una contea: all the — was at the ball, tutta la contea era al ballo ☆ — borough (o — council), consiglio di contea; — family, famiglia nobile (con antica residenza in provincia); — set, alta società provinciale; — town, capoluogo di contea.

coup [ku:], s. colpo (audace); impressione: he brought off a —, ha fatto un colpo ‖ — d'état, colpo di Stato; — de grâce, colpo di grazia; — de main, colpo di mano.

coupé [ˈku:pei], s. 1. «coupé» (vettura chiusa a quattro ruote) 2. (ferr.) mezzo scompartimento all'estremità di un vagone ☆ convertible —, (aut.) «cabriolet».

couple [ˈkʌpl], s. 1. coppia; paio: a — of books, un paio di libri; a — of friends, una coppia di amici; in a — of days; tra un paio di giorni; a married —, una coppia di sposi; to go, to hunt, to run in couples, andare, cacciare, correre in coppia; to work in couples, lavorare a coppia ‖ to have had a — (of drinks), (sl.) aver bevuto troppo 2. accoppiatoio (guinzaglio per due cani da caccia): thirty — of dogs, trenta coppie di cani 3. (fis.) coppia (di forze).

to **couple**, v.t.i. 1. accoppiare, accoppiarsi; appaiare 2. unire insieme, agganciare: to — two railway carriages, agganciare due carrozze ferroviarie ‖ to — up (o on) a carriage, agganciare una carrozza (al treno) 3. (mec.) calettare; accoppiare.

coupler [ˈkʌplə*], s. 1. (organo) tirante, pedale d'accoppiamento 2. (ferr.) attacco ☆ wire —, (elett.) gancio per unire fili.

couplet [ˈkʌplit], s. distico: heroic —, distico eroico.

coupling [ˈkʌpliŋ], s. 1. accoppiamento 2. associazione (d'idee) 3. (tec.) agganciamento, calettamento; accoppiamento; attacco; mezzo di agganciamento ☆ — -chain, — -hook, — -pin, (ferr.) catena, gancio, chiavarda di agganciamento.

coupon [ˈku:pɔn], s. 1. cedola, tagliando, scontrino 2. (sl. pol.) riconoscimento da parte del capo di un partito dei meriti di un candidato ☆ — candidate, candidato raccomandato ‖ — free-gift, (comm.) buono premi; international reply —, scontrino internazionale per risposta.

courage [ˈkʌridʒ], s. coraggio, ardire, audacia: to have the — of one's opinions, convictions, avere il coraggio delle proprie opinioni, convinzioni; to keep up one's —, non perdersi di coraggio; to lose —, perdersi di coraggio; to pluck (o to muster o to screw) up —, farsi coraggio; to take —, prendere coraggio ‖ Dutch —, (*fam.*) coraggio effimero (dato dall'alcool) ‖ *to take one's — in both hands*, prendere il coraggio a due mani.

courageous [kə'reidʒəs], *ag.* coraggioso, audace.

courageously [kə'reidʒəsli], *av.* coraggiosamente, audacemente, arditamente.

courageousness [kə'reidʒəsnis], *s.* coraggio.

courier ['kuriə*], *s.* **1.** corriere, messaggero **2.** domestico che organizza i viaggi del padrone (specialmente all'estero) **3.** corriere (giornale).

course [kɔ:s], *s.* **1.** corso (del tempo, degli avvenimenti, ecc.): *in the — of life, nature, time, a year, the discussion*, nel corso della vita, della natura, del tempo, di un anno, della discussione ‖ *as a matter of —*, va da sè che, naturalmente ‖ *by — of law*, (*dir.*) secondo la legge ‖ *in — of*, in via di: *the bridge is in — of construction*, il ponte è in costruzione ‖ *in due —*, a tempo debito ‖ *of —*, naturalmente, già, senza dubbio, beninteso **2.** corso (di lezioni, conferenze); serie, seguito (di cure, ecc.): *a — of injections*, una cura di iniezioni; *a — of public lectures*, un corso di conferenze pubbliche **3.** corso, linea, direzione, via: *he took to evil courses*, si diede a cattive abitudini; *several possible courses are open to him*, gli si aprono parecchie vie; *to hold (on) one's —*, mantenere la direzione scelta; *to select a — of conduct*, scegliere una linea di condotta **4.** portata (di pasti): *a three — lunch*, una colazione di tre portate **5.** (*comm.*) corso: *— of exchange*, corso dei cambi **6.** (*spor.*) circuito; percorso; pista; estensione di terreno **7.** (*aer. mar.*) rotta: *our — was due south*, la nostra rotta puntava verso il sud **8.** (*arch.*) corso di mattoni o pietre **9.** (*geol.*) filone; direzione di filone **10.** (*miner.*) galleria **11.** *pl.* (*fisiol.*) mestruazioni ☆ *golf- —*, campo di golf; *main —*, (*mar.*) vela maestra.

to **course**, *v.t.i.* **1.** inseguire, rincorrere **2.** far correre (cani da caccia) **3.** scorrere (di liquidi); colare: *the blood courses through the veins*, il sangue circola nelle vene **4.** correre, fare gare di corsa.

courser[1] ['kɔ:sə*], *s.* (*arc.*) corridore.

courser[2], *s.* (*poet.*) corsiero.

courser[3], *s.* (*ornit.*) cursore.

coursing ['kɔ:siŋ], *s.* **1.** caccia (con levrieri) **2.** (*spor.*) corsa di levrieri.

court [kɔ:t], *s.* **1.** corte, cortile **2.** caseggiato con abitazioni di lusso; (*amer.*) quartiere **3.** (*dir.*) corte, tribunale: *— of law* (o *— of justice*), tribunale; *to be ruled* (o *put*) *out of —*, essere allontanato dalla sala d'udienza; *to bring s.o. before the —*, trascinare qlcu. in tribunale; *to come before the —*, comparire innanzi alla Corte; *to settle a case* (o *quarrel*) *out of —*, comporre una controversia in via amichevole; *to take a case to —*, portare una controversia in tribunale **4.** corte (palazzo, famiglia, seguito di reali): *the Court of St. James*, la corte di San Giacomo; *to hold a —*, tenere un ricevimento a corte **5.** (*arc.*) castello, magione: *Hampton Court*, il castello di Hampton **6.** campo (da giuoco) **7.** corte, corteggiamento: *to make* (o *pay*) *— to s.o.*, fare la corte a qlcu. **8.** (*rar.*) vicolo cieco **9.** (*mil. mar.*) assemblea, consiglio: *— of inquiry*, (*mil.*) commissione d'inchiesta ☆ *—card*, (*a carte*) figura; *— -circular*, circolare di corte; *— -dress*, abito di corte; *— -room*, sala d'udienza ‖ *law —*, tribunale; *the Law Courts*, il Palazzo di Giustizia; *police- —*, tribunale di polizia; *tennis- —*, campo da tennis.

to **court**, *v.t.* **1.** corteggiare, far la corte a **2.** cercare, sollecitare (amicizia, favori, popolarità) **3.** offrirsi a, andare incontro a: *to — danger, defeat, disaster*, cercare un pericolo, una sconfitta, un disastro **4.** attirare: *to — s.o. into doing sthg.*, indurre qlcu. a fare ql.co.

courteous ['kə:tjəs], *ag.* cortese.

courteously ['kə:tjəsli], *av.* cortesemente.

courteousness ['kə:tjəsnis], *s.* cortesia.

courtesan [‚kɔ:ti'zæn], *s.* cortigiana, prostituta.

courtesy ['kə:tisi], *s.* **1.** cortesia, gentilezza: *exchange of courtesies*, scambio di gentilezze; *he did me the —*

— to ask my permission, mi fece la cortesia di chiedere il mio permesso ‖ *by* (o *as a matter of*) *—*, per cortesia: *programme presented by the — of the Brown Co.*, (*rad.*) programma offerto dalla Società Brown **2.** (*dir. inglese scoz.*) diritto del marito di usufruire di certi beni della moglie **3.** (*arc.*) inchino, riverenza ☆ *— -title*, titolo di cortesia.

courtier ['kɔ:tjə*], *s.* cortigiano.

courting ['kɔ:tiŋ], *s.* corteggiamento ‖ *to go a- —*, corteggiare.

courtliness ['kɔ:tlinis], *s.* cortesia, eleganza, urbanità.

courtly ['kɔ:tli], *ag.* **1.** cortigianesco; cerimonioso **2.** raffinato.

court-martial ['kɔ:t'mɑ:ʃəl], *pl.* **courts-martial** ['kɔ:ts'mɑ:ʃəl], *s.* (*mil.*) corte marziale, consiglio di guerra: *to be tried by —*, comparire davanti alla corte marziale.

to **court-martial**, *pass.p.p.* **court-martialled** ['kɔ:t'mɑ:ʃəld], *v.t.* fare comparire davanti alla corte marziale.

courtship ['kɔ:t-ʃip], *s.* corte, corteggiamento.

courtyard ['kɔ:t'jɑ:d], *s.* corte, cortile.

couscous ['kuskus], *s.* «cuscuss» (vivanda araba).

cousin ['kʌzn], *s.* **1.** cugino, cugina: *— once (twice, etc.) removed*, cugino in secondo (terzo, ecc.) grado **2.** cugino (titolo usato da sovrani, ecc.): *Our —, the King of France*, nostro cugino, il re di Francia ☆ *first —* (o *— german*), primo cugino; *second —*, cugino di secondo grado.

cousinhood ['kʌznhud], *s.* **1.** l'insieme dei cugini **2.** cuginanza.

cousinship ['kʌznʃip], *s.* cuginanza.

cove[1] [kouv], *s.* **1.** cavità di roccia; grotta, caverna **2.** piccola baia, insenatura **3.** (*amer.*) depressione di terreno, avvallamento **4.** (*arch.*) guscio, modanatura concava.

to **cove**[1], *v.t.* (*arch.*) piegare ad arco: *coved ceiling*, soffitto ad arco.

cove[2], *s.* (*sl.*) uomo, individuo: *a queer —*, un tipo strano.

coven ['kʌvin], *s.* (*scoz.*) congrega (generalmente di streghe).

covenant ['kʌvinənt], *s.* (*dir. pol. eccl.*) accordo solenne; convenzione, patto, contratto; alleanza ‖ *the Covenant of the League of Nations*, il Patto sociale della Società dalle Nazioni (1919) ‖ *National Covenant*, Convenzione Nazionale in Scozia (1638); *Solemn League and Covenant*, accordo fra i Parlamenti di Scozia e Inghilterra (1643).

to **covenant**, *v.t.i.* stipulare, convenire; impegnarsi: *to — to do sthg.*, convenire di fare ql.co.

covenantee [‚kʌvənən'ti:], *s.* (*dir.*) creditore.

covenanter ['kʌvinəntə*], *s.* **1.** (parte) contraente **2.** *Covenanter*, (*st.*) aderente al «National Covenant» (1638) e al «Solemn League and Covenant» (1643).

Covent Garden ['kʌvənt 'gɑ:dn], *s.* **1.** Covent Garden (mercato della frutta e verdura a Londra) **2.** Covent Garden (teatro dell'opera a Londra).

to **coventrate** ['kɔvəntreit], to **coventrize** ['kɔvəntraiz], *v.t.* (*aer.*) coventrizzare, distruggere con bombardamento a tappeto (zone industriali).

Coventry ['kɔvəntri], *no.pr.* (*geog.*) Coventry ‖ *to send s.o. to —*, (*fam.*) interrompere i rapporti con qlcu.

cover ['kʌvə*], *s.* **1.** coperta, copertura, tappeto **2.** cappuccio; coperchio; (*elett. mec.*) calotta (di protezione) **3.** copertina (di libro) ‖ *to read a book from — to —*, leggere un libro dal principio alla fine **4.** busta, plico: *under the same —*, nella stessa busta; *under separate —*, in plico a parte **5.** riparo, rifugio, ricovero: *— from fire*, (*mil.*) riparo dal fuoco; *under — of a tree*, al riparo di un albero; *the land offers no — for our troops*, il terreno non offre alcun riparo per le nostre truppe; *to break —*, uscire dal riparo (di selvaggina); *to give s.o. —*, offrire un ricovero a qlcu.; *to seek* (o *to take*) *—*, mettersi al coperto, al riparo; *to take* —, nascondersi (di selvaggina, nei boschi, ecc.) **6.** velo, mantello: *under (the)* — *of darkness* (o *under* — *of the night*), col favore della notte **7.** *fig.* pretesto, apparenza: *under* — *of friendship*, col pretesto dell'amicizia **8.** (*comm.*) copertura; caparra; fondi; margine: *full* —, garanzia piena **9.** coperto: *a dinner of ten covers*, un pranzo per dieci ☆ — *-charge*, (*neol.*) prezzo del coperto: *the* — *-charge was 100 liras*, il prezzo del coperto era di 100 lire ‖ *loose* — (*of a chair etc.*), fodera di (sedia, ecc.); *outer* —, (*aut.*) copertone.

to **cover**, *v.t.* **1.** coprire; ricoprire; rivestire (anche *fig.*): *covered with snow*, coperto di neve; *the snow covered the mountains*, la neve coprì le montagne; *to* — *a book*, ricoprire un libro; *to* — *oneself with (glory, etc.)* coprirsi di (gloria, ecc.); *to* — *s.o. with ridicule*, coprire qlcu. di ridicolo; *to be well covered*, essere ben coperto **2.** proteggere: *the frontier is covered by a chain of forts*, la frontiera è protetta da una catena di forti **3.** percorrere: *to* — *a distance*, percorrere una distanza **4.** nascondere, dissimulare: *he laughed to* — *his confusion*, rideva per nascondere il suo imbarazzo **5.** comprendere, includere: *in order to* — *all eventualities*, per coprire, per prepararsi a ogni eventualità **6.** (*comm.*) coprire: *to* — *a deficit*, colmare un deficit **7.** (*giornalismo*) descrivere, fare la cronaca di: *he covered the Paris Conference*, fece la cronaca della conferenza di Parigi **8.** accoppiarsi (generalmente di cavalli) **9.** (*spor.*) sostenere, star dietro a (un giocatore) **10.** *to* — *s.o. with a pistol*, tenere a bada qlcu. con la pistola **11.** *to* — **in**, ricoprire (un canale), riempire (una fossa) **12.** *to* — **over**, ricoprire, chiudere: *to* — *over a hole in the roof*, coprire un buco nel tetto **13.** *to* — **up**, coprire interamente; nascondere, dissimulare.

coverage ['kʌvəridʒ], *s.* **1.** (*amer. comm.*) riserva; copertura; (*assicurazioni*) copertura di rischi: *a 40% gold* — *of paper currency*, 40 % di copertura oro della carta moneta **2.** (*elett.*) copertura **3.** (*rad.*) zona di udibilità **4.** (*giornalismo*) esteso servizio d'informazioni ☆ — *diagram*, diagramma di copertura.

covering ['kʌvəriŋ], *ag.* che copre ‖ *s.* **1.** l'atto del coprire **2.** coperta; copertura, rivestimento ☆ — *forces*, (*mil.*) truppe di copertura; — *letter*, lettera di accompagnamento; — *note*, (*comm.*) garanzia.

coverlet ['kʌvəlit], *s.* copriletto.

covert ['kʌvət], *ag.* **1.** (*rar.*) coperto, nascosto; *fig.* celato, velato, finto: — *threats*, velate minacce **2.** (*dir.*) sotto tutela maritale ‖ *s.* ricovero, rifugio, nascondiglio ☆ — *-coat*, leggero soprabito corto.

covertly ['kʌvətli], *av.* nascostamente, segretamente.

coverture ['kʌvətjuə*], *s.* **1.** rifugio (anche *fig.*) **2.** copertura; coperta **3.** travestimento, velo (anche *fig.*).

to **covet** ['kʌvit], *v.t.* agognare, desiderare ardentemente (specialmente roba altrui).

covetable ['kʌvitəbl], *ag.* desiderabile.

coveted ['kʌvitid], *ag.* ambito; desiderato.

covetingly ['kʌvitiŋli], *av.* bramosamente.

covetous ['kʌvitəs], *ag.* desideroso; avido; avaro: — *glance*, sguardo di cupidigia; — *of glory*, bramoso di gloria.

covetously ['kʌvitəsli], *av.* cupidamente; avidamente.

covetousness ['kʌvitəsnis], *s.* cupidigia; avidità; avarizia.

covey ['kʌvi], *pl.* **coveys** ['kʌviz], *s.* **1.** covata, stormo (specialmente di pernici) **2.** (*fam.*) comitiva; gruppo.

covin ['kʌvin], *s.* (*dir.*) collusione; inganno.

coving ['kouviŋ], *s.* **1.** parte di edificio a volta, arcata **2.** *pl.* lati inclinati di un focolare.

covinous ['kʌvinəs], *ag.* (*dir.*) collusivo.

cow [kau], *pl.* **cows** [kauz], (*arc.*) **kine** [kain], *s.* **1.** vacca, mucca ‖ *the* — *with the iron tail*, (*scherz.*) la pompa usata per annacquare il latte ‖ *the time of the lean kine*, (*Bibbia*) il tempo delle vacche magre **2.** femmina (di grossi mammiferi) ☆ — *-bane*, cicuta acqua-

tica; — *bell*, campanaccio; — *-boy*, (*amer.*) bovaro; — *-catcher*, (*amer. ferr.*) cacciapietre; — *-fish*, vacca marina; — *-grass*, trifoglio di campo; — *-heel*, (*cuc.*) piedino di manzo; — *-house*; stalla; — *-keeper*, allevatore di bovini; — *-man*, vaccaro; (*amer.*) proprietario di fattorie; — *pox*, (*vet.*) vaiolo bovino; — *-puncher*, (*amer.*) custode di armenti; — *-shed*, stalla; — *-spanker*, (*austral.*) pastore di armenti ‖ *milch-* —, mucca; *fig.* miniera d'oro; *milking* —, mucca.

to **cow**, *v.t.* intimidire, intimorire: *to* — *a person into doing sthg.*, costringere una persona a fare ql.co. intimorendola; *to be cowed in s.o.'s presence*, essere intimidito dalla presenza di qlcu.; *to look cowed*, avere l'aria sottomessa.

coward ['kauəd], *s.* codardo, vile, vigliacco, pusillanime.

cowardice ['kauədis], **cowardliness** ['kauədlinis], *s.* codardia, viltà, vigliaccheria.

cowardly ['kauədli], *ag.* codardo, vile ‖ *av.* vilmente.

to **cower** ['kauə*], *v.i.* acquattarsi, ritrarsi, farsi piccino: *to* — *before s.o.*, tremare, farsi piccolo davanti a qlcu.

cowherd ['kauhə:d], *s.* vaccaro.

cowhide ['kauhaid], *s.* **1.** pelle bovina; cuoio **2.** (*amer.*) frusta di vacchetta.

to **cowhide**, *v.t.* (*amer.*) fustigare con una frusta di vacchetta.

cowish ['kauiʃ], *ag.* simile a mucca.

cowl[1] [kaul], *s.* **1.** cappuccio **2.** tonaca (da frate) ‖ *to take the* —, vestir la tonaca, farsi monaco ‖ *the* — *does not make the monk*, *prov.* l'abito non fa il monaco **3.** fumaiolo (di camino) **4.** (*aut. aer.*) cofano del motore.

to **cowl**[1], *v.t.* **1.** mettere la tonaca a **2.** incappucciare, mettere la copertura a (camino, fumaiolo).

cowl[2], *s.* recipiente a due anse (per liquidi) ☆ — *-staff*, bastone a cui è sospeso un recipiente, un cesto (portato a spalla da due uomini).

cowrie ['kauri], *s.* **1.** (*zool.*) cipride **2.** piccola conchiglia (usata come moneta in Africa, Asia meridionale).

cowslip ['kauslip], *s.* (*bot.*) primula gialla.

(to) **cox** [kɔks], *abbr.* di (to) **coxswain**.

coxa ['kɔksə], *pl.* **coxae** ['kɔksi:], *s.* (*anat.*) fianco.

coxal ['kɔksəl], *ag.* (*anat.*) del fianco.

coxcomb ['kɔkskoum], *s.* **1.** bellimbusto; zerbinotto **2.** (*st.*) berretto da buffone.

coxcombical [kɔks'kɔmikəl], *ag.* presuntuoso; vanitoso.

coxcombically [kɔks'kɔmikəli], *av.* presuntuosamente; vanitosamente.

coxcombry ['kɔkskoumri], *s.* fatuità; vanità; affettazione.

coxswain ['kɔkswein], *s.* (*mar.*) **1.** timoniere (di battello) **2.** sottufficiale comandante in assenza di ufficiale.

to **coxswain**, *v.t.* governare (un'imbarcazione).

coy [kɔi], *ag.* **1.** timido; riservato; modesto: *she is a* — *girl*, è una ragazza riservata; — *of speech*, riservato nel parlare **2.** appartato (di luogo).

coyish ['kɔiiʃ], *ag.* piuttosto riservato; piuttosto timido.

coyishly ['kɔiiʃli], *av.* in modo piuttosto timido, riservato.

coyly ['kɔili], *av.* timidamente; con riserbo.

coyness ['kɔinis], *s.* timidezza; riservatezza; modestia.

coyote ['kɔiout], *s.* (*amer. zool.*) lupo delle praterie.

coypu ['kɔipu:], *s.* (*zool.*) miopotamo.

coz [kʌz], *s.* (*arc. fam.*) cugino.

coze [kouz], *s.* (*fam.*) chiacchierata intima.

to **coze**, *v.i.* (*fam.*) chiacchierare.

to **cozen** ['kʌzn], *v.t.* (*letter.*) ingannare, gabbare; frodare: *to* — *s.o. into doing sthg.*, indurre qlcu. con artifici a fare ql.co.; *to* — *s.o. out of sthg.*, frodare qlcu. di ql.co.

cozenage ['kʌznidʒ], s. inganno.

cozier ['kouziə*], s. (arc.) ciabattino.

cozy, V. **cosy.**

crab[1] [kræb], s. 1. granchio (di mare) ‖ to catch a —, dare una palata a vuoto (con remo) 2. Crab, (astr.) Cancro 3. (mec.) verricello, argano ☆ — bucket, (mec.) benna; — faced, dall'espressione acida, bisbetico; — -louse, pidocchio inguinale.

to **crab**[1], pass.p.p. **crabbed** ['kræbid], v.t.i. 1. artigliarsi, lottare (di falchi) 2. (fam.) criticare; punzecchiare; avvilire; screditare; mettere i bastoni tra le ruote a: to — a scheme, bocciare un progetto 3. andare a pesca di granchi.

crab[2], s. 1. mela selvatica 2. (amer.) guastafeste; persona brontolona ☆ — -tree, melo selvatico.

to **crab**[2], v.t.i. 1. (aer. mar.) compensare la deriva con timone di direzione 2. (ind. tessile) cuocere, fissare il bollo 3. (sl. amer.) lagnarsi, brontolare.

crabbed ['kræbid], ag. 1. sgarbato, bisbetico, acido (di persona) 2. contorto, illeggibile (di stile, calligrafia) 3. contorto; nodoso (di ramo, bastone).

crabbedly ['kræbidli], av. aspramente; sgarbatamente; perversamente.

crabbedness ['kræbidnis], s. asprezza, acidità; intrattabilità; ruvidità (anche fig.).

crabbing[1] ['kræbiŋ], s. (ind. tessile) bollitura e avvolgimento (del tessuto sotto tensione) ☆ — machine, macchina per fissare la lucentezza del tessuto.

crabbing[2], s. pesca dei granchi.

crabbing[3], s. raccolta di mele selvatiche.

crabby ['kræbi], V. **crabbed** 1.

crablike ['kræblaik], ag. av. da granchio.

crabwise ['kræbwaiz], av. come un granchio: to walk —, camminare come un granchio, diagonalmente.

crack [kræk], ag. (fam.) scelto; di prim'ordine: — regiment, reggimento scelto; — shot, tiratore scelto ‖ s. 1. schianto; esplosione, detonazione; schiocco (di frusta) ‖ the — of doom, (le trombe del) Giudizio Universale ‖ — on the head, (fam.) scappellotto ‖ in a —, in un batter d'occhio; rottura; incrinatura; screpolatura; crepaccio; (metal.) cricca: there was a — in the wall, c'era una fenditura nel muro; this cup has a bad —, questa tazza ha una profonda incrinatura 3. voce fessa (nella pubertà) 4. (scoz.) chiacchierata: to have a — with s.o., far quattro chiacchiere con qlcu. 5. (scoz.) pl. notizia 6. (sl. amer.) vanteria; bugia 7. (sl.) scassinatore; furto con scasso 8. «crack» (cavallo di prim'ordine) ☆ — -brained, scervellato; tocco, picchiatello; — -jaw, (parola) difficile da pronunciare; — -voiced, dalla voce fessa.

to **crack**, v.t.i. 1. schiantare, schiantarsi; scricchiolare; esplodere; schioccare, far schioccare: a rifle cracked, partì un colpo di fucile; to — the joints of the fingers, far schioccare le dita 2. rompere, rompersi; fendersi; incrinare, incrinarsi; screpolare, screpolarsi: boiling water will — a glass, l'acqua bollente fa incrinare i bicchieri; he cracked his skull, si ruppe la testa; to — nuts, schiacciare le noci ‖ to — a bottle of wine with s.o., vuotare una bottiglia di vino con qlcu. 3. mutare, fendersi (di voce) 4. (scoz.) discorrere, chiacchierare 5. (arc.) dir fandonie, vanterie 6. raccontare, dire: to — a joke, raccontare una barzelletta 7. rovinare, guastare: to — s.o.'s credit, rovinare la reputazione di qlcu. 8. (sl.) scassinare ‖ to — a crib, entrare in una casa con scasso (a scopo di furto) 9. (chim.) sottomettere a piroscissione 10. to — on, (fam. amer.) imporre (una tassa) 11. to — up, fare a pezzi, andare in pezzi; (fam.) lodare, elogiare; precipitare (di aerei); fallire; avere un collasso: the firm cracked up, la ditta fallì; he cracked up, ebbe un collasso nervoso ‖ to — s.o., sthg. up to the nines, portare qlcu., ql.co. alle stelle.

crack, av. bruscamente; con uno schianto.

crack, inter. crac!, pum!.

crackajack ['krækə,dʒæk], ag. (sl. amer.) eccellente; abilissimo ‖ s. personaggio in gamba (in un determinato lavoro).

cracked [krækt], ag. 1. fesso (anche di voce): a — cup, una tazza fessa 2. scervellato: he is —, è pazzo.

cracker ['krækə*], s. 1. petardo 2. «cracker» (gallettina croccante) 3. (nut-) crackers, schiaccianoci 4. pl. (amer.) bigodini (per capelli) 5. (sl.) menzogna, fanfaronata 6. (sl. amer. spreg.) relitto umano (detto di quei bianchi degli Stati Uniti del Sud che vivono in miseria); crollo, collasso 7. — of cribs, scassinatore 8. — of jokes, burlone ☆ Christmas —, confezione natalizia a sorpresa, all'apertura della quale si produce uno scoppio.

crackerjack, V. **crackajack.**

cracking ['krækiŋ], ag. crepitante, scoppiettante ‖ s. 1. crepitio, scoppiettio; scricchiolio 2. fessura, fenditura; screpolatura 3. (chim.) piroscissione 4. (mec.) incrinatura, criccatura.

crackle ['krækl], s. 1. leggero scoppiettio; crepitio 2. screpolature; incrinature ☆ — -ware, — -china, ceramica, porcellana ricoperta di minuscole screpolature.

to **crackle**, v.t.i. 1. scoppiettare; scricchiolare; crepitare 2. screpolare, screpolarsi.

crackling ['krækliŋ], s. 1. scoppiettio, crepitio 2. pl. (cuc.) ciccioli, siccioli.

cracknel ['kræknl], s. biscotto croccante.

crackpot ['krækpot], ag. s. (sl. amer.) pazzo, picchiatello.

cracksman, pl. **cracksmen** ['kræksmən], s. (fam.) scassinatore.

cracky ['kræki], ag. 1. (fam.) picchiatello 2. fragile 3. screpolato, pieno di crepe.

Cracow ['krækou], no.pr. (geog.) Cracovia.

cradle ['kreidl], s. 1. culla (anche fig.): from, in the —, dall'infanzia, nell'infanzia; Greece was the — of western culture, la Grecia fu la culla della civiltà occidentale 2. (mec. aer. mar.) culla, intelaiatura di sostegno 3. (aut.) sdraio, carrellino 4. (edil.) centina 5. gabbia, alzacorpetto (su un letto d'ammalato) 6. (agr.) falce a rastrello 7. (miner.) crivello, vaglio (specialmente per sabbie aurifere) ☆ — song, ninna nanna ‖ starting —, (aer. mar.) culla di lancio.

to **cradle**, v.t. 1. mettere nella culla; cullare: to — a child in one's arms, cullare un bambino tra le braccia 2. allevare, educare: he was cradled in that idea, fu allevato con quell'idea 3. (mec.) sostenere, sollevare mediante intelaiatura (di sostegno) 4. (edil.) centinare 5. (agr.) falciare con falce a rastrello 6. (miner.) vagliare (specialmente sabbie aurifere).

cradling ['kreidliŋ], s. (edil.) centinatura per soffitti curvi.

craft [krɑːft], s. 1. abilità, arte; mestiere, professione: the — of the wood-carver, l'arte dell'intagliatore in legno; the builder's —, l'arte del costruttore ‖ the Craft, corporazione di artigiani; i membri di una corporazione; arts and crafts, arti e mestieri ‖ the gentle —, la pesca all'amo ‖ every man to his craft, prov. a ciascuno il suo mestiere 2. astuzia, inganno: he is full of —, è pieno di astuzia 3. (costrutto pl.) imbarcazione, barca di piccole dimensioni: — of all kind are in the harbour, imbarcazioni di ogni genere sono nel porto 4. aereo ☆ landing —, mezzi da sbarco; needle- —, arte del ricamo.

craftily ['krɑːftili], av. abilmente; astutamente.

craftiness ['krɑːftinis], s. astuzia.

craftsman, pl. **craftsmen** ['krɑːftsmən], s. artigiano; operaio.

craftsmanship ['krɑːftsmənʃip], s. 1. abilità d'artefice: of wonderful —, di meravigliosa esecuzione 2. padronanza del mestiere (di scrittore, ecc.).

crafty ['krɑːfti], ag. abile; astuto.

crag[1] [kræg], s. rupe, balza, roccia scoscesa.

crag[2], s. (scoz. dial.) collo.

cragged ['krægid], ag. roccioso; dirupato, scosceso.

craggedness ['krægidnis], **cragginess** ['kræginis], s. l'essere roccioso; ripidezza.

craggy ['krægi], ag. roccioso; dirupato, scosceso.

cragsman, *pl.* **cragsmen** ['krægzmən], *s.* rocciatore.

crake [kreik], *s.* **1.** (*ornit.*) corvo; cornacchia **2.** gracchiamento (del corvo).

to **crake**, *v.i.* gracchiare.

cram [kræm], *s.* **1.** scorpacciata **2.** (*sl. scolastico*) l'imbottirsi di nozioni (in vista di un esame) **3.** (*fam.*) calca, folla **4.** (*sl.*) bugia ☆ — -*full*, pieno zeppo.

to **cram**, *pass.p.p.* **crammed** [kræmd], *v.t.i.* **1.** ficcare, riempire, stipare: *he crammed the papers into his pocket*, si cacciò i documenti in tasca **2.** rimpinzare, ingozzare (anche *fig.*): *a book crammed with quotations*, un libro zeppo di citazioni; *to — (a subject) for an examination*, (*fam.*) imbottirsi di nozioni per un esame; *to — oneself with food*, rimpinzarsi di cibo **3.** ammassare, ammassarsi; stipare; accalcarsi: *we all crammed into a baggage van*, ci stipammo tutti in un bagagliaio.

crambo ['kræmbou], *s.* giuoco delle rime obbligate: *dumb* —, sciarada mimata.

crammer ['kræmə*], *s.* **1.** studente che sgobba (per un esame) **2.** ripetitore (per la preparazione di un esame) **3.** (*sl.*) bugia.

cramp[1] [kræmp], *ag.* rattrappito; contratto: — *handwriting*, scrittura indecifrabile; — *style*, stile impacciato, troppo conciso ‖ *s.* (*amer. gener. pl.*) crampo: *writer's, swimmer's* —, crampo dello scrittore, del nuotatore; *to be seized with* —, essere colto da un crampo.

to **cramp**[1], *v.t.* **1.** *fig.* paralizzare, bloccare: *shyness cramped his style*, la timidezza impacciava il suo stile **2.** causare crampi.

cramp[2], *s.* **1.** (*mec.*) — (-*iron*) morsetto **2.** (*artig.*) forma di legno (per fare scarpe).

to **cramp**[2], *v.t.i.* **1.** stringere, fissare con morsetto **2.** *fig.* mettere alle strette; torturare **3.** (*artig.*) fare (una scarpa) sulla forma.

crampon ['kræmpən], *s.* **1.** rampone **2.** *pl.* (*ind.*) braga a gancio, pinza per massi.

cran [kræn], *s.* « cran » (misura di capacità per la vendita di aringhe fresche = l. 170,3).

cranage ['kreinidʒ], *s.* (*comm.*) uso di gru; spese per uso di gru.

cranberry ['krænbəri], *s.* mirtillo.

to **cranch** [kra:ntʃ], *v.t.* schiacciare rumorosamente; sgretolare.

crane[1] [krein], *s.* **1.** (*ornit.*) gru **2.** (*mec.*) gru **3.** sifone ☆ — -*fly*, (*entom.*) tipula; — *hook*, gancio della gru; — *track*, rotaia della gru ‖ *quay* —, gru da porto; *travelling* —, gru a ponte; *unloading* —, gru da scaricamento; *water-* —, tubo per rifornire d'acqua la locomotiva.

to **crane**[1], *v.t.i.* **1.** (*mec.*) sollevare, abbassare mediante una gru **2.** allungare (il collo, la testa): *to — out, over, down*, sporgersi in fuori, in su, in giù **3.** fermarsi (di cavallo); esitare (davanti ad un ostacolo) (anche *fig.*): *to — at a difficulty*, esitare dinanzi ad una difficoltà; *to — at a hedge*, rifiutarsi di saltare una siepe (di cavallo).

crane[2], *s.* (*arc.*) cranio.

cranesbill ['kreinzbil], *s.* **1.** (specie di) geranio **2.** (*chir.*) pinze.

cranial ['kreinjəl], *ag.* cranico.

craniologist [‚kreini'ɔlədʒist], *s.* (*med.*) craniologo.

craniology [‚kreini'ɔlədʒi], *s.* (*med.*) craniologia.

craniometry [‚kreini'ɔmitri], *s.* (*med.*) craniometria.

cranium ['kreinjəm], *pl.* **crania** ['kreinjə], *s.* cranio.

crank[1] [kræŋk], *ag.* **1.** (*mec.*) piegato; disinnestato; che funziona male; instabile **2.** tortuoso; difficile; poco comprensibile ‖ *s.* (*mec.*) manovella, manubrio; gomito; leva ☆ — -*case*, (*mec.*) incastellatura; basamento; — *pin*, perno di biella; — -*shaft*, albero a gomiti, albero a manovella; (*ferr.*) asse.

to **crank**[1], *v.t.i.* **1.** (*mec.*) piegare a gomito **2.** fornire di manovella; fissare con manovella **3.** (*aut.*) mettere in moto con manovella ‖ *to — away*, continuare a girare la manovella; *to — up an engine, a car*, avviare un motore, un'automobile a mano (con manovella) **4.** (*cine.*) girare, riprendere: *to — a camera*, girare la manovella della macchina da presa **5.** serpeggiare.

crank[2], *ag.* (*mar.*) inclinato ☆ *a* — -*sided ship*, una nave che ha tendenza a capovolgersi.

crank[3], *s.* **1.** (*fam.*) persona eccentrica, maniaco; originale: *he was a regular* —, era un vero originale **2.** (*fam.*) mania **3.** arzigogolo; bisticcio; giro di parole ‖ *quips and cranks*, giuochi di parole.

to **crank**[4], *v.i.* stridere.

crankily ['kræŋkili], *av.* **1.** di cattivo umore, con mala grazia **2.** (*mec.*) in modo discontinuo.

crankiness ['kræŋkinis], *s.* **1.** carattere difficile; (*arc.*) eccentricità **2.** (*mec.*) cattivo funzionamento **3.** (*mar.*) instabilità (di nave).

crankle ['kræŋkl], *s.* voltata; curvatura; prominenza ad angolo.

to **crankle**, *v.i.* curvarsi; avvolgersi.

cranky ['kræŋki], *ag.* **1.** irritabile; eccentrico, capriccioso; ipocondriaco, sofferente **2.** non funzionante; instabile, malfermo.

crannied ['krænid], *ag.* screpolato, con fessure.

crannog ['krænəg], *s.* abitazione lacustre (in Scozia, Irlanda).

cranny ['kræni], *s.* **1.** screpolatura, fessura **2.** buco; nicchia.

to **cranny**, *v.i.* screpolarsi; fendersi (di legno).

crape [kreip], *s.* crespo ☆ — *band*, bracciale da lutto; — -*hanger*, (*sl. amer.*) pessimista.

to **crape**, *v.t.* **1.** coprire, vestire con crespo (in segno di lutto) **2.** arricciare (i capelli).

craped [kreipt], *ag.* crespo; arricciato.

craps [kræps], *s.pl.* (*amer.*) giuoco d'azzardo con dadi: *to shoot* —, giocare ai dadi.

crapulence ['kræpjuləns], *s.* crapula, intemperanza; dissolutezza.

crapulent ['kræpjulənt], **crapulous** ['kræpjuləs], *ag.* intemperante; vizioso, dissoluto.

crapy ['kreipi], *ag.* simile a crespo.

crash[1] [kræʃ], *s.* **1.** strepito, fracasso; scroscio, scoppio: *a — of thunder*, uno scoppio di tuono; *to fall with a* —, cadere con fracasso **2.** (*comm.*) catastrofe, crollo **3.** caduta; schiacciamento; urto **4.** (*aer.*) atterraggio precipitoso **5.** (*aut. ferr.*) scontro ☆ — -*dive*, immersione rapida di un sottomarino; — -*helmet*, (*neol.*) casco da guidatore; — -*landing*, (*neol.*) atterraggio improvviso ‖ *car* —, scontro automobilistico; *railway* —, scontro ferroviario.

to **crash**[1], *v.t.i.* **1.** precipitare, crollare con fracasso; abbattere, abbattersi **2.** scontrarsi con fracasso: *to — into*, sfondare, scontrare violentemente contro: *he crashed into a shop-window*, sfondò una vetrina ‖ *to — through*, passare rovinosamente attraverso **3.** *to — down*, cadere con fracasso; abbattere fragorosamente **4.** *to — in*, sprofondare, sprofondarsi: *the roof crashed in*, il tetto sprofondò.

crash[2], *s.* grossa tela da asciugamani.

crasis ['kreisis], *s.* (*gram.*) crasi.

crass [kræs], *ag.* grossolano, crasso: — *ignorance*, ignoranza crassa.

crassitude ['kræsitju:d], **crassness** ['kræsnis], *s.* grossolanità.

crassly ['kræsli], *av.* grossolanamente.

Crassus ['kræsəs], *no.pr.m.* (*st.*) Crasso.

cratch [krætʃ], *s.* rastrelliera, mangiatoia all'aperto.

crate [kreit], *s.* cassa, cesta da imballaggio.

crater ['kreitə*], *s.* **1.** (*geol.*) cratere **2.** (*st.*) vaso, anfora **3.** cavità (generalmente prodotta da bomba) ☆ *road-* —, cratere sulla sede stradale.

cratur ['kreitə*], *s.* (*sl. irl.*) whisky, acquavite.

cravat [krə'væt], *s.* (*arc.*) cravatta; fazzoletto da collo; sciarpa ☆ *hempen* —, (*iron.*) corda per impiccagione.

cravatted [krə'vætid], *ag.* (*arc.*) che indossa cravatta, fazzoletto da collo; sciarpa.

to **crave** [kreiv], *v.t.i.* chiedere con insistenza: *to — leave, permission*, chiedere licenza, permesso; *to — s.o.'s pardon*, chiedere perdono a qlcu.; *to — sthg. from* (o *of*) *s.o.*, implorare ql.co. da qlcu. ‖ *to — for* (o *after*) *sthg.*, desiderare ql.co. ardentemente.

craven ['kreivən], *ag.s.* vile, pusillanime, vigliacco, codardo ‖ *to cry*, arrendersi.

cravenly ['kreivənli], *av.* vilmente, codardamente.

cravenness ['kreivənnis], *s.* viltà, codardia.

craving ['kreiviŋ], *ag.* insaziabile; ardente: *— appetite*, appetito insaziabile; *— desire*, desiderio ardente ‖ *s.* forte desiderio; brama, voglia: *he has a — for strong drinks*, gli piacciono molto gli alcoolici.

craw [krɔ:], *s.* gozzo (di uccelli).

crawfish ['krɔ:fiʃ], *s.* (zool.) gambero d'acqua dolce.

crawl[1] [krɔ:l], *s.* **1.** movimento strisciante: *to go at a —*, avanzare molto lentamente **2.** (*nuoto*) « crawl ».

to **crawl**[1], *v.i.* **1.** strisciare; trascinarsi: *the snake crawled into a hole*, il serpente si infilò strisciando in un buco ‖ *to — in, out*, entrare, uscire strisciando **2.** andar carponi: *the child was at the crawling stage*, il bimbo era nell'età in cui si va carponi **3.** avanzare lentamente **4.** brulicare: *to — with vermin*, brulicare di insetti **5.** raccapricciare; aver la pelle d'oca: *the sight of those snakes made my flesh —*, la vista di quei serpenti mi fece accapponare la pelle.

crawl[2], *s.* vivaio subacqueo (per crostacei, tartarughe di mare, ecc.).

crawler ['krɔ:lə*], *s.c.* **1.** chi striscia (anche *fig.*) **2.** chi si muove lentamente ‖ *s.* **1.** (*fam.*) rettile **2.** (*fam.*) pidocchio **3.** (*fam.*) tassì che circola lentamente in attesa di clienti **4.** (*agr.*) trattore a cingoli **5.** *pl.* tuta per bambini piccoli.

crawly ['krɔ:li], *ag.* **1.** che si sente la pelle d'oca: *I feel —*, mi sento la pelle d'oca **2.** formicolante.

crayfish ['kreifiʃ], *s.* gambero (d'acqua dolce).

crayon ['kreiən], *s.* **1.** pastello: *drawn in —*, disegnato a pastello **2.** disegno a pastello; pastello **3.** (*elett.*) carbone (di lampada ad arco).

to **crayon**, *v.t.* **1.** disegnare a pastello **2.** abbozzare (un ritratto, un progetto).

craze [kreiz], *s.* **1.** mania; smania; voga: *a — for sthg.*, una mania per ql.co.; *to be the —*, essere in gran voga **2.** screpolatura; crepa.

to **craze**, *v.t.i.* **1.** fare ammattire; impazzire **2.** produrre screpolature; screpolarsi.

crazed [kreizd], *ag.* **1.** pazzo, folle **2.** dalla superficie screpolata.

crazily ['kreizili], *av.* pazzamente; insensatamente; follemente.

craziness ['kreizinis], *s.* **1.** pazzia, follia **2.** fragilità; instabilità; decrepitezza (di edifici, mobili).

crazy ['kreizi], *ag.* **1.** folle, pazzo: *— with fear, grief*, pazzo di terrore, dolore; *to drive* (o *send*) *s.o. —*, fare impazzire qlcu.; *to go —*, perdere la testa, impazzire ‖ *it was really a — show*, era veramente roba da matti **2.** entusiasta, maniaco: *to be — over* (o *about*) *s.o., sthg.*, essere entusiasta di qlcu., ql.co.: *he is — about music*, è pazzo per la musica; *to be — to do sthg.*, essere assai desideroso di fare ql.co. **3.** che minaccia di crollare, instabile; fragile **4.** composto di pezzi irregolari: *— pavement*, pavimento a mosaico irregolare.

creak [kri:k], *s.* cigolio; stridio.

to **creak**, *v.t.i.* **1.** cigolare; stridere; far cigolare; far stridere: *the door creaks*, la porta cigola sui cardini **2.** frinire.

creaky ['kri:ki], *ag.* stridente; cigolante.

cream [kri:m], *s.* **1.** panna; crema: *butter is made from —*, il burro è fatto dalla panna **2.** ogni materia densa ed untuosa **3.** color crema **4.** *fig.* crema; fior fiore: *the — of society*, il fior fiore della società **5.** *— of tartar*, (*chim.*) cremore di tartaro ☆ *— -bun*, pasticcino alla crema, alla panna; *— -cake*, torta alla crema; *— -cheese*, formaggio fresco e grasso; *— -coloured*, di color crema; *— -puff*, bignè — *separator*, (*mec.*)

scrematrice ‖ *boot- —*, lucido da scarpe; *cold- —*, crema emolliente ‖ *furniture —*, lucido per mobili ‖ *ice - —*, gelato ‖ *whipped- —*, panna montata.

to **cream**, *v.t.i.* **1.** scremare, spannare (anche *fig.*) **2.** aggiungere crema a **3.** coprirsi di crema (del latte) **4.** fare la spuma, spumeggiare (*p. e.* di birra) **5.** (*ind. gomma*) cremare.

creamer ['kri:mə*], *s.* **1.** bricchetto per crema **2.** (*mec.*) scrematrice.

creamery ['kri:məri], *s.* **1.** caseificio **2.** latteria ☆ *— butter*, burro industriale.

creaminess ['kri:minis], *s.* **1.** cremosità **2.** morbidezza vellutata.

creamy ['kri:mi], *ag.* **1.** ricco di crema, di panna; butirroso **2.** morbido, vellutato.

crease [kri:s], *s.* **1.** piega, piegatura; grinza: *the creases in a pair of trousers*, le pieghe di un paio di pantaloni; *to remove the creases from a piece of material*, togliere le pieghe a un pezzo di stoffa **2.** (*cricket*) linea bianca (sul terreno, per regolare la posizione dei giocatori).

to **crease**, *v.t.i.* **1.** fare pieghe a: *well-creased trousers* calzoni con la piega impeccabile **2.** sgualcirsi, raggrinzarsi: *this silk creases easily*, questa seta si sgualcisce facilmente.

creasy ['kri:si], *ag.* **1.** a pieghe **2.** spiegazzato.

to **create** [kri(:)'eit], *v.t.* **1.** creare: *to — a fashion*, lanciare una moda; *to — a part*, (*teat.*) creare una parte, un personaggio **2.** nominare: *he was created a knight*, fu nominato cavaliere **3.** produrre, suscitare, provocare: *to — a disturbance*, disturbare l'ordine pubblico; *to — a scandal*, creare, suscitare uno scandalo; *to — a vacuum*, produrre un vuoto.

creatine ['kri:ətain], *s.* (*chim.*) creatina.

creation [kri(:)'eiʃən], *s.* **1.** creazione, atto creativo: *the — of the world*, la creazione del mondo **2.** natura, universo; gli esseri creati: *the brute —*, gli animali **3.** creazione, prodotto, opera: *the latest creations*, le ultimissime creazioni della moda **4.** nomina.

creational [kri(:)'eiʃənl], *ag.* di creazione.

creationism [kri(:)'eiʃnizəm], *s.* (*fil.*) creazionismo.

creationist [kri(:)'eiʃnist], *s.* (*fil.*) seguace della teoria del creazionismo.

creative [kri(:)'eitiv], *ag.* creativo; produttivo.

creativeness [kri(:)'eitivnis], *s.* facoltà, potenza creatrice.

creator [kri(:)'eitə*], *s.* creatore ‖ *the Creator*, il Creatore.

creatress [kri(:)'eitris], *s.* creatrice.

creature ['kri:tʃə*], *s.* **1.** creatura, essere vivente: *dumb creatures*, gli animali; *God's creatures*, le creature di Dio ‖ *poor —*, poveretto, poveretta ‖ *not a — was to be seen*, non si vedeva anima viva **2.** protetto, favorito: *a — of the dictator*, una creatura del dittatore ‖ *the —*, (*sl. irl.*) bevanda alcoolica (specialmente whisky) ☆ *— comforts*, gli agi materiali: *to make provision for s.o.'s — comforts*, provvedere alla sicurezza materiale di qlcu.

creaturely ['kri:tʃəli], *ag.* di cosa creata; umano.

crèche [kreiʃ], *s.* **1.** nido, asilo infantile; brefotrofio **2.** presepio.

credence ['kri:dəns], *s.* **1.** credenza, fede; credito: *letter of —*, lettera di presentazione; *worthy of —*, degno di fede; *to give* (o *attach*) *— to sthg.*, prestare fede a ql.co. **2.** *— (-table)*, credenza (anche per arredi sacri).

credentials [kri'denʃəlz], *s.pl.* credenziali.

credibility [,kredi'biliti], *s.* credibilità.

credible ['kredəbl], *ag.* credibile: *it is hardly — that*, non è verosimile che.

credibleness ['kredəblnis], *s.* credibilità.

credibly ['kredəbli], *av.* credibilmente: *to be — informed of sthg.*, venire a conoscenza di ql.co. da una fonte sicura.

credit ['kredit], *s.* **1.** fiducia, fede: *a man of —*, un uomo di fiducia; *to give — to a report*, prestare fede ad una voce; *to place* (o *to put*) — *in*, aver fiducia in 2. credito, autorità, influenza, reputazione: *he has lost* — *with the public*, la sua reputazione presso il pubblico è diminuita; *to add to one's* —, aumentare la propria reputazione; *to use one's* — *in s.o.'s favour*, usare la propria autorità a favore di qlcu. 3. merito, onore: *he is a* — *to his parents*, fa onore ai suoi genitori; *he passed his examinations with* —, superò gli esami con onore; *it must be said, to his* —, *that*, si deve dire, a suo onore, che; *to do* — *to s.o.* (o *to do s.o.* —), fare onore a qlcu.; *to get* — *for another's work*, vedersi attribuire il merito del lavoro altrui; *to give* (s.o.) — *for*, attribuire merito (a qlcu.) per; *to take* — *for an action*, attribuirsi il merito di una azione 4. (*comm.*) credito, fido: *irrevocable* —, credito irrevocabile; *letter of* —, lettera di credito; *opening of* —, apertura di credito; *his* — *is good for a large sum*, gode di un grosso fido; *to give s.o.* —, far credito a qlcu; *to open a* —, aprire un credito; *to sell on* —, vendere a credito 5. (*amer. scuola*) certificato di promozione ☆ — *account*, conto creditori; — *balance*, saldo a credito attivo; — *institution*, istituto di credito; — *note*, nota di accreditato ‖ *bank* —, credito bancario; *working* —, credito di esercizio.

to **credit**, *v.t.* 1. credere, prestare fede a: *to* — *everything he says*, prestare fede a tutto quello che egli dice 2. attribuire: *to* — *s.o. with a quality*, attribuire una qualità a qlcu.: *he has not the talents you* — *him with*, egli non ha le doti che gli attribuisci; *I credited you with more sense*, ti attribuivo più senso comune 3. (*comm.*) accreditare: *to* — *a firm with the amount of...*, accreditare la somma di... ad una ditta; *to* — *a sum to s.o.*, accreditare una cifra a qlcu.

creditable ['kreditəbl], *ag.* stimabile; degno di elogio: *that's* — *to her*, ciò le fa onore.

creditably ['kreditəbli], *av.* in modo degno di stima; con onore.

creditor ['kreditə*], *s.* (*comm.*) creditore: *he is my* — *for...*, io gli devo... ☆ — *nation*, nazione creditrice; — *side* (*of an account*), l'attivo (di un conto) ‖ *secured* —, creditore privilegiato, garantito; *sundry creditors*, creditori diversi; *unsecured* —, creditore non garantito.

credo ['kri:dou], *s.* 1. (*teol.*) credo 2. credo, professione di fede.

credulity [kri'dju:liti], *s.* credulità.

credulous ['kredjuləs], *ag.* credulo.

credulously ['kredjuləsli], *av.* con credulità.

credulousness ['kredjuləsnis], *s.* credulità.

creed [kri:d], *s.* 1. (*teol.*) credo, simbolo, confessione di fede ‖ *The Apostles' Creed*, Credo, Simbolo apostolico 2. credenza religiosa, fede; credo: *political* —, credo politico.

creedless ['kri:dlis], *ag.* senza fede.

creek [kri:k], *s.* 1. insenatura, seno, cala 2. (*amer.*) affluente, immissario 3. (*amer.*) valletta fra monti.

creel[1] [kri:l], *s.* cesta per la pesca; nassa.

creel[2], *s.* (*ind. tessile*) rastrelliera.

creep [kri:p], *s.* 1. strisciamento 2. *pl.* brividi, pelle d'oca: *to give one the creeps*, far accapponare la pelle, far venire la pelle d'oca a qlcu. 3. (*geol. fis.*) scorrimento 4. (*mec.*) deformazione permanente ☆ — *-hole*, rifugio sotterraneo.

to **creep**, *pass.p.p.* **crept** [krept], *v.i.* 1. strisciare; arrampicarsi (di piante) 2. scorrere, spargersi, salire (di liquidi) 3. avanzare lentamente, furtivamente; insinuarsi: *the cat crept towards the mouse*, il gatto avanzò lentamente verso il topo; *fear crept over him*, la paura si insinuò in lui; *he crept into the room*, entrò furtivamente nella stanza; *to* — *into bed*, scivolare, infilarsi a letto; *to* — *into s.o.'s favour*, *fig.* insinuarsi nelle grazie di qualcuno 4. (*mec.*) deformarsi permanentemente 5. (*mar.*) dragare il fondo con ancorotto 6. *to* — *along*, avanzare strisciando, furtivamente 7. *to* — *away*, allontanarsi strisciando, furtivamente 8. *to* — *down*, **up**, scendere, salire furtivamente, lentamente: *the speed-*

ometer needle crept up to 80, l'ago del tachimetro salì lentamente fino a 80 9. *to* — **on**, avanzare lentamente: *old age is creeping on*, la vecchiaia avanza a passi lenti; *time creeps on*, il tempo passa insensibilmente.

creepage ['kri:pidʒ], *s.* (*elett.*) dispersione.

creeper ['kri:pə*], *s.* 1. rettile; verme; *fig.* persona strisciante, servile 2. (*bot.*) pianta rampicante 3. (*mar.*) grappino 4. rampone da ghiaccio.

creepy ['kri:pi], *ag.* 1. strisciante: *I could feel* — *things on my leg*, sentivo qualcosa strisciare sulla gamba 2. che dà i brividi, che fa rabbrividire: *to feel* —, sentirsi la pelle d'oca ☆ — *-crawly*, strisciante; che dà i brividi; — *-peppy*, (*neol. tv.*) telecamera portatile.

creese [kri:s], *s.* pugnale della Malesia.

to **eremate** [kri'meit], *v.t.* cremare.

cremation [kri'meiʃən], *s.* cremazione.

cremator [kri'meitə*], *s.* 1. chi esegue la cremazione 2. forno crematorio.

crematorium [,kremə'tɔ:riəm], *pl.* **crematoria** [,kremə'tɔ:riə], *s.* forno crematorio.

crematory ['kremətəri], *s.* crematoio, forno crematorio.

cremona[1] [kri'mounə], *s.* violino fabbricato a Cremona.

cremona[2], *s.* (*mus.*) cromorno.

crenate(d) ['kri:neit(id)], *ag.* (*bot. zool.*) dentellato, seghettato.

crenation [kri'neiʃən], **crenature** ['krenətʃə*], *s.* (*bot. zool.*) dentellatura.

crenel ['krenl], *s.* merlo; feritoia, spazio tra due merli.

crenel(l)ate ['krenileit], *ag.* merlato.

to **crenel(l)ate**, *v.t.* (*arch.*) merlare, fornire di merli.

crenel(l)ation [,kreni'leiʃən], *s.* (*arch.*) merlatura.

crenelle [kri'nel], *s.* merlo; feritoia; spazio fra due merli.

creole ['kri:oul], *ag.* creolo ‖ *s.c.* creolo, creola; (*amer.*) discendente dei coloni francesi ‖ *s.* il dialetto francese parlato dai creoli (specialmente a New Orleans).

creolin ['kri:əlin], *s.* (*ind. chim.*) creolina.

Creon ['kri:ɔn], *no.pr.m.* (*mit.*) Creonte.

creosote ['kriəsout], *s.* (*chim.*) creosoto.

crêpe [kreip], *s.* crespo; tessuto di seta ☆ — *-de -Chine*, crespo di Cina; — *paper*, carta crespata; — *rubber*, gomma crespata (per suole).

crepitant ['krepitənt], *ag.* crepitante.

to **crepitate** ['krepiteit], *v.i.* crepitare.

crepitation [,krepi'teiʃən], *s.* crepitio.

crept [krept], *pass.p.p.* di to **creep**.

crepuscular [kri'pʌskjulə*], *ag.* crepuscolare.

crepuscule ['krepəskju:l], *s.* crepuscolo.

crescendo [kri'ʃendou], *s.* (*mus.*) crescendo (anche *fig.*).

crescent ['kresnt], *ag.* 1. crescente 2. a mezzaluna; a semicerchio ‖ *the Crescent City*, New Orleans ‖ *s.* 1. luna crescente; (*rar.*) luna calante 2. mezzaluna (emblema turco) ‖ *the Crescent*, l'Impero turco 3. (*relig.*) Islamismo ‖ *the Cross and the Crescent*, la Croce o la Mezzaluna, il Cristianesimo e l'Islamismo 4. strada, lato di strada a semicerchio; fila di case disposte a semicerchio.

cress [kres], *s.* (*bot.*) crescione.

cresset ['kresit], *s.* torcia; lanterna.

Cressida ['kresidə], *no.pr.f.* (*lett.*) Criseide.

Cressy ['kresi], *no.pr.* (*geog.*) Crécy.

crest [krest], *s.* 1. cresta (di gallo) 2. ciuffo, ciuffetto di (uccello); criniera (di cavallo) 3. pennacchio; criniera; cimiero 4. cresta, cima (anche *fig.*) 5. (*arald.*) cimiero 6. (*arch.*) corona; linea di displuvio 7. (*elett. mec.*) cresta.

to **crest**, *v.t.i.* 1. ornare di pennacchio, cresta 2. servire da pennacchio, cresta a 3. giungere alla sommità di (colle, ecc.) 4. formare cresta (di onde).

crested ['krestid], *ag.* ornato di cresta, ciuffetto, pennacchio, cimiero, criniera ☆ — *note-paper*, carta da scrivere con stemma gentilizio.

crestfallen ['krest,fo:lən], *ag.* mortificato, umiliato; abbattuto.

cretaceous [kri'teifəs], *ag.* cretaceo.

Cretan ['kri:tən], *ag.s.c.* cretese.

Crete [kri:t], *no.pr.* (*geog.*) Creta, Candia.

cretic ['kri:tik], *ag.s.* (*poes.*) cretico.

to cretify ['kri:tifai], *v.t.* cretare, spalmare, imbrattare di creta.

cretin ['kretin], *s.* cretino.

cretinism ['kretinizəm], *s.* cretinismo.

to cretinize ['kretinaiz], *v.t.* incretinire.

cretinous ['kretinəs], *ag.* cretino.

cretonne [kre'ton], *s.* «cretonne».

Creusa [kri'u:zə], *no.pr.f.* (*lett.*) Creusa.

crevasse [kri'væs], *s.* crepaccio.

to crevasse, *v.i.* fendersi, spaccarsi.

crevice ['krevis], *s.* fessura, crepa, fenditura; interstizio.

crew [kru:], *s.* 1. (*mar. aer.*) equipaggio 2. squadra, gruppo (di operai); 3. (*spreg.*) banda, ciurma, combriccola ‖ *sorry* —, masnada ☆ *gun* —, (*artigl.*) i serventi a un pezzo di artiglieria; *train* —, (*amer.*) personale del treno.

crew, *pass.* di to **crow.**

crewel ['kru:il], *s.* lana da ricamo ☆ — *-needle*, ago da ricamo; — *-stitch*, punt'erba; — *-work*, ricamo in lana.

crib [krib], *s.* 1. rastrelliera, greppia 2. presepio 3. stalla; capanna 4. lettino a sbarre (per bambini); (*rar.*) culla 5. (*arch.*) puntellatura di sostegno; (*min.*) catasta di puntellamento 6. (*fam.*) piccolo furto; plagio 7. (*sl. scolastico*) bigino, traduttore.

to crib, *pass.p.p.* **cribbed** [kribd], *v.t.* 1. fornire di rastrelliera, di greppia 2. (*miner.*) puntellare 3. (*fam.*) rubacchiare; plagiare: *to* — *sthg. from s.o.*, rubacchiare ql.co. a qlcu. 4. (*sl. scolastico*) copiare: *to* — *an exercise from another boy*, copiare un compito da un compagno 5. (*arc.*) serrare, rinchiudere (in spazio limitato).

cribbage ['kribidʒ], *s.* «cribbage» (giuoco a carte).

cribriform ['kribrifo:m], *ag.* (*anat. bot.*) bucato, perforato.

crick¹ [krik], *s.* crampo: *a* — *in the neck*, torcicollo.

to crick¹, *v.t.* far venire un crampo a: *to* — *one's neck*, prendere il torcicollo.

to crick², *v.i.* frinire, stridere (di grilli).

cricket¹ ['krikit], *s.* grillo ☆ *house-* —, grillo domestico.

cricket², *s.* (*spor.*) «cricket» ‖ *that's not* —, (*fam.*) non è leale, non è sportivo.

to cricket², *v.i.* giocare al «cricket».

cricketer ['krikitə*], *s.* giocatore di «cricket».

cricoid ['kraikoid], *ag.* (*anat.*) cricoideo ‖ *s.* (*anat.*) cricoide.

crier ['krai-ə*], *s.* 1. banditore 2. chi piange molto ☆ *Court* —, usciere; *town-* —, banditore municipale.

crikey ['kraiki], *inter.* (*sl.*) caspita!.

crime [kraim], *s.* delitto; reato, crimine: *to charge with a* —, incolpare di un delitto 2. azione sconsiderata, peccato ☆ — *sheet*, (*mil.*) foglio delle punizioni.

to crime, *v.t.* (*mil.*) 1. incriminare 2. condannare.

Crimea [krai'miə], *no.pr.* (*geog.*) Crimea.

Crimean [krai'miən], *ag.* di Crimea.

crimeless ['kraimlis], *ag.* innocente.

criminal ['kriminl], *ag.* 1. criminale 2. penale: *to take* — *proceedings against s.o.*, intraprendere azione penale contro qlcu. ‖ *The Criminal Investigation Department*, (*fam. C.I.D.*) la polizia giudiziaria ‖ *s.c.* criminale, delinquente: *habitual* —, recidivo; pregiudicato ☆ — *action*, azione penale; — *law*, diritto penale; — *lawyer*, (avvocato) penalista.

criminalist ['kriminəlist], *s.* (*dir.*) penalista.

criminality [,krimi'næliti], *s.* criminalità.

criminally ['kriminəli], *av.* criminalmente.

to criminate ['krimineit], *v.t.* 1. (*dir.*) incriminare, accusare 2. (*dir.*) convincere di delitto: *to* — *oneself,*

fornire delle prove contro se stesso 3. biasimare; censurare.

crimination [,krimi'neifən], *s.* incriminazione, accusa.

criminative ['kriminətiv], **criminatory** ['kriminətəri], *ag.* incriminante, accusatorio.

crimine ['krimini], *inter.* (*arc.*) diamine!.

criminologist [,krimi'nolədʒist], *s.* criminologo.

criminology [,krimi'nolədʒi], *s.* criminologia.

criminous ['kriminəs], *ag.* (*dir.*) colpevole di delitto: — *clerck*, prete colpevole.

criminy ['krimini], *inter.* (*arc.*)diamine!.

crimp¹ [krimp], *s.* arrolatore fraudolento (di soldati, marinai).

to crimp¹, *v.t.* arrolare; far arrolare (con inganno).

crimp², *ag.* 1. friabile; fragile 2. arricciato.

crimp², *s.* 1. piega; pieghettatura (di stoffa) 2. arricciatura (di capelli).

to crimp², *v.t.i.* 1. piegare; pieghettare; sgualcirsi (di stoffe) 2. arricciare; increspare (capelli) 3. (*cuc.*) sventrare (pesce appena pescato perchè si indurisca) 4. comprimere; stringere; ridurre 5. modellare (cuoio per tomaia).

crimpy ['krimpi], *ag.* arricciato, increspato: — *hair*, capelli crespi.

crimson ['krimzn], *ag.* cremisino, cremisi ‖ *s.* cremisi; *fig.* rossore.

to crimson, *v.t.i.* 1. tingere di cremisi, di rosso 2. arrossire, farsi rosso.

cringe [krindʒ], *s.* atteggiamento ossequiente, servile.

to cringe, *v.i.* 1. farsi piccolo (per timore), acquattarsi, rannicchiarsi 2. *fig.* umiliarsi, piegare la schiena servilmente.

cringle ['kriŋgl], *s.* (*mar.*) gassa.

crinite ['krainait], *ag.* (*zool. bot.*) peloso.

crinkle ['kriŋkl], *s.* crespa, ruga, grinza.

to crinkle, *v.t.i.* 1. increspare, incresparsi; pieghettare; spiegazzare; arricciare, arricciarsi: *crinkled paper*, carta crespata 2. frusciare; crepitare.

crinkly ['kriŋkli], *ag.* 1. pieno di pieghe, spiegazzato 2. frusciante.

crinkum-crankum ['kriŋkəm'kræŋkəm], *s.* cosa ingarbugliata (anche *fig.*).

crinoid ['krainoid], *s.* (*zool.*) crinoide.

crinoline ['krinəli:n], *s.* crinolina.

cripes [kraips], *inter.* càspita!.

cripple ['kripl], *s.* 1. zoppo; storpio; sciancato 2. *fig.* incapace 3. impalcatura (per pulire, dipingere finestre) ☆ *war cripples*, mutilati di guerra.

to cripple, *v.t.i.* 1. storpiare; essere zoppo; zoppicare: *crippled foot*, piede zoppo; *crippled with rheumatism*, storpiato dai reumatismi; *he was crippled in the war*, fu mutilato durante la guerra ‖ *to* — *along*, avanzare zoppicando 2. *fig.* paralizzare.

Criseyde [kri'seidə], *no.pr.f.* (*lett.*) Criseide.

crisis ['kraisis], *pl.* **crises** ['kraisi:z], *s.* crisi ☆ *cabinet* —, (*pol.*) crisi ministeriale.

crisp [krisp], *ag.* 1. croccante, friabile 2. crespo, ricciuto 3. frizzante; tonificante (di aria) 4. vivo, incisivo (di stile, maniere).

to crisp, *v.t.i.* 1. rendere croccante 2. increspare (capelli), incresparsi (di capelli) 3. disseccarsi (di foglie).

crispate ['krispit], *ag.* 1. increspato 2. (*bot. zool.*) con i margini ondulati.

crispation [kris'peifən], *s.* 1. ondulazione 2. contrazione.

Crispin ['krispin], *no.pr.m.* Crispino ‖ **crispin,** *s.* (*arc.*) calzolaio.

crispness ['krispnis], *s.* 1. friabilità (di biscotto, ecc.) 2. cresposità (di capelli) 3. freddo intenso (di aria) 4. chiarezza, nitidezza (di stile, maniere).

crisps [krisps], *s.pl.* 1. (*potato-*) —, (*cuc.*) patatine fritte 2. (*sl.*) banconote.

crispy ['krispi], *ag.* 1. croccante (di biscotti) 2. crespo (di capelli) 3. frizzante (di aria).

criss-cross ['kriskros], *ag.* 1. incrociato; intersecato **2.** *fig.* stizzoso, irritabile (di persona) ‖ *s.* **1.** segno di croce (in luogo della firma) **2.** incrocio, rete: — *of wires*, incrocio di fili (*p.e.* elettrici).

to **criss-cross**, *v.t.i.* incrociare, incrociarsi; intersecare, intersecarsi: *brow criss-crossed with wrinkles*, fronte solcata di rughe.

criss-cross, *av.* a rovescio, di traverso, all'inverso: *everything is going* —, tutto va a rovescio.

cristate ['kristit], **cristated** [kris'teitid], *ag.* (*bot. zool.*) crestato.

criterion [krai'tiəriən], *pl.* **criteria** [krai'tiəriə], *s.* criterio, principio.

critic ['kritik], *s.* critico

critical ['kritikəl], *ag.* critico: — *situation*, situazione critica; *at a* — *moment of his life*, in un momento critico della sua vita ☆ — *age*, età critica; — *eye*, occhio critico; — *temperature*, (*fis.*) temperatura critica.

critically ['kritikəli], *av.* in modo critico.

criticaster [,kriti'kæstə*], *s.* critico da strapazzo.

criticism ['kritisizəm], *s.* **1.** critica **2.** esegesi **3.** (*fil.*) criticismo.

criticizable ['kritisaizəbl], *ag.* criticabile.

to **criticize** ['kritisaiz], *v.t.* **1.** criticare, fare la critica di **2.** censurare.

critique [kri'ti:k], *s.* **1.** critica **2.** recensione; saggio critico ‖ *Critique of Pure Reason*, (*fil.*) Critica della Ragion Pura.

croak [krouk], *s.* **1.** gracidamento; gracchiamento **2.** (*sl. amer.*) l'ultimo respiro: *to utter* —, (*sl.*) esalare l'ultimo respiro.

to **croak**, *v.t.i.* **1.** gracidare; gracchiare **2.** *fig.* brontolare; predire malanni **3.** (*sl.*) morire **4.** (*amer.*) uccidere.

croaker ['kroukə*], *s.* **1.** animale che gracchia, gracida **2.** *fig.* brontolone; uccello di malaugurio.

croaky ['krouki], *ag.* **1.** rauco **2.** gracidante.

Croat ['krouət], *ag.s.* croato.

Croatia [krou'eifjə], *no.pr.* (*geog.*) Croazia.

Croatian [krou'eifjən], *ag.* croato ‖ *s.c.* croato, croata ‖ *s.* lingua croata.

crochet ['kroufei], *s.* lavoro all'uncinetto ☆ — *-hook* (o — *-pin*), uncinetto.

to **crochet**, *v.t.* lavorare all'uncinetto.

crock[1] [krɔk], *s.* **1.** pentola, vaso (di terracotta); (*dial.*) pentola (di metallo) **2.** coccio di terracotta.

crock[2], *s.* **1.** persona vecchia, malandata **2.** ronzino **3.** pecora vecchia.

to **crock**[2], *v.t.i.* **1.** rendere inabile **2.** *to* — *up*, (*sl.*) ammalarsi.

crock[3], *s.* (*sl.*) sporcizia; fuliggine.

to **crock**[3], *v.t.* (*sl.*) sporcare, insudiciare (con fuliggine).

crockery ['krɔkəri], *s.* terraglia, terrecotte.

crocket ['krɔkit], *s.* (*arch.*) ornamento floreale agli angoli del frontone.

crocodile ['krɔkədail], *s.* coccodrillo ☆ — *tears*, *fig.* lacrime di coccodrillo.

crocodilian [,krɔkə'diljən], *ag.* di coccodrillo.

crocus ['kroukəs], *pl.* **crocuses** ['kroukəsiz], *s.* (*bot.*) croco.

Croesus ['kri:səs], *no.pr.m.* (*st.*) Creso ‖ **croesus**, *s.* creso, persona ricchissima.

croft[1] [krɔft], *s.* campicello; piccolo podere.

croft[2], *s.* (*rar.*) cripta, volta, caverna.

crofter ['krɔftə*], *s.* (*spec. scoz.*) affittuario di un piccolo podere.

cromlech ['krɔmlek], *s.* (*archeol.*) cromlech.

cromorne [krou'mɔ:n], *s.* (*mus.*) cromorno.

crone [kroun], *s.* **1.** (*spreg.*) vecchia donna rugosa **2.** pecora vecchia.

cronk [krɔŋk], *ag.* (*sl. australiano*) **1.** sospetto, disonesto (di affare) **2.** malfermo; in cattiva forma (di cavallo).

crony ['krouni], *s.* amico intimo: *an old* —, un vecchio amico.

crook [kruk], *s.* **1.** curva; curvatura; flessione: — *of the knee*, genuflessione **2.** gancio, uncino, raffio **3.** bastone da pastore; (*eccl.*) pastorale **4.** (*sl.*) truffatore,

ladro, imbroglione ‖ *by hook or by* —, (*fam.*) con qualunque mezzo, di riffa o di raffa ‖ *to get sthg. on the* —, (*sl.*) ottener ql.co. disonestamente.

to **crook**, *v.t.i.* curvare, curvarsi; piegare, piegarsi: *to* — *one's finger, arm*, piegare il dito, il braccio.

crookback ['krukbæk], *s.* gobba.

crookbacked ['krukbækt], *ag.* gobbo, curvo.

crooked ['krukid], *nel senso 4.* [krukt], *ag.* **1.** storto; curvo, curvato; contorto; deforme: — *legs*, gambe storte; *to wear one's hat* —, portare il cappello di traverso **2.** *fig.* tortuoso: — *reasoning*, ragionamento tortuoso **3.** *fig.* sleale, disonesto: — *counsels*, consigli disonesti **4.** a forma di gruccia (di bastone).

crookedly ['krukidli], *av.* **1.** tortuosamente; di sghembo **2.** indirettamente **3.** disonestamente, slealmente.

crookedness ['krukidnis], *s.* **1.** sinuosità, tortuosità (anche *fig.*) **2.** deformità fisica **3.** disonestà, slealtà.

croon [kru:n], *s.* canto sommesso, monotono ;cantilena.

to **croon**, *v.t.i.* cantare in tono basso, sommesso.

crooner ['kru:nə*], *s.* cantante di canzoni lente e sentimentali.

crop [krɔp], *s.* **1.** gozzo (di uccello) ‖ *neck and* —, completamente, del tutto **2.** manico di frustino **3.** raccolto, messe: *land out of* —, terra a maggese; *land under* (o *in*) —, terra coltivata; *second* —, secondo raccolto **4.** *fig.* raccolta, gruppo: *a* — *of lies*, (*fam.*) un sacco di bugie **5.** rapata (di capelli) **6.** marchio (di animali) **7.** (*metal.*) pezzo mozzato; spuntatura **8.** (*cuc.*) spalla (di animale) **9.** pelle intera conciata ☆ — *-eared*, dalle orecchie mozze ‖ *close* —, rapata a zero; *hunting-* —, frustino da caccia; *rice* —, raccolto del riso.

to **crop**, *pass.p.p.* **cropped** [krɔpt], *v.t.i.* **1.** tagliar via; spuntare; mozzare (orecchie, coda, ecc. ad animali); tosare; cimare (tessuti); *hair cropped close*, capelli tagliati a zero **2.** brucare: *the sheep were cropping the grass*, le pecore brucavano l'erba **3.** coltivare, seminare; produrre, dare un raccolto: *to* — *ten acres with wheat*, seminare dieci acri a grano **4.** *to* — *forth*, apparire, saltar fuori **5.** *to* — *out*, (*geol.*) affiorare; apparire **6.** *to* — *up*, (*geol.*) affiorare; *fig.* capitare, presentarsi, saltar fuori.

cropper[1] ['krɔpə*], *s.* **1.** potatore; tosatore; cimatore (di tessuti) **2.** coltivatore, mezzadro **3.** pianta che produce ☆ *good* —, *bad* —, pianta che dà un buono, un cattivo raccolto.

cropper[2], *s.* caduta, tombola: *to come a* —, fare una caduta; *to come a* — *in an examination*, cadere, far fiasco a un esame.

cropper[3], *s.* piccione gozzuto.

croppy ['krɔpi], *s.* (*st.*) ribelle irlandese del 1798 (coi capelli corti secondo la moda rivoluzionaria); persona con i capelli corti.

croquet ['kroukei], *s.* (*spor.*) «croquet», pallamaglio.

to **croquet**, *v.i.* giocare a pallamaglio.

croquette [krou'ket], *s.* «croquette», polpettina fritta.

crore [krɔ:*], *s.* (*ang.-in.*) dieci milioni di rupie.

crosier ['krouʒə*], *s.* (*eccl.*) pastorale.

cross [krɔs], *ag.* **1.** trasversale, obliquo; intersecante **2.** (*fam.*) imbronciato, bisbetico, di cattivo umore: *why are you so* — *with me?*, perchè sei così arrabbiato con me? ‖ *to be as* — *as two sticks* (o *as a bear with a sore head*), essere di pessimo umore **3.** opposto, avverso, contrario **4.** di razza mista.

cross, *s.* **1.** croce: *the stations of the Cross*, (*relig.*) la via crucis; *to make the sign of the* —, fare il segno della croce; *to sign with a* —, firmare con una croce ‖ *the George Cross*, la Croce di San Giorgio ‖ *Greek* —, Croce Greca ‖ *Maltese* —, Croce di Malta ‖ *The Red Cross*, la Croce Rossa ‖ *Southern Cross*, (*astr.*) Croce del Sud ‖ *The Victoria Cross*, la Croce della Regina

Vittoria || *on the* —, diagonalmente || *to take the* —, andar crociato **2.** pena, tribolazione; contrarietà: *to bear one's* —, (*fam.*) portare la propria croce **3.** incrocio di razze **4.** crocicchio, quadrivio **5.** taglio (sulla lettera « t »); sbieco: *on the* —, di sbieco, diagonalmente **6.** (*sl.*) imbroglio: *double* —, pasticcio.

to **cross**, *v.t.i.* **1.** fare il segno della croce: *to* — *oneself*, farsi il segno della croce **2.** incrociare, incrociarsi: *my letters crossed yours*, le nostre lettere si incrociarono; *to* — *one's legs*, accavallare le gambe; *to* — *swords*, incrociare le spade, battersi a duello; *fig.* entrare in conflitto **3.** attraversare: *to* — (*over*) *from Boulogne to Folkestone*, fare la traversata da Boulogne a Folkestone; *to* — *one's mind*, *fig.* venire in mente; *to* — *s.o.'s path*, trovarsi sulla strada di qlcu.; sbarrare il passo a qlcu. **4.** opporre, ostacolare: *he crossed me in everything*, mi ostacolò in tutto; *he has been crossed in love*, ha avuto amori contrastati; *to* — *s.o.'s plans*, contrariare qlcu., contrastare i piani di qlcu. **5.** (*biol.*) incrociare, incrociarsi: *to* — *breeds*, fare incroci di razze **6.** sbarrare: *a crossed cheque*, un assegno sbarrato; *to* — *one's t's*, fare il taglio alle t || *to* — *one's t's and dot one's i's*, *fig.* mettere i puntini sulle i **7.** *to* — **out, off**, cancellare, cancellare con un tratto di penna: *to* — *out words in a sentence*, cancellare parole da una frase.

cross, (*nei composti*): — *-bar*, traversa; — *-bearer*, crocifero; — *-bench*, banco trasversale (di deputato indipendente); — *-bencher*, membro indipendente (alla Camera dei Comuni); — *-country*, attraverso i campi: — *-country race*, corsa campestre; — *-eyed*, strabico; — *-fire*, (*mil.*) fuoco incrociato; — *-grain*, fibra trasversale (di legno); — *-grained*, a fibra torta, irregolare (di legno); perverso, intrattabile (di persona); — *-head(ing)*, sottotitolo (di giornale); (*mec.*) cappello; testa del pistone; — *-legged*, a gambe incrociate; — *-light*, luce incrociata; *fig.* descrizione di un soggetto da un altro punto di vista; — *-patch*, (*fam.*) borbottone, individuo malvagio, di cattivo carattere; — *-piece*, traversa; — *-purposes*, *pl.* contraddizione, propositi opposti; giuoco delle domande incrociate: *to be at* — *-purposes*, fraintendersi; avere piani opposti rivolti ad uno stesso scopo; — *-reference*, rinvio (da una parte di un libro ad altra); — *-road*, strada trasversale, incrocio: *at the* — *-roads*, *fig.* al bivio; — *-section*, (*tec.*) spaccato, sezione trasversale; (*radioattività*) sezione d'urto; rappresentanza, selezione, campione: — *-section of the working-class people of Wales*, rappresentanza della classe operaia del Galles; — *-stitch*, (*cucito*) punto a croce; — *-street*, via laterale; via trasversale; — *stroke*, tratto (di penna); colpo trasversale (tennis, ecc.); — *-talk*, (*rad.*) diafonia || *fiery* —, (*scoz.*) croce con le estremità bruciate, bagnate di sangue (emblema di sommossa); (*amer.*) croce di fuoco (simbolo del Ku-Klux-Klan).

crossbeam ['krɔsbi:m], *s.* (*edil.*) trave trasversale.

crossbelt ['krɔsbelt], *s.* cartucciera a tracolla.

crossbill ['krɔsbil], *s.* (*ornit.*) crociere.

crossbones ['krɔsbounz], *s.pl.* ossa incrociate: *skull and* —, teschio e ossa incrociate (emblema della morte).

crossbow ['krɔsbou], *s.* balestra.

crossbred ['krɔsbred], *ag.* incrociato (di razze).

crossbreed ['krɔsbri:d], *s.* incrocio (di razze).

crosscut ['krɔskʌt], *s.* **1.** taglio trasversale **2.** scorciatoia, sentiero trasversale ☆ — *-saw*, segone, sega da boscaiuolo.

crosse [krɔs], *s.* (*amer. spor.*) racchetta da « lacrosse » (specie di hockey).

cross-examination ['krɔsig,zæmi'neiʃən], *s.* (*dir.*) interrogatorio con contraddittorio.

to **cross-examine** ['krɔsig'zæmin], *v.t.* (*dir.*) interrogare in contraddittorio; sottoporre a controinterrogatorio.

cross-hatch ['krɔshætʃ], *s.* **1.** tratteggio **2.** (*ind. tessile*) trama incrociata.

to **cross-hatch**, *v.t.* tratteggiare.

crossing ['krɔsin], *s.* **1.** passaggio; traversata: *my first Channel* — *was rough*, la mia prima traversata della Manica fu tempestosa **2.** incrocio, sbarramento **3.** incrocio di razze **4.** opposizione, contraddizione ☆ *level* — (o *grade* —), (*amer.*) passaggio a livello; *underground* —, passaggio sotterraneo.

crosslet ['krɔslit], *s.* crocetta, piccola croce.

crossly ['krɔsli], *av.* di malumore, bruscamente.

crossness ['krɔsnis], *s.* malumore.

to **cross-question** ['krɔs'kwestʃən], *v.t.* (*dir.*) interrogare in contraddittorio; sottoporre a controinterrogatorio.

crosstrees ['krɔstri:z], *s.pl.* (*mar.*) crocette, barre ☆ *main* —, barre di maestra; *mizzen* —, barre di mezzana.

crosswise ['krɔswaiz], *av.* **1.** per traverso; di traverso **2.** a forma di croce.

crossword ['krɔswə:d], *s.* **1.** parole incrociate **2.** — (*puzzle*), cruciverba, giuoco delle parole incrociate.

crotch [krɔtʃ], *s.* **1.** (*bot.*) forca, biforcazione (di ramo) **2.** (*anat.*) inforcatura (del corpo).

crotched [krɔtʃt], *ag.* (*amer.*) biforcuto.

crotchet ['krɔtʃit], *s.* **1.** gancio, uncino, uncinetto **2.** *fig.* ghiribizzo, mania, capriccio **3.** (*mus.*) semiminima.

crotcheteer [,krɔtʃi'tiə*], *s.* individuo capriccioso, maniaco.

crotchety ['krɔtʃiti], *ag.* soggetto a ubbie, capriccioso, maniaco.

croton ['kroutən], *s.* (*bot.*) crotone.

crouch [krautʃ], *s.* l'accovacciarsi, il rannicchiarsi.

to **crouch**, *v.i.* **1.** accovacciarsi, rannicchiarsi, accoccolarsi: *the cat crouched on my lap*, il gatto mi si accoccolò in grembo; *the tiger crouched before springing*, la tigre si rannicchiò prima di saltare **2.** *fig.* piegarsi (per paura, timidezza, servilismo).

croup[1] [kru:p], *s.* groppa (specialmente di cavalli).

croup[2], *s.* (*patol.*) difterite.

croupier ['kru:piə*], *s.* **1.** « croupier » **2.** vicepresidente ad un pubblico banchetto.

crow[1] [krou], *s.* (*ornit.*) corvo; cornacchia || *as the* — *flies*, in linea retta, in linea d'aria || *a white* —, una mosca bianca || *to eat* —, mandar giù un rospo, subire un'umiliazione || *to have a* — *to pluck with s.o.*, aver qualcosa a ridire su qlcu. ☆ — *-bar*, (*tec.*) palanchino, piede di porco; — *'s-foot*, zampa di gallina, ruga; (*mil.*) tribolo; — *'s-nest*, (*mar.*) coffa, gabbia.

crow[2], *s.* **1.** canto del gallo: *to get up at cock's* —, alzarsi al canto del gallo **2.** grido di gioia (di bimbo).

to **crow**[2], *pass.* **crowed** [kroud], **crew** [kru:], *p.p.* **crowed**, *v.i.* **1.** cantare (del gallo) || *to* — *over s.o.*, cantar vittoria su qlcu. **2.** far gridolini di gioia (di bambini).

crowd[1] [kraud], *s.* **1.** folla, moltitudine: *in crowds*, in gran folla || *the* —, le masse, il popolo; *to follow* (o *to go with*) *the* —, fare quello che fanno gli altri || *to rise above the* —, *fig.* innalzarsi al disopra della folla **2.** massa, quantità, gran numero di cose: *a* — *of books and papers*, una massa di libri e carte; *a* — *of sails*, (*mar.*) una quantità di vele || *under a* — *of sails*, a vele spiegate **3.** (*fam. spreg.*) compagnia, cricca, combriccola: *I don't like any of that* —, non mi piace nessuno di quella compagnia ☆ — *scene*, (*cine.*) scena di massa.

to **crowd**[1], *v.t.i.* **1.** affollare, affollarsi; accalcarsi; riempire (di persone, cose): *crowded city*, città molto popolosa; *the pupils crowded round the teacher*, gli allievi si affollarono intorno all'insegnante; *to* — *a building with people*, affollare un edificio di gente; *to* — *people into a building*, ammassar gente in un edificio; *to* — *to a place*, affluire in folla ad un luogo **2.** (*sl. amer.*) sollecitare il pagamento di un debito **3.** *to* — **down**, scendere in massa **4.** *to* — **in**, entrare in massa; affollare: *ideas crowded in upon him*, le idee gli si affollarono alla mente **5.** *to* — **on** *sail*, (*mar.*) spiegare tutte le vele di una nave **6.** *to* — **out**, uscire in folla; lasciar fuori per troppa ressa, per mancanza di capienza: *many people were crowded out*, a causa della ressa molte persone dovettero rimanere fuori || *matter crowded out*, materiale giornalistico non pubblicato per mancanza di spazio **7.** *to* — **together**, stringersi insieme, raccogliersi (di folla) **8.** *to* — **up**, montare, salire in folla (sul tram, ecc.); (*amer.*) far salire (i prezzi).

crowd², s. antico strumento musicale celtico simile al violino.

crowdy ['kraudi], *ag.* affollato.

crowfoot ['krou-fut], *s.* **1.** (*bot.*) piè corvino **2.** (*mar.*) patta d'oca **3.** (*mil.*) tribolo.

crown [kraun], *s.* **1.** corona; ghirlanda, serto (anche *fig.*): *the martyr's* —, la corona del martirio; *royal* —, corona reale; *to succeed* (o *to come*) *to the* —, salire al trono; *to wear the* —, regnare || *the Crown*, la Corona, il potere sovrano **2.** corona (moneta): *half a* —, mezza corona **3.** cocuzzolo: *the* — *of a hat*, il cocuzzolo di un cappello || *from* — *to toe*, dalla testa ai piedi **4.** *fig.* coronamento, successo, raggiungimento: *the* — *of one's labours*, il coronamento delle proprie fatiche **5.** corona (di dente) **6.** (*arch.*) chiave **7.** (*min.*) cielo **8.** (*mar.*) diamante (di ancora) **9.** colmo (di strada) **10.** (*aer.*) corona (di paracadute) **11.** (*mec.*) testa **12.** volta (di fornace) || — *bar*, trave a corona armata; — *-cap*, (*neol.*) tappo a capsula; — *colony*, colonia dipendente dalla Corona; — *-imperial*, (*bot.*) corona imperiale; — *-lands*, terre demaniali; — *law*, diritto penale; — *-lawyer*, Pubblico Ministero; — *prince*, principe ereditario; — *wheel*, (*mec.*) corona a denti frontali.

to crown, *v.t.* **1.** incoronare: *to* — *s.o. king*, incoronare qlcu. re **2.** coronare, ricompensare: *his work was crowned with success*, la sua opera fu coronata da successo; *to be crowned with glory*, essere incoronato di gloria || *that crowns all!*, (*fam.*) non ci mancava che questo! || *to* — *all*, (*fam.*) per colmo (di fortuna, di disgrazia): *we lost the tickets and, to* — *all, we missed the train*, perdemmo i biglietti e, per colmo di sfortuna, anche il treno **3.** (*med.*) mettere una corona a (un dente) **4.** colmare (una strada) **5.** far dama, damare.

crowned [kraund], *ag.* (in)coronato ☆ *high, low -* — *hat*, cappello a cocuzzolo alto, basso; *high-* — *road*, strada a dorso di mulo.

crowning ['krauniŋ], *ag.* ultimo, finale; supremo: — *happiness, folly*, felicità, follia suprema || *s.* **1.** incoronazione; coronamento **2.** colmata (di strada).

crownless ['kraunlis], *ag.* senza corona.

crownlet ['kraunlit], *s.* coroncina, piccola corona.

crozier ['krouzə*], *s.* (*eccl.*) pastorale.

crucial ['kru:ʃəl], *ag.* **1.** cruciale, decisivo; critico **2.** (*anat. zool.*) crociato (di legamento); (*chir.*) incrociato, a forma di croce.

crucian ['kru:ʃən], *s.* (*ittiol.*) carassio.

cruciate ['kru:ʃiit], *ag.* (*bot. zool.*) crociforme.

crucible ['kru:sibl], *s.* **1.** crogiuolo **2.** *fig.* dura prova: *in the* —, a dura prova ☆ — *steel*, acciaio al crogiuolo.

crucifer ['kru:sifə*], *s.* **1.** (*eccl.*) crocifero **2.** (*bot.*) crocifera.

cruciferous [kru:'sifərəs], *ag.* **1.** crocifero **2.** (*bot.*) appartenente alle crocifere.

crucifier ['kru:sifaiə*], *s.* crocifissore.

crucifix ['kru:sifiks], *s.* crocifisso.

crucifixion [,kru:si'fikʃən], *s.* crocifissione || *the Crucifixion*, la Crocifissione.

cruciform ['kru:sifo:m], *ag.* crociforme.

to crucify ['kru:sifai], *v.t.* **1.** crocifiggere **2.** *fig.* mortificare.

crude [kru:d], *ag.* **1.** greggio, grezzo: — *oil*, petrolio grezzo **2.** informe; sommario; immaturo: — *ideas*, idee immature; — *method*, metodo sommario **3.** rozzo, primitivo; brutale: — *life in the forest*, vita primitiva nella foresta; — *manners*, modi rudi; — *statement of the facts*, esposizione brutale dei fatti **4.** (*fisiol.*) non digerito, non assimilato (di alimenti) **5.** (*med.*) non sviluppato (di morbo) **6.** — *form of a word*, (*gram.*) radice tematica di una parola.

crudely ['kru:dli], *av.* **1.** crudamente, rozzamente **2.** sommariamente.

crudeness ['kru:dnis], *V.* **crudity 1.**

crudity ['kru:diti], *s.* **1.** asprezza, mancanza di forma: *a book full of crudities*, un libro pieno di crudezze **2.** (*patol. arc.*) acidità (di stomaco).

cruel [kruəl], *ag.* crudele: *a* — *death*, una morte crudele; *a* — *master*, un padrone crudele || *she carried on something* —, (*sl.*) essa ci ha fatto una scena terribile; *it was* — *on him*, (*sl.*) è stato ben duro per lui.

cruelly ['kruəli], *av.* crudelmente.

cruelty ['kruəlti], *s.* crudeltà || *society for the prevention of* — *to animals*, società protettrice degli animali; *a piece of* —, una crudeltà.

cruet ['kru(:)it], *s.* ampolla ☆ — *-stand*, oliera.

cruise [kru:z], *s.* (*mar.*) crociera: *on a* —, in crociera; *to go on a* —, fare una crociera ☆ *around-the-world* —, crociera intorno al mondo.

to cruise, *v.i.* (*mar.*) incrociare; andare in crociera.

cruiser ['kru:zə*], *s.* **1.** (*mar.*) incrociatore; nave da crociera **2.** (*amer.*) automobile della polizia.

cruising ['kru:ziŋ], *ag.* (*mar.*) da crociera || *s.* crociera ☆ — *-speed*, velocità di crociera, velocità limitata; — *-taxi*, tassì libero che gira in cerca di clienti.

cruive [kru:v], *s.* (*mar.*) specie di nassa.

crumb [krʌm], *s.* **1.** briciola (anche *fig.*) **2.** mollica **3.** (*ind.*) grumo (della gomma) ☆ — *-brush*, spazzola per briciole; — *-tray*, paletta per briciole.

to crumb, *v.t.* **1.** sbriciolare **2.** (*cuc.*) impanare (costolette, ecc.).

crumble ['krʌmbl], *s.* (*rar.*) briciola.

to crumble, *v.t.i.* **1.** sbriciolare, sbriciolarsi (di pane, pietra, ecc.) **2.** *fig.* sgretolarsi; crollare; ridursi in polvere: *great empires have crumbled*, grandi imperi sono crollati.

crumbly ['krʌmbli], *ag.* friabile.

crumby ['krʌmi], *ag.* midolloso (di pane); soffice.

crummie, crummy ['krʌmi], *ag.* (*sl.*) **1.** paffutella, avvenente (di donna) **2.** agiato **3.** (*amer.*) meschino, disprezzabile || *s.* (*scoz.*) mucca con corna ricurve.

crump¹ [krʌmp], *ag.* (*scoz.*) fragile; friabile || *s.* (*scoz.*) fragilità; friabilità.

to crump¹, *v.t.* masticare rumorosamente (specialmente di cavalli, maiali).

crump² [krʌmp], *s.* **1.** colpo violento **2.** grave caduta **3.** detonazione **4.** (*sl. mil.*) proiettile esplosivo.

to crump², *v.t.* **1.** (*sl.*) colpire violentemente **2.** (*sl. mil.*) bombardare.

crumpet ['krʌmpit], *s.* **1.** pasticcino **2.** (*sl.*) testa || *to be off one's* —, essere balordo.

crumple ['krʌmpl], *s.* grinza; ruga.

to crumple, *v.t.i.* **1.** spiegazzare, spiegazzarsi; raggrinzire, raggrinzirsi: *to* — (*up*) *paper*, spiegazzare carta, farne una pallottola **2.** *to* — **up**, abbattere, abbattersi, accasciarsi; crollare; sfasciarsi: *the aeroplane crumpled up*, l'aeroplano si schiantò; *he crumpled up under the awful news*, si accasciò sotto il colpo della terribile notizia; *the opposition crumpled up*, l'opposizione crollò.

crumpled ['krʌmpld], *ag.* **1.** spiegazzato; raggrinzito **2.** ricurvo: *cow with* — *horns*, mucca con corna ricurve.

crunch [krʌntʃ], *s.* **1.** lo sgranocchiare rumorosamente **2.** sgretolio; scricchiolio (di ruote, ecc.).

to crunch, *v.t.i.* **1.** sgranocchiare rumorosamente **2.** scricchiolare, far scricchiolare: *we crunched* (*our way*) *through the snow to the station*, abbiamo raggiunto la stazione in mezzo alla neve che scricchiolava sotto i nostri passi.

crupper ['krʌpə*], s. **1.** groppiera, sottocoda **2.** groppa (di cavallo).

crural ['kruərəl], ag. (anat.) crurale.

crusade [kru:'seid], s. crociata (anche fig.): to go on a —, fare una crociata.

to **crusade**, v.i. fare una crociata (anche fig.).

crusader [kru:'seidə*], s. crociato.

cruse [kru:z], s. (arc. biblico) tazza; vaso di terracotta ‖ it is like a widow's —, (fam.) è il pozzo di San Patrizio.

crush [krʌʃ], s. **1.** frantumazione **2.** calca, folla, affollamento; riunione affollata **3.** (sl. amer.) infatuazione, cotta: to have a — on s.o., avere una cotta per qlcu. ☆ — -hat, gibus; — -room, (teat.) ridotto.

to **crush**, v.t.i. **1.** frantumare; triturare; torchiare (olive); pigiare (uva); accalcarsi, affollarsi; schiacciare, schiacciarsi (anche fig.): to — to pieces, stritolare ‖ please, — up a little !, per favore, fatemi un po' di posto! ‖ to — one's way through the crowd, aprirsi un varco tra la folla **2.** sgualcire **3.** fig. annientare; sconfiggere; schiantare: crushed with grief, schiantato dal dolore; she crushed him with a glance, ella lo annientò con uno sguardo; to — the enemy, annientare il nemico **4.** to — down, schiacciare; sbriciolare; fig. annientare, sottomettere: the enemy was crushed down by our victory, il nemico fu annientato dalla nostra vittoria; to make cement by crushing down stone, fare il cemento triturando la pietra **5.** to — in, entrare, far entrare a forza **6.** to — out, spremere (succo da un frutto); soffocare, sedare (un tumulto); aprirsi un varco, uscire a stento.

crusher ['krʌʃə*], s. **1.** (mec.) frantumatore meccanico; macinatrice, trituratrice; frantoio (per olive) **2.** (sl.) disgrazia, fulmine a ciel sereno: what a —!, che tegola! ☆ — clod —, (agr. mec.) frangizolle.

crushing ['krʌʃiŋ], ag. schiacciante (anche fig.): — defeat, sconfitta schiacciante ‖ s. forte pressione; schiacciamento; triturazione, frantumazione ☆ — -mill, frantoio (per olive); (mec.) macinatrice, trituratrice; — plant, impianto di frantumazione; — roll, (mec.) rullo a sagomare; — rolls, (mec.) frantoio a rulli; — test, prova di compressione.

crust [krʌst], s. **1.** crosta: a — of bread, una crosta di pane; the — of a burn, la crosta di una scottatura ‖ he's got a —!, ha una bella faccia tosta! ‖ the upper —, (scherz.) il fior fiore della società **2.** incrostazione: a — of ice, una incrostazione di ghiaccio ☆ milk —, (patol.) crosta lattea.

to **crust**, v.t.i. incrostare, incrostarsi; fare la crosta; coprire, coprirsi di croste: the ice crusted over during the night, si è formata una incrostazione di ghiaccio durante la notte.

Crustacea [krʌs'teiʃjə], s.pl. (zool.) crostacei.

crustacean [krʌs'teiʃjən], ag.s. (zool.) crostaceo.

crustaceous [krʌs'teiʃjəs], ag. (zool.) crostaceo.

crustation [krʌs'teiʃən], s. incrostazione.

crusted ['krʌstid], ag. **1.** crostoso: — over, coperto di croste **2.** grommato (di vino) **3.** fig. antiquato: a — theory, una teoria antiquata, superata.

crustily ['krʌstili], av. duramente; in tono irritato, bruscamente.

crustiness ['krʌstinis], s. **1.** durezza (della crosta) **2.** fig. umore nero, irritabilità.

crusty ['krʌsti], ag. **1.** crostoso (di pane) **2.** grommoso, vecchio (di vino) **3.** fig. burbero, irritabile, uggioso: a — old chap, un vecchio bisbetico.

crutch [krʌtʃ], s. **1.** gruccia, stampella; fig. puntello, sostegno: to go about (o to walk) on crutches, camminare con le grucce **2.** forcella (di ramo) **3.** inforcatura (del corpo, di calzoni) **4.** (mar.) candeliere a forca, forcola, forcaccio.

to **crutch**, v.t. sostenere, reggere (con grucce); puntellare (anche fig.).

crutched[1] [krʌtʃt], ag. che ha una gruccia.

crutched[2], ag. che porta una croce ☆ Crutchedfriars, frati della Santa Croce.

crux [krʌks], s. punto cruciale, difficoltà: that is the — of the matter, qui sta il nodo della questione.

cry [krai], s. **1.** grido: — of rage, grido di rabbia; angry cries from the mob, grida irate della plebaglia; to give (o to raise o to set up o to utter) a —, emettere un grido ‖ the cries of London, le grida di richiamo dei venditori ambulanti per le strade di Londra ‖ hue and —, inseguimento rumoroso; gli inseguitori; clamore, protesta pubblica ‖ much — and little wool, molto fumo e poco arrosto ‖ within — (of), a portata di voce (di) ‖ it is a far (o a long) — from here to…, c'è una bella distanza da qui a…; non è facile arrivare a ‖ to be in full —, abbaiare forte (dei cani da caccia): the pack is in full —, tutta la muta abbaia (anche fig.) **2.** lamento; pianto ‖ to have a good —, sfogarsi col pianto; to have one's — out, piangere tutte le proprie lacrime ☆ — -baby piagnucolone ‖ battle- —, grido di battaglia; war- —, grido di guerra.

to **cry**, v.t.i. **1.** gridare: to — aloud, gridare a gran voce; to — for help, implorare aiuto; to — for mercy, implorare grazia, misericordia; to — (un)to God, implorare, invocare Dio ‖ to — poverty, piangere miseria ‖ to — quits, dichiararsi reciprocamente soddisfatti **2.** piangere: to — bitter tears, piangere amaramente; to — for joy, piangere per la gioia; to — for sthg., chiedere ql.co. piangendo ‖ to — for the moon, chiedere l'impossibile ‖ to — one's eyes out, piangere tutte le proprie lacrime ‖ to — oneself to sleep, piangere tanto da addormentarsi ‖ to — over spilt milk, piangere sul latte versato, inutilmente **3.** to — down, screditare, deprezzare **4.** to — off, rinunziare a; disdire; svincolarsi da: to — off a contract, annullare, disdire un contratto **5.** to — out, gridare forte; alzare la voce; protestare: he cried out with pain, gridò per il dolore **6.** to — up, lodare.

crying ['kraiiŋ], ag. evidente, patente: a — injustice, un'ingiustizia patente; a — need, un bisogno urgente; a — shame, una vergogna evidente.

cryogen ['kraiodʒen], s. (chim.) criogeno.

cryolite ['kraioulait], s. (min.) criolite.

crypt [kript], s. (arch.) cripta.

cryptaesthesia [,kriptes'θi:ziə], s. criptestesia.

cryptic ['kriptik], ag. **1.** segreto, nascosto, ermetico; enigmatico **2.** (zool.) mimetico.

cryptogam ['kriptougæm], s. (bot.) crittogama.

cryptogamie [,kriptou'gæmik], **cryptogamous** [krip-'togəməs], ag. (bot.) crittogamo.

cryptogram ['kriptougræm], **cryptograph** ['kriptougra:f], s. crittogramma.

cryptographer [krip'togrəfə*], s. crittografo.

cryptographie [,kriptou'græfik], ag. crittografico.

cryptography [krip'togrəfi], s. crittografia.

crystal ['kristl], ag. cristallino ‖ s. **1.** cristallo: a necklace of crystals, una collana di cristalli **2.** oggetti di cristallo: silver and — shone on the dining-table, l'argenteria e la cristalleria splendevano sulla tavola da pranzo **3.** (amer.) vetro d'orologio ☆ — clear, cristallino; — detector, (rad.) rivelatore a cristallo, a galena; — factory, (fabbrica di) cristalleria; — -gazing, divinazione per mezzo di un globo di cristallo; — -glass, (vetro di) cristallo; — lattice, (min.) reticolo cristallino; — set, radio a galena; — work, cristalleria ‖ quartz —, (rad.) cristallo di quarzo; rock —, (min.) cristallo di rocca.

crystalline ['kristəlain], ag. cristallino (anche fig.) ‖ s. (anat.) cristallino — lens, (anat.) cristallino.

crystallizable ['kristəlaizəbl], ag. cristallizzabile.

crystallization [,kristəlai'zeiʃən], s. cristallizzazione.

to **crystallize** ['kristəlaiz], v.t.i. **1.** cristallizzare; fig. fossilizzarsi **2.** (cuc.) candire ☆ crystallized fruits, sugar, frutta candita, zucchero candito.

crystallographic(al) [,kristələ'græfik(əl)], ag. cristallografico.

crystallography [,kristə'logrəfi], s. cristallografia.

crystalloid ['kristəloid], ag. cristallino ‖ s. (fis. chim.) cristalloide.

cub¹ [kʌb], *s.* **1.** volpacchiotto; cucciolo (di animali selvatici) **2.** lupetto (giovane esploratore al disotto dei dieci anni) ‖ *s.c.* (*fam.*) ragazzaccio, ragazzaccia; *an unlicked* —, un ragazzaccio ineducato ☆ — *reporter*, (*amer.*) cronista principiante ‖ *bear* —, orsacchiotto; *lion* —, leoncino; *wolf* —, lupacchiotto.

to cub¹, *pass.p.p.* **cubbed** [kʌbd], *v.t.i.* partorire, figliare (di animali selvatici).

cub², *s.* recinto per bestiame; stalla.

Cuba [ˈkjuːbə], *no.pr.* (*geog.*) Cuba.

cubage [ˈkjuːbidʒ], *s.* cubatura.

Cuban [ˈkjuːbən], *ag.* cubano ‖ *s.c.* cubano, cubana.

cubature [ˈkjuːbətʃə*], *s.* cubatura.

cubbing [ˈkʌbiŋ], *s.* caccia alla volpe giovane.

cubbish [ˈkʌbiʃ], *ag.* da cucciolo; maleducato; goffo; inesperto.

cubby(-hole) [ˈkʌbi(houl)], *s.* angolo intimo, confortevole nascondiglio.

cube [kjuːb], *s.* cubo ☆ — *root*, (*mat.*) radice cubica.

to cube, *v.t.* **1.** (*mat.*) elevare al cubo; fare la cubatura di **2.** pavimentare (una via, ecc.) con blocchetti a forma di cubo.

cubic [ˈkjuːbik], *ag.* (*mat.*) cubico; (*min.*) isometrico ☆ — *foot*, piede cubo; — *measures*, misure di capacità; — *measurement*, cubatura.

cubical [ˈkjuːbikəl], *ag.* cubico, a forma di cubo.

cubicle [ˈkjuːbikl], *s.* cubicolo; piccola stanza.

cubiform [ˈkjuːbifɔːm], *ag.* cubiforme.

cubism [ˈkjuːbizəm], *s.* (*art.*) cubismo.

cubist [ˈkjuːbist], *ag.s.* (*art.*) cubista.

cubit [ˈkjuːbit], *s.* (*st.*) cubito (misura di lunghezza = cm. 45,72).

cubital [ˈkjuːbitl], *ag.* cubitale.

cuboid [ˈkjuːbɔid], *ag.* cuboide.

cucking-stool [ˈkʌkiŋstuːl], *s.* sedia su cui i colpevoli venivano posti alla berlina.

cuckold [ˈkʌkəld], *s.* becco, cornuto.

to cuckold, *v.t.* tradire, far becco (il marito).

cuckoo [ˈkuːkuː], *s.* **1.** (*ornit.*) cuculo **2.** semplicione, persona sciocca ☆ — *clock*, orologio a cucù; — *flower*, (*bot.*) crescione.

cucullate [ˈkjuːkʌlit], *ag.* (*bot. zool.*) a forma di cappuccio; incappucciato.

cucumber [ˈkjuːkʌmbə*], *s.* cetriolo ‖ *as cool as a* —, a sangue freddo, imperturbabile; fresco come una rosa ☆ — *tree*, (*amer. bot.*) magnolia.

cucurbit [kjuˈkəːbit], *s.* **1.** (*bot.*) cucurbita, zucca **2.** (*arc.*) cucurbita, caldaia dell'alambicco.

cucurbitaceous [kjuˌkəːbiˈteiʃəs], **cucurbital** [kjuˈkəːbitl], *ag.* (*bot.*) cucurbitaceo.

cud [kʌd], *s.* bolo alimentare (di ruminante): *to chew the* —, ruminare; *fig.* ruminare, meditare.

cudbear [ˈkʌdbɛə*], *s.* (*bot.*) oricello.

cuddle [ˈkʌdl], *s.* (*fam.*) abbraccio affettuoso.

to cuddle, *v.t.i.* **1.** stringere al seno; abbracciare con affetto: *to* — *a child in one's arms*, stringere un bambino fra le braccia **2.** *to* — *up*, stare rannicchiato: *to* — *up to s.o.*, rannicchiarsi vicino a qlcu.

cuddlesome [ˈkʌdlsəm], **cuddly** [ˈkʌdli], *ag.* che invita agli abbracci.

cuddy¹ [ˈkʌdi], *s.* (*st.*) regalia (dovuta dal contadino al signore).

cuddy², *s.* **1.** (*mar.*) cambusa, cucina **2.** (*mar.*) cabina di poppa **3.** armadio; ripostiglio; stanzino.

cuddy³, *s.* **1.** (*scoz.*) asino (anche *fig.*) **2.** (*mec.*) leva su treppiede per sollevare pietre.

cudgel [ˈkʌdʒəl], *s.* randello; bastone ‖ *to take up the cudgels for s.o.*, assumere le difese di qlcu. ☆ — *play*, lotta con i bastoni.

to cudgel, *pass.p.p.* **cudgelled** [ˈkʌdʒəld], *v.t.* randellare, battere: *to* — *s.o. to death*, randellare qlcu. a morte ‖ *to* — *one's brains*, *fig.* lambiccarsi il cervello.

cue¹ [kjuː], *s.* cu (la lettera *q*).

cue², *s.* **1.** (*teat. mus.*) battuta d'entrata **2.** suggerimento, imbeccata: *to give s.o. the* —, dare a qlcu.

l'imbeccata; *to take one's* — *from s.o.*, prendere l'imbeccata da qlcu., seguire la politica altrui **3.** (*arc.*) umore, vena.

cue³, *s.* **1.** stecca (da biliardo) **2.** codino, treccia (di capelli) ☆ — *rack*, (*biliardo*) porta-stecche; — *-tip*, (*biliardo*) punta (di cuoio) della stecca.

cueist [ˈkjuːist], *s.* giocatore di biliardo.

cuff¹ [kʌf], *s.* polsino (di camicia) ‖ *cuffs of trousers*, (*amer.*) risvolto dei pantaloni ‖ *to speak off the* —, improvvisare un discorso ☆ — *links*, gemelli da camicia.

cuff², *s.* pugno; schiaffo.

to cuff², *v.t.i.* schiaffeggiare; percuotere; fare a pugni.

Cufic [ˈkjuːfik], *ag.* (*st.*) cufico ‖ *s.* (*st.*) alfabeto, carattere cufico.

cuirass [kwiˈræs], *s.* corazza.

cuirassier [ˌkwirəˈsiə*], *s.* corazziere.

cuish [kwiʃ], *s.* (*st.*) cosciale.

cuisine [kwiˈ(ː)ziːn], *s.* cucina; modo di cucinare.

cuisse [kwis], *s.* (*st.*) cosciale.

cul-de-sac [ˈkuldəˈsæk], *s.* vicolo cieco (anche *fig.*).

culinary [ˈkʌlinəri], *ag.* culinario.

cull [kʌl], *s.* **1.** animale vecchio eliminato da un armento **2.** *pl.* (*amer.*) residuati, scarti.

to cull, *v.t.* **1.** cogliere **2.** scegliere, selezionare.

cullender [ˈkʌlində*], *s.* colino.

cullet [ˈkʌlit], *s.* vetro di rifiuto.

cully [ˈkʌli], *s.* **1.** (*rar.*) semplicione, minchione **2.** (*sl.*) amico, compagno.

culm¹ [kʌlm], *s.* **1.** polvere di carbon fossile **2.** antracite **3.** minerale scistoso contenente filoni di antracite impura.

culm², *s.* (*bot.*) culmo.

culminant [ˈkʌlminənt], *ag.* culminante: *the* — *point*, il punto culminante.

to culminate [ˈkʌlmineit], *v.i.* **1.** (*astr.*) culminare **2.** giungere al culmine; concludersi.

culmination [ˌkʌlmiˈneiʃən], *s.* **1.** (*astr.*) culminazione **2.** culmine, apogeo: *the* — *of glory*, l'apice della gloria; *the* — *of one's hopes*, il culmine delle proprie speranze.

culottes [kjuˈ(ː)lɔts], *s.pl.* gonna-pantalone.

culpability [ˌkʌlpəˈbiliti], *s.* colpevolezza.

culpable [ˈkʌlpəbl], *ag.* colpevole: — *negligence*, negligenza colpevole; *I hold you* —, ti ritengo colpevole.

culpableness [ˈkʌlpəblnis], *s.* colpevolezza.

culpably [ˈkʌlpəbli], *av.* colpevolmente.

culprit [ˈkʌlprit], *s.* **1.** accusato, imputato **2.** colpevole.

cult [kʌlt], *s.* culto; venerazione: *to make a* — *of sthg.*, (*fam.*) aver un culto per ql.co.

cultivable [ˈkʌltivəbl], *ag.* coltivabile.

to cultivate [ˈkʌltiveit], *v.t.* **1.** coltivare; valorizzare (terreni) **2.** *fig.* coltivare: *to* — *the mind, s.o.'s acquaintance*, coltivare la mente, la conoscenza di qlcu.

cultivated [ˈkʌltiveitid], *ag.* **1.** coltivato: — *land*, terra coltivata **2.** colto, fine, educato: *a* — *man*, un uomo fine, colto; *a* — *voice*, una voce garbata.

cultivation [ˌkʌltiˈveiʃən], *s.* **1.** coltivazione **2.** *fig.* cultura; raffinatezza.

cultivator [ˈkʌltiveitə*], *s.* **1.** coltivatore **2.** cultore (delle arti, ecc.): — *of the Muses*, amico delle Muse.

cultural [ˈkʌltʃərəl], *ag.* culturale.

culture [ˈkʌltʃə*], *s.* **1.** coltura, coltivazione (del suolo) **2.** allevamento, coltura (di api, bachi, perle) **3.** cultura (della mente): *the range of his* — *was immense*, era dotato di vastissima cultura ☆ — *pearl*, perla coltivata.

to culture, *v.t.* **1.** coltivare **2.** produrre una coltura di (bacilli, ecc.).

cultured [ˈkʌltʃəd], *ag.* colto, istruito, educato: *highly* — *man*, uomo assai colto.

culturist [ˈkʌltʃərist], *s.* culturista.

cultus [ˈkʌltəs], *s.* culto; venerazione.

culver [ˈkʌlvə*], *s.* colombo, piccione.

culverin [ˈkʌlvərin], *s.* (*st. mil.*) colubrina.

culvert [ˈkʌlvət], *s.* canale, condotto sotterraneo, fogna.

cum [kʌm], *prep.* (*lat.*) con: — *dividend*, (*comm.*) con dividendo; — *laude*, con lode: *to graduate* — *laude*, laurearsi con lode.

Cumae [ˈkjuːmiː], *no.pr.* (*geog.*) Cuma.

Cumaean [kjuˈmiːən], *ag.s.* cumano.

cumber [ˈkʌmbə*], *s.* **1.** ostacolo **2.** imbarazzo.

to cumber, *v.t.* **1.** ingombrare; ostacolare: *to* — *s.o. with parcels*, caricare qlcu. di pacchi **2.** imbarazzare.

cumbersome [ˈkʌmbəsəm], *ag.* ingombrante, incomodo.

cumbersomeness [ˈkʌmbəsəmnis], *s.* incomodità, ingombro.

Cumbrian [ˈkʌmbriən], *ag.s.c.* (abitante) del Cumberland ‖ *the* — *Mountains*, (*geog.*) i monti Cambrici.

cumbrous [ˈkʌmbrəs], *ag.* ingombrante, incomodo.

cumbrously [ˈkʌmbrəsli], *av.* in modo incomodo, ingombrante.

cumbrousness [ˈkʌmbrəsnis], *V.* **cumbersomeness.**

cumin [ˈkʌmin], *s.* (*bot.*) comino.

cummer [ˈkʌmə*], *s.* (*scoz.*) comare.

cummerbund [ˈkʌməbʌnd], *s.* (*ang.-in.*) sciarpa portata come cintura.

cumquat [ˈkʌmkwɔt], *s.* arancio nano giapponese.

cumshaw [ˈkʌmʃɔː], *s.* (*sl. orientale*) regalia, mancia.

cumulate [ˈkjuːmjulit], *ag.* accumulato, ammassato.

to cumulate, *v.t.i.* accumulare, accumularsi; ammassare, ammassarsi.

cumulative [ˈkjuːmjulətiv], *ag.* cumulativo.

cumulatively [ˈkjuːmjulətivli], *av.* cumulativamente.

cumulus [ˈkjuːmjuləs], *pl.* **cumuli** [ˈkjuːmjulai], *s.* **1.** cumulo **2.** cumulo, ammasso di nubi.

cunetator [kʌŋkˈteitə*], *s.* temporeggiatore.

cuneate [ˈkjuːniit], *ag.* cuneato.

cuneiform [ˈkjuːniifɔːm], *ag.* cuneiforme.

cunette [kjuˈnet], *s.* (*mil.*) cunetta (di trincea).

cunning [ˈkʌniŋ], *ag.* **1.** astuto, furbo; (*arc.*) abile **2.** (*amer.*) grazioso, delicato (di bambino, cagnolino) ‖ *s.* astuzia, furberia, accortezza; (*arc.*) abilità.

cunningly [ˈkʌniŋli], *av.* astutamente; abilmente.

cup [kʌp], *s.* **1.** tazza: — *and saucer*, tazza con piattino **2.** contenuto di una tazza: — *of tea*, una tazza di tè; (*amer.*) mezza pinta ‖ *the* — *is full*, la misura è colma ‖ *over one's cups*, mentre si beve ‖ *that is another* — *of tea*, (*fam.*) questo è un altro paio di maniche ‖ *that is my* — *of tea*, (*fam.*) questo è proprio quello che fa per me, che mi ci vuole ‖ *to be in one's cups*, essere un po' brillo **3.** (*eccl.*) calice; *fig.* calice, coppa: *the bitter* — *of life*, l'amaro calice della vita **4.** (*spor.*) coppa, trofeo **5.** (*bot.*) calice **6.** (*mec.*) coppa, scodellino, ghiera conica **7.** (*chir.*) coppetta ☆ — *-ball joint*, articolazione a rotelle; — *-bearer*, coppiere; — *-final*, finale di coppa, campionato ‖ *cider-* —, bevanda calda, gelata a base di sidro; *claret-* —, bevanda dolce a base di limone e vino rosso; *tea-* —, tazza da tè.

to cup, *pass.p.p.* **cupped** [kʌpt], *v.t.* **1.** (*chir.*) applicare coppette, ventose a **2.** far conca (con le mani) a: *with his chin cupped in his hand*, col mento appoggiato al cavo della mano; *to* — *one's hand round one's mouth, behind one's ear*, tenere la mano intorno alla bocca, dietro l'orecchio **3.** (*tec.*) rendere convesso, imbutire.

cupboard [ˈkʌbəd], *s.* credenza, armadio ‖ *skeleton in the* —, onta segreta di famiglia ☆ — *love*, amore interessato.

cupel [ˈkjuːpəl], *s.* (*metal.*) coppella.

to cupel, *v.t.* (*metal.*) coppellare.

cupellation [ˌkjuːpəˈleiʃən], *s.* (*metal.*) coppellazione.

cupful [ˈkʌpful], *s.* **1.** il contenuto di una tazza; tazza piena **2.** (*amer.*) mezza pinta.

Cupid [ˈkjuːpid], *no.pr.m.* (*mit.*) Cupido.

cupidity [kjuˈ(ː)piditi], *s.* cupidità, cupidigia.

cupola [ˈkjuːpələ], *s.* **1.** (*arch.*) cupola **2.** (*mar.*) torretta girevole **3.** — *(-furnace)*, (*metal.*) cubilotto.

cupping [ˈkʌpiŋ], *s.* (*chir.*) applicazione delle coppette ☆ — *glass*, coppetta di vetro.

cuprammonium [ˌkjuːprəˈmounjəm], *s.* (*chim.*) cuproammonio.

cupreous [ˈkjuːpriəs], *ag.* cupreo.

cupric [ˈkjuːprik], *ag.* (*chim.*) cuprico, ramico.

cupriferous [kjuˈ(ː)prifərəs], *ag.* cuprifero.

cuprite [ˈkjuːprait], *s.* (*min.*) cuprite.

cuproxide [kjuˈprɔksaid], *s.* (*chim.*) ossido di rame.

cupule [ˈkjuːpjuːl], *s.* (*bot.*) cupola.

cur [kəˑ*], *s.* **1.** cagnaccio **2.** mascalzone, screanzato; codardo.

curability [ˌkjuərəˈbiliti], *s.* curabilità.

curable [ˈkjuərəbl], *ag.* curabile.

Curaçao [ˌkjuərəˈsou], **Curaçoa** [ˌkjuərəˈsouə], *no. pr.* (*geog.*) Curaçao ‖ **curaçao, curaçoa,** *s.* « curaçao ».

curacy [ˈkjuərəsi], *s.* (*eccl.*) **1.** vicariato, cura **2.** benefici inerenti a un vicariato.

curare [kjuˈrɑːri], *s.* (*chim. farm.*) curaro.

to curarize [ˈkjuːrəraiz], *v.t.* somministrare curaro a.

curate [ˈkjuərit], *s.* **1.** (*eccl.*) curato, coadiutore **2.** (*scherz.*) piccolo attizzatoio.

curative [ˈkjuərətiv], *ag.* curativo.

curator [kjuəˈreitə*], *s.* **1.** direttore (di museo, istituzione universitaria, ecc.) **2.** (*dir.*) tutore (di minore); curatore (di incapace, fallito).

curatorship [kjuəˈreitəʃip], *s.* **1.** direzione (di museo, istituzione universitaria, ecc.) **2.** (*dir.*) tutela, curatela.

curatrix [kjuəˈreitriks], *s.* **1.** direttrice (di museo, istituzione universitaria, ecc.) **2.** (*dir.*) tutrice (di minore); curatrice (di incapace, fallito).

curb [kəˑb], *s.* **1.** barbazzale **2.** *fig.* freno: *to put a* — *on one's passions*, (*fam.*) porre un freno alle proprie passioni **3.** cordone di marciapiede, di strada **4.** (*amer.*) borsa **5.** (*vet.*) corba ☆ — *-bit*, morso della briglia; — *-chain*, barbazzale; — *-market*, (*amer.*) piccola borsa (mercato libero di titoli a New York); — *-roof*, tetto a mansarda.

to curb, *v.t.* **1.** mettere il morso a, frenare (un cavallo) **2.** *fig.* frenare; dominare; reprimere.

curcuma [ˈkəˑkjuːmə], *s.* (*bot.*) curcuma.

curd [kəˑd], *s.* giuncata, quagliata ☆ *soap curds*, grumi di sapone.

to curdle [ˈkəˑdl], *v.t.i.* **1.** cagliare; coagulare, coagularsi **2.** *fig.* agghiacciare, agghiacciarsi: *my blood curdled at the horrible sight*, mi si agghiacciò il sangue alla terribile vista.

curdy [ˈkəˑdi], *ag.* cagliato; coagulato.

cure¹ [kjuə*], *s.* **1.** cura: *to take a* —, fare una cura **2.** guarigione: *to effect a* —, operare una guarigione **3.** rimedio ‖ *the* — *is worse than the evil*, il rimedio è peggiore del male **4.** (*eccl.*) cura: — *of souls*, cura di anime **5.** vulcanizzazione (della gomma) ☆ — *-all*, panacea ‖ *cold-water* —, cura d'acqua fredda; *grape-* —, cura dell'uva; *rest-* —, cura di riposo.

to cure¹, *v.t.i.* **1.** curare; guarire; sanare: *to* — *a headache*, guarire un mal di testa; *to* — *s.o. of an illness*, guarire qlcu. di una malattia **2.** rimediare a: *to* — *an evil*, rimediare a un male **3.** salare; affumicare (carne, pesce) **4.** vulcanizzare (gomma), vulcanizzarsi.

cure², *s.c.* (*sl.*) persona strana, buffa.

cureless [ˈkjuəlis], *ag.* incurabile.

curer [ˈkjuərə*], *s.* **1.** guaritore **2.** salatore di cibi.

curette [kjuəˈret], *s.* (*chir.*) raschiatoio.

to curette, *v.t.i.* (*chir.*) eseguire un raschiamento (a).

curfew [ˈkəˑfjuː], *s.* coprifuoco: *to ring the* —, dare il segnale del coprifuoco ☆ — *-bell*, campana della sera.

curia [ˈkjuəriə], *s.* **1.** corte papale **2.** (*st. romana*) curia, senato **3.** (*st.*) corte di giustizia.

curial ['kjuəriəl], *ag.* curiale.

curialism ['kjuəriəlizəm], *s.* curialismo.

curie ['kjuəri], *s.* (*fis.*) curie ☆ — -*therapy*, (*med.*) curie terapia, radioterapia.

curing ['kjuəriŋ], *s.* **1.** guarigione **2.** conservazione di cibi **3.** vulcanizzazione.

curio ['kjuəriou], *pl.* **curios** ['kjuəriouz], *s.* curiosità; rarità; oggetto da collezione ☆ — -*dealer*, commerciante in oggetti rari; — *hunter*, collezionista di oggetti rari.

curiosity [,kjuəri'ɔsiti], *s.* **1.** curiosità; desiderio di sapere: *from* (o *out of*) —, per curiosità; *to burn with* (o *to die of*) —, ardere, morire dalla curiosità; *to satisfy one's* —, soddisfare la propria curiosità **2.** curiosità; oggetto raro, antico ☆ (*old*) — *shop*, bottega d'antiquario.

curious ['kjuəriəs], *ag.* **1.** curioso; desideroso di sapere: *I am* — *to know him*, sono curioso di conoscerlo **2.** curioso, strano, singolare: *a* — *mistake*, uno sbaglio strano; *a* — *object*, un oggetto singolare; *it is a* — *thing that*, è strano che **3.** *fig.* (*rar.*) diligente, minuzioso, scrupoloso **4.** erotico, pornografico.

curiously ['kjuəriəsli], *av.* **1.** curiosamente **2.** stranamente, singolarmente: — *enough*, strano a dirsi.

curiousness ['kjuəriəsnis], *s.* singolarità, stranezza.

curium ['kjuəriəm], *s.* (*chim.*) curio.

curl [kə:l], *s.* **1.** riccio, ricciolo: *how do you keep your hair in* —?, come fai a tenerti arricciati i capelli?; *to wear curls*, portare, avere i riccioli **2.** curva; ondulazione; voluta, spirale: — *of the lips*, smorfia di sdegno; — *of smoke from a cigarette*, spirale di fumo da una sigaretta **3.** malattia delle patate ☆ — -*paper*, diavoletto, bigodino di carta.

to curl, *v.t.i.* **1.** arricciare, arricciarsi: *to have one's hair curled*, farsi arricciare i capelli **2.** torcere, torcersi: *to* — *one's lips*, torcere le labbra **3.** sollevarsi in spire: *the smoke curls up(wards)*, il fumo si leva in spire **4.** (*sl.*) afflosciarsi **5.** giocare a «curling» **6.** *to* — *up*, corrugarsi, incresparsi, arricciarsi; raggomitolarsi: *to* — (*oneself*) *up in bed*, raggomitolarsi nel letto.

curler [kə:lə*], *s.* **1.** bigodino; ferro per arricciare i capelli **2.** giocatore di «curling».

curlew ['kə:lju:], *s.* (*ornit.*) chiurlo.

curliness ['kə:linis], *s.* arricciatura; ondulazione.

curling ['kə:liŋ], *s.* **1.** arricciatura (specialmente di capelli) **2.** «curling» (giuoco di bocce sul ghiaccio) ☆ — -*iron* (o — -*tongs*), ferro per arricciare; — -*pin*, forcina per arricciare.

curly ['kə:li], *ag.* ricciuto, riccio; a spirale; sinuoso ☆ — -*headed*, dalla testa ricciuta.

curmudgeon [kə:'mʌdʒən], *s.* bisbetico; spilorcio.

currach, curragh[1] ['kʌrə], *V.* **coracle.**

curragh[2], *s.* (*irl.*) terreno paludoso ‖ *the Curragh*, grande pianura del Kildare con campi di corse.

currant ['kʌrənt], *s.* **1.** uva passa di Corinto, sultanina **2.** ribes ☆ — -*bread*, pane con l'uva; *red* — *jelly*, gelatina di ribes rosso.

currency ['kʌrənsi], *s.* **1.** (*comm.*) circolazione monetaria; moneta legale, corrente; divisa, valuta: — *of a bill of exchange*, decorrenza di una cambiale; *payable in* —, pagabile in moneta corrente **2.** circolazione, corso; voga; credito: *to gain* —, accreditarsi (di un'idea); *to give* — *to a rumour*, mettere in circolazione una voce ☆ — *adjustment*, conguaglio monetario; — *note*, biglietto di banca ‖ *foreign* —, divisa estera; *gold* —, valuta aurea circolante; *legal* (*tender*) —, moneta legale corrente; *paper* —, valuta cartacea circolante.

current ['kʌrənt], *ag.* corrente (anche *comm.*): — *opinions*, opinioni correnti; — *word*, parola corrente; *the* — *year*, *reign*, *issue* (*of a periodical*), l'anno corrente, il regno attuale, il presente numero (di periodico); *to be* (o *to pass* o *to run*) —, aver corso, essere generalmente ammesso o valido.

current, *s.* **1.** corrente (anche *fig.*): *the* — *of events*, il corso degli avvenimenti: *a strong* — *of air*, una forte corrente d'aria; *he was swept away by the* —,

fu travolto dalla corrente; *to drift with the* —, lasciarsi portare dalla corrente; *to go against the* —, andare contro corrente **2.** (*elett.*) corrente.

current, (*nei composti*): — *account* (o *account* —), (*comm.*) conto corrente; — *coin*, moneta corrente; — *hand-writing*, scrittura in corsivo; — *price*, prezzo corrente ‖ *alternating* —, (*elett.*) corrente alternata; *direct* —, (*elett.*) corrente continua; *displacement* —, corrente di spostamento; *electric* —, corrente elettrica.

currently ['kʌrəntli], *av.* **1.** comunemente, generalmente: *it is* — *thought that*, generalmente si pensa che **2.** (*amer.*) attualmente, al presente: — *he is working with*, al presente lavora con.

curricle ['karikl], *s.* calessino.

curriculum [kə'rikjuləm], *pl.* **curricula** [kə'rikjulə], *s.* curriculum; corso, programma (di studi).

currier ['kʌriə*], *s.* conciatore.

currish ['kə:riʃ], *ag.* **1.** ringhioso, litigioso, brusco **2.** basso, ignobile, volgare; vile.

currishly ['kə:riʃli], *av.* bassamente, ignobilmente.

currishness ['kə:riʃnis], *s.* bassezza, volgarità.

curry[1] ['kʌri], *s.* (*cuc.*) « curry » (piatto di origine indiana) ☆ — -*powder*, polvere di radice di curcuma.

to curry[1], *v.t.* insaporire con la polvere di curcuma: *curried eggs*, uova alla curcuma, uova all'indiana.

to curry[2], *v.t.* **1.** strigliare **2.** conciare (cuoio) **3.** (*arc.*) adulare interessatamente: *to* — *favour with s.o.*, cercare di accattivarsi il favore di qlcu. con lusinghe.

curry-comb ['kʌri-koum], *s.* striglia.

curse [kə:s], *s.* **1.** maledizione, anatema; imprecazione, bestemmia: *to be under a* —, essere sotto il peso di una maledizione; *to call down curses upon s.o.*, lanciare, far ricadere maledizioni su qlcu.; *to utter a* —, bestemmiare ‖ *a* — *upon him!*, sia maledetto!; *maledizione a lui!* ‖ *not worth a* —, (*fam.*) non vale un fico secco ‖ *curses come home to roost*, le maledizioni ricadono su chi le lancia ‖ *I don't care* (o *give*) *a* — *for*, (*fam.*) non me ne importa un bel niente di **2.** disgrazia, sventura, calamità: *gambling is a* —, il giuoco d'azzardo è un malanno; *he is a* — *to his family*, è una disgrazia per la sua famiglia; *rabbits are a* — *in that country*, i conigli sono una calamità in quel paese ‖ — *of Scotland*, (*giuoco*) nove di quadri.

to curse, *v.t.i.* **1.** maledire: *cursed be he*, che egli sia maledetto; *to* — *the day one was born*, maledire il giorno della nascita di qlcu. **2.** scomunicare **3.** bestemmiare; imprecare: *he cursed loudly*, imprecò ad alta voce ‖ — (*it*)!, maledizione! **4.** affliggere: *he is cursed with a violent temper*, è afflitto da un carattere violento.

cursed ['kə:sid], *ag.* maledetto: *a* — *nuisance*, (*fam.*) una maledetta seccatura; *this* — *weather*, (*fam.*) questo tempo maledetto.

cursedly ['kə:sidli], *av.* (*fam.*) maledettamente.

cursedness ['kə:sidnis], *s.* **1.** maledizione **2.** (*fam.*) contrarietà: *the* — *of things*, la contrarietà delle cose.

cursive ['kə:siv], *ag.s.* corsivo (di calligrafia).

cursorial [kə:'sɔ:riəl], *ag.* atto a correre.

cursorily ['kə:sərili], *av.* rapidamente; superficialmente.

cursoriness ['kə:sərinis], *s.* rapidità; superficialità.

cursory ['kə:səri], *ag.* rapido, affrettato; superficiale ‖ *at a* — *glance*, a prima vista.

curst [kə:st], *pass. p.p.* (*arc.*) di to **curse.**

curt [kə:t], *ag.* brusco; secco; conciso: *a* — *answer*, una risposta secca; *to give s.o. a* — *reception*, ricevere qlcu. sgarbatamente.

to curtail [kə:'teil], *v.t.* **1.** accorciare, abbreviare (scritto, discorso); tagliare, troncare (opera, articolo) **2.** diminuire, limitare (autorità); privare: *to* — *s.o. of his privileges*, privare qlcu. dei suoi privilegi **3.** ridurre, limitare (le spese).

curtailment [kə:'teilmənt], *s.* **1.** raccorciamento, abbreviazione, riduzione (di libro, ecc.) **2.** diminuzione, limitazione (d'autorità); riduzione, restrizione (di spese).

curtail-step [kə:'teilstep], *s.* (*arch.*) gradino d'invito (primo gradino di una scala con gli orli arrotondati).

curtain ['kə:tn], *s.* **1.** tenda, tendina, cortina: *to draw the* —, tirare, aprire la tenda ‖ *to draw a* — *over sthg.*, *fig.* stendere un velo su ql.co. ‖ *to lift the* —, svelare **2.** (*teat.*) sipario, telone: *behind the* —, fra le quinte (anche *fig.*); *the* — *rises, falls* (o *drops*), il sipario si alza, cala ‖ —*!*, sipario! **3.** cortina: — *of fire, mist, smoke,* cortina di fuoco, nebbia, fumo **4.** (*arch.*) parete divisoria ☆ — -*call*, chiamata alla ribalta: *to take three* — -*calls*, essere chiamato tre volte alla ribalta; — -*fire*, cortina, barriera di fuoco; — -*lecture*, ramanzina a quattr'occhi; — -*raiser*, farsa, commediola d'apertura ‖ *bamboo* —, (*neol. pol.*) cortina di bambù; *fireproof* — (o *safety-* —), sipario (metallico) di sicurezza antincendio; *iron* —, (*pol.*) cortina di ferro.

to curtain, *v.t.* **1.** coprire, ornare con tende ‖ *to* — *off*, separare con tende **2.** *fig.* nascondere, velare.

curtilage ['kə:tilidʒ], *s.* (*dir. dial.*) cortile.

curtly ['kə:tli], *av.* brevemente; bruscamente.

curtness ['kə:tnis], *s.* asprezza (di parole); tono brusco; modi scortesi.

curts(e)y ['kə:tsi], *s.* riverenza, inchino (di donna): *to make* (o *to drop*) *a* —, fare un inchino, una riverenza; *to make one's* — *to s.o.*, fare la riverenza a qlcu. (specialmente a corte).

to curts(e)y, *v.i.* inchinarsi, fare una riverenza, un inchino: *she curtsied to the queen,* ella fece la riverenza, si inchinò alla regina.

curule ['kjuəru:l], *ag.* (*st. romana*) curule: — *chair,* sedia curule.

curvaceous [kə:'veiʃəs], *ag.* (*fam.*) curvilineo: *a* — *woman,* una donna tutta curve.

curvature ['kə:vətʃə*], *s.* curvatura; incurvamento: — *of the spine,* curvatura della spina dorsale.

curve [kə:v], *s.* **1.** curva, svolta: *banked* —, curva sopraelevata; *blind* —, (*amer.*) curva cieca; *dangerous* —, curva pericolosa **2.** diagramma **3.** (*elett. mat. fis. rad., ecc.*) curva.

to curve, *v.t.i.* curvare, curvarsi; piegare, piegarsi; descrivere una curva; svoltare (di strada).

curvet [kə:'vet], *s.* (*equitazione*) falcata, salto.

to curvet, *pass.p.p.* **curvetted** [kə:'vetid], *v.i.* (*equitazione*) fare una falcata.

curvilinear [,kə:vi'liniə*], *ag.* curvilineo.

curving ['kə:viŋ], *s.* curva, curvatura.

cuscus[1] ['kʌskʌs], *s.* (*zool.*) cusco.

cuscus[2], *s.* (*bot.*) radice aromatica di erba indiana.

cushat ['kʌʃət], *s.* (*ornit. dial. scoz.*) palombella.

cushion ['kuʃən], *s.* **1.** cuscino (da divano, ecc.) **2.** cuscinetto; imbottitura (di sponda di biliardo) ☆ — *space,* (*mec.*) cuscino (di vapore, aria); — -*tire,* (*aut.*) copertone semipneumatico.

to cushion, *v.t.* **1.** munire di cuscini, imbottire: *cushioned seat,* sedile imbottito **2.** (*biliardo*) mettere (la palla) vicino alla sponda **3.** (*mec.*) ammortizzare **4.** *fig.* soffocare (proteste, ecc.).

cushiony ['kuʃəni], *ag.* morbido; comodo.

cushy ['kuʃi], *ag.* (*sl.*) facile; comodo; piacevole: *a* — *job,* un impiego non impegnativo, facile.

cusp [kʌsp], *s.* **1.** (*geom.*) vertice, punta **2.** (*anat. arch.*) cuspide **3.** (*astr.*) corno di luna crescente.

cuspidal ['kʌspidəl], *ag.* (*arch.*) cuspidale.

cuspidate ['kʌspidit], **cuspidated** ['kʌspideitid], *ag.* (*bot. anat.*) cuspidato.

cuspidor(e) ['kʌspidə:*], *s.* (*amer.*) sputacchiera.

cuss [kʌs], *s.* **1.** (*sl. amer.*) maledizione ‖ *I don't care a* —, non m'importa un fico secco **2.** (*sl.*) tipo, individuo: *a queer old* —, uno strano tipo.

cussed ['kʌsid], *ag.* (*sl.*) **1.** maledetto **2.** ostinato.

cussedly ['kʌsidli], *av.* (*sl.*) **1.** maledettamente **2.** ostinatamente.

cussedness ['kʌsidnis], *s.* (*sl.*) perversità: *out of sheer* —, per puro spirito di malvagità.

custard ['kʌstəd], *s.* crema (di uova e latte) ☆ — -*apple,* (*bot.*) anona.

custodial [kʌs'toudjəl], *ag.* di custode, di guardiano.

custodian [kʌs'toudjən], **custodier** [kʌs'toudiə*], *s.c.* custode; guardiano, guardiana.

custody ['kʌstədi], *s.* **1.** custodia, vigilanza, cura: *in safe* —, sotto buona guardia, in luogo sicuro; *to grant* — *of a child to the mother,* affidare alla madre la custodia del figlio **2.** imprigionamento, arresto, detenzione: *to take s.o. into* —, arrestare qlcu.

custom ['kʌstəm], *s.* **1.** costume, consuetudine, abitudine, usanza: *the customs of a country,* le usanze di un paese; *according to* —, secondo le usanze; *it is a* — *with him to go,* è sua abitudine andare **2.** (*dir.*) diritto consuetudinario **3.** *pl.* dogana: *to clear one's luggage through the customs,* sdoganare i propri bagagli; *to pass* (o *to get through*) *the customs,* passare la dogana ‖ *International Customs Pass,* (*aut.*) trittico doganale **4.** (*comm.*) clientela: *we shall lose all our* —, perderemo tutta la nostra clientela ☆ — -*built,* (*amer.*) fuori serie, speciale: — -*built body,* (*aut.*) carrozzeria fuori serie; *customs duties,* dazio doganale; — -*house,* dogana: — -*house officer,* doganiere; — -*tailored suit,* abito su misura; — *tariff,* — *union,* tariffa, unione doganale.

customable ['kʌstəməbl], *ag.* soggetto a dogana.

customarily ['kʌstəmərili], *av.* abitualmente; solitamente; secondo le usanze.

customariness ['kʌstəmərinis], *s.* abitudine.

customary ['kʌstəməri], *ag.* abituale, d'uso comune, solito: *as is* —, come è d'uso; *splendour* — *to such occasions,* splendore abituale in tali occasioni ‖ *s.* raccolta delle consuetudini (di un luogo) ☆ — *law,* (*dir.*) diritto consuetudinario.

customer ['kʌstəmə*], *s.c.* (*comm.*) cliente; avventore ‖ *s.* (*sl.*) individuo, tipo: *queer, rum* —, tipo strano, curioso.

cut[1] [kʌt], *s.* **1.** taglio, ferita; colpo (di coltello, spada); sferzata; incisione: — *across the cheek,* sfregio alla guancia; *a* — *in one's finger,* una ferita al dito; *the surgeon made a small* — *in the finger,* il chirurgo fece una piccola incisione nel dito **2.** riduzione, taglio: *a* — *in prices,* una riduzione nei prezzi; *several cuts were made in that play,* furono fatti parecchi tagli a quella commedia **3.** taglio (di carne, stoffa): *a nice* — *of meat,* un bel pezzo di carne **4.** taglio, linea (di abito, capelli, pietra preziosa) **5.** (*danza*) sforbiciata **6.** (*spor.*) colpo secco, tagliato (a tennis, cricket) **7.** (*terr.*) strada scavata **8.** taglio, alzata (di mazzo di carte) **9.** (*tip.*) illustrazione, vignetta; incisione ‖ *see* —, vedi illustrazione **10.** (*mec. metal.*) taglio; intaglio, tacca: *rough* —, grosso taglio **11.** *fig.* osservazione, critica: *that was a* — *at me,* quello fu un attacco contro di me **12.** *to be a* — *above s.o.,* essere superiore a qlcu.: *she was a* — *above the other girls,* era di un livello sociale superiore alle altre ragazze ‖ *to give s.o. the* — *direct,* passare accanto a qlcu. fingendo di non riconoscerlo.

to cut[1], *pass.p.p.* **cut,** *v.t.i.* **1.** tagliare, tagliarsi: *cloth that cuts easily,* stoffa che si taglia facilmente; *knife that cuts like a razor,* coltello che taglia come un rasoio: *the wind* — *his face, fig.* il vento gli tagliava la faccia; *to* — *the hay,* tagliare il fieno; *to* — *in half, two, three, etc.,* tagliare a metà, in due, tre, ecc.; *to* — *in(to) pieces,* tagliare a pezzi; *to* — *into a tumor,* incidere un tumore; *to* — *one's finger,* tagliarsi un dito; *to* — *one's nails,* tagliarsi le unghie; *to* — *to pieces,* fare a pezzi: *to* — *an army to pieces,* decimare un esercito; *to* — *a play to pieces, fig.* demolire un lavoro teatrale; *to* — *the wedding cake,* tagliare la torta nuziale; *to have one's hair* —, farsi tagliare i capelli ‖ *to* — *it!,* scappa!, piantala! ‖ — *your kidding!,* basta con queste sciocchezze! ‖ *that cuts both ways,* (*fam.*) è un'arma a doppio taglio ‖ *this remark* — *him to the quick,* questa osservazione lo punse sul vivo ‖ *to* — *and come again,* (*fam.*) servirsi a sazietà ‖ *to* — *and run,* (*fam.*) darsela a gambe ‖ *to*

— *a caper* (o *capers*), fare capriole per la gioia; *to —
capers*, *fig.* giocare dei tiri; comportarsi in modo irresponsabile ‖ *to — a connection* (*with s.o.*), rompere
i rapporti (con qlcu.) ‖ *to — a dash* (o *a figure*), fare
un figurone ‖ *to — s.o., sthg. free*, liberare qlcu., ql.-
co. ‖ *to — the Gordian knot*, *fig.* tagliare il nodo gordiano ‖ *to — it fine*, riuscire, farcela per un pelo (a
fare ql.co.) ‖ *to — loose*, (*amer.*) emanciparsi: *to —
oneself loose from sthg.*, liberarsi da ql.co.; *to — sthg.
loose*, liberare ql.co. (tagliando fune, ecc.) ‖ *to — no
ice*, (*fam.*) fare poco effetto ‖ *to — sthg. open*, aprire
ql.co. ‖ *to — a person dead*, fingere di non vedere
una persona ‖ *to — a poor figure*, fare una brutta figura ‖ *to — the record*, (*spor.*) stabilire un nuovo primato ‖ *to — s.o. short*, interrompere qlcu.; *to —
*(*sthg.*) *short*, tagliare corto, accorciare (discorso, ecc.) ‖
to — through sthg., fendere ql.co., passare attraverso
ql.co.: *I — my way through the crowd*, mi feci strada tra la
folla ‖ *to — to the heart*, ferire al cuore ‖ *to — a tooth*,
mettere un dente: *the baby is cutting its teeth*, il bambino sta mettendo i denti ‖ *to — the whole concern*,
rinunciare all'affare ‖ *to — one's coat according to one's
cloth*, *prov.* fare il passo secondo la gamba **2.** (*comm.*)
ridurre: *to — losses*, ridurre le perdite; *to — prices
close*, ridurre i prezzi al minimo **3.** intagliare (vetro);
scolpire (caratteri su metalli, pietra); filettare (una
vite); (*amer.*) incidere (su disco, nastro) **4.** praticare
(un'apertura); scavare (un canale); (*miner.*) perforare: *to
— an opening in a wall*, praticare un'apertura in un
muro **5.** tagliare il mazzo (a carte) **6.** (*spor.*) tagliare (la palla, al tennis, cricket) **7.** urtarsi (di zampe
di cavallo) **8.** (*danza*) sforbiciare **9.** castrare **10.** *to
— about*, mutilare, rovinare, sfregiare (manoscritto,
statua, viso) **11.** *to — across*, tagliare di traverso;
andare di traverso: *this cuts across all my principles*,
questo va contro i miei principi **12.** *to — asunder*,
tagliare in due **13.** *to — away*, troncare, tagliare,
recidere; andarsene, svignarsela: *— away that loose
branch*, taglia quel ramo penzolante **14.** *to — back*,
(*comm.*) ridurre, interrompere (ordinazioni); (*cine.*)
ritornare al passato **15.** *to — down*, abbattere; tagliare,
recidere; (*mil.*) sterminare; ridurre (spese, costi, produzione); diminuire; accorciare, ridurre (abiti, discorsi,
opere, ecc.) **16.** *to — in*, entrare, rientrare (a carte);
intervenire (nella conversazione, ecc.); tagliare la strada **17.** *to — off*, tagliare; tagliar fuori; far cessare, interrompere; diseredare; (*sl.*) svignarsela, ritirarsi: *to
— off the enemy*, tagliar fuori il nemico; *to — off negotiation*, interrompere i negoziati; *to — off s.o.'s head*,
tagliar la testa a qlcu.; *to — off s.o.'s supplies*, tagliare i viveri a qlcu.; *to — oneself off from the world*,
ritirarsi dal mondo; *to be — off in the prime of life*,
essere stroncato nel fiore degli anni ‖ *to — s.o. off
with a shilling*, diseredare qlcu. **18.** *to — out*, ritagliare; intagliare; (*fam.*) superare, soppiantare; soffiare
il posto, l'impiego a; eliminare, sopprimere: *to —
out smoking*, cessare di fumare; *to — out details*, eliminare, ridurre i particolari; *to be — out for sthg.*, essere tagliato, portato per ql.co.: *he is — out for a
teacher*, ha la vocazione dell'insegnante; *to have one's
work — out*, aver lavoro a sufficienza, avere un compito difficile **19.** *to — up*, trinciare (pollo); sradicare
(alberi); rovinare (strada); far a pezzi (esercito, ecc.);
criticare aspramente ‖ *to — up well*, (*fam.*) lasciare
una grande sostanza in eredità ‖ *to — up rough*, arrabbiarsi: *he — up very rough about it*, ha preso la cosa
molto male ‖ *to be very — up by sthg.*, essere profondamente ferito da ql.co.

cut[1], (*nei composti*): — *-back*, (*cine.*) ritorno del-
l'azione ad un'epoca anteriore; (*comm.*) diminuzione,
riduzione (di ordinazioni); — *-in*, (*cine.*) sottotitolo,
scena di collegamento; (*elett.*) congiuntura ‖ *hair- —*,
taglio di capelli: *hair- — and shave*, barba e capelli;
prime —, pezzo (di carne) di prima scelta, primo taglio;
short- —, scorciatoia; *wage cuts*, riduzione dei salari.

cut[2], *s.*: *to draw cuts*, tirare a sorte.

cutaneous [kju(:)'teinjəs], *ag.* cutaneo.

cut-away ['kʌtəwei], *ag.* sezionato ‖ *s.* giacca del
tight ☆ — *drawing*, disegno a sezione verticale,
spaccato.

cutchery ['kʌtʃəri], **cutcherry** [kʌ'tʃeri], *s.* (*ang.-
in.*) **1.** tribunale **2.** ufficio.

cute [kju:t], *ag.* (*fam.*) **1.** abile, svelto, ingegnoso **2.** (*amer.*) attraente, grazioso.

cutely ['kju:tli], *av.* (*fam.*) abilmente, ingegnosamente.

cuteness ['kju:tnis], *s.* (*fam.*) abilità, ingegnosità;
intelligenza.

cuthbert ['kʌθbət], *s.* (*mil.*) imboscato.

cuticle ['kju:tikl], *s.* **1.** (*anat.*) cuticola, epidermide **2.** (*bot.*) cuticola, pellicola.

cuticular [kju(:)'tikjulə*], *ag.* cuticolare.

cutie ['kju:ti], *s.* (*sl. amer.*) ragazza elegante.

cutis ['kju:tis], *s.* (*anat.*) cute.

cutlass ['kʌtləs], *s.* (*gener. mar.*) corta sciabola.

cutler ['kʌtlə*], *s.* coltellinaio.

cutlery ['kʌtləri], *s.* **1.** mestiere del coltellinaio **2.** po-
sateria.

cutlet ['kʌtlit], *s.* costoletta.

cut-off ['kʌtɔ:f], *s.* **1.** (*amer.*) scorciatoia **2.** ritaglio
(di giornale) **3.** (*mec.*) otturatore, chiusura dell'ammissione **4.** (*cine.*) paravento di sicurezza (di proiettore) ☆ — *frequency*, (*rad.*) frequenza di interdizione,
frequenza di taglio; — *lever*, (*mec. aer.*) leva di
arresto.

cut-out ['kʌtaut], *s.* **1.** taglio (parte soppressa di
un'opera teatrale, ecc.); ritaglio (di film) **2.** (*elett.*) interruttore **3.** (*aut.*) valvola di scappamento libero.

cutpurse ['kʌtpə:s], *s.* tagliaborse, borsaiuolo.

cutter[1] ['kʌtə*], *s.* **1.** tagliatore (di abiti, gemme,
ecc.) **2.** (*mec.*) fresa ☆ *angular —*, fresa ad angolo;
concave —, fresa concava; *convex —*, fresa convessa;
dished —, coltello circolare; *facing —*, fresa a spianare; coltello; *shaving —*, coltello sbarbatore.

cutter[2], *s.* **1.** (*mar.*) •*cutter*• (canotto a vela, con un
albero e chiglia a coltello) **2.** (*amer. mar.*) lancia armata **3.** (*amer.*) slitta leggera trascinata da un cavallo
☆ *revenue —*, nave guardacoste.

cut-throat ['kʌtθrout], *ag.* accanito, spietato: —
competition, concorrenza accanita ‖ *s.* assassino; taglia-
gole.

cutting ['kʌtiŋ], *ag.* tagliente; *fig.* sferzante; pungente, mordace: — *irony*, ironia pungente; — *word*, parola mordace ‖ *s.* **1.** taglio; incisione **2.** ritaglio (di carta,
giornale); truciolo **3.** trincea (di strada, ferrovia) **4.** (*ind.
tessile*) cimatura **5.** (*comm.*) riduzione: — *of prices, wages*,
riduzione dei prezzi, dei salari **6.** (*chim.*) separazione **7.** (*agr.*) talea ☆ — *edge*, filo di lama ‖ *hair —*,
taglio dei capelli.

cuttle ['kʌtl], *s.*: — (*fish*), (*zool.*) seppia ☆ — *-bone*,
osso di seppia.

cutty ['kʌti], *ag.* corto, accorciato ‖ *s.* **1.** corta pipa
di terracotta **2.** (*scherz.*) ragazza capricciosa.

cutwater ['kʌt,wo:tə*], *s.* **1.** sprone (di ponte) **2.** (*mar.*)
tagliamare.

cutworm ['kʌtwə:m], *s.* (*entom.*) agrotide.

cyanamide ['saiənəmaid], *s.* (*chim.*) cianamide.

cyanate ['saiəneit], *s.* (*chim.*) cianato.

cyanic [sai'ænik], *ag.* (*chim.*) cianico.

cyanide ['saiənaid], *s.* (*chim.*) cianuro.

to cyanide, *v.t.* (*chim.*) trattare col cianuro.

cyanine ['saiənain], *s.* (*chim.*) cianina.

cyanite ['saiənait], *s.* (*min.*) cianite.

cyanogen [sai'ænədʒin], *s.* (*chim.*) cianogeno.

cyanosis [,saiə'nousis], *s.* (*patol.*) cianosi.

cyanotic [,saiə'nɔtik], *ag.* (*patol.*) cianotico.

Cybele ['sibəli], *no.pr.f.* (*mit.*) Cibele.

cybernetics [,saibə:'netiks], *s.* (*scient.*) cibernetica.

cycad ['saikəd], *s.* (*bot.*) cicadea.

Cyclades (the) ['siklədi:z], *no.pr.pl.* (*geog.*) Cicladi.

cyclamen ['sikləmən], *s.* (*bot.*) ciclamino.
cycle ['saikl], *s.* **1.** ciclo: *the — of the seasons*, il ciclo delle stagioni **2.** ciclo (di poemi): *the Arthurian —*, il ciclo Arturiano **3.** (*abbr.* di *bicycle*) biciclet- ta **4.** (*abbr.* di *tricycle*) triciclo ☆ *— -car*, motocar- rozzetta; *— track*, pista per ciclisti.
to **cycle**, *v.i.* **1.** svolgersi per cicli **2.** andare in bici- cletta.
cycler ['saiklə*], *s.c.* (*amer.*) ciclista.
cyclic(al) ['siklik(əl)], *ag.* ciclico ☆ *— novel*, ro- manzo fiume.
cycling ['saikliŋ], *s.* ciclismo.
cyclist ['saiklist], *s.c.* ciclista.
cycloid ['saikloid], *s.* (*geom.*) cicloide.
cycloidal [sai'kloidl], *ag.* (*geom.*) cicloidale.
cyclometer [sai'klɔmitə*], *s.* **1.** contachilome- tri **2.** strumento per misurare archi di cerchio.
cyclone ['saikloun], *s.* ciclone.
cyclonic(al) [sai'klɔnik(əl)], *ag.* ciclonico.
cyclop(a)edia [,saiklə'pi:djə], *s.* (*abbr.* di *encyclo- p(a)edia*) enciclopedia.
Cyclopean, Cyclopian [sai'kloupjən], *ag.* ciclopico.
Cyclops ['saiklɔps], *pl.* **Cyclopes** [sai'kloupi:z], *s.* (*mit.*) Ciclope.
cyclostyle ['saikləstail], *s.* ciclostile.
to **cyclostyle**, *v.t.* ciclostilare.
cyclotron ['saiklətrɔn], *s.* (*fis.*) ciclotrone.
cygnet ['signit], *s.* giovane cigno.
cylinder ['silində*], *s.* **1.** (*geom.*) cilindro **2.** (*mec.*) cilindro; rullo ☆ *— -barrel*, (*mec.*) canna del cilindro; *— (water) jacket*, camicia (d'acqua) di un cilindro; *— press*, (*tip.*) rotativa ‖ *six- — car*, (*aut.*) una sei cilindri.
cylindrical [si'lindrikəl], *ag.* cilindrico.
cylindriform [si'lindrifɔ:m], *ag.* cilindriforme.
cylindroid ['silindroid], *ag.* cilindroide.
cyma ['saimə], *s.* (*arch.*) gola.
cymbal ['simbəl], *s.* (*mus.*) piatto, cembalo.
cymbalist ['simbəlist], *s.* suonatore di piatti.
cymbalo ['simbəlou], *pl.* **cymbalos** ['simbəlouz], *s.* (*mus.*) cembalo, clavicembalo, spinetta.
Cymbeline ['simbili:n], *no.pr.m.* (*lett.*) Cimbelino.
cymbiform ['simbifɔ:m], *ag.* (*anat. bot.*) cimbiforme, a forma di navicella.
cymbocephalic [,simbəsi'fælik], *ag.* (*anat.*) cimbo- cefalico.
cyme [saim], *s.* (*bot.*) racemo, cima.

Cymric ['kimrik], *ag.* gallese.
cynic ['sinik], *ag.s.* cinico (anche *fil.*).
cynical ['sinikəl], *ag.* cinico.
cynically ['sinikəli], *av.* cinicamente.
cynicism ['sinisizəm], *s.* cinismo (anche *fil.*).
cynocephalus [,sainou'sefələs], *s.* (*mit. zool.*) cino- cefalo.
cynosure ['sinəzjuə*], *s.* **1.** (*astr.*) Orsa minore **2.** (*fam.*) centro, punto di mira: *the — of every eye*, il centro di tutti gli sguardi.
Cynthia ['sinθiə], *no.pr.f.* Cinzia.
(to) **cypher**, *V.* (to) **cipher**.
cypress ['saipris], *s.* cipresso.
Cyprian[1] ['sipriən], *ag.* cipriota ‖ *s.c.* cipriota ‖ *s.* persona licenziosa, prostituta, cortigiana.
Cyprian[2], *no.pr.m.* (*st. relig.*) Cipriano.
Cypriot ['sipriɔt], **Cypriote** ['sipriout], *ag.s.c.* ci- priota.
Cyprus ['saiprəs], *no.pr.* (*geog.*) Cipro.
Cyrano ['sirənou], *no.pr.m.* (*lett.*) Cirano.
Cyrenaic [,saiərə'neiik], *ag.s.* cirenaico.
Cyrenaica [,saiərə'neiikə], *no.pr.* (*geog.*) Cirenaica.
Cyril ['siril], *no.pr.m.* Cirillo.
Cyrillic [si'rilik], *ag.* cirillico.
Cyrus ['saiərəs], *no.pr.m.* Ciro.
cyst [sist], *s.* (*biol. patol.*) ciste, cisti.
cystic ['sistik], *ag.* (*biol. patol.*) cistico: *— tumor*, tumore cistico ☆ *— duct*, dotto cistico.
cystitis [sis'taitis], *s.* (*patol.*) cistite.
cystotomy [sis'tɔtəmi], *s.* (*chir.*) cistotomia.
Cythera [si'θiərə], *no.pr.* (*geog.*) Citera.
Cytherea [,siθə'ri(:)ə], *no.pr.f.* (*mit.*) Citerea, Venere.
Cytherean [,siθə'ri(:)ən], *ag.* di Citerea.
cytology [sai'tɔlədʒi], *s.* (*biol.*) citologia (studio delle cellule).
cytoplasm ['saitəplæzəm], *s.* (*biol.*) citoplasma.
cytostome ['saitəstoum], *s.* (*zool.*) citostoma.
czar [za:*], *s.* zar.
czarevitch ['za:rivitʃ], *s.* zarevic, figlio dello zar.
czarevna [za:'revnə], *s.* figlia dello zar.
czarina [za:'ri:nə], *s.* zarina.
czarism ['za:rizəm], *s.* zarismo.
Czech [tʃek], *ag.* ceco ‖ *s.c.* ceco, ceca.
Czecho-Slovak ['tʃekou'slouvæk], *ag.* cecoslovacco ‖ *s.c.* cecoslovacco, cecoslovacca.
Czecho-Slovakia ['tʃekou-slou'vækiə], *no.pr.* (*geog.*) Cecoslovacchia.

D

d [di:], *pl.* **d's, ds** [di:z], *s.* **1.** (*quarta lettera dell'alfabeto inglese*) d ‖ — *for David*, (*tel.*) d come Domodossola **2.** (*mus.*) re **3.** *d.* (*abbr. per lat. denarius*), « penny », « pence », soldo, soldi inglesi **4.** *d.* (*abbr. di died*) morto: *d. 1800*, morto nel 1800 · **5.** *d* — (*abbr. di damn*), maledizione; *d* — *d* (*abbr. di damned*), maledetto **6.** *D* (*cifra romana*), 500 **7.** a forma di D: *D joint*, (*mec.*) giunto a forma di D **8.** *D-day*, (*neol. mil.*) giorno predisposto per una operazione tattica (specialmente il 6 giugno 1944, data dello sbarco alleato in Normandia).

d', (*fam. abbr. di do*): *d'you know?*, sapete?.

'd, (*abbr. di had, should, would*): *I'd write*, scriverci; *I'd written*, avevo scritto.

dab[1] [dæb], *s.* **1.** tocco, colpo, colpettino; pugno; beccata: *a* — *in the eye*, un pugno nell'occhio **2.** macchia, schizzo; leggero strato (di vernice, burro, crema, ecc.): *a* — *of butter*, una spalmatina di burro; *a* — *of rouge*, un po' di rossetto; *dabs of mud*, zacchere di fango **3.** *pl.* (*fam.*) impronte digitali.

to dab[1], *pass.p.p.* **dabbed** [dæbd], *v.t.* **1.** toccare leggermente; tamponare: *to* — *one's eyes with a handkerchief*, passarsi un fazzoletto sugli occhi **2.** applicare; spalmare: *to* — *paint on sthg.*, stendere della vernice su ql.co.

dab[2], *s.* (*ittiol.*) pleuronettide.

dab[3], *s.* (*sl.*) esperto: *he's a* — *at maths*, è un cannone in matematica.

dabber ['dæbə*], *s.* **1.** (*tip.*) tampone per l'inchiostro **2.** spalmatore.

to dabble ['dæbl], *v.t.i.* inumidire, inumidirsi; guazzare: *to* — *one's hands in the water*, agitare le mani nell'acqua ‖ *to* — *in* (o *at*) *law, politics, medicine*, occuparsi, dilettarsi di legge, politica, medicina ‖ *to* — *on the Stock Exchange*, fare piccole operazioni in Borsa.

dabbler ['dæblə*], *s.* **1.** dilettante, chi si occupa di ql.co. come passatempo **2.** piccolo giocatore di Borsa.

dabchick ['dæbtʃik], *s.* **1.** (*ornit.*) svasso, colimbo **2.** (*mar.*) yacht che stazza cinque tonnellate o meno.

dace [deis], *s.* (*ittiol.*) lasca.

dachshund ['dækshund], *s.* (*zool.*) cane bassotto.

dacoit [də'kɔit], *s.* brigante (dell'India, della Birmania).

dacoity [də'kɔiti], *s.* azione brigantesca (in India, in Birmania).

dactyl ['dæktil], *s.* (*poes.*) dattilo.

dactylic [dæk'tilik], *ag.* (*poes.*) dattilico ‖ *s.* dattilo.

dad [dæd], **daddy** ['dædi], *s.* (*fam.*) babbo, papà ☆ *daddy-long-legs*, (*entom.*) tipula; (*amer. entom.*) falangio; (*fam.*) Papà Gambalunga.

dado ['deidou], *s.* (*arch.*) dado, plinto; zoccolo decorato (di parete).

dadoed ['deidoud], *ag.* con zoccolo decorato (di stanza).

daedal ['di:dl], **Daedalean, Daedalian** [di:'deiliən], *ag.* dedaleo, ingegnoso, abile; intricato.

Daedalus ['di:dələs], *no.pr.m.* (*mit.*) Dedalo.

daemon, *e derivati*, *V.* **demon**, *e derivati*.

to daff [dɑ:f], *v.t.* **1.** togliersi (indumenti, ecc.); gettar via **2.** mettere, gettare da parte.

daffodil ['dæfədil], *s.* (*bot.*) trombone, narciso selvatico; (*arc.*) asfodelo.

daft [dɑ:ft], *ag.* squilibrato, matto; scervellato: *he's gone clean* —, ha perduto il ben dell'intelletto.

dagger ['dægə*], *s.* **1.** stiletto, pugnale ‖ *to be at daggers drawn with s.o.*, (*fam.*) essere ai ferri corti con

qlcu. ‖ *to look daggers at s.o.*, guardare qlcu. con ostilità, lanciare uno sguardo furibondo a qlcu. **2.** (*tip.*) croce ☆ — *board*, (*mar.*) deriva a coltello.

dago ['deigou], *s.* (*amer. sl. spreg.*) individuo di razza latina (specialmente spagnolo, portoghese, italiano).

daguerreotype [də'geroutaip], *s.* (*foto.*) dagherrotipo.

daguerreotypy [də'geroutaipi], *s.* (*foto.*) dagherrotipia.

dahlia ['deiljə], *s.* (*bot.*) dalia.

dai [dai], *s.* (*ang.-in.*) balia, nutrice.

Dail Eireann [dail'ɛərən], *s.* Camera dei Deputati dell'Eire (Stato libero d'Irlanda).

daily ['deili], *ag.* del giorno, giornaliero, quotidiano: — *collections*, incassi giornalieri; — *newspaper*, quotidiano; *our* — *bread*, il nostro pane quotidiano ‖ *s.* **1.** (giornale) quotidiano **2.** (*fam.*) domestica a giornata.

daily, *av.* ogni giorno, giornalmente: *it happens* —, avviene tutti i giorni.

daintily ['deintili], *av.* delicatamente; con raffinatezza, con grazia.

daintiness ['deintinis], *s.* delicatezza; raffinatezza; squisitezza; ricercatezza.

dainty ['deinti], *ag.* **1.** raffinato; squisito; delicato; fragile; grazioso **2.** esigente; schizzinoso **3.** delizioso, squisito (di cibo) ‖ *s.* leccornia.

dairy ['dɛəri], *s.* **1.** latteria, cascina **2.** latteria (negozio) ☆ — *butter*, burro di cascina; — *farm*, fattoria con cascina; — *farming*, industria dei latticini.

dairying ['dɛəriiŋ], *s.* l'industria dei latticini.

dairymaid ['dɛərimeid], *s.* **1.** lattaia **2.** ragazza che lavora in una cascina.

dairyman, *pl.* **dairymen** ['dɛərimən], *s.* **1.** lattaio **2.** uomo che lavora in una cascina.

dais ['deiis], *s.* **1.** predella (piccola piattaforma per collocarvi un trono, ecc.) **2.** (*rar.*) baldacchino.

daisied ['deizid], *ag.* (*letter.*) cosparso di margherite.

daisy[1] ['deizi], *s.* **1.** margherita dei prati; pratolina **2.** (*sl.*) persona, cosa stupenda, straordinaria: *she is a* —, ella è una perla ☆ — *-chain*, ghirlanda di margheritine.

Daisy[2], *no.pr.f.* Margherita.

dale [deil], *s.* (*poet.*) valletta ☆ *dales-man*, valligiano.

Dalila [də'lailə], *no.pr.f.* (*Bibbia*) Dalila.

dalliance ['dæliəns], *s.* (*letter.*) **1.** amoreggiamento; armeggio amoroso **2.** indugio, esitazione.

to dally ['dæli], *v.i.* (*letter.*) **1.** scherzare, gingillarsi, trastullarsi: *to* — *with an idea*, trastullarsi con una idea; *to* — *with a woman's affections*, scherzare con i sentimenti di una donna **2.** sprecare tempo, indugiare, esitare: *to* — *over one's work*, perder tempo lavorando.

Dalmatia [dæl'meiʃjə], *no.pr.* (*geog.*) Dalmazia.

Dalmatian [dæl'meiʃjən], *ag.* dalmata ‖ *s.c.* dalmata ‖ *s.* (*zool.*) cane dalmata.

dalmatic [dæl'mætik], *s.* (*st. eccl.*) dalmatica.

daltonism ['dɔ:ltənizm], *s.* (*patol.*) daltonismo.

dam[1] [dæm], *s.* **1.** diga; argine; sbarramento **2.** complesso d'acqua contenuta da una diga **3.** (*metal.*) dama.

to dam[1], *pass.p.p.* **dammed** [dæmd], *v.t.* sbarrare; arginare; chiudere (con dighe).

dam[2], *s.* madre (specialmente di quadrupedi).

damage ['dæmidʒ], *s.* **1.** danno, guasto, avaria; *fig.* incomodo: *to my great* —, con mio grande danno; *to cause s.o.* —, dar fastidio a qlcu.; *to do* (o *cause*) *great* (o *much*) — *to*, causare molti danni a; *to pay for the* — *done*, pagare per i danni fatti **2.** *pl.* (*dir.*) indennizzo, risarcimento: *to be liable for damages*, essere ritenuto responsabile per i danni e gli interessi; *to sue s.o. for damages*, intentare un processo a qlcu. per risarcimento (di danni) **3.** (*fam.*) prezzo, costo ☆ *war damages*, danni di guerra.

to **damage**, *v.t.* **1.** danneggiare; avariare (merce); far subire dei danni a: *the fire damaged the pictures*, l'incendio danneggiò i quadri **2.** pregiudicare; nuocere a (reputazione): *his reputation was damaged by it*, la sua reputazione ne fu danneggiata.

damageable ['dæmidʒəbl], *ag.* danneggiabile; guastabile; avariabile.

damaged ['dæmidʒd], *ag.* avariato; guastato.

damaging ['dæmidʒiŋ], *ag.* dannoso, nocivo; pregiudizievole.

Damascene ['dæməsi:n], *ag.* **1.** damasceno, di Damasco **2.** damaschino ‖ *s.c.* abitanti di Damasco ‖ *s.* damaschinatura.

to **damascene**, *v.t.* (*metal.*) damaschinare, intarsiare.

damask ['dæməsk], *ag.* damaschino, damaschinato ‖ *s.* **1.** damasco (tessuto); metallo damaschinato **2.** — (*colour*), color rosa carico e cupo ☆ — -*prune*, prugna damascena; — -*rose*, (*bot.*) rosa damascena; — -*steel*, acciaio damaschinato.

to **damask**, *v.t.* **1.** damascare (tessuto) **2.** damaschinare **3.** colorare di rosa carico (guance, ecc.).

to **damaskeen** [,dæmə'ski:n], *V.* to **damascene**.

dame [deim], *s.f.* **1.** titolo di moglie di cavaliere o di baronetto, di donna insignita di un ordine cavalleresco: *Dame Nellie Melba*, Donna Nellie Melba **2.** (*arc.*) dama, signora, gentildonna: *an old* —, (*fam.*) una vecchia signora ‖ *Dame Nature, Fortune*, *fig.* la Natura, la Fortuna **3.** (*arc.*) maestra di scuola ☆ — -*school*, scuola elementare (del tipo anticamente tenuto da signore).

damfool ['dæm'ful], *s.* (*sl.*) cretino, sciocco.

dammar ['dæmə*], *s.* dammara (resina naturale).

damn [dæm], *s.* maledizione **2.** (*sl.*) un bel niente, nulla: *I don't care a* —, non mi importa un bel niente; *not to be worth a* —, non valere un fico secco.

to **damn**, *v.t.* **1.** dannare (anche *teol.*); condannare; censurare **2.** (spesso scritto *d* —) maledire; mandare all'inferno, imprecare: —!, maledizione!; — *it all!*, (*sl.*) maledizione!; — *the rain!*, sia maledetta la pioggia!; — *you!*, vai all'inferno!; *I'll be damned if I go!*, (*sl.*) non ci andrò nemmeno per sogno!; *well, I'm damned!*, (*sl.*) ci vuol tutta! **3.** rovinare; *fig.* disapprovare; (*teat.*) fischiare: *that is enough to* — *him*, ciò basta per rovinarlo.

damnable ['dæmnəbl], *ag.* **1.** dannabile; condannabile **2.** (*sl.*) maledetto; odioso; detestabile.

damnably ['dæmnəbli], *av.* **1.** in modo dannabile **2.** (*sl.*) odiosamente; detestabilmente.

damnation [dæm'neiʃən], *s.* **1.** dannazione **2.** (*teat.*) disapprovazione.

damnation, *inter.* (*sl.*) dannazione!, diavolo!.

damnatory ['dæmnətəri], *ag.* condannatorio.

damned [dæmd], *ag.* **1.** dannato ‖ *the* —, i dannati **2.** (*sl.*) (spesso scritto *d* — *d*) maledetto: *you* — *fool!*, maledetto cretino! ‖ *to do one's damnedest*, fare tutto il possibile **3.** disapprovato; (*teat.*) fischiato.

damned, *av.* (spesso scritto *d* — *d*) eccessivamente: *it was d* — *d hot*, faceva maledettamente caldo.

damnification [,dæmnifi'keiʃən], *s.* danno.

to **damnify** ['dæmnifai], *v.t.* (*dir. arc.*) danneggiare.

damning ['dæmiŋ], *ag.* **1.** che porta alla condanna, schiacciante: — *evidence*, prove schiaccianti **2.** che maledice ‖ *s.* **1.** condanna; dannazione **2.** maledizione.

Damocles ['dæməkli:z], *no.pr.m.* (*mit.*) Damocle ‖ *the Sword of* —, la spada di Damocle.

Damon ['deimən], *no.pr.m.* (*mit.*) Damone.

damp [dæmp], *ag.* umido; bagnato; molle; madido: — *climate*, clima umido; *a* — *forehead*, una fronte madida ‖ *s.* **1.** umidità (dell'aria, ecc.): *the evening* —,

l'umidità della sera **2.** nube di tristezza; depressione; scoraggiamento: *to cast a* — *over* (*s.o.*), avvolgere di un senso di tristezza, scoraggiare (qlcu.) ☆ — (-*proof*) *course*, strato impermeabile all'umidità ‖ *black* — (o *choke-* —), (gas di) acido carbonico; *fire-* —, grisù.

to **damp**, *v.t.i.* **1.** inumidire; bagnare ‖ *to* — *off*, marcire, perire per l'umidità (di pianta, germoglio) **2.** soffocare, estinguere; smorzare (fuoco, suono): *to* — *the appetite*, smorzare l'appetito; *to* — *down a fire*, soffocare, estinguere un incendio **3.** deprimere; scoraggiare: *nothing could* — *his spirits*, nulla poteva scoraggiarlo; *to* — *one's ardour*, raffreddare gli ardori **4.** (*mus.*) cessare (delle vibrazioni di una corda).

to **dampen** ['dæmpən], *V.* to **damp**.

dampener ['dæmpənə*], *s.* **1.** (*amer.*) aggeggio per inumidire la biancheria **2.** (*fam. fig.*) doccia fredda.

damper ['dæmpə*], *s.* **1.** (*fam.*) guastafeste; doccia fredda: *to cast a* — *on a party*, raggelare la compagnia **2.** pane senza lievito cotto nella cenere **3.** (*mus.*) smorzatoio (di pianoforte) **4.** (*mec.*) valvola di tiraggio (di camino); (*elett.*) smorzatore; (*aut.*) bloccasterzo **5.** spugnetta per francobolli.

damping ['dæmpiŋ], *s.* **1.** inumidimento **2.** (*elett. fis.*) smorzamento; (*mat.*) attenuazione.

dampish ['dæmpiʃ], *ag.* umidiccio.

dampishness ['dæmpiʃnis], *s.* leggera umidità.

dampness ['dæmpnis], *s.* umidità.

damsel ['dæmzəl], *s.* **1.** (*poet.*) fanciulla, damigella, donzella **2.** (*amer. sl.*) studentessa.

damson ['dæmzən], *s.* **1.** susina damascena **2.** color prugna ☆ — -*tree*, prugno damasceno.

dan [dæn], *s.* (*mar.*) piccola boa.

Danaë ['dæneii:], *no.pr.f.* (*mit.*) Danae.

Danaïdes [də'neidi:z], *no.pr.f.pl.* (*mit.*) Danaidi.

dance [dɑ:ns], *s.* **1.** danza, ballo: *may I have the next* — *with you?*, mi concede il prossimo ballo? ‖ *the Dance of Death*, danza macabra ‖ *to lead s.o. a* —, (*fam.*) mettere il bastone fra le ruote a qlcu.; dare del filo da torcere a qlcu. **2.** (festa da) ballo: *to give a* —, dare un ballo ☆ — -*band*, orchestrina da ballo; — -*hall*, sala da ballo (anche pubblica); — *hostess*, « entraineuse ».

to **dance**, *v.t.i.* **1.** danzare, ballare: *will you* — *with me?*, vuole ballare con me?; *to* — *in a circle*, ballare in tondo ‖ *to* — *along, in, out*, avanzare, entrare, uscire ballando ‖ *to* — *attendance on s.o.*, *fig.* stare alle costole di qlcu., far da cavalier servente (a una signora) ‖ *to* — *on nothing*, (*sl.*) essere impiccato ‖ *to* — *to s.o.'s piping*, (*fam.*) lasciarsi guidare da qlcu., adattarsi ai desideri di qlcu. **2.** saltare, far saltare; saltellare; agitarsi: *the leaves are dancing in the wind*, le foglie si agitano al vento; *to* — *a baby up and down*, far saltare un bambino tra le braccia; *to* — *for joy*, saltare dalla gioia **3.** fare una (figura di) danza (polka, minuetto, ecc.): *they danced a polka*, danzarono una polka **4.** *to* — *about*, saltellare, sgambettare **5.** *to* — *away*, continuare a ballare ‖ *to* — *away the time*, buttare via il proprio tempo in canti e danze.

danceable ['dɑ:nsəbl], *ag.* ballabile.

dancemusic ['dɑ:ns,mju:zik], *s.* musica da ballo.

dancer ['dɑ:nsə*], *s.c.* danzatore, danzatrice; ballerino, ballerina: *he's a good* — , egli balla bene ‖ *merry dancers*, l'aurora boreale.

dancing ['dɑ:nsiŋ], *ag.* danzante, ballante ‖ *s.* il ballo, la danza, l'arte della danza ☆ — -*girl*, danzatrice (di professione); — -*hall*, sala da ballo; — -*master*, maestro di ballo; — -*partner*, cavaliere, dama; — -*party*, festa danzante.

dandelion ['dændilaiən], *s.* (*bot.*) tarassico; (*pop.*) soffione, radichiella, dente di leone.

dander ['dændə*], *s.* (*sl.*) rabbia; spirito bellicoso: *to get s.o.'s* — *up*, fare arrabbiare ql.cu.

dandiacal [dæn'daiəkəl], *ag.* da, di damerino.

dandified ['dændifaid], *ag.* vestito con eleganza, azzimato (di persona); ricercato (di stile).

to **dandify** ['dændifai], *v.t.* vestire con eleganza, rendere ricercato (stile, maniere, ecc.).

to **dandle** ['dændl], *v.t.* far saltare (un bimbo) sulle ginocchia o tra le braccia.

dandruff ['dændrəf], *s.* forfora.

dandy[1] ['dændi], *ag.* elegante, affettato ‖ *s.* **1.** zerbinotto, elegantone **2.** (*amer. fam.*) ql.co. di magnifico, splendido **3.** (*mar.*) iolla, « yawl » **4.** — (*-roll*), (*tip.*) ballerino ☆ — *brush*, spazzola di osso di balena (per cavalli).

dandy[2], *s.*: — (*-fever*), (*patol.*) denga.

dandy[3], *s.* (*ang.-in.*) **1.** palanchino (in uso nelle zone montuose dell'India) **2.** battelliere (del Gange).

dandyish ['dændiiʃ], *ag.* vanesio, ricercato.

dandyism ['dændiizəm], *s.* maniere da zerbinotto, da damerino; ricercatezza ed eleganza nel vestire.

Dane [dein], *s.c.* danese ‖ *s.*: (*Great*) —, cane danese.

Danelagh, Danelaw ['deinlɔ:], *no.pr.* (*geog. st.*) Danelagh, Danelaw (zona dell'Inghilterra sotto la giurisdizione danese, IX e X sec.).

danewort ['deinwə:t], *s.* (*bot.*) ebbio; sambuco selvatico.

to **dang** [dæŋ], (*sl.*) per to **damn** **2.**

danger ['deindʒə*], *s.* pericolo: *a* — *to navigation,* un pericolo per la navigazione; *in* — *of* (*losing*) *one's life,* in pericolo di (perdere la) vita, di morte; *out of* —, fuori pericolo; *there is no* — *of his dying,* non c'è pericolo che muoia; *to be in* — *of,* correre il pericolo di ☆ — *-signal,* segnale di pericolo.

dangerous ['deindʒrəs], *ag.* pericoloso: *you are on* — *ground,* siete su un terreno pericoloso ‖ *to go to* — *lengths,* (*fam.*) passare la misura.

dangerously ['deindʒrəsli], *av.* pericolosamente; gravemente: — *ill,* gravemente ammalato.

dangerousness ['deindʒrəsnis], *s.* pericolo.

to **dangle** ['dæŋgl], *v.t.i.* **1.** (far) ciondolare, (far) penzolare: *to* — *one's arms,* far ciondolare le braccia **2.** *to* — *after* (o *round* o *about*) (*s.o.*), ronzare intorno (a una persona, come seguace o corteggiatore).

dangler ['dæŋglə*], *s.* cascamorto, donnaiuolo.

dangling ['dæŋgliŋ], *ag.* ciondolante ‖ *s.* il ciondolare.

Daniel ['dænjəl], *no.pr.m.* Daniele ‖ *s.* **1.** giudice retto **2.** libro di Daniele (nella Bibbia).

Danish ['deiniʃ], *ag.* danese ‖ *s.* lingua danese.

dank [dæŋk], *ag.* umido; malsano; fradicio: — *weather,* tempo umido.

dankish ['dæŋkiʃ], *ag.* umidiccio.

Dantean ['dæntiən], **Dantesque** [dæn'tesk], *ag.* dantesco.

Danube ['dænju:b], *no.pr.* (*geog.*) Danubio.

to **dap** [dæp], *pass.p.p.* **dapped** [dæpt], *v.t.i.* **1.** pescare facendo saltare l'esca sull'acqua; immergere leggermente l'esca **2.** saltare, far saltare (di palla) **3.** (*ind.*) preparare un incastro.

Daphne ['dæfni], *no.pr.f.* (*mit.*) Dafne ‖ **daphne,** *s.* (*bot.*) dafne.

Daphnis ['dæfnis], *no.pr.m.* (*lett.*) Dafni.

dapper ['dæpə*], *ag.* **1.** azzimato; attillato **2.** attivo, vivace: *a* — *little man,* un omino vivace.

dapple ['dæpl], *s.* chiazza (sulla pelle, sul mantello di cavallo, ecc.); macchia ☆ — *-grey,* leardo pomellato (di cavallo).

to **dapple,** *v.t.i.* chiazzare, chiazzarsi; macchiettare.

dappled ['dæpld], *ag.* chiazzato; pomellato.

darbies ['dɑ:biz], *s.pl.* (*sl.*) manette.

Darby ['dɑ:bi], *no.pr.m.*: — *and Joan,* (*fam.*) Filemone e Bauci (vecchi coniugi simbolo dell'amore coniugale).

dare [dɛə*], *pass.* **dared** [dɛəd], *rar.* **durst** [də:st], *v. dif.* (∇) (*pres. negativo forma contratta:* **daren't** [dɛənt]; *è usato generalmente nelle proposizioni interrogative, negative, dubitative e condizionali*) *osare:* — *you speak to me?,* osate parlarmi?; *how* — *he say such a thing?,* come osa egli dire una simile cosa.?; *I* — *not* (o *daren't*) *go,* non oso andare; *I don't know whether*

he — *come,* non so se egli osi venire ‖ *I* — *say,* credo bene, può darsi; è possibile, forse (*talvolta iron.*); *I* — *say that...,* suppongo che... ‖ to **dare,** *v.t.* (*seguito dall'inf. con o senza* to) **1.** *osare: don't* — (*to*) *speak to me!,* non osate parlarmi!; *he does not* — (*to*) *answer,* non osa rispondere; *he has never dared* (*to*) *come,* non ha mai osato venire **2.** *affrontare; rischiare, tentare: he would* — *any danger,* affronterebbe qualsiasi pericolo **3.** *sfidare: to* — *s.o. to do sthg.,* sfidare qlcu. a fare ql.co.: *I dared him to fight,* lo sfidai in combattimento.

dare-devil ['dɛə,devl], *s.* scavezzacollo; temerario.

darg [dɑ:g], *s.* (*scoz. dial.*) lavoro di una giornata.

daring ['dɛəriŋ], *ag.* audace; temerario ‖ *s.* audacia; temerarietà.

daringly ['dɛəriŋli], *av.* audacemente; con intrepidità.

Darius [də'raiəs], *no.pr.m.* Dario.

dark [dɑ:k], *ag.* **1.** scuro, buio; tenebroso: — *night,* notte fonda; *it is too* — *to read,* è troppo buio per leggere; *to get* —, farsi notte, annottare ‖ *the Dark Ages,* l'Alto Medioevo; *the Dark Continent,* il Continente Nero, l'Africa **2.** cupo (di colore): — *blue,* azzurro cupo **3.** bruno: — *eyes, hair,* occhi, capelli bruni **4.** *fig.* nero; triste: — *days,* giorni tristi; — *humour,* umore nero; *to see the* — *side of things,* vedere tutto nero **5.** *fig.* misterioso, segreto, sconosciuto; difficile da capire: *to keep sthg.* —, tenere celato ql.co. **6.** ignorante, ottuso: *to live in the darkest ignorance,* vivere nella più crassa ignoranza ☆ — *eyed,* dagli occhi scuri; — *horse,* vincitore imprevisto; persona le cui possibilità di successo sono sconosciute; (*fam.*) concorrente sconosciuto ma pericoloso; — *lantern,* lanterna cieca; — *race,* razza negra; — *-room,* (*foto.*) camera oscura; — *skinned,* dalla pelle nera.

dark, *s.* **1.** buio, oscurità, tenebre: *after* —, dopo il calar della notte; *at* —, al calar della notte; *before* —, prima che annotti; *in the* —, nell'oscurità, all'oscuro: *a leap in the* —, *fig.* un salto nel buio **2.** *fig.* ignoranza: *he is entirely in the* — *about that matter,* egli è completamente all'oscuro di quella faccenda; *to keep* (*s.o.*) *in the* —, tenere (qlcu.) all'oscuro.

to **darken** ['dɑ:kən], *v.t.i.* oscurare (stanza, ecc.); oscurarsi (del cielo, dell'avvenire, ecc.); far oscurare; imbrunire (di colori, ecc.): *his brow darkened,* la sua fronte s'oscurò ‖ *never* — *my doors again!,* non rimettere mai più piede in casa mia!

darkening ['dɑ:kniŋ], *s.* oscuramento; annerimento (di un dipinto, ecc.).

darkey ['dɑ:ki], *s.c.* (*fam.*) negro, negra.

darkish ['dɑ:kiʃ], *ag.* scuretto, un po' oscuro: — *hair,* capelli piuttosto scuri.

to **darkle** ['dɑ:kl], *v.i.* **1.** oscurarsi **2.** stare nascosto

darkling ['dɑ:kliŋ], *ag.* oscuro; cupo.

darkling, *av.* nell'oscurità.

darkly ['dɑ:kli], *av.* oscuramente.

darkness ['dɑ:knis], *s.* **1.** oscurità, tenebre: *because of the* —, a causa dell'oscurità; *complete* —, buio completo ‖ *the Prince of Darkness,* il principe delle tenebre, il diavolo **2.** tinta carica: — *of complexion,* colorito bruno.

darksome ['dɑ:ksəm], *ag.* (*arc. letter.*) fosco; cupo; tetro.

darky ['dɑ:ki], *s.c.* (*fam.*) negro, negra.

darling ['dɑ:liŋ], *ag.* caro, diletto ‖ *s.* prediletto, beniamino: *my* —, mio diletto, amor mio.

darn[1] [dɑ:n], *s.* rammendatura; rammendo.

to **darn**[1], *v.t.* rammendare.

darn[2], (*sl.*) per **damn**.

to **darn**[2], (*sl.*) per to **damn** **2.**

darnel ['dɑ:nl], *s.* (*bot.*) loglio.

darner ['dɑ:nə*], *s.c.* rammendatore, rammendatrice.

darning ['dɑ:niŋ], *s.* rammendo; l'arte del rammendare ☆ — *-ball,* palla, uovo per rammendare; — *-cotton,* cotone da rammendo; — *-needle,* ago da rammendo; — *-stitch,* punto rammendo; — *-wool,* lana da rammendo.

dart [dɑ:t], *s.* **1.** dardo, strale **2.** pungiglione (di insetto) **3.** slancio, movimento improvviso in avanti: *to make a (sudden) — on sthg.*, precipitarsi su ql.co. **4.** (*sartoria*) « pince », pieghina che finisce in nulla **5.** *pl.* (*giuoco*) specie di tirassegno con frecce metalliche (generalmente in locali pubblici).

to dart, *v.t.i.* **1.** dardeggiare (dei raggi, ecc.); scagliare, lanciare (anche *fig.*): *she darted an angry look at me*, ella mi lanciò uno sguardo irato **2.** lanciarsi (in avanti); volare (come una freccia); piombare su || *to — away*, fuggire come il vento; *to — in*, entrare come un bolide; *to — out*, uscire come un bolide; *to — past*, passare come una freccia **3.** fare una « pince », una pieghina, pieghine (su un indumento).

darter ['dɑ:tə*], *s.* **1.** scagliatore, arciere **2.** (*ornit.*) ploto; *pl.* famiglia di uccelli **3.** (*amer.*) pesciolini d'acqua dolce.

dartle ['dɑ:tl], *v.t.i.* (*rar.*) continuare a scagliare, a scagliarsi, a lanciare, a lanciarsi.

dartre ['dɑ:tə*], *s.* (*patol.*) herpes, erpete.

dartrous ['dɑ:trəs], *ag.* (*patol.*) erpetico.

Darwinian [dɑ:'winiən], *ag.s.* darwiniano.

Darwinism ['dɑ:winizəm], *s.* darwinismo.

Darwinist ['dɑ:winist], *s.* darwinista.

dash [dæʃ], *s.* **1.** slancio, impeto, foga: *troops full of —*, truppe piene di slancio; *to play with —*, (*mus.*) suonare con brio **2.** attacco, impeto: *to make a — at the enemy*, attaccare il nemico con impeto; *to make a — for sthg.*, buttarsi con impeto per raggiungere ql.co. **3.** sciabordio; tonfo (sull'acqua); colpo violento (anche *fig.*): *my hopes received a —*, le mie speranze ricevettero un colpo; *we could hear the — of oars*, potevamo udire il tonfo dei remi **4.** una piccola quantità; uno spruzzo; un goccio: *a — of colour*, una macchia di colore; *coffee with a — of brandy*, caffè con un goccio di cognac **5.** tratto di penna; (*tip.*) lineetta **6.** (*fam.*) *to cut a —*, fare una bella figura ☆ -*board*, (*aut.*) cruscotto.

to dash, *v.t.i.* **1.** cozzare, urtare violentemente; frantumare, frantumarsi; infrangere, infrangersi: *the car dashed into the wall*, l'auto cozzò contro il muro; *he dashed at his enemy*, si precipitò sul suo nemico; *the ship was dashed against a rock*, la nave cozzò contro una roccia; *to — sthg. to pieces*, fracassare ql.co. **2.** macchiare; spruzzare; inzaccherare: *dashed with pink*, screziato di rosa **3.** mescolare; adulterare: *to — wine with water*, mescolare l'acqua al vino **4.** buttar giù, scrivere senza cura **5.** *fig.* distruggere, rendere vano: *his hopes were dashed by this*, le sue speranze furono infrante da ciò **6.** (*fam.* per *to damn*) maledire **7.** *to — along*, lanciarsi in avanti, procedere a grande velocità **8.** *to — aside*, spingere, spingersi violentemente da parte **9.** *to — away*, schivare agilmente (ql.co.); darsela a gambe: *he dashed away a tear*, si asciugò furtivamente una lacrima **10.** *to — down*, abbattere, scaraventare per terra **11.** *to — in*, entrare precipitosamente; introdurre frettolosamente (*p.e.* dei dettagli in un bozzetto) **12.** *to — off*, buttar giù (una lettera, ecc.); eseguire (ql.co.) velocemente; scappar via **13.** *to — out*, precipitarsi fuori, (far) schizzar fuori: *to — out one's brains*, fracassarsi la testa.

dashed [dæʃt], *ag.* (eufemistico per *damned*) maledetto.

dasher ['dæʃə*], *s.* **1.** (*sl.*) individuo energico, brillante, elegante **2.** pestello (di zangola) **3.** (*amer. aut.*) cruscotto.

dashing ['dæʃiŋ], *ag.* **1.** impetuoso; pieno di slancio; focoso (di cavallo) **2.** ostentatamente elegante.

dashingly ['dæʃiŋli], *av.* **1.** impetuosamente; con slancio **2.** in modo ostentatamente elegante.

dastard ['dæstəd], *s.* vile, codardo; persona ignobile.

dastardliness ['dæstədlinis], *s.* codardia, viltà.

dastardly ['dæstədli], *ag.* vile, codardo; ignobile.

dasyure ['dæsijuə*], *s.* (*zool.*) dasiuro.

datable ['deitəbl], *ag.* databile.

date[1] [deit], *s.* (*bot.*) dattero.

date[2], *s.* **1.** data: *of early —*, di antica data; *under*

the — of May 3rd, alla data del 3 maggio; *up to this —*, sino a questa data; *to bear the — of*, portare la data di || *to —*, fino ad oggi: *interest to —*, interessi fino ad oggi || *up to —*, aggiornato; alla moda; (*comm.*) al corrente: *to be up to —*, essere al corrente; essere all'ultima moda; *to be up to — with payments*, (*comm.*) essere al corrente coi pagamenti; *to bring up to —*, modernizzare; *out of —* antiquato, fuori moda: *to be out of —*, essere antiquato, fuori moda **2.** epoca, periodo di tempo: *ruins of Roman —*, rovine dell'epoca romana **3.** (*comm.*) scadenza (*p. e.* di una cambiale): *at long, at short —*, a lunga, a breve scadenza; *due —*, data di scadenza, data stabilita; *three months after* (o *at three months'*) *—*, tre mesi dopo la scadenza **4.** (*amer.*) appuntamento; invito; impegno; persona con cui si ha un appuntamento: *to have, to make a — with s.o.*, avere, fissare un appuntamento con qlcu. ☆ -*line*, (*geog.*) linea di cambiamento di data.

to date[2], *v.t.i.* **1.** datare, mettere la data di, portare la data di: *dated*, in data; *the letter is dated from London, June 10th*, la lettera porta la data Londra, 10 giugno **2.** datare (da); risalire (a): *this church dates from* (o *back to*) *the 14th century*, questa chiesa risale al 14° secolo **3.** mostrare la propria età, essere invecchiato; essere fuori moda: *this car begins to —*, questa automobile è un po' fuori moda **4.** (*neol. amer.*) avere un appuntamento, fissare un appuntamento.

dateless ['deitlis], *ag.* **1.** senza data **2.** (*poet.*) eterno.

dater ['deitə*], *s.* timbro della data.

dating ['deitiŋ], *s.* **1.** timbratura **2.** (*amer.*) corteggiamento.

dative ['deitiv], *ag.* dativo || *s.* (*gram.*) dativo: *in the —*, al dativo ☆ *tutory —*, (*dir.*) tutela dativa.

datum ['deitəm], *pl.* **data** ['deitə], *s.* dato; elemento d'informazione; premessa; fatto, notizia ☆ -*level*, (*topografia*) piano di riferimento; *— -line*, (*topografia*) linea di riferimento; *— -point*, (*topografia*) punto di riferimento, caposaldo.

datura [də'tjuərə], *s.* (*bot.*) datura.

daub [dɔ:b], *s.* **1.** intonaco **2.** imbrattamento; sgorbio; pittura mal fatta.

to daub, *v.t.i.* **1.** intonacare (muri) **2.** imbrattare (tele); impiastrare, impiastricciare, impiastricciarsi: *she daubs her face with red*, essa si impiastra la faccia di rosso.

dauber ['dɔ:bə*], **daubster** ['dɔ:bstə*], *s.* **1.** imbrattatore, impiastratore **2.** imbrattatele.

dauby ['dɔ:bi], *ag.* **1.** vischioso **2.** imbrattato, dipinto male (di dipinti).

daughter ['dɔ:tə*], *s.* figlia, figliola || *a — of Eve*, (*fam.*) una figlia di Eva ☆ *— -in-law*, nuora || *God — -*, figlioccia; *grand- —*, nipote (di nonna, nonno); *only —*, figlia unica; *step- —*, figliastra.

daughterly ['dɔ:təli], *ag.* filiale, di figlia.

daunt [dɔ:nt], *s.* disco di legno per pressare le aringhe nei barili.

to daunt, *v.t.* **1.** intimidire: *he is never daunted*, non si scoraggia mai **2.** stipare (aringhe) in un barile.

dauntless ['dɔ:ntlis], *ag.* intrepido.

dauntlessly ['dɔ:ntlisli], *av.* intrepidamente.

dauntlessness ['dɔ:ntlisnis], *s.* intrepidezza.

Dauphin ['dɔ:fin], *s.* (*st. francese*) delfino.

Dauphiness ['dɔ:finis], *s.* (*st. francese*) delfina.

Dauphiny ['dɔ:fini], *no.pr.* (*geog.*) Delfinato.

davenport ['dævnpɔ:t], *s.* **1.** piccola scrivania (da salotto) **2.** (*amer.*) canapè; divano letto.

David ['deivid], *no. pr. m.* Davide.

davit ['dævit], *s.* (*mar.*) gru di imbarcazione ☆ *boat —*, (*mar.*) gru d'imbarcazione; *cat —*, (*mar.*) gru di capone; *fish —*, (*mar.*) gru del traversino; *paravane —*, (*mar.*) gru paramine.

davy[1] ['deivi], *s.*: *to take one's — that*, (*sl.*) giurare che.

Davy[2], *s.* lampada di Davy (di sicurezza per i minatori).

Davy[3], *no. pr. m. dim.* di **David**.

Davy Jones ['deivi'dʒounz], *s.* (*sl. mar.*) spirito maligno del mare: — *locker*, il fondo del mare, la tomba dei marinai.

daw [dɔ:], *V.* **jackdaw.**

to **dawdle** ['dɔ:dl], *v.t.i.* sprecare (il proprio tempo); oziare; gironzolare; bighellonare: *to — away one's time*, sciupare il tempo bighellonando.

dawdler ['dɔ:dlə*], *s.c.* perdigiorno.

dawn [dɔ:n], *s.* **1.** alba; aurora: *the rosy-fingered* —, l'aurora dalle rosee dita; *at* —, all'alba; *at early* —, alle prime luci del giorno; *from — till dark*, dall'alba al tramonto **2.** *fig.* alba; inizio, principio (della civiltà, ecc.): *the news brought a — of hope*, quella notizia portò un barlume di speranza.

to **dawn**, *v.i.* **1.** albeggiare; spuntare (dell'alba): *the day is dawning*, si fa giorno **2.** apparire (anche *fig.*): *I saw a smile dawning on her lips*, vidi spuntare un sorriso sulle sue labbra; *the truth dawned on him*, la verità cominciò ad apparirgli.

dawning ['dɔ:niŋ], *ag.* nascente ‖ *s.* l'albeggiare.

day [dei], *s.* **1.** giorno, giornata; momento: *a fine* —, un bel giorno, una bella giornata; *in the course of the* —, nel corso della giornata ‖ *— after* —, un giorno dopo l'altro; *— and night* (o *night and* —), giorno e notte, sempre; *— by* —, di giorno in giorno; *— in — out*, ogni giorno, senza tregua; *all — long* (o *all the* —), tutto il giorno; *by* —, di giorno ‖ *man of the* —, uomo del giorno ‖ *one* —, un giorno, un bel giorno, una volta; *some* —, un giorno o l'altro, un bel giorno ‖ *it will be a long — before I go there again*, ci vorrà del tempo prima che io ci vada di nuovo ‖ *she was a creature of a* —, ha avuto vita breve ‖ *to be on one's* —, (*fam.*) essere in forma ‖ *to end one's days*, (*fam.*) morire ‖ *to have one's* —, (*fam.*) avere un periodo di potere, di successo: *every dog has his* —, ognuno ha il suo raggio di sole; *I've had my* —, la mia ora di prosperità è passata **2.** giorno, luce del giorno: *before* —, prima dell'alba; *in broad* —, alla luce del giorno, in pieno giorno **3.** (*astr.*) giorno: *civil* —, giorno civile; *sidereal* —, giorno sidereo; *solar* —, giorno solare **4.** periodo di 24 ore; data: *what's the — of the month? it's the 3rd of May*, che giorno è? è il 3 maggio ‖ *the — after tomorrow*, dopodomani; *the — before yesterday*, avant'ieri; *every* —, ogni giorno, giornalmente; *every other* (o *second*) —, a giorni alterni; *from — to* —, di giorno in giorno; *in three days* (o *in three days' time*), fra tre giorni; *next* —, il giorno dopo; *one of these days*, uno di questi giorni, fra breve; *the other* —, l'altro giorno, alcuni giorni fa; *this* —, oggi stesso; *this — week, fortnight, month*, oggi otto, quindici, un mese; *to-* —, oggi; *to a* —, al giorno preciso: *two years ago to a* —, esattamente due anni oggi; *twice a* —, due volte al giorno ‖ *All Saints' Day*, Ognissanti; *Easter Day*, il giorno di Pasqua ‖ *let's make a — of it!*, spassiamocela! ‖ *to name the* —, fissare il giorno del matrimonio ‖ *to pass the time of — with s.o.*, salutare, dare il buongiorno a qlcu. **5.** giorno lavorativo: *to work by the* —, lavorare a giornata ‖ *— off*, giorno di riposo (di impiegati); *— out*, giorno di libera uscita (di domestica) ‖ *it's all in the —'s work*, (*fam.*) è una cosa abituale, capita a tutti **6.** età, tempo: *the good old days*, i bei tempi del passato; *in the days of old*, nei giorni andati, nel passato; *in the days to come*, nei giorni futuri; nel futuro **7.** (*mil.*) giornata, battaglia, lotta: *to win* (o *to carry*), *to lose the* —, vincere, perdere una battaglia ☆ *-blindness*, (*patol.*) nictalopia; *— -boarder*, semiconvittore; *— -book*, (*comm.*) brogliaccio; *— -boy*, allievo esterno; *— -fly*, (*entom.*) effimera; *— -girl*, allieva esterna; *— -labour*, lavoro a giornata; *— -labourer*, lavoratore, lavoratrice a giornata; *— -lily*, (*bot.*) emerocallide; *— -nurse*, bambinaia, infermiera (di giorno); *— -school*, scuola diurna; *— -work*, lavoro a giornata; *— -worker*, lavoratore, lavoratrice a giornata.

daybreak ['dei-breik], *s.* lo spuntar del giorno, alba: *at* —, allo spuntar del giorno.

daydream ['dei-dri:m], *s.* sogno ad occhi aperti, castelli in aria.

to **daydream**, *v.i.* sognare ad occhi aperti, fare castelli in aria.

daydreamer ['dei-dri:mə*], *s.c.* chi fa sogni ad occhi aperti.

daydreaming ['dei-dri:miŋ], *s.* il sognare ad occhi aperti, il fare castelli in aria.

daylight ['deilait], *s.* **1.** luce del giorno, giorno; alba: *before* —, prima del giorno; *by* —, di giorno; *in broad* —, in pieno giorno; *he was up at* —, era alzato all'alba ‖ *to burn* —, sprecare il tempo **2.** *fig.* chiarezza: *I begin to see* —, (*fam.*) comincio a vederci chiaro **3.** apertura, spazio libero ‖ *to let — into s.o.*, (*sl.*) pugnalare o fucilare qlcu. **4.** *pl.* (*arc.*) gli occhi ☆ *saving — time*, ora legale.

daylong ['deilɔŋ], *ag.* che dura tutta la giornata ‖ *av.* per tutta la giornata.

daytime ['dei-taim], *s.* il giorno, la giornata: *in the* —, di giorno, durante la giornata.

daze [deiz], *s.* sbalordimento; intontimento; stupore: *to be in a* —, essere istupidito, stupefatto, inebetito.

to **daze**, *v.t.* sbalordire, intontire; stupefare.

dazed [deizd], *ag.* stupefatto; inebetito (da un narcotico); intontito (da un colpo).

dazedly ['deizidli], *av.* con aria intontita, sbalordita.

dazzle ['dæzl], *s.* **1.** abbagliamento, accecamento **2.** (*mar. mil.*) mascheramento, mimetizzazione ☆ *— lamps* (o *lights*), (*aut.*) fari abbaglianti.

to **dazzle**, *v.t.* **1.** abbagliare: *dazzled with* (o *by*) *the light*, abbagliato dalla luce **2.** (*mar.*) mimetizzare: *to* — (o *paint*) *a ship*, (*mil.*) mascherare, mimetizzare una nave.

dazzlement ['dæzlmənt], *s.* abbagliamento.

dazzler ['dæzlə*], *s.* **1.** (*sl.*) cosa, persona che abbaglia **2.** colpo che stordisce.

dazzling ['dæzliŋ], *ag.* abbagliante: *— sky*, cielo radioso.

dazzlingly ['dæzliŋli], *av.* in modo abbagliante.

DDT ['di:di:'ti:], *s.* (*abbr.* di *diclorodifeniltricloroetano*) DDT.

deacon ['di:kən], *s.* **1.** (*eccl.*) diacono **2.** (*chiesa presbiteriana*) fabbriciere; anziano ☆ *— hide*, (*amer.*) pelle di vitello nato morto.

deaconess ['di:kənis], *s.f.* diaconessa.

deaconry ['di:kənri], *s.* diaconato.

deaconship ['di:kənʃip], *s.* diaconato, ufficio di diacono.

to **deactivate** [di'æktiveit], *v.t.* (*amer.mil.*) smobilitare.

dead [ded], *ag.* **1.** morto (*anche fig.*): *— colour*, colore morto; *the — hours*, le ore tranquille, la notte; *— language*, lingua morta; *— leaves*, foglie morte; *— market*, (*comm.*) mercato morto; *— season*, stagione morta; *— to the world*, morto per il mondo; *— with fright*, morto di paura ‖ *— and gone* (o *— and buried*), morto e sepolto ‖ *the Dead Sea*, il Mar Morto ‖ *as — as a doornail*, (*fam.*) morto stecchito; *he is — and done for*, (*fam.*) è bell'e spacciato; *my fingers feel — owing to the cold*, le mie dita sono insensibili per il freddo ‖ *to drop down* —, cadere a terra morto; *to fall* —, cadere morto; *to strike s.o.* —, colpire qlcu. a morte ‖ *— men tell no tales*, *prov.* i morti non parlano **2.** improvviso; completo; assoluto; esatto: *— calm*, calma assoluta; *— certainty*, certezza assoluta; *— secret*, segreto assoluto; *— silence*, silenzio di tomba; *— sleep*, sonno profondo; *— stop*, fermata brusca ‖ *to be — on time*, essere in perfetto orario ‖ *to be in — earnest*, fare proprio sul serio ‖ *to come to a — stop*, fermarsi di colpo, completamente.

dead, *s.* **1.** *the* —, i morti: *the Office for the* —, ufficio funebre; *to rise from the* —, risuscitare **2.** *fig.* cuore, profondità: *at — of night*, nel cuore della notte **3.** *pl.* (*miner.*) detriti, ganga.

dead, *av.* assolutamente; completamente; profondamente: — *asleep,* profondamente addormentato ‖ *to be* — *against sthg.,* essere assolutamente contrario a ql.co. ‖ *to go* — *slow,* procedere il più lentamente possibile ‖ *to stop* —, arrestarsi di colpo.

dead, (*nei composti*): — *-alive,* monotono, poco interessante (di luogo, occupazione, ecc.); — *angle,* (*mil.*) angolo morto; — *-ball,* (*tennis*) palla morta; — *-beat,* (*sl.*) completamente esaurito; — *broke,* squattrinato; — *-centre,* (*mec.*) punto morto; — *-drunk,* ubriaco fradicio; — *-eye,* (*mar.*) bigotta; — *-fire,* fuoco di S. Elmo; — *-freight,* (*comm.*) vuoto per pieno; — *-head,* chi viaggia, chi assiste ad uno spettacolo con biglietto omaggio; — *-house,* obitorio; — *-letter,* lettera non recapitata: *to become a* — *-letter,* cadere in disuso (di leggi, regole, ecc.); — *-light,* (*mar.*) oblò; — *-line,* linea non superabile; — *-load,* (*edil.*) carico fisso; — *-loss,* perdita completa; — *man,* morto; — *-men* (o *marines*), bottiglie vuote; — *money,* (*comm.*) denaro morto; — *-pan,* (*amer.*) viso senza espressione; — *-shot,* tiratore infallibile; — *tired,* stanco morto; — *-weight,* peso morto; (*mar.*) portata lorda; — *-wire,* (*elett.*) filo a terra; — *woman,* morta.

to deaden ['dednj], *v.t.i.* **1.** attutire (colpo, rumore, ecc.); affievolire, affievolirsi; indebolire, indebolirsi (di luce, ecc.); calmare, calmarsi (di dolore, ecc.); rendere insensibile **2.** isolare acusticamente.

deadener ['dednə*], *s.* ammorzatore ☆ *sound* —, isolante acustico.

deadening ['dedniŋ], *ag.* ammortizzante, smorzante ‖ *s.* **1.** ammortizzamento; isolamento acustico, insonorizzazione **2.** materiale insonorizzante; (*aut.*) antirombo.

deader ['dedə*], *s.* (*sl.*) cadavere.

deading ['dediŋ], *s.* (*tec.*) rivestimento; guarnizione.

deadliness ['dedlinis], *s.* velenosità.

deadlock ['dedlok], *s.* **1.** situazione insolubile, punto morto **2.** serratura a scatto.

deadly ['dedli], *ag.* **1.** mortale: — *insult,* insulto mortale **2.** implacabile: — *hatred,* odio implacabile **3.** (*fam.*) insopportabile, noioso: *a* — *party,* una festa noiosissima ☆ — *sin,* peccato mortale.

deadly, *av.* come la morte; mortalmente: — *pale,* pallido come un morto ‖ *in* — *earnest,* (*fam.*) proprio sul serio ‖ *it was* — *cold,* faceva un freddo da morire.

deadness ['dednis], *s.* **1.** torpore (di membra, ecc.); stasi (negli affari) **2.** indifferenza, insensibilità.

deaf [def], *ag.* sordo (anche *fig.*): — *and dumb,* sordomuto; — *in one ear,* sordo da un orecchio ‖ *as* — *as a* (*door-*) *post,* sordo come una talpa ‖ *to turn a* — *ear,* fare orecchi da mercante ‖ *there are none so* — *as those that will not hear,* *prov.* non c'è peggior sordo di chi non vuol udire ☆ — *-mute,* sordomuto, sordomuta.

to deafen ['defn], *v.t.* assordare, rendere sordo: *a deafening noise,* un rumore assordante.

deafness ['defnis], *s.* sordità.

deal[1] [di:l], *s.* quantità: *a great* —, *a good* — (*of time, money, etc.*), moltissimo (tempo, denaro, ecc.); *he is a good* — *better,* sta molto meglio; *to have a good* — *to do,* avere molto da fare ‖ *that's saying a good* —!, non è dire poco!.

deal[2], *s.* **1.** (*comm.*) affare, accordo: *to do a* — *with s.o.,* fare un affare con qlcu.; *to make a* —, venire ad un accordo ‖ *it's a* —, siamo d'accordo, affare fatto! ‖ *to give s.o. a fair* (o *square*) —, agire lealmente verso qlcu. **2.** (*pol.*) accordo: — *between parties,* accordo segreto tra partiti ‖ *New Deal,* « New Deal » (riforma economica attuata da Roosevelt nel 1932) **3.** (*carte*) il dare le carte; la mano: *whose* — *is it? your* —!, a chi tocca dare le carte? *to pass the* —, passare la mano ☆ *new* —, nuova gestione, organizzazione.

to deal[2], *pass.p.p.* **dealt** [delt], *v.t.i.* **1.** trattare; negoziare; mercanteggiare, contrattare; occuparsi: *I know*

how to — *with him,* so io come conviene trattarlo; *I refuse to* — *with him,* mi rifiuto di avere a che fare con lui; *to* — *generously with* (o *by*) *s.o.,* trattare qlcu. generosamente; *to* — *in* (*wool, etc.*), commerciare (in lana, ecc.); *to* — *with a piece of business,* trattare, combinare un affare; *to* — *with a situation,* affrontare una situazione; *to* — *with s.o.,* fare affari (o commerciare) con qlcu.; *to* — *with a subject,* occuparsi di, trattare un argomento; *man easy to* — *with,* uomo accomodante **2.** distribuire, ripartire, dispensare: *he was dealt four aces,* (*a carte*) gli son toccati quattro assi; *whose turn is it to* —?, (*a carte*) a chi tocca dare le carte?; *to* — *out gifts,* distribuire doni **3.** assestare (un colpo); *to* — *a blow at s.o.* (o *to* — *s.o. a blow*), assestare un colpo a qlcu.

deal[3], *s.* (asse di) legno d'abete o di pino ‖ *he can see through a* — *board,* (*fam.*) ha occhi di lince ☆ — *table,* una tavola (di assi) d'abete ‖ *red* —, abete rosso; *white* —, abete bianco.

dealer ['di:lə*], *s.* **1.** commerciante, negoziante: — *in wool,* negoziante in lana **2.** chi distribuisce le carte (da giuoco) ☆ *antique* —, antiquario; *double-* —, simulatore; *horse-* —, commerciante di cavalli; *retail* —, dettagliante; *wholesale* —, grossista; *wool* —, commerciante in lana.

dealing ['di:liŋ], *s.* **1.** commercio: — *in wool,* commercio della lana **2.** distribuzione (di doni, di carte da giuoco) **3.** *pl.* relazioni, rapporti: *to have dealings with s.o.,* avere rapporti con qlcu. **4.** condotta, modo di agire ☆ *double-* —, slealtà; doppiezza; *fair-* —, condotta leale; *underhand* —, condotta disonesta.

dealt [delt], *pass.p.p.* di to **deal.**

deambulation [di,æmbju'leifən], *s.* deambulazione.

deambulatory [di'æmbjulətəri], *ag.* deambulatorio.

dean[1] [di:n], *s.* **1.** (*eccl.*) decano; diacono; arciprete **2.** preside (di facoltà universitaria o di collegio universitario).

dean[2], *s.* valletta boscosa.

deanery ['di:nəri], *s.* decanato.

deanship ['di:nʃip], *s.* funzione di decano.

dear [diə*], *ag.* **1.** caro, amato, diletto: *my* — *children,* i miei cari bambini; *my* — *fellow,* caro amico; *he is* — *to me,* egli mi è caro; *to hold s.o.* —, voler bene a qlcu. ‖ *Dear Sir, Madam,* Egregio Signore, Gentile Signora; *My dearest Mary,* Mia carissima Maria (introduzione nelle lettere) ‖ *to run for* — *life,* correre a gambe levate **2.** caro, costoso: — *food,* cibo caro; *to get* —, *dearer,* diventare caro, rincarare ‖ *s.c.* caro. cara: *what a* —!, che cara persona!; *he's an old* —, è un carissimo uomo ‖ *help me there's a* —, (*fam.*) aiutami, su, da bravo.

dear, *av.* a caro prezzo; caro: *he sold his life* —, vendette la vita a caro prezzo.

dear, *inter.*: — —!, mio Dio!; — *me!,* ohimè!; *oh* — *me!,* o povero me!; *oh* — *no!,* certamente no!.

dearie ['diəri], *s.c.* (*fam.*) mio caro, mia cara.

dearish ['diəriʃ], *ag.* piuttosto costoso, caro.

dearly ['diəli], *av.* **1.** caramente, teneramente: *I love him* —, lo amo teneramente ‖ — *beloved brethren,* (*eccl.*) miei cari fratelli **2.** caro, a caro prezzo (anche *fig.*).

dearness ['diənis], *s.* **1.** tenerezza, affetto (per persone) **2.** caro prezzo, l'essere caro (di viveri).

dearth [də:θ], *s.* scarsità, penuria (di viveri, ecc.); povertà (di idee, ecc.).

deary ['diəri], *s.c.* (*fam.*) caro, cara.

death [deθ], *s.* morte, fine; *fig.* rovina, perdita: *the* — *of one's hopes, plans, ambitions,* il crollo delle proprie speranze, dei propri progetti, delle proprie ambizioni; *you 'll be the* — *of me!,* (*fam.*) sarai la mia rovina!; *your foolish boldness will be your* —, la tua folle audacia sarà la causa della tua rovina; *to be at* —*'s door,* essere in punto di morte; *to be burnt, frozen, starved to* —, morire bruciato, assiderato, di fame; *to bleed to* —, morire dissanguato; *to die a violent* —, morire di morte violenta; *to do s.o. to* —, *(arc.)* uccidere qlcu.; *to put s.o. to* —, condannare qlcu. a morte ‖ *as sure as* —, sicuro come due più due fa quattro ‖ *a fight to the* —, un combattimento all'ultimo sangue ‖ *tired (o bored) to* —, *(fam.)* stufo morto ‖ *to be in at the* —, *(caccia)* essere presenti all'uccisione della preda; *(fam.)* assistere al coronamento di un'impresa ‖ *to catch one's* — *of cold*, prendersi un malanno ‖ *to drink oneself to* —, accorciarsi la vita per il troppo bere ‖ *to snatch s.o. from the jaws of* —, strappare qlcu. alla morte **2.** *(dir.)* decesso: *proof of* —, constatazione di morte; *to notify a* —, notificare un decesso **3.** *pl.* necrologie ☆ — *adder*, *(zool.)* vipera; — *-bed*, letto di morte; — *-blow*, colpo mortale (anche *fig.*); —, *-chamber*, camera mortuaria; — *-duties*, *(dir.)* diritti di successione; —*'s-head*, teschio (simbolo di morte); — *-mask*, maschera mortuaria; — *-moth*, *(entom.)* atropo, testa di morto; — *-place*, luogo di morte; — *-rate*, mortalità; — *-rattle*, rantolo della morte; — *-stricken*, colpito a morte; — *-throes*, agonia; — *-trance*, *(med.)* letargo; — *-warrant*, ordine di esecuzione di sentenza di morte; — *-wound*, ferita mortale ‖ *the Black Death*, *(st.)* la Peste (del XIV sec.).

deathless ['deθlis], *ag.* immortale; eterno, imperituro.

deathlessly ['deθlisli], *av.* eternamente.

deathlessness ['deθlisnis], *s.* immortalità.

deathlike ['deθlaik], *ag.* simile alla morte, cadaverico: — *pallor*, pallore cadaverico.

deathly ['deθli], *ag.* *(letter.)* mortale; simile alla morte ‖ *av.* come la morte: — *pale*, pallido come la morte.

deb [deb], *(abbr. fam.)* di **débutante**.

débâcle [dei'bɑ:kl], *s.* **1.** sgelo repentino; rottura improvvisa del ghiaccio d'un fiume; forte corrente d'acqua che trascina blocchi di pietra e detriti **2.** *fig.* disastro, sfacelo, crollo.

to debar [di'bɑ:*], *pass.p.p.* **debarred** [di'bɑ:d], *v.t.* **1.** escludere, privare: *to* — *s.o. a right*, privare qlcu. di un diritto; *to* — *s.o. from sthg.*, escludere qlcu. da ql.co., privare qlcu. di ql.co. **2.** impedire, vietare; *to* — *s.o. from doing sthg.*, impedire a qlcu. di fare ql.co.

to debark [di'bɑ:k], *v.t.i.* sbarcare, fare uno sbarco.

debarkation [,di:bɑ:'keiʃən], *s.* sbarco.

to debase [di'beis], *v.t.* **1.** svilire, avvilire; abbassare, degradare: *to* — *oneself*, degradarsi **2.** svalutare, deprezzare (il valore del denaro, ecc.); falsificare (monete, usando leghe di basso valore).

debasement [di'beismənt], *s.* **1.** avvilimento; degradazione; abiezione **2.** svalutazione; falsificazione (di monete).

debaser [di'beisə*], *s.* falsificatore (di monete).

debasing [di'beisiŋ], *ag.* degradante, avvilente ‖ *s. V.* **debasement**.

debatable [di'beitəbl], *ag.* discutibile; contestabile.

debate [di'beit], *s.* dibattimento; dibattito (politico); discussione; contraddittorio, disputa: *the question is in* — (o *under* —), si sta discutendo la questione; *to open the* —, aprire il dibattito.

to debate, *v.t.i.* **1.** discutere; dibattere; disputare; sostenere una discussione; contestare: *a much debated question*, una questione molto dibattuta; *to* — *with s.o. on sthg.*, discutere con qlcu. su ql.co. **2.** considerare, ponderare, pensare: *I was debating whether to go to the seaside or to the mountains*, ero in dubbio se andare al mare o in montagna **3.** *(arc.)* riportare, conseguire (una vittoria).

debater [di'beitə*], *s.* argomentatore; oratore.

debating [di'beitiŋ], *s.* dibattito; discussione ☆ — *point*, argomento di discussione.

debauch [di'bɔ:tʃ], *s.* stravizio, bagordo; dissolutezza, sregolatezza: *to have a* —, fare un'orgia.

to debauch, *v.t.i.* **1.** pervertire, depravare, corrompere; traviare, sedurre (una donna) **2.** corrompere, viziare (gusto, ecc.); darsi alla dissolutezza.

debauchable [di'bɔ:tʃəbl], *ag.* corruttibile.

debauched [di'bɔ:tʃt], *ag.* corrotto.

debauchee [,debɔ:'tʃi:], *s.c.* persona pervertita, corrotta.

debaucher [di'bɔ:tʃə*] *s.* corruttore; seduttore.

debauchery [di'bɔ:tʃəri], *s.* dissolutezza; scostumatezza; pervertimento, corruzione: — *of youth*, *(dir.)* corruzione di minorenni.

debenture [di'bentʃə*], *s.* *(comm.)* obbligazione: *mortgage* —, obbligazione garantita da ipoteca.

debilitant [di'bilitənt], *ag.* *s.* debilitante.

to debilitate [di'biliteit], *v.t.* debilitare.

debilitation [di,bili'teiʃən], *s.* debilitazione.

debility [di'biliti], *s.* debolezza; astenia: — *of purpose*, irresolutezza.

debit ['debit], *s.* debito, dare: *to enter sthg. to the* — (*-side*) *of an account*, registrare ql.co. nel dare di un conto ☆ — *note*, nota di addebito.

to debit, *v.t.* addebitare: *to* — *a firm with a sum*, addebitare una somma ad una ditta; *to be debited to*, essere addebitato a, a carico di.

debitable ['debitəbl], *ag.* da addebitarsi a: *charge* — *to s.o.'s account*, spesa da addebitarsi a conto di qlcu.

debonair [,debə'nɛə*], *ag.* *(arc.)* gioviale; gaio; disinvolto; cortese.

Deborah ['debərə], *no.pr.f.* Debora.

to debouch [di'bautʃ], *v.i.* sfociare (di fiume), sboccare: *the army debouched into the plain*, l'esercito sboccò nella pianura.

debouchment [di'bautʃmənt], *s.* sbocco, sfociamento.

debris ['debri], *s.* detriti; rottami; avanzi; macerie.

debt [det], *s.* debito; *fig.* obbligo: — *of honour*, debito di giuoco; *to be in* — *to*, essere indebitato a, con; *to be out of* —, non avere più debiti; *to make debts, to get into* —, far dei debiti ☆ — *-collector*, esattore di crediti ‖ *bad debts*, crediti inesigibili; *book debts*, crediti chirografari.

debtor ['detə*], *s.c.* debitore, debitrice: *I am your* — *for (money, much kindness, etc.)*, sono vostro debitore per (denaro, le molte gentilezze fattemi, ecc.) ☆ — *account*, conto debitori; — *side*, *(comm.)* colonna del dare.

to debunk [di:'bʌŋk], *v.t.* *(fam.)* ridurre alle giuste proporzioni (una reputazione, un'istituzione, ecc.): *to* — *the cult of s.o.*, fare scendere qlcu. dal piedistallo.

to debus ['di:'bʌs], *v.t.i.* *(sl. mil.)* scaricare; (far) scendere (da autocarro, autobus).

début ['deibu:], *s.* debutto (di un artista); ingresso in società (di fanciulla): *to make one's* —, esordire.

débutant ['debju(:)tɑ:ŋ], *s.* esordiente.

débutante ['debju(:)tɑ:nt], *s.* debuttante (fanciulla che fa il suo ingresso in società; fanciulla presentata alla corte inglese).

decade ['dekeid], *s.* decade; decennio; decina.

decadence ['dekədəns], *s.* decadenza.

decadent ['dekədənt], *ag.* decadente ‖ *s.* *(letter.)* decadente.

decagon ['dekəgən], *s.* *(geom.)* decagono.

decagonal [de'kægənl], *ag.* *(geom.)* decagonale.

decagram(me) ['dekəgræm], *s.* decagrammo (misura di peso = 0.352 oz.).

decahedron [,dekə'hi:drən], *s.* *(geom.)* decaedro.

decalcification ['di:,kælsifi'keiʃən], *s.* *(patol.)* decalcificazione.

to decalcify [di:'kælsifai], *v.t.* *(patol.)* decalcificare.

decalitre ['dekə,li:tə*], *s.* decalitro (misura di capacità = 610.25 cu. in.).

decalogue ['dekələg], *s.* decalogo.

decametre ['dekə,mi:tə*], *s.* decametro (misura di lunghezza = 32.80 ft.).

to decamp [di'kæmp], *v.i.* **1.** *(mil.)* levar le tende **2.** *(fam.)* svignarsela.

decampment [di'kæmpmənt], *s.* **1.***(mil.)* il levar le tende **2.** *fig.* l'andarsene furtivamente.

to decant [di'kænt],*v.t.* decantare (liquidi), travasare.

decantation [ˌdiːkænˈteiʃən], s. decantazione, travasamento.

decanter [diˈkæntə*], s. caraffa.

decanterful [diˈkæntəful], s. il contenuto di una caraffa.

decanting [diˈkæntiŋ], s. (chim.) decantazione.

to **decapitate** [diˈkæpiteit], v.t. decapitare.

decapitation [diˌkæpiˈteiʃən], s. decapitazione.

decapod [ˈdekəpod], s. (zool.) decapodo.

decarbonization [diːˌkaːbənaiˈzeiʃən], s. (chim. metal.) decarburazione.

to **decarbonize** [diːˈkaːbənaiz], v.t. (chim. metal.) decarburare.

decarburization [diːˌkaːbjuəraiˈzeiʃən], s. (chim. metal.) decarburazione.

to **decarburize** [diːˈkaːbjuəraiz], v.t. (chim. metal.) decarburare.

decasualization [diːˌkæʒjuəlaiˈzeiʃən], s. eliminazione di lavoro avventizio.

to **decasualize** [diːˈkæʒjuəlaiz], v.t. eliminare la provvisorietà di (lavoro).

decasyllabic [ˈdekəsiˈlæbik], ag. (poes.) decasillabo.

decasyllable [ˈdekəsiləbl], ag. s. (poes.) decasillabo.

decay [diˈkei], s. 1. decadimento, decadenza (di paese, famiglia, arte, commercio) 2. deperimento, indebolimento (di salute): senile —, deperimento senile 3. perdita, rovina, sfacelo; disastro (di fortuna, ecc.): to fall into —, cadere in rovina 4. putrefazione; carie (di denti) 5. (fis.) disintegrazione (di sostanza radioattiva).

to **decay**, v.t.i. 1. decadere, far decadere; declinare (di nazione, famiglia, arte, commercio) 2. deperire, indebolirsi 3. andare in rovina; mandare in rovina; rovinare, crollare (di edifici, sostanze): decayed gentlewoman, signora decaduta 4. putrefarsi; cariarsi (di denti): decayed teeth, denti cariati.

decease [diˈsiːs], s. (dir.) decesso, morte.

to **decease**, v.i. decedere, morire.

deceased [diˈsiːst], ag. 1. (dir.) deceduto, defunto 2. appartenente a, di un defunto ‖ s.c. defunto, defunta ☆ — estate, il patrimonio del defunto.

deceit [diˈsiːt], s. 1. inganno; furberia; seduzione; illusione 2. (dir.) frode, truffa, dolo 3. falsità.

deceitful [diˈsiːtful], ag. ingannevole, delusorio, fallace; falso.

deceitfully [diˈsiːtfuli], av. in modo ingannevole; falsamente.

deceitfulness [diˈsiːtfulnis], s. inganno; falsità; fallacia.

deceivable [diˈsiːvəbl], ag. ingannabile, facile ad essere ingannato.

to **deceive** [diˈsiːv], v.t.i. 1. ingannare; imbrogliare; illudere; usare inganni: to — oneself, ingannarsi; illudersi 2. deludere.

deceiver [diˈsiːvə*], s.c. ingannatore, ingannatrice.

to **decelerate** [diːˈseləreit], v.t.i. (ferr., ecc.) rallentare; moderare la propria velocità.

deceleration [diːˌseləˈreiʃən], s. rallentamento; (fis. mec.) decelerazione, rallentamento.

decelerator [diːˈseləreitə*], s. (mec.) rallentatore.

December [diˈsembə*], s. 1. dicembre 2. (amer.) l'ultimo periodo (p.e. della vita).

decemvir [diˈsemvə*], s. (st.) decemviro.

decemvirate [diˈsemvirit], s. (st.) decemvirato.

decency [ˈdiːsnsi], s. 1. decenza; pudore; creanza; modestia: sense of —, pudore 2. pl. convenienze, decoro ☆ common decencies, le convenienze sociali.

decennary [diˈsenəri], ag. decennale ‖ s. decennio.

decennial [diˈsenjəl], ag.s. decennale.

decennially [diˈsenjəli], av. ogni dieci anni.

decennium [diˈsenjəm], pl. **decennia** [diˈsenjə], s. decennio.

decent [ˈdiːsnt], ag. 1. decente; modesto; conveniente: — clothes, abiti decenti 2. (fam.) moderato; discreto: — conditions, condizioni discrete; — house, casa decente; — language, linguaggio decente 3. (fam.) buono, soddisfacente: he's a — sort (o fellow o chap), è una persona per bene, un buon diavolo.

decently [ˈdiːsntli], av. decentemente; convenientemente; decorosamente.

decentralization [diːˌsentrəlaiˈzeiʃən], s. decentramento.

to **decentralize** [diːˈsentrəlaiz], v.t. decentrare.

deception [diˈsepʃən], s. inganno; frode; insidia; delusione.

deceptive [diˈseptiv], ag. ingannevole; illusorio; menzognero: appearances are—, le apparenze ingannano.

deceptively [diˈseptivli], av. in modo ingannevole; in modo menzognero.

deceptiveness [diˈseptivnis], s. carattere menzognero (di ql.co.); fallacia; falsità.

decibel [ˈdesibell], s. (elett.) decibel ☆ — meter, indicatore di decibel.

decidable [diˈsaidəbl], ag. che si può decidere.

to **decide** [diˈsaid], v.t.i. 1. decidere, prendere una decisione, stabilire; risolvere (questione, querela, ecc.): nothing has been decided yet, non c'è ancora nulla di deciso; to — s.o.'s fate, decidere il destino di qlcu.; to — to do sthg., decidere di fare ql.co.: I have decided to leave, ho deciso di partire ‖ to — against doing sthg., decidere, risolvere di non fare ql.co.; to — against s.o., sthg., pronunciarsi contro qlcu., ql.co. ‖ to — for (o in favour of) s.o., pronunciarsi in favore di qlcu. ‖ to — for oneself, decidere da sè ‖ to — on doing sthg., decidere di fare ql.co. ‖ to — (up)on sthg., decidere in merito a ql.co., stabilire ql.co.: have you decided on the price?, hai stabilito il prezzo?; the matter was soon decided on, la questione fu rapidamente risolta 2. (IV) indurre: to — s.o. to do sthg., indurre qlcu. a fare ql.co.

decided [diˈsaidid], ag. 1. deciso; risoluto: they are —, sono decisi 2. incontestabile, innegabile: a — difference, una differenza inconfutabile.

decidedly [diˈsaididli], av. 1. decisamente, risolutamente 2. indubbiamente.

decider [diˈsaidə*], s. 1. arbitro, giudice 2. partita decisiva.

deciding [diˈsaidiŋ], ag. decisivo: the — game, la partita decisiva.

deciduous [diˈsidjuəs], ag. caduco; (bot.) deciduo.

decigram(me) [ˈdesigræm], s. decigrammo (misura di peso = 1.543 gr.).

decilitre [ˈdesiˌliːtə*], s. decilitro (misura di capacità = 6.102 cu. in.).

decimal [ˈdesiməl], ag. decimale ‖ s. 1. decimale 2. pl. aritmetica decimale ☆ — point, (mat.) punto che divide le unità dai decimali; — system, sistema decimale ‖ recurring —, (mat.) numero decimale periodico.

to **decimate** [ˈdesimeit], v.t. decimare.

decimation [ˌdesiˈmeiʃən], s. decimazione.

decimetre [ˈdesiˌmiːtə*], s. decimetro (misura di lunghezza = 3.937 in.).

decipher [diˈsaifə*], s. decifrazione (di iscrizioni, geroglifici, ecc.).

to **decipher**, v.t. decifrare.

decipherable [diˈsaifərəbl], ag. decifrabile.

deciphering [diˈsaifəriŋ], **decipherment** [diˈsaifəmənt], s. decifrazione (di iscrizioni, geroglifici, ecc.).

decision [diˈsiʒən], s. 1. decisione: deliberazione; giudizio: final —, giudizio inappellabile 2. decisione, risoluzione: to come to (o to arrive at o to reach a) — (as to), giungere a una decisione (in merito a) 3. fig. risolutezza, fermezza: he acted with —, agì con fermezza.

decisive [diˈsaisiv], ag. 1. decisivo: — battle, battaglia decisiva 2. fermo, deciso: — manner, tone, modo, tono deciso.

decisively [diˈsaisivli], av. 1. in modo decisivo 2. decisamente.

decisiveness [diˈsaisivnis], s. 1. carattere decisivo (di un'esperienza, ecc.) 2. risolutezza; perentorietà.

Decius [′di:ʃjəs], *no.pr.m.* Decio.

deck [dek], *s.* **1.** (*mar.*) ponte, coperta: *to come* (o *to go*) *on* —, montare sul ponte ‖ *to clear the decks* (*for action*), sgombrare i ponti per entrare in azione (in guerra) **2.** (*mar. aer.*) piano, ponte, piattaforma **3.** (*amer.*) mazzo di carte da giuoco ☆ — -*boy*, mozzo di ponte; — -*cargo*, (*mar. comm.*) carico di coperta; — -*chair*, sedia a sdraio; — -*hand*, inserviente addetto al ponte; — -*house*, cabina di coperta; — -*passenger*, passeggero che viaggia sul ponte ‖ *flight* —, (*aer.*) ponte di volo, cabina piloti; *main* —, ponte di coperta; *middle* —, ponte di mezzo; *quarter* —, cassero di poppa; *top* —, imperiale (di autobus).

to deck, *v.t.* **1.** ornare, adornare; coprire, rivestire: *to* — *with flags*, imbandierare; *to* — *with flowers*, infiorare ‖ *to* — *oneself out*, mettersi in ghingheri **2.** (*mar.*) pontare: *to* — (*over, in*) *a ship*, mettere il ponte ad una nave.

decked [dekt], *ag.* (*mar.*) pontato ☆ *three-* — *ship*, nave a tre ponti; *double-* — *airliner*, (*aer.*) velivolo di linea a due ponti.

decker [′dekə*], *s.* mezzo di trasporto a piani ☆ *double-* —, (*aer.*) biplano; (*mar.*) nave a due ponti; (*fam.*) autobus, ecc. a due piani; *three-* —, (*mar.*) nave a tre ponti; (*fam. fig.*) romanzo in tre volumi.

decking [′dekiŋ], *s.* **1.** decorazione; sbandieramento (di navi, vie, ecc., generalmente con *out*) **2.** (*mar.*) coperta **3.** (*edil.*) impermeabilizzazione di una terrazza.

to declaim [di′kleim], *v.t.i.* **1.** declamare; arringare; recitare (versi) **2.** *to* — *against* (*s.o., sthg.*), protestare contro.

declaimer [di′kleimə*], *s.c.* declamatore, declamatrice.

declamation [ˌdeklə′meiʃən], *s.* declamazione; arringa; esercizio retorico.

declamatory [di′klæmətəri], *ag.* declamatorio.

declarant [di′klɛərənt], *s.c.* (*dir.*) dichiaratore, dichiaratrice.

declaration [ˌdeklə′reiʃən], *s.* dichiarazione: — *of income*, dichiarazione del reddito; — *of the poll*, scrutinio elettorale; — *of war*, dichiarazione di guerra ‖ *Declaration of Independence*, (*st. amer.*) Dichiarazione d'Indipendenza (4 luglio 1776); *Declaration of Rights*, Dichiarazione dei Diritti.

to declare [di′klɛə*], *v.t.i.* **1.** dichiarare; proclamare; render noto, fare una dichiarazione: *he was declared king*, fu proclamato re; *when will the results of the race be declared?*, quando saranno resi noti i risultati della corsa? ‖ *to* — *peace*, proclamare la pace; *to* — *a strike*, proclamare uno sciopero; *to* — *war* (*on, against s.o.*), dichiarare guerra a qlcu. **2.** (*IV*) dichiarare, dichiararsi; affermare, assicurare: *he declared he had seen you*, assicurò di averti visto; *to* — *oneself* (*to be*), dichiararsi: *I* — *myself* (*to be*) *innocent*, mi dichiaro innocente; *to* — *s.o.* (*to be*), dichiarare che qlcu. è: *I* — *him* (*to be*) *a traitor*, lo dichiaro traditore; *to* — *oneself*, dichiararsi (innamorato) ‖ *well, I* — *!*, oh, questa poi! **3.** *to* — *for, against* (*sthg.*), dichiararsi in favore di, contro **4.** *to* — (*a contract*) *off*, (*fam.*) rescindere, disdire (un contratto) **5.** (*dogana*) dichiarare: *have you anything to* —*?*, avete niente da dichiarare? **6.** (*giuoco delle carte*) dichiarare **7.** manifestarsi (di malattia).

declared [di′klɛəd], *ag.* dichiarato: *a* — *enemy*, un nemico dichiarato.

declaredly [di′klɛəridli], *av.* dichiaratamente, apertamente; formalmente.

declarer [di′klɛərə*], *s.c.* dichiaratore, dichiaratrice (giuoco del «bridge»).

declension [di′klenʃən], *s.* **1.** decadenza, declino (di un impero); alterazione; deviazione (del carattere) **2.** (*gram.*) declinazione.

declinable [di′klainəbl], *ag.* (*gram.*) declinabile.

declination [ˌdekli′neiʃən], *s.* **1.** inclinazione, pendio, pendenza **2.** (*astr.*) declinazione **3.** (*amer.*) rifiuto

☆ — *compass*, declinometro ‖ *magnetic* —, declinazione magnetica.

declinatory [di′klainətəri], *ag.* (*dir.*) che rifiuta: — *plea*, richiesta di incompetenza.

decline [di′klain], *s.* **1.** declino (di un giorno, una vita, un impero); decadenza, decadimento; tramonto; deperimento (della salute, ecc.): — *of* (o *in*) *prices*, ribasso dei prezzi; *to be on the* —, essere in ribasso (di prezzi), essere sul declinare (di persone) **2.** (*med.*) languore, consunzione: *to fall into a* —, perdere le forze, la salute, soffrire di consunzione.

to decline, *v.t.i.* **1.** (*II*) declinare; rifiutare cortesemente (invito, onore, offerta); schivare, evitare, esimersi da: *he declined the invitation with thanks*, egli ringraziò ma declinò l'invito; *to* — *battle*, (*mil.*) non accettare il combattimento; *to* — *to do* (o *to* — *doing*) *sthg.*, rifiutarsi di fare ql.co. **2.** (*gram.*) declinare (un nome) **3.** declinare; diminuire; calare; tramontare; venir meno, deperire (di giorno, sole, salute, influenza, impero, ecc.): *his strength was slowly declining*, le sue forze andavano diminuendo lentamente ‖ *to* — *from virtue*, deviare dalla virtù, dalla retta via **4.** (*comm.*) ribassare, essere in ribasso: *business is declining daily*, gli affari diminuiscono di giorno in giorno; *to* — *in price*, diminuire di prezzo **5.** inchinarsi, curvarsi verso il basso; essere in pendenza (di terreno) **6.** (*arc.*) chinare (la testa).

declining [di′klainiŋ], *ag.* declinante, nel (suo) declino: — *sun*, sole al tramonto; *in one's* — *years*, nel declinare della vita ‖ *s.* **1.** rifiuto (di un invito, ecc.) **2.** deperimento **3.** (*gram.*) declinazione, l'atto di declinare.

declinometer [ˌdekli′nɔmitə*], *s.* (*fis.*) declinometro.

declivitous [di′klivitəs], *ag.* in pendio, scosceso.

declivity [di′kliviti], *s.* pendio, declivio.

declivous [di′klaivəs], *ag.* declive, in pendenza.

to declutch [′di:′klʌtʃ], *v.i.* (*aut.*) disinnestarsi (di frizione).

decoction [di′kɔkʃən], *s.* **1.** (*farm.*) decozione (operazione per la quale si fa un decotto) **2.** decotto.

to decode [′di:′koud], *v.t.* decifrare.

decoherer [ˌdi:kou′hiərə*], *s.* (*rad.*) martelletto che stacca il coesore (per trasformare la frequenza delle radioonde).

to decollate [di′kɔleit], *v.t.* decapitare, decollare.

decollation [ˌdi:kɔ′leiʃən], *s.* decapitazione, decollazione.

décolleté [dei′kɔltei], *ag.* scollato (d'abito da signora) ‖ *s.* scollatura.

decolo(u)rization [di:ˌkʌlərai′zeiʃən], *s.* decolorazione.

to decolo(u)rize [di:′kʌləraiz], *v.t.* decolorare.

decolo(u)rizer [di:′kʌləraizə*], *s.* decolorante.

decomposable [ˌdi:-kəm′pouzəbl], *ag.* scomponibile.

to decompose [ˌdi:-kəm′pouz], *v.t.i.* **1.** decomporre, scomporre, scomporsi **2.** decomporsi, putrefarsi.

decomposer [ˌdi:-kəm′pouzə*], *s.* forza, agente che decompone.

decomposing [ˌdi:-kəm′pouziŋ], *ag.* **1.** che decompone **2.** in decomposizione, in putrefazione.

decomposite [di:′kɔmpəzit], *ag.* **1.** doppiamente composto **2.** (*bot.*) composito ‖ *s.* (*gram.*) parola doppiamente composta.

decomposition [ˌdi:-kɔmpə′ziʃən], *s.* **1.** decomposizione: *double* —, (*chim.*) doppia decomposizione **2.** alterazione, disintegrazione, putrefazione.

decompound [ˌdi:-kəm′paund], *V.* **decomposite**, *ag.*

to deconsecrate [′di:′kɔnsikreit], *v.t.* sconsacrare.

deconsecration [′di:ˌkɔnsi′kreiʃən], *s.* sconsacrazione.

to decontaminate [′di:-kən′tæmineit], *v.t.* togliere il contagio da (abiti, ambienti, ecc.).

decontamination [′di:-kən‚tæmi′neiʃən], *s.* azione di togliere il contagio.

to decontrol [′di:-kən′troul], *pass.p.p.* **decontrolled** [′di:-kən′trould], *v.t.* liberalizzare (il commercio, specialmente dal controllo governativo).

décor ['deikɔ:*], s. abbellimento, decorazione (di stanza, palcoscenico, ecc.).

to **decorate** ['dekəreit], v.t. **1.** decorare, ornare **2.** verniciare e tappezzare (un appartamento, ecc.) **3.** decorare (un militare, ecc.): *he was decorated with the George Cross*, ricevette la Croce di S. Giorgio.

decoration [,dekə'reiʃən], s. **1.** decorazione, ornamento; abbellimento (di strade, case, ecc.) **2.** decorazione, onorificenza || *Decoration Day*, (amer.) il 30 maggio (giorno in cui si depongono fiori sulle tombe dei caduti nella Guerra Civile) ☆ *war* —, decorazione di guerra.

decorative ['dekərətiv], ag. decorativo.

decorator ['dekəreitə*], s. decoratore; pittore decoratore (di appartamenti) ☆ *interior* —, arredatore, tappezziere in carta.

decorous ['dekərəs], ag. decoroso.

decorously ['dekərəsli], av. decorosamente.

to **decorticate** [di'kɔ:tikeit], v.t. scortecciare.

decortication [di,kɔ:ti'keiʃən], s. scortecciamento.

decorum [di'kɔ:rəm], s. buona creanza; senso della dignità.

decoy [di'kɔi], s. **1.** esca; richiamo **2.** adescatore; lusingatore; compare (di un truffatore) ☆ — *(-bird)*, (uccello da) richiamo; — *-duck*, anitra da richiamo; — *(-pond)*, capannuccia o reti preparate in una palude per la caccia delle anitre selvatiche.

to **decoy**, v.t. adescare; allettare; abbindolare; attirare: *to — s.o. into doing sthg.*, trascinare (con inganno) qlcu. a fare ql.co.; *to — s.o. into a trap*, attirare qlcu. in una trappola.

decrease ['di:kri:s], s. diminuzione; decrescimento; decrescenza: — *in value, in population*, diminuzione di valore, della popolazione; *to be on the* —, essere in diminuzione: *exports are on the* —, le esportazioni sono in diminuzione.

to **decrease** [di:'kri:s], v.t.i. diminuire; far diminuire; decrescere: *age decreases strength*, l'età diminuisce le forze; *my appetite has decreased*, il mio appetito è diminuito.

decreasing [di:'kri:siŋ], ag. decrescente: — *series*, (mat.) serie decrescenti.

decreasingly [di:'kri:siŋli], av. di meno in meno, in modo decrescente.

decree [di'kri:], s. decreto; editto; sentenza; ordinanza: *to issue a* —, promulgare un decreto ☆ — *nisi*, (dir.) sentenza provvisoria (di divorzio, ecc.).

to **decree**, v.t. decretare; ordinare; emettere un decreto.

decrement ['dekrimənt], s. diminuzione; (rad.) decremento.

decrepit [di'krepit], ag. decrepito.

to **decrepitate** [di'krepiteit], v.t.i. (chim.) decrepitare, calcinare.

decrepitation [di,krepi'teiʃən], s. (chim.) decrepitazione, calcinazione.

decrepitude [di'krepitju:d], s. decrepitezza.

decrescendo ['di:-kri'ʃendou], s. (mus.) decrescendo.

decrescent [di'kresnt], ag. decrescente: — *moon*, luna calante.

decretal [di'kri:tl], s. decretale, decreto papale || *the Gregorian Decretals*, le Decretali di Gregorio.

to **decry** [di'krai], v.t. denigrare; screditare.

decubitus [di'kju:bitəs], s. (med.) decubito.

decuman ['dekjumən], ag. **1.** decumano, immenso **2.** (st. romana) decumano: — *gate*, porta decumana ☆ — *wave*, (mar.) flutto decumano.

decumbent [di'kʌmbənt], ag. (zool. bot.) decombente; reclinato.

decuple ['dekjupl], ag. s. decuplo.

to **decuple**, v.t.i. decuplicare, decuplicarsi.

decurion [di'kjuəriən], s. (st.) decurione.

decury ['dekəri], s. (st.) decuria.

decussate [di'kʌsit], ag. (bot.) decussato, disposto traversalmente.

to **decussate** [di'kʌseit], v.t.i. incrociare, incrociarsi a forma di X; disporre traversalmente.

dedendum [di'dendəm], s. (mec.) dedendum.

to **dedicate** ['dedikeit], v.t. **1.** dedicare, consacrare (chiesa, ecc.); *to — oneself to s.o., to sthg.*, dedicarsi a qlcu., a ql.co. **2.** fare una dedica su (un libro, ecc.) **3.** (amer.) inaugurare (un edificio).

dedicatee [,dedikə'ti:], s.c. persona alla quale ql.co. è dedicata, consacrata.

dedication [,dedi'keiʃən], s. **1.** consacrazione **2.** dedica (su libro, ecc.).

dedicative ['dedikətiv], ag. dedicatorio.

dedicator ['dedikeitə*], s.c. dedicatore, dedicatrice.

dedicatory ['dedikətəri], ag. dedicatorio: — *letter*, lettera dedicatoria.

to **deduce** [di'dju:s], v.t. **1.** dedurre, desumere: *to — sthg. from a fact*, dedurre ql.co. da un fatto **2.** derivare, far discendere: *to — one's family from the Norman Conquest*, far discendere la propria famiglia dai tempi della Conquista Normanna.

deducible [di'dju:səbl], ag. deducibile.

to **deduct** [di'dʌkt], v.t. dedurre, detrarre, sottrarre, defalcare; togliere: *after deducting 10%*, dopo aver detratto il 10%; *to — a number, a sum*, detrarre, togliere un numero, una somma; *to — sthg. from the price*, defalcare ql.co. dal prezzo.

deduction [di'dʌkʃən], s. **1.** deduzione, sottrazione, trattenuta, defalco, ribasso **2.** deduzione, ragionamento deduttivo.

deductive [di'dʌktiv], ag. deduttivo.

deductively [di'dʌktivli], av. deduttivamente.

dee[1] [di:], s. **1.** di (la lettera *d*) **2.** a forma di D.

to **dee**[2], v.i. (scoz.) morire.

deed [di:d], s. **1.** azione, atto, fatto; gesta: *a — of valour*, un atto di valore; *deeds, not words*, fatti, non parole; *good deeds*, buone azioni; *in very* —, in realtà, di fatto **2.** (dir.) strumento, atto (notarile), scrittura legale: — *of gift, atto di donazione*; — *of partnership*, atto costitutivo (di società commerciale); *private* —, atto privato; *signature of a* —, sottoscrizione di un atto; *to draw a* —, redigere un atto ☆ — *-box*, cofanetto (per conservare documenti legali); — *-poll*, (dir.) atto unilaterale; contratto a titolo gratuito.

to **deed**, v.t. (amer. dir.) trasferire con atto legale.

to **deem** [di:m], v.t. giudicare, stimare, credere, considerare, pensare: *I — it an honour to serve you*, considero un onore il servirvi; *I do not — it necessary to go*, non credo sia necessario andare; *to — highly of s.o.*, aver un'alta opinione di qlcu.

deep [di:p], ag. **1.** profondo, alto; — *lake*, lago profondo; *a — wound*, una ferita profonda; *snow three feet* —, neve alta tre piedi; *he fell into a — hole*, cadde in una buca profonda || *to go off the — end*, (sl.) arrabbiarsi, perdere il controllo di sè **2.** largo, esteso: *the crowd was twenty* —, la folla si accalcava in venti file; *this land is 100 feet* —, questo terreno è largo 100 piedi **3.** fig. profondo; oscuro: *a — argument*, argomento astruso; *a — mystery*, un mistero profondo; — *sigh*, profondo sospiro; — *sorrow*, dolore profondo; — *thinker*, pensatore profondo **4.** sprofondato, immerso: — *in a book*, sprofondato in un libro; — *in love*, — *in debt*, — *in thought*, profondamente innamorato, affogato nei debiti, sprofondato nei pensieri; *in — waters*, in cattive acque || *a — one*, (sl.) un dritto **5.** cupo (di colore): — *red*, rosso cupo.

deep, s. **1.** (poet.) *the* —, il mare, l'oceano: *a monster out of the* —, un mostro marino **2.** gener. pl. abisso, profondità: *the ocean deeps*, gli abissi dell'oceano.

deep, av. profondamente: *with his hands — in his pockets*, con le mani affondate nelle tasche; *he went on dancing — into the night*, continuò a danzare fino a notte inoltrata; *to breathe* —, respirare profondamente; *to dig — for water*, scavare profondamente per cercare l'acqua; *to drink* —, bere abbondantemente || *still waters run* —, prov. le acque chete rovinano i ponti.

deep, (*nei composti*): — *-drawn,* profondo; — *-freeze,* (*neol.*) surgelamento; — *-laid,* segreto, complicato; — *-lying,* profondo; — *mourning,* lutto stretto; — *-read,* erudito; — *-rooted,* dalle radici profonde; *fig.* radicato; — *-sea,* alto mare; — *-seated,* profondamente stabilito; — *-set,* incavato, infossato ‖ *ankle-* —, *knee-* —, sprofondato fino alla caviglia, al ginocchio; *skin-* —, superficiale.

to deepen [ˈdiːpən], *v.t.i.* **1.** approfondire; scavare **2.** incupire, incupirsi (di colore) **3.** *fig.* approfondire, approfondirsi: *the silence deepened,* il silenzio si fece più profondo.

deeply [ˈdiːpli], *av.* profondamente: — *interesting,* profondamente interessante; *he fell* — *in love with her,* s'innamorò profondamente di lei; *I am* — *indebted to you,* ti sono profondamente obbligato; *I* — *regret,* mi dispiace profondamente; *to go* — *into sthg.,* penetrare a fondo in ql.co., approfondire ql.co.

deepness [ˈdiːpnis], *s.* **1.** profondità **2.** *fig.* astuzia.

deer [diə*], *s.* (*invariato al pl.*) cervo; daino ☆ — *-forest,* riserva di caccia al cervo; — *-hound,* grosso levriero usato per la caccia ai cervi; — *-lick,* (*amer.*) rocce coperte di sale (per attirare i cervi); — *-skin,* pelle di daino; — *-stalker,* cacciatore di cervi (con fucile); berretto da cacciatore ‖ *fallow* —, daino; *red* —, alce; *rein-* —, renna.

to deface [diˈfeis], *v.t.* **1.** sfigurare, sfregiare; mutilare; guastare (un'opera d'arte); rendere illeggibile **2.** cancellare, annullare (un francobollo).

defacement [diˈfeismənt], *s.* **1.** sfregio; mutilazione **2.** cancellazione; annullamento.

defacer [diˈfeisə*], *s.c.* sfregiatore, sfregiatrice; mutilatore, mutilatrice.

to defalcate [ˈdiːfælkeit], *v.i.* sottrarre beni; defalcare indebitamente.

defalcation [ˌdiːfælˈkeiʃən], *s.* defalco; appropriazione indebita (di beni dati in custodia); (*dir.*) concussione.

defalcator [ˈdiːfælkeitə*], *s.* chi commette appropriazione indebita; (*dir.*) concussionario.

defamation [ˌdefəˈmeiʃən], *s.* diffamazione, calunnia.

defamatory [diˈfæmətəri], *ag.* diffamatorio, calunnioso.

to defame [diˈfeim], *v.t.* diffamare, parlar male di.

defamer [diˈfeimə*], *s.c.* diffamatore, diffamatrice.

default [diˈfɔːlt], *s.* **1.** mancanza, difetto, omissione: *in* — *of,* in difetto di **2.** (*dir.*) mancata comparizione (in tribunale); contumacia: *judgement by* —, giudizio in contumacia **3.** (*comm.*) inadempienza: — *in paying,* inadempienza nei pagamenti; *not considered in* —, non considerato come inadempiente.

to default, *v.t.i.* **1.** (*dir.*) essere contumace, rendersi contumace **2.** condannare in contumacia **3.** venire meno agli obblighi; essere inadempiente.

defaulter [diˈfɔːltə*], *s.* **1.** (*dir.*) imputato contumace **2.** debitore moroso **3.** reo di appropriazione indebita **4.** (*mil.*) soldato punito, consegnato.

defeasance [diˈfiːzəns], *s.* (*dir.*) annullamento, abrogazione ☆ — *clause,* clausola risolutiva (di un contratto).

defeasible [diˈfiːzəbl], *ag.* (*dir.*) annullabile.

defeat [diˈfiːt], *s.* **1.** sconfitta, disfatta: *to suffer a* —, subire una sconfitta **2.** fallimento (di un progetto); insuccesso (di un'impresa).

to defeat, *v.t.* **1.** sconfiggere, sbaragliare; rovesciare **2.** far fallire (un progetto, ecc.); frustrare: *to* — *s.o.'s plans,* far fallire i piani di qlcu. **3.** (*dir.*) annullare.

defeatism [diˈfiːtizm], *s.* disfattismo.

defeatist [diˈfiːtist], *s.* disfattista.

to defecate [ˈdiːfikeit], *v.t.i.* **1.** (*fisiol. chim.*) defecare **2.** *fig.* purificare.

defecation [ˌdiːfiˈkeiʃən], *s.* (*fisiol. chim.*) defecazione.

defect [diˈfekt], *s.* **1.** difetto; imperfezione; mancanza; inconveniente: *bodily defects,* imperfezioni fisiche; *everyone has his defects,* ognuno ha i suoi difetti **2.** insufficienza; fallo.

defection [diˈfekʃən], *s.* defezione; abbandono; diserzione; (*relig.*) apostasia.

defective [diˈfektiv], *ag.* **1.** difettoso; imperfetto: — *memory,* memoria imperfetta; *to be* — *in sthg.,* mancare di ql.co. **2.** anormale: — *child,* bambino anormale **3.** (*gram.*) difettivo ‖ *s.* anormale, deficiente; sciocco: *a mental* —, un debole di mente.

defectively [diˈfektivli], *av.* difettosamente.

defectiveness [diˈfektivnis], *s.* difettosità.

defence [diˈfens], *s.* **1.** difesa, protezione: *line of* —, linea di difesa; *offence and* —, offesa e difesa; *to fight in* — *of one's country,* combattere per la difesa del proprio paese **2.** (*dir.*) arringa: *counsel for the* —, avvocato difensore (nelle cause civili); *in* — *of,* a difesa di; *to make a* — *against,* sostenere una difesa contro **3.** *pl.* (*mil.*) difese, fortificazioni, opere di difesa ☆ *self-* —, autodifesa.

defenceless [diˈfenslis], *ag.* senza difesa, indifeso.

defencelessness [diˈfenslisnis], *s.* incapacità, impossibilità di difendersi.

to defend [diˈfend], *v.t.i.* difendere, proteggere (anche *fig.*); fare una difesa: *they defended the town against the enemy,* difesero la città contro il nemico; *we had a stick to defend us from the dog,* avevamo un bastone per difenderci dal cane ‖ *God defend!,* che Dio ci aiuti!

defendant [diˈfendənt], *ag.s.* convenuto, imputato.

defender [diˈfendə*], *s.* difensore; (*spor.*) campione che difende il titolo ‖ *Defender of the Faith,* Difensore della Fede (titolo dei sovrani inglesi).

defenestration [diˌfenisˈtreiʃən], *s.* defenestrazione.

defense, (*amer.*) per **defence.**

defensibility [diˌfensiˈbiliti], *s.* difendibilità.

defensible [diˈfensəbl], *ag.* difensibile; giustificabile.

defensibly [diˈfensəbli], *av.* in modo da essere giustificato, da essere difeso.

defensive [diˈfensiv], *ag.* difensivo ‖ *s.* difensiva: *to be* (o *to stand*) *on the* —, stare sulla difensiva.

defensively [diˈfensivli], *av.* in modo difensivo.

to defer¹ [diˈfə*], *pass.p.p.* **deferred** [diˈfəːd], *v.t.i.* differire, rimandare, prorogare: *to* — *sthg. to a later date,* rimandare ql.co. a più tardi ☆ *deferred payment,* pagamento a rate; *deferred telegram,* telegramma differito.

to defer², *v.i.* essere deferente; rimettersi, sottomettersi (all'opinione, al giudizio altrui): *to* — *to s.o.'s opinions,* rimettersi alle opinioni di qlcu.

deference [ˈdefərəns], *s.* deferenza, rispetto: *in* (o *out of*) — *to,* per deferenza verso; *with all due* — *to you,* con tutto il rispetto che vi devo; *to show* — *to,* mostrare della deferenza verso.

deferent [ˈdefərənt], *ag.* **1.** (*anat.*) deferente: — *duct,* canale deferente **2.** (*rar.*) deferente, rispettoso.

deferential [ˌdefəˈrenʃəl], *ag.* deferente, rispettoso.

deferentially [ˌdefəˈrenʃəli], *av.* con deferenza.

deferment [diˈfəːmənt], *s.* differimento; dilazione; (*mil.*) rinvio della chiamata di leva.

defiance [diˈfaiəns], *s.* sfida: *in* — *of* (*the law, an order*), a dispetto di (una legge, un ordine); *he shouted* — *at the enemy,* lanciò una sfida al nemico; *to bid* — *to s.o.,* lanciare una sfida a qlcu.; trattare qlcu. con disprezzo; *to set s.o. at* —, sfidare qlcu., non rispettare (gli ordini, ecc. di) qlcu.

defiant [diˈfaiənt], *ag.* ardito, provocante, insolente.

defiantly [diˈfaiəntli], *av.* con tono provocante; con aria di sfida; arditamente.

deficiency [diˈfiʃənsi], *s.* **1.** deficienza, difetto, insufficienza **2.** (*comm.*) scoperto, disavanzo: *to make up a* —, colmare un disavanzo **3.** (*med.*) carenza (*in, of, di*): — *in vitamins,* carenza di vitamine.

deficient [diˈfiʃənt], *ag.* deficiente; difettoso; incompleto; insufficiente: *a mentally* — *person,* una persona mentalmente deficiente.

deficiently [diˈfiʃəntli], *av.* deficientemente; insufficientemente.

deficit ['defisit], *s.* (*comm.*) disavanzo, deficit: *to make up* (*good*) *the* —, colmare il disavanzo.

defier [di'faiə*], *s.c.* sfidante; provocatore, provocatrice.

to **defilade** [,defi'leid], *v.t.* (*mil.*) riparare (una fortificazione) dalla vista, dal tiro del nemico.

defile[1] ['di:fail], *s.* gola, stretto passo (attraverso cui le truppe possono procedere solo in fila).

to **defile**[1] [di'fail], *v.i.* (*mil.*) procedere, marciare in fila.

to **defile**[2], *v.t.* **1.** insozzare, lordare, contaminare; profanare **2.** violare; (*arc.*) violentare.

defilement [di'failmənt], *s.* contaminazione; profanazione.

defiler [di'failə*], *s.c.* contaminatore, contaminatrice; profanatore, profanatrice.

definable [di'fainəbl], *ag.* definibile, determinabile.

to **define** [di'fain], *v.t.* definire; determinare; delineare; delimitare: *to — one's position*, precisare la propria posizione (politica, ecc.) ☆ *well-defined*, ben definito, chiaramente disegnato.

definite ['definit], *ag.* **1.** definito; ben determinato, preciso, chiaro: — *answer*, risposta precisa; — *order*, *sale*, (*comm.*) ordinazione, vendita ferma **2.** (*gram.*) definito: — *article*, articolo definito, determinativo; *past* —, passato remoto.

definitely ['definitli], *av.* in modo preciso, ben determinato.

definiteness ['definitnis], *s.* natura precisa, definita; precisione; determinatezza.

definition [,defi'nifən], *s.* **1.** definizione **2.** (*eccl.*) decisione **3.** (*rad.*) fedeltà (nella riproduzione); (*foto. tv.*) nitidezza (dell'immagine).

definitive [di'finitiv], *ag.* definitivo; decisivo, finale.

definitively [di'finitivli], *av.* definitivamente, decisamente.

to **deflagrate** ['deflagreit], *v.t.i.* (*chim.*) deflagrare; far deflagrare.

deflagration [,deflə'greifən], *s.* (*chim.*) deflagrazione.

deflagrator ['deflagreitə*], *s.* deflagratore.

to **deflate** [di'fleit], *v.t.i.* **1.** sgonfiare, sgonfiarsi (pneumatico, di pneumatico) **2.** (*econ. pol.*) ridurre la carta moneta circolante.

deflation [di'fleifən], *s.* **1.** sgonfiamento (di pallone, pneumatico) **2.** (*econ. pol.*) deflazione **3.** (*geol.*) erosione dovuta ai venti.

deflationary [di'fleifnəri], *ag.* (*econ.*) deflazionistico.

deflationist [di'fleifnist], *s.* (*econ. pol.*) fautore della deflazione.

to **deflect** [di'flekt], *v.t.i.* deflettere; deviare, far deviare.

deflection [di'flekfən], *s.* deviazione; deformazione; flessione; incurvatura.

deflector [di'flektə*], *s.* (*mec.*) apparato deviatore; deflettore ☆ — *coils*, (*tv.*) bobine di deflessione elettromagnetica; — *plates*, (*tv.*) placche di deflessione.

deflexion, *V.* **deflection**.

defloration [,di:flɔ:'reifən], *s.* **1.** deflorazione, stupro **2.** florilegio letterario.

to **deflower** [di:'flauə*], *v.t.* **1.** deflorare, stuprare **2.** spogliare (una pianta, ecc.) dei fiori **3.** devastare, sciupare.

defluent ['deflu(:)ənt], *ag.* defluente.

defluxion [di'flʌkfən], *s.* **1.** deflusso **2.** (*patol.*) deflusso, flusso.

to **defoliate** [di'foulieit], *v.t.* spogliare; sfrondare, sfrondarsi (una pianta, di una pianta).

defoliation [di,fouli'eifən], *s.* il cadere delle foglie.

to **deforest** [di'forist], *v.t.* disboscare.

deforestation [di,foris'teifən], *s.* disboscamento.

to **deform** [di'fɔ:m], *v.t.* deformare; sfigurare; deturpare: *deformed by illness*, sfigurato dalla malattia.

deformation [,di:fɔ:'meifən], *s.* **1.** deformazione; alterazione **2.** (*patol.*) deformità; malformazione congenita ☆ *field* —, (*elett.*) torsione di campo.

deformed [di'fɔ:md], *ag.* deforme ☆ — *waves*, (*rad.*) onde sfasate.

deformity [di'fɔ:miti], *s.* **1.** deformità **2.** (*arc.*) bruttezza.

to **defraud** [di'frɔ:d], *v.t.* defraudare, frodare: *to — s.o. of sthg.*, defraudare qlcu. di ql.co.

defrauder [di'frɔ:də*], *s.* frodatore, defraudatore.

defrauding [di'frɔ:diŋ], *s.* frode.

to **defray** [di'frei], *v.t.* pagare: *to — the cost of sthg.*, coprire il costo di; *to — s.o.'s expenses*, rimborsare le spese a qlcu.

defrayable [di'freiəbl], *ag.* rimborsabile, a carico: *the upkeep of the roads is — by the town*, la manutenzione delle strade è a carico della città.

defrayal [di'freiəl], **defrayment** [di'freimənt], *s.* rimborso (spese).

to **defrock** [di:'frɔk], *v.t.* spretare.

to **defrost** [di:'frɔst], *v.t.* **1.** sgelare, disgelare (cibi) **2.** disgelare; sbrinare (il ghiaccio incrostatosi, *p.e.* su cella frigorifera) **3.** (*comm.*) sgelare (crediti, titoli, ecc.).

defroster [di:'frɔstə*], *s.* (*aut.*) riscaldatore, visiera termica.

deft [deft], *ag.* lesto; destro; agile; abile (specialmente di mani).

deftly ['deftli], *av.* destramente; abilmente.

deftness ['deftnis], *s.* destrezza; abilità: — *of touch*, abilità nell'usare il pennello.

defunct [di'fʌŋkt], *ag.* defunto, morto.

to **defy** [di'fai], *v.t.* **1.** sfidare; provocare: *I — you to do so*, vi sfido a fare ciò; *you must not — the law*, non dovete sfidare la legge **2.** offrire difficoltà insuperabili a: *the fortress defied all attacks*, la fortezza resistette a tutti gli attacchi; *the problem defied solution*, il problema non offriva nessuna soluzione; *to — description*, essere impossibile a descriversi.

degassing ['di:'gæsiŋ], *s.* **1.** degassificazione **2.** (*fonderia*) degassificazione.

degaussing ['di:'gausiŋ], *s.* (*elett. mar.*) smagnetizzazione.

degeneracy [di'dʒenərəsi], *s.* **1.** degenerazione; pervertimento **2.** (*rad.*) controreazione.

degenerate [di'dʒenərit], *ag.s.* degenerato.

to **degenerate** [di'dʒenəreit], *v.t.i.* **1.** degenerare: *thrift that degenerates into avarice*, senso dell'economia che degenera in avarizia **2.** (*arc.*) far degenerare.

degeneration [di,dʒenə'reifən], *s.* **1.** degenerazione **2.** (*rad.*) controreazione **3.** (*patol.*) degenerazione ☆ *black* —, melanismo; *fatty* —, (*patol.*) degenerazione grassa.

deglutition [,di:glu:'tifən], *s.* (*fisiol.*) deglutizione.

degradation [,degrə'deifən], *s.* **1.** degradazione; abbrutimento: *to live a life of* —, vivere nel fango **2.** (*fis. geol.*) degradazione.

to **degrade** [di'greid], *v.t.i.* **1.** degradare, degradarsi; avvilire, avvilirsi; degenerare: *to — man to the level of beasts*, abbassare gli uomini al livello delle bestie **2.** rimandare di un anno l'esame finale a Cambridge per il titolo di B. A.

degrading [di'greidiŋ], *ag.* degradante, avvilente.

degree [di'gri:], *s.* **1.** (*mat. fis. geog.*) grado: *a high — of humidity*, un alto grado di umidità; *the thermometer registers 15 degrees centigrade*, il termometro segna 15 gradi centigradi; *we were 30 degrees North*, ci trovavamo a 30 gradi latitudine Nord **2.** livello; grado: *a high — of culture*, un alto grado di cultura ‖ *by degrees*, a gradi, gradatamente; *in some* —, in una certa misura; *to a* —, (*fam.*) al più alto grado; *to a certain* (o *some*) —, fino ad un certo grado, punto; *to such a* — (*that*), a tal punto (che); *to a very large* —, con moltissima probabilità; *to what* —, quanto, fino a che punto **3.** rango, condizione: *a girl of high* —, una fanciulla di alto rango **4.** laurea, titolo: *a doctor's* —, dottorato; *a London* —, laurea dell'università di Londra; *to take one's* —, laurearsi **5.** (*gram.*) grado: — *of* *comparison*, grado di comparizione; *comparative* —, grado comparativo **6.** (*mat.*) grado: *equation of the second* —, equazione di secondo grado **7.** (*dir.*) grado: — *of relationship*, grado di parentela ☆ *first* — *murder*, (*amer.*) assassinio premeditato; *honorary* —, laurea ad honorem; *second* — *murder*, (*amer.*) omicidio preterintenzionale; *third* —, (*amer.*) interrogatorio di terzo grado.

degression [di'greʃən], *s.* diminuzione progressiva (del rapporto tra imposte e reddito).

degressive [di'gresiv], *ag.*: — *taxation*, tassazione progressiva.

to **dehisce** [di'his], *v.i.* (*bot.*) schiudersi (di semi, capsule, baccelli).

dehiscence [di'hisns], *s.* (*bot.*) deiscenza.

dehiscent [di'hisnt], *ag.* (*bot.*) deiscente.

dehortative [di'hɔ:tətiv], *ag.* (*rar.*) dissuasivo ‖ *s.* (*rar.*) consiglio che tende a dissuadere.

to **dehumanize** [di:'hju:mənaiz], *v.t.* disumanare.

dehumidification ['di:,hju:midifi'keiʃən], *s.* deumidificazione.

to **dehumidify** [,di:hju:'midifai], *v.t.* deumidificare.

to **dehydrate** [di:'haidreit], *v.t.* (*chim.*) disidratare.

dehydration [,di:hai'dreiʃən], *s.* (*chim.*) disidratazione.

deicer ['di:'aisə*], *s.* (*aer.*) dispositivo antighiaccio.

deicide ['di:isaid], *s.* **1.** deicida **2.** deicidio.

deification [,di:ifi'keiʃən], *s.* deificazione.

to **deify** ['di:ifai], *v.t.* deificare; divinizzare.

to **deign** [dein], *v.t.i.* degnare, degnarsi; accondiscendere: *she did not — me an answer*, essa non mi degnò di una risposta; *to — to do sthg.*, accondiscendere a fare ql.co.

deil [di:l], *s.* (*scoz.*) diavolo.

deionization ['di:,aiənai'zeiʃən], *s.* (*fis.*) deionizzazione.

deism ['di:izəm], *s.* deismo.

deist ['di:ist], *s.* deista.

deistic [di:'istik], *ag.* deistico.

deity ['di:iti], *s.* **1.** divinità, essenza divina **2.** dio, dea, divinità.

to **deject** [di'dʒekt], *v.t.* abbattere; scorare.

dejected [di'dʒektid], *ag.* abbattuto; scoraggiato.

dejectedly [di'dʒektidli], *av.* con aria scoraggiata; tristemente.

dejectedness [di'dʒektidnis], *s.* (*rar.*) abbattimento.

dejection [di'dʒekʃən], *s.* **1.** abbattimento, malinconia, tristezza **2.** (*fisiol.*) deiezione; escremento.

dekko ['dekou], *s.* (*sl. mil.*) sguardo, colpo d'occhio: *let's have a* —, fate vedere.

delaine [də'lein], *s.* mussola di lana.

to **delate** [di'leit], *v.t.* denunciare (una persona, un misfatto).

delation [di'leiʃən], *s.* delazione.

delator [di'leitə*], *s.c.* delatore, delatrice.

delay [di'lei], *s.* **1.** indugio; rinvio: *an hour's* —, un ritardo di un'ora; *without (further)* —, senza (ulteriore) ritardo, indugio; *to cause* —, causare ritardo; *to make no — in doing sthg.*, non ritardare a fare ql.co. **2.** (*comm. dir.*) proroga, dilazione: *to obtain a — in payment*, ottenere una proroga nel pagamento.

to **delay**, *v.t.i.* **1.** ritardare, ostacolare, rinviare, differire: *the train was delayed by the snow*, il ritardo del treno fu provocato dalla neve **2.** indugiare, indugiarsi; tardare, esitare, fermarsi: *to — in doing sthg.*, tardare, indugiare a far ql.co.

delayed [di'leid], *ag.* ritardato ☆ — *-action*, (*mec.*) ad azione ritardata.

delaying [di'leiiŋ], *ag.* che ritarda, che causa ritardo: — *action*, (*mil.*) azione ritardatrice, di disturbo ‖ *s.* ritardo.

del credere [del'kredəri], *ag. s.* (*comm.*) del credere.

to **dele** ['di:li(:)], *v.t.* (*tip.*) cancellare: —, cancella.

delectable [di'lektəbl], *ag.* (*letter.*) dilettevole; delizioso; piacevole.

delectableness [di'lektəblnis], *s.* (*letter.*) natura deliziosa (di ql.co.).

delectably [di'lektəbli], *av.* dilettevolmente.

delectation [,di:lek'teiʃən], *s.* diletto.

delectus [di'lektəs], *s.* raccolta di versioni latine o greche.

delegacy ['deligəsi], *s.* **1.** delegazione (atto del delegare) **2.** poteri del delegato **3.** commissione di delegati.

delegate ['deligit], *s.* delegato.

to **delegate** ['deligeit], *v.t.* delegare: *to — s.o. to do sthg.*, delegare qlcu. a fare ql.co.

delegation [,deli'geiʃən], *s.* **1.** delegazione (di diritti); delega **2.** (*amer.*) delegazione, commissione: *the American — was numerous*, la delegazione americana era numerosa.

to **delete** [di'li:t], *v.t.* **1.** cancellare (ql.co. di scritto, di stampato) **2.** annullare, sopprimere (parola, ecc.) (anche *fig.*).

deletion [di'li:ʃən], *s.* **1.** cancellatura (di parole) **2.** soppressione (*p.e.* di un paragrafo).

delf(t) [delf(t)], *s.* maiolica di Delft (Olanda).

Delia ['di:ljə], *no.pr.f.* Delia.

deliberate [di'libərit], *ag.* **1.** ponderato, cauto, prudente: — *action*, azione cauta; — *judgment*, giudizio ponderato **2.** intenzionale, premeditato: — *insult*, insulto voluto; — *lie*, menzogna premeditata.

to **deliberate** [di'libəreit], *v.t.i.* **1.** deliberare **2.** ponderare, riflettere; agire senza fretta.

deliberately [di'libəritli], *av.* **1.** deliberatamente, con proposito deliberato **2.** volutamente, con premeditazione.

deliberateness [di'libəritnis], *s.* **1.** ponderatezza; misura (nelle azioni) **2.** intenzione premeditata (di un insulto, ecc.).

deliberation [di,libə'reiʃən], *s.* **1.** decisione meditata: *after due* —, dopo la dovuta deliberazione, riflessione; *to act with* —, agire con riflessione, con ponderatezza **2.** deliberazione, dibattito (di un'assemblea).

deliberative [di'libərətiv], *ag.* **1.** deliberativo: *in a — moment*, in un momento di riflessione **2.** deliberante (assemblea, corpo, ecc.): — *assembly*, assemblea deliberante.

deliberatively [di'libərətivli], *av.* per deliberazione; in assemblea deliberante.

delicacy ['delikəsi], *s.* **1.** delicatezza, finezza (di qualità): *the — of her features*, la delicatezza dei suoi tratti; *the — of this design*, la delicatezza di questo disegno **2.** sensibilità (di sensi, sentimenti) **3.** debolezza, gracilità (di salute) **4.** difficoltà (di situazione politica) **5.** cibo ghiotto ☆ *table delicacies*, ghiottonerie.

delicate ['delikit], *ag.* **1.** delicato, fine (di qualità): *a — silk*, una seta fine **2.** sensibile (di sensi, sentimenti): *she has a — sense of smell*, ha un odorato fine **3.** debole, gracile (di salute) ‖ *to be in a — condition*, (*fam.*) essere in stato interessante **4.** difficile (di problema, situazione) ‖ *to tread on — ground*, (*fam.*) toccare argomenti delicati **5.** gustoso, raffinato (di cibo) ☆ — *-looking*, di aspetto gracile.

delicately ['delikitli], *av.* delicatamente.

delicateness ['delikitnis], *V.* **delicacy 1.**

delicatessen [,delikə'tesn], *s.pl.* ghiottonerie ☆ — *shop*, salumeria fine.

delicious [di'liʃəs], *ag.* delizioso; squisito: *what a — cake!*, che dolce delizioso!; *it smells* —, ha un profumo delizioso.

deliciously [di'liʃəsli], *av.* deliziosamente, squisitamente.

deliciousness [di'liʃəsnis], *s.* delizia; gusto squisito (di vivanda).

delict ['di:likt], *s.* (*dir.*) delitto: *in flagrant* —, in flagrante delitto.

delight [di'lait], *s.* **1.** delizia; delizie; diletto, piacere: *to be s.o.'s* —, essere la delizia di qlcu. **2.** gioia, contentezza: *to the great* — *of*, con grande gioia di; *to take* — *in doing* (o *to do*) *sthg.*, provare gioia, piacere nel fare ql.co.

to delight, *v.t.i.* **1.** deliziare; allettare, dilettare, incantare: *to* — *ears, eyes*, deliziare le orecchie, gli occhi **2.** provar piacere, compiacersi: *to* — *in sthg.*, dilettarsi di ql.co.; *to* — *in doing* (o *to do*) *sthg.*, provare gioia, piacere nel fare ql.co.

delighted [di'laitid], *ag.* **1.** incantato, ammirato: *to be* — *with s.o., with* (o *at*) *sthg.*, rallegrarsi alla vista di qlcu., per ql.co. **2.** lietissimo, felicissimo: — *to do sthg.*, lietissimo di fare ql.co.

delightedly [di'laitidli], *av.* con felicità, piacere, diletto.

delightful [di'laitful], *ag.* delizioso, dilettevole, molto piacevole: — *music, view*, musica, spettacolo che incanta.

delightfully [di'laitfəli], *av.* deliziosamente, molto piacevolmente: *she sings* —, ella canta deliziosamente.

delightsome [di'laitsəm], *ag.* (*arc. letter.*) piacevolissimo (di luogo).

Delilah [di'lailə], *no.pr.f.* (*Bibbia*) Dalila ‖ *s. fig.* tentatrice; donna di malaffare.

to delimit [di:'limit], **to delimitate** [di:'limiteit], *v.t.* delimitare (frontiere, ecc.).

delimitation [di,limi'teiʃən], *s.* delimitazione.

to delineate [di'linieit], *v.t.* delineare; tracciare; descrivere: *the mountains clearly delineated on the horizon*, le montagne si delineavano chiaramente all'orizzonte.

delineation [di,lini'eiʃən], *s.* delineazione; abbozzo; traccia, tracciato; disegno: — *of a character*, pittura di un carattere.

delineator [di'linieitə*], *s.* **1.** delineatore; disegnatore **2.** tracciatoio.

delinquency [di'liŋkwənsi], *s.* **1.** colpabilità, colpevolezza **2.** delinquenza; misfatto; delitto; traviamento: *juvenile* —, delinquenza minorile.

delinquent [di'liŋkwənt], *ag. s.* colpevole; delinquente; che, chi manca ai propri doveri ☆ — *taxes*, (*amer.*) imposte non pagate.

to deliquesce [,deli'kwes], *v.i.* (*chim. fis.*) liquefarsi, divenire liquido.

deliquescence [,deli'kwesns], *s.* (*chim.*) deliquescenza.

deliquescent [,deli'kwesnt], *ag* (*chim.*) deliquescente.

delirious [di'liriəs], *ag.* delirante, affetto da delirio; farneticante: — *with joy*, (*fam.*) pazzo di gioia; *to be* —, delirare; *to become* —, essere preso da delirio.

deliriously [di'liriəsli], *av.* in modo delirante; pazzamente.

delirium [di'liriəm], *s.* delirio; frenesia; furore ☆ — *tremens*, (*patol.*) delirium tremens.

to deliver [di'livə*], *v.t.* **1.** liberare, salvare: *to* — *oneself*, liberarsi: *to* — *oneself of an opinion*, *fig.* esprimere una opinione; *to* — *s.o. from death, captivity*, salvare qlcu. dalla morte, dalla cattività **2.** far partorire: *to be delivered of a child*, partorire ‖ *to* — *a woman* (*of a child*), assistere una donna nel parto **3.** consegnare: *to* — *s.o. into the hands of the enemy*, consegnare qlcu. in mano al nemico ‖ *to* — *oneself up to*, arrendersi a ‖ *to* — *over*, consegnare, cedere (una proprietà) **4.** consegnare, recapitare (lettere, pacchi, ecc.); trasmettere, consegnare (un messaggio); rilasciare (certificati, ecc.): *goods are delivered free, domicile, on board, to any address*, la merce viene consegnata gratis, a domicilio, a bordo, a qualsiasi indirizzo; *to* — *late*, effettuare la consegna in ritardo; *to* — *a lot of goods*, consegnare una partita di merci **5.** dare, vibrare (un colpo); fare (un attacco); lanciare (una palla) **6.** tenere, pronunciare (un discorso, ecc.) **7.** erogare.

deliverable [di'livərəbl], *ag.* (*comm.*) consegnabile.

deliverance [di'livərəns], *s.* **1.** liberazione **2.** (*fisiol.*) parto **3.** consegna **4.** dichiarazione, espressione enfatica (di opinione) **5.** (*dir. scoz.*) verdetto (della giuria).

deliverer [di'livərə*], *s.c.* **1.** liberatore, liberatrice; salvatore, salvatrice **2.** (*comm.*) chi consegna (merce, ecc.) **3.** chi esprime una data opinione.

delivery [di'livəri], *s.* **1.** (*arc.*) liberazione **2.** (*fisiol.*) parto **3.** (*mil.*) resa: — *of a town*, resa di una città **4.** consegna (di lettere, pacchi, merci, ecc.); distribuzione (di posta); svincolo: — *in bond*, (*comm.*) consegna in deposito franco; — *on rail*, consegna su vagone; — *to bearer*, consegna al latore; *cash on* — (*C. O. D.*), contro assegno; *check on* —, controllo alla consegna; *delay in* —, ritardo nella consegna; *times of* —, orario delle distribuzioni; *to effect* (o *to perform*) —, effettuare la consegna; *to get* —, ottenere la consegna; *to pay on* —, pagare alla consegna **5.** lancio (di una palla, ecc.); modo di lanciare **6.** il pronunciare (discorso, ecc.); dizione: *to have a good* —, saper pronunciare bene un discorso **7.** distribuzione, erogazione (di corrente elettrica, di acqua); materiale erogato, portata ☆ — -*charges*, spese di consegna; — -*man*, fattorino; — -*note*, bollettino di consegna; — -*order*, ordine di consegna; — *pipe outlet*, (*idraulica*) scarico del tubo di mandata; — *pressure* (o — *head*), (*idraulica*) pressione di mandata; — -*van*, furgoncino per consegne; — -*warrant*, ordine di consegna ‖ *due* —, consegna regolare; *express* (o *special*) —, consegna per espresso; *ex-quay* —, consegna sulla banchina; *forward* —, consegna a termine; *free* —, franco di consegna; *general* —, (*amer.*) (ufficio) fermo posta; *home* —, consegna a domicilio; *mail* —, distribuzione della corrispondenza; *non*- —, mancata consegna; *prompt* (o *ready* —), pronta consegna.

dell [del], *s.* valletta.

Delphi ['delfai], *no.pr.* (*geog.*) Delfo.

Delphian ['delfiən], **Delphic** ['delfik], *ag.* **1.** delfico, di Delfo **2.** *fig.* sibillino; ambiguo.

delphinium [del'finiəm], *s.* (*bot.*) fiorcappuccio.

delta ['deltə], *s.* **1.** delta (quarta lettera dell'alfabeto greco) **2.** (*geog.*) delta ☆ — *connection*, (*elett.*) triangolo; — -*metal*, metallo delta; — -*rays*, (*fis.*) raggi delta.

deltiology [,delti'olədʒi], *s.* (*amer.*) il raccogliere cartoline come passatempo.

to delude [di'lu:d], *v.t.* deludere; ingannare; indurre in errore: *to* — *oneself* (*with false hopes*), illudersi (con false speranze).

deluge ['delju:dʒ], *s.* diluvio (anche *fig.*): *a* — *of words*, un diluvio di parole ‖ *the Deluge*, il diluvio universale.

to deluge, *v.t.* inondare (anche *fig.*): *to be deluged with letters, questions, etc.*, essere sommerso da lettere, assalito da domande, ecc.

delusion [di'lu:ʒən], *s.* **1.** illusione; allucinazione; errore: *a fond* —, una dolce illusione; *to be under a* —, farsi illusioni, essere in errore **2.** inganno.

delusive [di'lu:siv], *ag.* illusorio, fallace; ingannevole.

delusively [di'lu:sivli], *av.* ingannevolmente.

delusiveness [di'lu:sivnis], *s.* illusorietà, fallacia.

delusory [di'lu:səri], *ag.* illusorio, fallace; ingannevole.

delve [delv], *s.* (*arc. poet.*) cavità (nel suolo); antro.

to delve, *v.t.i.* **1.** (*arc. poet.*) scavare (*to* — *up* (o *out*), esumare, disseppellire **2.** *fig.* far ricerche: *to* — *into the past*, rivangare il passato **3.** avvallarsi (di strada).

demagnetization ['di:,mægnitai'zeiʃən], *s.* demagnetizzazione.

to demagnetize ['di:'mægnitaiz], *v.t.* demagnetizzare.

demagogic [,demə'gogik], *ag.* demagogico.

demagogism ['deməgogizəm], *s.* demagogismo.

demagogue ['deməgog], *s.* demagogo.

demagogy ['deməgogi], *s.* demagogia.

demand [di'ma:nd], *s.* **1.** domanda, richiesta (anche *comm.*): *payable on* —, pagabile a presentazione, a vista; *supply and* —, domanda e offerta; *to be in great, little*

—, essere molto, poco richiesto; *to satisfy all demands*, soddisfare tutte le richieste **2.** esigenze: *the demands of the case*, le esigenze del caso; *to make great demands on s.o.'s patience, time, etc.*, esigere da qlcu. molta pazienza, molto tempo, ecc. ☆ — *bill*, *(comm.)* tratta a vista.

to **demand**, *v.t.* **1.** domandare, richiedere: *the policeman demanded his name*, il poliziotto chiese il suo nome; *this work demands patience*, questo lavoro richiede pazienza **2.** esigere, pretendere: *he demanded that I should go with him*, egli esigette che io andassi con lui; *he demands immediate payment*, egli esige pagamento immediato; *to* — *sthg. from* (o *of*) *s.o.*, esigere ql.co. da qlcu.

demandable [di'mɑːndəbl], *ag.* esigibile; che si può richiedere.

demandant [di'mɑːndənt], *s.c.* *(dir.)* attore.

demander [di'mɑːndə*], *s.c.* **1.** richiedente; compratore, compratrice **2.** *(dir.)* attore.

to **demarcate** ['diːmɑːkeit], *v.t.* **1.** demarcare, tracciare la linea di demarcazione di, delimitare (terreni, confini) **2.** *fig.* fare una distinzione (fra argomenti).

demarcation [,diːmɑː'keiʃən], *s.* demarcazione, delimitazione: *line of* —, linea di delimitazione.

to **dematerialize** ['diːmə'tiəriəlaiz], *v.t.i.* **1.** spiritualizzare, spiritualizzarsi **2.** *(spiritismo)* smaterializzare, smaterializzarsi.

to **demean**[1] [di'miːn], *v.r.*: *to* — *oneself* (solo con *av.*), comportarsi, condursi: *to* — *oneself honourably*, comportarsi onorevolmente.

to **demean**[2], *v.t.* abbassare, avvilire: *to* — *oneself*, abbassarsi, avvilirsi; *to* — *oneself to do sthg.*, abbassarsi a, degnarsi di fare ql.co.

demeanour [di'miːnə*], *s.* contegno, modo di comportarsi.

to **dement** [di'ment], *v.t.i.* ridurre alla demenza; far impazzire; impazzire.

demented [di'mentid], *ag.* demente; impazzito: *she was running like one* —, correva come una pazza.

dementedly [di'mentidli], *av.* come un demente.

dementia [di'menʃiə], *s.* *(patol.)* demenza ☆ — *praecox*, *(patol.)* demenza precoce.

demerit [diː'merit], *s.* demerito.

demesne [di'mein], *s.* **1.** dominio; possesso: — *of the Crown*, dominio della Corona **2.** proprietà terriera ☆ *state* —, proprietà terriera demaniale.

Demeter [di'miːtə*], *no.pr.f.* *(mit.)* Demetra.

Demetrius [di'miːtriəs], *no.pr.m.* Demetrio.

demigod ['demigɔd], *s.* semidio.

demijohn ['demidʒɔn], *s.* damigiana.

demilitarization ['diː,militərai'zeiʃən], *s.* smilitarizzazione.

to **demilitarize** ['diː'militəraiz], *v.t.* smilitarizzare.

demi-rep ['demirep], *s.* donna di dubbia onestà.

demisable [di'maizəbl], *ag.* *(dir.)* trasferibile, cedibile (terra, titoli).

demise [di'maiz], *s.* **1.** *(dir.)* cessazione; trasferimento (di valori, terre, ecc.); trasmissione (di titolo, corona nobiliare) **2.** *(dir.)* decesso, morte.

to **demise**, *v.t.* *(dir.)* trasferire, trasmettere; lasciare (per testamento), legare.

demisemiquaver ['demisemi,kweivə*], *s.* *(mus.)* biscroma.

demission [di'miʃən], *s.* **1.** abdicazione **2.** dimissione, rinuncia.

to **demit** [di'mit], *pass.p.p.* **demitted** [di'mitid], *v.t.i.* dimettere, dimettersi: *to* — *office*, dimettersi dal proprio ufficio.

demiurge ['diːmiəːdʒ], *s.* demiurgo.

to **demob** ['diː'mɔb], *pass.p.p.* **demobbed** ['diː'mɔbd], *v.t.* *(st. mil.)* smobilitare.

demobilization ['diː,moubilai'zeiʃən], *s.* *(mil.)* smobilitazione.

to **demobilize** [diː'moubilaiz], *v.t.i.* *(mil.)* smobilitare, smobilitarsi.

democracy [di'mɔkrəsi], *s.* democrazia.

democrat ['deməkræt], *s.* democratico; *(pol. amer.)* membro del partito democratico.

democratic [,demə'krætik], *ag.* democratico.

democratically [,demə'krætikəli], *av.* democraticamente.

democratism [di'mɔkrætizəm], *s.* teoria, sistema democratico.

democratization [di,mɔkrətai'zeiʃən], *s.* democratizzazione.

to **democratize** [di'mɔkrətaiz], *v.t.i.* democratizzare, democratizzarsi.

Democritus [di'mɔkritəs], *no.pr.m.* *(st. fil.)* Democrito.

Demogorgon ['diːmou'gɔːgən], *no.pr.m.* *(mit.)* Demogorgone.

demographer [di'mɔgrəfə*], *s.* studioso di demografia.

demographic [,diːmə'græfik], *ag.* demografico.

demography [di'mɔgrəfi], *s.* demografia.

to **demolish** [di'mɔliʃ], *v.t.* **1.** demolire, abbattere, distruggere (anche *fig.*) **2.** *(fam.)* divorare (cibo).

demolisher [di'mɔliʃə*], *s.c.* demolitore, demolitrice.

demolition [,demə'liʃən], *s.* demolizione.

demon ['diːmən], *s.* **1.** demone; demonio, diavolo ǁ *the Demon*, lo spirito maligno **2.** *(fam.)* genio, demonio (di persona abile): *he's a* — *at tennis*, è imbattibile al tennis.

demonetization [diː,mʌnitai'zeiʃən], *s.* svalutazione (di moneta, metalli).

to **demonetize** [diː'mʌnitaiz], *v.t.* svalutare (moneta).

demoniac [di'mouniæk], *ag.s.* demoniaco; indemoniato.

demoniacal [,diːmə'naiəkəl], *ag.* demoniaco.

demoniacally [,diːmə'naiəkəli], *av.* in modo demoniaco.

demonic [diː'mɔnik], *ag.* demonico, demoniaco.

demonism ['diːmənizəm], *s.* credenza nei demoni.

demonist ['diːmənist], *s.* chi crede nei demoni.

demonology [,diːmə'nɔlədʒi], *s.* demonologia.

demonry ['diːmənri], *s.* pratiche, influsso del demonio; stregoneria.

demonstrability [,demənstrə'biliti], *s.* dimostrabilità.

demonstrable ['demənstrəbl], *ag.* dimostrabile.

demonstrably ['demənstrəbli], *av.* in modo dimostrabile.

to **demonstrate** ['demənstreit], *v.t.i.* **1.** dimostrare; descrivere, spiegare **2.** *(pol.)* fare una dimostrazione; prendere parte ad una dimostrazione **3.** *(mil.)* fare una azione dimostrativa (per ingannare il nemico).

demonstration [,deməns'treiʃən], *s.* **1.** dimostrazione, prova: *practical* —, dimostrazione pratica **2.** dimostrazione, manifestazione (di sentimenti): *demonstrations of affection*, dimostrazione d'affetto **3.** dimostrazione, manifestazione (politica) **4.** *(mil.)* azione dimostrativa.

demonstrative [di'mɔnstrətiv], *ag.* **1.** dimostrativo; rivelatore **2.** espansivo **3.** *(gram.)* dimostrativo ǁ *s.* *(gram.)* aggettivo, pronome dimostrativo.

demonstratively [di'mɔnstrətivli], *av.* **1.** dimostrativamente **2.** con dimostrazioni d'affetto, gioia.

demonstrativeness [di'mɔnstrətivnis], *s.* **1.** dimostrazione (d'affetto, gioia, ecc.) **2.** carattere espansivo.

demonstrator ['demənstreitə*], *s.c.* **1.** dimostratore, dimostratrice **2.** assistente (di laboratorio scientifico) **3.** *(pol.)* dimostrante.

demoralization [di,mɔrəlai'zeiʃən], *s.* **1.** depravazione, corruzione **2.** demoralizzazione, scoramento.

to **demoralize** [di'mɔrəlaiz], *v.t.* **1.** depravare, corrompere **2.** demoralizzare; scoraggiare.

Demos ['diːmɔs], *s.* il popolo; la democrazia.

Demosthenes [di'mɔsθəniːz], *no.pr.m.* *(st. lett.)* Demostene.

to **demote** [di'mout], *v.t.* *(mil. amm.)* ridurre, far retrocedere ad un grado, ad una classe inferiore.

demotic [di(ː)'mɔtik], *ag.* **1.** popolare **2.** *(st.)* demotico.

demotion [di'mouʃən], *s.* (*mil.* a*mm.*) retrocessione ad un grado, ad una classe inferiore.

to **demount** [di'maunt], *v.t.* (*mec.*) togliere; smontare; disinstallare.

demulcent [di'mʌlsənt], *ag.s.* (*farm.*) sostanza emolliente.

demur [di'mə:*], *s.* **1.** esitazione; obiezione; difficoltà: *without* —, senza esitazione; *to make no* —, non opporre alcuna difficoltà **2.** (*dir.*) il sollevare eccezioni.

to **demur**, *pass.p.p.* **demurred** [di'mə:d], *v.i.* **1.** fare delle difficoltà; esitare; sollevare obiezioni: *he demurred at working on Sundays*, egli sollevò delle difficoltà a lavorare alla domenica **2.** (*dir.*) sollevare una eccezione.

demure [di'mjuə*], *ag.* modesto, contegnoso, riservato; pudico: — *look*, (*fam.*) aria da santarellina.

demurely [di'mjuəli], *av.* modestamente, con contegno, con riservatezza; pudicamente.

demureness [di'mjuənis], *s.* modestia; riservatezza; affettazione di candore; pudicizia.

demurrable [di'mə:rəbl], *ag.* (*spec. dir.*) confutabile; che si può infirmare.

demurrage [di'mʌridʒ], *s.* **1.** (*mar. comm.*) controstallia, soprastallia; indennità per controstallia **2.** ritardo, sosta **3.** ritenuta dedotta dalla Banca d'Inghilterra nel cambiare in valuta oro in barre ☆ — *days*, (*mar. comm.*) giorni di controstallia.

demurrer [di'mʌrə*], *s.* (*dir.*) eccezione (perentoria).

demy [di'mai], *pl.* **demies** [di'maiz], *s.* **1.** formato di carta (pollici 17¹/₂ × 22¹/₂ per carta da stampa; pollici 15¹/₂ × 20 per carta da scrivere) **2.** allievo borsista (nel Magdalen College, Oxford).

den [den], *s.* **1.** tana (di animali); antro, caverna, covo: — *of lions*, (*Bibbia*) fossa dei leoni; — *of thieves*, covo di ladri **2.** (*fam.*) stanzetta, studiolo; bugigattolo ☆ *opium* —, covo dei fumatori di oppio.

denarius [di'nɛəriəs], *s.* **1.** (*st. romana*) denaro **2.** *V.* d **3.**

denary [di'nəri], *ag.* (*arit.*) decimale.

denationalization [di'næʃnəlai'zeiʃən], *s.* perdita, privazione della nazionalità.

to **denationalize** [di:'næʃnəlaiz], *v.t.* privare della nazionalità, snazionalizzare.

denaturalization [di:,nætʃrəlai'zeiʃən], *s.* **1.** snaturalizzazione **2.** privazione del diritto di cittadino.

to **denaturalize** [di:'nætʃrəlaiz], *v.t.* **1.** snaturare **2.** privare del diritto di cittadino, della naturalizzazione.

denaturant [di:'neitʃrənt], *s.* (*chim.*) denaturante.

to **denaturate** [di:'neitʃreit], *V.* to **denature**.

denaturation [di:,neitʃə'reiʃən], *s.* (*chim.*) denaturazione.

to **denature** [di:'neitʃə*], to **denaturize** [di:'neitʃəraiz], *v.t.* (*chim.*) denaturare.

to **denazify** [di:'nɑ:tsifai], *v.t.* (*pol.*) denazificare.

dendrite ['dendrait], *s.* (*min.*) dendrite.

dendrochronology [,dendrəkrə'nɔlədʒi], *s.* dendrocronologia.

dendrology [den'drɔlədʒi], *s.* (*bot.*) dendrologia.

dene¹ [di:n], *s.* duna (specialmente vicino al mare).

dene², *s.* valletta boscosa.

dengue ['dɛŋgi], *s.:* — (*fever*), (*patol.*) denga.

deniable [di'naiəbl], *ag.* negabile.

denial [di'naiəl], *s.* **1.** diniego; rifiuto **2.** rinnegazione ☆ *self-* —, abnegazione.

denier¹ [di'nai-ə*], *s.c.* negatore, negatrice.

denier² [di'niə*], *nel senso* **2.** ['deniei], *s.* **1.** moneta francese **2.** (*ind. tessile*) denaro (unità di peso per filati sottili = g. 0,05).

to **denigrate** ['denigreit], *v.t.* denigrare.

denigration [,deni'greiʃən], *s.* denigrazione.

denigrator ['denigreitə*], *s.* denigratore.

denim ['denim], *s.* **1.** (*amer.*) tessuto di cotone ritorto (usato per tute, per coprire cuscini, ecc.) **2.** tuta.

Denis ['denis], *no.pr.m.* Dionigi.

Denise [də'ni:z], *no.pr.f.* Dionisia.

denizen ['denizn], *s.c.* **1.** (*poet.*) cittadino, cittadina; abitante: *denizens of the forest*, abitanti, ospiti della foresta **2.** straniero naturalizzato ‖ *s.* **1.** animale, pianta acclimatati **2.** parola (straniera) naturalizzata.

Denmark ['denmɑ:k], *no.pr.* (*geog.*) Danimarca.

to **denominate** [di'nɔmineit], *v.t.* denominare; chiamare.

denomination [di,nɔmi'neiʃən], *s.* **1.** denominazione; nome, definizione: *traitor is the right* — *for him*, il suo vero nome è traditore **2.** culto; setta; confessione **3.** (*arit.*) unità di misura **4.** (*comm.*) taglio (di titoli), valore (di monete).

denominational [di,nɔmi'neiʃənl], *ag.* confessionale; settario.

denominative [di'nɔminətiv], *ag.* denominativo.

denominator [di'nɔmineitə*], *s.* (*mat.*) denominatore.

denotation [,di:nou'teiʃən], *s.* **1.** indicazione: *denotations of an uneasy conscience*, segni di una coscienza agitata **2.** significato (di una parola); (*log.*) estensione (di un termine).

denotative [di:'noutətiv], *ag.* indicativo.

to **denote** [di'nout], *v.t.* denotare; significare; indicare: *his face denotes energy*, il suo viso denota energia.

to **denounce** [di'nauns], *v.t.* **1.** denunziare (un criminale); smascherare (un impostore): *to* — *s.o. as a coward*, denunziare qlcu. come codardo **2.** inveire contro; sollevarsi contro (un abuso) **3.** (*pol.*) denunziare: *to* — *a treaty*, denunziare un trattato.

denouncement [di'naunsmənt], *V.* **denunciation**.

denouncer [di'naunsə*], *s.c.* denunziatore, denunziatrice.

dense [dens], *ag.* **1.** denso, spesso, fitto; compatto **2.** ottuso, stupido **3.** (*foto.*) scuro, forte, opaco.

densely ['densli], *av.* **1.** densamente: — *populated*, densamente popolato **2.** ottusamente: — *ignorant*, ottuso e ignorante.

denseness ['densnis], *s.* **1.** densità, compattezza **2.** stupidità, ottusità.

densimeter [den'simitə*], *s.* (*chim.*) densimetro; (*fis.*) aerometro.

density ['densiti], *s.* **1.** densità (di popolazione, ecc.) **2.** (*fis.*) densità (di gas, ecc.) **3.** (*elett.*) intensità **4.** stupidità; ottusità **5.** (*foto.*) oscurità, opacità.

dent¹ [dent], *s.* incavo, ammaccatura, segno di un colpo: *the dents in a helmet*, le ammaccature in un elmetto.

to **dent¹**, *v.t.i.* intaccare; ammaccare, ammaccarsi.

dent², *s.* (*tec.*) tacca, dente.

dental ['dentl], *ag.* **1.** (*odontoiatria*) dentale **2.** (*fonet.*) dentale ‖ *s.* (consonante) dentale.

dentary ['dentəri], *ag.* (*anat.*) dentario.

dentate ['denteit], *ag.* (*bot.*) dentellato; (*zool.*) dentato.

dentation [den'teiʃən], *s.* dentellatura.

denticle ['dentikl], *s.* **1.** dentino **2.** (*arch.*) dentello.

denticular [den'tikjulə*], **denticulate** [den'tikjulit], **denticulated** [den'tikjuleitid], *ag.* dentellato; fornito di dentelli.

denticulation [den,tikju'leiʃən], *s.* (*arch.*) dentellatura.

dentiform ['dentifɔ:m], *ag.* a forma di dente.

dentifrice ['dentifris], *s.* dentifricio.

dentil ['dentil], *s.* (*arch.*) dentello.

dentine ['denti:n], *s.* (*anat.*) dentina.

dentist ['dentist], *s.* dentista.

dentistry ['dentistri], *s.* arte, professione del dentista.

dentition [den'tiʃən], *s.* dentizione.

denture ['dentʃə*], *s.* **1.** dentatura **2.** dentiera.

denudation [,di:nju(:)'deiʃən], *s.* **1.** denudazione **2.** (*geol.*) erosione.

to **denude** [di'nju:d], *v.t.* denudare.

denunciation [di,nʌnsi'eiʃən], *s.* **1.** denunzia, delazione (di complice, di abuso) **2.** condanna; accusa **3.** (*pol.*) denunzia (di tregua, trattato).

denunciator [di'nʌnsieitə*], *s.c.* denunziatore, denunziatrice.

to **deny** [di'nai], *v.t.* **1.** (I) negare; smentire: *I cannot — it*, non posso negarlo; *there is no denying the accusation that*, non si può smentire l'accusa che; *to — having done sthg.*, negare di aver fatto ql.co. **2.** negare, non riconoscere: *he denied God*, egli negava l'esistenza di Dio; *I cannot — my signature*, non posso non riconoscere la mia firma **3.** rifiutare, ricusare: *to — sthg. to s.o.* (o *s.o. sthg.*), rifiutare ql.co. a qlcu.: *the favour was denied* (*to*) *me*, il favore mi fu negato; *he denied me the favour*, egli mi negò il favore; *I was denied the favour*, mi fu rifiutato il favore ‖ *to — oneself*, sacrificarsi; *to — oneself sthg.*, privarsi di ql.co.

deodar ['diouda:*], *s.* (*bot.*) deodara, cedro dell'Imalaia.

deodorant [di:'oudərənt], *s.* sostanza deodorante.

deodorization [di:,oudərai'zeiʃən], *s.* (*chim.*) deodorizzazione.

to **deodorize** [di:'oudəraiz], *v.t.* (*chim.*) privare di odore, deodorare.

deodorizer [di:'oudəraizə*], *s.* (*chim.*) deodorante.

deontology [,di:on'tɔlədʒi], *s.* (*fil.*) deontologia.

deoxidation [di:,ɔksi'deiʃən], **deoxidization** [di:,ɔksidai'zeiʃən], *s.* (*chim.*) disossidazione.

to **deoxidize** [di:'ɔksidaiz], *v.t.* (*chim.*) disossidare.

to **depart** [di'pa:t], *v.i.* **1.** (*spec. letter.*) partire; andarsene: *to — from a place*, allontanarsi da, abbandonare un luogo **2.** *fig.* derogare: *to — from a custom*, perdere un'abitudine; *to — from one's word, promise*, non mantenere la propria parola, promessa **3.** (*poet. arc.*) morire, trapassare: *to — (from) this life*, morire.

departed [di'pa:tid], *ag.* passato, svanito: *— glory*, la gloria passata ‖ *the —*, il defunto, i defunti.

department [di'pa:tmənt], *s.* **1.** reparto **2.** ufficio, servizio; sezione **3.** (*amer.*) ministero, dicastero ‖ *the War Department*, il Ministero della Guerra **4.** (*geog.*) dipartimento ☆ *— store*, (*amer.*) grande magazzino ‖ *foreign language —*, sezione lingue straniere (università).

departmental [,di:pa:t'mentl], *ag.* dipartimentale; a sezione, a reparti ☆ *— store*, (*amer.*) grande magazzino.

departure [di'pa:tʃə*], *s.* **1.** partenza: *to take one's —*, andarsene, congedarsi **2.** (*arc.*) trapasso, morte **3.** *fig.* allontanamento: *— from a principle*, allontanamento da un principio **4.** tendenza, direzione: *a new —*, un nuovo orientamento.

to **depauperate** [di'pɔ:pəreit], *v.t.* depauperare, impoverire.

depauperation [di,pɔ:pə'reiʃən], *s.* impoverimento (di una regione, ecc.).

to **depauperize** ['di:'pɔ:pəraiz], *v.t.* **1.** trarre dall'indigenza; sollevare (una regione) dall'indigenza **2.** depauperare, impoverire.

to **depend** [di'pend], *v.i.* **1.** dipendere; essere subordinato: *health depends on good food*, la salute dipende dalla genuinità del cibo; *it all depends* (o *that depends*) *on circumstances*, dipende dalle circostanze; *it depends on the weather*, dipende dal tempo **2.** vivere sotto la protezione di qlcu., essere mantenuto da qlcu.: *children usually — on their parents for food*, i bambini generalmente sono mantenuti dai loro genitori **3.** contare, fare assegnamento: *he can never be depended on*, non si può mai far assegnamento su di lui; *I cannot — on his arriving to-day*, non posso essere sicuro che egl arrivi oggi; *she depends on her lessons (for a living)*, vive dando lezioni ‖ *— upon it*, puoi contarci, non c'è dubbio **4.** (*gram.*) dipendere da **5.** (*arc. poet.*) *to — from*, pendere da, scendere da.

dependability [di,pendə'biliti], *s.* fiducia: *— of a machine*, sicuro funzionamento di una macchina.

dependable [di'pendəbl], *ag.* fidato, sicuro.

dependableness [di'pendəblnis], *s.* fiducia.

dependably [di'pendəbli], *av.* in modo fidato.

dependant [di'pendənt], *ag. V.* **dependent** ‖ *s.* dipendente; persona a carico; domestico.

dependence [di'pendəns], *s.* **1.** dipendenza; subordinazione: *— on s.o., sthg.*, dipendenza da qlcu., ql.co. **2.** fiducia.

dependency [di'pendənsi], *s.* **1.** *V.* **dependence 2.** dipendenza (zona, regione sotto controllo straniero) **3.** *pl.* annessi, dipendenze (di podere, villa).

dependent [di'pendənt], *ag.* dipendente; a carico di: *he is — on his father*, è a carico di suo padre.

to **dephase** [di:'feiz], *v.t.* (*elett.*) sfasare (la corrente).

to **depict** [di'pikt], *v.t.* dipingere (anche *fig.*); descrivere, rappresentare: *terror was depicted on his face*, il terrore era dipinto sul suo viso.

depicter [di'piktə*], *s.* pittore; chi descrive; chi rappresenta.

depiction [di'pikʃən], *s.* pittura; rappresentazione.

depictor, *V.* **depicter**.

to **depilate** ['depileit], *v.t.* depilare.

depilation [,depi'leiʃən], *s.* depilazione.

depilatory [di'pilətəri], *ag. s.* depilatorio.

to **deplane** [di:'plein], *v.i.* scendere da un aereo.

to **deplenish** [di'pleniʃ], *v.t.* vuotare; sgombrare.

to **deplete** [di'pli:t], *v.t.* **1.** vuotare; esaurire (riserve, forze) **2.** (*med.*) decongestionare, scaricare.

depletion [di'pli:ʃən], *s.* **1.** esaurimento **2.** (*med.*) deplezione.

deplorable [di'plɔ:rəbl], *ag.* deplorabile.

deplorably [di'plɔ:rəbli], *av.* deplorabilmente.

to **deplore** [di'plɔ:*], *v.t.* deplorare; lamentarsi di: *he deplored his fate*, si lamentò della sua sorte.

to **deploy** [di'plɔi], *v.t.i.* (*mil.*) spiegare; spiegarsi.

deployment [di'plɔimənt], *s.* (*mil.*) spiegamento.

deplumation [,di:plu:'meiʃən], *s.* **1.** perdita delle penne **2.** perdita delle ciglia (per malattia).

depolarization ['di:,poulərai'zeiʃən], *s.* (*elett.*) depolarizzazione.

to **depolarize** [di:'pouləraiz], *v.t.* (*elett.*) depolarizzare.

depolarizer [di:'pouləraizə*], *s.* (*elett.*) depolarizzatore.

to **depone** [di'poun], *V.* to **depose**.

deponent [di'pounənt], *ag.* (*gram.*) deponente ‖ *s.* **1.** (*gram.*) verbo deponente **2.** (*dir.*) teste, testimone.

to **depopulate** [di:'pɔpjuleit], *v.t.i.* spopolare, spopolarsi.

depopulation [di:,pɔpju'leiʃən], *s.* spopolamento.

to **deport** [di'pɔ:t], *v.t.* **1.** deportare; esiliare; (*ang.-in.*) detenere (prigioniero politico) **2.** *to — oneself*, comportarsi.

deportation [,di:pɔ:'teiʃən], *s.* deportazione; espulsione; (*ang.-in.*) detenzione (per ragioni politiche).

deportee [,di:pɔ:'ti:], *s.* deportato; (*ang.-in.*) detenuto.

deportment [di'pɔ:tmənt], *s.* contegno, condotta.

to **depose** [di'pouz], *v.t.i.* **1.** deporre, destituire: *to — from the throne, an office*, deporre dal trono, destituire da una carica **2.** (*dir.*) deporre, testimoniare, fare una testimonianza.

deposit [di'pozit], *s.* **1.** (*comm.*) deposito, versamento: *— available at sight*, deposito disponibile, disponibilità a vista; *money on —*, denaro in deposito **2.** pegno; cauzione; acconto (di denaro): *to leave a — on sthg.*, versare una somma in acconto per ql.co.: *to leave a sum as —*, lasciare una somma come deposito; *to pay a —*, pagare un acconto, una cauzione **3.** (*geol.*) giacimento, sedimento; (*min.*) deposito; *pl.* detriti (di fiume) ☆ *— bank*, banca di deposito; *— fund*, fondo (cassa) depositi ‖ *guarantee —*, deposito cauzionale, cauzione; *irrevocable deposits*, depositi vincolati.

to **deposit**, *v.t.* **1.** depositare, affidare in deposito: *to — money with s.o., in a bank*, depositare denaro presso qlcu., in una banca **2.** depositare (sedimento) **3.** posare; deporre.

depositary [di'pozitəri], *s.* depositario.

deposition [ˌdepə'ziʃən], s. **1.** deposizione (di re) **2.** (dir.) deposizione, testimonianza **3.** deposito (di sedimento) **4.** the Deposition from the Cross, (art.) la deposizione dalla Croce.

depositor [di'pozitə*], s. depositante (di una banca): depositor's book, libretto nominativo (del depositante).

depository [di'pozitəri], s. deposito, magazzino ‖ s.c. depositario, depositaria.

depot ['depou], s. **1.** (mil.) deposito, magazzino; spaccio **2.** (amer.) stazione ferroviaria.

depravation [ˌdeprə'veiʃən], s. depravazione, corruzione (dell'anima, del gusto, ecc.).

to **deprave** [di'preiv], v.t. depravare, corrompere.

depraved [di'preivd], ag. depravato, corrotto.

depravity [di'præviti], s. (stato di) depravazione, pervertimento morale.

to **deprecate** ['deprikeit], v.t. **1.** disapprovare **2.** (arc.) deprecare, scongiurare.

deprecating ['deprikeitiŋ], ag. disapprovante.

deprecatingly ['deprikeitiŋli], av. con aria, tono di disapprovazione.

deprecation [ˌdepri'keiʃən], s. **1.** disapprovazione **2.** (arc.) deprecazione.

deprecative ['deprikeitiv], **deprecatory** ['deprikətəri], ag. **1.** che ha aria, tono, di disapprovazione **2.** (arc.) deprecativo, deprecatorio.

to **depreciate** [di'priːʃieit], v.t.i. svalutare, svalutarsi; deprezzare, deprezzarsi: to — in value through usage, diminuire di valore per effetto dell'uso.

depreciatingly [di'priːʃieitiŋli], av. con aria, tono sprezzante.

depreciation [di,priːʃi'eiʃən], s. svalutazione; deprezzamento; ammortamento: to suffer (o to undergo) a heavy —, subire un forte deprezzamento ☆ — account, conto deperimento; — allowance, — fund, quota di ammortamento.

depreciative [di'priːʃieitiv], ag. spregiativo; sprezzante.

depreciator [di'priːʃieitə*], s.c. spregiatore, spregiatrice; sprezzatore, sprezzatrice.

depreciatory [di'priːʃjətəri], ag. spregiativo; sprezzante ‖ — suffix, (gram.) suffisso peggiorativo.

to **depredate** ['deprideit], v.t. (rar.) depredare.

depredation [ˌdepri'deiʃən], s. saccheggio, rapina.

depredator ['deprideitə*], s. rapinatore, predone.

depredatory [di'predətəri], ag. caratterizzato da saccheggio, rapina: — expedition, spedizione a scopo di rapina.

to **depress** [di'pres], v.t. **1.** deprimere; avvilire **2.** (comm.) indebolire, far languire (affari, mercato); far abbassare (i prezzi) **3.** abbassare: to — one's voice, abbassare il tono della voce.

depressant [di'presənt], ag. s. (farm.) deprimente, sedativo.

depressed [di'prest], ag. **1.** depresso, triste, abbattuto: he is easily —, si abbatte facilmente **2.** (comm.) languente, calmo, depresso (di mercato, affari) **3.** (arch.) abbassato (di arco) ☆ — areas, (neol.) zone sottosviluppate, depresse; — classes, (pol.) le classi infime.

depressing [di'presiŋ], ag. sconfortante, deprimente, triste.

depression [di'preʃən], s. **1.** scoraggiamento, abbattimento **2.** (comm.) crisi, ristagno (negli affari) **3.** depressione, abbassamento: angle of —, angolo di depressione; full — of the pedal, (aut.) completa pressione del pedale.

depressor [di'presə*], s. **1.** (anat.) depressore (muscolo, nervo) **2.** (chim.) catalizzatore negativo **3.** (chir.) divaricatore.

deprivable [di'praivəbl], ag. revocabile.

deprival [di'praivəl], s. privazione.

deprivation [ˌdepri'veiʃən], s. **1.** privazione; perdita (di diritti, ecc.); revoca **2.** (eccl.) deposizione.

to **deprive** [di'praiv], v.t. **1.** privare, spogliare: to

— oneself, imporsi delle privazioni; to — s.o. of sthg., privare qlcu. di ql.co. **2.** (spec. eccl.) deporre.

depth [depθ], s. **1.** profondità (di fiume, ecc.): the well is ten feet in —, il pozzo ha dieci piedi di profondità **2.** profondità di pensiero, saggezza, cultura; intensità di sentimenti: he is a man of great —, è un uomo assai profondo; she showed a — of feeling that surprised everyone, dimostrava una profondità di sentimenti che stupiva tutti **3.** fondo: to be out of one's —, non toccare più il fondo (in acqua); fig. non esser all'altezza; to be within one's —, toccare il fondo (in acqua): to go (o get) beyond (o out of) one's —, arrivare in un punto dove non si tocca più il fondo (in acqua); fig. uscire dalla propria sfera (di competenza, ecc.) **4.** altezza (di acqua, neve, ecc.): the snow is two feet in —, la neve è alta due piedi **5.** intensità (di colore) **6.** (mar.) fondale **7.** gener. pl. profondità, abisso (anche fig.): in the depths of despair, nella disperazione più profonda; in the depths of one's heart, nel più profondo del cuore; in the depth(s) of winter, nel cuore dell'inverno, in pieno inverno ☆ — -charge, (mar.) bomba antisommergibile, di profondità; — -finder, (mar.) scandaglio.

depthless ['depθlis], ag. insondabile.

depthometer [dep'θomitə*], s. misuratore di profondità.

depurant ['depjurənt], ag.s. depurativo.

to **depurate** ['depjureit], v.t.i. depurare (p. e. il sangue); depurarsi.

depuration [ˌdepju'reiʃən], s. depurazione.

depurative ['depjureitiv], ag.s. depurativo.

deputation [ˌdepju(ː)'teiʃən], s. deputazione; delegazione.

to **depute** [di'pjuːt], v.t. deputare, delegare: to — powers to s.o., delegare poteri a qlcu.; to — s.o. to do sthg., delegare qlcu. a fare ql.co.

to **deputize** ['depjutaiz], v.i. sostituire, fare le veci di, fungere da delegato: the Home Secretary, deputizing for the Premier, replied..., il Ministro degli Interni, facente le veci del Primo Ministro, rispose ....

deputy ['depjuti], s. **1.** deputato, rappresentante ‖ Chamber of Deputies, Camera dei Deputati **2.** delegato, sostituto, supplente, aggiunto ☆ — -chairman, vice-presidente; — -judge, giudice supplente; — -manager, vice-direttore; — -mayor, vice-sindaco.

deputyship ['depjutiʃip], s. supplenza; delegazione.

to **deracinate** [di'ræsineit], v.t. sradicare, estirpare (anche fig.).

to **derail** [di'reil], v.t.i. (ferr.) far deragliare; (rar.) deragliare.

derailment [di'reilmənt], s. (ferr.) deragliamento.

to **derange** [di'reindʒ], v.t. **1.** sconcertare; scompigliare; sconvolgere (salute, spirito, mente, ecc.): to become, to be (mentally) deranged, diventare, essere pazzo **2.** guastare (una macchina).

derangement [di'reindʒmənt], s. **1.** scompiglio; sconvolgimento, confusione: — of mind, alienazione mentale **2.** guasto (ad una macchina).

to **deration** [di'ræʃən], v.t. togliere il tesseramento di.

deratization [diːˌrætai'zeiʃən], s. derattizzazione.

Derby ['dɑːbi, 'dəːbi], no.pr.(geog.) Derby ‖ s. **1.**(spor.) « derby » (corsa classica, per puledri di tre anni, che si corre ogni anno a Epsom, presso Londra, il primo mercoledì di giugno) **2.** — (hat), (amer.) bombetta, cappello duro ☆ — Day, il giorno in cui ha luogo il « derby »; — dog, (sl.) cane che attraversa la pista nel momento in cui corrono i cavalli; fig. osservazione, interruzione inopportuna.

derelict ['derilikt], ag. **1.** derelitto, abbandonato: a — ship, una nave abbandonata **2.** (amer.) negligente: to be — in one's duty, trascurare il proprio dovere ‖ s. **1.** persona o cosa abbandonata **2.** (mar.) relitto **3.** (amer.) persona negligente.

dereliction [ˌderi'likʃən], s. **1.** abbandono **2.** il ritirarsi del mare; terra così depositatasi **3.** trascuratezza, negligenza.

to **deride** [di'raid], *v.t.* deridere, schernire.

derider [di'raidə*], *s.c.* schernitore, schernitrice.

deridingly [di'raidiŋli], *V.* derisively.

derision [di'riʒən], *s.* **1.** derisione: *object of* —, oggetto di scherno **2.** oggetto di derisione: *he became the* — *of everybody*, divenne lo zimbello generale.

derisive [di'raisiv], *ag.* **1.** derisorio, derisivo: — *laughter*, riso ironico **2.** irrisorio: — *offer*, offerta irrisoria.

derisively [di'raisivli], *av.* derisoriamente, ironicamente.

derisory [di'raisəri], *V.* derisive.

derivable [di'raivəbl], *ag.* derivabile.

derivation [,deri'veiʃən], *s.* **1.** derivazione, deduzione (di una teoria); etimologia, origine (di una parola) **2.** (*med.*) trattamento derivativo.

derivative [di'rivətiv], *ag.* derivato ‖ *s.* **1.** (*gram.*) derivato **2.** (*chim.*) derivato **3.** (*mat.*) derivata **4.** (*mus.*) accordo derivato **5.** (medicamento) derivativo ☆ *rotary* —, (*aer.*) derivata di rotazione; *stability* —, (*aer.*) derivata di stabilità.

derivatively [di'rivətivli], *av.* per derivazione.

to **derive** [di'raiv], *v.t.i.* derivare: *he derives much pleasure from music*, egli trae molto piacere dalla musica; *to* — *consolation from*, trarre consolazione da; *to* — *a word from Latin*, derivare una parola dal latino.

derived [di'raivd], *ag.* derivato ☆ — *albumin* (o *proteine*), (*chim.*) albumina denaturata; — *circuit*, (*elett.*) circuito derivato; — *current*, (*elett.*) corrente derivata.

derm [də:m], **derma** ['də:mə], *s.* (*anat.*) derma.

dermal ['də:məl], *ag.* (*anat.*) cutaneo, dermico: — *sense*, sensibilità cutanea.

dermatitis [,də:mə'taitis], *s.* (*patol.*) dermatite.

dermatologist [,də:mə'tɔlədʒist] *s.* dermatologo.

dermatology [,də:mə'tɔlədʒi], *s.* (*med.*) dermatologia.

dermatosis [,də:mə'tousis], *s.* (*patol.*) dermatosi.

dermic ['də:mik], *V.* dermal.

dermographia [,də:mə'græfjə], **dermographism** [də'mɔgrəfizəm], *s.* (*med.*) dermografia, dermografismo.

to **dern** [də:n], (*sl. amer.*) per to **darn**[2].

to **derogate** ['derəgeit], *v.i.* **1.** derogare: *to* — *from one's position, dignity*, derogare al proprio rango, alla propria dignità **2.** (*arc.*) deprezzare, screditare; sminuire: *to* — *from a right*, sminuire un diritto.

derogation [,derə'geiʃən], *s.* **1.** derogazione, deroga: — *of a law*, deroga ad una legge **2.** (*arc.*) detrimento; scredito: — *from a right*, diminuzione di un diritto; *without* — (*from dignity, etc.*) senza detrimento (alla dignità, ecc.).

derogatory [di'rɔgətəri], *ag.* **1.** derogatorio **2.** sprezzante: *behaviour* — *to his education*, condotta indegna della sua educazione.

derrick ['derik], *s.* **1.** argano, gru **2.** (*mar.*) falcone **3.** (*miner.*) torre di sondaggio, di trivellazione **4.** (*mar.*) albero da carico, picco da carico: *derricks and rigging*, picchi da carico e attrezzatura.

derring-do ['deriŋ'du:], *s.* audacia, temerarietà.

derringer ['derindʒə*], *s.* (*amer.*) pistola a canna corta e di grosso calibro.

dervish ['də:viʃ], *s.* derviscio.

to **desalt** [di:'sɔ:lt], *v.t.* (*chim.*) desalificare.

to **descale** ['di:'skeil], *v.t.* (*ind.*) disincrostare.

descant ['deskænt], *s.* **1.** (*arc. mus.*) discanto **2.** (*arc.*) armonia; melodia; preludio **3.** disquisizione; commento.

to **descant** [dis'kænt], *v.t.* **1.** (*arc. mus.*) discantare **2.** discorrere, dissertare; commentare.

to **descend** [di'send], *v.t.i.* **1.** scendere, discendere: *the angel descended from heaven*, l'angelo scese dal cielo; *he descended the stairs, the hill*, egli scese le scale, la collina; *the path descends to the sea*, il sentiero scende al mare ‖ *to* — *on s.o.*, calare su, attaccare, assalire qlcu. ‖ *to* — *to s.o.'s level, to doing sthg.*, *fig.* abbassarsi al livello di qlcu., a fare ql.co. **2.** discendere,

trarre origine: *to* — (o *to be*) *descended from s.o.*, discendere da qlcu., trarre origine da qlcu. **3.** (*dir.*) passare, trasmettere (di proprietà, privilegio): *the land has always belonged to the family, descending from father to son*, la proprietà appartenne sempre alla famiglia, passando di padre in figlio.

descendable [di'sendəbl], *V.* descendible.

descendance [di'sendəns], *s.* **1.** discendenza, discendenti, posteri **2.** discendenza, origine, stirpe.

descendant [di'sendənt], *s.c.* discendente: *the descendants*, la discendenza, i posteri.

descendence, *V.* descendance.

descendent, *V.* descendant.

descendible [di'sendibl], *ag.* **1.** trasmissibile (di proprietà) **2.** (*rar.*) che può discendere.

descending [di'sendiŋ], *ag.* discendente ☆ — *scale*, (*mus.*) scala discendente.

descent [di'sent], *s.* **1.** scesa, discesa ‖ *the Descent from the Cross*, la Deposizione dalla Croce **2.** china, pendio: *a sharp* —, un pendio ripido **3.** caduta, abbassamento; rovina **4.** incursione; irruzione **5.** lignaggio, nascita: *he is a man of noble* —, è un uomo di alto lignaggio, discendenza **6.** (*dir.*) trasmissione (di beni).

describable [dis'kraibəbl], *ag.* descrivibile.

to **describe** [dis'kraib], *v.t.* **1.** descrivere, raccontare: *can you* — *it to me?*, potete descrivermelo?; *to* — *s.o., sthg. as*, rappresentare, descrivere qlcu., ql.co. come **2.** descrivere, tracciare (*p. e.* un cerchio).

describer [dis'kraibə*], *s.* descrittore.

description [dis'kripʃən], *s.* **1.** descrizione: *beyond* —, indescrivibile **2.** connotati: *to answer to the* —, rispondere ai connotati **3.** (*fam.*) genere, specie, tipo: *of any, of this* —, di qualsiasi, di questo genere.

descriptive [dis'kriptiv], *ag.* descrittivo ☆ — *catalogue*, catalogo ragionato; — *geometry*, geometria descrittiva.

descriptively [dis'kriptivli], *av.* in modo descrittivo.

to **descry** [dis'krai], *v.t.* scorgere; distinguere; riuscire a vedere (specialmente da lontano).

Desdemona [,dezdi'mounə], *no.pr.f.* (*lett.*) Desdemona.

to **desecrate** ['desikreit], *v.t.* profanare; sconsacrare.

desecration [,desi'kreiʃən], *s.* profanazione; sconsacrazione.

desecrator ['desikreitə*], *s.c.* profanatore, profanatrice.

to **desensitize** ['di:'sensitaiz], *v.t.* (*foto.*) desensibilizzare.

desensitizer ['di:'sensitaizə*], *s.* (*foto.*) desensibilizzatore.

desensitizing ['di:'sensitaiziŋ], *ag.* desensibilizzante ‖ *s.* desensibilizzazione.

desert[1] ['dezət], *ag.* deserto; desolato; arido, sterile: *a* — *island*, un'isola deserta ‖ *s.* deserto ‖ *the Sahara Desert*, il deserto del Sahara.

to **desert**[1] [di'zə:t], *v.t.i.* disertare; abbandonare (un luogo, un posto, una persona, ecc.): *he deserted*, (*mil.*) egli ha disertato; *he deserted his wife*, abbandonò sua moglie; *his courage deserted him*, il coraggio lo abbandonò; *poetry made him* — *the bar*, l'amore per la poesia lo allontanò dall'avvocatura.

desert[2] [di'zə:t], *s.* **1.** merito: *a place according to one's* —, un posto secondo il proprio merito **2.** *gener. pl.* compenso, mercede: *to get* (o *to obtain* o *to meet with*) *one's deserts*, aver ciò che si merita, essere ricompensato secondo i propri meriti: *he will only get his deserts*, ne riceverà solo la giusta ricompensa.

deserted [di'zə:tid], *ag.* deserto; disertato, abbandonato.

deserter [di'zə:tə*], *s.* **1.** (*mil.*) disertore **2.** fedifrago.

desertion [di'zə:ʃən], *s.* **1.** diserzione; defezione **2.** abbandono ☆ *wife* —, (*dir.*) abbandono del tetto coniugale (da parte del marito).

to **deserve** [di'zə:v], *v.t.* meritare, essere degno: *he deserves to be praised*, merita di essere lodato; *he richly* *deserves it!*, ben gli sta!; *she deserves hanging, to be hanged*, merita l'impiccaggione, di essere impiccata.

deservedly [di′zə:vidli], *av.* meritatamente; giustamente; degnamente.

deservedness [di′zə:vidnis], *s.* giustizia (di una punizione).

deserving [di′zə:viŋ], *ag.* meritevole, meritorio, degno: *a — case*, un caso meritorio, degno di interesse; *they are — of our esteem*, sono degni della nostra stima.

deservingly [di′zə:viŋli], *av.* meritatamente, degnamente.

déshabillé [,deizæ′bi:ei], *s.* veste da camera.

to desiccate [′desikeit], *v.t.* essiccare; stagionare.

desiccation [,desi′keiʃən], *s.* essiccazione.

desiccative [de′sikətiv], *ag.s.* essiccativo.

desiccator [′desikeitə*], *s.* essiccatore.

to desiderate [di′zidəreit], *v.t.* (*rar.*) sentire la mancanza di; considerare come desiderabile.

desiderative [di′zidərətiv], *ag.* desiderativo; (*gram.*) ottativo ‖ *s.* chi desidera.

desideratum [di,zidə′reitəm], *pl.* **desiderata** [di,zidə′reitə], *s.* desiderata, cose desiderate.

Desiderius [,dezi′di:riəs], *no.pr.m.* (*st.*) Desiderio.

design [di′zain], *s.* **1.** intenzione; scopo; proposito, intento: *by accident or —*, per caso o di proposito; *with this —*, con questo scopo; *I was unable to carry out my —*, fui incapace di realizzare il mio progetto; *to have designs on s.o.*, aver delle mire su qualcuno **2.** piano; progetto: *— of a novel, etc.*, canovaccio, trama di romanzo, ecc. **3.** disegno **4.** (*ind.*) forma; costruzione; tipo; progetto: *motor of faulty —*, motore di costruzione difettosa; *a ship of excellent —*, una nave di forma, tipo eccellente **5.** (*comm.*) modello: *our latest designs*, i nostri ultimi modelli ☆ *decorative —*, ornato; *— engineer*, (*neol.*) tecnico progettista.

to design, *v.t.i.* **1.** destinare, designare: *to — s.o. for sthg.*, destinare qlcu. a ql.co.: *his parents designed him for the army*, i suoi genitori lo destinarono alla carriera militare; *to — sthg. for s.o.*, destinare ql.co. a qlcu.: *we have designed this gift for you*, ti abbiamo destinato questo dono **2.** progettare, proporsi: *he designs to be a lawyer*, si propone di diventare avvocato; *to — to do* (o *doing*) *sthg.*, proporsi di fare ql.co. **3.** disegnare, fare disegni, schizzare: *she designs all her own dresses*, schizza i modelli di tutti i suoi abiti **4.** preparare; stabilire, deliberare, divisare.

designate [′dezignit], *ag.* (*segue sempre il sostantivo a cui si riferisce*) designato: *bishop —*, vescovo designato.

to designate [′dezigneit], *v.t.* **1.** designare, nominare: *to — s.o. as* (o *for*) *one's successor*, nominare qlcu. proprio successore; *to — s.o. to an office*, designare qlcu. ad un ufficio **2.** indicare, additare; chiamare **3.** indicare, mostrare: *his dress designated that he was a person of importance*, il suo abito rivelava che egli era una persona importante.

designation [,dezig′neiʃən], *s.* designazione.

designedly [di′zainidli], *av.* apposta, con intenzione, deliberatamente.

designer [di′zainə*], *s.c.* **1.** costumista; disegnatore, disegnatrice (di vestiti, ecc.); stilista (di macchine, ecc.); modellista **2.** intrigante ☆ *stage- —*, scenografo.

designing [di′zainiŋ], *ag.* intrigante, astuto ‖ *s.* disegno, creazione, studio (di macchina, nave, vestito, cappello, ecc.) ☆ *— department*, (*comm.*) ufficio studi, progetti.

designingly [di′zainiŋli], *av.* astutamente, di proposito.

to desilverize [di:′silvəraiz], *v.t.* disargentare (specialmente il piombo).

desipience [di′sipiəns], *s.* insipienza, fatuità.

desirability [di,zaiərə′biliti], **desirableness** [di′zaiərəblnis], *s.* **1.** l'essere desiderabile; attrattiva (di donna) **2.** vantaggio (di comportamento, ecc.).

desirable [di′zaiərəbl], *ag.* desiderabile; consigliabile; attraente; piacevole ‖ *s.* cosa desiderabile.

desirably [di′zaiərəbli], *av.* in modo desiderabile.

desire [di′zaiə*], *s.* **1.** desiderio, speranza; passione: *consumed with —*, consumato dal desiderio; *to have a — to do sthg.*, aver desiderio di fare ql.co. **2.** domanda, preghiera: *at* (o *by*) *s.o.'s —*, secondo il desiderio di qlcu. **3.** cosa desiderata: *I hope you will get your —*, spero che il vostro desiderio si realizzi.

to desire, *v.t.* **1.** desiderare fortemente (felicità, ecc.); volere, aver voglia di: *he desired that I should represent him* (o *he desired me to represent him*), desiderò che lo rappresentassi; *it leaves much to be desired*, ciò lascia molto a desiderare; *since you — it*, giacchè ci tenete; *to — to do sthg.*, desiderare di fare ql.co. **2.** domandare, chiedere: *to — s.o. to do sthg.*, pregare qlcu. di fare ql.co.; *to — sthg. of s.o.*, chiedere ql.co. a qlcu.

desirous [di′zaiərəs], *ag.* desideroso: *to be — of sthg.*, *of doing sthg.*, desiderare ql.co., di fare ql.co.

to desist [di′zist], *v.i.* desistere, cessare: *to — from sthg.*, rinunciare a ql.co.

desk [desk], *s.* **1.** scrivania, scrittoio **2.** (*comm.*) cassa: *pay at the —*, pagate alla cassa **3.** (*amer.*) ufficio; locale; reparto ‖ *the —*, il segretario di redazione **4.** (*amer.*) podio, pulpito ☆ *-lamp*, lampada da tavolo; *-pad*, cartella, blocco da tavolo ‖ *drawing- —*, tavolo da disegno; *information- —*, ufficio informazioni; *office- —*, tavolo da disegno; *pay- —*, (*comm.*) cassa; *school-master's —*, cattedra (di insegnante).

desolate [′desəlit], *ag.* **1.** desolato; sconsolato **2.** solitario, abbandonato; deserto, devastato (di luogo).

to desolate [′desəleit], *v.t.* **1.** abbandonare; rendere triste, affliggere (una persona) **2.** devastare, spopolare, rendere un luogo inabitabile.

desolately [′desəlitli], *av.* desolatamente.

desolateness [′desəlitnis], **desolation** [,desə′leiʃən], *s.* **1.** desolazione; devastazione (di un paese vinto, ecc.): *the fighting brought — to millions of homes*, la guerra portò la desolazione in milioni di case **2.** miseria; disperazione: *the — of the times*, la miseria dei tempi.

desolator [′desəleitə*], *s.* desolatore.

despair [dis′pɛə*], *s.* disperazione: *in —*, disperato; *to drive s.o. to —*, spingere qlcu. alla disperazione.

to despair, *v.i.* disperare: *the doctors — of saving his life*, i dottori disperano di salvargli la vita; *his life is despaired of*, si dispera della sua vita.

despairing [dis′pɛəriŋ], *ag.* disperato; che fa disperare: *a — situation*, una situazione disperata, *a — tone*, un tono disperato.

despairingly [dis′pɛəriŋli], *av.* disperatamente, senza speranza.

despatch, *V.* **dispatch**.

to despatch, *V.* **to dispatch**.

desperado [,despə′ra:dou], *pl.* **desperadoes** [,despə′ra:douz], *s.* uomo capace di tutto; disperato; bandito; furfante; fuorilegge.

desperate [′despərit], *ag.* **1.** disperato; senza speranza: *a — disease*, un morbo senza speranza **2.** funesto; estremo; terribile: *a — event*, un avvenimento funesto ‖ *— cases require — remedies*, a mali estremi, estremi rimedi **3.** furioso, accanito: *— energy*, la forza della disperazione.

desperately [′despəritli], *av.* **1.** disperatamente, con furore; a oltranza **2.** terribilmente **3.** furiosamente; accanitamente.

desperateness [′despəritnis], *s.* **1.** disperazione; stato disperato; accanimento **2.** inutilità: *the — of such an attempt*, l'inutilità di un tentativo simile.

desperation [,despə′reiʃən], *s.* disperazione: *to drive s.o. to —*, spingere qlcu. alla disperazione.

despicability [,despikə′biliti], *s.* spregevolezza.

despicable [′despikəbl], *ag.* disprezzabile; spregevole, meschino.

despicableness [′despikəblnis], *s.* spregevolezza.

despicably [ˈdespikəbli], *av.* con disprezzo; spregevolmente.

despisable [disˈpaizəbl], *V.* **despicable**.

despisal [disˈpaizəl], *s.* disprezzo.

to **despise** [disˈpaiz], *v.t.* disprezzare; spregiare.

despiser [disˈpaizə*], *s.c.* sprezzatore, sprezzatrice.

despisingly [disˈpaiziŋli], *av.* con disprezzo.

despite [disˈpait], *prep.* a dispetto di; malgrado; nonostante ‖ *in — of*, a dispetto di; *in his own —*, (*arc.*) suo malgrado.

despite, *s.* **1.** (*arc.*) dispetto; ripicco **2.** (*letter.*) avversione; rancore.

despiteful [disˈpaitful], *ag.* dispettoso; perfido; maligno.

despitefully [disˈpaitfuli], *av.* perfidamente; malignamente.

despitefulness [disˈpaitfulnis], *s.* dispetto; odio; malignità; perfidia.

to **despoil** [disˈpoil], *v.t.* spogliare; saccheggiare: *to — s.o. of sthg.* spogliare qlcu. di ql.co.

despoiler [disˈpoilə*], *s.* saccheggiatore; spogliatore.

despoilment [disˈpoilmənt], **despoliation** [dis,pouliˈeifən], *s.* spoliazione; depredazione.

despond [disˈpɔnd], *s.* (*arc.*) disperazione; abbattimento; scoraggiamento ‖ *the Slough of Despond*, (*lett.*) l'Abisso della Disperazione.

to **despond**, *v.i.* scoraggiarsi; lasciarsi abbattere.

despondency [disˈpɔndənsi], *s.* scoraggiamento; sconforto; accasciamento; abbattimento.

despondent [disˈpɔndənt], *ag.* scoraggiato; abbattuto; accasciato; depresso.

despondently [disˈpɔndəntli], **despondingly** [disˈpɔndiŋli], *av.* con aria scoraggiata, abbattuta.

despot [ˈdespɔt], *s.* tiranno; despota (anche *fig.*).

despotic [desˈpɔtik], *ag.* dispotico; arbitrario.

despotically [desˈpɔtikəli], *av.* dispoticamente; arbitrariamente.

despotism [ˈdespətizəm], *s.* dispotismo.

to **despumate** [ˈdespjumeit], *v.t.i.* togliere la schiuma da; spumeggiare.

despumation [,despjuˈmeifən], *s.* despumazione.

to **desquamate** [ˈdeskwəmeit], *v.i.* squamarsi.

desquamation [,deskwəˈmeifən], *s.* desquamazione.

dessert [diˈzə:t], *s.* « dessert », frutta, dolce (a fine pasto); (*amer.*) torte, budini: *at —*, alla frutta ☆ *— spoon, knife, and fork*, posate da frutta.

destination [,destiˈneifən], *s.* destinazione: *to reach one's —*, arrivare a destinazione.

to **destine** [ˈdestin], *v.t.* **1.** destinare, indirizzare: *he destined his son for the law*, egli destinò suo figlio allo studio della legge **2.** essere destinato: *he was destined to the navy*, egli era destinato a entrare in marina; *it was destined that*, era scritto che; *we were destined never to meet again*, eravamo destinati a non incontrarci più ‖ *to be destined for a place*, (*letter.*) essere diretto a un luogo.

destiny [ˈdestini], *s.* **1.** destino; sorte; fato **2.** (*mit.*): *Destiny*, il Destino; *the Destinies*, lo Parche.

destitute [ˈdestitju:t], *ag.* **1.** destituito, privo: *— of common sense*, privo di senso comune; *— of means*, senza mezzi **2.** indigente; povero ‖ *the —*, gli indigenti.

destitution [,destiˈtju:fən], *s.* **1.** povertà; miseria; privazione **2.** (*arc.*) destituzione; sospensione dall'impiego.

to **destroy** [disˈtrɔi], *v.t.* **1.** distruggere; sterminare; demolire **2.** uccidere; abbattere (un animale): *to — oneself*, uccidersi **3.** rendere inutile, annullare l'effetto di.

destroyable [disˈtrɔiəbl], *ag.* distruggibile.

destroyer [disˈtrɔiə*], *s.c.* distruttore, distruttrice ‖ *s.* (*mar.*) cacciatorpediniere ☆ *— tender*, nave appoggio per cacciatorpediniere ‖ *escort —*, cacciatorpediniere di scorta.

destroying [disˈtrɔiiŋ], *ag.* distruttore.

destructible [disˈtrʌktəbl], *ag.* distruttibile.

destruction [disˈtrʌkfən], *s.* **1.** distruzione; stermi-

nio **2.** rovina: *gambling was his —*, il giuoco fu la sua rovina.

destructive [disˈtrʌktiv], *ag.* distruttivo; rovinoso ‖ *s.* persona o cosa che mira alla distruzione.

destructively [disˈtrʌktivli], *av.* funestamente; rovinosamente.

destructiveness [disˈtrʌktivnis], *s.* **1.** potenza distruttiva **2.** mania distruttiva.

destructor [disˈtrʌktə*], *s.c.* distruttore; distruttrice ‖ *s.* (*tec.*) bruciatore (di rifiuti).

desuetude [diˈsju(:)itju:d], *s.* disuso, dissuetudine: *to fall into —*, cadere in disuso.

desulphurization [di:,sʌlfəraiˈzeifən], *s.* (*chim.*) desolforazione.

to **desulphurize** [di:ˈsʌlfəraiz], *v.t.* (*chim.*) desolforare, togliere lo zolfo a.

desultorily [ˈdesəltərili], *av.* saltuariamente; sconnessamente; senza ordine, senza metodo.

desultoriness [ˈdesəltərinis], *s.* discontinuità; sconnessione; mancanza di metodo.

desultory [ˈdesəltəri], *ag.* saltuario; irregolare; sconnesso, a sbalzi: *— reading*, letture occasionali.

to **desynonymize** [,di:siˈnɔnimaiz], *v.t.* differenziare il significato (di sinonimi).

to **detach** [diˈtætf], *v.t.* **1.** staccare, distaccare, separare (anche *fig.*): *to — a picture from the wall*, staccare un quadro dalla parete **2.** (*mil.*) distaccare (truppe, navi, ecc.).

detachability [di,tætfəˈbiliti], *V.* **detachableness**.

detachable [diˈtætfəbl], *ag.* staccabile; smontabile.

detachableness [diˈtætfəblnis], *s.* possibilità di separare, di smontare (le parti di una macchina, ecc.).

detached [diˈtætft], *ag.* **1.** disinteressato, distaccato, libero, senza pregiudizi: *a — mind*, una mente libera da pregiudizi; *a — opinion*, un'opinione disinteressata; *a — view*, un punto di vista obiettivo **2.** isolato: *— house*, casa isolata; *— post*, (*mil.*) posto distaccato ‖ *to live — from the world*, vivere lontano dal mondo ☆ *semi- — houses*, case generalmente costruite a due abitazioni con il solo muro divisorio in comune.

detachedly [diˈtætftli], *av.* **1.** separatamente; isolatamente **2.** con aria svogliata, noncurante.

detachedness [diˈtætftnis], *s.* **1.** separazione; isolamento **2.** svogliatezza, noncuranza.

detachment [diˈtætfmənt], *s.* **1.** distacco; separazione **2.** libertà (dello spirito, della mente); disinteressamento; indifferenza **3.** (*mil.*) distaccamento: *on —*, distaccato.

detail [ˈdi:teil], *s.* **1.** particolare; dettaglio: *in —*, dettagliatamente; *but that's a —!*, ma è una minuzia!; *to go to (o enter) into details*, entrare nei particolari **2.** (*mil.*) distaccamento; piccola azione; *pl.* ordine del giorno: *war of —*, guerriglia **3.** (*amer.*) piccolo gruppo: *details of police*, polizia a piccoli gruppi **4.** (*mec.*) pezzo componente.

to **detail**, *v.t.* **1.** esporre minuziosamente, raccontare punto per punto: *to — the facts*, descrivere minutamente i fatti **2.** (*mil.*) distaccare: *to — s.o. for a duty*, distaccare qlcu. per un servizio.

detailed [ˈdi:teild], *ag.* particolareggiato, dettagliato: *a — account*, un ragguaglio particolareggiato.

to **detain** [diˈtein], *v.t.* **1.** trattenere; detenere; custodire **2.** far ritardare: *the bad weather detained him*, il cattivo tempo lo fece ritardare.

detainee [,di:teiˈni:], *s.* confinato.

detainer [diˈteinə*], *s.* **1.** (*dir.*) detenzione di persona od oggetto **2.** (*dir.*) ordine di detenzione; ordine di incarcerazione.

detainment [diˈteinmənt], *s.* detenzione.

to **detect** [diˈtekt], *v.t.* **1.** scoprire; scovare: *to — s.o. in the act*, sorprendere qlcu. sul fatto **2.** intravvedere; percepire, discernere **3.** (*rad.*) rivelare; raddrizzare.

detectable [diˈtektəbl], **detectible** [diˈtektibl], *ag.* scopribile; discernibile, distinguibile.

detection [diˈtekfən], *s.* **1.** scoperta: *to escape —*, sfuggire alla ricerca **2.** (*rad. fis.*) rivelazione; raddrizzamento.

detective [di'tektiv], *ag.* rivelatore (di apparecchio) || *s.* investigatore; « detective », agente investigativo (della polizia) ☆ — *novel*, romanzo poliziesco || *private* —, investigatore privato.

detector [di'tektə*], *s.* **1.** chi scopre; inventore **2.** (*fis.*) rivelatore, misuratore; (*rad.*) detettore, rivelatore **3.** (*mec.*) livello **4.** (*elett.*) galvanometro direzionale.

detent [di'tent], *s.* (*mec.*) scattino (d'orologio); dente d'arresto, fermo.

detention [di'tenʃən], *s.* **1.** detenzione, prigionia; punizione (a scuola) **2.** ritardo inevitabile **3.** (*dir.*) detenzione (di una somma dovuta) ☆ — *allowance*, (*mil.*) indennità giornaliera; — *camp*, campo di internamento; — *house*, casa di correzione.

to **deter** [di'tə*], *pass.p.p.* **deterred** [di'tə:d], *v.t.* trattenere; scoraggiare; fermare, impedire: *nothing will* — *him*, nulla lo distoglierà; *to* — *s.o. from doing sthg.*, trattenere con la paura qlcu. dal fare ql.co.

to **deterge** [di'tə:dʒ], *v.t.* detergere (ferita, ecc.).

detergent [di'tə:dʒənt], *ag.s.* detergente; detersivo.

to **deteriorate** [di'tiəriəreit], *v.t.i.* deteriorare, deteriorarsi; diminuire; deprezzare, deprezzarsi.

deterioration [di,tiəriə'reiʃən], *s.* deterioramento.

deteriorative [di'tiəriə,reitiv], *ag.* deteriorante.

determent [di'tə:mənt], *s.* impedimento, azione dell'impedire; freno.

determinable [di'tə:minəbl], *ag.* **1.** determinabile **2.** (*dir.*) risolvibile (di contratto).

determinant [di'tə:minənt], *ag.* determinante || *s.* causa determinante.

determinate [di'tə:minit], *ag.* **1.** determinato; preciso; definito; definitivo **2.** risoluto.

to **determinate** [di'tə:mineit], *V.* to **determine**.

determinately [di'tə:minitli], *av.* con precisione; definitivamente.

determinateness [di'tə:minitnis], *s.* determinatezza.

determination [di,tə:mi'neiʃən], *s.* **1.** determinazione (di data, ecc.); delimitazione (di frontiera) **2.** determinazione, risoluzione, deliberazione; proposito: *to come to a* —, arrivare ad una decisione **3.** risolutezza: *air of* —, aria risoluta **4.** (*dir.*) sentenza **5.** (*fis.*) determinazione, tendenza ☆ *quantity* —, dosaggio (di ingredienti).

determinative [di'tə:minətiv], *ag.* **1.** determinativo, che determina **2.** (*gram.*) determinativo || *s.* ciò che determina (*p.e.* simbolo, attributo, articolo, ecc.).

to **determine** [di'tə:min], *v.t.i.* **1.** determinare, fissare: *circumstances may* — *a man's character*, le circostanze determinano talvolta il carattere dell'uomo **2.** (IV) risolvere, risolversi; decidere, decidersi, far decidere: *these thoughts will* — *me to go away*, questi pensieri mi decideranno ad andarmene; *to* — *to do* (*o on doing*) *sthg.*, decidere di far ql.co. **3.** stabilire esattamente: *to* — *the meaning of a word*, stabilire il significato di una parola **4.** scadere, terminare (di contratto, accordo, ecc.) **5.** *to* — *on*, fissarsi, ostinarsi su: *we had determined on a piano*, ci eravamo fissati su un pianoforte.

determined [di'tə:mind], *ag.* fermo, deciso, risoluto: *to be* — *to do sthg.*, essere deciso a fare ql.co.; *to be* — *on sthg.*, volere assolutamente ql.co.

determinedly [di'tə:mindli], *av.* risolutamente.

determinism [di'tə:minizəm], *s.* (*fil.*) determinismo.

determinist [di'tə:minist], *s.* (*fil.*) determinista.

deterrence [di'terəns], *s.* il distogliere col timore.

deterrent [di'terənt], *ag.* che trattiene; che dissuade || *s.* **1.** azione, fatto che trattiene, dissuade: *to act as a* — *of crime*, esercitare un effetto preventivo contro il reato **2.** (*neol.*) arma, specialmente atomica, così potente da dissuadere da eventuale aggressione.

detersion [di'tə:ʃən], *s.* detersione.

detersive [di'tə:siv], *ag.s.* detersivo.

to **detest** [di'test], *v.t.* (II) detestare, odiare: *I* — *him*, lo detesto; *we* — *being interrupted*, non possiamo sopportare di essere interrotti.

detestable [di'testəbl], *ag.* detestabile, odioso.

detestableness [di'testəblnis], *s.* odiosità.

detestably [di'testəbli], *av.* in modo detestabile, odioso.

detestation [,di:tes'teiʃən], *s.* **1.** odio: *to have* (*o to hold*) *sthg. in* —, detestare ql.co. **2.** cosa odiosa, orrore, abominio.

detester [di'testə*], *s.c.* chi detesta; chi aborrisce; nemico, nemica.

to **dethrone** [di'θroun], *v.t.* detronizzare.

dethronement [di'θrounmənt], *s.* deposizione (dal trono).

to **detonate** ['detouneit], *v.t.i.* detonare, fare detonare.

detonating ['detouneitiŋ], *ag.s.* detonante ☆ — *mixture*, miscela detonante.

detonation [,detou'neiʃən], *s.* detonazione, esplosione.

detonator ['detouneitə*], *s.* **1.** detonatore (di proiettile, bomba, ecc.) **2.** (*ferr.*) petardo, detonatore.

to **detort** [di'tɔ:t], *v.t.* (*arc.*) detorcere.

detour, détour ['deituə*], *s.* **1.** giro, via tortuosa; (*amer.*) deviazione (d'itinerario) **2.** digressione: *to make a* —, fare una digressione.

to **detour**, *v.t.i.* (*amer.*) deviare (di circolazione).

to **detoxicate** [di:'tɔksikeit], *v.t.* (*med.*) disintossicare.

to **detract** [di'trækt], *v.t.i.* diminuire; detrarre: *to* — *from s.o.'s merits*, diminuire i meriti di qlcu.; *to* — *sthg. from s.o.'s pleasure*, diminuire un po' il piacere di qlcu.

detractingly [di'træktiŋli], *av.* con detrazione.

detraction [di'trækʃən], *s.* detrazione; denigrazione; diffamazione.

detractive [di'træktiv], *ag.* diffamatorio; che toglie, che diminuisce, che detrae: *this is not* — *from his merits*, questo non diminuisce i suoi meriti.

detractor [di'træktə*], *s.* detrattore; donigratore.

to **detrain** [di:'trein], *v.t.i.* far scendere dal treno; scendere dal treno (*p.e.* truppe).

detriment ['detrimənt], *s.* detrimento; danno: *to the* — *of*, a detrimento, danno di; *without* — *to*, senza pregiudizio, danno per.

detrimental [,detri'mentl], *ag.* dannoso, nocivo; pregiudizievole.

detrimentally [,detri'mentəli], *av.* dannosamente, nocivamente.

detrition [di'triʃən], *s.* (*geol.*) corrosione per attrito.

detritus [di'traitəs], *s.* (*geol.*) detrito.

to **detrude** [di'tru:d], *v.t.* (*letter.*) detrudere.

to **detruncate** [di:'trʌŋkeit], *v.t.* troncare.

detumescence [,di:tju:'mesns], *s.* (*med.*) detumescenza.

to **detune** [di:'tju:n], *v.t.* (*rad.*) disintonizzare.

detuner [di:'tju:nə*], *s.* (*mec.*) silenziatore.

Deucalion [dju:(:)'keiljən], *no.pr.m.* (*mit.*) Deucalione.

deuce[1] [dju:s], *s.* **1.** due (di dadi, carte, domino) **2.** (*tennis*) 40 pari ☆ — *-ace*, due e uno (ai dadi); *fig.* cattiva sorte.

deuce[2], *s.* (*sl.*) diavolo, diamine: *go to the* —*!*, va' al diavolo!; *what the* — *does he mean?*, che diavolo vuol dire? || *he is the* — *of a liar*, egli è un bugiardo matricolato || *it's snowing like the* —, nevica che Dio la manda || *to play the* — *with s.o., sthg.*, rovinare qlcu., guastare ql.co.

deuced [dju:st], *ag.* (*sl.*) maledetto; diabolico; tremendo: — *hurry*, tremenda fretta; *what* — *weather!*, che tempo da lupi!.

deuced, *av.* (*sl.*) diabolicamente; tremendamente: *what* — *bad luck!*, che razza di sfortuna!.

deucedly ['dju:sidli], *av.* (*sl.*) diabolicamente; tremendamente.

to **deurbanize** [di:'ə:bənaiz], *v.t.* togliere il carattere metropolitano a (una zona, una regione, ecc.).

deuterium [dju(:)'tiəriəm], *s.* (*fis.*) deuterio, idrogeno pesante.

deuterogamist [ˌdju:tə'rɔgəmist], *s.c.* chi contrae un secondo matrimonio dopo la morte del primo coniuge.

deuterogamy [ˌdju:tə'rɔgəmi], *s.* il contrarre un secondo matrimonio dopo la morte del primo coniuge.

deuteron ['dju:tərən], *s.* (*fis.*) deuterone, deutone.

Deuteronomy [ˌdju:tə'rɔnəmi], *s.* (*Bibbia*) Deuteronomio.

deuteroscopy [ˌdju:tə'rɔskəpi], *s.* deuteroscopia.

devalorization [di:ˌvælərai'zeiʃən], *s.* (*econ.*) deprezzamento (della moneta).

to **devalorize** [di:'væləraiz], *v.t.* (*econ.*) deprezzare (la moneta).

to **devaluate** [di:'væljueit], *v.t.* (*econ.*) svalutare (la moneta).

devaluation [ˌdi:vælju'eiʃən], *s.* (*econ.*) svalutazione, (della moneta).

to **devalue** ['di:'vælju:], *V.* to **devaluate**.

to **devastate** ['devəsteit], *v.t.* devastare; rovinare; *the war had devastated the whole country*, la guerra aveva devastato l'intero paese.

devastating ['devəsteitiŋ], *ag.* **1.** rovinoso; devastante **2.** (*fam.*) grave (di argomento); fatale (di fascino).

devastatingly ['devəsteitiŋli], *av.* in modo da devastare: — *funny*, (*fam.*) da far ridere a crepapelle.

devastation [ˌdevəs'teiʃən], *s.* **1.** devastazione; rovina **2.** (*dir.*) dilapidazione.

devastator ['devəsteitə*], *s.c.* devastatore, devastatrice.

to **develop** [di'veləp], *v.t.i.* **1.** sviluppare, ampliare (le facoltà, un pensiero, un attacco, ecc.), svilupparsi; ampliarsi (del corpo, delle facoltà, ecc.): *his character is developing*, il suo carattere si sta formando; *plants — from seeds*, le piante si sviluppano dai semi; *seeds — into plants*, i semi si sviluppano in piante; *the story developed in the author's mind*, il racconto si sviluppò nella mente dell'autore **2.** valorizzare: *to — a district*, mettere in valore, valorizzare una regione **3.** generare: *to — heat*, generare calore **4.** contrarre (una malattia): *to — whooping cough*, contrarre la pertosse **5.** (*foto. mat.*) sviluppare **6.** (*miner.*) preparare **7.** (*amer.*) mostrar(si), rivelar(si): *it developed today that*, si è venuto a sapere oggi che; *to — a tendency to*, rivelare una tendenza verso.

developer [di'veləpə*], *s.* (*foto. chim.*) sviluppatore, rivelatore.

developing [di'veləpiŋ], *s.* **1.** sviluppo; valorizzazione; sfruttamento **2.** (*foto.*) sviluppo.

development [di'veləpmənt], *s.* **1.** sviluppo, evoluzione; accrescimento (del corpo, delle facoltà, ecc.): *the latest developments of the situation*, gli ultimi sviluppi della situazione; *a new —*, un fatto nuovo; *to await further developments*, aspettare gli ulteriori sviluppi (della situazione), attendere gli eventi **2.** valorizzazione, messa in valore (di una regione, ecc.) **3.** (*foto. mus.*) sviluppo **4.** (*miner.*) preparazione; spiegamento.

developmental [diˌveləp'mentl], *ag.* inerente allo sviluppo: — *ailments*, disturbi dello sviluppo.

to **devest** [di'vest], *V.* to **divest**.

deviate [di'viit], *ag.* (*amer.*) **1.** (*psicologia*) anormale **2.** traviato ‖ *s.* (*psicologia*) anormale.

to **deviate** ['di:vieit], *v.t.i.* deviare, far deviare.

deviation [ˌdi:vi'eiʃən], *s.* **1.** deviazione, scarto; *fig.* traviamento **2.** (*mar.*) dirottamento (di nave).

deviationism [ˌdi:vi'eiʃənizəm], *s.* (*pol.*) deviazionismo.

deviationist [ˌdi:vi'eiʃənist], *s.* (*pol.*) deviazionista.

deviator ['di:vieitə*], *s.* deviatore.

device [di'vais], *s.* **1.** mezzo, espediente; stratagemma, trovata **2.** *spec. pl.* capriccio, inclinazione: *to leave s.o. to his own devices*, lasciare qlcu. libero di

agire come vuole **3.** (*mec. elett.*) dispositivo, congegno, invenzione; (*fam.*) aggeggio **4.** (*arald.*) divisa; emblema, stemma.

devil ['devl], *s.* **1.** diavolo, demonio ‖ *go to the —!*, (*fam.*) vai al diavolo!; *he is a — of a man*, è un furbacchione, è uno che la sa lunga; *there is the — to pay*, (*fam.*) le conseguenze sono molto serie, ci sono gravi conseguenze in vista; *what the — are you doing?*, che diavolo stai facendo?; *to be between the — and the deep (blue) sea*, essere fra l'incudine e il martello; *to give the — his due*, rendere giustizia anche a chi non se la merita; *to paint the — blacker than he is*, dipingere il diavolo più brutto di quello che è; *to play the —*, fare il diavolo a quattro; *to play the (very) — with s.o.*, *sthg.*, fare molto male a qlcu., rovinare ql.co.; *to send s.o. to the —*, mandare qlcu. al diavolo; *talk of the — and he's sure to appear*, lupus in fabula; *to work like the —*, lavorare con accanimento **2.** spirito malvagio **3.** persona disgraziata: *poor —*, (*fam.*) povero diavolo ☆ — *-dodger*, (*sl.*) prete; — *-fish*, (*ittiol.*) razza; — *-like*, simile al diavolo; — *-may-care*, strafottente; — *-worship*, demonolatria; —*'s advocate*, avvocato del diavolo; —*'s bit*, (*bot.*) scabbiosa; —*'s bones*, dadi; —*'s books*, carte da giuoco; —*'s-milk*, (*bot.*) euforbia; —*'s tattoo*, il tamburellare (con dita o piedi) ‖ *dust-—*, (*Africa*) turbine di polvere; *printer's —*, apprendista di tipografia, fattorino; *she- —*, strega, donna cattiva.

to **devil**, *pass.p.p.* **devilled** ['devld], *v.t.i.* **1.** (*fam.*) far del lavoro per un altro (avvocato, scrittore) che lo fa poi passare per proprio **2.** cuocere alla graticola con spezie.

devilish ['deviliʃ], *ag.* diabolico.

devilishly ['deviliʃli], *av.* diabolicamente.

devilishness ['deviliʃnis], *s.* natura diabolica.

devilism ['devlizəm], *s.* satanismo.

devilment ['devlmənt], **devilry** ['devlri], **deviltry** ['devltri], *s.* diavoleria: *to be full of —*, avere il diavolo in corpo.

devious ['di:vjəs], *ag.* **1.** remoto, fuori mano **2.** tortuoso, serpeggiante **3.** erratico, vagante.

deviously ['di:vjəsli], *av.* in modo erratico, tortuoso.

deviousness ['di:vjəsnis], *s.* tortuosità (di sentiero, pensiero).

devisable [di'vaizəbl], *ag.* **1.** immaginabile **2.** (*dir.*) (bene immobile) trasmissibile (per testamento).

devise [di'vaiz], *s.* (*dir.*) **1.** disposizione testamentaria circa beni immobili **2.** legati di immobili.

to **devise**, *v.t.* **1.** escogitare; progettare, combinare (un progetto); inventare (un piano, un mezzo) **2.** (*dir.*) disporre per testamento (beni immobili); legare.

devisee [ˌdevi'zi:], *s.* (*dir.*) legatario, erede.

deviser [di'vaizə*], *s.c.* inventore, inventrice (di apparecchio, ecc.).

devising [di'vaiziŋ], *s.* **1.** invenzione **2.** (*dir.*) disposizione testamentaria.

devisor [ˌdevi'zo:*], *s.c.* (*dir.*) testatore, testatrice.

devitalization [di:ˌvaitəlai'zeiʃən], *s.* (*med.*) devitalizzazione.

to **devitalize** [di:'vaitəlaiz], *v.t.* **1.** (*med.*) devitalizzare **2.** indebolire.

to **devitrify** [di:'vitrifai], *v.t.* privare della qualità vitrea.

devoid [di'void], *ag.* privo, sprovvisto.

devoir [də'vwɔ:*], *s.* **1.** dovere **2.** *pl.* ossequio: *to pay one's devoirs to s.o.*, porgere i propri ossequi a qlcu.

to **devolute** ['devəlju:t], *v.t.* devolvere.

devolution [ˌdi:və'lu:ʃən], *s.* **1.** (*pol.*) delegazione del potere; trasmissione (di carica); decentramento amministrativo **2.** (*dir.*) devoluzione, trasmissione (di beni) **3.** (*biol.*) degenerazione.

to **devolve** [di'vɔlv], *v.t.i.* **1.** trasmettere; trasferire: *to — a duty, a responsability to* (o *upon*) *s.o.*, trasmettere a qlcu. un dovere, una responsabilità **2.** trasferirsi; cadere; incombere: *the duty devolved upon me to* *go there*, il dovere di andarci ricadde su di me **3.** (*dir.*) devolvere: *the house will — upon him*, sarà lui l'erede della casa.

Devonian [de'vounjən], *ag.* **1.** devoniano, del Devon **2.** (*geol.*) devoniano ‖ *s.c.* abitante del Devon ‖ *s.* (*geol.*) periodo, sistema devoniano.

to **devote** [di'vout], *v.t.* **1.** dedicare, consacrare: *he devoted his life to music, to helping the poor*, dedicò la vita alla musica, ad aiutare i poveri; *she devoted herself to study*, si dedicò allo studio; *to — oneself to the Muses*, votarsi al culto delle Muse **2.** votare, condannare alla rovina.

devoted [di'voutid], *ag.* **1.** devoto: *— friend*, amico devoto; *she is — to her children*, ella si dedica completamente ai suoi figli **2.** votato (a morte, rovina).

devotedly [di'voutidli], *av.* devotamente.

devotee [,devou'ti:], *s.* **1.** devoto; fedele **2.** fanatico, appassionato.

devotion [di'vouʃən], *s.* **1.** devozione; dedizione: *— to science*, dedizione alla scienza **2.** *gener. pl.* devozione, preghiera: *to be at one's devotions*, stare pregando, stare dicendo le proprie preghiere.

devotional [di'vouʃnl], *ag.* devoto, religioso, pio.

devotionally [di'vouʃnəli], *av.* con devozione.

to **devour** [di'vauə*], *v.t.* **1.** divorare (anche *fig.*): *devoured by terror*, in preda al terrore; *he devoured her with his eyes*, se la mangiava con gli occhi; *the lion devoured the deer*, il leone divorò il cervo; *to — a book*, divorare un libro **2.** dilapidare, mandare in rovina: *to — a fortune*, dilapidare una fortuna **3.** distruggere: *the fire devoured ten square miles of forest*, il fuoco distrusse dieci miglia quadrate di foresta.

devourer [di'vauərə*], *s.c.* chi divora.

devouring [di'vauəriŋ], *ag.* divorante; vorace.

devouringly [di'vauəriŋli], *av.* voracemente.

devout [di'vaut], *ag.* **1.** devoto, pio **2.** fervente, sincero: *a — supporter of the cause*, un fervente sostenitore della causa.

devoutly [di'vautli], *av.* **1.** devotamente **2.** sinceramente.

devoutness [di'vautnis], *s.* devozione, pietà.

dew [dju:], *s.* **1.** rugiada: *grass wet with —*, erba bagnata di rugiada **2.** *fig.* freschezza ☆ *— -berry*, (*bot.*) mora selvatica; *— -claw*, sperone (di cane, gallo, ecc.); *— -drop*, goccia di rugiada; *— -fall*, il cadere della rugiada; *— -pond*, stagno artificiale alimentato naturalmente; *— -worm*, lombrico ‖ *mountain —*, whisky distillato illegalmente in montagna.

to **dew**, *v.t.i.* **1.** *imp.* cadere (di rugiada) **2.** bagnare di rugiada **3.** imperlare; ingemmare, cospargere: *eyes dewed with tears*, occhi bagnati di lacrime.

dewan [di'wɑ:n], *s.* alto funzionario ministeriale (in India).

dewlap ['dju:læp], *s.* **1.** giogaia (di buoi) **2.** *fig.* pappagorgia, doppio mento.

dewlapped ['dju:læpt], *ag.* **1.** fornito di giogaia **2.** *fig.* con il doppio mento.

dewpoint ['dju:-point], *s.* (*fis.*) punto di rugiada, temperatura di condensazione.

dewy ['dju:i], *ag.* rugiadoso.

dexter ['dekstə*], *ag.* **1.** destro **2.** (*arald.*) destro (di scudo).

dexterity [deks'teriti], *s.* destrezza.

dexterous ['dekstərəs], *ag.* destro; abile.

dexterously ['dekstərəsli], *av.* con destrezza.

dexterousness ['dekstərəsnis], *s.* destrezza.

dextral ['dekstrəl], *ag.* destro.

dextrin(e) ['dekstrin], *s.* (*chim.*) destrina.

dextrorsal [deks'trɔ:səl], **dextrorse** [deks'trɔ:s], *ag.* (*bot.*) destrorso.

dextrose ['dekstrous], *s.* (*chim.*) destrosio.

dextrous ['dekstrəs], *ag.* destro; abile.

dextrously ['dekstrəsli], *av.* con destrezza.

dextrousness ['dekstrəsnis], *s.* destrezza.

dey[1] [dei], *s.f.* (*dial.*) lattaia; operaia di caseificio.

Dey[2], *s.* (*st.*) comandante dei giannizzeri di Algeri; governatore in Algeri, Tripoli.

dhobi ['doubi], *s.* (*ang.-in.*) lavandaio.

d(h)ow [dau], *s.* sambuco (imbarcazione usata nel Mar Rosso e nell'Oceano Indiano); nave araba adibita al trasporto degli schiavi.

diabetes [,daiə'bi:ti:z], *s.* (*patol.*) diabete.

diabetic [,daiə'betik], *ag.* (*patol.*) diabetico.

diablerie [di'ɑ:bləri], *s.* **1.** diavoleria **2.** negromanzia.

diabolic(al) [,daiə'bolik(əl)], *ag.* diabolico.

diabolically [,daiə'bolikəli], *av.* diabolicamente.

diabolism [dai'æbəlizəm], *s.* **1.** arte diabolica, magia nera **2.** culto del diavolo.

diabolo [di'ɑ:bəlou], *s.* (*giuoco*) diabolo.

diachylon [dai'ækilon], **diachylum** [dai'ækiləm], *s.* (*farm.*) diachilon (cerotto).

diaconal [dai'ækənl], *ag.* (*eccl.*) diaconale.

diaconate [dai'ækənit], *s.* (*eccl.*) diaconato.

diacoustics [,daiə'ku:stiks], *s.* (*fis.*) diacustica.

diacritic [,daiə'kritik], *ag.s.* (segno) diacritico.

diadem ['daiədem], *s.* diadema ☆ *— spider*, ragno comune.

diademed ['daiədemd], *ag.* cinto di diadema.

diadochi [dai'ædəkai], *s.pl.* (*st.*) diadochi.

diaeresis [dai'iərisis], *pl.* **diaereses** [dai'iərisi:z], *s.* dieresi.

to **diagnose** ['daiəgnouz], *v.t.i.* diagnosticare, fare una diagnosi.

diagnosis [,daiəg'nousis], *pl.* **diagnoses** [,daiəg'nousi:z], *s.* diagnosi.

diagnostic [,daiəg'nostik], *ag.* diagnostico.

diagnostically [,daiəg'nostikəli], *av.* diagnosticamente.

diagnostician [,daiəgnos'tiʃən], *s.* diagnostico.

diagonal [dai'ægənl], *ag. s.* diagonale.

diagonally [dai'ægənəli], *av.* diagonalmente.

diagram ['daiəgræm], *s.* diagramma, schema.

diagrammatic [,daiəgrə'mætik], *ag.* diagrammatico.

diagrammatically [,daiəgrə'mætikəli], *av.* diagrammaticamente, schematicamente.

dial ['daiəl], *s.* **1.** quadrante (di orologio) **2.** (*rad.*) scala parlante **3.** (*tel.*) disco combinatore **4.** (*compass*) —, (*mar.*) rosa dei venti **5.** (*miner.*) bussola **6.** (*sun-*) —, meridiana **7.** (*sl.*) faccia, muso ☆ *— -telephone*, telefono automatico.

to **dial**, *pass.p.p.* **dialled** ['daiəld], *v.t.* **1.** comporre il numero telefonico di: *to — the police*, telefonare alla polizia **2.** (*rad.*) cercare (una stazione).

dialect ['daiəlekt], *s.* dialetto.

dialectal [,daiə'lektl], *ag.* dialettale.

dialectally [,daiə'lektli], *av.* in modo dialettale.

dialectic [,daiə'lektik], *ag.* (*fil.*) dialettico ‖ *s.* (*fil.*) dialettica.

dialectical [,daiə'lektikəl], *ag.* (*fil.*) dialettico.

dialectically [,daiə'lektikəli], *av.* (*fil.*) dialetticamente.

dialectician [,daiəlek'tiʃən], *s.* **1.** (*fil.*) dialettico **2.** dialettologo, studioso di dialetti.

dialectics [,daiə'lektiks], *s.* (*fil.*) dialettica.

dialectologist [,daiəlek'tolədʒist], *s.* dialettologo, studioso di dialetti.

dialectology [,daiəlek'tolədʒi], *s.* dialettologia, studio dei dialetti.

dialogic [,daiə'lodʒik], *ag.* dialogico.

dialogism [dai'ælədʒizəm], *s.* dialogismo.

dialogist [dai'ælədʒist], *s.* dialogista.

dialogistic(al) [,daiələ'dʒistik(əl)], *ag.* dialogistico.

dialogue ['daiəlog], *s.* dialogo.

to **dialogue**, *v.t.i.* dialogare, sostenere un dialogo.

dialysis [dai'ælisis], *pl.* **dialyses** [dai'ælisi:z], *s.* (*fis.*) dialisi.

diamagnetic [,daiəmæg'netik], *ag.* (*elett.*) diamagnetico.

diamagnetism [,daiə'mægnitizəm], *s.* (*elett.*) diamagnetismo.

diamantiferous [ˌdaiəmənˈtifərəs], *ag.* diamantifero.

diameter [daiˈæmitə*], *s.* diametro.

diametral [daiˈæmitrəl], *ag.* diametrale.

diametrally [daiˈæmitrəli], *av.* diametralmente.

diametrical [ˌdaiəˈmetrikəl], *ag.* diametrale.

diametrically [ˌdaiəˈmetrikəli], *av.* diametralmente.

diamond [ˈdaiəmənd], *s.* **1.** diamante: *rough —*, diamante grezzo; *(fam.)* uomo rozzo in apparenza, ma buono, sincero ‖ *— cut —*, astuzia per astuzia **2.** losanga; rombo; *(carte)* quadri **3.** *(amer.)* campo da baseball **4.** *(tip.)* corpo 4¹/₂, diamante ☆ *— -bearing*, diamantifero; *— -field*, campo diamantifero; *— -panes*, vetri romboidali; *— -point*, punta di diamante; *— -snake*, serpente australiano; *— -wedding*, nozze di diamante ‖ *black diamonds*, *(fam.)* carbone; *cut —*, brillante; *glazier's —* (o *cutting —*), punta di diamante (per vetraio).

to **diamond**, *v.t.* indiamantare.

diamondiferous [ˌdaiəmənˈdifərəs], *ag.* diamantifero.

Diana [daiˈænə], *no.pr.f.* *(mit.)* Diana ‖ *s.* **1.** *(poet.)* la luna **2.** *(letter.)* cacciatrice; amazzone.

dianthus [daiˈænθəs], *s.* *(bot.)* dianto.

diapason [ˌdaiəˈpeisn], *s.* *(mus.)* diapason.

diaper [ˈdaiəpə*], *s.* **1.** tela damascata **2.** tovagliolo damascato; pannolino (specialmente per bambino) **3.** *(arch.)* pannello arabescato, a rombi ☆ *— rash*, sfogo dei lattanti; *— set*, completino per bimbo.

to **diaper**, *v.t.* **1.** damascare **2.** suddividere in rombi (una superficie) **3.** mettere un pannolino a (un bambino).

diaphanous [daiˈæfənəs], *ag.* trasparente; diafano.

diaphoresis [ˌdaiəfəˈriːsis], *s.* diaforesi.

diaphoretic [ˌdaiəfəˈretik], *ag.* sudorifero, diaforetico ‖ *s.* *(farm.)* sudorifero.

diaphragm [ˈdaiəfræm], *s.* diaframma; *(rad.)* membrana.

diaphragmatic [ˌdaiəfrægˈmætik], *ag.* diaframmatico.

diarist [ˈdaiərist], *s.* diarista, scrittore di diari.

to **diarize** [ˈdaiəraiz], *v.t.i.* fare il diario di; tenere un diario.

diarrhoea [ˌdaiəˈriə], *s.* *(patol.)* diarrea.

diary [ˈdaiəri], *s.* **1.** diario: *to keep, to post up a —*, tenere, aggiornare un diario **2.** agenda.

diastase [ˈdaiəsteis], *s.* *(chim.)* diastase.

diastasis [daiˈæstəsis], *s.* *(chir.)* diastasi.

diastole [daiˈæstəli], *s.* *(fisiol.)* diastole.

diathermie [ˌdaiəˈθəːmik], *ag.* **1.** *(med.)* diatermico **2.** *(fis.)* diatermano.

diathermy [ˈdaiəˌθəːmi], *s.* *(med.)* diatermia, marconiterapia.

diathesis [daiˈæθisis], *s.* *(med.)* diatesi.

diatomie [ˌdaiəˈtomik], *ag.* *(fis. chim.)* biatomico.

diatonic [ˌdaiəˈtonik], *ag.* *(mus.)* diatonico.

diatribe [ˈdaiətraib], *s.* diatriba.

to **dib** [dib], *pass.p.p.* **dibbed** [dibd], *V.* to **dap 1.**

dibble [ˈdibl], *s.* piuolo, piantatoio.

to **dibble**, *v.t.* fare buche nel terreno con un piantatoio per seminare, usare un piantatoio: *to — in potatoes*, piantare patate.

dibs [dibz], *s.pl.* **1.** ossetti (della zampa di pecora): *to play at —*, giocare agli ossetti (giuoco di bimbi) **2.** gettone (alle carte, ecc.) **3.** *(sl.)* denaro, spiccioli.

dice [dais], *pl.* di **die 1.**

to **dice**, *v.t.i.* **1.** giocare a dadi ‖ *to — away a fortune*, perdere una fortuna ai dadi **2.** tagliare a dadini *(p.e. legumi)* **3.** disegnare a scacchi.

dicer [ˈdaisə*], *s.* giocatore di dadi ‖ *—'s oath*, *(fam.)* promessa da marinaio.

dichotomy [diˈkɔtəmi], *s.* *(astr. bot.)* dicotomia.

dick[1], *s.* **1.** *(sl.)* frustino da cavallo **2.** *(amer.)* agente investigativo.

dick[2], *s.* *(sl.)* dichiarazione: *to take one's — that*, giurare che.

Dick[3] [dik], *no.pr.m. dim.* di **Richard**.

dickens [ˈdikinz], *s.* *(sl.)* diamine: *what the — are you doing?*, che diamine state facendo?.

Dickensian [diˈkenziən], *ag.* di Dickens, dickensiano ‖ *s.* ammiratore di Charles Dickens.

dicker[1] [ˈdikə*], *s.* *(comm.)* decina *(p.e. di pelli)*.

to **dicker**[1], *v.i.* *(sl. amer.)* commerciare, trafficare (in).

dicker[2], *s.* *(amer.)* affare di poco conto.

dickey, *V.* **dicky** *s.*

dicky [ˈdiki], *ag.* *(sl.)* male in arnese; malandato.

dicky, *s.* **1.** *(sl.)* asino, somarello **2.** grembiule di cuoio **3.** finto sparato di camicia; davantino; bavaglino **4.** sedile per cocchiere o autista; sedile posteriore per servitori (di carrozza) ☆ *— -bird*, uccellino.

dicotyledon [ˈdaiˌkɔtiˈliːdən], *s.* *(bot.)* dicotiledone.

dictagraph [ˈdiktəgrɑːf], *s.* dittografo.

dictaphone [ˈdiktəfoun], *s.* dittafono.

dictate [ˈdikteit], *s.* dettame; comando (specialmente di ragione, coscienza): *the dictates of conscience*, i dettami della coscienza.

to **dictate** [dikˈteit], *v.t.i.* dettare (anche *fig.*); *(fam.)* dettar legge: *business men — their letters*, gli uomini d'affari dettano la loro corrispondenza; *I will not be dictated to*, non voglio imposizioni; *to — terms to a defeated enemy*, dettare, imporre condizioni a un nemico sconfitto.

dictation [dikˈteiʃən], *s.* **1.** dettatura; dettato: *to do —*, fare il dettato **2.** ordine, comando, atto d'autorità.

dictator [dikˈteitə*], *s.* **1.** chi detta **2.** dittatore (anche *fig.*): *the — of fashion*, l'arbitro della moda.

dictatorial [ˌdiktəˈtɔːriəl], *ag.* dittatorio, dittatoriale.

dictatorially [ˌdiktəˈtɔːriəli], *av.* da dittatore.

dictatorship [dikˈteitəʃip], *s.* dittatura.

diction [ˈdikʃən], *s.* **1.** stile (di oratore) **2.** *(amer.)* dizione.

dictionary [ˈdikʃənri], *s.* dizionario ☆ *— -maker*, lessicografo; *— -making*, lessicografia.

dictograph [ˈdiktəgrɑːf], *s.* dittografo.

dictum [ˈdiktəm], *pl.* **dictums** [ˈdiktəmz], **dicta** [ˈdiktə], *s.* **1.** detto, massima, proverbio **2.** *(dir.)* sentenza non definitiva **3.** pronunciamento; affermazione.

did [did], *pass.* di to **do**.

didactic [diˈdæktik], *ag.* didattico.

didactically [diˈdæktikəli], *av.* didatticamente.

didactics [diˈdæktiks], *s.* didattica.

to **diddle** [ˈdidl], *v.t.* *(sl.)* **1.** gabbare, imbrogliare: *he diddled me out of £ 100*, mi ha soffiato cento sterline **2.** sciupare (il tempo) in sciocchezze.

Dido [ˈdaidou], *no.pr.f.* *(lett.)* Didone.

didymium [diˈdimiəm], *s.* *(chim.)* didimio.

Didymus [ˈdidiməs], *no.pr.m.* Didimo.

die[1] [dai], *pl.* **dies** [daiz], *nel senso* **1.** dice [dais], *s.* **1.** dado: *to play dice*, giocare a dadi ‖ *the — is cast*, il dado è tratto **2.** *pl.* *(arch.)* dado, plinto **3.** *pl.* *(tec.)* stampo, matrice; filiera, trafila ☆ *— -box*, bossolo (per dadi); *— -casting*, pressofusione; *— -sinker*, stampista, fabbricante di stampi, incisore di medaglie; *(macchina)* fresatrice per stampi.

to **die**[2], *v.i.* **1.** morire, perire: *his name will never —*, il suo nome non morirà mai; *his secret died with him*, si è portato il suo segreto nella tomba; *to — before one's time*, morire prematuramente; *to — a beggar, a martyr, a hero*, morire da mendicante, da martire, da eroe; *to — by one's hand*, morire di propria mano; *to — a dog's death*, morire come un cane; *to — from* (o *of*) *a wound*, morire in seguito a una ferita; *to — game*, morire con coraggio; *to — a glorious death*, fare una morte gloriosa; *to — happy, poor*, morire felice, povero; *to — hard*, morire lottando; *to — a natural death, in one's bed*, morire di morte naturale, nel proprio letto; *to — of* (di malattia, fame, dolore) ‖ *never say —*, non disperare, non cedere mai ‖ *to — in one's boots* (o *shoes*), morire sulla breccia **2.** *(fam. fig.)* morire: *to — with laughter* (o *of* o *with laughing*), morire dal ridere; *to be dying for sthg.*, *to do sthg.*, morire dalla voglia di ql.co., di fare ql.co.;

to be dying with curiosity, morire dalla curiosità 3. *to —* **away**, affievolirsi, svanire; sparire lentamente (di suono, visione, vento, ecc.) 4. *to —* **down**, abbassarsi, calare, venir meno (di fuoco, vento, suono) 5. *to —* **off**, morire (di foglie); morire uno dopo l'altro; estinguersi (di una famiglia, razza, ecc.) 6. *to —* **out**, estinguersi (di fuoco); deperire; scomparire (di abitudini, famiglia, ricordi).

to **die-cast** ['dai-kɑːst], *pass.p.p.* **die-cast**, *v.t.* (*mec.*) pressofondere, fondere sotto pressione.

die-hard ['dai-hɑːd], *ag.* che non si dà mai per vinto ‖ *s.* (*pol.*) conservatore intransigente.

dielectric [ˌdaiiˈlektrik], *ag.s.* dielettrico.

Diesel ['diːzəl], *no. pr.*: *— motor* (o *— engine*), motore Diesel; *— oil*, nafta (per motori Diesel); *— rail car*, automotrice Diesel.

diet[1] ['daiət], *s.* **1.** nutrimento, alimentazione **2.** (*med.*) dieta, regime: *to be on a —*, essere a dieta.

to **diet**[1], *v.t.* mettere a regime, a dieta; prescrivere una dieta a.

diet[2], *s.* (*pol.st.*) dieta, assemblea.

dietarian [ˌdaiəˈteəriən], *s.* chi sta a dieta.

dietary ['daiətəri], *ag.* dietetico ‖ *s.* regime, dieta (alimentare).

dietetic [ˌdaiiˈtetik], *ag.* dietetico.

dietetically [ˌdaiiˈtetikəli], *av.* dieteticamente.

dietetics [ˌdaiiˈtetiks], *s.* (*med.*) dietetica.

dietician [ˌdaiiˈtiʃən], *s.* dietologo.

to **differ** ['difə*], *v.i.* **1.** essere diverso, dissimile, differente: *I — from him in age*, sono di età diversa dalla sua; *she differed from her brother*, non assomigliava a suo fratello **2.** differire; non essere d'accordo: *I beg to —*, mi permetto di essere d'opinione diversa; *to — about sthg.*, non essere d'accordo in merito a ql.co.; *to — in opinion from* (o *with*) *s.o.*, differire in opinione da qlcu.: *we — in opinion from* (o *with*) *him*, la nostra opinione differisce dalla sua ‖ *to agree to —*, rimanere ciascuno della propria opinione.

difference ['difrəns], *s.* **1.** differenza: *the — between black and white*, la differenza fra bianco e nero; *what a — from...*, che differenza da...; *with the — that...*, con la differenza che...; *it makes a great —*, c'è una bella differenza; *to make no —*, non fare nessuna differenza **2.** (*mat.*) differenza: *the — between two and ten is eight*, la differenza fra due e dieci è otto; *to pay the —*, (*ferr.*) pagare il supplemento; *to split the —*, dividere a metà la differenza **3.** divario; divergenza; controversia: *to have a — with s.o. about sthg.*, avere una divergenza con qlcu. in merito a ql.co.; *to settle a —*, appianare una divergenza, mettersi d'accordo.

to **difference**, *v.t.* differenziare.

different ['difrənt], *ag.* **1.** differente, diverso; dissimile: *his ideas are — from mine*, le sue idee sono diverse dalle mie; *that is quite a — matter*, è tutt'altra cosa; *they are — in race*, sono di razza diversa; *things are now — than before*, le cose ora sono diverse da prima; *this colour is — from that one*, questo colore è differente da quello; *you can do this in a — way*, potete far questo in modo diverso **2.** vario: *at — times*, in varie epoche, in momenti diversi **3.** (*fam.*) speciale: *if you want sthg. of a — quality*, se vuoi ql.co. di qualità speciale.

differential [ˌdifəˈrenʃəl], *ag.s.* (*mat. aut.*) differenziale ☆ *— calculus*, (*mat.*) calcolo differenziale; *— gear*, (*mec. aut.*) differenziale; *— tariff*, (*comm. ferr.*) tariffa differenziale.

to **differentiate** [ˌdifəˈrenʃieit], *v.t.i.* differenziare, differenziarsi; essere, rendere differente.

differentiation [ˌdifərenʃiˈeiʃən], *s.* differenziazione; in modo vario.

differently ['difrəntli], *av.* differentemente, diversamente; in modo vario.

difficult ['difikəlt], *ag.* difficile (di lavoro, sforzo, strada, carriera, carattere, ecc.): *a — digestion*, una digestione laboriosa; *a — matter*, una questione, una faccenda difficile; *— to translate*, difficile da tradurre; *a question — to answer*, una domanda a cui è difficile

rispondere; *he is a person — to get on with*, è una persona con cui è difficile andar d'accordo; *it is — for me, I find it — to understand him*, mi è difficile capirlo, lo trovo difficile da capire; *that place is — of access*, quel luogo è di difficile accesso.

difficultly ['difikəltli], *av.* difficilmente.

difficulty ['difikəlti], *s.* **1.** difficoltà: *to have some — in doing sthg.*, aver qualche difficoltà a fare ql.co.: *I have great — in understanding spoken English*, mi è molto difficile capire l'inglese parlato **2.** ostacolo: *many difficulties*, molte difficoltà, molti ostacoli; *to get over* (o *to overcome*) *a —*, sormontare un ostacolo; *to make* (o *to raise*) *difficulties*, fare, opporre difficoltà, ostacoli; *to make no — about doing sthg.*, non fare nessuna difficoltà a fare ql.co. ‖ *that's the —*, (*fam.*) qui sta il busillis **3.** seccatura; imbarazzo: *to be in a —*, trovarsi in una situazione difficile; *to be in difficulties*, trovarsi a corto di denaro; *to get out of a —*, cavarsi da una situazione difficile.

diffidence ['difidəns], *s.* timidezza; modestia eccessiva; mancanza di fiducia in se stesso.

diffident ['difidənt], *ag.* timido; esitante; che manca di fiducia in se stesso: *I was — about writing to him*, esitavo a scrivergli; *to be —*, dubitare di se stesso.

diffidently ['difidəntli], *av.* timidamente; con qualche esitazione.

diffluent ['diflu(ː)ənt], *ag.* fluente.

to **diffract** [diˈfrækt], *v.t.* (*fis.*) diffrangere.

diffraction [diˈfrækʃən], *s.* (*fis.*) diffrazione.

diffuse [diˈfjuːs], *ag.* **1.** diffuso (di luce, ecc.) **2.** prolisso (di stile, ecc.).

to **diffuse** [diˈfjuːz], *v.t.i.* **1.** diffondere, diffondersi; spargere, spargersi; propagare, propagarsi (di luce, idea, notizia, ecc.) **2.** dilungarsi (in parole).

diffused [diˈfjuːzd], *ag.* diffuso ☆ *— lighting*, illuminazione a luce diffusa.

diffusedly [diˈfjuːzidli], *av.* ovunque, in ogni dove.

diffusely [diˈfjuːsli], *av.* **1.** ovunque **2.** diffusamente; in modo prolisso.

diffuseness [diˈfjuːsnis], *s.* prolissità (di stile).

diffuser [diˈfjuːzə*], *s.* (*tec.*) diffusore.

diffusibility [diˌfjuːzəˈbiliti], *s.* diffusibilità.

diffusible [diˈfjuːzəbl], *ag.* diffusibile.

diffusion [diˈfjuːʒən], *s.* **1.** propagazione; diffusione (di fluido, calore, luce, ecc.) **2.** prolissità (di stile).

diffusive [diˈfjuːsiv], *ag.* **1.** diffusivo **2.** prolisso; diffuso (di stile): *she was less — and more pointed than usual*, fu meno prolissa e più pungente del solito.

diffusively [diˈfjuːsivli], *av.* diffusamente.

dig [dig], *s.* **1.** vangata; scavo **2.** (*sl.*) urto; botta; spintone: *to give s.o. a — in the ribs*, dare una gomitata nelle costole a qlcu. **3.** (*fam.*) osservazione sarcastica: *to have a — at s.o.*, dare una stoccata a qualcuno **4.** (*sl. scolastico amer.*) secchione, sgobbone **5.** *pl.* (*sl.*) camera ammobiliata.

to **dig**, *pass.p.p.* **dug** [dʌg], *v.t.i.* **1.** vangare, lavorare la terra; scavare: *he digs in the garden*, vanga in giardino; *to — a hole*, scavare una buca ‖ *to — for*, scavare per trovare: *to — for gold*, scavare in cerca d'oro **2.** (*fam.*) dare un colpo, uno spintone: *to — s.o. in the ribs*, dare uno spintone nelle costole a qlcu. **3.** (*sl.*) alloggiare in camera ammobiliata **4.** (*sl. scolastico amer.*) secchiare, sgobbare **5.** *to — in*, penetrare scavando, affondare: *to — oneself in*, (*mil.*) trincerarsi; *to — one's nails in(to)*, affondare (le unghie) in ‖ *to — one's toes in*, tenersi saldo nelle proprie posizioni **6.** *to — out*, tirar fuori, estrarre con fatica: *he had to — the car out of the snow*, dovette liberare la macchina dalla neve; *these documents have been dug out of the archives*, *fig.* questi documenti sono stati disseppelliti dall'archivio **7.** *to — up*, dissodare (il terreno); scovare (informazioni, fatti); estrarre (dal terreno); *fig.* rivangare.

digest ['daidʒest], *s.* **1.** sommario, riassunto ‖ *Reader's Digest*, Selezione **2.** (*dir.*) digesto.

to **digest** [di'dʒest], *v.t.i.* **1.** (*fisiol.*) digerire, far digerire, essere digerito: *some foods — (o are digested) more easily than others*, alcuni cibi si digeriscono meglio di altri **2.** *fig.* assimilare: *have you digested everything that is important in that book?*, hai assimilato tutto quello che è importante in quel libro? **3.** tollerare: *to — an insult*, (*fam.*) tollerare un insulto **4.** (*arc.*) riassumere; riordinare; codificare.

digester [di'dʒestə*], *s.* **1.** chi redige sommari; redattore di sommari **2.** colui che digerisce: *to be a bad —*, avere una cattiva digestione **3.** (*farm.*) digestivo **4.** (*chim.*) digestore ☆ *Papin's —*, pentola di Papin.

digestibility [di,dʒestə'biliti], *s.* digeribilità.

digestible [di'dʒestəbl], *ag.* digeribile.

digestion [di'dʒestʃən], *s.* **1.** digestione: *to be easy, hard of —*, essere di facile, difficile digestione; *to have the — of an ostrich*, (*fam.*) avere uno stomaco di struzzo; *to have a poor —*, avere una cattiva digestione **2.** (*chim.*) digestione.

digestive [di'dʒestiv], *ag.* digestivo; digerente: *— system*, apparato digerente ∥ *s.* digestivo.

digger ['digə*], *s.* **1.** zappatore; sterratore, terraziere **2.** minatore: (*gold-*) *—*, cercatore d'oro **3.** (*sl.*) australiano, neozelandese **4.** (*mec.*) scavatrice, escavatrice; (*agr.*) scavapatate ☆ *grave- —*, becchino.

digging ['digiŋ], *s.* **1.** zappatura; scavo **2.** *gener. pl.* miniera d'oro; giacimento aurifero **3.** *pl.* (*sl.*) camera ammobiliata.

dight [dait], *ag.* (*arc.*) ornato.

digit ['didʒit], *s.* **1.** (*mat.*) numero semplice (dallo 0 al 9): *a number of eight digits*, un numero di otto cifre **2.** dito (misura di lunghezza = cm. 1,905) **3.** (*anat. zool.*) dito (di uomo, animale) **4.** (*astr.*) dodicesima parte del diametro (del sole, della luna).

digital ['didʒitl], *ag.* digitale; delle dita.

digitalin [,didʒi'teilin], *s.* (*farm.*) digitalina.

digitalis [,didʒi'teilis], *s.* (*bot.*) digitale.

digitate ['didʒitit], **digitated** ['didʒiteitid], *ag.* (*zool. bot.*) digitato.

digitigrade ['didʒiti,greid], *ag.s.* (*zool.*) digitigrado.

diglyph ['daiglif], *s.* (*arch.*) diglifo.

dignified ['dignifaid], *ag.* dignitoso; nobile; austero.

to **dignify** ['dignifai], *v.t.* **1.** conferire dignità a; nobilitare: *the little house was dignified with the name of "castle"*, quella piccola casa si fregiava del nome di « castello » **2.** onorare, esaltare.

dignitary ['dignitəri], *s.* dignitario; (*eccl.*) prelato.

dignity ['digniti], *s.* **1.** dignità: *the — of labour*, la dignità del lavoro; *air of —*, portamento dignitoso; *to be beneath one's — (to accept)*, essere al disotto della propria dignità, non abbassarsi (ad accettare); *to preserve one's —*, conservare la propria dignità; *to stand (up) on one's — (with s.o.)*, mantenere la propria dignità (nei confronti di qlcu.) **2.** rango, ufficio elevato **3.** dignitario: *the dignities of the State*, i dignitari dello Stato.

digraph ['daigrɑ:f], *s.* (*gram.*) digramma.

to **digress** [dai'gres], *v.i.* fare una digressione; perdersi in digressioni; deviare: *to — from*, allontanarsi da.

digression [dai'greʃən], *s.* digressione: *this by way of —*, questo per inciso.

digressive [dai'gresiv], *ag.* digressivo.

dihedron [dai'hi:drən], *s.* (*geom.*) diedro.

dik-dik ['dikdik], *s.* (*zool.*) piccola antilope africana.

dike [daik], *s.* **1.** diga, argine **2.** (*arc.*) fosso, canale **3.** (*geol.*) dicco, filone eruttivo.

to **dike**, *v.t.* arginare; proteggere con dighe.

to **dilacerate** [di'læsəreit], *v.t.* (*rar.*) lacerare.

dilaceration [di,læsə'reifən], *s.* (*rar.*) lacerazione.

to **dilapidate** [di'læpideit], *v.t.i.* dilapidare; mandare in rovina; cadere in rovina.

dilapidated [di'læpideitid], *ag.* decrepito; in rovina; a pezzi: *a — car*, un'automobile sconquassata.

dilapidation [di,læpi'deiʃən], *s.* dilapidazione (di una sostanza); sperpero; sfacelo; sconquassamento.

dilatability [dai,leitə'biliti], *s.* dilatabilità.

dilatable [dai'leitəbl], *ag.* dilatabile.

dilatation [,dailə'teiʃən], *s.* dilatazione.

dilatator ['dailəteitə*], *V.* **dilator.**

to **dilate** [dai'leit], *v.t.i.* dilatare; dilatarsi; diffondersi, dilungarsi: *to — (up)on a subject*, dilungarsi su un argomento.

dilation [dai'leiʃən], *s.* dilatazione.

dilator [dai'leitə*], *s.* **1.** (*anat.*) muscolo dilatatore **2.** (*med.*) dilatatore.

dilatorily ['dilətərili], *av.* lentamente, tardamente.

dilatoriness ['dilətərinis], *s.* lentezza, dilazione, ritardo.

dilatory ['dilətəri], *ag.* **1.** tardivo, lento (nell'agire) **2.** (*dir.*) dilatorio.

dilemma [di'lemə], *s.* **1.** dilemma: *the horns of the —*, i corni del dilemma **2.** (*fam.*) imbarazzo, incertezza: *to be in a —*, essere tra l'incudine e il martello.

dilettante [,dili'tænti], *pl.* **dilettanti** [,dili'tænti:], *s.* dilettante.

dilettantish [,dili'tæntiʃ], *ag.* da dilettante.

dilettantism [,dili'tæntizəm], *s.* dilettantismo.

dilettantist [,dili'tæntist], *ag.* da dilettante.

diligence[1] ['dilidʒəns], *s.* diligenza; assiduità; cura.

diligence[2] ['diliʒɑ:ns], *s.* diligenza, carrozza pubblica a cavalli.

diligent ['dilidʒənt], *ag.* diligente, assiduo; attivo; accurato.

diligently ['dilidʒəntli], *av.* diligentemente.

dill [dil], *s.* (*bot.*) aneto.

to **dilly-dally** ['dilidæli], *v.i.* (*fam.*) tentennare, titubare; gingillarsi, sciupare tempo.

diluent ['diljuənt], *ag.s.* (*chim. med.*) diluente.

dilute [dai'lju:t], *ag.* **1.** (*chim.*) diluito **2.** smorzato (di colore) **3.** *fig.* attenuato; all'acqua di rose **4.** debole; meschino.

to **dilute**, *v.t.* **1.** (*chim.*) diluire **2.** temperare, smorzare (colore) **3.** *fig.* attenuare, indebolire.

dilution [dai'lu:ʃən], *s.* diluzione; sostanza diluita ∥ *— of labour*, sostituzione di mano d'opera qualificata con personale non specializzato.

diluvial [dai'lu:vjəl], **diluvian** [dai'lu:vjən], *ag.* diluviale; diluviano.

diluvium [dai'lu:vjəm], *s.* diluvio.

dim [dim], *ag.* pallido (di luce); debole (di vista); sordo (di suono); vago, indistinto, appannato (di memoria); oscuro (di ambiente); ottuso (di intelligenza); smorzato (di tinte): *the — light of a candle*, la debole luce di una candela; *eyes — with tears*, occhi velati di lacrime; *to grow —*, oscurarsi, appannarsi ∥ *— out*, oscuramento parziale ∥ *— view*, (*neol.*) visione pessimistica ☆ *— sighted*, che ha la vista debole, offuscata.

to **dim**, *pass.p.p.* **dimmed** [dimd], *v.t.i.* oscurare, oscurarsi (di luce, ecc.); offuscare, offuscarsi; affievolire; indebolire, indebolirsi: *her eyes were dimmed with tears*, le si offuscarono gli occhi per le lacrime; *to — the headlights*, (*aut.*) commutare la luce abbagliante con quella antiabbagliante.

dime [daim], *s.* (*amer.*) moneta d'argento equivalente ad un decimo di dollaro ☆ *— novel*, romanzo da quattro soldi.

dimension [di'menʃən], *s.* **1.** *gener. pl.* dimensione; estensione; grandezza, misura: *the dimensions of a room*, la grandezza di una stanza; *of large dimensions*, di grandi dimensioni **2.** (*mec.*) quota **3.** (*mat.*) dimensione ∥ *the fourth —*, la quarta dimensione.

dimensional [di'menʃən], *ag.* **1.** di dimensione, dimensioni; che ha uno specificato numero di dimensioni: *three — space*, spazio a tre dimensioni **2.** (*fis.*) dimensionale.

dimensioned [di'menʃənd], *ag.* **1.** a dimensioni **2.** quotato (di disegno) ☆ *three- —*, tridimensionale, a tre dimensioni.

dimensionless [di'menʃənlis], *ag.* **1.** senza dimensioni **2.** illimitato, infinito.

dimerous ['dimərəs], *ag.* (*bot. entom.*) dimero.
dimeter ['dimitə*], *s.* (*poes.*) dimetro.
dimidiate [di'midiit], *ag.* dimezzato.
to diminish [di'miniʃ], *v.t.i.* **1.** diminuire, scemare; ridurre, ridursi; rimpicciolire, rimpicciolirsi; *fig.* degradare, umiliare **2.** (*arch.*) rastremare.
diminishable [di'miniʃəbl], *ag.* diminuibile.
diminished [di'miniʃt], *ag.* diminuito; ridotto: — *interval, fifth,* (*mus.*) intervallo diminuito, quinta diminuita.
diminishing [di'miniʃiŋ], *ag.* diminuente; calante; che fa diminuire, calare ‖ *s.* diminuzione; attenuazione.
diminishingly [di'miniʃiŋli], *av.* in modo da diminuire; *fig.* sfavorevolmente.
diminuendo [di,minju'endou], *s.* (*mus.*) diminuendo.
diminution [,dimi'nju:ʃən], *s.* **1.** diminuzione; riduzione **2.** (*arch.*) rastremazione.
diminutival [di,minju'taivəl], *ag.* (*gram.*) diminutivo.
diminutive [di'minjutiv], *ag.* (*fam.*) minuscolo; minuto; piccolo piccolo: *he was small, almost — in stature,* egli non era di alta statura, ma era anzi piccolo piccolo ‖ *s.* **1.** (*gram.*) diminutivo **2.** persona piccola.
diminutiveness [di'minjutivnis], *s.* piccolezza; esiguità.
dimissory ['dimisəri], *ag.* dimissorio ☆ — *letter,* (*eccl.*) lettera dimissoria.
dimity ['dimiti], *s.* **1.** tessuto di cotone rigato (per tendaggi, ecc.) **2.** (*arc.*) tessuto leggero di cotone.
dimly ['dimli], *av.* debolmente; indistintamente; oscuramente; imperfettamente.
dimmer ['dimə*], *s.* (*elett. aut.*) commutatore delle luci; (*cine. teat.*) oscuratore (di luce) ☆ *foot — switch,* (*aut.*) commutatore a pedale per luce anabbagliante.
dimming ['dimiŋ], *ag.* opacizzante, offuscante ‖ *s.* oscuramento; diminuzione dell'illuminazione.
dimmish ['dimiʃ], *ag.* piuttosto oscuro, piuttosto debole (di luce).
dimness ['dimnis], *s.* **1.** debolezza (d'illuminazione, di vista), oscurità (in una sala); offuscamento (d'intelligenza) **2.** *fig.* imprecisione di contorni (di un ricordo, ecc.).
dimorphism [dai'mɔ:fizəm], *s.* (*biol. fis.*) dimorfismo.
dimple ['dimpl], *s.* **1.** fossetta (di guancia, mento, braccio) **2.** increspamento, increspatura, piccola ondulazione (di acqua, terra).
to dimple, *v.t.i.* **1.** formarsi, crearsi (di fossette sorridendo): *her dimpled cheeks,* le sue guance illeggiadrite da fossette **2.** increspare, incresparsi (dell'acqua).
din [din], *s.* baccano, strepito, fracasso; tumulto: *the — of war,* lo strepito della guerra; *what a terrible —!,* che baccano terribile!.
to din, *pass.p.p.* **dinned** [dind], *v.t.i.* **1.** assordare; strepitare: *I had my ears dinned by hooters,* io ero assordato dalle sirene; *to — sthg. into s.o.'s ears,* ripetere ql.co. a qlcu. ad alta voce, far rintronare ql.co. nelle orecchie di qlcu. **2.** risuonare (di voce): *to — in s.o.'s ears,* rintronare, risuonare nelle orecchie di qlcu.
Dinah ['dainə], *no.pr.f.* Dina.
to dine [dain], *v.t.i.* **1.** pranzare: *to — on* (o *off*) *sthg.* (*meat, fish*), fare un pranzo a base di ql.co. (carne, pesce) ‖ *to — in,* pranzare a casa; *to — out,* pranzare fuori (casa) ‖ *to — with Duke Humphrey,* (*fam. arc.*) saltare il pranzo **2.** far pranzare, offrire un pranzo a: *we shall have to — them,* dovremo offrire loro un pranzo ‖ *the table dines twenty,* si può pranzare in venti intorno a questa tavola.
diner ['dainə*], *s.* **1.** commensale **2.** (*ferr.*) vagone ristorante ☆ — *out,* persona che pranza spesso fuori casa.
dinette [dai'net], *s.* (*neol. amer.*) saletta da pranzo; angolo del pranzo in una stanza.
to ding [diŋ], *v.t.i.* **1.** risuonare **2.** parlare con veemenza **3.** (*sl.*) fare entrare (un'idea) nella testa di qlcu.
ding-dong ['diŋ'dɔŋ], *ag.* oscillante: *a — race, fight,* corsa, combattimento di esito incerto ‖ *s.* **1.** dindon (di campane) **2.** oscillazione (d'opinione pubblica).

ding-dong, *av.* con persistente alternativa.
dingey, dinghy ['diŋgi], *s.* (*mar.*) «dinghy», lancia.
dinginess ['dindʒinis], *s.* aspetto scuro, triste, povero; sudiciume; trascuratezza.
dingle ['diŋgl], *s.* valletta ombrosa.
dingle-dangle ['diŋgl'dæŋgl], *av.* a penzoloni.
dingo ['diŋgou], *pl.* **dingoes** ['diŋgouz], *s.* (*zool.*) dingo.
dingy ['dindʒi], *ag.* scuro; triste; sporco; sbiadito, offuscato; povero; fosco: — *hotel,* albergo squallido e poco pulito; — *white,* bianco sporco.
dining ['dainiŋ], *s.* il pranzare ☆ — *-car,* (*ferr.*) carrozza ristorante; — *-hall,* sala da pranzo, refettorio; — *-room,* sala da pranzo; — *-table,* tavola da pranzo.
dinkum ['diŋkəm], *ag.* (*sl. austral.*) sincero; genuino; onesto ‖ *it is fair —,* è proprio vero ‖ *s.* (*austral.*) lavoro pesante, noioso.
dinky ['diŋki], *ag.* (*fam.*) carino, grazioso: *a — little hat,* un cappellino civettuolo.
dinna ['dinə], (*scoz.*) per *do not:* — *forget,* non dimenticare.
dinner ['dinə*], *s.* pranzo, desinare: *it is time for —,* è ora di andare a tavola; *to ask s.o. to —,* invitare qlcu. a pranzo; *to be at —,* essere a tavola; *to come for —,* arrivare per pranzo; *to come to —,* venire a pranzo; *to do — duty,* occuparsi della refezione scolastica; *to give a — (in honour of s.o., for s.o.),* dare un pranzo (in onore di qlcu.); *to go out to —,* pranzare fuori di casa; *to have —,* pranzare ☆ — *-bell,* campana annunciante il pranzo; — *-dance,* pranzo seguito da ballo; — *-jacket,* «smoking»; — *-party,* pranzo con invitati; i convitati; — *service* (o — *set*), servizio da tavola; — *-time,* l'ora del pranzo; — *-wagon,* carrello; — *wine,* vino da tavola.
dinnerless ['dinəlis], *ag.* che non ha pranzato: *to go —,* saltare il pranzo.
dinosaur ['dainəsɔ:*], *s.* (*paleont.*) dinosauro.
dint [dint], *s.* **1.** tacca, impronta, segno **2.** (*arc.*) violenza, forza: *by — of,* a forza di.
to dint, *v.t.* fare una tacca su; lasciare un segno, un'impronta su.
diocesan [dai'osisən], *ag.* (*eccl.*) diocesano ‖ *s.* **1.** (vescovo) diocesano **2.** membro di una diocesi.
diocese ['daiəsis], *s.* diocesi.
Diocletian [,daiə'kli:ʃən], *no.pr.m.* (*st.*) Diocleziano.
Diodorus [,daiə'dɔ:rəs], *no.pr.m.* (*st.*) Diodoro.
Diogenes [dai'ɔdʒini:z], *no.pr.m.* (*fil.*) Diogene ‖ — *Laertius,* (*st.*) Diogene Laerzio.
Diomed ['daiəmed], **Diomede** ['daiəmi:d], **Diomedes** [,daiə'mi:di:z], *no.pr.m.* (*mit.*) Diomede.
Dion ['daiən], *no.pr.m.* Dione ‖ *no.pr.f.* (*mit.*) Dione.
dionaea [,daiə'ni:ə], *s.* (*bot.*) dionea.
Dionysia [,daiə'niziə], *no.pr.f.* Dionisia ‖ *s. pl.* (*st.*) feste dionisiache.
Dionysiac [,daiə'niziæk], **Dionysian** [,daiə'niziən], *ag.* dionisiaco.
Dionysius [,daiə'nisiəs], *no.pr.m.* (*st.*) Dionigi.
Dionysus [,daiə'naisəs], *no.pr.m.* (*mit.*) Dioniso.
diopside [dai'ɔpsaid], *s.* (*min.*) diopside.
diopter [dai'ɔptə*], *s.* (*ott.*) diottria.
dioptric [dai'ɔptrik], *ag.* (*ott.*) diottrico ‖ *s.* (*ott.*) diottrica.
dioptrics [dai'ɔptriks], *s.* (*fis.*) diottrica.
diorama [,daiə'rɑ:mə], *s.* diorama.
Dioscuri (the) [,daiɔs'kju:rai], *no.pr.m.pl.* (*mit.*) Dioscuri.
diosmosis [,daiɔs'mousis], *s.* (*fis. chim.*) diosmosi.
dioxide [dai'ɔksaid], *s.* (*chim.*) biossido.
dip [dip], *s.* **1.** immersione, bagno, tuffo: — *in the sea,* bagno di mare; *to have* (*o to take*) *a —,* (*fam.*) fare un bagno, una nuotata ‖ *to have a — into a book,* (*fam.*) scorrere una libro rapidamente, dare una rapida occhiata ad un libro **2.** inclinazione (anche di ago magnetico); abbassamento (di terreno); (*min. geol.*) pendenza **3.** (*mar.*) posizione a mezz'asta (di bandiera):

flag at the —, bandiera a mezz'asta **4.** (*ind.*) soluzione, bagno **5.** (*aer.*) picchiata, tuffo **6.** candela (di sego) ☆ *hot* —, (*metal.*) immersione a caldo; *sheep-* —, bagno insetticida (per pecore).

to **dip**, *pass.p.p.* **dipped** [dipt], *v.t.i.* **1.** immergere, immergersi; bagnare, bagnarsi; tuffare, tuffarsi; intingere: *he dips his pen in the ink*, intinge la penna nell'inchiostro; *to* — *one's hand into sthg.*, immergere la mano in ql.co. ‖ *to* — *one's hand into one's purse*, spendere liberamente‖ *to* — *one's pen in gall*, intingere la propria penna nel fiele **2.** abbassare, abbassarsi: *to* — *a flag*, (*mil.*) abbassare la bandiera (in segno di saluto); *to* — *the head-lights*, (*aut.*) abbassare i fari **3.** (*aer.*) perdere improvvisamente quota **4.** *to* — *into*, cavar fuori: *to* — *into one's capital*, attingere al proprio capitale ‖ *to* — *into* (*a book, a subject*), sfogliare (un libro), studiare superficialmente (un argomento) **5.** *to* — *up*, attingere, cavar fuori.

dipetalous [dai'petələs], *ag.* (*bot.*) dipetalo.

diphase ['daifeiz], *ag.* (*elett.*) bifase.

diphenyl [dai'fenil], *s.* (*chim.*), difenile.

diphtheria [dif'θiəriə], *s.* (*patol.*) difterite.

diphtherial [dif'θiəriəl], **diphtheric** [dif'θerik], *ag.* (*patol.*) difterico.

diphtheroid ['difθərɔid], *ag.* (*patol.*) difteroide.

diphthong ['difθɔŋ], *s.* (*fonet.*) dittongo.

diphthongal [dif'θɔŋgəl], *ag.* (*fonet.*) di dittongo.

diploma [di'ploumə], *pl.* **diplomas** [di'plouməz], (*rar.*) **diplomata** [di'ploumətə], *s.* diploma.

diplomacy [di'plouməsi], *s.* **1.** diplomazia **2.** *fig.* tatto; accortezza.

diploma'd, diplomaed [di'plouməd], *ag.* diplomato, fornito di diploma.

diplomat ['dipləmæt], *s.* **1.** diplomatico **2.** *fig.* persona accorta e riservata.

diplomatic [,diplə'mætik], *ag.* **1.** diplomatico: *for* — *reasons*, per ragioni diplomatiche; *to enter the* — *service*, entrare in diplomazia, nella carriera diplomatica **2.** (*paleografia*) diplomatico ☆ — *body* (o *corps*), corpo diplomatico; — *ink*, (*chim.*) inchiostro simpatico.

diplomatically [,diplə'mætikəli], *av.* diplomaticamente.

diplomatics [,diplə'mætiks], *s.* **1.** diplomazia **2.** (*paleografia*) diplomatica.

diplomatist [di'ploumətist], *s.* diplomatico.

to **diplomatize** [di'ploumətaiz], *v.i.* fare della diplomazia; agire diplomaticamente.

Dipnoi ['dipnouai], *s. pl.* (*ittiol.*) dipnoi.

dipole ['dai-poul], *s.* (*tv.*) dipolo, antenna a dipolo.

dipper ['dipə*], *s.c.* **1.** chi immerge, chi si immerge; tuffatore, tuffatrice **2.** (*amer.*) mestola (piuttosto grande); (*artig. ind.*) cucchiaia; (*ind.*) macchina scavatrice **3.** (*amer. astr.*): *the Great Dipper*, l'Orsa Maggiore; *the Little Dipper*, l'Orsa Minore **4.** (*ornit.*) martin pescatore; acquaiola; cincia tuffatrice **5.** (*relig.*) anabattista.

dipping ['dipiŋ], *s.* **1.** immersione **2.** abbassamento; avvallamento; inclinazione ☆ — *-needle*, ago di inclinazione magnetica.

dippy ['dipi], *ag.* (*sl.*) pazzo.

dipsomania [,dipsou'meinjə], *s.* (*patol.*) dipsomania.

dipsomaniac [,dipsou'meiniæk], *ag.s.* (*patol.*) dipsomane; alcoolizzato.

Diptera ['diptərə], *s.pl.* (*entom.*) ditteri.

dipteral ['diptərəl], *s.* (*arch.*) dittero.

dipterous ['diptərəs], *ag.* (*entom.*) dell'ordine dei ditteri.

diptych ['diptik], *s.* dittico.

dire ['daiə*], *ag.* terribile, orrendo; disastroso; duro: — *poverty*, miseria nera; *to be in* — *need of help*, avere urgente bisogno di aiuto.

direct [di'rekt], *ag.* **1.** diretto; immediato: — *consequence*, conseguenza immediata; — *descendant*, discendente diretto **2.** schietto, franco, sincero: *a* — *answer*, una risposta franca; *a* — *way of doing things*, un modo di agire sincero ☆ — *action*, (*pol.*) azione

diretta; — *control*, (*mec.*) comando diretto; — *current*, (*elett.*) corrente continua; — *dialling*, (*tel.*) teleselezione; — *drive*, (*mec.*) presa diretta; — *evidence*, (*dir.*) prove dirette; — *method*, (*pedagogia*) metodo diretto; — *object*, — *speech*, (*gram.*) complemento, discorso diretto; — *taxes*, imposte dirette.

direct, *av.* diretto, direttamente: *I shall write to you* —, ti scriverò direttamente; *the train goes* — *to Rome*, il treno va diretto a Roma.

to **direct**, *v.t.i.* **1.** dirigere; amministrare; dare ordini: *who is directing the work?*, chi dirige i lavori? **2.** indirizzare (lettere, parole, ecc.) **3.** indicare (via, direzione): *can you* — *me to the post-office?*, può indicarmi la strada per andare alla posta? **4.** attirare; rivolgere; guidare: *to* — *one's course towards*, dirigere i propri passi verso; *to* — *s.o.'s attention to sthg.*, attirare l'attenzione di qlcu. su ql.co. **5.** ordinare (IV): *he directed his men to advance*, ordinò ai suoi uomini di avanzare ‖ *as directed*, secondo le istruzioni ricevute **6.** *to* — *the jury*, (*dir.*) istruire la giuria **7.** (*mus.*) dirigere.

direction [di'rekʃən], *s.* **1.** direzione; amministrazione: *under the* — *of*, sotto la direzione di; *to apply to the* —, rivolgersi alla direzione **2.** *gener. pl.* indirizzo di lettera **3.** senso, direzione, verso: *in the* — *of*, in direzione di; *in the opposite* —, nella direzione opposta; *to lose one's sense of* —, disorientarsi, perdere l'orientamento **4.** istruzione, indicazione: *full directions as to how (to use)*, indicazioni complete su come (si usa); *to comply with the detailed directions given*, conformarsi alle istruzioni particolareggiate ☆ — *-board* (o — *-plate*), indicatore stradale; — *-finder*, (*rad.*) radiogoniometro; — *-indicator*, (*aut.*) indicatore di direzione.

directional [di'rekʃənl], *ag.* **1.** (*rad.*) direzionale **2.** direttivo, dirigente ☆ — *aerial*, (*rad.*) antenna direzionale; — *wireless*, (*rad.*) radiogoniometria.

directive [di'rektiv], *ag.* direttivo: — *function*, funzione direttiva **3.** *s.* direttiva; istruzione, ordine.

directly [di'rektli], *av.* **1.** direttamente: — *concerned*, direttamente interessato; *a* — *opposite effect*, un effetto esattamente contrario; *he was coming* — *towards us*, veniva direttamente verso di noi **2.** subito, immediatamente: *I shall see him* —, lo vedrò subito.

directly, *cong.* (*fam.*) appena: *I shall see him* — *he comes*, lo vedrò appena verrà.

directness [di'rektnis], *s.* **1.** franchezza, sincerità **2.** sorgente diretta (di informazione).

director [di'rektə*], *s.* **1.** direttore; (*comm.*) amministratore, direttore, dirigente; membro del consiglio di amministrazione **2.** *board of directors*, consiglio di amministrazione **2.** (*eccl.*) direttore spirituale **3.** (*cine. teat. amer.*) regista; (*cine. inglese*) produttore **4.** (*tel.*) registratore **5.** (*mar.*) centrale di tiro ☆ *art* —, scenografo; *joint* —, condirettore; *sales* —, direttore commerciale.

directorate [di'rektərit], *s.* **1.** ufficio di direttore **2.** consiglio d'amministrazione.

directorial [,direk'tɔ:riəl], *ag.* direttivo.

directorship [di'rektəʃip], *s.* **1.** carica, funzioni di direttore, amministratore **2.** direttorato, amministrazione: *during his* —, nel corso della sua amministrazione.

directory [di'rektəri], *ag.* direttivo ‖ *s.* **1.** guida, annuario **2.** (*eccl.*) direttorio **3.** (*amer.*) consiglio d'amministrazione **4.** (*st. francese*) direttorio ☆ *city* —, *telephone* —, guida della città, elenco telefonico.

directress [di'rektris], *s.* direttrice.

directrix [di'rektriks], *pl.* **directrices** [,dairek'traisi:z], *s.* **1.** direttrice **2.** (*geom.*) direttrice.

direful ['daiəful], *ag.* orrendo, terribile; funesto: *to be in* — *want*, essere nella miseria più nera.

direfully ['daiəfuli], *av.* orrendamente, terribilmente; funestamente.

direfulness ['daiəfulnis], *s.* orrore; carattere funesto, spaventoso.

dirge [də:dʒ], *s.* inno, canto funebre.

to dirge, *v.i.* intonare un canto funebre.

dirigibility [ˌdiridʒi'biliti], *s.* dirigibilità.

dirigible ['diridʒəbl], *ag.* dirigibile ‖ *s.* (*aer.*) dirigibile; aeronave.

dirk [də:k], *s.* pugnale (degli Scozzesi e degli aspiranti di marina).

to dirk, *v.t.* pugnalare.

dirt [də:t], *s.* **1.** sporcizia, sudiciume; immondizia: *to live in a state of* —, vivere nella sporcizia; *to wash the* — *off*, lavar via la sporcizia ‖ *to be as cheap as* —, essere a prezzo bassissimo ‖ *to eat* —, *fig.* incassare (insulti, ecc.) ‖ *to fling* (o *to throw*) — *at s.o.*, calunniare qlcu., parlar male di qlcu. ‖ *to treat s.o. like* —, trattare qlcu. con disprezzo **2.** *fig.* sozzura, bruttura: *to talk* —, usare un linguaggio sboccato ☆ — *bed*, (*geol.*) strato sfatticcio; — *-eating*, (*patol.*) geofagia; — *road*, strada battuta (non asfaltata); — *-track*, (*spor.*) pista di cenere; — *waggon*, (*amer.*) carro delle immondizie.

dirtily ['də:tili], *av.* **1.** sporcamente, sudiciamente **2.** *fig.* bassamente; vilmente.

dirtiness ['də:tinis], *s.* **1.** sporcizia, sozzura **2.** *fig.* bassezza, viltà.

dirty ['də:ti], *ag.* **1.** sporco, sudicio; infangato: — *hands*, mani sporche; — *shoes*, scarpe infangate **2.** brutto; piovoso, tempestoso: *what* — *weather!*, che tempaccio! **3.** grossolano; sboccato; osceno: *a* — *story*, una storiella sboccata **4.** brutto; disonesto; sleale: — *business*, affare losco; — *money*, (*neol.*) denaro sudicio; — *trick*, (*sl.*) brutto scherzo: *to play s.o. a* — *trick*, giocare un brutto tiro a qlcu.; — *work*, azione disonesta, losca.

to dirty, *v.t.i.* sporcare; sporcarsi; insudiciare, insudiciarsi: *this cloth dirties easily*, questo tessuto si sporca facilmente; *you have dirtied your hands*, ti sei insudiciato le mani.

disability [ˌdisə'biliti], *s.* incapacità; impotenza; invalidità; (*dir.*) incapacità: *physical* —, infermità ☆ — *pension*, pensione d'invalidità.

to disable [dis'eibl], *v.t.* rendere incapace, inabile; storpiare; mutilare: *disabled soldier*, soldato invalido, mutilato; *to* — *s.o. from doing sthg.*, mettere qlcu. nell'impossibilità di fare ql.co.; (*dir.*) dichiarare qlcu. incapace di fare ql.co.

disablement [dis'eiblmənt], *s.* **1.** il rendere incapace, inabile (al lavoro) **2.** *V.* disability.

to disabuse [ˌdisə'bju:z], *v.t.* disingannare: *to* — *s.o. of sthg.*, disingannare qlcu. circa, su ql.co.

disaccord [ˌdisə'kɔ:d], *s.* disaccordo.

to disaccord, *v.i.* essere in disaccordo.

to disaccustom ['disə'kʌstəm], *v.t.* disabituare: *to* — *s.o. to doing sthg.*, disabituare qlcu. dal fare ql.co.

disadvantage [ˌdisəd'va:ntidʒ], *s.* svantaggio; perdita: *it is to your* —, è a vostro detrimento; *to be seen at a* —, essere visto in condizioni sfavorevoli; *to take s.o. at a* —, cogliere qlcu. alla sprovvista, in un momento sfavorevole.

disadvantageous [ˌdisædva:n'teidʒəs], *ag.* svantaggioso; sfavorevole.

disadvantageously [ˌdisædva:n'teidʒəsli], *av.* svantaggiosamente; sfavorevolmente.

to disaffect [ˌdisə'fekt], *v.t.* (*arc.*) disamorare; alienare; rendere maldisposto.

disaffected [ˌdisə'fektid], *ag.* maldisposto, malcontento.

disaffectedness [ˌdisə'fektidnis], **disaffection** [ˌdisə'fekʃən], *s.* **1.** disamore; disaffezione **2.** scontentezza.

to disaffirm [ˌdisə'fə:m], *v.t.* **1.** rinnegare; negare; contraddire **2.** (*dir.*) revocare, annullare, cassare.

disaffirmation [dis,æfə'meiʃən], *s.* (*dir.*) revocazione, annullamento.

to disafforest [ˌdisə'fɔrist], *v.t.* diboscare (un terreno).

disafforestation [ˌdisə,fɔris'teiʃən], *s.* diboscamento.

to disagree [ˌdisə'gri:], *v.i.* **1.** essere in disaccordo, non andar d'accordo: *we* — *on this subject*, su questo argomento non siamo d'accordo; *we* — *with you*, non siamo del vostro avviso **2.** non essere confacente, adatto: *onions* — *with me*, le cipolle mi restano sullo stomaco, mi sono indigeste; *sea air disagrees with her*, l'aria di mare non le si confà.

disagreeable [ˌdisə'griəbl], *ag.* sgradevole; spiacevole; antipatico: *how* — *you are to-day!*, come sei antipatico oggi! ‖ *s. gener. pl.* noia, fastidio.

disagreeableness [ˌdisə'griəblnis], *s.* sgradevolezza; spiacevolezza.

disagreeably [ˌdisə'griəbli], *av.* sgradevolmente; spiacevolmente.

disagreement [ˌdisə'gri:mənt], *s.* **1.** dissenso, dissapore, disaccordo; litigio: — *with s.o. on* (o *about*) *sthg.*, disaccordo con qlcu. per ql.co. **2.** differenza, discordanza.

to disallow [ˌdisə'lau], *v.t.* **1.** non permettere, rifiutare **2.** non ammettere; non riconoscere (privilegio, ipotesi, ecc.).

disallowance [ˌdisə'lau-əns], *s.* rifiuto; rifiuto di ammettere; divieto.

to disally [ˌdisə'lai], *v.t.* rompere, sciogliere (un'alleanza); (*arc.*) separare.

to disanchor [dis'æŋkə*], *v.t.* disancorare.

to disanimate [dis'ænimeit], *v.t.* disanimare.

to disannul [ˌdisə'nʌl], *pass.p.p.* **disannulled** [ˌdisə'nʌld], *v.t.* annullare completamente.

to disanoint [ˌdisə'nɔint], *v.t.* sconsacrare.

to disappear [ˌdisə'piə*], *v.i.* scomparire, svanire: *he disappeared from our sight*, scomparve alla nostra vista; *to* — *in the darkness*, svanire nell'oscurità; *to* — *into the crowd*, sparire, perdersi nella folla.

disappearance [ˌdisə'piərəns], *s.* sparizione, scomparsa.

to disappoint [ˌdisə'pɔint], *v.t.* **1.** deludere; frustrare (speranze); mancare a (una promessa): *don't* — *me*, mantieni la tua promessa; *to be disappointed in* (o *with*) *s.o.*, *in sthg.*, rimanere deluso di qlcu., ql.co. **2.** sconcertare, addolorare: *I am sorry I have disappointed you*, mi spiace di averti addolorato; *I was disappointed at not being able to see him*, rimasi addolorato di non averlo potuto vedere.

disappointed [ˌdisə'pɔintid], *ag.* deluso; insoddisfatto, scontento: — *ambition*, ambizione delusa; *a* — *man*, un uomo scontento.

disappointedly [ˌdisə'pɔintidli], *av.* con aria delusa, con tono triste.

disappointing [ˌdisə'pɔintiŋ], *ag.* deludente; scoraggiante; spiacevole; ingannevole: — *weather*, tempo brutto; *how* —!, che contrattempo!.

disappointingly [ˌdisə'pɔintiŋli], *av.* in modo deludente, scoraggiante.

disappointment [ˌdisə'pɔintmənt], *s.* **1.** delusione; disappunto: — *in love*, delusione d'amore; *to my* —, con mio disappunto **2.** contrattempo.

disapprobation [ˌdisæprou'beiʃən], *s.* disapprovazione.

disapprobative [dis'æproubeitiv], **disapprobatory** [dis'æproubeitəri], *ag.* disapprovante, riprensivo.

disapproval [ˌdisə'pru:vəl], *s.* disapprovazione.

to disapprove ['disə'pru:v], *v.t.i.* disapprovare; trovare a ridire: *we are sorry we must* — *your action*, ci dispiace di dover disapprovare la vostra azione; *to* — *of sthg.*, *s.o.*, trovare a ridire su ql.co., qlcu.

disapprovingly ['disə'pru:viŋli], *av.* con disapprovazione.

to disarm [dis'ɑ:m], *v.t.i.* **1.** disarmare, disarmarsi: *to* — *a soldier of his rifle*, disarmare un soldato del fucile **2.** *fig.* disarmare, calmare: *a disarming smile*, un sorriso disarmante.

disarmament [dis'ɑ:məmənt], **disarming** [dis'ɑ:miŋ], *s.* disarmo.

to disarrange ['disə'reindʒ], *v.t.* scomporre, scompigliare, mettere in disordine: *disarranged hair*, capelli arruffati.

disarrangement [ˌdisəˈreindʒmənt], s. disordine, scompiglio.

disarray [ˈdisəˈrei], s. disordine, scompiglio ‖ *in* —, semisvestito, in disordine.

to **disarray**, v.t. disorganizzare; scompigliare.

to **disarticulate** [ˈdisaˈtikjuleit], v.t. disarticolare; smembrare (pollo, ecc.); (*chir.*) amputare.

disarticulation [ˈdisaˌtikjuˈleiʃən], s. disarticolazione; (*chir.*) amputazione di una articolazione.

to **disassemble** [ˌdisəˈsembl], v.t. smontare (una macchina, ecc.).

disassembly [ˌdisəˈsembli], s. smontaggio (di macchina, ecc.).

disassimilation [ˌdisəˌsimiˈleiʃən], s. disassimilazione.

to **disassociate** [ˌdisəˈsouʃieit], V. to **dissociate**.

disassociation [ˌdisəˌsousiˈeiʃən], V. **dissociation**.

disaster [diˈzɑːstə*], s. disastro; calamità; sinistro; (*fam.*) guaio: *a public* —, una pubblica calamità; *our trip was a record of disasters*, la nostra gita fu un seguito di guai.

disastrous [diˈzɑːstrəs], ag. disastroso.

disastrously [diˈzɑːstrəsli], av. disastrosamente.

to **disavow** [ˈdisəˈvau], v.t. sconfessare, rinnegare (la propria fede, un'azione); ripudiare (la moglie, una dottrina).

disavowal [ˌdisəˈvau·əl], s. sconfessione; rinnegazione; disconoscimento.

to **disband** [disˈbænd], v.t.i. 1. disperdere, disperdersi, sbandare; sciogliere; accomiatare, congedare, licenziare: *the commission was disbanded*, la commissione fu sciolta 2. (*mil.*) sbandarsi; essere congedato.

disbandment [disˈbændmənt], s. dispersione; sbandamento; (*mil.*) congedo.

disbelief [ˈdisbiˈliːf], s. 1. incredulità 2. (*rel.*) miscredenza.

to **disbelieve** [ˈdisbiˈliːv], v.t.i. non credere, rifiutare di credere, non poter credere a: *I — his words*, rifiuto di credere alle sue parole; *to — in s.o., sthg.*, non credere a qlcu., in ql.co.

disbeliever [ˈdisbiˈliːvə*], s.c. incredulo, incredula; miscredente.

to **disbranch** [disˈbrɑːntʃ], v.t. spogliare (un albero) dei suoi rami.

to **disburden** [disˈbəːdn], v.t.i. scaricare, sgravare, sgravarsi; sbarazzare; sollevare, alleggerire, alleggerirsi: *to — one's heart to s.o.*, aprire il proprio cuore a qlcu.; *to — one's mind of (a secret)*, alleggerirsi l'animo di (un segreto); *to — one's wrath upon s.o.*, riversare la propria ira su qlcu.

to **disburse** [disˈbəːs], v.t. sborsare (denaro).

disbursement [disˈbəːsmənt], s. 1. sborso, pagamento 2. spese.

disc, V. **disk**.

discalced [disˈkælst], ag.: *Discalced Carmelites*, Carmelitani Scalzi.

discard [ˈdiskɑːd], s. 1. (*carte*) scarto 2. (*amer.*) scarto, rifiuto (di materiale, personale).

to **discard** [disˈkɑːd], v.t.i. 1. (*carte*) scartare, fare uno scarto 2. mettere, lasciare da parte; rinunciare a, abbandonare; smettere (indumenti).

discarnate [disˈkɑːnit], ag. (*arc. letter.*) scarnito: *— bones*, ossa scarnite; *— soul*, anima liberata dal corpo.

to **discern** [diˈsəːn], v.t.i. 1. percepire, comprendere, discernere, distinguere, scorgere: *to — s.o., sthg. in the distance*, scorgere qlcu., ql.co. in lontananza 2. (*arc.*) distinguere, far distinzione: *to — the difference between*, vedere la differenza fra.

discernible [diˈsəːnəbl], ag. visibile; discernibile.

discernibly [diˈsəːnibli], av. visibilmente.

discerning [diˈsəːniŋ], ag. perspicace, giudizioso; penetrante, sottile (di mente); sicuro (di gusto) ‖ s. discernimento; acume; oculatezza; sagacia; giudizio.

discernment [diˈsəːnmənt], s. discernimento; acume; oculatezza; sagacia; giudizio.

discharge [disˈtʃɑːdʒ], s. 1 scarico, lo scaricare (una nave): *the — of a ship*, lo scarico di una nave 2. scarica (di artiglieria, fucile, ecc.), sparo 3. (*fis.*) liberazione (di vapore, gas, ecc.); (*elett.*) scarica 4. (*med.*) suppurazione; essudazione 5. congedo; licenza; esonero; licenziamento (di operaio, ecc.): *— from the army*, congedo dall'esercito (p. e. dopo servizio attivo o perchè riformato); *— from hospital*, il dimettere dall'ospedale 6. (*dir.*) liberazione; assoluzione (di un accusato); (*comm.*) riabilitazione (di un fallito): *— from prison*, scarcerazione 7. adempimento (di un dovere): *he was perfect in the — of his duties*, fu perfetto nell'adempimento, nell'esercizio delle sue funzioni 8. pagamento (di un debito); quietanza: *— of all debts*, pagamento di tutti i debiti; *in full* —, a saldo di ogni avere 9. decolorazione ☆ *— lamp*, (*elett.*) lampada a elettroluminescenza; *— note*, (*mar.*) ordine di sbarco; *— pipe*, tubo di scarico; *— pressure*, (*elett.*) tensione di scarico.

to **discharge** [disˈtʃɑːdʒ], v.t.i. 1. scaricare (nave, cisterna, serbatoio, ecc.) 2. scaricarsi, scaricare (di fucile, ecc.) 3. (*elett.*) scaricare, scaricarsi (di una pila, ecc.) 4. sboccare, uscire (di vapore, gas, fumo, corso di acqua, ecc.) 5. (*med.*) suppurare 6. congedare; licenziare; esonerare; (*mil.*) riformare: *he was discharged for dishonesty*, egli fu licenziato per| disonestà; *the jury was discharged*, la giuria fu congedata; *to — for unfitness*, riformare per inabilità 7. liberare (prigionieri); riabilitare (un fallito); assolvere (un accusato): *discharged bankrupt*, (*comm.*) fallito riabilitato 8. compiere (un dovere) 9. (*comm.*) saldare (debiti) 10. decolorare: *to — the dye from a fabric*, decolorare un tessuto.

dischargeable [disˈtʃɑːdʒəbl], ag. 1. congedabile, riformabile (di soldato) 2. che si può riabilitare (di persona fallita) 3. pagabile (di debito).

dischargee [ˌdistʃɑːˈdʒiː], s. soldato congedato, riformato.

discharger [disˈtʃɑːdʒə*], s. (*elett., ecc.*) scaricatore.

disciple [diˈsaipl], s. discepolo ‖ *the Disciples*, i discepoli (di Gesù).

discipleship [diˈsaiplʃip], s. stato, qualità di discepolo.

disciplinable [ˈdisiplinəbl], ag. 1. disciplinabile 2. docile 3. punibile: *— offence*, offesa punibile.

disciplinal [ˈdisiplin], ag. disciplinare.

disciplinarian [ˌdisipliˈnɛəriən], s. disciplinatore; chi crede nella disciplina, la sa imporre.

disciplinary [ˈdisiplinəri], ag. disciplinare: *— punishment*, punizione disciplinare.

discipline [ˈdisiplin], s. 1. disciplina: *military* —, disciplina militare; *to enforce perfect* —, imporre una perfetta disciplina 2. (*arc.*) disciplina, insegnamento, materia di studio: *educated in the stern — of the classics*, educato nell'arduo apprendimento dei classici.

to **discipline**, v.t. 1. disciplinare; formare (carattere) 2. punire, castigare.

to **disclaim** [disˈkleim], v.t. 1. rifiutare di ammettere; non riconoscere: *I — your authority*, non riconosco la tua autorità 2. ripudiare, negare: *to — all responsibility*, declinare ogni responsabilità 3. (*dir.*) rinunciare a (un diritto).

disclaimer[1] [disˈkleimə*], s. 1. diniego, rifiuto 2.(*dir.*) rinuncia.

disclaimer[2], s.c. chi nega, rinuncia.

to **disclose** [disˈklouz], v.t. 1. svelare, scoprire: *to — a hidden treasure*, scoprire un tesoro nascosto 2. divulgare, propagare (un segreto, ecc.).

disclosure [disˈklouʒə*], s. 1. rivelazione (di un pensiero, ecc.); scoperta (di un tesoro, ecc.) 2. divulgazione, propagazione (d'un segreto, ecc.).

discobolus [disˈkobələs], pl. **discoboli** [disˈkobəlai], s. discobolo.

discography [disˈkogrəfi], s. discografia.

discoid [ˈdiskoid], ag. discoideo ‖ s. discoide.

to **discolor**, (*amer.*) per to **discolour**.

discloration, (*amer.*) per **disclouration**.

to **discolour** [dis'kʌlə*], *v.t.i.* **1.** decolorare; scolorire, scolorirsi, scolorare **2.** appannare, appannarsi; offuscare, offuscarsi.

discolouration [dis,kʌlə'reiʃən], *s.* **1.** scoloramento **2.** appannamento, offuscamento.

discolourment [dis'kʌləmənt], *s.* scoloramento.

to **discomfit** [dis'kʌmfit], *v.t.* **1.** (*letter.*) sconfiggere, mettere in rotta **2.** sconcertare, contrariare; frustrare.

discomfiture [dis'kʌmfitʃə*], *s.* **1.** (*letter.*) sconfitta **2.** sconcerto; turbamento.

discomfort [dis'kʌmfət], *s.* disagio; incomodo.

to **discomfort**, *v.t.* mettere a disagio; incomodare: *that speaker was discomforted by the smoke*, quell'oratore era messo a disagio dal fumo.

to **discommode** [,diskə'moud], *v.t.* **1.** scomodare; disturbare **2.** importunare.

discommodious [,diskə'moudjəs], *ag.* scomodo.

to **discompose** [,diskəm'pouz], *v.t.* **1.** scomporre, agitare, turbare: *discomposed face*, viso alterato **2.** scompigliare, disordinare.

discomposedly [,diskəm'pouzidli], *av.* scompostamente, in modo agitato; disordinatamente.

discomposingly [,diskəm'pouziŋli], *av.* in modo da portare turbamento, disordine.

discomposure [,diskəm'pouʒə*], *s.* scompostezza; agitazione; turbamento; alterazione (dei lineamenti).

to **disconcert** [,diskən'sə:t], *v.t.* **1.** sconcertare; turbare **2.** sconvolgere (piani, idee, ecc.).

disconcerting [,diskən'sə:tiŋ], *ag.* sconcertante.

disconcertingly [,diskən'sə:tiŋli], *av.* in modo sconcertante.

disconcertment [,diskən'sə:tmənt], *s.* **1.** sconcerto; turbamento **2.** confusione.

to **disconnect** [,diskə'nekt], *v.t.* **1.** sconnettere; disunire, separare; distaccare: *to — sthg. with* (o *from*) *sthg.*, separare ql.co. da ql.co. **2.** (*elett.*) disinserire, interrompere; (*mec.*) disinnestare: *to — the clutch*, (*aut.*) debraiare.

disconnected [,diskə'nektid], *ag.* **1.** sconnesso: — *speech, style*, discorso, stile sconnesso **2.** (*elett.*) disinserito; (*mec.*) disinnestato.

disconnectedly [,diskə'nektidli], *av.* sconnessamente.

disconnectedness [,diskə'nektidnis], *s.* incoerenza; sconnessione, mancanza di nesso (di idee, ecc.).

disconnecting [,diskə'nektiŋ], *s.* **1.** disgiunzione; sconnessione **2.** (*mec. elett.*) disinnesto.

disconnection, disconnexion [,diskə'nekʃən], *s.* **1.** disgiunzione, separazione; sconnessione **2.** (*mec. elett.*) disinnesto.

disconsolate [dis'kɔnsəlit], *ag.* sconsolato, afflitto, desolato, affranto; inconsolabile.

disconsolately [dis'kɔnsəlitli], *av.* sconsolatamente; inconsolabilmente.

discontent [,diskən'tent], *ag.* (*rar.*) scontento, malcontento, insoddisfatto ‖ *s.* scontento, malcontento.

to **discontent**, *v.t.* scontentare.

discontented [,diskən'tentid], *ag.* malcontento, insoddisfatto ‖ *the —*, i malcontenti.

discontentedly [,diskən'tentidli], *av.* in modo insoddisfatto.

discontentedness [,diskən'tentidnis], *s.* insoddisfazione; scontento, malcontento.

discontiguous [,diskən'tigjuəs], *ag.* disgiunto.

discontinuance [,diskən'tinjuəns], *s.* cessazione (di lavori, studi, ecc.); interruzione; rinuncia.

to **discontinue** [,diskən'tinju(:)], *v.t.i.* (I) cessare; interrompere, interrompersi: *the publication of this review will — at the end of...*, la pubblicazione di questa rivista cesserà alla fine di...; *to — doing sthg.*, cessare di fare ql.co.; *to — sthg.*, interrompere ql.co.

discontinuity ['dis,kɔnti'nju(:)iti], *s.* discontinuità; soluzione di continuità.

discontinuous ['diskən'tinjuəs], *ag.* discontinuo, interrotto; intermittente.

discontinuously ['diskən'tinjuəsli], *av.* senza continuità; in modo intermittente.

discophile ['diskəfil], *s.* (*amer.*) collezionista, appassionato di dischi.

discord ['diskɔ:d], *s.* **1.** discordia; contrasto: dissenso **2.** suono discordante (di voci, ecc.); (*mus.*) dissonanza; disarmonia.

to **discord** [dis'kɔ:d], *v.i.* **1.** dissentire, essere in disaccordo: *to — with* (o *from*) *s.o.*, essere in disaccordo con ql.cu. **2.** discordare (di suoni); (*mus.*) dissonare.

discordance [dis'kɔ:dəns], *s.* **1.** dissenso **2.** discordanza (di suoni, colori, ecc.).

discordant [dis'kɔ:dənt], *ag.* **1.** discorde, dissenziente **2.** discordante (di suoni); (*mus.*) dissonante.

discordantly [dis'kɔ:dəntli], *av.* **1.** in disaccordo **2.** disarmonicamente, in modo dissonante.

discount ['diskaunt], *s.* **1.** (*comm.*) sconto, ribasso, riduzione: *to make, to grant, to accord a — to s.o. on sthg.*, dare, concedere, accordare uno sconto a ql.cu. su ql.co. ‖ *at a —*, sottoprezzo; non ricercato, poco richiesto: *to sell at a —*, vendere in perdita **2.** *fig.* tara (a notizia esagerata) ☆ — *bank*, banca di sconto; — *rate*, tasso di sconto ‖ *bank —*, sconto di banca; *cash —*, sconto cassa; *sample —*, sconto sui campioni; *trade —*, sconto per i rivenditori.

to **discount**, *v.t.* **1.** (*comm.*) scontare **2.** *fig.* non dar credito a (notizia, ecc.); tenere in poco conto; far la tara a: — *half of what he says*, fa una tara della metà su quel che dice, devi credere solo la metà di quel che dice.

discountable [dis'kauntəbl], *ag.* **1.** (*comm.*) scontabile: — *bills*, cambiali scontabili **2.** *fig.* poco attendibile (di notizia, ecc.).

discountenance [dis'kauntinəns], *s.* (*rar.*) **1.** disapprovazione, critica **2.** opposizione, impedimento.

to **discountenance**, *v.t.* **1.** disapprovare, criticare; mettere in imbarazzo; svergognare **2.** opporsi a, cercare di impedire (un progetto, ecc.).

discounter [dis'kauntə*], *s.* (*comm.*) scontista.

discounting ['diskauntiŋ], *s.* sconto ☆ — *transaction*, operazione di sconto.

to **discourage** [dis'kʌridʒ], *v.t.* **1.** scoraggiare: *don't be discouraged*, non ti scoraggiare; *don't let one failure — you*, non scoraggiatevi per un insuccesso; *to become discouraged*, scoraggiarsi **2.** dissuadere: *I discouraged him from leaving today*, lo dissuasi dal partire oggi.

discouragement [dis'kʌridʒmənt], *s.* **1.** scoraggiamento: *to meet with —*, non incontrare incoraggiamento, provare disillusioni **2.** disapprovazione (di progetto, ecc.).

discouraging [dis'kʌridʒiŋ], *ag.* scoraggiante: — *reports*, notizie scoraggianti.

discouragingly [dis'kʌridʒiŋli], *av.* in modo scoraggiante.

discourse [dis'kɔ:s], *s.* **1.** (*letter.*) discorso, orazione, dissertazione **2.** (*arc.*) conversazione: *to hold — with s.o. on sthg.*, conferire con ql.cu. in merito a ql.co.

to **discourse**, *v.t.i.* **1.** (*letter.*) disser are: *to — (up)on a subject*, dissertare su un aromeno **2.** (*arc.*) conversare, intrattenersi su un argomeno **3.** (*arc.*) eseguire (musica).

discourteous [dis'kə:tjəs], *ag.* scortese.

discourteously [dis'kə:tjəsli], *av.* scortesemente.

discourtesy [dis'kə:tisi], *s.* scortesia.

to **discover** [dis'kʌvə*], *v.t.* **1.** scoprire; trovare: *we have discovered a good restaurant*, siamo riusciti a trovare un buon ristorante; *to — an island, gold, a new element*, scoprire un'isola, oro, un nuovo elemento ‖ *to be discovered at the rise of the curtain*, (*teat.*) essere in scena all'alzarsi del sipario **2.** scoprire, accorgersi, rendersi conto di: *I discovered how it was done*, mi resi conto di come era fatto; *I discovered that it was late*, mi accorsi che era tardi **3.** (*arc. letter.*) rivelare; far conoscere, divulgare: *he discovered the identity of the man*, rivelò l'identità dell'uomo; *to — oneself*, rivelarsi (*p.e.* un buon pianista).

discoverable [dis'kʌvərəbl], *ag.* **1.** scopribile **2.** evidente.

discoverer [dis'kʌvərə*], *s.c.* **1.** scopritore, scopritrice **2.** (*arc.*) rivelatore, rivelatrice (di segreto, complotto).

discovert [dis'kʌvət], *ag.* (*dir.*) senza tutela maritale (di nubile, vedova).

discovery [dis'kʌvəri], *s.* **1.** scoperta: *the — of America, of a new gas,* la scoperta dell'America, di un gas sconosciuto; *a voyage of —,* un viaggio di scoperta **2.** (*arc. letter.*) rivelazione (di segreto, ecc.) ‖ *to give — of documents,* (*dir.*) dare comunicazione di documenti.

discredit [dis'kredit], *s.* **1.** dubbio: *to throw — on a statement,* mettere in dubbio un'affermazione **2.** scredito, discredito: *disistima: to bring — on s.o.,* screditare qlcu.; *to fall into —,* cadere in discredito.

to discredit, *v.t.* **1.** non credere a, mettere in dubbio: *his theories were discredited by the scientists,* le sue teorie furono messe in dubbio dagli scienziati; *his words were discredited,* non si è creduto alle sue parole **2.** screditare, discreditare: *actions which — a banker,* azioni che screditano un banchiere.

discreditable [dis'kreditəbl], *ag.* indegno; disonorevole: *— conduct,* condotta indegna.

discreditably [dis'kreditəbli], *av.* indegnamente; disonorevolmente.

discreet [dis'kri:t], *ag.* prudente, discreto, riservato, cauto, circospetto: *— silence,* silenzio prudente; *— smile,* sorriso contenuto; *he is a very — person,* è una persona molto discreta, riservata.

discreetly [dis'kri:tli], *av.* prudentemente; con discrezione, con riservatezza.

discrepancy [dis'krepənsi], *s.* disaccordo; divario, differenza: *— between two accounts,* contraddizione fra due resoconti.

discrepant [dis'krepənt], *ag.* discrepante, discorde; diverso, differente.

discrete [dis'kri:t], *ag.* **1.** separato, distinto, diviso **2.** (*fil.*) astratto.

discreteness [dis'kri:tnis], *s.* **1.** separazione, distinzione **2.** (*fil.*) astrazione.

discretion [dis'kreʃən], *s.* **1.** discrezione, discernimento; arbitrio, libertà di azione: *the age of —,* l'età della ragione, della discrezione; *I leave it to your —,* ti lascio fare come meglio credi; *use your own —,* fai come meglio ti sembra ‖ *to surrender at —,* (*mil.*) arrendersi a discrezione **2.** saggezza, giudizio, prudenza: *to use —,* agire con giudizio, prudenza ‖ *— is the better part of valour,* (*scherz.*) è meglio non correre rischi inutili **3.** discrezione, riservatezza: *to rely entirely* (o *fully*) *on the — of s.o.,* contare pienamente sulla discrezione di qlcu.

discretionary [dis'kreʃnəri], *ag.* (*dir.*) discrezionale: *— power,* potere discrezionale.

discriminant [dis'kriminənt], *ag.s.* (*mat.*) discriminante.

discriminate [dis'kriminit], *ag.* **1.** discriminato, distinto **2.** giudizioso (di azione, condotta).

to discriminate [dis'krimineit], *v.t.i.* discriminare, discernere, distinguere, fare delle distinzioni, avere delle preferenze: *to — in favour of s.o.,* fare delle distinzioni in favore di qlcu.

discriminating [dis'krimineitiŋ], *ag.* **1.** giudizioso, perspicace; sagace ‖ *— ear,* orecchio fine **2.** distintivo, diverso **3.** (*dir.*) discriminante ☆ *— tariff,* tariffa differenziale.

discriminatingly [dis'krimineitiŋli], *av.* con discernimento.

discrimination [dis,krimi'neiʃən], *s.* **1.** discernimento, giudizio **2.** discriminazione, distinzione, differenziazione.

discriminative [dis'kriminətiv], *V.* discriminating.

to discrown [dis'kraun], *v.t.* detronizzare, deporre.

to disculpate [dis'kʌlpeit], *v.t.* discolpare.

discursive [dis'kə:siv], *ag.* **1.** saltuario, sconnesso **2.** raziocinativo, deduttivo.

discursively [dis'kə:sivli], *av.* **1.** saltuariamente, sconnessamente **2.** per deduzione.

discursiveness [dis'kə:sivnis], *s.* tendenza alla divagazione; incoerenza; prolissità.

discus ['diskəs], *s.* (*spor.*) disco.

to discuss [dis'kʌs], *v.t.* **1.** discutere, dibattere (una questione); trattare, studiare (un problema, ecc.): *to — a subject at large* (o *extensively*), discutere un argomento a fondo **2.** (*fam. scherz.*) centellinare; gustare.

discussible [dis'kʌsibl], *ag.* discutibile.

discussion [dis'kʌʃən], *s.* **1.** discussione, dibattito; disamina: *beyond —,* fuori discussione, indiscutibile; *hot —,* discussione vivace; *question under —,* questione in discussione; *the matter will soon come up for —,* il problema verrà presto discusso; *to enter into a — upon sthg.,* entrare in discussione circa qlco.; *to give up a —,* rinunziare a una discussione **2.** (*fam. scherz.*) assaporamento, centellino: *— of a bottle of wine,* il gustare una bottiglia di vino.

disdain [dis'dein], *s.* sdegno, disprezzo.

to disdain, *v.t.* sdegnare, disdegnare, disprezzare: *to — to do* (o *doing*) *sthg.,* disdegnare di fare qlco.

disdainful [dis'deinful], *ag.* sdegnoso; altero.

disdainfully [dis'deinfuli], *av.* sdegnosamente.

disease [di'zi:z], *s.* malattia, morbo, affezione, infermità: *— of the mind,* malattia mentale; *to die of —,* morire di malattia ☆ *— insurance,* assicurazione contro le malattie ‖ *blue —,* (*fam.*) cianosi, morbo blu; *foot-and-mouth —,* afta epizootica; *occupational —,* malattia del lavoro; *potato —,* malattia delle patate.

diseased [di'zi:zd], *ag.* **1.** malato: *— in body and mind,* malato di mente e di corpo ‖ *— meat,* carne contaminata **2.** *fig.* morboso.

to disembark [disim'ba:k], *v.t.i.* sbarcare.

disembarkation [,disemba:'keiʃən], *s.* sbarco.

to disembarrass ['disim'bærəs], *v.t.* **1.** togliere dall'imbarazzo; sgomberare **2.** disimpegnare, svincolare, liberare.

disembodiment ['disim'bodimənt], *s.* **1.** liberazione (dell'anima) dal corpo **2.** (*mil.*) congedo (di truppe).

to disembody ['disim'bodi], *v.t.* **1.** liberare dal corpo, disincarnare **2.** (*mil.*) congedare (truppe).

to disembogue [,disim'boug], *v.t.i.* **1.** scaricare, scaricarsi (di nave, ecc.) **2.** sboccare (di fiume) **3.** riversarsi (di folla).

to disembosom [,disim'buzəm], *v.t.i.* rivelare, rivelarsi: *to — oneself,* aprire il proprio cuore.

to disembowel [,disim'bauəl], *pass.p.p.* **disembowelled** [,disim'bauəld], *v.t.* sventrare, sbudellare.

to disembroil [,disim'broil], *v.t.* districare, chiarire, sbrogliare (un argomento, una questione).

to disenchant ['disin'tʃɑ:nt], *v.t.* disincantare; disilludere.

disenchantment [,disin'tʃɑ:ntmənt], *s.* disincanto; disillusione.

to disencumber ['disin'kʌmbə*], *v.t.* **1.** sgombrare, sbarazzare: *to — sthg. of, from sthg.,* sbarazzare qlco. di, da qlco. **2.** (*dir.*) sgravare, togliere un'ipoteca.

disencumbrance ['disin'kʌmbrəns], *s.* liberazione; sgombero.

to disendow ['disin'dau], *v.t.* espropriare (specialmente di beni della Chiesa).

disendowment ['disin'daumənt], *s.* espropriazione (specialmente di beni della Chiesa.)

to disengage ['disin'geidʒ], *v.t.i.* **1.** disimpegnare, disimpegnarsi; sbarazzare; svincolare, liberare: *to — oneself,* disimpegnarsi, liberarsi; *to — s.o. from sthg.,* liberare qlcu. da qlco. **2.** (*mec.*) disinnestare; disingranare; sbloccare **3.** (*scherma*) eseguire una cavazione.

disengaged ['disin'geidʒd], *ag.* **1.** libero; disimpegnato; disponibile; in grado di ricevere visitatori: *will you be — tomorrow?,* sarai libero, non avrai impegni domani? **2.** (*mec.*) disinnestato; disingranato; non in funzione.

disengagement [,disin'geidʒmənt], *s.* **1.** liberazione, svincolamento; sganciamento; disponibilità **2.** (*mec.*)

disinnesto **3.** rottura (di fidanzamento) **4.** _(scherma)_ cavazione.

disengaging [ˈdisinˈgeidʒiŋ], _ag._ (mec.) disinnestabile ‖ _s._ **1.** svincolamento; liberazione; (mil.) sganciamento **2.** (mec.) disinnesto ☆ — _gear_, (mcc.) apparecchio di disinnesto; — _movement_, (mil.) manovra di sganciamento.

to **disentail** [ˈdisinˈteil], _v.t._ (dir.) svincolare.

to **disentangle** [ˈdisinˈtæŋgl], _v.t.i._ districare, districarsi; sbrogliare, sbrogliarsi; _fig._ appianare (una divergenza): _this skein won't_ —, questa matassa non vuol sbrogliarsi.

disentanglement [ˌdisinˈtæŋglmənt], _s._ districamento, sbrogliamento (anche _fig._).

to **disentomb** [ˈdisinˈtuːm], _v.t._ dissotterrare, esumare.

disentombment [ˌdisinˈtuːmmənt], _s._ esumazione.

disequilibrium [disˌiːkwiˈlibriəm], _s._ squilibrio; instabilità.

to **disestablish** [ˈdisisˈtæbliʃ], _v.t._ privare (la Chiesa) del carattere di pubblica istituzione (da parte dello Stato).

disestablishment [ˈdisisˈtæbliʃmənt], _s._ separazione tra Stato e Chiesa (ad opera dello Stato).

diseur [ˌdiːˈzəː*], _s._ (teat.) dicitore.

diseuse [ˌdiːˈzəːz], _s._ (teat.) dicitrice.

disfavor, (amer.) per **disfavour**.

disfavour [ˈdisˈfeivə*], _s._ **1.** disfavore; disgrazia: _to be in_ — _with s.o._, non godere la simpatia di qlcu.; _to fall into_ —, cadere in disgrazia **2.** disapprovazione: _that has brought me into their_ —, ciò mi ha procurato la loro disapprovazione.

to **disfavour**, _v.t._ disapprovare; sfavorire.

to **disfeature** [disˈfiːtʃə*], _V._ to **disfigure**.

disfiguration [disˌfigjuəˈreiʃən], _V._ **disfigurement**.

to **disfigure** [disˈfigə*], _v.t._ sfigurare; deturpare; deformare; disonorare.

disfigured [disˈfigəd], _ag._ sfigurato; deturpato; deforme: — _face_, viso sfigurato.

disfigurement [disˈfigəmənt], _s._ deturpazione; deformazione; sfregio.

to **disforest** [disˈforist], _v.t._ diboscare.

to **disfranchise** [ˈdisˈfræntʃaiz], _v.t._ privare dei diritti civili; privare del diritto elettorale.

disfranchisement [disˈfræntʃizmənt], _s._ privazione dei diritti civili, del diritto elettorale.

to **disfrock** [disˈfrɔk], _v.t._ (eccl.) privare dell'uffizio, dell'abito sacerdotale.

to **disgorge** [disˈgɔːdʒ], _v.t._ **1.** vomitare, rigettare **2.** scaricarsi, riversarsi (di fiume) **3.** (sl.) vendere, restituire (il mal tolto).

disgrace [disˈgreis], _s._ **1.** vergogna; disonore; obbrobrio, ignominia: _he is a_ — _to his family_, egli è il disonore della sua famiglia; _there is no_ — _in doing so_, non è un disonore fare così **2.** disgrazia, sfavore: _the child is in_ —, il bambino è in castigo; _to be in_ —, essere in disgrazia, sfavore; _to fall into_ — _with s.o._, cadere in disgrazia di qlcu.

to **disgrace**, _v.t._ **1.** privare della protezione; destituire: _the courtier was disgraced for refusing to comply_, il cortigiano cadde in disgrazia per essersi rifiutato di ubbidire **2.** disonorare: _he has disgraced his family_, ha disonorato la sua famiglia.

disgraceful [disˈgreisful], _ag._ vergognoso, disonorevole, ignobile; scandaloso: — _behaviour_, comportamento vergognoso.

disgracefully [disˈgreisfuli], _av._ vergognosamente, disonorevolmente; scandalosamente.

disgracefulness [disˈgreisfulnis], _s._ vergogna; infamia, obbrobrio.

to **disgregate** [ˈdisgrigeit], _v.t._ disgregare.

disgruntled [disˈgrʌntld], _ag._ (fam.) malcontento, scontento; di cattivo umore.

disguise [disˈgaiz], _s._ **1.** travestimento: _in_ —, travestito; _in the_ — _of a policeman_, travestito da poliziotto ‖ _it may be a blessing in_ —, può essere che non

tutto il male venga per nuocere **2.** finzione; maschera: _under the_ — _of charity_, sotto la maschera della carità; _to throw off all_ —, togliersi la maschera.

to **disguise**, _v.t._ **1.** travestire; camuffare; mascherare: _she disguised herself as a gipsy_, si è travestita da zingara **2.** contraffare; dissimulare: _to_ — _one's sorrow_, dissimulare il proprio dolore; _to_ — _one's voice_, contraffare la propria voce.

disguisement [disˈgaizmənt], _V._ **disguise**.

disgust [disˈgʌst], _s._ disgusto; schifo, nausea; ripugnanza, avversione: — _at s.o.'s behaviour_, disgusto per il comportamento di qlcu.; _much to my_ —, con mia grande delusione, dispunto; _to hold sthg. in_ —, avere ripugnanza per ql.co.; _to turn away in_ —, voltare le spalle disgustato.

to **disgust**, _v.t._ **1.** disgustare, nauseare: _medicines that_ — _the palate_, medicine disgustose al palato **2.** indignare, spiacere a, offendere: _don't_ — _your teacher_, non dar dispiaceri al tuo insegnante; _he was disgusted at his friend's words_, si scandalizzò alle parole del suo amico; _his language disgusts me_, il suo modo di parlare mi disgusta; _to be disgusted at_ (o _by_ o _with_) _sthg._, essere indignato per ql.co.; _to be disgusted with s.o._, essere sdegnato con qlcu.

disgustedly [disˈgʌstidli], _av._ con disgusto.

disgustful [disˈgʌstful], **disgusting** [disˈgʌstiŋ], _ag._ disgustoso, ripugnante; nauseante.

disgustingly [disˈgʌstiŋli], _av._ disgustosamente; in modo nauseante.

dish[1] [diʃ], _s._ **1.** piatto (di portata): _to wash up the dishes_, rigovernare i piatti **2.** pietanza, piatto: _a_ — _of meat and vegetables_, un piatto di carne con verdura **3.** recipiente; (foto.) bacinella; (chim.) capsula **4.** cunetta (di campo, strada) **5.** tazza (di tè, ecc.) **6.** (radar) riflettore parabolico ☆ — _-cloth_, strofinaccio per i piatti; — _-cover_, copripiatto; — _-warmer_, scaldapiatti; — _-wash_ (o — _-water_), acqua di rigovernatura; — _-washer_, lavapiatti (persona, macchina); sguattero ‖ _dainty_ —, pietanza saporita, delicata; _standing_ —, piatto consueto; _fig._ il solito argomento; _vegetable_ —, legumiera.

to **dish**[1], _v.t._ **1.** scodellare, mettere (il cibo) nei piatti **2.** (sl.) battere, sconfiggere: _to_ — _one's adversaries_, battere i propri avversari ‖ _well, I'm dished!_, sono spacciato! **3.** (tec. mec.) imbutire **4.** _to_ — _up_, servire (un pasto); (fam.) presentare in modo attraente: _to_ — _up the dinner_, servire il pranzo; _to_ — _up well -known facts_, ripresentare fatti noti in una nuova veste.

to **dish**[2], _v.t._ (scoz.) spingere violentemente.

dishabille [ˌdisæˈbiːl], _s._ vestaglia: _in_ —, in veste succinta; in veste da casa.

to **dishabituate** [disha'bitjueit], _v.t._ disabituare.

disharmonious [ˌdisha:ˈmounjəs], _ag._ dissonante, discordante, disarmonico.

to **disharmonize** [ˈdisha:mənaiz], _v.t._ disarmonizzare.

disharmony [disˈha:məni], _s._ disarmonia, dissonanza.

to **dishearten** [disˈha:tn], _v.t._ scoraggiare; demoralizzare; _to become_ (o _to get_) _disheartened_, scoraggiarsi.

disheartening [disˈha:tniŋ], _ag._ scoraggiante: — _work_, lavoro ingrato.

disheartenment [disˈha:tnmənt], _s._ scoraggiamento.

to **dishevel** [diˈʃevəl], _v.t._ scapigliare, scarmigliare, arruffare; mettere in disordine.

dishevelled [diˈʃevəld], _ag._ arruffato, scapigliato, scarmigliato (di capelli); disordinato (di abiti).

dishevelment [diˈʃevəlmənt], _s._ scarmigliatura; disordine (di abiti).

dishful [ˈdiʃful], _s._ il contenuto di un piatto: _a_ — _of vegetables_, un piatto pieno di verdure.

dishonest [disˈɔnist], _ag._ disonesto; sleale.

dishonestly [disˈɔnistli], _av._ disonestamente; slealmente.

dishonesty [disˈɔnisti], _s._ disonestà; slealtà.

dishonor, (amer.) per **dishonour**.

to **dishonor**, (amer.) per to **dishonour**.

dishonour [dis'ɔnə*], *s.* **1.** disonore; vergogna; infamia: *to bring — on one's family*, disonorare la propria famiglia **2.** (*comm.*) mancato pagamento (di cambiale, assegno); mancata accettazione (di una cambiale) **3.** (*arc.*) affronto, insulto.

to dishonour, *v.t.* **1.** disonorare; sedurre (una donna) **2.** venir meno a, mancare a: *to — one's word*, venir meno alla propria parola **3.** (*comm.*) rifiutare di pagare; non accettare, lasciar cadere in protesto (un effetto) ☆ *dishonoured bill*, cambiale non pagata; *dishonoured check*, assegno a vuoto.

dishonourable [dis'ɔnərəbl], *ag.* disonorevole; disonorante.

dishonourableness [dis'ɔnərəblnis], *s.* carattere infamante (di un'azione).

dishonourably [dis'ɔnərəbli], *av.* in modo disonorevole, disonorante.

to dishorn [dis'hɔ:n], *v.t.* privare delle corna.

to dishorse [dis'hɔ:s], *v.t.* disarcionare.

to dishouse [dis'hauz], *v.t.* sfrattare; privare della casa.

disillusion [,disi'lu:ʒən], *s.* disinganno, disillusione.

to disillusion, **to disillusionize** [,disi'lu:ʒənaiz], *v.t.* disingannare, disilludere.

disillusionment [,disi'lu:ʒənmənt], *s.* disinganno, disillusione.

disinclination [,disinkli'neiʃən], *s.* ripugnanza, riluttanza; avversione: *a — for work*, avversione al lavoro; *to have a — to do sthg.*, avere ri uttanza a fare ql.co.

to disincline [disin'klain], *v.t.* distogliere da, allontanare da; togliere un desiderio a: *to — s.o. to sthg.*, *to do sthg.*, distogliere qlcu. da ql.co., dal fare ql.co.

to disincorporate [,disin'kɔ:pəreit], *v.t.* sciogliere (un ente); staccare da un ente; privare dei diritti propri di un ente.

to disinfect [,disin'fekt], *v.t.* disinfettare.

disinfectant [,disin'fektənt], *ag.s.* disinfettante.

disinfection [,disin'fekʃən], **disinfecting** [,disin'fektiŋ], *s.* disinfezione.

disinfector [,disin'fektə*], *s.* **1.** chi disinfetta **2.** disinfettante.

to disinfest [,disin'fest], *v.t.* disinfestare.

disinfestation ['disinfes'teiʃən], *s.* disinfestazione.

disinflation [,disin'fleiʃən], *s.* (*econ.*) deflazione.

disinflationary [,disin'fleiʃnəri], *ag.* (*econ.*) deflazionistico.

disingenuous [,disin'dʒenjuəs], *ag.* falso, finto, insincero; fraudolento.

disingenuously [,disin'dʒenjuəsli], *av.* falsamente; fraudolentemente.

disingenuousness [,disin'dʒenjuəsnis], *s.* insincerità; slealtà.

to disinherit ['disin'herit], *v.t.* diseredare.

disinheritance [,disin'heritəns], **disinheriting** ['disin'heritiŋ], *s.* il diseredare, diseredazione.

to disintegrate [dis'intigreit], *v.t.i.* disintegrare, disintegrarsi; disgregare, disgregarsi.

disintegration [dis,inti'greiʃən], *s.* disintegrazione; disgregazione.

disintegrator [dis'intigreitə*], *s.c.* disintegratore, disintegratrice; disgregatore, disgregatrice.

to disinter ['disin'tə:*], *pass. p.p.* **disinterred** ['disin'tə:d], *v.t.* dissotterrare; esumare.

to disinterest [dis'intrist], *v.t.* disinteressare: *to — oneself in a matter*, disinteressarsi di una questione.

disinterested [dis'intristid], *ag.* **1.** disinteressato, imparziale **2.** indifferente.

disinterestedly [dis'intristidli], *av.* **1.** disinteressatamente **2.** con indifferenza.

disinterestedness [dis'intristidnis], *s.* **1.** disinteresse **2.** indifferenza.

disinterment [,disin'tə:mənt], *s.* dissotterramento; esumazione.

to disjoin [dis'dʒɔin], *v.t.i.* disgiungere, disgiungersi; disunire, disunirsi; distaccare, distaccarsi.

to disjoint [dis'dʒɔint], *v.t.* **1.** disgiungere; slogare; disgregare; smembrare (anche *fig.*) **2.** (*chir.*) disarticolare.

disjointed [dis'dʒɔintid], *ag.* **1.** disgiunto; disarticolato; disgregato; smembrato **2.** sconnesso, incoerente (di stile, discorso, ecc.).

disjointedly [dis'dʒɔintidli], *av.* sconnessamente: *he writes —*, scrive in modo sconnesso.

disjointedness [dis'dʒɔintidnis], *s.* sconnessione, incoerenza (di stile, discorso, ecc.).

disjointing [dis'dʒɔintiŋ], *s.* **1.** separazione; smembramento; disgregamento **2.** (*chir.*) disarticolazione.

disjunct [dis'dʒʌŋkt], *ag.* disgiunto, separato.

disjunction [dis'dʒʌŋkʃən], *s.* disgiunzione, separazione.

disjunctive [dis'dʒʌŋktiv], *ag.* (*gram.*) disgiuntivo ‖ *s.* (*gram.*) particella, frase disgiuntiva.

disjunctively [dis'dʒʌŋktivli], *av.* disgiuntamente.

disk [disk], *s.* disco ☆ *— brake*, (*aut.*) freno a disco; *— coupling*, (*mec.*) accoppiamento a dischi; *— jockey*, (*amer.*) presentatore di un programma radiofonico di dischi; *— sanding*, (*ind.*) smerigliatura a dischi; *— saw*, sega circolare; *— signal*, segnale a disco; *— wheel*, ruota a disco ‖ *clutch —*, disco della frizione; *identity —*, (*mil.*) piastrina d'identità; *recording —* (o *phonograph —*), (*mus.*) disco; *sucking —*, ventosa, coppetta.

dislike [dis'laik], *s.* avversione; antipatia; ripugnanza: *likes and dislikes*, simpatie e antipatie; *to have a — of* (o *for*), aver un'avversione per; *to take* (o *to conceive*) *a — for* (o *to*), prendere in antipatia, prendere in uggia.

to dislike, *v.t.* (II) **1.** non piacere, non amare **2.** provare avversione, antipatia per; detestare: *he dislikes me and I — him*, io non gli piaccio ed egli non mi piace; *I — onions*, non mi piacciono le cipolle; *she does not — jazz*, non le dispiace il jazz; *to — doing* (o *to do*) *sthg.*, non amare, detestare di fare ql.co.

to dislocate ['disləkeit], *v.t.* **1.** mettere fuori posto; spostare; disorganizzare (circolazione stradale, traffico, ecc.) **2.** slogare, lussare: *dislocated shoulder*, spalla slogata; *he dislocated his foot*, si slogò un piede.

dislocation [,dislə'keiʃən], *s.* **1.** dislocazione, dislocamento **2.** disorganizzazione (degli affari, del traffico) **3.** slogatura, lussazione **4.** (*geol.*) dislocazione.

to dislodge [dis'lɔdʒ], *v.t.i.* **1.** sloggiare (il nemico, ecc.); scacciare; stanare (un animale dalla tana, ecc.) **2.** rimuovere, distaccare.

dislodg(e)ment [dis'lɔdʒmənt], *s.* **1.** sloggiamento; lo scacciare **2.** rimozione; il distaccarsi (*p. e.* di una pietra da un muro).

disloyal ['dis'lɔiəl], *ag.* sleale; infedele; perfido.

disloyally ['dis'lɔiəli], *av.* slealmente; senza fedeltà; perfidamente.

disloyalty ['dis'lɔiəlti], *s.* slealtà; infedeltà; perfidia.

dismal ['dizməl], *ag.* tetro, triste, fosco, lugubre: *— weather, face, outlook*, tempo, viso, prospettiva triste ‖ *the — science*, (*iron.*) l'economia politica.

dismals ['dizməlz], *s.pl.* malinconia: *to have the —*, (*sl.*) essere depresso.

dismally ['dizməli], *av.* lugubremente; tristemente.

dismalness ['dizməlnis], *s.* tristezza, malinconia; aspetto fosco, lugubre.

to dismantle [dis'mæntl], *v.t.* smantellare; demolire; spogliare; (*mar.*) disarmare.

dismantlement [dis'mæntlmənt], **dismantling** [dis'mæntliŋ], *s.* smantellamento; demolizione; (*mar.*) disarmo.

to dismast [dis'mɑ:st], *v.t.* disalberare (una nave).

dismay [dis'mei], *s.* costernazione; spavento; sgomento: *in (blank) —*, costernato; *to be filled with — at*, essere costernato da.

to dismay, *v.t.* costernare; spaventare; sgomentare: *I was dismayed at the news*, fui costernato dalla notizia; *nothing dismayed him*, nulla lo sgomentava.

to **dismember** [dis'membə*], v.t. smembrare.

dismemberment [dis'membəmənt], s. smembramento.

dismiss [dis'mis], s. (mil.) segnale di rompere le file, le righe.

to **dismiss**, v.t. **1.** congedare; licenziare; destituire, dimettere: *the master dismissed the class*, il maestro congedò la classe; *the prince dismissed us with a few gracious words*, il principe ci congedò con amabili parole; *to — the audience*, sciogliere l'adunanza; *to — an employee wrongfully*, licenziare un impiegato per motivi ingiustificati; *to — s.o. from the service*, (mil.) radiare qlcu. dai ranghi; *to — troops*, (mil.) mandare in congedo le truppe; *to be* (o *to get*) *dismissed the service*, (mar. mil.) essere esonerato dal servizio militare || *—l*, (mil.) rompete le file! **2.** bandire, scacciare, allontanare: *to — sthg. from one's thoughts* (o *one's mind*), bandire, scacciare ql.co. dai propri pensieri, dalla propria mente || *to — a ball to boundary*, (cricket) mandare la palla fuori dai limiti (da parte del battitore) **3.** mettere da parte, abbandonare; scartare (una proposta): *let us — the subject*, non parliamo più di questo argomento **4.** (dir.) rigettare, respingere (una domanda, un appello): *to — the accused*, prosciogliere l'imputato; *to — a case*, sollevare eccezione di inammissibilità; *to — a charge*, emettere ordinanza di non luogo a procedere.

dismissal [dis'misəl], s. **1.** congedo; licenziamento; destituzione, radiazione (da ruolo) **2.** (dir.) rinvio, rigetto: *— of a petition*, rigetto di una istanza **3.** (dir.) assoluzione.

dismissible [dis'misibl], ag. **1.** congedabile; licenziabile; che si può destituire **2.** (dir.) revocabile; rinviabile.

dismount ['dis'maunt], s. discesa (da cavallo, ecc.).

to **dismount**, v.t.i. **1.** scendere, smontare: *to — from a horse, a carriage*, scendere da cavallo, da una carrozza; *to — one's horse*, smontare da cavallo **2.** far scendere; buttare a terra: *the horse dismounted its rider*, il cavallo disarcionò il cavaliere **3.** (mil.) appiedare: *to — the cavalry*, appiedare la cavalleria **4.** (mec.) smontare; (artigl.) smontare, rendere inservibile (un cannone).

dismounted ['dis'mauntid], ag. appiedato ☆ *— cavalry*, cavalleria appiedata.

dismounting ['dis'mauntiŋ], s. **1.** discesa (da cavallo) **2.** (mec.) smontaggio, smontatura (di una macchina).

dismountable ['dis'mauntəbl], ag. smontabile.

disnatured ['dis'neitʃəd], ag. snaturato.

disobedience [.disə'bi:djəns], s. disubbidienza.

disobedient [disə'bi:djənt], ag. disubbidiente: *to be — to s.o.*, disubbidire a qlcu.

disobediently [.disə'bi:djəntli], av. disubbidientemente, da disubbidiente, con disubbidienza.

to **disobey** ['disə'bei], v.t. disubbidire (a); trasgredire: *don't — your mother, the law*, non disubbidire alla mamma, non trasgredire la legge; *she wouldn't be disobeyed*, non permetteva le si disubbidisse.

to **disoblige** ['disə'blaidʒ], v.t. usare scortesia verso; usare uno sgarbo a: *I am sorry to — you*, mi dispiace essere scortese verso di voi, di non potere soddisfare il vostro desiderio.

disobliging ['disə'blaidʒiŋ], ag. scortese, sgarbato.

disobligingly ['disə'blaidʒiŋli], av. scortesemente, sgarbatamente.

disobligingness ['disə'blaidʒiŋnis], s. scortesia.

disorder [dis'o:də*], s. **1.** disordine; confusione: *in —*, in disordine: *clothes in disorder*, abiti in disordine; *the enemy fled in —*, il nemico fuggì disordinatamente **2.** tumulto; sconcerto; disordine: *disorders in the capital*, disordini nella capitale **3.** indisposizione, disturbo (di digestione, ecc.): *nervous —*, disturbo nervoso.

to **disorder**, v.t. **1.** mettere in disordine, disordinare; turbare; scompigliare **2.** disturbare (lo stomaco, ecc.).

disordered [dis'o:dəd], ag. **1.** disordinato; scompigliato; disturbato; disorganizzato **2.** malato; morboso.

disorderliness [dis'o:dəlinis], s. **1.** mancanza d'ordine, disordine, confusione **2.** sregolatezza **3.** tumulto, turbolenza.

disorderly [dis'o:dəli], ag. **1.** disordinato, in disordine **2.** turbolento: *— crowd*, folla turbolenta **3.** disordinato, sregolato: *— conduct*, contegno sregolato, che non osserva le buone norme ☆ *— house*, (dir.) casa chiusa; casa da giuoco.

disordinate [dis'o:dinit]. ag. disordinato (anche fig.).

disorganic [.diso:'gænik], ag. disorganico.

disorganization [dis,o:gənai'zeiʃən], s. disorganizzazione.

to **disorganize** [dis'o:gənaiz], v.t. disorganizzare: *to become disorganized*, disorganizzarsi.

to **disorientate** [dis'o:rienteit], v.t. **1.** disorientare (anche fig.) **2.** orientare male; non orientare verso levante (una chiesa).

disorientation [dis,o:rien'teiʃən], s. disorientamento.

to **disown** [dis'oun], v.t. **1.** sconfessare; rinnegare; ripudiare; non riconoscere per proprio, disconoscere **2.** (arc.) negare (un fatto).

to **disoxidate** [dis'oksideit], v.t. (arc.) disossidare.

to **disparage** [dis'pæridʒ], v.t. **1.** deprezzare, sottovalutare, svilire **2.** screditare, denigrare.

disparagement [dis'pæridʒmənt], s. **1.** deprezzamento **2.** scredito; denigrazione.

disparager [dis'pæridʒə*], s.c. spregiatore, spregiatrice; detrattore, detrattrice.

disparaging [dis'pæridʒiŋ], ag. sprezzante; spregiativo; denigratorio.

disparagingly [dis'pæridʒiŋli], av. in modo spregiativo, denigratorio: *to speak — of s.o., sthg.*, parlare in modo denigratorio di qlcu., con dispregio di ql.co.

disparate ['dispərit], ag. disparato || s. gener. pl. cose disparate (che non ammettono confronti tra loro).

disparity [dis'pæriti], s. disparità, scarto; differenza: *— in age, rank, years, position*, differenza di età, rango, anni, posizione.

to **dispark** [dis'pa:k], v.t. **1.** aprire (un parco) al pubblico **2.** adibire (un parco) ad altri usi.

to **dispart** [dis'pa:t], v.t.i. **1.** (arc. letter.) fendere, fendersi; dividere, dividersi; separarsi: *the heavens disparted*, il cielo s'aprì **2.** distribuire.

dispassionate [dis'pæʃnit], ag. **1.** spassionato; calmo **2.** imparziale: *to take a — view of things*, giudicare le cose imparzialmente.

dispassionately [dis'pæʃnitli], av. **1.** spassionatamente; con calma **2.** con imparzialità.

dispassionateness [dis'pæʃnitnis], s. **1.** spassionatezza; calma **2.** imparzialità.

dispatch [dis'pætʃ], s. **1.** invio, spedizione: *the — of telegrams*, la spedizione dei telegrammi **2.** dispaccio (diplomatico, telegrafico, ecc.): *dispatches from everywhere*, dispacci da ogni luogo; *mention in dispatches*, (mil.) citazione all'ordine del giorno **3.** rapido disbrigo (di un affare); prontezza; celerità; sollecitudine: *with —*, prontamente; *with the utmost —*, con la massima celerità, sollecitudine **4.** esecuzione (di un criminale); il mandare a morte ☆ *-box*, valigia diplomatica; *-case*, busta per custodire dispacci, documenti; valigia diplomatica; *— note*, (comm.) bolletta di spedizione; *— rider*, (mil.) motociclista (che porta dispacci, ecc.); *— service*, (comm.) servizio dispacci; *— tube*, conduttura di posta pneumatica || *happy —*, karakiri, suicidio giapponese.

to **dispatch**, v.t. **1.** spedire, inviare; far partire (un corriere, un telegramma, ecc.): *to — a convoy*, mettere in moto un convoglio **2.** sbrigare (affari, ecc.) **3.** ingoiare (un pasto): *he soon dispatched his dinner*, trangugiò in fretta il pranzo **4.** spacciare, mandare all'altro mondo: *to — a wounded animal*, dare il colpo di grazia ad un animale ferito.

dispatcher [dis′pætʃə*], *s.* spedizioniere; mittente.

to **dispel** [dis′pel], *pass.p.p.* **dispelled** [dis′peld], *v.t.* dissipare; disperdere, cacciar via (nebbia, nubi; dubbi, timori, ecc.).

dispensable [dis′pensəbl], *ag.* **1.** non necessario **2.** (*eccl.*) che può ottenere dispensa **3.** (*amer.*) condonabile (di peccati, ecc.).

dispensary [dis′pensəri], *s.* (*med.*) dispensario.

dispensation [,dispen′seifən], *s.* **1.** dispensa, distribuzione (di ricompense, elemosine) **2.** amministrazione, governo (di cose umane) **3.** decreto, legge (della Provvidenza); legge religiosa: *the Mosaic —*, la legge mosaica **4.** esenzione (da tasse, ecc.), (*dir. eccl.*) dispensa.

dispensatory [dis′pensətəri], *ag.* che concede esenzione ‖ *s.* ricettario; farmacopea.

to **dispense** [dis′pens], *v.t.i.* **1.** dispensare, distribuire (carità, favori, ecc.) **2.** amministrare (sacramenti, giustizia) **3.** (*farm.*) preparare e distribuire (medicinali) **4.** (*dir. eccl.*) esimere, dispensare: *to — s.o. from sthg.*, *from doing sthg.*, dispensare, esimere qlcu. da ql.co., dal fare ql.co. **5.** *to — with* (*s.o.*, *sthg.*), fare a meno di: *to — with hand-labour*, eliminare il lavoro manuale.

dispenser [dis′pensə*], *s.c.* **1.** dispensiere, dispensiera **2.** farmacista ‖ *s.* dispensatore; amministratore (della legge, ecc.).

dispensing [dis′pensiŋ], *ag.* che dispensa ‖ *s.* **1.** il dispensare, distribuzione **2.** (*farm.*) preparazione (delle ricette) ☆ *— chemist*, farmacista autorizzato a preparare le ricette.

to **dispeople** [′dis′pi:pl], *v.t.* spopolare.

dispermous [dai′spə:məs], *ag.* (*bot.*) dispermo.

dispersal [dis′pə:səl], *V.* **dispersion.**

to **disperse** [dis′pə:s], *v.t.i.* **1.** disperdere, dispersi; spargere; sparpagliare; disseminare **2.** (*ott.*) decomporre (luce).

dispersedly [dis′pə:sidli], *av.* sparsamente; qua e là.

dispersion [dis′pə:ʃən], *s.* **1.** dispersione ‖ *the Dispersion*, (*st. ebraica*) la Diaspora **2.** diffusione (di calore, ecc.) **3.** (*ott. elett.*) dispersione ☆ *— pattern*, rosa di tiro.

dispersive [dis′pə:siv], *ag.* dispersivo.

dispersively [dis′pə:sivli], *av.* in modo dispersivo.

to **dispirit** [di′spirit], *v.t.* scoraggiare.

dispirited [di′spiritid], *ag.* scoraggiato; depresso; abbattuto.

dispiritedly [di′spiritidli], *av.* depressamente.

dispiriting [di′spiritiŋ], *ag.* scoraggiante; deprimente.

dispiteous [dis′pitiəs], *ag.* spietato, crudele.

to **displace** [dis′pleis], *v.t.* **1.** spostare, rimuovere; (*mar.*) dislocare **2.** destituire; sostituire: *to — s.o. by s.o. else*, sostituire qlcu. con qlcu. altro **3.** soppiantare; togliere slealmente il posto a ☆ *displaced person* (*D. P.*), profugo, rifugiato politico; deportato.

displaceable [dis′pleisəbl], *ag.* spostabile.

displacement [dis′pleismənt], *s.* **1.** spostamento; (*mar.*) dislocamento: *a ship of 8000 tons —*, una nave di 8000 tonnellate di dislocamento **2.** destituzione; sostituzione: *— of Brown by Smith*, sostituzione di Brown da parte di Smith ☆ *piston —*, cilindrata.

display [dis′plei], *s.* **1.** mostra; esibizione; esposizione **2.** ostentazione (di ricchezza, erudizione, ecc.): *to be fond of —*, amare mettersi in mostra; *to have a horror of —*, detestare ogni ostentazione **3.** (*tip.*) risalto dei caratteri ☆ *air —*, festa aeronautica; *fashion —*, sfilata di moda.

to **display**, *v.t.* **1.** mostrare; mettere in mostra; esporre (in vendita): *to — the flag*, esporre la bandiera; *to — a notice*, esporre un avviso **2.** mostrare, manifestare (coraggio, intelligenza, ecc.) **3.** ostentare, far mostra di **4.** rivelare (la propria ignoranza, ecc.) **5.** (*tip.*) stampare a caratteri ben visibili.

to **displease** [dis′pli:z], *v.t.* dispiacere a, recar dispiacere a; scontentare, seccare; offendere: *these things — my father*, queste cose dispiacciono a mio padre; *your behaviour displeases me*, il vostro contegno mi reca dispiacere, mi dispiace; *to be displeased at* (o *with*) *s.o.*, *sthg.*, essere malcontento di qlcu., ql.co.

displeasing [dis′pli:ziŋ], *ag.* spiacevole; sgradevole.

displeasingly [dis′pli:ziŋli], *av.* spiacevolmente; sgradevolmente.

displeasure [dis′pleʒə*], *s.* dispiacere; malcontento. scontento; corruccio; ira: *to incur s.o.'s —*, scontentare qlcu., rendere qlcu. malcontento.

to **displode** [dis′ploud], *v.t.i.* (*arc.*) esplodere, fare esplodere.

displosion [dis′plouʒən], *s.* (*arc.*) esplosione.

disponee [dis,pou′ni:], *s.* (*dir.*) cessionario.

to **disponge** [di′spʌndʒ], *v.t.* (*arc.*) spremere come da una spugna.

disport [dis′pɔ:t], *s.* (*arc.*) diporto, divertimento.

to **disport**, *v.i.r.* (*arc.*) spassarsela, divertirsi; folleggiare.

disportment [dis′pɔ:tmənt], *s.* (*arc.*) divertimento.

disposability [dis,pouzə′biliti], *s.* disponibilità.

disposable [dis′pouzəbl], *ag.* disponibile ‖ *— portion of property*, (*dir.*) beni disponibili per testamento.

disposal [dis′pouzəl], *s.* **1.** disposizione: *I am at your —*, sono ai vostri ordini; *to put* (o *to place*) *sthg. at s.o.'s —*, mettere ql.co. a disposizione di qlcu. **2.** sistemazione: *the — of some business*, la sistemazione di qualche faccenda **3.** eliminazione: *the — of household refuse*, la eliminazione dei rifiuti domestici; *the greatest difficulty was the — of the corpse*, la maggior difficoltà consisteva nello sbarazzarsi del cadavere **4.** (*comm.*) vendita; cessione **5.** (*dir.*) trasferimento; assegnazione (di proprietà per disposizione testamentaria) **6.** (*mil.*) disposizione, collocamento (di truppe) ☆ *bomb — unit*, (*mil.*) gruppo addetto al disinnescamento delle bombe.

to **dispose** [dis′pouz], *v.t.i.* **1.** disporre; combinare; distribuire; mettere in ordine (una casa, ecc.): *the general disposed his troops very well*, il generale distribuì molto bene le truppe; *I can — of my time as I like*, posso disporre del mio tempo come voglio; *to — oneself to sleep*, disporsi a dormire ‖ *man proposes, God disposes*, *prov.* l'uomo propone e Dio dispone **2.** disporre, rendere propenso: *the low salary did not — him to accept*, il misero stipendio lo rendeva poco propenso ad accettare **3.** *to — of* (*s.o.*, *sthg.*), disfarsi di, sbarazzarsi di, liberarsi di; (*comm.*) collocare, vendere; (*fam.*) mangiare, ingoiare: *all the goods were easily disposed of*, si collocò molto facilmente tutta la merce; *the dictator disposed of all his adversaries*, il dittatore si sbarazzò di tutti i suoi nemici; *he did not wish to — of the land*, non voleva vendere il terreno; *he quickly disposed of the dinner*, (*fam.*) ingoiò il pranzo in fretta e furia.

disposed [dis′pouzd], *ag.* disposto, intenzionato; incline: *do you feel — to go?*, vi sentite di andare?; *I am — for anything*, sono pronto a tutto; *to be — to*, essere portato a, incline a, aver tendenza a (pietà, obesità, ecc.); *to be — to do sthg.*, essere disposto a fare ql.co. ☆ *well —*, *ill —*, bene, male intenzionato: *to be well —*, *ill — towards s. o.*, essere bene, male intenzionato verso qlcu.

disposedly [dis′pouzidli], *av.* ordinatamente.

disposer [dis′pouzə*], *s.c.* **1.** chi dispone, chi ordina (le cose umane, ecc.) **2.** dispensatore, dispensatrice (di benefici, ecc.).

disposition [,dispə′ziʃən], *s.* **1.** disposizione, assestamento, ordine; (*mil.*) disposizione, schieramento (di truppe); (*dir.*) disposizione testamentaria **2.** disposizione, predisposizione, tendenza, inclinazione: *he has a — to jealousy*, è di temperamento geloso; *— to sorethroat, to catch cold*, tendenza al mal di gola, a raffreddarsi **3.** indole, temperamento: *she is of a kindly —*, ella è di indole gentile **4.** desiderio, intenzione (di fare ql.co.) **5.** *pl.* disposizioni, preparativi: *to take one's dispositions to do sthg.*, predisporsi a fare ql.co., prendere le proprie misure per fare ql.co.

to **dispossess** ['dispə'zes], *v.t.* **1.** spogliare, spossessare; spodestare; (*dir.*) espropriare **2.** (*arc.*) liberare: *to — s.o.* (*of an evil spirit*), liberare qlcu. da uno spirito maligno.

dispossession [,dispə'zeʃən], *s.* spogliazione; (*dir.*) esproprio, espropriazione.

dispossessor [,dispə'zesə*], *s.c.* espropriatore, espropriatrice.

dispraise [dis'preiz], *s.* denigrazione, critica, biasimo.

to **dispraise**, *v.t.* denigrare, criticare, biasimare.

dispraising [dis'preiziŋ], *ag.* denigrante.

dispraisingly [dis'preiziŋli], *av.* con tono di denigrazione, di critica, di biasimo.

disproof ['dis'pru:f], *s.* (*ret.*) confutazione.

disproportion ['disprə'pɔ:ʃən], *s.* sproporzione: — *in age*, divario di età.

disproportionate [,disprə'pɔ:ʃnit], *ag.* sproporzionato.

disproportionately [,disprə'pɔ:ʃnitli], *av.* sproporzionatamente.

disproportionateness [,disprə'pɔ:ʃnitnis], *s.* sproporzione.

disproportioned ['disprə'pɔ:ʃənd], *ag.* sproporzionato.

to **disprove** ['dis'pru:v], *p.p.* **disproved** ['dis'pru:vd], **disproven** ['dis'pru:vən], *v.t.* confutare; invalidare; contraddire; dimostrare la falsità di (una dichiarazione).

disputable [dis'pju:təbl], *ag.* disputabile, discutibile; contestabile.

disputably [dis'pju:təbli], *av.* discutibilmente.

disputant [dis'pju:tənt], *s.c.* disputatore, disputatrice.

disputation [,dispju(:)'teiʃən], *s.* disputa, discussione.

disputatious [,dispju(:)'teiʃəs], *ag.* litigioso; cavilloso; contenzioso.

disputatiousness [,dispju(:)'teiʃəsnis], *s.* cavillosità; contenziosità.

dispute [dis'pju:t], *s.* disputa, controversia, vertenza; (*dir.*) lite: — *at law*, vertenza giudiziaria; *case under* —, (*dir.*) causa in giudizio; *the matter in* —, la questione in discussione; *to avoid any further* —, evitare qualsiasi altra contestazione; *to bring into* —, mettere in discussione; *to settle a* —, appianare una controversia ‖ *beyond* (o *past* o *without*) —, indiscutibilmente, incontestabilmente.

to **dispute**, *v.t.i.* **1.** disputare, discutere; contrastare: *to — with* (o *against*) *s.o. on* (o *about*) *sthg.*, discutere con qlcu. su ql.co. **2.** contestare; contendere, contendersi: *to — (the possession of) sthg. with s.o.*, disputarsi ql.co. con qlcu.

disputer [dis'pju:tə*], *s.c.* disputatore, disputatrice.

disqualification [dis,kwolifi'keiʃən], *s.* **1.** incapacità, inabilità; (*dir.*) interdizione: — *from holding any public office*, interdizione dai pubblici uffici **2.** esclusione; (*spor.*) squalifica.

to **disqualify** [dis'kwolifai], *v.t.* **1.** rendere incapace; (*dir.*) interdire **2.** escludere; (*spor.*) squalificare: *to be disqualified from a competition*, essere escluso da un concorso, squalificato da una gara.

disqualifying [dis'kwolifaiiŋ], *ag.* **1.** che rende incapace, inabile **2.** esclusivo; (*spor.*) che squalifica ‖ *s.* **1.** interdizione **2.** (*spor.*) squalifica ☆ — *blow*, (*boxe*) colpo da squalifica.

disquiet [dis'kwaiət], *ag.* (*rar.*) inquieto, agitato ‖ *s.* inquietudine, ansietà, affanno.

to **disquiet(en)** [dis'kwaiət(n)], *v.t.* inquietare, turbare.

disquieting [dis'kwaiətiŋ], *ag.* inquietante, poco rassicurante.

disquietingly [dis'kwaiətiŋli], *av.* in modo inquietante, poco rassicurante.

disquietude [dis'kwaiitju:d], *s.* inquietudine, ansia; agitazione.

disquisition [,diskwi'ziʃən], *s.* **1.** disquisizione **2.** investigazione, inchiesta.

to **disrate** [dis'reit], *v.t.* degradare (anche *fig.*).

disregard ['disri'gɑ:d], *s.* noncuranza, disprezzo; inosservanza: — *of the law*, inosservanza della legge.

to **disregard**, *v.t.* ignorare; trascurare, non badare a, fare poco caso a, non curarsi di: *he disregarded my warning*, non si curò del mio avvertimento.

disregardful [,disri'gɑ:dful], *ag.* noncurante, inosservante.

disrelish [dis'reliʃ], *s.* disgusto, ripugnanza, avversione.

to **disrelish**, *v.t.* aver in uggia; provare disgusto, repugnanza, avversione per.

to **disremember** ['disri'membə*], *v.t.* (*dial.*) dimenticare, non ricordare.

disrepair ['disri'pɛə*], *s.* cattivo stato, sfacelo, rovina: *to fall into* —, cadere in rovina.

disreputable [dis'repjutəbl], *ag.* **1.** disonorevole, sconveniente (di azione) **2.** screditato, di cattiva fama, reputazione **3.** sciupato, logoro, stracciato: *a — old hat*, un vecchio cappellaccio ☆ — -*looking*, di aspetto losco.

disreputableness [dis'repjutəblnis], *s.* cattiva reputazione, cattiva fama.

disreputably [dis'repjutəbli], *av.* disonorevolmente, in modo disonorevole.

disrepute ['disri'pju:t], *s.* scredito; disistima; cattiva reputazione: *the hotel has fallen into* —, l'albergo si è acquistato una cattiva fama; *to bring s.o., sthg. into* —, rovinare la reputazione di qlcu., screditare ql.co.

disrespect ['disris'pekt], *s.* mancanza di rispetto, irriverenza: *to treat s.o. with* —, mancare di rispetto a qlcu.

disrespectful [,disris'pektful], *ag.* non rispettoso, sfacciato, irriverente: *to be — to s.o.*, mancare di rispetto a qlcu.

disrespectfully [,disris'pektfuli], *av.* senza il debito rispetto; irriverentemente: *to speak — of s.o.*, parlare senza rispetto di qlcu.

disrespectfulness [,disris'pektfulnis], *s.* mancanza di rispetto.

to **disrobe** ['dis'roub], *v.t.i.* svestire; svestirsi (anche *fig.*).

to **disroot** [dis'ru:t], *v.t.* sradicare; *fig.* sloggiare.

to **disrupt** [dis'rʌpt], *v.t.* **1.** rompere; spezzare, infrangere; spaccare **2.** smembrare (un impero, uno stato); far crollare (anche *fig.*).

disrupter [dis'rʌptə*], *s.* chi provoca rottura o crollo: *disrupters of society*, disorganizzatori della società.

disruption [dis'rʌpʃən], *s.* **1.** rottura, spaccatura **2.** smembramento; scisma; separazione ‖ *the Disruption*, scisma nella Chiesa Scozzese (1843).

disruptive [dis'rʌptiv], *ag.* **1.** dirompente; (*elett.*) disruptivo **2.** che smembra, disorganizza.

disruptor, *V.* **disrupter**.

dissatisfaction ['dis,sætis'fækʃən], *s.* insoddisfazione, malcontento.

to **dissatisfy** ['dis'sætisfai], *v.t.* non soddisfare; scontentare: *a dissatisfied man*, un uomo scontento; *I am dissatisfied with your work*, non sono soddisfatto del vostro lavoro; *you have dissatisfied me*, mi avete scontentato.

to **disseat** [dis'si:t], *v.t.* privare del seggio; rimuovere da un posto.

to **dissect** [di'sekt], *v.t.* **1.** sezionare, dissezionare (cadavere, pianta) **2.** *fig.* analizzare, sviscerare, trattare a fondo (un argomento, ecc.) **3.** *to — out*, (*chir.*) recidere.

dissecting [di'sektiŋ], *s.* **1.** sezionamento **2.** (*chir.*) recisione.

dissection [di'sekʃən], *s.* **1.** sezionamento, dissezione **2.** la parte sezionata.

dissector [di'sektə*], *s.* **1.** (*chir.*) dissettore, sezionatore **2.** (*chir.*) scalpello.

to **disseise, disseize** ['dis'si:z], *v.t.* espropriare.

disseisin, disseizin ['dis'si:zin], *s.* (*dir.*) espropriazione (ingiusta).

to **dissemble** [di'sembl], *v.t.i.* simulare, dissimulare; nascondere; passare sotto silenzio; fingere di non vedere: *it is no use to — the fact that,* è inutile nascondere, ignorare il fatto che.

dissembler [di'semblə*], *s.c.* simulatore, simulatrice; ipocrita.

dissembling [di'sembliŋ], *s.* dissimulazione; ipocrisia.

to **disseminate** [di'semineit], *v.t.* disseminare, seminare (grano, ecc.); *fig.* diffondere, divulgare (opinioni, ecc.).

dissemination [di,semi'neiʃən], *s.* disseminazione; *fig.* divulgazione (della verità, del Vangelo, ecc.).

disseminator [di'semineitə*], *s.c.* disseminatore, disseminatrice; *fig.* divulgatore, divulgatrice.

dissension [di'senʃən], *s.* divergenza; discordia ‖ *to sow —,* seminare zizzania.

dissent [di'sent], *s.* **1.** dissenso, dissentimento **2.** (*eccl.*) separazione, scisma **3.** *coll.* i dissidenti, gli scismatici (della Chiesa Anglicana).

to **dissent,** *v.i.* **1.** dissentire: *to — from s.o. about sthg.,* dissentire da qlcu. su ql.co. **2.** (*eccl.*) essere dissidente.

dissenter [di'sentə*], *s.* **1.** dissidente; dissenziente **2.** (*eccl.*) dissidente, persona che dissente dalla Chiesa Anglicana, dalla chiesa di Stato.

dissentient [di'senʃiənt], *ag.s.* dissidente.

dissenting [di'sentiŋ], *ag.* dissidente.

dissepiment [di'sepimənt], *s.* (*bot. zool.*) setto, diaframma.

to **dissert** [di'sə:t], to **dissertate** ['disə(:)teit], *v.i.* (*letter.*) dissertare.

dissertation [,disə(:)'teiʃən], *s.* dissertazione.

dissertationist [,disə(:)'teiʃnist], **dissertator** ['disə(:)teitə*], *s.* (*letter.*) dissertatore.

to **disserve** [dis'sə:v], *v.t.* rendere cattivo servizio a, disservire.

disservice ['dis'sə:vis], *s.* danno, cattivo servizio: *to do a — to s.o.* (o *to do s.o. a —*), fare un cattivo servizio a qlcu.

to **dissever** [dis'sevə*], *v.t.i.* separare, separarsi; disunire, disunirsi; dividere, distaccare.

disseverance [dis'sevərəns], *s.* separazione, divisione.

dissidence ['disidəns], *s.* dissidio; divergenza (di opinioni); disaccordo.

dissident ['disidənt], *ag. s.* dissidente.

dissimilar ['di'similə*], *ag.* dissimile, diverso.

dissimilarity [,disimi'læriti], *s.* dissomiglianza; (*ret.*) dissimilitudine, contrasto.

to **dissimilate** [di'simileit], *v.t.* (*linguistica*) dissimilare; rendere dissimile.

dissimilation ['disimi'leiʃən], *s.* **1.** (*linguistica*) dissimilazione **2.** (*zool. bot.*) catabolismo.

dissimilitude [,disi'militju:d], *V.* **dissimilarity.**

to **dissimulate** [di'simjuleit], *v.t.i.* dissimulare; fingere.

dissimulation [di,simju'leiʃən], *s.* dissimulazione; finzione.

dissimulator [di'simjuleitə*], *s.* dissimulatore.

to **dissipate** ['disipeit], *v.t.i.* **1.** dissipare, dissiparsi; dissolvere, dissolversi; disperdere, disperdersi: *the clouds dissipated soon,* le nuvole si dispersero presto **2.** sciupare, sprecare: *that man dissipated his time and money,* quell'uomo dissipò il suo tempo e il suo denaro **3.** condurre vita sregolata.

dissipated ['disipeitid], *ag.* dissipato; dissoluto: — *life,* vita dissipata, di piaceri; — *person,* persona dissoluta.

dissipation [,disi'peiʃən], *s.* **1.** dissipazione (di energia, denaro); dispersione (di calore, elettricità); disintegrazione; dissoluzione **2.** divertimento; distrazione **3.** dissipazione; dissolutezza; vita sregolata.

dissipative ['disipeitiv], *ag.* dispersivo.

dissipator ['disipeitə*], *s.* dispersore (di calore).

dissociable [di'souʃəbl], *ag.* (*chim.*) dissociabile.

to **dissocialize** [di'souʃəlaiz], *v.t.* rendere poco socievole, misantropo.

to **dissociate** [di'souʃieit], *v.t.i.* **1.** dissociare; disgiungere: *to — oneself from,* dissociarsi da, separarsi (in pensiero, atto) da **2.** (*chim. fis.*) dissociarsi (specialmente con il calore); dissociarsi **3.** (*psicologia*) sdoppiarsi (di personalità).

dissociation [di,sousi'eiʃən], *s.* **1.** dissociazione, separazione **2.** (*chim. fis.*) dissociazione **3.** (*psicologia*) sdoppiamento (della personalità) ☆ — *coefficient,* (*chim. fis.*) grado di dissociazione.

dissociative [di'souʃiətiv], *ag.* dissociativo.

dissolubility [di,sɔlju'biliti], *s.* dissolubilità.

dissoluble [di'sɔljubl], *ag.* dissolubile.

dissolute ['disəlu:t], *ag.* dissoluto, licenzioso.

dissolutely ['disəlu:tli], *av.* da dissoluto.

dissoluteness ['disəlu:tnis], *s.* dissolutezza.

dissolution [,disə'lu:ʃən], *s.* **1.** dissoluzione, liquefazione (di corpi, neve, ecc.) **2.** scioglimento (di matrimonio, Parlamento, società) **3.** decomposizione; disintegrazione; morte.

dissolvability [di,zɔlvə'biliti], *s.* dissolubilità.

dissolvable [di'zɔlvəbl], *ag.* dissolubile.

dissolve [di'zɔlv], *s.* (*cine.*) dissolvenza ☆ — *-in,* apertura in dissolvenza; — *-out,* chiusura in dissolvenza ‖ *lap —,* dissolvenza incrociata.

to **dissolve,** *v.t.i.* **1.** dissolvere, dissolversi; disciogliere, disciogliersi; disfarsi: *sugar dissolves in water,* lo zucchero si scioglie nell'acqua; *to — in tears,* sciogliersi in lacrime **2.** sciogliere, sciogliersi (di matrimonio, Parlamento, società) **3.** (*comm.*) annullare, rescindere **4.** disperdere, disperdersi (di folla) **5.** *fig.* dileguarsi, scomparire gradatamente ‖ *to — into thin air,* andare in fumo.

dissolvent [di'zɔlvənt], *ag.s.* dissolvente.

dissonance ['disənəns], *s.* (*mus.*) dissonanza.

dissonant ['disənənt], *ag.* (*mus.*) dissonante; discordante.

dissonantly ['disənəntli], *av.* in modo dissonante.

to **dissuade** [di'sweid], *v.t.* dissuadere, distogliere: *we dissuaded her from going there,* la dissuademmo dall'andarci.

dissuasion [di'sweiʒən], *s.* dissuasione.

dissuasive [di'sweisiv], *ag.* dissuasivo.

dissyllabic ['disi'læbik], *ag.* bisillabico, disillabo.

dissyllable [di'siləbl], *s.* bisillabo, disillabo.

dissymmetric ['disi'metrik], *ag.* asimmetrico.

dissymmetry ['di'simitri], *s,* asimmetria.

distaff ['dista:f], *s.* conocchia; rocca per filare ‖ *the — side,* il ramo femminile (di una famiglia).

distance ['distəns], *s.* **1.** distanza, lontananza: *the — between Milan and Pavia,* la distanza fra Milano e Pavia; *a — of ten miles,* una distanza di dieci miglia; (*at*) *a short —,* (a) breve distanza; *within striking —,* a portata di mano ‖ *from* (o *at*) *a —,* da lontano; *in the —,* in lontananza **2.** *fig.* riservatezza: — *of manners,* riserbo; *to keep one's —,* tenersi a distanza, mantenere le distanze; *to keep s.o. at a —,* tenere qlcu. a debita distanza **3.** distanza, intervallo di tempo: *at this — of time,* dopo tanto tempo; *to look back over a — of ten years,* riandare col pensiero agli ultimi dieci anni **4.** orizzonte, distanza visiva: *the countryside with its ample distances,* la campagna coi suoi vasti orizzonti ☆ *long- — call,* telefonata interurbana.

to **distance,** *v.t.* distanziare.

distant ['distənt], *ag.* **1.** distante, lontano: *a — town,* una città lontana; *a — view of Mont Blanc,* una veduta lontana del Monte Bianco; *ten miles —* (*from*), a dieci miglia (da) **2.** discosto, remoto, vago: — *ages,* epoche remote; *a — relation,* un parente lon

tano; *a — resemblance between*, una vaga rassomiglianza tra; *in the — future*, in un lontano avvenire **3.** riservato, freddo; altero: *a — manner*, modi poco cordiali; *a — nod*, un freddo cenno di saluto ☆ *— signal*,
(*ferr.*) segnale a distanza.

distantly ['dist*ə*ntli], *av.* in distanza; da lontano:
we are — related, siamo lontani parenti.

distaste ['dis'teist], *s.* ripugnanza; avversione; antipatia: *a — for hard work*, ripugnanza a un duro lavoro.

distasteful [dis'teistful], *ag.* repellente; disgustoso;
spiacevole.

distastefulness [dis'teistfulnis], *s.* l'essere repellente,
disgustoso.

distemper[1] [dis'temp*ə**], *s.* **1.** turbamento fisico,
mentale; indisposizione **2.** (*vet.*) cimurro.

to distemper[1], *v.t.* (*rar.*) far ammalare (fisicamente,
mentalmente): *a distempered mind*, una mente per-
turbata.

distemper[2], *s.* (*pitt.*) tempera.

to distemper[2], *v.t.* (*pitt.*) dipingere a tempera.

to distend [dis'tend], *v.t.i.* gonfiare, gonfiarsi (anche
fig.); allargare, allargarsi; dilatare, dilatarsi.

distensible [dis'tensibl], *ag.* dilatabile.

distension [dis'tenʃən], *s.* **1.** gonfiamento; gonfiezza **2.** (*patol.*) dilatazione.

distich ['distik], *s.* (*poes.*) distico.

distichous ['distikəs], *ag.* (*bot.*) distico.

to distil(l) [dis'til], *pass.p.p.* **distilled** [dis'tild],
v.t.i. **1.** stillare, essudare **2.** distillare.

distillable [dis'tiləbl], *ag.* distillabile.

distillate ['distilit], *s.* distillato.

distillation [,disti'leiʃən], *s.* distillazione.

distiller [dis'tilə*], *s.* distillatore.

distillery [dis'tiləri], *s.* distilleria.

distinct [dis'tiŋkt], *ag.* **1.** distinto, chiaro, definito:
— advantage, netto vantaggio; *a — improvement*, un
miglioramento notevole; *— sound*, suono chiaro **2.** distinto, separato, diverso: *two ideas quite — one from
the other*, due idee del tutto diverse l'una dall'altra.

distinction [dis'tiŋkʃən], *s.* **1.** distinzione: *without —*,
senza distinzione; *he was making a — without a difference*, egli voleva sottilizzare troppo, cercava il pelo
nell'uovo; *to draw distinctions*, distinguere; *to make no
— between*, non fare distinzione fra **2.** diversità, punto
di differenza: *the — between prose and poetry*, la diversità fra prosa e poesia **3.** elevatezza; raffinatezza:
people of —, gente distinta; *a writer of —*, uno scrittore raffinato **4.** distinzione, benemerenza; onorificenza.

distinctive [dis'tiŋktiv], *ag.* distintivo, atto a distinguere; caratteristico ☆ *— number*, numero di identificazione.

distinctively [dis'tiŋktivli], *av.* in modo caratteristico.

distinctiveness [dis'tiŋktivnis], *s.* distinzione, caratteristica.

distinctly [dis'tiŋktli], *av.* distintamente, chiaramente: *I — told him that*, gli dissi chiaramente che;
speak — please, parla con chiarezza, per favore.

distinctness [dis'tiŋktnis], *s.* chiarezza, precisione.

to distinguish [dis'tiŋgwiʃ], *v.t.i.* **1.** distinguere; fare
una distinzione: *to — between good and evil*, distinguere fra il bene e il male; *to — between two persons*,
fare una distinzione tra due persone; *to — one thing
from another*, distinguere una cosa da un'altra **2.** distinguere, discernere: *I cannot — him among the crowd*,
non posso vederlo tra la folla ‖ *to — oneself*, distinguersi, rendersi famoso: *he distinguished himself by
his bravery*, si distinse per il suo coraggio.

distinguishable |dis'tiŋgwiʃəbl], *ag.* distinguibile.

distinguished [dis'tiŋgwiʃ], *ag.* **1.** distinto, raffinato **2.** insigne, illustre: *a — writer, career*, uno scrittore illustre, una carriera brillante ☆ *— -looking*, dal-
l'aspetto distinto.

distinguishing [dis'tiŋgwiʃiŋ], *ag.* distinto, caratteristico, peculiare ☆ *— trait*, caratteristica.

to distort [dis'tɔ:t], *v.t.* **1.** distorcere, storcere: *face
distorted by rage*, viso alterato dall'ira; *to — one's eyes*,
storcere gli occhi **2.** svisare, alterare (notizie, informazioni) **3.** (*fis.*) distorcere; (*mec.*) deformare.

distortedly [dis'tɔ:tidli], *av.* **1.** distortamente **2.** alte-
ratamente.

distortion [dis'tɔ:ʃən], *s.* **1.** contorcimento; torsione;
distorsione **2.** stortura; deformazione; alterazione **3.** (*fis.*)
distorsione; (*mec.*) deformazione.

distortional [dis'tɔ:ʃənl], *ag.* **1.** di distorsione **2.** di
deformazione.

distortionist [dis'tɔ:ʃnist], *s.c.* contorsionista.

to distract [dis'trækt], *v.t.* **1.** distrarre, distogliere:
don't — my attention from my work, non distogliermi
dal mio lavoro **2.** stordire; turbare, sconvolgere; far
inquietare; far impazzire: *a distracted look*, uno sguardo turbato, confuso; *to drive s.o. distracted*, confondere
qlcu., far impazzire qlcu.

distractedly [dis'træktidli], *av.* follemente, perdutamente.

distractingly [dis'træktiŋli], *av.* in modo da far
impazzire.

distraction [dis'trækʃən], *s.* **1.** distrazione, disattenzione **2.** svago, divertimento **3.** confusione, follia, turbamento: *to drive (s.o.) to —*, spingere (qlcu.) alla
pazzia; *to love (s.o.) to —*, amare (qlcu.) alla follia.

to distrain [dis'trein], *v.i.* (*dir.*) fare un sequestro:
to — upon s.o.'s belongings for rent, sequestrare i beni di qlcu. per mancato pagamento dell'affitto.

distrainable [dis'treinəbl], *ag.* (*dir.*) sequestrabile.

distrainee [,distrei'ni:], *s.* (*dir.*) chi subisce un sequestro.

distrainer [dis'treinə*], *s.* (*dir.*) sequestrante.

distrainment [dis'treinmənt], *s.* (*dir.*) sequestro.

distrainor [,distrei'nɔ:*], *s.* (*dir.*) sequestrante.

distraint [dis'treint], *s.* (*dir.*) sequestro: *furniture
under —*, mobilia sotto sequestro.

distraught [dis'trɔ:t], *ag.* (*arc. letter.*) turbato; pazzo:
— with grief, pazzo di dolore.

distress [dis'tres], *s.* **1.** angoscia, angustia; preoccupazione, pena **2.** miseria, strettezza **3.** pericolo; difficoltà: *ship in —*, nave in pericolo **4.** (*dir.*) sequestro
☆ *— call* (o *— signal*), S.O.S., segnale di soccorso,
di pericolo; *— -gun*, (*mar.*) cannone per chiamare soccorso; *— -rocket*, (*mar.*) razzo per chiamare soccorso;
— -sale, asta pubblica dei beni sequestrati.

to distress, *v.t.* **1.** affliggere, angustiare; preoccupare **2.** tormentare **3.** (*dir.*) sequestrare.

distressed [dis'trest], *ag.* **1.** angustiato, afflitto **2.** indigente: *a — gentlewoman*, una signora decaduta.

distressful [dis'tresful], *ag.* **1.** penoso, doloroso **2.** (*arc.*) V. **distressed**.

distressing [dis'tresiŋ], *ag.* penoso, doloroso.

distressingly [dis'tresiŋli], *av.* penosamente, dolorosamente.

distributable [dis'tribjutəbl], *ag.* divisibile.

distributary [dis'tribjutəri], *s.* **1.** canale (di distribuzione) **2.** braccio, diramazione (di un fiume).

to distribute [dis'tribju(:)t], *v.t.* **1.** distribuire; assegnare; ripartire; dividere: *to — gifts to the needy*, distribuire doni ai bisognosi **2.** (*tip.*) scomporre ☆ *distributing centre*, centro di distribuzione.

distribution [,distri'bju:ʃən], *s.* **1.** distribuzione; ripartizione: *— of profits*, (*comm.*) ripartizione dei profitti **2.** (*tip.*) scomposizione.

distributive [dis'tribjutiv], *ag.* distributivo.

distributor [dis'tribjutə*], *s.c.* distributore, distributrice ‖ *s.* (*tip.*) scompositore.

district ['distrikt], *s.* **1.** distretto; quartiere, circondario; (*amer.*) circoscrizione ‖ *Metropolitan District Line*,
linea radiale della metropolitana londinese **2.** (*mil.*)
distretto; (*mar.*) dipartimento **3.** regione ‖ *the Lake
District*, la regione dei laghi del Cumberland ☆ *—
council*, consiglio distrettuale (amministrativo) ‖ *postal
—*, distretto postale.

to **district**, *v.t.* **1.** dividere in distretti **2.** (*amer.*) dividere in circoscrizioni elettorali.

distrust [dis'trʌst], *s.* diffidenza, sospetto, dubbio.

to **distrust**, *v.t.* diffidare di, non aver fiducia in: *I — him*, non ho fiducia in lui; *to — one's own eyes*, non credere ai propri occhi.

distrustful [dis'trʌstful], *ag.* diffidente, sospettoso.

distrustfully [dis'trʌstfuli], *av.* in modo diffidente, sospettoso.

to **disturb** [dis'tə:b], *v.t.* **1.** disturbare, incomodare: *I'm afraid of disturbing you*, temo d'importunarvi **2.** turbare, agitare: *to — the peace*, causare disordini, sommosse.

disturbance [dis'tə:bəns], *s.* **1.** agitazione, perturbazione (atmosferica) **2.** disordine, tumulto, confusione: *to make* (o *to create* o *to raise*) *a —*, provocare disordini **3.** inquietudine, irrequietezza.

disunion ['dis'ju:njən], *s.* disunione, separazione.

to **disunite** ['disju:'nait], *v.t.i.* disunire, disunirsi.

disuse ['dis'ju:s], *s.* disuso: *to fall into —*, cadere in disuso.

to **disuse** ['dis'ju:z], *v.t.* non usare più, cessare di usare.

disyllabic ['disi'læbik], *ag.* bisillabico.

disyllable [di'siləbl], *s.* bisillabo, disillabo.

ditch [ditʃ], *s.* fossato; trincea ‖ *to die in the last —*, difendersi fino all'ultimo sangue ‖ *the Ditch*, (*sl. aer.*) la Manica; il Mare del Nord; (*sl. amer.*) il Canale di Panama ☆ *— machine*, scavafossi; *— -water*, acqua stagnante: *as dull as — -water*, (*fam.*) noiosissimo, noioso da morire ‖ *antitank —*, (*mil.*) fosso anticarro.

to **ditch**, *v.t.i.* **1.** scavare fossi, canali (in un terreno, in un campo); prosciugare (scavando fossi) **2.** cadere in un fosso **3.** (*sl.*) piantare in asso **4.** (*amer.*) far deragliare (un treno) **5.** (*sl. aer.*) ammarare forzatamente.

ditcher ['ditʃə*], **1.** sterratore **2.** (*mec.*) affossatore, scavafossi, aratro per fossi.

ditheism ['daiθi(:)izm], *s.* (*st.*) diteismo.

dither [ˈdiðə*], *s.* (*fam.*) sovreccitazione: *to be in a —*, essere in uno stato di sovreccitazione ‖ *to have the dithers*, tremare come una foglia.

to **dither**, *v.i.* (*fam.*) **1.** tremare **2.** essere sovreccitato **3.** vacillare.

dithyramb ['diθiræmb], *s.* (*poes.*) ditirambo.

dithyrambic [ˌdiθiˈræmbik], *ag.* (*poes.*) ditirambico.

dittany ['ditəni], *s.* (*bot.*) dittamo.

ditto ['ditou], (*abbr. do.* o *dº*), *s.* idem, lo stesso, il medesimo ‖ *to say —*, (*fam.*) approvare, dire la stessa cosa: *I say — to that*, sono d'accordo su ciò ☆ *— marks*, virgolette ("), segno di ripetizione.

ditty ['diti], *s.* (*arc.*) breve canto; canzone rustica.

diuretic [ˌdaijuəˈretik], *ag. s.* diuretico.

diurnal [dai'ə:nl], *ag.* diurno; quotidiano.

diurnally [dai'ə:nəli], *av.* quotidianamente.

to **divagate** ['daivəgeit], *v.i.* **1.** divagare **2.** vagare.

divagation [ˌdaivəˈgeiʃən], *s.* divagazione.

divalent ['dai,veilənt], *ag.* (*chim.*) bivalente.

divan [di'væn], *s.* **1.** divano, ottomana **2.** (*st.*) divano, (sala del) consiglio di Stato in Turchia **3.** (*lett. orientale*) divano (raccolta di poesie) **4.** tabaccheria ☆ *— -bed*, divano-letto.

to **divaricate** [dai'værikeit], *v.i.* divergere, biforcarsi.

divarication [daiˌværiˈkeiʃən], *s.* divergenza; biforcazione.

dive [daiv], *s.* **1.** tuffo: *what a fine —!*, che bel tuffo! **2.** (*mar.*) immersione; (*aer.*) tuffo, picchiata **3.** (*fam.*) taverna, ristorante sotterraneo; (*amer.*) locale dove si servono alcoolici e si giuoca ☆ *— -bomber*, (*aer.*) bombardiere in picchiata; *— -bombing*, (*aer.*) bombardamento in picchiata; *— brakes*, (*aer.*) deflettori di picchiata ‖ *nose —*, (*aer.*) affondata, candela.

to **dive**, *v.i.* **1.** tuffarsi, immergersi (anche *fig.*): *to — for pearls*, tuffarsi per pescare perle; *to — into a lake*, tuffarsi in un lago ‖ *to — into a book*, immergersi nella lettura di un libro ‖ *to — into a mystery*, cercare

di penetrare un mistero ‖ *to — into one's pocket*, pescare nelle proprie tasche **2.** (*mar.*) immergersi; (*aer.*) lanciarsi in picchiata **3.** dileguarsi, sparire: *the pickpocket dived into a dark street*, il borsaiolo sparì in una strada buia.

diver ['daivə*], *s.* **1.** tuffatore; palombaro **2.** (*aer.*) velivolo in picchiata **3.** (*ornit.*) tuffolo, tuffetto.

to **diverge** [dai'və:dʒ], *v.i.* divergere.

divergence [dai'və:dʒəns], **divergency** [dai'və:dʒənsi], *s.* divergenza.

divergent [dai'və:dʒənt], *ag.* divergente.

divers ['daivə(:)z], *ag.* (*arc. scherz.*) più di uno, parecchi.

diverse [dai'və:s], *ag.* **1.** diverso, differente **2.** vario, mutevole.

diversely [dai'və:sli], *av.* diversamente.

diversification [daiˌvə:sifiˈkeiʃən], *s.* diversificazione.

to **diversify** [dai'və:sifai], *v.t.* diversificare, rendere diverso, differenziare.

diversion [dai'və:ʃən], *s.* **1.** diversione; derivazione **2.** *fig.* digressione **3.** divertimento, passatempo **4.** (*mil.*) diversione **5.** (*neol.*) deviazione (di strada) ☆ *— -cut*, (*ing.*) sfioratore.

diversionary [dai'və:ʃnəri], *ag.* diversivo; di, per diversione: *— landing*, (*mil.*) sbarco di diversione.

diversity [dai'və:siti], *s.* diversità: *— of opinion*, diversità d'opinione.

to **divert** [dai'və:t], *v.t.* **1.** deviare, stornare, cambiare la direzione di: *to — water from a river into rice-fields*, deviare l'acqua da un fiume nelle risaie **2.** sviare; distrarre; divertire: *a diverting book*, un libro divertente; *she has nothing to — herself*, non ha nulla con cui distrarsi **3.** (*mar.*) distogliere.

Dives ['daivi:z], *s.* il ricco Epulone; *fig.* ricco buontempone.

to **divest** [dai'vest], *v.t.* **1.** svestire, spogliare: *to — oneself of*, spogliarsi di; liberarsi di (idee, ricchezza ecc.) **2.** privare: *he was divested of his authority*, egli fu privato della sua autorità.

divestiture [dai'vestitʃə*], **divestment** [dai'vestmənt], *s.* spogliamento; spoliazione.

divide [di'vaid], *s.* (*amer.*) spartiacque, linea di displuvio ‖ *the Grand Divide*, le Montagne Rocciose.

to **divide**, *v.t.i.* **1.** dividere, dividersi, separare: *the river divides at its mouth forming a delta*, il fiume si divide alla foce formando un delta; *the river divides his land from mine*, il fiume separa la sua terra dalla mia **2.** (*arit.*) dividere, essere divisibile: *if you — 50 by 5 you get 10*, se dividi 50 per 5 ottieni 10; *9 divides by 3, 9 è divisibile per 3* **3.** dividere, distribuire, ripartire: *I shall — the profits with you*, dividerò i profitti con te; *the money was divided equally among the workers*, il denaro fu diviso in parti uguali fra i lavoratori **4.** dividere, mettere in gruppi diversi: *the old books were divided from the new ones*, i libri vecchi furono divisi da quelli nuovi **5.** diversificare: *opinions are divided on the matter*, le opinioni sull'argomento sono divise, divergono **6.** dividere, dividersi in due gruppi per procedere allo scrutinio dei voti (nel Parlamento britannico) **7.** *to — off*, separare **8.** *to — out*, distribuire, ripartire **9.** *to — up*, distribuire, smembrare, separare in tante parti.

divided [di'vaidid], *ag.* **1.** diviso; biforcuto **2.** graduato (di termometro, ecc.) ☆ *— skirt*, gonna-pantalone.

dividend ['dividend], *s.* **1.** (*arit.*) dividendo **2.** (*comm.*) dividendo: *ex, cum —*, senza, con dividendo (nella quotazione, ecc.) ☆ *— -warrant*, ordine per la riscossione del dividendo.

divider [di'vaidə*], *s.* chi divide; distributore ☆ *potential —*, (*elett.*) partitore di tensione.

dividers [di'vaidəz], *s.pl.* compasso a punte fisse.

dividual [di'vidjuəl], *ag.* (*rar.*) separato; separabile.

divination [ˌdiviˈneiʃən], *s.* **1.** divinazione, profezia **2.** intuizione.

divine [di'vain], *ag.* divino; *fig.* mirabile, perfetto ‖ *by — right*, per diritto divino ‖ *the Divine Comedy*, la Divina Commedia ‖ *s.* ecclesiastico; teologo ☆ — *service*, funzione sacra.

to **divine**, *v.t.i.* 1. divinare; indovinare; presagire; profetare 2. fare l'indovino; aver presagi.

divinely [di'vainli], *av.* divinamente.

diviner [di'vaino*], *s.* indovino, mago; divinatore; ☆ *water* —, rabdomante.

diving ['daiviŋ], *s.* il tuffarsi; tuffo; (*mar.*) immersione; (*aer.*) picchiata ☆ — *-bell*, campana da palombaro, campana subacquea; — *-board*, trampolino; — *compartment*, (*mar.*), cassa di compenso; — *-dress* (o — *suit*), scafandro; — *-helmet*, casco da palombaro.

divining [di'vainiŋ], *s.* divinazione ☆ — *-rod*, bacchetta divinatoria (dei rabdomanti).

divinity [di'viniti], *s.* 1. divinità (natura divina); dio 2. teologia: *Doctor of Divinity* (abbr. *D.D.*), dottore in teologia.

divinization [,divini'zeiʃən], *s.* divinizzazione.

to **divinize** ['divinaiz], *v.t.* divinizzare.

divisibility [di,vizi'biliti], *s.* divisibilità.

divisible [di'vizəbl], *ag.* divisibile.

division [di'viʒən], *s.* 1. divisione, confine, ciò che divide, separa: — *between my land and his*, confine tra la mia terra e la sua 2. (*mat.*) divisione 3. divisione, suddivisione, ripartizione, distribuzione: *the — of classes*, la divisione delle classi; — *of labour*, ripartizione del lavoro; *a fair* —, una divisione equa 4. discordia 5. (*amm. mil.*) divisione, reparto, sezione 6. separazione dei membri in due gruppi per procedere allo scrutinio dei voti (nel Parlamento Inglese): *the bill was passed without a* —, la legge fu approvata senza passare ai voti 7. graduazione (di un termometro).

divisional [di'viʒənl], *ag.* (*mil.*) di divisione ☆ — *rest*, turno di riposo nelle retrovie di una divisione.

divisionary [di'viʒənəri], *ag.* (*rar.*) di divisione.

divisor [di'vaizə*], *o.* (*mat.*) divisore.

divorce [di'vo:s], *s.* 1. divorzio: *to take* (o *to start*) — *proceedings*, iniziare le pratiche di divorzio 2. *fig.* separazione.

to **divorce**, *v.t.* 1. divorziare, far divorzio da: *the judge divorced Mr. and Mrs. Brown*, il giudice sentenziò il divorzio fra il Sig. e la Sig.ra Brown; *the king divorced the queen*, il re divorziò dalla regina; *she was divorced from her second husband*, divorziò dal suo secondo marito 2. *fig.* separare.

divorcé [di'vo:sei], *s.* divorziato.

divorcée [di'vo:sei], *s.* divorziata.

divorcee [di,vo:'si:], *s.c.* divorziato, divorziata.

divorcement [di'vo:smənt], *s.* 1. (*rar.*) divorzio 2. separazione; divario: *the — of the written from the spoken language*, il divario fra la lingua scritta e parlata.

divorcer [di'vo:sə*], *s.* chi divorzia, divorziante.

divot ['divət], *s.* 1. (*scoz.*) piota, zolla di terra erbosa 2. (*golf*) piota strappata da un colpo sbagliato.

to **divulgate** ['daivʌlgeit], *v.t.* divulgare, rendere noto.

divulgation [,daivʌl'geiʃən], *s.* divulgazione.

to **divulge** [dai'vʌldʒ], *v.t.* divulgare, diffondere; palesare; far conoscere.

divulgement [dai'vʌldʒmənt], **divulgence** [dai'vʌldʒəns], *s.* divulgazione.

divulsion [dai'vʌlʃən], *s.* strappo, separazione violenta.

Dixie[1] ['diksi], *s.* (*amer.*) 1. gli Stati del Sud 2. canzone dei Confederati nella Guerra Civile Americana.

dixie[2], *s.* (*sl. mil.*) pentola di ferro.

Dixie Land ['diksi,lænd], *V.* **Dixie**.

dixy ['diksi], *s.* (*sl. mil.*) pentola di ferro.

to **dizen** ['daizn], *v.t.* (*rar.*): *to — out* (o *up*), vestire sfarzosamente.

dizzily ['dizili], *av.* vertiginosamente; da far venire il capogiro.

dizziness ['dizinis], *s.* vertigine; capogiro; stordimento.

dizzy ['dizi], *ag.* 1. vertiginoso: *a — height*, un'altezza vertiginosa 2. preso da vertigine; stordito; confuso: *to feel* —, sentirsi girar la testa.

to **dizzy**, *v.t.* dare le vertigini a; far venire il capogiro a; stordire.

Djakarta [dʒə'ka:tə], *no.pr.* (*geog.*) Giacarta.

do. ['ditou], *abbr.* di **ditto**.

do[1] [dou], *s.* (*mus.*) la nota « do ».

do[2] [du:], *s.* 1. (*sl.*) inganno 2. (*fam.*) trattenimento.

to **do** [du: (*forma forte*), də, d (*forme deboli*)], *pass.* **did** [did], *p.p.* **done** [dʌn], *v.t.i.* (3ª *persona sing. pres. indic.* **does** [dʌz (*forma forte*), dəz, dz (*forme deboli*)], (*arc. poet.*) **doth** [dʌθ], **doeth** ['du(:)iθ]; 2ª *persona sing. pres. indic.* (*arc. poet.*) **dost** [dʌst], **doest** ['du(:)ist]; 2ª *persona sing. pass.* (*arc. poet.*) **didst** [didst]) 1. verbo ausiliare (V): — *you speak English?*, parlate l'inglese?; — *you not* (o *don't you*) *speak Italian?*, non parlate l'italiano?; *does he never visit you?*, non viene mai a trovarvi?; *he does not* (o *doesn't*) *speak English*, non parla l'inglese; *she did not* (o *didn't*) *go*, ella non andò; *didn't you go?*, non andaste?; *what — you — in the evening?*, che cosa fate di sera?; *who does not love music?*, chi non ama la musica? *I — not have time to see my friends*, (*amer.*) non ho tempo per vedere i miei amici; *I — not have that book*, (*amer.*) non ho quel libro; *when — you have dinner?*, a che ora pranzate? ‖ — *not* (o *don't*) *speak to me!*, non parlarmi!; — *not be so impatient!*, non essere così impaziente!; *don't let him know that...*, che egli non sappia che... ‖ (*enfatico*): *I — love music!*, come amo la musica!; *I did see him!*, l'ho visto davvero!; — *come with us!*, su, venite con noi!; — *be kind to us!*, via, siate gentili con noi! ‖ (*sostitutivo*): *he said he would pay and he did*, disse che avrebbe pagato e pagò; *she sings better than he does*, ella canta meglio di lui; *who saw him?, I did*, chi lo vide?, io 2. fare (*in senso generale, astratto, morale, intellettuale*), agire; eseguire; compiere, effettuare: — *something to help him*, fate qualche cosa per aiutarlo; *he always does his duty*, fa sempre il suo dovere; *he has too much to* —, ha troppo da fare; *I have nothing to* —, non ho nulla da fare; *what are you doing?*, che cosa stai facendo?; *what does he* —?, che cosa fa, quale è il suo mestiere, la sua professione?; *what he did was done well*, ciò che fece fu fatto bene; *what is to be done?*, che fare? che cosa si deve fare?; *to — a thing, something, anything*, fare una cosa, qualche cosa, qualsiasi cosa; *to — nothing*, non fare nulla; *to — all one can*, fare il possibile; *to — some, any, one's work*, fare del, qualsiasi, il proprio lavoro ‖ *done!*, accettato!, fatto! ‖ *have done!*, smettetela! finitela! ‖ *how — you* —?, piacere (nelle presentazioni) ‖ *I bet you I* —, scommetto che ce la farò ‖ *I shall — or die*, o la va o la spacca ‖ (*it is*) *easier said than done*, è più facile dirlo che farlo ‖ *no sooner said than done*, detto fatto ‖ *nothing doing!*, niente da fare! ‖ *to — better*, far meglio; migliorare (in salute, nel lavoro, ecc.) ‖ *to — business*, fare affari ‖ *to — good*, fare del bene, giovare ‖ *to — harm*, fare del male, nuocere ‖ *to — homage*, rendere omaggio ‖ *to — honour*, fare onore ‖ *to — ill*, fare male ‖ *to — justice*, rendere giustizia ‖ *to — one's best*, fare del proprio meglio ‖ *to — one's bit*, (*fam.*) adempiere i propri doveri ‖ *to — one's worst*, agire nel modo peggiore: *let him — his worst!*, faccia pure quello che vuole! ‖ *let him — right*, fare, agire bene: *you did right to refuse* (o *in refusing*), faceste bene a rifiutare ‖ *to — s.o. a favour, a kindness*, fare un favore, una cortesia a qlcu. ‖ *to — s.o. a good, a bad turn*, fare una buona, una cattiva azione verso qlcu. ‖ *to — a sum, a translation*, fare una somma, una traduzione ‖ *to — well*, comportarsi bene; star bene (di salute); cavarsela; guadagnare bene; crescere, svilupparsi: *he does himself well*, egli si tratta bene; *he did very well in Australia*, guadagnò bene in Australia; *roses — well here*, le rose crescono bene qui; *they did us well at that hotel*, in quell'albergo ci hanno trattato bene ‖ *to — wonders*, fare miracoli ‖ *to — wrong*, fare, agire male; errare: *you did wrong to trust* (o *in trusting*) *him*, avete fatto màle a fidarvi di lui ‖ *to be done*, essere finito, terminato, compiuto ‖ *to have done*, (I) aver finito: *have you done reading the newspaper?*, avete finito di leggere il giornale? ‖ *to have to — with s.o., sthg.*, avere a che fare con qlcu., ql.co.: *what have I to —with that?*, che c'entro io? ‖ *when in Rome — as the Romans —, prov.* paese che vai, usanza che trovi **3. bastare:** *that will —*, basta così; *that won't —*, non basterà; *we shall make it —*, lo faremo bastare; *will a thousand liras —?*, basteranno mille lire? **4. convenire, addirsi, star bene:** *— you think this will —?*, credete che questo andrà bene?; *it doesn't —!*, non va!; *it does not — to eat too much*, non è bene mangiar troppo; *that would never —!*, questa è una cosa che non va assolutamente!; *this room will — me*, questa stanza mi va (mi conviene) **5. pulire, rassettare, ordinare, mettere in ordine:** *to — the beds*, rifare i letti; *to — one's hair*, pettinarsi; *to — (up) a room*, rassettare una stanza **6. viaggiare; fare, compiere** (un viaggio): *the car did fifty miles an hour*, l'automobile fece cinquanta miglia all'ora; *we did the journey in ten hours*, facemmo il viaggio in dieci ore **7.** (*fam.*) **visitare** (città, galleria, ecc.): *did you — the British Museum?*, hai visto il Museo Britannico?; *have you done Rome yet?*, avete già visitato Roma?; *to — the sights of a city*, andare a vedere le cose interessanti di una città **8. ingannare, truffare:** *they did me!*, mi hanno ingannato! **9. recitare:** *he did Hamlet very well*, ha recitato molto bene la parte di Amleto **10.** *to — by (s.o., sthg.)*, (*generalmente nel passivo*) agire verso, trattare: *he did very well by me*, mi ha trattato molto bene; *he was hard done by*, fu trattato molto male ‖ *unto others as you would be done by*, fate agli altri ciò che desiderate sia fatto a voi stessi **11.** *to — for (s.o., sthg.)*, arrangiarsi; (*fam.*) fare i mestieri di casa per; sostituire, servire da; (*sl.*) far fuori: *he can — for himself*, si arrangia da solo; *how did he — for food on the desert island?*, in che modo riuscì a nutrirsi sull'isola deserta?; *I shall — for him!*, lo accopperò!; *she does for the old man*, ella cura la casa per il vecchio ‖ *to be done for*, essere spacciato, rovinato: *these boots are done for*, queste scarpe| non servono più **12.** *to — with (s.o., sthg.)*, (*generalmente con can, could*) essere soddisfatto di, avere abbastanza di; sopportare; passar sopra a: *can you — with cold meat for supper?*, vi soddisfa, va bene della carne fredda per cena?; *I can't — with his insolent ways*, non posso sopportare i suoi modi insolenti ‖ *he could — with a wash!*, non gli farebbe male lavarsi! ‖ *to have done with s.o., sthg.*, non voler più saperne di qlcu., ql.co.: *I have done with him*, non voglio più saperne di lui **13.** *to — without (s.o., sthg.)*, fare a meno di: *I cannot — without her*, non posso fare a meno di lei; *there is no more sugar and so I shall have to — without*, non c'è più zucchero e così dovrò farne a meno **14.** *to — away with (s.o., sthg.)*, togliere di mezzo, abolire; uccidere **15.** *to — in*, (*sl.*) rovinare, uccidere **16.** *to — out*, pulire, vuotare ‖ *to — out of*, (*fam.*) privare di, togliere con inganno: *he did me out of my job*, mi ha portato via l'impiego **17.** *to — over*, ricoprire (con una nuova mano di pittura, ecc.); rifare, rimaneggiare **18.** *to — up*, far su, fare un pacco; allacciare, abbottonare, agganciare; acconciare, mettere in ordine; rimettere a nuovo: *— up these books, please*, favorite fare un pacco di questi libri; *the house needs doing up* (o *to be done up*), la casa ha bisogno di essere rimessa a nuovo; *please — up my dress*, agganciami il vestito, per piacere ‖ *to be done up*, (*fam.*) essere stanchissimo.

to doat, *V.* **to dote.**

docile ['dousail, (*amer.*) 'dɔsil], *ag.* docile; trattabile.

docility [dou'siliti], *s.* docilità; mansuetudine.

dock[1] [dɔk], *s.* **1.** (*mar.*) « dock », bacino: *to be in —*, (*fam.*) essere in riparazione; *to go into —*, (*mar.*)

entrare in bacino **2.** *pl.* « docks » (insieme dei bacini, magazzini e annessi nei grandi porti commerciali) **3.** (*ferr.*) piano caricatore; marciapiede terminale ☆ *— -dues*, diritti di banchina; *— gate*, chiusa; *— -master*, capitano di porto; direttore dei « docks »; *— -worker*, scaricatore di porto ‖ *dry —* (o *graving —*), bacino di carenaggio; *loading- —*, (*fam.*) imbarcadero.

to dock[1], *v.t.i.* (*mar.*) **1.** fornire di bacinl **2.** entrare in bacino, attraccare.

dock[2], *s.* banco degli imputati ☆ *— brief*, (*dir.*) patrocinio gratuito.

dock[3], *s.* **1.** mozzicone, troncone (generalmente di coda di cavallo o di cane) **2.** sottocoda (di cavallo).

to dock[3], *v.t.i.* **1.** mozzare (la coda di un animale) **2.** ridurre, diminuire: *to — s.o. of his food*, lesinare sul cibo di qlcu.

dock[4], *s.* (*bot.*) romice, lapazio.

dockage ['dɔkidʒ], *s.* diritti di porto, di banchina.

docker ['dɔkə*], *s.* scaricatore; stivatore.

docket ['dɔkit], *s.* **1.** (*dir.*) ruolo (di cause), registro di sentenze **2.** sommario (di incartamenti, documenti) **3.** ricevuta di pagamento di dogana **4.** etichetta, cartellino.

to docket, *v.t.* **1.** (*dir.*) iscrivere nel registro delle sentenze **2.** scrivere per sommi capi il contenuto di (incartamenti, documenti) **3.** classificare (carte).

to dockize ['dɔkaiz], *v.t.* fornire di bacino, di banchine (un fiume).

dockyard ['dɔkja:d], *s.* (*mar.*) arsenale, cantiere ☆ *naval —*, porto militare.

doctor ['dɔktə*], *s.* **1.** medico, dottore: *ship's —*, medico di bordo; *to see a —*, consultare un medico; *to send for a —*, chiamare un dottore **2.** dottore (laureato): *Doctor of Law, Divinity, Literature*, dottore in legge, teologia, letteratura ‖ *Dr. Johnson*, il dott. Johnson **3.** (*sl. mar.*) cuoco ☆ *woman —*, dottoressa in medicina.

to doctor, *v.t.* (*fam.*) **1.** curare; medicare; castrare (gatto) **2.** aggiustare (macchinario, ecc.) **3.** adulterare (cibo); fatturare (bevande); falsificare (documenti, testimonianze, ecc.) **4.** addottorare, conferire una laurea a.

doctoral ['dɔktərəl], *ag.* dottorale.

doctorate ['dɔktərit], *s.* dottorato.

doctorial [dɔk'tɔ:riəl], *ag.* dottorale.

doctoring ['dɔktəriŋ], *s.* **1.** cura **2.** (*fam.*) professione di medico.

doctorship ['dɔktəʃip], *s.* dottorato.

doctrinaire [‚dɔktri'nεə*], *s.* dottrinario.

doctrinal [dɔk'train], *ag.* dottrinale.

doctrinally [dɔk'trainəli], *av.* dottrinalmente.

doctrinarian [‚dɔktri'nεəriən], *s.* dottrinario.

doctrinarianism [‚dɔktri'nεəriənizəm], *s.* dottrinarismo.

doctrine ['dɔktrin], *s.* dottrina.

document ['dɔkjumənt], *s.* documento; certificato; attestato: *cash against documents*, (*comm.*) pagamento a contanti contro documenti; *legal —*, atto autentico ☆ *— case*, borsa da avvocato.

to document ['dɔkjument], *v.t.* documentare.

documentary [‚dɔkju'mεntəri], *ag.* documentario ‖ *s.* (*cine.*) documentario ☆ *— credit*, (*comm.*) credito documentario; *— film*, (*cine.*) documentario.

documentation [‚dɔkjumen'teiʃən], *s.* documentazione ☆ *— office*, ufficio di documentazione.

dodder[1] ['dɔdə*], *s.* (*bot.*) cuscuta.

to dodder[2], *v.i.* **1.** tremare (per paralisi); vacillare, barcollare (per senilità) **2.** *to — along*, avanzare a tentoni.

doddered ['dɔdəd], *ag.* senza cima o rami (di alberi).

dodderer ['dɔdərə*], *s.* (*fam.*) vecchio cadente, debole, infermo.

doddery ['dɔdəri], *ag.* (*fam.*) tremante, barcollante.

dodecagon [dou'dekəgɔn], *s.* (*geom.*) dodecagono.

dodecahedron ['doudikə'hedrən], *s.* (*geom.*) dodecaedro.

Dodecanese (the) [ˌdoudikəˈniːz], *no.pr.* (*geog.*) Dodecaneso.

dodge [dɔdʒ], *s.* **1.** balzo, scarto improvviso; deviamento brusco **2.** (*sl.*) stratagemma; accorgimento; astuzia; inganno.

to dodge, *v.t.i.* **1.** scartare; scansare, scansarsi; deviare bruscamente: *to — the traffic*, scansare il traffico ǁ *to — about, in and out*, saltellare, saltare in qua e in là (per evitare ql.co.) ǁ *to — aside*, balzare di fianco ǁ *to — behind*, rimpiattarsi dietro **2.** *fig.* sfuggire; schivare; eludere: *to — the law*, eludere la legge; *to — military service*, farsi riformare **3.** ingannare, abbindolare; giocare.

dodger [ˈdɔdʒə*], *s.* **1.** (*fam.*) furbacchione; sornione **2.** (*amer.*) volantino reclamistico **3.** (*amer.*) focaccia di farina di granturco **4.** (*mar.*) riparo contro gli spruzzi sul ponte di una nave.

dodgy [ˈdɔdʒi], *ag.* elusivo; evasivo; ingannevole.

dodo [ˈdoudou], *s.* **1.** (*ornit.*) dronte **2.** *fig.* persona antiquata, vecchio fossile: *as old as the —*, vecchio come il cucco.

doe [dou], *s.* (*zool.*) **1.** daina **2.** femmina della lepre, del coniglio ☆ *— -skin*, pelle di daino, antilope, ecc.; tessuto di lana finissimo.

doer [ˈduː(ː)ə*], *s.c.* chi agisce, chi fa: *he is a —, not a talker*, egli non parla, agisce ☆ *evil- —*, malfattore.

does [dʌz (*forma forte*), dəz, dz (*forme deboli*)], **doest** [ˈduː(ː)ist], **doeth** [ˈduː(ː)iθ], *V.* **to do**.

to doff [dɔf], *v.t.* **1.** (*arc.*) cavare, togliersi (cappello, giacca) **2.** (*rar.*) abbandonare (abitudine, condizione) **3.** (*ind. tessile*) levare (le spole dai torcitori).

doffer [ˈdɔfə*], *s.* (*ind. tessile*) cilindro scaricatore.

dog [dɔg], *s.* **1.** cane ǁ *a — in the manger*, uno che impedisce agli altri di godere ciò che a lui non serve ǁ *a —'s chance*, (*fam.*) pochissima probabilità ǁ *the dogs of war*, (*poet.*) sterminio ǁ *the —'s letter*, la lettera «r» ǁ *the Greater, Lesser Dog*, (*astr.*) il Cane Maggiore, Minore ǁ *love me, love my —*, porta rispetto al cane per amore del padrone ǁ *to die a —'s death*, morire come un cane, una bestia ǁ *to give, to throw to the dogs*, gettare via ǁ *to go to the dogs*, (*fam.*) andare in malora ǁ *to help a lame — over a stile*, aiutare qlcu. che si trova in difficoltà ǁ *to lead, to live a —'s life*, fare una vita da cani ǁ *to lead. s.o. a —'s life*, perseguitare, tormentare qlcu., far fare a qlcu. una vita da cani ǁ *to put on (the) —*, (*sl. amer.*) darsi delle arie ǁ *to rain cats and dogs*, (*fam.*) piovere a dirotto ǁ *to throw discretion to the dogs*, mettere da parte ogni discrezione ǁ *every — has his day*, *prov.* ognuno ha il suo raggio di sole ǁ *let sleeping dogs lie*, *prov.* non svegliare il cane che dorme ǁ *a living — is better than a dead lion*, *prov.* meglio un asino vivo che un dottore morto **2.** maschio di certi animali **3.** (*sl.*) individuo, uomo; uomo indegno: *sly, lucky, gay —*, individuo furbo, fortunato, libertino ǁ *you —!*, cane! **4.** (*mec.*) gancio; rampone; grappa; dente d'arresto; tirante ☆ *— -berry*, (*bot.*) corniola; *— -cart*, calesse; *— -cheap*, molto a buon mercato; *— -collar*, collare per cani; (*sl.*) collarino (dei preti); *— -days*, giorni della canicola; *— -eared*, con orecchie alle pagine; *— -faced*, dal muso di cane; *— -fancier*, chi ama, si interessa di cani; *— -fight*, combattimento di cani; (*aer.*) combattimento accanito (generalmente tra caccia); *— -fox*, maschio della volpe; *— -headed*, cinocefalo; *— -kennel*, canile; *— -Latin*, latino maccheronico; *— -like*, simile ad un cane: *— -like devotion*, fedeltà simile a quella di un cane; *—'s -nose*, (*fam.*) bevanda di birra e gin; *— -racing*, corse di levrieri; *— -tired*, stanco morto; *— -violet*, viola canina; *— -weary*, stanco morto ǁ *fire-dogs*, alari; *hot —*, (*amer.*) panino con salsiccia; *house- —*, (*o watch- —*), cane da guardia; *lap- —*, cagnolino da salotto (di lusso); *sausage- —*, (*sl.*) cane bassotto; *sheep- —*, cane pastore; *sporting- —* (o *hunting- —*), cane da caccia; *top —*, (*fam.*) persona autorevole.

to dog, *pass.p.p.* **dogged** [dɔgd], *v.t.* **1.** seguire; pedinare; spiare: *to — s.o.'s footsteps*, pedinare qlcu. **2.** *fig.* perseguitare: *in the whole course of his life my grandfather was dogged by misfortune*, durante tutta la sua vita mio nonno fu perseguitato dalla sfortuna.

dogate [ˈdougeit], *s.* (*st.*) dogato.

dogbane [ˈdɔgbein], *s.* (*bot.*) apocinea, apocino canapino.

doge [doudʒ], *s.* (*st.*) doge: *—'s wife*, dogaressa.

dog-ear [ˈdɔgiə*] *s.* orecchia (alle pagine di un libro).

to dog-ear, *v.t.* fare le orecchie a (pagine di un libro, ecc.).

dogface [ˈdɔgfeis], *s.* (*sl. amer.*) fantaccino.

dogfish [ˈdɔgfiʃ], *s.* specie di pescecane; piccolo squalo.

dogged [ˈdɔgid], *ag.* ostinato; risoluto; tenace: *— resistance*, tenace resistenza.

doggedly [ˈdɔgidli], *av.* ostinatamente; tenacemente: *to work —*, lavorare senza posa.

doggedness [ˈdɔgidnis], *s.* ostinazione; tenacia; perseveranza.

dogger [ˈdɔgə*], *s.* (*mar.*) dogre.

doggerel [ˈdɔgərəl], *ag.* (*poet.*) pedestre, mediocre; imperfetto ǁ *s.* filastrocca; (*spreg.*) chitarronata.

doggie [ˈdɔgi], *s.* cagnolino (nel linguaggio infantile).

doggish [ˈdɔgiʃ], *ag.* da cane; cagnesco; ringhioso; brutale.

doggishly [ˈdɔgiʃli], *av.* brutalmente; ostilmente.

doggishness [ˈdɔgiʃnis], *s.* brutalità, sgarbatezza; ostilità.

doggo [ˈdɔgou], *av.*: *to lie —*, (*sl.*) fare il morto.

doggy [ˈdɔgi], *ag.* **1.** cagnesco, di cane **2.** (*fam.*) amante, conoscitore di cani **3.** (*fam.*) pretenzioso, azzimato ǁ *s.* cagnolino (nel linguaggio infantile).

dogma [ˈdɔgmə] *s.* dogma.

dogmatic [dɔgˈmætik], *ag.* dogmatico.

dogmatically [dɔgˈmætikəli], *av.* dogmaticamente.

dogmatics [dɔgˈmætiks], *s.* dogmatica.

dogmatism [ˈdɔgmətizəm], *s.* dogmatismo.

dogmatist [ˈdɔgmətist], *s.* dogmatista.

to dogmatize [ˈdɔgmətaiz], *v.i.* dogmatizzare.

do-gooder [ˈduːˈgudə*], *s.* (*iron. spreg.*) benefattore.

dogrose [ˈdɔg-rouz], *s.* rosa canina.

dogtooth [ˈdɔgtuːθ], *pl.* **dogteeth** [ˈdɔgtiːθ], *s.* **1.** dente canino **2.** ornamento architettonico medioevale a forma di piramide.

dog-watch [ˈdɔgwɔtʃ], *s.* (*mar.*) gaettone (turno di guardia).

dogwood [ˈdɔgwud], *s.* (*bot.*) corniolo.

doily [ˈdɔili], *s.* tovagliolino; sottocoppa.

doing [ˈduː(ː)iŋ], *s.* **1.** fare: *it is his —*, è opera, colpa sua; *that wants some —*, ce ne vuole per (riuscire a) fare ciò ǁ *there is great difference between — and saying*, c'è una bella differenza tra il dire e il fare **2.** *pl.* azioni, eventi, fatti, vicende; occupazione; attività: *the day's doings*, le occupazioni giornaliere; *tell me about your doings in America*, dimmi che cosa hai fatto in America **3.** *to give s.o. a —*, (*fam.*) fare una ramanzina a qlcu.

doit [dɔit], *s.* **1.** (*arc.*) piccola moneta olandese **2.** *fig.* nonnulla: *I don't care a —*, non m'importa un bel niente.

doldrums [ˈdɔldrəmz], *s.pl.* (*mar.*) zona delle calme equatoriali; *fig.* abbattimento, depressione: *to be in the —*, essere nella zona delle calme (di nave); essere di umor nero.

dole[1] [doul], *s.* **1.** sussidio, elemosina, dono caritatevole ǁ *to be on the —*, essere disoccupato; *to go on the —*, ricevere il sussidio di disoccupazione **2.** distribuzione (di sussidi, elemosina, ecc.) **3.** (*arc.*) parte; sorte ☆ *— unemployment*, sussidio di disoccupazione.

to dole[1], *v.t.* **1.** distribuire; dare in elemosina **2.** *to — out*, ripartire, distribuire con parsimonia.

dole[2], *s.* (*arc.*) duolo, dolore: *to make —*, lamentarsi.

dole[3], *s.* **1.** (*dir. scoz.*) dolo **2.** (*rar.*) inganno, frode.

doleful ['doulful], *ag.* triste; doloroso; afflitto.

dolefully ['doulfuli], *av.* tristemente; dolorosamente.

dolefulness ['doulfulnis], *s.* 1. tristezza; dolore 2. aspetto misero; carattere melanconico, deprimente.

dolichocephalic ['dolikouke'fælik], *ag.* (*anat.*) dolicocefalo.

dolina [do'li:na:], *s.* (*geol.*) dolina.

Doll[1] [dol], *no.pr.f.* dim. di **Dorothea.**

doll[2], *s.* 1. bambola, pupattola: *she has a face like a —*, ha un viso da bambola 2. (*sl. amer.*) ragazza; studentessa ☆ *— 's-house,* casa di bambola || *stuffed —,* bambola di pezza.

to doll[2], *v.t.i.* (*sl.*) vestire, vestirsi in modo lezioso, infantile: *to — oneself up,* agghindarsi.

dollar ['dolə*], *s.* 1. dollaro: *to worship the almighty —,* (*fam.*) divinizzare il denaro 2. (*sl.*) corona inglese ☆ *— area,* (*neol. econ.*) area del dollaro; *— diplomacy,* (*econ.*) politica a base di penetrazione economica; *— gap,* (*econ.*) deficit nella copertura in dollari; *— king,* riccone, finanziere americano; *— mark ($),* simbolo del dollaro; *— store,* magazzino al prezzo unico di un dollaro || *— half —,* mezzo dollaro.

dollop ['doləp], *s.* (*sl.*) pezzetto informe di cibo: *she put a — of butter on my bread,* ella mise un pezzo di burro sulla mia fetta di pane.

Dolly[1] [doli], *no.pr.f.* dim. di **Dorothea** ☆ *— Varden,* abito di mussola a fiori; cappello ornato di fiori; *— -bag,* borsa con cordoni.

dolly[2], *s.* 1. bambola (nel linguaggio infantile) 2. (*mec.*) mescolatore, controstampo 3. (*ind.*) curro, rullo; (*ferr.*) locomotore, locomotiva a scartamento ridotto; (*cine. tv.*) carrello, piattaforma mobile 4. pala da bucato ☆ *— -block,* (*metal.*) tassello; *— -pusher,* (*tv.*) carrellista; *— -shop,* (*mar. sl.*) bottega per forniture di marina (spesso serve da agenzia per prestiti su pegno); *— tub,* tinozza (da bucato, per lavaggio di minerali).

dolman ['dolmən], *s.* 1. « dolman » (lunga tunica usata dai Turchi) 2. « dolman » (cappa da signora, da ufficiale).

dolmen ['dolmen], *s.* (*archeol.*) dolmen.

dolomite ['doləmait], *s.* (*min.*) dolomite || *the Dolomites,* (*geog.*) le Dolomiti.

dolomitic [,dolə'mitik], *ag.* (*min.*) dolomitico.

dolor, (*amer.*) per **dolour.**

dolorous ['dolərəs], *ag.* (*poet. scherz.*) doloroso.

dolorously ['dolərəsli], *av.* dolorosamente.

dolose [dou'lous], *ag.* (*dir.*) doloso.

dolour ['doulə*], *s.* (*poet.*) dolore; tristezza; angoscia.

dolphin ['dolfin], *s.* 1. (*zool.*) delfino 2. (*ittiol.*) corifena 3. (*mar.*) boa di ormeggio ☆ *— mooring post,* (*mar.*) colonna d'alaggio; *— -striker,* (*mar.*) pennaccino.

dolt [doult], *s.* balordo; stupido; stolto.

doltish ['doultiʃ], *ag.* balordo; stupido; ottuso.

doltishness ['doultiʃnis], *s.* balordaggine; stupidità.

Dom [dom], *s.* (*titolo*) don.

domain [do'mein], *s.* 1. dominio; proprietà terriera 2. *fig.* dominio; sfera; campo; settore: *in the — of science,* nel campo della scienza.

domanial [do'meiniəl], *ag.* (*dir.*) demaniale.

dome [doum], *s.* 1. cupola; volta (anche *fig.*): *the — of heaven,* la volta celeste 2. (*poet.*) palazzo; casa padronale 3. (*mec. metal.*) duomo ☆ *— -lamp* (o *— -light*), lampadario; *— -shaped,* a forma di cupola.

domed [doumd], *ag.* a cupola.

Domesday (Book) ['du:mzdei (buk)], *s.* (*st.*) il grande Libro del Catasto d'Inghilterra (fatto compilare da Guglielmo il Conquistatore, 1086).

domestic [də'mestik], *ag.* 1. domestico, della casa, di famiglia: *— animal,* animale domestico; *— life,* vita di famiglia, di casa 2. interno, nazionale || *s.c.* domestico, domestica ☆ *— agency,* agenzia di collocamento per la servitù; *— commerce,* *— goods,* commercio, mercanzia nazionale; *— loan,* prestito interno; *— news,* notizie dall'interno; *— servant,* domestico, domestica; *— war,* guerra intestina.

domesticable [də'mestikəbl], *ag.* addomesticabile.

domestically [də'mestikəli], *av.* domesticamente.

to domesticate [də'mestikeit], *v.t.* 1. addomesticare; acclimatare: *animal that can be domesticated,* animale che può essere addomesticato 2. abituare alla vita di casa 3. civilizzare.

domestication [də,mesti'keiʃən], *s.* 1. addomesticamento; acclimatazione 2. attaccamento alla vita familiare 3. civilizzazione.

domesticity [,doumes'tisiti], *s.* 1. amore per il focolare domestico 2. *gener. pl.* lavori, doveri riguardanti la casa.

domett [dou'met], *s.* sorta di tessuto misto di lana e cotone.

domicile ['domisail], *s.* (*dir. comm.*) domicilio: *to elect — at a place,* eleggere il proprio domicilio in un luogo.

to domicile, *v.t.i.* 1. (*comm.*) domiciliare (un effetto): *bills domiciled in London,* effetti pagabili a Londra 2. stabilirsi, fissare domicilio, domiciliarsi; risiedere: *domiciled at Chester,* domiciliato a Chester.

domiciliary [,domi'siljəri], *ag.* domiciliare (visita, perquisizione).

to domiciliate [,domi'siljeit], *V.* to **domicile.**

domiciliation [,domisili'eiʃən], *s.* (*comm.*) dichiarazione di domicilio (per pagamento di effetti).

dominance ['dominəns], **dominancy** ['dominənsi], *s.* ascendente; predominio.

dominant ['dominənt], *ag.* dominante.

dominantly ['dominəntli], *av.* in modo dominante.

to dominate ['domineit], *v.t.i.* 1. dominare; prevalere; reggere: *to — (over) a people,* dominare un popolo 2. dominare, sovrastare: *the Alps — (over) the plain,* le Alpi sovrastano la pianura.

domination [,domi'neiʃən], *s.* 1. dominazione, dominio; ascendente 2. *pl.* (*teol.*) Dominazioni.

dominative ['domineitiv], *ag.* dominante; prevalente.

dominator ['domineitə*], *s.c.* dominatore, dominatrice.

to domineer [,domi'niə*], *v.i.* signoreggiare; fare il tiranno || *to — over s.o.,* tiranneggiare qlcu.

domineering [,domi'niəriŋ], *ag.* dispotico; autoritario; imperioso; prepotente.

domineeringly [,domi'niəriŋli], *av.* imperiosamente; con autorità; con prepotenza; con arroganza.

Dominic ['dominik], *no.pr.m.* Domenico.

dominical [də'minikəl], *ag.* (*eccl.*) domenicale; del Signore ☆ *the Dominical year,* il primo anno di Nostro Signore.

Dominican [də'minikən], *ag.* (*eccl.*) domenicano || *the — Republic,* la Repubblica Dominicana || *s.* (*eccl.*) domenicano.

dominie ['domini], *s.* (*scoz.*) pedagogo, maestro di scuola.

dominion [də'minjən], *s.* 1. dominio; impero; ascendente; autorità: *to be under s.o.'s —,* essere sottomesso a qlcu.; *to hold — over s.o.,* dominare qlcu. 2. « dominion » (paese autonomo membro del Commonwealth Britannico) || *the Dominion of Canada,* il Canada; *the Old Dominion,* (*amer.*) la Virginia 3. *pl.* (*teol.*) Dominazioni 4. (*dir.*) dominio.

domino ['dominou], *pl.* **dominoes** ['dominouz], *s.* 1. domino 2. persona che indossa il domino 3. *pl.* (giuoco del) domino 4. *pl.* (*sl.*) denti.

dominoed ['dominoud], *ag.* in domino (da ballo).

Domitian [də'miʃjən], *no.pr.m.* (*st.*) Domiziano.

don[1] [don], *s.* 1. don || *a Don Juan,* (*fam.*) un dongiovanni 2. membro di un collegio universitario (inglese); docente universitario 3. (*fam.*) asso, campione: *he is a great — at tennis,* è un asso del tennis.

to don[2], *pass.p.p.* **donned** [dond], *v.t.* indossare (divisa, ecc.): *to — the buskin,* (*letter.*) calzare il coturno.

dona(h) ['dounə], *s.* (*sl.*) donna; innamorata.

Donald ['donld], *n.pr.m.* Donaldo.

to donate [dou'neit], *v.t.* **1.** donare, elargire: *to —s.o. with sthg.*, fare dono di ql.co. a qlcu. **2.** (*med.*) donare (sangue).

donation [dou'neiʃən], *s.* donazione, dono, elargizione.

donative ['dounətiv], *s.* dono, donazione; donativo.

donator [dou'neitə*], *s.* (*dir.*) donatore.

donatory ['dounətəri], *s.* (*dir.*) donatario.

donatress [dou'neitris], *s.* (*dir.*) donatrice.

Donatus [dou'neitəs], *no.pr.m.* Donato.

done [dʌn], *pp.* di **to do** ‖ *ag.* cotto ☆ — *brown*, (*fam.*) ben cotto: *the fowls were — brown*, i polli furono ben rosolati ‖ *over-* —, troppo cotto; *under-* —, poco cotto.

donee [dou'ni:], *s.* (*dir.*) donatario.

donga ['dongə], *s.* crepaccio (in Sudafrica).

donjon ['dondʒən], *s.* (*archeol.*) dongione.

donkey ['donki], *s.* **1.** asino, ciuco, somaro **2.** (*fig. fam.*) asino, imbecille ☆ — *boiler*, caldaia ausiliaria, calderina; — *boy*, asinaio; — *-engine*, motore ausiliario; locomotiva di manovra; — *-pump*, (*mec.*) cavallino; — *race*, corsa degli asini.

donnish ['doniʃ], *ag.* pedantesco.

donor ['dounə*], *s.c.* **1.** (*dir.*) donatore, donatrice **2.** (*med.*) donatore, donatrice (di sangue).

don't [dount], *V.* **to do**.

doodle[1] ['du:dl], *s.* ghirigoro.

to doodle[1], *v.t.i.* fare ghirigori.

to doodle[2], *v.i.* (*scoz.*) suonare la cornamusa.

doodlebug ['du:dlbʌg], *s.* **1.** (*amer. entom.*) larva di formicaleone **2.** (*fam.*) bomba volante (a reazione e giroguidata) **3.** pendolo, pendolino (da radioestesista), bacchetta da rabdomante.

doolie, dooly ['du:li], *s.* lettiga per il trasporto di malati, feriti (in India).

doom [du:m], *s.* **1.** destino (funesto), sorte (triste): *he met his* —, ha trovato la morte **2.** perdita, rovina, distruzione; condanna: *his — is sealed*, il suo destino è segnato **3.** *the crack of* —, l'ultimo giudizio; *the day of* —, il giorno del Giudizio.

to doom, *v.t.* (*letter.*) condannare: *doomed town, man*, città votata alla distruzione, uomo perduto.

doomsday ['du:mzdei], *s.* **1.** (il giorno del) Giudizio Universale: *from now till* —, per sempre **2.** *Doomsday book*, *V.* **Domesday (Book)**.

door [do:*], *s.* **1.** porta, uscio: *the — opened, was opened*, la porta si aprì, venne aperta; *to close the — upon s.o.*, chiudere la porta in faccia a qlcu.; *to open, to close, to shut a* —, aprire, chiudere una porta ‖ *at death's* —, sulla soglia della morte ‖ *out of doors*, all'aperto ‖ *two, three doors off*, a due, tre porte di distanza ‖ *within doors*, in casa ‖ *to lay sthg. at s.o.'s* —, incolpare qlcu. di ql.co. ‖ *to open the — to*, *fig.* lasciare la porta aperta a ‖ *to show s.o. the* — (o *turn s.o. out of doors*), mettere qlcu. alla porta ‖ *to show s.o. to the* —, accompagnare qlcu. alla porta ‖ *to shut the — upon*, *fig.* rendere impossibile **2.** sportello, portiera (di vettura, ecc.) ☆ — *-bell*, campanello della porta; — *-case* (o — *frame*), telaio della porta; — *-keeper*, portinaio; — *-knocker*, battente; — *-man* (o — *porter*), portiere; — *-mat*, zerbino; — *-money*, (spesa di) ingresso; — *-plate*, targa sulla porta; — *-post*, stipite; — *-scraper*, raschietto per togliere il fango; — *-step*, gradino della porta; — *-way*, arco di porta ‖ *back-* —, porta posteriore; *black-* —, ospitalità negata; *folding-* —, porta a (due) battenti; *front* —, porta principale; *next-* —, porta, casa accanto; *revolving* —, porta girevole; *side-* —, porta laterale; *sliding* —, porta scorrevole.

doornail ['do:neil], *s.* borchia su porta ‖ (*as*) *dead as a* —, (*fam.*) morto stecchito.

dope [doup], *s.* **1.** lubrificante **2.** lacca, vernice (per aerei, veicoli) **3.** materiale assorbente (per esplosivi) **4.** narcotico, stupefacente; stimolante (somministrato a cavallo, cane per eccitarlo alla corsa) **5.** (*sl. amer.*) informazione segreta, previsione (ge-

neralmente sull'andamento probabile delle corse); falsa informazione: *to hand out the* —, far circolare notizie false ☆ — *-fiend*, morfinomane.

to dope, *v.t.* **1.** indurire con sostanza viscosa; laccare; verniciare **2.** (*sl.*) narcotizzare; mescolare narcotici a (bevande); drogare, somministrare stimolanti a (cavallo, cane da corsa) **3.** *to — out*, (*sl. amer.*) indovinare (il risultato di una corsa, ecc.): *he knew how to — out the winning horse*, sapeva indovinare quale sarebbe stato il cavallo vincitore.

doping ['doupiŋ], *s.* **1.** verniciatura **2.** il narcotizzare.

dopy ['doupi], *ag.* (*sl.*) inebetito (da narcotico).

dor [do:*], *s.* (*entom.*) **1.** calabrone **2.** geotrupe.

Dora ['do:rə], *no.pr.f.* Dora.

dorado [də'ra:dou], *s.* (*ittiol.*) corifena.

Dorian ['do:riən], *ag.* dorico ‖ *s.c.* abitante della Doride.

Doric ['dorik], *ag.s.* (dialetto) dorico.

dormant ['do:mənt], *ag.* **1.** addormentato; assopito (di passione, ecc.); inattivo (di vulcano); ibernante: *to lie* —, essere assopito; (*comm.*) stare inattivo **2.** caduto in disuso ☆ — *-law*, legge non applicabile; — *partner*, (*comm.*) socio occulto.

dormer ['do:mə*], *s.* — (*-window*), (*arc.*) abbaino.

dormitory ['do:mitri], *s.* **1.** dormitorio **2.** (*fam.*) i sobborghi di una metropoli **3.** (*amer.*) casa, alloggio per studenti.

dormouse ['do:maus], *pl.* **dormice** ['do:mais], *s.* (*zool.*) ghiro.

Dorothea [,dorə'θiə], **Dorothy** ['dorəθi], *no.pr.f.* Dorotea.

dorsal ['do:səl], *ag.* dorsale, del dorso.

dory[1] ['do:ri], *s.* pesce San Pietro.

dory[2], *s.* (*spec. amer.*) piccola barca da pesca a remi, a fondo piatto.

dosage ['dousidʒ], *s.* dosaggio, dosatura.

dose [dous], *s.* (*farm.*) dose: *to strengthen the* —, *fig.* rincarare la dose.

to dose, *v.t.* **1.** dosare (una medicina), somministrare a dosi ‖ *to — out a medicine to s.o.*, somministrare una medicina a qlcu. a piccole dosi **2.** adulterare (bevande); mescolare.

doss [dos], *s.* (*sl.*) letto (in dormitorio pubblico) ☆ — *-house*, dormitorio pubblico.

to doss, *v.i.* (*sl.*) dormire in un dormitorio pubblico.

dossal ['dosəl], *s.* dossale.

dossier ['dosiei], *s.* « dossier », incartamento.

dost [dʌst], *s.* « dost », incartamento.

dot[1] [dot], *s.* **1.** punto; puntino (di sospensione, sulla lettera i): *dots*, puntini puntini; *dots and dashes*, (*tel.*) punti e linee ‖ *he got there on the* —, (*fam.*) ci arrivò proprio in orario; *to be off one's dots*, essere un po' tocco, picchiatello **2.** (*mus.*) punto **3.** (*fam.*) bambinello, pupo.

to dot[1], *pass.p.p.* **dotted** ['dotid], *v.t.* **1.** mettere un punto sopra (la lettera i) ‖ *to — one's i's and cross one's t's*, mettere i puntini sugli i **2.** punteggiare: *dotted with*, punteggiato, cosparso, seminato di; *sign on the dotted line*, firmate sulla riga punteggiata; *fig.* acconsentite senza discutere **3.** (*mus.*) punteggiare.

dot[2], *s.* (*dir.*) dote.

dotage ['doutidʒ], *s.* **1.** rimbambimento: *he is in his* —, è un vecchio rimbambito **2.** infatuazione.

dotal ['doutl], *ag.* dotale, della dote.

dotard ['doutəd], *s.* vecchio rimbambito.

to dote [dout], *v.i.* **1.** essere rimbambito; essere stupido **2.** *to — (up)on s.o.*, amare qlcu. alla follia, adorare qlcu.; avere una mania per qlcu. ‖ *a doting mother*, una madre che adora i suoi figli (e li vizia).

doth [dʌθ], *V.* **to do**.

dotterel ['dotrəl], *s.* (*ornit.*) piviere tortolino.

dottle ['dotl], *s.* residuo di tabacco non fumato rimasto nella pipa.

dottrel ['dotrəl], *s.* (*ornit.*) piviere tortolino.

dotty ['doti], *ag.* **1.** punteggiato **2.** (*sl.*) tocco; rimbambito **3.** malfermo, traballante: *to be — on one's legs*, traballare, essere malsicuro sulle gambe.

double ['dʌbl], *ag.* **1.** doppio: *— knock*, due colpi (alla porta); *— whiskey*, doppio whiskey; *— work*, doppio lavoro ‖ *to run in — harness*, *(fam.)* essere sposato ‖ *to speak — Dutch*, *(fam.)* parlare confusamente **2.** doppio, messo a doppio: *to be bent —*, essere piegato in due **3.** doppio, due volte tanto: *I am — your age*, ho il doppio della tua età; *to pay —*, pagare il doppio (del valore) **4.** doppio, falso, ambiguo: *to play a — game*, fare il doppio giuoco **5.** *(tel.)* doppio: *dial seven- six- — seven*, chiama il 7677.

double, *s.* **1.** doppio: *twenty is the — of ten*, venti è il doppio di dieci ‖ *— or quits*, *(giuoco)* raddoppiare la posta o andare pari **2.** sosia; *(cine.)* controfigura **3.** *(tennis)* doppio: *men's, women's, mixed —*, doppio maschile, femminile, misto.

double, *av.* **1.** doppiamente, due volte tanto: *— as long as*, due volte più lungo di; *to be — as dear*, essere doppiamente caro; *to see —*, vedere doppio **2.** in due, a coppia: *to sleep, to ride —*, dormire in due, montare un cavallo in due.

to double, *v.t.i.* **1.** raddoppiare, moltiplicare per due ‖ *to — parts*, sostenere due ruoli (in un lavoro teatrale) **2.** *(mar.)* doppiare (un capo, ecc.) **3.** voltarsi; cambiare bruscamente direzione (di fiume, di lepre in corsa, ecc.) **4.** piegare in due: *to — one's fist*, piegare, stringere con forza il pugno (per combattere) **5.** *(mil.)* marciare a passo di carica **6.** *(cine.)* doppiare **7.** *to — back*, ripiegare; ritornare sui propri passi **8.** *to — down*, fare le orecchie a (una pagina) **9.** *to — up*, piegare, piegarsi (in due): *to — up with pain, laughter*, contorcersi dal dolore, dalle risa.

double, *(nei composti)*: *— -acting* (o *-action)*, *(mec.)* a doppia azione, a doppio effetto; *— -banked*, a doppio ordine di remi; *— -barrelled*, a doppia canna; doppio (di cognome); *fig.* ambiguo; *— -bass*, contrabbasso; *— -bedded*, a due letti; *— -breasted*, a doppio petto; *— -chin*, doppio mento, pappagorgia; *— -dealer*, *fig.* ingannatore; *— -dealing*, *fig.* inganno, duplicità; *— -decker*, *(mar.)* nave a due ponti; autobus, tram a due piani; *— -dyed*, tinto due volte; *fig.* matricolato: *— -dyed scoundrel*, furfante matricolato; *— -eagle*, *(amer.)* pezzo da venti dollari, aquila bifronte; *— -edged*, a doppio taglio (anche *fig.*); *— -entry*, *(comm.)* partita doppia; *— -faced*, *fig.* ipocrita; a due facce (di stoffa); *— -ganger*, spettro, fantasma; *— -geared*, *(mec.)* a doppio ingranaggio; *— -headed*, a due teste; *— -jointed*, snodato; *— march*, *(mil.)* passo di corsa: *— march!*, di corsa!; *— -meaning*, (a) doppio senso; *— -piston*, *(mec.)* stantuffo a doppio effetto; *— -pitch*, *(arch.)* a due falde; *— -quick*, (a) passo di carica; *— shaping machine*, *(mec.)* limatrice doppia.

double-cross ['dʌbl'krɔs], *s.* doppio giuoco.

to double-cross, *v.t.* *(sl.)* ingannare (i propri compagni); fare il doppio giuoco con (due parti in lotta).

double-lock ['dʌbl'lɔk], *s.* serratura doppia.

to double-lock, *v.t.* chiudere a doppia mandata.

doubleness ['dʌblnis], *s.* doppiezza; duplicità.

doubler ['dʌblə*], *s.* **1.** *(ind. tessile)* binatrice; addoppiatrice **2.** *(elett. rad.)* duplicatore.

doublet ['dʌblit], *s.* **1.** giubba, farsetto **2.** *(filologia)* allotropo **3.** *pl. (dadi)* doppioni **4.** *(fis.)* doppietto; *(ott.)* obiettivo doppio; sistema di due lenti **5.** *(rad.)* dipolo.

doubloon [dʌb'lu:n], *s.* *(arc.)* doblone (moneta spagnola).

doubly ['dʌbli], *av.* doppiamente ‖ *— so as*, tanto più che.

doubt [daut], *s.* dubbio, incertezza: *there is no — about it*, non c'è dubbio quanto a questo; *there is no room for —*, non c'è ragione di mettere in dubbio; *to have one's doubts about* (o *as to*) *sthg.*, avere, nutrire dubbi in merito a qlcu.; *to make no — of, that*, essere certo di, che; *to raise doubts*, sollevare dei dubbi ‖ *beyond (any) —*, certamente; *no —*, senza dubbio;

without (any) —, senza (alcun) dubbio ‖ *the benefit of the —*, *(dir.)* il beneficio del dubbio.

to doubt, *v.t.i.* dubitare, mettere in dubbio; esitare a credere; sospettare: *he doubted no more*, non dubitò più, non esitò più; *I — it*, ne dubito; *I do not — that he will come*, non dubito, sono sicuro che verrà; *to — one's eyes*, non credere ai propri occhi; *to — s.o., s.o.'s word*, dubitare di qlcu., della parola di qlcu.; *to — the truth of*, dubitare della verità di; *to — whether, that*, dubitare che.

doubtable ['dautəbl], *ag.* dubitabile.

doubter ['dautə*], *s.c.* persona dubbiosa; scettico, scettica.

doubtful ['dautful], *ag.* **1.** incerto, dubbio: *— result*, esito incerto; *in — taste*, di dubbio gusto; *he has a — character*, ha una dubbia reputazione **2.** dubbioso; esitante, irresoluto: *I am — (as to) what to do*, sono in dubbio sul da farsi.

doubtfully ['dautfuli], *av.* dubbiosamente.

doubtfulness ['dautfulnis], *s.* **1.** dubbiosità **2.** irresolutezza.

doubtless ['dautlis], *ag.* indubbio; certo; probabile.

doubtless, *av.* senza alcun dubbio, molto probabilmente.

doubtlessly ['dautlisli], *av.* indubbiamente.

douceur [,du:'sə:*], *s.* **1.** regalia, mancia **2.** *(fig. spreg.)* esca.

douche [du:ʃ], *s.* **1.** doccia **2.** irrigazione.

dough [dou], *s.* **1.** pasta (di pane, non ancora cotta) **2.** *(sl.)* quattrini ☆ *— -baked*, mezzo cotto; *fig.* corto di intelligenza.

doughboy ['doubɔi], *s.* **1.** pallottola di pasta (di pane) bollita **2.** *(sl. amer.)* fantaccino.

doughnut ['dounʌt], *s.* « krapfen », bombolone dolce.

doughtiness ['dautinis], *s.* *(scherz.)* prodezza.

doughty ['dauti], *ag.* *(scherz.)* prode, valoroso.

dour ['duə*], *ag.* *(scoz.)* **1.** austero, severo **2.** ostinato.

dourly ['duəli], *av.* *(scoz.)* **1.** austeramente **2.** con ostinazione.

dourness ['duənis], *s.* *(scoz.)* **1.** severità, austerità (di parola, di viso) **2.** ostinazione, durezza.

to douse¹ [daus], *v.t.* **1.** *(fam.)* gettare acqua su; bagnare **2.** tuffare, immergere (in acqua).

to douse², *v.t.* **1.** *(mar.)* ammainare (vele) **2.** *(sl.)* spegnere ‖ *— the glim!*, spegni la luce!.

dove¹ [dʌv], *s.* *(ornit.)* colomba; tortora; *(fam.)* piccione ‖ *the Dove*, lo Spirito Santo ‖ *my —*, *(fam.)* mia colomba, amor mio ☆ *— -colour*, color tortora; *— -cot(e)*, colombaia; piccionaia: *to flutter the — -cotes*, gettare scompiglio.

dove² [douv], *(amer.)* *pass.* di **to dive**.

dovetail ['dʌvteil], *s.* *(falegnameria)* incastro a coda di rondine.

to dovetail, *v.t.i.* **1.** *(falegnameria)* incastrare, calettare a coda di rondine **2.** *fig.* amalgamare, amalgamarsi: *to — two schemes together*, *(fam.)* collegare due iniziative.

dowager ['dauədʒə*], *s.* **1.** vedova (che gode di titolo o proprietà ereditati dal marito): *the queen and the queen —*, la regina e la regina madre **2.** *(fam.)* vecchia signora dall'aspetto austero.

dowdy ['daudi], *ag.* sciatto, trasandato ‖ *s.* donna trasandata, sciatta, mal vestita.

dower ['dauə*], *s.* **1.** *(dir.)* legittima (di vedova) **2.** dote (anche *fig.*).

to dower, *v.t.* **1.** assegnare una dote a (una sposa), un vitalizio a (una vedova) **2.** *fig.* dotare: *to be dowered with*, essere dotato di.

dowerless ['dauəlis], *ag.* senza dote.

dowlas ['dauləs], *s.* tela comune, robusta.

down¹ [daun], *s.* **1.** duna **2.** *pl.* colline (specialmente nel Sud dell'Inghilterra) ‖ *the Surrey Downs*, le Colline del Surrey **3.** *the Downs*, *(geog.)* la rada di Deal (nel Canale della Manica).

down², *s.* **1.** piumino, piuma **2.** lanugine; peluria ☆ — *-bed*, letto di piume.

down³, *ag.* **1.** diretto verso il basso **2.** abbattuto, depresso ‖ *s.* (*sl. fig.*) il basso: *the ups and downs of life*, gli alti e bassi della vita ‖ *to have a* — *on s.o.*, avere antipatia per qlcu., provare astio verso qlcu. ☆ — *-beat*, (*mus.*) tempo in battere; — *-draught*, corrente d'aria discendente; — *-leap*, salto in basso; — *-train*, treno che parte da un centro importante (generalmente da Londra).

to **down³**, *v.t.* abbattere; buttare a terra: *to* — *s.o.*, abbattere qlcu. ‖ *to* — *a drink*, (*sl.*) tracannare un bicchiere ‖ *to* — *tools*, cessare il lavoro; mettersi in sciopero.

down³, *av.* giù, in giù; in basso, abbasso; di sotto; a terra, per terra **1.** (con *to be*): *he is not* — *yet*, non è ancora sceso, è ancora di sopra; *she is* — *with fever*, è a letto con la febbre; *to be* —, essere abbattuto, a terra: *to hit a man when he is* —, colpire un uomo quando è già a terra ‖ *to be* — *and out*, (*fam.*) essere ridotto alla miseria ‖ *to be* — *at heels*, essere scalcagnato ‖ *to be* — *for £ 20*, essere quotato 20 sterline ‖ *to be* — *in the mouth*, essere depresso, triste **2.** (con altri verbi): *to burn* —, ridurre in cenere; *to calm* —, calmarsi gradatamente; *to come* —, scendere, venir giù: *to come* — *from Oxford*, rientrare (a casa) dall'università di Oxford; essersi laureato ad Oxford; *to die* —, spegnersi a poco a poco (di fuoco, entusiasmo, ecc.); *to fall* —, cadere in basso, scendere; *to go* — *from one's University*, lasciare l'università; *to hand* —, tramandare; *to kneel* —, inginocchiarsi; *to knock* —, abbattere (con un pugno, colpo, ecc.); *to let a person* —, abbandonare una persona nel momento del bisogno; *to lie* —, sdraiarsi, adagiarsi; *to look* —, abbassare gli occhi; *to look* — *on s.o.*, disprezzare qlcu.; *to pull* —, tirare giù (una tendina); demolire (un edificio); *to put* —, abbassare; *to put sthg.* —, metter giù ql.co.: *put it* — *to my account*, addebitamelo, passalo sul mio conto; *to bring* (o *to bring*) — *(an aircraft)*, abbattere (un aereo); *to sit* —, mettersi a sedere; *to wear* —, logorare; *to write sthg.* —, mettere ql.co. per iscritto **3.** (Fraseologia): —*!*, cuccia!, giù! (ad un cane); — *here*, qui, in queste vicinanze; — *there*, laggiù; — *to the ground*, (*fam.*) fino in fondo, interamente, completamente; — *to recent times*, fino ai nostri giorni; — *under*, agli antipodi; — *the wind*, in direzione del vento; — *with...!*, abbasso...!, a morte...! ‖ *cash* — (o *money* —), (*comm.*) pronta cassa, a contanti ‖ *face, head* —, con la faccia, la testa in giù; *further* —, più in basso; *up-side* —, alla rovescia, sottosopra ‖ *motion* — *for to-day*, mozione portata all'ordine del giorno.

down³, *prep.* giù per, verso (il basso, il fondo): *the tears ran* — *her face.* le lacrime le rigavano il volto; *to go* — *the street, the hill*, andar giù per la strada, la collina; *to go* — *the river*, scendere a valle ‖ — *town*, in città, (*amer.*) in centro.

downcast ['daunkɑːst], *ag.* **1.** scoraggiato, abbattuto: *to look* —, avere l'aria abbattuta **2.** rivolto verso il basso (di sguardo) ‖ *s.* (*miner.*) ventilazione.

downcome ['daunkʌm], *s.* **1.** sfacelo; disastro **2.** acquazzone.

downcomer ['daun,kʌmə*], *s.* (*ind.*) tubo di scarico.

downfall ['daunfɔːl], *s.* **1.** caduta, rovescio (di pioggia, ecc.) **2.** rovina; distruzione: *the* — *of all my hopes*, il crollo di tutte le mie speranze; *his* — *was caused by drink*, il bere lo rovinò.

downgrade ['daungreid], *s.* **1.** discesa (di linea ferroviaria) **2.** *fig.* declino: *to be on the* —, essere in declino, andar declinando.

to **downgrade**, *v.t.* (*amer.*) **1.** retrocedere; abbassare di grado, rango **2.** attribuire minor importanza a.

downhearted ['daun'hɑːtid], *ag.* scoraggiato, depresso, abbattuto.

downheartedly ['daun'hɑːtidli], *av.* con scoraggiamento.

downheartedness ['daun'hɑːtidnis], *s.* scoraggiamento, abbattimento morale.

downhill ['daun'hil], *ag.* discendente, declinante.

downhill, *s.* discesa; declivio; pendio.

downhill, *av.* in pendio: *to go* —, *fig.* andare declinando.

downiness ['dauninis], *s.* **1.** lanugine **2.** morbidezza.

Downing Street ['dauniŋ,striːt], *s.* (*fam.*) il governo inglese (dal nome della via dove si trova la residenza ufficiale del Primo Ministro).

downland ['daunlænd], *s.* regione collinosa.

downmost ['daunmoust], *ag.* il più basso.

downmost, *av.* in giù: *head* —, a testa in giù.

downpour ['daunpɔː*], *s.* acquazzone; diluvio; pioggia torrenziale.

downright ['daunrait], *ag.* vero, sincero, onesto ‖ *a* — *lie*, una bugia vera e propria; *a* — *man*, un uomo tutto d'un pezzo.

downright, *av.* completamente; nettamente; categoricamente: *he refused* —, rifiutò categoricamente.

downrightness ['daunraitnis], *s.* rettitudine, sincerità.

downstage ['daun'steidʒ], *ag.av.* (*teat.*) verso la ribalta.

downstairs ['daun'stɛəz], *ag.* di sotto, dabbasso ‖ *s.* pianterreno.

downstairs, *av.* giù: *to go* —, discendere le scale; *to wait* —, aspettare giù.

downstream ['daun'striːm], *av.* seguendo la corrente; a valle.

downtime ['dauntaim], *s.* (*mec. ind.*) tempo passivo.

downtrend ['daun,trend], *s.* (*econ.*) tendenza al ribasso.

downtrodden ['daun,trɔdn], *ag.* calpestato; oppresso.

downturn ['daun,təːn], *s.* (*spec. econ.*) abbassamento.

downward ['daunwəd], *ag.* giù, verso il basso: — *tendency, movement*, tendenza, movimento verso il basso.

downward(s) ['daunwəd(z)], *av.* verso il basso, in giù: *to look* —, abbassar gli occhi, guardare in basso.

downwash ['daun,wɔʃ], *s.* (*aer.*) deflessione.

downy¹ ['dauni], *ag.* ondulato (come le dune).

downy², *ag.* **1.** lanuginoso, coperto di peluria; vellutato **2.** molle, morbido **3.** (*sl.*) ben sveglio; conscio.

dowry ['dauəri], *s.* **1.** dote **2.** *fig.* dote, qualità.

to **dowse** [dauz], *v.i.* cercare acqua, minerali con la bacchetta divinatoria.

dowser ['dauzə*], *s.* **1.** rabdomante **2.** bacchetta divinatoria **3.** (*cine.*) schermo paraluce.

dowsing ['dauziŋ], *s.* rabdomanzia ☆ — *-rod*, bacchetta divinatoria.

doxological [,dɔksə'lɔdʒikəl], *ag.* (*eccl.*) di, relativo a dossologia.

doxology [dɔk'sɔlədʒi], *s.* (*eccl.*) dossologia.

doxy¹ ['dɔksi], *s.* (*sl.*) amante; donna di malaffare.

doxy², *s.* (*fam.*) opinione (generalmente teologica).

doyen ['dɔiən], *s.* decano.

doz [dʌz], *abbr.* di **dozen**.

doze [douz], *s.* sonnellino: *to fall into a* —, assopirsi; *to have a* —, fare un sonnellino.

to **doze**, *v.t.i.* **1.** sonnecchiare **2.** *to* — *away one's time*, passare il tempo sonnecchiando **3.** *to* — *off*, assopirsi.

dozed [douzd], *ag.* **1.** sonnolento; assopito **2.** marcio; tarlato (di legno).

dozen ['dʌzn], *s.* dozzina: *one, two, several* — *eggs*, una, due, parecchie dozzine di uova; *six* — *bottles of wine*, sei dozzine di bottiglie di vino; *dozens of people think as I do*, decine e decine di persone la pensano come me; *pack them in dozens*, imballatene dodici per volta; *to sell articles in dozens*, vendere articoli a dozzine ‖ *a baker's* —, una dozzina abbondante ‖ *to talk nineteen to the* —, (*fam.*) chiacchierare a non finire.

dozenth ['dʌznθ], *ag.* dodicesimo; (*fam.*) ennesimo: *I tell you for the* — *time*, ti dico per la ennesima volta.

drab¹ [dræb], *s.* **1.** donna sudicia, trasandata **2.** sgualdrina, prostituta.

to **drab**¹, *pass.p.p.* **drabbed** [dræbd], *v.i.* (*arc.*) frequentare donne di malaffare.

drab², *ag.* **1.** grigio, grigiastro, bruno grigiastro; « beige » **2.** scialbo; monotono ‖ *s.* **1.** monotonia, grigiore **2.** (*ind. tessile*) saglia grigia; tela naturale.

drabbet ['dræbit], *s.* (*ind. tessile*) saglia pesante di cotone.

to **drabble** ['dræbl], *v.t.i.* infangare, infangarsi.

drachm [dræm], **drachma** ['drækmə], *pl.* **drachmas** ['drækməz], **drachmae** ['drækmi:], *s.* **1.** dracma, dramma (misura di peso greca = g. 4,30) **2.** *V.* **dram 1.**

Draconian [drei'kounjən], **Draconic** [drei'kɔnik], *ag.* draconiano.

draff [dræf], *s.* feccia del vino; scorie del malto (nella lavorazione della birra).

draft, draught [drɑ:ft], *s.* **1.** (*generalmente draught*) tiro, trazione: *beasts of* —, bestie da tiro **2.** (*generalmente draught*) retata; gettata di reti **3.** (*generalmente draught*) dose (di medicina liquida); sorso; quantità di liquido: *beer on* — (o — *beer*), birra spillata (dalla botte); *to drink at a* (o *one*) —, bere in un solo sorso **4.** abbozzo; brutta copia; prima stesura di manoscritto; progetto (di legge, di contratto); (*arch. mec.*) disegno schematico; — *of an agreement*, schema di un contratto; *first* — *of a novel*, prima stesura di un romanzo **5.** (*generalmente draught*) corrente d'aria: *you are sitting in a* —, sei seduto in mezzo a una corrente d'aria **6.** (*comm.*) tratta; effetto; cambiale; assegno: — *at sight*, tratta a vista; *to make a* — *on s.o.*, spiccare tratta su qlcu. **7.** (*comm.*) buon peso, tolleranza **8.** (*mil.*) distaccamento; contingente; membro di un distaccamento o di un contingente **9.** (*mil. amer.*) coscrizione, leva **10.** (*mar.*) pescaggio; profondità di immersione di nave **11.** (*tip.*) prima bozza ☆ — *contract*, (*comm.*) progetto di contratto; *draught gauge*, (*mec.*) misuratore di tiraggio; — *-horse*, cavallo da tiro; — *scheme*, progetto: — *scheme for a railway*, progetto di una ferrovia ‖ *sight* —, (*comm.*) tratta a vista.

to **draft**, *v.t.* **1.** tirare **2.** disegnare; abbozzare; stendere la prima copia di; redigere (un processo verbale, un progetto di legge, ecc.): *to* — *a bill*, stendere un progetto di legge **3.** (*mil.*) distaccare (truppe, ecc.).

draftee [,drɑ:f'ti:], *s.* (*amer.*) coscritto.

drafter ['drɑ:ftə*], *s.* chi stende (documento); chi abbozza (progetti); redattore.

drafting ['drɑ:ftiŋ], *s.* stesura; redazione (di un progetto, legge, ecc.).

draftsman, *pl.* **draftsmen** ['drɑ:ftsmən], *s.* **1.** disegnatore **2.** *V.* **drafter.**

drag [dræg], *s.* **1.** (*agr.*) erpice pesante **2.** carrozza pesante a quattro cavalli; diligenza **3.** (*mar. miner.*) draga; scorticaria (rete a strascico); draia; carrello **4.** odore di selvaggina (artificialmente sparso sul terreno per addestrare i cani alla caccia); caccia fatta in questo modo (*p.e.* trascinando una volpe morta) **5.** (*mec.*) freno, cuneo d'arresto, martinicca **6.** *fig.* ostacolo, impedimento, peso: *his family has always been a* — *on him*, la sua famiglia gli è sempre stata di gran peso **7.** (*aer.*) resistenza aerodinamica ☆ — *-bar*, (*ferr.*) sbarra di trazione; — *-boat*, battello draga; — *-chain*, catena che connette i vagoni; — *-man*, pescatore a giacchio, alla scorticaria; — *-net*, giacchio, scorticaria (tipi di reti da pesca).

to **drag**, *pass.p.p.* **dragged** [drægd], *v.t.i.* **1.** trascinare, trascinarsi; tirare (con sforzo): *the conversation dragged*, la conversazione si trascinava, diventava monotona; *he could scarcely* — *himself along*, si trascinava avanti a mala pena; *the ship dragged her anchor*, la nave arava; *to* — *a heavy load*, trascinare un carico pesante; *to* — *one's feet*, strascicare i piedi **2.** (*agr.*) erpicare **3.** pescare a giacchio, a scorticaria **4.** procedere pesantemente, con stanchezza, monotonia **5.** (*mar.*) dragare; rastrellare; nettare (un fiume, un porto);

ricercare sotto l'acqua **6.** *to* — *about*, andare a zonzo; strascicarsi di qua e di là **7.** *to* — *away*, trascinare via; separare con forza: *to* — *s.o. away from*, separare qlcu. da **8.** *to* — *down*, tirare, trascinare verso il basso: *he has dragged his family down with him*, ha trascinato la sua famiglia con sè nella rovina **9.** *to* — *in*, trascinare a forza: *to* — *a subject in*, portare la conversazione su un dato argomento **10.** *to* — *on*, prolungare; tirar in lungo: *time drags on*, il tempo scorre lentamente; *to* — *on a wretched existence*, trascinare un'esistenza miserabile **11.** *to* — *out*, far uscire a forza: *to* — *s.o. out of bed*, tirare qlcu. fuori dal letto; *to* — *the truth out of s.o.*, strappare la verità a qlcu. **12.** *to* — *up*, tirare verso l'alto; (*fam.*) tirar fuori (una vecchia storia): *to* — *up a child*, (*fam.*) allevare un bimbo senza molte cure.

dragée [drɑ:'ʒei], *s.* cioccolatino; confetto.

dragging ['drægiŋ], *s.* il trascinare, il trascinarsi (dei piedi, dell'ancora, ecc.).

to **draggle** ['drægl], *v.t.i.* trascinare, trascinarsi nel fango; infangare, infangarsi; inzaccherare, inzaccherarsi.

draggle-tail ['dræglteil], *s.f.* donna sudicia e trascurata nel vestire.

dragline ['dræglain], *s.* (*mec.*) gru a cingoli ☆ — *excavator*, benna trascinata.

dragoman, *pl.* **dragomen** ['dræɡoumən], **dragomans** ['dræɡoumənz], *s.* dragomanno.

dragon ['drægən], *s.* **1.** drago, dragone ‖ *a* — *of virtue*, (*fam.*) donna di rigidi principi ‖ *the Dragon*, (*astr.*) il Dragone **2.** (*aer.*) pallone frenato **3.** (*mil.*) trattore ☆ — *'s-blood*, (*farm.*) sangue di drago; — *-fly*, (*entom.*) libellula; — *-tree*, (*bot.*) dracena.

dragon(n)ade [,drægə'neid], *s.* persecuzione (dei protestanti francesi sotto Luigi XIV).

dragoon [drə'gu:n], *s.* (*mil.*) dragone.

to **dragoon**, *v.t.* perseguitare; costringere con la forza: *to* — *s.o. into doing sthg.*, costringere qlcu. a fare ql.co.

drain [drein], *s.* **1.** canale di scolo; fogna, tubo di scarico **2.** (*med.*) tubo per drenaggio **3.** *fig.* perdita, fuga (d'energia, di denaro); esaurimento, impoverimento: — *of money*, diminuzione di capitali; — *on the resources*, esaurimento delle risorse **4.** (*fam.*) goccia (di bevanda): *leave me a* —!, lasciamene una goccia! ☆ — *-canal*, canale di evacuazione; — *cock*, (*mec.*) rubinetto di scarico; — *-pipe*, tubo di scolo; tubo di drenaggio; canale di scarico.

to **drain**, *v.t.i.* **1.** prosciugare, prosciugarsi (per mezzo di drenaggio); far sgocciolare; defluire gradatamente: *to be well, badly drained*, essere ben, mal fornito di fognatura **2.** (*miner.*) prosciugare **3.** *fig.* esaurire; dissanguare **4.** (*fam.*) scolare: *to* — *dry* (o *to the dregs*), bere fino all'ultima goccia.

drainable ['dreinəbl], *ag.* prosciugabile.

drainage ['dreinidʒ], *s.* **1.** fognatura; scolo; spurgo; scarico: — *of waters*, scolo delle acque **2.** drenaggio ☆ — *-area*, — *-basin*, area, bacino di drenaggio; — *-conduit*, canale di drenaggio.

drainer ['dreinə*], *s.* **1.** sterratore **2.** utensile per drenaggio **3.** colino; scolatoio.

draining ['dreiniŋ], *s.* **1.** scolatura; drenaggio; prosciugamento **2.** *pl.* scolatura (di bicchiere) ☆ — *shaft*, (*miner.*) pozzo di drenaggio.

drake¹ [dreik], *s.* nome comune ad alcune varietà di insetti usati come esca.

drake², *s.* (*ornit.*) maschio dell'anitra.

dram [dræm], *s.* **1.** dramma (unità di peso = g. 1,772) **2.** (*fam.*) goccia, bicchierino (di liquore).

drama ['drɑ:mə], *s.* (*teat.*) dramma ‖ *the* —, arte drammatica: letteratura drammatica: *a student of the* —, uno studioso di letteratura drammatica.

dramatic [drə'mætik], *ag.* drammatico (anche *fig.*) ☆ — *critic*, critico teatrale.

dramatically [drə'mætikəli], *av.* drammaticamente.

dramatics [drə'mætiks], *s.pl.* **1.** drammatica **2.** produzioni drammatiche di dilettanti.

dramatis personae ['drɑ:mətis-pə:'sounai], *s.pl.* (*teat.*) personaggi.

dramatist ['dræmətist], *s.* drammaturgo.

dramatization [,dræmətai'zeiʃən], *s.* il drammatizzare; il dar forma di dramma (a romanzo, ecc.).

to **dramatize** ['dræmətaiz], *v.t.i.* drammatizzare; prestarsi a riduzione drammatica.

dramaturgic [,dræmə'tə:dʒik], *ag.* di drammaturgo; di drammaturgia.

dramaturgist ['dræmə,tə:dʒist], *s.* drammaturgo.

dramaturgy ['dræmə,tə:dʒi], *s.* drammaturgia.

drank [dræŋk], *pass.* di to **drink**.

to **drape** [dreip], *v.t.* drappeggiare; ornare con drappo: *draped in mourning*, parato a lutto.

draper ['dreipə*], *s.* negoziante di tessuti.

draperied ['dreipərid], *ag.* coperto di drappi.

drapery ['dreipəri], *s.* **1.** tessuti **2.** drappeggi, tendaggi **3.** commercio di tessuti ☆ — *store*, negozio di tessuti.

draping ['dreipiŋ], *s.* drappeggio; panneggiamento.

drappy ['drɑ:pi], *s.* (*scoz.*) goccia (di liquore) ☆ *wee* —, goccino (di whiskey).

drastic ['dræstik], *ag.* **1.** (*med.*) drastico **2.** *fig.* drastico, energico.

draught, *V.* **draft**.

draughtboard ['drɑ:ftbɔ:d], *s.* scacchiera.

draughts [drɑ:fts], *s.pl.* giuoco della dama.

draughtsman, *pl.* **draughtsmen** ['drɑ:ftsmən], *s.* **1.** *V.* **draftsman 2.** (*dama*) pedina.

draughtsmanship ['drɑ:ftsmənʃip], *s.* l'arte del disegno industriale.

draughty ['drɑ:fti], *ag.* pieno di correnti d'aria.

draw [drɔ:], *s.* **1.** tiro, strattone, tirata; l'estrarre: *to be quick on the* —, essere veloce nell'estrarre (un'arma) **2.** *fig.* incentivo (a parlare, a sfogarsi) **3.** estrazione (di lotteria); tombola **4.** *fig.* attrazione: *this actress was a great* —, questa attrice costituiva una grande attrazione; *this week's* — *is ties*, (*comm.*) l'articolo della settimana sono le cravatte **5.** (*spor.*) partita nulla: *the game ended in a* —, la partita si concluse con punteggio pari **6.** (*arch.*) ala di ponte levatoio **7.** (*amer.*) piccolo canale naturale ☆ — *-stop*, (*mus.*) registro (di organo).

to **draw**, *pass.* **drew** [dru:], *p.p.* **drawn** [drɔ:n], *v.t.i.* **1.** tirare, tirarsi; trarre, trascinare; attirare; estrarre; attingere: *drawn by a locomotive*, trascinato da una locomotiva; *the chimney doesn't* — *well*, il camino ha poco tiraggio; *he drew the book towards himself*, avvicinò a sè il libro; *a pretty girl drew his eye*, una bella ragazza attirò il suo sguardo; *to* — *the blinds*, chiudere le imposte; *to* — *blood*, ferire; *to* — *a bow*, tendere un arco; *to* — *a breath*, respirare: *to* — *one's first, last breath*, nascere, morire; *to* — *a card*, estrarre una carta; *to* — *a confession from s.o.*, estorcere una confessione a qlcu.; *to* — *crowds*, attirare la folla; *to* — *lots*, tirare a sorte; *to* — *near*, avvicinare, avvicinarsi; *to* — *one's hat over one's eyes*, tirarsi il cappello sugli occhi; *to* — *one's sword*, sguainare la spada; *to* — *on one's capital*, attingere al proprio capitale; *to* — *on one's imagination*, ricorrere all'immaginazione; *to* — *a prize at a lottery*, vincere un premio alla lotteria; *to* — *profit from sthg.*, trarre profitto da ql.co.; *to* — *rein*, tirare le redini; *to* — *s.o. into conversation*, far entrare qlcu. nella conversazione; *to* — *s.o. into doing sthg.*, indurre qlcu. a fare ql.co.; *to* — *tears from s.o.*, strappare le lacrime a qlcu.; *to* — *vengeance upon oneself*, attirarsi una vendetta ‖ *to* — *a blank*, (*fam.*) restare con un pugno di mosche ‖ *to* — *a bead on s.o.*, (*amer.*) prendere di mira qlcu. ‖ *to* — *a game with s.o.*, (*spor.*) far pari con qlcu. ‖ *to* — *it mild*, non esagerare ‖ *to* — *the long bow*, esagerare; dirle grosse ‖ *to* — *rations*, (*mil.*) ritirare le razioni ‖ *to* — *tea*, far diventar forte il tè ‖ *to* — *s.o.'s teeth*, rendere innocuo

qlcu. ‖ *to feel drawn to s.o.*, sentirsi attratto verso qlcu. ‖ *to have a drawn face*, avere il volto contratto **2.** svuotare, sventrare: *sentenced to be hanged, drawn and quartered*, (*st.*) condannato ad essere impiccato, sventrato e squartato **3.** disegnare; tracciare (anche *fig.*): *to* — *a dash line*, tratteggiare; *to* — *a distinction between two things*, fare una distinzione fra due cose; *to* — *a dotted line*, punteggiare; *to* — *a full-length portrait*, disegnare un ritratto a figura intera; *to* — *a picture of s.o.*, fare il ritratto di qlcu.; *to* — *sthg. in ink, pencil*, disegnare ql.co. in inchiostro, a matita ‖ *to* — *it fine*, (*sl.*) essere molto preciso nel fare distinzioni ‖ *to* — *the line*, porre limiti **4.** allungare, stendere; (*ind. tessile*) stirare **5.** (*metal.*) trafilare; rinvenire **6.** (*ind. chim.*) estrarre **7.** (*comm.*) spiccare, emettere (tratta, ecc.): *to* — *at sight, at 30 days*, emettere a vista, a 30 giorni; *to* — *a bill* (o *draft*) *on*, emettere tratta su; *to* — *a cheque on a bank*, emettere un assegno su una banca **8.** *to* — **aside**, scostare, scostarsi **9.** *to* — **away**, distogliere; allontanarsi **10.** *to* — **back**, tirare, tirarsi indietro; ritirare (la mano): *it is too late to* — *back now*, (*fam.*) ora è troppo tardi per tirarsi indietro **11.** *to* — **down**, abbassare; fare scendere (anche *fig.*): *to* — *down wrath from heaven*, attirarsi la collera divina **12.** *to* — **forth**, tirar fuori, provocare (risa, elogi, proteste, ecc.) **13.** *to* — **forward**, avanzare, avvicinarsi **14.** *to* — **in**, ritirare, ritirarsi; tirar dentro; far entrare; accorciarsi; fare economie; *the days are drawing in*, le giornate si accorciano ‖ *to* — *in one's horns*, abbassare la cresta **15.** *to* — **off**, togliere, togliersi; ritirare, ritirarsi; deviare; spillare, travasare (liquidi) **16.** *to* — **on**, calzare, infilarsi; avanzare; avvicinarsi; attingere: *she drew on her gloves*, si infilò i guanti; *the ship drew on*, la nave avanzava; *summer was drawing on*, l'estate s'avvicinava **17.** *to* — **out**, aprire; estrarre; ritirare; prolungare; stendere; indurre a parlare; battere (metalli): *the speech drew out endlessly*, il discorso si prolungò all'infinito; *to try to* — *s.o. out*, tentare di far parlare qlcu. **18.** *to* — **round**, avvicinarsi **19.** *to* — **together**, riunire, riunirsi; far riunire: *the child's illness had drawn them together*, la malattia del bambino li aveva uniti **20.** *to* — **up**, alzarsi su; compilare; redigere; avvicinare, avvicinarsi; fermare, fermarsi: *the carriage drew up at the door*, la carrozza si fermò alla porta; *to* — *oneself up to one's full height*, raddrizzarsi in tutta la propria statura; *to* — *up in line*, allineare; *to* — *up with*, arrivare all'altezza di; raggiungere.

drawback ['drɔ:bæk], *s.* **1.** inconveniente; svantaggio; ostacolo: *a* — *to sthg.*, un ostacolo a ql.co. **2.** (*comm.*) «drawback» (restituzione di dogana o dazio, premio di esportazione) **3.** (*metal.*) parte smontabile.

drawbridge ['drɔ:bridʒ], *s.* ponte levatoio.

drawee [drɔ:'i:], *s.* (*comm.*) trattario.

drawer ['drɔ:ə*], *s.c.* **1.** chi tira, chi attinge (acqua); chi spilla (birra, vino) **2.** disegnatore, disegnatrice **3.** redattore, redattrice (di documenti) **4.** (*comm.*) traente ‖ [drɔ:*], *s.* cassetto: *chest of drawers*, cassettone ☆ — *pull*, maniglia di cassetto ‖ *cork* —, cavatappi; *nail* —, tenaglie.

drawers [drɔ:z], *s.pl.* mutandoni.

drawing ['drɔ:iŋ], *s.* **1.** disegno: *out of* —, mal disegnato **2.** il tirare; tiraggio, estrazione; *fig.* attrazione **3.** (*ind. tessile*) stiratura **4.** (*mec. metal.*) imbutitura; trafilatura **5.** (*comm.*) prelevamento di fondi ☆ — *-block*, blocco di carta; — *-board*, tavola per disegno; — *-master*, professore di disegno; — *-paper*, carta da disegno; — *-pen*, tiralinee; — *-pencil*, matita da disegno; — *-pin*, puntina da disegno; — *-table*, tavola allungabile ‖ *rough* —, schizzo.

drawing-room ['drɔiŋrum], *s.* **1.** salotto **2.** ricevimento **3.** (*amer. ferr.*) scompartimento salone.

drawl [drɔ:l], *s.* pronuncia strascicata.

to **drawl**, *v.t.i.* strascicare (la voce, le parole): *drawling voice*, voce strascicata; *to* — (*out*) *sthg.*, dire ql.co. con voce strascicata, con affettazione di pigrizia.

drawn [drɔ:n], *p.p.* di to **draw**.

dray [dreiʃ, s. **1.** carro pesante (senza sponde) **2.** (*amer.*) slitta per trasportare legname ☆ — *-horse*, cavallo da tiro; — *-man*, carrettiere.

dread [dred], *ag.* **1.** (*poet. letter.*) temibile, paventato **2.** venerabile, augusto ‖ *s.* timore, spavento, terrore; (*fam.*) fobia: *holy* —, sacro terrore; *to be, to live in* — *of s.o., of doing sthg.*, aver paura, vivere nel terrore di qlcu., di fare ql.co.; (*fam.*) aver una fobia per ql.co.

to **dread**, *v.t.* temere, aver paura di: *he dreads doing wrong* (o *to do wrong*), teme di far del male; *I* — *that he may fall ill*, temo che possa ammalarsi.

dreadful [ʹdredful], *ag.* terribile, spaventevole; terrificante; atroce: *a* — *storm*, una tempesta terribile; *it was sthg.* —, fu ql.co. di spaventoso ☆ *penny* —, romanzo giallo dell'epoca vittoriana.

dreadfully [ʹdredfuli], *av.* terribilmente, spaventosamente: — *tired*, (*fam.*) stanco morto; *he was* — *pale*, era pallidissimo; *I am* — *sorry*, mi spiace moltissimo.

dreadfulness [ʹdredfulnis], *s.* spaventosità.

dreadless [ʹdredlis], *ag.* intrepido.

dreadnought [ʹdrednɔ:t], *s.* **1.** chi nulla teme **2.** (*mar.*) « dreadnought », corazzata **3.** giaccone di pesante lana impermeabilizzata.

dream [dri:m], *s.* **1.** sogno: *sweet dreams*, sogni d'oro; *waking* —, sogno ad occhi aperti; *to awake from a bad* —, svegliarsi da un brutto sogno; *to dream a* —, (*letter.*) fare un sogno; *to have a* —, fare un sogno **2.** (*fam.*) sogno, meraviglia: *she was wearing a* — *of a dress!*, indossava un abito che era un sogno!.

to **dream**, *pass.p.p.* **dreamed** [dri:md], **dreamt** [dremt], *v.t.i.* **1.** sognare: *what did you* — *about?*, che cosa hai sognato? ‖ *to* — *away one's life, one's time, the hours, etc.*, passare sognando la propria vita, il proprio tempo, le ore, ecc. **2.** vagheggiare, fantasticare, immaginare: *never did I* — *that*, mai immaginavo che; *to* — *empty dreams*, fantasticare **3.** sognarsi; osare: *I shouldn't* — *of doing such a thing*, non mi sognerei mai di fare una cosa simile.

dreamer [ʹdri:mə*], *s.c.* sognatore, sognatrice; visionario, visionaria.

dreaminess [ʹdri:minis], *s.* stato di sogno.

dreamland [ʹdri:mlænd], *s.* terra dei sogni.

dreamless [ʹdri:mlis], *ag.* senza sogni.

dreamy [ʹdri:mi], *ag.* **1.** sognante, languido: — *eyes*, occhi sognanti **2.** vago: — *recollections*, ricordi vaghi.

drear [driə*], *V.* **dreary**.

drearily [ʹdriərili], *av.* tristemente; tetramente.

dreariness [ʹdriərinis], *s.* tristezza; monotonia; desolazione.

dreary [ʹdriəri], *ag.* triste; tetro; cupo: — *day*, giorno tetro; — *food*, alimentazione monotona; — *outlook*, previsione triste; — *speech*, discorso monotono, noioso.

dredge[1] [dredʒ], *s.* (*mec.*) draga ☆ — *-boat*, galleggiante per dragare; — *-net*, draga (rete) per la pesca; draga (cono di tela) ‖ *floating* —, draga galleggiante.

to **dredge**[1], *v.t.i.* dragare, scavare con la draga.

to **dredge**[2], *v.t.* (*cuc.*) cospargere, spargere, spolverizzare (di zucchero, ecc.): *to* — *meat with flour*, infarinare la carne.

dredger[1] [ʹdredʒə*], *s.* **1.** draga, battello usato per dragare **2.** chi lavora su una draga ☆ *mine* —, dragamine.

dredger[2], *s.* (*cuc.*) spargisale, spargizucchero.

to **dree** [dri:], *v.t.* (*arc. scoz.*) sopportare: *to* — *one's weird*, rassegnarsi alla propria sorte, subire il proprio destino.

dreggy [ʹdregi], *ag.* torbido, impuro.

dregs [dregz], *s.pl.* **1.** feccia, fondo (anche *fig.*): *the* — *of society*, la feccia, i bassifondi della società; *to*

drink the cup to the —, bere il calice fino all'ultima feccia; *fig.* soffrire tutto il soffribile **2.** (*chim.*) feccia, sedimento **3.** scorie.

drench [drentʃ], *s.* **1.** (*arc.*) pozione; veleno; medicina (somministrata per forza) **2.** (*vet.*) purga **3.** inzuppamento **4.** forte rovescio di pioggia.

to **drench**, *v.t.* **1.** bagnare, inzuppare: *drenched to the skin*, inzuppato fino alle ossa; *to get drenched with rain*, inzupparsi di pioggia **2.** far bere abbondantemente **3.** (*vet.*) somministrare una purga, una medicina a (un animale).

drencher [ʹdrentʃə*], *s.* **1.** acquazzone **2.** strumento per somministrare medicine alle bestie.

drenching [ʹdrentʃiŋ], *ag.* che inzuppa: *a* — *rain*, una pioggia che bagna fino alle ossa, penetrante ‖ *s.* **1.** inzuppamento **2.** rovescio di pioggia.

Dresden [ʹdrezdən], *no.pr.* (*geog.*) Dresda ☆ — *china*, porcellana di Sassonia.

dress [dres], *s.* **1.** abbigliamento: *articles of* —, articoli di abbigliamento ‖ *in full* —, in alta tenuta, in abito sfarzoso, in pompa magna ‖ *to talk* —, parlare di vestiti, di moda **2.** abito, vestito per signora, per bambini **3.** forma: *in a polished* —, in forma elegante ☆ — *-circle*, (*teat.*) prima galleria; — *-coat*, marsina; — *-designer*, figurinista; — *-hanger*, gruccia per abiti; — *length*, taglio d'abito; — *material*, stoffa per abiti; — *protector* (o — *shield*), sottascella; — *-rehearsal*, (*teat.*) prova generale (in costume); — *-suit*, abito da sera, da cerimonia ‖ *ball* —, abito da ballo; *evening* —, abito da sera; *morning* —, abito da mattina; *travelling* —, abito da viaggio; *walking* —, abito da passeggio.

to **dress**, *v.t.i.* **1.** vestire, vestirsi; abbigliare, abbigliarsi: *does one* — *in that hotel for dinner?*, ci si cambia in quell'albergo per il pranzo?; *he is too little to* — *himself*, è troppo piccolo per vestirsi da solo; *she dressed herself quickly*, si vestì in fretta; *well dressed*, ben vestito; *you take too long to* — (*yourself*), ti ci vuole troppo tempo a vestirti; *to be dressed in white, in silk*, esser vestito in bianco, di seta **2.** decorare, allestire; preparare: *to* — *one's hair*, pettinarsi, acconciarsi i capelli; *to* — *a ship*, (*mar.*) pavesare una nave; *to* — *a shop window*, decorare, allestire una vetrina **3.** (*mil.*) allinearsi, allineare (le file) **4.** (*med.*) curare, bendare: *to* — *a wound*, medicare una ferita **5.** (*cuc.*) preparare, guarnire (un piatto); condire: *to* — *a salad*, condire un'insalata **6.** (*tec.*) preparare; rifinire; dare l'appretto, la colla a; (*metal.*) lucidare; (*arch.*) intonacare (pareti); (*artig.*) conciare (pelli) **7.** *to* — *down*, (*fam.*) dare una lavata di capo a **8.** *to* — *out*, mettersi in ghingheri **9.** *to* — *up*, vestirsi sfarzosamente in maschera, in costume.

dresser[1] [ʹdresə*], *s.* **1.** assistente (di chirurgo) **2.** acconciatore **3.** (*teat.*) vestiarista **4.** (*tec.*) apparecchiatore; conciatore ☆ *hair* —, parrucchiere; *window* —, vetrinista.

dresser[2], *s.* **1.** credenza; dispensa **2.** (*amer.*) toletta.

dressing [ʹdresiŋ], *s.* **1.** abbigliamento; il vestire, l'atto di vestire; pettinatura **2.** allestimento **3.** (*mil.*) allineamento **4.** (*med.*) medicazione; l'occorrente per una medicazione **5.** (*cuc.*) condimento **6.** (*tec.*) preparazione; appretto ☆ — *-case*, borsa da toletta; — *down*, sgridata: *to give s.o. a good* — *down*, dare una bella lavata di capo a qlcu.; — *-gown*, vestaglia; — *-room*, spogliatoio; (*teat.*) camerino; — *-table*, tavola da toletta ‖ *salad* —, condimento per l'insalata; *window* —, allestimento delle vetrine.

dressmaker [ʹdres,meikə*], *s.* sarta (da donna).

dressmaking [ʹdres,meikiŋ], *s.* **1.** sartoria (per donna) **2.** confezioni (per donna).

dressy [ʹdresi], *ag.* **1.** ricercato nel vestire; elegante nell'abbigliamento (di persona) **2.** elegante, raffinato (di abito): *a* — *gown*, un abito elegante.

drew [dru:], *pass.* di to **draw**.

dribble [ʹdribl], *s.* **1.** gocciolamento; sbavamento **2.** (*calcio*) palleggio.

to **dribble**, *v.t.i.* **1.** stillare; gocciolare, far gocciolare; sbavare, emettere bava (di bimbi) **2.** (*calcio*) palleggiare, scartare, lavorare (la palla) con ripetuti colpi del piede.

dribbler ['driblə*], *s.* **1.** chi perde bava **2.** (*calcio*) palleggiatore.

dribblet ['driblit], *s.* piccola quantità, rata, quota: *in, by dribblets*, poco alla volta, in piccola quantità.

dribbling ['driblin], *V.* **dribble.**

driblet, *V.* **dribblet.**

dried [draid], *ag.* secco, essiccato: — *fruit*, frutta secca.

drier, *V.* **dryer.**

drift [drift], *s.* **1.** spinta, impulso (anche *fig.*): *the — of the current*, la spinta della corrente **2.** movimento progressivo; direzione, senso, velocità (di corrente); corso (di affari, eventi): *the — of labour into the towns*, il fluire progressivo della mano d'opera nelle città **3.** (*mar. aer.*) deriva, l'andare alla deriva **4.** (*geol.*) alluvione, terreno alluvionale ‖ *a — of rain*, una raffica di pioggia **5.** *fig.* significato, tenore (di conversazione, scritto): *I understood the — of what he said*, compresi dove voleva arrivare **6.** *fig.* il lasciar fare, il lasciarsi trasportare: *policy of —*, la politica del lasciar fare; *he was in a state of —*, non aveva idee sul da farsi ☆ — *-angle*, (*aer. mar.*) angolo di deriva; — *-net*, rete da pesca, tramaglio; — *-ice*, ghiaccio alla deriva; — *-wood*, pezzi di legno trasportati dalla corrente.

to **drift**, *v.t.i.* **1.** esser trasportato (dalla corrente, dal vento); andare alla deriva, lasciarsi trasportare; galleggiare: *drifting clouds*, nubi vaganti; *the ship had lost her rudder and was drifting about*, la nave aveva perso il timone ed andava alla deriva; *to — with the current*, esser trascinato dalla corrente; *to — down the river*, essere trasportato a valle dal fiume; *to — out to sea*, lasciarsi trasportare al largo **2.** *fig.* andare alla deriva, essere trascinato: *to — into vice*, abbandonarsi ai vizi **3.** sospingere, cacciare; ammucchiare, accumulare: *the wind drifted the snow in front of the door*, il vento ammucchiò la neve davanti alla porta **4.** (*aer.*) derivare **5.** *to — along*, andare avanti senza preoccupazioni **6.** *to — apart*, separarsi, perdersi a poco a poco di vista (di persone).

driftage ['driftidʒ], *s.* **1.** l'andare alla deriva **2.** (*mar. aer.*) deriva, deviazione (dalla rotta).

drifter ['driftə*], *s.* **1.** (*mar.*) motopeschereccio, peschereccio con tramaglio; dragamine **2.** pescatore con tramaglio **3.** (*min.*) perforatrice da cantiere.

driftless ['driftflis], *ag.* **1.** senza direzione; senza scopo **2.** senza deviazione.

drifty ['drifti], *ag.* **1.** tendente a deviare **2.** che tende ad ammucchiarsi.

drill[1] [dril], *s.* **1.** trapano; punta da trapano; perforatrice; sonda; trivella; (*med.*) trapano **2.** (*mil.*) esercitazione **3.** esercitazione scolastica (fisica, mentale) ☆ — *-bow*, archetto di trapano; — *-ground*, piazza d'armi; — *-hole*, foro di trivellazione; — *-press*, trapanatrice; — *-rod*, asta di sondaggio; — *-sergeant*, sergente istruttore ‖ *verb —*, esercitazione sui verbi; *pronunciation —*, esercizio di pronuncia.

to **drill**[1], *v.t.* **1.** trapanare; perforare; sondare (anche *med.*) **2.** (*mil.*) esercitare, addestrare; far esercitazioni **3.** far fare ginnastica a; istruire **4.** *fig.* istruire con rigore.

drill[2], *s.* **1.** (*agr. mec.*) seminatrice (a solchi regolari) **2.** solco della seminatrice **3.** fila di semi deposti con la seminatrice.

to **drill**[2], *v.t.* (*agr.*) seminare (con la seminatrice a solchi regolari).

drill[3], *s.* ruscelletto.

drill[4], *s.* traliccio di lino, di cotone.

drill[5], *s.* (*zool.*) drillo.

to **drill**[6], *v.t.i.* **1.** irretire **2.** svanire, scomparire per gradi.

driller ['drilə*], *s.* **1.** (macchina) perforatrice **2.** trapanatore, perforatore.

drilling ['drilin], *s.* **1.** (*mec.*) perforazione, trapanazione; trivellazione, sondaggio (per petrolio) **2.** (*mil.*) esercitazione **3.** esercitazione scolastica **4.** *pl.* trucioli di trapanatura ☆ — *-machine*, trapano, perforatrice; — *-ring*, sonda ‖ *machine —*, perforazione a macchina.

drily ['draili], *av.* **1.** seccamente **2.** alquanto ironicamente.

drink [drink], *s.* **1.** bevanda (generalmente alcoolica); (*med.*) pozione: *food and —*, cibo e bevande; *soft —*, bevanda analcoolica; *strong —*, bevanda alcoolica; *will you have a — ?*, volete bere ql.co.?; *to stand s.o. a —*, pagare da bere a qlcu. **2.** ubriachezza, alcoolismo: *to drive s.o. to —*, spingere qlcu. al bere; *to take to —*, darsi al bere ‖ *in —*, ubriaco; *on the —*, che beve molto; *to be the worse for —*, essere ubriaco; *to smell of —*, puzzare d'alcool **3.** (*sl. aer.*) il mare ☆ — *-money*, mancia; — *-offering*, libagione.

to **drink**, *pass.* **drank** [drænk], *p.p.* **drunk** [drʌnk], (*arc.*) **drunken** ['drʌnkən], *v.t.i.* **1.** bere: — *your soup*, mangia la minestra; *will you have sthg. to — ?*, vuoi ql.co. da bere?; *to — coffee*, bere caffè; *to — the waters*, fare una cura di acque; *to — s.o.'s health*, bere alla salute di qlcu. ‖ *fit to —*, potabile **2.** ubriacarsi, essere dedito al bere: *to — hard* (o *heavily*), bere moltissimo ‖ *to be drunk*, essere ubriaco; *to — like a fish*, bere come una spugna; *to — oneself drunk*, bere fino ad ubriacarsi; *to — oneself to death*, rovinarsi la salute a forza di bere; *to — s.o. under the table*, far bere qlcu. tanto da farlo finire sotto il tavolo **3.** *to — in*, assorbire, impregnarsi, inzupparsi di; *fig.* bere, ascoltare con rapimento (parole, musica, poesia, ecc.) **4.** *to — off*, tracannare, bere tutto d'un fiato **5.** *to — up*, bere fino in fondo, vuotare (un bicchiere).

drinkable ['drinkəbl], *ag.* bevibile, potabile.

drinker ['drinkə*], *s.* bevitore: *hard —*, forte bevitore.

drinking ['drinkin], *s.* **1.** il bere **2.** alcoolismo, ubriachezza ☆ — *-bout*, eccesso di ubriachezza; — *-fountain*, fontanella pubblica; — *-glass*, bicchiere; — *-saloon*, mescita; — *-song*, canzone bacchica; — *-trough*, abbeveratoio.

drip [drip], *s.* **1.** gocciolamento, stillicidio **2.** goccia **3.** (*arch.*) gocciolatoio ☆ — *-moulding* (o — *-stone*), gocciolatoio di pietra.

to **drip**, *pass.p.p.* **dripped** [dript], *v.t.i.* gocciolare, far gocciolare; stillare: *he was dripping sweat*, grondava (di) sudore; *the tap was dripping*, il rubinetto gocciolava.

dripping ['dripin], *ag.* gocciolante: — *with perspiration*, grondante di sudore ‖ *to be — wet*, essere inzuppato ‖ *s.* **1.** gocciolio; stillicidio **2.** sugo d'arrosto.

drive [draiv], *s.* **1.** passeggiata, gita (in carrozza, automobile): *an hour's —*, giro di un'ora; *we had a very pleasant —*, abbiamo fatto una bella gita; *to go for a —*, fare una gita in auto **2.** viale, strada carrozzabile (generalmente attraverso parco o giardino privato) **3.** (*caccia*) battuta, inseguimento **4.** spinta, urgenza, propulsione; iniziativa, energia: — *of business*, urgenza negli affari; *to have plenty of —*, aver molta iniziativa, energia **5.** (*cricket, golf, tennis*) forte colpo alla palla **6.** (*mec.*) movimento di propulsione; trasmissione; presa di moto; (*aut.*) guida **7.** (*miner.*) galleria in direzione lungobanco **8.** (*amer.*) sforzo speciale; campagna di propaganda ☆ *left-hand, right-hand —*, guida a sinistra, a destra.

to **drive**, *pass.* **drove** [drouv], *p.p.* **driven** ['drivn], *v.t.i.* **1.** andare (in veicolo); portare (in veicolo): *shall we — home, or walk?*, dobbiamo andare a casa in auto o a piedi?; *to — s.o. to town, into the country*, condurre (in veicolo) qlcu. in città, in campagna **2.** condurre, portare; trascinare; scacciare: *he drove his pigs to the market*, condusse i suoi maiali al mercato; *to — s.o. from the house*, scacciare qlcu. di casa **3.** guidare (cavallo, automobile, ecc.); far funzionare, azionare (una macchina): *he drives the engine*, egli aziona la macchina;

he drives his own car, egli guida la propria automobile; *the machinery is driven by steam*, il macchinario è azionato a vapore; *to — like mad*, (*fam.*) guidare come un pazzo, a forte andatura; *to — a pen*, (*iron.*) maneggiare una penna, scribacchiare **4.** *fig.* spingere, costringere, forzare: *he was driven to despair*, fu spinto alla disperazione; *to — one out of one's senses*, far perdere il senno a qlcu.; *to — s.o. into a corner*, metter qlcu. in una posizione difficile; *to — s.o. mad*, far impazzire qlcu. **5.** (*cricket, golf, tennis*) battere con energia (la palla) **6.** avanzare; spingersi: *the clouds drove across the sky*, le nubi avanzavano nel cielo **7.** esercitare con abilità (un commercio): *to — a bargain*, concludere un buon affare; *to — a roaring trade*, vendere con abilità e successo la propria merce **8.** *to — at* (*sthg.*), (*fam.*) tendere a, mirare a: *what are you driving at?*, che intenzioni hai? || *to let — at*, sparare verso; mirare un colpo (ad una palla) **9.** *to — through* (*sthg.*), passare attraverso (con forza); trafiggere: *to — a tunnel through a hill*, scavare una galleria in una collina **10.** *to — away, off*, scacciare, respingere; allontanarsi (in un veicolo) || *to — away at sthg.*, dedicarsi con lena a ql.co. **11.** *to — in*, spingere dentro, introdurre; *fig.* portare a conclusione; entrare (con un veicolo); accostarsi al marciapiede (di veicolo): *to — in a nail*, piantare, conficcare un chiodo **12.** *to — out*, cacciare (fuori): *to — the enemy out*, scacciare il nemico **13.** *to — under*, reprimere (un sentimento) **14.** *to — up*, avvicinarsi (in veicolo).

drive-in ['draiv,in], *ag.* (*amer.*) in cui si entra in automobile || *s.* (*neol. amer.*) « drive-in » (cinema, banca, negozio in cui i clienti vengono serviti senza scendere dall'automobile) ☆ — *movie house*, cinema all'aperto, in cui si può assistere allo spettacolo dalla propria automobile; — *restaurant*, ristorante in cui si è serviti senza scendere dall'automobile.

drivel ['drivl], *s.* **1.** bava **2.** ciancia; ciarla; *fig.* stupidaggine: *to talk —*, dire sciocchezze.

to **drivel**, *pass.p.p.* **drivelled** ['drivld], *v.i.* **1.** sbavare, emettere bava **2.** cianciare, ciarlare; dire sciocchezze: *he drivelled on*, continuava a dir sciocchezze.

driveller ['drivlə*], *s.* **1.** sbavone **2.** rimbecillito.

drivelling ['drivliŋ], *ag.* imbecille || — *idiot*, idiota.

driven ['drivn], *p.p.* di to **drive** || *ag.* **1.** sbattuto, spinto: *tempest- — ship*, nave sbattuta dalla tempesta **2.** (*mec.*) azionato; comandato; condotto ☆ *electric —*, azionato elettricamente.

driver ['draivə*], *s.* **1.** cocchiere, carrettiere; conducente, guidatore, autista **2.** (*ferr.*) macchinista **3.** guardiano, sorvegliante (di schiavi) **4.** (*mec.*) elemento motore, elemento conduttore **5.** (*rad.*) valvola pilota **6.** mazza da golf ☆ —*'s cab*, cabina del macchinista; —*'s licence*, patente di guida || *screw —*, cacciavite; *slave —*, negriero.

driveteria [,draivi'tiəriə], *s.* (*neol. amer.*) « drive-in » con tavola calda.

driveway ['draiv,wei], *s.* (*amer.*) viale carrozzabile.

driving ['draiviŋ], *ag.* **1.** (*mec.*) che spinge; di comando; che fa funzionare **2.** che sbatte; che sferza, sferzante: — *rain*, pioggia sferzante || *s.* **1.** (*aut.*) guida **2.** (*mec.*) comando, trasmissione; attacco ☆ — *-belt*, cinghia motrice; — *-gear*, ingranaggio conduttore; — *-mirror*, (*aut.*) specchietto retrovisivo; — *-power*, forza motrice; — *-pulley*, puleggia di comando; — *school*, scuola guida; — *-shaft*, albero motore, primario; — *-wheel*, ruota motrice; (*aut.*) volante (di guida).

drizzle ['drizl], *s.* pioggerella, pioggia fine e fitta.

to **drizzle**, *v.i.* piovigginare.

drizzly ['drizli], *ag.* piovigginoso.

drogher ['drougə*], *s.* battello costiero indiano.

drogue [droug], *s.* (*mar. aer.*) ancora galleggiante.

droit [droit], *s.* diritto.

droll [droul], *ag.* buffo, comico; ameno; strano || *s.* (*arc. letter.*) buffone.

drollery ['drouləri], *s.* buffoneria; scherzo; facezia.

drollness ['droulnis], *s.* carattere scherzoso, strano.

drolly ['drouli], *av.* facetamente; scherzosamente.

drome [droum], *s.* (*fam.*) aeroporto.

dromedary ['drʌmədəri], *s.* dromedario.

dromond ['drɔmənd], *s.* (*st.*) dromone (veloce nave da guerra).

drone [droun], *s.* **1.** (*entom.*) fuco; pecchione **2.** (*fam.*) fannullone **3.** (*aer. mar.*) aeroplano, nave teleguidata **4.** ronzio; suono ronzante (di motore); *fig.* tono monotono (di discorso, predica) **5.** (*mus.*) bordone.

to **drone**, *v.t.i.* **1.** ronzare; emettere suono monotono **2.** oziare || *to — one's life away*, vivere da fannullone, passare la vita senza far nulla **3.** biascicare: *to — (out) a prayer*, biascicare una preghiera.

droning ['drouniŋ], *ag.* ronzante || *s.* **1.** ronzio; suono monotono **2.** l'oziare.

droningly ['drouniŋli], *av.* con tono monotono.

to **drool** [dru:l], (*dial. amer.*) per to **drivel**.

droop [dru:p], *s.* **1.** posizione abbassata, piegata, incurvata (di testa, spalle) **2.** languore; accasciamento.

to **droop**, *v.t.i.* **1.** abbassare (occhi, capo); abbassarsi (di occhi) || *to — the colors*, (*amer. mil.*) salutare abbassando la bandiera **2.** languire, abbattersi (di persona, fiore, ecc.).

drooping ['dru:piŋ], *ag.* **1.** pendente, piegato in giù; abbassato (di occhi, baffi) **2.** languente, abbattuto (di spirito) || *s.* V. **droop**.

droopingly ['dru:piŋli], *av.* languidamente.

drop [drɔp], *s.* **1.** goccia: — *by —*, goccia a goccia; *to drink to the last —*, bere fino all'ultima goccia **2.** *pl.* (*med.*) medicina (a gocce) **3.** *pl.* (*arch.*) gocce **4.** *pl.* pastiglie, caramelline **5.** sorso, bicchiere (di liquido) **6.** discesa, caduta; diminuzione, abbassamento (di prezzi, temperatura, livello sociale, ecc.): *a sudden — in prices*, un calo improvviso nei prezzi **7.** (*aer. mil.*) lancio col paracadute **8.** trabocchetto della forca **9.** franatura, caduta di terra ☆ — *-bottle*, contagocce; — *-scene*, (*teat.*) sipario || *ear-drops*, orecchini a goccia.

to **drop**, *pass.p.p.* **dropped** [drɔpt], *v.t.i.* **1.** cadere (a gocce) **2.** cadere; lasciare, lasciarsi cadere: *don't — that vase*, non lasciar cadere quel vaso; *she dropped into an armchair*, si abbandonò in una poltrona; *to — anchor*, gettare l'àncora || *I am ready to —*, casco dalla stanchezza || *to — asleep*, addormentarsi || *to — a postcard, a line*, mandare una cartolina, mandare due righe, far sapere (per iscritto) **3.** *fig.* lasciar cadere (parola, osservazione) **4.** (*aer. mil.*) sganciare (bombe) **5.** diminuire, cadere (di vento, temperatura, prezzi, ecc.); (*mec.*) abbassare **6.** (*sl.*) perdere (denaro al giuoco) **7.** abbassare (occhi, voce) || *to — a curtsy*, fare un inchino **8.** deporre (passeggeri, pacchi) **9.** omettere, sopprimere: *to — one's h's*, non pronunciare l'h **10.** abbandonare; rinunciare a (progetto, abitudine, conoscenza) **11.** *to — across* (*s.o., sthg.*), incontrare per caso **12.** *to — into* (*a place*), entrare per caso in (un posto) **13.** *to — away*, andarsene alla spicciolata, uno dopo l'altro; sciogliersi (di famiglie) **14.** *to — behind*, rimanere indietro **15.** *to — in*, capitare per una breve visita **16.** *to — off*, andarsene a uno a uno, diminuire gradatamente; addormentarsi; distaccarsi (di foglie) **17.** *to — out*, scomparire; ritirarsi.

droplet ['drɔplit], *s.* gocciolina.

dropper ['drɔpə*], *s.* **1.** (*chim. med.*) tubo contagocce **2.** (*ind. tessile*) ponilamelle; guardiaordito ☆ — *in*, (*fam.*) ospite inatteso.

dropping ['drɔpiŋ], *s.* **1.** gocciolamento **2.** *pl.* escrementi (di animali).

dropsical ['drɔpsikəl], *ag.* (*patol.*) idropico.

dropsy ['drɔpsi], *s.* (*patol.*) idropisia.

dropwort ['drɔpwə:t], *s.* (*bot.*) filipendula.

drosera ['drɔsərə], *s.* (*bot.*) drosera.

droshky ['drɔʃki], **drosky** ['drɔski], *s.* leggera carrozza russa, aperta, a quattro ruote.

dross [drɔs], *s.* **1.** scoria di metalli **2.** materiale di scarto.

drossy ['drɔsi], *ag.* pieno di scorie; senza valore.

drought [draut], *s.* **1.** siccità **2.** (*arc.*) sete.

droughty ['drauti], *ag.* **1.** secco; arido **2.** sitibondo.

drouth [drauθ], (*arc. amer.*) per **drought**.

drove[1] [drouv], *s.* **1.** branco; gregge, mandria (in movimento); *fig.* turba, folla **2.** pista (per traffico pedonale o animale) **3.** piccolo canale d'irrigazione ☆ — *chisel*, scalpello per finitura; — *-road* (o — *-way*), pista.

to **drove**[1], *v.i.* fare il boaro, il mandriano.

drove[2], *pass.* di to **drive**.

drover ['drouvə*], *s.* boaro, mandriano; mercante di bestiame.

to **drown** [draun], *v.t.i.* **1.** annegare, annegarsi; affogare: *he drowned himself*, egli si annegò (volutamente); *he fell into the river and was drowned*, egli cadde nel fiume e si annegò (conseguenza non voluta); *he was drowned by his enemy*, egli fu fatto annegare dal suo nemico; *to* — *one's sorrow in drink*, (*fam.*) annegare il dolore nel vino || *to* — *the shamrock*, (*amer. irl.*) celebrare la festa di S. Patrizio bevendo **2.** sommergere; allagare || *to be drowned out*, essere cacciato di casa dalla piena **3.** coprire, smorzare, soffocare (suoni); offuscare (lo splendore, ecc.).

drowned [draund], *ag.* **1.** annegato: *a* — *man*, un annegato **2.** allagato, inondato ☆ — *dam*, pescaia, diga tracimante.

drowning ['drauniŋ], *s.* **1.** annegamento, affogamento **2.** allagamento, inondazione.

to **drowse** [drauz], *v.t.i.* assopire, assopirsi; essere assopito; sentire sonnolenza || *to* — *the time away*, passare il tempo a sonnecchiare.

drowsily ['drauzili], *av.* **1.** con aria sonnolenta **2.** in modo da indurre al sonno.

drowsiness ['drauzinis], *s.* sonnolenza, assopimento.

drowsy ['drauzi], *ag.* **1.** sonnolento; assopito **2.** che induce al sonno.

to **drub** [drʌb], *pass.p.p.* **drubbed** [drʌbd], *v.t.* picchiare, bastonare, dare una buona dose di legnate a || *to* — *sthg. into s.o.*, *out of s.o.*, far entrare ql.co. nella testa di qlcu., cavare ql.co. dalla testa di qlcu. a forza di legnate.

drubbing ['drʌbiŋ], *s.* bastonatura.

drudge [drʌdʒ], *s.c.* sgobbone, sgobbona.

to **drudge**, *v.i.* lavorare come un negro; sfacchinare.

drudgery ['drʌdʒəri], *s.* lavoro faticoso, ingrato.

drug [drʌg], *s.* **1.** sostanza medicinale, prodotto farmaceutico **2.** narcotico, stupefacente **3.** merce invendibile, passata di moda ☆ — *-addict* (o — *-fiend*), morfinomane; — *habit*, oppiomania, morfinomania, ecc.; — *-store*, (*amer.*) farmacia, negozio dove si vendono medicinali e bevande analcoliche; — *traffic*, traffico degli stupefacenti || *truth* —, siero della verità.

to **drug**, *pass.p.p.* **drugged** [drʌgd], *v.t.i.* **1.** adulterare con sostanze medicinali, ipnotiche, venefiche: *drugged cigarettes*, sigarette narcotizzate **2.** somministrare narcotici a, narcotizzare **3.** prendere narcotici.

drugget ['drʌgit], *s.* bigello; panno usato per fodera dei tappeti « moquette ».

druggist ['drʌgist], *s.* (*amer. scoz.*) farmacista; proprietario di un « drug-store ».

Druid ['dru(:)id], *s.* (*relig.*) druido (sacerdote degli antichi Celti).

Druidess ['dru(:)idis], *s.* (*relig.*) druidessa (sacerdotessa degli antichi Celti).

Druidical [dru(:)'idikəl], *ag.* (*relig.*) druidico.

Druidism ['dru(:)idizm], *s.* (*relig.*) druidismo.

drum [drʌm], *s.* **1.** (*mus. arch.*) tamburo: *to play the* —, suonare il tamburo **2.** (*mec.*) tamburo collettore (di caldaia) **3.** rullio del tamburo **4.** (*anat.*) timpano, membrana timpanica **5.** oggetto a forma di tamburo, rullo, cilindro, bidone ☆ — *-major*, tamburo maggiore; — *mixer*, (*mec.*) betoniera a tamburo; — *-stick*, bac-

chetta del tamburo || *big* —, grancassa; *kettle* —, timpano.

to **drum**, *pass.p.p.* **drummed** [drʌmd], *v.t.i.* **1.** suonare, battere il tamburo; tamburellare (sui vetri, sul tavolo) || *to* — *sthg. into s.o.'s head*, inculcare ql.co. nella mente di qlcu. **2.** *to* — *out*, (*mil.*) espellere (al suono del tamburo), degradare **3.** *to* — *up*, raccogliere (reclute, partigiani); (*amer.*) procurarsi (clienti); (*fam.*) fare appello a (amici): *to* — *up customers*, (*amer. comm.*) viaggiare per procurarsi clienti, fare propaganda.

drumfire ['drʌm,faiə*], *s.* (*artigl.*) fuoco tambureggiante di sbarramento.

drumfish ['drʌmfiʃ], *s.* (*ittiol.*) tamburo.

drumhead ['drʌmhed], *s.* **1.** pelle di tamburo **2.** (*anat.*) membrana del timpano **3.** (*mar.*) testa d'argano ☆ — *court-martial*, corte marziale (all'aperto) intorno ad un tamburo rovesciato; — *service*, funzione religiosa all'aperto.

drummer ['drʌmə*], *s.* **1.** (*mil.*) tamburino **2.** (*amer.*) viaggiatore di commercio; propagandista.

drunk [drʌŋk], *p.p.* di to **drink** || *ag. predicativo* **1.** ubriaco: *to be* —, essere ubriaco; *to get* —, ubriacarsi || *as* — *as a lord*, ubriaco fradicio **2.** *fig.* ebbro: — *with joy*, ebbro, pazzo di gioia || *s.* (*sl.*) ubriaco, ubriacone.

drunkard ['drʌŋkəd], *s.* ubriacone, beone.

drunken ['drʌŋkən], *p.p.* (*arc.*) di to **drink** || *ag.***1.**(*arc.*) ebbro, ubriaco; da ubriaco **2.** (*fis.*) inzuppato.

drunkenly ['drʌŋkənli], *av.* da ubriaco.

drunkenness ['drʌŋkənnis], *s.* ubriachezza; ebbrezza.

drupe [dru:p], *s.* (*bot.*) drupa.

Drury Lane ['druəri'lein], *s.* **1.** Drury Lane (strada di Londra famosa per i suoi teatri) **2.** (*abbr.* di *Drury Lane Theatre*), teatro Drury Lane.

druse [dru:z], *s.* (*min.*) drusa, geode.

dry [drai], *ag.* **1.** secco; asciutto; arido: — *eyed*, ad occhi asciutti, senza lacrime; — *facts*, i fatti puri e semplici; — *land*, terra arida; — *weather*, tempo asciutto; — *wood*, legna secca || *as* — *as a bone*, completamente secco || *to feel* —, aver sete **2.** monotono; arido, privo di interesse: — *reading*, lettura priva di interesse **3.** caustico, ironico **4.** (*metal.*) fragile; impuro; a grana grossa **5.** (*mil. amer.*) a salve, senza munizioni ☆ — *cleaning*, (*elett.*), batteria a secco; — *cleaning*, pulitura a secco; — *country*, (*amer.*) paese dove vige il proibizionismo; — *dock*, bacino di carenaggio; — *goods*, gli aridi; (*amer.*) tessuti; — *ice*, (*neol.*) ghiaccio secco; — *measure*, misura di capacità (per aridi); — *nurse*, balia asciutta; — *rot*, carie del legno; — (*stone*) *wall*, muro a secco.

to **dry**, *v.t.i.* **1.** seccare, far seccare **2.** asciugare, asciugarsi (di vestiti, lacrime): *to put sthg. out to* —, mettere fuori ql.co. ad asciugare **3.** (*ind.*) essiccare, asciugare, seccare **4.** *to* — *up*, asciugarsi completamente (anche *fig.*); (*fam.*) cessare di parlare: — *up!*, (*sl.*) stai zitto!.

dryad ['drai-əd], *s.* (*mit.*) driade.

dryasdust ['drai-əzdʌst], *ag.* arido, noioso, privo d'interesse || *s.* pedante; autore prolisso, pedante.

to **dry-clean** ['drai'kli:n], *v.t.* lavare a secco.

dryer ['draiə*], *s.* **1.** essiccatore; (*ind.*) essiccatoio **2.** (*chim.*) essiccativo ☆ *hair* —, « phon », asciugacapelli.

drying ['drai-iŋ], *ag.* essiccante; (*chim.*) essiccativo || *s.* l'asciugarsi; (*ind.*) essiccamento, essiccazione ☆ — *room*, (*ind.*) essiccatoio.

dryly ['draili], *av.* seccamente: *to answer* —, rispondere seccamente.

dryness ['drainis], *s.* **1.** siccità, aridità (di suolo, tempo) **2.** severità; causticità; aridità (di discorso, ecc.).

to **drysalt** ['drai'sɔ:lt], *v.t.* metter sotto sale, salare (carne, ecc. per conservarla).

drysalter ['drai,sɔ:ltə*], *s.* droghiere.

drysaltery ['drai,sɔ:ltəri], *s.* drogheria.

dry-shod ['drai'ʃɔd], *ag.av.* a piedi asciutti.

dual ['dju(:)əl], *ag.* doppio; duplice ‖ *s.* (*gram. greca*) duale, accoppiato ☆ — *carriage-way*, strada a doppia carreggiata.

dualism ['dju(:)əlizəm], *s.* **1.** (*fil.*) dualismo **2.** dualità.

dualist ['dju(:)əlist], *s.* (*fil.*) dualista.

dualistic [,dju(:)ə'listik], *ag.* dualistico.

duality [dju(:)'æliti], *s.* dualità.

to dub[1] [dʌb], *pass.p.p.* **dubbed** [dʌbd], *v.t.* **1.** (*arc.*) nominare, creare (cavaliere): *to — s.o. a knight,* creare qlcu. cavaliere **2.** (*fam.*) qualificare; dare un soprannome a **3.** (*tec.*) addobbare, ammorbidire (il cuoio) con grasso **4.** asciare (legno) **5.** rifinire il taglio a (una siepe).

to dub[2], *v.t.* (*cine.*) doppiare: *a film dubbed in French,* un film doppiato in francese; *to — English dialogue,* fare il doppiaggio del dialogo inglese.

dubbing[1] ['dʌbiŋ], *s.* (*ind.*) addobbamento (concia per ammorbidire il cuoio).

dubbing[2], *s.* (*cine.*) doppiaggio.

dubiety [dju(:)'baiəti], *s.* dubbiosità; incertezza.

dubious ['dju:bjəs], *ag.* **1.** dubbio; equivoco: — *character,* carattere poco chiaro **2.** esitante; incerto: *to be — of s.o.'s honesty,* aver dei dubbi sulla onestà di qlcu.; *to feel — as to,* sentirsi incerto in merito a, riguardo a.

dubiously ['dju:bjəsli], *av.* **1.** in modo dubbio; in modo incerto **2.** con esitazione.

dubiousness ['dju:bjəsnis], *s.* **1.** dubbiosità, incertezza **2.** carattere dubbio, equivoco.

dubitable ['dju:bitəbl], *ag.* (*letter.*) dubitabile.

to dubitate ['dju:biteit], *v.i.* (*letter.*) dubitare.

dubitation [,dju:bi'teiʃən], *s.* dubbio; esitazione.

dubitative ['dju:bitətiv], *ag.* **1.** dubitativo; esitante **2.** (*gram.*) dubitativo.

dubitatively ['dju:bitətivli], *av.* dubitativamente.

Dublin ['dʌblin], *no.pr.* (*geog.*) Dublino.

ducal ['dju:kəl], *ag.* ducale.

ducat ['dʌkət], *s.* ducato (moneta).

duchess ['dʌtʃis], *s.* duchessa.

duchy ['dʌtʃi], *s.* ducato (territorio).

duck[1] [dʌk], *s.* **1.** anitra: — *and green peas,* (*cuc.*) anitra arrosto con piselli ‖ *ducks and drakes,* rimbalzello: *to play ducks and drakes with one's money, life,* sperperare i propri denari, la propria vita ‖ *a fine day for young ducks,* giorno piovoso ‖ *in two shakes of a duck's tail,* in un batter d'occhio ‖ *that's like pouring water on a duck's back,* è tutta fatica sprecata ‖ *to take to sthg. like a — to water,* darsi a ql.co. senza esitazione, naturalmente, senza difficoltà **2.** (*fam.*) caro; cocco: *a — of a child,* un amore di bimbo; *you are a —!,* sei proprio cara! **3.** punteggio (specialmente al cricket): *to break one's —,* segnare il primo punto (al cricket) ‖ —*'s egg,* (*sl.*) zero ☆ —*-boards,* ponte di tavole; — *soup,* (*fam.*) cosa facile e (talvolta) rimunerativa ‖ *lame —,* (*fam.*) persona debole, minorata, in cattive acque; (*borsa*) speculatore moroso; (*amer. st. pol.*) membro non rieletto al Congresso, utilizzato come funzionario del governo; membro del Congresso non rieletto, ma in carica fino all'apertura del nuovo Congresso; *wild- —,* anitra selvatica.

duck[2], *s.* **1.** tuffo **2.** inchino.

to duck[2], *v.t.i.* **1.** tuffare, immergere nell'acqua per un momento; tuffarsi nell'acqua e venire subito a galla **2.** muoversi, piegarsi velocemente (per evitare di ricevere un colpo o di essere visto): *to — one's head,* abbassare improvvisamente la testa **3.** (*fam.*) inchinarsi (per salutare).

duck[3], *s.* **1.** tela olona, tela da vela **2.** *pl.* (*fam.*) calzoni di tela bianca.

duck[4], *s.* (*mil.*) veicolo anfibio.

duckbill ['dʌkbil], *s.* (*zool.*) ornitorinco.

ducker[1] ['dʌkə*], *s.* **1.** allevatore di anitre **2.** cacciatore di anitre.

ducker[2], *s.* **1.** chi si tuffa, si immerge **2.** (*ornit.*) strolaga; svasso.

ducking[1] ['dʌkiŋ], *s.* caccia di anitre selvatiche.

ducking[2], *s.* **1.** tuffo; immersione (anche involontaria) **2.** inchino.

duckling ['dʌkliŋ], *s.* anatroccolo.

duckweed ['dʌk-wi:d], *s.* (*bot.*) lente palustre.

ducky ['dʌki], *s.c.* (*fam.*) piccino mio, piccina mia; cuor mio.

duct [dʌkt], *s.* **1.** condotto; conduttura; (*tip.*) calamaio **2.** (*anat.*) canale, vaso (chilifero, linfatico, ecc.) **3.** (*bot.*) canale.

ductile ['dʌktail], *ag.* duttile; *fig.* docile.

ductility [dʌk'tiliti], *s.* duttilità; *fig.* docilità.

dud [dʌd], *ag.* senza energia; senza consistenza; inutile; futile; falso ‖ *s.* (*sl.*) **1.** *gener. pl.* cenci; stracci; indumenti, vestiti logori **2.** zuccone; persona incapace; persona che non val nulla **3.** (*mil.*) proiettile, bomba, razzo inesploso.

dude [dju:d], *s.* (*amer. fam.*) « dandy », zerbinotto ☆ — *ranch,* (*amer.*) fattoria dove alloggiano ospiti paganti.

dudeen [du:'di:n], *s.* (*irl.*) pipa corta di terracotta.

dudgeon ['dʌdʒən], *s.* collera, sdegno: *in high —,* indignatissimo.

due [dju:], *ag.* **1.** dovuto, da pagarsi: *to be —,* essere dovuto; *to fall* (o *to be*) —, (*comm.*) scadere, maturarsi (degli effetti): *the rent is — to-morrow,* l'affitto scade domani **2.** dovuto, adatto, conveniente: *after — consideration,* dopo la dovuta considerazione; *in — course,* a suo tempo, regolarmente; *in — time,* a tempo debito; *he has had his — reward,* ha avuto la ricompensa che gli spettava ‖ *I am — for a shave,* (*fam.*) è ora che mi faccia la barba **3.** *to be — to,* essere dovuto a, causato da: *the accident was — to,* il disastro fu dovuto a **4.** *to be —,* essere atteso; dovere: *the ship is — to-morrow,* la nave è attesa per domani; *they are — to speak this evening,* devono parlare questa sera.

due, *s.* **1.** il dovuto, il debito, il giusto; tributo; *to give a man his —,* dare ad uomo ciò che gli è giustamente dovuto ‖ *to give the devil his —,* dare a ciascuno quel che gli è dovuto **2.** *pl.* quota sociale (da pagarsi ad un circolo) ☆ *annual dues,* quote annuali; *dock dues,* diritti di magazzinaggio; *harbour dues,* diritti di porto; *town dues,* dazio.

due, *av.* direttamente, esattamente, precisamente (specialmente con punti cardinali): — *east,* in direzione est.

duel ['dju(:)əl], *s.* **1.** duello: *to fight a —,* battersi in duello **2.** *fig.* lotta, contestazione.

to duel, *pass.p.p.* **duelled** ['dju(:)əld], *v.i.* fare un duello, battersi in duello.

dueller ['dju(:)ələ*], *s.* duellante.

duelling ['dju(:)əliŋ], *s.* il duellare.

duellist ['dju(:)əlist], *s.* duellante.

duenna [dju(:)'enə], *s.* vecchia governante; dama di compagnia accompagnatrice di una ragazza (generalmente in Spagna).

duet [dju(:)'et], *s.* (*mus.*) duetto.

duff[1] [dʌf], *s.* (*fam.*) **1.** pasta di pane **2.** budino di farina.

to duff[2], *v.t.* **1.** (*sl.*) mettere a nuovo (abiti vecchi) **2.** (*austral.*) falsificare: *to — cattle,* cambiare il marchio al bestiame rubato.

to duff[3], *v.t.* (*spor.*) sbagliare (il colpo) (anche *fig.*).

duffel ['dʌfəl], *s.* **1.** (*fam.*) stoffa pesante; mollettone **2.** (*amer.*) equipaggiamento (per campeggio) ☆ — *coat,* « montgomery », giacchettone di lana.

duffer ['dʌfə*], *s.* **1.** (*fam.*) inetto; dappoco; ignorante **2.** venditore ambulante di merce di contrabbando **3.** (*austral.*) ladro di bestiame **4.** (*sl.*) cosa da poco, inutile.

duffle, *V.* **duffel**.

dug[1] [dʌg], *s.* **1.** capezzolo, mammella (di animale) **2.** *pl.* (*spreg.*) seno.

dug[2], *pass. p.p.* di *to* **dig**.

dugong ['du:gɔŋ], *s.* (*zool.*) dugongo.

dugout ['dʌgaut], *s.* **1.** canoa (ricavata da un tronco d'albero) **2.** rifugio; (*mil.*) ricovero sotterraneo, trincea **3.** (*mil. sl.*) ufficiale in pensione richiamato.

duke [dju:k], *s.* duca.

dukedom ['dju:kdəm], *s.* **1.** ducato (territorio governato da un duca) **2.** titolo, dignità di duca.

dulcamara [,dʌlkə'mɑ:rə], *s.* (*bot.*) dulcamara.

dulcet ['dʌlsit], *ag.* dolce, gradevole, soave (di suoni).

dulcification [,dʌlsifi'keiʃən], *s.* dolcificazione.

to **dulcify** ['dʌlsifai], *v.t.* dolcificare.

dulcimer ['dʌlsimə*], *s.* (*mus.*) salterio.

Dulcinea [,dʌlsi'niə], *no.pr.f.* (*lett.*) Dulcinea ‖ *s.* donna del cuore.

dulia [dju:'laiə], *s.* (*teol.*) dulia.

dull [dʌl], *ag.* **1.** tardo; lento; poco intelligente: *a — mind*, una mente tarda; *a — pupil*, un allievo ottuso; *to be — of hearing, of sight*, essere debole d'udito, di vista **2.** sordo; soffocato: *a — ache*, un dolore sordo; *a — sound*, un suono sordo, soffocato **3.** (*comm.*) fiacco: *the — season*, la stagione morta; *the market is —*, il mercato è fiacco **4.** triste, depresso: *to feel —*, sentirsi depresso, annoiato **5.** monotono, noioso, non interessante: *a — book, speech*, un libro tedioso, un discorso noioso; *— weather*, tempo uggioso ‖ *as — as ditch-water*, (*fam.*) noioso come una mosca **6.** non tagliente, spuntato: *a — knife*, un coltello non tagliente **7.** (*colore*) opaco, appannato, offuscato: *— light*, luce debole ☆ *— -brained*, dall'intelligenza ottusa; *— -eyed*, dall'occhio senza espressione; *— -witted*, d'intelligenza ottusa o tarda.

to **dull**, *v.t.i.* **1.** istupidirsi; istupidire; intorpidire (i sensi) **2.** spuntare (una lama) **3.** offuscare; rendere meno intenso; smorzare, indebolire: *to — pain by narcotics*, alleviare, calmare il dolore con narcotici.

dullard ['dʌləd], *s.c.* persona stupida, ottusa.

dullish ['dʌliʃ], *ag.* piuttosto noioso; un po' triste, tetro.

dullness ['dʌlnis], *s.* **1.** lentezza **2.** (*comm.*) fiacchezza, calma **3.** ottusità (di suono) **4.** noia; monotonia **5.** mancanza di luce, colore, vivacità, attrattiva.

dully ['dʌli], *av.* **1.** ottusamente; lentamente **2.** debolmente; senza energia **3.** in modo noioso, monotono.

dulness, *V.* **dullness.**

dulse [dʌls], *s.* (*scoz. irl.*) alga commestibile.

duly ['dju:li], *av.* **1.** debitamente: *members — appointed*, membri debitamente nominati; *I have — received...*, ho debitamente ricevuto... **2.** a tempo debito, in tempo utile: *you will — receive the money*, riceverete i denari a tempo debito.

duma ['du:mə], *s.* (*pol.*) duma.

dumb [dʌm], *ag.* **1.** muto: *— from birth* (o *born —*), muto dalla nascita; *deaf and —*, sordomuto ‖ *— as a fish* (o *as an oyster*), (*fam.*) muto come un pesce **2.** ammutolito, reticente: *to be struck — with astonishment, fear*, ammutolire per la sorpresa, il timore; *to strike s.o. —*, far ammutolire qlcu., ridurre qlcu. al silenzio **3.** mancante di suono **4.** (*amer. fam.*) stupido, ottuso ☆ *— fever*, (*patol.*) febbre intermittente; *— -piano*, pianoforte senza corde (usato per studio); *— -show*, (*teat.*) pantomima, scena muta; gesto muto; *— -waiter*, carrello; tavolino da tè a ripiani; (*amer.*) montavivande.

to **dumb**, *v.t.* attutire, render sordo (un suono).

dumb-bell ['dʌmbel], *s.* **1.** *pl.* peso; manubrio (per ginnastica) **2.** (*amer. sl.*) sciocco, imbecille.

to **dumbfound** [dʌm'faund], *v.t.* confondere, stordire; stupire: *dumbfounding news*, notizia stupefacente; *I was dumbfounded at the news*, rimasi attonito alla notizia; *the news dumbfounded me*, la notizia mi fece stupire, mi stordì.

dumbledore ['dʌmbl,dɔ:*], *s.* (*entom. dial.*) **1.** calabrone **2.** scarafaggio.

dumbly ['dʌmli], *av.* senza pronunciare parola; in silenzio: *he — accepted the verdict*, accettò il verdetto in silenzio.

dumbness ['dʌmnis], *s.* **1.** mutismo **2.** (*fam.*) silenzio.

dumdum ['dʌmdʌm], *s. — (bullet)*, (*mil.*) pallottola esplosiva dumdum.

dummy ['dʌmi], *ag.* **1.** muto, silenzioso **2.** falso, posticcio **3.** (*carte*) giocato con il morto ‖ *s.* **1.** (*fam.*) persona muta, silenziosa; (*lett.*) personaggio muto (nei drammi) **2.** fantoccio, manichino (da sarto, vetrina); falso pacchetto, scatola, ecc. **3.** uomo di paglia; prestanome **4.** (*carte*) morto (giocatore immaginario) **5.** (*tip.*) menabò **6.** (*ferr.*) locomotiva con condensatore **7.** (*sl. amer.*) persona scema, ottusa ☆ *— bomber*, (*aer.*) sagoma di bombardiere; *— box*, scatola da mostra: *in the shop-window there were all — boxes*, nella vetrina c'erano tutte scatole vuote, da mostra; *— cartridge*, (*mil.*) cartuccia a salve; *— bridge*, (*carte*) « bridge » col morto ‖ *baby's —*, tettarella, succhiotto.

dumose ['dju:mous], *ag.* spinoso; cespuglioso.

dump¹ [dʌmp], *s.* **1.** biglia di piombo (per giuoco di ragazzi) **2.** pasticca, caramella **3.** (*sl.*) soldo, centesimo; (*sl.*) quattrini: *it's not worth a —*, non vale un soldo **4.** individuo tozzo **5.** (*mar.*) bullone.

dump², *s.* buca profonda nel letto di un fiume.

dump³, *s.* **1.** colpo sordo (di ql.co. che cade pesantemente) **2.** mucchio; ammasso (di detriti, spazzatura, ecc.) **3.** luogo di scarico (di detriti, spazzatura, ecc.); (*miner.*) discarica **4.** (*amer. sl.*) asilo notturno; taverna; prigione **5.** (*comm.*) vendita sottocosto **6.** (*ammunition*) —, deposito di munizioni ☆ *— truck*, autocarro con cassone ribaltabile.

to **dump³**, *v.t.* **1.** scaricare (detriti, sabbia) **2.** formare una riserva, un deposito di (viveri, munizioni) **3.** (*comm.*) vendere sottocosto (a paese straniero) **4.** (*austral.*) pressare (lana) con pressa idraulica **5.** *to — down*, rovesciare con rumore sordo; sbarcare (indesiderabili).

dumper ['dʌmpə*], *s.* **1.** chi rovescia (alla rinfusa detriti, ecc.) **2.** (*aut.*) autoribaltabile; (*ferr.*) rovesciatore **3.** (*comm.*) esportatore di merce sottocosto.

dumpiness ['dʌmpinis], *s.* aspetto tarchiato.

dumping ['dʌmpiŋ], *s.* **1.** il rovesciare, lo scaricare (rifiuti) **2.** (*comm.*) « dumping » (esportazione di prodotti a prezzi rovinosi a scopo di concorrenza) ☆ *— -ground*, luogo di scarico; deposito di rifiuti.

dumpish ['dʌmpiʃ], *ag.* triste; abbattuto, depresso.

dumpishly ['dʌmpiʃli], *av.* tristemente; in modo depresso.

dumpishness ['dʌmpiʃnis], *s.* tristezza; abbattimento.

dumpling ['dʌmpliŋ], *s.* **1.** pallottola di pasta bollita (servita con carne, verdura) **2.** (*sl.*) persona, animale piccolo e rotondetto ☆ *apple —*, mela avvolta in uno strato di pasta e cotta al forno.

dumps [dʌmps], *s.pl.* (*fam.*) umor nero; depressione: *to be (down) in the —*, essere di cattivo umore.

dumpy¹ ['dʌmpi], *ag.* triste, abbattuto.

dumpy², *ag.* tarchiato ‖ *s.* **1.** persona tarchiata; animale dalle zampe corte **2.** *pl. the Dumpies*, (*fam.*) il diciannovesimo reggimento degli Ussari ☆ *— -level*, (*strum.*) livello da geometri, livello a cannocchiale.

dun¹ [dʌn], *ag.* bruno grigiastro opaco ‖ *s.* **1.** colore bruno grigiastro **2.** cavallo di colore bruno grigiastro **3.** (*pesca*) pupa; esca artificiale simile a pupa.

to **dun¹**, *pass.p.p.* **dunned** [dʌnd], *v.t.* **1.** render bruno, grigiastro **2.** salare (specialmente merluzzo).

dun², *s.* **1.** creditore importuno; esattore (di un debito) **2.** sollecitazione di pagamento.

to **dun²**, *v.t.* sollecitare con insistenza (un debitore): *to be dunned on all sides*, essere carico di debiti ☆ *dunning letter*, lettera che sollecita il pagamento di un debito.

dunce [dʌns], *s.* (*fam.*) ignorante; (*scolastico*) somaro, asino ☆ *—'s cap*, berretto d'asino.

duncedom ['dʌnsdəm], *s.* la categoria dei somari.

duncery ['dʌnsəri], *s.* stupidaggine; stoltezza.

to **dunch** [dʌnʃ], *v.t.* (*scoz.*) urtare, spingere coi gomiti.

Dunciad ['dʌnsiæd], *s.* (*lett.*) poema epico degli stolti; repubblica degli Stolti (dal poema epico di Pope).

dunder ['dʌndə*], s. feccia (delle canne da zucchero).

dunderhead ['dʌndəhed], s. (fam.) stupido.

dundreary [dʌn'drɪəri], s. (fam.) fedina, basetta.

dune [dju:n], s. duna.

dung [dʌŋ], s. 1. sterco, escrementi (specialmente di animali) 2. letame ☆ — -beetle, (entom.) scarabeo stercorario; — -cart, carretto per letame; — -fork, forca per letame.

to dung, v.t.i. 1. concimare 2. emettere escrementi.

dungaree [,dʌŋgə'ri:], s. 1. grossolana cotonina indiana 2. pl. tuta (generalmente blu, da operaio).

dungeon ['dʌndʒən], s. 1. dongione 2. cella, prigione sotterranea.

dunghill ['dʌŋhil], s. letamaio ‖ to raise s.o. from the —, (fam.) elevare qlcu. dal fango.

duniwassal ['du:ni'wɔsəl], s. (scoz.) gentiluomo appartenente ad un ramo cadetto di una grande famiglia.

to dunk [dʌŋk], v.t.i. (amer.) inzuppare (pane, biscotto) nel tè, latte, brodo.

Dunkerque, Dunkirk [dʌn'kə:k], no.pr. (geog.) Dunkerque ‖ s. fig. ritirata sotto bombardamento nemico.

dunlin ['dʌnlin], s. (ornit.) tringa alpina, piovanello.

Dunlop ['dʌnlɔp], s. formaggio molto grasso di Dunlop (Scozia).

dunnage ['dʌnidʒ], s. (mar.) paglietto; pagliuolo; (fam.) bagagli (di marinaio).

dunno [də'nou], (sl. abbr. di I don't know) non so.

dunnock ['dʌnək], s. (ornit.) sordone.

Dunsinane [dʌn'sinən, (in Shakespeare) 'dʌnsinein], no.pr. (geog.) Dunsinane (località scozzese dove fu sconfitto Macbeth).

dunt [dʌnt], s. 1. (scoz.) colpo, percossa 2. (scoz.) battito del cuore 3. (aer.) colpo che un aereo riceve da una corrente d'aria incontrata inaspettatamente.

to dunt, v.t.i. (scoz.) 1. battere, percuotere 2. battere violentemente (di cuore).

duodecennial [,dju(:)oudi'senjəl], ag. duodecennale.

duodecimal [,dju(:)ou'desiməl], ag. 1. dodicesimo 2. basato sul dodici ‖ s.pl. (mat.) sistema duodecimale, basato sul numero 12 (usato per piedi e pollici).

duodecimo [,dju(:)ou'desimou], s. (tip.) duodecimo, dodicesimo (formato di libro).

duodenal [,dju(:)ou'di:nl], ag. (anat.) duodenale ☆ — glands, ghiandole duodenali; — papilla, papilla duodenale; — ulcer, ulcera duodenale.

duodenary [,dju(:)ou'di:nəri], ag. (mat.) duodecimale.

duodenum [,dju(:)ou'di:nəm], s. (anat.) duodeno.

duologue ['djuəlɔg], s. dialogo (tra due persone).

dupable ['dju:pəbl], ag. ingannabile; mistificabile.

dupe [dju:p], s. gonzo; sempliciotto ‖ to be the ready — of s.o., lasciarsi facilmente gabbare da qlcu.

to dupe, v.t. ingannare; gabbare; abbindolare.

dupion ['dju:piən], s. doppione, bozzolo doppio formato da due bachi da seta.

duple ['dju:pl], ag. (mus.) doppio: — time, misura a due tempi.

duplex ['dju:pleks], ag. doppio; duplice ☆ — engine, (mec.) motore a due cilindri; — house, (amer.) casa per due famiglie; — operation, funzionamento in duplice.

duplicate ['dju:plikit], ag. doppio; di ricambio: — tyre, gomma di ricambio ‖ s. 1. duplicato: a letter in —, una lettera in duplicato, doppia copia 2. pezzo di ricambio 3. (gram.) sinonimo 4. (cine.) controtipo.

to duplicate ['dju:plikeit], v.t.i. 1. duplicare (documenti, ecc.) 2. (cine.) stampare un controtipo di.

duplicating ['dju:plikeitiŋ], s. 1. raddoppiamento; esecuzione di copia ☆ — machine, copialettere.

duplication [,dju:pli'keiʃən], s. raddoppiamento; riproduzione; duplicazione.

duplicator ['dju:plikeitə*], s. copialettere.

duplicity [dju(:)'plisiti], s. malafede; doppiezza.

durability [,djuərə'biliti], s. durabilità; durata: of prolonged —, di grande durata.

durable ['djuərəbl], ag. durevole; resistente.

durableness ['djuərəblnis], s. durabilità, durata.

durably ['djuərəbli], av. durevolmente.

dural ['djuərəl], **duralumin** [djuə'ræljumin], **duraluminium** [djuə,ræljum'minjəm], s. duralluminio.

duramen [djuə'reimen], s. (bot.) durame.

durance ['djuərəns], s. (poet.) prigionia.

duration [djuə'reiʃən], s. durata: — of copyright, durata dei diritti d'autore ☆ — form, (gram.) forma di durata.

durative ['djuərətiv], ag. (gram.) durativo.

durbar [də'ba:*], s. 1. ricevimento; luogo di ricevimento; sala delle udienze (in India) 2. corpo degli ufficiali in una corte indiana.

duress [djuə'res], s. 1. prigionia; arresto 2. costrizione; violenza: to act under —, cedere alla forza.

during ['djuəriŋ], prep. durante, nel corso di: — his life, durante la sua vita; — the winter, nel corso dell'inverno; killed — a brawl, ucciso in una rissa.

durst [də:st], pass. di to dare.

dusk [dʌsk], ag. (letter.) per dusky ‖ s. 1. oscurità, tenebre 2. crepuscolo: at —, all'imbrunire.

to dusk, v.t.i. (rar.) oscurare, oscurarsi; offuscare, offuscarsi; imbrunire.

duskiness ['dʌskinis], s. oscurità; colore scuro.

dusky ['dʌski], ag. 1. oscuro, fosco; fig. tetro, cupo 2. bruno (di colorito).

dust [dʌst], s. 1. polvere: to raise a cloud of —, sollevare una nube di polvere; to reduce sthg. to —, ridurre ql.co. in polvere ‖ to bite (o to lick) the —, mordere la polvere; cadere ferito, morto ‖ to humble oneself in the —, umiliarsi profondamente ‖ to raise (o to make) a —, fare tanto scalpore per nulla ‖ to shake the — off one's feet, andarsene indignato ‖ to throw — in a person's eyes, gettar la polvere negli occhi a qlcu. 2. (bot.) polline 3. ceneri (dei morti) 4. (gold-) —, (sl. amer.) denaro ☆ — -bin, pattumiera; — -bowl, (amer.) regione arida, polverosa, soggetta a siccità prolungata; — -cart, carro delle immondizie; — -coat (o — -cover o — -jacket), spolverina; — -pan, paletta per la spazzatura; — -storm, tempesta di polvere; — -wrapper (o — -jacket), sopracoperta (di libro, ecc.).

to dust, v.t.i. 1. (cuc.) cospargere: to — a cake with sugar, cospargere, spolverare un dolce con lo zucchero 2. impolverare, impolverarsi; ricoprire (ql.co.) di polvere 3. spolverare: to — s.o.'s coat for him, spolverare la giacca a qlcu.; fig. scuotere i panni a qlcu., spolverare le spalle a qlcu. (con un bastone) 4. ridurre in polvere.

duster ['dʌstə*], s. c. chi spolvera ‖ s. 1. strofinaccio, spolverino 2. (amer.) spolverina 3. (agr.) polverizzatore ☆ electric —, aspirapolvere elettrico.

dustiness ['dʌstinis], s. l'essere polveroso.

dusting ['dʌstiŋ], s. 1. lo spolverare 2. fig. bastonatura 3. (mar.) sballottamento.

dustman, pl. **dustmen** ['dʌstmən], s. 1. spazzino 2. il sonno (nel linguaggio infantile) ‖ the — is coming, (scherz.) arrivano i pisani, arriva il folletto serralocchi.

dusty ['dʌsti], ag. 1. polveroso, coperto di polvere: to get —, impolverarsi 2. arido, privo d'interesse; vago, indefinito ‖ it's not so —, (sl.) non c'è male, è discreto, abbastanza buono.

Dutch [dʌtʃ], ag. 1. olandese ‖ the —, gli olandesi ‖ this beats the —, è una cosa sorprendente ‖ to talk to s.o. like a — uncle, ammonire qlcu. paternamente 2. (arc.) tedesco ‖ s. 1. lingua olandese 2. (arc.) lingua tedesca ☆ — auction, asta pubblica in cui il banditore parte da un alto prezzo e lo abbassa finchè trova l'acquirente; — courage, coraggio dovuto al bere; — treat, trattenimento a cui si partecipa pagando alla romana.

Dutchman, pl. **Dutchmen** ['dʌtʃmən], s. (uomo) olandese.

Dutchwoman ['dʌtʃ,wumən], pl. **Dutchwomen** ['dʌtʃ,wimin], s. (donna) olandese.

duteous ['dju:tjəs], *V.* **dutiful**.
duteously ['dju:tjəsli], *av.* obbedientemente.
dutiable ['dju:tjəbl], *ag.* gravato di dazio; soggetto a dogana.
dutiful ['dju:tiful], *ag.* rispettoso, sottomesso, deferente: *a — husband*, un marito premuroso.
dutifully ['dju:tifuli], *av.* rispettosamente.
dutifulness ['dju:tifulnis], *s.* obbedienza, sottomissione.
duty ['dju:ti], *s.* **1.** ubbidienza, rispetto; ossequi: *to pay* (o *to present*) *one's — to s.o.*, presentare i propri ossequi a qlcu. **2.** dovere: *to do one's —*, fare il proprio dovere: *do your — come what may*, fa il tuo dovere qualsiasi cosa accada; *to do one's — by* (o *to*) *s.o.*, fare il proprio dovere verso qlcu. || *as in — bound*, come si deve **3.** (*gener. pl.*) funzioni; mansioni; compito, incarico: *the manager told me what my duties would be*, il direttore mi disse quali sarebbero state le mie incombenze **4.** servizio: *to be on, off —*, essere, non essere di servizio **5.** (*comm.*) dazio, dogana; diritto, tassa **6.** (*mec.*) rendimento di lavoro; (*elett.*) uso ☆ — *-free*, esente da dogana; — *-paid*, franco dogana || *death-duties*, tassa di successione; *excise —*, imposta di consumo; *stamp- —*, diritto di bollo; *succession duties*, imposta di successione.
duumvir [dju(:)'ʌmvə*], *pl.* **duumvirs** [dju(:)'ʌmvəz], **duumviri** [du:'umviri:], *s.* (*st. romana*) duumviro.
duumvirate [dju(:)'ʌmvirit], *s.* (*st. romana*) duumvirato.
dux [dʌks], *s.* **1.** capo **2.** (*spec. scoz.*) capoclasse.
dwale [dweil], *s.* (*bot.*) atropa, belladonna.
dwarf [dwo:f], *s.* nano ☆ — *-tree*, albero nano.
to dwarf, *v.t.* rimpicciolire; arrestare lo sviluppo di.
dwarfish ['dwo:fiʃ], *ag.* nano, di nano, da nano.
dwarfishly ['dwo:fiʃli], *av.* come un nano; da nano.
dwarfishness ['dwo:fiʃnis], *s.* (*patol.*) nanismo.
dwell [dwel], *s.* (*arc. mec.*) sosta, pausa.
to dwell, *pass.p.p.* **dwelt** [dwelt], (*amer.*) anche **dwelled** [dweld], *v.i.* **1.** dimorare, abitare: *to — in the country*, abitare in campagna **2.** restare; fissarsi; rimanere: *her memory dwells with me*, il suo ricordo rimane in me **3.** fermarsi; insistere; indugiare: *don't let your mind — on the past*, non lasciare che la tua mente si soffermi sul passato **4.** arrestarsi, esitare (di cavallo).
dweller ['dwelə*], *s.* **1.** abitante, abitatore **2.** cavallo che si arresta (prima del salto) ☆ *town- —*, cittadino.
dwelling ['dweliŋ], *s.* abitazione, residenza, dimora ☆ — *-house*, casa d'abitazione; — *-place*, dimora.
to dwindle ['dwindl], *v.i.* scemare, diminuire; deperire; restringersi, far restringere; *fig.* degenerare: *to — to nothing*, ridursi in nulla || *to — away*, diminuire poco alla volta (sino a scomparire).
dwindling ['dwindliŋ], *ag.* che diminuisce || *s.* diminuzione; deperimento.
dyad ['daiæd], *s.* (*mat.*) coppia; (*chim.*) elemento bivalente.
dyadie [dai'ædik], *ag.* (*chim.*) bivalente.
dye [dai], *s.* **1.** tinta, tintura: *fast —*, tinta solida ||

a scoundrel of the deepest —, (*fam.*) un furfante della peggior specie **2.** materia colorante, tintura **3.** — (*solution*), bagno di colore ☆ — *-house*, tintoria; — *-stuff*, materia colorante; — *-wood*, legno tintorio; — *-works*, tintoria.
to dye, *pass.p.p.* **dyed** [daid], *p.pr.* **dyeing** ['daiiŋ], *v.t.i.* **1.** tingere: *he dyes any kind of cloth*, tinge ogni genere di stoffa; *she dyes her hair brown*, si tinge i capelli color castano; *to — in the yarn*, tingere il filato; *to have a dress dyed*, farsi tingere un vestito **2.** tingersi: *this cloth dyes well*, questa stoffa si tinge bene, tiene bene la tintura ☆ *fast-dyed*, tinto a colori solidi; *piece-dyed*, tinto in pezza; *thread-dyed*, tinto in filato.
dyeing ['daiiŋ], *s.* il tingere; tintura.
dyer ['daiə*], *s.* tintore || *dyers and cleaners*, tintoria e lavanderia (negozio).
dying ['daiiŋ], *ag.* morente, moribondo, agonizzante: *the — day*, il giorno che muore; — *fire*, fuoco languente || *the —*, i morenti || *s.* agonia, morte ☆ — *bed*, letto di morte; — *breath*, l'ultimo respiro; — *day*, giorno della morte: *to one's — day*, fino al giorno della morte; — *oath*, l'ultimo giuramento; — *wish*, l'ultimo desiderio; — *words*, le ultime parole.
dyke, *V.* **dike**.
dynameter [dai'næmitə*], *s.* (*ott.*) dinametro.
dynamic [dai'næmik], *ag.* dinamico ☆ — *balancing*, (*mec.*) equilibratura dinamica.
dynamical [dai'næmikəl], *ag.s.* (principio) dinamico.
dynamically [dai'næmikəli], *av.* dinamicamente.
dynamics [dai'næmiks], *s.* dinamica.
dynamism ['dainəmizəm], *s.* dinamismo.
dynamist ['dainəmist], *s.* dinamista.
dynamitard ['dainəmita:d], *s.* dinamitardo.
dynamite ['dainəmait], *s.* dinamite.
to dynamite, *v.t.* far saltare con la dinamite.
dynamiter ['dainəmaitə*], *s.* dinamitardo.
dynamo ['dainəmou], *pl.* **dynamos** ['dainəmouz], *s.* (*elett.*) dinamo; generatore di corrente.
dynamometer [,dainə'mɔmitə*], *s.* dinamometro, misuratore di forza.
dynast ['dinəst], *s.* dinasta.
dynastic [di'næstik], *ag.* dinastico.
dynasty ['dinəsti], *s.* dinastia.
dyne [dain], *s.* (*fis.*) dina.
dyscrasia [dis'kreizjə], *s.* (*patol.*) discrasia.
dysenterie [,disn'terik], *ag.* (*patol.*) dissenterico.
dysentery ['disntri], *s.* (*patol.*) dissenteria.
dysmetria [dis'metriə], *s.* (*patol.*) dismetria.
dysorexia [,disə'reksiə], *s.* (*patol.*) disoressia.
dyspepsia [dis'pepsiə], *s.* (*patol.*) dispepsia.
dyspeptic [dis'peptik], *ag.* (*patol.*) dispeptico.
dysphagia [dis'feidʒiə], *s.* (*patol.*) disfagia.
dysphemia [dis'fi:miə], *s.* (*patol.*) balbuzie.
dysphonia [dis'founiə], *s.* (*patol.*) disfonia.
dyspnoea [dis'pni(:)ə], *s.* (*patol.*) dispnea.
dysprosium [dis'prousiəm], *s.* (*chim.*) disprosio.
dysuria [dis'juəriə], **dysury** ['disjuəri], *s.* (*patol.*) disuria.
dziggetai ['dzigitai], *s.* (*zool.*) emiono.

E

e [i:], *pl.* **es, e's** [i:z], *s.* **1.** (*quinta lettera dell'alfabeto inglese*) e ‖ — *for Edward,* (*tel.*) e come Empoli **2.** (*mus.*) mi.

'e, *pron.* (*sl.*) per **he.**

each [i:tʃ], *ag.* **ogni, ciascuno:** — *man,* — *woman,* ciascun uomo, ciascuna donna ‖ *pron.* **ognuno, ciascuno:** — *of us,* ciascuno di noi; — *and all of us,* proprio ciascuno di noi; *apples at a* (o *one*) *penny* —, mele ad un « penny » l'una; *give them two apples* —, date due mele a ciascuno di loro; *we* — *earn two pounds* (o *we earn two pounds* —), noi guadagnamo due sterline ciascuno ‖ **each other,** *pron. reciproco* **l'un l'altro** (*fra due*): *for* —, l'uno per l'altro; *they fought* —, si batterono l'un contro l'altro; *they looked into* —'*s eyes,* si guardarono negli occhi; *they love* —, si amano.

eager ['i:gə*], *ag.* **1.** ardente, appassionato: *an* — *hope,* una ardente speranza; *an* — *student of,* uno studioso appassionato di **2.** avido, desideroso; impaziente: — *for gain,* avido di guadagno; — *for knowledge,* desideroso di sapere; — *glance,* occhiata avida, ardente; *to be* — *to help,* essere desideroso, impaziente d'aiutare.

eagerly ['i:gəli] *av.* **1.** ardentemente: *to wish sthg.* —, desiderare ql.co. ardentemente **2.** avidamente: *to listen* —, ascoltare avidamente.

eagerness ['i:gənis], *s.* **1.** ardore; premura: *to show* — *in doing sthg.,* mostrare premura nel fare ql.co. **2.** impazienza: — *her* — *to go,* la sua ansia di andare **3.** brama, sete: — *for praise,* brama, sete di lode.

eagle ['i:gl], *s.* **1.** (*ornit.*) aquila **2.** (*arald.*) aquila: *double-headed* —, aquila bicipite; *imperial* —, aquila imperiale **3.** (*eccl.*) leggio a forma d'aquila **4.** (*amer.*) moneta da 10 dollari: *double* —, moneta da 20 dollari ☆ — *-eyed,* dagli occhi d'aquila; — *-hawk,* avvoltoio; — *-owl,* gran gufo, gufo reale, granduca.

eaglet ['i:glit], *s.* (*ornit.*) aquilotto.

eagre ['i:gə*], *s.* (*mar.*) calemma.

ear¹ [iə*], *s.* **1.** orecchio, orecchia: *a word in your* —, una parolina all'orecchio; *I pulled his ears,* gli ho dato una tiratina d'orecchi; *to speak in*(*to*) *s.o.'s* —, dire una cosa all'orecchio di qlcu. ‖ *over head and ears* (o *up to the ears*), fig. fin sopra i capelli ‖ *within* — *-shot,* a portata d'orecchio, di voce ‖ *walls have ears,* anche i muri hanno orecchi ‖ *to be all ears,* essere tutt'orecchi ‖ *to bring a storm* (o *a hornet's nest*) *about one's ears,* tirarsi addosso un'infinità di critiche ‖ *to cock* (o *to prick up*) *one's ears,* tendere l'orecchio ‖ *to drag in by the head and ears,* trascinare per forza ‖ *to give one's ears for sthg.,* fare qualsiasi sacrificio per ql.co. ‖ *to give* — *to s.o.* (o *to lend an* — *to s.o.* o *lend one's* — *to s.o.*), prestare orecchio a qlcu., ascoltare qlcu. ‖ *to go in at one* — *and out at the other,* entrare da un orecchio e uscire dall'altro ‖ *to have a good,* *a poor* — *for music,* avere, non avere orecchio per la musica ‖ *to have sharp ears,* avere l'udito fine ‖ *to keep one's ears open,* tenere le orecchie aperte ‖ *to play by* —, suonare a orecchio ‖ *to set people by the ears,* seminare zizzania ‖ *to turn a deaf* —, fare il sordo, fare orecchie da mercante ‖ *to win s.o.'s* —, attirare l'attenzione di qlcu. **2.** ansa (di vaso, ecc.) **3.** (*elett.*) attacco ☆ — *-ache,* mal d'orecchi (o — *splitting*), assordante; — *-drop,* (orecchino) pendente; — *-drum,* timpano; — *-flap,* lobo (dell'orecchio); — *-phone,* cuffia; — *-piercing,* penetrante, acuto;

— *-plug,* tappo per orecchi; — *-ring,* orecchino; — *-shell,* (*zool.*) orecchia marina; — *specialist,* otoiatra; — *-trumpet,* cornetto acustico; — *-wax,* cerume; — *witness,* testimone auricolare.

ear², *s.* spiga (di grano, ecc.).

to ear², *v.i.* (*agr.*) spigare, mettere la spiga.

eared¹ [iəd], *ag.* dalle orecchie ‖ *to listen open-* —, essere tutto orecchi ☆ *long-* —, dalle orecchie lunghe; *sharp-* —, dall'udito fine; *short-* —, dalle orecchie corte.

eared², *ag.* con spiga ☆ *full-* — *corn,* grano dalle spighe piene.

earing¹ ['iəriŋ], *s.* spigatura.

earing², *s.* (*mar.*) matafione.

earl [ə:l], *s.* titolo nobiliare inglese corrispondente a conte ‖ *Earl Marshal,* (*arald.*) presidente del Collegio Araldico inglese.

earldom ['ə:ldəm], *s.* **1.** contea **2.** dignità, titolo di conte.

earless¹ ['iəlis], *ag.* **1.** senza orecchie **2.** (*mus.*) senza orecchio, stonato.

earless², *ag.* senza spiga.

earliness ['ə:linis], *s.* **1.** le prime ore (del giorno, della notte) **2.** precocità (di morte, frutta, stagione).

early ['ə:li], *ag.* **1.** primo, della prima parte, del principio (di giorno, anno, vita, di qualsiasi tempo): — *childhood,* prima infanzia; — *English style,* stile primitivo inglese; *the* — *errors,* gli errori della giovinezza; *the* — *XV century,* i primi anni del XV secolo; — *remembrances,* ricordi d'infanzia; *in the* — *afternoon,* nel primo pomeriggio; *in the* — *morning,* di buon mattino; *in* — *summer,* all'inizio dell'estate; *in the* — *twenties,* negli anni immediatamente seguenti il 1920 **2.** mattiniero, mattutino: — *hours,* ore mattutine; *an* — *riser* (o *bird*), una persona mattiniera; *the* — *train,* il treno della mattina ‖ — *closing,* chiusura anticipata (di locali pubblici): — *closing day,* giorno in cui i negozi sono chiusi al pomeriggio ‖ *to keep* — *hours,* alzarsi e coricarsi presto ‖ *it is the* — *bird that catches the worm,* prov. chi dorme non piglia pesci **3.** primaticcio, prematuro: — *beans,* fagioli primaticci; — *death,* morte prematura; *an* — *spring,* primavera precoce **4.** remoto, antico: — *times,* tempi remoti; *the* — *writers,* gli antichi scrittori; *in the earliest times,* nei tempi più antichi **5.** prossimo: *at an* — *date,* ad una data prossima, prossimamente; *at an earlier date,* precedentemente; *at your earliest convenience,* (*comm.*) al più presto possibile; *to take an* — *opportunity to do sthg.,* fare ql.co. alla prima occasione, al più presto.

early, *av.* **1.** presto, di buon'ora, per tempo: — *in his career,* agli inizi della sua carriera; — *in life,* nei primi tempi della vita; — *in the month, in the year,* ai primi del mese, dell'anno; — *this morning,* nelle prime ore di questa mattina; *as* — *as the twelfth century,* fin dal dodicesimo secolo; *as* — *as you can,* appena puoi; *come* — *to lunch,* vieni presto a colazione; *to arrive five minutes too* —, arrivare con cinque minuti d'anticipo; *to die* —, morir giovane, prematuramente; *to rise* —, alzarsi presto, essere mattiniero **2.** al principio: — *in the list,* al principio della lista.

earmark ['iəmɑ:k], *s.* **1.** marchio di proprietà sull'orecchio (di animali) **2.** (*comm.*) contrassegno.

to earmark, *v.t.* **1.** apporre il marchio di proprietà sull'orecchio di (animali) **2.** (*comm.*) contrassegnare **3.** mettere da parte, accantonare; assegnare (fondi) a scopo speciale.

earmarking [ˈiəmɑːkiŋ], *s.* (*comm.*) assegnazione; accantonamento (di fondi per qualche operazione).

to **earn** [əːn], *v.t.* **1.** guadagnare (denaro): *he earns a lot of money*, guadagna molto denaro; *to — one's living by writing*, guadagnarsi da vivere scrivendo **2.** guadagnarsi, meritare, meritarsi (elogi, affetto, ecc.): *a well-earned rest*, un ben meritato riposo ☆ *earning capacity*, capacità di reddito, produttività finanziaria.

earnest[1] [ˈəːnist], *ag.* **1.** serio, zelante: *— worker*, lavoratore coscienzioso **2.** ardente, caloroso, fervido: *an — Christian*, un cristiano fervente; *— prayer*, fervida preghiera; *— request*, richiesta pressante ‖ *s.*: *in —*, sul serio, con perfetta convinzione: *are you in —?*, parli sul serio?, dici davvero?; *he is in real —*, è in buona fede; *he was very much in —*, ne era oltremodo convinto, se la prendeva a cuore; *it is snowing in real —*, nevica davvero.

earnest[2], *s.* **1.** (*comm. dir.*) caparra: *he gave an — to bind the bargain*, diede una caparra per vincolare il contratto **2.** *fig.* pegno, prova, garanzia: *an — of what is to follow*, un pegno di quel che seguirà ☆ *— -money*, caparra.

earnestly [ˈəːnistli], *av.* **1.** seriamente **2.** con ardore, con convinzione.

earnestness [ˈəːnistnis], *s.* **1.** serietà; gravità; zelo **2.** ardore, fervore.

earnings [ˈəːniŋz], *s.pl.* **1.** guadagno, guadagni; stipendio, salario; reddito: *taxes on professional —*, imposte sui redditi professionali **2.** (*comm. econ.*) utili ☆ *gross —*, utile lordo.

earth [əːθ], *s.* **1.** terra, mondo, globo terrestre: *the earth's crust*, la crosta terrestre; *on —*, sulla terra; *the — goes round the sun*, la terra gira intorno al sole ‖ *how, why, where on —...?*, come, perchè, dove mai...?; *what on — shall I do?*, cosa mai debbo fare?; *who on — said that?*, chi mai disse ciò? ‖ *come back to —*, (*fam.*) scendi dalle nuvole ‖ *as in heaven so in —*, come in cielo così in terra ‖ *to move heaven and —*, muovere cielo e terra **2.** terreno, suolo, terra: *— and sea, and sky*, terra, mare, cielo; *fat, heavy —*, terra grassa; *fill the hole with —*, riempi il buco di terra; *to till the —*, coltivare la terra **3.** (*chim.*) terra **4.** tana (di volpe, ecc.): *to run a fox to —*, inseguire, cacciare una volpe fino alla sua tana ‖ *to run sthg., s.o. to —*, scovare ql.co., qlcu. **5.** (*elett.*) massa, terra: *to put to —*, mettere a terra ‖ *— -bag*, (*mil.*) sacchetti di sabbia, terra; *— -bath*, (*med.*) fanghi; *— -born*, (*mit.*) nato dalla terra; umano, mortale; prodotto dalla terra; *— -bound*, (*letter.*) legato, attaccato alle cose terrene; *— -dam*, diga in terra; *— -fall*, frana; *— -house*, antica abitazione scavata nella terra; *— -hunger*, fame di terre; *— light*, luce riflessa della terra sulla luna; *— -nut*, (*bot.*) bulbocastano; *— -plate*, (*elett.*) piastra di terra; *— -worm*, lombrico ‖ *alkaline earths*, (*chim.*) terre alcaline; *rare earths*, (*chim.*) terre rare; *fire —*, terra refrattaria.

to **earth**, *v.t.i.* **1.** (*agr.*) interrare, coprire di terra: *the farmer earthed (up) the roots*, il contadino interrò le radici **2.** (*elett.*) mettere a terra **3.** (*caccia*) inseguire (una volpe) sino alla tana; rintanarsi (di volpe).

earthen [ˈəːθən], *ag.* di terra; di terracotta.

earthenware [ˈəːθənwɛə*], *s.* terraglia.

earthiness [ˈəːθinis], *V.* **earthliness**.

earthing [ˈəːθiŋ], *s.* (*elett. rad.*) messa a terra.

earthliness [ˈəːθlinis], *s.* **1.** terrenità **2.** mondanità, attaccamento ai beni terreni.

earthling [ˈəːθliŋ], *s.* abitante della terra, mortale.

earthly [ˈəːθli], *ag.* **1.** terrestre, della terra: *an — paradise*, un paradiso in terra **2.** (*fam.*) possibile; concepibile: *it has no — use*, non serve assolutamente a nulla; *there is no — hope, reason*, non v'è affatto spe-

ranza, ragione ☆ *— -minded*, mondano, attaccato alle cose di questo mondo.

earthquake [ˈəːθkweik], *s.* **1.** terremoto **2.** *fig.* sconquasso; rovesciamento (politico, ecc.) ☆ *— resisting*, antisismico; *— shock*, scossa sismica ‖ *submarine —*, maremoto.

earthward(s) [ˈəːθwəd(z)], *ag.av.* verso terra.

earthwork [ˈəːθ-wəːk], *s.* **1.** terrapieno; fortificazione **2.** sterramento ☆ *— labourer*, sterratore.

earthy [ˈəːθi], *ag.* **1.** terroso, di terra: *— taste*, sapore di terra **2.** terrestre **3.** (*fam.*) rozzo, grossolano (di persone).

earwig [ˈiəwig], *s.* (*entom.*) **1.** forfecchia **2.** (*amer. fam.*) millepiedi.

to **earwig**, *pass.p.p.* **earwigged** [ˈiəwigd], *v.t.* (*fam.*) **1.** tormentare, seccare **2.** insinuarsi presso; influenzare segretamente.

ease [iːz], *s.* **1.** tranquillità (di spirito); riposo, benessere: *a life of —*, una vita comoda; *a moment's —*, un momento di calma; *set your mind at —*, rassicurati, mettiti tranquillo; *to be at —*, aver l'animo tranquillo; *to be at one's —*, sentirsi a proprio agio; *to be ill at —*, essere ansioso, a disagio; *to take one's —*, mettersi a proprio agio, rilassarsi ‖ *stand at —!*, (*mil.*) riposo! **2.** facilità, agevolezza; naturalezza, disinvoltura: *with great — of manners*, con grande disinvoltura; *he did that hard work with —*, fece con facilità quel lavoro difficile; *to give — to one's style*, dare agilità al proprio stile **3.** sollievo, alleviamento **4.** (*sartoria*) morbidezza, ampiezza.

to **ease**, *v.t.i.* **1.** sollevare, alleviare; calmare, calmarsi; tranquillare; attenuare, attenuarsi: *his speech eased the situation*, il suo discorso ha prodotto una distensione; *the pain has eased*, il dolore si è attenuato **2.** liberare, alleggerire: *to — oneself of a burden*, liberarsi da un peso; *to — s.o. of his purse*, (*fam.*) alleggerire qlcu. del portafogli **3.** (*mar.*) mollare, allentare; mettere la barra sottovento: *— her!*, riducete la velocità! ‖ *to — away*, filare, mollare, calumare **4.** (*sartoria*) dare morbidezza, ampiezza a: *to — a sleeve*, dare ampiezza al giro di una manica **5.** *to — down*, diminuire, allentare **6.** *to — off*, allentare, allargare; alleggerirsi; rallentare (la velocità); rilassarsi; diventare meno opprimente **7.** *to — up*, rallentare; alleggerire, alleggerirsi.

easeful [ˈiːzful], *ag.* confortante; calmante, riposante.

easel [ˈiːzl], *s.* cavalletto; telaio.

easeless [ˈiːzlis], *ag.* **1.** senza conforto **2.** senza tranquillità.

easement [ˈiːzmənt], *s.* **1.** (*dir.*) servitù di passaggio; diritto d'uso **2.** (*ferr.*) raccordo **3.** (*arc.*) sollievo, conforto **4.** fabbricato annesso.

easily [ˈiːzili], *av.* **1.** facilmente: *— moved*, facile a commuoversi; *he is not — satisfied*, non si accontenta facilmente; *you can — imagine how...*, potete facilmente figurarvi come...; *to take life —*, prendere la vita come viene **2.** comodamente, agevolmente, senza difficoltà: *the car holds six people —*, l'auto porta comodamente sei persone; *he — got in first*, è arrivato primo senza difficoltà; *he is — forty*, ha i suoi bravi quarant'anni; *to live —*, vivere agiatamente.

easiness [ˈiːzinis], *s.* **1.** comodità, benessere **2.** grazia, agilità (di stile, ecc.) **3.** indifferenza **4.** facilità **5.** bontà, dolcezza (di carattere).

east [iːst], *ag.* orientale: *the — coast*, la costa orientale ‖ *s.* est, oriente, levante: *house facing (the) —*, casa esposta a est; *on the — (o to the —)*, all'est ‖ *the East*, l'Oriente, il Levante; (*amer.*) gli Stati dell'Est; *the East End*, il quartiere Orientale (il più povero di Londra); *the East Indies*, le Indie Orientali; *the Far, the Middle East*, l'Estremo, il Medio Oriente.

east, *av.* ad est, verso est, a oriente: *the ship sailed —*, la nave si diresse verso est ‖ *too far — is west*, gli estremi si toccano.

East Anglia [ˈiːstˈæŋgliə], *no.pr.* (*geog. st.*) East Anglia (uno dei regni della eptarchia anglosassone).

Easter ['i:stə*], s. Pasqua: *Thursday before* —, Giovedì santo‖ *to do one's* — *duty*, fare la Pasqua ☆ — *-Day*, domenica di Pasqua; — *-egg*, uovo pasquale; — *Eve*, Sabato santo; — *Island*, (geog.) isola di Pasqua; — *week*, la Settimana santa.

easterly ['i:stəli], ag. d'est, dall'est, orientale: — *wind*, vento dell'est ‖ s. vento dell'est.

easterly, av. ad est, verso est.

eastern ['i:stən], ag. dell'est, orientale: — *countries*, paesi orientali; — *religions*, religioni orientali ‖ s. 1. orientale 2. ortodosso, (persona) appartenente alla Chiesa ortodossa ☆ *the Eastern Church*, la Chiesa orientale ortodossa.

Eastertide ['i:stətaid], s. tempo pasquale.

easting ['i:stiŋ], s. (mar.) rotta verso est.

eastward ['i:stwəd], ag. ad est, verso est: — *position*, posizione verso est ‖ s. est: *to the* —, verso l'est, verso l'oriente.

eastward(s) ['i:stwədz], av. verso est, verso oriente.

easy ['i:zi], ag. 1. facile: *an* — *book*, un libro facile; — *method*, metodo semplice; — *money*, guadagno facile; — *of digestion*, facile a digerirsi; — *to enter*, di facile accesso; *within* — *reach* (o *distance*), facile a raggiungersi; *it is* — *to speak!*, è facile parlare! ‖ *as* — *as ABC* (o *as falling off a log* o *as shelling peas*), (fam.) facilissimo, infantile 2. agiato, comodo; tranquillo: — *life*, vita agiata, da papa; *with an* — *conscience*, con la coscienza tranquilla; *to make oneself* (o *one's mind*) — *about sthg.*, tranquillizzarsi, rassicurarsi su ql.co.; *to travel by* — *stages*, viaggiare a piccole tappe ‖ *stand* —!, (mil.) riposo! ‖ *to be in* — *street*, (fam.) essere nell'agiatezza 3. ampio, morbido (di abito, ecc.) 4. piacevole, disinvolto: — *gait*, andatura sciolta, disinvolta; — *manners*, modi piacevoli; — *style*, stile scorrevole; *a person* — *to get on with*, una persona con cui è facile andare d'accordo 5. (comm.): *by* — *payments* (o *on* — *terms*), con facilitazioni di pagamento; *cotton is* —, il cotone non è molto richiesto; *the market is* —, il mercato è tranquillo; *prices are getting easier*, i prezzi diventano accessibili.

easy, av. 1. facilmente: *I can do it easier than you*, lo posso fare più facilmente di te 2. comodamente ‖ *to take things* —, (fam.) prendere le cose come vengono: *take it* —!, non prendertela!

easygoing ['i:zi,gouiŋ], ag. 1. facilone; indolente: *an* — *man*, un uomo che se la prende comoda 2. sciolto nell'andatura (di cavalli).

to eat [i:t], pass. **ate** [et], arc. **eat**, p.p. **eaten** ['i:tn], v.t.i. 1. mangiare; prendere i pasti: *he lives to* —, vive per mangiare; *they* — *in the garden*, prendono i pasti in giardino; *to* — *bread*, mangiare pane ‖ *to* — *like a wolf*, mangiare come un lupo; *to* — *next to nothing*, mangiare come un uccellino; *to* — *oneself sick*, mangiare tanto da star male ‖ *to* — *one's heart out*, mangiarsi il fegato ‖ *to* — *one's words*, rimangiarsi la parola, ritrattare una precedente dichiarazione 2. rodere, corrodere; distruggere: *rust eats into iron*, la ruggine corrode il ferro 3. (fam. amer.) dar da mangiare a: *boarding-house that eats twenty*, pensione che dà da mangiare a venti persone 4. *to* — *away*, divorare; rodere; corrodere; attaccare (di acido): *the river has eaten away its banks*, il fiume ha corroso i suoi argini 5. *to* — *off*, consumare più di quanto si rende: *that horse eats its head off*, quel cavallo costa più a mantenerlo di quanto non renda; *to* — *off a field*, mangiare tutta l'erba di un campo 6. *to* — *up*, mangiar fino all'ultima briciola; consumare senza compenso, senza risultato: *to* — *up all s.o.'s time*, far perdere il tempo a qlcu.: *to be eaten up with sthg.*, essere divorato da ql.co.: *eaten up with envy*, divorato, roso dall'invidia.

eatable ['i:təbl], ag. mangereccio, commestibile.

eatables ['i:təblz], s.pl. vivande, viveri, commestibili.

eaten ['i:tn], p.p. di to **eat**.

eater ['i:tə*], s.c. mangiatore, mangiatrice; divoratore, divoratrice: *a good* —, un mangiatore, una buona

forchetta ‖ s. (neol.) frutta (specialmente mele) da consumarsi cruda.

eating ['i:tiŋ], ag. 1. che consuma, divora 2. fig. che corrode, rode ‖ s. il mangiare; cibo: *roast chicken is good* —, il pollo arrosto è una buona pietanza ☆ — *fruit*, frutta da tavola; — *-hall*, (amer.) refettorio; — *-house*, trattoria.

eats [i:ts], s.pl. (sl.) cibo; manicaretti.

eau [ou], s. (nei composti): — *-de-Cologne*, acqua di Colonia; — *-de-vie*, acquavite.

eaves [i:vz], s.pl. (arch.) gronda, cornicione.

to eavesdrop ['i:vzdrop], pass.p.p. **eavesdropped** ['i:vzdropt], v.i. origliare.

eavesdropper ['i:vz,dropə*], s.c. chi origlia.

ebb [eb], s. 1. riflusso, l'abbassarsi della marea: *the* — *and flow of the tide*, il flusso e il riflusso della marea 2. fig. declino, decadenza: *at a low* —, assai in basso, molto basso ☆ — *tide*, la bassa marea, riflusso.

to ebb, v.i. 1. rifluire (del mare) 2. fig. declinare; scemare; abbassarsi ‖ *to* — *away*, declinare, venir meno.

ebbing ['ebiŋ], ag. 1. rifluente 2. fig. in declino ‖ s. 1. riflusso 2. declino.

Ebenezer [,ebi'ni:zə*], no.pr.m. Ebenezer.

E-boat ['i:bout], s. (mar.) torpediniera motosilurante tedesca.

ebon ['ebən], ag. (poet.) d'ebano ‖ s. ebano.

ebonist ['ebənist], s. ebanista.

ebonite ['ebənait], s. ebanite.

to ebonize ['ebənaiz], v.t. rendere nero come ebano.

ebony ['ebəni], ag. nero, ebano: *the* — *keys on a piano*, i tasti neri di un pianoforte ‖ s. 1. ebano 2. colore ebano, nerissimo ‖ s.c. (amer.) negro, negra ☆ — *-tree*, (bot.) ebano.

Eboracum [i(:)'bɔrəkəm], no.pr. (geog. st.) York.

ebriety [i(:)'braiəti], s. ubriachezza, ebbrezza (anche fig.).

ebrious ['i(:)briəs], ag. ubriaco, ebbro (anche fig.).

ebullience [i'bʌljəns], **ebulliency** [i'bʌljənsi], s. 1. ebollizione 2. effervescenza (anche fig.).

ebullient [i'bʌljənt], ag. 1. in ebollizione 2. fig. esuberante, entusiasta, pieno di vita.

ebulliometer [i,bʌli'ɔmitə*], **ebullioscope** [i'bʌljə,skoup], s. (chim.) ebulliometro, ebullioscopio.

ebullioscopy [i,bʌli'ɔskəpi], s. (chim.) ebullioscopia.

ebullition [,ebə'liʃən], s. 1. (fis.) ebollizione 2. esuberanza; trasporto 3. accesso: scoppio improvviso (anche fig.).

eburnean [i'bə:niən], ag. eburneo.

eccentric [ik'sentrik], ag.s. 1. (geom. mec.) eccentrico 2. fig. eccentrico, stravagante, originale.

eccentrically [ik'sentrikəli], av. 1. (geom. mec.) eccentricamente 2. eccentricamente, in modo stravagante.

eccentricity [,eksen'trisiti], s. 1. (geom. mec.) eccentricità 2. fig. eccentricità, originalità, stravaganza: *to bear with s.o.'s eccentricities*, sopportare le eccentricità di qlcu.

ecchymosis [,eki'mousis], s. ecchimosi.

ecclesia [i'kli:zjə], s. ecclesia, assemblea, adunanza.

ecclesiast [i'kli:ziæst], s. ecclesiaste, predicatore.

Ecclesiastes [i,kli:zi'æsti:z], s. (Bibbia) Ecclesiaste.

ecclesiastic [i,kli:zi'æstik], ag.s. ecclesiastico.

ecclesiastical [i,kli:zi'æstikəl], ag. ecclesiastico.

ecclesiastically [i,kli:zi'æstikəli], av. ecclesiasticamente.

ecclesiasticism [i,kli:zi'æstisizəm], s. clericalismo.

echelon ['eʃəlɔn], s. 1. (mil.) scaglione 2. (mar.) formazione in linea di rilevamento.

to echelon, v.t. (mil.) scaglionare.

echidna [e'kidnə], s. (zool.) echidna.

echinoderm [i'kainoudə:m], s. (zool.) echinoderma.

echinus [e'kainəs], s. 1. (zool.) riccio di mare, echino 2. (arch.) echino.

echo ['ekou], pl. **echoes** ['ekouz], s. eco ‖ *to cheer to the* —, applaudire fragorosamente ‖ **Echo**, no.pr.f. (mit.) Eco.

to echo, v.t.i. 1. far eco a 2. echeggiare, risuonare.

echoless ['ekoulis], *ag.* senza eco ☆ — *studio*, (*cine.*) studio sordo, senza echi.

eclampsia [i'klæmpsiə], *s.* (*patol.*) eclampsia.

éclat ['eiklɑ:], *s.* splendore, gloria, gran successo.

eclectic [ek'lektik], *ag.s.* eclettico (anche *fil.*).

eclectically [ek'lektikəli], *av.* ecletticamente.

eclecticism [ek'lektisizəm], *s.* eclettismo (anche *fil.*).

eclipse [i'klips], *s.* **1.** (*astr.*) eclissi: *solar* —, eclissi di sole **2.** *fig.* periodo di oscurità: *his name is now suffering an* —, il suo nome subisce ora un periodo di oscurità ‖ *bird in* —, uccello in livrea invernale.

to eclipse, *v.t.* eclissare (anche *fig.*).

ecliptic [i'kliptik], *ag.* eclittico ‖ *s.* (*astr.*) eclittica.

eclogue ['eklɔg], *s.* (*poes.*) egloga.

ecology [i'kɔlədʒi], *s.* (*scient.*) ecologia.

economic [,i:kə'nɔmik], *ag.* (*econ. pol.*) economico: *the government's* — *policy*, la politica economica del governo.

economical [,i:kə'nɔmikəl], *ag.* **1.** economico, economo, parsimonioso: *an* — *woman*, una donna economa; *to be* — *of one's time*, non sciupare il proprio tempo **2.** (*arc. econ. pol.*) economico ☆ — *stove*, stufa economica.

economically [,i:kə'nɔmikəli], *av.* economicamente.

economics [,i:kə'nɔmiks], *s.* **1.** scienze economiche; economia politica **2.** sistema economico di un Paese.

economist [i(:)'kɔnəmist], *s.* **1.** economista **2.** persona economa **3.** (*arc. amm.*) economo.

economization [i(:),kɔnəmi'zeiʃən], *s.* economizzazione.

to economize [i(:)'kɔnəmaiz], *v.t.i.* economizzare, risparmiare (tempo, denaro, ecc.); fare economia: *to* — *on sthg.*, fare economia su ql.co.

economizer [i(:)'kɔnəmaizə*], *s.c.* chi economizza ‖ *s.* (*mec.*) economizzatore ☆ — *jet*, getto dell'economizzatore.

economy [i(:)'kɔnəmi], *s.* economia (anche *pol.*): *little economies*, piccole economie; *to disturb the* — *of Europe*, turbare l'economia dell'Europa; *to practise* —, economizzare ☆ *domestic* —, economia domestica; *planned* —, economia pianificata.

ecru ['ekru:], *ag.s.* (colore) greggio.

ecstasied ['ekstəsid], *ag.* in estasi, estasiato.

to ecstasize ['ekstəsaiz], *v.t.i.* **1.** mandare in estasi, estasiare **2.** andare in estasi.

ecstasy ['ekstəsi], *s.* **1.** estasi, rapimento, trasporto: *to be in an* — *of joy*, impazzire di gioia; *to be in ecstasies over sthg.*, andare in estasi, estasiarsi davanti a qualcosa **2.** (*med.*) « trance », sonno ipnotico.

ecstatic [eks'tætik], *ag.* estatico.

ecstatically [eks'tætikəli], *av.* estaticamente.

ectoderm ['ektoudə:m], *s.* (*biol.*) ectoderma.

ectoplasm ['ektouplæzəm], *s.* (*biol.*) (*metapsichica*) ectoplasma.

Ecuador [,ekwə'dɔ:*], *no.pr.* (*geog.*) Ecuador.

Ecuadorian [,ekwə'dɔ:riən], *ag.* ecuadoriano ‖ *s.c.* ecuadoriano, ecuadoriana.

ecumenic(al) [,i:kju(:)'menik(əl)], *ag.* (*eccl.*) ecumenico; universale.

ecumenicity [,i:kju(:)mi'nisiti], *s.* (*eccl.*) ecumenicità; universalità.

eczema ['eksimə], *s.* (*patol.*) eczema.

eczematous [ek'semətəs], *ag.* (*patol.*) eczematoso.

edacious [i'deiʃəs], *ag.* vorace.

edacity [i'dæsiti], *s.* voracità.

Edda ['edə], *no.pr.f.* Edda.

Eddie ['edi], *no.pr.m. dim.* di **Edgar, Edmund, Edward, Edwin.**

eddy ['edi], *s.* **1.** turbine (d'aria); vortice, mulinello (di acqua, vento, polvere) **2.** (*mar.*) gorgo, risucchio, remolo ☆ — *current*, (*elett.*) corrente parassita, di Foucault; — *flow*, (*idraulica*) moto turbolento.

to eddy, *v.t.i.* **1.** (far) turbinare (di vento, ecc.), mulinare **2.** (*mar.*) far risucchio, risucchiare.

eddying ['ediiŋ], *ag.* turbinoso; vorticoso ‖ *s.* turbinio.

edelweiss ['eidlvais], *s.* « edelweiss », stella alpina.

Eden ['i:dn], *s.* Eden: *the Garden of* —, l'Eden.

Edentata [,i:den'teitə], *s.pl.* (*zool.*) gli sdentati.

edentate [i'denteit], *ag.s.* (*zool.*) sdentato.

Edgar ['edgə*], *no.pr.m.* Edgardo.

edge [edʒ], *s.* **1.** bordo, orlo, margine, orlatura; labbro (di ferita): *at the water's* —, a fil d'acqua; *on the* — *of...*, sul punto di...; *rounded* —, orlo arrotondato; *to sit on the* — *of a chair*, sedere sull'orlo della sedia ‖ *to be* (o *to have one's nerves*) *on* —, avere i nervi a fior di pelle: *my nerves are all on* —, *fig.* ho i nervi a fior di pelle ‖ *to set on* —, irritare, urtare (i nervi): *to set one's teeth on* —, far allegare i denti; dare ai nervi **2.** limitare, margine; ciglio; sponda, riva: *the* — *of a precipice*, l'orlo di un precipizio; *the* — *of the road*, il ciglio della strada; *a hut on the* — *of a forest*, una capanna al limitare della foresta **3.** taglio (di lama), filo; spigolo; taglio della legatura (di libro); cresta (di montagne): *a knife with a sharp* —, un coltello molto affilato; *to put an* — *to a tool, on a blade*, affilare un arnese, una lama; *to take the* — *off a sword*, togliere il filo a una spada ‖ *words with an* —, *fig.* parole caustiche ‖ *it's the thin* — *of the wedge*, (*fam.*) è il primo passo che è pericoloso ‖ *to give an* — *to one's style*, *fig.* rendere tagliente il proprio stile ‖ *to give s.o. the* — *of one's tongue*, *fig.* dare una lavata di capo a qlcu. ‖ *to put to the* — *of a sword*, passare a fil di spada ‖ *to take the* — *off one's appetite*, *fig.* calmare la fame, fare uno spuntino; *to take the* — *off pleasure*, *fig.* guastare, rovinare il piacere ☆ — *definition*, (*tv.*) nitidezza dei contorni ‖ *blunted* —, filo smussato; *cutting* —, filo, taglio (di lama); *gilt* —, taglio dorato (di libro); *leading* —, (*aer.*) bordo d'attacco; (*rad.*) inizio dell'impulso; *trailing* —, (*aer.*) bordo di uscita, (*rad.*) termine dell'impulso.

to edge, *v.t.i.* **1.** bordare, fare un bordo a, orlare: *to* — *a handkerchief*, orlare un fazzoletto; *to* — *a road with poplars*, fiancheggiare una strada di pioppi **2.** affilare, arrotare; aguzzare (anche *fig.*): *to* — *the appetite*, (*fam.*) aguzzare l'appetito; *to* — *a knife*, affilare un coltello **3.** muovere, muoversi (poco a poco): *to* — *one's chair nearer*, accostare pian piano la propria sedia ‖ *to* — *oneself into a conversation*, intrufolarsi in una conversazione; *to* — (*one's way*) *into, out of a room*: entrare furtivamente in, uscire furtivamente da una stanza ‖ *to* — *one's way through the crowd*, farsi strada tra la folla ‖ *to* — *to the north*, (*mar.*) volgere (la rotta) al nord **4.** *to* — **away**, allontanarsi, sgattaiolare via; (*mar.*) aumentare gradatamente la distanza della nave **5.** *to* — **down**, (*mar.*) avvicinarsi gradatamente **6.** *to* — **off**, affilare (lama, ecc.); allontanarsi, filar via.

edged [edʒd], *ag.* affilato, tagliente, arrotato ‖ *to play with* — *tools*, (*fam.*) scherzare col fuoco ☆ *double* - —, a doppio taglio (anche *fig.*); *gilt*- —, dal taglio dorato (di libro, ecc.); *keen*- —, affilato, tagliente; *fig.* mordace; *sharp*- —, aguzzo, tagliente.

edgeless ['edʒlis], *ag.* **1.** senza bordo, orlo **2.** che non taglia; smussato; spuntato.

edgeways ['edʒweiz], **edgewise** ['edʒwaiz], *av.* **1.** di taglio, dalla parte del taglio, secondo il taglio: *to set* (o *to lay*) *a brick* —, mettere un mattone dalla parte del taglio ‖ *not to be able to get a word in* —, (*fam.*) non riuscire a infilare una parola (in un discorso) **2.** costa a costa.

edginess ['edʒinis], *s.* (*fam.*) nervosismo.

edging ['edʒiŋ], *s.* **1.** l'orlare, il bordare **2.** orlatura, bordo; sbieco, cordoncino, fettuccia (per orlatura); frangia ☆ — *shears*, cesoie per tagliare l'erba.

edgy ['edʒi], *ag.* **1.** affilato, tagliente **2.** stagliato (di roccia) **3.** dalle linee dure (di quadro) **4.** *fig.* angoloso; nervoso, irritabile.

edibility [,edi'biliti], *s.* mangiabilità.

edible ['edibl], *ag.* commestibile, mangereccio.

edibles ['ediblz], *s.pl.* commestibili.

edict ['i:dikt], *s.* editto.

edification [,edifi'keiʃən], *s.* (*spec. fig.*) edificazione.

edificatory ['edifikeitəri], *ag.* edificatorio.

edifice ['edifis], *s.* edificio (anche *fig.*): *the whole — of her hopes collapsed*, l'intero edificio delle sue speranze crollò.

edifier ['edifaiə*], *s.* (*gener. iron.*) edificatore.

to **edify** ['edifai], *v.t.* **1.** (*arc.*) costruire **2.** (*fig. iron.*) edificare, dar buon esempio a.

edifying ['edifaiiŋ], *ag.* edificante.

Edina [i'dainə], *no.pr.* (*geog. st.*) Edimburgo.

Edinburgh ['edinbərə], *no.pr.* (*geog.*) Edimburgo.

to **edit** ['edit], *v.t.* **1.** redigere, commentare, curare (un testo, per la pubblicazione): *edited by*, a cura di **2.** dirigere (giornale, rivista, ecc.): *edited by*, sotto la direzione di‖ *to — news for the public*, (*fam.*) manipolare le notizie del giorno per il gran pubblico.

Edith ['i:diθ], *no.pr.f.* Editta.

editing ['editiŋ], *s.* **1.** redazione (di un testo); commento (ad un testo) **2.** direzione (di giornale, ecc.): *— the news-paper took him the whole time*, la direzione del giornale occupava tutto il suo tempo.

edition [i'diʃən], *s.* edizione: *cheap —*, edizione economica; *final —*, ultima edizione (di giornale); *first, latest —*, prima, ultima edizione (di libri); *revised —*, edizione riveduta; *unabridged —*, edizione integrale‖ *he is a second — of his father*, è la copia di suo padre ☆ *pocket- —*, edizione tascabile.

editor ['editə*], *s.* **1.** commentatore (di un testo); curatore (di testo) **2.** (*giornalismo*) direttore; redattore: *— in chief*, redattore capo **3.** (*cine.*) tecnico del montaggio ☆ *associate —*, condirettore: *city —*, redattore finanziario; *economic —*, redattore economico; *financial —*, (*amer.*) redattore finanziario; *managing —*, direttore generale; *sporting —*, redattore sportivo.

editorial [,edi'tɔ:riəl], *ag.* editoriale‖ *s.* editoriale, articolo di fondo ☆ *— staff*, redazione (l'insieme dei redattori); *— office*, (ufficio di) redazione.

editorially [,edi'tɔ:riəli], *av.* in qualità di direttore, di redattore.

editorship ['editəʃip], *s.* **1.** direzione, redazione (di giornali, periodici, ecc.) **2.** funzione del direttore, del redattore.

editress ['editris], *s.f.* **1.** commentatrice (di un testo) **2.** (*giornalismo*) direttrice; redattrice.

Edmund ['edmənd], *no.pr.m.* Edmondo.

educable ['edjukəbl], *ag.* che può essere educato.

to **educate** ['edju(:)keit], *v.t.* **1.** istruire; educare: *she was educated in Italy*, ha compiuto i suoi studi in Italia; *to — one's son to a profession*, indirizzare il proprio figlio ad una professione **2.** ingentilire, affinare, esercitare: *to — one's memory*, esercitare la memoria; *to — s.o.'s taste*, affinare il gusto di qlcu. **3.** addestrare (animali).

educated ['edju(:)keitid], *ag.* **1.** istruito, colto: *indeed he is an — man!*, egli è una persona veramente colta! **2.** addestrato, ammaestrato (di animali) ☆ *self - — man*, autodidatta.

education [,edju(:)'keiʃən], *s.* **1.** cultura, educazione: *he received a liberal —*, egli ricevette un'educazione liberale **2.** istruzione, insegnamento‖ *Ministry of Education*, Ministro della Pubblica Istruzione **3.** addestramento (di animali) **4.** pedagogia ☆ *— acts*, leggi sull'istruzione; *elementary, secondary, non-state, university —*, istruzione elementare, secondaria, privata, universitaria; *free, compulsory —*, istruzione gratuita, obbligatoria.

educational [,edju(:)'keiʃənl], *ag.* educativo: *— film*, film educativo ☆ *— act*, (*amer.*) legge sull'istruzione.

educationally [,edju(:)'keiʃnəli], *av.* in modo educativo, istruttivo.

educationalist [,edju(:)'keiʃnəlist], **educationist** [,edju(:)'keiʃnist], *s.c.* educatore, educatrice; pedagogo; pedagogista.

educative ['edju(:)kətiv], *ag.* istruttivo, educativo.

educator ['edju(:)keitə*], *s.* educatore.

educatress ['edju(:)keitris], *s.* educatrice.

to **educe** [i(:)'dju:s], *v.t.* **1.** trarre, estrarre **2.** (*chim.*) liberare (un gas) **3.** dedurre.

educible [i(:)'dju:sibl], *ag.* **1.** che si può estrarre **2.** deducibile.

educt ['i:dʌkt], *s.* **1.** (*chim.*) prodotto della scomposizione **2.** (*fil.*) deduzione.

eduction [i(:)'dʌkʃən], *s.* **1.** estrazione **2.** (*fil.*) deduzione **3.** (*mec.*) emissione, scarico: *— of steam*, sprigionamento, esalazione di vapore ☆ *— -pipe, -valve*, tubo, valvola di scarico.

to **edulcorate** [i(:)'dʌlkəreit], *v.t.* **1.** dolcificare, addolcire **2.** (*chim.*) purificare.

edulcoration [i(:),dʌlkə'reiʃən], *s.* dolcificazione.

Edward ['edwəd], *no.pr.m.* Edoardo.

Edwardian [ed'wɔ:djən], *ag.* edoardiano: *— literature*, letteratura edoardiana‖ *the — Prayer-Book*, il libro di preghiere anglicano autorizzato da Edoardo VI.

ee [i:], *pl.* **een** [i:n], *s.* (*arc. poet. scoz.*) per **eye**.

'ee, *pron.* (*dial. abbr.* di *thee*) te: *thank'ee*, grazie a te.

eel [i:l], *s.* (*ittiol.*) anguilla: *stewed —*, (*cuc.*) anguilla marinata‖ *he is as slippery as an —*, (*fam.*) guizza di mano come un'anguilla ☆ *— -basket* (o *— -buck* o *— -pot* o *— -trap*), nassa (per anguille); *— -bed* (o *— -pond*), anguillara; *— -worm*, (*entom.*) anguillula.

e'en [i:n], *av.* (*poet.*) per **even**.

e'er [eə*], (*poet.*) per **ever**.

eerie, eery ['iəri], *ag.* **1.** strano, fantastico; misterioso; soprannaturale **2.** che ispira paura, che fa rabbrividire.

eerily ['iərili], *av.* **1.** stranamente, fantasticamente; misteriosamente **2.** paurosamente.

eeriness ['iərinis], *s.* paura superstiziosa, vago senso di timore.

to **efface** [i'feis], *v.t.* **1.** cancellare, obliterare (anche *fig.*): *inscriptions that are becoming effaced*, iscrizioni che vanno scomparendo **2.** eclissare, tenere in disparte: *to — oneself*, tenersi in disparte.

effaceable [i'feisəbl], *ag.* cancellabile.

effacement [i'feismənt], *s.* cancellamento, obliterazione ☆ *self- —*, il mettersi in disparte, lo scomparire nell'ombra.

effect [i'fekt], *s.* **1.** effetto, risultato, conseguenza: *the desired —*, il risultato voluto; *of no —*, senza risultato, di nessun effetto; *he is suffering from the effects of the heat*, soffre degli effetti del caldo; *the medicine will have a good — on him*, la medicina gli sarà di giovamento; *to bring* (o *to carry*) *sthg. into —*, effettuare ql.co.: *to give — to*, effettuare, mettere in esecuzione; *to go into —*, entrare in vigore, effettuarsi; *to have an — on s.o., sthg.*, produrre un effetto su qlcu., su ql.co.; *to put into —*, effettuare, mandare ad effetto; *to take* (o *to come into*) *—*, entrare in vigore: *law that takes* (o *comes into*) *— from today*, legge che entra in vigore a partire da oggi **2.** senso, significato; tenore (di lettera, documento, ecc.): *that is what he said, or words used to that —*, ecco ciò che ha detto, o ql.co. del genere; *we have made provisions to this —*, abbiamo preso disposizioni in questo senso **3.** effetto, impressione‖ *to do sthg. for —*, fare ql.co. per fare impressione, per farsi notare **4.** *pl.* indumenti, effetti personali, beni: *the dead man's effects were returned to the family*, gli oggetti personali del morto furono restituiti alla famiglia‖ *in —*, in realtà; *no effects*, (*comm.*) insolvibile (di assegno) ☆ *moonlight —*, effetto di luna; *sound -effects*, effetti acustici; *stage effects*, effetti scenici; *stop motion —*, (*cine.*) effetto Chaplin, effetto (comico) dovuto all'accelerazione.

to **effect**, *v.t.* effettuare, eseguire, compiere; realizzare: *to — a cure*, ottenere una guarigione; *to — an insurance*, (*comm.*) fare un'assicurazione; *to — one's purpose*, raggiungere il proprio scopo; *to — a payment, a sale*, effettuare un pagamento, una vendita; *to — a retreat*, (*mil.*) effettuare una ritirata‖ *to — an entrance*, forzare la porta, entrare di forza.

effectible [i'fektibl], *ag.* effettuabile.

effective [i'fektiv], *ag.* **1.** efficace: — *method,* metodo efficace **2.** effettivo, reale: — *money,* denaro reale; — *power,* rendimento effettivo **3.** ad effetto, che colpisce: — *phrase,* frase felice; — *picture,* quadro ad effetto **4.** (*mil.*) effettivo **5.** (*amer.*) in vigore: *the law becomes — today,* la legge entra in vigore oggi ‖ *s.* soldato.

effectively [i'fektivli], *av.* **1.** efficacemente, utilmente **2.** effettivamente, in realtà **3.** con effetto.

effectiveness [i'fektivnis], *s.* efficacia.

effectual [i'fektjuəl], *ag.* **1.** efficace **2.** (*dir.*) valido (di contratto, regolamento, ecc.).

effectuality [i,fektju'æliti], *s.* efficacia; validità.

effectually [i'fektjuəli], *av.* efficacemente.

effectualness [i'fektjuəlnis], *s.* efficacia.

to effectuate [i'fektjueit], *v.t.* effettuare.

effectuation [i,fektju'eifən], *s.* effettuazione.

effeminacy [i'feminəsi], *s.* effeminatezza.

effeminate [i'feminit], *ag.* effeminato: *to render s.o. —,* rendere qlcu. effeminato ‖ *s.* individuo effeminato.

to effeminate [i'femineit], *v.t.i.* rendere, diventare effeminato; infiacchire, snervare.

effeminately [i'feminitli], *av.* effeminatamente.

effeminateness [i'feminitnis], *s.* effeminatezza.

effendi [e'fendi], *s.* effendi (appellativo turco).

efferent ['efərənt], *ag.* (*fisiol.*) efferente.

to effervesce [,efə'ves], *v.i.* **1.** essere effervescente, entrare in effervescenza, spumare **2.** *fig.* essere allegro, vivace.

effervescence [,efə'vesns], *s.* **1.** effervescenza **2.** *fig.* eccitamento, agitazione.

effervescent [,efə'vesnt], *ag.* **1.** effervescente: — *beverages,* bibite effervescenti **2.** *fig.* vivace, spumeggiante (di persona).

effete [e'fi:t], *ag.* logoro; esaurito; indebolito; sterile: *an — civilization,* una civiltà che ha fatto il suo tempo.

effeteness [e'fi:tnis], *s.* logorio; esaurimento; scadimento; sterilità.

efficacious [,efi'keifəs], *ag.* efficace.

efficaciously [,efi'keifəsli], *av.* efficacemente.

efficaciousness [,efi'keifəsnis], **efficacity** [,efi'kæsiti], **efficacy** ['efikəsi], *s.* **1.** efficacia (di un rimedio); (*teol.*) efficacia (della grazia) **2.** rendimento (di una macchina).

efficiency [i'fifənsi], *s.* **1.** efficienza, rendimento totale **2.** capacità (di persona): — *of the workmen,* capacità professionale degli operai; *troops in a high state of —,* truppe in piena efficienza **3.** efficacia (di rimedio, ecc.) ☆ *commercial —,* rendimento economico; *energy —,* (*elett.*) rendimento in energia; *mechanical —,* rendimento meccanico; *over-all —,* (*mec.*) rendimento totale; *peak —,* (*ind.*) massimo rendimento; *unit —,* rendimento unitario; *yearly mean —,* rendimento medio annuale.

efficient [i'fifənt], *ag.* **1.** efficiente, di buono, alto rendimento: — *machine,* macchina ad alto rendimento **2.** abile, capace, quotato (di persona): *to be — in one's work,* essere attivo nel proprio compito **3.** (*fil.*) efficiente ☆ — *cause,* causa efficiente.

efficiently [i'fifəntli], *av.* **1.** efficientemente **2.** abilmente, con competenza **3.** efficacemente.

effigy ['efidʒi], *s.* effigie: *to burn, to hang s.o. in —,* bruciare, impiccare qlcu. in effigie.

to effloresce [,eflo:'res], *v.i.* **1.** (*letter.*) sbocciare, fiorire (anche *fig.*) **2.** (*chim.*) fare efflorescenza.

efflorescence [,eflo:'resns], *s.* **1.** (*bot.*) fioritura **2.** (*chim.*) efflorescenza **3.** (*patol.*) eruzione.

efflorescent [,eflo:'resnt], *ag.* **1.** (*bot.*) fiorente **2.** (*chim.*) efflorescente.

effluence ['efluəns], *s.* efflusso; emanazione.

effluent ['efluənt], *ag.* defluente; di scarico ‖ *s.* **1.** canale di scarico **2.** emissario.

effluvium [e'flu:vjəm], *pl.* **effluvia** [e'flu:vjə], *s.* effluvio; esalazione.

efflux ['eflʌks], *s.* efflusso; scolo; emanazione; decorso (del tempo).

effoliation [e,fouli'eifən], *s.* (*bot.*) sfogliatura.

effort ['efət], *s.* **1.** sforzo, fatica (anche *fig.*): — *of will,* sforzo di volontà; *make an —!,* (*fam.*) scuotiti!, sforzati!; *to make an — to succeed,* fare di tutto per, sforzarsi di riuscire **2.** (*fam.*) lavoro, opera: *has he seen your last —?,* ha visto il tuo ultimo lavoro?; *that's quite a good —,* non è per niente male, mi pare una cosa riuscita **3.** (*mec.*) sforzo ☆ *tractive —,* (*ferr.*) sforzo di trazione.

effortful ['efətful], *ag.* che costa sforzo, faticoso.

effortless ['efətlis], *ag.* **1.** che non fa sforzi; passivo **2.** senza sforzo, facile.

effrontery [e'frʌntəri], *s.* sfrontatezza; sfacciataggine.

to effulge [e'fʌldʒ], *v.t.i.* (*poet.*) risplendere, irraggiare.

effulgence [e'fʌldʒəns], *s.* splendore, fulgore (anche *fig.*).

effulgent [e'fʌldʒənt], *ag.* risplendente.

effuse [e'fju:s], *ag.* (*bot.*) effuso; sparso.

to effuse [e'fju:z], *v.t.i.* **1.** effondere, effondersi **2.** spargere, spargersi; versare, versarsi.

effusion [i'fju:ʒən], *s.* **1.** effusione, versamento (di sangue, ecc.) **2.** effusione, abbondanza; mancanza di freno: *poetical effusions,* (*fam.*) effusioni poetiche **3.** espansione (di gas, liquidi, ecc.).

effusive [i'fju:siv], *ag.* **1.** espansivo, esuberante: — *thanks,* ringraziamenti calorosi **2.** (*geol.*) effusivo: — *rock,* roccia effusiva.

effusively [i'fju:sivli], *av.* con effusione.

effusiveness [i'fju:sivnis], *s.* effusione, espansività.

eft[1] [eft], *ag.* (*arc. rar.*) pronto; adatto.

eft[2], *s.* (*zool.*) tritone crestato.

eftsoon(s) [eft'su:n(z)], *av.* (*arc. poet.*) subito dopo.

egad [i'gæd], *inter.* (*arc. abbr.* di *by God*) perdio!.

egality [i'gæliti], *s.* (*rar.*) uguaglianza.

egall ['i:gɔl], *ag.* (*arc.*) uguale.

Egeria [i(:)'dʒiəriə], *no.pr.f.* (*mit.*) Egeria.

Egeus ['i:dʒju:s, (*in Shakespeare*) i(:)'dʒi:əs], *no.pr.m.* (*mit.*) Egeo.

egg[1] [eg], *s.* **1.** uovo: *a bad —,* un uovo marcio; *fig.* un buono a nulla ‖ *good —,* (*sl.*) buon diavolo ‖ *the goose with the golden eggs,* la gallina dalle uova d'oro ‖ *old —!,* (*fam.*) vecchio mio! ‖ *as sure as eggs is eggs,* (*fam.*) sicuro come due più due fanno quattro ‖ *to kill a plot in the —,* soffocare un complotto sul nascere ‖ *to put all one's eggs in one basket,* rischiare il tutto per il tutto ‖ *to teach one's grandmother to suck eggs,* dare consigli a chi ne sa di più ‖ *to tread upon eggs, fig.* camminare sulle uova **2.** (*arch.*) ovolo **3.** (*neol. fam.*) bomba ☆ — *-and-spoon race,* corsa nella quale i concorrenti portano un uovo in un cucchiaio; — *-cup,* porta uovo; — *-flip* (o — *-nog*), bevanda preparata con birra ed uova; — *-glass,* clessidra (per le uova); — *-head,* (*neol. sl.*) intellettuale; — *-plant,* (*bot.*) melanzana; — *-shaped,* ovale; — *-shell,* guscio d'uovo; — *-spoon,* cucchiaio da uovo; — *-timer,* clessidra per cuocere le uova; — *-whisk,* frusta per montare uova ‖ *boiled —,* uovo alla coque; *fried —,* |uovo fritto; *hard-boiled —,* uovo sodo; *new-laid —,* uovo fresco; *poached —,* uovo in camicia; *scrambled eggs,* uova strapazzate.

to egg[1], *v.t.i.* **1.** coprire con rosso d'uovo **2.** lanciare uova marce contro **3.** raccogliere uova.

to egg[2], *v.t.*: — *to — on,* istigare, incitare.

egger ['egə*], *s.* (*entom.*) bombice della quercia.

eglantine ['eglantain], *s.* rosa canina.

eglatere ['eglə'tiə*], *s.* (*arc.*) rosa di macchia.

ego ['egou], *s.* (*fil.*) ego.

egocentric [,egou'sentrik], *ag.* egocentrico.

egocentrism [,egou'sentrizəm], *s.* egocentrismo.

egoism ['egouizəm], *s.* **1.** egoismo **2.** egotismo.

egoist ['egouist], *s.* egoista.

egoistic(al) [,egou'istik(əl)], *ag.* egoistico.

egoistically [,egou'istikəli], *av.* egoisticamente.

egotism ['egoutizəm], *s.* egotismo.

egotist ['egoutist], *s.* egotista.

egotistic(al) [ˌegou'tistik(əl)], *ag.* egotistico.
egotistically [ˌegou'tistikəli], *av.* egotisticamente.
to **egotize** ['egoutaiz], *v.i.* accentrare costantemente l'attenzione su di sè; autoesaltarsi.
egregious [i'gri:dʒəs], *ag.* **1.** (*arc.*) superiore **2.** (*spreg.*) grossolano: — *blunder*, errore marchiano.
egregiously [i'gri:dʒəsli], *av.* grossolanamente.
egregiousness [i'gri:dʒəsnis], *s.* enormità.
egress ['i:gres], *s.* **1.** uscita: *right of* —, diritto di uscita **2.** via d'uscita (anche *fig.*) **3.** (*astr.*) emersione da un'eclissi.
egression [i(:)'greʃən], *s.* uscita.
egret ['i:gret], *s.* **1.** (*ornit.*) egretta, airone bianco **2.** « aigrette », ciuffo **3.** (*bot.*) lanugine.
Egypt ['i:dʒipt], *no.pr.* (*geog.*) Egitto.
Egyptian [i'dʒipʃən], *ag.* egiziano ‖ *s.c.* egiziano, egiziana.
Egyptologist [ˌi:dʒip'tolədʒist], *s.* egittologo.
Egyptology [ˌi:dʒip'tolədʒi], *s.* egittologia.
eh [ei], *inter.* eh!, eh?, che cosa?.
eider ['aidə*], *s.* (— *-duck*), (*ornit.*) edredone, anatra dal piumino ☆ — *-down*, piuma fine; piumino; — *-quill*, piumino, trapunta.
eidograph ['aidougrɑ:f], *s.* pantografo.
eidolon [ai'doulon], *pl.* **eidolons** [ai'doulonz], **eidola** [ai'doulə], *s.* fantasma, spettro, immagine.
eight [eit], *ag.num.card.s.* **1.** otto: *a girl of* —, una bimba di otto anni ‖ *to have one over the* —, (*sl.*) prendere una sbornia **2.** (*aer. spor.*) otto (evoluzione): *horizontal* —, otto orizzontale; *to cut (figures) of eight*, fare degli otto sul ghiaccio **3.** (*spor.*) equipaggio a otto rematori ‖ *the Eights*, le regate ad Oxford e Cambridge per equipaggi a otto rematori ☆ — *-oar*, canotto ad otto rematori.
eighteen ['ei'ti:n], *ag.num.card.s.* diciotto.
eighteenmo [ei'ti:nmou], *ag.s.* (*tip.*) diciottesimo.
eighteenth ['ei'ti:nθ], *ag.num.ord.s.* diciottesimo, decimottavo.
eightfold ['eitfould], *ag.* ottuplo ‖ *av.* per otto volte.
eighth [eitθ], *ag.num.ord.s.* ottavo: *the* — (o *8th*) *of May*, l'otto maggio.
eighthly ['eitθli], *av.* in ottavo luogo.
eightieth ['eitiiθ], *ag.num.ord.s.* ottantesimo.
eightsome ['eitsəm], *s.* vivace danza scozzese eseguita da otto persone.
eighty ['eiti], *ag.num.card.s.* ottanta: *during the eighties*, negli anni tra il 1880 e il 1889; *she is in her eighties*, ella ha superato gli ottant'anni ‖ *the Eighty Club*, (*pol.*) associazione liberale fondata nel 1880.
Eileen ['aili:n], *no.pr.f.* (*irl.*) Elena.
Eire ['ɛərə], *no.pr.* (*geog. st.*) Irlanda.
eirenicon [ai'ri:nikon], *s.* irenica (dottrina che tratta della pace).
eisteddfod [ais'teðvod], *s.* « eisteddfod » (concorso di canto e di poesia tra gallesi o nel Galles).
either ['aiðə*, 'i:ðə*], *ag.* (o) **l'uno o l'altro** (*di due*); **ciascuno** (**dei due**); **tutti e due**: *at* — *end of this table*, all'una e all'altra estremità di questa tavola; *there are trees on* — *side of the street*, ci sono alberi su ciascun lato della strada; *there is no evidence* — *way*, non ci sono prove nè in un senso nè nell'altro; *without taking* — *side*, senza prendere le parti dell'uno o dell'altro ‖ — *way*, in un modo o nell'altro, in entrambi i modi ‖ *pron.*: — *of them may come*, può darsi che l'uno o l'altro venga; *I shall not punish* —, non punirò nè l'uno nè l'altro; *"Which of these two books do you want?"* "—", « Quale di questi due libri vuoi? » « O l'uno o l'altro » ‖ *not* ... — (= *neither*), nè l'uno nè l'altro: *I do not know* — (o *I know neither*), non conosco nè l'uno nè l'altro.
either, *av.* (*in frasi negative o interrogativo-negative*) **anche, pure, neanche, nemmeno, neppure:** *haven't you seen him* —?, neanche tu l'hai visto?; *if you do not go I will not go* —, se non vai tu non andrò nemmeno io ‖ *cong.* (*seguito da* or) **o, oppure:** *he is* — *in Rome*

or (*in*) *Milan*, è a Roma o a Milano; *I'll see him* — *to-day or tomorrow*, lo vedrò oggi o domani.
to **ejaculate** [i'dʒækjuleit], *v.t.* **1.** (*fisiol.*) eiaculare **2.** esclamare; dire all'improvviso.
ejaculation [i,dʒækju'leiʃən], *s.* **1.** (*fisiol.*) eiaculazione **2.** esclamazione **3.** (*eccl.*) giaculatoria.
ejaculatory [i'dʒækjulətəri], *a.* **1.** (*fisiol.*) eiaculatore **2.** esclamativo **3.** giaculatorio.
to **eject** [i(:)'dʒekt], *v.t.* **1.** gettare fuori; emettere, espellere **2.** (*dir.*) spossessare, sfrattare.
ejection [i(:)'dʒekʃən], *s.* **1.** espulsione, eiezione, deiezione **2.** *fig.* destituzione **3.** (*dir.*) sfratto **4.** eruzione (di vulcano) **5.** *pl.* materia scaricata, eiettata.
ejector [i(:)'dʒektə*], *s.* **1.** espulsore **2.** (*dir.*) colui che sfratta **3.** (*mec.*) estrattore; eiettore ☆ — *-seat*, (*neol. aer.*) sedile eiettabile.
to **eke**[1] [i:k], *v.t.*: *to* — **out**, aggiungere a; supplire all'insufficienza di: *to* — *out one's livelihood*, sbarcare il lunario.
eke[2], *av.* (*arc.*) anche, pure.
ekka ['ekɑ:], *s.* (*ang.-in.*) carro tirato da un solo cavallo, da un bue.
elaborate [i'læbərit], *ag.* elaborato; accurato; minuzioso.
to **elaborate** [i'læbəreit], *v.t.* **1.** elaborare; studiare **2.** sviluppare.
elaborately [i'læbəritli], *av.* elaboratamente; accuratamente.
elaborateness [i'læbəritnis], *s.* minuziosità; cura.
elaboration [i,læbə'reiʃən], *s.* elaborazione.
eland ['i:lənd], *s.* (*zool.*) antilope (del Sud Africa).
to **elapse** [i'læps], *v.i.* trascorrere, passare (del tempo): *years have elapsed since we met*, sono passati degli anni da quando ci incontrammo.
elastic [i'læstik], *ag.* elastico (anche *fig.*): *to be* —, avere della elasticità; avere capacità di ricupero ‖ *s.* elastico; fettuccia elastica ☆ — *band*, elastichino; fascia elastica.
elasticity [ˌelæs'tisiti], *s.* elasticità: — *to the torsion stress*, (*tec.*) elasticità allo sforzo di torsione.
to **elate** [i'leit], *v.t.* inebriare, esaltare; trasportare: *to be elated at the good news*, esultare per le buone notizie.
elate(d) [i'leit(id)], *ag.* (*rar.*) esaltato; esultante: *elated with victory*, esultante per la vittoria.
elation [i'leiʃən], *s.* esaltazione, ebbrezza (per un successo); esultanza; gioia, gaiezza.
elbow ['elbou], *s.* **1.** gomito: *at one's* —, accanto, vicino; *to be at s.o.'s elbows*, stare gomito a gomito con qlcu.; *to be out at elbows*, essere logoro (di abito); essere povero (di persona) ‖ *to be up to one's elbows in work*, (*fam.*) avere lavoro fin sopra i capelli ‖ *to crook the* — (o *to lift one's* —), (*fam.*) alzare il gomito **2.** (*mec.*) curva, gomito **3.** bracciuolo (di poltrona) ☆ — *-chair*, seggiola a bracciuoli; — *-grease*, *fig.* olio di gomito; — *-room*, spazio, agio.
to **elbow**, *v.t.i.* **1.** spingere con il gomito; dare gomitate, andare avanti a gomitate: *to* — *one's way through a crowd*, avanzare a gomitate in mezzo ad una folla; *to* — *a person out of the way*, allontanare una persona a gomitate **2.** formare gomito.
eld [eld], *s.* (*arc.*) **1.** vecchiaia **2.** antichità; il tempo che fu.
elder[1] ['eldə*], *ag.* (*comp.* di *old*) maggiore; più vecchio (tra due persone): *which is the* — *brother?*, quale è il maggiore dei due fratelli? ‖ *s.* **1.** maggiore (tra due), più vecchio, anziano ‖ *Pliny the Elder*, Plinio il Vecchio **2.** *pl.* antenati: *our elders*, i nostri antenati **3.** pastore, dignitario (specialmente presbiteriano).
elder[2], *s.* (*bot.*) sambuco ☆ — *-tree*, sambuco; — (*-flower*) *water*, infuso di fiori di sambuco; — (*-berry*) *wine*, vino di sambuco.
elderly ['eldəli], *ag.* attempato, anziano.
eldership ['eldəʃip], *s.* **1.** anzianità **2.** (*eccl.*) stato, dignità di anziano; gli anziani.

eldest ['eldist], *ag.* (*superl.* di *old*) maggiore (tra fratelli); primogenito.

El Dorado [,eldɔ'ra:dou], *s.* Eldorado (mitico paese sede d'ogni ricchezza e felicità).

eldritch ['eldritʃ], *ag.* (*scoz.*) soprannaturale; spaventoso.

Eleanor ['elinə*], **Eleonora** [,eliə'nɔ:rə], *no.pr.f.* Eleonora.

Eleazar [,eli'eizə*], *no.pr.m.* (*Bibbia*) Eleazaro.

elecampane [,elikæm'pein], *s.* (*bot.*) enula.

elect [i'lekt], *ag.* eletto, scelto ‖ *the —, God's —,* gli eletti, gli eletti di Dio ☆ *bishop —,* vescovo nominato, ma non ancora in funzione.

to elect, *v.t.* **1.** eleggere: *to — a member,* eleggere un deputato; *to — s.o. to the presidency,* eleggere qlcu. alla presidenza **2.** scegliere; decidersi: *he elected to be a doctor,* egli scelse la professione di medico; *to — domicile,* (*dir.*) eleggere domicilio.

election [i'lekʃən], *s.* **1.** elezione: *general —,* elezioni generali **2.** scelta; (*dir.*) opzione **3.** (*teol.*) elezione ☆ *— campaign,* campagna elettorale ‖ *by- —* (o *amer.* *special —*), elezione supplettiva (di un membro della Camera quando si rende vacante un seggio).

to electioneer [i,lekʃə'niə*], *v.i.* fare una campagna elettorale, fare propaganda elettorale.

electioneerer [i,lekʃə'niərə*], *s.* agente elettorale.

electioneering [i,lekʃə'niəriŋ], *s.* propaganda elettorale.

elective [i'lektiv], *ag.* **1.** elettivo; elettorale **2.** (*amer. scolastico*) facoltativo ☆ *— affinity,* (*chim.*) affinità elettiva.

electively [i'lektivli], *av.* elettivamente; per scelta.

electivity [i,lek'tiviti], *s.* eleggibilità.

elector [i'lektə*], *s.* elettore ‖ *the Elector of Hanover,* (*st.*) l'Elettore di Hannover.

electoral [i'lektərəl], *ag.* elettorale.

electorate [i'lektərit], *s.* **1.** (*st.*) elettorato **2.** elettori.

Electra [i'lektrə], *no.pr.f.* (*mit.*) Elettra ‖ *— complex,* (*psicanalisi*) complesso di Elettra.

electress [i'lektris], *s.* elettrice (anche *st.*).

electric [i'lektrik], *ag.* elettrico: *— energy,* energia elettrica; *— light,* luce elettrica ‖ *s.* sostanza vitrea, resinosa che sfregata si elettrizza ☆ *— battery,* (*elett.*) batteria elettrica; *— blanket,* (*neol.*) coperta elettrica; *— blue,* blu elettrico; *— chair,* sedia elettrica; *— eel,* (*ittiol.*) ginnoto; *— eye,* cellula fotoelettrica; *— meter,* contatore elettrico; *— shock, spark,* scossa, scintilla elettrica.

electrical [i'lektrikəl], *ag.* elettrico ☆ *— attraction,* attrazione elettrica.

electrically [i'lektrikəli], *av.* elettricamente: *— controlled,* a comando elettrico.

electrician [ilek'triʃən], *s.* elettricista.

electricity [ilek'trisiti], *s.* elettricità, energia elettrica: ☆ *magnetic —,* elettricità magnetica.

electrifiable [i'lektrifaiəbl], *ag.* elettrizzabile (anche *fig.*).

electrification [i,lektrifi'keiʃən], *s.* **1.** elettrificazione **2.** elettrizzazione.

electrified [i'lektrifaid], *ag.* **1.** elettrificato: *— railroad,* (*amer.*) ferrovia elettrificata **2.** elettrizzato (anche *fig.*).

to electrify [i'lektrifai], *v.t.* **1.** elettrificare **2.** elettrizzare (anche *fig.*).

electrifying [i'lektrifaiiŋ], *ag.* elettrizzante ‖ *s.* **1.** elettrificazione **2.** elettrizzazione (anche *fig.*).

electrization [i,lektri'zeiʃən], *s.* elettrizzazione.

to electrize [i'lektraiz], *v.t.* elettrizzare (anche *fig.*).

electroacoustics [i'lektrouə'ku:stiks], *s.* elettroacustica.

electrobiology [i'lektroubai'ɔlədʒi], *s.* elettrobiologia.

electrocardiogram [i'lektrou'ka:diəgræm], *s.* (*med.*) elettrocardiogramma.

electrocardiograph [i'lektrou'ka:diəgra:f], *s.* (*med.*) elettrocardiografo.

electrochemistry [i'lektrou'kemistri], *s.* elettrochimica.

to electrocute [i'lektrəkju:t], *v.t.* fulminare mediante elettricità; far morire sulla sedia elettrica.

electrocution [i,lektrə'kju:ʃən], *s.* elettroesecuzione.

electrode [i'lektroud], *s.* (*elett. rad.*) elettrodo; (*elett.*) piastra, placca ☆ *— force,* (*mec.*) forze dell'elettrodo, pressione sull'elettrodo; *— holder,* (*elett.*) portaelettrodo ‖ *control —,* (*elett.*) elettrodo regolatore; *modulator —,* (*tv.*) elettrodo regolatore; *passive —,* (*elett. chim.*) elettrodo indifferente; *starting —,* (*rad.*) anodo di accensione.

electrodynamics [i'lektroudai'næmiks], *s.* elettrodinamica.

electro-kinetics [i'lektroukai'netiks], *s.* elettrocinetica.

electrolier [i,lektrou'liə*], *s.* attacco, supporto per lampada elettrica.

to electrolyse [i'lektroulaiz], *v.t.* (*elett. chim.*) elettrolizzare.

electrolysis [ilek'trɔlisis], *s.* (*elett. chim.*) elettrolisi.

electrolyte [i'lektroulait], *s.* (*fis. chim.*) elettrolito.

electro-magnet [i'lektrou'mægnit], *s.* (*elett.*) elettromagnete, elettrocalamita.

electromagnetic [i'lektroumæg'netik], *ag.* (*elett.*) elettromagnetico ☆ *— theory,* teoria elettromagnetica; *— wave,* (*elett.*) onda elettromagnetica.

electro-magnetism [i'lektrou'mægnitizəm], *s.* (*elett.*) elettromagnetismo.

electrometallurgy [i'lektroume'tælədʒi], *s.* elettrometallurgia.

electrometer [ilek'trɔmitə*], *s.* (*elett.*) elettrometro.

electromotive [i'lektroumoutiv], *ag.* (*elett.*) elettromotore ☆ *— force,* forza elettromotrice.

electromotor [i'lektrou'moutə*], *s.* (*ind.*) motore elettrico; generatore di energia elettrica.

electron [i'lektron], *s.* (*fis. chim.*) elettrone ☆ *— camera,* (*tv.*) telecamera; *— flow,* (*elett.*) flusso elettronico; *— tube,* (*elett.*) valvola termoionica.

electronegative [i'lektrou'negətiv], *ag.* (*elett.*) elettronegativo.

electronic [ilek'trɔnik], *ag.* elettronico ☆ *— brain,* cervello elettronico; *— flash,* (*foto.*) lampo elettronico; *— switch,* (*rad.*) commutatore elettronico.

electronics [ilek'trɔniks], *s.* elettronica.

electrophorus [ilek'trɔfərəs], *s.* (*fis.*) elettroforo.

electrophysics [i'lektrou'fiziks], *s.* elettrofisica.

electro-physiology [i'lektrou,fizi'ɔlədʒi], *s.* elettrofisiologia.

electroplate [i'lektroupleit], *s.* (*ind.*) articoli placcati elettroliticamente, trattati con galvanostegia.

to electroplate, *v.t.* (*ind.*) placcare, trattare elettroliticamente, trattare con galvanostegia.

electropositive [i'lektrou'pozətiv], *ag.* (*elett. chim.*) elettropositivo.

electroscope [i'lektrəskoup], *s.* (*elett.*) elettroscopio.

electrostatics [i'lektrou'stætiks], *s.* elettrostatica.

electrotechnics [i'lektrou'tekniks], *s.* elettrotecnica.

electrotherapeutics [i'lektrouθerə'pju:tiks], **electrotherapy** [i'lektrou'θerəpi], *s.* (*med.*) elettroterapia.

electrothermal [i'lektrou'θə:məl], **electrothermic** [i'lektrou'θə:mik], *ag.* (*elett.*) elettrotermico.

electrothermy [i'lektrou'θə:mi], *s.* (*elett.*) elettrotermica.

electrotype [i'lektroutaip], *s.* (*tip.*) elettrotipo.

electrotypy [i'lektrou,taipi], *s.* (*tip.*) elettrotipia, galvanoplastica.

electrum [i'lektrəm], *s.* lega naturale di oro e argento.

electuary [i'lektjuəri], *s.* (*farm.*) elettuario.

eleemosynary [,elii'mɔsinəri], *ag.* **1.** caritatevole; gratuito **2.** che vive di elemosina.

elegance ['eligəns], **elegancy** ['eligənsi], *s.* eleganza.

elegant ['eligənt], *ag.* **1.** elegante, raffinato, di buon gusto **2.** (*sl.*) eccellente, di prim'ordine ‖ *s.* elegantone.

elegantly ['eligəntli], *av.* elegantemente.

elegiac [‚eli'dʒaiək], *ag.* (*poes.*) elegiaco.
elegiaes [‚eli'dʒaieks], *s.pl.* (*poes.*) versi elegiaci.
elegiast [e'li:dʒiæst], **elegist** ['elidʒist], *s.* poeta elegiaco.
elegy ['elidʒi], *s.* (*poes.*) elegia.
elektron [i'lektrɔn], *s.* (*metal.*) elektron.
element ['elimənt], *s.* 1. elemento: *the four elements*, i quattro elementi; *the fury of the elements*, la furia degli elementi ‖ *to be in, out of one's —*, essere nel, fuori del proprio elemento 2. principio costitutivo; parte di un tutto: *an — of truth*, un elemento di verità; *the personal —*, il fattore umano; *to reduce sthg. to its elements*, ridurre ql.co. ai suoi elementi 3. (*chim.*) elemento, corpo semplice; (*biol.*) cellula 4. *pl.* rudimenti: *elements of English grammar*, elementi di grammatica inglese.
elemental [‚eli'mentl], *ag.* 1. dei quattro elementi; delle forze naturali 2. elementare 3. fondamentale, essenziale.
elementary [‚eli'mentəri], *ag.* elementare, rudimentale: *— diagram*, diagramma schematico; *— school*, scuola elementare.
elemi ['elimi], *s.* elemi (tipo di resina).
elenchus [i'lenkəs], *pl.* **elenchi** [i'lenkai], *s.* (*fil.*) confutazione ‖ *Socratic —*, (*fil.*) maieutica.
elephant ['elifənt], *s.* elefante ‖ *a white —*, un elefante bianco; (*fam.*) cosa, oggetto di valore ma inutile e ingombrante ‖ *to see the —*, (*amer. fam.*) visitare i monumenti (di città, ecc.); girare il mondo ☆ *— -driver*, cornac; *—'s-ear*, (*bot.*) begonia ‖ *bull —*, elefante maschio; *calf —* (o *fam. baby —*), elefantino; *cow —* elefantessa.
elephantiasis [‚elifən'taiəsis],ˣ*s.* (*patol.*) elefantiasi.
elephantine [‚eli'fæntain], *ag.* elefantesco, elefantino.
Eleusinian [‚elju(:)'siniən], *ag.* eleusino, di Eleusi: *— mysteries*, (*relig.*) misteri eleusini.
Eleusis [e'lju(:)sis], *no.pr.* (*geog.*) Eleusi.
to elevate ['eliveit], *v.t.* 1. innalzare, elevare (anche *fig.*); alzare (occhi, voce) 2. esaltare 3. (*mil.*) puntare (un cannone).
elevated ['eliveitid], *ag.* 1. elevato: *— personage*, personaggio eminente ‖ *to be slightly —*, (*fam.*) essere un po' brillo 2. sopraelevato ☆ *— railway* (o *amer. — railroad*), ferrovia sopraelevata.
elevating ['eliveitiŋ], *ag.* 1. che eleva (lo spirito) 2. elevatore (di macchina) ‖ *s.* elevamento ☆ *— arc*, alzo (di armi da fuoco); *— gear*, dispositivo di elevazione; *— power*, (*aer.*) forza ascensionale.
elevation [‚eli'veiʃən], *s.* 1. elevazione, l'elevare (ad un rango più alto) 2. *the Elevation of the Host*, (*eccl.*) l'Elevazione dell'Ostia 3. (*mil.*) elevazione, angolo di elevazione 4. altezza (generalmente sopra il livello del mare); (*astr.*) altezza 5. collina, luogo alto, altitudine 6. disegno in proiezione ortogonale 7. (*mec.*) spostamento verticale 8. elevatezza (di pensiero, ecc.).
elevator ['eliveitə*], *s.* 1. ascensore; montacarichi, elevatore 2. (*anat.*) elevatorio, muscolo elevatore 3. (*calzoleria*) alzatacco interno 4. (*aer.*) equilibratore, timone di quota, profondità, impennaggio orizzontale 5. silos ☆ *— angle*, angolo di barra dell'equilibratore; *— bucket*, tazza per elevatore; *— easing*, colonna montante dell'elevatore; *— shaft*, pozzo dell'ascensore ‖ *belt —*, elevatore a nastro; *chain —*, elevatore a catena; *compressed-air —*, elevatore ad aria compressa; *pneumatic —*, elevatore pneumatico.
elevatory ['eliveitəri], *ag.* elevatore.
eleven [i'levn], *ag.num.card.s.* undici ‖ *an —*, (*spor.*) una squadra di undici giocatori.
elevens(es) [i'levnz(iz)], *s.* (*fam.*) spuntino a metà mattina.
eleventh [i'levnθ], *ag.num.ord.s.* undicesimo: *he was the — of his class*, era l'undicesimo della sua classe ‖ *at the — hour*, *fig.* appena in tempo, all'ultimo momento ☆ *— -hour*, dell'ultimo momento: *an — -hour change*, *fig.* un cambiamento fatto all'ultimo momento.

elevon ['elivɔn], *s.* (*neol. aer.*) elevone.
elf [elf], *pl.* **elves** [elvz], *s.* 1. (*mit.*) elfo, folletto 2. (*fam.*) bimbo vivacissimo, folletto ☆ *— -child*, bimbo sostituito dagli elfi; *— -lock*, (ciocca di) capelli arruffati.
elfin ['elfin], *ag.* di, da, simile ad elfo, folletto; incantato: *— landscape*, paesaggio incantato, da fiaba ‖ *s.* (*mit.*) elfo, folletto.
elfish ['elfiʃ], *ag.* 1. da elfo 2. vivace, birichino (di bimbo).
Elia(h) ['i:ljə], **Elias** [i'laiəs], *no.pr.m.* Elia.
to elicit [i'lisit], *v.t.* 1. scoprire (verità); trarre fuori; far confessare 2. attirare, provocare: *to — admiration*, provocare l'ammirazione; *to — an angry reply*, provocare una secca risposta.
elicitation [i‚lisi'teiʃən], *s.* deduzione; scoperta.
to elide [i'laid], *v.t.* elidere.
eligibility [‚elidʒə'biliti], *s.* eleggibilità.
eligible ['elidʒəbl], *ag.* 1. (*dir.*) eleggibile 2. desiderabile; vantaggioso: *— investment*, investimento vantaggioso; *an — young man*, un buon partito.
eligibleness ['elidʒəblnis], *s.* eleggibilità.
Elijah [i'laidʒə], *no.pr.m.* Elia.
eliminable [i'liminəbl], *ag.* eliminabile.
to eliminate [i'limineit], *v.t.* eliminare, togliere, scartare: *eliminating heats*, (*spor.*) (prove) eliminatorie; *to — a possibility*, scartare una possibilità.
elimination [i‚limi'neiʃən], *s.* eliminazione.
eliminative [i'liminətiv], *ag.* eliminatorio.
eliminator [i'limineitə*], *s.* chi, ciò che elimina.
eliminatory [i'liminətəri], *ag.* che elimina.
Elisabeth [i'lizəbəθ], *no.pr.f.* Elisabetta.
Elisha [i'laiʃə], *no.pr.m.* (*Bibbia*) Eliseo.
elision [i'liʒən], *s.* elisione.
élite [ei'li:t], *s.* « élite », il fior fiore della società.
elixir [i'liksə*], *s.* elisir.
Eliza [i'laizə], *no.pr.f.* Elisa.
Elizabeth [i'lizəbəθ], *no.pr.f.* Elisabetta.
Elizabethan [i‚lizə'bi:θən], *ag.* elisabettiano: *the — Age*, (*st.*) l'età elisabettiana ‖ *s.* elisabettiano.
elk, *pl.* **elk** [elk], **elks** [elks], *s.* (*zool.*) alce.
ell¹ [el], *s.* « ell » (misura di lunghezza = m. 1,143) ‖ *give him an inch and he'll take an —*, dàgli un dito e ti prenderà il braccio.
ell², *s.* 1. elle (la lettera *l*) 2. (*amer.*) ala di un edificio che forma con esso una L.
ellipse [i'lips], *s.* (*geom.*) ellisse.
ellipsis [i'lipsis], *pl.* **ellipses** [i'lipsi:z], *s.* (*gram.*) ellissi.
ellipsoid [i'lipsoid], *ag.* elissoidale ‖ *s.* (*geom.*) elissoide: *— of rotation*, elissoide di rotazione.
ellipsoidal [‚elip'soidl], *ag.* elissoidale.
elliptic(al) [i'liptik(əl)], *ag.* (*geom. gram.*) ellittico: *— arch*, (*arch.*) arco ellittico ☆ *— compass*, ellissografo.
elliptically [i'liptikəli], *av.* (*geom. gram.*) ellitticamente.
elm [elm], *s.* (*bot.*) olmo: *row of elms*, filare di olmi, olmaia ☆ *— -grove* (o *— -wood*), olmeto, olmaia; *— -sapling*, olmetto ‖ *gray —*, olmo bianco; *rock —*, olmo colorato.
elmy ['elmi], *av.* ricco di olmi.
elocution [‚elə'kju:ʃən], *s.* elocuzione; dizione.
elocutionary [‚elə'kju:ʃəri], *ag.* di elocuzione, di dizione; oratorio.
elocutionist [‚elə'kju:ʃnist], *s.* 1.˘ dicitore, declamatore 2. maestro di dizione.
éloge [ə'louʒ], *s.* discorso funebre.
Eloise [‚elou'i:z], *no.pr.f.* Eloisa.
elongate ['i:lɔŋgit], *ag.* (*bot. zool.*) oblungo, sottile, affusolato.
to elongate ['i:lɔŋgeit], *v.t.i.* 1. allungare, allungarsi; prolungare; (*bot.*) allungarsi, estendersi 2. (*astr.*) trovarsi in digressione.
elongation [‚i:lɔŋ'geiʃən], *s.* 1. allungamento; prolungamento (di linea) 2. (*astr.*) elongazione 3. (*mec.*,

ecc.) allungamento: — due to pull, allungamento dovuto alla trazione ☆ — test, prova di stiramento.

to **elope** [i'loup], v.i. fuggire (con un amante): to — with, fuggire con, farsi rapire da.

elopement [i'loupmənt], s. fuga (con un amante).

eloquence ['eləkwəns], s. eloquenza; retorica: Professor of —, professore di retorica.

eloquent ['eləkwənt], ag. eloquente (anche fig.): — look sguardo eloquente; to be naturally —, essere un oratore nato; to have an — tongue, essere buon parlatore.

eloquently ['eləkwəntli], av. eloquentemente.

else [els], av. (segue gli av. e i pron. interr., indef.) altro: give me something —, datemi qualcos'altro; nothing — was said, null'altro fu detto; this is somebody —'s book, questo è il libro di qualcun altro; was anybody — there?, c'era qualcun altro?; where — did you go?, dove altro andasti?; who — was there?, chi altro c'era? || (or) else, altrimenti, oppure: hurry up, (or) — we shall be late, spicciati, altrimenti facciamo tardi.

elsewhere ['els'wɛə*], av. altrove.

Elsie ['elsi], no.pr.f. Elisa.

to **elucidate** [i'lu:sideit], v.t. delucidare, spiegare.

elucidation [i,lu:si'deiʃən], s. delucidazione, spiegazione.

elucidative [i'lu:sideitiv], ag. delucidatorio.

elucidator [i'lu:sideitə*], s. delucidatore; esplicatore.

elucidatory [i'lu:sideitəri], ag. delucidatorio.

elucubration [i,lu:kju'breiʃən], s. elucubrazione.

to **elude** [i'lu:d], v.t. eludere, schivare, evitare; sfuggire, sottrarsi a: to — one's enemies, sfuggire ai propri nemici; to — payment of taxes, eludere il pagamento delle tasse; to — a promise, eludere una promessa.

elusion [i'lu:ʒən], s. elusione; l'evitare.

elusive [i'lu:siv], ag. 1. evasivo, ambiguo: — reply, risposta evasiva 2. sfuggevole, inafferrabile: an — criminal, un criminale inafferrabile.

elusory [i'lu:səri], ag. evasivo: — problem, problema che sfugge.

Elvira [el'vaiərə], no.pr.f. Elvira.

Elysian [i'liziən], ag. elisio; fig. felice, beato || the — Fields, (mit.) i Campi Elisi.

Elysium [i'liziəm], s. (mit.) gli Elisi; fig. luogo, condizione di completa felicità.

elytron ['elitron], pl. **elytra** ['elitrə], s. 1. elitra 2. (anat.) vagina.

Elzevir ['elzivi̯ə*], ag.s. (tip.) elzeviro.

'em [əm], abbr. di them.

to **emaciate** [i'meiʃieit], v.t. 1. far dimagrire; emaciare 2. impoverire (il suolo).

emaciated [i'meiʃieitid], ag. emaciato.

emaciation [i,meisi'eiʃən], s. dimagramento, emaciazione.

to **emanate** ['eməneit], v.i. emanare.

emanation [,emə'neiʃən], s. emanazione; effluvio.

to **emancipate** [i'mænsipeit], v.t. emancipare: an emancipated slave, woman, uno schiavo emancipato, una donna emancipata.

emancipation [i,mænsi'peiʃən], s. emancipazione.

emancipationist [i,mænsi'peiʃnist], s. 1. antischiavista 2. fautore dell'emancipazione (intellettuale, morale).

emancipator [i'mænsipeitə*], s.c. emancipatore, emancipatrice.

emancipist [i'mænsipist], s. (austral.) ex-forzato.

Emanuel [i'mænjuel], no.pr.m. Emanuele.

emasculate [i'mæskjulit], ag. 1. evirato 2. effeminato 3. fig. senza mordente (di stile).

to **emasculate** [i'mæskjuleit], v.t. 1. evirare 2. fig. snervare; impoverire (una lingua); togliere mordente a (uno stile); mutilare (un'opera letteraria).

emasculated [i'mæskjuleitid], V. emasculate.

emasculation [i,mæskju'leiʃən], s. 1. evirazione 2. fig. indebolimento; mutilazione (di opera letteraria).

to **embalm** [im'bɑ:m], v.t. 1. imbalsamare 2. profumare, rendere balsamica (aria) 3. fig. conservare (la memoria di qlcu., ecc.).

embalmer [im'bɑ:mə*], s. imbalsamatore.

embalmment [im'bɑ:mmənt], s. imbalsamazione.

to **embank** [im'bæŋk], v.t. arginare (fiumi, ecc.).

embankment [im'bæŋkmənt], s. 1. l'arginare 2. argine, diga; alzaia, strada lungo un fiume || Thames Embankment, Lungo Tamigi.

embarcation [,embɑ:'keiʃən], s. imbarco.

embargo [em'bɑ:gou], pl. **embargoes** [em'bɑ:gouz], s. 1. (mar.) embargo, fermo: to be under —, essere sotto sequestro; to impose (o to lay) an — on a ship, mettere l'embargo su una nave; to lift (o to take off) the — on a ship, togliere l'embargo ad una nave 2. proibizione, divieto, impedimento ☆ gold —, proibizione di cambiare cartamoneta in oro.

to **embargo**, v.t. mettere l'embargo a, imporre il fermo a, mettere sotto sequestro (navi, merci).

to **embark** [im'bɑ:k], v.t.i. 1. imbarcare (truppe, merci); imbarcarsi: to — for a voyage, imbarcarsi per un viaggio 2. fig. intraprendere, iniziare: to — on a business, intraprendere un commercio.

embarkation [,embɑ:'keiʃən], s. imbarco.

to **embarrass** [im'bærəs], v.t. mettere in imbarazzo, sconcertare; creare delle difficoltà a: to — s.o. with indiscreet questions, mettere in imbarazzo qlcu. con domande indiscrete; to be embarrassed, essere in imbarazzo: to be embarrassed for money (o to be in embarrassed circumstances), essere in difficoltà economiche, trovarsi in cattive acque.

embarrassing [im'bærəsiŋ], ag. 1. imbarazzante: an — situation, una situazione imbarazzante 2. dissestato.

embarrassingly [im'bærəsiŋli], av. in modo imbarazzante.

embarrassment [im'bærəsmənt], s. 1. imbarazzo, confusione 2. difficoltà: financial —, difficoltà finanziarie.

embassy ['embəsi], s. 1. ambasciata || the Italian Embassy in London, l'ambasciata italiana a Londra 2. ambasceria, missione diplomatica 3. ambasciata, messaggio ☆ special —, missione speciale.

to **embattle**[1] [im'bætl], v.t.i. |1. schierare (un esercito) in ordine di battaglia 2. (arc.) fortificare un castello.

to **embattle**[2], v.t. munire (edificio, mura) di merli, di bastioni.

embattled[1] [im'bætld], ag. 1. schierato (in battaglia) 2. coperto di truppe schierate in battaglia 3. fortificato.

embattled[2], ag. (arch.) merlato.

embattlement [im'bætlmənt], s. (arch.) merlatura.

to **embay**[1] [im'bei], v.t. 1. portare (una nave) in baia; costringere (una nave) a riparare in baia, trattenere (una nave) in baia (di vento, ecc.) 2. imprigionare, circondare: embayed by the ice, circondato dal ghiaccio.

to **embay**[2], v.t. (poet. arc.) bagnare.

embayment [im'beimənt], s. 1. baia 2. (fam.) parte rientrante (di baia, sala, ecc.).

to **embed** [im'bed], pass.p.p. **embedded** [im'bedid], v.t. (gener. al passivo) incassare; incastrare; conficcare (chiodo, ecc.); stones embedded in concrete, pietre cementate.

embedding [im'bediŋ], s. incassatura, incassamento.

to **embellish** [im'beliʃ], v.t. abbellire, ornare; infiorare, colorire (stile): to — a story, abbellire, colorire un racconto.

embellishment [im'beliʃmənt], s. 1. abbellimento 2. pl. miglioramenti, migliorie (a edifici, ecc.).

ember[1] ['embə*], s. 1. tizzone 2. gener. pl. brace; cenere ardente: the embers of a dying passion, i resti di una passione morente.

ember[2], ag. (nei composti): — -days, (eccl.) Quattro Tempora; — weeks, (eccl.) settimane delle Quattro Tempora.

ember[3], *s.* — (*-goose*), (*ornit.*) strolaga.

to **embezzle** [im'bezl], *v.t.* appropriarsi indebitamente di (denaro, ecc.).

embezzlement [im'bezlmənt], *s.* appropriazione indebita; malversazione.

embezzler [im'bezlə*], *s.* malversatore; prevaricatore; chi si appropria indebitamente.

to **embitter** [im'bitə*], *v.t.* **1.** rendere amaro (un liquido) **2.** *fig.* amareggiare, avvelenare; inasprire, esacerbare: *he was embittered by her refusal*, egli fu amareggiato dal suo rifiuto; *to — one's life*, amareggiarsi la vita.

embitterment [im'bitəmənt], *s.* amarezza; inasprimento.

to **emblaze**[1] [im'bleiz], *v.t.* illuminare; accendere.

to **emblaze**[2], to **emblazon** [im'bleizən], *v.t.* **1.** (*arald.*) blasonare, ornare con pezze araldiche **2.** celebrare, esaltare, portare alle stelle.

emblazonry [im'bleizənri], *s.* **1.** blasone **2.** pezze araldiche.

emblem ['embləm], *s.* emblema, simbolo (anche *fig.*): *the crown and sceptre are emblems of royalty*, la corona e lo scettro sono gli emblemi della regalità; *he was the — of honesty*, egli era il simbolo dell'onestà.

to **emblem**, *v.t.* simboleggiare, rappresentare.

emblematic(al) [,embli'mætik(əl)], *ag.* emblematico, simbolico: *the lion is — of strength*, il leone è l'emblema della forza.

to **emblematize** [em'blemətaiz], *v.t.* simboleggiare, rappresentare.

emblements ['emblmənts], *s.pl.* (*dir.*) **1.** proventi del raccolto **2.** prodotti della terra.

embodiment [im'bɔdimənt], *s.* incarnazione; personificazione.

to **embody** [im'bɔdi], *v.t.* **1.** incarnare, dar corpo a **2.** realizzare (un concetto); personificare (una qualità); applicare un principio a **3.** incorporare, includere: *article that embodies the following regulations*, articolo che comprende le seguenti disposizioni **4.** riunire, organizzare (truppe).

to **embog** [em'bɔg], *pass.p.p.* **embogged** [em'bɔgd], *v.t.* affondare, tuffare in un pantano (anche *fig.*).

to **emboil** [im'bɔil], *v.t.i.* (*poet.*) irritare; ardere d'ira.

to **embolden** [im'bouldən], *v.t.* incoraggiare, incitare.

embolism ['embəlizəm], *s.* **1.** (*patol.*) embolia **2.** (*astr.*) embolismo.

embolus ['embələs], *s.* (*patol.*) embolo.

to **embosom** [im'buzəm], *v.t.* **1.** stringere al seno **2.** *fig.* rinchiudere, circondare: *cottage embosomed in trees*, villetta circondata da alberi.

to **emboss** [im'bɔs], *v.t.* scolpire, stampare in rilievo; goffrare; sbalzare (metalli).

embossed [im'bɔst], *ag.* sbalzato, fatto in rilievo, goffrato ☆ — *rubber*, gomma goffrata; — *work*, lavoro in rilievo.

embosser [im'bɔsə*], *s.* **1.** goffratore **2.** (*mec.*) goffratrice.

embossing [im'bɔsiŋ], *s.* **1.** goffratura; lavoro di sbalzo **2.** (*tip.*) impressione a secco ☆ — *machine*, goffratrice.

embossment [im'bɔsmənt], *s.* rilievo ☆ — *-map*, mappa in rilievo.

embouchure [,ɔmbu'ʃuə*], *s.* **1.** imboccatura (di strumento a fiato) **2.** foce (di fiume).

to **embow** [im'bou], *v.t.* **1.** (*rar.*) piegare, curvare ad arco **2.** (*arch.*) coprire con un arco, una volta **3.** inglobare; inscrivere (anche *fig.*).

to **embowel** [im'bauəl], *pass.p.p.* **embowelled** [im-'bauəld], *v.t.* sbudellare (anche *fig.*).

embowelment [im'bauəlmənt], *s.* **1.** sbudellamento **2.** parte interna di una cosa.

to **embower** [im'bauə*], *v.t.* (*letter.*) rinchiudere, riparare (come in un pergolato).

embrace[1] [im'breis], *s.* **1.** abbraccio, amplesso **2.** rapporto sessuale.

to **embrace**[1], *v.t.i.* **1.** abbracciare, abbracciarsi: *they embraced*, s'abbracciarono **2.** abbracciare (carriera, causa, ecc.) **3.** abbracciare; comprendere: *a constituency that embraces several townships*, un collegio elettorale che comprende diversi centri abitati **4.** abbracciare (di sguardo): *from the terrace the eye embraces the whole valley*, dalla terrazza l'occhio abbraccia tutta la valle **5.** cogliere (occasione, opportunità).

to **embrace**[2], *v.t.* (*dir.*) subornare (giurati).

embracement [im'breismənt], *s.* **1.** abbraccio, stretta **2.** adozione, accettazione (di opinione, causa, ecc.).

embracer[1] [im'breisə*], *s.c.* chi abbraccia (anche *fig.*).

embracer[2], *s.c.* (*dir.*) subornatore, subornatrice.

embracery [im'breisəri], *s.* (*dir.*) subornazione.

embranchment [im'brɑ:ntʃmənt], *s.* biforcazione; diramazione.

to **embrangle** [im'bræŋgl], *v.t.* confondere, rendere perplesso.

embranglement [im'bræŋglmənt], *s.* confusione; perplessità.

embrasure [im'breiʒə*], *s.* **1.** (*arch.*) strombatura (di porta, finestra) **2.** (*mil.*) cannoniera; feritoia: *direct, oblique* —, cannoniera diretta, obliqua.

to **embreathe** [im'bri:ð], *v.t.i.* inspirare; inalare.

to **embrocate** ['embroukeit], *v.t.* (*med.*) embrocare.

embrocation [,embrou'keiʃən], *s.* (*farm.*) embrocazione, linimento; fomento.

embroglio [em'brouljou], *s.* imbroglio, pasticcio.

to **embroider** [im'brɔidə*], *v.t.* **1.** ricamare **2.** *fig.* ampliare, abbellire (un racconto, ecc.): *embroidered language*, linguaggio fiorito.

embroiderer [im'brɔidərə*], *s.c.* ricamatore, ricamatrice.

embroidery [im'brɔidəri], *s.* **1.** ricamo **2.** *fig.* ornamento, abbellimento ☆ — *frame*, telaio da ricamo; — *scissors*, forbici da ricamo.

to **embroil** [im'brɔil], *v.t.* **1.** imbrogliare, ingarbugliare; render inintelligibile ‖ *to — matters*, (*fam.*) imbrogliare le carte **2.** *to — a nation in a war*, coinvolgere una nazione in una guerra **3.** *to — s.o. with s.o.*, *fig.* fomentare la discordia, seminare zizzania tra due persone.

embroilment [im'brɔilmənt], *s.* **1.** imbroglio, garbuglio: *fearing new embroilments*, nel timore di nuove complicazioni **2.** *fig.* discordia.

to **embrown** [im'braun], *v.t.* (*poet.*) oscurare, imbrunire.

embryo ['embriou], *pl.* **embryos** ['embriouz], *s.* embrione: *in* —, in embrione; *barrister in* —, avvocato in erba; *plan still in* —, progetto ancora allo stato embrionale ☆ — *-sac*, (*bot.*) sacco embrionale.

embryogenesis [,embriou'dʒenisis], **embryogeny** [,embri'ɔdʒəni], *s.* (*biol.*) embriogenia.

embryology [,embri'ɔlədʒi], *s.* (*biol. fisiol.*) embriologia.

embryonic [,embri'ɔnik], *ag.* embrionale (anche *fig.*).

to **embus** [im'bʌs], *pass.p.p.* **embussed** [im'bʌst], *v.t.i.* (far) salire su un automezzo (specialmente truppe).

to **emend** [i(:)'mend], *v.t.* emendare, correggere (un testo, ecc.).

emendable [i(:)'mendəbl], *ag.* emendabile.

to **emendate** ['i:mendeit], *V.* to **emend**.

emendation [,i:men'deiʃən], *s.* **1.** emendazione, correzione **2.** variante proposta.

emendator ['i:mendeitə*], *s.* emendatore, correttore.

emendatory [i(:)'mendətəri], *ag.* emendativo, correttivo.

emerald ['emərəld], *s.* **1.** smeraldo; (colore) smeraldo ‖ *the Emerald Isle*, l'Isola di Smeraldo, la (verde) Irlanda **2.** (*tip.*) corpo 6½ ☆ — *-green*, verde smeraldo.

emeraldine ['emərəldain], *ag.* smeraldino ‖ *s.* (*chim.*) verde anilina.

to **emerge** [i'mə:dʒ], *v.i.* **1.** emergere, affiorare, apparire, sorgere: *the moon emerges from behind the clouds*, la luna appare di fra le nuvole; *on emerging from boyhood*, sul finire dell'adolescenza **2.** *fig.* risultare, apparire; essere chiaro: *from these facts it emerges that*, da questi fatti appare chiaro che.

emergence [i'mə:dʒəns], *s.* **1.** emersione **2.** apparizione improvvisa (di raggio luminoso, di teoria, ecc.).

emergency [i'mə:dʒənsi], *s.* emergenza; caso imprevisto; contingenza: *in case of* —, in caso di bisogno, di necessità; *to meet an* —, far fronte ad un caso urgente, ad una situazione critica; *to rise to the* —, essere, mostrarsi all'altezza della situazione ☆ — *-brake*, freno di sicurezza; — *bridge*, ponte provvisorio; — *camp*, campo di fortuna; — *-door*, — *-exit*, uscita di sicurezza; — *landing field*, (*aer.*) campo di fortuna; — *machine*, (*ind.*) macchina di riserva; — *man*, (*spor.*) riserva; — *means*, mezzi di fortuna; — *measures*, misure di sicurezza; — *stop*, (*elett. mec.*) arresto, blocco di emergenza.

emeritus [i(:)'meritəs], *ag.* emerito (di professore).

emersion [i(:)'mə:ʃən], *s.* emersione (anche *astr.*).

emery ['eməri], *s.* smeriglio ☆ — *-board*, limetta di carta smerigliata (per unghie); — *-cloth*, tela smeriglio; — *-dust*, — *-flour*, — *-powder*, polvere di smeriglio; — *-paper*, carta smerigliata; — *-rubbing*, smerigliatura; — *-stick*, lima a smeriglio; — *-wheel*, mola a smeriglio.

emetic [i'metik], *ag.s.* (*farm.*) emetico.

emetin ['emitin], *s.* (*chim.*) emetina.

emeu ['i:mju:], *s.* (*zool.*) emù.

emicant ['emikənt], *ag.* dardeggiante, lampeggiante.

emiction [i'mikʃən], *s.* minzione.

emigrant ['emigrənt], *ag.s.* emigrante ☆ — *runner*, agente di emigrazione clandestina.

to **emigrate** ['emigreit], *v.t.i.* **1.** (far) emigrare; (*amer.*) trasferirsi (in un altro Stato dell'Unione) **2.** (*fam.*) cambiare domicilio.

emigration [,emi'greiʃən], *s.* **1.** emigrazione **2.** (*fam.*) cambiamento di domicilio ☆ — *-agency*, agenzia di emigrazione; — *-law*, legge sull'emigrazione.

Emilia[1] [i'miliə], *no.pr.f.* Emilia.

Emilia[2], *no.pr.* (*geog.*) Emilia.

Emilian [i'mi:liən], *ag.* emiliano ‖ *s.c.* emiliano, emiliana ‖ *no.pr.m.* Emiliano.

Emilius [i'mi:liəs], *no.pr.m.* Emilio.

Emily ['emili], *no.pr.f.* Emilia.

eminence ['eminəns], *s.* **1.** luogo, parte eminente; altura **2.** (*anat.*) protuberanza, sporgenza **3.** *fig.* eminenza, eccellenza (d'ingegno, di grado); celebrità **4.** *Eminence*, (*eccl.*) Eminenza: *His, Your Eminence*, Sua, Vostra Eminenza ☆ *tyroid* —, pomo di Adamo.

eminent ['eminənt], *ag.* eminente (anche *fig.*): — *domain*, (*dir.*) dominio eminente; *to reach an* — *position*, pervenire ad una posizione eminente.

eminently ['eminəntli], *av.* eminentemente, per eccellenza.

emir [e'miə*], *s.* emiro.

emissary ['emisəri], *ag.* (*anat.*) escretorio, emissario: — *veins*, vene emissarie ‖ *s.* **1.** emissario, agente segreto; spia **2.** (*st. romana*) canale di scarico.

emission [i'miʃən], *s.* **1.** emissione, emanazione **2.** (*fisiol.*) emissione **3.** emissione (di carta monetata) **4.** (*fis.*) emissione ☆ *beam* —, (*rad.*) emissione direzionale; *electron* —, emissione elettronica.

emissive [i'misiv], *ag.* emissivo.

emissivity [,emi'siviti], *s.* (*fis.*) emissività.

to **emit** [i'mit], *pass.p.p.* **emitted** [i'mitid], *v.t.* **1.** emettere, emanare; esalare (odori); lanciare (grido) **2.** emettere (moneta, carta monetata) **3.** esprimere (un'opinione); dare (un consiglio) **4.** (*rad.*) trasmettere.

emitter [i'mitə*], *s.* trasmettitore ☆ — *valve*, valvola di emissione.

Emma ['emə], *no.pr.f.* Emma.

Emmanuel [i'mænjuəl], *no.pr.m.* Emanuele.

to **emmarble** [e'mɑ:bl], *v.t.* **1.** trasformare in marmo, pietrificare **2.** rappresentare in marmo; ornare con marmo.

emmenagogue [e'mi:nəgɔg], *s.* (*med.*) emmenagogo.

emmet ['emit], *s.* (*arc.*) formica.

emollient [i'mɔliənt], *ag.s.* emolliente.

emolument [i'mɔljumənt], *s.* remunerazione, salario: *emoluments of a Member of Parliament*, indennità parlamentare.

emotion [i'mouʃən], *s.* **1.** emozione; commozione; turbamento: *without showing the least* —, senza mostrare la minima emozione **2.** sensibilità; sentimento: *to appeal to the emotions*, fare appello ai sentimenti.

emotional [i'mouʃənl], *ag.* **1.** emotivo, impressionabile: *to be* —, essere impressionabile **2.** commovente, emozionante: *an* — *speech*, discorso commovente ☆ — *disturbances*, (*patol.*) disturbi emotivi.

emotionalism [i'mouʃnəlizəm], **emotionality** [i,mouʃə'næliti], *s.* impressionabilità, emotività.

emotionally [i'mouʃnəli], *av.* con emozione, in modo commosso.

emotive [i'moutiv], *ag.* **1.** commovente **2.** emotivo, impressionabile.

to **empanel** [im'pænl], *pass.p.p.* **empanelled** [im-'pænld], *v.t.* iscrivere in una lista, nell'albo di una professione: *to* — *a jury*, formare la lista della giuria.

empanelment [im'pænlmənt], *s.* iscrizione in una lista, nell'albo di una professione.

empathy ['empəθi], *s.* **1.** (*fil.*) empatia, intropatia; trasporto contemplativo **2.** (*patol.*) delirio sistematizzato.

Empedocles [em'pedəkli:z], *no.pr.m.* (*st. fil.*) Empedocle.

emperor ['empərə*], *s.* imperatore.

emphasis ['emfəsis], *s.* **1.** accentuazione, rilievo, evidenza: *to lay* — *on*, mettere in evidenza **2.** enfasi, vigore (di espressione): *oratorical* —, enfasi oratoria **3.** importanza: *too much* — *was placed on technique*, fu data troppa importanza alla tecnica.

to **emphasize** ['emfəsaiz], *v.t.* accentuare; dare rilievo a, mettere in evidenza; attirare l'attenzione su.

emphatic(al) [im'fætik(əl)], *ag.* accentuato; espressivo; enfatico: — *gesture*, gesto vigoroso; — *speaker*, oratore enfatico.

emphatically [im'fætikəli], *av.* enfaticamente; vigorosamente.

emphysema [,emfi'si:mə], *s.* (*patol.*) enfisema.

emphyteusis [,emfi'tju:sis], *s.* (*dir.*) enfiteusi.

emphyteutic [,emfi'tju:tik], *ag.* (*dir.*) enfiteutico.

empire ['empaiə*], *s.* impero: *Roman, British* —, impero romano, britannico ‖ *Empire City*, New York; *Empire Day*, festa nazionale britannica (24 maggio); *Empire State*, lo stato di New York.

empiric [em'pirik] *ag.* empirico ‖ *s.* empirista; ciarlatano.

empirical [em'pirikəl], *ag.* empirico.

empirically [em'pirikəli], *av.* empiricamente.

empiricism [em'pirisizəm], *s.* empirismo.

empiricist [em'pirisist], *s.* empirista.

emplacement [im'pleismənt], *s.* **1.** ubicazione **2.** (*mil.*) piazzuola.

employ [im'plɔi], *s.* impiego: *out of* —, senza impiego; *to be in the* — *of*, essere impiegato presso.

to **employ**, *v.t.* **1.** impiegare, adoperare, servirsi di: *he employed his spare time in fishing*, impiegava il suo tempo libero pescando **2.** impiegare, occupare, assumere al proprio servizio: *to* — *s.o. as secretary*, assumere qlcu. come segretario **3.** occuparsi: *to* — *oneself in doing sthg.*, occuparsi di ql.co.

employable [im'plɔiəbl], *ag.* impiegabile.

employee [,emplɔi'i:], (*amer.*) **employe** [em'plɔii:], *s.* impiegato, salariato.

employer [im'plɔiə*], *s.* principale, padrone, datore di lavoro.

employment [im'plɔimənt], *s.* impiego, occupazione, lavoro: *to be out of* —, essere senza impiego; *to give s.o.* —, dare un impiego a qlcu. ☆ — *bureau* (o — *agency*), ufficio di collocamento.

to **emplume** [em'plːum], *v.t.* impiumare.

to **empoison** [em'poizn], *v.t.* avvelenare.

emporium [em'poːriəm], *s.* **1.** centro commerciale **2.** (*fam.*) emporio, negozio.

to **empoverish**, *V.* to **impoverish**.

to **empower** [im'pauə*], *v.t.* **1.** autorizzare, dare pieni poteri a **2.** (*dir.*) dare la procura a.

empress ['empris], *s.* imperatrice.

emptier ['emptiə*], *s.* chi vuota.

emptiness ['emptinis], *s.* **1.** il vuoto **2.** vacuità, vuotezza; vanità.

emption ['empʃən], *s.* (*dir.*) acquisto: *right of* —, diritto di acquisto.

empty ['empti], *ag.* **1.** vuoto; deserto, disabitato: — *bottle*, bottiglia vuota; *an* — *building*, uno stabile disabitato; — *street*, strada deserta **2.** vacuo, vano, vuoto; privo di: *words* — *of meaning*, parole prive di significato, senza senso **3.** vacante: *an* — *chair*, cattedra vacante **4.** (*fam.*) vuoto, a digiuno: — *stomach*, stomaco vuoto: *to be taken on an* — *stomach*, da prendersi a digiuno; *to feel* —, aver lo stomaco vuoto, avere fame ‖ *s.* **1.** furgone vuoto; (*ferr.*) vagone merci vuoto; taxi vuoto; casa, appartamento vuoto **2.** *pl.* i vuoti: *to return the empties*, restituire i vuoti ☆ — -*handed*, a mani vuote; — -*headed*, scervellato — *prattler*, persona che parla a vuoto, a vanvera,

to **empty**, *v.t.i.* **1.** vuotare, vuotarsi; svuotare, svuotarsi; evacuare, sgombrare; versare; scaricare: *they have emptied my flat*, (*fam.*) hanno svaligiato il mio appartamento; *to* — *one's bowels*, (*med.*) evacuare gli intestini **2.** sfociare, sboccare (di fiume).

emptysis ['emptisis], *s.* (*med.*) emottisi.

to **empurple** [em'pəːpl], *v.t.* imporporare.

empyema [,empai'iːmə], *s.* (*patol.*) empiema.

empyreal [,empai'ri(ː)əl], *ag.* empireo; celeste.

empyrean [,empai'ri(ː)ən], *ag.* empireo; celeste ‖ *s.* empireo; cielo.

emu ['iːmjuː], *s.* (*zool.*) emù.

to **emulate** ['emjuleit], *v.t.* emulare, rivaleggiare con.

emulation [,emju'leiʃən], *s.* emulazione.

emulative ['emjulətiv], *ag.* emulo.

emulator ['emjuleitə*], *s.c.* emulatore, emulatrice.

emulous ['emjuləs], *ag.* **1.** emulo **2.** bramoso, desideroso.

emulously ['emjuləsli], *av.* con emulazione.

emulousness ['emjuləsnis], *s.* emulazione, rivalità.

to **emulsify** [i'mʌlsifai], *v.t.i.* emulsionare, emulsionarsi.

emulsion [i'mʌlʃən], *s.* emulsione☆ — *chamber*, (*mec.*) camera di emulsione.

to **emulsionize** [i'mʌlʃənaiz], *v.t.* emulsionare.

emulsive [i'mʌlsiv], *ag.* emulsivo.

emunctory [i'mʌŋktəri], *ag.* (*anat.*) emuntorio ‖ *s.* (*anat.*) organo emuntorio.

to **enable** [i'neibl], *v.t.* mettere in grado di; rendere capace di; (*dir.*) abilitare a: *this legacy enabled him to retire*, questa eredità gli permise di ritirarsi; *to* — *s.o. to do sthg.*, mettere qlcu. in grado di far ql.co.

to **enact** [i'nækt], *v.t.* **1.** (*dir.*) decretare, emanare (una legge); mettere in esecuzione: *as by law enacted*, a termine di legge; *be it further enacted that...*, si ordina inoltre che... **2.** recitare (una parte).

enactive [i'næktiv], *ag.* decretante.

enactment [i'næktmənt], *s.* **1.** promulgazione (di legge, decreto) **2.** legge, decreto.

enactor [i'næktə*], *s.* promulgatore (d'una legge).

enamel [i'næməl], *s.* **1.** lacca, smalto, vernice (per unghie, metalli, ecc.) **2.** smalto (dei denti) ☆ — *factory*, smalteria; — *paint*, vernice a smalto; — *ware*, vasellame smaltato; — *work*, smaltatura.

to **enamel**, *pass.p.p.* **enamelled** [i'næməld], *v.t.* **1.** smaltare **2.** (*poet.*) adornare con vari colori.

enamel(l)er [i'næmlə*], **enamellist** [i'næmlist], *s.* smaltatore, verniciatore.

to **enamour** [i'næmə*], *v.t.* (*gener. usato al p.p.*) fare innamorare; affascinare: *to be enamoured of* (o *with*) *s.o.*, essere innamorato di qlcu.

enantiopathy [e,nænti'opəθi], *s.* (*med.*) allopatia.

enarthrosis [,enaː'θrousis], *s.* (*anat.*) enartrosi.

encaenia [en'siːnjə], *s.* festa commemorativa della fondazione della città (specialmente a Oxford).

to **encage** [in'keidʒ], *v.t.* chiudere in gabbia.

to **encamp** [in'kæmp], *v.t.i.* accampare, accamparsi.

encampment [in'kæmpmənt], *s.* campeggio; accampamento.

to **encase** [in'keis], *v.t.* **1.** rinchiudere (in un astuccio, ecc.); custodire **2.** rivestire.

encasement [in'keismənt], *s.* rivestimento, custodia.

to **encash** [in'kæʃ], *v.t.* **1.** incassare (assegno, ecc.) **2.** realizzare, convertire in denaro.

encaustic [en'koːstik], *ag.* (*art.*) ad encausto ‖ *s.* (*art.*) encausto.

enceinte [aːn'sænt], *ag.* incinta, gravida ‖ *s.* (*mil.*) cinta (di mura, bastioni, ecc.).

encephalic [,enke'fælik], *ag.* (*anat.*) encefalico.

encephalitis [,enkefə'laitis], *s.* (*patol.*) encefalite: *hemorragic* —, encefalite emorragica; *pyogenic* —, encefalite purulenta.

to **enchain** [in'tʃein], *v.t.* incatenare.

to **enchant** [in'tʃaːnt], *v.t.* incantare, affascinare, ammaliare: *I'm enchanted with your singing*, il tuo canto mi affascina.

enchanter [in'tʃaːntə*], *s.* incantatore, mago.

enchanting [in'tʃaːntiŋ], *ag.* incantevole, affascinante.

enchantment [in'tʃaːntmənt], *s.* incanto; incantesimo; fascino.

enchantress [in'tʃaːntris], *s.* incantatrice, ammaliatrice.

to **enchase** [in'tʃeis], *v.t.* incastonare; *fig.* inserire; cesellare, scolpire.

enchiridion [,enkai'ridiən], *s.* manuale.

enchylema [,enki'liːmə], **enchyma** ['enkimə], *s.* (*biol.*) citolinfa.

to **encipher** [en'saifə*], *v.t.* **1.** cifrare (messaggio, dispaccio) **2.** cifrare, ricamare monogrammi su.

to **encircle** [in'səːkl], *v.t.* circondare, cingere.

encircling [in'səːkliŋ], **encirclement** [in'səːklmənt], *s.* accerchiamento.

to **enclasp** [in'klaːsp], *v.t.* abbracciare; stringere; afferrare.

enclave ['enkleiv], *s.* zona circondata da territori stranieri.

enclitic [in'klitik], *ag.* (*gram.*) enclitico ‖ *s.* enclitica.

to **enclose** [in'klouz], *v.t.* **1.** chiudere, racchiudere; cingere, cintare; circondare, avvolgere:‖ *to* — *a garden with a wall*, circondare un giardino con un muro **2.** accludere, includere, allegare, unire: *I'll* — *a cheque*, accluderò un assegno **3.** (*elett.*) incassare: *they enclosed the wires in the wall*, incassarono i fili nel muro.

enclosed [in'klouzd], *ag.* **1.** racchiuso; cinto, circondato; avvolto **2.** accluso, allegato: *the* — *letter*, la lettera acclusa; *please find* —, (*comm.*) abbiamo allegato.

enclosure [in'klouʒə*], *s.* **1.** recinto, luogo cintato **2.** recinto; staccionata **3.** (*comm.*) allegato: *three enclosures*, tre allegati **4.** clausura ☆ — *wall*, muro di cinta ‖ *barbed wire* —, recinto di filo spinato.

to **enclothe** [en'klouð], *v.t.* (*letter.*) rivestire.

to **encloud** [in'klaud], *v.t.* velare, oscurare con nubi.

encomiast [en'koumiæst], *s.* **1.** encomiasta, encomiatore **2.** adulatore.

encomiastic(al) [en,koumi'æstik(əl)], *ag.* **1.** encomiastico **2.** adulatorio.

encomiastically [en,koumi'æstikəli], *av.* **1.** encomiasticamente **2.** in modo adulatorio.

encomium [en'koumjəm], *s.* encomio, lode solenne.

to **encompass** [in'kʌmpəs], *v.t.* **1.** circondare, cingere **2.** racchiudere **3.** complottare, meditare.

encore [oŋˈkɔː*], *s.* (*teat.*) bis: *he got an* —, ebbe un bis; *she gave three encores*, ella concesse tre bis ‖ *inter.* (*teat.*) bis.

to encore, *v.t.* (*teat.*) chiedere un bis di.

encounter [inˈkauntə*], *s.* **1.** incontro (casuale) **2.** (*letter.*) scontro; lotta; duello.

to encounter, *v.t.* **1.** incontrare (difficoltà, ostacoli, nemici, ecc.) **2.** imbattersi in (amici, ecc.) **3.** affrontare (il nemico).

to encourage [inˈkʌridʒ], *v.t.* (IV) **1.** incoraggiare, incitare, spingere, animare **2.** appoggiare, favorire.

encouragement [inˈkʌridʒmənt], *s.* incoraggiamento.

encourager [inˈkʌridʒə*], *s.c.* incoraggiatrice, incoraggiatrice; sostenitore, sostenitrice; promotore, promotrice.

encouraging [inˈkʌridʒiŋ], *ag.* incoraggiante.

encouragingly [inˈkʌridʒiŋli], *av.* in modo incoraggiante.

to encrimson [inˈkrimzn], *v.t.* imporporare, arrossare.

to encroach [inˈkroutʃ], *v.i.*: *to* — (*up*)*on* (*sthg.*), usurpare; invadere; intaccare; (*dir.*) ledere; abusare: *the sea is encroaching upon the land*, il mare guadagna terreno; *to* — (*up*)*on s.o.'s land*, usurpare la terra di qlcu.; *to* — *upon s.o.'s time*, abusare del tempo di qlcu.

encroacher [inˈkroutʃə*], *s.c.* **1.** usurpatore, usurpatrice **2.** intruso, intrusa; persona importuna.

encroachingly [inˈkroutʃiŋli], *av.* abusivamente.

encroachment [inˈkroutʃmənt], *s.* **1.** usurpazione, invasione **2.** (*dir.*) lesione **3.** abuso.

to encrust [inˈkrʌst], *v.t.i.* **1.** incrostare, incrostarsi: *boiler encrusted with rust*, caldaia incrostata di ruggine **2.** incrostare, decorare con materiale prezioso: *to* — *ebony with mother of pearl*, incrostare ebano con madreperla.

encrustation [ˌinkrʌsˈteiʃən], *s.* incrostazione.

to encumber [inˈkʌmbə*], *v.t.* **1.** ingombrare, imbarazzare, impacciare, ostacolare: *that long skirt encumbered me while running*, quella lunga gonna mi impacciava nella corsa **2.** ingombrare, ostruire; caricare: *my table was encumbered with books*, il mio tavolo era ingombro di libri; *she is encumbered with parcels*, ella è carica di pacchi **3.** gravare, opprimere: *encumbered estate*, proprietà gravata d'ipoteche.

encumberment [inˈkʌmbəmənt], *s.* ingombro, impedimento.

encumbrance [inˈkʌmbrəns], *s.* **1.** ingombro, impedimento, impaccio; carico ‖ *without encumbrances*, senza figli **2.** debito; ipoteca.

encumbrancer [inˈkʌmbrənsə*], *s.* ipotecario.

to encurtain [inˈkəːtn], *v.t.* velare, coprire.

encyclic(al) [enˈsiklik(əl)], *ag.* (*eccl.*) enciclico ‖ *s.* (*eccl.*) enciclica.

encyclop(a)edia [enˌsaiklouˈpiːdjə], *s.* enciclopedia.

encyclop(a)edic(al) [enˌsaiklouˈpiːdik(əl)], *ag.* enciclopedico.

encyclop(a)edism [enˌsaiklouˈpiːdizəm], *s.* enciclopedismo.

encyclop(a)edist [enˌsaiklouˈpiːdist], *s.* enciclopedista.

to encyst [enˈsist], *v.t.i.* (*biol. patol.*) chiudere, chiudersi in una ciste.

end [end], *s.* **1.** estremità; fine, termine; orlo; capo; limite; confine: *the ends of a barrel*, i fondelli di un barile; *the* — *of a road*, la fine di una strada; — *to* —, con le estremità che si toccano; *the east, west* — *of a town*, la parte orientale, occidentale di una città; *the sea extends without* —, il mare si estende senza limite ‖ *no* —, senza limite: *no* — *of money, trouble*, moltissimo denaro, fastidio; *to be no* — *disappointed*, essere seccatissimo; *to think no* — *of s.o.*, avere un'altissima opinione di qlcu. ‖ *on* —, in piedi, diritto; di seguito: *three hours on* —, tre ore di fila; *his hair stood on* —, gli si rizzarono i capelli; *to stand on* —, star ritto (in piedi) ‖ *odds and ends*, cianfrusaglie ‖ *to be at a loose* —, essere disoccupato, non sapere che cosa fare ‖

to be at one's wit's —, essere perplesso, non sapere come cavarsela ‖ *to have the right* — *of the stick*, avere il coltello per il manico ‖ *to make both ends meet*, sbarcare il lunario **2.** fine (del mese, del lavoro, ecc.), termine, conclusione: *at the* —, alla fine, infine: *at the* — *of the year*, alla fine dell'anno; *in the* —, infine, insomma: *without* —, senza fine; *to come to an* —, finire, concludersi; *to make an* — *of sthg.* (o *to put an* — *to sthg.* o *to bring sthg. to an* —), finire, far cessare ql.co. ‖ *and there is an* — *of it*, ecco tutto ‖ *to be at the* — *of one's tether*, essere allo stremo delle proprie forze, non poterne più **3.** fine, morte, distruzione: *near his* —, morente; *a tragic* —, una fine tragica; *to make a good* —, fare una buona morte **4.** fine, scopo, mira, intento; risultato: *to the* — *that*, affinchè; *to this* —, a questo scopo; *the* — *justifies the means*, il fine giustifica i mezzi; *to gain one's* —, raggiungere il proprio scopo **5.** (*mar.*) prua ☆ — -*all*, fine completa; — *brain*, (*anat.*) telencefalo; — *carriage*, carrozza di coda; — *float* (o — *play*), (*mec.*) gioco assiale; — *lobe*, (*anat.*) lobo occipitale; — *mill*, (*mec.*) fresa a codolo; — -*on*, di fronte; — *organ*, (*anat.*) corpuscolo terminale; — -*paper*, (*tip.*) risguardo; — -*plate*, (*anat.*) placca motrice; — -*product*, (*ind.*) prodotto terminale ‖ *fag* - —, estremità sfilacciata (di corda, tessuto, ecc.); *fast* —, (*mec.*) radice; *nut* —, (*mec.*) gambo; *small*- —, (*mec.*) piede; *top* —, (*mec.*) estremità superiore.

to end, *v.t.i.* **1.** finire; concludere; giungere a termine: *he will* — *by doing it*, finirà per farlo; *in order to* — *the matter*, per concludere; *this state of things must* —, bisogna porre fine a questo stato di cose; *to* — *war*, finire la guerra ‖ *to* — *in smoke*, *fig.* finire in fumo ‖ *to* — *one's days in peace*, (*fam.*) finire i propri giorni in pace ‖ *to* — *off* (o *up*) *a speech*, concludere un discorso ‖ *to* — *up in prison*, finire in prigione.

to endanger [inˈdeindʒə*], *v.t.* **1.** mettere in pericolo; rischiare; compromettere; esporre (la vita, ecc.): *to* — *a country*, attentare alla sicurezza di un paese; *to* — *one's chances of success*, compromettere le proprie possibilità di successo **2.** ledere (interessi, ecc.).

to endear [inˈdiə*], *v.t.* affezionare, render caro: *to* — *oneself to one's friends*, rendersi caro ai propri amici.

endearing [inˈdiəriŋ], *ag.* tenero, affettuoso.

endearment [inˈdiəmənt], *s.* **1.** tenerezza, affetto, amorevolezza: *term of* —, vezzeggiativo **2.** vezzo, carezza **3.** fascino.

endeavo(u)r [inˈdevə*], *s.* sforzo, tentativo: *to make* (o *to use*) *every* —, fare ogni sforzo.

to endeavo(u)r, *v.t.i.* cercare, procurare; sforzarsi, tentare: *to* — *after sthg.*, sforzarsi per ql.co.; *to* — *to do sthg.*, sforzarsi di fare ql.co.

endemic [enˈdemik], *ag.* (*bot. patol.*) endemico ‖ *s.* (*bot. patol.*) endemia.

endemicity [ˌendiˈmisiti], **endemism** [ˈendimizəm], *s.* (*bot. patol.*) endemismo.

endermic [enˈdəːmik], *ag.* (*med.*) endermico.

endermically [enˈdəːmikəli], *av.* (*med.*) endermicamente.

ending [ˈendiŋ], *ag.* finale, ultimo ‖ *s.* **1.** fine, conclusione, termine; finale: *a happy* —, una felice conclusione **2.** (*gram.*) desinenza.

endive [ˈendiv], *s.* (*bot.*) indivia.

endless [ˈendlis], *ag.* senza fine, infinito, eterno, interminabile, continuo ☆ — *band* (o — *belt*), (*mec.*) nastro continuo, cinghia ad anello.

endlessly [ˈendlisli], *av.* continuamente, eternamente.

endlessness [ˈendlisnis], *s.* perpetuità, infinità: *the* — *of her complaints*, i suoi lamenti senza fine.

endlong [ˈendloŋ], *ag.* (*rar.*) perpendicolare.

endlong, *av.* **1.** longitudinalmente **2.** continuamente **3.** diritto ‖ *prep.* lungo.

endmost [ˈendmoust], *ag.* (*rar.*) il più remoto.

endocarditis [ˌendoukaːˈdaitis], *s.* (*patol.*) endocardite.

endocardium [‚endou'kɑ:diəm], *s.* (*anat.*) endocardio.

endocarp ['endouka:p], *s.* (*bot.*) endocarpo.

endocrane ['endoukrein], **endocranium** [‚endou-'kreinjəm], *s.* (*anat.*) endocranio.

endocrine ['endoukrain], *ag.* endocrino ☆ — *gland*, ghiandola endocrina.

endogamy [en'dogəmi], *s.* endogamia.

endogenetic [‚endoudʒi'netik], *ag.* endogeno: — *rock*, (*geol.*) roccia endogena.

endogeny [en'dodʒini], *s.* (*biol.*) endogenia, endogenesi.

endomorphism [‚endou'mɔ:fizəm], *s.* (*geol.*) endomorfismo.

endoplasm ['endouplæzəm], *s.* (*biol.*) endoplasma.

endopleura [‚endou'pluərə], *s.* (*bot.*) endopleura.

to **endorse** [in'dɔ:s], *v.t.* **1.** (*comm.*) girare; vistare; firmare: *to — a bill*, girare una cambiale; *to — a document*, vistare un documento; *to — in blank*, girare in bianco **2.** approvare, confermare; appoggiare; (*dir.*) approvare (ricorso, ecc.): *you — all I have done*, tu approvi tutto ciò che ho fatto.

endorsee [‚endo:'si:], *s.* (*comm.*) giratario.

endorsement [in'dɔ:smənt], *s.* **1.** (*comm.*) girata: *wording of the* —, dicitura della girata; *to transfer a bill by* —, trasferire una cambiale a mezzo girata **2.** approvazione; adesione ☆ *blank* —, girata in bianco: *qualified* —, girata condizionata.

endorser [in'dɔ:sə*], *s.* (*comm.*) girante: *next, prior* —, girante successivo, precedente.

endoscope ['endouskoup], *s.* (*chir.*) endoscopio.

endosmometer [‚endəz'mɔmitə*], *s.* (*fis.*) endosmometro.

endosmose ['endɔzmous], **endosmosis** [‚endəz'mousis], *s.* (*chim. fis. med.*) endosmosi.

endosperm ['endouspə:m], *s.* (*bot.*) endosperma.

endothermic [‚endou'θə:mik], *ag.* (*chim. mec.*) endotermico.

to **endow** [in'dau], *v.t.* **1.** dare in dote; dotare; sussidiare (scuola, ospedale, ecc.) **2.** *fig.* dotare, provvedere, fornire: *to — a person with powers*, conferire poteri ad una persona; *to be endowed by nature with beauty*, essere dotati di bellezza dalla natura.

endowed [in'daud], *ag.* **1.** dotato; sussidiato **2.** *fig.* dotato, provvisto, fornito: — *with a bright intelligence*, dotato di pronta intelligenza.

endowment [in'daumənt], *s.* **1.** dotazione; assegnazione, costituzione di dote; donazione **2.** *fig.* talento; dono naturale, dote ☆ — *fund*, fondo di dotazione; — *policy*, assicurazione dotale.

to **endue** [in'dju:], *v.t.* **1.** (*letter.*) conferire, dotare, investire: *to — s.o. with powers*, conferire poteri a qlcu. **2.** (*arc.*) vestire.

endurable [in'djuərəbl], *ag.* **1.** sopportabile, tollerabile **2.** (*letter.*) duraturo.

endurableness [in'djuərəblnis], *s.* sopportabilità.

endurably [in'djuərəbli], *av.* sopportabilmente.

endurance [in'djuərəns], *s.* **1.** resistenza, tolleranza, pazienza, sopportazione: *past* (*o beyond*) —, al di là di ogni sopportazione **2.** resistenza, durata; (*aer.*) durata (di volo) ☆ — *flight*, (*aer.*) volo di durata; — *limit*, (*mec.*) limite di fatica; — *strength*, (*mec.*) resistenza alla fatica; — *test*, (*mec.*) prova di durata.

to **endure** [in'djuə*], *v.t.i.* **1.** (II) tollerare, sopportare: *he won't be able to — that kind of life*, non potrà sopportare quel genere di vita **2.** durare, restare, continuare: *his work will* —, la sua opera vivrà.

enduring [in'djuəriŋ], *ag.* **1.** tollerante, paziente **2.** durevole, permanente, stabile.

enduringly [in'djuəriŋli], *av.* durevolmente.

Endymion [en'dimiən], *no.pr.m.* (*mit.*) Endimione.

endways ['endweiz], **endwise** ['endwaiz], *av.* **1.** in posizione eretta **2.** capo a capo **3.** longitudinalmente.

Eneas [i(:)'ni:æs], *no.pr.m.* Enea.

Eneid ['i:niid], *s.* (*lett.*) Eneide.

enema ['enimə], *s.* (*med.*) clistere.

enemy ['enimi], *ag.* nemico: — *aircraft*, aviazione

nemica; — *alien*, straniero nemico ‖ *s.* **1.** nemico; oppositore, avversario: *they were deadly enemies*, erano nemici mortali ‖ (*teol.*) *the Enemy*, il maligno, il demonio ‖ *how goes the —?*, (*amer. sl.*) che ora è? **2.** (*coll.*) *the* —, il nemico, le forze nemiche: *the — were forced to retreat*, il nemico fu costretto a ritirarsi.

energetic [‚enə'dʒetik], *ag.* **1.** energico: *he was an — man*, era un uomo energico, di polso **2.** energetico (di rimedio).

energetics [‚enə'dʒetiks.], *s.* energetica.

energetical [‚enə'dʒetikəl], *ag.* **1.** energico **2.** energetico (di rimedio).

energetically [‚enə'dʒetikəli], *av.* energicamente.

to **energize** ['enədʒaiz], *v.t.i.* **1.** infondere energia a, stimolare; (*letter.*) agire con vigore **2.** (*elett.*) eccitare, eccitarsi.

energumen [‚enə:'gju:men], *s.* **1.** energumeno, invasato **2.** fanatico; entusiasta.

energy ['enədʒi], *s.* **1.** energia, forza, vigore: *of no —*, senza energia; *to apply* (*o to devote*) *one's energies to a task*, dedicare le proprie energie a un compito; *to restore* (*o to recover*) *one's energies*, ricuperare le proprie energie ‖ *to have no —*, (*fam.*) non aver sangue nelle vene **2.** (*fis.*) energia: — *of friction*, lavoro di attrito; *atomic* —, energia atomica; *electrical* —, energia elettrica; *kinetic* —, forza viva, energia cinetica ☆ — *loss*, perdita di energia ‖ *binding* —, energia di legame; *strain* —, lavoro di deformazione.

enervate [i'nə:vit], *ag.* **1.** senza forza, senza vigore, snervato **2.** (*bot.*) senza nervatura.

to **enervate** ['enə:veit], *v.t.* snervare, indebolire, render fiacco.

enervation [‚enə:'veiʃən], *s.* **1.** inflacchimento, indebolimento **2.** mollezza.

to **enface** [in'feis], *v.t.* scrivere, stampare in alto (nella prima pagina) ☆ *enfaced paper*, prestiti indiani (pagabili a Londra).

to **enfeeble** [in'fi:bl], *v.t.* indebolire, debilitare, esaurire.

enfeeblement [in'fi:blmənt], *s.* indebolimento.

to **enfeoff** [in'fef], *v.t.* (*st.*) infeudare.

enfeoffment [in'fefmənt], *s.* (*st.*) infeudazione, infeudamento, investitura di un feudo.

to **enfetter** [in'fetə*], *v.t.* mettere in ceppi, incatenare (anche *fig.*).

enfilade [‚enfi'leid], *s.* (*mil.*) inflata.

to **enfilade**, *v.t.* (*mil.*) colpire con fuoco di fila, colpire d'inflata.

to **enfold** [in'fould], *v.t.* **1.** avvolgere **2.** cingere, abbracciare.

enfoldment [in'fouldmənt], *s.* avvolgimento.

to **enforce** [in'fɔ:s], *v.t.* **1.** imporre, far rispettare: *to — a law*, far rispettare una legge; *to — obedience*, farsi obbedire; *to — one's rights*, far valere i propri diritti; *to — one's will on s.o.*, imporre a qlcu. la propria volontà; *to — payment*, costringere (il debitore) al pagamento (del debito) **2.** far osservare, mettere in vigore (una legge) **3.** appoggiare, far valere (domanda, argomento, ecc.).

enforceable [in'fɔ:səbl], *ag.* **1.** applicabile, che può essere fatto valere **2.** (*dir.*) esecutorio.

enforced [in'fɔ:st], *ag.* imposto, forzato.

enforcedly [in'fɔ:sidli], *av.* forzatamente.

enforcement [in'fɔ:smənt], *s.* **1.** costrizione, imposizione **2.** (*dir.*) esecuzione, applicazione.

to **enframe** [in'freim], *v.t.* incorniciare.

to **enfranchise** [in'fræntʃaiz], *v.t.* **1.** affrancare (uno schiavo, un fondo) **2.** (*pol.*) accordare il diritto di suffragio a **3.** conferire un privilegio a.

enfranchisement [in'fræntʃizmənt], *s.* **1.** affrancamento (di schiavo, ecc.) **2.** diritto di suffragio.

to **engage** [in'geidʒ], *v.t.i.* **1.** impegnare, impegnarsi (moralmente): *to — oneself for dinner*, impegnarsi per il pranzo; *to — (oneself) to do sthg.*, impegnarsi a far ql.co. ‖ *to be engaged*, essere fidanzato: *are they already* *engaged?*, sono già fidanzati? **2.** assumere, prendere a servizio; ingaggiare: *that actor was engaged for the whole season*, quell'attore fu impegnato per tutta la stagione; *to — a servant*, assumere un domestico **3.** riservare, fissare (posto a teatro, camera, ecc.) **4.** attrarre, affascinare; trattenere l'attenzione; guadagnare, cattivarsi (l'affetto, ecc.) **5.** (*mil.*) ingaggiare, impegnare battaglia **6.** occupare, impegnare: *to — s.o. in conversation*, impegnare qlcu. in una conversazione; *to be engaged upon a novel*, essere occupato a scrivere un romanzo **7.** (*arch.*) incastrare; (*mec.*) ingranare, innestare (ruota dentata, ecc.) **8.** *to — for*, impegnarsi in, garantire, promettere: *it is more than I can — for*, è più di quel che posso garantire **9.** *to — in*, impegnarsi in: *the nations who were engaged in war*, le nazioni che presero parte alla guerra; *to — in battle*, ingaggiar battaglia; *to — in business*, mettersi negli affari; *to — in conversation, in discussion with s.o.*, prender parte a una conversazione, a una discussione con qlcu.; *to — in a dangerous speculation*, imbarcarsi in una speculazione pericolosa.

engaged [in'geidʒd], *ag.* **1.** impegnato: *are you —?*, sei impegnato, hai da fare?; *he is — in a difficult task*, è impegnato in un compito difficile; *I am — all day*, sono occupato tutto il giorno || *an — poet*, un poeta impegnato **2.** fidanzato: *the — couple*, i fidanzati **3.** preso, riservato, fissato, occupato (di posto, tavolo, auto, telefono, ecc.): *this seat is —*, questo posto è occupato **4.** (*mil.*) impegnato in combattimento **5.** (*mec.*) incastrato, ingranato, innestato.

engagement [in'geidʒmənt], *s.* **1.** impegno; promessa; appuntamento; contratto: *owing to a previous —*, a causa di un impegno precedente; *without —*, senza impegno; *to enter into an —*, prendere, assumere un impegno; *to have an —*, avere un impegno, un appuntamento; *to meet, to break an —*, fare onore, venir meno ad un impegno **2.** fidanzamento **3.** assunzione, impiego; arruolamento; reclutamento **4.** (*mil.*) scontro, azione, combattimento **5.** (*mec.*) incastratura ☆ *— -book*, agenda; *— -ring*, anello di fidanzamento || *labour — -sheet*, (*comm.*) modulo di assunzione.

engaging [in'geidʒiŋ], *ag.* attraente, avvincente, seducente: *to have an — manner*, avere dei modi seducenti.

engagingly [in'geidʒiŋli], *av.* in modo attraente: *to smile —*, sorridere in modo allettante.

to engaol [in'dʒeil], *v.t.* imprigionare.

to engarland [in'gɑ:lənd], *v.t.* inghirlandare.

to engender [in'dʒendə*], *v.t.* **1.** (*arch.*) generare, concepire **2.** produrre, causare, generare (sentimenti, malattie, ecc.).

to engild [in'gild], *v.t.* (*letter.*) indorare (anche *fig.*).

engine ['endʒin], *s.* **1.** macchina; motore: *to sit with one's face to the —*, sedersi nel senso della marcia **2.** (*arch.*) strumento, mezzo: *to employ every — at one's disposal*, usare di tutti i mezzi a propria disposizione **3.** (*ferr.*) locomotrice ☆ *— driver*, macchinista; *— room*, sala macchine; *— speed indicator*, contagiri motore || *air-cooled —*, motore raffreddato ad aria; *electric —* (o *motor —*), automotrice; *explosion —*, motore a scoppio; *fire- —*, auto-pompa; *four-stroke —*, motore a quattro tempi; *gas —*, motore a gas; *hot-air —*, motore ad aria calda; *internal-combustion —*, motore a combustione interna, motore a scoppio; *petrol —*, motore a benzina; *steam- —*, macchina a vapore, locomotiva.

engineer [ˌendʒi'niə*], *s.* **1.** ingegnere; tecnico **2.** (*mar.*) meccanico; (*amer.*) macchinista, tecnico meccanico **3.** (*mil.*) soldato del genio || *the Engineers*, il genio **4.** orditore, promotore: *the chief — of the scheme*, il principale promotore del progetto ☆ *chemical —*, ingegnere chimico; *consulting —*, consulente tecnico; *electrical —*, ingegnere elettrotecnico; *civil —*, ingegnere civile; *mechanical —*, ingegnere meccanico; *mining —*, ingegnere minerario; *naval —*, ingegnere navale; *sound —*, (*cine.*) tecnico del suono.

to engineer, *v.t.* **1.** costruire, progettare (ponti, strade, ecc.) **2.** (*fam.*) combinare; macchinare; progettare.

engineering [ˌendʒi'niəriŋ], *s.* **1.** ingegneria **2.** costruzione meccanica **3.** *fig.* macchinazioni, manovre ☆ *chemical —*, ingegneria chimica; *civil —*, ingegneria civile; *military —*, genio militare; *naval —*, genio navale; *road —*, ingegneria stradale; *radio —*, radiotecnica.

enginery ['endʒinəri], *s.* **1.** macchine, macchinario **2.** (*arc.*) macchinazioni **3.** funzionamento (di impresa).

to engird [in'gə:d], *v.t.* (*letter.*) circondare, cingere.

England ['iŋglənd], *no.pr.* (*geog.*) Inghilterra.

Englander ['iŋgləndə*], *s.c.* (*rar.*) inglese.

English ['iŋgliʃ], *ag.* inglese: *— history*, storia inglese || *the —*, gli inglesi || *the — Channel*, la Manica || *s.* la lingua inglese || *American —*, l'inglese come si parla in America; *British —*, (*amer.*) l'inglese come si parla in Inghilterra; *Middle —*, inglese medioevale; *Modern —*, inglese moderno; *Old —*, inglese antico, anglosassone; *Queen's —* (o *King's —*), l'inglese delle classi colte; *standard —*, l'inglese tipico || *what's the — for...?*, come si dice in inglese...? || *to speak in plain —*, parlare senza ambiguità, chiaramente ☆ *— born*, inglese di nascita; *— -speaking*, di lingua inglese: *— -speaking nations*, nazioni di lingua inglese.

to english, *v.t.* **1.** (*arc.*) tradurre in inglese **2.** anglicizzare.

Englisher ['iŋgliʃə*], *s.* **1.** (*rar.*) inglese **2.** chi traduce in inglese.

Englishism ['iŋgliʃizəm], *s.* **1.** caratteristiche inglesi; modo di vita inglese **2.** anglofilia.

Englishman, *pl.* **Englishmen** ['iŋgliʃmən], *s.* (uomo) inglese.

Englishry ['iŋgliʃri], *s.* **1.** la condizione di essere inglese **2.** quella parte della popolazione in Irlanda che è di origine inglese **3.** gli inglesi.

Englishwoman ['iŋgliʃˌwumən], *pl.* **Englishwomen** ['iŋgliʃˌwimin], *s.* (donna) inglese.

to engloom [in'glu:m], *v.t.* oscurare; rattristare.

to englut [in'glʌt], *v.t.* **1.** inghiottire; ingoiare **2.** ingozzare; saziare.

to engorge [in'gɔ:dʒ], *v.t.i.* **1.** ingurgitare, ingollare, ingollarsi; mangiare avidamente **2.** *to be engorged*, essere ingorgato; (*patol.*) essere congestionato.

engorgement [in'gɔ:dʒmənt], *s.* **1.** ingurgitamento **2.** (*patol.*) ingorgo, congestione.

to engrace [in'greis], *v.t.* aggraziare, rendere grazioso.

to engraft [in'grɑ:ft], *v.t.* **1.** (*bot.*) innestare **2.** *fig.* inserire; incorporare; inculcare (nella mente): *sound principles had been engrafted in him from his earliest childhood*, fin dalla prima infanzia gli avevano inculcato dei sani principi; *to — one scheme into another*, raccordare fra di loro due progetti **3.** (*chir.*) innestare (pelle).

engraftation [ˌiŋgrɑ:f'teiʃən], *s.* (*bot.*) innesto.

to engrail [in'greil], *v.t.* **1.** (*arald.*) dentellare **2.** ornare (una moneta) di granitura.

engrailment [in'greilmənt], *s.* granitura di una moneta.

to engrain [in'grein], *v.t.* **1.** tingere a forte tinta **2.** tingere allo stato grezzo **3.** *fig.* penetrare profondamente in.

to engrasp [in'grɑ:sp], *v.t.* abbracciare; afferrare.

to engrave [in'greiv], *v.t.* intagliare; scolpire; incidere (anche *fig.*): *engraved in my mind*, impresso nella mia mente.

engraver [in'greivə*], *s.* incisore ☆ *copperplate —*, (*mec.*) calcografo.

engraving [in'greiviŋ], *s.* **1.** arte dell'incisione, l'incidere **2.** incisione; stampa: *dealer of engravings*, mercante di stampe ☆ *wood —*, xilografia.

to engrieve [in'gri:v], *v.t.i.* addolorare, addolorarsi.

to engroove [in'gru:v], *v.t.* lavorare in solco; formare un solco in.

to **engross** [in'grous], *v.t.* **1.** copiare (un atto legale); redigere (un documento) a grandi caratteri **2.** assorbire (attenzione); prendere (tempo): *it will — your attention*, assorbirà la tua attenzione; *to become engrossed*, astrarsi **3.** (*arc. comm.*) incettare, accaparrare ‖ *to — the conversation*, accaparrarsi la conversazione.

engrosser [in'grouse*], *s.* amanuense.

engrossing [in'grousiŋ], *s.* incetta.

engrossment [in'grousmənt], *s.* **1.** (*dir.*) copiatura di documento **2.** assorbimento; accaparramento.

to **engulf** [in'gʌlf], *v.t.* ingolfare, inghiottire; inabissare: *to be engulfed in the sea*, essere inghiottito dal mare.

to **enhance** [in'hɑːns], *v.t.* accrescere, aumentare rincarare (prezzi); migliorare; intensificare: *his courage was enhanced by his success*, il successo accrebbe il suo coraggio; *to — the value of land*, valorizzare una terra.

enhancement [in'hɑːnsmənt], *s.* rialzo; elevazione; miglioramento; rincaro (di prezzi).

enharmonic [,enhɑː'mɔnik], *ag.* (*mus.*) enarmonico.

to **enhunger** [in'hʌŋɡə*], *v.t.* affamare.

enigma [i'niɡmə], *s.* **1.** enigma, enimma **2.** persona misteriosa.

enigmatic(al) [,eniɡ'mætik(əl)], *ag.* enigmatico.

enigmatically [,eniɡ'mætikəli], *av.* enigmaticamente.

enigmatist [i'niɡmətist], *s.* persona che si esprime per mezzo di enigmi.

to **enigmatize** [i'niɡmətaiz], *v.t.i.* **1.** simbolizzare, rendere enigmatico **2.** esprimersi per mezzo di enigmi.

to **enisle** [in'ail], *v.t.* isolare; segregare.

enjambment [in'dʒæmmənt], *s.* (*poes.*) « enjambement ».

to **enjoin** [in'dʒɔin], *v.t.* **1.** comandare; ingiungere; raccomandare: *to — prudence on s.o.*, raccomandare la prudenza a qlcu.; *to — (on) s.o. to do sthg.*, ingiungere a qlcu. di fare ql.co. **2.** (*dir. amer.*) proibire, interdire.

to **enjoy** [in'dʒɔi], *v.t.* (I) **1.** godere, gioire, esser felici di; assaporare, gustare, provar piacere in: *I enjoyed the concert*, ho gustato il concerto; *to — doing sthg.*, provar piacere nel fare ql.co.: *I — reading*, mi piace leggere; *to — oneself*, divertirsi **2.** godere del possesso, dell'uso di; possedere: *he enjoys her favours*, egli gode dei suoi favori; *to — good, poor health*, avere una salute florida, malferma.

enjoyable [in'dʒɔiəbl], *ag.* gradevole, piacevole, divertente: *we had a most — evening*, abbiamo trascorso una serata piacevolissima.

enjoyableness [in'dʒɔiəblnis], *s.* piacevolezza, amenità.

enjoyably [in'dʒɔiəbli], *av.* piacevolmente, gradevolmente.

enjoyment [in'dʒɔimənt], *s.* **1.** gioia, godimento, piacere **2.** (*dir.*) godimento (di un diritto).

to **enkindle** [in'kindl], *v.t.* **1.** *fig.* infiammare; eccitare; stimolare **2.** (*letter.*) accendere.

to **enlace** [in'leis], *v.t.* **1.** adornare con pizzi **2.** allacciare; stringere; abbracciare: *lovers enlaced in each other's arms*, amanti abbracciati.

to **enlarge** [in'lɑːdʒ], *v.t.i.* **1.** allargare, ampliare, ampliarsi; dilatare: *enlarged heart*, cuore dilatato; *enlarged pores*, pori] dilatati; *to — one's premises*, ingrandire il proprio negozio **2.** (*foto.*) ingrandire: *I'll get this photo enlarged*, farò ingrandire questa fotografia **3.** estendere, estendersi; allargare, allargarsi; espandersi, dilatarsi **4.** *to — upon (sthg.)*, dilungarsi su, sviluppare (un argomento) ☆ *enlarged ideas*, ampie vedute.

enlargement [in'lɑːdʒmənt], *s.* **1.** allargamento, amplificazione **2.** (*foto.*) ingrandimento **3.** (*med.*) ipertrofia (del cuore).

enlarger [in'lɑːdʒə*], *s.* (*foto.*) amplificatore, estensore.

to **enlighten** [in'laitn], *v.t.* rischiarare, illuminare (anche *fig.*); chiarire: *to — s.o. on a subject*, illuminare, istruire qlcu. su un argomento.

enlightenment [in'laitnmənt], *s.* spiegazione; schiarimento ‖ *the Age of Enlightenment*, (*st. lett.*) l'età dell'illuminismo.

to **enlink** [in'liŋk], *v.t.* unire, collegare (anche *fig.*): *to — sthg. with* (o *to*) *sthg.*, unire una cosa a un'altra.

to **enlist** [in'list], *v.t.i.* **1.** (*mil.*) arruolare, arruolarsi; ingaggiare, ingaggiarsi: *to — recruits*, arruolare delle reclute **2.** *fig.* ottenere l'appoggio di: *to — the services of s.o.*, assicurarsi i servigi, l'aiuto di qlcu. **3.** dare il proprio appoggio a, entrare al servizio di: *to — under the banner of liberty*, offrirsi per la causa della libertà ☆ *enlisted men*, soldati semplici.

enlistment [in'listmənt], *s.* (*mil.*) arruolamento, ingaggio.

to **enliven** [in'laivn], *v.t.* rianimare, rallegrare, ravvivare: *to — a discussion*, animare una discussione.

enlivener [in'laivnə*], *s.* persona, cosa che ravviva.

to **enmesh** [in'meʃ], *v.t.* irretire, inviluppare.

enmeshment [in'meʃmənt], *s.* irretimento.

enmity ['enmiti], *s.* ostilità, inimicizia: *to be at — with s.o.*, essere in cattivi rapporti con qlcu.

ennead ['eniəd], *s.* serie di nove (libri, discorsi, punti).

Ennius ['eniəs], *no.pr.m.* Ennio.

to **ennoble** [i'noubl], *v.t.* nobilitare, rendere nobile (anche *fig.*).

ennoblement [i'noublmənt], *s.* il nobilitare (anche *fig.*).

ennui [ɑː'nwiː], *s.* noia.

Enoch ['iːnɔk], *no.pr.m.* (*Bibbia*) Enoch.

enormity [i'nɔːmiti], *s.* mostruosità, malvagità.

enormous [i'nɔːməs], *ag.* enorme, immenso.

enormously [i'nɔːməsli], *av.* enormemente.

enormousness [i'nɔːməsnis], *s.* enormità.

enough [i'nʌf], *ag.* (*può seguire il s.*) sufficiente, bastante; abbastanza: *have you had — beer?*, hai avuto abbastanza birra?; *there was noise — to wake the dead*, c'era abbastanza rumore da svegliare un morto ‖ *av.* (*segue av. e ag.*) abbastanza, sufficientemente, discretamente; passabilmente: *is it hot —?*, è abbastanza caldo?; *she sings well —*, canta discretamente bene ‖ *sure —*, certamente ‖ *s.* il necessario; sufficienza: *he had — of everything*, era fornito a sufficienza di tutto; *he has — to live on*, ha abbastanza di che vivere; *I have had — of this*, ne ho avuto abbastanza; *to have — and to spare*, avere più che abbastanza ‖ *— of this!*, basta!, finitela! ‖ *more than —*, più che sufficiente ‖ *— is as good as a feast*, *prov.* chi si contenta gode.

to **enounce** [i(ː)'nauns], *v.t.* enunciare; pronunciare.

enouncement [i(ː)'naunsmənt], *s.* enunciazione.

enow [i'nau], (*arc. poet.*) per **enough** *ag. av.*

to **enquire**, *V.* to **inquire**.

enquiry, *V.* **inquiry**.

to **enrage** [in'reidʒ], *v.t.* far arrabbiare: *to be enraged at sthg.*, essere arrabbiato per ql.co.

to **enrapture** [in'ræptʃə*], *v.t.* rapire; estasiare; incantare: *to be enraptured with sthg.*, essere incantato da ql.co.

to **enrich** [in'ritʃ], *v.t.* **1.** arricchire **2.** *fig.* arricchire; abbellire, adornare: *the gallery was enriched with new pictures*, la galleria venne arricchita di nuovi quadri.

enrichment [in'ritʃmənt], *s.* arricchimento; abbellimento.

to **enrobe** [in'roub], *v.t.* vestire, ornare.

to **enrol** [in'roul], *pass.p.p.* **enrolled** [in'rould], *v.t.* **1.** arruolare (soldati), ingaggiare (operai); immatricolare; iscrivere: *to — s.o. as a member of a club*, iscrivere qlcu. a un club **2.** (*dir.*) registrare.

enrolment [in'roulmənt], *s.* **1.** arruolamento; iscrizione **2.** (*dir.*) registrazione.

enroute [ɑːn'ruːt], *av.* in viaggio; in cammino.

ens [enz], *pl.* **entia** ['enʃiə], *s.* (*fil.*) entità.

to **ensanguine** [in'sæŋɡwin], *v.t.* insanguinare (anche *fig.*), rinsanguare.

ensanguined [in'sæŋɡwind], *ag.* insanguinato.

to **ensconce** [in'skɔns], *v.t.* nascondere, rannicchiare; mettere al sicuro: *to — oneself behind the door*, nascondersi dietro la porta.

to **enshrine** [in'frain], *v.t.* rinchiudere (in un reliquiario); *fig.* conservare, serbare (come cosa sacra).

to **enshroud** [in'fraud], *v.t.* avvolgere; coprire completamente; nascondere.

ensiform ['ensifɔ:m], *ag.* (*bot.*) ensiforme.

ensign ['ensain], *s.* **1.** bandiera, stendardo; insegna, distintivo **2.** portabandiera, alfiere **3.** (*mar. amer.*) guardiamarina.

ensigncy ['ensainsi], **ensignship** ['ensainʃip], *s.* ufficio, grado d'alfiere.

ensilage ['ensilidʒ], *s.* **1.** (*agr.*) insilamento **2.** foraggio raccolto in silos.

to **ensilage**, to **ensile** [in'sail], *v.t.* insilare.

to **enslave** [in'sleiv], *v.t.* assoggettare, far schiavo (anche *fig.*).

enslavement [in'sleivmənt], *s.* servaggio, asservimento, schiavitù (anche *fig.*).

enslaver [in'sleivə*], *s.c.* chi fa schiavo (detto generalmente di donna che ammalia).

to **ensnare** [in'snɛə*], *v.t.* adescare; irretire; intrappolare (anche *fig.*).

to **ensorcel(l)** [in'sɔ:səl], *v.t.* stregare.

to **ensoul** [in'soul], *v.t.* animare, infondere un'anima in.

to **ensphere** [in'sfiə*], *v.t.* racchiudere; circondare.

to **ensue** [in'sju:], *v.t.i.* **1.** risultare, seguire, derivare; capitare, succedere (come conseguenza) **2.** (*arc.*) cercare di ottenere.

to **ensure** [in'ʃuə*], *v.t.* **1.** assicurare, garantire: *I cannot — her doing that*, non posso assicurare che ella lo faccia; *to — a prize*, garantire un premio **2.** (*comm.*) assicurare: *he ensured himself against* (o *from*) *risks*, si assicurò contro i rischi.

to **enswathe** [in'sweið], *v.t.* fasciare.

enswathement [in'sweiðmənt], *s.* fasciatura.

entablature [in'tæblətʃə*], *s.* (*arch.*) trabeazione.

entablement [in'teiblmənt], *s.* basamento di statua.

entail [in'teil], *s.* **1.** (*dir.*) assegnazione **2.** *fig.* eredità inalienabile.

to **entail**, *v.t.* **1.** (*dir.*) assegnare con delle limitazioni **2.** imporre, comportare, implicare: *this will — great expense on you*, questo comporterà una grossa spesa per voi.

entailer [in'teilə*], *s.* **1.** (*dir.*) chi lascia un'eredità inalienabile **2.** chi impone.

entailment [in'teilmənt], *s.* **1.** (*dir.*) assegnazione **2.** imposizione.

to **entangle** [in'tæŋgl], *v.t.* impigliare, imbrogliare, intralciare (anche *fig.*): *the rabbit got entangled in a snare*, il coniglio rimase impigliato in una trappola; *they entangled themselves with international spies*, furono coinvolti nello spionaggio internazionale.

entanglement [in'tæŋglmənt], *s.* **1.** groviglio, garbuglio; impiccio; ingarbugliamento; confusione **2.** *pl.* (*mil.*) reticolato.

entasis ['entəsis], *s.* (*arch.*) entasi.

entelechy [en'teləki], *s.* (*fil.*) entelechia.

to **entender** [in'tendə*], *v.t.* (*arc.*) intenerire; snervare.

to **enter** [in'tə*], *v.t.i.* **1.** entrare; penetrare: *— Iago*, (*teat.*) entra Iago; *the bullet entered his body*, la pallottola gli entrò nel corpo; *he entered the room*, egli entrò nella stanza **2.** entrare a far parte di: *to — a college, the Army, the Church*, entrare in un collegio, nell'esercito, prendere gli ordini religiosi **3.** iscrivere: *I want to — myself for the examinations*, desidero iscrivermi per gli esami; *to — a name on a list*, iscrivere un nome in un elenco **4.** (*comm.*) registare; prendere nota: *I shall — the engagement in my diary*, prenderò nota dell'impegno nella mia agenda **5.** *to — into* (*sthg.*), entrare; penetrare; prendere parte a; impegnarsi; capire: *to — into business*, entrare negli affari; *to — into conversation with s.o.*, iniziare una conversazione con qlcu.; *to — into details*, entrare in particolari; *to — into the spirit of the game*, entrare nello spirito del giuoco **6.** *to —*

(*up*)*on* (*sthg.*), iniziare, intraprendere (una carriera); lanciarsi (in una guerra); intavolare (una discussione); (*dir.*) entrare in possesso di (eredità, ecc.); *to — upon an office*, entrare in carica.

enterable ['entərəbl], *ag.* penetrabile; accessibile.

enteric [en'terik], *ag.* enterico, intestinale.

entering ['entəriŋ], *ag.* entrante ‖ *s.* **1.** entrata, ingresso **2.** ammissione; iscrizione (di studente) **3.** — (*up*), (*comm.*) registrazione: — *on the debit side*, registrazione in dare.

enteritis [,entə'raitis], *s.* (*patol.*) enterite.

enterocolitis [,entərouko'laitis], *s.* (*patol.*) enterocolite.

enterogastritis [,entərougæs'traitis], *s.* (*patol.*) gastroenterite.

enterolite ['entəroulait], *s.* (*patol.*) enterolite.

enteron ['entərɔn], *s.* (*anat.*) intestino.

enterorrhagia [,entərou'reidʒiə], *s.* (*patol.*) emorragia intestinale.

enterotomy [,entə'rɔtəmi], *s.* (*chir.*) enterotomia.

enterprise ['entəpraiz], *s.* **1.** impresa; avventura **2.** iniziativa, spirito intraprendente: *to show —*, mostrarsi pieno d'iniziativa, intraprendente.

to **enterprise**, *v.t.* (*arc.*) intraprendere.

enterpriser [,entə'praizə*], *s.* persona intraprendente.

enterprising ['entəpraiziŋ], *ag.* intraprendente.

enterprisingly ['entəpraiziŋli], *av.* in modo intraprendente.

to **entertain** [,entə'tein], *v.t.* **1.** ricevere; ospitare: *they — a great deal*, essi danno molti ricevimenti; *to — s.o. at* (o *to*) *lunch*, avere qlcu. a colazione **2.** intrattenere, divertire, deliziare: *he entertained his guests with witty stories*, intratteneva i suoi ospiti con aneddoti spiritosi **3.** carezzare (un'idea); avere, nutrire, concepire (dubbi, speranze, ecc.): *to — a hope*, accarezzare una speranza **4.** prendere in considerazione, accettare: *he could not — the proposal*, non potè prendere in considerazione la proposta **5.** tenere, mantenere (corrispondenza).

entertainer [,entə'teinə*], *s.c.* **1.** chi intrattiene, chi diverte (comico, canzonettista) **2.** chi ospita.

entertaining [,entə'teiniŋ], *ag.* divertente; piacevole.

entertainingly [,entə'teiniŋli], *av.* piacevolmente.

entertainment [,entə'teinmənt], *s.* **1.** trattenimento, divertimento; spettacolo **2.** ricevimento, festa **3.** divertimento, ilarità: *much to the — of his friends*, con gran divertimento degli amici **4.** trattamento: *this hotel is famous for its —*, questo albergo è famoso per il suo trattamento ‖ *extra pay* (o *extra sum*) *for* (*purposes of*) —, spese extra, di rappresentanza ☆ — *tax*, tassa sugli spettacoli.

to **enthral(l)** [in'θrɔ:l], *v.t.* **1.** *fig.* affascinare, incantare, ammaliare: *an enthralling book*, un libro che avvince **2.** (*letter.*) asservire, assoggettare.

enthralment [in'θrɔ:lmənt], *s.* **1.** incanto, malia **2.** (*letter.*) cattività, schiavitù.

to **enthrone** [in'θroun], *v.t.* **1.** metter sul trono, incoronare **2.** (*eccl.*) investire, insediare, intronizzare.

enthronement [in'θrounmənt], **enthronization** [in,θrouni'zeiʃən], *s.* investitura, intronizzazione.

to **enthuse** [in'θju:z], *v.t.i.* (*fam.*) entusiasmare, entusiasmarsi.

enthusiasm [in'θju:ziæzəm], *s.* entusiasmo: *he is easily moved to —*, si entusiasma facilmente.

enthusiast [in'θju:ziæst], *s.c.* entusiasta; appassionato, appassionata ☆ *music —*, appassionato di musica.

enthusiastic [in,θju:zi'æstik], *ag.* entusiastico: *to become — over sthg.*, entusiasmarsi per ql.co.

enthusiastically [in,θju:zi'æstikəli], *av.* entusiasticamente.

to **entice** [in'tais], *v.t.* sedurre; attirare; allettare; adescare: *they were all enticed by her uncommon beauty*, erano tutti attratti dalla sua non comune bellezza; *to — a young girl away from her home*, adescare una ragazza e indurla ad abbandonare la famiglia

enticement [in'taismənt], *s.* **1.** attrattiva; seduzione **2.** adescamento; istigazione.

enticer [in'taisə*], *s.c.* seduttore, seduttrice; adescatore, adescatrice.

enticing [in'taisiŋ], *ag.* seducente, attraente.

entire [in'taiə*], *ag.* **1.** intero, completo; indiviso, non frazionato: *an — delusion*, una completa delusione **2.** non castrato **3.** semplice, puro; sincero ‖ *s.* **1.** (*rar.*) l'intero, il tutto **2.** stallone **3.** specie di birra forte.

entirely [in'taiəli], *av.* interamente; completamente ‖ *— without foundation*, destituito di ogni fondamento.

entirety [in'taiəti], *s.* **1.** interezza, totalità; integrità: *to relate a story in its —*, raccontare una storia per intero **2.** (*dir.*) indivisibilità: *possession by entireties*, proprietà indivisibile.

to entitle [in'taitl], *v.t.* **1.** intitolare (un libro) **2.** dare un titolo a; *to — s.o. prince*, dare il titolo di principe a qlcu. **3.** concedere un diritto a, qualificare: *to be entitled to*, (*dir.*) aver diritto a.

entity ['entiti], *s.* entità ☆ *legal —*, (*dir.*) persona giuridica.

to entomb [in'tu:m], *v.t.* **1.** seppellire **2.** servire da tomba a (anche *fig.*).

entombment [in'tu:mmənt], *s.* inumazione, sepoltura.

entomological [,entəmə'lɔdʒikəl], *ag.* entomologico.

entomologist [,entə'mɔlədʒist], *s.* entomologo.

entomology [,entə'mɔlədʒi], *s.* entomologia.

entrails ['entreilz], *s.pl.* intestini, visceri: *the — of the earth*, *fig.* le viscere della terra.

to entrain [in'trein], *v.t.i.* salire, far salire in treno (specialmente truppe).

entrance[1] ['entrəns], *s.* **1.** accesso; entrata (l'atto di entrare): *actors must learn their exits and entrances carefully*, gli attori devono imparare attentamente le loro uscite ed entrate; *to make one's — into a room*, entrare in una stanza **2.** ammissione **3.** ingresso, porta, entrata ☆ *— examination*, esame d'ammissione; *—-fee* (o *— -money*), tassa d'ammissione; *— hall*, vestibolo ‖ *back —*, ingresso posteriore; *front —*, ingresso anteriore; *main —*, ingresso principale; *side —*, ingresso laterale.

to entrance[2] [in'trɑ:ns], *v.t.* **1.** ipnotizzare, mandare in « trance » **2.** mandare in estasi; estasiare.

entrancement [in'trɑ:nsmənt], *s.* estasi, rapimento; « trance ».

entrancing [in'trɑ:nsiŋ], *ag.* incantevole; che manda in estasi.

entrant ['entrənt], *s.c.* **1.** chi entra (in una stanza) **2.** chi inizia, abbraccia (una professione); debuttante **3.** (*spor.*) iscritto; concorrente, competitore: *— for the championship*, iscritto per il campionato.

to entrap [in'træp], *pass.p.p.* **entrapped** [in'træpt], *v.t.* prendere in trappola, truffare: *to — s.o. into doing sthg.*, raggirare qlcu. per fargli fare ql.co.

entrapment [in'træpmənt], *s.* intrappolamento (anche *fig.*).

to entreasure [in'treʒə*], *v.t.* custodire come un tesoro.

to entreat [in'tri:t], *v.t.* (IV) pregare, supplicare, chiedere insistentemente a: *to — a favour of s.o.*, chiedere un favore a qlcu.

entreatful [in'tri:tful], **entreating** [in'tri:tiŋ], *ag.* supplichevole, supplicante.

entreatingly [in'tri:tiŋli], *av.* insistentemente; in tono supplichevole, di preghiera.

entreaty [in'tri:ti], *s.* supplica, preghiera; istanza, petizione.

entrée ['ɔntrei], *s.* **1.** entrata, diritto di ammissione **2.** (*cuc.*) prima portata.

entremets ['ɔntrəmei], *s.* piatto di mezzo.

to entrench [in'trentʃ], *v.t.i.* **1.** trincerare, munire di trincee; fortificare (anche *fig.*): *to — oneself behind* (*sthg.*), trincerarsi dietro (ql.co.) **2.** *to — upon*, (*rar.*) usurpare, fare un'intrusione.

entrenchment [in'trentʃmənt], *s.* trincea, riparo; trinceramento.

entrepôt ['ɔntrəpou], *s.* **1.** magazzino **2.** centro commerciale.

entrepreneur [,ɔntrəprə'nə:*], *s.* **1.** (*teat.*) impresario **2.** (*pol. econ.*) imprenditore.

entresol ['ɔntrəsɔl], *s.* ammezzato, mezzanino.

entropion [en'troupion], *s.* (*patol.*) entropio.

entropy ['entrəpi], *s.* (*fis.*) entropia.

to entrust [in'trʌst], *v.t.* affidare; commettere, consegnare: *to — s.o. with a task*, affidare un compito a qlcu.: *he is entrusted with the sale*, la vendita è affidata a lui; *to — sthg. to s.o.*, affidare, dare in custodia ql.co. a qlcu.

entrustment [in'trʌstmənt], *s.* affidamento; confidamento; consegna.

entry ['entri], *s.* **1.** entrata: *the army made a triumphal —*, l'armata fece un ingresso trionfale; *to make one's —*, entrare (di attore, ecc.) **2.** ingresso, passaggio (stretto); entrata (di una miniera, caverna) **3.** (*dir.*) presa di possesso, insediamento **4.** (*comm.*) registrazione, dichiarazione, partita: *by single (double) —*, in partita semplice (doppia) **5.** (*comm.*) articolo, merce registrata **6.** (*spor.*) lista degli iscritti, dei concorrenti; iscrizione **7.** sbocco (di fiume) ☆ *— -way*, passaggio d'ingresso; *prime —*, dichiarazione di entrata (doganale) ‖ *transhipment —*, dichiarazione per il trasbordo; *warehousing —*, bolletta d'accompagnamento in deposito franco.

to entwine [in'twain], *v.t.i.* intrecciare, intrecciarsi; intessere, stringere, abbracciare : *to — with* (o *about* o *round*), intrecciare con, attorcigliarsi a.

to entwist [in'twist], *v.t.* avvincere; intrecciare; allacciare.

to enucleate [i'nju:klieit], *v.t.* **1.** spiegare; chiarire **2.** (*chir.*) estrarre, enucleare (un tumore, ecc.).

enucleation [i,nju:kli'eifən], *s.* **1.** spiegazione; chiarimento **2.** (*chir.*) estrazione, enucleazione (di un tumore, ecc.).

to enumerate [i'nju:məreit], *v.t.* enumerare, elencare, contare.

enumeration [i,nju:mə'reifən], *s.* enumerazione.

enumerative [i'nju:mərətiv], *ag.* enumerativo.

enumerator [i'nju:məreitə*], *s.* numeratore.

enunciable [i'nʌnfiəbl], *ag.* enunciabile.

to enunciate [i'nʌnsieit], *v.t.* **1.** enunciare, proclamare: *to — a new theory*, enunciare una nuova teoria **2.** pronunciare, articolare (parole, suoni).

enunciation [i,nʌnsi'eifən], *s.* **1.** enunciazione **2.** (*geom.*) enunciato **3.** pronuncia, articolazione.

enunciative [i'nʌnfiətiv], *ag.* enunciativo.

enunciator [i'nʌnsieitə*], *s.c.* enunciatore, enunciatrice.

to enure, *V.* to **inure**.

enuresis [,enju'ri:sis], *s.* (*patol.*) enuresi.

to envault [in'vɔ:lt], *v.t.* coprire con una volta.

to envelop [in'veləp], *v.t.* **1.** avviluppare, avvolgere (anche *fig.*): *the flames enveloped them*, le fiamme li avvolsero **2.** (*mil.*) circondare, accerchiare (il nemico).

envelope ['enviloup], *s.* **1.** busta, involucro, copertura (anche *fig.*): *stamped —*, busta affrancata; *torn —*, busta lacerata **2.** (*aer.*) involucro (di aerostato) **3.** (*biol. bot.*) involucro **4.** (*geom.*) inviluppo ☆ *pay —*, busta paga.

envelopment [in'veləpmənt], *s.* avvolgimento.

to envenom [in'venəm], *v.t.* **1.** avvelenare **2.** *fig.* avvelenare, amareggiare; corrompere.

enviable ['enviəbl], *ag.* invidiabile.

enviableness ['enviəblnis], *s.* invidiabilità.

enviably ['enviəbli], *av.* invidiabilmente.

envier ['enviə*], *s.* invidioso.

envious ['enviəs], *ag.* invidioso: *— looks*, occhiate d'invidia.

enviously ['enviəsli], *av.* invidiosamente, con invidia.

enviousness ['enviəsnis], *s.* invidia.

to **environ** [in'vaiərən], *v.t.* circondare; accerchiare, attorniare: *environed by* (o *with*) *enemies*, accerchiato da nemici; *that village was environed by* (o *with*) *forests*, quel villaggio era circondato di foreste.

environment [in'vaiərənmənt], *s.* ambiente; condizioni ambientali.

environs ['environz], *s.pl.* dintorni, sobborghi; vicinato.

to **envisage** [in'vizidʒ], *v.t.* **1.** guardare in faccia; affrontare (pericolo, ecc.) **2.** *fig.* considerare; immaginare: *I had not envisaged the matter in that light*, non avevo considerato la faccenda sotto questo punto di vista.

envisagement [in'vizidʒmənt], *s.* **1.** l'affrontare (pericolo, ecc.) **2.** *fig.* il considerare.

envoy[1] ['envoi], *s.* (*poes.*) congedo, commiato.

envoy[2], *s.* inviato, messo (diplomatico); ministro plenipotenziario.

envoyship ['envoiʃip], *s.* ufficio, carica di inviato.

envy ['envi], *s.* **1.** invidia, gelosia: *out of* —, per invidia; *to be green with* —, essere verde d'invidia; *to excite* (o *to raise*) —, suscitare l'invidia; *to feel* — *at* (o *of*) *sthg.*, provare invidia per ql.co. **2.** invidia, oggetto d'invidia: *she is the* — *of the town*, è l'(oggetto d') invidia di tutta la città.

to **envy**, *v.t.* (III) invidiare: *he envies their riches*, egli invidia la loro ricchezza; *to* — *s.o. sthg.*, invidiare ql.co. a qlcu.: *do not* — *anybody anything, neither the rich their wealth, nor the monarch his power*, non invidiare nulla a nessuno, non la ricchezza ai ricchi, non la potenza al monarca ǁ *it is better to be envied than pitied*, *prov.* meglio fare invidia che compassione.

to **enwind** [in'waind], *v.t.* (*poet.*) avviluppare, avvinghiare: *to* — *oneself*, avvilupparsi, avvinghiarsi.

to **enwomb** [in'wu:m], *v.t.* **1.** chiudere in seno; racchiudere (in petto, in cuore) **2.** (*arc.*) rendere pregna.

to **enwrap** [in'ræp], *pass.p.p.* **enwrapped** [in'ræpt], *v.t.* avvolgere, avviluppare (anche *fig.*): *to be enwrapped in thought*, essere immerso nella meditazione.

to **enwreathe** [in'ri:ð], *v.t.* **1.** incoronare, inghirlandare **2.** intrecciare.

enzootic [,enzou'ɔtik], *ag.* (*vet.*) enzootico ǁ *s.* (*vet.*) enzoozia.

enzooty [en'zouəti], *s.* (*vet.*) enzoozia.

enzyme ['enzaim], *s.* (*biol.*) enzima.

eocene ['i(:)ousi:n], *ag.* (*geol.*) eocenico ǁ *s.* (*geol.*) eocene.

Eolian, Eolic, *V.* Aeolian, Aeolic.

eolith ['i:ouliθ], *s.* eolite.

eolithic [,i:ou'liθik], *ag.* eolitico.

eon, *V.* aeon.

eozoic [,i:ou'zouik], *ag.* (*geol.*) eozoico.

epact ['i:pækt], *s.* (*astr.*) epatta.

Epaminondas [e,pæmi'nondæs], *no.pr.m.* (*st.*) Epaminonda.

eparch ['epɑ:k], *s.* eparco (prefetto dell'eparchia).

eparchy ['epɑ:ki], *s.* eparchia (specie di provincia dell'impero bizantino).

epaule [e'pɔ:l], *s.* (*mil.*) spalla di baluardo.

epaulement [e'pɔ:lmənt], *s.* spalliera di fortificazione a fianco di batteria.

epaulet(te) ['epoulet], *s.* (*mil.*) spallina: *to win one's epaulettes*, essere promosso ufficiale.

epergne [i'pə:n], *s.* centro ornamentale da tavola (con frutta, dolci, ecc.).

ephebe [e'fi:b], *s.* efebo.

ephemera [i'femərə], *s.* **1.** (*entom.*) effimera **2.** cosa effimera, di breve durata.

ephemeral [i'femərəl], *ag.* effimero, passeggero.

ephemerality [i,femə'ræliti], *s.* qualità di effimero.

ephemeris [i'feməris], *pl.* **ephemerides** [efi'meridi:z], *s.* **1.** (*astr.*) effemeride **2.** (*rar.*) diario **3.** (*rar.*) almanacco, calendario.

Ephesian [i'fi:ʒən], *ag.* efesino, efesio ǁ *s.c.* abitante di Efeso.

Ephesus ['efisəs], *no.pr.* (*geog.*) Efeso.

ephod ['i:fɔd], *s.* efod (paramento di sacerdote ebreo).

ephor ['efə*], *s.* (*st.*) eforo.

Ephraim ['i:freiim], *no.pr.m.* (*Bibbia*) Efraim.

epic ['epik], *ag.* epico ǁ *s.* poema epico, epopea.

epical ['epikəl], *ag.* epico.

epically ['opikəli], *av.* epicamente.

epicarp ['epikɑ:p], *s.* (*bot.*) epicarpo.

epicedium [,epi'si:djəm], *pl.* **epicedia** [,epi'si:djə], *s.* (*poes.*) epicedio.

epicene ['episi:n], *ag.* (*gram.*) epiceno ǁ *s.* ermafrodito.

epicentre ['episentə*], **epicentrum** [,epi'sentrəm], *s.* (*geol.*) epicentro.

Epictetus [,epik'ti:təs], *no.pr.m.* (*st. fil.*) Epitteto.

epicure ['epikjuə*], *s.* **1.** (*st. fil.*) (*rar.*) epicureo (anche *fig.*) **2.** buongustaio.

epicurean [,epikjuə'ri(:)ən], *ag.s.* (*st. fil.*) epicureo (anche *fig.*).

epicureanism [,epikjuə'ri(:)ənizəm], **epicurism** ['epikjuərizəm], *s.* (*st. fil.*) epicureismo.

Epicurus [,epi'kjuərəs], *no.pr.m.* (*st. fil.*) Epicuro.

epicycle ['episaikl], *s.* (*astr.*) epiciclo.

epicycloid ['epi'saiklɔid], *s.* (*geom.*) epicicloide.

epideictic [,epi'daiktik], *ag.* epidittico.

epidemic [,epi'demik], *ag.* epidemico, contagioso ǁ *s.* epidemia (anche *fig.*).

epidemical [,epi'demikəl], *ag.* epidemico.

epidemically [,epi'demikəli], *av.* epidemicamente, in modo contagioso.

epidemiology [,epi,di:mi'olədʒi], *s.* epidemiologia.

epidermal [,epi'də:məl], **epidermic** [,epi'də:mik], *ag.* (*anat.*) epidermico.

epidermis [,epi'də:mis], *s.* (*anat.*) epidermide.

epidiascope [,epi'daiəskoup], *s.* (*cine.*) epidiascopio.

epidote ['epidout], *s.* (*min.*) epidoto.

epigastric [,epi'gæstrik], *ag.* (*anat.*) epigastrico ☆ — *voice*, ventriloquia.

epigastrium [,epi'gæstriəm], *s.* (*anat.*) epigastrio, regione epigastrica.

epigenesis [,epi'dʒenisis], *s.* (*biol.*) epigenesi.

epigenesist [,epi'dʒenisist], *s.* (*biol.*) epigenista.

epigenetic [,epidʒi'netik], *ag.* (*biol.*) epigenetico.

epiglottis [,epi'glotis], *s.* (*anat.*) epiglottide.

epigone ['epigoun], *s.* epigono.

Epigoni [e'pigənai], *s.pl.* **1.** (*mit.*) epigoni **2.** (*lett.*) epigoni, decadenti.

epigram ['epigræm], *s.* (*poes.*) epigramma.

epigrammatic [,epigrə'mætik], *ag.* epigrammatico.

epigrammatically [,epigrə'mætikəli], *av.* in modo epigrammatico; concisamente.

epigrammatist [,epi'græmətist], *s.* epigrammista.

to **epigrammatize** [,epi'græmətaiz], *v.i.* fare, scrivere epigrammi.

epigraph ['epigrɑ:f], *s.* epigrafe.

epigrapher [e'pigrəfə*], *s.* epigrafista.

epigraphic [,epi'græfik], *ag.* epigrafico.

epigraphist [e'pigrəfist], *s.* epigrafista.

epigraphy [e'pigrəfi], *s.* epigrafia.

epilepsy ['epilepsi], *s.* (*patol.*) epilessia.

epileptic(al) [,epi'leptik(əl)], *ag.s.* (*patol.*) epilettico.

epilogist [i'pilədʒist], *s.* scrittore di epiloghi.

epilogue ['epilog], *s.* epilogo.

Epiphany [i'pifəni], *s.* (*eccl.*) Epifania.

epiphenomenon [,epifi'nominən], *s.* (*med.*) epifenomeno.

epiphysis [e'pifisis], *s.* (*anat.*) epifisi.

Epirot [i'paiərout], *ag. s.c.* epirota.

Epirus [e'paiərəs], *no.pr.* (*geog.*) Epiro.

episcopacy [i'piskəpəsi], *s.* episcopato: *the* — *of Belgium*, l'episcopato belga, tutti i vescovi belgi.

episcopal [i'piskəpəl], *ag.* episcopale, vescovile ǁ *the Episcopal Church*, la Chiesa Episcopale.

episcopalian [i,piskə'peiljən], *ag.* episcopale ǁ *s.* membro della Chiesa Episcopale.

episcopalianism [i,piskə'peiljənizəm], *s.* governo, dottrina episcopale.

episcopally [i'piskəpəli], *av.* episcopalmente.
episcopate [i'piskəpit], *s.* **1.** episcopato (carica) **2.** vescovado (sede).
episode ['episoud], *s.* episodio.
episodic(al) [,epi'sɔdik(əl)], *ag.* episodico.
episodically [,epi'sɔdikəli], *av.* episodicamente.
epispastic [,epi'spæstik], *ag.* (*farm.*) epispastico.
episperm ['epispə:m], *s.* (*bot.*) episperma.
epistaxis [,epi'stæksis], *s.* (*patol.*) epistassi.
epistemology [,episti:'mɔlədʒi], *s.* (*fil.*) epistemologia.
epistle [i'pisl], *s.* **1.** (*eccl.*) epistola **2.** (*scherz.*) lettera.
epistolary [i'pistələri], *ag.* epistolare (di stile, corrispondenza).
epistrophe [e'pistrəfi], *s.* (*ret.*) epistrofe.
epistyle ['epistail], *s.* (*arch.*) epistilio.
epitaph ['epita:f], *s.* epitaffio.
epitasis [e'pitəsis], *s.* (*teat.*) epitasi.
epithalamium [,epiθə'leimjəm], *s.* (*poes.*) epitalamio.
epithet ['epiθet], *s.* epiteto.
to **epithet,** *v.t.* (*rar.*) descrivere, definire per mezzo di epiteti.
epithetic(al) [,epi'θetik(əl)], *ag.* qualificativo.
epitome [i'pitəmi], *s.* epitome, riassunto, sommario; compendio.
epitomist [i'pitəmist], *s.* epitomatore.
to **epitomize** [i'pitəmaiz], *v.t.* compendiare, ridurre, riassumere.
epizoon [,epi'zouən], *pl.* **epizoa** [,epi'zouə], *s.*(*entom.*) insetto del gruppo degli epizoi.
epizootic [,epizou'ɔtik], *ag.* (*vet.*) epizootico ǁ *s.* (*vet.*) epizoozia.
epizooty [,epi'zouəti], *s.* (*vet.*) epizoozia.
epoch ['i:pɔk], *s.* epoca, età: *to make* (o *to mark*) *an* —, fare epoca ǁ *— -making* (o *— -marking*), che fa epoca (di scoperta, avvenimento).
epochal ['epɔkəl], *ag.* di un'epoca; che fa epoca.
epode ['epoud], *s.* (*poes.*) epodo.
eponym ['epounim], *s.* eponimo.
eponymous [i'pɔniməs], *ag.* eponimo.
epopee ['epoupi:], *s.* epopea.
epos ['epɔs], *s.* epos; epopea.
epsilon [ep'sailən], *s.* epsilon (lettera dell'alfabeto greco).
Epsom ['epsəm], *no.pr.* (*geog.*) Epsom ☆ — *salt,* sale purgativo, sale amaro, sale inglese.
equability [,ekwə'biliti], *s.* uguaglianza, uniformità.
equable ['ekwəbl], *ag.* uniforme, costante (umore, clima, ecc.).
equableness ['ekwəblnis], *s.* uguaglianza, uniformità.
equably ['ekwəbli], *av.* uniformemente.
equal ['i:kwəl], *ag.* **1.** uguale, simile; stesso; pari: *things of* — *value,* cose dello stesso valore; *on* — *terms,* a pari condizioni; *with* — *ease,* con la stessa facilità; *they are* — *in points,* (*spor.*) hanno lo stesso punteggio; *three times four is* — *to twelve,* tre per quattro fa dodici ǁ *to be* — *to doing sthg.,* avere la velleità, la capacità, la forza di far ql.co.; *to be* — *to the occasion,* essere all'altezza della situazione; *to be* — *to,* essere pari a, equivalere a: *he is* — *to his brother in goodness and virtue,* egli è pari a suo fratello in bontà e virtù; *to feel* — *to doing sthg.,* sentirsi (capace) di fare ql.co.; *to get* — *with s.o.,* (*fam.*) rendere pan per focaccia **2.** calmo; fermo; costante: *to keep an* — *mind,* mantenere la calma ǁ *s.* pari, simile: *your equals,* i tuoi pari; *he treated me as an* —, mi trattò da pari a pari; *to find one's* —, trovare il proprio simile ☆ — *mark,* (*arit.*) segno di uguaglianza.
to **equal,** *pass.p.p.* **equalled** ['i:kwəld], *v.t.* uguagliare: *there is nothing to* — *it,* non c'è nulla che lo possa eguagliare.
equality [i(:)'kwɔliti], *s.* uguaglianza, parità: *an* — *between two persons,* un'uguaglianza fra due persone; *on a footing of* — *with,* su un piede di parità con.
equalization [,i:kwəlai'zeiʃən], *s.* **1.** eguagliamento; (*amm.*) perequazione, livellamento: — *of wages,* li-

vellamento dei salari **2.** compensazione **3.** (*mec.*) livellamento, spianamento ☆ — *fund,* cassa di compensazione.
to **equalize** ['i:kwəlaiz], *v.t.i.* uguagliare, uguagliarsi; compensare, compensarsi; equiparare; uniformare, distribuire uniformemente; (*calcio, cricket, ecc.*) pareggiare: *to* — *accounts,* (*amm.*) far tornare i conti; *to* — *incomes,* equiparare le rendite.
equally ['i:kwəli], *av.* ugualmente; imparzialmente; uniformemente: *your friends are* — *clever,* i tuoi amici sono ugualmente intelligenti.
equanimity [,i:kwə'nimiti], *s.* equanimità; serenità; tranquillità (d'animo).
equanimous [i(:)'kwæniməs], *ag.* equanime.
to **equate** [i'kweit], *v.t.* **1.** rendere uguale; (*mat.*) uguagliare: *to* — *an expression to* (o *with*) *zero,* (*mat.*) uguagliare un'espressione a zero **2.** stabilire un parallelo tra, paragonare.
equation [i'kweiʃən], *s.* **1.** (*mat.*) equazione **2.** perequazione, pareggio **3.** (*amm.*) adeguato: *simple, compound* —, adeguato semplice, composto ☆ *simple, quadratic* —, equazione di primo, secondo grado.
equator [i'kweitə*], *s.* (*geog.*) equatore.
equatorial [,ekwə'tɔ:riəl], *ag.* (*geog.*) equatoriale.
equerry [i'kweri], *s.* scudiero; funzionario di corte.
equestrian [i'kwestriən], *ag.* equestre ǁ *s.* cavallerizzo.
equestrienne [i,kwestri'en], *s.* cavallerizza.
equiangular [,i:kwi'æŋgjulə*], *ag.* (*geom.*) equiangolo.
equidifferent ['i:kwi'difrənt], *ag.* equidifferente.
equidistant ['i:kwi'distənt], *ag.* (*geom.*) equidistante.
equilateral ['i:kwi'lætərəl], *ag.* (*geom.*) equilatero.
to **equilibrate** ['i:kwi'laibreit], *v.t.i.* equilibrare, equilibrarsi; far da contrappeso a; bilanciare, bilanciarsi.
equilibration [,i:kwilai'breiʃən], *s.* il mettere in equilibrio.
equilibrist [i(:)'kwilibrist], *s.c.* equilibrista.
equilibrium [,i:kwi'libriəm], *s.* equilibrio (anche *fig.*): *stable* —, equilibrio stabile; *want of* —, squilibrio; *to keep* (o *to maintain*) *one's* —, mantenersi in equilibrio.
equine ['i:kwain], *ag.* equino.
equinoctial [,i:kwi'nɔkʃəl], *ag.* equinoziale ǁ *s.* **1.** (*astr.*) linea dell'equinozio **2.** *pl.* venti, tempeste dell'equinozio.
equinox ['i:kwinɔks], *s.* (*astr.*) equinozio: *the precession of the equinoxes,* la precessione degli equinozi; *the vernal* —, l'equinozio di primavera.
to **equip** [i'kwip], *pass.p.p.* **equipped** [i'kwipt], *v.t.* **1.** equipaggiare, allestire; (*mar. mil.*) armare: *to* — *oneself for a long journey,* equipaggiarsi per un lungo viaggio **2.** fornire, ammobiliare, arredare (una casa); attrezzare (un'officina): *to be equipped with,* essere fornito di.
equipage ['ekwipidʒ], *s.* **1.** equipaggiamento; attrezzatura (per un viaggio) **2.** seguito (di un nobile); equipaggio (di carrozza).
equipment [i'kwipmənt], *s.* **1.** equipaggiamento; (*mar. mil.*) armamento **2.** attrezzatura (di stabilimento); (*elett.*) apparecchiatura **3.** (*ferr.*) materiale mobile ☆ *ancillary* —, corredo ausiliario; *antifire* —, equipaggiamento antincendio.
equipoise ['ekwipoiz], *s.* **1.** equilibrio (uguaglianza di peso e di forze) **2.** contrappeso.
to **equipoise,** *v.t.* **1.** bilanciare, equilibrare **2.** tenere in sospeso (mente, spirito).
equipollence [,i:kwi'pɔləns], **equipollency** [,i:kwi'pɔlənsi], *s.* equipollenza, equivalenza.
equipollent [,i:kwi'pɔlənt], *ag.* equipollente.
equiponderance [,i:kwi'pɔndərəns], *s.* equiponderanza.
equiponderant [,i:kwi'pɔndərənt], *ag.* equiponderante.
equiponderate [,i:kwi'pɔndəreit], *ag.* equiponderato.
to **equiponderate,** *v.t.i.* equiponderare.
equitable ['ekwitəbl], *ag.* equo, giusto; (*dir.*) valido.

equitableness ['ekwitəblnis], *s.* equità.

equitably ['ekwitəbli], *av.* equamente.

equitation [,ekwi'teiʃən], *s.* (*scherz.*) equitazione.

equity ['ekwiti], *s.* 1. giustizia, equità 2. (*dir.*) equità: — *of a statute*, spirito di una legge 3. *pl.* (*amm.*) azioni ordinarie (a reddito variabile) 4. *Equity*, sindacato degli attori ☆ — *securities*, (*amm.*) azioni ordinarie.

equivalence [i'kwivələns], *s.* equivalenza.

equivalent [i'kwivələnt], *ag.s.* equivalente.

equivalently [i'kwivələntli], *av.* equivalentemente.

equivocal [i'kwivəkəl], *ag.* 1. ambiguo, equivoco, dubbio: *she gave me an — answer*, mi diede una risposta ambigua 2. sospetto, losco: *an — transaction*, un losco affare.

equivocality [i,kwivə'kæliti], *V.* **equivocalness.**

equivocally [i'kwivəkəli], *av.* 1. ambiguamente, in modo equivoco, dubbio 2. in modo sospetto, losco.

equivocalness [i'kwivəkəlnis], *s.* 1. equivocità, ambiguità 2. equivoco.

to **equivocate** [i'kwivəkeit], *v.i.* equivocare; giocare sull'equivoco.

equivocation [i,kwivə'keiʃən], *s.* 1. l'equivocare, il giocare sulle parole 2. equivoco.

equivocator [i'kwivəkeitə*], *s.c.* chi giuoca sull'equivoco.

equivoke, equivoque ['ekwivouk], *s.* 1. giuoco di parole 2. ambiguità (d'espressione), doppio senso.

er [ʌ:, ə:], *inter.* èhm (suono indicante esitazione).

'er [ə:*], (*fam.*) per **her.**

era ['iərə], *s.* 1. era; epoca: *to mark an —*, caratterizzare un'epoca 2. data memorabile.

to **eradiate** [i'reidieit], *v.t.i.* 1. irraggiare, raggiare 2. irradiare.

eradiation [i,reidi'eiʃən], *s.* irradiazione, radiazione, irraggiamento.

eradicable [i'rædikəbl], *ag.* estirpabile, sradicabile.

to **eradicate** [i'rædikeit], *v.t.* sradicare, estirpare, svellere (anche *fig.*).

eradication [i,rædi'keiʃən], *s.* sradicamento, estirpazione (anche *fig.*).

erasable [i'reizəbl], *ag.* raschiabile; cancellabile, (anche *fig.*).

to **erase** [i'reiz], *v.t.* 1. raschiare; cancellare (anche *fig.*) 2. (*sl. amer.*) uccidere.

erasement [i'reizmənt], *V.* **erasion.**

eraser [i'reizə*], *s.c.* chi cancella ‖ *s.* raschietto; gomma (per cancellare) ☆ *ink-* —, gomma da inchiostro.

erasion [i'reiʒən], *s.* 1. raschiatura; cancellatura, obliterazione (anche *fig.*) 2. (*chir.*) raschiamento; abrasione.

Erasmian [i'ræzmiən], *ag.* (*st. lett.*) erasmiana.

Erasmus [i'ræzməs], *no.pr.m.* (*st. lett.*) Erasmo.

Erastian [i'ræstiən], *ag.s.* (*st. teol.*) (sostenitore) di Erasto.

Erastus [i'ræstəs], *no.pr.m.* (*st. teol.*) Erasto.

erasure [i'reiʒə*], *s.* raschiatura; cancellatura, obliterazione (anche *fig.*).

Erato ['erətou], *no.pr.f.* (*mit.*) Erato.

Eratosthenes [,erə'tosθəni:z], *no.pr.m.* (*st. mat.*) Eratostene.

ere [εə*], *prep.* (*poet. arc.*) prima di: — *this,* — *now,* prima d'ora, in precedenza ‖ *cong.* (*poet. arc.*) prima che; piuttosto che: — *I will leave her I die,* piuttosto che lasciarla muoio.

Erebus ['eribəs], *no.pr.* (*geog. mit.*) Erebo.

Erechtheum [,erek'θi(:)əm], *s.* (*archeol.*) Eretteo.

Erechtheus [i'rekθju:s], *no.pr.m.* (*mit.*) Eretteo.

erect [i'rekt], *ag.* 1. diritto, ritto; in piedi (di persona); verticale; irto (di capelli): *with head* —, a testa alta; *to stand* —, stare dritto, raddrizzarsi 2. *fig.* fermo; saldo.

to **erect,** *v.t.* 1. raddrizzare, rizzare 2. erigere, costruire; fondare (anche *fig.*) 3. (*mec.*) montare 4. (*ott.*) raddrizzare 5. (*geom.*) innalzare 6. (*fisiol.*) ergere.

erecter, *V.* **erector.**

erectile [i'rektail], *ag.* (*fisiol.*) erettile.

erection [i'rekʃən], *s.* 1. raddrizzamento 2. costruzione, erezione; fondazione (anche *fig.*) 3. (*mec.*) montaggio 4. (*fisiol.*) erezione.

erectly [i'rektli], *av.* in posizione eretta.

erectness [i'rektnis], *s.* posizione eretta.

erector [i'rektə*], *s. c.* chi erige, sostiene (anche *fig.*) ‖ *s.* 1. (*mec.*) montatore 2. (*ott.*) raddrizzatore 3. (*anat.*) erettore ☆ *-muscle*, muscolo erettore.

erelong [εə'lɔŋ], *av.* (*poet. arc.*) fra poco, quanto prima.

eremite ['erimait], *s.* (*poet.*) eremita.

eremitic(al) [,eri'mitik(əl)], *ag.* (*poet.*) eremitico.

erenow [εə'nau], *av.* (*poet. arc.*) già; prima d'ora.

erethism ['eriθizəm], *s.* (*patol.*) eretismo.

erewhile [εə'wail], *av.* (*poet. arc.*) poco tempo fa; poco tempo prima.

erg [ə:g], *s.* (*fis.*) erg, ergon.

ergatocracy [,ə:gə'tɔkrəsi], *s.* governo da parte dei lavoratori.

ergo ['ə:gou], *av.cong.* ergo, quindi, dunque.

ergon ['ə:gon], *s.* (*fis.*) erg, ergon.

ergot ['ə:gət], *s.* (*bot. farm.*) segale cornuta.

ergotine ['ə:gətin], *s.* (*chim.*) ergotina.

ergotism[1] ['ə:gətizəm], *s.* (*patol.*) ergotismo.

ergotism[2], *s.* argomentazione, discussione; conclusione logica.

Eridanus [i'ridənəs], *no.pr.* (*geog.*) Eridano.

Erin ['iərin], *no.pr.* (*geog. poet.*) Irlanda.

Erinyes [i'rinii:z], *no.pr.pl.* (*mit.*) Erinni.

eristic [e'ristik], *ag.* polemico ‖ *s.* 1. polemista 2. (*fil.*) eristica.

Eritrea [,eri'triə], *no.pr.* (*geog.*) Eritrea.

Eritrean [,eri'triən], *ag.* eritreo ‖ *s.c.* eritreo, eritrea.

erl-king ['ə:l-kiŋ], *s.* (*mit.*) il re degli elfi.

ermelin ['ə:milin], *V.* **ermine 1. 2.**

ermine ['ə:min], *s.* 1. (*zool.*) ermellino 2. pelliccia di ermellino 3. *fig.* carica di giudice: *to rise to the* —, (*fam.*) essere nominato giudice 4. (*arald.*) ermellino.

ermined ['ə:mind], *ag.* 1. rivestito, guarnito di ermellino 2. (*arald.*) ermellinato.

erne [ə:n], *s.* (*ornit.*) 1. aquila marina 2. aquila reale.

Ernest ['ə:nist], *no.pr.m.* Ernesto.

Ernestine ['ə:nisti:n], *no.pr.f.* Ernestina.

to **erode** [i'roud], *v.t.* erodere, corrodere, rodere; consumare; distruggere: *cliffs eroded by the sea*, scogliere erose dal mare.

Eros ['erɔs], *no.pr.m.* (*mit.*) Eros.

erosion [i'rouʒən], *s.* erosione, corrosione.

erosive [i'rousiv], *ag.* corrosivo, crosivo.

erotic [i'rɔtik], *ag.* erotico, amoroso ‖ *s.* poema erotico.

eroticism [e'rɔtisizəm], *s.* erotismo.

erotomania [e,routou'meinjə], *s.* (*patol.*) erotomania.

to **err** [ə:*], *v.i.* 1. commettere errori, sbagliare; peccare: *to* — *is human*, sbagliare è umano 2. errare, vagabondare: *to* — *from the straight path*, *fig.* allontanarsi dalla retta via.

errable [i'erəbl], *ag.* (*arc.*) soggetto ad errore.

errancy ['erənsi], *s.* l'errare; l'essere nell'errore.

errand ['erənd], *s.* 1. commissione: *I must go on an* —, devo fare una commissione; *to go on errands for s.o.*, andare a far commissioni per qlcu. 2. scopo: *what is his* —?, che scopo lo porta qui? ☆ *-boy*, fattorino; — *-girl*, piccinina.

errant ['erənt], *ag.* 1. errante 2. che sbaglia ☆ *knight* — — (*pl. knights*—), cavaliere errante.

errantly ['erəntli], *av.* a casaccio.

errantry ['erəntri], *s.* vagabondaggio; vita nomade dei cavalieri erranti.

erratic [i'rætik], *ag.* 1. (*geol. med.*) erratico 2. irregolare; intermittente: — *working of a machine*, rendimento ineguale di una macchina 3. eccentrico, strae vagante, capriccioso, bizzarro: — *way of life*, modo di vita eccentrico.

erratically [i'rætikəli], *av.* **1.** irregolarmente **2.** eccentricamente, capricciosamente.

erratum [e'rɑːtəm], *pl.* **errata** [e'rɑːtə] *s.* errore di stampa.

erring ['əːriŋ], *ag.* traviato; che si allontana dalla retta via.

erroneous [i'rounjəs], *ag.* erroneo: — *spelling*, ortografia sbagliata.

erroneously [i'rounjəsli], *av.* erroneamente.

erroneousness [i'rounjəsnis], *s.* erroneità; falsità (di una dottrina, ecc.).

error ['erə*], *s.* **1.** errore, sbaglio: *clerical —*, errore di trascrizione; *in —*, per sbaglio; *errors and omissions excepted (E. & O. E.)*, salvo errori ed omissioni; *you're a fool and no —*, (*sl.*) senza dubbio sei uno sciocco; *to make, to commit an —*, fare, commettere uno sbaglio **2.** errore, torto: *to be in —*, essere in errore, aver torto; *to run, to fall into —*, cadere in errore, incorrere in un errore **3.** peccato, colpa.

ersatz ['eəzæts], *s.* sostituto, surrogato.

Erse [əːs], *ag.s.* «Erse» (gaelico, delle montagne scozzesi e dell'Irlanda).

erstwhile ['əːst-wail], *av.* (*arc.*) tempo fa; prima.

erubescence [ˌeru(ː)'besns], *s.* erubescenza, rossore.

erubescent [ˌeru(ː)'besnt], *ag.* erubescente, arrossato.

to eruct [i'rʌkt], **to eructate** [i'rʌkteit], *v.t.i.* eruttare, ruttare.

eructation [ˌiːrʌk'teiʃən], *s.* eruttazione, rutto; *fig.* eruzione.

erudite ['eru(ː)dait], *ag.* erudito, dotto.

eruditely ['eru(ː)daitli], *av.* in modo erudito.

erudition [ˌeru(ː)'diʃən], *s.* erudizione.

to erupt [i'rʌpt], *v.i.* **1.** eruttare (di vulcano); entrare in eruzione **2.** spuntare (di denti).

eruption [i'rʌpʃən], *s.* **1.** eruzione **2.** scoppio (di guerra, passioni, ecc.) **3.** (*patol.*) eruzione **4.** (*fisiol.*) dentizione.

eruptive [i'rʌptiv], *ag.* (*patol. geol.*) eruttivo.

eruptively [i'rʌptivli], *av.* come in un'eruzione.

eruptiveness [i'rʌptivnis], *s.* natura eruttiva (di un vulcano, ecc.).

erysipelas [ˌeri'sipiləs], *s.* (*patol.*) risipola, erisipela.

erythema [ˌeri'θiːmə], *s.* (*patol.*) eritema.

Esau ['iːsɔː], *no.pr.m.* (*Bibbia*) Esaù.

escalade [ˌeskə'leid], *s.* (*mil.*) scalata.

to escalade, *v.t.* (*mil.*) scalare.

escalator ['eskəleitə*], *s.* scala mobile ☆ — *contract*, contratto a scala mobile.

escallop [is'kɔləp], *V.* scallop.

escapade [ˌeskə'peid], *s.* fuga; *fig.* scappata, scappatella.

escape¹ [is'keip], *s.* **1.** fuga, evasione (dal carcere, dai propri pensieri): *the prisoner's —*, la fuga del prigioniero **2.** scampo, salvezza ‖ *to have a narrow —*, cavarsela per miracolo **3.** (*ind.*) scappamento **4.** (*bot.*) pianta incolta ☆ — *door*, uscita di sicurezza; — *gas*, gas di scappamento; — *literature*, letteratura di evasione; — *pipe*, tubo di scappamento; — *valve*, valvola di scarico, di sicurezza ‖ *to — gas*, fuga di gas.

to escape¹, *v.t.i.* **1.** fuggire, evadere; scappare; svignarsela: *they escaped from prison*, evasero dalla prigione **2.** (I) evitare, scampare: *I'll try to — doing that work*, cercherò di evitare di fare quel lavoro ‖ *to — by the skin of one's teeth*, farcela per un pelo **3.** sfuggire (specialmente dalla mente): *his name escapes me*, mi sfugge il suo nome; *nothing escapes him!*, non gli sfugge nulla!; *a sigh escaped him*, gli sfuggì un sospiro.

escape², *s.* (*arch.*) fusto di colonna.

escapee [ˌeskə'piː], *s.* evaso.

escapement [is'keipmənt], *s.* (*mec.*) scappamento (specialmente di orologio).

escapism [is'keipizəm], *s.* evasione (dalla realtà).

escapist [is'keipist], *ag.* di evasione ‖ *s.* chi cerca di sfuggire alla realtà ☆ — *literature*, letteratura di evasione.

escarp [is'kɑːp], *s.* scarpata (anche *mil.*).

to escarp, *v.t.* (*mil.*) rendere erto; ridurre a scarpata; munire di scarpata.

escarpment [is'kɑːpmənt], *s.* scarpata.

eschalot ['eʃəlɔt], *s.* (*bot.*) scalogna.

eschar ['eskɑː*], *s.* (*patol.*) escara, crosta.

eschatological [ˌeskətə'lɔdʒikəl], *ag.* (*teol. fil.*) escatologico.

eschatology [ˌeskə'tɔlədʒi], *s.* (*teol. fil.*) escatologia.

escheat [is'tʃiːt], *s.* (*dir.*) proprietà caduca (che per mancanza di eredi diretti passa allo Stato); proprietà incamerata; incameramento.

to escheat, *v.t.* (*dir.*) **1.** confiscare (una proprietà) **2.** passare allo Stato (di proprietà).

to eschew [is'tʃuː], *v.t.* evitare; astenersi da, rifugire da: *you must — wine*, dovete evitare (di bere) il vino.

escort ['eskɔːt], *s.* **1.** (*mil. mar.*) scorta: *armed —*, scorta armata; *to conduct a prisoner under —*, scortare un prigioniero **2.** chi accompagna (per protezione, ecc.): — *to a lady*, accompagnatore di una signora in società ☆ — *planes*, aeroplani di scorta; — *vessel*, (*mar.*) avviso scorta.

to escort [is'kɔːt], *v.t.* scortare; accompagnare: *I will — you home*, ti accompagnerò fino a casa; *to — a lady*, accompagnare una signora in pubblico; *to — s.o. on horseback*, scortare qlcu. a cavallo.

escritoire [ˌeskri(ː)'twɑː*], *s.* scrittoio, scrivania.

escrow [es'krou], *s.* (*dir.*) atto depositato presso terzi.

escudo [es'kuːdou], *pl.* **escudos** [es'kuːdouz], *s.* scudo (moneta portoghese).

esculent ['eskjulənt], *ag.s.* commestibile.

escutcheon [is'kʌtʃən], *s.* **1.** (*arald.*) scudo: *a blot on one's —*, *fig.* una macchia sulla propria reputazione. ‖ — *of pretence*, (*arald.*) scudo sul quale un uomo porta le armi di sua moglie se erede o coerede **2.** (*mar.*) scudo di poppa **3.** (*mec.*) bocchetta **4.** borchia; targhetta.

Eskimo ['eskimou], *pl.* **Eskimoes** ['eskimouz], *s.c.* esquimese.

esophagus [iː(ː)'sɔfəgəs], *pl.* **esophagi** [iː(ː)'sɔfəgai], *s.* (*anat.*) esofago.

esoteric [ˌesou'terik], *ag.* **1.** (*fil.*) esoterico **2.** segreto, misterioso.

esoterically [ˌesou'terikəli], *av.* in modo esoterico.

espagnolette [ˌespɑːnjə'let], *s.* spagnoletta (di finestra).

espalier [is'pæljə*], *s.* **1.** spalliera (per piante) **2.** (*rar.*) albero o fila di alberi a spalliera.

to espalier, *v.t.* disporre a spalliera, proteggere con spalliera, fornire di spalliera (alberi).

esparto [is'pɑːtou], *s.* (*bot.*) sparto.

especial [is'peʃəl], *ag.* eccezionale, speciale.

especially [is'peʃəli], *av.* specialmente, particolarmente, soprattutto.

Esperantist [ˌespə'ræntist], *s.c.* esperantista.

Esperanto [ˌespə'ræntou], *s.* esperanto.

espial [is'paiəl], *s.* spiata (attraverso il buco della serratura, ecc.).

espionage [ˌespiə'nɑːʒ], *s.* spionaggio ☆ *counter- —*, controspionaggio.

esplanade [ˌesplə'neid], *s.* **1.** spianata; passeggiata **2.** (*mil.*) spianata.

espousal [is'pauzəl], *s.* (*arc.*) **1.** *pl.* sponsali, nozze **2.** adozione (di causa, idea).

to espouse [is'pauz], *v.t.* **1.** (*arc.*) sposare (generalmente detto di uomo) **2.** maritare (una figlia) **3.** *fig.* sposare, abbracciare (una causa, un'idea, ecc.).

espresso [es'presou], *s.* (*neol.*) **1.** macchina per caffè espresso **2.** — (*bar*), bar dove si beve caffè espresso.

esprit ['espriː], *s.* spirito.

to espy [is'pai], *v.t.* **1.** scorgere, intravvedere; spiare **2.** scoprire, notare.

Esquiline ['eskwilain], *no.pr.* (*geog.*) Esquilino.

Esquimau ['eskimou], *pl.* **Esquimaux** ['eskimouz], *s.c.* esquimese.

Esquire [is'kwaiə*], *s.* **1.** titolo di cortesia usato negli indirizzi: *John W. Brown, Esq.*, Egregio Signor John W. Brown. **2.** (*arc.*) scudiero.

ess [es], *s.* **1.** esse (la lettera *s*) **2.** ogni oggetto a forma di S.

essay ['esei], *s.* **1.** prova, saggio, esperimento; sforzo; tentativo **2.** (*lett.*) saggio; (*scuola*) componimento.

to essay [e'sei], *v.t.i.* provare; mettere alla prova: *to — (to do) sthg.*, esperimentare ql.co., tentare (di fare) ql.co.

essayist ['eseiist], *s.c.* saggista.

essence ['esns], *s.* **1.** essenza, elemento costitutivo: *the — of the matter*, il nocciolo della questione; *money is the — of business*, il denaro è l'anima degli affari **2.** (*chim.*) essenza, estratto.

Essene ['esi:n], *s.c.* (*relig. ebraica*) membro della setta degli esseni.

essential [i'senʃəl], *ag.* **1.** essenziale, sostanziale, fondamentale, principale; indispensabile **2.** (*chim.*) essenziale, puro || *s. gener. pl.* elemento essenziale ☆ *— oil*, (*chim.*) olio essenziale.

essentially [i'senʃəli], *av.* essenzialmente.

to establish [is'tæbliʃ], *v.t.* **1.** affermare (diritto, potere, ecc.); (*dir.*) confermare, ratificare (testamento, ecc.) **2.** instaurare, istituire (governo, sistema, ecc.): *the custom has been* (o *become*) *established to...*, si è introdotto l'uso di...; *to — close relations with s.o.*, stringere rapporti di amicizia con qlcu.; *to — a tax on sthg.*, mettere, imporre una tassa su ql.co. **3.** (*comm.*) fondare, costituire, istituire: *to — a business*, fondare una ditta **4.** stabilire, constatare, dimostrare; provare: *her honesty is well established*, la sua onestà è provata; *the law of gravity was established by Newton*, la legge di gravità fu enunciata da Newton; *they established his innocence*, dimostrarono la sua innocenza **5.** *to — oneself*, stabilirsi, installarsi (in campagna, casa).

established [is'tæbliʃt], *ag.* **1.** stabilito, affermato **2.** fondato, istituito, costituito: *— in 1885*, fondato nel 1885 || *the Established Church*, la religione di Stato **3.** dimostrato, provato.

establisher [is'tæbliʃə*], *s.* fondatore; consolidatore.

establishment [is'tæbliʃmənt], *s.* **1.** affermazione; conferma; (*dir.*) ratifica **2.** instaurazione, creazione, fondazione, costituzione **3.** stabilimento; azienda, casa **4.** personale (di una casa); (*mil. mar.*) personale effettivo **5.** *the* (*Church*) *Establishment*, la religione di Stato.

establishmentarian [is,tæbliʃmen'tɛəriən], *ag.s.* (persona) che sostiene il principio di una Chiesa regolata dalle leggi dello Stato.

estaminet [es,ta:mi:'nei], *s.* piccolo caffè, piccolo ristorante.

estate [is'teit], *s.* **1.** terra, proprietà, tenuta **2.** (*dir.*) beni, patrimonio, fortuna: *— and property*, situazione patrimoniale **3.** stato, ordine, gruppo politico || *the Fourth Estate*, (*scherz.*) il Quarto Stato (la stampa) || *the Third Estate*, (*st.*) il Terzo Stato || *the Three Estates of the Realm*, i tre poteri del regno (in Inghilterra) **4.** stato, condizione: *man's —*, l'età virile **5.** rango, condizione, classe sociale: *of high, low —*, di alta, bassa condizione (sociale) ☆ *— agent*, fattore; mediatore; *— car*, (*neol. aut.*) giardiniera; *— duty*, imposta sul patrimonio || *personal —*, beni mobili; *real —*, beni immobili.

estated [is'teitid], *ag.* possidente.

esteem [is'ti:m], *s.* stima, considerazione; deferenza: *to hold s.o. in high —*, aver grande stima di qlcu.; *to rise, to fall in s.o.'s —*, salire, decadere nella stima di qlcu.

to esteem, *v.t.* **1.** stimare, tenere in gran conto: *much as I — him*, per quanto lo stimi; *your father is greatly esteemed*, tuo padre è molto stimato || *your esteemed letter*, (*comm.*) la vostra pregiata lettera **2.** considerare, ritenere: *I — it* (*as*) *an honour*, lo considero un onore.

Esther ['estə*], *no.pr.f.* Ester.

esthete ['i:sθi:t], *s.* esteta.

esthetic, esthetics, *V.* **aesthetic, aesthetics.**

Est(h)onia [es'tounjə], *no.pr.* (*geog.*) Estonia.

Est(h)onian [es'tounjən], *ag.s.c.* estone || *s.* lingua estone.

estimable ['estiməbl], *ag.* stimabile, degno di stima: *he is not a very — person*, è una persona degna di poca stima.

estimably ['estiməbli], *av.* stimabilmente.

estimate ['estimit], *s.* **1.** stima, giudizio, valutazione, calcolo: *he has formed a correct — of that question*, ha valutato correttamente quella questione **2.** (*comm.*) preventivo, stima: *rough —*, valutazione approssimativa; *to make an —*, preventivare, fare un preventivo || *the Estimates*, il bilancio preventivo dello Stato.

to estimate ['estimeit], *v.t.* **1.** stimare, valutare; fare la stima di: *to — damages*, fare la stima dei danni **2.** preventivare: *estimated figure*, cifra preventivata.

estimation [,esti'meiʃən], *s.* **1.** stima, apprezzamento, valutazione, considerazione: *the — of the public*, la stima del pubblico; *to hold s.o. in —*, tenere qlcu. in grande considerazione **2.** opinione, giudizio: *in my —*, secondo me, a mio avviso.

estimative ['estimətiv], *ag.* estimativo.

estimator ['estimeitə*], *s.* perito, stimatore.

to estop [is'təp], *pass.p.p.* **estopped** [is'təpt], *v.t.* (*dir.*) ostacolare, sospendere, precludere: *he has been estopped from doing that*, gli è stato impedito di fare ciò.

estoppage [is'təpidʒ], *s.* (*dir.*) esclusione, impedimento.

estoppel [is'təpəl], *s.* (*dir.*) eccezione.

estovers [is'touvəz], *s.pl.* (*dir.*) legnatico: *common of —*, diritto di sboscamento.

estrade [es'tra:d], *s.* piattaforma, palco.

to estrange [is'treindʒ], *v.t.* alienare, alienarsi; allontanare: *his conduct has estranged all his friends*, la sua condotta gli ha alienato la stima di tutti i suoi amici; *to become estranged from s.o., sthg.*, staccarsi, allontanarsi da qlcu., ql.co.; *to live estranged from the world*, vivere ritirato dal mondo.

estrangement [is'treindʒmənt], *s.* alienazione, allontanamento; distacco; discordia.

estranger [is'treindʒə*], *s.* (*arc.*) straniero.

estray [is'trei], *s.* (*dir.*) animale randagio.

estreat [is'tri:t], *s.* (*dir.*) estratto, copia autenticata (di documento per procedimento penale).

to estreat, *v.t.* (*dir.*) fare un estratto, una copia autenticata di (documento).

estrich ['estritʃ], **estridge** ['estridʒ], *s.* (*arc.*) struzzo.

estuary ['estjuəri], *s.* estuario.

esurience [i'sjuəriəns], **esuriency** [i'sjuəriənsi], *s.* fame, cupidigia, voracità.

esurient [i'sjuəriənt], *ag.* famelico, affamato; bisognoso.

etacism ['eitəsizəm], *s.* (*linguistica*) etacismo.

etc. [it'setrə], (*abbr.* di *et coetera*; letto anche « *and so on* » o « *and so forth* ») eccetera.

etceteras [it'setrəz], *s.pl.* annessi e connessi.

to etch [etʃ], *v.t.i.* **1.** incidere all'acquaforte **2.** fare l'incisore **3.** (*mec.*) incidere, imprimere **4.** attaccare (chimicamente).

etcher ['etʃə*], *s.* acquafortista (incisore).

etching ['etʃiŋ], *s.* **1.** arte dell'incisione all'acquaforte **2.** incisione all'acquaforte, acquaforte **3.** (*mec.*) incisione **4.** attacco chimico ☆ *— -bath*, bagno d'incisione; *— figures*, (*metal.*) disegni di attacco; *— -ground* (o *— -varnish*), vernice all'asfalto; *— -machine*, macchina per incidere; *— -needle*, bulino.

Eteocles [i'ti:əkli:z], *no.pr.m.* (*mit.*) Eteocle.

eternal [i(:)'tə:nl], *ag.* **1.** eterno || *the Eternal City*, la Città Eterna, Roma **2.** (*fam.*) incessante, continuo || *s.: the Eternal*, l'Eterno, Dio.

to **eternalize** [i(:)'tə:nəlaiz], *v.t.* immortalare, rendere eterno, eternare.

eternally [i(:)'tə:nəli], *av.* eternamente.

eternity [i(:)'tə:niti], *s.* eternità (anche *fig.*): *she kept me waiting for an* —, mi fece attendere un'eternità ‖ *the eternities*, le verità eterne.

to **eternize** [i:'tə:naiz], *v.t.* immortalare, rendere eterno, eternare.

Etesian [i'ti:ʒjən], *ag.* etesio (di vento): — *winds*, etesi (venti del Mediterraneo).

ethane ['eθein], *s.* (*chim.*) etano.

ether ['i:θə*], *s.* **1.** (*chim. fis.*) etere: *cosmic* —, etere cosmico **2.** (*poet.*) *the* —, la volta eterea, la volta celeste.

ethereal [i(:)'θiəriəl], *ag.* **1.** etereo, inconsistente, leggero, impalpabile **2.** (*chim.*) etereo, volatile.

ethereality [i(:),θiəri'æliti], *s.* l'essere etereo, immateriale.

etherealization [i(:),θiəriəlai'zeiʃən], *s.* spiritualizzazione; eterizzazione.

to **etherealize** [i(:)'θiəriəlaiz], *v.t.* **1.** (*chim.*) eterizzare **2.** rendere etereo, immateriale.

etherification [,i:θərifi'keiʃən], *s.* (*chim.*) eterificazione.

etheriform ['i:θərifɔ:m], *ag.* eteriforme.

to **etherify** ['i:θərifai], *v.t.* (*chim.*) eterificare.

etherism ['i:θərizəm], *s.* (*med.*) eterismo.

etherization [,i:θərai'zeiʃən], *s.* (*med.*) eterizzazione.

to **etherize** ['i:θəraiz], *v.t.* **1.** (*med.*) eterizzare, anestetizzare **2.** (*chim.*) eterizzare.

etheromania [,i:θərə'meinjə], *s.* (*patol.*) eteromania.

ethic(al) ['eθik(əl)], *ag.* etico, morale.

ethically ['eθikəli], *av.* eticamente, moralmente.

ethics ['eθiks], *s.* etica, morale.

Ethiop ['i:θiop], *s.c.* (*arc.*) etiope.

Ethiopia [,i:θi'oupjə], *no.pr.* (*geog.*) Etiopia.

Ethiopian [,i:θi'oupjən], *ag.* etiopico ‖ *s.c.* **1.** etiope **2.** (*scherz.*) negro.

Ethiopic [,i:θi'opik], *ag.* etiopico.

ethnic(al) ['eθnik(əl)], *ag.* etnico.

ethnically ['eθnikəli], *av.* etnicamente.

ethnographer [eθ'nɔgrəfə*], *s.* etnografo.

ethnographic(al) [,eθnou'græfik(əl)], *ag.* etnografico.

ethnography [eθ'nɔgrəfi], *s.* etnografia.

ethnologic(al) [,eθnou'lɔdʒik(əl)], *ag.* etnologico.

ethnologically [,eθnou'lɔdʒikəli], *av.* etnologicamente.

ethnologist [eθ'nɔlədʒist], *s.* etnologo.

ethnology [eθ'nɔlədʒi], *s.* etnologia.

ethologic(al) [,i:θou'lɔdʒik(əl)], *ag.* riguardante l'etologia.

ethologist [i(:)'θɔlədʒist], *s.* etologo.

ethology [i(:)'θɔlədʒi], *s.* etologia.

ethos ['i:θɔs], *s.* carattere particolare (di popolo, sistema, ecc.).

ethyl ['eθil], *s.* (*chim.*) etile, etere comune, acido acetico.

ethylene ['eθili:n], *s.* (*chim.*) etilene.

ethylic [i'θilik], *ag.* (*chim.*) etilico.

to **etiolate** ['i:tiouleit], *v.t.i.* scolorire, sbiadire (di pianta); fare intristire (anche *fig.*).

etiolation [,i:tiou'leiʃən], *s.* scolorimento (di pianta); intristimento (anche *fig.*).

etiquette [,eti'ket], *s.* **1.** etichetta, cerimoniale, protocollo **2.** regole, usi convenzionali ☆ *court* —, cerimoniale di corte.

etna ['etnə], *s.* fornellino a spirito.

Eton ['i:tn], *no.pr.* (*geog.*) Eton (piccola città nel Buckinghamshire) ‖ — (*College*), Collegio di Eton ☆ — *blue*, (color) azzurro pallido; — *coat* (o *jacket*), giacchetta nera a vita; — *collar*, ampio colletto inamidato; — *crop*, taglio di capelli alla maschietta.

Etonian [i(:)'tounjən], *s.* allievo del Collegio di Eton.

Etruria [i'truəriə], *no.pr.* (*geog. st.*) Etruria.

Etrurian [i'truəriən]. **Etruscan** [i'trʌskən], *ag.* etrusco ‖ *s.c.* etrusco, etrusca ‖ *s.* lingua etrusca.

Etta ['etə], *no.pr.f. dim.* di Henrietta.

etui, etwee [e'twi:], *s.* astuccio (per aghi, ecc.).

etymologer [eti'mɔlədʒə*]. *s.* etimologo.

etymologic(al) [,etimə'lɔdʒik(əl)], *ag.* etimologico.

etymologically [,etimə'lɔdʒikəli], *av.* etimologicamente.

etymologist [,eti'mɔlədʒist], *s.c.* etimologista.

to **etymologize** [,eti'mɔlədʒaiz], *v.t.i.* **1.** dare, cercare l'etimologia di (una parola) **2.** occuparsi di etimologia.

etymology [,eti'mɔlədʒi], *s.* etimologia.

etymon ['etimon], *s.* etimo, radice (di una parola).

Euboea [ju:'biə], *no.pr.* (*geog.*) Eubea.

eucalyptus [,ju:kə'liptəs], *s.* (*bot.*) eucalipto.

Eucharist ['ju:kərist], *s.* (*eccl.*) Eucarestia: *to receive the* —, ricevere l'Eucarestia.

eucharistic(al) [,ju:kə'ristik(əl)], *ag.* eucaristico.

euchologion [,ju:kou'loudʒiɔn], *s.* (*relig. ortodossa*) eucologio (libro di preghiere rituali).

euchre ['ju:kə*], *s.* giuoco di carte americano.

to **euchre**, *v.t.* superare (l'avversario) alle carte (anche *fig.*): *to* — *s.o.*, mettere qlcu. in imbarazzo.

Euclid ['ju:klid], *no.pr.m.* **1.** (*st. mat.*) Euclide **2.** (*fam.*) geometria.

eud(a)emonism [ju:'di:mənizəm], *s.* (*fil.*) eudemonismo.

eudiometer [,ju:di'ɔmitə*], *s.* (*fis.*) eudiometro.

eudiometry [,ju:di'ɔmitri], *s.* (*fis.*) eudiometria.

Eugene [ju:'ʒein], *no.pr.m.* Eugenio.

Eugenia [ju:'dʒi:njə], *no.pr.f.* Eugenia.

eugenic [ju:'dʒenik], *ag.* eugenico.

eugenically [ju:'dʒenikəli], *av.* eugenicamente.

eugenics [ju:'dʒeniks], *s.* eugenetica.

Eugenius [ju:'dʒi:njəs], *no.pr.m.* Eugenio.

euhemerism [ju:'hi:mərizəm], *s.* (*fil.*) evemerismo.

Eulalia [ju:'leiljə], *no.pr.f.* Eulalia.

eulogic [ju:'lɔdʒik], *ag.* elogiativo.

eulogically [ju:'lɔdʒikəli]. *av.* elogiativamente.

eulogist ['ju:lədʒist], *s.* elogiatore, panegirista.

eulogistic(al) [,ju:lə'dʒistik(əl)], *ag.* laudativo.

eulogistically [,ju:lə'dʒistikəli], *av.* elogiativamente, laudativamente.

eulogium [ju:'loudʒjəm], *s.* elogio, panegirico: *to pronounce an* — *on s.o.*, fare il panegirico, le lodi di qlcu.

to **eulogize** ['ju:lədʒaiz], *v.t.* elogiare, lodare; fare il panegirico di.

eulogy ['ju:lədʒi], *s.* elogio, panegirico.

Eumenides [ju:'menidi:z], *no.pr.f.pl.* (*mit.*) Eumenidi.

Eunice ['ju:nis], *no.pr.f.* Eunice.

eunuch ['ju:nək], *s.* eunuco.

eupepsia [ju:'pepsia], **eupepsy** [ju:'pepsi], *s.* (*med.*) eupepsia.

eupeptic [ju:'peptik], *ag.* (*med.*) eupeptico.

Euphemia [ju:'fi:mjə], *no.pr.f.* Eufemia.

euphemism ['ju:fimizəm], *s.* (*ret.*) eufemismo.

euphemistic [,ju:fi'mistik], *ag.* (*ret.*) eufemistico.

euphemistically [,ju:fi'mistikəli], *av.* (*ret.*) eufemisticamente.

to **euphemize** ['ju:fimaiz], *v.t.i.* (*ret.*) esprimere per mezzo di eufemismi; usare eufemismi.

euphonic [ju:'fɔnik], *ag.* eufonico, armonioso.

euphonically [ju:'fɔnikəli], *av.* eufonicamente.

euphonious [ju:'founjəs], *ag.* eufonico, armonioso.

euphoniously [ju:'founjəsli], *av.* eufonicamente.

euphonium [ju:'founjəm], *s.* (*mus.*) eufonio.

to **euphonize** ['ju:fənaiz], *v.t.* rendere eufonico.

euphony ['ju:fəni], *s.* eufonia: *for the sake of* —, per eufonia.

euphorbia [ju:'fɔ:biə], *s.* (*bot.*) euforbia.

euphorbium [ju:'fɔ:biəm], *s.* (*bot.*) euforbio.

euphory ['ju:fəri], *s.* euforia.

Euphrasia [ju:'freiziə], *no.pr.f.* Eufrasia.

euphrasy ['ju:frəsi], *s.* (*bot.*) eufrasia.

Euphrates [ju:'freiti:z], *no.pr.* (*geog.*) Eufrate.

Euphrosyne [ju:'frɔzini:], *no.pr.f.* (*mit.*) Eufrosine.

euphuism ['ju:fju(:)izəm], *s.* **1.** (*lett.*) eufuismo **2.** (*fam.*) preziosità, affettazione (dello stile).

euphuist ['ju:fju(:)ist], *s.c.* chi scrive in modo affettato, ricercato.

euphuistic [,ju:fju(:)'istik], *ag.* prezioso, affettato.

euphuistically [,ju:fju(:)'istikəli], *av.* in modo ricercato, affettato.

Eurafrican [juə'ræfrikən], *s.c.* euroafricano, euroafricana.

Eurasia [juə'reiʒə], *no.pr.* (*geog.*) Eurasia.

Eurasian [juə'reiʒən], *ag.* eurasiano, eurasiatico ‖ *s.c.* eurasiano, eurasiana.

eurhythmic [ju:'riðmik], *ag.* euritmico.

eurhythmics [ju:'riðmiks], *s.* euritmia.

Euripides [juə'ripidi:z], *no.pr.m.* (*st. lett.*) Euripide.

Europa [juə'roupə], *no.pr.f.* (*mit.*) Europa.

Europe ['juərəp], *no.pr.* (*geog.*) Europa.

European [,juərə'pi(:)ən], *ag.* europeo ‖ *s.c.* europeo, europea.

Europeanism [,juərə'pi(:)ənizəm], *s.* europeismo.

to **Europeanize** [,juərə'pi(:)ənaiz], *v.t.* europeizzare: *to become Europeanized*, europeizzarsi.

Eurovision ['juərou,viʒən], *s.* (*tv.*) eurovisione.

Eurus ['juərəs], *s.* Euro (vento).

Euryalus [juə'raiələs], *no.pr.m.* (*lett.*) Eurialo.

Eurydice [juə'ridisi(:)], *no.pr.f.* (*mit.*) Euridice.

Eurypylus [juə'ripiləs], *no.pr.m.* (*lett.*) Euripilo.

Eusebius [ju:'si:bjəs], *no.pr.m.* (*st. relig.*) Eusebio.

Eustace ['ju:stəs], *no.pr.m.* Eustachio.

Eustachian [ju:s'teiʃjən], *ag.* d'Eustachio ☆ — *tube*, (*anat.*) tromba d'Eustachio; — *valve*, (*anat.*) valvola d'Eustachio.

Eustachius [ju:s'teikjəs], *no.pr.m.* (*st. med.*) Eustachio.

Euterpe [ju:'tə:pi], *no.pr.f.* (*mit.*) Euterpe.

euthanasia [,ju:θə'neiʒə], *s.* eutanasia.

Eutropius [ju:'troupjəs], *no.pr.m.* (*st. lett.*) Eutropio.

Euxine ['ju:ksain], *no.pr.* (*geog. st.*) Eusino.

Eva ['i:və], *no.pr.f.* Eva.

evacuant [i'vækjuənt], *ag.s.* (*farm.*) purgante.

to **evacuate** [i'vækjueit], *v.t.* **1.** evacuare, sfollare; (*mil.*) evacuare, ritirare (truppe) **2.** (*fisiol.*) evacuare.

evacuation [i,vækju'eiʃən], *s.* **1.** evacuazione, sfollamento; (*mil.*) ritiro **2.** (*fisiol.*) evacuazione.

evacuative [i'vækjueitiv], *ag.* (*farm.*) evacuante.

evacuee [i,vækju(:)'i:], *s.* sfollato.

to **evade** [i'veid], *v.t.* **1.** evitare, schivare, eludere, sottrarsi a: *he evaded the question*, eluse la domanda; *to — paying taxes*, eludere il pagamento delle tasse **2.** sconcertare (di cose).

to **evaluate** [i'væljueit], *v.t.* valutare.

evaluation [i,vælju'eiʃən], *s.* valutazione, apprezzamento.

Evander [i'vændə*], *no.pr.m.* Evandro.

to **evanesce** [,i:və'nes], *v.i.* (*spec. fig.*) svanire, sparire.

evanescence [,i:və'nesns], *s.* evanescenza, sparizione graduale.

evanescent [,i:və'nesnt], *ag.* **1.** evanescente **2.** (*mat.*) effimero, infinitesimale.

evanescently [,i:və'nesntli], *av.* in modo evanescente.

evangel [i'vændʒel], *s.* (*arc.*) **1.** vangelo **2.** dottrina, principio.

evangelic [,i:væn'dʒelik], *ag.* (*eccl.*) evangelico, conforme al Vangelo.

evangelical [,i:væn'dʒelikəl], *ag.* (*eccl.*) **1.** *V.* **evangelic 2.** appartenente alla Chiesa Evangelica, Protestante ‖ *s.* (*eccl.*) evangelico, protestante.

Evangelicalism [,i:væn'dʒelikəlizəm], *s.* Evangelicalismo, dottrina della Chiesa Evangelica.

evangelically [,i:væn'dʒelikəli], *av.* evangelicamente.

Evangeline [i'vændʒili:n], *no.pr.f.* Evangelina.

evangelism [i'vændʒilizəm], *s.* predicazione del Vangelo.

evangelist [i'vændʒilist], *s.* evangelista.

evangelistic [i,vændʒi'listik], *ag.* di evangelista.

evangelization [i,vændʒilai'zeiʃən], *s.* evangelizzazione.

to **evangelize** [i'vændʒilaiz], *v.t.* evangelizzare.

evaporable [i'væpərəbl], *ag.* evaporabile.

to **evaporate** [i'væpəreit], *v.t.i.* **1.** (*fis.*) evaporare, fare evaporare **2.** volatilizzarsi, evaporare (di profumi, ecc.) **3.** (*fam. fig.*) sparire, volatilizzarsi, morire.

evaporation [i,væpə'reiʃən], *s.* evaporazione, volatilizzazione.

evaporative [i'væpəreitiv], *ag.* evaporativo.

evaporator [i'væpəreitə*], *s.* evaporatore ☆ *vacuum* —, evaporatore a vuoto.

evasion [i'veiʒən], *s.* **1.** evasione **2.** sotterfugio, scusa, pretesto, scappatoia : *without evasions*, senza pretesti.

evasive [i'veisiv], *ag.* evasivo: *an — answer*, una risposta evasiva.

evasively [i'veisivli], *av.* evasivamente.

evasiveness [i'veisivnis], *s.* ambiguità, incertezza.

Eve [i:v], *no.pr.f.* (*Bibbia*) Eva ‖ *a daughter of —*, una figlia di Eva.

eve, *s.* **1.** vigilia (di una festa, ecc.): *on the — of peace*, alla vigilia della pace; *Christmas —*, la vigilia di Natale **2.** (*arc.*) sera: *at —*, di sera.

evection [i'vekʃən], *s.* (*astr.*) evezione.

Evelina [,evi'li:nə], **Eveline, Evelyn** ['i:vlin], *no.pr.f.* Evelina.

even ['i:vən], *ag.* **1.** uguale, uniforme, piano, piatto; regolare (di superficie): *the road is —*, la strada è piana; *to make —*, appianare (una superficie) **2.** uguale, uniforme, costante, regolare: *— breathing*, respiro regolare; *an — temper*, un umore costante **3.** uguale, stesso, pari (di distanza, altezza, quantità, ecc.): *the cars are — in the race*, nella corsa le macchine sono in parità ‖ *— with*, a livello di **4.** pari, uguale, equo: *an — bargain*, un affare giusto; *an — contest*, una contesa ad armi pari; *an — odds*, uguali probabilità; *to be — with s.o.*, essere alla pari con qlcu.; *to get — with s.o.*, prendere la rivincita su qlcu. **5.** pari (di numero): *— and odd*, pari e dispari ☆ *-aged*, della stessa età; *-handed*, imparziale; *-minded*, equilibrato; *-numbered*, avente i numeri pari; *-tempered*, di umore costante.

even, *av.* **1.** (*con comp.*) ancora: *the book is — more interesting than I thought*, il libro è ancora più interessante di quanto pensassi; *that would be — worse*, quello sarebbe ancor peggio **2.** perfino; anche: *— a child could do so*, anche un bambino potrebbe farlo: *— now is time*, anche ora c'è (ancora) tempo; *he never — spoke*, egli non ha neanche parlato ‖ *— if* (o *— though*), anche se; *— so*, anche se è così; *if —*, persino se; *not —*, neppure **3.** proprio: *— as he spoke she yawned*, proprio mentre egli parlava ella sbadigliava **4.** ugualmente, allo stesso modo: *the two children improved —*, i due bambini miglioravano ugualmente.

to **even**, *v.t.* **1.** appianare, livellare **2.** uguagliare, rendere uguale **3.** *to — up*, compensare esattamente, bilanciare ‖ *to — up on s.o.*, (*amer.*) prendersi la rivincita su qlcu.

evenfall ['i:vənfɔ:l], *s.* (*poet.*) crepuscolo.

evening[1] ['i:vniŋ], *s.* **1.** sera: *in the —*, di sera; *to spend the — with s.o.*, passare la sera con qlcu. ‖ *last —*, ieri sera; *Sunday —*, domenica sera; *to-morrow —*, domani sera **2.** serata (festa): *to make an — of it*, (*fam.*) passare una serata piacevole **3.** *fig.* fine, declino (della vita) ☆ *— dress*, abito da sera; *— paper*, giornale della sera; *— star*, Venere, la stella della sera ‖ *good —!*, buona sera!; *musical —*, serata musicale.

evening[2] ['i:vniŋ], *s.* **1.** uguagliamento; livellamento **2.** confronto.

evenly ['i:vənli], *av.* **1.** in modo uguale **2.** regolarmente, uniformemente **3.** imparzialmente, equamente.

evenness ['i:vənnis], *s.* **1.** uguaglianza; regolarità (di movimento, ritmo); uniformità **2.** serenità, calma **3.** imparzialità.

evensong ['i:vənsɔŋ], *s.* (*eccl.*) vespro || *at* —, al vespro.

event [i'vent], *s.* **1.** caso, eventualità: *at all events,* in ogni caso; *at any* —, in qualsiasi caso; *fortuitous* —, caso fortuito; *in the* — *of his death, of his refusing,* nell'eventualità della sua morte, che rifiuti; *in that* —, in tal caso **2.** avvenimento: *in the natural course of events,* nel corso naturale degli eventi; *it was a great* —, fu un grande avvenimento **3.** (*spor.*) prova; risultato, riuscita, esito: *I have entered my name for all events,* mi sono iscritto a tutte le prove.

eventful [i'ventful], *ag.* ricco di avvenimenti; memorabile; movimentato.

eventfulness [i'ventfulnis], *s.* ricchezza di avvenimenti.

eventide ['i:vəntaid], *s.* (*poet.*) sera.

eventless [i'ventlis], *ag.* privo di eventi, di avvenimenti.

eventration [,i:ven'treiʃən], *s.* sventramento.

eventual [i'ventjuəl], *ag.* **1.** finale, definitivo, conclusivo **2.** eventuale.

eventuality [i,ventju'æliti], *s.* eventualità, evenienza.

eventually [i'ventjuəli], *av.* alla fine; finalmente: *he will* — *marry her,* egli alla fine la sposerà.

to eventuate [i'ventjueit], *v.i.* risultare, risolversi; (*amer.*) accadere: *to* — *well, ill,* risolversi bene, male.

ever ['evə*], *av.* **1.** mai: *do you* — *miss the train?,* non ti capita mai di perdere il treno?; *have you* — *been to England?,* sei mai stato in Inghilterra?; *nothing* — *happens here,* qui non accade mai nulla; *when* — *did you lose it?,* quando mai l'hai perso?; *where* — *can he be?,* dove mai può essere?; *who* — *did that?,* chi mai fece ciò? || — *and again* (o — *and anon*), di tanto in tanto || *hardly* (o *scarcely*) —, quasi mai || *if* —, se mai || *more, less than* —, più, meno che mai || *why* — *not?,* perchè mai no? **2. sempre:** — *after* (o — *since*), da allora in poi; *for* — (o *for* — *and* —o *for* — *and a day*), per sempre; *he has been ill* — *since he has been here,* da quando si trova qui è sempre malato || *Yours* — (o *Ever yours*), sempre tuo (chiusa di lettera) **3.** (*fam. intensivo*): — *so much easier,* infinitamente più facile; *thank you* — *so much,* grazie mille volte || *come as soon as* — *you can,* vieni al più presto || *how* — *did you manage to do that?,* come diavolo sei riuscito a fare questo?; *what* — *shall we do?,* che diavolo faremo?.

Everest (Mount) ['evərist], *no.pr.* (*geóg.*) (Monte) Everest.

everglade ['evəgleid], *s.* (*amer.*) largo tratto di terreno paludoso.

evergreen ['evəgri:n], *ag.* semperverde || — *topic,* argomento sempre d'attualità || *s.* (*bot.*) sempreverde.

everlasting [,evə'la:stiŋ], *ag.* **1.** eterno; immortale; continuo; incessante; perenne **2.** (*bot.*) semprevivo || *s.* eternità || *the Everlasting,* l'Eterno, Dio.

everlastingly [,evə'la:stiŋli], *av.* eternamente; incessantemente.

everlastingness [,evə'la:stiŋnis], *s.* eternità, perpetuità.

everliving [,evə'liviŋ], *ag.* immortale, eterno.

evermore ['evə'mɔ:*], *av.* sempre, perpetuamente: *for* —, per sempre.

eversion [i'və:ʃən], *s.* (*patol. fisiol.*) eversione, rovesciamento.

to evert [i'və:t], *v.t.* (*chir.*) rovesciare.

every ['evri], *ag.* **1.** ogni, ciascuno, tutti: — *day,* ogni giorno, tutti i giorni; — *man for himself,* ciascuno per sè; si salvi chi può; — *time,* ogni volta; *he has read* — *book in the house,* ha letto tutti i libri di casa; *I shall meet* — *wish of yours,* soddisferò ogni

vostro desiderio; *I understood* — *word he said,* compresi ogni parola che egli disse || — *bit,* tutto, del tutto; — *bit as much...,* proprio tanto quanto... || — *few hours,* ogni poche ore; — *three days* (o — *third day*), ogni tre giorni || — *now and again,* di quando in quando; *ad intervalli;* — *now and then,* di quando in quando **2.** — *one,* ciascuno, ciascuna; tutti: — *one of them,* ognuno di essi, nessuno escluso; *almost* — *one of the critics,* quasi tutti i critici; *he has eaten* — *one of them,* li ha mangiati tutti **3.** — *other,* alterno; tutti gli altri: — *other boy,* tutti gli altri ragazzi; — *other day,* a giorni alterni.

everybody ['evribɔdi], *pron. indef.* **ognuno, tutti;** — *else,* tutti gli altri; — *says the same,* tutti dicono la stessa cosa.

everyday ['evridei], *ag.* quotidiano, di tutti i giorni ☆ — *clothes,* gli abiti di tutti i giorni; — *Italian,* l'italiano parlato; — *life,* la vita quotidiana.

everyhow ['evrihau], *av.* (*fam.*) in tutti i modi.

everyman ['evrimæn], *s.* ogni uomo; ognuno.

everyone ['evriwʌn], *V.* **everybody.**

everything ['evriθiŋ], *pron. indef.* **1. ogni cosa, tutto:** *he knows* —, sa tutto **2. tutto, cosa di massima importanza:** *she is* — *to me,* ella è la mia vita.

everyway ['evriwei], *av.* in ogni modo.

everywhen ['evriwen], *av.* in ogni momento, sempre.

everywhere ['evriweə*], *av.* ovunque, in ogni luogo.

to evict [i(:)'vikt], *v.t.* **1.** (*dir.*) evincere **2.** espellere, sfrattare.

eviction [i(:)'vikʃən], *s.* **1.** (*dir.*) evizione **2.** sfratto.

evidence ['evidəns], *s.* **1.** evidenza: *to acknowledge the* — *of the facts,* riconoscere l'evidenza dei fatti; *to be in* —, essere in vista, in evidenza (di persone) **2.** segno, attestazione, prova: *external* —, prova estrinseca; *internal* —, prova intrinseca; *there are evidences of overheating,* ci sono segni di surriscaldamento; *to give* — *of intelligence,* dar prova di intelligenza || *the Evidences of Christianity,* le prove del cristianesimo **3.** (*dir.*) testimonianza, deposizione: *false* —, falsa testimonianza; *oral, written* —, deposizione orale, scritta; *to be called in* —, essere chiamati a testimoniare; *to bear* (o *to give*) —, testimoniare, deporre **4.** *pl.* (*dir.*) testimoni: — *for the prosecution, for the defence,* testimoni d'accusa, a difesa || *to turn State's* (o *King's* o *Queen's*) —, deporre contro, denunciare i propri complici.

to evidence, *v.t.i.* **1.** provare, dimostrare, manifestare: *everybody evidenced the truth of what he said,* tutti provarono la verità di ciò che egli disse **2.** (*dir.*) testimoniare, deporre: *her cousin will* — *against her,* suo cugino testimonierà contro di lei.

evident ['evidənt], *ag.* evidente, chiaro, manifesto.

evidential [,evi'denʃəl], *ag.* probativo, indicativo.

evidently ['evidəntli], *av.* evidentemente, ovviamente.

evil ['i:vl], *ag.* **1.** cattivo, malvagio, perverso, peccaminoso: *an* — *tongue,* una mala lingua; (o — *repute,* di cattiva reputazione || *the Evil One,* il maligno, il demonio **2.** sfortunato, disgraziato: — *days,* tempi brutti: *to fall on* — *days,* trovarsi in cattive acque, essere in difficoltà || *s.* **1.** male, peccato: *to do* —, peccare, fare del male; *to return good for* —, rendere bene per male; *to speak* — *of,* parlar male di **2.** disgrazia, danno || *of two evils one must choose the less, prov.* tra due mali scegli il minore.

evil, *av.* male, malamente; malvagiamente.

evil, (*nei composti*): — *-doer* (o *-worker*), malfattore; — *-eye,* malocchio; — *-faced,* dall'aspetto cattivo; — *-favoured,* di brutto aspetto: *the poor girl is* — *-favoured,* la povera ragazza è assai bruttina; — *-living,* di costumi dissoluti; — *-looking,* losco; — *-minded,* male intenzionato; — *-smelling,* nauseabondo; — *-speaking,* maldicenza; maldicente.

evilly ['i:vili], *av.* male, malvagiamente: *to live* —, vivere nel vizio.

evilness ['i:vlnis], *s.* cattiveria, malvagità.

to **evince** [i'vins], *v.t.* **1.** dimostrare, provare, indicare: *this evinces clearly that...*, ciò dimostra chiaramente che... **2.** mostrare, manifestare, annunziare; testimoniare: *to — curiosity*, manifestare curiosità **3.** sopraffare, superare, vincere.

evincible [i'vinsəbl], *ag.* dimostrabile, provabile.
evincive [i'vinsiv], *ag.* dimostrativo, probativo.
to **evirate** ['i:vireit], *v.t.* castrare, evirare; *(fig.)* effeminare.
eviration [,evi'reiʃən], *s.* evirazione.
to **eviscerate** [i'visəreit], *v.t.* **1.** sventrare **2.** *fig.* togliere il contenuto a; indebolire, smidollare: *to — a law*, privare una legge del suo contenuto.
evisceration [i,visə'reiʃən], *s.* sventramento.
to **evite** [i'vait], *v.t.* *(arc.)* evitare, sfuggire.
to **evocate** ['evoukeit], *v.t.* evocare.
evocation [,evou'keiʃən], *s.* evocazione.
evocative [i'vokətiv], *ag.* evocatore.
evocator ['evoukeitə*], *s.c.* evocatore, evocatrice.
evocatory [i'vokətəri], *ag.* evocativo.
to **evoke** [i'vouk], *v.t.* **1.** evocare (spiriti, ricordi, ecc.) **2.** *(dir.)* impugnare.
evolute ['i:vəlu:t], *ag.* *(bot.)* sviluppato ‖ *s.* *(geom.)* evoluta.
evolution [,i:və'lu:ʃən], *s.* **1.** evoluzione, sviluppo: *the — of Eastern countries*, l'evoluzione dei paesi orientali **2.** *(scient.)* evoluzione ‖ *Theory of Evolution*, teoria dell'Evoluzione **3.** *(geom.)* evoluzione (di curva) **4.** *(mar. mil.)* evoluzione, manovra **5.** *(chim.)* sviluppo (di gas) **6.** *(mat.)* estrazione di radice.
evolutional [,i:və'lu:ʃənl], **evolutionary** [,i:və'lu:ʃnəri], *ag.* di evoluzione.
evolutionism [,i:və'lu:ʃənizəm], *s.* evoluzionismo.
evolutionist [,i:və'lu:ʃənist], *s.c.* evoluzionista.
evolutionistic [,i:və,lu:ʃə'nistik], *ag.* evoluzionistico.
evolutive ['evəlu:tiv], *ag.* evolutivo.
to **evolve** [i'volv], *v.t.i.* **1.** evolvere, evolversi, svolgere, sviluppare, svilupparsi: *to — from one's inner consciousness*, creare dal proprio intimo; *to — the powers of the mind*, sviluppare le facoltà mentali **2.** *(chim.)* sprigionare, sviluppare (gas, calore, ecc.).
evolvement [i'volvmənt], *V.* **evolution.**
evolvent [i'volvənt], *ag.* *(geom. mat.)* evolvente.
to **evulgate** [i'vʌlgeit], *v.t.* *(rar.)* divulgare.
evulsion [i'vʌlʃən], *s.* evulsione, estirpazione, estrazione.
ewe [ju:], *s.* pecora (femmina) ☆ *— -cheese*, cacio pecorino; *— -lamb*, agnella: *my one — -lamb*, *(fam.)* tesorino mio; *— -milk*, latte di pecora; *— -neck*, collo sottile e incavato (di cavallo).
ewer ['ju(:)ə*], *s.* brocca.
ex [eks], *prep.* *(comm.)* da, fuori da ☆ *— dividend*, senza dividendo; *— ship*, (merce) sbarcata dalla nave; *— store*, in, dal magazzino; *— wharf* (o *— quay*), franco banchina.
ex-, *prefisso*, ex, già, un tempo ☆ *— -emperor*, ex imperatore; *— -Prime-Minister*, ex primo ministro; *— -service-man*, ex combattente.
to **exacerbate** [eks'æsə(:)beit], *v.t.* esacerbare, inasprire, irritare.
exacerbation [eks,æsə(:)'beiʃən], *s.* **1.** esacerbamento; inasprimento; esasperazione **2.** *(med.)* esacerbazione, peggioramento.
exact [ig'zækt], *ag.* **1.** esatto, giusto: *the — word*, la parola giusta ‖ *the — sciences*, le scienze esatte **2.** stretto, rigoroso **3.** esatto, puntuale: *to be — in one's payments*, essere puntuale nei propri pagamenti.
to **exact**, *v.t.* **1.** esigere; estorcere: *to — fees*, esigere un onorario; *to — obedience from* (o *of) one's children*, esigere l'obbedienza dai propri figli **2.** richiedere, rendere necessario: *work that exacts very careful attention*, lavoro che richiede una grande attenzione.
exactable [ig'zæktəbl], *ag.* esigibile.
exacting [ig'zæktiŋ], *ag.* **1.** esigente: *he is an —*

teacher, è un insegnante esigente **2.** impegnativo: *this is an — job*, questo è un lavoro impegnativo ☆ *non - —*, non impegnativo.
exaction [ig'zækʃən], *s.* **1.** esazione; estorsione **2.** *(dir.)* concussione.
exactitude [ig'zæktitju:d], *s.* esattezza, precisione: *— in doing sthg.*, precisione nel fare ql.co.
exactly [ig'zæktli], *av.* esattamente, precisamente; giustamente; proprio così.
exactness [ig'zæktnis], *s.* esattezza, precisione: *— of reasoning*, rigore di ragionamento; *to aim at —*, aspirare all'esattezza.
exactor [ig'zæktə*], *s.c.* chi esige, estorce ‖ *s.* esattore.
to **exaggerate** [ig'zædʒəreit], *v.t.i.* esagerare; ingrandire, ampliare.
exaggerated [ig'zædʒəreitid], *ag.* esagerato: *to have an — opinion of oneself*, presumere di sè.
exaggeration [ig,zædʒə'reiʃən], *s.* esagerazione: *to indulge in exaggerations*, essere inclini ad esagerare.
exaggerative [ig'zædʒərətiv], *ag.* tendente all'esagerazione.
exaggerator [ig'zædʒəreitə*], *s.c.* esageratore, esageratrice.
exaggeratory [ig'zædʒərətəri], *V.* **exaggerative.**
to **exalt** [ig'zo:lt], *v.t.* **1.** innalzare, elevare (di grado): *to — bribery to system*, erigere la corruzione a sistema **2.** esaltare, lodare, vantare ‖ *to — s.o. to the skies*, portare qlcu. ai sette cieli **3.** intensificare (colori, ecc.).
exaltation [,egzo:l'teiʃən], *s.* **1.** innalzamento, elevazione (di grado) **2.** esaltazione, eccitazione **3.** *(astr.)* esaltazione.
exalted [ig'zo:ltid], *ag.* **1.** elevato (di grado, posizione, ecc.) **2.** esaltato, eccitato.
exam [ig'zæm], *(fam. abbr.)* di **examination 2.**
examinable [ig'zæminəbl], *ag.* esaminabile.
examinant [ig'zæminənt], *s.c.* esaminatore, esaminatrice.
examinate [ig'zæminit], *s.* chi sostiene un esame.
examination [ig,zæmi'neiʃən], *s.* **1.** esame, ispezione, verifica: *the matter is under —*, si sta esaminando la questione; *on — the signature was found to be false*, all'esame si scoprì che la firma era falsa **2.** esame: *an — in history* (o *a history —)*, esame di storia; *to enter for an —*, iscriversi ad un esame; *to fail in an —*, esser rimandato ad un esame; *to pass* (o *to get through) one's examinations*, superare gli esami; *to sit for an —* (o *to take an —)*, dare, sostenere un esame **3.** *(dir.)* interrogatorio, esame (di testimoni); istruzione (di un processo) ☆ *— -paper*, prova scritta, questionario scritto ‖ *competitive —*, (esame di) concorso; *cross- —*, *(dir.)* controinterrogatorio; *entrance —*, esame di ammissione; *post-mortem —*, *(med. dir.)* autopsia; *State —*, esame di Stato.
examinator [ig'zæmi,neitə*], *s.c.* esaminatore, esaminatrice.
examinatorial [ig,zæminə'to:riəl], **examinatory** [ig'zæminətəri], *ag.* esaminativo.
to **examine** [ig'zæmin], *v.t.i.* **1.** esaminare, ispezionare, verificare **2.** esaminare: *to — a candidate in French*, esaminare un candidato in francese **3.** *(dir.)* istruire (un processo) **4.** informarsi ☆ *examining-magistrate*, giudice istruttore.
examinee [ig,zæmi'ni:], *s.c.* candidato, candidata.
examiner [ig'zæminə*], *s.c.* ispettore, ispettrice; verificatore, verificatrice; esaminatore, esaminatrice: *board of examiners*, commissione d'esame.
example [ig'za:mpl], *s.* **1.** esempio; esemplare; tipo; modello: *for —*, per esempio; *this grammar contains many examples*, questa grammatica contiene molti esempi; *this is a good — of Milton's dramatic poetry*, questo è un bell'esempio della poesia drammatica di Milton; *to follow s.o.'s —*, seguire l'esempio di qlcu.; *to set* (o *to give) a good — to*, dare il buon esempio a **2.** avvertimento, lezione: *to make an — of s.o.*, dare

una punizione esemplare a qlcu. **3.** precedente: *without* (o *beyond*) —, senza pari, senza precedenti.

exanimate [ig′zænimit], *ag.* esanime.

exarch [′eksɑːk], *s.* (*st.*) esarca.

exarchate [′eksɑːkeit], *s.* (*st.*) esarcato.

to **exasperate** [ig′zɑːspəreit], *v.t.* **1.** peggiorare, aggravare, inasprire: *to — a situation, disease,* aggravare una situazione, malattia **2.** esasperare, eccitare, irritare: *he was exasperated at* (o *by*) *the children's noise,* era irritato dal baccano dei bambini **3.** provocare; spingere, indurre: *to — s.o. to ill,* spingere qlcu. al male.

exasperatingly [ig′zɑːspəreitiŋli], *av.* in modo esasperante, irritante.

exasperation [ig‚zɑːspə′reiʃən], *s.* **1.** peggioramento, inasprimento, aggravamento (di un dolore, ecc.) **2.** esasperazione, irritazione (di persona).

to **excavate** [′ekskəveit], *v.t.i.* scavare, fare scavi (anche *archeol.*).

excavation [‚ekskə′veiʃən], *s.* **1.** scavo, lo scavare **2.** fossa, buca.

excavator [′ekskəveitə*], *s.* **1.** (operaio) scavatore **2.** (*mec.*) escavatore, escavatrice ☆ *shovel* —, escavatore a cucchiaia; *steam* —, escavatore a vapore.

to **exceed** [ik′siːd], *v.t.i.* **1.** eccedere; oltrepassare; superare: *this exceeds the limit,* questo passa il limite **2.** superare, essere superiore a: *the outcome exceeded all our hopes,* il risultato superò tutte le nostre speranze; *twenty exceeds twelve by eight,* il venti supera il dodici di otto **3.** eccedere nel mangiare.

exceeding [ik′siːdiŋ], *ag.* esagerato, eccessivo.

exceedingly [ik′siːdiŋli], *av.* estremamente; troppo: *I am — grateful to you,* ti sono estremamente grato; *she is — made up,* ella è troppo truccata.

to **excel** [ik′sel], *pass.p.p.* **excelled** [ik′seld], *v.t.i.* **1.** primeggiare, essere eccellente, eccellere: *to — as a writer,* eccellere come scrittore; *to — in an art, at a game,* eccellere in un'arte, in un giuoco; *to — in* (o *at*) *doing sthg.,* eccellere nel fare ql.co. **2.** superare, essere superiore a: *to — s.o. at* (o *in*) *tennis,* essere superiore a qlcu. nel tennis.

excellence [′eksələns], *s.* **1.** eccellenza, perfezione **2.** pregio, merito; superiorità.

excellency [′eksələnsi], *s.* **1.** (*titolo*) eccellenza: *Your, His Excellency,* Vostra, Sua Eccellenza **2.** *V.* **excellence**.

excellent [′eksələnt], *ag.* eccellente, ottimo.

excellently [′eksələntli], *av.* in modo eccellente.

excelsior [ek′selsiɔ:*], *s.* (*amer.*) trucioli per imballaggio.

excelsior, *inter.* in alto, più in alto.

to **except** [ik′sept], *prep.* eccetto, tranne, eccettuato, ad eccezione di; salvo, all'infuori di: *all failed — him,* tutti furono bocciati tranne lui ‖ *— for,* tranne per, fatta eccezione di; *— that,* eccetto che, salvo che; *— when,* tranne quando ‖ *cong.* (*arc.*) a meno che: *— he be born again,* a meno che non nasca di nuovo.

to **except,** *v.t.i.* **1.** eccettuare, escludere: *present company excepted,* esclusi i presenti **2.** obiettare: *to — against s.o., sthg.,* fare obiezioni a qlcu., ql.co.

excepting [ik′septiŋ], *prep.* eccetto, tranne (usato dopo *not, without, always*): *we all are fallible not — you,* tutti possiamo sbagliare, te compreso.

exception [ik′sepʃən], *s.* **1.** eccezione: *with the — of,* ad eccezione di; *without —,* senza alcuna eccezione; *the — proves the rule,* l'eccezione conferma la regola; *to be an — to a rule,* essere l'eccezione ad una regola; *to make an — to a rule,* fare un'eccezione ad una regola **2.** obiezione: *to take — to sthg.,* trovare a ridire su ql.co., obiettare a ql.co.

exceptionable [ik′sepʃnəbl], *ag.* criticabile.

exceptional [ik′sepʃənl], *ag.* eccezionale, straordinario, d'eccezione; insolito.

exceptionality [ik‚sepʃə′næliti], *s.* eccezionalità.

exceptionally [ik′sepʃnəli], *ag.* eccezionalmente, in via eccezionale; straordinariamente.

excerpt [′eksəːpt], *s.* citazione; brano scelto.

to **excerpt** [ek′səːpt], *v.t.* citare; scegliere (brani).

excerption [ek′səːpʃən], *s.* scelta; citazione di passi.

excess [ik′ses], *s.* **1.** eccesso, intemperanza: *in —,* in eccesso; *he drinks to —,* beve troppo; *it was considered an — of cruelty,* fu considerato un eccesso di crudeltà; *to carry to —,* portare all'eccesso; *to commit excesses,* commettere degli eccessi, gozzovigliare **2.** eccedenza, sovrappiù; soprattassa: *— of labour,* sovrabbondanza di mano d'opera ☆ *— fare,* (*ferr.*) differenza (per cambio di classe, ecc.), supplemento; *— luggage,* (*aer. ferr.*) bagaglio eccedente; *— profits duty,* tassa sui soprapprofitti (*p.e.* di guerra).

excessive [ik′sesiv], *ag.* eccessivo, esagerato; smoderato; estremo: *— rain,* pioggia torrenziale; *— smoker,* fumatore smoderato; *I found his enthusiasm —,* trovai eccessivo il suo entusiasmo.

excessively [ik′sesivli], *av.* eccessivamente, esageratamente; smoderatamente.

excessiveness [ik′sesivnis], *s.* eccessività, smoderatezza.

exchange [iks′tʃeindʒ], *s.* **1.** cambio; scambio; baratto: *to give in — for,* dare in cambio di ‖ *— is no robbery, prov.* uno scambio non è furto **2.** (*finanza*) cambio: *— on London,* cambio su Londra; *foreign —,* cambio estero; *fluctuations of —,* oscillazioni del cambio; *par of —,* parità di cambio; *rate of —,* tasso di cambio, cambio ‖ *bill of —,* cambiale, tratta **3.** borsa, mercato: *on —,* in borsa **4.** (*tel.*) centrale, centralino ☆ *— broker,* agente di cambio; *— control,* (*neol.*) controllo del cambio; *— list,* bollettino dei cambi; *— office,* ufficio di cambio ‖ *corn —,* mercato del grano; *private —,* (*tel.*) centralino telefonico privato; *stock- —,* (*comm.*) borsa valori; *telephone —,* (*tel.*) centrale telefonica, centralino telefonico; *wool —,* (*comm.*) borsa della lana.

to **exchange,** *v.t.i.* **1.** cambiare; scambiare; barattare, permutare: *the two men exchanged their hats,* i due uomini si scambiarono il cappello ‖ *to — blows,* venire alle mani; *to — compliments,* farsi dei complimenti; *to — greetings,* scambiare saluti **2.** cambiare (denaro) **3.** passare: *to — from one regiment into another,* passare da un reggimento a un altro.

exchangeability [iks‚tʃeindʒə′biliti], *s.* possibilità di cambio, di scambio.

exchangeable [iks′tʃeindʒəbl], *ag.* scambiabile.

exchanger [iks′tʃeindʒə*], *s.* **1.** chi cambia **2.** (*finanza*) cambiavalute.

exchequer [iks′tʃekə*], *s.* **1.** Tesoro, Scacchiere, Erario, Fisco ‖ *Chancellor of the Exchequer,* Cancelliere dello Scacchiere, Ministro delle Finanze (in Inghilterra) **2.** risorse, entrate (di uno Stato, di un privato): *my — is low,* le mie entrate sono basse ☆ *— bill,* buono del Tesoro.

excisable [ek′saizəbl], *ag.* soggetto a dazio interno; soggetto a tributi indiretti.

excise[1] [ek′saiz], *s.* imposte indirette; dazio di consumo ☆ *— duty,* imposta sul consumo; *— law,* (*amer.*) legge sulla vendita delle bevande alcooliche; *— tax,* imposta sulle entrate indirette.

to **excise**[1], *v.t.* tassare, imporre un'imposta su (un prodotto).

to **excise**[2], *v.t.* (*chir.*) tagliar via, recidere; estirpare.

exciseman [ek′saizmæn], *pl.* **excisemen** [ek′saizmen], *s.* funzionario dell'ufficio imposte; daziere.

excision [ek′siʒən], *s.* (*chir.*) taglio, recisione; estirpazione.

excitability [ik‚saitə′biliti], *s.* eccitabilità.

excitable [ik′saitəbl], *ag.* eccitabile, emozionabile; emotivo.

excitant [′eksitənt], *ag.s.* (*farm.*) eccitante, stimolante.

excitation [‚eksi′teiʃən], *s.* eccitazione (anche *elett. fisiol.*) ☆ *— coil,* (*elett.*) avvolgimento di eccitazione ‖ *impulse —,* (*elett.*) eccitazione ad impulsi; *shunt —,* (*elett.*) eccitazione in derivazione.

excitative [ek'saitətiv], *ag.* eccitativo.

excitatory [ek'saitətəri], *ag.* (*med.*) eccitatore.

to **excite** [ik'sait], *v.t.* **1.** provocare, sollevare, far nascere (rivolta, sentimento); suscitare (interesse): *to — s.o.'s curiosity*, provocare la curiosità di qlcu. **2.** eccitare; animare; stimolare; infiammare: *everybody was excited by the news of his arrival*, tutti erano eccitati dalla notizia del suo arrivo; *to — s.o. to (do) sthg.*, stimolare, spingere qlcu. a (fare) ql.co.

excited [ik'saitid], *ag.* eccitato; commosso, turbato: *to get —*, eccitarsi, emozionarsi, animarsi.

excitedly [ik'saitidli], *av.* con eccitazione.

excitement [ik'saitmənt], *s.* agitazione, eccitazione, orgasmo; esaltazione: *the — of departure*, l'eccitazione della partenza; *to cause great —*, provocare grande agitazione.

exciter [ik'saitə*], *s.* **1.** eccitatore, istigatore (di rivolta, ecc.) **2.** (*elett.*) eccitatore, dinamo eccitatrice **3.** (*med.*) eccitante, stimolante.

exciting [ik'saitiŋ], *ag.* eccitante, emozionante: *an — competition*, una gara emozionante.

excitor, *V.* **exciter.**

to **exclaim** [iks'kleim], *v.t.i.* **1.** esclamare, gridare **2.** *to — at* (o *against*) (*s.o.*, *sthg.*), inveire contro.

exclamation [,eksklə'meiʃən], *s.* esclamazione: *note* (o *point*) *of —*, punto esclamativo ☆ *— mark* (o *— point*), (*amer.*) punto esclamativo.

exclamative [eks'klæmətiv], *ag.* esclamativo.

exclamatively [eks'klæmətivli], *av.* esclamativamente.

exclamatorily [eks'klæmətərili], *av.* esclamativamente.

exclamatory [eks'klæmətəri], *ag.* esclamativo.

to **exclude** [iks'klu:d], *v.t.* escludere; interdire, bandire: *to — all possibility of doubt*, scartare, escludere ogni possibilità di dubbio; *to — a person from a country*, vietare ad una persona l'ingresso in un paese; *to — s.o. from the sacraments*, rifiutare a qlcu. i sacramenti.

exclusion [iks'klu:ʒən], *s.* esclusione.

exclusive [iks'klu:siv], *ag.* **1.** che mantiene le distanze: *that man is — in his manner*, quell'uomo tiene le distanze con il suo modo di fare **2.** chiuso, scelto (di circolo, scuola, ecc.): *— social circle*, ambiente sociale chiuso; *he belongs to the most — club*, egli appartiene al più scelto club **3.** esclusivo: *— models*, modelli esclusivi; *— rights*, diritti esclusivi; *to have the — rights of* (o *in*) *sthg.*, avere l'esclusiva di ql.co. ‖ *— of*, escluso, eccettuato, senza contare: *crew of sixty — of officers*, un equipaggio di sessanta uomini senza contare gli ufficiali **4.** solo, unico: *it has been his — occupation for two years*, è la sua sola occupazione da due anni ‖ *s.* esclusivo, intransigente ☆ *— film*, film in esclusiva; *— interview*, intervista in esclusiva.

exclusively [iks'klu:sivli], *av.* esclusivamente.

exclusiveness [iks'klu:sivnis], *s.* esclusività.

exclusivism [iks'klu:sivizəm], *s.* esclusivismo.

exclusivist [iks'klu:sivist], *s.c.* esclusivista.

exclusory [iks'klu:səri], *V.* **exclusive.**

to **excogitate** [eks'kodʒiteit], *v.t.* pensare, architettare, escogitare.

excogitation [eks,kodʒi'teiʃən], *s.* escogitazione.

excogitative [eks'kodʒiteitiv], *ag.* escogitativo.

excommunicable [,ekskə'mju:nikəbl], *ag.* scomunicabile.

excommunicate [,ekskə'mju:nikit], *ag.* scomunicato ‖ *s.c.* scomunicato, scomunicata.

to **excommunicate** [,ekskə'mju:nikeit], *v.t.* scomunicare.

excommunication ['ekskə,mju:ni'keiʃən], *s.* scomunica.

excommunicative [,ekskə'mju:nikeitiv], *ag.* di scomunica.

excommunicator [ekskə'mju:nikeitə*], *s.* scomunicatore.

excommunicatory [,ekskə'mju:nikətəri], *ag.* di scomunica.

to **excoriate** [eks'ko:rieit], *v.t.* escoriare, scorticare.

excoriation [eks,ko:ri'eiʃən], *s.* escoriazione, scorticatura.

excrement ['ekskrimənt], *s.* escremento.

excremental [,ekskri'mentl], **excrementitial** [,ekskrimen'tiʃəl], **excrementitious** [,ekskrimen'tiʃəs], *ag.* escrementizio, fecale.

excrescence [iks'kresns], *s.* **1.** protuberanza; escrescenza, tumore **2.** *fig.* superfluità.

excrescent [iks'kresnt], *ag.* **1.** escrescente **2.** *fig.* superfluo, inutile **3.** (*gram.*) epentetico.

excreta [eks'kri:tə], *s.pl.* escrementi.

to **excrete** [eks'kri:t], *v.t.* espellere, secernere.

excretion [eks'kri:ʃən], *s.* escrezione, secrezione.

excretive [eks'kri:tiv], **excretory** [eks'kri:təri], *ag.* escretivo, escretorio.

to **excruciate** [iks'kru:ʃieit], *v.t.* (*letter.*) torturare, tormentare.

excruciating [iks'kru:ʃieitiŋ], *ag.* tormentoso, lancinante, atroce, straziante.

excruciatingly [iks'kru:ʃieitiŋli], *av.* tormentosamente, atrocemente.

excruciation [iks,kru:ʃi'eiʃən], *s.* tortura, supplizio, tormento.

excubant ['ekskjubənt], *ag.* in guardia.

to **exculpate** ['ekskʌlpeit], *v.t.* giustificare, scolpare, discolpare, assolvere.

exculpation [,ekskʌl'peiʃən], *s.* giustificazione, discolpa.

exculpatory [eks'kʌlpətəri], *ag.* giustificativo, che discolpa.

excurrent [eks'kʌrənt], *ag.* **1.** defluente **2.** arterioso (di sangue) **3.** (*bot.*) sporgente.

to **excurse** [iks'kə:s], *v.i.* (*rar.*) **1.** *fig.* divagare, far digressioni **2.** fare un'escursione.

excursion [iks'kə:ʃən], *s.* **1.** escursione, gita: *to make* (o *to go on*) *an —*, fare una gita **2.** (*astr.*) digressione **3.** (*mil. arc.*) sortita ☆ *— ticket*, biglietto festivo; *— train*, treno speciale per escursionisti, treno festivo.

excursionist [iks'kə:ʃnist], *s.c.* escursionista, gitante, turista.

to **excursionize** [iks'kə:ʃnaiz], *v.i.* (*fam.*) fare escursioni.

excursive [eks'kə:siv], *ag.* vago, digressivo; errante.

excursively [eks'kə:sivli], *av.* divagando, sconnessamente; senza metodo.

excursiveness [eks'kə:sivnis], *s.* divagazione; sconnessione; vagabondaggio.

excursus [eks'kə:səs], *pl.* **excursuses** [eks'kə:səsiz], *s.* **1.** «excursus», dissertazione **2.** (*fam.*) digressione.

excusability [iks,kju:zə'biliti], *s.* scusabilità.

excusable [iks'kju:zəbl], *ag.* scusabile, perdonabile, compatibile.

excusableness [iks'kju:zəblnis], *s.* scusabilità.

excusably [iks'kju:zəbli], *av.* scusabilmente.

excusatory [iks'kju:zətəri], *ag.* scusante, giustificativo.

excuse [iks'kju:s], *s.* **1.** scusa, giustificazione: *there is no possible — for his behaviour*, il suo contegno non ammette scusa alcuna ‖ *in — of*, a scusa di; *without —*, senza scusa; *ignorance of the law is no —*, l'ignoranza della legge non scusa **2.** scusa, pretesto: *to find an —*, trovare una scusa, un pretesto; *to look for an —*, cercare un pretesto ‖ *by way of —*, per scusa, come scusa.

to **excuse** [iks'kju:z], *v.t.* **1.** scusare; giustificare; compatire; perdonare: *— my saying so*, scusa, scusi se dico questo; *may I be excused?*, posso uscire?; *nothing can — you*, niente può scusarti; *to — oneself for*, scusarsi per ‖ *— me*, scusi; permesso **2.** esentare, dispensare dal fare: *excused from duty*, (*mar. mil.*) esente dal servizio.

exeat ['eksiæt], *s.* permesso di assentarsi (alle università di Oxford e Cambridge, nei collegi, ecc.).

execrable ['eksikrəbl], *ag.* esecrabile, abominevole, detestabile.

execrably ['eksikrəbli], *av.* in modo esecrabile, abominevole, detestabile.

to **execrate** ['eksikreit], *v.t.i.* **1.** esecrare, detestare **2.** maledire; lanciare imprecazioni.

execration [,eksi'kreiʃən], *s.* **1.** esecrazione **2.** maledizione.

execrative ['eksikreitiv], *ag.* esecratorio.

execratively ['eksikreitivli], *av.* in modo esecratorio.

execratory ['eksikreitəri], *ag.* esecratorio.

executable ['eksikju:təbl], *ag.* eseguibile.

executant [ig'zekjutənt], *s.c.* esecutore, esecutrice (specialmente di musica).

to **execute** ['eksikju:t], *v.t.* **1.** eseguire (ordine, comando); mettere in esecuzione: *he executed the captain's orders*, eseguì gli ordini del capitano; *to — a change of front*, (*mil.*) eseguire un cambiamento di fronte **2.** (*dir.*) eseguire; convalidare, rendere valido: *to — a judgment*, mettere in esecuzione una sentenza **3.** (*comm.*) adempiere, eseguire, mandare ad effetto: *to — an order readily*, dare pronta esecuzione ad un ordine **4.** giustiziare (un condannato) **5.** creare, eseguire (secondo un piano artistico): *he executed a statue in marble*, scolpì una statua di marmo **6.** interpretare; recitare; suonare: *the part of Hamlet was badly executed*, la parte di Amleto fu interpretata male.

executer ['eksikju:tə*], *s.* (*rar.*) esecutore.

execution [,eksi'kju:ʃən], *s.* **1.** compimento, esecuzione (di ordine, comando, ecc.); attuazione: *the — of his plan was a failure*, l'attuazione del suo progetto fu un insuccesso; *to carry sthg. into —*, mettere in esecuzione ql.co.; *to put sthg. in —*, dar corso a ql.co. **2.** (*mus.*) esecuzione: *a wonderful — of Beethoven's Ninth Symphony*, una meravigliosa esecuzione della Nona Sinfonia di Beethoven **3.** distruzione, effetto distruttivo (anche *fig.*): *the bomb did great — among the invaders*, la bomba portò la distruzione tra gli invasori; *her smiles did great —*, (*fam.*) i suoi sorrisi fecero strage **4.** esecuzione capitale **5.** (*dir.*) convalidazione **6.** (*dir.*) sequestro.

executioner [,eksi'kju:ʃnə*], *s.* boia, carnefice.

executive [ig'zekjutiv], *ag.* esecutivo ☆ *— committee*, comitato esecutivo; *— order*, decreto legge; *— powers*, poteri esecutivi; *— president*, presidente effettivo.

executive, *s.* **1.** potere esecutivo (di governo); direzione (di associazione) **2.** (*comm.*) dirigente, funzionario, amministratore ☆ *sales —*, direttore delle vendite.

executor [ig'zekjutə*], *s.* **1.** esecutore **2.** (*dir.*) esecutore testamentario ☆ *literary —*, chi cura la pubblicazione di opere postume.

executorship [ig'zekjutəʃip], *s.* **1.** (*dir.*) esecuzione testamentaria **2.** compito, funzione di esecutore.

executory [ig'zekjutəri], *ag.* esecutivo.

executrix [eg'zekjutriks], *pl.* **executrices** [eg'zekjutrisi:z], *s.* **1.** esecutrice **2.** (*dir.*) esecutrice testamentaria.

exedra ['eksidrə], *pl.* **exedrae** ['eksidri:], *s.* (*arch.*) esedra.

exegesis [,eksi'dʒi:sis], *s.* esegesi.

exegete ['eksidʒi:t] *s.* esegeta.

exegetic(al) [,eksi'dʒetik(əl)], *ag.* esegetico.

exegetically [,eksi'dʒetikəli], *av.* esegeticamente, in modo esegetico.

exegetics [,eksi'dʒetiks], *s.* esegetica.

exemplar [ig'zemplə*], *s.* esemplare, modello.

exemplarily [ig'zempləʔili], *av.* esemplarmente, in modo esemplare.

exemplariness [ig'zemplərinis], **exemplarity** [,egzem-'plæriti], *s.* esemplarità, l'essere esemplare.

exemplary [ig'zempləri], *ag.* **1.** esemplare; che serve da modello: *— conduct*, condotta esemplare **2.** che serve da ammonimento: *— punishment*, castigo che serve da ammonimento.

exemplifiable [ig'zemplifaiəbl], *ag.* esemplificabile.

exemplification [ig,zemplifi'keiʃən], *s.* **1.** esemplificazione **2.** (*dir.*) copia autentica (di atto).

to **exemplify** [ig'zemplifai], *v.t.* **1.** esemplificare, illustrare con esempi; servire d'esempio a **2.** (*dir.*) fare una copia autentica di: *exemplified copy*, copia autentica.

exempt [ig'zempt], *ag.* esente, dispensato, esonerato: *— from taxes*, esente da tasse ‖ *s.* persona esente (*p.e.* da tasse).

to **exempt**, *v.t.* esentare, esonerare: *to — s.o. from doing sthg.*, dispensare ql.cu. dal fare ql.co.

exemption [ig'zempʃən], *s.* esenzione, esonero, dispensa.

to **exenterate** [eg'zentəreit], *v.t.* *fig.* sviscerare.

exenteration [eg,zentə'reiʃən], *s.* *fig.* svisceramento.

exequatur [,eksi'kweitə*], *s.* (*lat.*) (*dir.*) exequatur.

exequies ['eksikwiz], *s.pl.* esequie, funerale.

exercisable ['eksəsaizəbl], *ag.* esercitabile (di diritto, autorità).

exercise ['eksəsaiz], *s.* **1.** esercizio; uso (di facoltà, privilegio, ecc.): *the — of patience*, l'esercizio della pazienza **2.** esercizio fisico, moto: *to take —*, fare del moto **3.** (*scuola*) esercizio, esercitazione, compito **4.** (*relig.*) esercizio: *religious exercises*, esercizi spirituali **5.** (*mil.*) esercitazione: *military exercises*, esercitazioni militari; manovre **6.** *pl.* (*amer.*) cerimonie: *opening exercises*, cerimonie d'apertura ☆ *-book*, quaderno ‖ *out-door —*, esercizio all'aria aperta.

to **exercise**, *v.t.i.* **1.** esercitare, usare; mettere in pratica, praticare: *to — one's rights, patience*, esercitare i propri diritti, la pazienza **2.** esercitare, esercitarsi; allenare, allenarsi: *he exercised his sons in swimming*, esercitò, allenò i suoi figli nel nuoto; *to — oneself*, esercitarsi, fare del moto; *to — s.o. in doing sthg.*, esercitare ql.cu. a fare ql.co. **3.** preoccupare, tormentare: *to be exercised over sthg.*, essere preoccupato per ql.co.

exerciser ['eksəsaizə*], *s.* **1.** colui che esercita (un diritto, ecc.) **2.** chi fa dell'esercizio fisico **3.** attrezzo ginnico.

exercitation [eg,zə:si'teiʃən], *s.* **1.** esercizio, uso (di una facoltà, ecc.) **2.** (*letter.*) dissertazione critica, esercizio oratorio.

exergue [ek'sə:g], *s.* esergo.

to **exert** [ig'zə:t], *v.t.* esercitare, fare uso di, impiegare: *to — a powerful influence on s.o.*, esercitare una forte pressione su ql.cu. ‖ *to — oneself (to do sthg.)*, sforzarsi, tentare (di fare ql.co.).

exertion [ig'zə:ʃən], *s.* **1.** esercizio (di autorità); uso, impiego **2.** sforzo; tentativo.

exertive [ig'zə:tiv], *ag.* che tende, incita allo sforzo, all'azione.

exes ['eksiz], *s.pl.* (*abbr.* *fam.* di *expenses*) spese; indennità, rimborso.

exeunt ['eksiʌnt], *3ª persona pl. pres. indic.* del *v. lat. exire*, (*teat.*) escono (di scena): *— omnes*, escono tutti.

to **exfoliate** [eks'foulieit], *v.t.i.* sfogliare, sfogliarsi; sfaldare, sfaldarsi; squamare, squamarsi (di pelle, vernice, corteccia, ecc.).

exfoliation [eks,fouli'eiʃən], *s.* **1.** sfogliamento, sfaldatura **2.** (*patol.*) desquamazione.

exhalant [eks'heilənt], *ag.* esalante.

exhalation [,ekshə'leiʃən], *s.* **1.** esalazione; evaporazione; effluvio **2.** (*patol.*) trasudato.

to **exhale** [eks'heil], *v.t.i.* esalare; emettere; emanare; evaporare; (*patol.*) trasudare.

exhaust [ig'zɔ:st], *s.* **1.** (*mec.*) scarico, scappamento **2.** gas di scappamento **3.** (apparato) aspiratore ☆ *— cone*, (*mec.*) cono di scarico; *— fan*, aspiratore; *— -pipe*, tubo di scarico; *— port*, (*mec.*) luce di scarico; *— ring*, (*aer. mec.*) collettore di scarico; *— silencer*, silenziatore; *— -valve*, valvola di scarico.

to **exhaust**, *v.t.i.* **1.** aspirare (aria, gas, ecc.) **2.** esaurire (anche *fig.*); stancare; sfinire: *to — oneself*, esaurirsi **3.** vuotare, fare il vuoto in: *to — a well*, vuotare un pozzo **4.** scaricarsi (di gas, vapore, ecc.).

exhausted [ig'zɔ:stid], *ag.* **1.** aspirato **2.** esaurito; esausto; spossato **3.** vuotato d'aria.

exhauster [ig'zɔ:stə*], *s.* aspiratore; ventilatore di scarico.

exhaustibility [ig,zɔːsti′biliti], s. capacità di essere scaricato, aspirato.

exhaustible [ig′zɔːstəbl], ag. esauribile; aspirabile.

exhausting [ig′zɔːstiŋ], ag. che esaurisce, che stanca ‖ s. aspirazione; esaurimento ☆ — power (of a chimney), tiraggio (di un camino).

exhaustion [ig′zɔːstʃən], s. 1. esaurimento: (state of) —, spossatezza 2. (fis.) aspirazione.

exhaustive [ig′zɔːstiv], ag. 1. esauriente; completo: — enquiry, ricerca approfondita 2. spossante.

exhaustively [ig′zɔːstivli], av. in modo esauriente: to study a subject —, studiare a fondo un argomento.

exhaustiveness [ig′zɔːstivnis], s. capacità di esaurire.

exhedra, V. **exedra**.

to **exheredate** [eks′herideit], v.t. (rar.) diseredare.

exheredation [eks,heri′deiʃən], s. (rar.) diseredazione.

exhibit [ig′zibit], s. 1. oggetto, raccolta di oggetti esposti in una mostra 2. (dir.) documento, oggetto (prodotto in giudizio).

to **exhibit**, v.t. 1. esibire, mostrare, rivelare (qualità, ecc.); esporre (quadri, ecc.); mettere in mostra (merci, ecc.) 2. (dir.) esibire, produrre (documenti, ecc.) 3. (arc.) somministrare (medicine).

exhibition [,eksi′biʃən], s. 1. presentazione (di documenti, ecc.) 2. esposizione, mostra: international —, mostra, esposizione internazionale ‖ to make an — of oneself, (fam.) dare spettacolo di sè 3. borsa di studio, sussidio 4. somministrazione (di medicine) ☆ — room, salone d'esposizione.

exhibitioner [,eksi′biʃnə*], s.c. chi usufruisce di una borsa di studio.

exhibitionism [,eksi′biʃnizəm], s. esibizionismo.

exhibitionist [,eksi′biʃnist], s.c. esibizionista.

exhibitor [ig′zibitə*], s.c. 1. espositore, espositrice 2. esibitore, esibitrice.

exhilarant [ig′zilərənt], ag. esilarante, ameno ‖ s. eccitante.

to **exhilarate** [ig′ziləreit], v.t. rallegrare; esilarare; rianimare.

exhilarating [ig′ziləreitiŋ], ag. esilarante.

exhilaration [ig,zilə′reiʃən], s. ilarità, allegria.

exhilarative [ig′zilərətiv], ag. esilarante.

to **exhort** [ig′zɔːt], v.t. (IV) esortare, ammonire; raccomandare vivamente a: to — s.o. to do sthg., esortare qlcu. a fare ql.co.

exhortation [,egzɔː′teiʃən], s. esortazione.

exhortative [ig′zɔːtətiv], **exhortatory** [ig′zɔːtətəri], ag. esortativo.

exhumation [,ekshjuː′meiʃən], s. esumazione.

to **exhume** [eks′hjuːm], v.t. esumare.

exigence [′eksidʒəns], **exigency** [′eksidʒənsi], s. 1. esigenza, necessità, bisogno: this meets the exigencies of our time, questo sopperisce alle necessità del nostro tempo 2. situazione critica, crisi, emergenza: he was reduced to exigency, si trovò in una situazione critica.

exigent [′eksidʒənt], ag. 1. pressante, urgente 2. esigente: — of praise, che esige lodi.

exigible [′eksidʒibl], ag. esigibile.

exiguity [,eksi′gju(:)iti], s. esiguità; scarsità.

exiguous [eg′zigjuəs], ag. esiguo; scarso.

exiguousness [eg′zigjuəsnis], s. esiguità; scarsità.

exile [′eksail], s. esilio; bando (anche fig.): to condemn s.o. to —, condannare qlcu. all'esilio; to go into —, andare in esilio, esiliarsi; to live in —, vivere in esilio; to send s.o. into —, mandare qlcu. in esilio, esiliare qlcu.

exile, s.c. esule; esiliato, esiliata.

to **exile**, v.t. esiliare; mettere al bando; scacciare: exiled from his country, esiliato, scacciato dalla patria; he was exiled for life, fu esiliato a vita.

exilic [eg′zilik], ag. relativo all'esilio (specialmente degli ebrei a Babilonia).

exility [eg′ziliti], s. tenuità; esilità; pochezza.

to **exist** [ig′zist], v.i. 1. esistere; vivere 2. mantenersi in vita.

existence [ig′zistəns], s. 1. esistenza, qualità di es-

sere, di esistere: in —, esistente; to call into —, far nascere; to come into —, nascere 2. esistenza, vita: to lead a happy —, condurre un'esistenza felice 3. (fil.) entità.

existent [ig′zistənt], ag. 1. esistente 2. attuale.

existential [,egzis′tenʃəl], ag. esistenziale.

existentialism [,egzis′tenʃəlizəm], s. (st. fil.) esistenzialismo.

existentialist [,egzis′tenʃəlist], ag.s. (fil.) esistenzialista.

existing [ig′zistiŋ], ag. 1. esistente 2. attuale: under (o in) — circumstances, nelle circostanze attuali.

exit [′eksit], s. 1. uscita; (teat.) uscita (di scena) 2. fig. fine, morte: to make one's —, morire ☆ emergency —, uscita di sicurezza.

exit, 3ª persona sing. pres. indic. del v. lat. exire, (teat.) esce (di scena): — Hamlet, Amleto esce.

ex-libris [eks′laibris], s. (lat.) «ex libris».

exodus [′eksədəs], s. esodo.

ex officio [,eksə′fiʃiou], l.av. (lat.) d'ufficio, di diritto.

exogamous [ek′sɔgəməs], ag. esogamo.

exogenous [ek′sɔdʒinəs], ag. (geol.) esogeno.

exon [′eksɔn], s. (st. inglese) ufficiale della Guardia del Re.

to **exonerate** [ig′zɔnəreit], v.t. 1. esonerare, dispensare 2. giustificare; discolpare; assolvere: they exonerated him from blame, lo assolsero da ogni biasimo.

exoneration [ig,zɔnə′reiʃən], s. 1. dispensa, esonero 2. giustificazione; assoluzione.

exonerative [ig′zɔnərətiv], ag. 1. che esonera 2. che assolve.

exophthalmos [,eksɔf′θælməs], **exophthalmus** [,eksɔf′θælməs], s. (patol.) esoftalmo.

exorable [′eksərəbl], ag. (rar.) esorabile.

exorableness [′eksərəblnis], s. (rar.) arrendevolezza alle preghiere.

exorbitance [ig′zɔːbitəns], s. esorbitanza, esagerazione, eccesso.

exorbitant [ig′zɔːbitənt], ag. esorbitante, eccessivo, esagerato.

exorbitantly [ig′zɔːbitəntli], av. in modo esorbitante, eccessivo; fuori misura.

to **exorbitate** [ig′zɔːbiteit], v.i. (arc.) esorbitare.

to **exorcise** [′eksɔːsaiz], v.t. esorcizzare; liberare dagli spiriti maligni.

exorciser [′eksɔːsaizə*], s.c. esorcista.

exorcism [′eksɔːsizəm], s. esorcismo.

exorcist [′eksɔːsist], s.c. esorcista.

exordial [ek′sɔːdjəl], ag. introduttivo, d'esordio.

exordium [ek′sɔːdjəm], pl. **exordia** [ek′sɔːdjə], **exordiums** [ek′sɔːdjəmz], s. esordio, prologo.

exosmose [′eksɔzmous], **exosmosis** [,eksɔz′mousis], s. (fis.) esosmosi.

exostosis [,eksɔs′tousis], s. (patol.) esostosi.

exoteric [,eksou′terik], ag. 1. (fil.) essoterico 2. popolare; comune: — opinion is that he will resign, è opinione comune che egli darà le dimissioni.

exotic [eg′zɔtik], ag. esotico ‖ s. pianta esotica.

exoticism [eg′zɔtisizəm], s. esotismo.

to **expand** [iks′pænd], v.t.i. 1. espandere, espandersi (di gas, ecc.); dilatare, dilatarsi (di metalli, ecc.); gonfiarsi; allargare, allargarsi; estendere, estendersi 2. fig. espandere, espandersi; allargare, allargarsi: trade expands, il commercio si estende; to — the minds of people, allargare la mente della gente 3. schiudere, schiudersi, aprirsi: the flower expanded, il fiore si schiuse 4. (fam.) divenire espansivo.

expander [iks′pændə*], s. (mec.) espansore, attrezzo per allargare; mandrino.

expanse [iks′pæns], s. spazio; distesa, estensione: the — of his brow, la spaziosità della sua fronte; the broad — of the ocean, l'ampia distesa dell'oceano ‖ the —, il firmamento.

expansibility [iks,pænsə′biliti], s. espansibilità; dilatabilità.

expansible [iks'pænsəbl], *ag.* estensibile; dilatabile; allargabile.

expansion [iks'pænʃən], *s.* **1.** espansione (di gas); allargamento; estensione; dilatazione (di metalli) **2.** (*comm.*) espansione, sviluppo **3.** (*alg.*) sviluppo (di equazione, di espressione) **4.** fioritura, sboccio ☆ — *joint,* (*mec.*) giunto di dilatazione ‖ *currency* —, (*econ.*) aumento della circolazione monetaria.

expansionism [iks'pænʃənizəm], *s.* (*pol.*) espansionismo.

expansionist [iks'pænʃənist], *s.* (*pol.*) espansionista.

expansive [iks'pænsiv], *ag.* **1.** espansivo; dilatabile; allargabile **2.** espansivo; esuberante (di persona) **3.** esteso, ampio.

expansively [iks'pænsivli], *av.* **1.** con espansione **2.** in modo espansivo **3.** estesamente, ampiamente.

expansiveness [iks'pænsivnis], *s.* **1.** espansione (di gas, ecc.) **2.** effusione.

ex parte ['eks'pɑ:ti], *ag.* (*lat.*) (*dir.*) unilaterale.

to expatiate [eks'peiʃieit], *v.i.* **1.** (*gener. fig.*) errare, vagabondare **2.** parlare, scrivere diffusamente.

expatiation [eks,peiʃi'eiʃən], *s.* **1.** dissertazione, lungo discorso **2.** prolissità.

expatiative [eks'peiʃjətiv], (*rar.*) per **expansive**.

expatiatory [eks'peiʃjətəri], *ag.* **1.** diffuso **2.** prolisso.

to expatriate [eks'pætrieit], *v.t.* spatriare, bandire, esiliare: *to* — *oneself,* espatriare, esulare; rinunciare alla propria nazionalità.

expatriation [eks,pætri'eiʃən], *s.* **1.** lo scacciare dalla patria; spatriamento **2.** espatrio.

to expect [iks'pekt], *v.t.* **1.** aspettare, aspettarsi; attendere: *I am waiting for the postman because I am expecting a letter from my husband,* aspetto il postino perchè attendo una lettera da mio marito; *I — he will write,* mi aspetto che scriverà; *I expected he would write,* mi aspettavo che scrivesse; *I expected you to lunch yesterday,* ti aspettavo ieri a colazione; *she is expecting a baby,* attende un bambino; *you are expected,* ti si attende (con ansia) ‖ *to — the worst,* aspettarsi il peggio **2.** (IV) aspettarsi, esigere, pretendere: *I — him to pay his debts at once,* esigo che egli paghi subito i suoi debiti; *I — them to do their duty,* esigo che essi facciano il loro dovere; *what do you —me to do?,* cosa pretendi che io faccia? **3.** aspettare, pensare, credere, supporre; sperare: *he is expected to come soon,* si pensa venga presto; *I — (so),* lo credo bene; *I — he has paid,* suppongo abbia pagato; *"Who has eaten all the cake?",* *"Oh, I — it was Tom",* «Chi ha mangiato tutta la torta?», «Oh, suppongo sia stato Tom».

expectable [iks'pektəbl], *ag.* prevedibile.

expectance [iks'pektəns], **expectancy** [iks'pektənsi], *s.* aspettativa, attesa; aspettazione.

expectant [iks'pektənt], *ag.* in attesa ‖ *s.* **1.** chi attende **2.** candidato ☆ — *mother,* donna gravida, incinta.

expectantly [iks'pektəntli], *av.* in attesa.

expectation [,ekspek'teiʃən], *s.* **1.** attesa, aspettativa; prospettiva: *beyond* —, al di là di ogni aspettativa; *in — of,* in attesa di; *to answer* (o *to come up to* o *to meet*) *one's expectations,* rispondere all'aspettativa; *to fall short of one's expectations,* non corrispondere all'aspettativa **2.** *pl.* speranze: *he disappointed her expectations,* egli deluse le sue speranze **3.** (*dir.*) prospettiva di eredità: *he has great expectations from his uncle,* ha grandi probabilità di ereditare dallo zio **4.** probabilità (di un avvenimento): — *of life,* probabilità di vita.

expectative [iks'pektətiv], *ag.* **1.** che forma oggetto di attesa **2.** (*dir.*) riversibile.

expecter [iks'pektə*], *s.* chi aspetta.

expectorant [eks'pektərənt], *ag.s.* (*farm.*) espettorante.

to expectorate [eks'pektəreit], *v.t.* espettorare.

expectoration [eks,pektə'reiʃən], *s.* espettorazione.

expedience [iks'pi:djəns], **expediency** [iks'pi:djənsi], *s.* **1.** convenienza; opportunità; vantaggio; utilità **2.** opportunismo.

expedient [iks'pi:djənt], *ag.* conveniente, vantaggioso, utile, opportuno ‖ *s.* espediente, ripiego; accorgimento, mezzo, invenzione: *to resort to expedients,* ricorrere ad espedienti.

expediently [iks'pi:djəntli] *av.* vantaggiosamente; utilmente.

to expedite ['ekspidait], *v.t.* **1.** accelerare; sbrigare; facilitare **2.** compiere con sollecitudine; (*comm.*) sollecitare.

expedition [,ekspi'diʃən], *s.* **1.** (*mil.*) spedizione, impresa: *to organize an* —, organizzare una spedizione **2.** prontezza, celerità; diligenza, sollecitudine: *to use* — *in doing sthg.,* fare ql.co. con prontezza, diligentemente.

expeditionary [,ekspi'diʃənəri], *ag.* (*mil.*) di spedizione ‖ *British Expeditionary Force* (*B.E.F.*), Corpo di Spedizione Britannico.

expeditionist [,ekspi'diʃənist], *s.* chi partecipa a una spedizione.

expeditious [,ekspi'diʃəs], *ag.* rapido, svelto, pronto, sollecito.

expeditiously [,ekspi'diʃəsli], *av.* rapidamente, prontamente, sollecitamente.

expeditiousness [,ekspi'diʃəsnis], *s.* prontezza, rapidità, celerità.

to expel [iks'pel], *pass.p.p.* **expelled** [iks'peld], *v.t.* espellere, cacciare, bandire: *they were expelled from the school,* furono espulsi dalla scuola.

expellent [iks'pelənt], *ag.* espellente.

expeller [iks'pelə*], *s.* (*mec.*) espulsore, estrattore.

to expend [iks'pend], *v.t.* **1.** spendere, impiegare, usare: *to* — *care in doing sthg.,* far ql.co. con la massima cura; *to* — *money on sthg.,* spendere denaro per ql.co.; *to — on doing sthg.,* spendere denaro per ql.co., per fare ql.co. **2.** consumare, esaurire: *to* — *energy on a work,* consumare le proprie energie, impegnarsi in un lavoro.

expendable [iks'pendəbl], *ag.* **1.** spendibile, usabile, consumabile **2.** (*mil.*) da abbandonarsi (in caso di necessità).

expendables [iks'pendəblz], *s.pl.* (*mil.*) materiale da abbandonarsi se necessario.

expenditure [iks'penditʃə*], *s.* **1.** dispendio, consumo **2.** spesa, somma spesa, sborso, uscita.

expense [iks'pens], *s.* **1.** spesa, sborso; (*comm.*) uscita: *I published it at my own* —, lo pubblicai a mie spese; *to put s.o. to* —, essere di onere, causare spese a qlcu.; *free of* —, gratis ‖ *they all laugh at his* —, ridono tutti alle sue spalle **2.** *fig.* sacrificio, prezzo: *at the* — *of his life,* a prezzo della vita **3.** *pl.* spese; indennità, rimborso ☆ *entertainment expenses,* spese di rappresentanza; *incidental expenses,* spese casuali; *overhead* (o *working*) *expenses,* spese generali; *travelling expenses,* indennità di viaggio.

expensive [iks'pensiv], *ag.* costoso, caro, dispendioso: *travelling is* —, i viaggi costano.

expensively [iks'pensivli], *av.* dispendiosamente, costosamente, con grande spesa.

expensiveness [iks'pensivnis], *s.* prezzo elevato, alto costo.

experience [iks'piəriəns], *s.* **1.** esperienza; pratica: *from* —, per esperienza; *practical* —, pratica; *has he had any previous* —?, ha mai lavorato in questo campo?; *to profit by* —, trar profitto dall'esperienza **2.** esperienza, incidente, avvenimento, avventura: *an unpleasant* —, una esperienza spiacevole; *he had interesting experiences in Africa,* ebbe interessanti avventure in Africa.

to experience, *v.t.* esperimentare, fare l'esperienza di; provare: *to* — *hard times,* attraversare tempi difficili, dure prove.

experienced [iks'piəriənst], *ag.* pratico, esperto, abile: *to be* — *in sthg.,* essere esperto di ql.co.

experienceless [iks'piəriənslis], *ag.* inesperto.

experiential [iks,piəri'enʃəl], *ag.* basato sull'esperienza, empirico.

experientialism [iks,piəri'enfəlizəm], *s.* sperimentalismo.

experientialist [iks,piəri'enfəlist], *s.c.* esperimentatore, esperimentatrice.

experiment [iks'perimənt], *s.* esperimento, prova: *by way of* —, a titolo di prova; *to make an* — *in chemistry*, fare un esperimento chimico.

to **experiment** [iks'periment], *v.t.i.* sperimentare, sottoporre a esperimento, provare: *to* — *on dogs*, far prove, esperimenti sui cani; *to* — *with new methods of teaching*, sperimentare nuovi metodi di insegnamento.

experimental [eks,peri'mentl], *ag.* sperimentale: — *farm*, fattoria sperimentale; — *target*, bersaglio sperimentale.

experimentalism [eks,peri'mentəlizəm], *s.* sperimentalismo.

experimentalist [eks,peri'mentəlist], *s.c.* sperimentalista.

to **experimentalize** [eks,peri'mentəlaiz], *v.i.* sperimentare, provare.

experimentally [eks,peri'mentəli], *av.* sperimentalmente, per esperienza.

experimentation [eks,perimen'teifən], *s.* lo sperimentare.

experimenter [eks'perimentə*], *s.c.* sperimentatore, sperimentatrice.

expert ['ekspə:t], *ag.* esperto, abile, competente || *s.* esperto, perito, competente, tecnico, specialista: *he is an* — *at such work*, egli è un vero tecnico di tale lavoro; *to pose as an* —, farsi passare per esperto ☆ *industrial* —, perito industriale.

expertise [,ekspə:'ti:z], *s.* abilità; conoscenza di esperti: *to develop* — *in*, impratichirsi in.

expertly ['ekspə:tli], *av.* abilmente, con perizia.

expertness ['ekspə:tnis], *s.* perizia, abilità, destrezza.

expiable ['ekspiəbl], *ag.* espiabile.

to **expiate** ['ekspieit], *v.t.* espiare.

expiation [,ekspi'eifən], *s.* espiazione: *in* — *of his crime*, per espiare il suo delitto.

expiator ['ekspieitə*], *s.c.* espiatore, espiatrice.

expiatory ['ekspiətəri], *ag.* espiatorio: — *of a sin*, che serve ad espiare un peccato.

expiration [,ekspaiə'reifən], *s.* **1.** fine, scadenza, termine: *date of* —, termine di scadenza **2.** (*fisiol. bot.*) espirazione.

expiratory [iks'paiərətəri], *ag.* espiratorio.

to **expire** [iks'paiə*], *v.t.i.* **1.** finire, scadere: *expired bill*, (*comm.*) cambiale scaduta; *the validity of this passport expires on the 15th of December*, questo passaporto scade il 15 dicembre **2.** spirare, morire; (*fam.*) svanire (della speranza): *he expired during the night*, è spirato durante la notte **3.** (*fisiol. bot.*) esalare, espirare: *we* — *the air from our lungs*, noi espiriamo l'aria dai polmoni.

expirer [iks'paiərə*], *s.c.* **1.** chi espira **2.** chi spira.

expiring [iks'paiəriŋ], *ag.* **1.** che scade, che cessa **2.** spirante, morente.

expiry [iks'paiəri], *s.* fine, cessazione, termine, scadenza.

to **expiscate** [eks'piskeit], *v.t.* **1.** (*scoz.*) ripescare **2.** *fig.* scoprire mediante esami minuziosi.

to **explain** [iks'plein], *v.t.i.* **1.** spiegare, dare una spiegazione, chiarire: *this will* — *to your mother*, questo sarà una spiegazione per tua madre; *will you please* — *this rule to me?*, mi spieghi, per piacere, questa regola? **2.** giustificarsi, spiegarsi: *please* — *yourself*, ti prego di giustificarti, spiegarti **3.** *to* — **away**, dar ragione di: *will you* — *away such an act?*, vuoi darmi ragione di un tale atto?

explainable [iks'pleinəbl], *ag.* spiegabile, giustificabile.

explainer [iks'pleinə*], *s.c.* chi spiega.

explanation [,eksplə'neifən], *s.* **1.** spiegazione, schiarimento, delucidazione: *to come to an* — *with s.o. about*

sthg., spiegarsi con qlcu. circa ql.co. **2.** giustificazione: *to give an* — *of sthg.*, fornire una giustificazione di ql.co.

explanatorily [iks'plænətərili], *av.* esplicativamente.

explanatory [iks'plænətəri], *ag.* esplicativo, chiarificatore.

expletive [eks'pli:tiv], *ag.* (*gram.*) espletivo, pleonastico || *s.* **1.** (*gram.*) particella espletiva **2.** (*fam.*) bestemmia.

expletory ['eksplitəri], *ag.* (*gram.*) espletivo.

explicable ['eksplikəbl], *ag.* spiegabile.

to **explicate** ['eksplikeit], *v.t.* **1.** (*log.*) sviluppare (principio, idea, ecc.) **2.** (*arc.*) spiegare.

explication [,ekspli'keifən], *s.* (*log.*) spiegazione, sviluppo, interpretazione (di principio, idea, ecc.).

explicative [eks'plikətiv], **explicatory** [eks'plikətəri], *ag.* esplicativo.

explicit [iks'plisit], *ag.* esplicito; categorico; chiaro; preciso: *to be more* — *in one's statements*, essere più chiaro nelle proprie affermazioni ☆ — *function*, (*mat.*) funzione esplicita.

explicitly [iks'plisitli], *av.* esplicitamente; categoricamente; con precisione.

explicitness [iks'plisitnis], *s.* chiarezza; precisione.

to **explode** [iks'ploud], *v.t.i.* **1.** esplodere, far esplodere; saltare, far saltare; scoppiare (anche *fig.*): *his anger exploded*, ebbe un accesso di collera; *to* — *with laughter*, scoppiare dalle risa **2.** screditare; smontare, demolire: *to* — *a superstition*, demolire una superstizione ☆ *exploded view*, (*mec.*) quadro pezzi smontati.

exploit ['eksploit], *s.* gesta; impresa; azione eroica.

to **exploit** [iks'ploit], *v.t.i.* **1.** utilizzare; sfruttare: *to* — *a mine*, sfruttare una miniera; *to* — *water-power*, utilizzare la forza idrica **2.** approfittare di, sfruttare (una persona): *to* — *the working class*, sfruttare i lavoratori.

exploitable [iks'ploitəbl], *ag.* sfruttabile; utilizzabile.

exploitation [,eksploi'teifən], *s.* sfruttamento; utilizzazione; valorizzazione.

exploiter [iks'ploitə*], *s.c.* **1.** chi sfrutta, valorizza (invenzione, idea, ecc.) **2.** sfruttatore, sfruttatrice (di persone, ecc.).

exploration [,eksplə:'reifən], *s.* esplorazione (anche *med.*).

explorative [eks'plə:rətiv], *ag.* esplorativo.

exploratory [eks'plə:rətəri], *ag.* esploratorio; esplorativo.

to **explore** [iks'plə:*], *v.t.* esplorare, visitare (anche *med.*).

explorer [iks'plə:rə*], *s.c.* esploratore, esploratrice || *s.* strumento di ricerca; (*med.*) specillo.

explosion [iks'plouʒən], *s.* esplosione, scoppio (anche *fig.*) ☆ — *bomb*, bomba calorimetrica; — *engine*, (*mec.*) motore a scoppio.

explosive [iks'plousiv], *ag.* **1.** (*artigl.*) esplosivo **2.** (*fonet.*) esplosivo (di consonante) **3.** che causa uno scoppio (anche *fig.*) || *s.* **1.** (*artigl.*) esplosivo: *high* —, alto esplosivo **2.** (*fonet.*) (consonante) esplosiva **3.** bomba (anche *fig.*) ☆ — *oil*, nitroglicerina.

explosively [iks'plousivli], *av.* in modo esplosivo.

explosiveness [iks'plousivnis], *s.* esplosività; carattere esplosivo.

exponent [eks'pounənt], *ag.* che divulga; che spiega || *s.* **1.** divulgatore; esponente: *every theory has its own exponents*, ogni teoria ha i suoi divulgatori **2.** interprete (anche *mus.*) **3.** (*mat.*) esponente, indice.

exponential [,ekspou'nenfəl], *ag.* (*mat.*) esponenziale.

export ['ekspə:t], *s.* **1.** esportazione **2.** *pl.* merci di esportazione ☆ — *trade*, commercio di esportazione.

to **export** [eks'pə:t], *v.t.* esportare.

exportable [eks'pə:təbl], *ag.* esportabile.

exportation [,ekspə:'teifən], *s.* esportazione.

exporter [eks'pə:tə*], *s.c.* esportatore, esportatrice.

to **expose** [iks'pouz], *v.t.* **1.** esporre, abbandonare (ai pericoli); lasciare (all'aria): *to* — *a new-born child*, abbandonare un neonato; *to* — *oneself (to danger)*, esporsi (al pericolo) || *not to be exposed to the air*, non esporre all'aria **2.** esporre, presentare, esibire (merci, quadri, ecc.): *to — the Blessed Sacrament*, esporre il Santissimo; *to be exposed to view*, essere esposto alla vista di tutti **3.** svelare, palesare, smascherare: *to — a secret, a fraud*, svelare un segreto, smascherare un'impostura **4.** (*foto.*) esporre, impressionare.

exposé [eks'pouzei], *s.* esposto, resoconto (specialmente di fatti disonoranti); denuncia, smascheramento.

exposed [iks'pouzd], *ag.* **1.** esposto, abbandonato; a nudo, allo scoperto: *— to the weather*, esposto alle intemperie; *not — to the wind*, al riparo dal vento; *to be —*, (*mil.*) essere allo scoperto **2.** smascherato **3.** (*foto.*) impressionato: *— plate*, lastra impressionata ☆ *— child*, esposito; trovatello, fanciullo abbandonato.

exposer [iks'pouzə*], *s.* espositore.

exposition [,ekspə'ziʃən], *s.* **1.** spiegazione, interpretazione, commento (di opera letteraria, ecc.) **2.** mostra, esposizione **3.** esposizione, abbandono (di fanciullo) **4.** esposizione (ai pericoli).

expositive [eks'pozitiv], *ag.* espositivo; descrittivo.

expositor [eks'pozitə*], *s.* commentatore, espositore.

to expostulate [iks'postjuleit], *v.i.* fare rimostranze; lagnarsi (in termini amichevoli): *to — with s.o. on* (o *about*) *sthg., for doing sthg.*, far rimostranze a qlcu. in merito a ql.co., per aver fatto ql.co.

expostulation [iks,postju'leiʃən], *s.* rimostranza, lagnanza.

expostulative [iks'postjulətiv], **expostulatory** [iks-'postjulətəri], *ag.* contenente rimostranze, lagnanze (di lettera, discorso).

exposure [iks'pouʒə*], *s.* **1.** esposizione (al freddo, al caldo, ai pericoli, ecc.): *her face was tanned from — to the sun*, aveva il viso abbronzato per essere rimasta al sole; *to die of —*, morire per assideramento **2.** abbandono (di neonato) **3.** mostra, esposizione (di merci, ecc.) **4.** smascheramento, denuncia, rivelazione (di delitto, menzogna, ecc.): *to threaten s.o. with —*, minacciare qlcu. di scandalo **5.** orientamento, esposizione: *house with southerly —*, casa esposta a sud **6.** (*foto.*) esposizione; tempo di esposizione, di posa ☆ *— meter*, (*foto.*) esposimetro ‖ *brief —*, (*foto.*) posa breve; *indecent —*, (*dir.*) oltraggio al pudore; *time- —*, (*foto.*) posa.

to expound [iks'paund], *v.t.* **1.** spiegare (teoria) **2.** interpretare (le Sacre Scritture).

expounder [iks'paundə*], *s.* commentatore.

express [iks'pres], *ag.* **1.** chiaro, preciso, esplicito: *it was his — wish*, era suo espresso desiderio **2.** espresso, diretto **3.** esatto, identico, fedele: *to be the — image of*, essere l'esatta immagine di ‖ *s.* **1.** espresso, corriere: *to send sthg. by —*, mandare ql.co. per espresso **2.** — (*train*), (treno) direttissimo ☆ *— agency* (o *— company*), (*amer.*) servizio corriere; *— delivery*, servizio postale espresso; *— letter*, espresso; *— wagon*, (*amer.*) furgone dei corrieri.

express, *av.* **1.** per espresso: *to send —*, mandare per espresso **2.** espressamente.

to express, *v.t.* **1.** esprimere, manifestare: *her smile expressed her joy*, il suo sorriso manifestò la sua gioia; *I cannot — myself in Italian*, non riesco a esprimermi in italiano; *to — one's heart-felt thanks to s.o.*, esprimere a qlcu. i propri sentiti ringraziamenti; *to — one's meaning in words*, esprimere a parole il proprio pensiero; *to — an opinion, a wish, surprise*, esprimere una opinione, un desiderio, sorpresa **2.** (*amer.*) mandare per corriere **3.** spremere: *to — juice out of a fruit*, spremere succo da un frutto.

expressible [iks'presəbl], *ag.* esprimibile.

expression [iks'preʃən], *s.* **1.** espressione, manifestazione: *beyond* (o *past*) *—*, impossibile ad esprimersi, inesprimibile; *to give — to one's feelings, will*, esprimere, manifestare i propri sentimenti, la propria volontà **2.** espressione (del viso, voce, ecc.): *a strange — on his face*, una strana espressione sul suo viso; *to read with —*, leggere con sentimento; *to sing with —*, can-

tare con espressione **3.** espressione, locuzione: *this — is not used in good English*, questa locuzione non si usa in buon inglese **4.** lo spremere (succo da frutto) **5.** (*alg.*) espressione.

expressional [iks'preʃənl], *ag.* relativo all'espressione.

expressionism [iks'preʃnizəm], *s.* (*st. art.*) espressionismo.

expressionist [iks'preʃnist], *s.* (*art.*) espressionista.

expressionless [iks'preʃənlis], *ag.* senza espressione, inespressivo; impassibile (di viso).

expressive [iks'presiv], *ag.* espressivo, significativo: *to give s.o. an — look*, rivolgere uno sguardo significativo a qlcu.

expressively [iks'presivli], *av.* espressivamente: *to look at s.o. —*, guardare qlcu. in modo espressivo.

expressiveness [iks'presivnis], *s.* forza, efficacia espressiva.

expressly [iks'presli], *av.* espressamente, chiaramente, apposta, a bella posta; esplicitamente.

expressman [iks'presmæn], *pl.* **expressmen** [iks'presmen], *s.* (*spec. amer.*) corriere, messo addetto al servizio corriere.

to expropriate [eks'prouprieit], *v.t.* espropriare: *to — s.o. from sthg.*, privare qlcu. di ql.co.

expropriation [eks,proupri'eiʃən], *s.* espropriazione.

to expugn [eks'pju:n], *v.t.* (*arc.*) espugnare.

expugnable [eks'pʌgnəbl], *ag.* (*arc.*) espugnabile.

expugnation [,ekspʌg'neiʃən], *s.* (*arc.*) espugnazione.

to expulse [eks'pʌls], *v.t.* (*rar.*) espellere.

expulsion [iks'pʌlʃən], *s.* espulsione.

expulsive [iks'pʌlsiv], *ag.* espulsivo (anche *fisiol.*).

expunction [iks'pʌŋkʃən], *s.* cancellatura.

to expunge [eks'pʌndʒ], *v.t.* espungere (passi da scritti, ecc.); togliere, cancellare, omettere.

to expurgate ['ekspə:geit], *v.t.* espurgare (uno scritto): *expurgated edition*, edizione espurgata.

expurgation [,ekspə:'geiʃən], *s.* espurgazione (di uno scritto).

expurgator [['ekspə:geitə*], *s.c.* espurgatore, espurgatrice (di scritti).

expurgatorial [eks,pə:gə'tɔ:riəl], **expurgatory** [eks-'pə:gətəri], *ag.* espurgatorio.

exquisite ['ekskwizit], *ag.* **1.** squisito: *— elegance*, eleganza squisita, raffinata **2.** acuto, vivo: *an — pain*, un dolore assai acuto; *— pleasure*, piacere vivo **3.** fine, sensibile: *to have an — ear for music*, avere un buon orecchio per la musica ‖ *s.* elegantone, bellimbusto.

exquisitely ['ekskwizitli], *av.* **1.** squisitamente **2.** acutamente, vivamente.

exquisiteness ['ekskwizitnis], *s.* **1.** squisitezza, finezza, ricercatezza **2.** intensità (di dolore, piacere, ecc.): *the — of his torments*, i suoi atroci tormenti **3.** finezza di udito.

exsanguine [eks'sæŋgwin], **exsanguinous** [eks'sæŋgwinəs], *ag.* esangue; anemico.

to exscind [ek'sind], *v.t.* recidere, tagliar via (anche *fig.*).

to exsect [ek'sekt], *v.t.* estirpare; recidere (anche *fig.*).

exsection [ek'sekʃən], *s.* estirpazione; recisione (anche *fig.*).

exsiccant [ek'sikənt], *ag.* essiccante.

to exsiccate ['eksikeit], *v.t.* essiccare; prosciugare; fare evaporare (una soluzione).

exsiccation [eksi'keiʃən], *s.* essiccazione; evaporazione (di una soluzione).

exsiccator ['eksikeitə*], *s.* (*chim.*) essiccatore.

extant [eks'tænt], *ag.* ancora esistente (di documenti, libri).

extemporaneous [eks,tempə'reinjəs], *ag.* improvvisato, estemporaneo.

extemporaneously [eks,tempə'reinjəsli], *av.* in modo improvvisato; estemporaneamente.

extemporaneousness [eks,tempə'reinjəsnis], *s.* estemporaneità.

extemporarily [iks'tempərərili], *av.* in modo improvviso; estemporaneamente.

extemporary [iks'tempərəri], *V.* **extemporaneous.**

extempore [eks'tempəri], *ag.* improvvisato: *to make an — speech*, fare un discorso improvvisato.

extempore, *av.* senza preparazione: *to speak —*, improvvisare un discorso.

extemporization [eks‚tcmpərai'zeiʃən], *s.* **1.** improvvisazione **2.** (*fam.*) improvvisata.

to **extemporize** [iks'tempəraiz], *v.t.i.* improvvisare; parlare estemporaneamente: *to — on the piano*, improvvisare al pianoforte.

extemporizer [iks'tempəraizə*], *s.c.* improvvisatore, improvvisatrice.

to **extend** [iks'tend], *v.t.i.* **1.** estendere, estendersi; tendere; allungare, allungarsi; allargare, ampliare: *an estate that extends over the hills to the sea*, una proprietà che si estende oltre le colline sino al mare; *that country has extended its frontiers*, quel paese ha esteso, allargato le sue frontiere; *to — one's arm*, stendere il braccio; *to — one's business, (comm.)* ampliare il proprio giro d'affari; *to — a road*, prolungare una strada **2.** prolungare; prorogare; protrarre, protrarsi: *his holidays were extended*, gli si prolungarono le vacanze; *research extending over many years*, ricerca protrattasi per molti anni; *to — the currency of a policy, (comm.)* estendere, prolungare la validità di una polizza di assicurazione **3.** manifestare; offrire; accordare: *he extended his kindness to me*, mi manifestò la sua gentilezza; *to — a welcome to s.o.*, dare il benvenuto a qlcu. **4.** (*mil.*) spiegare, spiegarsi: *to — forces*, spiegare le truppe **5.** (*dir.*) valutare; sequestrare (terreni).

extended [iks'tendid], *ag.* **1.** esteso, steso; allungato, ingrandito, ampliato **2.** prolungato **3.** (*mil.*) schierato, spiegato: *— order*, ordine spiegato **4.** (*dir.*) valutato; sequestrato (di terreno).

extendedly [iks'tendidli], *av.* estesamente.

extender [iks'tendə*], *s.* (*pitt.*) sostanza inerte, riempitivo.

extendible [iks'tendəbl], *ag.* estendibile, estensibile.

extensibility [iks‚tensə'biliti], *s.* estensibilità.

extensible [iks'tensəbl], *ag.* estensibile, allungabile.

extension [iks'tenʃən], *s.* **1.** estensione, allungamento; prolungamento, allargamento; ampliamento‖ *University Extension*, organizzazione che sotto l'egida di una università si occupa di istruzione popolare mediante corsi, conferenze, ecc. **2.** (*comm.*) proroga, dilazione (di pagamento); estensione (di credito) **3.** (*log.*) estensione (di una parola) **4.** parte aggiunta (a ferrovia, casa, ecc.) **5.** (*fisiol.*) stiramento di un arto ☆ *— telephone*, telefono interno.

extensive [iks'tensiv], *ag.* **1.** esteso, ampio, vasto; notevole: *— knowledge*, vasta, ampia conoscenza **2.** estensivo: *— agriculture*, coltura estensiva.

extensively [iks'tensivli], *av.* **1.** ampiamente **2.** estensivamente.

extensiveness [iks'tensivnis], *s.* larghezza, ampiezza.

extensor [iks'tensə*], *s.* (*anat.*) muscolo estensore.

extent [iks'tent], *s.* **1.** estensione; volume; limite; grado; lunghezza; dimensione: *to a certain —*, sino ad un certo grado; *to a great —*, in larga misura; *to what —?*, sino a che limite?, sin dove? **2.** (*dir.*) estimo; sequestro.

to **extenuate** [eks'tenjueit], *v.t.* **1.** attenuare: *extenuating circumstances*, circostanze attenuanti; *nothing can — his guilt*, nulla può attenuare la sua colpevolezza **2.** (*arc.*) estenuare, indebolire: *extenuated by fasting*, estenuato dal digiuno.

extenuation [eks‚tenju'eiʃən], *s.* **1.** attenuazione **2.** (*arc.*) indebolimento.

extenuative [eks'tenjuətiv], *ag.* **1.** attenuante **2.** (*arc.*) estenuante, deprimente ‖ *s.* (*dir.*) attenuante.

extenuatory [eks'tenjuətəri], *V.* **extenuative.**

exterior [eks'tiəriə*], *ag.* **1.** esterno, esteriore: *— angle*, (*geom.*) angolo esterno **2.** straniero ‖ *s.* **1.** l'esterno **2.** esteriorità, apparenza, aspetto: *a good woman with a rough —*, una buona donna dall'aspetto rude.

exteriority [eks‚tiəri'ɔriti], *s.* esteriorità, apparenza, parvenza.

exteriorization [eks‚tiəriərai'zeiʃən], *s.* esteriorizzazione.

to **exteriorize** [eks'tiəriəraiz], *v.t.* esteriorare; esternare, manifestare.

exteriorly [eks'tiəriəli], *av.* esteriormente; esternamente.

exterminable [eks'tə:minəbl], *ag.* sterminabile.

to **exterminate** [eks'tə:mineit], *v.t.* sradicare, estirpare, distruggere, sterminare: *the heresy was violently exterminated*, l'eresia fu estirpata in modo violento; *they were exterminated from that region*, furono sradicati da quella regione.

extermination [eks‚tə:mi'neiʃən], *s.* distruzione, sterminio.

exterminative [eks'tə:minətiv], *ag.* distruttivo; funesto.

exterminator [eks'tə:mineitə*], *s.c.* sterminatore, sterminatrice ‖ *s.* insetticida ☆ *ant- —*, insetticida per formiche.

exterminatory [eks'tə:minətəri], *ag.* sterminatore.

extern [eks'tə:n], *s.* esterno (allievo, medico).

external [eks'tə:nl], *ag.* **1.** esteriore, esterno: *the — world*, il mondo esterno; *for — use*, per uso esterno **2.** estero, straniero ‖ *s.* **1.** l'esterno **2.** *pl.* le circostanze esterne; aspetto esteriore; elementi non essenziali: *to judge by externals*, giudicare dall'apparenza ☆ *— evidence*, (*dir.*) prove tratte da elementi esterni; *— trade*, commercio con l'estero.

externality [‚eksta:'næliti], *s.* superficialità; esteriorità.

externalization [eks‚tə:nəlai'zeiʃən], *s.* l'esternare, il dare forma.

to **externalize** [eks'tə:nəlaiz], *v.t.* esternare, dare forma a.

externally [eks'tə:nəli], *av.* esternamente, secondo l'apparenza; esteriormente.

exterritorial ['eks‚teri'tɔ:riəl], *ag.* estraterritoriale.

exterritoriality [eks‚teri‚tɔ:ri'æliti], *s.* estraterritorialità.

extinct [iks'tiŋkt], *ag.* **1.** estinto, morto, scomparso: *an — family*, una famiglia estinta; *to become —*, estinguersi (di razza, ecc.) **2.** spento (di fuoco, speranza, ecc.): *an — volcano*, un vulcano spento **3.** abolito, caduto in disuso: *an — office*, carica abolita.

extinction [iks'tiŋkʃən], *s.* estinzione; annientamento.

extinctive [iks'tiŋktiv], *ag.* che estingue.

to **extinguish** [iks'tiŋgwiʃ], *v.t.* **1.** estinguere, spegnere: *to — a fire*, spegnere un incendio **2.** pagare, ammortizzare: *to — a debt*, pagare un debito **3.** soffocare; oscurare; eclissare; annientare: *all his ambitions were extinguished*, ogni sua ambizione fu soffocata.

extinguishable [iks'tiŋgwiʃəbl], *ag.* estinguibile.

extinguisher [iks'tiŋgwiʃə*], *s.c.* spegnitore, spegnitrice ‖ *s.* estintore; spegnitoio.

extinguishment [iks'tiŋgwiʃmənt], *s.* estinzione; soppressione; abolizione.

to **extirpate** ['ekstə:peit], *v.t.* estirpare, sradicare; distruggere (anche *fig.*).

extirpation [‚ekstə:'peiʃən], *s.* estirpazione, sradicamento; sterminio.

extirpator ['ekstə:peitə*], *s.c.* estirpatore, estirpatrice.

to **extol** [iks'tɔl], *pass.p.p.* **extolled** [iks'tɔld], *v.t.* (*letter.*) lodare, magnificare, esaltare: *to — s.o. to the skies*, innalzare qlcu. alle stelle.

extoller [iks'tɔlə*], *s.c.* lodatore, lodatrice.

extolment [iks'tɔlmənt], *s.* lode esagerata, panegirico.

to **extort** [iks'tɔ:t], *v.t.* estorcere, strappare; estrarre: *to — money from s.o.*, estorcere denaro a qlcu.; *to — a promise from s.o.*, strappare una promessa a qlcu.

extorter [iks'tɔ:tə*], *s.c.* chi estorce.

extortion [iks'tɔ:ʃən], *s.* estorsione.

extortionate [iks'tɔ:ʃnit], *ag.* **1.** eccessivo, esorbitante (di prezzi) **2.** oppressivo.

extortioner [iks'tɔ:ʃnə*], *s.c.* chi estorce danaro.

extra ['ekstrə], *ag.* straordinario, supplementare, aggiunto, in più, extra ‖ *s.* **1.** extra; cosa insolita; edizione straordinaria (di giornale) **2.** (*neol. teat. cine.*) comparsa ☆ — *binding*, rilegatura di lusso; — *current*, (*elett.*) extracorrente; — *fare*, supplemento (al biglietto); — *luggage*, eccedenza di bagaglio; — *postage*, soprattassa (di una lettera); — *pay for* — *work*, soprassoldo, compenso supplementare per lavoro straordinario.

extra, *av.* di più, in più; insolitamente ‖ *baths* —, i bagni sono extra, in più; *packing* —, imballaggio a parte ☆ — *-fine*, estrafino; — *-legal*, estralegale; — *-mundane*, ultraterreno; — *-mural*, fuori le mura (di una città); — *-special* (*edition*), ultima edizione (di gionali).

extract ['ekstrækt], *s.* **1.** estratto **2.** citazione, passo (da libro, giornale): *to make an* — *from an author*, citare un passo di un autore **3.** (*comm.*) stralcio, riproduzione parziale **4.** (*scoz.*) estratto, copia (da documento); copia autentica ☆ *meat* —, estratto di carne.

to **extract** [iks'trækt], *v.t.* **1.** estrarre, togliere, levare: *to* — *a bullet from a wound*, estrarre una pallottola da una ferita; *to* — *sthg. from s.o., from sthg.*, togliere ql.co. a qlcu., a ql.co.; *to* — *a tooth*, estrarre un dente **2.** estorcere: *to* — *money from s.o.*, estorcere denaro a qlcu. **3.** citare, scegliere: *to* — *a passage from a book*, scegliere, citare un passo da un libro **4.** (*mat.*) estrarre (la radice di un numero).

extractable [iks'træktəbl], *ag.* estraibile.

extraction [iks'trækʃən], *s.* **1.** estrazione **2.** origine, stirpe: *of low* —, di umile, bassa origine; *she is of German* —, ella è di origine tedesca.

extractive [iks'træktiv], *ag.* estrattivo ☆ — *industries*, industrie estrattive.

extractor [iks'træktə*], *s.* **1.** estrattore **2.** (*chir.*) forcipe.

extraditable ['ekstrədaitəbl], *ag.* (*dir.*) passibile di estradizione.

to **extradite** ['ekstrədait], *v.t.* (*dir.*) estradare; ottenere l'estradizione di.

extradition [,ekstrə'diʃən], *s.* (*dir.*) estradizione.

extrados [eks'treidəs], *s.* (*arch.*) estradosso.

extrajudicial ['ekstrədʒu(:)'diʃəl], *ag.* (*dir.*) extragiudiziale.

extrajudicially ['ekstrədʒu(:)'diʃəli], *av.* extragiudizialmente.

extraneous [eks'treinjəs], *ag.* estraneo; non essenziale; estrinseco: *to be* — *to the matter in hand*, non aver nulla a che fare con il problema in discussione.

extraneously [eks'treinjəsli], *av.* estraneamente; in modo non essenziale; estrinsecamente.

extraneousness [eks'treinjəsnis], *s.* mancanza di legame.

extraordinaries [iks'trɔ:dnriz], *s.pl.* (*arc. mil.*) soprassoldo.

extraordinarily [iks'trɔ:dnrili], *av.* straordinariamente; eccezionalmente.

extraordinariness [iks'trɔ:dnrinis], *s.* natura, cosa eccezionale, straordinaria; singolarità.

extraordinary [iks'trɔ:dnri], *ag.* straordinario; eccezionale, raro; strano; (*fam.*) fenomenale: — *beauty*, rara bellezza; — *event*, avvenimento straordinario; — *genius*, genio eccezionale ☆ *ambassador* —, ambasciatore straordinario.

extraparochial ['ekstrəpə'roukjəl], *ag.* al di fuori dei confini della parrocchia.

to **extrapolate** [eks'træpəleit], *v.t.* (*mat.*) estrapolare.

extrapolation [,ekstrəpou'leiʃən], *s.* (*mat.*) estrapolazione.

extrasensory ['ekstrə'sensəri], *ag.* (*neol.*) che va al di là dei sensi.

extraterritorial ['ekstrə,teri'tɔ:riəl], *ag.* estraterritoriale, che gode dei privilegi dell'estraterritorialità (di ambasciatore, ecc.).

extravagance [iks'trævigəns], *s.* **1.** prodigalità; dispendio esagerato: *a piece of* —, una spesa inutile **2.** stravaganza, bizzarria.

extravagant [iks'trævigənt], *ag.* **1.** prodigo **2.** stravagante, fuori del normale: *he has* — *tastes*, egli ha gusti stravaganti **3.** eccessivo, esorbitante: *hats at* — *prices*, cappelli a prezzi eccessivi **4.** smodato: — *laughter*, risata smodata.

extravagantly [iks'trævigəntli], *av.* **1.** prodigalmente **2.** in modo stravagante **3.** eccessivamente.

extravaganza [eks,trævə'gænzə], *s.* **1.** (*lett. mus.*) composizione bizzarra, fantasiosa **2.** linguaggio, comportamento stravagante.

to **extravagate** [eks'trævəgeit], *v.i.* (*rar.*) sviarsi; vagare.

to **extravasate** [eks'trævəseit], *v.t.i.* **1.** traboccare; far traboccare; travasare; cavare (sangue, ecc.) **2.** (*geol.*) sgorgare (di lava, ecc.).

extravasation [eks,trævə'seiʃən], *s.* **1.** travaso **2.** lo sgorgare (di lava, ecc.).

extreme [iks'tri:m], *ag.* **1.** estremo; ultimo: — *old age*, estrema vecchiaia **2.** grave: — *danger*, estremo pericolo **3.** severo, draconiano: *to take* — *measures*, prendere misure draconiane **4.** eccezionale: *an* — *case*, un caso eccezionale; — *patience*, pazienza eccezionale ☆ — *unction*, (*eccl.*) Estrema Unzione.

extreme, *s.* **1.** estremo, estremità, fine: *in the* —, all'estremo, eccessivamente ‖ *extremes meet*, gli estremi si toccano ‖ *to go to extremes*, andare, giungere agli estremi **2.** (*log. mat.*) estremo.

extremely [iks'tri:mli], *av.* estremamente; sommamente.

extremism [iks'tri:mizəm], *s.* (*pol.*) estremismo.

extremist [iks'tri:mist], *s.* (*pol.*) estremista.

extremity [iks'tremiti], *s.* **1.** estremità; colmo, eccesso: *to drive to extremities*, spingere agli estremi, sino in fondo **2.** imbarazzo; necessità; pericolo: *he is in great* —, si trova in grave imbarazzo **3.** *pl.* estremità (del corpo).

extricable ['ekstrikəbl], *ag.* che si può districare.

to **extricate** ['ekstrikeit], *v.t.* **1.** districare; liberare; sciogliere (anche *fig.*): *to* — *oneself from sthg.*, districarsi da ql.co., liberarsi di ql.co.; cavarsela da ql.co. **2.** (*chim.*) liberare (gas, calore): *to* — *heat*, liberare calore.

extrication [,ekstri'keiʃən], *s.* **1.** il togliere d'imbarazzo; il trarre d'impaccio **2.** liberazione (di un gas, ecc.).

extricator ['ekstrikeitə*], *s.c.* chi trae d'impaccio.

extrinsic [eks'trinsik], *ag.* estrinseco; esterno; non essenziale.

extrinsically [eks'trinsikəli], *av.* estrinsecamente.

extrorse [eks'trɔ:s], *ag.* (*bot.*) estrorso.

extroversion [,ekstrou'və:ʃən], *s.* estroversione.

extrovert ['ekstrouvə:t], *s.c.* estroverso, estroversa.

to **extrovert**, *v.t.* estrovertere.

to **extrude** [eks'tru:d], *v.t.* spingere fuori, espellere; estrudere.

extruder [eks'tru:də*], *s.* (*ind. mec.*) trafila; macchina a estrudere.

extrusion [eks'tru:ʒən], *s.* espulsione, lo spingere fuori; estrusione.

extrusive [eks'tru:siv], *ag.* estrusivo.

exuberance [ig'zju:bərəns], **exuberancy** [ig'zju:bərənsi], *s.* esuberanza.

exuberant [ig'zju:bərənt], *ag.* **1.** copioso, abbondante; lussureggiante: *plants with* — *foliage*, piante ricche di fogliame **2.** esuberante, pieno di vita: *an* — *person*, una persona piena di vita **3.** fertile (di mente, ecc.): *an* — *imagination*, un'immaginazione fertile **4.** pomposo (di stile).

exuberantly [ig'zju:bərəntli], *av.* **1.** copiosamente, abbondantemente **2.** in modo esuberante: — *healthy*, che scoppia di salute.

to **exuberate** [ig'zju:bəreit], *v.i.* essere esuberante; abbondare.

exudation [ˌeksjuˈdeiʃən], *s.* essudazione, trasudamento.

exudative [eksˈjuːdətiv], *ag.* essudante.

to **exude** [igˈzjuːd], *v.t.i.* essudare; trasudare, far trasudare.

to **exult** [igˈzʌlt], *v.i.* **1.** gioire, esultare **2.** cantar vittoria; trionfare: *to — over s.o.*, trionfare sopra qlcu.

exultance [igˈzʌltəns], **exultancy** [igˈzʌltənsi], *s.* gioia, esultanza.

exultant [igˈzʌltənt], *ag.* esultante; trionfante.

exultantly [igˈzʌltəntli], *av.* con esultanza.

exultation [ˌegzʌlˈteiʃən], *s.* esultanza.

exulting [igˈzʌltiŋ], *ag.* esultante.

exultingly [igˈzʌltiŋli], *ag.* con esultanza.

exuviae [igˈzjuːviiː], *s.pl.* spoglia (di serpi, ecc.); resti fossili.

to **exuviate** [igˈzjuːvieit], *v.t.i.* **1.** cambiar (pelle) **2.** gettar le spoglie (anche *fig.*).

exuviation [igˌzjuːviˈeiʃən], *s.* **1.** cambiamento di pelle **2.** il gettar le spoglie.

ex-voto [eksˈvoutou], *s.* (*lat.*) ex voto.

eyas [ˈaiəs], *s.* giovane falco (non ancora addestrato).

eye [ai], *s.* **1.** occhio; vista; sguardo: *black eyes*, occhi neri; (*fam.*) occhi pesti; *blind of one —*, cieco da un occhio; *bulging eyes*, occhi sporgenti; *don't strain your eyes*, non affaticarti gli occhi; *it was so interesting that I couldn't take my eyes off it*, era così interessante che non potevo distoglierne lo sguardo; *my eyes smart*, mi bruciano gli occhi; *with eyes starting out of one's head*, con gli occhi fuori dall'orbita; *to have keen eyes*, avere la vista acuta (anche *fig.*); *to keep one's eyes open*, tenere gli occhi aperti (anche *fig.*); *to screw up one's eyes*, strizzare gli occhi ‖ *an — for an —*, occhio per occhio ‖ *the — of day*, (*poet.*) il sole ‖ *— of the storm*, (*meteorologia*) centro del ciclone ‖ *in the — of the law*, dal punto di vista legale ‖ *in my eyes*, a parer mio ‖ *in a pig's —*, (*sl.*) mai ‖ *in the wind's —*, controvento ‖ *my —!* (o *my eyes!*), (*sl.*) perdinci!, davvero! ‖ *mind your —!*, sta' attento! ‖ *with an — to*, in considerazione di ‖ *that's all my — (and Betty Martin)*, sono tutte storie!, è fumo negli occhi! ‖ *she is the apple of his eyes*, è la pupilla dei suoi occhi ‖ *to be all eyes*, essere tutt'occhi, fissare attentamente ‖ *to be up to one's eyes in debt, work*, avere debiti, lavoro fin sopra i capelli ‖ *to catch* (o *to draw*) *s.o.'s —*, attirare l'attenzione di qlcu. ‖ *to close one's eyes to sthg.*, chiudere gli occhi di fronte a ql.co., rifiutarsi di constatare ql.co. ‖ *to cry one's eyes out*, struggersi in lacrime ‖ *to give a person the —*, (*sl. amer.*) guardare qlcu. con ammirazione ‖ *to have an — to everything*, avere occhi per tutto; *to have an — to business*, aver buon fiuto per gli affari ‖ *to keep an — on s.o., sthg.*, tenere d'occhio qlcu., ql.co. ‖ *to look through the corner of one's —*, guardare con la coda dell'occhio ‖ *to make* (o *to cast*) *sheep's eyes at s.o.*, fare gli occhi dolci a qlcu. ‖ *to open*

s.o.'s eyes to sthg., aprire gli occhi a qlcu. di fronte a ql.co., togliere le illusioni a qlcu. su ql.co. ‖ *to run one's eyes over* (o *through*) *sthg.*, scorrere velocemente ql.co. con lo sguardo ‖ *to see — to — with s.o.*, avere la stessa opinione di, andare d'accordo con qlcu. ‖ *to see sthg. with half an —*, capire ql.co. al volo ‖ *to set* (o *to clap*) *eyes on sthg.*, mettere gli occhi su ql.co. **2.** (*bot.*) gemma, bottone **3.** (*ornit.*) occhio, macchia (della coda di pavone) **4.** (*ind.*) occhio, occhiello; cruna (di ago); maglietta (di gancio); foro (di manico) **5.** (*mar.*) gassa, occhio di gassa; cubia, occhio di cubìa ☆ *— -ball*, (*anat.*) bulbo oculare; *— -opener*, fatto sorprendente, rivelatore; (*sl. amer.*) bevanda alcoolica (presa di primo mattino); *— -piece*, oculare (di cannocchiale); *— -pin*, (*mec.*) spina ad occhio; *— -shot*, campo visivo; *— -string*, (*anat.*) muscolo dell'occhio; *— -tooth*, (*anat.*) dente canino; *— -wash*, (*farm.*) collirio; (*sl.*) chiacchiere, inganno; *— -witness*, testimonio oculare ‖ *bull's- —*, (*mar.*) oblò; *electric —*, (*tv.*) cellula fotoelettrica; *glass- —*, occhio artificiale, di vetro; (*fam.*) monocolo, caramella; *screw- —*, (*carpenteria*) occhiello a vite.

to **eye**, *pass.p.p.* **eyed** [aid], *p.pr.* **eyeing** [ˈaiiŋ], *v.t.* guardare, osservare; sbirciare: *he eyed the money with greed*, lanciò uno sguardo rapace sul denaro; *to — s.o. up and down* (o *from head to foot*), squadrare qlcu. dall'alto in basso; *to — s.o. with suspicion*, guardare qlcu. con sospetto.

eyebright [ˈaibrait], *s.* (*bot.*) eufrasia.

eyebrow [ˈaibrau], *s.* sopracciglio: *to knit one's eyebrows*, aggrottare le sopracciglia.

eyed [aid], *ag.* **1.** dagli occhi **2.** macchiato ☆ *blue- —*, dagli occhi azzurri; *one- —*, guercio, monocolo; *squint- —*, dagli occhi strabici.

eyeglass [ˈaiglɑːs], *s.* lente; monocolo: *a pair of eyeglasses*, un paio di occhiali ☆ *rimless eyeglasses*, « pince-nez »; occhialino; binocolo.

eyehole [ˈaihoul], *s.* **1.** orbita, occhiaia **2.** buco, spiraglio.

eyelash [ˈailæʃ], *s.* ciglio: *she has long eyelashes*, ella ha le ciglia lunghe.

eyeless [ˈailis], *ag.* cieco.

eyelet [ˈailit], *s.* **1.** occhiello, asola; foro (per stringhe, ecc.) **2.** feritoia.

eyelid [ˈailid], *s.* palpebra ‖ *to escape by one's eyelids*, (*fam.*) scamparla bella; cavarsela per un pelo.

eyesight [ˈai-sait], *s.* vista, capacità visiva.

eyesore [ˈai-sɔː*], *s.* cosa brutta o spiacevole; cosa che offende la vista; (*fam.*) pugno nell'occhio.

eyot [ˈeiət], *s.* isolotto.

eyre [ɛə*], *s.* (*st. inglese*) **1.** corte ambulante **2.** sessione e itinerario di una corte ambulante.

eyrie [ˈaiəri], *s.* **1.** nido di uccelli da preda **2.** nidiata di uccelli da preda **3.** casa, castello sorgente su di un picco.

Ezekiel [iˈziːkjəl], *no.pr.m.* (*Bibbia*) Ezechiele.

Ezra [ˈezrə], *no.pr.m.* (*Bibbia*) Esdra.

F

f [ef], *pl.* **fs**, **f's** [efs], *s.* **1.** (*sesta lettera dell'alfabeto inglese*) f ‖ — *for Frederick*, (*tel.*) f come Firenze **2.** (*mus.*) fa.

fa [fɑ:], *s.* (*mus.*) fa.

Fabian[1] ['feibjən], *ag.* temporeggiatore: — *policy*, politica temporeggiatrice ‖ — *Society*, « Fabian Society » (associazione fautrice di un socialismo non rivoluzionario, fondata a Londra nel 1884) ‖ *s.* membro della « Fabian Society ».

Fabian[2], *no.pr.m.* Fabiano.

Fabius ['feibjəs], *no.pr.m.* (*st.*) Fabio.

fable ['feibl], *s.* **1.** fiaba; favola, apologo **2.** mito, leggenda **3.** fola, ciancia; frottola, fandonia; pura invenzione **4.** (*lett.*) intreccio.

to fable, *v.t.i.* **1.** (*arc. poet.*) favoleggiare **2.** raccontare frottole; inventare.

fabled ['feibld], *ag.* **1.** favoloso, mitico, leggendario **2.** inventato, irreale.

fabler ['feiblə*], *s.* favolista; favoleggiatore.

fabliau ['fæbliou], **fabliaux** ['fæbliouz], *s.* (*lett.*) « fabliau », favolello.

fabric ['fæbrik], *s.* **1.** tessuto **2.** (*ind.*) manufatto **3.** (*edil.*) intelaiatura **4.** edificio, struttura (anche *fig.*): *the whole — of society*, la intera struttura della società.

to fabricate ['fæbrikeit], *v.t.* **1.** inventare (una notizia); falsificare (un testamento, documento) **2.** (*rar.*) fabbricare, costruire.

fabrication [ˌfæbri'keiʃən], *s.* **1.** contraffazione, falsificazione; invenzione: *the — of a passport*, la falsificazione di un passaporto; *it is pure —*, è pura invenzione **2.** (*rar.*) fabbricazione, costruzione.

fabricator ['fæbrikeitə*], *s.* **1.** contraffattore; mentitore **2.** (*rar.*) costruttore.

Fabricius [fə'briʃəs], *no.pr.m.* (*st.*) Fabrizio.

fabulist ['fæbjulist], *s.* **1.** scrittore, narratore di favole **2.** bugiardo.

fabulosity [ˌfæbju'lɔsiti], *s.* favolosità.

fabulous ['fæbjuləs], *ag.* **1.** favoloso, leggendario, mitico: *the — ages*, le età mitiche **2.** *fig.* incredibile, favoloso, eccessivo: *a — price*, un prezzo favoloso.

fabulously ['fæbjulusli], *av.* favolosamente.

fabulousness ['fæbjuləsnis], *s.* favolosità.

façade [fə'sɑ:d], *s.* **1.** (*arch.*) facciata **2.** *fig.* facciata, apparenza.

face [feis], *s.* **1.** faccia, viso, volto: — *to — to* (o *with*), a faccia a faccia con; *in — of*, di fronte a; *in* (*the*) — *of*, a dispetto di; *to s.o.'s —*, in faccia, in presenza di qlcu., apertamente; *they shut the door in my —*, mi chiusero la porta in faccia; *to be unable to look s.o. in the —*, non riuscire a guardare in faccia qlcu.; *to show one's —*, farsi vedere; *to strike s.o. in the —*, colpire qlcu. in viso ‖ *a man with two faces*, un uomo dalla doppia personalità ‖ *to fly in the — of*, resistere a, sfidare ‖ *to look the facts in the —*, affrontare la realtà ‖ *to set one's — against sthg.*, opporsi a ql.co. **2.** apparenza, aspetto esteriore: *the — of things has changed*, l'aspetto delle cose è mutato ‖ *on the — of it*, giudicando dalle apparenze ‖ *to put a good* (o *brave*) — *on a bad business*, far buon viso a cattiva sorte **3.** sfrontatezza, impudenza, faccia tosta: *she had the — to tell me everything*, ella ha avuto la sfacciataggine di raccontarmi tutto ‖ *to have a brazen —*, (*fam.*) avere la faccia tosta **4.** facciata; faccia (di moneta, ecc.); quadrante: *the — of a* *building*, la facciata di un edificio; *the — of a coin*, diritto di una moneta; *the — of a watch*, il quadrante di un orologio; *a parallelepiped has six faces*, un parallelepipedo ha sei facce **5.** espressione del viso; smorfia ‖ *to pull faces*, far le boccacce; *to pull* (o *to make* o *to wear*) *a long —*, fare il broncio, essere serio, triste **6.** dignità, prestigio: *to lose one's —*, perdere la propria reputazione; *to save one's —*, salvare la faccia **7.** (*tip.*) occhio ☆ — -*ache*, nevralgia facciale; — -*card*, (*carte*) figura; — -*cream*, crema per il viso; — -*lifting*, plastica facciale (per eliminare le rughe); — -*plate*, (*mec.*) menabrida, disco del tornio; — -*powder*, cipria per il viso; — *value*, (*comm.*) valore nominale.

to face, *v.t.i.* **1.** fronteggiare, essere di fronte a, rimpetto a; essere esposto a: *he was facing me*, mi stava di fronte; *to be faced by*, trovarsi di fronte a **2.** affrontare, opporsi a: *to — danger*, affrontare il pericolo; *to — facts*, affrontare la realtà ‖ *to — the music*, (*sl.*) affrontare con coraggio una situazione difficile **3.** ricoprire, rivestire (una superficie): *to — a wall with tapestry*, ricoprire una parete di arazzi **4.** (*mil. amer.*) girare (nella direzione comandata): *about —!*, dietro front!; *left, right —!*, fronte sinist!, dest! **5.** (*carte*) voltare, scoprire (le carte) **6.** (*mec.*) sfacciare; spianare, lisciare **7.** *to — out*, affrontare (una difficoltà); non cedere.

faced [feist], *ag.* dalla faccia, dal viso ☆ *fair- —*, bello, chiaro di viso; *ugly- —*, brutto di viso.

facer ['feisə*], *s.* **1.** schiaffo (anche *fig.*) **2.** difficoltà, ostacolo **3.** utensile con cui sfacciare.

facet ['fæsit], *s.* sfaccettatura, faccetta (d'una gemma).

to facet, *v.t.* sfaccettare (una gemma).

facetiae [fə'si:ʃii:], *s.pl.* **1.** facezie, piacevolezze **2.** libri di carattere umoristico o piccante.

facetious [fə'si:ʃəs], *ag.* faceto, gaio, scherzoso.

facetiously [fə'si:ʃəsli], *av.* facetamente.

facetiousness [fə'si:ʃəsnis], *s.* lepidezza; scherzo.

facia ['feiʃə], *s.* insegna (di negozio).

facial ['feiʃəl], *ag.* facciale ‖ *s.* (*amer. fam.*) massaggio al viso ☆ — *angle*, angolo facciale.

facile ['fæsail], *ag.* **1.** facile, ottenuto facilmente **2.** destro, pronto: — *tongue*, lingua pronta **3.** accomodante; compiacente; arrendevole, remissivo: — *disposition*, indole remissiva.

to facilitate [fə'siliteit], *v.t.* agevolare, facilitare.

facilitation [fəˌsili'teiʃən], *s.* facilitazione.

facility [fə'siliti], *s.* **1.** facilità; capacità, destrezza, abilità: — *in speaking*, facilità di parola **2.** *pl.* occasioni, possibilità; facilitazioni: *facilities for travel*, facilitazioni di viaggio **3.** (*amer.*) arrendevolezza.

facing ['feisiŋ], *ag.* che sta di fronte ‖ *s.* **1.** rivestimento: — *of concrete*, rivestimento in calcestruzzo **2.** *pl.* (*mil.*) risvolti; mostrine **3.** *pl.* (*mil.*) cambiamento di direzione (nelle esercitazioni) ‖ *to go through one's facings*, (*rar.*) essere messo alla prova ‖ *to put s.o. through his facings*, mettere alla prova le qualità, la capacità di qlcu.

facinorous [fə'sinərəs], *ag.* facinoroso, scellerato.

facsimile [fæk'simili], *s.* **1.** facsimile, copia esatta **2.** (*rad. tv.*) teleriproduzione.

to facsimile, *v.t.* fare un facsimile di.

fact [fækt], *s.* **1.** fatto, azione: *an accomplished —*, un fatto compiuto; *caught in the —*, colto in flagrante **2.** realtà, verità, cosa provata: *the — of the matter is that...*, la verità, la realtà è che...; *it is necessary to* *distinguish — from fiction*, è necessario distinguere la realtà dalla fantasia; *tell me the facts*, dimmi come stanno veramente le cose, dimmi la verità ‖ *as a matter of* —, in verità, in effetti; *in* —, infatti, di fatto; *in point of* —, in realtà ☆ — *finding*, di inchiesta: — *finding board*, commissione di inchiesta.

faction ['fækʃən], *s.* **1.** fazione **2.** spirito di parte, partigianeria **3.** discordia, dissenso.

factional ['fækʃənl], *ag.* **1.** fazioso **2.** dissenziente.

factious ['fækʃəs], *ag.* fazioso, partigiano.

factiously ['fækʃəsli], *av.* faziosamente.

factiousness ['fækʃəsnis], *s.* spirito di parte.

factitious [fæk'tiʃəs], *ag.* fittizio; artificiale, falso.

factitiously [fæk'tiʃəsli], *av.* artificialmente.

factitiousness [fæk'tiʃəsnis], *s.* artificiosità.

factitive ['fæktitiv], *ag.* (*gram.*) causale, causativo.

factor ['fæktə*], *s.* **1.** fattore, agente, coefficiente: *it is the most important — in such circumstances*, è il fattore più importante in tali circostanze **2.** (*mat.*) fattore **3.** agente, commissionario; (*scoz.*) amministratore (di terre), intendente ☆ *exposure multiplying* —, (*foto.*) fattore di posa; *power* —, (*elett.*) fattore di potenza; *resonance* —, (*rad.*) coefficiente di risonanza; *safety* —, (*mec.*) coefficiente di sicurezza.

factorage ['fæktəridʒ], *s.* **1.** provvigione **2.** *coll.* gli agenti.

factorial[1] [fæk'tɔːriəl], *ag.* **1.** (*mat.*) relativo ai fattori, fattoriale **2.** relativo a un agente, a un commissionario ‖ *s.* (*mat.*) fattoriale.

factorial[2], (*rar.*) *ag.* relativo ad un'industria.

factory ['fæktəri], *s.* **1.** fabbrica; officina; stabilimento; manifattura ‖ *Factory Acts*, leggi sindacali **2.** filiale estera di azienda ☆ — *hand*, operaio; — *price*, prezzo di fabbrica; — *shop*, spaccio aziendale.

factotum [fæk'toutəm], *s.* factotum.

factual ['fæktjuəl], *ag.* effettivo, reale, positivo.

factum ['fæktəm], *pl.* **facta** ['fæktə], *s.* **1.** esposizione di fatti **2.** memoriale.

facula ['fækjulə], *pl.* **faculae** ['fækjuliː], *s.* (*astr.*) facella.

facultative ['fækəltətiv], *ag.* **1.** facoltativo **2.** contingente, casuale.

faculty ['fækəlti], *s.* **1.** facoltà (intellettuale); attitudine; capacità: *a — for music*, attitudine alla musica; *the faculties of hearing, seeing*, la facoltà di udire, di vedere; *he has the — of making friends easily*, ha la capacità di fare amicizie facilmente **2.** facoltà universitaria: *the Faculty of Law*, la facoltà di giurisprudenza ‖ *the Faculty*, (*fam.*) i medici; (*amer.*) il corpo insegnante **3.** (*dir.*) diritto, privilegio.

fad [fæd], *s.* **1.** mania; moda (bizzarra); entusiasmo passeggero: *she has a — for velvet curtains*, ha la mania delle tende di velluto **2.** capriccio: *he is full of fads*, è pieno di capricci.

faddiness ['fædinis], *V.* **faddishness**.

faddish ['fædiʃ], *ag.* **1.** bizzarro, fantastico **2.** capriccioso.

faddishness ['fædiʃnis], *s.* tendenza a seguire le proprie manie.

faddism ['fædizəm], *s.* abbandono completo alle proprie manie.

faddist ['fædist], *s.* maniaco.

faddy ['fædi], *ag.* **1.** capriccioso **2.** maniaco.

fade [feid], *s.* (*cine.*) dissolvenza; (*rad. tv.*) variazione graduale (di suono, immagine).

to **fade**, *v.t.i.* **1.** appassire, languire, perdere la freschezza; *fig.* perire, morire: *roses soon* —, le rose appassiscono presto **2.** sbiadire, scolorire, scolorirsi (di colori, stoffe, ecc.) **3.** scomparire, dileguarsi, svanire **4.** (*cine. rad. tv.*) variare gradualmente **5.** *to — in*, (*cine.*) aprire in dissolvenza; (*rad. tv.*) aumentare gradualmente di intensità **6.** *to — out*, (*cine.*) chiudere in dissolvenza; (*rad. tv.*) diminuire gradualmente di intensità.

faded ['feidid], *ag.* **1.** appassito **2.** scolorito, sbiadito.

fading ['feidiŋ], *ag.* **1.** che appassisce: — *flowers*, fiori che appassiscono **2.** che si scolora **3.** che si affievolisce (di luce) ‖ *s.* **1.** appassimento; *fig.* deperimento **2.** scolorimento **3.** (*rad.*) affievolimento di suono, evanescenza **4.** (*cine.*) dissolvenza.

fadingly ['feidiŋli], *av.* (*arc.*) languidamente; *fig.* fuggevolmente.

faecal ['fiːkəl], *ag.* fecale.

faeces ['fiːsiːz], *s.pl.* feci, escrementi.

faerie, faery ['feiəri], *ag.* (*arc.*) fatato; immaginario ‖ *s.* **1.** paese, regno delle fate **2.** (*rar.*) fata.

fag[1] [fæg], *s.* **1.** (*sl.*) fatica, lavoro pesante: *what a —!*, che fatica!, che sfacchinata! **2.** (*sl. scolastico*) studente giovane che deve fare servizi umili per uno studente anziano.

to **fag**[1], *pass.p.p.* **fagged** [fægd], *v.t.i.* **1.** sfacchinare, far sfacchinare: *to — (away) at (doing) sthg.*, affaticarsi a (far) ql.co.; *to — oneself*, logorarsi (col lavoro), affaticarsi, stancarsi **2.** (*sl. scolastico*) servire: *to — for a senior*, far servizi per uno studente anziano.

fag[2], *s.* (*sl.*) sigaretta.

fag[3], *s.* **1.** falla, imperfezione in un tessuto **2.** (*entom.*) zecca delle pecore.

fagging ['fægiŋ], *s.* **1.** lavoro faticoso **2.** (*sl. scolastico*) servizi fatti da studenti giovani per gli anziani.

fag(g)ot ['fægət], *s.* **1.** fascina, fastello **2.** (*metal.*) pacchetto di materiali ferrosi (da trattare, laminare) **3.** pietanza di fegato al forno ☆ — *vote*, voto manipolato (dato ad elettore che non ne avrebbe diritto).

to **fag(g)ot**, *v.t.i.* legare in fascina; far fascine.

fagottist [fə'gotist], *s.* (*mus.*) suonatore di fagotto.

fagotto [fə'gotou], *s.* (*mus.*) fagotto.

Fahrenheit ['færənhait], (*nei composti*): — *degree, temperature*, (*fis.*) grado, temperatura Fahrenheit.

faience [fai'ɑːns], *s.* terracotta; porcellana.

fail [feil], *s.* fallo: *without* —, senza fallo.

to **fail**, *v.t.i.* **1.** fallire (di piani, affari, ecc.); non riuscire: *all our plans failed*, tutti i nostri piani fallirono; *he failed in the examinations*, egli non superò gli esami; *we — to understand him*, non riusciamo a capirlo **2.** mancare, venire a mancare, far difetto, venir meno (anche *fig.*): *I shall not — to do all I can*, non mancherò di fare tutto ciò che mi sarà possibile; *my friend failed to keep his promise*, il mio amico venne meno alla promessa; *my memory failed me*, mi fallì la memoria; *water often fails in the dry season*, nella stagione asciutta manca spesso l'acqua; *words — me*, mi mancano le parole; *to — in one's duty*, mancare al proprio dovere ‖ *to — s.o.*, mancare ai propri impegni verso qlcu. **3.** diminuire, diventar debole: *his sight begins to* —, la sua vista comincia ad indebolirsi **4.** trascurare, dimenticare: *he never fails to write to his mother*, non manca mai di scrivere a sua madre **5.** (*comm.*) fallire: *several banks failed*, parecchie banche fallirono **6.** bocciare: *I failed him twice in grammar*, lo rimandai, bocciai due volte in grammatica.

failing ['feiliŋ], *ag.* debole, scarso (di vista, salute, ecc.): — *health*, salute cagionevole ‖ *s.* **1.** difetto, debolezza: *with all his failings*, con tutti i suoi difetti **2.** mancanza, errore, fallo: *his — in respect towards her*, la sua mancanza di rispetto verso di lei **3.** indebolimento (di vista, salute, ecc.) **4.** (*comm.*) fallimento.

failing, *prep.* in mancanza di: — *your direction to the contrary*, salvo vostra istruzione contraria.

faille [feil], *s.* faglia (tessuto di seta).

failure ['feiljə*], *s.* **1.** insuccesso, fallimento; (*teat.*) fiasco: — *in an examination did not discourage him*, la bocciatura in un esame non lo scoraggiò; *that plan was a* —, quel piano fu un fallimento **2.** incapacità: *his — to answer their questions*, la sua incapacità di rispondere alle loro domande **3.** mancanza, insufficienza **4.** mancanza, omissione: — *to obey rules*, la mancanza di obbedienza alle leggi **5.** indebolimento (di forze, ecc.) **6.** persona fallita: *he is a — as a lawyer*, come avvocato è un fallito **7.** (*comm.*) fallimento **8.** (*mec.*) avaria.

fain[1] [fein], *ag. predicativo* **1.** contento, allegro **2.** pronto, ben disposto **3.** costretto.

fain[1], *av.* (*arc.*) volentieri.

to **fain**[2], *v.i.*: *fains I do it* (o *fain I*), no!, neanche per sogno! (espressione di rifiuto infantile).

faineant ['feiniənt], *ag.s.* pigro, ozioso.

faint [feint], *ag.* **1.** debole; fiacco; appena percettibile (di luce, suono): *a — effort*, un debole sforzo; *a — hope*, una debole speranza; *I hear a — sound in the distance*, odo un debole suono in lontananza **2.** languido, debole, esangue: *she was — with hunger*, era debole per la fame; *to feel quite —*, sentirsi venir meno **3.** timido, pauroso **4.** vago, incerto: *I have not the faintest idea how* (*to do sthg.*), non ho la più pallida idea di come (fare ql.co.) **5.** soffocante, opprimente (di aria, profumo, ecc.): *— atmosphere*, atmosfera pesante, soffocante ☆ *— -heart*, codardo: *— -heart ne'er won fair lady*, *prov.* amante non sia chi coraggio non ha; *— -hearted*, pusillanime, timido; *— -heartedly*, poco coraggiosamente, timidamente; *— -heartedness*, timidezza, pusillanimità; *— lines*, rigatura (della carta).

faint, *s.* svenimento: *in a dead —*, assolutamente insensibile.

to **faint**, *v.i.* **1.** svenire, sentirsi mancare, sentirsi male: *the girl fainted*, la ragazza svenne; *to — from hunger*, venir meno dalla fame **2.** (*rar.*) indebolirsi; impallidire **3.** (*arc.*) perdersi di coraggio.

fainting ['feintiŋ], *ag.* che langue, che viene meno (di coraggio, voce, ecc.) || *s.* **1.** il venir meno, l'affievolirsi (di luce, suono, coraggio, ecc.) **2.** scoraggiamento.

faintish ['feintiʃ], *ag.* piuttosto debole.

faintly ['feintli], *av.* **1.** debolmente; vagamente **2.** languidamente **3.** timidamente.

faintness ['feintnis], *s.* **1.** debolezza; languore **2.** timidezza.

fair[1] [fɛə*], *ag.* **1.** giusto, onesto, leale, imparziale: *a — share*, una giusta parte (porzione); *it isn't — of you*, non è leale da parte tua || *by — means*, con mezzi onesti || *all's — in love and war*, in amore e in guerra tutto è lecito **2.** discreto, passabile **3.** probabile; favorevole: *the business is in a — way to succeed*, è molto probabile che l'affare riesca **4.** chiaro (di pelle); biondo (di capelli): *a — complexion*, una carnagione chiara **5.** sereno (di tempo); propizio (di vento) **6.** gentile, amabile, affabile **7.** pulito, nitido **8.** (*comm.*) libero **9.** (*arc. poet.*) bello, amabile ☆ *— -boding*, di buon auspicio; *— -copy*, bella copia; *— -faced*, di carnagione chiara; *— -fame*, buona fama; *— -field*, giuste condizioni; *— -haired* (o *— -headed*), biondo; *— -minded*, equanime; *— -play*, giustizia, condizioni uguali; comportamento leale; *— sex*, gentil sesso; *— -trade*, commercio libero; contrabbando; *— -wind*, vento favorevole; *— -weather*, *fig.* di circostanze favorevoli: *— -weather friend*, amico nel tempo felice.

fair[1], *av.* **1.** lealmente, giustamente, onestamente: *to fight —*, combattere secondo le regole; *to play —*, agire con lealtà **2.** con precisione: *to strike s.o. — on the chin*, colpire qlcu. dritto al mento **3.** (*arc.*) gentilmente: *to speak a person —*, parlare cortesemente, in modo persuasivo con una persona.

fair[1], *s.* **1.** il bello **2.** (*arc. poet.*) bella donna.

fair[2], *s.* fiera, mercato || *a day after the —*, troppo tardi ☆ *— -day*, giorno di fiera || *cattle —*, fiera del bestiame; *fancy —*, fiera di beneficenza; *fun —*, Luna Park; *sample —*, fiera campionaria; *world —*, esposizione universale.

fairing[1] ['fɛəriŋ], *s.* (*mar. aer.*) carenatura.

fairing[2], *s.* oggetto acquistato alla fiera.

fairish ['fɛəriʃ], *ag.* **1.** biondiccio (di capelli) **2.** passabile, mediocre **3.** alticcio; leggermente ubriaco.

fairly ['fɛəli], *av.* **1.** lealmente, onestamente; imparzialmente: *he treated me quite —*, mi trattò in modo del tutto leale **2.** abbastanza: *I am feeling — well*, mi sento benino; *I know him — well*, lo conosco abbastanza bene; *the play was*

— good, la commedia era abbastanza buona **3.** completamente: *we were — caught in the trap*, fummo completamente presi in trappola.

fairness ['fɛənis], *s.* **1.** bellezza **2.** color biondo; bianchezza, freschezza di carnagione **3.** imparzialità, equità; onestà; lealtà: *in all — I must say...*, in tutta franchezza devo dire... **4.** nitidezza.

fairway ['fɛəwei], *s.* canale navigabile.

fairy ['fɛəri], *ag.* **1.** di fata, delle fate; fatato, magico: *— forest*, foresta fatata; *— key*, chiave magica **2.** immaginario, fittizio || *s.* fata, maga; *fig.* ammaliatrice ☆ *— -lamp*, lampioncino alla veneziana; *— -ring*, circolo magico; *— -tale*, fiaba.

fairyland ['fɛərilænd], *s.* paese delle fate.

fairylike ['fɛərilaik], *ag.* simile a fata, da fata.

faith[1] [feiθ], *s.* **1.** fede; fiducia: *— in God*, fede in Dio; *I haven't much — in that man*, non ho molta fiducia in quell'uomo; *to put one's — in*, fidarsi di, porre fiducia in **2.** (*teol.*) fede, credo religioso: *the Christian —*, la fede cristiana **3.** lealtà, fedeltà || *in bad, good —*, in malafede, in buona fede; *in —*, in fede; *upon* (o *by*) *my —!*, in fede mia! **4.** promessa, garanzia || *to keep, to break one's —*, tener fede, venir meno alle proprie promesse ☆ *— -healer*, guaritore (con preghiere e suggestioni); *— -healing* (o *— -cure*), guarigione per suggestione.

Faith[2], *no.pr.f.* Fede.

faithful ['feiθful], *ag.* **1.** fedele, leale, costante: *a — friend*, un amico fedele || *the —*, i fedeli, i credenti **2.** degno di fiducia **3.** esatto, accurato, conforme a verità: *a — copy of the letter*, una copia esatta della lettera.

faithfully ['feiθfuli], *ag.* fedelmente, lealmente; letteralmente; formalmente || *Yours —*, distinti saluti.

faithfulness ['feiθfulnis], *s.* **1.** fedeltà, lealtà **2.** esattezza, precisione.

faithless ['feiθlis], *ag.* **1.** che non ha fede, senza fede **2.** sleale, perfido.

faithlessly ['feiθlisli], *av.* **1.** senza fede **2.** perfidamente, slealmente.

faithlessness ['feiθlisnis], *s.* **1.** mancanza di fede **2.** slealtà, perfidia.

faitour ['feitə*], *s.* (*arc.*) impostore.

fake[1] [feik], *s.* (*mar.*) duglia, giro di cavo.

to **fake**[1], *v.t.* (*mar.*) girare di cavo.

fake[2], *s.* (*sl.*) **1.** inganno, truffa **2.** notizia falsa; articolo falso, truccato.

to **fake**[2], *v.t.* (*sl.*) **1.** contraffare, falsificare; ingannare per mezzo di un trucco: *to — a painting*, falsificare un dipinto **2.** *to — up*, inventare (scuse, ecc.): *to — up a story*, inventare una storia.

fakement ['feikmənt], *s.* (*sl.*) **1.** truffa; inganno **2.** prodotto manipolato.

faker ['feikə*], *s.c.* (*sl.*) truffatore, truffatrice; falsificatore, falsificatrice.

fakir ['fɑ:kiə*], *s.* fachiro.

falbala ['fælbələ], *s.* falpalà.

falcade [fəl'kɑ:d], *s.* falcata.

falcate ['fælkeit], *ag.* (*anat. bot. zool.*) falcato.

falchion ['fɔ:ltʃən], *s.* scimitarra.

falciform ['fælsifɔ:m], *ag.* falciforme.

falcon ['fɔ:lkən], *s.* falcone ☆ *— house*, falconara.

falconer ['fɔ:lkənə*], *s.* falconiere.

falconet ['fɔ:lkənit], *s.* (*artigl.*) falconetto.

falconry ['fɔ:lkənri], *s.* falconeria.

falderal ['fældə'ræl], **falderol** ['fældə'rɔl], *s.* **1.** inezia, nonnulla **2.** (*arc.*) stornello.

faldstool ['fɔ:ldstu:l], *s.* **1.** (*eccl.*) faldistorio, panchettino episcopale **2.** inginocchiatoio.

Falernian [fə'lə:njən], *s.* Falerno (vino della Campania).

Falkland Islands ['fɔ:lklənd'ailəndz], *no.pr.* (*geog.*) Isole Falkland.

fall[1] [fɔ:l], *s.* **1.** caduta (anche *fig.*): *a — in prices*, un ribasso di prezzi; *a — in temperature*, un abbassamento di temperatura; *the — of an apple from a tree*, la caduta di una mela da un albero; *the — of day*, (*poet.*) il tramonto; *a — of snow*. una nevicata ‖ *to ride for a —*, (*fam.*) andare a rompicollo; agire inconsultamente ‖ *to try a — with s.o.*, provarsi nella lotta con qlcu. ‖ *dealing for —*, (*Borsa*) operazione al ribasso ‖ *the Fall* (*of Man*), la caduta dell'uomo **2.** (*amer.*) autunno **3.** *gener. pl.* cascata, cateratta: *the Niagara Falls*, le cascate del Niagara **4.** decadenza, rovina (di regno, ecc.): *the — of Troy*, la caduta di Troia **5.** declivio, discesa del terreno **6.** agnellatura **7.** (*mec.*) catena, cavo di comando, di manovra ☆ — *-trap*, trabocchetto.

to **fall**[1], *pass.* **fell** [fel], *p.p.* **fallen** ['fɔ:lən], *v.i.* **1.** cadere; abbattersi; crollare: *a big tree fell in the storm*, un grosso albero crollò durante la tempesta; *the book fell from the table to the floor*, il libro cadde dal tavolo sul pavimento; *he fell at my feet*, cadde ai miei piedi; *he fell into the well*, cadde nel pozzo; *he fell off* (o *from*) *the chair*, cadde dalla sedia; *he fell on his knees*, cadde in ginocchio; *he fell out of the window*, cadde dalla finestra; *mind you don't fall*, bada di non cadere; *to — full length*, cadere lungo disteso; *to — to pieces*, cadere in pezzi **2.** *fig.* cadere; decadere; diminuire (di vento, temperatura, prezzi, ecc.): *the accent falls on the last syllable*, l'accento cade sull'ultima sillaba; *Easter falls late this year*, quest'anno la Pasqua è alta; *a great fear fell upon me*, mi prese un grande terrore; *his vengeance fell on his enemies*, la sua vendetta cadde sui suoi nemici; *night is falling*, cade la sera; *not a word fell from his lips*, non pronunciò nemmeno una parola; *prices have fallen*, i prezzi sono diminuiti; *the wind fell*, il vento cadde; *to — in s.o.'s estimation*, perdere la stima di qlcu. ‖ *to — asleep*, addormentarsi; *to — in love*, innamorarsi; *to — ill*, ammalarsi **3.** soccombere; morire: *he fell in battle*, cadde combattendo; *to — into temptation*, soccombere alla tentazione **4.** inclinarsi (di terreno); scendere a valle (di fiume): *the Po falls into the Adriatic sea*, il Po sfocia nel mare Adriatico **5.** abbassarsi (di occhi): *her eyes fell*, ella abbassò gli occhi **6.** accadere per caso; toccare in sorte: *the expenses — on me*, la spesa è a mio carico; *to — to s.o.'s lot*, capitare in sorte a qlcu. **7.** dividersi: *his subject falls into three divisions*, la sua argomentazione si divide in tre parti ‖ **Seguito da prep. 8.** *to — behind*, rimanere indietro a; lasciarsi sorpassare da **9.** to — for, innamorarsi di, lasciarsi attrarre da: *he fell for her at once*, si innamorò subito di lei **10.** *to — into*, prendere (una posizione): *to — into a line*, (*mil.*) mettersi in riga; *to — into a habit*, prendere un'abitudine **11.** *to — (up)on*, gettarsi su, piombare su (nemico); imbattersi in; cavarsela **12.** *to — to*, cominciare a; mettersi a (lavoro) **13.** *to — under*, essere classificato fra, rientrare in; essere soggetto a **14.** *to — within*, essere incluso in: *it falls within article two*, è incluso nell'articolo due ‖ **Seguito da av. 15.** *to — astern*, (*mar.*) restare indietro **16.** *to — away*, allontanarsi; staccarsi; ribellarsi; deperire; dimagrire; cominciare a declinare (di terreno) **17.** *to — back*, ritirarsi ‖ *to — back (up)on*, ricorrere a; ripiegare su: *you can always — back on me*, puoi sempre ricorrere a me **18.** *to — behind*, rimanere indietro; indugiare **19.** *to — foul*, entrare in collisione; litigare **20.** *to — in*, (*mil.*) allinearsi, allinearsi; cadere, crollare (di edificio); scadere, maturare (di debito, contratto); essere disponibile (di terreno): *— in!*, (*mil.*) nei ranghi! ‖ *to — in with*, incontrare, imbattersi in; accordarsi con; conformarsi a: *in Rome I fell in with an old friend*, a Roma mi imbattei in un vecchio amico; *to — in with s.o.'s plans*, accettare, eseguire i progetti di qlcu. **21.** *to — off*, ritirarsi; ribellarsi; diminuire; sbiadire (di colori); (*mar.*) deviare sottovento **22.** *to — on*, buttarsi nella mischia; buttarsi con avidità sul cibo **23.** *to — out*, litigare; accadere; riuscir bene; (*mil.*) rompere le file: *things fell out well*, le cose riuscirono bene ‖ *to — out of*, rinunciare a (abitudini, ecc.) **24.** *to — short*, es-

sere insufficiente; avere spinta insufficiente (di missile) ‖ *to — short of*, non riuscire ad ottenere **25** *to — through*, fallire (di progetto) **26.** *to — to*, cominciare a combattere; cominciare a mangiare; chiudersi automaticamente (di cancello, ecc.).

fall[2], *s.* botola; trappola.

fall[3], *s.* **1.** grido dei balenieri quando la balena è avvistata o colpita dal ramponiere **2.** caccia alla balena.

fallacious [fə'leiʃəs], *ag.* fallace, erroneo.

fallaciously [fə'leiʃəsli], *av.* fallacemente.

fallaciousness [fə'leiʃəsnis], *s.* fallacia, inganno.

fallacy ['fæləsi], *s.* **1.** (*log.*) sofisma **2.** errore: *a current —*, un errore comune **3.** fallacia: *the — of senses*, la fallacia dei sensi.

fallal ['fæ'læl], *s. gener. pl.* falpalà, balza pieghettata, fronzolo.

fallen ['fɔ:lən], *p.p.* di to **fall**.

fallibility [,fæli'biliti], *s.* fallibilità.

fallible ['fæləbl], *ag.* fallibile.

fallibly ['fæləbli], *av.* in modo fallibile.

falling ['fɔ:liŋ], *ag.* cadente (anche *fig.*): *— empire*, impero in decadenza ‖ *s.* caduta, discesa (anche *fig.*) ☆ *— back*, deperimento; rivolta; apostasia; *— back*, (*mil.*) ripiegamento; *— in*, sprofondamento; crollo; *— off*, defezione; diminuzione; *— out*, dissidio; *— short*, deficienza, insufficienza; *— -sickness*, (*rar. patol.*) epilessia; *— -star*, stella cadente; *— -stone*, meteorite.

fall-out ['fɔ:l-aut], *s.* (*neol.*) pioggia radioattiva.

fallow[1] ['fælou], *ag.* fulvo ☆ *— -deer*, varietà di daino.

fallow[2], *ag.* (*agr.*) incolto: *to lie —*, rimanere incolto ‖ *s.* maggese ☆ *— field*, maggese.

to **fallow**[2], *v.t.* (*agr.*) **1.** arare **2.** maggesare.

fallowness ['fælounis], *s.* **1.** l'essere incolto (di terreno) **2.** ozio.

false [fɔ:ls], *ag.* **1.** falso, erroneo, sbagliato: *— imprisonment*, (*dir.*) imprigionamento illecito; *a — position*, una posizione falsa; *— pride*, falso orgoglio; *— start*, (*spor.*) falsa partenza; *— step*, passo falso **2.** ingannevole, mendace; infedele, perfido: *— swearing*, giuramento falso **3.** contraffatto, falsificato, artificiale, posticcio: *— beard*, barba posticcia; *a — coin*, una moneta falsa; *— teeth*, dentiera ‖ *to sail under — colours*, navigare sotto falsa bandiera; *fig.* mostrarsi sotto falso aspetto **4.** apparente, impropriamente chiamato così **5.** (*mus.*) stonato: *he struck a — note*, fece una stecca; *fig.* toccò un tasto falso ☆ *— acacia*, pseudoacacia; *— bottom*, doppio fondo; *— -faced*, ipocrita; *— -hearted*, perfido, sleale; *— keel*, (*mar.*) falsa chiglia, controchiglia.

to **false**, *v.t.* (*arc.*) **1.** ingannare **2.** falsificare.

false, *av.* falsamente ‖ *to play s.o. —*, ingannare qlcu.

falsehood ['fɔ:lshud], *s.* falsità; menzogna; frode: *to distinguish truth from —*, distinguere il vero dal falso.

falsely ['fɔ:lsli], *av.* falsamente.

falseness ['fɔ:lsnis], *s.* falsità; doppiezza; infedeltà.

falsetto [fɔ:l'setou], *pl.* **falsettos** [fɔ:l'setouz], *s.* (*mus.*) falsetto.

falsifiable ['fɔ:lsifaiəbl], *ag.* falsificabile.

falsification ['fɔ:lsifi'keiʃən], *s.* contraffazione; falsificazione.

falsifier ['fɔ:lsifaiə*], *s.* falsificatore; falsario.

to **falsify** ['fɔ:lsifai], *v.t.* **1.** falsificare, alterare, contraffare **2.** provare la falsità di; smentire (timori); deludere (speranze).

falsity ['fɔ:lsiti], *s.* **1.** menzogna; falsità **2.** scorrettezza, disonestà.

to **falter** ['fɔ:ltə*], *v.t.i.* **1.** barcollare, vacillare (di persona); essere irresoluto; tremare, esitare (di animo): *he never falters*, egli non esita mai **2.** balbettare **3.** *to — out*, dire balbettando: *he faltered out an excuse*, egli balbettò una scusa.

falterer ['fɔ:ltərə*], *s.* chi balbetta, si impappina.

faltering ['fɔ:ltəriŋ], *ag.* **1.** vacillante, barcollante (di persona): *a weak,* — *old woman,* una vecchia debole e tremante **2.** tremante, incerto (di voce) **3.** titubante, tentennante (di animo) ‖ *s.* debolezza; insufficienza.

falteringly ['fɔ:ltəriŋli], *av.* in modo barcollante; con esitazione.

famble ['fæmbl], *s.* (*sl.*) mano.

fame [feim], *s.* fama, rinomanza: *good* —, buona fama; *ill* —, cattiva fama; *to win* —, diventare famoso ‖ " *The House of Fame* ", (*lett.*) « La Casa della Fama ».

to fame, *v.t.* (*rar.*) rendere famoso.

famed [feimd], *ag.* rinomato, celebre: *to be* — *for sthg.,* essere famoso per ql.co. ☆ *world-* —, di fama mondiale.

fameless ['feimlis], *ag.* non famoso, comune.

familiar [fə'miljə*], *ag.* **1.** familiare; intimo: — *spirit,* folletto domestico; *to appear (quite)* — *with a subject,* apparire (molto) ferrato in un argomento; *to be* — (o *on* — *terms) with s.o.,* essere in rapporti familiari con qlcu.; *to be* — *with ᵀFrench,* conoscere bene il francese; *to make oneself* — *with sthg.,* imparare qualcosa **2.** conosciuto, usuale: *to be on* — *ground, fig.* trovarsi nel proprio elemento **3.** sfacciato, impudente ‖ *s.* **1.** amico intimo **2.** demone familiare.

familiarity [fə,mili'æriti], *s.* **1.** familiarità, intimità: *to treat s.o. with great* —, trattare qlcu. molto familiarmente **2.** conoscenza: — *with other peoples,* conoscenza di altri popoli **3.** impudenza, sfacciataggine, familiarità esagerata.

familiarization [fə,miljərai'zeiʃən], *s.* familiarità.

to familiarize [fə'miljəraiz], *v.t.* familiarizzare: *to* — *s.o. with sthg.,* far conoscere ql.co. a qlcu.

familiarly [fə'miljəli], *av.* familiarmente: *to treat s.o.* —, trattare qlcu. con familiarità.

family ['fæmili], *s.* **1.** famiglia: *the Brown* —, la famiglia Brown ‖ *the Holy Family,* la Sacra Famiglia ‖ *to be in the* — *way,* (*fam.*) essere incinta **2.** figli, prole: *a man of large* —, un padre di numerosa prole **3.** stirpe, discendenza **4.** famiglia, raggruppamento (di lingue, animali, piante, ecc.): *English belongs to the German* — *of languages,* l'inglese appartiene al gruppo delle lingue germaniche ☆ — *allowance,* assegni familiari; — *Bible,* Bibbia di famiglia (con le prime pagine in bianco su cui si segnano le date solenni della famiglia); — *boarding-house,* pensione familiare; — *butcher,* macellaio di famiglia; — *coach,* carrozza di famiglia; — *hotel,* albergo familiare; — *likeness,* somiglianza di famiglia; — *name,* cognome; — *tree,* albero genealogico; — *vault,* tomba di famiglia.

famine ['fæmin], *s.* carestia: *to die of* —, morire di fame ☆ — *prices,* prezzi elevati.

to famish ['fæmiʃ], *v.t.i.* **1.** morire di fame; essere affamato **2.** affamare, far morire di fame.

famished ['fæmiʃt], *ag.* affamato, famelico.

famishing ['fæmiʃiŋ], *ag.* affamato: *to be* —, (*fam.*) avere una fame da lupo.

famous ['feiməs], *s.* **1.** celebre, famoso: *town* — *for its monuments,* città famosa per i suoi monumenti **2.** (*fam.*) straordinario; ottimo: *he has a* — *appetite,* ha un appetito formidabile.

famously ['feiməsli], *av.* (*fam.*) splendidamente; a meraviglia.

famousness ['feiməsnis], *s.* celebrità, rinomanza.

famulus ['fæmjuləs], *pl.* **famuli** ['fæmjulai], *s.* **1.** famulo **2.** apprendista presso un mago.

fan¹ [fæn], *s.* **1.** ventaglio: *to arrange the fleet in* — *order,* (*mil.*) disporre la flotta a ventaglio **2.** (*poet.*) ala **3.** vaglio (per il grano) **4.** (*mec.*) ventilatore: *electric* —, ventilatore elettrico **5.** pala di mulino a vento; pala d'elica **6.** pinna caudale di balena ☆ — *turbine,* turboventilatore ‖ *alluvial* —, (*geol.*) conoide di deiezione.

to fan¹, *pass.p.p.* **fanned** [fænd], *v.t.i.* **1.** far vento a, sventolare: *to* — *oneself,* farsi vento; *to* — *the fire,* attizzare il fuoco (anche *fig.*); *to* — *the flame,* soffiare nel fuoco (anche *fig.*) **2.** (*agr.*) vagliare **3.** *to* — *out,* aprirsi a ventaglio (di truppe, ecc.).

fan², *s.c.* (*sl.*) tifoso, tifosa; appassionato, appassionata (di sport, ecc.); ammiratore, ammiratrice ☆ — *mail,* posta degli ammiratori (ad un attore, ecc.) ‖ *gramophone* —, discofilo.

fanatic [fə'nætik], *ag.s.* fanatico.

fanatical [fə'nætikəl], *ag.* fanatico.

fanatically [fə'nætikəli], *av.* fanaticamente.

fanaticism [fə'nætisizəm], *s.* fanatismo.

to fanaticize [fə'nætisaiz], *v.t.i.* **1.** rendere fanatico **2.** agire da fanatico.

fancied ['fænsid], *ag.* immaginario, fantastico.

fancier ['fænsiə*], *s.c.* amatore, amatrice; conoscitore, conoscitrice; allevatore, allevatrice ☆ *bird-* —, avicoltore; *rose-* —, conoscitore di rose.

fanciful ['fænsiful], *ag.* **1.** fantasioso, immaginoso **2.** immaginario, fantastico, chimerico.

fancifully ['fænsifuli], *av.* **1.** immaginosamente; fantasiosamente **2.** fantasticamente; in modo immaginario.

fancifulness ['fænsifulnis], *s.* **1.** fantasia; immaginazione **2.** fantasticheria, capriccio, ghiribizzo.

fancy ['fænsi], *ag.* **1.** immaginario, fantastico; capriccioso, stravagante **2.** decorato, elaborato, ricercato **3.** esorbitante, eccessivo **4.** (*amer.*) di qualità superiore ‖ *s.* **1.** fantasia, fantasticheria, immaginazione: *to strike s.o.'s* —, colpire la fantasia di qlcu. **2.** capriccio, ghiribizzo **3.** inclinazione, gusto; simpatia: *a passing* —, una simpatia passeggera; *to take a* — *to s.o., sthg.,* incapricciarsi per qlcu., ql.co. **4.** idea, supposizione arbitraria; *to have a* — *that...,* avere una vaga idea che... **5.** illusione: *he has a* — *that he can succeed in singing,* si illude di riuscire nel canto **6.** *the* —, gli appassionati dello sport (specialmente di pugilato) ☆ — *articles,* articoli fantasia; — *dog,* cane di lusso; — *-dress,* costume; — (-*dress*) *ball,* ballo in costume; — *fair,* fiera di beneficenza; — *food,* cibo di qualità superiore; — *-free,* non innamorato; — *price,* prezzo d'amatore; — *-shop,* negozio di lusso.

to fancy, *v.t.* **1.** (I) pensare, immaginare ‖ — *meeting you!,* chi avrebbe pensato di incontrarti!; — *now!* (o *just* — *that!*), chi l'avrebbe creduto!, che strano!, figurarsi!; *I* — *not,* non credo **2.** sentirsi attirato verso, aver desiderio di: *what do you* — *for dinner?,* cosa ti piacerebbe per cena? **3.** credere, supporre; illudersi; avere l'impressione: *he fancies that he can convince her,* s'illude di riuscire a convincerla; *I* — *I can go,* credo di poter andare; *I rather* — *that he won't come,* ho l'impressione che non verrà; *to* — *oneself,* avere un'alta opinione di sè **4.** fare allevamento di (uccelli, cani da salotto, ecc.); coltivare (piante pregiate).

fancying ['fænsiiŋ], *s.* allevamento di uccelli e piccoli animali pregiati; coltivazione di piante.

fandangle [fæn'dæŋgl], *s.* ornamento fantasioso.

fandango [fæn'dæŋgou], *s.* (*mus.*) fandango.

fane [fein], *s.* (*poet.*) fano, tempio.

fanfare ['fænfɛə*], *s.* fanfara.

fanfaronade [,fænfærə'na:d], *s.* **1.** fanfaronata, millanteria **2.** fanfara.

fang [fæŋ], *s.* **1.** zanna; dente canino **2.** dente velenoso (di serpente) **3.** *pl.* estremità velenose dei cheliceri del ragno **4.** radice dentaria **5.** (*mec.*) arpione.

to fang, *v.t.i.* **1.** (*rar.*) azzannare **2.** mettere in azione (una pompa).

fanged [fæŋd], *ag.* fornito di zanne.

fangless ['fæŋlis], *ag.* senza zanne.

fangle ['fæŋgl], *s.* (*rar.*) nuova moda, novità.

fanion ['fænjən], *s.* bandierina per segnalazioni.

fanlight ['fænlait], *s.* (*arch.*) lunetta.

fanner ['fænə*], *s.* ventilatore; macchina vagliatrice.

fanning ['fæniŋ], *s.* ventilazione.

Fanny ['fæni], *no.pr.f. dim.* di **Frances.**

fanon ['fænən], *s.* (*eccl.*) manipolo.

fantail ['fæn-teil], *s.* **1.** (*ornit.*) piccione con coda a ventaglio **2.** becco a gas con fiamma a ventaglio **3.** (*arch.*) struttura a ventaglio.

fantasia [fæn'teizjə], *s.* (*mus.*) fantasia.

fantasm, *V.* **phantasm.**

fantast ['fæntæst], *s.* visionario, sognatore.

fantastic(al) [fæn'tæstik(əl)], *ag.* 1. bizzarro, capriccioso, strano 2. (*rar.*) fantastico, immaginario.

fantastically [fæn'tæstikəli], *av.* 1. capricciosamente 2. fantasticamente.

fantasticalness [fæn'tæstikəlnis], *s.* bizzarria, eccentricità.

to fantasticate [fæn'tæstikeit], *v.i.* fantasticare.

fantasy ['fæntəsi], *s.* 1. fantasia, immaginazione 2. capriccio 3. prodotto della fantasia, visione 4. (*mus.*) fantasia.

faquir ['fɑ:kiə*], *s.* fachiro.

far [fɑ:*], *comp.* **farther** ['fɑ:ðə*], **further** ['fə:ðə*], *superl.* **farthest** ['fɑ:ðist], **furthest** ['fə:ðist], *ag.* 1. lontano, distante, discosto, remoto: *a — country,* un paese distante; *the — past,* il lontano passato ‖ *the Far East,* l'Estremo Oriente ‖ *his presents are few and — between,* i suoi regali sono ben rari ‖ *it is a — way (o cry) from here to...,* c'è una grande distanza da qui a... 2. (= *farther, further*) più distante; opposto: *the — bank of the river,* la riva opposta del fiume; *the — wall of the room,* la parete più distante della stanza ‖ *s.* luogo lontano: *do you come from —?,* vieni da un luogo lontano?.

far, *av.* 1. **lontano, distante, discosto:** *the house is not very — from here,* la casa non è molto distante da qui; *how — did you go?,* fin dove sei andato?; *how — is it from... to...?,* quanto c'è da... a...? ‖ *— and near* (o *— and wide*), dappertutto, per ogni dove, in capo al mondo; *— away* (o *off*), lontano ‖ *as — as,* fino a (di spazio); per quanto: *as — as the eye can see,* a perdita d'occhio; *as — as I know,* per quanto io sappia; *to go as — as Rome,* andare fino a Roma ‖ (*in*) *so — as,* per quanto: *so — as I know he is already busy enough,* per quel che so è già abbastanza occupato; *so —,* finora, fin qui: *so — and no further,* fin qui e non oltre; *so — so good,* sin qui va bene; *thus —,* fin qui ‖ *to go —, fig.* andar lontano, farsi un nome; *to go too —,* esagerare, eccedere: *this is going too —,* questo è un po' troppo 2. **lungi:** *— from,* lungi da: *— be it from me,* lungi da me, Dio me ne guardi; *— from it,* tutto al contrario; *I am — from denying that...,* son lungi dal negare che...; *this is — from perfect,* questo è lungi dall'essere perfetto 3. **di gran lunga, molto, assai:** *— better, worse, larger,* etc., di gran lunga migliore, peggiore, più grande, ecc.; *— different from...,* di gran lunga diverso da...; *by —* (o *— and away*), di molto, di gran lunga ☆ *—-away,* lontano; distratto; *—-fetched,* stiracchiato (di* racconto, ecc.); *—-flung,* ampio; d'ampio respiro; *—-gone,* molto ammalato; ubriaco; indebitato; *—-reaching,* di gran portata; *—-seeing,* preveggente; perspicace; prudente; *—-sighted,* presbite; *fig.* previdente.

farad ['færəd], *s.* (*fis.*) farad.

faradaic [,færə'deik], *ag.* (*fis.*) faradico.

farce [fɑ:s], *s.* (*teat.*) farsa; situazione farsesca, buffonata: *the discussions were a mere —,* i dibattiti furono una pura farsa.

to farce, *v.t.* (*arc. cuc.*) farcire (anche *fig.*).

farcical ['fɑ:sikəl], *ag.* (*teat.*) farsesco; burlesco, buffo, comico.

farcicality [,fɑ:si'kæliti], *s.* qualità farsesca.

farcically ['fɑ:sikəli], *av.* in modo farsesco; per burla.

farcy ['fɑ:si], *s.* (*patol.*) farcino ☆ *—-bud* (o *—-button*), (*patol.*) nodulo della morva.

fardel ['fɑ:dəl], *s.* (*arc.*) 1. fardello, fagotto 2. *fig.* peso; sventura ☆ *—-bag,* (*zool.*) omaso.

fare [fɛə*], *s.* 1. prezzo di una corsa (in treno, tram, autobus, ecc.): *fares will be raised next month,* le tariffe subiranno un aumento il mese prossimo 2. passeggero, cliente: *the taximan took his — to the station,* il tassista condusse il suo cliente alla stazione 3. vitto, cibo; viveri: *bill of —.* lista delle vivande; *good, bad —,*

vitto buono, cattivo ☆ *adult —* (o *full- —*), tariffa intera; *excess —,* supplemento (di tariffa); *half- —,* tariffa ridotta; *return —,* prezzo del biglietto di andata e ritorno; *single —,* prezzo del biglietto semplice.

to fare, *v.i.* 1. andare; vagare; viaggiare ‖ *— thee well,* (*poet.*) addio! ‖ *to — forth,* (*poet.*) partire 2. accadere, capitare; risultare: *he fared well in his business,* ebbe successo negli affari; *how fares it?,* (*fam.*) come vanno le cose?; *it has fared well, ill with him,* gli è andata bene, male 3. nutrirsi, essere nutriti: *to — well,* trattarsi bene (a tavola).

farewell ['fɛə'wel], *s.* congedo, commiato benaugurante: *to take one's —,* prendere congedo da qlcu.

farewell, *inter.* addio!: *— for ever,* addio per sempre.

farina [fə'rainə], *s.* 1. farina 2. (*bot.*) polline 3. (*chim.*) amido.

farinaceous [,færi'neiʃəs], *ag.* 1. farinaceo 2. amidaceo.

farinose ['færinous], *ag.* farinoso; infarinato.

farl [fɑ:l], *s.* (*scoz.*) focaccina di farina d'avena o di frumento.

farm[1] [fɑ:m], *s.* 1. fattoria; masseria; azienda agricola; tenuta, podere 2. nido d'infanzia 3. allevamento 4. (*st.*) canone d'affitto (di terreni, ecc.) ☆ *—-buildings,* edifici della fattoria; *— equipment,* materiale agricolo; *—-hand,* bracciante; *—-labourer,* bracciante; *—-servant,* lavorante domestico di fattoria; *—-stead,* cascina; *—-yard,* cortile di casa colonica, aia ‖ *chicken —,* allevamento di polli.

to farm[1], *v.t.i.* 1. coltivare: *he farms 200 acres,* egli coltiva 200 acri 2. fare l'agricoltore: *he is farming in Australia,* fa l'agricoltore in Australia 3. prendere, dare in appalto: *to — (out),* dare in appalto 4. tenere a pensione, assumere la cura di (specialmente bambini).

to farm[2], *v.t.* (*dial.*) vuotare, pulire.

farmable ['fɑ:məbll], *ag.* coltivabile.

farmer ['fɑ:mə*], *s.* 1. agricoltore; fattore; mezzadro; fittavolo; piantatore ‖ *"Old Farmer's Almanac",* «Almanacco degli Agricoltori» 2. esattore.

farmhouse ['fɑ:mhaus], *s.* casa colonica.

farming ['fɑ:miŋ], *s.* 1. il lavoro di una fattoria 2. il possedere, il dirigere una fattoria 3. agricoltura; coltivazione 4. il dare, prendere in affitto (terre, ecc.).

farmost ['fɑ:moust], *av.* lontanissimo; il più lontano.

faro ['fɛərou], *s.* (*carte*) faraone.

farouche [fə'ru:ʃ], *ag.* timido, ritroso.

farraginous [fə'reidʒinəs] *ag.* farraginoso.

farrago [fə'rɑ:gou], *s.* miscuglio, farragine.

farrier ['færiə*], *s.* 1. maniscalco 2. (*arc.*) veterinario; (*mil.*) ufficiale veterinario.

farriery ['færiəri], *s.* 1. lavoro del maniscalco 2. (*arc.*) veterinaria.

farrow ['færou], *s.* figliata, parto (di una scrofa).

to farrow, *v.t.i.* figliare (di scrofa).

fart [fɑ:t], *s.* (*volg.*) peto, scoreggia.

to fart, *v.i.* (*volg.*) emettere peti, scoreggiare.

farther ['fɑ:ðə*], *ag.* (*comp.* di **far**) 1. più lontano, più in là ‖ *on the — bank of the river,* sulla riva opposta del fiume 2. ulteriore, addizionale ‖ *av.* 1. di più, inoltre 2. oltre, più lontano: *— back,* più indietro; *— off,* più distante; *— on,* più avanti; *we could go no —,* non potevamo andare oltre ‖ *to wish s.o. —,* mandare qlcu. al diavolo.

to farther, *v.t.* (*rar.*) facilitare, far progredire.

farthermost ['fɑ:ðəmoust], *ag.* il più lontano (di luogo).

farthest ['fɑ:ðist], (*superl.* di **far**) *ag.* il più lontano: *at the —,* al più tardi; al più lontano; al massimo ‖ *av.* alla maggior distanza; al massimo.

farthing ['fɑ:ðiŋ], *s.* 1. quarto di «penny» 2. *fig.* cosa di nessun valore: *it does not matter a —,* non importa nulla; *it is not worth a (brass) —,* non vale un centesimo.

farthingale ['fɑ:ðiŋgeil], s. crinolina; guardinfante.
fasces ['fæsi:z], s. pl. (st. romana) fasci.
fascia ['feiʃə], nel senso 3. ['fæʃiə]; pl. **fasciae** ['feiʃii:], nel senso 1. **fascias** ['feiʃəz], s. 1. (arch.) fascia 2. (astr.) anello 3. (anat.) aponeurosi, membrana aponeurotica 4. benda, fascia.
fasciated ['fæʃieitid], ag. 1. (bot.) affastellato 2. striato.
fascicle ['fæsikl], s. 1. (bot.) mazzetto, ciuffo, cespo 2. fascicolo, dispensa.
fasciculation [fə,sikju'leiʃən], s. formazione di fascicoli.
fascicule ['fæsikju:l], V. **fascicle**.
to **fascinate** ['fæsineit], v.t. affascinare, ammaliare, incantare.
fascinating ['fæsineitiŋ], ag. incantatore, avvincente, ammaliatore, affascinante.
fascinatingly ['fæsineitiŋli], av. in modo affascinante, avvincente.
fascination [,fæsi'neiʃən], s. fascino, attrattiva, malia, incanto: the — of a phrase, l'incanto di una frase.
fascinator ['fæsineitə*], s.c. affascinatore, affascinatrice || s. (amer.) fisciù, scialletto.
fascine [fæ'si:n], s. (mil.) fascina ☆ — dwelling, palafitta.
fascism ['fæʃizəm], s. (pol.) fascismo.
fascist ['fæʃist], ag.s. 1. (pol.) fascista 2. reazionario.
fash [fæʃ], s. (scoz.) 1. noia, uggia 2. pena, preoccupazione.
to **fash**, v.t.i. (scoz.) 1. annoiare, seccare: to — oneself, annoiarsi 2. preoccuparsi, tormentarsi.
fashion ['fæʃən], s. 1. modo, maniera: after (o in) a —, in un certo modo; after the — of, alla maniera di, ad imitazione di; they behaved in a strange —, si comportarono in modo strano; to speak in a rude —, parlare in modo villano 2. abitudine, uso, usanza: she got up at eight o' clock, as was her —, si alzò alle otto, come d'abitudine 3. moda, foggia, stile, voga: in, out of —, alla moda, fuori moda; in the latest —, all'ultima moda; — changes every year, la moda cambia ogni anno; to be all the —, essere alla moda; to bring sthg. into —, lanciare la moda di ql.co.; to follow (o to be in) the —, seguire la moda; to set the —, creare la moda || a man of —, un uomo di mondo 4. usi convenzionali dell'alta società ☆ — -book (o — magazine), rivista di mode; — -plate, figurino di mode.
to **fashion**, v.t. foggiare, forgiare, formare, modellare: to — a boat out of a trunk, fare una barca da un tronco d'albero; to — clay into a jug, foggiare una brocca dall'argilla.
fashionable ['fæʃnəbl] , ag. 1. alla moda, di moda: green is very — this year, il verde è molto di moda quest'anno 2. elegante, distinto: — gentleman, uomo elegante, della buona società || the — circles, i salotti; the — world, il bel mondo, il gran mondo || s. persona elegante, alla moda ☆ — -looking, dall'aspetto elegante.
fashionableness ['fæʃnəblnis], s. eleganza, distinzione.
fashionably ['fæʃnəbli], av. alla moda, elegantemente.
fast¹ [fɑ:st], ag. 1. fermo, saldo, fisso; attaccato; solido, inalterabile: — colours, colori solidi; a — knot, un nodo stretto, saldo; make the boat —, legate bene la barca; the post is — in the ground, il palo è fisso nel terreno; to make the doors —, chiudere per bene a chiave le porte || hard and — rules, regolamenti di servizio || to take (a) — hold of, afferrare saldamente 2. fig. fedele, leale; provato: a — friend, un amico fedele 3. rapido, veloce, celere; in anticipo (di orologio): a — train, un treno diretto; a — trip, un viaggio rapido; the horse went at a — trot, il cavallo andava a trotto serrato; my watch is ten minutes —, il mio orologio è avanti di dieci minuti 4. fig. dissoluto, libertino, amante dei piaceri: the — set, quelli che fanno la bella vita, i gaudenti; a — woman, una donna di dubbia reputazione; he lives a — life, egli conduce una vita dissoluta.
fast¹, av. 1. fermamente; saldamente; fortemente; strettamente: — asleep, profondamente addormentato; — beside (o — by), (arc.) vicinissimo; hold — to the branch, tieni saldo al ramo; stand —, sta fermo; they bound him —, lo legarono stretto || to play — and loose (with), giocare a tiremmolla (con); fare il doppio giuoco 2. presto, velocemente, rapidamente: he ran as — as he could, corse alla maggiore velocità possibile; her tears fell —, pianse a calde lacrime; it is raining —, piove a dirotto; to talk —, parlare in fretta; to walk —, camminare veloce 3. in modo dissoluto: to live —, condurre una vita dissoluta.
fast², s. astinenza, digiuno: to break one's —, rompere il digiuno ☆ — -day, (eccl.) giorno di digiuno.
to **fast²**, v.i. digiunare; osservare il digiuno (anche eccl.).
fast³, s. (mar.) trozza.
to **fasten** ['fɑ:sn], v.t.i. 1. attaccare, legare, stringere (un nodo); allacciare, allacciarsi (di abito, scarpe): to — a dress, allacciare un vestito; to — (up) a parcel, legare un pacco 2. chiudere, chiudersi; sbarrare: the door will not —, non si riesce a chiudere la porta 3. fissare, fissarsi; concentrare, concentrarsi: to — one's attention upon a subject, concentrare l'attenzione su un argomento; to — one's eyes on s.o., fissare qlcu. con insistenza || to — a crime upon s.o., incolpare qlcu.; to — a nickname upon s.o., affibbiare un soprannome a qlcu. || to — (up)on a pretext, attaccarsi, appigliarsi a un pretesto 4. to — off, assicurare con un nodo 5. to — up, legare saldamente: to — up a dog, legare un cane alla catena.
fastener ['fɑ:snə*], s. chi, ciò che lega insieme; legaccio, laccio; chiusura, fermaglio: ☆ door —, chiavistello; paper, sample —, fermaglio per carta, per campioni; self-locking —, fermaglio automatico; snap —, bottoncino a pressione, automatico; zip —, chiusura lampo.
fastening ['fɑ:sniŋ], s. 1. legatura, fissaggio 2. gancio; chiavistello ☆ — screw, (mec.) vite di fissaggio.
faster ['fɑ:stə*], s.c. digiunatore, digiunatrice.
fasti ['fæsti:], s. pl. (st. romana) fasti.
fastidious [fæs'tidiəs], ag. 1. meticoloso, esigente, difficile da accontentare: she's very — about her dresses, è molto esigente in fatto di abiti 2. schizzinoso, schifiltoso; (fam.) pignolo.
fastidiously [fæs'tidiəsli], av. 1. meticolosamente 2. schifiltosamente.
fastidiousness [fæs'tidiəsnis], s. 1. meticolosità 2. schifiltosità; (fam.) pignoleria.
fastigiate [fæs'tidʒiit], ag. (arch. bot.) fastigiato.
fastness ['fɑ:stnis], s. 1. velocità, celerità 2. fermezza, saldezza, forza (anche fig.); solidità, inalterabilità (di colori) 3. fortezza, luogo fortificato (generalmente in montagna, di banditi).
fat [fæt], ag. 1. grasso, untuoso; oleoso: — meat, carne grassa 2. grasso, grosso, corpulento, pingue: to get (o to grow) —, ingrassare 3. fertile, ricco, proficuo: a — job, un lavoro ben rimunerato; — lands, terreni fertili || a — lot!, (sl.) un bel niente!; that's a — lot of help!, è un bell'aiuto! || to cut up —, (sl.) morire lasciando un patrimonio 4. stupido, ottuso ☆ — -brained, stupido; — -head, zuccone, testa dura; — -hen, (bot.) chenopodio.
fat, s. 1. grasso: animal, vegetable —, grasso animale, vegetale || the — is in the fire, (sl.) ormai il male è fatto 2. grasso, corpulenza: to put on —, ingrassare 3. fig. lusso, vita comoda: to live on the — of the land, vivere nella bambagia, nel lusso 4. (teat.) parte di rilievo ☆ wool —, (chim.) lanolina.
to **fat**, pass.p.p. **fatted** ['fætid], V. to **fatten**.
fatal ['feitl], ag. 1. fatale, inevitabile; necessario; destinato, voluto dal destino || the — sisters, (mit.) le Parche 2. decisivo, importante 3. funesto, mortale.
fatalism ['feitəlizəm], s. fatalismo.

fatalist ['feitəlist], *s.* fatalista.

fatalistic [,feitə'listik], *ag.* fatalistico.

fatality [fə'tæliti], *s.* **1.** fatalità; sottomissione al destino **2.** sfortuna, calamità **3.** morte accidentale.

fatally ['feitəli], *av.* **1.** fatalmente; inevitabilmente **2.** mortalmente.

fate [feit], *s.* **1.** fato, destino: *they wished to go to America but — decided where they should go,* desideravano andare in America ma il fato decise dove dovevano andare || *the Fates,* (*mit.*) le Parche || *as sure as —,* certissimo **2.** sorte: *the group captain was worried about the — of the airman,* il colonnello era preoccupato per la sorte dell'aviatore; *to leave s.o. to his —,* abbandonare qlcu. al suo destino **3.** (*solo sing.*) morte; distruzione: *to meet one's —,* essere uccisi.

to fate, *v.t.* (*gener.*) al *passivo*) stabilire, destinare: *it was fated (that)...,* fu stabilito (che)...; *to be fated to...,* essere destinato a....

fateful ['feitful], *ag.* **1.** profetico **2.** importante; decisivo; fatale **3.** mortale.

fatefulness ['feitfulnis], *s.* fatalità.

father ['fɑ:ðə*], *s.* **1.** padre: *he was a — to her,* le fece da padre || *like — like son,* tale il padre tale il figlio || *the child is — to the man,* nel bimbo c'è il germe dell'uomo **2.** *Father,* (*eccl.*) Padre: *the Father,* il Padre; *God the Father,* Dio Padre; *the Holy Father,* il Santo Padre, il Papa; *the most Reverend Father O'Brien,* il molto Reverendo Padre O'Brien || *the Fathers of the Church,* i Padri della Chiesa **3.** *pl.* gli anziani: *our fathers,* i nostri antenati || *the Pilgrim Fathers,* (*st. amer.*) i Padri Pellegrini ☆ *— confessor,* padre spirituale; *-in-law,* suocero || *adoptive —,* padre adottivo; *conscript fathers,* (*st. romana*) senatori; *god- —,* santolo; *step- —,* patrigno.

to father, *v.t.* **1.** procreare **2.** adottare (un bimbo) **3.** riconoscere la paternità di; *fig.* attribuire, addossarsi la paternità di (libro, progetto, ecc.).

fatherhood ['fɑ:ðəhud], *s.* paternità.

fatherland ['fɑ:ðəlænd], *s.* (madre) patria.

fatherless ['fɑ:ðəlis], *ag.* **1.** orfano di padre **2.** figlio di padre sconosciuto.

fatherlike ['fɑ:ðəlaik], *ag.* paterno || *av.* paternamente.

fatherliness ['fɑ:ðəlinis], *s.* amore, affetto paterno.

fatherly ['fɑ:ðəli], *ag.* paterno || *av.* paternamente.

fathom ['fæðəm], *s.* (*mar.*) braccio (misura di profondità = m. 1,829): *ten fathoms deep,* a dieci braccia di profondità, profondo dieci braccia.

to fathom, *v.t.* **1.** (*mar.*) scandagliare, misurare la profondità di **2.** *fig.* approfondire, penetrare, spiegare (questione, ecc.) **3.** (*arc.*) abbracciare.

fathomable ['fæðəməbl], *ag.* **1.** misurabile **2.** *fig.* spiegabile, comprensibile.

fathomless ['fæðəmlis], *ag.* **1.** incommensurabile **2.** *fig.* incomprensibile, impenetrabile.

fatidic(al) [fei'tidik(əl)], *ag.* fatidico.

fatidically [fei'tidikəli], *av.* fatidicamente.

fatigue [fə'ti:g], *s.* **1.** stanchezza, esaurimento **2.** fatica; lavoro faticoso, pesante **3.** (*mil.*) corvée **4.** (*metal.*) fatica ☆ *-dress,* tenuta di fatica; *— -duty,* (*mil.*) corvée; *— -party,* (*mil.*) distaccamento per servizio comandato.

to fatigue, *v.t.* **1.** affaticare, stancare: *to — oneself,* affaticarsi **2.** (*metal.*) affaticare.

fatigueless [fə'ti:glis], *ag.* non faticoso, non affaticante.

fatiguing [fə'ti:giŋ], *ag.* snervante, sfibrante.

fatiguingly [fə'ti:giŋli], *av.* in modo snervante.

fatling ['fætliŋ], *s.* animale da ingrasso.

fatly ['fætli], *av.* **1.** largamente, lautamente **2.** pesantemente, grevemente.

fatness ['fætnis], *s.* grassezza, pinguedine; corpulenza.

fatted ['fætid], *ag.: to kill the — calf, fig.* uccidere il vitello grasso; far festa a chi ritorna.

to fatten ['fætn], *v.t.i.* **1.** ingrassare, ingrassarsi (anche *fig.*) **2.** fertilizzare.

fattener ['fætnə*], *s.c.* ingrassatore, ingrassatrice || *s.* ciò che fa ingrassare.

fattening ['fætniŋ], *ag.* ingrassante || *s.* ingrassamento.

fattiness ['fætinis], *s.* grassezza; untuosità.

fattish ['fætiʃ], *ag.* grassoccio.

fatty ['fæti], *ag.* grasso, untuoso, oleoso: *— oil,* olio grasso; *— soil,* suolo grasso || *s.* bimbo grassoccio (usato al vocativo).

fatuitous [fə'tju(:)itəs], *ag.* fatuo.

fatuity [fə'tju(:)iti], *s.* fatuità.

fatuous ['fætjuəs], *ag.* fatuo ☆ *— fire,* fuoco fatuo.

fatuously ['fætjuəsli], *av.* in modo fatuo, fatuamente.

fatuousness ['fætjuəsnis], *s.* fatuità, stoltezza.

fatwitted ['fæt,witid], *ag.* ottuso, stupido.

faubourg ['fubuəg], *s.* sobborgo (generalmente di Parigi).

faucal ['fɔ:kəl], *ag.* (*fonet.*) gutturale.

fauces ['fɔ:si:z], *s.pl.* (*anat.*) fauci.

faucet ['fɔ:sit], *s.* (*amer.*) rubinetto; zipolo.

faugh [fɔ:], *inter.* puh!, eh, via!.

fault [fɔ:lt], *s.* **1.** mancanza, difetto, imperfezione: *to find — with s.o., sthg.,* trovare a ridire sul conto di qlcu., ql.co. **2.** fallo, errore; colpa, pecca: *at —,* colpevole: *to be at —,* essere colpevole; *to a —,* all'eccesso; *it is not my —,* non è colpa mia; *whose — is it?,* di chi è la colpa? **3.** (*geol.*) faglia **4.** (*elett.*) difetto d'impianto **5.** (*tennis, ecc.*) fallo ☆ *— -finder,* ipercritico, chi trova sempre da ridire; *— -finding,* critica pedante.

to fault, *v.t.i.* **1.** (*geol.*) spostare, spostarsi **2.** (*rar.*) biasimare **3.** (*arc.*) commettere una colpa.

faultage ['fɔ:ltidʒ], *s.* (*geol.*) faglia.

faultful ['fɔ:ltful], *ag.* pieno di difetti, di errori, di colpe.

faultily ['fɔ:ltili], *av.* difettosamente, imperfettamente; in modo censurabile.

faultiness ['fɔ:ltinis], *s.* imperfezione; manchevolezza; imprecisione.

faultless ['fɔ:ltlis], *ag.* senza difetto, impeccabile, irreprensibile; perfetto.

faultlessly ['fɔ:ltlisli], *av.* impeccabilmente; irreprensibilmente; perfettamente.

faultlessness ['fɔ:ltlisnis], *s.* impeccabilità, irreprensibilità; perfezione.

faulty ['fɔ:lti], *ag.* difettoso, imperfetto; censurabile: *— articulation,* pronuncia difettosa; *— construction of the sentence,* imperfetta costruzione della proposizione.

faun [fɔ:n], *s.* (*mit.*) fauno.

fauna ['fɔ:nə], *pl.* **faunae** ['fɔ:ni:], **faunas** ['fɔ:nəz], *s.* fauna.

faunal ['fɔ:nəl], *ag.* faunico.

faunist ['fɔ:nist], *s.* studioso della fauna.

Faunus ['fɔ:nəs], *no.pr.m.* (*mit.*) Fauno.

Faustina [fɔ:s'ti:nə], *no.pr.f.* Faustina.

Faustus ['fɔ:stəs], *no.pr.m.* Fausto.

fauteuil ['foutə:i], *s.* poltrona; poltrona di teatro.

fautor ['fɔtə*], *s.* fautore, favoreggiatore.

faux pas ['fou'pɑ:], *pl.* **faux pas** ['fou'pɑ:z], *s.* passo falso; imprudenza, errore.

Favonian [fə'vounjən], *ag.* (*meteorologia*) di favonio; *fig.* propizio, favorevole.

favour ['feivə*], *s.* **1.** favore; piacere; beneficio; dono: *this is a very great —,* questo è un grandissimo favore; *to ask a —,* chiedere un favore a qlcu.: *may I ask a — of you?,* posso chiederti un favore?; *to do s.o. a —,* fare un favore a qlcu.; *to receive a — from s.o.,* ricevere un dono da qlcu. **2.** grazia, buone grazie; approvazione: *by* (o *with*) *your —,* con il vostro permesso; *in — of,* in favore di; *to find — in s.o.'s eyes,* venir apprezzato da qlcu.; *to stand* (o *to be*) *high in s.o.'s —,* essere nelle buone grazie di qlcu.; *to win s.o.'s —,* conquistarsi i favori, la benevolenza di qlcu. **3.** parzialità; indulgenza: *he got that job by their — more than by his merit*, ottenne quel posto più per loro indulgenza che per merito suo **4.** (*comm.*) pregiata, stimata (lettera): *your — of the 17th inst.*, la vostra pregiata del 17 corr. **5.** distintivo; coccarda **6.** aiuto, vantaggio: *under — of night*, col favore della notte **7.** (*arc.*) lineamenti, fattezze.

to favour, *v.t.* **1.** favorire: *please — me with a prompt reply*, (*comm.*) abbiate la cortesia di rispondere al più presto; *to — s.o. with sthg.*, favorire qlcu. in ql.co.; *to be favoured by circumstances*, essere favorito dalle circostanze **2.** preferire, accordare preferenza a; sostenere (una teoria); confermare (un fatto): *I don't — your idea*, non approvo la vostra idea **3.** favoreggiare; avvantaggiare: *favoured by fortune*, favorito dalla fortuna; *the weather favoured our trip*, il tempo favorì la nostra gita **4.** (*fam.*) rassomigliare a: *she favours her father*, rassomiglia a suo padre.

favourable ['feivərəbl], *ag.* favorevole, propizio (di tempo, circostanze, ecc.): *the singer received a — reception*, il cantante ebbe un buon successo, fu ben accolto dal pubblico; *to look at s.o. with a — eye*, guardare qlcu. con occhio favorevole, benevolmente.

favourableness ['feivərəblnis], *s.* stato favorevole; benevolenza.

favourably ['feivərəbli], *av.* favorevolmente.

favoured ['feivəd], *ag.* favorito, privilegiato: *the — few*, i pochi privilegiati; *the most — nation*, la nazione più favorita ☆ *ill- —*, brutto, di brutto aspetto; *well- —*, bello, di bell'aspetto.

favourer ['feivərə*], *s.c.* chi favorisce; favoreggiatore, favoreggiatrice ‖ *s.* protettore; partigiano.

favouring ['feivəriŋ], *ag.* favorevole, propizio (di vento, circostanza, ecc.).

favouringly ['feivəriŋli], *av.* favorevolmente.

favourite ['feivərit], *ag.* preferito: *his — son* (*poet, book, etc.*), il figlio (poeta, libro, ecc.) preferito da lui ‖ *— son*, (*amer.*) figlio favorito (candidato presidenziale presentato da uno stato sebbene non abbia probabilità di essere eletto) ‖ *s.c.* favorito, favorita: *the king's —*, la favorita del re; *he is a general —*, tutti gli vogliono bene; *I bet on the —*, ho scommesso sul (cavallo) favorito.

favouritism ['feivəritizəm], *s.* favoritismo.

favourless ['feivəlis], *ag.* senza favore, considerato sfavorevole.

fawn[1] [fɔːn], *s.* **1.** (*zool.*) cerbiatto; daino **2.** colore fulvo ☆ *— -coloured*, di colore fulvo.

to fawn[1], *v.t.i.* figliare (di daini).

to fawn[2], *v.t.i.* **1.** dimostrare affetto per, far festa a: *my dog fawns (up)on me when I come home*, quando torno a casa il mio cane mi fa le feste **2.** *fig.* adulare, corteggiare servilmente.

fawner ['fɔːnə*], *s.c.* adulatore, adulatrice; persona strisciante, servile.

fawning ['fɔːniŋ], *ag.* strisciante ‖ *s.* servilismo, adulazione.

fawningly ['fɔːniŋli], *av.* servilmente; festosamente.

fay[1] [fei], *s.* (*arc.*) fede: *by my —!*, affè mia!.

fay[2], *s.* (*poet.*) fata.

fay[3], *s.* scoria.

to fay[3], *v.t.* (*dial.*) pulire.

to fay[4], *v.t.* unire a stretto contatto; (*amer.*) provare, modellare (in sartoria).

fealty ['fiːəlti], *s.* (*st.*) fedeltà (del vassallo al signore feudale): *to take oath of —*, fare giuramento di fedeltà.

fear [fiə*], *s.* **1.** paura, timore; apprensione; terrore: *the — of death*, il terrore della morte; *for — that*, per tema che; *wild with —*, pazzo di terrore; *there is no — of his escaping* (o *that he will escape*), non c'è pericolo che fugga; *to go in — of one's life*, temere per la propria vita; *to have fears for s.o.*, essere in apprensione per qlcu.; *to stand* (o *to be*) *in — of s.o., sthg.*, temere, tremare davanti a qlcu., per ql.co. ‖ *no — of my going*, (*fam.*) non c'è pericolo che ci vada ‖ *without — or favour*,

(*letter.*) in modo imparziale **2.** rispetto, timore (di Dio, della legge, ecc.) ‖ *to put the — of God into s.o.*, (*fam.*) dare una solenne lavata di capo a qlcu.

to fear, *v.t.i.* **1.** temere, aver paura: *he fears lest he should be discovered*, teme di essere scoperto; *I — I am late*, temo di essere in ritardo; *I — I have offended him*, temo di averlo offeso; *I — I shall be late*, temo che sarò in ritardo; *she fears to speak in his presence*, ha paura di parlare in sua presenza; *to — death*, temere la morte; *to — for s.o., sthg.*, essere in pensiero per qlcu., ql.co. ‖ *I — not*, non temo, non credo; *I — so*, temo di sì; *never —!*, niente paura! **2.** rispettare (le leggi); temere (Dio).

fearful ['fiəful], *ag.* **1.** terribile, spaventoso: *a — cry*, un grido spaventoso; *there was a — mess*, (*fam.*) c'era un disordine da non credersi **2.** pavido; timoroso, timido: *a — man*, un uomo pauroso.

fearfully ['fiəfəli], *av.* **1.** spaventosamente, paurosamente: *it's — hot!*, (*fam.*) fa tremendamente caldo! **2.** timidamente, timorosamente.

fearfulness ['fiəfulnis], *s.* **1.** aspetto terribile, terrificante **2.** timore; apprensione.

fearless ['fiəlis], *ag.* senza paura, intrepido, coraggioso: *she is — of the future*, non ha paura dell'avvenire.

fearlessly ['fiəlisli], *av.* senza paura; intrepidamente.

fearlessness ['fiəlisnis], *s.* intrepidezza, coraggio.

fearnought ['fiənɔːt], *s.* pesante stoffa di lana.

fearsome ['fiəsəm], *ag.* **1.** spaventoso, terrificante **2.** (*dial.*) timoroso, timido.

fearsomely ['fiəsəmli], *av.* spaventosamente.

fearsomeness ['fiəsəmnis], *V.* **fearfulness**.

feasibility [ˌfiːzə'biliti], *s.* **1.** fattibilità, praticabilità **2.** verosimiglianza, probabilità.

feasible ['fiːzəbl], *ag.* **1.** fattibile, possibile, realizzabile **2.** verosimile; probabile.

feasibleness ['fiːzəblnis], *V.* **feasibility**.

feasibly ['fiːzəbli], *av.* **1.** fattibilmente **2.** verosimilmente.

feast [fiːst], *s.* **1.** banchetto, convito, festino, pranzo ‖ *enough is as good as a —*, *prov.* il troppo stroppia **2.** (*eccl.*) festa, solennità **3.** *fig.* festa, gioia, gaudio.

to feast, *v.t.i.* **1.** festeggiare; banchettare ‖ *to — the night away*, passare la notte banchettando **2.** *fig.* pascersi; rallegrarsi (alla vista di): *to — one's eyes up(on) sthg.*, rallegrarsi gli occhi alla vista di ql.co. **3.** trattare in modo principesco, lussuoso.

feaster ['fiːstə*], *s.c.* convitato, convitata ‖ *s.* **1.** anfitrione **2.** *fig.* epicureo.

feastful ['fiːstful], *ag.* gioioso, festoso.

feat [fiːt], *ag.* (*arc.*) destro, abile; adatto ‖ *s.* azione, fatto insigne, gesta: *— of arms*, fatto d'arme; *— of engineering*, trionfo dell'ingegneria.

feather ['feðə*], *s.* **1.** penna, piuma ‖ *to show the white —*, *fig.* mostrarsi codardo **2.** piumaggio, penne ‖ *a — in one's cap*, (*fam.*) un motivo d'orgoglio ‖ *to be in full —*, essere in grande toletta ‖ *to be in high* (o *fine* o *good*) *—*, essere di ottimo umore **3.** (*mil.*) pennacchio **4.** *fig.* piuma, nonnulla, inezia **5.** specie, genere: *to be birds of a —*, (*fam.*) essere gente della stessa risma ‖ *birds of a — flock together*, *prov.* ogni simile ama il suo simile **6.** (*mar.*) scia (di periscopio) **7.** (*mec.*) flangia, aletta in argento; nervatura ☆ *— -bed*, letto di piume; *— -brain* (o *— -head*), cervello di gallina; *— -brained*, leggero, sventato; *— -edge*, (*mec.*) filo tagliente irregolare; (*ind.*) bava, sbavatura; (*artigl.*) spigolo acuto (di asse); (*ing.*) manto stradale; *— -stitch*, punto a lisca.

to feather, *v.t.i.* **1.** ornare, vestire, coprire di penne, piume; mettere penne a (una freccia): *to tar and — s.o.*, coprire qlcu. di catrame e piume (per punizione) ‖ *to — one's nest*, *fig.* arricchirsi **2.** muoversi come una piuma, fluttuare **3.** (*mar.*) spalare: *to — one's oars*, spalare i remi **4.** (*caccia*) colpire le piume di (un uccello, senza ucciderlo).

feathered ['feðəd], *ag.* 1. pennuto; ornato, coperto di piume 2. *fig.* alato, veloce 3. (*metal.*) granulare.

featheriness ['feðərinis], *s.* leggerezza; piumosità; *fig.* volubilità.

feathering ['feðəriŋ], *s.* 1. piumaggio, le piume 2. (*arch.*) ornamento a fogliami.

featherless ['feðəlis], *ag.* implume.

featherweight ['feðəweit], *s.* (*boxe*) peso piuma.

feathery ['feðəri], *ag.* soffice, leggero; piumato, pennuto.

featly ['fi:tli], *av.* (*arc.*) destramente, abilmente.

feature ['fi:tʃə*], *s.* 1. fattezza, lineamento 2. *pl.* fisionomia 3. configurazione, caratteristica: *geographical features*, configurazione geografica 4. (*teat. cine.*) attrattiva, « numero »: *the soprano was the — of the performance*, il soprano costituiva l'attrattiva della rappresentazione 5. (*giornalismo*) caratteristica, specialità: *foreign news is the main — of this week's number*, nel numero di questa settimana si dà il massimo rilievo alle notizie dall'estero ☆ — *film*, lungometraggio; *double-* — *program*, programma doppio.

to feature, *v.t.* 1. caratterizzare, distinguere; rivelare 2. (*teat. cine.*) mettere in evidenza, dare una parte importante a: *a film featuring Chaplin*, un film con Chaplin come protagonista.

featured ['fi:tʃəd], *ag.* formato, modellato; fornito di particolari lineamenti ☆ *hard-* —, dal viso duro.

featureless ['fi:tʃəlis], *ag.* privo di caratteristiche, di tratti distinti; poco interessante.

featurely ['fi:tʃəli], *ag.* caratteristico.

febricula [fi'brikjulə], *s.* febbriciattola.

febrifugal [fi'brifjugəl], *ag.* (*farm.*) febbrifugo.

febrifuge ['febrifju:dʒ], *s.* (*farm.*) febbrifugo.

febrile ['fi:brail], *ag.* febbrile.

February ['februəri], *s.* febbraio: *in* —, in febbraio.

fecal ['fi:kəl], *ag.* fecale.

feces ['fi:si:z], *s.pl.* feci, escrementi.

fecial ['fi:ʃəl], *ag.* (*st. romana*) feziale.

feck [fek], *s.* (*scoz.*) valore; vigore, energia.

feckless ['feklis], *ag.* (*scoz.*) debole, gracile; inetto, incapace.

fecklessly ['feklisli], *av.* (*scoz.*) senza energia; senza capacità.

fecklessness ['feklisnis], *s.* (*scoz.*) debolezza; inettitudine, incapacità.

fecula ['fekjulə], *s.* fecola.

feculence ['fekjuləns], *s.* 1. sedimento; feccia 2. fetidume; sporcizia.

feculent ['fekjulənt], *ag.* 1. torbido; limaccioso 2. fetido; sporco; ripugnante.

fecund ['fi:kənd], *ag.* fecondo, prolifico; produttivo, fertile.

to fecundate ['fi:kəndeit], *v.t.* fecondare; (*bot.*) impollinare.

fecundation [,fi:kən'deiʃən], *s.* fecondazione; fertilizzazione.

fecundity [fi'kʌnditi], *s.* fecondità; fertilità.

fed [fed], *pass.p.* di *to* **feed**.

federacy ['fedərəsi], *s.* federazione; alleanza.

federal ['fedərəl], *ag.* federale ‖ *the Federal City*, la Capitale Federale (Washington) ‖ *s.* *V.* **federalist**.

federalism ['fedərəlizəm], *s.* federalismo.

federalist ['fedərəlist], *s.* 1. federalista 2. (*st. amer.*) nordista.

to federalize ['fedərəlaiz], *v.t.* unire (stati) in una confederazione.

federate ['fedərit], *ag.* confederato (di stati, ecc.).

to federate ['fedəreit], *v.t.i.* confederare, confederarsi.

federation [,fedə'reiʃən], *s.* federazione, confederazione.

federative ['fedərətiv], *ag.* federativo.

federatively ['fedərətivli], *av.* in forma federativa.

Fedora [fi'dourə], *no.pr.f.* Fedora‖ **fedora**, *s.* (*amer.*) cappello molle di feltro.

fee [fi:], *s.* 1. emolumento; onorario; competenze: *a doctor's* —, l'onorario di un medico 2. tassa (di iscrizione, frequenza) 3. (*dir.*) proprietà ereditaria 4. (*st.*) feudo; beneficio feudale ☆ (*property held in*) — *-simple*, (*dir.*) proprietà assoluta; (*property held in*) — *-tail*, (*dir.*) (proprietà trasmessa) solo ad una particolare categoria di eredi ‖ *entrance-* —, biglietto di entrata; *registration* —, tassa di raccomandazione (di lettera, ecc.); tassa d'iscrizione; *tuition fees*, tasse di frequenza.

to fee, *v.t.* 1. pagare la parcella, l'onorario a; *to* — *a doctor*, pagare un dottore 2. assicurarsi i servigi di: *to* — *a lawyer*, assicurarsi i servigi di un avvocato.

feeble ['fi:bl], *ag.* debole, fiacco (di salute, polso, argomento, ecc.); infermo; vago, confuso (di luce, colore, suono): *a* — *person*, un infermo ☆ — *-minded*, debole di mente; — *-mindedness*, deficienza mentale.

feebleness ['fi:blnis], *s.* debolezza, spossatezza; infermità, invalidità.

feebly ['fi:bli], *av.* debolmente, senza forza.

feed [fi:d], *s.* 1. alimentazione, nutrimento (per animali; *scherz.* per persone) 2. (*fam.*) pasto ‖ *to be off one's* —, (*sl.*) non aver appetito; *to have a good* —, (*sl.*) fare una bella mangiata 3. pastura: *to be out at* —, pascolare 4. (*mec.*) avanzamento, alimentazione ☆ — *-pipe*, (*mec.*) tubo di rifornimento; — *-pump*, pompa di rifornimento.

to feed, *pass.p.p.* **fed** [fed], *v.t.i.* 1. nutrire, nutrirsi; cibare, cibarsi: *to* — *s.o. on sthg.*, nutrire qlcu. di ql.co. ‖ *to* — *a cold*, (*fam.*) mangiare molto per farsi passare il raffreddore 2. *fig.* nutrire, alimentare: *the news fed his hopes*, la notizia alimentò le sue speranze 3. pascere, nutrire (animali) 4. fornire, rifornire; (*mec.*) alimentare: *to* — *a machine with raw materials*, rifornire una macchina di materie prime 5. (*teat.*) dare la battuta a:_*to* — *an actor*, dare la battuta ad un attore 6. *to* — *up*, ingrassare: *to* — *up*, sottoporre qlcu. a superalimentazione; *to* — *up animals*, ingrassare animali per venderli ‖ *to be fed up*, (*sl.*) essere stufo, non poterne più: *I am fed up with everybody*, sono stufo di tutti.

feeder ['fi:də*], *s.* 1. chi, ciò che alimenta, nutre; allevatore (di bestiame) 2. mangiatore: *great* —, mangione 3. poppatoio; bavaglino 4. affluente 5. serbatoio; (*min.*) filone 6. (*elett.*) cavo di alimentazione 7. (*mec.*) alimentatore; spostatore 8. (*ferr.*) raccordo, linea secondaria 9. (*tip.*) mettifoglio.

feeding ['fi:diŋ], *ag.* nutriente ‖ *s.* 1. nutrizione, alimento 2. (*mec.*) alimentazione ☆ — *-bottle*, poppatoio; — *cup*, pipetta, tazza da ammalati ‖ *bottle-* —, allattamento artificiale.

fee-faw-fum ['fi:'fɔ:'fʌm], *inter.* ahm! (esclamazione con cui l'orco della favola esprime il suo istinto cannibalesco).

fee-faw-fum, *s.* spauracchio; storie, inezie: *it's all* —, sono tutte sciocchezze.

feel [fi:l], *s.* (*solo sing.*) tatto, tocco: *it is cold to the* —, è freddo al tatto; *to judge by the* — *of sthg.*, giudicare ql.co. toccandola.

to feel, *pass.p.p.* **felt** [felt], *v.t.i.* 1. (I, V, VI) sentire con il tatto, toccare: — *how soft this wool is*, senti quanto è soffice questa lana; — *whether the water is cold*, senti se l'acqua è fredda; *he felt my pulse*, egli mi tastò il polso; *I felt her hand trembling in mine*, sentii la sua mano tremare nella mia; *I felt his hand grip mine*, sentii la sua mano afferrare la mia ‖ *to* — *one's leg*, trovare una posizione sicura; *fig.* trovarsi a proprio agio ‖ *to* — *one's way*, procedere a tastoni, con cautela 2. sentire (fisicamente): *do you* — *pain?*, senti dolore?; *he feels the heat very much*, egli risente molto del caldo; *to* — *cold, hot*, aver freddo, caldo; *to* — *hungry, thirsty*, aver fame, sete 3. sentire, provare (un sentimento, ecc.): *I* — *angry*, sono arrabbiato; *I don't* — *much pity for them*, non sento molta pietà per loro ‖ *to — for s.o.*, aver simpatia per qlcu. ‖ *to — with s.o.*, condividere i sentimenti di qlcu. **4.** (VI) sentire, pensare, giudicare, considerare: *I — I am right*, sento di aver ragione; *I — myself called upon to help him*, penso che sia mio dovere aiutarlo; *I don't — he will win the race*, non penso che vincerà la corsa; *I don't — up to it*, non mi sento di far ciò **5.** sentirsi: *how are you feeling this morning?*, come ti senti stamane?; *to — certain, sad, well, ill, tired*, sentirsi sicuro, triste, bene, male, stanco; *to — giddy*, sentirsi girare la testa ‖ *I don't — quite the thing*, (*sl.*) non mi sento proprio bene ‖ *to — at sea*, sentirsi sperduto, non sapersi orientare ‖ *to — like*, (I) sentirsi disposto a (far ql.co.): *I don't — like doing this work*, non mi sento di fare questo lavoro ‖ *to — out of sorts*, sentirsi alquanto indisposto, non sentirsi del solito umore ‖ *not to — (quite) oneself*, non sentirsi bene: *he isn't feeling quite himself*, non si sente per niente bene **6.** (*con senso passivo*) risultare al tatto, dare al tatto l'impressione di: *this feels like iron*, al tatto questo sembra ferro; *velvet feels soft*, al tatto il velluto è morbido **7.** prevedere, aver la sensazione: *I — that sthg. dreadful will happen*, sento che accadrà ql.co. di terribile.

feeler ['fi:lə*], *s.* **1.** chi, che sente **2.** antenna (di insetti); baffi (di gatto); tentacolo **3.** notizia falsa diffusa per saggiare la reazione del pubblico: *to throw* (o *put*) *out a —*, (*fam.*) tastare il terreno, sondare l'opinione pubblica **4.** (*mec.*) sonda **5.** (*mil.*) esploratore ☆ *peace feelers*, (*fam.*) sondaggi di pace.

feeling ['fi:liŋ], *ag.* sensibile, che si commuove: *a — heart*, un cuore sensibile ‖ *s.* **1.** sentimento: *a — of happiness*, un senso di felicità **2.** sensazione; l'essere conscio: *I had a — that all was not well*, ebbi la sensazione che c'era ql.co. che non andava **3.** sensazione fisica: *a — of cold*, una sensazione di freddo; *there is no — in my arm*, il mio braccio ha perduto la sensibilità **4.** *pl.* sentimenti, emozioni; suscettibilità: *to hurt s.o.'s feelings*, urtare la suscettibilità di qlcu. **5.** interessamento: *to show — for the sufferings of others*, mostrare interessamento per le sofferenze altrui **6.** opinione: *the general — is against him*, l'opinione pubblica gli è contraria **7.** (*gener. con art. indef.*) sensibilità, capacità di apprezzare: *she has a deep — for natural beauty*, ha una sensibilità particolare per ogni forma di bellezza naturale.

feelingly ['fi:liŋli], *av.* con sentimento, con commozione.

feet [fi:t], *pl.* di **foot.**

to **feign** [fein], *v.t.i.* **1.** fingere, fingersi: *to — sick*, fingersi ammalato **2.** inventare (scuse, ecc.); falsificare (documenti, ecc.).

feigned [feind], *ag.* **1.** finto, simulato **2.** inventato; contraffatto ☆ *— hand*, scrittura contraffatta.

feignedly ['feinidli], *av.* con finzione, simulatamente.

feigner ['feinə*], *s.c.* simulatore, simulatrice.

feigning ['feiniŋ], *s.* finta, simulazione.

feint [feint], *ag.* **1.** *paper with — (o faint) lines*, (*comm.*) carta rigata; falsariga **2.** (*arc.*) V. **faint** ‖ *s.* **1.** (*mil.*) attacco simulato **2.** simulazione; (*spor.*) finta.

to **feint**, *v.i.* **1.** (*mil.*) fare un finto attacco **2.** (*spor.*) fare una finta.

feldspar ['feldspɑ:*], *s.* (*min.*) feldspato.

Felicia [fi'lisiə], *no.pr.f.* Felicia, Felicita.

felicide ['fi:lisaid], *s.* gatticidio.

to **felicitate** [fi'lisiteit], *v.t.* **1.** felicitarsi con, congratularsi con: *to — s.o. on sthg.*, felicitarsi con qlcu. di ql.co. **2.** (*rar.*) rendere felice.

felicitation [fi,lisi'teifən], *s.* felicitazione, congratulazione: *to offer s.o. one's felicitations*, fare le proprie felicitazioni a qlcu.

felicitous [fi'lisitəs], *ag.* **1.** adatto, appropriato, ben scelto: *a — phrase*, una frase felice; *a — quotation*, una citazione appropriata **2.** (*rar.*) felice, beato.

felicitously [fi'lisitəsli], *av.* felicemente.

felicity [fi'lisiti], *s.* **1.** felicità **2.** facoltà di esprimersi, di scrivere bene; espressione appropriata.

felid ['fi:lid], *ag.* felino.

feline ['fi:lain], *ag.s.* felino.

felinity [fi'liniti], *s.* astuzia felina.

Felix ['fi:liks], *no.pr.m.* Felice.

fell[1] [fel], *ag.* **1.** (*poet.*) feroce, terribile **2.** funesto.

fell[2], *s.* **1.** pelle d'animale; vello **2.** pellame.

fell[3], *s.* (*scoz.*) cresta rocciosa.

fell[4], *s.* **1.** legname abbattuto **2.** (*cucito*) ribattitura.

to **fell**[4], *v.t.* **1.** abbattere **2.** (*cucito*) ribattere.

fell[5], *s.* (*min.*) piombo allo stato grezzo.

fell[6], *pass.* di to **fall.**

fellah ['felə], *pl.* **fellaheen** ['feləhi:n], *s.* fellah, contadino egiziano.

feller ['felə*], *s.* taglialegna, tagliaboschi.

felling ['feliŋ], *s.* **1.** taglio d'un bosco **2.** (*cucito*) ribattitura **3.** macello (di bue).

fellness ['felnis], *s.* (*poet.*) crudeltà, ferocia.

felloe ['felou], *s.* gavello (settore di ruota).

fellow ['felou], *s.* **1.** persona, individuo; soggetto: *a decent —*, una persona a modo; *a good —*, un buon diavolo ‖ *my dear —!*, caro mio! ‖ *poor —!*, povero diavolo! **2.** compagno, camerata **3.** collega, membro (di società culturali) **4.** *Fellow*, membro di un « college » a Oxford, ecc.; laureato che gode di una borsa di studio (a durata limitata) **5.** compagno (di un paio): *I have lost the — of this glove*, ho perso il compagno di questo guanto ☆ *— -being*, simile; *— -boarder*, commensale; *— -citizen*, concittadino; *— -countryman*, compatriotta; *— -creature*, simile; *— -feeling*, comprensione, simpatia; *— -helper*, collaboratore; *— -prisoner*, compagno di prigionia; *— -soldier*, compagno d'armi; *— -student*, compagno di collegio, di studi; *— -traveller*, compagno di viaggio; simpatizzante di un partito politico (generalmente filo-comunista); *— -workman*, compagno di lavoro.

fellowship ['felouʃip], *s.* **1.** compagnia, socievolezza; amicizia **2.** associazione, corporazione **3.** (*università*) posizione; emolumento di un « fellow »; borsa di studio post-universitaria (generalmente per ricerche).

felly ['feli], *s.* gavello (settore di ruota).

felo-de-se ['fi:loudi:'si:], *s.c.* suicida.

felon[1] ['felən], *ag.* **1.** (*poet.*) crudele, malvagio **2.** (*dir.*) criminale ‖ *s.* (*dir.*) criminale.

felon[2], *s.* (*patol.*) patereccio, giradito.

felonious [fi'lounjəs], *ag.* **1.** perfido, malvagio **2.** (*dir.*) criminoso.

feloniously [fi'lounjəsli], *av.* **1.** perfidamente; malvagiamente **2.** (*dir.*) criminosamente.

feloniousness [fi'lounjəsnis], *s.* (*dir.*) criminosità.

felony ['feləni], *s.* **1.** (*dir.*) crimine **2.** (*st.*) fellonia.

felspar ['fel-spɑ:*], *s.* (*min.*) feldspato.

felt[1] [felt], *s.* **1.** feltro **2.** (*edil.*) materiale antiacustico **3.** (*ind. cartaria*) feltro ☆ *— hat*, cappello di feltro; *— packing*, guarnizione di feltro; *— washer*, (*mec.*) rondella di feltro ‖ *tarred —*, feltro catramato.

to **felt**[1], *v.t.i.* feltrare; infeltrire.

felt[2], *pass.p.p.* di to **feel.**

felting ['feltiŋ], *s.* feltratura.

felucca [fe'lʌkə], *s.* (*mar.*) feluca.

female ['fi:meil], *ag.* **1.** femminile, di sesso femminile: *— child*, bambina; *— companion*, compagna; *the — sex*, il sesso femminile **2.** *fig.* debole; di qualità inferiore **3.** (*mec.*) femmina: *— friction cone*, contro cono; *— screw*, madrevite ‖ *s.* **1.** femmina **2.** (*spreg.*) donna, ragazza.

feminality [,femi'næliti], *s.* qualità spiccatamente femminile; femminilità.

feminity [,femi'ni:iti], *s.* femminilità.

feminine ['feminin], *ag.* **1.** femminile, femminino; delicato, fine: *— curiosity*, curiosità femminile ‖ *the eternal —*, l'eterno femminino **2.** (*gram.*) femminile: *— gender*, genere femminile **3.** (*poes.*) debole, femminile.

— *caesurae*, cesura debole; — *rhyme*, rima femminile || *s.* **1.** femminile: *the* — *of actor is actress*, il femminile di attore è attrice **2.** (*fam.*) femmina.

femininely ['feminili], *av.* femminilmente.

feminineness ['femininnis], *s.* femminilità.

femininity [,femi'niniti], *s.* **1.** femminilità **2.** le donne.

feminism ['feminizam], *s.* femminismo.

feminist ['feminist], *s.c.* femminista.

feminity [fi'miniti], *s.* femminilità.

to **feminize** ['feminaiz], *v.t.i.* femminizzare, effeminare; rendere, diventare effeminato.

femoral ['femaral], *ag.* (*anat.*) femorale.

femur ['fi:ma*], *pl.* **femora** ['femara], *s.* (*anat.*) femore.

fen [fen], *s.* palude, maremma || *the Fens*, zona bassa e paludosa (del Cambridgeshire e del Lincolnshire) ☆ — *-berry*, (*bot.*) mirtillo; — *-cricket*, (*entom.*) grillotalpa; — *-fire*, fuoco fatuo.

fence [fens], *s.* **1.** recinto; steccato, stecconato, palizzata; cinta; siepe; barriera; riparo || *to come down on the right side of the* —, *fig.* mettersi dalla parte del vincitore; *to sit on the* —, *fig.* essere neutrale; essere indeciso **2.** scherma; *fig.* schermaglia **3.** (*sl.*) ricettatore **4.** (*mec.*) guida pezzo, guida di appoggio ☆ — *month* (o — *season* o — *time*), stagione in cui la caccia o la pesca sono chiuse || *lattice* —, recintazione a elementi incrociati.

to **fence**, *v.t.i.* **1.** cintare; fortificare; circondare con steccato: *to* — (*in*) *a piece of ground*, cintare un terreno; *to* — *a town*, fortificare una città **2.** tirar di scherma; *fig.* schermirsi, parare, evitare: *to* — *with a question*, eludere una domanda **3.** (*sl.*) fare il ricettatore **4.** (*equitazione*) saltare ostacoli.

fenceless ['fenslis], *ag.* (*poet.*) aperto, indifeso.

fencer ['fensa*], *s.* **1.** schermidore **2.** cavallo saltatore di ostacoli.

fencible ['fensibl], *s.* (*st. inglese*) guardia nazionale.

fencing ['fensin], *s.* **1.** materiale per cintare; cinta **2.** (*spor.*) scherma; *fig.* schermaglia **3.** (*sl.*) ricettazione ☆ — *gloves*, guanti da scherma; — *-master*, maestro di scherma.

to **fend** [fend], *v.t.i.* **1.** (*poet.*) difendere **2.** provvedere: *she can* — *for herself*, sa badare a se stessa **3.** *to* — *off*, parare, stornare: *to* — *off a blow*, parare un colpo.

fender ['fenda*], *s.* **1.** riparo, difesa **2.** paraurti; (*amer.*) parafango **3.** (*mar.*) parabordo **4.** parafuoco.

fenestra [fi'nestra], *s.* **1.** (*anat.*) canale (dell'orecchio) **2.** (*chir.*) finestra.

fenestrate [fi'nestrit], *ag.* (*bot. zool.*) perforato.

fenestration [,fenis'treifan], *s.* (*arch.*) disposizione e dimensionamento delle finestre, delle porte.

Fenian ['fi:njan], *ag.s.* feniano (membro di una associazione politica per l'emancipazione dell'Irlanda dal governo inglese).

fennel ['fenl], *s.* (*bot.*) finocchio ☆ — *-flower*, (*bot.*) nigella; — *-seed*, seme di finocchio.

fenny ['feni], *ag.* paludoso.

feoff [fef], *s.* feudo.

to **feoff**, *v.t.* (*dir.*) dare in feudo, in donazione a.

feoffee [fe'fi:], *s.c.* (*dir.*) donatario, donataria || — *in* (o *of*) *trust*, fidecommissario.

feoffer ['fefa*], *s.c.* (*dir.*) donatore, donatrice.

feoffment ['fefmant], *s.* **1.** investitura d'un feudo **2.** (*dir.*) donazione.

feoffor [fe'fo:*], *s.c.* (*dir.*) donatore, donatrice.

feracious [fa'reifas], *ag.* ferace, fertile.

feracity [fa'ræsiti], *s.* feracità, fecondità.

feral[1] ['fiaral], *ag.* **1.** ferale, mortale **2.** cupo, funereo.

feral[2], *ag.* ferino; selvaggio; brutale.

Ferdinand ['fa:dinand], *no.pr.m.* Ferdinando.

feretory ['feritari], *s.* **1.** (*eccl.*) reliquiario; cappella con reliquiario **2.** (*rar.*) feretro.

ferial ['fiarial], *ag.* feriale.

ferine ['fiarain], *ag.* ferino; selvaggio; brutale.

Feringhee [fa'ringi], *s.c.* (*ang.-in.*) europeo, europea.

ferment ['fa:ment], *s.* **1.** fermento; lievito **2.** fermentazione, effervescenza **3.** *fig.* fermento, agitazione, eccitazione, tumulto.

to **ferment** [fa(:)'ment], *v.t.i.* **1.** far fermentare, fermentare, lievitare **2.** *fig.* eccitare, fomentare; agitarsi.

fermentable [fa(:)'mentabl], *ag.* fermentabile.

fermentation [,fa:men'teifan], *s.* **1.** fermentazione **2.** *fig.* fermento, agitazione.

fermentative [fa:'mentativ], *ag.* fermentativo.

fern [fa:n], *s.* (*bot.*) felce.

fernery ['fa:nari], *s.* felceto, vivaio di felci.

ferny ['fa:ni], *ag.* coperto di felci.

ferocious [fa'roufas], *ag.* feroce; crudele.

ferociously [fa'roufasli], *av.* ferocemente; crudelmente.

ferocity [fa'rositi], *s.* ferocia; crudeltà.

ferox ['feroks], *s.* (*ittiol.*) trota di lago.

ferreous ['ferias], *ag.* ferroso; ferreo.

ferret[1] ['ferit], *s.* (*zool.*) furetto.

to **ferret**[1], *v.t.i.* **1.** cacciare (*p.e.* i conigli) col furetto **2.** *fig.* frugare **3.** *to* — *out*, scovare; scoprire.

ferret[2], *s.* nastro, fettuccia.

ferreter ['ferita*], *s.* **1.** cacciatore col furetto **2.** *fig.* investigatore; ficcanaso.

ferrety ['feriti], *ag.* di furetto.

ferriage ['ferid3], *s.* (prezzo di) trasporto in barca, traghetto.

ferric ['ferik], *ag.* (*chim.*) ferrico.

ferriferous [fe'riferas], *ag.* ferrifero.

ferro-concrete ['ferou'konkri:t], *s.* cemento armato.

ferrotype ['feroutaip], *s.* (*foto.*) ferrotipia.

ferrous ['feras], *ag.* (*chim.*) ferroso.

ferruginous [fe'ru:d3inas], *ag.* ferruginoso.

ferrule ['feru:l], *s.* (*mec.*) ghiera, boccola; bussola.

ferry ['feri], *s.* **1.** traghetto **2.** tassa dovuta per il traghetto ☆ — *-boat*, nave traghetto; — *-bridge*, ponte trasbordatore.

to **ferry**, *v.t.i.* **1.** traghettare: *to* — *across, over*, attraversare, traghettare; *to* — *s.o., sthg. across, over a river*, traghettare, far passare qlcu., ql.co. oltre un fiume **2.** (*aer.*) trasportare per via aerea.

ferryman, *pl.* **ferrymen** ['ferimen], *s.* traghettatore || *the Ferryman of the Styx*, (*poet.*) il Nocchiero dello Stige.

fertile ['fa:tail], *ag.* **1.** fertile (anche *fig.*) **2.** fertilizzante.

fertility [fa:'tiliti], *s.* fertilità.

fertilization [,fa:tilai'zeifan], *s.* il fertilizzare; fecondazione (di piante, animali).

to **fertilize** ['fa:tilaiz], *v.t.* fertilizzare; fecondare.

fertilizer ['fa:tilaiza*], *s.* concime, fertilizzante ☆ — *distributor*, (*agr.*) spandiconcime; — *drill*, (*agr.*) seminatrice con spandiconcime || *high grade* —, fertilizzante ad alto rendimento.

ferule ['feru:l], *s.* **1.** (*bot.*) ferula **2.** ferula, bacchetta.

fervency ['fa:vansi], *s.* fervore, ardore, zelo.

fervent ['fa:vant], *ag.* fervente, ardente; zelante.

fervently ['fa:vantli], *av.* con fervore.

ferventness ['fa:vantnis], *s.* fervore, ardore.

fervid ['fa:vid], *ag.* (*poet.*) ardente, fervido.

fervidly ['fa:vidli], *av.* ardentemente, fervidamente.

fervidness ['fa:vidnis], *s.* fervore, zelo, ardore.

fervor, (*amer.*) per **fervour**.

fervour ['fa:va*], *s.* **1.** ardore, calore intenso **2.** fervore, zelo.

Fescennine ['fesenain], *ag.* fescennino; osceno; scherzoso (di versi).

fescue ['feskju:], *s.* bacchetta (per indicare sulla lavagna, ecc.).

fesse[1] [fes], *s.* (*arald.*) fascia.

fesse[2], *s.* (*dial.*) azzurro pallido.

festal ['festl], *ag.* festivo; gaio; festoso || *s.* festa.

festally ['festali], *av.* gaiamente, festosamente.

fester ['festa*], *s.* ulcera superficiale; piaga dolorosa.

to **fester**, *v.t.i.* **1.** suppurare (di ferita); corrompersi **2.** *fig.* amareggiare, avvelenare.

festival ['festəvəl], *s.* **1.** giorno di festa; festa **2.** anniversario; celebrazione **3.** (*mus. cine., ecc.*) festival.
festive ['festiv], *ag.* **1.** festivo **2.** gioioso, festoso.
festively ['festivli], *av.* festosamente.
festiveness ['festivnis], *s.* allegria; festosità.
festivity [fes'tiviti], *s.* **1.** festività **2.** *pl.* festeggiamenti.
festoon [fes'tu:n], *s.* festone (di fiori, foglie, frutta).
to festoon, *v.t.* disporre a festoni; ornare di festoni.
fetal ['fi:tl], *ag.* fetale.
fetch[1] [fetʃ], *s.* **1.** l'andare a prendere; sforzo (per arrivare a): *a — of imagination*, uno sforzo di immaginazione **2.** giuoco; stratagemma; sofisma **3.** (*mar.*) distanza da percorrere; estensione, apertura (di golfo).
to fetch[1], *v.t.i.* **1.** andare a cercare, andare a prendere: *— me a chair, please*, vammi a prendere una sedia, ti prego; *to — water from a well*, attingere acqua ad un pozzo ‖ *to — and carry for s.o.*, scovare e riportare la selvaggina per qlcu. (di cani); far commissioni, sfacchinare per qlcu. **2.** far venire, tirare: *to — one's breath*, prendere fiato; *to — a sigh*, emettere un sospiro ‖ *to — s.o. a blow, a box on the ear*, (*fam.*) dare uno schiaffo, uno scappellotto a qlcu. **3.** (*comm.*) valere, fruttare: *English silver fetches high prices nowadays*, l'argenteria inglese è ora valutata molto **4.** (*fam.*) interessare; attirare, conquistare (lodi, ammirazione) **5.** (*mar.*) raggiungere (il porto, il molo); tenere la rotta; virare: *to — a ship to the quay*, attraccare una nave al molo **6.** *to — away*, portare, condurre via; (*mar.*) staccarsi; rotolare sul ponte (durante una tempesta) **7.** *to — back*, riportare **8.** *to — down*, far discendere; abbattere (avversari, prezzi, ecc.) **9.** *to — in*, far entrare, riportare dentro **10.** *to — out*, far uscire; far scomparire (macchie) **11.** *to — through*, arrivare in porto (anche *fig.*) **12.** *to — up*, far salire; vomitare, espettorare; arrestarsi; (*mar.*) giungere (in porto).
fetch[2], *s.* apparizione (di persona vivente).
fetcher ['fetʃə*], *s.* chi, che va a prendere.
fête [feit], *s.* festa; onomastico ☆ *— day*, onomastico.
to fête, *v.t.* festeggiare.
fetial ['fi:ʃəl], *ag.s.* (*st. romana*) feciale, feziale.
feticide ['fi:tisaid], *s.* feticidio, uccisione di feto.
fetid ['fetid], *ag.* fetido.
fetidity [fe'tiditi], *s.* fetore.
fetidly ['fetidli], *av.* fetidamente.
fetidness ['fetidnis], *s.* fetore.
fetish ['fi:tiʃ], *s.* feticcio; *fig.* idolo.
fetishism ['fi:tiʃizəm], *s.* feticismo; idolatria.
fetishist ['fi:tiʃist], *s.* feticista; idolatra.
fetishistic [ˌfi:ti'ʃistik], *ag.* feticistico.
fetlock ['fetlɔk], *s.* barbetta (di cavallo).
fetor ['fi:tə*], *s.* fetore.
fetter ['fetə*], *s. gener. pl.* **1.** ceppi, catene **2.** *fig.* legame; vincolo **3.** schiavitù.
to fetter, *v.t.* **1.** incatenare **2.** intralciare, ostacolare.
fetterless ['fetəlis], *ag.* libero (da legami), indipendente.
fetterlock ['fetəlɔk], *s.* pastoia.
fettle ['fetl], *s.* condizione, stato: *to be in fine* (o *good* o *high*) *—*, essere in buone condizioni (fisiche, morali).
to fettle, *v.t.i.* **1.** (*dial.*) preparare, sistemare **2.** (*metal.*) sbavare; rivestire, ricoprire (con materiale di protezione).
fetus ['fi:təs], *pl.* **fetuses** ['fi:təsiz], *s.* feto.
feu [fju:], *s.* (*scoz. dir.*) **1.** enfiteusi **2.** proprietà ad enfiteusi.
feud[1] [fju:d], *s.* antagonismo, ostilità (tra famiglie, «clan»): *deadly —*, guerra a morte; *to be at — with s.o.*, essere in contrasto con qlcu.
feud[2], *s.* (*st.*) feudo.
feudal ['fju:dl], *ag.* feudale.
feudalism ['fju:dəlizəm], *s.* feudalismo, feudalità.
feudalist ['fju:dəlist], *s.* rappresentante, fautore del feudalesimo.
feudality [fju:'dæliti], *s.* **1.** feudalesimo **2.** feudo.

to feudalize ['fju:dəlaiz], *v.t.* ridurre al sistema feudale.
feudally ['fju:dəli], *av.* feudalmente.
feudatory ['fju:dətəri], *ag.s.* feudatario.
feuilleton ['fə:itɔ:ŋ], *s.* appendice di giornale (dedicata a critica, letteratura, ecc.).
fever ['fi:və*], *s.* **1.** febbre: *to have a high —*, avere la febbre alta **2.** *fig.* febbre, eccitazione: *to be in a —*, avere la febbre, essere eccitato ☆ *— -heat*, (*patol.*) temperatura sopra il livello normale; *fig.* sovraeccitazione; *— -hospital*, ospedale per malattie contagiose; *— -trap*, luogo malsano, paludoso ‖ *child —*, febbre puerperale; *yellow —*, febbre gialla.
to fever, *v.t.* dar la febbre a.
feverfew ['fi:vəfju:], *s.* (*bot.*) camomilla, matricaria.
feverish ['fi:vəriʃ], *ag.* **1.** febbricitante: *to be —*, avere la febbre **2.** *fig.* eccitato, febbrile: *— activity*, attività febbrile.
feverishly ['fi:vəriʃli], *av.* febbrilmente (anche *fig.*).
feverishness ['fi:vəriʃnis], *s.* febbre febbrile.
few [fju:], *comp.* **fewer** ['fju:ə*], *superl.* **fewest** ['fju:ist], *ag.* **1.** pochi, qualche: *a man of — words*, un uomo di poche parole; *he has — friends*, ha pochi amici; *he has fewer relatives than I*, egli ha meno parenti di me; *she has no fewer than six furs*, non ha meno di sei pellicce; *she would call every — days*, le sue visite si susseguivano ad intervalli di pochi giorni **2.** *a —*, **alcuni**: *he has a — pictures*, possiede alcuni quadri; *he spoke a — words*, pronunciò alcune parole ‖ *pron. s.* **1.** **pochi**: *— can understand it*, pochi possono capirlo ‖ *the —*, la minoranza, gli eletti ‖ *some —*, alcuni ‖ *— know and fewer care*, *prov.* pochi sanno ed a meno importa **2.** *a —*, **alcuni**: *a — of them came*, alcuni di loro vennero; *send me a —*, mandamene alcuni ‖ *a good —*, un bel numero; *not a —*, non pochi, alcuni; *quite a —*, un numero considerevole.
fewness ['fju:nis], *s.* scarsità, scarsezza (di numero); numero ristretto (di persone, cose).
fey [fei], *ag.* (*scoz.*) **1.** condannato a morire; moribondo **2.** pazzo: *she is gone —*, è diventata pazza.
fez [fez], *s.* fez.
fiacre [fi'a:kə*], *s.* carrozza a quattro ruote.
fiancé [fi'a:nsei], *s.* fidanzato.
fiancée [fi'a:nsei], *s.* fidanzata.
fiasco [fi'æskou], *s.* fallimento, insuccesso, fiasco.
fiat ['faiæt], *s.* autorizzazione; decreto: *to give one's — to sthg.*, dare il proprio consenso per qualche cosa ☆ *— money*, (*amer. comm.*) carta moneta inconvertibile.
fib[1] [fib], *s.* fandonia, frottola, bugia.
to fib[1], *pass.p.p.* **fibbed** [fibd], *v.i.* raccontare frottole.
fib[2], *s.* (*boxe*) colpo.
to fib[2], *v.t.* (*boxe*) colpire, dare un colpo a, malmenare.
fibber ['fibə*], *s.* contafrottole.
fibbing ['fibiŋ], *s.* il raccontar frottole.
fiber, (*amer.*) per **fibre**.
fibre ['faibə*], *s.* **1.** (*anat. bot.*) fibra **2.** (*ind. tessile*) fibra: *artificial —*, fibra artificiale **3.** *fig.* fibra, natura, costituzione: *a man of coarse —*, un uomo grossolano, volgare ☆ *staple —*, fibra, fiocco.
fibreglass ['faibəgla:s], *s.* (*neol. ind.*) lana di vetro.
fibreless ['faibəlis], *ag.* senza fibra, senza forza.
fibriform ['faibrifɔ:m], *ag.* fibriforme.
fibril ['faibril], *s.* fibrilla.
fibrin ['faibrin], *s.* (*chim.*) fibrina.
fibroid ['faibroid], *ag.* di carattere fibroso ‖ *s.* (*patol.*) fibroma.
fibroin ['faibrouin], *s.* fibroina.
fibroma [fai'broumə], *s.* (*patol.*) fibroma.
fibrous ['faibrəs], *ag.* fibroso.
fibula ['fibjulə], *s.* **1.** (*anat.*) fibula **2.** fibbia, fermaglio.
fichu ['fi:ʃu:], *s.* scialletto, fazzoletto da collo.
fickle ['fikl], *ag.* incostante, volubile, variabile.
fickleness ['fiklnis], *s.* volubilità, incostanza.

fictile ['fɪktil], *ag.* fittile, d'argilla.

fiction ['fɪkʃən], *s.* **1.** prosa narrativa, novellistica: *works of* —, romanzi, novelle; *she prefers history to* —, preferisce la storia alla narrativa **2.** finzione, invenzione: *legal* —, (*dir.*) finzione legale; *truth is stranger than* — le cose vere sono più strane di quelle inventate.

fictional ['fɪkʃənl], *ag.* inventato, immaginario.

to fictionalize ['fɪkʃənəlaiz], *v.t.* romanzare.

fictionist ['fɪkʃənist], *s. c.* narratore, narratrice.

fictitious [fɪk'tiʃəs], *ag.* **1.** falso, contraffatto, simulato, fittizio: — *purchase*, acquisto simulato **2.** irreale, immaginario, fittizio.

fictitiously [fɪk'tiʃəsli], *av.* in modo fittizio.

fictitiousness [fɪk'tiʃəsnis], *s.* finzione.

fictive ['fɪktiv], *ag.* fittizio, finto, immaginario.

fid [fɪd], *s.* (*mar.*) **1.** caviglia per impiombare **2.** chiave dell'albero.

fiddle ['fɪdl], *s.* **1.** (*fam.*) violino ‖ *to be as fit as a* —, essere in ottime condizioni di salute e di spirito ‖ *to play second* — *to*, avere una parte secondaria in confronto a **2.** (*mar.*) tavola di rollio ☆ — *-bow*, archetto di violino; — *-bridge*, ponticello di violino; — *-case*, custodia per violino; — *-faddle*, chiacchiere, sciocchezze; — *-head*, (*mar.*) violino di bompresso.

fiddle, *inter.* sciocchezze!.

to fiddle, *v.t.i.* **1.** (*fam.*) suonare il, sul violino **2.** *fig.* divertirsi con sciocchezze; fare cose inutili; baloccarsi: *to* — *with one's watch-chain*, giocherellare con la catena dell'orologio ‖ *to* — *about*, trastullarsi, gingillarsi ‖ *to* — *away one's time*, perdere il tempo in sciocchezze.

to fiddle-faddle ['fɪdl,fædl], *v.i.* dire sciocchezze, gingillarsi, perdere il tempo.

fiddler ['fɪdlə*], *s.c.* (*fam.*) violinista ‖ *Fiddler's Green*, (*fam.*) paese di cuccagna (per marinai e vagabondi).

fiddlestick ['fɪdlstik], *s.* archetto (di violino) ‖ *fiddlesticks!*, sciocchezze!.

fiddling ['fɪdliŋ], *ag.* sciocco, fatuo; futile, insignificante.

fidelity [fɪ'deliti], *s.* **1.** fedeltà, lealtà **2.** accuratezza, esattezza, fedeltà: *the* — *of a translation*, la fedeltà di una traduzione ☆ *high*- — *record*, disco ad alta fedeltà.

fidget ['fɪdʒit], *s.* **1.** *gener. pl.* agitazione; irrequietezza; nervosismo **2.** persona nervosa, eccitabile.

to fidget, *v.t.i.* **1.** agitarsi; eccitarsi; muoversi con irrequietezza **2.** annoiare, dar fastidio a, irritare.

fidgetily ['fɪdʒitili], *av.* nervosamente, con irrequietezza.

fidgetiness ['fɪdʒitinis], *s.* irrequietezza, agitazione nervosa.

fidgety ['fɪdʒiti], *ag.* irrequieto; nervoso.

fidibus ['fɪdibəs], *s.* strisciolina di carta (per accendere la pipa, le candele, ecc.).

Fido ['faidou], *s.* (*abbr.* di *Fog Investigation Dispersal Operation*) (*aer.*) « Fido » (dispositivo antinebbia).

fiducial [fɪ'dju:fjəl], *ag.* **1.** (*teol.*) pertinente alla fede **2.** (*astr. geom., ecc.*) fiduciale: — *line*, (*astr. geom., ecc.*) linea fiduciale.

fiduciary [fɪ'dju:fjəri], *ag.* (*dir.*) fiduciario ‖ *s. c.* fiduciario, fiduciaria.

fie [fai], *inter.* oibò!: — *for shame!*, vergogna!; — *upon you!*, vergogna!.

fief [fi:f], *s.* (*st.*) feudo.

field [fi:ld], *s.* **1.** campo; campagna: — *of wheat*, campo di frumento; *in the open* —, in aperta campagna **2.** campo, terreno sportivo ‖ *the* —, i cavalli iscritti a una corsa (tranne il favorito) **3.** (*mil.*) campo di battaglia; campagna: — *of fire*, campo di tiro; *to hold the* —, tenere il campo; *to keep the* —, continuare una campagna; *to take the* — *against s.o.*, iniziare una campagna contro qlcu. **4.** campo, teatro d'azione; (*comm.*) mercato: *the* — *of art, politics*, il campo, il settore dell'arte, della politica; *the* — *of conjecture*, il campo delle ipotesi; *in this* —, in questo settore; *there is a great* — *for antiques in America*, l'America è un mer-

cato importante per le antichità **5.** (*arald.*) campo; (*art.*) sfondo: *depth of* —, (*foto.*) profondità di campo **6.** (*fis.*) campo, campo magnetico ☆ — *-allowance*, indennità di campagna, di guerra; — *-artillery*, artiglieria campale; — *-battery*, (*mil.*) batteria da campagna; — *-day*, (*mil.*) giorno di grandi manovre; — *-glass*, binocolo; — *-grey*, color grigio scuro; — *-gun*, cannone da campagna; — *-hospital*, ospedale da campo; — *-ice*, banchisa, ghiacci galleggianti; — *magnet*, (*elett.*) induttore; — *-marshal*, feldmaresciallo; — *-mouse*, topo di campagna; — *-officer*, ufficiale superiore; — *-sports*, caccia e pesca; — *-telephone*, (*mil.*) telefono da campo; — *-work*, fortificazione provvisoria ‖ *cricket* —, campo da « cricket »; *gold* —, giacimento aurifero; *pasture* —, pascolo; *strawberry* —, fragoleto.

to field, *v.t.i.* (*cricket*) cercare di prendere e rilanciare la palla.

fielder ['fi:ldə*], *s.* giocatore di « cricket » che rincorre e rilancia la palla.

fieldfare ['fi:ldfɛə*], *s.* (*ornit.*) tordella gazzina.

fieldpiece ['fi:ld,pi:s], *s.* (*mil.*) pezzo di artiglieria da campagna.

fieldsman, *pl.* **fieldsmen** ['fi:ldzmən], *V.* **fielder**.

fiend [fi:nd], *s.* **1.** demonio **2.** nemico mortale, malvagio ☆ *dope* —, (*fam.*) morfinomane; — *-like*, demoniaco, diabolico.

fiendish ['fi:ndiʃ], *ag.* diabolico, malvagio.

fiendishly ['fi:ndiʃli], *av.* diabolicamente, malvagiamente.

fiendishness ['fi:ndiʃnis], *s.* malvagità diabolica, diabolicità.

fierce [fiəs], *ag.* **1.** fiero; feroce; crudele; selvaggio: — *cat*, gatto selvatico; *a* — *cry*, un grido selvaggio **2.** ardente, eccessivo (anche *fig.*): — *heat*, calore ardente.

fiercely ['fiəsli], *av.* **1.** fieramente; ferocemente **2.** ardentemente; furiosamente.

fierceness ['fiəsnis], *s.* **1.** ferocia **2.** ardore, furia.

fierily ['faiərili], *av.* **1.** di fuoco **2.** *fig.* focosamente, ardentemente, impetuosamente.

fieriness ['faiərinis], *s.* **1.** calore **2.** *fig.* ardore, foga; irascibilità.

fiery ['faiəri], *ag.* **1.** di fuoco, igneo, infiammato **2.** *fig.* focoso, ardente, impetuoso: *he looked at them with* — *eyes*, li guardò con occhi fiammeggianti **3.** infiammabile (di gas): soggetto ad esplosione (di miniera).

fife [faif], *s.* piffero ☆ — *-major*, (*mil.*) sottufficiale, capobanda dei pifferi.

to fife, *v.t.i.* suonare il piffero; suonare col piffero.

fifer ['faifə*], *s.* **1.** piffero **2.** suonatore di piffero.

fifteen ['fif'ti:n], *ag.num.card.s.* quindici: *he is* —, ha quindici anni ‖ *the Fifteen*, (*st. inglese*) insurrezione giacobita del 1715.

fifteenth ['fif'ti:nθ], *ag.num.ord.s.* quindicesimo: *Louis the Fifteenth*, Luigi quindicesimo.

fifth [fifθ], *ag.num.ord.* quinto: *the* — *part*, la quinta parte; *Charles the Fifth*, Carlo Quinto ‖ — *column*, (*pol.*) la quinta colonna ‖ *Fifth Monarchy*, (*Bibbia*) il quinto impero; *Fifth Monarchy Men*, gruppo di puritani fanatici ‖ *to be the* — *wheel of a coach*, essere l'ultima ruota del carro ‖ *s.* **1.** quinto, quinta parte **2.** (*mus.*) quinta **3.** *pl.* materiale scadente **4.** (*amer.*) un quinto di gallone.

fifthly ['fifθli], *av.* in quinto luogo.

fiftieth ['fiftiiθ], *ag.num.ord.s.* cinquantesimo.

fifty ['fifti], *ag.num.card.s.* **1.** cinquanta: *in the fifties*, negli anni che vanno dal 50 al 60; *she is still in her fifties*, ella non ha ancora 60 anni **2.** numero indefinito elevato: *I have* — *things to tell you*, ho un mucchio di cose da dirti ☆ — *-fifty*, (*fam.*) a metà, diviso equamente; parte eguale; equa possibilità.

fiftyfold ['fiftifould], *ag.av.*, di, per cinquanta volte.

fig[1] [fig], *s.* **1.** fico **2.** *fig.* cosa di nessun valore: *I don't care a* — *for*, non me ne importa un fico di ‖ *to be under one's vine and* — *-tree*, essere tranquilli in casa propria ☆ — -*eater* (o *pecker*), (*ornit.*) beccafico; — -*leaf*, foglia di fico; — -*tree*, fico ‖ *Indian* —, fico d'India.

fig², *s.* **1.** vestito: *in full* —, in pompa magna **2.** condizione, forma.

fight [fait], *s.* **1.** combattimento, lotta, rissa: *to put up a good, poor* —, combattere con, senza coraggio **2.** *fig.* lotta, conflitto: *the* — *for life*, la lotta per la vita **3.** spirito combattivo: *there is no* — *left in her*, non vi è più spirito combattivo in lei; *to show* —, mostrare spirito combattivo, offrire resistenza ☆ *free* —, rissa, mischia; *sham* —, finta battaglia.

to **fight**, *pass.p.p.*, **fought** [fɔːt], *v.t.i.* **1.** combattere, battersi; dar battaglia; azzuffarsi, venire alle mani: *they fought the enemy away*, ricacciarono il nemico in battaglia; *they fought a good fight*, si batterono bene; *to* — *against* (o *with*), combattere contro; *to* — *for sthg.*, combattere per (ottenere) ql.co. ‖ *to* — *one's way* (*out*), aprirsi un varco con la forza ‖ *to* — *to a finish*, battersi sino ad un risultato decisivo **2.** *fig.* lottare, combattere: *to* — *the good fight*, combattere per una buona causa ‖ *to* — *shy of*, evitare, stare lontano da **3.** eccitare, spingere alla lotta: *to* — *cocks, dogs*, incitare galli, cani al combattimento **4.** manovrare (truppe, navi, in battaglia): *to* — *one's ships*, manovrare le proprie navi **5.** *to* — *down*, vincere, sconfiggere (anche *fig.*) **6.** *to* — *off*, scacciare (nemico, malattia) **7.** *to* — *out*, decidere (una contesa) con le armi: *to* — *it out*, battersi fino alla fine.

fighter [faitə*], *s.* **1.** combattente **2.** (*aer.*) caccia ☆ — -*bomber*, cacciabombardiere.

fighting [ˈfaitiŋ], *ag.* combattente ‖ *s.* combattimento; lotta; rissa ☆ — -*cock*, gallo da combattimento; *fig.* galletto; — *line*, (*mil.*) linea del fuoco, prima linea; — *men*, combattenti; — -*plane*, aereo da combattimento, da caccia.

figment [ˈfigmənt], *s.* finzione, invenzione: *figments of the mind*, immaginazioni.

figuline [ˈfigjulin], *ag.* figulino ‖ *s.* vaso di terracotta.

figurability [ˌfigjurəˈbiliti], *s.* figurabilità.

figurable [ˈfigjurəbl], *ag.* figurabile; immaginabile.

figural [ˈfigjurəl], *ag.* di figura.

figurant [ˈfigjurənt], *s.* (*teat.*) **1.** comparsa **2.** danzatore di balletto.

figurante [ˌfigjuˈrænti], *pl.* **figuranti** [ˌfigjuˈrænti:], *s.* (*teat.*) **1.** comparsa **2.** danzatrice di balletto.

figuration [ˌfigjuˈreiʃən], *s.* **1.** figurazione; configurazione **2.** allegoria **3.** (*mus.*) figurazione.

figurative [ˈfigjurətiv], *ag.* **1.** figurativo **2.** figurato; allegorico; simbolico; metaforico **3.** ornato, fiorito (di stile).

figuratively [ˈfigjurətivli], *av.* **1.** figurativamente **2.** figuratamente.

figurativeness [ˈfigjurətivnis], *s.* carattere figurato, metaforico.

figure [ˈfigə*], *s.* **1.** figura; forma; aspetto, sembianza: *an interesting historical* —, un'interessante figura storica; *plane, solid* —, (*geom.*) figura piana, solida ‖ *to cut a* —, fare un figurone; *to cut a poor, brilliant* —, fare brutta, bella figura ‖ *to keep one's* —, mantenere la linea **2.** raffigurazione; ritratto, statua: *the ceiling was covered with figures of trees and birds*, il soffitto era ricoperto di figure di alberi e uccelli **3.** (*mat.*) cifra, numero; ammontare, somma: *cheaper figures*, prezzi più bassi; *a high* —, un prezzo elevato; *round* —, cifra tonda **4.** illustrazione; diagramma; rappresentazione figurata dei segni zodiacali **5.** (*pattinaggio, danza*) figura **6.** (*gram. log. ret.*) figura **7.** (*mus.*) « leitmotiv » ☆ — -*caster*, astrologo; — -*dance*, ballo figurato.

to **figure**, *v.t.i.* **1.** raffigurare, rappresentare; foggiare; adornare con figure, disegni: *white figured in red*, bianco con disegni stampati in rosso **2.** immaginare, immaginarsi; figurarsi: *she figured he would give her a ride in his car*, si immaginava che egli le avrebbe fatto fare un giro nella sua automobile **3.** figurare,

apparire: *he figures as an honest man*, passa per un uomo onesto **4.** (*mat.*) scrivere in cifre **5.** eseguire una figura di danza **6.** simboleggiare; rappresentare con metafore, simboli, ecc. **7.** *to* — *out*, sommare; (*amer.*) calcolare **8.** *to* — *up*, calcolare.

figurehead [ˈfigəhed], *s.* **1.** (*mar.*) polena **2.** *fig.* prestanome, uomo di paglia **3.** (*scherz.*) viso, faccia.

figurine [ˈfigjuriːn], *s.* figurina, statuetta.

Fiji [fiːˈdʒiː], *no.pr.* (*geog.*) Isole Figi.

filament [ˈfiləmənt], *s.* **1.** filamento; fibrilla **2.** (*elett. bot.*) filamento ☆ — *circuit*, (*elett.*) circuito di filamento; — *lamp*, (*elett.*) lampada a filamento ‖ *silk* —, filo di seta.

filamentary [ˌfiləˈmentəri], **filamentous** [ˌfiləˈmentəs], *ag.* filamentoso.

filatory [ˈfilətəri], *s.* filatoio.

filature [ˈfilətʃə*], *s.* **1.** filatura **2.** filanda.

filbert [ˈfilbə(ː)t], *s.* (*bot.*) **1.** nocciola **2.** nocciolo.

filch [filtʃ], *s.* refurtiva.

to **filch**, *v.t.* rubacchiare; sgraffignare.

filcher [ˈfiltʃə*], *s.c.* ladruncolo, ladruncola.

filching [ˈfiltʃin], *s.* rubacchiamento.

file¹ [fail], *s.* **1.** lima **2.** (*sl.*) persona astuta: *he's a* —, è un volpone ☆ — -*cutter*, chi fa lime; — -*dust*, (*mec.*) limatura ‖ *knife* —, lima a coltello; *rasping* —, lima da legno.

to **file¹**, *v.t.* **1.** limare: *to* — *sthg. smooth*, levigare ql.co. con la lima **2.** *fig.* limare, perfezionare, correggere.

file², *s.* **1.** filza; schedario; archivio; raccolta di documenti, ecc.: *the* — *of the "Times"*, la raccolta del « Times »; *our, your* —, il vostro, il nostro numero di riferimento (in archivio); *to be on* —, trovarsi in archivio **2.** fila (di persone, di oggetti, ecc.): *in* —, (*mil.*) in fila per due; *in single* (o *Indian*) —, in fila indiana ‖ *the rank and* —, (*mil.*) soldati semplici e caporali **3.** (*arald.*) lambello ☆ — -*card*, cartellino, scheda; — -*copy*, copia da archiviare; — *holder*, raccoglitore; — -*leader*, capofila ‖ *correspondence* —, raccoglitore di corrispondenza; *paper-* —, raccoglitore (di documenti).

to **file²**, *v.t.i.* **1.** ordinare (documenti, ecc.); archiviare **2.** marciare in fila; far marciare in fila: *to* — *out of school*, uscire dalla scuola in fila **3.** *to* — *off*, allontanarsi marciando in fila.

to **file³**, *v.t.* **1.** sporcare, macchiare, insozzare **2.** *fig.* contaminare, disonorare.

filemot [ˈfilimət], *ag.s.* color foglia morta.

filer [ˈfailə*], *s.* limatore.

filial [ˈfiljəl], *ag.* filiale.

filially [ˈfiliəli], *av.* in modo filiale.

filiation [ˌfiliˈeiʃən], *s.* filiazione.

filibeg [ˈfilibeg], *s.* (*scoz.*) gonnellino.

filibuster [ˈfilibʌstə*], *s.* **1.** filibustiere **2.** (*pol. amer.*) ostruzionista.

to **filibuster**, *v.i.* **1.** agire da filibustiere **2.** (*pol. amer.*) fare ostruzionismo.

filibusterer [ˈfilibʌstərə*], *s.* (*pol. amer.*) ostruzionista.

filibustering [ˈfilibʌstəriŋ], *s.* (*pol. amer.*) ostruzionismo.

filiform [ˈfailifɔːm], *ag.* filiforme.

filigrane [ˈfiligrein], *s.* filigrana.

filigree [ˈfiligriː], *s.* filigrana ☆ — -*work*, lavoro in filigrana.

filigreed [ˈfiligriːd], *ag.* a filigrana, filigranato.

filing¹ [ˈfailin], *s.* **1.** limatura, il limare **2.** *pl.* limatura (di ferro, ecc.).

filing², *ag.* da archivio ‖ *s.* **1.** archiviazione, raccolta a schede **2.** (*mil.*) sfilata ☆ — *system*, sistema di raccolta a schede.

fill [fil], *s.* **1.** sazietà, sufficienza: *to one's* —, a sazietà; *eat your* —, mangia a sazietà; *to cry one's* —, piangere tutte le proprie lacrime; *to drink one's* —, bere a sazietà **2.** quanto basta per riempire ql.co.: *he helped himself to a* — *of tobacco*, egli si riempì la pipa di tabacco.

to fill, *v.t.i.* **1.** riempire, riempirsi; colmare; caricare; completare (anche *fig.*): *he filled his glass to the brim*, si riempì il bicchiere sino all'orlo; *his fame filled America*, la sua fama si diffuse per tutta America; *to — a tooth*, otturare un dente **2.** satollare, satollarsi; accontentare, accontentarsi; soddisfare **3.** occupare, coprire, tenere (carica, impiego, ecc.): *to — a part*, (*teat.*) interpretare una parte ‖ *to — s.o.'s shoes*, (*fam.*) succedere a qlcu., prendere il posto di qlcu. **4.** (*mar.*) gonfiarsi (di vele); imbarcare acqua **5.** (*comm.*) eseguire **6.** *to — in*, completare, compilare, riempire (modulo): *to — in the date*, inserire la data **7.** *to — out*, gonfiare, gonfiarsi; ingrassare, ingrassarsi; rimpolpare (anche *fig.*); versare **8.** *to — up*, riempire, colmare, completare; (*aer. aut.*) fare il pieno: *to — up a cheque*, riempire un assegno ‖ *to — s.o. up* (*with a tale*), (*fam.*) riempire la testa a qlcu. (con una storia).

filler ['filə*], *s.c.* addetto, addetta al carico, al riempimento di ql.co. ‖ *s.* **1.** cosa che riempie; pompetta (di stilografica); (*aut.*) riporto, bocchettone di riempimento, dispositivo di riempimento **2.** (*artig.*) stucco; (*pitt.*) fondo.

fillet ['filit], *s.* **1.** nastro, fascia **2.** (*cuc.*) filetto; fetta (di carne, pesce) **3.** (*arch.*) listello **4.** (*mec.*) raccordo concavo **5.** (*arald.*) partizione orizzontale (di uno scudo).

to fillet, *v.t.* **1.** (*arc.*) ornare di nastri **2.** (*cuc.*) tagliare (pesce, carne) a fette **3.** (*mec.*) raccordare.

filling ['filiŋ], *s.* **1.** riempitura; caricamento; otturazione **2.** (*odontoiatria*) mastice o altra sostanza usata per otturazioni **3.** (*cuc.*) impasto, ripieno usato per farcire i cib **4.** (*tessile*) trama ☆ *— funnel*, imbuto, *— station*, (*aut.*) stazione di rifornimento.

fillip ['filip], *s.* **1.** lo schioccare delle dita ‖ *not to be worth a —*, non valere nulla **2.** *fig.* stimolo rapido, improvviso.

to fillip, *v.t.i.* **1.** schioccare le dita **2.** *fig.* stimolare, eccitare.

fillister ['filistə*], *s.* (*strum. artig.*) incorsatoio.

filly ['fili], *s.* **1.** puledra **2.** (*fam.*) ragazza vispa ed allegra.

film [film], *s.* **1.** pellicola, strato sottile **2.** *fig.* velo: *a — of mist*, un velo di nebbia **3.** (*anat.*) membrana **4.** (*cine. foto.*) film, pellicola: *exposed —*, pellicola esposta, impressionata ‖ *to take* (o *to shoot*) *a —*, girare un film ☆ *— actor*, attore del cinema; *— -fan*, (*sl.*) patito del cinema; *— industry*, industria cinematografica; *— library*, cineteca; *— lover*, amante del cinema; *— -roll*, bobina; *— -script*, copione; *— -star*, divo, diva del cinema; *— strip*, filmina, pellicola diascopica; *— test*, provino cinematografico ‖ *colour —*, film a colori; *news —*, cinegiornale; *nonflam —*, pellicola infiammabile; *serial —*, film ad episodi; *silent —*, film muto; *slow motion —*, film al rallentatore; *sound —*, film sonoro; *talking —*, film parlato.

to film, *v.t.i.* **1.** coprire, coprirsi di una pellicola **2.** filmare, girare un film; riprodurre cinematograficamente: *this novel has been filmed*, questo romanzo è stato filmato.

filmland ['filmlænd], *s.* il mondo del cinema.

filmily ['filmili], *av.* in modo incerto, appannato.

filminess ['filminis], *s.* trasparenza, leggerezza.

filmy ['filmi], *ag.* nebbioso; appannato: *a — look*, uno sguardo annebbiato **2.** sottile, delicato.

filoselle ['filəsel], *s.* (*ind. tessile*) filaticcio.

filter ['filtə*], *s.* filtro ☆ *— -bed*, strato filtrante; *-paper*, carta da filtro; *— -tip*, filtro di sigaretta.

to filter, *v.t.i.* **1.** filtrare; distillare; depurare **2.** *fig.* purificare **3.** *fig.* trapelare, diffondersi: *the news soon filtered out* (o *through*), la notizia si diffuse presto.

filth [filθ], *s.* **1.** sozzura, sudiciume, immondizia **2.** corruzione morale **3.** linguaggio osceno.

filthily ['filθili], *av.* in modo sudicio, sozzo.

filthiness ['filθinis], *s.* **1.** sporcizia, sozzura **2.** corruzione morale; oscenità.

filthy ['filθi], *ag.* **1.** sporco, sudicio, sordido, sozzo **2.** *fig.* impuro, corrotto‖ *— lucre*, il vile denaro.

filtrate ['filtrit], *s.* liquido filtrato.

to filtrate ['filtreit], *V.* **to filter.**

filtration [fil'treiʃən], *s.* filtrazione.

fimbriate(d) ['fimbrieit(id)], *ag.* (*bot. zool.*) frangiato.

fin [fin], *s.* **1.** pinna (di pesce): *caudal, dorsal —*, pinna caudale, dorsale **2.** (*aer.*) piano stabilizzatore **3.** (*mec.*) aletta **4.** (*sl.*) mano, zampa: *tip us your —*, stringiamoci la mano.

finable ['fainəbl], *ag.* multabile.

final ['fainl], *ag.* **1.** finale, ultimo: *— chapter*, ultimo capitolo **2.** conclusivo, decisivo: *the — battle*, la battaglia decisiva ‖ *s.* **1.** (*spor.*) gara finale **2.** (anche *pl.*) esami finali **3.** (*fam.*) ultima edizione (di quotidiano).

finale [fi'nɑ:li], *s.* (*mus.*) finale.

finalist ['fainəlist], *s. c.* (*spor.*) finalista.

finality [fai'næliti], *s.* **1.** (*fil.*) finalità **2.** carattere definitivo.

finally ['fainəli], *av.* **1.** alla fine **2.** definitivamente.

finance [fai'næns], *s.* **1.** finanza **2.** *pl.* finanze; reddito.

to finance, *v.t.i.* **1.** finanziare **2.** maneggiare fondi.

financial [fai'nænʃəl], *ag.* finanziario ☆ *— year*, (*comm.*) esercizio finanziario.

financially [fai'nænʃəli], *av.* finanziariamente.

financier [fai'nænsiə*], *s.* **1.** finanziere **2.** finanziatore.

to financier, *v.t.i.* **1.** (*spreg.*) fare l'aggiotaggio **2.** (*amer.*) ingannare, truffare: *to — money out of s.o.*, imbrogliare qlcu.

finch [fintʃ], *s.* (*ornit.*) fringuello; cardellino.

find [faind], *s.* **1.** scoperta, ritrovamento: *this old book is a great —*, questo vecchio libro è una bella scoperta **2.** (*caccia*) scoperta (della preda); luogo in cui si trova sicuramente la preda (generalmente volpe).

to find, *pass.p.p.* **found** [faund], *v.t.* **1.** trovare, ritrovare, rintracciare (anche *fig.*): *at last the thirsty men found water*, alla fine gli assetati trovarono dell'acqua; *the dog found his way home*, il cane ritrovò la strada di casa; *has he found his books yet?*, ha già ritrovato i suoi libri?; *his works are to be found*, le sue opere sono reperibili; *to — one's bearings*, (*aer. fig.*) orientarsi; *to — one's way*, trovare la propria strada (anche *fig.*); *to — time*, trovar tempo ‖ *to — oneself*, scoprire la propria vocazione‖ *to — one's feet*, conquistarsi un posto nel mondo ‖ *to be found mentioned*, essere citato **2.** scoprire per caso, sorprendere: *she was found listening at the door*, la trovarono che origliava alla porta **3.** trovare, pensare, considerare, constatare: *as I have found to my sorrow*, come ho constatato con dolore; *to — it difficult, easy, impossible*, trovare difficile, facile, impossibile: *I — this book difficult to understand*, trovo questo libro difficile da capire ‖ *to — fault with sthg.*, *s.o.*, lamentarsi di, criticare ql.co., qlcu. **4.** fornire, provvedere: *you may be sure I won't — you money for your whims*, puoi star sicuro che non ti darò denari per i tuoi capricci; *to — in* (o *with*), fornire, provvedere di ‖ *all found*, tutto compreso **5.** *fig.* ottenere, incontrare: *it didn't — any favour with her*, non incontrò il suo gusto **6.** (*dir.*) dichiarare, giudicare: *any jury would — him guilty*, qualsiasi giuria lo dichiarerebbe colpevole **7.** *to — out*, scoprire, cercare di scoprire: *I shall — out all about her*, ne verrò a sapere vita, morte e miracoli‖ *to — s.o. out*, scoprire il vero carattere, le marachelle di qlcu.

findable ['faindəbl], *ag.* trovabile.

finder ['faində*], *s.c.* chi trova ‖ *s.* (*ott.*) mirino, traguardo; (*astr.*) cannocchiale cercatore.

finding ['faindiŋ], *s.* **1.** scoperta **2.** *pl.* (*amer.*) forniture, accessori di un artigiano **3.** (*dir.*) sentenza.

fine[1] [fain], *ag.* **1.** bello (di tempo, clima): *a — day*, una bella giornata; *— weather*, bel tempo ‖ *we are going wet or —*, andremo con qualunque tempo **2.** bello, eccellente, meraviglioso: *a — view*, una vista meravigliosa; *what a — girl!*, che bella ragazza! || *— arts*, belle arti || *he'll be punished one of these — days*, sarà punito un bel giorno || *that's —!*, (ciò va) benissimo! 3. buono; di qualità superiore; elevato (di sentimenti): *— feelings*, sentimenti elevati; *a — intellect*, una bella intelligenza, un bell'ingegno 4. fine, minuto, sottile, appuntito: *— pencil*, matita appuntita; *— sand*, sabbia fine 5. puro; raffinato; pregiato: *— workmanship*, lavorazione raffinata; *gold 18 carats —*, oro fino a 18 carati 6. elegante, distinto, raffinato: *you are looking very —!*, sei molto elegante! 7. sottile, acuto; raffinato: *a — distinction*, una distinzione sottile; *he has a — sense of the ridiculous*, egli ha uno spiccato senso del ridicolo.

fine[1], *av.* 1. bene; elegantemente: *that will suit me —*, *(fam.)* ciò mi va benone; *to talk —*, parlare con eleganza 2. *(fam.)* con margine minimo, di stretta misura.

to **fine**[1], *v.t.i.* 1. schiarire (birra, vino); diventare chiaro (di birra, vino) 2. *to —* **away, down, off**, assottigliare, assottigliarsi; affinarsi.

fine[1], *(nei composti)*: *— -drawer*, rammendatore, rammendatrice; *— -drawing*, rammendo invisibile; *— -fingered*, destro, lesto (di mano); *— -spoken*, che parla bene; *— -spun*, sottile, attenuato; *fig.* infondato.

fine[2], *s.* 1. multa, ammenda: *a heavy —*, una forte multa 2. *(dir.)* accomodamento finale tra le parti 3. *(dir. feudale)* somma pagata dal locatario o dal vassallo al padrone per ottenere concessioni 4. *(rar.)* fine, conclusione: *in —*, finalmente, in conclusione.

to **fine**[2], *v.t.i.* multare, pagare una multa.

fine[3], *s.* *(arc. irl.)* gruppo di famiglie, setta.

to **fine-draw** ['fain'dro:], *pass.* **fine-drew** ['fain'dru:], *p.p.* **fine-drawn** ['fain'dro:n], *v.t.* rammendare.

finely ['fainli], *av.* 1. bene; magnificamente, elegantemente 2. finemente, sottilmente; distintamente.

fineness ['fainnis] *s.* 1. bellezza, magnificenza 2. eleganza, distinzione 3. finitezza, finezza 4. titolo (di oro, argento, ecc,).

finery[1] ['fainəri], *s.* 1. eleganza un po' vistosa: *she was decked out in all her —*, era ornata di tutti i suoi fronzoli 2. *pl.* ornamento, fronzolo; abito vistoso.

finery[2], *s.* *(metal.)* forno di puddellaggio.

finesse [fi'nes], *s.* 1. finezza, sottigliezza 2. malizia, astuzia.

to **finesse**, *v.i.* usare astuzie; sottilizzare.

finger ['fingə*], *s.* 1. dito: *there are five fingers on each hand*: thumb, index — (o *forefinger*), middle —, ring —, little —, in ciascuna mano vi sono cinque dita: pollice, indice, medio, anulare, mignolo; *to eat sthg. with one's fingers*, mangiare ql.co. con le mani; *to lay* (o *to put*) *a — on sthg.*, toccare ql.co. || *the — of God*, *fig.* il dito di Dio || *with a wet —*, con facilità || *his fingers are all thumbs*, *fig.* egli è molto goffo || *to have a — in the pie*, *fig.* aver le mani in pasta || *to have sthg. on one's —-tips* (o *—-ends*), *fig.* avere ql.co. sulla punta delle dita, sapere alla perfezione ql.co. || *to keep one's fingers crossed*, toccar ferro (per scongiuro) || *to put one's — on sthg.*, *fig.* indicare il punto debole, mettere il dito sulla piaga || *to turn* (o *to twist*) *s.o. round one's little —*, *fig.* fare ciò che si vuole di qlcu. 2. ogni oggetto a forma di dito: *the — of a glove*, il dito di un guanto 3. quantità equivalente alla larghezza di un dito: *a — of whisky*, un dito di whisky 4. *(mec.)* lancetta; nottolino, dente; maschio, pistone ☆ *— -alphabet*, alfabeto dei muti, dattilologia; *— -bowl* (o *— glass*), vaschetta lavadita; *— -biscuit*, *(cuc.)* lingua di suocera; *— -board*, manico del violino; tastiera (di pianoforte, ecc.); *— -breadth*, tre quarti di pollice (= cm. 1,905); *— -mark*, ditata; *— -nail*, unghia (della mano); *— -plate*, placca di vetro, metallo (applicata alle porte per non insudiciarle); *— -post*, palo segnavia; *— -print*, impronta digitale; *— -print identification*, dattiloscopia; *— -stall*, copridito (di gomma).

to **finger**, *v.t.* 1. toccare con le dita, palpare 2. ru-

bacchiare 3. accettare (mance, ricompense) 4. toccare (tasti, corde) con le dita 5. *(mus.)* scrivere la diteggiatura di (un pezzo).

fingered ['fingəd], *ag.* dalle dita ☆ *light- —*, dalle mani lunghe; ladro.

fingering ['fingəriŋ], *s.* 1. *(mus.)* diteggiatura 2. lana grossa da calze.

fingerling ['fingəliŋ], *s.* 1. essere minuscolo 2. piccolo salmone.

finial ['fainiəl], *s.* *(arch.)* ornamento di pinnacolo (generalmente fiore crociforme).

finical ['finikəl], *ag.* 1. pignolo; meticoloso 2. affettato; ricercato; schizzinoso.

finically ['finikəli], *av.* 1. da pignolo 2. in modo affettato.

finicalness ['finikəlnis], *s.* meticolosità.

finickin ['finikin], **finicking** ['finikiŋ], **finicky** ['finiki], *ag.* 1. pignolo; meticoloso 2. affettato; ricercato; schizzinoso,

finis ['fainis], *s.* *(solo sing.)* fine, finis.

finish ['finiʃ], *s.* 1. *(solo sing.)* fine, compimento, conclusione: *to fight (it out) to a —*, combattere fino all'ultimo (anche *fig.*) 2. ultima tappa, volata finale (di corsa, caccia, ecc.): *to be in at the —*, *(caccia)* essere presente all'uccisione (della preda) 3. finezza, finitura (anche *fig.*): *his manners lack —*, i suoi modi non sono compiti 4. appretto (di tessuto).

to **finish**, *v.t.i.* 1. (I) finire; terminare; completare: *have you finished reading the newspaper?*, hai finito di leggere il giornale?; *he has finished his work*, ha finito il suo lavoro; *to —* (*up*) *with*, porre termine con, finire con: *the dinner finished* (*up*) *with a glass of champagne*, il pranzo si concluse con un bicchiere di champagne 2. distruggere; porre fine a: *to — sthg.* (*off* o *up*), *(fam.)* distruggere; mangiare tutto 3. rendere perfetto, completo 4. apprettare (tessuti) 5. *to — off*, dare l'ultimo tocco a, dare il colpo di grazia a.

finished ['finiʃt], *ag.* finito, perfetto, raffinato: *a — gentleman*, un perfetto gentiluomo; *a — performance of the Ninth Symphony*, una esecuzione perfetta della Nona Sinfonia.

finisher ['finiʃə*], *s.c.* chi finisce; rifinitore, rifinitrice; perfezionatore, perfezionatrice || *s.* 1. *(mec.)* finitrice 2. *fig.* colpo di grazia ☆ *— card*, *(mec.)* carda finitrice || *belt —*, *(mec.)* smerigliatrice a nastro.

finishing ['finiʃiŋ], *ag.* ultimo, che finisce || *s.* 1. finitura, rifinitura 2. appretto, finissaggio (di tessuti) ☆ *— school*, scuola di perfezionamento || *precision —*, *(mec.)* microfinitura.

finite ['fainait], *ag.* 1. circoscritto; limitato 2. *(gram.)* finito: *— verb*, verbo di modo finito || *s.* il finito, ciò che ha termine: *the — and the infinite*, il finito e l'infinito

finitely ['fainaitli], *av.* limitatamente, definitivamente.

finiteness ['fainaitnis], **finitude** ['fainitju:d], *s.* stato circoscritto, limitato.

fink [fiŋk], *s.* *(sl. amer.)* 1. delatore 2. crumiro.

Finland ['finlənd], *no.pr.* *(geog.)* Finlandia.

Finlander ['finləndə*], *s.c.* finlandese.

finless ['finlis], *ag.* senza pinne.

Finn [fin], *s.c.* finlandese.

finnan ['finən], *s.* merluzzo affumicato.

Finnic ['finik], *ag.* finlandese, finnico.

Finnish ['finiʃ], *ag.* finnico || *s.* la lingua finnica.

finny ['fini], *ag.* 1. provvisto di pinne 2. *(poet.)* relativo al pesce; pieno di pesci.

fiord [fjo:d], *s.* fiordo.

fiorin ['faiərin], *s.* *(bot.)* agrostide.

fir [fə:*], *s.* *(bot.)* abete ☆ *— -cone*, pigna; *— -needle*, ago d'abete; *— -tree*, abete; *— -wood*, abetaia.

fire ['faiə*], *s.* 1. fuoco, fiamma; *on —*, in fiamme; *to catch* (o *to take*) *—*, prendere fuoco; *to light a —*, accendere il fuoco; *to rouse* (o *to stir*) *the —*, attizzare il fuoco; *to set sthg. on —* (o *to set — to sthg.*), appiccare il fuoco a ql.co. || *St. Anthony's —*, *(patol.)* erpes zoster ‖ *to fall out of the frying-pan into the* —, cadere dalla padella nella brace ‖ *to set the Thames on* —, fare ql.co. di eccezionale ‖ *there's no smoke without* —, *prov.* non c'è fumo senza arrosto **2.** incendio: *he has insured his car against* —, ha assicurato l'automobile contro gli incendi **3.** (*artigl.*) tiro, fuoco: *under the enemy's* —, sotto il tiro del nemico; *to be between two fires*, essere tra due fuochi (anche *fig.*); *to cease, to open* —, cessare, aprire il fuoco **4.** *fig.* fuoco; ardore; entusiasmo; vigore: *on* —, eccitato ☆ — *-alarm*, allarme d'incendio; — *-ball*, globo di fuoco, meteorite; — *-balloon*, mongolfiera; — *-bomb*, bomba incendiaria; — *-brand*, tizzone; *fig.* tizzone della discordia; — *-brigade*, (corpo dei) pompieri; — *-bucket*, secchio per incendio; — *-cracker*, petardo; — *-drill*, esercitazione di pompieri; — *-eater*, mangiatore di fuoco, *fig.* attaccabrighe; — *-engine*, pompa antincendio; — *-escape*, uscita di sicurezza; — *-extinguisher*, estintore, pompa antincendio; — *-guard*, parafuoco; — *-hose*, manichetta, naspo; — *-irons*, paletta, molle, attizzatoio; — *-light*, luce del focolare; — *-office*, ufficio di assicurazione contro gli incendi; — *-plug*, bocca da incendio; — *-policy*, polizza di assicurazione contro incendi; — *-screen*, parafuoco; — *-station*, caserma dei pompieri; — *-step*, banchina di tiro; — *-stick*, legnetti per accendere il fuoco; — *-stone*, pietra refrattaria; — *-water*, (*amer.*) liquore alcoolico (rum, acquavite, whisky, ecc.); — *-work*, fuoco d'artificio; — *-worship*, adorazione del fuoco; — *-worshipper*, adoratore del fuoco.

to fire, *v.t.i.* **1.** dar fuoco, incendiare, incendiarsi, prender fuoco **2.** cuocere (mattoni); scaldare (caldaie); seccare (con calore) **3.** (*mil.*) far fuoco, sparare; far esplodere: *he fired (off) his gun*, fece fuoco col fucile; *to* — *at s.o.*, sparare contro qlcu.; *to* — *a salute*, sparare a salve **4.** *fig.* infiammare, infiammarsi; eccitare, eccitarsi; incollerirsi **5.** (*fam.*) licenziare; silurare **6.** *to* — *off*, tirare, sparare: *to* — *off a question at s.o.*, fare a qlcu. una domanda a bruciapelo **7.** *to* — *out*, (*amer.*) espellere, cacciare **8.** *to* — *up*, scattare, incollerirsi.

firebox ['faiəbɔks], *s.* focolaio, focolare (specialmente di caldaia).
firebrick ['faiəbrik], *s.* mattone refrattario.
fireclay ['faiə-klei], *s.* argilla refrattaria.
firedamp ['faiədæmp], *s.* (*miner.*) grisù.
firefly ['faiə-flai], *s.* (*entom.*) lucciola.
firelock ['faiəlɔk], *s.* fucile (di tipo antiquato).
fireman, *pl.* **firemen** ['faiəmən], *s.* **1.** vigile del fuoco, pompiere **2.** fochista.
fireplace ['faiə-pleis], *s.* focolare, caminetto.
fireproof ['faiə-pru:f], *ag.* incombustibile.
fireship ['faiə-ʃip], *s.* (*mar.*) brulotto.
fireside ['faiə-said], *s.* angolo del focolare.
firewood ['faiəwud], *s.* legna da ardere.
firing ['faiəriŋ], *s.* **1.** l'appiccare il fuoco; incendio **2.** il fare fuoco; tiro, sparo, scarica; fucilata; cannonata **3.** (*vet.*) cauterizzazione **4.** cottura (di mattoni, ceramiche) **5.** alimentazione, caricamento (di locomotiva, fornace, ecc.) ☆ — *-iron*, ferro per cauterizzare; — *-line*, linea di fuoco; — *-party* (o — *platoon* o — *squad*), plotone di esecuzione; — *-point*, (*chim. fis.*) punto di ionizzazione; — *-step*, banchina di tiro.
firkin ['fə:kin], *s.* **1.** «firkin» (misura di capacità = l. 40,91) **2.** barilotto (per burro, pesce, liquidi).
firm[1] [fə:m], *ag.* **1.** solido; compatto: — *ground*, un terreno compatto **2.** fisso, stabile: — *prices*, prezzi fissi; — *principles*, principi saldi **3.** deciso, risoluto, forte: — *character*, carattere deciso ‖ *av.* fermamente.
to firm[1], *v.t.i.* solidificare, solidificarsi, stabilizzare, stabilizzarsi.
firm[2], *s.* ditta; società; casa commerciale ☆ *long* —, banda di truffatori; *publishing* —, casa editrice.
firmament ['fə:məmənt], *s.* firmamento, cielo.
firmamental [,fə:mə'mentl], *ag.* del cielo, celeste.
firman [fə:'ma:n], *s.* (*st. turca*) firmano.
firmly ['fə:mli], *av.* **1.** fermamente: *I* — *believe that,*

credo fermamente che **2.** solidamente, saldamente: *he built his house* —, costruì solidamente la sua casa.
firmness ['fə:mnis], *s.* **1.** fermezza **2.** stabilità.
firn [fə:n], *s.* neve granulosa dei ghiacciai.
firry ['fə:ri], *ag.* **1.** di abete **2.** ricco di abeti.
first [fə:st], *ag.num.ord.* primo: *the* — *of June* (o *June the* — o *June 1st*), il primo di giugno; — *person*, (*gram.*) prima persona; *the* — *two, three days*, i primi due, tre giorni ‖ *the* — *men in the country*, gli uomini più importanti del paese ‖ *at* — *sight*, a prima vista ‖ *in the* — *place*, in primo luogo ‖ *First Lord of Admiralty*, ministro della Marina ‖ *Charles the First*, Carlo I ‖ *to do sthg.* — *thing*, fare ql.co. innanzitutto ‖ *av.* **1.** prima di tutto, per la prima volta, innanzitutto, per primo: — *of all*, prima di tutto; *America* —!, prima di tutto l'America; *ladies* —!, prima le signore; *I saw him* — *in London*, lo vidi per la prima volta a Londra ‖ — *and last*, in tutto e per tutto ‖ *to fall head* —, cadere a capofitto ‖ — *come* — *served, prov.* chi tardi arriva, male alloggia **2.** piuttosto: *when asked to betray his country, he said he would die* —, quando gli si chiese di tradire il suo paese, disse che piuttosto sarebbe morto ☆ — *-aid*, pronto soccorso; — *-born*, primogenito; — *-class* di prima qualità, ottimo: *this is* — *-class*, questa è di prima qualità; — *-class boxer*, campione di pugilato; — *-comer*, il primo venuto; — *-fruits*, primizie; i primi risultati (di lavoro); — *-hand*, di prima mano: *I heard that* — *-hand*, l'ho sentito di prima mano; — *lady*, (*amer.*) consorte del Presidente; — *name*, nome di battesimo; — *-nighter*, (*teat.*) frequentatore delle prime; — *-offender*, (*dir.*) imputato di primo reato; — *officer*, primo ufficiale; — *-rate*, ottimo.
first, *s.* **1.** il primo, la prima (persona, cosa): *the* — *in*, la prima persona ad entrare; *he was the* — *to speak*, fu il primo a parlare **2.** principio: *at* —, al principio, dapprima; *from the* —, dal principio; *from* — *to last*, dal principio alla fine **3.** (*scuola*) votazione di ottimo negli esami; *chi ricevè tale votazione* **4.** *pl.* (*comm.*) la migliore qualità di merce.
firstlings ['fə:stliŋz], *s. pl.* primizie.
firstly ['fə:stli], *av.* in primo luogo.
firth [fə:θ], *s.* (*scoz. geog.*) fiordo; estuario.
fisc [fisk], *s.* fisco.
fiscal ['fiskəl], *ag.* fiscale ‖ *s.* (*scoz.*) (procuratore) fiscale.
fiscally ['fiskəli], *av.* fiscalmente.
fish[1] [fiʃ], *pl.* **fishes** ['fiʃiz], *coll.* **fish**, *s.* **1.** pesce: — (*es*) *swim*, i pesci nuotano; *I caught a* —, *several* —, presi un pesce, parecchi pesci ‖ *the Fish(es)*, (*astr.*) i Pesci ‖ *he is like a* — *out of water*, (*fam.*) è come un pesce fuor d'acqua ‖ *he is neither* —, *flesh nor fowl*, non è nè carne nè pesce ‖ *he is a queer* —, (*sl.*) è un tipo strano, un originale ‖ *I've got other* — *to fry*, ho altri affari cui badare ‖ *to drink like a* —, bere come una spugna ‖ *to feed the fishes*, annegare; soffrire il mal di mare **2.** carne di pesce: *canned* —, pesce in scatola ☆ — *-ball* (o — *-cake*), (*cuc.*) polpettina di pesce; — *-bone*, lisca, spina di pesce; — *-breeding*, pescicultura; — *-carver*, coltello da pesce; — *-glue*, colla di pesce; — *-hook*, amo per la pesca; — *-knife and fork*, posate da pesce; — *-monger*, pescivendolo; — *-pond*, vivaio; — *-slice*, (*cuc.*) paletta per il pesce; — *-tail*, a coda di pesce; — *-torpedo*, (*mar.*) siluro a forma allungata.
to fish[1], *v.t.i.* **1.** pescare: *to* — *for trout*, pescare trote ‖ *to* — *in troubled waters*, *fig.* pescar nel torbido **2.** cercare di ottenere (informazioni, ecc.) senza averne l'aria: *to* — *for compliments*, cercare di farsi fare dei complimenti **3.** cercare, frugare **4.** *to* — *out*, tirar fuori; esaurire le risorse ittiche di (lago, fiume, con pesca intensiva): *she fished a coin out of her bag*, tirò fuori una moneta dalla borsa.
fish[2], *s.* (*mar.*) lapazza ☆ — *-joint*, (*mec.*) giunto a ganascia; — *-plate*, (*mec.*) coprigiunto.
to fish[2], *v.t.* **1.** (*mar.*) lapazzare **2.** (*mec.*) unire con giunto a ganascia.

fish[3], *s.* « fiche », gettone.

fish[4], *s.* **1.** il pescare **2.** (*mar.*) paranco ☆ — -*block*, (*mar.*) bozzello di calorna.

fisher ['fiʃə*], *s.* **1.** pescatore **2.** (*zool.*) martora della Virginia **3.** (*mar.*) peschereccio ☆ — *boat*, peschereccio; — *folk* (o — *people*), pescatori; — *woman*, pescivendola.

fisherman, *pl.* **fishermen** ['fiʃəmən], *s.* pescatore.

fishery ['fiʃəri], *s.* **1.** la pesca (l'industria) **2.** luogo dove si pesca; riserva di pesca **3.** licenza di pesca **4.** vivaio.

fishily ['fiʃili], *av.* **1.** da pesce **2.** (*sl.*) in modo equivoco.

fishiness ['fiʃinis], *s.* **1.** pescosità; il gusto, l'odore di pesce **2.** (*sl.*) carattere sospetto (di una cosa).

fishing ['fiʃiŋ], *ag.* di pesca, usato per la pesca ‖ *s.* pesca ☆ — -*gear* (o — -*tackle*), arnesi da pesca; — -*hook*, amo; — -*line*, lenza; — -*rod*, canna da pesca ‖ *deep-sea* —, pesca d'alto mare; *underwater* —, pesca subacquea.

fishwife ['fiʃwaif], *pl.* **fishwives** ['fiʃwaivz], *s.* pescivendola.

fishy ['fiʃi], *ag.* **1.** ricco di pesce, pescoso **2.** di pesce, che sa, odora di pesce: — *smell*, odore di pesce **3.** (*sl.*) equivoco, dubbio ☆ — *eye*, occhio di triglia.

fissile ['fisail], *ag.* fissile.

fission ['fiʃən], *s.* **1.** (*biol.*) scissione **2.** (*fis.*) fissione ☆ *nuclear* —, fissione nucleare.

fissionable ['fiʃnəbl], *ag.* (*biol. fis.*) fissile.

fissiparous [fi'sipərəs], *ag.* (*biol.*) fissiparo.

fissure ['fiʃə*], *s.* **1.** fessura (anche *anat.*) **2.** screpolatura **3.** (*bot.*) fenditura.

fist [fist], *s.* **1.** pugno: *his* — *was clenched on the paper*, il suo pugno era chiuso sulla carta **2.** (*fam.*) mano: *to give s.o. one's* —, porgere la mano a qlcu. ‖ *to make a good* — *of a job*, (*fam.*) fare bene un lavoro **3.** (*fam.*) calligrafia ☆ — -*law*, la legge del più forte ‖ *mailed* —, pugno.di ferro.

fistic(al) ['fistik(əl)], *ag.* (*scherz.*) pugilistico.

to fisticuff ['fistikʌf], *v.t.i.* prendere a pugni; battersi a pugni.

fisticuffs ['fistikʌfs], *s.pl.* pugilato; cazzottatura.

fistula ['fistjulə], *s.* **1.** (*patol.*) fistola **2.** (*zool.*) sfiatatoio (di balena, ecc.).

fistular ['fistjulə*], **fistulous** ['fistjuləs], *ag.* fistoloso.

fit[1] [fit], *comp.* **fitter** ['fitə*], *superl.* **fittest** ['fitist], *ag.* **1.** adatto, idoneo; capace, in grado; conveniente, opportuno, giusto: *he is* — *for nothing*, è un buono a nulla; *I am not* — *to be seen*, non sono presentabile; *that food is only* — *for a dog*, quello è cibo da cani; *your work is not* — *for publication*, il tuo lavoro non è pubblicabile **2.** pronto: *they were* — *for action*, erano pronti all'azione **3.** forte, in buona salute: — *for military service*, valido alle armi; *you're looking* —, (*fam.*) mi sembra che tu stia veramente bene; *to feel* —, sentirsi in forma, in efficienza ‖ *to be as* — *as a fiddle*, (*fam.*) essere sano come un pesce.

fit[1], *s.* **1.** aderenza, misura (di indumento): *it was a tight* —, era una misura un po' stretta; *fig.* era un momento difficile; *those shoes are a perfect* —, quelle scarpe calzano a pennello **2.** (*amer.*) preparazione, preparativo **3.** (*mec.*) accoppiamento ☆ — -*out*, equipaggiamento; — -*up*, (*teat.*) palcoscenico e scenari mobili, trasportabili.

to fit[1], *pass.p.p.* **fitted** ['fitid], *v.t.i.* **1.** adattare, adattarsi; accomodare, provare; addirsi, andar bene: *the tailor fitted my coat*, il sarto mi provò la giacca; *this dress fits you really well*, questo vestito ti sta veramente bene ‖ *to* — *for sthg.*, adattarsi a ql.co.: (*amer.*) prepararsi per ql.co.: *to* — *for college*, (*amer.*) prepararsi ad andare all'università **2.** *to* — **in**, andar bene, convenire; far quadrare **3.** *to* — **on**, provare (abiti) **4.** *to* — **out**, fornire, provvedere **5.** *to* — **up**, allestire, preparare, arredare.

fit[2], *s.* **1.** convulsione; parossismo; convulso ‖ *to give*

s.o. a —, *fig.* far venire un colpo a qlcu.: *she will have a* — *when you tell her*, (*fam.*) quando glielo dirai, le verrà un accidente **2.** attacco, accesso: *in a* — *of rage*, in un accesso di rabbia; *the* — *is now on her*, ella è in vena di, è disposta a fare ql.co.; *to be in fits of laughter*, avere un accesso di riso ‖ *by fits and starts*, a sbalzi, spasmodicamente.

fit[3], *s.* (*arc.*) canto; divisione di ballata o poema.

fitch[1] [fitʃ], *s.* (*bot.*) veccia.

fitch[2], *s.* **1.** pelle di puzzola **2.** pennello.

fitchew ['fitʃu:], *s.* (*zool.*) puzzola.

fitful ['fitful], *ag.* spasmodico; agitato; incostante; irregolare.

fitfully ['fitfuli], *av.* a sbalzi; irregolarmente.

fitfulness ['fitfulnis], *s.* variabilità, incostanza; irregolarità.

fitly ['fitli], *av.* appropriatamente, giustamente; convenientemente.

fitment ['fitmənt], *s.* mobile; mobilia ☆ *wardrobe* —, armadio incassato.

fitness ['fitnis], *s.* convenienza, appropriatezza, l'essere adatto.

fitter[1] ['fitə*], *s.* **1.** (*mec.*) aggiustatore; montatore **2.** (*sartoria*) chi esegue la prova di un abito.

fitter[2], *s.* (*dial.*) carbonaio.

fitting ['fitiŋ], *ag.* adatto; conveniente, confacente: *a* — *occasion*, un'occasione adatta ‖ *s.* **1.** adattamento, allestimento, prova **2.** (*gener. pl.*) accessori; equipaggiamento; suppellettili; mobili; arredi **3.** (*gener. pl. mec.*) guarnizione, attrezzo ☆ — -*out*, allestimento, (*mar.*) armamento; — -*room*, salottino di prova (sartoria).

fittingly ['fitiŋli], *av.* convenientemente.

fittingness ['fitiŋnis], *s.* convenienza.

five [faiv], *ag. num. card. s.* cinque ☆ — -*finger*, (*bot.*) cinquefoglie; (*ittiol.*) stella di mare; — *finger exercises*, (*mus.*) esercizi per le cinque dita; — -*o' clock* (*tea*), il tè pomeridiano; — -*ply*, a cinque fili (di lana).

fivefold ['faivfould], *ag.* quintuplo.

fivepence ['faifpəns], *s.* il valore di cinque « penny ».

fiver ['faivə*], *s.* (*sl.*) banconota da cinque sterline; (*amer.*) banconota da cinque dollari.

fives [faivz], *s.pl.* giuoco della palla al muro.

fix [fiks], *s.* **1.** difficoltà; dilemma: *to be in a* —, essere nei guai **2.** (*mar.*) punto nave; (*aer.*) punto determinato con rilevamenti ad incrocio.

to fix, *v.t.i.* **1.** fissare; montare; fermare; attaccare: *he fixed it with a nail*, lo fissò con un chiodo; *to* — *sthg. in one's memory*, fissarsi ql.co. nella mente **2.** attirare (l'attenzione): *that book fixed his attention*, quel libro attirò la sua attenzione **3.** stabilire, stabilirsi; designare; regolare: *to* — (*up*)*on sthg.*, fissare la propria scelta su, scegliere ql.co. **4.** (*cine. foto.*) fissare **5.** (*med.*) sterilizzare **6.** coagulare, coagularsi (di liquidi) **7.** (*fam.*) mettere nell'imbarazzo, conciare per le feste: *we've fixed him!*, l'abbiamo sistemato! **8.** *to* — **out**, equipaggiare, rifornire **9.** *to* — **up**, sistemare; concludere, regolare (affare); riparare (auto, apparecchio); equipaggiare, rifornire.

fixation [fik'seiʃən], *s.* **1.** fissazione **2.** solidificazione; coagulazione.

fixative ['fiksətiv], *ag.* fissativo ‖ *s.* **1.** (*pitt.*) fissativo **2.** fissatore, fissativo ☆ *denture* —, fissativo per dentiere.

fixature ['fiksətʃə*], *s.* brillantina.

fixed [fikst], *ag.* **1.** fisso, immobile **2.** stabilito, deciso, fissato, immutabile: — *prices*, prezzi fissi **3.** fisso, costante, ossessionato (di idea) **4.** (*chim.*) non volatile: — *oil*, olio fisso ☆ — -*air*, anidride carbonica; — *assets*, (*comm.*) immobilizzazioni; — -*interest securities*, titoli a reddito fisso; — *stars*, (*astr.*) stelle fisse.

fixedly ['fiksidli], *av.* immobilmente.

fixedness ['fiksidnis], *s.* immobilità.

fixer ['fiksə*], *s.* **1.** montatore **2.** (*chim.*) fissatore.

fixing ['fiksiŋ], s. 1. collocamento; messa in opera 2. lo stabilire 3. (chim. foto.) fissaggio 4. pl. (amer.) equipaggiamento; guarnizione (di vestiti, pietanza).

fixity ['fiksiti], s. 1. stabilità, fissità (di sguardo, ecc.) 2. (fis.) stabilità.

fixture ['fikstʃə*], s. 1. ciò che è fisso 2. pl. installazioni fisse (di casa, proprietà) 3. avvenimento sportivo con data fissata in precedenza 4. (fam.) persona che vive da molto tempo in un luogo; (scherz.) istituzione 5. impianto (di luce, gas, ecc.).

fixure ['fikʃə*], s. (arc.) stabilità; fissità.

fizgig ['fizgig], ag. volubile, capriccioso, mutevole ‖ s. 1. ragazza leggera 2. petardo.

fizz [fiz], s. 1. effervescenza; sibilo 2. vino, bevanda effervescente; (fam.) sciampagna.

to fizz, v.i. frizzare; spumeggiare; sibilare.

fizziness ['fizinis], s. effervescenza.

fizzle ['fizl], s. 1. suono sibilante 2. fiasco, fallimento.

to fizzle, v.i. 1. sibilare; spumeggiare (di vino) 2. to — out, fig. giungere a una conclusione insoddisfacente, far fiasco.

fizzy ['fizi], ag. effervescente, frizzante ‖ s. bevanda effervescente; (fam.) sciampagna.

fjord [fjo:d], s. fiordo.

to flabbergast ['flæbəgɑ:st], v.t. (fam.) sbalordire.

flabbily ['flæbili], av. 1. mollemente, fiaccidamente 2. debolmente; fiaccamente (di carattere, linguaggio).

flabbiness ['flæbinis], s. 1. mollezza; fiaccidezza 2. debolezza; fiacchezza (di carattere, linguaggio).

flabby ['flæbi], ag. 1. floscio, molle; vizzo 2. fiacco, debole (di carattere, linguaggio).

flabellate [flə'belit], ag. (bot. zool.) flabellato, flabelliforme.

flaccid ['flæksid], ag. 1. fiaccido, molle, rilassato, floscio 2. debole, irresoluto (di carattere, linguaggio).

flaccidly ['flæksidli], av. 1. fiaccidamente 2. irresolutamente.

flaccidness ['flaksidnis], s. fiaccidezza.

flacket ['flækit], s. (sl.) fiasco; bottiglia.

to flaff [flɑ:f], v.i. (scoz.) 1. sbattere le ali 2. agitarsi.

flag¹ [flæg], s. 1. (bot.) pianta della famiglia degli ireos 2. pl. tipo di erbaccia 3. foglia lunga e sottile (di certi fiori e cereali).

to flag¹, pass.p.p. **flagged** [flægd], v.t. 1. legare con giunchi 2. recidere, tagliare lo stelo di.

flag², s. 1. pietra per lastricare 2. pl. lastrico 3. (dial.) zolla erbosa ‖ — -stone, lastrico.

to flag², v.t. lastricare.

flag³, s. 1. bandiera, stendardo: — of truce, bandiera bianca; to dip one's —, abbassare la propria bandiera (in segno di saluto); to hoist one's —, issare la bandiera; to lower (o to strike) one's —, ammainare la bandiera (in segno di saluto o di resa) ‖ to keep the — flying, (fam.) non lasciarsi abbattere; mantenere alto l'onore (della casata) 2. (mar.) insegna, bandiera ammiraglia ‖ to hoist, to strike one's —, assumere, abbandonare il comando ‖ — of convenience, (neol.) bandiera di convenienza 3. (sl.) grembiule 4. coda di cane da caccia 5. (tip.) pesce ☆ — -bearer, portabandiera; — -boat, barca che segna il traguardo nelle gare nautiche; — -captain, capitano di nave ammiraglia; — -day, giorno nel quale si vendono per strada bandierine per beneficenza; — -lieutenant, aiutante di ammiraglio; — -officer, alto ufficiale, ammiraglio; — -ship, nave ammiraglia; — -station, stazione secondaria, con fermata facoltativa; — -wagging, (sl. mil.) segnalazioni fatte a mezzo di bandiere; — -waving, l'agitare bandiere; patriottismo superficiale ‖ black —, bandiera nera (dei pirati); red —, bandiera rossa (segno di pericolo, di sfida; simbolo del comunismo); white —, bandiera bianca; yellow — (o sick —), bandiera gialla (segno di epidemia a bordo di nave).

to flag³, v.t. 1. imbandierare, ornare con bandiere 2. segnalare con bandiere.

flag⁴, s. 1. pl. penne dell'ala (di uccello) 2. penne delle zampe di un falco.

to flag⁵, v.i. 1. pendere, penzolare 2. disseccarsi, appassire, avvizzire (di fiori, piante) 3. illanguidire, affievolirsi, svanire (di entusiasmo, interesse, ecc.).

flagellant ['flædʒilənt], ag. flagellante ‖ s.c. flagellatore, flagellatrice; penitente.

to flagellate ['flædʒeleit], v.t. flagellare.

flagellation [,flædʒe'leiʃən], s. flagellazione.

flagellator ['flædʒeleitə*], s.c. flagellatore, flagellatrice.

flagellum [flə'dʒeləm], pl. **flagella** [flə'dʒelə], s. (zool. bot.) flagello.

flageolet [,flædʒə'let], s. (mus.) zufolo.

flagginess ['flæginis], s. languidezza; debolezza.

flagging¹ ['flægiŋ], s. 1. il pavimentare con lastre di pietra 2. lastrico, pavimentazione.

flagging², s. indebolimento; languore.

flaggy¹ ['flægi], ag. ricco di piante di ireos.

flaggy², ag. languido, debole.

flagitious [flə'dʒiʃəs], ag. atroce, abominevole.

flagitiousness [flə'dʒiʃəsnis], s. atrocità, abominazione; infamia; ripugnanza.

flagon ['flægən], s. 1. bricco (generalmente con coperchio) 2. bottiglione da vino.

flagrancy ['fleigrənsi], s. flagranza.

flagrant ['fleigrənt], ag. flagrante, evidente.

flagrantly ['fleigrəntli], av. in flagrante.

flagstaff ['flægstɑ:f], **flagstick** ['flægstik], s. asta della bandiera.

flail [fleil], s. (agr.) correggiato.

to flail, v.t. (agr.) battere col correggiato; flagellare.

flair [flɛə*], s. fiuto, intuito; gusto: a — for languages, (fam.) facilità per le lingue.

flak [flæk], s. (mil.) fuoco contraereo, artiglieria antiaerea.

flake¹ [fleik], s. 1. fiocco (di neve, avena, lana, ecc.) 2. favilla 3. lamina, lastra; scaglia (di pesce) 4. (bot.) garofano coi petali screziati ☆ — -white, (pitt.) biacca.

to flake¹, v.t.i. 1. sfaldare, sfaldarsi 2. squamare, squamarsi 3. coprire di fiocchi; cadere in fiocchi.

flake², s. 1. piano su cui si mette il pesce a disseccare; grate su cui si stendono provviste 2. (mar.) rifugio contro l'acqua e il vento.

flaky ['fleiki], ag. 1. a falde 2. a scaglie, a lamine.

flam¹ [flæm], s. frottola, fandonia.

flam², s. segnale dato col tamburo.

flambeau ['flæmbou], pl. **flambeaus**, **flambeaux** ['flæmbouz], s. fiaccola.

flamboyant [flæm'boiənt], ag. 1. sgargiante; riccamente decorato 2. (arch.) fiammeggiante (di stile gotico).

flame [fleim], s. 1. fiamma, vampa; fuoco: to burst into —, divampare; to commit sthg. to the flames, dare ql.co. alle fiamme 2. splendore, sfolgorio 3. (fam.) la persona amata: he is my old —, è la mia vecchia fiamma ☆ — -projector (o — -thrower), lanciafiamme.

to flame, v.t.i. 1. fiammeggiare, ardere 2. prorompere (di passione) 3. splendere, sfolgorare 4. (med.) sterilizzare alla fiamma 5. to — out, fiammeggiare; prorompere (di passione): his anger flamed out, andò su tutte le furie 6. to — up, infiammarsi di collera; arrossire: the girl flamed up, la ragazza arrossì.

flameless ['fleimlis], ag. senza fiamma.

flamen ['fleimen], s. (st. romana) flamine.

flaming ['fleimiŋ], ag. 1. infuocato, ardente: — sun, sole ardente 2. di color acceso 3. eccessivo, esagerato 4. fig. violento, focoso, veemente: — enthusiasm, entusiasmo focoso ‖ s. combustione; incendio.

flamingly ['fleimiŋli], av. 1. esageratamente, eccessivamente 2. fig. violentemente, focosamente.

flamingo [flə'miŋgou], pl. **flamingo(e)s** [flə'miŋgouz], s. (ornit.) fenicottero.

flan [flæn], *s.* (*cuc.*) sformato.

flanconade ['flæŋkə,neid], *s.* (*scherma*) fianconata.

Flanders ['flɑːndəz], *no.pr.* (*geog.*) Fiandre || *the — poppy*, papavero simbolico dei caduti nella Grande Guerra.

flange [flænʤ], *s.* **1.** (*mec.*) flangia, bordo **2.** utensile per formare flange.

to flange, *v.t.* (*mec.*) bordare, flangiare.

flank [flæŋk], *s.* **1.** fianco, lato **2.** lato (di montagna, edificio) **3.** (*mil.*) fianco; *to attack on the —*, attaccare di fianco ☆ *— attack*, (*mil.*) attacco laterale.

to flank, *v.t.* **1.** fiancheggiare: *road flanked with trees*, strada fiancheggiata da alberi **2.** (*mil.*) attaccare il fianco di.

flanker ['flæŋkə*], *s.* (*mil.*) fianco.

flannel ['flænl], *ag.* di flanella || *s.* **1.** flanella **2.** *pl.* calzoni sportivi di flanella; completo sportivo ☆ *— shirt*, camicia di flanella.

flannelled ['flænld], *ag.* in abito sportivo.

flannellette [,flænl'et], *s.* flanella di cotone.

flannelly ['flænli], *ag.* di flanella.

flap [flæp], *s.* **1.** lembo; falda; risvolto; patta (di tasca); tesa (di cappello), linguetta (di busta); lobo (dell'orecchio); labbro (di una ferita) **2.** colpo leggero, colpo d'ala **3.** (*aer.*) deflettore ☆ *— -eared*, dalle orecchie penzoloni; *— jack*, portacipria; (*amer.*) frittella; *— -table*, tavolo ribaltabile; *— -valve*, (*mec.*) valvola a cerniera.

to flap, *pass.p.p.* **flapped** [flæpt], *v.t.i.* **1.** penzolare; ripiegare; ripiegarsi **2.** battere leggermente; aleggiare, battere le ali **3.** *to — away*, **off**, volar via sbattendo le ali; scacciare (mosche, ecc.).

flapdoodle ['flæp,duːdl], *s.* (*sl.*) sciocchezza.

flapped [flæpt], *ag.* **1.** floscio, pendente **2.** sbattuto, percosso.

flapper ['flæpə*], *s.* **1.** scacciamosche **2.** raganella per spaventare uccelli **3.** anatroccolo selvatico **4.** lembo; falda **5.** grossa pinna; coda di crostaceo **6.** *fig.* persona, cosa che stimola l'intelligenza, la memoria **7.** (*sl.*) ragazzina **8.** (*sl.*) mano.

flare [flɛə*], *s.* **1.** chiarore tremolante; fiammata improvvisa **2.** *fig.* ostentazione **3.** (*gener. mar.*) razzo, segnale luminoso **4.** (*tec.*) eruzione di gas naturale in combustione **5.** (*ott.*) interriflessione tra superfici di lenti **6.** (*mec.*) svasatura ☆ *— angle*, (*radar*) angolo di apertura; *— ghost*, (*ott.*) macchia di riflessione; *— -path*, (*aer.*) striscia illuminata per l'atterraggio; *— pistol*, pistola da segnalazione; *— signal*, segnale con razzo; *— -up*, scoppio (anche *fig.*) || *— parachute —*, (*aer.*) razzo illuminante munito di paracadute.

to flare, *v.t.i.* **1.** brillare di luce incerta; splendere **2.** allargarsi, stendersi all'infuori **3.** (*mec.*) svasare **4.** *to — up*, divampare, infiammarsi (anche *fig.*): *she flares up at the least thing*, si inquieta per un nonnulla.

flaring ['flɛərɪŋ], *ag.* **1.** abbagliante, sfolgorante **2.** (*mec.*) svasato.

flaringly ['flɛərɪŋli], *av.* in modo abbagliante, in modo sfolgorante.

flash[1] [flæʃ], *s.* stagno.

flash[2], *ag.* **1.** (*fam.*) vistoso, sgargiante **2.** falsificato, contraffatto: *— money*, moneta falsa **3.** dialettale, di gergo; volgare, triviale: *— language*, linguaggio triviale || *s.* **1.** lampo, sprazzo, baleno; bagliore improvviso, fiammata (anche *fig.*): *a — of genius*, un lampo di genio; *a — of hope*, un raggio di speranza; *a — of lightning*, un lampo; *in a —*, in un lampo || *— in the pan*, fuoco di paglia **2.** mostra, ostentazione **3.** rapida; chiusa **4.** (*tec.*) bavatura, sfrido **5.** (*cine.*) scena retrospettiva **6.** (*sl. giornalistico*) (messaggio) lampo, messaggio con precedenza assoluta ☆ *— -back*, (*cine.*) scena retrospettiva; (*tec.*) ritorno di fiamma; *— -card*, (*scuola*) cartellone dimostrativo; *— -house*, covo di ladri; bordello; *— -lamp*, (*foto.*) lampada per lampi di luce; *— -light*, (*mar.*) luce intermittente; (*foto.*) lampo di magnesio; *— -point*, (*fis.*) punto, temperatura di infiammabilità.

to flash[2], *v.t.i.* **1.** lampeggiare, dardeggiare, balenare (anche *fig.*): *his eyes flashed*, i suoi occhi mandavano lampi; *an idea flashed through my mind*, mi balenò un'idea **2.** proiettare, far luce (anche *fig.*): *he flashed a beam of light in her face*, le proiettò un fascio di luce in viso **3.** muovere, muoversi rapidamente **4.** diffondere (per telegrafo, radio, ecc.): *the news was flashed all over Europe*, le notizie furono diffuse in tutta Europa **5.** precipitarsi (di acqua); ingrossarsi (di fiume) **6.** (*fam.*) ostentare: *she flashed her jewels in my face*, ostentava i suoi gioielli davanti a me **7.** (*ind.*) applicare un sottile strato di vetro diversamente colorato **8.** *to — up*, **out**, infiammarsi, mostrare un'improvvisa passione.

flasher ['flæʃə*], *s.* **1.** (*mar.*) luce intermittente **2.** (*foto.*) lampo di magnesio **3.** (*mec.*) caldaia a rapida vaporizzazione.

flashily ['flæʃili], *av.* **1.** in modo brillante, vistoso, appariscente **2.** con ostentazione.

flashiness ['flæʃinis], *s.* volgarità, cattivo gusto.

flashing ['flæʃɪŋ], *ag.* risplendente, sfavillante, lampeggiante || *s.* **1.** luce scintillante; splendore, lucichio **2.** (*elett.*) scintillio **3.** (*edil.*) fandale, scossalina **4.** (*amer. aut.*) lampi luce ☆ *— -point*, (*fis.*) punto, temperatura di infiammabilità.

flashy ['flæʃi], *ag.* **1.** brillante, vistoso, appariscente **2.** ostentatore.

flask [flɑːsk], *s.* **1.** fiasco; fiasca, fiaschetta, borraccia **2.** (*mil.*) fiaschetta per polvere da sparo **3.** (*chim.*) beuta, pallone ☆ *suction —*, beuta di aspirazione; *thermos —*, termos.

flasket ['flɑːskit], *s.* **1.** fiaschetto; fiaschetta piccola **2.** cesta per biancheria da lavare **3.** (*arc.*) cesto, paniere.

flat[1] [flæt], *ag.* **1.** piatto, piano; liscio: *a — nose*, un naso camuso; *a floor must be —*, un pavimento deve essere piano, liscio; *the painting was — against the wall*, il quadro aderiva alla parete **2.** disteso; in posizione orizzontale: *the man was knocked —*, l'uomo fu steso a terra **3.** piatto, basso, poco profondo (di piatti, tegami, ecc.) **4.** scialbo, monotono, senza vita, senza interesse: *a — person*, una persona scialba; *in a — voice*, con voce monotona || *to fall —*, fallire, non riscuotere applausi **5.** depresso, avvilito: *he was feeling a bit —*, (*fam.*) era un po' giù di morale **6.** uniforme; invariabile: *he coloured those walls a — tint*, dipinse quelle pareti in una tinta uniforme **7.** assoluto, deciso, perentorio: *a — denial*, un rifiuto deciso; *he can't go, that's —*, (*fam.*) non può andare, questo è chiaro **8.** svanito (di vino, birra, ecc.) **9.** sgonfio (di pneumatico) **10.** (*mus.*) bemolle **11.** (*comm.*) inattivo, stagnante: *the market is —*, il mercato ristagna **12.** (*pitt.*) senza rilievo || *s.* **1.** superficie piana, parte piana di un oggetto **2.** pianura, terreno piatto; palude **3.** (*edil.*) tetto a terrazza **4.** (*min.*) vena **5.** (*mar.*) bassofondo **6.** (*mar.*) chiatta **7.** (*teat.*) fondale **8.** (*sl.*) persona stupida; zimbello **9.** (*mus.*) bemolle: *C —*, do bemolle ☆ *— aback*, sorpreso; *— -footed*, dai piedi piatti; dal fondo piatto; (*amer.*) risoluto; *— money*, (*amer.*) carta moneta; *— -race*, corsa piana, senza ostacoli.

to flat[1], *pass.p.p.* **flatted** ['flætid], *v.t.i.* **1.** appiattire **2.** coprire (una superficie) con una tinta opaca.

flat[1], *av.* (*rar.*) assolutamente, decisamente.

flat[2], *s.* **1.** appartamento **2.** piano di casa.

flatcar ['flætkɑ:*], *s.* (*amer. ferr.*) pianale, carro senza sponde.

flatfish ['flætfiʃ], *s.* (*ittiol.*) sogliola.

flatfoot ['flætfut], *s.* **1.** (*patol.*) piede piatto **2.** (*sl.*) poliziotto.

flathead ['flæthed], *s.* **1.** pellirossa **2.** (*fam.*) sciocco.

flatiron ['flæt,aiən], *s.* ferro da stiro.

flatlet ['flætlit], *s.* appartamentino.

flatly ['flætli], *av.* **1.** pianamente **2.** scialbamente **3.** recisamente; nettamente: *to say —*, dire recisamente.

flatness ['flætnis], *s.* **1.** pianezza **2.** scipitezza; monotonia **3.** l'essere deciso, netto (di rifiuto, ecc.).

to **flatten** ['flætn], *v.t.i.* **1.** rendere piano; appiattire, appiattirsi: *to — oneself against a wall*, addossarsi a un muro **2.** guastarsi, incerconire (di vino) **3.** *fig.* abbattere, abbattersi; prostrare **4.** smorzare; indebolire, indebolirsi (di colore, pittura) **5.** (*metal.*) laminare **6.** (*mus.*) bemollizzare (una nota) **7.** (*mar.*) bordare: *to — (in) a sail*, bordare una vela **8.** *to — out*, (*aer.*) riportare in linea normale di volo.

to **flatter** ['flætə*], *v.t.* **1.** adulare, lusingare: *the painter flattered her good looks*, il pittore accentuò la sua bellezza **2.** illudere, far sperare: *I — myself that he may come*, voglio sperare che possa venire **3.** compiacersi, vantarsi: *she flattered that she was as good as her sister*, si vantava di essere brava quanto sua sorella.

flatterer ['flætərə*], *s.c.* adulatore, adulatrice.

flattering ['flætəriŋ], *ag.* adulatorio, lusinghiero || *s.* adulazione.

flatteringly ['flætəriŋli], *av.* in modo lusinghiero: *he spoke — of his son*, fece l'elogio di suo figlio.

flattery ['flætəri], *s.* adulazione, lusinga.

flattie ['flæti], *s.* (*fam.*) film a due dimensioni.

flatting ['flætiŋ], *s.* **1.** appianamento **2.** (*pitt.*) smorzamento (di colori) **3.** (*metal.*) laminatura ☆ *— -mill*, laminatoio.

flattish ['flætiʃ], *ag.* **1.** piuttosto piano **2.** alquanto insipido.

flatulence ['flætjuləns], **flatulency** ['flætjulənsi], *s.* **1.** (*patol.*) flatulenza **2.** *fig.* vanità, vuoto (di stile, ecc.).

flatulent ['flætjulənt], *ag.* **1.** flatulento **2.** *fig.* vano; pretenzioso, pomposo (di stile, ecc.).

flatus ['fleitəs], *s.* (*patol.*) flatuosità.

flatways ['flætweiz], **flatwise** ['flætwaiz], *av.* in piano; piattamente.

flaunt [flɔ:nt], *s.* (*arc.*) ostentazione, sfoggio.

to **flaunt**, *v.t.i.* **1.** pavoneggiarsi; ostentare, sfoggiare **2.** sventolare.

flaunting ['flɔ:ntiŋ], *ag.* **1.** pomposo, sfarzoso **2.** sventolante (di bandiera, ecc.).

flauntingly ['flɔ:ntiŋli], *av.* sfarzosamente, pomposamente.

flautist ['flɔ:tist], *s.* (*mus.*) flautista.

flavescent [flei'vesənt], *ag.* tendente al giallo.

Flavia ['fleivjə], *no.pr.f.* Flavia.

Flavian ['fleivjən], *ag.* dei Flavi.

flavin ['fleivin], *s.* flavina.

Flavius ['fleivjəs], *no.pr.m.* Flavio.

(to) **flavor**, (*amer.*) per (to) **flavour**.

flavour ['fleivə*], *s.* **1.** gusto; fragranza; aroma; sapore **2.** *fig.* sapore, gusto: *the — of adventure*, il gusto dell'avventura.

to **flavour**, *v.t.* aromatizzare, profumare; dare gusto, sapore a.

flavoured ['fleivəd], *ag.* profumato; saporito, gustoso.

flavouring ['fleivəriŋ], *s.* condimento che dà sapore; aroma.

flavourless ['fleivəlis], *ag.* senza sapore, insipido.

flaw[1] [flɔ:], *s.* **1.** zolla erbosa **2.** screpolatura; incrinatura; fessura **3.** *fig.* macchia, magagna, pecca **4.** (*dir.*) vizio (in un documento, ecc.) **5.** (*mar.*) falla **6.** (*arc.*) frammento.

to **flaw**[1], *v.t.i.* screpolare, screpolarsi; incrinare, incrinarsi.

flaw[2], *s.* **1.** raffica di vento **2.** breve temporale.

to **flaw**[2], *v.t.i.* (*rar.*) soffiare a raffiche.

flawless ['flɔ:lis], *ag.* **1.** senza difetti; impeccabile, perfetto **2.** senza incrinature, senza fessure.

flawlessly ['flɔ:lisli], *av.* perfettamente.

flawlessness ['flɔ:lisnis], *s.* perfezione (di un articolo).

flawy ['flɔ:i], *ag.* **1.** screpolato **2.** difettoso.

flax [flæks], *s.* **1.** (*bot.*) lino **2.** fibre di lino **3.** tela di lino ☆ *— dresser*, cardatore di lino; *— -seed*, seme di lino || *raw —*, lino greggio.

flaxen ['flæksən], *ag.* **1.** di lino **2.** biondo (di capelli) ☆ *— -haired*, dai capelli chiarissimi.

to **flay** [flei], *v.t.* **1.** scorticare, pelare: *to be flayed alive*, essere scorticato vivo **2.** *fig.* criticare severamente **3.** *fig.* pelare (un compratore) ☆ *— -flint*, (individuo) esoso, avaro.

flayer ['fleiə*], *s.* **1.** scorticatore **2.** *fig.* critico severo **3.** *fig.* chi vende a caro prezzo.

flaying ['fleiiŋ], *s.* scorticamento.

flea [fli:], *s.* pulce || *to have a — in one's ear*, *fig.* avere dei sospetti ☆ *— -bag*, (*sl. mil.*) sacco a pelo; *— -bane* (o *— -wort*), (*bot.*) pulicaria; *— -bite*, morso della pulce; *fig.* inezia; *— -bitten*, morso dalle pulci; macchiato (specialmente di cavallo).

fleam [fli:m], *s.* (*vet.*) fiamma, strumento per salassi ad animali.

fleck [flek], *s.* **1.** macchia, chiazza; lentiggine **2.** scaglia; lamina; fiocco; granello di polvere.

to **fleck**, *v.t.* chiazzare, macchiare.

to **flecker** ['flekə*], *v.t.* macchiare; variegare.

fleckless ['fleklis], *ag.* senza macchia.

fled [fled], *pass.p.p.* di to **flee**.

to **fledge** [fledʒ], *v.t.i.* **1.** ricoprirsi di penne (di uccellini); aver cura di (un uccellino, fino a che sia in grado di volare) **2.** fornire di penne (frecce, ecc.).

fledged [fledʒd], *ag.* pennuto, piumato (di uccello).

fledgeless ['fledʒlis], *ag.* implume.

fledg(e)ling ['fledʒliŋ], *s.* **1.** uccellino **2.** *fig.* pivellino; poeta in erba.

to **flee** [fli:], *pass.p.p.* **fled** [fled], *v.t.i.* **1.** fuggire, scappare; abbandonare: *he had fled his native country*, aveva abbandonato la patria; *to — from*, scansare, evitare, sottrarsi a; *to — one's home*, abbandonare la propria casa **2.** svanire, sparire.

fleece [fli:s], *s.* **1.** vello || *the Order of the Golden Fleece*, l'Ordine del Toson d'oro **2.** oggetto dall'apparenza lanosa (nuvola, neve, ecc.) ☆ *— wool*, lana greggia.

to **fleece**, *v.t.* **1.** *fig.* spogliare (di denaro, di proprietà) **2.** (*rar.*) tosare.

fleeced [fli:st], *ag.* lanoso; velloso: *— with snow*, coperto da un mantello di neve.

fleeceless ['fli:slis], *ag.* privo di vello.

fleecer ['fli:sə*], *s.c.* (*sl.*) ladro, ladra.

fleecy ['fli:si], *ag.* **1.** lanoso, lanuto, velloso || *— clouds*, cielo a pecorelle **2.** crespo (di capelli).

fleer [fliə*], *s.* risata di scherno; osservazione ironica.

to **fleer**, *v.i.* ridere con impudenza; motteggiare: *to — at s.o.*, motteggiare, prendersi giuoco di qlcu.

fleerer ['fliərə*], *s.c.* burlone, burlona; motteggiatore, motteggiatrice.

fleet[1] [fli:t], *ag.* **1.** (*poet. letter.*) agile, rapido, leggero: *— of foot*, veloce nella corsa **2.** (*poet.*) evanescente, effimero, transitorio.

fleet[1], *s.* **1.** (*aer. mar.*) flotta: *aerial —*, flotta aerea || *Fleet Air Arm*, aviazione addetta alla Marina inglese || *the Home Fleet*, la flotta metropolitana **2.** gruppo, flottiglia, serie: *a — of fishing boats*, una flottiglia di pescherecci; *a — of locomotives*, una serie di locomotive; *a large — of cars*, un gran numero di automobili.

to **fleet**[1], *v.t.i.* **1.** galleggiare **2.** scorrere (di tempo, ruscello, ecc.) **3.** spostare, spostarsi; migrare, andarsene **4.** (*mar.*) sartiare.

fleet[2], *ag.* poco profondo (di acqua, solco, ecc.) || *s.* (*arc.*) ruscello; piccolo braccio di mare || *the Fleet*, il Fleet (affluente del Tamigi); (*sl.*) prigione per debiti || *Fleet Street*, Fleet Street (strada in cui si trovano molte redazioni di giornali, a Londra); *fig.* la stampa, il giornalismo inglese.

fleet[2], *av.* poco profondamente.

to **fleet**[3], *v.t.* schiumare, scremare (anche *fig.*).

fleeting ['fli:tiŋ], *ag.* fugace, passeggero, momentaneo, transitorio.

fleetingly ['fli:tiŋli], *av.* fugacemente, momentaneamente.

fleetly ['fli:tli], *av.* fuggevolmente, in modo transitorio.

fleetness ['fli:tnis], *s.* (*poet. letter.*) **1.** agilità, rapidità **2.** fugacità.

Fleming ['flemiŋ], *s.* fiammingo, abitante delle Fiandre.

Flemish ['flemiʃ], *ag.* fiammingo ‖ *s.* il fiammingo (lingua).

to **flench** [flentʃ], to **flense** [flens], *v.t.* **1.** fare a pezzi (una balena) **2.** scorticare (una foca).

flesh [fleʃ], *s.* **1.** carne: *to be in —*, essere in carne; *to lose —*, dimagrire; *to put on —*, ingrassare ‖ *— and blood*, il corpo umano; l'umanità ‖ *in the —*, in carne ed ossa ‖ *one's own — and blood*, i figli o i parenti più stretti ‖ *to go the way of all —*, morire ‖ *to make s.o.'s — creep*, far venire a qlcu. la pelle d'oca **2.** polpa (di frutta, ecc.) **3.** *fig.* la carne (in opposizione allo spirito): *the spirit is willing, but the — is weak*, lo spirito è forte, ma la carne è debole; *to mortify the —*, mortificare il corpo **4.** carnalità, appetiti sensuali: *the sins of the —*, i peccati carnali ☆ *— -colour*, color carne; *— -day*, giorno di grasso; *— -fly*, moscone della carne; *— pots*, *fig.* vita lussuosa e dispendiosa; *— tights*, calzamaglia color carne; *— -wound*, ferita superficiale.

to **flesh**, *v.t.* **1.** aizzare (cani da caccia) **2.** dare il battesimo di sangue a (truppe, spada) **3.** *fig.* saziare, soddisfare (vendetta, passione) **4.** infiammare con prospettive di successo **5.** scarnire (pelli).

flesher ['fleʃə*], *s.* (*scoz.*) macellaio.

fleshiness ['fleʃinis], *s.* carnosità; corpulenza; obesità.

fleshless ['fleʃlis], *ag.* scarno.

fleshliness ['fleʃlinis], *s.* carnalità; sensualità.

fleshlings ['fleʃliŋz], *s.pl.* (*teat.*) calzamaglia color carne

fleshly ['fleʃli], *ag.* **1.** carnale, lascivo, sensuale **2.** materiale; mortale.

fleshment ['fleʃmənt], *s.* (*rar.*) incitamento allo spargimento di sangue.

fleshy ['fleʃi], *ag.* **1.** grasso **2.** (*bot.*) polposo.

fleur-de-lis ['flə:də'li:], *pl.* **fleurs-de-lis** ['flə:də'li:z], *s.* (*bot. arald.*) fiordaliso; giglio.

fleuret ['fluərit], *s.* (*arch.*) ornamento a forma di fiore.

fleuron [ˌflə:'rɔ:n], *s.* (*arch.*) fiorone, rosone.

fleury ['fluəri], *ag.* (*arald.*) gigliato.

flew [flu:], *pass.* di to **fly**[1].

flews [flu:z], *s.pl.* labbri pendenti (di cane da caccia).

flex [fleks], *s.* (*elett.*) filo flessibile.

to **flex**, *v.t.i.* piegare, flettere, curvare (anche *fisiol.*); (*geol.*) piegare, piegarsi.

flexibility [ˌfleksə'biliti], *s.* **1.** flessibilità; elasticità **2.** pastosità, morbidezza (di voce) **3.** *fig.* arrendevolezza, docilità, compiacenza.

flexible ['fleksəbl], *ag.* **1.** flessibile, pieghevole **2.** pastosa (di voce) **3.** *fig.* trattabile; arrendevole, docile, compiacente: *— character*, carattere compiacente **4.** versatile.

flexibleness ['fleksəblnis], *V.* **flexibility**.

flexile ['fleksil], *ag.* **1.** flessibile, pieghevole **2.** *fig.* docile, arrendevole **3.** versatile.

flexility [flek'siliti], *s.* flessibilità.

flexion ['flekʃən], *s.* **1.** flessione, curvatura **2.** (*gram.*) flessione **3.** (*mat.*) curvatura **4.** curva.

flexor ['fleksə*], *s.* (*anat.*) muscolo flessore.

flexuosity [ˌfleksju'ɔsiti], *s.* flessuosità.

flexuous ['fleksjuəs], *ag.* flessuoso, sinuoso.

flexure ['flekʃə*], *s.* **1.** flessione; curvatura, curva **2.** (*mat.*) curvatura **3.** (*geol.*) flessura, piega monoclinale.

flibbertigibbet ['flibəti'dʒibit], *s.* (*fam.*) persona volubile, pettegola, frivola.

flick [flik], *s.* **1.** colpo (di frusta); schiocco; buffetto **2.** *pl.* (*sl.*) cinema ☆ *— -knife*, (*neol.*) coltello a molla.

to **flick**, *v.t.* **1.** colpire (con la frusta); dare un buffetto a **2.** *to — away*, *off*, far volare via con un colpetto.

flicker[1] ['flikə*], *s.* **1.** tremolio, guizzo, fremito **2.** (*tv.*) tremolio, sfarfallamento (di immagini).

to **flicker**[1], *v.i.* ondeggiare; tremolare (di luce, ecc.): svolazzare; guizzare; brillare debolmente.

flicker[2], *s.* (*ornit.*) picchio nord-americano.

flickering ['flikəriŋ], *ag.* vacillante; tremolante; guizzante ‖ *s.* **1.** ondeggiamento; movimento rapido; svolazzamento **2.** luce tremula, vacillante; tremolio.

flickeringly ['flikəriŋli], *av.* con tremolio; in modo vacillante.

flier, *V.* **flyer**.

flight[1] [flait], *s.* **1.** passaggio rapido; volo, volata; (*aer.*) volo; linea aerea: *a — over the Atlantic*, trasvolata dell'Atlantico; *in —*, durante il volo; *to wing one's —*, volare **2.** *fig.* slancio, ascesa, trasporto: *the — of imagination*, il volo dell'immaginazione **3.** stormo; sciame; squadriglia; nugolo **4.** rampa (di scale): *— of steps*, scalinata; *my room is two flights up*, la mia stanza si trova dopo la seconda rampa **5.** *fig.* arguzia, frizzo ☆ *— -commander*, comandante di squadriglia; *— -deck*, piattaforma di lancio; *— path*, traiettoria di volo ‖ *blind —*, volo cieco; *harassing —*, volo di disturbo; *non-stop —*, volo senza scalo; *test —*, volo di collaudo.

flight[2], *s.* fuga: *the — of time*, la fuga del tempo; *to put to —*, mettere in fuga; *to take (to) —*, darsi alla fuga.

flightily ['flaitili], *av.* leggermente; capricciosamente.

flightiness ['flaitinis], *s.* leggerezza (di carattere); incostanza; volubilità.

flighty ['flaiti], *ag.* frivolo, scervellato; incostante, volubile.

flim-flam ['flim-flæm], *s.* discorso inutile, senza senso; fandonia.

to **flimp** [flimp], *v.t.* (*sl.*): *to — s.o.*, borseggiare qlcu. mentre un compare lo urta.

flimsily ['flimzili], *av.* **1.** debolmente; leggermente **2.** frivolmente.

flimsiness ['flimzinis], *s.* **1.** mancanza di consistenza (di stoffa, carta, ecc.) **2.** *fig.* futilità, frivolezza, inconsistenza.

flimsy ['flimzi], *ag.* **1.** senza consistenza; leggero (di carta, stoffa, ecc.) **2.** superficiale, frivolo, sciocco; vano: *a — pretence*, una stupida pretesa ‖ *s.* **1.** carta velina **2.** (*sl.*) banconota.

to **flinch** [flintʃ], *v.i.* indietreggiare, ritrarsi (anche *fig.*): *he did not — from his duty*, egli non esitò a compiere il suo dovere; *he had his tooth out without flinching*, si fece strappare il dente senza paura.

flincher ['flintʃə*], *s.c.* chi indietreggia, si sottrae.

flinching ['flintʃiŋ], *s.* il ritirarsi; il sottrarsi.

flinchingly ['flintʃiŋli], *av.* ritirandosi; sottraendosi.

fling [fliŋ], *s.* **1.** getto, lancio; *fig.* tentativo: *to have a — at sthg.*, tentare di fare ql.co. **2.** beffa, sarcasmo: *to have a — at s.o.*, canzonare qlcu. **3.** danza movimentata: *Highland —*, vivace ballo scozzese **4.** impennata (di cavallo) **5.** periodo di svago e rilassamento: *to have one's —*, (*fam.*) godersela.

to **fling**, *pass.p.p.* **flung** [flʌŋ], *v.t.i.* **1.** gettare, gettarsi; lanciare, lanciarsi; scagliare, scagliarsi: *he flung his troops on the enemy*, egli scagliò le sue truppe contro il nemico; *she flung herself into her sister's arms*, si gettò nelle braccia di sua sorella; *to — one's money out of the window*, gettare il denaro dalla finestra ‖ *the windows were flung open*, le finestre furono spalancate con violenza ‖ *to — dirt at s.o.*, *fig.* macchiare la reputazione di qlcu. **2.** *to — away*, gettar via; sperperare **3.** *to — back*, respingere violentemente **4.** *to — down*, abbattere **5.** *to — off*, gettar via; sbarazzarsi di **6.** *to — out*, gettar fuori; mettere alla porta ‖ *to — out at s.o.*, ingiuriare qlcu. ‖ *to — out one's arms*, stendere, allargare le braccia **7.** *to — up*, gettare in aria; abbandonare: *to — up one's hands*, alzare le braccia al cielo; *to — up one's job*, lasciare il proprio impiego.

flint [flint], *s.* **1.** selce, silice **2.** pietra focaia; pietrina per accendisigari; pietra ‖ *to wring water from a —*, spremere acqua da una pietra; far miracoli ☆ — *-glass*, cristallo; — *-hearted*, *fig.* cuore di pietra; — *-lock*, fucile a pietra focaia.

flintiness ['flintinis], *s.* durezza (di cuore); spietatezza.

flinty ['flinti], *ag.* **1.** siliceo, petroso **2.** *fig.* duro, spietato.

flip¹ [flip], *s.* **1.** buffetto, colpetto **2.** (*sl.*) piccolo giro in aereo.

to flip¹, *pass.p.p.* **flipped** [flipt], *v.t.i.* **1.** colpire, dare un buffetto **2.** (far) schioccare (la frusta); agitare: *two eggs flipped with marsala*, due uova sbattute con marsala **3.** *to — through* (*sthg.*), (*fam.*) sfogliare (libro, ecc.).

flip², *s.* bevanda calda di acquavite, birra e zucchero ☆ *egg- —*, uova sbattute con acquavite, birra e zucchero.

flippancy ['flipənsi], *s.* mancanza di serietà, leggerezza; irriverenza; disinvoltura (nei modi, nel tono, ecc.).

flippant ['flipənt], *ag.* leggero, disinvolto, senza rispetto: *a — answer*, una risposta irriverente.

flippantly ['flipəntli], *av.* senza rispetto; in modo frivolo, leggero.

flipper ['flipə*], *s.* **1.** pinna, ala natatoria (di pinguino, foca, ecc.); pinna (di sommozzatore) **2.** (*sl.*) mano.

flipperty ['flipəti], *ag.* dondolante; pendente.

flirt [flə:t], *s.* **1.** movimento rapido (di ventaglio, ali, ecc.) **2.** vagheggino (di uomo); civetta (di donna) **3.** « flirt », amoreggiamento: *he used to be a — of mine*, è un mio vecchio « flirt ».

to flirt, *v.t.i.* **1.** muovere rapidamente: *to — a fan*, agitare rapidamente un ventaglio **2.** amoreggiare, civettare, « flirtare ».

flirtation [flə:'teiʃən], *s.* amoreggiamento, « flirt ».

flirtatious [flə:'teiʃəs], *ag.* incline al « flirt »; leggero, poco serio.

flit [flit], *s.* **1.** battito **2.** spostamento; (*scoz.*) trasloco.

to flit, *pass.p.p.* **flitted** ['flitid], *v.i.* **1.** volare, svolazzare; volteggiare (di uccello) **2.** andarsene; partire; sloggiare **3.** *fig.* scorrere, passare: *memories — through his mind*, i ricordi aleggiano nella sua mente; *the time flitted (away) in their company*, il tempo in loro compagnia passò rapidamente **4.** *to — off, out*, uscire rapidamente.

flitch [flitʃ], *s.* **1.** lardello; lardone **2.** pezzo di legno tagliato dalla parte esterna di un tronco d'albero ☆ — *-beam*, trave composta.

to flitch, *v.t.* tagliare in pezzi, a fette.

flitter ['flitə*], *s.* frullio (di ali) ☆ — *-mouse*, pipistrello.

to flitter, *v.i.* svolazzare; volteggiare.

flitting ['flitiŋ], *ag.* fuggitivo || *s.* volo; battito di ali.

flivver ['flivə*], *s.* (*sl. amer.*) **1.** fiasco, insuccesso **2.** automobile di poco prezzo, macinino.

flix [fliks], *s.* pelo, pelliccia di castoro (e di animali simili).

float [flout], *s.* **1.** (*rar.*) flusso **2.** massa galleggiante (di alghe, ghiaccio, ecc.) **3.** (*mar.*) galleggiante; sughero; gavitello **4.** (*teat.*) luci della ribalta **5.** lampada da notte **6.** carro (per sfilate e processioni) **7.** (*strum. artig.*) pialletto, taloccia, fratazzo; lima a taglio semplice **8.** (*mec.*) giuoco assiale **9.** (*aer.*) veleggio orizzontale.

to float, *v.t.i.* **1.** galleggiare, stare a galla; ondeggiare; fluttuare nell'aria: *the body floated away*, il corpo fu trascinato via dalla corrente || *to — down*, arrivare, discendere lentamente (*p. e.* sulla corrente di un fiume) **2.** far galleggiare, trasportare **3.** inondare, coprire d'acqua **4.** *fig.* venire in mente, fluttuare (nella memoria, dinanzi agli occhi): *memories floated before her mind*, i ricordi le fluttuavano nella memoria **5.** *fig.* spandersi, propagarsi (di notizie, fama) **6.** (*comm.*) costituire, promuovere (una società); lanciare (un'impresa); essere in circolazione.

floatable ['floutəbl], *ag.* **1.** che può galleggiare **2.** navigabile.

floatage ['floutidʒ], *s.* **1.** galleggiamento **2.** (*mar.*)

la parte della nave al disopra del livello dell'acqua; opera morta **3.** l'insieme delle navi (galleggianti) in un porto **4.** relitto.

floatation [flou'teiʃən], *s.* **1.** (*mar.*) flottazione; galleggiamento **2.** (*comm.*) lancio di una società, di un progetto, ecc. ☆ — *-cell*, (*min.*) celle di flottazione; — *-gear*, (*aer.*) carrello di emergenza per galleggiamento.

floater ['floutə*], *s.* **1.** galleggiante **2.** (*comm.*) promotore di società anonima.

floating ['floutiŋ], *ag.* **1.** fluttuante, galleggiante **2.** (*comm.*) oscillante, ondeggiante, fluttuante ☆ — *bridge*, (*mar.*) ponte galleggiante; — *capital*, (*comm.*) capitale circolante; — *charge, debt*, spesa, debito fluttuante; — *kidney*, (*patol.*) rene mobile; — *light*, (*mar.*) faro galleggiante; — *trade*, commercio riguardante i trasporti sul mare.

floatplane ['flout,plein], *s.* (*amer.*) idroplano con galleggianti portanti.

floccillation [,floksi'leiʃən], *s.* (*patol.*) carfologia.

floccose ['flokous], *ag.* (*bot.*) fioccoso, lanoso.

floccule ['flokju:l], *s.* fiocchetto.

flocculent ['flokjulənt], **flocculose** ['flokjulous], **flocculous** ['flokjuləs], *ag.* fioccoso.

flocculus ['flokjuləs], *pl.* **flocculi** ['flokjulai], *s.* **1.** fiocchetto, bioccolo **2.** (*anat.*) fiocculo.

flocceus ['flokəs], *pl.* **flocci** ['floksai], *s.* bioccolo.

flock¹ [flok], *s.* **1.** fiocco di lana, bioccolo **2.** *pl.* cascame di lana, di cotone **3.** *pl.* (*chim.*) precipitati ☆ — *-paper*, carta da tappezzeria ruvida.

to flock¹, *v.t.* riempire, imbottire con fiocco, cascame (di lana, cotone).

flock², *s.* **1.** gregge, stormo **2.** *fig.* gregge (i fedeli) **3.** gruppo, folla, turba.

to flock², *v.i.* affollarsi, accalcarsi: *to — together*, riunirsi, radunarsi.

flocky ['floki], *ag.* fioccoso.

floe [flou], *s.* banchisa, banco di ghiaccio galleggiante.

to flog [flog], *pass.p.p.* **flogged** [flogd], *v.t.* **1.** battere; fustigare, flagellare || *to — good manners into s.o.*, insegnare le buone maniere a qlcu. a suon di busse || *to — a dead horse*, *fig.* sprecare energia **2.** gettare la lenza ripetutamente su (un corso d'acqua) **3.** (*sl.*) sconfiggere, superare.

flogger ['flogə*], *s.c.* staffilatore, staffilatrice; fustigatore, fustigatrice.

flogging ['flogiŋ], *s.* staffilata; bastonatura: *he was given a good —*, gli dettero una buona bastonata.

flood [flʌd], *s.* **1.** inondazione, diluvio, piena (anche *fig.*): *a — of tears*, un fiume di lacrime; *a — of words*, un torrente di parole || *the Flood*, il diluvio universale **2.** flusso **3.** (*poet.*) corso d'acqua, fiume ☆ — *-tide*, flusso della marea.

to flood, *v.t.i.* **1.** inondare; irrigare; riempire (fiume, ecc.) fino a fare straripare; sommergere (anche *fig.*): *the table was flooded with papers*, la tavola era ricoperta di carte **2.** affluire.

floodgate ['flʌdgeit], *s.* paratoia, cateratta, chiusa.

floodlight ['flʌdlait], *s.* illuminazione con riflettore.

to floodlight, *pass.p.p.* **floodlit** ['flʌdlit], *v.t.* illuminare con riflettori; illuminare a giorno: *a floodlit palace*, palazzo illuminato a giorno.

floor [flɔ:*], *s.* **1.** pavimento, assito; solaio; — *of beaten earth*, pavimento di terra battuta **2.** piano (interno di un edificio) **3.** (*mar.*) platea; pagliolo; madiere **4.** fondo (di caverna) **5.** (*borsa*) sala delle negoziazioni **6.** emiciclo: *to hold the —*, tenere il bandolo della conversazione, accaparrarsi l'attenzione generale; *to take the —*, prender la parola in un dibattito **7.** (*econ.*) livello minimo (di prezzi, salari) ☆ — *-board*, (*mar.*) madiere; — *-cloth*, linoleum; straccio per lavare il pavimento; — *-joist*, (*edil.*) travetto, travicello; — *-layer*, pavimentatore; — *-line*, filo terra; — *-polisher*, lucidatore di pavimenti; (macchina) lucidatrice per pavimenti; — *-show*, (*neol.*) spettacolo di varietà sulla pista di un night-club; — *-sweeper*, (macchina) spazzatrice per pavimenti; — -*walker*, (*amer.*) ispettore (di grandi magazzini) ‖ *first-* —, primo piano; (*amer.*) pianterreno; *ground-* —, pianterreno; *second-* —, secondo piano; (*amer.*) primo piano.

to **floor**, *v.t.* **1.** pavimentare **2.** abbattere; gettare a terra (anche *fig.*) **3.** (*fam.*) superare, vincere ‖ *to — the paper*, (*sl. scolastico*) rispondere a tutte le domande (presentate al candidato su un foglio) **4.** (*sl. scolastico*) far sedere (chi non sa la lezione).

floorer ['flɔːrə*], *s.* **1.** colpo che abbatte **2.** (*sl. scolastico*) domanda difficile.

flooring ['flɔːriŋ], *s.* pavimento, tavolato, assito.

flop [flɔp], *s.* **1.** tonfo: *he fell with a — on a chair*, (*sl.*) egli cadde di schianto sulla sedia **2.** (*sl.*) fiasco, insuccesso **3.** (*sl. amer.*) letto.

to **flop**, *pass.p.p.* **flopped** [flɔpt], *v.t.i.* **1.** muoversi in modo sgraziato; lasciar cadere; gettare con noncuranza: *to —* (*along*), muoversi pesantemente; *to —* (*down*), lasciarsi cadere **2.** (*sl.*) fallire, far fiasco **3.** (*sl. amer.*) dormire **4.** (*amer.*) cambiare opinioni in politica.

flopover ['flɔp,ouvə*], *s.* (*tv.*) movimento verticale.

flopper ['flɔpə*], *s.* (*amer.*) chi passa ad altro partito politico.

floppy ['flɔpi], *ag.* **1.** floscio, molle: *do you like my — hat?*, ti piace il mio cappello floscio? **2.** trascurato, sgraziato: *she does look —!*, come è trascurata!.

Flora[1] ['flɔːrə], *no.pr.f.* Flora (anche *mit.*).

flora[2], *pl.* **floras** ['flɔːrəz], **florae** ['flɔːriː], *s.* flora.

floral ['flɔːrəl], *ag.* floreale.

Floréal ['flɔːriəl], *s.* (*st. francese*) floreale.

Florence ['flɔrəns], *no.pr.* (*geog.*) Firenze.

Florence, *no.pr.f.* Fiorenza.

Florentine ['flɔrəntain], *ag.* fiorentino ‖ *s.c.* fiorentino, fiorentina ‖ *s.* seta di lunga durata.

florescence [flɔː'resns], *s.* **1.** fioritura; inflorescenza **2.** periodo della fioritura **3.** *fig.* successo.

floret ['flɔːrit], *s.* (*bot.*) floscolo.

to **floriate** ['flɔːrieit], *v.t.* decorare con motivi floreali.

floricultural [,flɔːri'kʌltʃərəl], *ag.* relativo alla floricultura.

floriculture ['flɔːrikʌltʃə*], *s.* floricultura.

floriculturist [,flɔːri'kʌltʃərist], *s.* floricultore.

florid ['flɔrid], *ag.* **1.** florido; ben colorito **2.** appariscente, vistoso **3.** fiorito (di stile).

floridity [flɔ'riditi], *s.* floridezza.

floridly ['flɔridli], *av.* floridamente; fioritamente.

florilegium [flɔːri'liːdʒiəm], *pl.* **florilegia** [flɔːri'liːdʒiə], *s.* antologia.

florin ['flɔrin], *s.* fiorino; (*in Inghilterra*) moneta da due scellini.

florist ['flɔrist], *s.* fiorista; floricultore.

floss[1] [flɔs], *s.* **1.** lanuggine **2.** seta che circonda il bozzolo ☆ *-silk*, bavella.

floss[2], *s.* (*metal.*) scoria fusa galleggiante.

Flossie ['flɔsi], *no.pr.f. dim.* di **Florence**.

flossy ['flɔsi], *ag.* **1.** serico, leggero; spumoso **2.** (*sl. amer.*) vistoso, elegante.

flotilla [flou'tilə], *s.* (*mar.*) flottiglia.

flotsam ['flɔtsəm], *s.* **1.** relitti galleggianti sul mare ‖ *— and jetsam*, relitti galleggianti e merce gettata in mare per alleggerire una nave **2.** uova d'ostriche.

flounce[1] [flauns], *s.* gesto rapido.

to **flounce**[1], *v.i.* sussultare; agitarsi, dimenarsi ‖ *to — about*, andar su e giù con impazienza, ira, ecc.

flounce[2], *s.* falpalà, balza, volante (di gonna).

to **flounce**[2], *v.t.* ornare di falpalà.

flounder[1] ['flaundə*], *s.* (*ittiol.*) passerino.

flounder[2], *s.* movimento stentato; sforzo vano.

to **flounder**[2], *v.i.* **1.** muoversi faticosamente; agitarsi; (nel fango, nella neve) ‖ *to — about in the water*, dibattersi nell'acqua **2.** *fig.* sforzarsi, far cose con scarsi risultati.

flour ['flauə*], *s.* farina; fior di farina ☆ *-box*, spargitoio di farina; *— -mill*, mulino ‖ *potato- —*, fecola.

to **flour**, *v.t.* **1.** coprire, cospargere di farina, infarinare **2.** macinare.

flourish ['flʌriʃ], *s.* **1.** abbellimento; ornamento, svolazzo **2.** espressione fiorita (di linguaggio, stile) **3.** il roteare (di spada, ecc.) **4.** (*mus.*) rifioritura; squilli di tromba **5.** (*rar.*) vigore: *in full —*, in pieno vigore.

to **flourish**, *v.t.i.* **1.** prosperare, fiorire, essere in pieno rigoglio: *our business will —*, i nostri affari prospereranno; *these plants do not — in this climate*, queste piante non fioriscono in questo clima **2.** vivere, essere attivo: *Petrarch flourished in the 14th century*, il Petrarca fiorì nel XIV secolo **3.** usare uno stile fiorito **4.** fare ghirígori **5.** brandire (un'arma); agitare (braccio, ecc.) **6.** (*mus.*) eseguire abbellimenti.

flourishing ['flʌriʃiŋ], *ag.* **1.** pomposo **2.** *fig.* fiorente, prospero,

floury ['flauəri], *ag.* **1.** farinoso **2.** infarinato.

flout [flaut], *s.* motteggio; burla.

to **flout**, *v.t.i.* beffeggiare, motteggiare, burlare, burlarsi: *to —* (*at*) *s.o.*, burlarsi di qlcu.

flouter ['flautə*], *s.c.* beffatore, beffatrice.

flouting ['flautiŋ], *s.* canzonatura, burla.

floutingly ['flautiŋli], *av.* in modo canzonatorio.

flow [flou], *s.* (*solo sing.*) **1.** corrente, corso (d'acqua); flusso, fiotto: *— of capital*, (*comm.*) movimento, flusso dei capitali; *— of soul*, sfogo dell'animo; *— of spirits*, (*fam.*) allegria, ondata di gioia **2.** (*mar.*) flusso ☆ *grain —*, senso della fibra del legno.

to **flow**, *v.i.* **1.** scorrere, fluire (anche *fig.*); inondare; spargersi: *the river Thames flows in Southern England*, il Tamigi scorre nell'Inghilterra del Sud **2.** sgorgare: *warm tears flowed from her eyes*, calde lacrime le sgorgarono dagli occhi **3.** circolare (di sangue, persone, ecc.) **4.** ondeggiare; sventolare (di drappo); ricadere con morbidezza (di capelli) **5.** *to — from* (*sthg.*), derivare da, provenire da, essere il risultato di: *happiness doesn't — from money*, la felicità non proviene dal denaro **6.** *to — with* (*sthg.*), abbondare di ‖ *land flowing with milk and honey*, (*arc.*) paese dell'abbondanza **7.** *to — away*, scorrere (di liquido) **8.** *to — back*, risalire, rifluire.

flower ['flauə*], *s.* **1.** fiore: *a bunch of flowers*, un mazzo di fiori; *in —*, in fiore ‖ *no flowers by request*, si prega di non inviare fiori ‖ *to burst into —*, sbocciare, schiudersi **2.** *fig.* la parte migliore, il fior fiore: *the — of the nation's youth*, il fior fiore della gioventù della nazione; *to be in the — of one's age*, essere nel fiore degli anni **3.** *pl. fig.* ricercatezza: *flowers of speech*, i fiori della retorica **4.** *pl.* (*chim.*) fiore: *flowers of sulphur*, fiori di zolfo ☆ *-basket*, cestino di fiori; *— -bearing*, che produce fiori; *— -bed*, aiuola; *— -bud*, gemma; *— -cup*, (*bot.*) calice; *— -de-luce*, (*bot.*) ireos, giaggiolo; *— -dust*, polline; *— -girl*, fioraia; *— -holder*, portafiori; *— market*, mercato dei fiori; *— -piece*, quadro raffigurante fiori; *— -pot*, vaso da fiori; *— -show*, esposizione di fiori; *— -stalk*, stelo di fiore; *— -stand*, canestro da fiori; banco per la vendita di fiori; *— -work*, disegno a fiori ‖ *wild flowers*, fiori di campo.

to **flower**, *v.t.i.* **1.** fiorire, essere in fiore (anche *fig.*); produrre fiori **2.** ornare di fiori, di motivi floreali.

flowered ['flauəd], *ag.* **1.** fiorito: *white — plant*, pianta a fiori bianchi **2.** decorato con fiori, ornato di fiori, di motivi floreali.

flowerer ['flauərə*], *s.* (*bot.*) fanerogama.

floweret ['flauərit], *s.* (*poet.*) fiorellino.

floweriness ['flauərinis], *s.* stile fiorito; retorica.

flowering ['flauəriŋ], *ag.* in fiore, fiorito ‖ *s.* fioritura (di pianta) ☆ *— plants*, piante che producono fiori.

flowerless ['flauəlis], *ag.* senza fiori.

flowery ['flauəri], *ag.* **1.** fiorito, che ha molti fiori **2.** *fig.* fiorito, ornato: *— style*, stile fiorito.

flowing ['flouiŋ], *ag.* **1.** fluente, corrente: *— beard*, barba fluente; *— hair*, capelli fluenti, svolazzanti **2.** fluido, scorrevole (di stile, linee, contorni) ‖ *s.* corso, flusso (di fiume, ecc.); scolo (di acqua, metalli, ecc.) ☆ — *tide*, marea crescente, alta marea.

flowingly ['flouiŋli], *av.* scorrevolmente; facilmente.

flowingness ['flouiŋnis], *s.* fluidità di stile, di lingua.

flown[1] [floun], *ag.* 1. dai colori fusi 2. (*rar.*) gonfio, tronfio.

flown[2], *p.p.* di to **fly**.

flowsheet ['flouʃi:t], *s.* (*ind.*) diagramma del ciclo di lavorazione.

flu [flu:], *s.* (*fam. patol.*) influenza.

fluctuant ['flʌktjuənt], *ag.* 1. fluttuante, variabile 2. (*patol.*) fluttuante (di tumore, ecc.).

to **fluctuate** ['flʌktjueit], *v.i.* 1. fluttuare, ondeggiare, oscillare (di prezzo, ecc.) 2. *fig.* essere incerto, ondeggiare: *he fluctuated between hopes and fears*, egli ondeggiava tra speranze e timori.

fluctuation [,flʌktju'eiʃən], *s.* oscillazione, fluttuazione, variazione (di prezzi).

flue[1] [flu:], *s.* (*fam. patol.*) influenza.

flue[2], *s.* 1. cappa del camino; condotto d'aria calda 2. cannello della pipa ☆ — *-boiler*, caldaia a focolare interno; — *-pipe*, canna d'organo.

flue[3], *s.* rete da pesca.

flue[4], *s.* lanuggine.

flue[5], *s.* (*mar.*) patta.

to **flue**[6], *v.t.i.* allargarsi, far allargare (verso l'interno, l'esterno).

fluency ['flu(:)ənsi], *s.* fluidità, scorrevolezza, scioltezza (di lingua, ecc.); *to speak with* —, parlare correntemente.

fluent ['flu(:)ənt], *ag.* 1. fluente, fluido; scorrevole; spedito 2. dalla parola facile.

fluently ['flu(:)əntli], *av.* fluentemente; scorrevolmente; speditamente: *he speaks English* —, parla l'inglese speditamente.

fluff [flʌf], *s.* 1. peluria; lanugine ‖ *a bit of* —, (*sl.*) una donnina 2. (*sl. teat.*) parte imparata male.

to **fluff**, *v.t.* 1. scuotere (i capelli); arruffare (le penne) 2. (*teat.*) impaperarsi su (una parola, la propria parte).

fluffiness ['flʌfinis], *s.* leggerezza, morbidezza.

fluffy ['flʌfi], *ag.* 1. coperto di peluria, di lanugine 2. soffice, vaporoso: — *hair*, capelli vaporosi 3. (*teat.*) incerto (nel recitare) 4. (*sl.*) ubriaco; stonato.

fluid ['flu(:)id], *ag.* 1. fluido (anche *fig.*) 2. instabile, mutevole: — *opinions*, opinioni instabili ‖ *s.* fluido ☆ — *drive*, (*neol. mec.*) giunto idraulico.

to **fluidify** [flu(:)'idifai], *v.t.* render fluido.

fluidity [flu(:)'iditi], *s.* fluidità (anche *fig.*).

fluke[1] [flu:k], *s.* 1. (*ittiol.*) passerino 2. (*zool.*) distoma epatico 3. (*bot.*) tipo di patata ovale.

fluke[2], *s.* 1. (*mar.*) patta (di ancora, ecc.) 2. *pl.* coda di balena.

to **fluke**[2], *v.t.i.* 1. nuotare dando colpi di coda (di balena) 2. assicurare (una balena catturata).

fluke[3], *s.* 1. (*biliardo*) colpo fortunato 2. caso fortuito: *by a* —, per mero caso.

to **fluke**[3], *v.t.* 1. (*biliardo*) colpire (una palla) per caso 2. ottenere per puro caso.

fluky ['flu:ki], *ag.* 1. incerto; mutevole 2. fortuito.

flume [flu:m], *s.* 1. canale; condotto 2. torrente che scorre in fondo ad un burrone.

to **flume**, *v.t.i.* 1. trasportare per mezzo di canali artificiali 2. costruire canali artificiali.

flummery ['flʌməri], *s.* 1. budino alla crema 2. sciocchezza; complimento sciocco.

to **flummox** ['flʌməks], *v.t.* (*sl.*) smontare; sconcertare; meravigliare; confondere: *he isn't easily flummoxed*, non si lascia smontare facilmente.

flump [flʌmp], *s.* colpo sordo; tonfo.

to **flump**, *v.t.i.* fare un tonfo; muovere, muoversi pesantemente.

flung [flʌŋ], *pass.p.p.* di to **fling**.

flunkey ['flʌŋki] *pl.* **flunkeys** ['flʌŋkiz], *s.* 1. valletto; lacchè 2. parassita; persona servile.

flunkeydom ['flʌŋkidəm], *s.* mondo dei parassiti.

flunkeyism ['flʌŋkiizəm], *s.* servilismo; parassitismo.

fluor ['flu(:)ɔ:*], *s.* (*chim.*) fluoro ☆ — *-spar*, fluorite.

to **fluoresce** [fluə'res], *v.i.* essere, diventare fluorescente.

fluorescence [fluə'resns], *s.* fluorescenza.

fluorescent [fluə'resnt], *ag.* fluorescente: — *lamp*, lampada fluorescente; — *screen*, schermo fluorescente ☆ — *lighting*, illuminazione a fluorescenza.

to **fluoridize** ['fluəridaiz], *v.t.* (*chim.*) purificare (acque) con fluorina.

fluorine ['fluəri:n], *s.* (*chim.*) fluorina.

fluorite ['fluərait], *s.* (*min.*) fluorite.

fluorosis [fluə'rousis], *s.* (*patol.*) fluorosi.

flurry ['flʌri], *s.* 1. ventata; raffica; turbine 2. nervosismo, agitazione: *to be in a* —, essere agitato, confuso 3. le ultime convulsioni (di una balena).

to **flurry**, *v.t.* agitare, confondere (per rumore, fretta, ecc.): *to get flurried*, confondersi, perdere la testa.

flush[1] [flʌʃ], *ag.* 1. abbondante; traboccante, rigurgitante (di fiume) 2. pieno di vita 3. ben fornito (specialmente di denaro); prodigo: *to be* — (*of money*), (*fam.*) aver molto denaro; *he is* — *with his money*, spende con facilità 4. arrossito, arrossato 5. a livello; rasente: *to be* — *with*, essere rasente a.

flush[1], *s.* 1. improvviso flusso d'acqua, di sangue; vampa (al viso) 2. improvvisa abbondanza 3. colpo di sole 4. forte sentimento improvviso: *in the first* — *of victory*, nell'ebbrezza della vittoria 5. il germogliare (d'erba, fiori, ecc.) 6. nuovo vigore, freschezza: *the first* — *of spring*, il primo rigoglio della primavera ☆ — *tube*, tubo di scarico (d'acqua).

to **flush**[1], *v.t.i.* 1. lavare per mezzo di un forte getto 2. scorrere con forza e abbondanza; far scorrere abbondantemente; irrigare (un campo) 3. (*bot.*) buttare, (far) germogliare: *rain flushes the plants*, la pioggia fa germogliare le piante 4. affluire improvviso (di sangue); arrossire; far diventar rosso: *he flushed with pleasure*, arrossì di piacere 5. rianimare 6. livellare.

flush[2], *ag.* (*carte*) (di una mano) giocata dello stesso seme ‖ *s.* colore.

flush[3], *s.* improvviso levarsi a volo di uccelli.

to **flush**[3], *v.t.i.* volare via improvvisamente; far volare via.

flushed [flʌʃt], *ag.* rosso (in viso), accaldato; eccitato, agitato: — *with anger*, rosso di collera.

flusher ['flʌʃə*], *s.* addetto alla pulizia delle strade, fogne, ecc.

flushing ['flʌʃiŋ], *s.* 1. rossore; vampata 2. lavaggio con getti d'acqua.

fluster ['flʌstə*], *s.* eccitazione, agitazione: *to be all in a* —, essere agitato, confuso.

to **fluster**, *v.t.i.* 1. stordire; confondere; perdere, far perdere la testa (al troppo bere) 2. agitare, agitarsi; eccitare, eccitarsi; turbare, turbarsi.

flute [flu:t], *s.* 1. (*mus.*) flauto 2. increspatura 3. (*arch.*) scanalatura.

to **flute**, *v.t.i.* 1. suonare il flauto, suonare sul flauto 2. parlare dolcemente 3. scanalare.

fluted ['flu:tid], *ag.* 1. esile, flautato (di voci, suoni) 2. increspato 3. (*arch.*) scanalato.

fluting ['flu:tiŋ], *s.* 1. il suonare col flauto; il cantare dolcemente 2. increspatura, gala 3. (*arch.*) scanalatura.

flutist ['flu:tist], *s.* flautista.

flutter ['flʌtə*], *s.* 1. movimento rapido, battito: *with a* — *of wings*, con un battito d'ali 2. *fig.* stato di eccitazione, confusione ‖ *to make a* —, far colpo 3. (*sl.*) speculazione 4. (*aer.*) sbattimento, vibrazione 5. (*fis.*) oscillazione (di suono).

to **flutter**, *v.t.i.* 1. battere le ali 2. *fig.* eccitare, eccitarsi; sconvolgere, sconvolgersi; innervosire, innervosirsi; essere agitato 3. agitare; ondeggiare; muovere in modo rapido e irregolare: *to* — *a flag*, sventolare una bandiera ‖ *to* — *about*, svolazzare, muoversi in giro con agitazione.

fluttering ['flʌtəriŋ], *ag.* **1.** svolazzante; ondeggiante **2.** palpitante ‖ *s.* **1.** svolazzamento; battito **2.** tremito; palpitazione.

fluty ['flu:ti], *ag.* dal tono flautato, dolce.

fluvial ['flu:vjəl], **fluviatile** ['flu:vjətil], *ag.* fluviale.

flux [flʌks], *s* **1.** flusso (anche *fig.*); afflusso: — *and reflux*, flusso e riflusso (di marea) **2.** sbocco (di sangue); scarica, evacuazione (degli intestini) **3.** cambiamento costante, continuo: *to be in a state of* —, essere soggetto a frequenti mutamenti.

to **flux**, *v.t.i.* **1.** fondere, fondersi (di metalli) **2.** fluire.

fluxion ['flʌkʃən], *s.* **1.** (*patol.*) flussione **2.** (*mat.*) flussione di differenziale **3.** (*rar.*) movimento, cambiamento continuo.

fluxional ['flʌkʃənl], *ag.* variabile.

fluxionary ['flʌkʃəri], *ag.* variabile, incostante.

fly[1] [flai], *ag.* (*sl.*) svelto, sveglio; disinvolto.

fly[1], *pl.* **flies** [flaiz], *s.* **1.** volo: *on the* —, in volo **2.** striscia di stoffa per nascondere l'abbottonatura (di calzoni, ecc.) **3.** (*teat.*) spazio sopra il proscenio **4.** (*mec.*) volano **5.** carrozza, calesse ☆ — *-leaf*, pagina bianca all'inizio o alla fine di un libro; — *-wheel*, volano di macchina.

to **fly**[1], *pass.* **flew** [flu:], *p.p.* **flown** [floun], *v.t.i.* **1.** volare; trasportare in volo: *you have flown to more places*, avete volato di più; *some gossip was flying round*, *fig.* correvano le dicerie; *to* — *across the Pacific*, attraversare in volo il Pacifico; *to* — *blind*, (*aer.*) volare alla cieca; *to* — *from Rome to London*, volare da Roma a Londra; *to* — *s.o. to Berlin*, portare qlcu. in volo a Berlino ‖ *the bird has* (o *is*) *flown*, è uccel di bosco ‖ *to* — *high*, (*fam.*) essere ambizioso ‖ *to* — *in the face of s.o.*, *fig.* sfidare, disubbidire apertamente a qlcu. ‖ *to* — *into a rage*, incollerirsi ‖ *to* — *open*, spalancarsi con violenza **2.** svolazzare (di capelli); sventolare (di bandiera) ‖ *to* — *a flag*, battere una bandiera **3.** affrettarsi, muoversi correndo; volare (di tempo): *he flew to meet his mother*, corse incontro a sua madre; *she flew into the room*, entrò nella stanza di corsa; *time flies*, il tempo vola; *to* — *to s.o. for help*, ricorrere a qlcu. per aiuto; *to send s.o. flying*, cacciare via qlcu.; *to send sthg. flying*, fare volare ql.co.; *to* — *to arms*, correre alle armi **4.** far volare: *to fly a kite*, far volare un aquilone; *fig.* vedere che vento tira **5.** saltare, passare d'un balzo: *to* — *over a fence*, saltare una siepe **6.** rompersi improvvisamente; dileguarsi (di denaro): *to* — *in* (o *to*) *pieces*, volare in pezzi **7.** (*caccia*) librarsi all'attacco (di falco); cacciare con il falco **8.** (*mar.*) levarsi improvvisamente (di vento) **9.** *to* — *at* (*s.o.*, *sthg.*), attaccare improvvisamente ‖ *to let* — *at s.o.*, scaricare un fucile addosso a qlcu., attaccare qlcu. con sassi, con parole rabbiose **10.** *to* — *from* (*s.o.*, *sthg.*), volare via da; scappare da; evadere da **11.** *to* — *on* (*s.o.*, *sthg.*), assalire, slanciarsi su **12.** *to* — *about*, svolazzare, volare attorno **13.** *to* — *away*, volare via, fuggire ‖ *the devil* — *away with you!*, (*fam.*) che il diavolo ti porti! **14.** *to* — *back*, ritornare in volo; fare un salto indietro **15.** *to* — *down*, scendere volando **16.** *to* — *off*, volar via; fuggire, andarsene; (*aer.*) decollare **17.** *to* — *out*, fuggire, slanciarsi fuori; incollerirsi **18.** *to* — *up*, salire in volo.

fly[2], *pl.* **flies** [flaiz], *s.* **1.** mosca; (*dial.*) farfalla, zanzara ‖ *a* — *in amber*, una cosa rara ‖ *a* — *in the ointment*, una piccola pecca che guasta una cosa ottima ‖ *a* — *on the wheel*, persona tronfia ‖ *during the last war they died like flies*, durante l'ultima guerra morirono come mosche ‖ *there are no flies on him*, è una persona svelta, furba ‖ *to break a* — *on the wheel*, *fig.* sprecare le proprie energie **2.** (*pesca*) esca artificiale **3.** (*tip.*) ricevitore; macchina ricevitrice ☆ — *-blow*, uovo di mosca; — *-blown*, pieno di uova di mosche; *the meat is* — *-blown*, la carne è tutta insudiciata dalle mosche; — *-boat*, (*mar.*) nave leggera; — *-catcher*, (*ornit.*) uccello pigliamosche, muscicapa; — *-flap*, scacciamosche; — *-paper*, carta moschicida; — *-swatter*, scacciamosche ‖ *tsetse* —, mosca tsetse.

to **fly**[3], *pass.p.p.* **flied, flyed** [flaid], *v.i.* viaggiare in calesse, in carrozza.

flyer ['flai-ə*], *s.* **1.** volatile **2.** aviatore **3.** animale o mezzo di trasporto velocissimo **4.** (*spor.*) velocista **5.** (*mec.*) aletta **6.** salto di volata **7.** gradino; *pl.* rampa di scale.

flying ['flaiiŋ], *ag.* **1.** volante, che vola; ondeggiante ‖ *"The Flying Dutchman"*, «Il vascello fantasma» **2.** sventolante (di bandiera) ‖ *with* — *colours*, trionfalmente, con successo **3.** breve; rapido: *a* — *visit*, una visita breve **4.** (*mil.*) rapido, veloce **5.** provvisorio ☆ — *-boat*, idrovolante a scafo centrale; — *-bomb*, bomba volante; — *-bridge*, ponte provvisorio; — *-buttress*, (*arch.*) arco rampante; — *-dog*, vampiro; — *-field*, campo di aviazione; — *-fish*, (*ittiol.*) pesce volante, rondine di mare; — *-fox*, (*zool.*) rossetta; — *-man*, aviatore; — *-officer*, ufficiale d'aviazione; — *-pig*, (*sl.*) proiettile; — *-saucer*, (*neol.*) disco volante; — *-school*, (*aer.*) scuola di pilotaggio; — *-squadron*, squadrone mobile.

foal [foul], *s.* puledro (di cavallo, asino).

to **foal**, *v.t.i.* figliare (di cavalla, asina); mettere al mondo (un puledro di cavallo, asino).

foam [foum], *s.* **1.** schiuma (di mare, birra, ecc.) **2.** bava **3.** (*poet.*) mare ☆ — *rubber*, (*neol.*) gommapiuma.

to **foam**, *v.i.* **1.** spumeggiare, spumare **2.** far bava: *to* — *at the mouth*, avere la bava alla bocca; *to* — *with rage*, *fig.* essere furioso.

foaming ['foumiŋ], *ag.* spumeggiante, spumoso: *the* — *cup*, la coppa spumeggiante ‖ *s.* schiuma (alla bocca, ecc.).

foamless ['foumlis], *ag.* senza schiuma.

foamy ['foumi], *ag.* spumeggiante; schiumoso.

fob[1] [fob], *s.* **1.** taschino per l'orologio **2.** (*amer.*) piccola catena, nastro corto (per appendervi l'orologio).

to **fob**[1], *pass.p.p.* **fobbed** [fobd], *v.t.* intascare; mettere nel taschino (l'orologio).

fob[2], *s.* (*sl.*) trucco, astuzia.

to **fob**[2], *pass.p.p.* **fobbed**, *v.t.* gabbare, imbrogliare ‖ *to* — *sthg. off on s.o.*, appioppare ql.co. a qlcu.

focal ['foukəl], *ag.* (*ott.*) focale ☆ — *length*, (*ott.*) distanza focale; — *point*, (*ott.*) punto focale.

to **focalize** ['foukəlaiz], *v.t.* **1.** mettere a fuoco **2.** localizzare (una malattia).

focalization [,foukəlai'zeiʃən], *s.* **1.** messa a fuoco **2.** localizzazione (di malattia).

fo'c's'le ['fouksl], *contr.* di **forecastle.**

focus ['foukəs], *pl.* **focuses** ['foukəsiz], **foci** ['fousai], *s.* **1.** (*geom. fis.*) fuoco: *in* —, a fuoco; *out of* —, fuori fuoco, sfocato; *to bring into* —, mettere a fuoco **2.** centro (di attività, interesse): — *of earthquake*, epicentro di terremoto **3.** (*patol.*) focolare, focolaio.

to **focus**, *v.t.i.* **1.** (*fis.*) mettere a fuoco **2.** concentrare (attenzione, pensieri, ecc.) **3.** convergere (di luce, suono).

fodder ['fodə*], *s.* foraggio ☆ *gun-* —, (*sl.*) carne da cannone.

to **fodder**, *v.t.* dare il foraggio a (bestiame), foraggiare.

fodderer ['fodərə*], *s.c.* chi distribuisce il foraggio al bestiame.

foe [fou], *s.* (*letter.*) nemico, avversario (anche *fig.*): *to be a* — *to sthg.*, essere contrario a ql.co.

foeman, *pl.* **foemen** ['foumən], *s.* (*arc.*) nemico (in guerra).

foetal ['fi:tl], *ag.* fetale.

foeticide ['fi:tisaid], *s.* feticidio, uccisione di feto.

foetus ['fi:təs], *pl.* **foetuses** ['fi:təsiz], *s.* feto, embrione.

fog[1] [fog], *s.* **1.** (*agr.*) guaime; grumereccio **2.** (*scoz.*) muschio.

to **fog**[1], *pass.p.p.* **fogged** [fogd], *v.t.i.* **1.** (*agr.*) lasciare il guaime su (terreno); far pascolare (il bestiame) sul guaime **2.** (*scoz.*) ricoprirsi di muschio.

fog[2], *s.* **1.** nebbia, bruma (anche *fig.*): *thick* —, nebbia fitta; *wet* —, nebbia umida ‖ *to be in a* —, *fig.* essere sconcertati **2.** (*foto.*) velo, velatura ☆ — *-bank*, banco di nebbia; — -*bound*, avvolto nella nebbia; — -*horn*, (*mar.*) sirena da nebbia; — -*signal*, segnale da nebbia.

to **fog**[2],*v.t.i.* **1.** avviluppare, avvilupparsi nella nebbia **2.** *fig.* rendere perplesso **3.** (*foto.*) velare, velarsi.

fogey, *V.* **fogy.**

fogeydom, *V.* **fogydom.**

foggily ['fɔgili], *av.* indistintamente, confusamente.

fogginess ['fɔginis], *s.* nebbiosità (di tempo).

foggy ['fɔgi], *ag.* **1.** nebbioso (di tempo) **2.** oscuro, confuso (di idee, fotografie): *to have only a — idea of sthg.*, non avere che una vaga idea di ql.co.

fogle ['fougl], *s.* (*sl.*) fazzoletto di seta.

fogless ['fɔglis], *ag.* senza nebbia, limpido.

fogram ['fougræm], **fogrum** ['fougrəm], *ag.* antiquato, all'antica ‖ *s.*: (*old*) —, (*fam.*) persona all'antica.

fogy ['fougi], *s.*: (*old*) —, (*fam.*) persona all'antica.

fogydom ['fougidəm], **fogyism** ['fougiizəm], *s.* vecchiume; attaccamento a ciò che è antiquato.

foh [fo:], *inter.* puah!.

foible ['fɔibl], *s.* **1.** debolezza di carattere; lato, punto debole (d'una persona) **2.** debole (di lama di spada).

foil[1], *s.* **1.** foglia degli specchi; lamina di metallo (sotto una pietra preziosa per farla risaltare) **2.** *fig.* ciò che serve a mettere in risalto una cosa o persona: *an ugly old woman serves as a — to a pretty girl*, una brutta vecchia serve a far risaltare una bella ragazza **3.** (*arald.*) foglia **4.** (*arch.*) archetto di finestra gotica.

to **foil**[1], *v.t.* **1.** rivestire con lamina di metallo **2.** far risaltare, mettere in valore con contrasto **3.** (*arch.*) ornare (finestre gotiche) con archetti.

foil[2], *s.* (*arc.*) scacco, smacco, fiasco.

foil[3], *s.* traccia, pista (di animale braccato).

to **foil**[3], *v.t.i.* **1.** frustrare, sventare (attacco, tentativo, ecc.) **2.** (*caccia*) fare perdere la pista ai cani.

foil[4], *s.* **1.** fioretto da scherma **2.** *pl.* scherma.

foison ['fɔizn], *s.* **1.** (*arc.*) abbondanza; raccolto abbondante **2.** vigore, vitalità; *pl.* risorse.

foisonless ['fɔiznlis], *ag.* debole.

to **foist** [fɔist], *v.t.* **1.** rifilare, appioppare: *to — sthg. on s.o.*, rifilare ql.co. a qlcu. **2.** attribuire: *to — a book on s.o.*, attribuire un libro a qlcu. **3.** introdurre di soppiatto; interpolare, inserire.

fold[1] [fould], *s.* **1.** ovile: *to bring back a lost sheep to the —*, ricondurre all'ovile una pecora smarrita **2.** gregge **3.** *fig.* chiesa, congregazione di fedeli.

to **fold**[1], *v.t.* **1.** chiudere (il gregge) nell'ovile **2.** stabbiare (un terreno).

fold[2], *s.* **1.** piega, ripiegatura: *the folds of a skirt*, le pieghe di una gonna **2.** battente (di porta) **3.** spira (di serpente) **4.** (*geol.*) piega.

to **fold**[2], *v.t.i.* **1.** piegare, piegarsi: *I folded the letter*, piegai la lettera **2.** avvolgere: *the hills were folded in the mist*, le colline erano avvolte nella nebbia; *to — sthg. in paper*, avvolgere ql.co. nella carta **3.** abbracciare: *to — a person to one's breast*, stringere al cuore una persona **4.** incrociare (le braccia), congiungere (le mani): *he folded his arms*, incrociò le braccia **5.** *to — up*, ripiegare, avvolgere; (*sl. amer.*) fallire, far fiasco, cessare (produzione, pubblicazione): *to — up an umbrella*, chiudere un ombrello.

foldable ['fouldəbl], *ag.* pieghevole.

folder ['fouldə*], *s.* **1.** piegatore **2.** (*tip.*) piegafoglio **3.** volantino, manifestino pieghevole **4.** cartella **5.** pince-nez.

folding ['fouldiŋ], *ag.* ripiegabile; pieghevole ‖ *s.* **1.** piega; piegatura **2.** avvolgimento **3.** abbraccio **4.** l'incrociare (braccia, ecc.) **5.** (*geol.*) sistema di pieghe ☆ — *bed*, branda; — -*chair*, sedia pieghevole; — -*door*, porta a due battenti; — -*machine*, piegatrice meccanica; — -*screen*, paravento.

foliaceous [ˌfouli'eifəs], *ag.* foliaceo.

foliage ['fouliidʒ], *s.* fogliame (anche *art.*).

foliaged ['fouliidʒd], *ag.* coperto, fornito, decorato di fogliame.

foliar ['fouliə*], *ag.* di foglia.

foliate ['fouliit], *ag.* **1.** fronzuto; **2.** simile a foglia **3.** che ha un numero specificato di fogli.

to **foliate** ['foulieit], *v.t.i.* **1.** (*arch.*) ornare di archetti **2.** sfaldarsi, dividersi in fogli, lamine (di metalli, pietre) **3.** numerare i fogli (non le pagine) di un libro **4.** metter foglie.

foliation [ˌfouli'eifən], *s.* **1.** fogliazione **2.** riduzione (di metalli) in fogli, lamine **3.** numerazione di fogli (di libro) **4.** (*geol.*) stratificazione **5.** (*arch.*) decorazione ad archetti gotici.

folio ['fouliou], *pl.* **folios** ['fouliouz], *s.* **1.** (*tip.*) fo(g)lio: *in —*, in fo(g)lio **2.** (*contabilità*) due pagine opposte di un mastro **3.** numero di parole prese come unità di misura per stabilire la lunghezza di un documento (72 in Gran Bretagna; 100 negli Stati Uniti ☆ — *book*, libro in fo(g)lio ‖ *first —*, primo in fo(g)lio.

foliole ['foulioul], *s.* (*bot.*) fogliolina (di foglia composta).

folk [fouk], *nel senso* **1.** *pl.* anche **folk**, *s.* **1.** gente ‖ *my, your folks*, i miei, i tuoi (la mia, la tua famiglia): *how are the folks at home?*, come stanno i tuoi? **2.** (*arc.*) razza, popolo, nazione ☆ — -*dance*, antico ballo popolare; — -*song*, canzone popolare; — -*speech*, dialetto ‖ *country —*, (*gener. amer.*) gente di campagna; *fine —*, il bel mondo.

folklore ['fouk-lɔ:*], *s.* folclore; demopsicologia.

folklorist ['fouk,lɔ:rist], *s.* folclorista.

folksy ['fouksi], *ag.* (*fam. amer.*) socievole.

follicle ['fɔlikl], *s.* **1.** (*anat.*) follicolo **2.** (*bot.*) involucro **3.** (*entom.*) bozzolo.

follicular [fə'likjulə*], *ag.* follicolare.

follow ['fɔlou], *s.* **1.** (*biliardo*) colpo che lancia la palla dietro ad un'altra **2.** porzione supplementare (al ristorante) ☆ — -*my* -*leader*, gioco in cui tutti seguono i movimenti di un partecipante; — *through*, (*golf*) accompagnamento di un colpo; — *up*, (*fam.*) proseguimento, azione supplementare.

to **follow**, *v.t.i.* **1.** seguire; far seguire: — *his steps*, seguite le sue orme; *he followed one argument with another*, fece seguire un argomento all'altro; *they — the new theory*, hanno adottato la nuova teoria; *to — close*, seguire da presso ‖ *to — one's nose*, andare a casaccio, affidarsi alla fortuna **2.** andare lungo (una strada, ecc.): — *this road until you reach the school*, segui questa strada fino alla scuola **3.** esercitare (un mestiere, ecc.) **4.** afferrare (una spiegazione); seguire (un discorso): *can you — him?*, lo comprendi bene? **5.** succedere a (una persona nel grado, dignità): *to — one another*, succedersi **6.** imitare, prendere come esempio, agire in conformità a: *he follows his father's advice*, egli segue i consigli di suo padre **7.** risultare, derivare: *as follows*, come segue *it follows from this that*, ne consegue che ‖ *his reply doesn't — at all*, la sua risposta non significa nulla **8.** *to — on*, continuare, perseverare **9.** *to — out*, eseguire, perseguire (sino alla fine) **10.** *to — up*, perseguire (traccia, pista, ecc.); continuare (sino alla conclusione).

follower ['fɔlouə*], *s.c.* seguace, aderente; discepolo, discepola; partigiano, partigiana ‖ *s.* **1.** servitore **2.** (*mec.*) anello premistoppa; ruota comandata **3.** (*pop.*) innamorato, ammiratore, corteggiatore.

following ['fɔlouiŋ], *ag.* seguente, susseguente ‖ *s.* (*pol.*) sèguito, partito.

folly ['fɔli], *s.* follia; idea pazza; comportamento stravagante: *it would be the height of — to do that*, sarebbe la più grande follia far ciò.

to **foment** [fou'ment], *v.t.* **1.** (*med.*) applicare fomenti, impacchi caldi a **2.** fomentare, istigare.

fomentation [ˌfoumen'teifən], *s.* **1.** (*med.*) fomentazione **2.** istigazione.

fomenter [fou'mentə*], *s.c.* fomentatore, fomentatrice.

fond [fɔnd], *ag.* **1.** amante, appassionato; entusiasta ‖ *to be — of*, piacere: *I am — of going to the theatre*, mi piace andare a teatro; *she is very — of her children*, vuole molto bene ai suoi bambini **2.** affettuoso, tenero; premuroso; indulgente **3**. (*fam. arc.*) pazzo, insensato **4**. (*rar. arc.*) credulo, ingenuo.

fondant ['foundənt], *s*. (*cuc.*) fondente.

to fondle ['fondl], *v.t.i.* vezzeggiare; far moine a; baloccarsi: *to — a baby*, vezzeggiare un bambino.

fondler ['fondlə*], *s.c.* chi vezzeggia.

fondling ['fondliŋ], *ag*. lezioso, carezzevole (di sorriso) ‖ *s*. **1.** beniamino, prediletto **2.** blandizie; moine.

fondly ['fondli], *av*. **1.** appassionatamente **2.** amorevolmente, teneramente **3.** (*fam. arc.*) pazzamente; insensatamente, scioccamente **4.** ingenuamente.

fondness ['fondnis], *s*. **1.** tenerezza; passione **2.** amorevolezza, indulgenza eccessiva **3.** inclinazione, predisposizione, gusto: *— for languages*, predisposizione alle lingue.

font[1] [font], *s*. **1.** fonte battesimale **2.** acquasantiera **3.** (*poet.*) fonte, sorgente **4.** serbatoio per l'olio (in una lucerna).

font[2], *s*. (*tip.*) serie completa di caratteri.

fontal ['fontl], *ag*. **1.** primario, originale **2.** battesimale.

fontanel(le) [ˌfontə'nel], *s*. (*anat.*) fontanella.

food [fuːd], *s*. **1.** cibo, vitto; alimento, nutrimento: *rich —*, cibo sostanzioso; *he earns enough for his — and clothing*, guadagna abbastanza per mangiare e vestirsi ‖ *— for fishes*, gli annegati ‖ *— for powder*, (*mil.*) carne da cannone ‖ *— for worms*, i morti ‖ *to be off one's —*, soffrire di inappetenza **2.** pastura (di animali); linfa (di piante) **3.** *fig.* nutrimento, alimento: *mental —*, nutrimento dello spirito **4.** il mangiare: *— and drink*, mangiare e bere ☆ *-card*, tessera (di razionamento); *— -controller*, controllore degli approvvigionamenti; *— -stuffs*, cibarie, alimenti.

foodful ['fuːdful], *ag*. fertile, fecondo.

foodless ['fuːdlis], *ag*. **1.** senza cibo **2.** sterile (di paese).

fool[1] [fuːl], *ag*. (*scoz. amer.*) stupido, sciocco: *no more of your — ideas*, (*amer.*) basta con le tue idee stupide ‖ *s*. **1.** sciocco; stupido, imbecille: *born —* (o *hopeless —*), idiota perfetto; *to act* (o *to play) the —*, agire da sciocco, fare sciocchezze ‖ *—'s errand*, impresa senza successo; *—'s paradise*, sciocca illusione, felicità immaginaria ‖ *no — like an old —*, nessuno è più stolto d'un vecchio innamorato **2.** buffone (di corte): *—'s cap*, berretto a sonagli (da buffone); *to play the —*, fare buffonate **3.** vittima, zimbello: *don't make a — of me!*, non prendermi in giro!; *to make a — of oneself*, rendersi ridicolo; *to make a — of s.o.*, beffarsi di qlcu. ‖ *All Fool's Day*, il primo aprile.

to fool[1], *v.t.i.* **1.** far lo sciocco **2.** ingannare, truffare; farsi beffe di: *he fooled her out of her money*, le scroccò il denaro; *they fooled her into believing her guest was a princess*, le lecero credere che la sua ospite era una principessa **3.** *to — about* (o *around) all day long*, stare in ozio: *he fools about* (o *around) all day long*, sta in ozio tutto il giorno **4.** *to — away*, sciupare scioccamente: *to — money away*, sprecare denaro; *to — time away*, sciupare il tempo.

fool[2], *s*. dolce cremoso composto di frutta cotta e panna.

foolery ['fuːləri], *s*. **1.** follia **2.** sciocchezza; buffonata.

foolhardily ['fuːlˌhɑːdili], *av*. temerariamente, sconsideratamente.

foolhardiness ['fuːlˌhɑːdinis], *s*. folle temerarietà.

foolhardy ['fuːlˌhɑːdi], *ag*. temerario, sconsiderato.

foolish ['fuːliʃ], *ag*. sciocco, stolto, stupido; ridicolo, assurdo: *— thing*, sciocchezza.

foolishly ['fuːliʃli], *av*. scioccamente, stupidamente; ridicolmente.

foolishness ['fuːliʃnis], *s*. sciocchezza, insensatezza.

foolscap ['fuːlzkæp], *s*. carta formato protocollo.

foot [fut], *pl*. **feet** [fiːt], *nel senso 7.* **foots** [futs], *s*. **1.** piede; passo: *from head to —*, da capo a piedi; *on —*, a piedi; *on one's feet*, in piedi; *he was at her feet*, *fig.* egli era soggiogato da lei; *to have a heavy, light —,*

avere il passo pesante, leggero ‖ *— and mouth disease*, (*patol.*) afta epizootica ‖ *feet of clay*, *fig.* piedi di argilla ‖ *my —!*, (*sl.*) sciocchezze! ‖ *you are cutting off your —*, *fig.* ti stai dando la zappa sui piedi ‖ *to carry a person off his feet*, *fig.* entusiasmare una persona ‖ *to fall on one's feet*, essere fortunato, cavarsela bene ‖ *to find, to know the length of a person's —*, scoprire, conoscere il lato debole di una persona ‖ *to have one's — in the grave*, avere un piede nella fossa ‖ *to keep one's feet*, mantenersi in equilibrio ‖ *to put one's — down*, farsi valere, imporsi ‖ *to put one's best — forward*, mettersi al lavoro con lena; *fig.* allungare il passo ‖ *to put one's — in it*, (*fam.*) prendere un granchio; fare una « gaffe » ‖ *to set one's — on s.o.'s neck*, *fig.* mettere il piede sul collo a qlcu. ‖ *to set s.o., ql.co. on —*, rendere indipendente, stabile qlcu., ql.co. ‖ *to set sthg. on —*, iniziare ql.co.: *to set a business on —*, organizzare un affare, una ditta **2.** zampa; zoccolo (di cavallo): *the fore, hind feet*, le zampe anteriori, posteriori **3.** *fig.* piede; parte inferiore: *at —*, in calce; in fondo; *at the —*, ai piedi: *at the — of the class, list*, all'ultimo posto della classe, della lista; *at the — of the Cross*, ai piedi della Croce; *at the — of the hill*, ai piedi del colle **4.** piede (misura di lunghezza = cm. 30,48): *the water is five feet deep*, l'acqua è profonda cinque piedi **5.** (*mil. solo sing.*) fanteria: *— and horse*, fanteria e cavalleria **6.** (*poes.*) piede, divisione del verso **7.** (*chim.*) sedimenti, residui (specialmente di liquidi) ☆ *— bath*, pediluvio; vaschetta per pediluvio; *— pad*, grassatore; *— passenger*, pedone; *— pavement*, (*amer.*) marciapiede; *— pound*, (*mec.*) piede libbra; *— race*, (*spor.*) corsa podistica; *— warmer*, scaldino; *— cubic —*, piede cubico (misura di volume = dm.³ 28,318); *square —*, piede quadrato (misura di superficie = cm.² 929,03).

to foot, *v.t.i.* **1.** ballare (una quadriglia, ecc.); camminare ‖ *to — it*, (*fam.*) andare a piedi **2.** rifare un piede a (una calza) **3.** pagare: *to — the bill*, pagare il conto **4.** *to — up*, sommare: *to — up an account*, sommare un conto ‖ *to — up to*, ammontare a: *the expenses — up to £. 10*, le spese ammontano a L.st. 10.

football ['futbɔːl], *s*. pallone ☆ *association —*, giuoco del calcio; *Rugby —*, pallovale.

footballer ['futˌbɔːlə*], *s*. giocatore di calcio.

footboard ['futbɔːd], *s*. pedana (di carrozza); predellino (di veicolo).

footboy ['futbɔi], *s*. valletto, paggio.

footbridge ['futbridʒ], *s*. passerella, cavalcavia; ponte per soli pedoni.

footcloth ['futklɔθ], *s*. gualdrappa.

footed ['futid], *ag*. con i piedi; dai piedi ☆ *bare- —*, a piedi nudi; *four —*, a quattro zampe; quadrupede; *light- —*, dal passo leggero; *swift- —*, dal piede veloce.

footer ['futə*], *s*. **1.** (*sl.*) giuoco del calcio **2.** (*rar.*) pedone.

footfall ['futfɔːl], *s*. **1.** passo **2.** rumore di passo, pedata.

footgear ['futgiə*], *s*. (*fam.*) calzatura.

footguards ['futgɑːdz], *s.pl.* (*mil.*) guardie a piedi.

foothill ['futhil], *s*. collina bassa ai piedi di una catena montuosa.

foothold ['futhould], *s*. punto d'appoggio (anche *fig.*): *to get a —*, prender piede; *to lose one's —*, perdere l'equilibrio, scivolare.

footing ['futiŋ], *s*. **1.** (*solo sing.*) punto d'appoggio; posizione del piede: *to lose one's —*, perdere l'equilibrio; non trovare dove porre il piede **2.** *fig.* posizione: *a good — in society*, una buona posizione in società; *to be on a friendly —*, avere relazioni amichevoli con qlcu.; *to be on a war, a peace —*, essere sul piede di guerra, di pace **3.** (*arch.*) fondamento; allargamento (del muro) sul terreno **4.** *— up*, (*comm.*) l'assommare (cifre).

to footle ['fuːtl], *v.i.* (*sl.*) agire, parlare scioccamente.

footlights ['futlaits], *s. pl.* (*teat.*) luci della ribalta.

footman, *pl.* **footmen** ['futmən], *s.* **1.** soldato di fanteria **2.** lacchè; valletto; cameriere.

footmark ['futmɑːk], *s.* orma, impronta (di piede).

footnote ['futnout], *s.* poscritto; nota a piè di pagina, postilla.

footpath ['futpɑːθ], *s.* **1.** sentiero **2.** marciapiede.

footplate ['futpleit], *s.* (*ferr.*) pavimento di cabina (nella locomotiva).

footprint ['futprint], *s.* orma, impronta (di piede).

footrot ['futrɔt], *s.* (*vet.*) ulcera alle zampe (delle pecore, ecc.).

footrule ['fut-ruːl], *s.* regolo della lunghezza di un piede.

to foot-slog ['futslɔg], *pass.p.p.* **foot-slogged** ['fut-slɔgd], *v.i.* (*sl. mil.*) marciare.

footslogger ['fut‚slɔgə*], *s.* (*sl. mil.*) fantaccino.

footsore ['futsɔː*], *s.* indolenzimento dei piedi.

footstalk ['futstɔːk], *s.* (*bot.*) peduncolo, picciuolo.

footstep ['futstep], *s.* passo; orma: *to follow in s.o.'s footsteps*, seguire le orme di qlcu.

footstool ['futstuːl], *s.* sgabellino, posapiedi.

footway ['futwei], *s.* **1.** sentiero **2.** marciapiede.

footwear ['futwɛə*] *s.* calzatura.

fop [fɔp], **fopling** ['fɔpliŋ], *s.* vagheggino, bellimbusto; ganimede.

foppery ['fɔpəri], *s.* fatuità; affettazione, posa; frivolezza.

foppish ['fɔpiʃ], *ag.* fatuo, vanitoso; affettato; frivolo.

foppishly ['fɔpiʃli], *av.* con fatuità; affettatamente.

foppishness ['fɔpiʃnis], *s.* fatuità; affettazione, posa; frivolezza.

for [fɔː* (*forma forte*), fə* (*forma debole*)], *prep.* **1.** per, a favore di, a vantaggio di: *affection — children*, affetto per i bambini; *are you — or against this idea?*, siete pro o contro questa idea? *he built a house — himself*, egli si costruì una casa; *he did it — your good*, lo fece per il tuo bene; *he works — the ABC Company*, lavora per la società ABC; *I must see it — myself*, lo devo vedere per conto mio; *it is good — him that...*, è bene per lui che...; *sea air is good — the health*, l'aria di mare fa bene alla salute; *what can I do — you*, cosa posso fare per voi?; *to die — one's country*, morire per la patria || *to care — s.o.*, voler bene a qlcu.; aver cura di qlcu.; *to care — sthg.*, essere appassionato per ql.co.; interessarsi di ql.co. **2.** per, adatto a; destinato a; in direzione di: *a present — a good girl*, un regalo per una brava ragazza; *the train — Paris*, il treno per Parigi; *he is the man — the job*, (*fam.*) è l'uomo adatto per questo lavoro; *I have bought this book — you*, ho comperato questo libro per te; *is this letter — me?*, è per me questa lettera?; *smoking is bad — you*, il fumare ti nuoce; *to sail — Sidney*, salpare per Sidney || *it is not — you to reply*, non tocca a te rispondere || *to be fit — nothing*, non essere buono a nulla || *to be in — a good, bad time*, essere destinati a passarsela male: *they are in — it!*, ora se la vedranno bella! **3.** per, al prezzo di; in ricompensa di: *I paid ten shillings — this book*, ho pagato questo libro dieci scellini; *I would not do it — the world*, non lo farei per tutto il mondo. **4.** per, allo scopo di; come, da: *blinds — windows*, tendine per finestre; *a cure — toothache*, una cura per il mal di denti; *a machine — making sthg.*, una macchina per fabbricare ql.co.; *this large box will serve us — a table*, questa grande cassa ci servirà da tavolo; *this was built — a hospital*, questo fu costruito come ospedale || *— sale*, in vendita || *to come, to go — s.o.*, venire, andare a prendere qlcu.; *to go — a walk*, andare a fare una passeggiata; *to look — s.o., sthg.*, cercare qlcu., ql.co.; *to send — s.o.*, mandare a chiamare qlcu.; *to wait — s.o., sthg.*, aspettare qlcu., ql.co. **5.** per, a causa di: *he was arrested — stealing*, fu arrestato per aver rubato; *he was rewarded — saving the girl's life*, fu ricompensato per aver salvato la vita alla ragazza; *I could not see — the fog*, non potei vedere per la neb-

bia; *to suffer — love*, soffrire per amore || *— fear (that, of)*, per tema (che, di); *— love of*, per amore di; *— the sake of* (o *s.o.'s sake*), per considerazione, affetto, rispetto verso qlcu.; *— shame!*, vergogna!; *— want (o lack) of*, per mancanza di || *but —*, se non fosse per: *but — me, he...*, se non fosse per me, egli...; *but — my helping him, he...*, se non l'avessi aiutato, egli... || *what —?*, perchè?, per qual ragione?, a che pro? **6.** per, malgrado, nonostante: *— all his wealth he was unhappy*, nonostante tutta la sua ricchezza era infelice; *— one good action, he does ten bad ones*, per un'azione buona ne compie dieci cattive; *— such a young man, he plays the violin very well*, per (essere) un uomo così giovane, suona molto bene il violino; *he is tall — his age*, è alto per la sua età; *it is cold — August*, per (essere) agosto fa freddo || *— all*, malgrado, benchè, ad onta; *— all that*, ciò nonostante, pertanto || *— better or worse*, qualunque cosa accada, nella buona e nella cattiva sorte **7.** per, durante; da: *he hasn't been there — six years*, non ci va da sei anni; *I have been writing — an hour*, è un'ora che scrivo; *we stayed in Rome — a month*, ci fermammo a Roma per un mese || *— ever (and ever)*, per sempre, per l'eternità; *— good*, per sempre; *— life*, per tutta la vita; *— the present* (o *— the time being*), per ora **8.** per, con riferimento a; invece di: *— all* (o *aught*) *I know*, per quanto io sappia; *they spoke English so well that they were taken — Englishmen*, parlavano l'inglese così bene che furono scambiati per inglesi; *to take s.o.'s word — sthg.*, accettare la parola di qlcu. in merito a ql.co. || *as —*, quanto a: *as — me*, quanto a me; *as — my helping him*, (in) quanto a dargli il mio aiuto **9.** (*seguito da acc. e inf.*): *he stood aside — her to pass*, egli si scostò affinchè ella potesse passare; *I am waiting — you to help me*, aspetto che tu m'aiuti; *it is impossible — him to accept*, è impossibile che egli accetti.

for, *cong.* (*gener. letter.*) giacchè, poichè, perchè: *he's not allowed out, — he is not well*, non gli permettono di uscire, giacchè non sta bene; *wait a moment, — I have sthg. to do*, aspetta un momento, perchè ho ql.co. da fare.

forage ['fɔridʒ], *s.* foraggio ☆ *— -cap*, (*mil.*) bustina.

to forage, *v.t.i.* foraggiare; raccogliere foraggi; saccheggiare.

forasmuch [fərəz'mʌtʃ], *av.* (*arc. letter.*) in quanto che, visto che, poichè.

foray ['fɔrei], *s.* scorreria; incursione.

to foray, *v.t.i.* compiere un'incursione, una scorreria; saccheggiare.

forbade [fə'beid], *pass.* di to **forbid**.

forbear[1] ['fɔːbɛə*], *s. gener. pl.* antenati.

to forbear[2] [fɔː'bɛə*], *pass.* **forbore** [fɔː'bɔː*], *p.p.* **forborne** [fɔː'bɔːn], *v.t.i.* **1.** (I) astenersi (da); trattenersi (da); evitare: *to — (from) doing sthg.*, astenersi, guardarsi dal fare ql.co. **2.** essere indulgente, paziente: *to — with s.o.*, mostrarsi indulgente verso qlcu.

forbearance [fɔː'bɛərəns], *s.* **1.** pazienza, sopportazione, tolleranza: *to show — towards s.o.*, mostrare indulgenza verso qlcu. **2.** *— from doing sthg.* (o *to do sthg.*), l'astenersi dal fare ql.co.

forbearant [fɔː'bɛərənt], *ag.* paziente; tollerante.

forbearing [fɔː'bɛəriŋ], *ag.* paziente, indulgente; tollerante.

forbearingly [fɔː'bɛəriŋli], *av.* pazientemente; con tolleranza.

to forbid [fə'bid], *pass.* **forbade** [fə'beid], *p.p.* **forbidden** [fə'bidn], *v.t.* (III, IV) vietare, proibire; interdire; impedire: *the doctor has forbidden him wine*, il dottore gli ha proibito il vino; *his health forbids his taking on more work*, la sua salute gli impedisce di assumere altro lavoro; *the law forbids it*, la legge lo vieta; *to — a marriage*, proibire un matrimonio; *to — s.o. the house*, vietare a qlcu. l'accesso alla propria casa; *to — s.o. to do sthg.*, proibire a qlcu. di fare ql.co.: *I forbade him* *to go*, gli proibii di andare ‖ *fishing forbidden*, divieto di pesca‖ *God — !*, Dio ce ne guardi!.

forbiddance [fə'bidəns], *s.* proibizione, divieto.

forbidden [fə'bidn], *p.p.* di to **forbid** ‖ *ag.* proibito, vietato: — *weapons*, armi dichiarate fuori legge ☆ — *degrees*, (*dir.*) gradi di consanguineità che impediscono il matrimonio; — *fruit*, frutto proibito.

forbiddenly [fə'bidnli], *av.* illegalmente.

forbidding [fə'bidiŋ], *ag.* **1.** severo (di sguardo, apparenza, ecc.); minaccioso (di cielo, tempo) **2.** ripugnante; sgradevole.

forbiddingly [fə'bidiŋli], *av.* repulsivamente.

forbiddingness [fə'bidiŋnis], *s.* l'essere repulsivo.

forbore [fo:'bo:*], *pass.* di to **forbear**.

forborne [fo:'bo:n], *p.p.* di to **forbear**.

force[1] [fo:s], *s.* **1.** forza fisica; violenza; sforzo: *to yield to* —, piegarsi alla forza **2.** forza morale, mentale; potere di persuasione **3.** virtù; validità; efficacia (di argomento): *I do not see the — of learning these useless things*, non vedo l'utilità di apprendere queste cose inutili **4.** forza militare **5.** (*dir.*) forza, vigore: *to be, to remain in* —, essere, rimanere in vigore, valido; *to come into* —, entrare in vigore; *to put (a law) into* —, mettere in vigore (una legge) **6.** (atto di) forza, violenza: *forces of subversion*, forze disgregatrici **7.** (*fis. elett.*) forza, energia; causa di movimento; fonte di energia: — *of gravity*, forza di gravità; — *of inertia*, forza d'inerzia **8.** (*mec.*) pistone, stantuffo (di pompa) **9.** forza (esatto significato) di parola, documento ☆ — *pump*, (*mec.*) pompa di forza, a pistone ‖ *armed forces*, forze armate, esercito; *centrifugal* —, (*fis.*) forza centrifuga; *centripetal* —, (*fis.*) forza centripeta; *deflecting* —, (*aer.*) forza derivatrice; *land forces*, (*mil.*) effettivi terrestri; *landing forces*, truppe da sbarco; *lift* —, (*aer.*) forza portante; *the police* —, la polizia; *resultant* —, (*fis.*) (forza) risultante.

to force[1], *v.t.i.* **1.** forzare; fare violenza a; sforzare, sforzarsi: *to — a door*, forzare una porta; *to — an entry*, forzare, entrare con la forza; *to — open*, forzare per aprire; *to — the pace*, affrettare il passo; *to — plants*, forzare le piante (a produrre prima del tempo); *to — a smile*, sforzarsi di sorridere ‖ *to — sthg. on s.o.*, obbligare qlcu. a prendere, accettare ql.co.: *he forced his goods on me*, mi obbligò a prendere la sua merce **2.** (IV) *fig.* forzare, obbligare, costringere: *he forced me to go*, mi costrinse ad andare **3.** strappare, prendere per forza; estorcere: *to — tears from s.o.'s eyes*, strappare le lacrime a qlcu. **4.** *to — back*, respingere, far indietreggiare: *she forced back her tears*, ella ingoiò le lagrime **5.** *to — down*, far discendere: *to — down prices*, fare abbassare i prezzi **6.** *to — in*, conficcare, far entrare per forza **7.** *to — on*, far avanzare **8.** *to — out*, spinger fuori ‖ *to — out a few words of congratulation*, (*fam.*) felicitarsi a fior di labbra **9.** *to — up*, far salire.

force[2], *s.* (*scoz.*) cascata.

forced [fo:st], *ag.* **1.** forzato, inevitabile, obbligatorio: — *landing*, atterraggio forzato; — *march*, marcia forzata **2.** forzato; affettato, manierato: — *smile*, sorriso forzato **3.** (*bot.*) forzato: — *fruits and flowers*, frutta e fiori forzati ☆ — *labour*, lavoro forzato.

forcedly [fo:sidli], *av.* forzatamente.

forcedness [fo:sidnis], *s.* costrizione.

forceful [fo:sful], *ag.* forte; energico; violento.

forcefully [fo:sfuli], *av.* con forza; vigorosamente.

forcefulness [fo:sfulnis], *s.* forza; vigoria; impeto.

forceless [fo:slis], *ag.* debole, senza forza.

forceps, *pl.* **forceps** [fo:seps], *s.* (*chir.*) **1.** forcipe **2.** pinza (da dentista).

forcible [fo:səbl], *ag.* impetuoso, violento; energico: *a — entry into a house*, un'irruzione in una casa; *a — writer*, uno scrittore efficace.

forcibleness [fo:səblnis], *s.* forza, violenza; energia, vigore.

forcibly [fo:səbli], *av.* con forza, impetuosamente; energicamente, vigorosamente.

forcing [fo:siŋ], *s.* **1.** il forzare (una serratura, ecc.) **2.** (*bot.*) coltura forzata ☆ — *house*, serra.

forcite [fo:sait], *s.* tipo di dinamite.

ford [fo:d], *s.* guado.

to ford, *v.t.i.* passare a guado, guadare.

fordable [fo:dəbl], *ag.* guadabile.

fording [fo:diŋ], *s.* guado, il passare a guado.

fordless [fo:dlis], *ag.* senza guado.

fordone [fo:'dʌn], *ag.* esausto.

fore [fo:*], *ag.* anteriore: — *legs*, gambe anteriori ‖ *s.* (*mar.*) prua: *at the* —, sull'albero di trinchetto ‖ *to come to the* —, *fig.* venire alla ribalta, divenire d'attualità, sfondare.

fore, *inter.* (*golf*) attenzione davanti!.

fore, (*nei composti*): — *cited*, precitato; — *named*, suddetto.

fore-and-aft [fo:rən'ɑ:ft], *ag.* (*mar.*) longitudinale ‖ *av.* (*mar.*) da prua a poppa, per chiglia, longitudinalmente allo scafo ☆ — *sail*, vela di taglio.

forearm[1] [fo:'rɑ:m], *s.* avambraccio.

to forearm[2] [fo:r'ɑ:m], *v.t.* premunire; preparare contro un attacco, per un attacco.

forearmed [fo:r'ɑ:md], *ag.* premunito, avvertito ‖ *forewarned is* —, *prov.* uomo avvisato mezzo salvato.

forebear, *V.* **forbear**[1].

to forebode [fo:'boud], *v.t.* **1.** presagire (il male); presentire (qualche cosa di male) **2.** preannunziare: *these clouds — rain*, queste nuvole preannunziano pioggia **3.** (*rar.*) predire.

foreboding [fo:'boudiŋ], *s.* **1.** presagio (di male); presentimento (cattivo) **2.** (*rar.*) predizione.

forebodingly [fo:'boudiŋli], *av.* con presagio, con presentimento di mali.

forebrain [fo:'brein], *s.* (*anat.*) proencefalo.

forecabin [fo:'kæbin], *s.* cabina di prua.

forecast [fo:'kɑ:st], *pass.p.p.* di to **forecast** ‖ *s.* pronostico; previsione ☆ *weather* —, previsione del tempo.

to forecast, *pass.p.p.* **forecast**, *v.t.* prevedere, predire; pronosticare.

forecastle [fo:'fouksl], *s.* (*mar. abbr.* *fo'c's'le*) **1.** castello di prua **2.** parte di nave dove alloggia l'equipaggio (nelle navi mercantili).

forechosen [fo:'tʃouzn], *ag.* scelto in precedenza.

to foreclose [fo:'klouz], *v.t.* **1.** precludere, impedire **2.** (*dir.*) precludere il riscatto di (una ipoteca).

foreclosure [fo:'klouʒə*], *s.* **1.** esclusione **2.** (*dir.*) esclusione dal produrre eccezione in causa **3.** (*dir.*) il precludere il diritto di riscatto (di una ipoteca).

forecourt [fo:'ko:t], *s.* corte che sta davanti all'edificio.

to foredate [fo:'deit], *v.t.* antidatare.

foredeck [fo:'dek], *s.* parte anteriore della nave.

to foredoom [fo:'du:m], *v.t.* predestinare: *plan foredoomed to failure*, piano predestinato al fallimento.

forefather [fo:'fɑ:ðə*], *s.* antenato, avo.

to forefend, *V.* to **forfend**.

forefinger [fo:'fiŋgə*], *s.* indice (della mano).

forefoot [fo:'fut], *s.* zampa anteriore.

forefront [fo:'frʌnt], *s.* **1.** facciata **2.** (*mil.*) prima linea.

to foregather, *V.* to **forgather**.

to forego[1] [fo:'gou], *pass.* **forewent** [fo:'went], *p.p.* **foregone** [fo:'gon], *v.t.* precedere.

to forego[2], *V.* to **forgo**.

foregoer [fo:'gouə*], *s.* predecessore, precursore.

foregoing [fo:'gouiŋ], *ag.* precedente, anteriore: *from the* —, da quanto sopra.

foregone [fo:'gon], *ag.* **1.** passato **2.** sicuro, inevitabile: — *conclusion*, risultato inevitabile, decisione già scontata.

foreground [fo:'graund], *s.* (*foto.*) primo piano ‖ *that girl keeps herself in the* —, quella ragazza si mette molto in vista.

forehand [fo:'hænd], *s.* **1.** posizione superiore **2.** parte del cavallo dal garrese alla testa ☆ — *stroke*, (*tennis*) colpo diritto.

forehead ['forid], *s.* fronte.

foreign ['forin], *ag.* 1. forestiero; straniero; estero: — *money*, divisa estera || *the Foreign Office*, il Ministero degli Esteri britannico 2. *fig.* estraneo: *a* — *body*, un corpo estraneo; — *to the law*, estraneo alla legge; *his speech was* — *to the purpose*, il suo discorso era estraneo all'argomento.

foreigner ['forinə*], *s.c.* straniero, straniera; (*fam.*) forestiero, forestiera.

foreignness ['forinnis], *s.* l'essere straniero.

to forejudge [fo:'dʒʌdʒ], *v.t.* giudicare a priori.

to foreknow [fo:'nou], *pass.* **foreknew** [fo:'nju:], *p.p.* **foreknown** [fo:'noun], *v.t.* prevedere, sapere prima.

foreknowledge ['fo:'nolidʒ], *s.* prescienza, preconoscenza.

forel ['forəl], *s.* pergamena per ricoprire libri.

foreland ['fo:lənd], *s.* promontorio, capo; scogliera scoscesa; avanterra.

foreleg ['fo:leg], *s.* zampa anteriore.

forelock[1] ['fo:lok], *s.* (*mec.*) copiglia.

to forelock[1], *v.t.* fissare con copiglia.

forelock[2], *s.* ciuffo (sulla fronte) || *to take by the* —, *fig.* cogliere a volo: *to take time by the* —, approfittare dell'occasione.

foreman, *pl.* **foremen** ['fo:mən], *s.* 1. capo-officina; caposquadra; caporeparto; soprintendente 2. (*dir.*) capo dei giurati ☆ *printer's* —, proto.

foremast ['fo:ma:st], *s.* (*mar.*) albero di trinchetto.

forementioned [,fo:'menʃənd], *ag.* suddetto.

foremost ['fo:moust], *ag.* primo, principale: *the* — *writer of that period*, lo scrittore più importante di quel periodo || *av.* in prima fila; in testa; in primo luogo, anzitutto: *to fall head* —, cadere a testa in avanti || *first and* —, anzitutto.

forename ['fo:neim], *s.* nome di battesimo.

forenoon ['fo:nu:n], *s.* mattina, mattinata: *in the* —, prima di mezzogiorno.

forensic(al) [fə'rensik(əl)], *ag.* forense, del foro ☆ — *medicine*, medicina legale.

to foreordain ['fo:ro:'dein], *v.t.* predestinare.

foreordination [,fo:ro:di'neiʃən], *s.* predestinazione.

forepart ['fo:-pa:t], *s.* parte anteriore; principio.

forepeak ['fo:-pi:k], *s.* (*mar.*) gavone di prua.

to forereach [,fo:'ri:tʃ], *v.t.* passare, oltrepassare, superare.

to forerun [fo:'rʌn], *pass.* **foreran** [fo:'ræn], *p.p.* **forerun**, *v.t.* precedere, precorrere.

forerunner ['fo:,rʌnə*], *s.* 1. messaggero 2. precursore || *the Forerunner*, il Precursore (San Giovanni Battista).

foresail ['fo:seil], *s.* (*mar.*) vela di trinchetto.

to foresee [fo:'si:], *pass.* **foresaw** [fo:'so:], *p.p.* **foreseen** [fo:'si:n], *v.t.* prevedere.

foreseeable [fo:'si:əbl], *ag.* prevedibile.

to foreshadow [fo:'ʃædou], *v.t.* adombrare; presagire.

foreshore ['fo:-ʃo:*] *s.* lido; litorale.

to foreshorten [fo:'ʃo:tn], *v.t.* disegnare (figure) in prospettiva.

foreshortening [fo:'ʃo:tniŋ], *s.* scorcio.

foresight ['fo:-sait], *s.* 1. preveggenza 2. prudenza, previdenza 3. lettura altimetrica 4. mirino (di fucile).

foresighted ['fo:-saitid], **foresightful** ['fo:-saitful], *ag.* 1. preveggente 2. prudente, previdente.

foreskin ['fo:-skin], *s.* (*anat.*) prepuzio.

forest ['forist], *ag.* forestale; boschivo || *s.* 1. foresta, bosco: *high* (o *matured*) —, bosco d'alberi d'alto fusto || *the Black Forest*, la Foresta Nera 2. *fig.* selva: *a* — *of masts in a harbour*, una selva di alberi in un porto 3. riserva reale di caccia ☆ — *-guard*, guardia forestale.

to forest, *v.t.* coltivare a foresta, imboschire.

forestage ['foristidʒ], *s.* (*st.*) legnatico.

forestal ['foristl], *ag.* forestale.

to forestall [fo:'sto:l], *v.t.* 1. prevenire; anticipare: *to* — *a competitor*, prevenire un concorrente 2. (*st.*) accaparrare.

forestaller [fo:'sto:lə*], *s.* 1. chi previene 2. (*st.*) accaparratore.

forestalling [fo:'sto:liŋ], *s.* 1. anticipazione (di desideri) 2. (*st.*) accaparramento.

forestay ['fo:stei], *s.* (*mar.*) straglio di trinchetto.

forester ['foristə*], *s.* 1. guardia forestale 2. abitante di boschi, di foreste 3. animale di foresta 4. (*entom.*) zigena.

forestry ['foristri], *s.* 1. silvicultura: *school of* —, scuola forestale 2. foresta.

foretaste ['fo:-teist], *s.* pregustazione.

to foretaste [fo:'teist], *v.t.* pregustare.

to foretell [fo:'tel], *pass. p.p.* **foretold** [fo:'tould], *v.t.* predire, pronosticare.

foreteller [fo:'telə*], *s.c.* indovino, indovina.

foretelling [fo:'teliŋ], *s.* predizione, profezia.

to forethink [fo:'θiŋk], *pass.p.p.* **forethought** [fo:'θo:t], *v.t.* (*rar.*) premeditare; pronosticare.

forethought ['fo:-θo:t], *ag.* premeditato || *s.* 1. premeditazione 2. previdenza.

foretoken ['fo:,toukən], *s.* presagio; preannunzio; premonizione.

to foretoken [fo:'toukən], *v.t.* presagire; preannunziare.

foretop ['fo:-top], *s.* (*mar.*) coffa di trinchetto.

forever [fə'revə*], *av.* per sempre, eternamente.

to forewarn [fo:'wo:n], *v.t.* prevenire, avvertire.

forewarning ['fo:'wo:niŋ], *s.* premonizione, avvertimento.

forewoman ['fo:,wumən], *pl.* **forewomen** ['fo:,wimin], *s.* 1. direttrice (di cucitrici); prima lavorante 2. (*dir.*) capo di una giuria di donne.

foreword ['fo:wə:d], *s.* prefazione (di libro, ecc.).

forfeit ['fo:fit], *ag.* (*st. dir.*) perduto; confiscato; alienato || *s.* 1. perdita 2. ammenda, multa, penalità: *to pay the* —, pagare il fio; subire la pena 3. (*comm.*) rinuncia 4. (*giuoco*) penitenza; pegno: *to play forfeits*, giuocare a pegni.

to forfeit, *v.t.* perdere per confisca i propri diritti a; essere privato di; dover pagare (penalità, ecc.).

forfeitable ['fo:fitəbl], *ag.* confiscabile.

forfeiter ['fo:fitə*], *s.* chi perde ql.co. per confisca.

forfeiture ['fo:fitʃə*], *s.* 1. confisca; multa, penalità 2. perdita (per confisca) 3. oggetto confiscato.

to forfend [fo:'fend], *v.t.* 1. stornare, impedire; prevenire || *God* —!, Dio me ne guardi! 2. (*amer.*) proteggere; conservare.

to forgather [fo:'gæðə*], *v.i.* 1. adunarsi, raccogliersi 2. incontrarsi; fraternizzare.

forgave [fə'geiv], *pass.* di *to* **forgive**.

forge[1] [fo:dʒ], *s.* 1. fucina 2. fornace ☆ — *-bellows*, mantice; — *-hammer*, maglio.

to forge[1], *v.t.i.* 1. fucinare, forgiare 2. *fig.* fabbricare, inventare (scuse, ecc.) 3. (*dir.*) contraffare, falsificare (firme, ecc.).

to forge[2], *v.t.* 1. avanzare gradatamente, con difficoltà 2. (*mar.*) avanzare a tutta velocità; (*fam.*) farsi strada: *to* — *ahead*, essere in testa (in una gara).

forged [fo:dʒd], *ag.* 1. forgiato 2. (*dir.*) contraffatto, falsificato.

forger ['fo:dʒə*], *s.* 1. fabbro 2. contraffattore; falsario.

forgery ['fo:dʒəri], *s.* 1. contraffazione; falsificazione; alterazione: *to be guilty of* —, essere colpevole di falso 2. falso, documento contraffatto.

to forget [fə'get], *pass.* **forgot** [fə'got], *p.p.* **forgotten** [fə'gotn], (*arc.*) **forgot**, *v.t.i.* 1. dimenticare, dimenticarsi; non ricordare, non ricordarsi: *he forgets everything*, egli dimentica tutto; *he has forgotten his hat*, egli si è dimenticato il cappello; *I* — *whether I saw him*, non mi ricordo se l'ho veduto; *I* — *why he came*, non ricordo perchè sia venuto; *I* — *your name* *for the moment*, sul momento non ricordo il tuo nome; *I forgot I had already paid him*, mi ero dimenticato di averlo già pagato; *I forgot to pay him*, mi sono dimenticato di pagarlo; *I shall never — him*, non lo dimenticherò mai; *to — how, when, where, to do sthg.*, dimenticarsi come, quando, dove fare ql.co. || *forgive and —*, perdonate e dimenticate **2.** dimenticarsi, trascurare, omettere: *— about it!*, dimenticatevene!; *don't — to go there*, non trascurare, mancare di andarci; *you forgot to say*, tu non hai detto, hai trascurato di dire; *to — oneself*, (fam.) dimenticare se stessi; perdere la padronanza di sè; venir meno alla propria dignità ☆ *— -me-not*, (bot.) non ti scordar di me, miosotide: *— -me-not eyes*, occhi color pervinca; *never-to-be-forgotten*, memorabile, indimenticabile.

forgetful [fə'getful], *ag.* **1.** immemore **2.** negligente **3.** (poet.) che dà l'oblio.

forgetfully [fə'getfuli], *av.* **1.** smemoratamente **2.** negligentemente.

forgetfulness [fə'getfulnis], *s.* **1.** dimenticanza, oblio: *a moment of —*, un momento di smemorataggine **2.** negligenza.

forgettable [fə'getəbl], *ag.* dimenticabile.

forgetter [fə'getə*], *s.c.* chi dimentica.

forgetting [fə'getiŋ], *s.* (poet.) oblio.

forgettingly [fə'getiŋli], *av.* smemoratamente.

forgivable [fə'givəbl], *ag.* perdonabile.

to forgive [fə'giv], *pass.* **forgave** [fə'geiv], *p.p.* **forgiven** [fə'givn], *v.t.* perdonare, rimettere; condonare: *— me*, perdonami; *— my sins*, rimetti i miei peccati; *he was forgiven for stealing the fowls*, gli fu condonato il furto dei polli; *his sins were forgiven him*, gli furono perdonati i suoi peccati; *I shall — him his debts towards me*, gli condonerò i debiti verso di me; *please — me for my silence*, La prego di perdonare il mio silenzio; *please — us for not replying before*, La preghiamo di perdonarci per non aver risposto prima.

forgiveness [fə'givnis], *s.* **1.** perdono, remissione: *to ask for —*, chiedere perdono, scusa **2.** indulgenza, clemenza.

forgiving [fə'giviŋ], *ag.* clemente, pronto a perdonare, indulgente: *a — nature*, un carattere comprensivo.

forgivingly [fə'giviŋli], *av.* in modo comprensivo.

to forgo [fɔ:'gou], *pass.* **forwent** [fɔ:'went], *p.p.* **forgone** [fɔ:'gon], *v.t.* rinunziare a; privarsi di; far senza: *to — pleasures*, rinunciare ai divertimenti.

forgot [fə'got], *pass.* (arc.) *p.p.* di to **forget.**

forgotten [fə'gotn], *p.p.* di to **forget.**

fork [fɔ:k], *s.* **1.** forchetta **2.** (agr.) forca, forcone, tridente **3.** (mec.) forcella **4.** biforcazione: *— of a road*, biforcazione di una strada ☆ *— spanner*, (mec.) chiave a forcella || *crane —*, forca per gru; *spring —*, (mec.) forcella elastica; *swinging —*, (mec.) forcellone oscillante; *telescopic —*, (mec.) forcella a molleggio telescopico; *tuning- —*, (mus.) diapason.

to fork, *v.t.i.* **1.** biforcarsi (di tronco, strada, ecc.) **2.** (agr.) smuovere, trasportare con un forcone **3.** *to — out, over, up*, (sl.) pagare, tirar fuori: *he forked out the money at last!*, finalmente cacciò fuori i quattrini!.

forked [fɔ:kt], *ag.* forcuto, biforcuto; a forcella.

forkful [fɔ:kful], *s.* **1.** forchettata **2.** forcata.

forky [fɔ:ki], *ag.* forcuto, biforcuto.

forlorn [fə'lɔ:n], *ag.* **1.** abbandonato, trascurato, dimenticato **2.** in condizioni miserande; miserabile.

forlorn-hope [fə'lɔ:n,houp], *s.* **1.** missione disperata **2.** speranza vana, fallace.

form [fɔ:m], *s.* **1.** forma, immagine, aspetto, apparenza: *a dark — appeared*, apparve una forma scura; *to take —*, prendere, assumere forma || *without shape or —*, senza forma **2.** forma, tipo, sistema, specie, genere: *a — of madness*, una forma di pazzia; *a — of religion*, un sistema religioso; *literary —*, forma letteraria || *in sonata —*, nella forma di una sonata **3.** (gram.) forma: *singular —*, forma singolare **4.** mo-

dulo, scheda: *to fill in a —*, riempire un modulo **5.** formalità, modo di fare, etichetta: *good, bad —*, buone, cattive maniere; *for —'s sake*, per riguardo all'etichetta; *it is an ancient —*, è un modo antico **6.** forma, formula: *a — of prayer*, una forma di preghiera **7.** forma, stato di salute, di allenamento: *in, out of —*, in, giù di forma **8.** panca, banco **9.** classe (di scuole inglesi): *she is now in the second —*, ella è ora in seconda **10.** (tip.) forma (per stampa) **11.** (fil.) forma.

to form, *v.t.i.* **1.** formare, modellare; prendere forma, formarsi: *water forms ice when it freezes*, quando gela l'acqua forma il ghiaccio **2.** formare, istruire, educare: *to — a child's mind*, sviluppare la mente di un fanciullo **3.** (gram.) formare (il plurale, ecc.) **4.** formare; produrre, concepire; articolare: *to — an idea*, formulare un'idea; *to — long words*, articolare parole lunghe **5.** organizzare **6.** (mil.) disporre, disporsi: *to — (into) columns*, incolonnarsi.

formal ['fɔ:məl], *ag.* **1.** (log.) formale **2.** formale, positivo, esplicito: *a — denial*, un rifiuto esplicito **3.** in regola, preciso: *— report*, relazione precisa, ufficiale **4.** formale, cerimonioso; protocollare: *— manners*, maniere formali **5.** formalista: *he is always very —*, egli è sempre molto formalista ☆ *— dress*, abito da cerimonia.

formaldehyde [fɔ:'mældihaid], *s.* (chim.) formaldeide.

formalin ['fɔ:məlin], *s.* (chim.) formalina.

formalism ['fɔ:məlizəm], *s.* formalismo.

formalist ['fɔ:məlist], *s.c.* formalista.

formalistic [,fɔ:mə'listik], *ag.* formalistico.

formality [fɔ:'mæliti], *s.* formalità; convenzionalismo.

to formalize ['fɔ:məlaiz], *v.t.* **1.** dare forma a **2.** formalizzare.

formally ['fɔ:məli], *av.* **1.** formalmente **2.** nel modo prescritto **3.** con formalità, cerimoniosamente.

format ['fɔ:mæt], *s.* formato (di un libro).

formation [fɔ:'meiʃən], *s.* formazione (anche fig.).

formative ['fɔ:mətiv], *ag.* formativo, plastico: *— influence*, influenza formativa || *s.* (gram.) elemento usato nella formazione di vocaboli (prefisso, suffisso).

forme [fɔ:m], *s.* (tip.) forma.

former[1] [fɔ:mə*], *ag.* **1.** precedente; primo (di due): *I prefer the — alternative to the latter*, preferisco la prima alternativa alla seconda **2.** anteriore, precedente; antico: *my — pupils*, i miei antichi allievi; *she is a — friend of mine*, un tempo era mia amica.

former[1], *pron.* il primo (di due); il precedente; quello (come opposto di questo): *the — and the latter*, il primo e il secondo, quegli e questi.

former[2], *s.c.* chi forma; creatore, creatrice; artefice || *s.* stampo.

formerly ['fɔ:məli], *av.* anteriormente; in altri tempi, nel passato, tempo addietro.

formic ['fɔ:mik], *ag.* (chim.) formico.

formidable ['fɔ:midəbl], *ag.* **1.** spaventoso: *a — appearance*, un'apparenza spaventosa, minacciosa **2.** formidabile: *a — army*, un esercito formidabile.

formidably ['fɔ:midəbli], *av.* in modo formidabile.

forming ['fɔ:miŋ], *s.* formazione.

formless ['fɔ:mlis], *ag.* informe.

formula ['fɔ:mjulə], *pl.* **formulae** ['fɔ:mjuli:], **formulas** ['fɔ:mjuləz], *s.* formula.

to formularize ['fɔ:mjuləraiz], *v.t.* formulare.

formulary ['fɔ:mjuləri], *ag.* di formula, in formula || *s.* formulario.

to formulate ['fɔ:mjuleit], *v.t.* formulare.

formulation [,fɔ:mju'leiʃən], *s.* formulazione; esposizione esatta.

to fornicate ['fɔ:nikeit], *v.i.* fornicare.

fornication [,fɔ:ni'keiʃən], *s.* fornicazione.

fornicator ['fɔ:nikeitə*], *s.* fornicatore.

fornicatress ['fɔ:nikeitris], *s.* fornicatrice.

fornix ['fɔ:niks], *s.* (arch.) fornice.

to **forpine** [fə'pain], *v.i.* (*arc.*) consumarsi (per fame, ecc.).

to **forsake** [fə'seik], *pass.* **forsook** [fə'suk], *p.p.* **forsaken** [fə'seikən], *v.t.* **1.** abbandonare: *to — one's family*, abbandonare la propria famiglia **2.** rinunziare a: *to — bad habits*, rinunciare a cattive abitudini.

forsaken [fə'seikən], *p.p.* di to **forsake** ‖ *ag.* abbandonato, desolato.

forsaking [fə'seikiŋ], *s.* **1.** abbandono **2.** rinuncia.

forsook [fə'suk], *pass.* di to **forsake**.

forsooth [fə'su:θ], *av.* (*iron.*) veramente.

to **forspeak** [fə'spi:k], *pass.* **forspoke** [fə'spouk], *p.p.* **forspoken** [fə'spoukən], *v.t.* (*poet.*) **1.** impedire **2.** (*scoz.*) stregare.

to **forspend** [fə'spend], *pass.p.p.* **forspent** [fə'spent], *v.t.* (*rar.*) esaurire; spendere del tutto.

forspent [fə'spent], *pass.p.p.* di to **forspend** ‖ *ag.* esausto.

forspoke [fə'spouk], *pass.* di to **forspeak**.

forspoken [fə'spoukən], *p.p.* di to **forspeak**.

forswat [fɔ:'swɔt], *ag.* (*arc.*) coperto di sudore.

to **forswear** [fɔ:'swɛə*], *pass.* **forswore** [fɔ:'swɔ:*], *p.p.* **forsworn** [fɔ:'swɔ:n], *v.t.i.* **1.** abiurare; fare solenne promessa, giurare di rinunciare a: *to — smoking*, rinunciare al fumo **2.** spergiurare, giurare il falso.

fort [fɔ:t], *s.* **1.** (*mil.*) forte; posto fortificato **2.** (*st. amer.*) stazione commerciale fortificata.

fortalice [ˈfɔ:təlis], *s.* (*mil.*) fortilizio.

forte[1] [fɔ:t], *s.* **1.** attitudine spiccata, abilità particolare: *my — is mathematics*, il mio forte è la matematica **2.** forte (di lama di spada).

forte[2] [ˈfɔ:ti], *s.* (*mus.*) forte.

forth [fɔ:θ], *av.* **1.** avanti, innanzi: *from this day —*, d'ora in poi; *to go —*, uscire; avanzare; farsi vedere; *to set —*, mettersi in viaggio; *to walk —*, avanzare ‖ *and so —*, e così via **2.** fuori: *the trees put — new leaves in spring*, in primavera gli alberi germogliano ‖ *prep.* (*rar.*) fuori di.

forthcoming [fɔ:θ'kʌmiŋ], *ag.* approssimantesi; vicino, prossimo; pronto.

forthgoing [fɔ:θ'gouiŋ], *ag.* (*rar.*) entusiastico ‖ *s.* uscita.

forthright [fɔ:θ'rait], *ag.* **1.** che va diritto **2.** franco, sincero **3.** abile, decisivo ‖ *av.* direttamente.

forthwith [ˈfɔ:θ'wiθ], *av.* immediatamente, senz'altro.

fortieth [ˈfɔ:tiiθ], *ag. num. ord.* quarantesimo.

fortifiable [ˌfɔ:tifaiəbl], *ag.* fortificabile.

fortification [ˌfɔ:tifiˈkeiʃən], *s.* **1.** (*mil.*) fortificazione **2.** aumento dell'alcoolicità (di vini, liquori).

to **fortify** [ˈfɔ:tifai], *v.t.i.* **1.** (*mil.*) fortificare **2.** *fig.* rinvigorire, rinvigorirsi; incoraggiare **3.** aumentare l'alcoolicità di (vini, liquori).

Fortinbras [ˈfɔ:tinbræs], *no.pr.m.* (*lett.*) Fortebraccio.

fortissimo [fɔ:ˈtisimou], *s.* (*mus.*) fortissimo.

fortitude [ˈfɔ:titju:d], *s.* fortezza; forza d'animo; fermezza; coraggio.

fortlet [ˈfɔ:tlit], *s.* fortino.

fortnight [ˈfɔ:tnait], *s.* due settimane, quindicina: *a —'s holiday*, una vacanza di due settimane; *to-day —*, oggi a quindici; *within a —*, entro quindici giorni.

fortnightly [ˈfɔ:tˌnaitli], *ag.* quindicinale ‖ *av.* ogni due settimane, una volta ogni due settimane.

fortress [ˈfɔ:tris], *s.* **1.** fortezza, piazzaforte; difesa **2.** *fig.* appoggio, sostegno.

to **fortress**, *v.t.* **1.** fortificare **2.** *fig.* proteggere.

fortuitism [fɔ:ˈtju(:)itizəm], *s.* (*fil.*) casualismo.

fortuitist [fɔ:ˈtju(:)itist], *s.* (*fil.*) seguace del casualismo.

fortuitous [fɔ:ˈtju(:)itəs], *ag.* fortuito, casuale.

fortuitously [fɔ:ˈtju(:)itəsli], *av.* fortuitamente, casualmente.

fortuitousness [fɔ:ˈtju(:)itəsnis], **fortuity** [fɔ:ˈtju(:)iti], *s.* casualità; avvenimento fortuito.

fortunate [ˈfɔ:tʃnit], *ag.* **1.** fortunato: *I was — in my choice*, fui fortunato nella mia scelta **2.** propizio, favorevole: *— omen*, augurio propizio.

fortunately [ˈfɔ:tʃnitli], *av.* **1.** fortunatamente **2.** favorevolmente, con successo.

fortunateness [ˈfɔ:tʃnitnis], *s.* fortuna; successo.

fortune [ˈfɔ:tʃən], *s.* **1.** sorte, caso: *good, bad —*, fortuna, sfortuna; *piece of good —*, colpo fortunato ‖ *soldier of —*, soldato di ventura **2.** destino: *to have one's — told*, farsi predire il futuro ‖ *to try one's —*, fare un passo arrischiato **3.** fortuna **4.** ricchezza, dote, fortuna: *man of —*, uomo ricco; *to come into a —*, ereditare una fortuna; *to make a —*, farsi un patrimonio; *to marry a —*, sposare un'ereditiera ‖ *born to —*, nato con la camicia ☆ *— -hunter*, cacciatore di dote.

to **fortune**, *v.t.i.* (*arc. poet.*) **1.** dotare **2.** accadere, capitare: *it fortuned that*, accadde che.

fortuneless [ˈfɔ:tʃənlis], *ag.* **1.** sfortunato **2.** povero, senza beni.

to **fortune-tell** [ˈfɔ:tʃəntel], *pass.p.p.* **fortune-told** [ˈfɔ:tʃəntould], *v.i.* predire l'avvenire.

fortune-teller [ˈfɔ:tʃənˌtelə*], *s.c.* indovino, indovina; chiromante.

fortune-telling [ˈfɔ:tʃənˌteliŋ], *s.* predizione dell'avvenire.

forty [ˈfɔ:ti], *ag.s.* quaranta: *she is about —*, ella ha circa quarant'anni; *the forties*, gli anni dal 40 al 50 ‖ *to have — winks*, (*sl.*) fare un sonnellino, la siesta.

forum [ˈfɔ:rəm], *pl.* **fora** [ˈfɔ:rə], **forums** [ˈfɔ:rəmz], *s.* **1.** (*st. romana*) foro **2.** foro, tribunale **3.** luogo di pubblica discussione.

to **forwander** [fə'wɔndə*], *v.i.* (*arc.*) stancarsi vagando; vagare in lungo e in largo.

forward [ˈfɔ:wəd], *ag.* **1.** avanzato, in avanti: *— movement*, movimento in avanti, progressista; *— school*, scuola d'avanguardia **2.** precoce; primaticcio: *— winter*, inverno precoce **3.** ardito, presuntuoso, sfrontato, impertinente: *a — girl*, una ragazza impertinente **4.** pronto; sollecito; impaziente: *to be — to do sthg.*, essere sollecito nel fare ql.co., impaziente di fare ql.co. **5.** (*mar.*) prodiero **6.** (*comm.*) futuro ‖ *s.* (*calcio, hockey, ecc.*) attaccante ☆ *center —*, (*calcio, hockey, ecc.*) centrattacco.

forward(s) [ˈfɔ:wəd(z)], *av.* **1.** avanti, in avanti: *—!*, (*mil.*) avanti!; *from now —*, d'ora in avanti; *from that time —*, da quel giorno in poi, a partire da quel giorno; *we can't get any forwarder*, non possiamo andare oltre; *to bring —*, attirare l'attenzione su; *to date —*, (*comm.*) posdatare; (*to go*) *backwards and —*, (andare) avanti e indietro; *to look —*, pensare al futuro; *to move —*, (far) avanzare; *to move —*, (*calcio, hockey, ecc.*) giocare come centravanti; *to rush —*, precipitarsi avanti; *to set the clock —*, mettere avanti l'orologio; *to step —*, fare un passo avanti (da una fila); *to thrust oneself —*, mettersi in evidenza ‖ *to look — to*, non veder l'ora di, pregustare: *he looked — to seeing her again*, non vedeva l'ora di rivederla **2.** (*mar.*) a proravia.

to **forward**, *v.t.* **1.** promuovere, assistere, secondare (un progetto, ecc.) **2.** accelerare la crescita di (una pianta) **3.** far pervenire; mandare, spedire; inoltrare: *please —*, pregasi inoltrare (di lettera).

forwarder [ˈfɔ:wədə*], *s.c.* **1.** promotore, promotrice **2.** mittente ‖ *s.* spedizioniere.

forwarding [ˈfɔ:wədiŋ], *s.* spedizione ☆ *— agent*, (*comm.*) spedizioniere.

forwardly [ˈfɔ:wədli], *av.* **1.** prontamente; premurosamente **2.** arditamente; sfrontatamente.

forwardness [ˈfɔ:wədnis], *s.* **1.** premura; prontezza **2.** anticipo (di stagione, raccolto); precocità **3.** impertinenza; presunzione **4.** progresso (di un lavoro, ecc.).

forwent [fə'went], *pass.* di to **forgo**.

fossa [ˈfɔsə], *pl.* **fossae** [ˈfɔsi:], *s.* (*anat.*) fossa, cavità.

fosse [fɔs], *s.* **1.** (*anat.*) fossa, cavità **2.** (*mil.*) trincea.

fossil [ˈfɔsl], *ag.s.* **1.** fossile **2.** (*scherz.*) persona antiquata, dalle idee fossilizzate.

fossiliferous [ˌfɔsiˈlifərəs], *ag.* fossilifero.

fossilization [ˌfɔsilaiˈzeiʃən], *s.* fossilizzazione.

to **fossilize** [ˈfɔsilaiz], *v.t.i.* fossilizzare, fossilizzarsi (anche *fig.*).

fossor [ˈfɔsɔ*], *s.* (*st.*) fossore; becchino.

fossorial [fɔˈsɔːriɔl], *ag.* (*zool.*) scavatore.

foster [ˈfɔstə*], *s.* 1. cibo, nutrimento 2. tutela; protezione ☆ — -*brother*, fratello di latte; fratello adottivo; — -*child*, figlio adottivo; — -*father*, padre adottivo; tutore; — -*mother*, nutrice; madre adottiva; — -*sister*, sorella di latte; sorella adottiva.

to **foster**, *v.t.* 1. (*arc.*) allevare; (*fam.*) nutrire 2. favorire, incoraggiare (piani, opinioni, amicizia, ecc.); proteggere: *to — friendship between peoples*, incoraggiare l'amicizia fra i popoli.

fosterage [ˈfɔstəridʒ], *s.* 1. baliatico; allevamento 2. incoraggiamento.

fosterer [ˈfɔstərə*], *s.c.* 1. genitore adottivo, genitrice adottiva 2. protettore, protettrice; promotore, promotrice (di opere, affari, ecc.).

fosterling [ˈfɔstəliŋ], *s.* bimbo a balia; bimbo adottivo.

fought [fɔːt], *pass. p.p.* di to **fight**.

foul [faul], *ag.* 1. sporco, puzzolente: — *air*, aria viziata; — *breath*, alito cattivo 2. *fig.* sconcio, immondo, vergognoso; sleale: — *language*, linguaggio osceno; — *play*, intrigo, tradimento; (*spor.*) giuoco sleale ‖ *by fair means or* —, in un modo o nell'altro, con mezzi leciti o illeciti 3. pericoloso, tempestoso (di tempo); contrario (di vento) 4. ostruito, incrostato (di canna, camino, ecc.) 5. (*mar. amer.*) impigliato (di ancora); sporco: — *bottom*, carena sporca ‖ *to run — of another ship*, entrare in collisione con un'altra nave ☆ —*mouthed* (o — *spoken*), sboccato, osceno.

foul, *s.* 1. (*spor.*) fallo; atto irregolare 2. (*mar.*) collisione ‖ *through fair and* —, nella buona e cattiva fortuna.

to **foul**, *v.t.i.* 1. sporcare, sporcarsi; intorbidire, intorbidirsi; insozzare (anche *fig.*) 2. ostruirsi, otturarsi (di tubo, ecc.); impedire (il traffico) 3. (*mar.*) fare collisione, impigliarsi (di ancora, catena, ecc.): *the two boats fouled* (o *one boat fouled the other*), le due barche si urtarono.

foul, *av.* irregolarmente; slealmente: *to hit* —, (*boxe*) colpire basso (anche *fig.*) ‖ *to play s.o.* —, trattare qlcu. in modo sleale.

foulard [fuːˈlɑːd], *s.* « foulard » (stoffa e fazzoletto di seta).

foully [ˈfaulli], *av.* 1. sudiciamente 2. slealmente; vergognosamente; ignobilmente.

foulness [ˈfaulnis], *s.* 1. sporcizia, sozzura; *fig.* oscenità 2. puzzo 3. *fig.* cattiveria; perfidia; slealtà.

foumart [ˈfuːmɑːt], *s.* (*zool.*) puzzola.

found[1] [faund], *pass.p.p.* di to **find** ‖ *ag.* rifornito, mantenuto ‖ *our maid gets four pounds a week all* —, la nostra cameriera riceve quattro sterline alla settimana oltre al mantenimento.

to **found**[2], *v.t.i.* fondare (anche *fig.*); istituire (scuole, ecc.); costruire; stabilire: *founded on fact*, basato su fatti reali; *well, ill founded*, bene, mal fondato; *to — a family, a fortune*, mettere le basi di una famiglia, di un patrimonio; *to — one's opinion on*, basare la propria opinione su; *to — (oneself) on* (o *upon*) *s.o.*, basarsi su qlcu.

to **found**[3], *v.t.* fondere (metalli); gettare nella forma (metallo, vetro fuso).

foundation [faunˈdeiʃən], *s.* 1. fondazione; istituzione; fondazione benefica 2. (*arch.*) fondamenta 3. *fig.* fondamento, base, motivo, ragione: *the news has no* —, la notizia è priva di fondamento 4. (*cosmesi*) crema base ☆ — *stone*, prima pietra (di un edificio); *make -up* —, (*cosmesi*) fondo tinta.

foundationer [faunˈdeiʃnə*], *s.c.* (*scuola*) titolare di una borsa di studio.

founder[1] [ˈfaundə*], *s.* 1. fondatore (di istituto, ospedale, ecc.) 2. (*comm.*) promotore (di una società).

founder[2], *s.* fonditore (di metalli).

to **founder**[3], *v.t.i.* 1. affondare, affondarsi (di na-

ve) 2. sprofondare, crollare, sfasciarsi (di edificio, ecc.) 3. spossare, azzoppare (un cavallo).

foundling [ˈfaundliŋ], *s.c.* trovatello, trovatella ☆ — -*hospital*, brefotrofio.

foundress [ˈfaundris], *s.* fondatrice.

foundry [ˈfaundri], *s.* fonderia.

fount[1] [faunt], *s.* 1. (*poet. fig.*) sorgente, fonte 2. piccolo serbatoio (di lampada a olio, penna).

fount[2] [fɔnt], *s.* (*tip.*) serie di caratteri dello stesso tipo e dimensione.

fountain [ˈfauntin], *s.* 1. fontana, sorgente; getto d'acqua 2. *fig.* sorgente, origine ☆ — -*head*, sorgente (anche *fig.*); — -*pen*, penna stilografica.

four [fɔː*], *ag.s.num.card.* quattro: *the — corners of the earth*, gli angoli più remoti della Terra; *a party of* —, una comitiva di quattro persone ‖ *to walk on all fours*, camminare a quattro zampe, andare carponi ☆ — -*dimensional*, a quattro dimensioni; — -*footed*, quadrupede; — -*handed*, quadrumane; — -*in-hand* (o *couch and* —), tiro a quattro; — -*legged*, a quattro zampe, a quattro gambe; — -*pence*, somma di quattro pence; *one and* — -*pence*, uno scellino e quattro pence; — -*per-cents*, (*Borsa*) titoli al quattro per cento; — -*ply*, (lana) a quattro fili; — -*poster*, letto a (quattro) colonne; — -*seater*, vettura a quattro posti; — -*stroke*, a quattro tempi (di motore) — -*wheeler*, carrozza a quattro ruote.

fourfold [ˈfɔː-fould], *ag.av.* quadruplo, quattro volte.

fourgon [fuːˈgɔːn], *s.* furgone.

fourpenny [ˈfɔːpəni], *ag.* che vale quattro pence ‖ *s.* quattro pence (come valore).

fourscore [ˈfɔːˈskɔː*], *ag.* (*arc. letter.*) ottanta: *to be — and ten*, aver novant'anni.

foursome [ˈfɔːsəm], *s.* 1. (*spor.*) partita di golf giocata in quattro 2. (*fam.*) quattro persone, quartetto.

four-square [ˈfɔːˈskwɛə*], *ag.* con quattro lati uguali; *fig.* franco, saldo, deciso ‖ *av.* saldamente, decisamente.

fourteen [ˈfɔːˈtiːn], *ag.num.card.s.* quattordici.

fourteenth [ˈfɔːˈtiːnθ], *ag.num.ord.s.* quattordicesimo: *on the — of May*, il quattordici maggio.

fourth [fɔːθ], *ag.num.ord.* quarto ‖ *s.* 1. la quarta parte: *threefourths*, tre quarti ‖ *to make a* —, (*giuoco di carte*) fare il quarto 2. (*mus.*) quarta.

fourthly [ˈfɔːθli], *av.* in quarto luogo.

fowl [faul], *s.* 1. pollo; pollame 2. (*rar.*) volatile in genere: *the fowls of the air*, gli uccelli del cielo; *wild* —, uccelli selvatici ☆ — -*run*, pollaio; allevamento di polli.

to **fowl**, *v.i.* (*rar.*) andare a caccia di uccelli; uccellare (con reti).

fowler [ˈfaulə*], *s.* uccellatore.

fowling [ˈfauliŋ], *s.* uccellagione ☆ — -*piece*, fucile leggero da caccia.

fox [fɔks], *s.* 1. volpe ‖ *the Fox*, (*astr.*) la Volpe 2. *fig.* volpe, volpone, uomo astuto: *an old* —, una vecchia volpe; *a sly* (o *cunning*) —, un furbone 3. pelliccia di volpe 4. (*mar.*) treccia incatramata ☆ — -*brush*, coda di volpe; — -*cub*, volpacchiotto; — -*glove*, (*bot.*) digitale; — -*hunt*, caccia alla volpe; — -*hunter*, cacciatore di volpi; — -*hunting*, il cacciare la volpe; — -*tail*, coda di volpe; (*bot.*) alopecuro; — -*terrier*, (cane) « fox -terrier »: *wire-haired* — -*terrier*, « terrier » a pelo ruvido; — -*trot*, (*danza*) « fox-trot »; — -*wedge*, (*mec.*) zeppa, cuneo, bietta; controchiavetta ‖ *bitch-* —, volpe femmina; *dog-* —, volpe maschio; *flying-* —, (*zool.*) volpe volante; *sea-* —, (*ittiol.*) volpe di mare; *white* —, volpe polare.

to **fox**, *v.t.i.* 1. comportarsi, agire astutamente ‖ *to — about* (o *to go foxing round*), (*fam.*) mettere il naso dappertutto 2. scolorire (pagina di libro, stampa) con macchie: *foxed engraving*, stampa con macchie (di umidità, ecc.) 3. (*sl.*) ingannare.

foxhole [ˈfɔkshoul], *s.* 1. tana della volpe 2. (*mil.*) trincea, ricovero.

foxhound ['fɔkshaund], *s.* cane usato per la caccia alla volpe.

foxiness ['fɔksinis], *s.* **1.** astuzia **2.** colore rossastro.

foxy ['fɔksi], *ag.* **1.** astuto, volpino **2.** rossastro **3.** scolorito, sciupato **4.** inacidito, aspro.

foyer ['fɔiei], *s.* (*teat.*) ridotto.

foziness ['fouzinis], *s.* **1.** spugnosità **2.** *fig.* stupidaggine.

fracas ['fræka:], *s.* fracasso; lite rumorosa.

fraction ['frækʃən], *s.* **1.** frazione, parte, porzione **2.** (*mat.*) frazione: *decimal* —, frazione decimale **3.** (*eccl.*) frazione (eucaristica).

fractional ['frækʃnl], **fractionary** ['frækʃnəri], *ag.* frazionario.

to fractionate ['frækʃəneit], *v.t.* (*chim.*) sottoporre a distillazione frazionata.

fractionation [ˌfrækʃə'neiʃən], *s.* (*chim.*) frazionamento.

to fractionize ['frækʃənaiz], *v.t.* (*mat.*) frazionare.

fractious ['frækʃəs], *ag.* litigioso; permaloso; indisciplinato, indocile: *a — child*, un bambino permaloso.

fractiously ['frækʃəsli], *av.* litigiosamente; indisciplinatamente.

fractiousness ['frækʃəsnis], *s.* umore litigioso; permalosità; indocilità.

fracture ['fræktʃə*], *s.* **1.** frattura, rottura **2.** (*med.*) frattura: *compound* —, frattura composta; *to set a* —, ridurre una frattura **3.** (*geol.*) frattura **4.** (*filologia*) frattura ☆ — *plane*, (*geol.*) piano di frattura ‖ *rock* —, (*geol.*) litoclasi.

to fracture, *v.t.i.* spaccare, spaccarsi; rompere, rompersi; fratturare, fratturarsi: *he has fractured his leg*, si è fratturato la gamba.

fraenum ['fri:nəm], *pl.* **fraena** ['fri:nə], *s.* (*anat.*) frenulo.

fragile ['frædʒail], *ag.* fragile (di cose); debole, delicato (di persone).

fragility [frə'dʒiliti], *s.* fragilità (di cose); debolezza (di persone); delicatezza (di salute).

fragment ['frægmənt], *s.* **1.** frammento, pezzo, coccio **2.** (*lett.*) frammento, brano, passo.

fragmentarily ['frægməntərili], *av.* in modo frammentario.

fragmentariness ['frægməntərinis], *s.* frammentarietà.

fragmentary ['frægməntəri], *ag.* frammentario, incompleto.

fragmented ['frægməntid], *ag.* in frammenti.

fragrance ['freigrəns], **fragrancy** ['freigrənsi], *s.* fragranza; profumo.

fragrant ['freigrənt], *ag.* fragrante, odoroso; profumato.

fragrantly ['freigrəntli], *av.* in modo fragrante.

frail[1] [freil], *ag.* **1.** debole (di salute, moralità) **2.** fragile; *fig.* caduco, transitorio ‖ *s.* (*sl. amer.*) donna, ragazza.

frail[2], *s.* cestino di giunco (per la spedizione di frutta).

frailish ['freiliʃ], *ag.* **1.** deboluccio **2.** piuttosto fragile.

frailly ['freilli], *av.* **1.** debolmente **2.** fragilmente.

frailness ['freilnis], *s.* debolezza, fragilità.

frailty ['freilti], *s.* debolezza (di salute, morale) ‖ —, *thy name is woman*, fragilità, il tuo nome è donna.

fraise[1] [freiz], *s.* **1.** (*edil. mil.*) palizzata orizzontale o inclinata **2.** lattuga, gorgiera.

to fraise[1], *v.t.* (*edil. mil.*) munire di palizzata; difendere con una palizzata.

fraise[2], *s.* (*mec.*) fresa.

framboesia [fræm'bi:ziə], *s.* (*patol.*) frambesia.

frame [freim], *s.* **1.** struttura, armatura (d'ombrello, ecc.); ossatura, intelaiatura, telaio (di finestra, ecc.), telaio (da ricamo, di bicicletta); montatura (di occhiali): *the — of an aircraft*, il telaio di un aereo **2.** cornice, incorniciatura (di quadri) **3.** (*anat.*) struttura, ossa-

tura, scheletro; corpo **4.** *fig.* ordinamento; stato; disposizione: — *of reference*, teoria, base sistematica di principi e presupposti; *the* — *of society*, l'ordinamento della società; *out of* —, in disordine; *he is in a good* — *of mind*, è in una buona disposizione d'animo **5.** (*giardinaggio*) cassa a telaio, a vetri **6.** (*foto.*) fotogramma ☆ — *bridge*, ponte fatto con tavole di legno; — *-maker*, fabbricante di cornici; — *-up*, (*amer.*) complotto.

to frame, *v.t.i.* **1.** formare, dar forma a (un piano, una teoria) **2.** progettare (una casa) **3.** adattare, disporre; regolare: *to* — *sthg.* *to* (o *into*) *sthg.*, adattare ql.co. a ql.co. ‖ *she was framing well*, prometteva bene **4.** incorniciare: *curly hair framed her face*, capelli ricciuti le incorniciavano il viso; *to* — *a picture*, incorniciare un quadro **5.** comporre, preparare (un discorso, dei versi, ecc.) **6.** immaginare **7.** (*sl.*) montare un'accusa contro **8.** *to* — *up*, (*sl.*) alterare i risultati di (una competizione, ecc.): *a framed-up charge*, un'accusa falsa, architettata.

framer ['freimə*], *s.* **1.** artefice **2.** costruttore **3.** fabbricante di cornici.

framework ['freimwə:k], *s.* **1.** struttura, armatura, ossatura; carcassa; cornice, intelaiatura: *the* — *of a ship*, la carcassa di una nave; *the* — *of society*, *fig.* la struttura della società **2.** (*agr.*) ossatura, rami principali (di albero).

framing ['freimiŋ], *s.* **1.** armatura; cornice, incorniciatura; intelaiatura **2.** formazione **3.** concezione.

frampold ['fræmpould], *ag.* (*arc.*) bisbetico; litigioso.

franc [fræŋk], *s.* franco (moneta).

France [fra:ns], *no.pr.* (*geog.*) Francia.

Frances ['fra:nsis], *no.pr.f.* Francesca.

franchise ['fræntʃaiz], *s.* **1.** franchigia, immunità, privilegio **2.** diritto di voto, di cittadinanza **3.** (*amer.*) concessione (di appalto).

franchiser ['fræntʃaizə*], *s.* **1.** chi gode di una franchigia **2.** chi ha diritto di voto.

Francis ['fra:nsis], *no.pr.m.* Francesco.

Franciscan [fræn'siskən], *ag.s.* francescano.

francolin ['fræŋkoulin], *s.* (*ornit.*) francolino.

Francophil(e) ['fræŋkəfil], *ag.s.* francofilo.

Francophobe ['fræŋkəfoub], *ag.s.* francofobo.

franc tireur, *pl.* **francs tireurs** [ˌfra:ŋˌti:'rə:*], *s.* franco tiratore.

frangibility [ˌfrændʒi'biliti], *s.* frangibilità; fragilità.

frangible ['frændʒibl], *ag.* frangibile; fragile.

frangipane ['frændʒipein], *s.* **1.** (profumo di) gelsomino rosso **2.** frangipana **3.** dolce con crema e mandorle.

Frank[1] [fræŋk], *s.* franco (membro della tribù germanica): *the Franks*, i franchi.

Frank[2], *no.pr.m.* Franco.

frank[3], *ag.* franco, schietto; generoso.

frank[4], *s.* **1.** timbro, firma di franchigia **2.** busta, involucro che gode di franchigia.

to frank[4], *v.t.* **1.** (*arc.*) affrancare (una lettera, ecc.) **2.** esentare da pagamento.

frank[5], *s.* (*dial.*) airone.

frank[6], (*sl. amer.*) *abbr.* di **frankfurter**.

Frankfort, Frankfurt ['fræŋkfət], *no.pr.* (*geog.*) Francoforte.

Frankfurter ['fræŋkfətə*], *ag.s.c.* francofortese ‖ **frankfurt(er)**, *s.* (*amer. cuc.*) « Würstel » (salsiccia tedesca).

frankincense ['fræŋkinˌsens], *s.* incenso.

Frankish ['fræŋkiʃ], *ag.* franco, dei franchi ‖ *s.* lingua franca.

franklin ['fræŋklin], *s.* (*st. inglese*) proprietario terriero appartenente alla classe media.

frankly ['fræŋkli], *av.* francamente, sinceramente, apertamente.

frankness ['fræŋknis], *s.* franchezza, sincerità.

frantic ['fræntik], *ag.* frenetico ‖ — *with joy*, pazzo di gioia.

frantically ['fræntikəli], *av.* **1.** freneticamente; follemente **2.** spaventosamente; terribilmente: *I am — busy*, sono terribilmente occupato.

franticness ['fræntiknis], *s.* frenesia.

to **frap** [fræp], *pass.p.p.* **frapped** [fræpt], *v.t.* (*mar.*) rizzare.

frass [fræs], *s.* escremento di insetto.

fratch [frɑːtʃ], *s.* (*dial.*) litigio.

frater[1] ['freitə*], *s.* **1.** camerata, compagno fraterno **2.** frate.

frater[2], *s.* refettorio.

fraternal [frə'təːnl], *ag.* fraterno.

fraternally [frə'təːnəli], *av.* fraternamente.

fraternity [frə'təːniti], *s.* **1.** fraternità **2.** confraternita **3.** associazione (p.e. di giornalisti, studenti).

fraternization [ˌfrætənai'zeiʃən], *s.* affratellamento.

to **fraternize** ['frætənaiz], *v.i.* fraternizzare.

fratricidal [ˌfreitri'saidl], *ag.* fratricida.

fratricide[1] ['freitrisaid], *s.* fratricida.

fratricide[2], *s.* fratricidio.

fraud [frɔːd], *s.* **1.** frode, inganno: *to get money by —*, ottenere denaro con la frode **2.** (*fam.*) impostore, truffatore: *he was a —*, era un impostore.

fraudful ['frɔːdful], *ag.* ingannevole, pieno di frodi.

fraudfully ['frɔːdfuli], *av.* ingannevolmente.

fraudulence ['frɔːdjuləns], *s.* frode.

fraudulent ['frɔːdjulənt], *ag.* fraudolento, doloso, disonesto.

fraudulently ['frɔːdjuləntli], *av.* in modo fraudolento, dolosamente, disonestamente.

fraught [frɔːt], *ag.* **1.** (*arc.*) riempito; caricato: *ship — with goods*, nave carica di merci **2.** *fig.* pieno, ricco (di significato, conseguenze) || *s.* carico (di nave).

to **fraught**, *v.t.i.* (*arc.*) riempire; caricare; immagazzinare; formare il carico di una nave.

fraxinella [ˌfræksi'nelə], *s.* (*bot.*) frassinella.

fraxinus ['fræksinəs], *s.* (*bot.*) frassino.

fray[1] [frei], *s.* **1.** zuffa, rissa, mischia, lotta: *eager for the —*, (*letter.*) anelante alla lotta **2.** timore.

to **fray**[1], *v.t.i.* **1.** (*arc.*) azzuffarsi, lottare **2.** spaventare.

to **fray**[2], *v.t.i.* **1.** consumare, consumarsi; logorare, logorarsi; sfilacciare, sfilacciarsi (di stoffa): *to get frayed*, diventare liso **2.** sfregare, sfregarsi (di cervi, ecc.): *deer — their heads against trees*, i daini sfregano la testa contro gli alberi.

frazil ['freizil], *s.* (*amer.*) cristalli di ghiaccio nell'acqua.

frazzle ['fræzl], *s.* **1.** (*amer.*) logorio **2.** *fig.* esaurimento: *worn to a —*, ridotto a un cencio.

to **frazzle**, *v.t.i.* (*amer.*) **1.** logorare, logorarsi; consumare, consumarsi; ridurre a brandelli **2.** *fig.* stancare, stancarsi; esaurire, esaurirsi.

freak[1] [friːk], *s.* **1.** capriccio, ghiribizzo, ticchio **2.** fenomeno; anormalità: *a — of nature*, una anomalia della natura.

freak[2], *s.* macchiolina (di colore).

to **freak**[2], *v.t.* screziare.

freakful ['friːkful], **freakish** ['friːkiʃ], *ag.* capriccioso, bizzarro, stravagante.

freakishly ['friːkiʃli], *av.* capricciosamente, bizzarramente.

freakishness ['friːkiʃnis], *s.* capricciosità.

freaky ['friːki], *ag.* capriccioso, bizzarro, stravagante.

freckle ['frekl], *s.* lentiggine, efelide.

to **freckle**, *v.t.i.* coprire, coprirsi di lentiggini.

freckled ['frekld], **freckly** ['frekli], *ag.* lentigginoso.

Fred [fred], **Freddie, Freddy** ['fredi], *no.pr.m. dim.* di **Alfred, Frederick**.

Frederic(k) ['fredrik], *no.pr.m.* Federico.

free [friː], *comp.* **freer** ['friːə*], *superl.* **freest** ['friːist], *ag.* **1.** (*pol.*) libero, indipendente: *a — country*, un paese libero; *state that has become —*, stato che si è reso indipendente **2.** libero, sciolto da vincoli: *as — as the air*, libero come l'aria; *I did it of my own — will*, lo feci di mia spontanea volontà; *to set a*

prisoner, a slave —, liberare un prigioniero, uno schiavo; *to wrench oneself —*, liberarsi con uno sforzo violento **3.** libero, non controllato da regole: *— translation*, traduzione libera; *— verse*, verso libero || *to give s.o. a — rein*, dare carta bianca a qlcu. || *to make — use of sthg.*, fare libero uso di ql.co. || *to make — with s.o.*, prendersi delle libertà con qlcu. **4.** libero, gratuito: *— ticket*, biglietto gratuito; *admission —*, entrata libera **5.** (*comm.*) franco: *— alongside the ship* (*abbr. f.a.s.*), franco lungo bordo; *— of factory*, franco stabilimento; *— delivered*, franco consegna; *— in* (*abbr. f.i.*), franco spese entrata nella stiva; *— in and out* (*abbr. f.i.o.*), franco spese entrata e uscita dalla stiva; *— of average*, franco avaria; *— of income tax*, esente dalla tassa sul reddito; *— of postage*, franco di spese postali; *— on board* (*abbr. f.o.b.*), franco bordo; *— on rail* (*abbr. f.o.r.*), franco stazione ferroviaria; *— on truck* (*abbr. f.o.t.*), (*amer.*) franco vagone **6.** libero, non occupato: *a — afternoon*, un pomeriggio libero; *I am — this afternoon*, questo pomeriggio non ho impegni; *— moment*, momento libero; *is this table —?*, è libero questo tavolo?; *to have one's hands —*, avere le mani libere; *fig.* non avere lavoro fisso, impegnativo **7.** libero, separato, disgiunto || *the Free Churches*, le Chiese libere, non conformiste (in Inghilterra) **8.** spigliato; aggraziato: *— gestures and movements*, gesti e movimenti spigliati; *— style*, stile sciolto **9.** abbondante, copioso, generoso: *— flow of water*, corso d'acqua impetuoso; *to be — with one's money*, essere generoso col proprio denaro **10.** impudente, licenzioso, sconveniente: *to be somewhat — in one's conversation*, essere sconveniente nel parlare **11.** (*mec.*) folle, libero **12.** *— from*, libero da, esente: *a day — from wind*, una giornata senza vento ☆ *— and -easy*, anticonformista; *— -enterprise*, (*neol.*) liberismo economico; *— -hand*, a mano libera: *to get a — -hand*, avere il diritto di agire come si vuole; *— -handed*, liberale, generoso; *— -lance*, (*st.*) soldato mercenario; giornalista indipendente; *— -list*, (*comm.*) elenco della merce che non paga dogana; *— -love*, libero amore; *— -minded*, di larghe vedute; *— -port*, (*comm.*) porto franco; *— -speech*, libertà di parola; *— -spoken*, franco sincero, aperto nel parlare; *— -thought*, libertà di pensiero; *— -trade*, (*comm.*) libero scambio; *— -trader*, libero scambista; *— -wharf*, (*comm.*) franco banchina; *— -wheel*, (*mec.*) ruota libera; *— -will*, libero arbitrio.

to **free**, *v.t.* **1.** liberare: *to — an animal from a trap*, liberare un animale da una trappola; *to — a slave*, emancipare uno schiavo; *to — oneself from debts*, liberarsi dai debiti **2.** esentare; togliere restrizioni a, togliere tasse a: *to — coffee*, togliere la tassa sul caffè **3.** sbarazzare.

free, *av.* gratuitamente: *the gallery is open — on Saturdays*, l'ingresso alla galleria è gratis al sabato; *to get in —*, entrare gratis.

freebooter ['friːˌbuːtə*], *s.* pirata, predone.

freebooting ['friːˌbuːtiŋ], *s.* pirateria, saccheggio.

freeborn ['friːˈbɔːn], *ag.* che nasce libero con diritti civili e politici.

freedman ['friːdmæn], *pl.* **freedmen** ['friːdmen], *s.* schiavo liberato; (*st.*) liberto.

freedom ['friːdəm], *s.* **1.** libertà || *the four freedoms* (*of speech and expression, of worship, from want, from fear*), le quattro libertà (di parola e espressione, di fede e di culto, dal bisogno e dalla paura) **2.** libertà, franchigia || *Freedom of the Seas*, libertà dei mari || *to give s.o. the — of the house*, mettere la propria casa a disposizione di qlcu. **3.** franchezza, disinvoltura, scioltezza, facilità (di linguaggio): *to speak with —*, parlare con franchezza, con facilità **4.** familiarità, libertà (di modi): *to take freedoms with*, prendersi delle libertà con **5.** audacia di concezione; libertà (di mentalità) **6.** cittadinanza onoraria; immunità.

freehold ['friːhould], *s.* (*dir.*) proprietà fondiaria assoluta.

freely ['friːli], *av.* **1.** liberamente **2.** gratuitamente.

freeman ['fri:mæn], *pl.* **freemen** ['fri:men], *nel senso* **2.** ['fri:mən], *s.* **1.** uomo libero **2.** cittadino onorario: *a — of the City of Oxford*, cittadino onorario della città di Oxford.

freemartin ['fri:ˌmɑ:tin], *s.* vitella sterile gemella di un vitello.

freemason ['fri:ˌmeisn], *s.* (fra)massone.

freemasonry ['fri:ˌmeisnri], *s.* (fra)massoneria.

freeness ['fri:nis], *s.* (rar.) libertà.

freesia ['fri:zjə], *s.* (bot.) fresia.

freestone[1] ['fri:-stoun], *ag.* spiccatoio (di frutti) ‖ *s.* (bot.) frutto che si stacca facilmente dal nocciolo.

freestone[2], *s.* (min.) pietra da taglio.

freestyle ['fri:-stail], *s.* (spor.) gara di nuoto a stile libero.

freethinker ['fri:'θiŋkə*], *s.* libero pensatore.

freethinking ['fri:'θiŋkiŋ], *s.* libertà di pensiero.

freeze [fri:z], *s.* **1.** congelamento; gelo **2.** (econ. comm.) blocco, congelamento (di prezzi, salari).

to freeze, *pass.* **froze** [frouz], *p.p.* **frozen** ['frouzn], *v.t.i.* **1.** *imp.* gelare, essere freddo: *it is freezing to-night*, stasera fa molto freddo **2.** gelare (passare dallo stato liquido a quello solido); essere coperto di ghiaccio: *the lake was frozen over*, il lago era tutto gelato; *the ship was frozen in*, la nave restò prigioniera dei ghiacci; *the water froze*, l'acqua gelò **3.** sentir freddo, gelare: *I am freezing*, gelo dal freddo; *to — to death*, morire assiderato; (*fam.*) avere molto freddo **4.** *fig.* agghiacciare, agghiacciarsi: *my blood froze at the sight*, a quella vista mi si agghiacciò il sangue; *to — the blood*, agghiacciare il sangue **5.** rimanere attaccato (per il freddo); rimanere rigido, irrigidirsi: *his fingers froze on to his rifle*, le dita gli si incollarono al fucile per il freddo **6.** congelare (p.e. carne per conservarla) **7.** (econ. comm.) congelare, bloccare (prezzi, salari) **8.** *to — out*, escludere (da affari, competizioni, ecc.) ‖ *to be frozen out*, (sl.) scioperare per il freddo (di operai).

freezer ['fri:zə*], *s.* impianto refrigerante, cella frigorifera.

freezing ['fri:ziŋ], *ag.* glaciale (anche *fig.*) ‖ *s.* **1.** congelamento **2.** (econ. comm.) blocco, congelamento ☆ *— mixture*, miscela congelante; *— -point*, punto di congelamento: *below —-point*, zotto zero.

freight [freit], *s.* **1.** nolo, costo di trasporto; costo di noleggio (di nave, ecc.) **2.** carico **3.** trasporto (di merce) ☆ *— car*, (amer.) carro merci; *— plane*, aereo da trasporto; *— train*, (amer.) treno merci ‖ *dead —*, nolo vuoto per pieno; *paying —*, carico pagante.

to freight, *v.t.* **1.** noleggiare **2.** caricare (una nave) **3.** trasportare, spedire (merci, ecc.).

freightage ['freitidʒ], *s.* **1.** nolo, noleggio **2.** trasporto (di merce) via acqua, (amer.) via acqua, via terra **3.** costo di trasporto.

freighter ['freitə*], *s.* **1.** noleggiatore (di una nave) **2.** esportatore **3.** (amer.) consegnatario (di merce per trasporto via terra) **4.** nave da carico; (amer.) vagone merci.

freighting ['freitiŋ], *V.* **freightage**.

fremitus ['fremitəs], *s.* (invariato al pl.) (med.) fremito.

French [frentʃ], *ag.* francese ‖ *the —*, i francesi ‖ *to take — leave*, andarsene senza salutare, andarsene all'inglese ‖ *s.* il francese (lingua) ☆ *— -beans*, fagiolini verdi; *— -beaver*, pelle imitazione castoro; *— grey*, grigio rosato; *— -roll*, panino; *— -roof*, (arch.) tetto a mansarda; *— -window*, porta-finestra.

frenchification [ˌfrentʃifi'keiʃən], *s.* infranciosamento.

to frenchify ['frentʃifai], *v.t.i.* franceseggiare.

Frenchless ['frentʃlis], *ag.* che non sa il francese.

Frenchman, *pl.* **Frenchmen** ['frentʃmən], *s.* (uomo) francese.

Frenchwoman ['frentʃˌwumən], *pl.* **Frenchwomen** ['frentʃ wimin], *s.* (donna) francese.

frenchy ['frentʃi], *ag.* (spreg.) franceseggiante (di persona).

frenetic(al) [fri'netik(əl)], *ag.* frenetico; pazzo.

frenum, *V.* **fraenum**.

frenzied ['frenzid], *ag.* frenetico.

frenzy ['frenzi], *s.* **1.** frenesia, parossismo; *— of joy*, trasporto di gioia **2.** (patol.) delirio, pazzia.

frequency ['fri:kwənsi], *s.* **1.** frequenza, ripetizione continua **2.** (elett.) frequenza ☆ *— modulation*, (neol. rad.) modulazione di frequenza ‖ *high- —*, *low- —*, ad alta, bassa frequenza.

frequent ['fri:kwənt], *ag.* frequente; diffuso; numeroso: *— pulse*, (med.) polso frequente.

to frequent [fri'kwent], *v.t.* frequentare (teatri, caffè, ecc.): *an ill-frequented street*, una strada mal frequentata; *to — s.o.*, frequentare qlcu.

frequentable [fri'kwentəbl], *ag.* frequentabile, accessibile.

frequentation [ˌfri:kwen'teiʃən], *s.* il frequentare.

frequentative [fri'kwentətiv], *ag.* (gram.) frequentativo.

frequenter [fri'kwentə*], *s.c.* frequentatore, frequentatrice.

frequently ['fri:kwəntli], *av.* frequentemente, a brevi intervalli, sovente.

fresco ['freskou], *pl.* **frescos, frescoes** ['freskouz], *s.* (pitt.) affresco; arte dell'affresco.

fresh [freʃ], *ag.* **1.** fresco: *— eggs, milk, flowers*, uova, latte, fiori freschi **2.** nuovo, non usato: *a — sheet of paper*, un foglio bianco ‖ *to break — ground*, iniziare ql.co. di nuovo **3.** fresco, puro, freddo (di aria, ecc.): *he went for some — air*, uscì a respirare un po' di aria pura **4.** brillante, puro (di colori, carnagione, ecc.): *— colours*, colori brillanti; *— complexion*, carnagione splendente **5.** appena arrivato: *he is — from the country*, è appena arrivato dalla campagna **6.** vigoroso, fresco: *she is — even after six sets of tennis*, non è ancora stanca dopo sei partite di tennis **7.** non conservato: *— butter*, burro fresco (non conservato con sale) **8.** non salato, dolce: *— water*, acqua dolce **9.** *fig.* inesperto **10.** (sl.) brillo, alticcio; (amer.) insolente, arrogante ‖ *s.* **1.** il fresco (del mattino, della sera) **2.** sorgente d'acqua fresca ☆ *— -water*, d'acqua dolce: *he is a — -water sailer, fig.* è un marinaio d'acqua dolce.

fresh, *av.* di nuovo; recentemente; di fresco.

to freshen ['freʃn], *v.t.i.* **1.** rinfrescare, rinfrescarsi; diventare fresco; rinnovare: *the weather is freshening*, il tempo si va rinfrescando **2.** (far) perdere la salinità (a).

freshet ['freʃit], *s.* **1.** corrente d'acqua dolce che rifluisce nel mare **2.** piena di fiume.

freshish ['freʃiʃ], *ag.* freschetto.

freshly ['freʃli], *av.* **1.** in modo fresco **2.** recentemente **3.** vigorosamente.

freshman, *pl.* **freshmen** ['freʃmən], *s.* matricola d'università.

freshness ['freʃnis], *s.* **1.** freschezza **2.** novità (di avvenimento) **3.** vigoria **4.** inesperienza, ingenuità.

fret[1] [fret], *s.* inquietudine, irritazione: *to be in a —*, essere in (uno stato di) agitazione.

to fret[1], *pass. p.p.* **fretted** ['fretid], *v.t.i.* **1.** affliggersi, crucciarsi; inquietarsi; irritarsi: *the child is fretting for its mother*, il bimbo piagnucola perchè vuole la mamma; *to — over trifles*, irritarsi per cose futili ‖ *to — away one's life*, sciuparsi la vita inquietandosi **2.** rodere, rodersi: *rust has fretted the iron*, la ruggine ha corroso il ferro ‖ *to — and fume, fig.* mordere il freno **3.** incresparsi (di mare, ecc.) **4.** fermentare (di vino).

fret[2], *s.* **1.** (arch.) fregio; greca **2.** lavoro ad intaglio (p.e. nel legno) ☆ *— -saw*, sega da traforo; *— -work*, lavoro di traforo.

to fret[2], *v.t.* **1.** (arch.) ornare con greca **2.** traforare, intagliare (legno).

fret[3], *s.* (mus.) tasto (di chitarra, mandolino, ecc.).

to fret[3], *v.t.* (mus.) fornire (chitarra, ecc.) di tasti.

fretful ['fretful], *ag.* di cattivo umore; irritabile.

fretfully ['fretfuli], *av.* di cattivo umore; con irritazione.

fretfulness ['fretfulnis], *s.* cattivo umore; irritabilità.

fretting ['fretiŋ], *ag.* tormentoso; irritante ‖ *s.* tormento; irritazione.

fretty ['freti], *ag.* adorno di greche.

friability [,fraiə'biliti], *s.* friabilità.

friable ['fraiəbl], *ag.* friabile.

friableness ['fraiəblnis], *s.* friabilità.

friar ['fraiə*], *s.* **1.** frate, monaco **2.** (*tip.*) frate ☆ —'s balsam, (*chim.*) tintura di benzoino ‖ *Austin* - — (o *Augustinian* —), agostiniano; *Black-* —, domenicano; *Grey-* —, francescano; *White-* —, carmelitano.

friarly ['fraiəli], *ag.* di, da frate.

friary ['fraiəri], *s.* convento di frati.

fribble ['fribl], *s.* **1.** persona frivola **2.** frivolezza.

to fribble, *v.i.* baloccarsi, gingillarsi.

fribblish ['fribliʃ], *ag.* frivolo.

fricandeau ['frikəndou], *pl.* **fricandeaux** ['frikəndouz], *s.* (*cuc.*) fricandò.

fricassee [,frikə'si:], *s.* (*cuc.*) fricassea.

fricative ['frikətiv], *ag.* (*fonet.*) fricativo ‖ *s.* consonante fricativa.

friction ['frikʃən], *s.* **1.** (*med.*) frizione, massaggio **2.** (*mec. fis.*) sfregamento; frizione; attrito **3.** *fig.* attrito, antagonismo, divergenza ☆ — brake, (*mec.*) freno ad attrito; — clutch, (*aut.*) innesto a frizione; — -gearing, (*mec.*) trasmissione a ruote di frizione; — plate, (*mec.*) disco della frizione ‖ rolling —, (*mec.*) attrito volvente; single-pass —, (*ind.*) frizionatura ad un passaggio; skin —, attrito di superficie.

frictional ['frikʃənl], *ag.* di frizione; d'attrito.

frictionless ['frikʃənlis], *ag.* senza frizione, attrito.

Friday ['fraidi], *s.* venerdì: last —, venerdì scorso; a week last —, sono stati otto giorni venerdì; a week next —, venerdì otto; come next —, venite venerdì prossimo; come on —, venite venerdì; he comes on Fridays, viene il venerdì ‖ Good —, Venerdì Santo.

fridge [fridʒ], *s.* (*sl.*) frigorifero.

fried [fraid], *ag.* **1.** (*cuc.*) fritto **2.** (*sl. amer.*) ubriaco.

friend [frend], *s.c.* **1.** amico, amica: a — of the family, un amico di famiglia; a — of mine, un mio amico; a bosom —, un amico intimo; a man (o boy) —, un amico; a woman (o lady o girl) —, un'amica; to be friends (with), essere amici (di); to make friends again, riallacciare l'amicizia, rappacificarsi; to make friends with, fare amicizia con ‖ a — in need is a — indeed, prov. un vero amico si conosce nel bisogno **2.** protettore, protettrice: he was a — to our home for the poor, egli sosteneva il nostro asilo per i poveri **3.** Friend, (relig.) quacquero, quacquera: the Society of Friends, i quacqueri ‖ *s.* padrino, secondo (in duello).

friendless ['frendlis], *ag.* senza amici; abbandonato: to be completely —, essere solo al mondo.

friendlessness ['frendlisnis], *s.* mancanza di amicizie; abbandono, solitudine.

friendlily ['frendlili], *av.* (*rar.*) amichevolmente.

friendliness ['frendlinis], *s.* cordialità, benevolenza.

friendly ['frendli], *ag.* **1.** amichevole; amico: a — nation, una nazione amica; in a — manner (o way), amichevolmente, in modo amichevole; to be — with s.o., essere amico di qlcu.; to be on — terms, essere in relazioni amichevoli ‖ Friendly Society, società di mutuo soccorso **2.** propizio, favorevole; — winds, venti propizi; to give s.o. a — reception, fare una buona accoglienza a qlcu. ‖ *s.* indigeno amico.

friendly, *av.* amichevolmente.

friendship ['frendʃip], *s.* amicizia: a lifelong —, un'amicizia di tutta la vita; I did it out of —, l'ho fatto per amicizia.

frieze[1] [fri:z], *s.* rascia (panno di lana).

to frieze[1], *v.t.* (*ind. tessile*) ratinare.

frieze[2], *s.* (*arch.*) fregio.

frig [fridʒ], *s.* (*sl.*) frigorifero.

frigate ['frigit], *s.* (*mar.*) fregata ☆ — -bird, (*ornit.*) fregata.

fright [frait], *s.* **1.** paura; spavento: he was seized with —, la paura lo assalì; to die of —, morire di spavento; to get a —, spaventarsi; to give s.o. a —, spaventare qlcu.; to take — at, spaventarsi di **2.** (*fam.*) persona grottesca, ridicola, brutta: what a — she is!, quant'è brutta!.

to fright, *v.t.* (*poet.*) spaventare.

to frighten ['fraitn], *v.t.* spaventare, far paura a; terrorizzare: to — s.o. into, out of doing sthg., costringere qlcu. a fare, a non fare ql.co. facendogli paura ‖ to — to death, far morire di paura.

frightful ['fraitful], *ag.* **1.** spaventevole; terribile **2.** (*fam.*) brutto, orribile: what a — dress!, che brutto vestito!.

frightfully ['fraitfli], *av.* **1.** spaventevolmente; terribilmente **2.** orribilmente.

frightfulness ['fraitfulnis], *s.* spavento, terrore.

frigid ['fridʒid], *ag.* **1.** glaciale ‖ the — zone, la zona glaciale **2.** frigido, apatico; insipido **3.** freddo, formale: she gave us a — welcome, ella ci fece un'accoglienza fredda.

frigidity [fri'dʒiditi], *s.* **1.** freddezza **2.** frigidità, apatia **3.** formalismo.

frigidly ['fridʒidli], *av.* **1.** freddamente **2.** frigidamente, apaticamente **3.** formalmente.

frigidness ['fridʒidnis], *s.* frigidezza.

frill [fril], *s.* **1.** fronzolo; gala increspata ‖ to put on frills, (*sl.*) essere affettato, darsi delle arie **2.** (*di animale*) collare **3.** (*anat.*) mesenterio di animale **4.** (*foto.*) distacco (della gelatina).

to frill, *v.t.i.* **1.** ornare di gale, di increspature; arricciarsi, incresparsi **2.** (*foto.*) staccarsi (della gelatina).

frilled [frild], *ag.* ornato con gale; increspato.

frillies ['friliz], *s.pl.* (*fam.*) sottoveste con increspature, gale.

frilling ['friliŋ], *s.* **1.** increspatura **2.** (*foto.*) distacco (della gelatina).

frilly ['frili], *ag.* increspato, ornato di gale.

Frimaire [fri:'mɛə*], *s.* (*st. francese*) frimaio.

fringe [frindʒ], *s.* **1.** frangia **2.** frangetta (di capelli) **3.** orlo; bordo; limite; zona periferica: on the — of the desert, al limite del deserto **4.** (*foto.*) iridescenza.

to fringe, *v.t.* **1.** ornare con frangia **2.** orlare, limitare: a road fringed with poplars, una strada fiancheggiata da pioppi.

fringy ['frindʒi], *ag.* frangiato; ornato di frangia.

frippery ['fripəri], *s.* **1.** fronzoli (anche *fig.*); cianfrusaglie, ninnoli **2.** abiti fuori uso.

Frisco ['friskou], *no.pr.* (*geog.*) dim. di **San Francisco**.

frisette [fri'zet], *s.* frangetta (di capelli artificiali).

Frisian ['friziən], *ag.s.c.* frisone.

frisk [frisk], *s.* salto; capriola: with a — of his tail, con un colpo di coda (di cavallo, cane).

to frisk, *v.i.* saltellare, far capriole: the kittens were frisking about, i gattini facevano capriole.

frisket ['friskit], *s.* (*tip.*) fraschetta.

friskily ['friskili], *av.* gaiamente; vivacemente; con piccoli salti.

friskiness ['friskinis], *s.* allegria; vivacità; il saltellare gaiamente.

frisky ['friski], *ag.* gaio; vivace, saltellante: a — lamb, un agnellino zampettante.

frit [frit], *s.* **1.** vetro poroso **2.** (*artig.*) vetrina, fritta da smalto.

to frit, *pass.p.p.* **fritted** ['fritid], *v.t.* (*ind. vetraria*) calcinare; agglomerare.

frit-fly ['fritflai], *s.* (*entom.*) oscinide.

frith[1] [friθ], *s.* (*arc.*) tranquillità; sicurezza.

frith[2], *s.* **1.** (*rar.*) bosco, boscaglia; brughiera **2.** radura **3.** siepe; graticcio **4.** macchia, sottobosco.

to frith[2], *v.t.i.* (*dial.*) **1.** recingere con palizzata **2.** tagliare il sottobosco.

frith[3], *s.* estuario.

fritillary [fri'tiləri], *s.* (*bot.*) fritillaria.

fritt, *V.* **frit.**

fritter[1] ['fritə*], *s.* frittella (di mele, ecc.).

fritter[2], *s. gener. pl.* frammento.

to fritter[2], *v.t.* **1.** (*rar.*) tagliuzzare, ridurre in frammenti **2.** *to* — **away**, sciupare (denaro, energie, ecc.): *he fritters his time away*, spreca il tempo in cose inutili.

Fritz [frits], *s.* (*sl.*) soldato tedesco; aereo, sommergibile tedesco.

to frivol ['frivəl], *pass.p.p.* **frivolled** ['frivəld], *v.t.i.* **1.** frivoleggiare **2.** gingillarsi **3.** *to* — **away**, sprecare, sperperare (tempo, denaro).

frivolity [fri'voliti], *s.* frivolezza, leggerezza, vanità.

frivolous ['frivələs], *ag.* frivolo, leggero, vano.

frivolously ['frivələsli], *av.* frivolmente, con leggerezza.

frivolousness ['frivələsnis], *V.* **frivolity.**

friz(z)[1] [friz], *s.* ricciolo, riccioli; capelli ricci.

to friz(z)[1], *v.t.i.* **1.** arricciare, arricciarsi; increspare, incresparsi (di capelli) **2.** levigare (con pietra pomice) **3.** (*ind. tessile*) ratinare.

to frizz[2], *v.i.* sfrigolare.

frizzle[1] ['frizl], *s.* capelli ricci, crespi.

to frizzle[1], *v.t.i.* arricciare, arricciarsi (di capelli).

frizzle[2], *s.* acciarino (di arma da fuoco).

to frizzle[3], *v.t.i.* cuocere alla griglia; friggere; sfrigolare (di grassi, ecc.).

frizzly ['frizli], **frizzy** ['frizi], *ag.* crespo, riccio, ricciuto (di capelli).

fro [frou], *av.* (*usato solo nella l. av.*): *to and* —, avanti e indietro.

frock [frok], *s.* **1.** abito, vestito intero (da donna, bimbo) **2.** (*eccl.*) tonaca; *fig.* spirito sacerdotale **3.** giubbotto; grembialone (degli operai); giubba militare; maglia di marinaio ☆ — *-coat*, « redingote », finanziera.

to frock, *v.t.* rivestire dell'abito talare; ordinare.

frog[1] [frog], *s.* **1.** rana || *to have a* — *in one's throat*, avere la voce rauca **2.** (*patol.*) afta ☆ — *-eater*, (*spreg.*) francese; — *-fish* (o *fishing* —), rana pescatrice; — *-in-the throat*, raucedine; — *-tongue*, (*patol.*) ranula || *leap-* —, (*giuoco*) cavallina.

frog[2], *s.* fettone, forchetta (in zoccolo di cavallo).

frog[3], *s.* **1.** fermaglio, dragona (di spada) **2.** alamaro, allacciatura di giacca militare.

frog[4], *s.* (*ferr.*) cuore.

frogman, *pl.* **frogmen** ['frogmən], *s.* sommozzatore.

frolic ['frolik], *ag.* (*arc.*) scherzoso, allegro || *s.* scherzo, monelleria.

to frolic, *v.i.* fare scherzi; trastullarsi.

frolicsome ['froliksəm], *ag.* allegro, vivace, scherzoso, pazzerello.

frolicsomely ['froliksəmli], *av.* allegramente, vivacemente, scherzosamente.

frolicsomeness ['froliksəmnis], *s.* allegria, vivacità.

from [from (*forma forte*), frəm (*forma debole*)], *prep.* **1.** (*moto da luogo, separazione, allontanamento, decorrenza, distanza*) da: — *Monday onwards*, da lunedì in poi; — *one to five*, da uno a cinque; *the book fell* — *the table*, il libro cadde dal tavolo; *he has just arrived* — *Paris*, è appena arrivato da Parigi; *he parted* — *him*, si separò da lui; *how far is it* — *London to Dover?*, quanto c'è da Londra a Dover?; *she is absent* — *school*, è assente da scuola; *this train goes* — *Milan to Rome*, questo treno va da Milano a Roma; *to live far* — *towns*, vivere lontano dalle città || *to jump* — *over a wall*, saltar giù da un muro **2.** (*origine, provenienza*) da; da parte di: *a dress* — *Hartnell's*, un vestito della casa Hartnell; *perfumes* — *France*, profumi francesi; *cheese is made* — *milk*, il formaggio è fatto col latte; *his family is descended* — *Cavour*, la sua famiglia discende da Cavour; *I received a parcel* — *my friend*, ricevetti un pacco dal mio amico; *tell him* — *me*, digli da parte mia; *this word comes* — *Greek*, questa parola deriva dal greco; " *What country do you*

come — ? ", " — *China* ", « Da quale paese venite? », « *Dalla Cina* »; " *Where are you* — ? ", " — *Genoa* ", « Di dove siete? », « Di Genova »; *who(m) is that letter* — ?, da chi viene quella lettera? **3.** (*causa, ragione*) per, a motivo di, da: *pale* — *fright*, pallido dalla paura; *weak* — *hunger*, indebolito dalla fame; *to die* — *wounds*, morire per le ferite; *to speak* — *experience*, parlare per esperienza; *to suffer* — *gout, the cold*, soffrire per la gotta, per il freddo **4.** (*cambiamento*) da: *office-boy he became manager*, da fattorino divenne direttore **5.** (*Fraseologia*): — *afar*, da lontano; — *among*, fra; — *within*, — *without*, dal di dentro, dal di fuori || — *bad to worse*, di male in peggio; — *beginning to end* (o — *first to last*), dal principio alla fine; — *day to day*, di giorno in giorno; — *henceforth* (o — *now on*), d'ora innanzi; — *morning to night*, da mattina a sera; — *place to place*, da un luogo all'altro; — *time to time*, di quando in quando; — *top to toe*, da capo a piedi || *as* — *today*, (*comm.*) a datare da oggi || *to live* — *hand to mouth*, vivere alla giornata.

frond [frond], *s.* (*bot.*) fronda.

frondage ['frondidʒ], *s.* fogliame.

Fronde [fro:nd], *s.* **1.** (*st. francese*) fronda **2.** partito d'opposizione, ribelle.

frondose ['frondous], *ag.* frondoso.

front [frʌnt], *ag.* **1.** di fronte, davanti, anteriore: — *wheel*, ruota anteriore **2.** (*fonet.*) palatale, anteriore || *s.* **1.** parte anteriore; (*arch.*) facciata: *the* — *of the house*, la facciata della casa; *the* — *of the shirt*, lo sparato della camicia || *in* —, avanti, di fronte: *go in* —, andate avanti; *in* —, davanti a: *the house in* — *of the church*, la casa di fronte alla chiesa; *he was in* — *of me*, era davanti a me || *to come to the* —, *fig.* farsi conoscere, mettersi in evidenza **2.** (*mil. pol.*) fronte: *popular* —, fronte popolare; *to be sent to the* —, essere mandato al fronte **3.** passeggiata lungomare: *a house on the* —, una casa sul lungomare **4.** sfrontatezza: *to have the* — *to do sthg.*, avere la sfrontatezza di fare ql.co.; *to present* (o *to put*) *a bold* — *on a situation*, affrontare con coraggio una situazione **5.** (*poet.*) fronte; viso ☆ — *-bench*, seggio alla Camera dei Comuni occupato da ministri, ex-ministri; — *-carriage*, vettura di testa; — *-door*, porta d'entrata; — *-garden*, giardino davanti a una casa; — *-page*, prima pagina (di giornale, ecc.); — *-rank*, prima fila: *to be in the* — *-rank*, essere in prima fila; *fig.* essere ben noto ed importante; — *-ranker*, artista, ecc. di primo piano.

to front, *v.t.i.* **1.** essere situato in faccia, davanti (a); guardare (su):| *the windows* — (*upon*) *the garden*, le finestre guardano sul giardino **2.** opporsi a, affrontare **3.** (*arch.*) fare una (nuova) facciata a (un edificio).

frontage ['frʌntidʒ], *s.* **1.** esposizione d'una casa; terreno compreso tra la facciata di una casa e la strada **2.** (*arch.*) facciata **3.** veduta, prospetto.

frontal ['frʌntl], *ag.* frontale: — *attack*, attacco frontale || *s.* **1.** (*arch.*) facciata **2.** (*eccl.*) paliotto **3.** striscia, nastro posto sulla fronte **4.** — (*bone*), (*anat.*) osso frontale.

frontally ['frʌntəli], *av.* di fronte.

fronted ['frʌntid], *ag.* (*arch.*) munito di facciata.

frontier ['frʌntjə*], *s.* **1.** confine, frontiera **2.** (*amer.*) estremi limiti della civiltà (oltre i quali ci sono regioni inesplorate) **3.** *fig. gener. pl.* confini, limiti: *frontiers of knowledge*, limiti della conoscenza.

frontier(s)man, *pl.* **frontier(s)men** ['frʌntjə(z)mən], *s.* **1.** abitante di frontiera **2.** (*amer.*) pioniere.

frontispiece ['frʌntispi:s], *s.* **1.** (*arch.*) facciata; frontespizio **2.** (*tip.*) frontespizio **3.** (*sl. spec. boxe*) faccia.

to frontispiece, *v.t.* **1.** (*arch.*) munire di frontespizio **2.** (*tip.*) mettere come frontespizio.

frontless ['frʌntlis], *ag.* (*rar.*) sfacciato, sfrontato.

frontlet ['frʌntlit], *s.* **1.** benda per la fronte **2.** fronte di animale **3.** (*eccl.*) paliotto.

fronton ['frʌntən], *s.* (*arch.*) frontone.

frontward(s) ['frʌntwəd(z)],*av.*sul davanti; in avanti.

frore [frɔ:*], *ag.* (*poet.*) gelato, ghiacciato.

frost [frɔst], *s.* **1.** gelo; brina; depositi di ghiaccio ‖ *Jack Frost,* il Gelo (personificato) **2.** congelamento **3.** *fig.* freddezza **4.** (*sl.*) fiasco, insuccesso ☆ — *-bite,* (*patol.*) congelamento; — *-bitten,* (*patol.*) congelato; — *-nail,* rampone, chiodo da ghiaccio; — *-tender,* sensibile al freddo; — *-weed,* (*bot.*) eliantemo ‖ *black* —, freddo intenso senza brina; *hoar-* — (o *white* —), brina, brinata; *late* —, gelo primaverile.

to frost, *v.t.* **1.** far gelare (piante, ecc.); coprire di brina **2.** (*cuc.*) candire, glassare; congelare (cibi) **3.** smerigliare (vetro, ecc.) **4.** ferrare a ghiaccio (un cavallo) **5.** incanutire.

frosted ['frɔstid], *ag.* **1.** gelato; brinato **2.** (*cuc.*) glassato; congelato **3.** smerigliato.

frostily ['frɔstili], *av.* in modo glaciale, gelido.

frostiness ['frɔstinis], *s.* **1.** freddo glaciale **2.** *fig.* freddezza: *the — of my reception,* l'accoglienza gelida che mi è stata fatta.

frosting ['frɔstiŋ], *s.* **1.** (*cuc.*) glassatura **2.** smerigliatura.

frosty ['frɔsti], *ag.* gelato; *fig.* glaciale, gelido.

froth [frɔθ], *s.* **1.** schiuma (di birra, ecc.) **2.** *fig.* frivolezza; futilità (di discorso) ☆ — *-blower,* (*sl.*) bevitore di birra ‖ *sea-* —, spuma di mare.

to froth, *v.t.i.* far schiuma, (far) spumare: *the mad dog frothed at the mouth,* il cane idrofobo schiumava alla bocca.

frothily ['frɔθili], *av.* **1.** con spuma, schiuma; in modo spumeggiante **2.** frivolamente, futilmente.

frothiness ['frɔθinis], *s.* **1.** spumosità **2.** (*fam.*) futilità (di discorso).

frothy ['frɔθi], *ag.* **1.** schiumoso **2.** leggero (di tessuto) **3.** (*fam.*) frivolo, vuoto (di discorso).

frou-frou ['fru:-fru:], *s.* fruscio (specialmente di abiti).

frow [frau], *s.* (donna) olandese.

froward ['frouəd], *ag.* (*arc.*) ritroso, ostinato, ribelle.

frowardly ['frouədli], *av.* ostinatamente, da ribelle.

frowardness ['frouədnis], *s.* (*arc.*) ritrosità, indocilità.

frown [fraun], *s.* l'aggrottare delle ciglia; cipiglio, viso arcigno; occhiata di disapprovazione.

to frown, *v.t.i.* aggrottare le ciglia; guardare con un viso arcigno: — *at* (o *upon*) *s.o.,* guardare qlcu. in cagnesco; disapprovare qlcu.; *to* — *s.o. into silence* (o *to* — *s.o. down*), imporre il silenzio a qlcu. con una occhiata severa.

frowning ['frauniŋ], *ag.* **1.** accigliato, arcigno **2.** scuro, minaccioso (di cose) ‖ *s.* cipiglio.

frowningly ['frauniŋli], *av.* con cipiglio; minacciosamente.

frowst [fraust], *s.* (*fam.*) aria surriscaldata; tanfo di rinchiuso.

to frowst, *v.i.* stare in un locale dove l'aria è viziata.

frowsty ['frausti], *ag.* di cattivo odore, che sa di rinchiuso.

frowziness ['frauzinis], *s.* **1.** puzza di rinchiuso **2.** sporcizia.

frowzy ['frauzi], *ag.* (*sl.*) **1.** che puzza di rinchiuso **2.** mal tenuto, sporco.

froze [frouz], *pass.* di to **freeze.**

frozen ['frouzn], *p.p.* di to **freeze** ‖ *ag.* gelato, congelato, ghiacciato (anche *fig.*) ☆ — *capital,* (*econ.*) capitale bloccato; — *credits,* (*comm.*) crediti congelati; — *meat,* carne congelata.

fructed ['frʌktid], *ag.* (*arald.*) fruttifero.

Fructidor [,frju:kti:'dɔ:*], *s.* (*st. francese*) fruttidoro.

fructiferous [frʌk'tifərəs], *ag.* fruttifero.

fructification [,frʌktifi'keifən], *s.* **1.** fruttificazione **2.** organi riproduttori della pianta.

to fructify ['frʌktifai], *v.t.i.* **1.** fruttificare, produrre frutti (anche *fig.*) **2.** fecondare, fertilizzare.

fructose ['frʌktous], *s.* glucosio.

to fructuate ['frʌktjueit], *v.i.* fruttificare.

fructuation [,frʌktju'eifən], *s.* fruttificazione (anche *fig.*).

fructuous ['frʌktjuəs], *ag.* fruttuoso; fruttifero (anche *fig.*).

frugal ['fru:gəl], *ag.* **1.** frugale, parco, sobrio **2.** sobrio, economo (di persone): — *woman,* donna economa.

frugalist ['fru:gəlist], *s.c.* persona frugale.

frugality [fru(:)'gæliti], *s.* **1.** frugalità, sobrietà **2.** economia.

frugally ['fru:gəli], *av.* **1.** frugalmente, sobriamente **2.** economicamente.

frugiferous [fru(:)'dʒifərəs], *ag.* frugifero.

frugivorous [fru(:)'dʒivərəs], *ag.* (*zool.*) frugivoro.

fruit [fru:t], *s.* **1.** *gener. sing.* frutta: — *is good for children,* la frutta fa bene ai bambini; *do you eat much* —?, mangi molta frutta? **2.** frutto, prodotto della terra: *the fruits of the earth,* i diversi prodotti della terra **3.** organo riproduttore di una pianta **4.** *fig. gener. pl.* frutto, prodotto, risultato: *the fruits of labour,* i frutti del lavoro; *her knowledge was the fruit of much study,* la sua cultura era il frutto di lunghi studi **5.** (*Bibbia*) figli, discendenza ☆ — *-basket,* cestino per frutta; — *-bud,* (*bot.*) gemma fruttifera; — *-cake,* panfrutto; — *-flan,* torta di frutta; — *-grove,* frutteto; — *-grower,* frutticultore; — *-growing,* frutticultura; — *knife,* coltello da frutta; — *-preserving,* conservazione della frutta; — *salad,* macedonia di frutta; — *-tree,* albero da frutta ‖ *dry* —, frutta secca; *first* —, primizie; *wall-* —, frutto di spalliera.

to fruit, *v.t.i.* fruttificare, far fruttificare: *this tree fruits well,* questo albero dà buoni frutti.

fruitage ['fru:tidʒ], *s.* **1.** frutta **2.** *fig.* risultato, prodotto, conseguenza.

fruitarian [fru:'tɛəriən], *s.c.* chi si nutre di frutta.

fruiter ['fru:tə*], *s.* **1.** pianta da frutta **2.** nave per trasporto di frutta **3.** frutticultore.

fruiterer ['fru:tərə*], *s.* commerciante di frutta; fruttivendolo.

fruiteress ['fru:təris], *s.* fruttivendola.

fruitery ['fru:təri], *s.* (magazzino per la) frutta.

fruitful ['fru:tful], *ag.* **1.** fruttifero, fertile: *a* — *soil,* un terreno fertile; *a* — *tree,* un albero fruttifero **2.** (*letter.*) prolifico, fecondo **3.** redditizio, vantaggioso, rimunerativo: *a* — *plan,* un piano vantaggioso.

fruitfully ['fru:tfuli], *av.* fruttuosamente; vantaggiosamente.

fruitfulness ['fru:tfulnis], *s.* **1.** fertilità, fecondità (anche *fig.*) **2.** vantaggio, utilità.

fruition [fru(:)'ifən], *s.* realizzazione (di speranze); godimento, gioia (di possedere una cosa desiderata).

fruitless ['fru:tlis], *ag.* **1.** infruttuoso, sterile, arido (anche *fig.*) **2.** svantaggioso, inutile, vano.

fruitlessly ['fru:tlisli], *av.* **1.** sterilmente **2.** inutilmente.

fruitlessness ['fru:tlisnis], *s.* **1.** sterilità **2.** inutilità.

fruity ['fru:ti], *ag.* **1.** che sa di frutta; gustoso (di vino) **2.** (*fam.*) piccante; suggestivo.

frumentaceous [,fru:mən'teifəs], *ag.* frumentaceo.

frumentarious [,fru:mən'tɛəriəs], *ag.* frumentario.

frumentation [,fru:mən'teifən], *s.* (*st. romana*) frumentazione.

frumenty ['fru:mənti], *s.* (*cuc.*) frumento sbucciato e cotto nel latte.

frump [frʌmp], *s.* **1.** (*sl.*) donna vestita con abiti fuori moda, malvestita, trascurata **2.** *pl.* cattivo umore.

frumpish ['frʌmpif], **frumpy** ['frʌmpi], *ag.* **1.** trasandato, malvestito **2.** di brutto carattere, intrattabile.

to frustrate [frʌs'treit], *v.t.* deludere; ingannare; ostacolare, rendere inutile, vano (un piano, un progetto): *frustrated ambition,* ambizione delusa; *to* — *a plot,* impedire un complotto.

frustration [frʌs'treiʃən], frustrazione (di speranza); amara delusione.

frustrative ['frʌstreitiv], **frustratory** ['frʌstrətəri], *ag.* delusivo, fallace.

frustum ['frʌstəm], *pl.* **frusta** ['frʌstə], **frustums** ['frʌstəmz], *s.* (*geom.*) tronco (di solido).

frutex ['fru:teks], *s.* (*bot.*) frutice.

fruticose ['fru:tikous], *ag.* (*bot.*) fruticoso.

to **frutify** ['fru:tifai], *v.i.* (*arc. poet.*) fruttificare.

fry[1] [frai], *s.* **1.** (*cuc.*) fritto, frittura **2.** (*fam.*) eccitazione: *to be in a —,* essere smanioso.

to **fry**[1], *pass.p.p.* **fried** [fraid], *v.t.i.* friggere, far friggere: *fried eggs,* uova fritte; *to — fish,* friggere pesce; *to — with impatience, fig.* struggersi, essere impaziente ☆ *frying-pan,* padella: *to jump out of the frying-pan into the fire,* cadere dalla padella nella brace.

fry[2], *s.coll.* **1.** (*fam.*) avannotti; pesci appena nati **2.** piccoli (di animali multipari) **3.** persone, cose di nessuna importanza.

fuchsia ['fju:ʃə], *s.* (*bot.*) fucsia.

fucus ['fju:kəs], *pl.* **fuci** ['fju:sai], *s.* (*bot.*) fuco.

fuddle ['fʌdl], *s.* **1.** stato di confusione mentale, annebbiamento: *to be in a —,* essere annebbiato (per il troppo bere) **2.** (*fam.*) baldoria, gozzoviglia: *to go on the —,* gozzovigliare, far baldoria.

to **fuddle**, *v.t.i.* **1.** confondere, intontire, istupidire: *the wine has fuddled his brain,* il vino gli ha annebbiato il cervello **2.** (*fam.*) far baldoria, gozzovigliare.

fuddy-duddy ['fʌdi'dadi], *ag.* (*sl.*) pedante; criticone; reazionario ‖ *s.* (*sl.*) codino, retrogrado.

fudge [fʌdʒ], *s.* **1.** fandonia, frottola **2.** (*cuc.*) dolce caramellato con cioccolata **3.** notizia stampata all'ultimo momento.

to **fudge**, *v.t.i.* **1.** rattoppare, rappezzare, mettere insieme alla meglio **2.** *fig.* agire disonestamente, ingannare, truffare.

fudge, *inter.* sciocchezze!.

fudgy ['fʌdʒi], *ag.* **1.** irritabile **2.** goffo.

fuel ['fju:əl], *s.* **1.** combustibile, carburante: *liquid —,* (*aut.*) combustibile liquido **2.** *fig.* alimento, esca ‖ *to add — to the flame, fig.* soffiare sul fuoco ☆ *— oil,* nafta, olio pesante.

to **fuel**, *pass.p.p.* **fuelled** ['fju:əld], *v.t.i.* alimentare di combustibile (una fornace, ecc.); fornire di carburante; procurarsi combustibile: *fuelled from capacious tanks,* fornito di carburante da capaci cisterne.

fuelling ['fju:əliŋ], *s.* **1.** approvvigionamento **2.** *pl.* combustibili ☆ *— station,* posto di rifornimento (di combustibile).

fug [fʌg], *s.* (*fam.*) odore di stantio, di chiuso.

to **fug**, *pass.p.p.* **fugged** [fʌgd], *v.i.* (*fam.*) stare in un'atmosfera pesante, impura.

fugacious [fju(:)'geiʃəs], *ag.* fugace, fuggevole, effimero.

fugaciousness [fju(:)'geiʃəsnis], *s.* fuggevolezza.

fugacity [fju(:)'gæsiti], *s.* fugacità.

fuggy ['fʌgi], *ag.* (*fam.*) stantio.

fugitive ['fju:dʒitiv], *ag.* **1.** fuggitivo, fuggiasco **2.** passeggero, effimero, temporaneo, fugace ‖ *s.* **1.** fuggitivo, fuggiasco; disertore **2.** profugo, esiliato.

fugitively ['fju:dʒitivli], *av.* fuggevolmente.

fugitiveness ['fju:dʒitivnis], *s.* fuggevolezza.

fugleman, *pl.* **fuglemen** ['fju:glmən], *s.* **1.** (*mil. arc.*) capofila **2.** *fig.* guida; organizzatore; portavoce.

fugue [fju:g], *s.* (*mus.*) fuga.

to **fugue**, *v.i.* (*mus.*) comporre, eseguire una fuga.

fuguist ['fju:gist], *s.* (*mus*) compositore, esecutore di fughe.

fulcrum ['fʌlkrəm], *pl.* **fulcra** ['fʌlkrə], *s.* **1.** (*mec.*) fulcro. *pl.* (*bot.*) viticcio.

to **fulfil** [ful'fil], *pass.p.p.* **fulfilled** [ful'fild], *v.t.* **1.** soddisfare; esaudire; adempiere; ubbidire; compiere (una profezia): *to — an engagement,* mantenere un impegno; *to — the requirements,* corrispondere ai requisiti **2.** finire, completare (periodo, ecc.): *my days are fulfilled,* i miei giorni sono terminati.

fulfiller [ful'filə*], *s.c.* esecutore, esecutrice.

fulfilment [ful'filmənt], *s.* **1.** adempimento; realizzazione; esaudimento; esecuzione (di progetto) **2.** compimento (di periodo, ecc.).

fulgency ['fʌldʒənsi], *s.* fulgidezza.

fulgent ['fʌldʒənt], *ag.* (*poet.*) lucente; fulgido.

fulgently ['fʌldʒəntli], *av.* fulgidamente; fulgentemente.

fulgid ['fʌlgid], *ag.* fulgido.

fulgurant ['fʌlgjuərənt], *ag.* folgorante.

to **fulgurate** ['fʌlgjuəreit], *v.i.* folgorare; lampeggiare, balenare.

fulgurite ['fʌlgjuərait], *s.* (*geol.*) folgorite.

fulham ['fuləm], *s.* dado truccato.

fuliginous [fju:'lidʒinəs], *ag.* fuligginoso.

full[1] [ful], *ag.* **1.** pieno, colmo, ricolmo (anche *fig.*): *the box is — half —,* la scatola è piena, mezzo vuota; *fill your glass —,* riempi il bicchiere fino all'orlo; *my heart is too — for words, fig.* sono troppo emozionato per poter parlare ‖ *to be — up,* essere pieno zeppo: *the bus is — up,* l'autobus è al completo **2.** che ha abbondanza di, ricco di: *a lake — of fish,* un lago pieno di pesci **3.** intero, completo, che ha raggiunto il massimo: *— set of documents,* (*comm.*) serie completa di documenti; *in — bloom,* in piena fioritura; *to go at — speed, gallop,* andare a tutta velocità, a galoppo sfrenato; *to pay in —,* pagare a saldo di ogni avere; *to work — time,* lavorare ad orario pieno **4.** abbondante, copioso, ampio: *a — length novel,* un romanzo di ampia portata; *this dress should be fuller,* questo vestito dovrebbe essere più ampio **5.** sazio: *— stomach,* stomaco pieno **6.** assorbito, tutto preso da (pensiero, idea): *— of himself,* pieno di sè **7.** intenso (di colore, luce); sonoro (di suono); vigoroso (di moto).

full[1], *s.* **1.** pieno, pienezza; colmo **2.** il punto più alto **3.** il tutto, il totale; l'intero ‖ *in —,* completamente: *to write one's name in —,* scrivere il proprio nome per intero ‖ *to the —,* al massimo, completamente: *to enjoy oneself to the —,* divertirsi al massimo.

to **full**[1], *v.t.* rendere ampio; raccogliere in pieghe (abiti).

full[1], *av.* **1.** affatto, interamente **2.** direttamente, esattamente: *to hit s.o. — on his nose,* colpire qlcu. in pieno viso **3.** (*poet.*) molto, ben: *— many a time,* ben spesso.

full[1], (*nei composti*): *— age,* maggiore età; *— -aged,* maggiorenne; *— -back,* (*calcio*) portiere; *— -blooded,* vigoroso, appassionato; di razza pura; *— -blown,* completamente sbocciato; *fig.* in tutto il suo splendore; *— -bodied,* corpulento; *— -cargo,* carico completo di nave; *— -cream,* intero (di latte), *— dress,* abito da cerimonia; *— -face,* dal viso aperto; *— -fledged,* con tutte le penne (di uccello); *fig.* che ha raggiunto il massimo sviluppo: *a — fledged author,* un autore nel pieno della sua maturità; *— -gold standard,* (*econ.*) piena base aurea; *— -grown,* sviluppato, cresciuto; *— -hand,* (*poker*) « full » (tris e coppia); *— -house,* (*teat.*) tutto esaurito; *— -length,* in tutta la lunghezza; *— -moon,* luna piena; *— -mouthed,* dalla dentatura completa; dalla voce sonora; *— -page,* che occupa tutta la pagina; *— -pay,* salario intero; *— -risk,* (*assicurazioni*) pieno di rischio; *— -stop,* punto fermo; *— -size,* in grandezza naturale; *— -summed,* completo in ogni parte; *— -time,* orario completo; *— -voiced,* a gola spiegata.

to **full**[2], *v.t.* (*ind. tessile*) follare (panni).

fuller[1] ['fulə*], *s.* **1.** (*mec.*) presella **2.** scanalatura (specialmente d'un ferro di cavallo).

fuller[2], *s.* **1.** (*ind. tessile*) follatore **2.** follone ☆ *— 's earth,* argilla smectica.

fullness ['fulnis], *s.* pienezza; abbondanza (anche *fig.*); sazietà; ampiezza: *— of the heart,* cuore gonfio; *in the — of time,* a tempo opportuno, a cose mature.

fully ['fuli], *av.* **1.** completamente, interamente, ampiamente: *I — understand,* comprendo perfettamen-

te; *time — dedicated to*, tempo interamente dedicato
a **2.** non meno di, almeno (generalmente con numero):
there were — 10,000 people present, i presenti non erano
meno di 10.000.

fulmar ['fulmə*], *s.* (*ornit.*) procellaria glaciale.

fulminant ['fʌlminənt], *ag.* fulminante.

fulminate ['fʌlmineit], *s.* (*chim.*) fulminato.

to **fulminate**, *v.t.i.* **1.** fulminare; detonare **2.** imprecare, inveire: *to — against the present times*, imprecare contro il momento attuale.

fulmination [,fʌlmi'neiʃən], *s.* **1.** fulminazione **2.** imprecazione; denuncia.

fulminatory ['fʌlminətəri], *ag.* fulminatorio.

to **fulmine** ['fʌlmin], *v.t.i.* (*poet.*) fulminare; tuonare.

fulmineous [fʌl'minjəs], *ag.* (*arc.*) fulmineo.

fulminic [fʌl'minik], *ag.* (*chim.*) fulminico.

fulsome ['fulsəm], *ag.* esagerato, insincero, eccessivo; nauseante; basso.

fulsomely ['fulsəmli], *av.* disgustosamente; in modo
nauseante.

fulsomeness ['fulsəmnis], *s.* l'essere nauseante; bassezza.

Fulvia ['fʌlviə], *no.pr.f.* Fulvia.

fulvous ['fʌlvəs], *ag.* fulvo.

fumade [fju'meid], *s.* aringa affumicata.

fumarole ['fju:məroul], *s.* (*geol.*) fumarola.

to **fumble** ['fʌmbl], *v.t.i.* **1.** muovere le mani goffamente, nervosamente; cercare tastando; andare a tastoni: *he fumbled for the keyhole*, annaspò per trovare
il buco della serratura; *to — about in the dark*, camminare a tastoni nel buio; *to — in one's pocket* (*for a
key*), frugare in tasca (per trovarvi una chiave) **2.** maneggiare in modo maldestro: *to — a ball*, lasciarsi
sfuggire una palla.

fumbler ['fʌmblə*], *s.c.* persona maldestra, goffa.

fumblingly ['fʌmbliŋli], *av.* maldestramente; goffamente; con imperizia.

fume [fju:m], *s.* **1.** *gener. pl.* fumo, vapore, esalazione: *the fumes of incense*, il fumo dell'incenso; *the
fumes of wine*, i fumi del vino; *bad-smelling fumes*,
esalazioni graveolenti **2.** *fig.* stato di eccitazione: *to
be in a — of anxiety*, essere in grande ansia.

to **fume**, *v.t.i.* **1.** esalare fumo, vapore; sfumare **2.** (*fam.*) irritarsi, essere impaziente: *he fumed because he was kept waiting*, s'irritò perchè lo si fece
aspettare; *to fret and — (about trifles)*, essere impaziente (per inezie) **3.** affumicare (legno) per applicare
una patina: *fumed oak*, quercia patinata **4.** profumare
(con incenso, vapori, ecc.); sottoporre a vapori chimici.

to **fumigate** ['fju:migeit], *v.t.* **1.** suffumigare, fare
suffumigi a; purificare con fumi **2.** profumare.

fumigation [,fju:mi'geiʃən], *s.* suffumigio.

fun [fʌn], *s.* **1.** divertimento: *your friend is fond of
—*, al tuo amico piace divertirsi **2.** buffonata; burla,
scherzo: *for* (o *in*) *—*, per ridere, per scherzo; *to make
— of s.o.*, ridere di qlcu., canzonare qlcu. **3.** persona,
cosa divertente; lato ridicolo, buffo (di ql.co.): *I can't
see the — of it*, non ne capisco il lato buffo; *your friend
is great —*, il tuo amico è molto spassoso.

to **funambulate** [fju(:)'næmbjuleit], *v.i.* camminare
su una corda.

funambulism [fju(:)'næmbjulizəm], *s.* funambolismo.

funambulist [fju(:)'næmbjulist], *s.* funambolo.

function ['fʌŋkʃən], *s.* **1.** (*fisiol.*) funzione vitale **2.** scopo, funzione: *the — of education*, lo scopo del-
l'educazione **3.** *gener. pl.* incombenza, funzione: *to
discharge* (o *to perform* o *to fulfil*) *the functions of one's
office*, adempiere le funzioni, le incombenze del proprio ufficio; *to take up one's functions*, entrare in funzione, carica; *to resign one's functions*, dare le dimissioni **4.** cerimonia pubblica, religiosa **5.** (*mat.*) funzione.

to **function**, *v.i.* funzionare; fungere; adempiere ad
una funzione.

functional ['fʌŋkʃən], *ag.* funzionale.

functionally ['fʌŋkʃnəli], *av.* funzionalmente.

functionary ['fʌŋkʃnəri], *s.* funzionario.

functionless ['fʌŋkʃənlis], *ag.* privo di funzioni.

fund [fʌnd], *s.* **1.** fondo, riserva; capacità: *to have a
— of patience*, avere molta pazienza **2.** fondo, capitale, deposito **3.** *pl.* fondi pubblici, obbligazioni ☆ —
-holder, possessori di titoli di rendita || *provident funds*,
fondi di previdenza; *reserve —*, fondo di riserva;
sickness —, cassa malattia; *sinking —*, fondo d'ammortamento.

to **fund**, *v.t.* **1.** investire (denaro) in obbligazioni **2.** (*rar.*) accumulare **3.** consolidare (debiti).

fundament ['fʌndəmənt], *s.* natiche.

fundamental [,fʌndə'mentl], *ag.* fondamentale, essenziale; originale: *a — change*, cambiamento fonda-
mentale; *— rules*, regole fondamentali || *s.* **1.** principio
essenziale; base, fondamento **2.** (*mus.*) tonica.

fundamentalism [,fʌndə'mentəlizəm], *s.* stretta osservanza della tradizione religiosa protestante.

fundamentalist [,fʌndə'mentəlist], *ag.s.* rigido osservante della tradizione religiosa protestante.

fundamentally [,fʌndə'mentəli], *av.* fondamentalmente.

funeral ['fju:nərəl], *ag.* funereo; funebre || *s.* fune-
rale, esequie; corteo funebre: *to attend s.o.'s —*, assi-
stere al funerale di qlcu. || *none of your —*, (*sl.*) non
ti riguarda; *that's your —*, (*sl.*) è affar vostro ☆ — *oration*, orazione funebre; *— pile*, rogo; *— procession*,
corteo funebre; *— service*, ufficio dei defunti; *— train*,
convoglio funebre.

funerary ['fju:nərəri], **funereal** [fju(:)'niəriəl], *ag.*
(*poet.*) funereo, funebre, lugubre; sepolcrale.

fungible ['fʌndʒibl], *ag.* (*dir.*) fungibile.

fungicide ['fʌndʒisaid], *s.* fungicida.

fungiform ['fʌndʒifo:m], *ag.* fungiforme.

fungin ['fʌndʒin], *s.* (*bot.*) fungina.

fungosity [fʌŋ'gositi], *s.* (*patol.*) fungosità.

fungous ['fʌŋgəs], *ag.* (*bot. patol.*) fungoso.

fungus ['fʌŋgəs], *pl.* **fungi** ['fʌŋgai], **funguses** ['fʌŋ-
gəsiz], *s.* (*bot. patol.*) fungo: *edible —*, fungo commestibile.

funicle ['fju:nikl], *s.* (*anat. bot. zool.*) funicolo.

funicular [fju(:)'nikjulə*], *ag.* funicolare ☆ — *railway*, funicolare.

funiculus [fju(:)'nikjuləs], *pl.* **funiculi** [fju(:)'ni-
kjulai], *s.* (*anat. bot. zool.*) funicolo.

funk[1] [fʌŋk], *s.* (*sl.*) paura, timore, fifa: *to be in a
blue —*, avere una fifa blu, avere una paura del diavolo, avere la tremarella in corpo ☆ — *-hole*, (*sl. mil.*)
rifugio sotterraneo di trincea; imboscamento.

to **funk**[1], *v.t.i.* (*sl.*) **1.** avere la tremarella in corpo;
aver paura di: *to — s.o.*, *sthg.*, avere paura di qlcu.,
ql.co.; *to — to do* (o *doing*) *sthg.*, avere paura di fare
ql.co. **2.** cercare di ritrarsi da.

to **funk**[2], *v.t.i.* (*sl.*) **1.** avvolgere in una nube di
fumo **2.** fumare; emettere fumo.

funky ['fʌŋki], *ag.* (*sl.*) pauroso, spaventato: *to feel
—*, aver la tremarella.

funnel ['fʌnl], *s.* **1.** imbuto **2.** canna, gola (di camino) **3.** ciminiera (di nave, di locomotiva, ecc.) **4.** poz-
zo d'aereazione ☆ — *-shaped*, imbutiforme || *filtering
—*, imbuto a filtro.

funnelled ['fʌnld], *ag.* **1.** a forma d'imbuto **2.** munito di ciminiera.

funnily ['fʌnili], *av.* **1.** comicamente **2.** stranamente: *— enough....*, strano a dirsi....

funniment ['fʌnimənt], *s.* **1.** buffonata; scherzo **2.** stranezza.

funniness ['fʌninis], *s.* **1.** comicità; carattere divertente, faceto: *none of your —!*, basta con le vostre
spiritosaggini! **2.** stranezza, bizzarria.

funny[1] ['fʌni], *ag.* **1.** comico, buffo, divertente, faceto:
he is trying to be —, cerca di fare dello spirito; *it is
too — for words*, è veramente troppo buffo a dirsi; *you*

— *old thing!*, tu, simpatico buffone! **2.** strano, bizzarro, curioso, singolare: *what a — idea*, che idea strana!; *he is a — person*, è una persona stramba; *well, that's —*, ebbene, questo è curioso ☆ — -*bone*, punta del gomito, olecrano; — -*man*, (*teat. circo*) pagliaccio, comico, clown.

funny², *s.* **1.** (*mar.*) barca a un rematore **2.** *gener. pl.* (*sl. amer.*) pagina, giornale a fumetti.

fur [fə:*], *s.* **1.** pelo, pelame **2.** *gener. pl.* pelliccia; indumenti con guarnizioni di pelo **3.** animali con pelliccia **4.** patina linguale **5.** rivestimento, incrostazione, tartaro **6.** (*arald.*) pelliccia ☆ — -*bearer*, animale da pelliccia; — -*clad*, in pelliccia; — -*coat*, pelliccia; — -*collared*, con collo di pelliccia; — -*dresser*, pellicciaio, pellicciaia; — -*farming*, allevamento di animali da pelliccia; — -*lined*, foderato di pelliccia; — -*seal*, (*zool.*) lontra europea; — -*trade*, commercio di pellicce; — -*trimmed*, guarnito di pelliccia.

to fur, *pass.p.p.* **furred** [fə:d], *v.t.i.* **1.** fornire, guarnire, foderare di pelliccia; indossare una pelliccia: *she was furred to the eyes*, era completamente avvolta nella pelliccia **2.** (*med.*) formare patina su (lingua, denti) **3.** incrostare **4.** *to — up*, incrostarsi.

furbelow ['fə:bilou], *s.* **1.** balzana, falpalà **2.** *pl.* (*spreg.*) ornamenti pretenziosi.

to furbelow, *v.t.* ornare con falpalà.

to furbish ['fə:biʃ], *v.t.* **1.** lustrare, lucidare **2.** mettere a nuovo; rinfrescare; rinnovare: *she furbished (up) her Latin*, rinfrescò le sue cognizioni di latino.

furcate ['fə:kəit], *ag.* forcuto; biforcuto.

to furcate, *v.i.* biforcarsi.

furcation [fə:'keiʃən], *s.* biforcamento, biforcazione, bivio.

furfur ['fə:fə*], *pl.* **furfures** ['fə:fjuri:z], *s.* forfora.

furfuraceous [,fə:fju(:)'reiʃəs], *ag.* forforoso.

furious ['fjuəriəs], *ag.* furioso, adirato, furibondo: *to get* (o *to grow*) —, adirarsi ‖ *fast and — grew the fun*, il chiasso si fece tumultuoso ‖ *to go at a — pace*, correre a tutta velocità.

furiously ['fjuəriəsli], *av.* furiosamente.

to furl [fə:l], *v.t.i.* **1.** serrare (le vele) **2.** piegare, piegarsi; chiudere, chiudersi (di ombrello, ventaglio, tendine, ecc.) **3.** *to — away*, dissiparsi (di nuvole).

furlong ['fə:lɔŋ], *s.* « furlong » (misura di lunghezza = m. 201,16).

furlough ['fə:lou], *s.* (*mil.*) licenza, permesso; (*mar.*) franchigia: *to go home on —*, andare a casa in licenza.

to furlough, *v.t.* (*mil.*) accordare una licenza a, mandare in licenza.

furmety ['fə:miti], *V.* **frumenty**.

furnace ['fə:nis], *s.* **1.** (*metal.*) fornace, forno; focolare, camera di combustione **2.** caldaia del calorifero **3.** luogo caldissimo **4.** *fig.* prova difficile ☆ *air —*, forno a riverbero; *annealing —*, forno di ricottura; *blast —*, alto forno; *carbonizing* (o *carburizing*) —, forno di carburazione; *casehardening —*, forno di cementazione; *flowing —*, forno di colata; *hardening —*, forno di tempra; *house-heating —*, calorifero.

to furnace, *v.t.* scaldare in fornace, forno.

to furnish ['fə:niʃ], *v.t.* **1.** ammobiliare; arredare; allestire **2.** fornire, procurare: *the library was furnished with American books*, la biblioteca era fornita di libri americani; *to — an army with supplies*, approvvigionare un esercito; *to — s.o. with what he needs*, provvedere al fabbisogno di qlcu.

furnisher ['fə:niʃə*], *s.* fornitore (specialmente di mobili): — *to the Queen*, fornitore della regina ☆ *house —*, mobiliere.

furnishings ['fə:niʃiŋz], *s.pl.* arredamento, ammobiliamento (di una casa).

furniture ['fə:nitʃə*], *s.* (*solo sing.*) **1.** mobilio, mobili; arredi: — *and fittings*, mobili e arredi; *a piece of —*, un mobile: *that is a fine piece of —*, quello è un bel mobile; *this — is all old*, questi mobili sono tutti vecchi **2.** contenuto: — *of his pocket*, il suo denaro; — *of*

my shelves, i miei libri; — *of one's mind*, capacità mentale **3.** (*mar.*) attrezzatura **4.** (*tip.*) marginatura **5.** (*arc.*) equipaggiamento (di cavallo, cavaliere) ☆ — -*polisher*, lucidatore di mobili.

furore [fju'rɔ:ri], *s.* entusiastica ammirazione, furore: *to make* (o *to create*) *a —*, far furore.

furrier ['fʌriə*], *s.c.* pellicciaio, pellicciaia.

furring ['fə:riŋ], *s.* **1.** guarnizione, fodera di pelliccia **2.** (*mar.*) rivestitura delle plance **3.** tavole.

furrow ['fʌrou], *s.* **1.** solco **2.** scanalatura **3.** ruga profonda del viso **4.** scia ☆ — -*weed*, (*bot.*) zizzania.

to furrow, *v.t.* **1.** arare, solcare **2.** scanalare **3.** segnare di rughe.

furry ['fə:ri], *ag.* **1.** peloso **2.** di pelliccia; simile a pelliccia; coperto di, avvolto in pelliccia **3.** incrostato.

further ['fə:ðə*], *ag.* (*comp.* di **far**) **1.** più lontano ‖ *at the — end*, all'estremità più lontana **2.** nuovo, ulteriore, supplementare: *upon — consideration*, dopo ulteriore esame; *without — loss of time*, senza ulteriore perdita di tempo; *awaiting your — orders*, (*comm.*) in attesa di vostri nuovi ordini; *to go into — details*, entrare in più ampi dettagli ‖ *av.* **1.** oltre, più in là, più lontano **2.** ancora, in più, inoltre.

to further, *v.t.* favorire, secondare, incoraggiare.

furtherance ['fə:ðərəns], *s.* avanzamento, progresso.

furtherer ['fə:ðərə*], *s.c.* promotore, promotrice.

furthermore ['fə:ðə'mɔ:*], *av.* di più, inoltre.

furthermost ['fə:ðəmoust], *ag.* il più lontano.

furthersome ['fə:ðəsəm], *ag.* propizio; vantaggioso.

furthest ['fə:ðist], *ag.* (*superl.* di **far**) il più lontano; estremo: *the — limit I can go to*, *fig.* la mia estrema concessione ‖ *av.* alla più grande distanza; al massimo.

furtive ['fə:tiv], *ag.* furtivo, clandestino.

furtively ['fə:tivli], *av.* furtivamente, clandestinamente, di nascosto.

furuncle ['fjuərʌŋkl], *s.* foruncolo.

furuncular [fjuə'rʌŋkjulə*], **furunculous** [fjuə'rʌŋkjuləs], *ag.* (*patol.*) foruncoloso.

fury¹ ['fjuəri], *s.* **1.** furia, furore; violenza; collera: *the — of the wind*, la furia del vento ‖ *to get* (o *to fly*) *into a —*, montare su tutte le furie ‖ *to work like —*, lavorare con accanimento **2.** *fig.* donna violenta, maligna.

Fury², *s.* (*mit.*) Furia.

furze [fə:z], *s.* (*bot.*) ginestra spinosa, ginestrone.

furzy ['fə:zi], *ag.* (*bot.*) ricco, coperto di ginestre spinose.

fuscous ['fʌskəs], *ag.* scuro, fosco, cupo (di colore).

fuse¹ [fju:z], *s.* (*elett.*) valvola, fusibile ☆ — *block*, (*elett.*) portafusibile; — *box*, (*elett. aut.*) valvoliera; — *holder*, (*elett.*) portafusibile ‖ *box —*, (*elett.*) valvola; valvola a tabacchiera; *plug —*, (*elett.*) fusibile a tappo.

to fuse¹, *v.t.i.* **1.** fondere, fondersi (anche *fig.*) **2.** (*elett.*) saltare (di valvola).

fuse², *s.* **1.** (*mil.*) spoletta (di proiettile); detonatore **2.** miccia ☆ *clockwork —*, (*mil.*) spoletta ad orologeria; *concussion —*, (*mil.*) spoletta a percussione; *delayed-action —*, (*mil.*) spoletta a scoppio ritardato; *time- —*, (*mil.*) spoletta a tempo.

to fuse², *v.t.* munire di miccia, di spoletta, di detonatore.

fuse³, *s.* **1.** traccia, pista di animale **2.** *fig.* traccia.

fusee¹ [fju:'zi:], *s.* **1.** piramide (di orologio) **2.** fiammifero controvento **3.** soprosso (di cavallo).

fusee², *s.* schioppo.

fuselage ['fju:zila:ʒ], *s.* (*aer.*) fusoliera.

fusel-oil ['fju:zl'ɔil], *s.* (*chim.*) fuselolo, alcool amilico.

fusibility [,fju:zə'biliti], *s.* (*fis. metal.*) fusibilità.

fusible ['fju:zəbl], *ag.* (*fis. metal.*) fusibile ☆ — *metal*, metallo fusibile; — *plug*, (*elett.*) tappo fusibile.

fusiform ['fju:zifɔ:m], *ag.* fusiforme.

fusil¹ ['fju:zil], *s.* (*arald.*) rombo, fuso.

fusil², *s.* schioppo.

fusileer, fusilier [‚fju:zi'liə*], *s.* (*mil.*) fuciliere.

fusillade [‚fju:zi'leid], *s.* **1.** (*mil.*) fucilata **2.** fucilazione.

to **fusillade**, *v.t.* (*mil.*) **1.** assalire con fucileria **2.** passare per le armi.

fusion ['fju:ʒən], *s.* fusione (anche *fig.*): — *of metals, of races,* fusione di metalli, di razze ☆ — *point,* (*fis.*) punto di fusione.

fuss [fʌs], *s.* **1.** trambusto, confusione; chiasso, scalpore (per nulla): *to make a great — about nothing,* far molto rumore per nulla **2.** cerimonie, smancerie: *to make a — of s.o.,* colmare qlcu. di cortesie esagerate ☆ — *-pot,* (*sl.*) faccendone.

to **fuss**, *v.t.i.* **1.** affaccendarsi, agitarsi, preoccuparsi (per nulla); far confusione: *stop fussing!,* smettila di agitarti!; *to — over s.o.,* avere delle cure esagerate per qlcu. **2.** irritare, scocciare: *don't — me!,* non farmi arrabbiare!.

fusser ['fʌsə*], *s.* faccendone, arruffone.

fussily ['fʌsili], *av.* con inutile scalpore; con esagerata importanza; con eccessiva minuzia.

fussiness ['fʌsinis], *s.* tendenza a causar trambusto, a far confusione, chiasso.

fussy ['fʌsi], *ag.* **1.** faccendone; che fa confusione, chiasso (per nulla); che si preoccupa (per nulla) **2.** meticoloso, difficile da accontentare **3.** carico di fronzoli.

fust [fʌst], *s.* **1.** (*arch.*) fusto **2.** (*arc.*) odore di muffa.

to **fust**, *v.i.* (*arc.*) ammuffire; saper di muffa.

fustanella [‚fʌstə'nelə], *s.* fustanella.

fustian ['fʌstiən], *ag.* **1.** di fustagno **2.** *fig.* ampolloso **3.** di poco valore, misero, meschino ‖ *s.* **1.** fustagno **2.** *fig.* ampollosità, magniloquenza.

fustic ['fʌstik], *s.* **1.** (*bot.*) sommacco **2.** tintura derivata dal sommacco.

to **fustigate** ['fʌstigeit], *v.t.* (*scherz.*) fustigare.

fustigation [‚fʌsti'geifən], *s.* (*scherz.*) fustigazione.

fustiness ['fʌstinis], *s.* **1.** odore di muffa, tanfo **2.** *fig.* l'essere antiquato, fuori moda.

fusty ['fʌsti], *ag.* **1.** che sa di muffa, di rinchiuso; raffermo (di pane) **2.** *fig.* antiquato, sorpassato: — *ideas,* idee sorpassate.

futchel(l) ['fʌtfəl], *s.* pezzo di legno che sostiene le stanghe, l'asse di una vettura.

futhore ['fu:θɔ:k], *s.* alfabeto runico.

futile ['fju:tail], *ag.* futile, inutile, vano, frivolo.

futilely ['fju:tailli], *av.* futilmente, vanamente, frivolamente.

futility [fju(:)'tiliti], *s.* futilità, vanità, frivolezza.

futtock ['fʌtək], *s.* (*mar.*) scalmo, staminale ☆ — *-shrouds,* (*mar.*) rigge.

future ['fju:tfə*], *ag.* **1.** futuro: — *life,* vita futura; *my — wife,* la mia futura sposa **2.** (*gram.*) futuro: — *tense,* (tempo) futuro ‖ *s.* **1.** futuro, avvenire: *in* (o *in the* o *for the*) —, in avvenire; *in the near, distant* —, in un prossimo, lontano futuro; *he has a brilliant — before him,* lo attende un brillante avvenire **2.** (*gram.*) futuro: *verb in the* —, verbo al futuro **3.** *pl.* (*comm.*) merci vendute con consegna a termine; contratti per consegna a termine ☆ — *delivery,* (*comm.*) consegna a termine.

futureless ['fju:tfəlis], *ag.* senza futuro, senza avvenire.

futurism ['fju:tfərizəm], *s.* (*art.*) futurismo.

futurist ['fju:tfərist], *s.c.* (*art.*) futurista.

futuristic [‚fju:tfə'ristik], *ag.* (*art.*) futuristico.

futurition [‚fju:tju'rifən], *s.* (*fil. rar.*) futurazione.

futurity [fju(:)'tjuəriti], *s.* avvenire; avvenimenti futuri ☆ — *race,* (*amer.*) corsa (di cavalli) i cui concorrenti vengono selezionati molto tempo prima; — *stakes,* (*amer.*) somma di denaro offerta come premio per una « futurity race ».

fuze [fju:z], *s.* **1.** *V.* fuse¹ **2.** detonatore meccanico.

fuzee¹, *V.* fusee¹.

fuzee² [fju:'zi:] *s.* schioppo.

fuzz [fʌz], *s.* **1.** lanuggine, peluria **2.** polverio **3.** increspatura (di capelli): *a — of hair,* capelli gonfi e ricci ☆ — *-ball,* (*bot.*) vescia di lupo.

to **fuzz**, *v.t.i.* **1.** coprire, coprirsi di lanuggine **2.** coprire, coprirsi di polvere **3.** increspare, incresparsi (di capelli) **4.** sfilacciare, sfilacciarsi (di stoffa).

fuzzily ['fʌzili], *av.* confusamente, indistintamente.

fuzziness ['fʌzinis], *s.* **1.** increspatura (di capelli) **2.** (*foto.*) sfocatura.

fuzzy ['fʌzi], *ag.* **1.** coperto di lanuggine, peluria **2.** coperto di polvere **3.** increspato, gonfio (di capelli) **4.** sfrangiato, liso (di stoffa) **5.** confuso, indistinto **6.** (*foto.*) sfocato ☆ — *-minded,* dalle idee confuse; — *-wuzzy,* guerriero sudanese.

fylfot ['filfɔt], *s.* croce uncinata, svastica.

fyrd [fə:d], *s.* (*st. inglese*) forza militare di tutta la nazione anglo-sassone.

G

g [dʒi:], *pl.* **gs, g's** [dʒi:z], *s.* **1.** (*settima lettera dell'alfabeto inglese*) g ‖ — *for George*, (*tel.*) g come Genova **2.** (*mus.*) sol ☆ *G-clef*, (*mus.*) chiave di violino; *G-man*, (*amer. abbr.* di *Government-man*) agente federale.

gab¹ [gæb], *s.* bravata, millanteria.

to **gab¹**, *pass.p.p.* **gabbed** [gæbd], *v.i.* raccontare bravate, vantarsi.

gab², *s.* (*fam.*) chiacchiera; parlantina: *to have the gift of the* —, avere la parlantina sciolta.

to **gab²**, *v.i.* chiacchierare, parlare a vanvera.

gab³, *s.* (*mec.*) forcella, forchetta.

gab⁴, *s.* (*scoz.*) bocca.

gabardine [ˌgæbəˈdiːn], *s.* gabardina.

gabbart [ˈgæbət], *s.* (*mar.*) gabarra.

gabber¹ [ˈgæbə*], *s.* millantatore; gradasso.

gabber², *s.* chiacchierone.

gabble [ˈgæbl], *s.* barbugliamento, cicaleccio.

to **gabble**, *v.t.i.* barbugliare, borbottare; parlare, leggere in modo confuso ed affrettato: *to — one's part*, (*teat.*) recitare la propria parte senza intelligenza; *to — through a lesson*, recitare una lezione meccanicamente.

gabbler [ˈgæblə*], *s.* chiacchierone; barbuglione.

gabbro [ˈgæbrou], *s.* (*geol.*) gabbro, eufotide, granitone.

gabby [ˈgæbi], *ag.* (*amer. fam.*) garrulo, loquace.

gabelle [gəˈbel], *s.* gabella.

gaberdine [ˈgæbədiːn], *s.* **1.** palandrana **2.** gabardina.

gaberlunzie [ˌgæbəˈlʌnzi], *s.* (*scoz.*) mendicante vagabondo.

gabion [ˈgeibjən], *s.* (*mil.*) gabbione.

gabionade [ˈgeibjəneid], *s.* (*mil.*) gabbionata.

gabioned [ˈgeibjənd], *ag.* (*mil.*) fortificato con gabbioni.

gable [ˈgeibl], *s.* (*arch.*) timpano, frontone ☆ — *roof*, (*edil.*) tetto a due falde su timpano; — *wall*, (*arch.*) muro sormontato da un timpano.

gablet [ˈgeiblit], *s.* (*arch.*) timpano.

Gaboon [gəˈbuːn], *no.pr.* (*geog.*) Gabon.

Gabriel [ˈgeibriəl], *no.pr.m.* Gabriele.

gaby [ˈgeibi], *s.* (*fam. dial.*) sempliciotto.

gad¹ [gæd], *s.* **1.** punta metallica **2.** barra di metallo; lingotto **3.** (*miner.*) scalpello, barra a cuneo **4.** bacchetta, verga; bastone appuntito (da pastore) **5.** unità di misura per terreno a pascolo **6.** (*dial.*) canna da pesca.

to **gad¹**, *pass.p.p.* **gadded** [ˈgædid], *v.t.i.* **1.** munire di punta **2.** (*miner.*) usare la barra a cuneo, lo scalpello; rompere (la roccia) con la barra a cuneo.

gad², *s.*: *to be on* (o *upon*) *the* —, correre il mondo.

to **gad²**, *v.i.* **1.** bighellonare, vagabondare: *he's always gadding* (*about*), è sempre in viaggio, in movimento **2.** (*arc.*) crescere irregolarmente (di pianta).

gad³, *s.* (*mil.*) grossa fune intrecciata di fibre vegetali.

gad⁴, *inter.*: *by* —*!*, (*arc.*) perdio!.

gadabout [ˈgædəbaut], *ag.* vagabondo, scioperato ‖ *s.* bighellone, girandolone, vagabondo.

gadder¹ [ˈgædə*], *s.* (*miner.*) scalpello, barra a cuneo.

gadder², *s.* bighellone, vagabondo.

gaddi [gəˈdiː], *s.* **1.** trono di un capo indiano **2.** *fig.* regalità.

gaddingly [ˈgædiŋli], *av.* bighelloni.

gadfly [ˈgædflai], *s.* **1.** (*entom.*) tafano **2.** *fig.* persona irritante **3.** *fig.* impulso irresistibile.

gadge [gædʒ], *s.* (*rar.*) strumento di tortura.

gadget [ˈgædʒit], *s.* (*fam.*) **1.** congegno, dispositivo; arnese; piccola invenzione; accessorio di macchina **2.** gingillo, aggeggio: *give me that* —, dammi quel coso ☆ *knife-sharpening* —, arnese per affilare i coltelli.

Gadhelic [gæˈdelik], *V.* **Gaelic**.

gadi [gəˈdiː], *V.* **gaddi**.

gadoid [ˈgeidɔid], *ag.* (*ittiol.*) della famiglia dei gadidi ‖ *s.* (*ittiol.*) gado.

gadolinite [ˈgædəlinait], *s.* (*min.*) gadolinite.

gadroon [gəˈdruːn], *s.* **1.** cannoncino; increspatura **2.** (*arch.*) ovolo.

gadwall [ˈgædwɔːl], *s.* (*ornit.*) canapiglia.

Gael [geil], *s.* gaelico.

Gaelic [ˈgeilik], *ag.* gaelico ‖ *s.* lingua gaelica.

gaff¹ [gæf], *s.* **1.** (*pesca*) uncino, graffio; rampone; fiocina **2.** (*mar.*) picco ☆ — *sail*, (*mar.*) vela di randa; — *-top-sail*, (*mar.*) controranda.

to **gaff¹**, *v.t.* (*pesca*) uncinare, fiocinare, ramponare.

gaff², *s.* (*sl.*) sciocchezza; chiacchiera ‖ *to blow the* —, rivelare un segreto.

gaff³, *s.* (*sl.*) **1.** fiera **2.** (*penny*) —, ritrovo pubblico; teatro; varietà di infimo ordine.

to **gaff⁴**, *v.i.* (*sl.*) giocare d'azzardo; scommettere.

gaffe [gæf], *s.* gaffe, topica.

gaffer [ˈgæfə*], *s.* **1.** compare; vecchio **2.** mastro; caposquadra (di operai).

gag¹ [gæg], *s.* **1.** bavaglio **2.** (*chir.*) apribocca **3.** voto di chiusura (di un dibattito, in Parlamento) **4.** (*teat.*) improvvisazione di un attore in una commedia ☆ — *-bit*, morso molto robusto (per domare cavalli).

to **gag¹**, *pass.p.p.* **gagged** [gægd], *v.t.i.* **1.** imbavagliare (anche *fig.*): *to — the press*, (*fam.*) imbavagliare la stampa **2.** (*teat.*) improvvisare **3.** applicare il morso a (un cavallo da domare).

gag², *s.* **1.** (*sl.*) bugia, impostura **2.** (*teat.*) « gag », trovata geniale, motto di spirito, frizzo, battuta ☆ — *-man*, chi inventa frizzi (per film, commedie, ecc.); attore che si serve di motti, frizzi, ecc. nel recitare.

to **gag²**, *v.t.i.* **1.** (*sl.*) ingannare; darla a bere **2.** (*teat.*) improvvisare motti di spirito.

gaga [ˈgæguː], *s.* (*fam.*) **1.** gagà, bellimbusto **2.** rimbambito; debole di mente.

gage¹ [geidʒ], *s.* **1.** pegno; garanzia **2.** (*arc.*) sfida: *to throw down the* — *to s.o.*, sfidare qlcu.

to **gage¹**, *v.t.* **1.** dare in pegno **2.** (*arc.*) sfidare.

gage², *V.* **gauge 4**.

gage, *s. abbr.* di **greengage**.

gaggle [ˈgægl], *s.* branco di oche; (*fam.*) gruppo di donne.

to **gaggle**, *v.i.* schiamazzare (di oche).

gaiety [ˈgeiəti], *s.* **1.** gaiezza **2.** *pl.* divertimenti: *the gaieties of past times*, i divertimenti, le feste dei tempi passati.

gaily [ˈgeili], *av.* gaiamente.

gain¹ [gein], *s.* **1.** lucro; guadagno; vantaggio, profitto: *clear* —, guadagno netto; *the love of* —, l'amore del guadagno **2.** *pl.* guadagni: *a thief's ill-gotten gains*, i disonesti proventi di un ladro **3.** aumento, miglioramento: *a* — *in weight*, un aumento di peso; *a* — *to knowledge*, una conquista del sapere.

to **gain¹**, *v.t.i.* **1.** guadagnare; ottenere, vincere: *he gained an advantage over his competitors*, ottenne un vantaggio sui concorrenti; *to* — *ground*, guadagnare terreno; *fig.* fare progressi; *to — one's living by working*, guadagnarsi da vivere lavorando ‖ *to — the upper hand*, prendere il sopravvento **2.** giungere a; raggiungere: *to — the top of the mountain*, raggiungere la vetta della montagna **3.** *fig.* guadagnare, migliorare, beneficiare; fare progressi; aumentare (di peso): *this watch gains three minutes a day*, questo orologio va avanti tre minuti al giorno; *you have gained two pounds this summer*, sei aumentato due libbre quest'estate; *to — in popularity*, acquistare popolarità **4.** *to — (up)on*, (*s.o., sthg.*), sopraggiungere; raggiungere: *the sea is gaining on the land*, il mare corrode la costa.

gain², *s.* **1.** (*artig.*) tacca, intaglio **2.** (*miner.*) scavo trasversale ai lati di una galleria.

to gain², *v.t.* incastrare, congiungere a mortasa; fare delle tacche, degli intagli in (legno).

gainable ['geinəbl], *ag.* guadagnabile.

gainer ['geinə*], *s.c.* chi vince, guadagna.

gainful ['geinful], *ag.* lucroso, rimunerativo; vantaggioso.

gainings ['geiniŋz], *s.pl.* guadagni, profitti, utili.

to gainsay [gein'sei], *pass.p.p.* **gainsaid** [gein'seid], *v.t.* contraddire; negare: *argument that cannot be gainsaid*, argomento irrefutabile.

gainsayer [gein'seiə*], *s.* contraddittore; oppositore.

gainst, 'gainst [genst], (*poet.*) sta per **against**.

gait [geit], *s.* **1.** passo; andatura, portamento: *to have a graceful —*, camminare con grazia **2.** passo, andatura (di cavallo).

gaiter¹ ['geitə*], *s.* ghetta, uosa.

gaiter², *s.* (*bot.*) corniolo.

gal [gæl], *s.* (*sl.*) ragazza.

gala ['gɑːlə], *s.* gala ☆ *— day*, giorno di festa; *— -dress*, vestito di gala.

galactagogue [gə'læktəgog], *s.* (*med.*) galattagogo.

galactic [gə'læktik], *ag.* (*astr.*) galattico.

galactometer [,gælæk'tɔmitə*], *s.* galattometro.

galactose [gə'læktous], *s.* (*chim.*) galattosio.

galago [gə'leigou], *s.* (*zool.*) galagone.

galalith ['gæləliθ], *s.* (*min.*) galalite.

galanga [gə'læŋgə], *s.* (*bot.*) cipero.

galantine ['gæləntiːn], *s.* (*cuc.*) galantina.

Galatea [,gælə'tiə], *no.pr.f.* (*mit.*) Galatea ‖ **galatea**, *s.* stoffa di cotone a righe bianche e blu.

galaxy ['gæləksi], *s.* **1.** (*astr.*) galassia, Via Lattea **2.** *fig.* riunione di persone brillanti.

galbanum ['gælbənəm], *s.* (*bot.*) galbano.

gale¹ [geil], *s.* **1.** tempesta; colpo di vento; burrasca **2.** (*poet.*) brezza, zefiro **3.** scoppio di risa rumoroso.

gale², *s.* (*bot.*) mirica (*Myrica Gale*).

gale³, *s.* **1.** pigione **2.** tassa pagata per avere in concessione un terreno da scavare **3.** terreno dato in concessione.

galea ['geiliə], *s.* (*bot. entom. ornit.*) galea.

galeate ['gæliət], **galeated** ['gælieitid], *ag.* (*bot. entom. ornit.*) galeato.

galeeny [gə'liːni], *s.* gallina faraona.

Galen ['geilin], *no.pr.m.* (*st.*) Galeno ‖ **galen**, *s.* (*fam. scherz.*) dottore, medico.

galena [gə'liːnə], *s.* (*min.*) galena.

galenic¹ [gə'lenik], *ag.* (*st.*) galenico, di Galeno.

galenic², *ag.* (*min.*) galenico, che contiene galena.

galenism ['geilənizəm], *s.* (*st.*) dottrina di Galeno.

galenist ['geilənist], *s.* (*st.*) seguace di Galeno.

Galician [gə'liʃiən], *ag.* galiziano ‖ *s.c.* galiziano, galiziana.

Galilean [,gæli'li(ː)ən], *ag.* galileo ‖ *s.c.* galileo, galilea ‖ *the —*, il Galileo.

Galilee ['gælili:], *no.pr.* (*geog.*) Galilea ‖ **galilee**, *s.* (*arch.*) portico esterno, cappella di chiesa.

galingale ['gæliŋgeil], *s.* (*bot.*) cipero.

galipot ['gælipɔt], *s.* resina di pino.

gall¹ [gɔːl], *s.* **1.** bile, fiele (anche *fig.*): *— and wormwood*, amarezza e bile; *the — of life*, le amarezze della vita; *to dip one's pen in —*, intingere la penna nel

fiele; *to vent one's — on s.o.*, riversare il proprio livore su qlcu. **2.** (*ind.*) scorie nella fusione del vetro ☆ *— -bladder*, cistifellea; *— -stone*, calcolo biliare ‖ *ox —*, fiele di bue.

gall², *s.* **1.** scorticatura, escoriazione; pustola **2.** *fig.* ferita (all'amor proprio): *it left a — in his mind*, questo lo ha profondamente ferito **3.** difetto, imperfezione (in una stoffa) **4.** area sterile (di una prateria).

to gall², *v.t.i.* **1.** scorticare, irritare (una ferita) **2.** fregare **3.** *fig.* tormentare, aizzare, irritare, pungere; tormentarsi, rodersi.

gall³, *s.* (*bot.*) galla ☆ *— -fly*, (*entom.*) cinipe; *— -nut*, (*bot.*) noce di galla ‖ *oak- —*, galla della quercia.

to gall³, *v.t.* tingere con la galla della quercia.

gallant ['gælənt], *ag.* **1.** bravo, prode, valoroso **2.** bello; superbo **3.** cortese, galante; amoroso ‖ *s.* **1.** (*arc.*) galante, persona elegante; uomo di mondo; cavaliere **2.** amante; seduttore.

to gallant, *v.t.i.* **1.** far il galante; corteggiare; amoreggiare **2.** (*arc.*) scortare (una signora).

gallantly ['gæləntli], *av.* **1.** galantemente **2.** eroicamente.

gallantry ['gæləntri], *s.* **1.** galanteria **2.** nobiltà; spirito cavalleresco **3.** gentilezza; garbo **4.** coraggio, bravura **5.** atto, discorso amoroso **6.** intrigo amoroso.

galleon ['gæliən], *s.* (*mar.*) galeone.

gallery ['gæləri], *s.* **1.** galleria ‖ *Public Gallery* (o *Strangers' Gallery*), tribuna riservata al pubblico (ai Comuni **2.** (*teat.*) galleria, loggione; pubblico di galleria ‖ *to play to the —*, cercare d'incontrare il gusto del grosso pubblico **3.** passaggio coperto, galleria; portico; (*amer.*) balcone **4.** galleria, esposizione di quadri ☆ *— play*, lavoro teatrale di facile effetto ‖ *art- —*, galleria d'arte; *covered —*, androne; *picture- —*, galleria d'arte; *stern —*, (*mar.*) galleria di poppa.

galley ['gæli], *s.* **1.** (*mar.*) galera, galea **2.** (*mar.*) cambusa **3.** (*tip.*) vantaggio ☆ *— -proof*, (*tip.*) bozze in colonna; *— -slave*, galeotto, forzato; *fig.* sgobbone; *— -worm*, (*entom.*) millepiedi.

galliambic [,gæli'æmbik], *ag.s.* (*poes.*) (di) galliambo.

galliard ['gæljəd], *s.* (*danza*) gagliarda.

Gallic¹ ['gælik], *ag.* gallico, francese ‖ *s.* francese.

gallic², *ag.* (*chim.*) gallico: *— acid*, acido gallico.

Gallican ['gælikən], *ag.* (*eccl.*) gallicano ‖ *s.c.* gallicano, gallicana.

gallicanism ['gælikənizəm], *s.* (*eccl.*) gallicanismo.

gallicanist ['gælikənist], *s.c.* (*eccl.*) gallicanista.

gallice ['gælisi(ː)], *av.* in francese.

gallicism ['gælisizəm], *s.* gallicismo, francesismo.

to gallicize ['gælisaiz], *v.t.i.* gallicizzare, gallicizzarsi.

galligaskins ['gæli'gæskinz], *s.* (*scherz.*) brache, calzoni.

gallimaufry [,gæli'mɔːfri], *s.* guazzabuglio, confusione; mescolanza etereogenea.

gallinacean [,gæli'neiʃən], *ag.s.* gallinaceo.

gallinaceous [,gæli'neiʃəs], *ag.* gallinaceo.

galling ['gɔːliŋ], *ag.* irritante.

gallinule ['gælinjuːl], *s.* gallinella d'acqua.

Gallio ['gæliou], *no.pr.m.* (*st. romana*) Gallione ‖ *s.* (*fam.*) persona che evita responsabilità e fastidi.

galliot ['gæliət], *s.* galeotta; barcone olandese da carico, da pesca.

gallipot ['gælipɔt], *s.* vasetto di terracotta smaltata (per unguento).

gallium ['gæliəm], *s.* (*chim.*) gallio.

to gallivant [,gæli'vænt], *v.i.* **1.** amoreggiare **2.** gironzolare, vagare senza scopo.

galloglass ['gæləglɑːs], *s.* (*st.*) soldato celtico.

Gallomania [,gælou'meinjə], *s.* gallomania.

gallon ['gælən], *s.* gallone (misura di capacità = 1. 4,546 in Gran Bretagna; = 1. 3,785 negli Stati Uniti).

galloon [gə'luːn], *s.* gallone, nastro.

gallooned [gə'lu:nd], *ag.* gallonato, ornato di galloni.

gallop ['gæləp], *s.* **1.** galoppo: *at a* —, al galoppo; *at full* —, a briglia sciolta, a gran galoppo ‖ *to break into a* —, mettersi a galoppare, prendere il galoppo **2.** galoppata: *to have* (o *to go for*) *a* —, fare una galoppata ☆ *hand-* —, piccolo galoppo: *at hand-* —, al piccolo galoppo.

to **gallop**, *v.t.i.* **1.** (far) galoppare **2.** *fig.* parlare, lavorare in fretta: *to* — *over* (o *through*) *a book*, leggere un libro di volata **3.** progredire rapidamente (di malattia).

gallopade [,gælə'peid], *s.* (*danza*) galoppo.

galloper ['gæləpə*], *s.c.* galoppatore, galoppatrice ‖ *s.* (*mil.*) **1.** cannone leggero da campo **2.** aiutante di campo.

Gallophil ['gæləfil], **Gallophile** ['gæləfail], *ag.s.* gallofilo.

Gallophobe ['gæləfoub], *ag.s.* gallofobo.

Gallophobia [,gælə'foubiə], *s.* gallofobia.

galloping ['gæləpiŋ], *ag.* galoppante: — *consumption*, (*patol.*) tisi galoppante.

Gallovidian [,gælou'vidiən], *ag.s.c.* (abitante) del Galloway.

Galloway ['gæləwei], *no.pr.* (*geog.*) Galloway ‖ **galloway**, *s.* cavallino, mucca, bue del Galloway (Scozia).

gallows ['gælouz], *s.pl.* forca, patibolo; impiccagione: *crime worthy of the* —, delitto che merita la forca; *to hang s.o. on the* —, impiccare qlcu. ‖ *to miss the* — *by a hair's breadth*, cavarsela per il rotto della cuffia ☆ — *-bird*, (*sl.*) uomo, pezzo di galera; — *-free*, (*sl.*) avanzo di galera; — *look*, faccia patibolare; — *-tree*, forca.

Gallup-poll ['gæləp-poul], *s.* (*neol.*) sondaggio Gallup.

gally[1] ['gɔːli], *ag. gener. fig.* amaro come il fiele.

gally[2], *ag.* (*sl.*) **1.** che ha delle escoriazioni, delle scorticature **2.** squallido; umido (di territorio).

galoot [gə'lu:t], *s.* (*sl.*) soldato; marinaio; individuo goffo.

galop ['gæləp], *s.* (*danza*) galoppo.

to **galop**, *v.i.* danzare un galoppo.

galore [gə'lo:*], *s.* abbondanza, quantità.

galore, *av.* in quantità, in abbondanza, a profusione: *beef and ale* (*in*) —, carne e birra in quantità.

galosh [gə'lɔʃ], *s.* galoscia; soprascarpa.

to **galumph** [gə'lʌmf], *v.i.* camminare scompostamente per esultanza.

galvanic [gæl'vænik], *ag.* **1.** (*elett.*) galvanico **2.** *fig.* galvanizzante: *a* — *speech*, un discorso galvanizzante.

galvanism ['gælvənizəm], *s.* galvanismo.

to **galvanize** ['gælvənaiz], *v.t.* **1.** galvanizzare, elettrizzare (anche *fig.*): *to* — *into action*, spingere all'azione **2.** (*metal.*) galvanizzare; zincare.

galvanizer ['gælvənaizə*], *s.* (*elett.*) galvanizzatore.

galvanizing ['gælvənaiziŋ], *s.* (*elett.*) galvanizzazione.

galvanometer [,gælvə'nɔmitə*], *s.* (*elett.*) galvanometro.

galvanometric [,gælvənou'metrik], *ag.* (*elett.*) galvanometrico.

galvanoplastic [,gælvənou'plæstik], *ag.* (*chim.*) galvanoplastico.

galvanoplastics [,gælvənou'plæstiks], **galvanoplasty** [,gælvənou'plæsti], *s.* (*chim.*) galvanoplastica.

gam [gæm], *s.* (*mar.*) **1.** incontro di due, più baleniere **2.** branco di balene.

to **gam**, *pass.p.p.* **gammed** [gæmd], *v.i.* **1.** incontrarsi (di due, più baleniere) **2.** raggrupparsi in branco (di balene).

gamba ['gæmbə], *s.* (*mus.*) registro dell'organo con tono di violoncello.

gambado[1] [gæm'beidou], *pl.* **gambadoes** [gæm'beidouz], *s. gener. pl.* gambale, gambale da sella.

gambado[2], *pl.* **gambado(e)s**, *s.* **1.** salto (di cavallo) **2.** capriola, salto.

Gambia ['gæmbiə], *no.pr.* (*geog.*) Gambia.

gambit ['gæmbit], *s.* **1.** (*scacchi*) gambitto **2.** (*aer. mil.*) contatto tra aereo e sottomarino nemico.

gamble ['gæmbl], *s.* giuoco d'azzardo; *fig.* impresa rischiosa: *pure* —, pura speculazione; *everything's a* —, tutto dipende dalla fortuna.

to **gamble**, *v.t.i.* **1.** giocare d'azzardo; *fig.* arrischiare: *don't* — *with love*, non scherzare con l'amore; *he lost his fortune gambling on the Stock Exchange*, perse tutto il suo giocando in Borsa **2.** *to* — *away*, perdere al giuoco.

gambler ['gæmblə*], *s.c.* giocatore, giocatrice d'azzardo; *fig.* chi ama il rischio: — *on the Stock Exchange*, speculatore di Borsa.

gambling ['gæmbliŋ], *s.* giuoco d'azzardo ☆ — *-debts*, debiti di giuoco; — *-house*, casa da giuoco.

gamboge [gæm'bu:ʒ], *s.* varietà di gommagutta color arancione.

gambol ['gæmbəl], *s.* salto, capriola.

to **gambol**, *pass.p.p.* **gambolled** ['gæmbəld], *v.i.* saltare, fare capriole.

gambrel ['gæmbrəl], *s.* garretto di cavallo.

game[1] [geim], *ag.* **1.** ardito, coraggioso, risoluto: *a* — *little boy*, un ragazzo che ha del fegato; *to die* —, morire da eroe, combattendo fino all'ultimo **2.** pronto, disposto (a fare ql.co.): *she is* — *for anything, to do sthg.*, è pronta a tutto, a far ql.co.

game[1], *s.* **1.** giuoco (con regole): — *of tennis, football, baseball, cards, etc.*, giuoco del tennis, calcio, baseball, carte, ecc.; *he plays a good* — *at cards*, giuoca bene a carte ‖ *play the* —, *fig.* stai al giuoco; comportati correttamente ed onestamente ‖ *to have the* — *in one's hands*, essere sicuri del successo **2.** strumento per giocare; articolo sportivo: *this shop sells games*, questo negozio vende articoli da giuoco e da sport **3.** *pl.* prove agonistiche ‖ *the Olympic Games*, i Giuochi Olimpici **4.** giuoco, mano (in una partita): *to win three games in the first set*, vincere tre giuochi nella prima partita ‖ *to play a winning, losing* —, giocare una partita vinta, persa in partenza **5.** tiro, trucco, scherzo: *here is a* —*!*, questo è uno scherzo!; *you are having a* — *with me!*, vuoi burlarti di me! ‖ *the* — *is not worth the candle*, (*sl.*) il giuoco non vale la candela ‖ *the* — *is up*, il giuoco è finito, fallito ‖ *to make* — *of*, farsi beffe di **6.** *fig.* schema, progetto, piano d'azione: *what's his* —?, qual è il suo piano?; *to spoil s.o.'s* —, rovinare i piani di qlcu. **7.** *coll.* cacciagione, selvaggina ☆ — *-bag*, carniere; — *-laws*, leggi di caccia; — *-licence*, licenza di caccia; — *-preserver*, allevatore di selvaggina; *games -room*, sala di ricreazione; — *-tenant*, chi gode del diritto di caccia, di pesca ‖ *big* —, selvaggina grossa.

to **game**[1], *v.t.i.* **1.** giocare d'azzardo **2.** *to* — *away*, perdere al giuoco: *to* — *away money*, perdere denaro al giuoco; *to* — *away one's time*, sciupare il proprio tempo.

game[2], *ag.* zoppo, storpio, rattrappito.

gamecock ['geimkɔk], *s.* gallo da combattimento.

gamekeeper ['geim,ki:pə*], *s.* guardacaccia.

gamely ['geimli], *av.* coraggiosamente, arditamente.

gameness ['geimnis], *s.* coraggio, ardimento.

gamesome ['geimsəm], *ag.* scherzoso; allegro.

gamester ['geimstə*], *s.* giocatore d'azzardo.

gamete [gæ'mi:t], *s.* (*biol.*) gamete.

gamin ['gæmin], *s.* monello.

gaming ['geimiŋ], *s.* giuoco d'azzardo ☆ — *-debt*, debito di giuoco; — *-house*, bisca; — *-table*, tavolo da giuoco.

gamma ['gæmə], *s.* **1.** gamma **2.** (*entom.*) plusia ☆ — *rays*, (*fis.*) raggi gamma.

gammadion [gə'meidiən], *s.* croce formata da quattro gamma.

gammer ['gæmə*], *s.* (*fam.*) vecchia comare.

gammon[1] ['gæmən] *s.* **1.** parte più bassa di un prosciutto **2.** prosciutto affumicato, salato.

to **gammon**[1], *v.t.* affumicare, salare (prosciutto).

gammon[2], *s.* (*mar.*) trinca di bompresso.

to **gammon**[2], *v.t.* (*mar.*) trincare (il bompresso).

gammon[3], *s.* **1.** vittoria al giuoco del tric-trac, a tavola reale **2.** (*rar.*) giuoco del tric-trac.

to **gammon**³, *v.t.* battere, vincere al tric-trac.

gammon⁴, *s.* **1.** chiacchiere **2.** inganno, imbroglio ‖ *to give* —, (*sl.*) fare il palo ‖ *to keep s.o. in* —, (*sl.*) distrarre l'attenzione di qlcu. mentre un complice lo deruba.

to **gammon**⁴, *v.t.i.* **1.** chiacchierare **2.** fingere **3.** ingannare, farsi giuoco di.

gammon⁴, *inter.* sciocchezze!.

gammoning ['gæməniŋ], *s.* (*mar.*) trincatura di bompresso.

gamogenesis [,gæmə'dʒenisis], *s.* (*bot. zool.*) gamogenesi.

gamopetalous [,gæmə'petələs], *s.* (*bot.*) gamopetalo.

gamosepalous [,gæmə'sepələs], *s.* (*bot.*) gamosepalo.

gamp [gæmp], *s.* (*fam.*) ombrello.

gamut ['gæmət], *s.* **1.** (*st. mus.*) la nota più bassa della scala di Guido d'Arezzo; l'intera scala di Guido d'Arezzo **2.** (*mus.*) scala diatonica moderna **3.** (*mus.*) estensione di voce **4.** *fig.* gamma, gradazione; successione completa: — *of colours*, gamma di colori; *the whole* — *of feelings*, l'intera gamma dei sentimenti.

gamy ['geimi], *ag.* **1.** ricco di selvaggina **2.** che sa, che odora di selvaggina **3.** (*fam.*) coraggioso.

gan [gæn], *pass.* di to **gin**.

gander ['gændə*], *s.* **1.** (*ornit.*) papero **2.** sciocco, semplicione **3.** *to take a* —, (*amer.*) dare un'occhiata.

gang¹ [gæŋ], *s.* **1.** squadra (di operai, schiavi, prigionieri) **2.** banda (di malviventi); combriccola: *a* — *of thieves*, una banda di ladri **3.** serie, insieme di arnesi per un lavoro in comune **4.** (*dial.*) via, passaggio **5.** (*dial. scoz.*) pascolo ☆ — *-board* (o — *-plank*), ponticello di sbarco; — *-mill*, sega a lame multiple; — *press*, (*mec.*) pressa a matrici multiple.

to **gang**¹, *v.t.i.* formare una combriccola: *to* — (*up*) *with s.o.*, allearsi, formare una combriccola con qlcu. ‖ *to* — (*up*) *on s.o.*, attaccare qlcu. in banda.

to **gang**², *v.i.* (*scoz. dial.*) camminare; passeggiare.

ganger¹ ['gæŋə*], *s.* capo squadra di lavoratori.

ganger², *s.* **1.** chi cammina, viaggia a piedi **2.** cavallo dall'andatura veloce.

Ganges ['gændʒi:z], *no.pr.* (*geog.*) Gange.

Gangetic [gæn'dʒetik], *ag.* (*geog.*) del Gange.

gangland ['gæŋˌlænd], *s.* (*amer.*) zona dei banditi in una città.

gangliform ['gæŋglifɔ:m], *ag.* gangliforme.

ganglion ['gæŋgliən], *pl.* **ganglions** ['gæŋgliənz], **ganglia** ['gæŋgliə], *s.* **1.** (*anat.*) ganglio **2.** (*patol.*) tumore cistico dei tendini **3.** *fig.* centro di attività, di interessi.

ganglionic [,gæŋgli'ɔnik], *ag.* (*anat.*) relativo ai gangli.

gangrene ['gæŋgri:n], *s.* (*patol.*) cancrena.

to **gangrene**, *v.t.i.* mandare in cancrena; andare in cancrena; essere affetto da cancrena.

gangrenous ['gæŋgrinəs], *ag.* (*patol.*) cancrenoso.

gangster ['gæŋstə*], *s.* «gangster», bandito.

gangsterism ['gæŋstərizəm], *s.* banditismo, gangsterismo.

gangue [gæŋ], *s.* (*min.*) ganga.

gangway ['gæŋwei], *s.* **1.** passaggio (tra file di sedie, poltrone, ecc.); corsia; passaggio (che divide la Camera dei Comuni in diversi settori): — *please!*, (*fam.*) lasciare libero il passaggio, prego! ‖ *members above* —, sostenitori del governo; *members below* —, membri indipendenti **2.** (*mar.*) passerella (di sbarco, ecc.), passavanti.

gannet ['gænit], *s.* (*ornit.*) sula.

gannister ['gænistə*], *s.* **1.** roccia silicea **2.** (*ind.*) ganisto.

Ganoidei [gə'nɔidiai], *s.pl.* (*ittiol.*) ganoidi.

gantlet, *V.* **gauntlet**².

gantry ['gæntri], *s.* **1.** cavalletto **2.** piattaforma per gru, ecc.

Ganymede ['gænimi:d], *no.pr.m.* (*mit.*) Ganimede ‖ *s.* (*scherz.*) cameriere, coppiere.

gaol [dʒeil], *s.* prigione: *six months'* —, sei mesi di

prigione ☆ — *-bird*, avanzo di galera; — *-fever*, (*patol.*) febbre tifoidea.

to **gaol**, *v.t.* imprigionare, mettere in prigione.

gaoler ['dʒeilə*], *s.* carceriere.

gap [gæp], *s.* **1.** breccia, apertura; squarcio: *the sheep got out of the field through a* — *in the hedge*, il gregge uscì dal pascolo attraverso un buco nella siepe **2.** (*amer.*) gola, passo di montagna **3.** intervallo di tempo; distacco; interruzione; spazio vuoto: *there was a* — *in their conversation*, ci fu una pausa nella loro conversazione **4.** grande divergenza (di vedute, di simpatie): *a wide* — *between the views of the two statesmen*, un profonda divergenza di opinione fra i due statisti **5.** lacuna: *a* — *in one's learning*, una lacuna nella propria cultura ‖ *to bridge the* —, colmare la lacuna; *to fill (in)* (o *stop* o *supply*) *a* —, *fig.* chiudere una falla, fornire quanto manca ‖ *to reduce the* — *between...*, ridurre lo scarto tra... ‖ *to stand in the* — *of s.o.*, stare in difesa di qlcu. ☆ — *-toothed*, dai denti radi.

gape [geip], *s.* **1.** sbadiglio ‖ *the gapes*, (*vet.*) difterite dei polli **2.** sguardo fisso a bocca aperta **3.** apertura di bocca, di becco; parte di becco che si apre **4.** spaccatura, apertura.

to **gape**, *v.i.* **1.** sbadigliare **2.** spalancare la bocca; aprire il becco (di uccello); aprirsi (di ostriche, di ferita) **3.** rimànere a bocca aperta (per meraviglia): — *at s.o.*, guardare qlcu. a bocca aperta ‖ *to* — *for sthg.*, (*arc.*) desiderare ardentemente ql.co.

gaper ['geipə*], *s.c.* chi sbadiglia con frequenza.

gaping ['geipiŋ], *ag.* **1.** meravigliato, stupito: *a* — *gaze*, uno sguardo stupito **2.** aperto: *a* — *wound*, una ferita aperta ‖ *s.* **1.** sbadiglio **2.** contemplazione a bocca aperta.

gapingly ['geipiŋli], *av.* a bocca aperta.

gapped [gæpt], *ag.* avente il bordo dentellato.

gappy ['gæpi], *ag.* pieno di aperture, fenditure.

to **gar** [gɑ:*], *v.t.* (*scoz.*) costringere.

garage ['gærɑ:ʒ], *s.* «garage», autorimessa.

to **garage**, *v.t.* mettere, tenere in «garage».

garb [gɑ:b], *s.* costume; abito caratteristico: *a man in clerical* —, un uomo in abiti religiosi; *national* —, costume nazionale.

to **garb**, *v.t.* abbigliare, rivestire: *garbed all in black*, tutto vestito di nero.

garbage ['gɑ:bidʒ], *s.* **1.** rifiuti, immondizie **2.** cosa spregevole, senza valore ☆ — *-can*, porta-immondizie ‖ *literary* —, letteratura di second'ordine.

to **garble** ['gɑ:bl], *v.t.* **1.** troncare (un discorso, uno scritto) ad arte per alterarne il significato **2.** (*rar.*) scegliere il meglio da.

garbler ['gɑ:blə*], *s.* mutilatore (d'un testo).

garboil ['gɑ:bɔil], *s.* garbuglio; confusione.

garden ['gɑ:dn], *s.* **1.** *let's go into the* —, andiamo in giardino ‖ *to lead up the* —, (*sl.*) adescare, far deviare dalla retta via **2.** regione fertile **3.** *gener. pl.* giardini pubblici ☆ — *-bed*, aiuola; — *-party*, ricevimento in giardino; — *-stuff*, frutta e verdura ‖ *kitchen-* —, orto; *tea-* —, piantagione di tè; *zoological gardens*, giardino zoologico.

to **garden**, *v.t.i.* coltivare un giardino; fare del giardinaggio; coltivare a giardino.

gardener ['gɑ:dnə*], *s.c.* giardiniere, giardiniera.

gardenia [gɑ:'di:njə], *s.* (*bot.*) gardenia.

garefowl ['gɛəfaul], *s.* (*ornit.*) alca.

garfish ['gɑ:-fiʃ], *s.* **1.** (*ittiol.*) aguglia **2.** (*amer. ittiol.*) lepidosteo.

gargantuan [gɑ:'gæntjuən], *ag.* gigantesco, enorme.

gargarism ['gɑ:gərizəm], *s.* gargarismo.

to **gargarize** ['gɑ:gəraiz], *v.t.i.* gargarizzare; fare gargarismi.

garget ['gɑ:git], *s.* infiammazione alla gola o alle mammelle del bestiame.

gargle ['gɑ:gl], *s.* (*farm.*) liquido usato per gargarismi.

to **gargle**, *v.t.i.* far gargarismi; gargarizzare: *to* — *one's throat*, gargarizzarsi la gola.

gargoyle ['gɑ:gɔil], *s.* (*arch.*) doccione, grondone.

garial ['gɛəriəl], *s.* (*zool.*) gaviale.

garibaldi [ˌgæri'bɔ:ldi], *s.* blusa rossa ☆ — *biscuit*, dolce farcito con uva di Corinto.

garish ['gɛəriʃ], *ag.* **1.** abbagliante (di luce) **2.** appariscente, vistoso (di abito, decorazione, ecc.).

garishly ['gɛəriʃli], *av.* **1.** in modo abbagliante, accecante **2.** in modo appariscente.

garishness ['gɛəriʃnis], *s.* l'essere sgargiante, vistoso.

garland ['gɑ:lənd], *s.* **1.** ghirlanda, serto: *to win* (*o to carry away*) *the* —, riportare la palma **2.** (*arc.*) ghirlanda, antologia **3.** (*mar.*) grossa braca del timone.

to **garland**, *v.t.* inghirlandare.

garlic ['gɑ:lik], *s.* (*bot.*) aglio: *clove* (*o pig*) *of* —, spicchio d'aglio.

garlicky ['gɑ:liki], *ag.* che sa d'aglio.

garment ['gɑ:mənt], *s.* (*letter.*) **1.** capo di vestiario; *pl.* abiti **2.** copertura.

to **garment**, *v.t.* (*gener. al p.p.*) (*letter.*) rivestire; abbigliare.

garmentless ['gɑ:məntlis], *ag.* (*letter.*) svestito, spoglio.

garn [gɑ:n], *inter.* (*sl.*) va là!.

garner ['gɑ:nə*], *s.* **1.** (*letter.*) granaio **2.** *fig.* raccolta (di poesie).

to **garner**, *v.t.* (*letter.*) ammassare, raccogliere (anche *fig.*); depositare in un granaio: *memories garnered up in the heart*, ricordi che il cuore conserva.

garnet¹ ['gɑ:nit], *s.* (*min.*) granato.

garnet², *s.* (*mar.*) paranco.

garnish ['gɑ:niʃ], *s.* (*cuc.*) ornamento; guarnizione.

to **garnish**, *v.t.* **1.** (*cuc.*) adornare, guarnire **2.** (*dir.*) precettare: *to — a debtor*, diffidare un debitore a pagare non il suo creditore diretto ma il creditore di lui.

garnishee [ˌgɑ:ni'ʃi:], *s.* (*dir.*) sequestratario.

to **garnishee**, *v.t.* (*dir.*) sequestrare.

garnisher ['gɑ:niʃə*], *s.* (*dir.*) precettatore.

garnishing ['gɑ:niʃiŋ], *s.* **1.** guarnizione **2.** guarnizione (d'una pietanza) **3.** ornamento, fioritura (di stile).

garnishment ['gɑ:niʃmənt], *s.* **1.** ornamento, guarnizione **2.** (*dir.*) precetto: *to serve a* —, precettare.

garnishry ['gɑ:niʃri], *s.* ornamento.

garniture ['gɑ:nitʃə*], *s.* **1.** accessori **2.** guarnizione; ornamento (d'un abito); fioritura (di stile) **3.** (*cuc.*) ornamento, guarnizione.

garret¹ ['gærət], *s.* **1.** soffitta; solaio **2.** (*sl.*) testa.

to **garret²**, *v.t.* inserire schegge di sasso nelle fessure di (muratura grezza).

garreted ['gærətid], *ag.* **1.** fornito di abbaini **2.** alloggiato in abbaino.

garreteer [ˌgærə'tiə*], *s.c.* chi abita in un abbaino, in una soffitta.

garrison ['gærisn], *s.* (*mil.*) presidio; guarnigione ☆ — *town*, città di presidio.

to **garrison**, *v.t.* (*mil.*) presidiare; fornire di guarnigione.

garrot ['gærət], *s.* (*ornit.*) anitra marina.

garrotte [gə'rɔt], *s.* **1.** strangolamento **2.** garrotta (supplizio per strangolamento).

to **garrotte**, *v.t.* **1.** giustiziare strangolando **2.** strangolare a scopo di rapina.

garrulity [gæ'ru:liti], *s.* **1.** garrulità, loquacità **2.** verbosità (di stile).

garrulous ['gæruləs], *ag.* **1.** garrulo, loquace **2.** verboso (di stile).

garrulously ['gæruləsli], *av.* **1.** loquacemente **2.** verbosamente.

garter ['gɑ:tə*], *s.* giarrettiera ‖ *the Garter*, l'Ordine della Giarrettiera: *Knight of the Garter*, cavaliere dell'Ordine della Giarrettiera.

to **garter**, *v.t.* reggere con giarrettiere; mettere le giarrettiere a.

garth [gɑ:θ], *s.* (*arc.dial.*) recinto; praticello.

gas [gæs], *pl.* **gases** ['gæsiz], *s.* **1.** gas: *hydrogen and oxygen are gases*, l'idrogeno e l'ossigeno sono gas; *lighted with* —, illuminato a gas; *the — is laid on*,

la tubazione del gas è in funzione; *to turn on, off, up, down the* —, accendere, spegnere, alzare, abbassare il gas **2.** gas (usato come anestetico); gas esilarante **3.** (*mil.*) gas asfissiante; gas lagrimogeno **4.** (*fam.*) benzina: *to step on the* —, accelerare (anche *fig.*) **5.** (*min.*) idrocarburo di metano **6.** (*fam.*) ciance ☆ — *bag*, sacco, involucro contenente gas; (*aer.*) pallonetto; (*fam.*) chiacchierone; — *burner*, becco a gas; — *chamber*, camera a gas; — *cock* (o — *tap*), rubinetto del gas; — *cooker*, fornello a gas; — *fitter*, gassista; — *helmet*, maschera antigas; — *lamp*, lampada a gas; — *light*, luce a gas; — *man*, controllore del gas; — *mantle*, reticella a incandescenza; — *mask*, maschera antigas; — *meter*, contatore del gas; — *oil*, gasolio; — *oven*, forno a gas; — *pipe*, conduttura del gas; — *range*, fornello a gas; — *ring*, fiamma di fornello a gas; — *stove*, cucina a gas; — *works*, officina del gas ‖ *lighting* —, gas illuminante.

to **gas**, *pass.p.p.* **gassed** [gæst], *v.t.i.* **1.** fornire di gas **2.** (*mil.*) asfissiare con il gas **3.** (*ind. tessile*) bruciare **4.** (*fam.*) chiacchierare a vanvera.

Gascon ['gæskən], *s.c.* guascone.

gasconade [ˌgæskə'neid], *s.* guasconata, spacconata.

to **gasconade**, *v.i.* fare lo spaccone.

gasconader [ˌgæskə'neidə*], *s.c.* millantatore, millantatrice.

gaselier [ˌgæsə'liə*], *s.* lampadario a gas.

gaseous ['geizjəs], *ag.* gassoso.

gash¹ [gæʃ], *ag.* (*scoz.*) terrificante, spaventoso.

gash², *ag.* (*scoz.*) **1.** saggio, sagace **2.** ben vestito.

gash³, *s.* sfregio; incisione; ferita.

to **gash³**, *v.t.* sfregiare, tagliare, incidere.

gasification [ˌgæsifi'keiʃən], *s.* gassificazione.

gasiform ['gæsifɔ:m], *ag.* gassoso.

to **gasify** ['gæsifai], *v.t.* convertire in gas; volatilizzare.

gasket ['gæskit], *s.* **1.** (*mar.*) gaschetta, gerlo **2.** guarnizione (di tubi, ecc.).

gasogene ['gæzədʒi:n], *s.* gassogeno.

gasolene, gasoline ['gæsəli:n], *s.* **1.** gasolina, petrolio purificato **2.** (*amer.*) benzina per auto.

gasometer [gæ'sɔmitə*], *s.* gassometro.

gasp [gɑ:sp], *s.* respiro affannoso, rantolo, sussulto: *to be at one's last* —, essere all'ultimo respiro, in punto di morte.

to **gasp**, *v.t.i.* **1.** rimanere senza fiato; rimanere a bocca aperta **2.** ansare, respirare affannosamente: *to — for breath*, fare sforzi per respirare; *to — for life*, boccheggiare ‖ *I'm gasping for a drink*, (*fam.*) muoio dalla sete **3.** *to — out*, raccontare, dire affannosamente: *he gasped out his story*, raccontò affannosamente la sua storia.

gasper ['gɑ:spə*], *s.* (*sl.*) sigaretta di poco prezzo.

gaspingly ['gɑ:spiŋli], *av.* affannosamente.

gassy ['gæsi], *ag.* **1.** gassoso (anche di vino) **2.** chiacchierone, prolisso.

gasteropod ['gæstərəpɔd], *s.* (*zool.*) gasteropodo.

Gasteropoda [ˌgæstə'rɔpədə], *s.pl.* (*zool.*) gasteropodi.

gastralgia [gæs'trældʒiə], *s.* (*patol.*) gastralgia.

gastric ['gæstrik], *ag.* (*fisiol.*) gastrico ☆ — *fever*, febbre gastrica; — *juice*, (*fisiol.*) succo gastrico.

gastritis [gæs'traitis], *s.* (*patol.*) gastrite.

gastrology [gæs'trɔlədʒi], *s.* gastrologia.

gastronome ['gæstrənoum], **gastronomer** [gæs'trɔnəmə*], *s.* gastronomo.

gastronomic(al) [ˌgæstrə'nɔmik(əl)], *ag.* gastronomico.

gastronomically [ˌgæstrə'nɔmikəli], *av.* gastronomicamente.

gastronomist [gæs'trɔnəmist], *s.* gastronomo.

gastronomy [gæs'trɔnəmi], *s.* gastronomia.

gastrotomy [gæs'trɔtəmi], *s.* (*chir.*) gasterotomia.

gat [gæt], *s.* canale; passaggio tra banchi di sabbia.

gate¹ [geit], *s.* **1.** cancello; porta (di giardino, di città, ecc.); apertura ‖ *the — of heaven*, le porte del paradiso ‖

to get the —, (amer.) essere messo alla porta; to give s.o. the —, (amer.) congedare qlcu. **2.** barriera **3.** passo alpino **4.** (spor.) numero di entrate a pagamento, incasso realizzato con queste entrate ☆ — -bill (o — -fine), multa data agli studenti per ritardo nel rincasare (Oxford, Cambridge); — -by-pass switch, (elett.) interruttore di sicurezza; — -change gear, (aut.) leva di cambio a più velocità; — -house, portineria (di un parco); corpo di guardia; — -keeper, portiere; guardiano; cantoniere; — -keeper's lodge, (ferr.) casello; casa cantoniera; — -legged, (di tavola) a gambe mobili; — -money, prezzo d'ingresso; — -post, cardine (di porta, portone); — -valve, (mec.) saracinesca, valvola saracinesca.

to **gate**[1], v.t. punire (uno studente) togliendo il permesso di libera uscita (a Oxford e Cambridge).

gate[2], s. **1.** (scoz. dial.) via, sentiero **2.** vicolo (nelle denominazioni stradali) **3.** condotta, comportamento.

gate[3], s. (metal.) **1.** canale di colata **2.** colame.

to **gatecrash** ['geitkræʃ], v.t.i. (fam.) farsi largo; farsi largo per partecipare a (ricevimento, ecc.).

gatecrasher ['geit,kræʃə*], s.c. (fam.) intruso, intrusa (a ricevimento, ecc.).

gateless ['geit-lis], ag. senza porta.

gateway ['geit-wei], s. portone; entrata; passaggio.

gather ['gæðə*], s. gener. pl. pieghe, crespe (di abito) to **gather**, v.t.i. **1.** riunire, riunirsi; radunare; accumulare, accumularsi: tears gathered in his eyes, gli si riempirono gli occhi di lacrime; they soon gathered a crowd round them, in breve radunarono una folla intorno a loro **2.** cogliere, raccogliere: to — flowers, cogliere, raccogliere fiori || a rolling stone gathers no moss, prov. sasso che rotola non raccoglie muschio **3.** ottenere, acquistare gradatamente: to — ground, guadagnare terreno; to — oneself together, raccogliere le proprie energie; to — speed, aumentare di velocità; to — strength, riprendere forza; to — way, (mar.) cominciare a muoversi **4.** concludere, dedurre; capire: they could — at once that he was lying, capirono subito che mentiva **5.** venire a sapere; raccogliere (informazioni): I — he is ill, da quanto ho saputo, egli è ammalato **6.** riunire in pieghe, crespe **7.** (patol.) formare un ascesso || to — to a head, andare in suppurazione; maturare.

gatherer ['gæðərə*], s.c. raccoglitore, raccoglitrice.

gathering ['gæðəriŋ], s. **1.** riunione, assembramento; conciliabolo **2.** raccolta **3.** (patol.) gonfiore; ascesso.

gauche [gouʃ], ag. maldestro, goffo, senza tatto.

gaucherie ['gouʃəri(:)], s. goffaggine.

gaucho ['gautʃou], s. gaucho.

gaud [gɔːd], s. fronzolo.

gaudery ['gɔːdəri], s. eleganza vistosa.

gaudily ['gɔːdili], av. sfarzosamente.

gaudiness ['gɔːdinis], s. sfarzo; ostentazione, sfoggio; splendore.

gaudy ['gɔːdi], ag. sfarzoso; vistoso, appariscente; brillante.

gaudy, s. festa, trattenimento (specialmente nelle università inglesi).

gauge [geidʒ], s. **1.** misura; capacità: to take the — of, misurare; stimare **2.** calibro **3.** (ferr.) scartamento **4.** (mar.) posizione di nave rispetto al vento o ad altra nave **5.** (mar.) immersione, pescaggio ☆ broad —, (ferr.) scartamento normale; go —, not-go —, (mec.) calibro passa, calibro non passa; limit —, calibro differenziale; master — (o reference —), calibro campione; narrow —, (ferr.) scartamento ridotto; rain —, pluviometro; standard —, scartamento normale.

to **gauge**, v.t. **1.** misurare la capacità, il contenuto, il calibro di **2.** portare a un determinato grado (livello, misura) **3.** fig. stimare, giudicare.

gaugeable ['geidʒəbl], ag. misurabile.

gauger ['geidʒə*], s. collaudatore; incaricato di misurazioni.

gauging ['geidʒiŋ], s. **1.** calibratura **2.** verifica, misura **3.** intonaco di gesso e grassello di calce.

Gaul [gɔːl], no.pr. (geog. st.) Gallia || s.c. **1.** abitante della Gallia **2.** (poet. scherz.) francese.

Gaulish ['gɔːliʃ], ag. **1.** gallico **2.** (poet. scherz.) francese || s. lingua francese.

gault [gɔːlt], s. (geol.) strati d'argilla e marna.

Gaultheria [gɔːl'θiəriə], s. (bot.) gaultheria.

to **gaum** [gɔːm], v.t. imbrattare con sostanza appiccicaticcia.

gaunt [gɔːnt], ag. **1.** magro, scarno, sparuto **2.** dall'aspetto desolato.

gauntlet[1] ['gɔːntlit], s. **1.** guanto di guerriero medioevale || to fling (o to throw) down the —, gettare il guanto, sfidare; to pick (o to take) up the —, accettare la sfida **2.** guanto per automobilista.

gauntlet[2], s. (mil.) castigo per cui il punito doveva correre tra due file di commilitoni che lo battevano: to run the —, subire tale punizione; fig. essere sottoposto a severa critica.

gauntness ['gɔːntnis], s. magrezza.

gauss [gaus], s. (fis.) gauss (unità C.G.S. del campo magnetico).

gauze [gɔːz], s. **1.** (med.) garza: sterilized, antiseptic —, garza sterilizzata, antisettica **2.** velo, mussolina **3.** leggero velo di nebbia **4.** (foto.) velatino ☆ wire —, reticella metallica.

gauziness ['gɔːzinis], s. leggerezza, inconsistenza.

gauzy ['gɔːzi], ag. trasparente, simile a garza.

gave [geiv], pass. di to **give**.

gavel ['gævl], s. (amer.) martelletto (da banditore alle aste, da presidente di riunione).

gavelkind ['gævlkaind], s. (dir.) forma di proprietà, in uso soprattutto nel Kent, per cui le terre, alla morte del proprietario, erano divise in parti uguali tra i figli.

gavotte [gə'vɔt], s. gavotta.

Gawain ['gɑːwein], no.pr.m. (lett.) Galvano.

gawk [gɔːk], s.c. persona sciocca, goffa.

to **gawk**, v.i. (dial. amer.) guardare fissamente con aria sciocca: to — at s.o., guardare fissamente qlcu.

gawky ['gɔːki], ag. goffo, sgraziato; timido.

gay [gei], ag. **1.** gaio, allegro; giulivo; vivace **2.** vistoso; brillante **3.** fig. dissoluto: to lead a — life, condurre una vita dissoluta || to go —, (fam.) darsi alla pazza gioia **4.** (sl. amer.) sfrontato, impertinente.

gayety, V. **gaiety**.

gaysome ['geisəm], ag. (rar.) lieto, gaio.

Gaza ['gɑːzə], no.pr. (geogr.) Gaza.

gaze [geiz], s. sguardo fisso: to stand at —, restare in contemplazione.

to **gaze**, v.i. guardare fissamente: to — at (o on o upon) s.o., sthg., fissare qlcu., ql.co.

gazebo [gə'ziːbou], s. belvedere; balcone panoramico.

gazelle [gə'zel], s. (zool.) gazzella.

gazer ['geizə*], s.c. contemplatore, contemplatrice.

gazette [gə'zet], s. **1.** giornale ufficiale **2.** gazzetta (nei titoli di giornale) || the Westminster Gazette, la Gazzetta di Westminster **3.** (st.) giornale periodico.

to **gazette**, v.t. pubblicare nella gazzetta ufficiale || to be gazetted to a regiment, essere ufficialmente destinato a un reggimento.

gazetteer [,gæzi'tiə*], s. **1.** dizionario geografico **2.** (arc.) giornalista (specialmente se pagato dal governo).

gazing ['geiziŋ], ag. curioso || s. contemplazione ☆ — -stock, individuo esposto alla pubblica curiosità.

gazogene ['gæzədʒiːn], s. (aut.) gassogeno.

gazon [gə'zuːn], s. (arc.) zolla di terra erbosa.

gean [giːn], s. (bot.) amarasca.

gear [giə*], s. **1.** meccanismo, dispositivo **2.** (aut.) marcia; cambio di velocità: in —, in movimento, in marcia; out of —, in riposo, fermo, disingranato; fig. disturbato; to put in —, mettere in marcia, ingranare || — in neutral, cambio in folle **3.** ingranaggio (di ruote, ecc.) **4.** utensili da casa **5.** (mar.) attrezzatura di nave **6.** finimenti per animali da tiro **7.** (arc.) equipaggiamento ☆ — break, (amer.) — lever, leva del cambio; — -case, « carter » (di bicicletta, ecc.) ǁ *change* —, (*aut.*) cambio di velocità; *herring bone* —, (*mec.*) ingranaggio a freccia; *high-* —, (*aut.*) quarta velocità; *hunting* —, equipaggiamento da caccia; *landing* —, (*aer.*) carrello di atterraggio; *low-* —, (*aut.*) prima velocità; *ring* —, (*mec.*) corona dentata a dentatura interna; *steering* —, (*mar.*) agghiaccio, meccanismo di governo; *synchromesh* —, cambio sincronizzato.

to **gear**, *v.t.i.* 1. ingranare, ingranarsi ǁ *to* — *up*, *down*, aumentare, diminuire velocità (di auto, di produzione) 2. bardare (animali da tiro).

gearing ['giəriŋ], *s.* ingranaggio ☆ — *-down*, (*mec.*) riduzione (di giri); — *-up*, (*mec.*) moltiplicazione (di giri).

geek[1] [gek], *s.* (*dial.*) sempliciotto; matto.

geek[2], *s.* (*scoz.*) gesto di derisione; espressione di disprezzo.

to **geek**[2], *v.t.i.* (*scoz. dial.*) 1. schernire 2. scuotere la testa in segno di disprezzo.

gecko ['gekou], *pl.* **geckos**, **geckoes** ['gekouz], *s.* (*zool.*) geco.

gee [dʒi:], *inter.* 1. arri!, hop! 2. (*sl. amer.*) per Diana!, per Bacco!.

gee-gee ['dʒi:dʒi:], *s.* cavallo (nel linguaggio infantile) ǁ — *up!*, cavallino trotta trotta!.

geese [gi:s], *pl.* di **goose**.

geezer ['gi:zə*], *s.* (*sl.*) vecchio strano, eccentrico.

Gehenna [gi'henə], *s.* Geenna, inferno (anche *fig.*).

Geiger counter ['gaigə'kauntə*], *s.* (*fis.*) contatore Geiger.

geisha ['geiʃə], *s.* geisha.

geist [gaist], *s.* spirito; principio ispiratore.

gel [dʒel], *s.* (*chim.*) « gel » (soluzione colloidale semi-solida).

to **gel**, *pass.p.p.* **gelled** [dʒeld], *v.i.* coagularsi, passare allo stato semisolido.

gelastic [dʒi'læstik], *ag.* (*rar.*) incline al riso; risibile.

gelatine [,dʒelə'ti:n], *s.* gelatina ☆ — *solution*, soluzione gelatinosa ǁ *frosted* —, (*foto.*) gelatina cristallizzata.

to **gelatinize** [dʒi'lætinaiz], *v.t.i.* 1. gelatinizzare, gelatinizzarsi 2. (*foto.*) coprire con uno strato di gelatina.

gelatinoid [dʒi'lætinoid], *ag.* gelatinoso; gelatiniforme.

gelatinous [dʒi'lætinəs], *ag.* gelatinoso.

gelation [dʒi'leiʃən], *s.* congelamento.

geld[1] [geld], *s.* (*st.*) tributo dei proprietari terrieri ai sovrani anglo-sassoni.

to **geld**[1], *v.i.* (*st.*) pagare tributi.

to **geld**[2], *v.t.* 1. castrare (cavallo, ecc.) 2. indebolire (anche *fig.*).

gelding ['geldiŋ], *s.* cavallo castrato.

gelid ['dʒelid], *ag.* gelido (anche *fig.*).

gelidly ['dʒelidli], *av.* gelidamente.

gelidness ['dʒelidnis], *s.* gelidezza.

gelignite ['dʒelignait], *s.* (*chim.*) nitroglicerina.

gem [dʒem], *s.* 1. gemma, pietra preziosa 2. *fig.* perla: *a* — *of a wife*, una perla di moglie 3. (*sl. scolastico*) strafalcione, perla, errore madornale e ridicolo.

to **gem**, *pass.p.p.* **gemmed** [dʒemd], *v.t.* ingemmare.

geminate ['dʒeminit], *ag.* 1. accoppiato (foglie, colonne, ecc.) 2. (*gram.*) doppio (di lettere) ǁ *s.* consonante doppia.

to **geminate** ['dʒemineit], *v.t.* 1. appaiare 2. ripetere; fare un doppione di.

gemination [,dʒemi'neiʃən], *s.* geminazione, raddoppiamento.

Gemini ['dʒemini:], *s.pl.* (*astr.*) Gemelli, Castore e Polluce ǁ —!, (*arc. volg.*) mio Dio!.

geminous ['dʒeminəs], *ag.* doppio, gemello.

gemma ['dʒemə], *pl.* **gemmae** ['dʒemi:], *s.* 1. (*bot.*) gemma 2. (*di animali*) cellula agamica.

gemmate ['dʒemit], *ag.* (*bot.*) gemmato, che ha gemme.

to **gemmate** ['dʒemeit], *v.i.* gemmare, germogliare; riprodursi per gemmazione.

gemmation [dʒe'meiʃən], *s.* 1. (*bot.*) gemmazione, riproduzione delle gemme 2. (*zool.*) riproduzione cellulare organica.

gemmeous ['dʒemiəs], *ag.* gemmeo, di pietra preziosa.

gemmiferous [dʒe'mifərəs], *ag.* 1. che porta germogli, gemmifero 2. che produce pietre preziose.

gemmiparous [dʒe'mipərəs], *ag.* riproducentesi per gemmazione, a mezzo di gemme.

gemmology [dʒe'molədʒi], *s.* scienza delle gemme.

gemmule ['dʒemju:l], *s.* gemmula.

gemmy ['dʒemi], *ag.* coperto di gemme; splendente come gemma.

gemot [gi'mout], *s.* (*arc.*) assemblea.

gemsbok ['gemzbɔk], *s.* (*zool.*) antilope sud-africana.

gen [dʒen], *s.* (*biol.*) gene.

gendarme ['ʒɑ:ndɑ:m], *s.* poliziotto, gendarme.

gendarmerie ['ʒɑ:ndɑ:məri], *s.* gendarmeria.

gender ['dʒendə*], *s.* 1. (*gram.*) genere 2. (*scherz.*) sesso.

genderless ['dʒendəlis], *ag.* (*gram.*) di genere comune.

genealogical [,dʒi:njə'lɔdʒikəl], *ag.* genealogico ☆ — *-tree*, albero genealogico.

genealogist [,dʒi:ni'ælədʒist], *s.* genealogista.

to **genealogize** [,dʒini'ælədʒaiz], *v.t.i.* fare la genealogia di; occuparsi di genealogie.

genealogy [,dʒi:ni'ælədʒi], *s.* genealogia.

genera ['dʒenərə], *pl.* di **genus**.

generable ['dʒenərəbl], *ag.* generabile.

general ['dʒenərəl], *ag.* 1. generale, pubblico; comune; prevalente 2. vago, indefinito: *to have a* — *idea of the matter*, avere un'idea vaga della faccenda 3. capo, generale (dopo un titolo ufficiale) ǁ *s.* 1. (*mil.*) generale 2. capo (di ordini religiosi) 3. *pl.* (*rar.*) principi, nozioni generali 4. (*arc.*) pubblico ☆ — *-dealer*, commerciante in articoli varii; — *post-office*, posta centrale; — *practitioner*, medico generico; — *servant*, domestica tutto fare; — *strike*, sciopero generale ǁ *inspector-* —, ispettore generale.

generalissimo [,dʒenərə'lisimou], *s.* generalissimo.

generality [,dʒenə'ræliti], *s.* 1. generalità 2. indeterminatezza 3. maggioranza, la maggior parte.

generalization [,dʒenərəlai'zeiʃən], *s.* generalizzazione.

to **generalize** ['dʒenərəlaiz], *v.t.i.* 1. generalizzare 2. rendere di uso generale: *to* — *the use of a new invention*, rendere generale l'uso di una nuova invenzione.

generally ['dʒenərəli], *av.* generalmente, di solito.

generalship ['dʒenərəlʃip], *s.* 1. abilità militare; strategia 2. (*mil.*) generalato.

to **generate** ['dʒenəreit], *v.t.* generare, procreare; produrre.

generating ['dʒenəreitiŋ], *ag.* generante; generatore.

generation [,dʒenə'reiʃən], *s.* generazione (anche *biol.*): *the* — *of heat, electricity*, la produzione del calore, dell'elettricità; *spontaneous* —, generazione spontanea; *I have known them for three generations*, li conosco da tre generazioni ☆ *the rising* —, i giovani la nuova generazione.

generative ['dʒenərətiv], *ag.* generativo, produttivo.

generator ['dʒenəreitə*], *s.c.* generatore, generatrice.

generatrix ['dʒenəreitriks], *s.* (*geom.*) generatrice (di una superficie), linea generatrice.

generic [dʒi'nerik], *ag.* generico.

generically [dʒi'nerikəli], *av.* genericamente.

generosity [,dʒenə'rositi], *s.* generosità, liberalità, magnanimità.

generous ['dʒenərəs], *ag.* 1. generoso, munifico 2. fertile (di terreno) 3. abbondante, copioso.

generously ['dʒenərəsli], *av.* generosamente, abbondantemente, copiosamente.

generousness ['dʒenərəsnis], *s.* generosità.

genesis ['dʒenisis], *s.* genesi ǁ (*the Book of*) *Genesis*, Genesi (libro del Vecchio Testamento).

genet ['dʒenit], s. **1.** (zool.) genetta **2.** pelliccia di genetta.

genetic [dʒi'netik], ag. genetico.

genetically [dʒi'netikəli], av. geneticamente.

geneticist [dʒi'netisist], s. genetista.

genetics [dʒi'netiks], s. genetica.

geneva[1] [dʒi'ni:və], s. acquavite di ginepro.

Geneva[2], no.pr. (geogr.) Ginevra.

Genevan [dʒi'ni:vən], **Genevese** [,dʒeni'vi:z], ag. s. ginevrino.

Genevieve [,dʒenə'vi:v], no.pr.f. Genoveffa ‖ Saint — [,ʒenvi'eiv], Santa Genoveffa.

genial[1] ['dʒi:njəl], ag. **1.** gioviale; gentile; socievole **2.** mite (di clima) **3.** che dà conforto: — wine, vino generoso **4.** geniale, che ha talento **5.** geniale; nuziale ☆ — bed, (rar.) letto nuziale.

genial[2] [dʒi'naiəl], ag. (anat.) del mento.

geniality [,dʒi:ni'æliti], s. **1.** giovialità, gaiezza, buon umore **2.** mitezza (di clima, aria).

to **genialize** ['dʒi:niəlaiz], v.t. rendere amabile; rallegrare.

genially ['dʒi:njəli], av. giovialmente.

geniculate [dʒi'nikjulit], **geniculated** [dʒi'nikjuleitid], ag. (bot.) genicolato.

genie ['dʒi:ni], pl. **genii** ['dʒi:niai], s. (mit.) genio, spirito, demonio.

genista [dʒi'nistə], s. (bot.) ginestra.

genital ['dʒenitl], ag. genitale.

genitals ['dʒenitlz], s.pl. (anat.) organi genitali.

genitival [,dʒeni'taivəl], ag. (gram.) del genitivo.

genitive ['dʒenitiv], ag. s. (gram.) genitivo.

genitor ['dʒenitə*], s. (rar.) genitore.

genito-urinary [,dʒenitə'juərinəri], ag. (anat.) genito-urinario.

genitrix ['dʒenitriks], s. (rar.) genitrice.

genius ['dʒi:njəs], pl. **geniuses** ['dʒi:njəsiz], s. **1.** (solo sing.) genio, abilità, ingegno: man of —, uomo d'ingegno; work of —, opera di genio; he has a — for doing the wrong thing, ha la specialità di far le cose sbagliate; he is no —, (fam.) non è un'aquila; to have a — for geometry, aver del talento per la geometria **2.** genio, persona di genio: Einstein and Marconi were two of the greatest geniuses of all time, Einstein e Marconi furono dei più grandi geni di tutti i tempi; he is a mathematical —, è un genio matematico **3.** genio, spirito tutelare: she is his good —, ella è il suo angelo custode **4.** (gener. sing.) genio particolare, spirito (di luogo, nazione, epoca, razza, ecc.): the — of the 18th century, lo spirito del diciottesimo secolo; the French —, lo spirito dei francesi.

Genoa ['dʒenouə], no.pr. (geog.) Genova.

genocide ['dʒenousaid], s. genocidio.

Genoese [,dʒenou'i:z], ag.s.c. genovese.

genre [ʒɑ:nr], s. genere; stile, maniera.

gens [dʒenz], **gentes** ['dʒentiz], s. (lat.) stirpe, gente.

gent [dʒent], s. (pop.) abbr. di **gentleman**.

genteel [dʒen'ti:l], ag. **1.** (iron.) « snob », manieroso; che ha pretese di signorilità, distinzione **2.** (arc.) bennato; garbato; signorile; di qualità.

genteelism [dʒen'ti:lizəm], s. eufemismo.

genteelly [dʒen'ti:lli], av. **1.** (iron.) da snob, con pretese di signorilità **2.** (arc.) garbatamente; signorilmente.

gentian ['dʒenʃiən], s. (bot.) genziana.

gentianella [,dʒenʃiə'nelə], s. (bot.) genzianella.

gentile ['dʒentail], ag.s. gentile, pagano.

gentility [dʒen'tiliti], s. **1.** (gener. iron.) distinzione, nascita elevata, signorilità **2.** (arc.) gentilezza, cortesia.

gentle ['dʒentl], ag. **1.** nobile, distinto, di nobile famiglia **2.** gentile, garbato, cortese; grazioso **3.** mite; dolce; moderato: a — heat, un calore moderato **4.** facile, non faticoso, non violento ‖ s. larva di mosca usata come esca ☆ the — craft, la pesca con l'amo; the — sex, il gentil sesso.

to **gentle**, v.t. domare (cavalli); trattare (cavalli) fermamente ma con dolcezza.

gentlefolk(s) ['dʒentlfouk(s)], s.pl. gente della buona società ☆ distressed —, nobili decaduti.

gentlehood ['dʒentlhud], s. nobiltà di nascita.

gentleman, pl. **gentlemen** ['dʒentlmən], s. **1.** gentiluomo; persona distinta; signore; uomo: a perfect —, un perfetto gentiluomo; a — has called to see you, è venuto un uomo a cercarti ‖ ladies and gentlemen, signore e signori ‖ the old —, il vecchio; fig. il diavolo **2.** signore, possidente, proprietario: to lead a —'s life, vivere da signore **3.** (arc.) nobile, gentiluomo, uomo d'onore ‖ — -at-arms, membro della guardia del corpo del re; — at large, (arc.) gentiluomo di corte, senza speciali incarichi (scherz.) disoccupato; — in waiting, gentiluomo di servizio a corte; — -usher, usciere di palazzo ☆ —'s agreement, accordo leale, sulla parola; — -commoner, (st.) studente privilegiato (di Oxford, Cambridge); — farmer, gentiluomo di campagna.

gentlemanlike ['dʒentlmənlaik], ag. **1.** da gentiluomo; signorile, ben educato, distinto **2.** onorevole, nobile, della buona società.

gentlemanliness ['dʒentlmənlinis], s. signorilità.

gentlemanly ['dʒentlmənli], V. **gentlemanlike**.

gentleness ['dʒentlnis], s. gentilezza, cortesia, garbo; grazia; dolcezza.

gentlewoman ['dʒentl,wumən], pl. **gentlewomen** ['dʒentl,wimin], s. **1.** gentildonna **2.** signora.

gently ['dʒentli], av. con delicatezza, gentilmente; tranquillamente, dolcemente; gradualmente; senza far rumore: —!, fate piano!; the road sloped — to the sea, la strada declinava verso il mare.

gentry ['dʒentri], s. coll. classe gentilizia, possidenti (specialmente di campagna); piccola nobiltà; gente per bene; (scherz.) la gente ☆ the light-fingered —, (scherz.) i signori ladri.

to **genuflect** ['dʒenju(:)flekt], v.i. genuflettersi.

genuflection, **genuflexion** [,dʒenju(:)'flekʃən], s. genuflessione.

genuine ['dʒenjuin], ag. **1.** genuino; autentico: a — picture by Rubens, un Rubens autentico **2.** naturale; puro: a — diamond, un diamante puro **3.** sincero; schietto, leale: a — friend, un amico sincero.

genuinely ['dʒenjuinli], av. genuinamente.

genuineness ['dʒenjuinnis], s. **1.** autenticità **2.** sincerità, lealtà **3.** storicità (di un avvenimento).

genus ['dʒi:nəs], pl. **genera** ['dʒenərə], s. **1.** genere; classe, specie **2.** (biol.) genere ‖ the — Homo, la specie umana.

geocentric [,dʒi(:)ou'sentrik], ag. (astr.) geocentrico.

geode ['dʒi(:)oud], s. (min.) geode.

geodesic [,dʒi(:)ou'desik], ag. (geom.) geodetico.

geodesy [dʒi(:)'odisi], s. (geom.) geodesia.

geodetic [,dʒi(:)ou'detik], ag. (geom.) geodetico.

Geoffrey ['dʒefri], no.pr.m. Goffredo.

geognosy [dʒi'ognəsi], s. (geol.) geognosia.

geographer[4][dʒi'ogrəfə*], s. geografo.

geographic(al) [dʒiə'græfik(əl)], ag. geografico.

geographically [dʒiə'græfikəli], av. geograficamente.

geography [dʒi'ogrəfi], s. geografia.

geologic(al) [dʒiə'lodʒik(əl)], ag. geologico.

geologically [dʒiə'lodʒikəli], av. geologicamente.

geologist [dʒi'olədʒist], s. geologo.

to **geologize** [dʒi'olədʒaiz], v.t.i. far ricerche geologiche; studiare la geologia di (un luogo).

geology [dʒi'olədʒi], s. geologia.

geomancer ['dʒi:oumænsə*], s. geomante; indovino.

geomancy ['dʒi:oumænsi], s. geomanzia; magia.

geometer [dʒi'omitə*], s. **1.** geometra **2.** (entom.) geometrino.

geometric(al) [dʒiə'metrik(əl)], ag. geometrico.

geometrically [dʒiə'metrikəli], av. geometricamente.

geometrician [,dʒioume'triʃən], s. geometra.

geometry [dʒi'omitri], s. geometria.

geomys ['dʒi:əmis], s. (zool.) geomide.

George [dʒɔ:dʒ], no.pr.m. Giorgio ‖ Saint —, San Giorgio (patrono d'Inghilterra): St. —'s day, il giorno di S. Giorgio (23 aprile) ‖ *St.* —*'s cross*, la croce di S. Giorgio ‖ *s. (sl. aer.)* pilota automatico ☆ — *medal*, medaglia al valore civile.

georgette [dʒɔː'dʒet], *s. (tessile)* « georgette », crespo.

Georgia ['dʒɔːdʒjə], *no.pr.f.* Giorgia.

Georgian[1] ['dʒɔːdʒjən], *ag.* dell'epoca georgiana (XVIII sec.: Giorgio I, II, III; inizio del XX sec.: Giorgio V).

Georgian[2], *ag.* georgiano ‖ *s.c.* georgiano, georgiana (abitante del Caucaso e degli Stati Uniti) ‖ *s.* lingua georgiana.

Georgiana [,dʒɔːdʒi'ɑːnə], *no.pr.f.* Giorgiana.

georgic ['dʒɔːdʒik], *ag.* georgico ‖ **Georgics** ['dʒɔː-dʒiks], *s.pl. (lett.)* le Georgiche.

Gerald ['dʒerəld], *no.pr.m.* Gerardo, Gherardo.

Geraldine ['dʒerəldiːn], *no.pr.f.* Geraldina.

geranium [dʒi'reinjəm], *s. (bot.)* geranio.

Gerard ['dʒerɑːd], *no. pr. m.* Gherardo, Gerardo.

gerent ['dʒiərənt], *s.* gerente.

gerfalcon ['dʒɜː,fɔːlkən], *s. (ornit.)* girofalco.

geriatrics [,dʒeri'ætriks], **geriatry** ['dʒeriətri], *s. (med.)* geriatria.

germ [dʒɜːm], *s.* **1.** *(biol.)* germe; germoglio **2.** *fig.* principio, inizio: *in* —, in embrione ☆ — *warfare*, guerra batteriologica.

to **germ**, *v.i. fig.* sorgere, nascere.

german[1] ['dʒɜːmən], *ag.* germano ☆ *cousin* —, cugino germano, cugino di primo grado.

German[2], *ag.* tedesco: *the* — *language*, la lingua tedesca, il tedesco; *a* — *woman*, una tedesca ‖ *s.c.* tedesco, tedesca ‖ *s.* lingua tedesca ‖ *High, Low* —, alto, basso tedesco ☆ — *silver*, lega di rame, nickel e zinco; — *text*, *(tip.)* caratteri gotici.

germander [dʒɜː'mændə*], *s. (bot.)* camedrio, querciuola.

germane [dʒɜː'mein], *ag.* riguardante; concernente, pertinente: *question* — *to the subject*, questione pertinente all'argomento.

Germanic [dʒɜː'mænik], *ag.* germanico ‖ *s.* lingua germanica.

Germanism ['dʒɜːmənizəm], *s.* germanesimo.

Germanist ['dʒɜːmənist], *s.c.* germanista.

Germanity [dʒɜː'mæniti], *s.* germanesimo.

germanium [dʒɜː'meinjəm], *s. (chim.)* germanio.

Germanization [,dʒɜːmənai'zeiʃən], *s.* germanizzazione.

to **Germanize** ['dʒɜːmənaiz], *v.t.i.* **1.** tradurre in tedesco **2.** germanizzare, germanizzarsi.

Germanomania [,dʒɜːmənə'meinjə], *s.* germanomania.

Germanophil [dʒɜː'mænəfil], *s.* germanofilo.

Germanophobe [dʒɜː'mænəfoub], *s.* germanofobo.

Germanophobia [,dʒɜːmænə'foubjə], *s.* germanofobia.

Germany ['dʒɜːməni], *no.pr. (geog.)* Germania.

germicide ['dʒɜːmisaid], *ag. s.* germicida.

germinal[1] ['dʒɜːmin], *ag.* **1.** *(biol.)* germinale **2.** *fig.* in germe.

Germinal[2], *s. (st. francese)* germinale.

germinant ['dʒɜːminənt], *ag.* germinante.

to **germinate** ['dʒɜːmineit], *v.t.i.* **1.** *(biol.)* far germinare; germinare **2.** *fig.* produrre; nascere.

germination [,dʒɜːmi'neiʃən], *s. (biol.)* germinazione.

germinative ['dʒɜːmineitiv], *ag.* germinativo.

germinator ['dʒɜːmineitə*], *s.c.* germinatore, germinatrice; generatore, generatrice.

gerontocracy [,dʒerɔn'tɔkrəsi], *s.* gerontocrazia.

gerontologist [,dʒerɔn'tɔlədʒist], *s. (med.)* gerontologo.

gerontology [,dʒerɔn'tɔlədʒi], *s. (med.)* gerontologia.

Gerry ['dʒeri], *no.pr.m. dim.* di *Jeremy.*

gerrymander ['dʒerimændə*], *s. (pol.)* broglio elettorale.

to **gerrymander**, *v.t.i.* **1.** *(pol.)* brogliare (nelle elezioni) **2.** *(fam. amer.)* svisare (i fatti).

gerrymanderer ['dʒerimændərə*], *s. (pol.)* chi commette broglio elettorale.

Gertrude ['gɜːtruːd], *no.pr.f.* Geltrude.

Gerty ['gɜːti], *no.pr.f. dim.* di **Gertrude.**

gerund ['dʒerənd], *s. (gram.)* gerundio ☆ — *-grinder*, insegnante pedante.

gerundial [dʒi'rʌndiəl], *ag. (gram.)* gerundivo.

gerundive [dʒi'rʌndiv], *ag.s. (gram.)* gerundivo.

Gervase ['dʒɜːvəs], *no.pr.m.* Gervasio.

Geryon ['geriən], *no.pr.m. (mit.)* Gerione.

gesso ['dʒesoul], *s.* **1.** gesso per calchi **2.** calco in gesso.

gest[1] [dʒest], *s.pl.* **1.** *(arc.)* gesta, imprese **2.** *(st.)* canzone di gesta.

gest[2], *s. (arc.)* **1.** portamento, aspetto **2.** gesto.

gestation [dʒes'teiʃən], *s. (fisiol.)* gestazione.

gestatorial [,dʒestə'tɔːriəl], *ag.* gestatorio: — *chair*, *(eccl.)* sedia gestatoria.

to **gesticulate** [dʒes'tikjuleit], *v.t.i.* esprimere a gesti; gesticolare.

gesticulation [dʒes,tikju'leiʃən], *s.* gesticolazione; gesto.

gesticulator [dʒes'tikjuleitə*], *s.c.* chi gesticola.

gesticulatory [dʒes'tikjulətəri], *ag.* gesticolante.

gesture ['dʒestʃə*], *s.* **1.** gesto, movimento (della mano, ecc.) **2.** *fig.* gesto, atto: *a* — *of friendship*, un atto di amicizia **3.** il gestire: *this actor is a master of the art of* —, questo attore è maestro nell'arte del gestire.

to **gesture**, *v.t.i.* esprimere a gesti; gesticolare.

get [get], *s. (spec. sl.)* piccolo, nato (di animali).

to **get**, *pass.p.p.* **got** [gɔt], *p.p. (arc.* o talvolta *amer.)* **gotten** ['gɔtn], *v.t.i.* **1.** ottenere, ricevere; **acquistare, comprare; guadagnare; procurare, procurarsi:** *can you* — *me that book?*, puoi procurarmi quel libro?; *he got ten years in jail*, fu condannato a dieci anni di prigione; *I* — *my things at Simpson's*, mi rifornisco da Simpson; *she gets £ 700 a year*, guadagna 700 sterline all'anno; *she got it for £ 2*, l'ha comprato per 2 sterline; *to* — *admission free*, entrare gratis; *to* — *leave from s.o. to do sthg.*, ottenere da qlcu. il permesso di fare ql.co.; *to* — *sthg. for s.o.* (o *to* — *s.o, sthg.*), procurare ql.co. a qlcu. ‖ *you'll* — *it hot*, *(sl.)* riceverai una bella lavata di capo **2. prendere, cogliere, afferrare; comprendere:** *did you* — *the six-thirty train?*, hai preso il treno delle sei e trenta?; *do you* — *my meaning?*, mi capisci?; *got me?*, *(fam. amer.)* mi hai compreso?; *it always gets me to see a child crying*, mi colpisce sempre vedere piangere un bambino; *pains* — *me in my back*, mi prendono dei dolori alla schiena ‖ *she has got the upper hand*, ha preso il sopravvento ‖ *that's got him!*, l'ha lasciato di stucco! ‖ *we* — *London every evening*, prendiamo (radio) Londra tutte le sere ‖ *what's got her?*, che cosa ne è di lei? ‖ *you've got it!*, l'hai indovinata!, è proprio così! ‖ *to* — *by heart*, imparare a memoria **3. andare, arrivare:** *how long does it take to* — *to Sidney?*, quanto tempo ci vuole per andare a Sidney?; *when did you* — *here?*, quando sei arrivato? ‖ — *to hell!*, vai all'inferno! ‖ *to* — *aboard a train, etc.*, *(amer.)* salire su un treno, ecc. ‖ *to* — *to do sthg.*, *fig.* assuefarsi a, finire col fare ql.co. ‖ *to* — *there*, *(sl. amer.)* riuscire **4. divenire, diventare:** *to* — *better*, stare meglio, ristabilirsi (in salute); migliorare (di condizioni, cose); *to* — *drunk*, ubriacarsi; *to* — *fat*, ingrassare; *to* — *free*, liberarsi, disimpegnarsi; *to* — *ill*, ammalarsi; *to* — *married*, sposarsi; *to* — *ready*, prepararsi: *to* — *sthg. ready*, preparare ql.co.; *to* — *rid of sthg.*, sbarazzarsi di ql.co.; *to* — *sore about sthg.*, *(amer.)* andare in collera per ql.co.; *to* — *tired*, stancarsi; *to* — *wet*, bagnarsi **5. mettersi, cacciarsi:** *I shall* — *to bed*, mi metterò a letto; *if they* — *talking they never stop*, *(fam.)* se si mettono a parlare non si fermano più; *things have got going at last*, la faccenda si è messa finalmente in moto; *where has that book got to?*, dove si è cacciato quel libro? **6. fare avere, fare arrivare, portare, trasportare:** *aeroplanes* — *you to places quickly*, *(amer.)* l'aeroplano è un mezzo di trasporto celere; *how am I to* — *it for you?*, come posso procurartelo? **7.** (VI) **fare, farsi:** *I must — the work finished,* devo finire, far finire il lavoro; *why don't you — him arrested?*, perchè non lo fai arrestare?; *to — sthg. done, mended, etc.*, far fare, far riparare, ecc. ql.co. || *to — done with sthg.*, farla finita con ql.co. **8.** (IV) **indurre, convincere, persuadere:** *I hope to — her to sing*, spero di indurla a cantare || *that got him guessing*, (*sl. amer.*) gli mise una pulce nell'orecchio **9. to have got**, (*fam.*) avere, possedere; dovere: *have you got many friends?*, hai molti amici?; *what's that got to do with it?*, che c'entra quello?; *to have got to do sthg.*, dover fare ql.co.: *it has got to be done*, bisogna farlo; *you have got to do it*, devi farlo || **Seguito da prep. 10.** *to — across*, (far) attraversare **11.** *to — at*, riuscire a prendere; riuscire a capire; corrompere: *let me — at him!*, se mi capita a tiro!; *to — at a witness, the press*, corrompere un testimone, la stampa || *what are you getting at?*, (*fam.*) dove vuoi arrivare?, cosa vuoi insinuare? || *who(m) are you getting at?*, (*fam.*) con chi ce l'hai? **12.** *to — into*, (far) entrare in; penetrare in; salire in (carrozza, treno, ecc.); (*fam.*) indossare; confondere (la testa, di liquori): *to — into one's head*, *fig.* mettersi in testa; *to — into the way of doing sthg.*, prendere l'abitudine di fare ql.co., imparare a fare ql.co. **13.** *to — off*, scendere da (autobus, ecc.); allontanarsi da || *— off the grass!*, via dal prato! || *to — s.o., sthg. off one's hands*, sbarazzarsi di qlcu., di ql.co. **14.** *to — on*, montare a, in (cavallo, bicicletta) **15.** *to — over*, scavalcare, superare; (*sl.*) circuire: *he got over the fence*, egli scavalcò lo steccato; *he soon got over his illness*, ha superato in fretta la sua malattia **16.** *to — round*, aggirare, lusingare, adulare; eludere (leggi, ecc.) **17.** *to — through*, portare a termine; essere approvato in, da (di leggi, ecc.); far passare (il tempo, ecc.): *to — through a lot of work*, sbrigare molto lavoro **18.** *to — to*, cominciare || **Seguito da av. 19.** *to — about*, reggersi in piedi (dopo malattia); muoversi, circolare; diffondersi (di notizie): *it is getting about that...*, corre voce che... **20.** *to — abroad*, diffondersi (di notizie) **21.** *to — across*, far capire; aver successo: *to — a play across*, portare una commedia al successo **22.** *to — ahead*, superare; far progressi **23.** *to — along*, andare avanti; procedere; aver successo: *I'm getting along nicely*, me la passo abbastanza bene; *to — along with s.o.*, andar d'accordo con qlcu. || *— along (with you)!*, (*sl.*) vattene!; vuoi scherzare! **24.** *to — away*, allontanarsi, fuggire: *there is no getting away from the fact that...*, (*fam.*) non c'è dubbio che...; *to — s.o., sthg., away*, allontanare qlcu., rimuovere ql.co. || *to — away with sthg.*, (*fam.*) farla franca **25.** *to — back*, ritornare; recuperare || *to — one's own back on s.o.* (*amer.* *to — back at s.o.*), rendere la pariglia a qlcu. **26.** *to — behind*, rimanere indietro (nel lavoro, ecc.) **27.** *to — by*, passare **28.** *to — down*, (far) scendere; tirar giù || *to — down to facts*, venire ai fatti || *to — down to one's work*, mettersi a lavorare sul serio || *to — sthg. down on paper*, mettere ql.co. per iscritto **29.** *to — in*, (far) entrare, salire; arrivare (di treno); (*pol.*) essere eletto: *to — a boat in*, far entrare un'imbarcazione nel porto; *to — a word in*, interloquire || *to — in with s.o.*, stabilire rapporti di cordialità con qlcu. || *to — one's hand in*, farsi la mano (alla pesca, al tennis, ecc.) **30.** *to — off*, andarsene, partire || *to — off cheap*, cavarsela a buon mercato || *to — off to sleep*, addormentarsi || *to — s.o. off*, levare qlcu. dai guai: *his youth got him off*, la sua giovane età lo salvò || *to — sthg. off*, mandare, spedire ql.co. **31.** *to — on*, andare avanti, avvicinarsi; prosperare; far progressi: *he is getting on for forty*, si avvicina ai quaranta (anni); *they — on very well together*, vanno molto d'accordo || *how are you getting on?*, come va?, come te la cavi? **32.** *to — out*, (far) uscire; produrre: *I can't — the cork out*, non riesco a levare il turacciolo || *to — out of a habit*, *to — s.o. out of a habit*, *fig.* perdere, far perdere a qlcu. un'abitudine **33.** *to — over*, far passare sopra; aver successo; portare a termine: *the play*

failed to — over, (*fam.*) la commedia non ebbe successo **34.** *to — through*, (far) giungere a destinazione; superare un esame; essere approvato (di legge) || *to — through to s.o.*, ottenere la comunicazione telefonica con qlcu. || *to — through with s.o.*, non avere più niente da fare con qlcu. || *to — through with sthg.*, riuscire a fare, sopportare ql.co. **35.** *to — together*, riunire, riunirsi **36.** *to — under*, domare, dominare **37.** *to — up*, alzarsi; preparare; allestire: *everyone got up*, tutti si alzarono; *he got up a successful play*, mise in scena una commedia di successo || *to — (oneself) up*, farsi bello, pararsi a festa; truccarsi (il viso); travestirsi || *to — up steam*, mettere sotto pressione (anche *fig.*) || *to — up to*, arrivare fino a: *he got up to me*, mi raggiunse; *I got up to page 400*, sono arrivato a pagina 400.

get-at-able [get'ætəbl], *ag.* (*fam.*) accessibile, raggiungibile, ottenibile.

get-at-ableness [get'ætəblnis], *s.* (*fam.*) accessibilità.

getaway ['getəwei], *s.* **1.** fuga, evasione **2.** (*spor.*) partenza **3.** (*mec.*) avviamento.

get-off ['getɔ:f], *s.* (*aer.*) decollo.

get-out ['getaut], *s.* (*fam.*) evasione.

get-rich-quick ['get-ritʃ'kwik], *ag.* (*amer.* *fam.*) che promette mare e monti (di progetto).

gettable ['getəbl], *ag.* ottenibile.

getter ['getə*], *s.c.* (*fam.*) chi ottiene || *s.* (*elett.*) assorbitore ☆ *— -up*, promotore, promotrice; organizzatore, organizzatrice (di festa, ecc.); compilatore, compilatrice (di libro, ecc.) || *go- —*, (*sl. amer.*) arrivista.

get-up ['getʌp], *s.* **1.** abbigliamento, tenuta; truccatura **2.** presentazione (di libro, giornale, opera): *— of a play*, allestimento scenico di un'opera; *the general — of the book is attractive*, il libro si presenta molto bene **3.** (*amer.*) vigore, energia.

geum ['dʒi:əm], *s.* (*bot.*) erba cariofillacea.

gewgaw ['gju:gɔ:], *s.* ninnolo, gingillo; cianfrusaglia.

gey [gei], *av.* (*scoz.*) molto, considerevolmente.

geyser ['gaizə*], *nel senso* **2.** ['gi:zə*], *s.* **1.** (*geol.*) geyser **2.** scaldabagno.

Ghana ['gɑ:nə], *no.pr.* (*geog.*) Ghana.

Ghanaian [gɑ:'neiən], **Ghanian** ['gɑ:njən], *ag.s.c.* (abitante) del Ghana.

gharry ['gæri], *s.* (*ang.-in.*) vettura a cavalli indiana.

ghastlily ['gɑ:stlili], *av.* in modo spettrale; spaventosamente.

ghastliness ['gɑ:stlinis], *s.* **1.** aspetto spaventoso, sinistro; orrore **2.** pallore spettrale.

ghastly ['gɑ:stli], *ag.* **1.** orrendo, spaventoso **2.** spettrale, mortale: *— paleness*, pallore mortale; *he looks —*, sembra uno spettro.

ghastly, *av.* spaventosamente, orribilmente: *he is — pale*, è pallido come la morte.

Gha(u)ts (the) [gɔ:ts], *no.pr.* (*geog.*) monti Ghati || **ghа(u)t** [gɔ:t], *s.* (*ang.-in.*) **1.** catena di montagne; passo di montagna **2.** scala che porta all'approdo di un fiume.

ghee [gi:], *s.* (*ang.-in.*) burro semifluido.

Ghent [gent], *no.pr.* (*geog.*) Gand.

gherkin ['gə:kin], *s.* cetriolo.

ghetto ['getou], *pl.* **ghettos** ['getouz], *s.* **1.** ghetto, quartiere ebraico **2.** *fig.* isolamento; quartiere isolato.

ghost [goust], *s.* **1.** spirito || *the Holy Ghost*, lo Spirito Santo **2.** spirito, anima (dei morti) || *to give up the —*, rendere l'anima (a Dio) **3.** fantasma, spettro; apparizione || *the — of a chance*, (*fam.*) l'ombra di una probabilità ☆ *— -story*, racconto di spiriti; *— town*, città abbandonata; *— writer*, « negro » (scrittore anonimo che prepara materiale letterario per altri).

ghostlike ['goustlaik], *ag.* **1.** spettrale **2.** pallido, smunto.

ghostliness ['goustlinis], *s.* **1.** l'essere spettrale **2.** spiritualità.

ghostly ['goustli], *ag.* **1.** spettrale **2.** spirituale; religioso.

ghoul [gu:l], *s.* **1.** (*mit. orientale*) demone che divora i cadaveri **2.** *fig.* uomo rapace e crudele.

ghoulish ['gu:liʃ], *ag.* demoniaco; macabro.

Ghurka ['guəkə], *s.* Gurka (indigeno nepalese); soldato appartenente a reggimenti anglo-indiani con prevalenza di Gurka.

GI ['dʒi:'ai], *pl.* **GI's** ['dʒi:'aiz], *s.* (*amer. abbr. di Government Issue*) **1.** assegnazione di divise, rifornimenti, ecc. da parte del governo ai militari **2.** (*sl.amer.*) soldato degli U.S.A.

giant ['dʒaiənt], *s.* gigante (anche *fig.*).

giantess ['dʒaiəntis], *s.* gigantessa.

giantism ['dʒaiəntizəm], *s.* (*patol.*) gigantismo.

giaour ['dʒauə*], *s.* giaurro.

gib¹ [gib], *s.* (*fam.*) gatto (generalmente castrato).

gib², *s.* (*mec.*) lardone.

gibber ['dʒibə*], *s.* borbottio, farfuglio, parole confuse.

to **gibber**, *v.i.* borbottare, farfugliare, parlare in modo inarticolato e inintelligibile.

gibberish ['gibəriʃ], *s.* discorso inarticolato, inintelligibile.

gibbet ['dʒibit], *s.* **1.** patibolo, forca **2.** (*mec.*) braccio di gru.

to **gibbet**, *v.t.* **1.** impiccare; esporre sulla forca **2.** *fig.* mettere alla berlina.

gibbon ['gibən], *s.* (*zool.*) gibbone.

gibbous ['gibəs], *ag.* gibboso, gobbo.

gibbously ['gibəsli], *av.* con gibbosità.

gibbousness ['gibəsnis], *s.* gibbosità.

gibbosity [gi'bositi], *s.* gibbosità, gobba.

gibe [dʒaib], *s.* sarcasmo, scherno; beffa.

to **gibe**, *v.t.i.* schernire; beffare, beffarsi: *to — at s.o.*, beffarsi di qlcu.

giber ['dʒaibə*], *s.c.* schernitore, schernitrice; beffatore, beffatrice.

gibingly ['dʒaibiŋli], *av.* in modo beffardo; sarcasticamente.

giblets ['dʒiblits], *s.pl.* rigaglie (di oca, ecc.).

Gibraltar [dʒi'brɔ:ltə*], *no.pr.* (*geog.*) Gibilterra.

gibus ['dʒaibəs], *s.* gibus (cappello a cilindro pieghevole).

giddily ['gidili], *av.* storditamente, vertiginosamente.

giddiness ['gidinis], *s.* **1.** capogiro; vertigini **2.** *fig.* incostanza, frivolezza, storditezza.

giddy ['gidi], *ag.* **1.** stordito, preso da vertigini: *to feel —*, aver le vertigini **2.** vertiginoso; rapido: *a — height*, un'altezza vertiginosa **3.** frivolo, stordito, scervellato: *she is a — young thing*, è una svaporatella ‖ *to play the — goat*, (*sl.*) fare il buffone ☆ *— headed*, frastornato, scervellato.

to **giddy**, *v.t.i.* stordire; dar le vertigini a; essere preso da vertigini.

Gideon ['gidiən], *no.pr.m.* Gedeone.

gift [gift], *s.* **1.** dono; regalo **—**, regalo di nozze **2.** donazione: *deed of —*, contratto di donazione **3.** dote naturale, talento: *— for poetry*, inclinazione per la poesia ☆ *— -horse*, caval donato: *never look a — -horse in the mouth*, *prov.* a caval donato non si guarda in bocca.

to **gift**, *v.t.* **1.** dotare (*with*, di): *to be gifted with great talent*, essere dotato di grande talento **2.** (*scoz.*) regalare ‖ *to — sthg. away*, regalare qlco.

gifted ['giftid], *ag.* dotato, fornito di talento.

giftless ['giftlis], *ag.* privo di talento.

gig¹ [gig], *s.* **1.** barroccino, calessino **2.** (*mar.*) lancia; iole ☆ *— lamps*, fanali del barroccino; (*sl.*) occhiali.

to **gig¹**, *pass.p.p.* **gigged** [gigd], *v.i.* viaggiare in calessino.

gig², *s.* rampone, fiocina.

to **gig²**, *v.t.* ramponare, fiocinare.

gig³, *s.:* *— (-mill)*, (*ind. tessile*) garzatrice.

to **gig³**, *v.t.* (*ind. tessile*) garzare.

gig⁴, *s.* (*sl. amer.*) punizione.

to **gig⁴**, *v.t.* (*sl. amer.*) punire, dare una punizione a.

gigantean [,dʒaigæn'ti(:)ən], **gigantesque** [,dʒaigæn'tesk], **gigantic** [dʒai'gæntik], *ag.* gigantesco.

gigantically [dʒai'gæntikəli], *av.* gigantescamente, in modo gigantesco.

giggle ['gigl], *s.* **1.** risatina sciocca, affettata **2.** brevi scoppi di riso soffocato.

to **giggle**, *v.i.* **1.** ridere scioccamente, con affettazione **2.** far risatine soffocate.

giggler ['giglə*], *s.c.* chi ride scioccamente.

giglet ['giglit], **giglot** ['giglət], *s.* ragazza chiassosa.

gigolo ['ʒigəlou], *pl.* **gigolos** ['ʒigəlouz], *s.* gigolo.

gigot ['dʒigət], *s.* (*cuc.*) cosciotto di montone (generalmente arrostito).

gigue [ʒi:g], *s.* (*mus.*) giga.

Gilbert ['gilbət], *no.pr.m.* Gilberto.

gild, *V.* guild.

to **gild** [gild], *v.t.* **1.** dorare, indorare **2.** *fig.* indorare; abbellire; colorire: *to — the pill*, indorare la pillola.

gilded ['gildid], *ag.* dorato: *— spurs*, speroni dorati (emblema dei cavalieri) ‖ *the Gilded Chamber*, la Camera dei Lords ☆ *— youth*, gioventù dorata.

gilder ['gildə*], *s.c.* doratore, doratrice.

gilding ['gildiŋ], *s.* doratura (anche *fig.*).

Giles [dʒailz], *no.pr.m.* Egidio.

gill¹ [gil], *s. gener. pl.* **1.** branchia (di pesce) **2.** bargiglio **3.** lamelle (di funghi) **4.** pappagorgia ‖ *to look rosy about the gills*, aver un aspetto roseo e sano ☆ *— -net*, rete per pesci.

to **gill¹**, *v.t.* **1.** sbuzzare, pulire (pesci) **2.** mondare (funghi) **3.** pescare; prendere (pesci) nella rete.

gill², *s.* **1.** gola, burrone **2.** torrente, ruscello.

gill³, *s.* (*ind. tessile*) pettine, cardo.

to **gill³**, *v.t.* (*ind. tessile*) pettinare; cardare.

gill⁴ [dʒil], *s.* **1.** « gill » (misura di capacità = l. 0,142) **2.** recipiente contenente un quarto di pinta.

Gill⁵, *no.pr.f.* Gill ‖ *Jack and —*, un ragazzo e la sua ragazza.

gillie ['gili], *s.* (*scoz.*) servo, servitore.

gillyflower ['dʒili,flauə*], *s.* (*rar.*) garofano.

to **gilravage** [gil'rævidʒ], *v.i.* (*scoz.*) festeggiare, banchettare chiassosamente.

gilt¹ [gilt], *ag.* dorato: *— frame*, cornice dorata ‖ *s.* **1.** doratura (anche *fig.*) ‖ *to take the — off the ginger -bread*, (*fam.*) spogliare ql.co. di ogni attrattiva **2.** (*sl.*) oro; denaro ☆ *— -head*, pesce pagello.

gilt², *s.* (*dial.*) scrofa.

gimbals ['dʒimbəlz], *s.pl.* (*mar. mec.*) sospensione cardanica.

gimcrack ['dʒimkræk], *ag.* appariscente, vistoso; dozzinale, di poco pregio ‖ *s.* cianfrusaglia; oggetto vistoso, dozzinale ☆ *— ornaments*, ornamenti da quattro soldi.

gimcrackery ['dʒim,krækəri], *s.* paccottiglia, ciarpame.

gimcracky ['dʒim,kræki], *ag.* appariscente vistoso; dozzinale, di poco pregio.

gimlet ['gimlit], *s.* (*strum. artig.*) succhiello ☆ *— -eyed*, dalla vista molto acuta; *— -hole*, foro fatto con il succhiello.

to **gimlet**, *v.t.* succhiellare, forare col succhiello.

gimmick ['gimik], *s.* (*sl. amer.*) **1.** trucco (di prestigiatore) **2.** aggeggio, arnese.

gimp [gimp], *s.* **1.** cordoncino, spighetta in seta, in cotone **2.** lenza in seta rinforzata.

gin¹ [dʒin], *s.* gin, gineprella ☆ *— -drinker's liver*, (*patol.*) cirrosi epatica atrofica degli alcoolizzati; *— -fizz*, bevanda a base di gin, limone e seltz; *— -mill*, (*sl. amer.*) bar, spaccio di alcoolici; *— -shop*, taverna, bettola; *— -sling*, bevanda fredda americana a base di gin aromatizzato e addolcito; *— -soaked*, abbrutito dall'alcool; *— -trap*, (*sl.*) bocca.

gin², *s.* **1.** trappola (anche *fig.*) **2.** (*mec.*) argano, paranco; capra **3.** (*ind. tessile*) sgranatrice (di cotone) ☆ *— -block*, (*mar.*) paranco ad una o più pulegge; *— -pole*, (*mec.*) falcone ‖ *knife roller —*, (*ind. tessile*) sgranatrice a cilindri a coltelli.

to **gin**², *pass.p.p.* **ginned** [dʒind], *v.t.* **1.** intrappolare **2.** (*ind. tessile*) sgranare (cotone).

gin³, *s.* **1.** (*austral.*) donna indigena **2.** femmina del canguro.

gin⁴ [gin], *cong.* (*scoz. dial.*) se ‖ *prep.* (*scoz.*) entro.

to **gin**⁵, *pass.* **gan** [gæn], *v.t.i.* (*rar. arc.*) incominciare.

ging [giŋ], *V.* **gang**.

gingall [ˈdʒingɔːl], *s.* cannone a rotazione di piccolo calibro (in India, Cina).

ginger [ˈdʒindʒə*], *ag.* fulvo, rosso (di capelli) ‖ *s.* **1.** (*bot.*) zenzero ‖ — *shall be hot in the mouth*, fig. l'amore del piacere è immortale **2.** *fig.* vivacità, vitalità, energia: *she wants some* —, (*sl.*) manca di vivacità, non è certo un granello di pepe **3.** color fulvo, rossiccio ☆ — *-ale* (o — *-beer* o — *-pop*), bibita allo zenzero; — *-race*, (*bot.*) radice di zenzero.

to **ginger**, *v.t.* **1.** aromatizzare allo zenzero **2.** *to* — **up**, stimolare, incitare (anche *fig.*): *to* — *s.o. up*, scuotere, incitare qlcu.

gingerade [ˌdʒindʒərˈeid], *s.* bibita allo zenzero.

gingerbread [ˈdʒindʒəbred], *s.* pan di zenzero.

gingerly [ˈdʒindʒəli], *ag.* guardingo, cauto ‖ *av.* con precauzione; a passi felpati.

gingery [ˈdʒindʒəri], *ag.* **1.** che sa di zenzero; aromatizzato allo zenzero **2.** fulvo, rosso (di capelli).

gingham [ˈgiŋəm], *s.* **1.** percallina a righe o quadretti **2.** (*fam.*) ombrello.

gingili [ˈdʒindʒili], *s.* **1.** (*bot.*) giuggiolena, sesamo orientale **2.** — (*oil*), (*ind.*) olio di sesamo.

gingival [dʒinˈdʒaivəl], *ag.* (*anat.*) gengivale.

gingivitis [ˌdʒindʒiˈvaitis], *s.* (*patol.*) gengivite.

gingle, (*arc.*) per **jingle**.

ginglymus [ˈdʒiŋgliməs], *s.* (*anat.*) ginglimo.

gink [giŋk], *s.* (*sl.*) tipo, individuo.

ginkgo [ˈgiŋkou], *s.* (*bot.*) ginko.

ginseng [ˈdʒinseŋ], *s.* (*bot.*) ginseng.

to **gip** [gip], *pass.p.p.* **gipped** [gipt], *v.t.* pulire (pesce) per la conservazione.

gippo [ˈdʒipou], *s.* (*sl. mil.*) minestra; stufato; sugo.

gippy [ˈdʒipi], *s.* (*sl. mil.*) soldato egiziano.

gipsy [ˈdʒipsi], *s.c.* zingaro, zingara; gitano, gitana ☆ — *-rose*, (*bot.*) scabbiosa; — *wagon*, carrozzone degli zingari.

gipsydom [ˈdʒipsidəm], *s.* gli zingari; ambiente zingaresco.

to **gipsyfy** [ˈdʒipsifai], *v.t.i.* rendere zingaro; diventare zingaro.

gipsyhood [ˈdʒipsihud], *s.* natura, qualità di zingaro.

gipsyish [ˈdʒipsiiʃ], *ag.* zingaresco.

gipsyism [ˈdʒipsiizəm], *s.* natura, qualità di zingaro.

giraffe [dʒiˈrɑːf], *s.* giraffa.

girandole [ˈdʒirəndoul], *s.* **1.** girandola **2.** candelabro a braccia **3.** orecchino a pendente.

girasole [ˈdʒirəsoul], *s.* (*min.*) opale di fuoco.

to **gird**¹ [gəːd], *pass.p.p.* **girded** [ˈgəːdid], **girt** [gəːt], *v.t.* cingere, fasciare; circondare: *to* — (*on*) *a sword*, cingere la spada ‖ *to* — *up one's loins*, (*Bibbia*) prepararsi ad agire, alla lotta ☆ *sea-girt*, circondato dal mare: *a sea-girt fortress*, una fortezza circondata dal mare.

gird², *s.* (*dial.*) scarto; slancio **2.** beffa, scherno.

to **gird**², *v.i.* **1.** (*dial.*) muoversi rapidamente, precipitarsi; slanciarsi **2.** *fig.* farsi beffe: *to* — *at s.o.*, deridere, schernire qlcu.

girder [ˈgəːdə*], *s.* **1.** (*edil.*) trave maestra **2.** (*mec.*) sbarra; chiave ☆ — *-bridge*, ponte a travate; — *-rail*, (*ferr.*) rotaia a gola per tranvie.

girding¹ [ˈgəːdiŋ], *s.* azione del cingere.

girding², *s.* **1.** (*dial.*) slancio **2.** beffa.

girdle¹ [ˈgəːdl], *s.* **1.** cintura, fascia: — *of walls*, cerchia di mura **2.** busto leggero, ventriera **3.** linea divisoria delle due facce di un brillante **4.** (*arch.*) cintura, collarino (di colonna) ☆ *pelvic* —, (*anat.*) cintura pelvica; *shoulder* — (o *pectoral* —), (*anat.*) cingolo scapolare.

to **girdle**¹, *v.t.* **1.** cingere, fasciare **2.** racchiudere, cir-

condare **3.** incidere tutt'intorno (un albero per farlo morire o fruttificare maggiormente).

girdle², *s.* teglia di ferro per dolci.

girdler [ˈgəːdlə*], *s.* **1.** chi fa cinture **2.** chi circonda.

girkin [ˈgəːkin], *s.* cetriolo.

girl [gəːl], *s.* **1.** ragazza, bambina: *little* (o *young*) —, ragazzina; *his first child was not a boy, but a* —, il suo primo figlio non fu un maschio, ma una bambina ‖ *Girl Guide*, Giovane Esploratrice ‖ *old* —, (*fam.*) vecchia mia (termine affettivo) **2.** fanciulla, giovane donna: — *out of her teens*, giovane donna **3.** cameriera **4.** (*sl.*) fidanzata: *my cousin and his* —, mio cugino e la sua ragazza ☆ — *friend*, amica; innamorata ‖ *call-* —, (*sl.*) ragazza squillo; *cover* —, ragazza da copertina; *factory-* —, operaia; *flower* —, fioraia; *pick-up* —, peripatetica; *servant-* —, domestica; *shop-* —, commessa.

girlie [ˈgəːli], *s.* ragazzina.

girlhood [ˈgəːlhud], *s.* adolescenza (di ragazza): *in her* —, quand'era una ragazzina.

girlish [ˈgəːliʃ], *ag.* fanciullesco; di ragazza, da ragazza.

girlishly [ˈgəːliʃli], *av.* da ragazza, da ragazzina.

girlishness [ˈgəːliʃnis], *s.* modi, carattere, ingenuità di fanciulla.

to **girn** [gəːn], *v.i.* (*scoz.*) mostrare i denti.

Girondist [dʒiˈrondist], *ag.s.* (*st. francese*) girondino.

girt [gəːt], *s.* **1.** misurazione di superficie non piana **2.** circonferenza.

to **girt**, *V.* to **gird**¹.

girt, *pass.p.p.* di to **gird**¹.

girth [gəːθ], *s.* **1.** giro, circonferenza: *fifty inches in* —, cinquanta pollici di circonferenza **2.** cinghia, sottopancia ☆ *saddle-* —, cinghia della sella.

to **girth**, *v.t.i.* **1.** misurare (di circonferenza) **2.** cingere, circondare **3.** assicurare la sella a (un cavallo).

gist [dʒist], *s.* **1.** (*dir.*) base, fondamento **2.** perno: *the* — *of the question*, il nocciolo della questione.

gittern [ˈgitəːn], *s.* (*arc.*) cetra.

give [giv], *s.* **1.** elasticità **2.** rinunzia; arrendevolezza.

to **give**, *pass.* **gave** [geiv], *p.p.* **given** [ˈgivn], *v.t.i.* **1.** dare; offrire; distribuire, somministrare; rendere; pagare: *I* — *the boy an apple* (o *I* — *an apple to the boy*), dò una mela al ragazzo; *I have to* — *you a present and a word from him*, devo darti un suo regalo e comunicarti quanto mi ha detto; *I must* — *you your pill now*, ora devo darti la pillola; *I would* — *anything to know...*, (*fam.*) non so cosa darei per sapere...; *a pen was given to the girl* (o *the girl was given a pen*), diedero una penna alla ragazza; *shares giving 5 %*, azioni che rendono il 5 %; *they gave him the name of his grandfather*, gli diedero il nome del nonno; *they gave their lives for their country*, diedero la vita per la patria; *you gave it (to) him*, tu glielo desti ‖ *you will* — *me your cold*, mi attaccherai il raffreddore ‖ — *her my love!*, salutala affettuosamente da parte mia! ‖ — *me the good old times!*, (*fam.*) potessi tornare ai bei tempi passati! ‖ *he gave his son what for!*, (*sl.*) ha conciato il figlio per le feste! ‖ *I don't* — *a damn!*, (*sl.*) me ne infischio altamente! ‖ *what are you giving us?*, (*sl.*) che cosa ci volete dar a bere? ‖ *to* — *a chance* (o *sl. a break*), dare una possibilità ‖ *to* — *a dinner*, dare un pranzo ‖ *to* — *an injection*, fare un'iniezione ‖ *to* — *oneself to monastic life*, consacrarsi alla vita monastica; *to* — *oneself* (o *one's mind*) *to the study of*, darsi allo studio di ‖ *to* — *s.o. a hint*, accennare, dare un avvertimento, un suggerimento a qlcu. ‖ *to* — *and take*, fare concessioni reciproche ‖ *to* — *as good as one gets*, (*sl.*) rendere pan per focaccia ‖ *to* — *birth to*, dare alla luce, dar origine a (anche *fig.*) ‖ *to* — *a bound*, dare un balzo ‖ *to* — *currency to sthg.*, divulgare ql.co. ‖ *to* — *ear to sthg.*, prestare orecchio a ql.co. ‖ *to* — *evidence*, testimoniare: *to* — *evidence of sthg.*, dar prova di ql.co. ‖ *to* — *ground*, cedere terreno ‖ *to* — *heed to s.o., sthg.*, prestare attenzione, dar retta a qlcu., ql.co. ‖ *to* — *it to s.o.*, (*sl.*) punire qlcu. ‖ *to* — *a loud laugh*, scoppiare in una risata fragorosa ‖ *to — rise to*, provocare, causare ‖ *to — a sigh*, sospirare, dare un sospiro ‖ *to — s.o. a bit of one's mind*, (*fam.*) dirne quattro a qlcu. ‖ *to — s.o. a good dressing down*, (*sl.*) dare una bella lavata di capo, sonarle a qlcu. ‖ *to — s.o. a hand*, dare una mano a, aiutare qlcu. ‖ *to — s.o. joy*, (*fam.*) augurare felicità a qlcu. ‖ *to — s.o. the slip*, (*sl.*) piantare in asso qlcu. ‖ *to — s.o. to believe* (o *to understand*) *that*, far credere a qlcu. che ‖ *to — a toast for s.o.*, brindare, proporre un brindisi alla salute di qlcu. ‖ *to — tongue*, abbaiare (di cani); gridare, parlare a voce alta ‖ *to — vent to sthg.*, dare sfogo a ql.co. ‖ *to — way*, cedere, rompersi; abbandonarsi; ritirarsi; calare (di prezzi) **2.** (*mat.*) **dare come risultato; segnare:** *five plus three gives eight*, cinque più tre fa otto; *the thermometer gives thirty degrees*, il termometro segna trenta gradi **3. eseguire; cantare; rappresentare:** *to — a play*, dare una commedia; *to — a song*, cantare una canzone **4. dare accesso, guardare:** *this door gives into our garden*, questa porta dà nel nostro giardino; *the window gives (up)on the square*, la finestra guarda sulla piazza **5. cedere, allentarsi; addolcirsi** (di tempo): *the branches of that tree — but don't break*, i rami di quell'albero si piegano ma non si spezzano; *the frost is giving*, comincia il disgelo; *the ground gave under our feet*, il terreno cedette sotto i nostri passi **6.** *to — away*, dar via, disfarsi di; distribuire, consegnare; lasciarsi sfuggire; rivelare, tradire: *as chairman I was asked to — away the prizes*, come presidente mi fu chiesto di distribuire i premi; *don't — me away!*, non tradirmi!; *he has given away a good chance*, si è lasciato sfuggire una buona occasione ‖ *to — away the bride*, accompagnare la sposa all'altare ‖ *to — the show* (o *the game*) *away*, (*fam.*) rivelare i punti deboli di qlcu. **7.** *to — back*, rendere, restituire; riflettere (immagini): *this book must be given back on Saturday*, questo libro deve essere restituito sabato **8.** *to — forth*, render noto, divulgare; emettere **9.** *to — in*, cedere, arrendersi: *the enemy were forced to — in*, il nemico fu costretto alla resa; *he gave in to my opinion*, finì col darmi ragione ‖ *to — sthg. in*, consegnare ql.co. ‖ *to — in one's name*, iscriversi; farsi annunciare **10.** *to — off*, emettere; (*chim.*) liberare: *this coal gives off a thick smoke*, questo carbone sprigiona un fumo denso **11.** *to — out*, annunciare; distribuire; venir a mancare, esaurirsi, venir meno: *the candle was giving out*, la candela stava per spegnersi; *his strength gave out*, gli vennero a mancare le forze; *it was given out that he was ill*, si annunciò che era malato; *the teacher gave out the papers*, l'insegnante distribuì i compiti ‖ *to — oneself out as* (o *for* o *to be...*), farsi passare per: *she gave herself out to be a princess*, si fece passare per principessa **12.** *to — over*, smettere, cessare; abbandonare: *— over grumbling!*, smettila di borbottare!; *I hope the snow will — over*, spero smetterà di nevicare; *to — s.o. over*, abbandonare qlcu.; *to — sthg. over to s.o.*, consegnare ql.co. a qlcu. **13.** *to — up*, (I) smettere; cedere; consegnare; abbandonare: *you must — up smoking and drinking*, devi smettere di fumare e di bere; *the boy gave up his seat to the old lady*, il ragazzo cedette il posto alla vecchia signora; *the position was given up to the enemy*, la posizione fu abbandonata al nemico; *she was so late that we gave her up*, era così in ritardo che ormai non l'aspettavamo più; *the surgeon gave him up*, il chirurgo lo considerò spacciato; *they gave him up*, lo consegnarono alle autorità giudiziarie ‖ *to — oneself up*, costituirsi ‖ *to — oneself up to sthg.*, dedicarsi, darsi a ql.co.

give and take [ˈgivənˈteik], *s.* compromesso, concessione reciproca ☆ *a — policy*, politica di equo compromesso.

giveaway [ˈgivəwei], *ag.* a premio ‖ *s.* **1.** (*fam.*) tradimento **2.** (*amer.*) comunicazione, rivelazione involontaria ☆ *— show*, (*rad. tv.*) trasmissione a premi.

given [ˈgivn], *p.p.* di *to give* ‖ *ag.* convenuto; sta-

bilito; specificato; dato: *— to*, dedito a; *at a — time*, ad ora stabilita ☆ *— name*, (*amer.*) nome di battesimo.

giver [ˈgivə*], *s.c.* donatore, donatrice; dispensatore, dispensatrice.

giving [ˈgiviŋ], *s.* il dare; dono, donazione; elemosina ☆ *— out*, annuncio, dichiarazione; distribuzione.

gizzard [ˈgizəd], *s.* **1.** (*anat.*) ventriglio (di uccello) **2.** (*fam.*) stomaco: *to stick in one's —*, fig. rimanere sullo stomaco; non riuscire a tranguiare.

glabrous [ˈgleibrəs], *ag.* glabro, liscio.

glacé [ˈglæsei], *ag.* glacé.

glacial [ˈgleisjəl], *ag.* glaciale ☆ *— era*, era glaciale.

glacially [ˈgleisjəli], *ag.* glacialmente.

glaciated [ˈgleisieitid], *ag.* coperto di ghiaccio.

glaciation [ˌglæsiˈeiʃən], *s.* glaciazione.

glacier [ˈglæsjə*], *s.* ghiacciaio.

glacis [ˈglæsis], *pl.* **glacises** [ˈglæsisiz], *s.* terreno in pendio; spalto.

glad [glæd], *ag.* **1.** contento, felice: *I am — I went*, sono contento d'essere andato; *I am very — (of it)*, me ne rallegro molto; *I am very — to see you*, mi fa molto piacere vederti, sono felice di vederti **2.** allegro, lieto: *— tidings*, liete notizie **3.** (*sl.*) provocante, sgargiante: *—eye*, (*fam.*) sguardo gioioso, d'amore; *— rags*, (*fam.*) abiti della festa, abiti da sera.

to glad, *v.t.* (*arc.*) allietare.

to gladden [ˈglædn], *v.t.* rallegrare, ricreare, allietare, render contento.

glade [gleid], *s.* radura.

gladful [ˈglædful], *ag.* (*arc.*) contento, assai contento.

gladfulness [ˈglædfulnis], *s.* (*arc.*) contentezza.

gladiator [ˈglædieitə*], *s.* gladiatore.

gladiatorial [ˌglædiəˈtɔːriəl], *ag.* gladiatorio ☆ *— fights*, combattimenti di gladiatori.

gladiolus [ˌglædiˈouləs], *pl.* **gladioluses** [ˌglædiˈouləsiz], **gladioli** [ˌglædiˈoulai], *s.* (*bot.*) gladiolo.

gladly [ˈglædli], *av.* volentieri, con piacere.

gladness [ˈglædnis], *s.* contentezza, allegrezza, gioia.

gladsome [ˈglædsəm], *ag.* (*poet.*) contento, allegro, gaio.

gladsomely [ˈglædsəmli], *av.* (*poet.*) allegramente; con piacere.

gladsomeness [ˈglædsəmnis], *s.* (*poet.*) gioia, contentezza, allegrezza.

Gladstone [ˈglædstən], *s.*: *— (bag)*, valigia leggera a soffietto ☆ *— claret*, chiaretto francese a buon mercato.

glady [ˈgleidi], *ag.* ricco di radure.

Gladys [ˈglædis], *no.pr.f.* Gladys.

Glagolitic [ˌglægouˈlitik], *ag.* glagolitico.

glair [glɛə*], *s.* **1.** albume **2.** sostanze viscose usate per albuminare (carta, stoffa, ecc.).

to glair, *v.t.* albuminare; cospargere di albume.

glaireous [ˈglɛəriəs], **glairy** [ˈglɛəri], *ag.* simile ad albumina; viscido e trasparente.

glaive [gleiv], *s.* (*arc. poet.*) spada.

to glamorize [ˈglæməraiz], *v.t.* (*amer.*) **1.** rendere attraente, affascinante **2.** valorizzare al massimo (un'attrice).

glamorous [ˈglæmərəs], *ag.* affascinante; incantatore; attraente.

glamour [ˈglæmə*], *s.* **1.** incantesimo, malìa: *to cast a — over s.o.*, stregare ql.cu. **2.** fascino; prestigio: *the — of the stage*, il fascino del palcoscenico ☆ *— girl*, donna fatale, fatalona.

to glamour, *v.t.* incantare, stregare.

glance[1] [glɑːns], *s.* **1.** sguardo rapido; occhiata: *to give* (o *to take*) *a — at*, dare un'occhiata a ‖ *at (the) first —*, a prima vista **2.** bagliore, gibigiana **3.** colpo obliquo; rimbalzo.

to glance[1], *v.t.i.* **1.** gettare, lanciare uno sguardo: *to — at*, portare lo sguardo su, fig. fare allusione a; *to — one's eye* (o *to —*) *over a page*, scorrere rapidamente una pagina ‖ *to — up from one's work*, distogliere lo sguardo dal proprio lavoro **2.** alludere a; sfiorare (un argomento): *to — at a subject*, toccare fugacemente un argomento (cercando di evitarlo) || *to — off* (o *from*) *a subject*, sorvolare su di un argomento || *to — over a subject*, alludere ad un argomento 3. guizzare, balenare, scintillare 4. deviare; sfiorare: *the sword glanced off his armour*, la spada gli sfiorò l'armatura.

glance², *s.* minerale lucente per il contenuto metallico ☆ *— coal*, antracite || *cobalt —*, cobalto grigio; *copper —*, calcocite.

to glance², *v.t.* (*amer.*) spianare (metalli).

glancing ['glɑːnsiŋ], *ag.* fugace, rapido.

glancingly ['glɑːnsiŋli], *av.* fugacemente.

gland¹ [glænd], *s.* (*anat. bot.*) glandola ☆ *lacrimal —*, glandola lacrimaria; *lymphatic —*, glandola linfatica.

gland², *s.* (*bot.*) ghianda.

gland³, *s.* (*mec.*) pressatreccia; premistoppa.

glandered ['glændəd], *ag.* (*patol.*) affetto da morva.

glanders ['glændəz], *s.* (*patol.*) morva.

glanderous ['glændərəs], *ag.* (*patol.*) avente i caratteri della morva; affetto dalla morva.

glandiferous [glæn'difərəs], *ag.* (*bot.*) ghiandifero.

glandular ['glændjulə*], *ag.* (*anat.*) glandolare.

glandule ['glændjuːl], *s.* (*anat.*) glandoletta.

glandulous ['glændjuləs], *ag.* (*anat.*) glanduloso.

glare [glɛə*] *s.* 1. abbagliamento; luce abbagliante, accecante; riverbero: *the — of the sun on the water*, il riverbero del sole sull'acqua 2. sguardo truce e penetrante: *she looked at me with a —*, ella mi fissò con uno sguardo minaccioso.

to glare, *v.t.i.* 1. splendere di luce abbagliante 2. guardare con occhio torvo; esprimere (odio, disprezzo) con uno sguardo: *they were glaring at one another*, si guardarono in cagnesco.

glaring ['glɛəriŋ], *ag.* 1. abbagliante 2. evidente: *a — mistake*, un errore madornale ☆ *— headlights*, (*aut.*) fari abbaglianti.

glaringly ['glɛəriŋli], *av.* 1. con luce abbagliante 2. in modo evidente.

glaringness ['glɛəriŋnis], *s.* splendore abbagliante.

glary ['glɛəri], *ag.* 1. abbagliante 2. evidente.

glass [glɑːs], *s.* 1. vetro; cristallo; (*fam.*) specchio: *— breaks easily*, il vetro si rompe facilmente || *people who live in — houses shouldn't throw stones*, non criticare se non vuoi essere criticato 2. bicchiere; contenuto di un bicchiere: *he has had a — too much*, è un po' brillo 3. *pl.* occhiali: *to wear glasses*, portare gli occhiali 4. lente; telescopio; microscopio ☆ *— -blower*, soffiatore di vetro; *— -case*, vetrinetta, custodia di vetro; *— -cutter*, tagliatore di cristallo; vetraio; diamante tagliavetro; *— -door*, porta a vetri; *— -eye*, occhio di vetro; cecità (dei cavalli); *— -grinding*, smerigliatura del vetro; *— -house*, serra; studio fotografico a vetri; vetreria; (*fam.*) prigione militare; *— -man*, venditore, fabbricante di vetro; *— -painting*, pittura su vetro; *— -paper*, carta vetrata; *— -ware*, vetrerie, articoli di vetro; *— -works*, fabbrica di vetro || *eye- —*, monocolo, caramella; *field- —*, cannocchiale; *flint- —*, cristallo « flint »; *looking- —*, specchio: *to look at oneself in the looking- —*, specchiarsi; *magnifying- —*, lente d'ingrandimento; *opera-glasses*, binocolo da teatro; *plate- —*, cristallo (per vetrine, ecc.); *spun- —*, vetro filato; *wine —*, bicchiere per vino.

to glass, *v.t.* 1. specchiare; riflettere: *trees — themselves in the lake*, gli alberi si specchiano nel lago 2. (*rar.*) mettere i vetri a: *to — a window*, mettere i vetri ad una finestra 3. (*rar.*) rendere (l'occhio) vitreo 4. (*ind.*) levigare (pelli) 5. (*ind.*) imbottigliare (commestibili in recipienti di vetro per conservarli).

glassful ['glɑːsful], *s.* bicchiere pieno, il contenuto di un bicchiere.

glassily ['glɑːsili], *av.* con l'apparenza del vetro.

glassiness ['glɑːsinis], *s.* trasparenza; vetrosità.

glasswort ['glɑːs-wəːt], *s.* (*bot.*) salicornia.

glassy ['glɑːsi], *ag.* vitreo, simile al vetro; cristal-

lino, trasparente, limpido: *— eye*, occhio vitreo; *— water*, acqua limpida.

Glaswegian [glæs'wiːdʒən], *ag.s.c.* (abitante) di Glasgow.

glaucoma [glɔː'koumə], *s.* (*patol.*) glaucoma.

glaucous ['glɔːkəs], *ag.* 1. glauco 2. pruinoso (di frutti, foglie).

glaze¹ [gleiz], *s.* 1. (*ceramica*) mano di vernice trasparente pigmentata 2. superficie vetrosa 3. (*amer.*) rivestimento di ghiaccio 4. (*cuc.*) gelatina di copertura 5. (*sl.*) finestra.

to glaze¹, *v.t.i.* 1. fornire di vetro, mettere vetri a: *to — (in) a window*, mettere il vetro a una finestra 2. smaltare a vetrino; vetrificare: *to — pottery*, smaltare ceramiche 3. stendere una vernice trasparente su 4. levigare; lucidare 5. diventare vitreo (dell'occhio) ☆ *a glazed-in verandah*, una veranda chiusa da vetri.

to glaze², *v.i.* (*dial.*) guardare fissamente.

glazer ['gleizə*], *s.* verniciatore.

glazier ['gleiziə*], *s.* vetraio.

glazing ['gleiziŋ], *s.* 1. montaggio di vetri 2. vetrinatura 3. (*pitt.*) mano di vernice trasparente 4. lucidatura.

glazy ['gleizi], *ag.* simile a vetro; vitreo.

gleam [gliːm], *s.* barlume; sprazzo di luce: *a — of hope*, *fig.* un barlume di speranza.

to gleam, *v.i.* scintillare, luccicare, baluginare (anche *fig.*): *fury gleams in his eyes*, il furore lampeggia nei suoi occhi; *his knife gleamed in the dark*, il suo coltello brillava nel buio.

gleaming ['gliːmiŋ], *ag.* scintillante || *s.* bagliore.

gleamy ['gliːmi], *ag.* scintillante.

glean [gliːn], *s.* ciò che si è spigolato, raccolto.

to glean, *v.t.i.* 1. spigolare 2. *fig.* spigolare, raccogliere (notizie, fatti, ecc.).

gleaner ['gliːnə*], *s.c.* spigolatore, spigolatrice.

gleaning ['gliːniŋ], *s.* 1. spigolatura 2. *fig.* spigolatura, raccolta di notizie, fatti ecc.

glebe [gliːb], *s.* 1. (*poet.*) gleba, zolla; terra; campo 2. terreno facente parte di un beneficio ecclesiastico.

gledge [gledʒ], *s.* (*scoz.*) occhiata in tralice; sguardo astuto.

to gledge, *v.i.* (*scoz.*) guardare di traverso, in tralice; guardare astutamente.

glee [gliː], *s.* 1. allegria, gioia: *in high —*, al colmo della gioia 2. (*mus.*) canone (per sole voci maschili).

gleeful ['gliːful], *ag.* allegro, giulivo.

gleefully ['gliːfuli], *av.* gioiosamente; con gioia; allegramente.

gleeman, *pl.* **gleemen** ['gliːmən], *s.* (*st.*) menestrello.

gleep [gliːp], *s.* (da **G.L.E.E.P.**, sigla di *Graphite Low Energy Experimental Pile*), (*fis.*) la prima pila atomica inglese.

gleesome ['gliːsəm], *ag.* gioioso, allegro.

gleet [gliːt], *s.* (*patol.*) 1. uretrite cronica 2. (*rar.*) icore, sanie, pus.

gleety ['gliːti], *ag.* viscoso.

glen [glen], *s.* (*scoz.*) gola, forra.

glene ['gliːni(ː)], *s.* (*anat.*) 1. globo oculare; pupilla 2. glene, cavità articolare poco profonda.

glengarry [glen'gæri], *s.* tipo di berretto scozzese.

glenoid ['gliːnoid], *ag.* (*anat.*) glenoideo.

to gley [glai], *v.i.* (*scoz.*) guardare in tralice.

gleyed [glaid], *ag.* (*scoz.*) strabico.

gliadin ['glaiədin], *s.* (*chim.*) gliadina.

glib [glib], *ag.* 1. liscio, levigato (di superficie) 2. loquace, facondo; sciolto scorrevole (di discorso); pronto: *a — excuse*, una scusa pronta 3. sciolto, libero (di movimento).

to glib, *pass.p.p.* **glibbed** [glibd], *v.i.* parlare fluentemente.

glib, *av.* fluentemente.

glibly ['glibli], *av.* in modo sciolto, scorrevole; fluentemente.

glibness ['glibnis], *s.* **1.** facilità (di parola) **2.** scioltezza (di movimento).

glidder ['glidə*], **gliddery** ['glidəri], *ag.* (*dial.*) sdrucciolevole.

glide [glaid], *s.* **1.** sdrucciolamento, scivolata; passo strisciato (nella danza) **2.** (*mus.*) legamento **3.** (*fonet.*) suono transitorio degli organi vocali **4.** (*aer.*) volo librato, volo planato.

to **glide**, *v.t.i.* **1.** scorrere, far scorrere; sdrucciolare; scivolare, avanzare scivolando (anche *fig.*): *the boat is gliding away*, la barca si allontana scivolando; *to — into bad habits*, scivolare nelle cattive abitudini **2.** passare, far passare; trascorrere; volare (di tempo): *the days glided on*, i giorni passarono inavvertitamente; *he lets his life — away*, egli trascorre la vita in un ozio monotono.

glider ['glaidə*], *s.* **1.** (*aer.*) aliante **2.** aliantista **3.** (*mar.*) idroplano.

gliding ['glaidiŋ], *ag.* **1.** scorrevole; sdrucciolevole **2.** (*aer.*) che plana ☆ — *boat*, (*mar.*) idroscivolante; — *certificate*, (*aer.*) brevetto di volo a vela; — *landing*, (*aer.*) atterraggio a volo planato; — *machine*, (*aer.*) aliante.

gliding, *s.* (*aer.*) volo a vela.

glidingly ['glaidiŋli], *av.* scorrevolmente.

gliff [glif], *s.* (*scoz.*) **1.** occhiata, sguardo **2.** spavento improvviso.

glim [glim], *s.* (*sl.*) lume, candela, lanterna: *to douse the —*, spegnere la luce.

glimmer ['glimə*], *s.* barlume, raggio fioco; lucicchio, scintillio (dell'acqua, ecc.): — *of hope*, barlume di speranza; *the first — of dawn*, le prime luci dell'alba.

to **glimmer**, *v.i.* brillare, luccicare, tralucere.

glimmering ['gliməriŋ], *ag.* debole, fioco, tremolante (di luce) || *s.* **1.** barlume; luccichio, scintillio **2.** *fig.* barlume, pallida idea.

glimpse [glimps], *s.* **1.** visione, apparizione fugace: *to catch* (o *get*) *a — of sthg.*, vedere ql.co di sfuggita; *to show glimpses of sthg.*, *fig.* lasciare intravvedere ql.co. || *the glimpses of the moon*, (*letter.*) il mondo sublunare **2.** barlume, vaga idea: *he got a — of what had happened*, ebbe una pallida idea di ciò che era accaduto.

to **glimpse**, *v.t.i.* **1.** intravvedere, vedere di sfuggita; gettare uno sguardo: *to — at* (o *upon*) *sthg.*, gettare uno sguardo di sfuggita su ql.co. **2.** (*poet.*) albeggiare.

glint [glint], *s.* (*scoz.*) **1.** occhiata, sguardo **2.** scintillio, luccichio; lucentezza.

to **glint**, *v.i.* **1.** guardare in tralice **2.** *V.* to **glitter**.

glisk [glisk], *s.* **1.** (*scoz.*) apparizione **2.** lampo; occhiata **3.** barlume.

glissade [gli'sɑ:d], *s.* **1.** (*alpinismo*) scivolata su pendio nevoso **2.** (*danza*) passo strisciato.

to **glissade**, *v.i.* **1.** (*alpinismo*) scivolare su pendio nevoso **2.** (*danza*) eseguire un passo strisciato.

glisten ['glisn], *s.* scintillio, luccichio; lucentezza.

to **glisten**, *V.* to **glitter**.

to **glister** ['glistə*], *V.* to **glitter**.

glitter ['glitə*], *s.* scintillio, luccichio; lucentezza.

to **glitter**, *v.i.* brillare, scintillare, rifulgere: *the lake is glittering in the moonlight*, il lago scintilla al chiaro di luna || *all is not gold that glitters*, (*prov.*) non è tutt'oro quello che riluce.

glittering ['glitəriŋ], *ag.* scintillante, brillante; lucente: *uniform — with decorations*, un'uniforme scintillante di decorazioni || *s.* luccichio, scintillio.

glitteringly ['glitəriŋli], *av.* con scintillio, brillio.

gloam [gloum], *s.* luce crepuscolare; crepuscolo.

to **gloam**, *v.i.* (*scoz.*) imbrunire; oscurarsi.

gloaming ['gloumiŋ], *s.* crepuscolo, il cader della notte.

to **gloat** [glout], *v.i.* lanciare sguardi carichi di cupidigia, di gioia maligna: *the miser gloated over his gold*, l'avaro guardava avidamente il suo oro; *they seemed to — over our misfortunes*, sembravano godere delle nostre disgrazie.

gloatingly ['gloutiŋli], *av.* avidamente; intensamente.

global ['gloubəl], *ag.* globale.

globate ['gloubeit], *ag.* a forma di globo.

globe [gloub], *s.* **1.** globo, sfera; palla: — *of the eye*, globo dell'occhio **2.** pianeta; stella: *sole* || *the* (o *this*) —, la terra **3.** mappamondo ☆ — *-fish*, (*ittiol.*) pesce dei diodonti; — *-flower* (o — *-crowfoot*), (*bot.*) botton d'oro; — *-trotter*, giramondo || *celestial* —, globo celeste; *light* —, (*elett.*) diffusore a globo; *terrestrial* —, sfera terrestre.

globose ['gloubous], *ag.* rotondo, sferico.

globosity [glou'bositi], *s.* globosità.

globous ['gloubəs], **globular** ['globjulə*], *ag.* sferico, globoso.

globularity [,globju'læriti], *s.* globosità.

globularly ['globjuləli], *av.* in forma globulare.

globule ['globju:l], *s.* globulo; goccia.

globulin ['globjulin], *s.* (*chim. fisiol.*) globulina.

glomerate ['glomərit], *ag.* agglomerato; accumulato.

to **glomerate** ['gloməreit], *v.t.* (*arc.*) agglomerare.

glomerule ['gloməru:l], *s.* **1.** (*anat.*) glomerulo **2.** (*bot.*) inflorescenza cimosa.

gloom [glu:m], *s.* **1.** oscurità; buio; tenebre **2.** *fig.* tristezza; malinconia; depressione.

to **gloom**, *v.t.i.* **1.** oscurare, oscurarsi, offuscarsi; essere nuvoloso **2.** aver l'aria scontenta e abbattuta; rattristare, essere triste e depresso.

gloomily ['glu:mili], *av.* **1.** oscuramente **2.** malinconicamente, tristemente.

gloominess ['glu:minis], *s.* **1.** oscurità **2.** tristezza; malinconia.

gloomy ['glu:mi], *ag.* **1.** cupo, oscuro, tenebroso, tetro; lugubre; triste; malinconico: *Romanticism and its — heroes*, il Romanticismo ed i suoi eroi tenebrosi || *to see the — side of things*, veder nero, vedere le cose dal loro lato peggiore **2.** fosco; annuvolato: — *weather*, tempo oscuro.

glorification [,glo:rifi'keiʃən], *s.* glorificazione.

to **glorify** ['glo:rifai], *v.t.* glorificare.

gloriole ['glo:rioul], *s.* aureola.

glorious ['glo:riəs], *ag.* **1.** maestoso; glorioso, illustre: *the — reign of Queen Elizabeth*, il glorioso regno della Regina Elisabetta **2.** (*fam.*) delizioso, piacevole; stupendo, splendido (anche *iron.*): *a — sunrise*, una splendida alba; *what a — day!*, che giornata stupenda!; *what a — muddle!*, che bel pasticcio!.

gloriously ['glo:riəsli], *av.* **1.** gloriosamente **2.** splendidamente; deliziosamente.

gloriousness ['glo:riəsnis], *s.* l'essere glorioso; magnificenza.

glory ['glo:ri], *s.* **1.** gloria, onore, fama; motivo di vanto: *the glories of ancient Greece*, le glorie dell'antica Grecia; *the paths of — lead but to the grave*, i sentieri della gloria conducono soltanto alla tomba **2.** splendore, gloria, maestà; magnificenza: *the — of mountain scenery*, lo splendore di un panorama di montagna || *Old Glory*, la bandiera nazionale degli U.S.A. **3.** gloria, invocazione di lode, ringraziamento || — *to God in the highest*, gloria a Dio nel più alto dei Cieli **4.** splendore paradisiaco, gloria celeste: *to live with the Saints in* —, vivere nella gloria dei Santi || *to go to* —, (*sl.*) morire; *to send to* —, (*sl.*) uccidere **5.** aureola.

to **glory**, *v.i.* vantarsi; gloriarsi; insuperbirsi: *to — in doing sthg.*, gloriarsi di fare ql.co.; *to — in one's riches*, vantarsi delle proprie ricchezze.

glory-hole ['glo:rihoul], *s.* **1.** (*fam.*) ripostiglio di cianfrusaglie; cassetto; stanzino **2.** (*ind.*) spia, finestrino di fornace.

gloryingly ['glo:riiŋli], *av.* vanagloriosamente.

gloss[1] [glos], *s.* chiosa, glossa, commento; parafrasi.

to **gloss**[1], *v.t.* chiosare, interpretare; commentare.

gloss[2], *s.* **1.** lucentezza: *the — of satin*, la lucentezza del raso **2.** *fig.* apparenza esteriore: *a — of respectability*, una vernice di rispettabilità.

to **gloss**[2], *v.t.* **1.** lucidare, lustrare **2.** *fig.* rendere plausibile: *to — (over) one's errors*, rendere plausibili i propri errori.

glossarial [glɔ'sɛəriəl], *ag.* di, relativo a glossario.

glossarist ['glɔsərist], *s.* compilatore di glossario.

glossary ['glɔsəri], *s.* glossario; lessico.

glossator [glɔ'seitə*], *s.* glossatore, chiosatore.

glossily ['glɔsili], *av.* lucidamente, brillantemente, lucentemente.

glossiness ['glɔsinis], *s.* lucidezza, lucentezza.

glossitis [glɔ'saitis], *s.* (*patol.*) glossite.

glossographer [glɔ'sɔgrəfə*], *s.* glossatore, commentatore.

glossology [glɔ'sɔlədʒi], *s.* **1.** glossologia, glottologia; filologia comparata **2.** studio delle malattie della lingua.

glossy ['glɔsi], *ag.* lucido, brillante, lucente.

glottic ['glɔtik], *ag.* **1.** di lingua **2.** di glottologia.

glottis ['glɔtis], *s.* (*anat.*) glottide.

glottology [glɔ'tɔlədʒi], *s.* glottologia.

Gloucester ['glɔstə*], *s.* «Gloucester» (tipo di formaggio del Gloucestershire).

glove [glʌv], *s.* guanto: *it fits like a —,* calza come un guanto ‖ *to be hand in — with s.o.,* essere molto intimo con qlcu. ‖ *to take off the gloves to s.o.,* avere una seria contesa, discussione con qlcu. ‖ *to throw down the —,* sfidare ☆ *— -fight,* gara di pugilato; *— -maker,* guantaio; *— -stretcher,* allarga guanti ‖ *boxing —,* guantone da pugilato.

to glove, *v.t.* inguantare, mettere i guanti a.

gloved [glʌvd], *ag.* inguantato ☆ *white- —,* con, in guanti bianchi: *white- — hand,* mano inguantata di bianco.

gloveless ['glʌvlis], *ag.* senza guanti.

glover ['glʌvə*], *s.c.* guantaio, guantaia.

glow [glou], *s.* **1.** calore (del corpo): *to be in a —,* essere accaldato; *to feel a pleasant —,* sentire un piacevole calore per tutto il corpo **2.** fuoco, incandescenza: *in a —,* incandescente **3.** splendore, scintillio: *the — of the clouds at sunset,* lo splendore delle nubi al tramonto **4.** colorito vivo, sano: *— of health,* bel colorito, colorito sano; *a rich —,* un bel colore acceso **5.** *fig.* ardore, ira; passione: *the — of youth,* l'ardore della gioventù ☆ *— -lamp,* lampada incandescente; *— -worm,* lucciola.

to glow, *v.i.* **1.** essere infuocato, incandescente **2.** avvampare (per il caldo, per un'emozione, ecc.): *her cheeks glowed,* aveva il viso in fiamme **3.** risplendere, scintillare: *forests that — with autumn tints,* foreste che risplendono dei colori autunnali **4.** *fig.* ardere: *to — with pleasure,* ardere di piacere; *to — with zeal,* ardere di zelo.

glower ['glauə*], *s.* sguardo torvo, minaccioso.

to glower, *v.i.* fare un viso sdegnato, minaccioso: *he glowered at me,* egli mi guardò sdegnato.

gloweringly ['glauəriŋli], *av.* con sguardo torvo, minaccioso.

glowing ['glouiŋ], *ag.* **1.** incandescente, ardente: *— sky,* cielo di fuoco **2.** risplendente, raggiante **3.** entusiastico: *to paint in — colours,* descrivere con entusiasmo; *to speak in — terms of s.o.,* dire meraviglie di qlcu.

glowingly ['glouiŋli], *av.* con splendore; ardentemente; ferventemente.

gloxinia [glɔk'sinjə], *s.* (*bot.*) glossinia.

to gloze [glouz], *v.t.* velare con argomenti speciosi, palliare.

glozing ['glouziŋ], *s.* adulazione; discorso specioso.

Glubbdubdrib [,glʌbdʌb'drib], *no.pr.* (*geog. lett.*) Glubbdubdrib.

glucic ['glu:sik], *ag.* (*chim.*) di glucosio.

glucina [glu:'sainə], *s.* (*chim.*) glucina.

glucinum [glu:'sainəm], *s.* (*chim.*) glucinio.

glucose ['glu:kous], *s.* (*chim.*) glucosio, destrosio.

glue [glu:], *s.* colla, glutine ☆ *— -pot,* recipiente per sciogliere la colla ‖ *bone —,* colla d'ossa; *fish- —,* colla di pesce, ittiocolla.

to glue, *v.t.* **1.** incollare: *to — two pieces of wood together,* incollare due pezzi di legno **2.** *fig.* appiccicare,

attaccare: *he is always glued to his father,* è sempre appiccicato a suo padre; *his ear was glued to the key -hole,* stava ad origliare al buco della serratura.

gluer ['glu:ə*], *s.c.* chi incolla.

gluey ['glu(:)i], *ag.* colloso; appiccicaticcio; viscoso.

glueyness ['glu(:)inis], *s.* viscosità.

gluish ['glu(:)iʃ], *ag.* appiccicoso; viscoso.

glum [glʌm], *ag.* tetro; accigliato; depresso: *as — as a funeral,* (*fam.*) triste come un funerale.

glume [glu:m], *s.* (*bot.*) gluma.

glumly ['glʌmli], *av.* accigliatamente; con aria triste.

glumness ['glʌmnis], *s.* l'essere accigliato; tristezza.

glumpish ['glʌmpiʃ], *ag.* (*sl.*) piuttosto triste, cupo.

glumps [glʌmps], *s.pl.* (*sl.*) malumore, musoneria.

glut [glʌt], *s.* **1.** scorpacciata, eccesso (di cibo, ecc.) **2.** (*comm.*) sovrabbondanza, ingorgo, saturazione: *there is a — of these goods in the market,* il mercato è saturo di questa merce.

to glut, *pass.p.p.* **glutted** ['glʌtid], *v.t.i.* **1.** far fare una scorpacciata a; saziare, saziarsi; satollare, satollarsi: *to — oneself with,* saziarsi di **2.** *fig.* saziare, saziarsi; pascere, pascersi: *to — one's eyes,* saziare la vista **3.** (*comm.*) saturare (il mercato).

gluten ['glu:tən], *s.* glutine.

gluteus [glu:'ti:əs], *pl.* **glutei** [glu:'ti:ai], *s.* (*anat.*) gluteo.

to glutinate ['glu:tineit], *v.t.* attaccare con glutine.

to glutinize ['glu:tinaiz], *v.t.* rendere glutinoso.

glutinosity [,glu:ti'nɔsiti], *s.* glutinosità.

glutinous ['glu:tinəs], *ag.* glutinoso.

glutinousness ['glu:tinəsnis], *s.* glutinosità.

glutton ['glʌtn], *s.* **1.** goloso; ghiottone **2.** *fig.* smodatamente amante di: *he is a — for work,* non è mai stanco di lavorare; *she is a — of books,* è una divoratrice di libri **3.** (*zool.*) ghiottone.

to gluttonize ['glʌtnaiz], *v.i.* mangiare troppo, avidamente.

gluttonous ['glʌtnəs], *ag.* ghiotto; goloso; ingordo.

gluttony ['glʌtni], *s.* ghiottoneria; ingordigia.

glyceride ['glisəraid], *s.* (*chim.*) gliceride.

glycerin(e) [,glisə'ri:n], *s.* (*chim.*) glicerina.

glycogen ['glikoudʒen], *s.* (*biol.*) glicogeno.

glycol ['glaikɔl], *s.* (*chim.*) glicole.

glyconic [glai'kɔnik], *ag.s.* (*poes.*) gliconio.

glycosuria [,glaikou'sju:riə], *s.* (*patol.*) glicosuria.

glyph [glif], *s.* (*arch.*) glifo.

glyphography [gli'fɔgrəfi], *s.* glifografia.

glyptic ['gliptik], *ag.* (*art.*) glittico.

glyptics ['gliptiks], *s.* (*art.*) glittica.

glyptography [glip'tɔgrəfi], *s.* glittografia.

glyptotheca [,gliptə'θi:kə], *s.* glittoteca.

G-man ['dʒi:mæn], *pl.* **G-men** ['dʒi:men], *s.* (*amer. abbr.* di *Government-man*) agente investigativo (del Governo Federale).

gnaphalium [næ'feiljəm], *s.* (*bot.*) gnafalio.

to gnar [nɑ:*], *pass.p.p.* **gnarred** [nɑ:d], *v.i.* ringhiare; rumoreggiare.

gnarl¹ [nɑ:l], *s.* nodo (del legno).

gnarl², *s.* ringhio (di cane).

gnarled [nɑ:ld], *ag.* **1.** nodoso (di albero) **2.** rugoso, grinzoso; deformato.

to gnash [næʃ], *v.t.i.* digrignare (i denti).

gnashingly ['næʃiŋli], *av.* battendo i denti.

gnat [næt], *s.* **1.** (*entom.*) culice; (*amer.*) zanzara **2.** inezia ‖ *to strain at a —,* dare importanza a delle inezie.

gnathic ['næθik], *ag.* (*anat.*) mascellare.

to gnaw [nɔ:], *pass.* **gnawed** [nɔ:d], *p.p.* **gnawed, gnawn** [nɔ:n], *v.t.i.* **1.** rodere, rosicchiare: *the dog was gnawing (at o into) a bone,* il cane rodeva un osso **2.** mordere; corrodere, consumare **3.** *fig.* tormentare, consumare.

gnawer ['nɔ:ə*], *s.* roditore.

gnawing ['nɔ:iŋ], *ag.* rosicante; corrodente: *a — pain,* un dolore sordo.

gnawingly ['nɔ:iŋli], *av.* in modo corrodente.

gneiss [nais], *s.* (*min.*) gneis.

gnome[1] [noum], *s.* gnomo.

gnome[2] ['noumi:], *s.* (*lett.*) massima, sentenza; aforisma.

gnomic ['noumik], *ag.* (*lett.*) gnomico; sentenzioso: — *poets*, poeti gnomici.

gnomish ['noumiʃ], *ag.* di gnomo.

gnomon ['noumon], *s.* gnomone.

gnomonic [nou'monik], *ag.* gnomonico.

gnomonics [nou'moniks], *s.* gnomonica.

gnosis ['nousis], *s.* 1. (*fil.*) gnosi 2. gnosticismo.

gnostic ['nostik], *ag.* (*fil.*) gnostico ‖ **Gnostic,** *s.* gener. *pl.* gnostici (setta di eretici).

gnosticism ['nostisizəm], *s.* (*fil.*) gnosticismo.

gnu [nu:], *s.* (*zool.*) gnu.

go [gou], *pl.* **goes** [gouz], *s.* 1. l'atto di andare ‖ *on the* —, in movimento; in declino ‖ *it's all the* —, è in voga, è all'ultimo grido 2. (*fam.*) energia; attività; animazione: *to be full of* — (o *to have plenty of* —), essere pieno di energia 3. colpo; tentativo: *at one* —, in un sol colpo, tentativo; *to have a* — *at sthg.*, tentare di fare ql.co.: *have a* —*!*, prova! 4. (*fam.*) situazione imbarazzante: *what a* —*!*, che pasticcio!.

to go, *pass.* **went** [went], *p.p.* **gone** [gon], *v.t.i.* (*3ª persona sing.pres.* **goes** [gouz] 1. **andare, andarsene; partire; cessare; passare:** *he has gone to town, into the country, abroad*, è andato in città, in campagna, all'estero; *it is getting late, I must be going*, si fa tardi, me ne devo andare; *the lot went for twenty pounds*, il lotto fu aggiudicato per venti sterline; *to* — *by train, by car*, viaggiare in treno, in auto; *to* — *for a walk*, andare a fare una passeggiata; *to* — *hunting* (o *shooting*), *fishing*, andare a caccia, a pesca; *to* — *on foot, on horseback*, andare a piedi, a cavallo; *to* — *on a journey*, fare un viaggio; *to* — *to see s.o.* (o *to* — *and see s.o.*), andare a trovare qlcu. ‖ *as times* —, dati i tempi che corrono ‖ *the bank went*, la banca fallì ‖ *be gone!* (o *get you gone!*), vattene! ‖ *going! going! gone!*, uno, due, aggiudicato! (alle aste) ‖ *he is gone*, è morto ‖ *he is going fifteen*, va per i quindici anni ‖ *it goes without saying that*, è ovvio che ‖ *it's just gone twelve*, sono appena scoccate le dodici ‖ *that fuse went yesterday*, quella valvola è saltata ieri‧ ‖ *things have gone badly with him*, le cose gli sono andate male ‖ *this material is going cheap*, questa stoffa si vende a basso prezzo ‖ *twenty shillings* — *to the pound*, venti scellini fanno una sterlina ‖ *two weeks more to* — *and he'll be home again*, ancora due settimane e sarà di nuovo a casa ‖ *to* — *one's own way*, *fig.* seguire la propria inclinazione; *to* — *with the crowd*, seguire la maggioranza ‖ *to* — *it alone*, (*sl. amer.*) agire per proprio conto, da solo ‖ *to* — *to the bad*, finir male ‖ *to* — *to a better world* (o *to one's own place*), morire ‖ *to* — *to the devil*, andare al diavolo ‖ *to* — *to the dogs*, andare in rovina ‖ *to* — *to great lengths to do sthg.*, superare tutti gli ostacoli pur fare ql.co. ‖ *to* — *to law*, ricorrere alla legge ‖ *to* — *to war*, entrare in guerra ‖ *to keep the conversation, the fire going*, alimentare la conversazione, il fuoco 2. **divenire, farsi:** *to* — *communist*, diventar comunista; *to* — *dry*, asciugarsi; *to* — *mad*, impazzire; *to* — *native*, vivere da indigeno (di uomo bianco); *to* — *red*, arrossire; *to* — *white*, impallidire 3. **funzionare; aver corso** (di moneta): *do lire* — *here?*, ha corso la lira qui? ‖ *to* — *by steam*, andare a vapore; *to set an engine going*, far funzionare un motore ‖ **Seguito da prep.** 4. *to* — **about,** occuparsi di; mettersi a lavorare a: — *about your business*, bada ai fatti tuoi 5. *to* — **after,** corteggiare, correre dietro a; brigare per (un impiego, ecc.) 6. *to* — **against,** andar contro, opporsi a: *the judgement went against the plaintiff*, la sentenza diede torto al querelante 7. *to* — **at,** attaccare, assalire ‖ *to* — *at it hard*, mettercela tutta per fare ql.co. 8. *to* — **behind,** riesaminare: *to* — *behind a decision*, ritornare su una decisione 9. *to* — **by,** regolarsi su: *I shall entirely* — *by what my lawyers say*, mi regolerò interamente su quanto dicono i miei legali ‖ *to* — *by the name of*, andare sotto il nome di 10. *to* — **for,** andare a cercare; lanciarsi contro; sostenere la causa di; essere valutato: *they went for each other in the Court*, si diedero battaglia in tribunale; *to* — *for little*, essere stimato poco 11. *to* — **into,** addentrarsi; esaminare, studiare con cura: *to* — (*further*) *into a matter*, esaminare (ulteriormente) un problema 12. *to* — **off,** uscire da, deviare da: *to* — *off the beaten track*, *fig.* prendere una nuova strada; *to* — *off one's head*, *fig.* impazzire; *to* — *off the rails*, deragliare 13. *to* — **over,** esaminare; verificare (conti, motori, ecc.); ritoccare 14. *to* — **round,** girare; visitare; circondare: *to* — *round the town*, visitare la città 15. *to* — **through,** attraversare; esaminare minuziosamente; affrontare, subire (prove, processi, ecc.); eseguire per intero, portare a termine: *that book went through seven editions*, quel libro ebbe sette edizioni; *they will* — *through the trial*, affronteranno il processo 16. *to* — **with,** accompagnare, accompagnarsi con; intonarsi con (di colori, ecc.) ‖ **Seguito da av.** 17. *to* — **about,** andare in giro; circolare (di voci, ecc.); (*mar.*) virare di bordo: *there is a rumour going about that...*, corre voce che... 18. *to* — **ahead,** avanzare senza esitazioni; fare progressi 19. *to* — **along,** procedere, andare avanti ‖ — *along with you!*, fila!, vattene!; macchè!, ma va là!, non ci credo! 20. *to* — **ashore,** approdare 21. *to* — **astray,** deviare dal retto cammino 22. *to* — **away,** andarsene 23. *to* — **back,** ritornare, indietreggiare: *to* — *back on one's steps*, ritornare sui propri passi; *to* — *back on one's word*, mancare alla parola data 24. *to* — **by,** passare, scorrere: *as the years* — *by*, col passare degli anni 25. *to* — **down,** discendere, andar giù; cadere, soccombere; affondare (di nave); abbassarsi, calare (di temperatura, acqua, sole, ecc.) ‖ *that won't* — *down with me*, questa non la bevo ‖ *to* — *down* (*from the university*) lasciare l'università; ‖ *to* — *down in history*, passare alla storia 26. *to* — **far,** fare carriera 27. *to* — **forth,** essere pubblicato, uscire (di decreto, ecc.) 28. *to* — **forward,** avanzare, far progressi 29. *to* — **in,** entrare ‖ *to* — *in for*, dedicarsi a: *to* — *in for politics*, dedicarsi alla politica 30. *to* — **off,** partire; uscir di scena; morire; esplodere; scolorirsi ‖ *to* — *off into a faint*, svenire 31. *to* — **on,** (I) procedere, continuare; passare (di tempo); accadere: *as time went on, she became more impatient*, col passar del tempo, ella divenne più impaziente ‖ *to* — *on for*, avvicinarsi a: *he is going on for forty*, va per i quaranta 32. *to* — **out,** uscire, scomparire; terminare; abbassarsi (di marea): *out you* —*!*, fuori!; *to* — *out of fashion*, passare di moda; *to* — *out* (*on strike*), mettersi in sciopero 33. *to* — **over,** trasferirsi; cambiare partito, religione 34. *to* — **round,** compiere una deviazione; girare (di ruota, ecc.); diffondersi (di voci); far visita: *my head is going round*, mi gira la testa; *there is not enough to* — *round*, non ce n'è abbastanza per tutti (di cibo, ecc.) 35. *to* — **through,** concludersi: *to* — *through with*, portare a termine: *we have got to* — *through with it*, non ci resta che andare fino in fondo 36. *to* — **up,** montare, salire: *to* — *up to town*, andare in città; *to* — *up* (*to the university*), entrare all'università.

go, (*nei composti*): -*between*, intermediario; (*spreg.*) mezzano; — -*by: to give s.o.*, *sthg. the* — -*by*, sorpassare, oltrepassare qlcu., ql.co.; schivare, evitare, sottrarsi a qlcu., ql.co.; non tenere alcun conto di qlcu., ql.co.; fingere di non vedere qlcu.; — -*cart*, girello; carrozzella per bambini; — -*getter*, (*sl. amer.*) arrivista; persona senza scrupoli; — -*kart*, (*spor.*) «go-kart»; — -*off*, segnale di partenza.

goad [goud], *s.* 1. pungolo 2. *fig.* pungolo, stimolo; assillo.

to goad, *v.t.* 1. stimolare, pungolare 2. *fig.* pungere, spingere; incitare: *to* — *s.o. into doing sthg.*, spingere qlcu. a fare ql.co.

go-ahead ['gouəhed], *ag.* (*fam.*) intraprendente; all'avanguardia: — *business man*, uomo d'affari intraprendente ‖ *s.* (*neol.*) permesso di passare all'azione.

goal [goul], *s.* **1.** traguardo; barriera; termine **2.** fine, scopo, meta: *one's — in life*, lo scopo della propria vita **3.** (*calcio*) rete, porta: *to score* (o *to kick* o *to get*) *a —*, segnare una rete; *to win by two goals*, vincere per due reti **4.** (*st. romana*) colonna (nelle gare nel circo) ☆ — *-keeper*, (*calcio*) portiere; — *-kick*, (*calcio*) rimessa del portiere; — *-post*, palo della porta.

goalie ['gouli], *s.* (*fam. calcio*) **1.** portiere **2.** rete.

goat [gout] **1.** capra ‖ *the Goat*, (*astr.*) Capricorno ‖ *to get one's —*, (*sl.*) esasperare, irritare qlcu. ‖ *to play the giddy —*, (*fam.*) fare il pazzo, lo sciocco ‖ *to separate the sheep from the goats*, separare il bene dal male **2.** *fig.* satiro ☆ — *-god*, Pan; — *-herd*, capraio; — *'s beard*, (*bot.*) olmaria, regina dei prati; barba di capra; — *-skin*, pelle di capra; — *'s wool*, cosa inesistente.

goatee [gou'ti:], *s.* barbetta a punta.

goatish ['goutiʃ], *ag.* **1.** caprino, caprigno **2.** *fig.* libidinoso; lascivo.

goatishly ['goutiʃli], *av.* **1.** a guisa di capra **2.** *fig.* lascivamente.

goatishness ['goutiʃnis], *s.* **1.** odore caprino **2.** *fig.* lascivia.

goatling ['goutliŋ], *s.* capretto, capretta.

goatsucker ['gout,sʌkə*], *s.* (*ornit.*) caprimulgo.

goaty ['gouti], *V.* **goatish**.

gob¹ [gɔb], *s.* (*volg.*) sputo; grumo di bava.

to **gob¹**, *pass. p.p.* **gobbed** [gɔbd], *v.i.* (*volg.*) sputare.

gob², *s.* (*dial. sl.*) bocca.

gob³, *s.* (*dial.*) ciarle, chiacchiere.

gob⁴, *s.* (*miner.*) ripiena.

gob⁵, *s.* (*sl. amer.*) marinaio.

gobang [gou'bæŋ], *s.* giuoco giapponese e cinese.

gobbet ['gɔbit], *s.* (*arc.*) **1.** pezzo, boccone (specialmente di carne cruda) **2.** brano per traduzione.

gobble¹ ['gɔbl], *s.* (*golf*) colpo deciso che porta la palla in buca.

to **gobble²**, *v.t.* **1.** trangugiare in fretta; inghiottire rumorosamente **2.** (*sl. amer.*) afferrare, raccogliere, impadronirsi di.

to **gobble³**, *v.i.* gloglottare (di tacchino).

gobbledy-gook ['gɔbldi'guk], *s.* (*sl. amer.*) linguaggio involuto, pomposo (specialmente burocratico).

gobbler ['gɔblə*], *s.* tacchino.

gobelin ['goubəlin], *ag.* simile a gobelin, ad arazzo ‖ *s.* «gobelin», arazzo.

gobemouche [,gɔb'mu:ʃ], *s.* credulone.

goblet ['gɔblit], *s.* (*arc.*) **1.** bicchiere di vetro, metallo **2.** (*poet.*) calice, coppa **3.** (*comm.*) (bicchiere a) calice.

goblin ['gɔblin], *s.* demonio; spirito maligno; folletto.

gobo ['goubou], *s.* (*cine.*) pannello antisonoro.

goby ['goubi], *s.* (*ittiol.*) ghiozzo; gobione.

god [gɔd], *s.* **1.** divinità, dio ‖ *feast for the gods*, banchetto degno degli dei; *to worship false gods*, adorare false divinità, idoli **2.** idolo (persona, cosa in cui si riponga affetto smoderato): *to make a — of s.o.*, fare di qlcu. un idolo **3.** *pl.* (*teat.*) gli spettatori del loggione, loggione **4.** *God*, Dio: *to pray* (*to*) *God*, pregare Dio ‖ *God Almighty*, Dio Onnipotente (anche come esclamazione); *God forbid!*, Dio non voglia!; *God help me!*, Dio mi aiuti! ‖ *what in God's name are you doing?*, in nome di Dio, cosa fai? ☆ *God's acre*, cimitero; *God's book*, la Bibbia; *God-fearing*, timorato di Dio; *God-forsaken*, miserabile; abbandonato da Dio, sperduto (di luogo); *God-man*, Uomo-Dio, Cristo; — *-smith*, (*poet. arc.*) fabbricante di idoli ‖ *household gods*, i Penati.

godchild ['gɔdtʃaild], *pl.* **godchildren** ['gɔd,tʃildrən], *s.c.* figlioccio, figlioccia.

goddaughter ['gɔd,dɔ:tə*], *s.* figlioccia.

goddam ['gɔd,dæm], *ag. intensivo* (*volg. amer.*): *he is a — fool*, è un maledetto stupido.

goddess ['gɔdis], *s.* dea ‖ — *of corn*, Cerere; — *of heaven*, Giunone; — *of hell*, Proserpina; — *of love*, Venere.

godfather ['gɔd,fɑ:ðə*], *s.* padrino.

Godfrey ['gɔdfri], *no.pr.m.* Goffredo.

godhead ['gɔdhed], *s.* divinità.

Godiva [gə'daivə], *no.pr.f.* Godiva (nobildonna che ottenne dal marito, signore di Coventry, l'abolizione di una tassa cavalcando un cavallo bianco coperta soltanto dai suoi capelli).

godless ['gɔdlis], *ag.* **1.** ateo **2.** malvagio, empio.

godlessness ['gɔdlisnis], *s.* empietà.

godlike ['gɔdlaik], *ag.* divino, simile a Dio, a un dio.

godliness ['gɔdlinis], *s.* devozione; religiosità.

godly ['gɔdli], *ag.* religioso, pio, devoto.

godmother ['gɔd,mʌðə*], *s.* madrina.

godown ['goudaun], *s.* (*ang.-in.*) magazzino.

godsend ['gɔdsend], *s.* dono del cielo, benedizione; fortuna inaspettata: *it's a —*, (*fam.*) è una manna.

godship ['gɔdʃip], *s.* divinità.

godson ['gɔdsʌn], *s.* figlioccio.

godspeed ['gɔd'spi:d], *s.* successo, buona fortuna.

Godward(s) ['gɔdwəd(z)], *av.* verso Dio.

godwit ['gɔdwit], *s.* (*ornit.*) beccaccia d'acqua.

goer ['gouə*], *s.* **1.** chi va: *comers and goers*, chi va e chi viene **2.** camminatore, trottatore: *this horse is a good —*, questo cavallo corre bene **3.** (*fam.*) individuo energico ☆ *theatre- —*, frequentatore di teatro.

gofer ['goufə*], *s.* (*cuc.*) cialda.

goffer ['gɔfə*], *s.* **1.** ferro per arricciare, pieghettare **2.** volante arricciato, pieghettato.

to **goffer**, *v.t.* arricciare; pieghettare; stirare a cannoncini; goffrare (carta, cuoio, ecc.).

goffering ['gɔfəriŋ], *s.* **1.** arricciatura, pieghettatura; stiratura a cannoncini; goffratura (di carta, cuoio, ecc.) **2.** pieghe; cannoncini.

Gog and Magog ['gɔgən'meigɔg], *no.pr.* (*Bibbia*) Goga e Magoga.

goggle ['gɔgl], *ag.* stralunato, strabuzzato; sporgente (di occhi) ☆ — *-eyed*, dagli occhi bovini.

to **goggle**, *v.t.i.* **1.** stralunare, strabuzzare, roteare (gli occhi) **2.** sporgere, essere sporgenti (di occhi).

goggles ['gɔglz], *s.pl.* **1.** occhiali di protezione; (*sl.*) occhialoni rotondi **2.** (*vet.*) capogatto, capostorno ☆ *snow- —*, occhiali da neve.

Goidel ['gɔidil], *s.c.* celta.

Goidelic [gɔi'delik], *ag.* gaelico, celtico ‖ lingua gaelica, celtica.

going ['gouiŋ], *s.* **1.** partenza **2.** l'andare; il camminare ‖ *goings and comings*, viavai ‖ *to go while the — is good*, (*fam.*) battere il ferro finché è caldo, approfittare del momento favorevole **3.** condizione del terreno **4.** andatura, passo ☆ — *down*, discesa, calata, abbassamento (di titoli, temperatura); il decrescere (delle acque); tramonto (del sole); *goings on*, condotta, contegno (specialmente riprovevole).

goitre ['gɔitə*], *s.* (*patol.*) gozzo.

goitred ['gɔitəd], *ag.* (*patol.*) gozzuto.

goitrous ['gɔitrəs], *ag.* **1.** (*patol.*) affetto da gozzo **2.** simile a gozzo; di gozzo.

Golconda [gɔl'kɔndə], *no.pr.* (*st. geog.*) Golconda ‖ *s.* (*fig. letter.*) miniera di ricchezza.

gold [gould], *ag.* **1.** d'oro, aureo **2.** di colore giallo oro, dorato ‖ *s.* **1.** oro **2.** denaro, ricchezze **3.** colore giallo oro ☆ — *-beater*, battiloro; — *-brick*, lingotto d'oro; (*amer. fam.*) similoro; frode; — *-digger*, cercatore d'oro; — *-dust*, polvere d'oro; — *-foil*, — *-leaf*, oro laminato; — *-mine*, miniera d'oro, *fig.* fonte di ricchezza; — *-nugget*, pepita; — *-plate*, vasellame d'oro; — *-rush*, febbre dell'oro; — *-standard*, (*comm.*) base aurea; — *-thread*, (— *-wire*), filo d'oro; — *-washer*, chi libera l'oro dalla sabbia attraverso vari lavaggi; strumento per tali lavaggi ‖ *Dutch —*, similoro; *native — (o virgin —)*, oro vergine; *spun —*, oro filato.

Gold Coast ['gould'koust], *no.pr.* (*geog.*) Costa d'Oro.

golden ['gouldən], *ag.* **1.** d'oro; dorato: — *hair*, capelli biondo oro ‖ *the — age*, l'età dell'oro ‖ *Golden Horn*, (*geog.*) Corno d'Oro **2.** prezioso, importante: — *opportunity*, splendida occasione ☆ — *fleece*, vello d'oro; — *mean*, l'aurea mediocrità; il giusto mezzo; — *number*, (*astr.*) numero aureo; — *rule*, regola aurea; — *syrup*, melassa; — *wedding*, nozze d'oro.

goldfield ['gouldfi:ld], *s.* zona aurifera.

goldfinch ['gouldfintʃ], *s.* (*ornit.*) cardellino.

goldfish ['gouldfiʃ], *s.* (*ittiol.*) pesce rosso, ciprino.

goldilocks ['gouldi,loks], *s.* (*bot.*) ranuncolo.

goldsmith ['gouldsmiθ], *s.* orefice.

golf [golf], *s.* (*spor.*) « golf »: *a round of* —, una partita di golf ☆ — *-club*, circolo del golf; mazza da golf; — *-links*, campo di golf.

to golf, *v.i.* giuocare al golf.

golfer ['golfə*], *s.c.* giocatore, **giocatrice** di golf.

goliard ['gouljəd], *s.* goliardo.

goliardic [gou'ljɑ:dik], *ag.* goliardico.

Goliath [gə'laiəθ], *no.pr.m.* (*Bibbia*) Golia.

golliwog ['goliwog], *s.* bambolotto negro grottesco.

golly ['goli], *inter.* (*usata specialmente dai negri*): (*by*) —!, perdio!, per Bacco!.

golosh [gə'loʃ], *s.* galoscia, soprascarpa in gomma.

goluptious [gə'lʌpʃəs], *ag.* (*scherz.*) delizioso.

gombeen [gom'bi:n], *s.* usura ☆ — *man*, usuraio.

Gomorrah [gə'morə], *no.pr.* (*Bibbia*) Gomorra.

gondola ['gondələ], *s.* gondola; (*aer.*) navicella.

gondolier [,gondə'liə*], *s.* gondoliere.

gone [gon], *p.p.* di to **go** ‖ *ag.* **1.** andato, passato: *these five years* —, cinque anni fa, da cinque anni **2.** perduto, finito: — *case*, (*sl.*) caso disperato **3.** morto: *he is dead and* —, è morto e sepolto **4.** lontano, assente **5.** (*sl.*) innamorato: *to be* — *on s.o.*, essere innamorato di qlcu. ☆ *far* —, in uno stadio avanzato: *far* — *in drink*, ubriaco fradicio; *the disease was too far* —, la malattia era troppo avanzata.

goner ['gonə*], *s.* (*sl.*) persona morta; persona, cosa in stato disperato: *I'm a* —!, sono finito!.

Goneril ['gonəril], *no.pr.f.* (*lett.*) Gonerilla.

gonfalon ['gonfələn], *s.* gonfalone.

gonfalonier [,gonfələ'niə*], *s.* gonfaloniere.

gong [gon], *s.* gong.

to gong, *v.t.i.* **1.** suonare il gong **2.** intimare l'alt a (un automobilista) suonando (di polizia stradale).

Gongorism ['gongərizəm], *s.* (*st. lett.*) gongorismo.

goniometer [,gouni'omitə*], *s.* goniometro.

goniometric(al) [,gouniə'metrik(əl)], *ag.* goniometrico.

goniometry [,gouni'omitri], *s.* goniometria.

gonorrhea [,gonə'ri:ə], *s.* (*patol.*) gonorrea, blenorragia.

good [gud], *comp.* **better** ['betə*], *superl.* **best** [best], *ag.* **1.** buono; virtuoso, morale; gentile, benevolo: *how* — *of you*!, è molto gentile da parte tua!; *in* — *faith*, in buona fede; *in a* — *humour*, di buon umore; *he has a* — *name*, gode di una buona reputazione; *he is a* — *fellow*, è un buon diavolo; *to get into, to be in s.o.'s* — *graces* (o *books*), entrare, essere nelle buone grazie di qlcu.; *to live a* — *life*, vivere rettamente; *to say a* — *word*, dire una buona parola ‖ — *evening* (o *afternoon*), *morning*, *night*, buona sera, buon giorno, buona notte ‖ — *God!*, Dio mio!; — *gracious!* (o — *heavens!*), santo cielo! ‖ — *luck!*, buona fortuna! **2.** valido; abile, competente: *a* — *business man*, un abile uomo d'affari; *are you* — *for a ten mile walk?*, vi sentite in grado di fare dieci miglia a piedi?; *is the ticket still* —?, è ancora valido il biglietto?; *to be* — *at mathematics*, essere forte in matematica ‖ *to be a* — *sailor*, non soffrire il mal di mare ‖ *to make* —, adempiere; aver successo; risarcire, compensare **3.** grande, abbondante, considerevole: *a* — *deal of* (o *a* — *many*), una quantità considerevole di, un buon numero di; *I have been waiting for him a* — *while* (o *time*), lo sto aspettando da un bel po'; *I shall need a* — *hour to do that*, mi ci vorrà un'ora buona per farlo; *to have a* — *drink*, fare una bella bevuta ‖ *in* — *time*, per tempo **4.** bello, piacevole: *it is too* — *to be true*, è troppo bello per essere vero; *to have a* — *night*, dormir bene; *to have a* — *time*, divertirsi; *to put a* — *face on* ‖ *that's a* —

'un!, (*sl.*) questa si che è bella! **5.** *as* — *as*, (tanto) buono... quanto; praticamente: *he as* — *as told me I am a liar*, mi ha praticamente detto che sono un bugiardo; *this work is as* — *as done*, questo lavoro è praticamente finito ‖ *his word is as* — *as his bond*, ci si può fidare della sua parola; *to be as* — *as gold*, essere buono come un angelo (di bambini) ☆ — *-brother*, *-father*, *-mother*, *-sister*, *-son*, (*scoz. dial.*) cognato, suocero, suocera, cognata, genero; — *debts*, (*comm.*) crediti esigibili; — *-fellowship*, buona compagnia; socievolezza; *Good-Friday*, Venerdì Santo; — *-hearted*, di buon cuore; — *-humoured*, di buon umore; — *-looking*, di bell'aspetto; — *-nature*, bontà di cuore; — *-natured*, buono, di indole gentile; *the* — *people* (o — *folk*), le fate; — *-tempered*, di buon carattere, di buon temperamento; — *turn*, favore, atto di gentilezza.

good, *s.* **1.** bene; felicità, prosperità; virtù, moralità: *he is up to no* —, sta facendo ql.co. che non va; *it will do more* — *than harm*, farà più bene che male; *they deceived him for his* —, lo ingannarono per il suo bene ‖ *to do* —, fare del bene: *and much* — *did it do to me*, (*iron.*) e mi ha fatto molto bene; *much* — *may it do you!*, (*fam.*) buon pro ti faccia! ‖ *to become a power for* —, esercitare un'influenza salutare **2.** utilità, vantaggio: *is it any* — (*going*)? (I), vale la pena (di andare)?; *it's no* — *talking*, *your talking* (I), è inutile parlare, che parliate; *it is not a bit of* —, è proprio inutile; *what* — *is it?*, a che serve?; *what* — *will it do?*, a che servirà?; *what's the* — *of writing to him?*, a che serve scrivergli? ‖ *for* — (*and all*), per sempre: *he left her for* —, la lasciò per sempre ‖ *to the* —, all'attivo: *it's all to the* —, è tutto di guadagnato.

good, *inter.* bene!.

good-bye [gud'bai], *inter.s.* (*contr. di God be with you*) addio, arrivederci: *I must say* —, devo proprio salutarvi, andare.

good-for-nothing ['gudfə,nʌθiŋ], *ag.* inutile, senza valore ‖ *s.* buon a nulla: *he was a* —, era un inetto.

goodish ['gudiʃ], *ag.* **1.** discreto, abbastanza buono **2.** piuttosto grande: *it is a* — *step from here*, è a un buon tratto di strada da qui.

goodliness ['gudlinis], *s.* bellezza, avvenenza.

goodly ['gudli], *ag.* **1.** bello, avvenente **2.** ampio, grande, considerevole: *a* — *sum of money*, una bella somma di denaro.

goodman ['gudmæn], *pl.* **goodmen** ['gudmen], *s.* **1.** (*arc.*) capo famiglia **2.** (*scoz.*) marito.

goodness ['gudnis], *s.* **1.** virtù, bontà, gentilezza, benevolenza: — *of heart*, bontà di cuore; *please, have the* — *to help me*, per piacere, abbiate la gentilezza di aiutarmi **2.** l'essenza, il meglio (di ql.co.): *to extract all the* — *out of sthg.*, estrarre il meglio da ql.co. ‖ — *gracious!*, santo cielo!; — *knows!*, chissà!; — *me!* (*o my* —!), Dio mio!; *for* — *sake!*, per l'amor del cielo!; *I wish to* — *he would go!*, vorrei proprio che se ne andasse!.

goods [gudz], *s.pl.* (*comm.*) merci, merce; beni: — *on hand*, giacenza di magazzino; *to deliver the* —, consegnare la merce; (*fam. amer.*) adempiere i propri impegni ‖ — *and chattels*, (*dir.*) beni personali, masserizie ‖ *fine* — *in small parcels*, *prov.* in botte piccola sta buon vino ☆ — *-train*, treno merci ‖ *capital* —, beni di produzione; *consumer* —, beni di consumo; *manufactured* —, manufatti.

goodwife ['gudwaif], *pl.* **goodwives** ['gudwaivz], *s.* (*arc. scoz.*) padrona di casa; massaia; moglie.

goodwill ['gud'wil], *s.* **1.** benevolenza, favore: *to be in s.o.'s* —, essere nelle buone grazie di qlcu. **2.** zelo, buona volontà: *to set to work with* —, mettersi all'opera di buon animo **3.** (*comm.*) avviamento (di una ditta).

goody[1] ['gudi], *s.* buona donna; comare.

goody[2], *s.* chicca, caramella.

goody[2], *inter.* (*amer. fam.*) bene!; ottimo!; che bellezza!.

goody[3], **goody-goody** ['gudi'gudi], *ag.* (*fam.*) buono, troppo buono (per debolezza, sentimentalità, ecc.); *don't be* —, non essere tre volte buono ‖ *s.c.* (*amer.*)

santarellino, santarellina: *she played the* —, faceva la santarellina.

goof [gu:f], *s.c.* (*sl.*) persona sciocca, stupida.

to goof, *v.i.* (*sl.*) prendere un granchio.

goofy ['gu:fi], *ag.* (*sl.*) scemo, sciocco.

googly ['gu:gli], *s.* (*cricket*) lancio trasversale della palla.

gook [gu:k], *s.* (*sl. spreg.*) indigeno (di colore).

goon [gu:n], *s.* **1.** (*sl. amer.*) ostruzionista; crumiro **2.** (*sl.*) svanito; strampalato.

goosander [gu:'sændə*], *s.* (*ornit.*) marangone.

goose [gu:s], *pl.* **geese** [gi:s], *nel senso* **2. gooses** ['gu:siz], *s.* **1.** oca ‖ *all his geese are swans,* (*fam.*) egli magnifica ogni sua cosa ‖ *to kill the — that lays the golden eggs,* sacrificare per bisogno la fonte di un guadagno futuro **2.** ferro da stiro (per sarto) **3.** (*sl.*) stupido, sciocco ☆ — *-cap,* persona sciocca; — *-club,* associati a una lotteria il cui premio è l'oca natalizia; — *-flesh* (o — *-skin*), pelle d'oca; — *-neck,* (*mec.*) collo d'oca; — *-quill,* penna d'oca; — *-step,* passo dell'oca.

gooseberry ['guzbəri], *s.* **1.** (*bot.*) uva spina **2.** vino di uva spina **3.** « chaperon »: *to play* —, (*fam.*) tenere il lume, reggere il moccolo ☆ — *-bush,* arbusto d'uva spina; — *-fool,* crema di uva spina e panna.

gooseherd ['gu:shə:d], *s.c.* guardiano, guardiana di oche.

goosey ['gu:si], *s.* ochetta.

gopher[1] ['goufə*], *V.* **goffer.**

gopher[2], *s.* nome americano per diversi rosicanti.

goral ['gɔ:rəl], *s.* (*zool.*) antilope indiana.

gorbelly ['gɔ:beli], *s.* (*arc.*) persona corpulenta.

gorcrow ['gɔ:krou], *s.* (*ornit.*) corvo.

Gordian ['gɔ:djən], *ag.* — *knot,* (*mit.*) nodo gordiano; *fig.* problema difficile.

gore[1] [gɔ:*], *s.* sangue (rappreso, versato).

gore[2], *s.* **1.** zona, striscia di terreno a forma di cuneo **2.** « godet », gherone **3.** spicchio della superficie di un pallone, ombrello, vela, ecc.

to gore[2], *v.t.* tagliare in triangolo (stoffa, ecc.): *gored skirt,* gonna svasata, a « godet ».

to gore[3], *v.t.* colpire, ferire con le corna: *gored to death by a bull,* colpito a morte da un toro.

gorge[1] [gɔ:dʒ], *s.* **1.** (*letter.*) gola, fauci **2.** cibo appena ingerito ‖ *to make one's* — *rise,* disgustare, far venire la nausea **3.** gola di montagna **4.** (*mec.*) scanalatura della puleggia **5.** (*arch.*) gola.

to gorge[1], *v.t.i.* satollare; rimpinzare, rimpinzarsi; mangiare con ingordigia; inghiottire.

gorge[2], *s.* rimpinzata, scorpacciata.

gorgeous [['gɔ:dʒəs], *ag.* magnifico; fastoso, splendido; sgargiante.

gorgeously ['gɔ:dʒəsli], *av.* magnificamente; fastosamente, sontuosamente; in modo ricercato.

gorgeousness ['gɔ:dʒəsnis], *s.* magnificenza; fasto, splendore; ricercatezza.

gorget[1] ['gɔ:dʒit], *s.* **1.** (*st.*) gorgiera **2.** collarino (di uccello).

gorget[2], *s.* (*chir.*) sonda scanalata (per litotomia).

Gorgon ['gɔ:gən], *no.pr.f.* (*mit.*) Gorgone ‖ *s. fig.* mostro; donna repellente.

gorgonia [gɔ'gouniə], *pl.* **gorgoniae** [gɔ'gounii:], **gorgonias** [gɔ'gouniəz], *s.* (*ittiol.*) gorgonia.

gorgonian [gɔ'gouniən], *ag.* gorgoneo, di gorgone.

to gorgonize ['gɔ:gənaiz], *v.t.* pietrificare con lo sguardo.

gorgonzola [,gɔ:gən'zoulə], *s.* formaggio gorgonzola.

gorilla [gə'rilə], *s.* gorilla.

gorily ['gɔ:rili], *av.* sanguinosamente.

gormandize ['gɔ:məndaiz], *s.* ghiottoneria, golosità.

to gormandize, *v.t.i.* mangiare avidamente.

gormandizer ['gɔ:məndaizə*], *s.c.* ghiottone, ghiottona.

gorse [gɔ:s], *s.* ginestra spinosa, ginestrone.

Gorsedd ['gɔ:seð], *s.* **1.** riunione di bardi, druidi del Galles **2.** luogo di tale riunione.

gorsy ['gɔ:si], *ag.* coperto di ginestre spinose.

gory ['gɔ:ri], *ag.* **1.** insanguinato **2.** cruento.

gos [gɔs], *s.* (*ornit. abbr. di* goshawk) astore.

gosh [gɔʃ], *inter.* (*sl.*): (*by*) —!, perdinci!, perbacco!.

goshawk ['gɔshɔ:k], *s.* (*ornit.*) astore.

gosling ['gɔzliŋ], *s.* papero, paperino.

gospel ['gɔspəl], *s.* **1.** Vangelo ‖ *they have neither law nor* —, non hanno nè legge nè fede **2.** principio; verità religiosa, assoluta: *they take that for* (o *as*) —, lo credono come se fosse vangelo ☆ — *-oath,* giuramento fatto sulla Bibbia; — *-truth,* verità inconfutabile.

gospeller ['gɔspələ*], *s.* lettore del Vangelo durante il servizio religioso: *a hot* —, un ardente predicatore; uno zelante puritano.

gossamer ['gɔsəmə*], *ag.* leggero e sottile ‖ *s.* **1.** ragnatela; filo di ragnatela **2.** garza, tessuto finissimo.

gossamery ['gɔsəməri], *ag.* leggero; delicato; inconsistente.

gossan ['gɔzən], *s.* (*miner.*) cappello.

gossip ['gɔsip], *s. coll.* **1.** chiacchiera, pettegolezzo: *don't believe all the — you hear,* non credere a tutte le chiacchiere che senti **2.** chiacchierata: *to have a good — with a neighbour,* fare una bella chiacchierata con un vicino ‖ *s.c.* **1.** pettegolo, pettegola; ciarlone, ciarlona **2.** (*arc.*) vecchia conoscenza; compare, comare.

to gossip, *v.i.* chiacchierare; far pettegolezzi.

gossiper ['gɔsipə*], *s.c.* chiacchierone, chiacchierona; pettegolo, pettegola.

gossiping ['gɔsipiŋ], *s.* chiacchierio; il fare chiacchiere; pettegolezzo.

gossipry ['gɔsipri], *s.* **1.** chiacchierio, pettegolezzo **2.** (*coll.*) comari; pettegoli, pettegole.

gossipy ['gɔsipi], *ag.* chiacchierone; pettegolo.

gossoon [gɔ'su:n], *s.* (*irl.*) garzone; ragazzo.

got [gɔt], *pass.p.p.* di to **get.**

Goth [gɔθ], *s.* **1.** goto **2.** *fig.* barbaro, vandalo.

Gotham ['goutæm], *nel senso* **2.** ['gɔuðəm], *s.* **1.** tipica città di sciocchi: *wise man of* —, sciocco **2.** (*sl. amer.*) la città di New York.

Gothamite ['goutəmait], **Gothamist** ['goutəmist], *s.* semplicione, credulone.

Gothic ['gɔθik], *ag.* **1.** gotico **2.** *fig.* barbaro, rozzo **3.** (*arch.*) gotico, ogivale **4.** (*tip.*) gotico ‖ *s.* **1.** lingua gotica **2.** architettura gotica **3.** (*tip.*) carattere gotico.

gothically ['gɔθikəli], *av.* a guisa di gotico.

gothicism ['gɔθisizəm], *s.* **1.** stile gotico; goticismo **2.** rozzezza; barbarie.

to gothicize ['gɔθisaiz], *v.t.* rendere gotico, medievale.

gotta ['gɔtə], (*sl. amer. contr. di* have got to) devo: *I — go,* devo andare.

gotten ['gɔtn], *p.p.* (*arc. amer.*) di to **get.**

gouache [gu'a:ʃ], *s.* guazzo, pittura a guazzo.

gouge [gaudʒ], *s.* **1.** (*mec.*) sgorbia, scalpello tondo **2.** (*geol.*) coppe **3.** (*chir.*) sgorbia **4.** (*sl. amer.*) truffatore; truffa.

to gouge, *v.t.* **1.** (*mec.*) sgorbiare **2.** estrarre con la sgorbia **3.** (*sl. amer.*) ingannare; defraudare.

goulash ['gu:læʃ], *s.* (*cuc.*) « gulash ».

gourd [guəd], *s.* **1.** (*bot.*) pianta e frutto delle cucurbitacee (specie la zucca) **2.** zucca vuota (recipiente).

gourdiness ['guədinis], *s.* gonfiore (delle gambe di un cavallo).

gourdy ['guədi], *ag.* gonfio (delle gambe di un cavallo).

gourmand ['guəmənd], *ag.* goloso ‖ *s.* **1.** goloso, ghiottone **2.** buongustaio.

gourmandism ['guəməndizəm], *s.* **1.** ghiottoneria **2.** amore per la buona tavola.

gourmet ['guəmei], *s.* buongustaio; conoscitore (di vini, ecc.).

gout[1] [gaut], *s.* **1.** (*patol.*) gotta, podagra **2.** malattia del grano **3.** goccia (specialmente di sangue); macchia.

gout[2], *s.* canale (anche sotterraneo).

gout[3] [gu:], *s.* gusto.

goutiness ['gautinis], *s.* condizione di gottoso.

gouty ['gauti], *ag.* (*patol.*) gottoso.

to **govern** [ˈgʌvən], *v.t.i.* **1.** governare; amministrare: *the King reigns but does not —*, il re regna ma non governa **2.** regolare, influenzare: *you mustn't be governed by what other people say*, non devi lasciarti influenzare da ciò che dicono gli altri **3.** controllare: *she can't — herself*, ella non sa dominarsi; *to — one's passions*, controllare le proprie passioni **4.** (*gram.*) reggere: *to — the accusative*, reggere l'accusativo **5.** (*mec.*) regolare.

governable [ˈgʌvənəbl], *ag.* docile, sottomesso; governabile.

governance [ˈgʌvənəns], *s.* **1.** governo; direzione **2.** autorità, dominio.

governess [ˈgʌvənis], *s.* istitutrice.

governing [ˈgʌvəniŋ], *ag.* **1.** governante **2.** principale ☆ *— body*, corpo dirigente (di scuola, orfanotrofio, ecc.).

government [ˈgʌvnmənt], *s.* **1.** governo: *form of —*, regime **2.** ministero: *to form a —*, formare un ministero; *to serve on a —*, partecipare ad un ministero ‖ *Her Majesty's Government*, il governo di Sua Maestà (Britannica) **3.** forma di governo: *republican —*, governo repubblicano **4.** governatorato **5.** *for your —*, (*comm.*) per vostra norma ☆ *— -house*, residenza ufficiale del governatore; *— -offices*, uffici governativi; *— -securities*, titoli di stato.

governmental [ˌgʌvənˈmentl], *ag.* governativo; del governo.

governor [ˈgʌvənə*], *s.* **1.** governatore (d'una colonia, d'una fortezza, d'una prigione) **2.** (*fam.*) capo, padre; principale, padrone **3.** (*mec.*) regolatore ☆ *— -general*, governatore generale ‖ *speed- —*, [(*mec.*) regolatore di giri.

governorship [ˈgʌvənəʃip], *s.* **1.** la funzione di governatore **2.** governatorato.

gowan [ˈgau-ən], *s.* (*bot. scoz.*) margherita di prato.

gowk [gauk], *s.* **1.** (*ornit.*) cuculo **2.** semplicitotto, stupido.

to **gowl** [gaul], *v.i.* (*scoz.*) **1.** lamentarsi **2.** ululare (del vento).

gown [gaun], *s.* **1.** veste, abito (da donna) **2.** toga (degli universitari, dei magistrati, degli antichi romani, ecc.) ‖ *town and —*, i cittadini e i membri dell'università (a Cambridge e Oxford) ☆ *dressing- —* (o *morning- —*), veste da camera; *night- —*, camicia da notte; *tea- —*, abito da pomeriggio; *wedding- —*, abito da sposa.

to **gown**, *v.t.* rivestire con la toga.

gowned [gaund], *ag.* in toga, togato.

gownsman, *pl.* **gownsmen** [ˈgaunzmən], *s.* chi porta la toga (*p.e.* avvocato; giudice; membro di una università; sacerdote.

grab¹ [græb], *s.* **1.** presa; stretta; tentativo di afferrare ‖ *to be on the —*, (*fam.*) cercare di impadronirsi di ql.co. ‖ *to have* (o *to get*) *the — on*, (*sl.*) aver vantaggio su **2.** giuoco di carte per bambini **3.** (*mec.*) benna ☆ *— -bucket*, (*mec.*) benna; *— -crane*, (*mec.*) gru a benna.

to **grab¹**, *pass.p.p.* **grabbed** [græbd], *v.t.i.* **1.** acchiappare, afferrare; prendere avidamente e repentinamente: *he grabbed the letter*, afferrò la lettera; *to — at* (o *for*), cercare di afferrare **2.** arrestare, catturare **3.** (*mec.*) bloccare, ingranarsi **4.** (*ind.*) prendere con la benna.

grab², *s.* (*ang.-in.*) nave costiera a due alberi.

grabber [ˈgræbə*], *s.* (*spreg.*) accaparratore; arraffone ☆ *money- —*, persona dedita ad accumulare denaro.

to **grabble** [ˈgræbl], *v.i.* **1.** andare a tastoni; procedere a tastoni **2.** buttarsi per terra (a cercare ql.co.): *I was grabbling for my thimble*, cercavo per terra il mio ditale.

grabby [ˈgræbi], *s.* (*sl.*) fante.

grace¹ [greis], *s.* **1.** grazia, garbo, modi gentili: *to do sthg. with —, with a good, a bad —*, fare ql.co. con grazia, di buona grazia, di mala grazia **2.** *pl.* avvenenza, leggiadria: *a young lady full of pleasant graces*, una signorina molto avvenente ‖ *the three Graces,*

(*mit.*) le Tre Grazie **3.** favore: *to be in s.o.'s graces*, essere nelle grazie di qlcu.; *to fall out of — with s.o.*, perdere il favore di qlcu. **4.** grazia, perdono ‖ *Act of —*, amnistia, atto di clemenza **5.** (*teol.*) grazia divina: *in a state of —*, in stato di grazia ‖ *by the — of God*, per grazia di Dio **6.** (*comm.*) dilazione: *days of —*, giorni di grazia (dilazione concessa per pagamento di cambiali) **7.** breve preghiera prima, dopo i pasti: *to say —*, dire la preghiera a tavola **8.** (*mus.*) abbellimento, fioritura **9.** *Grace*, Grazia (titolo onorifico per duchi, arcivescovi): *His Grace the Duke of X*, sua Grazia il Duca di X ☆ *— -notes*, (*mus.*) note di passaggio; *— -stroke*, colpo di grazia.

to **grace¹**, *v.t.* adornare, abbellire; favorire; dotare; onorare: *to — the meeting with one's presence*, onorare il convegno della propria presenza; *to be graced with distinction*, avere il dono della distinzione.

Grace², *no.pr.f.* Grazia.

graced [greist], *ag.* **1.** aggraziato; raffinato **2.** virtuoso; casto.

graceful [ˈgreisful], *ag.* grazioso, leggiadro; gentile.

gracefully [ˈgreisfuli], *av.* graziosamente, con grazia; garbatamente.

gracefulness [ˈgreisfulnis], *s.* gentilezza; grazia; eleganza.

graceless [ˈgreislis], *ag.* **1.** sgraziato; sgarbato **2.** (*teol.*) non in stato di grazia **3.** depravato, scellerato.

gracelessly [ˈgreislisli], *av.* **1.** sgarbatamente **2.** sceleratamente.

gracelessness [ˈgreislisnis], *s.* **1.** mancanza di grazia; sgarbataggine **2.** perversità.

gracile [ˈgræsil], *ag.* gracile, esile; sottile ed aggraziato.

gracility [grəˈsiliti], *s.* **1.** gracilità, esilità; sottigliezza aggraziata **2.** semplicità disadorna (di stile).

gracious [ˈgreiʃəs], *ag.* **1.** condiscendente, clemente; benigno, buono, misericordioso; grazioso (di sovrano): *— and merciful God!*, Dio benigno e pietoso!; *our — Queen*, la nostra graziosa regina ‖ *good* (o *my*) *—!*, buon Dio!; *good —, no!*, nemmeno per sogno! **2.** (*poet.*) cortese, gentile **3.** (*arc.*) attraente.

graciously [ˈgreiʃəsli], *av.* benignamente; graziosamente; misericordiosamente.

graciousness [ˈgreiʃəsnis], *s.* benignità, indulgenza, condiscendenza; misericordia.

grackle [ˈgrækl], *s.* (*ornit.*) gracola.

to **gradate** [grəˈdeit], *v.t.i.* **1.** sfumare **2.** graduare.

gradatim [grəˈdeitim], *av.* (*lat.*) gradualmente.

gradation [grəˈdeiʃən], *s.* **1.** gradazione **2.** (*pitt.*) sfumatura **3.** (*filologia*) apofonia.

gradational [grəˈdeiʃənl], *ag.* graduale.

gradationally [grəˈdeiʃəli], *av.* gradualmente.

gradationed [grəˈdeiʃənd], *ag.* graduato.

grade [greid], *s.* **1.** grado; rango: *every — of society*, ogni grado sociale; *official grades*, gerarchia; *he has a high — of intelligence*, ha un alto livello di intelligenza; *the rank of captain is one — lower than that of major*, il rango di capitano è inferiore di un grado a quello di maggiore **2.** qualità **3.** (*amer.*) classe, anno (di scuola): *an elementary school in the Unites States has eight grades*, negli Stati Uniti la scuola elementare ha otto classi **4.** *amer.*) voto, classificazione **5.** (*amer.*) pendio, pendenza: *on the up, down —*, in salita, discesa (di ferrovia; livello, ecc.) ‖ *to make the —*, raggiungere la sommità di un pendio; *fig.* raggiungere la meta, superare le difficoltà **6.** ibrido, incrocio (di bestiame) **7.** (*zool.*) sottospecie **8.** (*mat.*) grado (di angolo) ☆ *— crossing*, (*amer.*) passaggio a livello; *— school*, scuola elementare; *— teacher*, insegnante elementare ‖ *leaf grades*, qualità di foglia (di tè).

to **grade**, *v.t.* **1.** graduare; classificare **2.** (*amer.*) classificare (a scuola) **3.** livellare (terreno, ecc.) **4.** selezionare (bestiame) **5.** sfumare (colore).

gradely [ˈgreidli], *ag.* (*dial.*) adatto, eccellente; conveniente ‖ *av.* bene; appropriatamente.

gradient ['greidjənt], *ag.* che sale, scende gradatamente (di linea ferroviaria) ‖ *s.* **1.** pendenza, inclinazione: *bad* (o *heavy*) —, pendenza forte; *good* —, pendenza dolce **2.** (*fis. elett.*, ecc.) gradiente ☆ *barometric* —, gradiente barometrico; *geothermal* —, (*geol.*) gradiente geotermico; *steady* —, (*ferr.*) livelletta.

gradin ['greidin], **gradine**[1] [grə'di:n], *s.* **1.** gradinata di anfiteatro **2.** gradino (di un altare).

gradine[2], *s.* gradina (scalpello da scultore).

grading ['greidiŋ], *s.* **1.** gradazione, classificazione; valutazione **2.** livellamento (di terreno) **3.** selezione (di bestiame) **4.** sfumatura (di colore).

gradual ['grædjuəl], *ag.* graduale ‖ *s.* (*eccl.*) graduale.

gradualism ['grædjuəlizəm], *s.* gradualismo.

graduality [,grædju'æliti], *s.* gradualità.

gradually ['grædjuəli], *av.* gradualmente, gradatamente.

gradualness ['grædjuəlnis], *s.* gradualità.

graduate ['grædjuit], *s.* **1.** laureato; (*amer.*)licenziato, diplomato **2.** (*chim.*) recipiente graduato ☆ — *nurse*, infermiera diplomata.

to **graduate** ['grædjueit], *v.t.i.* **1.** laurearsi; (*amer.*) licenziarsi (da istituti, scuole), diplomarsi: *he graduated at Oxford*, si laureò ad Oxford; *he graduated from a high school*, prese il diploma di scuola media superiore **2.** (*spec. amer.*) dare una laurea, un diploma a: *this university has graduated three hundred students*, questa università ha laureato trecento studenti **3.** graduare (termometro, recipiente, ecc.) **4.** proporzionare **5.** cambiarsi gradualmente.

graduated ['grædjueitid], *ag.* **1.** graduato **2.** graduale.

graduation [,grædju'eiʃən], *s.* **1.** laurea; (*amer.*) diploma, licenza **2.** graduazione **3.** *pl.* gradi (di un termometro, ecc.) ☆ — *ceremony*, (*amer.*) cerimonia della consegna delle lauree, dei diplomi; — *dress*, *gown*, abito, toga di laurea.

graduator ['grædjueitə*], *s.* strumento graduatore.

gradus ['greidəs], *s.* (*abbr.* di « Gradus ad Parnassum ») dizionario di prosodia classica.

Graecism ['gri:sizəm], *s.* grecismo; ellenismo.

to **Graecize** ['gri:saiz], *v.t.i.* grecizzare.

graffito [grɑ:'fi:tou], *pl.* **graffiti** [grɑ:'fi:ti:],*s.* graffito.

graft[1] [grɑ:ft], *s.* **1.** (*bot.*) innesto **2.** (*chir.*) innesto, trapianto.

to **graft**[1], *v.t.* **1.** (*bot.*) innestare **2.** *fig.* innestare, congiungere **3.** (*chir.*) trapiantare.

graft[2], *s.* **1.** badilata di terra **2.** vanga.

graft[3], *s.* (*sl. amer.*) concussione, corruzione politica.

to **graft**[3], *v.i.* (*sl. amer.*) fare illeciti guadagni (attraverso cariche pubbliche).

grafter[1] ['grɑ:ftə*], *s.* innestatore.

grafter[2], *s.* (*sl. amer.*) concussionario, chi trae illeciti guadagni da cariche pubbliche.

grail[1] [greil], *s.* (*eccl.*) graduale.

grail[2], *s.* « graal » (il sacro calice usato da Gesù nell'ultima cena).

grail[3], *s.* lima (per la fabbricazione di pettini).

grain[1] [grein], *s.* **1.** *coll. sing.* granaglie, cereali; grano, frumento; biada **2.** chicco, grano, granello (anche *fig.*): *a — of folly*, un pizzico di follia; *a — of mustard seed*, un granello di senape; *a — of rice*, un chicco di riso; *a — of sense*, un po' di buon senso; *with a — of salt*, (*fam.*) con discernimento, con un po' di sale in zucca **3.** grano (unità di peso = g.0,0648) **4.** venatura (di legno, pietra); grana (di pelle, cuoio, ecc.) **5.** (*metal. fis. foto.* ecc.) grana **6.** *fig.* inclinazione, tendenza: *it goes against the — for me to do it*, lo faccio proprio a malincuore **7.** grana, carminio di cocciniglia; (*poet.*) tinta, colore ☆ — *drill*, (*agr.*) seminatrice; — *export*, esportazione di cereali; — *harvester*, (*agr.*) mietitrice; — *oil*, (*chim.*) alcool di amile; — *refining*, (*metal.*) affinazione della grana; — *size*, (*metal.*) grossezza della grana.

to **grain**[1], *v.t.i.* **1.** (*agr.*) granire **2.** granulare **3.** tin-gere in grana **4.** zigrinare (cuoio, tela, ecc.) **5.** (*conceria*) pelare, depilare.

grain[2], *s.* **1.** (*dial.*) ramo **2.** (*dial.*) rebbio **3.** (*mar.*) *pl.* fiocina.

grainage[1] ['greinidʒ], *s.* **1.** tassa sul grano **2.** tumori alle gambe dei cavalli.

grainage[2], *s.* (*arc.*) tassa sul sale.

grained [greind], *ag.* **1.** a struttura granulare **2.** marezzato **3.** zigrinato: — *paper*, carta zigrinata ☆ *coarse-* —, (*metal.*) a grana grossa; *fine-* —, (*metal.*) a grana fine.

grainer ['greinə*], *s.* chi marmorizza.

graining ['greiniŋ], *s.* **1.** marezzatura **2.** (*conceria*) pelatura, depilazione **3.** granitura.

grainy ['greini], *ag.* **1.** granoso **2.** granuloso.

grakle ['grækl], *s.* (*ornit.*) gracola.

Gralle ['græli:], **Grallatores** [,grælə'tɔ:ri:z], *s.pl.* (*ornit.*) gralle, trampolieri.

grallatorial [,grælə'tɔ:riəl], *ag.* (*ornit.*) di gralle, di trampolieri.

gralloch ['grælɔk], *s.* interiora (di cervo, daino, ecc.).

to **gralloch**, *v.t.* sviscerare (cervo, daino, ecc.).

gram[1] [græm], *s.* cece.

gram[2], *s.* grammo (unità di peso = 15.432 gr.) ☆ — *-atom*, (*chim.*) grammoatomo; — *-molecule*, (*chim.*) grammomolecola, molecola.

grama ['grɑ:mə], *s.* varietà americana di erba da pascolo.

gramarye ['græməri], *s.* (*rar. arc.*) magia; chiromanzia; negromanzia.

gramercy [grə'mə:si], *inter.* (*arc.*) grazie.

graminaceous [,greimi'neiʃəs], *ag.* (*bot.*) graminaceo.

Gramineae [grə'minii:], *s.pl.* (*bot.*) graminacee.

gramineous [grei'miniəs], *ag.* (*bot.*) graminaceo.

graminivorous [,græmi'nivərəs], *ag.* erbivoro.

gramma ['græmə], *s.* varietà americana di erba da pascolo.

grammalogue ['græmələɔg], *s.* logogramma; stenogramma.

grammar ['græmə*], *s.* **1.** grammatica: *his — is shocking*, parla e scrive molto male **2.** testo grammaticale: *an English* —, una grammatica inglese ☆ — *-school*, scuola secondaria (specialmente ad indirizzo classico); (*st.*) scuola per lo studio delle lingue classiche; (*amer.*) scuola elementare.

grammarian [grə'mɛəriən], *s.* grammatico, filologo.

grammarless ['græməlis], *ag.* sgrammaticato.

grammatic(al) [grə'mætik(əl)], *ag.* grammaticale.

grammatically [grə'mætikəli], *av.* grammaticalmente.

grammaticaster [grə'mæti,kæstə*], *s.* (*spreg.*) grammaticastro.

to **grammaticize** [grə'mætisaiz], *v.t.i.* **1.** rendere grammaticale **2.** discutere di grammatica.

gramme [græm], *V.* **gram**[2].

gramophone ['græməfoun], *s.* grammofono: *to dance to the* —, ballare al suono del grammofono.

Grampians ['græmpjənz], *no.pr.pl.* (*geog.*) Grampiani.

grampus ['græmpəs], *s.* **1.** (*zool.*) orca **2.** chi ansima.

granadilla [,grænə'dilə], *s.* (*bot.*) granadiglia.

granary ['grænəri], *s.* granaio (anche *fig.*): *Russia is the — of Europe*, la Russia è il granaio d'Europa.

grand [grænd], *ag.* **1.** grande, superbo, grandioso, splendido, imponente: *to live in — style*, vivere con lusso **2.** celebre; importante; nobile: — *lady*, gran dama; — *manners*, *air*, tono, aria d'importanza ‖ *to do the* —, darsi delle arie **3.** nobile, sublime: *Lincoln had a — character*, Lincoln aveva un nobile carattere **4.** principale: *the — staircase*, scala principale, scalone d'onore **5.** intero, completo: *a — orchestra*, grande orchestra **6.** (*fam.*) magnifico, eccellente: *in — conditions*, in condizioni eccellenti; *to have a — time*, divertirsi molto **7.** *Grand*, *Gran* (nei titoli ufficiali): *Grand Duchy*, Granducato; *Grand Duke*, *Grand Duchess*, granduca sovrano, granduchessa sovrana ☆ — *-aunt*, prozia; — *-duke*, granduca; — *-duchess*, granduchessa; *Grand-*

Master, Gran Maestro (di ordine cavalleresco); — *-nephew*, — *-niece*, pronipote; — *-opera*, opera lirica; — *-piano*, piano a coda; — *total*, (*mat*.) totale assoluto; — *-uncle*, prozio.

grand, *s*. **1.** pianoforte **2.** (*sl*. *amer*.) biglietto da mille dollari.

grandam ['grændæm], *s*. (*arc*.) **1.** nonna; antenata **2.** donna vecchia.

grandchild ['græn-tʃaild], *pl*. **grandchildren** ['græn- ,tʃildrən], *s.c*. nipotino, nipotina; abiatico, abiatica.

granddad ['grændæd], *s*. (*fam*.) nonno.

granddaughter ['græn,dɔ:tə*], *s*. nipote, abiatica.

grandee [græn'di:], *s*. **1.** Grande di Spagna **2.** persona eminente.

grandeur ['grændʒə*], *s*. **1.** grandiosità, magnificenza, splendore, maestà: *the — of the Alps*, la grandiosità delle Alpi **2.** grandezza, nobiltà.

grandfather ['grænd,fa:ðə*], *s*. **1.** nonno **2.** antenato ☆ —('*s*)*-clock*, antico orologio a pendolo.

Grand Guignol [,gra:n,gi:'njɔ:l], *s*. Grand Guignol.

grandiloquence [græn'diləkwəns], *s*. grandiloquenza, magniloquenza.

grandiloquent [græn'diləkwənt], *ag*. magniloquente, ampolloso.

grandiloquently [græn'diləkwəntli], *av*. ampollosamente, enfaticamente.

grandiose ['grændious], *ag*. grandioso; pomposo.

grandiosely ['grændiousli], *av*. grandiosamente; ampollosamente.

grandiosity [,grændi'ositi], *s*. grandiosità; fastosità.

grandly ['grændli], *av*. grandiosamente; superbamente; magnificamente.

grandma ['grænma:], **grandmamma** ['grænmə,ma:], *s*. (*fam*.) nonna.

grandmother ['græn,mʌðə*], *s*. **1.** nonna ‖ *to teach one's — to suck eggs*, insegnare a volare agli uccelli, insegnare ai gatti ad arrampicare **2.** antenata.

to grandmother, *v.t*. **1.** essere la nonna di, trattare da nonna **2.** (*fam*.) vezzeggiare, coccolare.

grandmotherly ['græn,mʌðəli], *ag*.: — *legislation*, (*fam*.) legislazione troppo paterna.

grandness ['grændnis], *s*. grandezza, grandiosità.

grandpa ['grænpa:], **grandpapa** ['grænpə,pa:], *s*. (*fam*.) nonno.

grandparent ['græn,pɛərənt], *s.c*. nonno, nonna.

grandsire ['græn,saiə*], *s*. (*arc*.) **1.** nonno, antenato **2.** uomo anziano.

grandson ['grænsʌn], *s*. nipote, abiatico.

grandstand ['grændstænd], *s*. tribuna d'onore ☆ — *finish*, (*neol*. *spor*.) serrate finale.

grange [greindʒ], *s*. **1.** masseria, fattoria **2.** (*amer*.) sindacato di agricoltori.

granger ['greindʒə*], *s*. **1.** massaro, agricoltore **2.** (*amer*.) associato al sindacato agricoltori.

grangerism ['greindʒərizəm], *s*. illustrazione (di un libro) con vignette, disegni, ecc. ritagliate da altri libri.

to grangerize ['greindʒəraiz], *v.t*. illustrare (un libro) con stampe, figure ecc. ritagliate da un altro libro.

graniferous [grə'nifərəs], *ag*. granifero.

graniform ['grænifɔ:m], *ag*. graniforme.

granite ['grænit], *s*. (*geol*.) granito.

granitic [græ'nitik], *ag*. (*geol*.) granitico.

granitiform [græ'nitifɔ:m], *ag*. granitiforme.

granitoid ['grænitɔid], *ag*. (*geol*.) granitoide.

granivorous [grə'nivərəs], *ag*. granivoro.

grannom ['grænəm], *s*. (*pesca*) esca artificiale a forma di mosca.

granny ['græni], *s*. (*fam*.) nonnina.

granolithic [,grænou'liθik], *ag*. di cemento e granito.

grant [gra:nt], *s*. **1.** concessione; rilascio (di brevetti, permessi, ecc.) **2.** borsa di studio: *to receive a State —*, ottenere una borsa di studio statale **3.** (*dir*.) assegnazione; sovvenzione, allocazione, dono, cessione (di un bene); atto di donazione.

to grant, *v.t*. **1.** concedere, accordare; rilasciare (permessi, ecc.): *to — a pardon*, concedere la grazia; *to — a*

pension, assegnare una pensione; *to — a person permission to do sthg.*, dare a una persona il permesso di fare ql.co.; *to — a privilege to s.o.*, accordare un privilegio a qlcu. ‖ *God — that we get there alive*, voglia Iddio che ci arriviamo vivi **2.** ammettere, acconsentire; esaudire: *granted!*, va bene!, d'accordo!, l'ammetto!; *I — you are right*, ammetto che tu abbia ragione; *I — you that...*, sono d'accordo con te che... ‖ *to take (sthg.) for granted*, accettare (ql.co.) come vera **3.** cedere, trasmettere (proprietà, atti, ecc.).

grantable ['gra:ntəbl], *ag*. concedibile, accordabile.

grantee [gra:n'ti:], *s*. (*dir*.) concessionario; donatario; beneficiario.

Granth [grʌnt], *s*. scritture sacre dei Sikhs.

grantor [gra:n'tɔ:*], *s*. (*dir*.) concedente; donante.

granular ['grænjulə*], *ag*. granulare, granuloso.

granularity [,grænju'læriti], *s*. granulosità.

granulate ['grænjuleit], *ag*. granulato.

to granulate, *v.t.i*. **1.** granulare, granularsi; cristallizzare, cristallizzarsi; granire (una superficie) **2.** (*bot*.) fare i granelli, essere in granelli.

granulation [,grænju'leiʃən], *s*. granulazione; granitura.

granule ['grænju:l], *s*. granello, granulo.

granulite ['grænjulait], *s*. (*min*.) granulite.

granulous ['grænjuləs], *ag*. granuloso.

grape [greip], *s*. **1.** acino, chicco d'uva **2.** *pl*. uva: *a bunch of grapes*, un grappolo d'uva; *sour grapes*, uva acerba (anche *fig*.); *to gather grapes*, vendemmiare **3.** *pl*. (*vet*.) grappa (di cavalli) ☆ — *-cure*, cura dell'uva; — *-fruit*, pompelmo; — *-growing*, viticoltura; *forbici da uva*; — *-juice*, mosto; — *-scissors*, cesoie per viticoltura; — *-shot*, (*mil*.) mitraglia; — *-stone*, vinacciuolo; — *-sugar*, glucosio, destrosio; — *-vine*, vite ‖ *dessert grapes*, uva da tavola.

grapeless ['greiplis], *ag*. senza uva; senza aroma (di vino).

grapery ['greipəri], *s*. vigna; serra per uva.

graph [græf], *s*. grafico, diagramma ☆ — *paper*, carta millimetrata.

to graph, *v.t*. (*tec*.) tracciare il grafico di.

graphic ['græfik], *ag*. **1.** grafico **2.** *fig*. pittoresco: *a — description*, una descrizione vivace.

graphically ['græfikəli], *av*. **1.** graficamente **2.** pittorescamente.

graphite ['græfait], *s*. grafite ☆ — *crucible*, crogiuolo di grafite; — *rheostat*, resistenza di grafite; — *treated oil*, lubrificante grafitato.

graphiure ['græfjuə*], *s*. (*zool*.) grafiuro.

graphology [græ'fɔlədʒi], *s*. grafologia.

graphometer [græ'fɔmitə*], *s*. goniometro.

graphophone ['græfəfoun], *s*. grafofono.

graphospasm ['græfəspæzəm], *s*. grafospasmo, crampo degli scrivani.

grapnel ['græpnəl], *s*. (*mar*.) grappino.

grapple ['græpl], *s*. **1.** corpo a corpo **2.** (*mar*.) uncino, grappino.

to grapple, *v.t.i*. **1.** abbrancare, afferrare; impugnare **2.** lottare, combattere (anche *fig*.): *to — with an enemy, with a problem*, venire alle prese con un nemico, con un problema **3.** (*mar*.) uncinare ☆ *grappling-iron*, (*mar*.) grappino.

grapy ['greipi], *ag*. **1.** a grappolo; di, simile a uva **2.** (*vet*.) affetto da grappa.

grasp [gra:sp], *s*. **1.** stretta, presa: *to lose one's —*, lasciare la presa; *to wrest sthg. from s.o.'s —*, strappare ql.co. dalle mani di qlcu. **2.** manico, impugnatura **3.** potere, possesso, portata, comprensione: *it is beyond his —*, è al di là della sua comprensione.

to grasp, *v.t.i*. **1.** afferrare, prendere; impugnare; serrare, stringere; *to — s.o.'s hand*, afferrare qlcu. per la mano **2.** ‖ *to — the nettle*, (*fam*.) prendere il toro per le corna **2.** cercare di afferrare; aggrapparsi (anche *fig*.): *to — at*, cercare di aggrapparsi a; accettare con gioia; afferrare con avidità: *he grasped at the only* *chance he had*, si attaccò alla sua unica possibilità ‖ *to — the opportunity*, afferrare l'occasione ‖ — *all lose all*, *prov*. chi troppo vuole nulla stringe 3. comprendere, capire: *I can't — what you mean*, non riesco a capire che cosa tu voglia dire; *to — a fact, a meaning*, capire un fatto, un significato.

grasping ['grɑ:spiŋ], *ag*. 1. tenace 2. avido, cupido.

graspingly ['grɑ:spiŋli], *av*. 1. tenacemente 2. avidamente.

graspingness ['grɑ:spiŋnis], *s*. avidità, cupidigia.

grass [grɑ:s], *s*. 1. erba; prato; pascolo, pastura: *a blade of —*, un filo d'erba; *to be at —*, essere al pascolo; *fig*. essere in vacanza; *to send a horse out to —*, mandare un cavallo al pascolo ‖ *don't let the — grow under your feet*, *fig*. non perdere tempo ‖ *please, keep off the —*, è vietato calpestare il prato ‖ *to send s.o. to —*, stendere qlcu. a terra 2. graminacee 3. (*radar*) ondulazione 4. (*miner*.) superficie ☆ — *-cloth*, (tessuto di) seta vegetale; — *-green*, color verde prato; — *-plot*, prato artificiale; — *-roots*, (*neol*.) zone rurali di un paese; — *-snake*, biscia; — *-widow*, donna il cui marito è temporaneamente assente ‖ *sparrow- —*, (*fam. bot*.) asparago.

to grass, *v.t*. 1. coprire d'erba 2. stendere sul prato (tela, canapa) per il candeggio 3. abbattere, far cadere (persone, uccelli) 4. tirare (il pesce) a riva 5. (*miner*.) portare alla superficie.

grasshopper ['grɑ:s,hopə*], *s*. 1. (*entom*.) cavalletta 2. (*aer*.) « cicogna » 3. (*rad*.) cavalletto, trasmettitore meteorologico.

grassiness ['grɑ:sinis], *s*. l'essere erboso.

grassing ['grɑ:siŋ], *s*. 1. il mettere a erba, prato (un terreno) 2. (*ind. tessile*) candeggio al prato 3. il gettar di sella 4. l'abbattere (uccelli).

grassy ['grɑ:si], *ag*. erboso.

grate[1] [greit], *s*. 1. grata, griglia, inferriata 2. (*cuc*.) gratella, graticola.

to grate[1], *v.t*. fornire di grata.

to grate[2], *v.t.i*. 1. grattugiare: *grated cheese*, formaggio grattugiato 2. stridere; cigolare; digrignare: *the door grated on its hinges*, la porta cigolò sui cardini; *to — one's teeth*, digrignare i denti ‖ *those sounds — upon my ear*, quei suoni mi straziano le orecchie.

grateful ['greitful], *ag*. 1. grato, riconoscente 2. caro, gradito, piacevole.

gratefully ['greitfuli], *av*. 1. con gratitudine, riconoscenza 2. gradevolmente, piacevolmente.

gratefulness ['greitfulnis], *s*. 1. gratitudine, riconoscenza 2. gradevolezza, piacevolezza.

grater ['greitə*], *s*. grattugia.

graticulation [grə,tikju'leiʃən], *s*. retinatura (di disegno, quadro).

graticule ['grætikju:l], *s*. 1. (*pitt. disegno*) graticola 2. (*ott*.) reticolo.

gratification [,grætifi'keiʃən], *s*. 1. ricompensa; gratifica 2. piacere, diletto 3. soddisfacimento.

to gratify ['grætifai], *v.t*. 1. ricompensare; gratificare 2. appagare, soddisfare; dilettare; compiacere.

gratifying ['grætifaiiŋ], *ag*. soddisfacente; piacevole.

gratifyingly ['grætifaiiŋli], *av*. soddisfacentemente; piacevolmente.

gratin ['grætæŋ], *s*. (*cuc*.) « gratin ».

grating[1] ['greitiŋ], *ag*. 1. stridente, aspro, dissonante 2. spiacevole; urtante ‖ *s*. stridore.

grating[2], *s*. 1. grata, inferriata 2. (*ott*.) reticolo.

gratingly ['greitiŋli], *av*. 1. con stridore; in modo stridente 2. in modo spiacevole, urtante.

gratis ['greitis], *ag*. gratuito ‖ *av*. gratis.

gratitude ['grætitju:d], *s*. gratitudine, riconoscenza: — *to s.o. for sthg.*, gratitudine verso qlcu. per ql.co.

gratuitous [grə'tju(:)təs], *ag*. 1. gratuito 2. (*fam*.) gratuito, ingiustificato: *a — insult*, un insulto ingiustificato.

gratuitously [grə'tju(:)təsli], *av*. 1. gratuitamente 2. ingiustificatamente.

gratuitousness [grə'tju(:)itəsnis], *s*. gratuità.

gratuity [grə'tju(:)iti], *s*. gratifica; mancia.

gratulant ['grætjulənt], *ag*. congratulatorio.

to gratulate ['grætjuleit], *v.t*. (*rar*.) congratularsi con.

gratulation [,grætju'leiʃən], *s*. (*rar*.) congratulazione.

gratulatory ['grætjulətəri], *ag*. congratulatorio.

grave[1] [greiv], *nel senso* 2. [grɑ:v], *ag*. 1. grave, serio; dignitoso; solenne: — *news*, notizie gravi 2. (*gram*.) grave: — *accent*, accento grave ‖ *s*. 1. grave: *to pass from — to gay*, passar dal grave al gaio 2. (*gram*.) accento grave.

grave[2], *s*. 1. fossa, tomba, sepolcro ‖ *to have one's foot in the —*, avere un piede nella fossa; *to make s.o. turn in his —*, far rivoltare qlcu. nella fossa ‖ *fig*. morte, distruzione ☆ — *-clothes*, sudario; — *-stone*, lapide funeraria.

to grave[2], *pass*. **graved** [greivd], *p.p*. **graved, graven** ['greivən], *v.t*. 1. (*arc*.) seppellire 2. incavare; scolpire (anche *fig*.): *graven on one's memory*, scolpito nella memoria.

to grave[3], *v.t*. (*mar*.) pulire, grattare (la chiglia di una nave).

gravel ['grævəl], *s*. 1. ghiaia, ghiaietto 2. (*patol*.) renella ☆ — *-pit*, cava di ghiaia; — *-walk*, viale ghiaioso.

to gravel, *pass.p.p*. **gravelled** ['grævəld], *v.t*. 1. inghiaiare: *gravelled paths*, sentieri ghiaiosi; *to — a road*, inghiaiare una strada 2. *fig*. imbarazzare.

graveless ['greivlis], *ag*. senza tomba; insepolto.

gravelly ['grævli], *ag*. 1. ghiaioso; renoso 2. (*patol*.) che contiene renella, calcoloso.

gravely ['greivli], *av*. gravemente.

graven ['greivən], *p.p*. di to **grave**[2] ‖ *ag*. intagliato; scolpito ☆ — *image*, idolo.

graveness ['greivnis], *s*. gravità, serietà; dignità.

graver ['greivə*], *s*. 1. incisore; intagliatore 2. (*strum. artig*.) bulino.

graveyard ['greiv-jɑ:d], *s*. cimitero, camposanto ☆ — *school*, — *poetry*, scuola, poesia sepolcrale.

gravid ['grævid], *ag*. gravido.

graving[1] ['greiviŋ], *V*. **engraving**.

graving[2], *s*. (*mar*.) pulitura di nave; carenaggio ☆ — *-dock*, bacino di carenaggio.

to gravitate ['græviteit], *v.i*. gravitare (anche *fig*.): *to — to(wards) an idea*, gravitare intorno a un'idea.

gravitation [,grævi'teiʃən], *s*. (*fis*.) gravitazione.

gravity ['græviti], *s*. 1. gravità, serietà, austerità: *the — of the situation*, la gravità della situazione; *she couldn't keep her —*, non potè mantenersi seria, non potè fare a meno di ridere 2. (*fis*.) gravità: *center of —*, centro di gravità ☆ *specific —*, peso specifico.

gravure [grə'vjuə*], *s*. (*foto*.) fotoincisione.

gravy ['greivi], *s*. 1. sugo (di carne); salsa ☆ — *-beef*, girello; — *-boat*, salsiera.

gray, *V*. **grey**.

grayling ['greiliŋ], *s*. (*ittiol*.) temolo.

to graze[1] [greiz], *v.t.i*. 1. pascere, far pascolare, condurre al pascolo 2. pascolare, mangiare l'erba 3. tenere (un terreno) a pascolo.

graze[2], *s*. 1. tocco, colpo di striscio 2. scalfittura, escoriazione.

to graze[2], *v.t.i*. 1. sfiorare, rasentare: *the bullet grazed his arm*, il proiettile gli sfiorò il braccio; *to — against* (o *along* o *by*), andare, passare rasente 2. scalfire; escoriare.

grazier ['greizjə*], *s*. allevatore (di bestiame).

graziery ['greizjəri], *s*. allevamento (di bestiame).

grazing[1] ['greiziŋ], *s*. 1. pascolo, pastura 2. allevamento, pascolo di bestiame ☆ — *-land*, pascolo.

grazing[2], *ag*. radente.

grease [gri:s], *s*. 1. grasso, unto; grasso animale; sugna ‖ *in —* (o *in pride of —* o *in prime of —*), ben grasso (di selvaggina) 2. olio denso, lubrificante 3. (*ind*.) lana sudicia 4. (*vet*.) rappa, malandra (dei cavalli) 5. (*sl*.) discorsi, modi untuosi ☆ — *-cup*, (*mec*.) ingrassatore; — *-gun*, (*mec*.) pompa per ingrassaggio; — *-paint*, (*teat*.)

cerone; — -*proof*, pergamenata (di carta) ‖ *elbow-* —, (*scherz.*) olio di gomito.

to **grease** [gri:z], *v.t.* **1.** ungere, sporcare d'unto **2.** ungere, ingrassare, lubrificare ‖ *like greased lightning*, (*sl.*) rapidissimamente ‖ *to* — *the palm of s.o.*, *fig.* ungere, corrompere qlcu.; *to* — *the wheels*, *fig.* ungere le ruote **3.** attaccare la rappa, la malandra a (un cavallo).

greaser ['gri:zə*], *s.* **1.** ingrassatore **2.** (*sl. mar.*) macchinista **3.** (*sl. amer. spreg.*) messicano.

greasily ['gri:zili], *av.* untuosamente.

greasiness ['gri:zinis], *s.* **1.** grassume, untume; untuosità; oleosità; grassezza (di lana) **2.** *fig.* untuosità.

greasy ['gri:zi], *ag.* **1.** grasso; oleoso: —*wool*, lana grassa **2.** unto, macchiato, coperto di grasso **3.** scivoloso, sdrucciolevole (di strada) **4.** *fig.* untuoso **5.** che ha la rappa, la malandra (di cavallo) ☆ — *pole*, albero della cuccagna.

great [greit], *ag.* **1.** grande: — *A*, a grande, maiuscola; *a* — *company*, una compagnia numerosa; *a* — *friend of mine*, un mio grande amico; — *hopes*, grandi speranze; *the* — *men of the age*, i grandi dell'epoca; — *thoughts*, pensieri nobili, elevati; *he is a* — *hero*, *artist*, è un grande eroe, artista ‖ *the Great Armada*, la Grande Armata ‖ *the Great Bear*, l'Orsa Maggiore ‖ *the Great Powers*, le Grandi Potenze ‖ *the Great War*, la Grande Guerra ‖ *Frederick the Great*, Federico il Grande ‖ *the* — *unwashed*, la plebaglia ‖ *a* — *while ago*, molto tempo fa ‖ — *with child*, (*arc. dial.*) incinta ‖ *to reach a* — *age*, arrivare a tarda età **2.** (*con parole esprimenti numero, quantità*): *a* — *deal of money*, moltissimo denaro, una gran quantità di denaro; *a* — *many people*, moltissima gente; *he is a* — *deal better*, sta molto meglio ‖ *to a* — *extent* (o *in a* — *measure*), considerevolmente **3.** (*usato enfaticamente davanti ad ag.*): *a* — *big fish*, un grossissimo pesce; *a* — *big man*, un omone **4.** (*fam.*) divertente, splendido, fantastico: *that's a* — !, è fantastico!; *to have a* — *time*, divertirsi follemente **5.** (*usato predicativamente con prep.*): *to be* — *at doing sthg.*, essere bravo, abile nel fare ql.co.; *to be* — *in sthg.*, eccellere in ql.co.; *to be* — *on sthg.*, (*fam.*) essere appassionato di, avere la mania di ql.co. ☆ — -*aunt*, prozia; — -*grandchild*, — *grand daughter*, — -*grandson*, pronipote; — -*grandfather*, bisnonno; — -*grandmother*, bisnonna; — - — -*grandfather*, trisavolo; — - — -*grandmother*, trisavola; — -*hearted*, di gran cuore, magnanimo; — -*heartedness*, generosità, magnanimità; — -*nephew*, — -*niece*, pronipote; — *primer*, (*tip.*) carattere di corpo 18; — *toe*, alluce; — -*uncle*, prozio.

Great Britain ['greit'britn], *no.pr.* (*geog.*) Gran Bretagna.

greatcoat ['greit'kout], *s.* (*mil.*) cappotto pesante.

to **greaten** ['greitən], *v.t.i.* (*arc.*) ingrandire, crescere.

greatly ['greitli], *av.* **1.** molto: *she is* — *superior to me*, mi è di molto superiore; *we were* — *amused*, ci siamo divertiti molto **2.** nobilmente; generosamente.

greatness ['greitnis], *s.* **1.** grandezza, grossezza **2.** nobiltà, elevatezza (di pensiero); magnanimità **3.** forza (di passione, ecc.); gravità (di colpa, ecc.).

greave [gri:v], *s. spec. pl.* gambale (di armatura).

greaves [gri:vz], *s.pl.* (*cuc.*) ciccioli.

grebe [gri:b], *s.* (*ornit.*) colimbo.

Grecian ['gri:ʃən], *ag.* (*poet.*) greco: — *nose*, *profile*, naso, profilo greco ‖ — *gift*, dono che suscita diffidenza ‖ *s.c.* **1.** greco, greca **2.** ellenista ☆ — *knot*, pettinatura alla greca.

Greeism ['gri:sizəm], *s.* grecismo.

to **Grecize** ['gri:saiz], *v.t.i.* grecizzare.

Greece [gri:s], *no.pr.* (*geog.*) Grecia.

greed [gri:d], *s.* **1.** avidità, cupidigia, bramosia **2.** ingordigia; golosità.

greedily ['gri:dili], *av.* **1.** avidamente, cupidamente **2.** ingordamente; golosamente.

greediness ['gri:dinis], *s.* **1.** avidità **2.** ingordigia; golosità.

greedy ['gri:di], *ag.* **1.** avido; cupido: — *of gain*, avido di denaro; — *of honours*, avido di onori **2.** ingordo; goloso **3.** desideroso, bramoso (di fare ql.co.).

Greek [gri:k], *ag.* greco ‖ *the* — *Church*, la Chiesa ortodossa ‖ — *cross*, croce greca ‖ — *gift*, dono insidioso ‖ *at the* — *calends*, alle calende greche ‖ *s.c.* **1.** greco, greca **2.** imbroglione, imbrogliona ‖ *s.* lingua greca ‖ *it's all* — *to me*, non ci capisco niente, questo è arabo per me ☆ — *fret* (o — *key*), greca (ornamento).

green [gri:n], *ag.* **1.** verde **2.** verde, coperto di foglie ‖ *a* — *Christmas*, un Natale senza neve ‖ *he had* — *fingers*, era un abile giardiniere **3.** pallido, livido; *fig.* invidioso, geloso: *to be* — *with envy*, essere verde dall'invidia **4.** acerbo (di frutta); tenero (di verdura) **5.** *fig.* giovane, semplice, inesperto, ingenuo **6.** vigoroso, vegeto : *a* — *old age*, una vecchiaia vegeta **7.** recente: *a* — *wound*, una ferita ancora aperta.

green, *s.* **1.** colore verde **2.** vigore, giovinezza **3.** *pl.* verdura, erbaggi **4.** prato; prato pubblico; campo da golf.

to **green**, *v.t.i.* **1.** tingere in verde; coprire di verde; verdeggiare **2.** (*sl.*) beffare, canzonare.

green, (*nei composti*): — -*belt*, (*neol.*) zona verde (di centro urbano); — -*eyed*, dagli occhi verdi; *fig.* geloso; — -*fly*, (*entom.*) gorgoglione, pidocchio delle piante; — -*horn*, giovane inesperto; semplicciotto; — -*sickness*, (*patol.*) clorosi; — *table*, tavolo da giuoco; — -*tea*, tè verde.

greenback ['gri:nbæk], *s.* (*amer.*) biglietto di banca.

greener ['gri:nə*], *s.* (*sl.*) lavoratore inesperto, non specializzato.

greenery ['gri:nəri], *s.* **1.** vegetazione **2.** serra.

greenfinch ['gri:nfintʃ], *s.* (*ornit.*) verdone.

greengage ['gri:ngeidʒ], *s.* prugna Regina Claudia.

greengrocer ['gri:ngrousə*], *s.* erbivendolo.

greengrocery ['gri:ngrousəri], *s.* **1.** negozio di erbivendolo **2.** *pl.* frutta e verdura.

greenhouse ['gri:nhaus], *s.* **1.** serra **2.** (*neol.*) carlinga.

greening ['gri:niŋ], *s.* varietà di mela.

greenish ['gri:niʃ], *ag.* verdognolo, verdastro.

Greenland ['gri:nlənd], *no.pr.* (*geog.*) Groenlandia.

Greenlander ['gri:nləndə*], *s.c.* groenlandese.

greenlet ['gri:nlit], *s.* (*ornit.*) verdone.

greenly ['gri:nli], *av.* in modo immaturo, inesperto.

greenness ['gri:nnis], *s.* **1.** color verde **2.** acerbezza (di frutto); *fig.* immaturità **3.** *fig.* inesperienza, ingenuità **4.** vigore, gagliardia (di persona anziana).

greenroom ['gri:nrum], *s.* (*teat.*) camerino degli attori.

greenstone ['gri:n-stoun], *s.* (*min.*) nefrite; giada.

greensward ['gri:n-swo:d], *s.* erba; prato di parco o di giardino.

greenth [gri:nθ], *s.* (*rar.*) vegetazione.

Greenwich ['grinidʒ], *no.pr.* (*geog.*) Greenwich ☆ — (*mean*) *time*, ora di Greenwich.

greenwood ['gri:nwud], *s.* (*poet.*) foresta; bosco verde, frondoso.

greeny ['gri:ni], *ag.* verde.

to **greet**[1] [gri:t], *v.t.* **1.** salutare: *to* — *friends*, salutare amici **2.** offrirsi a (vista): *a new wonder greeted our eyes*, una nuova meraviglia si offerse ai nostri occhi.

to **greet**[2], *v.i.* (*scoz.*) piangere.

greeting ['gri:tiŋ], *s.* saluto: *best greetings to everybody*, i migliori saluti a tutti.

greffier ['grefiə*], *s.* cancelliere; notaio.

gregarious [gre'gɛəriəs], *ag.* **1.** (*zool.*) gregario **2.** (*fam.*) socievole: *a* — *group*, un gruppo di persone a cui piace far vita in comune **3.** (*bot.*) a ciuffi, a grappoli.

gregariously [gre'gɛəriəsli], *av.* in gruppo; in branco; in compagnia.

gregariousness [gre'gɛəriəsnis], *s.* **1.** (*biol.*) gregarismo **2.** socievolezza.

grege [greiʒ], *ag. s.* (di) colore tra beige e grigio.

Gregorian [gre'go:riən], *ag.* (canto, calendario) gregoriano ‖ *s.c.* gregoriano, gregoriana.

Gregory ['gregəri], *no.pr.m.* Gregorio.

Gregory-powder ['gregəri-,paudə*], *s.* (*farm.*) rabarbaro in polvere.

gremial ['gri:miəl], *s.* (*eccl.*) grembiale.

gremlin ['gremlin], *s.* spiritello maligno (specialmente dell'aria).

Grenada [gre'neidə], *no.pr.* (*geog.*) Grenada.

grenade [gri'neid], *s.* (*mil.*) granata.

grenadier [,grenə'diə*], *s.* **1.** granatiere **2.** (*ornit.*) ploceo.

grenadine[1] [,grenə'din], *s.* piatto di filetti di pollo o di vitello in gelatina.

grenadine[2], *s.* « grenadine » (organzino speciale).

grenadine[3], *s.* granatina (bibita).

Greta ['gri:tə], *no.pr.f.* Greta.

grew [gru:], *pass.* di to **grow**.

grey [grei], *ag.* **1.** grigio: — *day,* giornata grigia; *to turn* —, diventar grigio (di capelli); *to worry oneself* —, farsi venire i capelli bianchi (per dispiaceri) **2.** tetro, deprimente: *the future looks* —, il futuro si presenta grigio ‖ *s.* **1.** colore grigio: *to be dressed in* —, essere vestito di grigio **2.** (*ind. tessile*) filato o stoffa nel colore naturale **3.** cavallo grigio ‖ *the Scots Greys,* (*mil.*) il secondo reggimento dei dragoni **4.** pigmento grigio ☆ — *-coat,* (*amer.*) soldato confederato; — *-eyed,* dagli occhi grigi; — *friar,* francescano; — *-haired,* dai capelli grigi; — *matter,* (*anat.*) materia grigia.

to **grey**, *v.t.i.* **1.** rendere grigio, diventare grigio **2.** (*foto.*) velare.

greyhound ['greihaund], *s.* levriere.

greyish ['greiiʃ], *ag.* grigiastro.

greylag ['greilæg], *s.* oca selvatica.

greyness ['grei-nis], *s.* **1.** grigiore. **2.** tristezza.

greywacke ['greiwækə], *s.* (*geol.*) conglomerato.

grice [grais], *s.* (*scoz. arc.*) porcellino.

grid [grid], *s.* **1.** grata, griglia **2.** quadrettatura (di carta geografica) **3.** (*ind. tessile*) graticcio **4.** (*elett.*) rete a 132 KV o a 32 KV.

griddle ['gridl], *s.* **1.** teglia piatta da forno **2.** (*miner.*) vaglio.

to **griddle**, *v.t.* **1.** cucinare (in teglia) **2.** *to* — *out,* (*miner.*) vagliare.

gride [graid], *s.* stridore.

to **gride**, *v.i.* tagliare, raschiare, segare con stridore.

gridelin ['gridəlin], *s.* gridellino (colore).

gridiron ['grid,aiən], *s.* **1.** (*cuc.*) graticola **2.** (*mar.*) impalcatura di bacino di carenaggio **3.** (*teat.*) impalcatura sovrastante il palcoscenico **4.** (*amer.*) campo per il giuoco del calcio.

grief [gri:f], *s.* affanno, dolore, afflizione, angoscia: *to bring s.o. to* —, portare alla rovina qlcu.; *to come to* —, avere un incidente (automobilistico); cadere (da cavallo, ecc.); far fiasco; andare in rovina; *to die of* —, morire di dolore; *to give way to* —, abbandonarsi al dolore.

grievance ['gri:vəns], *s.* **1.** lagnanza; motivo di lagnanza: *to air one's grievances,* far sentire il proprio malcontento **2.** torto, ingiustizia.

grieve[1] [gri:v], *s.* (*scoz.*) fattore; soprintendente.

to **grieve**[2], *v.t.i.* affliggere, affliggersi; far dispiacere a, accorare, rattristare, rattristarsi.

grievingly ['gri:viŋli], *av.* con afflizione, con dolore.

grievous ['gri:vəs], *ag.* **1.** doloroso, penoso, crudele **2.** offensivo (di linguaggio) **3.** grave (di ferita, ecc.) **4.** insopportabile, gravoso.

grievously ['gri:vəsli], *av.* **1.** dolorosamente **2.** gravemente.

grievousness ['gri:vəsnis], *s.* **1.** dolore **2.** gravità (di una offesa, ecc.).

griffin[1] ['grifin], *s.* grifone.

griffin[2], *s.* (*sl. ang.-in.*) nuovo arrivato.

griffin[3], *s.* (*amer.*) mulatto.

griffon[1] ['grifən], *s.* (*zool.*) grifone (cane).

griffon[2], *s.* grifone.

grig [grig], *s.* **1.** piccola anguilla **2.** cavalletta **3.** (*fam.*) persona vivace.

grill[1] [gril], *s.* (*cuc.*) carne, pesce ai ferri ☆ — *room,* rosticceria.

grill[2], *s.* griglia, graticola.

to **grill**[2], *v.t.i.* **1.** (far) arrostire sulla graticola, cuocere ai ferri **2.** esporsi a forte calore, farsi arrostire (dal sole) **3.** *fig.* torturare **4.** (*amer.*) interrogare con severità.

grillage ['grilidʒ], *s.* (*arch.*) intelaiatura di fondazione.

grille [gril], *s.* **1.** griglia; inferriata **2.** incubatrice per pesci.

grilse [grils], *s.* (*ittiol.*) nome dato ad un salmone giovane che ritorna al fiume dal mare.

grim [grim], *ag.* feroce; severo; torvo; sinistro: — *mystery,* fosco mistero; — *smile,* sorriso sardonico.

grimace [gri'meis], *s.* **1.** smorfia **2.** affettazione.

to **grimace**, *v.i.* fare smorfie; fare moine.

grimalkin [gri'mælkin], *s.* **1.** vecchia gatta **2.** *fig.* megera.

grime [graim], *s.* sudiciume (di carbone, fuliggine).

to **grime**, *v.t.* insudiciare, sporcare.

griminess ['graiminis], *s.* sporcizia, sudiciume.

grimly ['grimli], *av.* con viso arcigno; trucemente; ferocemente; crudelmente.

grimness ['grimnis], *s.* viso truce; aspetto spaventevole; carattere, aspetto sinistro; inflessibilità; ferocia.

grimy ['graimi], *ag.* sudicio, sporco.

grin [grin], *s.* largo sorriso; sogghigno; smorfia.

to **grin**, *pass.p.p.* **grinned** [grind], *v.t.i.* far un largo sorriso; sogghignare: *to* — *and bear it,* far buon viso a cattivo giuoco ‖ *to* → *like a Cheshire cat,* ridacchiare frequentemente e scioccamente.

grind [graind], *s.* **1.** cigolio; scricchiolio; stridore **2.** lavoro lungo, pesante e monotono **3.** passeggiata igienica, scolastica **4.** (*fam. amer.*) sgobbone.

to **grind**, *pass.p.p.* **ground** [graund], *v.t.i.* **1.** macinare; maciullare; tritare; polverizzare; spezzarsi; frantumarsi **2.** (*mec.*) rettificare, molare; affilare; levigare **3.** far girare (macine); girare (una manovella) **4.** fregare; sfregarsi contro **5.** stringere, digrignare (denti) **6.** *fig.* schiacciare, opprimere **7.** (*fam.*) sgobbare.

grinder ['graində*], *s.* **1.** macina; molatrice; affilatrice; rettificatrice **2.** (*dente*) molare **3.** arrotino **4.** (*sl. amer.*) grosso panino farcito ‖ *s.c.* (*fam.*) insegnante; ripetitore, ripetitrice; sgobbone, sgobbona ☆ *organ* - —, sonatore di organetto.

grindery ['graindəri], *s.* **1.** materiale usato dai ciabattini **2.** bottega di arrotino.

grinding ['graindiŋ], *ag.* **1.** stridente **2.** opprimente **3.** doloroso, lacerante ‖ *s.* **1.** macinatura **2.** stridore (di denti) **3.** affilatura **4.** molatura, rettifica **5.** *fig.* oppressione.

grindstone ['graindstoun], *s.* macina, mola ‖ *to hold* (*o to keep*) *one's nose to the* —, lavorare senza posa.

gringo ['griŋgou], *s.* « gringo ».

grip[1] [grip], *s.* **1.** stretta, presa: *terror had them in its* —, essi erano in preda al terrore; *to come to grips,* venire alle prese (*with, con*) **2.** *fig.* padronanza; dominio; controllo: *to have a good* — *of the situation,* avere la situazione in pugno **3.** impugnatura, manico **4.** fitta di dolore **5.** (*amer.*) valigetta a mano.

to **grip**[1], *pass.p.p.* **gripped** [gript], *v.t.i.* **1.** afferrare strettamente (anche *fig.*) **2.** attirare l'attenzione di **3.** far presa.

grip[2], *s.* **1.** fossatello; solco di drenaggio **2.** grondaia.

to **grip**[2], *pass.p.p.* **gripped** [gript], *v.t.* solcare.

gripe [graip], *s.* **1.** presa; stretta **2.** (*mec.*) freno **3.** *fig.* presa, possesso; controllo **4.** *pl.* (*mar.*) rizze **5.** *pl.* (*patol.*) colica **6.** (*sl.*) usuraio **7.** (*fam. amer.*) lamentela, brontolio **8.** manico.

to **gripe**, *v.t.i.* **1.** prendere, stringere, afferrare, impugnare **2.** *fig.* opprimere, affliggere, irritare **3.** provocare coliche a **4.** (*mar.*) assicurare (l'ancora) con rizze **5.** (*fam. amer.*) brontolare.

griping ['graipiŋ], *ag.* **1.** avaro, rapace **2.** acuto, lancinante (di dolore) ‖ *s.* **1.** stretta, presa **2.** *fig.* oppressione **3.** (*patol.*) colica.

gripingly ['graipiŋli], *av.* avaramente; acutamente.

grippe [grip], *s.* (*patol.*) influenza.

gripper ['gripə*], *s.* pinza.

gripsack ['gripsæk], *s.* (*amer.*) valigia a mano.

griseous ['griziəs], *ag.* (*bot. zool.*) grigio perla, grigio azzurro, azzurrognolo.

grisette [gri'zet], *s.* grisetta, sartina francese (originariamente vestita di grigio).

griskin ['griskin], *s.* (*cuc.*) braciola di maiale.

grisliness ['grizlinis], *s.* orribilità, spaventosità.

grisly ['grizli], *ag.* (*letter.*) spaventoso, orribile; sinistro, macabro.

grist¹ [grist], *s.* **1.** grano, frumento, biada ‖ *to bring — to one's mill*, tirar l'acqua al proprio mulino, trarre vantaggio **2.** malto tritato (per la fabbricazione della birra) ☆ *— -mill*, mulino.

grist², *s.* spessore (di filo, corda, ecc.).

gristle ['grisl], *s.* (*anat.*) cartilagine.

gristly ['grisli], *ag.* (*anat.*) cartilaginoso.

grit [grit], *s.* **1.** graniglia; sabbia; arenaria **2.** grana, struttura **3.** (*fam.*) forza di carattere; resistenza; fierezza; energia: *a challenge to British —*, una sfida all'energia, alla forza di carattere degli inglesi.

to grit, *pass.p.p.* **gritted** ['gritid], *v.t.i.* digrignare (i denti); stridere.

grits [grits], *s.pl.* grossa farina d'avena.

gritstone ['gritstoun], *s.* (*geol.*) arenaria.

grittiness ['gritinis], *s.* l'essere sabbioso.

gritty ['griti], *ag.* ghiaioso, sabbioso; granuloso.

to grizzle¹ ['grizl], *v.i.* (*fam.*) piagnucolare.

to grizzle², *v.t.i.* (far) divenire grigio, brizzolato.

grizzly ['grizli], *ag.* grigio, brizzolato ‖ *s.* « grizzly » (orso grigio del Nord America).

groan [groun], *s.* **1.** gemito, lamento **2.** *pl.* mormorii (di disapprovazione).

to groan, *v.t.i.* **1.** gemere, lamentarsi; brontolare: *to — under tyranny*, gemere sotto il peso della tirannia ‖ *to — inwardly*, soffrire intimamente **2.** *to — for* (*sthg.*), desiderare ardentemente **3.** *to — down*, far tacere mormorando **4.** *to — out*, dire, raccontare tra i gemiti.

groaning ['grouniŋ], *ag.* lamentoso, gemente ‖ *s. coll.* gemito, gemiti; lamento, lamenti; mormorii.

groaningly ['grouniŋli], *av.* lamentosamente.

groat [grout], *s.* **1.** (*arc.*) « groat » (moneta inglese d'argento del valore di ⅓ di scellino) ‖ *it is not worth a —*, non vale un soldo **2.** somma insignificante.

groats [grouts], *s.pl.* fiocchi d'avena.

Grobian ['groubjən], *s.* persona goffamente e sciattamente vestita.

grocer ['grousə*], *s.* droghiere.

grocery ['grousəri], *s.* generi di drogheria; (*amer.*) drogheria (merce e bottega).

grog [grog], *s.* « grog » (tipo di ponce) ☆ *— -blossom*, bitorzolo (sul naso di un beone); *— -shop*, mescita, bar.

groggy ['grogi], *ag.* **1.** barcollante, brillo **2.** malfermo, vacillante (di sedie, tavoli).

grogram ['grogrəm], *s.* « grosgrain » (tessuto).

groin [groin], *s.* **1.** (*anat.*) inguine **2.** (*arch.*) unghia; costolone.

to groin, *v.t.* (*arch.*) costruire con costoloni.

gromwell ['gromwəl], *s.* (*bot.*) miglialsole.

groom [grum], *s.* **1.** staffiere, palafreniere **2.** gentiluomo di corte ‖ *— of the bedchamber*, cameriere segreto del re; *— of the stole*, gentiluomo addetto al guardaroba del re **3.** (*abbr.* di *bridegroom*) sposo.

to groom, *v.t.i.* **1.** governare, strigliare (cavalli) **2.** pulire, rassettare, riordinare **3.** (*amer. pol.*) istruire, fare pubblicità in favore di (candidato) ☆ *well-groomed*, accurato (di persona); di aspetto raffinato.

groomsman, *pl.* **groomsmen** ['grumzmən], *s.* testimone dello sposo.

groove [gru:v], *s.* **1.** scanalatura; incavo; solco; canale; (*min.*) galleria, pozzo **2.** *fig.* « routine », trantran **3.** (*anat.*) solco.

to groove, *v.t.* scanalare, incavare.

grooving ['gru:viŋ], *s.* **1.** scanalatura; (*mec.*) solcatura **2.** (*miner.*) escavazione.

grooviness ['gru:vinis], *s.* l'essere solcato, scanalato.

groovy ['gru:vi], *ag. fig.* che segue la corrente; dalla mentalità ristretta.

to grope [group], *v.i.* brancolare, andare a tastoni (anche *fig.*): *he groped his way to the door*, andò a tastoni fino alla porta; *to — for sthg.*, cercare ql.co. andando a tastoni.

gropingly ['groupiŋli], *av.* a tastoni.

grosbeak ['grousbi:k], *s.* (*ornit.*) frusone.

gross [grous], *ag.* **1.** volgare, rozzo, rustico: *— language*, linguaggio volgare; *— manners*, maniere rozze **2.** grossolano, madornale, evidente: *— mistake*, errore evidente, grossolano **3.** grasso, grosso, gonfio; pesante, grasso (di cibo) **4.** indecente, osceno **5.** ottuso (di sensi) **6.** lussureggiante, abbondante: *the — vegetation of the tropical jungle*, la vegetazione lussureggiante della giungla tropicale **7.** (*comm.*) lordo ‖ *s.* (*invariato al pl.*) **1.** (*solo sing.*) massa: *by the* (o *in the*) *—*, all'ingrosso, tutto compreso **2.** (*comm.*) grossa (dodici dozzine) ☆ *— amount*, totale lordo; *— feeder*, mangione (di cibi grossolani); *— weight*, peso lordo.

grossly ['grousli], *av.* **1.** grossolanamente; volgarmente **2.** approssimativamente **3.** abbondantemente.

grossness ['grousnis], *s.* **1.** grossolanità, volgarità; indecenza **2.** enormità.

grot [grot], *s.* (*poet.*) *abbr.* di **grotto**.

grotesque [grou'tesk], *ag.* **1.** (*art.*) grottesco **2.** stravagante, assurdo, bizzarro ‖ *s.* grottesco.

grotesquely [grou'teskli], *av.* bizzarramente, stranamente.

grotesqueness [grou'tesknis], *s.* bizzarria, stravaganza.

grotto ['grotou], *pl.* **grottos**, **grottoes** ['grotouz], *s.* (*geol.*) grotta; (*arch.*) grotta artificiale.

grouch [grautʃ], *s.* (*fam. amer.*) malumore, musoneria ‖ *s.c.* brontolone, brontolona.

to grouch, *v.i.* (*fam. amer.*) brontolare; essere di cattivo umore.

ground¹ [graund], *s.* **1.** superficie (della Terra) ‖ *above —*, vivo; *below —*, morto ‖ *it suits me to the —*, (*fam.*) mi va proprio bene ‖ *to fall to the —*, *fig.* fallire (di piani); essere deluso (di speranze) **2.** posizione, area; distanza, territorio (anche *fig.*): *he covered a lot of —*, ha percorso molta strada; *to be on one's own —*, conoscere bene l'argomento; essere sicuro del fatto proprio; *to be on sure —*, conoscere il terreno; andare a colpo sicuro; *to gain —*, guadagnare terreno; *to lose —*, perdere terreno ‖ *to shift one's —*, cambiare il proprio punto di vista, le proprie intenzioni ‖ *to stand one's —*, tener duro, testa **3.** suolo, terreno: *to till the —*, coltivare il suolo ‖ *forbidden —*, *fig.* argomento proibito; *to break fresh —*, coltivare un terreno incolto; *fig.* tentare ql.co. di nuovo **4.** terreno adibito ad un particolare uso **5.** fondo (di mare, fiume, lago): *to touch* (o *to take*) *—*, toccare il fondo, arenarsi (di nave) **6.** *gener. pl.* terreni, parchi, giardini (che circondano una casa) ‖ *house and grounds for sale*, casa e terreno in vendita **7.** *pl.* fondi, sedimenti **8.** *gener. pl.* motivi, ragioni, cause: *on the — of*, sotto pretesto di; *without —*, senza motivo; *I did it on personal grounds*, lo feci per motivi personali; *I have good ground(s) for having faith in him*, ho buone ragioni di avere fiducia in lui **9.** sfondo, campo (di disegno): *the — of a picture*, lo sfondo di un quadro **10.** (*elett.*) terra, massa ☆ *— -angling*, pesca con la lenza galleggiante; *— -ash*, frassino giovane; *— -bait*, esca che si getta sul fondo; *— crew*, (*aer.*) personale per servizio a terra; *— -fish*, pesce che vive sul fondo; *— -floor*, pianterreno; *— -game*, selvaggina (conigli, lepri, ecc.); *— -hog*, marmotta; formichiere; *— -ivy*, pianta simile a edera strisciante; *— -note*, nota fondamentale; *— -rent*, rendita fondiaria, affitto di terreni; *— -swell*, maremoto; *— work*, fondamento, base; — -zero, (neol. fis.) zero-terra ‖ coffee grounds, fondi di caffè; football —, campo di calcio.

to **ground**[1], v.t.i. **1.** fondare, fondarsi; basare, basarsi: to — a fact on (o in) sthg., basare un fatto su ql.co. ‖ — arms!, (mil.) pied'arm! **2.** arenarsi, incagliarsi (di nave); atterrare (di aereo) **3.** insegnare i primi elementi a: to — a pupil in Latin, insegnare i primi elementi di latino ad un allievo **4.** (elett.) mettere a terra (la corrente) **5.** preparare il fondo di (un quadro, un ricamo).

ground[2], pass.p.p. di to **grind** ‖ ag. **1.** macinato: — coffee, caffè macinato **2.** molato; levigato: — glass, vetro smerigliato, molato **3.** arrotato, affilato.

groundage ['graundidʒ], s. (mar.) diritto di porto.

grounded ['graundid], ag. basato, fondato; (elett.) legato alla terra ☆ ill- —, well- —, fig. infondato, fondato.

groundedly ['graundidli], av. ragionevolmente, fondatamente.

grounding ['graundiŋ], s. **1.** base, conoscenza: to have a good — in Latin, avere una buona conoscenza degli elementi del latino **2.** (mar.) arenamento; (aer.) atterraggio **3.** (amer. elett.) messa a terra **4.** sfondo; (pitt.) fondo, prima mano; (ind. tessile) fondo.

groundless ['graundlis], ag. infondato, senza ragione: — suspicions, sospetti infondati.

groundlessly ['graundlisli], av. infondatamente; senza ragione.

groundlessness ['graundlisnis], s. infondatezza; mancanza di basi.

groundling ['graundliŋ], s. **1.** pesce che vive sul fondo **2.** pianta rampicante; pianta nana **3.** (letter.) spettatore, lettore di gusti poco raffinati.

groundman ['graundmæn], pl. **groundmen** ['graundmen], s. **1.** addetto a scavi nel terreno **2.** inserviente dei campi sportivi **3.** meccanico di aeroplani.

groundsel ['graunsl], s. (bot.) senecione.

groundsman, pl. **groundsmen** ['graundzmen], V. **groundman**.

group [gru:p], s. **1.** gruppo, raggruppamento (di persone): literary —, cenacolo di letterati; to form a —, raggrupparsi **2.** (chim.) radicale; (elett.) gruppo **3.** (pitt. scult.) gruppo, insieme: harmonious — of colours, insieme armonioso di colori ☆ — -captain, (aer. inglese) colonnello d'aviazione.

to **group**, v.t.i. raggruppare, raggrupparsi; classificare.

groupage ['gru:pidʒ], **grouping** ['gru:piŋ], s. raggruppamento; combinazione (di colori).

grouse[1] [graus], s. (invariato al pl.) (ornit.) tetraone, gallo cedrone.

to **grouse**[1], v.i. andare a caccia di tetraoni.

grouse[2], s. (fam.) brontolio, borbottio.

to **grouse**[2], v.i. (fam.) brontolare, borbottare: to — at s.o., about sthg., brontolare contro qlcu., per ql.co.

grout[1] [graut], s. malta liquida, boiacca.

to **grout**[1], v.t. stuccare; rifinire con stucco.

to **grout**[2], v.t.i. grufolare.

grove [grouv], s. boschetto; vivaio (di piante) ☆ olive —, uliveto; orange —, aranceto.

to **grovel** ['grɔvl], pass.p.p. **grovelled** ['grɔvld], v.i. strisciare a terra; fig. umiliarsi: to — before (o to) s.o., (fam.) leccare i piedi a qlcu.

groveller ['grɔvlə*], s. essere strisciante (spec. fig.); leccapiedi, adulatore.

grovelling ['grɔvliŋ], ag. strisciante; fig. abietto ‖ s. strisciamento; fig. adulazione; prosternazione.

grovellingly ['grɔvliŋli], av. strisciando; fig. in modo strisciante, abietto.

to **grow** [grou], pass. **grew** [gru:], p.p. **grown** [groun], v.t.i. **1.** crescere, fiorire; svilupparsi: he has grown into a nice boy, si è fatto un simpatico ragazzo; rice grows well in Lombardy, il riso cresce bene in Lombardia; this custom has grown (up) much lately, questa abitudine si è molto diffusa recentemente ‖ you have grown so tall that you must now stop growing or you

will — out of all your clothes, sei tanto cresciuto in altezza che ora devi smettere di crescere o non avrai più abiti che ti vadano bene ‖ to — out of a habit, perdere un'abitudine con l'età **2.** aumentare; espandersi: Britain's power grew enormously in the 19th century, la Gran Bretagna accrebbe enormemente la sua potenza nel XIX secolo; to — in beauty, imbellire **3.** diventare, divenire gradualmente: to — angry, inquietarsi, irritarsi; to — bigger and bigger, ingrossare sempre più to — old, invecchiare; to — out of fashion, passare di moda; to — red, arrossire; to — tired, stancarsi **4.** coltivare; far(si) crescere: to — roses, coltivare delle rose; it's the fashion now for young men to — beards, è di moda ora per i giovani farsi crescere la barba **5.** to — (up)on (s.o.), aumentare l'influenza su; crescere nella stima di **6.** to — in, incarnarsi (di unghia) **7.** to — up, crescere, diventare adulto.

growable ['grouəbl], ag. coltivabile.

grower ['grouə*], s.c. coltivatore, coltivatrice ‖ s. pianta ☆ rapid —, slow —, pianta che cresce rapidamente, lentamente vine- —, viticultore.

growing ['grouiŋ], ag. crescente; che aumenta: a — danger, un pericolo crescente ‖ s. **1.** coltivazione (di piante) **2.** crescita ☆ corn- — area, zona produttrice di grano; — -pains, dolori.

growingly ['grouiŋli], av. con ritmo crescente.

growl [graul], s. brontolio; grugnito; ringhio.

to **growl**, v.t.i. brontolare; grugnire; ringhiare.

growler ['graulə*], s.c. brontolone, brontolona ‖ s. **1.** animale che ringhia o grugnisce **2.** (ittiol.) emulone **3.** (fam.) carrozza di piazza **4.** (sl. amer.) barile per birra della capacità di dieci galloni **5.** piccolo iceberg.

growlery ['grauləri], s. **1.** brontolio **2.** salotto privato.

growling ['grauliŋ], ag. ringhiante; che grugnisce; che brontola; brontolone ‖ s. ringhio; brontolio.

growlingly ['grauliŋli], av. con brontolii.

grown [groun], p.p. di to **grow** ‖ ag. cresciuto: a — man, un uomo fatto ☆ — -up, adulto.

growth [grouθ], s. **1.** crescita; aumento, sviluppo; progresso: the — of trade, l'aumento del commercio; a week's — of beard, una barba di una settimana; to reach full —, raggiungere il massimo sviluppo **2.** produzione; prodotto: apples of foreign —, mele di produzione straniera **3.** (med.) escrescenza.

groyne [grɔin], s. frangiflutti; pennello.

grub [grʌb], s. **1.** verme; lombrico **2.** larva **3.** (sl.) qualcosa da mangiare **4.** (sl. amer.) sgobbone; scribacchino.

to **grub**, pass.p.p. **grubbed** [grʌbd], v.t.i. **1.** zappare; scavare; dissodare; fig. scoprire **2.** (sl.) mangiare; dar da mangiare a **3.** sfacchinare, sgobbare **4.** to — along, vivacchiare.

grubber ['grʌbə*], s. **1.** (agr.) estirpatore, sarchio **2.** (sl.) mangione; sgobbone (a scuola).

to **grubble** ['grʌbl], v.t.i. **1.** cercare a tastoni **2.** brancolare.

grubby ['grʌbi], ag. **1.** pieno di vermi; bacato **2.** sporco.

Grub Street ['grʌb,stri:t], Grub Street (antica via di Londra abitata da letterati poveri perchè stipendiati da editori); (fam.) la bohème letteraria.

grudge [grʌdʒ], s. malanimo; rancore; invidia: to have a — against s.o., nutrire rancore contro qlcu.; I bear them no —, non provo alcun risentimento per loro ‖ to pay off old grudges, soddisfare vecchi rancori.

to **grudge**, v.t.i. **1.** dare a malincuore; permettere malvolentieri **2.** essere invidioso di: I do not — him his success, non gli invidio il suo successo **3.** (arc.) lagnarsi; brontolare.

grudgeful ['grʌdʒful], ag. sdegnato; incline al risentimento.

grudging ['grʌdʒiŋ], ag. **1.** riluttante **2.** avaro; invidioso: — of praise, avaro di lodi ‖ s. **1.** invidia; rancore **2.** avarizia.

grudgingly ['grʌdʒiŋli], *av.* a malincuore, malvolentieri.

to grue [gru:], *v.i.* (*scoz.*) rabbrividire; tremare d'orrore.

gruel [gruəl], *s.* farinata semiliquida d'avena, talvolta bollita nel latte ‖ *to give s.o. his —,* (*sl.*) darne un fracco a qlcu.

gruelling ['gruəliŋ], *ag.* (*sl.*) estenuante: *a — race,* una corsa faticosa ‖ *s.* (*sl.*) severa punizione; batosta.

gruesome ['gru:səm], *ag.* raccapricciante; macabro.

gruff [grʌf], *ag.* burbero; arcigno; rauco (di voce).

gruffly ['grʌfli], *av.* in modo burbero, arcigno; sgarbatamente; raucamente, con voce aspra.

gruffness ['grʌfnis], *s.* sgarbatezza; rudezza; tono burbero; viso arcigno; asprezza (di voce).

grum [grʌm], *ag.* 1. scontroso; corrucciato 2. rauco.

grumble ['grʌmbl], *s.* brontolio, borbottio; lagnanza.

to grumble, *v.t.i.* 1. brontolare, borbottare 2. lagnarsi, lamentarsi: *to — at s.o., about* (o *over*) *sthg.,* lagnarsi di qlcu., di ql.co. 3. borbottare, dire borbottando: *he grumbled* (*out*) *an answer,* borbottò una risposta.

grumbler ['grʌmblə*], *s.c.* brontolone, brontolona; borbottone, borbottona.

grumbling ['grʌmbliŋ], *ag.* che brontola, che sgrida ‖ *s.* brontolamento; lagnanza; sgridata.

grumblingly ['grʌmbliŋli], *av.* brontolando; sgridando.

grume [gru:m], *s.* coagulo; grumo.

grumly ['grʌmli], *av.* 1. in modo scontroso, sgarbato, arcigno 2. raucamente.

grumness ['grʌmnis], *s.* scontrosità.

grumous ['gru:məs], *ag.* grumoso.

grumpily ['grʌmpili], *av.* di cattivo umore.

grumpiness ['grʌmpinis], *s.* cattivo umore; irritabilità.

grumpish ['grʌmpiʃ], **grumpy** ['grʌmpi], *ag.* bisbetico; irritabile.

Grundy (Mrs.) ['grʌndi], *no.pr.f.* « Mrs. Grundy » (personificazione del più gretto convenzionalismo): *I don't care what Mrs. — says,* non me ne importa niente di quello che la gente dice di me.

Grundyism ['grʌndiizəm], *s.* gretto convenzionalismo.

grunt [grʌnt], *s.* 1. grugnito 2. brontolio, borbottio.

to grunt, *v.t.i.* 1. grugnire 2. borbottare, brontolare.

grunter ['grʌntə*], *s.* 1. porco 2. *fig.* brontolone.

gruntingly ['grʌntiŋli], *av.* brontolando.

gruntling ['grʌntliŋ], *s.* porcellino, maialino.

gruyère ['gru:jɛ*], *s.* gruviera (formaggio svizzero).

gryphon ['grifən], *s.* grifone.

guacharo ['gwa:tʃərou], *s.* (*ornit.*) guaciaro.

guaco ['gwa:kou], *s.* (*bot.*) guaco.

Guadeloupe [,gwa:də'lu:p], *no.pr.* (*geog.*) Guadalupa.

guaiacum ['gwaiəkəm], *s.* (*bot.*) guaiaco.

guana ['gwa:nə], *s.* (*zool.*) iguana; grossa lucertola.

guanaco [gwə'na:kou], *s.* (*zool.*) guanaco.

guaniferous [gwə'nifərəs], *ag.* che dà guano.

guano ['gwa:nou], *s.* guano.

guarana [gwə'ra:na:], *s.* (*farm.*) guarana.

guarantee [,gærən'ti:], *s.* 1. garanzia; pegno; cauzione; (*comm.*) avallo 2. garante, mallevadore: *to go — for s.o.,* rendersi garante per qlcu. ☆ *— bond,* cauzione; *— deposit,* deposito cauzionale ‖ *fidelity — insurance,* assicurazione contro i danni causati da infedeltà degli impiegati.

to guarantee, *v.t.* garantire, assicurare, farsi garante di: *to — a debt,* garantire un debito.

guarantor [,gærən'to:*], *s.* garante; (*comm.*) avallante.

guaranty ['gærənti], *V.* **guarantee** 1.

to guaranty, *V.* **to guarantee.**

guard [ga:d], *s.* 1. guardia, vigilanza; difesa: *the officer was on —,* l'ufficiale era di guardia; *to be on one's —,* stare in guardia; *to come off —,* smontare di guardia; *to go on* (o *to mount*) *—,* montare di guardia;

to keep —, fare la guardia; *to put s.o. on* (*his*) *—* (*against a danger*), premunire qlcu. (contro un pericolo); *to relieve —,* dare il cambio della guardia; *to run the —,* sfuggire alla guardia 2. posizione di guardia (scherma, pugilato, ecc.): *to take one's —,* mettersi in guardia 3. guardia; corpo di soldati; scorta: *— of honour,* guardia d'onore; *he was one of the old —,* apparteneva alla vecchia guardia 4. capotreno 5. sorvegliante; (*amer.*) secondino 6. custodia; protezione; riparo: *the — of a sword,* guardamano, guardia di una spada 7. (*med.*) correttivo 8. (*arch.*) parapetto ☆ *— -boat,* lancia di ronda; *-house,* (*mil.*) corpo di guardia; posto di polizia; *— -ring,* ferma anello; *— -room,* (*mil.*) corpo di guardia; cella per detenuti; *— -ship,* (*mar.*) nave vedetta; motovedetta; lancia portuale ‖ *advance- —,* avanguardia; *foot-guards,* guardie a piedi; *home- —,* milizia territoriale; *horse-guards,* guardie a cavallo; *rear- —,* retroguardia.

to guard, *v.t.i.* 1. custodire, proteggere; scortare; difendere: *to — s.o. from* (o *against*) *sthg.,* difendere qlcu. da ql.co.; *to — s.o. to his house,* scortare qlcu. fino a casa 2. *fig.* difendere, proteggere; sorvegliare: *to — one's reputation,* proteggere la propria reputazione; *to — one's words,* misurare le proprie parole 3. (*med.*) mescolare un correttivo a (un narcotico, ecc.) 4. stare in guardia; stare di sentinella.

guardant ['ga:dənt], *ag.* vigilante; in guardia ‖ *s.* (*arc.*) 1. guardiano 2. protettore.

guarded ['ga:did], *ag.* 1. prudente, misurato, circospetto: *— answer,* risposta cauta 2. scortato, guardato a vista: *— prisoner,* prigioniero scortato 3. munito di protezione.

guardedly ['ga:didli], *av.* guardingamente.

guardedness ['ga:didnis], *s.* cautela.

guardian ['ga:djən], *ag.* tutelare ‖ *s.c.* 1. guardiano-guardiana 2. amministratore, amministratrice ‖ *th. Board of Guardians,* (*st.*) comitato di pubblica assistenza 3. (*dir.*) tutore, tutrice; curatore, curatrice ‖ *se* (*eccl.*) padre guardiano ☆ *— angel,* angelo custode.

guardianship ['ga:djənʃip], *s.* (*dir.*) protezione; tutela; cura: *child under —,* minore sotto tutela.

guardless ['ga:dlis], *ag.* indifeso; senza protezione.

guardrail ['ga:d-reil], *s.* 1. (*riparo stradale*) guardavia; (*ferr.*) controrotaia 2. (*mar.*) battagliola.

guardsman, *pl.* **guardsmen** ['ga:dzmən], *s.* membro dei reggimenti della Guardia (specialmente ufficiale).

Guatemala [,gwæti'ma:lə], *no.pr.* (*geog.*) Guatemala.

guava ['gwa:və], *s.* (*bot.*) guava (pianta e frutto).

gubernation [,gju:bə'neiʃən], *s.* governo; regola.

gubernatorial [,gju:bənə'to:rjəl], *ag.* del governatore, governatoriale: *— election,* elezione del governatore.

gudgeon[1] ['gʌdʒən], *s.* 1. (*ittiol.*) ghiozzo 2. esca 3. *fig.* minchione, grullo; credulone.

gudgeon[2], *s.* (*mec.*) perno ☆ *— pin,* spinotto, perno di stantuffo ‖ *floating —,* perno flottante di stantuffo ‖ *rudder —,* (*aer. mar.*) femminella del timone.

Guelph [gwelf], *s.* (*st.*) guelfo.

Guelphic ['gwelfik], *ag.* (*st.*) guelfo.

guerdon ['gə:dən], *s.* (*poet.*) guiderdone.

to guerdon, *v.t.* (*poet.*) ricompensare.

guerilla, *V.* **guerrilla.**

Guernsey ['gə:nzi], *no.pr.* (*geog.*) Guernsey ‖ **guernsey,** *s.* 1. maglione di lana 2. mucca di razza Guernsey.

guerrilla [gə'rilə], *pl.* **guerrillas** [gə'riləz], *s.* 1. guerriglia 2. guerrigliere.

guess [ges], *s.* congettura, supposizione: *by —,* per ipotesi; *to give* (o *to have* o *to make*) *a —,* azzardare un'ipotesi ☆ *that's a good —,* (*fam.*) l'hai indovinata.

to guess, *v.t.i.* 1. congetturare, supporre: *I guessed her to be twenty,* le davo vent'anni 2. indovinare: *to — right, wrong,* indovinare, non indovinare 3. (*amer.*) credere: *I — she is right,* credo che abbia ragione.

guessable ['gesəbl], *ag.* 1. supponibile 2. indovinabile.

guesser ['gesə*], *s.c.* 1. chi fa congetture 2. indovino, indovina.

guessingly ['gesiŋli], *av.* per via di congetture.

guesswork ['gɛswə:k],¹ *s.* congettura; tentativo: *by* —, a lume di naso, a occhio e croce.

guest [gest], *s.c.* **1.** ospite, invitato, invitata: *we are expecting guests to lunch*, aspettiamo degli ospiti a colazione **2.** pensionante; cliente **3.** (*biol.*) parassita ☆ — -*chamber* (o — -*room*), camera degli ospiti; — -*house*, pensione, locanda; — -*rope*, (*mar.*) tonneggio; — -*towel*, asciugamano per ospiti ‖ *paying* —, ospite pagante; pensionante.

guffaw [gʌ'fɔ:], *s.* risata fragorosa.

to guffaw, *v.t.i.* **1.** ridere fragorosamente; sghignazzare **2.** fare, dire ridendo fragorosamente.

to guggle ['gʌgl], *V.* to gurgle.

Guiana [gi'ɑ:nə], *no.pr.* (*geog.*) Guiana: *British* — [gai'ænə], Guiana Britannica.

Guianese [,gaiə'ni:z], *ag.s. c.* (abitante) della Guiana.

guichet [,gi:ʃei], *s.* sportello di biglietteria.

guidable ['gaidəbl], *ag.* guidabile; docile.

guidance ['gaidəns], *s.* **1.** guida, direzione: *I owe much to his* —, devo molto ai suoi consigli **2.** indicazione, informazione: *for your* —, a titolo indicativo.

guide [gaid], *s.* **1.** guida; cicerone: *she acted as my* — *in London*, mi fece da cicerone a Londra **2.** guida; insegnamento: *let this event be a* — *to him*, che questo avvenimento gli sia d'esempio **3.** *fig.* consigliere, mentore: *he was my* — *during my youth*, mi guidò durante la giovinezza **4.** (*mil.*) guida **5.** guida (giovane esploratrice) **6.** — (-*book*), guida, manuale **7.** (*mar.*) nave guida **8.** (*mec.*) guida; (*rad.*) guida d'onda ☆ — -*post*, indicatore stradale; — -*rail*, (*ferr.*) terza rotaia; — -*rope*, (*aer.*) cavo pilota ‖ *alpine* —, guida alpina; *railway* - —, orario ferroviario; *wave*- —, (*rad.*) guida d'onda.

to guide, *v.t.* guidare, condurre; dirigere (anche *fig.*): *I will be guided by your advice*, seguirò il tuo consiglio.

guideless ['gaidlis], *ag.* senza guida.

guidon ['gaidən], *s.* guidone, pennone, stendardo.

guild [gild], *s.* corporazione; (*stor.*) gilda ‖ *the Guild-hall*, Palazzo delle Corporazioni (a Londra) ☆ — -*hall*, sede di corporazione; municipio.

guilder ['gildə*], *s.* (*st.*) «gulden», fiorino olandese.

guile [gail], *s.* insidia; astuzia; scaltrezza; frode.

guileful ['gailful], *ag.* insidioso; astuto, perfido.

guilefully ['gailfuli], *av.* insidiosamente; astutamente, perfidamente.

guilefulness ['gailfulnis], *s.* astuzia; perfidia.

guileless ['gaillis], *ag.* **1.** sincero, franco, schietto **2.** innocente; candido, ingenuo; semplice.

guilelessly ['gaillisli], *av.* **1.** sinceramente, francamente **2.** candidamente, ingenuamente.

guilelessness ['gaillisnis], *s.* **1.** sincerità, franchezza **2.** ingenuità; innocenza, candore.

guillemot ['gilimɔt], *s.* (*ornit.*) uria.

guillotine [,gilə'ti:n], *s.* **1.** ghigliottina **2.** (*ind. cartaria*) taglierina **3.** (*chir.*) tonsillotomo.

to guillotine, *v.t.* **1.** ghigliottinare, decapitare **2.** (*ind. cartaria*) tranciare con taglierina.

guilt [gilt], *s.* **1.** colpa, colpevolezza **2.** crimine, reato.

guiltily ['giltili], *av.* colpevolmente; come un colpevole, con aria colpevole.

guiltiness ['giltinis], *s.* colpevolezza.

guiltless ['giltlis], *ag.* **1.** innocente, senza colpa: *to hold* —, dichiarare innocente **2.** ignaro; privo: — *of French*, digiuno di francese ‖ *he is* — *of soap*, (*scherz.*) egli fa poco uso di sapone.

guiltlessly ['giltlisli], *av.* ingenuamente; con innocenza.

guiltlessness ['giltlisnis], *s.* innocenza.

guilty ['gilti], *ag.* **1.** colpevole; reo: *to find s.o.* —, *not* —, riconoscere qlcu. colpevole, innocente; *to plead* —, dichiararsi colpevole **2.** che si sente colpevole; turbato, tormentato da rimorsi: *a* — *conscience*, una coscienza tormentata.

Guinea ['gini], *no.pr.* (*geog.*) Guinea ‖ **guinea**, *s.* (*st.*) sterlina d'oro di Guinea; ghinea (unità di valore

pari a 21 scellini, si usa per onorari, beneficenza, premi) ☆ — -*fowl* (o — -*hen*), (*ornit.*) gallina faraona; — -*pig*, (*zool.*) procellino d'India; cavia.

Guinevere ['gwiniviə*], *no.pr.f.* Ginevra.

guipure [gi(:)'pjuə*], *s.* guipure (merletto di seta o di refe).

guise [gaiz], *s.* **1.** aspetto; apparenza esteriore **2.** falso aspetto, maschera: *under the* — *of friendship*, sotto la maschera dell'amicizia **3.** (*arc.*) stile, foggia; modo; guisa: *in the* — *of a monk*, in abito di monaco.

guitar [gi'tɑ:*], *s.* chitarra.

guitarist [gi'tɑ:rist], *s.c.* chitarrista.

gulch [gʌlʃ], *s.* (*amer.*) burrone (specialmente aurifero).

gules [gju:lz], *ag. s.* (*arald.*) (color) rosso.

gulf [gʌlf], *s.* **1.** golfo, insenatura ‖ *Gulf Stream*, la Corrente del Golfo **2.** abisso, precipizio **3.** vortice.

to gulf, *v.t.* inghiottire, assorbire.

gull¹ [gʌl], *s.* gabbiano.

gull², *s.* credulone, sempliciotto; sciocco.

to gull², *v.t.* darla a bere, truffare, ingannare.

gull³, *s.* (*dial.*) uccello senza penne (specialmente un piccolo papero).

gull⁴, *s.* forra.

to gull⁴, *v.t.i.* **1.** scanalare, erodere (di acqua) **2.** consumarsi, logorarsi.

guller ['gʌlə*], *s.* gabbamondo, impostore.

gullery ['gʌləri], *s.* (*arc.*) impostura.

gullet ['gʌlit], *s.* gola; esofago.

gullibility [,gʌli'biliti], *s.* credulità; ingenuità.

gullible ['gʌləbl], *ag.* credulo, credulone; ingenuo.

gullied ['gʌlid], *ag.* scanalato.

gullish ['gʌliʃ], *ag.* piuttosto credulo, sciocco.

Gulliver ['gʌlivə*], *no.pr.* (*lett.*) Gulliver.

gully¹ ['gʌli], *s.* **1.** burrone, gola (scavati dall'erosione) **2.** fognatura, condotto di scolo ☆ — -*drain*, cunetta; — *grating*, griglia di scarico; — -*hole*, tombino.

to gully¹, *v.t.* scavare canali, solchi di scolo in.

gully², *s.* largo coltello.

gulosity [gju'lɔsiti], *s.* (*rar.*) golosità.

gulp [gʌlp], *s.* **1.** atto, sforzo dell'ingoiare **2.** boccone; boccata; sorso: *to empty a glass at one* —, vuotare un bicchiere d'un fiato.

to gulp, *v.t.i.* **1.** inghiottire; trangugiare; mandar giù: *to* — (*down*) *a medicine*, trangugiare una medicina **2.** trattenere, soffocare; *fig.* inghiottire: *to* — *down one's rage*, soffocare la rabbia; *to* — *down* (o *back*) *one's tears*, inghiottire le lacrime.

gulpingly ['gʌlpiŋli], *av.* inghiottendo voracemente.

gum¹ [gʌm], *s.* (*gener. pl.*) gengive.

gum², *s.* **1.** gomma **2.** cispa **3.** gommosi (malattia delle piante da frutto) **4.** giuggiola **5.** *pl.* galosce ☆ — -*arabic*, gomma arabica; — -*boots*, (*amer.*) stivali di gomma; — -*dragon*, adragante; — -*elastic*, gomma elastica; — -*tree*, albero della gomma: *to be up* — -*tree*, (*fam.*) essere in difficoltà.

to gum², *pass.p.p.* **gummed** [gʌmd], *v.t.i.* **1.** ingommare, fissare con gomma **2.** secernere gomma **3.** (*sl. amer.*) imbrogliare, ingannare **4.** bloccare, bloccarsi; fermare, fermarsi (anche *fig.*).

gum³, *s.* (*dial. volg.*) Dio ‖ *by* —!, perdinci!; *my* —!, mio Dio!.

gumbo ['gʌmbou], *s.* (*amer.*) **1.** (*bot.*) ibisco **2.** zuppa ispessita con baccelli d'ibisco.

gumboil ['gʌmbɔil], *s.* (*patol.*) ascesso alla gengiva.

gumma ['gʌmə], *s.* (*patol.*) gomma.

gummatous ['gʌmətəs], *ag.* (*patol.*) gommoso.

gummiferous [gʌ'mifərəs], *ag.* (*bot.*) gommifero.

gumminess ['gʌminis], *s.* viscosità; gommosità.

gummy¹ ['gʌmi], *ag.* **1.** gommoso; vischioso; appiccicoso **2.** ricco di gomma **3.** gonfio (di gambe, caviglie).

gummy², *ag.* (*patol.*) gommoso.

gump [gʌmp], *s.* (*amer.*) sciocco, stupido.

gumption ['gʌmpʃən], *s.* **1.** (*fam.*) senso pratico; spirito d'iniziativa **2.** (*pitt.*) solvente per i colori.

gun [gʌn], *s.* **1.** cannone, bocca da fuoco, pezzo d'artiglieria: *a salute of six guns*, una salva di sei colpi; *to fire* (o *to discharge*) *a* —, sparare un colpo di cannone ‖ *a big* —, *fig.* un pezzo grosso ‖ *son of a* —, *fig.* briccone, mascalzone ‖ *sure as a* —, sicuro come due più due fa quattro ‖ *to blow great guns*, *fig.* soffiare forte (del vento) ‖ *to stand* (o *to stick*) *to one's guns*, tener duro (anche *fig.*) **2.** fucile, moschetto **3.** cacciatore, partecipante ad una partita di caccia: *a party of eight guns*, un gruppo di otto cacciatori **4.** (*amer.*) rivoltella ☆ — *-barrel*, canna di fucile; — *-boat*, (*mar.*) cannoniera; — *-carriage*, affusto di cannone, — *-case*, custodia per fucile; — *-dog*, cane da caccia; — *-drill*, (*mil.*) esercitazione ai pezzi; — *-fodder*, (*pop.*) carne da cannone; — *-layer*, (*artigl.*) puntatore; — *-room*, (*mar.*) quadrato dei sulbalterni; armeria; — *-runner*, contrabbandiere d'armi; — *-running*, contrabbando d'armi; — *-shy*, che teme gli spari (di cane da caccia); — *-sight*, (*artigl.*) congegno di mira ‖ *shot* —, fucile da caccia; *spray*-—, (*ind.*) pistola per verniciatura a spruzzo; *trench* —, (*artigl.*) lanciabombe, mortaio.

to gun, *pass.p.p.* **gunned** [gʌnd], *v.t.i.* (*amer.*) **1.** andare a caccia con fucile: *to go gunning for a thief*, inseguire armato un ladro **2.** freddare (con rivoltella).

guncotton [ˈgʌnˌkɔtn], *s.* (*chim.*) fulmicotone, nitrocotone.

gunfire [ˈgʌnˌfaiə*], *s.* **1.** sparatoria, tiro rapido; cannoneggiamento **2.** (*mar. mil.*) l'ora del mattino, della sera in cui viene sparato il colpo di cannone.

gunless [ˈgʌnlis], *ag.* senza cannoni.

gunman, *pl.* **gunmen** [ˈgʌnmən], *s.* (*sl. amer.*) bandito, rapinatore; terrorista.

gunmetal [ˈgʌnˌmetl], *s.* bronzo per cannoni.

gunnage [ˈgʌnidʒ], *s.* dotazione di cannoni di una nave da guerra.

gunned [gʌnd], *ag.* provvisto di cannoni.

gunnel [ˈgʌnl], *s.* (*mar.*) capo di banda, frisata.

gunner [ˈgʌnə*], *s.* artigliere; cannoniere ☆ —'s *mate*, aiuto cannoniere ‖ *machine* —, mitragliere.

gunnery [ˈgʌnəri], *s.* **1.** arte di costruire, maneggiare cannoni **2.** artiglieria **3.** fuoco d'artiglieria, cannoneggiamento.

gunning [ˈgʌniŋ], *s.* caccia: *to go out* —, andare a caccia.

gunny [ˈgʌni], *s.* **1.** rozza tela di iuta **2.** sacco.

gunpowder [ˈgʌnˌpaudə*], *s.* polvere nera da sparo, esplosivo ‖ *the Gunpowder Plot*, (*st. inglese*) la Congiura delle Polveri.

gunshot [ˈgʌnˌʃɔt], *s.* colpo di arma da fuoco ‖ *within a* —, a un tiro di schioppo ☆ — *wound*, ferita d'arma da fuoco.

gunsmith [ˈgʌnˌsmiθ], *s.* armaiuolo.

gunstock [ˈgʌnˌstɔk], *s.* fusto del fucile.

gunter [ˈgʌntə*], *s.* guntero (strumento per calcolo di logaritmi).

gunwale [ˈgʌnl], *s.* (*mar.*) capo di banda, frisata.

gup [gʌp], *s.* (*ang.-in.*) pettegolezzo; chiacchiera.

gurgitation [ˌgəːdʒiˈteiʃən], *s.* rigurgito.

gurgle [ˈgəːgl], *s.* gorgoglio; mormorio.

to gurgle, *v.i.* **1.** gorgogliare; mormorare (di ruscello) **2.** emettere suoni gutturali.

gurgling [ˈgəːgliŋ], *s.* gorgoglio; mormorio.

gurnard [ˈgəːnəd], **gurnet** [ˈgəːnit], *s.* (*ittiol.*) pesce capone.

gurrah [ˈgʌrɑː], *s.* recipiente di terracotta indiano.

gurry [ˈgʌri], *s.* fortino indiano.

guru [ˈguruː], *s.* (*ang.-in.*) « guru » (santone indiano).

Gus [gʌs], *no.pr.m.* dim. di **Gustavus**.

gush [gʌʃ], *s.* **1.** sgorgo; getto; fiotto; zampillo, ribollio (di acque): *a* — *of oil*, un getto di petrolio **2.** *fig.* effusione; torrènte (di parole, lacrime).

to gush, *v.t.i.* **1.** sgorgare; emettere a fiotti, versare: *the tears gushed into her eyes*, le si inondarono gli occhi di lacrime **2.** essere espansivo; intenerirsi: *girls often* —

over handsome film stars, le ragazze spesso si entusiasmano per i bei divi del cinema.

gusher [ˈgʌʃə*], *s.* **1.** persona esuberante, espansiva **2.** pozzo di petrolio ad eruzione spontanea.

gushing [ˈgʌʃiŋ], *ag.* **1.** zampillante; ribollente **2.** esuberante, espansivo: — *compliments*, complimenti calorosi.

gushy [ˈgʌʃi], *ag.* esuberante, espansivo.

gusset [ˈgʌsit], *s.* **1.** gherone **2.** fazzoletto ☆ — *plate*, (*edil.*) piastra nodale di testa.

Gussy [ˈgʌsi], *no.pr.m.* dim. di **Gustavus**.

gust[1] [gʌst], *s.* **1.** colpo di vento, raffica **2.** *fig.* impeto, scoppio (di passione, di collera).

gust[2], *s.* (*arc. poet.*) **1.** gusto **2.** apprezzamento **3.** aroma, sapore.

gustation [gʌsˈteiʃən], *s.* gustazione, degustazione.

gustative [ˈgʌstətiv], **gustatory** [ˈgʌstətəri], *ag.* gustatorio, gustativo.

Gustavus [gusˈtɑːvəs], *no.pr.m.* Gustavo.

gusto [ˈgʌstou], *s.* **1.** sapore speciale **2.** godimento, piacere; slancio, entusiasmo: *she does it really with* —, lo fa con evidente piacere.

gusty [ˈgʌsti], *ag.* ventoso; burrascoso, tempestoso.

gut [gʌt], *s.* **1.** *pl.* budella, intestini; parte di intestino **2.** (*mus.*) minugia **3.** stretto passaggio (di acque) **4.** *pl.* (*sl.*) coraggio; forza di carattere: *come now, put your guts into it!*, avanti, mettetecela tutta! ☆ — *-strings*, corda di minugia per violini ‖ *blind* —, (*anat.*) intestino cieco.

to gut, *pass.p.p.* **gutted** [ˈgʌtid], *v.t.* **1.** sventrare, sbudellare **2.** *fig.* distruggere, smantellare: *the house was gutted*, della casa non rimasero che le quattro mura.

gutta[1] [ˈgʌtə], *pl.* **guttae** [ˈgʌtiː], *s.* (*arch.*) goccia (di fregio ornamentale).

gutta[2](*-percha*) [ˈgʌtə(ˈpəːtʃə)], *s.* (*chim.*) guttaperca.

gutter [ˈgʌtə*], *s.* **1.** grondaia (di casa) **2.** cunetta **3.** condotto **4.** rigagnolo **5.** *fig.* la strada, i bassifondi: *language of the* —, linguaggio di strada; *to take a child out of the* —, togliere un bambino dalla strada ☆ — *-blood*, (*scoz.*) individuo di umili origini ‖ — *-snipe*, monello, ragazzo di strada.

to gutter, *v.t.i.* **1.** colare (di candela, ecc.) **2.** scanalare; fornire (una strada) di cunette; fornire (una casa) di grondaie **3.** scorrere a fiotti.

guttiferous [gʌˈtifərəs], *ag.* resinoso, gommifero.

to guttle [ˈgʌtl], *v.t.i.* mangiare avidamente; trangugiare.

guttler [ˈgʌtlə*], *s.c.* chi mangia avidamente.

guttural [ˈgʌtərəl], *ag. s.* gutturale.

gutturalism [ˈgʌtərəlizm], *s.* gutturalismo.

to gutturalize [ˈgʌtərəlaiz], *v.t.* **1.** rendere gutturale (un suono) **2.** pronunciare (un suono) con tono gutturale.

gutturally [ˈgʌtərəli], *av.* gutturalmente.

gutturalness [ˈgʌtərəlnis], *s.* gutturalità.

gutty [ˈgʌti], *s.* (*sl.*) palla da golf di guttaperca.

guy[1] [gai], *s.* corda, tirante di fissaggio; catena; (*mar.*) bozza ☆ — *-rope*, (*mar.*) tirante, fune, vento.

to guy[1], *v.t.* assicurare con una fune.

guy[2], *s.* **1.** fantoccio di Guy Fawkes (che si brucia in Inghilterra la notte del 5 novembre) **2.** spauracchio; maschera; persona vestita grottescamente **3.** (*sl. amer.*) tipo, individuo **4.** *to do a* —, (*sl.*) filarsela, svignarsela; *to give s.o. the* —, (*sl.*) sfuggire a qlcu.

to guy[2], *v.t.i.* **1.** portare il fantoccio di Guy Fawkes per le strade **2.** effigiare **3.** beffeggiare, mettere in ridicolo **4.** (*sl.*) svignarsela.

Guy[3], *no.pr.m.* Guido.

to guzzle [ˈgʌzl], *v.t.i.* gozzovigliare ‖ *to* — (*away*) *one's fortune*, sprecare denaro in gozzoviglie.

guzzler [ˈgʌzlə*], *s.* ubriacone; crapulone.

Gwen [gwen], *no.pr.f.* dim. di **Gwendolen**.

Gwendolen [ˈgwendəlin], *no.pr.f.* Guendalina.

gwyniad [ˈgwiniæd], *s.* (*ittiol.*) specie di salmone (« *Coregonus pennantii* »).

gybe [dʒaib], *s.* (*mar.*) fiocco.

to gybe, *v.t.i.* (*mar.*) orientare.

gyle [gail], *s.* **1.** quantità di birra fabbricata in una sola volta **2.** tino di fermentazione.

gym [dʒim], *s.* (*sl.*) *abbr.* di **gymnasium, gymnastics**.

gymkhana [dʒim'kɑ:nə], *s.* « gymkhana »; campo sportivo; riunione sportiva.

gymnasium [dʒim'neizjəm], *s.* **1.** palestra **2.** liceo classico (in Germania).

gymnast ['dʒimnæst], *s.* ginnasta.

gymnastic [dʒim'næstik], *ag.* ginnastico.

gymnastics [dʒim'næstiks], *s.* esercizi ginnici; ginnastica.

gymnastically [dʒim'næstikəli], *av.* da ginnasta.

gymnic ['dʒimnik], *ag.* ginnico.

gymnocarpous [,dʒimnə'kɑ:pəs], *ag.* (*bot.*) ginnocarpo.

gymnosophist [dʒim'nɔsəfist], *s.* ginnosofista.

gymnosophy [dʒim'nɔsəfi], *s.* ginnosofia.

gymnosperm ['dʒimnəspə:m], *s.* (*bot.*) gimnosperma.

gymnotus [dʒim'noutəs], *s.* (*ittiol.*) ginnoto.

gynaeceum [,dʒaini'si:əm], *s.* (*bot.*) gineceo.

gynaecocracy [,dʒaini'kɔ:krəsi], *s.* ginecocrazia.

gynaecological [,gainikə'lɔdʒikəl], *ag.* (*med.*) ginecologico.

gynaecologist [,gaini'kɔlədʒist], *s.* (*med.*) ginecologo.

gynaecology [,gaini'kɔlədʒi], *s.* (*med.*) ginecologia.

gynandrous [dʒai'nændrəs], *ag.* (*bot.*) ginandro.

gyp¹ [dʒip], *s.* **1.** servitore (a Cambridge, Durham) **2.** (*sl. amer.*) ladro; imbroglione.

to gyp¹, *pass.p.p.* **gypped** [dʒipt], *v.t.* (*sl. amer.*) a. gannare, imbrogliare: *he was charged with gypping the Government on his income tax*, fu accusato di truffare il Governo nella tassa sul reddito.

gyp², *s.*: *to give s.o. a —*, (*sl.*) darle sode a qlcu.

gypseous ['dʒipsiəs], *ag.* gessoso.

gypsum ['dʒipsəm], *s.* (*min.*) gesso idrato, pietra da gesso.

to gypsum, *v.t.* (*agr.*) ingessare, concimare col gesso.

gypsy, *V.* **gipsy**.

gyrate ['dʒaiərit], *ag.* (*bot.*) circinato.

to gyrate [,dʒaiə'reit], *v.i.* girare, turbinare.

gyration [,dʒaiə'reiʃən], *s.* vortice, movimento in tondo, a spirale.

gyratory ['dʒaiərətəri], *ag.* vorticoso, circolare.

gyre ['dʒaiə*], *s.* (*poet.*) **1.** giro **2.** movimento circolare.

gyroscope ['gaiərəskoup], *s.* (*mec.*) giroscopio.

gyrose ['dʒaiərous], *ag.* (*bot.*) piegato, ondulato.

gyrostabilizer [,gaiərou'steibilaizə*], *s.* (*neol. aer.*) girostabilizzatore.

gyrostat ['gaiəroustæt], *s.* (*fis.*) girostato.

gyrus ['dʒaiərəs], *s.* (*anat.*) circonvoluzione cerebrale.

gyte [gait], *ag.* (*scoz.*) fuori di sè, pazzo.

to gyve [dʒaiv], *v.t.* (*poet.*) incatenare, mettere in ceppi.

gyves [dʒaivz], *s.pl.* (*poet.*) catene, ceppi.

H

h [eitʃ], *pl.* **hs, h's** [ˈeitʃiz], *s. (ottava lettera dell'alfabeto inglese)* h ‖ — *for Harry,* (*tel.*) h come hotel ☆ *H -bomb,* (*neol. fis.*) bomba H.

ha [hɑː], *inter.* ah!.

haaf [hɑːf], *s.* zona di pesca in acque profonde (nel mare delle Shetland e delle Orkney).

habeas-corpus [ˈheibjəsˈkɔːpəs], *s.* (*dir.*) « habeas corpus » (legge che proibisce la detenzione arbitraria oltre il terzo giorno dall'arresto, in Gran Bretagna e negli Stati Uniti).

haberdasher [ˈhæbədæʃə*], *s.* **1.** merciaio **2.** (*amer.*) venditore di articoli di vestiario maschile.

haberdashery [ˈhæbədæʃəri], *s.* **1.** merceria **2.** (*amer.*) negozio di articoli di vestiario maschile.

habergeon [ˈhæbədʒən], *s.* usbergo.

habile [ˈhæbil], *ag.* (*letter.*) abile; capace.

habiliment [həˈbilimənt], *s.* abbigliamento, vestiario; *pl.* vestiario (generalmente da cerimonia, da parata).

to habilitate [həˈbiliteit], *v.i.* conseguire l'abilitazione (specialmente presso un'università tedesca).

habilitation [hə,biliˈteiʃən], *s.* abilitazione.

habit [ˈhæbit], *s.* **1.** abitudine: *out of —,* per abitudine; *to be in* (o *to have*) *the — of doing sthg.,* aver l'abitudine di fare ql.co.; *to break oneself of a —,* vincere un'abitudine; *to fall into bad habits,* prendere cattive abitudini; *to fall out of a —,* perdere un'abitudine; *to grow out of a —,* perdere un'abitudine con l'età **2.** temperamento, costituzione: *— of body,* costituzione fisica **3.** (*arc.*) abito (specialmente di religiosi) **4.** (*bot. zool.*) habitus ☆ *drug —,* abitudine di prendere sonniferi, stupefacenti; *riding- —,* abito da amazzone.

to habit, *v.t.* **1.** vestire **2.** (*arc.*) abitare.

habitability [,hæbitəˈbiliti], **habitableness** [ˈhæbitəblnis], *s.* abitabilità.

habitable [ˈhæbitəbl], *ag.* abitabile.

habitably [ˈhæbitəbli], *av.* in modo abitabile.

habitant [ˈhæbitənt], *s.c.* abitante.

habitat [ˈhæbitæt], *s.* (*bot. zool.*) « habitat ».

habitation [,hæbiˈteiʃən], *s.* abitazione; dimora.

habitual [həˈbitjuəl], *ag.* **1.** abituale, consueto **2.** inveterato.

habitually [həˈbitjuəli], *av.* abitualmente.

habitualness [həˈbitjuəlnis], *s.* abitudine.

to habituate [həˈbitjueit], *v.t.* abituare: *to — s.o. to doing sthg.,* abituare qlcu. a fare ql.co.

habituation [hə,bitjuˈeiʃən], *s.* l'abituare; l'abituarsi.

habitude [ˈhæbitjuːd], *s.* **1.** abitudine **2.** abito mentale; costituzione fisica; disposizione, temperamento.

hack[1] [hæk], *s.* **1.** tacca; incisione; ferita, taglio, escoriazione; (*calcio*) ferita da calcio allo stinco **2.** piccone, zappa, marra **3.** tosse secca ☆ *— sawing machine,* (*mec.*) segatrice alternativa, seghetto meccanico.

to hack[1], *v.t.i.* **1.** sminuzzare; tagliuzzare; stagliare ‖ *to — at s.o.,* colpire ripetutamente qlcu. (con arma da taglio) **2.** (*calcio*) colpire nello stinco **3.** tossire a colpi brevi e secchi.

hack[2], *s.* **1.** ronzino (da nolo) **2.** scribacchino; persona che sbriga il lavoro più pesante ☆ *— -writer,* scribacchino.

to hack[2], *v.t.i.* **1.** cavalcare al passo **2.** adoperare cavalli da nolo **3.** adibire a un lavoro pesante e mal retribuito **4.** rendere comune, trito; ridurre a semplice banalità.

hackle [ˈhækl], *s.* **1.** pettine (per cardare) **2.** penne

lunghe del collo (di gallo, uccello, ecc.) **3.** mosca artificiale (per la pesca).

to hackle, *v.t.* pettinare (canapa, lino).

hackler [ˈhæklə*], *s.* canapaio.

hacklet [ˈhæklit], *s.* (*ornit.*) puffino.

hackly [ˈhækli], *ag.* ruvido, scabro.

hackmatack [ˈhækmə,tæk], *s.* (*bot.*) larice americano.

hackney [ˈhækni], *s.* **1.** cavallo da nolo; ronzino **2.** vettura da nolo ☆ *— carriage* (o *— coach*), vettura da nolo.

to hackney, *v.t.* rendere comune, trito; ridurre a semplice banalità.

hackneyed [ˈhæknid], *ag.* trito, comune, molto usato (nel parlare): *— phrase,* frase fatta.

had [hæd (*forma forte*), həd, əd (*forme deboli*)], *pass. p.p.* di **to have.**

haddock [ˈhædək], *s.* (*ittiol.*) varietà di merluzzo (« *Gadus aeglefinus* »).

hade [heid], *s.* (*geol. miner.*) inclinazione (rispetto alla verticale).

to hade, *v.i.* (*geol. miner.*) inclinare (rispetto alla verticale).

Hades [ˈheidiːz], *s.* (*mit.*) Ade, Averno; inferno.

hadji [ˈhædʒi(ː)], *s.* maomettano che è stato in pellegrinaggio alla Mecca.

hadn't [ˈhædnt], (*abbr.* di *had not*) *V.* **to have.**

hae [hei], (*scoz.*) per **have.**

haecceity [hekˈsiːiti], *s.* (*fil.*) ecceità, individualità.

haemal [ˈhiːməl], *ag.* (*fisiol.*) del sangue; di vaso sanguigno.

haematemesis [,hiːməˈtemisis], *s.* (*patol.*) ematemesi.

haematic [hiˈmætik], *ag.* (*fisiol.*) ematico ‖ *s.* (*farm.*) rimedio antianemico.

haematin [ˈhiːmətin], *s.* (*fisiol.*) ematina.

heamatite [ˈhemətait], *s.* (*min.*) ematite.

haematozoon [,hiːmətəˈzouən], *pl.* **haematozoa** [,hiːmətəˈzouə], *s.* (*biol.*) ematozoo.

haematuria [,hiːməˈtjuəriə], *s.* (*patol.*) ematuria.

haemoglobin [,hiːmouˈgloubin], *s.* (*fisiol.*) emoglobina.

haemophilia [,hiːmouˈfiliə], *s.* (*patol.*) emofilia.

haemoptysis [hiˈmɔptisis], *s.* (*patol.*) emottisi.

haemorrhage [ˈheməridʒ], *s.* (*patol.*) emorragia.

haemorrhagic [,heməˈrædʒik], *ag.* (*patol.*) emorragico.

haemorrhoidal [,heməˈrɔidl], *ag.* (*patol.*) emorroidario.

haemorrhoids [ˈhemərɔidz], *s.pl.* (*patol.*) emorroidi.

haemostasia [,hiːmouˈsteiʒiə], *s.* (*med.*) emostasi.

haemostatic [,hiːmouˈstætik], *ag.* (*med.*) emostatico.

hafnium [ˈhæfnjəm], *s.* (*chim.*) afnio.

haft [hɑːft], *s.* manico; impugnatura (di coltello, pugnale, ascia, ecc.).

to haft, *v.t.* mettere il manico a (coltelli, ecc.).

hag[1] [hæg], *s.* **1.** strega, megera, vecchiaccia **2.** — (*fish*), (*ittiol.*) lampreda ☆ *— -born,* nato da strega; *— -ridden,* tormentato da incubi; *— -seed,* genia maledetta; *— -taper,* (*bot.*) verbasco; *— -weed,* ginestra; scopa (delle streghe).

hag[2], *s.* (*scoz.*) acquitrino, lama; torbiera.

hagberry [ˈhægberi], *s.* (*bot.*) pado, ciliegio a grappoli.

haggard [ˈhægəd], *ag.* **1.** sparuto, sofferente, macilento; disfatto, stravolto **2.** feroce, selvaggio, non addomesticato (di falco) ‖ *s.* **1.** falco non addomesticato **2.** *fig.* persona intrattabile, selvatica.

haggardly ['hægədli], *av.* **1.** con aria sofferente **2.** selvaticamente.

haggardness ['hægədnis], *s.* selvatichezza.

haggis ['hægis], *s.* (*scoz.*) guazzetto di frattaglie.

haggish ['hægiʃ], *ag.* da, di strega, megera.

to **haggle** ['hægl], *v.t.i.* **1.** tagliuzzare minutamente; lacerare **2.** disputare; cavillare: *to — about* (o *over*) *the price of sthg.*, mercanteggiare sul prezzo di ql.co.

haggler ['hæglə*], *s.c.* **1.** persona tirchia, che tira sul prezzo **2.** venditore, venditrice ambulante **3.** mendicante.

hagiarchy ['hægiɑ:ki], *s.* il regno dei santi.

hagiographer [,hægi'ogrəfə*], *s.* agiografo.

hagiographic(al) [,hægiə'græfik(əl)], *ag.* agiografico.

hagiography [,hægi'ogrəfi], *s.* agiografia.

hagiologist [,hægi'olədʒist], *s.* agiologo.

hagiology [,hægi'olədʒi], *s.* agiologia.

Hague (the) [heig], *no.pr.* (*geog.*) L'Aja.

hah [hɑ:], *inter.* ah!.

ha-ha[1] [hɑ(:)'hɑ:], *inter.* ah! ah! (esprimente ilarità).

ha-ha[2] ['hɑ:,hɑ:], *s.* fosso di cinta.

hai(c)k [haik], *s.* barracano.

hail[1] [heil], *s.* grandine ☆ — *-stones*, chicchi di grandine; — *-storm*, grandinata.

to **hail**[1], *v.t.i.* **1.** *imp.* grandinare **2.** *fig.* cadere, far cadere come grandine.

hail[2], *s.* segno di saluto ‖ *within* —, vicino, che si può chiamare alla voce ☆ — *-fellow-well-met with everybody*, (*fam.*) cordiale con tutti.

to **hail**[2], *v.t.i.* **1.** salutare, chiamare: *they hailed him* (*as*) *king*, lo salutarono (come) re ‖ *to — a cab, a taxi*, chiamare una vettura, un tassì che passa **2.** *to — from* (*a place*), venire da.

hail[2], *inter.* salve!, salute! ‖ *Hail Mary*, (*eccl.*) Ave Maria ‖ — *to thee blithe Spirit*, salve, spirito giocondo.

hair [hɛə*], *s.* **1.** *sing. coll.* capelli, capigliatura, chioma: *long fair* —, lunghi capelli biondi; *his — is grey*, i suoi capelli sono grigi; *she let down her* —, ella si sciolse i capelli; *she put up her* —, ella si raccolse i capelli sulla nuca; *to do one's* —, pettinarsi, mettersi in ordine i capelli; *to get* (o *to have*) *one's* — *cut*, farsi tagliare i capelli; *to lose one's* —, perdere i capelli; (*sl.*) inquietarsi; *to tear one's* —, strapparsi i capelli ‖ *to keep one's* — *on*, (*sl.*) mantenersi calmi ‖ *to make s.o.'s* — *stand on end*, far rizzare i capelli a qlcu. **2.** capello: *but the very hairs of your head are numbered*, (*Bibbia*) perfino i capelli del vostro capo sono contati; *he found a* — *in his soup*, trovò un capello nella minestra ‖ *to be exact to a* —, (*fam.*) essere estremamente precisi ‖ *to have s.o. by the short hairs*, tenere qlcu. in propria balìa ‖ *not to turn a* —, restare impassibile ‖ *to split hairs*, *fig.* spaccare un capello in quattro **3.** *pl.* (*arc. letter.*) chioma **4.** (anche *pl.*) pelo (di piante, uomini); pelame (di animali); crine; setola (di maiale): *that dog has a fine coat of* —, quel cane ha un bel pelo; *to remove s.o.'s superfluous hairs*, depilare qlcu.; *to stroke a cat against the* —, accarezzare un gatto contropelo ☆ — *-breadth*, spessore di un capello; distanza minima: *to have a* — *-breadth escape*, salvarsi per miracolo; — *-brush*, spazzola per capelli; — *-cut*, taglio dei capelli; — *-do* (o — *-dressing*), acconciatura; — *-dryer*, asciugacapelli, « phon »; — *-dye*, tintura per capelli; — *-grass*, agrostide (erba); — *-grip*, molletta per capelli; — *-line*, corda di crine; — *-net*, retina per capelli; — *-oil*, brillantina; — *-powder*, cipria per capelli; — *-restorer*, rigeneratore per capelli; — *-saloon*, (*amer.*) (negozio di) parrucchiere; — *-wash*, lozione per capelli; — *-wave*, (*neol.*) ondulazione.

haircloth ['hɛə-klɔθ], *s.* stoffa di crine (animale).

hairdresser ['hɛə,dresə*], *s.c.* parrucchiere, parrucchiera.

hairiness ['hɛərinis], *s.* pelosità; aspetto irsuto.

hairless ['hɛəlis], *ag.* **1.** senza capelli, calvo **2.** glabro; senza peli (di animali).

hairy ['hɛəri], *ag.* **1.** che ha molti capelli; peloso, irsuto; villoso **2.** (*astr.*) chiomato.

Haiti ['heiti], *no.pr.* (*geog.*) Haiti.

hake[1] [heik], *s.* (*ittiol.*) nasello.

hake[2], *s.* (*scoz.*) mensola, traliccio per far asciugare i formaggi, ecc.

hakim [hə'ki:m], *s.* (*in India*) medico.

Hal [hæl], *no.pr.m. dim.* di **Henry**.

halation [hə'leiʃən], *s.* (*foto.*) alone.

halberd ['hælbə(:)d], *s.* alabarda.

halberdier [,hælbə(:)'diə*], *s.* alabardiere.

halbert ['hælbə(:)t], *s.* alabarda.

halcyon ['hælsiən], *ag.* calmo (specialmente di giorni): — *days*, giorni calmi e felici ‖ *s.* (*ornit.*) alcione, martin pescatore.

hale[1] [heil], *ag.* robusto, gagliardo; sano; vegeto: — *and hearty*, arzillo e vegeto.

to **hale**[2], *v.t.* (*arc.*) trascinare, tirare a forza (anche *fig.*).

haleness ['heilnis], *s.* robustezza, vigoria.

half [hɑ:f], *ag.* mezzo: — *an apple*, mezza mela; — *a crown*, mezza corona; — (*an*) *hour*, mezz'ora.

half, *pl.* **halves** [hɑ:vz], *s.* metà, mezzo: — (*of*) *his men*, metà dei suoi uomini; *three and a* —, tre e mezzo; — *of the apples were bad*, metà delle mele erano marce; — *of the work was done*, metà del lavoro era fatto; *two halves make a whole*, due metà fanno un intero ‖ — *and* —, mezzo e mezzo; birra chiara e scura in eguale quantità ‖ *the first, second* —, (*spor.*) il primo, secondo tempo (di una partita) ‖ *one's better* —, (*scherz.*) la propria moglie, il proprio marito ‖ *to do things by halves*, far le cose a metà ‖ *to go halves with s.o. in sthg.*, fare a metà con qlcu. di ql.co.

half, *av.* mezzo, a mezzo, a metà: — *as much* (*many*) *again*, un'altra metà, un 50 % in più; *I — wish*, quasi quasi desidero ‖ *it is — past* (*amer. after*) *six*, sono le sei e mezzo ‖ *it is only — cooked*, è cotto solo a metà ‖ *not* —, (*sl.*) assai: *he didn't — swear*, bestemmiò con violenza ‖ *he is not — a bad fellow*, un buon diavolo.

half, (*nei composti*): — *-back*, (*calcio*) mediano; — *-baked*, non completamente cotto (anche *fig.*); — *-binding*, rilegatura con dorso in pelle; — *-blood*, consanguineità; — *-bred*, meticcio; — *-breed*, meticcio; animale di razza mista; — *-brother*, fratellastro; — *-caste*, figlio, figlia di padre europeo e di madre indiana; — *-crown*, moneta, pezzo da mezza corona; — *-dozen*, mezza dozzina; — *-holiday*, (giorno di) mezza festa; — *-hose*, calzini corti; — *-length*, di media lunghezza; ritratto a mezzo busto; — *-mast* (*high*), a mezz'asta (di bandiera); — *-measures*, misure insufficienti; mezze misure; — *-moon*, mezzaluna; — *-mourning*, mezzo lutto; — *-pay*, mezzo stipendio, stipendio ridotto; — *-price*, metà prezzo; — *-processed*, semilavorato; — *-seas-over*, mezzo brillo; — *-sister*, sorellastra; — *-size*, formato ridotto; — *-timer*, ragazzo che studia e lavora; — *-truth*, affermazione, informazione esatta solo in parte; — *-witted*, mezzo stupido; — *-year*, semestre; — *-yearly*, semestralmente ‖ *return* —, biglietto di ritorno.

halfpenny ['heipni], *pl. nel senso* **1.** **halfpennies** ['heipniz], *nel senso* **2.** **halfpence** ['heipəns], *s.* **1.** moneta di rame da mezzo penny: *give me two halfpennies for this penny*, dammi due mezzi penny in cambio di questo penny **2.** valore di mezzo penny: *three halfpence*, (valore di) un penny e mezzo ‖ *half-penny-worth* (o *fam. ha' p' orth*), ciò che costa, vale mezzo penny.

halfway ['hɑ:f'wei], *ag.av.* a mezza strada; in modo incompleto.

halibut ['hælibət], *s.* (*ittiol.*) passera, pianuzza.

hall [hɔ:l], *s.* **1.** sala, salone ‖ *to be born in marble halls*, nascere ricco **2.** refettorio; sala di ritrovo; sala per concerti **3.** tribunale (palazzo ed aula); municipio (palazzo) ‖ *Westminster Hall*, l'antica aula di Westminster, sede del Parlamento britannico **4.** anticamera, vestibolo, entrata **5.** casa dello studente; collegio universitario **6.** castello; palazzotto; casa signorile (in campagna) ☆ — *door*, porta, ingresso principale; — *mark*, punzonatura su oggetti d'oro e d'argento (per garanzia); — *porter*, portinaio ‖ *concert* —, sala da concerto; *waiting* —, sala d'aspetto.

halleluiah, hallelujah [ˌhæli'luːjə], *s. inter.* alleluia.

halliard, *V.* **halyard**.

hallo(a) [hə'lou], *inter.* (*fam.*) salve!; pronto! (al telefono).

halloo [hə'luː], *s.* grido (per richiamare l'attenzione, per incitare i cani).

to halloo, *v.t.i.* **1.** dire gridando ‖ *to* — *to s.o.*, chiamare qlcu. a gran voce **2.** gridare; incitare; aizzare (specialmente cani).

halloo, *inter.* ohé!.

hallow[1] ['hælou], *s.* **1.** santo **2.** *pl.* reliquie di santi.

to hallow[1], *v.t.* **1.** santificare, rendere santo; beatificare **2.** consacrare **3.** venerare **4.** santificare (giorni festivi).

hallow[2], *V.* **halloo** *s.*.

(to) hallow[2], *V.* (to) **halloo**.

Hallowe'en ['hælou'iːn], *s.* vigilia d'Ognissanti.

Hallowmas ['hæloumæs], *s.* Ognissanti.

to hallucinate [hə'luːsineit], *v.t.* allucinare.

hallucination [həˌluːsi'neiʃən], *s.* allucinazione; illusione.

hallucinative [hə'luːsinətiv], **hallucinatory** [hə'luːsinətəri], *ag.* allucinante; illusorio.

hallux ['hæləks], *pl.* **halluces** ['hæljusiːz], *s.* alluce.

hallway ['hɔlwei], *s.* (*amer.*) vestibolo; corridoio.

halo ['heilou], *pl.* **halos, haloes** ['heilouz], *s.* **1.** (*astr.*) alone **2.** aureola (anche *fig.*).

to halo, *v.t.* circondare di un'aureola.

halogen ['hæloudʒen], *s.* (*chim.*) alogeno.

haloid ['hæloid], *ag.* (*chim.*) aloide, saliforme ‖ *s.* (*chim.*) alogenuro.

halt[1] [hɔːlt], *ag.* (*arc.*) zoppo.

to halt[1], *v.i.* **1.** camminare vacillando **2.** esitare, mostrarsi esitante; parlare esitando: *halting speech*, discorso esitante **3.** (*arc.*) zoppicare.

halt[2], *s.* sosta, fermata, tappa: *to come to a* —, fermarsi.

to halt[2], *v.t.i.* **1.** fermare, fermarsi **2.** (*mil.*) far fare tappa a.

halter ['hɔːltə*], *s.* **1.** capestro **2.** cavezza.

to halter, *v.t.* **1.** impiccare **2.** mettere la cavezza a.

to halve [haːv], *v.t.* dividere a metà, ridurre alla metà.

halyard ['hæljəd], *s.* (*mar.*) drizza, ghindazzo, cavo buono.

ham[1] [hæm], *s.* **1.** (*anat.*) parte posteriore della coscia; *pl.* natiche **2.** prosciutto **3.** (*sl. amer.*) attore dilettante, inesperto; gigione ☆ — *actor*, attore da strapazzo.

to ham[1], *pass.p.p.* **hammed** [hæmd], *v.t.i.* (*sl. amer.*) recitare da dilettante; gigionare.

ham[2], *s.* (*st.*) villaggio.

Ham[3], *no.pr.m.* (*Bibbia*) Cam.

hamadryad [ˌhæmə'drai-əd], *s.* **1.** (*mit.*) amadriade, ninfa dei boschi **2.** (*zool.*) vipera dagli occhiali **3.** (*zool.*) amadriade.

Hamburg ['hæmbəːg], *no.pr.* (*geog.*) Amburgo ‖ **hamburg, hamburger** ['hæmbəːgə*], *s.* (*amer. cuc.*) polpetta di carne di manzo e cipolla tritata; panino farcito di tale polpetta.

hames [heimz], *s.pl.* anelli delle tirelle (di cavallo da tiro).

hamfatter ['hæmˌfætə*], *V.* **ham**[1] **3.**

Hamites ['hæmaits], *s.c.pl.* camiti.

Hamitic [hæ'mitik], *ag.* camitico.

hamlet ['hæmlit], *s.* piccolo villaggio; gruppo di casolari.

hammam ['hæmæm], *s.* bagno turco.

hammer ['hæmə*], *s.* **1.** martello; maglio ‖ *knight of the* —, fabbro ‖ *throwing the* —, (*spor.*) lancio del martello **2.** cane (di fucile) **3.** martelletto (di pianoforte) **4.** martello (di banditore ad aste pubbliche): *to bring to the* —, mettere all'asta; *to come under the* —, essere venduto all'asta **5.** (*anat.*) martelletto, ossicino dell'orecchio ☆ — *-and-tongs*, violentemente, con energia; — *-blow*, colpo di martello, di maglio; (*ferr.*)

martellamento (delle rotaie); — *-contact,* (*elett.*) contatto a martello; — *drill*, (*mec.*) martello perforatore; — *-fish*, pesce martello; — *-mill*, frangitutto, mulino a martelli; — *-thrower*, (*spor.*) lanciatore di martello; — *-toe*, dito a martello; — *-welding*, saldatura al maglio ‖ *brick* —, martello da muratore; *claw* —, martello da carpentiere; *forge* (o *power*) —, maglio; *glazier's* —, martello da vetraio.

to hammer, *v.t.i.* **1.** martellare ‖ *to* — (*away*) *at s.o.*, accanirsi contro qlcu. ‖ *to* — (*away*) *at sthg.*, lavorare sodo a ql.co. ‖ *to* — *into one's head*, mettersi bene in testa **2.** (*fam.*) sconfiggere duramente **3.** (*Borsa*) dichiarare fallito **4.** far scendere (i prezzi, per deprimere il mercato) **5.** *to* — *out*, avere in mente; progettare; organizzare; formulare.

hammering ['hæməriŋ], *s.* martellamento, martellatura; lavorazione al maglio ☆ — *-in*, (*mec.*) martellamento.

hammock ['hæmək], *s.* amaca.

hamper[1] ['hæmpə*], *s.* cesta, paniere.

hamper[2], *s.* (*mar.*) accessori ingombranti ☆ *top-* —, (*mar.*) sovrastruttura di ponte, ecc.

to hamper[2], *v.t.* imbarazzare; ostacolare; impedire i movimenti di.

Hampton Court ['hæmptənˌkɔːt], *s.* Hampton Court (antica residenza dei reali d'Inghilterra).

to hamshackle ['hæmˌʃækl], *v.t.* **1.** impastoiare (cavallo, bue, ecc.) **2.** *fig.* impedire.

hamster ['hæmstə*], *s.* (*zool.*) criceto.

hamstring ['hæm-striŋ], *s.* (*anat.*) tendine (delle gambe); tendine (delle zampe posteriori dei quadrupedi).

to hamstring, *v.t.* azzoppare (tagliando i tendini).

hand [hænd], *s.* **1.** mano: *the* — *of God*, *fig.* la mano, il dito di Dio; *piece for four hands*, (*mus.*) pezzo a quattro mani; *he has many children on his hands*, ha molti figli sulle spalle; *he is a good* — *at tennis*, è un valente giocatore di tennis; *it was the work of an enemy* —, fu opera di un nemico; *she has a light* — *at the piano*, suona il piano con mano leggera; *the work is now in your hands*, il lavoro è adesso in mani tue; *to ask for a lady's* —, chiedere la mano di una signorina; *to bind s.o.* — *and foot*, legare qlcu. mani e piedi (anche *fig.*); *to climb* — *over* —, arrampicarsi (specialmente su una fune) con una mano dopo l'altra; *to fight* — *to* —, combattere corpo a corpo; *to get out of hands*, diventare incontrollabile (di persone e cose); *to get sthg. off one's hands*, liberarsi di qlco.; *to have one's hands tied*, avere le mani legate; *to keep one's* — *in*, tenersi in esercizio; *to lay* (*violent*) *hands on s.o.*, mettere le mani addosso a qlcu.; *to lay hands on sthg.*, impadronirsi di ql.co.; *to lend a* —, dare una mano, aiutare; *to raise* (o *lift*) one's — *to* (o *against*) *s.o.*, colpire qlcu. o minacciare di farlo; *to shake hands with s.o.* (o *to shake s.o.'s* —), stringere la mano a qlcu.; *to take sthg. in* —, intraprendere ql.co. ‖ — *in* —, mano in mano: *they went away* — *in* —, se ne andarono via tenendosi per mano; *they work* — *in* —, lavorano in stretta collaborazione; ‖ *hands off!*, via le mani!, non toccare! ‖ *hands up!*, mani in alto! ‖ *at* —, vicino, prossimo; a portata di mano: *the examinations are at* —, gli esami sono prossimi; *to be at* — *when wanted*, essere disponibile all'occorrenza ‖ *in* —, a disposizione: *money in* —, denaro in riserva ‖ *to* —, (*comm.*) nelle (nostre) mani, in (nostro) possesso: *your letter has come to* —, (*comm.*) la vostra (lettera) è arrivata ‖ *to be* — *in* (o *and*) *glove with s.o.*, essere intimo di qlcu. ‖ *to go on one's hands and knees*, andare a quattro zampe, carponi ‖ *to make money* — *over fist*, (*sl.*) arricchirsi rapidamente ‖ *to put one's* — *to the plough*, mettersi al lavoro ‖ *to win hands down*, vincere a mani basse, con facilità **2.** operaio, lavoratore, membro dell'equipaggio di una nave: *all hands on deck!*, (*mar.*) tutti sul ponte!; *we are short of hands*, siamo a corto di personale; *we want two hundred hands more*, abbiamo bisogno ancora di duecento operai **3.** spanna (misura di lunghezza = cm. 10,16) **4.** lato, direzione: *on either* —, da entrambi i lati; *on the left* —, a sinistra; *on the other* —, d'altro lato, d'altronde; *on the right* —, a destra ‖ *on the one* — ..., *on the other* —..., da un lato ..., dall'altro lato... 5. calligrafia; firma: *a legible* —, una calligrafia chiara; *to set one's* — *to a deed*, apporre la propria firma a un documento 6. (*fam.*) lancetta dell'orologio 7. (*carte, biliardo*) mano, giro: *how many hands have you played?* quante mani avete giocato? 8. (*carte*) l'insieme delle carte che servono a un giocatore per una mano; un giocatore: *we want another* —, ci occorre un altro giocatore ☆ — *-ball*, (*spor.*) palla a mano, palla con cui si pratica tale giuoco; — *-barrow*, carrettino; — *-brake*, freno a mano; — *-grenade*, (*mil.*) bomba a mano; — *-knitted*, lavorato a maglia, a mano; — *-organ*, organetto di Barberia; — *-picked*, scelto singolarmente; colto a mano; — *spinning*, (*ind. tessile*) filatura a mano; — *steering*, (*mar.*) timone a mano; — *-woven*, tessuto a mano ‖ *first-* —, di prima mano: *a first-* — *news*, una notizia di prima mano; *second-* —, di seconda mano: *a second-* — *book*, un libro di seconda mano.

to **hand**, *v.t.* 1. porgere, rimettere, dare, passare: *please,* — *me that book*, per favore, porgimi quel libro 2. aiutare con la mano (a uscire, entrare): *he handed my wife into, out of the carriage*, aiutò mia moglie a salire, scendere dalla carrozza 3. *to* — **down**, trasmettere per successione, per tradizione; aiutare a scendere 4. *to* — **in**, consegnare ‖ *he has handed in his resignation*, ha rassegnato le dimissioni ‖ *to* — *in one's checks*, (*sl. amer.*) morire 5. *to* — **out**, distribuire 6. *to* — **over**, consegnare, rimettere: — *over what you have stolen*, fuori quel che hai rubato; *they handed him over to justice*, lo consegnarono alla giustizia.

handbag ['hændbæg], *s.* borsetta.
handbill¹ ['hændbil], *s.* coltello per potatura.
handbill², *s.* circolare, volantino; programma.
handbook ['hændbuk], *s.* manuale; guida.
handcuff ['hændkʌf], *s. gener. pl.* manette.
to **handcuff**, *v.t.* applicare le manette a.
handed ['hændid], *ag.* con, dalla mano ☆ *empty* -—, a mani vuote; *heavy-* —, dalla mano pesante; *left-* —, mancino; *two-* —, ambidestro.
handfeeding ['hænd,fi:diŋ], *s.* allattamento, allevamento artificiale.
handful ['hændful], *s.* 1. manciata, manata: *a* — *of coins*, una manata di monete 2. piccolo numero (di persone) 3. (*fam.*) persona, cosa difficile da trattarsi: *that child is a* —, è un bambino terribile.
handgrip ['hændgrip], *s.* 1. stretta di mano; morsa della mano 2. manopola (di bicicletta).
handicap ['hændikæp], *s.* 1. svantaggio, ostacolo; aggravio: *shyness is a* —, la timidezza è uno svantaggio 2. (*spor.*) «handicap», corsa pareggiata, corsa a composizione.
to **handicap**, *pass.p.p.* **handicapped** ['hændikæpt], *v.t.* 1. svantaggiare, ostacolare: *he is handicapped by ill-health*, è svantaggiato dalla cattiva salute 2. (*spor.*) assegnare l'«handicap» a (concorrente).
handicraft ['hændikrɑːft], *s.* 1. lavoro manuale; artigianato 2. abilità manuale.
handicraftsman, *pl.* **handicraftsmen** ['hændi,krɑːftsmən], *s.* artigiano.
handily ['hændili], *av.* 1. abilmente 2. comodamente; a portata di mano.
handiness ['hændinis], *s.* l'essere maneggevole, l'essere comodo (di arnesi, utensili); (*mar.*) manovrabilità.
handiwork ['hændiwəːk], *s.* lavoro fatto a mano ‖ *that's some of his* —, (*fam.*) qui ci ha messo la mano lui; ne ha fatto una delle sue.
handkerchief ['hæŋkətʃif], *s.* fazzoletto.
handle¹ ['hændl], *s.* 1. manico; impugnatura; maniglia; manovella; manubrio 2. *fig.* pretesto, occasione: *your behaviour is giving him a* — *against you*, il vostro contegno gli fornisce un'arma contro di voi 3. (*fam.*) titolo: *to have a* — *to one's name*, avere un titolo di

nobiltà ☆ — *-bar*, manubrio di bicicletta ‖ *door-* —, maniglia di una porta.
to **handle¹**, *v.t.* fornire di manico.
to **handle²**, *v.t.* 1. maneggiare, toccare con le mani: *you shouldn't* — *books with dirty hands*, non dovresti toccare i libri con le mani sporche 2. trattare, comportarsi verso: *she handles children well*, ci sa fare molto bene coi bambini; *to* — *roughly*, trattare senza riguardi 3. commerciare in, trattare: *he handles coffee*, egli commercia in caffè 4. trattare, discutere (un argomento) 5. (*mar.*) manovrare.
handler ['hændlə*], *s.* manipolatore.
handless ['hændlis], *ag.* 1. senza mani 2. *fig.* maldestro.
handling ['hændliŋ], *s.* 1. maneggiamento 2. trattamento, maniera di trattare: *rough* —, trattamento rozzo, senza riguardi; *skill in* —, abilità nel trattare.
handloom ['hændlu:m], *s.* telaio a mano.
handmade ['hænd'meid], *ag.* manufatto.
handmaid(en) ['hændmeid(n)], *s.* (*arc.*) serva.
handrail ['hænd-reil], *s.* corrimano; parapetto.
handsaw ['hændsɔ:], *s.* sega a mano.
handsel, *V.* **hansel**.
to **handsel**, *V. to* **hansel**.
handshake ['hændʃeik], *s.* stretta di mano.
handsome ['hænsəm], *ag.* 1. bello, ben fatto, di bell'aspetto (di uomo); imponente (di donna) 2. generoso, liberale: *a* — *present*, un dono generoso ‖ — *is that* —, *prov.* la generosità val più che la bellezza 3. considerevole: *a* — *fortune*, una fortuna considerevole.
handsomely ['hænsəmli], *av.* 1. elegantemente 2. generosamente: *he was* — *rewarded*, fu generosamente ricompensato.
handsomeness ['hænsəmnis], *s.* 1. bellezza; eleganza 2. generosità.
handwork ['hænd-wəːk], *V.* **handiwork**.
handwriting ['hænd,raitiŋ], *s.* calligrafia.
handy ['hændi], *ag.* 1. abile, destro (*at sthg., at, in doing sthg.*, in ql.co., a fare ql.co.): *that man is very* — *at his work*, quell'uomo è molto abile nel suo lavoro 2. utile; a portata di mano: *that tool will come in very* —, quell'arnese riuscirà molto utile; *to keep sthg.* —, tenere ql.co. a portata di mano 3. maneggevole; (*mar.*) manovriero ☆ — *-man*, uomo che sa fare un po' di tutto.

hang [hæŋ], *s.* 1. inclinazione; pendio 2. modo in cui una cosa pende, inclina: *the* — *of a coat, of a skirt*, il modo in cui cade una giacca, una sottana ‖ *I don't care a* —, (*sl.*) non me ne importa proprio nulla ‖ *I don't quite get the* — *of this*, (*fam.*) non so veramente da che parte prenderlo.
to **hang**, *pass.p.p.* **hung** [hʌŋ], *nel senso* 2. **hanged** [hæŋd] *v.t.i.* 1. appendere, attaccare, sospendere: *to* — *one's coat to a stand*, appendere il proprio cappotto a un attaccapanni; *to* — *the rudder*, (*mar.*) montare il timone; *to* — *sthg. on the wall*, appendere ql.co. al muro 2. impiccare; essere impiccato: *hanged, drawn and quartered*, impiccato e squartato; *he was hanged*, fu impiccato; *she hanged herself out of grief*, ella si impiccò per il dolore; *you shall* — *for it*, sarai impiccato per questo ‖ — *it!*, (*volg.*) all'inferno! ‖ *I'll be hanged if I know!*, che mi venga un accidente se lo so! 3. chinare, abbassare (la testa): *she hung her head*, ella chinò la testa 4. pendere, essere sospeso (anche *fig.*): *fruit hanging on a tree*, frutti appesi a un albero; *his clothes hung loose about him*, egli nuotava negli abiti; *a thick fog hangs over the airport*, una fitta nebbia avvolge l'aeroporto; *thing hangs on his answer*, tutto dipende dalla sua risposta ‖ *to* — *by a thread*, essere sospeso a un filo ‖ *to* — *fire*, *fig.* svolgersi lentamente (di eventi) ‖ *to* — *heavy*, passare lentamente (di tempo) 5. appoggiarsi, attaccarsi: *she was hanging on his arm*, ella si appoggiava pesantemente al suo braccio; *to* — *about s.o.'s neck*,

attaccarsi al collo di qlcu. **6.** *to* — **about**, andare oziando, ciondolare **7.** *to* — **back**, restare indietro; *fig.* esitare, essere ritroso **8.** *to* — **on**, stare attaccato; perseverare **9.** *to* — **out**, sporgersi **10.** *to* — **over**, star sospeso, minacciare, incombere **11.** *to* — **together**, associarsi, mantenersi uniti, collaborare **12.** *to* — **up**, appendere; rimandare; sospendere.

hang, (*nei composti*): — -*dog*, mascalzone; — -*out*, (*sl. amer.*) ritrovo, locale pubblico; — -*over*, (*sl.*) conseguenza; malessere, mal di capo (dopo una sbornia).

hangar ['hæŋə*], *s.* «hangar», aviorimessa.

hanger ['hæŋə*], *s.* **1.** persona che appende; (*arc.*) carnefice, boia **2.** gancio, uncino; catena del camino **3.** (*mec.*) staffa; supporto pendente; (*ferr.*) pendino, catena **4.** bosco sul fianco d'una collina **5.** coltellaccio; spadino ☆ — -*on*, seguace; dipendente; parassita; seccatore ‖ *bell*- —, cordoncino di campanello; *dress*- —, attaccapanni; *paper*- —, tappezziere; *pipe*- —, supporto a sospensione per tubi.

hanging ['hæŋiŋ], *ag.* pendente; sospeso ‖ *s.* **1.** impiccagione **2.** *gener. pl.* tappezzeria; arazzo ☆ — -*garden*, giardino pensile; — -*gutter*, grondaia; — -*wall*, (*miner.*) tetto.

hangman, *pl.* **hangmen** ['hæŋmən], *s.* boia, carnefice.

hang-nail ['hæŋneil], *s.* pipita.

hank [hæŋk], *s.* **1.** matassa, matassina (di filato) **2.** (*mar.*) anello, canestrello della randa.

to **hanker** ['kæŋkə*], *v.i.*: *to* — *after* (*sthg.*), desiderare ardentemente, ambire, agognare: *to* — *after praise*, desiderare la lode.

hankering ['hæŋkəriŋ], *s.* forte desiderio, brama.

hanky ['hæŋki], *s.* (*fam. abbr.* di *handkerchief*) fazzoletto.

hanky-panky ['hæŋkɪ'pæŋki], *s.* (*fam.*) frottola; imbroglio: *I think there is some* — *going on*, credo che ci sia qualcosa di poco chiaro.

Hanover ['hænəvə*], *no.pr.* (*geog.*) Hannover ‖ *House of* —, dinastia degli Hannover (da Giorgio I alla Regina Vittoria).

Hanoverian [,hænou'viəriən], *ag.* di Hannover ‖ *s.c.* **1.** cittadino, cittadina di Hannover **2.** membro, sostenitore della Casa di Hannover.

Hansard ['hænsəd], *s.* resoconto ufficiale dei dibattiti al Parlamento britannico.

to **Hansardize** ['hænsədaiz], *v.t.* mettere a confronto (un membro del Parlamento) con le precedenti dichiarazioni da lui fatte e registrate nel resoconto ufficiale dei dibattiti parlamentari.

Hanse [hæns], *no.pr.* (*st.*) «Hansa», Lega Anseatica.

Hanseatic [,hænsi'ætik], *ag.* anseatico.

hansel ['hænsəl], *s.* **1.** strenna **2.** (*comm.*) caparra **3.** inaugurazione **4.** assaggio.

to **hansel**, *pass.p.p.* **hanselled** ['hænsəld], *v.t.* **1.** dare una strenna a **2.** dare caparra a **3.** inaugurare **4.** saggiare, provare.

hansom(cab) ['hænsəm(kæb)], *s.* carrozza a due ruote col cocchiere dietro.

hap [hæp], *s.* (*arc.*) caso, destino: *by good* —, per buona fortuna.

to **hap**, *pass.p.p.* **happed** [hæpt], *v.i.* (*arc. rar.*) accadere per caso: *to* — *to do sthg.*, fare ql.co. per caso ‖ *to* — *on sthg.*, trovare ql.co. per caso.

haphazard ['hæp'hæzəd], *ag.* casuale ‖ *s.* caso: *at* (o *by*) —, per caso.

haphazard, *av.* casualmente; alla ventura.

hapless ['hæplis], *ag.* (*arc.*) sfortunato.

haplessly ['hæplisli], *av.* (*arc.*) sfortunatamente.

haply ['hæpli], *av.* (*arc.*) forse.

ha'p'orth ['heipəθ], *s.* (*fam. contr.* di *half-penny -worth*) (ciò che costa, vale mezzo penny.

to **happen** ['hæpən], *v.i.* **1.** avvenire, accadere, succedere: *how did the accident* —?, come accadde la disgrazia?; *I hope nothing will* — *to him*, spero che non gli succederà nulla; *whatever may* —, qualunque cosa avvenga, in ogni caso ‖ *as it happens*, per caso; preci-

samente: *as it happens I was in London when the war broke out*, io ero proprio a Londra quando scoppiò la guerra **2.** (*costruzione pers.*) darsi il caso, capitare; avere la fortuna di: *I happened to be out when he called me*, per caso ero fuori quando mi chiamò; *she happened to meet him*, le capitò di incontrarlo; *a taxi happened to be passing along and so I could catch my train*, per fortuna passò di lì un taxi e così potei prendere il treno **3.** *to* — (*up*)*on* (*s.o., sthg.*), trovare per caso, incontrare per caso.

happening ['hæpniŋ], *s.* avvenimento.

happily ['hæpili], *av.* fortunatamente; felicemente.

happiness ['hæpinis], *s.* felicità.

happy ['hæpi], *ag.* **1.** felice, contento; beato: *a marriage*, un matrimonio felice; *I shall be* — *to accept your invitation*, sarò assai lieto di accettare il vostro invito ‖ *to be as* — *as the day is long* (o *as a king* o *as a sandboy*), essere felice come una Pasqua **2.** adatto, felice: — *thought!*, buona idea! ☆ — -*go-lucky*, spensierato: *my brother is a* — -*go-lucky* (*fellow*), mio fratello prende il mondo come viene.

Hapsburg ['hæpsbə:g], *no.pr.* (*st.*) Asburgo.

hara-kiri ['hærə'kiri], *s.* carachiri.

harangue [hə'ræŋ], *s.* arringa; discorso.

to **harangue**, *v.t.i.* arringare; pronunciare un'arringa.

haranguer [hə'ræŋə*], *s.c.* arringatore, arringatrice.

haras ['hærəs], *s.* stabilimento di monta equina.

to **harass** ['hærəs], *v.t.* **1.** tormentare, molestare **2.** (*mil.*) bersagliare (il nemico) con continui attacchi.

harassing ['hærəsiŋ], *ag.* opprimente ‖ *s.* V. **harassment**.

harassment ['hærəsmənt], *s.* **1.** vessazione, tormento, molestia **2.** (*mil.*) bersagliare ininterrotto.

harbinger ['ha:bindʒə*], *s.c.* messaggero, messaggera; annunziatore, annunziatrice; precursore, precorritrice: *the swallow is the* — *of spring*, la rondine annuncia la primavera.

to **harbinger**, *v.t.* annunziare l'arrivo di.

to **harbor**, (*amer.*) per (to) **harbour**.

harbour ['ha:bə*], *s.* **1.** porto: *a natural, artificial* —, un porto naturale, artificiale **2.** *fig.* asilo, rifugio; ricetto **3.** tana d'animale ☆ — -*dues*, diritti portuali; — -*master*, capitano di porto; — -*office*, capitaneria di porto; — -*trust*, consorzio portuario ‖ *fishing* —, porto di pesca; *river*- —, porto di fiume; *sea*- —, porto di mare.

to **harbour**, *v.t.i.* **1.** accogliere, dare asilo a; rifugiarsi; trovare ricetto: *to* — *a criminal*, dare ricetto a un criminale **2.** *fig.* nutrire: *to* — *evil thoughts*, nutrire cattivi pensieri **3.** entrare in porto.

harbourage ['ha:bəridʒ], *s.* rifugio, asilo; ricetto.

harbourer ['ha:bərə*], *s.c.* ricettatore, ricettatrice (di ladri, ecc.); chi dà rifugio (anche *fig.*).

harbourless ['ha:bəlis], *ag.* **1.** senza rifugio, senza asilo **2.** (*mar.*) senza porto.

hard [ha:d], *ag.* **1.** duro: *as* — *as adamant*, duro come il diamante; *stone and glass are* — *substances*, la pietra e il vetro sono sostanze dure; *to become* (o *to get*) —, indurirsi; *to strike s.o. a* — *blow*, colpire duramente qlcu. ‖ *a* — *nut to crack*, *fig* un osso duro ‖ *to be as* — *as flint*, *fig.* avere un cuore di pietra ‖ *to be as* — *as nails*, *fig.* essere in buona forma fisica ‖ *to be* — *of hearing*, *fig.* essere duro d'orecchio **2.** duro; severo; spietato: — *heart*, cuore duro; — *luck*, sfortuna nera; — *times*, tempi duri; *to be* — *on s.o.*, essere severo con qlcu.; *to learn the* — *way*, imparare per esperienza ‖ — *and fast*, rigido (di regole) **3.** mero, puro e semplice: — *common sense*, semplice buon senso; — *facts*, meri fatti **4.** difficile; gravoso; problema difficile: — *problem*, problema difficile; — *to deal with*, intrattabile; — *to please*, incontentabile; — *to understand*, difficile da capire; *I found it* — *to accept*, l'accettarlo mi è stato difficile **5.** duro (di suono): — *consonants*, (*gram.*) consonanti dure; — *voice*, voce dura **6.** ruvido (al tatto): — *to the touch*, ruvido al tatto **7.** strenuo; vigoroso; accanito: —*drinker*, bevitore accanito; — *fight*, combattimento strenuo; — *gallop*, galoppo sostenuto; — *work*, lavoro accanito ‖ *to try one's hardest*, mettercela tutta **8.** rigido (di tempo): — *winter*, inverno rigido **9.** forte, alcoolico **10.** (*elett.*) a vuoto spinto; duro, ad alto potere penetrativo ☆ — *drink*, bevanda alcoolica; — *silk*, seta greggia; — *water*, (*chim.*) acqua dura.

hard, *s.* **1.** carreggiata in pendio su una spiaggia **2.** (*sl.*) lavoro forzato.

hard, *av.* **1.** energicamente, con grande forza; insistentemente; fissamente: *to beg* —, pregare con insistenza; *to look — at s.o.*, guardare fissamente qlcu.; *to pull a bell* —, suonare con energia; *to rain* —, piovere a dirotto; *to think* —, riflettere profondamente; *to try* —, provare e riprovare **2.** con difficoltà; duramente: *it comes — on him*, è dura per lui; *they study* —, essi studiano sodo; *to die* —, essere duro a morire; vendere cara la propria pelle ‖ *to be — up for an excuse*, essere a corto di scuse; *to be — up for money*, essere al verde **3.** vicino, accanto: *to follow — on* (o *after* o *behind*) *s.o.*, seguire qlcu. da vicino **4.** troppo: *he drinks* —, beve troppo.

hard, (*nei composti*): — -*boiled*, cotto, bollito fino a diventar duro; *fig.* incallito (dall'esperienza); — -*bought*, acquistato a fatica; — *cash*, denaro in contanti; — -*faced* (o — -*favoured*), brutto; — -*fisted*, *fig.* avaro; — *iron*, ghisa bianca; — -*headed*, *fig.* ostinato; — *lead*, piombo all'antimonio; — -*mouthed*, ribelle al morso; *fig.* ribelle; — -*set*, in bisogno; — -*soldered*, (*mec.*) saldato a forte; — *swearing*, spergiuro.

to **harden** ['hɑ:dn], *v.t.i.* **1.** indurire, indurirsi; temprare (anche *fig.*) **2.** irrobustire, irrobustirsi.

hardened ['hɑ:dnd], *ag.* indurito (anche *fig.*): — *heart*, cuore indurito ☆ *war-* —, agguerrito.

hardihood ['hɑ:dihud], *s.* ardire; coraggio.

hardily ['hɑ:dili], *av.* arditamente, audacemente.

hardiness ['hɑ:dinis], *s.* **1.** ardire **2.** robustezza; vigore; resistenza fisica.

hardish ['hɑ:diʃ], *ag.* **1.** piuttosto duro **2.** piuttosto difficile.

hardly ['hɑ:dli], *av.* **1.** a stento, a malapena, appena, difficilmente: *he will — be able to do it*, sarà difficile che lo possa fare; *I — know him*, lo conosco appena; *we had — arrived when* (o — *had we arrived when*), eravamo appena arrivati quando **2.** quasi: — *ever*, quasi mai: *he — ever came to see his mother*, non veniva quasi mai a trovare sua madre; — *anyone was present*, non c'era quasi nessuno; — *anything was done*, non si fece quasi nulla **3.** duramente, severamente.

hardness ['hɑ:dnis], *s.* **1.** durezza (anche *fig.*) **2.** (*fis.*) durezza di penetrazione ☆ — *gradient*, (*metal.*) gradiente di durezza.

hards [hɑ:dz], *s.pl.* lino, canapa grezzi; rifiuti di lino, canapa, stoppa.

hardship ['hɑ:dʃip], *s.* avversità; privazione; stento: *they bore every kind of* —, sopportarono privazioni d'ogni genere.

hardtack ['hɑ:d-tæk], *s.* galletta.

hardware ['hɑ:d-wɛə*], *s.* ferramenta.

hardy ['hɑ:di], *ag.* **1.** ardito, coraggioso **2.** robusto; resistente (specialmente di albero).

hare [hɛə*], *s.* lepre: *young* —, leprotto ‖ *he is as mad as a* (*March*) —, è matto da legare ‖ *to run with the — and hunt with the hounds*, tenere il piede in due scarpe, fare il doppio giuoco ‖ *first catch your* — (*then cook him*), *prov.* non dir quattro se non l'hai nel sacco ☆ — -*bell*, (*bot.*) convolvolo azzurro; campanellina; — -*brained*, scervellato, sventato; — *'s-foot*, (*bot.*) trifoglio dei campi; — -*hearted*, timido, pauroso; — -*hound*, cane da caccia; — -*lip*, labbro leporino.

harem ['hɛərem], *s.* harem.

haricot ['hærikou], *s.* **1.** (*cuc.*) guazzetto, ragù di montone **2.** — (*bean*), fagiolo.

to **hark** [hɑ:k], *v.t.i.* **1.** ascoltare (generalmente nell'imperativo): *hark!*, ascolta! **2.** *to — back*, ritornare

al punto di partenza (di cani da caccia per ritrovare la traccia); *fig.* tornare indietro (con il pensiero).

to **harken**, *V.* to **hearken**.

harl(e) [hɑ:l], *s.* barba (di penna).

Harlem ['hɑ:ləm], *s.* Harlem (quartiere negro di New York).

harlequin ['hɑ:likwin], *s.* **1.** arlecchino; buffone **2.** arlecchino (cane danese) **3.** (*ornit.*) moretta arlecchino (varietà di anatra).

harlequinade [,hɑ:likwi'neid], *s.* arlecchinata; scherzi e lazzi da arlecchino.

Harley Street ['hɑ:li,stri:t], *no.pr.* Harley Street (via di Londra dove abitano illustri medici); *fig.* i luminari della medicina.

harlot ['hɑ:lət], *s.* prostituta.

to **harlot**, *v.i.* esercitare la prostituzione.

harlotry ['hɑ:lətri], *s.* prostituzione.

harm [hɑ:m], *s.* torto; danno morale e fisico: *what — is there in it?*, che male c'è in ciò?; *to do — to s.o.*, danneggiare qlcu. ‖ *out of — 's way*, in luogo sicuro.

to **harm**, *v.t.* far male a; far torto a; nuocere a.

harmful ['hɑ:mful], *ag.* nocivo, dannoso.

harmfully ['hɑ:mfuli], *av.* in modo nocivo, dannoso.

harmfulness ['hɑ:mfulnis], *s.* l'essere nocivo.

harmless ['hɑ:mlis], *ag.* innocuo, inoffensivo.

harmlessly ['hɑ:mlisli], *av.* in modo innocuo.

harmlessness ['hɑ:mlisnis], *s.* l'essere innocuo.

harmonie [hɑ:'mɔnik], *ag.* **1.** armonico, armonioso (anche *mus.*) **2.** (*mat.*) in progressione ‖ **harmonies** [hɑ:'mɔniks], *s.* (*mus.*) armonica ☆ — *curve*, (*mat.*) sinusoide.

harmonica [hɑ:'mɔnikə], *s.* **1.** armonica **2.** armonica a bocca.

harmonically [hɑ:'mɔnikəli], *av.* armonicamente.

harmonicon [hɑ:'mɔnikən], *s.* armonica a bocca.

harmonious [hɑ:'mounjəs], *ag.* armonioso; *fig.* in armonia; (*mus.*) armonioso, melodioso.

harmoniously [hɑ:'mounjəsli], *av.* armoniosamente; in armonia, di buon accordo.

harmonist ['hɑ:mənist], *s.* armonista.

harmonium [hɑ:'mounjəm], *s.* (*mus.*) armonium.

harmonization [,hɑ:mənai'zeifən], *s.* armonizzamento.

to **harmonize** ['hɑ:mənaiz], *v.t.i.* armonizzare, armonizzarsi; mettere, mettersi d'accordo.

harmonizer ['hɑ:mənaizə*], *s.c.* armonizzatore, armonizzatrice.

harmony ['hɑ:məni], *s.* armonia, accordo (anche *mus.*): *in* —, in armonia, d'accordo; *to be in — with*, essere d'accordo con.

harness ['hɑ:nis], *s.* **1.** finimenti; *fig.* « routine » ‖ *die in* —, *fig.* morire sulla breccia ‖ *to hold in* —, *fig.* tenere imbrigliato ‖ *to put in* —, attaccare (cavalli) **2.** armatura ☆ — -*maker*, sellaio.

to **harness**, *v.t.* **1.** bardare; mettere i finimenti a ‖ *to — a horse to a carriage*, attaccare un cavallo ad una carrozza **2.** (*ing.*) imbrigliare: *to — a waterfall*, imbrigliare una cascata.

Harold ['hærəld], *no.pr.m.* Aroldo.

harp [hɑ:p], *s.* (*mus.*) arpa: *to strike* (o *to play*) *the* —, suonare l'arpa.

to **harp**, *v.i.* suonare l'arpa; arpeggiare ‖ *to be always harping on the same string*, *fig.* ripetere sempre la stessa cosa, toccare sempre lo stesso tasto.

harper ['hɑ:pə*], *s.c.* arpista.

harpist ['hɑ:pist], *s.c.* arpista (di professione).

harpoon [hɑ:'pu:n], *s.* rampone; fiocina.

to **harpoon**, *v.t.* colpire con la fiocina.

harpooner [hɑ:'pu:nə*], *s.* fiociniere; ramponiere.

harpsichord ['hɑ:psikɔ:d], *s.* (*mus.*) arpicordo; clavicembalo.

harpy ['hɑ:pi], *s.* **1.** (*mit.*) arpia ‖ *old* —, *fig.* (*fam.*) vecchia megera **2.** (*ornit.*) arpia.

harquebus ['hɑ:kwibəs], *s.* archibugio.

harquebusier [,hɑ:kwibəs'iə*], *s.* archibugiere.

harridan ['hæridən], *s.* vecchiaccia; strega.

harrier[1] ['hæriə*], *s.* **1.** (*arc.*) predatore, saccheggiatore **2.** (*ornit.*) albanella.

harrier[2], *s.* **1.** varietà di cane per la caccia alla lepre **2.** *pl.* insieme dei cani e dei cacciatori **3.** chi giuoca a « guardie e ladri » (giuoco infantile).

Harrovian [hə'rouvjən], *ag.* di Harrow ‖ *s.* allievo, ex-allievo della scuola di Harrow.

harrow[1] ['hærou], *s.* erpice ‖ *under the —,* *fig.* in ansia.

to harrow[1], *v.t.* **1.** erpicare **2.** tormentare.

to harrow[2], *v.t.* razziare, depredare.

Harrow[3], *no. pr.* (*geog.*) Harrow (piccola città del Middlesex) ‖ *— (school),* Scuola di Harrow.

harrowing ['hærouiŋ], *ag.* straziante.

harrowingly ['hærouiŋli], *av.* in modo straziante.

Harry[1] ['hæri], *no.pr.m. dim.* di **Henry** ‖ *Old —,* (*fam.*) il Diavolo: *to play Old —,* fare il diavolo a quattro.

to harry[2], *v.t.i.* **1.** saccheggiare **2.** tormentare.

harsh [hɑːʃ], *ag.* **1.** duro; ruvido **2.** aspro (al gusto) **3.** discordante (di suono) **4.** severo; rigoroso.

to harshen ['hɑːʃən], *v.t.* rendere duro, ruvido, aspro.

harshly ['hɑːʃli], *av.* aspramente, duramente.

harshness ['hɑːʃnis], *s.* asprezza; durezza; severità.

harslet ['hɑːslit], *s.* frattaglie.

hart [hɑːt], *s.* (*zool.*) cervo maschio.

harum-scarum ['hɛərəm'skɛərəm], *ag.* (*fam.*) stordito; sventato; irresponsabile ‖ *s.* (*fam.*) individuo irresponsabile, comportamento irresponsabile.

haruspex [hə'rʌspeks], *pl.* **haruspices** [hə'rʌspisiːz], *s.* (*st. romana*) aruspice.

Harvard ['hɑːvəd], *s.* Harvard (famosa università statunitense).

harvest ['hɑːvist], *s.* **1.** raccolto, messe: *to get in the —,* mettere al riparo il raccolto; *to reap the —,* mietere **2.** *fig.* frutti; prodotto ☆ *— -bug,* (*entom.*) tignuola dei raccolti; *— festival* (o *— thanksgiving*), cerimonia religiosa di ringraziamento per il raccolto; *— -home,* fine della mietitura; festa della mietitura; *— -moon,* luna di settembre; *— -mouse,* arvicola, topo dei campi.

to harvest, *v.t.i.* mietere, raccogliere.

harvester ['hɑːvistə*], *s.c.* mietitore, mietitrice ‖ *s.* **1.** mietitrice meccanica **2.** (*entom.*) tignuola dei raccolti ☆ *— -thresher,* mietitrebbia ‖ *forage —,* mietiforaggi.

has [hæz (*forma forte*), həz, əz (*forme deboli*)], 3ª persona *sing. pres. indic.* di **to have** ‖ *too right it —,* (*austral.*) ma è proprio così! ☆ *— -been,* uomo fallito, sorpassato.

hash [hæʃ], *s.* **1.** piatto di carne tagliata a pezzetti **2.** *fig.* mistura; mescolanza: *to make a — of sthg.,* (*fam.*) fare un pasticcio di ql.co. ‖ *to settle s.o.'s —,* (*fam.*) mettere qlcu. a posto, regolare i conti con qlcu.

to hash, *v.t.* tagliare (carne) a pezzetti.

hasheesh [hə'ʃiːʃ], **hashish** ['hæʃiʃ], *s.* hashish.

haslet ['heizlit], *s.* frattaglie (specialmente di maiale).

hasn't ['hæznt], (*contr.* di *has, not*) *V.* to **have** ‖ *not half it —!,* (*sl.*) proprio così!.

hasp [hɑːsp], *s.* **1.** cerniera di chiusura ad occhiello (solitamente con lucchetto) **2.** matassa di filo.

to hasp, *v.t.* chiudere con lucchetto.

hassock ['hæsək], *s.* **1.** inginocchiatoio (con cuscino); poggiapiedi **2.** zolla erbosa **3.** (*min.*) arenaria del Kent.

hastate ['hæsteit], *ag.* **1.** in forma di lancia **2.** (*bot.*) lanceolato.

haste [heist], *s.* fretta; rapidità: *he dressed in hot —,* si vestì in tutta fretta ‖ *make —!,* fa presto! ‖ *more — less speed,* *prov.* chi ha fretta vada adagio.

to haste, to hasten ['heisn], *v.t.i.* **1.** affrettare, affrettarsi, sbrigarsi; far premura a, sollecitare; accelerare ‖ *to — back, down, in, up,* affrettarsi a ritornare, scendere, entrare, salire **2.** *to — up: to — up to s.o.,* affrettarsi a raggiungere qlcu.

hastily ['heistili], *av.* **1.** frettolosamente **2.** precipitosamente, impetuosamente.

hastiness ['heistinis], *s.* **1.** fretta **2.** precipitazione; avventatezza **3.** irritabilità, irascibilità.

Hastings ['heistiŋz], *no.pr.* (*geog.*) Hastings (teatro della battaglia in cui Guglielmo il Conquistatore sconfisse i sassoni, 1066).

hasty ['heisti], *ag.* **1.** frettoloso, affrettato; rapido; pronto; spiccio: *to be — in doing sthg.,* fare ql.co. affrettatamente **2.** impetuoso, avventato; sconsiderato: *a — reply,* una risposta avventata **3.** irritabile, irascibile ☆ *— -tempered,* irritabile; *— -witted,* avventato.

hat [hæt], *s.* cappello: *hats off!,* giù il cappello!; *to put on, to take off one's —,* mettersi, togliersi il cappello; *to raise* (o *to lift*) *one's — to s.o.,* salutare qlcu. levandosi il cappello ‖ *— in hand,* con deferenza, servilmente ‖ *my —!,* (*sl.*) è impossibile! ‖ *to keep sthg. under one's —,* (*fam.*) mantenere il segreto su ql.co. ‖ *to send round the —,* fare una colletta ‖ *to talk through one's —,* (*sl.*) dire cose assurde; vantarsi ☆ *bowler- —,* bombetta; *high-* (o *silk- —* o *top- —*), cappello a cilindro; *opera- —,* « gibus », cilindro pieghevole; *red —,* cappello cardinalizio; *fig.* dignità di cardinale; *straw - —,* cappello di paglia.

hatable ['heitəbl], *ag.* odiabile; odioso.

hatband ['hætbænd], *s.* nastro da cappello.

hatbox ['hætboks], *s.* cappelliera.

hatbrush ['hætbrʌʃ], *s.* spazzola per cappelli.

hatch[1] [hætʃ], *s.* **1.** porta a ribalta; portello; mezza porta. *— (-way),* (*mar.*) boccaporto ‖ *under hatches,* (*mar.*) sotto coperta; fuori servizio; agli arresti; *fig.* nascosto; in stato di arresto; morto.

hatch[2], *s.* **1.** il nascere (di uccelli); l'uscire dall'uovo **2.** covata.

to hatch[2], *v.t.i.* **1.** covare **2.** far schiudere (uova) **3.** nascere (degli uccelli) ‖ *don't count the chickens before they are hatched,* *prov.* non dire quattro finchè non l'hai nel sacco **4.** *fig.* complottare; tramare.

hatch[3], *s.* linea incisa; tratteggio.

to hatch[3], *v.t.* incidere una serie di linee (generalmente parallele) su; tratteggiare.

hatrack ['hæt-ræk], *s.* rastrelliera per cappelli.

hatchery ['hætʃəri], *s.* vivaio.

hatchet ['hætʃit], *s.* accetta ‖ *to bury the —,* seppellire l'ascia di guerra, riconciliarsi; *to dig up the —,* dissotterrare l'ascia di guerra, riaprire le ostilità ☆ *— -faced,* dai lineamenti affilati.

to hate, *v.t.* (II,IV) **1.** odiare; avere in odio: *to — doing sthg.,* fare ql.co. con ripugnanza **2.** dispiacere immensamente: *he would — to be late,* non gli piacerebbe affatto essere in ritardo.

hateable ['heitəbl], *ag.* odiabile, odioso.

hateful ['heitful], *ag.* **1.** odioso, detestabile **2.** pieno di odio, di rancore.

hatefully ['heitfuli], *av.* odiosamente, con odio.

hatefulness ['heitfulnis], *s.* odiosità.

hater ['heitə*], *s.c.* odiatore, odiatrice; nemico, nemica.

hatful ['hætful], *s.* cappellata.

hath [hæθ], (*arc. letter.*) per **has.**

hatless ['hætlis], *ag.* senza cappello.

hatpin ['hætpin], *s.* spillone (da cappello).

hatrack ['hætræk], *s.* rastrelliera per cappelli.

hatred ['heitrid], *s.* odio; inimicizia; astio.

hatstand ['hæt-stænd], *s.* attaccapanni.

hatted ['hætid], *ag.* fornito di cappello.

hatter ['hætə*], *s.* cappellaio ‖ *as mad as a —,* pazzo da legare.

hauberk ['hɔːbəːk], *s.* (*st.*) usbergo.

haughtily ['hɔːtili], *av.* altezzosamente, arrogantemente; orgogliosamente.

haughtiness ['hɔːtinis], *s.* alterigia, boria; orgoglio.

haughty ['hɔːti], *ag.* altezzoso, arrogante; orgoglioso.

haul [hɔːl], *s.* **1.** trazione; tiro **2.** raccolta; retata: *a good —,* una buona retata (di pesce); *the police made a — (of them),* la polizia (ne) fece una retata **3.** *fig.* guadagno.

to haul, *v.t.i.* **1.** tirare; trainare; trasportare ‖ *to —*

s.o. *over* *the* *coals,* *fig.* criticare severamente ql-cu. **2.** (*mar.*) alare; stringere il vento ‖ *to — to port,* *to starboard,* accostare a sinistra, a dritta **3.** cambiare (di vento) **4.** *to —* **down,** (*mar.*) ammainare.

haulage [ˈhɔːlidʒ], *s.* **1.** trasporto (per trazione) **2.** costo del trasporto ☆ *— contractor,* imprenditore di trasporti.

haulier [ˈhɔːljə*], *s.* **1.** camionista; autotrasportatore **2.** (*miner.*) chi trascina i vagoncini.

haunch [hɔːntʃ], *s.* **1.** (*anat.*) anca; fianco **2.** coscia, quarto (di selvaggina) **3.** (*arch.*) fianco (di arco) ☆ *--bone,* osso iliaco.

haunt [hɔːnt], *s.* **1.** ricovero, ritiro; ritrovo, luogo frequentato assiduamente: *the — of criminals,* covo di ladri, della malavita; *my usual haunts,* i luoghi che frequento **2.** covo, tana; luogo dove gli animali bevono, si cibano abitualmente **3.** (*amer.*) fantasma.

to **haunt,** *v.t.* **1.** frequentare assiduamente **2.** perseguitare, ossessionare (di pensieri, ricordi, ecc.): *the memory of it haunted us for a long time,* il ricordo di ciò ci tormentò per molto tempo **3.** *to be haunted,* essere frequentato (da spettri): *that castle is haunted,* quel castello è abitato dai fantasmi.

haunted [ˈhɔːntid], *ag.* frequentato, perseguitato, infestato da apparizioni: *a — house,* una casa visitata dagli spettri.

haunter [ˈhɔːntə*], *s.* assiduo frequentatore (di teatri, taverne, ecc.).

haunting [ˈhɔːntiŋ], *ag.* che perseguita: *a — air,* una melodia che ricorre continuamente alla memoria.

hautboy [ˈouboi], *s.* **1.** (*mus.*) oboe **2.** (*bot.*) magiostra.

hauteur [ouˈtəː*], *s.* alterigia, superbia.

Havana [həˈvænə], *no.pr.* (*geog.*) Avana ‖ *s.* sigaro avana.

have [hæv] *s.* **1.** *gener. pl.* abbiente: *the haves and the — -nots,* (*fam.*) i ricchi ed i poveri; le nazioni ricche e quelle povere **2.** (*sl.*) truffa, imbroglio: *it's a —,* è un inganno.

to **have** [hæv (*forma forte*), həv, əv (*forme deboli*)], *pass.p.p.* **had** [hæd (*forma forte*), həd, əd (*forme deboli*)], *v.t.* (*have* davanti a *to* è spesso pronunciato [hæf]; 2ª *persona sing.* (*arc.*) *pres.* **hast** [hæst (*forma forte*), həst, əst (*forme deboli*)]; 3ª *persona sing.pres.* **has** [hæz (*forma forte*), həz, əz (*forme deboli*)], (*arc.*) **hath** [hæθ (*forma forte*), həθ, əθ (*forme deboli*)]; forme contratte: *he's* [hiːz] *= he has; it's* [its] *= it has; I've* [aiv] *= I have; I'd* [aid] *= I had; I haven't* [ˈhævnt] *= I have not; he hasn't* [ˈhæznt] *= he has not; I hadn't* [ˈhædnt] *= I had not*) **1.** (*ausiliare*) **avere, essere:** *— you not* (o *haven't you*) *seen him?,* non l'avete visto?; *I — not* (o *I haven't* o *I've not*) *seen him,* non l'ho visto ‖ *I — gone,* sono andato **2. avere, possedere:** *he had a dog,* possedeva un cane; *he has not a dog,* egli non possiede un cane ‖ *did the Romans — aeroplanes?,* i romani avevano aeroplani?; *do you — much time for reading?,* hai molto tempo da dedicare alla lettura? ‖ *how much money — you?* (o *fam. how much money — you got?* o *amer. how much money do you —?*), quanto denaro hai? **3. prendere; ottenere; ricevere:** *— you had his letter?,* hai ricevuto la sua lettera?; *I do not — coffee,* non prendo caffè; *will you — a cup of tea?,* prende una tazza di tè?; *to — one's wish,* ottenere ciò che si desidera ‖ *to be had at all grocers',* in vendita in tutte le drogherie **4. dovere:** *do you — to help him?,* dovete aiutarlo?; *I shall — to go,* dovrò andare ‖ *I don't — to go there,* non sono obbligato ad andarci; *I — not to go there,* non mi si permette di andarci **5.** (V, VI) **fare:** *I had it done by him,* lo feci fare da lui; *I must — my boots repaired,* devo farmi riparare le scarpe ‖ *— him come at once,* fallo venire subito; *I had him do it,* glielo feci fare **6.** (*seguito da* it) **sostenere, affermare, insistere:** *as the Poet has it,* come dice il Poeta; *he will — it that Timbuctoo is in America,* sostiene che Timbuctu si trova in America **7.** (**Fraseologia**): **had as well,** (V) tanto

varrebbe, sarebbe lo stesso: *we had as well stop,* tanto varrebbe che ci fermassimo ‖ **had better,** (V) sarebbe meglio che: *you had better go,* sarebbe meglio che tu andassi‖ **I had rather** (o **sooner**), (V) preferirei: *I had rather* (o *sooner*) *stop here than go,* preferirei fermarmi qui piuttosto che andare ‖ *he had it!,* (*sl. mil.*) è spacciato!, è stato ucciso! ‖ *he has no French,* non conosce il francese per nulla ‖ *I had as lief stay as go,* vorrei tanto rimanere quanto andare ‖ *I — no idea,* non saprei ‖ *I'm not having any,* non ne prendo; (*sl.*) non me la danno a bere; *I'm not to be had,* (*fam.*) non mi lascio ingannare facilmente ‖ *let them — it,* (*sl.*) dite loro quanto si meritano; conciateli per le feste ‖ *you — had it!,* l'hai voluto!, è finito!, chiuso! ‖ *you — me there!,* mi hai colto in fallo! ‖ *to — at s.o.,* attaccare qlcu. ‖ *to — a call to do sthg.,* avere motivo di fare ql.co. ‖ *to — the free run of a place,* andare e venire liberamente, farla da padroni in un luogo ‖ *to — a good time,* divertirsi ‖ *to — it out* (*with s.o.*), mettere fine ad una disputa (con qlcu.); *to — it over,* farla finita ‖ *to — no say in the matter,* non aver voce in capitolo ‖ *to — on,* avere indosso; (*sl.*) fare una scommessa su ‖ *to — a screw loose,* (*sl.*) essere svitato, un po' pazzo ‖ *to — s.o. in,* fare entrare qlcu. ‖ *to — s.o. in one's pocket,* avere qlcu. in tasca (controllarlo, dirigerlo) ‖ *to — s.o. up,* far comparire qlcu. in giudizio ‖ *to — tea and scandals,* fare pettegolezzi all'ora del tè ‖ *to — a tooth out,* farsi togliere un dente ‖ *to — the worst of the argument,* avere la peggio.

haven [ˈheivn], *s.* **1.** porto; rada **2.** *fig.* asilo, rifugio.

haversack [ˈhævəsæk], *s.* zaino, sacco da montagna.

havoc [ˈhævək], *s.* rovina; distruzione; strage: *to cry —,* dare l'ordine di strage; *to make — of* (o *to play — with* o *among*), distruggere, rovinare (anche *fig.*).

haw[1] [hɔː], *s.* recinto.

haw[2], *s.* (bacca di) biancospino.

haw[3], *s.* membrana nittitante (di cavallo, cane, ecc.).

haw[4], *inter.* **1.** ehm! (esclamazione di dubbio) **2.** ah, ah! (esclamazione di riso, scherno) ‖ *s.* sghignazzata.

to **haw**[4], *v.i.* dire « ehm! » (per esprimere esitazione).

haw-haw [ˈhɔːhɔː], *s.* sghignazzata.

to **haw-haw,** *v.i.* ridere fragorosamente, sguaiatamente; sghignazzare.

haw-haw, *inter.* ah, ah!.

hawk[1] [hɔːk], *s.* **1.** falco; sparviero ‖ *not to know a — from a handsaw,* non avere sufficiente discernimento ‖ *to have eyes like a —,* avere l'occhio di lince **2.** *fig.* avvoltoio, persona rapace ☆ *— -eyed,* di vista acuta; *— -moth,* (*entom.*) smerinto; *— -nosed,* dal naso aquilino.

to **hawk**[1], *v.t.i.* **1.** cacciare col falco **2.** assalire (la preda, di uccelli).

hawk[2], *s.* (*edil.*) sparviero, vassoio (di muratore).

to **hawk**[3], *v.t.i.* **1.** fare il venditore ambulante **2.** portare in giro (merci) per vendere **3.** *fig.* mettere in giro (notizie).

hawk[4], *s.* raschio.

to **hawk**[4], *v.i.* raschiarsi la gola.

hawker[1] [ˈhɔːkə*], *s.* falconiere.

hawker[2], *s.* venditore ambulante.

hawking [ˈhɔːkiŋ], *s.* caccia col falco.

hawse [hɔːz], *s.* (*mar.*) cubia, occhio di cubia.

hawser [ˈhɔːzə*], *s.* (*mar.*) gomena.

hawthorn [ˈhɔːθɔːn], *s.* biancospino.

hay[1] [hei], *s.* fieno; paglia: *to make —,* falciare ed esporre il fieno al sole ‖ *to make — of,* mettere in disordine ‖ *make — while the sun shines,* *prov.* batti il ferro quando è caldo ☆ *— -fever,* febbre del fieno; *— -field,* prato da falciare; *— -fork,* forcone per rivoltare il fieno; *— -harvest,* fienagione; *— -loft,* fienile; *— -making,* falciatura; *— -market,* mercato del fieno; *— -rick,* mucchio di fieno; *— -wire,* filo per legare il fieno; (*sl. amer.*) intrigo, cosa complicata: *to go — -wire,* eccitarsi.

to **hay**[1], *v.t.i.* **1.** coltivare a fieno **2.** rivoltare il fieno

hay[2], *s.* danza campestre.

haycock [ˈheikɔk], *s.* mucchio di fieno.

hayseed ['hei-si:d], *s.* **1.** seme di erba **2.** (*amer.*) persona rustica.

haystack ['hei-stæk], *s.* mucchio di fieno.

hay-ward ['heiwəd], *s.* guardia campestre.

hazard ['hæzəd], *s.* **1.** azzardo; caso; rischio, pericolo: *at all hazards*, ad ogni costo **2.** giuoco di dadi **3.** (*golf*) ostacolo naturale.

to hazard, *v.t.* azzardare; arrischiare.

hazardable ['hæzədəbl], *ag.* azzardabile.

hazardous ['hæzədəs], *ag.* rischioso, azzardato.

hazardously ['hæzədəsli], *av.* rischiosamente.

hazardousness ['hæzədəsnis], *s.* azzardo, rischio.

haze[1] [heiz], *s.* **1.** foschia; nebbia (prodotta dal calore) **2.** *fig.* oscurità, confusione mentale.

to haze[1], *v.t.i.* **1.** annebbiare **2.** (*fam.*) piovigginare.

to haze[2], *v.t.* **1.** (*mar.*) punire con lavori pesanti **2.** (*sl. scolastico amer.*) tormentare, fare scherzi a.

hazel[1] ['heizl], *s.* **1.** (*bot.*) nocciuolo; legno di nocciuolo **2.** colore nocciuola ☆ — *-nut*, nocciuola (frutto).

hazel[2], *s.* specie di pietra viva.

hazelly ['heizli], *ag.* di nocciuolo, di color nocciuola.

hazily ['heizili], *av.* confusamente, indistintamente.

haziness ['heizinis], *s.* **1.** nebbiosità; foschia **2.** confusione (di idee, ecc.): *the — of his knowledge*, la nebulosità della sua cultura.

hazy ['heizi], *ag.* **1.** nebbioso **2.** *fig.* indistinto, confuso: *— ideas*, idee confuse **3.** un po' brillo.

he [hi:], *pron. pers. 3ᵃ persona m. sing.* **1.** egli, lui, colui: *— is good*, egli è buono; *it is —*, è lui; *you are as good as —*, sei buono come lui, vali tanto quanto lui; *the dog barked, — (o it) had heard a noise*, il cane si mise ad abbaiare, aveva udito un rumore **2.** (*antecedente di pron. rel.*): *— of whom they spoke*, colui del quale essi parlarono; *— who comes*, colui che viene ‖ *att. indicante il sesso* (di animali): *a — -goat*, un caprone ‖ *a — -man*, (*amer.*) un vero uomo ‖ *s.* maschio: *it is a —!*, è un bambino, un maschio!.

head [hed], *s.* **1.** (*anat.*) testa: *— of hair*, folta capigliatura; *from — to foot*, da capo a piedi; *the horse won by a —*, il cavallo vinse per una testa; *I am taller by a —*, sono più alto di tutta una testa; *it cost him his —*, gli costò la testa; *wine went to his —*, il vino gli andò alla testa; *to nod one's —*, annuire col capo; *to set a price on s.o.'s —*, mettere una taglia sulla testa di qlcu.; *to shake one's —*, far cenno di no col capo; *to strike off s.o.'s —*, decapitare qlcu. ‖ *— over heels*, capovolto, a gambe levate; *fig.* alla rinfusa, in estrema confusione: *to be — over heels in love with s.o.*, essere innamorato di qlcu. alla follia ‖ *to be off one's —*, essere scemo, essere pazzo ‖ *to drag in a subject by the — and ears*, introdurre un argomento per forza ‖ *to beat s.o.'s — off*, (*fam.*) battere, vincere qlcu. ‖ *to give s.o. his —*, lasciare andare liberamente qlcu. ‖ *to keep one's —*, mantenersi calmi ‖ *to keep one's — above water*, mantenersi a galla (finanziariamente) ‖ *to make — against*, opporre resistenza a ‖ *to put (o to lay) heads together*, consultarsi ‖ *to sell a house over s.o.'s —*, vendere una casa senza avvertirne l'inquilino ‖ *to talk s.o.'s — off*, stordire qlcu. con chiacchiere ‖ *to walk with one's — in the air*, camminare a testa alta ‖ *two heads are better than one*, quattro occhi valgono più di due **2.** testa, intelligenza; immaginazione; volontà: *his clearness of — is well known to me*, conosco bene la sua lucidità di mente; *the thought came into my — that …*, mi venne l'idea che … ‖ *he made it out of his own —*, lo ha fatto di testa sua ‖ *his — is screwed on the right way*, è un uomo di buon senso ‖ *to have a good — for business*, essere tagliato per gli affari ‖ *to have a good — on one's shoulders*, aver la testa sulle spalle ‖ *to put sthg. into, out of s.o.'s —*, mettere in, togliere dalla testa ql.co. a qlcu. ‖ *to take it into one's — to do sthg.*, mettersi in testa di fare ql.co. **3.** capo, direttore, dirigente; posizione preminente: *— of a department*, capo-reparto; *at the — of a column of troops*, alla testa di una colonna di truppe; *to be at the — of*

the army, essere a capo dell'esercito **4.** individuo, persona: *the dinner cost five dollars a —*, il pranzo costò cinque dollari a testa **5.** parte alta di una cosa: *the — of a bed*, il capezzale di un letto; *a car with a folding —*, un'automobile decapottabile **6.** testa (di moneta): *heads or tails?*, testa o croce? ‖ *heads I win tails you lose*, in un modo o nell'altro vinco io ‖ *to be unable to make — nor tail of sthg.*, non riuscire a raccapezzarsi in ql.co. **7.** capo, unità di bestiame (invariato al *pl.*): *fifty — of cattle*, cinquanta capi di bestiame; *the park feeds about forty — of deer*, la riserva nutre circa quaranta cervi **8.** rubrica; intestazione; capitolo: *under separate heads*, in capitoli diversi **9.** sorgente; getto d'acqua soprelevato: *that mill has a good —*, quel mulino ha una buona sorgente **10.** promontorio, capo; estremità di una baia **11.** schiuma (di bibita); panna (di latte): *— on beer*, schiuma di birra; *bottle of milk without any —*, bottiglia di latte senza panna **12.** capocchia (di spillo, chiodo, zolfanello) ‖ *I don't care a pin's —*, (*fam.*) non me ne importa niente **13.** (*bot.*) infiorescenza a capolino **14.** punta purulenta di ascesso, foruncolo: *to come to a —*, suppurare (di ascesso); *fig.* giungere a una crisi decisiva **15.** (*mar.*) prora ☆ — *-band*, fascia sul capo; — *-cloth*, copricapo; — *-dress*, acconciatura; — *-first*, a capofitto; con la testa in giù; — *-foremost*, a capofitto; — *-hunter*, cacciatore di teste; — *-land*, promontorio, capo; — *-master*, — *-mistress*, direttore, direttrice di scuola; — *-money*, taglia; — *-note*, nota in testa a capitolo, pagina; — *-office*, (*comm.*) sede di una ditta; — *-on*, di fronte, uno di fronte all'altro; — *-phones*, (*rad.*) cuffia ricevente; — *-rest*, poggiatesta; — *-sea*, (*mar.*) corrente di fronte; — *-shake*, tentennamento del capo; — *-spring*, fonte; — *-stall*, testiera di una briglia; — *-station*, (*austral.*) abitazione in un grande allevamento di bestiame; — *-voice*, (*mus.*) voce di testa; falsetto; — *-water*, (*gener. pl.*) corso superiore di un fiume; — *-way*, abbrivio (specialmente di nave); *fig.* progresso; (*arch.*) altezza di un arco; (*ferr.*) intervallo tra due convogli; — *-wear*, copricapo; — *-wind*, (*mar.*) vento di prua; — *-word*, prima parola di un paragrafo; — *-work*, lavoro mentale; — *-worker*, intellettuale ‖ *crowned heads*, teste coronate.

to head, *v.t.i.* **1.** toccare, colpire con la testa: *to — the ball*, colpire la palla di testa (nel giuoco del calcio) **2.** dirigere, comandare, essere a capo di, in testa a: *he heads the firm*, è a capo della ditta; *to — the poll*, essere primo nello scrutinio **3.** dirigersi (verso): *to — for a place*, dirigersi verso un luogo; *to — south*, dirigersi verso sud **4.** intestare, intitolare: *to — a chapter, a letter*, intestare un capitolo, una lettera **5.** opporsi a, affrontare (un pericolo) **6.** venire a maturazione (di ascesso); accestire (di verdure); nascere (di fiume) **7.** *to — off*, bloccare; intercettare (fuggitivi); eludere (una domanda imbarazzante).

headache ['hedeik], *s.* mal di testa; *fig.* preoccupazione; guaio; problema difficile: *to have a splitting —*, avere un terribile mal di testa.

headachy ['hedeiki], *ag.* sofferente di mal di testa.

headed ['hedid], *ag.* munito di testa ☆ *fat —*, stupido; *hot —*, esaltato, (dalla) testa calda; *light —*, leggero, sventato; *pig —*, ostinato; *swollen —*, tronfio; *thick —*, ottuso; *wrong —*, caparbio, intrattabile.

header ['hedə*], *s.* **1.** tuffo, caduta con la testa in avanti **2.** (*ind.*) collettore; testata **3.** (*edil.*) mattone di punta **4.** comandante di baleniera.

headgear ['hedgiə*], *s.* **1.** copricapo **2.** finimenti della testa (di cavallo) **3.** (*miner.*) incastellatura di estrazione.

heading ['hedin], *s.* **1.** intestazione, titolo (di un capitolo) **2.** (*aer.*) rotta **3.** (*miner.*) cantiere di avanzamento.

headless ['hedlis], senza testa (anche *fig.*); sventato.

headlight ['hedlait], *s.* faro anteriore (d'automobile, ecc.): *to dim (o to dip) the headlights*, abbassare i fari ☆ *non-dazzle —*, (*aut.*) fanale anabbagliante.

headline ['hedlain], *s.* titolo, intestazione (di capitolo, articolo): *the large headlines*, i titoli a carattere bastone || *the headlines*, *(rad.)* sommario delle notizie più importanti.

headlong ['hedlɔŋ], *av.* a capofitto, precipitosamente: *to rush — into the fight*, buttarsi a capofitto nella mischia.

headman ['hedmæn], *nel senso* 2. ['hed'mæn], *pl.* **headmen** ['hedmen], *nel senso* 2. ['hed'men], *s.* 1. capo tribù 2. *(amer.)* caposquadra.

headmost ['hedmoust], *ag.* il primo, il più avanzato (di nave, ecc.).

headpiece ['hedpi:s], *s.* 1. elmo 2. testa; cervello; persona intelligente 3. *(tip.)* testata (incisa).

headquarters ['hed'kwɔ:təz], *s.pl.* 1. *(mil.)* quartier generale; centro di operazioni 2. centro, servizio centrale; direzione.

headship ['hedʃip], *s.* primato; autorità suprema; direzione.

headsman, *pl.* **headsmen** ['hedzmən] *s.* 1. carnefice 2. comandante di baleniera.

headstone ['hedstoun], *s.* 1. pietra tombale 2. *(edil.)* pietra angolare (anche *fig.*).

headstrong ['hedstrɔŋ], *ag.* ostinato, testardo.

heady ['hedi], *ag.* 1. violento, impetuoso; testardo 2. inebriante (di vino, profumo, ecc.).

to **heal** [hi:l], *v.t.i.* 1. guarire, curare, cicatrizzare, cicatrizzarsi: *the wound healed*, la ferita si cicatrizzò; *to — a sore*, guarire una piaga 2. *fig.* sanare: *to — a quarrel*, comporre un litigio ☆ — *-all*, panacea.

healer ['hi:lə*], *s.c.* guaritore, guaritrice.

healing ['hi:liŋ], *ag.* salutare; curativo || *s.* guarigione; cicatrizzazione.

health [helθ], *s.* 1. salute: *he looks the picture of —*, è il ritratto della salute; *his — broke down*, egli si è rovinata la salute; *to drink (to) s.o.'s —*, bere alla salute di qlcu. || *Health Insurance*, assicurazione contro le malattie || *Ministry of Health*, Ministero della Sanità || *National Health Service*, Servizio Sanitario Statale 2. salvezza, salute divina ☆ — *certificate*, certificato medico; — *-resort*, luogo di cura; — *-restoring*, che ridà salute; — *visitor*, ispettore sanitario.

healthful ['helθful], *ag.* 1. salubre, salutare 2. *(rar.)* sano.

healthfully ['helθfuli] *av.* in modo salubre, salutare.

healthfulness ['helθfulnis], *s.* 1. salubrità 2. *(rar.)* buona salute.

healthily ['helθili], *av.* salubremente; salutarmente.

healthiness ['helθinis], *s.* 1. salute 2. salubrità.

healthless ['helθlis], *ag.* *(rar.)* 1. ammalato, infermo 2. insalubre, malsano.

healthlessness ['helθlisnis], *s.* *(rar.)* 1. infermità 2. insalubrità.

healthsome ['helθsəm], *ag.* *(rar.)* salubre, salutare.

healthy ['helθi], *ag.* 1. sano; robusto 2. salutare, salubre ☆ — *-minded*, sano di mente.

heap [hi:p], *s.* 1. mucchio, cumulo; ammasso: *to put in a —*, accumulare || *struck all of a —*, *(fam.)* prostrato, depresso 2. *(fam.)* gran numero; molto: *heaps of books*, moltissimi libri; *heaps of love to you*, con tutto il mio affetto; *a — of trouble*, molto disturbo || *heaps of times*, un mucchio di volte || *he has got heaps*, *(fam.)* ne ha un mucchio (di soldi, ecc.).

to **heap**, *v.t.* 1. ammucchiare, accumulare, ammassare: *to — (up) bricks*, ammucchiare mattoni 2. riempire (anche *fig.*): *he has heaped me with benefits*, mi ha beneficato generosamente; *they heaped insults on him*, lo coprirono di ingiurie; *they heaped my plate with sausages*, mi riempirono il piatto di salsicce.

heaper ['hi:pə*], *s.c.* chi accumula.

heaps [hi:ps], *av.* *(fam.)* molto, infinitamente: *this is — better*, questo è infinitamente meglio.

to **hear** [hiə*], *pass.p.p.* **heard** [hə:d], *v.t.i.* 1. (I, V, VI) sentire, udire: *I can — her singing*, la sento cantare; *I heard him called a liar*, sentii che lo chiamavano bugiardo; *I never heard him speak so well*, non l'ho mai sentito parlare così bene || *—! —!*, (anche

iron.) bene!, bravo!, senti un po'! 2. sentir dire, venire a sapere: *I have heard it said*, l'ho sentito dire; *let me — from you soon*, fatemi aver presto vostre notizie; *hoping to — from you soon*, nella speranza di aver presto vostre notizie; *to — about s.o.*, avere notizie di qlcu. (indirettamente); *to — from one*, ricevere notizie da uno (direttamente); *to — of a person*, sentir parlare di una persona 3. (V) ascoltare: *you shall — me out!*, mi ascolterete finchè ho finito! 4. *(dir.)* dare udienza a.

hearable ['hiərəbl], *ag.* udibile.

heard [hə:d], *pass.p.p.* di to **hear**.

hearer ['hiərə*], *s.c.* chi ode, ascolta.

hearing ['hiəriŋ], *s.* 1. udito: *to be hard of —*, essere duro d'orecchio 2. udienza (anche *dir.*): *he granted me a —*, mi concesse un'udienza 3. attenzione; conoscenza: *give me a —!*, dammi ascolto!; *it came to my — that*, venni a sapere che.

to **hearken** ['hɑ:kən], *v.i.* *(letter.)* ascoltare; prestare attenzione.

hearsay ['hiəsei], *s.* diceria, voce: *by —*, per sentito dire.

hearse [hə:s], *s.* carro funebre ☆ — *-cloth*, drappo funebre.

heart [hɑ:t], *s.* 1. cuore (anche *fig.*): *he suffers from a weak —*, il suo cuore è debole || *— of gold*, cuor d'oro || *— of oak*, uomo coraggioso; *the British Hearts of Oak*, *(fam.)* la Marina Britannica || *to one's — content*, secondo i propri gusti || *have a —!*, abbi un po' di cuore!; *his — is in the right place*, è un uomo di cuore || *my — sank*, mi sentii mancare; *to break one's — over sthg.*, crucciarsi per ql.co.; *to break s.o.'s —*, spezzare il cuore a qlcu.; *to cry (o to sob) one's — out*, piangere disperatamente || *to have a — of stone*, avere un cuore di pietra || *to have one's — in one's boots*, avere paura || *to have one's — in one's mouth*, avere il cuore in gola || *to press (o to clasp) s.o. to one's —*, abbracciare qlcu. con trasporto || *to put one's — and soul (o to throw oneself — and soul) into sthg.*, darsi anima e corpo a ql.co. || *to wear one's — on one's sleeve*, agire, parlare a cuore aperto 2. *fig.* affetto; coraggio; interesse; desiderio; inclinazione: *at — he is not a bad fellow*, in fondo non è cattivo; *it does my — good*, ciò mi rallegra molto; *it goes against my — to*, *(arc.)* è estremamente a malincuore che; *she is a girl after my own —*, è il mio tipo di ragazza; *not to have the — to do sthg.*, non avere il coraggio di fare q.co.; *to be of good —*, stare contento, allegro || *to do sthg. with a light, heavy —*, fare ql.co. volentieri, a malincuore; *to do sthg. with half a —*, fare ql.co. senza slancio || *to find one's way into people's hearts*, guadagnarsi la simpatia della gente || *to give (o to lose) one's — to s.o.*, innamorarsi di qlcu. || *to have one's — in one's work*, dedicarsi con entusiasmo al proprio lavoro; *to have set one's — on sthg.*, *on doing sthg.*, avere posto il cuore a ql.co., voler fare assolutamente ql.co.; *to have sthg. at —*, tenere a ql.co. || *to learn by —*, imparare a memoria || *to lose —*, scoraggiarsi; *to pluck up (o to take) —*, prendere coraggio || *to put one's — into sthg.*, interessarsi vivamente a ql.co. || *to put s.o. in good —*, dar coraggio a qlcu. || *to set one's — at rest*, mettersi il cuore in pace || *to take the — out of s.o.*, scoraggiare qlcu. || *to take (o to lay) sthg. to —*, prendersi a cuore ql.co. || *kind hearts are more than coronets*, un cuore gentile vale più dei titoli 3. centro; *fig.* nocciolo, cuore, parte principale: *the — of a cabbage*, il cuore di un cavolo; *the — of the matter*, il nocciolo della faccenda; *in my — of hearts*, nel profondo del mio cuore 4. *(vezzeggiativo)* cuoricino 5. *pl.* *(carte)* cuori 6. *(mar.)* bigotta a canali ☆ — *attack*, *(patol.)* attacco cardiaco; — *-beat*, pulsazione; *fig.* emozione, batticuore; — *('s)-blood*, sangue del cuore; *fig.* anima, vita, vitalità; — *-break*, crepacuore; — *-breaking (o -rending)*, straziante; — *-broken*, desolato, straziato; — *-cam*, *(mec.)* camma a forma di cuore; — *-disease*, malattia di cuore; — *-easing*, confortante; — *failure*; *(patol.)* collasso cardiaco; — *-felt*, sincero, di cuore,

— -*free*, che ha il cuore libero; — -*grief*, profondo dolore; — -*heaviness*, depressione di spirito; — -*quake*, agitazione, batticuore; — -*searching*, esame di coscienza; —*'s-ease*, (*bot.*) viola del pensiero; — -*shaped*, a forma di cuore; — -*sick*, scoraggiato, triste; — -*some*, divertente, esilarante; — -*sore*, addolorato; — -*stirring*, commovente, eccitante; — -*strings*, *fig.* legami affettivi; — -*whole*, sincero; che ha il cuore libero; — -*wood*, (*bot.*) cuore del legno, duramen ‖ *athletic* — (o *enlarged* —), (*patol.*) cuore «atletico», ipertrofico.

heartache ['hɑːt-eik], *s.* angoscia, angustia, crepacuore, tristezza profonda.

heartburn ['hɑːtbəːn], *s.* bruciore di stomaco.

heartburning ['hɑːtbəːniŋ], *s.* gelosia; rancore.

hearted ['hɑːtid], *ag.* dal cuore, che ha il cuore ☆ *broken*- —, desolato; *chicken*- — (o *faint*- —), pauroso; *down*- —, depresso; *false*- —, falso; *half*- —, tiepido; esitante; *hard*- —, duro di cuore; *light*- —, dal cuore felice, spensierato; *lion*- —, dal cuore di leone; *sad*- —, triste; *single*- —, sincero; *soft*- —, tenero di cuore; *stout*- —, coraggioso; *warm*- —, di cuore, cordiale; *whole*- —, sincero, cordialissimo.

to **hearten** ['hɑːtn], *v.t.i.* incoraggiare, prender coraggio; rincuorare, rincuorarsi.

heartening ['hɑːtniŋ], *ag.* incoraggiante.

hearth [hɑːθ], *s.* **1.** focolare (anche *fig.*) **2.** (*metal.*) laboratorio; suola; letto di fusione; crogiuolo ☆ — -*rug*, tappeto steso davanti al focolare; — -*stone*, pietra del focolare; pietra pomice.

heartily ['hɑːtili], *av.* **1.** cordialmente **2.** vigorosamente **3.** abbondantemente.

heartiness ['hɑːtinis], *s.* **1.** cordialità; schiettezza **2.** vigoria.

heartless ['hɑːtlis], *ag.* senza cuore; insensibile.

heartlessly ['hɑːtlisli], *av.* crudelmente; insensibilmente.

heartlessness ['hɑːtlisnis], *s.* mancanza di cuore; insensibilità.

hearty ['hɑːti], *ag.* **1.** sincero; cordiale: *a* — *dislike*, una forte avversione **2.** sano; robusto; vegeto **3.** abbondante: *a* — *meal*, un pasto copioso, abbondante.

heat [hiːt], *s.* **1.** calore, caldo; calura: *sultry* —, caldo soffocante **2.** collera, animosità; entusiasmo: *the* — *of youth*, il fuoco della giovinezza; *in the* — *of the moment*, nella foga del momento; *he replied with some* —, replicò con vivacità **3.** (*spor.*) prova (singola di una serie) **4.** eccitazione sessuale (di animali, specialmente femmine) **5.** (*patol.*) eruzione, infiammazione ☆ — -*apoplexy*, (*patol.*) colpo di calore; — *barrier*, (*neol. aer.*) barriera del calore; — -*spot*, (*patol.*) macchia di calore (sulla pelle); — -*stroke*, (*patol.*) colpo di calore; — *treatment* (o — *cure*), (*med.*) termoterapia; — -*wave*, ondata di calore ‖ *constant*, *latent*, *specific* —, (*fis.*) calore costante, latente, specifico; *a dead* —, (*spor.*) una gara alla pari; *melting* —, (*fis.*) calore di fusione; *prickly*- —, (*patol.*) lichen; *qualifying* —, (*spor.*) prova eliminatoria.

to **heat**, *v.t.i.* scaldare, scaldarsi; riscaldare, riscaldarsi; animare, animarsi (anche *fig.*): *to* — *the imagination*, stimolare l'immaginazione.

heatedly ['hiːtidli], *av.* animatamente.

heater ['hiːtə*], *s.* riscaldatore; bollitore: *electric* —, radiatore, stufetta elettrica ☆ *electric immersion* —, (*elett.*) resistenza corazzata; *gas*- —, scaldabagno a gas.

heath [hiːθ], *s.* **1.** brughiera; landa **2.** (*bot.*) erica.

heathen ['hiːðən], *ag.* pagano: — *customs*, usanze pagane ‖ *s.c.* **1.** pagano, pagana: *the Saxons were heathens*, i sassoni erano pagani **2.** *the* —, i pagani **3.** persona rozza, primitiva, incivile.

heathendom ['hiːðəndəm], *s.* paganesimo; regioni dove regna il paganesimo.

heathenish ['hiːðəniʃ], *ag.* paganeggiante.

heathenishly ['hiːðəniʃli], *av.* paganamente.

heathenishness ['hiːðəniʃnis], **heathenism** ['hiːðənizəm], *s.* paganesimo.

to **heathenize** ['hiːðənaiz], *v.t.i.* **1.** rendere pagano **2.** paganeggiare.

heathenry ['hiːðənri], *s.* paganesimo.

heather ['heðə*], *ag.* violaceo ‖ *s.* (*bot.*) erica ‖ *to set the* — *on fire*, *fig.* dar fuoco alle polveri ‖ *to take to the* —, diventare un fuorilegge, darsi alla macchia.

heathery ['heðəri], *ag.* coperto di erica.

heathy ['hiːθi], *ag.* che abbonda di erica.

heating ['hiːtiŋ], *s.* riscaldamento ☆ — -*apparatus*, calorifero; — *element*, (*elett.*) resistenza; — -*power of fuel*, potere calorifico del combustibile ‖ *central* —, riscaldamento centrale.

heave [hiːv], *s.* **1.** sollevamento; sforzo (per sollevare ql.co.) **2.** rigonfiamento: *the* — *of the sea*, l'ondeggiare, il gonfiarsi del mare **3.** conato di vomito **4.** (*geol.*) componente orizzontale dello scorrimento **5.** *pl.* bolsaggine (di cavallo).

to **heave**, *pass.* **heaved** [hiːvd], **hove** [houv], *p.p.* **heaved**, *v.t.i.* **1.** sollevare, alzare (generalmente con sforzo): *to* — *high*, sollevare in alto ‖ *to* — (*up*), sollevare **2.** emettere: *to* — *a sigh*, emettere un sospiro **3.** (*mar.*) gettare; alare; inclinare; virare: *to* — *and set*, alzarsi e abbassarsi; *to* — *in sight*, (*mar.*) essere in vista, apparire all'orizzonte; *to* — *overboard*, gettare a mare; *to* — *to*, mettersi in panna ‖ — -*ho*, oh, issa! (grido di marinai nel sollevare un peso) **4.** sollevarsi (di mare); palpitare, ansare (di petto); avere conati di vomito; rivoltarsi (di stomaco).

heaven ['hevn], *s.* **1.** cielo, paradiso **2.** suprema felicità; stato di gioia ‖ *in the seventh* —, al settimo cielo, al colmo della felicità **3.** *Heaven*, Cielo; Dio: *for Heaven's sake*, per amor di Dio; *good Heavens!*, giusto cielo!; *thank Heaven!*, grazie a Dio! **4.** *gener. pl.* cielo; aria-orizzonte ☆ — -*born*, divino, celestiale; — -*fallen*, caduto dal cielo; — -*sent*, inviato dal cielo, provvidenziale.

heavenliness ['hevnlinis], *s.* divinità.

heavenly ['hevnli], *ag.* **1.** divino ‖ *the Heavenly City*, il Paradiso **2.** del cielo, celeste: — *bodies*, corpi celesti **3.** (*fam.*) delizioso, eccellente: *what* — *apples!*, che mele deliziose! ☆ — -*minded*, devoto.

heavenward ['hevnwəd], *ag.* rivolto al cielo.

heavenwards ['hevnwədz], *av.* verso il cielo.

heaver ['hiːvə*], *s.* **1.** sollevatore, elevatore; portatore; scaricatore (specialmente di porto) **2.** (*mar.*) barra.

heavily ['hevili], *av.* **1.** pesantemente, gravemente; molto: *he was* — *fined for speeding*, fu punito con una grossa multa per aver superato il limite di velocità **2.** profondamente **3.** con difficoltà.

heaviness ['hevinis], *s.* **1.** pesantezza **2.** abbattimento, avvilimento.

heaving ['hiːviŋ], *ag.* ondeggiante; palpitante ‖ *s.* gonfiamento; sollevamento; palpitazione.

heavy¹ ['hevi], *ag.* **1.** pesante: *a ship of* — *burden*, una nave da carico pesante; *I have* — *eyes*, ho sonno; *to grow* —, ingrassare, appesantirsi ‖ — *in hand*, difficile da condurre (cavallo) **2.** triste, grave, severo **3.** violento, forte: — *sea*, mare grosso **4.** fangoso; pesante (di terreno): — *road*, strada fangosa **5.** noioso (di produzione artistica e letteraria); (*teat.*) serio, triste **6.** indigesto; forte (di vino) **7.** plumbeo: — *sky*, cielo plumbeo **8.** gravoso (di spesa) ☆ — -*armed*, armato pesantemente; — *artillery*, artiglieria pesante; — -*handed*, maldestro; — -*headed*, stupido; — -*hearted*, triste.

heavy² ['hiːvi], *ag.* bolso (di cavallo).

heavyweight ['heviweit], *s.* (*spec. spor.*) peso massimo; (*fam. amer.*) grosso calibro.

hebdomad ['hebdəmæd], *s.* ebdomada.

hebdomadal [heb'dɔmədl], *ag.* ebdomadario, settimanale.

hebdomadary [heb'dɔmədəri], *ag.* ebdomadario, settimanale ‖ *s.* frate, canonico ebdomadario.

Hebe ['hiːbi(:)], *np.pr.f.* (*mit.*) Ebe.

to **hebetate** ['hebiteit], *v.t.i.* (far) inebetire, incretinire.

hebetude ['hebitjuːd], *s.* ebetismo, stupidità.

Hebraic [hiː(ː)'breiik], *ag.* ebraico.

Hebraically [hi(:)'breiikəli], *av.* all'ebraica.
Hebraism ['hi:breiizəm], *s.* ebraismo.
Hebraist ['hi:breiist], *s.c.* ebraista.
Hebraistic [,hi:brei'istik], *ag.* ebraico.
Hebraistically [,hi:brei'istikəli], *av.* al modo ebraico.
to **Hebraize** ['hi:breiaiz], *v.t.i.* ebraizzare.
Hebrew ['hi:bru:], *ag.* ebreo, ebraico, israelitico ‖ *s.c.* ebreo, ebrea, israelita ‖ *s.* lingua ebraica.
Hebrewess ['hi:bru:is], *s.* ebrea, israelita.
Hebrewism ['hi:bru:izəm], *s.* ebraismo.
Hebrides (the) ['hebridi:z], *no.pr.pl.* (*geog.*) (Isole) Ebridi.
Hecate ['hekəti(:)], *no.pr.f.* (*mit.*) Ecate.
hecatomb ['hekətoum], *s.* ecatombe.
heckle ['hekl], *V.* **hackle.**
to **heckle,** *v.t.* 1. pettinare (canapa, lino) 2. (*spec. pol.*) sottoporre a domande imbarazzanti.
hectare ['hekta:*], *s.* ettaro (misura di superficie = 2.471 a.).
hectic ['hektik], *ag.* 1. tisico, etico; febbricitante: — *cheeks,* (*poet.*) gote accaldate 2. (*fam.*) febbrile, agitato, movimentato: *a — life,* una vita movimentata ‖ *s.* 1. febbre tubercolare 2. rossore (caratteristico dei tisici) 3. (*rar.*) tisico.
hectically ['hektikəli], *av.* (*fam.*) febbrilmente.
hectogram(me) ['hektougræm], *s.* ettogrammo (misura di peso = 3.527 oz.).
hectograph ['hektougra:f], *s.* poligrafo.
hectolitre ['hektou,li:tə*], *s.* ettolitro (misura di capacità = 22 gal.).
hectometre ['hektou,mi:tə*], *s.* ettometro (misura di lunghezza = 109.36 yd.).
Hector ['hektə*], *no.pr.m.* Ettore ‖ **hector,** *s.* fanfarone, bravaccio, spaccone.
to **hector,** *v.t.i.* 1. fare lo spaccone, il bravaccio 2. strapazzare, malmenare; costringere con soprusi: *to — sthg. out of s.o.,* ottenere ql.co. da qlcu. con prepotenza.
Hecuba ['hekjubə], *no.pr.f.* (*lett.*) Ecuba.
he'd [hi:d], *contr.* di *he had, he would.*
heddle ['hedl], *s. gener. pl.* (*ind. tessile*) liccio ☆ — *-eye,* cappio di liccio; — *-hook,* infilacatene.
to **heddle,** *v.t.* (*ind. tessile*) far passare (le catene) nei licci.
hedge [hedʒ], *s.* 1. siepe 2. barriera (di difesa, protezione); riparo (anche *fig.*) ☆ — *-hyssop,* (*bot.*) graziola; — *-marriage,* matrimonio clandestino; — *-nettle,* (*bot.*) ortica; — *-parson* (o — *-priest*), parroco, prete di bassa estrazione e scarsa cultura; — *-school,* scuola all'aperto, scuola mediocre (per insegnamento); — *-writer,* scrittore mediocre.
to **hedge,** *v.t.i.* 1. chiudere, circondare con siepe, limitare (anche *fig.*): *to — (in) a garden,* circondare un giardino con una siepe ‖ *to — a bet,* scommettere pro e contro 2. evitare di compromettersi; essere elusivo.
hedgehog ['hedʒhɔg], *s.* riccio, porcospino (anche *fig.*).
hedgehoggy ['hedʒ,hɔgi], *ag.* (*fam.*) scontroso, intrattabile.
to **hedgehop** ['hedʒhɔp], *pass.p.p.* **hedgehopped** ['hedʒhɔpt], *v.t.i.* (*aer.*) volare, sorvolare a volo radente.
hedgerow ['hedʒrou], *s.* siepe (divisoria di campi, ecc.).
hedging ['hedʒiŋ], *s.* 1. il cintare con siepi; manutenzione di siepi 2. siepe di cinta 3. (*ippica*) scommessa pro e contro 4. (*comm.*) copertura con operazioni opposte, contropartita.
hedonic [hi'dɔnik], *ag.* che dà piacere.
hedonics [hi'dɔniks], *s.* edonismo, dottrina del piacere.
hedonism ['hi:dənizəm], *s.* edonismo.
hedonist ['hi:dənist], *s.c.* (*fil.*) edonista.
hedonistic [,hi:də'nistik], *ag.* edonistico.
heed [hi:d], *s.* attenzione, cura: *to give* (o *to pay*) — *to,* fare attenzione a; *to take* — *of,* badare a, prestare attenzione a: *to take no* — *of,* non badare a.
to **heed,** *v.t.* fare attenzione a, badare a; dar retta a.
heedful ['hi:dful], *ag.* attento, vigile.

heedfully ['hi:dfuli], *av.* attentamente, con cura.
heedfulness ['hi:dfulnis], *s.* attenzione; vigilanza; cura.
heedless ['hi:dlis], *ag.* stordito, sventato; disattento.
heedlessly ['hi:dlisli], *av.* senza cura; negligentemente; sventatamente.
heedlessness ['hi:dlisnis], *s.* trascuratezza; negligenza; disattenzione.
heedy ['hi:di], *ag.* (*poet.*) attento, cauto.
heehaw ['hi:'hɔ:], *s.* 1. raglio d'asino 2. risata forte, sciocca.
to **heehaw,** *v.i.* 1. ragliare 2. ridere forte, stupidamente.
heel[1] [hi:l], *s.* 1. calcagno, tallone: — *of Achilles,* *fig.* tallone d'Achille; *the — of Italy,* il tallone d'Italia ‖ *at* (o *on*) *s.o.'s heels,* alle calcagna di qlcu.; ‖ *down at —,* scalcagnato (di scarpa); trasandato, al verde (di persona) ‖ *to be under the — of,* essere sotto il dominio di ‖ *to cool* (o *to kick*) *one's heels,* aspettare a lungo ‖ *to show a clean pair of heels* (o *to take to one's heels*), alzare il tacco, svignarsela ‖ *to tread upon s.o.'s heels,* stare alle calcagna di qlcu. ‖ *to turn on one's heels,* voltarsi d'un tratto 2. calcagno (di calza); tacco (di scarpa); parte posteriore dello zoccolo (negli equini); *pl.* (*pop.*) zampa posteriore 3. sperone (degli uccelli) 4. (*mar.*) piede; calcagnolo; maschio; rabazza 5. (*ferr.*) calcio dello scambio 6. (*sl.*) mascalzone ☆ — *-tap,* sopratacco; residuo di liquido in fondo al bicchiere ‖ *rubber —,* tacco di gomma; *stiletto —,* tacco a spillo.
to **heel**[1], *v.t.i.* 1. battere il tacco 2. provvedere di tacco 3. essere alle calcagna di 4. armare (un gallo da combattimento) di sperone d'acciaio 5. (*rugby*) colpire (il pallone) di tacco 6. (*sl. amer.*) rifornire di ql.co. (specialmente di denaro, di un'arma).
heel[2], *s.* (*mar.*) sbandamento.
to **heel**[2], *v.t.i.* (*mar.*) ingavonare, sbandare.
heeling ['hi:liŋ], *s.* riparazione di tacchi.
heft [heft], *s.* (*dial.*) peso; sollevamento (di un peso).
to **heft,** *v.t.* sollevare soppesando.
hefty ['hefti], *ag.* forte, gagliardo, vigoroso.
Hegelian [hei'gi:ljən], *ag.* (*fil.*) hegeliano, di Hegel.
Hegelianism [hei'gi:ljənizəm], *s.* (*fil.*) hegelismo.
hegemonic [,hi(:)gi'mɔnik], *ag.* egemonico.
hegemony [hi(:)'geməni], *s.* egemonia.
hegira ['hedʒirə], *s.* (*st.*) egira.
heifer ['hefə*], *s.* giovenca.
heigh [hei], *inter.* ehi!, eh! ☆ — *-ho,* oh, ahimè!.
height [hait], *s.* 1. altezza: *a monument twelve feet in —,* un monumento alto dodici piedi; *what is your —?,* quanto sei alto? 2. altezza, altitudine (sopra il mare, l'orizzonte): *the village is at a considerable — above sea level,* il villaggio si trova a considerevole altitudine sul livello del mare 3. altura, collina: *the house stood on a —,* la casa sorgeva su un'altura 4. cima, sommità, il più alto grado (anche *fig.*): *the — of folly,* il colmo della pazzia; *the — of the season,* il culmine della stagione ☆ — *-sickness,* mal di montagna.
to **heighten** ['haitn], *v.t.i.* 1. innalzare, innalzarsi 2. accrescere, intensificare, aumentare: *to — one's interest in sthg.,* accrescere l'interesse per ql.co.
heinous ['heinəs], *ag.* odioso, atroce, nefando.
heinously ['heinəsli], *av.* odiosamente; in modo nefando (di delitto).
heinousness ['heinəsnis], *s.* odiosità, nefandezza.
heir [ɛə*], *s.* erede: — *to the Crown,* erede al trono; *the eldest son is usually the —,* il primogenito è generalmente l'erede ☆ — *apparent,* erede in linea diretta; — *-at-law,* erede legittimo, per diritto di sangue; — *-male,* erede maschio (solo per discendenza maschile); — *-presumptive,* erede presunto; — *under a will,* erede testamentario ‖ *sole —,* unico erede; erede universale.
heirdom ['ɛədəm], *s.* condizione di erede.
heiress ['ɛəris], *s.* erede; ereditiera.
heirless ['ɛəlis], *ag.* senza eredi.
heirloom ['ɛəlu:m], *s.* 1. (*dir.*) bene mobile d'famiglia

spettante all'erede legale **2.** cimelio di casa, oggetto appartenente da gran tempo ad una famiglia.

heirship ['ɛəʃip], *s.* condizione di erede.

helcoid ['helkoid], *ag.* (*patol.*) elcoide, ulcerisimile.

helcology [hel'kolədʒi], *s.* (*med.*) elcologia, studio dei fenomeni ulcerativi.

held [held], *pass.p.p.* di to **hold.**

Helen ['helin], **Helena** ['helinə], *no.pr.f.* Elena.

heliacal [hi(:)'laiəkəl], *ag.* (*astr.*) eliaco.

helianthus [,hi:li'ænθəs], *s.* (*bot.*) elianto.

helical ['helikəl], *ag.* spiraliforme.

helically ['helikəli], *av.* a spirale.

helicoid ['helikoid], **helicoidal** [,heli'koidəl], *ag.* elicoidale.

Helicon ['helikən], *no.pr.* (*geog. mit.*) Elicona.

Heliconian [,heli'kounian], *ag.* (*mit.*) eliconio.

helicopter ['helikoptə*], *s.* (*aer.*) elicottero: *the — took off from and landed on that roof,* l'elicottero decollò da quel tetto e vi atterrò di nuovo.

heliocentric(al) [,hi:liou'sentrik(əl)], *ag.* (*astr.*) eliocentrico.

heliochromy ['hi:liou,kroumi], *s.* (*foto.*) eliocromia.

heliograph ['hi:liougra:f], *s.* (*fis.*) eliografo.

heliography [,hi:li'ogrəfi], *s.* (*fis.*) eliografia.

heliogravure [,hi:liougrə'vjuə*], *s.* fotoincisione.

heliolatry [,hi:li'olətri], *s.* (*relig.*) eliolatria.

heliometer [,hi:li'omitə*], *s.* (*astr.*) eliometro.

Helios ['hi:lios], *no.pr.m.* (*mit.*) Elios.

helioscope ['hi:liəskoup], *s.* (*astr.*) elioscopio.

heliostat ['hi:lioustæt], *s.* (*fis.*) eliostato.

heliotherapy [,hi:liou'θerəpi], *s.* (*med.*) elioterapia.

heliotrope ['heljətroup], *s.* **1.** (*bot.*) eliotropio **2.** (*min.*) eliotropia.

heliotropic [,heljə'tropik], *ag.* (*bot.*) eliotropico.

heliotropism [,hi:li'otroupizəm], *s.* (*bot.*) eliotropismo.

heliotypy ['hi:liou,taipi], *s.* (*foto.*) eliotipia.

Heliozoa [,hi:liou'zouə], *s.* (*biol.*) eliozoi.

heliozoan [,hi:liou'zouən], *ag. s.* (*biol.*) (di) eliozoo.

heliport ['helipo:t], *s.* (*aer.*) eliporto.

helium ['hi:ljəm], *s.* (*chim.*) elio.

helix ['hi:liks], *pl.* **helixes** ['hi:liksiz], **helices** ['helisi:z], *s.* **1.** elica; spirale **2.** (*zool.*) elice **3.** (*anat.*) elice **4.** (*arch.*) elice, voluta.

hell [hel], *s.* **1.** inferno (anche *fig.*): *the gates of —,* le porte dell'inferno; *the pains of —,* le pene dell'inferno || *with him!,* vada all'inferno! || *— is let loose,* è un putiferio || *he made a — of a noise,* fece un fracasso d'inferno || *to make one's life a —,* rendere la propria vita un inferno || *to raise —,* (*amer.*) fare un putiferio || *to ride — for leather,* (*fam.*) andare a spron battuto || *to suffer — on earth,* patire l'inferno in terra || *to work like —,* lavorare con accanimento **2.** diavolo!: *what the — do I care?,* che diavolo me ne importa? ☆ — *-cat* (*o* *-hag*), megera.

he'll [hi:l], *contr.* di **he will, he shall.**

hellebore ['helibo:*], *s.* (*bot.*) elleboro.

Hellene ['heli:n], *s. c.* greco, greca.

Hellenic [he'li:nik], *ag.* ellenico, greco.

Hellenism ['helinizəm], *s.* ellenismo.

Hellenist ['helinist], *s.c.* ellenista.

Hellenistic [,heli'nistik], *ag.* ellenistico.

hellish ['heliʃ], *ag.* infernale.

hellishly ['heliʃli], *av.* diabolicamente.

hellishness ['heliʃnis], *s.* perversità, malvagità.

hello [he'lou], *inter.* pronto! (al telefono).

hello-girl ['helou'gə:l], *s.* (*amer.*) telefonista.

helluva ['heləvə], (*sl. amer. contr.* di *hell of a*) grande: *what a — responsibility!,* che tremenda responsabilità!; *to have a — good time,* divertirsi alla follia.

helm¹ [helm], *s.* (*arc.*) elmo, casco ☆ — *-cloud,* nuvola sovrastante la cima di un monte (vocabolo usato nella regione dei laghi inglesi).

to **helm**¹, *v.t.* (*poet.*) fornire di elmo.

helm², *s.* **1.** (*mar.*) timone **2.** *fig.* guida, direzione:

the — of state, il governo; *to shift the —,* girare il timone; *to take the —,* assumere il controllo.

to **helm**², *v.t. fig.* timoneggiare, guidare.

helm³, *s.* (*dial.*) paglia, gambi del grano.

helmet ['helmit], *s.* elmetto, casco ☆ *flying —,* casco da aviatore.

helmeted ['helmitid], *ag.* con l'elmo in capo.

Helminthes [hel'minθi: z], *s.* (*zool. patol.*) elminti.

helminthologist [,helmin'θolədʒist], *s.* elmintologo.

helminthology [,helmin'θolədʒi], *s.* elmintologia.

helmsman, *pl.* **helmsmen** ['helmzmən], *s.* timoniere.

Heloïse [,helou'i:z], *no.pr.f.* (*lett.*) Eloisa.

helot ['helət], *s.* (*st.*) ilota, schiavo.

helotry ['helətri], *s.* (*st.*) ilotia, schiavitù.

help [help], *s.* **1.** aiuto, soccorso: *thank you for your kind —,* grazie per il tuo cortese aiuto; *your work was of great — to me,* il tuo lavoro mi fu di grande aiuto; *to call for —,* invocare aiuto || *by — of,* col favore di: *by — of night,* col favore della notte || *past —,* perduto, irrecuperabile **2.** rimedio: *there is no — for it,* non c'è rimedio a ciò **3.** (*spec. amer.*) persona di servizio ☆ *lady —,* governante di casa; *mother's —,* bambinaia.

to **help,** *v.t.* **1.** (IV, V) aiutare, assistere; soccorrere; dare una mano a: *— me (to) do this, please,* aiutami a fare questo, per piacere; *— me to answer,* aiutami a rispondere; *the old woman was helped into the coach,* la vecchia fu aiutata a salire in carrozza; *she knows how to — herself,* sa come cavarsi d'impiccio || *—!,* aiuto! || *God helps him who helps himself, prov.* aiutati che Dio t'aiuta **2.** contribuire: *this helped to aggravate the offence,* ciò contribuì a rendere più grave la trasgressione **3.** servire (cibo): *may I — you to some meat?,* posso darti un po' di carne?; *to — oneself to (food),* servirsi di (cibo) **4.** (I) evitare, fare a meno di (costruito con *can, cannot*): *he couldn't — laughing,* non potè fare a meno di ridere; *I can't — going,* non posso far a meno di andare; *I can't — it,* non posso farci nulla; *it can't be helped,* è inevitabile **5.** to — **down,** aiutare a scendere **6.** to — **forward,** aiutare a procedere; dare una spinta a (un affare) **7.** to — **in,** aiutare a entrare, a salire (in vettura) **8.** to — **on,** aiutare a procedere || *to — s.o. on with his coat,* aiutare qlcu. a indossare il cappotto **9.** to — **out,** aiutare a uscire **10.** to — **over,** aiutare a sormontare (un ostacolo) **11.** to — **up,** aiutare a salire, ad alzarsi.

helper ['helpə*], *s.c.* aiutante; protettore, protettrice.

helpful ['helpful], *ag.* utile, giovevole, vantaggioso.

helpfully ['helpfuli], *av.* in modo giovevole, utilmente, vantaggiosamente.

helpfulness ['helpfulnis], *s.* utilità, giovamento.

helping ['helpiŋ], *s.* porzione (di cibo): *a second —,* una porzione, razione supplementare.

helpless ['helplis], *ag.* **1.** senza aiuto; indifeso; derelitto: *— and hopeless,* senza risorse; *a — child,* un bimbo derelitto **2.** debole, impotente.

helplessly ['helplisli], *av.* **1.** senza aiuto, senza risorse **2.** debolmente.

helplessness ['helplisnis], *s.* **1.** abbandono **2.** debolezza; impotenza **3.** mancanza d'iniziativa, di risorse.

helpmate ['helpmeit], **helpmeet** ['helpmi:t], *s.c.* collaboratore, collaboratrice; compagno, compagna (generalmente marito, moglie).

helter-skelter ['heltə'skeltə*], *av.* (*fam.*) confusamente, alla rinfusa.

helve [helv], *s.* manico (di arma, utensile).

Helvetia [hel'vi:ʃjə], *no.pr.* (*geog. letter.*) Elvezia.

Helvetian [hel'vi:ʃjən], *ag.* (*letter.*) elvetico || *s.c.* elvetico, elvetica.

Helvetic [hel'vetik], *ag.* (*letter.*) elvetico.

hem¹ [hem], *s.* orlo; bordo, bordura ☆ *open-work —,* orlo a giorno.

to **hem**¹, *pass.p.p.* **hemmed** [hemd], *v.t.* **1.** orlare **2.** *to — in, about, round,* rinchiudere; attorniare, circondare: *to — in an army,* accerchiare un esercito.

hem², *s.* ehm ‖ *inter.* ehm!; olà!.
hem², *inter.* ehm!; olà!.
to **hem²**, *pass.p.p.* **hemmed** [hemd], *v.i.* schiarirsi la voce; tossicchiare ‖ *to — and haw*, esprimere perplessità, esitare.
hem³, (*arc.*) per **them.**
hematic, *V.* **haematic.**
hematite ['hemətait], *s.* (*min.*) ematite.
hemeralopia [,hemərə'loupjə], *s.* (*patol.*) emeralopia.
hemianopsia [,hemiæ'nopsiə], *s.* (*patol.*) emianopsia.
hemicrania [,hemi'kreiniə], *s.* emicrania.
hemionus [hi'maiənəs], *s.* (*zool.*) emiono.
hemiplegia [,hemi'pli:dʒiə], *s.* (*patol.*) emiplegia.
hemiplegic [,hemi'pli:dʒik], *ag.* (*patol.*) emiplegico.
hemisphere ['hemisfiə*], *s.* emisfero.
hemispheric(al) [,hemi'sferik(əl)], *ag.* emisferico.
hemistich ['hemistik], *s.* (*poes.*) emistichio.
hemlock ['hemlɔk], *s.* (*bot.*) 1. cicuta 2. abete canadese.
hemorrhage ['heməridʒ], *s.* (*patol.*) emorragia.
hemorrhagic, *V.* **haemorrhagic.**
hemorrhoidal, *V.* **haemorrhoidal.**
hemorrhoids ['hemərɔidz], *s.pl.* (*patol.*) emorroidi.
hemostatic [,hemou'stætik], *ag.* (*med.*) emostatico.
hemp [hemp], *s.* 1. (*bot.*) canapa 2. (*scherz.*) corda per impiccare ☆ *— oil*, (*ind.*) olio di canapa; *— packing*, (*mec.*) guarnizione di canapa; *— rope*, canapo; *— -seed*, (*bot.*) seme di canapa.
hempen ['hempən], *ag.* di canapa, canapino.
hem-stitch ['hem-stitʃ], *s.* orlo a giorno.
to **hem-stitch**, *v.t.* fare l'orlo a giorno a.
hen [hen], *s.* 1. gallina 2. femmina (di uccelli) ☆ *— -bird*, uccello femmina; *— -coop*, stia; *— -hearted*, pusillanime, codardo; *— -house*, pollaio; *— -party*, riunione di donne sole; *— -roost*, pollaio ‖ *brood —*, chioccia; *guinea- —*, gallina faraona; *pea- —*, pavonessa.
henbane ['henbein], *s.* (*bot.*) giusquiamo.
hence [hens], *av.* 1. di qui a, da questo momento: *four months —*, di qui a quattro mesi 2. donde: *our surprise*, di qui la nostra sorpresa 3. (*arc.*) via di qui, lontano di qui: *— with you!*, va via!.
henceforth ['hens'fɔ:θ], **henceforward** ['hens'fɔ:wəd], *av.* d'ora innanzi, per l'avvenire.
henchman, *pl.* **henchmen** ['hentʃmən], *s.* 1. (*st.*) paggio 2. (*spec. pol.*) seguace, accolito.
hendecagon [hen'dekəgon], *s.* (*geom.*) endecagono.
hendecasyllabic ['hendekəsi'læbik], *ag.* (*poes.*) endecasillabico.
hendecasyllable ['hendekə,silæbl], *s.* (*poes.*) endecasillabo.
hendiadys [hen'daiədis], *s.* (*gram.*) endiadi.
henna ['henə], *s.* 1. (*bot.*) alcanna, « henné » 2. « henné » (tintura).
hennery ['henəri], *s.* pollaio.
henny ['heni], *ag.* simile a gallina; pennuto.
henpecked ['henpekt], *ag.* che si lascia dominare dalla moglie.
Henrietta [,henri'etə], *no.pr.f.* Enrica.
Henry ['henri], *no.pr.m.* Enrico.
hent [hent], *s.* 1. (*arc.*) presa 2. *fig.* intenzione.
to **hent**, *v.t.* 1. (*arc.*) prendere, acchiappare 2. afferrare, capire.
hepatic [hi'pætik], *ag.* (*med.*) epatico.
hepatitis [,hepə'taitis], *s.* (*patol.*) epatite.
hepatization [,hepətai'zeiʃən], *s.* (*patol.*) epatizzazione.
hepatogenous [,hepə'todʒinəs], *ag.* (*med.*) epatogeno.
heptachord ['heptəkɔ:d], *s.* (*mus.*) eptacordo.
heptad ['heptæd], *s.* 1. gruppo di sette 2. (*chim.*) atomo eptavalente.
heptagon ['heptəgən], *s.* (*geom.*) ettagono.
heptagonal [hep'tægənl], *ag.* (*geom.*) ettagonale.
heptahedron ['heptə'hedrən], *s.* (*geom.*) ettaedro.
heptameter [hep'tæmitə*], *s.* (*poes.*) ettametro.
heptarchy ['heptɑ:ki], *s.* eptarchia, governo a sette.

heptasyllabic [,heptəsi'læbik], *ag.* (*poes.*) eptasillabo, settenario.
Heptateuch ['heptətju:k], *s.* (*Bibbia*) Eptateuco.
her [hə:*], *ag.poss.* 3ª persona sing. (*riferito a possessore f.*) suo, sua, suoi, sue: *— books*, i suoi libri; *— father*, suo padre; *— mother*, sua madre; *— suit-cases*, le sue valigie ‖ *pron.pers.f.* 3ª persona sing. (*caso obliquo di she*) la, lei, le, colei, sè: *go with —*, andate con lei; *I saw —*, la vidi; *she took her little son with —*, portò il figlioletto con sè; *tell — I'm here*, ditele che sono qui; *tell — so*, diteglielo ‖ *it's —*, (*fam.*) è lei.
Heracles ['herəkli:z], *no.pr.m.* (*mit.*) Eracle.
herald ['herəld], *s.* 1. (*st.*) araldo 2. nunzio, messaggero; (*fig.*) precursore, foriero 3. araldista.
to **herald**, *v.t.* annunziare.
heraldic [he'rældik], *ag.* araldico.
heraldry ['herəldri], *s.* araldica.
herb [hə:b], *s.* 1. erba, pianta erbacea 2. (*cuc.*) erba, odore 3. pianta, erba medicinale ☆ *— -(of-)grace* (o *-of-repentance*), (*bot.*) ruta; *— -tea* (o *-water*), tisana, decotto di erbe.
herbaceous [hə:'beifəs], *ag.* erbaceo.
herbage ['hə:bidʒ], *s.* 1. vegetazione erbacea 2. (*dir.*) diritto di pascolo.
herbal ['hə:bəl], *ag.* di erba ‖ *s.* erbario (libro contenente descrizione di piante).
herbalist ['hə:bəlist], *s.* erborista.
herbarium [hə:'bɛəriəm], *pl.* **herbariums** [hə:'bɛəriəmz], **herbaria** [hə:'bɛəriə], *s.* erbario (raccolta classificata di erbe e piante disseccate).
Herbert ['hə:bət], *no.pr.m.* Erberto.
herbescent [hə:'besnt], *ag.* che diventa erba; che cresce come erba.
herbiferous [hə:'bifərəs], *ag.* erbifero, erboso.
herbivorous [hə:'bivərəs], *ag.* erbivoro.
herbless ['hə:blis], *ag.* senza erba, brullo.
herblet ['hə:blit], *s.* (*poet.*) erbetta.
herborist ['hə:bərist], *s.* erborista.
herborization [,hə:bərai'zeiʃən], *s.* erborizzazione.
to **herborize** ['hə:bəraiz], *v.i.* erborizzare.
herbose ['hə:bous], **herbous** ['hə:bəs], *ag.* erboso.
herby ['hə:bi], *ag.* erboso; erbaceo.
Herculaneum [,hə:kju'leinjəm], *no.pr.* (*geog.*) Ercolano.
Herculean [,hə:kju'li:(:)ən], *ag.* erculeo.
Hercules ['hə:kjuli:z], *no.pr.m.* (*mit.*) Ercole ‖ *s.* (*astr.*) costellazione di Ercole.
herd¹ [hə:d], *s.* 1. gregge, mandria 2. massa, moltitudine (di gente): *the —*, la massa, il popolo.
to **herd¹**, *v.t.i.* formare gregge, ammassarsi; riunire (il bestiame) in gregge: *to — together*, riunirsi in gregge (anche *fig.*).
herd², *s.* mandriano, pastore.
to **herd²**, *v.t.i.* condurre il bestiame; pascolare, pascere (il bestiame).
herdboy ['hə:dbɔi], *s.* aiuto mandriano.
herdsman, *pl.* **herdsmen** ['hə:dzmən], *s.* mandriano, pastore.
here [hiə*], *av.* qui, qua; *quaggiù: — and there*, qui e là; *— and there and everywhere*, ovunque; *— I am*, sono qui; *— are you!*, (*fam.*) ecco qui! (ciò che cerchi); *come —!*, vieni qui!; *look —!*, guarda, bada, sta' attento!; senti! ‖ *—!*, presente! ‖ *— goes!*, (*fam.*) ecco, si comincia! ‖ *—'s health to you!*, alla tua salute! ‖ *from —*, di qui; *up —*, qui su.
hereabout(s) ['hiərə,baut(s)], *av.* qui intorno, qui presso: *he does not belong —*, non è di queste parti.
hereafter [hiər'ɑ:ftə*], *s.* vita futura; l'al di là: *in the —*, all'altro mondo.
hereafter, *av.* d'ora innanzi, in futuro.
hereat [hiər'æt], *av.* (*arc.*) a ciò, su ciò, al che; quando avvenne questo.
hereby ['hiə'bai], *av.* 1. con questo mezzo 2. qui vicino.
hereditability [hi,reditə'biliti], *s.* ereditabilità.
hereditable [hi'reditəbl], *ag.* ereditabile.

hereditament [,heri'ditəmənt], *s.* (*dir.*) beni trasmissibili per eredità; eredità.

hereditarian [hi,redi'tɛəriən], *s.* sostenitore delle teorie sull'ereditarietà.

hereditarily [hi'reditərili], *av.* ereditariamente.

hereditariness [hi'reditərinis], *s.* ereditarietà.

hereditary [hi'reditəri], *ag.* ereditario.

hereditism [hi'reditizəm], **heredity** [hi'rediti], *s.* ereditarietà.

herein ['hiər'in], *av.* in questo; (*comm.*) nella presente (lettera).

hereinafter ['hiərin'ɑːftə*], *av.* dopo, più avanti (in questo documento).

hereinbefore ['hiərinbi'fɔ:*], *av.* prima, più sopra (in questo documento).

hereof [hiər'ɔv], *av.* (*arc.*) a questo riguardo; di ciò.

heresiarch [he'riːziɑːk], *s.* eresiarca.

heresy ['herəsi], *s.* eresia ☆ — -*hunter*, inquisitore.

heretic ['herətik], *ag.* eretico || *s.c.* eretico, eretica.

heretical [hi'retikəl], *ag.* eretico.

heretically [hi'retikəli], *av.* ereticamente.

to **hereticate** [hi'retikeit], *v.t.* (*rar.*) denunciare come eretico.

hereto ['hiə'tu:], *av.* (*comm. dir.*) a questo; con riferimento; allegato a questo.

heretofore ['hiətu'fɔ:*], *av.* (*dir.*) prima, prima d'ora: *as* —, come precedentemente.

hereunder [hiər'ʌndə*], *av.* qui sotto.

hereupon ['hiərə'pɔn], *av.* al che, in conseguenza di questo.

herewith ['hiə'wiô], *av.* qui accluso: *we are sending* —, con la presente vi inviamo.

heritable ['heritəbl], *ag.* ereditabile.

heritables ['heritəblz], *s.pl.* (*scoz. dir.*) proprietà ereditaria.

heritage ['heritidʒ], *s.* **1.** eredità; patrimonio (anche *fig.*) **2.** (*eccl.*) il popolo eletto; la Chiesa.

heritor ['heritə*], *s.c.* erede.

herma ['hə:mə], *s.* erma, statua.

Herman ['hə:mən], *no.pr.m.* Armando.

hermaphrodism [hə:'mæfrədizəm], *s.* ermafroditismo.

hermaphrodite [hə:'mæfrədait], *ag. s.* ermafrodito.

hermaphroditic(al) [hə:,mæfrə'ditik(əl)], *ag.* ermafrodito.

hermaphroditism [hə:'mæfrədaitizəm], *s.* ermafroditismo.

hermeneutic(al) [,hə:mi'nju:tik(əl)], *ag.* ermeneutico, interpretativo.

hermeneutics [,hə:mi'nju:tiks], *s.* ermeneutica.

Hermes ['hə:mi:z], *no.pr.m.* (*mit.*) Ermes, Mercurio.

hermetic [hə:'metik], *ag.* ermetico.

hermetically [hə:'metikəli], *av.* ermeticamente.

Hermione [hə:'maiəni], *no.pr.f.* (*mit.*) Ermione.

hermit ['hə:mit], *s.* eremita ☆ — -*crab*, (*zool.*) paguro.

hermitage ['hə:mitidʒ], *s.* **1.** eremo, eremitaggio **2.** *Hermitage*, varietà di vino francese.

hernia ['hə:njə], *s.* (*patol.*) ernia.

hernial ['hə:njəl], *ag.* erniario.

hero ['hiərou], *pl.* **heroes** ['hiərouz], *s.* **1.** eroe: *the* — *of heroes*, il sommo eroe **2.** protagonista (di commedia, romanzo); persona celebre — -*worship*, culto degli eroi.

Herod ['herəd], *no.pr.m.* (*st.*) Erode.

heroic [hi'rouik], *ag.* eroico, di eroe || *s.* **1.** verso eroico **2.** *pl.* frasi, linguaggio pomposo, retorico, stravagante ☆ — *couplet*, (*poes.*) distico di pentametri giambici a rima baciata; — *poetry*, poesia epica; — *verse*, (*poes.*) verso eroico || *mock-* —, eroicomico.

heroical [hi'rouikəl], *ag.* eroico, di eroe.

heroically [hi'rouikəli], *av.* eroicamente.

heroicalness [hi'rouikəlnis], *s.* eroicità.

heroicomic(al) [hi,roui'komik(əl)], *ag.* eroicomico.

to **heroify** [hi'rouifai], *v.t.* eroicizzare.

heroin ['herouin], *s.* (*chim.*) eroina.

heroine ['herouin], *s.* eroina.

heroism ['herouizəm], *s.* eroismo.

to **heroize** ['hiərouaiz],*v.t.i.* posare da eroe; eroicizzare.

heron ['herən], *s.* (*ornit.*) airone.

herpes ['hə:pi:z], *s.* (*patol.*) erpete.

herpetic [hə:'petik], *ag.* (*patol.*) erpetico.

herpetologist [,hə:pi'tolədʒist], *s.* erpetologo.

herpetology [,hə:pi'tolədʒi], *s.* erpetologia.

herring ['heriŋ], *s.* (*gener. invariato al pl.*) aringa: *kippered red* —, aringa affumicata || *to draw a red* — *across the track*, distogliere l'attenzione, creare un diversivo ☆ — -*bone*, a lisca di pesce; — -*bone stitch*, punto strega; — -*pond*, (*scherz.*) l'Atlantico del Nord.

hers [hə:z], *pron.poss.* (*riferito a possessore f.*) il suo, la sua, i suoi, le sue: *all these books are* —, tutti questi libri sono suoi; *this hat is mine and that is* —, questo cappello è mio e quello è suo; *your eyes are black and* — *are blue*, i tuoi occhi sono neri ed i suoi azzurri || *that sister of* —, quella sua sorella.

hersal ['hə:səl], (*arc.*) *abbr.* di **rehearsal.**

herself [hə:'self], *pron.* 3ª *persona sing.f.* **1.** *r.* si, sè, se stessa: *she hurt* —, si fece male; *she spoke of* —, ella parlò di sè || (*all*) *by* —, da sola **2.** (*enfatico*) **ella** stessa: *she told me* — (o *she* — *told me*), lei stessa me lo disse || *s.* ella stessa: *she was not* —, non era in sè.

Hertzian ['hə:tsiən], *ag.* (*fis.*) hertziano: — *waves*, onde hertziane.

he's [hi:z], *contr.* di *he is, he has.*

Hesiod ['hi:siəd], *no.pr.m.* (*st. lett.*) Esiodo.

hesitance ['hezitəns], **hesitancy** ['hezitənsi], *s.* esitazione, titubanza.

hesitant ['hezitənt], *ag.* esitante, titubante.

to **hesitate** ['heziteit], *v.i.* esitare, titubare.

hesitating ['heziteitiŋ], *ag.* esitante.

hesitatingly ['heziteitiŋli], *av.* con esitazione.

hesitation [,hezi'teiʃən], *s.* **1.** esitazione **2.** « hesitation » (*tipo di danza*) **3.** balbuzie.

hesitative ['heziteitiv], *ag.* incline all'esitazione.

hesitator ['heziteitə*], *s.* chi esita; chi è in dubbio.

hesitatory ['heziteitəri], *ag.* esitante.

Hesperian [hes'piəriən], *ag.* (*poet.*) esperio.

Hesperides [hes'peridi:z], *no.pr.pl.* (*mit.*) Esperidi.

hesperis ['hespəris], *s.* (*bot.*) esperide.

hesperornis [,hespə'rɔ:nis], *s.* (*paleont.*) esperornide.

Hesperus ['hespərəs], *no.pr.* (*astr. poet.*) Espero.

Hessian ['hesiən], *ag.* di Hesse || *s.c.* abitante di Hesse || *s.* **1.** tela rozza di canapa **2.** (*amer.*) mercenario ☆ — *boots*, tipo di stivaloni portati originariamente dalle truppe di Hesse; — *fly*, (*entom.*) cecidomia.

hest [hest], *s.* (*arc.*) comando, ordine.

hesternal [hes'tə:nl], *ag.* di ieri.

hetaera [hi'tiərə], *s.* (*st.*) etera.

hetaerism [hi'tiərizəm], *s.* concubinaggio.

heteroclite ['hetərouklait], *ag.* eteroclito, irregolare || *s.* sostantivo eteroclito; irregolare.

heterodox ['hetərədɔks], *ag.* eterodosso.

heterodoxy ['hetərədɔksi], *s.* eterodossia.

heterodyne ['hetərədain], *s.* (*rad.*) eterodina.

heterogeneity [,hetəroudʒi'ni:iti], *s.* eterogeneità.

heterogeneous ['hetərou'dʒi:njəs], *ag.* eterogeneo.

heterogeneousness ['hetərou'dʒi:njəsnis], *s.* eterogeneità.

heterogenesis [,hetərou'dʒenisis], *s.* (*biol.*) eterogenesi.

heteromorphic [,hetərou'mɔ:fik], *ag.* eteromorfo.

heteromorphism [,hetərou'mɔ:fizəm], *s.* eteromorfismo.

heteromorphous [,hetərou'mɔ:fəs], *ag.* eteromorfo.

heteronomous [,hetə'rɔnəməs], *ag.* eteronomo.

heteronomy [,hetə'rɔnəmi], *s.* eteronomia.

heterozygote [,hetərou'zaigout], *s.* (*biol.*) eterozigote.

Hetty ['heti], *no.pr.f. dim.* di **Henriette, Hester.**

heuristic [hjuə'ristik], *ag.* (*fil.*) euristico || *s.* (*fil.*) euristica.

to **hew** [hju:], *pass.* **hewed** [hju:d], *p.p.* **hewed, hewn** [hju:n], *v.t.* **1.** spaccare, fendere, tagliare (con l'ascia): *to — to pieces*, fare a pezzi ‖ *to — one's way (through...)*, farsi largo a fatica (attraverso...) **2.** *to — down*, abbattere **3.** *to — out*, sbozzare: *to — out a statue*, sbozzare una statua ‖ *to — out a career for oneself*, farsi una carriera con grandi sforzi.

hewer ['hju:ə*], *s.* **1.** tagliatore **2.** spaccalegna.

hewn [hju:n], *ag.* tagliato, sbozzato: *— timber, legname* rifilato.

hex [heks], *s.c.* (*amer.*) strega, stregone.

hexachord ['heksəko:d], *s.* (*mus.*) esacordo.

hexagon ['heksəgən], *s.* (*geom.*) esagono.

hexagonal [hek'sægənl], *ag.* (*geom.*) esagonale.

hexahedron ['heksə'hedrən], *s.* (*geom.*) esaedro.

hexameter [hek'sæmitə*], *s.* (*poès.*) esametro.

hexangular [hek'sængjulə*], *ag.* (*geom.*) esangolare.

hexapetalous [,heksə'petələs], *ag.* (*bot.*) esapetalo.

hexapod ['heksəpod], *ag.* (*entom.*) esapodo.

hexastich ['heksəstik], *s.* poesia, stanza di sei versi.

hexastyle ['hehsəstail], *ag.* (*arc.*) esastilo ‖ *s.* (*arch.*) edificio esastilo.

hey [hei], *inter.* eh!, eh!.

heyday ['heidei], *s.* (*solo sing.*) apogeo; epoca di maggiore prosperità; vigore: *in the — of his career*, all'apice della sua carriera; *in her —*, ai suoi bei giorni.

hey-day, *inter.* oh!, ih!.

hi [hai], *inter.* **1.** oh!, ih! (esprimente derisione, meraviglia) **2.** (*amer.*) ciao!.

hiatus [hai'eitəs], *s.* **1.** iato **2.** lacuna; interruzione.

hibernacle ['haibə:nikl], *s.* riparo per l'inverno.

hibernal [hai'bə:nl], *ag.* (*poet.*) invernale.

hibernant ['haibə:nənt], *ag.* ibernante.

to **hibernate** ['haibə:neit], *v.i.* **1.** svernare **2.** essere, rimanere in letargo invernale, in ibernazione.

hibernation [,haibə:'neiʃən], *s.* **1.** svernamento **2.** letargo, ibernazione.

Hibernia [hai'bə:njə], *no.pr.* (*st. geog.*) Irlanda.

Hibernian [hai'bə:njən], *ag.s.c.* (*st. geog.*) irlandese.

Hibernicism [hai'bə:nisizəm], *s.* espressione tipica irlandese.

hibiscus [hi'biskəs], *s.* (*bot.*) ibisco.

hiccough, hiccup ['hikʌp], *s.* singhiozzo, singulto.

to **hiccough**, to **hiccup**, *v.t.* **1.** avere il singhiozzo **2.** dire fra i singhiozzi.

hick [hik], *s.* (*amer. fam.*) provinciale, rusticone.

hickory ['hikəri], *s.* «hickory», noce d'America.

hickwall ['hikwo:l], *s.* (*ornit.*) picchio verde.

hid [hid], *pass. p.p.* di to **hide**[3].

hidalgo [hi'dælgou], *s.* «hidalgo», gentiluomo, nobile.

hidden ['hidn], *p.p.* di to **hide**[3] ‖ *ag.* **1.** nascosto; segreto: *— reserves*, riserve segrete **2.** sconosciuto.

hiddenly ['hidnli], *av.* nascostamente; segretamente.

hiddenmost ['hidnmoust], *ag.* il più recondito.

hide[1] [haid], *s.* **1.** cuoio, pelle: *to dress hides*, lavorare il cuoio **2.** (*scherz.*) pelle umana: *to save one's own —*, salvare la pelle **3.** frusta, scudiscio di cuoio ☆ *-bound*, ridotto a pelle ed ossa (di animali); *fig.* dalla mente ristretta, piena di pregiudizi.

to **hide**[1], *v.t.* **1.** spellare, scorticare **2.** (*sl.*) frustare.

hide[2], *s.* (*st.*) misura agraria equivalente a 48 ettari.

hide[3], *s.* nascondiglio ☆ *-and-seek*, giuoco del rimpiattino; *—away*, fuggiasco; nascondiglio.

to **hide**[3], *pass.* **hid** [hid], *p.p.* **hid, hidden** ['hidn], *v.t.i.* **1.** nascondere, nascondersi; celare, celarsi: *they hid behind the house*, si nascosero dietro la casa; *why do you — it from me?*, perchè me lo nascondi?; *to — one's face*, nascondersi il viso ‖ *to — (away) from s.o.*, nascondersi a qlcu. **2.** *to — out*, (*fam.*) star nascosto.

hideous ['hidiəs], *ag.* orrendo, spaventevole; odioso: *a — crime*, un orrendo delitto.

hideously ['hidiəsli], *av.* orrendamente.

hideousness ['hidiəsnis], *s.* aspetto orribile; odiosità.

hideout ['haidaut], *s.* nascondiglio.

hider ['haidə*], *s.c.* **1.** chi si nasconde **2.** dissimulatore, dissimulatrice.

hiding[1] ['haidiŋ], *s.* **1.** il nascondere **2.** *— (-place)*, nascondiglio.

hiding[2], *s.* (*sl.*) bastonatura: *to give s.o. a good —*, dare a qlcu. una buona bastonatura; rimproverare aspramente qlcu.

hidrotic [hi'drotik], *ag.s.* sudorifero.

to **hie** [hai], *v.i.* (*poet.*) affrettarsi; correre: *to — to a place*, correre in un luogo.

hiemal ['haiiməl], *ag.* (*poet.*) iemale, invernale.

hiems ['haiemz], *s.* (*poet.*) inverno.

hierarch ['haiəra:k], *s.* prelato.

hierarchic(al) [,haiə'ra:kik(əl)], *ag.* gerarchico.

hierarchism ['haiəra:kizəm], *s.* gerarchismo.

hierarchy ['haiəra:ki], *s.* gerarchia.

hieratic [,haiə'rætik], *ag.* ieratico.

hieroglyph ['haiərəglif], *s.* geroglifico.

hieroglyphic(al) [,haiərə'glifik(əl)], *ag.* geroglifico.

hieroglyphically [,haiərə'glifikəli], *av.* geroglificamente.

hierogram ['haiərougræm], *s.* gerogramma.

hierographic(al) [,haiərə'græfik(əl)], *ag.* gerografico.

Hieronymite [,haiə'ronimait], *s.* (*eccl.*) geronimita.

Hieronymus [,haiə'roniməs], *no.pr.m.* Geronimo; Gerolamo.

hierophant ['haiərəfænt], *s.* (*st. greca*) gerofante.

Hierosolymitan [,haiərə'solimaitən], *ag.* di Gerusalemme ‖ *s.* gerosolimitano.

to **higgle** ['higl], *v.i.* tirare sul prezzo.

higgledy-piggledy ['higldi'pigldi], *av.* alla rinfusa.

high [hai], *ag.* **1.** alto, elevato (anche *fig.*); principale; importante: *"How — is that building?"*, *"It is 100 feet (o foot) —"*, «Quanto è alto quell'edificio?», «È alto 100 piedi»; *she has a — mind*, ha uno spirito nobile; *to be — in office*, occupare una posizione importante; *to have a — opinion of s.o.*, avere un'alta opinione di qlcu.; *to set a — value on sthg.*, attribuire un alto valore a ql.co. ‖ *higher education*, istruzione superiore; *higher mathematics*, matematica superiore; *higher up the river*, a monte del fiume; *he belongs to the higher classes*, appartiene alla classe dirigente; *the sun is getting higher*, il sole avanza nel cielo; *to appoint s.o. to a higher post*, promuovere qlcu. di grado ‖ *in the highest degree*, al più alto grado; per eccellenza; *in the highest sense of the word*, nel senso più completo della parola ‖ *— and low*, i ricchi e i poveri ‖ *— sea*, mare grosso, agitato ‖ *— spirits*, spirito vivace, umore gaio ‖ *— stakes*, alta posta (in scommesse): *to play for — stakes*, scommettere forte ‖ *The Most High(est)*, l'Altissimo, Iddio ‖ *to be left — and dry*, essere lasciato in secco (di nave); *fig.* venire abbandonato senza aiuto ‖ *to speak of s.o. in — terms*, parlare di qlcu. in termini lusinghieri ‖ *to stand — with*, essere stimato da **2.** altezzoso, arrogante ‖ *with a — hand*, con arroganza arbitraria; *to be — and mighty*, essere arrogante, darsi delle arie; *to be on one's — horse* (o *to ride the — horse*), far l'arrogante **3.** forte, intenso (di luce, colore): *a — colour*, un colore acceso **4.** costoso, caro: *sugar is not — now*, lo zucchero non è caro ora **5.** pieno, avanzato (di tempo, stagione, ecc.): *— noon*, pieno meriggio; *— summer*, piena estate ‖ *it is — time for me to go*, è ora che me ne vada; *it is — time he earned sthg.*, sarebbe ora che cominciasse a guadagnare ql.co. **6.** alto, acuto (di suono): *he always speaks in a — voice*, parla sempre a voce alta **7.** troppo frollo, alterato (di carne); forte (di sapore): *this fish has a — smell*, questo pesce puzza ☆ *— -admiral*, grande ammiraglio; *— -altar*, altare maggiore; *— -blooded*, di sangue nobile; *— -board*, (*amer.*) trampolino; *— -born*, di alto lignaggio, nobile di nascita; *— -bred*, allevato nell'alta società; puro sangue (di cavallo); *-bridged*, arcuato (di naso); *— -chair*, seggiolone (per bambini); *High-Church*, Chiesa Alta (partizione della Chiesa Anglicana); *High-Churchman*, membro della Chiesa Alta; *— -class*, (*fam.*) di prim'ordine, di prima classe, eccellente; *— -coloured*, dal colore acceso; *— -court*, corte suprema; *— -day*, festa solenne;

giorno importante, memorabile; — *-explosive*, alto esplosivo; — *-fed*, ben nutrito; — *-fidelity*, (*neol. acu.*) alta fedeltà; — *-flier*, che vola in alto (di falco); ambizioso, che ama mettersi in vista (di persona); — *flown*, roboante, altisonante; — *-frequency*, (*elett.*) ad alta frequenza; *High German*, Alto Tedesco; — *-grade*, di alto grado (di funzionario, merce, minerale, ecc.); — *-handed*, arbitrario; violento, tirannico; — *-hearted*, pieno di coraggio; — *jump*, (*spor.*) salto in alto; — *-keyed*, (*mus.*) di tono alto; *fig.* sensibile; nervoso, con i nervi tesi; — *life*, (vita di) alta società; — *-light*, « clou », culmine; personalità: *the — -light of the performance*, il « clou » dello spettacolo; *the lights of the town*, le personalità della città; *High Mass*, Messa alta; — *-mettled*, focoso (di cavallo); intrepido (di cavaliere); — *-minded*, nobile d'animo, di pensiero; — *money*, (*amer. comm.*) denaro a tasso alto; — *-necked*, accollato (di abito, ecc.); — *-octane*, (*neol. ind. chim.*) ad alto numero di ottano; — *-pitched*, acuto (di suono); nobile (di pensiero); — *-power(ed)*, (*elett.*) ad alta potenza; — *-priced*, dal prezzo alto; — *-priest*, sommo sacerdote; *fig.* capo riconosciuto; — *-principled*, di alti princìpi; — *-raised* (o *-reared*), elevato, sopraelevato; — *-ranker*, persona elevata; — *-road*, strada maestra, strada principale, nazionale; *fig.* via facile, diretta; — *school*, (*amer.*) scuola media; — *sea*, mare aperto; — *-seasoned*, piccante, saporito; — *-souled*, di spirito nobile, elevato; — *-sounding*, sonoro; latisonante; — *-speed*, ad alta velocità; — *-spirited*, energico, audace, intrepido; vivace; — *-stepper*, cavallo che si impenna facilmente; persona coraggiosa; di grande intelligenza; *High Street*, strada principale; — *-tasted*, piccante; — *tea*, tè abbondante in sostituzione della cena; — *tension* (o — *voltage*), (*elett.*) alta tensione; — *-tide*, alta marea; (*rar.*) grande festa; — *-toned*, di tono elevato (anche *fig.*); — *-treason*, alto tradimento; — *-water*, alta marea.

high, *s.* **1.** ciò che sta in alto; il Cielo, l'Alto: *God on* —, Dio in Cielo **2.** (*meteorologia*) anticiclone, area di alta pressione.

high, *av.* **1.** alto, in alto (anche *fig.*): *he was flying at 3000 feet* —, volava a un'altezza di 3000 piedi; *to aim* —, mirare in alto; *to rise* — *in s.o.'s esteem*, crescere nella stima di qlcu. ‖ — *and low*, ovunque: *to search* (o *to hunt*) — *and low for sthg.*, cercare ql.co. per mare e per terra ‖ *to live* —, vivere nell'abbondanza, nell'agiatezza ‖ *to play, to stake* —, giocare, scommettere forte **2.** forte, fortemente: *to blow* —, soffiare violentemente (di vento); *to run* —, essere agitato (anche *fig.*): *popular feeling ran* —, il sentimento popolare era profondamente scosso; *the sea runs* —, il mare è agitato.

highball ['haibɔ:l], *s.* **1.** (*amer.*) whisky e soda con ghiaccio **2.** (*ferr.*) treno rapido; segnale di via libera.

highbrow ['hai-brau], *s.* intellettuale.

high-falutin ['hai-fə'lu:tin], **high-faluting** ['hai-fə'lu:tiŋ], *ag.* ampolloso ‖ *s.* discorso ampolloso.

highland ['hailənd], *s.* (*geog.*) regione montuosa ‖ *the Highlands*, la regione montuosa al nord della Scozia.

highlander ['hailəndə*], *s.* montanaro ‖ *Highlander*, abitante della regione montuosa al nord della Scozia.

highly ['haili], *av.* **1.** molto, estremamente, assai: — *amusing*, assai divertente; — *coloured*, di colore vivacissimo; — *paid*, pagato lautamente **2.** nobilmente, altamente: — *descended*, di alto lignaggio; *to think* — *of s.o.*, tenere qlcu. in molta considerazione.

highmost ['haimoust], *ag.* il più alto, altissimo.

highness ['hai-nis], *s.* **1.** altezza; elevatezza **2.** eccellenza; valore **3.** altezza (titolo) ‖ *His Royal Highness*, Sua Altezza Reale.

high-pressure ['hai'preʃə*], *ag.* **1.** ad alta pressione **2.** intenso; urgente ‖ *s.* alta, forte pressione.

hight [hait], *p.p. dall'arc. to* **hight** (*poet. scherz.*) detto; chiamato: *a maiden* — *Elaine*, una fanciulla chiamata Elena.

high-up ['haiʌp], *ag.* altolocato; importante ‖ *s.* (*fam.*) personaggio importante.

highway ['haiwei], *s.* **1.** strada maestra **2.** (*amer.*) autostrada: — *with six lanes*, autostrada con sei carreggiate **3.** (*mar.*) rotta.

highwayman, *pl.* **highwaymen** ['haiweimən], *s.* bandito, rapinatore.

to hijack ['haidʒæk], *v.t.* (*amer. fam.*) derubare (automobilisti) di alcoolici di contrabbando.

hijacker ['haidʒækə*], *s.* (*amer. fam.*) rapinatore di contrabbandieri di alcoolici (al tempo del proibizionismo).

hike [haik], *s.* (*fam.*) escursione a piedi in campagna; vagabondaggio.

to hike, *v.t.i.* **1.** fare un'escursione a piedi in campagna; vagabondare **2.** spingere; costringere a muoversi; issare.

hilarious [hi'lɛəriəs], *ag.* ilare; allegro.

hilariously [hi'lɛəriəsli], *av.* con ilarità; allegramente.

hilariousness [hi'lɛəriəsnis], **hilarity** [hi'læriti], *s.* ilarità; gaiezza; allegria.

Hilary ['hiləri], *no.pr. m.* Ilario.

hill [hil], *s.* collina; colle; altura: *steep* —, colle ripido ‖ *up* — *and down dale*, *fig.* per monti e per valli ☆ — *-folk*, montanari; setta dei Cameroniani scozzesi; elfi ed altri spiritelli della montagna e delle colline; — *-station*, (*ang.-in.*) luogo di cura o soggiorno in montagna ‖ *ant-* —, formicaio; *buried* —, rilievo sepolto, paleocatena.

hilliness ['hilinis], *s.* natura collinosa.

hillo ['hilou], *V.* **hallo(a)**.

hillock ['hilək], *s.* monticello, collinetta.

hillside ['hil'said], *s.* pendio.

hilltop ['hil'tɔp], *s.* sommità della collina.

hilly ['hili], *ag.* collinoso.

hilt [hilt], *s.* elsa ‖ *to prove up to the* —, provare, dimostrare pienamente.

hilum ['hailəm], *s.* (*bot.*) ilo.

him [him], *pron.pers.m.* 3ª *persona sing.* (*caso obliquo di he*) lo, lui, gli, colui, sè: *I heard* —, lo sentii; *tell* — *his friends are here*, digli che i suoi amici sono qui; *William took his daughter with* —, Guglielmo portò sua figlia con sè; *you may come along with* —, puoi venire con lui ‖ *it's* —, (*fam.*) è lui.

Himalaya [,himə'leiə], *no.pr.* (*geog.*) Imalaia.

Himalayan [,himə'leiən], *ag.* imalaiano ‖ *s.c.* imalaiano, imalaiana.

himself [him'self], *pron.* 3ª *persona sing.m.* **1.** *r.* si, sè, se stesso: *he cut* —, si tagliò ‖ (*all) by* —, da solo **2.** (*enfatico*) egli stesso: *he told me* — (o *he told me*), egli stesso me lo disse ‖ *s.* egli stesso: *he was not* —, non era in sè.

hind¹ [haind], *s.* (*zool.*) cerva; daina.

hind², *s.* **1.** contadino, villico; fattore **2.** (*scoz.*) bracciante agricolo (che ha cura di due cavalli e vive in una casetta della fattoria).

hind³, *ag.* posteriore, che è dietro ☆ — *-legs*, gambe, zampe posteriori; — *-quarters*, posteriore (di animali); — *-wheels*, ruote posteriori.

hinder ['haində*], *ag.* posteriore: *the* — *part*, la parte posteriore.

to hinder ['hində*], *v.t.i.* **1.** impedire: *they hindered him from doing his work*, gli impedirono di fare il proprio lavoro **2.** ostruire; imbarazzare, inceppare; ritardare: *lack of material hindered me in my research*, la mancanza di materiale mi ostacolò nella ricerca.

hindermost ['haindəmoust], *ag.* (*superl.* di *hind³*) ultimo; il più lontano ‖ *every one for himself and the Devil take the* —, ognuno per sè e Dio per tutti; si salvi chi può.

Hindi ['hin'di:], *ag.s.* (dialetto indiano) dell'India del Nord.

hindmost ['haindmoust], *V.* **hindermost**.

Hindoo ['hin'du:], *ag.s.c.* indù.

hindrance ['hindrəns], *s.* ostacolo; impaccio.

Hindu ['hin'du:], *ag.s.c.* indù.

Hinduism ['hindu(:)izəm], *s.* (*relig.*) induismo.

Hindustan [,hindu'sta:n], *no.pr.* (*geogr.*) Indostan.

Hindustanee, Hindustani [,hindu'sta:ni], *s.* dialetto indostano.

hinge [hindʒ], *s.* **1.** cardine; ganghero; cerniera: *a door off its hinges*, una porta scardinata ‖ *to be off one's hinges*, (*fam.*) essere fuori dai gangheri, essere sconvolto **2.** *fig.* perno, punto principale: *it is the — of the matter*, è il perno della faccenda ☆ *— -joint*, (*anat.*) ginglimo.

to hinge, *v.t.i.* **1.** munire di cardini; girare sui cardini **2.** *fig.* dipendere: *everything hinges on what he decides*, tutto dipende da ciò che deciderà.

hinny ['hini], *s.* (*zool.*) bardotto.

to hinny, *v.i.* nitrire.

hint [hint], *s.* **1.** cenno; accenno; avviso; menzione; allusione: *broad —*, allusione evidente; *gentle —*, lieve accenno; *to give a —*, fare un accenno, dare un suggerimento; *to take a —*, intendere a volo **2.** consiglio: *hints for housewives*, consigli per le massaie; *can you give me a —?*, puoi darmi un consiglio?.

to hint, *v.t.i.* accennare; suggerire; insinuare; alludere: *to — at sthg.*, lasciare intendere ql.co., lasciare intravvedere ql.co.

hinterland ['hintəlænd], *s.* retroterra.

hip[1] [hip] **1.** (*anat.*) anca, fianco: *to sway one's hips in walking*, camminare ancheggiando ‖ *to catch s.o. on the —*, sopraffare qlcu. ‖ *to have s.o. on the —*, (*fam.*) essere in vantaggio su qlcu. **2.** (*arch.*) spigolo del tetto ☆ *— -bath*, semicupio; *— -bone*, (*anat.*) osso iliaco; *— -flask*, fiaschetta per cognac; *— -joint*, (*anat.*) giuntura conofemorale; *— -pocket*, tasca posteriore (dei calzoni).

hip[2], *s.* (*bot.*) frutto della rosa canina.

hip[3], *s.* (*fam.*) ipocondria; depressione psichica; malinconia: *to have the —*, essere d'umor nero, malinconico.

to hip[3], *pass.p.p.* **hipped** [hipt], *v.t.* far venire la malinconia a, rattristare.

hip[4], *inter.*: *—, —, hurrah!*, evviva!.

hipparch ['hipɑːk], *s.* (*st. greca*) ipparco.

hipped [hipt], *ag.* (*fam.*) tetro, malinconico.

hippety-hoppety ['hipəti'hopəti], *av.* balzelloni.

hippish ['hipiʃ], *ag.* (*fam.*) depresso.

hippo ['hipou], *pl.* **hippos** ['hipouz], *s.* (*abbr.* di *hippopotamus*) ippopotamo.

hippocampus [,hipou'kæmpəs], *pl.* **hippocampi** [,hipou'kæmpai], *s.* **1.** (*mit.*) ippocampo **2.** (*ittiol.*) cavalluccio marino, ippocampo **3.** (*anat.*) ippocampo, sutura laterale del cervello.

hippocentaur [,hipou'sentɔ:*], *s.* (*mit.*) ippocentauro, centauro.

hippocrass ['hipoukræs], *s.* ippocrasso (vino drogato).

Hippocrates [hi'pokrəti:z], *no.pr.m.* (*st.*) Ippocrate.

hippocratic [,hipou'krætik], *ag.* ippocratico.

Hippocrene [,hipou'kri:ni(:)], *no.pr.* (*mit.*) Ippocrene (fontana sacra alle Muse).

hippodrome ['hipədroum], *s.* **1.** (*st. romana, greca*) ippodromo **2.** *Hippodrome*, teatro per varietà e spettacoli vari.

hippogriff, hippogriph ['hipougrif], *s.* (*mit.*) ippogrifo.

hippology [hi'polədʒi], *s.* ippologia.

Hippolyta [hi'politə], *no.pr.f.* (*mit.*) Ippolita.

hippopotamus [,hipə'potəməs], *pl.* **hippopotamuses** [,hipə'potəməsiz], **hippopotami** [,hipə'potəmai], *s.* ippopotamo.

hippuric [hi'pjuərik], *ag.* (*chim.*) ippurico ☆ *— acid*, acido ippurico.

hirable ['hairəbl], *ag.* da noleggio.

hircine ['hə:sain], *ag.* ircino, caprino, caprigno.

hircocervus [,hə:kou'sə:vəs], *s.* (*mit.*) ircocervo.

hire ['haiə*], *s.* **1.** affitto, nolo: *bicycles for —*, biciclette a nolo; *for —*, libero (di tassi); *on —*, in affitto, a nolo: *to let out horses on —*, noleggiare cavalli **2.** salario: *to work for —*, lavorare a salario ☆ *— -purchase* (o *— -system*), vendita a rate.

to hire, *v.t.* **1.** prendere a servizio, assumere: *she hired a waiter for the party*, assunse un servitore per il ricevimento **2.** affittare, dare a nolo.

hireling ['haiəliŋ], *s.* (*gener. spreg.*) persona prezzolata, venale; mercenario.

hirer ['haiərə*], *s.* noleggiatore; noleggino.

hiring ['haiəriŋ], *s.* affitto, noleggio.

hirsute ['hə:sju:t], *ag.* irsuto, ispido, irto.

hirsuteness ['hə:sju:tnis], *s.* pelosità.

hirundine [hi'rʌndain], *ag.* di rondine.

his [hiz] *ag.poss.* 3ª *persona sing.* (*riferito a possessore m.*) suo, sua, suoi, sue: *— birth*, la sua nascita; *— friends*, i suoi amici; *— hat*, il suo cappello; *— sisters*, le sue sorelle ‖ *pron.poss.* 3ª *persona sing.* (*riferito a possessore m.*) il suo, la sua, i suoi, le sue: *it is no business of —*, è una faccenda che non lo riguarda; *that car is —*, quell'auto è sua; *this is my coat, not —*, questo è il mio pastrano, non il suo ‖ *those friends of —*, quei suoi amici.

to hish [hiʃ], *V.* to **hiss**.

Hispanic [his'pænik], *ag.* ispanico.

Hispanist ['hispənist], *s.* ispanista.

hispid ['hispid], *ag.* ispido.

hispidity [his'piditi], *s.* ispidezza.

hiss [his], *s.* sibilo; fischio.

to hiss, *v.t.i.* **1.** sibilare **2.** fischiare ‖ *to — s.o. off* (o *away* o *down*), scacciare qlcu. con fischi: *the actress was hissed off the stage*, l'attrice fu fischiata e dovette abbandonare il palcoscenico.

hissing ['hisiŋ], *ag.* sibilante; fischiante ‖ *s.* sibilo; fischio.

hist [s:t], *inter.* sst!, zitto!, silenzio!.

histogenesis [,histou'dʒenisis], **histogeny** [his'todʒəni], *s.* (*biol.*) istogenia.

histologic(al) [,histə'lodʒik(əl)], *ag.* istologico.

histologist [his'tolədʒist], *s.* istologo.

histology [his'tolədʒi], *s.* istologia.

historian [his'tɔ:riən], *s.* storico.

historiated [his'tɔ:rieitid], *ag.* istoriato.

historie [his'tɔrik], *ag.* storico: *— present*, (*gram.*) presente storico.

historical [his'tɔrikəl], *ag.* storico (basato sulla storia): *— events*, avvenimenti storici; *— method*, metodo storico; *— novel*, romanzo storico.

historically [his'tɔrikəli], *av.* storicamente.

historicity [,histə'risiti], *s.* storicità.

historiette [his,tɔ:ri'et], *s.* storiella, raccontino.

historiographer [,histɔ:ri'ogrəfə*], *s.* storiografo.

historiographie(al) [his,tɔ:riə'græfik(əl)], *ag.* storiografico.

historiography [,histɔ:ri'ogrəfi], *s.* storiografia.

history ['histəri], *s.* storia ‖ *"History of English Literature"*, «Storia della letteratura inglese» ‖ *that's ancient —*, (*fam.*) sono cose passate ormai ‖ *to make —*, fare la storia ☆ *ancient —*, storia antica; *natural —*, storia naturale.

histrion ['histriən], *s.* istrione, commediante.

histrionic(al) [,histri'onik(əl)], *ag.* istrionico.

histrionically [,histri'onikəli], *av.* istrionicamente.

histrionicism [,histri'onisizəm], *s.* istrionismo.

histrionics [,histri'oniks], *s.pl.* teatralità, finzione teatrale: *it is mere — on her part*, è pura commedia da parte sua.

histrionism ['histriənizəm], *s.* istrionismo.

hit [hit], **1.** colpo, botta: *deadly —*, colpo mortale **2.** osservazione sarcastica **3.** caso fortunato: *a lucky —*, un colpo fortunato **4.** successo; commedia di successo: *the biggest hits of 1962*, i maggiori successi (canzoni, dischi, ecc.) del 1962; *she made quite a —*, ella ebbe un grande successo.

to hit, *pass.p.p.* **hit**, *v.t.i.* **1.** battere, colpire; picchiare: *he was — by the thief with a stone*, fu colpito dal ladro con un sasso; *to — a man in the face, in the nose, in the eye*, colpire un uomo in faccia, al naso, all'occhio; *to — a man on the head, on the forehead*, colpire un uomo sulla testa, sulla fronte; *to — s.o. a blow*, dare un pugno a qlcu., colpire qlcu. ‖ *to — below the belt*, colpire a tradimento, non rispettare le regole del giuoco ‖ *to — the bottle*, (*sl. amer.*) bere ‖ *to — the hay*, (*sl.*) andare a dormire ‖ *to — it*, *fig.* indovinare ‖ *to — the (right) nail on the head*, cogliere nel segno, indovinare **2.** urtare, venire a contatto; entrare in collisione: *they — against a rock*, urtarono contro una roccia, uno scoglio **3.** *fig.* toccare; colpire; ferire: *to — the mark*, dare nel segno; *to — s.o.'s pride*, ferire l'orgoglio di qlcu.; *to — a wrong note*, toccare una nota falsa ‖ *— or miss*, comunque ‖ *to — home*, centrare **4.** trovare, scoprire: *he did not — his stride until middle age*, non trovò il suo genere di attività fino alla tarda maturità; *to — the right path*, trovare la giusta strada ‖ *to — the jackpot*, (*fam.*) fare un colpo fortunatissimo **5.** (*mec.*) funzionare: *the engine is only hitting on three cylinders*, il motore va a soli tre cilindri **6.** *to — back*, difendersi, render pan per focaccia **7.** *to — off*, imitare ‖ *to — it off*, intendersela **8.** *to — out*, dare grandi colpi.

hitch [hitʃ], *s.* **1.** colpo, strattone; balzo repentino **2.** intoppo, ostacolo, difficoltà: *everything went off without a —*, tutto si svolse senza difficoltà **3.** (*mar.*) nodo **4.** (*sl. amer. mil.*) ferma, periodo di ferma **5.** (*sl. amer.*) gita col sistema dell'autostop.

to **hitch**, *v.t.i.* **1.** muovere, muoversi a sbalzi ‖ *to — (up) one's trousers*, aggiustarsi i pantaloni con un movimento brusco **2.** legare, attaccare: *to — a horse to a tree*, legare un cavallo ad un albero ‖ *to — one's waggon to a star*, entrare nella scia di persona altolocata **3.** rimanere impigliato: *my dress hitched on a nail*, il mio vestito rimase impigliato a un chiodo **4.** (*sl.*) fare l'autostop **5.** (*mar.*) legare con gomene; ammarare **6.** *to — up*, attaccare i cavalli alla carrozza.

to **hitchhike** [ˈhitʃhaik], *v.i.* (*sl.*) fare l'autostop, viaggiare con il sistema dell'autostop.

hitchhiker [ˈhitʃˌhaikə*], *s.c.* chi fa l'autostop.

hitchhiking [ˈhitʃˌhaikiŋ], *s.* autostop.

hither [ˈhiðə*], *av.* (*rar.*) qua; qui; in qua; per di qua; *— and thither*, qua e là.

hithermost [ˈhiðəmoust], *ag.* (*arc.*) il più vicino.

hitherto [ˈhiðəˈtu:], *av.* finora, fino adesso: *as —*, come per il passato.

hitherward [ˈhiðəwəd], *av.* in questa direzione.

hitter [ˈhitə*], *s.c.* chi colpisce.

hive [haiv], *s.* **1.** alveare (anche *fig.*); arnia: *the fair looked like a real —*, la fiera sembrava un vero formicaio **2.** sciame (anche *fig.*).

to **hive**, *v.t.i.* **1.** mettere, far entrare (api) nell'arnia **2.** immagazzinare (miele) nell'arnia **3.** vivere in comunità (come in un alveare).

hiver [ˈhaivə*], *s.* apicultore.

hives [haivz], *s.* (*patol.*) orticaria.

to **hizz** [hiz], *v.i.* (*rar.*) sibilare.

ho[1] [hou], *inter.* **1.** oh! (esclamazione di sorpresa, ammirazione, anche ironica) **2.** ohè!, olà! (esclamazione per attirare l'attenzione).

ho[2], *inter.* oh! (richiamo per fermare un animale).

ho[3], *inter.* issa! (grido di marinaio).

hoar [ho:*], *ag.* bianco; canuto ☆ *— -frost*, brina.

hoard [ho:d], *s.* **1.** gruzzolo, peculio; tesoro **2.** mucchio; scorta.

to **hoard**, *v.t.* ammassare, ammucchiare; tesaurizzare ‖ *he kept lots of recollections hoarded up in his heart*, custodiva gelosamente i suoi ricordi.

hoarder [ˈho:də*], *s.* incettatore.

hoarding [ˈho:diŋ], *s.* recinto provvisorio, palizzata (generalmente di cantiere edile) ☆ *advertisement —*, tabellone d'affissione.

hoariness [ˈho:rinis], *s.* **1.** candore (di capelli) **2.** vetustà; canizie.

hoarse [ho:s], *ag.* rauco; fioco: *to shout oneself —*, diventar rauco a forza di gridare.

hoarsely [ˈho:sli], *av.* raucamente.

hoarseness [ˈho:snis], *s.* raucedine.

hoary [ˈho:ri], *ag.* **1.** bianco; grigio; canuto **2.** vecchio; venerando.

hoax [houks], *s.* burla; canzonatura; tiro birbone: *to play a — on s.o.*, giocare un tiro a qlcu.

to **hoax**, *v.t.* burlare; canzonare.

hoaxer [ˈhouksə*], *s.c.* ingannatore, ingannatrice; burlone, burlona.

hoaxing [ˈhouksiŋ], *s.* inganno; burla.

hob[1] [hɔb], *s.* **1.** (*arc.*) pagliaccio, « clown » **2.** (*arc.*) elfo, folletto **3.** (*zool.*) furetto **4.** (*fam.*) birichinata; scherzo.

hob[2], *s.* **1.** mensola del focolare (per tenere in caldo le vivande) **2.** (*giuoco*) piastrella **3.** (*mec.*) creatore, fresa a vite ☆ *gear —*, creatore per ingranaggi; *master —*, stampiglia campione; *spline shaft —*, creatore per alberi scanalati; *spur —*, creatore per ingranaggi cilindrici; *worm gear —*, creatore per ruote elicoidali.

hobble [ˈhɔbl], *s.* **1.** zoppicamento **2.** imbarazzo, difficoltà **3.** pastoia ☆ *— skirt*, gonna strettissima.

to **hobble**, *v.t.i.* **1.** zoppicare; procedere a fatica (di discorso, poesia, ecc.) ‖ *to — along*, avanzare zoppicando **2.** mettere le pastoie a (un cavallo, ecc.).

hobbledehoy [ˈhɔbldiˈhɔi], *s.* adolescente ignorante, goffo; zoticone.

hobby[1] [ˈhɔbi], *s.* **1.** « hobby », svago preferito, passatempo: *my — is gardening*, il mio svago preferito è il giardinaggio **2.** cavallino ☆ *— -horse*, cavalluccio di legno.

hobby[2], *s.* (*ornit.*) falcone.

hobgoblin [ˈhɔbˌgoblin], *s.* **1.** folletto **2.** babau.

hobnail [ˈhɔbneil], *s.* **1.** grosso chiodo da scarpe, bulletta **2.** persona rustica.

hobnailed [ˈhɔbneild], *ag.* chiodato.

to **hobnob** [ˈhɔbnɔb], *pass.p.p.* **hobnobbed** [ˈhɔbnɔbd] *v.i.* **1.** bere insieme **2.** intrattenersi amichevolmente.

hobo [ˈhoubou], *pl.* **hobos**, **hoboes** [ˈhoubouz], *s.* (*amer.*) **1.** vagabondo **2.** lavoratore stagionale.

hoboy [ˈhouboi], *s.* (*mus.*) oboe.

Hobson's choice [ˈhɔbsnzˌtʃois], *l.* (*fam.*) offerta senza alternativa; scelta forzata.

hock[1] [hɔk], *s.* vino bianco del Reno.

hock[2], *s.* (*anat.*) garretto.

to **hock**[2], *v.t.* sgarettare, tagliare i garretti a.

hock[3], *s.* lenza.

hock[4], *s.*: *in —*, (*sl. amer.*) in prigione; in pegno; indebitato.

hockey[1] [ˈhɔki], *s.* (*arc.dial.*) festa del raccolto.

hockey[2], *s.* (*spor.*) « hockey », pallamaglio ☆ *ice - —*, « hockey » su ghiaccio.

to **hocus** [ˈhoukəs], *pass. p.p.* **hocussed** [ˈhoukəst], *v.t.* **1.** ingannare **2.** drogare.

hocus-pocus [ˈhoukəsˈpoukəs], *s.* **1.** gherminella **2.** formula magica.

hod [hɔd], *s.* (*edil.*) vassoio, sparviero.

hodden [ˈhɔdn], *s.* (*scoz.*) panno grossolano ☆ *— -grey*, abito rustico.

hodge [hɔdʒ], *s.* (*fam.*) tipico contadino inglese.

hodgepodge [ˈhɔdʒpɔdʒ], *s.* (*cuc.*) miscuglio di vari ingredienti.

hodiernal [ˌhoudiˈə:nl], *ag.* odierno.

hodman, *pl.* **hodmen** [ˈhɔdmən], *s.* manovale.

hodometer [hɔˈdɔmitə*], *s.* odometro.

hoe[1] [hou], *s.* (*dial.*) promontorio, roccia a picco.

hoe[2], *s.* zappa.

to **hoe**[2], *v.t.i.* zappare; estirpare (le erbacce) ‖ *to have a hard row to —*, *fig.* avere una gatta da pelare.

hog [hɔg], *s.* **1.** maiale, porco; *fig.* persona golosa o sudicia; porco ‖ *to go the whole —*, andare fino in fondo, fare le cose a fondo **2.** (*dial.*) pecora giovane avanti la prima tosatura **3.** (*mar.*) frettazza ☆ *— -mane*, criniera di cavallo tagliata molto corta; *— -pen*, porcile; *— -wash*, lavatura di piatti per i maiali; *fig.* cosa di nessun valore ‖ *road- —*, automobilista, ciclista indisciplinato.

to **hog**, *pass.p.p.* **hogged** [hɔgd], *v.t.i.* **1.** alzare, incurvare (la schiena, ecc.) **2.** tagliare (la criniera a un cavallo) **3.** *(fam.)* comportarsi in modo indisciplinato (per via).

hogback ['hɔg,bæk], *s.* **1.** schiena di maiale **2.** cresta di collina tondeggiante nel mezzo.

hogget ['hɔgit], *s.* pecora di un anno.

hoggin ['hɔgin], *s.* mescolanza di ghiaia ed argilla.

hoggish ['hɔgiʃ], *ag.* **1.** di porco **2.** *fig.* rozzo; bestiale **3.** avido; egoista.

hoggishness ['hɔgiʃnis], *s.* **1.** porcheria **2.** rozzezza **3.** avidità; egoismo.

hogmanay ['hɔgmənei], *s.* *(scoz.)* **1.** ultimo giorno dell'anno **2.** regali fatti ai bambini l'ultimo giorno dell'anno.

hog's-back ['hɔgz,bæk], *V.* **hogback**.

hogshead ['hɔgzhed], *s.* **1.** « hogshead » (misura di capacità = l. 238,5) **2.** barilotto (per tabacco, zucchero).

to **hoi(c)k** [hɔik], *v.t.i.* *(aer.)* far impennare; impennarsi; cabrare, far cabrare.

hoiks [hɔiks], *inter.* dai! dai! (per incitare i cani).

hoist [hɔist], *s.* **1.** *(mec.)* montacarichi; ascensore **2.** *(mar.)* ghinda **3.** *(fam.)* spinta verso l'alto: *to give s.o. a* —, dare una spinta a qlcu. (per aiutarlo a salire) ☆ *hand* —, paranco a mano.

to **hoist**, *v.t.* alzare, sollevare; issare: — *the anchor!*, levate l'ancora!; *to* — *the colours* (o *flag*), issare la bandiera.

hoist, *p.p.* *(dall'arc.* to **hoise**) *(poet.):* *to be* — *with one's own petard*, tirarsi la zappa sui piedi.

hoity-toity ['hɔiti'tɔiti], *ag.* **1.** pazzerello, capriccioso **2.** altero; arrogante; petulante ‖ *s.* *(rar.)* condotta riottosa.

hoity-toity, *inter.* ohibò!, vergogna!.

hokey-pokey ['houki'pouki], *s.* **1.** *(sl.)* gelato da passeggio, cono **2.** *V.* **hocus-pocus**.

hokum ['houkəm], *s.* **1.** *(sl. amer.)* ricerca di emozioni; sentimentalismo, appello al grosso pubblico **2.** sciocchezza; inganno.

hoky-poky, *V.* **hokey-pokey**.

hold[1] [hould], *s.* **1.** presa: *to catch* (o *to get* o *to take*) — *of*, afferrare; impossessarsi di; *to keep* — *of*, tenere in proprio possesso; mantenere la presa su **2.** *fig.* ascendente, influenza: *to have a* — *over* (o *on*) *s.o.*, avere un grande ascendente su qlcu. **3.** sostegno; punto d'appoggio: *the rock affords no* — *for hand or foot*, la roccia non offre nessun punto d'appoggio nè per le mani nè per i piedi **4.** rifugio; ricovero; tana **5.** fortezza; luogo di detenzione; cella di prigione ☆ — *-back*, ostacolo, impedimento.

to **hold**[1], *pass.* **held** [held], *p.p.* **held**, *(arc.)* **holden** ['houldən], *v.t.i.* **1.** tenere: *he was holding a book in his hands*, teneva un libro in mano **2.** tenere, mantenere; sostenere: — *yourself ready*, tieni pronto; *to* — *one's head high* (o *up*), andare a testa alta, procedere con fierezza ‖ *to* — *sthg. over s.o.*, usare ql.co. per intimidire qlcu. **3.** contenere: *these jugs* — *a pint each*, questi boccali contengono una pinta ciascuno ‖ *to* — *water*, resistere alle prove (di argomenti, progetti, ecc.) **4.** ritenere, credere, pensare: *to* — *in contempt, esteem, respect*, avere disprezzo, stima, rispetto per; *to* — *s.o. guilty*, ritenere qlcu. colpevole; *to* — *s.o. worthy*, ritenere qlcu. degno ‖ *to* — *dear*, aver caro **5.** trattenere: *he held his breath*, tratteneva il respiro ‖ *to* — *one's tongue*, tacere: — *your tongue*, sta' zitto ‖ *to* — *s.o. in hand*, tenere a bada qlcu. ‖ *to* — *s.o. to his promise*, obbligare qlcu. a mantenere la sua promessa **6.** *(mil.)* difendere; tenere: *to* — *a fort against the enemy*, difendere un forte contro il nemico ‖ *to* — *one's ground*, resistere, mantenere le proprie posizioni **7.** tenere, possedere; occupare (una carica): *to* — *shares in a business*, avere azioni in una ditta; *to* — *two offices at the same time*, occupare due cariche contemporaneamente **8.** tenere; dirigere: *to* — *a debate*, tenere un dibattito; *to* — *a feast*, organizzare una festa **9.** resistere, aggrapparsi: — *tight!*, tenetevi saldi!; *will this rope* —?, terrà questa corda? **10.** perdurare, continuare: — *hard!*, tieni duro!; aspetta!; *these laws*

still —, queste leggi sono sempre valide; *to* — *good*, restare valido **11.** *to* — *by* *(sthg.)*, mantenersi fedele a: *I* — *by what I said*, mantengo quello che ho detto **12.** *to* — *with* *(s.o., sthg.)*, partecipare per; approvare **13.** *to* — *aloof*, tenersi in disparte **14.** *to* — *back*, trattenere, trattenersi; esitare; indietreggiare; dissimulare **15.** *to* — *forth*, declamare in pubblico; fare una dissertazione **16.** *to* — *in*, imbrigliare; trattenere, trattenersi; restare in buone relazioni **17.** *to* — *off*, tenere, tenersi a distanza; astenersi **18.** *to* — *on*, non cedere, persistere, continuare: — *on!*, *(fam.tel.)* aspetta!, resta in linea! ‖ *to* — *on to*, aggrapparsi a: *he held on to a branch*, si aggrappò a un ramo **19.** *to* — *out*, offrire, porgere; *(mil.)* resistere: *they could* — *out no longer*, non poterono più resistere; *to* — *out a hand to s.o.*, dare una mano a qlcu., aiutare qlcu. **20.** *to* — *over*, ritardare, tenere in sospeso, posporre; *(comm.)* tenere in sospeso **21.** *to* — *together*, tenere insieme (due cose); tenersi uniti **22.** *to* — *up*, elevare; fermare, ostruire; ostacolare (il traffico); fermare per derubare ‖ *to* — *up to derision*, esporre alla derisione.

hold[2], *s.* *(mar.)* stiva.

holden ['houldən], *p.p.* *(arc.)* di to **hold**.

holder[1] ['houldə*], *s.c.* possessore, posseditrice; detentore, detentrice; proprietario, proprietaria ‖ *s.* **1.** sostegno, supporto **2.** dente canino; organo prensile di alcuni animali **3.** manico; maniglia; impugnatura; ecc. ☆ — *-forth*, predicatore, oratore; — *-up*, sostenitore, difensore ‖ *cigarette-* —, bocchino.

holder[2], *s.* *(mar.)* marinaio di stiva.

hold-fast ['houldfɑːst], *s.* **1.** rampone; uncino **2.** morsetto.

holding ['houldiŋ], *s.* **1.** presa; possesso **2.** podere, tenuta; patrimonio ☆ — *company*, società finanziaria.

hold-up ['houldʌp], *s.* **1.** intoppo (nel traffico), panna (di automobile) **2.** *(amer.)* rapina a mano armata **3.** *(fam. amer.)* sovraccarico ☆ — *-man*, *(amer.)* rapinatore.

hole [houl], *s.* **1.** foro; apertura, buco; breccia; spiraglio: *a* — *in a tooth*, un buco in un dente; *a* — *in a wall*, un'apertura in una parete; *road full of holes*, una strada piena di buche; *to have holes in one's stockings*, avere dei buchi nelle calze ‖ *a square peg in a round* —, *fig.* una persona inadatta al proprio ufficio ‖ *to make a* — *in sthg.*, fare un buco a ql.co.; attingere a ‖ *to put a* — *through s.o.*, ammazzare qlcu. ‖ *to put s.o. in a* —, *fig.* mettere qlcu. in una situazione spiacevole **2.** antro; tana, caverna; covo; luogo meschino, desolato: *the* — *of a badger*, la tana di un tasso; *what a* — *of a place!*, che postaccio! ‖ *to be like a rat in a* —, *fig.* trovarsi senza via d'uscita **3.** *(golf)* buca: *to win the first* —, guadagnare la prima buca ☆ *air-* —, *(mec.)* sfiatatoio; *arm-* —, ascella; imboccatura della manica; *black-* —, prigione sotterranea; *God-forsaken -* —, luogo sperduto; *hawse-* —, *(mar.)* occhio di cubia; *inspection* —, *(mec.)* foro di spia; *open* —, *(miner.)* pozzo non rivestito.

to **hole**, *v.t.i.* **1.** bucare, bucarsi **2.** ficcare in un buco **3.** *(golf)* fare una buca; lanciare in buca.

holiday ['hɔlədi], *s.* **1.** festa, giorno festivo; giorno di vacanza: *Easter Sunday is a* —, la domenica di Pasqua è vacanza; *to give s.o. a* —, dare vacanza a qlcu.; *to make* —, far festa; *to take a* —, prendersi una vacanza **2.** *(gener. pl.)* vacanze: *holidays in the country, at the seaside*, villeggiatura in campagna, al mare; *to be on one's holidays* (o *on* —), essere in vacanza ☆ — *clothes*, abiti della festa; — *-maker*, villeggiante; gitante; — *task*, compito delle vacanze ‖ *Christmas holidays*, vacanze natalizie.

holily ['houlili], *av.* *(rar.)* santamente.

holiness ['houlinis], *s.* santità ‖ *His Holiness*, Sua Santità.

holing ['houliŋ], *s.* perforazione; escavazione.

Holland ['hɔlənd], *no.pr.* *(geog.)* Olanda ‖ **holland**, *s.* tela di Olanda ☆ *brown* —, lino greggio.

Hollander ['hɔləndə*], s.c. olandese ‖ s. (mec.) olandese (macchina per cartiera).

Hollandish ['hɔləndiʃ], ag. (rar.) olandese.

hollands ['hɔləndz], s. — (gin), liquore (gin) olandese.

to **holler** ['hɔlə*], v.t.i. (st.amer.) urlare; gridare.

(to) **hollo** ['hɔlou], V. (to) **halloo**.

hollow ['hɔlou], ag. 1. cavo, concavo, vuoto; infossato: — cheeks, guance incavate; — tree, albero cavo 2. cupo, cavernoso; sordo, rauco (di suono): a — voice, una voce rauca; with a — sound, con un suono sordo 3. fig. falso, irreale; vacuo, vuoto: — promises, vane promesse; — victory, vittoria inutile ‖ s. cavo, cavità, buca; abisso; depressione; fosso: a — in the ground, una buca nel terreno; a wooded —, una valletta boscosa ☆ — -eyed, dagli occhi infossati; — -hearted, insincero; ingannatore.

to **hollow**, v.t.i. scavare, scavarsi; incavare, incavarsi: river banks are often hollowed (out) by rushing water, le rive dei fiumi sono spesso scavate dall'acqua corrente.

hollow, av. (fam.) completamente: to beat s.o. —, vincere, sorpassare qlcu. di gran lunga.

hollowly ['hɔlouli], av. falsamente.

hollowness ['hɔlounis], s. 1. cavità 2. timbro cavernoso (di voce) 3. fig. falsità, mancanza di sincerità.

holly ['hɔli], s. (bot.) agrifoglio.

hollyhock ['hɔlihɔk], s. (bot.) altea rosata.

holm[1] [houm], s. 1. isoletta (di fiume) 2. terreno alluvionale.

holm[2], s. (bot.) 1. agrifoglio 2. — (-oak), leccio.

holmium ['houlmiəm], s. (chim.) olmio.

holocaust ['hɔləkɔːst], s. olocausto.

Holofernes [,hɔlə'fəːniːz], no.pr.m. (Bibbia) Oloferne.

holograph ['hɔlɔgrɑːf], ag. s. (dir.) (documento) olografo.

holographic [,hɔlə'græfik], ag. (dir.) olografo.

holophrastic [,hɔlə'fræstik], ag. (ret.) olofrastico.

holothurian [,hɔlə'θjuəriən], s. (zool.) oloturia.

Holstein ['hɔlstain], no.pr. (geog.) Holstein ‖ **holstein**, s. bue, vacca di razza Holstein.

holster ['houlstə*], s. fondina da sella, da cintura.

holt [hoult], s. 1. (poet.) bosco 2. collina boscosa.

holy ['houli], ag. 1. santo, sacro, benedetto: this place is —, questo luogo è sacro ‖ the Holy Father, il Santo Padre ‖ the Holy Ghost (o Spirit), lo Spirito Santo ‖ the Holy Grail, il Santo Graal ‖ the Holy Land, la Terra Santa, la Palestina ‖ Holy Office, Sant'Uffizio ‖ the Holy of Holies, il Santo dei Santi ‖ the Holy Trinity, la Santissima Trinità ‖ Holy Week, Settimana Santa ‖ Holy Writ (o Bible), la Sacra Bibbia 2. (sl.) straordinario, notevole: he is a — terror, è un emerito seccatore, è insopportabile; to have a — fear of sthg., avere un sacro terrore di ql.co. ☆ — orders, ordini sacri; — water, acqua santa.

holystone ['houlistoun], s. pietra pomice (usata per pulire i ponti delle navi).

homage ['hɔmidʒ], s. 1. (st.) omaggio (del vassallo al signore) 2. omaggio, atto di deferenza: to pay — to, rendere omaggio a.

Homburg ['hɔmbəːg], no.pr. (geog.) Homburg ‖ s. — (-hat), cappello floscio (da uomo).

home [houm], s. 1. casa, dimora, abitazione, alloggio, residenza; focolare domestico; famiglia: at home, a casa; the pleasures of —, i piaceri della famiglia; he made his — in London, si è stabilito a Londra; I am not at — to anyone, non sono in casa per nessuno; I gave him a — (o I made a — for him), gli ho dato una casa, una famiglia; she wrote to me to make a — with her, mi scrisse di andare ad abitare con lei; there is no place like —, nessun posto è bello come casa propria ‖ —, sweet —!, casa, dolce casa! ‖ he is at — in (o with) any topic, tutti gli argomenti gli sono familiari ‖ it is a — from —, è una seconda casa ‖

nearer —, (fam.) più vicino: to take an example nearer — ..., senza andare a cercare tanto lontano... ‖ to be at — on Thursdays, ricevere il giovedì ‖ to eat s.o. out of house and —, vuotare la dispensa a qlcu.; mangiare a qlcu. fino all'ultimo soldo; vivere alle spalle di qlcu. ‖ to feel at —, sentirsi a proprio agio: I don't feel quite at —, mi sento un po' spaesato; I feel quite at — with them, con loro mi sento in famiglia ‖ to go to one's long (o last) —, fig. partire per l'ultima dimora ‖ to make oneself at —, fare come a casa propria, mettersi a proprio agio ‖ charity begins at —, prov. la carità incomincia a casa propria 2. patria, paese natale: at — and abroad, in patria e all'estero: our policy at — and abroad, la nostra politica interna e estera; we are exiles from —, siamo esuli dalla patria ‖ the Home Fleet, la flotta metropolitana; the Home Guard, la milizia territoriale ‖ the Home Office, il Ministero dell'Interno; the Home Secretary, il Ministro dell'Interno ‖ Home Rule, governo autonomo 3. asilo, rifugio; ospizio: — for the aged, ricovero per i vecchi; — of rest, casa di riposo; the island affords a — to myriads of birds, l'isola dà rifugio a miriadi di uccelli 4. (bot. zool.) « habitat », ambiente naturale: the — of fishes is water, l'elemento dei pesci è l'acqua 5. meta, traguardo, base, porta (in vari giuochi) ‖ the line for —, dirittura d'arrivo (nelle corse dei cavalli).

home, ag. domestico, casalingo; familiare; nazionale.

to **home**, v.t.i. 1. dirigersi verso casa, trovare la via di casa (specialmente di piccioni) 2. andare a casa, dirigere verso casa 3. dare una casa a.

home, av. 1. a casa; in patria: I saw her on her way —, la vidi diretta a casa; I took the child —, accompagnai il bambino a casa; is she — now?, è a casa ora?; let us walk —, rientriamo a piedi; send the children —, manda a casa i bambini; to arrive, to come, to go —, arrivare, venire, andare a casa; to be —, essere di ritorno (a casa) ‖ to bring a charge — to s.o., accusare qlcu. ‖ to bring sthg. — to s.o., aprire gli occhi a qlcu. ‖ it will come — to him some day, se ne renderà conto un giorno o l'altro ‖ that's nothing to write — about, non è niente di cui vantarsi ‖ to see s.o. —, accompagnare qlcu. a casa; to send s.o. — (from abroad), rimpatriare qlcu. 2. direttamente, al segno: the speech went —, il discorso andò a segno; to hit (o to strike) —, colpire nel segno 3. a fondo: to drive a nail —, conficcare un chiodo fino in fondo; to press a pedal —, (aut.) spingere a fondo un pedale; to screw a piece —, (mec.) avvitare a fondo un pezzo.

home, (nei composti): — -baked, cotto in casa (nel forno); — -born, indigeno, locale; — -bred, allevato in casa; — -brewed, fatta in casa (di birra); fig. combinato in famiglia; — -coming, ritorno al focolare; (amer.) raduno di ex-studenti; — -defence, difesa del territorio metropolitano; — -farm, azienda agricola che fa parte della casa padronale; — -fire, il focolare; — -folks, parenti; gente del proprio villaggio; — -grown, prodotto agricolo del paese; — -keeping, casalingo; sedentario; — -made, fatto in casa; — -manufacture, fabbricazione nazionale; — -market, mercato nazionale; — thrust, stoccata; — -town, città natia ; — trade, commercio interno.

homecraft ['houmkrɑːft], s. artigianato domestico.

homeland ['houmlænd], s. patria.

homeless ['houmlis], ag. senza casa.

homelessness ['houmlisnis], s. l'essere senza tetto (generalmente di persone).

homelike ['houmlaik], ag. domestico, familiare.

homelily ['houmlili], av. 1. familiarmente 2. modestamente; semplicemente.

homeliness ['houmlinis], s. 1. semplicità 2. mancanza di attrattiva.

homely ['houmli], ag. 1. semplice, modesto 2. domestico, familiare 3. scialbo (di viso).

Homer[1] ['houmə*], no.pr.m. (st. lett.) Omero.

homer[2], s. piccione viaggiatore.

Homeric [hou'merik], *ag.* omerico ‖ — *laughter*, risata omerica.

homesick ['houm-sik], *ag.* nostalgico.

homesickness ['houm-siknis], *s.* nostalgia.

homespun ['houm-spʌn], *ag.* **1.** di fabbricazione domestica **2.** semplice ‖ *s.* stoffa grossa tessuta in casa.

homestead ['houm-sted], *s.* **1.** fattoria e annessi **2.** (*amer.*) concessione di terra (da parte dello Stato).

to homestead, *v.t.* (*amer.*) entrare in possesso di (una concessione di terreno) col riconoscimento dello Stato.

homesteader ['houm,stedə*], *s.* **1.** colono **2.** (*amer.*) concessionario di un terreno (avuto dallo Stato).

homestretch ['houm'stretʃ], *s.* (*ippica*) dirittura d'arrivo.

homeward ['houmwəd], *ag.av.* (che si dirige) verso casa, verso la patria ☆ — *-bound*, diretto in patria (di nave, di viaggiatore).

homework ['houmwə:k], *s. coll.* compiti per casa.

homicidal [,həmi'saidl], *ag.* omicida.

homicide ['həmisaid], *s.* **1.** omicidio **2.** omicida.

homiletic [,həmi'letik], *ag.* (*eccl.*) omiletico.

homiletics [,həmi'letiks], *s.* (*eccl.*) omiletica.

homily ['həmili], *s.* (*eccl.*) omelia.

homing ['houmiŋ], *ag.* che va, che torna a casa ☆ — *-pigeon*, colombo viaggiatore.

homocentric [,həmou'sentrik], *ag.* (*geom.*) omocentrico.

homoeopathic [,houmjə'pæθik], *ag.* (*med.*) omeopatico.

homoeopathy [,houmi'əpəθi], *s.* (*med.*) omeopatia.

homogeneity [,həmoudʒe'ni:iti], *s.* omogeneità.

homogeneous [,həmə'dʒi:njəs], *ag.* omogeneo.

homogeneously [,həmə'dʒi:njəsli], *av.* omogeneamente.

homogeneousness [,həmə'dʒi:njəsnis], *s.* omogeneità.

homogenesis [,həmə'dʒenisis], *s.* (*biol.*) omogenesi.

homogeny [hou'mədʒini], *s.* (*biol.*) omogenia.

homograph ['həmougra:f], *s.* omografo.

to homologate [hou'mələgeit], *v.t.* omologare.

homologation [hou,mələ'geiʃən], *s.* omologazione.

homological [,həmə'lədʒikəl], *ag.* omologico.

to homologize [hou'mələdʒaiz], *v.t.i.* **1.** essere omologo, corrispondere **2.** omologare.

homologous [hə'mələgəs], *ag.* omologo.

homology [hə'mələdʒi], *s.* omologia.

homomorphic [,həmou'mɔ:fik], *ag.* omomorfo.

homonym ['həmənim], *s.* omonimo.

homonymous [hə'məniməs], *ag.* omonimo.

homonymy [hə'mənimi], *s.* omonimia.

homophone ['həməfoun], *s.* parola, lettera omofona.

homophonic [,həmou'fənik], *ag.* omofonico.

homophonous [hə'məfənəs], *ag.* omofono.

homophony [hə'məfəni], *s.* omofonia.

homosexual ['houmou'seksjuəl], *ag.* omosessuale.

homosexuality ['houmouseksju'æliti], *s.* omosessualità.

homuncle [hou'mʌŋkl], **homuncule** [hou'mʌŋkju:l]; **homunculus** [hou'mʌŋkjuləs], *pl.* **homunculi** [hou'mʌŋkjulai], *s.* **1.** omuncolo; ometto **2.** nano.

homy ['houmi], *ag.* casalingo, domestico.

Honduras [hən'djuərəs], *no.pr.* (*geog.*) Honduras.

hone[1] [houn], *s.* cote, pietra per affilare.

to hone[1], *v.t.* affilare; (*mec.*) levigare; smerigliare.

to hone[2], *v.i.* (*dial. amer.*) lamentarsi, gemere.

honest ['ənist], *ag.* **1.** onesto, integro, probo; rispettabile: *to turn* (o *to earn*) *an* — *penny*, guadagnarsi onestamente da vivere **2.** leale; sincero, veritiero: *tell me your* — *opinion*, dimmi sinceramente la tua opinione **3.** puro, genuino (di cose) **4.** (*arc.*) casta, virtuosa ‖ *to make an* — *woman of s.o.*, sposare una donna dopo averla compromessa.

honestly ['ənistli], *av.* **1.** onestamente **2.** lealmente; sinceramente **3.** (*arc.*) castamente.

honesty ['ənisti], *s.* **1.** onestà, probità; buona fede ‖

— *is the best policy*, l'onestà è la miglior politica **2.** lealtà; franchezza **3.** (*arc.*) castità **4.** (*bot.*) lunaria.

honey ['hʌni], *s.* **1.** miele; *fig.* dolcezza **2.** (*fam.*) tesoro, caro, cara ☆ — *-bag*, addome dell'ape; — *-bear*, (*zool.*) orsacchiotto; orso labiato; — *-bee*, pecchia; — *-dew*, melata; tabacco conciato con melassa; — *-guide*, (*ornit.*) uccello indicatore; — *-mouse*, (*zool.*) tarsipede; — *-mouthed*, mellifluo ‖ *virgin-* —, miele vergine; *wild* - —, miele grezzo.

honeyed ['hʌnid], *ag.* **1.** melato, coperto di miele; *fig.* dolce, sdolcinato **2.** adulatorio.

honeycomb ['hʌnikoum], *s.* **1.** favo **2.** falla (in un oggetto di metallo).

to honeycomb, *v.t.* crivellare.

honeyless ['hʌnilis], *ag.* senza miele.

honeymoon ['hʌnimu:n], *s.* luna di miele.

to honeymoon, *v.i.* trascorrere la luna di miele.

honeysuckle ['hʌni,sʌkl], *s.* (*bot.*) caprifoglio.

hong [həŋ], *s.* magazzino di deposito, fabbrica (in Cina, Giappone).

Hong-Kong [həŋ'kəŋ], *no.pr.* (*geog.*) Hong-Kong.

honied, *V.* **honeyed**.

honk [həŋk], *s.* **1.** grido dell'anitra selvatica **2.** suono di clacson.

to honk, *v.i.* **1.** anatrare (di anitra selvatica) **2.** suonare il clacson.

(to) honor, (*amer.*) per (to) **honour**.

honorarium [,ənə'rɛəriəm], *pl.* **honoraria** [,ənə'rɛəriə], **honorariums** [,ənə'rɛəriəmz], *s.* onorario.

honorary ['ənərəri], (*abbr.* **hon.**) *ag.* onorario; onorifico; non retribuito ☆ — *degree*, laurea ad honorem; — *member*, socio onorario.

honorific [,ənə'rifik], *ag.* onorifico ‖ *s.* formula di cortesia, di rispetto.

honour ['ənə*], *s.* **1.** onore, reputazione, buon nome: *code of* —, codice d'onore; *a debt of* —, un debito d'onore; *dinner in your* —, pranzo in vostro onore; *law of* —, legge d'onore; *word of* —, parola d'onore; *he has come off with* —, se l'è cavata con onore; *it is an affair of* —, è una questione d'onore; *to be on one's* —, essere legato dalla parola d'onore; *to lose one's* —, perdere il proprio onore ‖ *for* —, (*comm.*) per intervento ‖ *upon my* —, sul mio onore ‖ — *is at stake*, è in giuoco l'onore **2.** venerazione; stima, reverenza: *he did me the* — *of speaking to me*, mi fece l'onore di parlarmi; *they paid* — *to him*, gli resero onore; *to hold s.o. in great* —, tenere qlcu. in grande considerazione; *to show* — *to one's parents*, (*arc.*) mostrare rispetto per i propri genitori ‖ *guard of* —, guardia d'onore; *maid of* —, damigella d'onore **3.** *Honour*, Eccellenza (titolo di cortesia): *Your Honour*, Vostro Onore **4.** onore, gloria: *to be an* — *to one's country*, fare onore alla patria **5.** *pl.* onori; onorificenze; titoli; decorazioni: *last honours*, onoranze funebri; *military honours*, onori militari ‖ *with honours*, (*università*) con lode ‖ *to do the honours of the table, the house*, fare gli onori di tavola, casa **6.** (*carte*) onori: *honours are even*, gli onori sono pari **7.** reputazione; castità: *she held her* — *cheap*, non ebbe cura della propria reputazione ☆ — *-bright*, (*fam.*) parola d'onore; — *-point*, (*arald.*) punto sopra il centro dello scudo ‖ *birthday honours*, onorificenze concesse dal re in occasione del suo genetliaco.

to honour, *v.t.* **1.** onorare, fare onore a; glorificare; rispettare; venerare **2.** (*comm.*) accettare, pagare.

honourable ['ənərəbl], *ag.* **1.** stimato, onorevole; onorato **2.** *Honourable*, « Honourable » (titolo dato ai figli di un Pari, ai giudici, ai membri del governo) ‖ *Most Honourable*, « Most Honourable » (titolo spettante ai marchesi, ai membri del Consiglio della Corona) ‖ *Right Honourable*, « Right Honourable » (titolo spettante ai Pari di rango inferiore al marchesato).

honourableness ['ənərəblnis], *s.* onorabilità; probità.

honourably ['ənərəbli], *av.* onorevolmente.

honourless ['ənəlis], *ag.* senza onore, disonorato, infamato.

hood [hud], s. **1.** cappuccio; cappuccio di toga universitaria: *monk's* —, cappuccio di frate **2.** mantice (di carrozzella, calesse, ecc.); (*amer.*) cofano di automobile **3.** (*foto.*) paraluce ☆ — *fastener*, (*aut.*) fermacofano ‖ *armored* —, (*mil.*) cupola corazzata.

to hood, *v.t.* incappucciare, fornire di cappuccio.

hooded ['hudid], *ag.* **1.** incappucciato **2.** a cappuccio (di abito) **3.** (*poet.*) coperto; nascosto.

hoodless ['hudlis], *ag.* senza cappuccio.

hoodlum ['hudləm], s. (*sl. amer.*) teppista.

hoodoo ['hu:du:], s. **1.** sfortuna **2.** menagramo.

to hoodoo, *v.t.* portare sfortuna a, dare la iettatura a.

to hoodwink ['hudwiŋk], *v.t.* **1.** bendare gli occhi a **2.** (*fam.*) ingannare.

hooey ['hu:i], s. (*sl. amer.*) sciocchezza.

hoof [hu:f], *pl.* **hoofs** [hu:fs], **hooves** [hu:vz], s. **1.** zoccolo (di animale) **2.** (*scherz.*) piede ☆ — *mark*, impronta dello zoccolo di un cavallo ‖ *cloven* —, piede caprino.

to hoof, *v.t.i.* **1.** andare a piedi **2.** colpire con lo zoccolo (di animali) **3.** (*sl.*) prendere a calci ‖ *to* — *s.o. out*, scacciare qlcu. brutalmente.

hoofed [hu:ft], *ag.* (*zool.*) che ha zoccoli.

hoofless ['hu:flis], *ag.* (*zool.*) senza zoccoli.

hook [huk], s. **1.** uncino, gancio ‖ — *and eye*, allacciatura a gancio ‖ *by* — *or by crook*, per amore o per forza, di riffa o di raffa ‖ *on one's own* —, (*sl.*) per proprio conto ‖ *to be off the hooks*, (*arc.*) essere fuori dalla grazia di Dio ‖ *to drop off the hooks*, (*sl.*) morire ‖ *to take one's* —, (*sl.*) alzare i tacchi **2.** amo **3.** tagliola, trappola **4.** falce per grano **5.** (*mar.*) gola, ghirlanda **6.** ansa stretta (di fiume) **7.** promontorio, capo **8.** (*boxe*) gancio, « crochet » ☆ — *beaked*, dal becco ricurvo; — *-bill*, becco ricurvo; — *-mouth*, (*mec.*) apertura del gancio; — *-nose* (o — *-nosed*), dal naso adunco; — *-pocker*, attizzatoio; — *-spanner*, chiave a gancio; — *-up*, (*amer.*) (*rad.*) relais, schema; (*fam.*) legame, alleanza ‖ *boat* —, (*mar.*) gaffa, gancio d'accosto; *fish-* —, amo da pesca; *laying-* —, manubrio; *nail -* —, chiodo a gancio.

to hook, *v.t.i.* **1.** agganciarsi: *to* — (*up*) *a dress*, agganciare un abito **2.** prendere all'amo ‖ *to* — *a husband*, (*fam.*) pescare un marito **3.** (*mar.*) incocciare **4.** (*boxe*) colpire con un gancio **5.** (*sl.*) rubare.

hookah ['hukə], s. « narghilè », lunga pipa.

hooked [hukt], *ag.* **1.** fornito di uncini **2.** ricurvo, adunco ☆ — *cross*, croce uncinata.

hooker[1] ['hukə*], s. **1.** strumento ad uncino **2.** persona che usa strumenti ad uncino; (*min.*) operaio che aggancia i vagoni.

hooker[2], s. (*mar.*) peschereccio ad un albero.

hookey ['huki], s. fannullone; vagabondo ‖ *to play* —, marinare la scuola.

hooligan ['hu:ligən], s. giovinastro; teppista.

hooliganism ['hu:ligənizəm], s. teppismo.

hoop[1] [hu:p], s. **1.** collare; cerchio (di botte, di ruota, ecc.); cerchiatura (di fucile) **2.** cerchio (di ragazzi, di acrobati): *to go through the hoops*, passare attraverso il cerchio; *fig.* attraversare un momento difficile; *to trundle* (o *to drive*) *a* —, giocare al cerchio **3.** *gener. pl.* guardinfante; crinolina ☆ — *-ash*, (*bot.*) specie di frassino ‖ *barrel* —, cerchio di barile; *cask* —, cerchio di botte; *top-* —, (*mar.*) cerchio di gabbia.

to hoop[1], *v.t.* cerchiare (una botte, ecc.); circondare.

hoop[2], s. **1.** urlo, grido: *hoops of joy*, grida di gioia **2.** urlo della pertosse.

to hoop[2], *v.t.i.* **1.** urlare, gridare **2.** fare l'urlo tipico della pertosse ☆ *hooping-cough*, (*patol.*) pertosse.

hooper ['hu:pə*], s. bottaio.

hoopoe, hoopoo ['hu:pu:], s. (*ornit.*) upupa.

hoot [hu:t], s. **1.** grido della civetta **2.** rumore; schiamazzo **3.** fischio (di locomotiva) ‖ *I do not care a* — *for him*, (*sl. amer.*) non mi importa un bel niente di lui; *this is not worth a* —, ciò non vale nulla.

to hoot, *v.t.i.* **1.** urlare, gridare; fischiare; dare la

---

baia a ‖ *to* — *at s.o.*, fischiare qlcu.; *to* — *s.o. away*, far fuggire qlcu. con urla e fischi **2.** suonare il clacson; fischiare (di locomotiva) **3.** chiurlare; stridere (di civetta).

hooter ['hu:tə*], s. sirena; fischio di sirena; clacson.

hoots [hu:ts], *inter.* hu!, suvvia!.

hoove [hu:v], s. (*vet.*) meteorismo.

hop[1] [hɔp] s. (*bot.*) luppolo ☆ — *-bind* (o — *-bine*), stelo rampicante del luppolo; — *-field*, luppolaia; — *-picker*, raccoglitore di luppolo; — *-pole*, pertica da luppolo.

to hop[1], *pass.p.p.* **hopped** [hɔpt], *v.t.i.* **1.** aromatizzare, mescolare con luppolo **2.** raccogliere luppolo.

hop[2], s. **1.** salto (su una gamba sola); saltellamento ‖ *Hop-o'-my-thumb*, Pollicino; *fig.* persona piccolissima ‖ —, *skip, and jump*, (*spor.*) salto triplo ‖ *to be on the* —, essere in continuo movimento **2.** (*aer. fam.*) tappa **3.** (*fam.*) danza ☆ — *-scotch*, giuoco del mondo.

to hop[2], *v.t.i.* **1.** saltare (su una gamba sola), saltellare ‖ — *it!*, (*sl.*) sloggia!; *to* — *the twig* (o *the perch*), (*sl.*) sloggiare, andarsene; morire **2.** danzare **3.** *to* — *off*, (*aer. fam.*) partire, decollare.

Hope[1] [houp], *no.pr.f.* Speranza.

hope[2], s. speranza, fiducia; attesa, aspettativa: *it is past* (o *beyond*) —, non c'è più speranza; *to live in hopes* (*that*), vivere sperando (che) ‖ *while there's life there's* —, *prov.* finché c'è vita c'è speranza.

to hope[2], *v.t.i.* **1.** sperare, confidare, essere fiducioso; aspettarsi: *he had hoped for it a long time*, lo sperava da molto tempo; *I* — *he will arrive soon*, spero che arrivi presto; *I* — *I am right*, spero di aver ragione; *I* — *to go*, spero di andare; *to* — *against hope*, sperare senza ragione, fino all'ultimo; *to* — *for the best*, sperare per il meglio; *to* — *for sthg.*, sperare ql.co.; *to* — *in God*, sperare in Dio **2.** *to* — *on*, continuare a sperare.

hope[3], s. **1.** (*arc.*) terreno circondato da paludi **2.** (*scoz.*) valloncello **3.** (*scoz.*) braccio di mare.

hopeful ['houpful], *ag.* **1.** pieno di speranza, fiducioso **2.** promettente, che promette buoni risultati ‖ s. (*iron.*): *a young* —, un giovane promettente.

hopefully ['houpfuli], *av.* fiduciosamente, con buone speranze.

hopefulness ['houpfulnis], s. fiducia, buona speranza.

hopeless ['houplis], *ag.* senza speranza; disperato; irrimediabile: *to give sthg. up as* —, rinunciare a fare ql.co. perchè impossibile.

hopelessly ['houplisli], *av.* senza speranza; irrimediabilmente.

hopelessness ['houplisnis], s. disperazione; irreparabilità.

hopingly ['houpiŋli], *av.* speranzosamente, fiduciosamente.

hoplite ['hɔplait], s. (*st. greca*) oplita.

hopper[1] ['hɔpə*], s. **1.** persona od insetto che saltella **2.** (*agr.*) seminatoio **3.** (*strum. artig.*) tramoggia **4.** (*mar.*) chiatta per scarico di fango o ghiaia **5.** cavalletta di pianoforte.

hopper[2], *s.c.* raccoglitore, raccoglitrice di luppolo ‖ s. tino per la preparazione della birra.

hopping[1] ['hɔpiŋ], s. **1.** raccolta di luppolo **2.** mescolanza di malto e luppolo.

hopping[2], **1.** saltellamento **2.** danza; festa campestre.

hopple ['hɔpl], s. ceppi per cavalli.

to hopple, *v.t.* **1.** impastoiare **2.** mettere i ceppi a.

Horace ['hɔrəs], *no.pr.m.* Orazio.

horal ['hɔ:rəl], *ag.* orario, di ora.

Horatian [hɔ'reifiən], *ag.* (*lett. lat.*) di Orazio, oraziano.

horde [hɔ:d], s. **1.** orda **2.** truppa, banda, schiera.

horehound ['hɔ:haund], s. (*bot.*) mentastro; marrobbio.

horizon [hə'raizn], s. **1.** orizzonte: *on the* —, all'orizzonte; *the sun sank below the* —, il sole tramontò all'orizzonte **2.** *fig.* limite delle umane possibilità ☆ — *line*, linea dell'orizzonte.

horizontal [ˌhɔri'zɔntl], *ag.* orizzontale: *a — line,* una linea orizzontale ‖ *out of the —,* in posizione obliqua.

horizontality [ˌhɔrizɔn'tæliti], *s.* orizzontalità.

horizontally [ˌhɔri'zɔntəli], *av.* orizzontalmente.

hormone ['hɔːmoun], *s.* (*fisiol.*) ormone.

horn [hɔːn], *s.* **1.** corno, tentacolo; antenna: *horns of a stag,* corna di un cervo; *to shed* (o *to cast*) *its horns,* perdere le corna ‖ *— of plenty,* cornucopia ‖ *to draw in one's horns,* (*fam.*) ritirarsi, reprimere il proprio entusiasmo **2.** (*mus.*) corno; tromba (di fonografo); (*aut.*) clacson **3.** *fig.* alternativa: *to be on the horns of a dilemma,* essere al bivio ☆ *— -bill,* (*ornit.*) bucero; *— handle,* manico di corno: *knives often have — handles,* spesso i coltelli hanno manichi di corno; *— -mercury,* (*chim.*) calomelano; *— -owl,* (*ornit.*) gufo della Virginia; *— -rims* (o *— -rimmed glasses*), occhiali cerchiati di corno; *— -silver,* (*chim.*) cloruro d'argento ‖ *English —,* (*mus.*) corno inglese; *hunting —,* corno da caccia.

to horn, *v.t.i.* **1.** fornire di corna **2.** ferire, colpire con le corna **3.** (*mar.*) impostare perpendicolarmente alla linea della chiglia **4.** *to — in,* (*fam. amer.*) interferire, intromettersi; mettere il becco (in una conversazione).

hornbeam ['hɔːnbiːm], *s.* (*bot.*) carpine.

hornblende ['hɔːnblend], *s.* (*min.*) orneblenda.

hornbook ['hɔːnbuk], *s.* (*st.*) abbecedario.

horned [hɔːnd], *ag.* **1.** cornuto, fornito di corna **2.** a forma di corna ☆ *— -horse,* (*zool.*) gnu; *— -owl,* (*ornit.*) allocco; *— -snake* (o *viper*), (*zool.*) vipera cornuta.

horner ['hɔːnə*], *s.* **1.** lavorante, commerciante di oggetti di corno **2.** (*rar.*) suonatore di corno.

hornet ['hɔːnit], *s.* **1.** (*entom.*) vespa, calabrone; *fig.* persona fastidiosa ‖ *to stir up a nest of hornets,* suscitare un vespaio **2.** esca (per salmone).

horniness ['hɔːninis], *s.* **1.** callosità (delle mani) **2.** natura cornea.

hornish ['hɔːniʃ], *ag.* corneo.

hornless ['hɔːnlis], *ag.* senza corna.

hornlet ['hɔːnlit], *s.* piccolo corno.

hornpipe ['hɔːnpaip], *s.* **1.** (*arc.*) cornamusa **2.** danza vivace (di marinai).

hornwork ['hɔːn-wəːk], *s.* lavoro fatto in corno.

horny ['hɔːni], *ag.* **1.** calloso; indurito **2.** corneo **3.** cornuto ‖ *Auld Horny,* (*scoz.*) il Diavolo ☆ *— -handed,* dalle mani callose.

horography [hɔ'rɔgrəfi], *s.* l'arte dell'orologiaio.

horologe ['hɔrələdʒ], *s.* orologio.

horologer [hɔ'rɔlədʒə*], *s.* orologiaio.

horological [ˌhɔrə'lɔdʒikəl], *ag.* di orologio.

horologist [hɔ'rɔlədʒist], *s.* orologiaio.

horology[1] [hɔ'rɔlədʒi], *s.* (*eccl.*) libro d'ore.

horology[2], *s.* orologeria.

horoscope ['hɔrəskoup], *s.* oroscopo: *to cast a —,* fare un oroscopo.

horoscopic(al) [ˌhɔrə'skɔpik(əl)], *ag.* oroscopico.

horoscopy [hɔ'rɔskəpi], *s.* oroscopia.

horrent ['hɔrənt], *ag.* (*poet.*) irto.

horrible ['hɔrəbl], *ag.* **1.** orribile, orrendo: *a — cruelty,* una crudeltà spaventosa **2.** (*fam.*) eccessivo; spiacevole: *a — noise,* un rumore fastidioso.

horribleness ['hɔrəblnis], *s.* orribilità.

horribly ['hɔrəbli], *av.* orribilmente; (*fam.*) terribilmente: *it is — hot,* fa terribilmente caldo.

horrid ['hɔrid], *ag.* **1.** orrido, orrendo; spaventoso **2.** (*fam.*) eccessivo; spiacevole: *he said such — things!,* ne disse di tanto grosse!; *you're really — now,* adesso veramente esageri **3.** (*poet.*) ruvido; rozzo; ispido.

horridly ['hɔridli], *av.* orrendamente, spaventosamente.

horrific [hɔ'rifik], *ag.* orribile, orripilante.

horrification [ˌhɔrifi'keifən], *s.* (*scherz.*) orrore; cosa orripilante.

to horrify ['hɔrifai], *v.t.* **1.** atterrire, incutere terrore a **2.** scandalizzare; impressionare; offendere: *to be horrified at sthg.,* rimanere sconvolto, scandalizzato per ql.co.

horripilation [hɔˌripi'leifən], *s.* brivido; l'accapponarsi della pelle.

horror ['hɔrə*], *s.* **1.** orrore, spavento; disgusto: *to my —...,* con mio gran spavento...; *to have a — of doing sthg.,* avere in odio di fare ql.co. **2.** orrore, cosa orribile, spaventosa: *the horrors of war, of death,* gli orrori della guerra, della morte ‖ *Chamber of Horrors,* Camera degli Orrori **3.** *pl.* depressione con allucinazioni ☆ *— comic,* fumetto giallo; *— -stricken* (o *— -struck*), atterrito.

hors-d'oeuvre [ɔː'dəːvr], *s.* antipasto.

horse [hɔːs], *s.* **1.** cavallo: *to mount a —, to ride a —,* montare a cavallo, cavalcare ‖ *a — of another colour,* tutt'altra cosa ‖ *a dark —,* (*fig.*) un vincitore inaspettato; (*pol.*) candidato che viene sostenuto solo all'ultimo momento ‖ *to —!,* (*ordine mil.*) a cavallo! ‖ *I could eat a —,* ho una fame da lupo; *to eat like a —,* mangiare come un lupo ‖ *to flog a dead —,* sciupare energie inutilmente ‖ *to look a gift — in the mouth,* guardare in bocca a caval donato ‖ *to mount* (o *to ride*) *the high* (o *to get on one's high*) *—,* montar sul cavallo d'Orlando, darsi delle arie ‖ *to put the cart before the —,* *fig.* mettere il carro innanzi ai buoi ‖ *to work like a —,* lavorare come un mulo, con molta energia **2.** *coll.* cavalleria: *— and foot,* cavalleria e fanteria **3.** sgabello; cavalletto; (*spor.*) cavallo **4.** (*sl. studentesco*) traduttore, bigino **5.** (*sl. amer.*) mille dollari **6.** (*geol. min.*) ammasso sterile ☆ *— -bean,* (*bot.*) fava; *— -block,* staffa, predellino, montatoio; *— -box,* carro merci per trasporto di bestiame; *— -boy,* mozzo di stalla; *— -breaker,* domatore di cavalli; *— -chestnut,* (*bot.*) ippocastano; *— -cloth,* gualdrappa per cavalli; *— -coper* (o *— -dealer*), mercante di cavalli; *— -doctor,* veterinario; *— -fly,* (*entom.*) tafano; *horse-guards,* guardie a cavallo; *— -hair,* crine di cavallo; tessuto ruvido; *— -hide,* cuoio di cavallo; *— -laugh(ter),* risata grassa, riso smodato; *— -leech,* (*zool.*) sanguisuga; (*sl.*) individuo rapace; *— -marine,* (*fam. scherz.*) marinaio a cavallo, ammiraglio svizzero; pesce fuor d'acqua: *tell that to the — -marines,* (*fam.*) raccontalo al gatto; *— -opera,* (*sl.*) film « western »; *— -play,* giuoco scatenato; *— -pond,* abbeveratoio per cavalli; *— -power,* potenza in cavalli vapore; *— -race,* corsa ippica; *— -radish,* (*bot.*) rafano; *— -riding,* equitazione; *— -sense,* (*fam.*) buon senso; *— -shoe,* ferro di cavallo; *— -shoer,* maniscalco; *— -show,* mostra equina; concorso ippico; *— -tail,* (*bot.*) equiseto, coda di cavallo; *— -trading,* scambio di cavalli, *fig.* contrattazione; *— -trainer,* allenatore di cavalli ‖ *blood- —,* puro sangue; *draft- —,* cavallo da tiro; *pack- —,* cavallo da soma; *saddle- —,* cavallo da sella.

to horse, *v.t.i.* **1.** cavalcare, andare a cavallo **2.** fornire di cavalli (una carrozza, ecc.) **3.** frustare; fustigare **4.** trasportare (qlcu.) sul proprio dorso **5.** far coprire (una cavalla) **6.** (*sl. amer.*) deridere, prendersi giuoco di.

horseback ['hɔːsbæk], *s.* dorso di cavallo: *on —,* a (dorso di) cavallo.

horseflesh ['hɔːsfleʃ], *s.* carne di cavallo.

horseless ['hɔːslis], *ag.* senza cavallo.

horseman, *pl.* **horsemen** ['hɔːsmən], *s.* **1.** cavaliere **2.** esperto di cavalli.

horsemanship ['hɔːsmənʃip], *s.* **1.** equitazione **2.** ippologia.

horse-whip ['hɔːs-wip], *s.* frustino (da cavallo).

to horse-whip, *pass.p.p.* **horse-whipped** ['hɔːs-wipt], *v.t.* frustare.

horsy ['hɔːsi], *ag.* **1.** cavallino; equino **2.** che affetta le usanze dei fantini, degli stallieri ☆ *— clothes,* abiti sgargianti, vistosi.

hortative ['hɔːtətiv], *ag.* esortativo.

hortatory ['hɔːtətəri], *ag.* esortativo, incitante.

horticultural [ˌhɔːti'kʌltʃərəl], *ag.* attinente all'orticultura.

horticulture ['hɔːtikʌltʃə*], *s.* orticultura.

horticulturist [ˌhɔːtiˈkʌltʃərist], *s.* orticultore.

hosanna [houˈzænə], *s.* osanna.

hosanna, *inter.* osanna!.

hose [houz], *s.* 1. tubo flessibile; canna per innaffiare; (*mar.*) manica 2. *coll.* (*arc.*) calzamaglia 3. *coll.* (*comm.*) calze ☆ — *cover*, (*ind.*) copertura del tubo ‖ *air-* —, manica d'aria; *canvas* —, (*mar.*) manichetta di tela; *fire-* —- naspo, manichetta (antincendio); *half-* —, calzini; *radiator* —, (*aut.*) manicotto in gomma per radiatore; *rubber* —, (*mar.*) manichetta in gomma.

to **hose**, *v.t.* 1. provvedere di calze 2. bagnare, innaffiare con una canna.

hosier [ˈhouʒə*], *s.* commerciante in calze, maglieria.

hosiery [ˈhouʒəri], *s.* maglieria.

hospice [ˈhɔspis], *s.* alloggio; ospizio, ricovero (per poveri, ammalati).

hospitable [ˈhɔspitəbl], *ag.* ospitale.

hospitableness [ˈhɔspitəblnis], *s.* ospitalità.

hospitably [ˈhɔspitəbli], *av.* in modo ospitale.

hospital [ˈhɔspitl], *s.* 1. ospedale: *she is still in* —, è ancora all'ospedale ‖ *for* — *use*, per uso sanitario ‖ *to walk the hospitals*, fare internato (di studenti) 2. (*solo con no.pr.*) istituto di carità 3. (*st.*) Casa dei Cavalieri Ospitalieri ☆ — *fever*, (*patol.*) febbre nosocomiale; — *nurse*, infermiera d'ospedale; — *nursery*, reparto neonati; — *-ship*, nave ospedale; — *sister*, infermiera capo-reparto; — *staff*, personale ospedaliero; — *supply room*, dispensario d'ospedale ‖ *clearing* —, (*mil.*) ospedale di smistamento; *field-* —, (*mil.*) ospedale da campo.

hospitalism [ˈhɔspitəlizəm], *s.* (*spreg.*) metodi da ospedale.

hospitality [ˌhɔspiˈtæliti], *s.* ospitalità.

hospitalization [ˌhɔspitəliˈzeiʃən], *s.* 1. ricovero in ospedale 2. (*fam. amer.*) assicurazione ospedaliera.

to **hospitalize** [ˈhɔspitəlaiz], *v.t.* ricoverare, far ricoverare in ospedale: *to be hospitalized*, essere ricoverato in ospedale.

hospital(l)er [ˈhɔspitlə*], *s.* 1. frate ospitaliere: *Knights Hospitallers*, (*st.*) Cavalieri Ospitalieri 2. cappellano (in alcuni ospedali londinesi).

host¹ [houst], *s.* 1. folla, moltitudine ‖ *he is a* — *in himself*, è una persona che ne vale dieci 2. (*arc. poet.*) armata, schiera ‖ *heavenly hosts*, (*Bibbia*) le milizie celesti; *Lord God of the Hosts*, (*Bibbia*) Signore Dio degli Eserciti.

host², *s.* 1. ospite, anfitrione 2. oste; albergatore ‖ *to reckon without one's* —, fare i conti senza l'oste 3. (*biol.*) ospite.

Host, *s.* (*eccl.*) Ostia consacrata.

hostage [ˈhɔstidʒ], *s.* 1. ostaggio ‖ — *to fortune*, persona, cosa cara che si può perdere 2. pegno, garanzia.

hostel [ˈhɔstəl], *s.* 1. pensionato (per giovani, studenti, marinai, infermiere, ecc.) 2. (*arc.*) locanda ☆ *youth* —, ostello per la gioventù.

hostelry [ˈhɔstəlri], *s.* (*arc.*) locanda, osteria.

hostess [ˈhoustis], *s.* 1. ospite, padrona di casa 2. albergatrice, locandiera 3. « hostess », assistente di volo.

hostile [ˈhɔstail], *ag.* 1. (del) nemico: *the* — *army*, l'esercito nemico 2. ostile, nemico; antagonista ‖ *s.* 1. persona ostile 2. pellirossa ostile ai bianchi.

hostilely [ˈhɔstaili], *av.* in modo ostile.

hostility [hɔsˈtiliti], *s.* 1. inimicizia, ostilità; antagonismo 2. *pl.* (*mil.*) ostilità.

hosting [ˈhoustiŋ], *s.* (*arc.*) scontro armato.

hostler [ˈɔslə*], *s.* stalliere.

hot [hɔt], *ag.* 1. caldo; ardente: — *fire*, fuoco vivo; — *water*, acqua bollente; *fig.* turbamento, seccatura: *to be in* — *water*, *fig.* avere delle seccature; *to get into* — *water*, *fig.* mettersi nei guai; *to be* —, esser caldo (di cose); aver caldo (di persone); far caldo (di tempo); *to become* (o *to get* o *to grow*) —, riscaldarsi, cominciare ad aver caldo ‖ *to make things* (o *it*) *too* — *for s.o.*, rendere la vita intollerabile a qlcu. 2. forte, piccante (di cibi, bevande): *pepper and mustard are* —, il pepe e la se-

nape sono piccanti 3. violento, impetuoso, veemente, ardente; esaltato; iroso: *a* — *actor*, un valente attore; *a* — *competitor*, un concorrente formidabile; *a* — *temper*, un temperamento impetuoso; *to get* — *over an argument*, riscaldarsi per una questione 4. fresco, recente; nuovo: — *from the oven*, appena sfornato; *a* — *scent*, una traccia fresca; *they have* — *news for you*, hanno notizie fresche per te; (*amer.*) hanno notizie assai interessanti per te ‖ *piping hot*, caldo caldo, appena sfornato ‖ *to be* — *on the track of s.o.*, stare alle calcagna di qlcu. 5. (*elett.*) caldo, attivo; (*sl. amer.*) radioattivo: — *circuit*, circuito attivo 6. (*mus.*) eccitante, vivace: — *jazz*, « hot jazz » 7. (*sl. amer.*) rubato, contrabbandato di recente ☆ — *-blooded*, ardente, dal sangue ardente, dal sangue caldo; — *chair*, (*amer.*) sedia elettrica; — *-dog*, (*amer.*) panino imbottito con salsiccia e senape; — *-headed*, scalmanato, impulsivo; — *-plate*, (*elett.*) fornello, piastra riscaldante; — *stuff*, individuo volitivo, vigoroso; cosa straordinaria: — (*stuff*) *story*, storiella spinta, pepata; — *war*, guerra calda, conflitto armato; — *-water bottle*, borsa dell'acqua calda; — *-well*, (*ind.*) pozzo caldo.

hot, *av.* 1. ad alta temperatura ‖ *to blow* — *and cold*, contraddirsi, cambiare continuamente opinione ‖ *to go* — *all over*, avere delle vampate di caldo; *to go* — *and cold all over*, avere i brividi 2. *fig.* ardentemente; violentemente; rabbiosamente ‖ *give it him* —!, (*fam.*) digliene quattro!, dagli una bella strapazzata!.

hotbed [ˈhɔtbed], *s.* 1. (*floricultura, orticultura*) letto caldo 2. *fig.* focolaio: — *of corruption*, focolaio di corruzione.

hotchpotch [ˈhɔtʃpɔtʃ], *V.* **hodgepodge**.

hotel [houˈtel, ouˈtel], *s.* albergo ‖ *to put up at* (o *in*) *a* (o *an*) —, fermarsi in un albergo, soggiornarvi ☆ — *-keeper*, albergatore ‖ *private* —, pensione, albergo per famiglie; *residential* —, casa albergo; *temperance* —, albergo in cui sono proibiti gli alcoolici.

hotfoot [ˈhɔtfut], *av.* a gran velocità.

hothead [ˈhɔthed], *s.c.* testa calda; persona impulsiva, violenta.

hothouse [ˈhɔthaus], *s.* serra.

hotly [ˈhɔtli], *av.* caldamente; ardentemente; con veemenza.

hotness [ˈhɔtnis], *s.* calore; ardore; veemenza.

hotpot [ˈhɔtpɔt], *s.* spezzatino di carne con patate.

to **hotpress** [ˈhɔtpres], *v.t.* satinare (carta, stoffa).

hotspur [ˈhɔtspə(ː)*], *s.* testa calda; persona impulsiva, violenta.

Hottentot [ˈhɔtntɔt], *s.* 1. ottentotto 2. *fig.* barbaro, incivile.

howdah, *V.* **howdah**.

hough [hɔk], *s.* garretto.

to **hough**, *v.t.* azzoppare (un quadrupede) tagliando i tendini del garretto.

hound¹ [haund], *s.* 1. (*arc. poet.*) cane 2. bracco; segugio 3. *fig.* furfante ☆ — *bitch*, cagna da caccia.

to **hound¹**, *v.t.* 1. cacciare con i bracchi 2. *fig.* inseguire; perseguitare: *to* — *out of a place*, scacciare da un luogo; *to be hounded by one's creditors*, essere perseguitato dai propri creditori.

hound², *s.* (*tec.*) rinforzo laterale.

hour [ˈauə*], *s.* 1. ora: *an* — *ago*, un'ora fa; *an* — *and a half*, un'ora e mezzo; *a quarter of an* —, un quarto d'ora; *a three hours' journey*, un viaggio di tre ore, tre ore di viaggio; *ask the* —, chiedi che ore sono; *the church clock was striking the* — *as we got home*, battevano le ore al campanile della chiesa quando giungemmo a casa ‖ *you've given me a bad quarter of an* —, (*fam.*) mi hai fatto passare un brutto quarto d'ora 2. *pl.* orario ‖ *to keep good hours*, andare a letto presto; *to keep late hours*, andare a letto tardi; *to keep regular hours*, condurre una vita regolata 3. periodo; momento; occasione: *the hero of the* —, l'eroe del momento; *in a good, evil* —, in un momento buono, cattivo; *in the small hours of the night*, nel cuore della notte; *he spent his happiest hours in London*, trascorse il periodo più felice della sua vita a Londra ‖ *at the eleventh* —, all'ultimo momento **4.** (*astr.*) ora siderale **5.** (*eccl.*) ora canonica ‖ *Book of Hours*, libro d'ore ☆ — *-circle*, (*astr.*) cerchio orario; — *-glass*, clessidra; — *-hand*, lancetta delle ore ‖ *forty-* — *week*, settimana lavorativa li quaranta ore; *office hours*, orario d'ufficio; *rush* —, ora di punta; *school hours*, ore di lezione.

houri ['huəri], *s.* (*relig. musulmana*) uri.

hourly ['auəli], *ag.* **1.** continuo: *he lived in* — *dread of capture*, viveva nel continuo terrore di esser preso **2.** orario, all'ora: *her* — *wage was two shillings*, era pagata due scellini all'ora **3.** ad ogni ora: *an* — *bus service*, un servizio di autobus con partenze ad ogni ora.

hourly, *av.* **1.** continuamente **2.** ad ogni ora, una volta all'ora: *these pills must be taken* —, queste pillole devono essere ingerite ogni ora **3.** d'ora in ora: *his parents expect him* —, i suoi genitori lo attendono d'ora in ora, da un'ora all'altra.

house [haus], *pl.* **houses** ['hauziz], *s.* **1.** casa, dimora, abitazione: — *to* —, di casa in casa, di porta in porta; *at* (o *in* o *to*) *my* —, a casa mia, da me; *prefabricated* —, casa prefabbricata ‖ — *and home*, focolare domestico ‖ *like a* — *on fire*, con soprendente rapidità ‖ *to keep the* —, stare in casa; *to keep* — *for s.o.*, dirigere la casa per qlcu.; *to keep* — *together*, dividere la casa con qlcu.; *to keep open* —, essere molto ospitale ‖ *to move* —, traslocare **2.** albergo, pensione; taverna: — *of ill-fame*, casa di malaffare; *to have a drink on the* —, farsi offrire una consumazione dal proprietario di un locale **3.** clinica, ospedale; convento; pensionato per studenti: — *of correction*, casa di correzione; — *of God* (o *of prayer* o *of worship*), chiesa, cappella **4.** (*pol.*) edificio per assemblee, ecc. ‖ *the House of Commons* (o *the Lower House* o *fam. the House*), la Camera dei Comuni; *the House of Lords* (o *the Upper House*), la Camera dei Pari, la Camera Alta; *the Houses of Parliament*, il palazzo del Parlamento; *the House of Representatives*, (*amer.*) la Camera dei Rappresentanti **5.** casato, lignaggio, dinastia ‖ *the House of Windsor*, la dinastia dei Windsor **6.** teatro ‖ *full* —, tutto esaurito ‖ *to bring down the* —, *fig.* buttare giù il teatro (a forza di applausi) **7.** (*astrologia*) casa **8.** (*comm.*) ditta ☆ — *-agent*, mediatore di immobili; — *-boat*, casa galleggiante; — *-breaker*, scassinatore; uomo addetto alla demolizione delle case; — *-coat*, veste da casa, vestaglia da donna; — *-dinner*, pranzo per i soci (di un club); — *-doctor*, medico interno (di ospedale); — *-dog*, cane da guardia; — *-duty*, imposta sui fabbricati; — *-flag*, (*mar.*) bandiera (di compagnia mercantile); — *-flannel*, straccio per pavimenti; — *-fly*, mosca domestica; — *-leek*, (*bot.*) semprevivo; — *-maid*, cameriera; — *-mate*, (*fam.*) coabitante; — *-party*, week-end durante il quale gli ospiti rimangono in casa anche per dormire; — *-room*, posto, spazio (in casa); — *-surgeon*, chirurgo interno (di ospedale); — *-warming*, festa per l'inaugurazione di una casa ‖ *business* —, casa commerciale; *coffee-* —, caffè, bar; *country-* —, casa di campagna, villa; *fowl* —, pollaio; *public-* —, bar di tipo inglese; *tenement* —, casa popolare d'affitto.

to house [hauz], *v.t.i.* **1.** alloggiare, abitare; ricevere in casa; *fig.* offrire un rifugio a, rifugiarsi, proteggere, mettere al sicuro: *to* — *with s.o.*, abitare presso qlcu. **2.** immagazzinare **3.** incassare, coprire; (*mec.*) alloggiare, collocare; (*falegnameria*) incastrare ‖ *to* — *a mast*, (*mar.*) calare un albero.

houseful ['hausful], *s.* casa piena (di gente, ecc.) ‖ *a* — *of children*, una nidiata di bimbi.

household ['haushould], *s.* la famiglia (tutti quelli che vivono insieme compresi i domestici, ecc.) ‖ *Royal Household*, la famiglia reale ☆ — *bread*, pane casalingo; — *gods*, penati, lari; — *troops*, truppe al servizio del sovrano; — *word*, parola d'uso comune, familiare: *his name has become a* — *word*, il suo nome è sulla bocca di tutti.

householder ['haus,houldə*], *s.* **1.** chi vive in una casa; capofamiglia **2.** locatario di casa.

housekeeper ['haus,ki:pə*], *s.* **1.** guardiano (di una casa) **2.** governante; domestica **3.** donna di casa: *his wife is a good* —, sua moglie è una brava donna di casa.

housekeeping ['haus,ki:piŋ], *s.* il governo della casa, l'economia domestica ‖ *to set up* —, mettere su casa.

housel ['hauzl], *s.* (*rar. eccl.*) Eucarestia.

houseless ['hauslis], *ag.* senza casa; senza riparo.

houseling-cloth ['hauzliŋ-klɔθ], *s.* (*eccl.*) tovaglia per balaustra.

housemaid ['haus-meid], *s.* domestica, cameriera ☆ — *'s knee*, (*patol.*) borsite prepatellare; (*pop.*) ginocchio della lavandaia.

housemaster ['haus,mɑːstə*], *s.* professore incaricato del buon funzionamento di un pensionato per studenti annesso alla scuola in cui insegna (nelle scuole pubbliche inglesi).

housetop ['haus-tɔp], *s.* tetto (della casa) ‖ *to cry* (o *to proclaim*) *from the housetops*, (*fam.*) annunciare pubblicamente.

housewife ['haus-waif] *nel senso* **2.** ['hʌzif], *pl.* **housewives** ['haus-waivz] *nel senso* **2.** ['hʌzivz], *s.* **1.** massaia, casalinga, donna di casa **2.** astuccio da lavoro.

housewifely ['haus,waifli], *ag.* da (buona) massaia.

housewifery ['hauswifəri], *s.* economia domestica, governo della casa.

housework ['haus-wəːk], *s.* lavoro domestico.

housing[1] ['hauziŋ], *s.* **1.** il ricevere, l'accogliere, l'offrire riparo, rifugio **2.** rifugio, riparo; alloggio; abitazione **3.** proprietà immobiliare **4.** (*mec.*) corpo; carcassa; custodia; sostegno; gabbia **5.** (*aut.*) scatola (della frizione, dello sterzo) **6.** (*mar.*) parte sotto coperta; parte interna (di bompresso) ☆ — *estate*, quartiere residenziale; — *problem*, problema degli alloggi.

housing[2], *s.* **1.** gualdrappa **2.** *pl.* finimenti (di cavallo).

Houyhnhnm ['huihnəm], *s.* (*letter.*) « Houyhnhnm » (cavallo sapiente).

hove [houv], *abbr.* di *to* **behove**.

hove, *pass.* di *to* **heave**.

hovel[1] ['hɔvəl], *s.* **1.** tana **2.** baracca, tugurio.

to hovel[1], *pass.p.p.* **hovelled** ['hɔvəld], *v.t.* mettere al riparo in una baracca, in una casupola.

to hovel[2], *v.t.* portare (un vascello) in porto.

to hover ['hɔvə*], *v.i.* **1.** librarsi, svolazzare (di uccelli): *to* — *over*, librarsi sopra, sorvolare **2.** gironzolare: *to* — *about s.o.*, ronzare intorno a qlcu. **3.** *fig.* ondeggiare, oscillare **4.** (*aer.*) librarsi (di elicottero); volare a punto fisso.

how [hau], *av.* **1.** come, in che modo: — *can you remember so many words?*, come fai a ricordare tante parole?; — *did you do it?*, come l'hai fatto?; *tell me* — *you did it!*, dimmi come l'hai fatto! ‖ — *ever* (o — *on earth* o — *the deuce* o — *the devil* o — *the dickens*), come mai: — *the deuce can I tell?*, come posso dirlo? — *ever can you believe it?*, come ci puoi credere?; — *on earth did you know?*, come mai (lo) sapevi?; **2.** come (in quale stato di salute): — *are you*, — *is your father?*, come sta?, come sta suo padre? ‖ — *do you do?*, piacere di conoscerla! **3.** come (per chiedere un'opinione, una spiegazione, ecc.): — *now?*, allora, che significa?; — *so?*, come può essere?, vuoi spiegarti meglio?; — *about going to the pictures?*, che ne dici di andare al cinema?; — *come?*, (*amer.*) come?, come si spiega?; — *do you like it?*, ti piace?, ti va?; — *do you like this dress?*, ti piace questo vestito?; — *is that?*, come si spiega questo? **4.** come, fino a qual punto; **quanto** (in frasi interrogative ed esclamative): — *often a week?*, quante volte alla settimana?; — *far is it?*, quanto dista?, quanto è lontano?; — *long does it take to get there?*, quanto tempo ci vuole per andarci?; — *many books have you left?*, quanti libri vi restano?; — *many times did you see her?*, quante volte l'hai vista?; — *much is it?*, quanto costa?; — *much money do you require?*, quanto denaro ti occorre?; — *often do you go?*, ogni quanto ci vai?; — *old are you?*, quanti anni hai? ‖ — *foolish you are!*, come sei sciocco!; — *he snores!*, come russa!; — *time flies!* come vola il tempo!; — *very nice of you!*, come è gentile!, molt. gentile da parte tua! ‖ *s.* **il come, il modo** ‖ *cong. arc.*) **che:** *he told us* — *the King was ill*, ci disse che il re era ammalato ☆ — *-d'ye-do*, (*sl.*) situazione imbarazzante: *here is a pretty* — *-d'ye-do*, ecco un bell'imbroglio.

howbeit ['hau'bi:it], *cong.* (*arc.*) nondimeno.

howdah ['haudə], *s.* portantina fissata sul dorso di un elefante.

howdy ['haudi], *inter.* (*fam. contr.* di *how do you do?*) salve!; piacere di conoscerla.

however [hau'evə*], *av.* **1.** comunque, per quanto: — *wrong he may be, he...*, per quanto torto abbia, egli... **2.** però, tuttavia, ciò nonostante **3.** (*arc.*) in ogni caso ‖ *cong.* pure, nondimeno, tuttavia.

howitzer ['hauitsə*], *s.* (*mil.*) obice.

howl [haul], *s.* urlo, grido; ululato.

to **howl**, *v.t.i.* urlare, gridare; ululare ‖ *to* — *with laughter*, (*fam.*) ridere fragorosamente.

howler ['haulə*], *s.c.* urlatore, urlatrice; piagnone, piagnona ‖ *s.* **1.** (*fam.*) errore pacchiano, strafalcione **2.** scimmia.

howling ['hauliŋ], *ag.* **1.** urlante **2.** (*sl.*) terribile: *a* — *success*, un successo strepitoso.

howsoever [,hausou'evə*], *av.* (*arc.*) in qualsiasi modo, comunque.

hoy[1] [hɔi], *s.* nave da trasporto di piccolo cabotaggio.

hoy[2], *inter.* olà!, oh!.

to **hoy**[2], *v.t.* incitare.

hoyden ['hɔidn], *s.* monella; ragazza chiassosa: *she was a real* —, era un vero ragazzaccio.

hub [hʌb], *s.* **1.** mozzo di ruota **2.** *fig.* punto centrale: *Piccadilly Circus is the* — *of tho West End*, Piccadilly Circus è il cuore del West End.

hubble-bubble ['hʌbl,bʌbl], *s.* **1.** narghilè **2.** vocio.

hubbub ['hʌbʌb], *s.* tumulto, confusione; suono confuso di molte voci.

hubby ['hʌbi], *s.* (*fam. abbr. affettuosa* di *husband*) maritino.

Hubert ['hju:bə(:)t], *no.pr.m.* Uberto.

huckaback ['hʌkəbæk], *s.* grossa tela di lino, cotone (per asciugamani).

huckle ['hʌkl], *s.* anca; fianco ☆ — *-backed*, gobbo; — *-bone*, osso dell'anca.

huckleberry ['hʌklberi], *s.* (*amer.*) mirtillo.

huckster ['hʌkstə*], *s.* **1.** merciaiolo, venditore ambulante **2.** *fig.* persona meschina, venale **3.** (*amer. comm.*) agente pubblicitario; organizzatore di programmi radiotelevisivi.

to **huckster**, *v.t.i.* **1.** mercanteggiare, stiracchiare sul prezzo di **2.** vendere al minuto; commerciare in cose di poco prezzo.

huddle ['hʌdl], *s.* **1.** calca, folla, confusione **2.** (*amer.*) consultazione segreta.

to **huddle**, *v.t.i.* **1.** mettere assieme alla rinfusa; ammucchiare disordinatamente ‖ *to* — *oneself up*, raggomitolarsi, farsi piccino piccino **2.** affollarsi, accalcarsi: *to* — *together*, accalcarsi l'uno contro l'altro.

hue[1] [hju:], *s.* tinta, colore.

hue[2], *s.* clamore, grido.

to **hue**[2], *v.t.i.* gridare (specialmente a caccia); guidare con la voce; assalire con grida.

hue and cry ['hju:ən'krai], *s.* grido d'allarme (anche *fig.*): *to raise a* — *against s.o.*, fare opposizione contro qlcu. (*p.e.* un uomo politico).

hued [hju:d], *ag.* colorato, tinto.

huff [hʌf], *s.* **1.** stizza: *to be in a* —, essere di cattivo umore **2.** il soffiare una pedina (al giuoco della dama).

to **huff**, *v.t.i.* **1.** offendere, offendersi: *to be huffed*,

essere offeso **2.** maltrattare **3.** soffiare (al giuoco della dama): *to* — *a man at draughts*, soffiare una pedina **4.** (*rar.*) sbuffare.

huffily ['hʌfili], *av.* stizzosamente.

huffiness ['hʌfinis], *s.* **1.** suscettibilità; cattivo umore **2.** petulanza.

huffish ['hʌfiʃ], *ag.* **1.** suscettibile **2.** petulante.

huffishly ['hʌfiʃli], *av.* **1.** in modo suscettibile **2.** con petulanza.

huffishness ['hʌfiʃnis], *V.* **huffiness**.

huffy ['hʌfi], *ag.* **1.** suscettibile **2.** petulante.

hug [hʌg], *s.* abbraccio; stretta.

to **hug**, *pass.p.p.* **hugged** [hʌgd], *v.t.i.* **1.** abbracciare, abbracciarsi, stringere fra le braccia **2.** *fig.* abbracciare, restare attaccato a (un'idea, pregiudizio) **3.** (*mar.*) bordeggiare ‖ *to* — *the wind*, serrare il vento **4.** congratularsi: *to* — *oneself on* (o *for*) *sthg.*, congratularsi con se stesso per ql.co.

huge [hju:dʒ], *ag.* enorme; vasto, immenso; smisurato: *a* — *success, difference*, un immenso successo, una enorme differenza.

hugely ['hju:dʒli], *av.* immensamente; enormemente.

hugeness ['hju:dʒnis], *s.* grandezza smisurata.

hugeous ['hju:dʒəs], *ag.* (*gener. scherz.*) enorme.

hugger-mugger ['hʌgə,mʌgə*], *ag.* **1.** confuso **2.** segreto ‖ *s.* **1.** confusione, disordine **2.** segreto ‖ *in* —, in segreto.

to **hugger-mugger**, *v.t.i.* tener segreto; agire, parlare di nascosto.

hugger-mugger, *av.* **1.** in modo confuso **2.** in segreto.

Hugh [hju:], *no.pr.m.* Ugo.

huguenot ['hju:gənɔt], *s.* (*st.*) ugonotto.

huh [hʌ], *inter.* (*sl. amer.*) che dici?.

hulk [hʌlk], *s.* **1.** carcassa, scafo di nave smantellata (adibito a magazzeno) *2.pl.* (*st.*) galera **3.** (*mar.*) pontone **4.** *fig.* «vitellone», fannullone.

hulking ['hʌlkiŋ], *ag.* pesante, grosso; sgraziato.

hull[1] [hʌl], *s.* **1.** baccello; guscio **2.** copertura.

to **hull**[1], *v.t.* sgusciare; sgranare.

hull[2], *s.* (*mar. aer.*) scafo ☆ — *-down*, molto lontano (di nave il cui scafo è ancora invisibile).

to **hull**[2], *v.t.* forare (lo scafo di una nave) con una cannonata, siluro, ecc.

hullabaloo [,hʌləbə'lu:], *s.* tumulto, fracasso, baccano: *to make a* —, creare confusione; protestare a gran voce.

hullo ['hʌ'lou], *inter.* oh! (per indicare sorpresa); (*fam.*) salve!; (*tel.*) pronto!.

hully ['hʌli], *ag.* fornito di buccia; fornito di baccello.

hum[1] [hʌm], *s.* ronzio; mormorio: *the* — *of the conversation*, il mormorio della conversazione; *the* — *of bees*, il ronzio delle api.

to **hum**[1], *pass.p.p.* **hummed** [hʌmd], *v.t.i.* **1.** ronzare; mormorare: *the room hummed with voices*, nella stanza si udiva un ronzar di voci **2.** cantare a bocca chiusa. *humming chorus*, coro a bocca chiusa; *he hummed an old tune*, canticchiò un vecchio motivo **3.** barbugliare: *to* — *and haw*, nicchiare, esitare nel rispondere **4.** (*fam.*) essere attivo, vivace: *to make things* —, infondere energia, stimolare l'attività.

hum[2], *s.* (*sl.*) finzione, inganno.

to **hum**[2], *v.t.* (*sl.*) ingannare.

hum[3], *s.* (*sl.*) odore sgradevole.

to **hum**[3], *v.i.* (*sl.*) odorare sgradevolmente.

hum[4], *inter.* ehm!.

human ['hju:mən], *ag.* **1.** umano, relativo alla persona umana: *a* — *being*, un essere umano; — *nature*, la natura umana; — *weaknesses*, debolezze umane **2.** sensibile ‖ *s.* (*scherz.*) essere umano.

humane [hju(:)'mein], *ag.* **1.** umano, compassionevole, pietoso **2.** umanistico (di studi).

humanely [hju(:)'meinli], *av.* umanamente, pietosamente.

humaneness [hju(:)'meinnis], *s.* benevolenza, umanità.

humanism ['hju:mənizəm], *s.* **1.** (*lett.*) umanesimo **2.** (*fil.*) umanitarismo.

humanist ['hju:mənist], *s.* umanista, cultore degli studi classici.

humanistic [,hju:mə'nistik], *ag.* umanistico.

humanitarian [hju(:),mæni'tɛəriən], *ag.* filantropico, umanitario ‖ *s.* filantropo.

humanitarianism [hju(:),mæni'tɛəriənizəm], *s.* (*fil.*) umanitarismo; filantropia.

humanity [hju(:)'mæniti], *s.* **1.** umanità, il genere umano: *a crime against —,* un delitto contro l'umanità **2.** la natura umana **3.** bontà, benevolenza: *an act of —,* un atto d'umanità **4.** *the humanities,* le discipline classiche.

to humanize ['hju:mənaiz], *v.t.i.* **1.** rendere umano; acquisire sentimenti migliori, più benevoli **2.** adattare agli usi, alla natura umana.

humankind ['hju:mən'kaind], *V.* **mankind.**

humanlike ['hju:mənlaik], *ag.* simile all'uomo.

humanly ['hju:mənli], *av.* umanamente.

Humbert ['hʌmbə(:)t], *no.pr.m.* Umberto.

humble ['hʌmbl], *ag.* umile; modesto: *the — classes,* le classi umili; *in my — opinion,* secondo la mia umile opinione; *a — life,* una vita modesta; *a man of — birth,* un uomo di umili origini ‖ *your — servant,* vostro servo umilissimo ‖ *to eat — pie,* accettare un'umiliazione; scusarsi umilmente.

to humble, *v.t.* umiliare, avvilire: *to — oneself,* umiliarsi.

humble-bee ['hʌmblbi:], *s.* (*entom.*) calabrone.

humbleness ['hʌmblnis], *s.* umiltà.

humbling ['hʌmbliŋ], *ag.* umiliante ‖ *s.* umiliazione.

humblingly ['hʌmbliŋli], *av.* in modo umiliante.

humbly ['hʌmbli], *av.* umilmente.

humbug ['hʌmbʌg], *s.* **1.** frode, impostura, inganno ‖ *(that's all) —!,* (sono tutte sciocchezze! **2.** dolce alla menta ‖ *s.c.* impostore, impostora.

to humbug, *pass.p.p.* **humbugged** ['hʌmbʌgd], *v.t.i.* raccontar frottole; ingannare.

humbugger ['hʌm,bʌgə*], *s.c.* impostore, impostora.

humbuggery [hʌm'bʌgəri], *s.* impostura, inganno.

humdrum ['hʌmdrʌm], *ag.* noioso, tedioso, monotono: *a — life,* una vita monotona; *a — task,* un lavoro noioso ‖ *s.* **1.** monotonia, tedio **2.** persona monotona, abitudinaria.

to humdrum, *pass.p.p.* **humdrummed** ['hʌmdrʌmd], *v.i.* procedere con monotonia.

humeral ['hju:mərəl], *ag.* (*anat.*) omerale.

humerus ['hju:mərəs], *pl.* **humeri** ['hju:mərai], *s.* (*anat.*) omero.

humid ['hju:mid], *ag.* umido.

to humidify [hju(:)'midifai], *v.t.* inumidire.

humidity [hju(:)'miditi], *s.* umidità.

humidly ['hju:midli], *av.* con umidità.

humiliant [hju(:)'miliənt], *ag.* umiliante.

to humiliate [hju(:)'milieit], *v.t.* umiliare, mortificare.

humiliating [hju(:)'milieitiŋ], *ag.* umiliante.

humiliation [hju(:),mili'eiʃən], *s.* umiliazione, mortificazione.

humility [hju(:)'militi], *s.* umiltà; condizione modesta.

hummeler ['hʌmlə*], *s.* (*agr. dial.*) sbarbatrice.

humming ['hʌmiŋ], *ag.* **1.** ronzante **2.** (*fam.*) forte: *a — blow,* un colpo vigoroso ‖ *s.* ronzio; mormorio ☆ *— -bird,* (*ornit.*) colibrì; *— -top,* trottola.

hummock ['hʌmək], *s.* **1.** poggio, altura **2.** cresta di banchisa.

hummocky ['hʌməki], *ag.* ricco di alture.

humor, (*amer.*) *per* **humour.**

humoral ['hju:mərəl], *ag.* (*med.*) relativo agli umori ☆ *— pathology,* patologia umorale.

humorist ['hju:mərist], *s.* **1.** scrittore gaio, arguto; umorista **2.** persona faceta, allegra, spiritosa.

humoristic [,hju:mə'ristik], *ag.* umoristico.

humorous ['hju:mərəs], *ag.* **1.** arguto, dotato di senso dell'umorismo **2.** comico, divertente.

humorously ['hju:mərəsli], *av.* **1.** con arguzia, senso dell'umorismo **2.** in modo comico, divertente.

humorousness ['hju:mərəsnis], *s.* **1.** arguzia, senso dell'umorismo **2.** comicità.

humour ['hju:mə*], *s.* **1.** senso dell'umorismo: *broad —,* comicità grossolana; *he has no sense of —,* non ha nessun senso dell'umorismo **2.** umorismo, comicità: *the — of the situation,* il lato comico della situazione; *the story is full of —,* il racconto è pieno di umorismo **3.** umore, stato d'animo; inclinazione: *to be in the — for,* essere in vena di; *to be in the — to do sthg.,* aver voglia di fare ql.co.; *to be in a good, bad —,* essere di buon umore, di malumore; *to be out of — with s.o.,* essere malcontento di qlcu.; *to put s.o. out of —,* mettere qlcu. di cattivo umore ‖ *every man in his —,* ognuno secondo la propria inclinazione **4.** capriccio, fantasia: *when the — takes her,* quando le prende il capriccio **5.** (*fisiol.*) umore acqueo (dell'occhio) **6.** (*arc.*) umore, linfa; *fig.* indole, inclinazione dominante: *the cardinal humours,* i quattro principali umori umani.

to humour, *v.t.* compiacere, assecondare: *she's got to be humoured,* bisogna assecondarla.

humourless ['hju:məlis], *ag.* privo di senso dell'umorismo.

humoursome ['hju:məsəm], [*ag.* lunatico; petulante.

humoursomeness ['hju:məsəmnis], *s.* capricciosità; petulanza.

hump [hʌmp], *s.* **1.** gobba (nella schiena); gibbosità **2.** collinetta, cresta; (*sl. aer.*) catena montuosa da sorvolare **3.** *fig.* ostacolo, crisi da superare **4.** (*sl.*) depressione, malinconia: *it gives me the —,* mi dà la malinconia ☆ *— -backed,* gobbo.

to hump, *v.t.* **1.** curvare a forma di gobba **2.** (*sl.*) deprimere **3.** (*austral.*) caricarsi sulle spalle.

humpback ['hʌmpbæk], *s.* gobba; gibbosità ‖ *s.c.* gobbo, gobba.

humped [hʌmpt], *ag.* gibboso.

humph [hʌmf], *inter.* mah!, bah!, hm!, auff! (per indicare dubbio, malcontento).

humpless ['hʌmplis], *ag.* senza gobba.

humpty-dumpty ['hʌmpti'dʌmpti], *s.* (*scherz.*) persona grossa e tozza ‖ *Humpty-Dumpty,* (*fam.*) l'Uovo (protagonista di una famosa canzoncina infantile); persona che, una volta caduta in disgrazia, non può più riabilitarsi; cosa che, una volta rotta, non si può più riparare.

humpy ['hʌmpi], *ag.* **1.** gibboso **2.** (*sl.*) depresso, malinconico.

humus ['hju:məs], *s.* humus.

Hun [hʌn], *s.* **1.** unno **2.** *fig.* barbaro, distruttore **3.** (*spreg.*) prussiano, tedesco.

hunch [hʌntʃ], *s.* **1.** gobba, gibbosità **2.** (*sl. amer.*) idea, impressione, sospetto: *I have a — that he is not that kind of man,* ho proprio il sospetto che non sia quel genere di persona ☆ *— -player,* chi giuoca e spera nelle lotterie.

to hunch, *v.t.* piegare, incurvare a forma di gobba.

hunchback ['hʌntʃbæk], *s.c.* gobbo, gobba.

hunchbacked ['hʌntʃbækt], *ag.* gobbo.

hundred ['hʌndrəd], *ag.num.card.* cento: *a (o one) — men,* cento uomini; *a (o one) — and one women,* centouno donne; *six — books,* seicento libri; *two of them,* duecento di loro ‖ *a — percent efficient,* efficiente al cento per cento, al massimo ‖ *s.* **1.** centinaio: *by hundreds,* a centinaia; *hundreds and thousands,* centinaia e migliaia **2.** (*st. inglese*) suddivisione di una contea.

hundredfold ['hʌndrədfould], *ag.s.* centuplo.

hundredfold, *av.* cento volte.

hundredth ['hʌndrədθ], *ag.num.ord.s.* centesimo.

hundredweight ['hʌndrədweit], *s.* (*abbr. cwt*) « hundredweight » (misura di peso = kg. 50,80 in Gran Bretagna; = kg. 45,35 negli Stati Uniti).

hung [hʌŋ], *pass. p.p.* di to **hang.**

Hungarian [hʌŋ'gɛəriən], *ag. s.* ungherese.

Hungary ['hʌŋgəri], *no.pr.* (*geog.*) Ungheria.

hunger ['hʌŋgə*] *s.* 1. fame; appetito: *pangs of* —, stimoli della fame; *to die of* —, morire di fame; *to suffer* —, patire, soffrire la fame 2. *fig.* ingordigia; ardente desiderio: — *for money*, sete di denaro ☆ — -*march*, dimostrazione di protesta (di disoccupati); — -*strike*, sciopero della fame ‖ *air-* —, (*patol.*) dispnea.

to hunger, *v.t.i.* 1. aver fame 2. *fig.* bramare: *they* — *for* (o *after*) *freedom*, essi desiderano ardentemente d'essere liberi 3. affamare: *to* — *s.o. into submission*, costringere qlcu. a sottomettersi per fame.

hungerful ['hʌŋgəful], *ag.* affamato.

hungrily ['hʌŋgrili], *av.* 1. con grande appetito 2. *fig.* avidamente.

hungriness ['hʌŋgrinis], *s.* fame.

hungry ['hʌŋgri], *ag.* 1. affamato; famelico: *to be* —, aver fame; *to go* —, soffrire la fame ‖ *as* — *as a hunter*, famelico, affamato come un lupo 2. *fig.* bramoso: *to be* — *for glory*, essere assetato di gloria 3. povero, sterile (di terreno).

hunk [hʌŋk], *s.* grosso pezzo: *a* — *of bread and cheese*, un bel pezzo di pane e formaggio.

hunkers ['hʌŋkəz], *s.pl.*: *on one's* —, accosciato.

hunks [hʌŋks], *s.* avaraccio, pitocco.

hunky[1] ['hʌŋki], *s.* (*sl. amer.*) ungherese (termine di disprezzo per immigrati dall'Europa centro-orientale).

hunky[2], *ag.* (*sl. amer.*) buono, in buone condizioni ☆ — -*dory*, eccellente.

Hunnic ['hʌnik], **Hunnish** ['hʌniʃ], *ag.* 1. unnico 2. *fig.* barbaro distruttore 3. (*spreg.*) prussiano, tedesco.

hunt [hʌnt], *s.* 1. caccia: *to have a good* —, fare buona caccia 2. ricerca; inseguimento: *to have a* — *for a job*, cercare un impiego 3. insieme dei cacciatori; zona di caccia.

to hunt, *v.t.i.* 1. cacciare, andare a caccia: *wolves* — *in packs*, i lupi cacciano a branchi; *to* — *big game*, andare a caccia grossa 2. cercare affannosamente: *to* — (*for* o *after*) *gold*, cercare l'oro 2 *to* — *high and low*, cercare in lungo e in largo 3. inseguire; cacciar via, perseguitare: *to* — *a cat out of the kitchen*, scacciare il gatto dalla cucina; *to* — *down a thief*, dar la caccia a un ladro; *to* — *s.o. from* (o *out of*) *the country*, obbligare qlcu. a lasciare il paese 4. battere (una zona) cacciando ‖ *to* — *one's horse*, montare il proprio cavallo per la caccia 5. *to* — **out**, scovare 6. *to* — **up**, frugare, cercare.

hunter ['hʌntə*], *s.* 1. cacciatore (anche *fig.*) 2. cavallo da caccia; cane da caccia 3. orologio con calotta che ne protegge il quadrante ☆ —*'s-moon*, luna piena ‖ *fortune-* —, cacciatore di dote.

hunting ['hʌntiŋ], *s.* 1. caccia; il cacciare: *to go a-* —, andare a caccia ‖ *the happy* —*grounds*, il paradiso (per i pellirosse) 2. *fig.* ricerca ☆ — -*box* (o — -*lodge* o — -*seat*), casino da caccia; — -*crop* (o — -*whip*), frustino da caccia; — -*field* (o — -*ground*), terreno di caccia; — -*horn*, corno da caccia; — -*knife* (o — -*sword*), coltello da caccia; — -*tide*, stagione della caccia ‖ *husband-* —, (*scherz.*) caccia al marito.

huntress ['hʌntris], *s.* cacciatrice.

huntsman, *pl.* **huntsmen** ['hʌntsmən], *s.* 1. cacciatore 2. capocaccia.

hurdle ['hə:dl], *s.* 1. graticcio; barriera 2. ostacolo (anche *fig.*) 3. carretta su cui i traditori venivano portati al supplizio ☆ — -*race* (o *hurdles*), corsa ad ostacoli.

to hurdle, *v.t.i.* 1. cintare (con graticci) 2. partecipare a una corsa ad ostacoli; saltare (un ostacolo); *fig.* superare (una difficoltà).

hurdler ['hə:dlə*], *s.* 1. chi fa graticci 2. chi partecipa a una corsa ad ostacoli.

hurdy-gurdy ['hə:di,gə:di], *s.* (*fam.*) organetto a manovella.

hurl [hə:l], *s.* lancio violento.

to hurl, *v.t.* lanciare, gettare con violenza, scagliare (anche *fig.*): *he was hurled from the throne*, fu sbalzato dal trono; *to* — *defiance*, sfidare; *to* — *reproaches, stones*, lanciare rimproveri, pietre; *to* — *sthg. at s.o.*, lanciare ql.co. contro qlcu.

hurler ['hə:lə*], *s.* lanciatore.

hurley ['hə:li], *s.* 1. hockey irlandese 2. mazza da hockey irlandese.

hurly ['hə:li], *s.* subbuglio, chiasso ☆ — -*burly*, scompiglio, subbuglio.

hurrah [hu'rɑ:], *s.* urrah ‖ *inter.* urrah!.

to hurrah, *v.i.* gridare urrah.

hurray [hu'rei], *s.* urrah ‖ *inter.* urrah!.

hurricane ['hʌrikən], *s.* uragano; ciclone (anche *fig.*): *a* — *of applause*, un uragano di applausi.

hurried ['hʌrid], *ag.* affrettato, precipitoso, frettoloso.

hurriedly ['hʌridli], *av.* precipitosamente, in gran fretta, affrettatamente.

hurriedness ['hʌridnis], *s.* precipitazione, fretta.

hurry ['hʌri], *s.* fretta, precipitazione; urgenza, premura: *the* — *of modern life*, la fretta della vita moderna; *no* — *!*, non c'è fretta!; *to be in a great* —, aver molta fretta; *to be in no* —, non aver fretta ‖ *they will not ask us to dinner again in a* —, (*fam.*) non ci inviteranno di nuovo volentieri a pranzo; *you will not beat that in a* —, (*fam.*) non supererete ciò facilmente; *you won't see him again in a* —, (*fam.*) ci vorrà del tempo prima di rivederlo.

to hurry, *v.t.i.* 1. affrettare, affrettarsi; precipitarsi; sollecitare, spronare: *he hurried me to work*, mi sollecitò a lavorare; *he was hurried into doing his work*, egli fu spronato a fare il suo lavoro; *I hurried them on*, feci loro premura 2. *to* — **along**, camminare in fretta 3. *to* — **away**, andarsene precipitosamente 4. *to* — **up**, far premura ‖ — *up!*, (*fam.*) sbrigati!, affrettati!.

hurryingly ['hʌriiŋli], *av.* precipitosamente, in fretta.

hurry-scurry ['hʌri'skʌri], *s.* disordine, confusione.

hurry-scurry, *av.* in disordine, in grande confusione.

hurst [hə:st], *s.* 1. banco di sabbia 2. collina; altura boscosa; macchia.

hurt [hə:t], *s.* 1. lesione, ferita 2. *fig.* danno, offesa.

to hurt, *pass.p.p.* **hurt**, *v.t.i.* 1. dolere: *my ankle hurts*, mi duole la caviglia; *this shoe hurts* (*me*), questa scarpa mi fa male; *to get* —, venir ferito, ricevere un colpo; farsi male 2. offendere, recar dolore a: *nothing hurts like the truth*, niente offende quanto la verità; *to* — *s.o.'s feelings*, offendere i sentimenti di qlcu. 3. danneggiare: *it won't* — *to postpone it for a few days*, non ci sarà alcun danno a rimandarlo di alcuni giorni; *to* — *s.o.'s interests*, danneggiare gli interessi di qlcu.

hurtful ['hə:tful], *ag.* 1. dannoso, nocivo 2. ingiurioso, offensivo.

hurtfully ['hə:tfuli], *av.* 1. dannosamente 2. in modo ingiurioso, offensivo.

hurtfulness ['hə:tfulnis], *s.* perniciosità, dannosità.

to hurtle ['hə:tl], *v.t.i.* (*arc.*) scagliare, scagliarsi; precipitarsi: *he came hurtling out*, si precipitò fuori come un bolide.

hurtless ['hə:tlis], *ag.* (*arc.*) innocuo, inoffensivo.

husband ['hʌzbənd], *s.m.* 1. marito, sposo 2. (*arc.*) uomo economo: *good, bad* —, buono, cattivo amministratore.

to husband, *v.t.* 1. amministrare con parsimonia; risparmiare, usare con economia 2. (*arc.*) coltivare (terreno) 3. (*poet. scherz.*) procurare marito a 4. (*rar.*) sposare.

husbandless ['hʌzbəndlis], *ag.* senza marito.

husbandman, *pl.* **husbandmen** ['hʌzbəndmən], *s.* agricoltore, fattore.

husbandry ['hʌzbəndri], *s.* 1. agricoltura; coltivazione 2. frugalità, economia; amministrazione domestica: *good, bad* —, buona, cattiva amministrazione.

hush [hʌʃ], *s.* silenzio, calma: *the* — *before the storm*, la quiete prima della tempesta ☆ — -*money*, prezzo del silenzio.

hush, *inter.* zitto!, silenzio!.

to **hush**, v.t.i. **1.** far tacere; imporre silenzio a; tacere; far silenzio **2.** fig. calmare **3.** to — **up**, soffocare (uno scandalo).

hushaby ['hʌʃəbai], inter. fa' la nanna!.

hush-hush ['hʌʃ'hʌʃ], ag. segreto, segretissimo.

to **hush-hush**, v.t. ridurre al silenzio.

husk[1] [hʌsk], s. **1.** (bot.) guscio; baccello; loppa **2.** fig. involucro (senza valore).

to **husk**[1], v.t. sgusciare; sbucciare; mondare.

husk[2], s. (vet.) tosse.

to **husk**[2], v.i. (vet.) tossire.

husked [hʌskt], ag sbucciato; sgusciato; mondato.

huskily ['hʌskili], av. con voce rauca; fiocamente.

huskiness ['hʌskinis], s. raucedine.

husking ['hʌskiŋ], s. **1.** scartocciatura del granturco **2.** (amer.) « husking » (festa campestre in tale occasione).

husky[1] ['hʌski], ag. **1.** rugoso, secco **2.** velato, rauco (di voce) **3.** (amer. fam.) robusto, forte || s. (amer. fam.) persona robusta.

husky[2], s. **1.** esquimese (abitante, lingua) **2.** cane esquimese.

hussar [hu'zɑ:*], s. (mil.) ussaro.

hussif ['husif], V. **housewife 2.**

hussy ['hʌsi], s. **1.** donna leggera, da poco **2.** ragazza impertinente: a gossiping —, una chiacchierona.

hustings ['hʌstiŋz], s. **1.** operazioni elettorali **2.** (amer.) tribuna elettorale.

hustle ['hʌsl], s. (solo sing.) **1.** spinta, spintone **2.** fretta **3.** andirivieni.

hustler ['hʌslə*], s. persona attiva, energica.

hut [hʌt], s. **1.** capanna; casupola **2.** rifugio alpino **3.** baracca militare.

to **hut**, pass.p.p. **hutted** ['hʌtid], v.t.i. fare alloggiare, alloggiare in una baracca.

hutch [hʌtʃ], s. **1.** conigliera; gabbia **2.** baracca, casupola **3.** (miner.) vagoncino.

hutment ['hʌtmənt], s. (mil.) baraccamento.

huzza [hu'zɑ:], inter. evviva!, urrah!.

to **huzza**, v.t.i. **1.** gridare urrah! **2.** acclamare freneticamente.

hyacinth ['haiəsinθ], s. (bot.) giacinto.

hyacinthine [,haiə'sinθain], ag. (bot.) di giacinto.

Hyades ['haiədi:z], no.pr.pl. (astr.) Iadi, Gallinelle.

hyaena [hai'i:nə], s. (zool.) iena.

hyaline ['haiəlin], ag. ialino, cristallino, vitreo.

hyalite ['haiəlait], s. (min.) ialite.

hyaloid ['haiəlɔid], ag. (anat.) ialoideo, vitreo, trasparente ☆ — membrane, membrana ialoidea dell'occhio.

hybrid ['haibrid], ag. (bot. zool.) ibrido; eterogeneo: — corn, granturco ibrido || s. (bot. zool.) ibrido.

hybridism ['haibridizəm], **hybridity** [hai'briditi], s. ibridismo.

to **hybridize** ['haibridaiz], v.t.i. (bot. zool.) rendere, diventare ibrido.

hydatid ['haidətid], s. (patol.) idatide.

hydra ['haidrə], s. **1.** (mit.) idra (anche fig.) **2.** (zool.) idra.

hydrangea [hai'dreindʒə], s. (bot.) ortensia.

hydrant ['haidrənt], s. idrante.

hydrargyrum [hai'drɑ:dʒirəm], s. (chim.) mercurio.

hydrate ['haidreit], s. (chim.) idrato.

to **hydrate**, v.t. (chim.) idratare.

hydration [hai'dreiʃən], s. (chim.) idratazione.

hydraulic [hai'drɔ:lik], ag. idraulico ☆ — cement, cemento idraulico; — lime, calce idraulica; — press, pressa idraulica.

hydraulically [hai'drɔ:likəli], av. con mezzi idraulici.

hydraulician [,haidrɔ:'liʃən], s. perito idraulico.

hydraulics [hai'drɔ:liks], s. (fis.) idraulica.

hydric ['haidrik], ag. (chim.) di idrogeno, contenente idrogeno.

hydro ['haidrou], abbr. di **hydropathic.**

hydroairplane [,haidrou'ɛə-plein], V. **hydroplane.**

hydrobromic [,haidrou'broumik], ag. (chim.) idrobromico.

hydrocarbon ['haidrou'kɑ:bən], s. (chim.) idrocarburo.

hydrochlorate ['haidrou'klɔ:rit], s. (chim.) idroclorato.

hydrochloric ['haidrə'klɔrik], ag. (chim.) cloridrico: — acid, acido cloridrico.

hydrodynamic ['haidroudai'næmik], ag. (fis.) idrodinamico.

hydrodynamics ['haidroudai'næmiks], s. (fis.) idrodinamica.

hydroelectric [,haidroui'lektrik], ag. idroelettrico: — power, station, forza, centrale idroelettrica.

hydrogen ['haidridʒən], s. (chim.) idrogeno ☆ — bomb, bomba all'idrogeno; — peroxide, acqua ossigenata; — sulphide, idrogeno solforato || heavy —, idrogeno pesante, deuterio.

to **hydrogenate** [hai'drɔdʒəneit], to **hydrogenize** ['haidroudʒənaiz], v.t. (chim.) idrogenare.

hydrogenous [hai'drɔdʒinəs], ag. (chim.) che contiene idrogeno.

hydrographer [hai'drɔgrəfə*], s. idrografo.

hydrographic(al) [,haidrou'græfik(əl)], ag. idrografico.

hydrography [hai'drɔgrəfi], s. idrografia.

hydrokinetics [,haidroukai'netiks], s. (fis.) idrocinetica.

hydrology [hai'drɔlədʒi], s. idrologia.

hydrolysis [hai'drɔlisis], s. (chim.) idrolisi.

hydromania [,haidrou'meinjə], s. (patol.) idromania.

hydromechanics ['haidroumi'kæniks], s. idromeccanica.

hydromel ['haidroumel], s. idromele.

hydrometer [hai'drɔmitə*], s. (fis.) idrometro.

hydrometric(al) [,haidrou'metrik(əl)], ag. (fis.) idrometrico.

hydrometry [hai'drɔmitri], s. (fis.) idrometria.

hydropathic [,haidrə'pæθik], ag. (med.) idroterapico || s. stabilimento, centro idroterapico.

hydropathy [hai'drɔpəθi], s. (med.) idroterapia.

hydrophobia [,haidrə'foubjə], s. (patol.) idrofobia.

hydrophobic [,haidrə'foubik], ag. (patol.) idrofobo.

hydrophone ['haidrəfoun], s. (mar.) idrofono.

hydrophyte ['haidrəfait], s. (bot.) idrofite, alga.

hydropic [hai'drɔpik], ag. (patol.) idropico.

hydroplane ['haidrouplein], s. (aer.) idrovolante, idroplano.

hydropneumatic [,haidrounju(:)'mætik], ag. (fis.) idropneumatico.

hydroponics [,haidrou'pɔniks], s. (chim.) idroponica.

hydropsy ['haidrɔpsi], s. (patol.) idropisia.

hydroquinone ['haidroukwi'noun], s. (chim. foto.) idrochinone.

hydroscope ['haidrəskoup], s. (mar.) idroscopio.

hydrosphere ['haidrousfiə*], s. idrosfera.

hydrostat ['haidroustæt], s. idrostato, regolatore di livello.

hydrostatic(al) [,haidrou'stætik(əl)], ag. idrostatico.

hydrostatically [,haidrou'stætikəli], av. idrostaticamente.

hydrostatics [,haidrou'stætiks], s. idrostatica.

hydrotherapeutic [,haidrou,θerə'pju:tik], ag. (med.) idroterapeutico.

hydrotherapeutics [,haidrou,θerə'pju:tiks], s. (med.) idroterapeutica, idroterapia.

hydrothermal [,haidrou'θə:məl], ag. idrotermale.

hydrotropism [hai'drɔtrəpizəm], s. (bot.) idrotropismo.

hydrous ['haidrəs], ag. acquoso.

Hydrozoa [,haidrə'zouə], s.pl. (zool.) idrozoi.

hyena [hai'i:nə], s. (zool.) iena.

Hygeia [hai'dʒi(:)ə], no.pr.f. (mit.) Igea.

hygeian [hai'dʒi(:)ən], ag. **1.** di Igea **2.** salutare; igienico.

hygiene ['haidʒi:n], s. igiene.

hygienic(al) [hai'dʒi:nik(əl)], *ag.* igienico.
hygienically [hai'dʒi:nikəli], *av.* igienicamente.
hygienics [hai'dʒi:niks], *s.* igiene (scienza).
hygienist ['haidʒinist], *s.* igienista.
hygrology [hai'grolədʒi], *s.* (*fis.*) igrologia.
hygrometer [hai'grəmitə*], *s.* (*fis.*) igrometro ☆ *hair* —, igrometro a capello; *dew-point* —, igrometro a condensazione.
hygrometric(al) [,haigrou'metrik(əl)], *ag.* (*fis.*) igrometrico.
hygrometry [hai'grəmitri], *s.* (*fis.*) igrometria.
hygroscope ['haigrəskoup], *s.* (*fis.*) igroscopio.
hygroscopic [,haigrou'skɔpik], *ag.* (*fis.*) igroscopico.
hylomorphism [,hailou'mɔ:fizəm], *s.* (*fil.*) ilomorfismo.
Hymen ['haimen], *no.pr.m.* (*mit.*) Imene ‖ **hymen**, *s.* (*anat.*) imene.
hymeneal [,haime'ni(:)əl], **hymenean** [,haime'ni(:)ən], *ag.* **1.** di Imene **2.** nuziale.
Hymenoptera [,haimə'nɔptərə], *s.pl.* (*entom.*) gli imenotteri.
hymenopterous [,haimə'nɔptərəs], *ag.* (*entom.*) imenottero.
hymn [him], *s.* inno, canto di lode.
to **hymn**, *v.t.i.* lodare (Dio) con inni; cantare inni.
hymnal ['himnəl], *ag.* di inno ‖ *s.* collezione, libro di inni.
hymnary ['himnəri], *s.* (*eccl.*) innario.
hymnic ['himnik], *ag.* di inno.
hymnody ['himnədi], *s.* innodia.
hymnographer [him'nɔgrəfə*], *s.* innografo.
hymnologist [him'nɔlədʒist], *s.* innologo.
hymnology [him'nɔlədʒi], *s.* innologia.
hyoid ['haiɔid], *ag.s.* (*anat.*) ioide.
hyoscine ['haiousain], *s.* (*chim.*) ioscina.
hyoscyamine [,haiou'saiəmain], *s.* (*chim.*) iosciamina.
hypaethral [hai'pi:θrəl], *ag.* (*arch.*) ipetro.
hypallage [hai'pæləgi(:)], *s.* (*ret.*) ipallage.
hyperacute ['haipərə'kju:t], *ag.* iperacuto.
hyperaemia [,haipə'ri:mjə], *s.* iperemia.
hyperaesthesia [,haipəres'θi:zjə],*s.*(*patol.*) iperestesia.
hyperbatic [,haipə(:)'bætik], *ag.* (*ret.*) iperbatico.
hyperbatically [,haipə(:)'bætikəli], *av.* (*ret.*) iperbaticamente.
hyperbaton [hai'pə:bətɔn], *s.* (*ret.*) iperbato.
hyperbola [hai'pə:bələ], *s.* (*geom.*) iperbole.
hyperbole [hai'pə:bəli], *s.* (*ret.*) iperbole.
hyperbolic(al) [,haipə(:)'bɔlik(əl)], *ag.* iperbolico.
hyperbolically [,haipə(:)'bɔlikəli], *av.* iperbolicamente.
hyperbolism [hai'pə:bəlizəm], *s.* (*ret.*) iperboleggiamento.
hyperbolist [hai'pə:bəlist], *s.* iperboleggiatore.
to **hyperbolize** [hai'pə:bəlaiz], *v.t.i.* iperboleggiare; esagerare.
hyperborean [,haipə(:)bɔ:'ri(:)ən], *ag.s.* iperboreo.
hypercatalectic [,haipə,kætə'lektik], *ag.* (*poes.*) ipercatalettico.
hypercritic ['haipə(:)'kritik], *s.* (*arc.*) ipercritico.
hypercritic(al) ['haipə(:)'kritik(əl)], *ag.* ipercritico.
hypercriticism ['haipə(:)'kritisizəm], *s.*ipercriticismo.
Hyperion [hai'piəriən], *no.pr.m.* (*mit.*) Iperione.
hypermeter [hai'pə:mitə*], *s.* (*poes.*) (verso)ipermetro.
hypermetric(al) [,haipə(:)'metrik(əl)], *ag.* (*poes.*)ipermetro.
hypermetropia [,haipə(:)mi'troupiə], *s.* (*patol.*) ipermetropia.
hyperplasia [,haipə(:)'pleiziə], *s.* (*patol.*) iperplasia.
hypersensitive ['haipə(:)'sensitiv], *ag.* ipersensitivo.
hypersonic [,haipə(:)'sɔnik], *ag.* supersonico: — *speed*, velocità supersonica.
hyperspace ['haipə(:)'speis], *s.* (*geom.*) iperspazio.
hypersthene ['haipə(:)sθi:n], *s.* (*min.*) iperstene.
hypersthenia [,haipə(:)'sθi:niə], *s.* (*patol.*) iperstenia.
hypersthenic [,haipə(:)'sθenik], *ag.* (*min. patol.*) iperstenico.

hypertension [,haipə(:)'tenʃən],*s.*(*patol.*)ipertensione.
hyperthyroidism [,haipə(:)'θairɔidizəm], *s.* (*patol.*) ipertiroidismo.
hypertrophic [,haipə(:)'trɔfik], **hypertrophied** [hai'pə:trɔfid], *ag.* (*patol.*) ipertrofico.
hypertrophy [hai'pə:trɔfi], *s.* (*patol.*) ipertrofia.
hyphen ['haifən], *s.* **1.** lineetta d'unione **2.** (*tip.*) divisione.
to **hyphen(ate)** ['haifən(eit)], *v.t.* unire (due parole) con una lineetta d'unione ‖ *hyphenated American*, (*amer. spreg.*) straniero naturalizzato americano.
hypnosis [hip'nousis], *s.* ipnosi.
hypnotic [hip'nɔtik], *ag.* ipnotico ‖ *s.* (*farm.*) narcotico.
hypnotism ['hipnətizəm], *s.* ipnotismo.
hypnotist ['hipnətist], *s.c.* ipnotizzatore, ipnotizzatrice.
hypnotization [,hipnətai'zeiʃən], *s.* ipnotizzazione.
to **hypnotize** ['hipnətaiz], *v.t.* ipnotizzare.
hypnotizer ['hipnətaizə*], *s.c.* ipnotizzatore, ipnotizzatrice.
hypnum ['hipnəm], *s.* (*bot.*) ipno.
hypocaust ['haipəkɔ:st], *s.* (*archeol.*) ipocausto.
hypochondria [,haipou'kɔndriə], *s.* (*patol.*) ipocondria.
hypochondriac [,haipou'kɔndriæk], *ag.* (*patol.*) ipocondriaco ‖ *s.c.* ipocondriaco, ipocondriaca.
hypochondriacal [,haipoukɔn'draiəkəl], *ag.* (*patol.*) ipocondriaco.
hypochondriasis [,haipoukɔn'draiəsis], *s.* (*patol.*) ipocondria.
hypocrisy [hi'pɔkrəsi], *s.* ipocrisia.
hypocrite ['hipəkrit], *s.c.* ipocrita.
hypocritic(al) [,hipə'kritik(əl)], *ag.* ipocrita.
hypocritically [,hipə'kritikəli], *av.* ipocritamente.
hypoderma [,haipə'də:mə], *s.* (*entom. bot.*) ipoderma.
hypodermic [,haipə'də:mik], *ag.* ipodermico: — *syringe*, siringa ipodermica.
hypogastrium [,haipə'gæstriəm], *s.* (*anat.*) ipogastrio.
hypogeal [,haipə'dʒi:əl], *ag.* (*arch.*) ipogeo; sotterraneo.
hypogeum [,haipə'dʒi:əm], *s.* (*arch.*) ipogeo; sotterraneo.
hypostasis [hai'pɔstəsis], *s.* (*teol. fil. patol.*) ipostasi.
hypostyle ['haipoustail], *ag.* (*arch.*) ipostilo.
hyposulphite [,haipou'sʌlfait], *s.* (*chim.*) iposolfito.
hyposulphurous [,haipə'sʌlfjuərəs], *ag.* (*chim.*) iposolforoso.
hyposulphuric [,haipəsʌl'fjuərik], *ag.* (*chim.*) iposolforico.
hypotenuse [hai'pɔtinju:z], *s.* (*geom.*) ipotenusa.
hypothec [hai'pɔθik], *s.* (*dir.*) ipoteca.
hypothecary [hai'pɔθikəri], *ag.* (*dir.*) ipotecario.
to **hypothecate** [hai'pɔθikeit], *v.t.* (*dir.*) ipotecare.
hypothecation [hai,pɔθi'keiʃən], *s.* (*dir.*) l'ipotecare.
hypothecator [hai'pɔθikeitə*], *s.* (*dir.*) ipotecario.
hypothesis [hai'pɔθisis], *pl.* **hypotheses** [hai'pɔθisi:z], *s.* ipotesi.
to **hypothesize** [hai'pɔθisaiz], *v.t.i.* fare ipotesi; supporre.
hypothetic(al) [,haipou'θetik(əl)], *ag.* ipotetico.
hypothetically [,haipou'θetikəli], *av.* ipoteticamente.
hypotyposis [,haipoutai'pousis], *s.* (*ret.*) ipotiposi.
hypsometer [hip'sɔmitə*], *s.* ipsometro.
hyrax ['haiəræks], *s.* (*zool.*) irace.
hyson ['haisn], *s.* tè verde cinese.
hyssop ['hisəp], *s.* (*bot.*) issopo.
hysteresis [,histə'ri:sis], *s.* (*fis.*) isteresi.
hysteria [his'tiəriə], *s.* (*patol.*) isterismo.
hysteric(al) [his'terik(əl)], *ag.* (*patol.*) isterico.
hysterically [his'terikəli], *av.* (*patol.*) istericamente.
hysterics [his'teriks], *s.pl.* (*patol.*) attacco isterico; convulsioni isteriche: *to fall* (o *to go*) *into* —, avere un attacco, una crisi di nervi.
hysterotomy [,histə'rɔtəmi], *s.* (*chir.*) isterotomia.

I

i [ai], *pl.* **is**, **i's** [aiz], *s.* **1.** (*nona lettera dell'alfabeto inglese*) i ‖ *to dot one's i's*, mettere i puntini sugli i ‖ — *for Isaac*, (*tel.*) i come Imola **2.** I, (*cifra romana*) 1.

I, *pron.pers.* 1ª *persona sing. nom.* **io:** — *think, therefore* — *am*, penso, dunque esisto ‖ *am* — *not...?* (o *fam. aren't* — ...?), non sono io...?; *it is* —, sono io ‖ *s. the* —, (*fil.*) l'io.

Iago [i'ɑːgou], *no.pr.m.* (*lett.*) Iago.

iamb ['aiæmb], *s.* (*poes.*) giambo.

iambic [ai'æmbik], *ag.* (*poes.*) giambico ‖ *s.* (*poes.*) verso giambico.

iambographer [,aiæm'bɔgrəfə*], *s.* scrittore di giambi.

iambus [ai'æmbəs], *s.* (*poes.*) giambo.

Ian [iən], *no.pr.m.* (*scoz.*) Giovanni.

ib. [ib], *av.* (*abbr. di ibidem*) nello stesso luogo.

Iberia [ai'biəriə], *no.pr.* (*geog.*) Iberia.

Iberian [ai'biəriən], *ag.* iberico ‖ *s.* ibero.

ibex ['aibeks], *pl.* **ibexes** ['aibeksiz], *s.* (*zool.*) stambecco.

ibid. ['iːbid], *av.* (*abbr. di ibidem*) nello stesso luogo.

ibidem [i'baidem], *av.* nello stesso luogo.

ibis ['aibis], *pl.* **ibises** ['aibisiz], *s.* (*ornit.*) ibis, ibi.

Icarian [ai'kɛəriən], *ag.* (*mit.*) icario, di Icaro.

Icarus ['aikərəs], *no.pr.m.* (*mit.*) Icaro.

ice [ais], *s.* ghiaccio: *floating* —, ghiaccio galleggiante; *thick, thin* —, ghiaccio spesso, sottile; *my feet are like* —, hoi piedi di ghiaccio ‖ *to be on thin* —, fig. toccare un argomento delicato ‖ *to break the* —, fig. rompere il ghiaccio ‖ *to cut no* — *with s.o.*, (*amer. fig.*) non fare impressione su qlcu. ☆ — *-age*, era glaciale; — *-axe*, piccozza da alpinisti; — *-bank* (o — *-field* o — *floe*), banchiglia; — *-breaker*, nave rompighiaccio; — *-bound*, chiuso tra i ghiacci; — *-box* (o — *-chest*), ghiacciaia; — *-brick*, ghiaccio in blocchi; — *-cold*, freddo come il ghiaccio; — *-cream*, gelato; — *-fall*, cascata di seracchi; — *-hockey*, disco sul ghiaccio; — *-rink*, pista di pattinaggio; — *-run*, pista del toboga ‖ *dry* —, (*chim.*) ghiaccio secco.

to ice, *v.t.* **1.** ghiacciare, congelare **2.** (*cuc.*) glassare.

iceberg ['aisbəːg], *s.* « iceberg », massa di ghiaccio galleggiante, montagna di ghiaccio.

iceboat ['aisbout], *s.* nave rompighiaccio.

Iceland ['aislənd], *no. pr.* (*geog.*) Islanda.

Icelander ['aisləndə*], *s.c.* islandese.

Icelandic [ais'lændik], *ag.* islandese ‖ *s.* lingua islandese.

iceman ['aismæn], *pl.* **icemen** ['aismen], *s.* **1.** venditore di ghiaccio; gelataio **2.** alpinista.

icepack ['ais-pæk], *s.* « pack », banco di ghiaccio.

ichneumon [ik'njuːmən], *s.* (*zool. entom.*) icneumone.

ichnographic(al) [,iknə'græfik(əl)], *ag.* icnografico.

ichnographically [,iknə'græfikəli], *av.* icnograficamente.

ichnography [ik'nɔgrəfi], *s.* icnografia.

ichthyological [,ikθiou'lɔdʒikəl], *ag.* ittiologico.

ichthyologist [,ikθi'ɔlədʒist], *s.* ittiologo.

ichthyology [,ikθi'ɔlədʒi], *s.* ittiologia.

ichthyophagist [,ikθi'ɔfədʒist], *s.* ittiofago.

ichthyophagy [,ikθi'ɔfədʒi], *s.* ittiofagia.

ichthyosaurus [,ikθiə'sɔːrəs], *s.* (*paleont.*) ittiosauro.

icicle ['aisikl], *s.* ghiacciuolo.

icily ['aisili], *av.* gelidamente.

iciness ['aisinis], *s.* gelidezza.

icing ['aisiŋ], *ag.* (*cuc.*) glassato ‖ *s.* (*cuc.*) glassa.

icon ['aikɔn], *s.* (*eccl.*) icona.

iconic [ai'kɔnik], *ag.* (*eccl.*) iconico.

iconoclast [ai'kɔnəklæst], *s.* iconoclasta.

iconoclastic [ai,kɔnə'klæstik], *ag.* iconoclastico.

iconographic [ai,kɔnə'græfik], *ag.* iconografico.

iconography [,aikə'nɔgrəfi], *s.* iconografia.

iconology [,aikə'nɔlədʒi], *s.* iconologia.

iconoscope [ai'kɔnəskoup], *s.* (*tv.*) iconoscopio ☆ *image* —, iconoscopio ad immagine.

icosahedron ['aikəsə'hedrən], *s.* (*geom.*) icosaedro.

icteric(al) [ik'terik(əl)], *ag.* (*patol.*) itterico.

icterus ['iktərəs], *s.* **1.** (*patol.*) itterizia **2.** (*ornit.*) ittero.

ictus ['iktəs], *s.* **1.** (*poes.*) arsi **2.** (*patol.*) ictus, apoplessia **3.** (*med.*) battito.

icy ['aisi], *ag.* gelido, gelato; ghiacciato: — *road*, strada ghiacciata; *an* — *wind was blowing*, soffiava un vento gelido.

id. [id], *av.* (*abbr. di idem*) idem.

I'd [aid], *contr. di I had, I should, I would*.

Ida ['aidə], *no.pr.f.* Ida.

idea [ai'diə], *s.* **1.** idea, concetto, pensiero; opinione; impressione: *he hit upon the* — *of doing sthg.*, gli venne l'idea di fare ql.co.; *he is a man full of ideas*, è un uomo pieno di idee; *I have an* — *that he will accept*, credo che accetterà; *I've got an* — *that I have seen him before*, ho l'impressione di averlo visto prima; *I've no* —, non saprei; *that's a good* —!, che bell'idea!; *this gives you a good* — *of what we can do*, questo vi dà un'idea esatta di ciò che sappiamo fare **2.** intenzione: *I have no* — *of going*, non ho nessuna intenzione di andare **3.** (*iron.*) idea; fantasia, capriccio: *what an* —!, che bella idea!; *to get ideas into one's head*, farsi delle idee ‖ *the young* —, la mente (anima, fantasia) dei bimbi.

ideal [ai'diəl], *ag.* ideale: *an* — *life*, una vita ideale; — *weather*, tempo ideale ‖ *s.* ideale: *to realize one's ideals*, realizzare i propri ideali.

idealess [ai'diəlis], *ag.* senza idee.

idealism [ai'diəlizəm], *s.* (*fil.*) idealismo.

idealist [ai'diəlist], *s.* idealista.

idealistic [ai,diə'listik], *ag.* idealistico.

ideality [,aidi'æliti], *s.* idealità.

idealization [ai,diəlai'zeiʃən], *s.* idealizzazione.

to idealize [ai'diəlaiz], *v.t.i.* idealizzare.

ideally [ai'diəli], *av.* idealmente.

idem ['aidem], *av.* (*lat.*) idem.

identic [ai'dentik], *ag.* identico (specialmente in diplomazia): — *note*, nota identica.

identical [ai'dentikəl], *ag.* identico, uguale: *A is* — *with B* (o *A and B are* —), A e B sono identici.

identically [ai'dentikəli], *av.* identicamente.

identicalness [ai'dentikəlnis], *s.* identicità.

identifiable [ai'dentifaiəbl], *ag.* identificabile.

identification [ai,dentifi'keiʃən], *s.* identificazione, riconoscimento ☆ — *mark*, contrassegno.

to identify [ai'dentifai], *v.t.* identificare: *to* — *oneself with*, identificarsi, associarsi strettamente con.

identity [ai'dentiti], *s.* identità: *to prove one's* —, farsi riconoscere con prove ☆ — *card*, carta di identità; — *disc* (o — *disk*), (*mil.*) piastrina di riconoscimento.

ideogram ['idiougræm], **ideograph** ['idiougrɑːf], *s.* ideogramma.

ideographic(al) [,idiou'græfik(əl)], *ag.* ideografico.

ideographically [,idiou'græfikəli], *av.* ideograficamente.

ideography [‚idi'ɔgrəfi], *s.* ideografia.
ideologic(al) [‚aidiə'lɔdʒik(əl)], *ag.* ideologico.
ideologist [‚aidi'ɔlədʒist], *s.* ideologo.
ideology [‚aidi'ɔlədʒi], *s.* ideologia.
Ides [aidz], *s.pl.* Idi (nel calendario romano).
idest [id'est], *l. av. (lat. abbr. i.e.*, pronunciata anche *that is* [ðət'iz]) cioè.
idiocy ['idiəsi], *s. (patol.)* idiozia, cretinismo, ebetismo.
idiom ['idiəm], *s.* **1.** idiotismo; costruzione, locuzione particolare di una lingua, di un autore **2.** idioma; dialetto.
idiomatic(al) [‚idiə'mætik(əl)], *ag.* idiomatico.
idiomatically [‚idiə'mætikəli], *av.* idiomaticamente.
idiopathy [‚idi'ɔpəθi], *s. (patol.)* idiopatia.
idiosyncrasy [‚idiə'sinkrəsi], *s.* idiosincrasia.
idiosyncratic [‚idiəsin'krætik], *ag.* che soffre di idiosincrasie.
idiot ['idiət], *s.* idiota, cretino, ebete.
idiotic(al) [‚idi'ɔtik(əl)], *ag.* idiota, ebete.
idiotically [‚idi'ɔtikəli], *av.* da idiota, da ebete.
idiotish ['idiətiʃ], *ag.* idiota.
idiotism ['idiətizəm], *s.* idiozia.
idle ['aidl], *ag.* **1.** pigro, ozioso, disoccupato, sfaccendato: *— hours,* ore d'ozio; *— period,* periodo inattivo: *owing to the strike the machines are* —, le macchine sono ferme a causa dello sciopero; *to be (o to stand)* —, stare senza far niente **2.** inutile, vano, senza scopo: *— tears,* lacrime vane; *it is — to expect him to pay for us,* è inutile aspettarsi che egli paghi per noi **3.** frivolo, futile: *an — tale,* un racconto futile; *— words,* parole futili, oziose ☆ *— wheel,* (*mec.*) ingranaggio di rinvio.
to **idle**, *v.t.i.* oziare; sciupare, sprecare: *to — time away,* perdere il tempo oziando.
idleness ['aidlnis], *s.* **1.** pigrizia; ozio; indolenza; inattività: *lo live in* —, vivere nell'ozio, senza lavorare **2.** inutilità, futilità.
idler ['aidlə*], *s.* pigro, ozioso; poltrone; indolente.
idless ['aidlis], (*arc.*) per **idleness**.
idly ['aidli], *av.* **1.** pigramente, oziosamente; indolentemente **2.** inutilmente.
idocrase ['aidoʊkreis], *s.* (*min.*) idocrasio, vesuvianite.
idol ['aidl], *s.* idolo.
idolater [ai'dɔlətə*], *s.* idolatra.
idolatress [ai'dɔlətris], *s.* donna idolatra.
to **idolatrize** [ai'dɔlətraiz], *v.t.* idolatrare.
idolatrous [ai'dɔlətrəs], *ag.* idolatrico, da idolatra.
idolatrously [ai'dɔlətrəsli], *av.* con idolatria, da idolatra.
idolatry [ai'dɔlətri], *s.* idolatria.
idolism ['aidəlizəm], *s.* idolatria.
idolist ['aidəlist], *s.* idolatra.
idolization [‚aidəlai'zeiʃən], *s.* **1.** l'adorare come idolo **2.** l'essere idolatrato.
to **idolize** ['aidəlaiz], *v.t.i.* idolatrare, idoleggiare, fare un idolo di; adorare idoli.
idolizer ['aidəlaizə*], *s.c.* idolatra.
Idomeneus [ai'dɔminju:s], *no.pr.m. (mit.)* Idomeneo.
idyl(l) ['idil], *s. (poes.)* idillio.
idyllic [ai'dilik], *ag.* idillico, pastorale.
idyllically [ai'dilikəli], *av.* in modo idillico.
idyllist ['aidilist], *s.* scrittore di idilli.
if [if], *cong.* **1.** (*condizione*) se: *— it does not rain, we shall go,* se non pioverà, andremo; *— (it is) possible, necessary, we...,* se (è) possibile, necessario, noi...; *come and get your books — you want them,* vieni a prendere i tuoi libri se ne hai bisogno **2.** anche se, **supposto che**: *— I am wrong, you are wrong too,* se ho torto io, hai torto anche tu **3.** (*nella lingua parlata si trova* **if** *usato sovente invece di* **whether**): *I don't know — he is at home,* non so se sia in casa **4.** *as —,* **come se**: *as — you didn't know!,* come se tu non lo sapessi!; *he is walking as — he were very tired,* cammina come se fosse molto stanco **5.** (**Fraseologia**): *— anything,* se

mai: *— anything, she is uglier than her sister,* ella è se mai più brutta di sua sorella ‖ *— at all,* se mai, se per caso ‖ *— only,* se solo: *— only I knew!,* se solo lo sapessi!.
igloo ['iglu:], *s.* igloo.
Ignatia [ig'neiʃjə], *no.pr.f.* Ignazia.
Ignatius [ig'neiʃjəs], *no.pr.m.* Ignazio.
igneous ['igniəs], *ag.* igneo.
igniferous [ig'nifərəs], *ag.* ignifero.
ignis-fatuus ['ignis'fætjuəs], *pl.* **ignes-fatui** ['ignis-'fætjuai], *s.* fuoco fatuo.
ignitable [ig'naitəbl], *ag.* infiammabile.
to **ignite** [ig'nait], *v.t.i.* **1.** accendere, accendersi; infiammare, dar fuoco a; prender fuoco **2.** (*chim.*) calcinare; incenerire; sottoporre all'azione del fuoco.
ignition [ig'niʃən], *s.* ignizione; accensione ☆ *— (lock) key,* (*aut.*) chiavetta dell'accensione.
ignobility [‚ignoʊ'biliti], *s.* ignobilità, bassezza.
ignoble [ig'noubl], *ag.* ignobile, turpe, disonorevole.
ignobleness [ig'noublnis], *s.* ignobilità, bassezza.
ignobly [ig'noubli], *av.* ignobilmente.
ignominious [‚ignə'miniəs], *ag.* ignominioso, infamante.
ignominiously [‚ignə'miniəsli], *av.* ignominiosamente.
ignominy ['ignəmini], *s.* ignominia, infamia.
ignoramus [‚ignə'reiməs], *s.* ignorante, ignorantone.
ignorance ['ignərəns], *s.* ignoranza: *out of* —, per ignoranza.
ignorant ['ignərənt], *ag.* **1.** ignorante; illetterato **2.** ignaro: *to be* — *of,* ignorare.
ignorantly ['ignərəntli], *av.* per ignoranza.
ignoration [‚ignə'reiʃən], *s.* il fingere di non conoscere, l'ignorare.
to **ignore** [ig'nɔ:*], *v.t.* **1.** ignorare, trascurare: *he ignored my remark,* finse di non sentire la mia osservazione; *to — the facts,* non tenere nessun conto dei fatti **2.** fingere di non conoscere, non voler riconoscere: *they always — him,* fingono sempre di non riconoscerlo **2.** (*dir.*) dichiarare non luogo a procedere.
iguana [i'gwa:nə], *s. (zool.)* iguana.
iguanodon [i'gwa:nədɔn], *s. (paleont.)* iguanodonte.
ilex ['aileks], *pl.* **ilexes** ['aileksiz], *s. (bot.)* elce, leccio.
iliac ['iliæk], *ag. (anat.)* iliaco.
Iliad ['iliəd], *s. (lett.)* Iliade.
Ilium ['iliəm], *no.pr. (st.)* Ilio.
ilk [ilk], *ag. (scoz.)* stesso ‖ *of that* —, della stessa famiglia, dello stesso luogo, ecc.
I'll [ail], *contr. di I will, I shall.*
ill [il], *comp.* **worse** [wə:s], *superl.* **worst** [wə:st], *ag.* **1.** ammalato: *he was — with a fever,* era affetto da una forma febbrile; *to be* —, essere ammalato; *to fall (o get o be taken)* —, ammalarsi; *to feel* —, sentirsi male **2.** cattivo; nocivo, dannoso; malaugurato: *— deed,* cattiva azione ‖ *to do s.o. an — turn,* rendere a qlcu. un cattivo servizio ‖ *— weeds grow apace,* prov. l'erba cattiva cresce in fretta ‖ *it's an — wind that blows nobody any good,* prov. non tutto il male viene per nuocere **3.** deficiente, difettoso ‖ *s.* **1.** male: *to do* —, fare del male; *to speak, think — of s.o.,* parlare, pensar male di qlcu. **2.** danno, torto; *pl.* avversità: *the ills of this life,* le avversità di questa vita.
ill, *av.* male, malamente; malauguratamente; sfavorevolmente.
ill, (nei composti): *— -advised,* sconsiderato; *— -bred,* maleducato; *— -conditioned,* in cattive condizioni (di salute, stato); *— -disposed,* malevolo; *— -fated,* sfortunato; *— -favoured,* sgraziato, brutto, deforme; *— -gotten,* male acquisto: *— -gotten gains,* guadagni illeciti; *— -health,* cattiva salute; *— -humoured,* bisbetico; *— -judged,* non opportuno; imprudente; *— -mannered,* maleducato; *— -natured,* di carattere difficile; *— -omened,* di cattivo augurio; *— -repute,* cattiva reputazione; *— -starred,* nato sotto una cattiva stella; *— -tempered,* di cattivo carattere; *— -timed,* inopportuno;

— *-treated* (*o* — *-used*), maltrattato; — *-wisher*, che augura male agli altri.

illation [i'leiʃən], *s.* illazione.

illative [i'leitiv], *ag.* illativo ‖ *s.* parola o clausola illativa.

illatively [i'leitivli], *av.* conclusivamente.

illegal [i'li:gəl], *ag.* illegale; illecito.

illegality [,ili(:)'gæliti], *s.* illegalità.

illegally [i'li:gəli], *av.* illegalmente.

illegibility [i,ledʒi'biliti], *s.* illeggibilità.

illegible [i'ledʒəbl], *ag.* illeggibile.

illegibly [i'ledʒəbli], *av.* in modo illeggibile.

illegitimacy [,ili'dʒitiməsi], *s.* illegittimità.

illegitimate [,ili'dʒitimit], *ag.* illegittimo; illegale; bastardo.

to **illegitimate** [,ili'dʒitimeit], *v.t.* dichiarare illegittimo.

illegitimately [,ili'dʒitimitli], *av.* illegittimamente.

illiberal [i'libərəl], *ag.* illiberale; poco generoso; meschino; gretto.

illiberality [i,libə'ræliti], *s.* illiberalità; ingenerosità; grettezza.

illiberally [i'libərəli], *av.* senza liberalità; meschinamente; grettamente.

illicit [i'lisit], *ag.* illecito; vieto.

illicitly [i'lisitli], *av.* illecitamente.

illicitness [i'lisitnis], *s.* l'essere illecito.

illimitable [i'limitəbl], *ag.* illimitato, sconfinato.

illimitableness [i'limitəblnis], *s.* illimitatezza.

illimitably [i'limitəbli], *av.* illimitatamente.

illimitation [i,limi'teiʃən], *s.* illimitazione.

illimited [i'limitid], *ag.* illimitato.

illiteracy [i'litərəsi], *s.* analfabetismo; mancanza di cultura.

illiterate [i'litərit], *ag.* analfabeta; ignorante ‖ *s.c.* analfabeta; ignorante.

illiterateness [i'litəritnis], *s.* analfabetismo.

illness [ˈilnis], *s.* malattia; indisposizione: *to be absent through* —, essere assente per malattia.

illogical [i'lɔdʒikəl], *ag.* illogico.

illogicality [,ilɔdʒi'kæliti], *s.* illogicità.

illogically [i'lɔdʒikəli], *av.* illogicamente, con poco raziocinio.

illogicalness [i'lɔdʒikəlnis], *s.* illogicità.

illth [ilθ], *s.* (*rar.*) cattivo stato; bisogno.

to **illude** [i'lju:d], *v.t.* (*rar.*) illudere; ingannare; eludere.

to **illume** [i'lju:m], *v.t.* (*poet.*) illuminare (anche *fig.*).

illuminable [i'lju:minəbl], *ag.* illuminabile.

illuminant [i'lju:minənt], *ag.* illuminante ‖ *s.* lume.

to **illuminate** [i'lju:mineit], *v.t.* 1. illuminare; rischiarare (anche *fig.*) 2. miniare 3. illuminare a festa (edifici, strade, ecc.).

illuminating [i'lju:mineitiŋ], *ag.* chiarificante, illuminante (anche *fig.*).

illumination [i,lju:mi'neiʃən], *s.* 1. illuminazione (anche *fig.*); (*gener. pl.*) luminaria 2. miniatura 3. ispirazione divina.

illuminative [i'lju:minətiv], *ag.* illuminativo.

illuminator [i'lju:mineitə*], *s.c.* 1. illuminatore, illuminatrice 2. miniatore, miniatrice.

to **illumine** [i'lju:min], *v.t.* rischiarare, illuminare (anche *fig.*).

illuminism [i'lju:(:)minizəm], *s.* (*st. fil.*) illuminismo.

illuminist [i'lju:(:)minist], *s.* (*st. fil.*) illuminista.

illusion [i'lu:ʒən], *s.* 1. illusione; inganno 2. tulle leggerissimo.

illusionism [i'lu:ʒənizəm], *s.* illusionismo.

illusionist [i'lu:ʒənist], *s.* illusionista.

illusive [i'lu:siv], *ag.* illusorio; ingannevole.

illusively [i'lu:sivli], *av.* illusoriamente.

illusiveness [i'lu:sivnis], *s.* illusorietà.

illusory [i'lu:səri], *ag.* illusorio.

to **illustrate** [ˈiləstreit], *v.t.* 1. spiegare; delucidare; esemplificare 2. illustrare (con incisioni, disegni): *illustrated weekly*, rivista settimanale illustrata.

illustration [,iləs'treiʃən], *s.* 1. esempio; spiegazione 2. illustrazione, disegno.

illustrative ['iləstreitiv], *ag.* illustrativo, esplicativo.

illustratively ['iləstreitivli], *av.* in modo illustrativo, esplicativo.

illustrator ['iləstreitə*], *s.c.* 1. illustratore, illustratrice 2. esplicatore, esplicatrice.

illustrious [i'lʌstriəs], *ag.* illustre, celebre.

illustriously [i'lʌstriəsli], *av.* illustremente.

illustriousness [i'lʌstriəsnis], *s.* fama, celebrità.

illy [ˈili], *av.* (*rar.*) male.

Illyria [i'liriə], *no.pr.* (*geog. st.*) Illiria.

Illyrian [i'liriən], *ag.* illirico ‖ *s.c.* abitante dell'Illiria ‖ *s.* lingua illirica.

Ilus [ˈailəs], *no.pr.m.* (*mit.*) Ilo.

I'm [aim], *contr.* di *I am.*

'im [im], (*volg.*) *abbr.* di *him.*

image [ˈimidʒ], *s.* 1. immagine, effigie; idolo 2. (*foto.*) immagine 3. somiglianza, ritratto: *she is the living* — *of her mother*, ella è il ritratto di sua madre 4. idea, concetto ☆ — *-worship*, culto delle immagini, idolatria.

to **image**, *v.t.* 1. immaginare, immaginarsi 2. descrivere; rappresentare, figurare: *to* — *sthg. to oneself*, figurarsi ql.co. 3. riflettere su.

imageless [ˈimidʒlis], *ag.* privo d'immagini.

imagery [ˈimidʒəri], *s.* 1. immagini 2. (*ret.*) immagine; metafora; linguaggio figurato 3. statuaria; lavoro d'intaglio.

imaginable [i'mædʒinəbl], *ag.* immaginabile.

imaginableness [i'mædʒinəblnis], *s.* immaginabilità.

imaginary [i'mædʒinəri], *ag.* immaginario.

imagination [i,mædʒi'neiʃən], *s.* immaginazione; fantasia.

imaginative [i'mædʒinətiv], *ag.* immaginativo; fantasioso.

imaginatively [i'mædʒinətivli], *av.* immaginativamente.

imaginativeness [i'mædʒinətivnis], *s.* immaginativa; inventiva.

to **imagine** [i'mædʒin], *v.t.i.* immaginare, immaginarsi; farsi un'idea, figurarsi: — *meeting you here!*, chi avrebbe mai pensato di incontrarti qui!; *he imagined himself lost*, si credeva perduto; *I cannot* — *what he will do now*, non posso immaginarmi che cosa farà ora; *I imagined him as a very proud man*, me lo figuravo un uomo molto fiero; *just* —..., puoi ben' immaginare...; *try to* — *my position*, cerca di farti un'idea della mia posizione.

imaginer [i'mædʒinə*], *s.c.* immaginatore, immaginatrice.

imagining [i'mædʒiniŋ], *s.* immaginazione: *these are all vain imaginings*, queste sono tutte vane chimere.

imagism [ˈimidʒizəm], *s.* (*lett.*) immaginismo.

imago [i'meigou], *pl.* **imagines** [i'meidʒini:z], **imagos** [i'meigouz], *s.* imagine (forma definitiva di insetto).

imam [i'mɑ:m], *s.* (*relig. maomettana*) imano.

imbecile [ˈimbisi:l], *ag.s.* imbecille, sciocco, scemo; debole (anche fisicamente).

imbecilely [ˈimbisi:lli], *av.* da imbecille.

imbecility [,imbi'siliti], *s.* imbecillità; debolezza.

to **imbibe** [im'baib], *v.t.* 1. assorbire, assimilare (idee): *he imbibed the most absurd ideas*, assorbì le idee più assurde 2. bere, assorbire, imbeversi di: *the earth imbibed the water*, la terra assorbì l'acqua.

imbiber [im'baibə*], *s.c.* bevitore, bevitrice.

imbibition [,imbi'biʃən], *s.* (*fis.*) assorbimento; imbibizione.

imbricate [ˈimbrikit], *ag.* embricato, imbricato (anche *bot. zool.*).

to **imbricate** [ˈimbrikeit], *v.t.* sistemare (tegole, embrici) in ordine sovrapposto.

imbrication [,imbri'keiʃən], *s.* sovrapposizione di tegole.

imbroglio [im'brouliou], *s.* imbroglio; pasticcio.

to **imbrue** [im'bru:], *v.t.* (*arc. letter.*) intridere; imbrattare, macchiare: *his sword was imbrued with blood*, la sua spada era imbrattata di sangue.

to imbrute [im'bru:t], *v.t.i.* abbrutire, abbrutirsi.

to imbue [im'bju:], *v.t.* 1. imbevere, impregnare (di umidità, colore) 2. *fig.* impregnare: *they imbued him with love for honesty*, gli inculcarono, instillarono l'amore all'onestà.

imitability [,imitə'biliti], *s.* imitabilità.

imitable ['imitəbl], *ag.* imitabile.

imitant ['imitənt], *ag.* imitante.

to imitate ['imiteit], *v.t.* imitare; contraffare.

imitation [,imi'teiʃən], *s.* imitazione; copia, contraffazione: *beware of imitations*, diffidate delle imitazioni ☆ — *jewelry*, gioielli falsi; — *leather*, finta pelle.

imitative ['imitətiv], *ag.* imitativo, imitante; contraffatto; simulato.

imitatively ['imitətivli], *av.* imitativamente; per imitazione.

imitator ['imiteitə*], *s.c.* imitatore, imitatrice; contraffattore, contraffattrice.

immaculate [i'mækjulit], *ag.* 1. immacolato, incontaminato, puro ‖ *the Immaculate Conception*, l'Immacolata Concezione 2. *(fam.)* impeccabile.

immaculately [i'mækjulitli], *av.* senza macchia.

immaculateness [i'mækjulitnis], *s.* 1. purezza; biancore; l'essere immacolato 2. *(fam.)* impeccabilità.

immane [i'mein], *ag.* 1. *(arc.)* immane, tremendo 2. feroce, crudele.

immanely [i'meinli], *av.* 1. terribilmente 2. crudelmente.

immanence ['imənəns], **immanency** ['imənənsi], *s.* *(fil.)* immanenza.

immanent ['imənənt], *ag.* *(fil.)* immanente.

Immanuel [i'mænjuəl], *no.pr.m.* Emanuele ‖ *s.* *(Bibbia)* Emmanuele.

immaterial [,imə'tiəriəl], *ag.* 1. immateriale, incorporeo 2. senza importanza, non importante: — *objections*, obiezioni senza importanza.

immaterialism [,imə'tiəriəlizəm], *s.* *(fil.)* immaterialismo; spiritualismo.

immaterialist [,imə'tiəriəlist], *s.* *(fil.)* immaterialista; spiritualista.

immateriality ['imə,tiəri'æliti], *s.* immaterialità.

to immaterialize [,imə'tiəriəlaiz], *v.t.* 1. render immateriale 2. togliere importanza a.

immaterially [,imə'tiəriəli], *av.* 1. immaterialmente 2. irrilevantemente.

immature [,imə'tjuə*], *ag.* 1. immaturo, prematuro: — *death*, morte prematura 2. incompleto.

immaturely [,imə'tjuəli], *av.* immaturamente.

immaturity [,imə'tjuəriti], *s.* immaturità.

immeasurability [i,meʒərə'biliti], *s.* incommensurabilità; immensità.

immeasurable [i'meʒərəbl], *ag.* incommensurabile; immenso.

immeasurableness [i'meʒərəblnis], *s.* incommensurabilità; immensità.

immeasurably [i'meʒərəbli], *av.* incommensurabilmente; immensamente.

immediacy [i'mi:djəsi], *s.* 1. immediatezza 2. rapporto diretto.

immediate [i'mi:djət], *ag.* 1. immediato, istantaneo: *the — future*, l'immediato futuro; *the effect was —*, l'effetto fu istantaneo; *in the — vicinity*, nelle immediate vicinanze; *to take — action*, prendere provvedimenti immediati: *for — delivery*, per consegna immediata, urgente 2. diretto: — *information*, informazioni dirette; *he is in — contact with the Premier*, è in contatto diretto con il primo ministro.

immediately [i'mi:djətli], *av.* 1. immediatamente, subito, istantaneamente 2. direttamente.

immediateness [i'mi:djətnis], *s.* immediatezza, subitaneità, istantaneità.

immemorial [,imi'mɔ:riəl], *ag.* immemorabile; molto vecchio: *from time —*, da tempo immemorabile.

immemorially [,imi'mɔ:riəli], *av.* da tempo immemorabile.

immense [i'mens], *ag.* 1. immenso, smisurato 2. *(sl.)* ottimo, eccellente.

immensely [i'mensli], *av.* immensamente, smisuratamente; *(fam.)* moltissimo.

immenseness [i'mensnis], **immensity** [i'mensiti], *s.* immensità.

immensurability [i,menʃurə'biliti], *s.* immensurabilità.

immensurable [i'menʃurəbl], *ag.* immensurabile.

immensurableness [i'menʃurəblnis], *s.* immensurabilità.

to immerge [i'mə:dʒ], *v.t.i.* immergere, immergersi.

immeritous [i'meritəs], *ag.* *(arc.)* immeritevole.

to immerse [i'mə:s], *v.t.* 1. immergere, tuffare (anche *fig.*): *he immersed his head in water*, egli immerse la testa nell'acqua; *he was immersed in study*, era immerso nello studio; *to be immersed in one's thoughts*, essere immerso nei propri pensieri 2. battezzare per immersione.

immersion [i'mə:ʃən], *s.* 1. immersione (anche *fig.*) 2. battesimo (per immersione) 3. *(astr.)* eclissi ☆ — *heater*, *(elett.)* riscaldatore ad immersione.

immigrant ['imigrənt], *ag.s.* immigrante.

to immigrate ['imigreit], *v.t.i.* immigrare; importare (persone) come immigranti.

immigration [,imi'greiʃən], *s.* immigrazione.

imminence ['iminəns], *s.* 1. imminenza 2. pericolo sovrastante.

imminent ['iminənt], *ag.* imminente, prossimo.

imminently ['iminəntli], *av.* imminentemente.

to immingle [i'miŋgl], *v.t.i.* mescolare, mescolarsi.

immiscibility [i,misi'biliti], *s.* impossibilità a mescolarsi.

immitigable [i'mitigəbl], *ag.* non mitigabile, implacabile.

immixible [i'miksibl], *ag.* che non può essere mischiato.

immixture [i'mikstʃə*], *s.* 1. mescolanza 2. l'essere coinvolto (in un affare, ecc.).

immobile [i'moubail], *ag.* immobile; immoto (anche *fig*); stazionario.

immobility [,imou'biliti], *s.* immobilità.

immobilization [i,moubilai'zeiʃən], *s.* immobilizzazione.

to immobilize [i'moubilaiz], *v.t.* 1. immobilizzare 2. mettere, tener fuori dalla circolazione; *fig.* mettere, tener fuori dal giro d'azione.

immoderate [i'mɔdərit], *ag.* smodato, eccessivo.

immoderately [i'mɔdəritli], *av.* smodatamente, eccessivamente.

immoderation ['i,mɔdə'reiʃən], *s.* smoderatezza, eccesso; intemperanza.

immodest [i'mɔdist], *ag.* 1. immodesto; impudico 2. impertinente; impudente.

immodestly [i'mɔdistli], *av.* 1. immodestamente; impudicamente 2. impertinentemente; impudentemente.

immodesty [i'mɔdisti], *s.* 1. immodestia; impudicizia; indecenza 2. impertinenza, impudenza.

to immolate ['imouleit], *v.t.* immolare.

immolation [,imou'leiʃən], *s.* immolazione.

immolator ['imouleitə*], *s.c.* chi immola.

immoral [i'mɔrəl], *ag.* immorale; dissoluto; licenzioso.

immorality [,imə'ræliti], *s.* immoralità; dissolutezza; licenziosità.

immorally [i'mɔrəli], *av.* in modo immorale; in modo dissoluto.

immortal [i'mɔ:tl], *ag.* immortale; perenne (anche *fig.*) ‖ *s.* immortale.

immortality [,imɔ:'tæliti], *s.* immortalità; perpetuità.

immortalization [i,mɔ:təlai'zeiʃən], *s.* l'immortalare.

to immortalize [i'mɔ:təlaiz], *v.t.* immortalare.

immortally [i'mɔ:təli], *av.* immortalmente; perpetuamente.

immortelle [,imɔ:'tel], *s.* *(bot.)* semprevivo.

immovability [i‚mu:və'biliti], *s.* 1. immobilità 2. immutabilità 3. inamovibilità.

immovable [i'mu:vəbl], *ag.* 1. immobile; inamovibile, immutabile 2. impassibile 3. (*dir.*) inamovibile; immobiliare ☆ — *properties*, beni immobili.

immovableness [i'mu:vəblnis], *s.* 1. immobilità 2. immutabilità 3. inamovibilità.

immovables [i'mu:vəblz], *s.pl.* (*dir.*) beni immobili.

immovably [i'mu:vəbli], *av.* 1. immobilmente 2. impassibilmente.

immune [i'mju:n], *ag.* 1. immune; libero da obblighi; esente (anche *fig.*) 2. (*med.*) immune ☆ — *body*, anticorpo; — *protein*, antitossina.

immunity [i'mju:niti], *s.* 1. (*amm.*) esenzione; privilegio: *diplomatic* —, immunità diplomatica 2. immunità (da contagio, da pericolo).

immunization [‚imju(:)nai'zeiʃən], *s.* immunizzazione.

to **immunize** ['imju(:)naiz], *v.t.* (*med.*) immunizzare.

to **immure** [i'mjuə*], *v.t.* 1. murare, circondare con muri ‖ *to* — *oneself*, rinchiudersi 2. imprigionare.

immurement [i'mjuəmənt], *s.* imprigionamento.

immutability [i‚mju:tə'biliti], *s.* immutabilità; invariabilità.

immutable [i'mju:təbl], *ag.* immutabile; invariabile.

immutableness [i'mju:təblnis], *V.* **immutability**.

immutably [i'mju:təbli], *av.* immutabilmente.

Imogen ['imoudʒən], *no.pr.f.* Imogene.

imp [imp], *s.* diavoletto, demonietto; bimbo capriccioso e vivace.

impact ['impækt], *s.* 1. urto, cozzo; collisione 2. (*mil.*) impatto (di missile) 3. (*psicologia*) contatto, urto ☆ — *strength*, (*arch.*) resilienza, resistenza dinamica.

to **impact** [im'pækt], *v.t.* 1. comprimere; conficcare; incastrare 2. urtare, cozzare 3. *fig.* imprimere.

impaction [im'pækʃən], *s.* compressione, pressione.

impair[1] [im'pɛə*], *ag.* dispari.

to **impair**[2], *v.t.* 1. indebolire: *his energy is being impaired by old age*, la vecchiaia indebolisce la sua energia 2. deteriorare, danneggiare, menomare: *his health was seriously impaired*, la sua salute fu seriamente danneggiata.

impaired [im'pɛəd], *ag.* 1. indebolito 2. deteriorato, danneggiato; menomato.

impairment [im'pɛəmənt], *s.* 1. indebolimento 2. deterioramento, danno, menomazione.

to **impale** [im'peil], *v.t.* 1. impalare 2. recingere (con una palizzata).

impalement [im'peilmənt], *s.* 1. impalatura 2. terreno rinchiuso con una palizzata.

impalpability [im‚pælpə'biliti], *s.* 1. impalpabilità 2. inafferrabilità.

impalpable [im'pælpəbl], *ag.* 1. impalpabile 2. inafferrabile.

impalpably [im'pælpəbli], *av.* impalpabilmente.

impaludism [im'pælju(:)dizəm], *s.* (*patol.*) paludismo, malaria.

impanate [im'peinit], *ag.* (*teol.*) impanato.

impanation [‚impə'neiʃən], *s.* (*teol.*) impanazione.

to **imparadise** [im'pærədais], *v.t.* 1. rendere completamente felice 2. rendere (un luogo) simile a paradiso.

imparisyllabic ['im‚pærisi'læbik], *ag.s.* imparisillabo.

imparity [im'pæriti], *s.* imparità.

to **impark** [im'pɑ:k], *v.t.* rinchiudere (animali) in luogo cinato; cintare (un terreno) per farne un parco.

imparkation [‚impɑ:'keiʃən], *s.* palizzata.

to **impart** [im'pɑ:t], *v.t.* 1. impartire: *to* — *knowledge*, impartire nozioni 2. dare, conferire (coraggio, ecc.) 3. comunicare, informare; rivelare 4. distribuire, dividere: *let the rich* — *to those who are not rich*, dividano i ricchi con coloro che non sono ricchi.

impartation [‚impɑ:'teiʃən], *s.* comunicazione, trasmissione (di notizie, ecc.).

impartial [im'pɑ:ʃəl], *ag.* giusto, imparziale, disinteressato.

impartiality ['im‚pɑ:ʃi'æliti], *s.* imparzialità, equità.

impartially [im'pɑ:ʃəli], *av.* imparzialmente, equamente.

impartible [im'pɑ:tibl], *ag.* indivisibile.

impartment [im'pɑ:tmənt], *s.* assegnazione; distribuzione: comunicazione.

impassability ['im‚pɑ:sə'biliti], *s.* invalicabilità; impraticabilità.

impassable [im'pɑ:səbl], *ag.* invalicabile; impraticabile; inguadabile.

impassableness [im'pɑ:səblnis], *s.* invalicabilità; impraticabilità.

impasse [æm'pɑ:s], *s.* vicolo cieco, via senza uscita (anche *fig.*).

impassibility ['im‚pæsi'biliti], *s.* impassibilità, imperturbabilità; insensibilità.

impassible [im'pæsibl], *ag.* impassibile, imperturbabile; insensibile.

impassibleness [im'pæsiblnis], *s.* impassibilità, imperturbabilità; insensibilità.

impassibly [im'pæsibli], *av.* impassibilmente.

to **impassion** [im'pæʃən], *v.t.* appassionare, eccitare.

impassionate [im'pæʃənit], *ag.* eccitato; commosso.

impassioned [im'pæʃənd], *ag.* veemente; caloroso; eccitato.

impassive [im'pæsiv], *ag.* impassibile; insensibile.

impassively [im'pæsivli], *av.* impassibilmente, imperturbabilmente; insensibilmente.

impassiveness [im'pæsivnis], *s.* impassibilità, imperturbabilità; insensibilità.

to **impaste** [im'peist], *v.t.* impastare (anche *pitt.*).

impasto [im'pɑ:stou], *s.* (*pitt.*) impasto.

impatience [im'peiʃəns], *s.* 1. impazienza, irrequietezza, smania 2. avversione, disgusto, intolleranza: — *of sthg.*, intolleranza di ql.co.; *his* — *of contradiction was well known*, tutti sapevano che non poteva sopportare d'essere contraddetto.

impatient [im'peiʃənt], *ag.* 1. impaziente, irrequieto, smanioso 2. intollerante: *to be* — *of advice*, non poter sopportare i consigli; *to grow* (o *to get*) —, perdere la pazienza.

impatiently [im'peiʃəntli], *av.* 1. impazientemente, con irrequietezza, smaniosamente 2. con intolleranza.

impavid [im'pævid], *ag.* impavido.

impavidly [im'pævidli], *av.* coraggiosamente.

to **impawn** [im'pɔ:n], *v.t.* depositare come garanzia; impegnare.

to **impeach** [im'pi:tʃ], *v.t.* 1. (*dir.*) imputare; accusare, mettere in stato d'accusa; denunziare; incriminare: *to* — *s.o. for high treason*, accusare qlcu. di alto tradimento; *to* — *s.o. with*, *of a crime*, accusare qlcu. di un delitto 2. biasimare, censurare.

impeachable [im'pi:tʃəbl], *ag.* accusabile, denunziabile, incolpabile, incriminabile.

impeacher [im'pi:tʃə*], *s.* (*dir.*) accusatore.

impeachment [im'pi:tʃmənt], *s.* 1. accusa, imputazione, incriminazione 2. denigrazione.

to **impearl** [im'pə:l], *v.t.i.* imperlare, imperlarsi (anche *fig.*).

impeccability [im‚pekə'biliti], *s.* impeccabilità.

impeccable [im'pekəbl], *ag.* impeccabile.

impecuniosity [‚im-pi‚kju:ni'ositi], *s.* mancanza di denaro; povertà, indigenza.

impecunious [‚im-pi'kju:njəs], *ag.* senza denaro; povero, indigente.

to **impede** [im'pi:d], *v.t.* impedire; ostacolare; intralciare; ritardare.

impediment [im'pedimənt], *s.* 1. impedimento; ostacolo; difficoltà: *an* — *in one's speech*, un difetto di pronuncia; *let me not to the marriage of true minds admit impediments*, non sarà che alle nozze di animi costanti io ammetta impedimenti 2. *pl.* (*spec. mil.*) impedimenta, bagagli.

impedimental [im‚pedi'mentl], *ag.* che causa impedimento.

impeditive [im'peditiv], *ag.* impeditivo.

to **impel** [im'pel], *pass.p.p.* **impelled** [im'peld], *v.t.* (IV) **1.** incitare, stimolare, spingere: *poverty impelled him to crime*, la povertà lo spinse al delitto **2.** costringere, forzare.

impellent [im'pelənt], *ag.* impellente ‖ *s.* movente; incentivo, stimolo.

impeller [im'pelə*], *s.c.* istigatore, istigatrice ‖ *s.* **1.** movente **2.** (*mec.*) ventola, girante.

to **impend** [im'pend], *v.i.* sovrastare, incombere; essere imminente: *impending dangers*, pericoli incombenti.

impendence [im'pendəns], *s.* ciò che incombe; imminenza.

impendent [im'pendənt], *ag.* sovrastante, incombente; imminente.

impenetrability [im‚penitrə'biliti], *s.* impenetrabilità.

impenetrable [im'penitrəbl], *ag.* impenetrabile.

impenetrably [im'penitrəbli], *av.* impenetrabilmente.

impenitence [im'penitəns], *s.* impenitenza.

impenitent [im'penitənt], *ag. s.* (individuo) impenitente, incorreggibile: *an — gambler*, un giocatore impenitente.

impenitently [im'penitəntli], *av.* in modo impenitente, incorreggibilmente.

imperatival [im‚perə'taivəl], *ag.* (*gram.*) relativo al modo imperativo.

imperative [im'perətiv], *ag.* **1.** imperativo; perentorio; urgente; obbligatorio **2.** (*gram.*) imperativo: *— mood*, modo imperativo ‖ *s.* (*gram.*) imperativo ‖ *categorical —*, (*fil.*) imperativo categorico.

imperatively [im'perətivli], *av.* imperiosamente; perentoriamente.

imperativeness [im'perotivnis], *s.* imperiosità.

imperator [‚impə'rɑ:to:*], *s.* (anche *st. romana*) imperatore.

imperatorial [im‚perə'tɔ:riəl], *ag.* **1.** imperiale **2.** imperatorio.

imperceptible [‚im-pə'septəbl], *ag.* impercettibile.

imperceptibleness [‚im-pə'septəblnis], *s.* impercettibilità.

imperceptibly [‚im-pə'septəbli], *av.* impercettibilmente.

impercipient [‚impə:'sipiənt], *ag.* mancante di percezione.

imperfect [im'pə:fikt], *ag.* **1.** imperfetto; difettoso, mancante, incompleto, incompiuto: *to leave sthg. —*, lasciare ql.co. incompleto **2.** (*gram.*) imperfetto: *— tense*, tempo imperfetto ‖ *s.* (*gram.*) imperfetto.

imperfection [‚im-pə'fekʃən], *s.* imperfezione; incompiutezza; difetto.

imperfectly [im'pə:fiktli], *av.* imperfettamente; incompiutamente; difettosamente.

imperfectness [im'pə:fiktnis], *s.* l'essere imperfetto; imperfezione.

imperforable [im'pə:fərəbl], *ag.* imperforabile.

imperforate [im'pə:fərit], *ag.* non perforato.

imperial [im'piəriəl], *ag.* **1.** imperiale: *— prince*, principe imperiale ‖ *His, Her Imperial Majesty*, Sua Maestà Imperiale **2.** supremo; maestoso, grandioso ‖ *s.* **1.** pizzo, pizzetto **2.** imperiale (cassa per bagagli sul tetto di una vettura); tetto di vettura, di autobus **3.** imperiale (moneta russa) ☆ *— preference*, dogana ridotta per merci provenienti dai paesi dell'Impero Britannico.

imperialism [im'piəriəlizəm], *s.* imperialismo.

imperialist [im'piəriəlist], *s.* imperialista.

imperialistic [im‚piəriə'listik], *ag.* imperialistico.

imperiality [im‚piəri'æliti], *s.* imperialità.

to **imperialize** [im'piəriəlaiz], *v.t.* rendere imperiale.

to **imperil** [im'peril], *pass.p.p.* **imperilled** [im'perild], *v.t.* mettere in pericolo; mettere a repentaglio.

imperious [im'piəriəs], *ag.* **1.** imperioso; prepotente; arrogante **2.** urgente: *an — need*, una necessità impellente.

imperiously [im'piəriəsli], *av.* imperiosamente; prepotentemente; arrogantemente.

imperiousness [im'piəriəsnis], *s.* **1.** imperiosità; prepotenza; arroganza **2.** urgenza.

imperishability [im‚periʃə'biliti], *s.* indistruttibilità.

imperishable [im'periʃəbl], *ag.* indistruttibile; imperituro.

imperishableness [im'periʃəblnis], *s.* indistruttibilità; l'essere imperituro.

imperishably [im'periʃəbli], *av.* indistruttibilmente.

imperium [im'piəriəm], *pl.* **imperia** [im'piəriə], *s.* **1.** impero; comando, potere assoluto **2.** (*dir.*) diritto di prim'ordine.

impermanence [im'pə:mənəns], *s.* temporaneità, caducità, precarietà.

impermanent [im'pə:mənənt], *ag.* temporaneo, caduco, precario.

impermeability [im‚pə:mjə'biliti], *s.* impermeabilità.

impermeable [im'pə:mjəbl], *ag.* impermeabile.

impermeably [im'pə:mjəbli], *av.* in modo impermeabile.

impermissible [‚impə'misibl], *ag.* non permissibile.

imperscriptible [‚impə'skriptibl], *ag.* imprescrittibile.

impersonal [im'pə:snl], *ag.* **1.** impersonale; senza personalità, senza carattere **2.** (*gram.*) impersonale: *— verb*, verbo impersonale.

impersonality [im‚pə:sə'næliti], *s.* l'essere impersonale; mancanza di personalità.

impersonally [im'pə:snəli], *av.* impersonalmente.

impersonate [im'pə:sənit], *ag.* personificato.

to **impersonate** [im'pə:səneit], *v.t.* interpretare; impersonare.

impersonation [im‚pə:sə'neiʃən], *s.* **1.** personificazione **2.** interpretazione teatrale (di un personaggio) **3.** l'assumere una personalità fittizia.

impersonative [im'pə:sənətiv], *ag.* impersonante.

impersonator [im'pə:səneitə*], *s.* **1.** chi personifica **2.** (*teat.*) interprete **3.** chi assume una personalità fittizia.

to **impersonify** [‚impə:'sonifai], *v.t.* impersonare.

impertinence [im'pə:tinəns], *s.* **1.** impertinenza; impudenza **2.** futilità; stravaganza **3.** (*dir.*) impertinenza.

impertinent [im'pə:tinənt], *ag.* **1.** impertinente **2.** inappropriato; (*dir.*) non pertinente.

impertinently [im'pə:tinəntli], *av.* **1.** impertinentemente **2.** in modo non appropriato.

imperturbability ['im-pə(:)‚tə:bə'biliti], *s.* imperturbabilità; calma.

imperturbable [‚im-pə(:)'tə:bəbl], *ag.* imperturbabile; calmo.

imperturbably [‚im-pə(:)'tə:bəbli], *av.* imperturbabilmente; con calma.

imperturbation [‚im-pə(:)tə(:)'beiʃən], *s.* imperturbabilità; calma.

inperviable [im'pə:viəbl], *ag.* impervio.

impervious [im'pə:vjəs], *ag.* **1.** impervio; impenetrabile; inaccessibile (anche *fig.*): *— to reason*, sordo alla ragione **2.** impermeabile: *— to water*, impermeabile all'acqua.

imperviously [im'pə:vjəsli], *av.* imperviamente.

imperviousness [im'pə:vjəsnis], *s.* impenetrabilità; impermeabilità.

impetigenous [‚impi'tidʒinəs], *ag.* (*patol.*) impetiginoso.

impetigo [‚impi'taigou], *s.* (*patol.*) impetigine.

to **impetrate** ['impitreit], *v.t.* impetrare; (*rar.*) implorare.

impetration [‚impi'treiʃən], *s.* impetrazione.

impetrative ['impitreitiv], *ag.* impetrativo.

impetratory ['impitreitəri], *ag.* impetratorio.

impetuosity [im‚petju'ositi], *s.* impetuosità; violenza; passionalità.

impetuous [im'petjuəs], *ag.* impetuoso; violento; passionale.

impetuously [im'petjuəsli], *av.* impetuosamente.

impetuousness [im'petjuəsnis], *V.* **impetuosity**.

impetus ['impitəs], *s.* impeto, impulso (anche *fig.*).

impiety [im'paiəti], *s.* irriverenza; empietà; malvagità.

to **impinge** [im'pindʒ], *v.t.i.* 1. urtare, colpire 2. venire in urto: *to — on* (o *upon*) *sthg.*, venire in urto con ql.co. 3. violare; intromettersi illegalmente: *to — upon s.o.'s authority*, violare l'autorità di qlcu.

impingement [im'pindʒmənt], *s.* 1. colpo; spinta; urto 2. violazione.

impious ['impiəs], *ag.* irreligioso; empio, malvagio.

impiously ['impiəsli], *av.* empiamente.

impiousness ['impiəsnis], *s.* empietà.

impish ['impiʃ], *ag.* birichino; malizioso; indiavolato.

impishness ['impiʃnis], *s.* carattere malizioso, birichino.

impiteous [im'pitiəs], *ag.* (*poet.*) spietato.

implaceability [im,plækə'biliti], *s.* implacabilità.

implacable [im'plækəbl], *ag.* implacabile.

implacably [im'plækəbli], *av.* implacabilmente.

implant ['im-plɑ:nt], *s.* (*amer. med.*) trapianto.

to **implant** [im'plɑ:nt], *v.t.* 1. piantare, fissare 2. inculcare, instillare, imprimere (idee, ecc.).

implantation [,im-plɑ:n'teiʃən], *s.* 1. impianto 2. inculcazione (di idee, ecc.).

implausible [im'plɔ:zibl], *ag.* non plausibile.

to **impleach** [im'pli:tʃ], *v.t.* (*poet.*) intrecciare.

to **impledge** [im'pledʒ], *v.t.* dare in pegno.

implement ['implimənt], *s.* 1. utensile, apparecchio 2. mobile; articolo di vestiario; *pl.* attrezzi, masserizie 3. (*dir.*) adempimento.

to **implement** ['implimənt], *v.t.* compiere, effettuare; rendere effettivo (un contratto, ecc.); completare.

impletion [im'pli:ʃən], *s.* riempimento; pienezza.

to **implicate** ['implikeit], *v.t.* implicare, coinvolgere: *he was implicated in a crime*, fu coinvolto in un delitto.

implication [,impli'keiʃən], *s.* 1. implicazione: *by —*, implicitamente, per induzione 2. insinuazione.

implicative [im'plikətiv], *ag.* implicante.

implicit [im'plisit], *ag.* implicito: *— faith in*, fede implicita in; *— obedience*, ubbidienza assoluta.

implicitly [im'plisitli], *av.* implicitamente.

implicitness [im'plisitnis], *s.* l'essere implicito.

implied [im'plaid], *ag.* implicito; tacito.

imploration [,implə'reiʃən], *s.* implorazione.

to **implore** [im'plɔ:*], *v.t.* (IV) implorare, supplicare.

implorer [im'plɔ:rə*], *s.* (*rar.*) imploratore; postulante.

imploring [im'plɔ:riŋ], *ag.* supplichevole; supplicante.

imploringly [im'plɔ:riŋli], *av.* in tono supplichevole.

impluvium [im'plu:viəm], *pl.* **impluvia** [im'plu:viə], *s.* (*arch. romana*) impluvio.

to **imply** [im'plai], *v.t.* implicare; significare, voler dire; insinuare.

to **impocket** [im'pɔkit], *v.t.* intascare.

impolicy [im'pɔlisi], *s.* 1. cattiva politica 2. goffaggine; inopportunità.

impolite [,im-pə'lait], *ag.* scortese, ineducato.

impolitely [,im-pə'laitli], *av.* scortesemente.

impoliteness [,im-pə'laitnis], *s.* scortesia.

impolitic [im'pɔlitik], *ag.* 1. impolitico 2. inopportuno; imprudente; malaccorto.

imponderability [im,pɔndərə'biliti], *s.* imponderabilità.

imponderable [im'pɔndərəbl], *ag.* imponderabile; *fig.* inestimabile.

imponderableness [im'pɔndərəblnis], *s.* imponderabilità.

to **impone** [im'poun], *v.t.i.* imporre; scommettere su.

import ['impɔ:t], *s.* 1. importanza; peso; entità; valore: *of great —*, di grande importanza 2. significato, senso: *what is the — of his words?*, quale è il significato delle sue parole? 3. *gener. pl.* (*comm.*) importazione;

articolo d'importazione ☆ — *certificate*, certificato di importazione; — *duty*, dazio di importazione; — *quay*, banchina di scarico.

to **import** [im'pɔ:t], *v.t.i.* 1. essere importante; interessare 2. indicare; significare: *what do his words —?*, che cosa significano le sue parole? 3. (*comm.*) importare, introdurre: *to — goods (from one country into another)*, importare merci (da un paese in un altro).

importable [im'pɔ:təbl], *ag.* importabile.

importance [im'pɔ:təns], *s.* importanza; entità; rilievo; peso: *it is of — that*, è importante che; *to attach — to sthg.*, attribuire importanza a ql.co.

important [im'pɔ:tənt], *ag.* importante; rilevante.

importantly [im'pɔ:təntli], *av.* in modo importante.

importation [,impɔ:'teiʃən], *s.* importazione.

importer [im'pɔ:tə*], *s.* importatore.

importless [im'pɔ:tlis], *ag.* (*arc.*) senza importanza.

importunate [im'pɔ:tjunit], *ag.* 1. importuno, molesto; insistente 2. urgente (di affari).

importunately [im'pɔ:tjunitli], *av.* importunamente; insistentemente.

importunateness [im'pɔ:tjunitnis], *s.* importunità; insistenza.

importune [im'pɔ:tju:n], *V.* **importunate**.

to **importune**, *v.t.* importunare, molestare.

importunely [im'pɔ:tju:nli], *av.* insistentemente; importunamente.

importuner [im'pɔ:tju:nə*], *s.c.* importunatore, importunatrice; molestatore, molestatrice.

importunity [,impɔ:'tju:niti], *s.* importunità; insistenza.

to **impose** [im'pouz], *v.t.i.* 1. imporre, imporsi (con l'autorità); prescrivere; comandare: *to — a tax on*, imporre una tassa su 2. (*tip.*) ordinare pagine composte 3. (*eccl.*) imporre le mani, benedire 4. *to — (up)on* (*s.o.*), ingannare: *they imposed upon his kindness*, hanno abusato della sua gentilezza; *to let oneself be imposed upon*, lasciarsi ingannare.

imposing [im'pouziŋ], *ag.* maestoso, grandioso, imponente.

imposingly [im'pouziŋli], *av.* maestosamente, grandiosamente.

imposingness [im'pouziŋnis], *s.* imponenza.

imposition [,impə'ziʃən], *s.* 1. imposizione; soverchieria, prepotenza 2. (*eccl.*) imposizione 3. imposta, tassa 4. (*sl. scolastico*) penso 5. inganno.

impossibility [im,pɔsə'biliti], *s.* impossibilità.

impossible [im'pɔsəbl], *ag.* 1. impossibile: *it's — for me to go*, mi è impossibile andare 2. (*fam.*) strano; assurdo; stravagante; intollerabile.

impossibly [im'pɔsəbli], *av.* impossibilmente: *— exacting*, oltremodo esigente.

impost[1] ['impoust], *s.* 1. imposta; tassa; dazio di entrata 2. (*sl. spor.*) handicap.

impost[2], *s.* (*arch.*) imposta.

to **impost(h)umate** [im'pɔstjumeit], *v.t.i.* (*rar. patol.*) impostemire.

impost(h)umation [im,pɔstju'meiʃən], *s.* (*patol.*) apostema.

to **impost(h)ume** [im'pɔstju:m], *v.t.i.* (*rar. patol.*) impostemire.

impostor [im'pɔstə*], *s.* impostore; imbroglione.

imposture [im'pɔstʃə*], *s.* impostura; inganno; frode.

impot ['impɔt], *s.* (*sl. scolastico*) penso.

impotence ['impətəns], **impotency** ['impətənsi], *s.* 1. impotenza; incapacità; debolezza 2. (*dir. patol.*) impotenza.

impotent ['impətənt], *ag.* 1. impotente; debole; inetto, incapace 2. (*dir. patol.*) impotente.

impotently ['impətəntli], *av.* 1. impotentemente; debolmente 2. (*dir. patol.*) impotentemente.

to **impound** [im'paund], *v.t.* 1. sequestrare (persone, beni); rinchiudere (bestiame in un recinto) 2. raccogliere (acque) 3. (*dir.*) confiscare.

to **impoverish** [im'pɔvəriʃ], *v.t.* impoverire; esaurire.

impoverishment [im'povərifmənt], *s.* impoverimento; esaurimento.

impracticability [im,præktikə'biliti], *s.* **1.** inattuabilità (di progetti, ecc.) **2.** impraticabilità (di strade) **3.** intrattabilità (di persone).

impracticable [im'præktikəbl], *ag.* **1.** inattuabile, impossibile (di progetti, ecc.) **2.** impraticabile (di strade) **3.** intrattàbile (di persone).

impracticableness [im'præktikəblnis], *V.* **impracticability.**

impracticably [im'præktikəbli], *av.* impraticabilmente.

to **imprecate** ['imprikeit], *v.t.* imprecare: *to — curses upon s.o.*, lanciare maledizioni contro qlcu.

imprecation [,impri'keifən], *s.* imprecazione; maledizione.

imprecatory ['imprikeitəri], *ag.* imprecatorio, imprecativo; maledicente.

imprecise [,impri'sais], *ag.* (*rar.*) impreciso.

imprecision [,impri'siʒən], *s.* (*rar.*) imprecisione.

to **impregn** [im'pri:n], (*poet.*) per to **impregnate.**

impregnability [im,pregnə'biliti], *s.* inespugnabilità.

impregnable [im'pregnəbl], *ag.* **1.** inespugnabile (di fortezza, ecc.) **2.** *fig.* insuperabile, incrollabile.

impregnably [im'pregnəbli], *av.* **1.** in modo inespugnabile **2.** insuperabilmente.

impregnate [im'pregnit], *ag.* **1.** impregnato, imbevuto **2.** (*biol.*) pregno, fecondato.

to **impregnate** ['impregneit], *v.t.* **1.** (*biol.*) fecondare **2.** fertilizzare, rendere fecondo **3.** impregnare, saturare, imbevere (anche *fig.*): *his shirt was impregnated with sweat*, la sua camicia era impregnata di sudore.

impregnated ['impregneitid], *ag.* **1.** (*biol.*) pregno, gravido; *fig.* pieno **2.** imbevuto.

impregnation [,impreg'neifən], *s.* **1.** (*biol.*) fecondazione **2.** impregnazione.

impresario [,impre'sa:riou], *pl.* **impresarios** [,impre-'sa:riouz], *s.* (*teat. rad. tv.*) impresario.

imprescriptibility [,impri,skripti'biliti], *s.* imprescrittibilità.

imprescriptible [,impri'skriptibl], *ag.* imprescrittibile.

impress[1] ['impres], *s.* impressione; marchio; stampo; *fig.* impronta.

to **impress**[1] [im'pres], *v.t.* **1.** (*tip.*) stampare; imprimere **2.** *fig.* imprimere, inculcare (idee, sentimenti, ecc.): *he impressed the idea on her mind*, fissò quella idea nella mente di lei **3.** impressionare: *he went away much impressed*, andò via molto impressionato; *they will — you with their cleverness*, sarete impressionati dalla loro abilità.

to **impress**[2], *v.t.* **1.** (*mar. mil.*) arruolare forzatamente **2.** requisire (merci, ecc.).

impressibility [im,presi'biliti], *s.* **1.** impressionabilità (anche *fig.*) **2.** suscettibilità.

impressible [im'presəbl], *ag.* **1.** (*tip.*) imprimibile; stampabile **2.** impressionabile **3.** suscettibile.

impressibly [im'presəbli], *av.* in modo impressionabile; in modo suscettibile.

impression [im'prefən], *s.* **1.** impressione, impronta **2.** (*tip.*) ristampa: *sixth — of the third edition*, sesta ristampa della terza edizione **3.** *fig.* impressione; idea: *a strong, a vague —*, un'impressione profonda, vaga; *under the — that...*, sotto l'impressione che...; *to create an —*, dare un'impressione.

impressionability [im,prefnə'biliti], *s.* **1.** impressionabilità **2.** sensibilità.

impressionable [im'prefnəbl], *ag.* **1.** impressionabile **2.** sensibile.

impressionism [im'prefnizəm], *s.* (*st. art.*) impressionismo.

impressionist [im'prefnist], *s.c.* (*art.*) impressionista.

impressionistic [im,prefə'nistik], *ag.* (*art.*) impressionistico.

impressive [im'presiv], *ag.* **1.** impressionante; imponente; commovente **2.** solenne.

impressively [im'presivli], *av.* **1.** in modo impressionante **2.** solennemente.

impressiveness [im'presivnis], *s.* **1.** imponenza **2.** solennità.

impressment [im'presmənt], *s.* **1.** (*mil.*) arruolamento (d'ufficio); (*mar.*) leva forzata **2.** requisizione (di merci, viveri, ecc.) **3.** *fig.* spinta.

imprest ['imprest], *s.* prestito concesso a pubblico funzionario.

imprimatur [,impri'meitə*], *s.* (*lat.*) imprimatur; *fig.* approvazione.

imprint ['im-print], *s.* **1.** impressione; impronta **2.** (*tip.*) stampa: *no —*, senza indicazione dell'editore; *publisher's —*, stampato da, coi tipi di.

to **imprint** [im'print], *v.t.* stampare; imprimere (anche *fig.*): *to — sthg. in the mind, on the memory of s.o.*, imprimere ql.co. nella mente, nella memoria di qlcu.

to **imprison** [im'prizn], *v.t.* imprigionare, incarcerare; *fig.* rinchiudere; relegare; confinare.

imprisonment [im'priznmənt], *s.* **1.** incarceramento, arresto; carcerazione **2.** prigionia, reclusione.

improbability [im,probə'biliti], *s.* improbabilità; inverosimiglianza.

improbable [im'probəbl], *ag.* improbabile; inverosimile.

improbably [im'probəbli], *av.* improbabilmente; inverosimilmente.

improbity [im'proubiti], *s.* malvagità; disonestà.

impromptu [im'promptju:], *ag.* improvvisato, estemporaneo ‖ *s.* (*mus. lett.*) improvvisazione ‖ *av.* all'improvviso, estemporaneamente.

improper [im'propə*], *ag.* **1.** improprio, disadatto **2.** erroneo, scorretto **3.** sconveniente; indecente.

improperly [im'propəli], *av.* **1.** impropriamente **2.** erroneamente, scorrettamente **3.** sconvenientemente.

impropriate [im'proupriit], *ag.* dato in proprietà; (*dir. eccl.*) secolarizzato (di beneficio).

to **impropriate** [im'prouprieit], *v.t.* appropriarsi indebitamente di; (*dir. eccl.*) secolarizzare (benefici ecclesiastici); concedere (benefici ecclesiastici).

impropriation [im,proupri'eifən], *s.* (*dir. eccl.*) secolarizzazione (di benefici, ecc.).

impropriator [im'prouprieitə*], *s.* (*dir. eccl.*) laico investito di benefici ecclesiastici.

impropriety [,im-prə'praiəti], *s.* **1.** improprietà **2.** scorrettezza; sconvenienza.

improvability [im,pru:və'biliti], *s.* suscettibilità di miglioramento, di valorizzazione.

improvable [im'pru:vəbl], *ag.* **1.** perfezionabile, suscettibile di miglioramento **2.** bonificabile.

improvableness [im'pru:vəblnis], *s.* perfettibilità.

improvably [im'pru:vəbli], *av.* in modo perfettibile, valorizzabile.

to **improve** [im'pru:v], *v.t.i.* **1.** migliorare, perfezionare, perfezionarsi; far progredire; fare progressi: *he is improving in health*, migliora in salute; *his manners are improving*, i suoi modi migliorano; *my French has improved*, il mio francese è migliorato; *wine improves with age*, il vino migliora con gli anni; *your young sister has improved*, la tua sorellina si è fatta graziosa; *to — in one's studies*, migliorare negli studi; *to — upon sthg.*, apportare delle migliorie; *to — with use*, migliorare con l'uso ‖ *to — on s.o.'s offer*, (*comm.*) superare l'offerta di qlcu. **2.** approfittare di, approfittarsi di: *to — the occasion, the opportunity*, approfittare dell'occasione, dell'opportunità **3.** coltivare, valorizzare (terreno); far fruttare (denaro).

improvement [im'pru:vmənt], *s.* **1.** miglioramento; miglioria; perfezionamento; progresso: *— in health*, miglioramento di salute; *open to —*, suscettibile di miglioramento; *no — seems possible*, non sembra possibile alcun miglioramento; *there is need of — in your studies*, c'è bisogno di miglioramento nei tuoi studi; *this book is an — on* (o *over*) *his former works*, questo libro supera le sue opere precedenti; *to effect improvements in sthg.*, effettuare miglioramenti in ql.co. **2.** bonifica, valorizzazione (di terreno).

improver [im'pru:və*], *s.c* **1.** perfezionatore, perfezionatrice **2.** apprendista

improvidence [im'prɔvidəns], *s.* imprevidenza.

improvident [im'prɔvidənt], *ag.* imprevidente.

improvidently [im'prɔvidəntli], *av.* imprevidentemente, senza previdenza.

improving [im'pru:viŋ], *s.* miglioramento.

improvingly [im'pru:viŋli], *av.* in modo da far migliorare, da valorizzare.

to **improvisate** [im'prɔvizeit], *v.t.* improvvisare.

improvisation [,imprəvai'zeiʃən], *s.* improvvisazione.

improvisator [im'prɔvizeitə*], *s.* improvvisatore.

improvisatorial [im,prɔvizə'tɔ:riəl], **improvisatory** [,imprə'vaizətəri], *ag.* improvvisante.

improvisatrice [,improu,vi:za:'tri:tʃei], *s.* improvvisatrice.

to **improvise** ['imprəvaiz], *v.t.i.* improvvisare; preparare in fretta: *he can — good music*, sa improvvisare buona musica; *to — a meal*, preparare in fretta un pasto.

improviser ['imprəvaizə*], *s.c.* improvvisatore, improvvisatrice.

imprudence [im'pru:dəns], *s.* imprudenza.

imprudent [im'pru:dənt], *ag.* imprudente, incauto.

imprudently [im'pru:dəntli], *av.* imprudentemente, incautamente.

impudence ['impjudəns], *s.* impudenza, sfrontatezza.

impudent ['impjudənt], *ag.* impudente, sfrontato.

impudently ['impjudəntli], *av.* impudentemente, sfrontatamente.

impudicity [,impju'disiti], *s.* impudicizia.

to **impugn** [im'pju:n], *v.t.* impugnare; oppugnare; contrastare; contraddire.

impugnable [im'pʌgnəbl], *ag.* impugnabile; oppugnabile.

impugner [im'pju:nə*], *s.* oppositore; antagonista.

impugnment [im'pju:nmənt], *s.* impugnazione; attacco; sfida.

impuissance [im'pju(:)isns], *s.* impotenza; debolezza.

impuissant [im'pju(:)isnt], *ag.* impotente; debole.

impulse ['impʌls], *s.* impulso; impeto; stimolo; urto; spinta: *to act on —*, agire d'impulso; *to feel an — to do sthg.*, sentirsi spinto a fare ql.co. ☆ *current —*, (*elett.*) impulso di corrente.

impulsion [im'pʌlʃən], *s.* impulso; spinta; impeto; stimolo.

impulsive [im'pʌlsiv], *ag.* **1.** impulsivo **2.** (*mec.*) propulsore.

impulsively [im'pʌlsivli], *av.* impulsivamente; per impulso.

impulsiveness [im'pʌlsivnis], **impulsivity** [,impʌl'siviti], *s.* impulsività.

impunity [im'pju:niti], *s.* impunità.

impure [im'pjuə*], *ag.* **1.** impuro; contaminato; adulterato **2.** impudico.

impurely [im'pjuəli], *av.* **1.** impuramente **2.** impudicamente.

impurity [im'pjuəriti], *s.* **1.** impurità, contaminazione **2.** impudicizia **3.** *pl.* corpi estranei, impurità.

to **impurple** [im'pə:pl], *v.t.* (*arc.*) imporporare.

imputability [im,pju:tə'biliti], *s.* imputabilità.

imputable [im'pju:təbl], *ag.* imputabile, attribuibile.

imputableness [im'pju:təblnis], *s.* imputabilità.

imputably [im'pju:təbli], *av.* con imputazione.

imputation [,impju(:)'teiʃən], *s.* imputazione.

imputative [im'pju:tətiv], *ag.* d'imputazione.

to **impute** [im'pju:t], *v.t.* imputare, attribuire (colpe, ecc.): *the mistake was imputed to him*, l'errore fu imputato a lui.

in [in], *av.prep.* **a, in, dentro, entro; durante; tra, fra; con, per 1.** (**luogo**): *— China*, in Cina; *— the country*, in campagna; *— the streets of London*, nelle strade di Londra; *I saw it — the newspaper*, lo vidi sul giornale **2.** (**tempo**): *— the daytime*, *— the morning*, *— the night*, durante il giorno, di mattina, di notte; *— summer*, *— August*, nell'estate, in agosto; *— the 20th century*, nel ventesimo secolo; *— 1915*, nel 1915 ‖ *— a week*, fra una settimana; *I shall finish this work — two hours*, terminerò questo lavoro fra due ore **3.** (**stato, condizione, circostanze, ecc.**): *he is — danger*, egli è in pericolo; *he is — a good humour, a bad temper*, egli è di buon umore, di cattivo umore; *he works — the export business*, egli lavora nel commercio delle esportazioni; *she is — love*, ella è innamorata; *to go out — the snow*, uscire nella neve **4.** (**relazione, riferimento**): *— my opinion*, secondo la mia opinione; *blind — the eye*, cieco da un occhio; *the books, four — number*, i libri, quattro di numero; *once — three years*, una volta ogni tre anni; *one — a hundred*, uno su cento **5.** (**maniera, modo di vestire, scopo, ecc.**): *— a muffled voice*, con voce soffocata; *to write — English*, scrivere in inglese; *to write — ink*, scrivere con inchiostro ‖ *he appeared — a brown suit*, egli apparve in un abito marrone; *he was — slippers*, era in ciabatte; *she was dressed — white*, ella era vestita di bianco ‖ *— honour of*, in onore di; *— order that*, affinchè, in modo che; *— reply to*, in risposta a **6.** (**dopo certi verbi** e per tradurre **mentre, all'atto di**): *he succeeded — winning*, è riuscito a vincere ‖ *to drop —*, fare una breve visita; *to give —*, cedere, arrendersi; *to go —*, entrare (andare dentro) ‖ *— crossing the street he was run over*, nell'attraversare la strada fu travolto; *— studying Latin, you must remember...*, studiando (nello studiare) il latino, dovete ricordare... **7.** (**con to be**): *to be —*, essere in casa, essere arrivato, ecc.: *he is always — and out (of the house)*, egli è sempre dentro e fuori (di casa), va e viene continuamente; *he is — with the best people*, è in relazione con la migliore società; *the labour party is —*, il partito laburista è al potere; *the spring is —*, la primavera è arrivata ‖ *to be — for*, esser destinato a: *he is — for trouble*, gli capiterà qualche guaio ‖ *to be — great hopes*, avere grandi speranze ‖ *to be — the wrong*, essere dalla parte del torto **8.** (**Fraseologia**): *— all*, in tutto; *— fact*, infatti, in effetto; *— that*, in quanto che; *— with you!*, su, entrate!.

in, *ag.* interno ‖ *s.* **1.** (*pol.*) membro del partito al potere ‖ *the ins and outs*, i membri del partito al potere e quelli all'opposizione **2.** i dettagli, ogni particolare: *he knows the ins and outs of the problem*, conosce tutti i particolari del problema.

inability [,inə'biliti], *s.* inabilità; incapacità.

inaccessibility ['inæk,sesə'biliti], *s.* inaccessibilità; irraggiungibilità.

inaccessible [,inæk'sesəbl], *ag.* inaccessibile; irraggiungibile; inavvicinabile.

inaccessibleness [,inæk'sesəblnis], *V.* **inaccessibility**.

inaccessibly [,inæk'sesəbli], *av.* inaccessibilmente.

inaccuracy [in'ækjurəsi], *s.* inesattezza, imprecisione; sbaglio: *— of a translation*, imprecisione di una traduzione; *work full of inaccuracies*, lavoro pieno di inesattezze.

inaccurate [in'ækjurit], *ag.* inesatto, impreciso; sbagliato.

inaccurately [in'ækjuritli], *av.* in modo impreciso, inesattamente.

inaction [in'ækʃən], *s.* **1.** inazione, inattività, inoperosità; ozio **2.** (*chim. fis.*) inerzia.

inactive [in'æktiv], *ag.* **1.** inerte, inattivo, inoperoso; ozioso **2.** (*chim. fis.*) inerte, inattivo.

inactively [in'æktivli], *av.* inattivamente, inoperosamente.

inactivity [,inæk'tiviti], *s.* **1.** inattività, inoperosità ozio, indolenza, passività **2.** (*chim. fis.*) inerzia.

inadaptable [,inə'dæptəbl], *ag.* (*rar.*) inadattabile.

inadaptability ['inə,dæptə'biliti], *s.* inadattabilità

inadequacy [in'ædikwəsi], *s.* inadeguatezza; insufficienza (anche *med.*).

inadequate [in'ædikwit], *ag.* inadeguato; insufficiente.

inadequately [in'ædikwitli], *av.* inadeguatamente; insufficientemente.

inadequateness [in'ædikwitnis], *V.* **inadequacy.**

inadhesive [,inəd'hi:siv], *ag.* che non aderisce.

inadmissibility ['inəd,misə'biliti], *s.* inammissibilità.

inadmissible [,inəd'misəbl], *ag.* inammissibile.

inadvertence [,inəd'və:təns], **inadvertency** [,inəd-'və:tənsi], *s.* inavvertenza, disattenzione, sbadataggine.

inadvertent [,inəd'və:tənt], *ag.* **1.** disattento, sbadato **2.** involontario (di azione, ecc.).

inadvertently [,inəd'və:təntli], *av.* **1.** disattentamente, sbadatamente **2.** inavvertitamente.

inaidable [in'eidəbl], *ag.* (*poet. arc.*) che non può essere aiutato.

inalienability [in,eiljənə'biliti], *s.* inalienabilità.

inalienable [in'eiljənəbl], *ag.* inalienabile.

inalterability [in,ɔ:ltərə'biliti], *s.* inalterabilità; immutabilità.

inalterable [in'ɔ:ltərəbl], *ag.* inalterabile; immutabile.

inalterably [in'ɔ:ltərəbli], *av.* inalterabilmente.

inane [i'nein], *ag.* **1.** vuoto, vacuo **2.** insensato, sciocco ‖ *s.* vuoto, vacuità (anche *fig.*).

inanely [i'neinli], *av.* insensatamente; vuotamente.

inanimate [in'ænimit], *ag.* **1.** inanimato; esanime: — *beings*, esseri inanimati; — *nature*, mondo inanimato **2.** privo di vivacità, fiacco: — *conversation*, conversazione fiacca.

inanimately [in'ænimitli], *av.* inanimatamente.

inanimateness [in'ænimitnis], **inanimation** [in,æni-'meiʃən], *s.* immobilità; mancanza di vita.

inanition [,inə'niʃən], *s.* inanizione.

inanity [i'næniti], *s.* inanità; vacuità (anche *fig.*).

inappeasable [,inə'pi:zəbl], *ag.* implacabile; che non si può calmare, pacificare.

inappellable [,inə'peləbl], *ag.* inappellabile.

inappetence [in'æpitəns], *s.* inappetenza.

inapplicability ['in,æplikə'biliti], *s.* inapplicabilità; l'essere inadatto.

inapplicable [in'æplikəbl], *ag.* inapplicabile; inadatto.

inapplication [in,æpli'keiʃən], *s.* **1.** indolenza; negligenza **2.** inapplicabilità.

inapposite [in'æpəzit], *ag.* improprio, fuori luogo; non appropriato; non pertinente.

inappositely [in'æpəzitli], *av.* impropriamente, male a proposito; fuori luogo.

inappreciable [,inə'pri:ʃəbl], *ag.* **1.** impercettibile, trascurabile **2.** inapprezzabile.

inappreciably [,inə'pri:ʃəbli], *av.* **1.** impercettibilmente, trascurabilmente **2.** in modo non apprezzabile.

inappreciation [,inə,pri:ʃi'eiʃən], *s.* incapacità di apprezzare.

inappreciative [,inə'pri:ʃiətiv], *ag.* che non apprezza.

inapprehensible [,inæpri'hensəbl], *ag.* incomprensibile; inafferrabile.

inapprehension [,inæpri'henʃən], *s.* incomprensibilità.

inapprehensive [,inæpri'hensiv], *ag.* che non comprende.

inapproachable [,inə'proutʃəbl], *ag.* inavvicinabile; inaccessibile.

inapproachably [,inə'proutʃəbli], *av.* inaccessibilmente.

inappropriate [,inə'proupriit], *ag.* non appropriato, improprio: *utterly* — *to the existing situation*, assolutamente incompatibile con la situazione attuale.

inappropriately [,inə'proupriitli], *av.* impropriamente.

inapt [in'æpt], *ag.* **1.** inadatto **2.** inabile, maldestro.

inaptitude [in'æptitju:d], *s.* inattitudine, incapacità.

inaptly [in'æptli], *av.* in modo inadatto.

inaptness [in'æptnis], *s.* inattitudine, incapacità.

inarable [in'ærəbl], *ag.* inarabile.

to **inarch** [in'ɑ:tʃ], *v.t.* (*agr.*) innestare per approssimazione.

inarching [in'ɑ:tʃiŋ], *s.* (*agr.*) innesto per approssimazione.

to **inarm** [in'ɑ:m], *v.t.* (*poet.*) abbracciare.

inarticulate [,inɑ:'tikjulit], *ag.* **1.** inarticolato; indistinto (di suono, voce); muto **2.** (*zool.*) disarticolato.

inarticulately [,inɑ:'tikjulitli], *av.* indistintamente.

inarticulateness [,inɑ:'tikjulitnis], *s.* **1.** poca chiarezza nei suoni, nel parlare; afonia **2.** disarticolazione.

inartificial [in,ɑ:ti'fiʃəl], *ag.* **1.** non artistico **2.** semplice, naturale.

inartificiality [in,ɑ:tifiʃi'æliti], *s.* naturalezza.

inartificially [in,ɑ:ti'fiʃəli], *av.* naturalmente, semplicemente.

inartistic [,inɑ:'tistik], *ag.* **1.** non portato all'arte **2.** non artistico.

inartistically [,inɑ:'tistikəli], *av.* senza arte.

inasmuch [inəz'mʌtʃ], *av.* **1.** (*arc.*) parimenti **2.** — *as*, visto che, considerando che, poichè, dacchè, in quanto che.

inattention [,inə'tenʃən], *s.* **1.** disattenzione; distrazione; sbadataggine **2.** trascuratezza, negligenza: — *to one's business*, negligenza nei propri affari.

inattentive [,inə'tentiv], *ag.* **1.** disattento; distratto; sbadato **2.** negligente.

inattentively [,inə'tentivli], *av.* **1.** distrattamente; sbadatamente **2.** trascuratamente, negligentemente.

inattentiveness [,inə'tentivnis], *s.* disattenzione.

inaudibility [in,ɔ:də'biliti], *s.* impercettibilità; inafferrabilità (di suono); debolezza (di voce).

inaudible [in'ɔ:dəbl], *ag.* impercettibile; inafferrabile: *the noise rendered his words* — *to us*, il rumore ci impedì di afferrare le sue parole.

inaudibly [in'ɔ:dəbli], *av.* in modo non udibile.

inaugural [i'nɔ:gjurəl], *ag.* inaugurale ‖ *s.* (*amer.*) discorso inaugurale.

to **inaugurate** [i'nɔ:gjureit], *v.t.* inaugurare.

inauguration [i,nɔ:gju'reiʃən], *s.* inaugurazione ‖ *Inauguration Day*, (*amer.*) giornata in cui il nuovo Presidente assume i poteri.

inaugurator [i'nɔ:gjureitə*], *s.c.* chi inaugura.

inauguratory [i'nɔ:gjureitəri], *ag.* inaugurale.

inauspicious [,inɔ:s'piʃəs], *ag.* infausto, funesto, malaugurato.

inauspiciously [,inɔ:s'piʃəsli], *av.* infaustamente, funestamente, malauguratamente.

inauspiciousness [,inɔ:s'piʃəsnis], *s.* cattivi auspici; malaugurio.

inboard ['in'bɔ:d], *ag.* (*mar.*) interno, entrobordo: — *cabin*, cabina interna.

inboard, *av.* internamente, entrobordo: *to take the anchor* —, ritirare l'àncora.

inborn ['in'bɔ:n], *ag.* innato, congenito.

to **inbreathe** ['in'bri:ð], *v.t.* inspirare (anche *fig.*).

inbred ['in'bred], *ag.* **1.** innato, congenito **2.** consanguineo (di cavalli, ecc.).

inbreeding ['in'bri:diŋ], *s.* incrocio tra animali, piante affini.

Inca ['iŋkə], *s.* (*st. peruviana*) Inca.

incalculability [in,kælkjulə'biliti], *s.* incalcolabilità; imprevedibilità.

incalculable [in'kælkjuləbl], *ag.* incalcolabile; imprevedibile; incerto (di persona, carattere).

incalculably [in'kælkjuləbli], *av.* incalcolabilmente; imprevidibilmente.

to **incandesce** [,inkæn'des], *v.t.i.* ardere, far ardere; essere incandescente, rendere incandescente.

incandescence [,inkæn'desns], *s.* incandescenza.

incandescent [,inkæn'desnt], *ag.* incandescente ☆ — *burner*, becco incandescente; — *lamp*, lampada a incandescenza.

incantation [,inkæn'teiʃən], *s.* incantesimo; magia.

incapability [in,keipə'biliti], *s.* **1.** incapacità; inettitudine; inabilità **2.** (*dir.*) incapacità.

incapable [in'keipəbl], *ag.* **1.** incapace; inetto; inabile: — *of speech*, incapace di parlare; — *of doing sthg.*, incapace di fare ql.co. **2.** (*dir.*) inabilitato: *to have s.o. declared* — *of managing his own affairs*, fare interdire qlcu.

incapably [in'keipəbli], *av.* inettamente: *to act* —, dare prova di incapacità ‖ — *drunk*, ubriaco fradicio.

to **incapacitate** [,inkə'pæsiteit], *v.t.* **1.** inabilitare, rendere incapace: *to* — *s.o. for work*, inabilitare qlcu. al lavoro; *to* — *s.o. from doing sthg.*, rendere qlcu. inabile a fare ql.co. **2.** (*dir.*) dichiarare incapace; privare di potere; inabilitare.

incapacitation ['inkə,pæsi'teiʃən], *s.* **1.** inabilità, incapacità **2.** (*dir.*) inabilitazione.

incapacity [,inkə'pæsiti], *s.* **1.** incapacità, inabilità; incompetenza: — *for doing sthg.* (o *to do sthg.*), incapacità di fare ql.co. **2.** (*dir.*) inabilità, incapacità legale.

to **incarcerate** [in'kɑːsəreit], *v.t.* imprigionare (anche *fig.*).

incarceration [in,kɑːsə'reiʃən], *s.* **1.** incarcerazione **2.** (*patol.*) strozzamento (di ernia).

incarcerator [in'kɑːsəreitə*], *s.* imprigionatore.

incarnadine [in'kɑːnədain], *ag.* color carne; color cremisi.

to **incarnadine**, *v.t.* (*poet.*) tingere di color carne, di color cremisi.

incarnate [in'kɑːnit], *ag.* incarnato, personificato: *to become* —, incarnarsi.

to **incarnate** ['inkɑːneit], *v.t.* **1.** incarnare; personificare **2.** concretare, realizzare.

incarnation [,inkɑː'neiʃən], *s.* incarnazione, personificazione.

incatenation [in,kæti'neiʃən], *s.* incatenamento.

incautious [in'kɔːʃəs], *ag.* incauto; imprudente; sconsiderato: — *words*, parole imprudenti.

incautiously [in'kɔːʃəsli], *av.* incautamente; imprudentemente; sconsideratamente.

incautiousness [in'kɔːʃəsnis], *s.* imprudenza; sconsideratezza; avventatezza.

incelebrity [,insi'lebriti], *s.* mancanza di celebrità.

incendiarism [in'sendjəriəm], *s.* **1.** incendio doloso **2.** *fig.* sobillazione, attività sediziosa.

incendiary [in'sendjəri], *ag.* **1.** incendiario **2.** *fig.* incendiario; sovversivo, sedizioso (di discorso, proposito, ecc.) ‖ *s.* incendiario; sovversivo ☆ — *bomb*, bomba incendiaria.

incense[1] ['insens], *s.* **1.** incenso **2.** *fig.* incensamento, adulazione.

to **incense**[1], *v.t.* incensare (anche *fig.*); profumare di incenso.

to **incense**[2] [in'sens], *v.t.* provocare, irritare; esasperare: *to* — *s.o. against s.o.*, istigare, incitare qlcu. contro qlcu. ‖ *to become* (o *to grow*) *incensed* (*against, at, with s.o.*), irritarsi (contro qlcu.).

incensement [in'sensmənt], *s.* esasperazione; ira.

incensory ['insensəri], *s.* (*eccl.*) turibolo.

incentive [in'sentiv], *ag.* stimolante ‖ *s.* incentivo, stimolo; movente, motivo.

to **incept** [in'sept], *v.t.* (*rar.*) iniziare, cominciare.

inception [in'sepʃən], *s.* principio, inizio.

inceptive [in'septiv], *ag.* iniziale; (*gram.*) incoativo ‖ *s.* (*gram.*) verbo incoativo.

incertain [in'sɔːtn], *ag.* (*arc.*) incerto.

incertitude [in'sɔːtitjuːd], *s.* incertezza, indecisione; dubbio.

incessant [in'sesnt], *ag.* incessante, continuo.

incessantly [in'sesntli], *av.* incessantemente.

incessantness [in'sesntnis], *s.* continuità.

incest ['insest], *s.* incesto.

incestuous [in'sestjuəs], *ag.* incestuoso.

incestuously [in'sestjuəsli], *av.* incestuosamente.

inch[1] [intʃ], *s.* **1.** pollice (misura di lunghezza = cm. 2,54) **2.** *fig.* piccola quantità, cosa da poco, inezia ‖ — *by* — (o *by inches*), a poco a poco, gradatamente, lentamente ‖ *an* — *of cold iron*, un colpo di pugnale ‖

a king in every — (o *every* — *a king*), re da capo a piedi ‖ *within an* — *of*, quasi a, a un pelo da: *he was flogged within an* — *of his life*, fu quasi fustigato a morte ‖ *not to give way an* —, non cedere per nulla ‖ *give him an* — *and he will take an ell*, se gli date un dito si prende un braccio **3.** *pl.* statura: *a man of your inches*, un uomo della tua statura ☆ *cubic* —, pollice cubico (misura di volume = cm.^{3} 16,388); *square* —, pollice quadrato (misura di superficie = cm.^{2} 6,4516).

to **inch**[1], *v.t.i.* muovere, muoversi gradatamente: *to* — *one's way forward*, spingersi avanti poco alla volta.

inch[2], *s.* (*scoz.*) isolotto.

inched [intʃt], *ag.* segnato con divisioni per pollici.

inchoate ['inkoueit], *ag.* appena cominciato; rudimentale; incipiente ☆ — *crimes*, (*dir.*) delitti non perfetti.

to **inchoate**, *v.t.* cominciare; originare.

inchoation [,inkou'eiʃən], *s.* principio; incipienza; fase iniziale.

inchoative ['inkoueitiv],*ag.* (*gram.*)incoativo; iniziale.

incidence [in'insidəns], *s.* **1.** incidenza (anche *geom.*): *angle of* —, angolo di incidenza **2.** raggio di azione, di influenza.

incident ['insidənt], *ag.* **1.** fortuito; probabile; inerente **2.** (*fis.*) incidente ‖ *s.* **1.** caso; avvenimento **2.** episodio, frammento, brano (di commedia, componimento poetico, ecc.) **3.** (*dir.*) servitù, privilegio (inerente a una proprietà).

incidental [,insi'dentl], *ag.* **1.** fortuito; casuale, accidentale; secondario **2.** (*gram.*) incidentale ‖ *s.* caso fortuito; eventualità.

incidentally [,insi'dentli], *av.* incidentalmente; casualmente.

to **incinerate** [in'sinəreit], *v.t.* incenerire; cremare.

incineration [in,sinə'reiʃən], *s.* incenerimento; cremazione.

incinerator [in'sinəreitə*], *s.* forno per rifiuti; (*amer.*) forno crematorio.

incipience [in'sipiəns], **incipiency** [in'sipiənsi], *s.* incipienza, inizio, principio.

incipient [in'sipiənt], *ag.* incipiente: *an* — *tumour*, un tumore allo stadio iniziale.

to **incise** [in'saiz], *v.t.* incidere; intagliare.

incised [in'saizd], *ag.* inciso; intagliato; (*bot.*) frastagliato; seghettato (di ali).

incision [in'siʒən], *s.* incisione; taglio; intaglio.

incisive [in'saisiv], *ag.* **1.** incisivo, tagliente **2.** *fig.* sarcastico; acuto; penetrante ‖ *s.* (dente) incisivo ☆ — *teeth*, denti incisivi.

incisively [in'saisivli], *av.* **1.** in modo incisivo **2.** *fig.* acutamente.

incisiveness [in'saisivnis], *s.* tono incisivo; acutezza.

incisor [in'saizə*], *s.* (dente) incisivo.

incisorial [,insai'sɔːriəl], **incisory** [in'saisəri], *ag.* incisorio.

incisure [in'siʒə*], *s.* taglio, incisione; fessura, fenditura.

incitant ['insitənt], *ag.s.* eccitante; stimolante.

incitation [,insai'teiʃən], *s.* (*rar.*) incitamento; incentivo, stimolo.

to **incite** [in'sait], *v.t.* incitare, spronare; istigare.

incitement [in'saitmənt], *s.* incitamento; istigazione; incoraggiamento; incentivo, stimolo.

inciter [in'saitə*], *s.* incitatore.

inciting [in'saitiŋ], *ag.* incitante; stimolante.

incitingly [in'saitiŋli], *av.* in modo incitante.

incivility [,insi'viliti], *s.* villania; maleducazione.

incivism ['insivizəm], *s.* mancanza di senso civico.

inclemency [in'klemənsi], *s.* inclemenza; rigore, rigidità (di clima).

inclement [in'klemənt], *ag.* inclemente; rigido (di clima, ecc.).

inclemently [in'kleməntli], *av.* inclementemente.

inclinable [in'klainəbl], *ag.* incline, propenso, proclive.

inclination [,inkli'neiʃən], *s.* **1.** inclinazione, tendenza, disposizione; predilezione: *to have an — for sthg., towards s.o.,* avere inclinazione per ql.co., essere attratti da qlcu.; *to have a great — to do sthg.,* essere molto portati a fare ql.co. **2.** pendio; china, declivio.

incline [in'klain], *s.* **1.** pendenza; pendio; declivio **2.** (*geom.*) piano inclinato.

to incline, *v.t.i.* **1.** inclinare, piegare: *to — one's head (in prayer),* chinare il capo (nella preghiera); *to — one's ear to s.o.,* ascoltare con benevolenza qlcu. **2.** tendere (di colori); *fig.* tendere, propendere, essere proclive: *red that inclines to pink,* rosso che tende al rosa; *to be inclined to think that...,* esser propenso a pensare che...; *to feel inclined for a walk, a drink,* aver desiderio di fare una passeggiata, di bere una bibita.

inclined [in'klaind], *ag.* **1.** inclinato: *— plane,* piano inclinato **2.** *fig.* tendente, propenso, proclive.

inclining [in'klainiŋ], *s.* **1.** inclinazione **2.** *fig.* tendenza.

inclinometer [,inkli'nomitə*], *s.* (*fis. mar. aer.*) inclinometro.

to inclip [in'klip], *v.t.* (*arc.*) circondare; abbracciare.

to inclose, *V.* **to enclose.**

inclosure, *V.* **enclosure.**

to include [in'klu:d], *v.t.* includere; comprendere: *he included them all in his invitation,* incluse tutti nel suo invito ‖ *price including taxes,* prezzo tasse comprese; *up to and including 31st December,* a tutto il 31 dicembre.

inclusion [in'klu:ʒən], *s.* inclusione.

inclusive [in'klu:siv], *ag.* compreso; inclusivo; comprendente ‖ *— of,* comprensivo di ☆ *— terms,* tutto compreso (negli alberghi).

inclusively [in'klu:sivli], *av.* inclusivamente.

incoercible [,inkou'ə:sibl], *ag.* incoercibile.

incog [in'kog], *ag.s.* (*abbr. scherz.* di *incognito*) incognito ‖ *av.* in incognito: *to travel —,* viaggiare in incognito.

incogitable [in'kodʒitəbl], *ag.* inconcepibile, impensabile.

incognito [in'kognitou], *ag. s.* incognito ‖ *av.* in incognito.

incognizable [in'kognizəbl], *ag.* inconoscibile.

incognizant [in'kognizənt], *ag.* inconscio.

incognoscibility ['inkog,nosi'biliti], *s.* inconoscibilità.

incognoscible [,inkog'nosibl], *ag.* inconoscibile.

incoherence [,inkou'hiərəns], **incoherency** [,inkou-'hiərənsi], *s.* incoerenza; incongruità; inconsistenza.

incoherent [,inkou'hiərənt], *ag.* incoerente; incongruo; inconsistente.

incoherently [,inkou'hiərəntli], *av.* incoerentemente.

incohesive [,inkou'hi:siv], *ag.* non coesivo.

incombustibility ['inkəm,bʌstə'biliti], *s.* incombustibilità.

incombustible [,inkəm'bʌstəbl], *ag.* incombustibile.

incombustibly [,inkəm'bʌstəbli], *av.* in modo incombustibile.

income ['inkəm], *s.* rendita; reddito; entrata ☆ *— -tax,* imposta sul reddito ‖ *upper — brackets,* (*amer.*) gli alti strati della società.

incomer ['in,kʌmə*], *s.* **1.** chi entra; immigrante **2.** successore **3.** invasore; intruso.

incoming ['in,kʌmiŋ], *ag.* entrante; chi, che succede ad altri: *the — tenant,* il nuovo affittuario ‖ *s.* **1.** entrata, ingresso: *the — and outgoing of the tide,* il flusso e riflusso della marea **2.** *pl.* rendite, entrate.

incommensurability ['inkə,menʃərə'biliti], *s.* incommensurabilità; smisuratezza.

incommensurable [,inkə'menʃərəbl], *ag.* incommensurabile; smisurato.

incommensurably [,inkə'menʃərəbli], *av.* incommensurabilmente; smisuratamente.

incommensurate [,inkə'menʃərit], *ag.* **1.** non paragonabile **2.** sproporzionato; inadeguato.

to incommode [,inkə'moud], *v.t.* incomodare, disturbare, infastidire.

incommodious [,inkə'moudjəs], *ag.* incomodo, scomodo.

incommodiousness [,inkə'moudjəsnis], *s.* scomodità.

incommodity [,inkə'moditi], *s.* scomodità.

incommunicability ['inkə,mju:nikə'biliti], *s.* incomunicabilità.

incommunicable [,inkə'mju:nikəbl], *ag.* **1.** incomunicabile **2.** ineffabile, indicibile.

incommunicableness [,inkə'mju:nikəblnis], *s.* incomunicabilità.

incommunicably [,inkə'mju:nikəbli], *av.* incomunicabilmente.

incommunicating [,inkə'mju:nikeitiŋ], *ag.* senza comunicazione.

incommunicative [,inkə'mju:nikətiv], *ag.* riservato; poco comunicativo.

incommunicatively [,inkə'mju:nikətivli], *av.* senza comunicativa; con riservatezza.

incommunicativeness [,inkə'mju:nikətivnis], *s.* riservatezza; riserbo.

incommutability ['inkə,mju:tə'biliti], *s.* incommutabilità; immutabilità.

incommutable [,inkə'mju:təbl], *ag.* incommutabile; immutabile.

incommutableness [,inkə'mju:təblnis], *s.* incommutabilità; immutabilità.

incommutably [,inkə'mju:təbli], *av.* incommutabilmente; immutabilmente.

incompact [,inkəm'pækt], *ag.* non compatto; *fig.* disgregato.

incomparability [in,kompərə'biliti], *s.* incomparabilità, impareggiabilità.

incomparable [in'kompərəbl], *ag.* incomparabile, impareggiabile.

incomparableness [in'kompərəblnis], *s.* incomparabilità, impareggiabilità.

incomparably [in'kompərəbli], *av.* incomparabilmente, impareggiabilmente.

incompatibility ['inkəm,pætə'biliti], *s.* incompatibilità: *— of character,* incompatibilità di carattere.

incompatible [,inkəm'pætəbl], *ag.* incompatibile.

incompatibly [,inkəm'pætəbli], *av.* incompatibilmente.

incompetence [in'kompitəns], **incompetency** [in-'kompitənsi], *s.* incompetenza; incapacità.

incompetent [in'kompitənt], *ag.* incompetente; incapace.

incompetently [in'kompitəntli], *av.* incompetentemente.

incomplete [,inkəm'pli:t], *ag.* incompleto; imperfetto.

incompletely [,inkəm'pli:tli], *av.* incompletamente; imperfettamente.

incompleteness [,inkəm'pli:tnis], **incompletion** [,inkəm'pli:ʃən], *s.* incompletezza; imperfezione.

incompliance [,inkəm'plaiəns], *s.* scompiacenza.

incompliant [,inkəm'plaiənt], *ag.* scompiacente.

incomprehensibility [in,komprihensə'biliti], *s.* incomprensibilità.

incomprehensible [in,kompri'hensəbl], *ag.* incomprensibile; inconcepibile; inintelligibile; (*teol.*) illimitato ‖ *the Three Incomprehensibles,* (*rar.*) la Trinità.

incomprehensibleness [in,kompri'hensəblnis], **incomprehensibly** [in,kompri'hensəbli], *s.* incomprensibilità.

incomprehension [in,kompri'henʃən], *s.* incomprensione.

incompressibility ['inkəm,presə'biliti], *s.* incompressibilità.

incompressible [,inkəm'presəbl], *ag.* incompressibile.

incomputable [,inkəm'pju:təbl], *ag.* incalcolabile.

inconceivability [ˈinkən,siːvəˈbiliti], *s.* inconcepibilità.

inconceivable [ˌinkənˈsiːvəbl], *ag.* inconcepibile; (*fam.*) incredibile; straordinario; inaudito.

inconceivably [ˌinkənˈsiːvəbli], *av.* inconcepibilmente; incredibilmente; straordinariamente.

inconclusive [ˌinkənˈkluːsiv], *ag.* inconcludente, sconclusionato.

inconclusively [ˌinkənˈkluːsivli], *av.* inconcludentemente.

inconclusiveness [ˌinkənˈkluːsivnis], *s.* inconcludenza.

incondensability [ˌinkən,densəˈbiliti], *s.* non condensabilità.

incondensable [ˌinkənˈdensəbl], *ag.* che non si può condensare.

incondite [inˈkɔndit], *ag.* **1.** mal composto; mal costruito (di romanzo, ecc.) **2.** rozzo, grossolano.

incongruence [inˈkɔŋgruəns], **incongruity** [ˌinkənˈgru(ː)iti], *s.* incongruità; assurdità; incoerenza.

incongruous [inˈkɔŋgruəs], *ag.* incongruo; assurdo; incoerente.

incongruously [inˈkɔŋgruəsli], *av.* incongruentemente; assurdamente; incoerentemente.

incongruousness [inˈkɔŋgruəsnis], *V.* **incongruence.**

inconscient [inˈkɔnʃənt], **inconscious** [inˈkɔnʃəs], *ag.* inconscio.

inconsecutive [ˌinkənˈsekjutiv], *ag.* inconseguente.

inconsecutively [ˌinkənˈsekjutivli], *av.* inconseguentemente; illogicamente.

inconsecutiveness [ˌinkənˈsekjutivnis], *s.* inconseguenza; illogicità.

inconsequence [inˈkɔnsikwəns], *s.* inconseguenza; incongruenza; illogicità.

inconsequent [inˈkɔnsikwənt], *ag.* inconseguente; incongruente; illogico; sconnesso; non pertinente.

inconsequential [in,kɔnsiˈkwenʃəl], *ag.* **1.** inconseguente; incoerente; illogico **2.** (*amer.*) irrilevante; senza conseguenze.

inconsequentiality [in,kɔnsi,kwenʃiˈæliti], *s.* **1.** inconseguenza; incongruenza; illogicità **2.** (*amer.*) irrilevanza.

inconsequentially [in,kɔnsiˈkwenʃəli], *av.* incongruentemente; illogicamente.

inconsiderable [ˌinkənˈsidərəbl], *ag.* trascurabile; insignificante.

inconsiderate [ˌinkənˈsidərit], *ag.* **1.** sconsiderato, imprudente, precipitoso, avventato **2.** indiscreto, senza riguardi.

inconsiderately [ˌinkənˈsidəritli], *av.* **1.** sconsideratamente **2.** senza riguardi.

inconsiderateness [ˌinkənˈsidəritnis], *s.* **1.** sconsideratezza **2.** mancanza di riguardo.

inconsideration [ˈinkən,sidəˈreiʃən], *s.* **1.** sconsiderazione; irriflessione **2.** mancanza di riguardo.

inconsistence [ˌinkənˈsistəns], **inconsistency** [ˌinkənˈsistənsi], *s.* inconsistenza; incoerenza; incompatibilità.

inconsistent [ˌinkənˈsistənt], *ag.* inconsistente; incoerente; incompatibile.

inconsistently [ˌinkənˈsistəntli], *av.* in modo inconsistente; incompatibilmente.

inconsolable [ˌinkənˈsouləbl], *ag.* inconsolabile.

inconsolably [ˌinkənˈsouləbli], *av.* inconsolabilmente.

inconsonance [inˈkɔnsənəns], *s.* disarmonia; discordanza.

inconsonant [inˈkɔnsənənt], *ag.* non in armonia; discorde: *to be — with*, non essere d'accordo con.

inconsonantly [inˈkɔnsənəntli], *av.* non armonicamente; in modo discorde.

inconspicuous [ˌinkənˈspikjuəs], *ag.* incospicuo; insignificante: — *flower*, fiore che si vede appena.

inconspicuously [ˌinkənˈspikjuəsli], *av.* in modo insignificante; in modo non appariscente.

inconspicuousness [ˌinkənˈspikjuəsnis], *s.* l'essere insignificante; il passare inosservato.

inconstancy [inˈkɔnstənsi], *s.* incostanza; instabilità; variabilità.

inconstant [inˈkɔnstənt], *ag.* incostante; instabile; variabile.

inconstantly [inˈkɔnstəntli], *av.* incostantemente; instabilmente; mutabilmente.

inconsumable [ˌinkənˈsjuːməbl], *ag.* inconsumabile, inesauribile, non deteriorabile.

incontestability [ˈinkən,testəˈbiliti] *s.* incontestabilità.

incontestable [ˌinkənˈtestəbl], *ag.* incontestabile.

incontestably [ˌinkənˈtestəbli], *av.* incontestabilmente.

incontiguous [ˌinkənˈtigjuəs], *ag.* non contiguo; separato.

incontinence [inˈkɔntinəns], *s.* incontinenza; smoderatezza.

incontinent [inˈkɔntinənt], *ag.* incontinente; smoderato.

incontinently [inˈkɔntinəntli], *av.* **1.** (*arc.*) subito, immediatamente **2.** intemperatamente, smoderatamente.

incontrollable [ˌinkənˈtrouləbl], *ag.* incontrollabile.

incontrollably [ˌinkənˈtrouləbli], *av.* in modo incontrollabile.

incontrovertible [ˈinkɔntrəˈvəːtəbl], *ag.* incontrovertibile; incontestabile.

incontrovertibly [ˈinkɔntrəˈvəːtəbli], *av.* incontrovertibilmente; incontestabilmente.

inconvenience [ˌinkənˈviːnjəns], *s.* **1.** noia; disturbo: *without the slightest —*, senza il minimo disturbo; *I am putting you to great —*, vi do molto disturbo **2.** scomodità.

to **inconvenience**, *v.t.* incomodare, disturbare: *are you sure I shall not — you?*, sei sicuro che non ti disturberò?.

inconvenient [ˌinkənˈviːnjənt], *ag.* incomodo, che reca disturbo: *if it is not — to you*, se non vi reca disturbo.

inconveniently [ˌinkənˈviːnjəntli], *av.* inopportunamente, sconvenientemente: *to arrive —*, arrivare in un momento inopportuno.

inconversable [ˌinkənˈvəːsəbl], *ag.* riservato; poco comunicativo.

inconversant [ˌinkənˈvəːsənt], *ag.* (*arc.*) non versato.

inconvertibility [ˈinkən,vəːtəˈbiliti], *s.* inconvertibilità.

inconvertible [ˌinkənˈvəːtəbl], *ag.* inconvertibile ☆ — *paper currency*, carta moneta che non può essere convertita in moneta metallica.

inconvertibly [ˌinkənˈvəːtəbli], *av.* inconvertibilmente.

inconvincible [ˌinkənˈvinsəbl], *ag.* inconvincibile.

incoordinate [ˌinkouˈɔːdnit], *ag.* non coordinato.

incoordination [ˌinkou,ɔːdiˈneiʃən], *s.* mancanza di coordinazione.

incoronate [inˈkɔrənit], *ag.* incoronato.

incorporate [inˈkɔːpərit], *ag.* **1.** unito in corporazione; che forma una corporazione **2.** privo di corpo.

to **incorporate** [inˈkɔːpəreit], *v.t.i.* **1.** incorporare, incorporarsi; fondere; unirsi, associarsi: *to — one bank with another*, fondere una banca con un'altra **2.** costituire (una società commerciale); erigere in municipalità.

incorporated [inˈkɔːpəreitid], *ag.* **1.** incorporato; unito (in corporazione) **2.** costituito, eretto in ente: — *company*, associazione eretta in ente commerciale; società costituita, autorizzata; (*amer.*) società per azioni.

incorporation [in,kɔːpəˈreiʃən], *s.* **1.** incorporazione **2.** costituzione di una società; erezione in municipalità.

incorporator [inˈkɔːpəreitə*], *s.c.* incorporatore, incorporatrice.

incorporeal [,inkɔ:'pɔ:riəl], *ag.* incorporeo.
incorporeality [,inkɔ:,pɔ:ri'æliti], *s.* incorporeità.
incorporeally [,inkɔ:'pɔ:riəli], *av.* incorporeamente.
incorporeity [in,kɔ:pə'ri:iti], *s.* incorporeità.
incorrect [,inkə'rekt], *ag.* inesatto, scorretto.
incorrectly [,inkə'rektli], *av.* inesattamente, scorrettamente.
incorrectness [,inkə'rektnis], *s.* inesattezza, scorrettezza.
incorrigibility [in,kɔridʒə'biliti], *s.* incorreggibilità.
incorrigible [in'kɔridʒəbl], *ag.* incorreggibile.
incorrigibly [in'kɔridʒəbli], *av.* incorreggibilmente.
incorrodible [,inkə'roudəbl], *ag.* che non si può corrodere; inattaccabile (dagli acidi).
incorrupt [,inkə'rʌpt], *ag.* **1.** incorrotto, puro; integro **2.** incorrotto, corretto (di lingua, testo).
incorruptibility ['inkə,rʌptə'biliti], *s.* incorruttibilità.
incorruptible [,inkə'rʌptəbl], *ag.* incorruttibile.
incorruptibleness [,inkə'rʌptəblnis], *s.* incorruttibilità.
incorruptibly [,inkə'rʌptəbli], *av.* incorruttibilmente.
incorruption [,inkə'rʌpʃən], *s.* (*arc.*) l'essere incorrotto.
incorruptly [,inkə'rʌptli], *av.* incorrottamente.
incrassate [in'kræsit], *ag.* (*bot. zool.*) grosso; gonfio.
to incrassate [in'kræseit], *v.t.* inspessire, inspessirsi; infittire, infittirsi.
increasable [in'kri:səbl], *ag.* aumentabile.
increase ['inkri:s], *s.* accrescimento, aumento; incremento; aggiunta: — *in value, prices*, aumento di valore, di prezzi; *to be on the* —, essere in aumento.
to increase [in'kri:s], *v.t.i.* accrescere, accrescersi, crescere; aumentare, aumentarsi; ingrandire, ingrandirsi, svilupparsi: *increased cost of living*, rincaro della vita; *they will* — *their efforts*, raddoppieranno i loro sforzi; *to* — *fourfold, tenfold*, quadruplicarsi, decuplicarsi; *to* — *in power, size, value*, aumentare di potenza, di misura, di valore; *to* — *speed to a hundred miles*, aumentare la velocità a cento miglia.
increaseful [in'kri:sful], *ag.* (*arc.*) fruttifero.
increasing [in'kri:siŋ], *ag.* che aumenta, crescente ‖ *s.* aumento.
increasingly [in'kri:siŋli], *av.* in aumento; sempre più.
incredibility [in,kredi'biliti], *s.* incredibilità.
incredible [in'kredəbl], *ag.* incredibile.
incredibly [in'kredəbli], *av.* incredibilmente.
incredulity [,inkri'dju:liti], *s.* incredulità.
incredulous [in'kredjuləs], *ag.* incredulo.
incredulously [in'kredjuləsli], *av.* con incredulità.
incredulousness [in'kredjuləsnis], *s.* incredulità.
incremation [,inkri'meiʃən], *s.* (*rar.*) cremazione.
increment ['inkrimənt], *s.* incremento; profitto: *unearned* —, profitto congiunturale (di azioni, ecc.).
incremental [,inkri'mentl], *ag.* che dà incremento.
increscent [in'kresnt], *ag.* crescente (della Luna).
incretion [in'kri:ʃən], *s.* (*fisiol.*) secrezione interna, endocrina; ormone.
to incriminate [in'krimineit], *v.t.* incriminare, incolpare.
incrimination [in,krimi'neiʃən], *s.* incriminazione.
incriminatory [in'kriminətəri], *ag.* incriminante.
incrustation [,inkrʌs'teiʃən], *s.* **1.** incrostazione **2.** rivestimento.
to incubate ['inkjubeit], *v.t.i.* covare; *fig.* meditare.
incubation [,inkju'beiʃən], *s.* incubazione (anche di malattia).
incubative ['inkjubeitiv], *ag.* di incubazione.
incubator ['inkjubeitə*], *s.* incubatrice.
incubatory ['inkjubeitəri], *ag.* di incubazione.
incubus ['inkjubəs], *pl.* **incubi** ['inkjubai], **incubuses** ['inkjubəsiz], *s.* **1.** incubo; *fig.* oppressione **2.** (*arc.*) demonio, spirito maligno.
to inculcate ['inkʌlkeit], *v.t.* inculcare: *to* — *sthg.*

upon s.o., in (o *upon*) *s.o.'s mind*, inculcare ql.co. a qlcu., nella mente di qlcu.
inculcation [,inkʌl'keiʃən], *s.* inculcazione.
inculcator ['inkʌlkeitə*], *s.* inculcatore.
inculpable [in'kʌlpəbl], *ag.* incolpevole, innocente.
to inculpate ['inkʌlpeit], *v.t.* **1.** accusare; biasimare **2.** incolpare, incriminare.
inculpation [,inkʌl'peiʃən], *s.* l'incolpare.
inculpatory [in'kʌlpətəri], *ag.* accusatore, d'accusa — *witness*, testimone d'accusa.
incult [in'kʌlt], *ag.* (*rar.*) incolto.
incumbency [in'kʌmbənsi], *s.* **1.** l'essere incombente **2.** incombenza, incarico **3.** (*eccl.*) possesso di un beneficio.
incumbent [in'kʌmbənt], *ag.* incombente; obbligatorio: *it is* — *on you to do so*, tocca a voi fare questo ‖ *s.* **1.** (*eccl.*) beneficiario **2.** (*arc.*) titolare.
incunabulum [,inkju(:)'næbjuləm], *pl.* **incunabula** [,inkju(:)'næbjulə], *s.* **1.** incunabulo **2.** *pl.* gli inizi.
to incur [in'kə:*], *pass.p.p.* **incurred** [in'kə:d], *v.t.* **1.** incorrere in: *to* — *debts*, contrarre debiti **2.** esporsi a: *to* — *expenses*, esporsi a' spese **3.** attirarsi: *to* — *hatred*, attirarsi odio.
incurability [in,kjuərə'biliti], *s.* incurabilità.
incurable [in'kjuərəbl], *ag.* incurabile.
incurableness [in'kjuərəblnis], *s.* incurabilità.
incurably [in'kjuərəbli], *av.* incurabilmente.
incuriosity [,inkjuəri'ɔsiti], *s.* mancanza di curiosità; indifferenza; negligenza.
incurious [in'kjuəriəs], *ag.* **1.** non curioso; indifferente **2.** negligente **3.** trascurabile.
incuriously [in'kjuəriəsli], *av.* indifferentemente; negligentemente.
incursion [in'kə:ʃən], *s.* scorreria, incursione: *to make an* — *into an enemy's country*, fare un'incursione nel paese nemico.
incursive [in'kə:siv], *ag.* d'incursione.
incurvate [in'kə:vit], *ag.* curvo; incurvato.
to incurvate ['inkə:veit], *v.t.i.* incurvare, incurvarsi.
incurvation [,inkə:'veiʃən], *s.* incurvatura, incurvamento.
incurvature [in'kə:vətʃə*], *s.* curvatura, incurvatura.
to incurve [in'kə:v], *v.t.i.* incurvare, incurvarsi.
incus ['inkəs], *s.* (*anat.*) incudine.
incuse [in'kju:z], *ag.* incuso, impresso (di figure su monete) ‖ *s.* incuso, figura impressa.
to incuse [in'kju:z], *v.t.* fregiare (una moneta) con una figura.
incut ['inkʌt], *ag.* inserito.
Ind [ind], *no.pr.* (*geog.*) (*arc. poet.*) India.
to indagate ['indəgeit], *v.t.* indagare.
indagation [,ində'geiʃən], *s.* (*arc.*) indagine.
indagative ['indəgeitiv], *ag.* (*arc.*) indagatore.
indebted [in'detid], *ag.* **1.** (*comm.*) indebitato: — *to*, debitore di; *heavily* — *to a bank*, fortemente indebitato con una banca **2.** obbligato: *I am* — *to all of you for your help*, mi sento molto obbligato con voi tutti per il vostro aiuto.
indebtedness [in'detidnis], *s.* l'essere indebitato con; debito (anche *fig.*): *our* — *to Greece*, il nostro debito con la Grecia.
indecency [in'di:snsi], *s.* indecenza; sconvenienza: *public act of* —, (*dir.*) oltraggio al pudore.
indecent [in'di:snt], *ag.* indecente, indecoroso, sconveniente.
indecently [in'di:sntli], *av.* indecentemente, sconvenientemente.
indeciduous [,indi'sidjuəs], *ag.* (*bot.*) sempreverde, non deciduo.
indecipherable [,indi'saifərəbl], *ag.* indecifrabile.
indecision [,indi'siʒən], *s.* indecisione; irresolutezza, esitazione.
indecisive [,indi'saisiv], *ag.* indeciso; irresoluto, esitante; non concludente; non decisivo.
indecisively [,indi'saisivli], *av.* in maniera non decisiva; con indecisione.

indecisiveness [ˌindi'saisivnis], *s.* indecisione, incertezza.

indeclinable [ˌindi'klainəbl], *ag.* (*gram.*) indeclinabile.

indeclinably [ˌindi'klainəbli], *av.* indeclinabilmente.

indecomposable ['in,di:kəm'pouzəbl], *ag.* indecomponibile.

indecorous [in'dekərəs], *ag.* indecoroso; disdicevole; sconveniente.

indecorously [in'dekərəsli], *av.* indecorosamente; sconvenientemente.

indecorousness [in'dekərəsnis], *s.* mancanza di decoro; sconvenienza.

indecorum [ˌindi'kɔ:rəm], *s.* mancanza di decoro; sconvenienza; atto indecoroso.

indeed [in'di:d], *av.* 1. di fatti, in verità, veramente: *and* —..., e infatti ...; *I am very glad* —, sono proprio molto contento; *thank you very much* —, ti ringrazio moltissimo; *you are right* —, hai veramente ragione 2. anzi; per meglio dire: *it is past midnight,* — *it is one o' clock,* è mezzanotte passata, anzi è la una. **indeed,** *inter.* davvero: *fine people* —*!,* (*iron.*) della bella gente davvero!; *no,* —*!,* no, davvero!, questo poi no!; *yes* —*!,* si, davvero!; ma certamente!.

indefatigability ['indi,fætigə'biliti], *s.* infaticabilità.

indefatigable [ˌindi'fætigəbl], *ag.* infaticabile, instancabile, indefesso.

indefatigableness [ˌindi'fætigəblnis], *s.* infaticabilità, instancabilità.

indefatigably [ˌindi'fætigəbli], *av.* indefessamente, instancabilmente.

indefeasibility ['indi,fi:zə'biliti], *s.* irrevocabilità; imprescrittibilità.

indefeasible [ˌindi'fi:zəbl], *ag.* irrevocabile; imprescrittibile.

indefeasibly [ˌindi'fi:zəbli], *av.* irrevocabilmente; imprescrittibilmente.

indefectible [ˌindi'fektibl], *ag.* indefettibile.

indefensibility ['indi,fensə'biliti], *s.* insostenibilità (di argomento, ecc.).

indefensible [ˌindi'fensəbl], *ag.* indifendibile; insostenibile; inscusabile.

indefinable [ˌindi'fainəbl], *ag.* indefinibile.

indefinable [ˌindi'fainəbl], *av.* indefinibilmente.

indefinably [in'definit], *ag.* 1. indefinito, vago: *to leave a point* —, lasciare un punto in sospeso 2. indeterminato, illimitato: —*[leave,* (*mil.*) congedo illimitato 3. (*gram.*) indefinito: — *pronoun,* pronome indefinito.

indefinitely [in'definitli], *av.* 1. indefinitamente, vagamente 2. indeterminatamente, illimitatamente: *to postpone sthg.* —, rimandare ql.co. alle calende greche.

indefiniteness [in'definitnis], *s.* indefinitezza; indeterminatezza.

indehiscent [ˌindi'hisənt], *ag.* (*bot.*) indeiscente.

indelibility [in,deli'biliti], *s.* indelebilità.

indelible [in'delibl], *ag.* indelebile, incancellabile: — *ink,* inchiostro indelebile; — *pencil,* matita copiativa.

indelibly [in'delibli], *av.* indelebilmente.

indelicacy [in'delikəsi], *s.* 1. indelicatezza 2. sconvenienza.

indelicate [in'delikit], *ag.* 1. indelicato; sgarbato 2. sconveniente; grossolano.

indelicately [in'delikitli], *av.* 1. indelicatamente; sgarbatamente 2. sconvenientemente.

indemnification [in,demnifi'keiʃən], *s.* indennizzo, risarcimento.

to **indemnify** [in'demnifai], *v.t.* 1. indennizzare, risarcire 2. assicurare: *to* — *s.o. against* (o *from*) *sthg.,* assicurare qlcu. contro ql.co.

indemnitor [in'demnitə*], *s.* assicuratore; indennizzatore.

indemnity [in'demniti], *s.* 1. indennità, risarcimento 2. assicurazione (contro perdite, danni, ecc.) 3. esenzione ☆ *war* —, indennità di guerra.

indemonstrability ['indi,mɔnstrə'biliti], *s.* indimostrabilità.

indemonstrable [in'demənstrəbl], *ag.* indimostrabile.

indent[1] ['indent], *s.* 1. (*mec.*) dentellatura; tacca 2. (*tip.*) capoverso 3. (*comm.*) ordinazione di merci (dall'estero) 4. ordine di requisizione (di merci).

to **indent**[1] [in'dent], *v.t.i.* 1.(*mec.*) dentellare, intaccare; frastagliare, formare insenature; incidere, solcare 2. separare (le due copie di un documento) 3. (*tip.*) iniziare (un paragrafo) a distanza dal margine 4. (*comm.*) ordinare (merci): *to* — *upon s.o. for sthg.,* passare un ordine di ql.co. a qlcu. 5. requisire (merci): fare una requisizione.

indent[2], *s.* incavo, incavatura.

to **indent**[2], *v.t.* incavare; intagliare.

indentation [ˌinden'teiʃən], *s.* 1. intaccatura, tacca, dentellatura; incisione, intaglio 2. (*tip.*) capoverso.

indented [in'dentid], *ag.* intaccato, dentellato; frastagliato.

indention [in'denʃən], *s.* (*tip.*) capoverso.

indenture [in'dentʃə*], *s.* 1. dentellatura, intaglio 2. (*dir.*) contratto 3. inventario.

to **indenture,** *v.t.* 1. legare con un contratto 2. mettere a bottega.

independence [ˌindi'pendəns], *s.* indipendenza; autonomia ‖ *Independence Day,* anniversario della proclamazione dell'indipendenza americana (4 luglio 1776).

independency [ˌindi'pendənsi], *s.* 1. stato autonomo 2. indipendenza di mezzi 3. congregazionalismo (dottrina che afferma l'indipendenza di ogni comunità in materia di fede e di disciplina ecclesiastica).

independent [ˌindi'pendənt], *ag.* 1. indipendente; autonomo: *to be* — *of s.o., of sthg.,* non dipendere da alcuno, da alcuna cosa 2. benestante, agiato ‖ *s.* (*pol. eccl.*) indipendente.

independently [ˌindi'pendəntli], *av.* indipendentemente; separatamente.

indescribable [ˌindis'kraibəbl], *ag.* indescrivibile.

indescribables [ˌindis'kraibəblz], *s.pl.* 1. cose indescrivibili 2. (*sl.*) pantaloni.

indescribably [ˌindis'kraibəbli], *av.* indescrivibilmente.

indestructibility ['indis,trʌktə'biliti], *s.* indistruttibilità.

indestructible [ˌindis'trʌktəbl], *ag.* indistruttibile.

indestructibly [ˌindis'trʌktəbli], *av.* indistruttibilmente.

indeterminable [ˌindi'tə:minəbl], *ag.* indeterminabile.

indeterminableness [ˌindi'tə:minəblnis], *s.* indeterminabilità.

indeterminably [ˌindi'tə:minəbli], *av.* indeterminabilmente.

indeterminate [ˌindi'tə:minit], *ag.* indeterminato.

indeterminately [ˌindi'tə:minitli], *av.* indeterminatamente.

indeterminateness [ˌindi'tə:minitnis], *s.* indeterminatezza.

indetermination ['indi,tə:mi'neiʃən], *s.* indeterminazione; irresolutezza.

indeterminism [ˌindi'tə:minizəm], *s.* (*fil.*) indeterminismo.

indeterminist [ˌindi'tə:minist], *s.* (*fil.*) indeterminista.

index ['indeks], *pl.* **indexes** ['indeksiz], **indices** ['indisi:z], *s.* 1. il dito indice 2. indice alfabetico (di libro, ecc.); rubrica; lista; tavola 3. (*chim.fis.mec., ecc.*) indice 4. (*mat.*) esponente 5. (*tip.*) segno 6. *the Index,* l'indice dei libri proibiti ☆ *living* (o *cost of living*) —, l'indice del costo della vita; *production* —, (*comm.*) coefficiente di produzione.

to **index,** *v.t.* 1. comporre un indice di, rubricare 2. (*mec.*) graduare 3. mettere (un libro) all'Indice.

indexless ['indekslis], *ag.* privo di indice.

India ['indjə], *no.pr.* (*geog.*) India ☆ — *ink,* inchiostro di China; — *paper,* carta d'India; — *-rubber,* cauccìù; gomma per cancellare.

Indiaman, *pl.* **Indiamen** ['indjəmən], *s.* (*st.*) nave per il commercio con l'India.

Indian ['indjən], *ag.* indiano ‖ *s.c.* indiano, indiana ‖ *Red Indians* (o *Copper Indians*), pellirosse ☆ — *corn*, granoturco; — *fig*, fico d'India; — *file*, fila indiana; — *fire*, bengala; — *ink*, inchiostro di China; — *summer*, estate di S. Martino; — *weed*, tabacco.

indicant·['indikənt], *ag.* indicativo.

to **indicate** ['indikeit], *v.t.* **1.** indicare: *to* — *sthg.* *with the hand*, indicare ql.co. con la mano **2.** segnalare: *to* — *a book to s.o.*, segnalare un libro a qlcu. **3.** indicare, denotare, esprimere: *face that indicates energy*, viso che esprime energia.

indication [,indi'keiʃən], *s.* **1.** indicazione **2.** segno; indizio.

indicative [in'dikətiv], *ag.* **1.** (*gram.*) indicativo **2.** — *of*, indicativo, che indica: *smile* — *of pleasure*, sorriso che denota piacere ‖ *s.* (*gram.*) modo indicativo.

indicatively [in'dikətivli], *av.* indicativamente.

indicator ['indikeitə*], *s.* (*tec. chim.*, ecc.) indicatore ☆ *airspeed* —, (*aer.*) indicatore di velocità, anemometro; *height* —, (*aer.*) indicatore di quota; *mileage* —, contachilometri.

indicatory [in'dikətəri], *ag.* indicativo.

to **indict** [in'dait], *v.t.* (*dir.*) accusare, mettere in stato d'accusa; imputare: *to* — *for an offence*, accusare di un'offesa; *to stand indicted*, essere accusato.

indictable [in'daitəbl], *ag.* (*dir.*) accusabile; imputabile: *an* — *offence*, un atto passibile di pena.

indictee [,indai'ti:], *s.c.* imputato, imputata.

indicter [in'daitə*], *s.* (*dir.*) attore, accusatore: *to assume the role of* —, costituirsi parte civile.

indiction [in'dikʃən], *s.* (*st.*) indizione.

indictment [in'daitmənt], *s.* (*dir.*) accusa; imputazione: *bill of* —, atto d'accusa.

Indies (the) ['indiz], *no.pr.pl.* (*geog.*) Indie: *the East* —, le Indie Orientali; *the West* —, le Indie Occidentali.

indifference [in'difrəns], *s.* **1.** indifferenza; apatia: — *towards* (o *to*) *art*, mancanza d'interesse per l'arte **2.** mancanza di valore, di significato: *a matter of* —, una cosa di nessuna importanza.

indifferent [in'difrənt], *ag.* **1.** indifferente, incurante; apatico: *his praise is* — *to me*, i suoi elogi non mi fanno nè caldo nè freddo **2.** neutrale, imparziale: *we cannot remain* — *in this dispute*, non possiamo rimanere neutrali in questo dibattito **3.** (*chim. elett.*) neutro **4.** mediocre; scadente: *his English is* —, il suo inglese è mediocre **5.** poco importante, privo di conseguenze.

indifferentiated [,indifə'renʃieitid], *ag.* (*rar.*) indifferenziato.

indifferentism [in'difrəntizəm], *s.* (*pol. relig.*) indifferentismo.

indifferentist [in'difrəntist], *s.* (*pol. relig.*) indifferentista.

indifferently [in'difrəntli], *av.* **1.** indifferentemente **2.** imparzialmente **3.** mediocremente **4.** in un modo qualunque.

indigence ['indidʒəns], **indigency** ['indidʒənsi], *s.* indigenza.

indigene ['indidʒi:n], *s.* indigeno.

indigenous [in'didʒinəs], *ag.* indigeno.

indigenously [in'didʒinəsli], *av.* da indigeno.

indigent ['indidʒənt], *ag.* indigente, bisognoso.

indigently ['indidʒəntli], *av.* poveramente.

indigested [,indi'dʒestid], *ag.* **1.** indigesto **2.** *fig.* confuso, caotico.

indigestibility ['indi,dʒestə'biliti], *s.* indigeribilità.

indigestible [,indi'dʒestəbl], *ag.* **1.** indigeribile, indigesto **2.** caotico, non ordinabile.

indigestion [,indi'dʒestʃən], *s.* (*patol.*) dispepsia.

indigestive [,indi'dʒestiv], *ag.* (*patol.*) dispeptico.

indign [in'dain], *ag.* (*poet.*) indegno, vergognoso.

indignance [in'dignəns], *s.* (*rar.*) indignazione.

indignant [in'dignənt], *ag.* indignato, sdegnato.

indignantly [in'dignəntli], *av.* con indignazione, con sdegno.

indignation [,indig'neiʃən], *s.* indignazione, sdegno: *to feel strong* — *against* (o *with*) *s.o.*, sentire una forte indignazione per qlcu. ☆ — *-meeting*, comizio di protesta.

indignity [in'digniti], *s.* **1.** trattamento indegno **2.** disprezzo; offesa.

indigo ['indigou], *s.* indaco ☆ — *-plant*, (*bot.*) indigofera.

indirect [,indi'rekt], *ag.* **1.** traverso, tortuoso: *an* — *road*, una strada tortuosa **2.** *fig.* indiretto; secondario: *an* — *result*, un risultato secondario; *to make an* — *reference to s.o.*, alludere indirettamente a qlcu. **3.** (*gram.*) indiretto: — *speech*, discorso indiretto ☆ — *taxes*, imposte indirette.

indirection [,indi'rekʃən], *s.* *fig.* mezzi indiretti; inganno; raggiro: *by* —, con l'inganno.

indirectly [,indi'rektli], *av.* indirettamente.

indirectness [,indi'rektnis], *s.* disonestà; slealtà.

indiscernible [,indi'sə:nəbl], *ag.* indiscernibile, indistinguibile.

indiscernibly [,indi'sə:nəbli], *av.* indiscernibilmente, indistinguibilmente.

indisciplinable [in'disiplinəbl], *ag.* indisciplinabile.

indiscipline [in'disiplin], *s.* indisciplina.

indiscoverable [,indis'kʌvərəbl], *ag.* che non può essere scoperto.

indiscreet [,indis'kri:t], *ag.* sconsiderato; incauto; sbadato; indiscreto.

indiscreetly [,indis'kri:tli], *av.* sconsideratamente; incautamente; indiscretamente.

indiscreetness [,indis'kri:tnis], *s.* inopportunità; sconsideratezza; indiscretezza.

indiscrete [,indis'kri:t], *ag.* inscindibile; compatto.

indiscretion [,indis'kreʃən], *s.* sconsideratezza; imprudenza; indiscrezione.

indiscriminate [,indis'kriminit], *ag.* **1.** indiscriminato; confuso, non differenziato: *to give* — *praise to sthg.*, lodare ql.co. senza discriminazione **2.** che non fa distinzioni: *an* — *reader*, uno che legge un po' di tutto.

indiscriminately [,indis'kriminitli], *av.* confusamente; a casaccio, senza distinzione.

indiscriminating [,indis'krimineitiŋ], *ag.* **1.** non differenziato **2.** che non fa distinzioni.

indiscrimination ['indis,krimi'neiʃən], *s.* **1.** confusione **2.** mancanza di discernimento.

indiscriminative [,indis'kriminətiv], *ag.* **1.** non differenziato **2.** che non fa distinzioni.

indispensability ['indis,pensə'biliti], *s.* indispensabilità.

indispensable [,indis'pensəbl], *ag.* indispensabile; essenziale, necessario.

indispensableness [,indis'pensəblnis], *s.* indispensabilità.

indispensably [,indis'pensəbli], *av.* indispensabilmente, necessariamente.

to **indispose** [,indis'pouz], *v.t.* **1.** indisporre, distogliere: *to* — *s.o. towards sthg.*, to do sthg., rendere qlcu. mal disposto verso ql.co., a fare ql.co.; *to* — *s.o. from sthg.*, distogliere qlcu. da ql.co. **2.** *fig.* inabilitare: *to* — *s.o. for sthg.* (o *for doing sthg.* o *to do sthg.*), rendere qlcu. incapace a ql.co. (o a fare ql.co.) **3.** rendere malato, indisposto.

indisposed [,indis'pouzd], *ag.* **1.** indisposto **2.** maldisposto; contrario: — *to do sthg.*, maldisposto a fare ql.co.

indisposedness [,indis'pouzidnis], **indisposition** [,indispə'ziʃən], *s.* **1.** avversione **2.** poca inclinazione **3.** indisposizione, malessere.

indisputable [,indis'pju:təbl], *ag.* **1.** indiscutibile; certo **2.** (*fil.*) apodittico.

indisputableness [,indis'pju:təblnis], **indisputability** ['indispju:tə'biliti], *s.* indiscutibilità; certezza.

indisputably [,indis'pju:təbli], *av.* indiscutibilmente.

indisputed [,indis'pju:tid], *ag.* incontestato, indiscusso.

indissociable [,indi'souʃjəbl], *ag.* inseparabile.
indissolubility ['indi,sɔlju'biliti], *s.* indissolubilità.
indissoluble [,indi'sɔljubl], *ag.* indissolubile: *an — bond*, un legame indissolubile.
indissolubleness [,indi'sɔljublnls], *s.* indissolubilità.
indissolubly [,indi'sɔljubli], *av.* indissolubilmente.
indissolvable [,indi'sɔlvəbl], *ag.* (*arc.*) indissolubile.
indistinct [,indis'tiŋkt], *ag.* indistinto, confuso; oscuro.
indistinction [,indis'tiŋkʃən], *s.* (*rar.*) confusione.
indistinctive [,indis'tiŋktiv], *ag.* che non distingue.
indistinctively [,indis'tiŋktivli], *av.* indistintamente.
indistinctly [,indis'tiŋktli], *av.* indistintamente, confusamente, vagamente.
indistinctness [,indis'tiŋktnis], *s.* confusione; mancanza di chiarezza.
indistinguishable [,indis'tiŋgwiʃəbl], *ag.* indistinguibile; impercettibile: — *to the naked eye*, impercettibile a occhio nudo.
indistinguishableness [,indis'tiŋgwiʃəblnis], *s.* indistinguibilità.
indistinguishably [,indis'tiŋgwiʃəbli], *av.* indistinguibilmente.
indistributable [,indis'tribjutəbl], *ag.* indistribuibile.
to indite [in'dait], *v.t.* redigere, comporre (in prosa, in versi) (anche *scherz.*).
inditement [in'daitmənt], *s.* (*arc.*) redazione, composizione.
indivertible [,indi'və:tibl], *ag.* che non si può far deviare.
individual [,indi'vidjuəl], *ag.* 1. singolo, individuale: — *member*, singolo membro; — *station*, (*rad.*) stazione singola 2. particolare; caratteristico ‖ *s.* individuo.
individualism [,indi'vidjuəlizəm], *s.* 1. (*fil. pol.*) individualismo 2. egoismo.
individualist [,indi'vidjuəlist], *s.* (*fil. pol.*) individualista.
individualistic [,indi,vidjuə'listik], *ag.* individualistico.
individuality [,indi,vidju'æliti], *s.* individualità; peculiarità.
individualization [,indi,vidjuəlai'zeiʃən], *s.* individualizzazione.
to individualize [,indi'vidjuəlaiz], *v.t.* 1. individualizzare, caratterizzare 2. specificare.
individually [,indi'vidjuəli], *av.* individualmente; isolatamente, separatamente.
to individuate [,indi'vidjueit], *v.t.* individuare.
individuation [,individju'eiʃən], *s.* individuazione.
indivisibility ['indi,vizi'biliti], *s.* indivisibilità.
indivisible [,indi'vizəbl], *ag.* indivisibile, inseparabile.
indivisibly [,indi'vizəbli], *av.* indivisibilmente, inseparabilmente.
Indo-Aryan ['indou'ɛəriən], *ag.* indo-ariano ‖ *s.* lingua indo-ariana.
Indo-China ['indou'tʃainə], *no.pr.* (*geog.*) Indocina.
Indo-Chinese ['indou-tʃai'ni:z], *ag.s.c.* indocinese.
indocile [in'dousail], *ag.* indocile.
indocility [,indou'siliti], *s.* indocilità.
to indoctrinate [in'dɔktrineit], *v.t.* addottrinare: *to — s.o. with an idea*, addottrinare qlcu. in un'idea.
indoctrination [in,dɔktri'neiʃən], *s.* addottrinamento; istruzione: *political —*, istruzione politica.
Indo-European ['indou,juərə'pi(:)ən], *ag.* indo-europeo ‖ *s.* lingua indo-europea.
Indo-Germanic ['indoudʒə:'mænik], *ag.* indo-germanico ‖ *s.* lingua indo-germanica.
indolence ['indələns], *s.* 1. indolenza, pigrizia 2. (*med.*) insensibilità.
indolent ['indələnt], *ag.* 1. indolente, infingardo, pigro 2. (*med.*) indolore: — *tumour*, tumore indolore.
indolently ['indələntli], *av.* indolentemente.
indomitable [in'dɔmitəbl], *ag.* indomabile; indomito; ferreo.

indomitably [in'dɔmitəbli], *av.* indomabilmente; indomitamente.
Indonesia [,indou'ni:zjə], *no.pr.* (*geog.*) Indonesia.
Indonesian [,indou'ni:zjən], *ag.* indonesiano ‖ *s.c.* indonesiano, indonesiana.
indoor ['indɔ:*], *ag.* situato in casa; eseguito, da eseguirsi in casa ☆ — *game*, un giuoco da farsi in casa; giuoco di società; *the — poor*, i ricoverati poveri (di ospedale, ospizio, ecc.); — *relief*, assistenza data ai ricoverati.
indoors [in'dɔ:z], *av.* in casa; al coperto; all'interno: — *and out*, dentro e fuori; *to stay, to go —*, rimanere, andare a casa.
indorsation [,indo:'seiʃən], *s.* 1. (*comm.*) girata 2. conferma, approvazione.
to indorse, *V.* to **endorse**.
indorsee [,indo:'si:], *s.* (*comm.*) giratario.
indraught ['in-drɑ:ft], *s.* corrente (d'aria, d'acqua) verso l'interno.
indrawn ['in'drɔ:n], *ag.* introverso, chiuso in se stesso (di persona).
to indrench [in'drentʃ], *v.t.* (*arc. poet.*) bagnare, inzuppare ;immergere; imbevere.
indri ['indri], *s.* (*zool.*) indri.
indubious [in'dju:bjəs], *ag.* (*arc.*) indubbio, certo.
indubitable [in'dju:bitəbl], *ag.* indubitabile.
indubitableness [in'dju:bitəblnis], *s.* indubitabilità.
indubitably [in'dju:bitəbli], *av.* indubitabilmente.
to induce [in'dju:s], *v.t.* (IV) 1. indurre; persuadere: *to — s.o. to do sthg.*, persuadere qlcu. a fare ql.co. 2. produrre, causare: *his illness was induced by overwork*, la sua malattia fu causata dal troppo lavoro 3. (*elett.*) indurre: *induced current*, corrente indotta.
inducement [in'dju:smənt], *s.* 1. allettamento, lusinga 2. istigazione; incentivo.
inducer [in'dju:sə*], *s.c.* istigatore, istigatrice; allettatore, allettatrice.
inducibile [in'dju:sibl], *ag.* che può essere indotto.
to induct [in'dʌkt], *v.t.* 1. investire, mettere in possesso ufficiale (di carica, beneficio, ecc.): *to — s.o. to a benefice*, mettere qlcu. in possesso di un beneficio 2. introdurre; installare: *to — s.o. into a room*, (*rar.*) introdurre qlcu. in una stanza 3. iniziare; introdurre 4. (*elett.*) indurre 5. (*mil. amer.*) arruolare.
inductance [in'dʌktəns], *s.* (*elett.*) induttanza.
inductile [in'dʌktail], *ag.* (*metal.*) non duttile.
inductility [,indʌk'tiliti], *s.* (*metal.*) mancanza di duttilità.
induction [in'dʌkʃən], *s.* 1. induzione: — *of facts*, induzione dei fatti; *by —*, per induzione 2. (*elett. fis. mat.*) induzione: *aerodynamic —*, induzione aerodinamica; *electromagnetic —*, induzione elettromagnetica; *electrostatic —*, induzione elettrostatica; *mutual —*, induzione mutua 3. entrata; insediamento, presa di possesso (di carica); investitura: — *of a judge*, investitura di un giudice 4. (*med.*) causa, ragione di una malattia 5. (*arc.*) preambolo, introduzione, prologo ☆ — *coil*, rocchetto Ruhmkorff, bobina d'induzione; — *motor*, motore asincrono, a induzione.
inductive [in'dʌktiv], *ag.* induttivo.
inductively [in'dʌktivli], *av.* per induzione.
inductiveness [in'dʌktivnis], *s.* induttività.
inductor [in'dʌktə*], *s.* 1. chi investe (qlcu.) di una carica, beneficio, ecc. 2. (*elett.*) induttore.
to indue, *V.* to **endue**.
to indulge [in'dʌldʒ], *v.t.i.* 1. essere indulgente con; viziare: *she indulges her children too much*, è troppo indulgente verso i suoi bambini ‖ *to — s.o. with sthg.*, regalare ql.co. a qlcu. 2. *fig.* carezzare; abbandonarsi a (speranze): *to — the hope*, abbandonarsi alla speranza 3. permettersi; concedersi; darsi a, lasciarsi andare a: *he never indulges in a holiday*, non si concede mai una vacanza; *ladies like to — in a little gossip*, alle signore piace permettersi qualche pettegolezzo; *to — in strong*

language, dire parolacce ‖ *I rather think he indulges too much,* mi pare che beva un po' troppo **4.** (*comm.*) concedere una proroga a **5.** (*relig.*) concedere un'indulgenza a.

indulgence [in'dʌldʒəns], *s.* **1.** indulgenza; compiacenza; favore: *a mother's — to her child,* l'indulgenza di una madre verso il suo bambino; *you grant him every —,* gli concedi tutto **2.** l'abbandonarsi a: *— in sin,* l'abbandonarsi al peccato; *to allow oneself the — of a glass of wine,* concedersi il piacere di un bicchiere di vino **3.** (*comm.*) proroga **4.** (*teol.*) indulgenza: *plenary —,* indulgenza plenaria.

indulgenced [in'dʌldʒənst], *ag.* che dà indulgenza.

indulgent [in'dʌldʒənt], *ag.* indulgente; condiscendente; benevolo.

indulgently [in'dʌldʒəntli], *av.* con indulgenza.

indulger [in'dʌldʒə*], *s.c.* chi indulge.

induline ['indjulain], *s.* (*chim.*) indolina.

indult [in'dʌlt], *s.* indulto.

to **indurate** ['indjuəreit], *v.t.i.* indurire, indurirsi; irrigidire, irrigidirsi (anche *fig.*).

induration [,indjuə'reiʃən], *s.* indurimento; irrigidimento.

indurative ['indjuəreitiv], *ag.* che serve a indurire.

Indus ['indəs], *no.pr.* (*geog. astr.*) Indo.

indusium [in'dju:ziəm], *s.* **1.** (*bot.*) indusio **2.** involucro che protegge la larva di un insetto.

industrial [in'dʌstriəl], *ag.* industriale ‖ *s.* **1.** persona che lavora nell'industria **2.** *pl.* (*comm.*) azioni di ditte industriali ☆ *— design* « industrial design », estetica e funzionalità del prodotto; *— exhibition, fair,* esposizione, fiera industriale; *— maintenance,* organizzazione industriale per i sussidi ai disoccupati; *— school,* scuola industriale; *— unit,* (*econ. pol.*) fabbrica.

industrialism [in'dʌstriəlizəm], *s.* industrialismo.

industrialist [in'dʌstriəlist], *s.* industriale; lavoratore dell'industria.

industrialization [in,dʌstriəlai'zeiʃən], *s.* industrializzazione.

to **industrialize** [in'dʌstriəlaiz], *v.t.* industrializzare.

industrially [in'dʌstriəli], *av.* industrialmente.

industrious [in'dʌstriəs], *ag.* operoso, laborioso, industrioso, attivo.

industriously [in'dʌstriəsli], *av.* laboriosamente, diligentemente.

industriousness [in'dʌstriəsnis], *s.* operosità, laboriosità, industriosità.

industry ['indəstri], *s.* **1.** industria; manifattura **2.** diligenza, operosità: *his success was due to his —,* il suo successo era dovuto alla sua operosità ☆ *cottage —,* artigianato; *cotton —,* industria del cotone.

to **indwell** [in'dwel], *pass.p.p.* **indwelt** ['in'dwelt], *v.t.i.* **1.** risiedere in, abitare in **2.** essere continuamente presente.

indweller ['in,dwelə*], *s.c.* abitante.

indwelt ['in'dwelt], *pass p.p.* di to **indwell**.

to **inearth** [in'ə:θ], *v.t.* (*poet.*) interrare, seppellire.

inebriant [i'ni:briənt], *ag.* inebriante ‖ *s.* sostanza inebriante.

inebriate [i'ni:briit], *ag. s.* ubriaco.

to **inebriate** [i'ni:brieit], *v.t.* ubriacare; inebriare.

inebriation [i,ni:bri'eiʃən], **inebriety** [,ini(:)'braiəti], *s.* ubriachezza.

inebrious [i'ni:briəs], *ag.* (*rar.*) **1.** ubriaco **2.** inebriante.

inedible [in'edibl], *ag.* immangiabile.

inedited [in'editid], *ag.* inedito.

ineffable [in'efəbl], *ag.* ineffabile.

ineffableness [in'efəblnis], *s.* ineffabilità.

ineffably [in'efəbli], *av.* ineffabilmente.

ineffaceable [,ini'feisəbl], *ag.* incancellabile, indelebile.

ineffaceably [,ini'feisəbli], *av.* incancellabilmente, indelebilmente.

ineffective [,ini'fektiv], *ag.* **1.** inefficace; di scarso effetto artistico **2.** incapace; inefficiente (di persona).

ineffectively [,ini'fektivli], *av.* inefficacemente.

ineffectiveness [,ini'fektivnis], *s.* inefficacia.

ineffectual [,ini'fektjuəl], *ag.* **1.** inutile, vano **2.** incapace (di persona).

ineffectually [,ini'fektjuəli], *av.* inutilmente; inefficacemente.

ineffectualness [,ini'fektjuəlnis], *s.* inefficacia; inutilità.

inefficacious [,inefi'keiʃəs], *ag.* inefficace.

inefficaciously [,inefi'keiʃəsli], *av.* inefficacemente.

inefficaciousness [,inefi'keiʃəsnis], **inefficacity** [,inefi'kæsiti], **inefficacy** [in'efikəsi], *s.* inefficacia.

inefficiency [,ini'fiʃənsi], *s.* inefficienza; inefficacia; incapacità (professionale).

inefficient [,ini'fiʃənt], *ag.* inefficiente; inefficace; incapace.

inefficiently [,ini'fiʃəntli], *av.* inefficientemente; inefficacemente; senza capacità.

inelastic [,ini'læstik], *ag.* non elastico; *fig.* inflessibile.

inelasticity [,inilæs'tisiti], *s.* mancanza di elasticità; *fig.* inflessibilità.

inelegance [in'eligəns], **inelegancy** [in'eligənsi], *s.* ineleganza; rozzezza.

inelegant [in'eligənt], *ag.* inelegante; rozzo.

inelegantly [in'eligəntli], *av.* inelegantemente; rozzamente.

ineligibility [in,elidʒə'biliti], *s.* ineleggibilità.

ineligible [in'elidʒəbl], *ag.* ineleggibile.

ineligibly [in'elidʒəbli], *av.* in modo non eleggibile.

ineloquent [in'eləkwənt], *ag.* ineloquente.

ineluctable [,ini'lʌktəbl], *ag.* ineluttabile, inevitabile.

inenarrable [,ini'nærəbl], *ag.* (*arc.*) inenarrabile.

inept [i'nept], *ag.* **1.** inetto, inabile, incapace **2.** fatuo, sciocco (di risposta, ecc.).

ineptitude [i'neptitju:d], *s.* **1.** inettitudine, incapacità **2.** fatuità, stoltezza.

ineptly [i'neptli], *av.* **1.** inettamente **2.** fatuamente.

ineptness [i'neptnis], *s.* inettitudine.

inequable [in'i(:)kwəbl], *ag.* non uniforme; mutevole.

inequality [,ini(:)'kwɔliti], *s.* **1.** ineguaglianza, disuguaglianza (di misura, grado, circostanze, ecc.) **2.** irregolarità.

inequitable [in'ekwitəbl], *ag.* ingiusto; sleale.

inequitably [in'ekwitəbli], *av.* ingiustamente; slealmente.

inequity [in'ekwiti], *s.* ingiustizia; slealtà.

ineradicable [,ini'rædikəbl], *ag.* inestirpabile.

ineradicably [,ini'rædikəbli], *av.* in modo inestirpabile.

inerrability [in,erə'biliti], *s.* infallibilità.

inerrable [in'erəbl], *ag.* infallibile.

inerrably [in'erəbli], *av.* infallibilmente.

inerrant [in'erənt], *ag.* **1.** che non erra **2.** (*astr.*) fisso.

inert [i'nə:t], *ag.* **1.** (*fis. chim.*) inerte **2.** apatico, indolente.

inertia [i'nə:ʃjə], *s.* **1.** (*fis.*) inerzia **2.** apatia, indolenza.

inertial [i'nə:ʃəl], *ag.* inerte.

inertly [i'nə:tli], *av.* senza movimento.

inertness [i'nə:tnis], *s.* **1.** apatia, indolenza **2.** (*fis.*) inerzia.

inerudite [in'eru(:)dait], *ag.* inerudito.

Ines ['ainez], *no.pr.f.* Ines.

inescapable [,inis'keipəbl], *ag.* inevitabile.

inessential ['ini'senʃəl], *ag.* **1.** non essenziale **2.** (*rar.*) immateriale.

inestimable [in'estiməbl], *ag.* inestimabile; incalcolabile.

inestimably [in'estiməbli], *av.* inestimabilmente; incalcolabilmente.

inevitability [in,evitə'biliti], *s.* inevitabilità.

inevitable [in'evitəbl], *ag.* inevitabile; immancabile; (*fam.*) solito: *the — late-comer,* il solito (o l'immancabile) ritardatario.

inevitableness [in'evitəblnis], *s.* inevitabilità.

inevitably [in'evitəbli], *av.* inevitabilmente; immancabilmente.

inexact [ˌinig'zækt], *ag.* inesatto, inaccurato, impreciso.

inexactitude [ˌinig'zæktitju:d], *s.* inesattezza, imprecisione.

inexactly [ˌinig'zæktli], *av.* inesattamente.

inexactness [ˌinig'zæktnis], *V.* **inexactitude.**

inexcusability ['iniks‚kju:zə'biliti], *s.* inescusabilità.

inexcusable [ˌiniks'kju:zəbl], *ag.* imperdonabile, ingiustificabile.

inexcusableness [ˌiniks'kju:zəblnis], *s.* inescusabilità.

inexcusably [ˌiniks'kju:zəbli], *av.* ingiustificabilmente.

inexecutable [in'eksikju:təbl], *ag.* ineseguibile.

inexecution [in‚eksi'kju:ʃən], *s.* mancata esecuzione.

inexhaustibility ['inig‚zo:stə'biliti], *s.* **1.** inesauribilità **2.** instancabilità, infaticabilità.

inexhaustible [ˌinig'zo:stəbl], *ag.* **1.** inesauribile **2.** instancabile, infaticabile.

inexhaustibleness [ˌinig'zo:stəblnis], *s.* inesauribilità.

inexhaustibly [ˌinig'zo:stəbli], *av.* **1.** inesauribilmente **2.** instancabilmente, infaticabilmente.

inexistence¹ [ˌinig'zistəns], *s.* (*fil.*) immanenza; l'essere immanente.

inexistence², *s.* (*rar.*) inesistenza.

inexistent¹ [ˌinig'zistənt], *ag.* (*fil.*) immanente.

inexistent², *ag.* inesistente.

inexorability [in‚eksərə'biliti], *s.* inesorabilità.

inexorable [in'eksərəbl], *ag.* inesorabile, implacabile, inflessibile.

inexorableness [in'eksərəblnis], *s.* inesorabilità, implacabilità.

inexorably [in'eksərəbli], *av.* inesorabilmente, implacabilmente, inflessibilmente.

inexpectant [ˌiniks'pektənt], *ag.* che non aspetta.

inexpedience [ˌiniks'pi:djəns], **inexpediency** [ˌiniks'pi:djənsi], *s.* inopportunità.

inexpedient [ˌiniks'pi:djənt], *ag.* inopportuno; svantaggioso.

inexpediently [ˌiniks'pi:djəntli], *av.* inopportunamente; svantaggiosamente.

inexpensive [ˌiniks'pensiv], *ag.* poco costoso, economico, a buon mercato.

inexpensively [ˌiniks'pensivli], *av.* a basso prezzo, a buon mercato.

inexpensiveness [ˌiniks'pensivnis], *s.* basso prezzo, basso costo.

inexperience [ˌiniks'piəriəns], *s.* inesperienza; imperizia.

inexperienced [ˌiniks'piəriənst], *ag.* inesperto, senza esperienza: — *in doing sthg.*, inesperto nel fare ql.co.

inexpert [ˌineks'pə:t], *ag.* inesperto; inabile.

inexpertly [ˌineks'pə:tli], *av.* inespertamente.

inexpertness [ˌineks'pə:tnis], *s.* imperizia; inabilità.

inexpiable [in'ekspiəbl], *ag.* **1.** inespiabile **2.** (*arc.*) implacabile.

inexpiableness [in'ekspiəblnis], *s.* **1.** inespiabilità **2.** (*arc.*) implacabilità.

inexpiably [in'ekspiəbli], *av.* **1.** inespiabilmente **2.** (*arc.*) implacabilmente.

inexplicability [in‚eksplikə'biliti], *s.* inspiegabilità.

inexplicable [in'eksplikəbl], *ag.* inesplicabile, inspiegabile.

inexplicably [in'eksplikəbli], *av.* inesplicabilmente, inspiegabilmente.

inexplicit [ˌiniks'plisit], *ag.* non esplicito, non chiaro.

inexplorable [ˌiniks'plo:rəbl], *ag.* inesplorabile; impenetrabile.

inexplosive [ˌiniks'plousiv], *ag.* inesplosibile.

inexpressible [ˌiniks'presəbl], *ag.* inesprimibile, indicibile.

inexpressibles [ˌiniks'presəblz], *s.pl.* (*scherz.*) calzoni.

inexpressibly [ˌiniks'presəbli], *av.* inesprimibilmente; indicibilmente.

inexpressive [ˌiniks'presiv], *ag.* inespressivo.

inexpressively [ˌiniks'presivli], *av.* scialbamente; senza espressione.

inexpressiveness [ˌiniks'presivnis], *s.* mancanza di espressione.

inexpugnable [ˌiniks'pʌgnəbl], *ag.* inespugnabile (anche *fig.*).

inexpugnably [ˌiniks'pʌgnəbli], *av.* inespugnabilmente (anche *fig.*).

inextended [ˌiniks'tendid], *ag.* inesteso.

inextensible [ˌiniks'tensəbl], *ag.* inestensibile.

inextension [ˌiniks'tenʃən], *s.* inestensione.

inextinguishable [ˌiniks'tiŋgwiʃəbl], *ag.* inestinguibile.

inextinguishably [ˌiniks'tiŋgwiʃəbli], *av.* inestinguibilmente.

inextricable [in'ekstrikəbl], *ag.* inestricabile.

inextricableness [in'ekstrikəblnis], *s.* inestricabilità.

inextricably [in'ekstrikəbli], *av.* inestricabilmente.

infall ['info:l], *s.* (*rar.*) scorreria, incursione.

infallibilist [in'fælibilist], *s. c.* (*teol.*) infallibilista.

infallibility [in‚fælə'biliti], *s.* infallibilità.

infallible [in'fæləbl], *ag.* infallibile.

infallibly [in'fæləbli], *av.* infallibilmente.

to **infamize** ['infəmaiz], *v.t.* infamare.

infamous ['infəməs], *ag.* infame, abominevole, malfamato ☆ — *person*, (*amer. dir.*) persona privata dei diritti civili.

infamously ['infəməsli], *av.* infamemente, abominevolmente.

infamy ['infəmi], *s.* **1.** infamia, scelleratezza, disonore: *to be guilty of an* —, commettere un'infamia **2.** (*dir.*) l'essere privato dei diritti civili.

infancy ['infənsi], *s.* **1.** prima infanzia, infanzia: *from* —, dalla più tenera età **2.** (*dir.*) minorità **3.** *fig.* infanzia, il periodo iniziale: — *of a nation*, infanzia di una nazione.

infant¹ ['infənt], *ag.* **1.** infantile **2.** *fig.* nuovo, nascente: — *civilization*, civiltà nascente ‖ *s.* **1.** neonato, bambino, infante ‖ *the Infant Jesus*, il Bambino Gesù **2.** (*dir.*) minorenne ☆ — *-like*, puerile, come un bambino; — *school*, asilo infantile.

infant², *s.c.* infante, infanta (di Spagna, Portogallo).

infanta [in'fæntə], *s.* infanta (di Spagna, Portogallo).

infante [in'fænti], *s.* infante (di Spagna, Portogallo).

infanticide¹ [in'fæntisaid], *s.c.* infanticida.

infanticide², *s.* (*dir.*) infanticidio.

infantile ['infəntail], *ag.* infantile, puerile ☆ — *paralysis*, (*patol.*) poliomielite.

infantilism [in'fæntilizəm], *s.* (*patol.*) infantilismo.

infantine ['infəntain], *V.* **infantile.**

infantry ['infəntri], *s.* (*mil.*) fanteria: — *of the line*, fanteria di linea ☆ — *-man*, fante ‖ *light* —, fanteria leggera; *mounted* —, fanteria a cavallo.

infarct [in'fa:kt], **infarction** [in'fa:kʃən], *s.* (*patol.*) infarto.

to **infatuate** [in'fætjueit], *v.t.* infatuare; affascinare: *he is infatuated with music*, egli è un fanatico della musica.

infatuatedly [in'fætjueitidli], *av.* con infatuazione.

infatuation [in‚fætju'eiʃən], *s.* infatuazione: *to have an* — *for s.o.*, aver un'infatuazione per qlcu.

infaust [in'fo:st], *ag.* (*rar.*) infausto.

to **infect** [in'fekt], *v.t.* **1.** infettare; contagiare (anche *fig.*): *all of them were infected with enthusiasm*, furono tutti presi da entusiasmo **2.** (*fonet.*) alterare, modificare (il suono della sillaba vicina).

infection [in'fekʃən], *s.* **1.** infezione; contagio; *fig.* contaminazione **2.** (*dir.*) vizio (di contratto) **3.** (*gram.*) alterazione del suono di una sillaba.

infectious [in'fekʃəs], *ag.* **1.** infettivo, contagioso (anche *fig.*): — *laughter,* ilarità contagiosa **2.** pestilenziale, malsano (di aria, ecc.).

infectiously [in'fekʃəsli], *av.* contagiosamente.

infectiousness [in'fekʃəsnis], *s.* natura contagiosa; contagio (anche *fig.*).

infective [in'fektiv], *ag.* infettivo, contagioso (anche *fig.*).

infectiveness [in'fektivnis], **infectivity** [ˌinfek'tiviti], *s.* l'essere infettivo, contagioso.

infector [in'fektə*], *s.* chi infetta; *fig.* chi contamina.

infecund [in'fi:kənd], *ag.* infecondo.

infecundity [ˌinfi'kʌnditi], *s.* infecondità.

infelicitous [ˌinfi'lisitəs], *ag.* **1.** infelice (di matrimonio) **2.** improprio (di espressione, ecc.).

infelicity [ˌinfi'lisiti], *s.* **1.** infelicità; sventura **2.** improprietà, infelicità (di un'espressione, ecc.) **3.** topica, granchio, gaffe.

infelonious [ˌinfi'lounjəs], *ag.* non malvagio.

infelt ['in-felt], *ag.* profondo, intimo; sentito.

infeoffment [in'fefmənt], *s.* (*scoz.*) infeudamento.

to **infer** [in'fə:*], *pass.p.p.* **inferred** [in'fə:d], *v.t.i.* **1.** inferire, dedurre; concludere; tirare delle conclusioni, arguire, supporre: *it is inferred that ...,* si suppone che ...; *to — sthg. from sthg.,* dedurre ql.co. da ql.co.: *from what do you — that?,* da che cosa lo deduci? **2.** implicare: *a picture infers the existence of a painter,* un quadro implica l'esistenza di un pittore.

inferable [in'fə:rəbl], *ag.* deducibile.

inference ['infərəns], *s.* inferenza, deduzione; conclusione: *to draw an — from sthg.,* trarre una conclusione da ql.co.

inferential [ˌinfə'renʃəl], *ag.* deduttivo: — *proofs,* prove deduttive.

inferentially [ˌinfə'renʃəli], *av.* deduttivamente.

inferior [in'fiəriə*], *ag.* inferiore: — *piece of work,* lavoro scadente; *to be — to s.o. in merit,* essere inferiore a qlcu. per merito ‖ *s.* inferiore; subalterno.

inferiority [inˌfiəri'oriti], *s.* inferiorità ☆ — *complex,* (*psicanalisi*) complesso d'inferiorità.

inferiorly [in'fiəriəli], *av.* inferiormente.

infernal [in'fə:nl], *ag.* **1.** infernale: — *powers,* potenze infernali **2.** *fig.* diabolico, infernale: — *machine,* macchina infernale; — *row,* rumore infernale.

infernality [ˌinfə'næliti], *s.* infernalità.

infernally [in'fə:nəli], *av.* infernalmente: *it is — hot,* fa un caldo d'inferno; *it is — lonely here,* ci si sente terribilmente soli qui.

inferno [in'fə:nou], *pl.* **infernos** [in'fə:nouz], *s.* inferno ‖ *Dante's Inferno,* l'Inferno di Dante.

infertile [in'fə:tail], *ag.* sterile, infecondo.

infertility [ˌinfə:'tiliti], *s.* sterilità, infecondità.

to **infest** [in'fest], *v.t.* infestare: *the roads were infested with highwaymen,* le strade erano infestate da briganti.

infestation [ˌinfes'teiʃən], *s.* infestamento.

infeudation [ˌinfju'deiʃən], *s.* infeudamento.

infidel ['infidəl], *ag.s.* infedele; miscredente.

infidelity [ˌinfi'deliti], *s.* miscredenza; infedeltà; slealtà: *conjugal —,* infedeltà coniugale.

infield ['in-fi:ld], *s.* terreno coltivo; terreno arato.

infighting ['inˌfaitiŋ], *s.* lotta corpo a corpo.

to **infilter** [in'filtə*], *v.t.* filtrare, fare filtrare.

to **infiltrate** ['infiltreit], *v.t.i.* infiltrare, infiltrarsi.

infiltration [ˌinfil'treiʃən], *s.* infiltrazione.

infinite ['infinit], *ag.* **1.** infinito, illimitato; immenso **2.** (*con s.pl.*) (*arc.*) moltissimi, innumerevoli: — *times,* un'infinità di volte **3.** (*gram.*) infinito, indefinito: — *verb,* verbo indefinito ‖ *s.* infinito (anche *mat.*) ‖ *The Infinite,* l'Infinito, Dio.

infinitely ['infinitli], *av.* infinitamente, all'infinito.

infiniteness ['infinitnis], *s.* infinità; immensità.

infinitesimal [ˌinfini'tesiməl], *ag.* infinitesimo; (*mat.*)

infinitesimale ‖ *s.* quantità infinitesimale; (*mat.*) un infinitesimo ☆ — *calculus,* calcolo infinitesimale.

infinitesimally [ˌinfini'tesiməli], *av.* in modo infinitesimale.

infinitival [inˌfini'taivəl], *ag.* (*gram.*) infinitivo.

infinitive [in'finitiv], *ag.s.* (*gram.*) infinito: *in the —,* all'infinito.

infinitude [in'finitju:d], *s.* infinità.

infinity [in'finiti], *s.* **1.** infinità; immensità **2.** (*foto. mat.*) infinito: *to —,* all'infinito.

infirm [in'fə:m], *ag.* **1.** infermo; debole; cagionevole, malaticcio **2.** irresoluto, incerto: *to be — of purpose,* (*arc.*) essere irresoluto.

infirmarian [ˌinfə'mɛəriən], *s.c.* infermiere, infermiera (nei monasteri).

infirmary [in'fə:məri], *s.* ambulatorio; infermeria; ospedale.

infirmity [in'fə:miti], *s.* **1.** infermità; debolezza **2.** irresolutezza; mancanza di volontà.

infirmly [in'fə:mli], *av.* **1.** debolmente **2.** incostantemente; instabilmente.

to **infix** [in'fiks], *v.t.* **1.** infiggere, conficcare **2.** *fig.* imprimere (nella mente) **3.** (*gram.*) inserire.

to **inflame** [in'fleim], *v.t.i.* **1.** infiammare, infiammarsi; ardere; accendere (anche *fig.*): *hay inflames very easily,* il fieno s'infiamma, prende fuoco molto facilmente; *to — discord,* attizzare la discordia; *to be inflamed with passion,* ardere d'amore **2.** (*patol.*) infiammarsi.

inflamer [in'fleimə*], *s.c.* suscitatore, suscitatrice (di passioni, ecc.) ‖ *s.* ciò che infiamma (anche *fig.*).

inflammability [inˌflæmə'biliti], *s.* infiammabilità.

inflammable [in'flæməbl], *ag.* infiammabile (anche *fig.*).

inflammableness [in'flæməblnis], *s.* infiammabilità.

inflammation [ˌinflə'meiʃən], *s.* **1.** (*patol.*) infiammazione **2.** l'infiammare, l'infiammarsi; il prendere fuoco (anche *fig.*).

inflammatory [in'flæmətəri], *ag.* **1.** (*patol.*) infiammatorio **2.** *fig.* infiammatorio: — *speeches,* discorsi che infiammano, che eccitano (*p.e.* alla rivolta).

to **inflate** [in'fleit], *v.t.i.* **1.** gonfiare, gonfiarsi (anche *fig.*): *to — s.o. with pride,* gonfiare qlcu. di orgoglio **2.** enfiare **3.** (*econ.*) provocare l'inflazione; inflazionare (moneta).

inflated [in'fleitid], *ag.* **1.** gonfio (anche *fig.*) **2.** enfiato **3.** *fig.* ampolloso, altisonante, declamatorio (di stile) **4.** (*comm.*) esagerato (di prezzi).

inflater [in'fleitə*], *s.* pompa per pneumatici.

inflation [in'fleiʃən], *s.* **1.** gonfiatura (anche *fig.*) **2.** (*patol.*) enfiagione, gonfiore **3.** ampollosità (di stile) **4.** (*econ.*) inflazione.

inflationist [in'fleiʃənist], *s.* (*comm.*) inflazionista.

inflatus [in'fleitəs], *s.* (*rar.*) inspirazione.

to **inflect** [in'flekt], *v.t.* **1.** flettere, piegare, curvare **2.** (*gram.*) flettere **3.** (*fis.*) inflettere **4.** modulare (la voce) **5.** (*mus.*) alterare (una nota) mediante semitoni.

inflection, *V.* **inflexion.**

inflective [in'flektiv], *ag.* (*gram.*) flessivo.

inflexibility [inˌfleksə'biliti], *s.* inflessibilità.

inflexible [in'fleksəbl], *ag.* inflessibile.

inflexibleness [in'fleksəblnis], *s.* inflessibilità.

inflexibly [in'fleksəbli], *av.* inflessibilmente.

inflexion [in'flekʃən], *s.* **1.** inflessione; flessione **2.** (*mus.*) alterazione (di nota).

inflexional [in'flekʃənl], *ag.* (*gram.*) flessivo.

to **inflict** [in'flikt], *v.t.* infliggere: *to — oneself (o one's company) on s.o.,* (*fam.*) infliggere la propria compagnia a qlcu.; *to — a punishment on s.o.,* infliggere una punizione a qlcu.

infliction [in'flikʃən], *s.* **1.** l'infliggere (una pena, ecc.) **2.** noia; fastidio.

inflorescence [ˌinflo'resns], *s.* (*bot.*) inflorescenza.

inflow ['in-flou], *s.* afflusso.

influence ['influəns], *s.* **1.** influsso; influenza; ascendente: *to exert one's — upon s.o.*, esercitare il proprio ascendente su qlcu. **2.** (*elett.*) induzione.

to **influence**, *v.t.* influenzare, avere influenza su: *he easily influences his friends*, egli esercita un forte ascendente sui suoi amici.

influent ['influənt], *ag.s.* (*geog.*) affluente.

influential [,influ'enʃəl], *ag.* influente, autorevole.

influentially [,influ'enʃəli], *av.* autorevolmente.

influenza [,influ'enzə], *s.* (*patol.*) influenza.

influx ['inflʌks], *s.* **1.** affluenza (di gente, acqua, ecc.) **2.** (*geog.*) confluenza.

inform¹ [in'fɔ:m], *ag.* informe.

to **inform²**, *v.t.i.* **1.** informare, dare informazioni; far sapere, annunciare: *can you — me when...?*, puoi farmi sapere quando...?; *I am informed that...*, mi si informa che...; *I informed the police*, informai la polizia; *to — s.o. about sthg.*, informare qlcu. di ql.co.; *to — s.o. of sthg.*, informare, avvisare qlcu. di ql.co.: *he informed me of his work*, mi ha messo al corrente del suo lavoro **2.** imprimere forma a; guidare; ispirare: *to — s.o. with a feeling*, ispirare un sentimento a qlcu. **3.** *to — against* (*s.o.*), denunziare.

informal [in'fɔ:ml], *ag.* **1.** non ufficiale; senza formalità, senza pretese, alla buona: *an — conversation between two ambassadors*, una presa di contatto tra due ambasciatori; *an — dinner*, un pranzo alla buona; *an — visit*, una visita senza cerimonie **2.** (*dir.*) irregolare, non legale.

informality [,infɔ:'mæliti], *s.* **1.** assenza di formalità; tono, carattere intimo: *I like the — of your dinners*, mi piace il tono intimo dei tuoi pranzi **2.** (*dir.*) vizio di forma, irregolarità.

informally [in'fɔ:məli], *av.* **1.** senza formalità, alla buona **2.** (*dir.*) irregolarmente.

informant [in'fɔ:mənt], *s.c.* **1.** informatore, informatrice **2.** (*dir.*) accusatore, accusatrice.

information [,infə'meiʃən], *s.* (*usato soltanto al sing.*) **1.** informazioni, notizie, ragguagli: *that's an interesting piece of —*, questa è un'informazione interessante; *to get — about, on, sthg., s.o.*, ottenere informazioni in merito a ql.co., a qlcu. ‖ *for your —*, a titolo d'informazione ‖ *the Ministry of Information*, il Ministero delle Informazioni **2.** conoscenza; scienza; sapere: *he showed a certain desire for —*, dimostra un certo desiderio di sapere **3.** (*dir.*) accusa, denunzia: *— against s.o.*, denunzia contro qlcu. ☆ *— bureau*, ufficio informazioni.

informative [in'fɔ:mətiv], **informatory** [in'fɔ:mətəri], *ag.* informativo; istruttivo.

informed [in'fɔ:md], *ag.* istruito ☆ *well- —*, colto.

informer [in'fɔ:mə*], *s.* (*dir.*) accusatore, denunziatore: *a common —*, delatore, spia (della polizia) ‖ *to turn —*, fare la spia.

infortune [in'fɔ:tʃən], *s.* (*arc.*) sfortuna.

infracostal [,infrə'kɔstl], *ag.* (*anat.*) intercostale.

to **infract** [in'frækt], *v.t.* infrangere.

infraction [in'frækʃən], *s.* infrazione; trasgressione (di una legge, ecc.); violazione (di un patto, ecc.).

infractor [in'fræktə*], *s.* violatore, trasgressore.

infragrant [in'freigrənt], *ag.* malodorante.

infrangibility [in,frændʒi'biliti], *s.* infrangibilità.

infrangible [in'frændʒibl], *ag.* **1.** infrangibile; *fig.* inviolabile **2.** (*fis.*) non fissionabile.

infraorbital [,infrə'ɔ:bitl], *ag.* (*anat.*) infraorbitale.

infrared ['infrə'red], *ag.* (*fis.*) infrarosso.

infrascapular [,infrə'skæpjulə*], *ag.* (*anat.*) infrascapolare.

infra-structure ['infrə,strʌktʃə*], *s.* substrato.

infrequency [in'fri:kwənsi], *s.* infrequenza, rarità.

infrequent [in'fri:kwənt], *ag.* infrequente, raro.

infrequently [in'fri:kwəntli], *av.* raramente: *not —*, abbastanza spesso.

to **infringe** [in'frindʒ], *v.t.i.* **1.** trasgredire, violare (una legge, ecc.): *to — copyright*, violare le leggi sui diritti d'autore **2.** contraffare: *to — a patent*, contraffare

un brevetto **3.** *to — upon* (*sthg.*) usurpare: *how could he — upon your rights?*, come ha potuto usurpare i vostri diritti?.

infringement [in'frindʒmənt], *s.* **1.** infrazione, violazione (di legge, ecc.) **2.** contraffazione (di brevetto).

infringer [in'frindʒə*], *s.* **1.** trasgressore **2.** contraffattore.

infructuous [in'frʌktjuəs], *ag.* infruttuoso.

infructuously [in'frʌktjuəsli], *av.* infruttuosamente.

to **infumate** ['infjumeit], *v.t.* affumicare.

infumation [,infju'meiʃən], *s.* affumicamento.

infundibular [,infʌn'dibjulə*], *ag.* (*anat. zool.*) a forma di imbuto.

to **infuriate** [in'fjuərieit], *v.t.* rendere furioso, far infuriare.

to **infuse** [in'fju:z], *v.t.i.* **1.** versare; *fig.* infondere: *to — courage into s.o.*, infondere coraggio a qlcu. **2.** fare un infuso di (tè, erbe, ecc.); mettere, stare in infusione: *let it — for five minutes*, lascialo in infusione per cinque minuti.

infuser [in'fju:zə*], *s.* infonditore; infuso.

infusibility [in,fju:zi'biliti], *s.* infusibilità.

infusible [in'fju:zəbl], *ag.* infusibile.

infusion [in'fju:ʒən], *s.* infusione; decotto, infuso.

infusive [in'fju:siv], *ag.* innato.

infusoria [,infju:'zo:riə], *s.pl.* (*zool.*) infusori.

infusorial [,infju:'zo:riəl], *ag.* (*zool.*) di infusori.

ingate ['ingeit], *s.* ingresso, entrata.

ingathering ['in,gæðəriŋ], *s.* raccolto.

to **ingeminate** [in'dʒemineit], *v.t.* reiterare.

to **ingenerate** [in'dʒenəreit], *v.t.* ingenerare, procreare.

ingenious [in'dʒi:njəs], *ag.* ingegnoso, abile; (*arc.*) d'ingegno; geniale.

ingeniously [in'dʒi:njəsli], *av.* ingegnosamente; abilmente.

ingeniousness [in'dʒi:njəsnis], *V.* **ingenuity.**

ingénue [,ænʒei'nju:], *s.* (*teat.*) ingenua.

ingenuity [,indʒi'nju(:)iti], *s.* **1.** ingegnosità; abilità inventiva: *to tax one's — in order to do sthg.*, ingegnarsi a fare ql.co. **2.** (*rar.*) ingenuità.

ingenuous [in'dʒenjuəs], *ag.* **1.** sincero, franco **2.** ingenuo; semplice; candido.

ingenuously [in'dʒenjuəsli], *av.* **1.** sinceramente **2.** ingenuamente; semplicemente; candidamente.

ingenuousness [in'dʒenjuəsnis], *s.* ingenuità; candore; semplicità.

to **ingest** [in'dʒest], *v.t.* ingerire.

ingestion [in'dʒestʃən], *s.* ingerimento.

ingle ['ingl], *s.* fiamma; fuoco; focolare ☆ *— -nook*, cantuccio presso il focolare.

to **inglobe** [in'gloub], *v.t.* (*arc.*) inglobare.

inglorious [in'glo:riəs], *ag.* **1.** umile, oscuro; sconosciuto **2.** disonorevole, ignominioso.

ingloriously [in'glo:riəsli], *av.* ingloriosamente, vergognosamente, ignominiosamente.

ingloriousness [in'glo:riəsnis], *s.* **1.** disonore, ignominia **2.** oscurità.

ingluvies [in'glu:vii:z], *s.* ingluvie (gozzo di uccello).

ingoing ['in'gouiŋ], *ag.* entrante ‖ *s.* (*arc.*) entrata.

ingot ['ingət], *s.* lingotto (d'oro, d'argento); pane (di qualsiasi metallo) ☆ *— iron*, ferro fuso.

to **ingot**, *v.t.* fondere in lingotti, in pani.

to **ingraft** [in'gra:ft], *v.t.* innestare; inculcare.

ingrain ['in'grein], *ag.* **1.** tinto in filato, prima della lavorazione **2.** *V.* **ingrained.**

ingrained [in'greind], *ag.* radicato; inveterato (di abitudini, pregiudizi, ecc.).

ingrate [in'greit], *ag.s.* (*arc.*) ingrato.

ingrateful [in'greitful], *ag.* ingrato; sgradevole.

to **ingratiate** [in'greiʃieit], *v.t.* ingraziare: *to — oneself with a person*, ingraziarsi qlcu.

ingratitude [in'grætitju:d], *s.* ingratitudine.

ingravescence [,ingrə'vesns], *s.* peggioramento (di malattia).

ingravescent [‚ingrə'vesnt], *ag.* che va aggravandosi (di malattia).

ingredient [in'gri:djənt], *s.* ingrediente; elemento.

ingress ['ingres], *s.* (*dir. astr.*) ingresso, entrata.

ingrowing ['in‚grouiŋ], *ag.* che cresce internamente: — (*toe-*)*nail*, unghia incarnita.

ingrowth ['in‚grouθ], *s.* **1.** crescita verso l'interno **2.** ciò che cresce internamente.

inguinal ['iŋgwinl], *ag.* (*anat.*) inguinale.

to **ingurgitate** [in'gə:dʒiteit], *v.t.* ingurgitare, ingollare, inghiottire (anche *fig.*).

ingurgitation [in‚gə:dʒi'teiʃən], *s.* ingurgitamento, inghiottimento.

to **inhabit** [in'hæbit], *v.t.* abitare; dimorare in (anche *fig.*): they — *a large house*, occupano una grande casa.

inhabitable [in'hæbitəbl], *ag.* abitabile.

inhabitance [in'hæbitəns], **inhabitancy** [in'hæbitənsi], *s.* (*dir.*) domicilio; residenza.

inhabitant [in'hæbitənt], *s.* abitante.

inhabitation [in‚hæbi'teiʃən], *s.* abitazione.

inhalant [in'heilənt], *ag.* inalante.

inhalation [‚inhə'leiʃən], *s.* inalazione; inspirazione, aspirazione (di fumo, ecc.).

to **inhale** [in'heil], *v.t.* inalare; aspirare (fumo, ecc.).

inhaler [in'heilə*], *s.* **1.** inalatore **2.** persona che aspira (fumo, ecc.).

inharmonic [‚inhɑ:'mɔnik], **inharmonious** [‚inhɑ:-'mounjəs], *ag.* disarmonico, discordante.

inharmoniously [‚inhɑ:'mounjəsli], *av.* disarmonicamente, senza armonia.

inharmoniousness [‚inhɑ:'mounjəsnis], *s.* disarmonia, discordanza.

inharmony [in'hɑ:məni], *s.* disarmonia.

to **inhere** [in'hiə*], *v.i.* essere inerente; appartenere.

inherence [in'hiərəns], *s.* inerenza; appartenenza.

inherent [in'hiərənt], *ag.* inerente; intrinseco; connesso.

inherently [in'hiərəntli], *av.* inerentemente.

to **inherit** [in'herit], *v.t.i.* ereditare: *she inherited from him*, ella fu la sua erede; *to* — *sthg. from s.o.*, ereditare ql.co. da qlcu.

inheritability [in‚heritə'biliti], *s.* **1.** ereditarietà **2.** (*dir.*) diritto di eredità.

inheritable [in'heritəbl], *ag.* **1.** ereditabile **2.** (*dir.*) avente diritti di erede.

inheritableness [in'heritəblnis], *V.* **inheritability.**

inheritance [in'heritəns], *s.* eredità; successione: *to come into an* —, ricevere un'eredità.

inheritor [in'heritə*], *s.* erede.

inheritress [in'heritris], **inheritrix** [in'heritriks], *s.* erede; ereditiera.

inhesion [in'hi:ʒən], *s.* inerenza.

to **inhibit** [in'hibit] *v.t.* **1.** inibire; trattenere, reprimere (sentimenti): *an inhibited person*, una persona inibita **2.** proibire, impedire: *to* — *s.o. from doing sthg.*, proibire a qlcu. di fare ql.co. **3.** (*dir. eccl.*) interdire: *inhibited priest*, prete interdetto.

inhibition [‚inhi'biʃən], *s.* **1.** inibizione **2.** (*dir. eccl.*) proibizione **3.** (*eccl.*) interdizione.

inhibitory [in'hibitəri], *ag.* inibitorio (anche *fisiol.*).

inholder [in'houldə*], *s.* (*arc.*) affittuario.

to **inhoop** [in'hu:p], *v.t.* (*arc.*) chiudere come in un cerchio.

inhospitable [in'hɔspitəbl], *ag.* inospitale.

inhospitableness [in'hɔspitəblnis], *s.* inospitalità.

inhospitably [in'hɔspitəbli], *av.* inospitalmente; in modo inospitale.

inhospitality ['in‚hɔspi'tæliti], *s.* inospitalità.

inhuman [in'hju:mən], *ag.* inumano, barbaro, brutale: — *laws*, leggi crudeli.

inhumanity [‚inhju(:)'mæniti], *s.* inumanità, crudeltà, barbarie.

inhumanly [in'hju:mənli], *av.* inumanamente, crudelmente, barbaramente.

inhumation [‚inhju(:)'meiʃən], *s.* inumazione, seppellimento.

to **inhume** [in'hju:m], *v.t.* inumare, seppellire.

inimical [i'nimikəl], *ag.* **1.** nemico; ostile: *to be* — *to s.o.*, osteggiare qlcu. **2.** dannoso.

inimically [i'nimikəli], *av.* **1.** ostilmente **2.** dannosamente.

inimitability [i‚nimitə'biliti], *s.* inimitabilità.

inimitable [i'nimitəbl], *ag.* inimitabile.

inimitableness [i'nimitəblnis], *s.* inimitabilità.

inimitably [i'nimitəbli], *av.* inimitabilmente, in modo inimitabile.

iniquitous [i'nikwitəs], *ag.* iniquo, malvagio; ingiusto.

iniquitously [i'nikwitəsli], *av.* iniquamente, malvagiamente; ingiustamente.

iniquity [i'nikwiti], *s.* iniquità, malvagità; ingiustizia.

initial [i'niʃəl], *ag.* iniziale: — *expenses*, spese iniziali; — *stage*, stadio iniziale ‖ *s.* iniziale; sigla; monogramma.

to **initial**, *pass.p.p.* **initialled** [i'niʃəld], *v.t.* firmare con le iniziali; siglare; parafare.

initially [i'niʃəli], *av.* inizialmente.

initiate [i'niʃiit], *ag.s.* iniziato.

to **initiate** [i'niʃieit], *v.t.* **1.** cominciare; istituire, dar origine a **2.** iniziare: *to* — *s.o. in* (o *to*) *sthg.*, iniziare qlcu. a ql.co.: *to* — *s.o. in an art, a science*, iniziare qlcu. a un'arte, una scienza; *to* — *s.o. into a secret society*, ammettere qlcu. in una società segreta.

initiation [i‚niʃi'eiʃən], *s.* **1.** inizio **2.** iniziazione.

initiative [i'niʃiətiv], *ag.* iniziativo, introduttivo ‖ *s.* iniziativa: *to do sthg. on one's own* —, fare ql.co. di propria iniziativa; *to lack* —, mancare di iniziativa; *to show* —, mostrare iniziativa; *to take the* — *in doing sthg.*, prendere l'iniziativa nel fare ql.co.

initiator [i'niʃieitə*], *s.* **1.** iniziatore, chi comincia, lancia (una moda, ecc.) **2.** iniziatore (a misteri, ecc.).

initiatory [i'niʃiətəri], *ag.* iniziale; preparatorio, preliminare ☆ — *steps*, preliminari.

initiatress [i'niʃieitris], **initiatrix** [i‚niʃi'eitriks], *s.* iniziatrice.

to **inject** [in'dʒekt], *v.t.* immettere; (*med.*) iniettare: *to* — *intramuscularly*, iniettare per via intramuscolare; *to* — *intravenously*, iniettare per endovena; *to* — *s.o.'s arm with sthg.*, iniettare ql.co. nel braccio di qlcu.

injection [in'dʒekʃən], *s.* iniezione (anche *mec. ind.*): *hypodermic* —, iniezione sottocutanea, ipodermica; *to give, have an* —, fare, farsi fare un'iniezione ☆ — *-cock*, (*mec.*) rubinetto d'iniezione; — *-pipe*, tubo d'iniezione.

injector [in'dʒektə*], *s.* (*mec.*) iniettore.

to **injelly** [in'dʒeli], *v.t.* (*rar.*) mettere in gelatina.

to **injoint** [in'dʒɔint], *v.t.* unire, congiungere.

injudicial [‚indʒu(:)'diʃəl], *ag.* extragiudiziale.

injudicious [‚indʒu(:)'diʃəs], *ag.* poco giudizioso; avventato, sconsiderato.

injudiciously [‚indʒu(:)'diʃəsli], *av.* poco saggiamente; avventatamente, sconsideratamente.

injudiciousness [‚indʒu(:)'diʃəsnis], *s.* mancanza di giudizio; imprudenza.

Injun ['indʒən], *s.* (*amer. fam.* per *Red Indian*) pellirossa ‖ *honest* —!, (*sl. scolastico*) parola d'onore!.

to **injunct** [in'dʒʌŋkt], *v.t.* (*fam.*) ingiungere.

injunction [in'dʒʌŋkʃən], *s.* ingiunzione, ordine.

to **injure** ['indʒə*], *v.t.* **1.** nuocere; ledere, danneggiare; far torto a, far male a: *to* — *one's health*, danneggiare la propria salute; *to* — *s.o.'s reputation*, ledere la reputazione di qlcu. **2.** *fig.* ingiuriare, offendere ‖ *to* — *oneself*, (*fam.*) darsi la zappa sui piedi **3.** ferire: *fatally injured*, mortalmente ferito **4.** (*comm. mar.*) avariare (merce).

injured ['indʒəd], *ag.* **1.** danneggiato, leso: *the* —

party, (dir.) la parte lesa 2. avariato: — cotton, cotone di scarto 3. fig. oltraggiato 4. ferito.

injurer ['indʒərə*], s.c. 1. chi offende, nuoce 2. feritore, feritrice.

injurious [in'dʒuəriəs], ag. 1. nocivo, dannoso; lesivo: — of s.o.'s interests, lesivo degli interessi di qlcu.; — to the health, nocivo alla salute 2. fig. ingiurioso, oltraggioso.

injuriously [in'dʒuəriəsli], av. 1. nocivamente, dannosamente; lesivamente 2. fig. ingiuriosamente 3. ingiustamente, a torto.

injuriousness [in'dʒuəriəsnis], s. 1. l'esser nocivo, dannosità 2. fig. oltraggio 3. fig. ingiustizia.

injury ['indʒəri], s. 1. male, torto; danno, lesione: — to one's reputation, danno alla propria reputazione; to the — of s.o., a danno di qlcu.; to do s.o. an —, far torto a qlcu. 2. ferita, lesione: insurance against injuries to workmen, assicurazione contro infortuni sul lavoro; to suffer injuries to one's head, subire lesioni alla testa 3. (comm. mar.) avaria.

injustice [in'dʒʌstis], s. ingiustizia: flagrant pieces (o cases) of —, ingiustizie flagranti; to do s.o. an —, fare un'ingiustizia a qlcu.

ink [iŋk], s. 1. inchiostro ‖ to sling —, scrivere (articoli); guadagnarsi la vita scrivendo; scrivere articoli ingiuriosi 2. nero (di seppia, ecc.) ☆ — (o -sac), tasca del nero (di seppia, ecc.); — -bottle, bottiglia da inchiostro; — -eraser, gomma da inchiostro; — -feed, sebatoio (di penna stilografica); — -fish, seppia; — -pad, tampone per inchiostro; — -pot, calamaio; — -well, calamaio infisso (in scrittoio, banco di scuola) ‖ copying —, inchiostro copiativo; Indian — (o China —), inchiostro di China; marking —, inchiostro indelebile; printing —, inchiostro da stampa; sympathetic —, inchiostro simpatico.

to ink, v.t. 1. imbrattar d'inchiostro: the boys' hands were inked, le mani dei ragazzi erano impiastricciate d'inchiostro 2. (tip.) inchiostrare 3. to — in, passare a penna 4. to — out, cancellare (parola, ecc.) con l'inchiostro 5. to — up, impregnare, coprire d'inchiostro.

inker ['iŋkə*], s. (tip.) rullo inchiostratore.

inkholder ['iŋk-houldə*], (arc.) **inkhorn** ['iŋk-hɔ:n], s. calamaio.

inkiness ['iŋkinis], s. 1. nero d'inchiostro 2. nerezza d'inchiostro.

inkless ['iŋklis], ag. senza inchiostro.

inkling ['iŋkliŋ], s. indizio, avviso, sospetto: not an — of..., non il minimo sospetto di...; he had an — of the truth, ebbe sentore della verità; to give s.o. an — of sthg., dare a qlcu. un indizio di ql.co.

inkstand ['iŋkstænd], s. calamaio da scrittoio.

inky ['iŋki], ag. 1. d'inchiostro, nero come l'inchiostro 2. macchiato d'inchiostro.

to inlace [in'leis], V. to **enlace**.

inlaid ['in'leid], pass.p.p. di to **inlay** ‖ ag. intarsiato: the sky was — with stars, il cielo era cosparso di stelle ☆ — work, intarsio.

inland ['inlənd], ag. interno (di paese) ‖ s. interno (di un paese); retroterra ☆ — sea, mare interno; — trade, commercio interno; — revenue, fisco.

inland [in'lænd], av. all'interno, nell'interno, verso l'interno; nell'entroterra.

inlander ['inləndə*], s.c. abitante dell'interno (di un paese).

in-law ['inlɔ:], s. (fam.) parente acquisito, affine.

inlay ['inlei], s. intarsio, intarsiatura.

to inlay [in'lei], pass.p.p. **inlaid** ['in'leid], v.t. intarsiare.

inlayer ['in'leiə*], s. intarsiatore.

inlaying ['in'leiiŋ], s. intarsio, intarsiatura.

inlet ['inlet], s. 1. (geog.) piccola baia; piccola insenatura 2. inserzione 3. (mec.) ammissione, apertura ☆ — port, foro di ammissione; — stroke, fase di aspirazione; — valve, valvola di ammissione ‖ air —, presa d'aria.

to inlock [in'lɔk], v.t. (arc. scoz.) rinchiudere.

inly ['inli], ag. (poet.) interno; intimo; segreto ‖ av. (poet.) internamente; intimamente, nel cuore.

inlying ['in,laiiŋ], ag. posto nell'interno (di un paese).

inmate ['inmeit], s. 1. inquilino; coinquilino 2. ospite; persona alloggiata in un istituto, manicomio, ecc.

inmeats ['inmi:ts], s.pl. (dial. cuc.) interiora.

inmost ['inmoust], ag. interiore; intimo; il più segreto; il più profondo: our — thoughts, i nostri pensieri più reconditi.

inn [in], s. alberghetto; osteria; locanda: to keep an —, tenere una locanda ‖ — of court, scuola di legge; the Inns of Court, Collegi degli Avvocati (a Londra) ☆ — -holder (o — keeper), locandiere, oste; albergatore; — yard, cortile d'albergo, di locanda.

innate ['i'neit], ag. innato: — ideas, idee innate.

innately ['i'neitli], av. istintivamente.

innateness ['i'neitnis], s. l'essere innato, istintivo.

innavigable [i'nævigəbl], ag. non navigabile.

innavigably [i'nævigəbli], av. in modo non navigabile.

inner ['inə*], ag. interiore, interno; fig. intimo, segreto: — emotions, emozioni intime; — court, retro corte ‖ the — man, l'anima, lo spirito; (scherz.) lo stomaco: to refresh one's — man, nutrirsi, mangiare ‖ s. linee di bersaglio vicine al centro; colpo che prende il centro del bersaglio ☆ — tube, camera d'aria.

innermost ['inəmoust], V. **inmost**.

to innervate ['inə:veit], v.t. (anat. fisiol.) rinvigorire.

innervation [,inə:'veiʃən], s. (anat. fisiol.) innervazione.

to innerve [i'nə:v], v.t. rinvigorire.

inning ['iniŋ], s. 1. raccolto 2. sistemazione del raccolto in luogo chiuso 3. pl. (cricket) turno d'un giocatore per colpire la palla 4. pl. fig. periodo di preminenza (di partito politico, di gruppo di persone, di persona).

innocence ['inəsns], **innocency** ['inəsnsi], s. innocenza; purezza; semplicità.

innocent ['inəsnt], ag. 1. innocente; puro ‖ — of, (fam.) privo: window — of glass, finestra senza vetri 2. ingenuo; sciocco ‖ s. 1. innocente 2. sciocco.

Innocent, no.pr.m. Innocente.

innocently ['inəsntli], av. innocentemente, senza malizia.

innocuity [,inou'kju:iti], s. innocuità.

innocuous [i'nɔkjuəs], ag. innocuo.

innocuously [i'nɔkjuəsli], av. innocuamente.

innocuousness [i'nɔkjuəsnis], s. innocuità.

innominable [i'nɔminəbl], ag. innominabile.

innominables [i'nɔminəblz], s.pl. (scherz.) calzoni.

innominate [i'nɔminit], ag. 1. innominato 2. (anat.) innominato; anonimo ☆ — artery, arteria anonima; — bone, osso dell'anca; — vein, vena anonima.

to innovate ['inouveit], v.i. fare innovazioni; introdurre novità.

innovation [,inou'veiʃən], s. innovazione; novità.

innovator ['inouveitə*], s. innovatore.

innoxious [i'nɔkʃəs], ag. innocuo.

innoxiously [i'nɔkʃəsli], av. innocuamente, inoffensivamente.

innoxiousness [i'nɔkʃəsnis], s. innocuità, natura inoffensiva.

innuendo [,inju(:)'endou], s. insinuazione, allusione (generalmente maligna).

innumerability [i,nju:mərə'biliti], s. innumerabilità.

innumerable [i'nju:mərəbl], ag. innumerevole.

innumerableness [i'nju:mərəblnis], s. innumerabilità.

innumerably [i'nju:mərəbli], av. innumerevolmente.

innutrition [,inju(:)'triʃən], s. denutrizione.

innutritious [,inju(:)'triʃəs], ag. poco nutriente.

inobservable [,inəb'zə:vəbl], ag. inosservabile.

inobservance [,inəb'zə:vəns], s. 1. inosservanza (di legge, ecc.) 2. disattenzione.

inobservant [,inəb'zə:vənt], *ag.* 1. inosservante 2. disattento.

inobtrusive [,inəb'tru:siv], *V.* **unobtrusive.**

inoccupation ['in,ɔkju'peiʃən], *s.* mancanza di occupazione.

inoculable [i'nɔkjuləbl], *ag.* inoculabile.

to inoculate [i'nɔkjuleit], *v.t.* 1. (*med.*) inoculare; vaccinare: *he was inoculated against typhus,* lo vaccinarono contro il tifo; *to — s.o. with the germs of a disease,* inoculare a qlcu. i germi di una malattia 2. (*agr.*) innestare 3. inculcare: *to — s.o. with ideas,* inculcare delle idee a qlcu.

inoculation [i,nɔkju'leiʃən], *s.* 1. (*med.*) inoculazione 2. (*agr.*) innesto.

inoculative [i'nɔkjuleitiv], *ag.* da inoculare.

inoculator [i'nɔkjuleitə*], *s.* 1. inoculatore 2. innestatore.

inodorous [in'oudərəs], *ag.* inodoro.

inoffensive [,inə'fensiv], *ag.* inoffensivo.

inoffensively [,inə'fensivli], *av.* inoffensivamente.

inoffensiveness [,inə'fensivnis], *s.* carattere inoffensivo.

inofficial [,inə'fiʃəl], *ag.* (*rar.*) non ufficiale.

inofficious [,inə'fiʃəs], *ag.* 1. senza funzione 2. (*dir.*) contrario al diritto naturale.

inoperable [in'ɔpərəbl], *ag.* (*med.*) non operabile.

inoperative [in'ɔpərətiv], *ag.* inefficace.

inopportune [in'ɔpətju:n], *ag.* inopportuno, intempestivo.

inopportunely [in'ɔpətju:nli], *av.* inopportunamente, male a proposito.

inopportuneness [in'ɔpətju:nnis], **inopportunity** [,inəpə'tju:niti], *s.* inopportunità.

inordinancy [i'nɔ:dinənsi], *s.* (*rar.*) smoderatezza, intemperanza.

inordinate [i'nɔ:dinit], *ag.* eccessivo, smoderato; sregolato.

inordinately [i'nɔ:dinitli], *av.* eccessivamente, smoderatamente; sregolatamente.

inordinateness [i'nɔ:dinitnis], *s.* smoderatezza, intemperanza.

inorganic [,inɔ:'gænik], *ag.* inorganico ☆ *— chemistry,* chimica inorganica.

inorganically [,inɔ:'gænikəli], *av.* inorganicamente.

inorganization [in,ɔ:gənai'zeiʃən], *s.* disorganizzazione.

inornate [i'nɔ:nit], *ag.* disadorno.

to inosculate [i'nɔskjuleit], *v.t.i.* 1. (*chir.*) unire per anastomosi 2. (*anat.*) inoscularsi, anastomizzarsi.

inosculation [i,nɔskju'leiʃən], *s.* (*anat.*) inoscolazione, anastomosi.

in-patient ['in,peiʃənt], *s.* degente; ammalato ricoverato all'ospedale.

inpouring ['in,pɔ:riŋ], *ag.* affluente ‖ *s.* afflusso.

input ['in-put], *s.* (*mec. elett.*) potenza, energia assorbita; alimentazione; entrata ☆ *— circuit,* circuito di alimentazione; *— energy,* energia immessa; *— transformer,* trasformatore d'entrata.

inquest ['inkwest], *s.* 1. inchiesta, interrogatorio: *Coroner's —,* inchiesta giudiziaria in caso di morte improvvisa; *to hold an — on a body,* procedere a una inchiesta per determinare la causa di morte di qlcu. ‖ *great* (o *last*), *—,* giudizio universale 2. giuria.

inquiet [in'kwaiət], *ag.* inquieto.

to inquiet, *v.t.* (*rar.*) disturbare.

inquietude [in'kwaiitju:d], *s.* inquietudine.

to inquire [in'kwaiə*], *v.t.i.* 1. chiedere, domandare: *they inquired what he knew about the matter,* presero da lui informazioni sulla faccenda; *you had better — the way of s.o.,* sarebbe meglio che tu chiedessi la strada a qlcu.; *to — whether,* domandare se ‖ *to — about, after s.o.,* chiedere notizie, informarsi su qlcu.; *to — for,* chiedere: *he inquired for a pair of shoes,* egli chiese un paio di scarpe 2. *to — into* (*sthg.*), indagare, cercare di saper ql.co. su una faccenda.

inquirer [in'kwaiərə*], *s.c.* investigatore, investigatrice; indagatore, indagatrice.

inquiring [in'kwaiəriŋ], *ag.* curioso, indagatore, investigatore: *— glance,* sguardo indagatore; *— mind,* mente avida di sapere.

inquiringly [in'kwaiəriŋli], *av.* interrogativamente, con sguardo indagatore: *to look — at s.o.,* interrogare qlcu. con lo sguardo.

inquiry [in'kwaiəri], *s.* 1. domanda, interrogazione, informazione: *on — I learnt...,* dopo debite informazioni ho saputo...; *to make inquiries about sthg.,* assumere informazioni su ql.co. 2. (*dir.*) inchiesta: *court of —,* commissione d'inchiesta; *to hold an — into,* procedere ad una inchiesta su; *to learn sthg. by —,* venire a sapere ql.co. con un'inchiesta ☆ *— office,* ufficio informazioni; *— operator,* (*tel.*) operatrice per informazioni.

inquisition [,inkwi'ziʃən], *s.* ricerca, investigazione; (*dir.*) inchiesta, perquisizione ‖ *the Inquisition,* (*st.*) l'Inquisizione.

inquisitional [,inkwi'ziʃənl], *ag.* inquisitorio.

inquisitive [in'kwizitiv], *ag.* indagatore; curioso; indiscreto: *— women,* donne curiose.

inquisitively [in'kwizitivli], *av.* curiosamente; indiscretamente.

inquisitiveness [in'kwizitivnis], *s.* curiosità; indiscrezione.

inquisitor [in'kwizitə*], *s.* 1. (*dir.*) magistrato inquirente 2. (*eccl.*) inquisitore ‖ *Inquisitor General,* Capo dell'Inquisizione di Spagna; *Grand Inquisitor,* Grande Inquisitore.

inquisitorial [in,kwizi'tɔ:riəl], *ag.* inquisitorio.

inquisitorially [in,kwizi'tɔ:riəli], *av.* in modo inquisitorio.

inquisitress [in'kwizitris], *s.* inquisitrice.

inroad ['inroud], *s.* 1. (*mil.*) incursione, invasione, scorreria, irruzione 2. *fig.* intromissione abusiva, usurpazione ‖ *this work makes inroads* (*up*)*on my time,* questo lavoro mi prende troppo tempo.

inrush ['inrʌʃ], *s.* irruzione (anche *fig.*); afflusso (d'aria, gas, ecc.).

to insalivate [in'sæliveit], *v.t.* (*fisiol.*) insalivare.

insalivation [in,sæli'veiʃən], *s.* (*fisiol.*) insalivazione.

insalubrious [,in-sə'lu:briəs], *ag.* insalubre, malsano.

insalubrity [,in-sə'lu:briti], *s.* insalubrità.

insalutary [in'sæljutəri], *ag.* insalubre.

insanable [in'seinəbl], *ag.* (*arc.*) insanabile.

insane [in'sein], *ag.* 1. pazzo, insano, alienato 2. *fig.* insensato, insano, folle (di desiderio, ecc.) ☆ *— asylum,* (*rar.*) manicomio.

insanely [in'seinli], *av.* pazzamente, follemente.

insaneness [in'seinnis], *s.* carattere insensato, insano (di azione, desiderio, ecc.).

insanitary [in'sænitəri], *ag.* insalubre, antigienico, malsano.

insanity [in'sæniti], *s.* 1. insania, pazzia, alienazione mentale 2. follia, stoltezza (di desiderio, azione, ecc.).

insatiability [in,seiʃjə'biliti], *s.* insaziabilità.

insatiable [in'seiʃjəbl], *ag.* insaziabile (anche *fig.*).

insatiableness [in'seiʃjəblnis], *s.* insaziabilità.

insatiably [in'seiʃjəbli], *av.* insaziabilmente.

insatiate [in'seiʃiit], *ag.* insaziabile.

insatiety [,insə'taiəti], *s.* (*arc.*) insaziabilità.

inscient ['inʃiənt], *ag.* ignaro, inconsapevole.

inscribable [in'skraibəbl], *ag.* inscrivibile.

to inscribe [in'skraib], *v.t.* 1. iscrivere 2. incidere, scolpire: *to — a name on a tomb* (o *to — a tomb with a name*), incidere un nome su di una tomba 3. *fig.* scolpire (nella mente, ecc.) 4. dedicare: *to — a work to s.o.,* dedicare un'opera a qlcu. 5. (*geom.*) inscrivere 6. (*comm.*) emettere titoli nominativi ☆ *inscribed stock,* titoli nominativi.

inscription [in'skripʃən], *s.* 1. iscrizione (su moneta, ecc.) 2. epitaffio 3. dedica (di libro).

inscriptional [in'skripʃənl], *ag.* di iscrizione; (*arc.*) che porta un'iscrizione.

inscriptive [in'skriptiv], *ag.* di iscrizione.

inscrutability [in,skru:tə'biliti], *s.* inscrutabilità, impenetrabilità.

inscrutable [in'skru:təbl], *ag.* inscrutabile, impenetrabile.

inscrutableness [in'skru:təblnis], *V.* inscrutability.

inscrutably [in'skru:təbli], *av.* impenetrabilmente.

to **insculp** [in'skʌlp], *v.t.* (*poet. arc.*) scolpire; incidere.

insculpture [in'skʌlptʃə*], *s.* (*arc.*) scultura; incisione.

insect ['insekt], *s.* **1.** insetto **2.** *fig.* persona spregevole ☆ — *-collector*, entomologo; — *-eater*, insettivoro; — *-powder*, polvere insetticida.

insectarium [,insek'tɛəriəm], *s.* insettario.

insecticidal [in,sekti'saidl], *ag.* insetticida.

insecticide [in'sektisaid], *s.* insetticida.

insectiform [in'sektifɔ:m], *ag.* a forma d'insetto.

insectifuge [in'sektifju:dʒ], *ag.* insettifugo.

insection [in'sekʃən], *s.* incisione.

insectivora [,insek'tivərə], *s.pl.* (*zool.*) insettivori.

insectivorous [,insek'tivərəs], *ag.* insettivoro.

insecure [,in-si'kjuə*], *ag.* **1.** malsicuro, malfermo, instabile, pericoloso (di terreno, ecc.): *to be in an — position*, essere in una posizione critica **2.** incerto, dubbioso.

insecurely [,in-si'kjuəli], *av.* **1.** instabilmente, senza sicurezza: *the King was — seated on the throne*, (*fam.*) il re sedeva su di un trono malsicuro **2.** in modo incerto, dubbioso.

insecurity [,in-si'kjuəriti], *s.* **1.** instabilità, mancanza di sicurezza; pericolo **2.** incertezza.

insemination [in,semi'neiʃən], *s.* (*med.*) fecondazione: *artificial —*, fecondazione artificiale.

insensate [in'senseit], *ag.* **1.** insensibile (di persona, corpo, materia) **2.** insensato (di progetto, desiderio).

insensately [in'senseitli], *av.* **1.** insensibilmente **2.** insensatamente.

insensateness [in'senseitnis], *s.* **1.** insensibilità **2.** insensatezza.

insensibility [in,sensə'biliti], *s.* **1.** incoscienza: *in a state of —*, in uno stato di incoscienza; *to fall into a state of —*, perdere la conoscenza, cadere in deliquio **2.** insensibilità; indifferenza.

insensible [in'sensəbl], *ag.* **1.** svenuto, in uno stato di incoscienza **2.** insensibile (anche *fig.*); indifferente, apatico: *when your hands are frozen they become —*, quando le mani sono gelate diventano insensibili **3.** inconsapevole: *to be — of*, non accorgersi di **4.** impercettibile: *by — degrees*, impercettibilmente.

insensibleness [in'sensəblnis], *V.* insensibility.

insensibly [in'sensəbli], *av.* insensibilmente, impercettibilmente, a poco a poco.

insensitive [in'sensitiv], *ag.* insensibile: *— to friendship*, insensibile all'amicizia.

insensitiveness [in'sensitivnis], *s.* insensibilità.

insentient [in'senʃiənt], *ag.* insensibile; inanimato.

inseparability [in,sepərə'biliti], *s.* inseparabilità.

inseparable [in'sepərəbl], *ag.* inseparabile.

inseparableness [in'sepərəblnis], *s.* inseparabilità.

inseparably [in'sepərəbli], *av.* inseparabilmente.

inseparate [in'sepərit], *ag.* inseparato.

insert ['insə:t], *s.* inserzione; codicillo (a legge, decreto); aggiunta (a manoscritto, documento, ecc.); (*amer.*) circolare, volantino (inserito in un libro, rivista, ecc.) ☆ *cork —*, (*mec.*) guarnizione in sughero.

to **insert** [in'sə:t], *v.t.* inserire; introdurre: *to — an advertisement*, fare un'inserzione (su un giornale); *to — a coin in a slot-machine*, introdurre una moneta in un distributore automatico; *to — a condition*, *a clause in an act*, inserire una condizione, una clausola in un atto.

insertion [in'sə:ʃən], *s.* inserzione (anche su un giornale); aggiunta; (*anat. bot. tip.*) inserzione ☆ *lace- —*, applicazione in pizzo.

inset ['in-set], *s.* **1.** (*tip.*) pagina aggiunta ad un libro; cartina, illustrazione di particolare inserita nel margine di una più grande **2.** pezzo di stoffa inserito in un indumento (per allargarlo, adornarlo).

to **inset** ['in-set], *pass.p.p.* **inset, insetted** ['in'setid], *v.t.* inserire.

inseverable [in'sevərəbl], *ag.* inseparabile.

inshore ['in'ʃɔ:*], *ag.av.* vicino, verso la riva.

inside ['in'said], *ag.* interno, interiore ‖ *s.* interno: *the door opened on the —*, la porta si apriva verso l'interno; *the dressmaker turned the overcoat — out*, la sarta rivoltò il soprabito; *to turn one's pockets — out*, rovesciare le tasche ‖ *I spent the — of a week there*, vi ho passato meno di una settimana ☆ *— address*, (*comm.*) indirizzo interno; *— -drive car*, automobile a guida interna; *— information*, (*fam.*) informazioni private, confidenziali.

inside, *av.* internamente; dentro: *come —*, vieni dentro, entra ‖ *— and out*, dentro e fuori ‖ *— of a week*, (*fam.*) in meno di una settimana.

inside, *prep.* nell'interno, entro: *don't let the dog come — the house*, non lasciare entrare il cane in casa.

insider ['in'saidə*], *s.c.* **1.** chi è addentro (*p.e.* in un segreto); iniziato, iniziata **2.** chi si trova in un luogo.

insidious [in'sidiəs], *ag.* insidioso; ingannevole; capzioso: *an — disease*, una malattia insidiosa.

insidiously [in'sidiəsli], *av.* insidiosamente.

insidiousness [in'sidiəsnis], *s.* l'essere insidioso.

insight ['insait], *s.* intuito; penetrazione; capacità d'osservazione: *a man of —*, un uomo d'intuito; *to get an — into sthg.*, riuscire a vedere a fondo in ql.co.; *to have great — into sthg.*, comprendere a fondo ql.co.

insignia [in'signiə], *s.pl.* insegne, distintivi.

insignificance [,insig'nifikəns], *s.* insulsaggine; futilità; piccolezza.

insignificant [,insig'nifikənt], *ag.* insignificante; privo di senso; trascurabile: *an — little man*, un ometto insignificante.

insincere [,insin'siə*], *ag.* insincero, falso.

insincerely [,insin'siəli], *av.* senza sincerità, falsamente.

insincerity [,insin'seriti], *s.* insincerità, falsità; ipocrisia.

to **insinuate** [in'sinjueit], *v.t.* **1.** insinuare: *to — oneself into s.o.'s favour*, insinuarsi nelle grazie di qlcu., ingraziarsi qlcu. **2.** introdurre: *to — sthg. into a place*, introdurre ql.co. in un luogo **3.** insinuare, suggerire indirettamente: *to — that a man is a liar*, insinuare che un uomo è un bugiardo.

insinuating [in'sinjueitiŋ], *ag.* insinuante.

insinuation [in,sinju'eiʃən], *s.* insinuazione.

insinuative [in'sinjueitiv], *ag.* insinuante.

insinuator [in'sinjueitə*], *s.c.* chi insinua.

insipid [in'sipid], *ag.* **1.** insipido **2.** *fig.* insulso, sciocco; privo di interesse.

insipidity [,insi'piditi], *s.* **1.** insipidezza **2.** *fig.* insulsaggine.

insipidly [in'sipidli], *av.* **1.** insipidamente **2.** *fig.* insulsamente; scioccamente.

insipidness [in'sipidnis], *s.* *V.* insipidity.

insipience [in'sipiəns], *s.* insipienza.

insipient [in'sipiənt], *ag.* insipiente.

to **insist** [in'sist], *v.i.* insistere; persistere ‖ *to — on*, insistere per, perché, su: *he insists on the importance of sthg.*, insiste sull'importanza di ql.co.; *I — on his going*, insisto perché egli vada; *they — on your being present* (o *on your presence*), insistono sulla necessità della tua presenza; *they will — on knowing the truth*, insisteranno per sapere la verità.

insistence [in'sistəns], **insistency** [in'sistənsi], *s.* insistenza.

insistent [in'sistənt], *ag.* insistente.

insistently [in'sistəntli], *av.* insistentemente.

insisture [in'sistʃə*], s. (arc.) persistenza.

insobriety [ˌinsou'braiəti], s. intemperanza.

insociable [in'souʃəbl], ag. taciturno; insocievole.

to **insolate** ['insouleit], v.t. insolare, soleggiare, esporre al sole.

insolation [ˌinsou'leiʃən], s. insolazione.

insole ['insoul], s. suola interna; sottopiede.

insolence ['insələns], s. insolenza, impertinenza, arroganza.

insolent ['insələnt], ag. insolente, impertinente, arrogante.

insolently ['insələntli], av. insolentemente, impertinentemente, arrogantemente.

insolidity [ˌinsə'liditi], s. mancanza di solidità.

insolubility [inˌsɔlju'biliti], s. insolubilità.

insoluble [in'sɔljubl], ag. insolubile: an — problem, substance, un problema, una sostanza insolubile.

insolubly [in'sɔljubli], av. insolubilmente.

insolvable [in'sɔlvəbl], ag. insolubile.

insolvency [in'sɔlvənsi], s. insolvenza, insolvibilità.

insolvent [in'sɔlvənt], ag. insolvente ‖ s. debitore insolvente.

insomnia [in'sɔmniə], s. insonnia.

insomnious [in'sɔmniəs], ag. insonne.

insomuch [ˌinsou'mʌtʃ], av. fino al punto, tanto: — as, visto che; — that, fino al punto che, tanto che.

insooth [in'su:θ], av. (poet.) in verità.

insouciance [in'su:sjəns], s. noncuranza; spensieratezza.

insouciant [in'su:sjənt], ag. noncurante; spensierato.

to **inspan** [in'spæn], pass.p.p. **inspanned** [in'spænd], v.t. 1. attaccare a un veicolo (buoi, cavalli) 2. attrezzare (un carro).

to **inspect** [in'spekt], v.t. ispezionare, esaminare, verificare; sorvegliare, sovraintendere (lavori); (mec.) collaudare, controllare.

inspection [in'spekʃən], s. ispezione, verifica; sorveglianza; (mec.) controllo, collaudo.

inspective [in'spektiv], ag. ispettivo.

inspector [in'spektə*], s. ispettore, verificatore; sovraintendente, sorvegliante; (mec.) collaudatore ☆ woman —, ispettrice; police —, ispettore di polizia.

inspectoral [in'spektərəl], ag. relativo ad ispettore, ispezione.

inspectorate [in'spektərit], s. ispettorato.

inspectorial [ˌinspek'tɔːriəl], V. **inspectoral**.

inspectorship [in'spektəʃip], s. ispettorato, sovraintendenza.

inspectress [in'spektris], s. ispettrice.

inspirable [in'spaiərəbl], ag. inspirabile.

inspiration [ˌinspə'reiʃən], s. 1. inspirazione, aspirazione (dell'aria, ecc.) 2. fig. ispirazione: divine —, ispirazione divina; poetic —, vena poetica; to draw — from nature, trarre ispirazione dalla natura; to have a sudden —, aver un'improvvisa ispirazione.

inspirational [ˌinspə'reiʃənl], ag. inspiratorio; prodotto da inspirazione.

inspirator ['inspəreitə*], s. inspiratore, aspiratore.

inspiratory [in'spaiərətəri], ag. inspiratore.

to **inspire** [in'spaiə*], v.t. 1. inspirare, aspirare 2. fig. ispirare, infondere: an inspiring example, un esempio ispiratore; to — s.o. with hope (o — hope into s.o.), ispirare, infondere speranza in qlcu.; to — a thought. a feeling in (to) s.o., ispirare un'idea, un sentimento a qlcu.

inspired [in'spaiəd], ag. 1. inspirato, aspirato 2. ispirato: an inspired poet, preacher, un poeta, predicatore ispirato 3. suggerito da persona influente (p.e. di articolo di giornale).

inspirer [in'spaiərə*], s. c. ispiratore, ispiratrice.

to **inspirit** [in'spirit], v.t. 1. animare (anche fig.) 2. incoraggiare: to — s.o. to do sthg., an action, incoraggiare qlcu. a fare ql.co., ad un'azione.

to **inspissate** [in'spiseit], v.t. inspessire; condensare.

inspissation [ˌinspi'seiʃən], s. (fisiol.) inspessimento.

inst. ['instənt], ag. (comm. abbr. di instant) del corrente mese: 5th inst., il 5 c.m.

instability [ˌinstə'biliti], s. instabilità.

to **install** [in'stɔːl], v.t. 1. installare; impiantare; insediare; collocare: to — new light fixtures, installare nuove apparecchiature elettriche; to — oneself in a new house, installarsi in una casa nuova 2. investire (di una dignità): to — a bishop, investire un vescovo.

installation [ˌinstə'leiʃən], s. 1. insediamento (p.e. di un vescovo) 2. (ind.) impianto; installazione; messa in opera ☆ electric light —, impianto della luce elettrica.

instalment [in'stɔːlmənt], s. 1. acconto; rata: to pay by instalments, (comm.) pagare a rate 2. puntata (di una pubblicazione) ☆ — -plan, sistema di vendita con pagamenti rateali; — -selling, vendita a rate.

instance ['instəns], s. 1. esempio: for —, per esempio 2. fatto, caso: in the first —, in primo luogo; in many instances, in molti casi; in your —, nel vostro caso 3. (dir.) istanza, richiesta, sollecitazione: at the — of, per richiesta di; court of the first —, tribunale di prima istanza.

to **instance**, v.t. citare ad esempio, addurre ad esempio.

instancy ['instənsi], s. urgenza; insistenza; pressione.

instant ['instənt], ag. 1. urgente: — need, bisogno urgente 2. imminente 3. (comm.) del corrente mese ‖ s. istante, momento: at this very —, in questo stesso momento; in an —, fra un momento; on the —, subito; I went that —, andai in quel momento preciso ‖ the —, non appena che: I told you the — I knew, te lo dissi non appena lo seppi.

instantaneity [inˌstæntə'ni:iti], s. istantaneità.

instantaneous [ˌinstən'teinjəs], ag. istantaneo.

instantaneously [ˌinstən'teinjəsli], av. istantaneamente.

instantaneousness [ˌinstən'teinjəsnis], s. istantaneità.

instanter [in'stæntə*], av. (scherz.) subito, all'istante.

instantly ['instəntli], av. all'istante, immediatamente, subito ‖ cong. non appena che.

to **instar** [in'stɑː*], pass.p.p. **instarred** [in'stɑːd], v.t. costellare, adornare di stelle.

to **instate** [in'steit], v.t. (dir.) insediare, collocare.

instauration [ˌinstɔː(ː)'reiʃən], s. restaurazione; rinnovamento.

instaurator ['instɔː(ː)reitə*], s.c. restauratore, restauratrice; rinnovatore, rinnovatrice.

instead [in'sted], av. invece, anzi, anziché: — of this, invece di questo; — of going, invece di andare ‖ this will do —, questo servirà al posto di quello.

instep ['in-step], s. 1. (anat.) collo del piede: foot with a high —, piede con il collo alto 2. collo di scarpa ☆ — -raiser, fiosso ortopedico.

to **instigate** ['instigeit], v.t. istigare, incitare: to — workers to go on strike, incitare i lavoratori a mettersi in sciopero.

instigation [ˌinsti'geiʃən], s. istigazione, incitamento: at (o by) — of s.o., per istigazione di qlcu.

instigator ['instigeitə*], s.c. istigatore, istigatrice.

to **instil(l)** [in'stil], pass.p.p. **instilled** [in'stild], v.t. instillare; fig. infondere, inculcare: to — an idea, a feeling into s.o., inculcare un'idea, un sentimento in qlcu.

instillation [ˌinsti'leiʃən], **instilment** [in'stilmənt], s. instillamento, l'instillare (anche fig.).

instinct [in'stiŋkt], ag. imbevuto; pieno.

instinct ['instiŋkt], s. istinto; impulso; capacità istintiva: an — for (doing) sthg., un istinto per (fare) ql.co.; by (o from) —, per istinto; to act on —, agire per puro istinto.

instinctive [in'stiŋktiv], ag. istintivo; impulsivo; spontaneo.

instinctively [in'stiŋktivli], av. istintivamente; impulsivamente; spontaneamente.

institute ['institju:t], *s.* **1.** istituto(culturale, scientifico, sociale, ecc.); (*amer.*) corso di specializzazione: *banking, research, technical* —, istituto bancario, di ricerche, tecnico **2.** *pl.* istituzione, regola ‖ *the Institutes of Justinian*, le Istituzioni di Giustiniano.

to institute, *v.t.* **1.** istituire, stabilire (una legge, una regola) **2.** fondare (una società) **3.** (*dir.*) istituire, intentare: *to* — (*legal*) *proceedings* (o *an action*) *against s.o.*, intentare un processo contro qlcu. **4.** (*dir.*) nominare; investire: *to* — *s.o. heir*, nominare qlcu. erede; *to* — *s.o. to a benefice*, (*eccl.*) investire qlcu. di un beneficio.

institution [,insti'tju:ʃən], *s.* **1.** istituzione, ente, associazione: *charitable* —, istituto di beneficenza **2.** (*fam.*) istituzione: *La Scala Theatre is a national* —, il Teatro alla Scala è una istituzione nazionale **3.** istituzione, creazione (di uno Stato, di una banca) **4.** (*eccl.*) nomina.

institutional [,insti'tju:ʃən], *ag.* istituzionale.
institutive ['insti,tju:tiv], *ag.* istitutivo.
institutor ['insti,tju:tə*], *s.* istitutore; fondatore; organizzatore.
institutress ['insti,tju:tris], **institutrix** [,insti'tju:triks], *s.* (*rar.*) istitutrice; fondatrice.

to instruct [in'strʌkt], *v.t.* **1.** istruire; insegnare: *to* — *s.o. in sthg.*, istruire qlcu. in ql.co.; *to* — *a solicitor*, (*dir.*) dare istruzioni ad un avvocato **2.** informare: *to* — *s.o. that*, informare qlcu. che **3.** (IV) incaricare; dare ordini a: *to* — *s.o. to do sthg.*, dare ordini a qlcu. di far ql.co.; *to be instructed* (*to do sthg.*), esser incaricato (di fare ql.co.).

instructible [in'strʌktəbl], *ag.* (*rar.*) istruibile.
instruction [in'strʌkʃən], *s.* **1.** istruzione; insegnamento **2.** *pl.* disposizioni, ordini; (*mil.*) consegne: *official instructions*, prescrizioni d'autorità.
instructional [in'strʌkʃən], *ag.* educativo.
instructive [in'strʌktiv], *ag.* istruttivo.
instructively [in'strʌktivli], *av.* istruttivamente.
instructor [in'strʌktə*], *s.* istruttore; maestro; precettore; (*amer.*) lettore (d'università); (*mil.*) istruttore ☆ *sergeant* —, sergente istruttore.
instructress [in'strʌktris], *s.* istitutrice; maestra.
instrument ['instrumənt], *s.* **1.** (*mec.*) strumento; apparecchio; meccanismo **2.** (*mus.*) strumento **3.** *fig.* agente, mezzo: *she was but the* — *of God*, non era che lo strumento di Dio **4.** (*comm.*) documento; titolo: — *of credit*, titolo di credito **5.** (*dir.*) atto giuridico; documento ufficiale ☆ *controlling* —, strumento di comando; *indicating* —, strumento indicatore; *string* —, strumento a corde; *wind* —, strumento a fiato.
to instrument, *v.t.* **1.** (*mus.*) strumentare, orchestrare (un'opera, ecc.) **2.** (*dir.*) redigere un atto, un documento ufficiale.
instrumental [,instru'mentl], *ag.* **1.** strumentale: — *errors*, errori strumentali **2.** attivo; utile: *to be* — *in doing sthg.*, contribuire a fare ql.co **3.** (*mus.*) strumentale **4.** (*gram.*) strumentale: *the* — *case*, il caso strumentale ‖ *s.* (*gram.*) caso strumentale.
instrumentalist [,instru'mentəlist], *s.* (*mus.*) strumentista; concertista.
instrumentality [,instrumen'tæliti], *s.* mezzo; aiuto (per riuscire in un intento): *to obtain sthg. through the* — *of s.o.*, ottenere ql.co. con l'aiuto di qlcu.
instrumentally [,instru'mentəli], *av.* istrumentalmente.
instrumentation [,instrumen'teiʃən], *s.* **1.** (*mus.*) strumentazione; orchestrazione **2.** uso di strumenti scientifici, chirurgici **3.** mezzo; aiuto.
insubordinate [,insə'bɔ:dnit], *ag.* insubordinato; indisciplinato.
insubordination ['insə,bɔ:di'neiʃən], *s.* insubordinazione; indisciplinatezza.
insubstantial [,in-səb'stænʃəl], *ag.* incorporeo; inconsistente (anche *fig.*).
insufferable [in'sʌfərəbl], *ag.* insopportabile.
insufferably [in'sʌfərəbli], *av.* insopportabilmente.

insufficience [,insə'fiʃəns], **insufficiency** [,insə'fiʃənsi], *s.* insufficienza, inadeguatezza.
insufficient [,insə'fiʃənt], *ag.* insufficiente, inadeguato.
insufficiently [,insə'fiʃəntli], *av.* insufficientemente, inadeguatamente.
to insufflate ['insʌfleit], *v.t.* **1.** insufflare **2.** (*med.*) inalare; curare con inalazioni.
insufflation [,insʌ'fleiʃən], *s.* **1.** insufflazione **2.** (*med.*) inalazione.
insufflator [,insʌ'fleitə*], *s.* **1.** apparecchio soffiatore **2.** (*med.*) inalatore.
insular ['insjulə*], *ag.* **1.** insulare **2.** *fig.* di mentalità ristretta; pieno di pregiudizi.
insularism ['insjulərizəm], **insularity** [,insju'læriti], *s.* **1.** insularità **2.** *fig.* ristrettezza mentale.
insularly ['insjuləli], *av.* **1.** secondo le abitudini, la mentalità degli isolani **2.** con ristrettezza di vedute.
to insulate ['insjuleit], *v.t.* **1.** trasformare (una terra) in isola **2.** isolare, separare **3.** (*elett.*) isolare.
insulation [,insju'leiʃən], *s.* **1.** isolamento **2.** (*elett.*) (materiale) isolante; isolamento ☆ *heat* —, isolamento termico.
insulator ['insjuleitə*], *s.* (*elett.*) isolatore ☆ *high-tension* —, isolatore per alta tensione; *telephone type* —, isolatore per linee telefoniche.
insulin ['insjulin], *s.* (*farm.*) insulina.
insulse [in'sʌls], *ag.* (*arc.*) insulso.
insult ['insʌlt], *s.* insulto, offesa, ingiuria.
to insult [in'sʌlt], *v.t.* insultare, offendere, ingiuriare.
insultable [in'sʌltəbl], *ag.* (*rar.*) insultabile.
insulter [in'sʌltə*], *s.* chi insulta, offende, ingiuria.
insulting [in'sʌltiŋ], *ag.* insultante, offensivo, ingiurioso.
insultingly [in'sʌltiŋli], *av.* in modo insultante, insolentemente, oltraggiosamente.
insultment [in'sʌltmənt], *s.* (*rar.*) insulto.
insuperability [in,sju:pərə'biliti], *s.* insuperabilità.
insuperable [in'sju:pərəbl], *ag.* insuperabile, insormontabile.
insuperably [in'sju:pərəbli], *av.* insuperabilmente, insormontabilmente.
insupportable [,in-sə'pɔ:təbl], *ag.* insopportabile.
insupportableness [,in-sə'pɔ:təblnis], *s.* insopportabilità.
insuppressible [,in-sə'presəbl], *ag.* insopprimibile.
insuppressibly [,in-sə'presəbli], *av.* insopprimibilmente.
insuppressive [,in-sə presiv], *ag.* (*rar.*) insopprimibile.
insurable [in'ʃuərəbl], *ag.* assicurabile.
insurance [in'ʃuərəns], *s.* assicurazione ☆ — *agent*, agente di assicurazione; — *company*, compagnia di assicurazione; — *policy*, polizza di assicurazione; — *premium*, premio di assicurazione ‖ *fire, life* — *company*, compagnia di assicurazione contro il fuoco, sulla vita; *unemployment* —, assicurazione contro la disoccupazione.
insurant [in'ʃuərənt], *s.* assicurato.
to insure [in'ʃuə*], *v.t.* **1.** assicurare: *to* — *sthg. against fire, etc.*, assicurare ql.co. contro gli incendi, ecc. **2.** garantire, assicurare (*p.e.* il buon esito di un progetto).
insured [in'ʃuəd], *ag.s.* assicurato.
insurer [in'ʃuərə*], *s.* (*comm.*) assicuratore (persona, ditta).
insurgence [in'sə:dʒəns], **insurgency** [in'sə:dʒənsi], *s.* insurrezione; rivolta.
insurgent [in'sə:dʒənt], *ag.s.* insorto, rivoluzionario.
insurmountability ['insə(:),mauntə'biliti], *s.* insormontabilità.
insurmountable [,insə(:)'mauntəbl], *ag.* insuperabile, insormontabile.
insurmountably [,insə(:)'mauntəbli], *av.* insuperabilmente, insormontabilmente.
insurrection [,insə'rekʃən], *s.* insurrezione, rivolta: *to rise in* —, insorgere.

insurrectional [ˌinsəˈrekʃən]], **insurrectionary** [ˌinsəˈrekʃnəri], *ag.* insurrezionale.

insurrectionist [ˌinsəˈrekʃnist], *s.* insorto, ribelle, rivoltoso.

insusceptibility [ˈin-sə,septəˈbiliti], *s.* mancanza di suscettibilità.

insusceptible [ˌin-səˈseptəbl], *ag.* non suscettibile.

to **inswathe** [inˈsweið], *v.t.* bendare, fasciare.

intact [inˈtækt], *ag.* intatto; intero, integro.

intactness [inˈtæktnis], *s.* integrità.

intagliated [inˈtæljeitid], *ag.* intagliato.

intaglio [inˈtaːliou], *pl.* **intaglios** [inˈtaːliouz], *s.* intaglio; incisione.

intake [ˈin-teik], *s.* 1. presa (idraulica, ecc.); immissione (d'acqua, ecc.); aspirazione (di motore, pompa, ecc.) 2. (*miner.*) pozzo d'aerazione 3. (*mec.*) energia assorbita 4. strozzatura (di tubo, ecc.) 5. nuovo acquisto ☆ — *valve*, valvola di aspirazione.

intangibility [in,tændʒəˈbiliti], *s.* intangibilità; *fig.* l'essere inafferrabile.

intangible [inˈtændʒəbl], *ag.* intangibile; *fig.* inafferrabile.

intangibly [inˈtændʒəbli], *av.* intangibilmente; *fig.* inafferrabilmente.

integer [ˈintidʒə*], *s.* 1.(*mat.*) numero intero 2. tutto, insieme, cosa completa in se stessa.

integral [ˈintigrəl], *ag.* integrale, completo, intero; (*metal.*) massiccio, in un solo pezzo: — *calculus*, (*mat.*) calcolo integrale ‖ *s.* (*mat.*) integrale.

integrality [ˌintiˈgræliti], *s.* integralità.

integrally [ˈintigrəli], *av.* integralmente.

integrant [ˈintigrənt], *ag.* integrante.

integrate [ˈintigrit], *ag.* integrale, intero.

to **integrate** [ˈintigreit], *v.t.* integrare, completare; (*mat.*) integrare.

integration [ˌintiˈgreiʃən], *s.* integrazione (anche *pol.*).

integrative [ˈintigreitiv], *ag.* integrativo.

integrator [ˈintigreitə*], *s.* integratore.

integrity [inˈtegriti], *s.* integrità; probità.

integument [inˈtegjumənt], *s.* (*anat. bot.*) tegumento.

integumentary [in,tegjuˈmentəri], *ag.* (*anat. bot.*) tegumentario.

intellect [ˈintilekt], *s.* 1. intelletto; intelligenza: — *distinguishes man from the animals*, l'intelletto distingue l'uomo dagli animali 2. persona di grande intelletto: *the intellect(s) of the age*, le migliori menti dell'epoca.

intellection [ˌintiˈlekʃən], *s.* intellezione.

intellective [ˌintiˈlektiv], *ag.* intellettivo.

intellectual [ˌintiˈlektjuəl], *ag.s.* intellettuale.

intellectualism [ˌintiˈlektjuəlizəm], *s.* 1. intellettualismo 2. (*fil.*) razionalismo.

intellectualist [ˌintiˈlektjuəlist], *s.* 1. intellettualista 2. (*fil.*) razionalista.

intellectuality [ˈinti,lektjuˈæliti], *s.* intellettualità.

intellectually [ˌintiˈlektjuəli], *av.* intellettualmente.

intelligence [inˈtelidʒəns], *s.* (*solo sing.*) 1. intelligenza: *a boy who shows very little* —, un ragazzo che mostra poca intelligenza 2. intesa: *a glance of* —, uno sguardo d'intesa 3. sagacia; perspicacia: *person of good* —, persona dalla mente sagace 4. informazioni; notizie: *to give, to receive* — *of sthg.*, dare, ricevere notizie di ql.co. ‖ *Intelligence Department*, (*mil. mar.*) Ufficio Informazioni ‖ *Intelligence Service*, servizio segreto britannico di informazioni ☆ — *office*, ufficio informazioni e statistiche; — *quotient*, quoziente di intelligenza; — *test*, « test » di intelligenza.

intelligencer [inˈtelidʒənsə*], *s.* informatore, spia; agente segreto.

intelligent [inˈtelidʒənt], *ag.* 1. intelligente 2. informato.

intelligential [in,teliˈdʒenʃəl], *ag.* 1. relativo all'intelligenza 2. che informa.

intelligently [inˈtelidʒəntli], *av.* intelligentemente.

intelligentsia [in,teliˈdʒəntsiə], *s.coll.* intellettuali classe colta (di una nazione).

intelligibility [in,telidʒəˈbiliti], *s.* intelligibilità; comprensibilità; chiarezza.

intelligible [inˈtelidʒəbl], *ag.* intelligibile; comprensibile; chiaro.

intelligibleness [inˈtelidʒəblnis], *s.* intelligibilità; comprensibilità; chiarezza.

intelligibly [inˈtelidʒəbli], *av.* intelligibilmente.

intemperance [inˈtempərəns], *s.* 1. intemperanza; smoderatezza, eccesso, abuso 2. (*amer.*) alcoolismo.

intemperate [inˈtempərit], *ag.* 1. smoderato, sfrenato, violento 2. dedito al bere 3. rigido (di clima).

intemperately [inˈtempəritli], *av.* smoderatamente.

intemperateness [inˈtempəritnis], *s.* intemperanza, smoderatezza.

to **intend** [inˈtend], *v.t.* 1. (II, IV) intendere, aver l'intenzione di, prefiggersi, aver per scopo, proporsi: *I don't* — *him to go for me*, non intendo che egli vada per me; *to* — *to do* (o *doing*) *a thing*, proporsi di fare una cosa 2. destinare, designare: *we* — *our son for the army*, vogliamo che nostro figlio entri nell'esercito 3. voler dire, significare: *what do you* — *by these words?*, che cosa intendi dire con queste parole? 4. (*arc.*) tendere, volgere: *they* — *their thoughts homeward*, i loro pensieri volgono verso casa.

intendancy [inˈtendənsi], *s.* intendenza; sovraintendenza.

intendant [inˈtendənt], *s.* intendente; sovraintendente.

intended [inˈtendid], *ag.* progettato; premeditato; deliberato ‖ *s.c.* (*fam.*) fidanzato, fidanzata; promesso sposo, promessa sposa.

intendedly [inˈtendidli], *av.* deliberatamente.

intendment [inˈtendmənt], *s.* (*dir.*) significato esatto quale è stato fissato dalla legge.

to **intenerate** [inˈtenəreit], *v.t.* (*rar.*) ammorbidire; rendere tenero (anche *fig.*).

to **intensate** [inˈtenseit], *v.t.* (*rar.*) intensificare.

intense [inˈtens], *ag.* intenso; *fig.* ardente; veemente; profondo: — *pain*, dolore acuto; — *young woman*, (*fam.*) ragazza emotiva, ipersensibile.

intensely [inˈtensli], *av.* intensamente; vivamente; profondamente; eccessivamente.

intenseness [inˈtensnis], *V.* **intensity**.

intensification [in,tensifiˈkeiʃən], *s.* intensificazione.

to **intensify** [inˈtensifai], *v.t.i.* 1. intensificare, intensificarsi; rafforzare, rafforzarsi 2. (*foto.*) rinforzare.

intension [inˈtenʃən], *s.* 1. tensione 2. risolutezza; determinazione.

intensity [inˈtensiti], *s.* 1. intensità (di calore, suono, ecc.) 2. *fig.* indefessità (di studio, lavoro) 3. veemenza (di linguaggio); vigore 4. (*foto.*) forza, intensità.

intensive [inˈtensiv], *ag.* 1. intenso; intensivo; concentrato 2. (*gram.*) intensivo, enfatico 3. *fig.* tenace, indefesso.

intensively [inˈtensivli], *av.* intensamente; intensivamente.

intensiveness [inˈtensivnis], *s.* intensività.

intent [inˈtent], *ag.* 1. intento, dedito: *to be* — *on sthg.*, essere tutto intento a ql.co. 2. deciso: *to be* — *on doing sthg.*, essere deciso a fare ql.co. 3. ardente; accanito: — *gaze*, sguardo profondo, ardente ‖ *s.* intenzione, scopo, proposito: *to do sthg. with* —, fare ql.co. con un (certo) scopo in vista; *to shoot with* — *to kill*, sparare col deliberato scopo di uccidere ‖ *to all intents and purposes*, virtualmente; effettivamente; a tutti i riguardi.

intention [inˈtenʃən], *s.* 1. intenzione, scopo, mira, disegno: — *of*, intenzione di: *I have no* — *of going*, non ho nessuna intenzione di andare; *what are his intentions?*, che intenzioni ha?; *to court a woman with honorable intentions*, (*fam.*) fare la corte ad una donna con intenzioni matrimoniali; *to grasp s.o.'s* —, afferrare il pensiero di qlcu. ‖ *the road to hell is paved* *with good intentions, prov.* la strada per l'inferno è pavimentata di buone intenzioni **2.** (*dir.*) concezione: *primary, secondary intentions,* concetti primari, secondari **3.** (*eccl.*) intenzione (per cui si celebra la Messa) **4.** (*med.*) intenzione: *healing (of a wound) by the first, second* —, cura diretta con effetto immediato, con effetto secondario.

intentional [in'tenʃən]], *ag.* intenzionale; premeditato; volontario.

intentionally [in'tenʃnəli], *av.* intenzionalmente; premeditatamente; volontariamente.

intentioned [in'tenʃənd], *ag.* intenzionato ☆ *ill-* —, male intenzionato; *well-* —, bene intenzionato.

intently [in'tentli], *av.* intensamente.

intentness [in'tentnis], *s.* intensità; applicazione.

to **inter** [in'tə:*], *pass.p.p.* **interred** [in'tə:d], *v.t.* seppellire, sotterrare.

interact[1] ['intərækt], *s.* (*teat.*) intermezzo; intervallo.

to **interact**[2] [,intər'ækt], *v.i.* esercitare un'azione reciproca.

interaction [,intər'ækʃən], *s.* azione reciproca.

to **interblend** ['intə(:)'blend], *v.t.i.* mescolare, mescolarsi; fondere, fondersi.

to **interbreed** ['intə(:)'bri:d], *pass.p.p.* **interbred** ['intə(:)'bred], *v.t.i.* incrociare, incrociarsi (di animali di razza diversa)

interealary [in'tə:kələri], *ag.* **1.** intercalato **2.** interpolato.

to **intercalate** [in'tə:kəleit], *v.t.* **1.** intercalare **2.** interpolare.

intercalation [in,tə:kə'leiʃən], *s.* **1.** l'intercalare **2.** l'interpolare.

to **intercede** [,intə(:)'si:d], *v.i.* intercedere: *I will* — *for you with your uncle,* intercederò per te presso tuo zio.

interceder [,intə(:)'si:də*], *s.c.* intercessore, interceditrice; intermediario, intermediaria.

intercellular [,intə(:)'seljulə*], *ag.* (*biol.*) intercellulare.

intercept ['intə(:)sept], *s.* **1.** messaggio intercettato **2.** (*geom.*) segmento.

to **intercept** [,intə(:)'sept], *v.t.* intercettare, interrompere (comunicazioni, ecc.); arrestare, fermare: *to* — *s.o.'s retreat,* tagliare la ritirata a qlcu.

intercepter [,intə(:)'septə*], *s.* **1.** intercettatore **2.** (*neol. aer.*) caccia intercettatore.

interception [,intə(:)'sepʃən], *s.* intercettamento; interruzione.

interceptive [,intə(:)'septiv], *ag.* intercettivo.

interceptor [,intə'septə*], *V.* **intercepter**.

intercession [,intə'seʃən], *s.* intercessione.

intercessional [,intə'seʃən]], *ag.* di intercessione.

intercessor [,intə'sesə*], *V.* **interceder**.

intercessorial [,intəse'sɔ:riəl], *ag.* intercedente.

intercessory [,intə'sesəri], *ag.* intercedente.

interchange ['intə(:)'tʃeindʒ], *s.* **1.** scambio; baratto **2.** avvicendamento.

to **interchange** [,intə(:)'tʃeindʒ], *v.t.i.* **1.** scambiare, scambiarsi; barattare **2.** avvicendare, avvicendarsi; alternare, alternarsi.

interchangeability ['intə(:),tʃeindʒə'biliti], *s.* scambievolezza; intercambiabilità.

interchangeable [,intə(:)'tʃeindʒəbl], *ag.* scambievole; intercambiabile.

interchangeableness [,intə(:)'tʃeindʒəblnis], *s.* scambievolezza; intercambiabilità.

interchangeably [,intə(:)'tʃeindʒəbli], *av.* scambievolmente, vicendevolmente.

intercollegiate ['intə(:)kə'li:dʒiit], *ag.* fra collegi: — *games,* giuochi fra differenti collegi.

intercolonial ['intə(:)kə'lounjəl], *ag.* intercoloniale.

intercolumn [,intə(:)'kɔləm], *s.* (*arch.*) intercolunnio.

intercolumnar [,intə(:)kə'lʌmnə*], *ag.* (*arch.*) intercolonnare.

intercolumniation ['intə(:)kə,lʌmni'eiʃən], *s.* (*arch.*) intercolunnio.

intercom ['intə(:)kəm], *s.* (*tel.*) citofono.

to **intercommune** [,intə(:)kə'mju:n], *v.i.* (*rar.*) comunicare reciprocamente.

intercommunicable [,intə(:)kə'mju:nikəbl], *ag.* intercomunicabile.

to **intercommunicate** [,intə(:)kə'mju:nikeit], *v.i.* essere intercomunicante; comunicare (mutualmente).

intercommunication ['intə(:)kə,mju:ni'keiʃən], *s.* comunicazione reciproca; l'essere intercomunicante.

intercommunion [,intə(:)kə'mju:njən], *s.* comunione reciproca.

intercommunity [,intə(:)kə'mju:niti], *s.* comunanza.

intercomparison [,intə(:)kəm'pærisn], *s.* paragone, confronto.

to **interconnect** ['intə(:)kə'nekt], *v.t.* collegare.

intercontinental [,intə(:),kɔnti'nentl], *ag.* intercontinentale.

intercostal [,intə(:)'kɔstl], *ag.* (*anat.*) intercostale.

intercourse ['intə(:)kɔ:s], *s.* relazione, rapporto, rapporti: *our* — *with you,* i nostri rapporti con voi; *right of free* —, diritto di libero scambio; *sexual* —, rapporti sessuali; *to have (o to hold)* — *with s.o.,* avere rapporti con qlcu. ☆ *business* —, rapporti d'affari.

intercross ['intə(:)krɔs], *s.* incrocio; ibridazione.

to **intercross** [,intə(:)'krɔs], *v.t.i.* incrociare, incrociarsi.

intercurrence [,intə(:)'kʌrəns], *s.* intercorrenza.

intercurrent [,intə(:)'kʌrənt], *ag.* intercorrente.

to **interdepend** [,intə(:)di'pend], *v.i.* dipendere l'uno dall'altro.

interdependence [,intə(:)di'pendəns], *s.* interdipendenza.

interdependent [,intə(:)di'pendənt], *ag.* interdipendente.

interdict ['intə(:)dikt], *s.* proibizione, divieto; (*dir.*) interdizione; (*eccl.*) interdetto.

to **interdict** [,intə(:)'dikt], *v.t.* proibire, vietare; (*dir.*) interdire; (*eccl.*) colpire con l'interdetto.

interdiction [,intə(:)'dikʃən], *V.* **interdict**.

interdictive [,intə(:)'diktiv], **interdictory** [,intə(:)-'diktəri], *ag.* interdittorio.

interest ['intrist], *s.* **1.** interesse, partecipazione: — *in foreign companies,* partecipazioni in società estere; *companies in which we hold* —, società nelle quali siamo interessati; *he has an* — *in our business,* è interessato nella nostra azienda **2.** interesse; vantaggio; profitto: *in the* — *of truth,* nell'interesse della verità; *it is to your* — *to go,* è tuo interesse, vantaggio andare; *to look after one's own* —, badare ai propri interessi **3.** interesse, interessamento, sollecitudine: *his great* — *is music,* il suo maggiore interesse è la musica; *this has no* — *for us,* questo non ci interessa; *we heard with* — *that...,* con interesse abbiamo appreso che...; *to take an* — *in,* interessarsi di, a **4.** (*comm.*) interesse: — *on delayed payment,* interesse di mora; *at compound* —, all'interesse composto; *at 3%* —, all'interesse del 3%; *at what* — *did he lend you the money?,* a quale interesse ti ha prestato il denaro? || *with* —, (*fam.*) ad usura: *to repay an injury with* —, restituire ad usura un'offesa ricevuta.

to **interest,** *v.t.* **1.** interessare; destare attenzione, interesse: *does that* — *you?,* ti interessa?; *to* — *oneself in sthg.,* prender parte a ql.co. **2.** (*comm.*) dare un interesse.

interested ['intristid], *ag.* interessato: *an* — *look,* uno sguardo interessato; — *motives,* motivi interessati || *those* —, gli interessati.

interestedly ['intristidli], *av.* interessatamente.

interestedness ['intristidnis], *s.* interesse, interessamento.

interesting ['intristiŋ], *ag.* interessante; che attira l'attenzione: *what an* — *story!,* che storia emozionante! || *to be in an* — *condition,* essere in stato interessante.

interestingly ['intristiŋli], *av.* in modo interessante.

interfacial [,intə'feifəl], *ag.* (*geom.*) interfacciale.

to **interfere** [,intə'fiə*], *v.i.* **1.** impedire, ostacolare; interferire: *you mustn't let pleasure — with business*, non permettere che il piacere ostacoli il lavoro **2.** interferire, intromettersi, interporsi, ingerirsi, immischiarsi: *I never — in a debate*, non intervengo mai in una discussione; *their cousin will — between them*, il cugino si intrometterà fra loro; *they must not —*, non devono immischiarsene; *why did he — with that matter?*, perchè si immischiò in quella faccenda? **3.** urtarsi, scontrarsi; venire a conflitto **4.** urtarsi (di gambe di cavallo) **5.** (*fis.*) interferire.

interference [,intə'fiərəns], *s.* **1.** interferenza, intromissione, interposizione, ingerenza **2.** collisione **3.** (*elett. fis. rad.*) interferenza: *— from foreign broadcasting stations*, (*rad.*) interferenza di stazioni estere **4.** (*spor.*) intervento.

interferer [,intə'fiərə*], *s.c.* chi si intromette, si immischia (nei fatti altrui); ficcanaso.

interfering [,intə'fiəriŋ], *ag.* interferente.

interferingly [,intə'fiəriŋli], *av.* con interferenza.

interfluent [in'tə:flu(:)ənt], *ag.* scorrente in mezzo; mescolantesi senza sforzo.

interfoliaceous ['intə(:),fouli'eifəs], *ag.* (*bot.*) interfogliaceo.

to **interfuse** [,intə(:)'fju:z], *v.t.i.* **1.** spargere **2.** infondere; permeare; penetrare **3.** fondere, fondersi; mescolare, mescolarsi.

interfusion [,intə(:)'fju:ʒən], *s.* fusione; mescolanza.

to **intergrade** [,intə(:)'greid], *v.i.* trasformarsi gradualmente.

intergrowth ['intə(:),grouθ], *s.* crescita interna.

interim ['intərim], *ag.* (*lat.*) provvisorio, temporaneo; (*pol.*) interino, interinale ‖ *s.* interim, intervallo di tempo; (*pol.*) interinato ‖ *in the —*, nel frattempo ☆ *— dividend*, (*comm.*) dividendo in acconto; *— ministry*, ministero interinale.

interim, *av.* (*lat.*) nel frattempo.

interior [in'tiəriə*], *ag.* **1.** interiore, interno: *— angle*, (*geom.*) angolo interno **2.** interno, lontano dalla costa, dalla frontiera: *— lands*, regioni interne **3.** (*pol.*) interno: *— economy*, economia interna ‖ *s.* interno (di paese, casa, ecc.) ‖ *Department of the Interior*, (*pol.*) Ministero degli Interni ☆ *— decorator*, arredatore.

interiority [in,tiəri'oriti], *s.* (*rar.*) interiorità.

interiorly [in'tiəriəli], *av.* interiormente.

interjacent [,intə(:)'dʒeisənt], *ag.* intermedio.

to **interject** [,intə(:)'dʒekt], *v.t.* interferire; interloquire: *she interjected a question*, ella interloquì con una domanda.

interjection [,intə(:)'dʒekʃən], *s.* **1.** (*gram.*) interiezione **2.** *fig.* intromissione.

interjectional [,intə(:)'dʒekʃənl], *ag.* interiettivo.

interjectionally [,intə(:)'dʒekʃnəli], *av.* a mo' di interiezione.

to **interjoin** [,intə(:)'dʒɔin], *v.t.* (*arc.*) congiungere.

to **interknit** [,intə(:)'nit], *pass.p.p.* **interknitted** [,intə(:)'nitid], *v.t.i.* intrecciare, intrecciarsi.

to **interlace** [,intə(:)'leis], *v.t.i.* allacciare, allacciarsi; intrecciare, intrecciarsi (anche *fig.*) ☆ *interlaced* (o *interlacing*) *scanning*, (*tv.*) analisi interlineata.

interlacement [,intə(:)'leismənt], *s.* intreccio, viluppo (anche *fig.*).

to **interlard** [,intə(:)'la:d], *v.t.* **1.** infiorare (scritto, discorso) con parole straniere, ridondanti **2.** (*cuc. rar.*) lardellare.

to **interleave** [,intə(:)'li:v], *v.t.* interfogliare.

to **interline**[1] [,intə(:)'lain], *v.t.* interlineare.

to **interline**[2], *v.t.* foderare con ovattina (giacca, soprabito).

interlinear [,intə(:)'liniə*], *ag.* interlineare.

interlineation ['intə(:),lini'eiʃən], *s.* interlineazione.

to **interlink** [,intə(:)'liŋk], *v.t.* unire, concatenare.

to **interlocate** [,intə(:)lou'keit], *v.t.* interporre.

interlock ['intə(:)lɔk], *s.* (*cine.*) **1.** sincronizzazione **2.** apparecchio di sincronizzazione.

to **interlock** [,intə(:)'lɔk], *v.t.i.* **1.** unire, unirsi; congiungere, congiungersi; allacciare, allacciarsi **2.** (*ferr. mec.*) rendere interdipendenti **3.** (*cine.*) sincronizzare.

interlocution [,intə(:)lou'kju:ʃən], *s.* interlocuzione.

interlocutor [,intə(:)'lɔkjutə*], *s.* **1.** interlocutore **2.** (*dir.*) giudizio provvisorio.

interlocutory [,intə(:)'lɔkjutəri], *ag.* **1.** in forma di dialogo **2.** (*dir.*) interlocutorio ‖ *s.* (*dir.*) sentenza interlocutoria.

interlocutress [,intə(:)'lɔkjutris], **interlocutrix** [,intə(:)'lɔkjutriks], *s.* interlocutrice.

to **interlope** [,intə(:)'loup], *v.t.i.* immischiare, immischiarsi.

interloper ['intə(:)loupə*], *s.* **1.** intruso **2.** (*arc.*) commerciante non autorizzato **3.** nave contrabbandiera.

interlude ['intə(:)lu:d], *s.* **1.** intervallo **2.** (*mus.*) intermezzo, interludio **3.** (*st. lett.*) breve rappresentazione drammatica, mimica.

intermarriage [,intə(:)'mæridʒ], *s.* **1.** matrimonio fra membri di famiglie, razze diverse **2.** matrimonio fra consanguinei.

to **intermarry** ['intə(:)'mæri], *v.i.* imparentarsi (con altre tribù, famiglie, ecc.) per mezzo di matrimonio.

to **intermeddle** [,intə(:)'medl], *v.i.* intromettersi, ingerirsi, immischiarsi: *to — with* (o *in*) *what is not one's business*, occuparsi dei fatti altrui.

intermeddler [,intə(:)'medlə*], *s.c.* ficcanaso, intrigante.

intermeddling [,intə(:)'medliŋ], *s.* intromissione, ingerenza inopportuna, inframmettenza.

intermediacy [,intə(:)'mi:djəsi], *s.* l'essere intermedio.

intermedial [,intə(:)'mi:djəl], *ag.* (*arc.*) intermedio.

intermediary [,intə(:)'mi:djəri], *ag.* intermedio; intermediario ‖ *s.* mediatore, intermediario.

intermediate [,intə(:)'mi:djət], *ag.* intermedio, frapposto ‖ *s.* **1.** mediatore **2.** cosa intermedia ☆ *— bearing*, (*mec.*) cuscinetto intermedio; *— brake control*, (*aut.*) rimando dei freni; *— circuit*, (*rad.*) circuito intermedio; *— examinations*, esami catenaccio alla fine del biennio (nelle università inglesi); *— forging*, (*metal.*) sbozzatura a caldo; *— gear*, (*mec.*) ingranaggio di rinvio; *— landing*, (*aer.*) scalo aereo intermedio; *— shaft*, (*mec.*) albero di rinvio.

to **intermediate** [,intə(:)'mi:dieit], *v.i.* interporsi, fare da mediatore.

intermediately [,intə(:)'mi:djətli], *av.* per mezzo d'intermediario; indirettamente.

intermediation ['intə(:),mi:di'eiʃən], *s.* mediazione.

intermedium [,intə(:)'mi:djəm], *pl.* **intermedia** [,intə(:)'mi:djə], **intermediums** [,intə(:)'mi:djəmz], *s.* **1.** mezzo; strumento **2.** (*anat.*) osso intermedio nel carpo e nel tarso.

interment [in'tə:mənt], *s.* sepoltura.

intermezzo [,intə(:)'metsou], *pl.* **intermezzi** [,intə(:)'metsi(:)], **intermezzos** [,intə(:)'metsouz], *s.* (*mus. teat.*) intermezzo.

intermigration [,intə(:)mai'greiʃən], *s.* emigrazione scambievole.

interminable [in'tə:minəbl], *ag.* interminabile.

interminableness [in'tə:minəblnis], *s.* interminabilità.

interminably [in'tə:minəbli], *av.* interminabilmente.

to **intermingle** [,intə(:)'miŋgl], *v.t.i.* mescolare, mescolarsi; mischiare, mischiarsi.

intermission [,intə(:)'miʃən], *s.* sospensione, pausa, interruzione, sosta, intervallo: *without —*, senza sosta, senza intervallo.

to **intermit** [,intə(:)'mit], *pass.p.p.* **intermitted** [,intə(:)'mitid], *v.t.i.* sospendere; interrompere, interrompersi; arrestarsi, fermarsi; rendere intermittente.

intermittence [,intə(:)'mitəns], **intermittency** [,intə(:)'mitənsi], *s.* intermittenza.

intermittent [ˌintə(:)'mitənt], *ag.* intermittente: — *fever*, (*patol.*) febbre intermittente.

intermittently [ˌintə(:)'mitəntli], *av.* in modo intermittente.

intermitting [ˌintə(:)'mitiŋ], *ag.* intermittente.

to **intermix** [ˌintə(:)'miks], *v.t.i.* mescolare, mescolarsi; frammischiare, frammischiarsi.

intern [in'tə:n], *s.* 1. medico interno 2. internato.

to **intern**, *v.t.* internare.

internal [in'tə:nl], *ag.* interno, interiore; intrinseco; *fig.* intimo; soggettivo: — *injuries*, (*patol.*) lesioni interne ☆ — -*combustion*, (*aut.*) combustione interna: — -*combustion engine*, motore a scoppio.

internality [ˌintə(:)'næliti], *s.* qualità di interno.

internally [in'tə:nəli], *av.* internamente; *fig.* intimamente; soggettivamente.

international [ˌintə(:)'næʃənl], *ag.* internazionale ‖ *s.* competitore in gare internazionali (generalmente atletiche) ‖ *International*, Internazionale: *first, second, third International*, (*pol.*) prima, seconda, terza Internazionale.

internationalism [ˌintə(:)'næʃṇəlizəm], *s.* internazionalismo.

internationalist [ˌintə(:)'næʃṇəlist], *s.* internazionalista.

internationality ['intə(:),næʃə'næliti], *s.* internazionalità.

internationalization ['intə(:),næʃṇəlai'zeiʃən], *s.* internazionalizzazione.

to **internationalize** [ˌintə(:)'næʃṇəlaiz], *v.t.* internazionalizza e.

internationally [ˌintə(:)'næʃṇəli], *av.* internazionalmente.

internecine [ˌintə(:)'ni:sain], *ag.* micidiale.

internee [ˌintə'ni:], *s.* internato; prigioniero.

internment [in'tə:nmənt], *s.* internamento ☆ — *camp*, campo di concentramento.

internode ['intə(:)noud], *s.* (*bot.*) internodio.

internuncial [ˌintə(:)'nʌnʃəl], *ag.* di correlazione.

internunciary [ˌintə(:)'nʌnʃəri], *ag.* (*eccl.*) di internunzio.

internuncio [ˌintə(:)'nʌnʃiou], *s.* (*eccl.*) internunzio.

interoceanic ['intə(:)r,ouʃi'ænik], *ag.* interoceanico.

interocular [ˌintə(:)r'ɔkjulə*], *ag.* (*anat.*) interoculare.

to **interosculate** [ˌintə(:)r'ɔskjuleit], *v.i.* 1. mescolarsi, confondersi 2. (*biol.*) avere caratteri comuni.

to **interpage** [ˌintə(:)'peidʒ], *v.t.* interfogliare.

interparietal [ˌintə(:)pə'raiitl], *ag.* (*anat.*) interparietale.

to **interpellate** [in'tə:peleit], *v.t.* fare una interpellanza (in Parlamento).

interpellation [in,tə:pe'leiʃən], *s.* interpellanza.

interpellator [ˌintə:pe'leitə*], *s.* interpellante.

to **interpenetrate** [ˌintə(:)'penitreit], *v.t.i.* compenetrare, compenetrarsi.

interpenetration ['intə(:),peni'treiʃən], *s.* compenetrazione.

interphone ['intə(:)foun], *s.* citofono.

interplanetary [ˌintə(:)'plænitəri], *ag.* interplanetario.

interplay ['intə(:)'plei], *s.* azione reciproca ‖ — *of colours*, giuoco di colori.

interpolar [ˌintə(:)'poulə*], *ag.* interpolare.

to **interpolate** [in'tə:pouleit], *v.t.* inserire; interpolare: *interpolated clause*, (*gram.*) inciso; *to — a function*, (*mat.*) interpolare una funzione.

interpolation [in,tə:pou'leiʃən], *s.* 1. (*gram. mat.*) interpolazione 2. (*chir.*) trapianto di un tessuto.

interpolator [in'tə:pouleitə*], *s.c.* interpolatore, interpolatrice.

interposal [ˌintə(:)'pouzl], *s.* intervento; mediazione; interferenza.

to **interpose** [ˌintə(:)'pouz], *v.t.i.* interporre, interporsi; frammettersi; intervenire; interferire.

interposer [ˌintə(:)'pouzə*], *s.c.* mediatore, mediatrice.

interposition [in,tə:pə'ziʃən], *s.* interposizione; intervento; interferenza.

to **interpret** [in'tə:prit], *v.t.i.* 1. interpretare; decifrare; spiegare 2. fare l'interprete.

interpretable [in'tə:pritəbl], *ag.* interpretabile.

interpretation [in,tə:pri'teiʃən], *s.* interpretazione.

interpretative [in'tə:pritətiv], *ag.* interpretativo.

interpretatively [in'tə:pritətivli], *av.* interpretativamente.

interpreter [in'tə:pritə*], *s.* interprete: *a literary masterpiece needs no* —, un capolavoro letterario non ha bisogno di interprete; *to act as — to s.o.*, fare da interprete a qlcu.

interpretership [in'tə:pritəʃip], *s.* lavoro di interprete.

interpretress [in'tə:pritris], *s.* interprete (donna).

interprovincial [ˌintə(:)prə'vinʃəl], *ag.* interprovinciale.

interpunction [ˌintə(:)'pʌŋkʃən], *s.* interpunzione.

interracial [ˌintə(:)'reiʃəl], *ag.* 1. comune a varie razze 2. *fra razze*: — *marriage*, matrimonio fra individui di razze diverse.

interregnum [ˌintə'regnəm], *s.* 1. interregno 2. *fig.* intervallo, pausa.

interrelation ['intə(:)ri'leiʃən], *s.* relazione, rapporto.

interrelationship ['intə(:)ri'leiʃənʃip], *s.* interdipendenza.

interrex ['intə(:)reks], *s.* interrè.

to **interrogate** [in'terəgeit], *v.t.i.* interrogare; far delle domande.

interrogation [in,terə'geiʃən], *s.* interrogazione: ☆ — -*mark*, punto interrogativo.

interrogative [ˌintə'rɔgətiv], *ag.* interrogativo ‖ *s.* interrogativo, parola interrogativa.

interrogatively [ˌintə'rɔgətivli], *av.* interrogativamente.

interrogator [in'terəgeitə*], *s.c.* esaminatore, esaminatrice; inquisitore, inquisitrice.

interrogatory [ˌintə'rɔgətəri], *ag.* interrogativo; inquisitivo ‖ *s.* domanda, interrogazione; (*dir.*) interrogatorio.

to **interrupt** [ˌintə'rʌpt], *v.t.* interrompere.

interruptedly [ˌintə'rʌptidli], *av.* con interruzioni.

interrupter [ˌintə'rʌptə*], *s.c.* chi interrompe ‖ *s.* (*elett.*) interruttore.

interruption [ˌintə'rʌpʃən], *s.* interruzione.

interruptive [ˌintə'rʌptiv], *ag.* interrompente.

interruptively [ˌintə'rʌptivli], *av.* in modo da interrompere.

interscapular [ˌintə(:)'skæpjulə*], *ag.* (*anat.*) interscapolare.

to **intersect** [ˌintə(:)'sekt], *v.t.i.* intersecare, intersecarsi; incrociare, incrociarsi; tagliare, tagliarsi: *intersected with canals*, intersecato da canali.

intersecting [ˌintə(:)'sektiŋ], *ag.* intersecante: *two intersecting lines*, (*geom.*) due linee che s'intersecano.

intersection [ˌintə(:)'sekʃən], *s.* intersecazione.

intersectional [ˌintə(:)'sekʃənl], *ag.* intersecatorio.

intersidereal [ˌintə(:)sai'diəriəl], *ag.* infrasidereo, interstellare.

intersocial [ˌintə(:)'souʃəl], *ag.* intersociale.

interspace ['intə(:)'speis], *s.* spazio, intervallo.

to **intersperse** [ˌintə(:)'spə:s], *v.t.* cospargere, disseminare; spargere, spargere qua e là.

interspersion [ˌintə(:)'spə:ʃən], *s.* cospargimento.

interspinal [ˌintə(:)'spainl], **interspinous** [ˌintə(:)'spainəs], *ag.* (*anat.*) interspinale.

interstate ['intə(:),steit], *ag.* (*amer.*) fra stati: — *commerce*, commercio fra gli stati di un governo federale.

interstellar [ˌintə(:)'stelə*], *ag.* interstellare.

interstice [in'tə:stis], *s.* interstizio.

interstitial [ˌintə(:)'stiʃəl], *ag.* interstiziale.

to **intertangle** [ˌintə(:)'tæŋgl], *v.t.* ingarbugliare; intrecciare insieme.

intertribal [ˌintə(:)'traibəl], *ag.* fra tribù.

intertrigo [ˌintə(:)'traigou], *s.* (*patol.*) intertrigine.

intertropical [ˌintə(:)'trɔpikəl], *ag.* intertropicale.

to **intertwine** [ˌintə(:)'twain], *v.t.i.* attorcigliare, attorcigliarsi; intrecciare, intrecciarsi.

intertwiningly [ˌintə(:)'twainiŋli], *av.* in modo da intrecciarsi.

to **intertwist** [ˌintə(:)'twist], *V.* to **intertwine**.

interurban [ˌintə(:)'ə:bən], *ag.* interurbano.

interval ['intəvəl], *s.* intervallo: *at intervals*, ad intervalli.

intervale ['intəveil], *s.* (*amer.*) tratto di terreno piano (fra due colline o lungo un fiume).

intervallic [ˌintə(:)'vælik], *ag.* di intervallo.

to **intervene** [ˌintə(:)'vi:n], *v.i.* **1.** intervenire, frapporsi, intromettersi (anche *dir.*): *to — between two persons*, intromettersi fra due persone; *to — in sthg.*, intervenire in ql.co. **2.** accadere, sopravvenire.

intervener [ˌintə(:)'vi:nə*], *s.c.* chi interviene; (*dir.*) chi interviene in una causa in cui prima non aveva parte.

intervenient [ˌintə(:)'vinjənt], *ag.* interveniente.

intervening [ˌintə(:)'vi:niŋ], *ag.* interveniente; intermedio; intercorrente: *in the — time*, nel frattempo ‖ *s.* intervento; interposizione.

intervention [ˌintə(:)'venʃən], *s.* intervento; mediazione; interferenza: *surgical —*, (*med.*) intervento chirurgico.

interventionist [ˌintə(:)'venʃənist], *s.* (*pol.*) interventista.

intervertebral [ˌintə(:)'və:tibrəl], *ag.* (*anat.*) intervertebrale.

interview ['intəvju:], *s.* intervista, abboccamento: *he went up for an — with the minister*, si recò a un'intervista con il ministro; *she refused to give the journalists any —*, ella rifiutò di concedere interviste ai giornalisti.

to **interview**, *v.t.* intervistare; abboccarsi con.

interviewed ['intəvju:d], *ag.* intervistato.

interviewer ['intəvju:ə*], *s.c.* intervistatore, intervistatrice.

intervocalic [ˌintə(:)vou'kælik], *ag.* intervocalico.

to **intervolve** [ˌintə(:)'vɔlv], *v.t.* avvolgere, avvolgersi.

inter-war [ˌintə(:)'wɔ:*], *ag. attributivo* tra due guerre: *the — years*, gli anni tra le due guerre.

to **interweave** [ˌintə(:)'wi:v], *pass.* **interwove** [ˌintə(:)'wouv], *p.p.* **interwoven** [ˌintə(:)'wouvən], *v.t.* intessere, tessere; intrecciare; frammischiare: *interwoven with gold*, intessuto d'oro.

to **interwind** [ˌintə(:)'waind], *pass.pp.* **interwound** [ˌintə(:)'waund], *v.t.* **1.** avvolgere insieme **2.** *fig.* unire intimamente.

intestable [in'testəbl], *ag.* (*dir.*) intestabile, che non ha facoltà di far testamento o di beneficiare di esso.

intestacy [in'testəsi], *s.* (*dir.*) successione ab intestato.

intestate [in'testit], *ag.* (*dir.*) intestato: *to die —*, morire intestato.

intestinal [in'testinl], *ag.* intestinale.

intestine [in'testin] *ag.* intestino, interno: *— wars*, guerre intestine ‖ *s. gener. pl.* (*anat.*) intestino.

intil [in'til], *prep.* (*scoz.*) per **in**, **into**, **unto**.

intimacy ['intiməsi], *s.* intimità.

intimate ['intimit], *ag.* intimo; essenziale, intrinseco: *an — friend*, un amico intimo; *an — knowledge of the subject*, una profonda conoscenza dell'argomento ‖ *s.* amico intimo.

to **intimate** ['intimeit], *v.t.* **1.** intimare; notificare; dichiarare **2.** implicare; accennare; suggerire.

intimately ['intimitli], *av.* intimamente; familiarmente.

intimation [ˌinti'meiʃən], *s.* **1.** intimazione, avviso **2.** preannunzio; indicazione; segno: *— of immortality*, presagio di immortalità.

to **intimidate** [in'timideit], *v.t.* intimidire; intimorire.

intimidation [in,timi'deiʃən], *s.* intimidazione.

intimidator [in'timideitə*], *s.c.* chi intimidisce.

intimidatory [in'timideitəri], *ag.* intimidatorio.

intimity [in'timiti], *s.* intimità; vita privata.

to **intitule** [in'titju:l], *v.t.* intitolare.

into ['intu], *prep.* **in**, **dentro**, **entro** **1.** (*generalmente verso un luogo chiuso o l'interno di una cosa*): *let us go — the library*, andiamo in biblioteca; *pour the wine — a bottle*, versa il vino in una bottiglia ‖ *to take sthg. — consideration*, tenere debito conto di ql.co. ‖ *to work far — the night*, lavorare fino a tarda notte **2.** (*esprimente cambiamento, risultato*): *he grew — a man*, divenne un uomo; *to change sthg. — sthg. else*, cambiare ql.co. in ql.co. d'altro.

intoed ['intoud], *ag.* (*patol.*) valgo (di piede).

intolerable [in'tɔlərəbl], *ag.* intollerabile, insopportabile.

intolerableness [in'tɔlərəblnis], *s.* intollerabilità, insopportabilità.

intolerably [in'tɔlərəbli], *av.* intollerabilmente, insopportabilmente.

intolerance [in'tɔlərəns], *s.* intolleranza.

intolerant [in'tɔlərənt], *ag.* intollerante: *to be — of sthg.*, non saper sopportare ql.co. ‖ *s.* intollerante.

intolerantly [in'tɔlərəntli], *av.* intollerantemente.

to **intomb** [in'tu:m], *v.t.* seppellire.

to **intonate** ['intouneit], *v.t.* intonare.

intonation [ˌintou'neiʃən], *s.* **1.** intonazione **2.** accento, modulazione della voce **3.** cadenza, ritmo (di una lingua): *English — is quite the opposite of Italian —*, il ritmo della lingua inglese è del tutto opposto a quello dell'italiano.

to **intone** [in'toun], *v.t.* intonare; recitare cantando (salmi, preghiere, ecc.).

intoning [in'touniŋ], *s.* intonazione.

intoxicant [in'tɔksikənt], *ag.* inebriante; intossicante ‖ *s.* bevanda alcoolica, liquore.

to **intoxicate** [in'tɔksikeit], *v.t.* **1.** ubriacare, inebriare **2.** *fig.* eccitare.

intoxicating [in'tɔksikeitiŋ], *ag.* inebriante.

intoxication [in,tɔksi'keiʃən], *s.* **1.** ubriachezza, ebbrezza **2.** eccitazione.

intracellular [ˌintrə'seljulə*], *ag.* intercellulare.

intractable [in'træktəbl], *ag.* intrattabile; indocile.

intractableness [in'træktəblnis], *s.* intrattabilità; indocilità.

intractably [in'træktəbli], *av.* in modo intrattabile; ostinatamente.

intrados [in'treidos], *s.* (*arch.*) intradosso.

intransigence [in'trænsidʒəns], *s.* intransigenza.

intransigent [in'trænsidʒənt], *ag.s.* intransigente.

intransigentism [in'trænsidʒəntizəm], *s.* (*pol.*) intransigenza.

intransitive [in'trænsitiv], *ag.s.* (*gram.*) intransitivo.

intransitively [in'trænsitivli], *av.* intransitivamente.

intransmissible [ˌintræns'misibl], *ag.* non trasmissibile.

intransmutable [ˌintræns'mju:təbl], *ag.* immutabile.

intrant ['intrənt], *s.c.* **1.** chi entra (in un collegio, associazione, ecc.) **2.** (*eccl.*) novizio, novizia.

intravenous [ˌintrə'vi:nəs], *ag.* (*med.*) endovenoso.

to **intreasure** [in'treʒə*], *v.t.* (*arc.*) tesaurizzare.

to **intrench**, *V.* to **entrench**.

intrepid [in'trepid], *ag.* intrepido; impavido.

intrepidity [ˌintri'piditi], *s.* intrepidezza.

intricacy ['intrikəsi], *s.* confusione; complicazione; *fig.* labirinto.

intricate ['intrikit], *ag.* intricato; complicato; confuso.

intricately ['intrikitli], *av.* intricatamente; in modo complicato; confusamente.

intricateness ['intrikitnis], *V.* **intricacy**.

intrigant ['intrigənt], *s.c.* intrigante.

intrigue [in'tri:g], *s.* **1.** intrigo; raggiro **2.** (*teat.*)

intreccio: *comedy of* —, commedia d'intreccio 3. amore illecito ☆ *love* —, tresca.

to **intrigue,** *v.t.i.* **1.** intrigare: *to* — *with s.o.*, intrigare con qlcu. **2.** interessare; affascinare: *the puzzle intrigued her*, l'enigma l'affascinava **3.** avere una tresca: *to* — *with s.o.*, avere una tresca con qlcu.

intriguer [in'tri:gə*], *s.c.* intrigante.

intriguing [in'tri:giŋ], *ag.* **1.** intrigante **2.** interessante: *it is an* — *problem*, è un problema affascinante.

intrinse [in'trins], *ag.* intricato; involuto.

intrinsic [in'trinsik], *ag.* intrinseco; essenziale: — *value of a man, a coin*, valore reale di un uomo, di una moneta.

intrinsicality [in,trinsi'kæliti], *s.* intrinsichezza.

intrinsically [in'trinsikəli], *av.* intrinsecamente.

intrinsicate [in'trinsikit], *ag.* (*rar.*) intricato; involuto.

to **introduce** [,intrə'dju:s], *v.t.* **1.** introdurre, far entrare: *to* — *an idea, a system*, introdurre un'idea, un sistema; *to* — *Italian goods into foreign countries*, introdurre merce italiana in paesi stranieri; *to* — *sthg. into some place*, introdurre ql.co. in qualche luogo **2.** presentare, far conoscere: *to* — *oneself*, presentarsi; *to* — *s.o. to s.o. else*, presentare qlcu. a qlcu. altro; *to* — *to public notice*, far conoscere al pubblico ‖ *the bill was introduced before Parliament*, il progetto di legge fu presentato al Parlamento.

introducer [,intrə'dju:sə*], *s.c.* introduttore, introduttrice; presentatore, presentatrice.

introduction [,intrə'dʌkʃən], *s.* **1.** introduzione (di libro) **2.** presentazione: *letter of* —, lettera di presentazione **3.** manuale elementare.

introductive [,intrə'dʌktiv], *ag.* introduttivo.

introductorily [,intrə'dʌktərili], *av.* introduttivamente.

introductory [,intrə'dʌktəri], *ag.* introduttivo; preliminare: *to be* — *to*, servire d'introduzione a.

introit ['introit], *s.* (*eccl.*) introito.

intromission [,introu'miʃən], *s.* **1.** interferenza **2.** (*med.*) inserimento **3.** (*fis.*) intromissione.

to **intromit** [,introu'mit], *pass.p.p.* **intromitted** [,introu'mitid], *v.t.* (*arc.*) **1.** far entrare, lasciar entrare **2.** introdurre.

intromitter [,introu'mitə*], *s.c.* chi si intromette.

introrse [in'tro:s], *ag.* (*bot.*) introrso.

to **introspect** [,introu'spekt], *v.i.* autoesaminarsi.

introspection [,introu'spekʃən], *s.* introspezione.

introspective [,introu'spektiv], *ag.* introspettivo.

introspectively [,introu'spektivli], *av.* in modo introspettivo.

introspectiveness [,introu'spektivnis], *s.* tendenza all'introspezione.

introversion [,introu'və:ʃən], *s.* introversione (anche *psicologia*).

introvert ['introuvə:t], *ag.* introvertito ‖ *s.c.* introvertito, introvertita.

to **introvert** [,introu'və:t], *v.t.* **1.** introvertire; rivolgere (la mente, il pensiero) su se stesso **2.** (*zool.*) far rientrare, ritirare (un organo).

to **intrude** [in'tru:d], *v.t.i.* imporre, imporsi; intromettersi arbitrariamente: *I hope I am not intruding*, spero che il mio intervento non sia fuori luogo; *to* — *one's views upon s.o.*, (*fam.*) imporre le proprie opinioni a qlcu.; *to* — *upon a person's privacy*, disturbare l'intimità di una persona.

intruder [in'tru:də*], *s.c.* intruso, intrusa; seccatore, seccatrice ‖ *s.* (*aer.*) apparecchio di disturbo.

intrusion [in'tru:ʒən], *s.* **1.** intrusione **2.** (*geol.*) intrusione (di rocce plutoniche) **3.** usurpazione (di carica, di beneficio, di proprietà).

intrusionist [in'tru:ʒənist], *s.* intruso.

intrusive [in'tru:siv], *ag.* **1.** intruso; importuno, invadente **2.** (*geol.*) intrusivo.

intrusively [in'tru:sivli], *av.* da intruso; inopportunamente.

intrusiveness [in'tru:sivnis], *s.* carattere importuno, indiscreto; importunità, indiscrezione.

to **intubate** ['intju(:)beit], *v.t.* (*chir.*) intubare.

to **intuit** [in'tju(:)it], *v.t.i.* intuire; avere intuito.

intuition [,intju(:)'iʃən], *s.* intuizione, intuito.

intuitional [,intju(:)'iʃən], *ag.* intuitivo.

intuitionalism [,intju(:)'iʃənəlizəm], *s.* (*fil.*) intuizionismo.

intuitive [in'tju(:)itiv], *ag.* intuitivo.

intuitively [in'tju(:)itivli], *av.* intuitivamente.

intuitiveness [in'tju(:)itivnis], *s.* intuito.

intuitivism [in'tju(:)itivizəm], *s.* (*fil.*) intuizionismo.

to **intumesce** [,intju(:)'mes], *v.i.* tumefarsi.

intumescence [,intju(:)'mesns], *s.* intumescenza.

intumescent [,intju(:)'mesnt], *ag.* intumescente; tumefatto; enfiato.

intussusception [,intəssə'sepʃən], *s.* (*patol. fisiol.*) intussuscezione.

inulin ['injulin], *s.* (*chim.*) inulina.

inunction [in'ʌŋkʃən], *s.* **1.** applicazione di pomata, unguento **2.** pomata, unguento.

to **inundate** ['inʌndeit], *v.t.* inondare (anche *fig.*): *to* — *a land with water*, inondare d'acqua una regione; *to* — *a person with letters*, inondare una persona di lettere.

inundation [,inʌn'deiʃən], *s.* inondazione.

inurbane [,inə:'bein], *ag.* inurbano; scortese.

inurbanely [,inə:'beinli], *av.* inurbanamente; scortesemente.

inurbanity [,inə:'bæniti], *s.* inurbanità; scortesia.

to **inure** [i'njuə*], *v.t.i.* **1.** abituare; avvezzare; assuefare: *to* — *oneself to sthg., to hard work*, abituarsi a ql.co., al lavoro duro; *to be inured to cold* essere assuefatto al freddo **2.** (*dir.*) entrare in vigore (di legge, ecc.).

inurement [i'njuəmənt], *s.* assuefazione; abitudine.

to **inurn** [i'nə:n], *v.t.* mettere (le ceneri) in un'urna; seppellire.

inutile [i'nju:til], *ag.* inutile.

inutility [,inju(:)'tiliti], *s.* inutilità.

inutterable [in'ʌtərəbl], *ag.* inesprimibile; impronunciabile.

to **invade** [in'veid], *v.t.* **1.** invadere, assalire (anche *fig.*): *the city was invaded by tourists*, la città fu invasa da turisti **2.** violare: *to* — *s.o.'s rights*, violare i diritti di qlcu.

invader [in'veidə*], *s.c.* **1.** chi invade **2.** violatore, violatrice.

to **invaginate** [in'vægineit], *v.t.* **1.** invaginare **2.** fare rientrare.

invagination [in,vægi'neiʃən], *s.* (*chir.*) invaginazione.

invalid[1] ['invəli:d], *ag.s.* invalido, infermo; debole.

to **invalid**[1] [,invə'li:d], *v.t.i.* rendere invalido; dichiarare inabile per invalidità; (*mil.*) riformare; entrar nella lista degli invalidi: *he was invalided out of the army*, fu dimesso dall'esercito per invalidità.

invalid[2] [in'vælid], *ag.* (*dir.*) non valevole, nullo.

to **invalidate** [in'vælideit], *v.t.* infirmare, annullare; (*dir.*) invalidare (testamento).

invalidation [in,væli'deiʃən], *s.* invalidazione, invalidamento.

invalidity [,invə'liditi], *s.* invalidità.

invalidly [in'vælidli], *av.* senza validità.

invaluable [in'væljuəbl], *ag.* inestimabile; senza prezzo.

invaluably [in'væljuəbli], *av.* inestimabilmente.

invar [in'va:*], *s.* (*metal.*) invar.

invariability [in,vɛəriə'biliti], *s.* invariabiltà.

invariable [in'vɛəriəbl], *ag.* **1.** invariabile, immutabile **2.** (*mat.*) costante.

invariably [in'vɛəriəbli], *av.* invariabilmente.

invasion [in'veiʒən], *s.* **1.** invasione; *fig.* intrusione **2.** (*med.*) inizio (di malattia) **3.** violazione (di diritti).

invasive [in'veisiv], *ag.* di invasione; *fig.* invadente: — *war*, guerra d'invasione.

invective [in'vektiv], s. invettiva; insulto, ingiuria.

invectively [in'vektivli], av. invettivamente; ingiuriosamente.

to **inveigh** [in'vei], v.i. inveire: to — against, inveire contro.

to **inveigle** [in'vi:gl], v.t. allettare; tentare; sedurre: to — s.o. into doing sthg., indurre qlcu. a fare ql.co.

inveiglement [in'vi:glmənt], s. allettamento; adescamento; seduzione.

inveigler [in'vi:glə*], s.c. seduttore, seduttrice; tentatore, tentatrice.

invendibility [in,vendi'biliti], s. invendibilità.

invendible [in'vendəbl], ag. (rar.) invendibile.

to **invent** [in'vent], v.t. 1. inventare 2. (arc.) trovare, scoprire.

invention [in'venʃən], s. 1. invenzione, scoperta; (dir.) invenzione brevettabile || the Invention of the Cross, (st.) l'Invenzione della Croce 2. artificio, inganno 3. (mus.) invenzione 4. inventiva.

inventive [in'ventiv], ag. inventivo.

inventively [in'ventivli], av. inventivamente.

inventiveness [in'ventivnis], s. inventiva, fantasia.

inventor [in'ventə*], s. inventore.

inventory ['invəntri], s. inventario: to draw up an —, fare un inventario.

to **inventory**, v.t. far l'inventario, inventariare.

inventress [in'ventris], s. inventrice.

inveracious [,invə'reiʃəs], ag. insincero, mendace.

inveracity [,invə'ræsiti], s. insincerità, mendacia.

Inverness [,invə'nes], no.pr. (geog.) Inverness ☆ — overcoat, soprabito con mantellina.

inverse ['in'və:s], ag. inverso, opposto: in — order, in ordine inverso; in — ratio, in ragione inversa || s. inverso, opposto.

inversely ['in'və:sli], ag. inversamente.

inversion [in'və:ʃən], s. inversione, capovolgimento.

inversive [in'və:siv], s. insincerità, mendacia.

invert ['invə:t], ag. (chim.) invertito || s. 1. (edil.) arco invertito 2. invertito, omosessuale ☆ — soap, sapone disinfettante; — sugar, zucchero invertito.

to **invert** [in'və:t], v.t. invertire, capovolgere.

Invertebrata [in,və:ti'bra:tə], s.pl. gli invertebrati.

invertebrate [in'və:tibrit], ag. invertebrato; fig. fiacco, inetto || s. invertebrato.

invertebrated [in'və:tibreitid], ag. invertebrato.

inverted [in'və:tid], ag. invertito, rovesciato, capovolto ☆ — commas, virgolette.

invertedly [in'və:tidli], av. in ordine inverso.

inverter [in'və:tə*], s. (elett.) convertitore.

to **invest** [in'vest], v.t.i. 1. vestire, rivestire (anche fig.) 2. conferire (una carica, una dignità); investire: he was invested with a high rank, fu investito di un'alta carica 3. investire (capitali); fare un investimento: tell me how I might — my money, dimmi come potrei investire il mio denaro || I'll — in a new hat, (fam.) comprerò un cappello nuovo.

investigable [in'vestigəbl], ag. investigabile.

to **investigate** [in'vestigeit], v.t investigare, indagare.

investigation [in,vesti'geiʃən], s. investigazione, indagine.

investigative [in'vestigeitiv], ag. investigativo.

investigator [in'vestigeitə*], s.c. investigatore, investigatrice.

investigatory [in'vestigeitəri], ag. indagatore, investigativo.

investiture [in'vestitʃə*], s. 1. investitura 2. (arc.) copertura, rivestimento.

investment [in'vestmənt], s. 1. (comm.) investimento (di capitali) 2. (mil.) investimento, assedio ☆ — trust, società finanziaria di investimento.

investor [in'vestə*], s.c. investitore, investitrice.

inveteracy [in'vetərəsi], s. l'essere radicato, inveterato; (med.) cronicità, inguaribilità.

inveterate [in'vetərit], ag. inveterato, radicato; ac-

canito: an — disease, un male inguaribile; an — smoker, un fumatore accanito.

inveterately [in'vetəritli], av. ostinatamente.

invidious [in'vidiəs], ag. irritante; odioso; spiacevole; ingiusto: — comparison, confronto odioso.

invidiously [in'vidiəsli], av. malignamente; odiosamente; sgradevolmente.

invidiousness [in'vidiəsnis], s. malignità; odiosità.

to **invigilate** [in'vidʒileit], v.i. sorvegliare i candidati (durante un esame).

invigilation [in,vidʒi'leiʃən], s. sorveglianza, assistenza (specialmente agli esami).

invigilator [in'vidʒileitə*], s.c. sorvegliante, assistente (specialmente agli esami).

to **invigorate** [in'vigəreit], v.t. rinvigorire, rinforzare; rianimare.

invigorating [in'vigəreitiŋ], ag. rinforzante, rinvigorente: — air, aria salubre, corroborante.

invigoration [in,vigə'reiʃən], s. rinvigorimento.

invigorative [in'vigərətiv], ag. rinforzante.

invigorator [in'vigəreitə*], s. ricostituente.

invincibility [in,vinsi'biliti], s. invincibilità.

invincible [in'vinsəbl], ag. invincibile.

invincibly [in'vinsəbli], av. invincibilmente.

inviolability [in,vaiələ'biliti], s. inviolabilità.

inviolable [in'vaiələbl], ag. inviolabile.

inviolableness [in'vaiələblnis], s. inviolabilità.

inviolably [in'vaiələbli], av. inviolabilmente.

inviolacy [in'vaiələsi], s. l'essere inviolato (di una legge, di un santuario).

inviolate [in'vaiəlit], ag. inviolato, intatto.

inviolately [in'vaiəlitli], av. inviolatamente.

inviolateness [in'vaiəlitnis], s. condizione di inviolato.

invisibility [in,vizə'biliti], s. invisibilità.

invisible [in'vizəbl], ag. invisibile || the —, il mondo invisibile; Dio ☆ — exports, esportazioni invisibili.

invisibleness [in'vizəblnis], s. invisibilità.

invisibly [in'vizəbli], av. invisibilmente.

invitation [,invi'teiʃən], s. invito: he declined my —, rifiutò il mio invito; to send out invitations to a dinner, mandare inviti per un pranzo.

invitatory [in'vaitətəri], ag. invitativo; invitante.

invite [in'vait], s. 1. (fam.) invito 2. (scherma) invito.

to **invite**, v.t. 1. (IV) invitare: to — in, invitare ad entrare; to — s.o. to dinner, invitare qlcu. a pranzo 2. (IV) indurre 3. provocare: it is better not to — criticism, è meglio non provocare, non esporsi a critiche 4. to — in, invitare ad entrare 5. to — out, invitare a uscire.

invitement [in'vaitmənt], s. (rar.) invito.

inviter [in'vaitə*], s.c. chi invita, ospita.

inviting [in'vaitiŋ], ag. invitante; seducente.

invitingly [in'vaitiŋli], av. in modo invitante, seducente, attraente.

invitingness [in'vaitiŋnis], s. l'essere invitante, seducente.

to **invocate** ['invoukeit], v.t. invocare.

invocation [,invou'keiʃən], s. invocazione.

invocative [in'vokətiv], ag. invocativo.

invocatory [in'vokətəri], ag. invocativo; invocante.

invoice ['invois], s. (comm.) fattura ☆ — book, libro fatture; — clerk, fatturista; — price, prezzo di fattura.

to **invoice**, v.t. (comm.) fatturare.

to **invoke** [in'vouk], v.t. 1. invocare; chiedere: to — s.o.'s aid, chiedere aiuto a qlcu. 2. evocare (spiriti) con esorcismi 3. appellarsi a: to — s.o.'s authority, appellarsi all'autorità di qlcu.

involucre ['invəlu:kə*], s. (anat. bot.) involucro; rivestimento.

involuntarily [in'vɔləntərili], av. involontariamente.

involuntariness [in'vɔləntərinis], s. involontarietà.

involuntary [in'vɔləntəri], ag. involontario.

involute ['invəlu:t], ag. 1. involuto; intricato 2. a spirale (anche bot.) 3. (geom. mec.) evolvente || s. 1. (rar.)

cosa involuta **2.** (*geom.*) evolvente, sviluppante.

involution [ˌinvəˈluːʃən], *s.* **1.** involuzione, avvolgimento **2.** imbroglio, complicazione, intrico **3.** (*biol. patol.*) involuzione **4.** (*mat.*) elevazione a potenza.

to **involve** [inˈvɔlv], *v.t.* **1.** avviluppare, avvolgere (a spirale), attorcigliare **2.** complicare, rendere intricato: *an involved style,* uno stile involuto **3.** coinvolgere, compromettere, implicare: *she was involved in the crime,* ella fu coinvolta nel delitto **4.** portare come conseguenza, comportare: *expansion in business involves expenditure,* lo sviluppo degli affari comporta spese; *the war has involved an enormous increase in the national debt,* la guerra ha portato come conseguenza un enorme aumento del debito nazionale **5.** (*mat.*) elevare a potenza.

involvement [inˈvɔlvmənt], *s.* **1.** complicazione; confusione **2.** implicazione **3.** strettezza finanziaria.

invulnerability [inˌvʌlnərəˈbiliti], *s.* invulnerabilità.

invulnerable [inˈvʌlnərəbl], *ag.* invulnerabile.

invulnerableness [inˈvʌlnərəblnis], *s.* invulnerabilità.

invulnerate [inˈvʌlnərit], *ag.* (*arc.*) invulnerato.

inward [ˈinwəd], *ag.* interiore; interno; *fig.* intimo ‖ *s.* **1.** (*rar.*) l'interno, la parte interna; *fig.* l'intimo **2.** *pl.* viscere.

inward, *V.* **inwards.**

inwardly [ˈinwədli], *av.* internamente; interiormente; *fig.* intimamente.

inwardness [ˈinwədnis], *s.* interiorità, spiritualità; profondità (di sentimenti, ecc.).

inwards [ˈinwədz], *av.* **1.** verso l'interno **2.** internamente; interiormente; intimamente.

to **inweave** [ˈinˈwiːv], *pass.* **inwove** [ˈinˈwouv], *p.p.* **inwoven** [ˈinˈwouvən], *v.t.* tessere, intessere; intrecciare (anche *fig.*).

inwit [ˈinwit], *s.* (*arc.*) coscienza.

to **inwreathe** [inˈriːð], *v.t.* inghirlandare.

inwrought [ˈinˈrɔːt], *ag.* **1.** intessuto (anche *fig.*); ricamato, lavorato **2.** *fig.* unito intimamente.

Io [ˈaiou], *no.pr.f.* (*mit.*) Io.

iodate [ˈaiədeit], *s.* (*chim.*) iodato.

iodic [aiˈɔdik], *ag.* (*chim.*) iodico.

iodide [ˈaiədaid], *s.* (*chim.*) ioduro.

iodine [ˈaiədiːn], *s.* (*chim.*) iodio.

iodism [ˈaiədizəm], *s.* (*patol.*) iodismo.

to **iodize** [ˈaiədaiz], *v.t.* (*chim.*) iodare.

iodoform [aiˈɔdəfɔːm], *s.* (*chim.*) iodoformio.

iolite [ˈaiəlait], *s.* (*min.*) iolito.

ion [ˈaiən], *s.* (*fis.*) ione.

Ionian [aiˈounjən], *ag.s.* (*geog.*) Ionio.

Ionic [aiˈɔnik], *ag.* ionico: — *order,* (*arch.*) ordine ionico.

ionium [aiˈouniəm], *s.* (*chim.*) ionio.

ionization [ˌaiənaiˈzeiʃən], *s.* (*fis. chim.*) ionizzazione.

to **ionize** [ˈaiənaiz], *v.t.* (*fis.*) ionizzare.

ionosphere [aiˈɔnəsfiə*], *s.* ionosfera.

iota [aiˈoutə], *s.* **1.** iota (nona lettera dell'alfabeto greco) **2.** *fig.* un nonnulla; un nulla.

iotacism [aiˈoutəsizəm], *s.* (*linguistica*) iotacismo.

IOU [ˈaiouˈjuː], (*contr.* di *I owe you*) io vi devo (dichiarazione di debito).

ipecacuanha [ˌipikækjuˈænə], *s.* (*bot. farm.*) ipecacuana.

Iphigenia [iˌfidʒiˈnaiə], *no.pr.f.* (*mit.*) Ifigenia.

iracund [ˈairəkʌnd], *ag.* iracondo.

irade [iˈrɑːdei], *s.* « iradè » (ordine emanato dal sultano dei Turchi).

Irak [iˈrɑːk], *no. pr.* (*geog.*) Irak.

Iraki [iˈrɑːki], *ag.* iracheno ‖ *s.c.* iracheno, irachena ‖ *the Irakis,* gli iracheni.

Iran [iˈrɑːn], *no. pr.* (*geog.*) Iran.

Iranian [iˈreinjən], *ag.* iranico, persiano ‖ *s.c.* persiano, persiana ‖ *s.* lingue iraniche.

Iraq [iˈrɑːk], *no.pr.* (*geog.*) Irak.

Iraqi [iˈrɑːki], *V.* **Iraki.**

irascibility [iˌræsiˈbiliti], *s.* irascibilità, iracondia; irritabilità.

irascible [iˈræsibl], *ag.* irascibile, iracóndo; irritabile

irascibly [iˈræsibli], *av.* iracondamente.

irate [aiˈreit], *ag.* irato, arrabbiato.

ire [ˈaiə*], *s.* (*poet.*) ira, collera.

ireful [ˈaiəful], *ag.* (*poet.*) adirato, furioso, infuriato .

irefully [ˈaiəfuli], *av.* iratamente.

Ireland [ˈaiələnd], *no.pr.* (*geog.*) Irlanda.

Irenaeus [ˌairiˈniːəs], *no.pr.m.* (*st. relig.*) Ireneo.

Irene [aiˈriːni], *no.pr.f.* Irene.

irenic(al) [aiˈriːnik(əl)], *ag.* pacifico, conciliatore.

irenics [aiˈriːniks], *s.* irenica (dottrina che tratta della conciliazione fra le chiese cristiane).

Iridaceae [ˌairiˈdeisiiː], *s.pl.* (*bot.*) iridacee.

iridal [ˈairidl], *ag.* iridato.

iridescence [ˌiriˈdesns], *s.* iridescenza.

iridescent [ˌiriˈdesnt], *ag.* iridescente.

iridium [aiˈridiəm], *s.* (*chim.*) iridio.

to **iridize** [ˈairidaiz], *v.t.* iridare, rendere iridescente.

Iris [ˈaiəris], *no.pr.f.* Iride ‖ **iris,** *s.* **1.** (*anat.*) iride **2.** (*bot.*) iris, giaggiolo.

irisated [ˈairiseitid], *ag.* iridato.

Irish [ˈaiəriʃ], *ag.* irlandese, gaelico ‖ *the —,* gli irlandesi ‖ *s.* **1.** lingua irlandese, gaelico **2.** (*fam.*) scoppio d'ira.

Irishism [ˈaiəriʃizəm], *s.* carattere, tratto particolare degli irlandesi.

Irishman, *pl.* **Irishmen** [ˈaiəriʃmən], *s.* (uomo) irlandese.

Irishwoman [ˈaiəriʃˌwumən], *pl.* **Irishwomen** [ˈaiəriʃˌwimin], *s.* (donna) irlandese.

iritis [aiˈraitis], *s.* (*patol.*) irite.

to **irk** [əːk], *v.t.* ripugnare; infastidire; annoiare: *it irks me to do sthg.,* mi ripugna fare ql.co.

irksome [ˈəːksəm], *ag.* noioso; fastidioso, molesto; tedioso.

irksomely [ˈəːksəmli], *av.* fastidiosamente, tediosamente.

irksomeness [ˈəːksəmnis], *s.* noia, tedio.

iron [ˈaiən], *ag.* di ferro; in ferro; ferreo (anche *fig.*); ferruginoso; color ferro ‖ *s.* **1.** ferro ‖ — *age,* età del ferro ‖ *Iron Crown,* corona ferrea ‖ *the Iron Duke,* il Duca di ferro (detto del Duca di Wellington) ‖ *a man of —,* un uomo di ferro ‖ *to have too many irons in the fire,* avere troppa carne al fuoco ‖ *to strike while the — is hot,* battere il ferro mentre è caldo **2.** ferro da stiro; oggetto, strumento di ferro **3.** *pl.* catene, ceppi **4.** (*spor.*) mazza da golf **5.** (*farm.*) tonico a base di ferro **6.** (*sl.*) rivoltella, pistola ☆ ‖ — -*bound,* cinto di ferro: — -*bound coast,* costa rocciosa; — -*curtain,* cortina di ferro; — -*foundry,* ferriera, fonderia; — -*grey,* grigio ferro; — -*handed,* dal pugno di ferro; — -*hearted,* dal cuore di pietra; — *horse,* (*scherz.*) locomotiva, bicicletta; — *industry,* industria metallurgica; — *lung,* (*med.*) polmone d'acciaio; — -*ore,* minerale di ferro; — *rations,* (*mil.*) razioni di riserva; — *scrap,* rottami di ferro; — *sheet,* lamiera di ferro; — *wire,* filo di ferro ‖ *cast-* —, ghisa; *chilled* —, ghisa temprata; *crisping -* —, ferro per arricciare i capelli; *galvanized* —, ferro zincato; *pig* —, ghisa d'altoforno, di prima fusione; *sheet-* —, ferro in lamiera; *wrought-* —, ferro battuto.

to **iron,** *v.t.* **1.** stirare **2.** rivestire di ferro **3.** ferrare.

ironclad [ˈaiənklæd], *ag.* corazzato ‖ *s.* (*mar.*) corazzata.

ironer [ˈaiənə*], *s.c.* stiratore, stiratrice.

ironic(al) [aiˈrɔnik(əl)], *ag.* ironico.

ironically [aiˈrɔnikəli], *av.* ironicamente.

ironing [ˈaiəniŋ], *s.* stiratura.

ironist [ˈaiənist], *s.* (*neol.*) ironista.

ironmaster [ˈaiənˌmɑːstə*], *s.* padrone di ferriera.

ironmonger [ˈaiənˌmʌŋgə*], *s.* negoziante in ferramenta.

ironmongery [ˈaiənˌmʌŋgəri], *s.* ferramenta; negozio di ferramenta.

ironmould ['aiənmould], *s.* macchia di ruggine.

ironside ['aiən-said], *s.* **1.** (*arc.*) uomo coraggio-so **2.** corazzata **3.** *pl.* (*st.*) la cavalleria di Cromwell.

ironsmith ['aiənsmiθ], *s.* fabbro ferraio.

ironstone ['aiən-stoun], *s.* minerale di ferro.

ironware ['aiənwɛə*], *s.* ferramenta.

ironwork ['aiənwə:k], *s.* **1.** armatura di ferro; lavoro in ferro **2.** *pl.* ferriera.

irony[1] ['aiəni], *ag.* di ferro, ferreo.

irony[2] ['aiərəni], *s.* ironia: *the — of fate*, l'ironia della sorte.

Iroquois ['irəkwoiz], *s.c.* irochese.

irradiance [i'reidjəns], *s.* irradiamento, irradiazione.

irradiant [i'reidjənt], *ag.* irradiante.

to **irradiate** [i'reidieit], *v.t.i.* **1.** irradiare; rischiarare, illuminare **2.** (*med.*) irradiare **3.** *fig.* risplendere.

irradiation [i,reidi'eiʃən], *s.* **1.** irraggiamento; illuminazione (spirituale, intellettuale); splendore **2.** (*med.*) irradiazione.

irradiative [i'reidieitiv], *ag.* irradiante.

irradiator [i'reidieitə*], *s.* irradiatore.

to **irradicate** [i'rædikeit], *v.t.* (*rar.*) radicare.

irrational [i'ræʃənl], *ag.* irrazionale; irragionevole; illogico, assurdo ‖ *s.* (*mat.*) numero irrazionale.

irrationality [i,ræʃə'næliti], *s* irrazionalità; irragionevolezza; assurdità.

irrationally [i'ræʃnəli], *av.* irrazionalmente; assurdamente.

irrealizable [i'riəlaizəbl], *ag.* irrealizzabile.

irrebuttable [,iri'bʌtəbl], *ag.* (*dir.*) irrefragabile, irrefutabile (di testimonianza, ecc.).

irreciprocal [,iri'siprəkəl], *ag.* non reciproco.

irreclaimable [,iri'kleiməbl], *ag.* **1.** irreparabile, irrimediabile; incorreggibile; irrecuperabile; irrevocabile **2.** non bonificabile.

irrecognizable [i'rekəgnaizəbl], *ag.* irriconoscibile.

irreconcilable [i'rekənsailəbl], *ag.* irreconciliabile.

irreconcilableness [i'rekənsailəblnis], *s.* inconciliabilità; incompatibilità.

irrecoverable [,iri'kʌvərəbl], *ag.* irrecuperabile; irreparabile.

irrecoverably [,iri'kʌvərəbli], *av.* irreparabilmente; senza rimedio.

irrecusable [,iri'kju:səbl], *ag.* irrecusabile.

irredeemability ['iri,di:mə'biliti], *s.* irredimibilità.

irredeemable ['iri,di:məbl], *ag.* irredimibile.

irredeemableness [,iri'di:məblnis], *s.* irredimibilità.

irredeemably [,iri'di:məbli], *av.* in modo irredimibile.

irredentism [,iri'dentizəm], *s.* irredentismo.

irredentist [,iri'dentist], *s.c.* irredentista.

irreducibility ['iri,dju:si'biliti], *s.* irriducibilità.

irreducible [,iri'dju:səbl], *ag.* irriducibile.

irreducibleness [,iri'dju:səblnis], *s.* irriducibilità.

irreflection [,iri'flekʃən], *s.* irriflessione.

irreflective [,iri'flektiv], *ag.* irriflessivo.

irrefragability [i,refrəgə'biliti], *s.* irrefragabilità.

irrefragable [i'refrəgəbl], *ag.* irrefragabile, innegabile.

irrefragably [i'refrəgəbli], *av.* irrefragabilmente.

irrefrangible [,iri'frændʒibl], *ag.* irrefrangibile.

irrefutable [i'refjutəbl], *ag.* irrefutabile.

irrefutably [i'refjutəbli], *av.* irrefutabilmente.

irregular [i'regjulə*], *ag.* **1.** irregolare; anormale **2.** sregolato (di costumi, ecc.): — *life*, vita sregolata **3.** (*gram.*) irregolare: — *verb*, verbo irregolare **4.** asimmetrico; non uniforme: — *shape*, forma irregolare, asimmetrica ‖ *s.* **1.** (*eccl.*) irregolare **2.** *pl.* (*mil.*) truppe irregolari.

irregularity [i,regju'læriti], *s.* irregolarità.

irregularly [i'regjuləli], *av.* irregolarmente.

irrelative [i'relətiv], *ag.* senza relazione, connessione.

irrelatively [i'relətivli], *av.* senza relazione, connessione.

irrelevance [i'relivəns], **irrelevancy** [i'relivənsi], *s.* non pertinenza; ciò che non è pertinente.

irrelevant [i'relivənt], *ag.* non appropriato, non pertinente, estraneo: *to make — remarks*, divagare.

irrelevantly [i'relivəntli], *av.* non appropriatamente, senza pertinenza.

irreligion [,iri'lidʒən], *s.* irreligione.

irreligious [,iri'lidʒəs], *ag.* irreligioso.

irreligiously [,iri'lidʒəsli], *av.* irreligiosamente.

irreligiousness [,iri'lidʒəsnis], *s.* irreligiosità.

irremediable [,iri'mi:djəbl], *ag.* irrimediabile, irreparabile.

irremediableness [,iri'mi:djəblnis], *s.* irrimediabilità.

irremediably [,iri'mi:djəbii], *av.* irrimediabilmente, irreparabilmente.

irremissible [,iri'misibl], *ag.* irremissibile; imperdonabile.

irremissibleness [,iri'misiblnis], *s.* irremissibilità; imperdonabilità.

irremissibly [,iri'misibli], *av.* irremissibilmente.

irremovability ['iri,mu:və'biliti], *s.* irremovibilità; inamovibilità.

irremovable [,iri'mu:vəbl], *ag.* irremovibile; inamovibile.

irremovably [,iri'mu:vəbli], *av.* irremovibilmente.

irreparability [i,repərə'biliti], *s.* irreparabilità; irrimediabilità.

irreparable [i'repərəbl], *ag.* irreparabile; irrimediabile.

irreparableness [i'repərəblnis], *s.* irreparabilità.

irreparably [i'repərəbli], *av.* irreparabilmente; irrimediabilmente.

irrepealable [,iri'pi:ləbl], *ag.* inabrogabile.

irreplaceable [,iri'pleisəbl], *ag.* insostituibile.

irreprehensible [i,repri'hensibl], *ag.* irreprensibile.

irreprehensibleness [i,repri'hensiblnis], *s.* irreprensibilità.

irreprehensibly [i,repri'hensibli], *av.* irreprensibilmente.

irrepressible [,iri'presəbl], *ag.* irreprimibile, irrefrenabile.

irrepressibleness [,iri'presəblnis], *s.* il non poter reprimere, frenare.

irrepressibly [,iri'presəbli], *av.* irreprimibilmente.

irreproachable [,iri'proutʃəbl], *ag.* irreprensibile, incensurabile; corretto: — *dress*, vestito impeccabile; *he was always — in his conduct*, il suo contegno è sempre stato irreprensibile.

irreproachableness [,iri'proutʃəblnis], *s.* irreprensibilità; correttezza.

irreproachably [,iri'proutʃəbli], *av.* irreprensibilmente, incensurabilmente; correttamente.

irreprovable [,iri'pru:vəbl], *ag.* irreprensibile.

irresistance [,iri'zistəns], *s.* mancanza di resistenza.

irresistibility ['iri,zistə'biliti], *s.* irresistibilità.

irresistible [,iri'zistəbl], *ag.* irresistibile.

irresistibleness [,iri'zistəblnis], *s.* irresistibilità.

irresistibly [,iri'zistəbli], *av.* irresistibilmente.

irresoluble [,iri'zɔljubl], *ag.* irresolubile.

irresolute [i'rezəlu:t], *ag.* irresoluto, indeciso, incerto, dubbioso: *to be —*, esitare, non sapere cosa fare.

irresolutely [i'rezəlu:tli], *av.* in modo irresoluto.

irresoluteness [i'rezəlu:tnis], **irresolution** ['irezə-'lu:ʃən], *s.* irresolutezza, indecisione: *the — of the human heart*, l'irresolutezza del cuore umano.

irresolvable [,iri'zɔlvəbl], *ag.* insolubile.

irrespective [,iri'spektiv], *ag.* senza riguardo a; noncurante: *he rushed forward to help — of consequences*, egli corse in aiuto noncurante delle conseguenze; *they go to the cinema — of what film is being shown*, vanno al cinema senza preoccuparsi del film in programma.

irrespectively [,iris'pektivli], *av.* con noncuranza.

irrespirable [i'respirəbl], *ag.* irrespirabile.

irresponsibility ['iris,pɔnsə'biliti], *s.* irresponsabilità, mancanza di senso di responsabilità.

irresponsible [,iris'pɔnsəbl], *ag.* **1.** irresponsabile **2.** (*comm.*) insolvibile.

irresponsibly [ˌiris'pɔnsəbli], *av.* in modo irresponsabile.

irresponsive [ˌiris'pɔnsiv], *ag.* che non risponde, che non reagisce; insensibile.

irretention [ˌiri'tenʃən], *s.* (*patol.*) irritenzione (urinaria).

irretentive [ˌiri'tentiv], *ag.* incapace a trattenere; che non ritiene: — *memory*, memoria labile.

irretrievability ['iriˌtri:və'biliti], *s.* irrecuperabilità; irreparabilità.

irretrievable [ˌiri'tri:vəbl], *ag.* irricuperabile; irrimediabile.

irretrievably [ˌiri'tri:vəbli], *av.* irrimediabilmente.

irreverence [i'revərəns], *s.* irriverenza; insolenza; empietà.

irreverent [i'revərənt], *ag.* irriverente, insolente; empio.

irreverently [i'revərəntli], *av.* irriverentemente.

irreversibility ['iriˌvə:sə'biliti], *s.* irreversibilità; immutabilità.

irreversible [ˌiri'və:səbl], *ag.* immutabile; irreversibile.

irreversibly [ˌiri'və:səbli], *av.* immutabilmente.

irrevocability [iˌrevəkə'biliti], *s.* irrevocabilità.

irrevocable [i'revəkəbl], *ag.* irrevocabile.

irrevocableness [i'revəkəblnis], *s.* irrevocabilità.

irrevocably [i'revəkəbli], *av.* irrevocabilmente.

to **irrigate** ['irigeit], *v.t.* irrigare; bagnare; irrorare.

irrigation [ˌiri'geiʃən], *s.* irrigazione (anche *med.*).

irrigator ['irigeitə*], *s.* irrigatore (anche *med.*).

irriguous [i'rigjuəs], *ag.* irriguo.

irritability [ˌiritə'biliti], *s.* 1. irritabilità; permalosità 2. (*med.*) riflesso.

irritable ['iritəbl], *ag.* irritabile; eccitabile; permaloso.

irritably ['iritəbli], *av.* irritabilmente.

irritancy[1] ['iritənsi], *s.* irritazione, fastidio.

irritancy[2], *s.* (*dir.*) annullamento.

irritant ['iritənt], *ag.s.* irritante.

to **irritate**[1] ['iriteit], *v.t.* irritare; eccitare i riflessi di.

to **irritate**[2], *v.t.* (*dir. scoz.*) annullare.

irritating ['iriteitiŋ], *ag.* irritante.

irritatingly ['iriteitiŋli], *av.* in modo irritante.

irritation [ˌiri'teiʃən], *s.* irritazione.

irritative ['iriteitiv], *ag.* (*med.*) irritante.

irruption [i'rʌpʃən], *s.* irruzione; invasione.

irruptive [i'rʌptiv], *ag.* irrompente.

is [iz (*forma forte*), z, s (*forme deboli*)], *3ª pers. sing. indic. pres.* di to **be.**

Isaac ['aizək], *no.pr.m.* Isacco.

Isabel[1] ['izəbel], **Isabella**[1] [ˌizə'belə], *no.pr.f.* Isabella.

isabel[2], **isabella**[2], *ag.s.* (color) isabella.

isagogic [ˌaisə'gɔdʒik], *ag.* isagogico.

isagogics [ˌaisə'gɔdʒiks], *s.* isagoge.

Isaiah [ai'zaiə], *no.pr.m.* (*Bibbia*) Isaia.

isatin ['aisətin], *s.* (*chim.*) isatina.

Iscariot [is'kæriət], *no.pr.m.* Iscariota (soprannome di Giuda) ‖ *s.* traditore.

ischiadic [ˌiski'ædik], *ag.* (*anat.*) ischiatico.

ischialgia [ˌiski'ældʒiə], *s.* (*patol.*) ischialgia.

ischium ['iskiəm], *pl.* **ischia** ['iskiə] *s.* (*anat.*) ischio.

Iseult [i:'zu:lt], *no.pr.f.* Isotta.

Ishmael ['iʃmeiəl], *no.pr.m.* (*Bibbia*) Ismaele.

Ishmaelite ['iʃmiəlait], *s.c.* (*relig.*) ismaelita.

Isidore ['izidɔ:*], *no.pr.m.* Isidoro.

isinglass ['aiziŋglɑ:s], *s.* 1. colla di pesce 2. (*min. fam.*) mica.

Isis ['aisis], *no.pr.f.* (*mit.*) Iside.

Islam ['izlɑ:m], *s.* (*relig.*) Islamismo.

Islamic [iz'læmik], *ag.* islamico, maomettano.

Islamism ['iskiəm], *s.* (*relig.*) islamismo.

Islamite ['izləmait], *s.c.* (*relig.*) islamita.

island ['ailənd], *s.* 1. isola 2. (*mar.*) isola, sovrastruttura laterale (di una nave portaerei) 3. salvagente (nella strada) 4. isolato (di case) 5. (*fisiol.*) isola.

islander ['ailəndə*], *s.c.* isolano, isolana.

isle [ail], *s.* 1. (*poet.*) isola 2. *Isle*, isola (in nomi geografici di isole piccole): *Isle of Wight*, isola di Wight 3. isolato (di case).

islesman, **pl.* **islesmen ['ailzmən], *s.* isolano.

islet ['ailit], *s.* isolotto.

ism ['izəm], *s.* (*fam. peggiorativo*) dottrina, teoria: *I profess no* —, non parteggio per alcuna dottrina.

isn't ['iznt], *contr.* di *is not.*

isobar ['aisoubɑ:*], *s.* 1. (*meteorologia*) linea isobara 2. (*chim.*) isobaro.

isobaric [ˌaisou'bærik], *ag.* (*meteorologia, chim.*) isobaro.

isochromatic [ˌaisoukrou'mætik], *ag.* isocromatico.

isochronism [ai'sɔkrənizəm], *s.* isocronismo.

isochronous [ai'sɔkrənəs], *ag.* isocrono.

isoclinal [ˌaisou'klainl], *ag.* isoclino.

Isocrates [ai'sɔkrəti:z], *no.pr.m.* (*st.*) Isocrate.

isogamy [ai'sɔgəmi], *s.* (*bot.*) isogamia.

isogonal [ai'sɔgənl], *ag.* isogono ‖ *s.* linea isogona.

isolable ['aisələbl], *ag.* isolabile.

to **isolate** ['aisəleit], *v.t.* isolare; separare.

isolation [ˌaisə'leiʃən], *s.* isolamento.

isolationism [ˌaisə'leiʃnizəm], *s.* (*pol.*) isolazionismo.

isolationist [ˌaisə'leiʃnist], *s.* (*pol.*) isolazionista.

isolator ['aisəleitə*], *s.* (*elett.*) isolatore.

Isolda, Isolde [i'zɔldə], *no.pr.f.* Isotta.

isomer ['aisoumə*], *s.* (*chim.*) isomero.

isomeric [ˌaisou'merik], *ag.* (*chim.*) isomerico.

isomerism [ai'sɔmərizəm], *s.* (*chim.*) isomeria.

isomerization [aiˌsɔməri'zeiʃən], *s.* (*chim.*) isomerizzazione.

isometric(al) [ˌaisou'metrik(əl)], *ag.* (*geom.*) isometrico ‖ *s.* curva isometrica.

isomorphism [ˌaisou'mɔ:fizəm], *s.* isomorfismo.

isomorphous [ˌaisou'mɔ:fəs], *ag.* isomorfo.

isonomy [ai'sɔnəmi], *s.* isonomia.

isopathy [ai'sɔpəθi], *s.* (*med.*) isopatia.

isoperimetry [ˌaisoupə'rimitri], *s.* (*geom.*) isoperimetria.

isosceles [ai'sɔsili:z], *ag.* (*geom.*) isoscele.

isotherm ['aisouθə:m], *s.* (*meteorologia*) isoterma.

isothermal [ˌaisou'θə:məl], *ag.* isotermico ‖ *s.* (*meteorologia*) isoterma.

isotope ['aisoutoup], *s.* (*chim.*) isotopo.

isotopic [ˌaisou'tɔpik], *ag.* (*chim.*) isotopico.

isotopy [ai'sɔtəpi], *s.* (*chim.*) isotopia.

isotron ['aisoutrɔn], *s.* (*fis. atomica*) isotrone.

Israel ['izreiəl], *no.pr.* 1. Israele, il popolo ebraico 2. (*st.*) il regno di Israele 3. (*geog.*) lo Stato di Israele.

Israeli [iz'reili], *ag.* israeliano ‖ *s.c.* israeliano, israeliana.

Israelite ['izriəlait], *s.c.* israelita.

Israelitish ['izriəlaitiʃ], *ag.* israelitico.

issei ['i:'sei], *s.* americano di origine giapponese.

issuable ['isju(:)əbl], *ag.* 1. emissibile 2. suscettibile di contesa legale.

issue ['isju:], *s.* 1. uscita; sbocco; foce (di fiume): *the issues from the underground*, le uscite della metropolitana 2. conclusione, risultato, esito: *I suppose that will be the* — *of the matter*, credo che andrà a finire così; *to bring matters to an* —, portare una faccenda a conclusione 3. (*spec. dir.*) stirpe, discendenza, prole: *to die without* —, morire senza prole 4. (*dir.*) punto in discussione, questione, problema: *agreement on four issues*, accordo su quattro punti; *to dodge the real* —, eludere il vero problema; *to state an* —, porre una questione ‖ *at* —, in discussione ‖ *to join* —, (*dir.*) venire a discussione: *to join* — *with s.o. about sthg.*, discutere con qlcu. in merito a ql.co. 5. emissione (di moneta, francobolli, ecc.) 6. promulgazione (di decreti) 7. pubblicazione (di libri, giornali, ecc.): *as stated in to-day's* —, come è detto nell'edizione di oggi 8. (*med.*) sbocco 9. rendita (di terre, capitale, ecc.) ☆ — *bank*, istituto di emissione; — *price*, prezzo di emissione.

to **issue**, *v.t.i.* 1. uscire: *blood issued from the wound*, il sangue sgorgò dalla ferita **2.** emettere: *to — paper money*, emettere carta moneta **3.** pubblicare: *book to be issued*, libro che sarà pubblicato; *to — a bulletin*, pubblicare un bollettino **4.** rilasciare: *to — a passport*, rilasciare un passaporto **5.** spedire, inoltrare **6.** (*mil.*) fornire: *to — the soldiers with articles of equipment*, fornire l'equipaggiamento ai soldati **7.** *to — from* (*s.o., sthg.*), discendere, aver origine **8.** *to — in* (*sthg.*), risultare, finire.

issueless ['isju:lis], *ag.* senza prole, senza discendenza: *the king died —*, il re morì senza lasciare discendenti diretti.

issuer ['isju(:)ə*], *s.* **1.** chi emette **2.** chi pubblica.

isthmian ['isθmiən], *ag.* istmico.

isthmus ['isməs], *s.* istmo.

istle ['istli], *s.* fibra sintetica ottenuta dall'agave.

it[1] [it], *pron. 3ª persona n. sing.* **1.** *nom.* esso, essa: *the flat is small, but — is nice*, l'appartamento è piccolo, ma è grazioso; *I saw her baby, — is very strong*, ho visto il suo bambino, è molto robusto **2.** (*caso obliquo*) **lo, la, ciò, gli, le, ne, ci, sè:** *bring the child and give — a drink*, porta qui il bambino e dagli da bere; *I don't believe —*, non ci credo; *I don't remember —*, non me ne ricordo; *she is not stupid, far from —*, è ben lontana dall'essere stupida, è tutt'altro che stupida; *to fall into —*, caderci dentro **3.** (*soggetto di v. impers.*): *— doesn't matter*, non importa; *— is four o' clock*, sono le quattro; *— is raining*, piove; *— was the 22nd of March*, era il 22 marzo; *that's —!*, è proprio così!; "*Who is —?*", "*It is I (o me)*", «Chi è?», «Sono io» **4.** (*ogg. indef. di v. o prep.*): *confound —!*, all'inferno!; *now for —!*, e adesso coraggio!; *I feel the better for —*, me ne sento sollevato; *to ask for —*, cercar guai; *to face —*, fronteggiare la situazione; *to lord — over s.o.*, trattare qlcu. dall'alto in basso; *to rough —*, aver la vita difficile **5.** (*usato per anticipare una frase*): *his attitude made — difficult to reach an agreement*, il suo atteggiamento rese difficile il raggiungere un'intesa; *I hardly thought — likely that...*, ritenevo poco probabile che... **6.** (*fam.*) il non plus ultra **7.** (*fam.*) «sex appeal», fascino **8.** (*in giuochi di bambini*) «chi sta sotto».

it,[2] *s.* (*fam. abbr. di Italian vermouth*) vermouth: *gin and —*, gin e vermouth.

itacism ['i:təsizəm], *s.* (*fonet.*) itacismo.

Italian [i'tæljən], *ag.* italiano ‖ *s.c.* italiano, italiana ‖ *s.* lingua italiana.

Italianate [i'tæljənit], *ag.* italianizzato.

to Italianate [i'tæljəneit], *v.t.* italianizzare.

Italianism [i'tæljənizəm], *s.* **1.** italianità **2.** italianismo.

to Italianize [i'tæljənaiz], *v.t.i.* **1.** italianizzare **2.** far l'italiano, aver tendenze italianizzanti.

Italic [i'tælik], *ag.* italico ☆ *italic type*, (*tip.*) carattere corsivo.

to italicize [i'tælisaiz], *v.t.* (*tip.*) stampare in corsivo; sottolineare (in manoscritto).

italics [i'tæliks], *s.pl.* (*tip.*) corsivo.

Italiot [i'tæliot], **Italiote** [i'tæliout], *s.c.* (*st.*) italiota.

Italy ['itəli], *no.pr.* (*geog.*) Italia.

itch [itʃ], *s.* **1.** (*patol.*) rogna; scabbia **2.** prurito **3.** *fig.* voglia, desiderio irresistibile ☆ *— -mite*, (*entom.*) acaro della scabbia ‖ *baker's —*, (*patol.*) psoriasi; *barber's —*, (*patol.*) sicosi.

to itch, *v.i.* **1.** prudere, pizzicare; sentir prurito: *scratch yourself if you —*, grattati se senti prurito **2.** aver voglia: *he itched to tell them the news*, moriva dalla voglia di dir loro le notizie: *she is itching to be off*, (*fam.*) le scottano i piedi (desidera uscire).

itchiness ['itʃinis], *s.* prurito.

itching ['itʃiŋ], *s.* **1.** prurito **2.** (*fam.*) voglia, smania.

itchy ['itʃi], *ag.* **1.** rognoso **2.** che prude; affetto da prurito.

item ['aitem], *s.* **1.** (*comm.*) voce; registrazione; scritturazione; dettaglio; articolo: *— of a balance sheet*, voce del bilancio; *— of a contract*, articolo di un contratto ‖ *items on the agenda (of a meeting)*, questioni all'ordine del giorno (di un'assemblea) **2.** (*teat.*) numero: *the last — on the programme*: l'ultimo numero del programma ☆ *news items*, (*giornalismo*) notizie.

item, *av.* anche; parimenti.

to itemize ['aitemaiz], *v.t.* dettagliare: *to — a bill*, dettagliare un conto.

iterance ['itərəns], *s.* ripetizione; reiterazione.

to iterate ['itəreit], *v.t.* reiterare; ripetere.

iteration [,itə'reiʃən], *s.* ripetizione; iterazione.

iterative ['itərətiv], *ag.* iterativo.

Ithaca ['iθəkə], *no.pr.* (*geog. st.*) Itaca.

ithyphallic [,iθi'fælik], *ag.s.* (*poes.*) itifallico.

itinerancy [i'tinərənsi], *s.* l'andare di luogo in luogo (specialmente per predicare, tener conferenze).

itinerant [i'tinərənt], *ag.* ambulante; errante; viaggiante: *an — preacher*, un predicatore errante.

itinerary [ai'tinərəri], *ag.* inerente ai viaggi ‖ *s.* itinerario.

to itinerate [i'tinəreit], *v.i.* viaggiare, andare di luogo in luogo (specialmente per tenere conferenze, prediche, ecc.).

its [its], *ag.poss.* (*riferito a cose, animali*) **suo, sua, suoi, sue, ne:** *I'll take the baby with me, get — clothes ready, please*, porterò il bambino con me, prepara i suoi indumenti, per piacere; *that dog is ill, look at — nose*, quel cane è malato, guarda il suo naso; *that table was too high so I had — legs cut*, quel tavolo era troppo alto, così ne feci accorciare le gambe.

it's [its], *contr. di it is, it has*.

itself [it'self], *pron. 3ª persona n. sing.* **1.** *r.* si, sè, se stesso, se stessa: *the fox hid — in its den*, la volpe si nascose nella sua tana ‖ (*all*) *by —*, da solo: *a mother shouldn't leave her baby by — for long*, una madre non dovrebbe lasciare il suo bambino solo a lungo **2.** (*enfatico*) stesso, stessa: *he was generosity —*, era la generosità stessa ‖ *s.* esso stesso, essa stessa: *the dog is not — to-day*, il cane non sta bene oggi.

Ivanhoe ['aivənhou], *no.pr.m.* (*lett.*) Ivanoe.

I've [aiv], *contr. di I have*.

ivied ['aivid], *ag.* coperto di edera.

ivory ['aivəri], *s.* avorio ‖ *Ivory Coast*, (*geog.*) Costa d'Avorio.

ivy ['aivi], *s.* edera.

ixia ['iksiə], *s.* (*bot.*) issia, vischio.

Ixion [ik'saiən], *no.pr.m.* (*mit.*) Issione.

izard ['izəd], *s.* camoscio dei Pirenei.

izzard ['izəd], *s.* (*arc.*) lettera zeta.

izzat ['izət], *s.* (*ang.-in.*) onore; reputazione; decoro.

J

j [dʒei], *pl.* **j**, **j's** [dʒeiz], (*decima lettera dell'alfabeto inglese*) j ‖ — *for Jack*, (*tel.*) j come jersey.

jab [dʒæb], *s.* **1.** stilettata; stoccata; baionettata **2.** pugno improvviso.

to **jab**, *pass.p.p.* **jabbed** [dʒæbd], *v.t.* **1.** conficcare: *to — a thing into a place*, conficcare una cosa in un posto **2.** dare una stoccata, un colpo secco **3.** pugnalare.

jabber [ˈdʒæbə*], *s.* **1.** borbottamento, brontolamento **2.** ciarla; chiacchiera.

to **jabber**, *v.t.i.* **1.** farfugliare, borbottare, brontolare **2.** ciarlare, chiacchierare.

jabberer [ˈdʒæbərə*], *s.c.* **1.** chi barbuglia **2.** ciarlone, ciarlona.

jabbering [ˈdʒæbəriŋ], *s.* **1.** barbugliamento **2.** ciancia, chiacchiera.

jabble [ˈdʒæbl], *s.* (*scoz.*) tremolio (nell'acqua).

to **jabble**, *v.t.i.* (*scoz.*) schizzare.

jabiru [ˈdʒæbiru:], *s.* (*ornit.*) mitteria americana.

jaborandi [ˌdʒæbəˈrændi], *s.* (*bot.*) foglie secche dello iaborandi.

jabot [ˈʒæbou], *s.* (*abbigliamento*) « jabot ».

jacamar [ˈdʒækəmə*], *s.* (*ornit.*) giacamaro; galbula verde.

jacinth [ˈdʒæsinθ], *s.* (*min.*) giacinto.

Jack[1] [dʒæk], *no.pr.m.* (*fam.*) dim. di **John** ‖ — *Frost*, Mastro Gelo (nelle fiabe) ‖ — *-in-the-box*, scatola con fantoccio a molla ‖ — *-in office*, piccolo funzionario presuntuoso ‖ — *ketch*, boia ‖ — *-o'-lantern*, fuoco fatuo ‖ — *-of-all-trades*, factotum ‖ — *-of-all -trades-and-master-of-none*, chi sa fare tutto, ma nulla a fondo, superficialone ‖ — *-Tar*, marinaio ‖ *before you can say* — *Robinson*, improvvisamente, in un batter d'occhio.

jack[2], *s.* **1.** uomo di fatica, manovale; (*fam.*) marinaio **2.** (*carte da giuoco*) fante **3.** girarrosto **4.** (*mec.*) cricco, martinetto; (*elett. tel.*) presa **5.** maschio di alcuni animali: — *hare*, lepre maschio ☆ — *frame*, macchina per grossa filatura; — *knife*, coltello a serramanico; — *towel*, bandinella ‖ *boot*- —, cavastivali; *screw* —, binda a vite.

to **jack**[2], *v.t.* **1.** sollevare con un martinetto **2.** *to — up*, abbandonare (un'impresa, ecc.).

jack[3], *s.* bandiera di nave: *to have a — up*, battere bandiera ‖ *Union Jack*, bandiera britannica ☆ — *staff*, pennone. (per bandiera sulla nave).

jack[4], *s.* (*st.*) **1.** cotta d'arme; giaco **2.** (*black*) —, borraccia.

jack[5], *s.* (*bot.*) artocarpo (albero e frutto).

jackal [ˈdʒækɔ:l], *s.* sciacallo (anche *fig.*).

to **jackal**, *v.i.* compiere lavori disonesti (per conto di qlcu.).

jackanapes [ˈdʒækəneips], *s.* **1.** (*arc.*) scimmia **2.** sfacciatello; vanesio.

jackaroo [ˈdʒækəru:], *s.* (*sl. austral.*) colono appena arrivato.

jackass [ˈdʒækæs], *s.* **1.** somaro **2.** (*iron.*) stupido ☆ *laughing* —, (*ornit.*) dacelide.

jackdaw [ˈdʒækdɔ:], *s.* cornacchia.

jackeroo, *V.* **jackaroo**.

jacket [ˈdʒækit], *s.* **1.** giacchetta; casacca; giubba ‖ *to dust a person's* —, percuotere qlcu. **2.** rivestimento protettivo; isolante; copertina di libro **3.** buccia: *potatoes boiled in their jackets*, patate cotte con la buccia ☆ *blue* —, marinaio; *dinner* —, smoking.

to **jacket**, *v.t.* rivestire con materiale isolante, involucro protettivo.

jacketed [ˈdʒækitid], *ag.* rivestito con materiale isolante, con involucro protettivo.

jackplane [ˈdʒækplein], *s.* pialla per sgrossare.

jackpot [ˈdʒækpɔt], *s.* (*poker*) posta ‖ *to hit the* —, aver successo, riuscire.

jackpudding [dʒækˈpudiŋ], *s.* buffone.

Jacky [ˈdʒæki], *no.pr.m.* dim. di **Jack**.

Jacob [ˈdʒeikəb], *no.pr.m.* Giacobbe ‖ *Jacob's ladder*, (*Bibbia*) scala di Giacobbe; (*bot.*) polemonia; (*mar.*) biscaglina.

Jacobean [ˌdʒækəˈbi(:)ən], *ag.* del regno, del tempo di Giacomo I d'Inghilterra (1603-25) ‖ *s.* scrittore, uomo politico del tempo di Giacomo I.

Jacobin[1] [ˈdʒækəbin], *s.* (*st.*) giacobino.

jacobin[2], *s.* (*ornit.*) colombo dal cappuccio.

jacobinic(al) [ˌdʒækəˈbinik(əl)], *ag.* giacobino.

Jacobinism [ˈdʒækəbinizəm], *s.* (*st.*) giacobinismo.

to **jacobinize** [ˈdʒækəbinaiz], *v.t.* rendere giacobino.

Jacobite [ˈdʒækəbait], *s.* (*st.*) giacobita; seguace di Giacomo II d'Inghilterra (1685-1688).

jacobitie(al) [ˌdʒækəˈbitik(əl)], *ag.* di giacobita.

Jacobitism [ˈdʒækəbaitizəm], *s.* **1.** principi politici dei seguaci di Giacomo II Stuart **2.** principi della setta eutichiana.

jacobus [dʒəˈkoubəs], *s.* moneta d'oro del valore di 20-24 scellini, coniata durante il regno di Giacomo I.

jaconet [ˈdʒækənit], *s.* giaconetta.

jacquard [dʒəˈkɑːd], *s.* (*ind. tessile*) jacquard.

Jacqueline [ˈdʒækliːn], *no.pr.f.* Giacomina.

jactation [dʒækˈteiʃən], *s.* ostentazione.

jactitation [ˌdʒæktiˈteiʃən], *s.* **1.** (*patol.*) barcollamento; agitazione motoria **2.** (*dir.*) falsa dichiarazione (a detrimento di altri) **3.** ostentazione.

to **jaculate** [ˈdʒækjuleit], *v.t.* lanciare, gettare.

jaculation [ˌdʒækjuˈleiʃən], *s.* lancio.

jaculator [ˈdʒækjuleitə*], *s.* lanciatore.

jade[1] [dʒeid], *s.* **1.** giada **2.** color verde giada.

jade[2], *s.* **1.** cavallo; ronzino **2.** donnaccia, megera ‖ *a saucy* —, una ragazzetta impertinente.

to **jade**[2], *v.t.i.* **1.** ridurre male un cavallo **2.** sfinire; logorare; logorarsi; stancarsi.

jaded [ˈdʒeidid], *ag.* stanco, sfinito; logoro.

jadeite [ˈdʒeidait], *s.* (*min.*) giadeite.

jadish [ˈdʒeidiʃ], *ag.* **1.** sfinito, stanco **2.** scostumato (di donna).

jaeger [ˈjeigə*], *s.* **1.** cacciatore tedesco, svizzero **2.** (*mil.*) fuciliere tedesco, austriaco **3.** gabbiano **4.** stoffa di pura lana.

Jael [ˈdʒeiəl], *no.pr.f.* (*Bibbia*) Giaele.

Jaffa [ˈdʒæfə], *no.pr.* (*geog.*) Giaffa ☆ — *orange*, arancia palestinese.

jag[1] [dʒæg], *s.* **1.** punta di roccia **2.** dente (di sega, ecc.) **3.** frastaglio.

to **jag**[1], *pass.p.p.* **jagged** [dʒægd], *v.t.* frastagliare; dentellare; intaccare.

jag[2], *s.* (*sl.*) sbornia.

jagged [ˈdʒægid], *ag.* **1.** frastagliato; dentellato; intaccato; tagliuzzato; ineguale: — *outline of a coast*, profilo frastagliato di una costa **2.** (*bot.*) lanceolato.

jaggedly [ˈdʒægidli], *av.* a dentellature, a sporgenze.

jaggedness [ˈdʒægidnis], *s.* **1.** frastagliamento; dentellatura **2.** ineguaglianza; scabrosità, rugosità.

jagger[1] ['dʒægə*], s. rotellina dentata.

jagger[2], s. 1. venditore ambulante 2. (miner.) vagonista.

jaggery ['dʒægəri], s. zucchero scuro estratto dalla linfa del cocco.

jaggy ['dʒægi], V. **jagged**.

Jago ['dʒeigou], no.pr.m. (lett.) Jago.

jaguar ['dʒægjuə*], s. (zool.) giaguaro.

Jahave(h) ['jɑ:vei], no.pr.m. (Bibbia) Javè.

(to) **jail**, V. (to) **gaol**.

jailer, V. **gaoler**.

Jain [dʒein], s. (relig.) seguace del giainismo.

Jainism ['dʒeinizəm], s. (st. relig.) giainismo.

jake [dʒeik], ag. (sl. amer.) bello, ottimo, di prima qualità ‖ s. (sl. amer.) denaro (specialmente in contanti) ‖ that will be a —, benissimo.

jalap ['dʒæləp], s. (bot.) gialappa.

jalousie ['ʒælu(:)zi:], s. imposta (per finestra).

jam[1] [dʒæm], s. 1. stretta; compressione 2. (mec.) arresto, inceppamento 3. intralcio, ingorgo nel traffico 4. (sl.) pasticcio, difficoltà ☆ traffic- —, ingorgo (di circolazione).

to **jam**[1], pass.p.p. **jammed** [dʒæmd], v.t.i. 1. comprimere, premere, schiacciare, serrare, pigiare: I jammed all my clothes into a suitcase and hurried away, stipai tutti i miei abiti in una valigia e me ne andai in fretta 2. bloccare, bloccarsi: owing to a breakdown on the road all the traffic was jammed for an hour, in seguito a un guasto lungo la strada il traffico rimase bloccato per un'ora 3. (mar.) puntellare 4. (rad.) disturbare, causare interferenze nelle trasmissioni 5. (sl. amer.) improvvisare (in jazz).

jam[2], s. conserva di frutta, marmellata ☆ — -jar (o — -pot), barattolo per marmellata.

Jamaica [dʒə'meikə], no.pr. (geog.) Giamaica ☆ — -bark, (bot.) scorza d'albero della Cina; — -pepper, pepe, droghe della Giamaica.

Jamaican [dʒə'meikən], ag. giamaicano ‖ s.c. giamaicano, giamaicana.

jamb [dʒæm], s. stipite; montante ☆ — stone, stipite in pietra.

jamboree [,dʒæmbə'ri:], s. 1. riunione internazionale, intersezionale di boy-scouts 2. (sl.) allegra riunione; baldoria.

James [dʒeimz], no.pr.m. Giacomo.

jammy ['dʒæmi], ag. attaccaticcio, appiccicoso.

to **jampack** ['dʒæm'pæk], v.t. (amer.) gremire.

jampan ['dʒæmpæn], s. portantina a quattro portatori.

jampanee [,dʒæmpə'ni:], s. portatore di portantina.

Jane [dʒein], no.pr.f. Gianna.

Janet ['dʒænit], no.pr.f. dim. di **Jane**.

jangle ['dʒæŋgl], s. 1. (arc.) disputa, alterco, baruffa 2. suono stonato, stridente.

to **jangle**, v.t.i. 1. altercare, litigare 2. stonare 3. (far) emettere suoni stridenti, stonati.

jangler ['dʒæŋglə*], s. 1. persona litigiosa, attaccabrighe 2. (mar.) campanella.

jangling ['dʒæŋgliŋ], s. 1. rissa, contesa, baruffa, alterco 2. chiacchiere, ciance 3. suono aspro; scampanellata.

janitor ['dʒænitə*], s. portiere; portinaio; custode.

janizary ['dʒænizəri], s. (st.) giannizzero.

jannock ['dʒænək], ag. (dial.) retto, onesto; genuino.

Jansenism ['dʒænsnizəm], s. (st.) giansenismo.

Jansenist ['dʒænsnist], s.c. (st.) giansenista.

jantily ['dʒɑ:ntili], av. gaiamente, vivacemente.

jantiness ['dʒɑ:ntinis], s. gaiezza, vivacità.

janty ['dʒɑ:nti], ag. gaio, vivace.

January ['dʒænjuəri], s. gennaio.

Janus ['dʒeinəs], no.pr.m. (mit.) Giano.

Jap [dʒæp], ag. s.c. (fam.) giapponese.

Japan [dʒə'pæn], no.pr. (geog.) Giappone.

japan, s. 1. lacca giapponese 2. oggetto di lacca.

to **japan**, pass.p.p. **japanned** [dʒə'pænd], v.t. laccare.

Japanese [,dʒæpə'ni:z], ag.s.c. giapponese ‖ s. lingua giapponese.

japanner [dʒə'pænə*], s. laccatore, verniciatore.

jape [dʒeip], s. scherzo, tiro birbone; giuoco di parole.

to **jape**, v.i. scherzare; giocare un tiro.

Japheth ['dʒeifiθ], no.pr.m. (Bibbia) Iafet.

Japonic [dʒə'pɔnik], ag. giapponese.

japonica [dʒə'pɔnikə], s. (bot.) pero, cotogno del Giappone.

Jaques [dʒeiks], no.pr.m. (lett.) Jaques.

jar[1] [dʒɑ:*], s. 1. rumore aspro; dissonanza; discordanza; stridio 2. alterco; discordia ☆ family jars, beghe di famiglia.

to **jar**[1], pass.p.p. **jarred** [dʒɑ:d], v.t.i. 1. discordare, far discordare; vibrare, far vibrare; stridere, far stridere; stonare 2. non essere d'accordo; disputare, contendere: their opinions —, le loro opinioni sono in conflitto ‖ to — on a person's nerves, urtare i nervi a qlcu.

jar[2], s. giara, orcio; secchio; brocca; vaso (di terra, di vetro) ☆ electrical — (o Leyden —), (fis.) bottiglia di Leida.

jar[3], s. (fam.): on the —, socchiuso: the door is on the —, la porta è socchiusa.

jardinière [,ʒɑ:di'njɛə*], s. 1. vaso da fiori 2. piatto di verdure miste.

jarful ['dʒɑ:-ful], s. il contenuto di un vaso.

jargon[1] ['dʒɑ:gən], s. 1. gergo, linguaggio professionale; lingua parlata in modo incomprensibile 2. cinguettio di uccelli.

jargon[2], s. (min.) giargone.

jarl [jɑ:l], s. (st.) capo danese o scandinavo.

jarring ['dʒɑ:riŋ], ag. 1. discorde; stridente; stonato 2. che scuote ‖ s. 1. scuotimento 2. discordia; contrasto 3. dissonanza.

jarringly ['dʒɑ:riŋli], av. in modo stridente, contrastante, discorde.

jarvey ['dʒɑ:vi], s. (sl.) fiaccheraio.

jasey ['dʒeizi], s. (sl.) parrucca (generalmente di lana).

jasmin(e) ['dʒæsmin], s. (bot.) gelsomino.

Jasmine, no.pr.f. Gelsomina.

Jason ['dʒeisn], no.pr.m. (mit.) Giasone.

jasper[1] ['dʒæspə*], s. (min.) diaspro.

Jasper[2], no.pr.m. Gaspare.

Jat [dʒɑ:t], s. membro di una tribù del Nord-ovest dell'India.

jaundice ['dʒɔ:ndis], s. 1. (patol.) itterizia 2. fig. pregiudizio; ostilità; gelosia.

to **jaundice**, v.t. (spec. fig.) far venire l'itterizia; render geloso, invidioso.

jaundiced ['dʒɔ:ndist], ag. (patol.) itterico; (fam.) geloso, invidioso.

jaunt [dʒɔ:nt], s. scampagnata, gita, passeggiata.

to **jaunt**, v.i. andare a spasso; fare una gita.

jauntily ['dʒɔ:ntili], av. 1. vivacemente, briosamente 2. in modo disinvolto, baldanzoso 3. elegantemente.

jauntiness ['dʒɔ:ntinis], s. 1. allegria, gaiezza, vivacità 2. disinvoltura, baldanza.

jaunting ['dʒɔ:ntiŋ], ag. girovago; ambulante.

jaunty ['dʒɔ:nti], ag. 1. gaio, vivace, brioso 2. disinvolto; baldanzoso 3. elegante.

jaup [dʒɔ:p], s. (scoz.) zacchera, pillacchera.

to **jaup**, v.t. (scoz.) inzaccherare.

Java ['dʒɑ:və], no.pr. (geog.) Giava.

Javan ['dʒɑ:vən], ag. s.c. giavanese.

Javanese [,dʒɑ:və'ni:z], ag.s.c. giavanese.

javel ['dʒævl], s. uomo da nulla; furfante.

javelin ['dʒævlin], s. giavellotto; dardo.

jaw [dʒɔ:], s. 1. (anat.) mascella; mandibola; (fam.) ganascia; fauci: lower —, mascella inferiore; upper —, mascella superiore ‖ he had better hold his —, (sl.) farebbe meglio a chiudere il becco 2. pl. stretta; gola; spaccatura 3. (mec.) morsa; ganascia 4. (sl.) chiacchiere, ciarle; parole offensive, litigiose ☆ — -bone, (anat.) mascella; osso mandibolare; — -breaker, (sl.) parola

difficile da pronunciare; (*mec.*) frantoio a mascelle;
— -*tooth*, molare.

to **jaw**, *v.t.i.* **1.** (*sl.*) parlare, ciarlare in modo noioso, offensivo **2.** (*sl.*) ammonire; far la predica a.

jawed [dʒɔːd], *ag.* che ha mascelle.

jay [dʒei], *s.* **1.** (*ornit.*) ghiandaia **2.** *fig.* chiacchierone insolente; sempliciotto.

to **jaywalk** ['dʒeiwɔːk], *v.i.* (*fam.*) attraversare la via distrattamente.

jaywalker ['dʒei,wɔːkə*], *s.* (*fam.*) pedone distratto.

jazz [dʒæz], *ag.* **1.** discordante **2.** vistoso **3.** sgarbato **4.** burlesco ‖ *s.* « jazz » (musica, danza): *cool* —, « jazz » freddo; *hot* —, « jazz » caldo ☆ — -*band*, orchestra di suonatori di « jazz ».

to **jazz**, *v.t.i.* **1.** suonare, ballare il « jazz » **2.** adattare (musica) al ritmo di « jazz » **3.** *to* — *up*, (*sl. amer.*) rendere vivace.

jealous ['dʒeləs], *ag.* geloso; sospettoso; invidioso: *to be* — *of s.o.*, essere geloso di qlcu.

jealously ['dʒeləsli], *av.* gelosamente; sospettosamente; invidiosamente.

jealousness ['dʒeləsnis], **jealousy** ['dʒeləsi], *s.* gelosia; invidia; sospetto.

Jean[1] [dʒiːn], *no.pr.f.* Giovanna.

jean[2] [dʒein], *s.* **1.** traliccio **2.** *pl.* calzoni, tuta di tela grossa.

jeep [dʒiːp], *s.* (*aut. mil.*) « jeep », camionetta.

jeer[1] [dʒiə*], *s.* burla; beffa; scherno.

to **jeer**[1], *v.t.i.* burlare; schernire; prendersi gioco: *they all jeered at the poor boy*, tutti quanti canzonarono il povero ragazzo ‖ *to* — *an actor off the stage*, costringere con scherno un attore ad abbandonare la scena.

jeer[2], *s.* (*mar.*) drizza di pennone.

jeerer ['dʒiərə*], *s.c.* schernitore, schernitrice; dileggiatore, dileggiatrice.

jeering ['dʒiəriŋ], *ag.* beffardo; canzonatorio ‖ *s.* canzonatura.

jeeringly ['dʒiəriŋli], *av.* beffardamente; in modo canzonatorio.

Jeffrey ['dʒefri], *no.pr.m.* Goffredo.

Jehoshaphat [dʒi'hɔʃəfæt] *no.pr.m.* (*Bibbia*) Giosafatte.

Jehovah [dʒi'houvə], *no.pr.m.* (*Bibbia*) Jeova.

jehu ['dʒiːhjuː], *s.* (*scherz.*) guidatore (spericolato).

jejune [dʒi'dʒuːn], *ag.* **1.** magro; sterile; arido (di terreno) **2.** privo d'interesse.

jejunely [dʒi'dʒuːnli], *av.* aridamente; sterilmente.

jejuneness [dʒi'dʒuːnnis], *s.* **1.** penuria; scarsezza; magrezza; aridità; sterilità **2.** l'esser privo d'interesse.

jejunum [dʒi'dʒuːnəm], *s.* (*anat.*) digiuno, intestino tenue secondo.

to **jell** [dʒel], *v.t.i.* **1.** (*fam. amer.*) per *to* **elly** **2.** *fig.* solidificarsi, cristallizzarsi.

jellied ['dʒelid], *ag.* in gelatina.

jelly ['dʒeli], *s.* gelatina (anche di frutta) ☆ — -*bag*, sacchetto-filtro per gelatina; — -*broth*, brodo ristretto; ‖ *raspberry-* —, gelatina di lamponi.

to **jelly**, *v.t.i.* **1.** congelarsi, rapprendersi; far congelare; ridurre, ridursi in gelatina **2.** mettere in gelatina.

jellyfish ['dʒelifiʃ], *s.* (*zool.*) medusa.

jemadar ['dʒemədɑː*], *s.* ufficiale dell'esercito anglo-indiano; capo-poliziotto.

jemina [dʒi'mainə], *s.* **1.** cravatta con nodo fatto **2.** *pl.* stivali con elastico laterale.

jemmy ['dʒemi], *s.* **1.** pastrano **2.** grimaldello **3.** (*sl.*) testa di pecora al forno.

jennet ['dʒenit], *s.* cavallino spagnolo.

jenneting ['dʒenitiŋ], *s.* mela di S. Giovanni.

jenny ['dʒeni], *s.* **1.** femmina di vari animali **2.** (*mec.*) gru mobile; (*ind.*) filatoio ‖ — -*wren*, (*pop.*) scricciolo.

Jenny, *no.pr.f. dim.* di **Jane**.

to **jeopardize** ['dʒepədaiz], *v.t.* mettere a repentaglio; mettere in pericolo; arrischiare: *to* — *one's life*, mettere a repentaglio la propria vita.

jeopardous ['dʒepədəs], *ag.* rischioso; arrischiato.

jeopardy ['dʒepədi], *s.* rischio, pericolo: *to put sthg. in* —, mettere ql.co. a repentaglio.

Jephthah ['dʒefθə], *no.pr.m.* (*Bibbia*) Jefte.

jerboa [dʒəː'bouə], *s.* (*zool.*) topo delle piramidi.

jereed, *V.* **jerid**.

jeremiad [,dʒeri'maiəd], *s.* geremiade.

Jeremiah [,dʒeri'maiə], *no.pr.m.* (*Bibbia*) Geremia.

Jeremy ['dʒerimi], *no.pr.m.* Geremia.

Jericho ['dʒerikou], *no.pr.* (*geog.st.*) Gerico ‖ *go to* —, (*sl.*) va' a farti benedire.

jerid [dʒə'riːd], *s.* **1.** giavellotto usato dai cavalieri persiani ed arabi **2.** giuoco in cui è usato il « jerid ».

jerk[1] [dʒəːk], *s.* **1.** strattone; scatto; balzo ‖ *in a* —, in un baleno **2.** spinta; colpo **3.** sussulto; spasmo; tic nervoso; contorsione **4.** discorso breve ed arguto ☆ *ankle-* —, (*med.*) riflesso tendineo della caviglia; *knee-* —, (*med.*) riflesso patellare; *physical jerks*, (*fam.*) ginnastica da camera.

to **jerk**[1], *v.t.i.* **1.** dare uno strattone; scattare, sobbalzare; balzare; sussultare **2.** dare una spinta, un colpo, un urto a **3.** *to* — **along**, avanzare, far avanzare a scatti **4.** *to* — **back**, spingere indietro; indietreggiare di colpo **5.** *to* — **out**, parlare a scatti ‖ *to* — *sthg. out of s.o.'s hand*, far saltar via ql.co. dalla mano di qlcu. (con un urto) **6.** *to* — **up**, raddrizzare di colpo.

jerk[2], *s.* carne essiccata al sole.

to **jerk**[2], *v.t.* far essiccare (la carne) al sole.

jerkily ['dʒəːkili], *av.* a scosse; a salti.

jerkin ['dʒəːkin], *s.* giustacuore.

jerkiness ['dʒəːkinis], *s.* **1.** strattone, sobbalzo **2.** spinta, urto.

jerky ['dʒəːki], *ag.* traballante, sussultante.

Jeroboam [,dʒerə'bouəm], *no.pr.m.* (*Bibbia*) Geroboamo ‖ **jeroboam** *s.* **1.** bottiglione **2.** grossa coppa.

Jerome ['dʒerəm], *no.pr.m.* Gerolamo.

to **jerque** [dʒəːk], *v.t.* ispezionare (un bastimento) per motivi doganali.

jerquer ['dʒəːkə*], *s.* ispettore doganale.

Jerry ['dʒeri], *no.pr.m. dim.* di **Jeremy** ‖ **jerry**, *s.* **1.** (*sl.*) soldato tedesco **2.** (*sl.*) vaso da notte ☆ — -*builder*, costruttore di case economiche e brutte, per speculazione; — -*built*, costruito con materiale scadente; — -*shop*, (*sl.*) osteria, bettola.

Jersey ['dʒəːzi], *no.pr.* (*geog.*) Jersey (isola della Manica) ‖ **jersey**, *s.* **1.** camicetta a maglia con maniche **2.** maglia sportiva **3.** razza pregiata di bestiame.

Jerusalem [dʒə'ruːsələm], *no.pr.* (*geog.*) Gerusalemme ‖ *s.* — (*pony*), (*scherz.*) asinello ☆ — *artichoke*, (*bot.*) topinamburo.

jess [dʒes], *s.* geto.

to **jess**, *v.t.* mettere il geto a (falcone).

jessamine ['dʒesəmin], *s.* (*bot.*) gelsomino.

Jesse ['dʒesi], *no.pr.m.* (*Bibbia*) Jesse ‖ *tree of* —, albero di Jesse (albero genealogico in cui è rappresentata la discendenza di Cristo da Jesse).

Jessica ['dʒesikə], *no.pr.f.* Gessica.

jest [dʒest], *s.* **1.** scherzo, arguzia, facezia, motteggio, beffa: *it was said in a* —, fu detto per scherzo ‖ *half in* —, *half in earnest*, tra il serio e il faceto; *there's many a true word spoken in* —, scherzando Arlecchino si confessa **2.** zimbello: *he is a standing* —, è lo zimbello di tutti ☆ — -*book*, raccolta di facezie.

to **jest**, *v.i.* scherzare; dir delle facezie; prendersi gioco, farsi beffe.

jester ['dʒestə*], *s.c.* burlone, burlona; freddurista ‖ *s.* (*st.*) buffone, menestrello.

jestful ['dʒestful], *ag.* incline allo scherzo, alle burle.

jesting ['dʒestiŋ], *ag.* scherzoso, canzonatorio, frizzante ‖ *s.* scherzo, burla, beffa, frizzo.

jestingly ['dʒestiŋli], *av.* per scherzo, per burla.

Jesuit ['dʒezjuit], *s.* **1.** gesuita **2.** (*spreg.*) ipocrita; individuo astuto.

Jesuitical [,dʒezju'itikəl], *ag.* **1.** gesuitico, da gesuita **2.** (*spreg.*) ipocrita, scaltro, astuto.

Jesuitically [,dʒezju'itikəli], *av.* gesuiticamente.

Jesuitism ['dʒezjuitizəm], **1.** gesuitismo **2.** (*spreg.*) astuzia, scaltrezza, ipocrisia.

to **jesuitize** ['dʒesjuitaiz], *v.t.i.* **1.** instillare principi gesuitici **2.** fare il gesuita.

Jesuitry ['dʒezjuitri], *V.* **Jesuitism**.

Jesus ['dʒi:zəs], *no.pr.m.* Gesù.

jet[1] [dʒet], *ag.* color giaietto, nero lucido ‖ *s.* giaietto ☆ — *-black*, nero lucente.

jet[2], *s.* **1.** getto; spruzzo, zampillo **2.** (*chim.*) becco **3.** spruzzatore **4.** aviogetto ☆ — *engine*, (*aer.*) motore a reazione; — *liner*, aereo (di linea) a reazione; — *pipe*, tubo di scarico; (*zool.*) sfiatatoio (di cetacei); — *plane*, aviogetto, aeroplano a reazione; — *propelled plane*, aeroplano a reazione; — *propulsion*, propulsione a getto ‖ *fuel* —, getto del carburante; *gas* —, becco a gas.

to **jet**[2], *pass.p.p.* **jetted** ['dʒetid], *v.t.i.* slanciarsi; sprizzare; emettere un getto; zampillare, far zampillare; schizzare, far schizzare.

jetsam ['dʒetsəm], *s.* (*mar.*) relitti di mare.

jettison ['dʒetisn], *s.* **1.** (*aer.*) scarico rapido **2.** (*mar.*) scarico in mare del carico.

to **jettison**, *v.t.* **1.** gettare in mare (un carico) **2.** *fig.* disfarsi di.

jetton ['dʒetən], *s.* gettone con impressa una sigla, un motto.

jetty[1] ['dʒeti], *ag.* di giaietto, nero come il giaietto.

jetty[2], *s.* (*mar.*) molo, gettata: *landing* —, imbarcadero.

Jew [dʒu:], *s.* ebreo; israelita; giudeo ‖ *the wandering* —, l'Ebreo errante ☆ — *-baiting*, persecuzione antisemita; —*'s ear*, (*bot.*) fungo detto orecchio di Giuda; —*'s-harp*, (*mus.*) trigono.

jewel ['dʒu:əl], *s.* **1.** gioiello, gioia (anche *fig.*): *a — of a car*, un gioiello di automobile; *she is a — of a servant*, è una perla di cameriera **2.** (*orologeria*) rubino ☆ — *-box*, custodia, astuccio per gioielli; — *-case*, cofanetto per i gioielli.

to **jewel**, *pass.p.p.* **jewelled** ['dʒu:əld], *v.t.* ingemmare, ornare di pietre preziose.

jeweller ['dʒu:ələ*], *s.* gioielliere.

jewelled ['dʒu:əld], *ag.* ingemmato, ornato di pietre preziose: *a — robe*, una tunica tempestata di pietre preziose.

jeweller ['dʒu:ələ*], *s.* gioielliere.

jewellery, jewelry ['dʒu:əlri], *s.* gioielli; commercio delle gemme.

Jewess ['dʒu(:)is], *s.* ebrea, israelita.

Jewish ['dʒu(:)iʃ], *ag.* ebreo, ebraico, giudaico, israelitico.

Jewishly ['dʒu(:)iʃli], *av.* da ebreo, da giudeo.

Jewry ['dʒuəri], *s.* **1.** gli ebrei **2.** ghetto.

Jezebel ['dʒezəbl], *no.pr.f.* (*Bibbia*) Gezabele ‖ *s. fig.* megera; donna ambiziosa e crudele.

jib[1] [dʒib], *s.* **1.** (*mar.*) fiocco **2.** (*mec.*) braccio (di gru, di argano) ‖ *the cut of one's* —, (*sl.*) l'aspetto esteriore, il modo di vestire di qlcu. ☆ — *-boom*, (*mar.*) asta di fiocco.

to **jib**[1], *pass.p.p.* **jibbed** [dʒibd], *v.t.i.* (*mar.*) orientare; girare (detto di vele).

to **jib**[2], *pass.p.p.* **jibbed**, *v.i.* **1.** recalcitrare; impuntarsi **2.** *to — at* (*s.o., sthg.*), mostrare repugnanza a, per.

jibber ['dʒibə*], *s.* cavallo recalcitrante.

jibbings ['dʒibinz], *s.pl.* ultimo latte munto da una mucca.

jib-door ['dʒibdɔ:*], *s.* usciuolo dissimulato nel muro.

(to) **jibe**, *V.* (to) **gibe**.

jiff [dʒif], **jiffy** ['dʒifi], *s.* (*fam.*) momento: *in a* —, in un batter d'occhio; *wait a* —, aspetta un momento.

jig[1] [dʒig], *s.* **1.** giga (aria e ballo) **2.** (*miner.*) crivello oscillante **3.** (*mec.*) maschera; maschera di montaggio.

to **jig**[1], *pass.p.p.* **jigged** [dʒigd], *v.t.i.* **1.** ballar la giga **2.** agitarsi: *to — up and down*, saltare su e giù **3.** (*mec.*) lavorare con maschere, con attrezzature **4.** (*miner.*) crivellare.

jig[2], *s.* (*sl. amer.*) negro.

jigger[1] ['dʒigə*], *s.* **1.** (*miner.*) crivello **2.** (*mar.*) bozzello, paranco a coda **3.** (*fam.*) aggeggio **4.** (*mec.*) gru idraulica.

jigger[2], *s.* (*entom.*) pulce tropicale.

to **jiggle** ['dʒigl], *v.t.i.* muovere, muoversi con piccoli scatti.

jigot ['dʒigət], *s.* cosciotto di montone.

jigsaw ['dʒigsɔ:], *s.* sega da traforo ☆ — *puzzle*, giuoco di pazienza; *fig.* mosaico.

jilt [dʒilt], *s.* civetta, donna leggera.

to **jilt**, *v.t.* piantare in asso (un innamorato) dopo averlo incoraggiato.

Jim [dʒim], *no.pr.m. dim.* di **James**.

Jim Crow ['dʒimkrou], *s.* **1.** (*sl. amer.*) negro **2.** discriminazione razziale (specialmente contro i negri) **3.** *jim-crow*, (*mec.*) (martinetto) piegarotaie.

jimjams ['dʒimdʒæmz], *s.pl.* (*sl.*) delirium tremens.

Jimmy ['dʒimi], *no.pr.m. dim.* di **James**.

to **jimmy**, *v.t.* (*amer.*) scassinare.

jingle ['dʒingl], *s.* **1.** tintinnio **2.** cantilena, ripetizione monotona; allitterazione.

to **jingle**, *v.t.i.* **1.** far tintinnare; tintinnare **2.** essere pieno di cantilene, di allitterazioni (di scritto).

jingo ['dʒingou], *ag.* **1.** fanatico, sciovinista **2.** volgare, violento ‖ *s.* (*pl.* **jingoes** ['dʒingouz]), sciovinista, nazionalista fanatico ‖ *by* —!, per Bacco!.

jingoism ['dʒingouizəm], *s.* sciovinismo.

jink [dʒink], *s.* (*scoz.*) **1.** movimento elusivo **2.** *pl.* chiasso, allegria ☆ *high-jinks*, baldoria.

to **jink**, *v.t.i.* (*scoz.*) **1.** muoversi rapidamente; sfuggire, schivare, eludere **2.** (*sl. aer.*) far evoluzioni, manovre (per evitare il fuoco antiaereo).

jinn [dʒin], *pl.* di **jinnee**.

jinnee [dʒi'ni:], *pl.* **jinn** [dʒin], *s.* (*mit. araba*) genio, demone.

jinricksha [dʒin'rikʃə], **jinrikisha** [dʒin'rikiʃə], *s.* risciò.

jinx [dʒinks], *s.* (*sl. amer.*) iettatore, menagramo.

to **jitter** ['dʒitə*], *v.i.* (*sl. amer.*) essere nervoso, agitato; agire nervosamente.

jitterbug ['dʒitəbʌg], *s.* (*sl. amer.*) giovane fanatico di danze a ritmo violento.

to **jitterbug**, *pass.p.p.* **jitterbugged** ['dʒitəbʌgd], *v.i.* (*sl. amer.*) suonare musica fortemente ritmata; abbandonarsi a danze molto ritmate.

jitteriness ['dʒitərinis], *s.* nervosismo.

jitters ['dʒitəz], *s.pl.* (*sl.*) nervosismo, agitazione: *to have the* —, avere i nervi a fior di pelle; essere agitato.

jittery ['dʒitəri], *ag.* nervoso ‖ *to grow* —, diventar nervoso, innervosirsi.

jiu-jitsu [dʒju:'dʒitsu:], *s.* « jiu-jitsu » (lotta giapponese).

jive [dʒaiv], *s.* **1.** « jive » (musica, danza sincopata molto veloce) **2.** gergo degli appassionati degli « jive ».

Jo [dʒou], *no.pr.m.f. dim.* di **Joseph, Josephine**.

Joachim ['jouəkim], *no.pr.m.* Gioacchino.

Joan [dʒoun], **Joanna** [dʒou'ænə], *no.pr.f.* Giovanna.

job[1] [dʒɔb], *s.* **1.** mansione; lavoro; impiego; impresa: *permanent* —, impiego stabile; *can you give me a* —?, potete darmi un lavoro?; *it is not my* —, non è affar mio; *to be out of a* —, essere disoccupato; *to be paid by the* —, essere pagato a cottimo; *to give sthg. up as a bad* —, rinunziare a un'impresa impossibile; *to make the best of a difficult* —, cavarsela bene in un'impresa difficile **2.** (*fam.*) faccenda; situazione: *a pretty* —!, (*iron.*) bell'affare!; *that's a good, a bad* —, è una bella cosa, è una brutta faccenda ‖ *that's a* —!, è proprio quel che ci vuole! **3.** cavallo, carrozza presa, data a nolo ☆ — *evaluation*, valutazione delle mansioni; — *lot*, (*comm.*) lotto di merce; occasione ‖ *full-time* —, impiego a orario completo ‖ *odd jobs*, piccoli lavori vari; *odd — man*, uomo assunto per lavoretti vari ‖ *part-time* —, impiego a mezza giornata.

to **job**[1], *pass.p.p.* **jobbed** [dʒɔbd], *v.t.i.* **1.** fare lavori **2.** dare lavori in appalto **3.** lavorare a cottimo **4.** comprare, vendere all'ingrosso **5.** trattare affari come mediatore **6.** commettere peculato; lasciarsi corrompere **7.** noleggiare (cavallo, carrozza).

job², *s.* **1.** strappata di morso **2.** colpo dato con qualcosa di appuntito.

to job², *v.t.i.* **1.** pungere; pungolare; stimolare **2.** colpire, dare un colpo: *he jobbed my nose*, *(sl.)* mi ha dato un colpo sul naso; *to — at sthg.*, colpire ql.co.

Job³ [dʒoub], *no.pr.m.* *(Bibbia)* Giobbe.

jobation [dʒou'beiʃən], *s.* *(fam.)* strapazzata, paternale.

jobber ['dʒɔbə*], *s.* **1.** noleggiatore **2.** lavoratore a cottimo **3.** trafficante disonesto **4.** *(comm.)* speculatore in borsa **5.** *(amer.)* grossista.

jobbery ['dʒɔbəri], *s.* baratteria, peculato.

jobbing ['dʒɔbiŋ], *s.* **1.** cottimo **2.** noleggio **3.** speculazione.

jobholder ['dʒɔb,houldə*], *s.* **1.** impiegato regolare **2.** *(amer.)* funzionario governativo.

Jocasta [dʒə'kæstə], *no.pr.f.* *(mit.)* Giocasta.

Jocelyn ['dʒɔslin], *no.pr.m.* Gioscellino.

jockey ['dʒɔki], *s.* **1.** fantino **2.** mediatore di cavalli **3.** furbo; ingannatore; briccone ☆ *disk —*, *(sl. rad.)* annunciatore radiofonico di programma registrato.

to jockey, *v.t.i.* **1.** ingannare; truffare; intrigare **2.** *(mar.)* mandrare: *the yachts were jockeying for the breeze*, gli « yachts » mandravano per avere il vento.

jockeyship ['dʒɔkiʃip], *s.* professione di fantino.

joeko ['dʒɔkou], *s.* scimpanzè.

jocose [dʒə'kous], *ag.* giocoso; faceto; gioviale.

jocosely [dʒə'kousli], *av.* scherzosamente; in modo faceto; giovialmente.

jocoseness [dʒə'kousnis], *s.* giocondità; umore faceto.

jocosity [dʒou'kɔsiti], *s.* giocondità; atto, detto faceto.

jocular ['dʒɔkjulə*], *ag.* giocoso; scherzoso; lepido.

jocularity [,dʒɔkju'læriti], *s.* lepidezza; spirito.

jocularly ['dʒɔkjuləli], *av.* scherzosamente; giovialmente.

joculator ['dʒɔkjuleitə*], *s.* *(arc.)* giocoliere; buffone di professione.

jocund ['dʒɔkənd], *ag.* giocondo; giulivo; gaio.

jocundity [dʒou'kʌnditi], *s.* giocondità; allegria; gaiezza.

jocundly ['dʒɔkəndli], *av.* giocondamente.

jocundness ['dʒɔkəndnis], *s.* giocondità; gaiezza.

jodel ['joudl], *s.* *(mus.)* canto alla tirolese (con passaggi in falsetto).

to jodel, *pass.p.p.* **jodelled** ['joudld], *v.t.i.* *(mus.)* cantare alla tirolese.

jodhpurs ['dʒɔdpuəz], *s.pl.* calzoni da cavallerizzo.

Joe [dʒou], *no.pr.m.* di *Joseph* ǁ — *Miller*, *fig.* scherzo vecchio, conosciuto ǁ *not for —*, *(sl.)* neanche per sogno.

joey ['dʒoui], *s.* *(austral.)* cangurino.

jog¹ [dʒɔg], *s.* **1.** spinta, urto; gomitata **2.** scossa; sballottamento **3.** andatura lenta e monotona ☆ — *-trot*, trotto regolare, mezzo trotto; andatura lenta e monotona.

to jog¹, *pass.p.p.* **jogged** [dʒɔgd], *v.t.i.* **1.** spingere, urtare; dar di gomito **2.** scuotere leggermente; sballottare: *to — s.o.'s memory*, rinfrescare la memoria a qlcu. **3.** avanzare lentamente, avviarsi, muoversi a rilento **4.** *to — along*, andare al piccolo trotto; seguire il solito trantran.

jog², *s.* *(amer.)* **1.** rientro, nicchia (in una parete). **2.** sporgenza (in una parete).

jogger ['dʒɔgə*], *s.* **1.** chi, che avanza a scatti **2.** *(fam.)* piccolo omnibus a cavalli **3.** *(mec.)* dispositivo che avanza ad intermittenza.

joggle¹ ['dʒɔgl], *s.* *(arch.)* gorgia, dente per evitare lo scorrimento di una giunzione o di un giunto.

to joggle¹, *v.t.* **1.** *(arch.)* sfalsare **2.** *(mec.)* fissare con grani.

joggle², *s.* scatto; scossetta.

to joggle², *v.t.i.* **1.** scuotere, far muovere a scatti; muoversi a scatti **2.** *(mec.)* spostare a scatti, a intermittenza.

John [dʒɔn], *no.pr.m.* Giovanni ǁ — *Bull*, « John Bull » (personificazione della nazione inglese); inglese tipico; — *Bullism*, carattere, gesto tipicamente inglese ǁ — *Doe*, *(dir.)* persona fittizia.

Johnian ['dʒounjən], *s.* membro, studente del collegio di St. John a Cambridge.

Johnnie, Johnny ['dʒɔni], *no.pr.m.* dim. di **John** ǁ — *Raw*, recluta, novizio.

johnny, *s.* **1.** zerbinotto, perdigiorno **2.** *(sl. amer.)* poliziotto **3.** *(sl. amer.)* — *cake*, *(amer.)* focaccia di granoturco; *(austral.)* focaccia di grano.

join [dʒɔin], *s.* giuntura, congiunzione.

to join, *v.t.i.* (III) **1.** unire, unirsi (anche *fig.*); collegare; legare; riunire; congiungere, congiungersi: *the roads —*, le strade si congiungono; *to — hands with s.o.*, prendere qlcu. per mano; unirsi a qlcu.; *to — in the conversation*, unirsi alla conversazione ǁ *to — the great majority*, morire **2.** essere contiguo: *the house joins the church*, la casa è contigua alla chiesa **3.** raggiungere: *he will — me next week*, egli mi raggiungerà la settimana ventura; *you are to — your regiment*, dovete raggiungere il vostro reggimento **4.** *to — in*, entrare a far parte del gruppo **5.** *to — up*, *(mil.)* arruolarsi.

joinder ['dʒɔində*], *s.* *(dir.)* unione, congiunzione.

joiner ['dʒɔinə*], *s.* falegname; fabbricante di mobili ☆ — *bench*, banco da falegname; — *-work*, lavoro di falegnameria.

joinery ['dʒɔinəri], *s.* falegnameria.

joining ['dʒɔiniŋ], *s.* congiunzione; unione.

joint [dʒɔint], *ag.* unito; aggiunto; indiviso; associato ǁ *during their — lives*, *(dir.)* finché sono tutti vivi ☆ — *account*, *(comm.)* conto di partecipazione; — *author*, coautore; collaboratore; — *-heir*, *(dir.)* coerede; — *industrial committee*, comitato misto di produzione; — *-stock*, *(comm.)* capitale sociale; — *-stock bank*, banca per azioni; — *-stock company*, società per azioni; — *-tenancy*, comproprietà; — *-tenant*, comproprietario.

joint, *s.* **1.** congiunzione, giuntura, congiuntura; aggiunta **2.** trancio di carne per arrosto **3.** *(mec.)* giunto, giunzione **4.** *(anat.)* articolazione; giuntura **5.** *(bot.)* congiunzione, nodo **6.** *(geol.)* fessura **7.** *(sl. amer.)* luogo di riunione; rivendita di liquori (specialmente non autorizzata) **8.** *(sl. amer.)* locale; edificio ☆ *universal —*, *(mec.)* giunto universale, giunto cardanico ǁ *elbow —*, *(anat.)* articolazione del gomito.

to joint, *v.t.* **1.** congiungere, unire, far combaciare **2.** *(mec.)* fare giunzioni, connettere; rendere snodato; raccordare.

jointed ['dʒɔintid], *ag.* che ha giunture, articolazioni.

jointer ['dʒɔintə*], *s.* *(artig.)* pialla; *(agr.)* avanvomere, coltello.

jointing ['dʒɔintiŋ], *s.* giunzione ☆ — *-rule*, squadra da muratore.

jointly ['dʒɔintli], *av.* unitamente; collettivamente: — *and severally*, congiuntamente e separatamente.

jointress ['dʒɔintris], *s.* vedova che vive del reddito del patrimonio assegnatole all'atto del matrimonio.

jointure ['dʒɔintʃə*], *s.* patrimonio assegnato ad una donna all'atto del matrimonio, perchè ne usufruisca in caso di vedovanza.

to jointure, *v.t.* assegnare a (una donna) un patrimonio di cui potrà godere solo dopo la morte del marito.

joist [dʒɔist], *s.* *(arch.)* travetto, travicello.

to joist, *v.t.* *(arch.)* munire di travetti, travicelli.

joke [dʒouk], *s.* scherzo; facezia; canzonatura; burla; tiro: *a poor —*, uno scherzo di cattivo gusto; *a practical —*, un tiro mancino, una beffa: *to play a practical — on s.o.*, giocare una beffa a qlcu.; *he loves cracking jokes*, gli piace dir facezie; *it is no —*, è un affar serio; *my brother can't see a —*, mio fratello non ha il senso dell'umorismo.

to joke, *v.t.i.* burlarsi; canzonare; scherzare: *don't — about it*, non prenderlo come uno scherzo.

joker ['dʒoukə*], *s.* **1.** burlone, tipo ameno **2.** (*sl.*) individuo; tipo **3.** matta (nel giuoco delle carte).

jokingly ['dʒoukiŋli], *av.* per scherzo, ridendo.

jollification [,dʒolifi'keiʃən], *s.* allegria, ilarità.

to jollify ['dʒolifai], *v.t.i.* essere, tenere allegro.

jollily ['dʒolili], *av.* (*fam.*) allegramente.

jolliness ['dʒolinis], **jollity** ['dʒoliti], *s.* allegria, ilarità.

jolly ['dʒoli], *ag.* allegro, gaio; vivace; ameno; alticcio: *a — fellow*, un giovialone, un tipo ameno ‖ *the — god*, Bacco ‖ *s.* (*sl.*) (marinaio della) Regia Marina.

to jolly, *v.t.* (*fam.*) **1.** adulare **2.** prendersi giuoco di.

jolly, *av.* (*fam.*) molto, moltissimo: *he is a — good fellow*, è un ottimo ragazzo; *you — well must*, tu devi proprio.

jollyboat ['dʒolibout], *s.* iole; piccola lancia.

jolt [dʒoult], *s.* scossa; sobbalzo; sbalzo.

to jolt, *v.t.i.* far sobbalzare; scuotere; sobbalzare.

joltingly ['dʒoultiŋli], *av.* sobbalzando, a scosse.

jolty ['dʒoulti], *ag.* che va a scosse, sobbalzando.

Jonah ['dʒounə], *no.pr.m.* (*Bibbia*) Giona ‖ *s.* iettatore.

Jonas ['dʒounəs], *no.pr.m.* (*Bibbia*) Giona.

Jonathan ['dʒonəθən], *no.pr.m.* Gionata ‖ (*Brother*) —, personificazione del popolo americano.

jongleur [ʒɔ:ŋ'glə:*], *s.* giullare; menestrello.

jonquil ['dʒoŋkwil], *s.* (*bot.*) giunchiglia; narciso.

Jordan ['dʒo:dn], *no.pr.* (*geog.*) **1.** Giordano **2.** Giordania.

Jordanian [dʒo:'deinjən], *ag.* giordano ‖ *s.* giordanico.

jorum ['dʒo:rəm], *s.* **1.** tazza; boccale **2.** ponce.

Joseph¹ ['dʒouzif], *no.pr.m.* Giuseppe.

joseph², *s.* costume da amazzone del XVIII sec.

Josephine ['dʒouzifi:n], *no.pr.f.* Giuseppina.

Josephus [dʒou'si:fəs], *no.pr.m.* Giuseppe.

josh [dʒoʃ], *s.* (*sl.*) scherzo bonario; canzonatura.

to josh, *v.t.i.* (*sl.*) scherzare; canzonare.

josher ['dʒoʃə*], *s.* (*sl.*) burlone.

Joshua ['dʒoʃwə], *no.pr.m.* Giosuè.

Josiah [dʒou'saiə], *no.pr.m.* (*Bibbia*) Giosia.

joskin ['dʒoskin], *s.* (*sl.*) zoticone.

joss [dʒos], *s.* idolo cinese ☆ *— -house*, tempio cinese; *— -stick*, bastoncino profumato da bruciarsi nei templi cinesi.

josser ['dʒosə*], *s.* (*sl.*) **1.** sciocco **2.** individuo.

jostle ['dʒosl], *s.* forte spinta; gomitata; urto.

to jostle, *v.t.i.* **1.** spingere; dar di gomito; farsi strada a gomitate: *he went out jostling everybody*, uscì facendosi strada a gomitate **2.** investire; scontrarsi.

jot [dʒot], *s.* iota: *I don't care a —*, non me ne importa nulla.

to jot, *pass.p.p.* **jotted** ['dʒotid], *v.t.* prendere nota di: *he jotted down a few lines*, buttò giù due righe di appunti.

jotting ['dʒotiŋ], *s.* annotazione.

jougs [dʒu:gz], *s.* (*scoz.*) gogna.

joule [dʒu:l], *s.* (*elett.*) joule.

to jounce [dʒauns], *v.t.i.* scuotere; sobbalzare, far sobbalzare.

journal ['dʒə:nl], *s.* **1.** giornale; periodico; rivista **2.** diario **3.** (*mar.*) giornale di bordo **4.** (*comm.*) giornale **5.** (*mec.*) zona supportata (di albero, di perno, ecc.).

journalese [,dʒə:nə'li:z], *s.* gergo giornalistico.

journalism ['dʒə:nəlizəm], *s.* giornalismo.

journalist ['dʒə:nəlist], *s.* giornalista.

journalistic [,dʒə:nə'listik], *ag.* giornalistico.

to journalize ['dʒə:nəlaiz], *v.t.i.* **1.** (*comm.*) mettere a giornale **2.** tenere un diario **3.** fare del giornalismo.

journey ['dʒə:ni], *s.* viaggio (generalmente per terra); escursione: *the —'s end*, la fine del viaggio, *the — out,*

il viaggio di andata; *— there and back*, andata e ritorno; *a week's —*, un viaggio di una settimana; *to be on a —*, essere in viaggio; *to go on* (o *to go for*) *a —*, mettersi in viaggio; *to make* (o *to take*) *a —*, fare un viaggio ‖ *by short journeys*, a tappe ☆ *— -work*, lavoro a giornata; lavoro letterario mal retribuito.

to journey, *v.i.* fare un viaggio, viaggiare.

journeyman, *pl.* **journeymen** ['dʒə:nimən], *s.* (*st.*) **1.** operaio qualificato **2.** operaio a giornata.

joust [dʒaust], *s.* (*st.*) torneo; giostra.

to joust, *v.i.* torneare; giostrare; partecipare a un torneo.

Jove [dʒouv], *no.pr.m.* **1.** (*mit.*) Giove ‖ *by —!*, per Giove! **2.** (*astr.*) Giove.

jovial ['dʒouvjəl], *ag.* gioviale; festevole; allegro.

joviality [,dʒouvi'æliti], *s.* giovialità, gaiezza.

jovially ['dʒouvjəli], *av.* giovialmente; gaiamente.

jovialness ['dʒouvjəlnis], *s.* giovialità.

Jovian ['dʒouvjən], *ag.* di Giove; simile a Giove.

jowl¹ [dʒaul], *s.* **1.** mascella **2.** guancia ‖ *cheek by —,* vicinissimo, guancia a guancia.

jowl², *s.* **1.** gozzo **2.** giogaia (dei bovini).

jowl³, *s.* (*cuc.*) testa e parte anteriore di salmone, storione.

joy¹ [dʒoi], *s.* gioia; gaiezza; contentezza ‖ *to be beside oneself with —*, non stare in sè dalla gioia; *to jump for —*, saltare dalla gioia ☆ *— -bells*, campane a festa; *— -ride*, (*sl.*) gita in automobile (generalmente rubata); *— -stick*, (*sl.*) leva di comando di aeroplano.

to joy¹, *v.t.i.* (*poet.*) rallegrare, rallegrarsi; allietare; godere: *I — to see you so happy* (o *in your happiness*), mi rallegro della tua felicità.

Joy², *no.pr.f.* Gioia.

joyance ['dʒoiəns], *s.* (*poet.*) gioia; letizia.

joyful ['dʒoiful], *ag.* gaio; giulivo; felice; allegro.

joyfully ['dʒoifuli], *av.* gioiosamente; gaiamente; allegramente.

joyfulness ['dʒoifulnis], *s.* gioia; gaiezza, allegria.

joyless ['dʒoilis], *ag.* senza gioia, triste; mesto, cupo.

joylessly ['dʒoilisli], *av.* senza gioia, tristemente; mestamente, cupamente.

joylessness ['dʒoilisnis], *s.* tristezza; mestizia.

joyous ['dʒoiəs], *ag.* gioioso; gaio; festevole.

joyously ['dʒoiəsli], *av.* gioiosamente; gaiamente.

joyousness ['dʒoiəsnis], *s.* gioia; allegria.

jr. ['dʒu:njə*], *abbr. di* **junior**.

Juan ['dʒu(:)ən], *no.pr.m.* Giovanni ‖ *Don —*, Don Giovanni.

jubilant ['dʒu:bilənt], *ag.* giubilante; trionfante; esultante.

jubilantly ['dʒu:biləntli], *av.* con esultanza.

to jubilate ['dʒu:bileit], *v.i.* giubilare; esultare.

jubilation [,dʒu:bi'leiʃən], *s.* giubilo.

jubilee ['dʒu:bili:], *s.* **1.** giubileo: *to keep a —*, celebrare un giubileo ‖ *Diamond Jubilee*, il sessantesimo anniversario di regno (1897) della Regina Vittoria **2.** cinquantenario **3.** *fig.* giubilo; allegria ☆ *silver —*, nozze d'argento.

Judaea [dʒu:'diə], *no.pr.* (*geog. st.*) Giudea.

Judah ['dʒu:də], *no.pr.m.* Giuda.

Judaic [dʒu(:)'deiik], *ag.* giudaico, ebraico.

Judaism ['dʒu:deiizəm], *s.* giudaismo.

judaist ['dʒu:deiist], *s.* seguace delle dottrine giudaiche.

to judaize ['dʒu:deiaiz], *v.t.i.* seguire, rendere conforme a costumi, riti giudaici.

Judas ['dʒu:dəs], **Jude** [dʒu:d], *no.pr.m.* Giuda ‖ *— Iscariot*, Giuda Iscariota ‖ *— Maccabaeus*, Giuda Maccabeo ☆ *— kiss*, bacio di Giuda; *— tree*, (*bot.*) albero di Giuda.

Judean [dʒu:'diən], *ag. s.c.* (abitante) della Giudea.

judge [dʒʌdʒ], *s.* **1.** giudice ‖ *Judge-Advocate-General*, (*amer.*) presidente del Tribunale militare di Cassazione; *— of Appeal*, presidente della Corte di Appello o di Cassazione ‖ *Judges*, « Giudici » (libro del Vecchio Testamento) **2.** arbitro: — *at a flower show*, membro della giuria di una mostra di fiori **3.** conoscitore, intenditore: *I am not a good* — *of wine*, non sono un conoscitore di vini.

to **judge**, *v.t.i.* **1.** fare da giudice; giudicare: *I will* — *him by his deeds*, lo giudicherò dai suoi atti; *to* — *by* (o *from*) *appearances*, giudicare dalle apparenze **2.** considerare, supporre, stimare: *we judged it better to accept*, abbiamo considerato fosse meglio accettare.

judgement [ˈdʒʌdʒmənt], *s.* **1.** giudizio ‖ *the Day of Judgement*, il Giorno del Giudizio; *the Last Judgement*, il Giudizio finale **2.** sentenza; decisione; verdetto: *the* — *against him*, la sentenza contraria a lui; *to pass*, *give*, *deliver* — *on*, pronunziare una sentenza, un giudizio su **3.** punizione divina (anche *scherz.*): *it is a* — *on you*, è un castigo di Dio per te **4.** parere, giudizio: *in my* —, a mio giudizio, secondo me, a parer mio **5.** discernimento: *excellent* — *in choosing*, eccellente discernimento nella scelta ☆ — *-hall*, aula di tribunale; — *-seat*, banco dei giudici; tribunale.

judgeship [ˈdʒʌdʒʃip], *s.* carica di giudice.

judgment, *V.* **judgement.**

judicable [ˈdʒuːdikəbl], *ag.* che deve essere giudicato, giudicabile.

judicatory [ˈdʒuːdikətəri], *ag.* giudiziario, concernente un giudizio; che offre una base per un giudizio ‖ *s.* (*scoz.*) tribunale.

judicature [ˈdʒuːdikətʃə*], *s.* giustizia; giurisdizione ‖ *Supreme Court of Judicature*, Corte Suprema di Giustizia.

judicial [dʒu(ː)ˈdiʃəl], *ag.* **1.** giudiziale; giudiziario; giuridico **2.** imparziale ☆ — *assembly*, assemblea di giudizio; — *murder*, delitto giudiziario; — *separation*, separazione legale.

judicially [dʒu(ː)ˈdiʃəli], *av.* **1.** giudizialmente; giuridicamente **2.** imparzialmente **3.** con discernimento.

judiciary [dʒu(ː)ˈdiʃəri], *ag.* giudiziario ‖ *s.* magistratura.

judicious [dʒu(ː)ˈdiʃəs], *ag.* giudizioso; prudente.

judiciously [dʒu(ː)ˈdiʃəsli], *av.* giudiziosamente; prudentemente.

judiciousness [dʒu(ː)ˈdiʃəsnis], *s.* assennatezza; prudenza.

Judith [ˈdʒuːdiθ], *no.pr.f.* Giuditta.

judo [ˈdʒuːdou], *s.* « judo » (lotta giapponese).

Judy [ˈdʒuːdi], *no.pr.f.* Giuditta ‖ *Punch and* —, Pulcinella e sua moglie.

jug¹ [dʒʌg], *s.* **1.** boccale: *a* — *of ale*, un boccale di birra ‖ *Toby* —, boccale caratteristico (di ceramica figurata) **2.** brocca; bricco; caraffa; anfora: *a* — *of water*, una brocca d'acqua **3.** (*sl.*) prigione ☆ *milk-* —, lattiera; *water-* —, brocca per l'acqua.

to **jug¹**, *pass.p.p.* **jugged** [dʒʌgd], *v.t.* **1.** (*cuc.*) brasare, cuocere in salmì: *jugged hare*, lepre in salmì **2.** (*sl.*) imprigionare, mettere in gattabuia.

jug², *s.* nota di uccello (specialmente usignolo).

to **jug²**, *v.i.* cantare di uccello (specialmente usignolo).

jugate [ˈdʒuːgit], *ag.* (*bot.*) che ha foglioline disposte a coppia.

juger [ˈdʒuːdʒə*], *pl.* **jugers** [ˈdʒuːdʒəz]; **jugerum** [ˈdʒuːdʒərəm], *pl.* **jugera** [ˈdʒuːdʒərə], *s.* (*agr. st.*) iugero (misura di superficie = are 25,2).

juggins [ˈdʒʌginz], *s.* (*sl.*) semplicione.

juggle [ˈdʒʌgl], *s.* **1.** giuoco di prestigio, di destrezza **2.** *fig.* truffa, raggiro.

to **juggle**, *v.t.i.* **1.** fare il prestigiatore, fare giuochi di destrezza **2.** *fig.* truffare; svisare (i fatti).

juggler [ˈdʒʌglə*], *s.* **1.** giocoliere **2.** impostore.

jugglery [ˈdʒʌgləri], *s.* **1.** giuoco di prestigio **2.** *fig.* truffa, raggiro.

juggling [ˈdʒʌgliŋ], *ag.* **1.** di giocoliere **2.** *fig.* raggiratore ‖ *s.* *V.* **jugglery.**

jugglingly [ˈdʒʌgliŋli], *av.* con inganno, con raggiri.

Jugoslav [ˈjuːgouˈslɑːv], *ag.* iugoslavo ‖ *s.c.* iugoslavo, iugoslava ‖ *s.* lingua iugoslava.

Jugoslavia [ˈjuːgouˈslɑːvjə], *no.pr.* (*geog.*) Iugoslavia.

jugular [ˈdʒʌgjulə*], *ag.s.* (*anat.*) giugulare: *the* — *veins*, le vene giugulari.

to **jugulate** [ˈdʒuːgjuleit], *v.t.* giugulare, scannare.

juice [dʒuːs], *s.* **1.** succo (di frutta, ecc.) **2.** (*anat.*) succo gastrico **3.** (*sl.*) benzina; elettricità.

juiceless [ˈdʒuːslis], *ag.* senza succo.

juiciness [ˈdʒuːsinis], *s.* succosità.

juicy [ˈdʒuːsi], *ag.* **1.** sugoso, succoso **2.** piovoso, umido (di tempo) **3.** interessante; vivace; piccante.

ju-jitsu [dʒuːˈdʒitsuː], *s.* « ju-jitsu » (lotta giapponese).

jujube [ˈdʒuːdʒuː(ː)b], *s.* **1.** (*bot.*) giuggiola **2.** (*fam.*) giuggiola, pasticca di gomma ☆ — *-tree*, giuggiolo.

juke-box [ˈdʒuːkbɔks], *s.* (*sl. amer.*) « juke-box » (grammofono automatico a gettoni).

julep [ˈdʒuːlep], *s.* **1.** (*farm.*) giulebbe **2.** bibita alcoolica con ghiaccio ☆ *mint* —, bibita alla menta.

Julia [ˈdʒuːljə], *no.pr.f.* Giulia.

Julian¹ [ˈdʒuːljən], *ag.* giuliano, relativo a Giulio Cesare: — *Calendar*, calendario giuliano ‖ (*the*) — *Alps*, (le) Alpi Giulie.

Julian², *no.pr.m.* (*st.*) Giuliano.

Juliana [ˌdʒuːliˈɑːnə], *no.pr.f.* Giuliana.

Juliet [ˈdʒuːljət], *no.pr.f.* Giulietta.

Julius [ˈdʒuːljəs], *no.pr.m.* (*st.*) Giulio.

July [dʒuː(ː)ˈlai], *s.* luglio.

jumart [ˈdʒuːmɑːt], *s.* (*mit.*) ippotoro.

jumbal [ˈdʒuːmbl], *s.* ciambella.

jumble¹ [ˈdʒʌmbl], *s.* **1.** guazzabuglio, miscuglio **2.** scossone **3.** (*fam.*) gita in carrozza ☆ — *-sale*, vendita di merci varie per beneficenza; — *-shop*, bazar.

to **jumble¹**, *v.t.i.* mescolare; confondere; mettere alla rinfusa; mescolarsi (confusamente).

jumble², *s.* ciambella.

jumblingly [ˈdʒʌmbliŋli], *av.* confusamente.

jumbo [ˈdʒʌmbou], *s.* colosso; persona grossa e goffa; *fig.* elefante.

jump [dʒʌmp], *s.* **1.** salto, balzo; scarto; sussulto **2.** salto, balzo (dei prezzi) **3.** *pl.* (*fam. patol.*) delirium tremens ☆ *long* —, (*spor.*) salto in lungo; *running* —, salto con rincorsa; *standing* —, salto.

to **jump**, *v.t.i.* **1.** saltare, superare con un salto; scavalcare; passar sopra; passare al di là ‖ *to* — *from the frying pan into the fire*, cadere dalla padella nella brace ‖ *to* — *the track*, (*ferr.*) deragliare **2.** far saltare (*p.e.* un bimbo sulle ginocchia) **3.** trasalire, sussultare ‖ *to* — *out of one's skin*, fare un salto (per la paura, per la gioia) **4.** fare un salto (di prezzi), rincarare: *prices have jumped* (*up*) *five shillings*, i prezzi hanno subito un aumento di cinque scellini **5.** *fig.* saltare: *to* — *to conclusions*, arrivare troppo presto a delle conclusioni **6.** (*bridge*) saltare; (*dama*) mangiare **7.** (*sl.*) attaccare; prendere di sorpresa ‖ *to* — *a claim*, usurpare i diritti di qlcu. su un terreno **8.** *to* — *at* (*sthg.*), precipitarsi a, su: *to* — *at an offer*, accettare un'offerta con entusiasmo **9.** *to* — *on* (*s.o.*), (*fam.*) sgridare **10.** *to* — *about*, essere sempre in moto **11.** *to* — *in*, saltar dentro **12.** *to* — *off*, (*mil.*) iniziare un attacco.

jumper¹ [ˈdʒʌmpə*], *s.* **1.** (*relig.*) membro di setta metodista gallese, il cui rituale includeva dei balzi **2.** saltatore ☆ *counter-* —, (*fam. spreg.*) bottegaio.

jumper², *s.* **1.** camiciotto da marinaio **2.** maglione; casacchina (da donna, da infilarsi dalla testa).

jumpiness [ˈdʒʌmpinis], *s.* nervosismo.

jumping [ˈdʒʌmpiŋ], *ag.* saltatore ☆ — *board*, trampolino; — *-deer*, varietà di cervo del Nord America; — *-jack*, fantoccio legato a un elastico; — *-off -place*, (*amer.*) l'estremo limite del mondo civile.

jumpy [ˈdʒʌmpi], *ag.* nervoso, eccitato.

juncaceous [dʒʌŋˈkeiʃəs], *ag.* giuncaceo.

junction [ˈdʒʌŋkʃən], *s.* **1.** congiunzione, punto di riunione 2. nodo ferroviario ‖ *Clapham* —, nodo di Clapham (il più importante a sud di Londra).

juncture ['dʒʌŋktʃə*], *s.* **1.** (*anat.*) articolazione **2.** *fig.* congiuntura; frangente, momento critico: *at this* —, in questo frangente.

juncus ['dʒʌŋkəs], *s.* giunco.

June [dʒu:n], *s.* giugno.

jungle ['dʒʌŋgl], *s.* giungla.

jungli ['dʒʌŋgli], *ag.* indigeno ‖ *s.* indigeno, abitante della giungla.

jungly ['dʒʌŋgli], *ag.* della giungla.

junior ['dʒu:njə*], *ag.* **1.** minore, di secondaria importanza **2.** (*abbr. jun. jr.*) cadetto; iuniore **3.** il più giovane (di due fratelli, a scuola): *Brown* —, il fratello minore di *Brown senior* ‖ *s.* chi è più giovane, chi ha posizione, grado inferiore: *he is my* —, è più giovane di me ☆ — *partner*, (*comm.*) socio giovane.

juniorate ['dʒu:njərit], *s.* corso biennale che precede l'ammissione al sacerdozio (nella Compagnia di Gesù).

juniority [,dʒu:ni'ɔriti], *s.* minorità.

juniper ['dʒu:nipə*], *s.* (*bot.*) ginepro.

Junius ['dʒu:njəs], *no.pr.m.* Giunio.

junk[1] ['dʒʌŋk], *s.* **1.** gomena vecchia tagliata per farne stoppa **2.** (*mar.*) carne salata **3.** avanzo; rifiuto ☆ — *-bottle*, (*amer.*) bottiglia di vetro spesso verde o nero; — *-dealer*, (*arc.*) negoziante di articoli marinareschi; — *-ring*, (*mec.*) anello di guarnizione; — *-shop*, (*arc.*) negozio di utensili marinareschi.

to **junk**[1], *v.t.* **1.** ridurre a stoppa **2.** scartare.

junk[2], *s.* (*mar.*) giunca.

junket ['dʒʌŋkit], *s.* **1.** (*cuc.*) giuncata **2.** festa; banchetto **3.** escursione; picnic.

to **junket**, *v.t.* **1.** banchettare **2.** fare un'escursione.

junketing ['dʒʌŋkitiŋ], *s.* festa; banchetto.

Juno ['dʒu:nou], *no.pr.f.* (*mit.*) Giunone ‖ *s. fig.* donna maestosa.

Junoesque [,dʒu:nou'esk], *ag.* giunonico.

junta ['dʒʌntə], *s.* (*amm.*) giunta (in Spagna e Italia).

junto ['dʒʌntou], *pl.* **juntos** ['dʒʌntouz], *s.* fazione; lega.

jupe [ʒu:p], *s.* gonna.

Jupiter ['dʒu:pitə*], *no.pr.m.* (*mit. astr.*) Giove.

jural ['dʒuərəl], *ag.* giuridico, legale.

jurassic [dʒu'ræsik], *ag.* (*geol.*) giurassico.

jurat ['dʒuəræt], *s.* **1.** funzionario pubblico **2.** magistrato delle isole normanne.

juridic(al) [dʒuə'ridikəl], *ag.* giuridico: — *regulation*, disciplina giuridica.

juridically [dʒuə'ridikəli], *av.* giuridicamente.

jurisconsult ['dʒuəriskən,sʌlt], *s.* giurista, giureconsulto.

jurisdiction [,dʒuəris'dikʃən], *s.* giurisdizione.

jurisdictional [,dʒuəris'dikʃənl], *ag.* giurisdizionale.

jurisprudence ['dʒuəris,pru:dəns], *s.* giurisprudenza.

jurisprudent ['dʒuəris,pru:dənt], *ag.* pratico della legge ‖ *s.* giurisperito, giurisprudente.

jurisprudential [,dʒuərispru(:)'denʃəl], *ag.* legale, relativo alla giurisprudenza.

jurist ['dʒuərist], *s.* giurista.

juristic(al) [dʒuə'ristik(əl)], *ag.* giuristico, giuridico.

juror ['dʒuərə*], *s.* giurato, membro della giuria.

jury ['dʒuəri], *s.* giuria, giurì: *the foreman of a* —, il presidente della giuria; *to be* (*up*)*on the* —, essere membro della giuria ☆ — *-box*, banco della giuria.

juryman, *pl.* **jurymen** ['dʒuərimən], *s.* giurato.

jurymast ['dʒuərimɑ:st], *s.* (*mar.*) albero di fortuna.

jus [dʒʌs], *s.* il diritto.

jussive ['dʒʌsiv], *ag.* (*gram.*) imperativo.

just [dʒʌst], *ag.* **1.** giusto; onesto; retto; imparziale, equo: *to be* — *to s.o.*, essere giusto verso qlcu **2.** dovuto, debito; corretto; preciso: — *proportions*, giuste proporzioni; — *resentment*, giusto risentimento **3.** adeguato; meritato: *a* — *reward*, una giusta ricompensa.

just, *av.* **1.** proprio; esattamente; appunto: — *in the nick of time*, proprio al momento buono, giusto in

tempo; — *now*, proprio ora; — *so*, proprio così; — *then*, proprio allora; — *as we came in*, proprio mentre entravamo; — *to please me*, proprio per farmi piacere; *it is* —, (*fam.*) è proprio splendido **2.** soltanto, solamente, appena: — *enough*, appena abbastanza; — *in case*, nel caso che; — *a little*, soltanto un pochino; — *a moment, please*, un momento, per favore; — *one*, soltanto uno; — *listen to him!*, ma statelo a sentire!; — *to see her*, soltanto per vederla **3.** or ora: *he has* — *gone out*, è uscito or ora.

(to) **just**, *V.* (to) **joust**.

justice ['dʒʌstis], *s.* **1.** (*dir.*) giustizia: *the robber was brought to* —, il ladro fu processato e condannato **2.** giustizia, imparzialità: *we must do* — *to him*, dobbiamo rendergli giustizia **2.** giudice, magistrato ‖ *Justice of the Peace*, Giudice di Pace ‖ *Chief Justice, Lord Chief Justice*, Presidente della Corte; *Mr. Justice Lavin*, il signor giudice Lavin.

justiceship ['dʒʌstisʃip], *s.* magistratura.

justiciable [dʒʌs'tiʃiəbl], *ag.* processabile.

justiciar [dʒʌs'tiʃiɑ:*], *s.* (*st.*) alto funzionario, giudice.

justiciary [dʒʌs'tiʃiəri], *ag.* giudiziario ‖ *s.* giudice; (*st.*) alto funzionario, giudice.

justifiability [,dʒʌstifaiə'biliti], *V.* **justifiableness**.

justifiable ['dʒʌstifaiəbl], *ag.* giustificabile; legittimo ☆ — *homicide*, omicidio per legittima difesa.

justifiableness ['dʒʌstifaiəblnis], *s.* legittimità (di difesa).

justifiably ['dʒʌstifaiəbli], *av.* in modo giustificabile; legittimamente.

justification [,dʒʌstifi'keiʃən], *s.* **1.** giustificazione **2.** (*tip.*) allineamento.

justificative ['dʒʌstifikeitiv], *ag.* giustificativo.

justificator ['dʒʌstifikeitə*], *s.* **1.** giustificatore, difensore **2.** vendicatore.

justificatory ['dʒʌstifikeitəri], *ag.* giustificativo.

justifier ['dʒʌstifaiə*], *s.c.* giustificatore, giustificatrice.

to **justify** ['dʒʌstifai], *v.t.* **1.** (*dir.*) giustificare; difendere; perdonare; assolvere **2.** (*teol.*) assolvere, rimettere i peccati a **3.** (*tip.*) allineare.

justifying ['dʒʌstifaiiŋ], *ag.* giustificante.

Justin ['dʒʌstin], *no.pr.m.* Giustino.

Justina [dʒʌs'tainə], *no.pr.f.* Giustina.

Justinian [dʒʌs'tiniən], *no.pr.m.* (*st.*) Giustiniano.

to **justle** ['dʒʌsl], *V.* to **jostle**.

justly ['dʒʌstli], *av.* giustamente; esattamente; rettamente; a buon diritto.

justness ['dʒʌstnis], *s.* **1.** giustizia **2.** precisione, esattezza.

Justus ['dʒʌstəs], *no.pr.m.* Giusto.

jut [dʒʌt], *s.* sporgenza ☆ — *-window*, finestra sporgente, ad aggetto.

to **jut**, *pass.p.p.* **jutted** ['dʒʌtid], *v.i.* **1.** sporgersi, protendersi **2.** (*edil.*) aggettare.

Jute[1] [dʒu:t], *s.c.* (*st.*) iuto (della tribù degli iuti).

jute[2], *s.* iuta (pianta e fibra).

jutting ['dʒʌtiŋ], *ag.* sporgente, aggettante.

juttingly ['dʒʌtiŋli], *av.* con sporgenza, con aggetto.

to **jutty** ['dʒʌti], *v.i.* (*edil.*) aggettare.

Juvenal ['dʒu:vinl], *no.pr.m.* (*st. lett.*) Giovenale.

juvenescence [,dʒu:vi'nesns], *s.* adolescenza.

juvenescent [,dʒu:vi'nesnt], *ag.* adolescente.

juvenile ['dʒu:vinail], *ag.* giovane, giovanile ‖ *s.* **1.** giovane, ragazzo **2.** *pl.* libri per ragazzi ☆ — *court*, tribunale dei minorenni; — *offender*, imputato minorenne.

juvenilely ['dʒu:vinailli], *av.* giovanilmente.

juvenileness ['dʒu:vinailnis], *V.* **juvenility**.

juvenilia [,dʒu:vi'niliə], *s.pl.* opere giovanili (di un autore).

juvenility [,dʒu:vi'niliti], *s.* giovinezza, aspetto giovanile.

to **juxtapose** ['dʒʌkstəpouz], *v.t.* affiancare.

juxtaposition [,dʒʌkstəpə'ziʃən], *s.* l'affiancare, il mettere a contatto: *in* —, contiguo, a contatto.

K

k [kei], *pl.* ks, k's [keiz], *s.* (*undicesima lettera del-l'alfabeto inglese*) k ‖ — *for king*, (*tel.*) k come kursaal.

kaaba ['kɑːbə], *s.* (*relig. islamica*) caaba, caba.

kaama ['kɑːmə], *s.* (*zool.*) antilope del Sud Africa.

kab(b)ala [kə'bɑːlə], *s.* cabala.

Kabyle [kə'bail], *s.c.* berbero, berbera della Tunisia, dell'Algeria ‖ *s.* dialetto berbero.

kaddish ['kædiʃ], *s.* (*relig. ebraica*) «kaddish» (preghiera per i defunti).

kadi ['kɑːdi], *s.* cadì.

Kaffir ['kæfə*], *ag.* cafro ‖ *s.c.* 1. cafro, cafra 2. nativo, nativa del Kafiristan (in Asia) ‖ *s. pl.* azioni delle miniere sudafricane.

kafila ['kɑːfilə], *s.* cafila (carovana araba).

Kafir, *V.* Kaffir.

kago ['kɑːgou], *s.* palanchino giapponese in vimini.

kail [keil], *s.* (*bot.*) cavolo riccio ‖ — -*yard school*, gruppo di narratori fine '800 che descrissero, spesso servendosi di forme dialettali, la vita rurale scozzese ☆ — -*yard*, orto; *Scotch* —, (zuppa di) cavolo rosso.

kainite ['kainait], *s.* (*min.*) kainite.

kaiser ['kaizə*], *s.* « kaiser » (titolo dell'imperatore di Germania).

kaiserism ['kaizərizəm], *s.* imperialismo prussiano.

kajawah [kə'dʒɑːwə], *s.* (*ang.-in.*) lettiga per donne portata a dorso di cammello.

kaka ['kɑːkə], *s.* (*ornit.*) nestore.

kakapo ['kɑːkəpou], *s.* (*ornit.*) strigope.

kakemono [,kæki'mounou], *s.* « kakemono » (pittura giapponese su seta).

kaki ['kɑːki], *s.* 1. (*bot.*) kaki 2. color kaki.

kakistocracy [,kækis'tɔkrəsi], *s.* governo dei cittadini peggiori.

kalaazar ['kɑːlɑːɑː'zɑː*], *s.* violenta febbre malarica di genere tropicale.

kale, *V.* kail.

kaleidophone [kə'laidəfoun], *s.* caleidofonio.

kaleidoscope [kə'laidəskoup], *s.* caleidescopio.

kaleidoscopical [kə,laidə'skɔpikəl], *ag.* caleidoscopico.

kaleidoscopically [kə,laidə'skɔpikəli], *av.* come un caleidoscopio.

kalends ['kælendz], *s.pl.* calende.

kali ['kæli], *s.* (*bot.*) cali.

Kalmuck ['kælmʌk], *ag.* calmucco ‖ *s.c.* calmucco, calmucca ‖ *s.* 1. lingua dei calmucchi 2. (*ind. tessile*) calmucco, pannolana.

kalong ['kɑːlɔŋ], *s.* (*zool.*) pteropo.

Kama ['kɑːmə], *s.* dio indù dell'amore.

Kamerun ['kæməruːn], *no.pr.* (*geog.*) Camerun.

kami ['kɑːmi], *s.* 1. « kami » (titolo nobiliare giapponese) 2. divinità (nello scintoismo).

kampong ['kɑːmpɔŋ], *s.* villaggio malese.

Kanaka ['kænəkə], *s.* 1. havaiano 2. indigeno bracciante in Australia.

kangaroo [,kæŋgə'ruː], *s.* 1. canguro 2. *pl.* (*sl.*) azioni, azionisti delle miniere australiane ☆ — -*rat*, piccolo marsupiale australiano; — -*thorn*, (*bot.*) acacia armata.

Kantian ['kæntiən], *ag.* kantiano.

Kantism ['kæntizəm], *s.* (*fil.*) kantismo.

Kantist ['kæntist], *s.* kantista.

kaolin ['keiəlin], *s.* (*min.*) caolino.

kapok ['keipɔk], *s.* capoc.

kappa ['kæpə], *s.* cappa (lettera dell'alfabeto greco).

kaput [kɑː'puːt], *ag.* (*sl.*) «kaput», disfatto; finito.

karma ['kɑːmə], *s.* (*relig. buddista*) «karma» (il complesso delle azioni di un individuo in uno dei successivi periodi della sua esistenza).

kaross [kə'rɔs], *s.* mantello di pelli d'animali usato dagli indigeni del Sud Africa.

karroo [kə'ruː], *s.* altipiano desertico a fondo argilloso (nel Sud Africa).

kartel ['kɑːtl], *s.* letto in legno nei vagoni per bestiame del Sud Africa.

karting ['kɑːtiŋ], *s.* kartismo (lo sport del «go-kart»).

Kashmir [kæʃ'miə*], *no.pr.* (*geog.*) Cachemire.

Kashmiri [kæʃ'miəri], *s.c.* nativo, nativa del Cachemire ‖ *s.* lingua del Cachemire.

katabasis [kə'tæbəsis], *s.* catabasi.

katabolism [kə'tæbəlizəm], *s.* (*biol.*) catabolismo.

Kate [keit], *no.pr.f. dim.* di Katharina.

Katharina [,kæθə'riːnə], Katharine, Katherine ['kæθərin], Kathleen [kæθ'liːn], *no.pr.f.* Caterina.

kathode ['kæθoud], *s.* (*elett.*) catodo.

Katie ['keiti], *no.pr.f. dim.* di Katherine.

katydid ['keitidid], *s.* (*entom.*) grossa cavalletta verde (comune in America).

kauri, kaury ['kauri], *s.* (*bot.*) « kauri ».

kava ['kɑːvə], *s.* 1. (*bot.*) «kava» 2. bevanda fatta con la «kava».

kavass [kə'vɑːs], *s.* 1. gendarme turco, guardia 2. messaggero turco.

Kay [kei], *no.pr.f. dim.* di Katharina.

kayak ['kaiæk], *s.* caiacco (canoa esquimese).

kea ['keiə], *s.* (*ornit.*) nestore.

keb [keb], *s.* (*scoz.*) pecora che ha abortito.

keck [kek], *s.* (*sl.*) conato di vomito.

to keck, *v.i.* 1. (*sl.*) avere nausea, conati di vomito 2. *fig.* provar disgusto 3. to — at (*sthg.*), rigettare.

keckle ['kekl], *V.* cackle.

kedge [kedʒ], *s.* (*mar.*) ancorotto.

to kedge, *v.t.i.* (*mar.*) tonneggiare.

kedgeree [,kedʒə'riː], *s.* « kedgeree » (pietanza indiana di riso, uova, cipolle e aromi).

keech [kiːtʃ], *s.* (*sl.*) pezzo di grasso congelato.

keek [kiːk], *s.* (*scoz.*) atto dello spiare.

to keek, *v.i.* (*scoz.*) spiare.

keel[1] [kiːl], *s.* 1. (*mar.*) chiglia, carena 2. (*poet.*) nave ☆ — -*block*, (*mar.*) taccata; — *line*, (*mar.*) linea di chiglia ‖ *false* —, (*mar.*) sotto-chiglia.

to keel[1], *v.t.i.* (*mar.*) 1. carenare 2. to — over, rovesciare, rovesciarsi; *fig.* sconvolgere (persone, ecc.).

keel[2], *s.* chiatta (per il trasporto del carbone).

to keelhaul ['kiːlhɔːl], *v.t.* 1. (*mar.*) rinchiudere (un marinaio) nella cala (per punizione) 2. strapazzare, rimproverare aspramente (un dipendente).

keeling ['kiːliŋ], *s.* (*scoz.*) merluzzo.

Keeling Islands ['kiːliŋ'ailəndz], *no.pr.pl.* (*geog.*) Isole Cocos.

keelman, keelmen ['kiːlmən], *s.* chi trasporta il carbone su chiatte.

keelson ['kelsn], *s.* (*mar.*) paramezzale; controchiglia.

keen[1] [kiːn], *ag.* 1. aguzzo, acuminato; affilato, tagliente: *a* — *razor*, un rasoio affilato 2. pungente, vivo, penetrante (di freddo, aria, ecc.); acuto (di suono) 3. vivo, forte, intenso: *a* — *appetite*, un appetito vorace; *a* — *disappointment*, una forte delusione; — *satire*, satira mordace; *a — sorrow*, un amaro dolore 4. appassionato, accanito: *a — golfer*, un appassionato del golf; *they are — competitors*, si fanno una concorrenza spietata; *to be — on sthg.*, essere entusiasta, appassionato di ql.co. ‖ *— us mustard*, *(fam.)* entusiasta 5. perspicace, sottile; acuto, penetrante (di sguardo); fine (d'orecchio): *a — intelligence*, un'intelligenza acuta; *to have a — ear*, avere l'orecchio fine ‖ *to have a — eye for a bargain*, avere il senso degli affari, aver buon naso per gli affari 6. avido: *— on truth*, assetato di verità 7. minimo, di concorrenza (di prezzi) ☆ *— -edged*, tagliente, ben affilato; *— -eyed*, dalla vista acuta; perspicace; *— -scented*, dall'olfatto fine (di cane da caccia); *— -set*, affamato; *— -sighted*, dalla vista acuta.

keen², *s.* *(irl.)* lamento funebre.

to **keen²**, *v.t.i.* *(irl.)* cantare un lamento funebre; lamentarsi dolorosamente; piangere (un morto) con lamenti funebri.

keener ['ki:nǝ*], *s.* prefica, lamentatrice.

keenly ['ki:nli], *av.* 1. in modo penetrante, pungente 2. dolorosamente, profondamente 3. vivamente, aspramente: *— disputed point*, questione vivamente discussa 4. con acume, perspicacia 5. avidamente: *to listen —*, ascoltare avidamente 6. *(comm.)* al minimo: *to quote —*, ridurre i prezzi al minimo.

keenness ['ki:nnis], *s.* 1. sottigliezza (di lama, ecc.) 2. intensità, rigore (di freddo, ecc.) 3. ardore, zelo, passione; intensità: *— on doing sthg.*, vivo desiderio di fare ql.co. 4. acume, perspicacia; acutezza (di vista); finezza (di udito).

keep [ki:p], *s.* 1. sostentamento, mantenimento: *to earn one's —*, guadagnare da vivere, mantenersi 2. torrione, maschio (di castello); *(fam.)* prigione, gattabuia 3. *for keeps*, *(sl.)* sempre, per sempre; per davvero 4. *(mec.)* cappello.

to **keep**, *pass.p.p.* **kept** [kept], *v.t.i.* 1. tenere; mantenere, conservare, custodire: *do you want to — the drinks for later?*, vuoi tenere le bibite per più tardi!?; *she keeps her jewels under lock and key*, tiene i gioielli sotto chiave; *you may — this*, puoi tenerlo; *to — one's balance*, mantenersi in equilibrio (anche *fig.*); *to — one's way*, proseguire per la propria strada; *to — peace*, mantenere la buona armonia; *to — the peace*, mantenere l'ordine pubblico, la pace; *to — s.o. spellbound*, *fig.* tenere qlcu. avvinto; *to — s.o. waiting, standing*, fare aspettare qlcu., tenere qlcu. in piedi; *to — sthg. in mind*, tenere a mente ql.co.; *to — sthg. to oneself*, tenere ql.co. per sè; *to — time*, *(mus.)* tenere il tempo ‖ *— your head*, non perdere la testa ‖ *to — bad hours*, far tardi (la sera) ‖ *to — the ball rolling*, *fig.* tener viva la conversazione ‖ *to — good, bad time*, funzionare bene, male (di orologio) ‖ *to — to the house*, restare in casa ‖ *to — one's bed*, stare, essere costretto a letto ‖ *to — one's countenance*, controllarsi, mantenersi calmo, serio ‖ *to — one's ground*, tener duro, non cedere ‖ *to — one's temper*, non adirarsi ‖ *to — oneself to oneself*, starsene per proprio conto ‖ *to — open house*, tener corte bandita, essere molto ospitale ‖ *to — track of s.o.*, non perdere di vista qlcu.; *(fam.)* seguire il progresso di qlcu.; *to — track of sthg.*, seguire il corso (di ql.co.) ‖ *to — watch (o an eye) on*, tener d'occhio 2. mantenere; esercire, gestire; amministrare: *he has a large family to —*, deve mantenere una famiglia numerosa; *he keeps four servants and two cars*, ha quattro domestici e due macchine; *she keeps house for him*, gli tiene la casa; *to — the books*, *(comm.)* tenere la contabilità; *to — oneself in clothes, in food*, pagarsi il vestiario, il vitto; *to — a shop*, esercire un negozio 3. tenere, trattenere: *he kept me late*, mi ha trattenuto fino a tardi; *I kept him for dinner*, lo trattenni a pranzo; *nothing keeps me in Italy*, non c'è nulla che mi trattenga in Italia 4. osservare, rispettare, tener fede a: *to — the Commandments*, osservare i Comandamenti; *to — the law*, rispettare la legge; *to — one's word*, mantenere la parola 5. festeggiare, cele-

brare: *to — Christmas*, festeggiare il Natale; *to — one's birthday*, festeggiare il proprio compleanno 6. vigilare, custodire; proteggere; *(mil.)* difendere: *God — you!*, Dio ti protegga!; *to — the goal*, *(spor.)* difendere la rete 7. stare, restare: *— where you are*, rimani dove sei; *to — afloat*, galleggiare; *to — aloof*, tenersi in disparte, non immischiarsi; *to — awake*, star sveglio; *to — cool*, *fig.* mantenersi calmo; *to — fit*, mantenersi in forma; *to — in touch with s.o.*, tenersi in contatto con qlcu.; *to — on good terms with s.o.*, mantenersi in buoni rapporti con qlcu.; *to — quiet*, restar tranquillo; *to — standing*, stare in piedi; *to — well (o in good health)*, mantenersi in buona salute 8. (I) continuare: *— along the river*, segui la riva del fiume; *to — at work (o working)*, continuare il lavoro; *to — doing sthg.*, continuare a, non smettere di fare ql.co. 9. vendere: *do you — the ''Times'' ?*, avete il «Times»? 10. conservarsi (di cibo): *eggs don't — long*, le uova non si conservano a lungo 11. *to — from (doing)*, impedire di; trattenersi da: *— him from running away*, impedisci gli di scappare; *I couldn't — from laughing*, non potei trattenermi dal ridere 12. *to — off (sthg.)*, evitare ‖ *— off the grass*, è vietato calpestare l'erba 13. *to — to (sthg.)*, attenersi a: *he keeps to a strict diet*, egli si attiene a una dieta rigorosa; *to — to the left, right*, tenere la sinistra, la destra ‖ *to — to the north*, dirigersi verso il nord 14. *to — away*, tener(si) lontano: *— away from here*, sta' lontano da qui 15. *to — back*, tenere indietro, trattenere; tenersi indietro; svisare (fatti); celare (la verità): *— back!*, sta' indietro!; *to — back one's tears*, trattenere le lagrime 16. *to — behind*, tenere, stare indietro 17. *to — down*, tenere, stare giù; contenere, reprimere; mantenere basso (un prezzo) 18. *to — in*, tenere chiuso, rinchiuso (in casa, ecc.); restare in casa; trattenere, contenere (sentimenti, ecc.); mantenere vivo (un fuoco); *to — a pupil in*, trattenere a scuola un allievo (per punizione) ‖ *to — one's hand in*, tenersi in esercizio 19. *to — off*, tener lontano; tenersi lontano, in disparte 20. *to — on* (I), continuare, proseguire, andare avanti; continuare a tenere: *— your hat on*, non toglierti il cappello; *the dog keeps on barking*, il cane non fa che abbaiare; *don't — on saying the same things over and over again*, non ripetere sempre le stesse cose; *she kept her old servant on*, continuò a tenere il suo vecchio servitore ‖ *to — on at s.o.*, *(fam.)* molestare, tormentare qlcu. 21. *to — out*, non lasciar entrare, passare; tenersi lontano, al di fuori: *these shoes don't — out the wet*, queste scarpe non sono impermeabili ‖ *— out of danger!*, stai lontano dal pericolo!; *to — out of a quarrel*, non immischiarsi in una disputa 22. *to — together*, unire, tenere insieme; restare uniti, insieme 23. *to — under*, tenere a freno (passioni); tenere sottomesso (un popolo); domare (un incendio) 24. *to — up*, tenere su, sostenere; tenere alto, diritto; conservare; mantenere; mantenere efficiente; continuare; tenere, rimanere alzato: *— up your courage*, non scoraggiarti; *he kept me up all night*, mi fece stare alzato tutta la notte; *you should — up your Italian*, dovresti mantenerti in esercizio con l'italiano ‖ *to — one's end up*, non scoraggiarsi ‖ *to — up appearances*, salvare le apparenze ‖ *to — up with s.o.*, mantenere i rapporti con qlcu.; stare al passo con qlcu.

keeper ['ki:pǝ*], *s.* 1. guardiano, custode, sorvegliante; intendente: *— of a prison*, carceriere ‖ *Keeper of the Great Seal*, Guardasigilli 2. ferma-anello 3. *(elett.)* àncora; armatura 4. frutto, cibo che si mantiene ☆ *boarding-house —*, padrone, padrona di una pensione; *lighthouse- —*, guardiano del faro.

keeping ['ki:piŋ], *s.* 1. guardia, sorveglianza: *in safe —*, sotto sicura custodia 2. mantenimento; conservazione 3. osservanza (di regole); adempimento (di promesse) 4. incombenza, ufficio, carica 5. armonia, accordo: *to be in, out of — with*, essere, non essere in armonia con: *his acts are out of — with his promises*, le sue azioni mal si accordano con le sue promesse; *this carpet is in — with the curtains*, questo tappeto si armonizza con le tende.

keepsake ['kiːpseik], *s.* oggetto ricordo; pegno.

kef [kef], *s.* **1.** canapa indiana fumata o masticata come narcotico **2.** stato di torpore e indolenza prodotto dal fumare o masticare canapa indiana.

keffiyeh [ke'fiːjei], *s.* fazzoletto portato in testa da beduini e arabi.

kefir ['kefə*], *s.* liquore effervescente.

keg [keg], *s.* barilotto (per brandy, aringhe, ecc.).

kelp [kelp], *s.* **1.** (*bot.*) fuco **2.** soda greggia (estratta dal fuco).

kelpie, kelpy ['kelpi], *s.* (*scoz.*) spirito acquatico maligno (che si presenta generalmente sotto forma di cavallo).

kelson, *V.* **keelson**.

kelt[1] [kelt], *s.* (*ittiol.*) trota di mare, salmone che ha deposto le uova.

Kelt[2], **Keltic**, *V.* **Celt, Celtic**.

kemp [kemp], *s.* (*ind. tessile*) pelo ruvido della lana.

kempy ['kempi], *ag.* dal pelo ruvido (di lana).

ken [ken], *s.* (*letter.*) conoscenza; percezione; comprensione: *out of* (o *beyond* o *outside*) *one's* —, fuori dell'ambito, al di là della propria comprensione; *within one's* —, nell'ambito della propria conoscenza.

to ken, *pass.* **kent** [kent], **kenned** [kend], *p.p.* **kent**, (*scoz.*) *V.* **to know**.

kennel[1] ['kenl], *s.* **1.** canile **2.** (*fam.*) covo, tana **3.** muta (di cani) **4.** *pl.* allevamento di cani.

to kennel[1], *pass.p.p.* **kennelled** ['kenld], *v.t.i.* **1.** portare al canile; tenere in un canile **2.** vivere in un canile, in una tana.

kennel[2], *s.* rigagnolo; cunetta.

Kensington ['kenziŋtən], *s.* Kensington (quartiere di Londra).

kent [kent], *pass.p.p.* di to ken.

Kent, *no.pr.* (*geog.*) Kent, contea del Kent: *man of* —, nativo della parte orientale del Kent.

Kentish ['kentiʃ], *ag.* della contea del Kent ☆ — -man, nativo della parte occidentale del Kent.

kentledge ['kentlidʒ], *s.* (*mar.*) zavorra di pani di ghisa.

Kenya ['kiːnjə], *no.pr.* (*geog.*) Kenia.

kepi ['keipi], *s.* cheppì.

kept [kept], *pass.p.p.* di to keep ‖ *ag.* mantenuto ☆ — *mistress*, mantenuta.

keratin ['kerətin], *s.* (*chim.*) cheratina.

keratose ['kerətous], *ag.* (*chim.*) corneo.

kerb, *V.* **curb**.

kerbstone ['kəːbstoun], *s.* cordonatura del marciapiede.

kerchief ['kəːtʃif], *s.* **1.** fazzoletto da collo, da testa **2.** (*poet.*) fazzoletto da naso.

kerf [kəːf], *s.* taglio; intaccatura.

kermes ['kəːmiz], *s.* (*entom. chim.*) chermes.

kermess ['kəːmis], *s.* chermessa.

kern[1] [kəːn], *s.* **1.** (*st. scoz. irl.*) fante **2.** *fig.* contadino; zoticone.

kern[2], *s.* (*tip.*) sporgenza.

kernel ['kəːnl], *s.* **1.** mandorla; gheriglio **2.** seme, chicco (di frumento, ecc.) **3.** *fig.* essenza, nucleo.

kernelly ['kəːnəli], *ag.* pieno di mandorle o di gherigli.

kerosene ['kerəsiːn], *s.* petrolio raffinato ☆ — *stove*, stufa a petrolio.

kersey ['kəːzi], *s.* rozzo tessuto di lana.

kestrel ['kestrəl], *s.* (*ornit.*) gheppio.

ket [ket], *s.* (*scoz.*) carogna; rifiuto.

ketch [ketʃ], *s.* (*mar.*) tartana.

ketchup ['ketʃəp], *s.* « ketchup » (salsa piccante).

ketone ['kiːtoun], *s.* (*chim.*) chetone.

kettle ['ketl], *s.* bollitore; bricco ‖ *a pretty — of fish*, *fig.* un bel pasticcio ☆ — -*holder*, presa (per ma-

nichi di bollitori, pentole, ecc.) ‖ *camp*- —, (*mil.*) marmitta; *giant's* —, (*geol.*) marmitta dei giganti; *tea* - —, bricco (per bollirvi l'acqua del tè).

kettledrum ['ketldrʌm], *s.* (*mus.*) timpano.

kettledrummer ['ketl,drʌmə*], *s.* (*mus.*) timpanista.

kevel ['kevl], *s.* (*mar.*) caviglia (per assicurare i cavi).

key[1] [kiː], *s.* **1.** chiave (anche *fig.*): *Gibraltar, the — to the Mediterranean*, Gibilterra, chiave del Mediterraneo; *he left the — in the lock*, lasciò la chiave nella serratura; *it was the — of his success*, fu la chiave del suo successo ‖ *to have* (o *to get*) *the — of the street*, essere lasciato a ciel sereno; essere senza tetto ‖ *to hold the keys of one's own fate*, essere padrone del proprio destino **2.** tasto (di macchina per scrivere, ecc.) **3.** (*mus.*) chiave: *the — of D major*, la chiave di re maggiore **4.** *fig.* tono (di pensiero, discorso): *to speak in a high* —, parlare in tono elevato **5.** (*mec.*) bietta; chiavetta **6.** interpretazione, soluzione (di testo, enigma, ecc.) **7.** *pl.* autorità ecclesiastica: *power of the keys*, il potere dell'autorità ecclesiastica ☆ — -*industry*, industria chiave; — -*man*, personalità importante; — -*money*, buonuscita; — -*note*, (*mus.*) nota fondamentale; — -*ring*, anello portachiavi.

to key[1], *v.t.* **1.** (*mec.*) inchiavettare **2.** (*mus.*) accordare **3.** *to* — *up*, *fig.* rianimare, stimolare.

key[2], *s.* isoletta o scogliera poco elevata sul mare.

key[3], *s.* (*arc.*) molo.

keyboard ['kiːbɔːd], *s.* tastiera (di piano, macchina per scrivere, ecc.).

keyed [kiːd], *ag.* **1.** munito di chiave **2.** (*mus.*) a tasti **3.** (*mec.*) inchiavettato **4.** (*rad.*) modulato **5.** — *up*, (*fam.*) entusiasta.

keyhole ['kiːhoul], *s.* buco della serratura.

keying ['kiːiŋ], *s.* **1.** (*mus.*) accordatura **2.** (*mec.*) inchiavettatura **3.** (*rad.*) manipolazione.

keyless ['kiːlis], *ag.* senza chiave.

keystone ['kiːstoun], *s.* (*arch.*) chiave di volta (anche *fig.*).

khaki ['kɑːki], *ag.* cachi ‖ *s.* stoffa cachi (per divise militari).

khaki, *av.* con spirito guerriero.

khalifa [kɑː'liːfə], *s.* califfo.

khalifat [kɑːliːfæt], *s.* califfato.

khan[1] [kɑːn], *s.* can.

khan[2], *s.* caravanserraglio.

khanate ['kæneit], *s.* (*st.*) canato.

Khartum [kɑːˈtuːm], *no.pr.* (*geog.*) Cartum.

kheda ['kedə], *s.* (*ang. - in.*) recinto per catturare elefanti.

Khedive [ki'diːv], *s.* kedivè.

khilafat ['kiːləfæt], *s.* califfato.

Kibbutz [ki'buːts], *pl.* **Kibbutzim** [ki:'buːtsim], *s.* (*neol.*) « Kibbutz » (comunità agricola israeliana).

kibble[1] ['kibl], *s.* (*miner.*) secchia di ferro.

to kibble[2], *v.t.* macinare a grani grossi.

kibe [kaib], *s.* gelone ulcerato; fiacca (generalmente di piede) ‖ *to gall* (o *to tread*) *on s.o.'s kibes*, *fig.* pestare i piedi a qlcu.

kibitka [ki'bitkə], *s.* **1.** tenda circolare tartara **2.** slitta russa coperta.

kibitzer ['kibitsə*], *s.* (*sl. amer.*) ficcanaso.

kibosh ['kaiboʃ], *s.* (*sl.*) sciocchezza ‖ *to put the — on*, ridurre al silenzio, mettere fine a.

kick[1] [kik], *s.* **1.** calcio; pedata ‖ *a good, bad* —, (*calcio*) un buon, cattivo calciatore ‖ *to get the* —, (*sl.*) esser licenziato ‖ *to get more kicks than halfpence*, ricevere più calci che carezze **2.** (*fam.*) effetto stimolante, eccitante: *a drink with a — in it*, una bevanda eccitante, che rianima **3.** (*fam.*) forza: *he has no — left in him*, è completamente a terra **4.** (*mil.*) rinculo ☆ — -*off*, (*calcio*) calcio d'inizio: *from the — - off*, fin dall'inizio; — -*up*, (*sl.*) rumore, baccano ‖ *corner* —, (*calcio*) calcio d'angolo; *penalty* —, (*calcio*) calcio di rigore.

to kick[1], *v.t.i.* **1.** dar calci; tirar calci; spingere col piede; spingere a calci: *to — s.o. downstairs*, scaraventare qlcu. dalle scale; *to — s.o. out*, buttar fuori qlcu.; *to — sthg. over*, buttare per aria ql.co. con un calcio ‖ *to — the bucket*, (*sl.*) tirare le cuoia, morire ‖ *to — one's heels*, attendere a lungo, far anticamera **2.** recalcitrare; lagnarsi; opporsi: *he always kicks at everything*, protesta sempre per tutto; *to — against s.o.*, ribellarsi a, contro qlcu. **3.** rinculare (di armi) **4.** *to — back*, reagire in modo inatteso e violento **5.** *to — off*, gettar via; (*calcio*) dare il calcio d'inizio: *to — off one's shoes*, liberarsi delle scarpe con un calcio **6.** *to — up*, sollevare: *to — up its heels*, scalciare (di cavallo); *to — up a row, a fuss*, (*fam.*) piantare una grana, scatenare un putiferio.

kick², *s.* fondo di bottiglia rientrante.

kicker ['kikə*], *s.* **1.** calciatore **2.** cavallo che tira calci.

kickshaw ['kikʃɔ:], *s.* **1.** dolce; pietanza ricercata **2.** nonnulla, inezia; giocattolo.

kid¹ [kid], *s.* **1.** capretto; pelle e carne di capretto ‖ *the Kids*, (*astr.*) i Capretti (tre piccole stelle nell'Auriga) **2.** (*sl.*) bimbo, ragazzino: *you bad —!*, cattivo bambino! ☆ *— -gloves*, guanti di pelle di capretto: *to handle s.o. with — -gloves*, (*fam.*) trattare qlcu. coi guanti.

to kid¹, *pass.p.p.* **kidded** ['kidid], *v.t.i.* partorire (di capra).

kid², *s.* ciotola (per marinai).

kid³, *s.* (*sl.*) scherzo; imbroglio.

to kid³, *v.t.* (*sl.*) prendere in giro; illudere; raccontar storie a: *to — oneself*, farsi delle illusioni, montarsi la testa.

kidder ['kidə*], *s.c.* (*sl.*) burlone, burlona.

kiddle ['kidl], *s.* pescaia.

kiddy ['kidi], *s.c.* (*sl.*) ragazzino, ragazzina.

to kidnap ['kidnæp], *pass.p.p.* **kidnapped** ['kidnæpt], *v.t.* rapire (specialmente bambini).

kidnapper ['kid,næpə*], *s.* rapitore (di bambino).

kidnapping ['kid,næpiŋ], *s.* ratto (di bambino).

kidney ['kidni], *s.* **1.** (*anat.*) rene; rognone: *stones in the kidneys*, (*patol.*) calcoli renali **2.** temperamento; natura: *a man of that —*, un uomo di quella tempra.

kief [kif], *V.* **kef.**

kier [kiə*], *s.* (*ind. tessile*) caldaia, recipiente (per il trattamento dei tessuti prima del candeggio).

kilderkin ['kildəkin], *s.* barilotto (misura di capacità = l. 81,83).

Kilimanjaro [,kilimən'dʒɑ:rou], *no.pr.* (*geog.*) Kilimangiaro.

kill [kil], *s.* (solo *sing.*) **1.** uccisione **2.** cacciagione.

to kill, *v.t.i.* **1.** uccidere, ammazzare (anche *fig.*); far morire; spingere alla morte: *ten men were killed in action*, dieci uomini furono uccisi in combattimento; *to — oneself*, uccidersi: *he killed himself with work*, *fig.* si ammazzò a forza di lavorare ‖ *he's got up to —*, (*fam.*) è vestito molto elegantemente ‖ *to — by inches*, far morire goccia a goccia ‖ *to — in cool blood*, ammazzare a sangue freddo ‖ *to — time*, ammazzare il tempo ‖ *to — two birds with one stone*, prendere due piccioni con una fava **2.** distruggere; sopprimere (anche *fig.*): *he killed all my hopes*, ha distrutto tutte le mie speranze; *to — a passage*, sopprimere un passo (di una pubblicazione) **3.** respingere, bocciare: *to — a bill in Parliament*, respingere una legge in Parlamento; *to — a proposal*, respingere, bocciare una proposta **4.** *fig.* soffocare, opprimere: *to — with kindness*, soffocare di gentilezze **5.** neutralizzare (colori); smorzare (suoni); (*metal.*) calmare (acciaio) **6.** (*tip.*) cancellare una o più parole; rompere la composizione **7.** *to — off*, disfarsi di, liberarsi da.

killeow ['kilkau], *s.* **1.** macellaio **2.** smargiasso, prepotente.

killer ['kilə*], *s.c.* chi uccide; assassino, assassina ☆ *— whale*, (*zool.*) orca marina ‖ *lady- —*, dongiovanni.

killick ['kilik], *s.* ancorotto.

killing ['kiliŋ], *ag.* **1.** mortale, micidiale; distruttivo **2.** (*fam.*) affascinante **3.** (*fam.*) irresistibilmente buffo, ridicolo ‖ *s.* assassinio; uccisione, carneficina.

killingly ['kiliŋli], *av.* in modo irresistibile, affascinante.

killjoy ['kildʒɔi], *s.* guastafeste.

killock ['kilək], *s.* ancorotto.

kill-time ['kiltaim], *s.* passatempo.

kiln [kiln], *s.* (*ind. edil.*) fornace, forno ☆ *brick- —*, forno da mattoni; *lime- —*, forno da calce.

kilo ['ki:lou], *s.* chilogrammo (misura di peso = 2.204 lb.).

kilocycle ['kilou,saikl], *s.* (*rad.*) chilociclo.

kilogram(me) ['kiləgræm], *V.* **kilo.**

kiloliter, kilolitre ['kilou,li:tə*], *s.* chilolitro (misura di capacità = 35.315 cu. ft.)

kilometer, kilometre ['kilə,mi:tə*], *s.* chilometro (misura di lunghezza = 0.621 mi.)

kilowatt ['kiləwɔt], *s.* (*elett.*) chilowatt.

kilt [kilt], *s.* « kilt » (gonnellino degli scozzesi).

to kilt, *v.t.* **1.** pieghettare (una gonna) **2.** rialzare, raccogliere (la gonna).

kilter ['kiltə*], *s.* (*fam.*) buono stato; buon ordine.

kiltie ['kilti], *s.* (*fam.*) soldato scozzese.

kimmer ['kimə*], *s.* (*scoz.*) comare.

kimono [ki'mounou], *s.* chimono.

kin [kin], *ag.* consanguineo; affine (anche *fig.*): *— souls*, anime gemelle ‖ *s.* **1.** (*rar.*) ceppo, stirpe **2.** parenti, congiunti: *next of —*, parente prossimo; *of — to*, affine a ‖ *kith and —*, amici, parenti, conoscenti.

kinchin ['kintʃin], *s.c.* (*sl.*) bimbo, bimba ☆ *— -cove*, ragazzo; *— -lay*, furto di denaro a bambini; *— -mort*, ragazza.

kincob ['kiŋkəb], *s.* damasco indiano ricamato d'oro, d'argento.

kind¹ [kaind], *ag.* gentile; benevolo; indulgente: *very — of you*, molto gentile da parte vostra; *be so — as to inform us*, siate così cortese da informarci; *they are — people*, sono persone gentili; *was he — to you?*, fu gentile con te? ‖ *— regards*, cordiali saluti, ossequi (nelle lettere) ☆ *— -hearted*, di cuore buono, gentile; *— -heartedness*, bontà di cuore, di animo; benevolenza.

kind², *s.* **1.** specie, razza: *the human —*, il genere umano **2.** genere, tipo, qualità: *nothing of the —*, nulla del genere; *he is a — of writer*, è una specie di scrittore; *the trees formed a — of arch*, gli alberi formavano come un arco; *what — of tree is this?*, che specie di albero è questo? ‖ *— of*, (*fam.*) quasi, pressappoco; piuttosto: *I — of expected it*, quasi me lo aspettavo **3.** natura; carattere: *to act after one's —*, agire secondo la propria natura, il proprio carattere ‖ *payment in —*, pagamento in natura **4.** *in —*, nello stesso modo: *to repay s.o. in —*, ripagare qlcu. della stessa moneta.

kindergarten ['kində,gɑ:tn], *s.* scuola materna, giardino d'infanzia.

kindergartener ['kində,gɑ:tnə*], *s.* **1.** maestra giardiniera **2.** bimbo che frequenta l'asilo.

to kindle ['kindl], *v.t.i.* **1.** accendere, accendersi; incendiare, incendiarsi; prendere fuoco **2.** *fig.* eccitare; provocare: *to — s.o. to do sthg.*, eccitare qlcu. a fare qualcosa.

kindler ['kindlə*], *s.c.* provocatore, provocatrice.

kindliness ['kaindlinis], *s.* gentilezza; bontà, amorevolezza; dolcezza.

kindling ['kindliŋ], *s.* **1.** accensione **2.** legna minuta (per accendere un fuoco).

kindly ['kaindli], *ag.* gentile, benevolo, generoso, mite: *— advice*, consiglio benevolo; *— wind*, venticello.

kindly, *av.* gentilmente, per favore, per cortesia: *— let me know*, favorite farmi sapere; *will you — tell me the time?*, mi dice l'ora, per favore? ‖ *to take — to s.o.*, nutrire amicizia per qlcu. ‖ *to take sthg. —*, prendere ql.co. in buona parte.

kindness ['kaindnis], *s.* **1.** gentilezza; bontà, benevolenza ‖ *out of* —, per gentilezza **2.** favore, piacere: *to do s.o. a* —, fare un piacere a qlcu.

kindred ['kindrid], *ag.* imparentato; affine, analogo, simile: — *souls*, anime gemelle ‖ *s.* **1.** parentela; *fig.* affinità: *the ties of* —, i legami di parentela **2.** *coll.* parenti.

kine [kain], *pl.* (*arc.*) di **cow**.

kinematic(al) [,kaini'mætik(əl)], *ag.* (*fis.*) cinematico.

kinematics [,kaini'mætiks], *s.* (*fis.*) cinematica.

kinematograph [,kaini'mætəgrɑ:f], *V.* **cinematograph**.

kinematographic [,kaini,mætə'græfik], *V.* **cinematographic**.

kinematography [,kainimə'tɔgrəfi], *V.* **cinematography**

kinetic [kai'netik], *ag.* (*fis.*) cinetico.

kinetics [kai'netiks], *s.* (*fis.*) cinetica.

king [kiŋ], *s.* **1.** re, sovrano, monarca: *the kings and queens of England*, i sovrani britannici; *the* — *of beasts*, il re degli animali ‖ *King George VI*, Re Giorgio Sesto ‖ *the King of Kings*, il Re dei Re ‖ *the three Kings*, i Re Magi **2.** magnati **3.** (*dama*) dama; (*carte, scacchi*) re ☆ — -*bird*, (*ornit.*) paradisea; — -*bolt*, (*mec.*) perno; — -*craft*, arte del governare; *King-of -arms*, (*arald.*) primo araldo; — -*pin*, (*mec.*) perno di sterzaggio; *King's English*, la lingua inglese ufficiale; *King's evidence*, (*dir.*) testimone d'accusa contro un complice; —'*s -evil*, (*patol.*) scrofola; —'*s highway*, strada maestra; —'*s man*, realista; doganiere; —'*s -spear*, (*bot.*) asfodelo ‖ *oil* —, magnate del petrolio.

to king, *v.t.i.* eleggere (qlcu.) re; fare il re ‖ *to* — *it*, (*fam.*) fare il despota.

kingcup ['kiŋ-kʌp], *s.* (*bot.*) ranuncolo, botton d'oro.

kingdom ['kiŋdəm], *s.* regno, reame (anche *fig.*); *the vegetable* —, il regno vegetale; *the kitchen is the cook's* —, la cucina è il regno della cuoca ‖ *the United Kingdom*, il Regno Unito ☆ — -*come*, (*fam.*) mondo dell'al di là.

kingdomed ['kiŋdəmd], *ag.* costituito in reame; diviso in reami.

kingfisher ['kiŋ,fiʃə*], *s.* (*ornit.*) martin pescatore; alcione.

kinghood ['kiŋhud], *s.* regalità; dignità regale.

kinglet ['kiŋlit], *s.* **1.** (*iron.*) reuccio **2.** (*ornit.*) liù.

kinglihood ['kiŋlihud], *s.* regalità.

kingliness ['kiŋlinis], *s.* regalità, carattere regale.

kingly ['kiŋli], *ag.* regale, regio.

kingpost ['kiŋpoust], *s.* (*edil.*) monaco, ometto.

kingship ['kiŋʃip], *s.* regalità; potere sovrano.

kink[1] [kiŋk], *s.* **1.** nodo; cappio; (*mar.*) cocca **2.** *fig.* grillo, ghiribizzo, ticchio: *she has got a* — *in her brain*, ha dei grilli per la testa.

to kink[1], *v.t.i.* annodare, annodarsi; attorcigliare, attorcigliarsi.

kink[2], *s.* accesso di tosse o di riso che toglie il respiro.

to kink[2], *v.i.* ridere convulsamente; ansimare.

kinkajou ['kiŋkədʒu:], *s.* (*zool.*) procione del Messico.

kinless ['kinlis], *ag.* solo, senza parenti.

kino ['ki:nou], *s.* « kino » (resina usata in farmacia e tintoria).

kinsfolk ['kinzfouk], *s.pl.* parenti; parentela.

kinship ['kinʃip], *s.* **1.** parentela: *the call of* —, la voce del sangue **2.** affinità (di carattere, ecc.).

kinsman, *pl.* **kinsmen** ['kinzmən], *s.* parente, congiunto: — *by father's side*, parente per parte di padre.

kinswoman ['kinz,wumən], *pl.* **kinswomen** ['kinz,wimin], *s.* parente, congiunta.

kiosk [ki'ɔsk], *s.* chiosco, edicola.

kip[1] [kip], *s.* pelle di animale giovane.

kip[2], *s.* (*sl.*) **1.** locanda; camera, letto a pigione **2.** casa malfamata.

to kip[2], *pass.p.p.* **kipped** [kipt], *v.i.* (*sl.*) andare a letto; dormire.

kipper ['kipə*], *s.* **1.** salmone maschio **2.** aringa, salmone affumicato **3.** (*sl.*) individuo.

to kipper, *v.t.* affumicare (pesce).

kirk [kə:k], *s.* (*scoz.*) chiesa.

kirsch [kiəʃ], **kirschwasser** ['kiəʃ,vɑ:sə*], *s.* « kirschwasser » (grappa di ciliege).

kirtle ['kə:tl], *s.* (*arc.*) **1.** giubbetto, tunica (da uomo) **2.** gonna; sottoveste.

kismet ['kismet], *s.* destino.

kiss [kis], *s.* **1.** bacio: *treacherous* —, bacio di Giuda; *to blow* (*o to send*) *s.o. a kiss*, mandare un bacio a qlcu.; *to give a* —, dare un bacio **2.** (*biliardo*) rimpallo **3.** zuccherino.

to kiss, *v.t.i.* **1.** baciare: *he kissed her hand*, le baciò la mano; *to* — *each other, one another*, baciarsi; *to* — *on the forehead*, baciare in fronte ‖ *the waves* — *the shore*, le onde lambiscono la riva ‖ *to* — *away tears*, asciugare le lacrime con baci ‖ *to* — *the Book*, baciare la Bibbia; pronunciare un solenne giuramento ‖ *to* — *the dust* (*o the ground*), mordere la polvere; essere umiliato; essere ucciso ‖ *to* — *goodbye*, accomiatarsi con un bacio ‖ *to* — *one's hand to s.o.*, mandare un bacio con la mano a qlcu. ‖ *to* — *the rod*, accettare con rassegnazione un castigo **2.** (*biliardo*) rimpallare.

kissing ['kisiŋ], *ag.* che bacia; che tocca ‖ *s.* il baciare ☆ — -*crust*, parte morbida della crosta del pane cotto a contatto con altro pane.

kit[1] [kit], *s.* **1.** secchio; cassetta; borsa; cesta **2.** utensili, attrezzi **3.** equipaggiamento; corredo: *to pack up one's* —, fare i bagagli ☆ — -*bag*, sacca sportiva, sacco militare ‖ *flight tool* —, (*aer.*) corredo degli attrezzi di volo; *tool* —, borsa utensili.

to kit[1], *pass.p.p.* **kitted** ['kitid], *v.t.* mettere in cassette o ceste (specialmente pesce per il mercato).

kit[2], *abbr.* di **kitten**.

Kit[3], *no.pr.f. dim.* di **Catherine**.

Kit[4], *no.pr.m. dim.* di **Christopher**.

kit[5], *s.* (*rar.*) violino in miniatura.

Kitcat ['kitkæt], *no.pr.* Kitcat (nome di una associazione letteraria fondata sotto il regno di Giacomo II, i cui membri erano del partito whig) ‖ **kitcat**, *s.* (*pitt.*) ritratto a mezzo busto.

kitchen ['kitʃin], *s.* cucina ☆ — -*battery* (o — -*utensils* o — -*ware*), utensili da cucina; — *boy*, sguattero; — *garden*, orto, orticello; — -*maid* (o — -*wench*), sguattera; — *range*, fornello; — *sink*, acquaio.

kitchener ['kitʃinə*], *s.* **1.** cuciniere; cuoco di monastero **2.** fornello.

kitchenette [,kitʃi'net], *s.* cucinino.

kite [kait], *s.* **1.** (*ornit.*) nibbio **2.** *fig.* persona avida **3.** aquilone, cervo volante: *to fly a* —, lanciare un aquilone; *fig.* saggiare l'opinione pubblica **4.** (*aer.*) aliante; (*pallone*) drago **5.** (*mar.*) divergenti per dragaggio **6.** (*sl. comm.*) cambiale di comodo ☆ — -*balloon*, (*mil.*) pallone drago.

to kite, *v.t.i.* **1.** volare; far volare come un aquilone **2.** (*comm.*) convertire in cambiale di comodo.

kith [kiθ], *s.*: — *and kin*, amici e parenti; *to have neither* — *nor kin*, essere solo al mondo.

kitten ['kitn], *s.* gattino, micino.

to kitten, *v.t.i.* figliare (della gatta).

kittenish ['kitniʃ], *ag.* da gattino; vivace; che ama giocare; smorfioso: — *grace*, grazia felina.

kittiwake ['kitiweik], *s.* (*ornit.*) gabbiano.

kittle ['kitl], *ag.* difficile; instabile, mutevole; intrattabile: *women are* — *cattle*, le donne sono mutevoli.

to kittle, *v.t.* **1.** (*scoz.*) solleticare; divertire **2.** rendere perplesso.

kittul [ki'tu:l], *s.* varietà di palma; fibra che se ne deriva.

kitty[1] ['kiti], *s.* (*fam.*) gattino, micio.

kitty[2], *s.* (*carte*) « pool ».

Kitty[3], *no.pr.f. dim.* di **Catherine**.

kiwi ['ki:wi(:)], *s.* (*ornit.*) atterige.

klaxon ['klæksn], *s.* (*aut.*) clackson, tromba.

klepht [kleft], *s.* « clefta », guerrigliero greco, albanese.

kleptomania [,kleptou'meinjə], *s.* cleptomania.

kleptomaniac [,kleptou'meiniæk], *ag.s.* cleptomane.

klieglight ['kli:glait], *s.* (*cine.*) riflettore ad arco.

klipspringer ['klip,spriŋə*], *s.* (*zool.*) saltarupi.

kloof [klu:f], *s.* burrone.

knack [næk], *s.* **1.** abilità, destrezza acquisite: *translating is easy when you have the — of it,* tradurre è facile quando si acquista abilità con l'esercizio **2.** dispositivo ingegnoso; scherzo ben congegnato.

knacker[1] ['nækə*], *s.* nacchera; cosa che produce rumore simile a quello delle nacchere.

knacker[2], *s.* **1.** chi commercia, macella cavalli inabili **2.** chi compra case, navi, ecc. per utilizzarne il materiale.

knackiness ['nækinis], *s.* abilità, ingegnosità.

knackish ['nækiʃ], **knacky** ['næki], *ag.* abile; ingegnoso; astuto.

knag [næg], *s.* nodo, nocchio (nel legno).

knagginess ['næginis], *s.* nodosità (del legno).

knaggy ['nægi], *ag.* nodoso; rugoso.

to knap [næp], *pass.p.p.* **knapped** [næpt], *v.t.* spaccare (pietre, ecc.).

knapper ['næpə*], *s.* spaccapietre.

knapsack ['næpsæk], *s.* zaino.

knapweed ['næpwi:d], *s.* (*bot.*) centaurea.

knar [na:*], *s.* nodo, nocchio (nel legno).

knarred [na:d], *ag.* nodoso, pieno di nodi (di albero).

knave [neiv], *s.* **1.** furfante, briccone, cattivo soggetto: *he is an arrant —,* è un furfante matricolato **2.** (*carte*) fante.

knavery ['neivəri], *s.* disonestà; frode; mariuoleria, briccanata.

knavish ['neiviʃ], *ag.* disonesto; losco; malvagio.

knavishly ['neiviʃli], *av.* disonestamente, da briccone, da furfante.

knavishness ['neiviʃnis], *s.* disonestà; bricconeria.

to knead [ni:d], *v.t.* **1.** impastare; intridere; mescolare **2.** massaggiare.

kneadable ['ni:dəbl], *ag.* impastabile; mescolabile.

kneader ['ni:də*], *s.c.* chi impasta || *s.* (*ind.*) macchina impastatrice.

kneading ['ni:diŋ], *s.* impastatura; impasto ☆ — -trough, madia; (*ind.*) gramolatrice.

knee [ni:], *s.* **1.** ginocchio: *on one's knees,* in ginocchio || *on the knees of the gods,* in grembo agli dei; *fig.* ancora incerto || *to bend one's — to,* piegare il ginocchio, umiliarsi davanti a; *to bring s.o. to his knees,* ridurre qlcu. a completa sottomissione **2.** tubo a gomito **3.** (*arch.*) curva, gomito **4.** (*mar.*) bracciuolo **5.** (*mec.*) sostegno di caldaia ☆ — -cap, ginocchiera; (*anat.*) rotula; — -deep (o — -high), che arriva fino al ginocchio; — -joint, giuntura del ginocchio; — -piece, ginocchiera (di armatura); — swell, (*mus.*) leva di organo.

to kneel [ni:l], *pass.p.p.* **knelt** [nelt], (*amer.* talvolta *reg.*), *v.i.* inginocchiarsi, genuflettersi: *to — on one knee,* mettere un ginocchio a terra.

kneeler ['ni:lə*], *s.c.* chi si inginocchia || *s.* inginocchiatoio.

knell [nel], *s.* **1.** suono di campana; rintocco funebre, campana a morto **2.** presagio di morte.

to knell, *v.t.i.* **1.** (*arc.*) suonare (di campane); suonare a morto **2.** *fig.* suonare come triste presagio **3.** *fig.* annunciare; chiamare a raccolta.

knelt [nelt], *pass.p.p.* di to **kneel.**

knew [nju:], *pass.* di to **know.**

Knickerbocker ['nikəbɔkə*], *s.* cittadino di New York || *knickerbockers,* calzoni alla zuava.

knickers ['nikəz], *s.pl.* (*fam. abbr.* di *knickerbockers*) **1.** calzoni alla zuava **2.** mutandine (da donna).

knick-knack ['niknæk], *s.* **1.** gingillo, ninnolo; cianfrusaglia; aggeggio **2.** (*fam.*) bocconcino **3.** *pl.* soprammobili.

knick-knackery ['nik,nækəri], *s.* cianfrusaglie; ninnoli; inezie.

knife [naif], *pl.* **knives** [naivz], *s.* **1.** coltello: *a silver —,* un coltello d'argento || *war to the —,* guerra ad oltranza, guerra senza quartiere || *before he could say —,* in un batter d'occhio || *to have one's — into s.o.,* avercela a morte con qlcu. **2.** (*chir.*) bisturi || *to have horror of the —,* avere terrore del bisturi ☆ — -and-fork, buona forchetta: *to play a good — -and-fork,* essere una buona forchetta; — -basket, porta posate; — -blade, lama del coltello; — -edge, lama, filo della lama; *fig.* cresta di roccia; — -grinder, arrotino; — -rest, posaposate || *carving- —,* trinciante; *chopping- —,* grosso coltello da macellaio; *erasing- —,* raschietto; *paper- —,* tagliacarte; *paring- —,* scarnitoio; *pen- —,* temperino; *pruning- —,* falcetto; *table - —,* coltello da tavola.

to knife, *v.t.* **1.** tagliare **2.** pugnalare; accoltellare, ferire (con coltello); (*amer. fam.*) *fig.* pugnalare alla schiena.

knight [nait], *s.* **1.** cavaliere || *— of the Garter,* cavaliere dell'ordine della Giarrettiera; *— of the shire,* (*st.*) membro del Parlamento inglese rappresentante una contea || *Knight Hospitaller,* cavaliere di Malta || *— of the brush,* (*scherz.*) pittore; *— of industry,* (*spreg.*) cavaliere d'industria, avventuriero, imbroglione; *— of the needle,* (*scherz.*) sarto; *— of the pestle,* (*scherz.*) farmacista; *— of the road,* (*iron.*) vagabondo; bandito; *— of St. Crispin,* (*scherz.*) calzolaio **2.** (*scacchi*) cavallo ☆ — -bachelor, cavaliere (che ha il solo titolo senza appartenere a nessun ordine); — -errant, cavaliere errante; — -heads, (*mar.*) apostoli.

to knight, *v.t.* crear cavaliere.

knightage ['naitidʒ], *s.* classe dei cavalieri.

knighthood ['naithud], *s.* **1.** rango, dignità di cavaliere **2.** cavalleria **3.** compagnia di cavalieri.

knightless ['naitlis], *ag.* (*poet.*) indegno di un cavaliere.

knightlike ['naitlaik], *V.* **knightly.**

knightliness ['naitlinis], *s.* virtù, carattere cavalleresco.

knightly ['naitli], *ag.* cavalleresco, da cavaliere || *av.* cavallerescamente.

Knightsbridge ['naitsbridʒ], *s.* Knightsbridge (strada, quartiere elegante di Londra).

to knit [nit], *pass.p.p.* **knitted** ['nitid], **knit,** *v.t.i.* **1.** lavorare a maglia, sferruzzare: *to — socks,* fare la calza **2.** corrugare (la fronte): *to — one's brows,* aggrottare le ciglia **3.** saldare, saldarsi: *the bone is knitting,* l'osso si salda **4.** *fig.* unire, unirsi; congiungere, congiungersi: *they were — together by common interests,* erano uniti da comuni interessi **5.** *to — up,* rammendare (a punto maglia); *fig.* concludere ☆ *well- —,* solido, robusto: *a well- frame,* una struttura solida, una corporatura robusta.

knitter ['nitə*], *s.* **1.** chi lavora a maglia; magliaia **2.** telaio per maglieria ☆ *circular —,* (*ind. tessile*) telaio circolare per maglieria; *straight —,* (*ind. tessile*) telaio rettilineo per maglieria.

knitting ['nitiŋ], *s.* lavoro a maglia; lavorazione a maglia ☆ — -needles (o — -pins), ferri da calza; — -machine, macchina per maglieria.

knittle ['nitl], *s.* aghetto.

knitwear ['nitwɛə*], *s.* maglieria; indumenti a maglia.

knives [naivz], *pl.* di **knife.**

knob [nɔb], *s.* **1.** protuberanza, bozza, bernoccolo; nodo (del legno) **2.** pomo (di bastone, porta, ecc.); manopola (di radio, ecc.) **3.** zolletta (di zucchero); pezzo (di carbone) **4.** (*sl.*) testa, zucca.

to knob, *pass.p.p.* **knobbed** [nɔbd], *v.t.i.* **1.** sporgere; formare protuberanze **2.** fornire di protuberanze.

knobbed [nɔbd], *ag.* nodoso; fornito di protuberanze.

knobbiness ['nɔbinis], *s.* nodosità.

knobble ['nɔbl], *s.* pomolo.

knobby ['nɔbi], *ag.* nodoso; bitorzoluto.

knock [nɔk], *s.* **1.** colpo, urto; percossa; il bussare (alla porta): *I recognized his* —, riconobbi il suo modo di bussare ‖ *to take the* —, (*sl.*) subire una batosta finanziaria **2.** (*mec.*) detonazione; battito in testa ☆ — *-about*, (*sl. teat.*) rappresentazione rumorosa; da fatica (di abiti); — *-down*, decisivo; che butta a terra; minimo (di prezzi); — *-kneed*, che ha le gambe ad X; — *-out*, colpo di grazia; (*boxe*) « knock-out » (il mettere fuori combattimento); (*sl.*) individuo eccezionale; cosa straordinaria.

to **knock**, *v.t.i.* **1.** urtare, colpire, cozzare; dare un urto, dare un colpo; bussare; *fig.* fare una forte impressione su: *he knocked at my door*, bussò alla mia porta; *his sudden departure knocked me on the head*, la sua improvvisa partenza mi turbò profondamente; *what knocks me is his impudence*, quello che mi colpisce è la sua impudenza; *to* — *against*, collidere con; imbattersi in **2.** (*sl. amer.*) criticare **3.** (*mec.*) detonare; battere in testa **4.** *to* — *about*, bistrattare, malmenare; vagabondare, far vita randagia **5.** *to* — *down*, abbattere; rovesciare; aggiudicare, assegnare un oggetto in un'asta; (*fam.*) ridurre, ribassare i prezzi; smontare macchinari (per facilitarne il trasporto) **6.** *to* — *in*, affondare; far penetrare colpendo con forza **7.** *to* — *off*, smettere di lavorare; far cadere; (*fam.*) detrarre (dal prezzo): *he knocked me off ten dollars*, mi detrasse dieci dollari **8.** *to* — *out*, metter fuori combattimento, sopraffare (anche *fig.*); vuotare battendo (una pipa) **9.** *to* — *together*, mettere insieme in tutta fretta **10.** *to* — *under*, sottomettersi, riconoscersi vinto **11.** *to* — *up*, spingere su con un colpo; svegliare; sfinire: *to be knocked up*, essere sfinito.

knocker ['nɔkə*], *s.* battente ‖ *up to the* —, (*sl.*) alla perfezione ‖ *s.c.* chi picchia, urta, batte.

knocking ['nɔkiŋ], *s.* **1.** strepito, rumore, fracasso **2.** (*mec.*) detonazione **3.** (*aut.*) battito in testa.

knoll[1] [noul], *s.* poggio, collinetta.

to **knoll**[2], *V.* to knell.

knop [nɔp], *s.* **1.** (*arc.*) per knob **2.** bocciuolo **3.** (*ind. tessile*) ☆ — *yarn*, filato « bouclé ».

knot[1] [nɔt], *s.* **1.** nodo; groviglio, viluppo: *to tie* (o *to make*) *a* —, fare un nodo **2.** (*mar.*) nodo, miglio marino: *my motor boat makes* (o *does*) *five knots an hour*, il mio motoscafo fa cinque nodi all'ora **3.** *fig.* difficoltà, problema ‖ *Gordian* —, nodo gordiano ‖ *to tie oneself in knots*, cacciarsi nei guai **4.** *fig.* nocciolo, punto essenziale **5.** gallone; coccarda; nastro ornamentale **6.** (*patol.*) tumore; bitorzolo; gonfiore; (*anat.*) ganglio **7.** gruppo di persone, di cose ☆ — *-grass*, gramigna ‖ *love-* —, nodo d'amore; *running-* — (o *slip-* —), nodo scorsoio.

to **knot**[1], *pass.p.p.* **knotted** ['nɔtid], *v.t.i.* annodare, annodarsi; aggrovigliare, aggrovigliarsi; legare; unire strettamente: *to* — *a parcel*, legare un pacco; *to get knotted*, aggrovigliarsi ‖ *to* — *one's brows*, aggrottare la fronte.

knot[2], *s.* (*ornit.*) piovanello.

knotberry ['nɔtbəri], *s.* (*bot.*) rovo.

knotless ['nɔtlis], *ag.* senza nodi.

knotted ['nɔtid], *ag.* nodoso; intrecciato; intricato; ingarbugliato.

knottiness ['nɔtinis], *s.* **1.** nodosità; *fig.* difficoltà **2.** garbuglio, intrigo.

knotting ['nɔtiŋ], *s.* **1.** l'annodare **2.** (*ricamo*) macramè **3.** (*pitt.*) vernice alla gommalacca.

knotty ['nɔti], *ag.* **1.** nodoso **2.** *fig.* difficile; scabroso, intricato: — *point*, questione spinosa.

knout [naut], *s.* « knut », sferza, gatto a nove code.

to **knout**, *v.t.* fustigare.

know [nou], *s.* conoscenza, informazione ‖ *to be in the* —, (*sl.*) essere informato ☆ — *-all*, sapientone; — *-how*, (*sl.*) conoscenza pratica, abilità tecnica; — *-nothing*, ignorante, agnostico.

to **know**, *pass.* **knew** [nju:], *p.p.* **known** [noun], *v.t.* **1.** riconoscere, distinguere: *I knew him for a Spaniard*, riconobbi in lui uno spagnolo; *they knew him*

by his voice, lo riconobbero dalla voce; *you wouldn't* — *her from a native*, non la si distinguerebbe da una del luogo; *to* — *good from evil*, distinguere il bene dal male ‖ *I don't* — *him from Adam!*, mai visto prima d'ora! **2.** conoscere (persona, luogo); essere in intimità (con qlcu.): *I don't* — *London*, non conosco Londra; *she is not a woman to* —, non è donna da frequentare; *to make oneself known*, farsi conoscere ‖ *to* — *s.o. inside out*, conoscere qlcu. a fondo **3.** (IV, V) conoscere, sapere (per informazione, esperienza): *as far as I* —, per quel che ne so; *how do I* —?, come faccio a saperlo?; *I* — *I am right*, so di aver ragione; *I have known it to happen*, so che succede; *to* — *by name, not by sight*, conoscere di nome, non di vista; *to* — *for a fact that*, saper per certo che; *to* — *how to do sthg.*, saper fare ql.co.; *to* — *one's own mind*, sapere ciò che si vuole ‖ *don't I* — *it!*, a chi lo dici! ‖ *Goodness knows!*, chi lo sa! ‖ *he has never known sickness*, è sano come un pesce ‖ *he is rather clever and doesn't he* — *it!*, non manca di intelligenza e lo sa fin troppo bene! ‖ *not if I* — *it!*, per nulla al mondo! ‖ *you* — *best*, tu ne sei il miglior giudice ‖ *to* — *better*, saperla lunga: *they ought to have known better*, non avrebbero dovuto essere così ingenui ‖ *to* — *more than one says*, saperne più di quanto si dica ‖ *to* — *on which side one's bread is buttered*, (*fam.*) conoscere bene il proprio interesse ‖ *to* — *the ropes*, (*fam.*) conoscere i segreti, le stuzie ‖ *to* — *a thing or two*, (*fam.*) saperla lunga ‖ *to get to* — *sthg.*, apprendere, venire a sapere ql.co. **4.** conoscere, sapere (per dottrina): *he knows English well*, conosce bene l'inglese; *she didn't* — *botany*, non conosceva la botanica **5.** (*arc.*) avere rapporti sessuali con **6.** *to* — *about* (*s.o., sthg.*), essere al corrente di, essere informato su: *do you* — *about it?*, sei al corrente della faccenda?; *what do you* — *about that?*, (*amer.*) cosa hai da dire in proposito? **7.** *to* — *of* (*s.o., sthg.*), aver sentito parlare di: *not that I* — *of*, no, che io sappia.

knowable ['nouəbl], *ag.* **1.** comprensibile; apprendibile **2.** riconoscibile.

knowableness ['nouəblnis], *s.* l'essere comprensibile, apprendibile, riconoscibile.

knower ['nouə*], *ag.* conoscitore; intenditore.

knowing ['nouiŋ], *ag.* **1.** istruito: *to assume a air*, prendere un'aria saputa; *to pretend to be very* —, far finta di saperla lunga **2.** intelligente, abile, esperto, oculato, accorto.

knowingly ['nouiŋli], *av.* **1.** coscientemente; intenzionalmente **2.** accortamente; astutamente.

knowingness ['nouiŋnis], *s.* abilità; accortezza.

knowledge ['nɔlidʒ], *s.* **1.** conoscenza, cognizione, consapevolezza: *not in my* —, fuori dell'ambito della mia conoscenza; *without my* —, a mia insaputa; *he has no* — *of it*, non ne sa niente; *it has come to my* — *that*, sono venuto a sapere che; *to keep sthg. from s.o.'s* —, nascondere ql.co. a qlcu.; *to speak with full* —, parlare con cognizione di causa **2.** sapere, scienza: *his* — *is immense*, il suo sapere è immenso; *to have a* — *of several languages*, conoscere diverse lingue ‖ *the tree of* — *of good and evil*, (*Bibbia*) l'albero della scienza del bene e del male ‖ — *is power*, *prov.* sapere è potere.

knowledgeable ['nɔlidʒəbl], *ag.* (*fam.*) **1.** intelligente **2.** bene informato.

known [noun], *p.p.* di to know ‖ *ag.* saputo, conosciuto; noto: *he is* — *to everyone, everywhere*, è conosciuto da tutti, ovunque; *it is* — *to everybody that*, è noto a tutti che, tutti sanno che; *a place* — *to me alone*, un posto noto solo a me; *the son is better* — *than his father for his generosity*, il figlio è più conosciuto del padre per la sua generosità.

knuckle ['nʌkl], *s.* **1.** (*anat.*) nocca; articolazione, giuntura; falange **2.** (*cuc.*) garretto ☆ — *-bone*, falange; — *-duster*, pugno di ferro; — *-joint*, (*mec.*) giunto a cerniera.

to **knuckle**, *v.t.i.* **1.** colpire, premere con le nocche **2.** *to* — *down*, cedere, sottomettersi.

knurl [nə:l], s. (*mec.*) godronatura, zigrinatura.

to **knurl,** *v.t.* (*mec.*) godronare, zigrinare.

knurr [nə:*], s. **1.** escrescenza, nodo (in tronco d'albero) **2.** (*spor.*) palla di legno.

koala [kou'ɑ:lə], s. (*zool.*) «koala» (marsupiale australiano).

kobold ['kəbould], s. (*mit. nordica*) coboldo.

kodak ['koudæk], s. kodak (macchina fotografica).

to **kodak,** *v.t.* **1.** fotografare (con una kodak) **2.** *fig.* descrivere vividamente.

koel ['kouil], s. (*ornit.*) cuculo indiano o australiano.

kohinoor ['kouinuə*], s. «kohinoor» (famoso diamante).

kohl [koul], s. polvere orientale per scurire le palpebre.

kohlrabi ['koul'rɑ:bi], s. (*bot.*) cavolrapa.

kola ['koulə], s. (*bot.*) cola.

kolinsky [kə'linski], s. pelliccia di visone siberiano.

Konrad ['kɔnræd], *no.pr.m.* Corrado.

koodoo ['ku:du:], s. (*zool.*) antilope del Sud Africa.

kopje ['kɔpi], s. collinetta (nel Sud Africa).

Koran [kɔ'rɑ:n], s. Corano.

Koranic [kɔ'rænik], *ag.* del Corano.

Korea [kə'riə], *no.pr.* (*geog.*) Corea.

Korean [kə'riən], *ag.* coreano ‖ *s.c.* coreano, coreana.

kosher ['kouʃə*], *ag.* puro, lecito (di cibo, secondo la religione ebraica) ‖ *s.* cibo permesso dalla religione ebraica.

kotow ['kou'tau], s. inchino cerimonioso (alla cinese).

to **kotow,** *v.i.* inchinarsi; comportarsi ossequiosamente (alla cinese).

koumiss ['ku:mis], s. liquore estratto dal latte di cavalla fermentato.

kourbash ['kuəbæʃ], s. frusta di pelle (usata in Turchia ed Egitto).

Kowloon [kau'lu:n], *no.pr.* (*geog.*) Kowloon.

kraal [krɑ:l], s. **1.** villaggio sudafricano **2.** recinto per bestiame.

krait [krait], s. serpente indiano velenoso.

kraken ['krɑ:kən], s. (*mit. nordica*) mostro marino.

Kremlin ['kremlin], s. Cremlino.

kris [kri:s], s. «kriss» (pugnale malese).

krone ['krounə], s. corona (moneta danese, norvegese, svedese).

krypton ['kripton], s. (*chim.*) cripto, cripton.

Kublai Khan ['kublai'kɑ:n], *no.pr.m.* (*lett.*) Kublai Khan.

kudos ['kju:dɔs], s. (*sl.*) gloria; fama.

Ku-klux-klan ['kju:-klʌks'klæn], s. (*amer.*) «Ku-klux-klan» (associazione segreta che si formò negli stati del Sud dopo la guerra civile per lottare contro l'influenza dei negri).

kukri ['kukri], s. largo coltello indiano.

Kurdistan ['kurdistɑ:n], *no.pr.* (*geog.*) Curdistan.

kyanite ['kaiənait], s. (*min.*) cianite.

to **kyanize** ['kaiənaiz], *v.t.* impregnare (il legno) di sublimato corrosivo per preservarlo.

kyle [kail], s. (*scoz.*) stretto canale tra due isole.

kyloe ['kailou], s. (*scoz.*) bovino di razza piccola, con lunghe corna.

kymograph ['kaiməgrɑ:f], s. **1.** (*fis.*) chimografo **2.** registratore dei movimenti rotatori (di aereo in volo).

L

l [el], *pl.* ls, l's [elz], *s.* 1. (*dodicesima lettera dell'alfabeto inglese*) l ‖ — *for Lucy*, (*tel.*) l come Livorno 2. oggetto, isolato di case a forma di L 3. *l.* (*abbr.* del *lat. libra*), « pound », libbra 4. L (*cifra romana*), 50 5. L (*abbr. di Learner*), scuola guida (sull'automobile di chi impara a guidare).

la [lɑ:], *s.* (*mus.*) la.

laager ['lɑ:gə*], *s.* accampamento (generalmente formato da carri disposti a cerchio).

to laager, *v.t.i.* accampare, accamparsi; disporre in cerchio difensivo (i carri) per accamparsi.

labarum ['læbərəm], *s.* labaro.

labdacism ['læbdəsizəm], *s.* labdacismo.

labefaction [,læbi'fækʃən], *s.* indebolimento.

label ['leibl], *s.* 1. etichetta, cartellino; marca; *fig.* (*spreg.*) soprannome; definizione 2. (*arch.*) modanatura in aggetto (su portale, finestra); gocciolatoio 3. (*dir.*) poscritto, codicillo 4. (*arald.*) lambello.

to label, *pass.p.p.* labelled ['leibld], *v.t.* 1. (*comm.*) contromarcare; mettere le etichette a 2. classificare, definire.

labellum [lə'beləm], *pl.* labella [lə'belə],] *s.* (*bot.*) labello.

labial ['leibjəl], *ag.s.* labiale.

labialism ['leibjəlizəm], *s.* labialismo.

labialization [,leibiəlai'zeiʃən], *s.* labializzazione.

to labialize ['leibiəlaiz], *v.t.* (*fonet.*) rendere labiale.

labiate ['leibiit], *ag.s.* (*bot.*) labiata.

labile ['leibil], *ag.* (*chim. fis.*) instabile.

labiodental ['leibiou'dentl], *ag.s.* (*fonet.*) labiodentale.

labium ['leibiəm], *pl.* labia ['leibiə], *s.* (*anat. bot.*) labbro.

laboratorial [,læbərə'tɔ:riəl], *ag.* di laboratorio.

laboratory [lə'bɔrətəri], *s.* 1. (*chim. farm., ecc.*) laboratorio 2. (*metal.*) suola (di fornace).

laborious [lə'bɔ:riəs], *ag.* 1. laborioso; faticoso; arduo 2. laborioso; operoso; solerte.

laboriously [lə'bɔ:riəsli], *av.* laboriosamente.

laboriousness [lə'bɔ:riəsnis], *s.* 1. laboriosità 2. difficoltà; fatica.

labour ['leibə*], *s.* 1. lavoro (fisico, mentale): *lost* —, sforzi vani, fatica sprecata 2. fatica, compito ‖ — *of Hercules*, fatica d'Ercole ‖ — *of love*, lavoro fatto per proprio diletto 3. i lavoratori, la classe operaia ‖ *Labour and Capital*, capitale e lavoro ‖ *Labour Exchange*, ufficio collocamento ‖ *Labour leader*, organizzatore sindacale; *Labour Party*, partito laburista; *Labour Union*, sindacato dei lavoratori 4. doglie (del parto), travaglio: *to be in* —, avere le doglie ☆ *hand*- —, lavoro manuale; *hard* —, lavori forzati; *skilled* —, mano d'opera specializzata.

to labour, *v.t.i.* 1. lavorare, faticare ‖ *to* — *at*, lavorare a, affaticarsi a, occuparsi di ‖ *to* — *under*, soffrire per, essere oppresso da 2. avanzare a fatica (anche *fig.*); lottare (per uno scopo) 3. elaborare 4. rullare pesantemente (di nave) 5. (*arc.*) lavorare (la terra), arare.

laboured ['leibəd], *ag.* 1. elaborato: — *style*, stile elaborato, pesante 2. *fig.* penoso: — *breathing*, respiro affannoso.

labourer ['leibərə*], *s.* uomo di fatica; manovale ☆ *agricultural* —, bracciante, contadino.

labouring ['leibəriŋ], *ag.* 1. laborioso, operoso 2. laborioso, faticoso.

labourist ['leibərist], labourite ['leibərait], *s.* (*pol.*) laburista.

laboursome ['leibəsəm], *ag.* (*arc.*) faticoso, laborioso.

labrose ['leibrous], *ag.* dalle grosse labbra.

labrum ['leibrəm], *pl.* labra ['leibrə], *s.* labbro.

laburnum [lə'bə:nəm], *s.* (*bot.*) avorno, ornello.

labyrinth ['læbərinθ], *s.* 1. labirinto (anche *anat. mec.*) 2. *fig.* ginepraio ☆ — *fish*, (*ittiol.*) labirintici.

labyrinthal [,læbə'rinθəl], *ag.* labirinteo.

labyrinthiform [,læbə'rinθifɔ:m], *ag.* a forma di labirinto.

labyrinthine [,læbə'rinθain], *ag.* labirintico.

labyrinthodon [,læbi'rinθədon], *s.* (*paleont.*) labirintodonte.

lac[1] [læk], *s.* lacca.

lac[2], *s.* (*ang.-in.*) centomila ‖ *a* — *of rupees*, un numero rilevante di rupie.

Laccadive ['lækədiv], *no.pr.* (*geog.*) (isole) Laccadive.

lace [leis], *s.* 1. laccio, stringa 2. pizzo, trina, merletto 3. gallone, passamaneria: *gold*, *silver* —, gallone d'oro, d'argento ☆ — *collar*, colletto di pizzo; — *-glass*, vetro filigranato; — *-maker*, — *-worker*, merlettaia, fabbricante di pizzi; — *trimming*, guarnizione in pizzo; — *-work*, merletto, trina; gallone ‖ *pillow*-—, tombolo; *shoe-laces*, lacci per scarpe.

to lace, *v.t.i.* 1. allacciare, allacciarsi 2. guarnire di merletti; gallonare.

Lacedaemon [,læsi'di:mən], *no.pr.* (*geog. st.*) Lacedemone.

lacerable ['læsərəbl], *ag.* lacerabile.

lacerate ['læsərit], *ag.* lacerato.

to lacerate ['læsəreit], *v.t.* lacerare, strappare (anche *fig.*).

laceration [,læsə'reiʃən], *s.* lacerazione, strappo.

lacerative ['læsərətiv], *ag.* lacerante.

laches ['leitʃiz], *s.* (*dir.*) negligenza, morosità.

Lachesis ['lækisis], *no.pr.f.* (*mit.*) Lachesi.

lachrymal ['lækriməl], *ag.* (*anat.*) lacrimale ☆ — *gland*, ghiandola lacrimale.

lachrymation [,lækri'meiʃən], *s.* lacrimazione.

lachrymatory ['lækrimətəri], *ag.* lacrimogeno *s.* 1. (*archeol.*) lacrimatoio 2. (*scherz.*) fazzoletto.

lachrymose ['lækrimous], *ag.* lacrimoso.

lack [læk], *s.* insufficienza; mancanza; penuria; assenza: — *of evidence*, insufficienza, mancanza di prove; — *of food*, mancanza di cibo; *for* — *of*, causa l'assenza di; *his* — *of sense*, la sua mancanza di buon senso; *to be in* — *of*, essere a corto di.

to lack, *v.t.i.* 1. mancare di: *that king lacked authority*, quel re mancava di autorità; *these accounts* — *precision*, questi conti mancano di precisione 2. occorrere, aver bisogno, essere mancante: *money is lacking for this plan*, occorre, manca denaro per questo progetto.

lackadaisical [,lækə'deizikəl], *ag.* 1. apatico, pigro 2. sentimentale; lezioso, affettato.

lackadaisically [,lækə'deizikəli], *av.* languidamente, affettatamente.

lackadaisicalness [,lækə'deizikəlnis], *s.* affettazione; sentimentalismo.

lacker ['lækə*], *s.* 1. lacca 2. oggetto laccato.

to lacker, *v.t.* laccare, verniciare.

lackey ['læki], *s.* 1. lacchè, staffiere 2. *fig.* adulatore.

to lackey, *v.t.* servire (anche *fig.*).

lackland ['læklænd], *ag.s.* (persona) senza terra.

laconic [lə'kɔnik], *ag.* laconico; breve; conciso.
laconically [lə'kɔnikəli], *av.* laconicamente.
laconicism [lə'kɔnisizəm], *s.* laconicismo.
lacquer ['lækə*], *s.* **1.** lacca **2.** oggetto laccato.
to lacquer, *v.t.* laccare, verniciare.
lacquerer ['lækərə*], *s.* laccatore, verniciatore.
lacquering ['lækəriŋ], *s.* verniciatura, laccatura.
lacquey ['læki], *s.* **1.** lacchè, staffiere **2.** *fig.* adulatore.
to lacquey, *v.t.* **1.** servire **2.** *fig.* adulare.
lacrosse [lə'krɔs], *s.* « lacrosse » (giuoco canadese praticato con racchetta e palla).
Lactantius [læk'tænʃjəs], *no.pr.m.* (*st. lett.*) Lattanzio.
lactate ['læktit], *s.* (*chim.*) lattato.
lactation [læk'teifən], *s.* **1.** lattazione **2.** allattamento.
lacteal ['læktiəl], *ag.* latteo ☆ — *fever*, febbre lattea.
lacteals ['læktiəlz], *s.pl.* (*anat.*) vasi chiliferi.
lacteous ['læktiəs], *ag.* latteo.
lactescence [læk'tesns], *s.* lattescenza.
lactescent [læk'tesnt], *ag.* lattescente.
lactic ['læktik], *ag.* lattico ☆ — *acid*, acido lattico.
lactiferous [læk'tifərəs], *ag.* lattifero.
lactometer [læk'tɔmitə*], *s.* lattometro.
lactoscope ['læktouskoup], *s.* lattoscopio.
lactose ['læktous], *s.* (*chim.*) lattosio.
lacuna [lə'kju:nə], *pl.* **lacunae** [lə'kju:ni:], **lacunas** [lə'kju:nəz], *s.* lacuna, vuoto, mancanza.
lacunar [lə'kju:nə*], *ag.* lacunoso ‖ *s.* soffitto a cassettoni; lacunare.
lacunary [lə'kju:nəri], **lacunose** [lə'kju:nous], *ag.* lacunoso.
lacustrian [lə'kʌstriən], *ag.* lacustre ‖ *s.* abitante di città lacustre.
lacustrine [lə'kʌstrain], *ag.* lacustre.
lacy ['leisi], *ag.* simile a, come pizzo.
lad [læd], *s.* giovinetto, ragazzo.
ladder ['lædə*], *s.* **1.** scala a piuoli **2.** smagliatura (di calza, di tessuto a maglia) **3.** *fig.* scala sociale: *to be at, to reach the top of the —*, essere, giungere alla sommità della scala sociale ☆ *aerial- —* (o *extension —*), scala porta; *rope- —*, scala di corda.
to ladder, *v.t.i.* **1.** munire di scala **2.** smagliarsi.
laddie ['lædi], *s.* (*scoz.*) ragazzino.
to lade [leid], *pass.* **laded** ['leidid], *p.p.* **laden** ['leidn], *v.t.* caricare (una nave).
laden ['leidn], *p.p.* di to **lade** ‖ *ag.* **1.** caricato **2.** *fig.* oppresso: *he was — with sorrow*, era oppresso dal dolore.
Ladin [lə'di:n], *s.* ladino, romancio.
lading ['leidiŋ], *s.* carico: *bill of —*, (*comm.*) polizza di carico ☆ — *operations*, operazioni di carico.
Ladino [la:'di:nou], *s.* ladino (gergo degli ebrei spagnoli) ‖ *s.c.* meticcio, meticcia.
ladle ['leidl], *s.* **1.** mestolo **2.** (*metal.*) cucchiaione; siviera, secchione di colata ☆ *soup —*, cucchiaione da minestra.
to ladle, *v.t.* versare, distribuire con un mestolo: *to — out soup*, scodellare, servire la minestra.
ladleful ['leidlful], *s.* mestolata; cucchiaiata.
lady ['leidi], *s.* **1.** signora: *the — of the house*, la padrona di casa; *old —*, vecchia signora; *she looks a —*, ha l'aria distinta ‖ *Ladies and Gentlemen*, signore e signori **2.** *Lady*, « Lady » (moglie, figlia di barone, conte, marchese, ecc.): *Lady Blessington can't accept your invitation*, Lady Blessington non può accettare il vostro invito ‖ *My Lady*, signora **3.** sovrana: — *of the manor*, castellana; *our sovereign —*, la nostra sovrana ‖ *Lady Bountiful*, (*lett. fig.*) fata benefica **4.** *Our Lady*, la Madonna ‖ *Lady-altar*, altare della Madonna; *Lady -Chapel*, Cappella della Madonna; *Lady Day*, giorno dell'Annunciazione **5.** moglie; (*fam.*) fidanzata: *my young —*, (*fam.*) la mia bella; *officers and their ladies*, gli ufficiali e le loro mogli **6.** (*usato attributivamente indica dignità, professione con riferimento a donna*): — *clerk*, impiegata; — *doctor*, dottoressa; — *reader*, let-

trice ☆ — *-help*, governante di casa; — *-in waiting*, dama di corte; — *-killer*, rubacuori; — *-love*, donna amata; —*'s-maid*, cameriera particolare della signora; *ladies' man*, damerino ‖ *young —*, signorina.
ladybird ['leidibə:d], **ladybug** ['leidibʌg], *s.* (*entom.*) coccinella.
ladylike ['leidilaik], *ag.* **1.** signorile, adatto a una signora **2.** effeminato.
ladyship ['leidiʃip], *s.* **1.** rango, posizione di una nobildonna **2.** *Ladyship*, Signoria, Eccellenza: *did Your Ladyship call?*, la Signoria Vostra ha chiamato?; *Her Ladyship can't receive you today*, Sua Eccellenza non può riceverla oggi.
Laertes [lei'ə:ti:z], *no.pr.m.* (*lett.*) Laerte.
Laetitia [li'tiʃiə], *no.pr.f.* Letizia.
laevorotatory [,li:vou'routətəri], *ag.* (*chim.*) levogiro.
laevulose ['li:vjulous], *s.* (*chim.*) levulosio.
lag[1] [læg], *s.* ritardo, intervallo ‖ *angle of —*, (*mec.*) angolo di ritardo.
to lag[1], *pass.p.p.* **lagged** [lægd], *v.t.i.* ritardare; avanzare troppo lentamente: ‖ *to — behind*, restare indietro.
lag[2], *s.* (*tec.*) rivestimento isolante; bordatura.
to lag[2], *v.t.* (*tec.*) rivestire con materiale isolante.
lag[3], *s.* (*sl.*) forzato, condannato: *an old —*, un galeotto di professione.
to lag[3], *v.t.* (*sl.*) condannare, deportare; arrestare.
lager ['la:gə*], *s.* birra chiara (di tipo tedesco).
laggard ['lægəd], *ag.s.* (individuo) tardo, pigro, inerte.
lagging[1] ['lægiŋ], *ag.* pigro; lento.
lagging[2], *s.* rivestimento isolante.
laggingly ['lægiŋli], *av.* lentamente; pigramente.
lagoon, lagune [lə'gu:n], *s.* laguna.
laic(al) ['leiik(əl)], *ag.* laico, secolare.
laically ['leiikəli], *av.* laicamente; da laico.
to laicize ['leisaiz], *v.t.* laicizzare, rendere laico.
laid [leid], *pass.p.p.* di to **lay**.
lain [lein], *p.p.* di to **lie**.
lair [lεə*], *s.* **1.** tana, covo (di animali) **2.** riparo (per bestiame) **3.** (*fam.*) rifugio, stanzino, studiolo.
laird [lεəd], *s.* (*scoz.*) proprietario terriero.
laity ['leiiti], *s.* **1.** stato secolare; i laici **2.** i profani, gli inesperti.
lake[1] [leik], *s.* lago ‖ *Lake Como*, il Lago di Como ‖ *the Lake District*, la regione dei laghi (in Inghilterra); *the Lake School* (o *the Lake Poets*), i poeti laghisti ‖ *the Great Lakes*, i grandi laghi nordamericani ☆ *salt —*, lago salato.
lake[2], *s.* rosso lacca.
Lakeland ['leik-lænd], *no.pr.* (*geog.*) la regione dei laghi nell'Inghilterra Settentrionale.
lakeless ['leiklis], *ag.* senza laghi.
lakelet ['leiklit], *s.* laghetto.
lakh [la:k], *V.* **lac**[2].
lakist ['leikist], *s.* (*st. lett.*) laghista.
laky ['leiki], *ag.* di lago, lacustre.
lallation [læ'leifən], *s.* (*linguistica*) lallazione.
to lam [læm], *pass.p.p.* **lammed** [læmd], *v.t.* (*sl.*) colpire, bastonare: *to — sthg. into s.o.*, (*sl. scolastico*) cacciar ql.co. in testa a qlcu. a suon di bastone.
lama[1] ['la:mə], *s.* (*relig. buddista*) lama.
lama[2], *V.* **llama**.
Lamaism ['la:məizm], *s.* (*relig. buddista*) lamaismo.
Lamaist ['la:məist], *s.* (*relig. buddista*) seguace del lamaismo.
lamasery ['la:məsəri], *s.* (*relig. buddista*) monastero tibetano.
lamb [læm], *s.* **1.** agnello ‖ *wolf in —'s skin*, *fig.* lupo in veste di agnello **2.** *fig.* bimbo, persona innocente ☆ —*'s-wool*, lana fine di prima qualità; *Persian —*, agnellino persiano.
to lamb, *v.t.i.* figliare; nascere (di pecora).
to lambaste [læm'beist], *v.t.* **1.** battere, sferzare **2.** (*sl. amer.*) riprovare; accusare.

lambda ['læmdə], *s.* lambda (lettera dell'alfabeto greco).

lambdacism ['læmdəsizəm], *s.* lambdacismo.

lambdoid ['læmdɔid], **lambdoidal** [læm'dɔidl], *ag.* a forma di lambda ☆ — *suture*, (*med.*) sutura lambdoidea.

lambency ['læmbənsi], *s.* scintillio (anche *fig.*).

lambent ['læmbənt], *ag.* 1. che lambisce, che sfiora (di fiamma, ecc.) 2. scintillante; *fig.* sottile.

Lambert ['læmbə(:)t], *no.pr.m.* Lamberto.

lambkin ['læmkin], *s.* agnellino.

lamblike ['læmlaik], *ag.* di agnello; come un agnello.

lambskin ['læm-skin], *s.* pelle d'agnello.

lame [leim], *ag.* 1. zoppo; zoppicante, storpio: *to go* —, (mettersi a) zoppicare 2. *fig.* zoppicante, imperfetto, debole: *a* — *excuse*, una cattiva scusa; — *verses*, versi difettosi ☆ — *duck*, *fig.* invalido, fallito.

to lame, *v.t.i.* storpiare; azzoppare; zoppicare.

lamella [lə'melə], *pl.* **lamellae** [lə'meli:], *s.* (*bot. zool.*) lamella.

lamellar [lə'melə*], *ag.* lamellare.

lamellate ['læmelit], **lamellated** ['læmeleitid], *ag.* lamellato.

lamellose [lə'melous], *ag.* lamelloso.

lamely ['leimli], *av.* 1. zoppicando 2. *fig.* imperfettamente, debolmente.

lameness ['leimnis], *s.* 1. claudicazione, zoppaggine 2. *fig.* imperfezione, debolezza.

lament [lə'ment], *s.* 1. lamento 2. elegia funebre.

to lament, *v.t.i.* lamentare, lamentarsi, dolersi; rimpiangere: *to* — *one's lot*, lagnarsi della propria sorte.

lamentable ['læməntəbl], *ag.* lamentevole; deplorevole.

lamentably ['læməntəbli], *av.* lamentevolmente; deplorevolmente.

lamentation [,læmen'teiʃən] *s.* lamento, lamentazione.

lamented [lə'mentid], *ag.* deplorato, compianto: *your late* — *friend*, il tuo compianto amico.

lamentingly [lə'mentiŋli], *av.* lamentosamente.

lametta [lə'metə], *s.* lamina, filo (d'oro, d'argento, ecc.).

lamia ['leimiə], *s.* (*mit.*) lamia.

lamina ['læminə], *pl.* **laminae** ['læmini:], *s.* 1. lamina, foglia, piastra di metallo 2. (*bot.*) lamina, lobo 3. (*geol.*) strato.

to laminate ['læmineit], *v.t.i.* (*metal.*) laminare; ridurre in lamine; coprire di lamine; dividersi in lamine.

lamination [,læmi'neiʃən], *s.* 1. (*metal.*) laminazione 2. (*mec. fis.*) lamina; (*elett.*) lamierino magnetico 3. struttura lamelliforme (anche *geol.*).

Lammas ['læməs], *s.* (*st. relig.*) primo d'agosto (festa del raccolto) ‖ *at latter* —, alle calende greche.

lammergeyer ['læməgaiə*], *s.* (*ornit.*) gipeto, avvoltoio barbuto.

lamp [læmp], *s.* 1. lampada, lampadina; lucerna; fanale: *an electric* —, una lampadina elettrica 2. (*poet.*) sole; luna; stella 3. *fig.* lume (dell'intelletto); fonte di speranza ☆ — *-black*, nerofumo; — *-chimney*, tubo di lampada ad olio; — *-oil*, olio da ardere, petrolio; — *-post*, sostegno del lampione stradale: *between you and me and the* — *-post*, (*fam.*) in gran segreto; *what a* — *-post he is!*, (*sl.*) che spilungone!; — *-shade*, paralume ‖ *bicycle* —, fanale da bicicletta; *ceiling* —, lampadario; *oil* —, lampada ad olio; *pilot* —, lampada spia; *reading* — (o *table* —), lampada da tavolo, portatile; *spirit* —, lampada a spirito.

to lamp, *v.t.i.* 1. brillare 2. illuminare; dotare di lampade 3. (*sl.*) guardare.

lampas[1] ['læmpəz], *s.* (*vet.*) lampasco.

lampas[2] ['læmpəs], *s.* (*ind. tessile*) lampasso.

lampern ['læmpə:n], *s.* (*ittiol.*) lampreda di fiume.

lampion ['læmpiən], *s.* lampioncino in vetro colorato per luminarie.

lamplight ['læmp-lait], *s.* luce artificiale.

lamplighter ['læmp-laitə*], *s.* lampionaio.

lampoon [læm'pu:n], *s.* libello; pasquinata, satira.

to lampoon, *v.t.* satireggiare; scrivere una satira, una pasquinata per.

lampooner [læm'pu:nə*], **lampoonist** [læm'pu:nist], *s.* libellista, scrittore di satire.

lamprey ['læmpri], *s.* (*ittiol.*) lampreda.

Lancaster ['læŋkəstə*], *no.pr.* (*geog.*) Lancaster ‖ *the House of* —, la dinastia dei Lancaster.

Lancastrian [læŋ'kæstriən], *ag.* della Casa di Lancaster ‖ *s.c.* 1. abitante del Lancashire, di Lancaster 2. appartenente alla Casa di Lancaster.

lance [la:ns], *s.* 1. lancia 2. (*mar.*) fiocina, rampone ☆ — *-jack*, (*sl. mil.*) caporale; — *-sergeant*, caporale che fa le veci di un sergente.

to lance, *v.t.* 1. ferire con una lancia 2. (*chir.*) incidere col bisturi.

lancelet ['la:nslit], *s.* (*ittiol.*) anfiosso.

Lancelot ['la:nslət], *no.pr.m.* (*lett.*) Lancillotto.

lanceolate ['la:nsiəlit], *ag.* (*bot.*) lanceolato, fatto a forma di lancia.

lancer ['la:nsə*], *s.* 1. (*mil.*) lanciere 2. *pl.* i lancieri (musica, danza).

lancet ['la:nsit], *s.* 1. (*chir.*) bisturi 2. — (*window*), finestra ad ogiva ☆ — *arch*, arco a sesto acuto.

lanceted ['la:nsitid], *ag.* (*arch.*) a sesto acuto.

lancinating ['la:nsineitiŋ], *ag.* lancinante, acuto.

land [lænd], *s.* 1. terra ferma: *to reach* —, raggiungere la terra ferma; *to travel by* —, viaggiare per terra 2. paese, contrada: *a barren* —, un paese squallido 3. campagna; terreno: *cultivated* —, terra coltivata; *to go, to work on the* —, diventare, essere agricoltore 4. proprietà, dominio: *to own acres of* —, avere dei beni al sole ‖ *houses and lands*, case e terreni (proprietà) 5. (*mec.*) pieno, parte in rilievo fra le rigature (di fucile) ☆ — *-agent*, intendente, agente; amministratore di campagne; (*amer.*) agente per la compravendita di terreni; — *-breeze*, vento di terra; — *-force*, esercito; — *-girl*, ragazza di fattoria; — *-grabber*, accaparratore di terre; — *-holder*, proprietario terriero; fittabile; possidente; — *-locked*, chiuso, circondato da terre; mediterraneo; — *-lubber*, (*mar. spreg.*) abitante di terra ferma; — *-office*, ufficio del catasto; — *-owner*, proprietario di terre; — *-rover*, (*neol.*) specie di jeep; — *-slide*, frana; (*pol.*) vittoria schiacciante; — *-surveying*, agrimensura; — *-surveyor*, agrimensore; — *-tax*, imposta fondiaria ‖ *native* —, patria; *no man's* —, (*mil.*) terra di nessuno.

to land, *v.t.i.* 1. sbarcare, approdare, fare approdare; (*aer.*) atterrare: *they landed at Genoa*, sbarcarono a Genova 2. porre, porsi (in una determinata situazione): *that landed me in great difficulties*, ciò mi pose in grandi difficoltà ‖ *to* — *on one's feet*, (*fam.*) cadere in piedi; *fig.* cavarsi d'impaccio 3. vincere, riuscire a procurarsi: *they landed a few hundred pounds*, guadagnarono, vinsero alcune centinaia di lire sterline; *to* — *a fish*, pescare un pesce 4. assestare, allungare (uno schiaffo, ecc.): *to* — *s.o. a blow in the face*, colpire qlcu. con un pugno in viso.

landau ['lændɔ:], *s.* landò.

landed ['lændid], *ag.* fondiario ☆ — *estate*, proprietà fondiaria.

landfall ['lændfɔ:l], *s.* (*mar.*) approdo.

landgrave ['lændgreiv], *s.* (*st.*) langravio.

landing ['lændiŋ], *s.* 1. sbarco, approdo; (*aer.*) atterraggio; luogo di sbarco: *to effect a* —, effettuare uno sbarco 2. pianerottolo ☆ — *-craft*, mezzi da sbarco; — *-net*, negossa (rete da pesca); — *-place*, approdo; — *speed*, velocità d'atterraggio; — *-stage*, pontile di sbarco; scalandrone; — *-strip*, pista d'atterraggio; — *ticket*, contrassegno per lo sbarco; — *wire*, (*aer.*) controdiagonale.

landlady ['læn,leidi], *s.* 1. proprietaria di immobili, padrona di casa 2. affittacamere, albergatrice, ostessa.

landless ['lændlis], *ag.* senza terreni; che non ha beni immobili.

landlord ['lænlɔːd], *s.* **1.** padrone di casa, affitta-camere **2.** albergatore, oste **3.** proprietario di terre.

landman, *pl.* **landmen** ['lændmən], *s.* **1.** contadino **2.** (*rar.*) abitante di terra ferma.

landmark ['lændmɑːk], *s.* **1.** punto di riferimento: *the church on the hilltop was a well-known* —, la chiesa sulla collina era un noto punto di riferimento **2.** *fig.* pietra miliare: *landmarks in the history of civilization*, pietre miliari nella storia della civiltà; *to be a* —, fare epoca **3.** pietra di confine.

landocracy [lænd'ɔkrəsi], *s.* (*scherz.*) plutocrazia terriera.

landocrat ['lændəkræt], *s.* (*scherz.*) plutocrate terriero.

landscape ['lænskeip], *s.* paesaggio ☆ — *-gardening* (*art.*) studio della disposizione dei giardini; — *-painter*, (*pitt.*) paesista; — *-painting*, (*pitt.*) paesaggio.

landslip ['lændslip], *s.* frana.

landsman, *pl.* **landsmen** ['lændzmən], *s.* uomo di terra ferma.

landward ['lændwəd], **landwards** ['lændwədz], *av.* (*mar.*) verso terra.

lane [lein], *s.* **1.** viottolo, sentiero; stradicciola; vicolo: *in this district there are many lanes*, in questa regione ci sono molti viottoli || *the red* —, (*fam.*) la gola || *it is a long* — *that has no turning*, *prov.* il tempo arriva per chi lo sa aspettare **2.** passaggio fra due ali di gente: *to make a* — *for s.o. to pass through*, fare ala per lasciare passare qlcu. **3.** (*mar.*) rotta **4.** (*elett.*) corsia ☆ *air-* —, corridoio aereo; *blind-* — vicolo cieco; *four* — *motor road*, autostrada a quattro corsie; *landing-* —, sentiero di atterraggio; *sea-* —, rotta marittima.

Lanfranc ['lænfræŋk], *no.pr.m.* Lanfranco.

langrage ['læŋgridʒ], *s.* (*mil. arc.*) mitraglia.

lang-syne ['læŋ'sain], *av.* (*scoz.*) molto tempo fa || *s.* il tempo passato.

language ['læŋgwidʒ], *s.* **1.** lingua, facoltà di parlare: *do animals possess* —?, gli animali possono parlare? **2.** lingua, idioma: *a dead* —, una lingua morta; *a living* —, una lingua viva **3.** modo di esprimersi: *literary* —, linguaggio letterario; — *of flowers*, linguaggio dei fiori; *to use bad* —, usare un linguaggio sboccato ☆ *finger* —, linguaggio dei muti.

languaged ['læŋgwidʒd], *ag.* esperto in una o più lingue; espresso in una lingua ☆ *many-* —, che conosce molte lingue, poliglotta.

languescent [læŋ'gwesənt], *ag.* languente.

languid ['læŋgwid], *ag.* languido; fiacco: *to be* — *about sthg.*, non avere entusiasmo per ql.co.; *to give s.o. a* — *look*, guardare qlcu. languidamente.

languidly ['læŋgwidli], *av.* languidamente; fiaccamente.

languidness ['læŋgwidnis], *s.* languidezza; fiacchezza.

languish ['læŋgwiʃ], *s.* languore; sguardo tenero.

to languish, *v.i.* **1.** languire, illanguidire; indebolirsi: *the roses are languishing*, le rose stanno appassendo; *they made him* — *with hunger*, gli fecero patire la fame **2.** struggersi.

languishingly ['læŋgwiʃiŋli], *ag.* languido: *they exchanged* — *looks*, si scambiarono occhiate languide.

languishingly ['læŋgwiʃiŋli], *av.* languidamente.

languishment ['læŋgwiʃmənt], *s.* languore.

languor ['læŋgə*], *s.* **1.** languore, debolezza; aspetto languido **2.** indifferenza **3.** afa.

languorous ['læŋgərəs], *ag.* languido.

langur [lʌŋ'guə*], *s.* (*zool.*) entello.

laniary ['læniəri], *ag.* (*zool.*) lacerante, tagliente || *s.* dente canino.

laniferous [lei'nifərəs], *ag.* lanifero.

lank [læŋk], *ag.* **1.** magro, sottile, scarno **2.** diritto, non arricciato: — *hair*, capelli lisci.

lankiness ['læŋkinis], *s.* eccessiva magrezza.

lanky ['læŋki], *ag.* alto e magro; scarno, sparuto.

lanner ['lænə*], *s.* (*ornit.*) lanario.

lanolin(e) ['lænəliːn], *s.* lanolina.

lansquenet ['lɑːnskənet], *s.* (*st.*) lanzichenecco.

lantern ['læntən], *s.* **1.** lanterna, fanale **2.** (*mar.*) lanterna; faro **3.** (*arch.*) lucernario, cupolino, lanterna ☆ — *lecture*, conferenza con proiezioni || *dark* —, lanterna cieca; *magic* —, lanterna magica.

lanuginous [lə'njuːdʒinəs], *ag.* lanuginoso.

lanyard ['lænjəd], *s.* **1.** (*mar.*) cordone (portato al collo per fischietto, ecc.) **2.** (*mar.*) cima, drizza.

Laocoon [lei'ɔkouən], *no.pr.m.* (*mit.*) Laocoonte.

Laodamia [ˌleioudə'maiə], *no.pr.f.* (*mit.*) Laodamia.

Laodicea [ˌleioudi'siə], *no.pr.* (*geog.*) Laodicea.

Laomedon [lei'ɔmidon], *no.pr.m.* (*mit.*) Laomedonte.

Laos [lauz], *no.pr.* (*geog.*) Laos.

Laotian ['lauʃiən], *ag.* laotiano || *s.c.* abitante del Laos.

lap[1] [læp], *s.* **1.** grembo, seno: *to sit on* (o *in*) *s.o.'s* —, sedere in grembo a, sulle ginocchia di qlcu. || *in the* — *of luxury*, nel lusso || *it is in the* — *of Providence*, Dio solo lo sa, è nelle mani di Dio **2.** (*arc.*) lobo (d'orecchio, fegato, polmone) **3.** conca, valletta fra due colline **4.** lembo, falda, balza ☆ — *-dog*, cane da salotto.

lap[2], *s.* **1.** parte sovrapposta a un'altra **2.** giro, avvolgimento (di filo) **3.** (*ind. tessile*) falda (d'ovatta); tela **4.** (*spor.*) giro di circuito, di pista: *to be on the last* —, essere in vista del traguardo ☆ — *-dissolve*, (*tv.*) dissolvenza graduale; — *-joint*, giunto a sovrapposizione; — *-machine*, (*ind. tessile*) avvolgitore; — *-roll*, (*ind. tessile*) rullo avvolgitore; — *welding*, (*metal.*) saldatura a sovrapposizione || *half-* —, (*metal.*) giunto a sovrapposizione.

to lap[2], *pass.p.p.* **lapped** [læpt], *v.t.i.* **1.** piegare, avvolgere; ricoprire: *lapped in flannel*, avvolto in soffice lana **2.** ripiegare, ripiegarsi; sovrapporre, sovrapporsi; (*mec. metal.*) incastrare, fare un giunto a sovrapposizione **3.** (*ind. tessile*) infaldare, avvolgere **4.** (*spor.*) superare uno (concorrente) di uno o più giri **5.** *to* — *over*, sovrapporre, sovrapporsi; sormontare; *fig.* estendersi oltre un certo limite.

lap[3], *s.* **1.** broda, brodaglia (per animali); (*sl.*) bibita, liquore; sorso (di ql.co.) **2.** il lappare (di cani) **3.** sciabordio.

to lap[3], *v.t.i.* **1.** bere avidamente, rumorosamente; lambire, lappare **2.** sciabordare ☆ *lapping waves*, maretta.

lap[4], *s.* **1.** mola per preziosi **2.** bacchetta (per pulire il fucile).

to lap[4], *v.t.* levigare, molare (acciaio, preziosi, ecc.).

laparotomy [ˌlæpə'rɔtəmi], *s.* (*chir.*) laparatomia.

lapel [lə'pell], *s.* risvolto (di giacca, soprabito).

lapelled [lə'peld], *ag.* che ha risvolto, con risvolto.

lapful ['læpful], *s.* grembialata.

lapicide ['læpisaid], *s.* scalpellino; marmista.

lapidary ['læpidəri], *ag.* lapidario || *s.* lapidario.

to lapidate ['læpideit], *v.t.* lapidare.

lapidation [ˌlæpi'deiʃən], *s.* lapidazione.

lapidescent [ˌlæpi'desənt], *ag.* lapidescente.

lapidification [lə,pidifi'keiʃən], *s.* pietrificazione.

to lapidify [lə'pidifai], *v.t.i.* pietrificare; pietrificarsi.

lapis-lazuli [ˌlæpis'læʒjulai], *s.* (*min.*) lapislazzuli.

Lapithae ['læpiθiː], *s.pl.* (*mit.*) Lapiti.

Lapland ['læplænd], *no.pr.* (*geog.*) Lapponia.

Laplander ['læplændə*], *s.c.* lappone.

Laplandish ['læplændiʃ], *ag.* lappone.

Lapp [læp], *ag.* lappone || *s.c.* lappone || *s.* lingua lappone.

lappet ['læpit], *s.* **1.** falda; risvolto **2.** (*eccl.*) manipolo; bendone (di mitra) **3.** lobo (di orecchio); bargigli (di tacchino) **4.** copriserratura.

Lappie ['læpik], **Lappish** ['læpiʃ], *ag.* lappone || *s.* lingua lappone.

Lapponian [læ'pouniən], *ag.s.c.* lappone.

lapse [læps], *s.* **1.** errore, sbaglio; passo falso; scorrettezza (anche *fig.*) **2.** intervallo, lasso: *a long* — *of time*, un lungo lasso di tempo **3.** (*dir.*) prescrizione estintiva.

to **lapse**, *v.i.* **1.** mancare, venir meno; errare **2.** *fig.* scivolare, cadere: *to — into bad habits*, abbandonarsi a cattive abitudini **3.** (*dir.*) cadere in prescrizione.

Laputa [lə'pju:tə], *no.pr.* (*lett.*) Laputa.

lapwing ['læpwiŋ], *s.* (*ornit.*) pavoncella.

lar [lɑ:*], *pl.* **lares** ['lɛəri:z], *s.* (*mit.*) lare.

larboard ['lɑ:bəd], *s.* (*mar.*) babordo.

larcenist ['lɑ:snist], *s.* (*dir.*) ladruncolo.

larceny ['lɑ:sni], *s.* (*dir.*) furto, ladrocinio.

larch [lɑ:tʃ], *s.* (*bot.*) larice.

to **lard**, *v.t.* **1.** ungere con lardo; lardellare **2.** arricchire (discorso, scritto).

lardaceous [lɑ:'deifəs], *ag.* (*patol.*) lardaceo.

larder ['lɑ:də*], *s.* dispensa, credenza.

larderer ['lɑ:dərə*], *s.* dispensiere.

lardy ['lɑ:di], *ag.* lardaceo.

lardy-dardy ['lɑ:di'dɑ:di], *ag.* (*sl.*) affettato; ostentatamente languido.

large [lɑ:dʒ], *ag.* **1.** grande; largo; vasto, spazioso (anche *fig.*): *— discretion*, grande discrezione; *— family*, famiglia numerosa, *— powers*, ampi poteri; *— views*, ampie vedute; *it's a — sum*, è una somma considerevole ‖ *as — as life*, al naturale, (*fam.*) come se niente fosse ‖ *on a — scale*, su vasta scala **2.** generoso, liberale: *they have been very —*, sono stati molto generosi **3.** (*mar.*) favorevole (di vento) **4.** (*rar.*) prolisso, lungo ☆ *— -hearted*, generoso; *— -heartedness*, generosità; *— -limbed*, forte, nerboruto; *— -minded*, di larghe vedute; *— -sized*, di grandi dimensioni.

large, *s.: in —*, su vasta scala; *people at —*, la gente in genere, la gran massa; *to be at —*, essere in libertà; *to scatter imputations at —*, fare delle imputazioni a caso; *to set at —*, dare la libertà; *to talk at —*, parlare a vanvera.

large, *av.: to sail —*, (*mar.*) salpare col vento in poppa.

largely ['lɑ:dʒli], *av.* largamente, in gran misura.

to **largen** ['lɑ:dʒən], *v.t.i.* (*poet.*) allargare, allargarsi.

largeness ['lɑ:dʒnis], *s.* **1.** larghezza, grandezza; estensione; ampiezza: *— of views*, larghezza di vedute **2.** generosità.

largess(e) ['lɑ:dʒes], *s.* **1.** donazione **2.** liberalità.

largish ['lɑ:dʒiʃ], *ag.* piuttosto largo, abbondante.

larghetto [lɑ:'getou], *s.* (*mus.*) larghetto.

largo ['lɑ:gou], *s.* (*mus.*) largo.

lariat ['læriət], *s.* «lazo», laccio.

lark¹ [lɑ:k], *s.* (*ornit.*) allodola.

lark², *s.* (*fam.*) burla, scherzo; incidente comico ‖ *what a —!*, che spasso! ‖ *to have a —*, fare una burla.

to **lark²**, *v.i.* fare delle burle; scherzare.

larkspur ['lɑ:k-spə:*], *s.* (*bot.*) consolida reale.

larky ['lɑ:ki], *ag.* gaio, spensierato; burlone.

larrikin ['lærikin], *s.* (*austral.*) monello.

larva ['lɑ:və], *pl.* **larvae** ['lɑ:vi] *s.* (*entom.*) larva **2.** larva; spettro, fantasma.

larval ['lɑ:vəl], *ag.* (*entom.*) larvale.

larvate ['lɑ:veit], *ag.* larvato.

laryngeal [,lærin'dʒi(:)əl], *ag.* (*anat.*) laringeo.

laryngitis [,lærin'dʒaitis], *s.* (*patol.*) laringite.

laryngologist [,læriŋ'gɔlədʒist], *s.* laringologo.

laryngology [,læriŋ'gɔlədʒi], *s.* laringologia.

laryngoscope [lə'riŋgəskoup], *s.* laringoscopio.

laryngoscopy [,læriŋ'gɔskəpi], *s.* laringoscopia.

laryngotomy [,læriŋ'gɔtəmi], *s.* (*chir.*) laringotomia.

larynx ['læriŋks], *s.* (*anat.*) laringe.

Lascar ['læskə*], *s.* (*angl.-in.*) marinaio indigeno; artigliere, attendente indigeno.

lascivious [lə'siviəs], *ag.* lascivo, lussurioso.

lasciviously [lə'siviəsli], *av.* lascivamente.

lasciviousness [lə'siviəsnis], *s.* lascivia.

lash¹ [læʃ], *s.* **1.** parte flessibile della frusta **2.** frustata (anche *fig.*) ☆ (*eye*)- —, ciglio.

to **lash¹**, *v.t.i.* **1.** frustare; sferzare, colpire; staffilare (anche *fig.*): *he lashed his horse*, egli frustò il cavallo ‖ *to — at*, castigare, sferzare; *to — at vice*, inveire contro

il vizio **2.** agitare, agitarsi; infuriarsi: *the lion lashed its tail*, il leone agitò la coda; *to — oneself into a fury*, andar su tutte le furie **3.** infrangersi (di onde) **4.** *to — out*, sferrare calci (di cavallo); lanciarsi violentemente; parlare, rimproverare rabbiosamente: *the horse lashed out at me*, il cavallo mi sferrò un calcio.

to **lash²**, *v.t.* (*mar.*) legare.

lasher ['læʃə*], *s.* **1.** sferzatore **2.** (*mar.*) corda, cavo **3.** acqua che passa sopra una diga; diga **4.** bacino ai piedi di una diga.

lashing¹ ['læʃiŋ], *s.* **1.** frustata; staffilata **2.** *pl.* (*fam.*) abbondanza: *strawberries with lashings of cream*, fragole con moltissima panna.

lashing², *s.* legatura, allacciatura.

lass [læs], *s.* **1.** ragazza, ragazzetta **2.** innamorata **3.** (*scoz.*) servetta.

lassie ['læsi], *s. dim.* di **lass**.

lassitude ['læsitju:d], *s.* stanchezza; accasciamento; apatia.

lasso ['læsou], *pl.* **lassos, lassoes** ['læsouz], *s.* laccio.

to **lasso**, *v.t.* prendere col laccio.

last¹ [lɑ:st], *ag.* (*superl.* di *late*) **1.** ultimo (di posizione): *the — two persons*, le ultime due persone ‖ *— but not least*, ultimo ma non meno importante; ‖ *the — but one*, il penultimo ‖ *the Last Day*, il Giorno del Giudizio ‖ *the — straw*, il colmo, la goccia che fa traboccare il vaso ‖ *to be on one's — legs*, (*fam.*) essere vicini alla morte; essere all'estremo delle proprie risorse **2.** ultimo, scorso, più recente: *— night*, la notte scorsa, ieri sera; *— week year*, la settimana scorsa, l'anno scorso; *in the — fortnight*, negli ultimi quindici giorni; *on Monday — (o — Monday)*, lunedì scorso; *the night before —*, l'altro ieri sera, due sere fa **3.** ultimo, il meno desiderato, il più impensato: *it was the — thing I wanted to do*, era l'ultima cosa che volessi fare; *it was the — thing I was thinking of*, era l'ultima cosa a cui pensassi **4.** ultimo, definitivo: *the — word has not yet been said*, non si è ancora detta l'ultima parola **5.** massimo, estremo: *it's a matter of the — importance*, è una faccenda della massima importanza ‖ *s.* **1.** fino: *at — (o at long —)*, alla fine; *to the —*, fino all'ultimo: *to hold on to the —*, resistere sino alla fine **2.** (sta per *— person, thing, etc.*): *the — of the Stuarts*, l'ultimo degli Stuart; *the — to leave were my parents*, gli ultimi ad andarsene furono i miei genitori; *when was your — born?*, quando nacque il tuo ultimo figlio? **3.** (sta per *— day, moments, etc.*): *to breathe one's —*, morire **4.** (sta per *— letter, book, mention, etc.*): *did you read his —?*, hai letto la sua ultima lettera? **5.** (**Fraseologia**): *thank god, we have seen the — of him*, grazie al cielo, ce ne siamo liberati; *that was the — I saw of her*, non l'ho più rivista; *we haven't heard the — of it*, ne sentiremo ancora parlare ‖ *av.* **1.** ultimo, in ultimo, per ultimo: *which boy came in —?*, quale ragazzo arrivò ultimo? **2.** l'ultma volta: *when did you see him —?*, quando l'hai visto l'ultima volta? **3.** alla fine, finalmente.

last², *s.* (*rar.*) continuazione, durata.

to **last²**, *v.i.* durare; conservarsi; resistere: *how long did the performance —?*, quanto durò la rappresentazione?; *this material is sure not to — long*, è certo che questa stoffa non durerà a lungo.

last³, *s.* forma di scarpa.

to **last³**, *v.t.* mettere in forma (una scarpa).

last⁴, *s.* lasta (misura di peso e capacità variabile).

lastage ['lɑ:stidʒ], *s.* **1.** tassa portuale (per avere il permesso di caricare una nave) **2.** tassa per commercianti (che partecipano ad un mercato, ad una fiera).

lasting ['lɑ:stiŋ], *ag.* durevole, duraturo; permanente ‖ *s.* durata.

lastingly ['lɑ:stiŋli], *av.* durevolmente; permanentemente; perpetuamente.

lastingness ['lɑ:stiŋnis], *s.* durabilità.

latch [lætʃ], *s.* **1.** saliscendi, chiavistello; nottola **2.** serratura con scatto a molla.

to **latch**, *v.t.* chiudere con saliscendi.

latchkey ['lætʃkiː], *s.* chiave per serrature a molla.

late [leit], *comp.* **later** ['leitə*], *irr.* **latter** ['lætə*], *superl.* **latest** ['leitist], *irr.* **last** [lɑːst], *ag.* **1.** in ritardo, tardi: *don't be — !*, non far tardi!; *is it so — ?*, è così tardi?; *now it's too —*, ora è troppo tardi; *the plane was twenty minutes —*, l'aereo aveva venti minuti di ritardo **2.** tardo, avanzato, inoltrato: *in the — after-noon*, nel tardo pomeriggio; *in the — twenties*, negli anni immediatamente precedenti il 1930; *the hour is —*, l'ora è tarda; *to keep — hours*, rientrare ad ore tarde, fare le ore piccole **3.** tardivo: *— snowfalls*, nevicate tardive **4.** precedente; ex; defunto, fu: *the — mayor*, l'ex sindaco; *her — husband*, il suo defunto marito **5.** recente: *the — rains*, le piogge recenti ‖ *of — years*, in questi ultimi anni ‖ *av.* tardi, in ritardo; recentemente: *— in the night*, a notte inoltrata; *I arrived —*, arrivai in ritardo; *to sit up —*, stare alzato fino a tardi ‖ *of —*, da poco, da qualche tempo ‖ *it is better — than never*, *prov.* meglio tardi che mai.

lately ['leitli], *av.* recentemente; ultimamente: *till —*, fino a poco tempo fa.

latency ['leitənsi], *s.* latenza.

lateness ['leitnis], *s.* **1.** indugio, ritardo **2.** tempo, epoca avanzata; data, epoca recente.

latent ['leitənt], *ag.* nascosto; segreto; latente.

latently ['leitəntli], *av.* latentemente.

later ['leitə*], *ag.* (*comp.* di *late*) posteriore; ulteriore; più recente: *— events*, avvenimenti ulteriori, successivi; *at a — date than her marriage*, a una data posteriore al suo matrimonio ‖ *av.* più tardi, dopo; più recentemente: *— on*, poi, più tardi; *a moment —*, un momento più tardi; *see you — !*, (*fam.*) a più tardi!; *sooner or —*, prima o poi.

lateral ['lætərəl], *ag.* laterale ‖ *s.* parte laterale.

Lateran ['lætərən], *ag.* lateranense ‖ *s.* Laterano.

laterite ['lætərait], *s.* (*geol.*) laterite.

latest ['leitist], *ag.* (*superl.* di *late*) ultimo; recentissimo: *— novelties*, le ultime novità; *in the — fashion*, all'ultima moda; *here is the — news*, ecco le ultime notizie ‖ *at (the) —*, al più tardi ‖ *that is the —*, è l'ultima novità; (*fam.*) è il colmo.

latex ['leiteks], *s.* (*bot.*) lattice.

lath [lɑːθ], *s.* canniccio; assicella; stecca ‖ *as thin as a —*, magro come un chiodo ☆ *— -house*, (*agr.*) riparo, capanna di cannicci; *— -work*, incannicciatura.

to **lath**, *v.t.* ricoprire, mettere cannicci a.

lathe [leið], *s.* (*mec.*) tornio ☆ *— -bed*, bancale del tornio; *— -carrier* (o *-dog*), brida ‖ *bench —*, tornio da banco; *chuck —*, tornio frontale; *extension gap —*, tornio a collo d'oca, a doppio banco; *wood turning —*, tornio da legno.

lather ['lɑːðə*], *s.* **1.** schiuma (di sapone) **2.** sudore schiumoso (di cavallo).

to **lather**, *v.t.i.* **1.** coprire di schiuma; insaponare **2.** far schiuma, schiumare.

lathering ['lɑːðəriŋ], *s.* battitura; frustatura.

lathing ['lɑːθiŋ], *s.* incannicciatura.

lathy ['lɑːθi], *ag.* simile a uno stecco (di persona).

Latin ['lætin], *ag.* latino: *— people*, popolo latino ‖ *s.c.* latino, latina ‖ *s.* lingua latina ☆ *— -American*, sud-americano; *— Church*, Chiesa Cattolica; *— -cross*, croce latina ‖ *dog —*, latino maccheronico; *thieves —*, gergo dei ladri.

Latinism ['lætinizəm], *s.* latinismo.

Latinist ['lætinist], *s.c.* latinista.

Latinity [lə'tiniti], *s.* latinità.

Latinization [ˌlætinai'zeifən] *s.* latinizzazione.

to **Latinize** ['lætinaiz], *v.t.i.* latinizzare, latinizzarsi.

latitude ['lætitjuːd], *s.* **1.** latitudine: *degree of —*, grado di latitudine **2.** *pl.* regioni, climi **3.** *fig.* larghezza, spazio; libertà: *to allow a certain —*, permettere una certa libertà ☆ *high latitudes*, regioni dell'estremo Nord o Sud; *North —*, latitudine settentrionale.

latitudinal [ˌlæti'tjuːdinl], *ag.* latitudinale.

latitudinarian ['læti,tjuːdi'nɛəriən], *ag.* latitudinario, rio ‖ *s.* (*eccl.*) partigiano della tolleranza religiosa nella Chiesa Anglicana.

Latona [lə'tounə], *no.pr.f.* (*mit.*) Latona.

latrine [lə'triːn], *s.* latrina.

latter ['lætə*], *ag.* (*comp.* di *late*) posteriore; ultimo, più recente; quest'ultimo; secondo: *the — half of the century*, la seconda metà del secolo; *in these — days*, in questi ultimi tempi; ai nostri giorni ‖ *latter -day Saints*, i mormoni ‖ *— end*, parte finale (di vita, epoca, ecc.) ‖ *pron.* l'ultimo (di due): *the former and the —*, quegli e questi.

latterly ['lætəli], *av.* ultimamente; recentemente.

lattice ['lætis], *s.* grata, traliccio ☆ *— -window*, finestra con grata, con vetri a piombo; *— -work*, intelaiatura a traliccio.

latticed ['lætist], *ag.* munito di grata, traliccio.

Latvia ['lætviə], *no.pr.* (*geog.*) Lettonia.

Latvian ['lætviən], *ag.s.c.* lettone.

laud [lɔːd], *s.* (*poet.*) **1.** lode **2.** *pl.* (*eccl. poes.*) laudi.

to **laud**, *v.t.* (*rar.*) lodare.

laudability [ˌlɔːdə'biliti], *s.* lodabilità.

laudable ['lɔːdəbl], *ag.* lodevole.

laudably ['lɔːdəbli], *av.* lodevolmente.

laudanum ['lɔːdnəm], *s.* (*farm.*) laudano.

laudation [lɔː'deifən], *s.* lode.

laudative ['lɔːdətiv], *ag.* laudativo.

laudator [lɔː'deitə*], *s.c.* lodatore, lodatrice.

laudatory ['lɔːdətəri], *ag.* lodativo, laudatorio.

laugh [lɑːf], *s.* riso; risata; ilarità: *a hearty —*, una risata cordiale; *a loud —*, una risata sonora; *now he had the — on his side*, poteva ben ridere ora; *to break into a —*, scoppiare a ridere, ridere a denti stretti; *to give a forced —*, ridere forzatamente, ridere verde; *to have a good —*, fare una bella risata; *to join in the —*, partecipare all'allegria generale; *to raise a —*, eccitare, destare ilarità ‖ *to have the — of s.o.*, (*fam.*) ridere a spese di qlcu.

to **laugh**, *v.t.i.*, **1.** ridere: *he laughed heartily*, rise di cuore; *she laughed a hearty laugh*, rise di cuore; *she laughed herself helpless*, rise a crepapelle; *you make me —*, mi fai proprio ridere ‖ *I soon made him — on the wrong side of his face*, gli feci passare subito la voglia di ridere ‖ *to — in a person's face*, ridere in faccia a qlcu. ‖ *to — up one's sleeve*, ridere sotto i baffi ‖ *to — to scorn*, trattare con disprezzo ‖ *— on Friday, cry on Sunday*, *prov.* chi ride il venerdì piange la domenica ‖ *he laughs best who laughs last*, *prov.* ride bene chi ride ultimo **2.** *to — at* (*s.o.*), ridere di, burlarsi di: *he was laughed at*, fu deriso; *I — at your anger*, della tua collera me ne rido **3.** *to — away*, dissipare, allontanare ridendo: *she laughed away his doubts*, scherzando riuscì a dissipare i dubbi di lui **4.** *to — off*, buttarla in ridere: *she always manages to — off embarrassing situations*, in situazioni imbarazzanti riesce sempre a cavarsela con spirito **5.** *to — out*, distogliere deridendo: *I laughed him out of his fright*, con una bella risata gli feci passare la paura **6.** *to — over*, discutere ridendo.

laughable ['lɑːfəbl], *ag.* comico, divertente; piacevole; ridicolo.

laughableness ['lɑːfəblnis], *s.* comicità.

laughably ['lɑːfəbli], *av.* ridicolmente.

laugher ['lɑːfə*], *s.c.* chi ride; burlone, burlona.

laughing ['lɑːfiŋ], *ag.* che ride, allegro: *— eyes*, occhi ridenti ‖ *it is no — matter*, non c'è niente da ridere ‖ *s.* risata: *not so much — and talking, please*, basta con le chiacchiere e le risate ☆ *— -gas*, gas esilarante; *— -stock*, zimbello.

laughingly ['lɑːfiŋli], *av.* con risa, in modo ridente.

laughter ['lɑːftə*], *s.* (*solo sing.*) il ridere, riso; ilarità; risata: *burst of —*, scoppio di riso; *a fit of —*, riso irrefrenabile; *roar of —*, risa sfrenate; *to break (o to burst) into —*, scoppiare a ridere, ridere a crepapelle ‖ *to die with —*, morire dal ridere.

launce [lɑːns], s. (ittiol.) ammocete.

Launcelot ['lɑːnslət], no.pr.m. (lett.) Lancellotto.

launch[1] [lɔːntʃ], s. **1.** (mar.) varo **2.** l'alzarsi a volo (di uccelli) **3.** (missilistica) lancio.

to **launch**[1], v.t.i. **1.** lanciare, lanciarsi (anche fig.): to — a missile, lanciare un missile; to — threats against s.o., lanciare minacce contro qlcu. **2.** (mar.) varare: to — a ship, varare una nave **3.** to — out, varare; incominciare da capo: to — out into expense, darsi alle spese; to — out on a new enterprise, imbarcarsi in una nuova impresa ‖ he's launching out!, si lancia! (si dà alle spese per farsi notare) ☆ launching-carriage, (aer.) carrello di lancio; launching-site, (aer.) pista di lancio.

launch[2], s. **1.** scialuppa **2.** motolancia.

launcher ['lɔːntʃə*], s. (mil.) dispositivo di lancio.

to **launder** ['lɔːndə*], v.t.i. lavare e stirare, fare il bucato: these sheets — well, queste lenzuola si lavano bene ☆ freshly-laundered, di bucato: freshly-laundered sheets, lenzuola di bucato.

launderer ['lɔːndərə*], s. lavandaio.

launderette [ˌlɔːndə'ret], s. lavanderia attrezzata con lavatrici automatiche (dove il cliente fa da sè il proprio bucato).

laundress ['lɔːndris], s. lavandaia; stiratrice.

laundry ['lɔːndri], s. **1.** lavanderia **2.** bucato ☆ — -maid, lavandaia; — -man, lavandaio.

Laura ['lɔːrə], no.pr.f. Laura.

laureate ['lɔːriit], ag. coronato d'alloro ‖ the Poet Laureate, il poeta laureato (in Inghilterra).

laureateship ['lɔːriitʃip], s. titolo, ufficio di poeta laureato (in Inghilterra).

laureation [ˌlɔːri'eiʃən], s. conferimento del titolo di poeta laureato (in Inghilterra).

laurel ['lɔrəl], s. **1.** (bot.) lauro, alloro **2.** gener. pl. fig. onore; vittoria: to look to one's laurels, cercare di mantenere la propria alta posizione; to reap (o to win) —, mietere allori; to rest on one's laurels, riposarsi sugli allori.

to **laurel**, pass.p.p. **laurelled** ['lɔrəld], v.t. coronare d'alloro.

Laurence ['lɔrəns], no.pr.m. Lorenzo.

Laurentian [lɔ'renʃən], ag. laurenziano.

lauriferous [lɔ'rifərəs], ag. laurifero.

lauwine ['lɔːwin], s. slavina; valanga.

lava ['lɑːvə], s. lava.

lavabo [lə'veibou], pl. **lavaboes** [lə'veibouz], s. (eccl.) lavabo.

lavatory ['lævətəri], s. gabinetto, cesso ☆ — chain, catena (del gabinetto).

to **lave** [leiv], v.t.i. (poet.) lavare, lavarsi; bagnare, bagnarsi; scorrere (di acque).

lavender ['lævində*], s. (bot.) lavanda ☆ — -water, acqua di lavanda.

laver[1] ['leivə*], s. (bot.) lattuga di mare.

laver[2], s. **1.** (poet.) bacinella, catino **2.** fig. fonte battesimale.

Lavinia [lə'viniə], no.pr.f. Lavinia.

lavish ['læviʃ], ag. **1.** prodigo, generoso: to be — in giving one's money, essere prodigo del proprio denaro; to be — of one's praise, essere generoso di lodi **2.** abbondante, profuso: — expenses, grosse spese.

to **lavish**, v.t. prodigare, profondere: to — sthg. on s.o., dare generosamente ql.co. a qlcu.

lavishly ['læviʃli], av. **1.** generosamente, prodigamente **2.** profusamente.

lavishment ['læviʃmənt], s. (rar.) prodigalità.

lavishness ['læviʃnis], s. prodigalità.

law [lɔː], s. **1.** legge; decreto legge; ordinanza: breach of —, violazione di legge; the king's will is —, la volontà del re è legge; what he says is —, (fam.) la sua parola è legge; to be —, aver forza di legge; to carry out a — (o to put a — into force), far osservare una legge; to lay down the —, dettar legge; to pass a —, passare una legge; to repeal a —, abrogare una legge ‖ to have one — for the rich and another for the poor, aver due pesi e due misure **2.** the —, la legge: the — allows, forbids, la legge consente, proibisce; to keep the —, osservare la legge ‖ the limb of the —, (fam.) poliziotto **3.** professione legale: to be in the —, avere uno studio di avvocato; to go in for the —, dedicarsi all'avvocatura; to practise —, esercitare l'avvocatura ‖ the —, gli avvocati **4.** giustizia: to go to — against s.o., procedere per vie legali contro qlcu.; to have recourse to the —, ricorrere alle vie legali ‖ to be at —, essere in causa **5.** legge, principio: Grimm's, Newton's —, legge di Grimm, di Newton; Kepler's laws, le leggi di Keplero **6.** legge morale: the divine —, la legge divina ‖ the Law, la Legge, il Decalogo **7.** (spor.) regola; vantaggio: to give fair —, (caccia) dare vantaggio a ☆ -abiding, osservante della legge; — -book, testo di diritto; — -breaker, violatore della legge; — -calf, rilegatura in pelle di libri di legge; — -court, tribunale; — -day, giorno di udienza (di tribunale); — -faculty, facoltà di giurisprudenza; — -list, annuario di giurisprudenza; — -lord, lord presidente al lavoro legislativo alla Camera dei Lords; — -maker, legislatore; — -merchant, diritto mercantile; — -monger, azzeccagarbugli; — -student, studente in giurisprudenza; — -term, termine legale; — -writer, giurista ‖ canon- —, diritto canonico; brother-in- —, cognato; civil —, dritto civile; commercial —, diritto commerciale; daughter-in- —, nuora; father-in- —, suocero; golf laws, le regole del golf; international —, diritto internazionale; martial —, legge marziale; mother-in- —, suocera; sister-in- —, cognata.

lawful ['lɔːful], ag. legale; legittimo; lecito, permesso, consentito: the — owner, il legittimo proprietario; a — system, un sistema legale ‖ — wife, moglie legittima.

lawfully ['lɔːfuli], av. secondo la legge, legittimamente: — married, legalmente sposato.

lawfulness ['lɔːfulnis], s. legalità; legittimità.

lawgiver ['lɔːˌgivə*], s. legislatore.

lawgiving ['lɔːˌgiviŋ], ag. che detta legge.

lawine [lɑ'viːnə], pl. **lawinen** [lɑ'viːnən], s. slavina.

lawk(s) [lɔːk(s)], inter. (volg.) oh, Dio!.

lawless ['lɔːlis], ag. **1.** senza legge; illegale; arbitrario **2.** sregolato, sfrenato.

lawlessly ['lɔːlisli], av. **1.** illegalmente; arbitrariamente **2.** sfrenatamente.

lawlessness ['lɔːlisnis], s. **1.** illegalità; arbitrio; licenza **2.** sfrenatezza, sregolatezza.

lawn[1] [lɔːn], s. prato rasato ☆ — -mower, falciatrice per prati; — -tennis, tennis su prato.

lawn[2], s. (tela) batista.

lawny[1] ['lɔːni], ag. erboso, a tappeto verde.

lawny[2], ag. di (tela) batista; simile a (tela) batista.

Lawrence ['lɔrəns], no.pr.m. Lorenzo ‖ the St. —, (geog.) il S. Lorenzo: the St. — Waterway, il Canale del San Lorenzo.

lawsuit ['lɔː-sjuːt], s. causa, processo.

lawyer ['lɔːjə*], s. avvocato, giurista: a good —, un buon conoscitore delle leggi ☆ — -like, da avvocato, avvocatesco; poor man's —, patrocinio gratuito.

lax[1] [læks], ag. **1.** trascurato, negligente, inesatto **2.** molle, fiacco, rilassato: — discipline, disciplina rilassata.

lax[2], s. (ittiol.) salmone.

laxative ['læksətiv], ag.s. (farm.) lassativo.

laxist ['læksist], s. (fil.) lassista.

laxity ['læksiti], s. **1.** mollezza, fiacchezza; negligenza **2.** rilassatezza.

laxness ['læksnis], s. rilassamento, fiacchezza.

lay[1] [lei], ag. **1.** laico, secolare **2.** profano, non dotto (specialmente in legge, in medicina): to his — mind the judge had been too hard, ai suoi occhi di profano il giudice era stato troppo severo ☆ — -brother, -sister, converso, conversa; — -clerk, cantore; — -man, laico, secolare; dilettante, profano; — -reader, predicatore laico.

lay[2], *s.* **1.** configurazione, disposizione: — *of the land*, configurazione del terreno **2.** (*sl.*) campo, genere di affari: *it is not my —*, non è il mio campo **3.** (*mar.*) commettitura (di corde) **4.** (*tip.*) disposizione (di pagine di stampa) **5.** percentuale sugli utili (generalmente nella caccia alle balene) **6.** (*dial.*) tassa, imposta **7.** ostricaio, luogo di coltura delle ostriche **8.** tana.

to **lay**[2], *pass.p.p.* **laid** [leid], *v.t.i.* **1.** posare, collocare; stendere, adagiare; mettersi a letto: *he laid his head on the table*, posò il capo sul tavolo || *to — apart*, mettere da parte, serbare || *to — bare*, mettere a nudo, rivelare || *to — by the heels*, imprigionare || *to — claim to*, avanzare diritti su || *to — dead*, uccidere, stendere morto || *to — hands on*, impadronirsi di, mettere le mani addosso a; (*eccl.*) imporre le mani: *I cannot — my hands upon my cap*, non riesco a trovare il mio berretto; *to — violent hands on oneself*, suicidarsi || *to — heads together*, discutere (un piano) insieme || *to — hold of*, impadronirsi di || *to — the hounds on scent*, mettere i cani sulla traccia || *to — low*, abbattere || *to — open*, mettere a nudo, rivelare || *to — siege to*, porre l'assedio a || *to — snares*, tendere insidie || *to — s.o. under obbligation* (*to s.o.*), rendere qlcu. obbligato, in debito (verso qlcu.) || *to — sthg. at the door of s.o.*, attribuire ql.co. a qlcu. || *to — stress on*, accentuare, dare importanza a || *to — to rest* (o *to sleep*), mettere a dormire; *fig.* seppellire **2.** deporre (uova) **3.** disporre, preparare: *to — the fire*, preparare il fuoco; *to — the table*, apparecchiare la tavola **4.** acquietare, calmare; abbattere; far sparire: *what can I do to — your doubts?*, cosa posso fare per dissipare i tuoi dubbi?; *to — a spirit*, esorcizzare uno spirito **5.** sottoporre (fatti, informazioni): *to — data before s.o.*, sottoporre dei dati di fatto a qlcu. **6.** infliggere (un castigo); imporre (regole, tasse): *to — sthg. to the charge of s.o.*, accusare qlcu. di ql.co.; *to — a tax on sthg.*, imporre una tassa su ql.co. **7.** aver luogo (di azione): *the scene is laid in Milan*, la scena si svolge a Milano **8.** (*mar.*) stendere colori, intonacare: *to — colours on a canvas*, stendere colori su una tela; *to — the floor with a carpet*, coprire il pavimento con un tappeto **9.** progettare; applicarsi con sforzo: *his plans had long been laid*, il suo piano era stato pensato a lungo **10.** scommettere, fare una scommessa; giocare (denaro): *to — money on a horse*, scommettere su un cavallo; *to — a wager*, scommettere, fare una scommessa **11.** (*mil.*) puntare (un'arma da fuoco) **12.** (*mar.*) commettere **13.** (*agr.*) margottare **14.** *to — the land*, (*mar.*) perdere di vista la terra **15.** (*tip.*) disporre le pagine (per la stampa) **16.** *to — into* (*s.o.*), (*sl.*) bastonare, picchiare, rimproverare **17.** *to — aside* (o *away* o *by*), mettere da parte, serbare; economizzare; abbandonare (un progetto, abitudini, ecc.) **18.** *to — down*, mettere a terra; deporre; progettare; mettere in costruzione; convertire a pascolo (un terreno); formulare (regola, legge, ecc.); scommettere: *to — down Chianti*, mettere il Chianti in cantina; *to — down a condition*, stabilire una condizione; *to — down one's arms*, deporre le armi; *to — down one's cards*, scoprire le proprie carte; *to — down one's life*, sacrificare la propria vita; *to — down a ship*, impostare una nave; *to — oneself down*, coricarsi **19.** *to — in*, mettere in serbo **20.** *to — off*, (*sl.*) prendersi un riposo; (*amer.*) licenziare **21.** *to — on*, applicare; sovrapporre; coprire; installare; picchiare; mettere (i cani) sulla traccia: *to — on plaster*, intonacare; *to — on the water, the gas*, installare l'acqua, il gas || *to — it on thick*, adulare esageratamente || *to — on a good supper*, (*fam.*) improvvisare una buona cenetta **22.** *to — out*, stendere; tracciare schema, piano (di giardino, ecc.); spendere: *they will be obliged to — out a big sum*, saranno obbligati a sborsare una grossa somma; *to — out a page*, (*tip.*) impaginare || *to — s.o. out*, (*fam.*) mettere fuori combattimento qlcu. || *to — out a corpse*, comporre un cadavere **23.** *to — to*, (*mar.*) essere alla cappa **24.** *to — up*, mettere in serbo, accumulare; obbligare a stare a letto; (*mar.*) mettere in disarmo una nave: *to be laid up*, essere allettato.

lay[3], *s.* (*poes.*) lai.

lay[4], *pass.* di *to* **lie**.

lay-by ['leibai], *s.* **1.** piazzuola (lungo una strada); punto di sbarco (lungo un fiume) **2.** economie, risparmi.

lay-days ['leideiz], *s. pl.* (*comm.*) stallia.

layer ['leiə*], *s.* **1.** strato (anche *geol.*): *a — of clay*, uno strato di argilla **2.** (*agr.*) margotta, propaggine **3.** (gallina) ovaiola: *is this hen a good —?*, fa molte uova questa gallina? **4.** (*mil.*) puntatore **5.** (*foto.*) strato (di emulsione) **6.** *pl.* zone di grano allettato **7.** *layers and backers*, scommettitori (su cavalli) ☆ — *-cake*, dolce a strati.

to **layer** ['leə*], *v.t.i.* **1.** (*agr.*) propagginare, margottare **2.** (*agr.*) prostrarsi, allettarsi (di grano).

layering ['leəriŋ], *s.* **1.** (*ind. ferr. elett.*) strato; posa, messa in opera **2.** (*edil.*) rinzaffo **3.** covata; uova deposte **4.** (*mil.*) puntamento.

layette [lei'et], *s.* corredino da neonato.

lay-figure ['lei'figə*], *s.* **1.** (*art.*) manichino **2.** fantoccio (anche *fig.*).

laying ['leiiŋ], *V.* **layering**.

laylock ['leilək], *s.* (*bot. pop.*) lilla, serenella.

lay-off ['leiɔf], *s.* (*amer.*) licenziamento temporaneo.

lay-out ['leiaut], *s.* **1.** disposizione, ordinamento; tracciato, schema, pianta (di città, giardino, ecc.): *general —*, disegno, piano di massima **2.** (*tip.*) impaginazione **3.** piazzuola (lungo una strada) **4.** (*amer.*) organizzazione (di persone) ☆ — *man*, (*tip.*) impaginatore.

laystall ['leistɔ:l], *s.* immondezzaio.

lazar ['læzə*], *s.* (*arc.*) lazzaro, straccione; lebbroso ☆ — *-house*, lebbrosario, lazzaretto.

lazaret [,læzə'ret], **lazaretto** [,læzə'retou], *s.* **1.** lazzaretto **2.** (*mar.*) interponte.

Lazarus ['læzərəs], *no.pr.m.* Lazzaro || *s.* mendico.

laze [leiz], *s.* (*fam.*) pigrizia; ozio.

to **laze**, *v.t.i.* (*fam.*) fare il pigro, trascorrere (il tempo) in ozio: *he's been lazing all day*, ha ciondolato tutto il giorno || *to — away one's life*, trascorrere la vita pigramente.

lazily ['leizili], *av.* pigramente, indolentemente.

laziness ['leizinis], *s.* pigrizia, indolenza, poltroneria.

lazuli ['læzjulai], *s.* (*min.*) lapislazzuli.

lazulite ['læzjulait], *s.* (*min.*) lazulite.

lazy ['leizi], *ag.* pigro, indolente, neghittoso: *a — fellow*, un fannullone; *to be — over one's work*, essere pigro nel proprio lavoro ☆ — *-bones* (o — *-boots*), (*fam.*) pigrone, poltrone.

to **lazy**, *v.i.* impigrire, impoltronirsi.

lea[1] [li:], *s.* (*poet.*) prato; prateria.

lea[2], *ag.* (*agr.*) a maggese || *s.* maggese.

lea[3], *s.* matassa (misura di lunghezza per il cotone e la seta = m. 109,7).

leach [li:tʃ], *s.:* — *-trough* (o — *-tub*), colatoio (per bucato).

to **leach**, *v.t.* **1.** (*chim. geol.*) lisciviare **2.** (*edil.*) percolare.

lead[1] [led], *s.* **1.** piombo || *an ounce of —*, *fig.* una pallottola **2.** grafite **3.** (*dial.*) pentolone, calderone **4.** (*mar.*) piombo per scandaglio: *to heave the —*, scandagliare **5.** *pl.* lamiere di piombo (per tetti) || *the Leads of Venice*, (*st.*) i Piombi di Venezia **6.** (*tip.*) interlinea ☆ — *acetate*, (*chim.*) acetato di piombo; — *alloy*, lega di piombo; — *coating*, impiombatura; — *glance*, (*min.*) galena; — *line*, (*mar.*) sagola per scandaglio; — *monoxide*, (*chim.*) litargirio; — *ore*, minerale di piombo; — *-paint* (o *red- —*), (*chim.*) minio; — *-pencil*, matita di grafite; — *-poisoning*, (*patol.*) saturnismo; — *shots*, pallini di piombo || *hard —*, piombo antimoniale; *sounding- —*, (*mar.*) piombo per scandagliare; *white- —*, (*pitt.*) biacca.

to **lead**[1], *v.t.i.* **1.** impiombare; piombare **2.** (*tip.*) interlineare **3.** incrostarsi di piombo (di armi da fuoco).

lead² [li:d], *s.* **1.** comando, guida; direzione: *to follow s.o.'s* —, lasciarsi guidare da qlcu.; *to give s.o. a* —, instradare qlcu.; *to take the* —, marciare alla testa; (*spor.*) essere il primo; *to take the* — *in a conversation*, avere parte eminente in una conversazione; *to take the* — *of* (o *over*) *s.o.*, dominare qlcu. **2.** (*teat.*) parte principale di una commedia; primo attore **3.** (*carte*) mano: *whose* — *is it?*, a chi la mano?; *your* —*!*, sei di mano tu! **4.** guinzaglio: *dogs must be kept on a* —, i cani devono essere tenuti al guinzaglio **5.** corso d'acqua artificiale (per mulini); canale fra i ghiacci **6.** (*miner.*) filone; deposito di sabbia aurifera (sul letto di un fiume) **7.** (*elett.*) conduttore isolato; anticipo di fase **8.** (*mec.*) passo (di vite); precessione **9.** (*giornalismo*) testata di articolo ☆ — *-nut*, (*mec.*) madrevite; — *-screw*, (*mec.*) vite madre; — *violin*, primo violino ‖ *down* —, (*rad.*) coda (di antenna); *juvenile* —, primo attor giovane.

to lead², *pass.p.p.* **led** [led], *v.t.i.* **1.** condurre, guidare; capeggiare; dirigere: *the lights led me to the house*, le luci mi guidarono alla casa; *Oxford led by two lengths*, conduceva Oxford per due lunghezze; *to* — *by the hand*, condurre per mano; *to* — *the dance*, condurre la danza; *to* — *s.o. a dance*, *fig.* dar del filo da torcere a qlcu.; *to* — *an expedition*, capeggiare una spedizione; *to* — *an orchestra*, dirigere un'orchestra; *to* — *to the altar*, condurre all'altare; *to* — *the way*, mostrare il cammino; *fig.* guidare ‖ *to* — (*s.o.*) *astray*, sviare (qlcu.) ‖ *to* — *s.o. by the nose*, menare qlcu. per il naso **2.** guidare (un cieco) per mano; condurre (un cavallo) per la briglia; tenere (un cane) al guinzaglio **3.** condurre (di strada, ecc.): *door that leads into the garden*, porta che dà sul giardino; *where does this street* — *to?*, dove conduce questa strada? ‖ *all roads* — *to Rome*, tutte le strade conducono a Roma **4.** (IV) indurre, spingere: *he led me to suppose that...*, mi indusse a supporre che...; *he was led into vice*, fu spinto al vizio; *to* — *s.o. into temptation*, indurre qlcu. in tentazione; *to be led by one's instincts*, seguire il proprio istinto **5.** trascorrere; passare (il tempo) in un determinato modo: *they* — *a miserable life*, trascinano una vita miserabile; *to* — *a double life*, condurre una doppia vita **6.** (*carte*) essere di mano **7.** (*elett.*) essere in anticipo **8.** *to* — *about*, condurre in giro, menare a spasso **9.** *to* — **away**, condur via; *fig.* trascinare: *he was led away by his enthusiasm*, fu trascinato dal suo entusiasmo **10.** *to* — **back**, ricondurre (anche *fig.*) **11.** *to* — **off**, cominciare; guidare **12.** *to* — **on**, condurre, guidare; trascinare; *fig.* incoraggiare: *to* — *the army on to victory*, guidare l'esercito alla vittoria; *to* — *s.o. on to talk*, incoraggiare qlcu. a parlare **13.** *to* — **out**, far uscire, condurre fuori **14.** *to* — **up**, far salire (qlcu.); far avanzare; dare accesso (di scala, ecc.) ‖ *to* — *up to*, condurre gradatamente a; servire da introduzione a.

leaded ['ledid], *ag.* **1.** piombato **2.** (*tip.*) interlineato.

leaden ['ledn], *ag.* **1.** di piombo **2.** *fig.* pesante; inerte, tardo **3.** plumbeo (di colore) ☆ — *-hearted*, dal cuore di piombo, insensibile.

leader ['li:də*], *s.* **1.** capo, guida, comandante; dirigente; capopartito: — *of the opposition in the House of Commons*, capo dell'opposizione alla Camera dei Comuni **2.** avvocato principale (in una causa) **3.** (*spor.*) capitano (di una squadra) **4.** (*mus.*) primo violino **5.** cavallo di testa **6.** (*anat.*) tendine **7.** (*giornalismo*) editoriale, articolo di fondo **8.** (*tip.*) puntini di guida **9.** (*arch.*) pluviale **10.** (*miner.*) vena secondaria **11.** (*mec.*) conduttore **12.** (*foto. cine.*) linguetta iniziale (di pellicola).

leaderette [,li:də'ret], *s.* (*giornalismo*) breve editoriale.

leaderless ['li:dəlis], *ag.* senza capo, senza guida.

leadership ['li:dəʃip], *s.* direzione; comando.

leading¹ ['ledin], *s.* **1.** impiombatura **2.** lavoro in piombo.

leading² ['li:diŋ], *ag.* dominante, sovrastante; prin-

cipale; primo: *the* — *surgeon in Birmingham*, il primo chirurgo di Birmingham; *to play a* — *part in an affair*, avere una parte dominante in un affare ‖ *s.* **1.** guida; direzione **2.** *fig.* esempio; influenza ☆ — *-actor*, *lady*, primo attore, prima attrice; — *-article*, articolo di fondo; — *-business*, (*teat.*) la parte principale; — *-power*, forza motrice; — *-rein*, briglia; — *-strings*, bretelle per sorreggere i bambini: *to be in* — *strings*, *fig.* essere sotto tutela.

leadsman, *pl.* **leadsmen** ['ledzmən], *s.* (*mar.*) scandagliatore.

leadwork ['ledwə:k], *s.* **1.** impiombatura **2.** lavoro in piombo.

leaf¹ [li:f], *pl.* **leaves** [li:vz], *s.* **1.** foglia; *coll.* fogliame: *many trees shed their leaves in autumn*, molti alberi perdono le foglie in autunno **2.** foglio: *a book with a hundred pages has fifty leaves*, un libro di cento pagine ha cinquanta fogli ‖ *to take a* — *out of s.o.'s book*, *fig.* seguire l'esempio di qlcu. ‖ *to turn over a new* —, *fig.* cambiare vita, cominciare da capo **3.** foglia (di metallo), lamina **4.** asse (per allungare un tavolo); ribalta; battente (di porta) **5.** (*mec.*) paletta (di ruota) ☆ — *-blight*, ruggine delle foglie; — *-bud*, germoglio (di foglia); — *-green*, clorofilla; verde prato (colore); — *-insect*, fillio; — *-mould*, terriccio; — *-shaped*, a forma di foglia; — *stalk*, picciuolo; — *-tobacco*, tabacco in foglie.

to leaf¹, *v.t.i.* **1.** mettere le foglie **2.** sfogliare: *to* — (*through*) *a book*, (*amer.*) sfogliare un libro.

leaf², *s.* (*sl. mil.*) congedo, licenza.

leafage ['li:fidʒ], *s.* fogliame.

leafed [li:ft], *ag.* coperto di foglie.

leafiness ['li:finis], *s.* ricchezza di foglie, abbondanza di fogliame.

leafless | ['li:f-lis], *ag.* senza foglie; sfrondato.

leaflessness ['li:flisnis], *s.* mancanza di foglie.

leaflet ['li:f-lit], *s.* **1.** fogliolina **2.** volantino, manifestino.

leafy ['li:fi], *ag.* coperto di foglie, fronzuto.

league¹ [li:g], *s.* lega, unione; fazione: *the League of Nations*, la Società delle Nazioni; *in* — *with*, alleato di; *to join* (*in*) *a* —, allearsi, far lega.

to league¹, *v.t.i.* allearsi, confederarsi, far lega con.

league², *s.* lega (misura itineraria = km. 4,83; misura marina = km. 5,56).

leaguer¹ ['li:gə*], *s.* alleato, membro di lega, confederato.

leaguer², *s.* **1.** campo d'assedio; esercito d'assedio **2.** assedio.

Leah [liə], *no.pr.f.* Lia, Lea.

leak [li:k], *s.* **1.** fessura, apertura; (*mar.*) falla **2.** perdita, fuga (di gas); (*elett.*) dispersione **3.** *fig.* trapelamento (di notizie) ☆ — *-detector*, rivelatore di fuga (di gas); — *-finder*, (*aer.*) cercafughe.

to leak, *v.i.* **1.** perdere, colare, far acqua; lasciar uscire un liquido: *the boat is leaking*, la barca fa acqua; *the roof leaked*, entrava acqua dal tetto **2.** *to* — **out**, spandersi, trapelare: *the news has leaked out*, la notizia è trapelata.

leakage ['li:kidʒ], *s.* **1.** colatura; scolo; stillamento (di liquido): *stopper allowing no* —, tappo a perfetta tenuta **2.** infiltrazione; dispersione **3.** (*comm.*) sconto (per deterioramento, perdita di merce).

leakiness ['li:kinis], *s.* **1.** presenza di fessure, di falle **2.** il perdere, lasciar uscire (da fessura, falla).

leaky ['li:ki], *ag.* **1.** che cola; che perde **2.** (*fam.*) chiacchierone.

leal [li:l], *ag.* (*scozz. poet.*) leale; onesto.

lean¹ [li:n], *s.* inclinazione.

to lean¹, *pass.p.p.* **leaned**, **leant** [lent], *v.t.i.* **1.** pendere; inclinare, inclinarsi: *that tower leans*, quella torre pende **2.** appoggiarsi, fare appoggiare: *don't* — *against that wall*, non appoggiarti a quella parete; *she leaned upon my arm*, si appoggiò al mio braccio **3.** sporgersi:

she leaned out of the window, si sporse dalla finestra **4.** *fig.* dipendere da, appoggiarsi (per consiglio): *he leaned on his friend's advice*, si affidò al consiglio del suo amico **5.** tendere, avere un'inclinazione: *he generally leans towards fatalism*, tende ad essere fatalista.

lean², *ag.* **1.** magro, scarno, smunto (di persona): *to be as — as a lath* (*o as a rake*), essere magro come un chiodo; *to grow —*, dimagrire **2.** povero, improduttivo, sterile: *— crop*, raccolto scarso; *— years*, anni di carestia **3.** magra (di carne) ‖ *s.* **1.** la parte magra (di carne) **2.** lavoro mal retribuito ☆ *— -witted*, povero di spirito.

Leander [li(:)'ændə*], *no.pr.m.* (*lett.*) Leandro.

leaning ['li:niŋ], *ag.* pendente; inclinato ‖ *the Leaning Tower of Pisa*, la Torre pendente di Pisa ‖ *s.* **1.** l'appoggiarsi, l'atto di appoggiarsi **2.** *fig.* inclinazione, propensione.

leanly ['li:nli], *av.* magramente; stentatamente.

leanness ['li:nnis], *s.* magrezza; estenuazione.

lean-to ['li:n'tu:], *ag.* (tetto) appoggiato a un muro ‖ *s.* baracca, tetto, tettoia appoggiata ad altro edificio.

leap¹ [li:p], *s.* **1.** salto, balzo: *at a —*, con un salto; *to take a —*, spiccare un salto ‖ *a — in the dark*, un salto nel buio ‖ *by leaps and bounds*, a balzelloni; con straordinaria rapidità; a passi da gigante **2.** *fig.* cambiamento repentino **3.** monta (di animali) **4.** magra (di fiumi); salto d'acqua **5.** (*mus.*) intervallo ☆ *— -frog*, (*giuoco*) cavalletta; *— -year*, anno bisestile.

to leap¹, *pass.p.p.* **leaped, leapt** [lept], *v.t.i.* **1.** balzare, lanciarsi; saltare, far saltare: *they leapt on their enemies*, balzarono sui nemici; *to — for joy*, balzare, saltare dalla gioia; *to — to one's feet*, balzare in piedi **2.** *to — over* (*sthg.*), scavalcare con un salto **3.** *to — about*, saltellare qua e là **4.** *to — out*, uscire con un balzo **5.** *to — up*, sussultare: *to — up with indignation*, sussultare per l'indignazione.

leap², *s.* **1.** cestello, canestro **2.** nassa.

leaper ['li:pə*], *s.c.* saltatore, saltatrice.

leaping ['li:piŋ], *s.* salto, balzo.

to learn [lə:n], *pass.p.p.* **learnt** [lə:nt], **learned** [lə:nd], *v.t.i.* **1.** imparare; istruirsi; studiare: *to — a lesson*, imparare una lezione; *to — to write*, imparare a scrivere ‖ *to — by heart*, imparare a memoria **2.** venire a sapere, sentire da: *I learnt of his death the other day*, appresi la notizia della sua morte l'altro giorno; *on enquiring, I learnt that...*, informandomi sono venuto a sapere che... **3.** ricevere istruzioni: *to — how to do sthg.*, imparare a fare ql.co.

learnable ['lə:nəbl], *ag.* apprendibile.

learned ['lə:nid], *ag.* dotto, istruito, erudito: *a — man*, un dotto, un erudito.

learnedly ['lə:nidli], *av.* dottamente, eruditamente.

learnedness ['lə:nidnis], *s.* istruzione; erudizione.

learner ['lə:nə*], *s.c.* chi impara; scolaro, scolara; allievo, allieva; apprendista.

learning ['lə:niŋ], *s.* cultura; erudizione; sapere; istruzione ‖ *the new —*, (*st.*) il Rinascimento.

lease¹ [li:s], *s.* **1.** contratto d'affitto; locazione (di terra, fabbricato): *on —*, in affitto: *he holds the land on —*, ha il terreno in affitto **2.** durata, termine (di contratto) ‖ *a new — of life*, *fig.* nuove prospettive di vita ☆ *Lend-Lease Act*, legge noleggio e prestito (legge americana promovente gli aiuti agli Alleati - 1941).

to lease¹, *v.t.* affittare, dare in affitto.

lease², *s.* (*ind. tessile*) invergatura (dei fili dell'ordito) ☆ *— bar*, bacchetta d'invergatura.

leasehold ['li:should], *s.* **1.** proprietà in affitto **2.** durata di un contratto di affitto.

leaseholder ['li:s‚houldə*], *s.* locatario, affittuario.

leash [li:ʃ], *s.* guinzaglio; legaccio: *a dog on the —*, un cane al guinzaglio; *to hold in —*, *fig.* controllare, tenere a freno.

to leash, *v.t.* tenere, legare al guinzaglio.

leasing ['li:siŋ], *s.* (*arc. dial.*) menzogna, bugia.

least [li:st], *ag.* (*superl. irr.* di *little*) **il più piccolo, il minimo:** *he did not have the — chance*, non ebbe la minima opportunità; *Mary is not the — bit musical*, Maria non ha alcun senso musicale; *there wasn't the least wind*, non c'era un alito di vento ‖ *last but not —*, ultimo ma non il meno importante ‖ *(the) —*, **(il) meno:** *not in the — (degree)*, per niente; *a pound (the) very —*, una libbra al minimo; *it does not matter in the —*, non importa affatto, per niente; *you can at — try*, potete per lo meno provare; *to say the — of it*, per non dir di più ‖ *av. (the) —*, **(il) meno; minimamente:** *the — happy*, il meno felice; *— of all*, meno di tutti; tanto meno, soprattutto: *— of all would I...*, soprattutto non vorrei...; *don't tell anyone, — of all your sister*, non lo dire a nessuno e tanto meno a tua sorella; *she deserves it — of all*, ella lo merita meno di tutti.

leastways ['li:stweiz], **leastwise** ['li:stwaiz], *av.* (*dial. pop.*) in ogni caso; o per lo meno.

leat [li:t], *s.* gora; canale di derivazione; condotto.

leather ['leðə*], *s.* **1.** cuoio; pelle **2.** oggetto (*o* parte di esso) in cuoio, pelle; cinghia (di staffa); cuoio (di stecca da biliardo); pelle di daino (per pulire); ecc. **3.** *pl.* pantaloni, gambali (di cuoio) **4.** (*sl.*) palla da cricket, pallone da football **5.** (*sl.*) pelle, epidermide ☆ *— -back*, dorso (di libro), schienale in pelle; *— -back*, tartaruga marina; *— -bottle*, otre; *— -bound*, rilegato in pelle; *— -cloth* (*o American —*), tela cerata; *— -dresser*, conciatore, conciapelli; *— -dressing*, concia di pelli; *— gloves*, guanti di pelle; *fancy — goods*, articoli di pelletteria; *— -head*, *fig.* testa di legno; *— -jacket*, pesci dalla pelle spessa (monocanto, ecc.); (*entom.*) larva della tipula; *— -neck*, (*amer. sl.*) marinaio; *— -paper*, carta marocchina; *— shoes*, scarpe di pelle ‖ *dressed —* (*o tanned —*), cuoio conciato; *imitation —*, pelle finta; *pegamoide*; *Morocco —*, marocchino; *patent —*, coppale, vernice; *undressed —* (*o rough —*), cuoio greggio; *white —*, cuoio allumato.

to leather, *v.t.* **1.** applicare cuoio, pelle a; rilegare, coprire in pelle ‖ *to become leathered*, indurirsi **2.** (*sl.*) conciare per le feste, picchiare di santa ragione.

leatherette [‚leðə'ret], *s.* pelle finta; pegamoide.

leathering ['leðəriŋ], *s.* (*sl.*) bastonatura, sacco di legnate.

leathern ['leðə(:)n], *ag.* di cuoio, di pelle.

leatheroid ['leðəroid], *s.* fibra vulcanizzata.

leathery ['leðəri], *ag.* coriaceo.

leave¹ [li:v], *s.* **1.** permesso, autorizzazione: *by* (*o with*) *your —*, col vostro permesso: *without a "with your —"* (*o without a "by your —"*), (*fam.*) senza chiedere permesso ‖ *to take — to do sthg.*, permettersi di fare ql.co. **2.** licenza, congedo: *he is on —*, è in licenza; *he got a six months' —*, ottenne un congedo di sei mesi **3.** congedo, commiato: *to take — of s.o.*, prendere congedo, accomiatarsi da qlcu.; *to take one's —*, prendere congedo, accomiatarsi ‖ *to be out on ticket of —*, essere in libertà provvisoria ‖ *to take — of one's senses*, impazzire ‖ *to take French —*, (*fam.*) andarsene all'inglese ☆ *— -taking*, addio, commiato ‖ *sick- —*, congedo per ragioni di salute.

to leave¹, *pass.p.p.* **left** [left], *v.t.i.* **1.** lasciare, abbandonare: *he left his books on the table*, lasciò i suoi libri sul tavolo; *he left a wife and three children*, lasciò moglie e tre figli; *she had been left a widow at thirty*, era rimasta vedova a trent'anni; *why did you — your old friends?*, perchè hai abbandonato i tuoi vecchi amici?; *to — the table*, alzarsi da tavola; *to — s.o. free to do sthg.*, lasciar libero qlcu. di fare ql.co.; *to — s.o. in the lurch*, lasciare qlcu. in difficoltà ‖ *it leaves me cold* (*o cool*), mi lascia indifferente, non mi fa nè caldo nè freddo ‖ *it leaves much to be desired*, lascia molto a desiderare ‖ *left to myself, I should act differently*, se dipendesse da me, mi comporterei diversamente ‖ *let us — it at that*, non parliamone più ‖ *to — hold of*, lasciare andare ‖ *to — sthg. unsaid*, tacere ql.co., passare ql.co. sotto silenzio ‖ *to* — *s.o., sthg. alone,* lasciare in pace, lasciar qlcu., lasciar stare, non immischiarsi in ql.co. **2.** partire; lasciare un luogo; uscire: *at what time did he* —?, a che ora è partito?; *he has just left,* è appena uscito, partito; *he left two days ago for New York,* è partito per New York due giorni fa; *I* — *home at 9 o' clock,* esco di casa alle nove; *on leaving the theatre...,* uscendo da teatro...; *she never leaves the house,* non esce mai di casa ‖ *to* — *the road,* uscire di strada (di automobile, ecc.); *to* — *the track* (o *the rails*), (*ferr.*) deragliare **3.** affidare, consegnare: — *it to her,* lascia fare a lei; (*has*) *anything* (*been*) *left for me?,* non c'è nulla per me?; *I* — *it to you,* mi rimetto a te; *I* — *the matter in your hands,* affido la cosa a te; *to* — *in charge,* lasciare in custodia; *to* — *sthg. to time,* affidare ql.co. al tempo; *to* — *word with s.o.,* affidare ql.co. a qlcu.; *to* — *word with s.o.,* lasciar detto a qlcu. ‖ *to be left till called for,* da consegnare su richiesta **4.** lasciare in testamento: *he left all his money to charity,* lasciò tutto il suo denaro in beneficenza **5.** *to be left,* restare, rimanere: *there is no bread left,* non c'è più pane **6.** *to* — *about,* lasciare in giro, in disordine **7.** *to* — *behind,* dimenticare, tralasciare, lasciarsi dietro: *he left the keys behind,* ha dimenticato le chiavi **8.** *to* — *off* (I) finire, smettere, cessare, smettere (abiti): — *off!,* smettila!, finiscila!; — *off shouting,* smettila di gridare; *to* — *off business,* ritirarsi dagli affari **9.** *to* — *out,* trascurare, tralasciare: *nothing was left out to please her,* nulla fu trascurato per farla contenta **10.** *to* — *over,* lasciare in sospeso; avanzare.

to **leave**², *V.* to **leaf**¹.

leaved [li:vd], *ag.* **1.** frondoso, fronzuto **2.** a due battenti (di porta) **3.** allungabile (di tavola).

leaven ['levn], *s.* **1.** lievito **2.** *fig.* fermento.

to **leaven,** *v.t.* **1.** far lievitare, fermentare **2.** (*fam.*) impregnare; modificare, trasformare.

leaving ['li:viŋ], *s.* **1.** partenza **2.** *pl.* avanzi; rifiuti ☆ — *certificate,* certificato di studi; — *examination,* esame di licenza.

Lebanese [,lebə'ni:z], *ag.s.c.* libanese.

Lebanon ['lebənən], *no.pr.* (*geog.*) Libano.

lecher ['letʃə*], *s.* libertino.

lecherous ['letʃərəs], *ag.* lascivo; libertino.

lecherously ['letʃərəsli], *av.* lascivamente; da libertino.

lechery ['letʃəri], *s.* lascivia; libertinaggio.

lectern ['lektə(:)n], *s.* (*eccl.*) leggio.

lection ['lekʃən], *s.* **1.** (*eccl.*) lezione **2.** variante (di un testo).

lectionary ['lekʃnəri], *s.* (*eccl.*) lezionale.

lector ['lektɔ:*], *s.* lettore (anche *eccl.*).

lecture ['lektʃə*], *s.* **1.** conferenza; lezione (di tipo universitario): *we follow* (o *attend*) *lectures on the Romantic Period,* seguiamo un corso di lezioni sul periodo romantico; *to give* (o *to deliver*) *a* —, tenere una conferenza **2.** sgridata, ramanzina: *did he read you a good* —?, ti ha fatto una bella paternale? ☆ — -*hall* (o — -*room*), sala da conferenze; aula universitaria.

to **lecture,** *v.t.i.* **1.** fare una conferenza per; tenere un corso di pubbliche lezioni o conferenze **2.** ammonire, fare una paternale a.

lecturer ['lektʃərə*], *s.c.* **1.** conferenziere, conferenziera **2.** lettore, lettrice universitaria ‖ *s.* predicatore.

lectureship ['lektʃəʃip], *s.* **1.** carica di lettore (universitario) **2.** ciclo di conferenze.

led [led], *pass.p.p.* di to **lead.**

Leda ['li:də], *no.pr.f.* (*mit.*) Leda.

ledge [ledʒ], *s.* **1.** prominenza; sporgenza; sponda **2.** scoglio (a fior d'acqua) **3.** (*miner.*) vena ☆ *window* — , davanzale di finestra.

ledger ['ledʒə*], *s.* **1.** (*comm.*) libro mastro **2.** pietra tombale **3.** (*arch.*) traversa ☆ — -*bait,* esca fissa; — -*board,* corrimano; — -*line,* (*mus.*) rigo supplementare; — -*paper,* carta di medio spessore.

ledgy ['ledʒi], *ag.* pieno di sporgenze.

lee¹ [li:], *ag.* (*mar.*) sottovento ‖ *Lee Islands,* (*geog.*) Isole Sottovento ‖ *s.* (*mar.*) luogo tranquillo, riparato dal vento; *fig.* rifugio ☆ -*shore,* (*mar.*) costa di sottovento; — -*side,* (*mar.*) sottovento; — -*tide,* marea nella stessa direzione del vento.

lee², *s. gener. pl.* sedimento, feccia, fondo (di vino, liquore) ‖ *the lees of society,* (*fam.*) la feccia della società ‖ *to drink a cup to the lees, fig.* bere il calice sino alla feccia.

leech¹ [li:tʃ], *s.* **1.** (*zool.*) sanguisuga, mignatta **2.** (*med.*) coppette **3.** *fig.* usuraio: *he sticks to you like a* —, ti si appiccica come una mignatta.

leech², *s.* (*arc.*) chirurgo, medico.

leech³, *s.* (*mar.*) caduta, colonna (di vela) ☆ -*lines,* caricaboline.

leek [li:k], *s.* **1.** (*bot.*) porro **2.** porro (emblema del Galles).

leer¹ [liə*], *s.* occhiata bieca; occhiata maliziosa.

to **leer**¹, *v.i.* guardar di traverso, biecamente, con cattive intenzioni; guardar con occhio malizioso: *to* — *at s.o.,* guardare qlcu. di traverso.

leer², *s.* forno di ricottura del vetro.

leer³, *ag.* (*dial.*) affamato.

leeringly ['liəriŋli], *av.* di sottecchi.

leery ['liəri], *ag.* (*sl.*) astuto.

leeward ['li:wəd], *ag.av.* sottovento ☆ — -*tide,* marea nella medesima direzione del vento.

Leeward Islands (the) ['li:wəd'ailəndz], *no.pr.* (*geog.*) Isole Sottovento.

leewardly ['li:wədli], *ag.* (*mar.*) che tende a muoversi sottovento.

leeway ['li:wei], *s.* **1.** (*mar. aer.*) deriva, scarroccio; angolo di deriva: *to make* —, scarrocciare **2.** *fig.* ritardo; perdita di tempo; *to make up* —, rifarsi del tempo perduto.

left¹ [left], *ag.* sinistro, manco: — *hand,* mano sinistra ‖ *s.* sinistra: *to* (o *on*) *the* —, a sinistra: *he was seated on your* —, sedeva alla tua sinistra ‖ *the Left,* (*pol.*) la sinistra ☆ — -*hand,* lato sinistro; — -*handed,* mancino; goffo; ambiguo: *a* — -*handed marriage,* un matrimonio morganatico; — -*handiness,* goffaggine; — -*winger,* (*fam.*) aderente, simpatizzante della sinistra.

left², *pass.p.p.* di to **leave** ☆ — -*luggage,* deposito bagagli; — -*off,* scartato, messo da parte: — -*offs,* abiti smessi; — -*over,* lasciato in sospeso.

leftism ['leftizəm], *s.* politica di sinistra.

leftist ['leftist], *ag.* (*pol.*) appartenente alla sinistra ‖ *s.c.* membro della sinistra; progressista.

leftward ['leftwəd], *ag.* verso sinistra.

leftward(s) ['leftwəd(z)], *av.* verso sinistra.

leg [leg], *s.* **1.** gamba: *wooden* —, gamba di legno; *a dog has four legs,* un cane ha quattro gambe; *to stretch one's legs,* sgranchirsi le gambe ‖ *on one's legs,* in piedi ‖ *to be all legs,* essere tutto gambe ‖ *to be on one's last* —, (*fam.*) essere ridotti alla disperazione ‖ *to feel* (o *to find*) *one's legs,* muovere i primi passi ‖ *to have good* (*walking*) *legs* (o *a good* —), essere un buon camminatore ‖ *to keep one's legs,* mantenersi in piedi ‖ *not to have a* — *to stand on,* non avere nessuna scusa convincente ‖ *to pull s.o.'s* —, canzonare, prendere in giro qlcu. ‖ *to run s.o. off his legs,* tenere qlcu. costantemente occupato ‖ *to set s.o. on his legs,* rimettere qlcu. in piedi (in salute) ‖ *to shake a* —, (*sl.*) ballare ‖ *to take to one's legs,* darsela a gambe **2.** coscia (di pollo), cosciotto: — *of mutton,* cosciotto di montone **3.** gamba, piede (di tavolo, sedia, ecc.) **4.** gambale (di stivale) **5.** (*amer.*) tappa (di viaggio, volo, ecc.): *first* —, prima tappa; *the last 200 mile* — *of his journey,* le 200 miglia dell'ultima tappa del suo viaggio **6.** (*mar.*) bordata **7.** (*geom.*) lato (di triangolo) ☆ — -*bail,* (*fam.*) evasione; — -*pull,* (*fam.*) presa in giro, canzonatura; — -*up,* (*fam.*) aiuto (a salire): *to give one a* — -*up,* aiutare qlcu. a salire (anche *fig.*).

to **leg**, *pass.p.p.* **legged** [legd], *v.t.i.* **1.** camminare in fretta; correre velocemente: *we have to — it back*, dobbiamo tornarcene a piedi in tutta fretta **2.** spingere coi piedi.

legacy ['legəsi], *s.* legato, lascito; eredità: *to leave a —*, fare un legato, lasciare in eredità ☆ — *-hunter*, chi va a caccia di eredità.

legal ['li:gəl], *ag.* **1.** legale, legittimo, lecito **2.** secondo la legge ☆ — *tender*, denaro a corso legale.

legalism ['li:gəlizəm], *s.* legalismo; stretta aderenza alla legge.

legality [li(:)'gæliti], *s.* legalità.

legalization [,li:gəlai'zeiʃən], *s.* legalizzazione.

to **legalize** ['li:gəlaiz], *v.t.* legalizzare, autenticare.

legally ['li:gəli], *av.* legalmente, secondo la legge.

legate ['legit], *s.* legato papale.

legatee [,legə'ti:], *s.* (*dir.*) legatario.

legateship ['legitʃip], *s.* legazione (anche *eccl.*).

legatine ['legətain], *ag.* di legato (pontificio).

legation [li'geiʃən], *s.* legazione.

legator [li'geitə*], *s.* (*dir.*) testatore.

legend ['ledʒənd], *s.* **1.** leggenda, mito, favola ‖ *the Golden Legend*, la Leggenda Aurea **2.** leggenda, motto, iscrizione (di moneta, ecc.).

legendary ['ledʒəndəri], *ag.* leggendario, favoloso, mitico: — *stories* (o *tales*), storie leggendarie, leggende ‖ *s.* leggendario.

legendry ['ledʒəndri], *s. coll.* insieme di leggende.

legerdemain ['ledʒədə'mein], *s.* giuochi di prestigio; prestidigitazione; giuoco di mano; artificio.

legged [legd], *ag.* che ha gambe ☆ *bandy-* —, dalle gambe storte; *one-* —, *two-* —, a una gamba, a due gambe; *short-* —, dalle gambe corte.

legginess ['leginis], *s.* esagerata lunghezza di gambe.

leggings ['leginz], *s.pl.* ghette, uose; gambali.

leggy ['legi], *ag.* (*fam.*) dalle gambe lunghe (specialmente di bambini, cagnolini, puledri).

Leghorn ['leg'ho:n], *come s.* [le'go:n], *no.pr.* (*geog.*) Livorno ‖ **leghorn**, *s.* **1.** cappello di paglia di Firenze **2.** gallina livornese.

legibility [,ledʒi'biliti], *s.* leggibilità.

legible ['ledʒəbl], *ag.* leggibile.

legibly ['ledʒəbli], *av.* in modo leggibile.

legion ['li:dʒən], *s.* **1.** legione ‖ *the Legion of Honour*, la Legion d'Onore ‖ *Legion of Merit*, (*mil. amer.*) decorazione a valore ‖ *the British Legion*, associazione britannica degli ex-combattenti ‖ *the Foreign Legion*, la Legione Straniera **2.** schiera, moltitudine, folla.

legionary ['li:dʒənəri], *ag.* **1.** legionario **2.** innumerevole ‖ *s.* legionario.

to **legislate** ['ledʒisleit], *v.t.i.* **1.** fare, decretare delle leggi **2.** trasformare per mezzo di leggi.

legislation [,ledʒis'leiʃən], *s.* legislazione.

legislative ['ledʒislətiv], *ag.* legislativo.

legislatively ['ledʒislətivli], *av.* legislativamente.

legislator ['ledʒisleitə*], *s.* legislatore.

legislatorial [,ledʒisli'to:riəl], *ag.* legislativo.

legislatress ['ledʒisleitris], **legislatrix** [,ledʒis'leitriks], *s.* (*arc.*) legislatrice.

legislature ['ledʒisleitʃə*], *s.* **1.** legislatura **2.** corpo legislativo.

legist ['li:dʒist], *s.* (*dir.*) legista.

legitimacy [li'dʒitiməsi], *s.* legittimità, legalità.

legitimate [li'dʒitimit], *ag.* legittimo (anche *fig.*); legale.

to **legitimate** [li'dʒitimeit], *v.t.* legittimare; giustificare.

legitimately [li'dʒitimitli], *av.* legittimamente, a buon diritto.

legitimation [li,dʒiti'meiʃən], *s.* legittimazione.

to **legitimatize** [li'dʒitimətaiz], *v.t.* legittimare.

legitimism [li'dʒitimizəm], *s.* (*st.*) legittimismo.

legitimist [li'dʒitimist], *s.* (*st.*) legittimista.

to **legitimize** [li'dʒitimaiz], *v.t.* rendere legittimo, legittimare.

legume ['legju:m], **legumen** [li'gju:mən], *s.* (*bot.*) legume.

leguminous [le'gju:minəs], *ag.* (*bot.*) leguminoso.

lei [lei], *s.* « lei », ghirlanda di fiori (delle Hawaii).

leister ['li:stə*], *s.* fiocina, tridente.

leisure ['leʒə*], *s.* agio; ozio; tempo a disposizione: *at your —*, a vostro agio, con comodo; *to be at —*, aver agio, avere tempo ☆ — *hours*, — *time*, ore d'ozio, tempo di riposo.

leisured ['leʒəd], *ag. attributivo* sfaccendato ☆ — *classes*, classi agiate.

leisurely ['leʒəli], *ag.* fatto con comodo, con agio.

leisurely, *av.* con comodo, con agio.

leit-motiv ['laitmou,ti:f], *s.* (*mus.*) « leitmotiv », motivo guida (anche *fig.*).

leman ['lemən], *s.c.* (*arc.*) amante sleale.

lemma ['lemə], *pl.* **lemmas** ['leməz], **lemmata** ['lemətə], *s.* lemma.

lemming ['lemiŋ], *s.* (*zool.*) « lemming » (topo artico).

lemon ['lemən], *s.* **1.** limone ‖ *the answer's a —*, (*fam.*) non si capisce niente: *we have studied the problem thoroughly but the answer's a —*, abbiamo studiato a fondo il problema ma invano ‖ *that's a — for me!*, (*sl. amer.*) questa è una doccia fredda per me! **2.** (colore) giallo limone ☆ — *-juice*, spremuta di limone, succo di limone; — *-peel*, scorza di limone; — *-squash*, limonata; — *-squeezer*, spremi-limoni; — *-tree*, limone (albero); — *yellow*, giallo limone.

lemonade [,lemə'neid], *s.* limonata ☆ *fizzy —*, gassosa; *still —*, limonata.

lemonish ['leməniʃ], *ag.* simile a limone.

lemony ['leməni], *ag.* che ha profumo, sapore di limone.

lemur ['li:mə*], *pl.* **lemurs** ['li:məz], **lemures** ['lemjuriz], *s.* **1.** (*zool.*) lemure **2.** *pl.* (*mit.*) lemuri.

to **lend** [lend], *pass.p.p.* **lent** [lent], *v.t.i.* prestare, fare dei prestiti: — *me a book*, prestami un libro; *to — money at interest*, prestar danaro a interesse ‖ *to — aid, a hand*, prestare aiuto, are una mano; *to — ear* (o *an ear* o *one's ears*) *to*, prestare ascolto a ‖ *to — oneself to an ugly business*, prestarsi ad un affare losco.

lendable ['lendəbl], *ag.* prestabile.

lender ['lendə*], *s.c.* prestatore, prestatrice.

lending ['lendiŋ], *s.* prestito ☆ — *library*, biblioteca circolante.

length [leŋθ], *s.* **1.** lunghezza, estensione: *river that is 200 miles in —*, fiume lungo 200 miglia; *to be four yards in —*, misurare quattro iarde; *to go the — of the street*, arrivare fino in fondo alla strada; *to win by a —*, vincere per una lunghezza ‖ *at arm's —*, alla distanza di un braccio: *to keep s.o. at arm's —*, *fig.* tenere qlcu. a debita distanza; *at full —*, lungo disteso; *fig.* per esteso **2.** durata, spazio di tempo: *to make a stay of some —*, fare un soggiorno abbastanza prolungato ‖ *at —*, alla fine, finalmente, a lungo **3.** pezzo (di corda, nastro); taglio (di stoffa); tratto, troncone (di tubo) **4.** (*poes.*) quantità (di sillaba) ☆ *short- —*, (*cine.*) cortometraggio.

to **lengthen** ['leŋθən], *v.t.i.* **1.** allungare, allungarsi; stendere: *the days — in March*, in marzo le giornate si allungano **2.** far aumentare, accrescere **3.** *fig.* prolungare: *to — out a story*, prolungare un racconto.

lengthening ['leŋθəniŋ], *s.* allungamento; prolungamento.

lengthily ['leŋθili], *av.* prolissamente.

lengthiness ['leŋθinis], *s.* lungaggine, prolissità.

lengthwise ['leŋθwaiz], *av.* per il lungo, longitudinalmente.

lengthy ['leŋθi], *ag.* lungo, prolisso.

lenience ['li:njəns], **leniency** ['li:njənsi], *s.* indulgenza, benevolenza; clemenza.

lenient ['li:njənt], *ag.* indulgente, benevolo; clemente.

leniently ['li:njəntli], *av.* con indulgenza, benevolmente.

to **lenify** ['li:nifai], *v.t.* (*rar.*) lenire.

lenitive ['lenitiv], *ag.* lenitivo, calmante ‖ *s.* lenitivo, palliativo.

lenity ['leniti], *s.* indulgenza, clemenza, mitezza.

leno ['li:nou], *s.* linone (stoffa).

lens [lenz], *pl.* **lenses** ['lenziz], *s.* **1.** (*ott.*) lente: *convex, concave* —, lente convessa, concava; *speed of* —, massima apertura **2.** (*foto.*) obiettivo: *speed of* —, massima apertura di obiettivo ☆ — *-holder,* porta-obiettivo; — *-shutter,* otturatore (d'obiettivo); — *turret,* torretta portaobiettivi (di cinepresa) ‖ *crystalline* —, (*anat.*) cristallino; *double-convex* —, lente biconvessa; *fixed-focus* —, obiettivo a fuoco fisso; *projection* —, obiettivo da proiezione; *telephoto* —, telelente; teleobiettivo; *wide-angle* —, obiettivo grandangolare.

lensed [lenzd], *ag.* munito di lenti.

lensless ['lenzlis], *ag.* senza lenti.

lent [lent], *pass.p.p.* di to **lend**.

Lent, *s.* **1.** (*eccl.*) quaresima: *the first Sunday in* —, la prima domenica di quaresima; *to keep* —, fare quaresima ‖ *Mid-* —, mezza quaresima **2.** (*arc.*) primavera **3.** *pl.* regate di primavera (a Cambridge) ☆ *lent-lily,* narciso selvatico; — *term,* secondo trimestre dell'anno scolastico.

Lenten ['lentən], *ag.* quaresimale: — *fare,* vitto quaresimale ☆ — *face,* (*fam.*) faccia da quaresima.

lenticular [len'tikjulə*], *ag.* lenticolare.

lentigo [len'taigou], *pl.* **lentigines** [len'tigini:z], *s.* lentiggine.

lentil ['lentil], *s.* (*bot.*) lente, lenticchia.

lentisk ['lentisk], *s.* (*bot.*) lentisco, lentischio.

lentitude ['lentitju:d], *s.* indolenza.

lentoid ['lentoid], *ag.* lentiforme.

Leo ['li(:)ou], *no.pr.m.* Leone ‖ *the* —, (*astr.*) il Leone.

Leonard ['lenəd], *no.pr.m.* Leonardo.

Leonidas [li(:)'onidæs], *no.pr.m.* (*st. greca*) Leonida.

leonine[1] ['li(:)ənain], *ag.* leonino, di leone.

Leonine[2], *ag.* **1.** di papa Leone: — *city,* città leonina **2.** (*poes.*) leonino: — *verse,* verso leonino ‖ *s.* (*poes.*) verso leonino.

Leonora ,li(:)ə'nɔ:rə], *no.pr.f.* Leonora.

leopard ['lepəd], *s.* leopardo; gattopardo ☆ *American* —, giaguaro; *hunting* —, ghepardo; *snow* —, lonza.

leopardess ['lepədis], *s.* femmina del leopardo.

Leopold ['liəpould], *no.pr.m.* Leopoldo.

leper ['lepə*], *s.* (*patol.*) lebbroso.

lepered ['lepəd], *ag.* (*patol.*) lebbroso, colpito dalla lebbra.

lepid ['lepid], *ag.* lepido; piacevole.

lepidopter [,lepi'dɔptə*], *s.* (*entom.*) lepidottero.

Lepidoptera [,lepi'dɔptərə], *s. pl.* (*entom.*) i lepidotteri.

lepidopterous [,lepi'dɔptərəs], *ag.* (*entom.*) dei lepidotteri.

Lepidus ['lepidəs], *no.pr.m.* (*st. romana*) Lepido.

leporine ['lepərain], *ag.* leporino.

leprechaun ['leprəkɔ:n], *s.* (*irl.*) folletto, gnomo (che rivela tesori nascosti).

leprose ['leprous], *ag.* (*bot.*) squamoso, scaglioso.

leprosery ['leprəsəri], *s.* lebbrosario.

leprosy ['leprəsi], *s.* (*patol.*) lebbra.

leprous ['leprəs], *ag.* **1.** (*patol.*) lebbroso **2.** simile alla lebbra.

Lesbia ['lezbiə], *no.pr.f.* (*lett.*) Lesbia.

Lesbian ['lezbiən], *ag.* **1.** di Lesbo **2.** lesbico ‖ *s.* lesbica.

Lesbos ['lezbɔs], *no.pr.* (*geòg.*) Lesbo.

lese-majesty ['li:z'mædʒisti], *s.* (*dir.*) delitto di lesa maestà.

lesion ['li:ʒən], *s.* lesione.

less [les], (*comp.* di *little*) *ag.* **minore, più piccolo, meno:** — *light, please!,* abbassate la luce, per favore!; *drink* — *water,* bevi meno acqua; *it is of* — *importance than I thought,* è meno importante di quanto io credessi; *ten is* — *than twelve,* dieci è meno di dodici; *to grow* —, rimpicciolirsi, scemare ‖ *Napoleon*

the Less, Napoleone terzo ‖ *s.* **meno;** *he said much* — *than he knew,* disse molto meno di quanto non sapesse; *some have more, others* —, alcuni hanno di più, altri di meno; *you cannot get it for* —, non puoi averlo a meno ‖ *in* — *than an hour,* in meno di un'ora; *in* — *than no time,* in men che non si dica ‖ *so much the* — *to do,* tanto meno da fare ‖ *av.* **meno:** *one man* —, un uomo di meno; *the* — *you dream of it the better,* meno ci pensi meglio è; *drink* —, bevi meno; *he is* — *rich than his friend,* è meno ricco del suo amico ‖ *more or* —, più o meno ‖ *no* —, non meno; *niente meno che: he is no* — *daring than I,* non è meno coraggioso di me; *they have six cars, no* — *!,* hanno niente meno che sei automobili! ‖ *none the* —, nondimeno ‖ *nothing* — *than,* niente di meno che ‖ *so much the* —, tanto meno ‖ *still* — (o *even* —), ancora meno ‖ *prep.* **meno:** *a month* — *two days,* un mese meno due giorni; *purchase price* — *10 %,* prezzo d'acquisto con sconto del 10 %.

lessee [le'si:], *s.* (*dir.*) affittuario, locatario.

to lessen ['lesn], *v.t.i.* diminuire; abbassare, abbassarsi; scemare: *to* — *oneself,* abbassarsi, umiliarsi.

lessening ['lesniŋ], *s.* diminuzione; attenuazione.

lesser ['lesə*], *ag. attributivo* minore; inferiore; più piccolo: *the* — *evil,* il male minore; *in a* — *degree,* in minor grado ‖ *of two evils choose the* —, *prov.* dei due mali scegli il minore.

lesson ['lesn], *s.* **1.** lezione (anche *fig.*): *let her fate be a* — *to you,* che la sua sorte sia una lezione per te; *to deliver a* — *to a class,* far lezione a una scolaresca; *to do, to go over one's lessons,* preparare, ripassare le lezioni; *to say* (o *to recite*) *one's* —, recitare la lezione **2.** (*eccl.*) lezione.

to lesson, *v.t.* rimproverare, ammonire.

lessor ['lesɔ:*], *s.* (*dir.*) locatore.

lest [lest], *cong.* per paura che, per tema, per timore di: — *she should go away,* per tema che ella dovesse partire.

let[1] [let], *s.* affitto, l'affittare.

to let[1], *pass.p.p.* **let,** *v.t.i.* (III, IV, V) **1.** (V) permettere, lasciare; far sì che, far sì che: — *him do what he likes,* lasciagli fare quello che vuole; — *me know when you can come,* fammi sapere quando puoi venire; — *me tell you that,* lascia che ti dica che; *the authorities* — *no one go on board,* le autorità non permettono a nessuno di recarsi a bordo; *could you* — *me have it tomorrow?,* potreste farmelo avere per domani?; *he* — *himself be cheated,* si lasciò imbrogliare ‖ *to* — *alone,* non fare attenzione; lasciare in pace ‖ *to* — *blood,* (*med.*) salassare ‖ *to* — *bygones be bygones,* dimenticare il passato ‖ *to* — *fall,* lasciar cadere ‖ *to* — *fly,* sparlare; parlare volgarmente ‖ *to* — *the grass grow under one's feet,* perdere del tempo prezioso ‖ *to* — *loose,* allentare, sciogliere; liberare; rallentare ‖ *to* — *oneself go,* abbandonarsi; lasciarsi andare ‖ *to* — *s.o. stew in his own juice,* lasciar cuocere qlcu. nel suo brodo **2.** (*ausiliare dell'imperativo per la 1ª e 3ª persona sing. pl.*): — *it be,* sia pure; — *me see,* vediamo; — *us go,* andiamo **3.** affittare, affittarsi: *this flat lets for 40,000 lire a month,* questo appartamento si affitta a 40.000 lire al mese ‖ *house to* —, casa da affittare **4.** *to* — *into* (*sthg.*), lasciare entrare; far penetrare, introdurre; iniziare a; attaccare: *to* — *s.o. into a secret,* mettere a parte qlcu. di un segreto **5.** *to* — **down,** abbassare; far scendere; sciogliere (capelli, ecc.); allungare (abiti, ecc.) ‖ *to* — *s.o. down,* abbandonare qlcu. nei guai; deludere qlcu.: — *him down gently,* dirgli di no senza ferirlo; *I won't* — *you down,* puoi contare su di me **6.** *to* — **in,** lasciare entrare, fare entrare; incastrare, inserire; causare una perdita; imbrogliare; (*sl.*) coinvolgere: *he was* — *in for £ 500,* perse 500 sterline **7.** *to* — **off,** far partire (un colpo di fucile, ecc.); lasciar andare; perdonare: *he was* — *off with a fine,* se la cavò con una multa ‖ *to* — *off steam,* sfogarsi ‖ *to* — *s.o. off from doing sthg.,* dispensare qlcu. dal fare ql.co. **8.** to — **on**, lasciar capire; (*sl.*) rivelare un segreto; (*amer. sl.*) far finta di **9.** to — **out**, lasciar uscire; lasciare, lasciarsi sfuggire; mettere in libertà, rilasciare; affittare; (*mar.*) allentare ‖ *he — the cat out of the bag*, egli rivelò il segreto ‖ *to — out at s.o.*, dirne quattro a qlcu. ‖ *to — out at s.o. with one's foot, fist*, dare un calcio, un pugno a qlcu. **10.** to — **through**, lasciar passare: *to — s.o. through an exam*, promuovere qlcu. ad un esame **11.** to — **up**, far salire; (*amer. fam.*) diminuire; cessare.

let², *s.* **1.** (*arc.*) ostacolo, impedimento: *without — or hindrance*, senza impedimenti **2.** (*tennis*) colpo nullo. to **let²**, *pass.p.p.* **letted** ['letid], **let**, *v.t.* (*arc.*) ostacolare, impedire.

let-down ['let'daun], *s.* (*fam.*) disappunto, delusione.

lethal ['li:θəl], *ag.* letale: — *weapons*, armi letali.

lethargic(al) [le'θɑːdʒik(əl)], *ag.* letargico.

lethargically [le'θɑːdʒikəli], *av.* (come) in letargo.

to **lethargize** ['leθədʒaiz], *v.t.* far cadere in letargo.

lethargy ['leθədʒi], *s.* letargo.

Lethe ['li:θi(:)], *no.pr.* (*mit.*) Lete ‖ *s.* oblio, dimenticanza.

lethean [li'θiːən], *ag.* leteo.

letheon ['li:θiən], *s.* (*chim.*) etere (solforico).

let-in ['let'in], *s.* (*fam.*) truffa; mistificazione.

Leto ['li:tou], *no.pr.f.* (*mit.*) Latona.

Lett [let], *s.c.* lettone.

letter¹ ['letə*], *s.* **1.** lettera dell'alfabeto ‖ *in the — and spirit*, nella forma e nella sostanza; *to the —*, alla lettera, esattamente **2.** lettera, epistola ‖ — *of attorney*, procura; — *of credit*, lettera di credito **3.** (*tip.*) carattere: *capital, small* —, lettera maiuscola, minuscola **4.** *pl.* lettere; letteratura; *a man of letters*, un uomo di lettere ‖ *the republic* (o *the commonwealth*) *of letters*, la repubblica delle lettere ‖ — -*balance*, pesalettere; — -*bearer*, latore (di una lettera); — -*bill*, (*comm.*) polizza; — -*book*, copialettere, — -*box*, cassetta postale; — -*card*, biglietto postale; — -*head*, intestazione di lettera; — -*paper*, carta da lettera; — -*perfect*, (*teat.*) di attore che conosce la parte a perfezione; — -*writer*, autore di lettere, copialettere ‖ *dead* —, lettera non recapitata; *registered* —, (lettera) raccomandata.

to **letter¹**, *v.t.* **1.** imprimere il titolo su (copertina di libro); imprimere lettere **2.** classificare secondo l'ordine alfabetico.

letter², *s.c.* chi affitta.

lettered ['letəd], *ag.* **1.** letterato, dotto **2.** marcato con lettere: — *paper*, carta intestata.

lettering ['letəriŋ], *s.* **1.** titolo (su una rilegatura), iscrizione **2.** lettere impresse.

letterless ['letəlis], *ag.* illetterato.

letterpress ['letə-pres], *s.* parte stampata (escluse le illustrazioni).

Lettic ['letik], *ag.* lettone ‖ *s.* lettone (lingua).

letting ['letiŋ], *s.* affitto; l'affittare.

Lettish ['letiʃ], *ag.* lettone ‖ *s.* lettone (lingua).

lettuce ['letis], *s.* (*bot.*) lattuga.

let-up ['let'ʌp], *s.* **1.** diminuzione **2.** cessazione.

leucine ['lju:sin], *s.* (*chim.*) leucina.

leuciscus [lju:'siskəs], *s.* (*ittiol.*) leucisco.

leucite ['lju:sait], *s.* (*min.*) leucite.

leucocyte ['lju:kəsait], *s.* (*biol.*) leucocito.

leucocythaemia [,lju:kousi'θimiə], *s.* (*patol.*) leucemia.

leucoma [lju:'koumə], *s.* (*patol.*) leucoma.

leucopathy [lju:'kɔpəθi], *s.* (*patol.*) leucopatia; (*med.*) acromasia, albinismo.

leucorrhea [,lju:kə'riːə], *s.* (*patol.*) leucorrea.

leucosis [lju:'kousis], *s.* (*patol.*) leucosi.

leukemia [lju:'ki:miə], *s.* (*patol.*) leucemia.

levant¹ ['levənt], *come s.* [li'vænt], *ag.* orientale, levantino ‖ *s.* **1.** vento di levante **2.** *the Levant*, il Levante ‖ *the Levant Company*, (*st.*) la Compagnia del Levante.

to **levant²** [li'vænt], *v.i.* fuggire per debiti (specialmente di giuoco).

Levanter [li'væntə*], *s.c.* levantino, levantina ‖ *s.* vento di levante.

Levantine ['levəntain], *ag.* levantino.

levator [li'veitə*], *s.* **1.** (*anat.*) muscolo elevatore **2.** (*chir.*) leva.

levee¹ ['levi], *s.* (*spec. amer.*) diga, argine (di fiume). to **levee¹**, *v.t.* (*spec. amer.*) arginare (un fiume).

levee², *s.* **1.** (*st.*) udienza mattutina (di sovrano) **2.** udienza pomeridiana (di sovrano, presidente, ecc.) riservata a soli uomini: *to hold a —*, dare udienza.

level ['levl], *ag.* **1.** livellato, piatto, piano; uniforme; orizzontale: — *ground*, terreno piano; *to make —*, spianare, livellare **2.** a livello: — *with the ground*, a livello di terra; — *with the water*, a flor d'acqua **3.** equilibrato; regolato, regolare: — *life*, vita regolata; *to have a — head*, essere equilibrato; *to keep a — head*, conservare il proprio sangue freddo ‖ *to do one's — best*, fare tutto il possibile ‖ *s.* **1.** spianata; superficie piana, uguale ‖ *on the —*, (*fig.*) onestamente, in buona fede **2.** livello (anche *fig.*): *on a — with*, a livello con; *to be on a — with s.o.*, essere sullo stesso piano di qlcu.; *to find one's —*, trovare il proprio ambiente; *to rise to the — of s.o.*, innalzarsi al livello di qlcu. **3.** livella ☆ — -*headed*, equilibrato, con la testa quadrata; — -*crossing*, passaggio a livello ‖ *plumb- —*, (*edil.*) archipenzolo; *sea- —*, livello del mare: *how high are we above sea- —?*, a che altezza siamo sopra il livello del mare?.

to **level**, *pass.p.p.* **levelled** ['levld], *v.t.i.* **1.** (anche *fig.*) livellare; spianare, pareggiare; uguagliare: *death levels all men*, la morte eguaglia tutti gli uomini; *to — a town to the ground*, radere al suolo una città **2.** puntare (fucile, ecc.); prendere di mira: *he levelled his gun against* (o *at*) *a person*, puntò il fucile contro una persona; *to — sarcasm, accusations against* (o *at*) *s.o.*, *fig.* dirigere dei sarcasmi, delle accuse contro qlcu. **3.** *to — away*, uguagliare; abolire (distinzioni sociali, ecc.) **4.** *to — down*, livellare (muri); abbassare allo stesso livello **5.** *to — up*, innalzare allo stesso livello; livellare (terreno).

leveller ['levələ*], *s.* **1.** chi livella, livellatore **2.** (*pol.*) chi è fautore dell'uguaglianza.

levelling ['levliŋ], *s.* **1.** livellamento; spianamento; livellazione **2.** (*artigl.*) puntamento, mira ☆ — -*instrument*, livello a cannocchiale; livella; — -*staff*, stadia.

levelly ['levli], *av.* (*rar.*) uniformemente.

levelness ['levlnis], *s.* **1.** uniformità (di superficie livellata) **2.** parità di livello **3.** *fig.* equilibrio: *his — of head was perfect*, aveva un perfetto equilibrio mentale.

lever ['liːvə*], *s.* **1.** (*mec.*) manubrio **2.** (*mec.*) leva: — *of a balance*, braccio d'una bilancia; *fulcrum of a —*, fulcro d'una leva **3.** *fig.* stimolo, incitamento ☆ — -*arm*, (*mec.*) braccio di leva ‖ *brake- —*, (*aut.*) leva del freno; *cocking —*, (*mil.*) leva di caricamento; *gear —*, (*aut.*) leva del cambio di velocità; *hand —*, leva a mano; *release —*, (*mec.*) leva di disimpegno; *spark- —*, accensione; *standard- —*, leva regolatrice; *starting —*, leva di avviamento, della messa in marcia; *steering- —*, leva di direzione; *two-armed —*, (*mec.*) leva a due bracci.

to **lever**, *v.t.i.* dar leva; far leva; alzare, rimuovere con leva.

leverage ['liːvəridʒ], *s.* (*mec.*) **1.** azione di una leva; modo di applicare una leva **2.** sistema di leve **3.** potenza di una leva **4.** *fig.* potere, influenza.

leveret ['levərit], *s.* leprotto.

Levi ['liːvai], *no.pr.m.* (*Bibbia*) Levi.

leviable ['leviəbl], *ag.* imponibile (di tasse).

leviathan [li'vaiəθən], *s.* (*Bibbia*) leviathan.

levigable ['levigəbl], *ag.* levigabile.

to **levigate** ['levigeit], *v.t.* **1.** porfirizzare; polverizzare **2.** impastare.

levigation [,levi'geiʃən], *s.* levigazione; polverizzazione.

levin ['levin], *s.* (*poet.*) bagliore, lampo.

levirate ['li:virit], *s.* (*st. ebraica*) levirato.

to **levitate** ['leviteit], *v.t.i.* (*spiritismo*) (fare) alzare in aria; alzarsi in aria; fluttuare in aria.

levitation [.levi'teiʃən], *s.* (*spiritismo*) levitazione.

Levite ['li:vait], *s.* (*Bibbia*) levita.

Levitic(al) [li'vitik(əl)], *ag.* (*Bibbia*) levitico.

Leviticus [li'vitikəs], *s.* (*Bibbia*) Levitico.

levity ['leviti], *s.* **1.** leggerezza, incostanza; frivolezza; spensieratezza **2.** leggerezza (di peso).

levorotatory [.li:vou'routətəri], *ag.* (*chim.*) levogiro.

levulose ['levjulous], *s.* (*chim.*) levulosio.

levy ['levi], *s.* **1.** (*mil.*) leva, arruolamento: — *in mass*, leva in massa **2.** imposta, tributo.

to **levy**, *v.t.* **1.** arruolare: *to — an army*, adunare, riunire un'armata ‖ *to — war upon* (o *against*), far guerra a **2.** imporre (una tassa, un tributo) ‖ *to — blackmail*, fare un ricatto.

lewd [lu:d], *ag.* **1.** impudico; indecente; immondo; lascivo **2.** (*arc.*) vile; ignobile.

lewdly ['lu:dli], *av.* **1.** impudicamente; indecentemente; lascivamente **2.** (*arc.*) vilmente; spregevolmente.

lewdness ['lu:dnis], *s.* **1.** impudicizia; indecenza; lascivia **2.** (*arc.*) viltà; spregevolezza.

Lewis[1] ['lu(:)is], *no.pr.m.* Luigi.

lewis[2], *s.* (*edil.*) campanella da ingessatura, ulivella.

lexical ['leksikəl], *ag.* lessicale.

lexicographer [.leksi'kɔgrəfə*], *s.* lessicografo.

lexicographic(al) [.leksikou'græfik(əl)], *ag.* lessicografico.

lexicography [.leksi'kɔgrəfi], *s.* lessicografia.

lexicology [.leksi'kɔlədʒi], *s.* lessicologia.

lexicon ['leksikən], *s.* lessico, dizionario (specialmente di lingue antiche).

ley [li:], *s.* (*poet.*) prato; terreno erboso.

Leyden ['laidn], *no.pr.* (*geog.*) Leida ☆ — *jar*, (*fis.*) bottiglia di Leida.

liability [.laiə'biliti], *s.* **1.** obbligo: *the — for military service*, l'obbligo del servizio militare **2.** disposizione, tendenza: *to have a — to catch cold*, essere soggetto ai raffreddori **3.** (*dir.*) responsabilità **4.** *pl.* (*comm.*) passività, debiti; impegni commerciali: *assets and liabilities*, attivo e passivo; *to meet one's liabilities*, soddisfare ai propri impegni ☆ *limited —*, (*comm.*) responsabilità limitata; *several —*, responsabilità separata.

liable ['laiəbl] *ag.* **1.** soggetto, esposto: — *to a fine*, passibile di multa; *all men are — to make mistakes*, tutti sono soggetti a fare errori; *he is — to rheumatism*, è soggetto ai reumatismi **2.** (*dir.*) responsabile: *you are — for the damage*, siete responsabili del danno; *to hold a person —*, tenere una persona responsabile.

liaison [li(:)'eizən], *s.* **1.** legame; unione; relazione illecita **2.** (*mil.*) collegamento **3.** (*fonet.*) legamento ☆ — *officer*, ufficiale di collegamento.

liana [li'ɑ:nə], *s.* (*bot.*) liana.

liar ['laiə*], *s.c.* mentitore, mentitrice; bugiardo, bugiarda.

liard ['laiəd], *ag.* grigio, leardo.

lias ['laiəs], *s.* (*geol.*) « lias », giurassico nero.

liassic [lai'æsik], *ag.* (*geol.*) liassico.

libant ['laibənt], *ag.* che liba.

to **libate** [lai'beit], *v.t.* libare.

libation [lai'beiʃən], *s.* libagione.

libel ['laibəl], *s.* **1.** libello; calunnia, diffamazione **2.** (*dir.*) libello; querela.

to **libel**, *pass.p.p.* **libelled** ['laibəld], *v.t.* **1.** diffamare con libelli; calunniare **2.** (*dir.*) denunciare, sporgere querela.

libel(l)er ['laiblə*], *s.c.* diffamatore, diffamatrice; libellista.

libel(l)ous ['laibləs], *ag.* diffamatorio, infamatorio, calunnioso.

libellously ['laibləsli], *av.* con libelli.

liberal ['libərəl], *ag.* **1.** liberale, senza pregiudizi:

— *views*, idee liberali **2.** generoso, prodigo; abbondante, ampio: — *of advice*, prodigo di consigli; — *supply of food*, alimentazione abbondante **3.** umanistico: — *education*, educazione umanistica ‖ *Liberal Arts*, Arti liberali **4.** (*pol.*) liberale ‖ *s.* (*pol.*) liberale ‖ *the Liberals*, i liberali.

liberalism ['libərəlizəm], *s.* (*st. pol.*) liberalismo; principi politici dei liberali.

liberalist ['libərəlist], *s.c.* liberalista.

liberality [.libə'ræliti], *s.* liberalità, generosità.

liberalization [.libərəlai'zeiʃən], *s.* il rendere liberale.

to **liberalize** ['libərəlaiz], *v.t.i.* rendere liberale; liberalizzarsi.

liberally ['libərəli], *av.* liberalmente, largamente, generosamente.

to **liberate** ['libəreit], *v.t.* **1.** affrancare (uno schiavo); mettere in libertà; far libero **2.** (*chim.*) liberare (gas, ecc.).

liberation [.libə'reiʃən], *s.* liberazione, affrancamento.

liberator ['libəreitə*], *s.c.* liberatore, liberatrice.

Liberia [lai'biəriə], *no.pr.* (*geog.*) Liberia.

libertarian [.libə(:)'tɛəriən], *s.c.* fautore, fautrice del libero arbitrio.

libertarianism [.libə(:)'tɛəriənizəm], *s.* (*teol.*) dottrina del libero arbitrio.

libertine ['libə(:)tain], *ag.* libertino ‖ *s.* **1.** (*spreg.*) libero pensatore **2.** libertino.

libertinism ['libətinizəm], *s.* **1.** libertinaggio, dissolutezza, sregolatezza **2.** libero pensiero.

liberty ['libəti], *s.* **1.** libertà; permesso, licenza: — *of conscience, of speech, of the press*, libertà di coscienza, di parola, di stampa; — *of thought*, libertà di pensiero; *they leave me full —*, mi lasciano piena libertà; *they set the prisoners at —*, misero in libertà i prigionieri; *you are at — to believe*, sei libero di credere **2.** libertà, confidenza: *he took the — to joke with her*, si prese la libertà di scherzare con lei; *I took the — of using your telephone*, mi sono permesso di usare il tuo telefono; *to take liberties with s.o.*, prendersi, permettersi delle libertà con qlcu. **3.** *pl.* privilegi ☆ — *man*, marinaio che ha il permesso di scendere a terra.

libidinous [li'bidinəs], *ag.* libidinoso, lascivo.

libidinously [li'bidinəsli], *av.* libidinosamente, lascivamente.

libido [li'bi:dou], *s.* libidine, lascivia.

libra ['laibrə], *pl.* **librae** ['laibri:], *s.* **1.** (*st. romana*) libbra (misura di peso = g. 326) **2.** lira sterlina (usato solo nell'*abbr.* £ [paund(z)]) **3.** libbra (peso) (usato solo nell'*abbr. lb.* [paund(z)]) ‖ **Libra**, *no.pr.* (*astr.*) Libra.

librarian [lai'brɛəriən], *s.c.* bibliotecario, bibliotecaria.

librarianship [lai'brɛəriənʃip], *s.* ufficio, carica di bibliotecario.

library ['laibrəri], *s.* biblioteca (collezione di libri, sala di lettura) ‖ *walking —*, persona molto erudita ☆ *circulating —*, biblioteca circolante; *film —*, cineteca; *free —*, biblioteca pubblica; *lending —*, biblioteca che dà libri in prestito; *newspaper —*, emeroteca; *record —*, discoteca.

to **librate** ['laibreit], *v.i.* oscillare, librarsi, bilanciarsi.

libration [lai'breiʃən], *s.* oscillazione; (*astr.*) librazione.

libratory ['laibrətəri], *ag.* oscillatorio.

librettist [li'bretist], *s.* (*teat.*) librettista.

libretto [li'bretou], *pl.* **librettos** [li'bretouz], **libretti** [li'breti(:)], *s.* (*teat.*) libretto (d'opera).

Libya ['libiə], *no.pr.* (*geog.*) Libia.

Libyan ['libiən], *ag.* libico: — *Desert*, Deserto Libico.

lice [lais], *pl.* di **louse**.

licence ['laisəns], *s.* **1.** permesso, licenza: *under — of the author*, col permesso dell'autore **2.** (*amm.*) licenza, autorizzazione; patente; (*eccl.*) dispensa (di pubblicazioni matrimoniali) **3.** *fig.* sregolatezza, scostumatezza **4.** libertà, licenza (poetica) ☆ — *holder*, chi è munito di permesso, patente, ecc. || *dramatic —*, permesso di rappresentazione; *driving —*, patente automobilistica; *import —*, permesso di importazione; *marriage- —*, permesso di contrarre matrimonio; *off- —*, permesso di vendere esclusivamente bevande da trasportare altrove; *on- —*, permesso di consumare le bevande sul luogo; *shooting —*, licenza di caccia.

to licence, *v.t.* autorizzare, accordare una licenza, un privilegio, una patente a.

licenceless ['laisənslis], *ag.* privo di licenza.

to license, *V.* to **licence.**

licensed ['laisənst], *ag.* autorizzato, patentato: *— victualler*, rivenditore autorizzato di vino, liquori, ecc.

licensee [,laisən'si:], *s.* chi possiede una autorizzazione.

licenser ['laisənsə*], *s.* **1.** che concede licenze, permessi **2.** censore (di teatro, stampa, ecc.).

licentiate [lai'senʃiit], *s.* licenziato, diplomato presso un'università.

licentious [lai'senʃəs], *ag.* licenzioso, scostumato.

licentiously [lai'senʃəsli], *av.* licenziosamente.

licentiousness [lai'senʃəsnis], *s.* dissolutezza.

lich [litʃ], *s.* (*rar.*) cadavere ☆ *— -gate*, portico coperto all'entrata di cimitero ove si posava la bara in attesa del sacerdote; *— -house*, obitorio; *— -owl*, civetta.

lichen ['laiken], *s.* **1.** (*bot.*) lichene **2.** (*patol.*) lichene, impettigine.

lichened ['laikend], *ag.* coperto di licheni.

licit ['lisit], *ag.* lecito.

licitly ['lisitli], *av.* lecitamente.

lick [lik], *s.* **1.** leccata, leccatura: *to give s.o. a —*, leccare qlcu. || *a — and a promise*, pulizia spiccia e sommaria **2.** (*sl.*) piccola quantità: *he won't do a — of work*, (*amer.*) non fa niente di niente **3.** (*sl.*) colpo forte: *a — in the face*, manrovescio **4.** (*sl.*) passo: *at a great —*, a passo veloce ☆ *salt- —*, (*amer.*) località dove gli animali vanno a leccare il sale (naturale o depostovi a tale scopo).

to lick, *v.t.t.* **1.** leccare: *the dog licked my hand*, il cane mi leccò la mano; *to — one's fingers*, leccarsi le dita || *to — the dust*, mordere la polvere || *to — into shape*, (*fam.*) dar forma, foggiare, rendere presentabile || *to — s.o.'s shoes*, essere servili verso qlcu. || *to — up* (o *off*), pulire leccando **2.** lambire, essere lambente (di onde, fiamme) **3.** (*sl.*) battere, superare, sconfiggere: *they licked me*, mi avevano battuto **4.** (*sl.*) bastonare **5.** (*sl.*) affrettarsi.

licker ['likə*], *s.c.* chi lecca.

lickerish ['likəriʃ],᷄ *ag.* ghiotto, avido.

licking ['likiŋ], *s.* **1.** leccata **2.** (*sl.*) sconfitta **3.** (*sl.*) bastonatura.

lickspittle ['lik,spitl], *s.* leccapiedi, parassita.

licorice ['likəris], *s.* liquirizia.

lictor ['liktə*], *s.* (*st. romana*) littore.

lid [lid], *s.* **1.** coperchio; copertura || *that puts the — on it!*, (*sl.*) questo è il colmo!, non mancava che questo! **2.** (*bot.*) opercolo **3.** (*sl.*) cappello, copricapo **4.** (*fig. amer.*) restrizione ☆ *eye- —*, palpebra.

lidded ['lidid], *ag.* munito di coperchio ☆ *heavy - — eyes*, occhi dalle palpebre pesanti.

lido ['li:dou], *s.* piscina pubblica scoperta.

lie¹ [lai], *s.* **1.** menzogna, bugia: *a pack of lies*, un tessuto di menzogne; *white —*, bugia innocente; *to tell a —*, dire una bugia || *to act a —* agire slealmente **2.** the *—*, smentita: *to give the — to sthg.*, smentire il.co., fare una smentita; *to give s.o. the —*, smentire qlcu. ☆ *— -detector*, (*neol.*) macchina della verità.

to lie¹, *pass.p.p.* **lied** [laid], *p.pr.* **lying** ['laiiŋ], *v.t.i.* **1.** mentire, dir bugie: *you're lying!*, tu menti!; *to — to s.o.*, mentire a qlcu. || *you — in your teeth* (o *throat*), (*scherz.*) tu menti per la gola || *to — away s.o.'s reputation*, rovinare la reputazione di qlcu. con menzogne || *to — oneself, s.o. into trouble*, mettersi, mettere qlcu. nei pasticci con menzogne; *to — oneself,*

s.o. out of trouble, trarsi, trarre qlcu. d'impaccio con menzogne **2.** ingannare (di cose, apparenza).

lie², *s.* **1.** posizione, disposizione: *the — of the land*, la configurazione del terreno; *fig.* la situazione degli affari **2.** tana, covo ☆ *— -abed*, dormiglione.

to lie², *pass.* **lay** [lei], *p.p.* **lain** [lein], *p.pr.* **lying** ['laiiŋ], *v.i.* **1.** giacere, stare disteso, sdraiato: *we found him lying ill in bed*, lo trovammo a letto ammalato || *he lies with his fathers*, è sepolto nella tomba di famiglia || *to — asleep*, essere addormentato; *to — doggo*, (*sl.*) stare disteso immobile || *let sleeping dogs —*, *prov.* non svegliare il can che dorme **2.** essere situato, posto; trovarsi (anche *fig.*): *he has money lying at the bank*, ha del denaro in banca; *he knows where his interest lies*, sa bene dov'è il suo interesse; *to — at anchor*, (*mar.*) essere all'ancora; *to — in prison*, essere in prigione || *as far as in me lies*, per quel che sta in me; *it lies whith you to do that*, sta a te fare questo || *to find out how the land lies*, scoprire come stanno le cose || *to — idle*, rimanere inoperoso || *to — in wait*, essere in attesa, in agguato || *to — in the way*, essere di ostacolo, d'impedimento || *to — low*, rannicchiarsi; essere prostrato; essere morto; (*sl.*) starsene zitto, non intromettersi || *to — lurking*, essere appiattato || *to — on hand*, rimanere invenduto || *to — open to*, essere esposto a || *to — out of one's money*, non essere pagati || *to — waste*, rimanere incolto (di terreno) **3.** estendersi, allargarsi (anche *fig.*): *a happy future lay before her*, un lieto futuro l'attendeva; *a vast plain lay before us*, una vasta pianura si estendeva dinanzi a noi **4.** (*dir.*) essere accettabile, sostenibile: *no action will —*, nessun atto sarà valido **5.** (*arc.*) dimorare, alloggiare **6.** *to — about*, essere sparso qua e là, in disordine **7.** *to — by*, essere inattivo; tenersi in disparte; (*mar.*) essere alla cappa **8.** *to — down*, coricarsi; sottomettersi senza protestare: *he took it lying down*, subì la situazione senza protestare **9.** *to — in*, partorire **10.** *to — off*, (*mar.*) stare al largo **11.** *to — over*, differire: *the motion was allowed to — over*, la mozione fu aggiornata **12.** *to — to*, (*mar.*) essere alla cappa **13.** *to — up*, tenere il letto; rimanere inattivo; (*mar.*) essere in porto.

lief [li:f], *av.* (*letter.*) volentieri; piuttosto: *I had* (o *would*) *as — stay as go*, andare o restare mi è indifferente; *I would liefer stay than go*, preferirei restare piuttosto che andare.

liege [li:dʒ], *ag.* ligio, fido, fedele || *s.* **1.** vassallo, dipendente **2.** signore ☆ *— lord*, sovrano.

liegeman ['li:dʒmæn], *pl.* **liegemen** ['li:dʒmen], *s.* vassallo; seguace fedele.

lien [liən], *s.* (*dir.*) pegno, diritto di pegno; garanzia: *to establish a —*, fissare un pegno.

lieu [lju:], *s.* luogo: *in — of*, invece di.

lieutenancy [lef'tenənsi], *s.* luogotenenza.

lieutenant [(*mil.*) lef'tenənt, (*mar.*) le'tenənt, (*amer.*) lju'tenənt], *s.* luogotenente, tenente ☆ *— -general*, tenente generale; *— -governor*, vice governatore.

lieutenantship [lef'tenəntʃip], *s.* luogotenenza.

life [laif], *pl.* **lives** [laivz], *s.* **1.** vita; esistenza; lo stato di essere vivo: *in —*, in vita; *Shakespeare's — in London*, la vita di Shakespeare a Londra; *— is sweet*, la vita è dolce; *a great number of lives were lost*, ci fu un gran numero di morti; *he ran for his* (o *dear*) *—*, cercò la salvezza nella fuga; *the war took a heavy toll of lives*, la guerra ha falciato molte vite; *to bring to — (again)*, far rinvenire, rianimare; *to keep in —*, mantenere in vita; *to lose one's —*, perdere la vita; *to take a person's —*, uccidere una persona || *the — everlasting, the everlasting —*, la vita ultraterrena || *expectation of —*, (*amm. comm.*) media normale della vita || *for the — of me*, per nulla al mondo || *not on your —*, assolutamente no || *the cat has nine lives*, il gatto ha nove vite; *he has as many lives as a cat*, ha la pelle dura || *it is a matter of — and death*, è questione di vita o di morte || *not in my — will you enter this house*, finchè sarò vivo non entrerai in questa casa ‖ *upon my — I did not do it*, ti do la mia parola che non l'ho fatto io ‖ *while there is — there is hope*, *prov.* finchè c'è vita c'è speranza **2.** modo di vivere; attività sociale; società: *a flat —*, una vita monotona; *way of —*, modo di vivere; *to lead a happy —*, fare la bella vita ‖ *to have the time of one's —*, divertirsi come non mai ‖ *to keep — and soul together*, vivere stentatamente ‖ *to lead a cat and dog —*, vivere come cane e gatto ‖ *to see —*, vedere il mondo **3.** biografia: *Plutarch's Lives*, Le Vite di Plutarco **4.** vigore, energia, vivacità: *Doris was the — and soul of the party*, Doris era l'anima della compagnia **5.** realtà; forma, modello vivente: *statue the size of —*, statua a grandezza naturale; *a picture taken from —*, un quadro preso dal vero ‖ *as large as —*, al naturale; *(fam.)* in persona; senza dubbio ‖ *to the —*, al naturale ☆ *— -belt*, cintura di salvataggio; *— -blood*, *(poet.)* fluido vitale; sangue; *— -everlasting*, *(bot.)* sempreviso; *— -guard*, guardia del corpo; *(amer.)* bagnino; *— -giving*, vivificante; *— -insurance* (o *— assurance*), assicurazione sulla vita; *— -interest*, reddito vitalizio; *— -jacket*, cintura di salvataggio; *— -line*, *(mar.)* sagola di salvataggio; linea di comunicazione vitale; *— -preserver*, salvagente; bastone sfollagente; *— -rent*, rendita vitalizia; *— -sentence*, ergastolo; *— -tenancy*, affitto vita natural durante; *— -weary*, stanco della vita; *— -work*, opera principale; lavoro di una vita intera ‖ *country —*, *town —*, vita di campagna, di città; *high —*, mondo elegante; alta società.

lifeboat ['laifbout], *s.* scialuppa di salvataggio ☆ *— man*, marinaio addetto a una stazione di salvataggio.

lifeless ['laif-lis], *ag.* **1.** senza vita **2.** senza vigore.

lifelessly ['laif-lisli], *av.* **1.** senza vita **2.** senza vigore.

lifelessness ['laif-lisnis], *s.* **1.** mancanza di vita; insensibilità **2.** apatia.

lifelike ['laif-laik], *ag.* vivido, realistico, che dà l'impressione della vita.

lifelong ['laif-lɔŋ], *ag.* che dura tutta la vita.

lifer ['laifə*], *s.* *(sl.)* **1.** ergastolano **2.** (condanna all') ergastolo.

lifetime ['laiftaim], *s.* durata della vita; la vita tutta intera.

lift [lift], *s.* **1.** il sollevare, l'innalzare **2.** ascensore, montacarichi **3.** *(mec.)* alzata; *(aer.)* portanza **4.** sopratacco **5.** *(fam.)* passaggio (su un veicolo): *to give s.o. a —*, dare un passaggio a qlcu.; *can I give you a —?*, posso darle un passaggio? ☆ *— boy* (o *— man*), addetto all'ascensore ‖ *dinner —* (o *service —*), montavivande; *ski —*, « ski-lift », sciovia.

to lift, *v.t.i.* **1.** alzare, alzarsi; sollevare, sollevarsi; levare, innalzare (anche *fig.*): *the mist begins to —*, la nebbia comincia a diradarsi; *the tide will — the boat*, la marea alzerà la barca; *the wind lifted him off his feet*, il vento lo sollevò per aria; *to — a hand against s.o.*, alzare la mano contro qlcu.; *to — a hand to do sthg.*, fare uno sforzo per compiere ql.co.; *to — one's hat*, salutare togliendosi il cappello; *to — one's head*, alzare, rialzare la testa (anche *fig.*); *to — up the hand*, giurare ‖ *the rain is lifting*, il tempo si schiarisce **2.** rubare; plagiare: *to — a passage from an author*, plagiare un passo d'un autore **3.** *(amer.)* estinguere un'ipoteca **4.** fare un intervento di chirurgia plastica a (una parte del corpo).

lifter ['liftə*], *s.* **1.** chi solleva, innalza **2.** *(mec.)* elevatore **3.** ☆ *— -rod*, *(mec.)* asta di punteria ‖ *valve- —*, *(mec.)* alzavalvole.

lifting ['liftiŋ], *s.* **1.** sollevamento, elevazione; alzata **2.** *(artigl.)* allungamento (di tiro) **3.** furto ☆ *— -eye*, *(mar.)* vite ad occhio; *— -gear*, meccanismo di sollevamento; *— -lug*, gancio di sollevamento; *— -plate*, placca di estrazione (in una fonderia); *— -power*, portata di una gru ‖ *— shop*, taccheggio.

ligament ['ligəmənt], *s.* *(anat.)* legamento.

ligamental [,ligə'mentl], **ligamentary** [,ligə'mentə-

ri], **ligamentous** [,ligə'mentəs], *ag.* legamentoso, di legamento.

ligature ['ligətʃuə*], *s.* *(chir. mus. tip.)* legatura.

light[1] [lait], *ag.* **1.** chiaro, rischiarato **2.** chiaro (di colore); biondo (di capelli): *— blue*, blu chiaro; *— brown*, castano chiaro ‖ *the — blues*, *(spor.)* gli studenti di Cambridge ‖ *s.* **1.** luce, splendore, chiarore, bagliore: *a — in the distance*, una luce in lontananza; *by the — of the sun*, alla luce del sole; *northern lights*, aurora boreale; *to be —*, far giorno; *to come to —*, manifestarsi, venire alla luce; *to put on* (o *to turn on) the —*, accendere la luce; *to put out* (o *to turn off* o *to switch off) the —*, spegnere la luce; *to see the —*, *(ret.)* nascere ‖ *to stand in one's own —*, farsi ombra; *fig.* danneggiarsi; *to stand in s.o.'s —*, *fig.* fare ombra a qlcu. **2.** luce, chiarezza, conoscenza; illuminazione mentale: *I was beginning to see —*, la luce si fece nella mia mente; *to bring to —*, scoprire, svelare; *to throw — upon a fact*, spiegare un fatto **3.** lume, lanterna, lampada; fanale; *(mar.)* faro (anche *fig.*): *the —*, l'illuminazione, la luce elettrica; *Dante was the — of his time*, Dante fu il faro luminoso dei suoi tempi; *to carry a — in one's hand*, portare una lampada in mano ‖ *the City of Light*, Parigi **4.** fuoco, fiamma (anche *fig.*): luminaria: *will you give me a —?*, mi fai accendere (la sigaretta)?; *you should have seen the — in her eye!*, se tu avessi visto la fiamma nei suoi occhi!; *to set to —*, appiccare fuoco a **5.** luce, apparenza: *in a bad —*, in cattiva luce; *in its true —*, nella sua vera luce; *I do not look upon it in that —*, non vedo la cosa sotto questo aspetto; *put it in a good —*, fallo apparire in buona luce **6.** *pl.* abilità; possibilità **7.** *(pitt.)* chiaro: *— and shade*, chiaroscuro **8.** finestra, lucernario, vetrata, vetro: *this room has three lights*, questa stanza ha tre finestre **9.** *(poet.)* vista **10.** *pl.* *(sl.)* occhi **11.** *(teol.)* illuminazione ☆ *— -beam*, raggio di luce, fascio di luce; *— effects*, effetti di luce; *— -fastness*, solidità alla luce; *— -range*, portata luminosa; *— -spot*, macchia di luce; *— -tight*, inaccessibile alla luce; *— -year*, *(astr.)* anno luce ‖ *blue lights*, fuochi del Bengala; *flash- —*, torcia elettrica; « flash » (di apparecchio fotografico); *half- —*, mezza luce; *parking- —*, *(aut.)* luce di posizione; *rear* (o *tail)- —*, *(aut.)* fanale posteriore; *riding lights*, *(mar.)* fanali di fonda; *stern- —*, *(mar.)* fanale di poppa; *traffic lights*, semaforo; *wing landing —*, *(aer.)* proiettore alare di atterraggio.

to light[1], *pass.p.p.* **lighted** ['laitid], **lit** [lit], *v.t.i.* **1.** accendere, accendersi: *she lighted* (o *lit) a cigarette*, ella accese una sigaretta **2.** illuminare, rischiarare, rischiararsi (anche *fig.*); far lume a: *— the doctor out*, fa' lume al dottore mentre esce; *his face lighted up*, il suo viso si illuminò **3.** *fig.* animare, accendere, infiammare.

light[2], *ag.* **1.** leggero, non pesante; semplice, facile; piacevole: *— beer*, birra leggera; *— bread*, pane lievitato; *— diet*, dieta leggera; *— music*, musica leggera; *she has a wonderfully — hand*, ha un tocco straordinariamente leggero ‖ *to be a — sleeper*, avere il sonno leggero **2.** non importante, insignificante: *— talk*, discorsi fatui; *to make — of*, non dare importanza a **3.** frivolo; incostante, volubile: *— a woman*, una donna leggera **4.** agile, svelto; leggero (anche *fig.*): *— fingers*, dita leste, leggere; *— of foot*, agile nella corsa; *with a — heart*, a cuor leggero ☆ *— -armed*, armato alla leggera; *— cavalry*, *(mil.)* cavalleria leggera; *— -fingered*, lesto di mano; ladro; *— -foot(ed)*, agile, lesto; *— -handed*, che ha la mano leggera, dal guanto di velluto; *— -headed*, folle, scervellato; delirante; *— -headedness*, delirio; storditaggine; *— -hearted*, allegro, gaio; *— -heartedness*, allegria, gaiezza; *— -infantry*, fanteria leggera; *— -minded*, frivolo, volubile, leggero; *— -mindedness*, frivolezza, volubilità, leggerezza; *— o'-love*, donna leggera; *— -spirited*, leggero, giulivo, gaio.

to light[2], *v.t.i.* **1.** alleggerire; *(mar.)* scaricare (nave) **2.** *(arc.)* scendere, smontare: *to — from*, scendere da **3.** posarsi, cadere su (di uccelli, insetti) **4.** *to —* (*up*)*on* (*s.o.*, *sthg.*), imbattersi in ‖ *to — on one's feet*, cadere in piedi (anche *fig.*).

lightable ['laitəbl], *ag.* illuminabile.

to lighten[1] ['laitn], *v.t.i.* **1.** alleggerire, alleggerirsi; sgravare, sgravarsi **2.** mitigare, alleviare: *to — a sorrow*, alleviare un dolore.

to lighten[2], *v.t.i.* **1.** illuminare, illuminarsi; accendere, accendersi (anche *fig.*): *his eyes lightened* (*up*), i suoi occhi si illuminarono **2.** rischiararsi, schiarirsi (di tempo) **3.** *imp.* lampeggiare: *it thundered and lightened*, tuonò e lampeggiò.

lightening[1] ['laitņiŋ], *s.* alleggerimento

lightening[2], *s.* lo schiarirsi (del tempo).

lighter[1] ['laitə*], *s.* (*mar.*) chiatta, maona, bettolina.

lighter[2], *s.* accenditore; accendisigaro, accendino ☆ *cigar- —*, accendisigaro; *cigarette- —*, accendino.

lighterage ['laitəridȝ], *s.* **1.** (*mar.*) scarico con chiatte **2.** (*mar.*) spese per trasporto su chiatte.

lighterman, *pl.* **lightermen** ['laitəmən], *s.* (*mar.*) scaricatore di chiatte; chiattaiuolo.

lighthouse ['laithaus], *s.* faro ☆ *— keeper*, guardiano di faro.

lighting ['laitiŋ], *s.* **1.** accensione (di lampade); illuminazione **2.** luce (di un quadro) ☆ *—-up time*, l'orario fissato per accendere le luci.

lightless ['laitlis], *ag.* privo di luce, oscuro.

lightly ['laitli], *av.* **1.** leggermente; alla leggera: *you behaved very —*, hai agito molto leggermente **2.** allegramente; agilmente **3.** poco; un poco.

lightness[1] ['laitnis], *s.* **1.** leggerezza **2.** agilità **3.** gaiezza.

lightness[2], *s.* illuminazione.

lightning ['laitniŋ], *s.* fulmine, saetta; lampo; *fig.* lampo: *as quick as —*, veloce come il lampo; *to strike with —*, fulminare ☆ *— arrester*, (*elett.*) scaricatore per sovratensioni di carattere atmosferico; *—-conductor* (o *—-rod*), parafulmine; *— grounding switch*, (*rad.*) commutatore antenna terra; *— speed*, velocità fulminea; *— strike*, sciopero improvviso.

lightship ['lait-ʃip], *s.* (*mar.*) battello-faro.

lightsome[1] ['laitsəm], *ag.* **1.** leggero; grazioso; elegante **2.** ridente; allegro **3.** frivolo **4.** agile.

lightsome[2], *ag.* luminoso, arioso (di edificio).

lightsomely[1] ['laitsəmli], *av.* **1.** leggermente **2.** allegramente **3.** agilmente.

lightsomely[2], *av.* luminosamente.

lightsomeness[1] ['laitsəmnis], *s.* **1.** leggerezza; eleganza **2.** gaiezza **3.** frivolezza **4.** agilità.

lightsomeness[2], *s.* luminosità (di edificio).

lightweight ['lait-weit], *s.* **1.** (*boxe*) peso leggero **2.** (*sl. amer.*) persona di nessuna importanza **3.** indumento leggero.

lightwood ['lait-wud], *s.* legno leggero per bruciare (specialmente resinoso, di pino).

lign-aloes [,lain'ælouz], *s.* (*bot.*) aloè.

ligneous ['ligniəs], *ag.* ligneo, legnaceo, legnoso.

ligniferous [lig'nifərəs], *ag.* che produce legno.

lignification [,lignifi'keiʃən], *s.* lignificazione.

to lignify ['lignifai], *v.t.i.* trasformare in legno; lignificare.

lignite ['lignait], *s.* (*min.*) lignite.

lignum-vitae ['lignəm'vaiti:], *s.* (*bot.*) guaiaco.

Liguria [li'gjuəriə], *no.pr.* (*geog.*) Liguria.

Ligurian [li'gjuəriən], *ag.s.c.* ligure.

like [laik], *ag.* **1.** simile, somigliante; uguale, pari, pale: *— signs*, (*alg.*) segni uguali; *in — manner*, parinenti; *he gave her something — a hundred pounds*, le diede ql.co. come cento sterline; *I know people — that*, conosco gente così; *there is nothing — a good swim*, non c'è niente di meglio di una bella nuotata; *to be —*, rassomigliare; avere gli stessi gusti: *what is he —?*, he tipo è?; *to be — each other*, rassomigliarsi ‖ *that's more — it!*, questo va meglio! ‖ *that's something —ain!*, questo sì che si chiama piovere!; *they are as*

— as two peas, si somigliano come due gocce d'acqua ‖ *— father, — son* (o *masterman*), *prov.* tale padre, tale figlio **2. caratteristico, proprio di, tipico di:** *it is — me* (o *that is just — me*), io sono fatto così; *it is just — him to say so*, è da lui dire questo; *that is just — a woman!*, questo è tipicamente femminile! **3.** (*arc.*) **probabile:** *he is — to succeed*, è probabile che riuscirà; *it is — we shall see him no more*, è probabile che non lo vedremo più **4.** (usato predicativamente, *spec.* in unione con *to feel*, *to look*): *I don't feel — going, working*, non mi sento di andare, di lavorare; *I feel — some tea*, prenderei volentieri una tazza di tè; *it looks — rain* (o *raining*), sembra che voglia piovere.

like, *s.* **1. simile, pari, uguale:** *did you ever hear the —* (*of it*)*?*, hai mai sentito una cosa simile?; *I never saw his —*, non ho mai visto un individuo come lui; *you and the likes of you*, (*fam.*) tu e i tuoi pari; *to do the —*, fare lo stesso ‖ *and the —*, e simili, e così via ‖ *to give — for —*, rendere pan per focaccia ‖ *— attracts —*, *prov.* chi si somiglia si piglia **2.** *spec. pl.* **gusto, preferenza:** *likes and dislikes*, gusti, simpatie e antipatie.

to like, *v.t.i.* (costruzione *pers.*) (II) **1.** piacere, aver simpatia per; amare; gradire; preferire; aver voglia: *do you — wine?*, ti piace il vino?; *how do you — my dress?*, ti piace il mio vestito?; *"How do you — your tea?", "I — it strong"*, «Come preferisci il tè? », «Mi piace forte»; *I — music*, amo la musica; *some — to take the bus, others the tram*, alcuni preferiscono prendere l'autobus, altri il tram; *these plants don't — damp*, queste piante temono l'umidità ‖ *to — best*, preferire (tra più di due): *this is the kind of music I — best*, questo è il tipo di musica che preferisco; *to — better*, preferire (tra due): *I — better hunting than fishing*, preferisco la caccia alla pesca ‖ *I — strawberries, but they don't — me*, (*fam.*) mi piacciono le fragole ma non mi fanno bene ‖ *well, I — that!*, questa sì che è bella! **2.** (IV) volere, desiderare: *as you —*, come vuoi; *if you —*, se vuoi, se lo desideri; *he thinks he can do anything he likes*, crede di poter fare tutto ciò che vuole; *I can do as I — with him*, con lui posso fare ciò che voglio; *I should — you to know*, vorrei che tu sapessi; *take as many as you —*, prendine quanti ne vuoi; *when you — we can go home*, quando vuoi possiamo andare a casa; *would you — some bread?*, (*fam.*) vuoi del pane? ‖ *whether he likes it or not*, volente o nolente.

like, *av.* **1.** *— enough* (o *very —*), probabilmente **2.** (idiotismo) piuttosto; quasi: *he looked angry —*, sembrava arrabbiato; *I stumbled —*, inciampai ‖ *cong.* (idiotismo per *as*) come: *do — I do*, fa' come me; *rain is falling — in February*, piove come in febbraio ‖ *prep.* come, alla maniera di, similmente a: *he ran — a madman*, correva come un pazzo; *I can't do it — you*, non posso farlo come te ‖ *don't leave me — that*, non lasciarmi così ‖ *it is raining — anything*, piove a più non posso; *they swore — anything*, bestemmiavano come turchi ‖ *it will fit you — a glove*, ti calzerà come un guanto ‖ *to smoke — a chimney*, fumare come un turco.

likeable ['laikəbl], *ag.* simpatico, piacevole, attraente.

likelihood ['laiklihud], *s.* verosimiglianza; probabilità: *in all —*, con tutta probabilità.

likely ['laikli], *ag.* **1.** verosimile; probabile: *he is not — to come*, non è probabile che egli venga **2.** adatto; conveniente: *this is the most — place for camping*, questo è il luogo più adatto per il campeggio; *this is the likeliest place to find oysters*, questo è il luogo più adatto per trovare ostriche **3.** promettente: *a — young man*, un giovane promettente ‖ *av.* verosimilmente; probabilmente: *most* (o *very*) *—*, con tutta probabilità; *he will succeed as — as not*, può darsi che riesca come che non riesca.

to liken ['laikən], *v.t.* **1.** paragonare **2.** (*rar.*) rendere simile a.

likeness ['laiknis], s. **1.** somiglianza, rassomiglianza: *a close —*, una grande rassomiglianza; *the portrait is a poor —*, il ritratto è poco somigliante **2.** immagine, apparenza, sembianza, aspetto: *he is an enemy in the — of a friend*, è un nemico nelle sembianze di amico **3.** ritratto: *to draw* (o *to take*) *s.o.'s —*, fare il ritratto di qlcu.; *to have one's — taken*, farsi fotografare, farsi fare un ritratto.

likewise ['laik-waiz], av. **1.** parimenti; similmente; allo stesso modo; così: *to do —*, fare altrettanto **2.** anche, inoltre.

liking ['laikiŋ], s. gusto, preferenza, predilezione; gradimento: *is this cigar to your —?*, questo sigaro è di tuo gusto?; *to have a — for s.o., sthg.*, avere simpatia per qlcu., preferenza per ql.co., *to take a — for* (o *to*) *sthg.*, prendere gusto a ql.co.

lilac ['lailək], ag. lilla: *a — hat*, un cappello color lilla ‖ s. **1.** (bot.) lilla, serenella: *a bunch of —*, un mazzo di lilla **2.** (color) lilla ☆ *-bush*, arboscelli di lilla.

liliaceous [,lili'eifəs], ag. (bot.) gigliaceo, liliaceo.

Lilian ['liliən], no.pr.f. Liliana.

Lilliput ['lilipʌt], no.pr. (lett.) Lilliput.

Lilliputian [,lili'pju:fjən], ag. lilliputiano; minuscolo (di persona, cosa) ‖ s.c. lilliputiano, lilliputiana; persona piccola.

lilt [lilt], s. **1.** canzonetta ben ritmata **2.** ritmo accentuato, cadenza.

to **lilt**, v.t.i. **1.** cantare dolcemente **2.** cantare con ritmo.

lily ['lili], ag. bianco, pallido ‖ s. giglio: fig. candore, purezza di giglio; *white as a —*, bianco come un giglio ☆ *-iron*, tipo di fiocina; *— -livered*, codardo; *— of the valley*, (bot.) mughetto; *— -white*, candido come il giglio ‖ *Madonna- —* (o *white —*), giglio della Madonna; *tiger- —*, giglio rosso; *water- —*, ninfea.

limaceous [lai'meifəs], ag. di lumaca.

limax ['laimæks], s. lumaca.

limb[1] [lim], s. **1.** arto, membro; ala: *the lower limbs*, gli arti inferiori ‖ *— of the law*, (iron.) rappresentante della legge ‖ *to escape with life and limbs*, fig. rimanere sano e salvo; (fam.) scamparla bella **2.** ramo; ala (di edificio); braccio (di croce): *— of a tree*, ramo d'albero **3.** (fam.) diavoletto: *a — of Satan!*, birbantello!.

to **limb**[1], v.t. smembrare.

limb[2], s. (scient. astr.) orlo, contorno; orlo graduato (di quadrante, ecc.); (bot.) contorno di petalo, foglia.

limbed [limd], ag. che ha membra ☆ *long- —*, dalle gambe lunghe; *strong- —*, tarchiato, nerboruto.

limber[1] ['limbə*], s. **1.** (artigl.) avantreno **2.** (arc. dial.) timone; stanga (di veicolo).

to **limber**[1], v.t. (artigl.) attaccare all'avantreno.

limber[2], ag. **1.** agile **2.** flessibile, pieghevole; fig. arrendevole.

to **limber**[2], v.t. rendere flessibile, pieghevole; fig. rendere arrendevole ‖ *to — up*, (spor.) scaldarsi i muscoli, mettersi in forma.

limberness ['limbənis], s. flessibilità.

limbless ['limlis], ag senza membra.

Limbo, limbo ['limbou], s. **1.** (teol.) limbo **2.** prigione **3.** (fam.) luogo per persone, cose dimenticate, abbandonate.

Limbus ['limbəs], s. (teol.) limbo.

lime[1] [laim], s. **1.** calce: *milk of —*, latte di calce **2.** calcina **3.** pania, vischio ☆ *-wash*, lavaggio con acqua di calce; *— -water*, acqua di calce ‖ *bird- —*, pania; *quick- —*, calce viva; *slaked —*, calce spenta.

to **lime**[1], v.t. **1.** (spec. fig.) cementare **2.** invischiare, impaniare, tendere panie a (anche fig.).

lime[2], s. (bot.) cedro ☆ *— -juice*, succo di cedro.

lime[3], s. (bot.) tiglio.

limekiln ['laimkiln], s. fornace da calce.

limelight ['laimlait], s. luce fortissima; (teat.) luce della ribalta (anche fig.): *a politician now in the —*, un uomo politico ora assai in vista.

limen ['laimen], s. (psicologia) limen.

limer ['laimə*], s. **1.** imbianchino **2.** spazzola per imbiancare ‖ s.c. chi invischia.

Limerick ['limərik], no.pr. (geog.) Limerick ‖ s. (poes.) «limerick» (stanza di cinque versi, caratterizzata da toni umoristici e spesso assurdi).

limestone ['laimstoun], s. (min.) calcare.

limit ['limit], s. limite; confine (anche fig.): *within limits*, con moderazione; *without —*, senza limite; *to set limits to*, fissare un limite a; fig. porre dei limiti ‖ *that's the —!*, (sl.) questo è il colmo!.

to **limit**, v.t. **1.** limitare: *rain that limits the view*, pioggia che limita la visuale **2.** fig. porre termine a; frenare **3.** confinare.

limitable ['limitəbl], ag. limitabile.

limitary ['limitəri], ag. **1.** limitato, ristretto **2.** limitativo; restrittivo **3.** che è situato alla frontiera.

limitation [,limi'teifən], s. **1.** limitazione, restrizione **2.** inabilità **3.** (dir.) termine di prescrizione.

limitative ['limitətiv], ag. limitativo.

limited ['limitid], ag. limitato; ristretto ☆ *— company*, (comm.) società a responsabilità limitata; *— monarchy*, monarchia costituzionale, parlamentare.

limitedly ['limitidli], av. limitatamente.

limitless ['limitlis], ag. senza limiti; illimitato.

limitrophe ['limitrouf], ag. limitrofo.

to **limn** [lim], v.t. (arc.) dipingere; miniare.

limner ['limnə*], s. (arc.) pittore; miniatore.

limnology [lim'nolədʒi], s. limnologia.

limonite ['laimənait], s. (min.) limonite.

limousine ['limu(:)zi:n], s. (aut.) «limousine», berlina.

limp[1] [limp], s. zoppicamento.

to **limp**[1], v.i. **1.** zoppicare, camminare zoppicando: *the wounded soldiers limped off*, i soldati feriti s'allontanarono zoppicando **2.** avanzare con fatica e lentamente (di nave danneggiata, ecc.).

limp[2], ag. **1.** flessibile, molle **2.** debole; fiacco; facilmente influenzabile: *to feel as — as a rag*, sentirsi debole come uno straccio.

limpet ['limpit], s. **1.** (zool.) patella **2.** (scherz.) persona, funzionario eccessivamente attaccato alla sua carica.

limpid ['limpid], ag. limpido; chiaro; trasparente.

limpidity [lim'piditi], s. limpidezza; trasparenza.

limpidly ['limpidli], av. limpidamente; chiaramente.

limpidness ['limpidnis], s. limpidezza.

limping ['limpiŋ], ag. zoppicante ‖ s. zoppicamento.

limpingly ['limpiŋli], av. zoppicando, zoppiconi.

limply ['limpli], av. **1.** flessibilmente **2.** debolmente; fiaccamente.

limpness ['limpnis], s. **1.** flessibilità, pieghevolezza **2.** debolezza; fiacchezza.

limy ['laimi], ag. **1.** viscoso, glutinoso **2.** calcareo.

linage ['lainidʒ], s. (tip.) **1.** numero di righe di composizione **2.** pagamento in rapporto al numero di righe.

linchpin ['lintfpin], s. (mec.) acciarino (di ruota).

linden ['lindən], s. (bot.) tiglio.

line[1] [lain], s. **1.** linea, tratto, riga: *a straight — from A to B*, una linea retta da A a B; *the — of life*, la linea della vita **2.** pl. contorni; lineamenti: *the severe lines of the castle*, le linee severe del castello **3.** ruga: *there are lines on his forehead*, ci sono delle rughe sulla sua fronte **4.** filo, cordicella, corda, fune: *she hung the linen on the —*, stese la biancheria sulla corda **5.** riga; verso: *new —*, a capo; *to drop a —*, scrivere due righe **6.** la dodicesima parte di un pollice (misura di lunghezza = mm. 2,12) **7.** (spor.) linea: *has the ball crossed the —?*, la palla ha passato la riga? **8.** *the Line*, l'equatore: *to cross the —*, attraversare l'equatore **9.** linea di demarcazione; frontiera, confine; fig. limite: *to draw a —*, stabilire un confine un limite **10.** linea (di comunicazione): *— of communication*, linea di comunicazione; *the — is engaged*, (tel.) la linea è occupata **11.** (mar.) linea (di navigazione), compagnia, società di navigazione: *the Cunard Line*, la compagnia Cunard **12.** (mil.) riga, fila; linea (d fortificazioni, di combattimento): — *of fire*, linea del fuoco; *all along the* —, su tutta la linea; *to fall out of* —, rompere le righe || *to toe the* —, mettersi in linea; *fig.* sottomettersi alla disciplina **13.** fila (di persone o di cose); coda: *to stand in* (*a*) —, far la coda || *to fall* (o *to come*) *into* — *with s.o.'s ideas*, *fig.* conformarsi alle idee di qlcu. **14.** linea, stirpe, discendenza: *a long* — *of kings*, una lunga successione di re; *to come of a good* —, appartenere ad una buona famiglia **15.** linea di condotta; criterio: *this building is constructed on modern lines*, questo edificio è costruito con criteri moderni; *we shall take the* — *of least resistance*, sceglieremo il sistema più facile; *to proceed along certain lines*, seguire una certa linea di condotta; *to take up a* — *of one's own*, seguire una propria direttiva **16.** attività; mestiere; ramo: *his* — *of business is selling hats*, la sua attività è vendere cappelli; *sport is not in his* —, lo sport non rientra nelle sue attività; *what is your* —?, qual è la tua attività? **17.** moda, foggia; linea: *we are trying a new* — *this year*, lanceremo una nuova moda quest'anno **18.** *pl.* parte di un attore ☆ — *-engraving*, incisione || *air-* —, linea di navigazione aerea; *branch* —, (*ferr.*) linea secondaria; *down-* —, (*ferr.*) linea in partenza da Londra; *fishing* —, lenza; *front-* —, linea del fronte; *lightning* —, parafulmine; *loop-* —, (*ferr.*) diversione, linea di scambio; *marriage-lines*, certificato di matrimonio; *party-* —, (*tel.*) duplex; *shipping* —, compagnia di navigazione; *up-* —, (*ferr.*) linea per Londra.

to line¹, *v.t.i.* **1.** rigare; delineare; segnare: *pain had lined her face*, il suo viso era segnato dal dolore **2.** fiancheggiare: *the streets were lined with trees*, le strade erano fiancheggiate da alberi; *they lined the street with troops*, allinearono le truppe lungo la strada **3.** *to* — *in*, abbozzare **4.** *to* — *off*, tracciare **5.** *to* — *out*, allinearsi (di due squadre); mettere in linea (piante) **6.** *to* — *through*, depennare con una linea (una parola) **7.** *to* — *up*, allinear(si), mettersi in fila: *the soldiers lined up*, i soldati si allinearono.

line², *s.* (*rar.*) **1.** filato di lino **2.** tessuto di lino.

to line², *v.t.* **1.** rinforzare; foderare: *the gloves were lined with fur*, i guanti erano foderati di pelliccia **2.** riempire (stomaco, tasche, ecc.) || *to* — *one's pocket* (o *purse*), fare denaro (specialmente in modo disonesto).

to line³, *v.t.* coprire, montare (di cani, ecc.).

lineage ['liniidʒ], *s.* lignaggio, stirpe; pedigree.

lineal ['liniəl], *ag.* in linea diretta: *a* — *descendant*, *heir*, un discendente, erede diretto.

lineally ['liniəli], *av.* direttamente.

lineament ['liniəmənt], *s.* lineamento; caratteristica: *every* —, ogni lineamento; *the actress had beautiful lineaments*, l'attrice aveva dei bei lineamenti.

linear ['liniə*], *ag.* lineare: — *equation*, equazione di primo grado; — *leaf*, foglia lineare.

linearly ['liniəli], *av.* linearmente.

lineate ['liniit], *ag.* lineato.

lineman, *pl.* **linemen** ['lainmən], *s.* guardafili.

linen ['linin], *ag.* di lino || *s.* **1.** filato o tela di lino **2.** biancheria || *wash your dirty* — *at home!*, i panni sudici lavali a casa tua! ☆ — *-draper*, negoziante di telerie; *table-* —, biancheria da tavola.

liner¹ ['lainə*], *s.c.* chi traccia linee || *s.* **1.** (*mar.*) transatlantico, nave di linea **2.** (*aer.*) aereo di linea **3.** giornalista, pubblicista pagato un tanto la riga ☆ *air-* —, grosso aeroplano di linea.

liner², *s. c.* chi fa, applica fodere interne || *s.* (*mec.*) spessore; canna; camicia (smontabile).

linesman, *pl.* **linesmen** ['lainzmən], *s.* **1.** soldato di prima linea **2.** guardafili **3.** (*spor.*) guardalinea.

ling¹ [liŋ], *s.* (*ittiol.*) molva.

ling², *s.* (*bot.*) erica.

to linger ['liŋgə*], *v.t.i.* indugiare; tirare in lungo; protrarsi; trascorrere (il tempo) in indugi: *a beggar was lingering about the park*, un mendicante bighello-

nava per il parco; *don't* — *over your breakfast*, non tirare in lungo la colazione; *he lingered on his favourite subject*, indugiò sul suo argomento preferito || *the poor man lingered out his last days*, il pover'uomo trascinava a stento i suoi ultimi giorni.

lingerer ['liŋgərə*], *s.c.* ritardatario, ritardataria.

lingerie ['lænʒəri:], *s.* biancheria per signora.

lingering ['liŋgəriŋ], *ag.* **1.** lento; *a* — *agony*, una lenta agonia **2.** indugiante: *a* — *look*, uno sguardo che si indugia || *s.* ritardo; lentezza; il protrarsi.

lingeringly ['liŋgəriŋli], *av.* lentamente.

lingo ['liŋgou], *pl.* **lingoes** ['liŋgouz], *s.* (*spreg.*) linguaggio; gergo particolare; lingua straniera ☆ *card -sharpers'* —, il gergo dei bari.

lingua franca ['liŋgwə'fræŋkə], *s.* lingua franca (specialmente quella parlata nel Levante).

lingual ['liŋgwəl], *ag.* **1.** (*anat. gram.*) linguale **2.** linguistico || *s.* linguale (consonante).

linguiform ['liŋgwifɔ:m], *ag.* linguiforme.

linguist ['liŋgwist], *s.c.* **1.** poliglotta: *he is no* —, fa fatica ad imparare le lingue **2.** linguista.

linguistic [liŋ'gwistik], *ag.* linguistico ☆ — *atlas*, atlante linguistico.

linguistically [liŋ'gwistikəli], *av.* linguisticamente.

linguistics [liŋ'gwistiks], *s.* linguistica.

lingula ['liŋgjulə], *pl.* **lingulae** ['liŋgjuli:], *s.* (*anat. zool.*) lingula.

lingulate ['liŋgjuleit], *ag.* a forma di lingua.

lingy ['lindʒi], *ag.* coperto di erica.

liniment ['linimənt], *s.* (*med.*) linimento.

lining¹ ['lainiŋ], *s.* **1.** rigatura **2.** allineamento.

lining², *s.* **1.** fodera; interno || *every cloud has a silver* —, *prov.* non tutto il male viene per nuocere **2.** materiale per rivestimento interno; (*elett.*) rivestimento isolante; (*mec.*) incamiciatura ☆ — *paper*, carta per tappezzeria, rivestimenti.

link¹ [liŋk], *s.* **1.** anello, maglia (di catena) **2.** «link» (misura di lunghezza = cm. 20,12) **3.** *fig.* vincolo, legame; concatenazione; congiunzione || *the missing* —, lacuna; (*biol.*) ipotetico anello di congiunzione **4.** (*mec.*) comando articolato ☆ — *-up*, collegamento || *air* —, collegamento aereo; *cuff-links*, gemelli da polso.

to link¹, *v.t.i.* **1.** vincolare; collegare, collegarsi; concatenare, concatenarsi; unire: *these facts are closely linked together*, questi fatti sono strettamente collegati **2.** (*mec.*) collegare **3.** *to* — *in*, *up with* (*sthg.*), unirsi a.

link², *s.* (*arc.*) torcia, fiaccola.

links [liŋks], *s.pl.* **1.** (*scoz.*) dune **2.** (*con costruzione sing.*) campo da golf.

Linnaean [li'ni:(ə)n], *ag.* (*bot.*) linneano, di Linneo || *s.* seguace di Linneo.

Linnaeus [li'ni:(ə)s], *no.pr.m.* Linneo.

linnet ['linit], *s.* (*ornit.*) fanello.

linoleum [li'nouljəm], *s.* linoleum.

linotype ['lainoutaip], *s.* (*tip.*) linotipo ☆ — *-operator*, linotipista.

linotypist ['lainou,taipist], *s.* linotipista.

linsang ['linsæŋ], *s.* (*zool.*) zibetto del Borneo.

linseed ['linsi:d], *s.* semi di lino; linosa ☆ — *-oil*, olio di semi di lino.

linsey-woolsey ['linzi'wulzi], *s.* mezzalana (tessuto misto di lana e cotone).

linstock ['linstɔk], *s.* (*mil.*) miccia.

lint [lint], *s.* (*chir.*) filaccia, garza.

lintel ['lintl], *s.* (*arch.*) architrave; mensola (di caminetto).

liny ['laini], *ag.* pieno di linee; rugoso.

lion ['laiən], *s.* **1.** leone: —*'s cub* (o *whelp*), leoncino || *Lion*, (*astr.*) Leone || *a* — *in the path* (o *in the way*), un ostacolo tremendo || —*'s share*, *fig.* la parte del leone || *the British Lion*, (*arald.*) il Leone Britannico (emblema nazionale) || *to put one's head into the* —*'s mouth*, incorrere in gravi pericoli || *to twist the* —*'s tail*, *fig.* torcere la coda al leone (si dice dei giornalisti americani che attaccano l'Inghilterra) **2.** *fig.* leone, persona coraggiosa **3.** celebrità: *the* — *of the day,* la celebrità del giorno; *to make a* — *of s.o.*, incensare qlcu. **4.** *pl.* curiosità, bellezze di un luogo: *to see, to show the lions of a place,* visitare, mostrare le curiosità, le bellezze naturali di un luogo ☆ *Lion-heart,* (*st.*) Cuor di Leone (detto di Riccardo I); — *-hearted,* coraggioso; — *-like,* leonino; feroce.

Lionel ['laiənl], *no.pr.m.* Lionello.

lioness ['laiənis], *s.* leonessa.

lionism ['laiənizəm], *s.* **1.** visita ai monumenti di un luogo **2.** il trattare (qlcu.) come una celebrità.

to **lionize** ['laiənaiz], *v.t.i.* **1.** vedere, mostrare le bellezze, le curiosità di un luogo **2.** considerare (qlcu.) come una celebrità; atteggiarsi a celebrità; essere la celebrità del momento.

lip [lip], *s.* **1.** labbro: *thick lips,* labbra grosse; *but let him open his lips!*, ma lasciagli aprir bocca!; *he hung on her lips, fig.* pendeva dalle sue labbra; *he licked his lips,* si leccò le labbra; *it just escaped my lips,* mi è sfuggito (nel parlare); *she bit her lips,* si morse le labbra ‖ *to curl one's lips,* atteggiare le labbra a disprezzo; *to purse* (o *to screw up*) *one's lips,* serrare le labbra; *to smack one's lips over sthg.*, far schioccare le labbra per ql.co. **2.** orlo, bordo, margine; labbro (di ferita) **3.** (*sl.*) sfacciataggine, insolenza; discorsi sboccati: *none of your* —*!*, non esser così sfacciato! **4.** (*bot. anat.*) lobo, labbro **5.** filo, taglio ☆ — *-Christian,* bigotto; — *-homage,* complimento insincero; — *-language,* linguaggio delle labbra (per sordomuti); — *-teeth consonants,* consonanti labio-dentali; — *-reading,* metodo orale (per sordomuti); — *-salve,* burro di cacao; *fig.* lusinga; — *-service,* mancanza di sincerità; rispetto non sentito; — *-stick,* rossetto, matita per labbra; — *-wisdom,* saggezza a parole ‖ *lower* — (o *under* —), labbro inferiore; *upper* —, labbro superiore: *stiff upper* —, *fig.* orgoglio, ostinazione, risolutezza.

to **lip**, *pass.p.p.* **lipped** [lipt], *v.t.* **1.** toccare con le labbra; imboccare (strumento a fiato) **2.** lambire, sfiorare (di acqua) **3.** sussurrare, mormorare **4.** (*golf*) spingere la palla fino all'orlo della (buca); (della palla) raggiungere l'orlo della (buca) senza cadervi dentro.

lipless ['liplis], *ag.* senza labbra.

liplet ['liplit], *s.* labbruzzo.

lipoid ['lipɔid], *ag.s.* (*biol. chim.*) lipoide.

lipoma [li'poumə], *s.* (*patol.*) lipoma.

lipped [lipt], *ag.* (*bot.*) labiato.

to **lippen** ['lipn], *v.t.i.* (*scoz.*) fidarsi; confidare in.

lipper ['lipə*], *s.* increspatura (del mare).

to **liquate** ['laikweit], *v.t.* (*fis. metal.*) fondere.

liquation [li'kweiʃən], *s.* (*fis. metal.*) liquazione.

liquefacient [,likwi'feiʃənt], *ag.* liquefaciente.

liquefaction [,likwi'fækʃən], *s.* liquefazione.

liquefiable ['likwifaiəbl], *ag.* fondibile.

liquefier ['likwifaiə*], *s.* **1.** (*ind.*) apparecchio per liquefare **2.** (*chim. fis.*) sostanza liquefaciente.

to **liquefy** ['likwifai], *v.t.i.* liquefare, liquefarsi; fondere; sciogliersi.

liquescency [li'kwisənsi], *s.* (*fis.*) liquescenza.

liquescent [li'kwisənt], *ag.* (*fis.*) liquescente.

liqueur [li'kjuə*], *s.* rosolio ☆ — *brandy,* «brandy» di qualità fine; — *-glass,* bicchierino da liquore.

liquid ['likwid], *ag.* **1.** liquido: *to reduce sthg. to a* — *state,* liquefare ql.co. **2.** chiaro, trasparente: *a* — *sky,* un cielo chiaro **3.** fluente, armonioso: — *lines,* versi armoniosi **4.** fluttuante, instabile: — *convictions,* convinzioni instabili **5.** (*comm.*) liquido ‖ *s.* **1.** liquido **2.** (*gram.*) liquida (consonante) **3.** (*comm.*) denaro liquido ☆ — *air,* (*chim.*) aria liquida; — *assets,* disponibilità finanziarie; — *fire,* (*mil.*) petrolio infiammato; — *measure,* misura di capacità per liquidi.

to **liquidate** ['likwideit], *v.t.i.* **1.** (*comm.*) liquidare, svendere **2.** (*comm.*) liquidare, saldare, pagare **3.** *fig.* liberarsi di; (*sl.*) finire, distruggere; uccidere.

liquidation [,likwi'deiʃən], *s.* (*comm.*) liquidazione: *to go into* —, andare in liquidazione.

liquidator ['likwideitə*], *s.* (*comm.*) liquidatore.

liquidity [li'kwiditi], *s.* **1.** liquidità **2.** limpidezza.

to **liquidize** ['likwidaiz], *v.t.* rendere liquido.

liquidly ['likwidli], *av.* liquidamente.

liquidness ['likwidnis], *s.* liquidezza.

liquor ['likə*], *s.* **1.** sostanza liquida; brodo; soluzione **2.** bevanda alcoolica ‖ *to be in* —, essere ubriaco; *to be under the influence of* —, essere brillo ☆ — *laws,* leggi che limitano l'uso di bevande alcooliche ‖ *malt* —, birra.

to **liquor**, *v.t.i.* **1.** ingrassare (scarpe, pelle) **2.** imbevere, immergere **3.** *to* — *up,* (*sl.*) bere ql.co. di alcoolico ‖ *to* — *s.o. up,* far ubriacare qlcu.

liquorice ['likəris], *s.* liquirizia.

liquorish ['likəriʃ], *ag.* amante dei liquori.

lira ['liərə], *pl.* **lire** ['liəri], **liras** ['liərəz], *s.* lira (moneta italiana).

liriodendron [,liriə'dendrən], *s.* (*bot.*) liriodendro.

Lisa ['li:zə], *no.pr.f.* Lisa.

Lisbet ['lizbit], **Lisbeth** ['lizbəθ], *no.pr.f. dim.* di **Elizabeth**.

Lisbon ['lizbən], *no.pr.* (*geog.*) Lisbona.

Lisle [lail], *no.pr.* (*geog.*) Lilla.

lisp [lisp], *s.* **1.** pronuncia blesa **2.** fruscio (di foglie); mormorio (di acque).

to **lisp**, *v.i.* parlare bleso (dire *th* per *s*).

lisping ['lispiŋ], *ag.* bleso ‖ *s.* pronuncia blesa.

lissom(e) ['lisəm], *ag.* agile; pieghevole, flessibile.

lissom(e)ness ['lisəmnis], *s.* pieghevolezza, flessibilità.

list[1] [list], *s.* **1.** lista, elenco, catalogo ‖ *the* —, elenco dei titoli ammessi alle contrattazioni (in borsa) ‖ *the free* —, (*comm.*) elenco delle merci esenti da dogana; (*teat.*) elenco dei «portoghesi» **2.** (*mil.*) ruolo ☆ *active* —, (*mil.*) ruolo attivo; *waiting-* —, elenco di candidati.

to **list**[1], *v.t.* **1.** elencare, catalogare **2.** (*mil.*) arrolare.

list[2], *s.* **1.** (*ind. tessile*) cimosa, vivagno **2.** lista, striscia **3.** (*arch.*) listello **4.** confine, frontiera **5.** *pl.* recinto, palizzata ‖ *to enter the lists,* entrare in lizza **6.** (*amer.*) solco.

to **list**[2], *v.t.* **1.** listare **2.** tagliare a listelli.

list[3], *s.* (*mar.*) sbandamento.

to **list**[3], *v.i.* (*mar.*) sbandare.

to **list**[4], *v.t.i.* (*arc. poet.*) ascoltare, prestare attenzione.

to **list**[5], *v.t.i.* (*arc.*) aver voglia; desiderare: *the wind bloweth where it listeth,* il vento soffia dove vuole.

to **listen** ['lisn], *v.i.* **1.** ascoltare, prestare ascolto (anche *fig.*): *to* — *to s.o.*, ascoltare qlcu.: *he would not* — *to me,* si rifiutò di darmi ascolto; *his advice must be listened to,* bisogna seguire i suoi consigli ‖ *to* — *for the sound of a bell,* stare ad ascoltare se suona un campanello **2.** *to* — *in,* captare una comunicazione, una trasmissione; ascoltare la radio.

listener ['lisnə*], *s.c.* ascoltatore, ascoltatrice: *to be a good* —, saper ascoltare (dimostrando interesse e comprensione) ☆ — *-in,* radioascoltatore.

listening ['lisniŋ], *s.* l'ascoltare ☆ — *-post,* (*mil.*) posto di ascolto.

lister[1] ['listə*], *s.* chi registra; chi fa una lista.

lister[2], *s.* (*amer.*) aratro assolcatore ☆ — *drill,* aratro-seminatrice.

listerine ['listəri:n], *s.* (*farm.*) soluzione antisettica.

to **listerize** ['listəraiz], *v.t.* (*med.*) curare (una ferita) secondo i metodi di Lister.

listful ['listful], *ag.* (*arc.*) attento.

listing[1] ['listiŋ], *s.* (*ind. tessile*) cimosa, vivagno.

listing[2], *s.* (*amer.*) il fare una lista.

listless ['listlis], *ag.* disattento, sbadato, distratto **2.** svogliato; indifferente.

listlessly ['listlisli], *av.* **1.** sbadatamente, distrattamente **2.** svogliatamente; con indifferenza.

listlessness ['listlisnis], *s.* **1.** trascuratezza **2.** svogliatezza; indifferenza.

lit [lit], *pass. p.p.* di to **light**.

litany ['litəni], *s.* (*eccl.*) litania.

literacy ['litərəsi], *s.* il saper leggere e scrivere; grado di istruzione.

literal ['litərəl], *ag.* **1.** di lettera alfabetica: — *error*, refuso, errore di stampa **2.** letterale: — *translation*, traduzione letterale **3.** conforme alla realtà; testuale: — *truth*, verità testuale **4.** prosaico, privo di immaginazione: *he is a* — *person*, è una persona priva di immaginazione ‖ *s.* errore di stampa.

literalism ['litərəlizəm], *s.* interpretazione puramente letterale.

literalist ['litərəlist], *s.* chi si attiene all'interpretazione puramente letterale.

to **literalize** ['litərəlaiz], *v.t.* interpretare in senso letterale (metafore, ecc.).

literally ['litərəli], *av.* letteralmente: *he was* — *mad with delight*, era letteralmente pazzo di gioia; *to translate* —, tradurre letteralmente.

literarily ['litərərili], *av.* letterariamente.

literary ['litərəri], *ag.* letterario: *a* — *magazine*, una rivista letteraria; — *property*, proprietà letteraria; — *style*, stile letterario ☆ *a* — *man*, un letterato.

literate ['litərit], *ag.* **1.** letterato **2.** capace di leggere e scrivere ‖ *s.* **1.** letterato **2.** chi sa leggere e scrivere **3.** candidato agli ordini sacri anglicani che non ha frequentato una università.

literati [,litə'rɑːtiː], *s.pl.* (*lat.*) i letterati; i dotti.

literatim [,litə'rɑːtim], *av.* (*lat.*) lettera per lettera, letteralmente; testualmente.

literator ['litəreitə*], *s.* letterato.

literature ['litərit∫ə*], *s.* **1.** letteratura; opere letterarie **2.** studi letterari; carriera letteraria **3.** (*fam.*) scritti, opuscoli (intorno a un dato soggetto) ☆ *advertising* —, opuscoli pubblicitari.

lithantrax [li'θæntræks], *s.* (*min.*) litantrace.

litharge ['liθɑːdʒ], *s.* (*chim.*) litargirio.

lithe [laið], *ag.* agile; svelto; flessibile: — *movements*, movimenti agili.

lithely ['laiðli], *av.* agilmente; flessibilmente.

litheness ['laiðnis], *s.* agilità; flessibilità.

lither ['liðə*], *ag.* **1.** flessibile, cedevole **2.** (*dial.*) pigro.

lithesome ['laiðsəm], *V.* **lissom(e)**.

lithia ['liθiə], *s.* (*chim.*) litina.

lithiasis [li'θaiəsis], *s.* (*patol.*) litiasi.

lithie ['liθik], *ag.* (*chim.*) litico.

lithium ['liθiəm], *s.* (*chim.*) litio.

lithograph ['liθəgrɑːf], *s.* litografia, riproduzione litografica.

to **lithograph**, *v.t.* litografare.

lithographer [li'θɔgrəfə*], *s.* litografo.

lithographic(al) [,liθə'græfik(əl)], *ag.* litografico.

lithographically [,liθə'græfikəli], *av.* litograficamente.

lithography [li'θɔgrəfi], *s.* (processo, arte della) litografia.

lithoid ['liθɔid], *ag.* (*geol.*) litoide.

lithological [,liθə'lɔdʒikəl], *ag.* (*geol.*) litologico.

lithologist [li'θɔlədʒist], *s.* litologo.

lithology [li'θɔlədʒi], *s.* **1.** (*geol.*) litologia **2.** (*med.*) studio della calcolosi.

lithomancy ['liθəmænsi], *s.* litomanzia.

lithomarge ['liθəmɑːdʒ], *s.* (*geol.*) litomarga.

lithophane ['liθəfein], *s.* (*artig.*) litofania.

lithophyte ['liθəfait], *s.* (*min.*) litofito.

lithosphere ['liθousfiə*], *s.* (*geol.*) litosfera.

lithotomic(al) [,liθə'tɔmik(əl)], *ag.* (*chir.*) litotomico.

lithotomy [li'θɔtəmi], *s.* (*chir.*) litotomia.

lithotrity [li'θɔtriti], *s.* (*chir.*) litotripsia.

Lithuania [,liθju(ː)'einjə], *no.pr.* (*geog.*) Lituania.

Lithuanian [,liθju(ː)'einjən], *ag.* lituano ‖ *s.c.* lituano, lituana ‖ *s.* lituano (lingua).

litigant ['litigənt], *ag.s.* (*dir.*) contendente: — *parties*, le parti contendenti.

to **litigate** ['litigeit], *v.t.i.* (*dir.*) **1.** essere in causa **2.** contestare (in un processo).

litigation [,liti'gei∫ən], *s.* (*dir.*) lite; causa.

litigious [li'tidʒəs], *ag.* (*dir.*) contenzioso; litigioso.

litigiously [li'tidʒəsli], *av.* (*dir.*) contenziosamente.

litigiousness [li'tidʒəsnis], *s.* (*dir.*) contenziosità.

litmus ['litməs], *s.* (*chim.*) tornasole, laccamuffa ☆ — *paper*, (*chim.*) cartina di tornasole.

litotes ['laitoutiːz], *s.* (*ret.*) litote.

litre ['liːtə*], *s.* litro (unità di capacità = 61.025 cu. in.).

litter ['litə*], *s.* **1.** lettiga; barella **2.** strame, lettiera **3.** rifiuti; immondizie **4.** disordine **5.** figliata.

to **litter**, *v.t.i.* **1.** stendere paglia, strame; preparare la lettiera **2.** sparpagliare; mettere in disordine (carte, oggetti usati, inutili) **3.** proliferare (di animali).

little ['litl], *comp.* **less** [les], **lesser** ['lesə*], *superl.* **least** [liːst], *ag.* **1.** piccolo, piccino: — *boy*, — *girl*, ragazzino, ragazzina; *his* — *room*, la sua stanzetta; *come here, my* — *man!*, vieni qui, ometto mio! (a un bambino) ‖ *the* — *ones*, i bambini, i piccoli ‖ *the Little Bear*, (*astr.*) l'Orsa Minore ‖ — *Mary*, (*fam.*) lo stomaco; *the* — *people*, le fate ‖ — *and good*, *prov.* nelle botti piccole sta il vino buono **2.** corto, breve: *come with me a* — *way*, vieni con me per un breve tratto di strada; *wait a* — *while*, aspetta un istante, un momentino **3.** poco: — *fever*, poca febbre; — *or much bread*, poco o molto pane; *he has* — *money*, ha poco denaro; *you gave me not a* — *trouble*, mi desti non poco fastidio **4.** insignificante; esiguo; meschino: *for so* — *a matter*, per così poca cosa; *a man with a* — *mind*, un uomo dalla mente meschina; *I know your* — *ways*, conosco i tuoi mezzucci **5.** (con art. indef.) un po' di: *he has a* — *money*, ha un po' di denaro; *I'd like a* — *more cake*, vorrei ancora un po' di dolce; *make a* — *less noise, please!*, fate un po' meno rumore, per favore! ☆ — *finger*, mignolo; — *-go*, (*fam.*) primo esame di baccalaureato (all'università di Cambridge).

little, *s.* poco, piccola cosa, piccola quantità: *a* — *makes him laugh*, un'inezia lo fa ridere; *I'll take a* —, ne prenderò un po'; *she did what* — *she could*, fece quel poco che potè; *she knows a* — *of everything*, sa un po' di tutto; *to eat* — *or nothing*, mangiare poco o nulla ‖ *after a* —, for *a* —, dopo un po', per un po' (di tempo) ‖ *in* —, in piccolo (formato) ‖ *every* — *helps*, tutto fa brodo ‖ *I see very* — *of him*, lo vedo pochissimo, non lo vedo mai ‖ *to come to* —, non riuscire gran che ‖ *to think* — *of s.o.*, non tenere in gran cónto qlcu., aver poca stima di qlcu. ‖ *to think* — *of sthg.*, non dar peso a, minimizzare ql.co.

little, *av.* **1.** poco: — *known*, poco conosciuto; *I see them very* —, li vedo raramente; *it is* — *better*, ciò non vale granchè di più; *she reached home in* — *more than an hour*, andò a casa in poco più di un'ora ‖ — *by* —, a poco a poco ‖ *as* — *as possible*, il meno possibile **2.** affatto: *he* — *thinks that*, non pensa affatto che, è lontano dal pensare che **3.** (con art. indef.) piuttosto, alquanto: *she was a* — *afraid*, era piuttosto spaventata; *these shoes are a* — *too large*, queste scarpe sono un po' troppo grandi.

littleness ['litlnis], *s.* **1.** piccola quantità **2.** piccolezza, meschinità.

littoral ['litərəl], *ag.s.* litorale.

liturgic [li'təːdʒik], *ag.* (*eccl.*) liturgico.

liturgical [li'təːdʒikəl], *ag.* (*eccl.*) liturgico.

liturgically [li'təːdʒikəli], *av.* (*eccl.*) liturgicamente.

liturgics [li'təːdʒiks], *s.* (*eccl.*) studio e interpretazione delle liturgie.

liturgist ['litə(ː)dʒist], *s.* (*eccl.*) liturgista.

liturgy ['litə(ː)dʒi], *s.* (*eccl.st. greca*) liturgia.

live [laiv], *ag.* **1.** vivo, vivente: *sale of* — *eels*, si vendono anguille vive **2.** ardente: — *coals*, carboni ardenti **3.** non usato; carico (di proiettile) **4.** ricco di energia, attività, interesse: *a — question*, una questione di attualità **5.** (*elett.*) sotto tensione ☆ *— -axle*, (*mec.*) assale mobile, asse motore; *— -bait*, esca viva; *— -born*, nato vivo; *— -cartridge*, cartuccia carica; *— rock*, roccia viva; *— -shell*, proiettile inesploso; *— -stock*, bestiame; *— -wire*, (*elett.*) filo di tensione; *fig.* persona attiva, energica.

to live [liv], *v.t.i.* **1.** vivere, esistere: *as long as he lives*, finchè vive, vita natural durante; *I wish I could — that lovely day again!*, vorrei poter rivivere quella giornata indimenticabile!; *they lived an honest life*; vissero onestamente ‖ *they lived through the war*, sopravvissero alla guerra ‖ *to — and let —*, vivere e lasciar vivere ‖ *to — close*, vivere stentatamente ‖ *to — a double life*, vivere una doppia vita ‖ *to — a retired life*, vivere appartato, in solitudine ‖ *to — up to one's principles*, vivere secondo i propri principi **2.** vivere, abitare, dimorare, stare: *he lived in Milan*, abitava a Milano .**3.** vivere, sostentarsi: *to — on sthg.*, vivere di ql.co.: *he lives on his income*, vive di rendita; *she seems to — on air*, sembra che viva d'aria ‖ *to — by one's wits*, vivere d'espedienti ‖ *to — from hand to mouth*, vivere alla giornata **4.** *to — down*, (far) dimenticare: *to — down one's past*, far dimenticare col tempo il proprio passato **5.** *to — in*, risiedere, essere interno (di medici, alunni, ecc.): *all pupils — in*, tutti gli scolari sono interni; *their maid lived in*, avevano una domestica fissa **6.** *to — on*, continuare a vivere, perdurare: *his fame will — on*, la sua fama non morirà **7.** *to — out*, essere esterno (di medici, di alunni, ecc.); sopravvivere a: *maid-servant living out*, donna a mezzo servizio; *she lived out her serious illness*, sopravvisse alla sua grave malattia.

livelihood ['laivlihud], *s.* mezzi di sussistenza: *she earns her — by teaching*, essa si guadagna la vita con l'insegnamento; *to deprive s.o. of his —*, togliere il pane di bocca a qlcu.

liveliness ['laivlinis], *s.* vivacità, animazione; brio.

livelong ['livloŋ], *ag.* (*poet.*) lungo; intero: *I work the — day*, lavoro tutto il santo giorno.

livelong, *s.* (*bot.*) faragello.

lively ['laivli], *ag.* **1.** vivo, vivace; animato, movimentato; allegro: *a — child*, un bimbo pieno di vita **2.** vivo, intenso (di colore) **3.** realistico: *a — novel*, un romanzo realistico ‖ *to make things — for s.o.*, (*fam.*) rendere la vita dura a qlcu.

to liven ['laivn], *v.t.i.* ravvivare, animare, animarsi: *to — up the conversation*, animare la conversazione.

liveness ['laivnis], *s.* vivacità, animazione.

liver[1] ['livə*], *s.* (*anat.*) fegato ☆ *— -colour*, color rosso bruno; *— -complaint*, malattia di fegato; *— -stone*, (*patol.*) calcoli al fegato.

liver[2], *s.* persona che conduce un particolare genere di vita ☆ *fast —*, gaudente; *loose —*, libertino.

liveried ['livərid], *ag.* che porta una livrea.

liverish ['livəriʃ], *ag.* **1.** (*fam.*) malato di fegato, bilioso **2.** *fig.* irritabile, iracondo.

Liverpudlian [,livə'pʌdliən], *ag.s.c.* (abitante) di Liverpool.

livery[1] ['livəri], *ag.* **1.** (*fam.*) malato di fegato; bilioso **2.** *fig.* irritabile, iracondo.

livery[2], *s.* **1.** livrea; costume (di corporazioni londinesi) ‖ *in —*, in livrea; *out of —*, in abiti borghesi **2.** (*poet. letter.*) abito; apparenza: *birds in their winter —*, uccelli nel loro abito invernale **3.** stallaggio **4.** (*dir.*) passaggio di proprietà: *to sue one's —*, chiedere di entrare in possesso dei propri beni (di minorenni) ☆ *— -company*, corporazione (londinese); *— -horse*, cavallo da noleggio; *— -servant*, valletto; *— -stable*, stallaggio, stallatico.

liveryman, *pl.* **liverymen** ['livərimən], *s.* **1.** membro di una corporazione (londinese) **2.** noleggiatore di cavalli.

livid ['livid], *ag.* **1.** livido, bluastro **2.** (*fam.*) furioso, incollerito.

lividity [li'viditi], *s.* lividezza.

lividly ['lividli], *av.* di colore livido, lividamente.

living ['liviŋ], *ag.* **1.** vivo, vivente, esistente: *— or dead*, vivo o morto; *no — man could write better*, nessuno al mondo potrebbe scrivere meglio; *not a — soul could be seen*, non si poteva vedere anima viva ‖ *the —*, i viventi ‖ *within — memory*, a memoria d'uomo **2.** vivo, profondo, forte: *a — faith*, una fede profonda **3.** esatto, perfetto (di rassomiglianza) **4.** perenne (di corsi d'acqua) ‖ *s.* **1.** mezzo di mantenimento, di sostentamento: *to earn* (o *to make*) *a — as a cook*, guadagnarsi da vivere come cuoco **2.** modo di vivere; linea di condotta: *the art of —*, l'arte di vivere; *plain —*, vita semplice, modesta **3.** (*eccl.*) beneficio ☆ *— -room*, (stanza di) soggiorno; *— space*, spazio vitale; *— wage*, (*econ.*) salario sufficiente per vivere.

Livy ['livi], *no.pr.m.* (*st. lett.*) (Tito) Livio.

to lixiviate [lik'sivieit], *v.t.* (*chim. ind.*) lisciviare.

lixiviation [lik,sivi'eiʃən], *s.* lisciviazione.

lixivium [lik'siviəm], *s.* lisciva.

Liza ['laizə], *no.pr.f. dim.* di **Elizabeth.**

lizard ['lizəd], *s.* lucertola.

Lizzie ['lizi], *no.pr.f. dim.* di **Elizabeth.**

'll [l], *fam. contr.* di **shall, will.**

llama ['lɑ:mə], *s.* **1.** (*zool.*) lama **2.** tessuto di pelo di lama.

Lloyd's [loidz], *s.* (*mar.*) « Lloyd » (compagnia di assicuratori a Londra) ☆ *— list*, giornale del movimento marittimo; *— register*, registro delle navi con le loro caratteristiche.

lo [lou], *inter.* (*arc.*) ecco!, guarda!.

loach [loutʃ], *s.* pesciolino d'acqua dolce.

load [loud], *s.* **1.** carico, peso (anche *fig.*): *a heavy —*, un carico pesante; *to get a — off one's chest*, (*fam.*) sfogarsi; *to take a — off s.o.'s mind*, togliere a qlcu. un gran peso dal cuore; *to take in a —*, fare il carico ‖ *loads of...*, (*fam.*) un sacco di..., una gran quantità di... **2.** (*mec.*) carico, pressione **3.** (*elett.*) carica, tensione ☆ *— factor*, (*elett.*) fattore di carico; *— line*, (*mar.*) linea a pieno carico; *— voltage*, (*elett.*) tensione di carico ‖ *cart —*, carrettata.

to load, *v.t.i.* **1.** caricare, caricarsi; colmare (anche *fig.*): *air loaded with carbon*, aria carica di carbonio; *a table loaded with food*, una tavola colma di cibarie; *he loaded her with gifts*, la colmò di regali; *his stomach was loaded with food*, (*volg.*) aveva lo stomaco imbarazzato; *they 'll — me with reproaches*, mi soffocheranno di rimproveri; *to — a cart with hay*, caricare un carro di fieno; *to — a gun*, caricare un fucile; *to — a ship with goods*, caricare una nave di merci, fare il carico; *to — s.o. with parcels*, caricare qlcu. di pacchi **2.** appesantire, zavorrare (con piombo): *to — the dice*, falsare i dadi **3.** alterare, adulterare (vino) **4.** (*Borsa*) comprare azioni in gran quantità ⌊**5.** (*assicurazioni*) aumentare il premio.

loaded ['loudid], *ag.* **1.** carico; caricato: *a — cart*, un carretto carico; *a — revolver*, una rivoltella carica **2.** impiombato: *a — cane*, un bastone impiombato **3.** (*sl. amer.*) ubriaco **4.** (*sl. amer.*) pieno di soldi.

loader ['loudə*], *s.* **1.** caricatore **2.** servo che carica i fucili (a caccia).

loading ['loudiŋ], *s.* carico, caricamento ☆ *— -coil*, (*elett.*) bobina di induzione; *— station*, stazione di caricamento.

loadstar ['loudstɑ:*], *s.* **1.** (*astr.*) stella polare **2.** *fig.* principio fondamentale.

loadstone ['loudstoun], *s.* (*min.*) magnetite.

loaf[1] [louf], *pl.* **loaves** [louvz], *s.* **1.** pane in cassetta, pan « carrè »; pagnotta: *a — (of bread), please*, un pan « carrè », per favore ‖ *half a —* *is better than no bread*, *prov.* meglio poco che nulla **2.** (*bot.*) grumolo, cuore (di lattuga, ecc.) **3.** (*sl.*) testa, capoccia: *use your —!*, fa' funzionare un po' la tua capoccia! ☆ *— -sugar*, zucchero in zollette ‖ *meat —*, polpettone; *sugar- —*, pan di zucchero.

loaf², s. (solo sing.) (fam.) l'oziare, il far niente.

to **loaf²**, v.i. (fam.) oziare: to — through life, passare la vita oziando.

loafer ['loufə*], s. 1. (fam.) poltrone, fannullone 2. scarpa da riposo.

loam [loum], s. 1. terra grassa, suolo fertile 2. argilla per mattoni, da plasmare.

to **loam**, v.t. ricoprire di terriccio.

loamy ['loumi], ag. 1. argilloso 2. grasso, fertile.

loan [loun], s. 1. prestito, mutuo: the contractors of a —, i sottoscrittori di un prestito; forced (o compulsory) —, prestito forzoso; on —, a prestito; patriotic —, prestito patriottico; public —, prestito pubblico; secured —, prestito garantito; unsecured —, prestito allo scoperto; to ask for the — of sthg., chiedere ql.co. in prestito; to contract a —, contrarre un prestito; to issue (o to raise) a —, emettere un prestito; to put out on —, dare a prestito, prestare 2. il dare a prestito ☆ — -collection, esposizione d'oggetti d'arte ricevuti in prestito; — -office, cassa prestiti, ufficio prestiti; — -shark, usuraio; — -society, istituto di prestito; — word, barbarismo || loyalty —, prestito patriottico; mortgage- —, mutuo ipotecario; war —, prestito di guerra.

to **loan**, v.t. (amer.) prestare, dare a prestito.

loanable ['lounəbl], ag. che può essere prestato.

loanee [lou'ni:], s.c. chi riceve un prestito.

loaner ['lounə*], s.c. prestatore, prestatrice.

loath [louθ], ag. riluttante, restio, mal disposto: she was — to go, era riluttante ad andarsene || nothing —, molto volentieri.

to **loathe** [louð], v.t. detestare, odiare, aborrire: I simply — that man, ho una vera avversione per quell'individuo; to — doing sthg., avere ripugnanza a fare ql.co.

loathful ['louðful], ag. (rar.) nauseante, disgustoso.

loathing ['louðiŋ], s. disgusto; ripugnanza.

loathingly ['louðiŋli], av. con disgusto, con ripugnanza.

loathly ['louðli], ag. (arc. lett.) nauseante, disgustoso.

loathsome ['louðsəm], ag. 1. odioso, detestabile 2. nauseante, disgustoso.

loathsomely ['louðsəmli], av. in modo nauseante, disgustoso.

loathsomeness ['louðsəmnis], s. l'essere nauseante, disgustoso.

lob¹ [lob], ag. sgarbato; rozzo, goffo || s. 1. (dial.) individuo rozzo, contadino 2. (dial. miner.) pepita (d'oro) 3. mistura, miscuglio denso (nella fabbricazione della birra) ☆ —'s pound, prigione; fig. difficoltà.

lob², s. (miner.) filone a gradini.

lob³, s. 1. palla lanciata in alto 2. (tennis) pallonetto.

to **lob³**, pass.p.p. **lobbed** [lobd], v.t.i. 1. passeggiare, muoversi, correre pesantemente 2. lanciare la palla in alto 3. (tennis) fare pallonetti.

lobar ['loubə*], ag. lobare.

lobate ['loubeit], ag. (bot.) lobato.

lobby ['lobi], s. 1. anticamera; corridoio 2. (teat.) ridotto 3. corridoio del Parlamento 4. (amer.) sostenitore di uomini politici.

to **lobby**, v.t.i. (pol.) frequentare i corridoi del Parlamento per cercare d'influenzarne i membri: to — a bill through, far passare un progetto di legge per mezzo di intrighi.

lobbyist ['lobiist], s. (pol. amer.) intrigante.

lobe [loub], s. lobo.

lobed [loubd], ag. lobato.

lobeless ['loublis], ag. privo di lobi.

lobelia [lou'bi:ljə] s. (bot. farm.) lobelia.

loblolly ['lobloli], s. (arc.) pozione ☆ — boy, (mar.) assistente del medico di bordo.

lobscouse ['lobskaus], s. (mar.) pietanza di carne con galletta e verdura.

lobster ['lobstə*], s. 1. aragosta 2. (spreg.) soldato inglese ☆ — -pot, nassa da aragoste.

lobular ['lobjulə*], ag. lobulare.

lobule ['lobju:l], s. lobulo.

lobworm ['lobwə:m], s. (zool.) arenicola.

local ['loukəl], ag. 1. locale, del luogo: the — post office, l'ufficio postale del luogo || Local, Città (negli indirizzi) 2. locale, parziale, ristretto: a — anaesthetic, anestesia locale; a — disease, una malattia localizzata || s. 1. abitante, professionista, predicatore del luogo 2. treno, autobus locale 3. — (news) novità locali 4. — (public-house), (fam.) taverna, osteria 5. — (examinations), esami organizzati da una università e sostenuti in sedi diverse ☆ — colour, colore locale; — time, ora locale.

localism ['loukəlizəm], s. 1. idiotismo, termine locale; usanza locale 2. campanilismo; provincialismo.

locality [lou'kæliti], s. 1. località; luogo; posizione: people from these localities, gente del luogo 2. aspetto, caratteristiche di un luogo || to have a good bump for —, (fam.) avere un forte senso d'orientamento.

localization [,loukəlai'zeifən], s. localizzazione.

to **localize** ['loukəlaiz], v.t. 1. localizzare, circoscrivere 2. rivestire delle caratteristiche di un luogo.

locally ['loukəli], av. localmente.

to **locate** [lou'keit], v.t. 1. individuare: to — the enemy's headquarters, individuare il quartier generale nemico 2. situare, collocare: our offices are located on the second floor, i nostri uffici sono situati al secondo piano 3. indicare, mostrare la posizione di.

location [lou'keifən], s. 1. posizione, sito: a suitable — for a new school, una posizione adatta per una nuova scuola 2. (comm.) locazione, contratto d'affitto 3. (cine.) «set» all'aperto.

locative ['lokətiv], ag.s. (gram.) (caso) locativo.

loch [lok], s. 1. (scoz.) lago 2. braccio di mare lungo e stretto.

Lochness ['loknis], no.pr. (geog.) Lochness.

lock¹ [lok], s. 1. ciocca, ricciolo: — of hair, ciocca di capelli 2. fastello: — of hay, fastello di fieno 3. fiocco: — of wool, fiocco di lana.

lock², s. 1. serratura, toppa || —, stock and barrel, completamente || under — and key, sotto chiave, chiuso 2. diga; chiusa; cateratta 3. otturatore di fucile 4. (mec.) chiavetta, copiglia; freno, bloccaggio (di ruota) 5. (ing.) camera di equilibrio 6. ingorgo di vetture ☆ — -chain, catena per bloccare una ruota; — -gate, diga; — -hospital, ospedale dermosifilopatico; — -jaw, (patol.) tetano, trisma; — -keeper, guardiano delle chiuse || double —, serratura a doppia mandata; Yale —, serratura Yale.

to **lock²**, v.t.i. 1. serrare; sprangare; chiudere a chiave; essere fornito di serrature: does this trunk —?, si chiude a chiave questo baule?; his hands were tightly locked, le sue mani erano strettamente serrate || to — the stable door after the horse has been stolen, prov. chiudere la stalla quando i buoi sono scappati 2. imprigionare 3. (mec.) incantarsi, incepparsi: the wheels locked, le ruote si incepparono 4. fornire (canali, ecc.) di chiuse 5. custodire nella mente; tenere in serbo 6. to — away, rinchiudere, riporre sotto chiave: to have a memory locked away in one's mind, custodire un ricordo nella mente 7. to — in, rinchiudere, mettere sotto chiave 8. to — out, chiudere fuori, chiudere la porta in faccia (a qlcu.); fare una serrata: they locked him out, lo chiusero fuori di casa 9. to — up, mettere al sicuro; chiudere sotto chiave; rinchiudere in prigione, manicomio, ecc.; chiudere casa.

lockage ['lokidʒ], s. 1. passaggio di una chiusa 2. diritti di passaggio di una chiusa.

locker ['lokə*], s. 1. armadio, armadietto a chiave || to go to Davy Jones's —, (sl. mar.) andare a fondo, annegare 2. (mar.) bauletto, cassone 3. persona, cosa che chiude.

locket ['lokit], s. medaglione (da portare al collo).

Lockian ['lokjən], ag. di Locke; relativo alla filosofia di Locke.

lockless ['lɔklis], *ag.* **1.** senza serrature **2.** senza chiuse (di canale, ecc.).

lockman, *pl.* **lockmen** ['lɔkmən], *s.* guardiano di chiuse.

lockout ['lɔkaut], *s.* serrata.

locksman, *pl.* **locksmen** ['lɔksmən], *s.* guardiano di chiuse.

locksmith ['lɔk-smiθ], *s.* fabbro; magnano.

locomobile [,loukə'moubil], *ag.* che può spostarsi ‖ *s.* locomobile.

to **locomote** ['loukəmout], *v.i.* (*biol.*) muoversi da un luogo ad un altro.

locomotion [,loukə'mouʃən], *s.* locomozione.

locomotive ['loukə,moutiv], *ag.* locomotivo; locomotore ‖ *s.* (*ferr.*) locomotiva ☆ — *engine*, (*ferr.*) locomotiva; — *organs*, (*anat.*) organi locomotori.

locomotor [,loukə'moutə*], *ag.* locomotore ☆ — *ataxy*, (*patol.*) atassia locomotrice.

loculus ['lɔkjuləs], *pl.* **loculi** ['lɔkjulai], *s.* **1.** (*zool. bot. anat.*) alveolo **2.** loculo (di catacombe).

locum-tenency ['loukəm'ti:nənsi], *s.* supplenza, interinato.

locum-tenens ['loukəm'ti:nenz], *s.* interino, supplente; vicario: *he acted as — for the local doctor*, sostituì il medico condotto.

locus ['loukəs], *pl.* **loci** ['lousai], *s.* **1.** località, posizione **2.** (*mat.*) luogo ☆ — *classicus*, passo celebre di un libro; — *communis*, luogo comune.

locust ['loukəst], *s.* **1.** (*entom.*) locusta, cavalletta **2.** *fig.* persona vorace ☆ — *-bean*, (*bot.*) carruba; — *-tree*, (*bot.*) carrubo; robinia ‖ *migratory* —, cavalletta migratoria.

locution [lou'kju:ʃən], *s.* locuzione.

locutory ['lɔkjutəri], *s.* **1.** parlatorio **2.** grata (di parlatorio).

lode [loud], *s.* (*min.*) vena; filone.

lodestar, *V.* **loadstar.**

lodestone ['loudstoun], *s.* (*min.*) magnetite.

lodge [lɔdʒ], *s.* **1.** (*arc.*) casetta **2.** portineria **3.** padiglione di caccia **4.** tana (del castoro, della lontra) **5.** (*amer.*) tenda; *fig.* nucleo familiare di pellirosse **6.** loggia massonica.

to **lodge,** *v.t.i.* **1.** alloggiare, dare asilo, ospitare; essere alloggiato, ospitato: *where are you lodging now?*, dove alloggiate ora?; *who lodges them?*, chi li ospita? **2.** entrare, far entrare; piantare, piantarsi: *the bullet lodged in his brain*, la pallottola gli si piantò nel cervello **3.** collocare; mettere al sicuro; depositare: *to — one's money in a bank*, depositare il proprio denaro in una banca **4.** *fig.* porre, depositare, affidare: *destiny lodges in the hands of God*, il destino è nelle mani di Dio **5.** (*dir.*) presentare, sporgere querela.

lodgement ['lɔdʒmənt], *s.* **1.** (*mil.*) posizione stabile: *to effect* (o *to make*) *a —*, conquistare una posizione stabile **2.** (*comm.*) versamento, deposito **3.** deposito, intoppo (in un tubo, ecc.) **4.** (*rar.*) alloggio.

lodger ['lɔdʒə*], *s.* inquilino, pigionante.

lodging ['lɔdʒiŋ], *s.* **1.** alloggio, dimora: *a night's —*, alloggio per una notte **2.** *gener. pl.* camere in affitto, appartamento ammobiliato ‖ *board and —*, vitto e alloggio ☆ — *-house*, pensione; — *-house keeper*, affittacamere ‖ *furnished lodgings*, camere ammobiliate.

lodgment, *V.* **lodgement.**

loess ['louis], *s.* (*geol.*) loess.

loft [lɔft], *s.* **1.** attico; soffitta, solaio **2.** piccionaia **3.** cantoria (di chiesa); galleria ☆ *hay-* —, fienile.

to **loft,** *v.t.* **1.** (*golf*) colpire (la palla) in modo da farle fare un'ampia curva in altezza **2.** tenere (piccioni) in piccionaia.

lofter ['lɔftə*], *s.* bastone da golf.

loftily ['lɔftili], *av.* **1.** in posizione elevata; *fig.* nobilmente **2.** altezzosamente.

loftiness ['lɔftinis], *s.* **1.** altezza, elevatezza; *fig.* nobiltà, grandezza; dignità **2.** superbia.

lofty ['lɔfti], *ag.* **1.** alto, elevato; *fig.* nobile: — *ideals*, alti ideali; — *mountain*, montagna elevata; — *sentiments*, nobili sentimenti **2.** orgoglioso, altero.

log [lɔg], *s.* **1.** ceppo, ciocco ‖ *King Log*, il Re Travicello ‖ *roll my — and I'll roll yours*, una mano lava l'altra ‖ *to fall like a —*, cadere pesantemente **2.** (*mar.*) solcometro: *to sail by the —*, calcolare la posizione della nave con il solcometro ☆ — *-book*, giornale di bordo; — *-cabin*, capanna di legno; — *-canoe*, canoa scavata in un tronco d'albero; — *-house*, (*amer.*) prigione; — *-juice*, (*sl.*) vino manipolato; — *-rolling*, trasporto dei ceppi facendoli rotolare; *fig.* mutuo soccorso (specialmente in politica).

to **log,** *pass.p.p.* **logged** [lɔgd], *v.t.i.* **1.** abbattere alberi; fare legname; disboscare (una regione) **2.** (*mar.*) registrare sul giornale di bordo.

log, *abbr.* di **logarithm.**

logaoedic [,logə'i:dik], *ag.s.* (*poes.*) (verso) logaedico.

logarithm ['lɔgəriθm], *s.* (*mat.*) logaritmo.

logarithmic(al) [,lɔgə'riθmik(əl)], *ag.* logaritmico.

logger ['lɔgə*], *s.* taglialegna.

loggerhead ['lɔgəhed], *s.* **1.** (*arc.*) stupido; testone **2.** mestolo per pece, ecc. **3.** tartaruga marina **4.** *at loggerheads*, in disaccordo, in controversia: *to be at loggerheads with s.o.*, essere in lite con qlcu.

loggia ['lɔdʒə], *pl.* **loggias** ['lɔdʒəz], **loggie** ['lɔdʒei], *s.* (*arch.*) loggia.

logging ['lɔgiŋ], *s.* **1.** taglio del legname **2.** registrazione sul giornale di bordo.

logic ['lɔdʒik], *s.* logica; concatenamento.

logical ['lɔdʒikəl], *ag.* logico.

logicality [,lɔdʒi'kæliti], *s.* logicità.

logically ['lɔdʒikəli], *av.* logicamente.

logician [lou'dʒiʃən], *s.c.* chi sa di logica; ragionatore, ragionatrice.

logie ['lougi], *s.* (*teat.*) orpello, ornamento di latta.

logistic(al) [lou'dʒistik(əl)], *ag.* logistico.

logistics [lou'dʒistiks], *s.pl.* (*mil.*) logistica.

logogram ['lɔgougræm], *s.* logogramma.

logographer [lə'gɔgrəfə*], *s.* (*lett. greca*) logografo.

logographic(al) [,lɔgou'græfik(əl)], *ag.* logografico.

logography [lə'gɔgrəfi], *ag.* logografia.

logogriph ['lɔgəgrif], *s.* logogrifo.

logomachy [lə'gɔməki], *s.* logomachia.

Logos ['lɔgɔs], *s.* (*teol.*) Logos, il Verbo.

logotype ['lɔgoutaip], *s.* (*tip.*) logotipo.

logwood ['lɔgwud], *s.* (*bot.*) campeggio.

loin [lɔin], *s.* **1.** (*cuc.*) lonza, lombo, lombata **2.** *pl.* (*anat.*) (le) reni; (*poet.*) fianchi, lombi: *sprung from the loins of*, discendente da ‖ *to gird up one's loins*, cingersi i lombi, apprestarsi (a sforzo, viaggio) ☆ — *-cloth*, fascia che cinge i fianchi.

loir ['lɔiə*], *s.* (*zool.*) ghiro.

to **loiter** ['lɔitə*], *v.t.i.* indugiare; bighellonare, gironzolare; trascorrere (il tempo) in ozio: *he loitered on his way home from school*, andò bighellonando nel tornare a casa da scuola ‖ *to — the hours away*, passare le ore oziando.

loiterer ['lɔitərə*], *s.c.* bighellone, bighellona; pigrone, pigrona; perdigiorno.

loitering ['lɔitəriŋ], *s.* l'indugiare; l'andare a zonzo.

loiteringly ['lɔitəriŋli], *av.* con indugio; lentamente; indolentemente.

to **loll** [lɔl], *v.t.i.* **1.** pendere; (far) penzolare, ciondolare: *the dog lolled his tongue out*, il cane lasciò penzolare la lingua **2.** stendersi, adagiarsi pigramente: *to — about*, starsene in panciolle, oziare.

Lollard ['lɔləd], *s.* (*st.*) lollardo (seguace di Wycliffe).

lollipop ['lɔlipɔp], *s.* lecca-lecca.

to **lollop** ['lɔləp], *v.i.* **1.** bighellonare **2.** camminare, avanzare goffamente.

lolly ['lɔli], *s.* **1.** lecca-lecca **2.** (*sl.*) denaro.

Lombard ['lɔmbəd], *ag.s.c.* **1.** lombardo, lombarda: — *-Street*, Lombard-Street (strada di Londra originariamente abitata da banchieri lombardi, in cui ora risiedono le principali banche della città) *fig.* il mercato finanziario della City ‖ *it's — Street to a China orange*, (*fam.*) niente da fare!, troppa disparità di forze **2.** (*st.*) longobardo, longobarda.

Lombardic [lɔm'bɑːdik], *ag.* **1.** lombardo **2.** (*st.*) longobardo **3.** (*arch.*) lombardesco.

Lombardy ['lɔmbədi], *no.pr.* (*geog.*) Lombardia.

London ['lʌndən], *no.pr.* (*geog.*) Londra ☆ — *pride*, (*bot.*) sassifraga ombrosa; (*fam.*) garofano.

Londoner ['lʌndənə*], *s.c.* londinese.

Londonese [ˌlʌndə'niːz], *ag.* londinese ‖ *s.* dialetto londinese.

to **londonize** ['lʌndənaiz], *v.t.* rendere londinese.

lone [loun], *ag.* **1.** (*letter.*) solitario, solo, isolato: *a — pine*, un pino solitario ‖ *the Lone Star State*, (*amer.*) il Texas ‖ *to play a — hand*, (*carte*) giocare una mano da solo; *fig.* fare ql.co. da solo **2.** (*scherz.*) nubile; vedova.

loneliness ['lounlinis], *s.* **1.** solitudine, isolamento **2.** malinconia.

lonely ['lounli], *ag.* **1.** solo; isolato; solitario: *a — traveller*, un viaggiatore solitario; *a — village*, un villaggio isolato **2.** malinconico, depresso.

lonesome ['lounsəm], *ag.* **1.** solitario; abbandonato; fuor di mano **2.** malinconico.

lonesomely ['lounsəmli], *av.* **1.** in modo solitario **2.** malinconicamente.

lonesomeness ['lounsəmnis], *s.* **1.** solitudine; isolamento **2.** malinconia, depressione.

long [lɔŋ], *ag.* **1.** lungo: *— in the leg, in the arm*, di gamba lunga, di braccia lunghe; *a — journey*, un lungo viaggio; *a — time ago*, molto tempo fa; *the garden is twenty feet —*, il giardino è lungo sei metri e mezzo; *it is a — time since I saw her*, è molto tempo che non la vedo; *it takes a — time*, ci vuole molto tempo; *the nights are getting longer*, le notti si allungano; *that's a — step forward*, *fig.* è un gran passo avanti; *they are a — time coming*, tardano molto; *to make a — arm for sthg.*, allungare il braccio per prendere ql.co.; *to make sthg. longer*, allungare ql.co.; *to take the longest way round*, fare la strada più lunga ‖ *— drink*, bibita allungata ‖ *— memory*, memoria tenace ‖ *at the longest*, al massimo ‖ *by a — way* (o *fam. by a — chalk*), di gran lunga ‖ *face as — as a fiddle*, faccia da funerale ‖ *friend of — standing*, amico di vecchia data ‖ *gun at — range*, cannone a lunga portata ‖ *in the — run*, a lungo andare ‖ *three — miles*, tre buone miglia ‖ *it is as broad as it is —*, (*fam.*) è lo stesso ‖ *it will be a — day before...*, ce ne vorrà prima che... ‖ *to be — in the tooth*, (*fam.*) non esser più tanto giovane ‖ *to have a — head*, esser perspicace, scaltro ‖ *to have — sight*, avere la vista lunga, essere presbite ‖ *to have a — tongue*, *fig.* avere la lingua lunga ‖ *to have a — wind*, avere molto fiato in corpo ‖ *to make a — nose at s.o.*, fare marameo a qlcu. ‖ *to pull a — face*, fare il viso lungo, imbronciato ‖ *to take a — chance*, rischiare molto ‖ *to take — views*, *fig.* guardare lontano **2.** (*fonet.*) lungo (di vocale) **3.** numeroso: *a — family*, una famiglia numerosa **4.** ingente; elevato: *a — price*, un prezzo elevato ‖ *s.* **1.** molto tempo: *he hasn't — to live*, non ha molto tempo da vivere; *he will be away for —*, starà via molto tempo; *I had only — enough to do the work*, avevo appena il tempo per fare il lavoro; *it will not take —*, non ci vorrà molto tempo ‖ *before* (o *ere*) *—*, fra breve ‖ *he knows the — and the short of it*, ne conosce tutti i particolari **2.** (*fonet.*) vocale lunga: *longs and shorts*, vocali lunghe e brevi.

to **long**, *v.i.* desiderare fortemente, morire dalla voglia; non vedere l'ora, essere impaziente: *I am longing to go to London*, ho gran desiderio di andare a Londra ‖ *to — for sthg.*, desiderare ardentemente, aver molta voglia di ql.co.: *she longs for home*, ha molta nostalgia di casa sua.

long, *av.* lungamente, per lungo tempo, a lungo: *— after, before*, molto tempo dopo, prima; (*not*) —

ago, (*non*) molto tempo fa; *all* (*the*) *day —*, per tutto il giorno; *how —?*, quanto tempo?: *how — does it take to go to...?*, quanto tempo ci vuole per andare a...?; *not —*, non molto tempo; (*not*) *so —*, (*non*) tanto tempo, (*not*) *too —*, (*non*) troppo tempo; *not very —*, pochissimo tempo; *as* (*so*) *— as*, fino a, purchè; *does this play last —?*, dura molto questa commedia?; *he does not work any longer with us*, non lavora più con noi; *he was not — coming*, non tardò a venire; *I am sorry you cannot stay longer*, mi spiace che tu non possa fermarti più a lungo; *is it — since you saw her?*, è molto tempo che non la vedi? ‖ *— live the King!*, viva il Re! ‖ *so —!*, (*fam.*) arrivederci! ‖ *she was not to be — for this world*, non aveva molto da vivere.

long, (*nei composti*): *— -bow*, arco: *to draw the — -bow*, raccontar frottole; *— -distance*, a lunga distanza; *— -distance call*, (*amer.*) telefonata interurbana; *— -dozen*, tredici; *— -headed*, dolicocefalo; *fig.* sagace, acuto; *— home*, *fig.* l'ultima dimora; *— jump*, (*spor.*) salto in lungo; *— -legged*, dalle gambe lunghe; *— measure*, misura di lunghezza; *— odds*, (*sl. ippica*) quota alta: *to lay — odds on*, puntare forte su; *— -playing* (*record*), (*neol. mus.*) microsolco; *— primer*, (*tip.*) (carattere) corpo 10; *— pull*, un abbondante bicchiere di birra; *— purse*, portafoglio ben fornito; *— range*, a lunga portata (cannone, missile); *— -sighted*, prevesggente; *— -term*, (*neol.*) a lunga scadenza; *— vacation*, vacanze estive (dei tribunali, università inglesi); *— waves*, (*rad.*) onde lunghe; *— -winded*, prolisso.

longanimity [ˌlɔŋgə'nimiti], *s.* longanimità.

longanimous [lɔŋ'gæniməs], *ag.* longanime.

longboat ['lɔŋbout], *s.* (*mar.*) lancia, scialuppa.

longeron ['lɔndʒərən], *s.* (*aer.*) longherone.

longeval [lɔn'dʒiːvəl], *ag.* longevo.

longevity [lɔn'dʒeviti], *s.* longevità.

longhand ['lɔŋhænd], *s.* la scrittura ordinaria (contrapposta alla stenografia e alla dattilografia).

longicorn ['lɔndʒikɔːn], *ag.s.* (coleottero) longicorne.

longimetric [ˌlɔndʒi'metrik], *ag.* (*geom.*) longimetrico.

longimetry [lɔn'dʒimitri], *s.* (*geom.*) longimetria.

longing ['lɔŋiŋ], *ag.* bramoso, smanioso: *a — look*, uno sguardo di desiderio ‖ *s.* brama, vivo desiderio; *a great — for peace*, un gran desiderio di pace.

longingly ['lɔŋiŋli], *av.* con vivo desiderio: *to look — at sthg.*, covare ql.co. con gli occhi.

longish ['lɔŋiʃ], *ag.* lunghetto, alquanto lungo.

longitude ['lɔndʒitjuːd], *s.* longitudine.

longitudinal [ˌlɔndʒi'tjuːdinl], *ag.* longitudinale.

longitudinally [ˌlɔndʒi'tjuːdinəli], *av.* longitudinalmente.

Longobard ['lɔŋgəbɑːd], *s.* (*st.*) longobardo.

longshore ['lɔŋʃɔː*], *ag.* che si trova, è attiguo a riva.

longshoreman, *pl.* **longshoremen** ['lɔŋʃɔːmən], *s.* scaricatore di porto.

longsome ['lɔŋsəm], *ag.* noioso, prolungato sino alla noia.

longways ['lɔŋweiz], **longwise** ['lɔŋwaiz], *av.* per il lungo.

looby ['luːbi], *s.* sciocco, gonzo.

(to) **loof** [luːf], *V.* (to) **luff.**

loofah ['luːfɑː], *s.* (*bot.*) luffa ☆ — *hand*, guanto di spugna vegetale (usato per toeletta).

look [luk], *s.* **1.** sguardo, occhiata, colpo d'occhio: *he gave her a pleased —*, la guardò con compiacenza; *I had a good — at it*, l'ho esaminato attentamente; *let me have a — at you*, lascia che ti guardi; *to cast* (o *to direct*) *a — at s.o.*, lanciare un'occhiata a qualcuno **2.** espressione; aspetto: *a — of pleasure*, un'espressione di piacere; *I don't like his looks* (o *the — of him*), il suo aspetto non mi piace; *this town has an American —*, questa sembra una città americana; *an ugly — came into his eyes*, nei suoi occhi balenò un'espressione di cattiveria; *to judge by looks*, giudicare dalle apparenze **3.** *pl.* bella cera, bellezza: *she had looks but no money*, era bella ma non aveva danaro.

to **look**, *v.t.i.* **1.** guardare: — *(and see) what time it is*, *(fam.)* guarda che ora è; — *where you are going*, guarda dove vai; — *who is here!*, guarda chi c'è!; *to — the other way*, guardare altrove; *to — s.o. in the face*, guardare qlcu. in viso ‖ — *before you leap*, *prov.* prima di agire pensaci ‖ *to — one's last on sthg.*, dare un'ultima occhiata a ql.co. **2.** sembrare, aver l'aria di, apparire; dimostrare: *business looks promising*, la situazione finanziaria promette bene; *he looked fine in uniform*, la divisa gli donava; *he looks as if (o as though) he wanted to...*, ha l'aria di volere...; *she looks about thirty*, dimostra una trentina d'anni; *to — happy*, aver l'aria felice; *to — ill, well*, avere una brutta, bella cera; *to — one's age*, dimostrare la propria età ‖ — *sharp (o alive)!*, sbrigati! ‖ *you're looking off colour*, hai l'aria di non star troppo bene ‖ *to — black*, apparire adirato, accigliato; *to — blue*, essere triste, di cattivo umore ‖ *to — like*, assomigliare a; minacciare di; promettere; aver l'aria di: *does he — like jesting?*, ha l'aria di scherzare?; *he looks like his father*, assomiglia al padre; *it looks like rain*, sembra che voglia piovere; *she looks like winning*, è probabile che vinca; *what does he — like?*, che tipo è? ‖ *to — one's best*, essere in gran forma, apparire in piena bellezza ‖ *to — small*, aver l'aria mogia: *to make s.o. — small*, mortificare qlcu. **3.** esprimere con lo sguardo: *to — compassion*, esprimere compassione con lo sguardo ‖ *she looked daggers at her rival*, lanciò sguardi pieni d'odio alla rivale **4.** guardare, essere esposto, situato: *which way does the house —?*, come è esposta la casa? **Seguito da prep. 5.** *to — about*, guardarsi in giro, cercare di orientarsi **6.** *to — after*, badare a, sorvegliare; occuparsi di; seguire con lo sguardo; cercare: *to — after one's interests*, badare ai propri interessi **7.** *to — at*, guardare, osservare; considerare: — *at the success of that actor!*, considera il successo di quell'attore!; *she doesn't like being looked at*, non le piace essere guardata; *we looked at him working*, l'osservammo mentre lavorava ‖ *she won't — at it*, ella non ne vuol sapere **8.** *to — down: to — down one's nose at*, *(fam.)* guardare con disprezzo **9.** *to — for*, cercare, aspettarsi: *I never looked for such a result as this*, non mi sarei mai aspettato un simile risultato; *who(m) are you looking for?*, chi cerchi? **10.** *to — into*, esaminare a fondo: *the matter will be looked into*, la questione sarà esaminata a fondo **11.** *to — on*, considerare: *I — on him as my son*, lo considero mio figlio ‖ *to — on(to)*, essere prospiciente a, dare su **12.** *to — over*, dare una scorsa a; esaminare; lasciar correre **13.** *to — through*, guardare attraverso; trasparire; scorrere, sfogliare **14.** *to — to*, aver cura di; occuparsi di; badare a; contare su; mirare a: *I looked to you for help*, contavo sul tuo aiuto **15.** *to — towards*, essere esposto a, guardare verso a; *(fam.)* bere alla salute **16.** *to — upon*, considerare, stimare: *she is looked upon as a great pianist*, è considerata una grande pianista. **Seguito da av. 17.** *to — about*, stare in guardia; cercare: *I was looking about for a job*, ero in cerca di un lavoro **18.** *to — ahead*, *fig.* guardare al futuro ‖ — *ahead!*, attenzione! guarda dove vai! (detto a un rematore) **19.** *to — back*, *fig.* ricordare; *(fam.)* cessare di progredire: *I — back to my youth*, ricordo la mia giovinezza; *since that day he never looked back*, da quel giorno ha continuato a progredire **20.** *to — down*, soggiogare con un'occhiata; *(comm.)* essere in, tendere al ribasso ‖ *to — down (up)on s.o.*, guardare con disprezzo qlcu. **21.** *to — forward to*, non veder l'ora di: *I am looking forward to going away*, non vedo l'ora di andarmene **22.** *to — in*, fare una visitina: *we looked in at his house*, abbiamo fatto una breve visita a casa sua **23.** *to — on*, essere, fare da spettatore: *help me instead of looking on*, aiutami invece di stare a guardare ‖ *to — on with s.o.*, leggere insieme a qlcu. (da uno stesso libro, ecc.) **24.** *to — out*, guardare fuori; stare in guardia, in attesa; scegliere: — *out!*, sta' attento! **25.** *to — over*, esami-

nare, verificare **26.** *to — round*, esaminare, considerare: *don't make a hurried decision*, — *round well first*, non prendere decisioni affrettate, prima considera bene il pro e il contro **27.** *to — through*, esaminare attentamente, scrutare: *we looked him through and through*, lo scrutammo attentamente **28.** *to — up*; alzare gli occhi; *(comm.)* tendere al rialzo, migliorare; consultare (orario, dizionario, ecc.); fare una breve visita: — *me up when you have time*, passa da me quando hai tempo; *business is looking up*, la situazione finanziaria migliora ‖ *to — s.o. up and down*, squadrare qlcu. ‖ *to — up to*, rispettare, venerare: *the teacher was looked up to by all his pupils*, l'insegnante era rispettato da tutti gli scolari.

look, (nei composti): — *-in*, visitina; *(spor.)* probabilità di successo; — *-over*, esame, rassegna; — *-see*, *(fam.)* sguardo, esame; — *-up*, *(fam.)* breve visita.

looker ['luːk*], **looker-on** ['lukər'on], *s.c.* spettatore, spettatrice; astante.

looking ['lukin], *ag.s.* (solo nei composti): — *back*, retrospezione; — *-down*, disprezzo: — *-down on s.o.*, disprezzo per qlcu.; — *-for*, ricerca; — *-glass*, specchio; — *-over*, esame ‖ *good-* —, di bell'aspetto; *queer-* —, dall'aria bizzarra, dall'aspetto singolare.

lookout ['luk'aut], *s.* **1.** vigilanza, guardia: *to keep a* — *(for)*, stare in guardia (per) **2.** *(mil.)* osservatorio **3.** vista panoramica **4.** *fig.* prospettiva, probabilità: *it's a bad* — *for him*, *(fam.)* è una brutta prospettiva per lui.

loom[1] [luːm], *s.* **1.** telaio per tessitura **2.** tessitura ☆ *hand* —, telaio a mano; *power* —, telaio meccanico; *treadle* —, telaio a pedali.

to **loom**[1], *v.t.* *(rar.)* mettere a telaio; tessere.

loom[2], *s.* *(ornit.)* uria.

loom[3], *s.* fusto (del remo).

loom[4], *s.* *(mar.)* vaga apparizione della terra all'orizzonte.

to **loom**[4], *v.i.* **1.** apparire in lontananza; mostrarsi indistintamente **2.** *fig.* mostrarsi alla mente.

loon[1] [luːn], *s.* *(scoz.)* fannullone.

loon[2], *s.* *(ornit.)* tuffolo.

loony ['luːni], *ag.* *(sl.)* pazzo, mentecatto.

loop[1] [luːp], *s.* **1.** cappio; nodo scorsoio **2.** occhiello metallico; gancio **3.** alamaro **4.** punto a maglia, all'uncinetto **5.** *(ferr. tel.)* linea di raccordo **6.** *(aer.)* gran volta, cerchio della morte: *to loop the* —, fare il cerchio della morte.

to **loop**[1], *v.t.i.* **1.** fare un cappio **2.** annodare; affibbiare.

loop[2], *s.* *(metal.)* lingotto incandescente.

looper ['luːpə*], *s.* **1.** dispositivo per asole (in macchine da cucire) **2.** *(entom.)* geometrino.

loophole ['luːphoul], *s.* **1.** *(mil.)* feritoia **2.** *fig.* scappatoia.

to **loophole**, *v.t.* aprire feritoie, munire di feritoie.

loopy ['luːpi], *ag.* ingannevole, falso.

loose [luːs], *ag.* **1.** sciolto, libero, staccato, slegato: — *hair*, capelli sciolti; *to be* —, essere sciolto, libero; *to come* —, disfarsi, sciogliersi; *to get* —, slacciarsi; *to let* —, staccare, liberare, dar libero corso a ‖ *a* — *tongue*, una lingua sciolta ‖ *with a* — *rein*, con redini lente; *fig.* con indulgenza ‖ *to break* —, evadere ‖ *to pack up* —, imballare merce sciolta **2.** ampio, largo (di abiti) **3.** vago, non ben definito: *a* — *statement*, una dichiarazione approssimativa; *a* — *translation*, una traduzione libera **4.** *fig.* licenzioso, dissoluto ‖ *to be on the* —, divertirsi smodatamente **5.** non accurato, poco esatto: *a* — *ball*, *(cricket)* una palla mal lanciata **6.** allentato, dondolante: *a* — *tooth*, un dente che dondola ‖ *to have a screw* —, *(fam.)* mancare di una rotella ☆ — *bowels*, *(patol.)* dissenteria; — *-box*, « box » (per i cavalli); — *-cover*, fodera staccabile (di poltrona, ecc.); — *cough*, tosse catarrosa.

loose, *s.* libertà, libera espressione: *to give* — *to one's feelings*, dar libera espressione ai propri sentimenti.

to **loose**, *v.t.i.* **1.** sciogliere, sciogliersi; slacciare, slacciarsi; slegare, snodare **2.** *fig.* liberare, lasciar andare **3.** scoccare, lanciare (frecce, ecc.) || *to — off*, (*sl. mil.*) sparare una raffica di mitragliatrice **4.** (*mar.*) mollare gli ormeggi.

loosely ['lu:sli], *av.* **1.** mollemente; scioltamente **2.** vagamente **3.** dissolutamente **4.** inesattamente.

to **loosen** ['lu:sn], *v.t.i.* **1.** sciogliere, sciogliersi; slegare, slegarsi; allentare, allentarsi: *to — discipline*, allentare la disciplina; *to — one's grip*, allentare la presa; *to — a screw*, allentare una vite; *to — s.o.'s tongue*, far sciogliere la lingua a qlcu. **2.** *fig.* rilassare, rilassarsi.

loosener ['lu:snə*], *s.* (*farm.*) lassativo.

looseness ['lu:snis], *s.* **1.** scioltezza **2.** ampiezza (di abiti, ecc.) **3.** *fig.* rilassamento **4.** libertinaggio **5.** imprecisione (di stile, linguaggio, ecc.).

loot [lu:t], *s.* bottino.

to **loot**, *v.t.i.* saccheggiare; darsi ai saccheggi.

lop[1] [lɔp], *s.* potatura; rami potati.

to **lop**[1], *pass.p.p.* **lopped** [lɔpt], *v.t.* potare; tagliare; mozzare (membra, testa): *to — off branches*, potare dei rami.

lop[2], *s.* (*mar.*) maretta.

to **lop**[2], *v.i.* rompersi in piccole onde.

lop[3], *s.* coniglio dalle orecchie pendenti.

to **lop**[3], *v.i.* pendere, penzolare, ciondolare.

lope [loup], *s.* lungo salto, balzo.

to **lope**, *v.i.* muoversi a lunghi balzi.

Lophobranchii [ˌlɔfə'bræŋkiai], *s.pl.* (*ittiol.*) lofobranchi.

lopper ['lɔpə*], *s.* potatore.

lopping ['lɔpiŋ], *s.* potatura.

loppy[1] ['lɔpi], *ag.* (*mar.*) a piccole onde.

loppy[2], *ag.* pendente.

lopsided ['lɔp'saidid], *ag.* pendente; sbilenco; asimmetrico, più piccolo da una parte; male equilibrato.

loquacious [lou'kweiʃəs], *ag.* loquace; garrulo.

loquaciously [lou'kweiʃəsli], *av.* loquacemente.

loquaciousness [lou'kweiʃəsnis], **loquacity** [lou'kwæsiti], *s.* loquacità.

loquat ['loukwæt], *s.* (*bot.*) **1.** nespola **2.** nespolo del Giappone.

lord [lɔ:d], *s.* **1.** signore, capo, sovrano; (*scherz.*) marito: *the — of the manor*, il signore del castello || *our sovereign — the King*, il nostro signore sovrano, il re **2.** *Lord*, (*eccl.*) Iddio: *our Lord*, nostro Signore: *the year of our Lord 1960*, A. D. 1960 || (*oh*) *Lord!*, Signore, mio Dio! || *the Lord's Day*, la domenica; *the Lord's Prayer*, il Paternostro; *the Lord's Supper*, l'Eucarestia **3.** *Lord*, Pari: *Lord in waiting*, gentiluomo di corte || *the House of Lords* (o *fam.* the *Lords*), la Camera Alta, dei Lords **4.** *Lord*, Lord (titolo di alti funzionari): *Lord Chamberlain*, Gran Ciambellano; *Lord Chancellor*, Gran Cancelliere; *Lord Provost*, (*scoz.*) Sindaco; *Lord Mayor* (*of London, etc.*), il Sindaco (di Londra, ecc.); *the Lords of the Admiralty*, gli alti funzionari dell'Ammiragliato **5.** *Lord*, Lord (titolo nobiliare di conte, marchese, ecc.) || *My Lord*, signore || *as drunk as a —*, ubriaco fradicio; *to act the —*, assumere un contegno altezzoso; *to drink like a —*, bere come un otre; *to live like a —*, condurre una vita dispendiosa.

to **lord**, *v.t.i.* **1.** dominare || *to — it*, (*fam.*) atteggiarsi a gran signore; *to — it over s.o.*, tiranneggiare qlcu.; volersi imporre a qlcu. **2.** (*rar.*) elevare alla dignità di Lord.

lordliness ['lɔ:dlinis], *s.* **1.** dignità; alterigia **2.** sfarzo, magnificenza.

lordling ['lɔ:dliŋ], *s.* (*spreg.*) signorotto, tirannello.

lordly ['lɔ:dli], *ag.* **1.** signorile, di, da gran signore **2.** altero, disdegnoso.

lordly, *av.* in modo degno di un lord; dignitosamente.

lordship ['lɔ:dʃip], *s.* **1.** signoria; autorità; dignità di signore **2.** proprietà terriera, possedimento **3.** *Lordship*, Signoria, Eccellenza (titolo onorifico preceduto da *ag.*

poss.): *did Your Lordship ring?*, la Signoria Vostra ha suonato?; *His Lordship is not in at present*, Sua Eccellenza non è in casa in questo momento.

lore [lɔ:*], *s.* **1.** insieme di fatti e credenze tradizionali di, intorno a una comunità, un popolo: *Irish —*, le tradizioni degli irlandesi **2.** (*poet. arc.*) scienza, sapere; erudizione.

lorgnette [lɔ:'njet], *s.* **1.** occhialino **2.** binocolo da teatro.

lorica [lə'raikə], *s.* lorica.

loricate ['lɔrikeit], *ag.* (*zool.*) loricato.

lorikeet [ˌlɔri'ki:t], *s.* (*ornit.*) lorichetto.

loriner ['lɔrinə*], *s.* chi fabbrica speroni.

loriot ['lɔriət], *s.* (*ornit.*) rigogolo.

loris ['lɔ:ris], *s.* (*zool.*) lori, lori gracile.

lorn [lɔ:n], *ag.* (*love-*) *—*, (*poet. scherz.*) derelitto, abbandonato: *a — widow*, una vedova desolata.

lorry ['lɔri], *s.* (*motor*) *—*, autocarro, camion ☆ *—-driver*, camionista; *— hopping*, (*sl.*) autostop (praticato fermando camion).

lory ['lɔ:ri], *s.* (*ornit.*) lorichetto.

losable ['lu:zəbl], *ag.* perdibile.

to **lose** [lu:z], *pass.p.p.* **lost** [lɔst], *v.t.i.* **1.** perdere, far perdere, subire una perdita (anche *fig.*): *he lost the key*, perse la chiave; *that mistake lost him his job*, quello sbaglio gli fece perdere il posto; *they lost a thousand pounds over that deal*, persero mille sterline in quell'affare; *to — ground*, perdere terreno; *to — heavily*, perdere una forte somma; *to — a patient*, non riuscire a salvare un malato; *to — weight*, diminuire di peso || *to — heart*, scoraggiarsi || *to — in public esteem*, scadere nella pubblica stima || *to — one's character*, perdere la propria reputazione || *to — one's temper*, andare in collera **2.** smarrire, smarrirsi; perdersi: *he was lost in the crowd*, si perse nella folla; *to — oneself* (o *to — one's way* o *to get lost*), smarrirsi || *to — one's place*, perdere il segno (in un libro, ecc.) || *to — sight of*, perdere di vista || *to be lost at sea*, perire in un naufragio **3.** sprecare, sciupare: *he lost his labour*, la sua fu fatica sprecata; *I can't afford to — any time*, non posso perdere tempo; *my hint was lost upon him*, il mio consiglio fu sprecato con lui **4.** ritardare (di orologio): *my watch loses two minutes a day*, il mio orologio ritarda due minuti al giorno **5.** essere sconfitto.

losel ['louzl], *s.* (*arc.*) fannullone, buono a nulla.

loser ['lu:zə*], *s.c.* chi perde, perdente: *to be a —*, perdere, essere in perdita; *to be a good —*, saper perdere.

losing ['lu:ziŋ], *ag.* perdente: *a — game*, un giuoco, un'impresa senza probabilità di riuscita || *s.* perdita.

loss [lɔs], *s.* **1.** perdita: *— of appetite*, inappetenza || *profits and losses*, (*comm.*) profitti e perdite || *to be at a —*, essere imbarazzato, non saper che fare **2.** svantaggio, scapito, danno, rovina.

lost [lɔst], *pass.p.p.* di to **lose** || *ag.* **1.** perduto, smarrito; rovinato; dannato: *a — cause*, una causa persa; *to give s.o. up for* (o *as*) *—*, perdere la speranza di trovare, di salvare qlcu. || *to look —* (o *to seem —*), aver un'aria spaesata **2.** *— to*, insensibile a: *he is — to all sense of decency*, non ha il minimo senso di pudore ☆ *— property office*, ufficio oggetti smarriti; *— souls*, le anime dannate.

lot [lɔt], *s.* **1.** sorte, destino, fortuna; caso: *by —*, a sorte, a caso; *a happy —*, *fig.* una buona stella; *it's my — to do it*, tocca a me farlo || *a bad —*, un individuo fuorviato, sviato || *to cast* (o *to draw*) *lots*, trarre, estrarre a sorte || *to fall to s.o.'s —*, toccare in sorte a qlcu. **2.** lotto (di terreno, ecc.) **3.** parte, quota (di imposta) **4.** (*comm.*) partita, lotto **5.** (*fam.*) quantità (di persone, cose, ecc.): *lots of friends*, moltissimi amici; *it'll do you a — of good*, ti farà molto bene || *I saw quite a — of him in London*, l'ho visto assai spesso a Londra || *what a — of time you waste!*, quanto tempo sprechi!.

to **lot**, *pass.p.p.* **lotted** ['lɔtid], *v.t.* dividere in lotti.

loth, *V.* **loath**.

Lothario [lou'θɑ:riou], *no.pr.m.* (*lett.*) Lotario ‖ *s. fig.* vitaiuolo; libertino: *to be a gay —*, fare la bella vita.

lotion ['louʃən], *s.* lozione.

lottery ['lɔtəri], *s.* **1.** lotteria **2.** *fig.* caso, probabilità: *marriage is a —*, il matrimonio è un salto nel buio ☆ — *prize*, premio della lotteria; — *ticket*, biglietto della lotteria; — *-wheel*, ruota della fortuna.

lotto ['lɔtou], *s.* tombola.

lotus ['loutəs], *s.* (*bot.*) loto ☆ — *-eaters*, (*mit.*) lotofagi.

loud [laud], *ag.* **1.** forte, alto; sonoro; fragoroso: *in a — voice*, ad alta voce **2.** sgargiante, vistoso (di colori, vestiti): *a — colour*, un colore violento **3.** rumoroso, volgare (di persona): — *manners*, modi volgari ☆ — *-speaker*, altoparlante.

loud, *av.* ad alta voce; rumorosamente: *don't talk so —*, non parlare così ad alta voce ‖ *to laugh — and long*, ridere a crepapelle.

to louden ['laudn], *v.t.i.* **1.** alzare, accrescere (voce, ecc.) **2.** diventare volgare (di persona).

loudly ['laudli], *V.* **loud**.

loudness ['laudnis], *s.* **1.** frastuono, strepito **2.** vistosità; volgarità.

lough [lɔk], *s.* (*irl.*) **1.** lago **2.** braccio di mare.

Louis ['lu(:)is], *no.pr.m.* Luigi.

Louisa [lu(:)'i:zə], **Louise** [lu(:)'i:z], *no.pr.f.* Luisa, Luigia.

lounder ['lu:ndə*], *s.* (*scoz.*) percossa.

to lounder, *v.t.* (*scoz.*) percuotere.

lounge [laundʒ], *s.* **1.** il bighellonare; l'andare a zonzo **2.** lo stare in panciolle **3.** ridotto (di teatro); sala d'albergo; (*fam.*) salotto **4.** agrippina ☆ — *-lizard*, (*sl.*) gigolo; — *-suit*, abito maschile da passeggio.

to lounge, *v.i.* **1.** bighellonare, gironzolare: *to — about*, andare a zonzo **2.** poltrire, stare in panciolle: *to — in a bed*, poltrire a letto.

lounger ['laundʒə*], *s.c.* fannullone, fannullona.

lounging ['laundʒiŋ], *ag.* ozioso.

loungingly ['laundʒinli], *av.* oziosamente.

lour ['lauə*], *s.* **1.** cipiglio **2.** oscuramento (di cielo); minaccia di tempesta.

to lour, *v.i.* **1.** aggrottare le ciglia ‖ *to — at* (o *on* o *upon*) *s.o.*, guardare qlcu. minacciosamente **2.** apparire minaccioso, oscurarsi (di cielo, ecc.).

louring ['lauəriŋ], *ag.* accigliato; minaccioso.

louringly ['lauərinli], *av.* minacciosamente: — *the clouds gathered*, le nubi si ammucchiavano minacciose.

loury ['lauəri], *ag.* accigliato; minaccioso; cupo.

louse [laus], *pl.* **lice** [lais], *s.* pidocchio.

to louse, *v.t.* spidocchiare.

lousy ['lauzi], *ag.* **1.** pidocchioso **2.** *fig.* abietto; vile ‖ *what — weather!*, (*sl.*) che tempo schifoso! ‖ *you are a — fellow*, (*sl.*) sei un pezzente.

lout [laut], *s.* zoticone.

loutish ['lautiʃ], *ag.* grossolano, rustico.

loutishly ['lautiʃli], *av.* grossolanamente; rusticamente.

loutishness ['lautiʃnis], *s.* grossolanità; rustichezza.

louver, louvre ['lu:və*], *s.* **1.** (*arch. medioevale*) abbaino, lucernario **2.** (*aut.*) feritoia per ventilazione; sfinestratura.

lovable ['lʌvəbl], *ag.* amabile; simpatico.

lovableness ['lʌvəblnis], *s.* amabilità.

lovably ['lʌvəbli], *av.* amabilmente; simpaticamente.

love [lʌv], *s.* **1.** devozione; affetto; tenerezza: *the — of God*, l'amore di Dio; *for the — of s.o.* (o *sthg.*), per amor di qlcu. (o di ql.co.), per qlcu. (o ql.co.); *out of —*, per amore; *the — you bear me*, l'affetto che mi porti ‖ *not to be had for — nor money*, impossibile a ottenersi ‖ *there is no — lost between them*, si detestano ‖ *to give* (o *to send*) *one's — to s.o.*, mandare saluti affettuosi a qlcu. **2.** interesse, passione: — *of learning*, amore del sapere; *a labour of —*, un lavoro piacevole; *he has a great — for football*, ha una gran passione per il calcio **3.** amore; passione: *in — with*, inna-

morato di; *to fall in — with s.o.*, innamorarsi, invaghirsi di qlcu.; *to make — to*, amoreggiare con, far la corte a ‖ — *in a cottage*, un cuore e una capanna ‖ *all is fair in — and war*, tutto è lecito in amore e in guerra **4.** persona amata: *my —*, amore mio; *here I am, —!*, eccomi, amor mio!; *mind the step, —!*, (*fam.*) attenta allo scalino, cara!, guarda dove metti i piedi!; *what a — she is!*, che amore!, che carina!, che cara! ‖ *he is an old —*, è una cara persona **5.** *Love*, (*mit.*) Amore, Cupido **6.** (*spor.*) zero: — *all*, zero a zero ☆ — *-affair*, relazione amorosa; intrigo amoroso; — *-apple*, (*arc.*) pomodoro; — *-child*, figlio naturale; — *-feast*, (*relig.*) agape; — *-game*, (*spor.*) cappotto; — *-in-a-mist*, (*bot.*) fiore del finocchio; — *-in-idleness*, (*bot.*) viola del pensiero; — *-knot*, nodo d'amore; — *-letter*, lettera d'amore; — *-making*, il corteggiare, l'amoreggiare; — *-match*, matrimonio d'amore; — *-philtre* (o *-potion*), filtro d'amore; — *-shaft*, freccia, dardo di Cupido; — *-song*, romanza, canzone d'amore; — *-story*, romanzo, storia d'amore.

to love, *v.t.* **1.** amare; essere innamorato di; adorare: *she loves her father*, ella ama suo padre; *your cousin loves you very much*, tuo cugino ti vuol molto bene; *to — each other, one another*, amarsi (l'un l'altro); *to — God*, amare, adorare Dio ‖ *it is better to have loved and lost, than never to have loved at all*, *prov.* meglio un amor perduto che non aver amato; — *me, — my dog*, *prov.* prendi l'amico tuo col difetto suo **2.** (II, IV) (*fam.*) provare piacere in; dilettarsi di: *Ann loves comforts*, Anna ama le comodità; *he simply loves to find mistakes*, egli è proprio felice di trovare degli errori; *I — music*, mi piace la musica; *I'd — him to come with us*, mi piacerebbe che venisse con noi; *she loves reading*, le piace leggere.

lovebird ['lʌvbə:d], *s.* pappagallino verde africano.

loveless ['lʌvlis], *ag.* senza amore; che non ama; non amato.

lovelessy ['lʌvlisli], *av.* senza amore.

lovelessness ['lʌvlisnis], *s.* mancanza di amore.

lovelily ['lʌvlili], *av.* leggiadramente, graziosamente.

loveliness ['lʌvlinis], *s.* avvenenza, leggiadria, beltà (di donna); bellezza (di paesaggio).

lovelock ['lʌvlɔk], *s.* tirabaci.

lovelorn ['lʌvlɔ:n], *ag.* abbandonato; che si strugge d'amore.

lovelornness ['lʌvlɔ:nnis], *s.* desolazione, sconforto.

lovely ['lʌvli], *ag.* **1.** bello, grazioso; attraente: *what a — necklace!*, che bella collana!; *what a — woman!*, che donna deliziosa! **2.** (*fam.*) divertente: *we had a — time*, ci siamo divertiti un mondo; *it is a — game*, è un giuoco divertente.

lover ['lʌvə*], *s.* **1.** amante; innamorato; pretendente; fidanzato: *a lovers' lane*, un sentiero da innamorati; *they were lovers*, si amavano **2.** amatore; amico: — *of learning*, amante dello studio; — *of music*, appassionato di musica.

loverless ['lʌvəlis], *ag.* senza amante; senza innamorato.

loverlike ['lʌvəlaik], **loverly** ['lʌvəli], *ag.* di, da amante ‖ *av.* come un amante.

lovesick ['lʌvsik], *ag.* malato, consumato d'amore.

loving ['lʌviŋ], *ag.* **1.** affezionato; amoroso: — *parents*, genitori amorosi **2.** d'amore, d'amicizia: — *act*, un atto d'amore, d'amicizia ☆ — *-cup*, grande coppa da cui, nei conviti, tutti bevevano in segno di amicizia; — *-kindness*, bontà; affetto ‖ *home- —*, amante della casa.

lovingly ['lʌviŋli], *av.* affettuosamente, amorosamente, teneramente.

lovingness ['lʌviŋnis], *s.* affettuosità, tenerezza.

low[1] [lou], *ag.* **1.** basso, piccolo: *she has a — forehead*, ha la fronte bassa; *their prices are extremely —*, hanno dei prezzi ottimi ‖ *Low-Church*, Chiesa Bassa (corrente della Chiesa Anglicana) ‖ *the Lower Chamber* (o *House*), la Camera dei Comuni ‖ *Low Sunday*, Do-

menica in Albis **2.** basso, poco profondo: *the tide is —
at 6 o'clock,* la marea è bassa alle 6 ‖ *in — water, fig.* al
verde **3.** basso, debole: — *note,* nota bassa; *in a —
voice,* sottovoce **4.** umile; non importante; poco civilizzato: *he comes of a — family,* discende da famiglia
umile; *he has a — position,* occupa una posizione
modesta; *that was a — tribe,* era un tribù poco civi-
lizzata **5.** volgare, triviale; poco onorevole: — *comedy,*
commedia grossolana, d'effetto; *to have — manners,*
aver modi volgari; *to use — language,* usare linguaggio volgare ‖ *a — dog,* (*sl.*) un poco di buono **6.** debole;
abbattuto: *a — pulse,* un polso debole; *to be in —
spirits,* essere giù di morale **7.** sfavorevole: *I expressed
a — opinion of his work,* ho dato un parere sfavorevole sul suo lavoro **8.** scarso: — *diet,* nutrimento
scarso, dieta ☆ - - -*bred,* volgare; maleducato; — -*brow,*
(individuo) poco evoluto; — -*browed,* dalla fronte
bassa; — -*down,* (*sl.*) basso, disonorevole (*sl. amer.*)
fatti, notizie confidenziali; — -*gear,* (*aut.*) prima velocità (di cambio); — *mass,* messa bassa; — -*necked,*
scollato (di abito); — -*pressure,* bassa pressione; —
-*spirited,* depresso; — -*tide* (o — -*water*), bassa marea.

low¹, *av.* **1.** in basso, abbasso: *to bow —,* fare un
profondo inchino; *to fall —,* cadere in basso, decadere;
to lie —, giacere disteso; tenersi nascosto ‖ *to be laid
—,* essere abbattuto, ucciso; essere costretto a letto ‖
to run —, esaurirsi (di rifornimento, denari, ecc.):
our funds were running —, scarseggiavano di fondi **2.** a voce bassa, sommessamente: *to speak —,* parlare a voce bassa **3.** a basso prezzo: *they played very
—,* giocavano con poste modeste; *to buy —,* comprare
a buon mercato.

low², *s.* muggito, mugghio.

to low², *v.t.i.* muggire; esprimere muggendo.

to lower¹ ['louə*], *v.t.i.* **1.** abbassare: *to — a ceiling,*
abbassare un soffitto; *to — one's voice,* abbassare la
voce ‖ *to — a sandwich and a glass of beer,* (*fam.*)
mangiare un boccone e bere un sorso **2.** *fig.* abbattere, abbattersi; umiliare, umiliarsi **3.** ribassare, far
calare (i prezzi); diminuire, calare (di prezzi): *the stocks
lowered in price,* le azioni erano in ribasso **4.** indebolire; scemare: *her resistance is lowered by such a diet,*
la sua resistenza è indebolita da quella dieta **5.** (*mar.*)
ammainare.

(to) lower², *V.* (to) **lour.**

lowering ['louərin], *s.* abbassamento; ribasso; diminuzione (di prezzo, ecc.).

loweringly ['lauərinli], *av.* foscamente; con viso
arcigno; con aria minacciosa.

lowermost ['louəmoust], *ag.* (*superl. irr.* di *low*)
il più basso.

lowland ['loulənd], *s.* pianura; terreno pianeggiante.

lowlander ['louləndə*], *s. c.* **1.** abitante della pianura **2.** *Lowlander,* scozzese della Scozia meridionale.

Lowlands ['loulədz], *no.pr.pl.* (*geog.*) Scozia meridionale.

lowlihood ['loulihud], *s.* condizione umile.

lowlily ['loulili], *av.* umilmente.

lowliness ['loulinis], *s.* umiltà; *fig.* modestia.

lowly ['louli], *ag.* basso; *fig.* umile, modesto.

lowly, *av.* umilmente, modestamente.

lown [loun], *ag.* (*scoz.*) tranquillo, calmo, riparato.

lowness ['lounis], *s.* **1.** depressione, tristezza **2.** gravità (di suono); tono basso (di voce) **3.** debolezza (di
rumore) **4.** modicità (di prezzo).

lowringly, *V.* **loweringly.**

loxodromics [,loksou'dromiks], *s.* (*mar. mat.*) los-
sodromia.

loyal ['loiəl], *ag.* leale, fedele (al sovrano): — *party,*
partito di Corte.

loyalist ['loiəlist], *s.* suddito fedele.

loyally ['loiəli], *av.* lealmente, fedelmente.

loyalty ['loiəlti], *s.* lealtà, fedeltà (al sovrano, al governo).

lozenge ['lozindʒ], *s.* **1.** (*geom.*) rombo **2.** (*arald.*)
losanga **3.** pasticca, pastiglia.

lozenged ['lozindʒd], *ag.* a losanga.

lubber ['lʌbə*], *s.* **1.** villanzone, zotico **2.** marinaio
d'acqua dolce.

lubberlike ['lʌbəlaik], *ag.* goffo.

lubberliness ['lʌbəlinis], *s.* goffaggine, balordaggine.

lubberly ['lʌbəli], *ag.* goffo; grossolano, villano.

lubberly, *av.* goffamente, grossolanamente.

lubricant ['lu:brikənt], *ag.s.* lubrificante.

to lubricate ['lu:brikeit], *v.t.* lubrificare.

lubrication [,lu:bri'keiʃən], *s.* lubrificazione.

lubricator ['lu:brikeitə*], *s.* lubrificatore.

lubricious [lu:'briʃəs], *ag.* lubrico.

lubricity [lu:'brisiti], *s.* **1.** viscosità (di un lubrificante) **2.** *fig.* lubricità.

Lucan ['lu:kən], *no.pr.m.* (*st. lett.*) Lucano.

Lucania [lu:'keinjə], *no.pr.* (*geog.*) Lucania.

lucarne [lu:'ka:n], *s.* abbaino.

Lucas ['lu:kəs], *no.pr.m.* Luca.

luce [lju:s], *s.* (*ittiol.*) luccio.

lucency ['lu:snsi], *s.* lucentezza, luminosità.

lucent ['lu:snt], *ag.* lucente, splendente, luminoso.

lucern(e) [lu:'sə:n], *s.* erba medica.

Lucerne, *no.pr.* (*geog.*) Lucerna.

Lucian ['lu:sjən], *no.pr.m.* Luciano.

lucid ['lu:sid], *ag.* **1.** chiaro: — *style,* stile chiaro **2.** lucido (di mente): *a — interval,* intervallo di
lucidità **3.** (*poet.*) luminoso, brillante, trasparente.

lucidity [lu:'siditi], *s.* **1.** chiarezza **2.** lucidità di
mente **3.** (*poet.*) limpidezza, trasparenza.

lucidly ['lu:sidli], *av.* lucidamente.

Lucie ['lu:si], *no.pr.f.* Lucia.

Lucifer ['lu:sifə*], *no.pr.m.* **1.** Lucifero **2.** (*astr.*) Lucifero ‖ **lucifer,** (*rar.*) zolfanello.

lucifugous [lu:'sifjugəs], *ag.* lucifugo.

Lucilius [lu:'siliəs], *no.pr.m.* Lucilio.

Lucius ['lu:sjəs], *no.pr.m.* Lucio.

luck [lʌk], *s.* **1.** ventura, sorte, caso: *bad* (o *ill*) —,
sfortuna; *good —,* buona ventura; *to try one's —,* tentare la sorte ‖ *just my —!,* sono sfortunato, come al
solito! ‖ *worse —!,* sfortunatamente ‖ *he is down
on his —,* (*fam.*) è scalognato **2.** buona fortuna, buona
sorte: *a run of —,* una serie di successi; *I'm doing it
for —,* lo faccio perchè mi porti fortuna; *to have the
— to,* aver la fortuna di ‖ *good — to you!,* buona fortuna a te! ‖ *to be in —, out of —,* essere fortunato,
sfortunato.

luckily ['lʌkili], *av.* fortunatamente, per buona sorte.

luckiness ['lʌkinis], *s.* fortuna; buona sorte.

luckless ['lʌklis], *ag.* sfortunato.

lucklessly ['lʌklisli], *av.* sfortunatamente.

lucklessness ['lʌklisnis], *s.* sfortuna.

lucky ['lʌki], *ag.* fortunato; favorevole: *a — chance,*
un'occasione favorevole; *a — hit,* un successo inaspettato; *how —!,* che fortuna!; *to be —,* essere fortunato,
portare fortuna; *to be born —,* (*fam.*) esser nato con
la camicia ‖ — *bargee* (o — *beggar*)*!,* beato te!; *you're
a — dog!,* te fortunato! (congratulazioni a un pretendente accettato) ☆ — *pig* (o — *stone*), portafortuna.

lucrative ['lu:krətiv], *ag.* lucrativo; profittevole.

lucratively ['lu:krətivli], *av.* lucrosamente; con profitto.

lucre ['lu:kə*], *s.* (*spreg.*) lucro, guadagno.

Lucrece [lu:'kri:s], **Lucretia** [lu:'kri:fjə], *no.pr.f.* Lucrezia.

Lucretius [lu:'kri:fjəs], *no.pr.m.* (*st. lett.*) Lucrezio.

to lucubrate ['lu:kju(:)breit], *v.i.* scrivere delle elu-
cubrazioni.

lucubration [,lu:kju(:)'breifən], *s.* elucubrazione.

luculent ['lu:kjulənt], *ag.* chiaro, lampante.

luculently ['lu:kjuləntli], *av.* chiaramente.

Lucullus [lu:'kʌləs], *no.pr.m.* (*st.*) Lucullo.

lucumo ['lu:kju(:)mou], *s.* (*st. etrusca*) lucumone.

Lucy ['lu:si], *no.pr.f.* Lucia.

Lud [lʌd], *no.pr.m.* (*mit. nordica*) Lud.

ludicrous ['lu:dikrəs], *ag.* ridicolo, comico.

ludicrously ['lu:dikrəsli], *av.* comicamente.

ludicrousness ['lu:dikrəsnis], *s.* ridicolezza, comicità.

lues ['lu:i:z], *s.* (*patol.*) lue.

luetic ['lu'etik], *ag.* (*patol.*) luetico.

luff [lʌf], *s.* (*mar.*) **1.** orzata **2.** caduta prodiera.

to luff, *v.i.* **1.** (*mar.*) orzare **2.** (*mec.*) alzare, abbassare (il braccio di una gru).

lug[1] [lʌg], *s.* **1.** paraorecchi (di berretto) **2.** (*scoz. fam.*) lobo dell'orecchio; orecchio **3.** manico (di brocca) **4.** (*mec.*) aggetto; aletta **5.** (*elett.*) capocorda.

lug[2], *s.* (*zool.*) arenicola.

lug[3], *s.* strappata, tirata.

to lug[3], *pass.p.p.* **lugged** [lʌdg], *v.t.i.* **1.** tirare, trascinare: *to — at sthg.*, tirare violentemente ql.co. **2.** *fig.* introdurre a sproposito un argomento in un discorso.

lug[4], *V.* **lugsail.**

luggage ['lʌgidʒ], *s.* (*solo sing.*) bagaglio ☆ — *-ticket*, scontrino di bagaglio; — *-van*, bagagliaio.

lugger ['lʌgə*], *s.* (*mar.*) trabaccolo.

lugsail ['lʌgseil], *s.* (*mar.*) vela al quarto, al terzo.

lugubrious [lu:'gju:briəs], *ag.* lugubre, tetro, cupo.

lugubriousness [lu:'gju:briəsnis], *s.* carattere lugubre, triste.

Luke [lu:k], *no.pr.m.* Luca.

lukewarm ['lu:k-wɔ:m], *ag.* **1.** tiepido **2.** *fig.* indifferente; senza entusiasmo ‖ *s.* persona indifferente.

lukewarmness ['lu:k-wɔ:mnis], *s.* **1.** tiepidezza **2.** indifferenza; mancanza di entusiasmo.

lull [lʌl], *s.* bonaccia, calma; momento di calma: *the — after the tempest*, la quiete dopo la tempesta.

to lull, *v.t.i.* **1.** cullare: *to — a baby to sleep*, far addormentare un bimbo cullandolo **2.** calmare, calmarsi, acquietare, acquietarsi (anche *fig.*).

lullaby ['lʌləbai], *s.* **1.** ninna-nanna, cantilena **2.** (*poet.*) mormorio (di vento negli alberi, di acqua che scorre).

to lullaby, *v.t.* ninnare.

lumbago [lʌm'beigou], *s.* (*patol.*) lombaggine.

lumbar ['lʌmbə*], *ag.* (*anat.*) lombare.

lumber[1] ['lʌmbə*], *s.* **1.** cianfrusaglie; mobili di scarto; *fig.* guazzabuglio **2.** (*amer.*) legname; legno da costruzione ☆ — *-jack*, boscaiolo; — *-mill*, segheria; — *-room*, ripostiglio; — *-yard*, deposito di legname ‖ *asbestos —*, eternit, fibrocemento.

to lumber[1], *v.t.i.* **1.** ammassare, accatastare; ingombrare (con cianfrusaglie) **2.** (*amer.*) tagliare legname per la vendita.

to lumber[2], *v.i.* muoversi pesantemente e rumorosamente: *the cart lumbered along*, il carro avanzava pesantemente.

lumberer, *s.* **1.** (*amer.*) commerciante in legname **2.** rigattiere.

lumbering[1] ['lʌmbəriŋ], *s.* (*amer.*) commercio di legname.

lumbering[2], *ag.* che si muove pesantemente.

lumberman, *pl.* **lumbermen** ['lʌmbəmən], *s.* **1.** boscaiolo **2.** commerciante in legname.

luminary ['lu:minəri], *s.* **1.** astro, corpo luminoso **2.** *fig.* luminare, personalità di gran rilievo.

luminosity [,lu:mi'nositi], *s.* luminosità.

luminous ['lu:minəs], *ag.* **1.** luminoso, fulgente, smagliante: *a — smile*, un sorriso luminoso; *a — substance*, una sostanza luminosa **2.** chiaro, facile da capire: *a — explanation*, una spiegazione chiara; *a — remark*, un'osservazione intelligente.

luminously ['lu:minəsli], *av.* luminosamente.

luminousness ['lu:minəsnis], *s.* **1.** luminosità **2.** lucidità; chiarezza.

lummy ['lʌmi], *ag.* (*fam.*) eccellente, di prim'ordine.

lump[1] [lʌmp], *s.* **1.** massa informe; mucchio, cumulo; grumo; zolla, zolletta: *a — of sugar*, una zolletta di zucchero ‖ *a — in the throat*, *fig.* un nodo in gola **2.** protuberanza; gonfiore; bernoccolo **3.** (*comm.*) blocco: *in*

the —, in blocco; *to sell in the —*, vendere in blocco **4.** persona goffa, ottusa **5.** (*metal.*) massello ☆ — *sum*, somma globale.

to lump[1], *v.t.i.* **1.** raggrumarsi (di sostanze) **2.** mettere, considerare in blocco; ammassare; trattare senza distinzione: *he lumped persons together*, egli considerava tutti alla stessa tregua **3.** puntare (denaro) su una sola cosa.

lump[2], *s.* (*ittiol.*) lumpo.

to lump[3], *v.t.* (*fam.*) sopportare controvoglia: *if you don't like it, you will have to — it*, se non ti va, dovrai ingoiarla ugualmente.

lumper ['lʌmpə*], *s.* **1.** scaricatore di porto **2.** piccolo appaltatore.

lumpily ['lʌmpili], *av.* **1.** con grumi, protuberanze **2.** con increspature (di mare).

lumpiness ['lʌmpinis], *s.* **1.** tendenza a raggrumarsi **2.** l'essere raggrumato, coperto di protuberanze **3.** l'essere increspato (di mare).

lumpish ['lʌmpiʃ], *ag.* goffo, pesante; ottuso.

lumpishly ['lʌmpiʃli], *av.* goffamente, pesantemente.

lumpishness ['lʌmpiʃnis], *s.* goffaggine, pesantezza; ottusità.

lumpy ['lʌmpi], *ag.* **1.** grumoso, granuloso; pieno di protuberanze **2.** increspato (di mare) **3.** pesante; ottuso (di persona).

lunacy ['lu:nəsi], *s.* pazzia; demenza.

lunar ['lu:nə*], *ag.* lunare ☆ — *eclipse*, eclisse lunare.

lunarian [lu:'nɛəriən], *s.* **1.** selenita, abitante della Luna **2.** astronomo specialista dei fenomeni lunari.

lunate ['lu:neit], *ag.* lunato.

lunatic ['lu:nətik], *ag.* **1.** pazzo, alienato **2.** di pazzo; da pazzo ‖ *s.* pazzo, alienato ☆ — *asylum*, manicomio; — *fringe*, (*neol.*) membri più estremisti ed eccentrici di una comunità.

lunation [lu:'neiʃən], *s.* (*astr.*) lunazione.

lunch [lʌntʃ], **luncheon** ['lʌntʃən], *s.* seconda colazione; pasto del mezzogiorno; (*amer.*) spuntino ☆ *quick - —* (*o counter —*), « tavola calda ».

to lunch, *v.t.i.* **1.** fare la seconda colazione; (*amer.*) fare uno spuntino **2.** preparare la colazione per.

lune [lu:n], *s.* (*geom.*) lunula.

lunette [lu:'net], *s.* (*arch.*) lunetta.

lung [lʌŋ], *s.* **1.** (*anat.*) polmone ‖ *to have good lungs*, avere una voce forte **2.** *fig.* zona verde, parco: *the lungs of a city*, i parchi di una città ☆ — *disease*, malattia polmonare; — *-fish*, (*ittiol.*) dipnoo ‖ *iron —*, (*med.*) polmone d'acciaio.

lunge[1] [lʌndʒ], *s.* **1.** (*scherma*) stoccata: *to make a full —*, fare un affondo **2.** rapido movimento in avanti.

to lunge[1], *v.i.* **1.** (*scherma*) dare un stoccata **2.** fare un rapido movimento in avanti.

lunge[2], *s.* **1.** lunga corda legata al cavallo per allenarlo a girare in tondo **2.** pista circolare (per allenare i cavalli).

to lunge[2], *v.t.i.* far girare (un cavallo) in tondo; girare in tondo (di cavallo).

lungless ['lʌŋlis], *ag.* senza polmoni.

lungwort ['lʌŋwɔ:t], *s.* (*bot.*) polmonaria.

lunisolar [,lu:ni'soulə*], *ag.* lunisolare.

lupin(e) ['lu:pin], *s.* (*bot.*) lupino.

lupine ['lu:pain], *ag.* di lupo.

lupoid ['lu:pɔid], *ag.* (*patol.*) lupoide, della natura del lupus.

lupous ['lu:pəs], *ag.* (*patol.*) luposo, della natura del lupus.

lupus ['lu:pəs], *s.* (*patol.*) lupus.

lurch[1] [lə:tʃ], *s.* **1.** (*mar.*) violento e improvviso rollio **2.** barcollamento.

to lurch[1], *v.i.* **1.** (*mar.*) rollare all'improvviso e violentemente **2.** barcollare.

lurch[2], *s.* (*arc.*) situazione difficile, impiccio: *to leave s.o. in the —*, lasciare qualcuno nelle peste.

to **lurch**[2], *v.t.* (*arc.*) **1.** (*carte*) dare cappotto a **2.** lasciare in difficoltà.

lurch[3], (*arc.*) *s.* agguato, imboscata: *to lie at* (o *on* o *upon the*) —, stare in agguato.

to **lurch**[3], *v.i.* (*arc.*) stare in agguato.

lurcher ['lə:tʃə*], *s.* **1.** ladro; spia **2.** cane bastardo (incrocio tra levriero e pastore scozzese).

lure [ljuə*], *s.* **1.** esca; logoro (per falconi) **2.** *fig.* esca, allettamento, lusinga.

to **lure**, *v.t.* **1.** richiamare (il falcone) col logoro **2.** *fig.* adescare, allettare; attirare: *to* — *s.o. away from a duty*, distogliere qlcu. da un dovere (con lusinghe, ecc.); *to* — *s.o. into doing sthg.*, indurre qlcu. a fare ql.co.; *to be lured on to destruction*, lasciarsi trascinare alla rovina.

lurid ['ljuərid], *ag.* **1.** spettrale, fosco, sinistro; livido, scialbo, pallido (di colore): *a* — *sky*, un cielo fosco; *to cast a* — *light on sthg.*, *fig.* gettare una luce sinistra su ql.co. **2.** cupreo, rosseggiante; molto colorito (di linguaggio): — *flames*, fiamme rosseggianti.

luridly ['ljuəridli], *av.* in modo spettrale, fosco, sinistro.

luridness ['ljuəridnis], *s.* spettralità, lividezza; carattere, natura sinistra.

lurk [lə:k], *s.* nascondiglio ‖ *on the* —, spiando.

to **lurk**, *v.i.* **1.** nascondersi, rimanere nascosto; appiattarsi: *who is that man lurking in the shadow?*, chi è quell'uomo in agguato nell'ombra? **2.** *fig.* essere latente: *there was some doubt lurking in her mind*, ella nutriva un vago dubbio ☆ *lurking-place*, nascondiglio.

luscious ['lʌʃəs], *ag.* **1.** dolce, profumato, succulento: — *grapes*, uva dolcissima **2.** piacevole, delizioso: — *music*, musica deliziosa **3.** ridondante; immaginoso (di stile, linguaggio).

lusciously ['lʌʃəsli], *av.* **1.** dolcissimamente **2.** in modo piacevole **3.** in modo ridondante, immaginoso (di stile, linguaggio).

lusciousness ['lʌʃəsnis], *s.* **1.** saporosità, dolcezza estrema **2.** carattere, natura piacevole **3.** ridondanza, immaginosità (di stile, linguaggio).

lush[1] [lʌʃ], *ag.* **1.** lussureggiante (di vegetazione) **2.** succoso (di frutta).

lush[2], *s.* (*sl.*) bevanda alcoolica.

to **lush**[2], *v.t.i.* (*sl.*) **1.** offrire bevande alcooliche a **2.** far uso di alcoolici.

lushy ['lʌʃi], *ag.* (*sl.*) ubriaco.

lust [lʌst], *s.* **1.** lussuria, sensualità; concupiscenza **2.** brama, avidità: — *of power*, sete di potere.

to **lust**, *v.i.*: *to* — *after, for* (*s.o.*, *sthg.*), concupire, bramare; aver sete di: *to* — *for riches*, aver sete di ricchezze.

lustful ['lʌstful], *ag.* **1.** sensuale, libidinoso **2.** bramoso.

lustfully ['lʌstfuli], *av.* **1.** sensualmente, libidinosamente **2.** avidamente, bramosamente.

lustfulness ['lʌstfulnis], *s.* **1.** sensualità, libidine, lascivia **2.** brama, cupidigia.

lustihood ['lʌstihud], *s.* vigoria, robustezza, gagliardia.

lustily ['lʌstili], *av.* vigorosamente, gagliardamente.

lustiness ['lʌstinis], *s.* vigoria, robustezza, gagliardia.

lustless ['lʌstlis], *ag.* non concupiscente; che non ha brame sensuali.

lustral ['lʌstrəl], *ag.* lustrale.

lustration [lʌs'treiʃən], *s.* lustrazione.

lustre[1] ['lʌstə*], *s.* **1.** lucidezza, lucentezza; luminosità: *the* — *of pearls*, la lucentezza delle perle **2.** lustro, splendore (anche *fig.*): *the* — *of one's name*, il lustro del proprio nome **3.** goccia di lampadario **4.** lampadario a gocce **5.** lustrina (stoffa).

to **lustre**[1], *v.t.i.* lucidare.

lustre[2], *s.* lustro.

lustreless ['lʌstəlis], *av.* senza lucidezza; senza splendore (anche *fig.*).

lustrine ['lʌstrin], *s.* lustrina (stoffa).

lustrous ['lʌstrəs], *ag.* lucido, luminoso, splendente.

lustrously ['lʌstrəsli], *av.* luminosamente.

lustrum ['lʌstrəm] *pl.* **lustrums** ['lʌstrəmz], **lustra** ['lʌstrə], *s.* lustro.

lusty ['lʌsti], *ag.* vigoroso, robusto, gagliardo.

lutanist ['lju:tənist], *s.c.* (*mus.*) liutista.

lute[1] [lu:t], *s.* (*mus.*) liuto.

lute[2], *s.* luto.

to **lute**[2], *v.t.* lutare, cementare con il luto.

luteolin ['lju:tiəlin], *s.* (*chim.*) luteolina.

luteolus [lju'ti:ələs], *ag.* luteo, tendente al color giallo dorato.

luteous ['lju:tiəs], *ag.* luteo, di color giallo dorato.

lutestring ['lju:tstriŋ], *s.* lustrino (stoffa).

Lutetian [lju'ti:ʃən], *ag.* luteziano (abitante di Parigi, antica Lutetia).

Luther ['lu:θə*], *no.pr.m.* (*st. relig.*) Lutero.

Lutheran ['lu:θərən], *ag.* (*relig.*) luterano ‖ *s.c.* luterano, luterana.

Lutheranism ['lu:θərənizəm], *s.* (*relig.*) luteranesimo.

lutist ['lu:tist], *s.* **1.** (*mus.*) liutista, suonatore di liuto **2.** liutaio.

to **luxate** ['lʌkseit], *v.t.* (*med.*) lussare.

luxation [lʌk'seiʃən], *s.* (*med.*) lussazione.

Luxemburg ['lʌksəmbə:g], *no.pr.* (*geog.*) Lussemburgo.

luxuriance [lʌg'zjuəriəns], **luxuriancy** [lʌg'zjuəriənsi], *s.* **1.** carattere lussureggiante, esuberante (di linguaggio) **2.** stato lussureggiante, rigoglioso (in natura).

luxuriant [lʌg'zjuəriənt], *ag.* **1.** lussureggiante, ridondante (di linguaggio) **2.** lussureggiante, rigoglioso (della natura).

luxuriantly [lʌg'zjuəriəntli], *av.* **1.** in modo lussureggiante, ridondante (di linguaggio) **2.** in modo lussureggiante, rigoglioso (della natura).

to **luxuriate** [lʌg'zjuərieit], *v.i.* **1.** lussureggiare, prosperare rigogliosamente **2.** trovare godimento, godersela: *to* — *in sthg.*, deliziarsi, godere di ql.co.

luxurious [lʌg'zjuəriəs], *ag.* **1.** sontuoso, fastoso **2.** che ama il lusso, il fasto.

luxuriously [lʌg'zjuəriəsli], *av.* sontuosamente, lussuosamente.

luxuriousness [lʌg'zjuəriəsnis], *s.* **1.** sfarzo, lusso **2.** amore per il lusso.

luxury ['lʌkʃəri], *s.* **1.** lusso; fasto, sontuosità: *to live in* —, vivere nel lusso **2.** oggetto di lusso, prodotto raro e squisito: *fruit is a* — *for them*, la frutta è un lusso per loro **3.** piacere: *the* — *of a cigar*, il piacere di un sigaro.

lycanthrope ['laikənθroup], *s.* (*patol.*) licantropo.

lycanthropy [lai'kænθrəpi], *s.* (*patol.*) licantropia.

Lyceum [lai'siəm], *s.* **1.** (*fil.*) Liceo (sede della scuola aristotelica) **2.** centro di cultura umanistica.

lychnis ['liknis], *s.* (*bot.*) licnide.

Lycidas ['lisidæs], *no.pr.m.* (*lett.*) Licida.

lycopodium [,laikə'poudjəm], *s.* (*bot.*) licopodio.

lyddite ['lidait], *s.* (*chim.*) liddite.

Lydia ['lidiə], *no.pr.f.* Lidia.

Lydian ['lidiən], *ag.* **1.** lidio **2.** (*st. mus.*) lidio (uno de tre modi fondamentali dell'antica musica greca): — *airs*, melodie lidie ‖ *s.* lidio (abitante della Lidia).

lye [lai], *s.* **1.** lisciva **2.** (*chim.*) soluzione alcalina.

lying[1] ['laiiŋ], *ag.* menzognero, bugiardo ‖ *s.* il dir bugie.

lying[2], *ag.* giacente; situato ‖ *s.* il giacere ☆ — *-in*, degenza in clinica (di partorienti); — *-in hospital*, clinica ginecologica.

lyke-wake ['laik-weik], *s.* (*arc.*) veglia funebre.

lymph [limf], *s.* **1.** linfa **2.** vaccino **3.** (*poet.*) acqua pura.

lymphatic [lim'fætik], *ag.* linfatico (anche *fisiol.*) ‖ *s.* (*anat.*) vaso linfatico.

lymphatism [ˈlimfətizəm], *s.* (*patol.*) linfatismo.
lymphoma [limˈfoumə], *s.* (*patol.*) linfoma.
limphous [ˈlimfəs], *ag.* (*fisiol.*) linfatico.
lyncean [linˈsiːən], *ag.* **1.** di lince **2.** dagli occhi di lince.
to lynch [lintʃ], *v.t.* linciare.
lynch-law [ˈlintʃlɔ:], *s.* linciaggio.
lynx [liŋks], *s.* (*zool.*) lince ☆ — -*eyed*, dagli occhi di lince, dalla vista acuta.
Lyonesse [ˌlaiəˈnes], *no.pr.* (*lett.*) Lyonesse (poesie delle leggende arturiane).
Lyra [ˈlaiərə], *no.pr.* (*astr.*) Lira.
lyre [ˈlaiə*], *s.* **1.** (*mus.*) lira **2.** *the* —, *fig.* la poesia **3.** (*astr.*) Lira ☆ — -*bird*, (*ornit.*) uccello lira.
lyric [ˈlirik], *ag.* lirico: — *poetry*, poesia lirica ‖ *s.* lirica; poema lirico; versi lirici.

lyrical [ˈlirikəl], *ag.* lirico.
lyrically [ˈlirikəli], *av.* liricamente.
lyricism [ˈlirisizəm], *s.* lirismo.
lyricist [ˈlirisist], *s.* poeta lirico.
lyriform [ˈlaiəriˌfɔ:m], *ag.* liriforme.
lyrism [ˈlirizəm], *s.* lirismo.
lyrist [ˈlaiərist], *nel senso* **2.** [ˈlirist], *s.* **1.** suonatore di lira **2.** poeta lirico.
Lysander [laiˈsændə*], *no.pr.m.* (*st. lett.*) Lisandro.
Lysias [ˈlisiæs], *no.pr.m.* (*st. lett.*) Lisia.
Lysippus [laiˈsipəs], *no.pr.m.* (*st. scult.*) Lisippo.
lysis [ˈlaisis], *s.* (*chim. med.*) lisi.
Lysistratus [laiˈsistrətəs], *no.pr.m.* (*st.*) Lisistrato.
lysol [ˈlaisol], *s.* (*farm.*) lisolo.
lyssa [ˈlisə], *s.* (*patol.*) lissa, idrofobia.

M

m [em], *pl.* ms, m's [emz], *s.* 1. (*tredicesima lettera dell'alfabeto inglese*) m ‖ — *for Mary*, (*tel.*) m come Milano 2. '*m*, (*volg.*) *abbr.* di *madam*: *yes'm*, sissignora 3. *M* (*cifra romana*), 1000.

ma [mɑ:], *s. abbr.* di mamma[1].

ma'am [mæm], *s.* (*contr.* di *madam*) 1. signora (vocativo usato per le dame della famiglia reale) 2. maestra di scuola.

Mab [mæb], *no.pr.f.* (*mit.*) Mab (regina delle fate).

Mac [mæk], *prefisso* (*di cognomi scozzesi; significa* figlio di): *James Macpherson lived in the XVIII century*, James Macpherson visse nel XVIII secolo.

macabre [mə'kɑ:br], *ag.* macabro.

macaco [mə'keikou], *pl.* macacos [mə'keikouz], *s.* (*zool.*) macaco.

macadam [mə'kædəm], *s.* macadam (tipo di massicciata stradale).

macadamization [mə,kædəmai'zeiʃən], *s.* pavimentazione stradale a macadam.

to macadamize [mə'kædəmaiz], *v.t.* macadamizzare, pavimentare a macadam.

Macao [mə'kau], *no.pr.* (*geog.*) Macao.

macaroni [,mækə'rouni], *s.* 1. (solo *sing.*) maccheroni 2. (*arc.*) damerino; zerbinotto.

macaronic [,mækə'rɔnik], *ag.* (*poes.*) maccheronico ‖ *s.* (*lett.*) maccheronea.

macaroon [,mækə'ru:n], *s.* amaretto.

Macassar [mə'kæsə*], *no.pr.* (*geog.*) Macassar ‖ macassar, *s.* olio per capelli.

macaw[1] [mə'kɔ:], *s.* (*ornit.*) macao, ara.

macaw[2], *s.* (*bot.*) palma indiana.

Maccabean [,mækə'bi:ən], *ag.* (*Bibbia*) maccabeo.

Maccabees ['mækəbi:z], *s.pl.* (*Bibbia*) Maccabei.

Maccabeus [,mækə'bi:əs], *no.pr.m.* (*Bibbia*) Maccabeo.

maccaboy ['mækəbɔi], *s.* macuba (tabacco da fiuto).

mace[1] [meis], *s.* 1. (*st.*) mazza 2. mazza (simbolo dell'autorità) 3. (specie di) stecca da biliardo ☆ — -bearer, mazziere.

mace[2], *s.* (*chim.*) macis.

macedoine [,mæsə'dwa:n], *s.* (*cuc.*) macedonia.

Macedonia [,mæsi'dounjə], *no.pr.* (*geog.*) Macedonia.

Macedonian [,mæsi'dounjən], *ag.s.c.* macedone ‖ *s.* lingua macedone.

to macerate ['mæsəreit], *v.t.i.* macerare, macerarsi (anche *fig.*).

maceration [,mæsə'reiʃən], *s.* macerazione, maceramento (anche *fig.*).

Mach (number) [mɑ:k('nʌmbə*)], *s.* (*fis.*) (numero di) Mach.

machete [mə'tʃeiti], *s.* « machete » (coltello usato in America del Sud anche come arma).

Machiavelli [,mækiə'veli], *no.pr.* (*st.*) Machiavelli ‖ *s.* machiavello; uomo astuto.

Machiavellian [,mækiə'veliən], *ag.* machiavellico; *fig.* astuto.

Machiavellism [,mækiə'velizəm], *s.* machiavellismo.

machicolation [mə,tʃikə'leiʃən], *s.* (*arch. mil.*) caditoia, piombatoio.

to machinate ['mækineit], *v.t.i.* macchinare; tramare; complottare.

machination [,mæki'neiʃən], *s.* macchinazione; congiura, trama.

machinator ['mækineitə*], *s.c.* macchinatore, macchinatrice; intrigante.

machine [mə'ʃi:n], *s.* 1. macchina (anche *fig.*): *to be a mere* —, essere un automa 2. (*spec. pol. amer.*) organo direttivo di partito: *the Democratic* —, l'esecutivo del partito democratico 3. (*spec. scoz.*) veicolo (auto, bicicletta, aeroplano, ecc.) ☆ — -gun, mitragliatrice; — -gunner, mitragliere; — -hour, ora di lavoro di macchina; — -made, fatto a macchina; *fig.* stereotipato; — -maker, costruttore di macchine; — -oil, olio per macchina; — -tool, macchina utensile; — -work, lavoro a macchina ‖ adding- — (o calculating- —), macchina calcolatrice; boring- —, alesatrice; dishwashing- —, lavastoviglie; milling- —, fresatrice; planing- —, piallatrice; ploughing- —, aratrice; printing- —, macchina per stampare; punching- —, punzonatrice; sewing- —, macchina per cucire; slot- —, distributore automatico; sowing- —, seminatrice; threshing- —, trebbiatrice; weighing- —, pesatrice, bilancia automatica.

to machine, *v.t.i.* lavorare alla macchina.

to machine-gun [mə'ʃi:ngʌn], *pass.p.p.* machine -gunned [mə'ʃi:ngʌnd], *v.t.* mitragliare.

machinery [mə'ʃi:nəri], *s.* 1. macchinario 2. (*mec.*) congegno, meccanismo 3. *fig.* macchina, organizzazione: *the — of Government*, la macchina, l'organizzazione dello Stato; *if we do that, we shall put the whole — in motion*, se facciamo questo metteremo in moto tutto il meccanismo (gli organi competenti, interessati) 4. (*lett.*) macchinismo, intervento delle potenze soprannaturali ☆ — seating, collocazione, installazione del macchinario ‖ driving — (o propelling —), apparecchio, congegno motore.

machining [mə'ʃi:niŋ], *s.* 1. (*tec.*) lavorazione a macchina 2. (*tip.*) stampa a macchina ☆ — allowance, (*metal.*) sovrametallo; — down, (*metal.*) riduzione, assottigliamento (del pezzo); — time, tempo di lavorazione di macchina.

machinist [mə'ʃi:nist], *s.* 1. macchinista 2. operaio; meccanico specializzato.

mack [mæk], *abbr.* di mackintosh 1.

mackerel ['mækrəl], *s.* (*ittiol.*) maccarello, sgombro ☆ — sky, cielo a pecorelle.

mackintosh ['mækintəʃ], *s.* 1. (soprabito) impermeabile 2. tessuto gommato, impermeabilizzato.

macrocephalic [,mækrousi'fælik], macrocephalous [,mækrou'sefələs], *ag.* macrocefalo.

macrocosm ['mækrəkəzəm], *s.* macrocosmo.

macrocosmic [,mækro'kozmik], *ag.* macrocosmico.

macrodactyl [,mækrə'dæktil], *ag.s.* (*zool.*) macrodattilo.

macrology [mə'krɔlədʒi], *s.* macrologia.

macron ['mækrɔn], *s.* segno di allungamento su vocale.

macropod ['mækrəpɔd], *ag.* macropode.

macropterous [mə'krɔptərəs], *ag.* che ha lunghe ali.

macroscopic [,mækrou'skɔpik], *ag.* macroscopico.

macula ['mækjulə], *pl.* maculae ['mækjuli:], *s.* macchia (specialmente solare).

to maculate ['mækjuleit], *v.t.* maculare.

maculation [,mækju'leiʃən], *s.* maculamento.

maculose ['mækjulous], *ag.* maculato.

mad [mæd], *ag.* 1. pazzo, matto, folle: *to become* (o *to go* o *to run*) —, ammattire, diventar matto; *to drive* (o *to send*) *s.o.* —, fare impazzire qlcu. ‖ *to be as — as a hatter* (o *as a March hare*), essere matto da legare 2. (*fam.*) furioso, arrabbiato, furente: *they were — about missing the train*, erano furenti di aver perduto il treno; *to be*

— *with s.o.*, essere arrabbiato con qlcu. **3.** idrofobo, arrabbiato (di cane) **4.** *fig.* appassionato, fanatico: — *with joy*, pazzo di gioia; *she is — on dancing*, va pazza per il ballo; *to be — on music*, andar pazzo per la musica ‖ *like —*, come un pazzo ‖ *to have a — time*, divertirsi pazzamente ☆ — *-doctor*, alienista.

to mad, *v.t.i.* (*rar.*) fare impazzire; essere, agire da pazzo.

Madagascar [ˌmædəˈgæskə*], *no.pr.* (*geog.*) Madagascar.

madam [ˈmædəm], *s.* signora (al vocativo).

madapollam [ˌmædəˈpɔləm], *s.* (tela) madapolam.

madarosis [ˌmædəˈrousis], *s.* (*patol.*) madarosi.

madcap [ˈmædkæp], *s.* scervellato, testa matta.

to madden [ˈmædn], *v.t.i.* **1.** far impazzire; diventar matto **2.** *fig.* disperarsi; far disperare; far inquietare; render furioso.

maddening [ˈmædniŋ], *ag.* **1.** che fa impazzire **2.** *fig.* irritante; esasperante.

madder [ˈmædə*], *s.* (*bot.*) robbia.

madding [ˈmædiŋ], *ag.* folle; pazzo; furioso.

maddingly [ˈmædiŋli], *av.* follemente; furiosamente.

made [meid], *pass.p.p.* di **to make** ‖ *ag.* fatto, lavorato, confezionato; composto ☆ — *man*, un arrivato; — *over*, (*amer.*) rimesso a nuovo, rinnovato; — *up*, alterato, truccato; (*arc.*) completo: *it is a — up story*, è una frottola; *she is — up*, è tutta truccata ‖ *hand- —*, fatto a mano; *home- —*, fatto in casa; *ready- —*, fatto, confezionato (di abiti).

Madeira [məˈdiərə], *no.pr.* (*geog.*) Madera ‖ *s.* (vino di) Madera ☆ — *nut*, (*amer.*) noce.

Madge [mædʒ], *no.pr.f. dim.* di **Margaret**.

madhouse [ˈmædhaus], *s.* manicomio (anche *fig.*).

madly [ˈmædli], *av.* **1.** pazzamente, furiosamente **2.** *fig.* alla follia, perdutamente.

madman, *pl.* **madmen** [ˈmædmən], *s.* alienato, pazzo; insensato.

madness [ˈmædnis], *s.* **1.** pazzia, demenza: *it is sheer — to go out in this weather*, è pazzia uscire con questo tempo ‖ *midsummer —*, il colmo della pazzia **2.** (*fam.*) ira; furore, rabbia **3.** idrofobia, rabbia.

madonna [məˈdɔnə], *s.* (*pitt. scult.*) Madonna.

madrepore [ˌmædriˈpo:*], *s.* (*zool.*) madrepora.

madrigal [ˈmædrigəl], *s.* (*poes.*) madrigale.

madwoman [ˈmædˌwumən], *pl.* **madwomen** [ˈmædˌwimin], *s.* pazza.

Maecenas [miˈ(:)ˈsiːnæs], *no.pr.m.* (*st. lett.*) Mecenate ‖ *s.* mecenate.

maelstrom [ˈmeilstroum], *s.* **1.** « maelstrom » (vortice nelle acque norvegesi) **2.** turbine, vortice (anche *fig.*).

maenad [ˈmiːnæd], *s.* (*mit.*) menade, baccante (anche *fig.*).

Mae West [ˈmeiˈwest], *s.* (*sl.*) cintura di salvataggio (per aviatori).

to maffick [ˈmæfik], *v.i.* darsi ad entusiastiche, sfrenate manifestazioni pubbliche.

magazine [ˌmægəˈziːn], *s.* **1.** magazzino, deposito (di armi, viveri in tempo di guerra); (*mil.*) polveriera; (*mar.*) santabarbara; serbatoio **2.** periodico, rivista **3.** caricatore (di arma) ☆ — *-camera*, macchina fotografica a magazzino; — *-rifle*, fucile a ripetizione.

Magdalen [ˈmægdəlin], **Magdalene** [ˌmægdəˈliːni], *no.pr.f.* Maddalena ‖ *Magdalen* [ˈmɔːdlin] *College*, «Magdalen College» (Oxford); *Magdalene* [ˈmɔːdlin] *College*, «Magdalene College» (Cambridge) ‖ *s.* prostituta redenta.

mage [meidʒ], *s.* (*arc.*) **1.** mago **2.** sapiente.

Magellan [məˈgelən], *no.pr.* (*st.*) Magellano.

magenta [məˈdʒentə], *ag.s.* (color) magenta.

Maggie [ˈmægi], *no.pr.f. dim.* di **Margaret**.

maggot [ˈmægət], *s.* **1.** (*entom.*) larva **2.** *fig.* idea fissa, capriccio, ubbia: *to have a — in one's head*, avere un'idea fissa.

maggoty [ˈmægəti], *ag.* **1.** guasto, bacato **2.** *fig.* capriccioso, strambo.

magi [ˈmeidʒai], *pl.* di **magus**.

magic [ˈmædʒik], *ag.* magico; fatato: — *mirror*, specchio magico ‖ *s.* magia; incantesimo ‖ *like —*, come per incanto ☆ — *lantern*, lanterna magica; — *square*, quadrato magico ‖ *black —*, magia nera; *white —*, magia bianca.

magical [ˈmædʒikəl], *ag.* magico.

magically [ˈmædʒikəli], *av.* per magia, magicamente.

magician [məˈdʒiʃən], *s.c.* mago, maga; stregone, strega.

magilp, *V.* **megilp**.

magisterial [ˌmædʒisˈtiəriəl], *ag.* **1.** di magistrato: *in his — capacity*, nella sua qualità di magistrato **2.** autorizzato **3.** autoritario, dispotico **4.** autorevole.

magisterially [ˌmædʒisˈtiəriəli], *av.* **1.** da magistrato **2.** con autorizzazione **3.** autoritariamente, dispoticamente **4.** autorevolmente.

magistery [ˈmædʒistəri], *s.* (*farm. chim.*) magistero.

magistracy [ˈmædʒistrəsi], *s.* magistratura.

magistral [məˈdʒistrəl], *ag.* **1.** (*rar.*) magistrale, di maestro **2.** (*farm.*) magistrale, secondo prescrizione medica ☆ — *staff*, corpo insegnante.

magistrate [ˈmædʒistrit], *s.* magistrato ‖ *Police Court Magistrate*, giudice conciliatore.

magistrateship [ˈmædʒistritʃip], **magistrature** [ˈmædʒistrətjuə*], *s.* magistratura.

magma [ˈmægmə], *pl.* **magmata** [ˈmægmətə], **magmas** [ˈmægməz], *s.* (*geol.*) magma.

Magna Charta [ˈmægnəˈkaːtə], *s.* **1.** (*st.*) Magna Carta (1215) **2.** *fig.* qualsiasi costituzione secondo principi liberali.

magnanimity [ˌmægnəˈnimiti], *s.* magnanimità.

magnanimous [mægˈnænimøs], *ag.* magnanimo.

magnanimously [mægˈnænimøsli], *av.* magnanimamente.

magnate [ˈmægneit], *s.* **1.** (*st.*) magnate; maggiorente **2.** grande industriale ☆ *oil —*, magnate del petrolio.

magnesia [mægˈniːʃə], *s.* (*chim. farm.*) magnesia: *milk of —*, latte di magnesia.

magnesian [mægˈniːʃən], *ag.* (*chim.*) magnesiaco.

magnesium [mægˈniːzjəm], *s.* (*chim.*) magnesio.

magnet [ˈmægnit], *s.* magnete, calamita (anche *fig.*); elettromagnete ☆ — *core*, nucleo magnetico ‖ *blowout —*, (*elett.*) magnete antiarco, rompiarco; *brake —*, (*elett.*) magnete freno; *field —*, elettromagnete di campo, di statore; *horse-shoe —*, calamita a ferro di cavallo; *lifting —*, elettromagnete di sollevamento; *permanent —*, (*elett.*) magnete permanente; *releasing —*, elettrocalamita, magnete di scatto.

magnetic(al) [mægˈnetik(əl)], *ag.* magnetico; *fig.* attraente, affascinante: — *fluid*, fluido magnetico; *a — glance*, uno sguardo magnetico; *a — personality*, una personalità attraente ☆ — *circuit*, (*elett.*) circuito magnetico; — *compass*, (*ind.*) bussola magnetica; — *equator*, equatore magnetico; — *field*, (*elett. fis.*) campo magnetico; — *induction*, induzione magnetica; — *iron sheet*, (*metal.*) lamierino magnetico; — *needle*, (*mec. fis.*) ago magnetico, calamitato; — *poles*, poli magnetici (della Terra); — *recorder*, magnetofono; — *tape*, *wire*, nastro, filo magnetico.

magnetically [mægˈnetikəli], *ag.* magneticamente (anche *fig.*).

magnetics [mægˈnetiks], *s.* magnetismo.

magnetism [ˈmægnitizəm], *s.* magnetismo; *fig.* attrazione, fascino ☆ *animal —*, magnetismo animale; ipnotismo; *residual —*, (*elett.*) magnetismo residuo.

magnetist [ˈmægnitist], *s.* ipnotizzatore; magnetizzatore.

magnetite [ˈmægnitait], *s.* (*min.*) magnetite.

magnetization [ˌmægnitaiˈzeiʃən], *s.* (*elett. fis.*) magnetizzazione; forza d'attrazione (anche *fig.*).

to magnetize [ˈmægnitaiz], *v.t.* magnetizzare (anche *fig.*).

magneto [mægˈniːtou], *s.* (*elett.*) magnete ‖ *there is sthg. wrong with the —*, (*aut.*) l'avviamento non funziona

☆ *hand starting* —, (*elett.*) magnete per avviamento.
magnetometer [,mægni'tɔmitə*], *s.* magnetometro.
magnetron ['mægnitrɔn], *s.* (*rad.*) « magnetron »: *tunable* —, « magnetron » sintonizzabile.
magnifie(al) [mæg'nifik(əl)], *ag.* (*arc.*) magnifico; splendido; sublime.
magnifically [mæg'nifikəli], *av.* (*arc.*) magnificamente; splendidamente.
Magnificat [mæg'nifikæt], *s.* (*eccl.*) Magnificat.
magnification [,mægnifi'keiʃən], *s.* **1.** esaltazione; lode **2.** (*ott.*) ingrandimento.
magnificence [mæg'nifisns], *s.* magnificenza.
magnificent [mæg'nifisnt], *ag.* magnifico; splendido; sontuoso.
magnificently [mæg'nifisntli], *av.* magnificamente; splendidamente; sontuosamente.
magnifico [mæg'nifikou], *s.* (*st.*) magnifico (titolo onorifico specialmente riferito ai Signori veneziani).
magnifier ['mægnifaiə*], *s.c.* esaltatore, esaltatrice, magnificatore, magnificatrice || *s.* (*ott.*) lente d'ingrandimento.
to **magnify** ['mægnifai], *v.t.* **1.** magnificare, esaltare **2.** (*ott.*) ingrandire ☆ *magnifying glass*, lente d'ingrandimento.
magniloquence [mæg'niləkwəns], *s.* magniloquenza.
magniloquent [mæg'niləkwənt], *ag.* magniloquente.
magniloquently [mæg'niləkwəntli], *av.* in modo magniloquente.
magnitude ['mægnitju:d], *s.* **1.** importanza **2.** grandezza: *a star of the first* —, una stella di prima grandezza.
magnolia [mæg'nouljə], *s.* (*bot.*) magnolia.
magnum ['mægnəm], *s.* bottiglione della capacità di l. 2,28 (per vini o liquori).
magpie ['mægpai], *s.* **1.** (*ornit.*) gazza **2.** *fig.* persona pettegola **3.** (colpo che raggiunge il) penultimo cerchio di un bersaglio **4.** (*sl.*) mezzo penny.
magus ['meigəs], *pl.* **magi** ['meidʒai], *s.* **1.** antico prete persiano **2.** stregone || *the Magi*, i Re Magi.
Magyar ['mægjɑ:*], *ag.* magiaro || *s.c.* magiaro, magiara || *s.* lingua magiara.
maharaja(h) [,mɑ:hə'rɑ:dʒə], *s.* maragià.
maharanee [,mɑ:hə'rɑ:ni:], *s.* consorte di maragià.
mahatma [mə'hɑ:tmə], *s.* « mahatma », asceta, saggio dotato di grandissimi meriti (in India).
Mahdi ['mɑ:di(:)], *s.* (*relig. musulmana*) « Mahdi ».
mahlstick ['mɔ:l-stik], *s.* (*pitt.*) appoggiamano.
mahogany [mə'hɔgəni], *s.* **1.** mogano (pianta, legno) || *the* —, (*fam.*) la tavola da pranzo **2.** color mogano.
Mahomet [mə'hɔmit], *no.pr.m.* (*st. relig.*) Maometto.
Mahometan [mə'hɔmitən], *ag.* maomettano || *s.c.* maomettano, maomettana.
Mahound [mə'haund], *no.pr.m.* Maometto.
mahout [mə'haut], *s.* guidatore di elefanti.
maid [meid], *s.* **1.** (*poet.*) ragazza, fanciulla; vergine: — *of honour*, damigella d'onore || *the Maid of Orleans*, la Pulzella d'Orléans **2.** domestica || — *in waiting*, (*arc.*) ancella ☆ — *of-all-work*, donna tutto fare || *chamber* —, cameriera (d'albergo); *old* —, (*fam.*) zitella.
maiden ['meidn], *ag.* **1.** virgineo, verginale; *fig.* fresco, puro: — *modesty*, ritrosia, pudore verginale **2.** nubile: — *aunt*, zia nubile; (*fam.*) vecchia zia; — *name*, cognome da nubile **3.** primo, esordiente: — *horse*, cavallo che non ha mai vinto; — *speech*, il primo discorso di un uomo politico; — *trip* (o *voyage*), primo viaggio (di una nave) || *s.* **1.** (*letter.*) fanciulla, giovinetta; vergine **2.** zitella **3.** (*st. scoz.*) ghigliottina.
maidenhair ['meidnhɛə*], *s.* (*bot.*) capelvenere.
maidenhead ['meidnhed], *s.* **1.** verginità **2.** (*anat.*) imene.
maidenhood ['meidnhud], *s.* l'essere nubile; verginità.
maidenish ['meidniʃ], *ag.* di fanciulla; di vergine.
maidenlike ['meidnlaik], *V.* **maidenly**.

maidenliness ['meidnlinis], *s.* modestia; pudore; ritrosia.
maidenly ['meidnli], *ag.* verginale, casto; modesto || *av.* castamente, pudicamente; modestamente: *she blushed* —, arrossì pudicamente.
maidish ['meidiʃ], *ag.* di fanciulla; di vergine.
maidless ['meidlis], *ag.* senza domestica: *she was* — *and overworked*, non aveva domestica ed era sovraccarica di lavoro.
maidly ['meidli], *ag.* somigliante a fanciulla.
maidservant ['meid,sə:vənt], *s.* cameriera, domestica.
maieutic [mei'ju:tik], *ag.* che serve a chiarire idee latenti.
maieutics [mei'ju:tiks], *s.* (*st. fil.*) maieutica.
maigre ['meigə*], *ag.* magro (di cibo).
mail[1] [meil], *s.* **1.** posta, corrispondenza: *he does all his* — *himself*, sbriga personalmente tutta la sua corrispondenza; *will you answer the* — *for me?*, vuoi rispondere alla posta per me? **2.** posta, servizio postale || *the Indian Mail*, la Valigia delle Indie ☆ — *-bag*, sacco per la posta; — *boat*, (battello) postale; — *-box*, (*amer.*) cassetta per la posta; — *-coach*, diligenza postale; — *order*, ordinazione (di merci) per corrispondenza; — *order catalogue*, catalogo per la vendita per corrispondenza; — *-train*, treno postale; — *-van*, furgone postale || *air-* —, posta aerea; *outward* —, corrispondenza in partenza.
to **mail**[1],*v.t.* mandare per posta ☆ *mailing list*, elenco di indirizzi per invio di materiale pubblicitario: *we shall be glad to have you on our mailing list*, saremo lieti d'inviarvi i nostri cataloghi e listini.
mail[2], *s.* maglia (di ferro): *coat of* —, cotta di maglia.
mailable ['meiləbl], *ag.* spedibile.
maim [meim], *s.* mutilazione; storpiamento.
to **maim**, *v.t.* mutilare; storpiare; paralizzare (anche *fig.*).
maimed [meimd], *ag.* mutilato; storpiato || *the* —, gli storpi: *the halt and the* —, (*letter. arc.*) gli zoppi e gli storpi.
maimedness ['meimdnis], *s.* mutilazione.
main[1] [mein], *ag.* principale, più importante; essenziale; capitale: *the* — *features of a speech*, i tratti salienti di un discorso || *the* — *body*, (*mil.*) il grosso dell'esercito || *the* — *issue*, il nocciolo della questione || *in the* —, (*amer.*) principalmente || *to have an eye to the* — *chance*, curare i propri interessi.
main[1], *s.* **1.** (*poet.*) mare; oceano || *the Spanish Main*, (*st.*) il Mar delle Antille; terre, coste sul Mar delle Antille (una volta sotto dominio spagnolo) **2.** (*tec.*) conduttura, tubatura principale **3.** l'essenziale: *in the* —, in complesso **4.** (*arc.*) forza || *with might and* —, con tutte le energie, con tutte le forze.
main[1], (*nei composti*): — *-course*, (*mar.*) vela maestra; — *-deck*, (*mar.*) ponte di batteria; — *office*, (*comm.*) direzione centrale, sede; — *road*, strada maestra; — *royal sail*, (*mar.*) controvelaccio; — *-top-gallant-mast*, (*mar.*) alberetto di velaccio; — *top-gallant-yard*, (*mar.*) pennone di gran velaccio; — *top sail*, gabbia di maestra; *mains-operated set*, (*rad.*) apparecchio radio a corrente elettrica.
main[2], *s.* **1.** (*dadi*) numeri dal 5 al 9 **2.** combattimento tra galli.
mainbrace ['meinbreis], *s.* (*mar.*) corda del pennone di maestra.
mainland ['meinlənd], *s.* terra ferma; continente.
mainly ['meinli], *av.* **1.** principalmente, soprattutto **2.** nel complesso.
mainmast ['meinmɑ:st], *s.* (*mar.*) albero maestro.
mainor ['meinə*], *s.* (*dir.*) refurtiva.
mains [meinz], *s.* (*scoz.*) fattoria principale.
mainsail ['meinseil], *s.* (*mar.*) vela maestra.
mainspring ['mein-spriŋ], *s.* **1.** molla principale **2.** *fig.* movente principale.
mainstay ['mein-stei], *s.* **1.** (*mar.*) straglio di maestra **2.** *fig.* appoggio, sostegno; fondamento.

to **maintain** [men'tein], *v.t.* **1.** mantenere: *they maintained her family for a long time*, mantennero la sua famiglia a lungo; *to — the speed*, mantenere la velocità **2.** conservare, difendere: *I — my ground*, (*fam.*) mantengo le mie posizioni; *they maintained their positions*, (*mil.*) conservarono le loro posizioni **3.** pretendere, asserire, affermare: *he maintains that it is true*, egli afferma che ciò è vero.

maintainable [men'teinəbl], *ag.* **1.** mantenibile **2.** difendibile.

maintainer [men'teinə*], *s.* mantenitore.

maintenance ['meintinəns], *s.* **1.** mantenimento, sostentamento **2.** assistenza **3.** (*dir.*) alimenti **4.** (*mec.*) manutenzione **5.** difesa (dei propri diritti) ☆ — *charge* (o — *cost*), spese di manutenzione; — *staff*, personale di sorveglianza; gli addetti alla manutenzione.

maintop ['mein-tɔp], *s.* (*mar.*) coffa di maestra.

mainyard ['mein-jɑ:d], *s.* (*mar.*) pennone di maestra.

Mainz [maints], *no.pr.* (*geog.*) Magonza.

maisonnette [,meizə'net], *s.* appartamentino.

maistry ['meistri], *s.* (*ang.-in.*) capo operaio.

maize [meiz], *s.* **1.** granoturco, mais **2.** (colore) giallo.

majestic(al) [mə'dʒestik(əl)], *ag.* maestoso; augusto.

majestically [mə'dʒestikəli], *av.* maestosamente.

majesticalness [mə'dʒestikəlnis], *s.* maestosità.

majesty ['mædʒisti], *s.* **1.** maestà: *His, Her, Your Majesty*, Sua, Vostra Maestà; *Their Majesties*, le Loro Maestà **2.** grandezza, maestà.

majolica [mə'jɔlikə], *s.* maiolica.

major[1] ['meidʒə*], *ag.* **1.** maggiore, superiore, più importante; — *course*, — *subject*, (*amer.*) corso di studi, materia più importante; — *operation*, intervento chirurgico grave; *the — part*, la maggior parte; — *road*, strada principale; *the — writers*, i maggiori, i più grandi scrittori **2.** (*mus.*) in tono maggiore **3.** il maggiore (di due fratelli, a scuola): *Brown —*, il fratello maggiore di *Brown minor* ‖ *s.* **1.** (*dir.*) maggiorenne **2.** (*amer. scolastico*) disciplina di specializzazione ☆ — *scale*, (*mus.*) scala maggiore.

to **major**[1], *v.i.* (*amer. scolastico*) specializzarsi: *to — in chemistry*, specializzarsi in chimica.

major[2], *s.* (*mil.*) maggiore.

majorat [,mɑ:ʒə'rɑ:], *s.* (*dir.*) maggiorasco.

Majorca [mə'dʒɔ:kə], *no.pr.* (*geog.*) Maiorca.

majordomo ['meidʒə'doumou], *s.* (*rar.*) maggiordomo.

majority [mə'dʒɔriti], *s.* **1.** maggioranza: *absolute —*, maggioranza assoluta; *to win by a handsome —*, vincere con una forte maggioranza (una battaglia elettorale) ‖ *to join the —*, raggiungere il numero dei più, morire **2.** maggiore età: *to attain one's —*, diventare maggiorenne.

majorship ['meidʒəʃip], *s.* (*mil.*) grado di maggiore.

majuscule ['mædʒəskju:l], *ag.* maiuscolo ‖ *s.* lettera maiuscola.

make [meik], *s.* **1.** fattura, forma, struttura; fabbricazione, marca; taglio: *cars of all makes*, auto di tutte le marche; *a house of flimsy —*, una casa di fragile struttura; *of good, solid —*, di buona, robusta fattura; *of Italian —*, di fabbricazione italiana; *of our own —*, di nostra fabbricazione ‖ *to be on the —*, (*sl.*) cercare di far denaro **2.** costituzione fisica, morale: *a man of feeble —*, un uomo di costituzione gracile; un uomo debole di carattere **3.** (*elett.*) chiusura (del circuito): *at —*, in circuito.

to **make**, *pass.p.p.* **made** [meid], *v.t.i.* **1.** fare; creare; fabbricare, formare; costruire, produrre; comporre; preparare: *God made the world*, Dio creò il mondo; *a joiner made this table*, un falegname ha costruito questa tavola; *the table is made of wood*, la tavola è fatta di legno; *will you — tea for us, please?*, ci prepari il tè, per favore?; *wine is made from grapes*, il vino è fatto con l'uva; *to — a bed*, rifare un letto; *to — faces*, far

smorfie; *to — a noise*, far rumore; *to — peace, war*, far pace, guerra; *to — trouble*, dar noia ‖ *I only just made it*, ce l'ho fatta per un pelo; *they will never — it*, non ce la faranno (mai) ‖ *I can — nothing of it*, non ci capisco nulla; *what do you — of this?*, cosa ne pensi? ‖ *to — the best of sthg.*, trarre il massimo vantaggio da ql.co.: *to — the best of a bad bargain*, fare buon viso a cattiva sorte; *to — the best of one's way*, procedere il più velocemente possibile ‖ *to — bold* (*to do sthg.*), permettersi, prendersi la libertà (di fare ql.co.) ‖ *to — cards*, mescolare le carte ‖ *to — a clean breast of*, vuotare il sacco, fare una completa confessione ‖ *to — do with sthg.* (o *sthg. do*), arrangiarsi con ql.co.: *the students must — do with the books they have*, gli studenti debbono arrangiarsi con i libri che hanno ‖ *to — fun of*, farsi giuoco di ‖ *to — a fuss*, esagerare, fare storie ‖ *to — a go*, spuntarla, aver successo; *to — a go of sthg.*, portare al successo ql.co. ‖ *to — a habit of doing sthg.*, prender l'abitudine di fare ql.co., abituarsi a fare ql.co. ‖ *to — haste*, affrettarsi ‖ *to — head against s.o.*, tener testa a qlcu. ‖ *to — inquiries*, assumere informazioni ‖ *to — love to s.o.*, fare la corte a qlcu. ‖ *to — the most of sthg.*, profittare al massimo di ql.co.: *the most of your stay in England*, cerca di trarre il maggior vantaggio possibile dal tuo soggiorno in Inghilterra ‖ *to — much, little* (o *light*) *of s.o., sthg.*, dare molta, poca importanza a qlcu., ql.co. ‖ *to — no bones about sthg.*, (*fam.*) agire senza esitazione ‖ *to — sail*, (*mar.*) fare vela ‖ *to — (a) shift*, cavarsela alla meno peggio ‖ *to — short* (o *quiet*) *work of sthg.*, finire rapidamente ql.co.; liberarsi di ql.co. ‖ *to — way to*, far largo a **2.** far divenire: *to — s.o. king*, creare qlcu. re ‖ *to — a fool of s.o.*, farsi beffe di qlcu.; *to — a fool of oneself*, rendersi ridicolo ‖ *to — hay of sthg.*, (*fam.*) creare disordine in ql.co. **3.** rendere: *to — beautiful*, render bello; *to — clear*, chiarire, render chiaro; *to — fast*, legare, assicurare; *to — free*, liberare; *to — free with*, prendersi troppa libertà con; *to — ready*, preparare; *to — useless*, rendere inutile ‖ *to — good*, adempiere, mantenere, compensare, risarcire; (*fam.*) far carriera, riuscire (nella vita, ecc.): *he will — his word good*, manterrà la parola; *he will — it up to you*, ti risarcirà, ti compenserà ‖ *to — it hot for s.o.*, (*fam.*) rendere la vita difficile a qlcu. ‖ *to — merry*, far festa, baldoria **4.** (V, VI) far fare; obbligare a; costringere a; far sì che, che: *he made me do what he liked*, mi fece fare ciò che voleva; *I made him confess*, lo obbligai a confessare; *he can — himself understood*, si fa capire; *she made herself loved by everybody*, fece amare da tutti; *you — me laugh!*, mi fai ridere! ‖ *to — both ends meet*, sbarcare il lunario **5.** acquistare; guadagnare: *to — friends with s.o.*, fare amicizia con qlcu.; *to — money*, far denaro, guadagnare ‖ *to — a bit*, (*fam.*) far la cresta sulla spesa ‖ *to — hay while the sun shines*, battere il ferro finchè è caldo **6.** raggiungere, arrivare; (*mar.*) avvistare: *we could — land at last*, finalmente avvistammo la terra **7.** coprire (una distanza); avviarsi, dirigersi: *he made the distance in few minutes*, fece tutta la strada in pochi minuti **8.** *to — for (a place)*, dirigersi verso: *we are making for town* siamo diretti in città **9.** *to — into* (*sthg.*), volgere in, tradurre in: *can you — it into Italian?*, sai tradurlo in italiano? **10.** *to — away*, andarsene ‖ *to — away with s.o., oneself*, ammazzare qlcu., ammazzarsi **11.** *to — back*, ritornare **12.** *to — down*, ridurre (un abito): *her mother used to — down her elder sister's dresses for her*, sua madre aveva l'abitudine di adattarle gli abiti della sorella maggiore **13.** *to — off*, svignarsela; andarsene in fretta: *he made off with the cash*, se n'è andato coi quattrini **14.** *to — out*, redigere, scorgere; decifrare; capire, interpretare; (*comm.*) emettere, rilasciare (un assegno): *I can't — this story out*, non riesco a capire questa faccenda; *you — him out braver than he is*, tu lo credi, lo descrivi più coraggioso di quanto egli non sia **15.** *to — over*, trasferire, passare a; (*amer.*) rifare, accomodare: *before he died he made the firm* *over to his son*, prima di morire cedette la ditta al figlio **16.** *to* — **up**, appianare, comporre (una lite, ecc.); fare, preparare (anche *fig.*); truccare, truccarsi; (*tip.*) impaginare: *he will* — *up an excuse*, troverà una scusa || *to* — *up for*, compensare per: *to* — *up for lost time*, riguadagnare il tempo perduto || *to* — *up one's mind*, decidersi || *to* — *up to*, adulare; salire (di marea).

make-believe ['meikbi,li:v], *s.* finzione: *don't trust him, it is all* —, non fidarti di lui, son tutte finzioni.

to **make-believe**, *v.i.* far finta (specialmente nel linguaggio infantile): *let's* — *you are an old lady*, facciamo finta che tu sia una vecchia signora.

make-peace ['meikpi:s], *s.* paciere.

maker ['meikə*], *s.* **1.** fattore, creatore, artefice; fabbricante; costruttore **2.** *Maker*, Dio, il Creatore; *our Maker, the Maker of all*, il Creatore **3.** (*bridge*) dichiarante, il primo che parla ☆ — *-up*, (*teat.*) truccatore; (*tip.*) impaginatore.

makeshift ['meikʃift], *ag.* improvvisato, di fortuna, di ripiego: *a* — *agreement*, un accordo improvvisato; *a* — *dinner*, un pranzo di ripiego || *s.* espediente, accorgimento di fortuna, ripiego: *this is only a* —, questo è solo un ripiego, un espediente.

make-up ['meikʌp], *s.* **1.** composizione; confezione (di abiti); insieme di elementi: *I don't like the* — *of the new football team*, non mi piace la formazione della nuova squadra di calcio **2.** disposizione; temperamento; comportamento: *there was sthg. unusual in his* —, c'era un che d'insolito nel suo comportamento **3.** truccatura, cosmetici (di donne, attori): *I don't like your* —, *it is too showy*, non mi piace il tuo trucco, è troppo vistoso; *this* — *is first-rate*, questi cosmetici sono ottimi **4.** (*tip.*) impaginazione.

make-weight ['meik-weit], *s.* complemento del peso; aggiunta, supplemento (anche *fig.*) || *as a* —, (*fam.*) tanto per far numero.

making ['meikiŋ], *s.* **1.** fattura, lavorazione; confezione: *all my own* —, fatto tutto da me; *so much for the* —, tanto per la fattura, la fabbricazione; *things that go in the* — *of it*, cose occorrenti per farlo **2.** sviluppo, formazione: *doing military service has been the* — *of him*, facendo il servizio militare egli si è maturato **3.** *gener. pl. fig.* l'occorrente, il necessario: *she has not the makings of a good wife*, non ha la stoffa della buona moglie **4.** (*elett.*) apertura (di circuito): — *and breaking*, apertura e chiusura (di circuito).

Malacca [mə'lækə], *no.pr.* (*geog.*) Malacca ☆ — *-cane*, canna da passeggio.

Malachi ['mæləkai], *no.pr.m.* (*Bibbia*) Malachia.

malachite ['mæləkait], *s.* (*min.*) malachite.

maladdress [,mælə'dres], *s.* goffaggine.

maladjusted ['mælə'dʒʌstid], *ag.* disadatto, incapace di inserirsi (in una società, un ambiente).

maladjustment ['mælə'dʒʌstmənt], *s.* **1.** inadattabilità, incapacità di adattamento (a un ambiente, a un lavoro) **2.** assestamento, accomodamento difettoso **3.** (*mec.*) regolazione difettosa.

maladministration ['mæləd,minis'treiʃən], *s.* cattiva amministrazione; malgoverno.

maladroit ['mælə'drɔit], *ag.* goffo, maldestro; incapace.

maladroitly ['mælə'drɔitli], *av.* goffamente, maldestramente.

maladroitness ['mælə'drɔitnis], *s.* goffaggine.

malady ['mælədi], *s.* malattia (anche *fig.*).

Malaga ['mæləgə], *no.pr.* (*geog.*) Malaga || *s.* vino di Malaga.

Malagasy [,mælə'gæsi], *ag.* malgascio; del Madagascar || *s.c.* malgascio, malgascia || *s.* lingua malgascia.

malaise [mæ'leiz], *s.* malessere.

malanders ['mæləndəz], *s.pl.* (*vet.*) malandre.

malapert ['mæləpə:t], *ag.s.* (*arc.*) impertinente, sfacciato.

malaprop ['mæləprɔp], *s.* strafalcione.

malapropism ['mæləprɔpizəm], *s.* papera, strafalcione a ripetizione.

malapropos ['mæl'æprəpou], *ag.* inopportuno || *s.* **1.** sproposito **2.** accidente.

malapropos, *av.* inopportunamente.

malar ['meilə*], *ag.* (*anat.*) malare, zigomatico || *s.* zigomo.

malaria [mə'lɛəriə], *s.* (*patol.*) malaria.

malarial [mə'lɛəriəl], *ag.* malarico.

Malay [mə'lei], *no.pr.* (*geog.*) Malesia || *ag.s.c.* malese || — *Archipelago*, Arcipelago Malese; — *Peninsula*, Penisola Malese.

Malaya [mə'leiə], *no.pr.* (*geog.*) Malacca || — *Federation*, Federazione degli Stati Malesi.

Malayalam [,mæli'ɑ:ləm], *s.* lingua del Malabar.

Malayan [mə'leiən], *ag.s.c.* malese || *s.* lingua malese.

malconformation ['mæl,kɔnfɔ:'meiʃən], *s.* conformazione imperfetta.

malcontent ['mælkən,tent], *ag.s.* malcontento, scontento.

Maldive Islands (the) ['mɔ:ldiv'ailəndz], *no.pr.* (*geog.*) le Isole Maldive.

male [meil], *ag.* maschio; maschile, di sesso maschile: — *child*, figlio maschio; — *choir*, coro maschile || *s.* maschio ☆ — *-fern*, (*bot.*) felce maschia; — *screw*, (*mec.*) vite maschia; — *ward*, corsia degli uomini.

malediction [,mæli'dikʃən], *s.* maledizione.

maledictory [,mæli'diktəri], *ag.* maldicente.

malefaction [,mæli'fækʃən], *s.* (*arc.*) misfatto.

malefactor ['mælifæktə*], *s.* malfattore; criminale.

malefic [mə'lefik], *ag.* malefico; maligno.

malefically [mə'lefikəli], *av.* maleficamente.

malefice ['mælifis], *s.* (*arc.*) maleficio.

maleficence [mə'lefisns], *s.* malvagità.

maleficent [mə'lefisnt], *ag.* malefico; dannoso.

malengin(e) [,mælen'dʒi:n], *s.* (*arc.*) inganno.

malevolence [mə'levələns], *s.* malevolenza; malanimo.

malevolent [mə'levələnt], *ag.* malevolo.

malevolently [mə'levələntli], *av.* in modo malevolo.

malfeasance [mæl'fi:zəns], *s.* **1.** atto criminale **2.** condotta scorretta.

malformation ['mælfɔ:'meiʃən], *s.* conformazione difettosa; (*anat.*) deformità.

malformed [mæl'fɔ:md], *ag.* malformato; deforme.

malic ['mælik], *ag.* (*chim.*) malico.

malice ['mælis], *s.* **1.** malizia; malignità: *out of* —, per malizia, per malignità **2.** livore, astio: *to bear* — *to* (*o towards*), covare astio, rancore per, verso ☆ — *prepense*, (*dir.*) premeditazione.

malicious [mə'liʃəs], *ag.* **1.** maligno, malevolo **2.** (*dir.*) doloso, premeditato.

maliciously [mə'liʃəsli], *av.* **1.** con malevolenza; malignamente **2.** (*dir.*) dolosamente.

maliciousness [mə'liʃəsnis], *s.* malignità, malanimo.

malign [mə'lain], *ag.* malefico, maligno; nocivo: — *disease*, morbo maligno; — *influence*, influsso malefico.

to **malign**, *v.t.* malignare su; diffamare: *I've heard you maligned in every way*, (*fam.*) me ne hanno dette di tutti i colori sul tuo conto.

malignancy [mə'lignənsi], *s.* **1.** malignità, malvagità **2.** (*med.*) indole maligna (di malattia).

malignant [mə'lignənt], *ag.* maligno, malevolo: — *tumour*, tumore maligno.

malignantly [mə'lignəntli], *av.* malignamente, con malevolenza.

maligner [mə'lainə*], *s.c.* calunniatore, calunniatrice; diffamatore, diffamatrice.

malignity [mə'ligniti], *s.* **1.** malignità, malvagità **2.** (*med.*) indole maligna (di malattia).

malignly [mə'lainli], *av.* malignamente.

to **malinger** [mə'lingə*], *v.i.* fingersi ammalato; darsi malato (per farsi esonerare dal lavoro).

malingerer [mə'lingərə*], *s.* chi si finge ammalato (per farsi esonerare dal lavoro); simulatore.

malingery [mə'lingəri], *s.* simulazione di malattia (per farsi esonerare dal lavoro).

malison ['mælizn], *s.* (*arc.*) maledizione.

mall [mɔːl], s. viale, passeggiata ‖ *the Mall*, [mel], ‹the Mall›, passeggiata nel parco di St. James (a Londra).

mallard ['mæləd], s. mallardo, anatra selvatica.

malleability [ˌmæliə'biliti], s. malleabilità.

malleable ['mæliəbl], ag. **1.** (*metal.*) malleabile **2.** *fig.* docile, arrendevole.

malleableness ['mæliəblnis], s. malleabilità.

to **malleate** ['mælieit], v.t. lavorare a colpi di martello; spianare col martello.

malleolar [mə'liːələ*], ag. (*anat.*) malleolare.

malleolus [mə'liːələs], pl. **malleoli** [mə'liːəlai], s. (*anat.*) malleolo.

malleus ['mæliəs], s. (*anat.*) malleo.

mallet ['mælit], s. martello di legno, mazzuolo.

mallow ['mælou], s. (*bot.*) malva.

malm [mɑːm], s. **1.** «malm» (rocce calcaree bianche o rosse) **2.** tipo di mattone.

malmaison [mæl'meizɔːŋ], s. (*bot.*) «malmaison» (varietà di garofano).

malmsey ['mɑːmzi], s. malvasia (vino).

malnutrition ['mælnjuː(ː)'triʃən], s. malnutrizione, alimentazione insufficiente o errata; denutrizione.

malodorous [mæ'loudərəs], ag. puzzolente.

malpractice ['mæl'præktis], s. **1.** azione disonesta; pratica illecita **2.** cura sbagliata.

malt [mɔːlt], s. malto, orzo tallito ☆ — *-house*, distilleria di malto; — *liquor*, liquore di malto, birra.

to **malt**, v.t.i. far germogliare (l'orzo); tallire.

Malta ['mɔːltə], no.pr. (*geog.*) Malta.

Maltese [mɔːl'tiːz], ag. maltese ‖ — *cross*, croce di Malta; — *knight*, cavaliere di Malta ‖ s.c. (*invariato al pl.*) maltese ‖ s. lingua maltese ☆ — *dog*, cane maltese.

maltha ['mælθə], s. malta, bitume viscoso.

Malthusian [mæl'θjuːzjən], ag. maltusiano.

Malthusianism [mæl'θjuːzjənizəm], s. maltusianesimo.

malting ['mɔːltiŋ], s. fabbrica di malto.

maltose ['mɔːltous], s. (*chim.*) maltosio.

to **maltreat** [mæl'triːt], v.t. maltrattare, malmenare.

maltreatment [mæl'triːtmənt], s. maltrattamento.

maltster ['mɔːltstə*], s. chi prepara il malto.

malvaceous [mæl'veiʃəs], ag. (*bot.*) malvaceo.

malversation [ˌmælvə'seiʃən], s. (*dir.*) malversazione.

mama [mə'mɑː], s. mamma.

mambo ['mɑːmbou], s. (*neol.*) mambo (musica, danza).

mamelon ['mæmələn], s. (*geog.*) mammellone.

Mameluke ['mæmiluːk], s. (*st.*) Mammalucco.

Mamie ['meimi], no.pr.f. (*amer.*) dim. di **Mary**.

mamilla [mæ'milə], pl. **mamillae** [mæ'miliː], s. capezzolo.

mamillary ['mæmiləri], ag. mammillare.

mamillate(d) ['mæmileit(id)], ag. fornito di capezzoli.

mamma¹ [mə'mɑː], s. mamma.

mamma² ['mæmə], pl. **mammae** ['mæmiː], s. mammella.

mammal ['mæməl], s. mammifero.

Mammalia [mæ'meiljə], s.pl. i mammiferi.

mammalian [mæ'meiljən], s. e ag. mammifero.

mammaliferous [ˌmæmə'lifərəs], ag. (*geol.*) che contiene resti di mammifero.

mammalogic(al) [ˌmæmə'lɔdʒik(əl)], ag. mammalogico.

mammalogist [mæ'mælədʒist], s. studioso della mammalogia.

mammalogy [mæ'mælədʒi], s. mammalogia.

mammary ['mæməri], ag. mammario.

to **mammer** ['mæmə*], v.t.i. (*poet. arc.*) **1.** esitare; balbettare **2.** vacillare.

mammiferous [mæ'mifərəs], ag. mammifero.

to **mammock**, v.t. fare a pezzi, fare a brandelli.

Mammon ['mæmən], no.pr. (*mit.*) Mammone ‖ **mammon**, s. *fig.* mammona, la ricchezza.

mammonish ['mæməniʃ], ag. **1.** avido di ricchezza **2.** fatto per avidità di denaro.

mammoth ['mæməθ], ag. enorme, mastodontico ‖ s. (*paleont.*) mammut ☆ — *-tree*, (*bot.*) sequoia.

mammy ['mæmi], s. **1.** mammina **2.** (*amer.*) bambinaia negra.

man [mæn], pl. **men** [men], s. **1.** uomo: *God was made* —, Dio si fece uomo; *he is no longer a boy, he is a* —, non è più un ragazzo, è un uomo **2.** persona, essere umano; umanità: — *is mortal*, gli uomini sono mortali; — *is weak*, l'uomo, la carne è debole; *all men must die*, tutti gli uomini devono morire; *he is the very* — *I want*, è proprio la persona che mi occorre ‖ *the* — *in the street, the common* —, l'uomo della strada, l'uomo medio ‖ — *of letters*, uomo di lettere ‖ — *of straw*, uomo di paglia ‖ — *of the world*, uomo di mondo ‖ *men say that*, si dice che ‖ *old* —, vecchio mio: *it is long since I saw you, old* —, è un pezzo che non ci vediamo, mio caro ‖ *quick*, —*!*, su, svelto! ‖ *small* —, piccolo commerciante ‖ *to a* —, tutti: *they answered yes to a* —, risposero tutti di sì ‖ *I am your* —, (*fam.*) sono d'accordo, accetto, faccio proprio al caso tuo **3.** servo, domestico; fattorino; operaio; (*st.*) vassallo: *I shall send my* — *to fetch it*, manderò il mio servo a prenderlo; *the men went on strike*, i lavoratori scioperarono **4.** marito: *they live as* — *and wife*, vivono come marito e moglie **5.** (*calcio*) giocatore **6.** studente; laureato: *he is a Cambridge* —, è uno studente di Cambridge, ha studiato a Cambridge **7.** gener. pl. soldato, soldati, la truppa: *officers, N.C.O.'s and men*, ufficiali, sottufficiali e soldati **8.** pedina ☆ — *-at-arms*, (*st.*) armigero; — *-eater*, cannibale; pescecane, squalo; — *-hour*, ora lavorativa; — *-of-war*, nave da guerra; — *-power*, mano d'opera effettiva, potenziale umano; — *-servant*, servitore ‖ *twelfth* —, giocatore di riserva.

to **man**, pass.p.p. **manned** [mænd], v.t. **1.** (*mil.*) munire (di uomini, di truppa); presidiare; (*mar.*) equipaggiare: *fresh troops were sent to* — *the town*, furono mandate truppe di rincalzo a presidiare la città; *the ship was fully rigged and manned*, la nave era completamente attrezzata ed equipaggiata **2.** far funzionare, mettere in azione: *we had to* — *the pumps*, dovemmo far funzionare le pompe **3.** *to* — *oneself*, farsi coraggio: *you will have to* — *yourself for the occasion*, dovrai farti animo per l'occasione.

manacle ['mænəkl], s. gener. pl. **1.** manetta **2.** *fig.* restrizione, freno.

to **manacle**, v.t. **1.** ammanettare, mettere le manette a **2.** *fig.* trattenere; ostacolare.

manage ['mænidʒ], s. (*arc.*) maneggio; scuola di equitazione.

to **manage**, v.t.i. **1.** dirigere, amministare: *to* — *a theatre, a hotel, a business enterprise*, dirigere un teatro, un albergo, un'impresa commerciale **2.** saper trattare (con riguardo): *he does not know how to* — *his wife*, egli non sa trattare la moglie, non sa prenderla per il suo verso; *you must* — *him*, devi trattarlo con riguardo **3.** maneggiare (uno strumento); manovrare: *to* — *a canoe*, condurre una canoa **4.** domare: *to* — *a horse*, domare un cavallo **5.** cavarsela, venire a capo di; riuscire; fare in modo di: *I am glad he managed to do it*, sono lieto che ci sia riuscito, che se la sia cavata; *if you can* — *to see him*, se puoi fare in modo di vederlo; *perhaps we can* — *with what we have*, può darsi che ce la facciamo con quanto abbiamo; *we'll* — *without it*, ne faremo a meno ‖ *can you* — *another ice-cream?*, (*fam.*) ce la fai a mangiare un altro gelato?, che ne diresti di un altro gelato?

manageability [ˌmænidʒə'biliti], **manageableness** ['mænidʒəblnis], s. **1.** trattabilità; docilità **2.** maneggiabilità.

manageable ['mænidʒəbl], ag. **1.** trattabile; docile **2.** maneggevole (di cosa) **3.** fattibile; agevole.

manageably ['mænidʒəbli], av. **1.** docilmente **2.** maneggevolmente.

management ['mænidʒmənt], s. **1.** direzione, gestione, amministrazione: *bad* (o *ill*), *good, wise* — *of a* *firm*, cattiva, buona, saggia amministrazione di una ditta; *under his — the firm prospered*, sotto la sua direzione la ditta prosperò **2.** *coll.* la direzione, i dirigenti: *the — cannot be held responsible*, la direzione non può essere tenuta responsabile; *the strife between labour and — was very hard*, la contesa fra mano d'opera e dirigenti fu molto aspra **3.** governo, cura: *the — of a horse is exacting*, il governo, la cura di un cavallo è impegnativa **4.** astuzia, abilità; maneggio, intrigo: *all his managements availed him nothing*, tutti i suoi intrighi non gli fruttarono nulla.

manager ['mænidʒə*], *s.* **1.** direttore; gestore, gerente; procuratore; (*dir.*) curatore di fallimento: *general —*, direttore generale **2.** (*teat.*) impresario ‖ *s.c.* organizzatore, organizzatrice; amministratore, amministratrice: *he is quite a —*, è uno che sa amministrare bene; *she is a good —*, è una brava massaia ☆ *assistant- —* (o *vice- —*), vicedirettore; *planning- —*, capo servizio impianti; *production —*, direttore di produzione; *sales —*, direttore commerciale; *works —*, direttore di fabbrica.

manageress ['mænidʒəres], *s.* padrona (d'albergo); direttrice; economa.

managerial [,mænə'dʒiəriəl], *ag.* di direttore, direttivo: *— class*, classe dirigente; *— responsibilities*, responsabilità direttive.

managership ['mænidʒəʃip], *s.* direzione; gerenza; amministrazione.

managing ['mænidʒiŋ], *ag.* dirigente, che amministra ☆ *— director*, consigliere delegato; *— partner*, socio gerente.

manakin ['mænəkin], *s.* (*ornit.*) manachino.

manatee [,mænə'ti:], *s.* (*ittiol.*) lamantino.

Manchester ['mæntʃistə*], *no.pr.* (*geog.*) Manchester ☆ *— School*, (*econ.*) Scuola di Manchester (fautrice del libero scambio).

manchineel [,mæntʃi'ni:l], *s.* (*bot.*) mancinella.

Manchu [mæn'tʃu:], *ag.s.c.* mancese, manciù ‖ *s.* lingua della Manciuria.

Manchuria [mæn'tʃuəriə], *no.pr.* (*geog.*) Manciuria.

maneiple ['mænsipl], *s.* economo (di collegio, ecc.).

Mancunian [mæn'kju:niən], *ag.s.c.* **1.** (abitante) di Manchester **2.** (membro) della Scuola di Manchester.

mandarin[1] ['mændərin], *s.* **1.** mandarino; dignitario cinese **2.** lingua mandarina, cinese letterario ☆ *— duck*, anitra mandarino.

mandarin[2], *s.* **1.** (*bot.*) mandarino **2.** (color) mandarino **3.** liquore di mandarino.

mandatary ['mændətəri], *s.* (*dir.*) mandatario.

mandate ['mændeit], *s.* (*dir. pol. relig.*) mandato; ordine, comando ☆ *— -holder*, mandatario.

to mandate, *v.t.* affidare ad un mandatario: *mandated colonies*, colonie sotto mandato.

mandator [mæn'deitə*], *s.* (*dir.*) mandante.

mandatory ['mændətəri], *ag.* (*dir.*) che contiene un mandato; ingiuntivo: *— States*, Stati mandatari ‖ *s.* (*dir.*) mandatario.

mandible ['mændibl], *s.* (*anat.*) mandibola.

mandibular [mæn'dibjulə*], *ag.* mandibolare.

mandola [mæn'doulə], *s.* (*mus.*) mandola.

mandolin ['mændəlin], **mandoline** [,mændə'li:n], *s.* (*mus.*) mandolino.

mandolinist ['mændəlinist], *s.* mandolinista.

mandragora [mæn'drægərə], **mandrake** ['mændreik], *s.* (*bot.*) mandragora.

mandrel ['mændrəl], *s.* (*metal.*) anima metallica; (*mec.*) mandrino.

mandrill ['mændril], *s.* (*zool.*) mandrillo.

manducable ['mændjukəbl], *ag.* masticabile; mangiabile.

to manducate ['mændjukeit],*v.t.*masticare; mangiare.

manducation [,mændju'keiʃən],*s.*masticazione; manducazione.

mane [mein], *s.* **1.** criniera (di leone, cavallo, ecc.) **2.** *fig.* zazzera.

maned [meind], *ag.* dalla criniera: *brown- —*, dalla bruna criniera, zazzera.

manège [mæ'nei3], *s.* **1.** maneggio; cavallerizza **2.** equitazione.

maneless ['meinlis], *ag.* senza criniera.

manes ['mɑːneiz], *s.pl.* (*mit.*) mani.

(to) **maneuver**, (*amer.*) per (to) **manoeuvre**.

Manfred ['mænfred], *no.pr.m.* Manfredi.

manful ['mænful], *ag.* valoroso, audace; virile.

manfully ['mænfuli], *av.* valorosamente, audacemente; risolutamente; virilmente.

manfulness ['mænfulnis], *s.* valore, ardire.

manganese [,mæŋgə'ni:z], *s.* (*min.*) manganese ☆ *— steel*, acciaio al manganese.

manganic [mæŋ'gænik], *ag.* (*min.*) manganico.

manganite [mæŋgənait], *s.* (*min.*) manganite.

mange [mein3], *s.* rogna, scabbia.

mangel(-wurzel) ['mæŋgl('wə:zl)], *s.* bietola da foraggio.

manger ['mein3ə*], *s.* mangiatoia, greppia ‖ *a dog in the —*, chi impedisce ad altri di godere ciò che è inutile a lui.

mangle[1] ['mæŋgl], *s.* (*artig. ind.*) mangano ☆ *— wheel*, (*mec.*) guida dentata per trasformare un moto circolare in alternativo; (*ind. tessile*) ruota a lanterna.

to mangle[1], *v.t.* (*artig. ind.*) passare al mangano, manganare (panni).

to mangle[2], *v.t.* **1.** lacerare, mutilare **2.** *fig.* storpiare (parole, lingua, citazioni).

mangler[1] ['mæŋglə*], *s.* (*artig. ind.*) **1.** manganatore **2.** (macchina) manganatrice.

mangler[2], *s.* **1.** laceratore **2.** chi storpia (parole, lingua, citazioni).

mangling[1] ['mæŋgliŋ], *s.* (*artig. ind.*) manganatura: *have you done the —?*, hai passato i panni al mangano?

mangling[2], *s.* **1.** lacerazione, mutilazione **2.** storpiatura (di parola, lingua).

mango ['mæŋgou], *pl.* **mango(e)s** ['mæŋgouz], *s.* (*bot.*) mango (albero, frutto).

mangold ['mæŋgəld], *s.* bietola da foraggio.

mangonel ['mæŋgənel], *s.* (*st.*) mangano.

mangostan ['mæŋgoustən], **mangosteen** ['mæŋgousti:n], *s.* (*bot.*) **1.** mangosta **2.** mangostano.

mangrove ['mæŋgrouv], *s.* (*bot.*) mangrovia.

mangy ['mein3i], *ag.* **1.** rognoso, scabbioso: *a — dog*, un cane rognoso **2.** cencioso, miserabile.

to manhandle ['mæn,hændl], *v.t.* **1.** manovrare, muovere a mano (carrelli, ecc.) **2.** (*fam.*) maltrattare, trattare brutalmente.

Manhattan [mæn'hætən], *no.pr.* (*geog.*) Manhattan ‖ **manhattan**, *s.* « manhattan », cocktail di vermut, whisky e amaro.

manhole ['mænhoul], *s.* **1.** botola, bocca di accesso (di tombino, pozzetto, ecc.) **2.** passo d'uomo (di carro armato); (*mar.*) boccaportella ☆ *— lid*, tombino.

manhood ['mænhud], *s.* **1.** umanità, natura umana **2.** virilità, età virile **3.** vigore, coraggio **4.** tutti gli uomini (di una nazione).

mania ['meinjə], *s.* **1.** pazzia **2.** eccessivo entusiasmo; mania.

maniac ['meiniæk], *ag.s.* **1.** matto; pazzo furioso **2.** *fig.* maniaco.

maniacal [mə'naiəkəl], *ag.* maniaco: *— fury*, furia maniaca.

maniacally [mə'naiəkəli], *av.* da maniaco.

manichee ['mæni'ki:], *s.* (*st. relig.*) manicheo.

manicheism ['mæni,ki:izəm], *s.* (*st.relig.*) manicheismo.

manicure ['mænikjuə*], *s.* **1.** cura delle unghie, delle mani **2.** manicure.

to manicure, *v.t.* curare le unghie, le mani.

manicurist ['mænikjuərist], *s.* manicure.

manifest ['mænifest], *ag.* manifesto, evidente, ovvio: *his intentions were —*, le sue intenzioni erano chiare ‖ *s.* (*comm. mar.*) manifesto, nota di carico.

to **manifest**, *v.t.i.* **1.** manifestare, rivelare; mostrare: *he soon manifested himself for the rogue he was*, si rivelò ben presto il furfante che era; *she manifested her regret at my not arriving*, manifestò il suo rincrescimento per il mio mancato arrivo; *to — itself*, manifestarsi **2.** manifestarsi, apparire (di uno spirito) **3.** fare manifestazioni pubbliche: *the Labour Party manifested against the Bill*, il partito laborista fece manifestazioni pubbliche contro il progetto di legge **4.** (*comm. mar.*) far figurare sul bollettino doganale.

manifestation [ˌmænifes'teiʃən], *s.* **1.** manifestazione; dimostrazione: *his silence was a — of cowardice*, il suo silenzio fu una manifestazione di codardia **2.** dimostrazione pubblica; *there was a public — against the Government*, vi fu una dimostrazione pubblica contro il governo ☆ *mass —*, dimostrazione di massa.

manifestative [ˌmæni'festətiv], *ag.* manifestativo.

manifestly ['mænifestli], *av.* chiaramente; ovviamente; manifestamente.

manifestness ['mænifestnis], *s.* evidenza.

manifesto [ˌmæni'festou], *pl.* **manifestos, manifestoes** [ˌmæni'festouz], *s.* proclama; bando.

manifold ['mænifould], *ag.* molteplice; multiforme; numeroso; vario: *under — aspects*, sotto molteplici aspetti.

manifold, *s.* **1.** (*fil.*) molteplicità **2.** (*mec.*) collettore **3.** copia a poligrafo ☆ *— -pressure*, (*aer.*) pressione di alimentazione; *— -writer*, poligrafo.

to **manifold**, *v.t.* poligrafare.

manifoldly ['mænifouldli], *av.* molteplicemente; in modo multiforme; variamente.

manifoldness ['mænifouldnis], *s.* molteplicità; varietà.

manikin ['mænikin], *s.* **1.** omiciattolo, nanerottolo **2.** manichino; modello del corpo umano **3.** (*ornit.*) mànachino.

manilla[1] [mə'nilə], *s.* braccialetto di metallo (usato da tribù africane anche come moneta).

Manilla[2], *no.pr.* (*geog.*) Manilla ‖ **manilla**, *s.* **1.** manila (fibra tessile) **2.** sigaro di Manilla ☆ *— hemp*, canapa di Manilla; *— paper*, carta da imballo.

manioc ['mæniɔk], *s.* **1.** (*bot.*) manioca **2.** (*cuc.*) tapioca.

maniple ['mænipl], *s.* **1.** (*st. romana*) manipolo **2.** (*eccl.*) manipolo (nel paramento liturgico).

to **manipulate** [mə'nipjuleit], *v.t.* **1.** manipolare; maneggiare; trattare con abilità **2.** *fig.* influenzare.

manipulation [məˌnipju'leiʃən], *s.* manipolazione.

manipulative [mə'nipjuleitiv], *ag.* di manipolazione; fatto per mezzo di manipolazione.

manipulator [mə'nipjuleitə*], *s.* **1.** manipolatore **2.** intrigante, imbroglione **3.** (*comm.*) aggiotatore.

manipulatory [mə'nipjulətəri], *V.* **manipulative**.

manitou ['mænitu:], *s.* spirito buono o maligno; cosa avente un potere soprannaturale (nel linguaggio degli indiani d'America).

mankind [mæn'kaind], *nel senso* **2.** ['mænkaind], *s.* **1.** il genere umano, gli uomini; l'umanità **2.** sesso maschile.

manlike ['mænlaik], *ag.* **1.** di, da uomo, maschile; virile (di donna) **2.** antropomorfo (di animali): *the — apes*, scimmie antropoidi.

manliness ['mænlinis], *s.* virilità; mascolinità.

manly ['mænli], *ag.* maschio; virile: *a — voice*, una voce maschia.

manna ['mænə], *s.* manna (anche *fig.*) ☆ *— sugar*, (*farm.*) mannite.

mannequin ['mænikin], *s.c.* indossatore, indossatrice ‖ *s.* manichino ☆ *— parade*, sfilata di modelle.

manner ['mænə*], *s.* **1.** maniera, modo; guisa: *in a queer —*, in modo strano; *do it in this —*, fallo in questa maniera ‖ *by no — of means*, in nessun modo ‖ *in a —*, in un certo modo, fino ad un certo punto ‖ *in a — of speaking*, per così dire ‖ *in like —*, parimenti, similmente ‖ *that boy plays the piano as (if) to the — born*, quel ragazzo suona il pianoforte come se non avesse

fatto altro dalla nascita **2.** contegno, atteggiamento: *her modest —*, il suo contegno modesto; *I don't like his — to his teacher*, non mi piace il suo atteggiamento verso il suo insegnante **3.** (*lett. pitt.*) stile, maniera: *after the — of*, secondo lo stile di; *he has a — of his own*, ha uno stile inconfondibile **4.** *pl.* modi, maniere: *bad manners*, cattive maniere; *he has no manners*, è uno zoticone, non ha educazione; *I'll teach him manners*, gli insegnerò io l'educazione **5.** *pl.* usanze, abitudini: *such were the manners of the time*, tali erano le usanze del tempo **6.** (*arc.*) specie, sorta, genere, tipo: *all — of people were there*, c'era ogni sorta di gente; *what — of man is he?*, che tipo d'uomo è? ☆ *road-manners*, cortesia stradale.

mannered ['mænəd], *ag.* manierato, lezioso, affettato: *— style*, stile ricercato ☆ *bad- —*, maleducato; *kind- —*, gentile; *rough- —*, rude; *well- —*, beneducato.

mannerism ['mænərizəm], *s.* **1.** leziosaggine; manierismo; affettazione **2.** (*fam.*) abitudine; ticchio.

mannerist ['mænərist], *s.* manierista.

manneristic(al) [ˌmænə'ristik(əl)], *ag.* manierato.

manneristically [ˌmænə'ristikəli], *av.* manieratamente.

mannerless ['mænəlis], *ag.* maleducato.

mannerliness ['mænəlinis], *s.* cortesia, educazione.

mannerly ['mænəli], *ag.* cortese, educato.

mannish ['mæniʃ], *ag.* maschile; poco femminile: *she wears a — style of dress*, ella porta vestiti di stile maschile; *what a — way to thread a needle!*, che modo poco femminile di infilare un ago!.

mannishness ['mæniʃnis], *s.* mascolinità.

mannite ['mænait], *s.* (*farm.*) mannite.

manoeuvrability [məˌnu:vrə'biliti], *s.* manovrabilità.

manoeuvre [mə'nu:və*], *s.* (*mil. mar.*) manovra.

to **manoeuvre**, *v.t.i.* **1.** (*mil. mar.*) fare le manovre; far fare le manovre a **2.** *fig.* manovrare; fare in modo di; usare astuzie, stratagemmi: *they'll — him into doing it*, con l'astuzia lo persuaderanno a farlo.

manoeuvrer [mə'nu:vərə*], *s.* **1.** stratega **2.** (*fam.*) intrigante.

manometer [mə'nɔmitə*], *s.* manometro.

manor ['mænə*], *s.* grande proprietà terriera; (*st.*) feudo ☆ *— -house*, maniero; castello; residenza signorile di campagna.

manorial [mə'nɔ:riəl], *ag.* feudale.

mansard ['mænsəd], *s.* mansarda ☆ *— roof*, mansarda (in Scozia).

manse [mæns], *s.* presbiterio (residenza del pastore, specialmente in Scozia).

mansion ['mænʃən], *s.* **1.** castello; palazzo; (*arc.*) dimora ‖ *Mansion House*, Mansion House (residenza ufficiale del sindaco di Londra) **2.** *pl.* casa ad appartamenti ☆ *— -house*, maniero; castello; residenza signorile di campagna.

manslaughter ['mænˌslɔ:tə*], *s.* (*dir.*) omicidio colposo, preterintenzionale ☆ *voluntary —*, omicidio volontario, premeditato.

mansuetude ['mænswitju:d], *s.* (*arc.*) mansuetudine.

mantel ['mæntl], *V.* **mantelpiece, mantelshelf, manteltree**.

mantelet ['mæntlit], *s.* **1.** mantellina **2.** (*mil.*) copertura di protezione (di cannone).

mantelpiece ['mæntlpi:s], *s.* caminetto; mensola; cappa di caminetto ☆ *— clock*, pendola, orologio da caminetto.

mantelshelf ['mæntlʃelf], *s.* mensola di camino, caminetto.

manteltree ['mæntltri:], *s.* architrave di camino, caminetto.

mantic ['mæntik], *ag.* profetico.

mantilla [mæn'tilə], *s.* mantiglia.

mantis ['mæntis], *s.* (*entom.*) mantide ☆ *praying —*, mantide religiosa.

mantissa [mæn'tisə], *s.* **1.** (*mat.*) mantissa **2.** *fig.* aggiunta superflua.

mantle ['mæntl], *s.* **1.** mantello, cappa **2.** *fig.* manto:
a — of ivy, un manto di edera; *a — of weeds covered
the pond*, lo stagno era ricoperto da uno strato di
erbe **3.** reticella Auer (per lampade a gas) **4.** (*edil.*)
manto **5.** mantello (dei molluschi).

to **mantle**, *v.t.i.* **1.** ammantare; avviluppare, coprire, avvolgere: *wall mantled with ivy*, muro tappezzato di edera **2.** spumeggiare (di liquidi) **3.** tingersi, coprirsi (di colore): *her face mantled with blushes*, ella arrossì

mantlet, *V.* **mantelet**.

mantology [mæn'tɔlədʒi], *s.* mantica.

mantrap ['mæn-træp], *s.* trabocchetto, trappola.

Mantua[1] ['mæntjuə], *no.pr.* (*geog.*) Mantova.

mantua[2], *s.* manto ☆ — *-maker*, sarta (per donna).

Mantuan ['mæntjuən], *ag.* mantovano || *the — Swan*,
il Cigno di Mantova (Virgilio) || *s.c.* mantovano, man-
tovana.

manual ['mænjuəl], *ag.* manuale; fatto a mano; azionato a mano: — *fire-engine*, pompa antincendi azio-
nata a mano; — *labour* (o *work*), lavoro manuale ||
s. **1.** manuale (libro) **2.** tastiera d'organo ☆ — *alphabet*,
alfabeto muto; — *exercise*, maneggio delle armi.

Manuel ['mænjuel], *no.pr.m.* Manuele.

manufactory [,mænju'fæktəri], *s.* fabbrica, stabilimento.

manufacture [,mænju'fæktʃə*], *s.* **1.** manifattura;
lavorazione; fabbricazione **2.** manufatto, prodotto
☆ *cotton* —, industria cotoniera; lavorazione del cotone.

to **manufacture**, *v.t.* **1.** fabbricare; confezionare **2.** *fig.* fabbricare, inventare: *to — news*, fabbricare
notizie.

manufacturer [,mænju'fæktʃərə*], *s.* **1.** fabbricante **2.** industriale.

manufacturing [,mænju'fæktʃəriŋ], *ag.* **1.** manifat-
turiero **2.** industriale: — *town*, città industriale || *s.*
fabbricazione; confezione.

manumission [,mænju'miʃən], *s.* (*st.*) manomissione,
affrancamento, emancipazione.

to **manumit** [,mænju'mit], *pass.p.p.* **manumitted**
[,mænju'mitid], *v.t.* (*sl.*) manomettere, affrancare, emancipare.

manure [mə'njuə*], *s.* concime, letame ☆ — *spreader*,
(*agr. mec.*) spandiconcime || *green* —, (*agr.*) sovescio.

to **manure**, *v.t.* concimare, fertilizzare.

manurer [mə'njuərə*], *s.* concimatore.

manurial [mə'njuəriəl], *ag.* concimante.

manuring [mə'njuəriŋ], *s.* concimazione.

manuscript ['mænjuskript], *ag.* manoscritto || *s.*
manoscritto: *to have poems in* —, avere delle poesie
manoscritte.

Manx [mæŋks], *ag.* (*geog.*) dell'isola di Man || *s.c.pl.*
abitanti dell'isola di Man || *s.* lingua dell'isola di Man
☆ — *cat*, gatto senza coda (dell'isola di Man).

Manxman, *pl.* **Manxmen** ['mæŋksmən], **Manx-
woman** ['mæŋks,wumən], *pl.* **Manxwomen** ['mæŋks-
,wimin], *s.* abitante dell'isola di Man.

many ['meni], *comp.* **more** [mɔ:*], *superl.* **most**
[moust], *ag.* **molti, un gran numero di; più di uno:** —
books, molti libri; — *a man*, più di un uomo, molti
uomini; — *times* (o *a time*), molte volte; *ever so* —
opportunities, moltissime occasioni; *how — hours?*,
quante ore?; *not so — children*, non tanti bambini ||
give me as — stamps again, mi dia ancora altrettanti
francobolli; *I have as — books as you*, ho tanti libri
quanti ne hai tu || *pron.* **molti:** — *of them are not in
to-day*, molti di loro sono assenti; *give me as* —, dammene altrettanti; *there was one too* — *of them*, ce n'era
uno di troppo || *s.* molti, molte persone: *a great* —
(o *a good* —), un gran numero, moltissimi || *the* —, la
moltitudine, la folla ☆ — *-coloured*, multicolore; —
-headed, dalle molte teste; — *-sided*, multilaterale; *fig.*
versatile; complesso: *a — -sided activity*, un'attività
molteplice; *a — -sided question*, una questione complessa.

Maori ['mauri], *ag. s.c.* maori (indigeno della Nuova
Zelanda) || *s.* lingua dei maori.

map [mæp], *s.* carta geografica; mappa: — *of the
world*, mappamondo || *to be on, off the* —, (*fam.*) essere,
non essere attuale ☆ — *-maker*, cartografo || *outline* —
(o *skeleton* —), carta muta.

to **map**, *pass.p.p.* **mapped** [mæpt], *v.t.* **1.** disegnare,
tracciare una carta geografica di **2.** *to — out*, progettare: *he did not — out a course of actions*, egli non tracciò un piano d'azione.

maple ['meipl], *s.* (*bot.*) acero ☆ — *-sugar*, zucchero
d'acero; — *syrup*, sciroppo di zucchero d'acero ||
great —, (*bot.*) sicomoro; *rock* — (o *sugar* —), acero
da zucchero.

to **mar** [mɑ:*], *pass.p.p.* **marred** [mɑ:d], *v.t.* **1.** gua-
stare; rovinare || *to make or* — *s.o.*, fare la fortuna di
qlcu. o rovinarlo per sempre **2.** alterare, sfigurare:
his face was marred by smallpox, by a long nose, il suo
volto era sfigurato dal vaiuolo, da un naso troppo lungo.

marabou ['mærəbu:], *s.* (*ornit.*) marabù.

marabout ['mærəbu:t], *s.* **1.** marabutto (santone
musulmano) **2.** tomba di marabutto.

maraschino [,mærəs'ki:nou], *s.* maraschino.

marasmus [mə'ræzməs], *s.* (*patol.*) marasma.

Marathon ['mærəθən], *no.pr.* (*geog. st.*) Maratona
☆ — *race*, (*spor.*) maratona.

to **maraud** [mə'rɔ:d], *v.t.i.* fare scorrerie; predare,
rubare; saccheggiare: *to — (up)on a place, (up)on a
population*, saccheggiare un luogo, predare una popolazione.

marauder [mə'rɔ:də*], *s.* grassatore; predatore.

marauding [mə'rɔ:diŋ], *ag.* di grassatore; predone ||
s. scorreria; razzia; saccheggio.

marble ['mɑ:bl], *s.* **1.** marmo: *a cross of* —, una
croce di marmo; *a heart of* —, *fig.* un cuore di pietra **2.** pallina (di vetro, argilla, ecc.): *to play marbles*,
giocare alle palline **3.** *pl.* statue marmoree ☆ —
-breasted (o — *-hearted*), crudele, insensibile; — *-constant*,
irremovibile; — *-cutter*, marmista; — *-edged*, coi margini marmorizzati (di libro); — *industry*, industria marmifera; — *-paper*, carta marmorizzata; — *-quarry*,
cava di marmo || *clouded* —, marmo variegato; *glass*
—, pallina di vetro.

to **marble**, *v.t.* marmorizzare; marezzare.

marbled ['mɑ:bld], *ag.* marmoreo; ricoperto di
marmo.

marbling ['mɑ:bliŋ], *s.* marmorizzazione.

marc [mɑ:k], *s.* sansa; vinaccia; residuo di frutta
spremuta.

marcasite ['mɑ:kəsait], *s.* (*min.*) marcassite.

Marcellus [mɑ:'seləs], *no.pr.m.* (*st. romana*) Marcello.

marcescent [mɑ:'sesənt], *ag.* marcescente (di piante).

March[1] [mɑ:tʃ], *s.* marzo: *in* —, nel mese di
marzo ☆ — *hare* lepre marzolina; (*fig. fam.*) tipo originale, stravagan,e; — *winds*, venti di marzo.

march[2], *s.* **1.** frontiera, confine **2.** *gener. pl.* (*st.*) regione di confine (in particolare quella tra Inghilterra
e Scozia) **3.** limiti, confini di una tenuta, di una proprietà ☆ — *-stone*, pietra di confine.

to **march**[2], *v.i.* confinare: *to — with another country*,
avere una frontiera comune con un altro paese; *to —
with another estate*, confinare con un'altra proprietà.

march[3], *s.* **1.** (*mil.*) marcia; passo di marcia: *a day's*
—, una giornata di marcia; *on the* —, in marcia **2.** (*mus.*)
marcia **3.** *fig.* progresso, cammino: — *of events*, lo svolgersi degli eventi; — *of progress*, il cammino del progresso; *the — of time*, il corso del tempo ☆ — *orders*,
(*mil.*) ordini di marcia; — *past*, sfilata (di truppe);
corteo; *dead-* — (o *funeral-* —), (*mus.*) marcia funebre;
double —, (*mil.*) passo di carica; *forced* —, (*mil.*) marcia
forzata; *parade* — (o *slow* —), passo di parata; *quick*
—, passo di corsa; *route* —, esercitazione di marcia,
wedding —, (*mus.*) marcia nuziale.

to **march**[3], *v.t.i.* **1.** (anche *mil.*) marciare; far
marciare; mettersi in marcia || *quick* —!, avanti,

marsch! **2.** *fig.* avanzare, progredire, fare passi avanti (di imprese, eventi) **3.** *to* — **along**, avanzare, procedere **4.** *to* — **away**, partire; (fare) allontanare **5.** *to* — **in**, entrare (marciando); presentarsi: *I am sure he will* — *in, one of these days*, sono sicuro che lo vedremo capitare qui, uno di questi giorni **6.** *to* — **off**, mettersi in marcia **7.** *to* — **on**, continuare la propria strada **8.** *to* — **out**, uscire (marciando) **9.** *to* — **past**, passare in rivista **10.** *to* — **up**, avanzare.

marching ['mɑ:tʃiŋ], *ag.* **1.** in marcia, marciante **2.** di marcia: *in* — *order*, (*mil.*) in ordine di marcia ☆ — *orders*, (*mil.*) ordine di partenza; ruolino di marcia.

marchioness ['mɑ:ʃənis], *s.* marchesa.

marchpane ['mɑ:tʃpein], *s.* marzapane.

to **marconi** [mɑ:'kouni], *v.t.i.* (*rar.*) marconigrafare.

marconigram [mɑ:'kounigræm], *s.* marconigramma.

Marcus ['mɑ:kəs], *no.pr.m.* Marco.

Mardi-gras ['mɑ:di'grɑ:], *s.* martedì grasso.

mare [mɛə*], *s.* cavalla, giumenta, puledra: *grey* —, cavalla storna ‖ *a* —*'s nest*, una scoperta deludente ‖ *Shanks's* —, il cavallo di San Francesco ‖ *the grey* — *is the better horse*, è la moglie che porta i pantaloni.

mare's-tail ['mɛəzteil], *s.* **1.** (*zool.*) equiseto, coda di cavallo **2.** cirro (nuvola).

Margaret ['mɑ:gərit], *no.pr.f.* Margherita.

margarine [,mɑ:dʒə'ri:n], *s.* (*cuc.*) margarina.

margarite[1] ['mɑ:gərait], *s.* perla.

margarite[2], *s.* (*min.*) margherita.

margay ['mɑ:gei], *s.* (*zool.*) marguai.

marge[1] [mɑ:dʒ], *s.* (*cuc. fam.*) margarina.

marge[2], **margin** ['mɑ:dʒin], *s.* **1.** margine, orlo, bordo; vivagno **2.** (*comm.*) margine; (*Borsa*) somma versata per coprire eventuali perdite.

to **margin**, *v.t.* **1.** marginare, provvedere di margine **2.** fare note in margine a **3.** (*comm.*) fare un deposito di garanzia per.

marginal ['mɑ:dʒinl], *ag.* marginale; di confine ☆ — *case*, caso limite; — *notes*, note in margine; — *stop*, marginatore (di macchina per scrivere); — *tribes*, tribù di confine.

marginalia [,mɑ:dʒi'neiljə], *s.pl.* note marginali.

marginally ['mɑ:dʒinəli], *av.* in margine.

to **marginate** ['mɑ:dʒineit], *v.t.* fornire di margine.

Margot ['mɑ:gou], *no.pr.f.* dim. di **Margaret**.

margrave ['mɑ:greiv], *s.* (*st.*) margravio.

margravine ['mɑ:grəvi:n], *s.* (*st.*) margravia.

marguerite [,mɑ:gə'ri:t], *s.* (*bot.*) margherita.

Maria [mə'raiə], *no.pr.f.* Maria ‖ *black* —, (*fam.*) (furgone) cellulare.

Marian[1] ['mɛəriən], *ag.* **1.** mariano (della Vergine) **2.** di Maria Tudor; di Maria Stuart ‖ *s.* (*st.*) seguace di Maria Tudor; seguace di Maria Stuart.

Marian[2], *no.pr.f.* Marianna.

Marie ['mɑ:ri], *no.pr.f.* Maria.

marigold ['mærigould], *s.* (*bot.*) calendula.

marijuana [,mæri'wɑ:nə], *s.* marijuana.

marimba [mə'rimbə], *s.* (*mus.*) marimba (strumento di origine africana).

marinade [,mæri'neid], *s.* (*cuc.*) salsa di aceto e spezie.

to **marinade**, *v.t.* marinare.

marine [mə'ri:n], *ag.* **1.** marino; marittimo, del mare **2.** navale; di marina ‖ *s.* **1.** marina ‖ *the Ministry of Marine*, Ministero della Marina **2.** fuciliere di marina **3.** *pl.* fanteria di marina ‖ *tell that to the* (*horse-*)*marines*, raccontalo al gatto **4.** (*pitt.*) marina ☆ — *insurance*, assicurazione marittima; — *officer*, ufficiale di marina; — *stores*, negozio di forniture per navi; rigatteria ‖ *merchant* — (o *mercantile* —), marina mercantile.

mariner ['mærinə*], *s.* (*arc.*) marinaio; navigatore ☆ —*'s card*, rosa dei venti; — *'s compass*, bussola ‖ *master* —, capitano di una nave mercantile.

Marinism [mə'ri:nizəm], *s.* (*st. lett.*) marinismo.

Marinist [mə'ri:nist], *s.* (*st. lett.*) marinista.

Mariolatry [,mɛəri'olətri], *s.* (*teol.*) mariolatria.

marionette [,mæriə'net], *s.* marionetta.

marish ['mæriʃ], *ag.* paludoso.

marital [mə'raitl], *ag.* maritale; coniugale.

maritally [mə'raitəli], *av.* maritalmente.

maritime ['mæritaim], *ag.* marittimo, marino; di mare ☆ — *law*, diritto marittimo.

Marius ['mɛəriəs], *no.pr.m.* Mario.

marjoram ['mɑ:dʒərəm], *s.* (*bot.*) maggiorana.

Marjorie, Marjory ['mɑ:dʒəri], *no.pr.f.* dim. di **Margaret**.

mark[1] [mɑ:k], *s.* **1.** segno, traccia, indicazione; impronta; marchio: — *of age*, segno, indice di vecchiaia; — *of esteem, of love*, segno, pegno di stima, di amore; *the* — *of a foot*, l'impronta di un piede; *who made these dirty marks on my book?*, chi ha fatto questi segnacci sul libro?; *to bear marks of suffering on one's face*, portare i segni della sofferenza sul volto; *to leave one's* —, lasciare traccia di sè ‖ *I don't feel up to the* —, non mi sento bene ‖ (*God*) *save the* —!, con licenza parlando, mi si perdoni l'espressione! ‖ *to be up to the* —, *fig.* essere all'altezza (di un compito) ‖ *to make one's* —, farsi strada, acquistare fama **2.** bersaglio (anche *fig.*): *to be near, over, under, wide of the* —, aver colpito vicino, sopra, sotto, lontano dal bersaglio; *to hit the* —, far centro; *to miss the* —, mancare il bersaglio **3.** segno di interpunzione **4.** (*scuola*) voto; valutazione: *to have bad, good marks*, avere voti brutti, belli **5.** marchio, marca, etichetta **6.** (*spor.*) segnale, linea di partenza; *on the* —!, pronti!; *to be off the* —, essere partito (di podista, corridore, ecc.) **7.** *fig.* importanza, distinzione: *man of* —, persona notevole, importante; *person, thing of great, of little* —, persona, cosa di grande, di poca importanza **8.** segno particolare, caratteristica fisica: *that horse has a white* — *on its head*, quel cavallo ha una macchia bianca sulla testa **9.** (*st.*) marca (territorio posseduto dalla comunità di un villaggio presso gli antichi Germani) **10.** croce (firma degli analfabeti) ☆ *draught* —, marca di pescaggio; *examination* —, voto d'esame; *exclamation-* —, punto esclamativo; *finger-* —, ditata; *hall-* —, marchio (a garanzia di metalli pregiati); *high-water-* —, livello di piena; *interrogation* (o *question*) —, punto interrogativo; *press* —, collocazione (di un libro in biblioteca); *quotation marks*, virgolette; *tide-* —, linea di alta marea.

to **mark**[1], *v.t.* **1.** marcare, segnare; contrassegnare; classificare; indicare (prezzi): *I am afraid he plays with marked cards*, temo che giuochi con carte segnate; *she marked my handkerchiefs*, mi ha messo la cifra sui fazzoletti; *these eggs are marked " fresh " and " new-laid " at different prices*, quelle uova sono segnate « fresche » e « da bere » a prezzi diversi; *to* — (*points in*) *a game*, marcare i punti in un giuoco ‖ *to* — *the rhythm*, battere il tempo ‖ *to* — *time*, segnare il passo (anche *fig.*); (*mil.*) batter la fiacca **2.** dare i voti a: *I have some exercises to* —, devo correggere e dare il voto ad alcuni compiti **3.** scegliere, designare, destinare: *he will* — *you for the job*, sceglierà, indicherà te per quel lavoro; *that horse is marked for slaughtering*, quel cavallo è destinato al macello **4.** mostrare; rivelare; manifestare: *he used to* — *his approval openly*, era solito manifestare la sua approvazione apertamente **5.** osservare, notare, fare attenzione a: — *my words!*, bada alle mie parole!; — *where the bomb fell*, osserva il punto dove è caduta la bomba **6.** *to* — **down**, svalorizzare (merci); prendere nota di: — *that down*, prendi nota di questo **7.** *to* — **off**, **out**, delimitare, separare; distinguere (anche *fig.*): *his dress marked him off* (*o out*) *from the rest*, i suoi abiti lo distinguevano dagli altri; *we had to* — *off* (*o out*) *a tennis-court*, dovemmo tracciare i limiti di un campo di tennis.

mark[2], *s.* marco (moneta tedesca).

Mark[3], *no.pr.m.* Marco.

marked [mɑ:kt], *ag*. **1.** segnato, contrassegnato ‖ *he is a — man*, è un individuo dal destino segnato **2.** marcato, notevole: — *difference*, differenza marcata; *to have a very — foreign accent*, avere un forte accento straniero.

markedly [ˈmɑːkidli], *av*. segnatamente.

marker [ˈmɑːkə*], *s*. **1.** chi segna i punti fatti (al giuoco) **2.** segnalibro **3.** (*amer*.) lapide commemorativa.

market [ˈmɑːkit], *s*. **1.** mercato; luogo di vendita: *the cook went to — to buy food for the family*, la cuoca andò al mercato a far la spesa per la famiglia; *the next — is on the 15th*, il prossimo giorno di mercato sarà il 15 ‖ *to bring one's eggs to the wrong —*, *fig*. picchiare alla porta sbagliata **2.** (*comm*.) mercato; compravendita: *his house is in the —*, la sua casa è in vendita; *to be in the — for sthg.*, essere sul mercato per fare acquisti; *to be put into* (o *on*) *the —*, essere messo in vendita ‖ *he makes a — of his honour*, vende il suo onore, fa traffico del suo onore ‖ *to be a good — value*, essere un buon affare ☆ — *-day*, giorno di mercato; — *-garden*, orto (per la vendita al mercato); — *-gardener*, ortolano; — *-place* (o — *-square*), piazza del mercato; — *-price*, prezzo corrente; — *-town*, città sede di mercato ‖ *black-* —, borsa nera; *brisk-* —, (*comm*.) mercato attivo; *home* —, *overseas* —, mercato interno, d'oltremare; *labour* —, mercato della mano d'opera; *money -* —, (*econ*.) borsa; *open-* —, mercato libero; *spot-* —, (*comm*.) mercato del pronto.

to market, *v.t.i.* **1.** comperare, vendere al mercato **2.** introdurre, lanciare sul mercato.

marketable [ˈmɑːkitəbl], *ag*. vendibile; smerciabile; corrente.

marketer [ˈmɑːkitə*], *s.c.* chi porta, vende merci al mercato.

marketing [ˈmɑːkitiŋ], *s*. **1.** compra-vendita ‖ *Marketing Board*, ufficio controllo vendite **2.** (*econ*.) «marketing» (tecnica delle ricerche di mercato) ☆ *free* —, libera trattazione.

marking [ˈmɑːkiŋ], *ag*. che marca, che segna ‖ *s. gener. pl*. macchia, segno; traccia ☆ — *-ink*, inchiostro indelebile.

marksman, *pl*. **marksmen** [ˈmɑːksmən], *s*. **1.** tiratore scelto **2.** analfabeta (che firma con la croce).

marksmanship [ˈmɑːksmənʃip], *s*. abilità nel, precisione di tiro.

marl [mɑːl], *s*. (*geol*.) marga, marna, terra grassa ☆ — *-pit*, cava di marna.

to marl, *v.t.* marnare, concimare con marna.

marline [ˈmɑːlin], *s*. (*mar*.) merlino.

marm [mɑːm], *s*. (*amer.contr.* di *madam*) maestra di scuola.

marmalade [ˈmɑːməleid], *s*. marmellata (d'arance, di limoni).

marmite [ˈmɑːmait], *s*. estratto di lievito di birra.

marmoreal [mɑːˈmɔːriəl], *ag*. marmoreo.

marmoset [ˈmɑːmozet], *s*. (*zool*.) uistiti, apale.

marmot [ˈmɑːmət], *s*. (*zool*.) marmotta.

Maronite [ˈmærənait], *s.c.* (*st. relig*.) maronita.

maroon[1] [məˈruːn], *ag*. marrone rossastro ‖ *s*. **1.** il colore castano **2.** castagnola (sorta di fuoco d'artificio).

maroon[2], *s.c.* **1.** negro, negra delle Indie Occidentali **2.** chi è abbandonato in luogo deserto.

to maroon[2], *v.t.i.* **1.** abbandonare qlcu. in luogo deserto **2.** oziare **3.** (*amer*.) fare un campeggio.

marplot [ˈmɑː-plɔt], *s*. chi intromettendosi impedisce un progetto.

marque [mɑːk], *s.*: *letters of* —, (*st*.) permesso di armare navi per predare navi mercantili nemiche.

marquee [mɑːˈkiː], *s*. grande tenda.

Marquesas Islands (the) [mɑːˈkeisæsˈailəndz], *no.pr. pl*. (*geog*.) Isole Marchesi.

marquess [ˈmɑːkwis], *s*. marchese.

marquetry [ˈmɑːkitri], *s*. intarsio.

marquis [ˈmɑːkwis], *s*. marchese.

marquisate [ˈmɑːkwizit], *s*. marchesato.

marquise [mɑːˈkiːz], *s*. **1.** marchesa, consorte di marchese (non inglese) **2.** «marquise» (montatura allungata di anello, gemma).

marriage [ˈmæridʒ], *s*. **1.** matrimonio; nozze: *to give, to take in —*, dare, prendere in moglie **2.** *fig*. legame, unione, fusione: *the — of true minds*, l'unione di animi sinceri; — *of words and music*, la fusione di parole e musica ☆ — *articles*, contratto di matrimonio; — *-licence*, dispensa di matrimonio; — *-lines*, certificato di matrimonio; — *service*, cerimonia nuziale; — *tie*, vincolo coniugale.

marriageable [ˈmæridʒəbl], *ag*. **1.** in età da marito, da moglie **2.** adatto al matrimonio.

married [ˈmærid], *ag*. **1.** sposato, ammogliato: — *man*, uomo ammogliato; — *woman*, donna sposata; *to get —*, sposarsi **2.** coniugale, inerente al matrimonio ☆ *a — couple*, una coppia di coniugi; — *life*, vita coniugale; — *love*, amore coniugale.

marrow[1] [ˈmærou], *s*. **1.** midollo ‖ *to be frozen to the —*, essere gelati fino alle ossa **2.** *fig*. essenza; quintessenza **3.** (*vegetable*) —, zucca ‖ *the pith and — of a statement*, la quintessenza di una dichiarazione ☆ — *-bone*, osso con midollo; — *-squash*, (*amer*.) zucchina ‖ *spinal* —, midollo spinale.

marrow[2], *s*. (*dial*.) **1.** compagno; consorte **2.** simile, pari.

marrowfat [ˈmæroufæt], *s*. specie pregiata di pisello.

marrowless [ˈmæroulis], *ag*. senza midollo.

marrowy [ˈmæroui], *ag*. midolloso.

to marry[1] [ˈmæri], *pass.p.p.* **married** [ˈmærid], *v.t.i.* **1.** sposare, sposarsi; ammogliarsi, maritarsi: *he married a beautiful girl*, egli sposò una bella ragazza; *she didn't — until she was thirty*, ella non si sposò fino ai trent'anni; *to — again*, risposarsi ‖ *to — into a family*, imparentarsi con una famiglia **2.** accasare: *she has married off all her daughters*, ella ha accasato tutte le sue figlie **3.** unire in matrimonio: *a priest married them*, un sacerdote li sposò.

marry[2], *inter*. (*arc*.) diamine!.

Mars [mɑːz], *no.pr.m.* (*mit*.) Marte ‖ *no.pr.* (*astr*.) Marte.

Marsala [mɑːˈsɑːlə], *no.pr.* (*geog*.) Marsala ‖ *s*. vino marsala.

Marseillaise [ˌmɑːsəˈleiz], *s*. marsigliese (inno).

Marseilles [mɑːˈseilz], *no.pr.* (*geog*.) Marsiglia.

marsh [mɑːʃ], *s*. palude, acquitrino ☆ — *-fever*, (*patol*.) malaria; — *-gas*, gas metano; — *-mallow*, (*bot*.) altea, malva; caramella gelatinosa; — *-marigold*, (*bot*.) fiorrancio delle paludi.

marshal [ˈmɑːʃəl], *s*. **1.** (*mil*.) maresciallo ‖ *Air -Marshal*, maresciallo dell'aria; *Earl Marshal*, gran maresciallo; *Field-Marshal*, feldmaresciallo **2.** maestro di cerimonie, cerimoniere **3.** (*amer*.) maresciallo (di polizia, dei pompieri).

to marshal, *pass.p.p.* **marshalled** [ˈmɑːʃəld], *v.t.i.* **1.** assegnare i posti a; disporre in ordine: *to — facts*, disporre i fatti in buon ordine; *to — two coats of arms in one shield*, (*arald*.) disporre due blasoni su uno scudo **2.** (*mil*.) schierare, schierarsi; ordinare: *they marshalled in front of him*, si schierarono di fronte a lui **3.** condurre (una persona) cerimoniosamente: *to — s.o. into a room*, introdurre cerimoniosamente qlcu. in una stanza.

marshalling [ˈmɑːʃəliŋ], *s*. **1.** schieramento; ordinamento **2.** (*ferr*.) smistamento ☆ — *yard*, stazione di smistamento.

marshy [ˈmɑːʃi], *ag*. paludoso, acquitrinoso.

marsupial [mɑːˈsjuːpjəl], *ag.s.* (*zool*.) marsupiale.

marsupium [mɑːˈsjuːpjəm], *s*. marsupio.

mart[1] [mɑːt], *s*. **1.** (*poet*.) mercato; fiera; emporio; sala di vendita all'incanto **2.** centro commerciale.

mart[2], *s*. (*zool*.) martora.

martel [ˈmɑːtel], *s*. (*arc*.) martello da guerra.

martello [mɑːˈtelou], *s*. (*st*.) torre (per difesa costiera) ☆ — *towers*, torri martello (in Corsica, Sardegna).

marten [ˈmɑːtin], *s*. (*zool*.) martora.

Martha ['mɑːθə], *no.pr.f.* Marta.

martial ['mɑːʃəl], *ag.* 1. marziale, guerresco 2. (*astr. mit.*) di Marte 3. (*chim.*) marziale, ferruginoso ☆ — *law*, legge marziale ‖ *court-* —, corte marziale.

martially ['mɑːʃəli], *av.* in modo marziale.

Martian ['mɑːʃjən], *ag.* di Marte ‖ *s.* marziano.

Martin ['mɑːtin], *no.pr.m.* Martino ‖ *St.* —*'s Summer*, l'estate di S. Martino.

martin, *s.* (*house*) —, (*ornit.*) rondicchio.

martinet[1] [,mɑːti'net], *s.* (*mil.*) ufficiale rigoroso nella disciplina ‖ *he, she is a* —*!*, egli, ella è proprio un caporale!.

martinet[2], *s.* (*st.*) balista.

martingale ['mɑːtiŋgeil], *s.* 1. martingala (per cavallo) 2. (*mar.*) controstraglio del bastone di fiocco.

Martini[1] [mɑː'tiːni], *s.* Martini (aperitivo).

Martini[2], *s.* fucile del tipo « Martini-Henry ».

Martinique [,mɑːti'niːk], *no.pr.* (*geog.*) Martinica.

Martinmas ['mɑːtinməs], *s.* festa di San Martino.

martlet ['mɑːtlit], *s.* 1. (*ornit.*) rondone 2. (*arald.*) merlotto.

martyr ['mɑːtə*], *s.* martire, vittima (anche *fig.*): *to be a* — *to rheumatism*, essere vittima dei reumatismi; *to make a* — *of oneself*, fare la vittima, atteggiarsi a martire; *to make a* — *of s.o.*, presentare qlcu. con l'aureola del martirio.

to **martyr**, *v.t.* martoriare, martirizzare; condannare al martirio.

martyrdom ['mɑːtədəm], *s.* martirio.

to **martyrize** ['mɑːtəraiz], *v.t.i.* martirizzare; tormentare; (*rar.*) rendersi martire: *she will* — *herself over that*, si tormenterà senza fine per quello.

martyrologie(al) [,mɑːtirə'lɔdʒik(əl)], *ag.* di martirologio.

martyrologist [,mɑːti'rɔlədʒist], *s.* autore di martirologi.

martirology [,mɑːti'rɔlədʒi], *s.* martirologio.

martyry ['mɑːtiri], *s.* (*arch.*) martirio (tempio dedicato a un martire).

marvel ['mɑːvəl], *s.* 1. meraviglia; cosa, esempio meraviglioso: *what a* —*!*, che meraviglia! 2. (*arc.*) stupore.

to **marvel**, *pass.p.p.* **marvelled** ['mɑːvəld], *v.i.* meravigliarsi, stupirsi, essere sorpresi: *they marvelled at his courage*, si stupirono del suo coraggio; *to* — *that, how, why*, meravigliarsi che, come, perchè.

marvellous ['mɑːviləs], *ag.* meraviglioso; incredibile; stupefacente ‖ *s.* prodigio; cosa meravigliosa, incredibile: *the* — *is that he is coming back*, la cosa più stupefacente è che ritorna; *he doesn't believe in the* —, non crede ai prodigi.

marvellously ['mɑːviləsli], *av.* meravigliosamente.

marvellousness ['mɑːviləsnis], *s.* natura meravigliosa (di un avvenimento, una guarigione, ecc.).

Marxian ['mɑːksjən], *ag.s.c.* (*pol.*) marxista.

Marxism ['mɑːksizəm], *s.* (*pol.*) marxismo.

Marxist ['mɑːksist], *ag.s.c.* (*pol.*) marxista.

Mary ['mɛəri], *no.pr.f.* Maria.

marzipan [,mɑːzi'pæn], *s.* marzapane.

mascara [mæs'kɑːrə], *s.* cosmetico per ciglia.

mascot ['mæskət], *s.c.* mascotte, portafortuna.

masculine ['mɑːskjulin], *ag.* 1. (*gram.*) di genere maschile 2. mascolino, maschile; *fig.* maschio, virile ‖ *s.* 1. parola di genere [maschile 2. (*gram.*) il genere maschile.

masculinely ['mɑːskjulinli], *av.* maschilmente, virilmente.

masculineness ['mæskjulinnis], **masculinity** [,mæskju'liniti], *s.* mascolinità.

mash[1] [mæʃ], *s.* 1. miscuglio, mistura (di acqua e malto per fare birra) 2. beverone (per cavalli) 3. (*cuc.*) purè passato 4. miscuglio, mescolanza.

to **mash**[1] *v.t.* 1. mescolare, mischiare (specialmente acqua e malto) 2. schiacciare, impastare 3. (*iron.*) guastare, sciupare.

mash[2] *s.* (*sl.*) persona ammirata, amata.

to **mash**[2], *v.t.* (*sl.*) suscitare ammirazione in; far innamorare: *to be mashed on*, essere innamorato di.

mashed [mæʃt], *ag.* 1. mescolato, mischiato 2. (*cuc.*) schiacciato: — *potatoes*, purè di patate.

masher[1] ['mæʃə*], *s.* (*cuc.*) utensile per schiacciare ☆ *potato* —, schiacciapatate.

masher[2], *s.* (*sl.*) damerino, rubacuori.

mashie ['mæʃi], *s.* tipo di mazza da golf.

mask [mɑːsk], *s.* 1. maschera ‖ *with the* — *off*, a viso scoperto 2. schermo di protezione del viso 3. *fig.* maschera, finzione; espressione del viso di un attore: *tragic* —, maschera tragica; *under the* — *of friendship*, sotto la maschera dell'amicizia 4. (*arch.*) mascherone 5. (*foto.*) mascherino ☆ *carnival-* —, maschera carnevalesca; *death-* —, maschera mortuaria; *gas-* —, maschera antigas.

to **mask**, *v.t.* 1. mascherare: *to* — *one's face*, mascherarsi 2. *fig.* mascherare, nascondere, celare: *to* — *one's feelings*, celare i propri sentimenti 3. (*foto.*) mettere un mascherino a 4. (*mil.*) coprire, mascherare: *to* — *one's own batteries*, coprire le proprie batterie.

masked [mɑːskt], *ag.* 1. mascherato 2. *fig.* dissimulato: *his hatred was* — *under a veil of friendliness*, il suo odio era mascherato sotto una parvenza di amicizia ☆ — *-ball*, ballo mascherato.

masker ['mɑːskə*], *s.* 1. (*teat.*) maschera 2. chi è mascherato.

masochism ['mæzəkizəm], *s.* (*patol.*) masochismo.

mason ['meisn], *s.* 1. muratore 2. franco muratore; massone.

to **mason**, *v.t.* costruire, rinforzare con mattoni.

masonic [mə'sɔnik], *ag.* massonico; relativo alla massoneria.

masonry ['meisnri], *s.* 1. arte, professione del muratore 2. costruzione in muratura 3. (*st.*) massoneria.

masque [mɑːsk], *s.* 1. rappresentazione allegorica, mitologica (muta in origine, in seguito con dialogo e musica) 2. testo per « masque ».

masquerade [,mæskə'reid], *s.* 1. mascherata; ballo mascherato 2. finzione; montatura.

to **masquerade**, *v.i.* 1. mascherarsi 2. *fig.* presentarsi sotto mentite spoglie: *he masqueraded as a doctor*, si fece passare per medico.

masquerader [,mæskə'reidə*], *s.c.* chi prende parte ad una mascherata.

mass[1] [mæs], *s.* messa: — *for a person's soul*, messa in suffragio di qlcu.; *to go to* —, andare a messa ☆ — *-book*, libro da messa, messale ‖ *high* —, messa solenne; *low* —, messa bassa.

mass[2], *s.* 1. massa; gran numero; quantità: *there were masses of roses in their garden*, nel loro giardino c'erano rose a profusione 2. folla, massa; maggioranza: *the* (*great*) — *of*, la maggioranza di; *the* — *must be educated*, bisogna educare la massa 3. (*fis. chim.*) massa ☆ — *attack*, (*mil.*) attacco in massa; — *-meeting*, adunata popolare, comizio; — *number*, (*fis.*) numero di massa; — *observation*, (*sociologia*) studio dei fenomeni di massa; — *-production*, (*ind.*) produzione in serie ‖ *isotopic* —, (*fis.*) massa isotopica; *rest* —, (*fis.*) massa di riposo.

to **mass**[2], *v.t.i.* ammassare, ammassarsi: *troops were massed along the river*, furono ammassate truppe lungo il fiume.

massacre ['mæsəkə*], *s.* massacro, strage.

to **massacre**, *v.t.* massacrare, trucidare.

massage ['mæsɑːʒ], *s.* massaggio.

to **massage**, *v.t.* massaggiare.

masseter [mæ'siːtə*], *s.* (*anat.*) massetere.

masseur [mæ'sə:*], *s.* massaggiatore.

masseuse [mæ'sə:z], *s.* massaggiatrice.

massif ['mæsiːf], *s.* massiccio (montagnoso).

massiness ['mæsinis], *s.* solidità; pesantezza.

massive ['mæsiv], *ag.* **1.** massiccio; forte; solido: *a — building*, una costruzione massiccia **2.** (*farm.*) massivo: *in — doses*, in dosi massive **3.** *fig.* potente; solido: *a — mind*, un'intelligenza potente **4.** di massa, in massa: *a — protest*, una protesta in massa **5.** (*geol.*) compatto, non stratificato, omogeneo ☆ — *yold*, oro massiccio.

massively ['mæsivli], *av.* in forma compatta, massiccia.

massiveness ['mæsivnis], *s.* compattezza; solidità.

massy ['mæsi], *ag.* compatto; massiccio; imponente.

mast¹ [mɑ:st], *s.* **1.** (*mar.*) albero: *to be at the —*, essere di guardia in coffa; *to send to —*, mandare in coffa ‖ *to sail before the —*, essere marinaio semplice **2.** (*aer.*) antenna radio ☆ — *-coat*, (*mar.*) cappa della mastra d'albero; — *-head*, (*mar.*) colombiere, testa d'albero; — *heel*, (*mar.*) piede d'albero; — *hole*, (*mar.*) mastra d'albero; — *rigging*, (*mar.*) attrezzatura dell'albero ‖ *lower —*, (*mar.*) albero maggiore; *mizzen- —*, albero di mezzana; *topgallant —*, (*mar.*) alberetto.

to mast¹, *v.t.* (*mar.*) alberare.

mast², *s.* ghianda, bacca (specialmente usata come foraggio).

masted ['mɑ:stid], *ag.* (*mar.*) alberato ☆ *three- —*, a tre alberi.

master¹ ['mɑ:stə*], *s.* **1.** padrone; signore; proprietario: *where is your —?*, dov'è il signore? ‖ *to be one's own —*, essere indipendente; non dover nulla a nessuno ‖ *to be, to remain — of the field*, essere, restare padrone del campo (anche *fig.*) **2.** padroncino, signorino (prefisso servile, di cortesia) ‖ *Master John*, il signorino John **3.** maestro (chi eccelle in particolari qualità): *he is a — of irony*, è maestro nell'ironia **4.** grande artista, pittore ‖ *the old masters*, i grandi pittori (dal XIII al XVII secolo) **5.** maestro; artigiano; esperto **6.** maestro; insegnante, professore (non universitario); direttore di collegio universitario ‖ *the Master*, il Cristo, il Maestro **7.** (incaricato): *Master of Ceremonies*, maestro di cerimonia; — *of ceremonies*, (*amer. tv.*) presentatore; — *of hounds*, gran maestro di caccia; capocaccia; *Master of the Rolls*, magistrato britannico della Corte d'Appello (responsabile degli Archivi dell'Alta Corte di Giustizia) **8.** (*mar.*) capitano (di nave mercantile) **9.** (titolo accademico superiore a « Bachelor »): *Master of Arts*, laureato in lettere ☆ — *-at-arms*, (*mar.*) commissario di bordo; — *builder*, capomastro; — *catalogue*, (*comm.*) catalogo generale; — *cylinder*, (*mec.*) cilindro principale; — *-hand*, mano maestra; — *-key*, chiave maestra, chiave comune; — *-mechanic*, capo meccanico; — *-rod*, (*mec.*) biella madre; — *switch*, (*elett.*) interruttore principale, generale; — *-wheel*, (*mec.*) ruota di comando; — *-wort*, (*bot.*) angelica ‖ *fencing —*, maestro di scherma; *music —*, maestro di musica.

to master¹, *v.t.* **1.** approfondire (studi, ecc.); conoscere a fondo: *to — a foreign language*, conoscere alla perfezione una lingua straniera **2.** eseguire alla perfezione **3.** avere la meglio, sopraffare; vincere, vincersi; sottomettere: *he could not — himself*, non potè dominarsi; *she is mastered by her husband*, è dominata da suo marito; *to — one's temper*, dominare la propria ira.

master², *s.* nave a più alberi.

masterdom ['mɑ:stədəm], *s.* padronanza; supremazia.

masterful ['mɑ:stəful], *ag.* **1.** autoritario, imperioso **2.** abile, destro.

masterfully ['mɑ:stəfuli], *av.* imperiosamente.

masterfulness ['mɑ:stəfulnis], *s.* imperiosità; autorità dominante.

masterhood ['mɑ:stəhud], *s.* padronanza; autorità.

masterless ['mɑ:stəlis], *ag.* **1.** senza padrone **2.** incontrollato.

masterliness ['mɑ:stəlinis], *s.* maestria; abilità da maestro.

masterly ['mɑ:stəli], *ag.* magistrale; da maestro: *in a — manner*, magistralmente.

masterpiece ['mɑ:stəpi:s], *s.* capolavoro.

mastership ['mɑ:stəʃip], *s.* **1.** valentia; abilità; maestria **2.** autorità; superiorità; dominio.

masterstroke ['mɑ:stə-strouk], *s.* colpo magistrale.

mastery ['mɑ:stəri], *s.* **1.** maestria; conoscenza profonda; padronanza **2.** supremazia, signoria.

mastic ['mæstik], *s.* **1.** (*bot.*) lentischio **2.** mastice.

masticability [,mæstikə'biliti], *s.* masticabilità.

to masticate ['mæstikeit], *v.t.* **1.** masticare **2.** (*ind.*) masticare, plastificare.

mastication [,mæsti'keiʃən], *s.* masticazione (anche *ind.*).

masticator ['mæstikeitə*], *s.* **1.** masticatore **2.** (*ind.*) macchina masticatrice **3.** (*ind.*) operaio addetto alla masticatrice.

masticatory ['mæstikətəri], *ag.* masticatorio.

mastiff ['mæstif], *s.* mastino.

mastitis [mæs'taitis], *s.* (*patol.*) mastite.

mastodon ['mæstədɔn], *s.* (*paleont.*) mastodonte.

mastodontic [,mæstə'dɔntik], *ag.* mastodontico.

mastoid ['mæstɔid], *ag.* mastoideo ‖ *s.* **1.** (*anat.*) mastoide **2.** (*fam. patol.*) mastoidite.

to masturbate ['mæstəbeit], *v.i.* (*patol.*) masturbarsi.

masturbation [,mæstə'beiʃən], *s.* (*patol.*) masturbazione.

mat¹ [mæt], *s.* **1.** stuoia, stoino ‖ *on the —*, (*sl.*) nei guai **2.** sottopiatto, sottovaso **3.** (*mar.*) paglietto ☆ *door- —*, zerbino.

to mat¹, *pass.p.p.* **matted** ['mætid], *v.t.i.* **1.** intrecciare **2.** coprire con stuoie **3.** arruffare, arruffarsi.

mat², *ag.* opaco ‖ *s.* **1.** filetto d'oro matto all'interno di una cornice **2.** superficie di metallo non brunito **3.** (*tip.*) matrice ☆ — *paper*, carta patinata opaca.

to mat², *v.t.* rendere opaca (una superficie di metallo o di vetro); smerigliare.

matador ['mætədə:*], *s.* matador.

match¹ [mætʃ], *s.* **1.** avversario, competitore: *he has found more than his —*, ha trovato un rivale che gli terrà testa; *he is no — for him*, è assai più debole di lui, non può competere con lui; *to find (o to meet) one's —*, incontrare un degno avversario **2.** (*spor.*) gara; partita; incontro; lotta **3.** (l')uguale, (il) simile; (il) riscontro: *I cannot find the — to this vase*, non riesco a trovare il compagno di questo vaso **4.** matrimonio; partito: *a good —*, un buon partito; *to make a — of it*, combinare un matrimonio ☆ — *-maker*, paraninfo, paraninfa ‖ *boxing —*, incontro di pugilato; *foot-ball —*, partita di calcio; *return —*, partita di calcio di ritorno.

to match¹, *v.t.i.* **1.** maritare, dare in matrimonio **2.** accoppiarsi (di animali); accoppiare, appaiare **3.** (*arc.*) rivaleggiare; lottare; misurarsi: *no one can — with them*, nessuno può rivaleggiare con loro **4.** opporre: *to — one person against another*, opporre una persona a un'altra **5.** accordarsi, uniformarsi, armonizzare: *these colours — well*, questi colori si accompagnano bene; *these ribbons — with your dress*, questi nastri armonizzano con il tuo vestito **5.** pareggiare, uguagliare.

match², *s.* fiammifero ☆ — *-book*, bustina di fiammiferi; — *-box*, scatola di fiammiferi ‖ *safety —*, fiammifero svedese.

to match², *v.t.* fumigare (vini, liquori) bruciando fiammiferi.

matchable ['mætʃəbl], *ag.* accoppiabile, accompagnabile; uguagliabile.

matchboard ['mætʃbɔ:d], *s.* (*falegnameria*) perlina.

matchet ['mætʃit], *s.* (*amer.*) coltellaccio.

matching ['mætʃiŋ], *s.* **1.** (*metal.*) centratura (degli stampi) **2.** *pl.* lana scelta ☆ — *impedance*, (*elett.*) impedenza di adattamento; — *-transformer*, (*rad.*) trasformatore di adattamento.

matchless ['mætʃlis], *ag.* impareggiabile, senza pari.

matchlessly ['mætʃlisli], *av.* incomparabilmente.

matchlessness ['mætʃlisnis], *s.* incomparabilità.

matchlock ['mætʃlɔk], *s.* (*arc.*) fucile a miccia.

matchwood ['mætʃwud], *s.* schegge di legno ‖ *to make — of sthg.*, fare a pezzi ql.co.

mate[1] [meit], *s.c.* **1.** compagno, compagna; uno dei due membri di una coppia **2.** aiuto, assistente: *cook's —*, sottocuoco ‖ *s.* **1.** (*mar.*) secondo; ufficiale in seconda **2.** (*pop.*) amico, « capo »: *say, —, where do you get in?*, ehi, capo, da che parte si entra? ☆ *play —*, compagno di giuochi; *room —*, compagno di camera; *school —*, compagno di scuola.

to mate[1], *v.t.i.* **1.** accoppiare, accoppiarsi (di animali) **2.** (*fam.*) unire, unirsi in matrimonio.

mate[2], *s.* scacco matto.

to mate[2], *v.t.i.* dare scacco matto (a): *to — in four*, dare scacco matto in quattro mosse.

mateless ['meitlis], *ag.* senza compagno.

mater ['meitə*], *s.*: *the —*, (*sl. studentesco*) la madre, la mamma ☆ *dura —*, (*anat.*) pachimeninge; *pia —*, (*anat.*) pia madre.

material [mə'tiəriəl], *ag.* **1.** materiale: *— phenomena*, fenomeni materiali; *gross — soul*, anima grossolana e rozza **2.** sostanziale, importante; essenziale, principale: *a — point of the business*, un punto essenziale della faccenda.

material, *s.* **1.** materiale; materia: *the workmanship is better than the —*, la lavorazione è migliore del materiale **2.** stoffa, tessuto: *what — is it?*, che genere di stoffa è? **3.** *pl.* articoli, accessori ☆ *raw materials*, materie prime; *writing materials*, l'occorrente per scrivere.

materialism [mə'tiəriəlizəm], *s.* materialismo.

materialist [mə'tiəriəlist], *s.* materialista.

materialistic [mə,tiəriə'listik], *ag.* materialistico.

materiality [mə,tiəri'æliti], *s.* materialità.

materialization [mə,tiəriəlai'zeiʃən], *s.* materializzazione.

to materialize [mə'tiəriəlaiz], *v.t.i.* **1.** materializzare, materializzarsi; dar corpo a; prender corpo **2.** *fig.* avverarsi: *our plans did not —*, i nostri piani non si sono avverati.

materially [mə'tiəriəli], *av.* **1.** materialmente; fisicamente **2.** sostanzialmente, essenzialmente.

materialness [mə'tiəriəlnis], *s.* materialità.

materia medica [mə'tiəriə'medikə], *s.* farmacologia.

maternal [mə'tə:nl], *ag.* materno.

maternally [mə'tə:nəli], *av.* maternamente.

maternity [mə'tə:niti], *s.* maternità ☆ *— centre*, consultorio per gestanti; *— hospital*, maternità (ospedale).

matey ['meiti], *ag.* (*fam.*) amichevole, cordiale; socievole.

mathematic(al) [,mæθi'mætik(ə)l], *ag.* matematico; di matematica: *— certainty*, certezza matematica.

mathematically [,mæθi'mætikəli], *av.* matematicamente.

mathematician [,mæθimə'tiʃən], *s.* matematico.

mathematics [,mæθi'mætiks], *s.* matematica: *applied —*, matematica applicata.

Mathilda [mə'tildə], *no.pr.f.* Matilde.

maths [mæθs], (*fam. contr.*) di **mathematics**.

Matilda [mə'tildə], *no.pr.f.* Matilde.

matin ['mætin], *ag.* mattutino, del mattino.

matinal ['mætin], *ag.* mattutino.

matinée [mætinei], *s.* (*teat.*) « matinée », mattinata.

matins ['mætinz], *s. pl.* **1.** (*eccl.*) mattutino: *the bell was ringing to —*, la campana suonava il mattutino **2.** (*poet.*) canto mattutino degli uccelli.

matrass ['mætrəs], *s.* (*chim.*) matraccio (recipiente di vetro per analisi).

matriarch ['meitriɑ:k], *s.* (*scherz.*) madre, donna che predomina (in una famiglia, in un gruppo sociale).

matriarchal [,meitri'ɑ:kəl], *ag.* matriarcale.

matriarchy ['meitriɑ:ki], *s.* matriarcato.

matric [mə'trik], *abbr. fam.* di **matriculation**.

matrice ['meitris], *V.* **matrix**.

matrices ['meitrisi:z], *pl.* di **matrix**.

matricidal ['meitri,saidl], *ag.* matricida.

matricide ['meitrisaid], *s.c.* matricida ‖ *s.* matricidio.

to matriculate [mə'trikjuleit], *v.t.i.* immatricolare, immatricolarsi (all'università).

matriculation [mə,trikju'leiʃən], *s.* **1.** immatricolazione (all'università) **2.** esame di ammissione all'università.

matrimonial [,mætri'mounjəl], *ag.* matrimoniale, coniugale.

matrimonially [,mætri'mounjəli], *av.* matrimonialmente.

matrimony ['mætriməni], *s.* matrimonio.

matrix ['meitriks], *pl.* **matrixes** ['meitriksiz], **matrices** ['meitrisi:z], *s.* **1.** matrice **2.** stampo, forma **3.** (*anat.*) utero **4.** (*biol.*) sostanza intercellulare di un tessuto **5.** (*geol.*) ganga.

matron ['meitrən], *s.* **1.** matrona, madre di famiglia **2.** capo infermiera; direttrice; governante.

matronage ['meitrənidʒ], *s.* condizione, qualità di matrona.

matronal ['meitrənl], *ag.* **1.** matronale **2.** grave; severo; autorevole.

matronhood ['meitrənhud], *s.* matronato.

matronly ['meitrənli], *ag.* **1.** matronale **2.** grave; severo; autorevole.

matronly, *av.* matronalmente.

matronship ['meitrənʃip], *s.* direzione.

matted ['mætid], *ag.* **1.** coperto di stuoie, di paglia **2.** intrecciato; aggrovigliato, arruffato; infelpato: *— hair*, capelli arruffati; *— wool*, lana infeltrita; *my dog's hair became —*, il pelo del mio cane si arruffò.

matter ['mætə*], *s.* **1.** faccenda, affare; argomento: *I have a serious — to attend to*, devo occuparmi di una faccenda seria; *to enter upon the —*, entrare in argomento; *to look into a —*, occuparsi di una cosa ‖ *the — in the hand*, l'argomento in questione ‖ *a — of course*, una faccenda di ordinaria amministrazione ‖ *as a — of fact*, in realtà ‖ *for that —* (o *for the — of that*), per quanto riguarda ciò ‖ *in the — of*, a proposito di, in quanto a ‖ *no laughing —*, una faccenda seria ‖ *to take matters easy*, prendere le cose alla leggera **2.** importanza: *it is* (o *makes*) *no —*, non importa, non fa nulla ‖ *no — how*, non importa come, comunque; *no — where*, dovunque; *what —?*, che importa? **3.** difficoltà, guaio: *what is the — with him?*, che ha?, non si sente bene?; *there is nothing the* (o *nothing is the*) *with him*, non ha nulla, sta bene **4.** materia, sostanza: *gaseous, liquid, solid, vegetable —*, materia gassosa, liquida, solida, vegetale ‖ *mind and —*, spirito e materia **5.** *fig.* materia, contenuto: *the — in your novel is excellent, but the style is deplorable*, il contenuto del tuo romanzo è eccellente, ma lo stile è deplorevole **6.** (*patol.*) pus, materia ☆ *printed —*, giornali, libri, stampati; *reading —*, materiale per lettura.

to matter, *v.i.* **1.** importare, premere: *it does not —*, non importa; *it little* (o *hardly*) *matters that*, importa, conta poco che; *it will — to them, if not to you*, importerà a loro, se non a te; *what does it —?*, che importa? **2.** (*patol.*) suppurare, spurgare.

matterful ['mætəful], *ag.* **1.** ricco di contenuto (di libro, ecc.) **2.** forte, energico.

Matterhorn (the) ['mætəhɔ:n], *no.pr.* (*geog.*) Monte Cervino.

matterless ['mætəlis], *ag.* **1.** (*rar.*) immateriale **2.** non importante.

matter-of-fact ['mætərəv'fækt], *ag.* pratico, positivo (di persona).

matter-of-factness ['mætərəv'fæktnis], *s.* praticità: *all his actions were characterized by —*, tutte le sue azioni erano improntate a praticità.

mattery ['mætəri], *ag.* purulento.

Matthew ['mæθju:], *no.pr.m.* Matteo.

Matthias [mə'θaiəs], *no.pr.m.* Mattia.

matting[1] ['mætiŋ], *s.* **1.** stuoia, stoino **2.** materiale per stuoie.

matting[2], *s.* **1.** opacità (di metallo prezioso); superficie opaca **2.** profilatura in oro opaco (di quadro).

mattins, *V.* **matins**.

mattock ['mætək], *s.* zappa, zappone; piccone.

mattoid ['mætoid], *s.* mattoide.

mattress ['mætris], *s.* materasso ☆ *spring-* —, materasso a molle; *straw* —, pagliericcio.

to **maturate** ['mætjureit], *v.t.i.* (*med.*) portare a maturazione, far suppurare; suppurare.

maturation [,mætju'reifən], *s.* **1.** maturazione **2.** (*patol.*) suppurazione.

maturative [mə'tjuərətiv], *ag.* **1.** maturativo **2.** (*patol.*) suppurativo.

mature [mə'tjuə*], *ag.* **1.** maturo (anche *fig.*) **2.** completo; perfezionato (di piano, progetto) **3.** (*comm.*) in scadenza; scaduto.

to **mature**, *v.t.i.* **1.** (far) maturare (anche *fig.*) **2.** completare; perfezionare (piano, progetto) **3.** (*comm.*) giungere alla scadenza, scadere.

maturely [mə'tjuəli], *av.* con maturità; ponderatamente.

matureness [mə'tjuənis], **maturity** [mə'tjuəriti], *s.* **1.** maturità (anche *fig.*) **2.** completezza (di piano, progetto) **3.** (*comm.*) scadenza: *credit at long* —, credito a lunga scadenza.

matutinal [,mætju(:)'tainl], *ag.* mattutino.

matutine ['mætju(:)tain], *ag.* mattutino.

maty ['meiti], *ag.* socievole; amichevole, cordiale.

maud [mo:d], *s.* sorta di « plaid » usato dai pastori scozzesi; coperta da viaggio di tal tipo.

Maud(e) [mo:d], *no.pr.f. dim.* di **Matilda, Magdalen.**

maudlin ['mo:dlin], *ag.* sdolcinato, scioccamente sentimentale; querulo, piagnucoloso (di ubriaco).

maudlinism ['mo:dlinizəm], *s.* tono querulo, piagnucoloso (di ubriaco).

maugre ['mo:gə*], *prep.* (*arc.*) malgrado.

maul [mo:l], *s.* mazza, maglio.

to **maul**, *v.t.* **1.** battere; maltrattare (anche *fig.*): *don't* — *the dog*, smetti di maltrattare il cane **2.** bistrattare; danneggiare con la critica: *that picture was mauled by the critics*, quel quadro fu bistrattato dai critici **3.** (*amer.*) spezzare a colpi di maglio.

mauley ['mo:li], *s.* (*sl.*) pugno; mano.

maulstick ['mo:l-stik], *s.* (*pitt.*) appoggiamano.

maund [mo:nd], *s.* « maund » (misura di peso variabile in uso in India e nell'Asia occidentale).

to **maunder** ['mo:ndə*], *v.i.* **1.** parlare a vanvera, borbottare **2.** muoversi, agire senza mèta.

Maundy ['mo:ndi], *s.* (*eccl.*) cerimonia della lavanda dei piedi ai poveri (che si effettua il Giovedì Santo) ‖ — *money*, elemosina distribuita nell'Abbazia di Westminster, per conto del re, il Giovedì Santo; — *Thursday*, Giovedì Santo.

Maurice ['moris], *no.pr.m.* Maurizio.

Mauritius [mə'rifəs], *no.pr.* (*geog.*) Maurizio (isola).

mauser ['mauzə*], *s.* « mauser » (tipo di fucile, pistola).

mausoleum [,mo:sə'liəm], *s.* mausoleo.

mauve [mouv], *ag.s.* (color) malva.

mauveine ['mouvin], *s.* (*chim.*) malveina.

maverick ['mævərik], *s.* (*amer.*) **1.** capo di bestiame non marchiato **2.** *fig.* persona indipendente, individualista.

mavis ['meivis], *s.* (*poet.*) tordo.

mavourneen [mə'vuəni:n], *s. inter.* (*irl.*) tesoro mio; caro, cara.

maw[1] [mo:], *s.* **1.** stomaco (di ruminanti); (*scherz.*) stomaco (di uomini) **2.** gozzo (di uccelli).

maw[2], *s.* (*ornit.*) gabbiano.

mawk [mo:k], *s.* (*entom.*) larva.

mawkish ['mo:kif], *ag.* **1.** dal sapore nauseante **2.** sdolcinato; lezioso; sentimentale: *a* — *song*, una canzone sdolcinata, sentimentale.

mawkishly ['mo:kifli], *av.* sdolcinatamente; con sentimentalismo.

mawkishness ['mo:kifnis], *s.* **1.** sapore nauseante **2.** sdolcinatezza; sentimentalismo.

mawseed ['mo:si:d], *s.* seme di papavero.

Max [mæks], *no.pr.m. dim.* di **Maximilian.**

maxilla [mæk'silə], *pl.* **maxillae** [mæk'sili:], *s.* mascella (generalmente superiore).

maxillary [mæk'siləri], *ag.* mascellare.

maxim[1] ['mæksim], *s.* massima; sentenza; norma, principio di condotta: *it was a* — *of his to help his neighbour*, era sua norma aiutare il prossimo ☆ — *-monger*, chi fa sfoggio di massime.

Maxim[2], *s.* — (*-gun*), mitragliatrice « Maxim ».

maximal ['mæksiməl], *ag.* del massimo valore; massimo.

maximalist ['mæksiməlist], *s.* massimalista.

Maximilian [,mæksi'miljən], *no.pr.m.* Massimiliano.

maximally ['mæksiməli], *av.* massimamente.

to **maximize** ['mæksimaiz], *v.t.* elevare, alzare al massimo grado.

maximum ['mæksiməm], *pl.* **maxima** ['mæksimə], **maximums** ['mæksiməmz], *ag.* massimo: *the* — *price*, il massimo prezzo; — *speed per hour*, velocità oraria massima; *the* — *weight*, il peso massimo ‖ *s.* il massimo, la maggior quantità: *at the examination he got fifty-five marks out of a* — *of a hundred*, all'esame riportò la votazione di cinquantacinque su cento; *the enthusiasm was at its* —, l'entusiasmo aveva raggiunto il più alto grado ☆ — *and minimum thermometer*, termometro a massima e minima; — *duration*, (*aut. aer.*) autonomia.

Maximus ['mæksiməs], *no.pr.m.* (*st.*) Massimo.

May[1] [mei], *s.* **1.** maggio **2.** *fig.* giovinezza, primavera (della vita): *in the* — *of life*, nel fiore della vita **3.** *pl.* sessione d'esami estiva (a Cambridge) **4.** *pl.* regate universitarie sul Tamigi ☆ *may-beetle* (o *may-bug*), (*entom.*) maggiolino; *may-bloom* (o *may-blossom*), (*bot.*) biancospino; — *-dew*, rugiada di maggio (che secondo un'antica credenza schiariva la biancheria e i volti); — *lady* (o — *-queen*), regina di maggio; *may-lily*, (*bot.*) mughetto.

May[2], *no.pr.f. dim.* di **Mary.**

may[3] [mei, me (*forme forti*), mi, mə (*forme deboli*)], *v. difettivo* (V); (*indic. congiunt. pres.* **may**; *indic. congiunt. pass. e condiz.* **might** [mait]; *2*[a] *persona sing. pres. indic.* (*poet.*) **mayest** ['meiist], **mayst** [meist]; *forme negative:* **may not** [mei not], **might not** [mait not]; *forme contratte:* **mayn't** [meint], **mightn't** ['maitnt]) **1.** (*esprimente permesso*): — *I smoke?*, posso fumare?; *if I* — *say so*, se mi è concesso dirlo; *you* — *come when you like*, puoi venire quando vuoi **2.** (*esprimente probabilità*): *he* — *come to-morrow*, può darsi che venga domani; *how old* — *she be?*, quanti anni avrà?; *I wonder what I* — *have done to hurt him*, mi domando che cosa avrò mai fatto per urtarlo; *it* —, *might be that...*, può darsi, potrebbe darsi che...; *they* — *go*, può darsi che vadano; *we* —, *might as well go to the theatre*, tanto vale, varrebbe andare a teatro; *you might have read it!*, avresti potuto leggerlo! ‖ *be that as it* —, avvenga quello che avvenga, qualunque cosa accada ‖ *he recognized her, as well he might, seeing that...*, la riconobbe, e non c'è da meravigliarsi, visto che... ‖ *that's as* — *be*, secondo, dipende **3.** (*esprimente scopo, desiderio, timore*): *eat that you* — *live*, mangia per vivere; *I hope he* — *come tomorrow*, spero che possa venire domani; *I was afraid he might have killed her*, temevo che l'avesse uccisa; *wire to him that he* — *know when we arrive*, telegrafagli affinchè sappia quando arriveremo **4.** (*esprimente augurio*): — *you be happy!*, che tu possa essere felice!; — *you succeed!*, che tu possa avere successo!.

Mayan ['ma:jən], *ag.* (*st. amer.*) maya.

maybe ['meibi:], *av.* forse, probabilmente; può darsi che.

Mayday ['meidei], *s.* primo di maggio; (*st.*) calendimaggio.

Mayfair ['mei-fɛə*], *no.pr.* Mayfair (quartiere aristocratico di Londra) ☆ — *manners*, modi aristocratici.

mayflower ['mei,flauə*], *s.* 1. biancospino; fiore primaverile 2. *Mayflower*, (*st.*) « Mayflower » (nave che portò i « Pilgrim Fathers » in America) || — *compact*, primo abbozzo di costituzione americana.

mayfly ['mei-flai], *s.* (*entom.*) effimera.

mayhap ['meihæp], *av.* (*arc.*) forse.

mayhem ['meihem], *s.* (*amer. st. dir.*) mutilazione: *damage and* —, danni e lesioni; *to commit — on s.o.*, storpiare qlcu.

maying ['meiiŋ], *s.*: *to go (a-)* —, festeggiare il primo maggio.

mayn't [meint], *contr.* di *may not*.

mayonnaise [,meiə'neiz], *s.* (*cuc.*) maionese.

mayor [mɛə*], *s.* sindaco: *the Lord Mayor of London*, il sindaco di Londra ☆ *deputy* —, vicesindaco.

mayoral ['mɛərəl], *ag.* di sindaco.

mayoralty ['mɛərəlti], *s.* sindacato (dignità e ufficio di sindaco).

mayoress ['mɛəris], *s.* moglie del sindaco.

maypole ['mei-poul], *s.* maio (palo ornato di nastri e fiori intorno al quale i giovani solevano danzare nelle feste di calendimaggio).

mazard¹ ['mæzəd], *s.* (*arc.*) testa; viso.

mazard², *s.* ciliegia acquaiola.

mazarine [,mæzə'ri:n], *ag.s.* (colore) blu scuro.

Mazdaism ['mæzdiizəm], *s.* mazdeismo (religione iranica).

maze [meiz], *s.* labirinto, dedalo; *fig.* complicazione; perplessità: *to be in a* —, essere disorientato, confuso; *to get into, out of a* —, cacciarsi in, togliersi da un imbroglio.

to maze, *v.t.* confondere, disorientare.

mazer ['meizə*], *s.* (*st.*) largo boccale in legno duro.

mazily ['meizili], *av.* confusamente; perplessamente.

maziness ['meizinis], *s.* confusione; perplessità.

mazurka [mə'zə:kə], *s.* mazurca.

mazy ['meizi], *ag.* 1. sinuoso 2. complesso, intricato.

me [mi], *pron. pers.* 1ᵃ *persona sing.* (*caso obliquo di I*) me, mi: *call — at seven*, svegliami alle sette; *give — a kiss*, dammi un bacio; *will you come with —?*, volete venire con me? || *dear —!*, (*fam.*) povero me! || *I laid — down*, (*arc.*) mi sono coricato || *it's —*, (*fam.*) sono io.

mead¹ [mi:d], *s.* idromele.

mead², *poet.* per **meadow**.

meadow ['medou], *s.* prato, prateria ☆ — *-lark*, allodola mattolina; — *-mushroom*, fungo prataiolo; — *-saffron*, (*bot.*) colchico; — *-sweet*, (*bot.*) olmaria.

meager (*amer.*) per **meagre**.

meagre ['mi:gə*], *ag.* 1. magro, scarno 2. scarso, insufficiente; frugale; povero: — *information*, scarse informazioni; *a — meal*, un pasto molto frugale; — *style*, stile povero, disadorno.

meagrely ['mi:gəli], *av.* scarsamente; poveramente.

meagreness ['mi:gənis], *s.* 1. magrezza 2. scarsità; frugalità; povertà.

meal¹ [mi:l], *s.* farina (non di frumento) ☆ — *-chest*, madia; — *-moth*, (*entom.*) piralide; — *-worm*, (*entom.*) tenebrione mugnaio || *Indian* —, farina di mais; *linseed* —, farina di lino; *oat-* —, farina d'avena.

to meal¹, *v.t.i.* 1. macinare, ridurre in farina 2. infarinare 3. dare farina.

meal², *s.* 1. pasto: *a poor* —, un magro pasto; *a square* —, un pasto sostanzioso; *three meals a day*, tre pasti al giorno; *where do you take (o have) your meals?*, dove prendi i pasti?; *to make a — of sthg.*, cibarsi di ql.co. 2. quantità di latte data da una mucca ad ogni mungitura ☆ — *-time*, l'ora dei pasti.

to meal², *v.i.* prendere un pasto, mangiare.

mealie ['mi:li], *s. gener. pl.* granoturco; mais.

mealiness ['mi:linis], *s.* farinosità.

mealy ['mi:li], *ag.* 1. simile a farina; cosparso di farina; farinoso: — *potatoes*, patate farinose 2. pallido (di carnagione) 3. chiazzato (di cavallo) ☆ — *-mouthed*, mellifluo; insincero.

mean¹ [mi:n], *ag.* 1. basso, spregevole; volgare, triviale: *he is of — birth*, è di bassi natali; *this is a — insinuation*, questa è una vile insinuazione 2. mediocre, dappoco: *a man of — intelligence*, un uomo di mediocre intelligenza; *no* —, molto abile, bravo, non dappoco: *no — scholar*, studioso di valore; *to have no — opinion of*, avere un'alta opinione di 3. gretto, meschino, spilorcio: *he's very* —, è molto gretto 4. (*fam.*) sgarbato, villano: *don't be so —!*, non esser così sgarbato!; *what a — thing to do, to say*, che atto villano!, che scortesia!.

mean², *ag.* medio, intermedio: — *temperature*, temperatura media.

mean², *s.* 1. media; mezzo, punto medio || *the happy* —, il giusto mezzo 2. *pl.* (*gener. costruzione sing.*) mezzo; strumento: *means of communication*, mezzi di comunicazione; *I must find the means to do it*, devo trovare il mezzo per farlo; *to find (a) means of doing sthg.*, trovare il mezzo per fare ql.co. || *by all means*, con ogni mezzo; *ad ogni costo*; ma certo! || *by fair means or foul*, con qualsiasi mezzo; *by means of*, per mezzo di || *by no means*, ben lungi da, affatto: *this is by no means an easy matter*, questa è ben lungi dall'essere una faccenda semplice || *by some means or other*, in qualche modo 3. *pl.* mezzi economici, risorse finanziarie: *a man of means*, un uomo agiato; *he always lived beyond his means*, ha sempre speso più di quello che guadagnava; *she lives on her own means*, ella vive del suo ☆ *means test*, accertamento per il rilascio del certificato di nullatenenza || *golden* —, (*geom.*) sezione aurea.

to mean³, *pass.p.p.* **meant** [ment], *v.t.i.* 1. (IV) intendere, significare, voler dire: *he, she means a lot to me*, egli, ella significa, è tutto per me; *I — him to obey*, intendo che egli ubbidisca; *I — what I* —, intendo dire ciò che ho detto; *I didn't — what you think*, non volevo dire quello che pensi tu; *I meant her to come to us*, intendevo che ella venisse da noi; *I never say what I don't* —, non dico mai quello che non penso; *what does this word* —?, che cosa significa questa parola?; *what do you — by that?*, che cosa intendi dire con ciò?; (*fam.*) che cosa credi di dire, di fare? 2. (II, IV) proporsi, aver l'intenzione, far conto di: *he means to go as soon as possible*, intende andare al più presto possibile; *they meant it for a joke*, volevano fare uno scherzo; *they meant no harm*, non volevano fare del male; *what do they — to do?*, che intendono fare?; *to — business*, far sul serio; *to — mischief*, avere pessime intenzioni; *to — well (to, by s.o.)*, essere animato da buoni sentimenti (verso qlcu.) 3. destinare, riserbare, assegnare: *he was meant for a doctor*, era nato per fare il medico; *I meant it as a present for you*, lo serbavo come regalo per te; *the letter was not meant for him*, la lettera non era destinata a lui.

Meander [mi'ændə*], *no.pr.* (*geog. st.*) Meandro || **meander**, *s.* 1. *gener. pl.* meandro, tortuosità, ansa (anche *fig.*) 2. (*art.*) meandro.

to meander, *v.i.* serpeggiare; vagare; *fig.* divagare.

meandering [mi'ændəriŋ], *ag.* sinuoso, serpeggiante.

meandrous [mi'ændrəs], *ag.* sinuoso, tortuoso.

meaning ['mi:niŋ], *ag.* 1. disposto, intenzionato 2. significativo: *a — look*, uno sguardo significativo ☆ *well* —, che ha buone intenzioni.

meaning, *s.* 1. senso, significato: *what's the — of this?*, che cosa significa questo?, (*fam.*) che cosa state combinando? 2. pensiero, idea: *if you understand my* —, se capite la mia idea, se esprimo bene il mio pensiero 3. disegno, intento: *his — was to do it himself*, la sua intenzione era di farlo egli stesso.

meaningless ['mi:niŋlis], *ag.* insignificante; senza senso; senza motivo.

meaningly ['mi:niŋli], *av.* in modo significativo; eloquentemente: *she looked at her mother* —, rivolse alla madre un'occhiata eloquente.

meanly ['mi:nli], *av.* 1. meschinamente; avaramente 2. umilmente; poveramente 3. (*fam.*) sgarbatamente.

meanness ['mi:nnis], *s.* **1.** meschinità; mediocrità: *the — of his daily life*, lo squallore della sua vita di ogni iorno **2.** grettezza (di animo) **3.** (*fam.*) maleducazione; volgarità ‖ *a piece of —*, una bella villanata.

meant [ment], *pass.p.p.* di to **mean**.

meantime ['mi:n'taim], **meanwhile** ['mi:n'wail], *s.* frattempo: *in the —*, nel frattempo ‖ *av.* intanto.

measles ['mi:zlz], *s.* **1.** morbillo **2.** (*vet.*) cisticher-chiasi, tenia dei suini ✩ *German —*, rosolìa.

measly ['mi:zli], *ag.* **1.** morbilloso **2.** che ha contratto la tenia (detto di suino) **3.** (*sl.*) meschino, senza valore: *he is a — old man*, è un vecchio tirchio; *they gave me a — pound*, mi diedero una miserabile sterlina.

measurable ['meʒərəbl], *ag.* misurabile: *within — distance of success*, *fig.* a due passi dal successo.

measurableness ['meʒərəblnis], *s.* misurabilità.

measurably ['meʒərəbli], *av.* **1.** sensibilmente **2.** moderatamente.

measure ['meʒə*], *s.* **1.** misura, dimensione; quantità; peso; *fig.* capacità, portata, limite: *the — of an agreement*, la portata di un accordo; *beyond* (o *out of*) —, oltre misura, esageratamente; *a dress made to —*, un abito fatto su misura; *full*, *short —*, misura completa, scarsa; *in a great* (o *large*) —, in gran parte; *in some —*, in parte, fino a un certo punto; *words do not always give the — of our feelings*, le parole non danno sempre la misura dei nostri sentimenti; *to set measures to sthg.*, porre dei limiti a ql.co.; *to take s.o.'s —*, prendere le misure a qlcu.; giudicare il carattere, l'abilità di qlcu. ‖ *to take the — of s.o.'s foot*, valutare la capacità di qlcu. **2.** misura (strumento per misurare, unità di misura, sistema di misura): *an inch is a — of length*, un pollice è una misura di lunghezza **3.** provvedimento; precauzione: *a wise —*, un saggio provvedimento; *to take measures*, prendere provvedimenti; *to take legal measures*, adire le vie legali ‖ *— for —*, occhio per occhio **4.** (*arit.*) divisore **5.** (*poes.*) metro; ritmo; (*mus.*) battuta; tempo; (*arc.*) danza **6.** (*geol.*) strato ✩ *chest-—*, circonferenza toracica; *folding —*, metro snodato; *greatest common —*, (*arit.*) massimo comun divisore; *liquid —*, misura di capacità; *tape-—*, rotella metrica, metro a nastro.

to measure, *v.t.i.* **1.** misurare; prender le misure; avere una certa misura: *he measured three yards of that cloth*, misurò tre iarde di quella stoffa; *the tailor measured me for a new suit*, il sarto mi prese le misure per un abito nuovo ‖ *to — one's length*, (*fam.*) cadere lungo disteso **2.** esaminare; valutare, confrontare; misurarsi: *you ought to — your strength before attempting anything new*, dovresti valutare bene le tue forze prima di tentare una cosa nuova; *to — (oneself) with* (o *by*) *s.o.*, *sthg.*, misurarsi con qlcu., ql.co.: *he only measured it with his eye*, l'ha misurato così ad occhio e croce; *he tried to — himself with him*, volle misurarsi con lui; *I can't — my strength with his*, non posso misurare le mie forze con le sue; *you should not — her love by yours*, non dovresti misurare il suo amore basandoti sul tuo **3.** (*poet.*) coprire una distanza **4.** *to — out*, misurare; distribuire; versare **5.** *to — up to* (*s.o.*, *sthg.*), (*amer.*) raggiungere, essere all'altezza di.

measured ['meʒəd], *ag.* **1.** misurato; esatto; moderato, controllato: *— language*, linguaggio moderato; *in no — words*, in termini eccessivi **2.** cadenzato, ritmico: *— tread*, passo cadenzato.

measureless ['meʒəlis], *ag.* incommensurabile, smisurato, immenso.

measurement ['meʒəmənt], *s.* **1.** misura, grandezza, volume, dimensione **2.** *pl.* misure, dati precisi ✩ *hip*, *waist —*, circonferenza (dei) fianchi, (della) vita.

measuring ['meʒəriŋ], *s.* misurazione; (*chim.*) dosatura, dosaggio ✩ *— appliances*, strumenti per rilievi metrici; *— cylinder*, *— glass*, cilindro, vetro graduato; *— range*, campo di misura; *— stick*, asta di misurazione; *— tape*, nastro metrico.

meat [mi:t], *s.* **1.** carne **2.** (*arc.*) cibo, nutrimento (anche *fig.*): *— and drink*, cibo e bevanda; *the — of his story*, la sostanza del suo racconto ‖ *one man's — is another man's poison*, *prov.* ciò che giova all'uno nuoce all'altro **3.** (*arc.*) pasto: *before*, *after —*, prima, dopo il pasto ✩ *— fly*, mosca della carne; *— -pie*, pasticcio di carne; *— -safe*, moscaiola; *— -tea*, spuntino in cui oltre al tè viene servita carne ‖ *boiled —*, lesso; *canned —* (o *tinned —*), carne in scatola; *frozen —*, carne congelata; *minced —*, carne trita; *roast —*, arrosto; *salted —*, carne insaccata.

meatus [mi'eitəs], *pl.* **meatuses** [mi'eitəsiz], *s.* (*anat.*) meato.

meaty ['mi:ti], *ag.* **1.** polposo, carnoso **2.** *fig.* denso, sostanzioso.

Mecca ['mekə], *no.pr.* (*geog.*) Mecca ‖ *s.* *fig.* luogo ove si aspira andare.

meccano [me'ka:nou], *s.* meccano.

mechanic [mi'kænik], *s.* **1.** meccanico **2.** operaio; artigiano ✩ *dental —*, odontotecnico; *filling-station —*, garagista; *motor —*, autista-meccanico.

mechanical [mi'kænikəl], *ag.* **1.** meccanico: *— power*, forza meccanica; *— skill*, abilità, capacità meccanica, tecnica **2.** automatico **3.** istintivo, meccanico: *a — gesture*, un gesto istintivo **4.** (*mil.*) motorizzato ✩ *— device*, dispositivo automatico; *— engineer*, ingegnere meccanico; *— transport*, trasporto motorizzato.

mechanically [mi'kænikəli], *av.* **1.** meccanicamente **2.** per abitudine, macchinalmente ✩ *— operated*, a comando automatico.

mechanicalness [mi'kænikəlnis], *s.* meccanicità.

mechanician [,mekə'niʃən], *s.* meccanico.

mechanics [mi'kæniks], *s.* **1.** meccanica **2.** meccanismo (del corpo umano, ecc.) ✩ *analytical*, *pure —*, meccanica analitica, razionale.

mechanism ['mekənizəm], *s.* **1.** meccanismo, congegno **2.** tecnica: *he could not master the — of piano playing*, non riusciva a rendersi padrone della tecnica del pianoforte **3.** (*fil.*) meccanismo.

mechanist ['mekənist], *s.* meccanico.

mechanization [,mekənai'zeiʃən], *s.* meccanizzazione.

to mechanize ['mekənaiz], *v.t.* meccanizzare; render meccanico ✩ *mechanized troops*, truppe motorizzate.

mechanology [,mekə'nolədʒi], *s.* meccanologia.

Mechlin, Mecklin ['meklin], *no.pr.* (*geog.*) Malines ‖ *s.* *— (lace)*, merletto di Malines.

meconic [mi'konik], *ag.* (*chim.*) meconico.

meconin ['mi:kənin], *s.* (*chim.*) meconina.

meconium [mi'kouniəm], *s.* (*fisiol.*) meconio.

med [med], *s.* (*sl.*) studente in medicina.

medal ['medl], *s.* medaglia ‖ *the reverse of the —*, il rovescio della medaglia.

medalist ['medlist], *s.* **1.** medagliaio; medaglista **2.** persona decorata con una medaglia.

medalled ['medld], *ag.* decorato, fregiato di medaglie.

medallic [mi'dælik], *ag.* di medaglia; raffigurato su medaglia.

medallion [mi'dæljən], *s.* medaglione.

medallist, *V.* **medalist**.

to meddle ['medl], *v.i.* **1.** immischiarsi, intromettersi, interferire: *don't — with my books, please!*, non toccare i miei libri, per piacere!; *he is always meddling with* (o *in*) *other people's business*, s'impiccia sempre dei fatti altrui; *to — with sthg.*, immischiarsi in ql.co. **2.** aver a che fare: *I advise you not to — with that man*, ti consiglio di non aver a che fare con quell'uomo.

meddler ['medlə*], *s.* intrigante, ficcanaso.

meddlesome ['medlsəm], *ag.* importuno, indiscreto.

meddlesomeness ['medlsəmnis], *s.* ingerenza (negli affari altrui).

meddling ['medliŋ], *ag.* importuno ‖ *s.* **1.** ingerenza, interferenza: *his — with it spoiled everything*, il suo intervento mandò tutto all'aria **2.** mene, intrighi, raggiri: *with all his — he couldn't get the job*, con tutte le sue mene non è riuscito ad ottenere il posto.

Mede [mi:d], *s.c.* (*st.*) abitante della Media ‖ *it is like the laws of the Medes and Persians*, è una legge immutabile.

Medea [mi'diə], *no.pr.f.* (*mit.*) Medea.

Media ['mediə], *no.pr.* (*geog. st.*) Media.

mediacy ['mi:diəsi], *s.* (*log. fis.*) stato, qualità intermedia.

mediaeval [,medi'i:vəl], *ag.* medioevale.

medial ['mi:djəl], *ag.* **1.** medio; mediano **2.** (*anat.*) mediale ☆ — *malleolus*, malleolo mediale.

median[1] ['mi:djən], *ag.* (*anat. bot. geom.*) mediano ‖ *s.* **1.** (*anat.*) nervo mediano; vena mediana **2.** (*statistica*) valore mediano **3.** (*geom.*) mediana, linea mediana ☆ — *lobe*, lobo medio (del polmone).

Median[2], *ag.* della Media; dei medi ‖ *s.* medo (abitante, lingua).

mediant ['mi:djənt], *s.* (*mus.*) mediante.

mediastinum [,mi:diəs'tainəm], *s.* (*anat.*) mediastino ☆ — *cerebri*, falce cerebrale.

mediate ['mi:diit], *ag.* mediato; indiretto: — *collection of tax*, esazione di un tributo fatto presso il produttore o l'intermediario; — *testimony*, (*dir.*) testimonianza per procura.

to mediate ['mi:dieit], *v.t.i.* **1.** (*comm.*) far da intermediario; conseguire con la mediazione **2.** interporsi; pacificare **3.** far da legame (di cose).

mediately ['mi:diitli], *av.* mediatamente; indirettamente.

mediation [,mi:di'eiʃən], *s.* mediazione; intercessione; intervento; tramite: *through the — of Mr. Casoli*, tramite il signor Casoli; *he has offered his — with...*, egli ha offerto i suoi buoni uffici presso....

to mediatize ['mi:diətaiz], *v.t.i.* **1.** (*st. tedesca*) annettere (uno stato minore) a uno maggiore (salvaguardando alcuni diritti del primo) **2.** (*st.*) ridurre un vassallo da immediato a mediato (nel Sacro Romano Impero) **3.** fare da mediatore.

mediator ['mi:dieitə*], *s.* **1.** (*comm.*) mediatore **2.** intercessore; paciere.

mediatorial [,mi:diə'to:riəl], *ag.* **1.** di mediatore **2.** di paciere; di intercessore.

mediatorship ['mi:dieitəʃip], *s.* ufficio di mediatore.

mediatress ['mi:dieitris], **mediatrix** [,mi:di'eitriks], *pl.* **mediatrices** [,mi:dii'traisi:z], *s.* mediatrice; interceditrice.

medic ['medik], *ag.* (*poet.*) *abbr.* di **medical** ‖ *s.* (*sl. amer.*) **1.** studente in medicina **2.** medico.

medicable ['medikəbl], *ag.* medicabile.

medical ['medikəl], *ag.* **1.** medico; della medicina: *he requires — treatment*, egli necessita di cure mediche; *your father should have — attention*, vostro padre dovrebbe farsi curare da un medico **2.** (*rar.*) medicinale ‖ *s.* (*fam.*) studente in medicina; — *board*, consiglio di sanità; corpo medico (di ospedale); — *corps*, (*mil.*) Corpo sanitario; — *jurisprudence*, medicina legale; — *man*, (medico) generico; — *officer*, ufficiale sanitario: *to pass the — officer*, (*mil.*) passare la visita medica; — *pathology*, patologia medica; — *store*, materiale sanitario; — *student*, studente in medicina.

medically ['medikəli], *av.* **1.** da medico: — *speaking...*, parlando da medico...; — *viewed*, dal punto di vista medico **2.** per mezzo di medicine; per mezzo della medicina.

medicament [me'dikəmənt], *s.* medicamento, farmaco, medicina.

medicamental [,medikə'mentl], *ag.* medicamentoso.

medicaster ['medikæstə*], *s.* medicastro.

to medicate ['medikeit], *v.t.* medicare, curare.

medicated ['medikeitid], *ag.* medicato.

medication [,medi'keiʃən], *s.* medicazione; cura.

medicative ['medikətiv], *ag.* medicamentoso, curativo.

Medicean [,medi'tʃi(:)ən], *ag.* (*st.*) mediceo.

medicinal [me'disinl], *ag.s.* medicinale.

medicinally [me'disinəli], *av.* medicinalmente.

medicine ['medsin], *s.* **1.** medicina, farmaco: *it was a good — for him*, è stata una medicina salutare per lui ‖ *to swallow* (o *to take*) *one's —*, *fig.* ingoiare un boccone amaro, una pillola **2.** scienza medica **3.** sortilegio, incantesimo, stregoneria **3.** (*fam.*) purga: *to take —*, purgarsi ☆ — *chest*, armadietto, cassetta farmaceutica; — *-man*, stregone.

to medicine, *v.t.* (*arc.*) somministrare medicine, curare con medicine.

medick ['mi:dik], *s.* (*bot.*) erba medica.

medico ['medikou], *pl.* **medicos** ['medikouz], *s.* (*scherz.*) medico.

medieval [,medi'i:vəl], *ag.* medioevale.

medievalism [,medi'i:vəlizəm], *s.* medievalismo.

medievalist [,medi'i:vəlist], *s.* cultore di studi medioevali.

mediocre ['mi:dioukə*], *ag.* mediocre.

mediocrity [,mi:di'okriti], *s.* mediocrità.

to meditate ['mediteit], *v.t.i.* **1.** progettare; macchinare, tramare: *he meditated revenge*, egli macchinava la vendetta **2.** meditare, riflettere: *to — on* (o *upon*) *sthg.*, meditare su ql.co.

meditation [,medi'teiʃən], *s.* meditazione; riflessione.

meditative ['meditətiv], *ag.* meditativo; pensoso.

meditatively ['meditətivli], *av.* meditatamente, con riflessione.

meditativeness ['meditətivnis], *s.* inclinazione alla meditazione.

Mediterranean [,meditə'reinjən], *ag.* mediterraneo: *the — (Sea)*, il (mare) Mediterraneo; — *race*, razza mediterranea ☆ — *fever*, (*patol.*) febbre maltese.

medium ['mi:djəm], *ag.* medio ☆ — *-powered car*, automobile di media cilindrata; — *shot*, (*cine.*) campo medio; (*tv.*) ripresa media; — *-sized*, di grandezza media; — *speed*, velocità media; — *steel*, (*metal.*) acciaio naturale; — *voltage*, (*elett.*) tensione media; — *waves*, (*rad.*) onde medie.

medium, *pl.* **mediums** ['mi:djəmz], **media** ['mi:djə], *s.* **1.** mezzo, strumento: *through the — of*, per mezzo di: *through the — of the press*, tramite la stampa **2.** mezzo, elemento: *water is the natural — of fish*, l'acqua è l'elemento naturale dei pesci **3.** mezzo; punto, termine medio ‖ — *of exchange*, (*pol. finanziaria*) media dei cambi ‖ *to stick to a happy —*, serbare il giusto mezzo **4.** (*spiritismo*) medium **5.** (*pitt.*) liquido solvente ☆ *advertising —*, mezzo pubblicitario; *culture —*, (*biol.*) brodo di coltura; *circulating —*, (*econ.*) agente circolante; *agente monetario*.

mediumistic [,mi:djə'mistik], *ag.* medianico.

medlar ['medlə*], *s.* (*bot.*) nespola ☆ — *-tree*, nespolo.

medley ['medli], *ag.* misto, eterogeneo ‖ *s.* **1.** miscuglio; guazzabuglio **2.** (*lett.*) miscellanea **3.** (*mus.*) « pot-pourri », selezione di pezzi.

to medley ['medli], *v.t.* mescolare.

medulla [me'dʌlə], *s.* (*anat. bot.*) midollo.

medullary [mi'dʌləri], *ag.* midollare ☆ — *anaesthesia*, anestesia spinale; — *sheath*, guaina midollare.

Medusa [mi'dju:zə], *no.pr.f.* (*mit.*) Medusa ‖ **medusa**, *pl.* **medusae** [mi'dju:zi:], *s.* (*zool.*) medusa.

medusan [mi'dju:zən], *ag.* (*zool.*) di medusa.

medusoid [mi'dju:sɔid], *ag.* (*zool.*) simile a medusa.

meed [mi:d], *s.* (*poet.*) ricompensa, premio: — *of praise*, tributo di elogio.

meek [mi:k], *ag.* docile, mansueto, mite; umile: *as — as a lamb* (o *as — as Moses*), mansueto come un agnello ☆ — *-eyed*, dallo sguardo mansueto; — *-hearted*, di carattere dolce.

meekly ['mi:kli], *av.* docilmente; mitemente.

meekness ['mi:knis], *s.* dolcezza; mansuetudine.

meerschaum ['miəʃəm], *s.* (*min.*) sepiolite, schiuma di mare ☆ — *pipe*, pipa di schiuma.

meet¹ [mi:t], *ag.* (*arc.*) idoneo, adatto, conveniente.

meet², *s.* **1.** partita di caccia **2.** riunione sportiva.

to meet², *pass.p.p.* **met** [met], *v.t.i.* **1.** incontrare, incontrarsi; riunire, riunirsi; scontrarsi: *she met us with a hearty smile*, ci venne incontro con un sorriso cordiale; *they met by chance*, si incontrarono per caso; *we are to* — *again soon*, ci incontreremo ancora presto; *we shall* — *you as far as possible*, *fig.* vi verremo incontro il più possibile **2.** fare la conoscenza (di): *we have already met*, ci conosciamo già; *we knew him by sight, but had never met him*, lo conoscevamo (di) vista, ma non avevamo mai fatto la sua conoscenza **3.** andare a prendere: *we met them at the station*, andammo a prenderli alla stazione **4.** far onore (a impegni); far fronte (a spese); soddisfare; rispondere a; pagare: *has he not met his engagements?*, non ha fatto fronte ai suoi impegni?; *to* — *the case*, essere adeguato al caso; *to* — *a draft*, (*comm.*) pagare una tratta; *to* — *a necessity*, rispondere a un bisogno; *to* — *s.o.'s wishes*, venire incontro ai desideri di qlcu. ‖ *to* — *half-way*, venire ad un compromesso **5.** toccare, venire in contatto con; incontrare: *his hand met hers*, la sua mano incontrò quella di lei; *to* — *s.o.'s eye*, incontrare lo sguardo di qlcu. ‖ *to* — *the eye*, attirare l'attenzione ‖ *to make both ends* —, sbarcare il lunario **6.** *to* — *with* (*s.o., sthg.*), imbattersi in, essere colto da; subire: *he has met with an accident*, gli è capitata una disgrazia; *she met with her friend*, si imbatté nella sua amica; *we met with a storm*, fummo colti da un temporale.

meeting ['mi:tiŋ], *s.* **1.** riunione, convegno, raduno; assemblea, seduta: — *of creditors*, assemblea dei creditori; *a* — *took place last week*, la settimana scorsa ci fu un raduno; *to address the* —, prender la parola (a un raduno); *to call a* — *of the shareholders*, convocare gli azionisti; *to put a resolution to the* —, (*pol.*) sottoporre una mozione all'approvazione dell'assemblea **2.** duello **3.** incontro; incrocio: *at the* — *of the rivers*, alla confluenza dei due fiumi; *I didn't like him at first* —, non mi piacque al primo incontro ☆ — *-house*, luogo di riunione dei quaccheri; — *-place*, luogo di riunione; — *-point*, (*geom.*) punto d'intersezione.

meetly ['mi:tli], *av.* (*arc.*) convenientemente, propriamente.

meetness ['mi:tnis], *s.* (*arc.*) conformità, convenienza.

Meg [meg], *no.pr.f. dim.* di **Margaret**.

megacephalic [,megəsi'fælik], **megacephalous** [,megə'sefələs], *ag.* (*patol.*) megalocefalo.

megacycle ['megə,saikl], *s.* (*rad.*) megaciclo.

megalith ['megəliθ], *s.* (*archeol.*) megalito.

megalithic [,megə'liθik], *ag.* (*archeol.*) megalitico.

megalomania ['megəlou'meinjə], *s.* megalomania.

megalomaniac ['megəlou'meiniæk], *ag.* di megalomania; di megalomane ‖ *s.c.* megalomane.

megalosaurus [,megəlou'sɔ:rəs], *s.* (*paleont.*) megalosauro.

megaphone ['megəfoun], *s.* megafono.

megapod ['megəpɒd], **megapode** ['megəpoud], *s.* (*ornit.*) megapodo.

megatherium [,megə'θiəriəm], *pl.* **megatheria** [,megə'θiəriə], *s.* (*paleont.*) megaterio.

megaton ['megətʌn], *s.* (*fis. atomica*) megaton.

megass(e) [me'gæs], *s.* residuo fibroso della canna da zucchero.

megawatt ['megəwɒt], *s.* (*elett.*) megawatt.

megger ['megə*], *s.* (*elett.*) «megger», megaohmetro.

megilp [mə'gilp], *s.* (*art.*) solvente liquido per colori a olio.

megrim ['mi:grim], *s.* **1.** emicrania; vertigine **2.** *pl.* cattivo umore; depressione **3.** *pl.* (*vet.*) capostorno.

meiosis [mai'ousis], *s.* **1.** (*ret.*) litote **2.** (*biol.*) meiosi.

melancholia [,melən'kouljə], *s.* melanconia, depressione psichica.

melancholic [,melən'kɒlik], *ag.* melanconico; triste, abbattuto; psichicamente depresso.

melancholy ['melənkəli], *ag.* malinconico, triste ‖ *s.* malinconia; depressione; tristezza.

Melanesia [,melə'ni:zjə], *no.pr.* (*geog.*) Melanesia.

Melanesian [,melə'ni:zjən], *ag.* melanesiano, della Melanesia.

melanism ['melənizəm], *s.* (*fisiol. patol.*) melanismo.

melanosis [,melə'nousiz], *s.* (*patol.*) melanismo.

melanuria [,melə'njuəriə], *s.* (*patol.*) melanuria.

Melchizedek [mel'kizədek], *no.pr.m.* (*st.*) Melchisedec.

Meleager [,meli'eigə*], *no.pr.m.* (*mit.*) Meleagro.

mêlée ['melei], *s.* mischia, confusione.

Meliboeus [,meli'bi:əs], *no.pr.m.* (*lett.*) Melibeo.

melic ['melik], *ag.* (*poes.*) melico.

melinite ['melinait], *s.* melinite (esplosivo).

to meliorate ['mi:ljəreit], *V.* **to ameliorate**.

melioration [,mi:ljə'reifən], *V.* **amelioration**.

mellay, (*arc.*) per **mêlée**.

mellifero s [me'lifərəs], *ag.* mellifero.

mellifluence [me'lifluəns], *s.* mellifluità.

mellifluous [me'lifluəs], *ag.* melliffuo.

mellifluously [me'lifluəsli], *av.* mellifluamente.

mellow ['melou], *ag.* **1.** succoso, maturo (di frutta); stagionato; amabile (di vino) **2.** *fig.* comprensivo; pacato (di persona) **3.** *fig.* pastoso, pieno, caldo (di luce, suono, colore) **4.** ricco, ubertoso, fertile (di terreno) **5.** (*fam.*) allegro, gioviale; un po' brillo.

to mellow, *v.t.i.* **1.** maturare, far maturare; stagionare, stagionarsi (di frutta, vino, ecc.) **2.** *fig.* maturarsi, addolcirsi (di persona) **3.** diventare ricco, dolce, pastoso (di luce, suono, colore) **4.** (*fam.*) essere un po' brillo.

mellowness ['melounis], *s.* **1.** succosità, maturità, dolcezza (di frutta, vino, ecc.) **2.** *fig.* dolcezza; comprensione; maturità (di persona) **3.** *fig.* ricchezza, pastosità (di luce, suono, colore) **4.** ricchezza, fertilità, ubertosità (di terreno) **5.** (*fam.*) giovialità; leggera ebbrezza.

melodeon [mi'loudiən], *s.* (*mus.*) melodion.

melodic [mi'lɒdik], *ag.* melodico, di melodia.

melodion [mi'loudiən], *s.* (*mus.*) melodion.

melodious [mi'loudjəs], *ag.* melodioso.

melodiously [mi'loudjəsli], *av.* melodiosamente.

melodiousness [mi'loudjəsnis], *s.* melodiosità.

melodist ['meloudist], *s.* (*mus.*) melodista.

to melodize ['melədaiz], *v.t.i.* **1.** fare delle melodie **2.** rendere melodioso **3.** mettere in musica.

melodrama ['melə,drɑ:mə], *s.* **1.** melodramma **2.** dramma a lieto fine **3.** *fig.* melodramma.

melodramatic [,meloudrə'mætik], *ag.* melodrammatico.

melodramatically [,meloudrə'mætikəli], *av.* in modo melodrammatico.

melodramatist [,melou'dræmətist], *s.* autore di melodrammi.

melody ['melədi], *s.* **1.** melodia; canto; aria: *old Irish melodies*, vecchie arie irlandesi **2.** (*mus.*) tema, canto; melodia: *he should not emphasize the* — *so much*, non dovrebbe dare tanto rilievo al canto.

melon ['melən], *s.* **1.** melone, popone **2.** (*fam. amer.*) grosso margine di profitti (da dividere fra soci): *the boss gets a big cut from the* —, (*fam.*) il principale si prende una bella fetta di torta ☆ — *-cutting*, (*amer.*) distribuzione dei profitti; — *-shaped*, a forma di melone ‖ *water-* —, anguria.

Melos ['mi:lɒs], *no.pr.* (*geog.*) Milo.

Melpomene [mel'pɒmini(:)], *no.pr.f.* (*mit.*) Melpomene.

melt [melt], *s.* **1.** fusione; colata (di metallo fuso): *on the* —, in fusione **2.** scioglimento.

to melt, *pass.* **melted** ['meltid], *p.p.* **melted**, (*arc.*) **molten** ['moultən], *v.t.i.* **1.** liquefare, liquefarsi: *the sun will soon* — *the snow*, il sole scioglierà presto la neve; *these sweets* — *in the mouth*, questi dolci si sciolgono in bocca **2.** addolcire, intenerire, intenerirsi; sciogliersi: *it will — even his heart*, ciò intenerirà perfino lui; *she melted into tears*, si sciolse in lacrime **3.** *to* — **away**, sciogliersi completamente (di neve); disperdersi (di folla): *the clouds melted away*, le nuvole svanirono; *his anger was melting away*, la sua collera svaniva; *his money is melting away*, il suo denaro svanisce **4.** *to* — **down**, fondere (oggetti) per utilizzarne il metallo: *to* — *down silver spoons*, fondere dei cucchiai d'argento.

melter ['meltə*], *s.* fonditore.

melting ['meltiŋ], *ag.* **1.** che fonde, che fa fondere; che si scioglie **2.** *fig.* struggente; che intenerisce, commovente: *he spoke in a* — *voice*, parlò con voce commossa ‖ *s.* fusione; sostanza fusa; scioglimento ☆ — *-point*, (*fis.*) punto di fusione; — *-pot*, crogiuolo: *the U. S. are a* — *-pot of races*, gli Stati Uniti sono un crogiuolo di razze; *to put back into the* — *-pot*, *fig.* rimettere in discussione; riesaminare.

meltingly ['meltiŋli], *av.* teneramente.

melton ['meltən], *s.* «melton» (stoffa di lana da uomo).

member ['membə*], *s.* **1.** socio, membro: *ordinary* — (*of an association*), socio ordinario; *to become a* — *of an association*, diventare membro di una associazione ‖ — *of Congress*, (*M.C.*) membro del Congresso Americano ‖ — *of Parliament*, (*M.P.*) deputato al Parlamento Britannico **2.** (*anat.*) membro ‖ *the unruly* —, (*fam.*) lingua **3.** parte, pezzo, elemento (di macchina, di struttura, ecc.) ☆ *cross* —, (*mec.*) traversa; *side* —, (*mec.*) longherone.

membership ['membəʃip], *s.* **1.** l'insieme dei membri (di una associazione): *the* —*of T.C.I. is over one million*, i soci del T.C.I. superano il milione **2.** funzione di membro: *he has all the qualifications for* —, ha tutti i titoli per essere eletto socio ☆ — *card*, tessera di associazione.

membranaceous [,membrə'neiʃəs], *ag.* membranaceo.

membrane ['membrein], *s.* (*anat. bot.*) membrana.

membraneous [mem'breinjəs], **membranous** [mem-'breinəs], *ag.* membranoso.

memento [mi'mentou], *s.* **1.** memento, oggetto ricordo **2.** (*eccl.*) memento.

memo ['mi:mou], *V.* **memorandum**.

memoir ['memwɑ:*], *s.* **1.** saggio; monografia **2.** *pl.* memorie, ricordi ‖ *Churchill's " War Memoirs "*, « Le memorie di guerra » di Churchill.

memoirist ['memwɑ:rist], *s.* memorialista.

memorability [,memərə'biliti], *s.* memorabilità.

memorable ['memərəbl], *ag.* memorabile; indimenticabile.

memorably ['memərəbli], *av.* memorabilmente.

memorandum [,memə'rændəm], *pl.* **memoranda** [,memə'rændə], **memorandums** [,memə'rændəmz], *s.* memorandum, appunto ☆ — *-book* (o — *-sheet*), taccuino, agenda; — *-pad* (o — *-tablet*), blocco, blocchetto per appunti.

memorial [mi'mɔ:riəl], *ag.* **1.** commemorativo ‖ *Memorial-Day*, giornata della Rimembranza (festa nazionale degli Stati Uniti) **2.** (*rar. arc.*) memorabile ‖ *s.* **1.** monumento, cippo: *a* — *of*, un ricordo, un segno commemorativo di **2.** memoriale, libro di memorie **3.** *gener. pl.* memoriale, raccolta di documenti **4.** memoriale, supplica ☆ — *tablet*, lapide, targa commemorativa ‖ *war* —, monumento ai Caduti.

memorialist [mi'mɔ:riəlist], *s.c.* chi rivolge una petizione, postulante ‖ *s.* memorialista, scrittore di memorie.

to memorialize [mi'mɔ:riəlaiz], *v.t.* **1.** commemorare **2.** presentare una petizione a.

to memorize ['meməraiz], *v.t.* imparare a memoria; affidare al ricordo.

memory ['meməri], *s.* **1.** memoria: *within living* —, a memoria d'uomo; *if my* — *serves me well*, se ben mi ricordo; *speaking from* —, per quanto, fin dove ricordo; *to have a good, bad* —, avere una buona, cattiva memoria ‖ *to the best of my* —, per quanto mi ricordo **2.** ricordo, memoria: *in* — *of*, a ricordo di; *of blessed* —, di buona memoria; *to keep s.o.'s* — *alive*, tener vivo il ricordo di qlcu.

Memphis ['memfis], *no.pr.* (*geog. st.*) Menfi.

mem-sahib ['mem,sɑ:hib], *s.* (*ang.-in.*) signora europea.

men [men], *pl.* di **man**.

menace ['menəs], *s.* minaccia.

to menace, *v.t.* minacciare.

menacing ['menəsiŋ], *ag.* minaccioso, torvo.

menacingly ['menəsiŋli], *av.* minacciosamente.

ménage [me'nɑ:ʒ], *s.* «ménage», governo della casa.

menagerie [mi'nædʒəri], *s.* **1.** serraglio **2.** (*sl. teat.*) orchestra.

mend [mend], *s.* rattoppo, rammendo ‖ *to be on the* —, migliorare di salute, di condizione.

to mend, *v.t.i.* **1.** riparare; accomodare, aggiustare; rammendare: *to* — *stockings*, rammendare calze ‖ *to* — *the fire*, alimentare il fuoco **2.** *fig.* correggere, correggersi; emendare, emendarsi: *he will never* —, non si correggerà mai; *things will* —, le cose si aggiusteranno; *to* — *one's pace*, affrettare il passo; *to* — *one's ways*, correggersi ‖ *it is never too late to* —, *prov.* non è mai troppo tardi per correggersi ‖ *least said soonest mended*, *prov.* un bel tacer non fu mai scritto **3.** migliorare, ristabilirsi (in salute): *his health is slowly mending*, la sua salute migliora lentamente.

mendacious [men'deiʃəs], *ag.* mendace, menzognero.

mendaciously [men'deiʃəsli], *av.* in modo menzognero, mendacemente.

mendacity [men'dæsiti], *s.* **1.** abitudine di, tendenza a mentire: *I can't bear his* —, non posso sopportare la sua abitudine di mentire **2.** bugia, menzogna.

Mendelism ['mendəlizəm], *s.* (*biol.*) mendelismo.

mender ['mendə*], *s.c.* riparatore, riparatrice; rammendatore, rammendatrice.

mendicancy ['mendikənsi], *s.* — mendicità.

mendicant ['mendikənt], *ag.* mendicante: — *friars*, frati mendicanti ‖ *s.c.* mendicante.

mendicity [men'disiti], *s.* mendicità.

mending ['mendiŋ], *s.* **1.** riparazione; rammendo: *invisible* —, rammendo invisibile **2.** panni da ramendare: *that's the* — *I have to do*, quella è la roba che devo rammendare ☆ — *cotton*, — *wool*, cotone, lana da rammendo; — *outfit*, astuccio da lavoro ‖ *road* —, lavori stradali (di manutenzione).

Menelaus [,meni'leiəs], *no.pr.m.* (*mit.*) Menelao.

menhir ['menhiə*], *s.* (*archeol.*) pietra monumentale.

menial ['mi:njəl], *ag.* **1.** servile (di lavoro) **2.** che fa lavori servili (di persona) ‖ *s.* servo.

meningeal [mi'nindʒiəl], *ag.* meningeo.

meningitis [,menin'dʒaitis], *s.* (*patol.*) meningite.

meningocele [mi'niŋgousi:l], *s.* (*patol.*) meningocele.

meninx ['mi:niŋks], *pl.* **meninges** [mi'nindʒi:z], *s.* (*anat.*) meninge.

meniscus [mi'niskəs], *s.* (*anat. geom. fis.*) menisco.

menology [mi'nɔlədʒi], *s.* (*eccl.*) menologio.

menopause ['menoupɔ:z], *s.* (*fisiol.*) menopausa.

menorrhagia [,menou'reidʒiə], *s.* (*patol.*) menorragia.

menorrhea [,menou'ri:ə], *s.* (*fisiol.*) menorrea.

mensal[1] ['mensəl], *ag.* mensile.

mensal[2], *ag.* della mensa.

menses ['mensi:z], *s.pl.* (*fisiol.*) mestruazioni.

Menshevik ['menʃəvik], *s.* (*st. russa*) menscevico.

menstrual ['menstruəl], *ag.* **1.** (*fisiol.*) mestruale **2.** (*astr.*) mensile.

menstruation [,menstru'eiʃən], *s.* mestruazione.

mensurability [,menʃurə'biliti], *s.* misurabilità.

mensurable ['menʃurəbl], *ag.* **1.** misurabile **2.** (*mus.*) ritmico.

mensural ['menʃurəl], *ag.* di misura.

mensuration [,menʃuə'reiʃən], *s.* misurazione.

mental[1] ['mentl], *ag.* **1.** mentale, intellettuale: — *activities*, attività intellettuali; — *arithmetic*, calcolo mentale **2.** (*patol.*) mentale: *a — case* (o — *patient*), un malato di mente; — *disease*, malattia mentale ‖ *he is —*, (*sl.*) è un po' tocco ☆ — *defective* (o — *deficient*), deficiente; — *-hospital*, manicomio; — *specialist*, alienista; — *sphere*, campo intellettuale.

mental², *ag.* (*anat.*) mentale, del mento.

mentality [men'tæliti], *s.* **1.** potere intellettuale, intelligenza: *a person of average —*, una persona di media intelligenza **2.** mentalità.

mentally ['mentəli], *av.* mentalmente ☆ — *defective* (o — *deficient*), (bambino) deficiente, dallo sviluppo mentale ritardato.

mentation [men'teiʃən], *s.* lavorio mentale; stato mentale.

menthol ['menθɔl], *s.* (*farm.*) mentolo.

mention ['menʃən], *s.* menzione, citazione, allusione: *no — was made of it*, non ne fu fatto cenno ☆ *honourable —*, menzione d'onore.

to **mention**, *v.t.* accennare a, nominare, far menzione di: *above, before, under mentioned*, già citato, sopraddetto, sottocitato; *he said he would — it to him*, disse che gliene avrebbe parlato; *I must also — that*, devo anche dire, render noto che; *it was not mentioned in the paper*, il giornale non ne faceva cenno; *not to —* (o *without mentioning*), senza contare, senza dire nulla di; *she didn't — her father*, non ha parlato del padre ‖ *don't — it*, prego, si figuri, non c'è di che: *" Thank you so much ! ", " Please don't — it ! "*, « Grazie mille ! », « Ma Le pare, non c'è di che! ».

mentionable ['menʃənəbl], *ag.* menzionabile.

mentor ['mento:*], *s.* mentore, consigliere, guida.

menu ['menju:], *s.* ∗ menu ∗, lista delle vivande.

Mephistophelean [ˌmefistə'fi:liən], *ag.* mefistofelico.

Mephistopheles [ˌmefis'tɔfili:z], *no.pr.m.* Mefistofele ‖ *s. fig.* persona malvagia, satanica.

Mephistophelian [ˌmefistə'fi:liən], *ag.* mefistofelico.

mephitic [me'fitik], *ag.* mefitico.

mephitis [me'faitis], *s.* mefite.

mercantile ['mə:kəntail], *ag.* **1.** mercantile, commerciale **2.** mercenario, venale ☆ — *marine*, marina mercantile.

mercantilism ['mə:kəntailizəm], *s.* mercantilismo.

Mercator [mə:'keito:*], *no.pr.* (*st.*) Mercatore (geografo fiammingo) ‖ *—'s chart* (o *projection*), proiezione di Mercatore.

mercenarily ['mə:sinərili], *av.* da mercenario; venalmente.

mercenariness ['mə:sinərinis], *s.* venalità.

mercenary ['məsi:nəri], *ag.* mercenario, venale: *— motives*, motivi venali ‖ *s.* soldato mercenario.

mercer ['mə:sə*], *s.* negoziante di stoffe (specialmente seterie).

to **mercerize** ['mə:səraiz], *v.t.* (*tec.*) mercerizzare.

mercery ['mə:səri], *s.* **1.** commercio di seterie **2.** *coll.* seterie.

merchandise ['mə:tʃəndaiz], *s.* merce, mercanzia.

to **merchandise**, *v.t.i.* commerciare.

merchant ['mə:tʃənt], *s.* **1.** mercante, commerciante (specialmente all'ingrosso) ‖ *Company of Merchant Tailors*, (*st.*) corporazione dei sarti mercanti **2.** (*spec. amer.*) bottegaio, negoziante ☆ — *prince*, mercante molto facoltoso; — *service*, marina mercantile; — *ship*, nave mercantile.

merchantable ['mə:tʃəntəbl], *ag.* commerciabile.

merchantman, *pl.* **merchantmen** ['mə:tʃəntmən], *s.* **1.** (*arc.*) commerciante **2.** nave mercantile.

Mercia ['mə:ʃə], *no.pr.* (*geog. st.*) Mercia (uno dei regni della eptarchia anglosassone).

merciful ['mə:siful], *ag.* pietoso, misericordioso.

mercifully ['mə:sifuli], *av.* misericordiosamente.

mercifulness ['mə:sifulnis], *s.* misericordia, pietà.

to **mercify** ['mə:sifai], *v.t.* usare misericordia a, avere pietà di.

merciless ['mə:silis], *ag.* spietato, crudele.

mercilessly ['mə:silisli], *av.* spietatamente.

mercilessness ['mə:silisnis], *s.* spietatezza, crudeltà.

mercurial [mə:'kjuəriəl], *ag.* **1.** *Mercurial*, (*astr. mit.*) di Mercurio, mercuriale **2.** *fig.* vivace, attivo, pronto **3.** (*farm.*) mercuriale ‖ *s.* medicinale a base di mercurio.

mercurialism [mə:'kjuəriəlizəm], *s.* (*patol.*) mercurialismo.

mercuriality [mə:ˌkjuəri'æliti], *s.* vivacità, prontezza.

to **mercurialize** [mə:'kjuəriəlaiz], *v.t.* **1.** curare, trattare con mercurio **2.** rendere vivace, attivo, pronto.

mercuric [mə:'kjuərik], *ag.* (*chim.*) mercurico.

to **mercurify** [mə:'kjuərifai], *v.t.* estrarre mercurio da; mescolare, combinare con mercurio.

mercurous [mə:'kiurəs], *ag.* (*chim.*) mercurioso.

Mercury [mə:'kjuri], *no.pr.m.* (*mit.*) Mercurio ‖ *no.pr.* (*astr.*) Mercurio ‖ *mercury*, *s.* **1.** (*chim.*) mercurio ‖ *the — is rising*, il barometro sale, il tempo va migliorando; *fig.* le cose vanno meglio **2.** messaggero **3.** *fig.* vivacità, argento vivo **4.** (*bot.*) marcorella.

Mercutio [mə:'kju:fjou], *no.pr.m.* (*lett.*) Mercuzio.

mercy ['mə:si], *s.* **1.** misericordia, clemenza, pietà, compassione, carità: *divine —*, la misericordia divina; *God's infinite —*, l'infinita misericordia di Dio; *sisters of —*, suore di carità; *without —*, senza pietà; *works of —*, opere di carità; *to crave for —*, implorare pietà; *to find — with s.o.*, essere perdonato da qlcu.; *to have — upon s.o.* (o *to show — to s.o.*), dimostrare misericordia per qlcu. ‖ — *upon us !*, misericordia! **2.** grazia, mercè: *at the — of the waves*, alla mercè dei flutti; *what a — that you have met him !*, che fortuna che tu l'abbia incontrato!; *to be — (o to lie) at s.o.'s —*, essere alla mercè di qlcu.; *to be thankful for small mercies*, essere grato di ogni beneficio ☆ — *-seat*, (*Bibbia*) propiziatorio; *fig.* il Cristo, il Propiziatore; il trono di Dio; — *-slaying*, uccisione indolore (di animali).

mere¹ [miə*], *ag.* **1.** mero, puro, pretto: *a — coincidence*, una mera coincidenza **2.** mero, semplice; solo: *he is a — child*, è soltanto un bambino; *it is a question of a — £. 50*, si tratta di sole 50 sterline.

mere², *s.* laghetto; stagno.

mere³, *s.* (*arc.*) confine.

to **mere³**, *v.t.* (*arc.*) delimitare, segnare un confine a.

merely ['miəli], *av.* meramente, semplicemente, puramente; soltanto: *the invitation is — formal*, l'invito è puramente formale.

merestone ['miə-stoun], *s.* pietra miliare; confine.

meretricious [ˌmeri'triʃəs], *ag.* **1.** di meretrice **2.** vistoso; pomposo (di stile letterario).

meretriciously [ˌmeri'triʃəsli], *av.* **1.** da meretrice **2.** vistosamente; pomposamente.

meretriciousness [ˌmeri'triʃəsnis], *s.* **1.** qualità di meretrice **2.** vistosità; ampollosità: *the — of his style*, gli orpelli del suo stile.

meretrix ['meritriks], *pl.* **meretrices** [ˌmeri'traisi:z], *s.* (*letter.*) meretrice.

merganser [mə:'gænsə*], *s.* (*ornit.*) smergo, mergone.

to **merge** [mə:dʒ], *v.t.i.* **1.** immergersi, assorbire, essere assorbito: *twilight merged into darkness*, la luce del crepuscolo si spense nell'oscurità **2.** fondere, fondersi, amalgamarsi; incorporare: *the small banks were merged into one large organization*, le piccole banche furono fuse in una sola grande organizzazione.

merger ['mə:dʒə*], *s.* **1.** assorbimento **2.** fusione, incorporamento (di imprese commerciali, industriali).

merging ['mə:dʒiŋ], *s.* **1.** fusione **2.** assorbimento.

meridian [mə'ridiən], *ag.* **1.** meridiano, di mezzogiorno **2.** *fig.* culminante ‖ *s.* **1.** (*geog.*) meridiano **2.** *fig.* apogeo, culmine: *in the — of life*, nel fiore degli anni **3.** (*arc.*) siesta.

meridional [mə'ridiənl], *ag.* **1.** meridionale **2.** (*geog. mar.*) di meridiano ‖ *s.* meridionale, abitante del Sud (specialmente francese) ☆ — *distance*, distanza in longitudine.

meridionality [məˌridiə'næliti], s. qualità di meridionale; l'essere meridionale.

meridionally [mə'ridiənəli], av. meridionalmente; a sud, a mezzogiorno.

meringue [mə'ræŋ], s. meringa.

merino [mə'ri:nou], ag. di merino   s. 1. (zool.) merino 2. tessuto, lana di merino.

meristem ['meristem], s. (bot.) meristema.

merit ['merit], s. merito; pregio; valore: *a man of —*, un uomo che ha dei meriti, un uomo di valore; *it has great merits*, ha gran pregi; *we shall decide the question on its merits*, decideremo la questione valutandone i pro e i contro; *to make a — of sthg.*, farsi merito di ql.co., farsi vanto di ql.co. || *to go into the merits of a case*, (dir.) entrare in merito a, discutere una causa.

to **merit**, v.t. meritare; esser degno di.

meritorious [ˌmeri'tɔ:riəs], ag. meritorio, meritevole.

meritoriously [ˌmeri'tɔ:riəsli], av. meritevolmente.

meritoriousness [ˌmeri'tɔ:riəsnis], s. l'essere meritorio.

Merlin[1] ['mə:lin], no.pr.m. (lett.) Merlino.

merlin[2], s. (ornit.) smeriglio.

merlon ['mə:lən], s. (edil. mil.) merlone.

mermaid ['mə:meid], **mermaiden** ['mə:meidn], s. sirena.

merman ['mə:mæn], pl. **mermen** ['mə:men], s. tritone.

Merovaeus [ˌmerou'vi:əs], no.pr.m. (st.) Meroveo.

Merovingian [ˌmerou'vindʒiən], ag.s. (st.) merovingio.

merrily ['merili], av. gaiamente, allegramente.

merriness ['merinis], s. gaiezza, allegria.

merriment ['merimənt], s. gaiezza, allegria.

merry[1] ['meri], ag. 1. gaio, allegro, giocondo: *— as a lark* (o *— as a cricket*), allegro come un passero; *to be —*, essere allegro, (fam.) essere un po' brillo || *— Christmas!*, buon Natale! || *the more, the merrier*, più siamo, tanto meglio è (in feste, riunioni) || *to make —*, far festa, stare allegri || *to make — over s.o.*, *sthg.*, burlarsi di, prendersi giuoco di ql.co., qlcu. 2. (arc.) piacevole, amabile, dolce: *— England*, la dolce Inghilterra; *the — month of May*, il dolce mese di maggio ☆ *— -andrew*, pagliaccio, buffone; *— -go-round*, giostra, carosello (anche fig.).

merry[2], s. (bot.) visciola, amarena.

merrymaking ['meriˌmeikiŋ], s. festa, divertimento.

merrythought ['meriθɔ:t], s. (fam.) forcella (osso dello sterno del pollo) [il nome deriva dal giuoco di contendersi la parte più lunga: viene esaudito il desiderio della persona a cui essa resta].

Mersey ['mə:zi], no.pr. (geog.) Mersey.

mersion ['mə:ʃən], s. (rar.) immersione.

merycism ['merisizəm], s. (patol.) mericismo.

mesa ['meisə], s. altipiano roccioso.

mésalliance [me'zæliəns], s. «mésalliance» (matrimonio tra due persone di diversa classe sociale).

meseems [mi'si:mz], v.imp. (arc.) mi sembra.

mesenteric [ˌmesen'terik], ag. mesenterico.

mesenteritis [meˌsentə'raitis], s. (patol.) mesenterite.

mesentery ['mezəntəri], s. (anat.) mesentero.

mesh [meʃ], s. 1. maglia, interstizio (di una rete); pl. rete (anche fig.): *to be caught in s.o.'s meshes*, cadere, essere preso nella rete di qlcu. 2. (tec.) maglia, rete: *a 40 — screen*, un vaglio a 40 maglie per pollice lineare 3. (mec.) presa, ingranamento: *in —*, ingranato 4. (elett.) maglia 5. (fisiol.) struttura retiforme ☆ *— -connection*, collegamento poligonale; *constant — gear*, ingranaggio di presa continua.

to **mesh**, v.t.i. 1. (rar.) prender nella rete (anche fig.) 2. (mec.) ingranare.

meshy ['meʃi], ag. a rete.

mesial ['mi:zjəl], ag. mediano.

mesially ['mi:zjəli], av. nel mezzo.

meshing ['meʃiŋ], s. 1. ingranamento 2. graticcio ☆ *— gear*, ingranaggio accoppiato || *wire —*, reticolato di filo di ferro.

mesmeric [mez'merik], ag. mesmerico.

mesmerism ['mezmərizəm], s. mesmerismo.

mesmerist ['mezmərist], s. 1. seguace del mesmerismo 2. ipnotizzatore.

mesmerization [ˌmezməri'zeiʃən], s. mesmerizzazione.

to **mesmerize** ['mezməraiz], v.t. ipnotizzare.

mesne [mi:n], ag. (st. dir.) intermedio ☆ *— lord*, (st.) valvassore.

mesocarp ['mesoukɑ:p], s. mesocarpo.

meson ['mi:zɔn], s. (fis.) mesone.

mesophyll ['mesoufil], s. (bot.) mesofillo.

mesotron ['mesətrɔn], s. (fis.) mesotrone.

mesozoic [ˌmesou'zouik], ag. (geol.) mesozoico.

mess [mes], s. 1. (arc.) piatto, porzione 2. gruppo di persone che prendono un pasto in comune; (mar. mil.) mensa: *the new officer was introduced to the —*, il nuovo ufficiale fu presentato ai compagni di mensa 3. confusione, disordine; imbroglio, pasticcio: *what a —!*, che pasticcio!; *the room was in a —*, la stanza era in gran disordine; *to be in a nice —*, essere in un bel pasticcio; *to clear up the —*, rimettere in ordine; *to make a — of sthg.*, rovinare, buttare all'aria ql.co. ☆ *— -boy*, garzone di mensa, cameriere; *— jacket*, giacca da mensa (indossata dagli ufficiali); *— -tin*, gavetta || *officers' —*, mensa ufficiali, circolo ufficiali.

to **mess**, v.t.i. 1. mettere in disordine, fare confusione; imbrogliare: *they — up everything they meddle with*, creano disordine in tutte le cose in cui si immischiano; *to — (up) a business*, mandare a monte un affare 2. (gener. mil.) mangiare alla stessa tavola: *the five young men decided to — together*, i cinque giovani decisero di far mensa comune 3. *to — about*, bighellonare, perdersi in cose inutili.

message ['mesidʒ], s. 1. messaggio, ambasciata: *to leave a — for s.o.*, lasciare un messaggio per qlcu. 2. commissione || *to run messages*, fare commissioni || *to send s.o. on a —*, mandare qlcu. a fare una commissione 3. fig. profezia; messaggio ☆ *drop —*, messaggio paracadutato; *wireless —*, messaggio radio; *written -telephone —*, fonogramma.

to **message**, v.t. mandare come messaggio, trasmettere con segnalazioni, ecc.

messenger ['mesindʒə*], s. 1. messaggero 2. *— (-boy)*, fattorino ☆ *— cable*, (ind.) corda portante.

Messiah [mi'saiə], s. Messia.

Messiahship [mi'saiəʃip], s. dignità di Messia.

Messianic [ˌmesi'ænik], ag. messianico.

Messias [mi'saiəs], s. Messia.

Messidor [ˌmesi'dɔ:*], s. (st. francese) messidoro.

messmate ['mesmeit], s. compagno di mensa.

Messrs. ['mesəz], s.pl. signori: *— Brown and Co.*, (comm.) Spett. Ditta Brown e C.

messuage ['meswidʒ], s. (dir.) podere (casa e terreni).

messy ['mesi], ag. confuso, in disordine.

mestizo [mes'ti:zou], s. meticcio (dell'America centro-meridionale).

met [met], pass.p.p. di to meet.

metabasis [me'tæbəsis], s. (med.) metabasi.

metabolic [ˌmetə'bɔlik], ag. (biol. fisiol.) metabolico, pertinente al metabolismo ☆ *— -rate*, metabolismo.

metabolism [me'tæbəlizəm], s. (biol. fisiol.) metabolismo.

metacarpal [ˌmetə'kɑ:pəl], ag. (anat.) metacarpale.

metacarpus [ˌmetə'kɑ:pəs], s. (anat.) metacarpo.

metachronism [me'tækrənizəm], s. (ret.) metacronismo.

metage ['mi:tidʒ], s. 1. misurazione; pesatura 2. imposta sul peso.

metal ['metl], s. 1. metallo: *precious* (o *noble*) *—*, metallo prezioso; *to convert the ore into —*, estrarre il metallo da un minerale 2. (road-) *—*, brecciame, pietrisco 3. vetro fuso 4. (mil.) carro armato 5. potenza delle bocche da fuoco di una nave 6. pl. rotaie: *to leave* (o *to jump*) *the metals*, deragliare 7. pl. (tip.) caratteri ☆ *— -worker*, operaio metallurgico || *base —*, metallo base; *bell-* —, bronzo per campane; *wrought-* —, metallo lavorato, martellato.

to **metal**, *pass.p.p.* **metalled** ['metld], *v.t.* **1.** rivestire di metallo **2.** macadamizzare (una strada); inghiaiare (una linea ferroviaria).

metalepsis [,metə'lepsis], *s.* (*ret.*) metalessi.

metalled ['metld], *ag.* **1.** rivestito di metallo **2.** macadamizzato (di strada); inghiaiato (di linea ferroviaria).

metallic [mi'tælik], *ag.* metallico, di metallo ☆ — *currency*, moneta metallica.

metalliferous [,metə'lifərəs], *ag.* metallifero.

metalliform [mi'tælifɔ:m], *ag.* metalliforme.

metalling ['metliŋ], *s.* pietrisco (per opere stradali).

metallist ['metəlist], *s.* **1.** (*rar.*) operaio metallurgico **2.** (*econ. pol.*) sostenitore del sistema monetario metallico.

metallization [,metəlai'zeiʃən], *s.* **1.** (*fis.*) metallizzazione **2.** vulcanizzazione.

to **metallize** ['metəlaiz], *v.t.* **1.** (*fis.*) metallizzare **2.** vulconizzare.

metallography [,metə'lɔɡrəfi], *s.* metallografia.

metalloid ['metəloid], *ag.* (*min.*) metalloidico, simile a metallo ‖ *s.* (*min.*) metalloide.

metallurgic(al) [,metə'lə:dʒik(əl)], *ag.* metallurgico.

metallurgist [me'tælədʒist], *s.* operaio metallurgico.

metallurgy [me'tælədʒi], *s.* metallurgia.

metamorphic [,metə'mɔ:fik], *ag.* metamorfico.

metamorphism [,metə'mɔ:fizəm], *s.* (*geol.*) metamorfismo.

to **metamorphose** [,metə'mɔ:fouz], *v.t.* metamorfosare, trasformare.

metamorphosis [,metə'mɔ:fəsis], *pl.* **metamorphoses** [,metə'mɔ:fəsi:z], *s.* metamorfosi; trasformazione.

metaphor ['metəfə*], *s.* (*ret.*) metafora.

metaphoric(al) [,metə'fɔrik(əl)], *ag.* (*ret.*) metaforico.

metaphorically [,metə'fɔrikəli], *av.* (*ret.*) metaforicamente; sotto metafora.

metaphrase ['metəfreiz], *s.* **1.** (*ret.*) metafrasi; esposizione (di un testo) con altre parole **2.** traduzione letterale, parola per parola.

to **metaphrase**, *v.t.* **1.** esporre (un testo) con altre parole **2.** tradurre letteralmente, parola per parola.

metaphrastic [,metə'fræstik], *ag.* (*ret.*) metafrastico.

metaphysic [,metə'fizik], *V.* **metaphysics**.

metaphysic(al) [,metə'fizik(əl)], *ag.* **1.** (*fil.*) metafisico; ontologico **2.** astruso; astratto; troppo sottile **3.** soprannaturale; trascendentale.

metaphysically [,metə'fizikəli], *av.* **1.** metafisicamente **2.** astrusamente **3.** in modo soprannaturale.

metaphysician [,metəfi'ziʃən], *s.* (*fil.*) metafisico.

metaphysics [,metə'fiziks], *s.* (*fil.*) metafisica; ontologia.

metaplasm ['metəplæzəm], *s.* (*biol.*) metaplasma.

metapsychic(al) [,metə'saikik(əl)], *ag.* metapsichico.

metapsychics [,metə'saikiks], *s.* metapsichica.

metastasis [me'tæstəsis], *s.* (*patol.*) metastasi.

metastatic [,metə'stætik], *ag.* (*patol.*) metastatico ☆ — *abscess*, ascesso metastatico; — *ophthalmia*, oftalmia simpatica.

metatarsal [,metə'tɑ:səl], *ag.* (*anat.*) del metatarso.

metatarsus [,metə'tɑ:səs], *s.* (*anat.*) metatarso.

metathesis [me'tæθəsis], *pl.* **metatheses** [me'tæθəsi:z], *s.* **1.** (*gram.*) metatesi **2.** (*chim.*) sostituzione **3.** (*patol.*) metastasi.

metayage [me'teijidʒ], *s.* mezzadria.

metayer [me'teijə*], *s.* mezzadro.

mete[1] [mi:t], *s.* (*poet.*) misura.

to **mete**[1], *v.t.* (*poet.*) **1.** misurare **2.** *to* — **out**, dare (una ricompensa, una punizione); distribuire, ripartire.

mete[2], *s.* confine, limite; pietra di confine ‖ *metes and bounds*, (*dir.*) limiti e confini.

metempsychosis [,metempsi'kousis], *pl.* **metempsychoses** [,metempsi'kousi:z], *s.* metempsicosi.

meteor ['mi:tjə*], *s.* **1.** (*astr.*) meteora **2.** meteora, fenomeno atmosferico **3.** *fig.* cosa fugace.

meteoric [,mi:ti'ɔrik], *ag.* **1.** (*astr.*) meteorico, relativo a meteora **2.** meteorologico: — *agents*, agenti metereologici **3.** *fig.* transitorio.

meteorism ['mi:tiərizəm], *s.* (*patol.*) meteorismo.

meteorite ['mi:tjərait], *s.* meteorite, aereolito.

meteorograph ['mi:tiərəɡrɑ:f], *s.* meteorografo.

meteorologic(al) [,mi:tjərɔ'lɔdʒik(əl)], *ag.* meteorologico.

meteorologist [,mi:tjə'rɔlədʒist], *s.* meteorologo.

meteorology [,mi:tjə'rɔlədʒi], *s.* meteorologia.

meter[1] ['mi:tə*], *s.* contatore, misuratore; (*fam.*) tassametro ☆ *air* —, anemometro; *airflow* —, flussometro; *altitude* —, altimetro; *current* —, amperometro; *electric* — (o *electricity* —), contatore dell'elettricità; *gas-* —, contatore del gas; *slot-* —, contatore a moneta.

to **meter**[1], *v.t.* **1.** misurare; controllare **2.** dosare.

meter[2], (*amer.*) per **metre**[2].

meterage ['mi:təridʒ], *s.* misurazione a contatore.

methane ['meθein], *s.* (*chim.*) metano ☆ — *pipeline*, metanodotto.

metheglin [me'θeɡlin], *s.* (*arc.*) idromele aromatizzato.

methinks [mi'θiŋks], *pass.* **methought** [mi'θɔ:t], *v.imp.* (*arc.*) mi pare, mi sembra: — *you are wrong*, mi sembra che tu abbia torto.

method ['meθəd], *s.* **1.** metodo; modo, maniera: — *of payment*, modalità di pagamento; *a sure* —, un metodo sicuro **2.** ordine; regolarità; disposizione regolare; classificazione: *with* —, con ordine ‖ *there is* — *in his madness*, non è così matto come sembra.

methodic(al) [mi'θɔdik(əl)], *ag.* metodico; ordinato.

methodically [mi'θɔdikəli], *av.* metodicamente.

Methodism ['meθədizəm], *s.* (*relig.*) metodismo.

methodist ['meθədist], *s.c.* **1.** (*relig.*) metodista; (*spreg.*) persona di rigide vedute religiose **2.** chi si attiene scrupolosamente ad un metodo.

methodistic(al) [,meθə'distik(əl)], *ag.* (*relig.*) di, proprio del metodismo; di metodista.

to **methodize** ['meθədaiz], *v.t.* metodizzare; ordinare.

methodology [,meθə'dɔlədʒi], *s.* metodologia.

methought [mi'θɔ:t], *pass.* di **methinks**.

Methusalem [mi'θju:zələm], **Methuselah** [mi'θju:zələ], *no.pr.m.* (*Bibbia*) Matusalemme.

methyl ['meθil], *s.* (*chim.*) metile ☆ — *alcohol*, alcool metilico.

to **methylate** ['meθileit], *v.t.* (*chim.*) metilare, mescolare con metile: *methylated spirit*, alcool denaturato.

methylene ['meθili:n], *s.* (*chim.*) metilene.

methylic [mi'θilik], *ag.* (*chim.*) metilico.

meticulosity [mi,tikju'lɔsiti], *s.* meticolosità.

meticulous [mi'tikjuləs], *ag.* meticoloso; timoroso di sbagliare.

meticulously [mi'tikjuləsli], *av.* meticolosamente.

métier ['meitjei], *s.* occupazione, mestiere, professione.

metis ['meitis], *s.* meticcio.

metonymic(al) [,metə'nimik(əl)], *ag.* (*ret.*) metonimico.

metonymically [,metə'nimikəli], *av.* (*ret.*) metonimicamente.

metonymy [mi'tɔnimi], *s.* (*ret.*) metonimia.

metope ['metoup], *s.* (*arch.*) metope.

metoposcopist [,metou'pɔskəpist], *s.* metoposcopo.

metoposcopy [,metou'pɔskəpi], *s.* metoposcopia.

metre[1] ['mi:tə*], *s.* **1.** (*poes.*) metro **2.** metrica, prosodia **3.** componimento in versi **4.** (*mus.*) tempo.

to **metre**[1], *v.t.i.* comporre in versi; verseggiare.

metre[2], *s.* metro (unità di lunghezza = 39.37 in.) ☆ *cubic* —, metro cubo (misura di volume = 1.308 cu. yd.); *square* —, metro quadrato (misura di superficie = 1.196 sq. yd.).

metric[1] ['metrik], *ag.* (*poes.*) metrico.

metric[2], *ag.* metrico (di misura lineare) ☆ — *geometry*, geometria metrica; — *system*, sistema metrico decimale.

metrical ['metrikəl], *ag.* metrico (di misura lineare).

metrically ['metrikəli], *av.* metricamente; in metri.

metrics ['metriks], s. metrica, prosodia.

metrist ['metrist], s. versificatore, rimatore.

metrological [,metrə'lɔdʒikəl], ag. (fis.) metrologico.

metrology [me'trɔlədʒi], s. (fis.) metrologia.

metronome ['metrənoum], s. (mus.) metronomo.

metropolis [mi'trɔpəlis], s. metropoli.

metropolitan [,metrə'pɔlitən], ag. metropolitano ‖ the Metropolitan Area, i ventotto settori di Londra (la City esclusa) ‖ s. 1. abitante di una metropoli 2. (eccl.) vescovo metropolitano.

mettle ['metl], s. 1. animo, ardore, coraggio: full of —, pieno di foga, di coraggio ‖ to be on one's —, impegnarsi a fondo, voler dar prova del proprio valore; to put s.o. on his —, mettere qlcu. alla prova 2. carattere, tempra, temperamento: he showed the — he was made of, (fam.) mostrò di che tempra era.

mettled ['metld], mettlesome ['metlsəm], ag. 1. vivace, coraggioso; ardente (di persona) 2. focoso (di cavallo) ☆ high- — horse, cavallo assai focoso.

mew¹ [mju:], s. (ornit.) gabbiano.

to mew¹, v.t.i. (arc.) mutare (le penne).

mew², s. 1. gabbia per falchi 2. (rar.) tana, nascondiglio.

to mew², v.t. 1. rinchiudere (in gabbia) 2. rinchiudere, segregare; confinare.

mew³, s. il miagolare; miagolio.

to mew³, v.i. miagolare; stridere.

mew³, inter. miao! (suono onomatopeico).

mewing ['mju:iŋ], s. miagolio (del gatto); stridio (del gabbiano).

to mewl [mju:l], v.i. 1. miagolare 2. vagire (di neonati); gemere.

mews [mju:z], s. 1. (st.) scuderie reali a Londra 2. quartiere ove sorgono le scuderie cittadine.

Mexican ['meksikən], ag. messicano ‖ s.c. messicano, messicana.

Mexico ['meksikou], no.pr. (geog.) Messico ‖ Gulf of —, Golfo del Messico.

mezzanine ['mezəni:n], s. 1. mezzanino; ammezzato 2. (teat.) piano sotto il palcoscenico.

mezzo¹ ['medzou], s. abbr. di mezzo-soprano.

mezzo², s. abbr. di mezzotint.

mezzo-soprano ['medzousə'prɑ:nou], s. (mus.) mezzosoprano.

mezzotint ['medzoutint], s. 1. (art.) mezzatinta 2. (tip.) zincotipia a mezzatinta.

to mezzotint, v.t. incidere a mezzatinta.

mi [mi:], s. mi (nota musicale).

miaow [mi(:)'au], s. miao (verso del gatto).

to miaow, v.i. miagolare.

miasma [mi'æzmə], s. miasma, esalazione mefitica.

miasmal [mi'æzməl], miasmatic [miəz'mætik], ag. miasmatico.

(to) miaul [mi'ɔ:l], V. (to) miaow.

mica ['maikə], s. (min.) mica.

micaceous [mai'keiʃəs], ag. (min.) micaceo.

Micah ['maikə], no.pr.m. (Bibbia) Michea.

mice [mais], pl. di mouse.

Michael ['maikl], no.pr.m. Michele.

Michaelmas ['miklməs], s. festa di San Michele ☆ — -daisy, (bot.) aster.

to miche [mitʃ], v.i. (dial.) nascondersi; vagabondare; marinare la scuola.

Michelangelesque [,maikəl,ændʒə'lesk], ag. (art.) michelangiolesco.

Michelangelo [,maikəl'ændʒilou], no.pr.m. Michelangelo.

Michigander [,miʃi'gændə*], s.c. abitante del Michigan.

Mick [mik], no.pr.m. dim. di Michael ‖ s. (sl. amer.) irlandese.

Mickey Mouse ['miki'maus], no.pr.m. Topolino ‖ s. (sl. aer.) sganciabombe.

mickle ['mikl], s. (arc. scoz.) grande quantità ‖ many a little makes a —, prov. molti pochi fanno assai.

microbe ['maikroub], s. microbo.

microbial [mai'kroubiəl], ag. microbico, batterico.

microbiologist [,maikroubai'ɔlədʒist], s. batteriologo.

microbiology [,maikroubai'ɔlədʒi], s. microbiologia.

microcephalus ['maikrou'kefələs], ag. (patol.) microcefalo.

microcosm ['maikroukozəm], s. microcosmo.

microfilm ['maikroufilm], s. (foto.) microfilm.

micrographer [mai'krɔgrəfə*], s. micrografo.

micrographic [,maikrou'græfik], ag. micrografico.

micrography [mai'krɔgrəfi], s. micrografia.

microgroove ['maikrougru:v], s. microsolco.

micrology [mai'krɔlədʒi], s. micrologia.

micrometer [mai'krɔmitə*], s. micrometro.

micrometry [mai'krɔmitri], s. micrometria.

micron ['maikrɔn], s. micron (unità di lunghezza = 0.000039 in.).

Micronesian [,maikrou'ni:ʃən], ag.s.c. (abitante) della Micronesia.

microorganism ['maikrou'ɔ:gənizəm], s. microrganismo.

microphone ['maikrəfoun], s. (rad.) microfono.

microscope ['maikrəskoup], s. (scient.) microscopio.

microscopic(al) [,maikrəs'kɔpik(əl)], ag. microscopico: — examination, esame al microscopio; — lens, lente d'ingrandimento.

microscopically [,maikrəs'kɔpikəli], av. microscopicamente.

microscopist [mai'krɔskəpist], s. microscopista.

microscopy [mai'krɔskəpi], s. microscopia.

microseismograph [,maikrou'saizməgrɑ:f], s. (scient.) microsismografo.

microtome ['maikrətoum], s. (scient.) microtomo ☆ — section, sezione microscopica ottenuta col microtomo.

microwave ['maikrəweiv], s. (rad.) microonda ☆ — -beam, fascio di microonde.

micturition [,miktju'riʃən], s. (fisiol.) minzione.

mid [mid], ag. medio, in mezzo: from — August to — October, dalla metà di agosto alla metà di ottobre; a woman in her — fifties, una donna sui cinquantacinque anni ☆ — -air, tra cielo e terra: — -air stunts, (aer.) acrobazie a bassa quota; — -European, dell'Europa centrale; — -gut, (anat.) ileo; — -leg, a mezza gamba; — Lent, mezza quaresima; — -sea, mare aperto; — -Victorian, caratteristico della metà dell'epoca vittoriana.

mid, V. amid.

Midas ['maidæs], no.pr.m. (mit.) Mida.

midbrain ['midbrein], s. (anat.) mesencefalo.

midday ['middei], s. mezzogiorno ☆ the — meal, il pasto di mezzogiorno.

midden ['midn], s. (dial.) mucchio di letame ☆ — -pit, concimaia.

middle ['midl], ag. attributivo medio; intermedio, situato nel mezzo ‖ Middle Ages, Medioevo ‖ the Middle East, il Medio Oriente ‖ Middle English, l'inglese parlato fra il 1200 e il 1500 circa ‖ Middle Kingdom, la Cina ‖ Middle West, gli Stati della Prateria (U.S.A.) ‖ s. 1. mezzo, centro: in the — of his speech, nel bel mezzo del suo discorso; in the — of the room, nel centro della stanza 2. cintola, vita: he was up to his — in snow, la neve gli arrivava alla cintola ‖ I've got a pain in my —, (fam.) ho male di pancia ☆ — -aged, di mezza età; — article, (sl.) articolo di carattere letterario, elzeviro; — class, la borghesia; della borghesia; — finger, (dito) medio; — ground, (pitt.) secondo piano; — -sized, di misura media; — term, (fil.) termine medio (di sillogismo); — voice, (gram.) voce media (dei verbi greci); — -watch, (mar.) secondo turno di guardia.

to middle, v.t. 1. (tec.) porre, collocare nel mezzo, nel centro 2. (calcio) rimandare (il pallone) al centro 3. (mar.) piegare (una vela) in due.

middleman ['midlmæn], pl. middlemen ['midlmen]

s. **1.** (*comm.*) intermediario, mediatore **2.** (*irl.*) latifondista che affitta piccoli lotti di terreno.

middlemost ['midlmoust], *V.* **midmost** *ag.*

middling ['midliŋ], *ag.* **1.** medio (di grandezza, qualità, grado, ecc.) **2.** passabile **3.** che gode discreta salute **4.** (*comm.*) corrente, mediocre.

middling, *av.* discretamente, passabilmente: — *good,* discretamente buono.

middlings ['midliŋz], *s.pl.* **1.** merci di qualità corrente **2.** semolino **3.** (*min.*) minerale di media frantumazione.

midge [midʒ], *s.* **1.** (*entom.*) moscerino **2.** persona molto piccola.

midget ['midʒit], *s.* **1.** persona piccolissima; nano **2.** cosa piccolissima: — *wireless set,* apparecchio radio tascabile.

midland ['midlənd], *ag.* centrale; interno.

Midlands (the) ['midləndz], *s.pl.* contee dell'Inghilterra centrale.

midmost ['midmoust], *ag.* il più vicino al centro ‖ *s.* il centro.

midmost, *av.* nel bel mezzo.

midmost, *prep.* nel bel mezzo di.

midnight ['midnait], *s.* mezzanotte; notte fonda ‖ *to burn the — oil,* lavorare, scrivere durante la notte, vegliare lavorando ☆ — *gloom,* tenebre notturne; — *sun,* il sole di mezzanotte.

midrib ['midrib], *s.* (*bot.*) venatura centrale (d'una foglia).

midriff ['midrif], *s.* **1.** (*anat.*) diaframma **2.** (*fam. neol.*) corpetto attillato e scollato.

midship ['midʃip], *s.* (*mar.*) parte centrale della nave ☆ — *section,* sezione maestra.

midshipman, *pl.* **midshipmen** ['midʃipmən], *s.* **1.** (*mar.*) guardia marina **2.** (*amer.*) allievo dell'Accademia Navale.

midships ['midʃips], *av.* nel mezzo della nave.

midst [midst], *s.* mezzo, centro: *in the — of,* nel mezzo di, durante; *in our —,* fra noi.

midst, *av.* nel mezzo: *first, —, and last,* da principio, a mezzo, infine ‖ *prep.* (*poet.*) in mezzo, tra.

midsummer ['mid.sʌmə*], *s.* il pieno, il cuore dell'estate; il solstizio d'estate ‖ *"A Midsummer Night's Dream",* (*lett.*) « Sogno di una notte di mezz'estate » ☆ — *day,* il giorno di S. Giovanni (24 giugno).

midway ['mid'wei], *ag.* (*rar. poet.*) posto a mezza via ‖ *s.* (*amer.*) viale centrale di una esposizione, di un parco di divertimento.

midway, *av.* a mezza strada; a metà distanza: — *up the hill,* a mezza costa; *the house stands — between the river and the church,* la casa si trova a mezza via tra il fiume e la chiesa.

mid-week ['midwi:k], *ag.* di metà settimana.

midwife ['midwaif], *pl.* **midwives** ['midwaivz], *s.* levatrice.

midwifery ['midwifəri], *s.* arte, professione di levatrice; ostetricia.

midwinter ['mid'wintə*], *s.* il pieno, il cuore dell'inverno; il solstizio d'inverno.

mien [mi:n], *s.* (*letter.*) aspetto, portamento, aria (di una persona).

miff [mif], *s.* (*fam.*) broncio, picca; battibecco: *to get in a —,* stizzirsi.

to miff, *v.t.i.* (*fam.*) offendere, offendersi: *to be miffed,* essere offeso; tenere il broncio.

miffy ['mifi], *ag.* (*fam.*) suscettibile.

might [mait], *s.* potere, potenza; forza: *God's —,* la potenza di Dio; *to work with all one's —,* lavorare con tutte le forze ‖ *with — and main,* con tutte le forze ‖ *— is right,* prov. la ragione è del più forte.

might, *pass.* di **may.**

mightful ['maitful], *ag.* (*poet.*) potente; forte.

might-have-been ['maithəv.bi:n], *s.* **1.** ciò che avrebbe potuto essere, occasione perduta: *he kept talking of —,* continuava a parlare di ciò che avrebbe

potuto essere **2.** (individuo) fallito: *as a writer, he was a —,* come scrittore, era un fallito.

mightily ['maitili], *av.* **1.** potentemente; fortemente **2.** (*fam.*) estremamente: *he was — happy,* toccava il cielo con un dito.

mightiness ['maitinis], *s.* potenza, potere ‖ *His, Your (High) —,* (*iron.*) Sua, Vostra altezza.

mightn't ['maitnt], *contr.* di *might not.*

mighty ['maiti], *ag.* **1.** potente, possente; forte **2.** massiccio; imponente ‖ *the —,* i potenti.

mighty, *av.* (*fam.*) molto, assai, estremamente: *I'm — proud of you,* sono molto fiero di te; *it's — nice of you!,* è proprio bello da parte tua!.

mignonette [.minjə'net], *s.* **1.** (*bot.*) reseda **2.** « mignonette » (sorta di pizzo).

migraine ['migrein], *s.* emicrania.

migrant ['maigrənt], *ag.* migratore; emigrante ‖ *s.c.* migratore, migratrice; emigrante.

to migrate [mai'greit], *v.i.* emigrare; trasmigrare.

migration [mai'greiʃən], *s.* **1.** migrazione; emigrazione **2.** (*chim.*) emigrazione (di atomi da una molecola all'altra).

migrator [mai'greitə*], *s.c.* migratore, migratrice; emigrante.

migratory ['maigrətəri], *ag.* **1.** migratore; nomade **2.** viaggiatore, di passo (di uccelli, ecc.) **3.** migratorio.

mikado [mi'kɑ:dou], *s.* mikado (titolo dato all'imperatore del Giappone).

Mike [maik], *no.pr.m. dim.* di **Michael** ‖ *for the love of —!,* per l'amor del cielo!.

mike¹, *s.* (*sl.*) ozio; pigrizia: *to be on the —,* oziare.

to mike¹, *v.i.* (*sl.*) oziare.

mike², *s.* (*abbr. fam.* di *microphone*) microfono ☆ — *stew,* sibilo del microfono.

mil [mil], *s.* mille (unità di lunghezza = mm. 0,0254); millesimo convenzionale: *per —,* per mille, al mille.

Milady [mi'leidi], *s.* « milady », mia signora.

milage ['mailidʒ], *s.* **1.** distanza in miglia **2.** spese di viaggio, di trasporto per miglia ☆ — *recorder,* contachilometri.

Milan [mi'læn], *no.pr.* (*geog.*) Milano.

Milanese [.milə'ni:z], *ag.s.c.* milanese.

milch [miltʃ], *ag.* da latte ☆ — *-cow,* mucca da latte; *fig.* fonte di denaro, di guadagno: *his uncle George is the — -cow of the family,* suo zio Giorgio è la provvidenza per tutta la famiglia.

mild [maild], *ag.* **1.** dolce, moderato; gentile: *a — answer,* una risposta gentile; *a — climate,* un clima mite; *a — disposition,* un carattere dolce, mite; *a — punishment,* una moderata punizione **2.** dolce, leggero (di cibo, bevanda, tabacco): — *beer,* birra leggera; — *cheese,* formaggio dolce **3.** blando (di medicina).

to milden ['maildən], *v.t.i.* mitigare, rendere mite; mitigarsi, diventare mite.

mildew ['mildju:], *s.* muffa; ruggine (delle graminacee); oidio (della vite).

to mildew, *v.t.i.* procurar la muffa, la ruggine, l'oidio a; ammuffire; coprirsi di ruggine (delle graminacee); coprirsi di oidio (della vite).

mildewy ['mildju:i], *ag.* ammuffito, coperto di muffa.

mildly ['maildli], *av.* dolcemente; moderatamente.

mildness ['maildnis], *s.* dolcezza; mitezza; moderazione.

mile [mail], *s.* **1.** miglio (misura di lunghezza = km. 1,6093) ‖ *no modern writer comes (o is) within miles of Dante, fig.* nessuno scrittore moderno può essere anche lontanamente paragonato a Dante; *to be miles better than..., fig.* valere infinitamente di più di...; *to be miles from thinking that, fig.* essere a mille miglia dal pensare che **2.** corsa di un miglio ☆ *square —,* miglio quadrato (misura di superficie = km². 2,5885).

mileage, *V.* **milage.**

miler ['mailə*], *s.* cavallo, individuo allenato per corse sul miglio.

Milesian¹ [mai'li:zjən], *ag.s.c.* (abitante) di Mileto.

Milesian[2], *ag.s.c.* irlandese.
milestone ['mail-stoun], *s.* pietra miliare.
milfoil ['milfoil], *s.* (*bot.*) millefoglio.
miliary ['miliəri], *ag.* (*patol.*) migliare, simile a grani di miglio ☆ — *fever*, febbre migliare.
milieu ['mi:ljə:], *s.* (*letter.*) ambiente.
militancy ['militənsi], *s.* 1. inclinazione, tendenza alla lotta 2. (*pol.*) attivismo.
militant ['militənt], *ag.* 1. militante || *the Church* —, (*eccl.*) la Chiesa militante 2. (*pol.*) attivo, militante || *s.* (*pol.*) attivista.
militarily ['militərili], *av.* militarmente.
militarism ['militərizəm], *s.* militarismo.
militarist ['militərist], *s.* militarista.
militarization ['militərai'zeiʃən], *s.* militarizzazione.
to **militarize** ['militəraiz], *v.t.* militarizzare.
military ['militəri], *ag.* militare; guerresco: — *men*, i militari; — *preparations*, preparazioni belliche || *s. coll.* (*the*) —, i militari, l'esercito, la truppa.
to **militate** ['militeit], *v.i.* 1. *fig.* militare || *to* — *against sthg.*, opporsi a ql.co.; *to* — *in favour of sthg.*, sostenere ql.co. 2. (*arc.*) militare, combattere.
militia [mi'liʃə], *s.* milizia, guardia nazionale.
militiaman, *pl.* **militiamen** [mi'liʃəmən], *s.* milite.
milk [milk], *s.* latte || *land of* — *and honey*, paese della cuccagna || *to come home with the* —, rientrare alle ore piccole || *it is no use crying over spilt* —, *prov.* è inutile piangere sul latte versato ☆ — *-and-water*, insipido; all'acqua di rose; — *-bar*, bar dove si vendono solo analcoolici; — *-cow*, mucca lattifera; — *-crust*, (*patol.*) crosta lattea; — *-dentition*, denti di latte; — *diet*, dieta lattea; — *-fever*, (*patol.*) febbre lattea; — *float*, furgone del latte; — *-glass*, (*ind.*) opalina; — *-punch*, punch al latte; — *run*, (*sl. mil. amer.*) missione di volo spesso ripetuta; — *-shake*, frullato di latte; — *-sugar*, (*chim.*) lattosio; — *-tooth*, dente di latte; — *-walk*, giro giornaliero del lattivendolo; — *-white*, bianco come il latte; (*tec.*) lattescente || *new* —, latte appena munto; *skim* —, latte scremato; *whole* —, latte intero.
to **milk**, *v.t.i.* 1. mungere: *to* — *a cow*, mungere una mucca || *to* — *the bull* (o *the ram*), *fig.* tentare ql.co. di impossibile, cavar sangue da una rapa 2. estrarre, cavare (liquido, da piante, animali): *to* — *venom from a snake*, estrarre il veleno da un serpente 3. *fig.* sfruttare (una persona) 4. produrre latte: *the cows are milking well now*, le mucche producono molto latte ora 5. (*fam.*) captare (messaggi su un circuito telefonico, telegrafico, ecc.).
milker ['milkə*], *s.c.* mungitore, mungitrice || *s.* (mucca) produttrice di latte ☆ *mechanical* —, mungitrice meccanica.
milkily ['milkili], *av.* 1. con aspetto lattiginoso 2. gentilmente; effeminatamente.
milkiness ['milkinis], *s.* 1. lattescenza 2. gentilezza; effeminatezza.
milking ['milkiŋ], *s.* 1. mungitura 2. (*tel.*) intercezione ☆ — *machine*, mungitrice; — *-time*, ora della mungitura.
milkmaid ['milkmeid], *s.* mungitrice; operaia di caseificio.
milkman, *pl.* **milkmen** ['milkmən], *s.* lattaio, lattivendolo.
milksop ['milksɔp], *s.* (*fam.*) uomo debole, effeminato.
milkweed ['milkwi:d], *s.* pianta appartenente alla famiglia delle asclepiadacee.
milkwoman ['milk,wumən], *pl.* **milkwomen** ['milk,wimin], *s.* lattaia.
milkwort ['milk-wə:t], *s.* (*bot.*) poligala.
milky ['milki], *ag.* 1. latteo; lattiginoso || *the Milky Way*, (*astr.*) la Via Lattea 2. *fig.* gentile; effeminato.
mill[1] [mil], *s.* 1. mulino || *all is grist that comes to his* —, trae profitto da tutto || *God's* — *grinds slow but sure*, *prov.* Dio non paga il sabato || *to bring grist to the* —, *fig.* tirar l'acqua al proprio mulino || *to put*,

to go through the —, *fig.* mettere, essere messo a dura prova; farne passare, passarne di tutti i colori 2. opificio, fabbrica, stabilimento 3. macinino; utensile per macinare, tritare; frullatore 4. (*ind.*) mescolatore (di gomma); (*ind. tessile*) molazza; (*mec.*) fresa; (*mec.*) laminatoio; treno 5. incontro di pugilato ☆ — *-hand*, operaio di fabbrica; — *-owner*, proprietario di mulino; — *-wheel*, ruota di mulino || *coffee-* —, macinino da caffè; *cotton-* —, cotonificio; *oil-* —, oleificio; *paper-* —, cartiera; *pepper-* —, macinino del pepe; *powder-* —, polverificio; *rolling-* —, (*mec.*) laminatoio; *saw-* —, segheria; *sugar -* —, zuccherificio; *water-* —, mulino ad acqua.
to **mill**[1], *v.t.i.* 1. macinare; tritare; frantumare: *to* — *grain*, macinare il grano; *to* — *ore*, frantumare minerali 2. (*ind.*) follare (panni); (*mec.*) fresare; coniare (monete); segare; laminare in barre 3. sbattere, frullare: *to* — *chocolate*, frullare la cioccolata 4. (*sl.*) fare a pugni con; picchiare 5. circolare disordinatamente; assieparsi (di bestiame, folla).
mill[2], *s.* (*amer.*) millesimo di dollaro.
millboard ['milbɔ:d], *s.* cartone doppio, pressato.
milldam ['mildæm], *s.* chiusa di mulino.
milled [mild], *ag.* 1. macinato, tritato, frantumato 2. (*ind.*) follato; (*mec.*) fresato; coniato (di moneta) 3. frullato, sbattuto.
millenarian [,mili'nɛəriən], *ag.s.* millenario.
millenarianism [,mili'nɛəriənizəm], *s.* (*st. relig.*) millenarismo.
millenary [mi'lenəri], *ag.* millenario || *s.* millennio.
millennial [mi'leniəl], *ag.* del millennio.
millennium [mi'leniəm], *s.* 1. millennio 2. *fig.* periodo di buon governo e prosperità.
millepede ['milipi:d], *s.* (*entom.*) millepiedi.
millepore ['milipɔ:*], *s.* (*zool.*) milleporide.
miller ['milə*], *s.* 1. mugnaio 2. (*mec.*) fresatrice 3. operaio fresatore 4. (*entom.*) maggiolino ☆ —'s *thumb*, (*ittiol.*) ghiozzo.
millesimal [mi'lesiməl], *ag.s.* millesimo.
millet ['milit], *s.* (*bot.*) miglio.
milliard ['miljɑ:d], *s.* 1. miliardo 2. (*amer.*) bilione.
milliary ['miljəri], *ag.* miliare || *s.* (*archeol.*) pietra miliare.
milligram(me) ['miligræm], *s.* milligrammo (misura di peso = 0.015 gr.).
millilitre ['mili,li:tə*], *s.* millilitro (misura di capacità = 0.061 cu. in.).
millimetre ['mili,mi:tə*], *s.* millimetro (misura di lunghezza = 0.039 in.).
milliner ['milinə*], *s.* 1. modista 2. (*arc.*) venditore di articoli di moda (specialmente importati da Milano) ☆ *man* —, *fig.* uomo dedito a occupazioni frivole.
millinery ['milinəri], *s.* 1. modisteria 2. articoli di modisteria.
milling ['miliŋ], *s.* 1. macinatura 2. (*mec.*) fresatura.
million ['miljən], *s.* milione: *a* (o *one*) — *men*, un milione di uomini || *the* —, *fig.* la folla || *that man is worth millions*, è un arcimilionario.
millionaire [,miljə'nɛə*], *s.* milionario.
millionairess [,miljə'nɛəris], *s.* milionaria.
millionary ['miljənəri], *ag.* milionario.
millionfold ['miljənfould], *ag.* di un milione di volte.
millionfold, *av.* un milione di volte.
millionth ['miljənθ], *ag.s.* milionesimo.
millipede ['milipi:d], *s.* (*entom.*) millepiedi.
millocrat ['miləkræt], *s.* ricco industriale.
millpond ['mil-pɔnd], *s.* gora di mulino.
millrace ['mil-reis], *s.* corrente che aziona un mulino.
millstone ['mil-stoun], *s.* 1. pietra da mulino, macina || *to be between the upper and nether* —, *fig.* essere fra l'incudine e il martello || *to see through a* —, avere il dono della chiaroveggenza 2. *fig.* peso, gravame.
millwright ['mil-rait], *s.* disegnatore, costruttore di mulini.
Milord [mi'lɔ:*], *s.* « milord », mio signore.

milt [milt], *s.* **1.** (*anat.*) milza **2.** latte di pesce.

to milt, *v.t.* fecondare (di pesce maschio).

milter ['miltə*], *s.* pesce maschio (nel periodo della fecondazione).

Miltiades [mil'taiədi:z], *no.pr.m.* (*st.*) Milziade.

Miltonian [mil'touniən], **Miltonic** [mil'tɔnik], *ag.* miltoniano.

Miltonically [mil'tɔnikəli], *av.* nello stile di Milton.

mime ['maim], *s.* **1.** (*teat.*) mimo (rappresentazione, attore) **2.** buffone, istrione, imitatore.

to mime, *v.i.* (*teat.*) mimare.

mimeograph ['mimiəgra:f], *s.* (*tec.*) ciclostile.

to mimeograph, *v.t.* ciclostilare.

mimesis [mi'mi:sis], *s.* (*biol.*) mimesi.

mimetic(al) [mi'metik(əl)], *ag.* mimetico.

mimetically [mi'metikəli], *av.* mimeticamente, in modo imitativo.

mimic ['mimik], *ag.* **1.** imitativo: — *coloration*, colorazione mimetica; — *skill*, abilità imitativa || *the* — *art*, la mimica **2.** falso, contraffatto: *a* — *battle*, una battaglia per burla || *s.* **1.** mimo; imitatore **2.** contraffazione, imitazione.

to mimic, *pass.p.p.* **mimicked** ['mimikt], *v.t.* **1.** imitare; contraffare; scimmiottare: *she can* — *the actresses very well*, essa sa imitare molto bene le grandi attrici **2.** imitare; assomigliare molto a: *wood painted to* — *marble*, legno dipinto ad imitazione del marmo.

mimicker ['mimikə*], *s.c.* imitatore, imitatrice; contraffattore, contraffattrice.

mimicry ['mimikri], *s.* **1.** mimesi; imitazione; parodia **2.** mimetismo: *protective* —, mimetismo protettivo **3.** mimica.

miminy-piminy ['mimini'pimini], *ag.* affettato; pretenzioso; sdolcinato.

mimosa [mi'mouzə], *s.* (*bot.*) mimosa.

mimulus ['mimjuləs], *s.* (*bot.*) mimolo.

mina[1] ['mainə], *pl.* **minae** ['maini:], *s.* (*st.*) mina (moneta greca del valore di 100 dracme).

mina[2], *s.* passeraceo d'Oriente.

minacious [mi'neiʃəs], *ag.* minaccioso.

minaciously [mi'neiʃəsli], *av.* minacciosamente.

minacity [mi'næsiti], *s.* minacciosità.

minar [mi'na:*], *s.* **1.** faro **2.** torre.

minaret ['minəret], *s.* minareto.

minatory ['minətəri], *ag.* minatorio; minaccioso.

mince [mins], *s.* carne tritata ☆ — *-pie*, pasticcio di frutta secca e carne tritata.

to mince, *v.t.i.* **1.** tritare, tagliuzzare **2.** abbreviare, tagliare una parte di (discorso, ecc.) **3.** *fig.* attenuare; mitigare: *not to* — *matters*, parlare con franchezza **4.** parlare, pronunciare con affettazione: *to* — *one's words*, parlare con affettazione **5.** camminare a passettini, in modo affettato.

minced [minst], *ag.* sminuzzato, tritato.

mincemeat ['mins-mi:t], *s.* **1.** carne tritata **2.** composta mista di frutta secca, mele, ecc. || *to make* — *of sthg.*, *s.o.*, *fig.* fare polpette di, demolire ql.co., qlcu.

mincer ['minsə*], *s.* tritacarne.

mincing ['minsiŋ], *ag.* affettato; smorfioso: — *gait*, portamento affettato.

mincingly ['minsiŋli], *av.* con ostentazione.

mind [maind], *s.* **1.** memoria, facoltà di ricordare || *time out of* —, tempo immemorabile; *to bear* (o *to keep*) *in* —, tenere a mente, ricordare; *to bring* (o *to recall*) *sthg. to s.o.'s* —, far ricordare, rammentare ql.co. a qlcu.; *to call* (o *to bring*) *sthg. to* —, ricordare ql.co.; *to pass* (o *to go*) *out of s.o.'s* —, essere dimenticato da qlcu.; *to put s.o. in* — *of sthg.*, far ricordare ql.co. a qlcu. || *out of sight, out of* —, *prov.* lontan dagli occhi, lontan dal cuore **2.** mente, intelletto; spirito; animo: *a penetrating* —, una mente acuta; *a sound* —, uno spirito sano; una mente equilibrata || *the Mind*, Dio || *frame, state of* —, umore, stato d'animo || *peace of* —, serenità, tranquillità || *presence of* —, presenza di spirito || *turn of* —, mentalità, modo di vedere le cose ||

he keeps his — *on it*, ci pensa continuamente; *she took her* — *off it*, ella cessò di pensarci; *you must give your* — *to it*, devi fare attenzione a ciò || *it is a load* (o *a weight*) *off my* —, mi sono tolto un pensiero; *she has sthg. on her* —, ha ql.co. che la preoccupa **3.** opinione, parere, idea; intenzione || *to my* —, secondo me || *to be in two minds*, esitare; *not to know one's own* —, essere indeciso || *to be of a person's* —, essere d'accordo con una persona; *to be of a* (o *one*) —, essere dello stesso parere || *to change one's* —, cambiare opinione || *to give* (*s.o.*) *a piece* (o *a bit*) *of one's* —, esprimere chiaramente (a qlcu.) cosa si pensa (di lui); *to speak one's* —, esprimere chiaramente il proprio parere; *to tell s.o. one's* —, dire a qlcu. ciò che si pensa || *to have a good* (o *great*) — *to*, avere la ferma intenzione di || *to make up one's* —, decidersi **4.** senno, giudizio, ragione || *to be in one's right* —, essere sano di mente; *to be out of one's* —, essere sconvolto, fuori di sè, essere pazzo **5.** mente, intelligenza: *he was one of the great minds of the age*, egli fu una delle grandi menti dell'epoca ☆ — *-cure* (o — *-healing*), (*med.*) psicoterapia; — *-reading*, lettura del pensiero.

to mind, *v.t.i.* **1.** badare a, occuparsi di; aver cura di, accudire a, sorvegliare: — *the baby for me*, bada al mio bambino; *he ought to* — *his own business*, dovrebbe badare ai fatti suoi **2.** fare attenzione (a): —*!*, attenzione!; — *the step*, attenzione allo scalino; — *what I tell you*, fa' attenzione a ciò che ti dico; — *what you are about!*, bada a quello che fai!; — *you!*, bada!; — *you don't fall*, attento a non cadere || — *your eye!*, (*sl.*) attenti!, badate! || — *your head on...*, bada a non battere il capo contro... **3.** (I) importare; spiacere; garbare (*spec. interr. o neg.*): *do you* — *draughts?*, ti dan noia le correnti d'aria?; *do you* — *my smoking?*, le spiace se fumo?; *I don't* — *trying*, sono disposto a provare; *I should not* — *a glass of whisky*, non mi spiacerebbe un bicchierino di whisky; *if you don't* —, *I'll come tomorrow*, se non vi spiace, verrò domani; *if you don't* — *my saying so*, se mi permettete di dirlo, se non vi spiace ch'io lo dica, col vostro permesso direi... || *never* —*!*, non importa!: *never* — *the cost*, la spesa non importa **4.** considerare, osservare, notare: *they won't* — *us*, non baderanno a noi **5.** obbedire (a); seguire i consigli di: *he never minded his mother's advice*, egli non si curò mai dei consigli di sua madre **6.** (*arc.*) ricordare.

minded ['maindid], *ag.* incline, disposto, portato; del parere: *do it if you are so* —, fatelo, se siete di quel parere || *absent-* —, distratto; *acute-* —, sagace; *atom* - —, cosciente dell'importanza dell'energia atomica: *we must make people atom-* —, dobbiamo far capire alla gente l'importanza dell'energia atomica; *book-* —, che ama i libri; *broad-* —, di ampie vedute; *evil-* —, diabolico; *free-* —, senza preoccupazioni, spensierato; *high* - —, di nobili sentimenti; *narrow-* —, di idee ristrette; *right-* —, di mente retta, ben pensante; *strong-* —, deciso, energico.

mindedly ['maindidli], *av.* (*nei composti*): *absent-* —, distrattamente; *open-* —, con ampie vedute: *he spoke open-* — *of the thing*, parlò della cosa spregiudicatamente; *simple-* —, ingenuamente; *strong-* —, decisamente, con energia.

mindedness ['maindidnis], *s.* inclinazione, disposizione.

mindful ['maindful], *ag.* memore: *to be* — *of one's duties*, essere memore dei propri doveri; *to be* — *of one's good name*, difendere il proprio buon nome.

mindfully ['maindfuli], *av.* premurosamente; attentamente.

mindfulness ['maindfulnis], *s.* attenzione; diligenza, cura.

mindless ['maindlis], *ag.* **1.** disattento, noncurante: *to be* — *of danger*, essere noncurante del pericolo **2.** senza spirito; stupido.

mine[1] [main], *pron.poss.* *1ª persona sing.* **il mio, la mia, i miei, le mie**: *your books and* —, i vostri libri ed i miei; *this book is* —, questo libro è mio ‖ *a book of* —, un mio libro ‖ — *own*, (*arc.*) il mio proprio ‖ *ag. poss.* (*arc. poet.*) **mio, mia, miei, mie.**

mine[2], *s.* 1. miniera 2. *fig.* fonte; miniera: *he is a — of information,* è una miniera di notizie 3. (*mil. mar.*) mina: *to spring* (o *to touch off*) *a* —, far brillare una mina ☆ — *detector*, (*mil.*) rilevatore di mine; — *-field*, (*mil.*) campo minato; — *-layer*, (*mar.*) nave posamine; — *-shaft*, pozzo di miniera; — *-sweeper*, (*mar.*) dragamine; — *ventilation*, aerazione della miniera; — *-worker*, minatore ‖ *coal-* —, miniera di carbone; *drift* —, miniera con accesso a pozzo; *gold-* —, miniera d'oro; *strip* —, miniera a cielo aperto.

to **mine**[2], *v.t.i.* 1. scavare 2. (*miner.*) estrarre 3. (*mil.*) minare, posare mine in 4. *fig.* minare, indebolire: *drink is mining his health,* l'alcool gli sta rovinando la salute.

miner ['maɪnə*], *s.* minatore.

mineral ['mɪnərəl], *ag.* minerale ‖ *s.* minerale ☆ — *oil*, (*ind.*) olio minerale; — *pitch*, asfalto; — *water*, acqua minerale; — *wool*, (*ind.*) cotone silicato.

mineralist ['mɪnərəlɪst], *s.* mineralista.

mineralization [,mɪnərəlaɪ'zeɪʃən], *s.* mineralizzazione.

to **mineralize** ['mɪnərəlaɪz], *v.t.i.* 1. mineralizzare 2. andare a cercare minerali.

mineralizer ['mɪnərəlaɪzə*], *ag.* mineralizzatore.

mineralogic(al) [,mɪnərə'lɒdʒɪk(əl)], *ag.* mineralogico.

mineralogist [,mɪnə'rælədʒɪst], *s.* mineralogista.

mineralogy [,mɪnə'rælədʒɪ], *s.* mineralogia.

Minerva [mɪ'nɜːvə], *no.pr.f.* (*mit.*) Minerva.

minever, *V.* miniver.

mingle ['mɪŋgl], *s.* (*rar.*) mescolanza, miscuglio.

to **mingle,** *v.t.i.* mescolare, mescolarsi; confondere, confondersi; unirsi: *he mingled with his students,* si unì ai suoi studenti; *they mingled their tears,* piansero insieme; *to — in the crowd,* confondersi nella folla.

mingle-mangle ['mɪŋgl'mæŋgl], *s.* confusione, disordine; accozzaglia; guazzabuglio.

to **mingle-mangle,** *v.t.* mescolare confusamente; creare confusione, disordine in.

mingling ['mɪŋglɪŋ], *s.* mescolanza, miscuglio.

mingy ['mɪndʒɪ], *s.* (*fam.*) avaro, tirchio; meschino.

miniature ['mɪnjətʃə*], *ag.* in miniatura, in scala ridotta: *our pond is a — lake,* il nostro stagno è un lago in miniatura ‖ *s.* miniatura: *to paint in* —, far miniature ‖ *in* —, in miniatura, in scala ridotta: *the family is society in* —, la famiglia è la società in miniatura ☆ — *camera*, (*foto.*) microcamera; — *model*, (*cine.*) modello in scala ridotta; — *painting*, (*pitt.*) miniatura; — *tube*, (*rad.*) valvola miniatura.

to **miniature,** *v.t.* 1. miniare 2. rappresentare in scala ridotta, in miniatura.

miniaturist ['mɪnjətʃuərɪst], *s.c.* miniatore, miniatrice; miniaturista.

to **minify** ['mɪnɪfaɪ], *v.t.* rimpicciolire; minimizzare.

minikin ['mɪnɪkɪn], *ag.* 1. minuscolo (di cosa); grazioso, delicato 2. (*iron.*) affettato ‖ *s.* 1. (*vezzeggiativo*) ometto; donnina, bamboletta 2. (*tip.*) diamante.

minim ['mɪnɪm], *s.* 1. (*mus.*) minima 2. (*farm.*) goccia (unità di capacità = ml. 0,059) 3. persona, animale, cosa minuscola 4. *pl.* minimi (ordine di frati francescani)

minimal ['mɪnɪml], *ag.* minimo.

minimization [,mɪnɪmaɪ'zeɪʃən], *s.* riduzione al minimo.

to **minimize** ['mɪnɪmaɪz], *v.t.* minimizzare; ridurre al minimo; attribuire poca importanza a, sminuire: *to — an accident,* minimizzare l'importanza di un incidente.

minimum ['mɪnɪməm], *pl.* **minima** ['mɪnɪmə], *s.* minimo: *with the — of inconvenience,* col minimo di disturbo ☆ — *price,* prezzo minimo; — *wage,* salario minimo.

minimus ['mɪnɪməs], *ag.* il più giovane (di almeno tre fratelli, a scuola): *Brown* —, il più giovane dei Brown.

mining ['maɪnɪŋ], *ag.* minerario ‖ *s.* 1. scavo 2. (*miner.*) estrazione 3. (*mil.*) posa di mine ☆ — *claim,* concessione di miniere; — *company,* società mineraria; — *engineer,* ingegnere minerario; — *equipment,* attrezzatura mineraria; — *-hole,* foro di mina; — *industry,* industria mineraria; — *-ship,* nave posamine.

minion ['mɪnjən], *s.* 1. (*arc.*) favorito, beniamino: — *of fortune,* favorito dalla fortuna 2. (*spreg.*) schiavo; dipendente dai modi servili 3. (*tip.*) carattere di stampa (corpo 7).

to **minish** ['mɪnɪʃ], *v.t.i.* (*arc.*) diminuire.

minister ['mɪnɪstə*], *s.* 1. ministro; segretario ‖ *the Prime Minister,* il primo ministro 2. (*eccl.*) ministro (del culto); superiore (di alcuni ordini di religiosi) 3. rappresentante, incaricato.

to **minister,** *v.t.i.* 1. portare aiuto; dare assistenza (ad ammalati, ecc.); venire incontro: *the nurse ministered to the wants of the sick man,* l'infermiera assisteva l'ammalato; *the soldiers ministered to the victims of the earthquake,* i soldati soccorsero le vittime del terremoto ‖ *she ministered to his vanity,* *fig.* ella lusingava la sua vanità 2. (*eccl.*) officiare; rivestire dignità di ministro 3. (*arc.*) fornire, somministrare.

ministerial [,mɪnɪs'tɪərɪəl], *ag.* 1. ministeriale 2. dipendente, accessorio: *this is — to that,* questo contribuisce a quello; questo è accessorio a, dipendente da quello 3. sacerdotale ☆ — *benches,* il banco del governo; il Gabinetto; i sostenitori del governo in carica.

ministerialist [,mɪnɪs'tɪərɪəlɪst], *ag.* ministeriale.

ministrant ['mɪnɪstrənt], *s.* 1. chi provvede 2. (*eccl.*) celebrante.

ministration [,mɪnɪs'treɪʃən], *s.* 1. (*eccl.*) ministero; cura spirituale 2. cura; assistenza: *thanks to the ministrations of his nurse, he recovered,* guarì grazie alle cure della sua infermiera.

ministrative ['mɪnɪstreɪtɪv], *ag.* che aiuta, che somministra.

ministrator ['mɪnɪstreɪtə*], *s.* ministratore, somministratore.

ministress ['mɪnɪstrɪs], *s.* ministratrice, somministratrice.

ministry ['mɪnɪstrɪ], *s.* 1. ministero (ufficio, opera) 2. ministero (i ministri di Stato) 3. sacerdozio 4. clero.

minium ['mɪnɪəm], *s.* (*chim.*) minio.

miniver ['mɪnɪvə*], *s.* 1. vaio 2. (*fam.*) pelo di ermellino o altro animale, purchè bianco.

mink [mɪŋk], *s.* visone (animale e pelliccia).

Minnie[1] ['mɪnɪ], *no.pr.f. dim.* di Wilhelmine.

minnie[2], *s.* (*sl. mil.*) 1. lanciabombe 2. bomba.

minnow ['mɪnoʊ], *s.* pesciolino d'acqua dolce ‖ *a triton among the minnows,* un gigante fra i pigmei.

Minoan [mɪ'noʊən], *ag.* (*archeol.*) minoico.

minor ['maɪnə*], *ag.* 1. minore, di secondaria importanza: *he was a — poet,* era un poeta minore 2. (*mus.*) in tono minore 3. il più giovane (di due fratelli, a scuola): *Brown* —, il minore dei Brown ‖ *s.* 1. (*dir.*) minorenne 2. (*fil.*) premessa minore 3. (*eccl.*) frate minore ☆ — *diameter,* (*mec.*) diametro interno; — *scale,* (*mus.*) scala minore.

Minorca [mɪ'nɔːkə], *no.pr.* (*geog.*) Minorca.

minorite ['maɪnəraɪt], *s.* frate francescano, frate minore, minorita.

minority [mai'nɒrɪtɪ], *s.* 1. (*dir.*) età minore 2. minoranza.

Minos ['maɪnɒs], *no.pr.m.* (*mit.*) Minosse.

Minotaur ['maɪnətɔː*], *no.pr.m.* (*mit.*) Minotauro.

minster ['mɪnstə*], *s.* 1. chiesa di una abbazia, di un monastero 2. cattedrale ‖ *York Minster,* la cattedrale di York.

minstrel ['mɪnstrəl], *s.* 1. menestrello, giullare 2. (*poet.*) poeta, musicista 3. *pl.* suonatori ambulanti (generalmente bianchi travestiti da negri).

minstrelsy ['mɪnstrəlsi], *s.* 1. canto, musica dei menestrelli 2. poesia giullaresca.

mint[1] [mint], s. **1.** zecca **2.** forte somma **3.** *fig.* miniera, fonte ☆ — *-man*, coniatore; — *-mark*, marchio di zecca; — *-master*, direttore della zecca.

to **mint**[1], *v.t.* coniare (anche *fig.*).

mint[2], s. (*bot.*) menta ☆ — *-julep*, sciroppo di menta; — *-sauce*, salsa alla menta; — *-sling*, (*amer.*) bevanda alcoolica alla menta.

mintage ['mintidʒ], s. diritto di battere moneta; coniatura (anche *fig.*).

minter ['mintə*], s. coniatore.

minuend ['minjuend], s. (*mat.*) minuendo.

minuet [,minju'et], s. (*mus.*) minuetto.

minus ['mainəs], a. **1.** (*mat.*) meno **2.** (*mat.*) negativo: *-3 x² is a — quantity*, -3 x² è una quantità negativa ‖ s. (*mat.*) meno ☆ *the — sign*, il segno meno.

minus, *prep.* **1.** meno: *9 — 5 is 4*, 9 meno 5 dà 4 **2.** (*fam.*) senza: *he came back — an eye*, ritornò privo di un occhio.

minuscule [mi'nʌskju:l], a. minuscolo, piccolo ‖ s. lettera minuscola; carattere minuscolo (anche *tip.*).

minute[1] [mai'nju:t], a. **1.** minuto, minuscolo: — *particles of dust*, minuscoli granelli di polvere **2.** minuzioso, preciso: *a — description*, una descrizione minuziosa, precisa.

minute[2] ['minit], s. **1.** minuto (primo): *five minutes to six*, le sei meno cinque; *to be five minutes late*, essere in ritardo di cinque minuti **2.** breve spazio di tempo, istante, momento: *I'll come in a —*, vengo subito; *wait a —*, aspetta un momento ‖ *the — (that)*, non appena: *I'll tell you the — he gets here*, te lo dirò non appena arriverà ‖ *to the —*, puntuale: *the train left at five o'clock to the —*, il treno partì alle cinque in punto **3.** (*geom.*) la sessantesima parte di un grado **4.** nota, appunto, minuta: *to take a — of sthg.*, prendere nota di ql.co. **5.** *pl.* processo verbale: *to keep the minutes of the meetings*, tenere i verbali delle riunioni ☆ — *-book*, registro dei verbali; — *-gun*, cannone che spara ad intervalli di un minuto (per lutto o per invocare aiuto); — *-hand*, lancetta dei minuti.

to **minute**[2], *v.t.* **1.** stendere una minuta, un verbale: *to — sthg. down*, prendere nota, atto di ql.co. **2.** (*spor.*) cronometrare.

minutely[1] [mai'nju:tli], *av.* minuziosamente, dettagliatamente.

minutely[2] ['minitli], *a.* che accade ogni minuto; continuo, incessante ‖ *av.* di minuto in minuto.

minuteness [mai'nju:tnis], s. **1.** piccolezza, minutezza **2.** precisione estrema, minuziosità, meticolosità.

minutia [mai'nju:ʃiə], *pl.* **minutiae** [mai'nju:ʃii:], s. *gener.pl.* minuzia, piccolo particolare.

minx [miŋks], s. pettegola; sfacciatella; civetta.

Miocene ['maiəsi:n], a. (*geol.*) miocenico ‖ s. (*geol.*) miocene.

mirable ['mairəbl], a. (*poet.*) mirabile.

miracle ['mirəkl], s. **1.** miracolo; prodigio: *the miracles of Christ*, i miracoli di Cristo; *that surgeon can work miracles*, quel chirurgo può fare miracoli; *to work a —*, fare un miracolo **2.** (*teat.*) miracolo (sacra rappresentazione medievale) ☆ — *-play*, (*st. teat.*) miracolo.

miraculous [mi'rækjuləs], a. miracoloso, soprannaturale; straordinario.

miraculously [mi'rækjuləsli], *av.* miracolosamente.

miraculousness [mi'rækjuləsnis], s. miracolosità.

mirage ['mira:ʒ], s. miraggio.

Miranda [mi'rændə], *no.pr.f.* Miranda.

mire ['maiə*], s. fango, melma; pantano: *to sink into the —*, affondare nel fango ‖ *to be in the —*, *fig.* essere in difficoltà ‖ *to drag s.o. (o s.o.'s name) through the —*, *fig.* trascinare ql.cu. nel fango.

to **mire**, *v.t.i.* **1.** infangare, inzaccherare; sporcare di fango; affondare nel fango **2.** *fig.* mettere in difficoltà; insozzare.

Miriam ['miriəm], *no.pr.f.* Miriam.

miriness ['maiərinis], s. fangosità.

mirror ['mirə*], s. specchio (anche *fig.*) ☆ *driving-* — (o *rear view-* —), (*aut.*) specchietto retrovisore; *magic* —, specchio magico ‖ — *writing*, scrittura a specchio.

to **mirror**, *v.t.* **1.** riflettere, specchiare **2.** *fig.* rispecchiare: *his writings — his times*, i suoi scritti rispecchiano la sua epoca, i suoi tempi.

mirth [mə:θ], s. allegria, gioia, giubilo ☆ — *-provoking*, che suscita l'ilarità.

mirthful ['mə:θful], a. allegro, gioioso, gaio.

mirthfully ['mə:θfuli], *av.* allegramente, gioiosamente.

mirthfulness ['mə:θfulnis], s. allegria, gioia, gaiezza.

mirthless ['mə:θlis], a. senza allegria, triste, cupo.

miry ['maiəri], a. **1.** fangoso, melmoso **2.** *fig.* vile, abietto.

misadventure ['misəd'ventʃə*], s. disavventura, infortunio ‖ *homicide by —*, omicidio preterintenzionale.

misadventured ['misəd'ventʃəd], a. sfortunato.

misadventurous ['misəd'ventʃərəs], a. sfortunato.

misadvertence ['misəd'və:təns], s. inavvertenza.

to **misadvise** ['misəd'vaiz], *v.t.* consigliare male.

misadvised ['misəd'vaizd], a. (*arc.*) malconsigliato.

misalliance ['misə'laiəns], s. « mésalliance » (matrimonio fra due persone di diversa classe sociale).

misallied ['misə'laid], a. mal sposato (con persona di classe inferiore).

misanthrope ['mizənθroup], s. misantropo.

misanthropic(al) [,mizən'θrɔpik(əl)], a. misantropico.

misanthropist [mi'zænθrəpist], s. misantropo.

misanthropy [mi'zænθrəpi], s. misantropia.

misapplication ['mis,æpli'keiʃən], s. applicazione erronea; uso erroneo.

to **misapply** ['misə'plai], *v.t.* applicar male, usare erroneamente.

misappreciated ['misə'pri:ʃieitid], a. misconosciuto.

misappreciation ['misə,pri:ʃi'eiʃən], s. misconoscimento, disistima.

to **misapprehend** ['mis,æpri'hend], *v.t.* fraintendere.

misapprehension ['mis,æpri'henʃən], s. malinteso, equivoco, errata interpretazione.

misapprehensive ['mis,æpri'hensiv], a. che mal comprende.

misapprehensively ['mis,æpri'hensivli], *av.* per errore.

to **misappropriate** ['misə'prouprieit], *v.t.* appropriarsi indebitamente di; stornare (fondi, somme).

misappropriation ['misə,proupri'eiʃən], s. appropriazione indebita; storno (di somme).

to **misarrange** ['misə'reindʒ], *v.t.* disporre in ordine errato.

misarrangement ['misə'reindʒmənt], s. ordinamento errato; ordine sbagliato.

to **misbecome** ['misbi'kʌm], *pass.* **misbecame** ['misbi'keim], *p.p.* **misbecome**, *v.t.* essere inadatto a, non conveniente a.

misbecoming ['misbi'kʌmiŋ], a. inadatto, non conveniente.

misbegotten ['misbi'gɔtn], a. **1.** illegittimo, bastardo **2.** (*fam.*) mal concepito, deforme **3.** strampalato; scombinato: *this is one of his — ideas* questa è una delle sue idee strampalate.

to **misbehave** ['misbi'heiv], *v.t.i.*: *to — (oneself)*, comportarsi male.

misbehaved ['misbi'heivd], a. (*poet.*) ineducato.

misbehaviour ['misbi'heivjə*], s. cattivo contegno.

misbelief ['misbi'li:f], s. falsa credenza; miscredenza; eresia.

to **misbelieve** ['misbi'li:v], *v.i.* avere una falsa credenza; credere in una falsa dottrina.

misbeliever ['misbi'li:və*], s. miscredente.

misbelieving ['misbi'li:viŋ], a. miscredente.

to **misbeseem** ['misbi'si:m], *V.* to **misbecome**.

misbirth ['mis'bə:θ], s. (*arc.*) aborto.

misborn ['mis'bɔːn], *ag.* **1.** abortivo **2.** deforme dalla nascita **3.** illegittimo.

to **miscalculate** ['mis'kælkjuleit], *v.t.i.* calcolar male.

miscalculation ['mis,kælkju'leiʃən], *s.* calcolo errato.

to **miscall** ['mis'kɔːl], *v.t.* **1.** chiamare impropriamente, con nome sbagliato **2.** insultare.

miscarriage ['mis'kæridʒ], *s.* **1.** disguido, smarrimento (postale): — *of goods*, smarrimento di merce; *in case of* —, in caso di disguido **2.** (*med. fam.*) aborto **3.** insuccesso, fiasco; errore: — *of justice*, errore giudiziario.

to **miscarry** [mis'kæri], *v.i.* **1.** smarrirsi; non giungere a destinazione (di merce, lettera, ecc.) **2.** (*med.*) abortire **3.** fallire; venir meno: *all his plans miscarried*, tutti i suoi piani fallirono.

miscasting ['mis'kɑːstiŋ], *s.* **1.** errore di calcolo **2.** (*teat.*) errata distribuzione delle parti.

miscegenation [,misidʒi'neiʃən], *s.* incrocio di razze (specialmente tra la bianca e la negra).

miscellanea [,misi'leinjə], *s.pl.* miscellanea; raccolta di scritti vari.

miscellaneous [,misi'leinjəs], *ag.* **1.** miscellaneo; misto; eterogeneo **2.** versatile, multiforme.

miscellaneously [,misi'leinjəsli], *av.* in modo eterogeneo.

miscellanist [mi'selənist], *s.* autore di miscellanea.

miscellany [mi'seləni], *s.* **1.** *pl.* raccolta di miscellanea; miscellanea **2.** mescolanza.

mischance [mis'tʃɑːns], *s.* disdetta; sfortuna; disgrazia: *by* —, per disgrazia; per sfortuna.

to **mischance**, *v.i.* (*arc.*) accadere per disgrazia.

mischancy [mis'tʃɑːnsi], *ag.* (*scoz.*) sfortunato; pericoloso.

mischief ['mis-tʃif], *s.* **1.** danno, torto, male: *the — of it is that...*, il guaio è che...; *to do s.o. a* —, far torto, far del male a qlcu.; *to keep out of* —, tenersi lontano dai fastidi; (*fam.*) non far guai; *to make* —, creare discordia, metter male **2.** malizia; cattiveria; furberia: *he looked at her, his eyes full of* —, egli la guardò con occhi maliziosi; *she did that out of pure* —, l'ha fatto per pura cattiveria; *there's no* — *in her*, non è maliziosa ‖ *where the* — *have you been?*, (*rar.*) dove diavolo siete stati? **3.** (*fam.*) cattivello, birbante, birba, diavolo, diavoletto: *he is a little* —!, è una birba! **4.** birichinata, marachella: *he is up to some* —, sta meditando un brutto tiro; *she is in* —, sta combinandone una delle sue ☆ — *-maker*, attaccabrighe, seminatore di zizzania, linguaccia; — *-making*, maldicente.

mischievous ['mis-tʃivəs], *ag.* **1.** nocivo (di cose) **2.** malizioso; molesto, noioso (di persone) **3.** (*fam.*) vivace, furbo, birichino ‖ *she is as* — *as a monkey*, è dispettosa come una scimmietta.

mischievously ['mis-tʃivəsli], *av.* **1.** nocivamente **2.** maliziosamente; in modo molesto **3.** (*fam.*) furbescamente.

mischievousness ['mis-tʃivəsnis], *s.* **1.** l'essere nocivo **2.** malizia; molestia **3.** (*fam.*) furbizia.

miscible ['misibl], *ag.* (*arc.*) mescolabile.

to **miscolour** ['mis'kʌlə*], *v.t.* presentare sotto falsa luce; svisare.

to **miscomprehend** ['mis,kɔmpri'hend], *v.t.* fraintendere.

miscomprehension ['mis,kɔmpri'henʃən], *s.* fraintendimento.

to **misconceive** ['miskən'siːv], *v.t.i.* formarsi un'idea sbagliata; fraintendere.

misconception ['miskən'sepʃən], *s.* concetto erroneo; fraintendimento.

misconduct [mis'kɔndəkt], *s.* **1.** cattiva amministrazione **2.** cattiva condotta **3.** adulterio.

to **misconduct** ['miskən'dʌkt], *v.t.* **1.** dirigere, amministrare male: *to* — *one's business* (o *one's affairs*), amministrare male i propri affari **2.** *to* — *oneself*, comportarsi male; commettere adulterio.

misconjecture ['miskən'dʒektʃə*], *s.* (*rar.*) congettura sbagliata.

to **misconjecture**, *v.t.i.* (*rar.*) far congetture sbagliate.

misconstruction ['miskəns'trʌkʃən], *s.* **1.** falsa interpretazione, fraintendimento **2.** (*gram.*) costruzione sbagliata.

to **misconstrue** ['miskən'struː], *v.t.* **1.** interpretare male, fraintendere **2.** (*gram.*) costruire male (una frase).

miscopy ['mis'kɔpi], *s.* errore di copiatura.

to **miscopy**, *v.t.* copiare erroneamente.

miscount ['mis'kaunt], *s.* conteggio erroneo; addizione sbagliata (specialmente di voti).

to **miscount**, *v.t.i.* sbagliare un conto; contar male.

miscreance ['miskriəns], *s.* miscredenza.

miscreant ['miskriənt], *ag.* (*arc.*) eretico; miscredente ‖ *s.* (*arc.*) **1.** eretico **2.** furfante.

miscreated ['miskri(ː)'eitid], *ag.* malconformato; deforme.

miscreation ['miskri(ː)'eiʃən], *s.* malconformazione; deformità.

miscue ['mis'kjuː], *s.* (*biliardo*) colpo sbagliato.

misdate ['mis'deit], *s.* data sbagliata.

to **misdate**, *v.t.* datare erroneamente.

misdeal ['mis'diːl], *s.* (*carte*) distribuzione errata.

to **misdeal**, *pass.p.p.* **misdealt** ['mis'delt], *v.t.i.* (*carte*) distribuire male, fare errori nella distribuzione.

misdeed ['mis'diːd], *s.* misfatto.

to **misdeem** ['mis'diːm], *v.t.i.* **1.** (*arc.poet.*) giudicare male; avere un'opinione sbagliata **2.** confondere (una persona con un'altra).

to **misdemean** [,misdi'miːn], *v.t.i.*: *to* — (*oneself*), comportarsi male.

misdemeanant [,misdi'miːnənt], *s.c.* (*dir.*) colpevole, delinquente.

misdemeanour [,misdi'miːnə*], *s.* **1.** (*dir.*) misfatto; atto contrario alla legge **2.** cattiva condotta.

to **misdescribe** ['misdis'kraib], *v.t.* descrivere in modo inesatto.

misdescription ['misdis'kripʃən], *s.* (*dir.*) descrizione inesatta (di un articolo di commercio).

to **misdirect** ['misdi'rekt], *v.t.* mandare in direzione sbagliata; dare un indirizzo sbagliato a (anche *fig.*): *to* — *s.o.'s studies*, dare una direzione errata agli studi di qlcu.

misdirection ['misdi'rekʃən], *s.* indicazione sbagliata; informazione sbagliata; indirizzo errato.

misdoing ['mis'du(ː)iŋ], *s.* misfatto.

to **misdoubt** ['mis'daut], *v.t.i.* (*arc.*) dubitare; sospettare.

to **misemploy** ['misim'plɔi], *v.t.* impiegare, usare erroneamente.

misemployment ['misim'plɔimənt], *s.* impiego, uso erroneo.

mise-en-scène ['miːzɔn'sein], *s.* **1.** (*teat.*) regìa, allestimento scenico **2.** *fig.* messa in scena, scena.

miser ['maizə*], *s.* avaro, taccagno, spilorcio.

miserable ['mizərəbl], *ag.* **1.** triste, infelice; avvilito: *he was in a* — *mood*, egli era molto avvilito; *to feel* —, sentirsi depresso **2.** deprimente, spiacevole, penoso: — *journey*, viaggio penoso; *what* — *weather!*, che tempo orribile! **3.** miserabile, misero, povero, pietoso: *a* — *meal*, un pasto insufficiente; — *salary*, salario irrisorio; *five* — *pounds*, cinque miserabili sterline; *they lived in a* — *slum*, vivevano in un miserabile tugurio **4.** meschino, da poco: *it was a* — *result*, fu un meschino risultato.

miserableness ['mizərəblnis], *s.* **1.** abbattimento, sconforto **2.** stato di miseria.

miserably ['mizərəbli], *av.* miserevolmente; miseramente: *to die* —, morire miseramente.

Miserere [,mizə'riəri], *s.* **1.** (*eccl. mus.*) miserere **2.** V **misericord**.

misericord [mi'zerikɔːd], *s.* **1.** (*eccl.*) stanza di monastero dove erano permesse certe infrazioni alle regole **2.** (*arch.*) mensola d'appoggio sotto il sedile ribal tabile dello stallo (nel coro) **3**. (*st.*) misericordia (pugnale).

miserliness ['maizəlinis], *s.* avarizia, taccagneria, spilorceria.

miserly ['maizəli], *ag.* avaro, taccagno, spilorcio; sordido.

misery ['mizəri], *s.* **1.** sofferenza; infelicità; tormento: *to put an animal out of its* —, dare il colpo di grazia a un animale; *to put s.o. out of* —, liberare qlcu. dalle sofferenze **2.** indigenza, povertà: *to live in* — *and want*, vivere in estrema indigenza **3.** *pl.* avversità.

misesteem ['misi'sti:m], *s.* disistima, mancanza di rispetto.

to **misestimate** ['mis'estimeit], *v.t.* stimare, giudicare erroneamente.

misfeasance [mis'fi:zəns], *s.* (*dir.*) infrazione alla legge; abuso d'autorità.

misfire ['mis'faiə*], *s.* **1.** mina mancata **2.** (*aut.*) accensione difettosa **3.** mattone malcotto.

to **misfire**, *v.i.* **1.** far cilecca (di mina o arma da fuoco) **2.** (*aut.*) dare accensioni irregolari **3.** *fig.* (*fam.*) fallire il colpo.

misfit ['misfit], *s.* **1.** abito, indumento che non si adatta bene **2.** *fig.* pesce fuor d'acqua.

misfortune [mis'fo:tʃən], *s.* sventura, sfortuna; disgrazia: *to suffer* —, subire una disgrazia || *misfortunes never come singly*, *prov.* le disgrazie non vengono mai sole.

to **misgive** [mis'giv], *pass.* **misgave** [mis'geiv], *p.p.* **misgiven** [mis'givn], *v.t.i.* **1.** ispirare diffidenza o sospetto a **2.** far presentire disgrazie a: *his mind misgave him that sthg. was going to happen*, il cuore gli diceva che ql.co. stava per accadere **3.** essere apprensivo.

misgiving [mis'givin], *s.* **1.** apprensione, timore **2.** cattivo presentimento: *I have a* — *that I am going to have a bad time*, ho il presentimento che me la passerò male.

to **misgovern** ['mis'gʌvən], *v.t.* governare, amministrare male, disonestamente.

misgovernment [mis'gʌvənmənt], *s.* malgoverno, cattiva amministrazione.

misguidance ['mis'gaidəns], *s.* **1.** direzione sbagliata **2.** traviamento.

to **misguide** ['mis'gaid], *v.t.* **1.** guidar male **2.** traviare, sviare.

misguided ['mis'gaidid], *ag.* **1.** fuorviato; infatuato: *he was ruined by his* — *enthusiasm*, la sua infatuazione, il suo eccesso di entusiasmo fu causa della sua rovina **2.** scriteriato: *poor* — *boy*, povero scriteriato; povero illuso.

to **mishandle** ['mis'hændl], *v.t.* trattare male, maltrattare.

mishap ['mishæp], *s.* **1.** infortunio; disgrazia **2.** contrattempo; peripezia: *after many mishaps*, dopo molte peripezie.

to **mishear** ['mis'hiə*], *pass.p.p.* **misheard** ['mis'hə:d], *v.t.* udire male, fraintendere.

mishit ['mishit], *s.* colpo sbagliato.

to **mishit**, *pass.p.p.* **mishit**, *v.t.* colpire male (una palla).

mishmash ['miʃmæʃ], *s.* confusione.

to **misinform** ['misin'fo:m], *v.t.* informare male; fuorviare.

misinformation ['mis,infə'meiʃən], *s.* informazione sbagliata.

misintelligence ['misin'telidʒəns], *s.* **1.** malinteso; disaccordo **2.** (*rar.*) mancanza di intelligenza.

to **misinterpret** ['misin'tə:prit], *v.t.* interpretare male.

misinterpretation ['misin,tə:pri'teiʃən], *s.* interpretazione erronea.

to **misjudge** ['mis'dʒʌdʒ], *v.t.i.* giudicare male; farsi un'opinione sbagliata di.

misjudgement ['mis'dʒʌdʒmənt], *s.* giudizio erroneo.

to **misknow** ['mis'nou], *pass.* **misknew** ['mis'nju:], *p.p.* **misknown** ['mis'noun], *v.t.* conoscere male; capire in modo sbagliato.

misknowledge ['mis'nolidʒ], *s.* conoscenza sbagliata.

to **mislay** [mis'lei], *pass.p.p.* **mislaid** [mis'leid], *v.t.* collocare in un posto sbagliato; smarrire (un oggetto).

to **mislead** [mis'li:d], *pass.p.p.* **misled** [mis'led], *v.t.* **1.** sviare, traviare **2.** ingannare.

mislike [mis'laik], *s.* **1.** avversione, antipatia **2.** disapprovazione.

to **mislike**, *v.t.* sentire avversione, antipatia per; disapprovare.

misluck [mis'lʌk], *s.* sfortuna.

to **misluck**, *v.i.* avere sfortuna.

to **mismanage** ['mis'mænidʒ], *v.t.* dirigere male, amministrare male.

mismanagement ['mis'mænidʒmənt], *s.* cattiva direzione, cattiva amministrazione.

to **mismate** [mis'meit], *v.t.i.* accoppiare, accoppiarsi erroneamente.

mismated [mis'meitid], *ag.* male accoppiato.

to **misname** [mis'neim], *v.t.* nominare, chiamare impropriamente.

misnomer ['mis'noumə*], *s.* **1.** errore di nome **2.** definizione non appropriata: *painters by* — *called masters*, pittori poco appropriatamente chiamati maestri.

to **misobserve** ['misəb'zə:v], *v.t.i.* osservare male.

misogamist [mi'sogəmist], *s.* misogamo.

misogamy [mi'sogəmi], *s.* misogamia.

misogynist [mai'sodʒinist], *s.* misogino.

mispickel ['mispikəl], *s.* (*min.*) arsenopirite.

to **misplace** ['mis'pleis], *v.t.* **1.** collocar male (affetto, confidenza): *his affection was misplaced*, il suo amore non era rivolto a persona degna di lui **2.** collocare fuori posto (libro, quadro, ecc.): *she misplaced the pictures*, ella appese i quadri al posto sbagliato.

misplacement ['mis'pleismənt], *s.* **1.** spostamento **2.** il collocare fuori posto.

to **misplease** ['mis'pli:z], *v.t.* dispiacere a.

misprint ['mis'print], *s.* errore di stampa, refuso.

to **misprint**, *v.t.* stampare con molti refusi: *this word is misprinted*, c'è un errore di stampa in questa parola.

misprision[1] [mis'priʒən], *s.* **1.** (*dir.*) omissione di denuncia, di referto: — *of felony, of treason*, mancata denuncia di un delitto, di alto tradimento **2.** (*arc.*) errore di interpretazione.

misprision[2], *s.* (*arc.*) **1.** disistima **2.** errore di valutazione.

to **misprize** ['mis'praiz], *v.t.* **1.** disprezzare **2.** misconoscere.

to **mispronounce** ['misprə'nauns], *v.t.* pronunciare in modo erroneo, storpiare.

mispronounciation ['misprə,nʌnsi'eiʃən], *s.* pronuncia scorretta; errore di pronuncia.

misquotation ['miskwou'teiʃən], *s.* citazione erronea.

to **misquote** ['mis'kwout], *v.t.* citare erroneamente.

to **misread** [mis'ri:d], *pass.p.p.* **misread** ['mis'red], *v.t.* **1.** leggere erroneamente **2.** interpretare erroneamente: *to* — *s.o.'s feelings*, sbagliarsi sui sentimenti di qlcu.

misreading ['mis'ri:diŋ], *s.* falsa interpretazione.

to **misrepresent** ['mis,repri'zent], *v.t.* rappresentare erroneamente; travisare; dare un'idea sbagliata di.

misrepresentation ['mis,reprizen'teiʃən], *s.* **1.** esposizione erronea, svisata **2.** (*dir.*) falsa dichiarazione.

misrule ['mis'ru:l], *s.* malgoverno; cattiva amministrazione; disordine, confusione.

to **misrule**, *v.t.* governare male.

miss[1] [mis], *s.* **1.** colpo mancato; perdita || *a lucky* —, una via d'uscita fortunata || *to give sthg. a* —, trascurare, evitare ql.co. || *a* — *is as good as a mile*, *prov.* per un punto Martin perse la cappa **2.** difetto, assenza, mancanza || *he is no great* —, si può far benissimo a meno di lui.

to **miss**[1], *v.t.i.* **1.** mancare (il colpo): *to* — *the target*, mancare il bersaglio || *to* — *the mark*, *fig.* fallire nei propri intenti **2.** perdere (il treno, un'occasione, ecc.): *you will* — *your train*, perderete il treno; *to* — *the* *bus*, perderete l'autobus; *fig.* perdere l'occasione, arrivare troppo tardi; **3.** non riuscire a prendere; sbagliare; fallire; non afferrare, non capire: *he missed the ball*, non riuscì ad afferrare la palla; *he missed his footing*, mise il piede in fallo; *when you speak so quickly, I — several words*, quando parlate così in fretta, perdo parecchie parole ‖ *to — the point*, non afferrare l'essenziale **4.** tralasciare, omettere: *he missed the meal*, saltò il pasto; *he never misses a foot-ball match*, non manca mai alla partita di calcio; *you have missed out a whole paragraph*, hai tralasciato un intero paragrafo **5.** (I) mancare poco che, rischiare di: *he just missed being killed*, poco mancò che fosse ucciso **6.** notare la mancanza, la sparizione di; notare l'assenza di; *fig.* sentire la mancanza di: *I — some papers that were here on my desk*, mi mancano alcune carte che erano qui sulla scrivania; *we missed each other in the crowd*, ci perdemmo di vista tra la folla; *we shall — him badly*, sentiremo molto la sua mancanza; *when did you — your necklace?*, quando ti sei accorta che ti mancava la collana?.

miss², *s.* **1.** signorina: *Miss Jane Smith*, la signorina Giovanna Smith ‖ *the Misses Brown* (o *the Miss Browns*), le sorelle Brown ‖ *Miss Brown*, la maggiore delle sorelle Brown **2.** *Miss*, « Miss » (titolo dato a donna vincitrice di concorso, ecc.): *Miss Europe 1962*, Miss Europa 1962 **3.** (*pop.*) signorina (usato come vocativo da inferiori, subordinati): *good evening, — !*, buona sera, signorina!.

miss³, *s.* (*carte*) giro supplementare.

missal ['misəl], *s.* (*eccl.*) messale.

to **missay** ['mis'sei], *pass.p.p.* **missaid** ['mis'sed], *v.i.* parlar male.

missel ['mizəl], *s.* (*ornit.*) tordella.

to **misset** ['mis'set], *pass.p.p.* **misset**, *v.t.* collocar male.

misshape ['mis'ʃeip], *s.* deformità.

to **misshape**, *v.t.* deformare.

misshapen ['mis'ʃeipən], *ag.* **1.** deforme, malformato **2.** sformato.

missile ['misail], *ag.* di, da tiro, da lancio ‖ *s.* missile, proiettile ☆ *ballistic —*, missile balistico; *guided - —*, missile teleguidato.

missing ['misiŋ], *ag.* smarrito, mancante: *the child is —*, non si trova il bambino; *he has been — for two days*, siamo senza sue notizie da due giorni; *where did you find the — book?*, dove hai trovato il libro che mancava? ‖ *s.* disperso: *the —*, i dispersi; *he was reported —*, fu dato per disperso.

mission ['miʃən], *s.* **1.** missione: *on a — in missione*: *he was sent on a — to Paris*, fu mandato in missione a Parigi; *she thinks her — in life is to help him*, pensa che la sua missione nella vita sia di aiutarlo **2.** missione, sede di missionari: *foreign missions*, missioni straniere; *the — lies to the north of the village*, la missione si trova a nord del villaggio ☆ *trade —*, missione commerciale: *a trade — to South America*, una missione commerciale per l'America del Sud.

missionary ['miʃnəri], *ag.* inerente, relativo alle missioni, ai missionari: *a — meeting*, incontro, adunanza riguardante le missioni ‖ *s.* missionario ☆ *— box*, cassetta per l'elemosina delle missioni.

missioner ['miʃnə*], *s.* missionario (specialmente preposto alle opere di una parrocchia).

missis ['misiz], *s.* **1.** (*pop.* per *Mrs.*) signora, padrona: *the — is out*, la padrona non c'è **2.** (*pop. scherz.*) moglie.

missive ['misiv], *s.* lettera ufficiale; (*scherz.*) missiva, lettera.

to **misspell** ['mis'pel], *pass.p.p.* **misspelled, misspelt** ['mis'pelt], *v.t.* sbagliare l'ortografia di: *this word is misspelt*, l'ortografia di questa parola è sbagliata; *you misspelled this word*, hai scritto male questa parola.

to **misspend** ['mis'spend], *pass.p.p.* **misspent** ['mis'spent], *v.t.* dissipare; spendere, impiegare male (tempo, denaro): *a misspent life*, una vita sprecata.

to **misstate** ['mis'steit], *v.t.* dichiarare, esporre inesattamente.

misstatement ['mis'steitmənt], *s.* dichiarazione inesatta; descrizione inesatta.

misstep ['mis'step], *s.* passo falso (anche *fig.*).

to **missuit** ['mis'sju:t], *v.t.* non convenire a, non essere adatto a.

missus ['misəs], *V.* missis.

missy ['misi], *s.* (*dim. pop.* di *miss*) signorinella.

mist [mist], *s.* **1.** bruma, foschia; caligine; pioggia leggera: *the hills were hidden in —*, le colline erano avvolte nella foschia **2.** appannamento (dei vetri); velo (davanti agli occhi): *to have a — before one's eyes*, avere un velo davanti agli occhi.

to **mist**, *v.t.i.* appannare, appannarsi: *her eyes misted*, le si velarono gli occhi (d² lacrime); *the river was slowly misting*, lenta la bruma andava coprendo il fiume; *steam mists glass*, il vapore appanna il vetro.

mistakable ['mis'teikəbl], *ag.* suscettibile d'errore; confondibile: *twins are easily — for each other*, è facile scambiare un gemello per l'altro.

mistake [mis'teik], *s.* **1.** sbaglio, fallo, errore; svista: *it was a tragical —*, fu un tragico errore; *make no —*, bada di non far errori; *no —, it was wrong*, senza dubbio, era sbagliato; *your translation is full of mistakes*, la tua traduzione è piena di errori **2.** (*fam.*) granchio, strafalcione, cantonata.

to **mistake**, *pass.* **mistook** [mis'tuk], *p.p.* **mistaken** [mis'teikən], *v.t.i.* **1.** confondere, scambiare: *mind you do not — your way*, sta'attento a non sbagliare strada; *she mistook George for his brother*, scambiò Giorgio per suo fratello **2.** non intendere, non comprendere: *you — my words*, non capisci le mie parole, quello che voglio dire **3.** errare, sbagliare: *there is no mistaking the fact that*, non si può sbagliare sul fatto che.

mistaken [mis'teikən], *p.p.* di to **mistake** ‖ *ag.* **1.** in errore: *to be —*, sbagliare, sbagliarsi; *to be — about* (o *in*) *s.o., sthg.*, sbagliarsi in merito a qlcu., ql.co. **2.** erroneo, sbagliato; confuso; male interpretato: *a — belief, idea*, una credenza, un'idea falsa, sbagliata; *— identity*, errore di persona; *— statement*, dichiarazione male interpretata; dichiarazione errata; *— zeal*, zelo fuori posto.

mister ['mistə*], *s.* **1.** signore (*abbr.* Mr.): *Mr. Jones*, il signor Jones ‖ *Mr. Chairman*, Signor Presidente **2.** (*pop.*) signore (usato come vocativo da inferiori, subordinati): *what is the time, —?*, che ora è, signore?.

to **mister**, *v.t.* chiamare « signore »: *don't — me!*, non chiamatemi signore!.

mistful ['mistful], *ag.* nebbioso.

mistigris ['mistigris], *s.* (*carte*) matta.

mistily ['mistili], *av.* nebbiosamente; nebulosamente.

to **mistime** ['mis'taim], *v.t.* dire, fare intempestivamente, fuori luogo.

mistiness ['mistinis], *s.* **1.** brumosità, foschia, nebbiosità; appannamento: *the — on the windscreen*, l'appannamento del parabrezza **2.** *fig.* poca chiarezza, oscurità: *the — of his style*, l'oscurità del suo stile.

mistletoe ['misltou], *s.* vischio.

mistook [mis'tuk], *pass.* di to **mistake**.

mistral ['mistrəl], *s.* maestrale.

to **mistranslate** ['mistræns'leit], *v.t.* tradurre malamente; interpretare scorrettamente; travisare il senso di (una frase).

mistranslation ['mistræns'leiʃən], *s.* traduzione erronea; errore nel tradurre.

to **mistreat** ['mis'tri:t], *v.t.* maltrattare.

mistreatment ['mis'tri:tmənt], *s.* maltrattamento.

mistress ['mistris], *s.* **1.** padrona, signora (anche *fig.*): *she is her own —*, è padrona di se stessa; *she is the — of the situation*, ella domina la situazione; *Venice was once the — of the Adriatic*, Venezia era un tempo la signora dell'Adriatico; *where is your —?*, dov'è la padrona? *Mistress of the Robes*, (*arc.*) guardarobiera della regina **3.** maestra, esperta (in un'arte): *a — of needle work*, un'esperta nei lavori di cucito **4.** insegnante **5.** amante; mantenuta **6.** *Mistress*, signora (*abbr.* *Mrs.*): *Mrs. Smith*, la signora Smith ☆ *a history* —, un'insegnante di storia.

mistrial ['mis'traiəl], *s.* **1.** errore giudiziario **2.** sentenza viziata da errore di giudizio o di procedura.

mistrust ['mis'trʌst], *s.* diffidenza; sfiducia; sospetto.

to **mistrust**, *v.t.* diffidare di; sospettar di.

mistrustful ['mis'trʌstful], *ag.* diffidente; sospettoso.

mistrustfully ['mis'trʌstfuli], *av.* con diffidenza; sospettosamente.

mistrustfulness ['mis'trʌstfulnis], *s.* diffidenza; sospetto.

mistrustless ['mis'trʌstlis], *ag.* fiducioso.

misty ['misti], *ag.* **1.** nebbioso; pieno di vapori: — *weather*, tempo nebbioso **2.** oscuro; vago, indistinto: — *recollection*, ricordo confuso, vago.

to **misunderstand** ['misʌndə'stænd], *pass.p.p.* **misunderstood** ['misʌndə'stud], *v.t.* **1.** capir male, fraintendere **2.** ingannarsi su, sbagliarsi su.

misunderstanding ['misʌndə'stændiŋ], *s.* **1.** malinteso, equivoco **2.** dissapore, disaccordo.

misunderstood ['misʌndə'stud], *pass.p.p.* di to **misunderstand** ‖ *ag.* **1.** male interpretato **2.** incompreso (di persona): *she felt — in her family*, si sentiva incompresa nella sua famiglia.

misusage ['mis'ju:zidʒ], *s.* **1.** uso errato **2.** cattivo trattamento.

misuse ['mis'ju:s], *s.* abuso; cattivo uso: — *of authority*, abuso di autorità.

to **misuse** ['mis'ju:z], *v.t.* **1.** usar male, fare un cattivo uso di; abusare di **2.** maltrattare.

misventure ['mis'ventʃə*], *s.* (*arc.*) disavventura.

to **miswrite** ['mis'rait], *pass.* **miswrote** ['mis'rout], *p.p.* **miswritten** ['mis'ritn], *v.t.* scrivere scorrettamente.

mite[1] [mait], *s.* (*entom.*) baco ☆ *cheese-* —, baco del formaggio.

mite[2], *s.* **1.** soldino, obolo (moneta): *to offer one's* —, dare il proprio obolo **2.** bimbo, piccino: *he was a — of a child*, era alto come un soldo di cacio **3.** oggetto piccino; piccola quantità: *there is not a — left*, non c'è più neanche una briciola.

Mithra ['miθrə], **Mithras** ['miθræs], *no.pr.m.* (*mit.*) Mitra.

mithridate ['miθrideit], *s.* (*arc.*) antidoto, contravveleno; rimedio (contro malattie infettive).

Mithridates [,miθri'deiti:z], *no.pr.m.* (*st.*) Mitridate.

to **mithridatize** ['miθrideitaiz], *v.t.* immunizzare contro un veleno somministrandone dosi graduali.

to **mitigate** ['mitigeit], *v.t.* mitigare, lenire; temperare.

mitigation [,miti'geiʃən], *s.* alleviamento; attenuazione.

mitigatory ['mitigeitəri], *ag.* mitigativo; palliativo.

mitosis [mi'tousis], *pl.* **mitoses** [mi'tousi:z], *s.* (*biol.*) mitosi, cariocinesi.

mitraille [mi'treil], *s.* mitraglia.

mitrailleuse [,mitrai'ə:z], *s.* tipo di mitraglia.

mitral ['maitrəl], *ag.* mitrale ☆ — *valve*, (*anat.*) valvola mitrale.

mitre[1] ['maitə*], *s.* **1.** mitra (specie di turbante) **2.** (*eccl.*) mitra, mitria; *fig.* dignità di vescovo **3.** nome di taverne, locande.

to **mitre**[1], *v.t.* (*eccl.*) mitriare.

mitre[2], *s.* (*tec.*) giunto ad angolo ☆ — *gears*, (*mec.*) ingranaggi conici; — *-square*, (*strum. artig.*) squadra zoppa (a 45°); — *valve*, (*mec.*) valvola con sede a 45°.

to **mitre**[2], *v.t.* **1.** (*tec.*) tagliare (asse, lastra, ecc.) a ugnatura **2.** giungere (parti) ad angolo.

mitt [mit], (*amer.*) **mitten** ['mitn], *s.* **1.** manopola (guanto avente solo la divisione per il pollice); mezzo guanto **2.** *pl.* (*boxe*) guantoni **3.** congedo: *to get the* —, (*sl.*) essere licenziato; essere piantato dall'innamorata ‖ *to give the (frozen)* —, (*sl.*) lasciar in asso, abbandonare l'innamorato; licenziare.

mittimus ['mitiməs], *s.* **1.** (*dir.*) mandato di cattu-

ra **2.** (*fam.*) licenziamento: *to get one's* —, essere licenziato; ricevere il foglio di via.

mity ['maiti], *ag.* coi bachi (di formaggio, ecc.).

to **mix** [miks], *v.t.i.* **1.** mescolare, mescolarsi: *he mixed cocktails for everybody*, preparò i coktails per tutti; *she mixed the salad*, condì l'insalata **2.** armonizzare (di colori): *black mixes well with any colour*, il nero si accompagna bene, si sposa bene con qualsiasi colore **3.** associare, associarsi: *she likes to — with artists*, le piace frequentare gli artisti **4.** incrociare (negli allevamenti) **5.** *to — up*, mescolare completamente; confondere, confondersi: *he is mixing everything up*, sta facendo una gran confusione; *to be mixed up*, essere coinvolto, implicato (in azioni poco oneste).

mixed [mikst], *ag.* **1.** misto; mescolato **2.** eterogeneo; non selezionato; promiscuo: *a — company*, una compagnia mista, eterogenea; *a — school*, una scuola mista **3.** (*fam.*) confuso, sconcertato: *now, don't get* —, non far confusione, non perdere la testa **4.** (*mat.*) misto (di numero) ☆ — *-grill*, misto di carne ai ferri; *a — -up kid*, (*fam.*) ragazzo disorientato, spostato.

mixedly ['mikstli], *av.* confusamente; alla rinfusa.

mixedness ['mikstnis], *s.* **1.** mescolanza **2.** promiscuità **3.** (*fam.*) confusione.

mixer ['miksə*], *s.c.* (*fam.*) persona socievole: *he is a bad* —, è un orso; *she is a good* —, è affabile con tutti ‖ *s.* **1.** (*cinc.*) tecnico del missaggio **2.** (*mcc.*) agitatore, mescolatore **3.** (*rad.*) variatore di frequenza.

mixture ['mikstʃə*], *s.* **1.** mescolanza, miscuglio, misto: *a — of humour and tragedy*, un misto di umorismo e tragedia **2.** (*farm.*) mistura **3.** (*chim.*) miscuglio; miscela (di carburante, ecc.) ☆ *explosive* —, (*aut.*) miscela esplosiva; *freezing* —, miscela frigorifera.

mix-up ['miks'ʌp], *s.* **1.** confusione **2.** baruffa; tumulto.

mizzen ['mizn], *ag.* (*mar.*) di mezzana ‖ *s.* (*mar.*) mezzana ☆ — *-mast*, albero di mezzana, — *-sail*, vela di mezzana.

mizzle[1] ['mizl], *s.* pioggerella.

to **mizzle**[1], *v. imp.* piovigginare.

to **mizzle**[2], *v.i.* (*sl.*) svignarsela.

mizzly ['mizli], *ag.* piovigginoso.

mnemonic [ni(:)'mɔnik], *ag.* mnemonico.

mnemonics [ni(:)'mɔniks], *s.* mnemonica.

Mnemosyne [ni:'mɔzini:], *no.pr.f.* (*mit.*) Mnemosine.

mnemotechnics [,ni:mə'tekniks], *s.* mnemotecnica.

mo[1] [mou], *s.* (*sl. abbr.* di *moment*) momento: *half a* —!, un momento!.

mo[2], (*arc.*) per **more**.

Moabite ['mouəbait], *ag.s.c.* (*st. biblica*) moabita.

moan [moun], *s.* gemito, lamento; pianto.

to **moan**, *v.t.i.* **1.** gemere (anche del vento); lamentarsi: *he moaned yes*, gemette sì, emise un flebile sì; *she moaned an apology*, chiese scusa piagnucolando **2.** (*poet.*) lamentare, lamentarsi; piangere su.

moanful ['mounful], *ag.* lamentoso; dolente; querulo.

moat [mout], *s.* fosso, fossato.

to **moat**, *v.t.* cingere di fossato.

moated ['moutid], *ag.* cinto di fossato.

mob[1] [mob], *s.* **1.** folla, ressa, calca **2.** popolino; plebe, plebaglia: *to gather into a* —, affollarsi ☆ — *-law*, legge imposta dalla plebaglia; — *oratory*, oratoria da comizio, da tribuno; — *psychology*, psicologia delle masse ‖ *swell* —, (*sl.*) ladri in guanti gialli.

to **mob**[1], *pass.p.p.* **mobbed** [mobd], *v.t.i.* **1.** assalire; malmenare; aggredire: *the crowd wanted to — the house*, la folla voleva assalire la casa; *the thief was mobbed*, il ladro fu malmenato dalla folla **2.** affollare, affollarsi, accalcarsi: *police rescues film-star mobbed by the crowd*, la polizia libera la diva pressata dalla folla **3.** (*rar.*) mescolarsi alla folla: *he likes to — with the crowd*, gli piace partecipare a manifestazioni popolari.

mob[2], *s.* **1.** (*rar. arc.*) donna licenziosa **2.** vestaglia per signora, *négligé* **3.** — *(-cap)*, cuffia (da donna) con pizzi e volanti.

mobile ['moubail], *ag.* **1.** mobile, movibile, spostabile: — *troops*, (*mil.*) truppe mobili **2.** *fig.* instabile, variabile, volubile ‖ *s.* (*neol.scult.*) composizione mobile.

mobility [mou'biliti], *s.* **1.** mobilità: *the — of his features*, la mobilità del suo viso **2.** *fig.* volubilità.

mobilization [ˌmoubilai'zeiʃən], *s.* (*mil.*) mobilitazione.

to **mobilize** ['moubilaiz], *v.t.* (*mil.*) mobilitare.

moccasin ['mɔkəsin], *s.* mocassino.

mocha[1] ['moukə], *s.* (caffè) moca ☆ — *cake*, torta al caffè.

mocha[2], *s.* (*min.*) pietra di moka (varietà dell'agata).

mock [mɔk], *ag.* **1.** ironico; scherzoso; burlesco **2.** finto ‖ *s.* **1.** (*arc.*) derisione, scherno; burla: *to make a — of s.o, sthg.*, deridere qlcu., ql.co. **2.** imitazione, cosa finta ☆ *a — battle*, una finta battaglia; — *-heroic*, eroicomico; — *-modesty*, falsa modestia; — *moon*, paraselene; — *sun*, parelio; — *turtle soup*, (*cuc.*) finto brodo di tartaruga; — *-up*, (*tec.*) simulacro, manichino; modello dimostrativo.

to **mock,** *v.t.i.* **1.** deludere, ingannare: *a mirage mocked the travellers*, un miraggio ingannò i viaggiatori **2.** sfidare, sprezzare **3.** deridere, canzonare, schernire, motteggiare **4.** rendere vano **5.** *to — at* (*s.o.*, *sthg.*), burlarsi di: *he mocked at her fears*, egli rise delle sue paure.

mockable ['mɔkəbl], *ag.* che può essere deriso.

mocker ['mɔkə*], *s.c.* chi deride, chi beffa; burlone, burlona.

mockery ['mɔkəri], *s.* **1.** derisione, ironia, scherno: *with her usual —*, con la sua solita ironia **2.** beffa, inganno: *life is a —, he said*, la vita è un inganno, egli disse **3.** contraffazione.

mocking ['mɔkiŋ], *ag.* beffardo, ironico, sarcastico: *a — laugh*, un riso beffardo ☆ — *bird*, (*ornit.*) mimo, tordo beffeggiatore.

mockingly ['mɔkiŋli], *av.* in modo ironico, beffardo.

modal ['moudl], *ag.* (*log. gram.*) modale ☆ — *legacy*, (*dir.*) legato condizionale.

modalism ['moudəlizəm], *s.* modalismo.

modality [mou'dæliti], *s.* modalità.

mode [moud], *s.* **1.** modo, maniera **2.** foggia, costume, usanza **3.** (*fil. gram.*) modo **4.** (*mus.*) modo, tono.

model ['mɔdl], *ag.* modello, che serve da modello: *a — wife*, una moglie modello.

model, *s.* **1.** modello: *a — of an aeroplane*, un modello di aeroplano; *constructed after* (o *on* o *upon*) —, costruito secondo il modello ‖ *the latest Paris models*, gli ultimi modelli di Parigi **2.** *fig.* copia: *she's a perfect — of her grandmother*, è la copia esatta di sua nonna **3.** *fig.* modello, campione, esempio: *to be taken as a —*, essere preso ad esempio **4.** (*pitt.*) modella: *she was working as a —*, lavorava come modella **5.** indossatrice ☆ *current —*, (modello) di serie; *plastic —*, (*arch.*) plastico; *special —*, (modello) fuori serie; *working- —*, modello funzionante.

to **model,** *pass.p.p.* **modelled** ['mɔdld], *v.t.* **1.** modellare, formare, costruire: *to — a hand in clay*, modellare una mano con la creta **2.** scolpire, dipingere al modo di: *his painting is modelled after* (o *on* o *upon*) *the old masters*, la sua pittura si rifà ai grandi pittori del passato **3.** *fig.* imitare, tenere d'esempio.

modeller ['mɔdlə*], *s.* **1.** modellatore **2.** modellista.

modelling ['mɔdliŋ], *s.* **1.** modellatura **2.** creazione di modelli.

Modena ['mɔdinə], *no.pr.* (*geog.*) Modena ‖ **modena**, *s.* (color) rosso scuro.

moderate ['mɔdərit], *ag.* **1.** moderato; misurato; modico: — *prices*, prezzi modici; — *talent*, scarso talento; *he had a — appetite*, aveva poco appetito **2.** temperato, moderato (del tempo): *a — wind*, un vento moderato ‖ *s.* (*pol.*) moderato.

to **moderate** ['mɔdəreit], *v.t.i.* **1.** moderare, moderarsi, temperare: *to — one's pretensions*, moderare le proprie pretese **2.** calmarsi, mitigarsi (del tempo): *the*

tempest is moderating, la tempesta si sta calmando **3.** calmare.

moderately ['mɔdəritli], *av.* moderatamente; modicamente; sobriamente.

moderateness ['mɔdəritnis], *s.* moderatezza, sobrietà; modicità.

moderation [ˌmɔdə'reiʃən], *s.* **1.** moderazione; sobrietà: *in —*, moderatamente, senza eccessi **2.** *pl.* primo esame pubblico per la laurea in lettere a Oxford.

moderator ['mɔdəreitə*], *s.* **1.** arbitro; mediatore **2.** presidente (di un'assemblea) **3.** ministro (nella Chiesa presbiteriana) ‖ *Moderator of the Church of Scotland*, capo della Chiesa presbiteriana di Scozia **4.** esaminatore (a Cambridge, a Oxford) **5.** (*fis. atomica*) moderatore, rallentatore **6.** (*mec.*) regolatore, equilibratore.

moderatrix [ˌmɔdə'reitriks], *s.* moderatrice.

modern ['mɔdən], *ag.* **1.** moderno, recente: — *history*, storia moderna; — *times*, tempi presenti **2.** aggiornato ‖ *s.* **1.** persona vivente nei tempi moderni **2.** persona moderna (di gusto, vedute) **3.** (*tip.*) romano moderno ☆ — *school*, scuola secondaria (con indirizzo pratico).

modernism ['mɔdə(:)nizəm], *s.* **1.** maniera, forma, usanza moderna; vedute moderne **2.** neologismo **3.** (*teol.*) modernismo.

modernist ['mɔdə(:)nist], *s.* **1.** amante delle novità, della modernità **2.** (*teol.*) modernista.

modernity [mɔ'də:niti], *s.* modernità.

modernization [ˌmɔdə(:)nai'zeiʃən], *s.* rimodernamento; aggiornamento: *technical —*, aggiornamento tecnico; *a plan of — for the capital has been proposed*, è stato proposto un nuovo progetto di pianificazione della capitale.

to **modernize** ['mɔdə(:)naiz], *v.t.i.* **1.** modernizzare, ammodernare, rimodernare **2.** adottare sistemi moderni.

modernizer ['mɔdə(:)naizə*], *s.c.* **1.** rimodernatore, rimodernatrice **2.** innovatore, innovatrice.

modernly ['mɔdənli], *av.* modernamente; nei tempi moderni.

modernness ['mɔdənnis], *s.* modernità.

modest ['mɔdist], *ag.* **1.** modesto, riservato: *he was — about his achievements*, egli era modesto a proposito dei suoi successi **2.** pudico: *she is too — to speak about her illness*, è troppo pudica per parlare della sua malattia **3.** modesto, moderato; modico: *at a — computation*, secondo un calcolo moderato; *my demands are quite —*, le mie richieste sono proprio modeste **4.** senza pretese.

modestly ['mɔdistli], *av.* **1.** modestamente **2.** pudicamente, castamente **3.** modicamente **4.** senza pretese.

modesty ['mɔdisti], *s.* **1.** modestia; riserbo; timidezza: — *is rare*, la modestia è rara **2.** pudore; onestà **3.** moderatezza; modicità **4.** semplicità.

modicum ['mɔdikəm], *s.* piccola quantità (di cibo, ecc.).

modifiability [ˌmɔdifaiə'biliti], *s.* modificabilità.

modifiable ['mɔdifaiəbl], *ag.* modificabile.

modification [ˌmɔdifi'keiʃən], *s.* modificazione, modifica: *to make modifications in sthg.*, apportare delle modifiche a ql.co.

modificative ['mɔdifikeitiv], *ag.* modificativo.

modificatory ['mɔdifikeitəri], *ag.* modificante.

modified ['mɔdifaid], *ag.* **1.** modificato, mutato **2.** attenuato, mitigato: — *penalty*, (*dir.*) pena mitigata.

modifier ['mɔdifaiə*], *s.c.* modificatore, modificatrice ‖ *s.* (*ind. chim.*) agente modificante.

to **modify** ['mɔdifai], *v.t.* **1.** modificare, correggere; mutare, cambiare: *he was obliged to — his plans*, fu costretto a modificare i suoi piani **2.** addolcire; attenuare, mitigare (una pena): *his character was modified by misfortune*, le avversità gli addolcirono il carattere **3.** (*gram.*) modificare.

modillion [mou'diljən], *s.* (*arch.*) modiglione.

modish ['moudiʃ], *ag.* 1. affettato 2. ridicolo, stravagante 3. (*arc.*) alla moda.

modishly ['moudiʃli], *av.* 1. con affettazione, ostentazione 2. in modo bizzarro, stravagante 3. (*arc.*) alla moda.

modishness ['moudiʃnis], *s.* l'essere schiavi della moda; eleganza affettata.

modiste [mou'di:st], *s.* modista; sarta (di lusso).

mods [mɔdz], (*sl. scolastico*) *abbr.* di **moderation** 2.

to **modulate** ['mɔdjuleit], *v.t.i.* (*mus. elett. rad.*) modulare.

modulation [,mɔdju'leiʃən], *s.* (*mus. elett. rad.*) modulazione ☆ — *-meter*, modulometro ‖ *amplitude-* — (*abbr. A. M.*), modulazione di ampiezza; *frequency-* — (*abbr. F. M.*), modulazione di frequenza; *outphasing-* —, modulazione per sfasamento.

modulator ['mɔdjuleitə*], *s.c.* (*mus.*) modulatore, modulatrice ‖ *s.* (*mus.*) libro dei solfeggi.

module ['mɔdju:l], *s.* (*arch.*) modulo.

modulus ['mɔdjuləs], *pl.* **moduli** ['mɔdjulai], *s.* (*mat. mec.*) modulo, coefficiente: — *of efficiency*, coefficiente di rendimento; — *of rupture*, resistenza alla flessione ☆ *section* —, modulo di resistenza.

modus vivendi ['mɔdəsvi(:)'vendi:], *s.* 1. sistema di vita 2. modus vivendi, accordo reciproco.

moe [mou], (*arc.*) per **more**.

mofette [mou'fet], *s.* (*geol.*) mofeta, putizza.

mofussil [mou'fʌsil], *s.* (*ang.-in.*) località campestre.

Mogul [mou'gʌl], *ag.* mogol, mongolo ‖ *s.* 1. mogol, mongolo ‖ *the Great* (o *Grand*) —, il Gran Mogol 2. (*amer.*) personaggio importante, magnate 3. (*amer.*) tipo di locomotiva 4. *pl.* carte da giuoco della miglior qualità.

mohair ['mouheə*], *s.* 1. « mohair » (pelo di capra d'Angora) 2. filato, tessuto di « mohair ».

Mohammed [mou'hæmed], *no.pr.m.* (*st. relig.*) Maometto.

Mohammedan [mou'hæmidən], *ag.* (*st. relig.*) maomettano ‖ *s.c.* maomettano, maomettana.

Mohammedanism [mou'hæmidənizəm], *s.* (*st. relig.*) maomettismo, islamismo.

to **Mohammedanize** [mou'hæmidənaiz], *v.t.* convertire al maomettismo.

Mohican ['mouikən], *ag.s.* moicano ‖ " *The Last of the Mohicans* ", (*lett.*) « L'ultimo dei Moicani ».

moidore ['mɔido:*], *s.* (*st.*) moidoro (moneta d'oro portoghese e brasiliana).

moiety ['mɔiəti], *s.* 1. (*dir.*) metà, mezzo 2. una delle due frazioni (di un tutto).

to **moil** [mɔil], *v.i.* affaticarsi, sfacchinare: *to toil and* —, sfacchinare duramente.

moire [mwɑ:], *s.* « moire », moerro, tessuto marezzato.

moiré ['mwɑ:rei], *ag.* « moiré », marezzato (di stoffe, metalli) ‖ *s.* marezzatura.

moist [mɔist], *ag.* 1. umido, bagnato: — *with dew*, rorido, rugiadoso; *her eyes grew* —, le si riempirono gli occhi di lacrime 2. piovoso 3. (*med.*) essudante, madido.

to **moisten** ['mɔisn], *v.t.i.* umettare, inumidire, inumidirsi: *her eyes moistened*, le si inumidirono gli occhi (di lacrime).

moistness ['mɔistnis], *s.* umidità.

moisture ['mɔistʃə*], *s.* 1. vapore umido: *it is dangerous to drive when* — *settles on the windscreen*, è pericoloso guidare col parabrezza appannato 2. umore (degli alberi) ☆ — *expansion*, rigonfiamento (di legname, ecc.) dovuto all'umidità; — *tester*, (*tec.*) misuratore di umidità.

moits [mɔits], *s.pl.* (*ind.*) corpi estranei vegetali nella lana, ecc.).

moke [mouk], *s.* (*sl.*) asino.

moko ['moukou], *s.* sistema di tatuaggio dei maori.

molar[1] ['moulə*], *ag.s.*: — (*tooth*), (*anat.*) (dente) molare.

molar[2], *ag.* 1. che appartiene alla massa 2. (*chim.*) molare ☆ — *dilution*, diluizione molare.

molasses [mə'læsiz], *s.* melassa.

mold, *V.* **mould**[1].

Moldavian [mɔl'deivjən], *ag.* moldavo, della Moldavia ‖ *s.c.* moldavo, moldava, abitante della Moldavia.

to **molder**, *V.* to **moulder**.

mole[1] [moul], *s.* 1. neo 2. piccola escrescenza.

mole[2], *s.* 1. talpa ‖ *as blind as a* —, cieco come una talpa 2. *fig.* chi lavora al buio; chi vede imperfettamente ☆ — *-cricket*, (*entom.*) grillotalpa; — *-eyed*, miope; quasi cieco; — *-track*, cunicolo scavato dalla talpa.

mole[3], *s.* 1. molo, diga, frangiflutti 2. mole, mausoleo romano.

mole[4], *s.* (*chim.*) grammo-molecola.

molecular [mou'lekjulə*], *ag.* (*chim. fis.*) molecolare: — *volume*, *weight*, (*chim.*) volume, peso molecolare.

molecularity [mou,lekju'læriti], *s.* (*chim. fis.*) molecolarità.

molecule ['mɔlikju:l], *s.* 1. (*chim. fis.*) molecola 2. piccola quantità, particella.

molehill ['moulhil], *s.* cumulo di terra sopra la tana della talpa ‖ *to make a mountain out of a* —, *fig.* far d'una mosca un elefante.

moleskin ['moul-skin], *s.* 1. pelle, pelliccia di talpa 2. fustagno di qualità superiore 3. *pl.* pantaloni di fustagno.

to **molest** [mou'lest], *v.t.* molestare, vessare, infastidire.

molestation [,moules'teiʃən], *s.* molestia, tormento.

molester [mou'lestə*], *s.* molestatore.

Molinism ['mɔlinizəm], *s.* (*st. relig.*) molinismo.

Moll[1] [mɔl], *no.pr.f. dim.* di **Mary**.

moll[2], *s.* (*sl.*) prostituta, donna di malaffare.

mollifiable ['mɔlifaiəbl], *ag.* 1. che può essere ammorbidito 2. *fig.* placabile.

mollification [,mɔlifi'keiʃən], *s.* 1. ammollimento 2. *fig.* raddolcimento; rabbonimento.

mollifier ['mɔlifaiə*], *s.* 1. (*med.*) emolliente, calmante 2. *fig.* paciere.

to **mollify** ['mɔlifai], *v.t.* 1. ammorbidire 2. *fig.* addolcire, placare.

mollifying ['mɔlifaiiŋ], *ag.* 1. che ammorbidisce 2. *fig.* calmante; dolce: *in a* — *tone*, con un tono dolce ‖ *s.* 1. ammollimento 2. *fig.* raddolcimento; rabbonimento.

mollusc ['mɔləsk], *s.* mollusco.

molluscoid [mɔ'lʌskɔid], *ag.s.* molluscoide.

molluscous [mɔ'lʌskəs], *ag.* relativo a mollusco.

molluscum [mɔ'lʌskəm], *s.* (*patol.*) mollusco.

mollusk ['mɔləsk], *s.* mollusco.

Molly[1] ['mɔli], *no.pr.f. dim.* di **Mary** ‖ *a Miss* —, un pulcino nella stoppa, un pulcino bagnato.

molly[2], *s.* uomo, giovane effeminato.

mollycoddle ['mɔlikɔdl], *s.* 1. giovane, uomo effeminato 2. (*fam.*) cocco di mamma.

to **mollycoddle**, *v.t.* viziare, coccolare (bambino, ecc.).

Moloch ['moulɔk], *no.pr.m.* Moloc (dio fenicio) ‖ **moloch**, *s.* 1. moloc, ente malefico 2. (*zool.*) moloc.

molossian [mə'lɔsiən], *ag.s.* (*st.*) molosso ☆ — *dog* (o — *hound*), (*zool.*) molosso.

molossus [mə'lɔsəs], *s.* (*poes.*) molosso.

molten ['moultən], *p.p.* (*arc.*) di to **melt** ‖ *ag.* liquefatto, fuso (di metalli).

moly ['mouli], *s.* 1. (*mit. bot.*) moli 2. (*bot.*) aglio selvatico.

molybdenite [mɔ'libdinait], *s.* (*min.*) molibdenite.

molybdenum [mɔ'libdinəm], *s.* (*chim.*) molibdeno.

moment ['moumənt], *s.* 1. momento, istante, attimo, minuto: *he never wastes a* —, non perde mai un'istante ‖ *at any* —, da un momento all'altro; *at the present* —, ora, adesso; *in a* —, tra un momento, quasi subito; *the man of the* —, l'uomo del momento; *not for a* —!, mai!; *to the* —, puntualmente 2. importanza, peso: *a decision of great, little, no* —, una decisione di grande, poca, nessuna importanza **3.** (*fis. mec.*) momento ☆ *damping* —, (*aer.*) momento smorzante; *nosedive* —, (*aer.*) momento di picchiata.

momentarily ['mouməntərili], *av.* **1.** momentaneamente **2.** da un momento all'altro.

momentariness ['mouməntərinis], *s.* transitorietà.

momentary ['moumәntəri], *ag.* momentaneo, passeggero, transitorio.

momently ['moumәntli], *av.* **1.** a momenti, in un momento, da un momento all'altro **2.** momentaneamente.

momentous [mou'mentəs], *ag.* importante, grave: *on this* — *occasion*, in questa importante occasione.

momentously [mou'mentəsli], *av.* gravemente.

momentousness [mou'mentəsnis], *s.* importanza.

momentum [mou'mentəm], *pl.* **momenta** [mou-'mentə], *s.* **1.** (*mec. fis.*) quantità di moto **2.** velocità acquisita; *fig.* impeto, slancio: *to gather* —, aumentare di velocità (*p. e. di caduta*).

Momus ['mouməs], *no.pr.m.* (*mit.*) Momo ‖ *s.* critico malevolo.

momism ['mɔmizəm], *s.* (*neol. amer. psicologia*) mammismo.

monachal ['mɔnəkəl], *ag.* monacale; monastico.

monachism ['mɔnəkizəm], *s.* monachesimo.

Monaco ['mɔnəkou], *no.pr.* (*geog.*) (Principato di) Monaco.

monad ['mɔnæd], *s.* (*biol. chim. fil.*) monade.

monadelph ['mɔnədelf], *s.* (*bot.*) pianta monadelfa.

monadelphous [,mɔnə'delfəs], *ag.* (*bot.*) monadelfo.

monadic [mɔ'nædik], *ag.* monadico.

monadism ['mɔnədizəm], *s.* (*fil.*) monadismo.

monandrous [mɔ'nændrəs], *ag.* (*bot.*) monandro.

monarch ['mɔnək], *s.* **1.** monarca, sovrano (anche *fig.*) **2.** (*entom.*) danaide.

monarchal [mɔ'nɑ:kəl], *ag.* regale; di, da, monarca.

monarchie(al) [mɔ'nɑ:kik(əl)], *ag.* monarchico.

monarchically [mɔ'nɑ:kikəli], *av.* monarchicamente.

monarchism ['mɔnəkizəm], *s.* lealismo monarchico.

monarchist ['mɔnəkist], *s.* (*pol.*) monarchico.

monarchy ['mɔnəki], *s.* **1.** monarchia: *absolute* —, monarchia assoluta; *constitutional, limited* —, monarchia costituzionale **2.** (*rar.*) regno, reame.

monastery ['mɔnəstəri], *s.* monastero, convento.

monastic [mə'næstik], *s.* monaco.

monastic(al) [mə'næstik(əl)], *ag.* monastico.

monastically [mə'næstikəli], *av.* monasticamente.

monasticism [mə'næstisizəm], *s.* monachismo; vita monastica.

monatomie [,mɔnə'tɔmik], *ag.* **1.** (*chim.*) monoatomico **2.** (*chim.*) monovalente.

Monday ['mʌndi], *s.* lunedì: *we meet on Mondays*, ci vediamo al lunedì ‖ *Black* —, (*arc.*) lunedì dopo Pasqua; (*sl. scolastico*) il lunedì dopo una lunga vacanza ‖ *Easter* —, il lunedì dell'Angelo.

Mondayish ['mʌndiiʃ], *ag.* (*scherz.*) che ha il male del lunedì (di chi è svogliato dopo un giorno di festa).

monde [mɔnd], *s.* **1.** mondo elegante; società mondana **2.** ambiente, mondo **3.** globo (simbolo di regalità).

mondial ['mɔndiəl], *ag.* mondiale.

monetary ['mʌnitəri], *ag.* monetario ☆ —*unit*, unità monetaria.

monetization [,mʌnitai'zeiʃən], *s.* monetazione.

to **monetize** ['mʌnitaiz], *v.t.* monetizzare; fissare il valore monetario di.

money ['mʌni], *s.* **1.** denaro, moneta, valuta: *he does not like to part with his* —, è attaccato al denaro; *he keeps his boy short of* —, tiene suo figlio a corto di denaro; *it is a bargain for the* —, a quel prezzo è un affare; *to bank* —, depositare denaro in banca; *to get in* —, incassare denaro; *to make* —, far denaro, arricchirsi; *to put* — *to interest*, dar denaro ad interesse ‖ *your* — *or your life!*, o la borsa o la vita! *—makes the mare to go*, il denaro può tutto ‖ *there is* — *in it*, è un buon affare ‖ *to be rolling in* —, nuotare

nell'oro ‖ *to come into* —, ereditare ‖ *to get one's* — *worth*, spendere bene il proprio denaro ‖ *to marry* —, fare un matrimonio d'interesse ‖ *time is* —, 'prov. il tempo è denaro **2.** *pl.* fondi: *moneys paid out*, versamenti effettuati ☆ — *-bag*, borsa (di esattore, ecc.) per riporvi il denaro; *pl.* (*fam.*) ricchezze; *fig.* riccone; — *-bill*, decreto legge finanziario; — *-box*, salvadanaio; — *-broker* (o — *-changer* o — *-dealer*), cambiavalute; — *grubber*, avaro; strozzino; — *-lender*, usuraio; — *-market*, borsa valori; — *-order*, vaglia, mandato, ordine di pagamento; — *-payment*, pagamento in denaro; — *-spinner*, ragno portafortuna; *fig.* speculatore ‖ *bad* — (o *base* — o *counterfeit* —), moneta falsa; *current* —, valuta corrente; *earnest* —, caparra; *hard* —, (*amer.*) denaro contante, moneta metallica; *paper* — (o *soft* —), (*amer.*) valuta cartacea; *public moneys*, fondi pubblici, tesoro pubblico; *ready* —, denaro contante: *to pay (down) in ready* —, pagare in contanti; *specie* —, valuta metallica.

moneyed ['mʌnid], *ag.* **1.** monetato **2.** danaroso, ricco: — *man*, ricco; capitalista ☆ — *assistance*, aiuti in denaro; — *corporation*, (*amer.*) ente autorizzato a trattare con denaro, istituto di credito; — *interest*, il capitale; le classi abbienti.

moneyer ['mʌniə*], *s.* zecchiere.

moneyless ['mʌnilis], *ag.* senza denaro; povero.

monger ['mʌngə*], *s.* mercante, venditore ☆ *ballad-* —, canzonettista; *cheese-* —, formaggiaio; *fish-* —, pescivendolo; *iron-* —, venditore di ferramenta; *news-* —, (*spreg.*) pettegolo, spacciatore di notizie; *scandal-* —, (*spreg.*) seminatore di scandali; *slander-* —, malalingua, maldicente; *strike-* —, (*spreg.*) fomentatore di scioperi; *war-* —, (*spreg.*) guerrafondaio.

Mongol ['mɔngɔl], *ag.* mongolo ‖ *s.c.* mongolo, mongola ‖ *s.* lingua mongolica.

Mongolian [mɔn'gouljən], *ag.* mongolo ‖ *s.* lingua mongolica.

Mongolic [mɔn'gɔlik], *ag.* mongolico.

mongolism ['mɔngɔlizəm], *s.* (*patol.*) mongolismo.

mongoloid ['mɔngəlɔid], *ag. s.* mongoloide.

mongoose ['mɔngu:s], *s.* (*zool.*) mangusta.

mongrel ['mʌngrəl], *ag.* misto, ibrido; meticcio ‖ *s.* **1.** cane bastardo **2.** (*spreg.*) persona di sangue misto **3.** (*bot. zool.*) incrocio ☆ — *cur*, (*zool.*) botolo.

mongrelism ['mʌngrəlizəm], *s.* imbastardimento.

to **mongrelize** ['mʌngrəlaiz], *v.t.* imbastardire.

monial ['mouniəl], *V.* **mullion**.

Monica ['mɔnikə], *no.pr.f.* Monica.

moniliform [mɔ'nilifɔ:m], *ag.* moniliforme.

monism ['mɔnizəm], *s.* (*fil.*) monismo.

monist ['mɔnist], *s.* (*fil.*) monista.

monistic [mɔ'nistik], *ag.* (*fil.*) monistico.

monition [mou'niʃən], *s.* **1.** ammonizione **2.** (*dir.*) citazione.

monitor ['mɔnitə*], *s.* **1.** consigliere, monitore **2.** capoclasse **3.** (*zool.*) varano **4.** (*elett.*) monitore, dispositivo di controllo, avvisatore **5.** (*mar.*) monitore, pontone armato corazzato **6.** (*fis.*) apparecchio portatile di controllo della radioattività **7.** (*rad. tv.*) monitor ☆ — *-roof*, (*arch. ferr.*) lanternino; — *-room*, cabina fonica di controllo del suono ‖ *wave* —, (*elett.*) oscilloscopio (per il controllo delle forme d'onda).

to **monitor**, *v.t.* **1.** (*rad. tv.*) controllare **2.** (*fis.*) provare, determinare (intensità radioattiva).

monitorily [ˈmɔnitərili], *av.* in modo da ammonire.

monitoring phone ['mɔnitəriŋ,foun], *s.* telefono inserito per ascoltare segretamente le conversazioni.

monitoring service ['mɔnitəriŋ,sə:vis], *s.* servizio di ascolto delle radio straniere.

monitory ['mɔnitəri], *ag.* **1.** ammonitore; che mette in guardia, consiglia **2.** (*eccl.*) monitorio ‖ *s.* (*eccl.*) monitorio.

monitress ['mɔnitris], *s.* **1.** ammonitrice **2.** (*allieva*) capoclasse.

monk [mʌŋk], *s.* monaco, frate ‖ *the cowl does not*

make the —, *prov.* l'abito non fa il monaco ☆ — *-fish,* (*ittiol.*) squadro; rana pescatrice; — *-seal,* (*zool.*) foca monaca, —*'s hood,* (*bot.*) aconito || *black* —, benedettino; *white* —, cistercense.

monkery ['mʌŋkəri], *s.* **1.** (*spreg.*) vita monastica **2.** i religiosi in genere **3.** comunità di religiosi; monastero.

monkey ['mʌŋki], *s.* **1.** scimmia, scimmiotto || *to get* (o *to put*) *s.o.'s* — *up,* (*sl.*) fare andare qlcu. in bestia; *to have one's* — *up,* (*sl.*) essere di malumore **2.** (*scherz.*) persona, bambino vivace e dispettoso: *you, young* —*!,* tu, scimmiottino! **3.** (*tec.*) mazza battente **4.** (*sl.*) 500 sterline; (*amer.*) 500 dollari ☆ — *-bread,* (*bot.*) frutto del baobab; — *-business,* imbroglio, pasticcio; — *-chatter,* (*rad.*) interferenza, bisbiglio; — *-flower,* (*bot.*) mimulo; — *-jacket,* giubbetto, giacca corta e attillata; — *-like,* scimmiesco; — *-nut,* arachide; — *-puzzle,* (*bot.*) araucaria; — *-tricks,* burle; — *-wrench* (o — *-spanner*), chiave inglese a rullino.

to **monkey,** *v.t.i.* **1.** scimmiottare || *to* — *s.o. out of sthg.,* sottrarre (con astuzia) ql.co. a qlcu. **2.** fare scherzi di cattivo genere **3.** *to* — (*about*) *with sthg.,* maneggiare maldestramente ql.co.: *stop monkeying* (*about*) *with those tools!,* non scassare quegli arnesi!.

monkeyish ['mʌŋkiiʃ], *ag.* scimmiesco.
monkeyishness ['mʌŋkiiʃnis], *s.* natura scimmiesca.
monkhood ['mʌŋkhud], *s.* monacato.
monkish ['mʌŋkiʃ], *ag.* monastico; (*spreg.*) monacale.
monkship ['mʌŋkʃip], *s.* monachesimo.
monobasic [,mɔnou'beisik], *ag.* (*chim.*) monobasico.
monoblepsis [,mɔnou'blepsis], *s.* (*patol.*) monoblepsia.
monobloc ['mɔnoublɔk], *s.* (*mec.*) monoblocco.
monocarpie [,mɔnou'ka:pik], **monocarpous** [,mɔnou'ka:pəs], *ag.* (*bot.*) monocarpico.
monocentric [,mɔnou'sentrik], *ag.* monocentrico.
monocephalous [,mɔnou'sefələs], *ag.* (*bot.*) monocefalo.
monochord ['mɔnoukɔ:d], *s.* **1.** (*mus.*) monocordo **2.** (*tel.*) monocorda.
monochromatic [,mɔnəkrə'mætik], *ag.* monocromatico.
monochrome ['mɔnəkroum], *ag.* monocromatico || *s.* (*pitt.*) monocroma; monocromia.
monocle ['mɔnɔkl], *s.* monocolo, caramella.
monoclinal [,mɔnou'klainl], *ag.* (*geol.*) monoclino.
monocline ['mɔnəklain], *s.* (*geol.*) strato monoclino.
monoclinic [,mɔnou'klinik], *ag.* (*min.*) monoclino (di cristalli).
monocotyledon [,mɔnou,kɔti'li:dən], *s.* (*bot.*) monocotiledone.
monocotyledonous ['mɔnou,kɔti'li:dənəs], *ag.* (*bot.*) monocotiledone.
monocular [mə'nɔkjulə*], *ag.* monoculare.
monodactylous [,mɔnou'dæktiləs], *ag.* (*zool.*) monodattilo.
monodic [mə'nɔdik], *ag.* (*mus.*) monodico.
monodist ['mɔnədist], *s.* (*mus.*) chi scrive, canta monodie.
monody ['mɔnədi], *s.* (*mus.*) monodia.
monogamic [,mɔnou'gæmik], *ag.* monogamico.
monogamist [mɔ'nɔgəmist], *s.* fautore della monogamia.
monogamous [mɔ'nɔgəməs], *ag.* monogamo.
monogamy [mɔ'nɔgəmi], *s.* monogamia.
monogenesis [,mɔnou'dʒenisis], *s.* monogenesi.
monogenetic [,mɔnou'dʒi'netik], *ag.* monogenetico.
monogram ['mɔnəgræm], *s.* monogramma.
monogrammatic(al) [,mɔnougrə'mætik(əl)], *ag.* monogrammatico.
monograph ['mɔnəgrɑ:f], *s.* monografia.
to **monograph,** *v.t.* scrivere una monografia su.
monographer [mə'nɔgrəfə*], *s.* monografista.
monographic(al) [,mɔnou'græfik(əl)], *ag.* monografico.
monographist [mə'nɔgrɑ:fist], *s.* monografista.
monography [mə'nɔgrəfi], *s.* (*rar.*) monografia.

Monogynia [,mɔnou'dʒiniə], *s.pl.* (*bot.*) monoginie
monogynian [,mɔnou'dʒinien], **monogynous** [mə'nɔdʒinəs], *ag.* (*bot.*) monogino.
monolith ['mɔnouliθ], *s.* **1.** monolito **2.** *fig.* cosa, istituzione solida e compatta.
monolithic [,mɔnou'liθik], *ag.* **1.** monolitico **2.** *fig.* solido, compatto: *a* — *state,* uno stato accentratore.
to **monologize** [mə'nɔlədʒaiz], *v.i.* dire monologhi; parlare in soliloquio.
monologue ['mɔnələg], *s.* monologo: *mental, subconscious* —, monologo interiore.
monomania ['mɔnou'meinjə], *s.* (*patol.*) monomania.
monomaniac [,mɔnou'meiniæk], *ag.* (*patol.*) monomaniaco || *s.* (*patol.*) monomane.
monometallic [,mɔnoumi'tælik], *ag.* monometallico.
monometallism [,mɔnou'metəlizəm], *s.* (*econ.*) monometallismo (impiego di un solo metallo prezioso come moneta legale).
monometallist [,mɔnou'metəlist], *s.* (*econ.*) fautore del monometallismo.
monometer [mə'nɔmitə*], *ag.* (*poes.*) monometro || *s.* (*poes.*) verso monometro; composizione in versi monometri.
monometric [,mɔnou'metrik], *ag.* (*min.*) monometrico.
monomial [mə'noumiəl], *ag.* (*alg.*) di monomio || *s.* (*alg.*) monomio.
monomorphic [,mɔnou'mɔ:fik], **monomorphous** [,mɔnou'mɔ:fəs], *ag.* monomorfo.
monopetalous [,mɔnou'petələs], *ag.* (*bot.*) monopetalo.
monophthong ['mɔnəfθɔŋ], *s.* (*fonet.*) monottongo.
Monophysite [mə'nɔfisait], *s.* (*st. relig.*) monofisita.
monoplane ['mɔnouplein], *s.* (*aer.*) monoplano.
monoplegia [,mɔnou'pli:dʒiə], *s.* (*patol.*) monoplegia.
monopolism [mə'nɔpəlizəm], *s.* sistema, politica di monopolio, di accaparramento.
monopolist [mə'nɔpəlist], *s.* **1.** monopolista; incettatore; accaparratore **2.** fautore della politica dei monopoli.
monopolization [mə,nɔpəlai'zeiʃən], *s.* **1.** monopolizzazione **2.** accaparramento.
to **monopolize** [mə'nɔpəlaiz], *v.t.* monopolizzare, accaparrare (anche *fig.*): *don't* — *the conversation!,* non monopolizzare la conversazione!.
monopolizer [mə'nɔpəlaizə*], *s.* **1.** *V.* **monopolist 2.** (*fam.*) chi non lascia parlare gli altri.
monopoly [mə'nɔpəli], *s.* **1.** monopolio: *to have the* — (*of*) *on*) *sthg.,* avere il monopolio di qualcosa **2.** possesso esclusivo (anche *fig.*).
monopolylogue [,mɔnou'pɔliləg], *s.* rappresentazione in cui un solo attore fa molte parti.
monorail ['mɔnoureil], *ag.* a una rotaia || *s.* monorotaia.
monorefringent [,mɔnouri'frindʒənt], *s.* (*fis.*) monorifrangente.
monorhyme ['mɔnəraim], *s.* (*poes.*) componimento monorimo.
monosepalous [,mɔnə'sepələs], *ag.* (*bot.*) monosepalo.
monospermous [,mɔnə'spə:məs], *ag.* (*bot.*) monospermo.
monostich ['mɔnoustik], *s.* (*poes.*) monostichio.
monostrophic [,mɔnou'strɔfik], *ag.* (*poes.*) monostrofico.
monosyllabic(al) ['mɔnəsi'læbik(əl)], *ag.* monosillabo, monosillabico.
monosyllable ['mɔnə,siləbl], *s.* monosillabo.
monotheism ['mɔnouθi:,izəm], *s.* (*relig.*) monoteismo.
monotheist ['mɔnouθi:,ist], *s.* (*relig.*) monoteista.
monotheistic ['mɔnouθi:,istik], *ag.* (*relig.*) monoteistico.
monotone ['mɔnətoun], *ag.* monotono || *s.* **1.** tono di voce uniforme, senza modulazioni **2.** (*mus.*) serie di suoni dello stesso tono.
to **monotone,** *v.t.i.* recitare, cantare, parlare in tono uniforme.

monotonic [ˌmɔnə'tɔnik], *ag.* (*mus.*) monotonico, monocorde.

monotonous [mə'nɔtnəs], *ag.* monotono, noioso; uniforme.

monotonously [mə'nɔtnəsli], *av.* in modo monotono.

monotonousness [mə'nɔtnəsnis], **monotony** [mə'nɔtni], *s.* monotonia; uniformità.

monotype ['mɔnətaip], *s.* (*tip.*) monotipo.

monovalent ['mɔnouˌveilənt], *ag.* (*chim.*) monovalente.

monoxide [mɔ'nɔksaid], *s.* (*chim.*) monossido.

Monroeism [mən'rouizəm], *s.* (*pol. amer.*) dottrina di Monroe.

monsignor [mɔn'si:njə*], **monsignore** [ˌmɔnsi'njɔ:rei], *s.* (*eccl.*) monsignore.

monsoon [mɔn'su:n], *s.* monsone ☆ *dry* —, monsone invernale; *wet* —, monsone estivo.

monster ['mɔnstə*], *ag.* gigantesco, colossale ‖ *s.* mostro (anche *fig.*): *a* — *of cruelty*, un mostro di crudeltà; *Beowulf killed the* —, Beowulf uccise il mostro.

monstrance ['mɔnstrəns], *s.* (*eccl.*) ostensorio.

monstrosity [mɔns'trɔsiti], *s.* mostruosità.

monstrous ['mɔnstrəs], *ag.* **1.** mostruoso, deforme **2.** enorme **3.** atroce, mostruoso: *it is* — *that...*, è mostruoso che... **4.** assurdo, incredibile.

monstrous, *av.* (*arc.*) molto, estremamente: — *wise*, di una saggezza prodigiosa.

monstrously ['mɔnstrəsli], *av.* **1.** mostruosamente **2.** enormemente **3.** prodigiosamente.

monstrousness ['mɔnstrəsnis], *s.* mostruosità.

montage [mɔn'tɑ:ʒ], *s.* (*cine.*) montaggio.

Montagnard [ˌmɔ:ntɑ:'njɑ:*], *s.* (*st.*) montagnardo.

Montagu(e) ['mɔntəgju:], *no.pr.* (*lett.*) Montecchi.

Montanan [mɔn'tænən], *ag.s.* (abitante) dello stato del Montana.

Mont Blanc [mɔ:m'blɑ:ŋ], *no.pr.*(*geog.*) Monte Bianco.

Mont Cenis [ˌmɔ:nsə'ni:], *no.pr.* (*geog.*) Moncenisio.

Monte Carlo [ˌmɔnti'kɑ:lou], *no.pr.* (*geog.*) Montecarlo.

Montenegrin [ˌmɔnti'ni:grin], *ag.* montenegrino ‖ *s.c.* montenegrino, montenegrina.

Montenegro [ˌmɔnti'ni:grou], *no.pr.* (*geog.*) Montenegro.

month [mʌnθ], *s.* mese: *bill at three months*, (*comm.*) cambiale a tre mesi; *from* — *to* —, di mese in mese; *this day* —, fra un mese; *this day* — *ago*, è un mese oggi; *what day of the* — *is this?*, in che giorno del mese siamo?; *to hire a room by the* —, affittare una stanza a mese ‖ *a* — *of Sundays*, (*scherz.*) un'eternità ☆ *calendar* —, mese civile; *current* —, corrente mese; *lunar* —, mese lunare ‖ —*'s pay*, mensile, paga.

monthly ['mʌnθli], *ag.* mensile ‖ *s.* **1.** rivista mensile **2.** (*nurse*), infermiera (che assiste una madre per un mese dopo il parto).

monthly, *av.* mensilmente.

monticule ['mɔntikju:l], *s.* monticello; cumulo; piccola sporgenza.

monture ['mɔntʃə*], *s.* montatura (di anelli, ecc.).

monument ['mɔnjumənt], *s.* **1.** monumento ‖ *the Monument*, colonna commemorativa dell'incendio di Londra (1666) **2.** monumento funebre **3.** documento.

to monument ['mɔnjument], *v.t.* erigere (un monumento) a commemorazione di.

monumental [ˌmɔnju'mentl], *ag.* monumentale, colossale, imponente ☆ — *mason*, marmista (per pietre tombali).

monumentally [ˌmɔnju'mentəli], *av.* in modo imponente.

moo [mu:], *s.* muggito, mugghio.

to moo, *v.i.* muggire, mugghiare.

mooch [mu:tʃ], *s.* (*sl. dial.*) pigrizia, fiacca ‖ *to be on the* —, batter la fiacca; oziare in attesa di fare un furto.

to mooch, *v.t.i.* (*sl. dial.*) **1.** oziare **2.** rubare: *he's mooched my cap*, mi ha sgraffignato il berretto **3.** *to* — *about*, *along*, vagabondare, gironzolare.

mood¹ [mu:d], *s.* (*gram.*) modo: *subjunctive* —, modo congiuntivo.

mood², *s.* **1.** umore, stato d'animo: *to be in a good*, *in a bad* —, essere di buono, di cattivo umore; *to be in the* — *to do sthg.*, sentirsi disposto a fare ql.co.: *to feel in no laughing* —, non aver nessuna voglia di ridere **2.** *pl.* ubbie, capricci: *he has moods*, è pieno di capricci, è lunatico; *he is in one of his moods*, (*fam.*) ha la luna, è di malumore.

moodily ['mu:dili], *av.* di malumore; con fare imbronciato.

moodiness ['mu:dinis], *s.* umore nero; tristezza, malinconia.

moody ['mu:di], *ag.* di malumore, d'umore nero; triste; pensoso: *to be* —, avere la luna.

moolvi(e) ['mu:lvi(:)], *s.* dotto (fra i maomettani dell'India).

moon [mu:n], *s.* **1.** luna: *by the light of the* —, al chiaro di luna ‖ *to cry for the* —, desiderare l'impossibile ‖ *to promise s.o. the* — *and stars*, promettere mari e monti a qlcu. **2.** (*astr.*) satellite: *the planet Jupiter has nine moons*, Giove ha nove satelliti **3.** (*poet.*) mese ‖ *once in a blue* —, ad ogni morte di vescovo ☆ — *-beam*, raggio di luna; — *-blind*, affetto da oftalmia periodica; — *-fish*, (*ittiol.*) pesce luna; — *-flower*, margherita, occhio di bue; — *-glade*, riflesso della luna sull'acqua; — *-goddess*, divinità lunare; — *-madness*, follia; — *-raker* (o — *-sail*), (*mar.*) uccellina; — *-stone* (*min.*) lunaria ‖ *full-* —, luna piena; *half-* —, mezzaluna.

to moon, *v.t.i.* **1.** esporre ai raggi lunari **2.** muoversi come un satellite **3.** guardare con aria trasognata **4.** perdere (tempo) sognando: *to* — *away a whole day*, perdere un'intera giornata sognando **5.** (*neol.*) allunare.

mooncalf ['mu:nkɑ:f], *s.* **1.** imbecille, idiota **2.** essere deforme; aborto **3.** persona stramba, lunatica.

mooned [mu:nd], *ag.* lunato, a forma di luna.

mooner ['mu:nə*], *s.* bighellone.

moonface ['mu:nfeis], *s.* faccia da luna piena.

moonfaced ['mu:nfeist], *ag.* dalla faccia tonda, di luna piena.

moonish ['mu:niʃ], *ag.* capriccioso, mutevole.

moonless ['mu:nlis], *ag.* senza luna: *a* — *night*, una notte senza luna, buia.

moonlight ['mu:nlait], *ag.* illuminato dalla luna ‖ *s.* chiaro di luna: *by* —, al chiaro di luna ☆ — *flitting*, trasloco effettuato di notte per non pagare l'affitto; — *walk*, passeggiata al chiaro di luna.

moonlighter ['mu:nˌlaitə*], *s.* **1.** (*fam.*) chi compie azioni clandestine di notte **2.** (*amer.*) distillatore clandestino di alcoolici **3.** (*irl. st.*) terrorista (che agiva di notte nelle campagne).

moonlit ['mu:nlit], *ag.* illuminato dalla luna.

moonset ['mu:nset], *s.* tramonto della luna.

moonshine ['mu:n-ʃain], *s.* **1.** chiaro di luna **2.** discorso senza significato; fantasie; sciocchezze **3.** alcool di contrabbando.

moonshiner ['mu:n-ʃainə*], *s.* (*sl. amer.*) contrabbandiere di alcoolici; distillatore clandestino di alcoolici.

moonshiny ['mu:n-ʃaini], *ag.* **1.** illuminato dalla luna **2.** fantastico, immaginario.

moonstricken ['mu:n-strikən], **moonstruck** ['mun-strʌk], *ag.* pazzoide; lunatico.

moony ['mu:ni], *ag.* **1.** lunare; a forma di mezzaluna **2.** svagato, sognante, distratto **3.** (*sl.*) brillo.

moor¹ [muə*], *s.* brughiera, landa.

moor², *V.* **moorage**.

to moor², *v.t.* (*mar.*) ormeggiare; ancorare.

Moor³, *s.* moro; marocchino; saraceno.

moorage ['muəridʒ], *s.* (*mar.*) **1.** ormeggio **2.** diritti, tassa di ancoraggio.

moorcock ['muə-kɔk], **moorfowl** ['muə-faul], *s.* gallo di brughiera.

moorhen ['muəhen], *s.* gallina di brughiera.

mooring ['muəriŋ], *s.* (*mar.*) **1.** ormeggio; ammarraggio **2**. *pl.* ormeggi; luogo dove la nave ha fissato gli ormeggi: *ship at her moorings*, nave agli ormeggi ☆ — *buoy*, boa d'ormeggio; — *pile*, (*mar.*) palo d'ormeggio; — *rope*, cavo d'ormeggio.

moorish[1] ['muəriʃ], *ag.* di brughiera; sterile, incolto.

Moorish[2], *ag.* moro, moresco.

moorland ['muələnd], *s.* landa, brughiera.

moory ['muəri], *ag.* **1**. paludoso **2**. di brughiera.

moose [mu:s], *s.* (*amer. zool.*) alce.

moot [mu:t], *ag.* discutibile; dubbio, non sicuro ‖ *s.* **1**. (*st.*) assemblea popolare **2**. processo fittizio a scopo di esercitazione (tenuto dagli studenti in legge) ☆ — *case*, (*dir.*) questione controversa; — *-hall*, camera di consiglio; — *-hill*, collina dove si tenevano le assemblee; — *point*, punto controverso.

to **moot**, *v.t.i.* disputare, sollevare (discussioni).

mop[1] [mɔp], *s.* **1**. scopa di stracci, di filacce **2**. (*mar.*) radazza **3**. zazzera; capigliatura arruffata: — *of hair*, ciuffo arruffato di capelli ☆ — *-headed*, che ha i capelli arruffati ‖ *dish* —, strofinaccio per lavare i piatti; *window* —, straccio per pulire i vetri.

to **mop**[1], *pass.p.p.* **mopped** [mɔpt], *v.t.* **1**. pulire, asciugare (un pavimento) ‖ *to* — *the floor with*, (*sl. mil.*) avere una superiorità schiacciante su **2**. asciugare, detergere: *to* — *one's brow*, asciugarsi il sudore della fronte **3**. *to* — *up*, asciugare, prosciugare; (*sl.*) assorbire (guadagni, ecc.); (*mil.*) rastrellare: *to* — *up the trenches*, rastrellare le trincee.

mop[2], *s.* smorfia ‖ *mops and mows*, boccacce.

to **mop**[2], *v.i.* fare smorfie, boccacce.

mope [moup], *s.* **1**. persona melanconica **2**. musone **3**. *pl.* depressione di spirito: *to suffer from* (*a fit of*) *the mopes*, veder tutto nero.

to **mope**, *v.t.i.* avvilire, avvilirsi; rattristare, rattristarsi.

moped [moupt], *s.* (*neol.*) micromotore.

mopish ['moupiʃ], *ag.* **1**. avvilito, triste **2**. apatico.

mopishly ['moupiʃli], *av.* **1**. mestamente, tristemente **2**. con aria tediata.

mopishness ['moupiʃnis], *s.* **1**. tristezza; avvilimento **2**. tedio, insoddisfazione **3**. musoneria.

moppet ['mɔpit], *s.* **1**. (*arc.*) bambola di stoffa **2**. (*scherz.*) bambola, bambolina.

mopus ['moupəs], *s.* (*sl.*) denaro; monetina.

moquette [mɔ'ket], *s.* « moquette » (tappeto a metratura).

mora ['mɔːrə], *s.* (*giuoco*) morra.

moraine [mɔ'rein], *s.* (*geol.*) morena.

morainic [mɔ'reinik], *ag.* (*geol.*) morenico.

moral ['mɔrəl], *ag.* **1**. morale: — *certainty*, certezza morale; — *courage*, coraggio morale; — *law*, legge morale; — *sense*, senso morale; — *victory*, vittoria morale **2**. serio; onesto; virtuoso: *she leads a very* — *life*, conduce una vita onesta ‖ *s.* **1**. morale: *to draw* (*o to point*) *the* — *of a tale*, trarre la morale da una favola **2**. *pl.* moralità, costumi: *a person of good morals*, una persona di buoni costumi; *she has no morals*, non ha principi morali ☆ — *philosophy*, etica.

morale [mɔ'raːl] *s.* il morale, lo stato d'animo: *the* — *of the troops was very high*, il morale delle truppe era altissimo.

moralism ['mɔrəlizəm], *s.* moralismo.

moralist ['mɔrəlist], *s.* **1**. moralista **2**. che insegna, pratica la morale.

moralistic [,mɔrə'listik], *ag.* moralistico.

morality [mɔ'ræliti], *s.* **1**. morale, moralità **2**. *pl.* principii di etica **3**. sistema di morale: *commercial* —, moralità commerciale **4**. (*st. teat.*) moralità, rappresentazione drammatica allegorica.

moralization [,mɔrəlai'zeiʃən], *s.* moralizzazione.

to **moralize** ['mɔrəlaiz], *v.t.i.* **1**. moralizzare; render morale **2**. trarre la morale da.

moralizer ['mɔrəlaizə*], *s.c.* moralizzatore, moralizzatrice.

morally ['mɔrəli], *av.* moralmente.

morass [mə'ræs], *s.* palude; acquitrino; pantano.

morassic [mə'ræsik], **morassy** [mə'ræsi], *ag.* paludoso; acquitrinoso.

morat ['mɔːrət], *s.* bevanda di miele e succo di more.

moratorium [,mɔrə'tɔːriəm], *pl.* **moratoria** [,mɔrə'tɔːriə], **moratoriums** [,mɔrə'tɔːriəmz], *s.* (*dir.*) moratoria.

moratory ['mɔrətəri], *ag.* (*dir.*) moratorio.

Moravia [mə'reivjə], *no.pr.* (*geog.*) Moravia.

Moravian [mə'reivjən], *ag.* (*geog. st. relig.*) moravo ‖ *s.c.* moravo, morava.

morbid ['mɔːbid], *ag.* **1**. *fig.* morboso: — *fear*, fobia; — *thoughts*, pensieri morbosi **2**. (*patol.*) morboso, malato, malsano; patologico ☆ — *anatomy*, anatomia patologica.

morbidity [mɔː'biditi], *s.* **1**. morbosità **2**. stato patologico **3**. percentuale di malati.

morbidly ['mɔːbidli], *av.* morbosamente.

morbidness ['mɔːbidnis], *V.* **morbidity 1**. **2**.

morbiferous [mɔː'bifərəs], *ag.* morbifero.

morbilli [mɔː'bilai], *s.pl.* (*patol.*) morbillo.

morbilliform [mɔː'bilifɔːm], *ag.* (*patol.*) morbilloso; di morbillo.

morbillous [mɔː'biləs], *ag.* (*patol.*) morbilloso; di morbillo.

mordacious [mɔː'deiʃəs], *ag.* mordace, caustico.

mordacity [mɔː'dæsiti], **mordancy** ['mɔːdənsi], *s.* mordacità, causticità.

mordant ['mɔːdənt], *ag.* **1**. pungente, sarcastico: *a* — *remark*, un'osservazione sarcastica **2**. acuto: *a* — *pain*, un dolore acuto **3**. (*chim.*) corrosivo ‖ *s.* (*chim.*) mordente.

mordanting ['mɔːdəntiŋ], *s.* mordenzatura.

mordantly ['mɔːdəntli], *av.* mordacemente; sarcasticamente.

Mordecai [,mɔːdi'keiai], *no.pr.m.* (*Bibbia*) Mardocheo.

mordent ['mɔːdənt], *s.* (*mus.*) mordente.

more [mɔː*], *ag.* (*comp.* di *much, many*) più, di più, una maggior quantità di; un maggior numero di: — *policemen are required*, ci vuole un maggior numero di poliziotti; *he has* — *money than we thought*, ha più denaro di quanto credessimo; *she has* — *friends than I have*, ella ha più amici di me; *there is nothing* — *to be said*, non c'è più nulla da dire; *will you have some* — *sugar?*, volete ancora un po' di zucchero? ‖ *what* — *do you want?*, che vuoi di più?.

more, *pron.indef.s.* **una maggior quantità, un numero maggiore**: — *than one person has come*, è venuta più di una persona; *he cannot give* —, non può darne di più; *I hope to hear* — *of them*, spero di avere altre loro notizie; *I hope to learn* — *about you*, spero di apprendere di più sul tuo conto; *that's* — *than enough*, è più che abbastanza ‖ *he is forty and* —, ha quarant'anni e anche di più ‖ *the* — *they have the* — *they want*, *prov.* l'appetito vien mangiando.

more, *av.* **1**. **maggiormente, più, di più**: *he should walk* — *and eat less*, dovrebbe camminare di più e mangiare meno; *to attend* — *to details*, fare più attenzione ai dettagli ‖ — *and* —, sempre più: *he studies* — *and* —, egli studia sempre di più ‖ — *or less*, più o meno ‖ *neither* — *nor less than*, nè più nè meno che, di: *I want you to do neither* — *nor less than I told you to*, desidero che tu faccia nè più nè meno di quanto ti ho detto ‖ *never* —, mai più ‖ *no* —, non più: *the days that are no* —, i giorni del passato ‖ *so much the* — *that*, tanto più che ‖ *the* — *one studies the* — *one learns*, più si studia più si impara **2**. (*a formare il comp. di ag. e av.*): — *easily*, più facilmente; *please speak* — *clearly*, per favore parla più chiaramente; *she is* — *beautiful than her sister*, è più bella di sua sorella ‖ *the exercise you are translating is* — *long than hard*, l'esercizio che traduci è più lungo che difficile **3**. **ancora, di più**: *once* —, ancora una volta.

moreen [mɔː'riːn], *s.* stoffa per tende; damasco di lana, di cotone; di lana.

morel[1] [mɔ'rel], *s.* (*bot.*) erba morella; dulcamara; belladonna.

morel[2], *s.* (*bot.*) marasca.

morel[3], *s.* (*bot.*) morchella.

morello [mə'relou], *s.* (*bot.*) marasca.
moreover [mɔ:'rouvə*], *av.* **1.** oltre a ciò, inoltre **2.** d'altronde, d'altra parte.
Moresque [mɔ'resk], *ag.* moresco.
morganatic [,mɔ:gə'nætik], *ag.* morganatico.
morganatically [,mɔ:gə'nætikəli], *av.* morganaticamente.
morgue¹ [mɔ:g], *s.* **1.** (*spec. amer.*) « morgue », obitorio **2.** (*sl. giornalistico amer.*) archivio di materiale (di consultazione): — *of 30,000 photographs*, un archivio di 30.000 fotografie.
morgue², *s.* (*letter.*) comportamento altezzoso.
moribund ['mɔribʌnd], *ag.s.* morente, moribondo.
morion¹ ['mɔriən], *s.* morione (antico elmo).
morion², *s.* (*min.*) morione, quarzo nero.
Morisco [mə'riskou], *ag.* moresco || *s.* **1.** (*st.*) moro (di Spagna) **2.** meticcio ispano-messicano || **morisco,** *s.* danza moresca.
Mormon ['mɔ:mən], *s.c.* (*relig.*) mormone.
Mormonism ['mɔ:mənizəm], *s.* (*relig.*) mormonismo.
morn [mɔ:n], *s.* (*poet.*) mattino.
morning ['mɔ:niŋ], *s.* mattino, mattinata; (*poet.*) alba: *good* —, buon giorno; *I have a* — *off*, ho una mattinata libera; *I'll come in the* —, verrò di mattina ☆ — *call*, visita di primo pomeriggio; — *coat*, abito da cerimonia; — *concert*, concerto pomeridiano; — -*dress*, abito da mattino; — -*glory*, (*bot.*) convolvolo, vilucchio; — *performance*, (*teat.*) « matinée », mattinata; — -*prayer*, preghiera mattutina; — -*star*, la stella del mattino, il pianeta Venere; — -*watch*, (*mar.*) turno di guardia del mattino.
Moroccan [mə'rɔkən], *ag.* marocchino || *s.c.* marocchino, marocchina.
Morocco [mə'rɔkou], *no.pr.* (*geog.*) Marocco || **morocco,** *s.* marocchino (pelle).
moron ['mɔ:rɔn], *s.* **1.** deficiente, idiota **2.** (*fam.*) degenerato.
morose [mə'rous], *ag.* tetro, cupo; imbronciato, scontento; non socievole: *he bore a* — *look on his face*, aveva un'espressione scontenta.
morosely [mə'rousli], *av.* tetramente, cupamente; con aria scontenta.
moroseness [mə'rousnis], **morosity** [mə'rɔsiti], *s.* tetraggine, malinconia; musoneria.
morpheme ['mɔ:fi:m], *s.* (*linguistica*) morfema.
Morpheus ['mɔ:fju:s], *no.pr.m.* (*mit.*) Morfeo || *to be in the arms of* —, *fig.* essere in braccio a Morfeo.
morphia ['mɔ:fjə], **morphine** ['mɔ:fi:n], *s.* (*chim.*) morfina.
morphinism ['mɔ:finizəm], *s.* (*patol.*) morfinismo.
morphinomania [,mɔ:finou'meinjə], *s.* (*patol.*) morfinomania.
morphinomaniac [,mɔ:finou'meinjæk], *ag. s.* (*patol.*) morfinomane.
morphologic(al) [,mɔ:fə'lɔdʒik(əl)], *ag.* morfologico.
morphologically [,mɔ:fə'lɔdʒikəli], *av.* morfologicamente.
morphology [mɔ:'fɔlədʒi], *s.* morfologia.
morra ['mɔrə], *s.* (*giuoco*) morra.
Morris¹ ['mɔris], *no.pr.m.* Maurizio.
morris², *ag.s.* (*nei composti*): — -*dance*, danza campestre inglese; — -*pike*, picca moresca.
to morris², *v.i.* danzare.
morrow ['mɔrou], *s.* (*poet.*) domani, l'indomani: *on the* — *of*, il giorno dopo di.
morse¹ [mɔ:s], *s.* (*zool.*) tricheco, cavallo marino.
morse², *s.* gibula, fermaglio del piviale.
Morse³, (*nei composti*): — *alphabet* (o — *code*), (*tel.*) alfabeto Morse; — *signals*, (*tel.*) segnali Morse; — *taper*, (*mec.*) conicità Morse; — *telegraph*, telegrafo Morse.
morsel ['mɔ:səl], *s.* pezzo, pezzetto; boccone; tozzo: *a dainty* —, un bocconcino prelibato.
mort¹ [mɔ:t], *s.* **1.** (*caccia*) ♦hallalì♦ **2.** carogna, animale morto; (*scherz.*) cadavere (di persona) ☆ — -*bell*, campana a morto; — *cloth*, drappo funebre.

mort², *s.* (*dial.*) un mucchio, un gran numero: *I had a* — *of things to do*, avevo un sacco di cose da fare.
mortal ['mɔ:tl], *ag.* **1.** mortale, soggetto alla morte: *all men are* —, tutti gli uomini sono mortali **2.** mortale, letale; funesto: *a* — *wound*, una ferita mortale **3.** implacabile: — *enemies*, nemici acerrimi **4.** (*sl.*) interminabile, uggioso: *the rain fell for seven* — *days*, la pioggia cadde per sette interminabili giorni **5.** (*sl.*) molto; grande: *she was in a* — *hurry*, aveva moltissima fretta || *s.* mortale; (*scher.*) persona.
mortality [mɔ:'tæliti], *s.* mortalità || *the* —, (*arc.*) i mortali.
mortally ['mɔ:təli], *av.* **1.** mortalmente, a morte **2.** molto: *I felt* — *tired*, ero stanco morto.
mortar¹ ['mɔ:tə*], *s.* mortaio (anche *artigl.*).
mortar², *s.* calcina, malta ☆ — -*board*, giornello (di muratore); (*fig. fam.*) tocco accademico degli universitari inglesi e americani || *lime* —, malta di calce.
to mortar², *v.t.* mescolare e fissare con malta.
mortgage ['mɔ:gidʒ], *s.* ipoteca: *the* — *was paid off*, l'ipoteca fu estinta; *covered with* —, ipotecato; *encumbered with heavy mortgages*, gravato da forti ipoteche: *to borrow on* —, prendere a prestito su garanzia ipotecaria; *to redeem from* —, liberare da ipoteca ☆ — *bond*, obbligazione ipotecaria; — *credit, debt*, credito, debito ipotecario; — *deed*, contratto d'ipoteca.
to mortgage, *v.t.* ipotecare || *he mortgaged his word*, (*fam.*) egli impegnò la sua parola.
mortgagee [,mɔ:gə'dʒi:], *s.* creditore ipotecario.
mortgager [,mɔ:gidʒə*], **mortgagor** [,mɔ:gə'dʒɔ:*], *s.* debitore ipotecario.
mortice ['mɔ:tis], *s.* (*carpenteria*) mortasa.
mortician [mɔ:'tiʃən], *s.* (*amer.*) imprenditore di pompe funebri; necroforo.
mortification [,mɔ:tifi'keiʃən], *s.* **1.** mortificazione (anche *fig.*) **2.** (*patol.*) cancrena, necrosi.
mortified ['mɔ:tifaid], *ag.* **1.** mortificato, umiliato **2.** (*patol.*) incancrenito.
mortifier ['mɔ:tifaiə*], *s.* mortificatore.
to mortify ['mɔ:tifai], *v.t.i.* **1.** mortificare, mortificarsi; dominare: *to* — *the flesh*, mortificare la carne **2.** umiliare, mortificare: *they wanted to* — *her*, volevano umiliarla **3.** (*patol.*) incancrenire, incancrenirsi.
mortifying ['mɔ:tifaiiŋ], *ag.* mortificante, umiliante || *s.* mortificazione (di passioni, ecc.).
mortifyingly ['mɔ:tifaiiŋli], *av.* in modo mortificante.
mortise ['mɔ:tis], *s.* (*carpenteria*) mortasa.
to mortise, *v.t.* (*carpenteria*) congiungere a mortasa; incastrare.
mortmain ['mɔ:tmein], *s.* (*dir.*) manomorta: *goods in* —, beni di manomorta.
mortuary ['mɔ:tjuəri], *ag.* mortuario || *s.* **1.** camera mortuaria **2.** (*dir. eccl.*) diritto di decima sui patrimoni dei defunti.
mosaic¹ [mə'zeiik], *ag.* musivo, di, in mosaico || *s.* **1.** mosaico **2.** (*foto. tv.*) mosaico aerofotografico, mosaico planimetrico, rilevamento fotopanoramico ☆ — *gold*, (*chim.*) solfuro di stagno, oro musivo; — *plate*, (*tv.*) mosaico fotoelettrico.
to mosaic¹, *v.t.* adornare di mosaici; comporre a mosaico.
Mosaic², *ag.* (*Bibbia*) mosaico: — *Law*, legge mosaica.
mosaicist [mə'zeiisist], *s.* mosaicista.
moschatel [,mɔskə'tel], *s.* (*bot.*) erba fumaria.
Moscow ['mɔskou], *no.pr.* (*geog.*) Mosca.
moselle [mə'zel], *s.* vino bianco della Mosella.
Moses ['mouziz], *no.pr.m.* (*Bibbia*) Mosè || *s.* usuraio.
to mosey ['mouzi], *v.i.* (*sl. amer.*) andarsene || *to* — *along*, andarsene lemme lemme.
Moslem ['mɔzlem], *ag.* musulmano || *s.c.* musulmano, musulmana.
mosque [mɔsk], *s.* moschea.
mosquito [məs'ki:tou], *pl.* **mosquito(e)s** [məs'ki:touz], zanzara ☆ — -*bite*, puntura di zanzara; — -*boat,*

(*mar.*) motosilurante, mas; — *-curtain* (o — *-net*), zanzariera; — *-netting*, garza per zanzariera.

moss [mɔs], *s.* **1.** terreno acquitrinoso **2.** torbiera **3.** muschio ☆ — *back*, (*amer. st.*) imboscato; (*sl. amer.*) conservatore a oltranza; persona di idee antiquate; — *-clad* (o — *-grown*), coperto di muschio; — *-land*, torbiera; — *-rose*, (*bot.*) rosa muschiata; — *-stitch*, punto riso (nel lavoro a maglia).

to **moss**, *v.t.* ricoprire di muschio.

mossy ['mɔsi], *ag.* di muschio; muscoso, coperto di muschio.

most [moust], *ag.* (*superl.* di *much*, *many*) il più, **la maggior parte**, il **maggior numero di**, il **massimo**, il **più grande**: — *men are liars*, la maggior parte degli uomini sono bugiardi; *who won the — times?*, chi ha vinto il maggior numero di volte? ‖ *for the — part*, per la maggior parte; il più sovente, quasi sempre; *in — cases*, nella maggior parte dei casi.

most, *pron.indef.s.* **Il massimo; la maggior quantità**, il **maggior numero**: — *of us*, la maggior parte di noi; — *of it is a lie*, la maggior parte di ciò è falso; *she spends — of her time reading*, dedica alla lettura la maggior parte del suo tempo; *they did the — they could*, fecero il massimo che poterono; *they were kinder than —*, furono più gentili degli altri ‖ *at (the) —*, al più, tutt'al più, al massimo ‖ *to make the — of sthg.*, trarre il massimo, trarre il meglio da ql.co.: *he doesn't know how to make the — of himself*, non sa farsi valere; *he makes the — of his time*, sa sfruttare al massimo il suo tempo.

most, *av.* **1.** (*a formare il* **superl.** *di ag. e av.*): *the — beautiful woman I know*, la più bella donna che io conosca; *the — boring film of the season*, il film più noioso della stagione **2. molto, estremamente:** — *likely*, molto probabilmente; *that's — strange*, è molto strano **3. maggiormente, al massimo:** *that's what I like —*, questo è ciò che preferisco; *those who run (the) — will get the prize*, chi correrà di più avrà il premio **4.** (*amer. dial.*) *V.* **almost.**

mostly ['moustli], *av.* per lo più, soprattutto, generalmente: *I am — out in the morning*, sono quasi sempre fuori al mattino.

mot [mou], *s.* parola arguta; frizzo; motto di spirito.

mote[1] [mout], *s.* granellino di polvere; pagliuzza ‖ *to behold the — in one's brother's eye*, vedere la festuca nell'occhio altrui.

mote[2], (*arc. per may, must*): *so — it be*, così possa essere, così sia, amen.

motel ['moutel], *s.* (*neol.*) « motel », albergo per automobilisti.

motet [mou'tet], *s.* (*mus.*) mottetto.

moth [mɔθ], *s.* (*entom.*) **1.** falena ‖ *she is rather like a — round a candle flame*, è come una farfalla vicino al fuoco; è frivola **2.** tignuola, tarma ☆ — *-balls*, palline antitarma; — *-eaten*, roso, tarlato; *fig.* antiquato; — *-hunter*, (*ornit.*) caprimulgo.

mother[1] ['mʌðə*], *s.* **1.** madre, mamma: *she has become a —*, ha avuto un figlio ‖ *Mother's Day*, la giornata, la festa della mamma **2.** *Mother*, (*eccl.*) superiora: *the Mother Superior*, la madre superiora; *Reverend Mother*, reverenda madre **3.** (*fam.*) appellativo premesso al cognome di donna anziana di classe inferiore: *Mother Jones*, la vecchia Jones **4.** *fig.* origine: *pride is the — of ignorance*, la superbia è la madre dell'ignoranza ☆ *Mother Carey's chicken*, (*ornit.*) procellaria; — *-cell*, (*biol.*) cellula madre; *Mother-Church*, la Chiesa Madre; — *-country*, madrepatria; — *-earth*, madreterra; *to kiss — earth*, (*scherz.*) cadere; — *-in-law*, suocera; — *-of-pearl*, madreperla; — *-right*, successione in linea femminile; matriarcato; — *-tongue*, madre lingua; — *-wit*, buon senso.

to **mother**[1], *v.t.* **1.** dar vita a **2.** proteggere, curare come una madre; dichiararsi la madre di: *to — a child (up) on s.o.*, attribuire a qlcu. la maternità di un bambino.

mother[2], *s.* madre dell'aceto.

to **mother**[2], *v.i.* fermentare (di aceto).

mothercraft ['mʌðəkrɑ:ft], *s.* puericultura.

motherhood ['mʌðəhud], *s.* maternità.

mothering ['mʌðəriŋ], *s.* cure materne ‖ *Mothering Sunday*, quarta domenica di Quaresima; (*amer.*) seconda domenica di maggio (in cui i figli fanno per consuetudine regali alla madre).

motherless ['mʌðəlis], *ag.* orfano di madre.

motherliness ['mʌðəlinis], *s.* tenerezza materna; atteggiamento materno.

motherly ['mʌðəli], *ag.* materno; degno di una madre: *she treated him in a — way*, ella lo trattava maternamente.

motherly, *av.* maternamente.

mothery ['mʌðəri], *ag.* inacidito, fiorito (di vino, ecc.).

mothproof ['mɔθ,pru:f], *ag.* inattaccabile dalle tarme ☆ — *-processed*, sottoposto a trattamento antitarma (di tessuto).

mothy ['mɔθi], *ag.* tarmato.

motif [mou'tif], *s.* **1.** particolare dominante, idea predominante (di un'opera artistica): *horses are that painter's favourite —*, i cavalli sono il tema preferito di quel pittore **2.** (*mus.*) motivo **3.** guarnizione, ricamo, applicazione: *the blouse had a — in gold braid*, la camicetta aveva una guarnizione in spighetta dorata.

motile ['moutil], *s.* (*bot. zool.*) mobile, capace di movimento.

motion ['mouʃən], *s.* **1.** moto, movimento: *they must study the laws of —*, devono studiare le leggi del moto; *to put (o to set) sthg. in —*, mettere in moto, avviare ql.co. **2.** gesto, atto; andatura: *it was a pleasure to watch her graceful motions*, era un piacere osservare con che grazia ella si muoveva **3.** mozione, proposta, petizione: *nobody supported the — and it was not carried*, nessuno appoggiò la proposta ed essa non fu approvata ‖ — *of no-confidence*, mozione di sfiducia **4.** (*fisiol.*) scarica (di feci) ☆ — *-picture*, pellicola cinematografica; — *-picture theatre*, sala cinematografica ‖ *perpetual —*, (*fis.*) moto perpetuo.

to **motion**, *v.t.i.* far segno (a); far cenno (a); invitare (coi gesti): *he motioned me to a chair*, mi invitò a sedere; *he motioned them away*, fece loro cenno di allontanarsi.

motionless ['mouʃənlis], *ag.* senza moto, immobile.

to **motivate** ['moutiveit], *v.t.* **1.** motivare, dare un motivo a **2.** causare **3.** stimolare, spronare.

motivation [,mouti'veiʃən], *s.* **1.** motivazione **2.** motivo, movente **3.** stimolo.

motive ['moutiv], *ag.* motore ☆ — *power*, forza motrice.

motive, *s.* motivo, movente; causa; ragione: *interest is a powerful —*, l'interesse è un forte movente; *to have a — in doing sthg.*, avere un motivo per fare ql.co.

to **motive**, *V.* to **motivate**.

motiveless ['moutivlis], *ag.* senza motivo.

motivelessly ['moutivlisli], *av.* senza motivo.

motivity [mou'tiviti], *s.* (*mec.*) energia cinetica.

motley ['mɔtli], *ag.* **1.** screziato; variegato; variopinto **2.** eterogeneo: *a — crowd*, una folla eterogenea ‖ *s.* **1.** miscuglio eterogeneo **2.** (*st.*) abito variopinto (dei buffoni di corte): *to wear the —*, *fig.* fare il buffone.

motor ['moutə*], *ag.* motore, motorio ‖ *s.* motore (apparecchio generatore di forza motrice) ☆ — *-bicycle* (o — *bike*), motocicletta; — *-boat*, motobarca; — *-bus*, autobus; — *-car*, automobile; — *-coach*, torpedone; — *-cycle*, motocicletta; — *-cyclist*, motociclista; — *-driven*, azionato a motore; — *generator*, (*elett.*) dinamo generatrice; — *-lorry*, autocarro; — *nerves*, (*anat.*) nervi motori; — *-road* (o — *-way*), autostrada; — *-scooter*, motoretta; — *-ship*, motonave; — *-trawler*, motopeschereccio; — *vehicle*, automezzo ‖ *auxiliary —*, motore ausiliario; *four-stroke*, *two-stroke —*, motore a quattro, a due tempi; *variable speed —*, motore a velocità regolabile.

to **motor**, *v.t.i.* **1.** andare in automobile; guidare (un'automobile) **2.** accompagnare in automobile.

motorcade ['moutəkeid], *s.* (*amer.*) sfilata di automobili: *a ten-car —*, una sfilata di dieci automobili.

motorial [mou'tɔ:riəl], *ag.* motorio.

motoring ['moutəriŋ], *s.* automobilismo.

motorist ['moutərist], *s.* automobilista.

motorization [‚moutəri'zeiʃən], *s.* motorizzazione.

to **motorize** ['moutəraiz], *v.t.* motorizzare.

motory ['moutəri], *ag.* (anat.) motore; motorio.

mottle ['motl], *s.* screziatura, venatura, chiazza ☆ — *faced*, dal volto chiazzato.

to **mottle**, *v.t.* screziare, venare, chiazzare (di colori diversi).

mottled ['motld], *ag.* screziato, venato, chiazzato ☆ — *iron*, (metal.) ghisa trotata.

motto ['mɔtou], *pl.* **mottoes** ['mɔtouz], *s.* **1.** motto; epigramma **2.** aforismo, detto ‖ *cracker* —, frase sentimentale (come se ne trovano nell'involucro dei cioccolatini) **3.** epigrafe (in un libro) **4.** (mus.) motivo.

moufflon ['mu:flon], *s.* (zool.) muflone.

moujik ['mu:ʒik], *s.* « mugik », contadino russo.

mould[1] [mould], *s.* terriccio ☆ — *-board*, vomere d'aratro.

to **mould**[1], *v.t.* (rar.) coprire di terriccio.

mould[2], *s.* **1.** forma; stampo; modello (anche fig.): *cast in the same* —, di carattere identico; *a man of heroic* —, un uomo di tempra eroica; *he is of a different* — *from his brother*, è di tutt'altro stampo che suo fratello **2.** (cuc.) stampo; vivanda cucinata nello stampo (budini, ecc.) **3.** (metal.) forma **4.** (mar. aut.) sagoma **5.** (mec.) matrice **6.** (edil.) cassaforma (nella tecnica del cemento armato) **7.** (arch.) modanatura **8.** (geol.) impronta (di fossile) ☆ *permanent* —, (metal.) forma permanente; *plaster* —, (metal.) forma in gesso; *semipermanent* —, (metal.) forma semipermanente.

to **mould**[2], *v.t.* **1.** foggiare; modellare, plasmare (anche fig.): *he moulded the statue out of* (o *in*) *clay*, modellò la statua in argilla; *to* — *s.o.'s character*, plasmare il carattere di qlcu.; *to* — *upon a pattern*, foggiare secondo un modello **2.** (metal.) formare, costruire la forma di **3.** fare le forme del (pane).

mould[3], *s.* muffa ☆ *blue* —, muffa di formaggi (del tipo gorgonzola); *penicillin* —, muffa della penicillina.

to **mould**[3], *v.t.i.* (amer.) fare ammuffire; ammuffire, ammuffirsi (anche fig.).

mouldable ['mouldəbl], *ag.* modellabile; plasmabile; fondibile.

to **moulder** ['mouldə*], *v.t.i.* ridurre in polvere, sgretolarsi, cadere in rovina: *a mouldering building*, un edificio cadente; *to* — *in idleness*, fig. abbrutirsi, inebetirsi nell'ozio.

mouldiness ['mouldinis], *s.* l'essere ammuffito (anche fig.): *there is a certain* — *in his last books*, i suoi ultimi libri sanno un po' di stantio.

moulding ['mouldiŋ], *s.* **1.** modellatura; azione del modellare **2.** (metal.) getto; fusione **3.** (arch.) modanatura **4.** spec.‖ *pl.* (arch.) cornice; cornicione ☆ — *box*, (metal.) staffa; — *machine*, (mec.) macchina a formare; — *sand*, (metal.) sabbia per fonderia ‖ *compression* —, stampaggio a pressione (di materie plastiche): *dry* —, (metal.) formatura a secco; *greensand* —, (metal.) formatura in verde; *injection* —, stampaggio ad iniezione (di materie plastiche).

mouldy ['mouldi], *ag.* ammuffito (anche fig.): *I feel* —, mi sento a terra: *to go* —, ammuffire; *to smell* —, odorare di muffa, di stantio.

moult [moult], *s.* muda (di uccelli).

to **moult**, *v.t.i.* mudare (di uccelli); fig. rinnovarsi; mutar costume.

moulting ['moultiŋ], *s.* muda (di uccelli).

mound[1] [maund], *s.* tumulo, mucchio; monticello, collinetta; (rar.) terrapieno, argine.

to **mound**[1], *v.t.i.* circondare con una siepe; fortificare con argine; formare tumoli.

mound[2], *s.* (arald.) globo.

mount[1] [maunt], *s.* **1.** (poet. o usato davanti ai no. pr. sing.) monte, montagna: *Mt. Blanc*, il Monte Bian-

co; *the Sermon on the Mount*, il Sermone della Montagna **2.** (mil.) terrapieno **3.** (anat.) monte.

to **mount**[1], *v.t.i.* **1.** (anche fig.) salire; ascendere; affluire: *he is bound to* — *the throne*, è destinato a salire al trono; *his blood mounted*, arrossì, gli affluì il sangue al viso; *to* — *a hill*, salire su una collina; *to* — *a ladder*, salire su una scala ‖ *to* — (*on, upon*) *a chair*, montare in cattedra, fig. fare il saccente ‖ *to* — *guard over sthg.*, (mil.) fare la guardia a ql.co. **2.** ammontare: *the bill mounts up to fifty pounds*, il conto ammonta a cinquanta sterline **3.** montare, fare montare a cavallo **4.** incastonare; incorniciare: *I had my sapphire mounted*, ho fatto montare il mio zaffiro **5.** mettere in scena: *who mounted the play?*, chi ha organizzato la recita? **6.** (artigl.) mettere in posizione: *they mounted the gun*, misero il cannone in posizione di tiro.

mount[2], *s.* **1.** cavalcatura: *my* — *was a donkey*, la mia cavalcatura era un asino **2.** (ippica) monta (del fantino) **3.** intelaiatura; supporto **4.** (mec.) incastellatura di sostegno **5.** (artigl.) affusto (di cannone) **6.** (ott.) montatura (di lenti); vetrini ed accessori per microscopia **7.** montatura; incorniciatura (di ritratti, ecc.) ☆ *engine* —, (aer.) castello motore.

mountain ['mauntin], *s.* **1.** montagna, monte ‖ *the Rocky Mountains*, le Montagne Rocciose **2.** fig. (fam.) monte, mucchio: *a* — *of difficulties*, un monte di difficoltà ‖ *he makes a* — *of every mole-hill*, ingigantisce ogni cosa, affoga in un bicchier d'acqua **3.** *the Mountain*, (st. francese) la Montagna ☆ — *-ash*, (bot.) sorbo selvatico; — *-blue*, (min.) malachite turchina; — *-cat*, gatto selvatico; — *-chain* (o — *range*), catena di montagne; — *-high*, altissimo; — *-sickness*, mal di montagna; — *system*, sistema montuoso.

mountained ['mauntind], *ag.* montagnoso.

mountaineer [‚maunti'niə*], *s.* **1.** montanaro **2.** alpinista, scalatore.

to **mountaineer**, *v.i.* fare dell'alpinismo.

mountaineering [‚maunti'niəriŋ], *s.* alpinismo.

mountainous ['mauntinəs], *ag.* **1.** montuoso **2.** fig. enorme.

mountainousness ['mauntinəsnis], *s.* **1.** montuosità **2.** fig. (rar.) enormità.

mountebank ['mauntibæŋk], *s.* ciarlatano; saltimbanco.

mountebankery ['maunti‚bæŋkəri], **mountebankism** ['maunti‚bæŋkizəm], *s.* ‚ciarlataneria.

mounted ['mauntid], *ag.* **1.** a cavallo **2.** montato: *a* — *telescope*, un telescopio montato ☆ — *police*, *troops*, polizia, truppe, a cavallo.

mounter ['mauntə*], *s.* **1.** montatore **2.** chi mette in opera.

mountie ['maunti], *s.* (amer.) poliziotto canadese a cavallo.

mounting ['mauntiŋ], *s.* **1.** montatura (di gemma, quadro, apparecchio) **2.** (tec.) supporto; montaggio **3.** (teat.) messa in scena; allestimento **4.** ascensione, salita ☆ — *-block*, (ippica) montatoio.

to **mourn** [mɔ:n], *v.t.i.* **1.** piangere; deplorare, lamentare:‖ *she mourns over her father's death*, ella piange la morte di suo padre **2.** vestire a lutto; portare il lutto: *whom do they* — *for?*, per chi portano il lutto? **3.** tubare (di colombi).

mourner ['mɔ:nə*], *s.c.* chi è in lutto; chi accompagna un funerale ‖ *s.* (arc.) prefica.

mournful ['mɔ:nful], *ag.* lugubre, triste, funereo: — *face*, volto triste; (fam.) faccia da funerale.

mournfully ['mɔ:nfuli], *av.* lugubremente, tristemente.

mournfulness ['mɔ:nfulnis], *s.* tristezza, malinconia: *the* — *of that desolate plain*, l'aspetto malinconico di quella pianura desolata.

mourning ['mɔ:niŋ], *s.* **1.** dolore, cordoglio, afflizione **2.** lutto: *to go into* —, mettere, smettere il lutto; *to wear* — *for s.o.*, portare il lutto per qlcu. ‖ *eye in* —, (scherz.) occhio pesto; *nails in* —

(scherz.) unghie a lutto ☆ — -*band*, fascia da lutto; — -*paper*, carta listata a lutto ‖ *deep-* —, lutto stretto; *half-* —, mezzo lutto.

mouse [maus], *pl.* **mice** [mais], *s.* **1.** sorcio, topo: *young* —, topolino ‖ *he is as poor as a church* —, è povero in canna **2.** *fig.* persona timida, ritrosa; *(fam. amer.)* topino, topolino, tesoro **3.** contrappeso (di finestre a ghigliottina) **4.** *(mar.)* ringrosso, legatura al gancio **5.** *(fam.)* occhio livido ☆ — -*colour*, color grigio topo; — -*ear*, *(bot.)* miosiotide; — -*hole*, piccola tana, piccolo buco; — -*trap*, trappola per topi; *fig.* trabocchetto; *(scherz.)* casetta ‖ *field-* —, topo di campagna; *house-* —, topolino, topo comune.

to mouse [mauz], *v.i.* cacciare, prendere sorci: *my cat mouses well*, il mio gatto è abile nel dar la caccia ai topi.

mouser ['mauzə*], *s.* **1.** cacciatore di sorci: *that cat is a good* —, quel gatto è un abile cacciatore di topi **2.** *(sl.)* investigatore.

mousseline ['mu:sli:n], *s.* mussola.

moustache [məs'ta:ʃ], *s.* baffi.

moustached [məs'ta:ʃt], *ag.* baffuto.

mousy ['mausi], *ag.* **1.** grigio topo **2.** infestato dai topi **3.** maleodorante (per la presenza di topi) **4.** quieto, timido, silenzioso (di persona).

mouth [mauθ], *s.* **1.** bocca: *with a pipe in his* —, con la pipa in bocca; *the news spread from* — *to* —, la notizia correva di bocca in bocca; *this sounds strange in your* —, questo è strano detto da te ‖ *down in* (o *at*) *the* —, depresso, abbattuto ‖ *useless* —, mangiapane a ufo ‖ *he stopped his* —, lo fece tacere; *stop your* —*!*, chiudi il becco!‖ *I made him laugh on the wrong side of his* —, gli ho fatto passare la voglia di ridere ‖ *to give* — to, esprimere ‖ *to live from hand to* —, vivere alla giornata ‖ *to make s.o.'s* — *water*, far venire l'acquolina in bocca a qlcu. ‖ *to put words into s.o.'s* —, suggerire a qlcu. ciò che deve dire ‖ *to take the words out of s.o.'s* —, rubare le parole di bocca a qlcù. ‖ *don't look a gift horse in the* —, *prov.* a caval donato non si guarda in bocca **2.** bocca, fauci, gola (di animale) ‖ *to have sthg.* (*straight*) *from the horse's* —, *(fam.)* avere informazioni dirette, da fonti sicure **3.** orifizio; apertura; ingresso, entrata; bocca, foce: *the dark* — *of the tunnel*, l'imbocco buio della galleria; *the pitcher's* —, la bocca del vaso; *the river's* —, la foce del fiume **4.** smorfia, boccaccia: *to make mouths at s.o.*, fare smorfie a qlcu. ‖ *to make a poor* —, piangere miseria **5.** *(fam.)* discorso impudente; sfacciataggine, impertinenza: *none of your* —*!*, zitto, impertinente! ☆ — -*filling*, altisonante, enfatico; — -*organ*, armonica a bocca.

to mouth [mauð], *v.t.i.* **1.** parlare con tono enfatico, declamare: *you needn't* — *your words, just speak*, non occorre che declami quel che hai da dire, parla normalmente **2.** prendere con la bocca **3.** fare le boccacce **4.** abituare (un cavallo) al morso **5.** sfociare (di fiume) **6.** *(tec.)* fare l'imboccatura a un recipiente.

mouthable ['mauðəbl], *ag.* declamabile, che suona bene.

mouthed [mauðd], *ag. (nei composti)*: *clean-* —, *fig.* dal parlare onesto; *foul-* —, *fig.* dal linguaggio volgare, indecente; *full-* —, dalle labbra grosse; *fig.* dalla voce sonora; *many-* —, *(tec.)* a molte bocche; *mealy-* —, dal parlare melato; *open-* —, a bocca aperta; *single-* —, *(tec.)* a una sola bocca.

mouther ['mauðə*], *s. (scherz.)* oratore; declamatore.

mouthful ['mauθful], *s.* **1.** boccone; piccola quantità **2.** *(fam.)* parola lunga; frase molto roboante **3.** *(sl. amer.)* osservazione appropriata: *you've said a* —*!*, l'hai detta giusta!.

mouthing ['mauðiŋ], *s.* **1.** declamazione; tono declamatorio, ampolloso **2.** *pl.* smorfie.

mouthless ['mauθlis], *ag.* senza bocca, senza apertura.

mouthpiece ['mauθpi:s], *s.* **1.** bocchino (di pipa) **2.** imboccatura (di strumento a fiato) **3.** *fig.* portavoce: *he was the* — *of his party*, era il portavoce del

suo partito **4.** *(tec.)* portavoce, ricevitore (di microfono, telefono, ecc.).

mouthy ['mauði], *ag.* **1.** linguacciuto, chiacchierone **2.** enfatico, ampolloso.

movability [,mu:və'biliti], *s.* mobilità.

movable ['mu:vəbl], *ag.* movibile, mobile: — *feasts*, feste mobili.

movableness ['mu:vəblnis], *s.* mobilità.

movables ['mu:vəblz], *s.pl. (dir.)* beni mobili.

movably ['mu:vəbli], *av.* mobilmente.

move [mu:v], *s.* **1.** movimento: *to make a* — *towards sthg.*, fare un movimento verso ql.co. ‖ *to be on the* —, essere in stato di attività, in movimento ‖ *to get a* — *on*, *(sl.)* spicciarsi, affrettarsi ‖ *to make a* —, muoversi, cambiar posto; cominciare ad agire **2.** *fig.* mossa, azione, procedimento: *a bad* —, *a false* —, una manovra sbagliata, un passo falso; *what is the next* —*?*, che si fa ora?, che cosa dobbiamo fare? ‖ *he is up to a* — *or two*, ha più di una freccia al suo arco **3.** mossa (al giuoco): *to make a* —, fare una mossa **4.** trasloco.

to move, *v.t.i.* **1.** muovere, spostare, rimuovere; trasferire (funzionario, ecc.); agitare, scuotere; mettere in marcia, in movimento: *I moved my chair near the fire*, avvicinai la sedia al fuoco; *turbines are moved by water-power*, le turbine sono messe in moto dalla forza idraulica; *the wind moved the trees*, il vento scuoteva gli alberi; *to* — *sthg. from its place*, cambiare di posto a ql.co. ‖ *to* — *heaven and earth*, *fig.* muovere cielo e terra **2.** muoversi, spostarsi, camminare; circolare; avanzare: *the crowd was moving in the streets*, la folla circolava per le strade; *the earth moves round the sun*, la Terra gira intorno al Sole; *keep moving!*, circolate!; *the procession began moving slowly through the streets*, la processione cominciò lentamente a sfilare per le strade; *why do you* — *so much, can't you keep still?*, perchè ti muovi tanto, non puoi stare fermo?; *to* — *one step*, muoversi di un passo; *to* — *towards, from a place*, dirigersi verso, allontanarsi da un luogo ‖ *this article is not moving*, *(fam.)* questo prodotto non ha smercio **3.** trasferirsi, traslocare: *we* — (*house*) *at the end of March*, traslochiamo alla fine di marzo; *to* — *into town*, trasferirsi in città **4.** *(giuoco)* muovere (pedina); fare una mossa: *the bishop moves diagonally*, l'alfiere muove in diagonale; *it is for you to* —, tocca a te **5.** commuovere, muovere a; intenerire: *her sufferings moved him deeply*, le sue sofferenze lo commossero profondamente; *to* — *s.o. to anger*, provocare la collera di qlcu.; *to* — *s.o. to tears*, commuovere qlcu. fino alle lacrime **6.** incitare, spronare, spingere; far cambiare idea a: *he was moved to act*, fu spinto ad agire; *nothing will* — *him*, niente gli farà cambiare idea **7.** proporre; chiedere; far domanda, ricorso: *I* — *that*, propongo, chiedo che; *to* — *for a new trial*, far ricorso per un nuovo processo; *to* — *a resolution*, proporre una mozione **8.** far progressi, avanzare: *my work moves slowly*, il mio lavoro procede lentamente **9.** agire **10.** *(med.)* evacuare (gli intestini) **11.** *(mar.)* tonneggiare **12.** *(mec.)* aver giuoco, giocare **13.** *to* — *about*, andare e venire **14.** *to* — *along*, avanzare **15.** *to* — *away*, allontanare, allontanarsi **16.** *to* — *back*, (far) indietreggiare **17.** *to* — *down*, discendere **18.** *to* — *forward*, (far) avanzare **19.** *to* — *in*, traslocare (i mobili) in un nuovo alloggio; entrare in **20.** *to* — *off*, allontanarsi, partire; mettersi in moto **21.** *to* — *on*, (far) circolare **22.** *to* — *out*, (far) uscire, (far) sloggiare; traslocare; sgomberare **23.** *to* — *up*, (far) salire.

movement ['mu:vmənt], *s.* **1.** movimento, moto (anche *fig.*); gesto: *the religious* —, il movimento religioso; *she lay there without a* —, ella giaceva immobile **2.** movimento; marcia; manovra **3.** impulso, moto: *a* — *of anger*, un moto d'ira **4.** meccanismo **5.** *(comm.)* oscillazione (del mercato) **6.** *(mus.)* movimento **7.** *(med.)* evacuazione.

mover ['mu:və*], *s.* **1.** animatore, anima; promotore: *he is the prime* — *of the firm*, è l'anima dell'azienda ‖

the Prime Mover, il Primo Motore, Dio **2.** *(mec.)* (forza) motrice **3.** autore di una mozione, proponente.

movie ['muːvi], *s.* **1.** *(sl. amer.)* film muto **2.** *pl.* *(sl.)* cinema ☆ — *camera*, cinepresa; — *goer*, frequentatore di cinema; — *maker*, produttore cinematografico; — *man*, operatore; — *star*, stella del cinema.

movieland ['muːvilænd], *s.* *(sl. amer.)* cinelandia.

moving ['muːviŋ], *ag.* **1.** commovente; patetico, toccante: — *scene*, scena patetica **2.** mobile; in movimento, in marcia: *a* — *train*, un treno in moto **3.** che dà moto, impulso: *the* — *ideas of the age*, le idee che diedero impulso all'epoca ‖ *s.* **1.** spostamento; trasferimento **2.** trasloco: *he arrived during our* —, arrivò durante il nostro trasloco ☆ — *-coil*, *(elett.)* a bobina mobile; *(rad.)* magnetodinamico; — *-day*, giorno di trasloco; giorno in cui scade il contratto di affitto; — *in*, ingresso nella nuova abitazione; — *man*, *(amer.)* imballatore, manovale specializzato; — *period*, *(cine.)* fase di movimento, scatto; — *pictures*, cinematografo; — *staircase* (o — *stairs*), scala mobile.

movingly ['muːviŋli], *av.* in modo commovente.

mow[1] [mou], *s.* **1.** *(dial. amer.)* covone, mucchio di fieno, di cereali (in un granaio) **2.** luogo in un granaio ove si ripone grano, fieno, ecc.

to **mow**[1], *v.t.* *(dial.)* accatastare, ammassare in covoni.

to **mow**[2], *pass.* **mowed** [moud], *p.p.* **mown** [moun], *v.t.* **1.** falciare (erba); mietere (grano, ecc.) **2.** *fig.* sterminare (animali, nemici, ecc.).

mow[3] [mau], *s.* *(dial. letter.)* smorfia; boccaccia.

to **mow**[3], *v.i.* fare boccacce.

mower ['mouə*], *s.c.* falciatore, falciatrice; mietitore, mietitrice ‖ *s.* *(mec.)* falciatrice ☆ *motor* —, falciatrice meccanica.

mowing ['mouiŋ], *s.* falciatura; mietitura ☆ — *-grass*, erba da taglio; — *-machine*, falciatrice meccanica; *lawn* — *-machine*, falciatrice da prati.

mown [moun], *p.p.* di to **mow**.

Mozambique [,mouzəm'biːk], *no.pr.* *(geog.)* Mozambico.

Mozarab [mouz'ærəb], *s.* *(st.)* mozarabo.

Mozarabic [mouz'ærəbik], *ag.* *(st.)* mozarabico.

Mr. ['mistə*], *abbr.* di **Mister 1.**

Mrs. ['misiz], *abbr.* di **Mistress 6.**

much [mʌtʃ], *comp.* **more** [mɔ:*], *superl.* **most** [moust], *pl.* **many** ['meni], *ag.* **molto**; *(arc.)* grande, considerevole: *did you have* — *rain?*, avete avuto molta pioggia?; *he drank too* — *wine*, bevve troppo vino; *how* — *bread is there?*, quanto pane c'è?; *she earns so* — *money*, guadagna tanto denaro ‖ *to be too* — *for s.o.*, essere troppo (superiore, difficile, ecc.) per qlcu.

much, *s.* **molto**; **gran quantità, gran parte**: — *of the food went bad*, gran parte del cibo andò a male; *he hasn't* — *to do*, non ha molto da fare; *there is not* — *to see*, non c'è gran che da vedere ‖ *so* — *for that*, basta (con ciò), chiudiamo l'argomento ‖ *so* — *per cent*, tanto per cento ‖ *I don't see* — *of him nowadays*, non lo vedo molto di questi tempi ‖ *it is not worth* — (o *fam. it is not up to* —), non vale gran che; *she is not* — *of an artist*, non è una grande artista, come artista non vale un gran che ‖ *I will say this* — *for him*, dirò tutto ciò in suo favore ‖ *the skirt is that too long* —, la gonna è troppo lunga di tanto ‖ *that is so* — *to the good*, è tanto di guadagnato ‖ *to make* — *of s.o.*, far festa a qlcu.; stimare qlcu.; adulare qlcu.: *they made* — *of the actor when he arrived*, fecero una grande accoglienza all'attore al suo arrivo; *they make* — *of him as an abstract painter*, lo stimano molto come pittore astratto; *to make* — *of sthg.*, attribuire molta importanza a qlco.; trarre gran vantaggio da qlco.: *I do not make* — *of that book*, non mi soddisfa molto quel libro; *the newspapers made* — *of the new underground*, i giornali hanno parlato molto della nuova metropolitana ‖ *to think* — *of s.o., sthg.*, avere una grande opinione di qlcu., qlco. ‖ *to think too* — *of oneself*, darsi troppa importanza, essere

troppo pieno di sè ‖ — *will have more*, prov. l'appetito vien mangiando ‖ *too* — *is as bad as none at all*, prov. il troppo stroppia.

much, *av.* **1.** **molto, assai; di gran lunga**: *he* — *regrets*, gli rincresce molto; *it is* — *better*, *worse*, è molto meglio, peggio; *it is* — *the best*, è di gran lunga il migliore; *she talks too* —, ella parla troppo; *she would like it very* —, le piacerebbe moltissimo; *this novel is* — *more interesting*, questo romanzo è molto più interessante ‖ — *to my astonishment*, con mia grande meraviglia ‖ — *as*, per quanto: — *as I like him, I cannot do what you ask*, per quanto io abbia simpatia per lui, non posso fare quello che mi chiedi ‖ *as* —, altrettanto, tanto ‖ *as* — *as*, tanto, quanto: *I love him as* — *as I love her*, amo lui quanto lei; *it is as* — *as saying that*, tanto vale dire che ‖ *how* —?, quanto (costa)? ‖ *so* —, tanto: *thank you so* —, grazie tanto ‖ *so* — *the better*, tanto meglio; *so* — *the less*, tanto meno; *so* — *the worse*, tanto peggio **2.** **pressappoco**: — *of a size*, pressappoco della stessa misura; *it is* — *the same*, è pressappoco lo stesso.

much, *(nei composti)*: — *-admired*, ammirato da tutti; — *-advertised*, molto reclamizzato, lanciato; — *discussed*, controverso, molto discusso; — *sought*, molto richiesto, ricercato.

muchness ['mʌtʃnis], *s.*: *it is much of a* —, *prov.* se non è zuppa è pan bagnato.

mucilage ['mjuːsilidʒ], *s.* mucillaggine; colla liquida.

mucilaginous [,mjuːsi'lædʒinəs], *ag.* mucillagginoso.

muck[1] [mʌk], *s.* **1.** letame, concime **2.** terriccio; melma **3.** fradiciume, mucchio di verdura, di frutta fradicia **4.** *fig.* *(fam.)* oscenità; porcheria; notizie scandalose; cose senza valore: *I am afraid he writes* —, temo che scriva cose senza valore; *the lunch was an awful* —, la colazione era una porcheria; *you should not read that* —, non dovresti leggere quelle sconcezze; *to rake up* —, sollevare scandali, raccogliere notizie piccanti **5.** confusione: *to make a* — *of sthg.*, abborracciare ql.co.; creare confusione in ql.co. ☆ — *-heap* (o — *-hill*), letamaio, concimaia; — *-rake*, rastrello per il letame; — *-worm*, larva di scarabeo stercorario, verme di letamaio; *fig.* monello di strada.

to **muck**[1], *v.t.i.* **1.** concimare **2.** insudiciare **3.** pulire, spazzolare (una stalla, ecc.) **4.** *about*, *(sl.)* bighellonare; lavoricchiare; gingillarsi **5.** *to* — *in*, *(sl.)* andare ad abitare, dividere la stessa camera **6.** *to* — *up*, *(sl.)* abborracciare (un lavoro).

muck[2], *V.* **amuck.**

mucker[1] ['mʌkə*], *s.* *(sl.)* **1.** capitombolo: *to come a* —, misurare il pavimento, cadere lungo disteso; *fig.* cadere, fallire **2.** *fig.* disgrazia; rovina ‖ *to go a* — *on sthg.* (o *over the purchase of sthg.*), fare spese pazze per una cosa che non le vale.

mucker[2], *s.* **1.** *(amer.)* riformatore fanatico **2.** ipocrita **3.** persona zotica, villana.

muckiness ['mʌkinis], *s.* sudiciume, sporcizia.

to **muck-rake** ['mʌk-reik], *v.i.* *(amer. fam.)* raccogliere e divulgare scandali.

mucky ['mʌki], *ag.* sudicio; imbrattato, infangato.

mucosity [mju'kɔsiti], *s.* mucosità.

mucous ['mjuːkəs], *ag.* mucoso; viscoso ☆ — *membrane*, *(anat.)* mucosa.

mucousness ['mjuːkəsnis], *s.* mucosità.

mucus ['mjuːkəs], *s.* muco.

mud [mʌd], *s.* **1.** fango, melma, mota: *to get stuck in the* —, impantanarsi **2.** *fig.* calunnia, insulto ‖ *to fling* (o *to throw*) — *at s.o.*, insultare, calunniare qlcu. **3.** residui melmosi; fango (di caldaia) ☆ — *-barge* (o — *-lighter*), barcone con draga (per il trasporto della mota); — *-bath*, *(med.)* fangature; — *-flap*, paraspruzzi (di bicicletta); — *-guard*, *(aut.)* parafango; — *-pie*, forma di terra, di sabbia (fatta da bambini per giuoco).

to **mud**, *pass.p.p.* **mudded** ['mʌdid], *v.t.i.* **1.** infangare **2.** rendere torbido **3.** riposare nel fango (di anguille, pesci, ecc.).

mudded ['mʌdid], *ag.* infangato, sporco di fango, inzaccherato: — *all over*, tutto infangato, inzaccherato.

muddily ['mʌdili], *av.* torbidamente; confusamente.

muddiness ['mʌdinis], *s.* **1.** fangosità; torbidezza **2.** *fig.* confusione: — *of mind*, mancanza di chiarezza nel pensiero.

muddle ['mʌdl], *s.* confusione, disordine; pasticcio: *to be in a* —, essere in un pasticcio, in un imbroglio; *to make a* — *of sthg.*, fare una gran confusione a proposito di una cosa.

to muddle, *v.t.i.* **1.** far confusione, confondere; creare disordine tra (anche *fig.*): *he muddled my papers so badly!*, ha messo una tale confusione tra le mie carte!; *she muddled an answer*, si confuse nel rispondere || *don't* — *things up*, non complicare le cose **2.** intontire: *a drop of whisky is enough to* — *him*, una goccia di whisky gli dà subito alla testa **3.** *to* — *along, on,* (*fam.*) tirare avanti alla meglio **4.** *to* — *through,* (*fam.*) cavarsela alla meno peggio, arrabattarsi.

muddled ['mʌdld], *ag.* **1.** disordinato, in disordine; confuso (anche *fig.*): *all his things were* — *up*, tutte le sue cose erano in disordine; *he felt* —, si sentì turbato **2.** alticcio, brillo: *he is* — (*with drink*), è un po' brillo, non ha la testa a posto.

muddleheaded ['mʌdl,hedid], *ag.* confusionario.

muddler ['mʌdlə*], *s.* pasticcione, confusionario.

muddling ['mʌdliŋ], *ag.* **1.** confusionario **2.** che rende perplesso, dubbioso, esitante: *it's a* — *business*, è una faccenda che non mi sembra chiara.

muddy ['mʌdi], *ag.* **1.** fangoso, melmoso: *a* — *road*, una strada fangosa; *this water tastes* —, quest'acqua sa di fango **2.** infangato, imbrattato: *his clothes were* —, i suoi abiti erano infangati **3.** torbido; opaco: *a* — *voice*, una voce opaca; *this coffee is too* — *for my liking*, questo caffè è troppo torbido per i miei gusti **4.** *fig.* poco chiaro, confuso.

to muddy, *v.t.i.* **1.** infangare, infangarsi; inzaccherare, inzaccherarsi **2.** *fig.* confondere.

muezzin [mu(:)'ezin], *s.* muezzino.

muff[1] [mʌf], *s.* manicotto (anche *tec.*).

muff[2], *s.* **1.** (*fam.*) persona maldestra; scimunito, babbeo **2.** azione fallita, mancata (specialmente *spor.*): *to make a* — *of a catch, a business*, mancare il colpo, far fallire un'impresa.

to muff[2], *v.t.i.* (*sl.*) fallire (il colpo); far cilecca, fiasco.

muffin ['mʌfin], *s.* **1.** « muffin » (tartina da tè) **2.** piattino.

muffineer [,mʌfi'niə*], *s.* **1.** piatto con coperchio per tenere caldi i «muffins» **2.** spargisale; spargizucchero.

muffle[1] ['mʌfl], *s.* **1.** guantone **2.** (*tec.*) muffola ☆ — *-furnace*, (*tec.*) forno a muffola.

to muffle[1], *v.t.* **1.** avvolgere; imbacuccare: *it was so bitterly cold that he muffled himself up to his eyes*, faceva così freddo che si imbacuccò fino alle orecchie **2.** smorzare; soffocare (suoni, rumori): *the snow muffled all sounds*, la neve smorzava ogni rumore **3.** imbavagliare.

muffle[2], *s.* labbro superiore e naso (di ruminante, di roditore).

muffled ['mʌfld], *ag.* **1.** imbacuccato, ben coperto **2.** attutito, smorzato (di suoni, rumori).

muffler ['mʌflə*], *s.* **1.** sciarpa pesante **2.** guantone da pugilato **3.** feltro (nel pianoforte) **4.** (*tec.*) silenziatore; marmitta (di scarico).

mufti[1] ['mʌfti], *s.* muftì, giureconsulto islamico.

mufti[2], *s.* abito civile: *in* —, in borghese.

mug[1] [mʌg], *s.* **1.** bicchierone, boccale, coppa **2.** bibita rinfrescante.

mug[2], *s.* (*sl.*) muso: *ugly* —, grinta, ceffo **2.** (*amer.*) connotati; dati segnaletici (di delinquenti).

to mug[2], *pass.p.p.* **mugged** [mʌgd], *v.t.i.* **1.** (*sl. teat.*) fare una smorfia **2.** (*amer.*) fotografare (specialmente delinquenti) **3.** *to* — *up*, dipingersi il viso, truccarsi.

mug[3], *s.* (*sl.*) babbeo, gonzo.

mug[4], *s.* (*sl.*) **1.** esame **2.** sgobbone.

to mug[4], *v.t.i.* (*sl.*) sgobbare, studiare con grande impegno: *she mugged up her maths in three weeks*, sgobbò tre settimane per la matematica.

mugginess ['mʌginis], *s.* **1.** aria umidiccia e pesante; afa **2.** aria viziata, odore di rinchiuso, di stantìo.

muggins ['mʌginz], *s.* **1.** babbeo, scimunito, semplicotto **2.** variante del giuoco del domino **3.** vari giuochi infantili alle carte (rubamazzo, l'uomo nero, ecc.).

muggy ['mʌgi], *ag.* **1.** afoso; umido; opprimente (del tempo) **2.** che sa di rinchiuso: *it was* — *inside*, c'era odor di rinchiuso all'interno.

mugweed ['mʌgwi:d], **mugwort** ['mʌgwə:t], *s.* (*bot.*) artemisia.

mugwump ['mʌgwʌmp], *s.* **1.** (*amer. pol.*) indipendente **2.** (*sl.*) pezzo grosso, persona che si crede molto importante.

mulatto [mju(:)'lætou], *pl.* **mulattos** [mju(:)'lætouz], *ag.s.* mulatto.

mulattress [mju(:)'lætris], *s.* mulatta.

mulberry ['mʌlbəri], *ag.* morato || *s.* **1.** mora; mora di gelso **2.** gelso **3.** (*mil.*) porto artificiale per truppe da sbarco ☆ — *-bush*, girotondo; — *-faced*, viso chiazzato; — *-tree*, gelso.

mulch [mʌlʃ], *s.* riparo di paglia, foglie, terriccio intorno alle radici di una pianta.

to mulch, *v.t.* riparare (le radici di una pianta) con paglia, foglie, terriccio.

mule[1] [mju:l], *s.c.* mulo, mula (anche *fig.*): *as obstinate as a* —, testardo come un mulo; *on a* —, a dorso di mulo || *s.* **1.** ibrido **2.** (*ind. tessile*) filatoio intermittente ☆ — *canary*, canarino ibrido.

mule[2], *s.* pianella, ciabatta.

muleteer [,mju:li'tiə*], *s.* mulattiere.

muliebrity [,mju:li'ebriti], *s.* **1.** femminilità **2.** effeminatezza.

mulish ['mju:liʃ], *ag.* **1.** di, da mulo **2.** ostinato, testardo.

mulishly ['mju:liʃli], *av.* ostinatamente.

mulishness ['mju:liʃnis], *s.* ostinatezza, testardaggine.

mull[1] [mʌl], *s.* **1.** mussola leggera **2.** garza di cotone, di lino per rilegatura.

mull[2], *s.* (*scoz.*) promontorio.

mull[3], *s.* (*fam.*) confusione: *to make a* — *of sthg.*, far confusione in ql.co.: (*spor.*) mancare il colpo.

to mull[3], *v.t.* **1.** non riuscire in, far fiasco in; fallire (il colpo) **2.** *to* — *over* (*sthg.*), (*fam. amer.*) rimuginare.

to mull[4], *v.t.* scaldare (vino) con zucchero e aromi.

mullein ['mʌlin], *s.* (*bot.*) verbasco, tasso barbasso.

muller ['mʌlə*], *s.* **1.** pietra, pestello (del mortaio) **2.** (*tec.*) mescolatore a molazza, molazza **3.** (*arc.*) recipiente per scaldare il vino.

mullet[1] ['mʌlit], *s.* (*ittiol.*) **1.** triglia **2.** muggine.

mullet[2], *s.* (*arald.*) stella a cinque punte.

mulligrubs ['mʌligrʌbz], *s.pl.* **1.** depressione, malinconia **2.** (*fam.*) mal di stomaco.

mulling ['mʌliŋ], *s.* (*tec.*) molazzatura.

mullion ['mʌliən], *s.* (*arch.*) montante; colonnina divisoria di una finestra a più luci.

mullioned ['mʌliənd], *ag.* (*arch.*) a più luci.

mullock ['mʌlək], *s.* **1.** (*austral.*) roccia non aurifera **2.** detriti di rocce aurifere **3.** (*fam.*) roba di scarto.

mulsh, *V.* mulch.

multangular [mʌl'tæŋgjulə*], *ag.* pluriangolare.

multeity [mʌl'ti:iti], *s.* molteplicità.

multicolour ['mʌlti,kʌlə*], *ag.* multicolore.

multicylinder ['mʌlti,silində*], *ag.* a più cilindri.

multifarious [,mʌlti'fɛəriəs], *ag.* vario; variato; multiforme; molteplice.

multifariousness [,mʌlti'fɛəriəsnis], *s.* varietà; molteplicità.

multifoil ['mʌltifoil], *ag.* (*arch.*) a sei o più lobi.

multiform ['mʌltifɔ:m], *ag.* multiforme, vario.

multiformity [,mʌlti'fɔ:miti], *s.* multiformità, molteplicità di forme; pluriformità.

multilateral ['mʌlti'lætərəl], *ag.* multilaterale.

multiloquy [mʌl'tiləkwi], *s.* loquacità; moltiloquio.

multimillionaire ['mʌltimiljə'nɛə*], *s.* multimilionario.

multinomial ['mʌlti'noumiəl], *ag.s.* (*mat.*) polinomio.

multiparous [mʌl'tipərəs], *ag.* multiparo.

multiple ['mʌltipl], *ag.* multiplo; molteplice: — *interests*, interessi molteplici ‖ *s.* **1.** (*mat.*) multiplo **2.** (*elett.*) parallelo: *running in* —, marcia in parallelo ☆ — *current generator*, generatrice polimorfa; — *fabric*, tessuto multiplo; — *line*, (*elett.*) linea multipla; — *store* (o — *shop*), negozio a catena ‖ *least common* — (*L.C.M*), (*mat.*) minimo comune multiplo (M.C.M.).

multiplex ['mʌltipleks], *ag.* multiplo; molteplice ‖ *s.* **1.** telegrafo multiplo; sistema di trasmissione contemporanea sullo stesso circuito **2.** (*rad. tv.*) sistema di trasmissione contemporanea sulla stessa onda ☆ — *telegraphy*, telegrafia multipla.

multiplicable ['mʌltiplikəbl], *ag.* moltiplicabile.

multiplicand [,mʌltipli'kænd], *s.* (*arit.*) moltiplicando.

multiplication [,mʌltipli'keiʃən], *s.* (*arit.*) moltiplicazione ☆ — *table*, tavola pitagorica.

multiplicative [,mʌlti'plikətiv], *ag.* moltiplicativo, che serve a moltiplicare.

multiplicator ['mʌltiplikeitə*], *s.* (*arit. elett.*) moltiplicatore.

multiplicity [,mʌlti'plisiti], *s.* molteplicità; grande numero di: *the* — *of his excuses was a clear sign of his unwillingness*, il grande numero, la varietà delle sue scuse era chiaro indizio della sua malavoglia.

multiplier ['mʌltiplaiə*], *s.* (*arit. elett.*) moltiplicatore ☆ *electron* —, moltiplicatore elettronico; *frequency* —, (*rad.*) moltiplicatore di frequenza.

to multiply ['mʌltiplai], *v.t.i.* **1.** moltiplicare: *to* — *five by six*, moltiplicare cinque per sei **2.** moltiplicarsi, riprodursi; crescere: *rabbits* — *rapidly*, i conigli si moltiplicano rapidamente **3.** (*arc.*) ingrandire (immagini, suoni).

multiplying ['mʌltiplaiiŋ], *ag.* moltiplicante ‖ *s.* moltiplicazione: *the* — *of deadly weapons does not seem to make for peace*, il moltiplicarsi di armi letali non sembra avere come obiettivo la pace ☆ — *factor*, fattore di moltiplicazione; (*foto.*) fattore di posa; — *lens*, (*ott.*) lente d'ingrandimento.

multipolar ['mʌlti'poulə*], *ag.* (*elett.*) multipolare.

multisyllable ['mʌlti'siləbl], *ag.* multisillabo, polisillabo.

multitude ['mʌltitju:d], *s.* **1.** moltitudine, massa, folla: *this film will appeal to the* —, questo film piacerà alla massa **2.** molteplicità; gran numero: *the* — *of his occupations*, la molteplicità dei suoi impegni.

multitudinous [,mʌlti'tju:dinəs], *ag.* **1.** molto numeroso, innumerevole **2.** svariato; molteplice **3.** vasto; immenso: *the* — *seas*, i vasti mari.

multitudinously [,mʌlti'tju:dinəsli], *av.* in modo svariato, molteplice.

multitudinousness [,mʌlti'tju:dinəsnis], *s.* **1.** molteplicità **2.** vastità; immensità.

multivalence [mʌl'tivələns], *s.* (*chim.*) polivalenza.

multivalent [mʌl'tivələnt], *ag.* (*chim.*) polivalente.

multiwall ['mʌlti'wɔ:l], *ag.* (*tec.*) a pareti multiple ☆ — *bag*, (*ind.*) sacco a pareti multiple.

multure ['mʌltʃə*], *s.* **1.** prezzo della macinazione (del grano al molino) **2.** (*rar.*) macinazione.

mum[1] [mʌm], *ag.* zitto, riservato: *to be* — *on sthg.*, tacere su ql.co.; *to keep* —, tacere, non proferire parola ‖ *s.* (*arc.*) persona silenziosa.

to mum[1], *pass.pp.* **mummed** [mʌmd], *v.i.* **1.** mimare, fare il mimo **2.** camuffarsi; mascherarsi.

mum[1], *inter.* zitto!, silenzio! ‖ —'*s the word!*, acqua in bocca!.

mum[2], *s.* (*fam.*) mammina.

mum[3], *s.* (*pop.*) *contr.* di **ma'am**.

mumble ['mʌmbl], *s.* borbottio; mormorio indistinto.

to mumble, *v.t.i.* mormorare; borbottare; biascicare: *to* — *a prayer*, biascicare una preghiera.

mumbler ['mʌmblə*], *s.c.* brontolone, brontolona.

mumbling ['mʌmbliŋ], *ag.* che borbotta, biascica: *a* — *old man*, un vecchio sdentato ‖ *s. V.* **mumble**.

mumblingly ['mʌmbliŋli], *av.* indistintamente.

Mumbo Jumbo ['mʌmbou'dʒʌmbou], *s.* **1.** «Mumbo Jumbo» (feticcio africano) **2.** *fig.* idolo; oggetto di feticismo.

mummer ['mʌmə*], *s.* **1.** (*st.*) mimo **2.** (*spreg.*) guitto.

mummery ['mʌməri], *s.* **1.** buffonata, mascherata **2.** cerimoniale ridicolo.

mummification [,mʌmifi'keiʃən], *s.* **1.** mummificazione **2.** (*patol.*) gangrena secca.

to mummify ['mʌmifai], *v.t.* mummificare.

mummy[1] ['mʌmi], *s.* **1.** mummia (anche *fig.*) **2.** pigmento marrone bruciato **3.** poltiglia: *to beat s.o. to a* —, (*fam.*) bastonare ql.cu. di santa ragione; *to beat sthg. to a* —, ridurre ql.co. in polvere, in poltiglia ☆ — -*case*, sarcofago.

mummy[2], *s.* (*fam.*) mammetta, mammina.

to mump[1] [mʌmp], *v.i.* **1.** assumere un aspetto contrito; tenere il broncio **2.** biascicare, mormorare.

to mump[2], *v.t.i.* mendicare.

mumper ['mʌmpə*], *s.* mendicante.

mumpish ['mʌmpiʃ], *ag.* di cattivo umore; depresso.

mumps [mʌmps], *s.* **1.** (*patol.*) parotite epidemica; (*fam.*) orecchioni **2.** (*fam.*) broncio, luna: *to have the* —, aver la luna.

to munch [mʌntʃ], *v.t.i.* biascicare; sgranocchiare; ruminare: *to* — (*away*) *biscuits*, sgranocchiare biscotti.

mundane ['mʌndein], *ag.* **1.** terrestre; mondano **2.** cosmico; universale.

mundanely ['mʌndeinli], *av.* **1.** mondanamente **2.** cosmicamente; universalmente.

mundaneness ['mʌndeinnis], **mundanity** [mʌn'dæniti], *s.* mondanità.

mundification [,mʌndifi'keiʃən], *s.* disinfezione; purificazione.

to mundify ['mʌndifai], *v.t.* detergere; disinfettare; purificare.

mungo ['mʌŋgou], *s.* (*ind. laniera*) lana meccanica di seconda qualità; tessuto grossolano di lana (ricavato da stracci).

Munich ['mju:nik], *no.pr.* (*geog.*) Monaco (di Baviera).

municipal [mju(:)'nisipəl], *ag.* municipale ☆ — *law*, (*dir.*) legislazione municipale.

municipality [,mju(:)nisi'pæliti], *s.* municipalità.

municipalism [mju(:)'nisipəlizəm], *s.* **1.** municipalismo **2.** campanilismo.

municipalist [mju(:)'nisipəlist], *s.* campanilista.

municipalization [mju(:),nisipəlai'zeiʃən], *s.* municipalizzazione.

to municipalize [mju(:)'nisipəlaiz], *v.t.* municipalizzare.

municipally [mju(:)'nisipəli], *av.* municipalmente.

munificence [mju(:)'nifisns], *s.* munificenza.

munificent [mju(:)'nifisnt], *ag.* munifico, generoso.

munificently [mju(:)'nifisntli], *av.* generosamente, con munificenza.

muniment ['mju:nimənt], *s.gener.pl.* (*dir.*) atto; documento ☆ — -*house* (o — -*room*), archivio notarile.

munition [mju(:)'niʃən], *s.* **1.** fortificazione; difesa **2.** *pl.* munizioni; armi: *munitions of war*, munizioni di guerra ‖ *Ministry of Munitions*, Ministero dei Rifornimenti e Approvvigionamenti ☆ — -*factory*, fabbrica di munizioni; — -*worker*, operaio in una fabbrica di munizioni.

to munition, *v.t.* fornire di munizioni, armare (nave, esercito, ecc.).

munitioneer [mju(:),niʃə'niə*], **munitioner** [mju(:)'niʃənə*], *s.* operaio di una fabbrica di munizioni.

munnion ['mʌnjən], *V.* **mullion.**

muntjak ['mʌntdʒæk], *s.* (*zool.*) « muntjak » (piccolo daino asiatico).

Muntz [mʌnts], *s.* metallo Muntz.

muræna [mju'ri:nə], *s.* (*ittiol.*) murena.

mural ['mjuərəl], *ag.* murale ‖ *s.* pittura, decorazione murale; affresco.

murder ['mə:də*], *s.* **1.** (*dir.*) assassinio; omicidio: — *in the first degree*, (*amer.*) omicidio di primo grado: — *in the second degree*, (*amer.*) omicidio di secondo grado; *wilful* —, omicidio premeditato **2.** (*fam.*) fattaccio, delitto; segreto ‖ —!, aiuto!, che cosa mai ho fatto! ‖ *the — is out!*, il segreto è scoperto! ‖ *the exam was sheer* —!, (*fam.*) l'esame fu un vero macello! ‖ *he can get away with* —!, (*fam.*) se la cava sempre! ‖ *to cry blue* —, urlare a squarciagola ‖ —, *will out*, *prov.* ogni nodo viene al pettine ☆ — *-case*, processo per assassinio.

to murder, *v.t.i.* **1.** assassinare, uccidere **2.** *fig.* distruggere; massacrare; sciupare: *that girl can but this difficult sonata*, quella ragazza non può che massacrare questa difficile sonata.

murderer ['mə:dərə*], *s.* assassino, omicida.

murderess ['mə:dəris], *s.* assassina.

murderous ['mə:dərəs], *ag.* omicida; feroce; sanguinario: — *war*, guerra omicida; *I felt simply* —, (*scherz.*) mi sentivo addirittura capace di uccidere.

murderously ['mə:dərəsli], *av.* crudelmente; sanguinariamente: *to assault* —, assalire con intenzioni omicide.

murex ['mjuəreks], *pl.* **murices** ['mjuərisi:z], *s.* (*zool.*) murice.

muriate ['mjuəriit], *s.* (*chim.*) muriato, cloruro.

muriatic [,mjuəri'ætik], *ag.* (*chim.*) muriatico, cloridrico.

murk [mə:k], *ag.* **1.** (*arc. poet.*) oscuro, tenebroso **2.** denso (di oscurità).

murkily ['mə:kili], *av.* oscuramente, tetramente.

murkiness ['mə:kinis], *s.* **1.** oscurità, tenebre, buio **2.** densità; torbidezza.

murky ['mə:ki], *ag.* **1.** oscuro, tenebroso, fosco **2.** denso (di oscurità).

murmur ['mə:mə*], *s.* **1.** mormorio, sussurro **2.** borbottio, borbottamento: *she has swallowed it without a* —, (*fam.*) ha ingoiato la pillola senza fiatare **3.** (*patol.*) soffio.

to murmur, *v.t.i.* **1.** sussurrare, mormorare: *he murmured her name*, mormorò il suo nome; *the wind murmured through the leaves*, il vento sussurrava tra le foglie **2.** borbottare, brontolare; criticare, trovare da ridire: *he murmured at* (o *against*) *her coming late*, brontolò per il suo ritardo.

murmurer ['mə:mərə*], *s.c.* brontolone, brontolona; mormoratore, mormoratrice.

murmuring ['mə:məriŋ], *s.* **1.** *ag.* mormorante, sussurrante **2.** borbottante ‖ *s.* **1.** mormorio, sussurro **2.** brontolio; lagnanza.

murmuringly ['mə:məriŋli], *av.* **1.** con mormorii **2.** con brontolii.

murmurous ['mə:mərəs], *ag.* pieno di mormorii.

murphy ['mə:fi], *s.* (*sl.*) patata.

murrain ['mʌrin], *s.* **1.** (*vet.*) epizoozia **2.** (*arc.*) peste, malanno ‖ *a — on him!*, che il malanno se lo porti!.

murrey ['mʌri], *ag.s.* (*arc.*) (colore) morato, rossoviolaceo.

musa ['mju:zə], *s.* (*bot.*) musa.

muscadel [,mʌskə'del], *s.* moscato (uva, vino).

muscadine ['mʌskədain], *s.* uva moscata.

muscardine [mʌs'kɑ:di(:)n], *s.* (*vet.*) calcino.

muscat ['mʌskət], **muscatel** [,mʌskə'tel], *s.* moscato (uva, vino).

muscle ['mʌsl], *s.* **1.** (*anat.*) muscolo: *he stood without moving a* —, egli stava immobile **2.** muscolatura; forza muscolare ☆ — *-bound*, coi muscoli induriti per eccesso di fatica.

to muscle, *v.i.* (*amer.*) penetrare a forza, aprirsi un varco; intromettersi a viva forza (anche *fig.*): *to — in a matter*, immischiarsi in una questione.

muscled ['mʌsld], *ag.* muscoloso ☆ *strong-* —, *weak-* —, dai muscoli robusti, deboli.

muscleless ['mʌsllis], *ag.* fiacco, molle, senza nerbo.

muscling ['mʌsliŋ], *s.* muscolatura.

museology [mʌs'kɔlədʒi], *s.* briologia.

muscosity [mʌs'kɔsiti], *s.* abbondanza di muschio.

Muscovite[1] ['mʌskəvait], *ag.s.c.* moscovita.

muscovite[2], *s.* (*min.*) mica.

Muscovy ['mʌskəvi], *no.pr.* (*geog. st.*) Moscovia.

muscular ['mʌskjulə*], *ag.* muscolare; muscoloso: *a — man*, un uomo muscoloso ☆ — *injection*, iniezione intramuscolare.

muscularity [,mʌskju'læriti], *s.* muscolosità, vigore muscolare.

musculature ['mʌskjulətʃə*], *s.* (*anat.*) muscolatura, sistema muscolare.

Muse[1] [mju:z], *no.pr.f.* (*mit.*) Musa ‖ *the* —, la Musa; l'ispirazione poetica; *pl.* le arti liberali.

muse[2], *s.* (*arc.*) meditazione, contemplazione: *to fall into a — over sthg.*, meditare su qualcosa.

to muse[2], *v.i.* riflettere, pensare, meditare; fantasticare: *he muses over memories of the past*, è assorto nei ricordi del passato.

muser ['mju:zə*], *s.c.* sognatore, sognatrice.

musette [mju(:)'zet], *s.* **1.** « musette » (strumento simile alla zampogna) **2.** ballo popolare francese.

museum [mju(:)'ziəm], *s.* museo ☆ — *-piece*, pezzo da museo.

mush[1] [mʌʃ], *s.* **1.** polpa, sostanza molle, soffice **2.** (*amer.*) farinata, specie di polenta **3.** *fig.* sdolcinatura, leziosaggine.

mush[2], *s.* **1.** *abbr.* di **mushroom 2.** (*sl.*) ombrello.

mush[3], *s.* (*amer.*) viaggio sulla neve con slitta (trascinata dai cani).

to mush[3], *v.i.* (*amer.*) viaggiare sulla neve con slitta (trascinata dai cani).

mushroom ['mʌʃrum], *s.* **1.** (*bot.*) fungo mangereccio **2.** *fig.* arricchito **3.** (*fam.*) grande cappello di paglia da donna ☆ — *growth*, *fig.* sviluppo subitaneo.

to mushroom, *v.i.* **1.** raccogliere funghi: *to go mushrooming*, andar per funghi **2.** schiacciarsi (di proiettili) **3.** (*amer.*) dilagare (di fuoco).

mushy ['mʌʃi], *ag.* **1.** spappolato (di cibo, ecc.); molle, infrollito **2.** sdolcinato, sentimentale.

music ['mju:zik], *s.* musica: *academy* (o *college*) *of* —, conservatorio; *to compose*, *write* —, comporre, scrivere musica; *to play without* —, suonare a memoria; *to set to* —, mettere in musica ‖ *to face the* —, *fig.* affrontare le critiche, una sfuriata ☆ — *-book*, libro di musica; — *-case*, cartella da musica; — *-drama*, dramma musicale; — *-hall*, caffè concerto; — *-holder*, leggio; — *-master*, *mistress* (o *-teacher*), insegnante di musica; — *-paper*, carta pentagrammata; — *-room*, sala da musica; — *-school*, scuola di musica; — *-stand*, leggio; — *-stool*, sgabello da pianoforte ‖ *rough* —, baccano, chiasso.

musical ['mju:zikəl], *ag.* **1.** musicale, melodioso, armonioso: *a — sound*, un suono melodioso **2.** appassionato di musica: *these young people are not* —, questi giovani non amano la musica ☆ — *comedy*, commedia musicale; operetta; — *director*, direttore d'orchestra; — *glasses*, armonica.

musicale [,mju:zi'kæl], *s.* (*amer.*) serata, mattinata musicale.

musicality [,mju:zi'kæliti], *s.* musicalità.

musically ['mju:zikəli], *av.* musicalmente.

musicalness ['mju:zikəlnis], *s.* musicalità.

musician [mju(:)'ziʃən], *s.* musicista (esecutore, compositore); musicante ☆ *street* —, suonatore ambulante.

musicologist [,mju:zi'kɔlədʒist], *s.* musicologo.

musicology [,mju:zi'kɔlədʒi], *s.* musicologia.

musing ['mju:ziŋ], *s.* meditabondo; riflessivo ‖ *s.* **1.** meditazione, contemplazione **2.** fantasticheria.

musingly ['mju:ziŋli], *av.* pensosamente.

musk [mʌsk], *s.* (*chim.*) muschio ☆ — *-deer,* (*zool.*) mosco; — *-gland,* glandola che secerne il muschio; — *-ox,* bue muschiato; — *-rat,* topo muschiato; — *-rose,* rosa muschiata.

musket ['mʌskit], *s.* moschetto, fucile.

musketeer [,mʌski'tiə*], *s.* moschettiere.

musketry ['mʌskitri], *s.* **1.** moschetteria, fucileria **2.** (*mil.*) tiro; abilità di tiro; scuola di tiro.

muskiness ['mʌskinis], *s.* odore di muschio.

musky ['mʌski], *ag.* muschiato: — *smell,* odore di muschio; odor di selvatico.

Muslim ['muslim], *ag.* musulmano ‖ *s.c.* musulmano, musulmana.

muslin ['mʌzlin], *ag.* di mussola ‖ *s.* **1.** mussola ‖ *bit of —,* (*fam.*) donna, ragazza **2.** (*mar. sl.*) vele, tende.

muslined ['mʌzlind], *ag.* vestito di mussola.

musquash ['mʌs-kwɔʃ], *s.* **1.** topo muschiato **2.** pelliccia di topo muschiato.

muss [mʌs], *s.* (*amer. fam.*) disordine, scompiglio; pasticcio.

to muss, *v.t.* (*amer. fam.*) arruffare, scompigliare, mettere in disordine: *to — (up) one's dress,* sgualcirsi il vestito.

mussel ['mʌsl], *s.* (*zool.*) mitilo, muscolo, cozza, mollusco ☆ — *-plum,* prugna nera; — *-scalp,* banco di molluschi; — *-shell,* conchiglia di mollusco.

Mussulman ['mʌslmən], *ag.* musulmano ‖ *s.c.* musulmano, musulmana.

mussy ['mʌsi], *ag.* (*amer.*) in disordine; sgualcito; sporco.

must[1] [mʌst], *s.* mosto.

must[2], *s.* **1.** muffa **2.** odor di muffa.

to must[2], *v.t.i.* ammuffire, fare ammuffire.

must[3], *ag.* eccitato (di elefante, cammello): — *elephant,* elefante infuriato ‖ *s.* eccitazione periodica e pericolosa (di elefante, cammello).

must[4], *s.* (*fam.*) cosa che deve essere assolutamente fatta, ottenuta, considerata: *be here every night: it is a —,* sii qui ogni sera: è una cosa che devi fare assolutamente.

must[4] [mʌst (*forma forte*), məst, məs (*forme deboli*)], *v.* difettivo (V); *indic. congiunt. pres.* **must;** *forma negativa:* **must not** [mʌst nɔt] *forma contratta:* **mustn't** ['mʌsnt] **1.** (*esprimente dovere, obbligo, necessità*): — *you really do it?,* devi proprio farlo?; *he — be here in time if he wants to catch his train,* deve essere qui per tempo se vuole prendere il treno; *she — go now,* è necessario che ella vada ora; *these writings — be regarded as literary documents,* questi scritti devono essere considerati documenti letterari; *you — study more,* devi studiare di più ‖ *the play, you — know, was very successful,* la commedia, devi sapere, ebbe un gran successo ‖ *the reader — understand that...,* il lettore capirà che... **2.** (*esprimente supposizione, probabilità*): *Ann — be rich,* Anna deve essere ricca; *he — be about twenty,* deve avere circa vent'anni; *he — be very strong to do that,* deve essere ben forte per far ciò; *the phone is ringing, it — be George,* il telefono sta squillando, deve essere Giorgio; *when he said that, he — have known it was not true,* quando disse ciò doveva sapere che non era vero **3.** (*esprimente certezza, inevitabilità*): *I understand that I — appear guilty,* mi rendo conto che devo sembrare colpevole; *if she had looked carefully, she — have seen the train approaching,* se avesse fatto attenzione, avrebbe certamente visto giungere il treno; *you — know him!,* non puoi non conoscerlo!.

mustang ['mʌstæn], *s.* (*zool.*) mustango.

mustard ['mʌstəd], *s.* **1.** (*bot.*) senape **2.** (*cuc.*) mostarda, senape **3.** (*sl.*) cosa piccante; persona arguta ☆ — *-gas,* (*chim.*) iprite; — *-plaster,* senapismo; —

-pot, mostardiera; — *-poultice,* cataplasma alla senape; — *seed,* seme di senape.

Mustelidae [mʌs'telidi:], *s. pl.* (*zool.*) mustelidi.

muster ['mʌstə*], *s.* **1.** (*mil.*) adunata; rivista: *to make (o to take) — of troops,* passare le truppe in rivista ‖ *to pass —,* riuscire accettabile; essere all'altezza: *she looked at her shoes and thought they would pass —,* si guardò le scarpe e pensò che potevano andare **2.** assemblea, riunione; assembramento ‖ *to turn out in full —,* presentarsi al gran completo **3.** (*comm.*) campione ☆ — *parade,* (*fam.*) ispezione; — *-roll,* ruolo, ruolino; (*mar.*) appello.

to muster, *v.t.i.* **1.** (*mil.*) passare in rivista, in rassegna; (*mar.*) fare l'appello **2.** radunare, radunarsi ‖ *they mustered (up) their courage,* presero il coraggio a due mani.

mustiness ['mʌstinis], *s.* **1.** muffa **2.** odor di muffa.

musty ['mʌsti], *ag.* **1.** ammuffito; stantio; rancido **2.** vecchio, superato **3.** (*amer.*) tedioso; noioso; apatico.

mutability [,mju:tə'biliti], *s.* mutabilità.

mutable ['mju:təbl], *ag.* mutabile, mutevole.

mutableness ['mju:təblnis], *s.* mutabilità.

mutably ['mju:təbli], *av.* mutabilmente.

mutation [mju(:)'teiʃən], *s.* **1.** cambiamento, alterazione **2.** (*biol. mus.*) mutazione **3.** metafonia.

mute[1] [mju:t], *ag.* **1.** muto; silenzioso; taciturno: *he was — with surprise,* restò ammutolito per la sorpresa ‖ *as a fish,* (*fam.*) muto come un pesce ‖ — *of malice,* (*dir.*) reticente **2.** (*fonet.*) muto: — *consonant,* consonante muta ‖ *s.* **1.** muto **2.** (*fonet.*) lettera muta **3.** (*mus.*) sordina ‖ *with the — on,* in sordina **4.** (*rar.*) piagnone **5.** (*teat.*) comparsa ☆ *deaf —,* sordomuto.

to mute[1], *v.t.* (*mus.*) mettere la sordina a.

mute[2], *s.* sterco (di uccelli).

to mute[2], *v.i.* evacuare (di uccelli).

to mute[3], *v.t.* controllare la fermentazione del (mosto).

mutely ['mju:tli], *av.* da muto; silenziosamente.

muteness ['mju:tnis], *s.* mutismo; silenziosità.

to mutilate ['mju:tileit], *v.t.* mutilare, storpiare; troncare.

mutilated ['mju:tileitid], *ag.* mutilato; mutilo.

mutilation [,mju:ti'leiʃən], *s.* mutilazione; troncamento.

mutilator ['mju:tileitə*], *s.c.* mutilatore, mutilatrice.

mutineer [,mju:ti'niə*], *s.* ammutinato, ribelle.

mutinous ['mju:tinəs], *ag.* ammutinato, rivoltoso; ribelle, sedizioso: — *behaviour,* condotta ribelle.

mutinously ['mju:tinəsli], *av.* sediziosamente.

mutinousness ['mju:tinəsnis], *s.* ammutinamento; spirito ribelle.

mutiny ['mju:tini], *s.* ammutinamento, rivolta.

to mutiny, *v.i.* ammutinarsi: *to — against s.o., sthg.,* ribellarsi a qlcu., a ql.co.

mutism ['mju:tizəm], *s.* mutismo.

mutt [mʌt], *s.* (*sl. amer.*) **1.** semplicciotto, babbeo **2.** cane bastardo.

mutter ['mʌtə*], *s.* mormorio; brontolamento.

to mutter, *v.t.i.* mormorare; bisbigliare; borbottare, brontolare; rumoreggiare (di tuono): *to — at (o against) s.o.,* mormorare contro qlcu.

mutterer ['mʌtərə*], *s.c.* brontolone, brontolona.

muttering ['mʌtəriŋ], *s.* mormorio; borbottio; brontolio (anche di tuono): *hostile mutterings,* ostilità sorda.

mutteringly ['mʌtəriŋli], *av.* borbottando, brontolando.

mutton ['mʌtn], *s.* **1.** carne di montone; castrato: *leg of —,* cosciotto di montone ‖ *dead as —,* morto stecchito ‖ *to eat one's — with,* pranzare con **2.** (*scherz.*) pecora — *dressed like lamb,* (*fam.*) donna anziana che s'atteggia a giovinetta ‖ *let us return to our muttons,* torniamo a bomba ☆ — *-chop* (o — *-cutlet*), costoletta di montone: — *-chop whiskers,* favoriti, scopettoni; — *fat*, grasso di montone; — *-head*, (*fam.*) sempliciotto, babbeo, scimunito.

mutual ['mju:tjuəl], *ag.* **1.** mutuo, reciproco: — *benefit*, vantaggio reciproco; — *love*, affetto reciproco; *on* — *terms*, alla pari **2.** comune: *our* — *friend*, il nostro comune amico ☆ — *inductance*, (*elett.*) induttanza neutra; — *insurance*, mutua assicurazione.

mutualism ['mju:tjuolizəm], *s.* mutualismo.

mutuality [,mju:tju'æliti], *s.* mutualità, reciprocità.

mutually ['mju:tjuəli], *av.* mutuamente, reciprocamente.

mutule ['mju:tju:l], *s.* (*arch.*) modiglione.

muzzily ['mʌzili], *av.* con intontimento; da inebetito.

muzziness ['mʌzinis], *s.* intontimento, inebetimento.

muzzle ['mʌzl], *s.* **1.** muso di animale **2.** museruola **3.** bocca, imboccatura (di armi da fuoco, ecc.) ☆ — *-loader*, fucile, cannone ad avancarica; — *-velocity*, velocità iniziale (di proiettile).

to **muzzle**, *v.t.i.* **1.** mettere la museruola **2.** *fig.* imbavagliare, impedire di parlare a: *to* — *the press*, (*fam.*) imbavagliare la stampa **3.** (*mar.*) abbassare (una vela).

muzzy ['mʌzi], *ag.* **1.** inebetito; confuso; vago (di idee) **2.** (*fam.*) instupidito dall'alcool.

my [mai], *ag. poss. 1ª persona sing.* mio, mia, miei, mie: — *book*, il mio libro; — *daughters*, le mie figlie ‖ *it is* — *turn*, tocca a me.

my, *inter.*: — (*eye*) *!*, acciderba!, accipicchia!.

myalgia [mai'ældʒiə], *s.* (*patol.*) mialgia.

myall ['maiəl], *s.* (*bot.*) acacia australiana.

mycelium [mai'si:liəm], *s.* (*bot.*) micelio.

Mycenae [mai'si:ni(:)], *no.pr.* (*st. geog.*) Micene.

Mycenaean [mai'si:niən], *ag.* (*st. archeol.*) miceneo, micenico.

mycetology [,maisi'tolədʒi], *s.* micologia, micetologia.

mycologic(al) [,maikou'lodʒik(əl)], *ag.* micologico.

mycology [mai'kolədʒi], *s.* micologia, micetologia.

mycosis [mai'kousis], *s.* (*patol.*) micosi ☆ — *cutis*, dermatomicosi; — *-favosa*, favo, tigna favosa; — *intestinalis*, (*patol.*) antrace.

mycotic [mai'kotik], *ag.* (*patol.*) micotico,

myelitis [,maiə'laitis], *s.* (*patol.*) mielite.

mygale ['migəli:], *s.* (*zool.*) migale.

mylodon ['mailədon], *s.* (*paleont.*) milodonte.

myocarditis [,maiouka:'daitis], *s.* (*patol.*) miocardite.

myocardium [,maiou'ka:diəm], *s.* (*anat.*) miocardio.

myology [mai'olədʒi], *s.* (*anat.*) miologia.

myoma [mai'oumə], *s.* (*patol.*) mioma.

myope ['maioup], *s.* miope.

myopia [mai'oupjə], *s.* miopia.

myopic [mai'opik], *ag.* miope.

myopy ['maioupi], *s.* miopia.

myosis [mai'ousis], *s.* (*patol.*) miosi.

myosote ['maiəsout], **myosotis** [,maiə'soutis], *s.* (*bot.*) miosotide, non-ti-scordar-di-me.

myriad ['miriəd], *ag.* (*poet. ret.*) innumerevole ‖ *s.* miriade.

myriapod ['miriəpod], *s.* (*zool.*) miriapodo.

Myriapoda [,miri'æpədə], *s.pl.* (*zool.*) miriapodi.

Myrmidon ['mə:midən], *s.* (*mit. gr.*) mirmidone ‖ **myrmidon**, *s.* sbirro: — *of the law*, poliziotto.

myrobalan [mai'robələn], *s.* (*bot.*) mirobolano, mirabolano.

myrrh¹ [mə:*], *s.* mirra.

myrrh², *s.* (*bot.*) laserpizio.

Myrrha ['mirə], *no.pr.f.* (*mit.*) Mirra.

myrrhie ['mə:rik], *ag.* mirrico.

myrtaceous [mə:'teiʃəs], *ag.* (*bot.*) mirteo, di mirto.

myrtle ['mə:tl], *s.* (*bot.*) mirto, mortella.

myself [mai'self], *pron. 1ª persona sing.* **1.** *r.* io stesso, mi, me stesso: *I am enjoying* — *very much*, mi sto divertendo molto; *I am not speaking for* —, non parlo

per me; *I have hurt* —, mi son fatto male; *it concerns nobody but* —, non riguarda altri che me; *I was speaking to* —, parlavo tra me e me ‖ *I want to go there by* —, voglio andarci da solo **2.** (*enfatico*) io stesso: *I did it* —, l'ho fatto proprio io; *I*, —, *do not believe it*, in quanto a me, non lo credo; *I* — *said so*, fui io a dirlo; *I said so* —, l'ho detto io stesso; *I want to go* —, voglio andare di persona ‖ *s.* io stesso: *I am not* (*quite*) —, non sono io, non mi sento bene; *I am quite* — *again*, mi sono completamente rimesso.

mystagogic(al) [,mistə'godʒik(əl)], *ag.* (*st. greca*) mistagogico, di mistagogia.

mystagogy ['mistəgodʒi], *s.* (*st. greca*) mistagogia.

mysterious [mis'tiəriəs], *ag.* misterioso; occulto, segreto: *a* — *business*, un affare misterioso; *there was* — *talk of him*, correvano voci strane sul suo conto.

mysteriously [mis'tiəriəsli], *av.* misteriosamente; occultamente, segretamente: *to behave* —, comportarsi misteriosamente, con aria di mistero.

mysteriousness [mis'tiəriəsnis], *s.* misteriosità, mistero.

mystery¹ ['mistəri], *s.* **1.** mistero, enigma, arcano, segreto: *the mysteries of biology*, gli arcani della biologia; *the crime was wrapped in* —, il delitto era avvolto nel mistero; *they don't make a* — *of it*, essi non ne fanno un segreto **2.** (*teol.*) mistero, verità di fede ‖ *the Holy Mysteries*, la Santa Eucarestia **3.** *pl.* (*st.*) misteri, riti religiosi **4.** (*st. teat.*) sacra rappresentazione; mistero.

mystery², *s.* (*arc.*) mestiere ‖ *arts and mysteries*, arti e mestieri.

mystic(al) ['mistik(əl)], *ag.* **1.** mistico **2.** misterioso; occulto; magico: *the* — *hour of midnight*, l'ora misteriosa della mezzanotte ‖ *s.* mistico.

mystically ['mistikəli], *av.* misticamente.

mysticalness ['mistikəlnis], **mysticism** ['mistisizəm], *s.* misticismo.

to **mysticize** ['mistisaiz], *v.t.* rendere mistico.

mystification [,mistifi'keiʃən], *s.* **1.** mistificazione, inganno; burla **2.** confusione di idee.

mystificator ['mistifikeitə*], *s.* (*rar.*) mistificatore.

to **mystify** ['mistifai], *v.t.* **1.** mistificare; ingannare, imbrogliare **2.** confondere le idee di; disorientare: *I was mystified by that torrent of words*, fui stordito da quel torrente di parole **3.** avvolgere nel mistero; fare un mistero di.

mystique [mis'ti:k], *s.* **1.** mistica **2.** fanatismo.

myth [miθ], *s.* mito.

mythic(al) ['miθik(əl)], *ag.* **1.** mitico: — *heroes*, eroi mitici **2.** immaginario: — *wealth*, ricchezze immaginarie.

mythically ['miθikəli], *av.* miticamente.

to **mythicize** ['miθisaiz], *v.t.* **1.** volgere in mito **2.** interpretare mitologicamente.

mythographer [mi'θogrəfə*], *s.* mitografo.

mythography [mi'θogrəfi], *s.* mitografia.

mythologic(al) [,miθə'lodʒik(əl)], *ag.* **1.** mitologico **2.** irreale, immaginario.

mythologically [,miθə'lodʒikəli], *av.* mitologicamente.

mythologist [mi'θolədʒist], *s.* mitologo, mitologista.

to **mythologize** [mi'θolədʒaiz], *v.t.i.* **1.** studiare, interpretare miti **2.** spiegare (fenomeni, fatti) trattandoli come miti.

mythology [mi'θolədʒi], *s.* mitologia: *Greek* —, mitologia Greca; *the mythologies of primitive races*, la mitologia delle razze primitive.

mythus ['maiθəs], *s.* mito.

mytilus ['mitiləs], *s.* (*zool.*) mitilo.

myxoedema [,miksou'di:mə], *s.* (*patol.*) mixedema.

myxoma [miks'oumə], *s.* (*patol.*) mixoma.

myxomatosis [,miksoumə'tousis], *s.* (*patol.*) mixomatosi.

N

n [en], *pl.* **ns, n's** [enz], *s.* **1.** (*quattordicesima lettera dell'alfabeto inglese*) n ‖ — *for Nellie,* (*tel.*) n come Napoli **2.** (*mat.*) numero indefinito: *b to the nth* (*power*) *is written* b^n, b all'ennesima potenza si scrive b^n.

to **nab** [næb], *pass.p.p.* **nabbed** [næbd], *v.t.* (*sl.*) afferrare; arraffare; agguantare; catturare: *he nabbed a watch, and so got nabbed by a cop,* egli arraffò un orologio e così si fece agguantare da un poliziotto.

nabob ['neibɔb], *s.* nababbo (anche *fig.*).

nacelle [nə'sel], *s.* (*aer.*) carlinga; navicella (di dirigibile).

nacre ['neikə*], *s.* **1.** madreperla **2.** mollusco che produce madreperla.

nacreous ['neikriəs], **nacrous** ['neikrəs], *ag.* madreperlaceo.

nadir ['neidiə*], *s.* **1.** (*astr.*) nadir **2.** *fig.* punto di massima depressione.

naevus ['ni:vəs], *pl.* **naevi** ['ni:vai], *s.* voglia, macchia della pelle.

nag[1] [næg], *s.* cavallino; (*fam.*) cavallo da sella.

nag[2], *s.* brontolio, brontolamento.

to **nag**[2], *pass.p.p.* **nagged** [nægd], *v.t.i.* brontolare; infastidire; tormentare: *a nagging wife,* una moglie brontolona; *she was always nagging at him,* lo tormentava con continui rimbrotti; *to — to death,* infastidire a morte.

nagger ['nægə*], *s.* brontolone.

nagging ['nægiŋ], *s.* rimprovero.

nagor ['neigo:*], *s.* (*zool.*) antilope.

naiad ['naiæd], *s.* (*mit.*) naiade.

naif [nɑ:'i:f], *ag.* ingenuo, semplice, non sofisticato.

nail [neil], *s.* **1.** unghia; artiglio: *to bite one's nails,* mordersi le unghie; *to pare one's nails,* tagliarsi le unghie ‖ *nails in mourning,* (*scherz.*) unghie listate a lutto, unghie sporche **2.** chiodo ‖ *a — in s.o.'s coffin, fig.* un chiodo della bara di qlcu., un contributo alla fine, alla rovina di qlcu. ‖ (*as*) *hard as nails,* robustissimo, spietato; (*as*) *right as nails,* giustissimo; sanissimo ‖ *to drive the — home,* giungere ad una conclusione ‖ *to hit the — on the head,* colpire nel segno **3.** « nail » (misura di lunghezza = cm. 5,715) ☆ — *-brush,* spazzolino da unghie; — *-file,* lima da unghie; — *-polish,* smalto per unghie; — *-scissors,* forbicine da unghie.

to **nail,** *v.t.* **1.** inchiodare: *to — together,* fissare insieme con chiodi ‖ *to — one's colours to the mast, fig.* perseverare, irrigidirsi sulle proprie posizioni ‖ *to — a lie to the barn-door* (o *to the counter*), *fig.* dimostrare la falsità di un'affermazione **2.** munire di chiodi, chiodare: *if he is going to do any climbing, he should have his boots nailed,* se ha l'intenzione di fare dell'alpinismo, dovrebbe farsi mettere dei chiodi alle scarpe **3.** fissare, trattenere (l'attenzione, ecc.), impegnare (una persona) **4.** *to — down,* fissare con chiodi ‖ *to — s.o. down to,* mettere qlcu. con le spalle al muro: *this argument nailed him down to his promise,* questo argomento lo impegnò a mantenere la promessa data **5.** *to — up,* chiudere con chiodi; inchiodare, condannare (una porta, ecc.).

nailer ['neilə*], *s.* **1.** fabbricante di chiodi **2.** (*sl.*) campione: *he is a — at tennis,* giuoca benissimo a tennis.

nailery ['neiləri], *s.* fabbrica di chiodi.

nailing ['neiliŋ], *ag.* (*sl.*) magnifico, splendido, eccellente.

naïve [nɑ:'i:v], *ag.* ingenuo, semplice, non sofisticato.

naïvely [nɑ:'i:vli], *av.* ingenuamente.

naiveté [nɑ:'i:vtei], **naïvety** [nɑ:'i:vti], *s.* ingenuità.

naked ['neikid], *ag.* **1.** nudo, spogliato, scoperto: — *sword,* spada sguainata; *the child was stripped —,* il bimbo fu spogliato completamente; *he was as — as his mother bore him,* era nudo come mamma lo fece ‖ *to the — eye,* a occhio nudo **2.** spoglio, indifeso, senza armi **3.** semplice, genuino, puro, senza ornamenti: *I want to know the — truth,* voglio sapere la verità pura e semplice.

nakedly ['neikidli], *av.* **1.** a nudo; senza difesa **2.** *fig.* evidentemente.

nakedness ['neikidnis], *s.* **1.** nudità **2.** *fig.* evidenza **3.** miseria, povertà (di spirito, ecc.).

namby-pamby ['næmbi'pæmbi], *ag.* scioccamente sentimentale; grazioso e sciocco ‖ *s.* **1.** discorso, scritto sciocco, insulso **2.** persona graziosa e sciocca, insulsa.

name [neim], *s.* **1.** nome; generalità: *she called him by —,* lo chiamò per nome; *to have nothing to one's —,* non possedere nulla ‖ *in the — of God,* in nome di Dio ‖ *give it him in my —,* daglielo a nome mio ‖ *to put one's — down for,* porre la propria candidatura a **2.** fama, reputazione: *he has an ill —,* ha una cattiva reputazione; *he soon made a — for himself,* egli presto si distinse, si fece un nome; *that physician has a — for honesty,* quel medico è noto per la sua onestà **3.** (*gram.*) nome, sostantivo **4.** *pl. fig.* ingiurie, insolenze: *they called him names,* lo coprirono di ingiurie ☆ — *-day,* onomastico; — *-plate,* targhetta (sulla porta) ‖ *Christian —* (o *amer. first —* o *given —*), nome di battesimo; *full —,* generalità; *he gave his full —,* diede il suo nome e cognome; *last —,* cognome.

to **name,** *v.t.* **1.** nominare, dare un nome a: *how did they — him?,* come lo chiamarono? **2.** designare: *he was named mayor,* fu nominato, scelto come sindaco **3.** fissare, scegliere: — *your price,* dite la vostra cifra.

nameable ['neiməbl], *ag.* nominabile.

nameless ['neimlis], *ag.* **1.** senza nome, innominato; anonimo, ignoto **2.** innominabile, indescrivibile; abominevole.

namelessly ['neimlisli], *av.* anonimamente, senza nome.

namely ['neimli], *av.* cioè, vale a dire.

namesake ['neim-seik], *s.* omonimo: *we are namesakes,* abbiamo lo stesso nome.

Nancy ['nænsi], *no.pr.f. dim.* di **Agnes, Anne.**

nankeen [næŋ'ki:n], *s.* **1.** anchina (tela) **2.** *pl.* pantaloni di anchina.

Nannie ['næni], *no.pr.f. dim.* di **Anne.**

nanny ['næni], *s.* bambinaia, balia ☆ — *-goat,* capra.

Naomi ['neiəmi], *no.pr.f.* Noemi.

nap[1] [næp], *s.* siesta, sonnellino: *to take a —,* fare un sonnellino, schiacciare un pisolino.

to **nap**[1], *pass.p.p.* **napped** [næpt], *v.i.* schiacciare un sonnellino, sonnecchiare ‖ *to catch s.o. napping,* prendere qlcu. alla sprovvista.

nap[2], *s.* **1.** pelo (di panno e di altre stoffe pelose) **2.** (*bot.*) lanuggine, peluria.

to **nap**[2], *v.t.* cardare; felpare; spazzolare contropelo (una stoffa).

napalm ['neipɑ:m], *s.* (*chim. mil.*) « napalm » (miscela esplosiva).

nape [neip], *s.* nuca.

napery ['neipəri], *s.* (*arc.*) biancheria da tavola.

naphtha ['næfθə], *s*. nafta.
naphthalene ['næfθəli:n], *s*. naftalina.
to naphthalize ['næfθəlaiz], *v.t*. trattare alla nafta.
naphthol ['næfθɔl], *s*. (*chim. farm.*) naftolo.
napkin ['næpkin], *s*. **1.** tovagliolo **2.** pannolino (per bambini) **3.** (*scoz.*) fazzoletto ‖ *to lay up in a —*, *fig.* trascurare, non far uso di ☆ *— -ring*, anello per tovagliolo.
Naples ['neiplz], *no.pr.* (*geog.*) Napoli.
napless ['næplis], *ag.* senza pelo (di tessuto).
Napoleon [nə'pouljən], *no.pr.m.* Napoleone ‖ **napoleon**, *s*. **1.** napoleone (moneta d'oro da venti franchi) **2.** specie di stivale da caccia **3.** (*carte*) napoleone.
Napoleonic [nə,pouli'ɔnik], *ag.* napoleonico.
nappiness ['næpinis], *s*. pelosità.
nappy[1] ['næpi], *ag.* peloso.
nappy[2], *ag.* **1.** schiumoso; forte (di birra) **2.** brillo.
nappy[3], *s*. pannolino (per bambini).
narcissism [nɑ:'sisizəm], *s*. narcisismo.
Narcissus [nɑ:'sisəs], *no.pr.m.* (*mit.*) Narciso ‖ **narcissus**, *pl*. **narcissi** [nɑ:'sisai], **narcissuses** [nɑ:'sisəsiz], *s*. (*bot.*) narciso.
narcolepsy ['nɑ:kəlepsi], *s*. (*patol.*) narcolessia.
narcosis [nɑ:'kousis], *s*. narcosi.
narcotic [nɑ:'kɔtik], *ag. s*. narcotico.
narcotine ['nɑ:kətin], *s*. narcotina.
narcotism ['nɑ:kətizəm], *s*. narcosi.
narcotist ['nɑ:kətist], *s*. persona dedita ai narcotici.
narcotization [,nɑ:kətai'zeiʃən], *s*. narcotizzazione.
to narcotize ['nɑ:kətaiz], *v.t*. narcotizzare.
nard [nɑ:d], *s*. **1.** (*bot.*) nardo **2.** nardo (balsamo).
nares [nɛəz], *s.pl*. narici.
narghile ['nɑ:gili], *s*. «narghilè» (pipa orientale).
narrable ['nœrəbl], *ag.* narrabile.
to narrate [næ'reit], *v.t*. narrare, raccontare.
narration [næ'reiʃən], *s*. narrazione, racconto, descrizione.
narrative ['nœrətiv], *ag.* narrativo ‖ *s*. resoconto, narrazione.
narratively ['nœrətivli], *av.* narrativamente.
narrator [næ'reitə*], *s*. narratore.
narrow ['nœrou], *ag.* **1.** stretto, angusto, limitato, ristretto (anche *fig.*): *a — circle of friends*, una ristretta cerchia di amici; *a — majority*, una scarsa maggioranza; *my bathroom is —*, la mia stanza da bagno è stretta; *what does this word mean in the narrowest sense?*, che cosa significa letteralmente questa parola?; *to have a — escape*, salvarsi per miracolo ‖ *the — seas*, i canali d'Irlanda e d'Inghilterra **2.** esatto, minuzioso, rigoroso: *a — inspection*, un'ispezione minuziosa ‖ *s*. **1.** stretta (di valle, passo, ecc.) **2.** *gener. pl*. stretto ☆ *— -gauge*, (*ferr.*) a scartamento ridotto; *— -minded*, di idee ristrette; retrogrado; *— -mindedness*, ristrettezza di mente, di idee; povertà, meschinità (di spirito).
to narrow, *v.t.i*. stringere, stringersi; limitare, limitarsi; ridurre; contrarsi: *he narrowed the argument*, limitò la discussione; *the river narrows*, il fiume si restringe ‖ *to — down*, limitare, limitarsi.
narrowly ['nœrouli], *av.* **1.** a stento; *fig.* poveramente **2.** da vicino; a fondo, minuziosamente.
narrowness ['nœrounis], *s*. **1.** strettezza, esiguità, limitatezza **2.** precisione, meticolosità.
narthex ['nɑ:θeks], *s*. (*arch.*) nartece.
narwhal ['nɑ:wəl], *s*. (*zool.*) narvalo.
nasal ['neizəl], *ag.* (*anat.*) nasale: *the — sounds*, i suoni nasali ‖ *s* **1.** suono nasale **2.** nasale (di elmetto) **3.** (*anat.*) osso nasale ☆ *the — cavity*, cavità nasale; *the — fossae*, fosse nasali; *the — organ*, il naso; *the — septum*, il setto nasale.
nasality [nei'zæliti], *s*. tono nasale (di voce).
nasalization [,neizəlai'zeiʃən], *s*. nasalizzazione.
to nasalize ['neizəlaiz], *v.t.i*. nasalizzare; parlare con voce nasale.
nasally ['neizəli], *av.* nasalmente.

nascency ['næsnsi], *s*. nascita; origine.
nascent ['næsnt], *ag.* **1.** nascente **2.** (*chim.*) nascente (di gas che si libera da un composto).
nasofrontal [,neisou'frʌntl], *ag.* nasofrontale.
nastily ['nɑ:stili], *av.* **1.** sgradevolmente, in modo disgustoso **2.** con cattiveria **3.** (*spec. amer.*) sudiciamente; in modo osceno.
nastiness ['nɑ:stinis], *s*. **1.** cattivo gusto **2.** cattiveria (di persone) **3.** (*spec. amer.*) sporcizia; oscenità; indecenza.
nasturtium [nəs'tə:ʃəm], *s*. (*bot.*) nasturzio.
nasty ['nɑ:sti], *ag.* **1.** sporco; sgradevole; disgustoso, ripugnante **2.** pericoloso; cattivo, tempestoso (di tempo): *a — illness*, una malattia pericolosa; *the sea is —*, il mare è cattivo, agitato **3.** osceno, indecente **4.** cattivo, dispettoso: *a — temper*, un cattivo carattere ‖ *a — one*, (*fam.*) un colpo mancino.
natal ['neitl], *ag.* natale.
natality [nə'tæliti], *s*. natalità; (*rar.*) nativtà.
natant ['neitənt], *ag.* natante.
natation [nei'teiʃən], *s*. nuoto.
natatorial [,neitə'tɔ:riəl], **natatory** ['neitətəri], *ag.* natatorio, relativo al nuoto.
nates ['neiti:z], *s.pl*. (*anat.*) **1.** natiche **2.** tubercoli quadrigemelli anteriori.
Nathan ['neiθən], *no.pr.m.* Nathan.
Nathaniel [nə'θænjəl], *no.pr.m.* Nataniele.
natheless ['neiθlis], *av.* (*arc.*) nondimeno, tuttavia.
nation ['neiʃən], *s*. nazione; popolo ‖ *the United Nations Organization* (*U.N.O.*), l'Organizzazione delle Nazioni Unite (N.U., O.N.U.).
national ['næʃənl], *ag.* nazionale: *— anthem*, inno nazionale ‖ *National Gallery*, Galleria Nazionale ☆ *— debt*, debito pubblico; *— insurance*, assicurazione di previdenza sociale; *— service*, servizio militare.
nationalism ['næʃnəlizəm], *s*. nazionalismo; patriottismo.
nationalist ['næʃnəlist], *s*. nazionalista.
nationality [,næʃə'næliti], *s*. **1.** nazionalità; carattere nazionale: *people of all nationalities*, gente di ogni nazionalità **2.** patriottismo.
nationalization [,næʃnəlai'zeiʃən], *s*. **1.** nazionalizzazione **2.** naturalizzazione.
to nationalize ['næʃnəlaiz], *v.t*. **1.** nazionalizzare **2.** naturalizzare (stranieri): *he was nationalized*, si naturalizzò.
nationally ['næʃnəli], *av.* nazionalmente.
nationals ['næʃənlz], *s.pl*. compatriotti: *one's —*, i propri compatriotti.
native ['neitiv], *ag.* **1.** innato: *— wit*, intelligenza innata; *her — modesty*, la sua innata modestia **2.** naturale, semplice **3.** nativo, natio; indigeno, originario; primitivo: *— customs*, usanze primitive; *— language*, lingua materna; *my — land*, la mia terra natia **4.** (*min.*) nativo, puro: *— gold*, oro puro ‖ *s*. **1.** nativo: *he speaks English like a —*, parla inglese come uno del luogo **2.** indigeno (persona, animale, prodotto); persona di razza non europea: *to go —*, (*fam.*) vivere da indigeno (di uomo bianco) **3.** persona nata sotto un determinato segno dello zodiaco **4.** ostrica coltivata artificialmente in Gran Bretagna ☆ *— -born*, nativo.
natively ['neitivli], *av.* spontaneamente.
nativeness ['neitivnis], *s*. naturalezza.
nativity [nə'tiviti], *s*. **1.** nascita; natività ‖ *the Nativity*, il Natale **2.** oroscopo: *to cast s.o.'s —*, trarre l'oroscopo di qlcu.
natron ['neitrən], *s*. (*chim.*) natron, carbonato di sodio.
to natter ['nætə*], *v.i*. (*dial.*) agitarsi, irritarsi.
natterjack ['nætədʒæk], *s*. rospo.
nattery ['nætəri], *ag.* querulo, lagnoso.
nattily ['nætili], *av.* **1.** ordinatamente; accuratamente; elegantemente **2.** abilmente, destramente.
nattiness ['nætinis], *s*. **1.** ordine; accuratezza; eleganza **2.** abilità, destrezza.

natty ['næti], *ag.* **1.** ordinato; accurato; elegante **2.** a-bile, destro.

natural ['nætʃrəl], *ag.* **1.** naturale; fisico: — *death*, morte naturale **2.** genuino, semplice; spontaneo: *he spoke in quite a — voice*, ha parlato con voce per nulla affettata **3.** istintivo; innato: — *gift*, dono innato; *it comes — to me*, lo faccio senza sforzo alcuno; *they are — enemies*, sono nemici per istinto **4.** bastardo, illegittimo: — *child*, figlio naturale, illegittimo **5.** (*mus.*) naturale, bequadro: — *note*, nota naturale ☆ — *history*, storia naturale; — *law*, legge di natura; — *order*, (*bot.*) classificazione naturale; — *philosophy*, fisica, filosofia naturale; — *religion*, religione naturale; — *science*, scienze naturali.

natural, *s.* **1.** persona corta d'intelletto **2.** (*mus.*) nota naturale; bequadro.

naturalism ['nætʃrəlizəm], *s.* naturalismo.

naturalist ['nætʃrəlist], *ag.* naturalistico.

naturalist, *s.* **1.** naturalista **2.** seguace del naturalismo **3.** commerciante di animali **4.** imbalsamatore (di animali), tassidermista.

naturalistic [,nætʃrə'listik], *ag.* naturalistico.

naturalistically [,nætʃrə'listikəli], *av.* naturalisticamente.

naturalization [,nætʃrəlai'zeiʃən], *s.* **1.** naturalizzazione, naturalità **2.** acclimatamento (di piante, animali).

to **naturalize** ['nætʃrəlaiz], *v.t.i.* **1.** naturalizzare; naturalizzarsi **2.** adottare, accettare (costumi, espressioni, ecc. di paesi stranieri) **3.** acclimatare (animali, piante di paesi stranieri) **4.** occuparsi di storia naturale.

naturalized ['nætʃrəlaizd], *ag.* **1.** naturalizzato **2.** a-dottato **3.** acclimatato.

naturally ['nætʃrəli], *av.* naturalmente; istintivamente; per natura.

nature ['neitʃə*], *s.* **1.** natura: *against —*, contro natura; *by —*, per natura; *human —*, la natura umana; *love for —*, amore per la natura; *state of —*, stato naturale **2.** carattere, temperamento; costituzione; essenza; disposizione, inclinazione: *good —*, bontà, buon carattere; *ill —*, cattiveria, cattivo carattere **3.** la vita fisica dell'uomo **4.** tipo, specie, genere: *I dislike things of this —*, non mi piacciono cose di questo genere.

natured ['neitʃəd], *ag.* per natura, di [natura ☆ *good- —*, buono, di buon carattere; *ill- —*, cattivo, di cattivo carattere; *simple- —*, semplice, di carattere semplice.

naturism ['neitʃərizəm], *s.* (*neol.*) naturismo, nudismo.

naught [nɔːt], *ag.* (*arc.*) senza valore; inutile ‖ *s.* (*arc.*) niente; (*arit.*) zero: *to set s.o., sthg. at —*, non tenere in alcun conto, disprezzare qlcu., ql.co.

naughtily ['nɔːtili], *av.* con cattiveria; con impertinenza; con disubbidienza (specialmente di bambini).

naughtiness ['nɔːtinis], *s.* cattiveria; impertinenza; disubbidienza (specialmente di bambini).

naughty ['nɔːti], *ag.* **1.** cattivo; impertinente; disubbidiente (specialmente di bambini): *you — child !*, cattivello!, birichino! **2.** salace; indecente.

Nauru [nɑː'uːruː], *no.pr.* (*geog.*) Nauru.

nausea ['nɔːsjə], *s.* **1.** nausea **2.** disgusto, avversione.

nauseant ['nɔːsjənt], *ag.* nauseante.

to **nauseate** ['nɔːsieit], *v.t.i.* disgustare, stomacare; nauseare; provar nausea; essere nauseato: *he was nauseated at it*, egli ne fu nauseato.

nauseating ['nɔːsieitiŋ], *ag.* nauseante, nauseabondo, disgustoso.

nauseation [,nɔːsi'eiʃən], *s.* il sentir nausea.

nauseous ['nɔːsjəs], *ag.* nauseabondo, disgustoso.

nauseousness ['nɔːsjəsnis], *s.* carattere disgustoso, nauseabondo, l'essere nauseante.

nautic(al) ['nɔːtik(əl)], *ag.* nautico, marino, navale ☆ — *almanac*, effemeride, almanacco nautico; — *mile*, miglio marittimo (misura di lunghezza = m. 1853,2); — *science*, nautica.

nautilus ['nɔːtiləs], *pl.* **nautiluses** ['nɔːtiləsiz], **nautili** ['nɔːtilai], *s.* (*zool.*) nautilo.

naval ['neivəl], *ag.* navale, marittimo ☆ — *academy*, accademia navale; — *forces*, marina da guerra; — *officer*, ufficiale di marina; (*amer.*) funzionario delle dogane nei porti; — *power*, potenza navale; — *station* (o — *base*), base navale, porto militare; — *vessel*, nave da guerra.

nave[1] [neiv], *s.* mozzo di ruota.

nave[2], *s.* (*arch.*) navata (di chiesa).

navel ['neivəl], *s.* **1.** (*anat.*) ombelico **2.** *fig.* centro ☆ — *cord* (o — *string*), cordone ombelicale; — *orange*, varietà di arancia (con depressione alla sommità).

navicert ['nævisəːt], *s.* permesso di trasporto (per merci su nave in tempo di guerra).

navigability [,nævigə'biliti], *s.* navigabilità.

navigable ['nævigəbl], *ag.* navigabile: *the ship was not in a — condition*, la nave non era in condizioni di poter tenere il mare.

navigableness ['nævigəblnis], *s.* navigabilità.

to **navigate** ['nævigeit], *v.t.i.* **1.** navigare; veleggiare **2.** regolare la rotta di (nave o aeroplano).

navigation [,nævi'geiʃən], *s.* **1.** navigazione ‖ *navigation act*, (*st.*) atto di navigazione **2.** rotta ☆ — *company*, compagnia di navigazione; — *lights*, (*aer. mar.*) fanali di via; — *officier*, ufficiale di rotta; — *school*, istituto nautico ‖ *air —*, navigazione aerea; *inland —*, navigazione interna; *pressure —*, (*aer.*) navigazione barometrica; *river —*, navigazione fluviale.

navigator ['nævigeitə*], *s.* **1.** navigatore; ufficiale di rotta **2.** (*rar.*) sterratore ☆ — *'s compartment*, (*aer.*) cabina di navigazione.

navvy ['nævi], *s.* sterratore.

navy ['neivi], *s.* **1.** (*poet.*) flotta **2.** marina da guerra: *the Royal Navy*, la marina da guerra inglese ☆ — *blue*, blu marina; — *board*, consiglio d'ammiragliato della marina; — *league*, lega navale; — *list*, lista degli ufficiali, ecc. di marina; — *yard*, (*amer.*) arsenale.

nawab [nə'wɑːb], *s.* vicerè indiano; nababbo (anche *fig.*).

nay [nei], *av.* **1.** (*arc.*) no **2.** anzi, non solo; di più; inoltre, anche: *it was beautiful, — wonderful*, era bello, anzi meraviglioso.

nay, *s.* no; rifiuto; diniego: *yea and —*, incertezza, indecisione; *to say s.o. —*, negare ql.co. a qlcu.; contraddire qlcu.

Nazarene [,næzə'riːn], *ag.s.* nazzareno ‖ *the —*, il Nazzareno, Gesù.

Nazareth ['næzəriθ], *no.pr.* (*geog.*) Nazaret.

Nazarite[1] ['næzərait], *s.c.* nazzareno, nazzarena.

Nazarite[2], *s.* ebreo che ha pronunciato voti di astinenza.

naze [neiz], *s.* promontorio, capo.

Nazi ['nɑːtsi], *ag.s.c.* nazista.

ne [nei], *av.* (*arc.*) non.

neap[1] [niːp], *ag.* minimo (di marea) ‖ *s.* bassa marea.

to **neap**[1], *v.t.i.* abbassarsi (della marea) ‖ *to be neaped*, non poter prendere il largo per la bassa marea.

neap[2], *s.* **1.** (*amer.*) stanga di un carro **2.** supporto per la stanga di un veicolo.

Neapolitan [niə'pɔlitən], *ag.* napoletano ‖ *s.c.* napoletano, napoletana ☆ — *ice-cream*, cassata.

near [niə*], *ag.* **1.** vicino, prossimo; imminente: *a — miss*, un colpo mancato per un pelo; *in the — distance*, (anche *mil.*) in primo piano; *he has made a — guess*, ha quasi indovinato ‖ *the Near East*, il Levante ‖ *he was almost killed, it was a — thing !*, fu quasi ucciso, l'ha scampata bella! **2.** affine; intimo, stretto: *a — race*, una razza affine; — *relations*, parenti stretti; *a — resemblance*, una notevole rassomiglianza ‖ *our — and dear*, i nostri cari **3.** fedele, esatto: *a — translation*, una traduzione fedele; *a — work*, un lavoro delicato, di precisione **4.** economo; avaro, tirchio: *she is rather — with her money*, è piuttosto tirchia col suo denaro **5.** breve: *the nearest road*, la strada più breve **6.** di, a sinistra (del traffico in Inghilterra): *the — wheel*, la ruota di sinistra; *to keep the — side*, tenere la sinistra ☆ — -sighted, miope; — -sightedness, miopia.

near, av. **1. vicino, presso:** *he came — to doing* (o *to do*) *it,* fu sul punto di farlo; *he came, drew — to me,* mi si avvicinò; *it was very — to Easter,* si era sotto Pasqua ‖ — *at hand,* a portata di mano; vicinissimo ‖ — *by,* non lontano **2. quasi, circa:** *it lasted — one month,* durò circa un mese ‖ *prep.* **vicino a, presso a:** *come — me,* vienimi vicino; *he came — doing it,* fu sul punto di farlo; *he has a house — the lake,* ha una casa vicino al lago; *sit down — her,* siediti vicino a lei.

to **near,** v.t.i. avvicinare, avvicinarsi; approssimarsi: *the storm nears,* il temporale si avvicina; *they were nearing the land,* si avvicinavano alla terra.

nearby ['niəbai], ag.av.prep. assai vicino.

nearly ['niəli], av. **1. quasi:** — *always,* quasi sempre; *not* —, affatto, tutt'altro che; *it's — ten o'clock,* sono quasi le dieci **2. strettamente; da vicino:** *the matter concerns me* —, la faccenda mi riguarda da vicino; — *related to,* stretto parente di.

nearness ['niənis], s. **1. vicinanza, prossimità; intimità:** — *of relationship,* parentela stretta **2. fedeltà, esattezza** (di traduzioni) **3. parsimonia, economia.**

neat[1] [ni:t], ag. **1. pulito, lindo; ordinato:** *a — room,* una stanza linda, bene ordinata **2. grazioso, armonioso:** *she has a very — figure,* ha una figura armoniosa, molto graziosa **3. semplice, di buon gusto:** *a — dress,* un abito semplice, di buon gusto **4. chiaro; conciso, acuto, epigrammatico** (di pensiero, stile, ecc.): *she gave a very — answer,* diede una risposta veramente acuta **5. puro, non diluito** (di bevande alcooliche): — *vermouth, whisky,* vermouth, whisky liscio, senza seltz **6. abile, destro 7. accurato** ☆ — *-handed,* svelto.

neat[2], s.(invariato al pl.) **1.** (rar.) bovino **2.** coll. bovini ☆ — *-herd,* bovaro; — *-house,* stalla per bovini; — *'s leather,* vacchetta.

neath [ni:θ], prep. (poet.) sotto, al di sotto di.

neatly ['ni:tli], av. **1. lindamente, ordinatamente 2. graziosamente, armoniosamente 3. con semplicità, buon gusto 4. concisamente, acutamente 5. abilmente, destramente 6. accuratamente.**

neatness ['ni:tnis], s. **1. pulizia, ordine 2. grazia, armonia, eleganza 3. semplicità, buon gusto 4. chiarezza, concisione, acutezza 5. abilità, destrezza 6. accuratezza.**

neb [neb], s. (scoz.) **1. naso 2. becco 3. beccuccio** (di teiera, ecc.) **4. punta** (di penna, matita).

Nebuchadnezzar [ˌnebjukəd'nezə*], no.pr.m. (st.) Nabucodonosor.

nebula ['nebjulə], pl. **nebulae** ['nebjuli:], s. (astr.) nebulosa.

nebular ['nebjulə*], ag. (astr.) nebulare ☆ — *hypothesis, (astr.)* ipotesi nebulare.

nebulosity [ˌnebju'lositi], s. nebulosità.

nebulous ['nebjuləs], ag. **1.** (astr.) nebulare **2. nuvoloso 3.** fig. nebuloso, vago, indistinto.

nebulousness ['nebjuləsnis], s. nebulosità.

necessarian [ˌnesi'sɛəriən], ag.s. (fil.) determinista.

necessarianism [ˌnesi'sɛəriənizəm], s. (fil.) determinismo.

necessarily ['nesisərili], av. necessariamente.

necessary ['nesisəri], ag. **1. necessario, indispensabile:** *it is — for him to come here,* è necessario che egli venga qui; *it is — that you should obey him,* voi dovete ubbidirgli; *not to do more than is absolutely* —, non fare che lo stretto necessario; *to make it — for s.o. to do sthg.,* mettere qlcu. nella necessità di fare ql.co. **2. essenziale:** *water is — for life,* l'acqua è un elemento essenziale per vivere **3. inevitabile:** *war seems to be a — evil in this world,* sembra che la guerra sia un male inevitabile di questo mondo ‖ s. gener. pl. il necessario; cosa necessaria, necessità: *the necessaries of life,* il necessario per vivere ‖ *to do the* —, (sl.) pagare il conto ‖ *to find, to provide the* —, (sl.) trovare, provvedere il denaro necessario.

necessitarian [niˌsesi'tɛəriən], ag.s. (fil.) determinista.

necessitarianism [niˌsesi'tɛəriənizəm], s. (fil.) determinismo.

to **necessitate** [ni'sesiteit], v.t. **1. rendere necessario:** *the increase in population necessitates a greater food supply,* l'aumento di popolazione richiede un maggior rifornimento di viveri **2.** (rar.) costringere.

necessitous [ni'sesitəs], ag. povero, bisognoso, indigente: *to be in — circumstances,* essere nell'indigenza, in strettezze.

necessitously [ni'sesitəsli], av. poveramente; in modo miserabile.

necessitousness [ni'sesitəsnis], s. miseria, indigenza; necessità, bisogno; penuria.

necessity [ni'sesiti], s. **1. necessità:** *a — of life,* una necessità della vita; *by* (o *from* o *out of*) —, per necessità, per forza di cose: *to do sthg. out of* —, fare ql.co. per necessità; *case of absolute* —, caso di forza maggiore; *there was no — for you to treat him so cruelly,* non era necessario che tu lo trattassi così duramente; *to be under the — of doing sthg.,* essere costretti a fare ql.co. ‖ *doctrine of* —, (fil.) determinismo ‖ *of* —, necessariamente, inevitabilmente ‖ — *is the mother of invention,* prov. la necessità è il miglior maestro ‖ — *knows no law,* prov. la necessità non ha legge ‖ *to make a virtue of* —, prov. fare di necessità virtù **2. bisogno assoluto, urgenza:** *the doctor asked us not to call him except in case of* —, il dottore ci pregò di non chiamarlo tranne in caso di urgenza **3. cosa necessaria, indispensabile:** *food and warmth are necessities,* il cibo e il calore sono indispensabili **4. miseria, indigenza, bisogno, povertà:** *to be in* —, essere in povertà, miseria.

neck [nek], s. **1. collo:** *to break one's* —, rompersi il collo; *to risk one's* —, rischiare la vita; *to save one's* —, salvarsi dal capestro; *fig.* salvar la pelle; *to win by a* —, *(ippica)* vincere per un'incollatura ‖ — *and crop,* a capofitto, completamente ‖ — *and* —, uguali, testa a testa (in una corsa di cavalli) ‖ — *or nothing,* tutto per tutto ‖ *to be up to one's — in work,* essere soffocato dal lavoro ‖ *to get it in the* —, (sl.) ricevere un duro colpo **2. collo di bottiglia 3.** (mec. metal. rad.) collo **4.** (aer.) manica, appendice tubolare **5.** (geol.) « neck », diatrema, canale di esplosione (di vulcano) **6.** (geog.) istmo; lingua (di terra); gola (di montagna); braccio (di mare) **7.** (arch.) fregio (di colonna) ☆ — *-band,* collaretto, listino del collo (di camicia); colletto a giro ‖ *stiff* —, torcicollo; fig. ostinazione.

to **neck,** v.t.i. **1. colpire al collo** (per tramortire, uccidere); decapitare **2.** (sl. amer.) sbaciucchiare, sbaciucchiarsi.

necked [nekt], ag. dal collo ☆ *bull- —,* dal collo taurino; *high- —, low- —,* dal collo alto, basso; *stiff- —,* fig. ostinato.

neckerchief ['nekətʃif], s. fazzoletto da collo.

necking ['nekiŋ], s. **1.** (arch.) collarino **2.** (sl. amer.) lo sbaciucchiarsi.

necklace ['neklis], s. collana, vezzo.

necklet ['neklit], s. **1. collo, colletto di pelliccia,** di stoffa **2.** (amer.) collana.

neckline ['neklain], s. scollatura: *long* —, scollatura pronunciata.

necktie ['nek-tai], s. cravatta ☆ — *party,* (sl. amer.) impiccagione.

neckwear ['nek-wɛə*], s. colletti, cravatte, ecc.

necrologic(al) [ˌnekrou'lodʒik(ə)l], ag. necrologico.

necrologist [ne'krolədʒist], s. necrologista.

necrology [ne'krolədʒi], s. **1. necrologia 2. necrologio.**

necromancer ['nekroumænsə*], s.c. chi esercita la negromanzia.

necromancy ['nekroumænsi], s. negromanzia.

necromantic [ˌnekrou'mæntik], ag. negromantico.

necrophilism [neˈkrɔfilizəm], s. (patol.) necrofilia.
necrophobia [ˌnekrouˈfoubiə], s. necrofobia.
necrophorus [neˈkrɔfərəs], s. (entom.) necroforo.
necropolis [neˈkrɔpəlis], s. necropoli.
necropsy [neˈkrɔpsi], s. necroscopia.
necroscopic(al) [ˌnekrouˈskɔpik(əl)], ag. necroscopico.
necroscopy [neˈkrɔskəpi], s. necroscopia.
necrosis [neˈkrousis], s. (patol.) necrosi, cancrena.
necrotic [neˈkrɔtik], ag. (patol.) necrotico.
nectar [ˈnektə*], s. (bot. mit.) nettare.
nectarean [nekˈtɛəriən], ag. nettareo.
nectared [ˈnektəd], ag. imbevuto di nettare.
nectareous [nekˈtɛəriəs], ag. nettareo.
nectarium [nekˈtɛəriəm], pl. **nectaria** [nekˈtɛəriə], s. proboscide (di insetti).
nectary [ˈnektəri], s. 1. (bot.) nettario 2. proboscide (di insetti).
Ned [ned], no.pr.m. dim. di **Edmund, Edward.**
Neddy [ˈnedi], no.pr.m. dim. di **Edmund, Edward** ‖ s. (fam.) asino, somaro.
née [nei], ag. nata, per nascita: Mrs. Brown, — Whyle, la signora Brown, nata Whyle.
need [ni:d], s. 1. necessità, bisogno: there is no — to do so, non c'è bisogno di fare così; what have you — of?, di che cosa avete bisogno? ‖ if — be, se c'è bisogno, necessità; if — were, se ci fosse la necessità ‖ a friend in — is a friend indeed, prov. nel bisogno si conoscono gli amici 2. il necessario; esigenza: he attends to his father's needs, egli provvede alle necessità di suo padre; his needs are few, egli non ha molte esigenze 3. miseria, indigenza, povertà.
to need, v.t.i. (costruzione pers.) 1. (seguito da inf.) essere obbligato; essere necessario, occorrere: does he — to work so hard?, è necessario che lavori così tanto?; she doesn't — to wait, non occorre che ella aspetti; we didn't — to hurry, non occorreva che ci affrettassimo (e non ci siamo affrettati) 2. (seguito da compl. oggetto, gerundio o inf. passivo) aver bisogno di, abbisognare di; richiedere, occorrere: she needs a hundred pounds, le occorrono cento sterline; this floor needs cleaning (o to be cleaned), questo pavimento ha bisogno di una pulita 3. essere nel bisogno ‖ need, v. dif. (V) (pres. negativo forma contratta: **needn't** [ˈni:dnt]; costruzione pers.; è usato generalmente in frasi interrogative e negative seguito da inf.) essere obbligato; essere necessario; occorrere: — he work so hard?, è necessario che lavori così tanto?; she — not wait, non occorre che ella aspetti; we — not have hurried, non occorreva che ci affrettassimo (e invece ci siamo affrettati)
needful [ˈni:dful], ag. 1. necessario, indispensabile 2. (rar.) bisognoso ‖ the —, il necessario; (sl.) il denaro (occorrente); to do the —, fare il necessario; (calcio) segnare (conducendo a termine un'azione).
needfully [ˈni:dfuli], av. necessariamente.
needfulness [ˈni:dfulnis], s. necessità, bisogno.
needily [ˈni:dili], av. (arc.) poveramente, in grande necessità.
neediness [ˈni:dinis], s. bisogno; povertà, indigenza.
needle [ˈni:dl], s. 1. ago (da cucire, chirurgico, magnetico, di pino, ecc.) ‖ needles and pins, formicolio ‖ it's like looking for a — in a bottle of hay, è come cercare un ago in un pagliaio ‖ she is as sharp as a —, è arguta e intelligente ‖ to have the needle, (sl.) avere una crisi di nervi 2. puntina di grammofono 3. obelisco; picco roccioso 4. cristallo a forma d'ago ☆ — -bath, doccia filiforme; — -book, porta aghi; — -case, agoraio; — -craft, arte del ricamo; —'s eye, cruna dell'ago: as small as a —'s eye, piccolo come la cruna di un ago; — -fish, (ittiol.) aguglia; — -gun, fucile ad ago ‖ compass- —, ago di bussola; crochet- —, uncinetto; darning - —, ago da rammendo; knitting- —, ferro da calza; packing- —, ago da imballaggio.
to needle, v.t.i. 1. cucire; pungere (con ago) 2. irritare; provocare; punzecchiare 3. cristallizzarsi in aghi 4. (sl. amer.) rafforzare (aggiungendo alcool).

needleful [ˈni:dlful], s. gugliata.
needless [ˈni:dlis], ag. inutile, superfluo.
needlessly [ˈni:dlisli], av. senza necessità.
needlessness [ˈni:dlisnis], s. superfluità, inutilità.
needlewoman [ˈni:dlˌwumən], **needlewomen** [ˈni:dlˌwimin], s. cucitrice.
needlework [ˈni:dlwə:k], s. lavoro ad ago.
needn't [ˈni:dnt], contr. di **need not.**
needs [ni:dz], av. (si usa soltanto prima e dopo must come rafforzativo) necessariamente; assolutamente: I must — go, devo andare assolutamente.
needy [ˈni:di], ag. povero, indigente, bisognoso.
ne'er [nɛə*], av. (contr. poet. di never) mai ☆ a — -do-well, un buono a nulla.
nefandous [niˈfændəs], ag. nefando; infame.
nefarious [niˈfɛəriəs], ag. nefasto; scellerato; atroce.
nefariously [niˈfɛəriəsli], av. atrocemente.
nefariousness [niˈfɛəriəsnis], s. nefandezza; atrocità.
to negate [niˈgeit], v.t. 1. negare 2. annullare.
negation [niˈgeiʃən], s. 1. negazione 2. (gram.) proposizione negativa.
negationist [niˈgeiʃənist], s. negatore.
negative [ˈnegətiv], ag. negativo: — evidence, testimonianza negativa; — numbers, (alg.) numeri negativi; — quantity, (alg.) quantità negativa; — pole, (elett.) polo negativo ‖ s. 1. negazione: he returned us a —, ci rispose di no; nay is a —, no è una negazione; two negatives make an affirmative, due negazioni affermano 2. qualità negativa, mancanza: his character is made up of negatives, il suo carattere è pieno di qualità negative 3. diritto di veto 4. (foto.) negativa.
to negative, v.t. 1. rifiutare, negare; respingere 2. provare il contrario di 3. neutralizzare.
negatively [ˈnegətivli], av. negativamente.
negativeness [ˈnegətivnis], s. l'essere negativo.
neglect [niˈglekt], s. 1. trascuratezza, negligenza: out of — (o from — o through —), per negligenza 2. dimenticanza.
to neglect, v.t. (II) trascurare; disdegnare; tralasciare: he neglects looking after such details, egli disdegna di occuparsi di tali particolari.
neglectable [niˈglektəbl], ag. trascurabile.
neglectedness [niˈglektidnis], s. trascuratezza.
neglecter [niˈglektə*], s. negligente; trascurato.
neglectful [niˈglektful], ag. negligente; noncurante.
neglectfully [niˈglektfuli], av. negligentemente.
neglectfulness [niˈglektfulnis], s. negligenza, noncuranza.
negligence [ˈneglidʒəns], s. negligenza; trascuratezza; indifferenza.
negligent [ˈneglidʒənt], ag. negligente; trascurato; indifferente.
negligently [ˈneglidʒəntli], av. negligentemente; indifferentemente.
negligible [ˈneglidʒəbl], ag. trascurabile.
negligibly [ˈneglidʒəbli], av. in modo trascurabile.
negotiability [niˌgouʃjəˈbiliti], s. (comm.) negoziabilità.
negotiable [niˈgouʃjəbl], ag. (comm.) negoziabile.
negotiant [niˈgouʃiənt], s. (rar.) negoziatore.
to negotiate [niˈgouʃieit], v.t.i. 1. negoziare, trattare; commerciare: to be allowed to — with foreigners, avere il permesso di commerciare con stranieri 2. (sl.) superare, passare: he could not — that difficult climb, non potè superare quella difficile scalata.
negotiation [niˌgouʃiˈeiʃən], s. trattativa.
negotiator [niˈgouʃieitə*], s. (rar.) negoziatore.
negotiatress [niˈgouʃiətris], **negotiatrix** [niˈgouʃiətriks], s. negoziatrice.
negress [ˈni:gris], s. negra.
negrillo [neˈgrilou], s. negrillo.
negrito [neˈgri:tou], s. negrito.
negro [ˈni:grou], pl. **negroes** [ˈni:grouz], ag.s. negro, moro ☆ — ant, (entom.) formica nera; — minstrels,

suonatori, cantanti negri; — *spirituals*, canti religiosi dei negri d'America.

negrohead ['ni:grou-hed], *s.* 1. tabacco forte 2. gomma scadente.

negroid ['ni:grɔid], *ag.* negroide.

Negus¹ ['ni:gəs], *s.* negus, imperatore d'Etiopia.

negus², *s.* bevanda calda di acqua, vino e zucchero.

Nehemiah [,ni:i'maiə], *no.pr.m.* (*Bibbia*) Neemia.

neigh [nei], *s.* nitrito.

to **neigh**, *v.i.* nitrire.

neighbour ['neibə*], *s.* vicino; prossimo: *his — at table*, il suo vicino di tavola; *I think he does not love his — enough*, credo che egli non ami abbastanza il suo prossimo; *is she a good — to you?*, è una buona vicina per voi?; *a lady, a — of mine, told me*, una signora, mia vicina, mi disse ☆ *next-door —*, il vicino della casa accanto.

to **neighbour**, *v.t.i.* 1. essere vicini di casa; essere in rapporti di buon vicinato 2. essere contiguo (a) (di terreno) 3. avvicinare.

neighbourhood ['neibəhud], *s.* 1. i vicini; vicinato 2. paraggi, dintorni; vicinanza: *everybody in the — knows him*, nei dintorni lo conoscono tutti || *in the —*, (*fam.*) circa: *in the — of fifteen pounds, of forty miles*, circa 15 sterline, 40 miglia.

neighbouring ['neibəriŋ], *ag.* vicino, contiguo.

neighbourliness ['neibəlinis], *s.* socievolezza, cortesia, cordialità.

neighbourly ['neibəli], *ag.* da buon vicino; cordiale, gentile, socievole || *av.* da buon vicino; gentilmente, socievolmente.

neighbourship ['neibəʃip], *s.* vicinanza; rapporti di buon vicinato.

neither ['naiðə*, 'ni:ðə*], *ag.* nè l'uno nè l'altro: *— performance was interesting*, nè l'una nè l'altra rappresentazione furono interessanti || *pron.* nè l'uno nè l'altro; nessuno (tra due): *— of them knows about it*, nè l'uno nè l'altro (di loro) lo sa.

neither, *av.* (*seguito da* nor) nè: *— I nor he is American*, nè io nè lui siamo Americani; *he is — intelligent, nor good*, non è nè intelligente, nè buono || *cong.* **neppure, nemmeno**: " *I don't know* ", " *— do I* ", « Non lo so », « Neppure io »; *if she doesn't come, — shall I*, se ella non viene, non verrò neppure io; *you know not, — can you guess*, (*arc.*) non sapete, e nemmeno potete indovinarlo.

nekton ['nekton], *s.* necton.

Nellie, Nelly ['neli], *no.pr.f.* dim. di **Ellen, Eleanor**.

nelly ['neli], *s.* (*ornit.*) grande procellaria.

nelumbium [ni'lʌmbiəm], *s.* (*bot.*) nelumbio.

Nemathelminthes [,neməθel'minθi:z], *s. pl.* (*zool.*) i nematelminti.

Nemesis ['nemisis], *no.pr.f.* (*mit.*) Nemesi (dea della vendetta) || **nemesis**, *pl.* **nemeses** ['nemisi:z], *s.* nemesi.

nemoral ['nemərəl], *ag.* boschereccio.

nenuphar ['nenjufa:*], *s.* (*bot.*) ninfea.

neodymium [,ni(:)ou'dimiəm], *s.* (*chim.*) neodimio.

neolithic [,ni(:)ou'liθik], *ag.* (*geol.*) neolitico.

neologian [,ni(:)ou'loudʒjən], *s.* neologo.

neologism [ni(:)'ɔlədʒizəm], *s.* neologismo.

to **neologize** [ni(:)'ɔlədʒaiz], *v.i.* coniare, introdurre neologismi.

neology [ni(:)'ɔlədʒi], *s.* neologia.

neon ['ni:ən], *s.* (*chim.*) neon ☆ *— lights*, luci al neon; *— signs*, insegne al neon.

neophron ['ni(:)oufron], *s.* avvoltoio bianco egiziano.

neophyte ['ni(:)oufait], *s.* neofito.

neoplasm ['ni(:)ouplæzəm], *s.* (*patol.*) neoplasma.

neoplastic [,ni(:)ou'plæstik], *ag.* (*patol.*) neoplastico.

neoplasty ['ni(:)ou,plæsti], *s.* chirurgia plastica.

Neoplatonic [,ni(:)ouplə'tɔnik], *ag.* (*fil.*) neoplatonico.

Neoplatonism [,ni(:)ou'pleitənizəm], *s.* (*fil.*) neoplatonismo.

Neoplatonist [,ni(:)ou'pleitənist], *s.* (*fil.*) neoplatonico.

neoprene ['ni(:)oupri:n], *s.* (*neol. chim.*) neoprene.

neoteric [,ni(:)ou'terik], *ag.s.* neoterico.

neozoic [,ni(:)ou'zouik], *ag.* (*geol.*) neozoico.

Nepal [ni'pɔ:l], *no.pr.* (*geog.*) Nepal.

Nepalese [,nepo:'li:z], *ag.s.c.* nepalese.

nepenthe [ne'penθi], **nepenthes** [ne'penθi:z], *s.* (*mit. bot.*) nepente.

nephew ['nevju(:)], *s.* nipote, nipotino (di zio).

nephology [ne'fɔlədʒi], *s.* studio delle nubi.

nephritic [ni'fritik], *ag.* (*patol.*) nefritico.

nephritis [ne'fraitis], *s.* (*patol.*) nefrite.

nepotic [ni'pɔtik], *ag.* nepotistico.

nepotism ['nepotizəm], *s.* nepotismo.

nepotist ['nepotist], *s.* nepotista.

Neptune ['neptju:n], *no.pr.m.* (*mit. astr.*) Nettuno.

Neptunian [nep'tju:njən], *ag.* (*mit. astr. geol.*) nettuniano.

neptunium [nep'tju:njəm], *s.* (*chim.*) nettunio.

Nereid ['niəriid], *s.* (*mit.*) Nereide || **nereid**, *s.* (*zool.*) nereide.

Nereus ['niərju:s], *no.pr.m.* (*mit.*) Nereo.

Nero ['niərou], *no.pr.m.* (*st.*) Nerone.

nervate ['nə:veit], *ag.* (*bot.*) nervato.

nervation [nə:'veiʃən], *s.* (*bot.*) nervatura.

nerve [nə:v], *s.* 1. (*anat.*) nervo; (*poet.*) tendine: *he has got steel nerves*, ha dei nervi di acciaio; *she had a fit of nerves*, ebbe una crisi di nervi; *that difficult work strained his nerves*, quel difficile lavoro lo esaurì; *that girl gets on my nerves*, quella ragazza mi dà sui nervi; *to strain every —, fig.* fare ogni sforzo possibile || *war of nerves*, guerra psicologica 2. (*bot. zool.*) nervatura 3. forza, energia; sangue freddo: *a man of —*, un uomo coraggioso; *to lose one's —*, perdere il proprio sangue freddo 4. (*fam.*) sfrontatezza, audacia ☆ *— -cell*, neurone; *— -centre*, centro nervoso; *— pain*, nevralgia; *— -racking*, irritante, esasperante; *— -specialist*, neurologo.

to **nerve**, *v.t.* 1. tonificare, rinvigorire 2. *fig.* incoraggiare: *to — oneself*, farsi coraggio, riprendersi.

nerved [nə:vd], *ag.* 1. (*bot.*) nervato 2. rinvigorito

nerveless [nə:'vlis], *ag.* 1. snervato, inerte, indolente, fiacco 2. prolisso (di stile) 3. (*bot.*) senza nervature 4. (*anat. zool.*) senza nervi.

nervelessness ['nə:vlisnis], *s.* snervatezza.

nervine ['nə:vi:n], *ag.s.* (*farm.*) nervino.

nervous ['nə:vəs], *ag.* 1. nervoso, di nervi 2. forte, vigoroso, nerboruto; conciso (di stile) 3. nervoso, agitato; timido, apprensivo: *I must own that I felt rather —*, devo ammettere che mi sentivo alquanto agitato ☆ *— breakdown*, esaurimento nervoso; *— prostration*, (*patol.*) nevrastenia; *— system*, (*anat.*) sistema nervoso.

nervously ['nə:vəsli], *av.* 1. nervosamente 2. timidamente.

nervousness ['nə:vəsnis], *s.* 1. nervosismo, irritabilità, stato di agitazione 2. timidezza.

nervure ['nə:vjuə*], *s.* (*bot. zool.*) nervatura.

nervy ['nə:vi], *ag.* 1. (*poet.*) muscoloso, forte 2. (*sl.*) isterico; nervoso: *I was feeling —*, mi sentivo i nervi scoperti 3. (*sl.*) sfacciato, impudente: *I would call that — on his side*, la riterrei una bella sfacciataggine da parte sua.

nescience ['nesiəns], *s.* nescienza, ignoranza.

nescient ['nesiənt], *ag.s.* 1. ignorante 2. agnostico.

ness [nes], *s.* promontorio; capo.

nest [nest], *s.* 1. nido; covo 2. *fig.* covo, tana: *they fell into a — of spies*, caddero in un covo di spie 3. casa; letto: *to foul one's own —*, parlar male della propria casa || *she feathered her —*, si fece un bel gruzzolo con mezzi poco onesti 4. colonia di uccelli, insetti, ecc. 5. serie di oggetti in scala di grandezza che possono essere contenuti uno nell'altro: *— of tables*, tavolini tipo cicogna 6. (*mar.*) coffa 7. (*mec.*) gruppo compatto 8. (*min. geol.*) tasca ☆ *— -egg*, nidiandolo (uovo lasciato nel nido per richiamo alle galline); *fig.* richiamo, esca; somma di denaro messa da parte per il futuro.

to **nest**, *v.t.i.* 1. fare il nido, nidificare: *the swallows* *nested under my roof*, le rondini nidificarono sotto il mio tetto **2.** inserire l'uno nell'altro: *nested boxes*, scatole inserite l'una nell'altra.

   to **nestle** ['nesl], *v.t.i.* **1.** annidarsi, stabilirsi: *they nestled in a little villa*, si stabilirono in una villetta **2.** rifugiarsi, accoccolarsi: *she nestled among the cushions*, ella si accoccolò tra i cuscini **3.** stringersi affettuosamente a, nascondere (il viso, la testa): *the child nestled his face against his mother's shoulders*, il bimbo nascose il viso contro la spalla di sua madre.

   nestling ['neslin], *s.* uccellino di nido.

   Nestor ['nestɔ:*], *no.pr.m.* (*lett.*) Nestore ‖ *s.* vecchio saggio.

   net¹ [net], *ag.* netto: — *price*, prezzo netto; — *profit*, guadagno netto; — *weight*, peso netto.

   net², *s.* **1.** rete: *to spread a —*, tendere la rete **2.** *fig.* laccio, trappola: *to be caught in the —*, essere preso in trappola **3.** (*ferr. rad. tel.*) rete **4.** pizzo, tulle ☆ — *fishing*, pesca con la rete; — *-play*, (tennis) giuoco a rete ‖ *Brussels —*, pizzo di Bruxelles; *butterfly- —*, rete da farfalle; *fishing- —*, rete da pesca; *game —*, rete da caccia; *hair- —*, retina per capelli.

   to **net**², *pass.p.p.* **netted** ['netid], *v.t.i.* **1.** coprire con reti, cintare con reti **2.** catturare con reti; pescare con rete **3.** lavorare a rete; fare reti **4.** mandar (la palla) in rete.

   netful ['netful], *s.* retata.

   nether ['neðə*], *ag.* (*arc. o scherz.*) più basso, inferiore ‖ *the — person*, le gambe ‖ *the — world*, l'inferno.

   Netherlander ['neðələndə*], *s.c.* abitante dei Paesi Bassi.

   Netherlandish ['neðə,lændiʃ], *ag.* dei Paesi Bassi.

   Netherlands ['neðələndz], *no.pr.pl.* (*geog.*) Paesi Bassi.

   nethermost ['neðəmoust], *ag.* il più basso.

   netting ['netin], *s.* reticella (di maglia, spago); reticolato.

   nettle ['netl], *s.* (*bot.*) ortica.

   to **nettle**, *v.t.* **1.** pungere (di ortica); orticheggiare: *her hands were badly nettled*, le sue mani erano tutte punte dalle ortiche **2.** *fig.* ferire: *he was nettled at her remark*, si sentì punto sul vivo alla sua osservazione.

   nettlerash ['netlræʃ], *s.* (*patol.*) orticaria.

   network ['net-wə:k], *s.* **1.** rete; reticolato **2.** (*neol. rad.*) rete.

   neume [nju:m], *s.* (*mus.*) neuma.

   neural ['njuərəl], *ag.* (*anat.*) neurale.

   neuralgia [njuə'rældʒə], *s.* (*patol.*) nevralgia.

   neuralgic [njuə'rældʒik], *ag.* (*patol.*) nevralgico.

   neurasthenia [,njuərəs'θi:njə], *s.* (*patol.*) neurastenia, nevrastenia.

   neurasthenic [,njuərəs'θenik], *ag.* nevrastenico.

   neurasthenically [,njuərəs'θenikəli], *av.* da nevrastenico.

   neurine ['njuərain], *s.* (*anat.*) tessuto nervoso.

   neuritis [njuə'raitis], *s.* (*patol.*) nevrite.

   neurological [,njuərə'lɔdʒikəl], *ag.* (*med.*) neurologico.

   neurologist [njuə'rɔlədʒist], *s.* (*med.*) neurologo.

   neurology [njuə'rɔlədʒi], *s.* (*med.*) neurologia.

   neuron ['njuərɔn], *s.* (*fisiol.*) neurone.

   neuropath ['njuərəpæθ], *s.c.* (*patol.*) neuropatico, neuropatica.

   neuropathist [njuə'rɔpəθist], *s.* (*med.*) neurologo.

   neuropathology [,njuərəpə'θɔlədʒi], *s.* (*med.*) neuropatologia.

   neuropathy [njuə'rɔpəθi], *s.* (*patol.*) neuropatia.

   neurosis [njuə'rousis], *s.* (*patol.*) neurosi, nevrosi ☆ *cardiac —*, nevrosi cardiaca.

   neurotic [njuə'rɔtik], *ag.* nervoso; neuropatico ‖ *s.* neurotico; neuropatico.

   neurotically [njuə'rɔtikəli], *av.* da neuropatico.

   neuter ['nju:tə*], *ag.* **1.** (*gram.*) neutro; intransitivo (di verbo) **2.** (*rar.*) neutrale: *he stood —*, egli era

neutrale **3.** (*bot. entom.*) neutro ‖ *s.* **1.** parola neutra; neutro **2.** persona neutrale **3.** animale castrato; insetto femmina sessualmente non sviluppato.

   neutral ['nju:trəl], *ag.* **1.** neutrale: *Brazil was —*, il Brasile era neutrale **2.** neutro, indeterminato: — *tint*, tinta neutra; *he is a — sort of person*, egli è un essere insignificante ‖ *s.* stato, persona neutrale.

   neutralist ['nju:trəlist], *s.* neutralista.

   neutrality [nju(:)'træliti], *s.* neutralità.

   neutralization [,nju:trəlai'zeiʃən], *s.* neutralizzazione.

   to **neutralize** ['nju:trəlaiz], *v.t.* **1.** neutralizzare; render vano; annullare **2.** dichiarare neutrale.

   neutralizer ['nju:trəlaizə*], *s.* neutralizzatore.

   neutrally ['nju:trəli], *av.* in modo neutrale.

   neutron ['nju:trɔn], *s.* (*fis.*) neutrone.

   névé ['neivei], *s.* nevaio.

   never ['nevə*], *av.* **1.** mai, giammai: *I have — read such an exciting book*, non ho mai letto un libro così emozionante; *you — shut the door when you go out*, non chiudi mai la porta quando esci ‖ — *a*, nessuno, neppure uno: *he answered — a word*, non rispose parola alcuna ‖ — *again* (o *more*), mai più ‖ — *mind!*, non importa! ‖ *now or —*, adesso o mai più ‖ *well, I —!*, non l'avrei mai immaginato! ‖ — *is a long day*, prima di dire « mai », pensaci! **2.** — *!*, (*fam.*) non può essere: " *He has already left* ", " — *!* ", « È già partito! », « Non può essere! » ☆ — *-ending*, eterno, senza fine: *ours is — -ending job*, il nostro è un lavoro senza fine.

   nevermore ['nevə'mɔ:*], *av.* mai più.

   nevertheless [,nevəðə'les], *av. cong.* tuttavia, nonostante, ciò nondimeno: *the boy was punished, — he did not repent*, il ragazzo fu punito, tuttavia non si pentì.

   Nevill(e) ['nevil], *no.pr.m.* Neville.

   new [nju:], *ag.* nuovo, novello, recente: — *potatoes, wine, cheese*, patate novelle, vino nuovo, formaggio fresco; *he was a — boy in the school*, era un allievo nuovo nella scuola; *he will lead a — life*, condurrà una nuova vita; *I am — to this kind of work*, sono nuovo a questo genere di lavoro ‖ *the — learning*, (*st. lett.*) il Rinascimento ‖ *New Testament*, Nuovo Testamento ‖ *the New World*, il Nuovo Mondo ‖ *New Year*, l'anno nuovo; *New Year's Day*, Capodanno; *New Year's Eve*, il 31 dicembre ☆ — *chums*, emigranti appena arrivati in Australia; — *moon*, luna nuova; *the — woman*, la donna moderna ‖ *brand —*, nuovo di zecca; *ever —*, sempre nuovo, sempre rinnovantesi.

   new, *av.* recentemente; appena; or ora ☆ — *-blown*, appena sbocciato; — *-born*, neonato; — *-built*, appena costruito; — *-come*, appena arrivato; — *-comer*, nuovo venuto; — *-fashioned*, all'ultima moda; — *-laid eggs*, uova fresche; — *-made*, appena fatto; — *-married*, appena sposato.

   New Caledonia ['nju:,kæli'dounjə], *no.pr.* (*geog.*) Nuova Caledonia.

   Newcastle ['nju:,ka:sl], *no.pr.* (*geog.*) Newcastle ‖ *to carry coals to —*, portare acqua al mare.

   newel ['nju:(:)əl], *s.* colonna (su cui poggia una scala a chiocciola); pilastro (ad inizio di scala).

   New England [nju:'inglənd], *no.pr.* (*geog.*) Nuova Inghilterra.

   newfangled ['nju:,fæŋgld], *ag.* amante del nuovo; (*spreg.*) di nuovo conio.

   newfangledness ['nju:,fæŋgldnis], *s.* amore per il nuovo.

   Newfoundland [,nju:fənd'lænd], *no.pr.* (*geog.*) Terranova.

   New Guinea [nju:'gini], *no.pr.* (*geog.*) Nuova Guinea.

   New Hebrides (the) [nju:'hebridi:z], *no.pr. pl.* (*geog.*) Nuove Ebridi.

   newish ['nju:iʃ], *ag.* piuttosto nuovo.

   newly ['nju:li], *av.* recentemente; nuovamente.

   newlywed ['nju:li,wed], *s.* (*amer.*) persona appena sposata.

   newness ['nju:nis], *s.* novità.

news [nju:z], *s.* nuove; notizie; avviso: — *in brief*, notizie in breve; *latest* —, ultimissime; *official* —, comunicato ufficiale; *he told me an interesting piece of* —, mi raccontò un'interessante notizia; *there is no sure* —, mancano notizie sicure; *what is the* —*?*, che notizie ci sono? ‖ *this is in the* —, (*fam.*) se ne parla nella stampa ☆ — *-agency*, agenzia d'informazioni; — *-agent* (o — *-dealer*), giornalaio; — *-boy* (o — *-vendor* o — *-man* o — *-hawk*), (*amer.*) strillone; — *-hen*, (*amer. scherz.*) donna giornalista; — *-man*, (*amer.*) giornalaio; giornalista; — *-print*, carta da giornale; — *-reader* (o — *-caster*), (*amer.*) radiocronista; — *-reel*, cinegiornale; — *-stand*, edicola; — *-writer*, cronista.

newsless ['nju:zlis], *ag.* senza notizie.

newsmonger ['nju:z,mʌŋgə*], *s.* persona pettegola e curiosa: *he is a regular* —, è un vero gazzettino.

New South Wales ['nju:sauθ'weilz], *no.pr.* (*geog.*) Nuova Galles del Sud.

newspaper ['nju:s,peipə*], *s.* giornale, quotidiano ☆ — *-man*, giornalista.

newsworthy ['nju:z,wə:ði], *ag.* (*amer.*) tempestivo, importante, interessante.

newsy ['nju:zi], *ag.* (*fam.*) ricco di notizie, pettegolo.

newt [nju:t], *s.* (*zool.*) tritone.

Newtonian [nju:(:)'tounjən], *ag.* di Newton ‖ *s.* seguace di Newton.

New York ['nju:'jɔ:k], *no.pr.* (*geog.*) Nuova York.

New Yorker ['nju:'jɔ:kə*], *s.* nuovayorchese.

New Zealand [nju:'zi:lənd], *no.pr.* (*geog.*) Nuova Zelanda.

New Zealander [nju:'zi:ləndə*], *s.* neozelandese.

next [nekst], *ag.* **1.** (*di spazio, ordine, ecc.*) **prossimo, vicino, più vicino; contiguo:** *the* — *room*, la stanza accanto; *the* — *stop is yours*, la prossima fermata è la vostra; *the* — *town is twenty miles from here*, la città più vicina è a 20 miglia; *I want gloves the* — *larger size*, voglio dei guanti di una misura più grande ‖ — *door*, porta a porta ‖ *what* —, *please?*, e poi?; (*a un cliente*) che altro desidera, prego? ‖ *the* — *best thing would be to...*, in mancanza di ciò, il meglio sarebbe... **2.** (*di tempo*) **prossimo, venturo, futuro; seguente:** — *April* (o *in April* —), il prossimo aprile; — *week*, la prossima settimana; *the* — *week*, la settimana dopo; *will you return* — *year?*, tornerete l'anno venturo? ‖ *I will stop the* — *policeman I meet*, fermerò il primo vigile che incontro ‖ *s.* **persona, cosa più vicina, seguente:** — *of kin*, parente stretto; —, *please!*, avanti il primo!; *in his* — *he will describe his new house*, nella prossima lettera egli descriverà la sua nuova casa.

next, *av.* **dopo, in seguito, poi; la prossima volta:** — *they read the letters*, poi essi lessero le lettere; *Florence is the most beautiful Italian town*, — *to Rome*, dopo Roma, Firenze è la più bella città d'Italia; *shall we do what* —*?*, e adesso che altro dobbiamo fare?; *when you come* —, quando vieni la prossima volta ‖ — *to impossible*, quasi impossibile; — *to nothing*, quasi niente ‖ *prep.* **presso a, accanto a:** *they were standing* — *the window*, — *her*, erano in piedi accanto alla finestra, accanto a lei.

nexus ['neksəs], *s.* nesso; legame ☆ *casual* —, nesso causale.

Niagara [nai'ægərə], *no.pr.* (*geog.*) Niagara ‖ — *Falls*, Cascate del Niagara.

nib[1] [nib], *s.* **1.** pennino **2.** *pl.* grani di cacao pestati.

to nib[1], *pass.p.p.* **nibbed** [nibd], *v.t.* appuntire (una penna d'oca); mettere il pennino a.

to nib[2], *v.t.i.* (*dial.*) mordicchiare, mangiucchiare.

nibble ['nibl], *s.* morso; il mordicchiare.

to nibble, *v.t.i.* **1.** mordicchiare, sgranocchiare, rosicchiare: *he nibbled (at) a biscuit*, sgranocchiò un biscotto **2.** abboccare (di pesci) **3.** brucare **4.** (*fam.*) muovere critiche, borbottare: *to* — *at sthg.*, criticare ql.co.

nibbler ['niblə*], *s.c.* roditore, roditrice.

nibs [nibz], *s.*: *His* —, (*sl. scherz.*) Sua grazia.

Nicaragua [,nikə'rægjuə], *no.pr.* (*geog.*) Nicaragua.

Nice[1] [ni:s], *no.pr.* (*geog.*) Nizza.

nice[2] [nais], *ag.* **1.** piacevole; bello; simpatico: *what a* — *dress!*, che bel vestito!; *how* — *it is in here!*, come si sta bene qui dentro! ‖ *we are in a* — *mess*, (*fam.*) siamo in un bel pasticcio **2.** buono, gustoso: *what a* — *cake!*, che buon dolce! **3.** accurato, minuzioso; sottile; esatto, corretto: *a* — *shade of meaning*, una sottile sfumatura di significato; *he has a* — *judgement*, egli ha un sottile senso critico **4.** difficile; delicato; schizzinoso: *you must not be so* — *about everything*, non devi essere così difficile da accontentare ☆ — *-looking*, grazioso, attraente.

nicely ['naisli], *av.* **1.** esattamente: *this will do* —, questo andrà proprio bene **2.** piacevolmente; delicatamente; amabilmente; elegantemente.

Nicene [nai'si:n], *ag.* di Nicea ‖ — *Creed*, (*relig.*) il Credo, simbolo di Nicea.

niceness ['naisnis], *s.* **1.** esattezza, scrupolosità, sottigliezza **2.** delicatezza **3.** piacevolezza; fascino.

nicety ['naisiti], *s.* **1.** finezza, sottigliezza; precisione, accuratezza ‖ *to a* —, alla perfezione, al punto esatto: *the roast-veal was done to a* —, l'arrosto di vitello era cotto a puntino **2.** *pl.* minuzie: *the niceties of a language*, le finezze di una lingua.

niche [nitʃ], *s.* nicchia.

Nicholas ['nikələs], *no.pr.m.* Nicola, Niccolò.

Nick [nik], *no.pr.m. dim.* di **Nicholas** ‖ (*Old*) —, il Diavolo.

nick, *s.* **1.** tacca, intaccatura; intaglio **2.** (*dadi*) colpo decisivo **3.** momento critico, momento opportuno: *he came just in the* — *of time*, capitò proprio al momento opportuno.

to nick, *v.t.i.* **1.** intaccare; intagliare **2.** indovinare, colpire nel segno; cogliere (la stagione, il tempo opportuno) **3.** prendere appena in tempo (treno, ecc.) **4.** (*sl.*) catturare (un delinquente).

nickel ['nikl], *s.* **1.** (*min.*) nichel, nichelio **2.** moneta di nichel; (*amer.*) moneta da cinque « cents » ☆ — *-silver*, alpacca, argentone; — *-steel*, acciaio al nichel.

to nickel, *v.t.* nichelare.

nicker ['nikə*], *s.* **1.** intagliatore; chi fa una intaccatura **2.** teppista che infrangeva i vetri delle finestre lanciandovi contro monete di rame (al principio del 1700).

nick-nack, *V.* **knick-knack.**

nickname ['nikneim], *s.* soprannome; vezzeggiativo.

to nickname, *v.t.* soprannominare.

Nicobars (the) ['nikouba:z], *no.pr.* (*geog.*) Isole Nicobare.

Nicodemus [,nikə'di:məs], *no.pr.m.* (*Bibbia*) Nicodemo.

Nicomedes [,nikə'mi:di:z], *no.pr.m.* (*st.*) Nicomede.

nicotian [ni'kouʃən], *ag.* di tabacco ‖ *s.* fumatore.

nicotine ['nikəti:n], *s.* (*chim.*) nicotina.

nicotinism ['nikəti:nizəm], *s.* (*patol.*) nicotinismo.

to nicotinize ['nikəti:naiz], *v.t.* intossicare con nicotina; impregnare di nicotina.

to nictate ['nikteit], *v.i.* batter le palpebre ☆ *nic(ti)tating membrane*, membrana nittitante (di uccelli e altri animali).

nictation [nik'teiʃən], *s.* nittitazione.

to nictitate ['niktiteit], *V.* to **nictate.**

nictitation [,nikti'teiʃən], *V.* nictation.

niddering ['nidəriŋ], *ag.s.* (*arc.*) codardo, vile.

niddle-noddle ['nidl,nodl], *ag.* vacillante; tentennante.

to niddle-noddle, *v.t.i.* tentennare; vacillare; dondolare, dondolarsi.

to nidificate ['nidifikeit], *v.i.* nidificare.

nidification [,nidifi'keiʃən], *s.* nidificazione.

to nidify ['nidifai], *v.i.* nidificare.

to nid-nod ['nid,nod], *pass.p.p.* **nid-nodded** ['nid,nodid], *v.i.* accennare continuamente col capo.

nidus ['naidəs], *pl.* **nidi** ['naidai], **niduses** ['naidəsiz], *s.* **1.** nido (d'insetti) **2.** luogo favorevole allo sviluppo delle spore **3.** focolaio (di malattie, dottrine, ecc.).

niece [ni:s], *s.* nipote, nipotina (di zio).

niello [ni'elou], *pl.* **nielli** [ni'eli], **niellos** [ni'elouz], *s.* (*artig.*) niello.

nigella [nai'dʒelə*], *s.* (*bot.*) nigella.

Niger ['naidʒə*], *no.pr.* (*geog.*) Niger.

Nigeria [nai'dʒiəriə], *no.pr.* (*geog.*) Nigeria.

Nigerian [nai'dʒiəriən], *ag.s.c.* (abitante) della Nigeria.

niggard ['nigəd], *ag.s.* avaro, spilorcio.

niggardliness ['nigədlinis], *s.* avarizia, spilorceria.

niggardly ['nigədli], *ag.* avaro, spilorcio, tirchio; gretto, meschino.

niggardly, *av.* con avarizia; grettamente, meschinamente.

nigger ['nigə*], *s.* **1.** (*spreg.*) negro ‖ *a — in the fence* (o *woodpile*), (*sl.*) punto oscuro, cosa non chiara **2.** (*entom.*) bruco nero della rapa **3.** (colore) marrone scuro **4.** (*foto.*) bandiera ☆ *— melody*, melodia negra; *— song*, canto negro.

niggerdom ['nigədəm], *s.* i negri, l'insieme dei negri.

to niggle ['nigl], *v.i.* gingillarsi, perder tempo in minuzie.

niggler ['niglə*], *s.* pedante, persona minuziosa.

niggling ['niglin], *ag.* **1.** minuzioso **2.** frivolo, superficiale.

nigh [nai], (*poet.*) comp. **nigher** ['naiə*], (*arc.*) **near** [niə*]; *superl.* **nighest** ['naiist], (*arc.*) **next** [nekst], *ag.* **1.** vicino **2.** diretto, breve **3.** sinistro (di animale, veicolo) ‖ *av.* vicino; quasi ‖ *prep.* vicino a: *the bridge that stood — it*, il ponte che si ergeva vicino.

to nigh, *v.t.i.* (*arc.*) avvicinare, avvicinarsi.

nighly ['naili], *av.* vicino; quasi.

night [nait], *s.* **1.** notte, sera: *— and day*, notte e giorno, sempre; *at —*, di notte; *by —, in the —*, di notte, durante la notte; *from morning till —*, dalla mattina alla sera; *to have a good, bad —*, passare una buona, cattiva notte ‖ *the — before last*, l'altra sera; *last —*, ieri sera ‖ *the last — of a play*, l'ultima rappresentazione di una commedia ‖ *to make a — of it*, passare la notte facendo baldoria ‖ *to turn — into day*, far della notte giorno **2.** buio, oscurità, tenebre; *fig.* ignoranza ☆ *— -bird*, uccello notturno; *fig.* nottambulo; *— -blindness*, (*patol.*) nictalopia; *— -chair* (o *— stool*), seggetta; *— -club*, locale notturno; *— -crawler*, (*amer.*) lombrico; *— -dress*, camicia da notte (da donna); *— -flight*, volo notturno; *— -glass*, binocolo notturno da marina; *— -gown*, camicia da notte (da donna, bambino); *— -hag*, strega; incubo; *— -hawk*, (*ornit.*) nottolone; *— -lamp* (o *— -light*), lampada velata da notte; *— -line*, lenza con esche lasciata nell'acqua di notte; *— -out*, serata di festa; serata di permesso dei domestici; *— -porter*, portiere di notte; *— -school*, scuola serale; *— -shift*, turno di notte; *— -shirt*, camicia da notte (da uomo); *— -soil*, contenuto delle fogne; *— -stick*, (*amer.*) grosso bastone da poliziotto; *— -suit*, pigiama; *— -table*, comodino; *— -tide*, (*poet.*) notte; *— -walker*, nottambulo; passeggiatrice; *— -watch*, (periodo di) guardia notturna; *— -watchman*, sentinella notturna; guardiano notturno; *— -wear*, indumenti da notte; *— -work*, lavoro notturno ‖ *good- —*, buona notte: *to say good- — to s.o.*, *to wish* (o *to bid*) *s.o. good- —*, dire, augurare buona notte a qlcu.

nightcap ['naitkæp], *s.* berretto da notte.

nighted ['naitid], *ag.* sorpreso dalla notte.

nightfall ['naitfɔ:l], *s.* tramonto, crepuscolo.

nightfire ['nait,faiə*], *s.* fuoco notturno; fuoco fatuo.

nightingale ['naitingeil], *s.* (*ornit.*) usignolo.

nightjar ['naitdʒɑ:*], *s.* (*ornit.*) nottolone, succiacapre.

nightlong ['naitlon], *ag.* che dura tutta la notte.

nightlong, *av.* durante tutta la notte.

nightly ['naitli], *ag.* notturno, di notte; di ogni notte: *— performance*, rappresentazione che si replica tutte le sere.

nightly, *av.* di notte, nottetempo; ogni notte.

nightmare ['naitmɛə*], *s.* **1.** incubo (anche *fig.*): *he*

is the — of the family, è l'incubo della famiglia **2.** incubo (spirito maligno).

nightpiece ['naitpi:s], *s.* « notturno », dipinto che rappresenta una scena notturna.

nights [naits], *av.* (*sl. amer.*) di notte: *his work kept him from sleeping —*, il lavoro gli impediva di dormire la notte.

nightshade ['nait-ʃeid], *s.* (*bot.*) solano ☆ *deadly —*, (*bot.*) belladonna; *woody —*, (*bot.*) dulcamara.

nightward ['naitwəd], *ag.* notturno, che va verso la notte.

nighty ['naiti], *s.* (*dim. fam.*) camicia da notte (per donna, bimbo).

nigrescence [nai'gresəns], *s.* **1.** l'annerirsi **2.** nerezza (specialmente di pelle, capelli, occhi).

nigrescent [nai'gresənt], *ag.* nerastro.

nigritude ['nigritju:d], *s.* nerezza (anche *fig.*).

nihilism ['naiilizəm], *s.* (*fil. pol.*) nichilismo.

nihilist ['naiilist], *s.* (*fil. pol.*) nichilista.

nihility [nai'hiliti], *s.* **1.** il nulla **2.** cosa da nulla.

Nike ['naiki:], *no.pr.f.* (*mit.*) Nike.

nil [nil], *s.* **1.** nulla **2.** (*spor.*) zero.

Nile [nail], *no.pr.* (*geog.*) Nilo.

nilgai ['ni:lgai], *s.* (*zool.*) nilgau.

Nilotic [nai'lotik], *ag.* nilotico, del Nilo.

nimble ['nimbl], *ag.* **1.** agile, leggero; svelto: *goats are very — in climbing‖ among the rocks*, le capre sono molto agili nell'arrampicarsi tra le rocce **2.** intelligente, versatile; sveglio, pronto: *a — mind*, una mente sveglia; *a — reply*, una risposta pronta ☆ *— -fingered*, di mano lesta; *— -footed*, svelto, agile.

nimbleness ['nimblnis], *s.* **1.** agilità, leggerezza; flessuosità; sveltezza **2.** prontezza, agilità (di mente, ecc.).

nimbly ['nimbli], *av.* **1.** agilmente, leggermente; lestamente **2.** prontamente.

nimbus ['nimbəs], *pl.* **nimbi** ['nimbai], **nimbuses** ['nimbəsiz], *s.* **1.** nimbo, aureola **2.** nembo, nuvolone.

niminy-piminy ['nimini'pimini], *ag.* affettato, ricercato.

Nimrod ['nimrod], *no.pr.m.* (*Bibbia*) Nembrotte ‖ **nimrod**, *s. fig.* cacciatore.

Nina ['ni:nə], *no.pr.f.* dim. di **Ann.**

nincompoop ['ninkəmpu:p], *s.* sciocco, sempliciotto.

nine [nain], *ag.num.card.s.* nove: *— of us*, nove di noi; *— times out of ten*, nove volte su dieci, quasi sempre; *he will be — next birthday*, va per i nove anni ‖ *the Nine*, le Muse ‖ *a — days' wonder*, un fuoco di paglia ‖ *to the nines*, alla perfezione: *to be dressed up to the nines*, essere vestito di tutto punto ‖ *to cast out the nines*, (*arit.*) fare la prova del nove.

ninefold ['nainfould], *ag.* **1.** nove volte tanto **2.** che ha nove parti.

ninepence ['nainpəns], *s.* (valore di) nove penny, 3/4 di scellino.

ninepenny ['nainpəni], *ag.* attributivo da nove penny.

ninepins ['nain-pinz], *s.pl.* birilli ‖ *to go down like —*, cadere come dei birilli.

nineteen ['nain'ti:n], *ag.num.card.s.* diciannove ‖ *to talk — to the dozen*, parlare continuamente.

nineteenth ['nain'ti:nθ], *ag.num.ord.* diciannovesimo, decimonono.

nineties ['naintiz], *s.pl.* gli anni, i gradi del termometro tra 89 e 99; novantina: *an old woman in her —*, una vecchia di oltre novant'anni ‖ *the naughty —*, gli anni scapestrati tra il 1890 e il 1900.

ninetieth ['naintiθ], *ag.num.ord.s.* novantesimo.

ninety ['nainti], *ag.num.card.s.* novanta ‖ *say — -nine!*, (*med.*) dica trentatrè !.

Nineveh ['ninivi], *no.pr.* (*geog.*) Ninive.

ninish ['nainiʃ], *ag.* circa nove.

ninny ['nini], *s.* sempliciotto; sciocco.

ninth [nainθ], *ag.num.ord.* nono ‖ *s.* **1.** nono **2.** (*mus.*) nona.

ninthly ['nainθli], *av.* in nono luogo.

Ninus ['nainəs], *no.pr.m.* (*mit.*) Nino.

Niobe ['naiəbi], *no.pr.f.* (*mit.*) Niobe ‖ *fig.* madre sventurata.

niobium [nai'oubiəm], *s.* (*chim.*) niobio.

nip[1] [nip], *s.* **1.** pizzicotto; morso **2.** stretta; presa **3.** il morso (del gelo, del freddo): *the — of the early morning*, il freddo mordente del primo mattino **4.** (*mec.*) bloccaggio; interferenza **5.** (*mar.*) volta, cocca.

to **nip**[1], *pass.p.p.* **nipped** [nipt], *v.t.i.* **1.** pizzicare; pungere; mordere (anche di vento, freddo, ecc.): *her arm was nipped black and blue*, il suo braccio era livido per i pizzicotti; *the wind nips hard this morning*, il vento è molto pungente questa mattina **2.** stroncare, rovinare, distruggere (dell'effetto del gelo sulle piante e *fig.*): *my hopes were nipped in the bud*, le mie speranze furono stroncate sul nascere; *nipped by the cold*, distrutto dal freddo ‖ *to — a flower in the bud*, *fig.* recidere un fiore in boccio **3.** — **in**, entrare velocemente (precedendo qlcu.); *fig.* interrompere una conversazione **4.** — **off**, tagliare; strappare via; squagliarsela **5.** — **out**, tirar fuori con prontezza (revolver, ecc.); andarsene, uscire in fretta: *he nipped in and out of the traffic*, si destreggiò bene in mezzo al traffico **6.** — **up**, raccogliere lestamente; salire con agilità.

nip[2], *s.* sorso, piccola quantità di bevanda alcoolica.

to **nip**[2], *v.t.i.* **1.** sorseggiare (una bevanda acoolica) **2.** bere spesso e volentieri alcoolici.

Nip, (*sl. mil.*) *abbr.* di **Nipponian**.

nipper[1] ['nipə*], *s.* **1.** ragazzo, fattorino; (*fam.*) monello, ragazzo **2.** *pl.* pinze; pinzette; tenaglie; forcipe; ecc. **3.** *pl.* chela **4.** (*sl.*) « pince-nez ».

nipper[2], *s.* persona che beve volentieri.

nipping ['nipiŋ], *ag.* **1.** pungente; frizzante; tagliente; sarcastico **2.** che distrugge (di gelo, ecc.).

nippingly ['nipiŋli], *av.* con tono pungente, sarcastico.

nipple ['nipl], *s.* **1.** capezzolo **2.** copri capezzoli (durante l'allattamento) **3.** tettarella **4.** cocuzzolo (di montagna), mammellone **5.** (*mec.*) rubinetto di regolazione, di arresto **6.** (*mec.*) cappuccio per valvola, capezzolo ☆ — -*wort*, (*bot.*) lassana.

Nippon ['nipɔn], *no.pr.* (*geog.*) Giappone.

Nipponian [ni'pouniən], *ag.* giapponese.

nippy ['nipi], *ag.* **1.** pungente **2.** (*sl.*) agile, svelto: *tell him to be — about it*, digli di sbrigarsi.

nirvana [niə'va:nə], *s.* (*relig. indù*) nirvana.

Nisus ['naisəs], *no.pr.m.* (*lett.*) Niso.

nit [nit], *s.* **1.** lendine; uovo di parassita **2.** pidocchio.

nitrate ['naitreit], *s.* (*chim.*) nitrato: — *of potash*, nitrato di potassio, salnitro ☆ — *fertilizers*, fertilizzanti all'azoto.

nitre ['naitə*], *s.* (*chim.*) nitrato di potassio, salnitro.

nitric ['naitrik], *ag.* nitrico: — *acid*, acido nitrico.

to **nitrify** ['naitrifai], *v.t.* **1.** convertire in nitro **2.** fertilizzare con nitrati (terreno).

nitrite ['naitrait], *s.* (*chim.*) nitrito.

nitrogen ['naitridʒən], *s.* (*chim.*) azoto.

nitrogenous [nai'trɔdʒinəs], *ag.* azotato.

nitro-glycerin(e) ['naitrou-glisə'ri:n], *s.* (*chim.*) nitroglicerina.

nitrous ['naitrəs], *ag.* (*chim.*) nitroso ☆ — *oxide*, protossido d'azoto.

nitwit ['nitwit], *s.* (*sl.*) stupido, imbecille.

nitwitted ['nit,witid], *ag.* di scarsa intelligenza.

niveous ['niviəs], *ag.* niveo.

Nivôse [ni:'vouz], *s.* (*st. francese*) nevoso.

nix[1] [niks], *inter. s.* (*sl.*) « ssst... » (per avvertire i compagni dell'arrivo del maestro, padrone, poliziotto).

nix[2], *s.* (*mit. nordica*) elfo delle acque.

nix[3], *s.* (*sl.*) nulla, niente da fare.

nixie ['niksi], *s.* (*mit. nordica*) fatina delle acque.

Nizam [nai'zæm], *s.* **1.** (*st.*) « Nizam », sovrano di Hyderabad **2.** soldato dell'esercito turco.

no [nou], *ag.* **nessuno**: *there is — hope whatever*, non c'è speranza alcuna ‖ — *doubt*, certamente ‖ — *end*

of, (*fam.*) innumerevoli ‖ — *one*, nessuno ‖ — *smoking*, vietato fumare ‖ *in less than — time*, prestissimo ‖ *affairs of — small matter were discussed*, si discussero faccende di non poco conto ‖ *he is — poet*, non è poeta ‖ *it is — go*, è inutile ‖ *it is — joke*, non è uno scherzo ‖ — *one person could do it*, una persona da sola non potrebbe farlo ‖ *s.*; *pl.* **noes** [nouz] **1.** **no**: *I will not take — for an answer*, non accetterò un rifiuto; *two noes make a yes*, due negazioni affermano **2.** *pl.* coloro che votano contro; voti contrari: *the noes have it*, ha vinto l'opposizione; la maggioranza è sfavorevole ‖ *av.* **1. no**: *"Have you seen him?"*, *"No, I haven't"*, « L'hai veduto?», «No, non l'ho veduto»; *to say —*, dire di no, negare ‖ *whether or —*, in tutti i modi **2.** (*seguito da un comp.*) **non**, **in nessun modo**, **punto**, **affatto**: — *later (than)*, non più tardi (di); — *longer (than)*, non più (di); — *more*, niente più; non più; mai più; — *sooner*, non appena: — *sooner said than done*, detto fatto; — *such*, niente di simile.

Noah ['nouə], *no.pr.m.* (*Bibbia*) Noè.

Noachian [nou'eikiən], *ag.* di Noè.

nob[1] [nɔb], *s.* (*sl.*) **1.** testa **2.** fante (al giuoco del cribbage).

to **nob**[1], *pass.p.p.* **nobbed** [nɔbd], *v.t.* (*boxe*) colpire al capo.

nob[2], *s.* (*sl.*) persona ricca, aristocratica.

to **nobble** ['nɔbl], *v.t.* (*sl.*) **1.** drogare (un cavallo) (per impedirgli di vincere) **2.** corrompere (con denaro) **3.** catturare (un delinquente) **4.** impadronirsi in modo illegale di.

nobby ['nɔbi], *ag.* (*sl.*) elegante.

nobiliary [nou'biljəri], *ag.* nobiliare ☆ — *particle*, particella nobiliare.

nobility [nou'biliti], *s.* **1.** nobiltà (classe sociale): *the Venetian —*, la nobiltà veneziana **2.** nobiltà, distinzione, elevatezza: — *of mind*, elevatezza di mente.

noble ['noubl], *ag.* **1.** nobile, aristocratico: *to be of — birth*, essere di nobile nascita **2.** nobile, sublime, elevato; generoso (di sentimenti, ecc.): *a — action*, una nobile azione; *a — soul*, un'anima nobile, generosa **3.** superbo, grandioso (di monumenti, proporzioni, ecc.): *a — building*, un edificio grandioso ‖ *to do things on a — scale*, fare le cose in grande **4.** (*metal.*) nobile, prezioso ‖ *s.* **1.** nobile, aristocratico **2.** « noble » (antica moneta d'oro del valore di 6 s. 8 d.) ☆ — *-minded*, di sentimenti elevati; — *mindedness*, nobiltà di sentimenti.

nobleman, *pl.* **noblemen** ['noublmən], *s.* nobiluomo.

nobleness ['noublnis], *s.* **1.** nobiltà (di nascita) **2.** nobiltà, magnanimità, generosità (d'animo, ecc.) **3.** proporzioni superbe, grandiose, dimensioni impressionanti.

noblesse [nou'bles], *s.* la nobiltà, i nobili (specialmente di paese straniero).

noblewoman ['noubl,wumən], *pl.* **noblewomen** ['noubl,wimin], *s.* nobildonna.

nobly ['noubli], *av.* **1.** nobilmente **2.** magnificamente.

nobody ['noubədi], *pron.indef.* nessuno: *there was — there*, non c'era nessuno; — *would have believed it*, nessuno l'avrebbe creduto ‖ *s.*; *pl.* **nobodies** ['noubədiz] persona che non conta, nullità, zero: *he is but a —*, è una persona trascurabile; *they were treated as mere nobodies*, furono trattati come nullità.

nock [nɔk], *s.* cocca (di freccia).

to **nock**, *v.t.* scoccare (una freccia).

noctambulant [nɔk'tæmbjulənt], *ag.* **1.** nottambulo **2.** sonnambulo.

noctambulism [nɔk'tæmbjulizəm], *s.* **1.** nottambulismo **2.** sonnambulismo.

noctambulist [nɔk'tæmbjulist], *s.* **1.** nottambulo **2.** sonnambulo.

noctiluca [,nɔkti'lju:kə], *pl.* **noctilucae** [,nɔkti'lju:si:], *s.* (*zool.*) nottiluca.

noctua ['nɔktjuə], *s.* (*entom.*) nottua.

noctule ['nɔktju:l], *s.* (*zool.*) nottola.

nocturnal [nɔk'tə:nl], *ag.* notturno; di notte.

nocturnals [nɔk'tə:nlz], *s.pl.* uccelli notturni.

nocturne ['nɔktə:n], s. (mus. pitt.) notturno.
nocuous ['nɔkjuəs], ag. nocivo.
nocuously ['nɔkjuəsli], av. nocivamente.
nod [nɔd], s. 1. cenno del capo (di saluto, assenso, ecc.): she gave him a little —, ella gli fece un piccolo cenno col capo 2. inclinazione del capo nel sonno 3. ordine, comando: they were all at his —, erano tutti ai suoi ordini || the land of Nod, il regno dei sogni: to go to the land of Nod, assopirsi, partire per il regno dei sogni.
to **nod**, pass.p.p. **nodded** ['nɔdid], v.t.i. 1. annuire col capo; chinare il capo (per saluto, ecc.): I just — to them, lo conosco appena; she nodded yes, ella accennò di sì 2. chinare il capo nel sonno; sonnecchiare, assopirsi: they both were nodding by the fire, entrambi sonnecchiavano accanto al fuoco || Homer sometimes nods, anche il buon Omero talvolta sonnecchia 3. essere inclinato (di edifici, ecc.) 4. svolazzare (di piume) 5. ordinare, comandare con un solo cenno del capo.
nodal ['noudl], ag. di nodo.
nodding ['nɔdiŋ], ag. 1. chinato; inclinato; piegato in avanti 2. svolazzante: — plumes, pennacchi svolazzanti || s. cenno del capo || a — acquaintance, una conoscenza vaga, superficiale, persona conosciuta solo di vista.
noddle ['nɔdl], s. (scherz.) testa; zucca: to get sthg. into one's —, mettersi in testa ql.co.
to **noddle**, v.t. dondolare, scuotere (la testa).
noddy ['nɔdi], s. sciocco, gonzo.
node [noud], s. 1. (bot.) nodo 2. (patol.) nodosità, indurimento 3. (astr. fis. elett.) nodo 4. (geom.) punto doppio 5. centro, punto d'incontro.
nodical ['noudikəl], ag. (astr.) nodale.
nodiform ['noudifɔ:m], ag. a forma di nodo.
nodose [nou'dous], ag. nodoso.
nodosity [nou'dɔsiti], s. nodosità; protuberanza.
nodular ['nɔdjulə*], **nodulated** ['nɔdjuleitid], ag. nodoso; a forma di nodo.
nodulation [,nɔdju'leiʃən], s. formazione di nodi; insieme di nodi.
nodule ['nɔdju:l], s. (geol. anat. bot.) nodulo.
nodulose [,nɔdju'lous], **nodulous** ['nɔdjuləs], ag. (bot. anat. geol.) a noduli.
nodulus ['nɔdjuləs], s. (geol. anat. bot.) nodulo.
nodus ['noudəs], pl. **nodi** ['noudai], s. intoppo, difficoltà, complicazione.
Noel[1] ['nouəl], no.pr.m. Natale.
Noel[2], V. **Nowel**.
noetic [nou'etik], ag. noetico || s. (fil.) noetica.
nog [nɔg], s. 1. piuolo; tassello 2. nodo (di tronco, ramo).
to **nog**, pass.p.p. **nogged** [nɔgd], v.t. 1. fissare con piuoli, tasselli 2. costruire con travature di legno e mattoni.
noggin ['nɔgin], s. 1. piccolo boccale 2. « noggin » (misura di capacità = l. 0,142).
nohow [nou'hau], av. 1. in nessun modo 2. (fam.) fuori posto: he felt all —, si sentiva tutto scombussolato.
noil [nɔil], s. (ind. tessile) cascáme di pettinatura.
noise [nɔiz], s. rumore; fragore; chiasso; schiamazzo: a deafening — came from his room, dalla sua stanza veniva un chiasso assordante; to make a lot of — about a novel, fare molto chiasso intorno ad un romanzo || a big —, (sl.) un pezzo grosso, un personaggio importante || to make a — in the world, far parlare molto di sè ☆ — meter, (acu.) fonometro || background —, (acu.) rumore di fondo; needle —, (acu.) fruscio della puntina (su un disco).
to **noise**, v.t.i. 1. divulgare, diffondere, rendere pubblico 2. (rar.) far rumore.
noiseful ['nɔizful], ag. rumoroso.
noiseless ['nɔizlis], ag. senza rumore, silenzioso: — typewriter, macchina per scrivere silenziosa; with — tread, con passo felpato.
noiselessly ['nɔizlisli], av. senza rumore, silenziosamente.
noiselessness ['nɔizlisnis], s. silenzio; quiete, tranquillità.

noisette [nwɑ:'zet], s.gener.pl. (cuc.) messicano.
noisily ['nɔizili], av. rumorosamente, con fracasso.
noisiness ['nɔizinis], s. 1. chiasso, rumore 2. turbolenza (dei bambini).
noisome ['nɔisəm], ag. 1. nocivo; malsano 2. fetido; disgustoso.
noisomely ['nɔisəmli], av. 1. in modo nocivo 2. in modo disgustoso.
noisomeness ['nɔisəmnis], s. 1. l'essere nocivo 2. miasma; fetore.
noisy ['nɔizi], ag. 1. rumoroso fragoroso; turbolento: a — child, un bimbo turbolento; a — street, una strada rumorosa 2. fig. vistoso, chiassoso: a — colour, un colore vistoso, chiassoso.
nomad ['nɔməd], ag.s. nomade.
nomadic [nou'mædik], ag. nomade, di nomade.
nomadism ['nɔmədizm], s. nomadismo.
to **nomadize** ['nɔmədaiz], v.i. condurre vita nomade.
no-man's-land ['noumænzlænd], s. terra di nessuno.
nome[1] [noum], s. (st.) nomo (divisione territoriale dell'antico Egitto).
nome[2], s. (st. mus.) nomo (forma di composizione musicale greca).
nome[3], s. (mat.) nomo (membro di una quantità composta).
nomenclator ['noumənkleitə*], s. 1. classificatore, nomenclatore 2. (st. romana) nomenclatore.
nomenclature [nou'menklətʃə*], s. nomenclatura, terminologia.
nomic ['noumik], ag. convenzionale; solito; ordinario.
nominable ['nɔminəbl], ag. degno di essere nominato.
nominal ['nɔminl], ag. nominale; non effettivo; simbolico: — fee, pagamento simbolico; — value, valore nominale.
nominalism ['nɔminəlizəm], s. (fil.) nominalismo.
nominalist ['nɔminəlist], s. (fil.) nominalista, seguace del nominalismo.
nominalistic [,nɔminə'listik], ag. nominalistico.
nominally ['nɔminəli], av. nominalmente.
to **nominate** ['nɔmineit], v.t. 1. nominare; qualificare; designare, proporre per elezione: he was nominated for Parliament, fu proposto come candidato al Parlamento 2. (arc.) chiamare per nome.
nominately ['nɔminitli], av. particolarmente; (arc.) per nome.
nomination [,nɔmi'neiʃən], s. nomina, designazione; elezione.
nominative ['nɔminətiv], ag. s. (gram.) nominativo.
nominator ['nɔmineitə*], s. nominatore, designatore.
nominee [,nɔmi'ni:], s. persona nominata; candidato proposto, presentato.
non-acceptance ['nɔnək'septəns], s. mancata accettazione.
nonage ['nounidʒ], s. 1. (dir.) minorità 2. (fam.) mancanza di maturità.
nonagenarian [,nounədʒi'nɛəriən], ag.s. nonagenario.
nonagesimal [,nɔnə'dʒesiml], ag. nonagesimo.
non-aligned ['nɔnə'laind], ag. non allineato || — countries, (neol. pol.) paesi non impegnati.
non-appearance ['nɔnə'piərəns], s. (dir.) contumacia.
non-belligerency ['nɔnbi'lidʒərənsi], s. (pol.) non-belligeranza.
nonce [nɔns], s. (rar.) (tempo) presente; occasione: for the —, per l'occasione ☆ — -word, parola coniata per un'occasione.
non-certifiable ['nɔn'sə:tifaiəbl], s. non provabile, non documentabile.
nonchalance ['nɔnʃələns], s. noncuranza; indifferenza.
nonchalant ['nɔnʃələnt], ag. noncurante; indifferente.
nonchalantly ['nɔnʃələntli], av. indifferentemente; con noncuranza.
non-claim ['nɔnkleim], s. (dir.) mancato ricorso (entro il termine legale).

non-collegiate ['nɔnkə'li:dʒiit], *s.* studente universitario esterno.

non-commissioned officer ['nɔnkə'miʃənd'ofisə*], *s.* (*abbr.* N.C.O.) sottufficiale.

non-committal ['nɔnkə'mitl], *ag.* non impegnativo, vago: *a — answer*, una risposta non impegnativa.

non-conducting ['nɔnkən'dʌktiŋ], *ag.* (*fis.*) coibente, isolante, non conduttore.

non-conductor ['nɔnkən,dʌktə*], *s.* (*fis.*) coibente, isolante.

non-conformist ['nɔnkən'fɔ:mist], *ag.s.* (*st. relig.*) anticonformista (in Scozia XVII sec.); (*gener.*) dissidente (da una Chiesa costituita).

non-conformity ['nɔnkən'fɔ:miti], *s.* (*st. relig.*) anticonformismo (in Scozia XVII sec.); (*gener.*) dissidenza (da una Chiesa costituita).

non-content ['nɔnkən'tent], *s.* **1.** chi dà voto negativo (alla Camera dei Lords) **2.** malcontento.

non-cooperation ['nɔnkou,ɔpə'reiʃən], *s.* (*pol.*) rifiuto di cooperare.

non-delivery ['nɔndi'livəri], *s.* mancata consegna.

nondescript ['nɔndiskript], *ag.* non classificabile; qualunque ‖ *s.* persona, cosa difficilmente classificabile.

none [nʌn], *pron. indef.* nessuno, niuno, non uno: *— but your parents have accepted*, soltanto i tuoi genitori hanno accettato; *— can imagine it*, nessuno può immaginarlo; *— of us is* (o *are*) *strong enough*, nessuno di noi è abbastanza forte ‖ *av.* **affatto, niente affatto, punto:** *he is — the wiser*, non ne sa certo più di prima; *the price is — too high*, il prezzo non è affatto troppo alto ‖ *— the less*, non di meno ‖ *ag.* (*rar. arc.*) nessuno, niuno: *thou shalt have — other gods but me*, non avrai altro Dio all'infuori di Me; *to make of — effect*, invalidare.

non-effective ['nɔni'fektiv], *ag.* inefficace ‖ *s.* (*mil.*) non in servizio effettivo.

non-ego ['nɔn'egou], *s.* (*fil.*) non-io.

nonentity [nɔ'nentiti], *s.* **1.** inesistenza **2.** persona, cosa insignificante.

Nones [nounz], *s.pl.* **1.** (*calendario romano*) none **2.** (*eccl.*) nona.

nonesuch ['nʌnsʌtʃ], *ag.* senza pari, senza paragone ‖ *s.* **1.** cosa, persona senza pari, senza paragone **2.** (*bot.*) erba medica.

non-existence ['nɔnig'zistəns], *s.* inesistenza.

nonfading ['nɔn'feidiŋ], *ag.* resistente alla luce, che non si scolora, solido (di colore).

non-feasance ['nɔn'fi:zəns], *s.* (*dir.*) trasgressione; omissione.

non-feasant ['nɔn'fi:zənt], *s.* (*dir.*) trasgressore.

non-flammable ['nɔn'flæməbl], *ag.* incombustibile, ininfiammabile.

non-fraternization ['nɔn,frætənai'zeiʃən], *s.* proibizione di fraternizzare.

non-human ['nɔn'hju:mən], *ag.* non umano; inumano.

non-intervention ['nɔn,intə(:)'venʃən], *s.* non intervento; non interventismo.

non-juring ['nɔn'dʒuəriŋ], *ag.* che rifiuta di prestare giuramento.

non-juror ['nɔn'dʒuərə*], *s.* (*st.*) chi rifiutava di prestare giuramento a re Guglielmo d'Orange.

non-logical ['nɔn'lɔdʒikəl], *ag.* illogico.

non-member ['nɔn'membə*], *s.* non socio: *open to non-members*, aperto al pubblico.

non-metal ['nɔn'metl], *s.* (*chim.*) metalloide.

non-moral ['nɔn'mɔrəl], *ag.* **1.** amorale **2.** che non riguarda la morale.

non-natural ['nɔn'nætʃrəl], *ag.* non naturale.

non-official ['nɔnə'fiʃəl], *ag.* **1.** ufficioso **2.** supplementare: *— hours*, ore di lavoro straordinario.

nonpareil ['nɔnpərel], *ag.* unico, impareggiabile ‖ *s.* **1.** persona, cosa impareggiabile **2.** (*tip.*) carattere di corpo sei.

nonplus ['nɔn'plʌs], *s.* perplessità, imbarazzo: *he was at a —*, non sapeva assolutamente che cosa fare.

to **nonplus**, *pass.p.p.* **nonplussed** ['nɔn'plʌst], *v.t.* rendere perplessi; imbarazzare.

non-resident ['nɔn'rezidənt], *ag.s.* **1.** chi, che non risiede nel luogo ove svolge le sue mansioni: *— clergyman*, sacerdote che abita fuori parrocchia; *— maid*, donna di servizio a giornata; *— master*, maestro esterno; *— medical officer*, medico esterno **2.** (persona) di passaggio: *hotel open to non-residents*, albergo che offre i suoi servizi anche a persone che non pernottano.

non-resistance ['nɔnri'zistəns], *s.* resistenza passiva.

nonsense ['nɔnsəns], *s.* **1.** assurdità; sciocchezza: *he kept on talking —*, continuò a dire sciocchezze **2.** filastrocca (senza nè capo nè coda) ☆ *— rhymes*, filastrocca in versi.

nonsense, *inter.* ma no!; sciocchezze!; ma va!.

nonsensical [nɔn'sensikəl], *ag.* assurdo; sciocco; strampalato.

nonsensically [nɔn'sensikəli], *av.* assurdamente; stupidamente.

nonsensicalness [nɔn'sensikəlnis], *s.* stramberia; assurdità.

non-stop ['nɔn'stɔp], *ag.* continuo; ininterrotto ‖ *av.* di continuo; ininterrottamente.

nonsuit ['nɔn'sju:t], *s.* (*dir.*) non luogo a procedere.

to **nonsuit** *v.t.* (*dir.*) mettere fuori ruolo.

non-transferable ['nɔntræns'fə:rəbl], *ag.* personale, non trasferibile.

non-white ['nɔn'wait], *ag.s.c.* (persona) di sangue misto.

noodle[1] ['nu:dl], *s.* sciocco; gonzo; minchione.

noodle[2], *s. gener. pl.* (*cuc.*) taglierini (da brodo).

nook [nuk], *s.* **1.** cantuccio, angolo: *they explored every — and corner*, esplorarono tutti gli angoli **2.** ripostiglio.

noon [nu:n], *s.* mezzodì, mezzogiorno.

noonday ['nu:ndei], **noontide** ['nu:n-taid], *ag.* di mezzogiorno ‖ *s.* mezzogiorno; giorno pieno.

noose [nu:s], *s.* **1.** nodo scorsoio, cappio; trappola (anche *fig.*) **2.** (*scherz.*) legame matrimoniale.

to **noose**, *v.t.* accalappiare, prendere in trappola.

nope [noup], *av.* (*sl. amer.*) no.

nor [nɔ:*], *cong.* nè, neppure, nemmeno: *— did I think of it*, non ci pensai neppure; *he is neither good — bad, — clever*, non è nè buono, nè cattivo, nè intelligente; *she was neither young — beautiful*, non era nè giovane nè bella ‖ *— good — bad*, (*arc.*) nè buono nè cattivo.

nor', *abbr.* di **north**.

Nora(h) ['nɔ:rə], *no.pr.f.* Nora.

Nordic ['nɔ:dik], *ag.* nordico, scandinavo, teutonico.

noria ['nɔ:riə], *s.* (*mec.*) noria.

norland ['nɔ:lənd], *s.* paese nordico.

norlander ['nɔ:ləndə*], *s.* abitante del nord.

norm [nɔ:m], *s.* **1.** tipo; modello **2.** norma: *— of Catholic worship*, norma del culto cattolico.

normal ['nɔ:məl], *ag.* **1.** (*geom.*) perpendicolare, normale **2.** normale, regolare, logico ‖ *Normal School*, scuola di perfezionamento per maestri ‖ *s.* **1.** (*geom.*) (linea) perpendicolare **2.** norma.

normalcy ['nɔ:məlsi], **normality** [nɔ:'mæliti], *s.* normalità.

normalization [,nɔ:məlai'zeiʃən], *s.* normalizzazione.

to **normalize** ['nɔ:məlaiz], *v.t.* normalizzare.

normally ['nɔ:məli], *av.* normalmente.

Norman[1] ['nɔmən], *ag.* normanno: *— style*, stile romanico, normanno ‖ *the — Conquest*, (*st.*) la conquista normanna dell'Inghilterra (1066) ‖ *s.c.* normanno, normanna.

norman[2], *s.* (*mar.*) cariglione.

Normandy ['nɔ:məndi], *no.pr.* (*geog.*) Normandia.

normanesque [,nɔ:mə'nesk], *ag.* in stile romanico normanno.

Normanism ['nɔ:mənizəm], *s.* dominio dei normanni; cultura e civiltà normanne.

Normanization [,nɔ:mənai'zeiʃən], *s.* normannizzazione.

to **normanize** ['nɔ:mənaiz], *v.t.i.* porre sotto il dominio e l'influsso normanno; sottoporsi a, uniformarsi agli usi dei normanni.

normative ['nɔ:mətiv], *ag.* normativo.

Norn [nɔ:n], **Norna** ['nɔ:nə], *no.pr.f.* (*mit.*) Norna.

Norse [nɔ:s], *ag.s.c.* norvegese ‖ *s.* lingua norvegese.

Norseland ['nɔ:slənd], *no.pr.* (*geog. st.*) Norvegia.

Norseman, *pl.* **Norsemen** ['nɔ:smən], *s.* norvegese.

Norsk [nɔ:sk], *ag.s.c.* norvegese ‖ *s.* lingua norvegese.

north [nɔ:θ], *ag.* del nord, nordico, settentrionale, artico; situato verso nord; esposto al nord: *a — room*, una stanza esposta a tramontana; — *wind*, vento di tramontana ‖ *North America*, America del Nord ‖ *North Country*, le zone settentrionali dell'Inghilterra ‖ *the North Sea*, il Mare del Nord ‖ *s.* **1.** nord, settentrione, parte settentrionale di una regione **2.** vento del nord ☆ — *-countryman*, settentrionale (inglese); — *-east*, nord-est; — *-eastern*, di nord-est; — *-eastwards*, verso nord-est; — *-polar*, del polo nord; — *-west*, nord ovest; — *-western*, di nord-ovest; — *-westwards*, verso nord-ovest.

north, *av.* a nord, verso nord: — *of*, a nord di; *it lies —*, è esposto a nord.

north-eastward [nɔ:θ'i:stwəd], *ag.* a, di nord-est ‖ *s.* nord-est ‖ *av.* verso nord-est.

northerly ['nɔ:ðəli], *ag.* del nord; settentrionale ‖ *av.* a nord, verso nord.

northern ['nɔ:ðən], *ag.* nordico, settentrionale; artico ‖ *s. V.* **northerner** ☆ — *lights*, aurora boreale.

northerner ['nɔ:ðənə*], *s.c.* **1.** abitante del nord **2.** (*amer.*) nordista.

northernmost ['nɔ:ðənmoust], *ag.* il più a nord.

northing ['nɔ:θiŋ], *s.* (*mar.*) distanza percorsa verso il nord; deviazione verso nord.

Northland ['nɔ:θlənd], *s.* (*poet.*) regioni settentrionali ☆ — *latitude*, latitudine nord.

Northman, *pl.* **Northmen** ['nɔ:θmən], *s.* scandinavo; svedese; norvegese.

northmost ['nɔ:θmoust], *ag.* il più a nord.

Northumbria [nɔ:'θʌmbriə], *no.pr.* (*geog. st.*) Northumbria (uno dei regni della eptarchia anglosassone).

Northumbrian [nɔ:'θʌmbriən], *ag.* appartenente all'antica Northumbria; del Northumberland (Contea a nord del fiume Humber) ‖ *s.* abitante, dialetto dell'antica Northumbria; abitante del Northumberland.

northward ['nɔ:θwəd], *ag.* settentrionale, verso nord ‖ *s.* nord, direzione nord ‖ *av.* verso il nord.

northwardly ['nɔ:θwədli], *ag.* in posizione, direzione nord ‖ *av.* verso il nord.

northwards ['nɔ:θwədz], *av.* in direzione nord.

north-westward ['nɔ:θ'westwəd], *ag.* a, di nord -ovest ‖ *s.* nord-ovest ‖ *av.* verso nord-ovest.

Norway ['nɔ:wei], *no.pr.* (*geog.*) Norvegia.

Norwegian [nɔ:'wi:dʒən], *ag.s.c.* norvegese ‖ *s.* lingua norvegese.

nor'-wester [nɔ:'westə*], *s.* (*contr.* di *north-wester*) **1.** forte vento di nord-ovest **2.** bicchiere di liquore forte **3.** cappuccio impermeabile da marinaio.

nose [nouz], *s.* **1.** naso: *he blew his —*, si soffiò il naso; *he has a snub —*, ha il naso camuso; *to speak through one's —*, parlare nel naso ‖ *by a —*, con un piccolissimo margine (in corse di cavalli, ecc.) ‖ *let us count noses*, contiamo quanti siamo ‖ *she snapped his — off*, *fig.* gli rispose seccamente ‖ *to follow one's —*, andare avanti diritto, essere guidati dall'istinto ‖ *to lead by the —*, menare per il naso ‖ *to pay through the —*, pagare un prezzo esorbitante ‖ *to poke one's — into*, ficcare il naso in ‖ *to put s.o.'s — out of joint*, giocare un brutto tiro a qlcu. ‖ *to turn up one's — at s.o.*, *sthg.*, arricciare il naso davanti a qlcu., ql.co. **2.** muso (di animali); parte anteriore di aeroplani, navi **3.** odorato; fiuto; sagacia: *to have a good —*, aver fiuto, aver buon naso **4.** becco (di storta); volata (di cannone); apertura (di tubo, ecc.) **5.** (*sl.*) spia ☆ — *-bag*, sacchetta per foraggio (sospesa al muso dei cavalli); —

-band, tirante (della briglia); — *-dive*, (*aer.*) picchiata in candela; — *-ring*, anello da naso.

to **nose**, *v.t.i.* **1.** fiutare, odorare: *he noses a job in everything*, ha un fiuto straordinario per gli affari; *to — at sthg.*, fiutare ql.co. **2.** ficcare il naso: *he nosed into my business*, ficcò il naso negli affari miei **3.** *to — after*, *for* (*sthg.*), cercare ql.co. **4.** *to — down*, (*aer.*) discendere in picchiata **5.** *to — out*, scoprire **6.** *to — up*, (*aer.*) prendere quota.

nosed [nouzd], *ag.* (*solo nei composti*): *big- —*, che ha il naso grosso; *snub- —*, dal naso camuso.

to **nosedive** ['nouzdaiv], *v.i.* (*aer.*) scendere in picchiata.

nosegay ['nouzgei], *s.* mazzolino di fiori.

noseless ['nouzlis], *ag.* senza naso.

noser ['nouzə*], *s.* forte vento che soffia in faccia.

nosey ['nouzi], *ag.* **1.** nasuto **2.** nasale **3.** di odore sgradevole **4.** (*fam.*) indiscreto, ficcanaso ‖ *s.* **1.** nasone, persona dal naso grande **2.** ficcanaso.

nosing ['nouziŋ], *s.* **1.** (*edil.*) sporgenza; estremità della pila di un ponte, taglia-acqua **2.** striscia di metallo protettiva (di gradino) **3.** (*ferr.*) serpeggiamento.

nosology [nə'sɔlədʒi], *s.* nosologia.

nostalgia [nɔs'tældʒiə], *s.* nostalgia.

nostalgic [nɔs'tældʒik], *ag.* nostalgico.

nostril ['nɔstril],*s.* (*anat.*) narice ‖ *to stink in somebody's nostrils*, (*volg.*) essere odioso a qlcu.

nostrum ['nɔstrəm], *s.* panacea (anche *fig.*).

nosy, *V.* **nosey.**

not [nɔt], *av.* **1.** **non**, **no**; **niente**, **punto**: — *knowing him...*, non conoscendolo...; *did you — say so?*, non l'hai detto?; *he is — older than I*, egli non è più vecchio di me; *I think —*, penso di no; *tell him — to go*, digli di non andare **2.** (*contratto in* n't *si unisce ai verbi ausiliari e difettivi*): *don't you know?*, non sapete?; *hasn't he told you?*, non ve lo ha detto?; *I won't go*, non voglio andare; *I wouldn't mind going*, non mi spiacerebbe andare; *she isn't rich*, non è ricca **3.** (**Fraseologia**): — *any later*, non più tardi, non oltre ‖ — *at all*, niente affatto ‖ — *bad*, non c'è male ‖ — *but*, non è che non: — *but I believe him to be an honest man*, non già che io non lo creda un uomo onesto ‖ — *in the least*, niente affatto ‖ — *much*, non molto ‖ — *that*, non che ‖ *" Will he ever come? ", " — he! "*, «Verrà mai?», «Lui?, no davvero!».

notability [,noutə'biliti], *s.* **1.** notabilità, cospicuità **2.** persona autorevole.

notable ['noutəbl], *ag.* **1.** degno di nota, notevole; rilevante; insigne **2.** (*chim.*) percettibile, sensibile **3.** (*dial.*) attiva, laboriosa (di donna di casa) ‖ *s.* persona eminente; notabile ‖ *Assembly of Notables*, (*st. francese*) assemblea dei Notabili.

notableness ['noutəblnis], *s.* **1.** notabilità, cospicuità **2.** persona autorevole.

notably ['noutəbli], *av.* notevolmente; considerevolmente; sensibilmente.

notarial [nou'tɛəriəl], *ag.* notarile, di notaio.

notarially [nou'tɛəriəli], *av.* per via notarile.

to **notarize** ['noutəraiz], *v.t.* (*amer.*) legalizzare (da parte di un notaio).

notary ['noutəri], *s.* notaio: *before a —*, davanti al notaio ☆ — *public*, notaio.

notation [nou'teifən], *s.* **1.** (*mus.*) notazione **2.** (*mat.*) numerazione.

notch [nɔtʃ], *s.* **1.** (*mec.*) tacca, dentellatura, incavo a V **2.** intaglio **3.** (*geog. spec. amer.*) passo fra monti.

to **notch**, *v.t.* **1.** (*mec.*) fare delle tacche; dentellare **2.** intagliare.

note [nout], *s.* **1.** (*mus.*) nota; tono: *to sing* (o *to play*) *a false —*, prendere una nota falsa; *to strike the —*, dare la nota ‖ *speech that hits the right —*, discorso che cade a proposito **2.** marchio, segno: — *of infamy*, marchio d'infamia **3.** (*tip.*) segno, punto: — *of exclamation*, punto esclamativo, — *of interrogation*, punto interrogativo **4.** nota, appunto: *to speak from notes*, parlare seguendo appunti, consultare delle note nel parlare; *to take — of a declaration*, prendere atto di una dichiarazione **5**. commento; chiosa: *critical notes on a work*, commento critico su di un'opera; *to write* (o *to make*) *notes on a text*, commentare un testo **6**. biglietto, letterina: *I wrote off a — to her at once*, le ho mandato subito un biglietto **7**. (*comm.*) cedola; acconto; polizza di pagamento: *— of hand*, cambiale **8**. banconota **9**. rinomanza; distinzione; importanza: *nothing of —*, niente d'importante; *all the men of — I know*, tutte le persone importanti che conosco; *it is worthy of — that*, conviene notare che ☆ — *-paper*, carta da lettere ‖ *bibliographical —*, nota bibliografica; *diplomatic —*, nota diplomatica; *half —*, (*mus.*) semitono.

to **note**, *v.t.* notare, prendere nota di; osservare; marcare: *to — sthg.* (*down*), registrare ql.co.

notebook ['noutbuk], *s.* taccuino.

noted ['noutid], *ag.* **1**. eminente, illustre, celebre (di persona) **2**. rimarchevole, degno di nota (di cosa).

notedly ['noutidli], *av.* con attenzione.

notehead ['nouthed], *s.* intestazione.

noteless ['noutlis], *ag.* privo di interesse; poco notevole.

notelet ['noutlit], *s.* noterella; breve annotazione.

noter ['noutə*], *s.c.* osservatore, osservatrice.

noteworthiness ['nout,wə:ðinis], *s.* importanza.

noteworthy ['nout,wə:ði], *ag.* notevole.

nothing ['nʌθiŋ], *pron. indef.* nulla, niente, nessuna cosa: *— new, good*, niente di nuovo, di buono; *less than —*, meno di niente; *he could do — else but obey*, non potè fare a meno di obbedire; *there is — doing*, non c'è niente da fare; *this is — but the truth*, questa non è che la pura verità; *this is — to him*, questo è nulla per lui; *to have — to do with*, non avere niente a che fare con ‖ *as if — at all was the matter*, come se niente fosse ‖ *to be —*, essere ateo, agnostico ‖ *to dance on —*, essere impiccato ‖ *to make — of sthg.*, prendere ql.co. alla leggera ‖ *— venture — win*, prov. chi non risica non rosica ‖ *s.* **1**. (*arit.*) zero **2**. niente; bagattella, cosa da nulla: *he is a mere —*, è uno zero, una nullità; *he whispered sweet nothings to her*, le sussurrava dolci paroline; *to come to —*, risultare inutile, andare in fumo ‖ *much ado about —*, molto rumore per nulla ‖ *av.* **niente affatto, per nulla**: *this helps us —*, ciò non ci giova per niente; *this house is — near large enough for us*, questa casa non è assolutamente abbastanza grande per noi; *we should have been — the worse for it*, non ci avrebbe fatto per nulla male.

nothingness ['nʌθiŋnis], *s.* **1**. inesistenza; il nulla: *God created the world out of —*, Dio creò il mondo dal nulla **2**. nullità.

notice ['noutis], *s.* **1**. avviso, avvertimento: *public —*, avviso al pubblico; *till further —*, fino a nuovo avviso; *to give s.o. — of one's intentions*, avvertire qlcu. delle proprie intenzioni; *to send a —*, mandare un avviso **2**. (*dir.*) intimazione; notifica: *— of measures about to be taken*, notifica dei provvedimenti che saranno presi; *to serve a — on s.o.*, notificare un mandato di arresto a qlcu. **3**. preavviso; disdetta; licenziamento: *at short —*, con breve preavviso; *to give — (to quit)*, dare disdetta: *to give a servant —*, licenziare; *to give a week's —*, dare una settimana di preavviso **4**. attenzione; cura; osservazione: *take —!*, attenzione!; *who brought it to your —?*, chi te l'ha fatto osservare?; *to come into —*, attrarre l'attenzione; *to take — of sthg.*, osservare ql.co., fare attenzione a ql.co.; occuparsi di ql.co.; accorgersi di ql.co. **5**. articolo, recensione ☆ — *-board*, tabellone (per affissi); cartello pubblicitario.

to **notice**, *v.t.* **1**. osservare **2**. (I, V) osservare, fare attenzione a; badare a, occuparsi di; notare: *did you — her new ring?*, avete osservato il suo nuovo anello?; *she would get herself noticed*, ci teneva ad attirare l'attenzione su di sè **3**. avere attenzioni, riguardi, cortesie per, verso **4**. (*giornalismo*) recensire.

noticeable ['noutisəbl], *ag.* **1**. notevole **2**. percettibile.

noticeably ['noutisəbli], *av.* notevolmente.

notifiable ['noutifaiəbl], *ag.* da denunciarsi: *a — disease*, una malattia da dichiarare alla Sanità.

notification [,noutifi'keiʃən], *s.* notificazione, notifica.

to **notify** ['noutifai], *v.t.* notificare, far sapere: *to — s.o. of sthg.*, notificare ql.co. a qlcu.: *please, — me of the date of your arrival*, per favore, fammi sapere la data del tuo arrivo.

notion ['nouʃən], *s.* **1**. (*fil.*) nozione, concetto **2**. idea, opinione; teoria: *I haven't the haziest — of what he means*, non ho la più vaga idea di quello che intende dire; *it is a common — that*, è opinione comune che; *to take up a —*, mettersi in testa ql.co. **3**. intenzione, progetto: *I have no — of resigning*, non ho intenzione di dimettermi **4**. *pl.* (*amer.*) piccoli oggetti utili a poco prezzo; piccole invenzioni ingegnose.

notional ['nouʃənl], *ag.* **1**. immaginario, chimerico **2**. speculativo **3**. (*amer.*) bizzarro; fantastico.

notionally ['nouʃnəli], *av.* speculativamente.

notoriety [,noutə'raiəti], *s.* notorietà.

notorious [nou'tɔ:riəs], *ag.* **1**. noto, conosciuto, manifesto, notorio; evidente: *a ship — for ill-luck*, una nave conosciuta per la sua cattiva fortuna **2**. famigerato: *a — smuggler*, un famigerato contrabbandiere.

notoriously [nou'tɔ:riəsli], *av.* notoriamente.

notus ['noutəs], *s.* (*poet.*) noto (vento).

notwithstanding [,notwiθ'stændiŋ], *av.* (*arc.*) nondimeno ‖ *cong.* (*arc.*) benchè ‖ *prep.* nonostante, malgrado: *— his resistance*, nonostante la sua resistenza; *this —*, nonostante questo.

nougat ['nu:ga:], *s.* torrone.

nought [no:t], *s.* **1**. nulla ‖ *to bring to —*, rovinare; *to come to —*, rovinarsi **2**. (*arit.*) zero.

noumenon ['naumənon], *pl.* **noumena** ['naumənə], *s.* (*fil.*) noumeno.

noun [naun], *s.* (*gram.*) nome, sostantivo.

to **nourish** ['nʌriʃ], *v.t.* **1**. nutrire, alimentare: *he nourished his dog on* (o *with*) *meat*, egli nutriva il suo cane con carne **2**. *fig.* nutrire, accarezzare (speranza, ecc.).

nourishable ['nʌriʃəbl], *ag.* nutribile.

nourishing ['nʌriʃiŋ], *ag.* nutriente, nutritivo.

nourishment ['nʌriʃmənt], *s.* nutrimento.

nous [naus], *s.* **1**. (*fil.*) intelletto **2**. (*sl.*) senso comune; accortezza.

Nova Scotia ['nouvə'skouʃə], *no.pr.* (*geog.*) Nuova Scozia.

novel[1] ['novəl], *ag.* novello, nuovo; insolito.

novel[2], *s.* **1**. romanzo: *biographical —*, biografia romanzata **2**. (*arc.*) novella (in raccolte quali il «Decamerone») **3**. *pl.* (*dir.*) Novelle (nel Codice di Giustiniano) ☆ — *-writer*, romanziere ‖ *cycle- —*, romanzo fiume; *detective- —*, romanzo poliziesco.

novelette [,novə'let], *s.* **1**. romanzo breve **2**. (*mus.*) novelletta.

novelist ['novəlist], *s.* romanziere.

to **novelize** ['novəlaiz], *v.t.* romanzare.

novelty ['novəlti], *s.* novità.

November [nou'vembə*], *s.* novembre.

novennial [nou'veniəl], *ag.* novennale.

novercal [nou'və:kəl], *ag.* di matrigna.

novice ['novis], *s.* **1**. (*eccl.*) novizio **2**. apprendista: *to be a — in* (o *at*) *sthg.*, essere apprendista in ql.co.

noviceship ['novisʃip], *s.* noviziato.

noviciate, novitiate [nou'viʃiit], *s.* **1**. (*eccl.*) noviziato: *to go through one's —*, fare il noviziato **2**. apprendistato, tirocinio.

novocaine [,nouvə'kein], *s.* (*farm.*) novocaina.

now [nau], *av.* **1**. ora, adesso; attualmente; al presente: *— or never!*, ora o mai!; *— loud, and — low*, ora forte, ora piano ‖ *just —*, proprio ora. ‖ *— and again* (o *— and then*), di quando in quando **2**. subito, immediatamente: *he is going to come —*, verrà immediatamente **3**. allora: *it was — clear that...*, allora risultò chiaro che... **4. ebbene; a dire il vero:** —, *it is a shame*, ebbene, è una vergogna ‖ *cong.* **ora che:** — *you mention it*, *I remember*, ora che lo dici, me ne ricordo.

now, *s.* il presente ‖ *by* —, ormai: *he should be here by* —, dovrebbe essere qui ormai ‖ *from* — *on* (o *scherz. from* — *till doomsday*), d'ora innanzi.

nowaday ['nauədei], *ag. attributivo* del giorno d'oggi, d'oggigiorno.

nowadays ['nauədeiz], *av.* al giorno d'oggi, oggigiorno ‖ *s.* oggigiorno.

Nowel[1] [nou'el], *inter.s.* (arc.) Natale (nelle cantilene e nei canti natalizi).

nowel[2] ['nouel], *s.* (metal.) fondo, staffa inferiore.

nowhere ['nouweə*], *s.* luogo inesistente: *he came out of* —, apparve misteriosamente.

nowhere, *av.* in nessun luogo ‖ *to be* —, (spor.) non riuscire, fallire; non entrare in classifica (in gare, concorsi).

nowise ['nouwaiz], *av.* in nessun modo; niente affatto.

noxious ['nokʃəs], *ag.* nocivo, dannoso; malsano: — *gases*, gas nocivi.

noxiously ['nokʃəsli], *av.* nocivamente, in modo dannoso, malsano.

noxiousness ['nokʃəsnis], *s.* l'essere nocivo, dannoso, malsano.

noyance ['noiəns], *s.* (arc.) noia, fastidio, seccatura.

nozzle ['nozl], *s.* **1.** becco, beccuccio (di teiera, tubo, pompa); boccaglio, lancia (in pompa antincendio) **2.** (sl.) naso; muso.

n't [nt], *V.* not 2.

nuance [nju(:)'ɑ:ns], *s.* sfumatura (anche *fig.*).

nub [nʌb], **nubble** ['nʌbl], *s.* **1.** piccolo pezzo (specialmente di carbone) **2.** protuberanza; nodo **3.** (amer.) nocciolo, essenziale (di ql.co.).

nubbly ['nʌbli], *ag.* nodoso, pieno di protuberanze.

nubiferous [nju'bifərəs], *ag.* nubifero.

nubile ['nju:bil], *ag.* nubile.

nubility [nju'biliti], *s.* stato, condizione di nubile.

nubilous ['nju:biləs], *ag.* nuvoloso; nebbioso.

nucleal ['nju:kliəl], **nuclear** ['nju:kliə*], *ag.* (fis.) nucleare ☆ — *chain reaction*, reazione nucleare a catena; — *energy*, energia nucleare; — *physics*, fisica nucleare; — *reactor*, reattore nucleare; — *warfare*, guerra atomica.

nucleate ['nju:kliit], *ag.* avente un nucleo.

to nucleate ['nju:klieit], *v.t.i.* raccogliere, raccogliersi in un nucleo.

nucleated [,nju:kli'eitid], *ag.* avente un nucleo.

nucleation [,nju:kli'eifən], *s.* formazione di un nucleo.

nucleiform ['nju:klii,fo:m], *ag.* a forma di nucleo.

nuclein ['nju:kliin], *s.* (chim.) nucleina.

nucleolar [nju'kli:ələ*], *ag.* (biol.) di, della natura di un nucleolo.

nucleolate(d) ['nju:kliəleit(id)], *ag.* avente un nucleo, un nucleolo.

nucleole ['nju:klioul], *s.* (biol.) nucleolo.

nucleolus [nju'kli:ələs], *pl.* **nucleoli** [nju'kli:əlai], *s.* (biol.) nucleolo.

nucleon ['nju:klioun], *s.* (fis. chim.) nucleone (protone, neutrone nel nucleo atomico).

nucleonics [,nju:kli'oniks], *s.* (fis.) fisica nucleare.

nucleus ['nju:kliəs], *pl.* **nuclei** ['nju:kliai], *s.* **1.** (astr. biol. chim. fis.) nucleo **2.** nocciolo **3.** centro.

nude [nju:d], *ag.* **1.** nudo, spoglio; *fig.* semplice **2.** (dir.) senza valore, nullo ‖ *s.* (pitt. scult.) nudo: *a study from the* —, un nudo dal vero.

nudely ['nju:dli], *av.* nudamente.

nudeness ['nju:dnis], *s.* **1.** nudità **2.** (pitt. scult.) nudo.

nudge [nʌdʒ], *s.* gomitata; colpetto (per richiamare l'attenzione).

to nudge, *v.t.* dare una gomitata, un colpetto a (per richiamare l'attenzione).

nudism ['nju:dizəm], *s.* nudismo.

nudist ['nju:dist], *s.* nudista.

nudity ['nju:diti], *s.* **1.** nudità **2.** (pitt. scult.) nudo.

nugatory ['nju:gətəri], *ag.* **1.** futile, vano, frivolo **2.** (dir.) nullo, non valido.

nugget ['nʌgit], *s.* pepita d'oro.

nuisance ['nju:sns], *s.* **1.** noia, seccatura, fastidio, incomodità; *fig.* supplizio, flagello: *her child is an awful* —, il suo bimbo è un vero flagello **2.** danno; violazione di leggi e regolamenti ‖ *commit no* —, vietato lordare, arrecare danni ☆ — *raid*, incursione di disturbo.

null [nʌl], *ag.* **1.** nullo, insignificante **2.** (dir.) nullo, non valido ‖ — *and void*, senza valore legale.

to null, *v.t.* annullare.

nullification [,nʌlifi'keifən], *s.* annullamento: *the* — *of a law*, l'abrogazione di una legge.

nullifier ['nʌlifaiə*], *s.* annullatore.

to nullify ['nʌlifai], *v.t.* annullare; (dir.) privare di validità.

nullipore ['nʌlipɔ:*], *s.* (bot.) nullipora.

nullity ['nʌliti], *s.* **1.** il non essere valido **2.** nullità: *he is a* —, egli è una nullità ☆ — *suit*, (dir.) processo per annullamento di matrimonio.

numb [nʌm], *ag.* **1.** intorpidito, intirizzito: — *with cold*, intirizzito dal freddo **2.** insensibile; tramortito; intontito: — *with grief*, paralizzato dal dolore ☆ — *-fish*, (ittiol.) torpedine.

to numb[1], *v.t.* **1.** intorpidire, intirizzire **2.** *fig.* paralizzare; istupidire.

number ['nʌmbə*], *s.* **1.** numero, cifra (abbr. No., pl. Nos.): *cardinal* —, numero cardinale; *decimal* —, numero decimale; *even numbers*, numeri pari; *odd numbers*, numeri dispari; *his pictures are twenty in* —, i suoi quadri ammontano a venti ‖ *Numbers*, Numeri (quarto libro dell'Antico Testamento) ‖ — *one*, (sl.) se stesso ‖ *No. 10* (*Downing Street*), Downing Street N. 10 (residenza del Primo Ministro britannico a Londra) ‖ *the science of numbers*, la scienza dei numeri, l'aritmetica ‖ *his* — *went up*, (sl.) morì; *to lose the* — *of one's mess*, morire **2.** numero, quantità: *a large* —, un gran numero; *a small* — *came*, venne poca gente; *they made up a* —, facevano numero; *they won by numbers*, vinsero perché più numerosi **3.** (gram.) numero: *the plural* —, il (numero) plurale **4.** numero (di fascicolo, dispensa, giornale): *have you got yesterday's* — *of "The Times"?*, hai il numero di ieri del « Times »? **5.** (ind. tessile) titolo **6.** *pl.* (poes.) versi; piedi **7.** (mus.) note ☆ — *board*, tavoletta di numerazione; — *plate*, (aut.) targa ‖ *back* —, numero arretrato (di giornale); *registration* —, numero di matricola.

to number, *v.t.* **1.** contare, numerare; calcolare: *his days are numbered*, ha i giorni contati **2.** annoverare: *I* — *her among my friends*, la annovero tra i miei amici **3.** ammontare a: *the population numbered one million*, la popolazione ammontava ad un milione **4.** (ind. tessile) titolare.

numberer ['nʌmbərə*], *s.c.* numeratore, numeratrice.

numberless ['nʌmbəlis], *ag.* innumerevole.

numbly ['nʌmli], *av.* come intirizzito, intorpidito.

numbness ['nʌmnis], *s.* torpore; intorpidimento (anche *fig.*).

numdah ['nʌmdɑ:], *s.* (ang.-in.) feltro per sella.

numerability [,nju:mərə'biliti], *s.* numerabilità.

numerable ['nju:mərəbl], *ag.* calcolabile, numerabile.

numerableness ['nju:mərəblnis], *s.* numerabilità.

numeral ['nju:mərəl], *ag. s.* (gram.) numerale.

numerally ['nju:mərəli], *av.* numericamente.

to numerate ['nju:məreit], *v.t.* contare, numerare.

numeration [,nju:mə'reifən], *s.* numerazione.

numerator ['nju:məreitə*], *s.* (arit.) numeratore.

numerical [nju(:)'merikəl], *ag.* numerico, numerale.

numerically [nju(:)'merikəli], *av.* numericamente.

numerosity [,nju:mə'rositi], *s.* numerosità.

numerous ['nju:mərəs], *ag.* **1.** numeroso **2.** (ret.) armonioso (di verso).

numerously ['nju:mərəsli], *av.* in gran numero.

numerousness ['nju:mərəsnis], *s.* **1.** numerosità **2.** armonia (di versi, ecc.).

numismatic [,nju:miz'mætik], *ag.* numismatico.

numismatics [ˌnjuːmizˈmætiks], s. numismatica.
numismatist [njuː(ː)ˈmizmətist], s. numismatico.
numismatology [njuː(ː)ˌmizməˈtɔlədʒi], s. numismatica.
nummary [ˈnʌməri], **nummulary** [ˈnʌmjuləri], ag. monetario, relativo alla moneta.
nummulite [ˈnʌmjulait], s. (paleont.) nummolite.
numskull [ˈnʌmskʌl], s. testa dura, stupido.
numskulled [ˈnʌmskʌld], ag. stupido, tardo.
nun [nʌn], s. 1. monaca, suora: to become a —, farsi suora 2. piccione dal cappuccio ☆ —'s thread, cotone da cucito; —'s veiling, flanella, mussola di lana.
nun-buoy [ˈnʌnbɔi], s. boa, gavitello a doppio cono.
nunciature [ˈnʌnʃiətʃə*], s. (eccl.) nunziatura.
nuncio [ˈnʌnʃiou], s. (eccl.) nunzio ‖ Papal Nuncio, Nunzio apostolico, pontificio.
to nuncupate [ˈnʌnkjupeit], v.t. (dir.) esprimere verbalmente (le proprie volontà testamentarie).
nuncupation [ˌnʌnkjuˈpeiʃən], s. (dir.) nuncupazione.
nuncupative [ˈnʌnkjupeitiv], ag. (dir.) nuncupativo: — will, testamento nuncupativo.
nunhood [ˈnʌnhud], s. monacato (di religiosa).
nunlike [ˈnʌnlaik], ag. monacale (di religiosa).
nunnery [ˈnʌnəri], s. convento (di monache).
nunship [ˈnʌnʃip], s. monacato (di religiosa).
nunnish [ˈnʌniʃ], ag. monacale (di religiosa).
nuphar [ˈnjuːfə*], s. (bot.) nenufaria, ninfea.
nuptial [ˈnʌpʃəl], ag. nuziale☆ — ring, anello nuziale.
nuptials [ˈnʌpʃəlz], s. pl. nozze, sponsali.
Nuremberg [ˈnjuərəmbəːg], no.pr. (geog.) Norimberga.
nurse [nəːs], s. 1. nutrice, balia; bambinaia: to put (out) to —, mettere a balia 2. infermiera 3. (entom.) ape operaia ☆ — -child, bimbo a balia ‖ district —, visitatrice sanitaria; dry- —, balia asciutta.
to nurse, v.t. 1. allattare, nutrire: a mother should — her baby for eight months, una madre dovrebbe allattare il suo piccolo per otto mesi 2. allevare: he was nursed in luxury, fu allevato nel lusso 3. fig. alimentare, nutrire; incoraggiare (sentimenti): he nursed a secret hope, nutriva una segreta speranza 4. cullare, stringersi al seno: they drove home again, the girl nursing her new doll, tornarono a casa in carrozza, con la bimba che si stringeva al petto la bambola nuova 5. curare (ammalati): I shall — him back to health, le mie cure gli renderanno la salute.
nursery [ˈnəːsri], s. 1. camera dei bambini 2. asilo, scuola materna 3. vivaio ☆ — -maid, bambinaia; — tale, favola, racconto per bambini ‖ day —, (amer.) nido per bambini.
nurseryman, pl. **nurserymen** [ˈnəːsrimən], s. orticoltore.
nursing [ˈnəːsiŋ], ag. 1. che allatta, nutre 2. che cura ‖ s. 1. allattamento 2. il curare, il nutrire (anche fig.) 3. professione di infermiera: to go in for —, farsi infermiera ☆ — -house (o — home), casa di cura.
nursling [ˈnəːsliŋ], s. 1. bimbo a balia, lattante, poppante 2. malato (curato da un'infermiera) 3. allievo; giovane agli inizi della carriera.
nurture [ˈnəːtʃə*], s. 1. vitto, nutrimento 2. fig. nutrimento; disciplina, educazione: — of the mind, nutrimento dello spirito.

to nurture, v.t. 1. nutrire, allevare 2. fig. educare.
nut [nʌt], s. 1. noce, nocciuola: to crack a —, rompere una noce ‖ oh, nuts!, storie! ‖ a hard — to crack, un osso duro, una gatta da pelare ‖ to find a blind —, rimanere delusi 2. (mec.) dado 3. (mar.) mazza d'ancora 4. (sl.) elegantone, gagà 5. (sl.) testa: my poor —!, la mia povera testa!; to go off one's —, impazzire ☆ — cake, dolce di noci; — -gall, galla di quercia; — hook, bacchio; fig. ladro di frutta; — -oil, olio di noce; — -tree, noce, nocciuolo; — -wrench, (mec.) chiave per dadi ‖ check —, (mec.) controdado; earth - —, arachide; stop —, (mec.) dado di sicurezza; wing —, (mec.) dado ad alette.
to nut, pass.p.p. **nutted** [ˈnʌtid], v.i. cercare, raccogliere noci: he went nutting, andò a raccogliere noci.
to nutate [njuːˈteit], v.i. (rar.) penzolare; chinarsi.
nutation [njuːˈteiʃən], s. (astr. mec. bot.) nutazione.
nutcracker [ˈnʌˌkrækə*], s. 1. gener. pl. schiaccianoci 2. (ornit.) ghiandaia nocciolaia; picchio 3. pl. (sl.) bazza sdentata; denti.
nuthatch [ˈnʌthætʃ], s. (ornit.) picchio.
nutmeg [ˈnʌtmeg], s. noce moscata ☆ — grater, grattugia per spezie; — liver, fegato cirrotico; — -tree, noce moscata (albero).
nutria [ˈnjuːtriə], s. (zool.) nutria.
nutrient [ˈnjuːtriənt], ag. nutriente ‖ s. sostanza nutriente.
nutriment [ˈnjuːtrimənt], s. nutrimento, cibo.
nutrition [njuː(ː)ˈtriʃən], s. nutrizione, alimentazione.
nutritious [njuː(ː)ˈtriʃəs], ag. nutriente, nutritivo.
nutritiously [njuː(ː)ˈtriʃəsli], av. in modo nutriente, nutritivo.
nutritiousness [njuː(ː)ˈtriʃəsnis], s. efficacia nutritiva.
nutritive [ˈnjuːtritiv], ag. nutritivo ‖ s. cibo nutriente.
nutritively [ˈnjuːtritivli], av. in modo nutritivo.
nuts [nʌts], ag. (sl.) pazzo; svitato: he is —, (fam.) ha le pigne in testa; I'm — on Chopin, vado pazzo per Chopin.
nutshell [ˈnʌt-ʃel], s. guscio di noce ‖ in a —, in poche parole.
nutty [ˈnʌti], ag. 1. che sa di noce 2. con molte noci 3. (sl.) entusiasta, innamorato 4. (amer. sl.) pazzo.
nux vomica [ˈnʌksˈvɔmikə], s. (bot. farm.) noce vomica.
to nuzzle [ˈnʌzl], v.t.i. 1. frugare (col muso); andare annusando (di animali); toccare col naso 2. rannicchiarsi (vicino a ql.co., qlcu.).
Nyasa [ˈnjæsə], no.pr. (geog.) (lago) Niassa ‖ ag.s.c. (abitante) del Niassa.
Nyasaland [ˈnjæsəlænd], no.pr. (geog.) Niassa.
nyctalops [ˈniktələps], s. (patol.) nictalopo.
nylon [ˈnailən], s. 1. nailon 2. pl. (fam.) calze, indumento di nailon: a sale of nylons, vendita di indumenti di nailon ☆ — stockings, calze di nailon.
nymph [nimf], s. 1. (mit. poet.) ninfa 2. (entom.) ninfa, crisalide.
nymphaea [nimˈfiːə], s. (bot.) ninfea.
nymphal [ˈnimfəl], ag. ninfale, di ninfa.
nymphet [ˈnimˈfet], s. (neol.) ninfetta.
nymphomania [ˌnimfəˈmeinjə], s. (patol.) ninfomania.
nystagmus [nisˈtægməs], s. (patol.) nistagmo.

O

o [ou], *pl.* o's, oes, os [ouz], *s.* 1. (*quindicesima lettera dell'alfabeto inglese*) o ‖ — *for Oliver,* (*tel.*) o come Otranto 2. zero: *my 'phone number is three one* — *two,* il mio numero telefonico è tre, uno, zero, due 3. qualunque cosa a forma di circoletto.

o, *inter.* oh!: — *me!,* ahimè!; — *dear me!,* oh me misero!.

o' [ə], *prep.* 1. (*abbr.* di *of*): *five* — *clock tea,* il tè delle cinque; *man-* — *-war,* (*mil.*) nave da guerra 2. (*abbr.* di *on*): *he dreams of it* — *nights,* se lo sogna persino di notte.

O' [ou], *prefisso* (*di cognomi irlandesi; significa* discendente di): *Eugene O'Neill was a great playwright,* Eugene O'Neill fu un grande drammaturgo.

oaf [ouf], *pl.* oafs [oufs], oaves [ouvz], *s.* 1. (*arc.*) figlio di elfi; bimbo sostituito ad un altro dalle fate 2. bimbo idiota, imbecille 3. zoticone, sempliciotto; individuo goffo, rozzo.

oafish ['oufiʃ], *ag.* stupido, balordo.

oafishness ['oufiʃnis], *s.* stupidità, balordaggine.

oak [ouk], *s.* 1. quercia ‖ *the Royal Oak,* la quercia in cui si nascose Carlo II quando sfuggì all'inseguimento di Cromwell (1651) ‖ *the Oaks,* corsa di puledre di tre anni (a Epsom) 2. porta esterna (di appartamento nelle università inglesi): *to sport one's* —, (*sl.*) chiudersi nel proprio appartamento per non ricevere visite ☆ — *-apple,* galla (di quercia): — *-apple Day,* 29 maggio (anniversario della Restaurazione di Carlo II, 1660); — *-bark,* corteccia di quercia, tannino; — *-button,* galla; — *-grove,* querceto, querceta; — *-pest,* (*entom.*) filossera della quercia; — *-timber,* legno di quercia, rovere; — *-tree,* quercia; — *-wood,* querceto; legno di quercia, rovere ‖ *cork-* —, quercia da sughero.

oaken ['oukən], *ag.* (*arc.*) di legno di quercia.

oaklet ['ouklit], *s.* (*bot.*) querciola.

oakum ['oukəm], *s.* stoppa.

oar [ɔ:*], *s.* remo ‖ *to be chained to the* —, lavorare come una bestia da soma ‖ *to pull a good* —, essere un buon rematore ‖ *to put in one's* —, intervenire a sproposito, impicciarsi di ql.co. ‖ *to rest on one's oars,* *fig.* dormire sugli allori, sospendere il lavoro ☆ — *-blade,* pala di remo; — *-handle,* impugnatura di remo ‖ *four-* —, imbarcazione a quattro remi; *pair-* —, imbarcazione a due remi.

to oar, *v.t.i.* remare; sospingere coi remi: *they oared the boat towards the shore,* sospinsero la barca verso la riva a forza di remi ‖ *we oared our arms,* agitammo le braccia (a guisa di remi).

oarage ['ɔ:ridʒ], *s.* remata.

oarless ['ɔ:lis], *ag.* senza remi.

oarsman, *pl.* oarsmen ['ɔ:zmən], *s.* rematore.

oarsmanship ['ɔ:zmənʃip], *s.* l'arte del remare.

oarswoman ['ɔ:z,wumən], *pl.* oarswomen ['ɔ:z,wimin], *s.* rematrice.

oary ['ɔ:ri], *ag.* a forma di remo, simile a remo; fornito di remi.

oasis [ou'eisis], *pl.* oases [ou'eisi:z], *s.* oasi.

oast [oust], *s.* forno per asciugare il luppolo.

oat [out], *s.* gener.pl. avena ‖ *to feel one's oats,* (*sl. amer.*) sentirsi in forma; sentirsi importante ‖ *to sow one's wild oats,* *fig.* correre la cavallina 2. (*poet.*) zampogna ☆ — *-cake,* focaccia di farina d'avena; — *-meal,* farina d'avena ‖ *wild* —, avena selvatica.

oaten ['outn], *ag.* d'avena.

oath [ouθ], *pl.* oaths [ouðz],*s.* 1. giuramento: *I'll take my* — *on it,* ci giurerei; *fig.* metterei la mano sul fuoco; *to break one's* —, venir meno al proprio giuramento; *to release* (o *to relieve) s.o. from his* —, liberare qlcu. dal giuramento; *to swear an* —, fare, prestare giuramento 2. bestemmia; imprecazione: *he gave a terrible* —, proferì un'atroce bestemmia ☆ — *-breaker,* spergiuro.

Obadiah [,oubə'daiə], *no.pr.m.* (*Bibbia*) Abdia.

obduracy ['ɔbdjurəsi], *s.* 1. indurimento (di cuore); inesorabilità, inflessibilità 2. ostinazione; impenitenza.

obdurate ['ɔbdjurit], *ag.* 1. indurito; inesorabile, inflessibile 2. ostinato; impenitente; *fig.* incallito.

obdurately ['ɔbdjuritli], *av.* 1.inesorabilmente 2. ostinatamente.

obdurateness ['ɔbdjuritnis], *s.* 1. durezza; resistenza 2. ostinatezza.

obedience [ə'bi:djəns], *s.* 1. ubbidienza; osservanza; sottomissione: — *to the will of s.o.,* sottomissione alla volontà di qlcu.; *to compel* — *from s.o.,* costringere qlcu. all'ubbidienza; *to enforce* — *to the law,* far rispettare la legge 2. giurisdizione: *the Roman* —, la giurisdizione della Chiesa di Roma.

obedient [ə'bi:djənt], *ag.* obbediente, docile, sottomesso.

obediently [ə'bi:djəntli], *av.* ubbidientemente.

obeisance [ou'beisəns], *s.* 1. (*arc.*) inchino, riverenza; saluto rispettoso 2. deferenza; omaggio: *to do* (o *to make* o *to pay*) — *to s.o.,* rendere omaggio a qlcu., inchinarsi a qlcu.

obelisk ['ɔbilisk], *s.* 1. (*arch.*) obelisco 2. (*tip.*) obelo, asterisco.

to obelize ['ɔbilaiz], *v.t.* segnare, contrassegnare con obelo, con asterisco.

obelus ['ɔbiləs], *pl.* obeli ['ɔbilai], *s.* (*tip.*) obelo, asterisco.

Oberon ['oubərən], *no.pr.m.* (*mit.*) Oberon.

obese [ou'bi:s], *ag.* obeso.

obeseness [ou'bi:snis], obesity [ou'bi:siti], *s.* obesità.

to obey [ə'bei], *v.t.i.* (III) ubbidire; essere sottomesso; cedere: *she can make herself obeyed,* ella sa farsi ubbidire; *we must* — *the law,* dobbiamo sottometterci alle leggi.

obeyingly [ə'beiiŋli], *av.* ubbidientemente.

to obfuscate ['ɔbfʌskeit], *v.t.* 1. offuscare 2. confondere, disorientare; sbalordire.

obfuscation [,ɔbfʌs'keiʃən], *s.* offuscamento (anche *fig.*).

obiter ['ɔbitə*], *av.* incidentalmente.

obituarist [ə'bitjuərist], *s.* necrologista.

obituary [ə'bitjuəri], *ag.* necrologico ‖ *s.* necrologia.

object ['ɔbdʒikt], *s.* 1. oggetto; argomento, materia: *the* — *looked at under the microscope,* l'oggetto esaminato al microscopio; *the Bible had been the* — *of his study,* la Bibbia aveva formato la materia dei suoi studi 2. scopo, fine; obiettivo: *with the same* — *in view,* con la stessa intenzione; *to have sthg. for* (o *as*) *an* —, avere ql.co. come scopo 3. (*gram.*) oggetto: *direct, indirect* —, oggetto diretto, indiretto 4. persona, cosa di aspetto scostante o ridicolo: *what an* — *she looked in those old rags!,* come stava male con quei vecchi cenci! ☆ — *-glass,* (*foto.*) obiettivo.

to object [əb'dʒekt], *v.t.i.* obiettare, fare delle obiezioni; opporsi a; protestare contro: *I objected that there was no time*, obiettai che non c'era tempo; *what have you got to — against her?*, cosa hai da obiettare contro di lei?, che cosa le rimproveri?; *to — to doing sthg.*, rifiutarsi di fare ql.co.; *I don't — to waiting*, non m'importa aspettare.

objectification [ɔb,dʒektifi'keiʃən], *s.* (*fil.*) oggettivazione.

to **objectify** [ɔb'dʒektifai], *v.t.* (*fil.*) oggettivare.

objection [əb'dʒekʃən], *s.* **1.** obiezione: *to raise an —*, sollevare un'obiezione **2.** avversione: *he has a strong — to getting up early*, sente una forte avversione ad alzarsi presto; *we have a strong — to him*, sentiamo una profonda avversione per lui **3.** inconveniente; ostacolo: *that presents objections*, ciò offre degli inconvenienti.

objectionable [əb'dʒekʃnəbl], *ag.* **1.** biasimevole; reprensibile **2.** sgradevole, ripugnante.

objective [ɔb'dʒektiv], *ag.* **1.** (*fil. gram.*) oggettivo: *— case*, caso oggettivo **2.** obiettivo ‖ *s.* **1.** (*foto. mil.*) obiettivo **2.** (*gram.*) caso oggettivo.

objectively [əb'dʒektivli], *av.* **1.** (*gram.*) oggettivamente **2.** obiettivamente.

objectiveness [əb'dʒektivnis], *s.* **1.** oggettività **2.** obiettività.

objectivism [ɔb'dʒektivizəm], *s.* (*fil.*) oggettivismo.

objectivity [,ɔbdʒek'tiviti], *V.* **objectiveness**.

objectless [ɔbdʒiktlis], *ag.* senza oggetto; senza scopo.

objector [əb'dʒektə*], *s.* confutatore; oppositore ☆ *conscientious —*, obiettore di coscienza.

oblate[1] ['ɔbleit], *ag.* (*geom.*) schiacciato ai poli.

oblate[2], *s.* (*eccl.*) oblato.

oblation [ou'bleiʃən], *s.* (*eccl.*) oblazione ‖ *the great —*, il sacramento dell'Eucarestia.

obligant ['ɔbligənt], *s.* (*dir.*) debitore.

to **obligate** ['ɔbligeit], *v.t.* (*dir.*) obbligare, costringere.

obligation [,ɔbli'geiʃən], *s.* **1.** obbligo; dovere; impegno: *without —*, (*comm.*) senza impegno; *to be under an — to s.o.*, aver un obbligo verso qlcu.; *to hold oneself under an —*, sentirsi obbligato; *to lay* (o *to put*) *s.o. under an — to do sthg.*, obbligare qlcu. a fare ql.co. (per gratitudine); *to meet one's obligations*, tener fede ai propri impegni; *to repay an —*, ricambiare un favore **2.** (*dir.*) obbligazione.

obligatorily [ɔ'bligətərili], *av.* obbligatoriamente.

obligatoriness [ɔ'bligətərinis], *s.* obbligatorietà.

obligatory [ɔ'bligətəri], *ag.* obbligatorio: *to make it — (up)on s.o. to do sthg.*, obbligare qlcu. a fare ql.co.

to **oblige** [ə'blaidʒ], *v.t.* **1.** (IV) obbligare, costringere: *the law obliges parents to send their children to school*, la legge obbliga i genitori a mandare a scuola i loro figli; *to be obliged to do sthg.*, essere obbligato a, dover fare ql.co. **2.** fare un favore a, fare cosa grata a: *please — me by closing the door*, fammi il favore di chiudere la porta; *to be obliged to s.o.*, essere grato a qlcu. ‖ *to go out obliging*, (*sl.*) andare a fare servizi a ore.

obligee [,ɔbli'dʒi:], *s.* (*dir.*) creditore; beneficiario.

obliging [ə'blaidʒiŋ], *ag.* cortese; compiacente.

obligingly [ə'blaidʒiŋli], *av.* cortesemente; compiacentemente.

obligingness [ə'blaidʒiŋnis], *s.* cortesia; compiacenza.

obligor [,ɔbli'gɔ:*], *s.* (*dir.*) debitore.

oblique [ə'bli:k], *ag.* **1.** inclinato, obliquo: *— angle*, (*geom.*) angolo non retto; *— plane*, (*geom.*) piano inclinato **2.** (*gram. ret.*) indiretto: *— case*, caso indiretto; *— oration* (o *speech*), discorso indiretto **3.** *fig.* evasivo; contorto; indiretto: *— ways*, mezzi indiretti.

to **oblique**, *v.i.* **1.** essere, diventare obliquo (di linea, piano, ecc.) **2.** (*mil.*) avanzare obliquamente.

obliquely [ə'bli:kli], *av.* **1.** obliquamente **2.** indirettamente.

obliqueness [ə'bli:knis], **obliquity** [ə'blikwiti],

s. **1.** obliquità **2.** *fig.* mancanza di franchezza, di dirittura.

to **obliterate** [ə'blitəreit], *v.t.* cancellare (anche *fig.*): *little by little every recollection of it was obliterated*, a poco a poco se ne cancellò ogni ricordo; *to — one's signature*, cancellare la propria firma.

obliteration [ə,blitə'reiʃən], *s.* cancellatura; distruzione; estinzione.

oblivion [ə'bliviən], *s.* oblio, dimenticanza: *to fall into —*, cadere in dimenticanza, in disuso; *to rescue s.o., sthg. from —*, salvare qlcu., ql.co. dall'oblio ‖ *Act* (o *Bill*) *of Oblivion*, (legge d') amnistia.

oblivious [ə'bliviəs], *ag.* dimentico; immemore.

obliviously [ə'bliviəsli], *av.* con oblio.

obliviousness [ə'bliviəsnis], *s.* oblio.

oblong ['ɔblɔŋ], *ag.* oblungo, bislungo ‖ *s.* figura, oggetto di forma oblunga; (*geom.*) rettangolo.

obloquy ['ɔbləkwi], *s.* **1.** calunnia, ingiuria **2.** cattiva reputazione; disonore; onta.

obmutescence [,ɔbmju'tesəns], *s.* silenzio ostinato.

obmutescent [,ɔbmju'tesənt], *ag.* muto; silenzioso.

obnoxious [əb'nɔkʃəs], *ag.* **1.** odioso, detestabile; biasimevole; sgradevole **2.** (*dir.*) responsabile.

obnoxiousness [əb'nɔkʃəsnis], *s.* **1.** odiosità; sgradevolezza **2.** (*dir.*) responsabilità.

oboe ['oubou], *s.* (*mus.*) oboe.

obol ['ɔbɔl], **obolus** ['ɔbələs], *pl.* **oboli** ['ɔbəlai], *s.* obolo (moneta d'argento dell'antica Grecia).

obscene [ɔb'si:n], *ag.* osceno.

obscenely [ɔb'si:nli], *av.* oscenamente.

obsceneness [ɔb'si:nnis], **obscenity** [ɔb'si:niti], *s.* oscenità; linguaggio osceno.

obscurant [ɔb'skjuərənt], *s.* oscurantista.

obscurantism [,ɔbskju'ræntizəm], *s.* oscurantismo.

obscurantist [,ɔbskju'ræntist], *ag.* di oscurantismo ‖ *s.* oscurantista.

obscuration [,ɔbskjuə'reiʃən], *s.* **1.** oscuramento **2.** (*astr.*) eclissi **3.** *fig.* offuscamento (della vista, ecc.).

obscure [əb'skjuə*], *ag.* **1.** oscuro, tenebroso **2.** *fig.* oscuro; vago; incerto: *the meaning is —*, il significato è oscuro **3.** nascosto; poco noto: *he is an — writer*, è uno scrittore poco noto ‖ *s.* oscurità, tenebra.

to **obscure**, *v.t.* **1.** oscurare; offuscare **2.** nascondere.

obscurely [əb'skjuəli], *av.* oscuramente.

obscureness [əb'skjuənis], *s.* oscurità (di stile).

obscurity [əb'skjuəriti], *s.* oscurità (di stile, nascita, notte, ecc.).

to **obsecrate** ['ɔbsikreit], *v.t.* (*rar.*) pregare, supplicare (una persona); mendicare (una cosa).

obsecration [,ɔbsi'kreiʃən], *s.* **1.** preghiera; supplica; istanza **2.** (*ret.*) ossecrazione.

obsequies ['ɔbsikwiz], *s. pl.* esequie, funerali.

obsequious [əb'si:kwiəs], *ag.* ossequioso; servile.

obsequiously [əb'si:kwiəsli], *av.* ossequiosamente.

obsequiousness [əb'si:kwiəsnis], *s.* ossequiosità.

observable [əb'zə:vəbl], *ag.* **1.** visibile; percettibile; sensibile **2.** notevole **3.** che si deve osservare.

observance [əb'zə:vəns], **observancy** [əb'zə:vənsi], *s.* **1.** osservanza, adempimento (di doveri, legge, ecc.); pratica (di abitudini, riti, ecc.) **2.** (*eccl.*) regola.

observant [əb'zə:vənt], *ag.* **1.** osservante; rispettoso **2.** attento ‖ *s. Observant*, (*eccl.*) francescano osservante.

Observantine [əb'zə:vəntin], *s.* **1.** osservante (frate minore) **2.** carmelitano.

observation [,ɔbzə(:)'veiʃən], *s.* osservazione: *he's under —*, è sorvegliato; (*med.*) è in osservazione; *to escape s.o.'s —*, sfuggire all'attenzione di qlcu. ☆ *— car*, (*ferr.*) vagone panoramico; *— post* (o *post of —*), posto di osservazione.

observatory [əb'zə:vətri], *s.* osservatorio, specola.

to **observe** [əb'zə:v], *v.t.i.* **1.** osservare; praticare, *he observes his religion scrupulously*, pratica con scrupolo la religione **2.** (I, V) notare, osservare; rilevare; considerare; esaminare.

observer [əb'zə:və*], *s.c.* osservatore, osservatrice ‖ *s. (mil.)* vedetta; osservatore (su aerei).

observing [əb'zə:viŋ], *ag.* 1. attento 2. osservante.

observingly [əb'zə:viŋli], *av.* attentamente.

to obsess [əb'ses], *v.t.* ossessionare, perseguitare.

obsession [əb'seʃən], *s.* ossessione.

obsessive [əb'sesiv], *ag.* ossessivo.

obsidian [əb'sidiən], *s. (min.)* ossidiana.

obsolescence [,ɔbsə'lesns], *s.* tendenza a cadere in disuso.

obsolescent [,ɔbsə'lesnt], *ag.* che sta cadendo in disuso; antiquato.

obsolete ['ɔbsəli:t], *ag.* 1. antiquato, fuori moda, disusato; *(scherz.)* antidiluviano 2. *(biol.)* rudimentale.

obsoleteness ['ɔbsəli:tnis], *s.* 1. l'essere antiquato, in disuso 2. *(biol.)* deficienza di sviluppo.

obstacle ['ɔbstəkl], *s.* ostacolo, difficoltà, impedimento: *you are sure to meet with lots of obstacles*, incontrerete certo una quantità di ostacoli ☆ — *-race*, corsa ad ostacoli.

obstetric(al) [ɔb'stetrik(əl)], *ag. (med.)* ostetrico.

obstetrician [,ɔbste'triʃən], *s. (med.)* ostetrico.

obstetrics [ɔb'stetriks], *s. (med.)* ostetricia.

obstinacy ['ɔbstinəsi], *s.* ostinazione, caparbietà.

obstinate ['ɔbstinit], *ag.* ostinato, caparbio.

obstinately ['ɔbstinitli], *av.* ostinatamente.

obstinateness ['ɔbstinitnis], *s.* ostinatezza.

obstreperous [əb'strepərəs], *ag.* assordante, rumoroso; turbolento.

obstreperously [əb'strepərəsli], *av.* in modo assordante; rumorosamente.

obstriction [əb'strikʃən], *s. (rar.)* costrizione.

to obstruct [əb'strʌkt], *v.t.* 1. ostruire, otturare, ingorgare 2. ritardare, impedire (progresso, attività, ecc.); fare ostruzionismo a (un progetto di legge, ecc.).

obstruction [əb'strʌkʃən], *s.* ostacolo, impedimento; ostruzione; intasamento; ingorgo; *(pol.)* ostruzionismo; *(patol.)* ostruzione.

obstructionism [əb'strʌkʃənizəm], *s.* ostruzionismo.

obstructionist [əb'strʌkʃənist], *s.* ostruzionista.

obstructive [əb'strʌktiv], *ag.* ostruente; ostruttivo; ostruzionista.

obstructively [əb'strʌktivli], *av.* in modo da ostruire; con fine ostruzionistico.

obstruent ['ɔbstruənt], *ag.s.* (sostanza) ostruente.

to obtain [əb'tein], *v.t.i.* 1. ottenere, far ottenere; raggiungere, conseguire; procurare 2. prevalere, diffondersi, stabilirsi: *peace will* —, la pace prevarrà.

obtainable [əb'teinəbl], *ag.* ottenibile; raggiungibile.

obtaining [əb'teiniŋ], *(rar.)* obtainment [əb'teinmənt], *s.* conseguimento, raggiungimento.

obtected [əb'tektid], *ag. (entom.)* rinchiuso in involucro chitinoso.

to obtrude [əb'tru:d], *v.t.i.* imporre, imporsi (di idee, opinioni, ecc.); importunare, intromettersi: *he obtruded upon our attention*, si impose alla nostra attenzione; *they — their ideas*, essi impongono le proprie idee.

obtruder [əb'tru:də*], *s.* intruso; importuno.

to obtruncate [əb'trʌŋkeit], *v.t.* troncare; tagliare la testa, la cima di.

obtrusion [əb'tru:ʒən], *s.* intrusione.

obtrusive [əb'tru:siv], *ag.* intruso, importuno.

obtrusively [əb'tru:sivli], *av.* da intruso; importunamente.

obtrusiveness [əb'tru:sivnis], *s.* intrusione; invadenza.

obtundent [əb'tʌndənt], *ag.* ottundente ‖ *s.* sedativo.

to obturate ['ɔbtjuəreit], *v.t.* otturare, ostruire.

obturation [,ɔbtjuə'reiʃən], *s.* otturazione.

obturator ['ɔbtjureitə*], *s.* otturatore.

obtuse [əb'tju:s], *ag.* 1. ottuso (anche *geom.*) 2. *fig.* ottuso, poco intelligente 3. sordo (di dolore, ecc.).

obtusely [əb'tju:sli], *av.* 1. ottusamente 2. *fig.* stupidamente.

obtuseness [əb'tju:snis], *s.* 1. ottusità 2. *fig.* stupidità.

obtusity [əb'tju:siti], *s.* ottusità.

obverse ['ɔbvə:s], *ag.* opposto, inverso ‖ *s.* 1. retto (di medaglia, moneta, pagina, ecc.) 2. opposto, inverso: *the — of the truth*, l'opposto della verità.

obversely [ɔb'və:sli], *av.* inversamente; in opposizione.

to obviate ['ɔbvieit], *v.t.* ovviare; impedire.

obvious ['ɔbviəs], *ag.* ovvio, chiaro, evidente.

obviously ['ɔbviəsli], *av.* ovviamente, evidentemente.

obviousness ['ɔbviəsnis], *s.* chiarezza, evidenza.

occasion [ə'keiʒən], *s.* 1. occasione; opportunità: *to take* (o *to seize*) *the* —, approfittare dell'occasione 2. causa, motivo, ragione: *there is no — to be angry*, non è il caso di andare in collera 3. occorrenza, occasione: *as — requires*, al bisogno ‖ *to rise to the* —, essere all'altezza della situazione 4. *pl.* affari: *one's lawful occasions*, i propri affari legali.

to occasion, *v.t.* cagionare, causare; determinare.

occasional [ə'keiʒənl], *ag.* occasionale, casuale, accidentale; d'occasione (di poesia, ecc.).

occasionalism [ə'keiʒnəlizəm], *s. (fil.)* occasionalismo.

occasionally [ə'keiʒnəli], *av.* occasionalmente, casualmente; di quando in quando.

Occident ['ɔksidənt], *s. (poet.)* Occidente.

occidental [,ɔksi'dentl], *ag.* occidentale.

occidentalism [,ɔksi'dentəlizəm], *s.* occidentalismo, modi e costumi occidentali.

occidentalist [,ɔksi'dentəlist], *s.* occidentalista, fautore, studioso della civiltà occidentale.

to occidentalize [,ɔksi'dentəlaiz], *v.t.* occidentalizzare.

occidentally [,ɔksi'dentəli], *av.* all'occidentale.

occipital [ɔk'sipitl], *ag. (anat.)* occipitale.

occiput ['ɔksipʌt], *s. (anat.)* occipite.

to occlude [ɔ'klu:d], *v.t.i.* 1. occludere; chiudere; chiudersi; interrompere il flusso di 2. *(chim.)* assorbire, trattenere (gas, liquidi).

occlusion [ɔ'klu:ʒən], *s.* occlusione.

occult [ɔ'kʌlt], *ag.* occulto, segreto; misterioso.

to occult, *v.t.i.* occultare; nascondere, nascondersi.

occultation [ɔkəl'teiʃən], *s.* occultamento.

occulted [ɔ'kʌltid], *ag.* occulto; nascosto.

occultism ['ɔkəltizəm], *s.* occultismo.

occultist ['ɔkəltist], *s.* occultista.

occultly [ɔ'kʌltli], *av.* occultamente.

occultness [ɔ'kʌltnis], *s.* occultezza, segretezza.

occupancy ['ɔkjupənsi], *s.* presa di possesso, occupazione.

occupant ['ɔkjupənt], *s.* occupante; locatario.

occupation [,ɔkju'peiʃən], *s.* 1. occupazione, presa di possesso 2. impiego; professione; lavoro: *what is he by* —? (o *what is his* —?), qual è la sua professione?; ☆ — *troops*, truppe, esercito d'occupazione.

occupational [,ɔkju(:)'peiʃənl], *ag.* professionale ☆ — *disease*, malattia del lavoro.

occupier ['ɔkjupaiə*], *s.* occupante; locatario.

to occupy ['ɔkjupai], *v.t.* 1. occupare; prendere possesso di: *Mr. Smith occupies an important position in the Ministry of Education*, il signor Smith occupa un posto importante al Ministero della Pubblica Istruzione; *she occupied herself with* (o *in*) *charities*, ella si occupava di opere di carità 2. impiegare: *why did he not — himself?*, perchè non si è impiegato?.

to occur [ə'kə:*], *pass.p.p.* occurred [ə'kə:d], *v.i.* 1. accadere, capitare, succedere; sopravvenire: *that seldom occurs*, ciò avviene raramente 2. venire in mente: *it suddenly occurred to him that...*, gli venne in mente d'improvviso che... 3. ricorrere: *this sentence very often occurs in his speech*, questa frase ricorre spesso nei suoi discorsi.

occurrence [ə'kʌrəns], *s.* evento, avvenimento: *such accidents are unfortunately of frequent* —, tali incidenti purtroppo accadono spesso.

ocean [ou∫ən], *s.* **1.** oceano **2.** immensità; spazio immenso ☆ — *bill of lading*, (*mar. comm.*) polizza di carico per trasporto oceanico; — *-going*, d'alto mare; — *lane*, rotta oceanica; — *palace*, transatlantico di lusso; — *-river*, grande fiume navigabile; — *tramp*, « carretta », nave da carico.

Oceania [,ou∫i'einjə], *no.pr.* (*geog.*) Oceania.

Oceanian [,ou∫i'einjən], *ag.* dell'Oceania ‖ *s.c.* nativo, nativa dell'Oceania.

oceanic [,ou∫i'ænik], *ag.* **1.** oceanico **2.** pelagico (di flora e fauna marina).

Oceanid [ou'si:ənid], *pl.* **Oceanids** [ou'si:ənidz], **Oceanides** [,ousi'ænidi:z], *s.* (*mit.*) Oceanina (ninfa).

oceanography [,ou∫jə'nɔgrəfi], *s.* oceanografia.

Oceanus [ou'si:ənəs], *no.pr.m.* (*mit.*) Oceano.

ocellus [ou'seləs], **ocelli** [ou'selai], *s.* (*entom.*) ocello.

ocelot ['ousilɔt], *s.* (*zool.*) ocelot.

ochlocracy [ɔk'lɔkrəsi], *s.* (*rar.*) oclocrazia.

ochre ['oukə*], *s.* **1.** (*min.*) ocra **2.** color ocra **3.** (*sl.*) denaro.

ochreous ['oukriəs], **ochroid** ['oukrɔid], **ochrous** ['oukrəs], **ochry** ['oukəri], *ag.* ocraceo.

o'clock [ə'klɔk], *contr.* di *of the clock*: *it is six* —, sono le sei.

octachord ['ɔktəkɔ:d], *s.* (*mus.*) **1.** ottacordo **2.** scala diatonica.

octad ['ɔktæd], *s.* **1.** gruppo di otto **2.** (*chim.*) corpo, elemento ottovalente.

octagon ['ɔktəgən], *s.* (*geom.*) ottagono.

octagonal [ɔk'tægənəl], *ag.* ottangolare, ottagonale.

octahedron [ɔktə'hedrən], *s.* (*geom.*) ottaedro.

octameter [ɔk'tæmitə*], *s.* (*poes.*) ottametro.

octan ['ɔktən], *ag.* (*patol.*) ottanario.

octane ['ɔktein], *s.* (*chim.*) ottano.

octangle ['ɔktæŋgl], *ag.* ottangolare ‖ *s.* (*geom.*) ottagono.

octangular [ɔk'tæŋgjulə*], *ag.* ottangolare.

octant ['ɔktənt], *s.* (*geom. astr. mat.*) ottante.

octapodie [,ɔktə'pɔdik], *ag.* (*poes.*) di otto piedi.

octapody [ɔk'tæpədi], *s.* (*poes.*) verso di otto piedi.

octastyle ['ɔktəstail], *s.* edificio, portico ottastilo.

octavalent [ɔk'tævələnt], *ag.* (*chim.*) ottovalente.

octave ['ɔktiv], *s.* **1.** ottava (otto giorni) **2.** (*mus. poes.*) ottava **3.** piccolo barile per vino ☆ — *-flute*, (*mus.*) ottavino.

Octavia [ɔk'teivjə], *no.pr.f.* Ottavia.

Octavian [ɔk'teivjən], *no.pr.m.* (*st. romana*) Ottaviano.

Octavius [ɔk'teivjəs], *no.pr.m.* Ottavio.

octavo [ɔk'teivou], *ag.* (*tip.*) in-ottavo ‖ *s.* (*pl.* **octavos** [ɔk'teivouz]), (*tip.*) (volume) in ottavo.

octennial [ɔk'tenjəl], *ag.* **1.** che dura otto anni **2.** che si ripete ogni otto anni.

octet, octette [ɔk'tet], *s.* **1.** (*mus.*) ottetto **2.** (*poes.*) gruppo di otto versi (specialmente le prime due quartine del sonetto).

octillion [ɔk'tiljən], *s.* ottilione [(*inglese*) unità seguita da 48 zeri, (*amer.*) unità seguita da 27 zeri].

October [ɔk'toubə*], *s.* ottobre: *in* —, in ottobre; *on the seventh of* —, il sette ottobre.

octobrachiate ['ɔktou'breikiit], *ag.* a otto bracci; a otto raggi.

octodecimo ['ɔktou'desimou], *ag.* (*tip.*) in-diciottesimo ‖ *s.* (*tip.*) (volume) in diciottesimo.

octodentate ['ɔktou'denteit], *ag.* che ha otto denti.

octogenarian [,ɔktoudʒi'nɛəriən], *ag. s.* ottuagenario.

octogenary [ɔk'tɔdʒinəri], *ag.* ottuagenario.

octohedron ['ɔktou'hedrən], *s.* (*geom.*) ottaedro.

octolateral ['ɔktou'lætərəl], *ag.* che ha otto lati.

octonal ['ɔktən], *ag.* che procede di otto in otto.

octonarian [,ɔktou'nɛəriən], *ag.* di otto sillabe ‖ *s.* ottonario, verso di otto sillabe.

octonary ['ɔktounəri], *ag.* di otto; di otto in otto ‖ *s.* gruppo di otto; strofa di otto versi.

octopetalous [,ɔktou'petələs], *ag.* (*bot.*) ottopetalo.

Octopoda [ɔk'tɔpədə], *s.pl.* (*zool.*) ottopodi.

octopus ['ɔktəpəs], *pl.* **octopodes** [ɔk'toupədi:z], **octopuses** ['ɔktəpəsiz], *s.* **1.** (*zool.*) polipo; piovra **2.** *fig.* forza tentacolare.

octoroon [,ɔktə'ru:n], *s.* persona che ha un ottavo di sangue negro.

octosyllabic ['ɔktousi'læbik], *ag.* (*poes.*) ottosillabico ‖ *s.* verso ottosillabico, ottonario.

octosyllable ['ɔktou,siləbl], *ag.* (*poes.*) ottosillabico ‖ *s.* **1.** verso ottosillabico, ottonario **2.** parola ottosillabica.

octroi ['ɔktrwɑ:], *s.* dazio.

octuple ['ɔktju(:)pl], *ag.* ottuplo.

to **octuple**, *v.t.* moltiplicare per otto.

octyl ['ɔktil], *s.* (*chim.*) octile.

octylic [ɔk'tilik], *ag.* (*chim.*) octilico.

ocular ['ɔkjulə*], *ag. s.* oculare.

ocularly ['ɔkjuləli], *av.* ocularmente.

oculate ['ɔkjulit], **oculated** ['ɔkjuleitid], *ag.* maculato.

oculiform ['ɔkjulifɔ:m], *ag.* oculiforme.

oculist ['ɔkjulist], *s.* (*med.*) oculista.

oculistic [,ɔkju'listik], *ag.* (*med.*) oculistico.

odal ['oudl], *ag.* (*dir.*) allodiale ‖ *s.* (*dir.*) allodio.

odalisque ['oudəlisk], *s.* odalisca.

odd [ɔd], *ag.* **1.** dispari: *seven and nine are* — *numbers*, il sette e il nove sono numeri dispari ‖ *to play* (*at*) *even or* —, giocare a pari o dispari **2.** spaiato, scompagnato: *an* — *shoe*, una scarpa spaiata; *two* — *volumes of an encyclopaedia*, due volumi scompagnati di una enciclopedia **3.** in soprappiù, in soprannumero: *an* — *player*, un giocatore in più ‖ *ten pounds* —, dieci sterline e rotti **4.** di resto, restante: *that is the* — *money of the pound-note you gave me*, questo è il resto della sterlina che mi hai dato **5.** occasionale, saltuario, libero (di tempo): *he picks up* — *jobs*, egli accetta lavori saltuari; *to do sthg. at* — *moments*, fare ql.co. a tempo perso **6.** inaspettato, impensato: *in some* — *corner*, in un angolo impensato **7.** bizzarro, originale, strano: — *his remembering me!*, strano che si ricordi di me!; *an* — *kind of person*, un tipo strampalato, eccentrico; *what an* — *hat!*, che strano cappello! ‖ *s.* cosa extra, eccezionale; (*golf*) colpo extra ☆ — *-come-short*, rimasuglio; — *-come -shortly*, un giorno o l'altro; tra qualche giorno; — *game*, (*tennis, carte, ecc.*) bella; — *-looking*, strano; — *-man-out*, eliminazione fra più persone; chi viene eliminato; — *-shaped*, di forma strana.

oddity ['ɔditi], *s.* **1.** singolarità; stranezza; originalità **2.** (persona) originale: *he is an* —, è un originale **3.** cosa bizzarra, curiosità; avvenimento strano.

oddly ['ɔdli], *av.* stranamente: — *enough*, piuttosto stranamente.

oddments ['ɔdmənts], *s.pl.* (*comm.*) scampoli; fondi di magazzino: *great annual sale of* — *and remnants*, grande vendita annuale di scampoli e rimanenze.

oddness ['ɔdnis], *s.* **1.** disparità **2.** singolarità; stranezza; bizzarria.

odds [ɔdz], *s.pl.* (*talvolta con costruzione sing.*) **1.** differenza; disuguaglianza: *what's the* —?, che importa? **2.** disaccordo, contrasto: *to be at* — *with s.o.*, essere in disaccordo con qlcu.; *to set at* —, seminar zizzania **3.** pronostico, probabilità: *the* — *are in your favour*, *against you*, il pronostico è in vostro favore, in vostro sfavore **4.** vantaggio iniziale (concesso per uguagliare le parti in gara): *they will not give you any* —, essi non vi daranno nessun vantaggio **5.** posta (nelle scommesse): *the* — *are ten to one*, la posta è di dieci a uno ‖ — *and ends*, oggetti vari, rimasugli, avanzi.

ode [oud], *s.* (*poes.*) ode.

odeum [ou'di(:)əm], *pl.* **odeums** [ou'di(:)əmz], **odea** [ou'di(:)ə], *s.* auditorio.

Odin ['oudin], *no.pr.m.* (*mit. nordica*) Odino.

odious ['oudjəs], *ag.* odioso, detestabile.

odiously ['oudjəsli], *av.* odiosamente.

odiousness ['oudjəsnis], *s.* odiosità.

odium ['oudjəm], *s.* **1.** odio; biasimo generale **2.** odiosità.

Odoacer [ˌɔdou'eisə*], *no.pr.m.* (*st.*) Odoacre.
odometer [ou'dɔmitə*], *s.* (*mec.*) odometro.
odontalgia [ˌɔdon'tældʒiə], *s.* (*patol.*) odontalgia.
odontalgic [ˌɔdon'tældʒik], *ag.s.* odontalgico.
odontalgy [ˌɔdon'tældʒi], *s.* (*patol.*) odontalgia.
odontological [əˌdɔntə'lɔdʒikəl], *ag.* odontologico.
odontologist [ˌɔdon'tɔlədʒist], *s.* odontoiatra.
odontology [ˌɔdon'tɔlədʒi], *s.* odontologia.
odoriferous [ˌoudə'rifərəs], *ag.* odorifero, profumato.
odoriferously [ˌoudə'rifərəsli], *av.* profumatamente; odorosamente.
odoriferousness [ˌoudə'rifərəsnis], *s.* profumo; fragranza.
odorous ['oudərəs], *ag.* (*poet.*) odoroso, fragrante.
odorously ['oudərəsli], *V.* **odoriferously**.
odorousness ['oudərəsnis], *s.* odorosità; profumo.
odour ['oudə*], *s.* **1.** odore; profumo, olezzo, fragranza **2.** *fig.* traccia, sentore; reputazione: favore.
odourless ['ōudəlis], *ag.* inodoro.
Odysseus [ə'disju:s], *no.pr.m.* (*lett.*) Odisseo.
Odyssey ['ɔdisi], *s.* **1.** Odissea **2.** *fig.* serie di peripezie, avventure.
oecology [i:'kɔlədʒi], *s.* ecologia.
oecumenical [ˌi:kju(:)'menikəl], *ag.* (*eccl.*) ecumenico; universale: — *council*, concilio ecumenico.
oecumenicity [ˌi:kju(:)mi'nisiti], *s.* ecumenicità.
oedema [i(:)'di:mə], *s.* (*patol.*) edema.
oedematous [i(:)'demətəs], *ag.* (*patol.*) edematoso.
Oedipus ['i:dipəs], *no.pr.m.* (*mit.*) Edipo ☆ — *complex*, (*psicanalisi*) complesso di Edipo.
oenological [ˌi:nə'lɔdʒikəl], *ag.* enologico.
oenologist [i:'nɔlədʒist], *s.* enologo.
oenology [i:'nɔlədʒi], *s.* enologia.
Oenone [i(:)'nouni(:)], *no.pr.* (*mit.*) Enone.
o'er ['ouə*], *av.prep.* (*poet.*) per **over**.
oesophageal [ˌi:sou'frædʒiəl], *ag.* (*anat.*) esofageo.
oesophagitis [ˌi:soufə'dʒaitis], *s.* (*patol.*) infiammazione dell'esofago.
oesophagus [i:'sɔfəgəs], *s.* (*anat.*) esofago.
oestrum ['i:strəm], **oestrus** ['i:strəs], *s.* **1.** (*entom.*) estro **2.** *fig.* stimolo; impeto, impulso **3.** (*fisiol.*) calore (negli animali).
of [ɔv (*forma forte*), əv (*forma debole*)], *prep.* **1.** (*indicante specificazione, causa, materia, età, qualità, argomento, ecc.*) di: *a child — seven*, un bambino di sette anni; *the City — New York*, la città di Nuova York; *the lyrics — Shelley*, le liriche di Shelley; *a man — tact*, un uomo di tatto; *he died — pneumonia*, morì di polmonite; *to do sthg. — necessity*, fare ql.co. per necessità ‖ *because —* (o *on account —*), a causa di ‖ *days — yore* (o *old*), giorni lontani ‖ *a fool — a man*, uno sciocco **2.** (*partitivo e dopo un superl. rel.*) di: *the best — friends*, il migliore degli amici; *a child — his*, un suo figlio; *few — them*, pochi di loro; *the whole — it*, tutto quanto **3.** (*retto da ag.*): *guilty —*, colpevole di; *nice — you*, gentile da parte vostra; *was it right — me to come?*, ho fatto bene a venire? **4.** (*in espressioni di tempo*) **a, in:** — *an evening*, a morning, a Sunday, al mattino, alla sera, alla domenica; — *late years*, in questi ultimi anni **5.** (*amer.* per *to*): *a quarter — ten*, le dieci meno un quarto.
off [ɔ:f], *av.* **1. lontano, distante; via; fuori:** *a few miles —*, ad alcune miglia di distanza; *further —*, più lontano; *a long way —*, a grande distanza, molto lontano; *the children are — to school*, i ragazzi stanno per andare a scuola; *the girl is — to-day*, la ragazza è assente oggi; *to keep s.o. —*, tenere qlcu. a distanza ‖ — *and on*, di tanto in tanto ‖ — *with his head!*, tagliategli la testa! ‖ — *with that dog!*, portate via quel cane! ‖ — *with you!*, vattene! ‖ *hats — !*, giù il cappello! ‖ *right* (o *straight*) —, immediatamente **2. completamente:** *to drink —*, bere tutto; *to pay — a debt*, pagare interamente un debito **3.** (*con* to *be*): *chicken is —*, il pollo è esaurito; *the concert is —*, il concerto è sospeso; *the light is —*, la luce è spenta; *the motor is —*, il motore è fermo; *the play is —*, la commedia

non è più in cartellone; *the profits are — this year*, quest'anno i redditi sono inferiori; *the water is —*, hanno tolto l'acqua; *to be badly* (o *poorly*) —, *to be well —*, essere in cattive, in buone condizioni finanziarie **4.** (*con altri verbi*): *to fall —*, cadere; diminuire; declinare; deperire; appassire: *all the leaves have fallen —*, tutte le foglie sono cadute; *to go —* (*to sleep*), addormentarsi; *to sail —*, (*mar.*) andare al largo; *to see s.o. —*, salutare qlcu. alla partenza; *to set —*, partire; mettere in rilievo; *to shake — sthg.*, scuotersi ql.co. di dosso; *to take sthg. —*, togliersi ql.co. di dosso; *to throw — reserves*, abbandonare ogni reticenza; *to turn — the gas*, chiudere, togliere il gas.
off, *prep.* **via da; fuori da; lontano da; giù da:** *the cat stole the meat — the dish*, il gatto rubò la carne dal piatto; *she cut a slice — it*, ne tagliò una fetta; *she fell — the ladder*, cadde giù dalla scala; *she took the cover — the dish*, tolse il coperchio dal piatto ‖ — *the beaten track*, in regioni sconosciute; *fig.* fuori del comune; — *the cape*, (*mar.*) al largo del capo; — *duty*, fuori servizio; — *the map*, (*sl.*) scomparso, sparito; — *the mark*, fuori bersaglio; — *one's head*, (*fam.*) fuori di sè, matto; — *the record information*, informazioni ufficiose, confidenziali ‖ *6d. — the price*, una riduzione di 6 penny sul prezzo.
off, *ag.* **1.** destro; più distante; esterno: *the — horse*, il cavallo di destra (in un tiro a due); *on the — side of the wall*, sul lato esterno della parete **2.** lontano; improbabile: *there is an — chance that...*, c'è poca probabilità che... **3.** secondario: *an — street*, una strada secondaria **4.** libero, vuoto: *an — day*, un giorno di libertà, di riposo; *the — season*, la stagione morta **5.** non fresco (di cibi, ecc.): *this egg is a bit —*, quest'uovo non è fresco ‖ *s.* (*cricket*) lato esterno (del campo) ‖ *I have my offs and ons*, ho i miei alti e bassi.
to off, *v.t.* (*fam.*) annunciare l'intenzione di annullare (un impegno, accordo, ecc.).
off, (*nei composti*): — -*beat*, insolito; non convenzionale; eccentrico; — -*print*, (*tip.*) estratto (di rivista, ecc.); — -*stage*, fra le quinte; — -*time*, fuori orario.
Offa ['ɔfə], *no.pr.m.* (*mil. nordica*) Offa.
offal ['ɔfəl], *s.* **1.** (*cuc.*) frattaglie; regaglie **2.** rimasugli; briciole; avanzi; rifiuti.
offence [ə'fens], *s.* **1.** offesa; ingiuria: *no — meant*, sia detto senza offesa; *there's no — in it*, non c'è niente di male; *to cause — to s.o.*, offendere qlcu.; *to take — at sthg.*, offendersi di ql.co. **2.** (*teol.*) colpa, peccato **3.** (*dir.*) delitto; infrazione: *to commit an — against the law*, commettere un'infrazione alla legge **4.** scandalo: *rock of —*, pietra dello scandalo **5.** (*mil.*) offesa, attacco.
offenceless [ə'fenslis], *ag.* **1.** inoffensivo; innocuo **2.** innocente.
to offend [ə'fend], *v.t.i.* **1.** offendere, far torto a, oltraggiare: *sorry if you are offended*, mi spiace che tu sia offeso **2.** (*arc.*) scandalizzare: *if thy right hand offends thee, cut it off*, se la mano destra ti dà scandalo, tagliala via **3.** peccare **4.** (*dir.*) commettere infrazioni: *to — against the law*, infrangere la legge.
offender [ə'fendə*], *s.* peccatore; colpevole; (*dir.*) delinquente; trasgressore; criminale.
offending [ə'fendiŋ], *ag.* offensivo.
offensive [ə'fensiv], *ag.* **1.** offensivo; insultante; ingiurioso: — *answer*, risposta insultante **2.** ripugnante, nauseabondo; sgradevole; nocivo ‖ *s.* (*mil.*) offensiva.
offensively [ə'fensivli], *av.* **1.** offensivamente; ingiuriosamente **2.** sgradevolmente.
offensiveness [ə'fensivnis], *s.* **1.** aggressività; insolenza **2.** sgradevolezza.
offer ['ɔfə*], *s.* **1.** offerta: *to close with an —*, (*comm.*) accettare un'offerta; *to make an — of sthg. to s.o.*, fare una offerta di ql.co. a qlcu. ‖ *goods on —*, (*comm.*) merce in vendita **2.** proposta: — *of marriage*, proposta di matrimonio **3.** (*rar.*) tentativo.
to offer, *v.t.i.* **1.** offrire, offrirsi; proporre; esporre: — (*up*) *your prayers to God*, elevate le vostre preghiere

a Dio; *I was offered a new contract*, mi offersero un nuovo contratto; *they offered us their opinions*, ci esposero le loro opinioni **2.** presentare, presentarsi: *as opportunity offers*, quando si presenti l'occasione **3.** tentare, cercare: *he offered to strike me*, tentò di colpirmi **4.** scegliere come materia d'esame: *she offered Italian as her main subject*, scelse l'italiano come materia base.

offerer ['ɔfərə*], *s.* offerente: *to the highest* —, al miglior offerente.

offering ['ɔfəriŋ], *s.* offerta; sacrificio; oblazione.

offertory ['ɔfətəri], *s.* **1.** (*eccl.*) offertorio **2.** elemosina raccolta in chiesa durante un servizio religioso.

offhand ['ɔːf'hænd], *ag.* **1.** casuale; improvvisato; estemporaneo; — *speech*, discorso improvvisato **2.** disinvolto; sbrigativo, brusco; alla buona ‖ *av.* **1.** lì per lì; all'improvviso **2.** senza cerimonie, complimenti; in modo disinvolto, sbrigativo.

offhanded ['ɔːf'hændid], *V.* **offhand** *ag.*

offhandedly ['ɔːf'hændidli], *V.* **offhand** *av.*

offhandedness ['ɔːf'hændidnis], *s.* disinvoltura; modi bruschi, sbrigativi, alla buona.

office ['ɔfis], *s.* **1.** servizio, ufficio: *by the good offices of*, coi buoni uffici di; *they did me an ill* —, mi resero un cattivo servizio **2.** dovere, funzione: *to do the* — *of*, far la funzione di **3.** impiego, carica: *the* — *of President*, la carica di Presidente; *to be in* —, essere in carica; *to come into* (o *to enter upon*) —, entrare in carica; *to leave* (o *to resign*) —, dare le dimissioni ‖ *Jack-in-* —, impiegato che si dà arie **4.** *Office*, Ministero ‖ *Foreign Office, Home Office, War Office*, Ministero degli Esteri, dell'Interno, della Guerra ‖ *the Holy Office*, l'Inquisizione **5.** ufficio (locale, serie di locali) **6.** (*eccl.*) uffizio, ufficio: — *for the dead*, ufficio funebre; *to say the* —, dire l'uffizio **7.** (*sl.*) avviso, segnale **8.** *pl.* stanze di servizio ☆ — *bearer*, funzionario; — *boy*, fattorino ‖ — *box*, botteghino (del teatro); *head managing* —, direzione.

officer ['ɔfisə*], *s.* **1.** ufficiale, agente, funzionario **2.** ufficiale (dell'esercito, marina, aviazione) **3.** *High Officer*, gran dignitario (in un ordine cavalleresco) ☆ *commissioned* —, ufficiale per nomina; *custom-house* —, funzionario delle dogane; *flying* —, tenente pilota; *liaison* —, ufficiale di collegamento; *municipal* —, ufficiale municipale; *police* —, funzionario di polizia.

to officer, *v.t.* **1.** provvedere di ufficiali **2.** (*quasi sempre passivo*) comandare come ufficiale: *to be well officered*, essere comandato da buoni ufficiali.

official [ə'fiʃəl], *ag.* **1.** ufficiale, autorizzato; pubblico: *his* — *duties keep him busy*, le sue funzioni ufficiali lo tengono occupato; *is the news* —?, è ufficiale la notizia? **2.** (*farm.*) ufficiale, ‖ *s.* **1.** ufficiale (civile); funzionario; impiegato **2.** giudice, alto funzionario della Corte Episcopale Anglicana.

officialdom [ə'fiʃəldəm], **officialism** [ə'fiʃəlizəm], *s.* **1.** burocrazia **2.** qualità di pubblico ufficiale.

officialese [ə,fiʃə'liːz], *s.* gergo burocratico.

officially [ə'fiʃəli], *av.* ufficialmente.

officiant [ə'fiʃənt], *s.* ufficiante, celebrante.

to officiate [ə'fiʃieit], *v.i.* **1.** esercitare funzioni: *to* — *as host, as hostess*, esercitare le funzioni di ospite, di padrona di casa ‖ *to* — *for*, sostituire temporaneamente: *I officiated for him during his illness*, l'ho sostituito durante la sua malattia **2.** (*eccl.*) ufficiare.

officinal [,ɔfi'sain], *ag.* (*farm.*) farmaceutico, officinale.

officious [ə'fiʃəs], *ag.* **1.** intrigante, inframmettente, invadente **2.** ufficioso **3.** (*arc.*) servizievole; premuroso.

officiously [ə'fiʃəsli], *av.* **1.** in modo intrigante, inopportunamente **2.** ufficiosamente **3.** premurosamente.

officiousness [ə'fiʃəsnis], *s.* **1.** invadenza; intromissione, inframmettenza **2.** ufficiosità **3.** premura.

offing ['ɔfiŋ], *s.* (*mar.*) **1.** largo: *the sea was rough in the* —, il mare era agitato al largo; *to gain* (o *to get*) *an* —, prendere il largo; *to keep an* —, tenere il largo; *to stand for the* —, battere il largo ‖ *in the* —, (*fam.*) vicino, in vista: *a good job in the* —, un buon posto

in vista **2.** distanza dalla costa: *the ship had ten miles'* —, la nave era a una distanza di dieci miglia dalla costa.

offish ['ɔfiʃ], *ag.* (*fam.*) riservato, distante, poco comunicativo; compassato.

offscourings ['ɔːf,skauəriŋz], *s.pl.* rifiuti, scarti; feccia; immondizia.

offset ['ɔːfset], *s.* **1.** equivalente, compenso **2.** sperone (di montagna, collina) **3.** (*bot.*) germoglio, pollone; *fig.* rampollo; — *of a noble family*, rampollo di una nobile famiglia **4.** (*arch.*) risega **5.** (*geom.*) ordinata **6.** (*mec.*) deviazione; disassamento **7.** (*elett.*) linea di deviazione, secondaria **8.** (*tip.*) «offset», fotolito ☆ — *printing*, stampa «offset», fotolitografia; — *process*, metodo di stampa «offset», fotolito.

to offset, *pass. p.p.* **offset**, *v.t.i.* **1.** controbilanciare, contrapporre, fronteggiare **2.** germogliare; ramificare, ramificarsi **3.** (*mec.*) decentrare, deviare **4.** (*tip.*) stampare a «offset», a fotolito.

offshoot ['ɔːfʃuːt], *s.* **1.** germoglio; ramo; *fig.* rampollo; ramo cadetto (di una famiglia) **2.** derivato.

offshore ['ɔːf'ʃɔ:*], *ag.* **1.** di terra: — *wind*, vento di terra **2.** lontano dalla costa ‖ *av.* al largo, verso il largo.

offside ['ɔːf'said], *s.* fuori giuoco (calcio, ecc.).

offspring ['ɔːfspriŋ], *s.* **1.** *coll.* prole; progenie; discendenza: *she has six* —, ha sei figli **2.** *fig.* frutto, prodotto.

offward ['ɔːfwəd], *av.* (*mar.*) al largo.

oft [ɔːft], *av.* (*poet. tranne nei composti*) spesso ☆ — *recurring*, che capita spesso; — *told*, narrato e rinarrato.

often ['ɔːfn], *av.* spesso, sovente, frequentemente: *how* —?, quante volte?; *once too* —, una volta di troppo ☆ — *as not*, tante volte sì quante no.

oftentimes ['ɔːfntaimz], **ofttimes** ['ɔːftaimz], *av.* (*arc.*) spesso, spesse volte.

ogee ['oudʒiː], *s.* **1.** (*arch.*) modanatura a S **2.** (*arch.*) gola diritta o rovescia ☆ — *arch*, arco ogivale; — *window*, finestra ogivale.

ogham ['ɔgəm], *s.* **1.** «ogham» (antico alfabeto britannico e irlandese) **2.** iscrizione in «ogham» **3.** lettera di alfabeto «ogham».

ogival [ou'dʒaivl], *ag.* (*arch.*) ogivale, a sesto acuto.

ogive ['oudʒaiv], *s.* (*arch.*) ogiva, sesto acuto.

ogle ['ougl], *s.* occhiata, sguardo amoroso.

to ogle, *v.t.i.* **1.** guardare amorosamente; lanciare sguardi amorosi a; vagheggiare **2.** ammiccare; guardare sottecchi.

ogler ['ouglə*], *s.* vagheggiatore, vagheggino.

ogre ['ougə*], *s.* orco.

ogress ['ougris], *s.* orchessa.

ogrish ['ougriʃ], *ag.* di orco; simile ad orco.

oh [ou], *inter.* oh!, ah!.

ohm [oum], *s.* (*elett.*) «ohm» (unità di resistenza) ‖ *Ohm's law*, la legge di Ohm.

oho [ou'hou], *inter.* oh!, oh!, evviva!.

oil [ɔil], *s.* **1.** olio: — *and vinegar*, olio e aceto; *fig.* cose inconciliabili; — *burns well*, l'olio brucia bene ‖ *work that smells of* —, *fig.* opera elaborata che rivela lo sforzo ‖ *to burn the midnight* —, *fig.* lavorare fino a tarda notte ‖ *to pour* — *on the flames*, *fig.* versare olio sul fuoco; *to pour* — *on troubled waters*, *fig.* gettare acqua sul fuoco, calmare dissensi **2.** petrolio: *to strike* —, trovare il petrolio; *fig.* arricchire improvvisamente; avere successo ☆ — *beetle*, (*entom.*) meloe proscarabeo; — *bird*, (*ornit.*) guaciaro; — *cake*, (*agr. ind.*) panello di sansa; — *can*, recipiente di latta per olio lubrificante; — *cloth*, tela cerata; — *colour*, (*pitt.*) colore a olio; — *concession*, concessione petrolifera; — *field*, campo petrolifero; — *film*, velo d'olio — *lamp*, lampada ad olio; — *mill*, oleificio; frantoio; — *nut*, (*bot.*) noce da olio; — *of vitriol*, acido solforico fumante; — *painting*, pittura, dipinto a olio; — *palm*, palma da cui si estrae l'olio; — *paper*, carta oleata; — *plant*, — *seed*, pianta, seme oleoso; — *silk*, seta impermeabilizzata; — -skin, tela impermeabile; pl. giacca e pantaloni di tela impermeabile; — -soap, sapone all'olio; — well, pozzo petrolifero || castor —, olio di ricino; coal-tar —, olio di catrame; cod-liver —, olio di fegato di merluzzo; crude —, petrolio greggio; fuel —, nafta; hemp —, olio di canapa; holy —, olio santo; lamp —, olio da ardere; linseed —, olio di lino; lubricating —, olio lubrificante; mineral —, olio minerale; olive —, olio d'oliva; paraffin —, olio di paraffina; sperm — , (ind.) olio di spermaceti; tallow —, olio di sego; vegetable —, olio vegetale; volatile —, (chim.) olio essenziale.

to **oil**, v.t.i. **1.** ungere; lubrificare; ingrassare: to — the wheels, ungere le ruote (anche fig.) || to — one's tongue, fare l'adulatore || to — s.o.'s hand, corrompère qlcu. **2.** diventare oleoso; fondersi (di burro, ecc.) **3.** (mar.) fare il pieno di nafta.

oiler ['oilə*], s. **1.** oliatore, lubrificatore **2.** persona che lubrifica (motori, ecc.) **3.** (mar.) nave cisterna; nave alimentata a nafta **4.** (sl.) individuo viscido, mellifluo.

oilery ['oiləri], s. oli; commercio degli oli; rivendita d'olio.

oiliness ['oilinis], s. untuosità (anche fig.).

oiling ['oilin], s. lubrificazione; oliatura (di lana).

oilman, pl. **oilmen** ['oilmən], s. **1.** negoziante di oli **2.** negoziante di colori **3.** persona addetta alla lubrificazione di macchine **4.** addetto alle ricerche petrolifere.

oily ['oili], ag. oleoso; fig. untuoso.

ointment ['ointmənt], s. unguento; pomata ☆ mercurial —, (farm.) unguento mercuriale; zinc —, (farm.) pomata all'ossido di zinco.

O.K., OK. ['ou'kei], ag.av. (fam.) bene; tutto bene, benissimo: every thing is —, tutto va bene; the totals are —, i conti sono esatti.

to **O.K.**, pass.p.p. **O.K.'d** ['ou'keid], v.t. (fam.) approvare, acconsentire a: to — an order, approvare una ordinazione.

okapi [ou'ka:pi], s. (zool.) okapi.

okay, V. O.K.

okra ['okrə], s. (bot.) abelmosco.

old [ould], comp. **older** ['ouldə*], **elder** ['eldə*], superl. **oldest** ['ouldist], **eldest** ['eldist], ag. **1.** vecchio; antico; antiquato: — age, vecchiaia; — bachelor, scapolone; — maid, zitella; — man, vecchio: one's — man, (fam.) il proprio padre, il proprio marito; — woman, vecchia: one's — woman, (fam.) la propria moglie; the good — times, il buon tempo antico; of the — school, di vecchio stampo; to be ... years —, avere ... anni: "How — was his eldest brother?", "He was thirty", «Quanti anni aveva suo fratello maggiore?», «Aveva trent'anni»; to call up one's — memories, rinvangare il passato; to grow —, invecchiare; to look —, sembrare vecchio; — bean, (sl.) mio caro; — boy (o — chap o — fellow o — man), vecchio mio, caro mio || Old English, la lingua anglosassone (sino al 1066) || Old Glory, la bandiera statunitense || Old Harry (o Old Nick o the Old One o Old Scratch), il diavolo || — hat, (sl.) antiquato || the Old Lady of Threadneedle Street, (scherz.) la Banca d'Inghilterra || the Old Testament, il Vecchio Testamento || Old Tom, qualità forte di gin || to be as — as the hills (o as — as Methuselah), essere vecchio come Matusalemme **2.** esperto; scaltro || — in crime, pregiudicato || s. **1.** tempo passato: days of —, tempi antichi **2.** the —, i vecchi ☆ — bird, volpone; — -clothes man, rigattiere; — -clothes shop, bottega del rigattiere; — -fashioned, antiquato; — -fogyish, da vecchio bacucco; — -gentlemanly, da gentiluomo di vecchio stampo; — -gold, color oro vecchio; — hand, esperto; — man's beard, (bot.) clematide, vitalba; — school tie, cravatta coi colori della propria scuola; fig. fedeltà alle vecchie tradizioni; — stager, persona di lunga esperienza; — -time, vecchiotto, d'altri tempi; — -womanish, proprio di una vecchia; — -world, anti-

quato, d'altri tempi; del vecchio mondo; dell'antichità.

olden ['ouldən], ag. (arc. poet.) vecchio, antico: in — time(s), nei tempi antichi.

to **olden**, v.t.i. invecchiare; far invecchiare.

oldish ['ouldiʃ], ag. attempato, piuttosto vecchio.

oldness ['ouldnis], s. vecchiaia; antichità.

oldster ['ouldstə*], s. persona che sta invecchiando.

oleaginous [,ouli'ædʒinəs], ag. oleoso; untuoso (anche fig.).

oleander [,ouli'ændə*], s. (bot.) oleandro.

oleaster [,ouli'æstə*], s. (bot.) oleastro.

oleic ['ouliik], ag. (chim.) oleico.

olein(e) ['ouliin], s. oleina.

oleograph ['ouliougra:f], **oleography** [,ouli'ografi], s. (chim.) oleografia.

oleomargarine ['ouliou,ma:dʒə'ri:n], s. (cuc.) oleomargarina.

oleometer [,ouli'omitə*], s. (chim.) oleometro.

oleose ['oulious], **oleous** ['ouliəs], ag. (rar.) oleoso.

olfaction [ol'fækʃən], s. olfatto.

olfactory [ol'fæktəri], ag. olfattivo, olfattorio || s. gener.pl. organo dell'olfatto.

Olga ['olgə]. no.pr.f. Olga.

olibanum [ə'libənəm], s. olibano, incenso.

olid ['olid], ag. fetido.

oligaemia [,oli'gæmiə], s. (patol.) oligoemia.

oligarch ['oliga:k], s. oligarca.

oligarchic(al) [,oli'ga:kik(əl)], ag. oligarchico.

oligarchically [,oli'ga:kikəli], av. oligarchicamente.

oligarchy ['oliga:ki], s. oligarchia.

oligocene [ə'ligousi:n], ag. (geol.) oligocene.

olio ['ouliou], pl. **olios** ['ouliouz], s. **1.** (cuc.) spezzatino **2.** miscuglio, mescolanza.

oliphant ['olifənt], s. (letter.) olifante, corno d'avorio.

olivaceous [,oli'veiʃəs], ag. olivastro, verde oliva.

olivary ['oliveri], ag. (anat.) olivale, olivare ☆ — bodies, corpi olivali.

olive ['oliv], ag. d'oliva; d'olivo; olivastro || s. **1.** olivo **2.** oliva **3.** qualsiasi oggetto a forma di oliva **4.** pl. messicani, involtini di carne ripieni ☆ — -branch, ramo d'olivo: to hold out the — -branch, far profferte di riconciliazione; — -coloured, olivastro; — -crown, corona d'olivo; — -green, verde oliva; — -grove, boschetto d'olivi; — -oil, olio d'oliva; — -season, stagione del raccolto delle olive; — -skinned, pelle olivastra; — -tree, olivo; — -wood, legno d'olivo; — -yard, uliveto.

oliver[1] ['olivə*], s. (mec.) martello a pedale.

Oliver[2], no.pr.m. Oliviero.

olivet ['olivet], s. **1.** perla d'imitazione **2.** bottone di forma ovale.

Olivetan [,oli'vi:tən], s. (eccl.) olivetano.

Olivia [ə'liviə], no.pr.f. Olivia.

Olivier [ə'liviə*], no.pr.m. Oliviero.

olivine [,oli'vi:n], s. (min.) olivina.

ology ['olədʒi], s. (scherz.) scienza.

Olympia [ou'limpiə], no.pr.f Olimpia.

Olympiad [ou'limpiæd], s. Olimpiade.

Olympian [ou'limpiən], ag. olimpico, dell'Olimpo || s.c. divinità dell'Olimpo; olimpionico, olimpionica.

Olympic [ou'limpik], ag. olimpico, di Olimpia: the — games, i giuochi olimpici.

Olympus [ou'limpəs], no.pr. **1.** (mit. geog.) Olimpo **2.** Olimpo **3.** fig. paradiso.

omasum [ou'meisəm], s. (anat.) omaso.

ombre ['ombə*], s. ombra (giuoco di carte).

omega ['oumigə], s. **1.** omega (ultima lettera dell'alfabeto greco) **2.** fig. l'ultimo della serie; conclusione.

omelet(te) ['omlit], s. frittata || you cannot make an — without breaking eggs, prov. con niente non si fa niente.

omen ['oumen], s. pronostico, auspicio, augurio, presagio: bird of good, ill —, uccello di buon augurio, di malaugurio.

to **omen**, v.t. presagire, divinare.

omentum [ou'mentəm], *pl.* **omenta** [ou'mentə], *s.* (*anat.*) omento.

omicron [ou'maikrən], *s.* omicron (lettera dell'alfabeto greco).

ominous ['ominəs], *ag.* sinistro, infausto; di cattivo augurio; minaccioso; inquietante.

ominously ['ominəsli], *av.* in modo sinistro.

ominousness ['ominəsnis], *s.* aspetto, carattere sinistro.

omissible [ou'misibl], *ag.* trascurabile.

omission [ou'miʃən], *s.* omissione; negligenza; dimenticanza: *sins of* —, peccati di omissione.

omissive [ou'misiv], *ag.* di omissione.

to **omit** [ou'mit], *pass.p.p.* **omitted** [ou'mitid], *v.t.* (II) omettere, tralasciare, trascurare; dimenticare: *he omitted the last words*, omise le ultime parole; *she omitted to do* (o *doing*) *it*, ella si dimenticò di farlo.

omnibus ['omnibəs], *ag.* che include tutto, che comprende molti casi o argomenti ‖ *s.* (*pl.* **omnibuses** ['omnibəsiz]), **1.** (*gener. abbr.* **bus**) autobus, omnibus **2.** — (*volume*), volume contenente tutte o gran parte delle opere di un autore ☆ — *clause*, clausola riguardante svariati argomenti; — *train*, accelerato.

omnifarious [,omni'fɛəriəs], *ag.* d'ogni genere.

omniformity [,omni'fo:miti], *s.* capacità di assumere ogni forma.

omnipotence [om'nipətəns], *s.* onnipotenza.

omnipotent [om'nipətənt], *ag.* onnipotente.

omnipresence ['omni'prezəns], *s.* onnipresenza.

omnipresent ['omni'prezənt], *ag.* onnipresente.

omniscience [om'nisiəns], *s.* onniscienza.

omniscient [om'nisiənt], *ag.* onnisciente ‖ *the Omniscient*, Dio.

omnium ['omniəm], *s.* (*finanze*) insieme dei valori che garantiscono un prestito.

omnivorous [om'nivərəs], *ag.* onnivoro (anche *fig.*): *an* — *reader*, uno che legge di tutto.

omoplate ['ouməpleit], *s.* (*rar.*) omoplata, scapola.

omphalos ['omfələs], *pl.* **omphali** ['omfolai], *s.* **1.** ombelico **2.** punto centrale.

on [on (*forma forte*), ən (*forma debole*)], *prep.* **1.** su, sopra; presso: — *the table*, sul tavolo; *a house* — *the river*, una casa sul fiume; *he sat* — *a stool*, sedette su uno sgabello; *he threw it* — *the floor*, lo gettò sul pavimento; *he had no money* —, non aveva denaro con sè; *I read it* — *page four*, l'ho letto a pagina quattro ‖ *to put money* — *a horse*, puntare su un cavallo **2.** (*direzione*) **su, verso**: *to march* — *Paris*, marciare su Parigi **3.** (*argomento*) su, di: *an essay* — *history*, un'esercitazione di storia; *a lecture* — *Freud*, una conferenza su Freud **4.** (*in espressioni di tempo*) **a**: — *arriving we found him*, all'arrivo lo trovammo; — *the death of his father*, alla morte di suo padre; *I am leaving* — *Friday*, partirò venerdì **5.** (**Fraseologia**): — *account of*, a causa di, per; — *board ship*, a bordo; — *the chain*, alla catena; — *the cheap*, a buon mercato; in economia; — *duty*, in servizio; — *fire*, in fiamme; — *foot*, a piedi; — *holiday*, in vacanza; — *horseback*, a cavallo; — *the instant*, sull'istante; — *the minute*, puntualissimo; — *my honour*, sul mio onore; — *purpose*, di proposito; — *the right, the left*, a destra, a sinistra; — *sale*, in vendita; — *the way*, in cammino, cammin facendo; — *the whole*, tutto sommato ‖ *payable* — *sight*, (*comm.*) pagabile a vista ‖ *I am here* — *business*, sono qui per affari; *this round of beer is* — *me*, (*fam.*) queste birre le pago io ‖ *to buy sthg.* — *bad terms*, comprare ql.co. a condizioni svantaggiose; *to go* — *strike*, mettersi in sciopero; *to live* — *one's private income*, vivere di rendita.

on, *av.* **1.** su, sopra; indosso: *put it* —, mettilo, indossalo; *put* — *your hat*, mettiti il cappello; *what had she got* —?, come era vestita?; *to have nothing* —, non aver niente addosso, essere nudo ‖ *to be* —, essere proiettato, essere rappresentato (di film, lavoro teatrale, ecc.), essere in scena (di attore): *what's on at*

the *Capitol*?, cosa danno al Capitol?; *who is* — *as Hamlet?*, chi fa la parte di Amleto? **2. avanti** (*indicante progresso o continuità d'azione*): *and* — *they went*, ed essi continuarono ad avanzare; *move* — *please*, circolate; *read* —, continua a leggere ‖ *and so* —, e così via, eccetera ‖ *off and* —, a intervalli **3. verso**: *to keep an aircraft nose* — *to the wind*, tenere un aereo in direzione contraria al vento **4.** (*in espressione di tempo*): *from that day* —, da quel giorno in poi; *later* —, più tardi ‖ *well* — *in years*, di età avanzata **5.** (*indicante funzionamento, ecc.*): *the gas is* —, il gas è acceso; *the machine was* —, la macchina era in funzione; *to put* (o *to turn*) — *the tap*, aprire il rubinetto; *to switch* — *the radio*, accendere la radio.

on, *ag.* **1.** (*cricket*) a sinistra (del campo): *drive to the* — *side*, colpo avanti a sinistra **2.** in forma (di atleta, ecc.): *it was not one of his* — *days*, non era in uno dei suoi giorni migliori ‖ *s.* (*cricket*) lato sinistro (del campo) ☆ — *consumption*, consumazione sul posto (di alcoolici, ecc.); — *-licence*, licenza per vendere alcoolici da consumarsi sul posto.

onager ['onəgə*], *pl.* **onagers** ['onəgəz], **onagri** ['onəgrai], *s.* **1.** (*zool.*) onagro **2.** (*mil.*) catapulta.

onanism ['ounənizəm], *s.* onanismo.

onanist ['ounənist], *s.* onanista.

onanistic [,ounə'nistik], *ag.* onanistico.

once [wʌns], *av.* **1.** una volta: — *for all*, una volta per sempre; — *in a while*, una volta ogni tanto; — *a month*, una volta al mese; — *more*, ancora una volta; — *or twice*, una volta o due; *I've read it more than* —, l'ho letto più di una volta ‖ *when* — *he understands...*, una volta che ha capito... **2.** una volta, anticamente: — *when I was young*, un tempo, quando ero giovane ‖ — *upon a time*, c'era una volta ‖ *my* — *master*, il mio padrone di una volta **3.** *at* —, subito, all'istante; nello stesso tempo: *all at* —, tutto, tutti in una volta; *at* — *stern and tender*, severo e nello stesso tempo affettuoso ☆ — *-famous*, una volta famoso; — *-loved*, una volta amato.

once, *cong.* una volta che, se appena: — *he hesitates, we have him*, se appena esita, è in mano nostra.

once, *s.* una volta: *for* —, *for this* —, per una, per questa volta; — *is enough for him*, una volta gli basta ☆ — *-over*, rapido sguardo d'insieme; (*sl.*) occhiata scrutatrice: *to give s.o. the* — *-over*, squadrare qlcu. da capo a piedi.

oncology [oŋ'kolədʒi], *s.* (*med.*) oncologia.

on-coming ['on,kʌmiŋ], *ag.* prossimo, futuro, che si avvicina, imminente ‖ *s.* avvicinamento; prossimità.

one [wʌn], *ag.num.card.* uno: — *man in a hundred*, un uomo su cento; *a hundred, a thousand and* —, cento uno, mille uno; *twenty-* — (o *arc.* — *and twenty*), ventuno; *she comes* — *day out of two*, viene un giorno sì e un giorno no; *speaking from* — *expert to another*, parlando tra specialisti ‖ *ag. indef.* uno, un certo: *he went out* — *stormy evening in January*, uscì in una notte tempestosa di gennaio ‖ *ag.* solo, unico; stesso, medesimo: *all in* — *direction*, tutti nella stessa direzione; *like* — *man*, come un solo uomo; *with* — *voice*, ad una (sola) voce; *all gave* — *answer*, tutti diedero la stessa risposta; *the* — *and only person who can do that*, l'unica persona che può farlo; *the* — *way to do it*, l'unico modo per farlo ‖ *I am* — *with you*, sono del tuo stesso parere.

one, *pl.* **ones** [wʌnz], *pron. dimostrativo* **questo, quello, codesto**: *the best* —, il migliore, la migliore; *this picture is finer than the* — *I have*, questo quadro è più bello di quello che ho ‖ *"What apples would you like, Madam?", "The ones over there"*, « Che qualità di mele desidera, signora ? », « Quelle laggiù »; *which* — *do you prefer?*, quale preferisci? ‖ *the Evil One*, il Maligno; *the Holy One*, l'Eterno ‖ *the little ones*, i bambini; i piccoli (di animali) ‖ *pron. indef.* **1.** uno, una; l'uno, l'una: — *after another*, uno dopo l'altro; — *by* —, uno a uno; *any* — *of us*, uno qualunque di noi; *each* — *of them*, ciascuno di loro; *he behaves like* — *frenzied*, si comporta come un pazzo; *I haven't a pen, have you got* — *?*, non ho la penna, ne hai una tu?; *no* — *likes to think so*, a nessuno piace pensare così; *some* — *says*, qlcu. dice ‖ — *Mr. Stevens*, un certo signor Stevens 2. (*costruzione imp.*) **uno, qualcuno**, si: *if* — *could only know the future*, se solo si potesse conoscere il futuro ‖ *one's*, (suo) proprio: *to do things one's own way*, fare a modo proprio.

one, *ag. num. card. s.* **1.** uno, unità: *eleven is written with two ones*, l'undici è scritto con due uno ‖ *chapter* —, capitolo primo ‖ *to be at* — *with s.o.*, essere d'accordo con qlcu. ‖ *to make* —, (*maglieria*) crescere un punto, fare un aumento **2.** *the One*, (*fil.*) l'Assoluto, il Principio Primo, l'Uno.

one, (*nei composti*): — -*eyed*, monocolo, guercio; — -*horse*, a un cavallo; — -*legged*, con una gamba sola; — -*sided*, unilaterale; — -*sidedness*, unilateralità; — -*track*, a un solo binario: *a* — -*track mind*, *fig.* una mente unilaterale, che ha orizzonti limitati.

onefold [ˈwʌnfould], *ag.* semplice, singolo.

oneirocritic [ou,naiərouˈkritik], *ag.s.* (di) chi interpreta il futuro attraverso i sogni.

oneirocriticism [ou,naiərouˈkritisizəm], *s.* divinazione attraverso i sogni.

oneiromancy [ouˈnaiəroumænsi], *s.* oniromanzia.

oneness [ˈwʌnnis], *s.* unicità, unità; identità; unione, accordo (di idee, opinioni, ecc.).

oner [ˈwʌnə*], *s.* **1.** tipo unico nel suo genere ‖ *a* — *at sthg.*, (*sl.*) un asso in ql.co. **2.** (*sl.*) colpo forte **3.** (*sl.*) bugia, menzogna.

onerary [ˈonərəri], *ag.* adatto al trasporto di pesi ‖ *s.* nave da trasporto.

onerous [ˈonərəs], *ag.* oneroso, gravoso.

onerously [ˈonərəsli], *av.* gravosamente.

onerousness [ˈonərəsnis], *s.* onerosità.

oneself [wʌnˈself], *pron. r.* se stesso: *to comb* —, pettinarsi; *to keep to* —, tenersi appartato ‖ *by* —, da solo.

onfall [ˈonfɔːl], *s.* assalto.

ongoings [ˈon,gouiŋz], *s.pl.* comportamento, condotta.

onion [ˈʌnjən], *s.* **1.** (*bot.*) cipolla **2.** (*sl.*) abitante delle Bermude **3.** (*sl.*) testa: *off one's* —, fuori di sé ☆ — -*marble*, (*min.*) marmo cipollino; — -*skin*, carta lucida, sottile ‖ *spring*- —, cipollina.

oniony [ˈʌnjəni], *ag.* che sa di cipolla.

onliness [ˈounlinis], *s.* **1.** solitudine **2.** unicità.

onlooker [ˈon,lukə*], *s.c.* spettatore, spettatrice.

only [ˈounli], *ag.* solo, unico: *his* — *novel*, il suo unico romanzo; *are you an* — *child?*, sei figlio unico?; *you are the* — *girl I ever admired*, sei l'unica ragazza che abbia mai ammirato.

only, *av.* solo, soltanto, solamente, unicamente: — *a few of them*, soltanto alcuni di loro; — *once*, soltanto una volta; *if* — *it would stop raining!*, se soltanto cessasse di piovere! ‖ — *just*, proprio, veramente: *we were* — *just in time*, arrivammo appena in tempo ‖ — *too pleased*, contentissimo, soddisfattissimo ‖ *Ladies* —, riservato alle signore.

only, *cong.* ma, però, eccetto che: — *that you'd be bored*, *I'd tell you everything*, solo se non fosse per non seccarti, ti racconterei tutto; *the girl is pretty*, — *too tall*, la ragazza è graziosa, ma troppo alta; *he does well*, — *that he is nervy*, fa bene, ma è molto nervoso.

onomastic [,onouˈmæstik], *ag.* onomastico.

onomasticon [,onouˈmæstikən], *s.* vocabolario di nomi di persona.

onomatology [,onouməˈtolədʒi], *s.* terminologia.

onomatop [ouˈnomətop], **onomatope** [ouˈnomətoup], *s.* parola onomatopeica.

onomatopoeia [,onoumætouˈpi(ː)ə], *s.* (*ret.*) onomatopeia.

onomatopoeic [,onoumætouˈpiːik], **onomatopoetic** [,onou,mætoupouˈetik], *ag.* (*ret.*) onomatopeico.

onrush [ˈonrʌʃ], *s.* attacco, assalto.

onrushing [ˈon,rʌʃiŋ], *ag.* impetuoso.

onset [ˈonset], **onslaught** [ˈonslɔːt], *s.* **1.** (*poet.*) assalto, attacco **2.** inizio, partenza.

onto [ˈontu], *prep.* sopra, su.

ontogenesis [,ontəˈdʒenisis], *s.* ontogenesi.

ontogenetic [,ontədʒiˈnetik], *ag.* ontogenetico.

ontological [,ontəˈlodʒikəl], *ag.* (*fil.*) ontologico.

ontologically [,ontəˈlodʒikəli], *av.* (*fil*) ontologicamente.

ontology [onˈtolədʒi], *s.* (*fil.*) ontologia.

onus [ˈounəs], *s.* peso, carico; dovere, obbligo; responsabilità ‖ — *probandi*, (*dir.*) onere della prova.

onward [ˈonwəd], *ag.* avanzato; progressivo.

onward(s) [ˈonwəd(z)], *av.* avanti; in avanti; in là; oltre; progressivamente.

onychia [ouˈnikiə], *s.* (*patol.*) onichia.

onyx [ˈoniks], *s.* **1.** (*min.*) onice **2.** (*patol.*) presenza di pus tra gli strati della cornea.

oodles [ˈuːdlz], *s.pl.* (*sl.*) un sacco, una gran quantità.

oof [uːf], *s.* (*sl.*) denaro; ricchezza ☆ — *bird*, fonte di denaro, persona ricca.

oofless [ˈuːflis], *ag.* **1.** senza soldi, povero.

oofy [ˈuːfi], *ag.* ricco.

oogenesis [,ouəˈdʒenisis], *s.* (*biol.*) oogenesi.

oolite [ˈouəlait], *s.* (*geol.*) oolite.

oolitic [,ouəˈlitik], *ag.* (*geol.*) oolitico.

oology [ouˈolədʒi], *s.* (*ornit.*) oologia.

oom [uːm], *s.* (*Sud Africa*) zio ‖ *Oom Paul*, « Oom Paul », il presidente dei Boeri Paul Krüger.

ooze[1] [uːz], *s.* **1.** melma, fango; fanghiglia **2.** (*geol.*) materiale calcareo.

ooze[2], *s.* **1.** (*tec.*) liquido per concia **2.** trasudazione; infiltrazione; il fluire lentamente.

to ooze[2], *v.t.i.* **1.** fluire, colare lentamente; trasudare, stillare: *tears were oozing from her eyes*, le lacrime le scendevano lentamente dagli occhi **2.** *to* — *away* (o *amer.* **along**), scomparire lentamente: *her courage oozed away*, ella si perse d'animo **3.** *to* — *out*, trapelare; (*sl. amer.*) squagliarsela: *the news oozed out*, la notizia trapelò.

oozy [ˈuːzi], *ag.* **1.** melmoso **2.** fangoso.

opacity [ouˈpæsiti], *s.* **1.** opacità **2.** *fig.* oscurità (di significato, ecc.); ottusità mentale.

opah [ˈoupə], *s.* pesce luna.

opal [ˈoupəl], *s.* (*min.*) opale.

opalescence [,oupəˈlesns], *s.* opalescenza.

opalescent [,oupəˈlesnt], **opalesque** [,oupəˈlesk], *ag.* opalescente.

opaline [ˈoupəlain], *come s.* [ˈoupəliːn], *ag.* opalino ‖ *s.* « opaline » (vetro simile all'opale).

opaque [ouˈpeik], *ag.* **1.** opaco **2.** *fig.* ottuso.

opaqueness [ouˈpeiknis], *V.* **opacity.**

to ope [oup], *v.t.i.* (*poet.*) aprire, aprirsi.

open [ˈoupən], *ag.* **1.** aperto; dischiuso, sbocciato; libero, non ostruito; esposto; accessibile; suscettibile: *an* — *river*, un fiume libero (da ghiacci, ecc.); *in the* — *country*, in aperta campagna; *with* — *arms*, a braccia aperte; *fig.* calorosamente; *the book lay on the table*, il libro stava aperto sul tavolo; *the door was flung* —, la porta fu aperta con violenza; *the flowers were all* —, i fiori erano tutti sbocciati ‖ *the* — *door*, politica delle porte aperte ‖ — *weather*, tempo sereno; — *winter*, inverno mite ‖ *to lay oneself* — *to criticism*, lasciare il fianco scoperto alle critiche **2.** (*aperto al*) pubblico; vacante: *an* — *competition*, una gara aperta a tutti; *the* — *season (for fishing, shooting)*, la stagione aperta (per la pesca, la caccia); *the job is still* —, l'impiego è ancora vacante; *museum* — *to the public*, museo aperto al pubblico ‖ *to try in the* — *court*, (*dir.*) fare un processo a porte aperte **3.** *fig.* aperto; sincero; franco, dichiarato; — *to advice*, pronto ad accettare consigli; *to keep an* — *mind on sthg.*, non avere preconcetti su ql.co. **4.** pubblico, manifesto, non segreto: — *scandal*, scandalo pubblico ☆ —

account, conto aperto, conto corrente; — *-air*, l'aria aperta, l'aperto: — *-air school*, scuola all'aperto; — *-armed*, (che accoglie) a braccia aperte; — *car*, automobile scoperta; — *cast*, miniera all'aperto; — *-cheque*, assegno non sbarrato; — *-contract*, contratto in sospeso; — *-earcd*, con le orecchie aperte, attento; — *-eyed*, con gli occhi spalancati; — *-handed*, generoso; — *-handedness*, generosità; — *-hearted*, espansivo; generoso; — *house*, ospitalità: *to keep* — *house*, essere ospitale; — *letter*, lettera aperta (a un giornale); — *market*, mercato libero; — *mill*, (*ind.*) mescolatore aperto; — *-minded*, di larghe vedute; — *-mindedness*, larghezza di vedute; — *mouthed*, a bocca aperta; — *necked*, scollato (di abito); — *question*, questione in sospeso; — *sea*, mare aperto; — *secret*, segreto di Pulcinella; — *shop*, (*amer.*) azienda che impiega anche chi non fa parte di un sindacato; — *town*, città aperta; — *verdict*, (*dir.*) non luogo a procedere; — *-work*, punto a giorno, lavoro a traforo.

to **open**, *v.t.i.* **1.** aprire, aprirsi; schiudere, schiudersi; dissuggellare: *the bank opens at ten*, la banca apre alle dieci; *the doctor opened the abscess*, il dottore incise l'ascesso; *the flowers are opening*, i fiori stanno sbocciando; *he opened the door wide into the garden*, spalancò la porta verso il giardino; *the two rooms — into one another*, le due camere sono comunicanti; *the windows — on to the sea*, le finestre danno sul mare; *to — a box*, aprire una scatola; *to — a hole in a wall*, fare un buco nel muro; *to — a new road through the forest*, aprire una nuova strada nella foresta; *to — one's hand, a newspaper*, aprire la mano, un giornale; *to — one's shop*, aprire il negozio; *to — the ranks*, (*mil.*) aprire le file || *to — the door to a disease, fig.* lasciar via libera ad una malattia || *to — s.o.'s eyes, fig.* aprire gli occhi a qlcu. || *to — one's heart, mind, fig.* aprire il proprio cuore, far conoscere i propri pensieri **2.** aprire, iniziare: *the show opened with a song*, la rappresentazione ebbe inizio con una canzone; *to — an account at a bank*, aprire un conto in banca; *to — a debate*, aprire un dibattito; *to — fire on the enemy*, (*mil.*) aprire il fuoco sul nemico; *to — (out) a new shop*, aprire un nuovo negozio **3.** aprire, inaugurare: *the Queen opened Parliament*, la regina inaugurò la sessione del Parlamento **4.** (*caccia*) fare cagnara **5.** *to — out*, aprire, stendere, spiegare: *he opened out a map*, spiegò una mappa **6.** *to — up*, aprire (un cammino, una miniera, ecc.).

opencast ['oupǝnka:st], *s.* (*miner.*) scavo a cielo aperto.

opener ['oupnǝ*], *s.* chi, che apre ☆ *bottle-* —, apribottiglie; *can-* — (o *tin-* —), apriscatole.

opening ['oupniŋ], *ag.* che si apre; nascente; che inizia || *s.* **1.** principio; esordio; apertura; inaugurazione **2.** radura; schiarita (nel cielo) **3.** foro, bocca; apertura; breccia; luce, larghezza **4.** occasione favorevole.

openly ['oupnli], *av.* apertamente, francamente; pubblicamente.

openness ['oupnnis], *s.* **1.** l'essere aperto; esposizione (di un terreno) **2.** *fig.* franchezza; apertura (mentale); chiarezza.

opera ['opǝrǝ], *pl.* **operas** ['opǝrǝz], *s.* (*teat.*) opera: ☆ — *-bouffe*, opera buffa; — *-cloak*, mantello da sera; — *-girl*, ballerina d'opera; — *-glass*, binocolo; — *-hat*, cappello a cilindro con molle; gibus; — *-house*, teatro dell'opera.

operable ['opǝrǝbl], *ag.* operabile.

operant ['opǝrǝnt], *ag.* operante, operativo || *s.* operatore; chi opera.

to **operate** ['opǝreit], *v.t.i.* **1.** operare, agire, aver effetto, produrre: *atomic energy operates changes in matter*, l'energia atomica produce mutamenti nella materia; *this law operates to our disadvantage*, questa legge opera a nostro svantaggio **2.** funzionare, essere in funzione, far funzionare: *he operated a big machine*,

egli faceva funzionare una grossa macchina; *the lift was not operating properly*, l'ascensore non funzionava bene **3.** (*chir.*) fare un'operazione: *he was operated on for appendicitis*, egli fu operato di appendicite **4.** (*mil. comm.*) fare delle operazioni **5.** amministrare, gestire; sfruttare (miniera, ecc.).

operatic [,opǝ'rætik], *ag.* di opera, lirico.

operating ['opǝreitiŋ], *ag.* operante || *s.* **1.** funzionamento; azione **2.** esercizio (di miniera, ecc.) **3.** (*chir.*) operazione ☆ — *-room*, sala operatoria.

operation [,opǝ'reiʃǝn], *s.* **1.** effetto; azione; vigore; attività: *in full* —, in piena attività; *to come into* —, entrare in vigore **2.** (*chir. mat. mil. comm.*) operazione: *base of operations*, (*mil.*) base di operazioni; *a mathematical* —, un'operazione matematica; *to perform an — on s.o.*, (*chir.*) operare qlcu. **3.** (*mec.*) funzionamento.

operational [,opǝ'reiʃǝn], *ag.* (*mil.*) relativo ad operazioni ☆ — *training*, addestramento militare.

operative ['opǝrǝtiv], *ag.* **1.** attivo; efficace: *this law will be — as from...*, questa legge entrerà in vigore dal... **2.** (*chir.*) operatorio **3.** pratico || *s.c.* artigiano, artigiana; operaio (meccanico), operaia (meccanica).

operatively ['opǝrǝtivli], *av.* attivamente, efficacemente.

operator ['opǝreitǝ*], *s.* **1.** agente **2.** persona che fa funzionare un apparecchio; (*cine.*) operatore **3.** (*chir.*) operatore ☆ *telephone* —, telefonista.

operculum [ou'pǝ:kjulǝm], *pl.* **opercula** [ou'pǝ:kjulǝ], *s.* (*bot. zool.*) opercolo.

operetta [,opǝ'retǝ], *pl.* **operettas** [,opǝ'retǝz], *s.* (*teat.*) operetta.

operose ['opǝrous], *ag.* operoso, diligente.

operosely ['opǝrousli], *av.* operosamente, diligentemente.

operoseness ['opǝrousnis], **operosity** [,opǝ'rositi], *s.* operosità, attività, diligenza, zelo.

Ophelia [o'fi:ljǝ], *no. pr. f.* (*lett.*) Ofelia.

ophicleide ['ofiklaid], *s.* (*mus.*) oficleide.

Ophidia [o'fidiǝ], *s.pl.* (*zool.*) ofidi.

ophidian [o'fidiǝn], (*zool.*) *ag.* degli ofidi || *s.* ofide.

ophiology [,ofi'olǝdʒi], *s.* ofiologia.

ophite ['ofait], *s.* (*min.*) serpentino, ofite.

ophiuran [,ofi'juǝrǝn], *s.* (*zool.*) ofiura.

ophthalmia [of'θælmiǝ], *s.* (*patol.*) oftalmia.

ophthalmic [of'θælmik], *ag.* oftalmico.

ophthalmologist [,ofθæl'molǝdʒist], *s.* oculista.

ophthalmology [,ofθæl'molǝdʒi], *s.* oftalmologia.

ophthalmoscope [of'θælmouskoup], *s.* oftalmoscopio.

ophthalmoscopy [,ofθæl'moskǝpi], *s.* oftalmoscopia.

ophthalmotomy [,ofθæl'motǝmi], *s.* oftalmotomia.

opiate ['oupiit], *ag.* oppiato, oppiaceo; soporifero (anche *fig.*) || *s.* narcotico, sonnifero.

to **opiate** ['oupieit], *v.t.* oppiare.

opinable [ou'painǝbl], *ag.* opinabile.

to **opine** [ou'pain], *v.t.* opinare, pensare.

opinion [ǝ'pinjǝn], *s.* **1.** opinione, parere, giudizio: *in his* —, secondo lui; *in my* —, secondo me; *a matter of* —, una cosa discutibile; *to act up to one's opinions*, agire secondo le proprie idee; *to ask s.o.'s* —, chiedere il parere di qlcu.; *to give one's* —, esprimere il proprio parere; *to take counsel's* —, consultare un avvocato **2.** stima: *a high* —, un alto concetto; *I have no — of those people*, non ho alcuna stima per quella gente.

opinionated [ǝ'pinjǝneitid], *ag.* ostinato, tenace; dogmatico.

opinionatedness [ǝ'pinjǝneitidnis], *s.* ostinazione; fermo attaccamento alle proprie idee.

opinionative [ǝ'pinjǝneitiv], *ag.* ostinato, tenace; dogmatico.

opinionatively [ǝ'pinjǝneitivli], *av.* ostinatamente, tenacemente; dogmaticamente.

opinionativeness [ǝ'pinjǝneitivnis], ostinazione; fermo attaccamento alle proprie idee.

opinioned [ǝ'pinjǝnd], *ag.* ostinato, tenace; dogmatico.

opinionist [ǝ'pinjǝnist], *s.* settario.

opisometer [ˌɔpi'sɔmitə*], s. curvimetro.

opisthodome [ou'pisθoudoum], **opisthodomos** [ˌɔpis-'θɔdoumɔs], s. (arch.) opistodomo.

opisthograph [ou'pisθougrɑːf], s. pergamena, lapide scritta da ambo le parti.

opium ['oupjəm], s. oppio ☆ — -den, fumeria d'oppio; — -eater, masticatore, mangiatore d'oppio; — -smoker, fumatore d'oppio.

opiumism ['oupjəmizəm], s. (patol.) oppiomania.

to opiumize ['oupjəmaiz], v.t. oppiare.

opopanax [ou'pɔpənæks], s. (bot.) opoponaco.

opossum [ə'pɔsəm], s. (zool.) opossum.

oppidan ['ɔpidən], ag. (rar.) cittadino ‖ s. 1. (rar.) cittadino 2. allievo esterno (del collegio di Eton).

to oppilate ['ɔpileit], v.t. (med.) oppilare.

oppilation [ˌɔpi'leiʃən], s. (med.) oppilazione.

opponency [ə'pounənsi], s. opposizione.

opponent [ə'pounənt], ag. (rar.) contrario, opposto ‖ s. avversario, antagonista: he is my — in this game, egli è il mio avversario in questo giuoco ☆ — muscle, (anat.) muscolo oppositore (della mano).

opportune ['ɔpətjuːn], ag. opportuno; tempestivo, a proposito.

opportunely ['ɔpətjuːnli], av. opportunamente; a tempo; a proposito.

opportuneness ['ɔpətjuːnnis], s. opportunità; tempestività.

opportunism ['ɔpətjuːnizəm], s. opportunismo.

opportunist ['ɔpətjuːnist], s. opportunista.

opportunistic [ˌɔpətjuː'nistik], ag. opportunistico.

opportunity [ˌɔpə'tjuːniti], s. occasione; opportunità: possibilità: a golden — occurred to me, mi si presentò un affare d'oro; have you ever had the — of speaking to him?, hai mai avuto la possibilità di parlargli?; he took (o availed himself of) the — to go to London, colse l'occasione per andare a Londra ‖ — makes the thief, prov. l'occasione fa l'uomo ladro.

opposable [ə'pouzəbl], ag. opponibile.

to oppose [ə'pouz], v.t. opporre, opporsi a; contrapporre; contrastare; essere contrario a; obiettare a: he opposed the majority motion, egli si oppose alla mozione della maggioranza; to fury we'll — patience, alla furia opporremo la pazienza.

opposed [ə'pouzd], ag. 1. ostile, avverso: he is — to that scheme, egli è contrario a quel progetto; the press was — to the Government, la stampa era ostile al governo 2. opposto: country life as — to town life offers some advantages, la vita di campagna offre alcuni vantaggi rispetto alla vita di città.

opposer [ə'pouzə*], s. oppositore; avversario; antagonista.

opposite ['ɔpəzit], ag. 1. opposto, contrario: the — sex, l'altro sesso; they went away in — directions, se ne andarono in direzioni opposte 2. opposto, di faccia, di fronte: the house —, la casa di fronte ‖ s. opposto: I am just the — of my brother, io sono tutto l'opposto di mio fratello ☆ — number, corrispondente in grado, simile.

opposite, av. dirimpetto, di fronte: there was a theatre —, dirimpetto c'era un teatro ‖ prep. di fronte a, dirimpetto a: the garden — my house, il giardino di fronte a casa mia; they live — us, vivono di fronte, dirimpetto a noi.

oppositely ['ɔpəzitli], av. (gener. bot.) opposta-mente.

oppositeness ['ɔpəzitnis], s. situazione opposta; opposizione.

opposition [ˌɔpə'ziʃən], s. 1. opposizione; ostacolo: there was no — on her side, non ci fu opposizione da parte sua; they met with unexpected —, incontrarono inattesa resistenza 2. (pol.) opposizione: the leader of the —, il capo dell'opposizione 3. (astr.) opposizione: the planet is in —, il pianeta è in opposizione (al sole) 4. (comm.) concorrenza.

oppositional [ˌɔpə'ziʃənl], ag. (rar.) antitetico, contrastante.

oppositive [ə'pɔzitiv], ag. (rar.) antitetico, contra-stante.

to oppress [ə'pres], v.t. 1. opprimere; tiranneggiare (vinti, sudditi) 2. opprimere, gravare, angustiare: I feel oppressed, mi sento oppresso.

oppression [ə'preʃən], s. 1. oppressione 2. fig. ab-battimento.

oppressive [ə'presiv], ag. oppressivo, opprimente; pesante.

oppressively [ə'presivli], av. in modo opprimente; tirannicamente.

oppressor [ə'presə*], s. oppressore.

opprobrious [ə'proubriəs], ag. obbrobrioso; in-famante; ingiurioso.

opprobriously [ə'proubriəsli], av. obbrobriosamente; ingiuriosamente.

opprobriousness [ə'proubriəsnis], s. obbrobriosità; obbrobrio; vituperio; ignominia.

opprobrium [ə'proubriəm], s. obbrobrio; vituperio.

to oppugn [ɔ'pjuːn], v.t. oppugnare; combattere (un principio, ecc.).

oppugnant [ɔ'pʌgnənt], ag. ostile; contrario ‖ s. antagonista; avversario.

oppugnation [ˌɔpʌg'neiʃən], s. (rar.) opposizione; re-sistenza.

oppugner [ɔ'pjuːnə*], s. oppositore.

to opt [ɔpt], v.i. optare.

optative ['ɔptətiv], ag. (gram.) ottativo ‖ s. (gram.) il modo ottativo.

optic ['ɔptik], ag. ottico ‖ s. (scherz.) occhio ☆ — angle, angolo ottico; — nerve, nervo ottico.

optical ['ɔptikəl], ag. ottico: — illusion, illusione ottica; — instrument, strumento ottico.

optically ['ɔptikəli], av. otticamente.

optician [ɔp'tiʃən], s. ottico (chi vende lenti).

optics ['ɔptiks], s. (fis.) ottica.

optimate ['ɔptimit], s. ottimate; nobile, aristocratico.

optimism ['ɔptimizəm], s. ottimismo.

optimist ['ɔptimist], ag. ottimistico ‖ s. ottimista.

optimistic [ˌɔpti'mistik], ag. ottimistico.

optimistically [ˌɔpti'mistikəli], av. ottimistica-mente.

to optimize ['ɔptimaiz], v.i. essere ottimista.

optimum ['ɔptiməm], s. 1. (biol.) optimum (la con-dizione più favorevole per la crescita, riproduzione, ecc.) 2. la condizione migliore.

option ['ɔpʃən], s. 1. opzione; scelta: to have no — but, non aver altra scelta che, non potere fare altro che, dovere; to make one's —, fare la propria scelta ‖ at the — of, con la facoltà di 2. (Borsa) opzione.

optional ['ɔpʃənl], ag. facoltativo.

optionally ['ɔpʃnəli], av. facoltativamente.

optometer [ɔp'tɔmitə*], s. (ott.) optometro.

opulence ['ɔpjuləns], s. opulenza; ricchezza.

opulent ['ɔpjulənt], ag. opulento; ricco.

opulently ['ɔpjuləntli], av. in modo opulento, ricco.

opuntia [ou'pʌnʃiə], s. (bot.) opunzia, fico d'India.

opus ['oupəs], s. (solo sing.) opera, composizione musicale.

opuscule [ɔ'pʌskjuːl], (lat.) **opusculum** [ɔ'pʌskjuləm], pl. **opuscula** [ɔ'pʌskjulə], s. (mus. lett.) opera minore.

or[1] [ɔː*], s. (arald.) oro; colore giallo.

or[2], cong. 1. o, od, oppure: either one — the other, o l'uno o l'altro; white — grey, bianco o grigio; make haste — you'll be late, fai presto, altrimenti sarai in ritardo; they put it on the table — somewhere, l'hanno messo sul tavolo o da qualche parte; whether he stays — goes, sia che egli rimanga o vada; will she be in — not?, sarà in casa o no? ‖ — else, altrimenti ‖ a pound — so, una sterlina circa 2. (con negazione) nè: no voice — other sound was to be heard, non si udivano nè voci, nè altro rumore.

or[3], prep. cong. (arc.) prima che.

oracle ['ɔrəkl], s. oracolo (anche fig.): the Delphic —, l'oracolo di Delfo; to talk like an —, parlare come un oracolo ‖ *to work the* —, *fig.* ottenere ql.co. per mezzo di segrete influenze.

oracular [ɔ'rækjulə*], *ag.* **1.** di oracolo; profetico **2.** ambiguo, misterioso.

oracularly [ɔ'rækjuləli], *av.* profeticamente.

oracularness [ɔ'rækjulənis], **oraculousness** [ɔ'rækjuləsnis], *s.* **1.** tono, autorità da oracolo **2.** oscurità, ambiguità da oracolo.

oral ['ɔːrəl], *ag.* orale ‖ *s.* esame orale, l'orale.

orally ['ɔːrəli], *av.* **1.** oralmente **2.** (*med.*) per via orale.

orange[1] ['ɔrindʒ], *ag.* di colore arancio; simile all'arancio ‖ *s.* arancia; arancio (albero, colore) ☆ — -blossom, fiore d'arancio; — -flower, fiore d'arancio: — -flower water, essenza di fiori d'arancio; — -grove, arancio; — juice, succo d'arancia; — marmalade, marmellata d'arance; — -peel, scorza d'arancia; — pekoe, qualità pregiata di tè scuro; — squash, spremuta d'arancia.

Orange[2], *no.pr.* (*geog.*) Orange ‖ *s.* **1.** appartenente alla famiglia d'Orange **2.** — (*man*), (*st.*) partigiano del protestantesimo in Irlanda.

orangeade ['ɔrindʒ'eid], *s.* aranciata.

orangery ['ɔrindʒəri], *s.* **1.** aranceto **2.** aranciera, serra per aranci.

orang-(o)utang ['ɔːrəŋ'uːtæŋ], *s.* (*zool.*) orangutan.

orant ['ourent], *s.* (*pitt.*) orante.

to **orate** [ɔː'reit], *v.i.* (*scherz.*) arringare; fare un discorso.

oration [ɔː'reiʃən], *s.* **1.** discorso **2.** orazione, preghiera **3.** (*gram.*) discorso: *direct* —, discorso diretto ☆ *funeral* —, orazione funebre.

orator ['ɔrətə*], *s.* oratore.

oratorial [,ɔrə'tɔːriəl], *ag.* (*rar.*) oratorio.

oratorian [,ɔrə'tɔːriən], *s.* padre oratoriano.

oratorical [,ɔrə'tɔrikəl], *ag.* oratorio; ampolloso.

oratorically [,ɔrə'tɔrikəli], *av.* oratoriamente, in tono oratorio, ampolloso.

oratorio [,ɔrə'tɔːriou], *s.* (*mus.*) oratorio.

oratory[1] ['ɔrətəri], *s.* **1.** oratorio, piccola cappella **2.** *Oratory*, Oratorio (ordine religioso fondato da S. Filippo Neri).

oratory[2], *s.* arte oratoria; eloquenza: *flight of* —, voli d'oratoria ☆ *forensic* —, oratoria forense.

oratress ['ɔrətris], *s.* oratrice.

orb [ɔːb], *s.* **1.** cerchio **2.** globo, sfera **3.** (*astr.*) orbita **4.** (*poet.*) occhio.

to **orb**, *v.t.i.* **1.** circoscrivere in un'orbita **2.** formare un cerchio.

orbed [ɔːbd], *ag.* **1.** circolare **2.** sferico ☆ *full-moon*, luna piena.

orbicular [ɔː'bikiulə*], *ag.* sferico; (*anat.*) orbiculare, anulare ☆ — *bone*, ossicino che forma la parte laterale dell'incudine; — *ligament*, ligamento anulare del radio; — *process*, processo lenticolare dell'incudine.

orbit ['ɔːbit], *s.* **1.** (*anat. astr.*) orbita **2.** *fig.* zona di influenza, di attività, orbita.

orbital ['ɔːbitl], *ag.* relativo all'orbita, orbitale.

orby ['ɔːbi], *ag.* (*poet. rar.*) **1.** a forma di orbita, sferico; che si muove in un'orbita **2.** di, da corpo celeste.

orc [ɔːk], *s.* (*zool.*) orca marina.

Orcadian [ɔː'keidjən], *ag.* delle Isole Orcadi ‖ *s. c.* abitante delle Isole Orcadi.

orchard ['ɔːtʃəd], *s.* frutteto.

orcharding ['ɔːtʃədiŋ], *s.* **1.** orticoltura **2.** terreni coltivati a frutta.

orchardist ['ɔːtʃədist], **orchardman**, *pl.* **orchardmen** ['ɔːtʃədmən], *s.* frutticoltore.

orchestic [ɔː'kestik], *ag.* attinente alla danza.

orchestics [ɔː'kestiks], *s.* l'arte della danza.

orchestra ['ɔːkistrə], *s.* orchestra (anche nel significato di spazio riservato ai musici) ☆ — *circle*, (*amer.*) recinto per l'orchestra; — *stalls*, le prime file di poltrone ‖ *string* —, orchestra d'archi.

orchestral [ɔː'kestrəl], *ag.* orchestrale ☆ — *score*, partitura.

to **orchestrate** ['ɔːkistreit], *v.t.* (*mus.*) orchestrare.

orchestration [,ɔːkes'treiʃən], *s.* (*mus.*) orchestrazione; strumentazione.

orchestrina [,ɔːkis'triːnə], **orchestrion** [ɔː'kestriən], *s.* (*mus.*) ‹ orchestrion › (specie di organo portatile).

orchid ['ɔːkid], *s.* (*bot.*) orchidea.

orchidaceous [,ɔːki'deiʃəs], *ag.* (*bot.*) orchidaceo.

orchil ['ɔːtʃil], *s.* (*chim.*) orcina; (*bot.*) oricello.

orchis ['ɔːkis], *s.* (*bot.*) orchidea.

orchitis [ɔː'kaitis], *s.* (*patol.*) orchite.

orcin ['ɔːsin], *s.* (*chim.*) orcina.

to **ordain** [ɔː'dein], *v.t.* **1.** (*eccl.*) ordinare, consacrare: *he was ordained priest*, fu consacrato sacerdote **2.** decretare, stabilire, ordinare: *what the laws* —, ciò che ordinano le leggi **3.** predestinare (di Dio, fato, ecc.): *God ordained Death as our lot*, Dio ci predestinò alla morte; *it was ordained that they should be parted*, era destino che essi dovessero separarsi.

ordainable [ɔː'deinəbl], *ag.* che può prendere gli ordini sacri.

ordainer [ɔː'deinə*], *s.* **1.** (*eccl.*) chi ordina, chi consacra **2.** chi comanda.

ordainment [ɔː'deinmənt], *s.* (*rar.*) decreto.

ordeal [ɔː'diːl], *s.* (*st.*) ordalia, giudizio di Dio; *fig.* dura prova: — *by fire*, prova del fuoco.

order ['ɔːdə*], *s.* **1.** ordine: *in* —, in ordine; *was his passport in* —?, il suo passaporto era in regola?; *in working* —, in efficienza, in funzione; *to put out of* —, mettere in disordine **2.** classe, categoria (di persone): *all orders of men*, tutte le classi sociali **3.** successione, sequela: *in alphabetical* —, in ordine alfabetico **4.** ordine cavalleresco ‖ *the Order of the Thistle*, l'Ordine del Cardo (in Scozia) ‖ *the Dominican Order*, l'Ordine dei Domenicani **5.** (*teol.*) gerarchia angelica **6.** *pl.* (*eccl.*) ordine, sacramento dell'ordine: *his brother was in holy orders*, suo fratello era sacerdote **7.** ordine naturale; ordinamento; sistema **8.** comando; ingiunzione; consegna: *the officer's* — *was to let nobody through*, la consegna dell'ufficiale era di non lasciar passare nessuno **9.** (*arch.*) ordine: *the Doric* —, l'ordine Dorico **10.** (*bot. zool.*) ordine, classe, suddivisione **11.** (*mil.*) ordine; uniforme, tenuta; — *of battle*, ordine di battaglia; *in close* —, in ordine serrato **12.** (*comm.*) ordine, ordinazione, commissione, mandato: *he has given us an* — *for five tons*, ci ha fatto un'ordinazione di cinque tonnellate ‖ *made to* —, eseguito su ordinazione; *on* —, in ordinazione **13.** scopo, fine, intenzione: *in* — *that he may come*, affinché venga; *in* — *to do sthg.*, allo scopo di fare ql.co. ☆ — -*paper*, testo dell'ordine del giorno (del Parlamento inglese) ‖ *postal* —, vaglia postale; *repeat* —, ordine rinnovato; *standing* —, ordine fisso; *trial* —, ordine di prova.

to **order**, *v.t.* **1.** ordinare, riordinare: *I must* — *my papers*, devo riordinare le mie carte **2.** (IV) comandare, ordinare, ingiungere; disporre; regolare; prescrivere: *the doctor ordered a change of air for her*, il dottore le prescrisse un cambiamento d'aria; *I was ordered to do it at once*, mi fu ingiunto di farlo subito **3.** (*comm.*) ordinare; commissionare; far fare: *he has ordered a new winter suit*, si è fatto fare un nuovo abito invernale **4.** (*eccl.*) ordinare: *he was ordered deacon*, fu consacrato diacono **5.** *to* — **about**, mandare da destra a sinistra, da un luogo ad un altro **6.** *to* — **away**, mandar via **7.** *to* — **back**, richiamare **8.** *to* — **down**, far discendere **9.** *to* — **in**, far entrare **10.** *to* — **off**, mandar via **11.** *to* — **out**, far uscire **12.** *to* — **up**, far salire.

orderer ['ɔːdərə*], *s.* capo, comandante.

ordering ['ɔːdəriŋ], *s.* **1.** ordinamento; disposizione **2.** (*eccl.*) ordinazione.

orderless ['ɔːdəlis], *ag.* disordinato.

orderliness ['ɔːdəlinis], *s.* **1.** ordine, regolarità, metodo **2.** disciplina, buona condotta.

orderly ['ɔːdəli], *ag.* ordinato, regolato, metodico; tranquillo, disciplinato ‖ *s.* **1.** (*mil.*) attendente, ordinanza 2. inserviente (d'ospedale) ☆ — *officer*, (*mil.*) ufficiale di giornata; — *room*, (*mil.*) sala di rapporto.

ordinal ['ɔ:dinl], *ag.* 1. (*mat.*) ordinale 2. (*zool. bot.*) appartenente ad un ordine ‖ *s.* 1. numero ordinale 2. (*eccl.*) ordinale.

ordinance ['ɔ:dinəns], *s.* 1. ordinanza, legge, decreto 2. (*eccl.*) rito.

ordinand [,ɔ:di'nænd], *s.* (*eccl.*) ordinando.

ordinarily ['ɔ:dnrili], *av.* ordinariamente, di solito.

ordinary ['ɔ:dnri], *ag.* 1. ordinario, consueto, solito; comune: *he read the* — *prayer*, lesse la solita preghiera 2. comune, mediocre; (*spreg.*) comune, dozzinale, di cattivo gusto: *a small and* — *flat*, un appartamentino dozzinale ‖ *s.* 1. condizione ordinaria, normale: *a person out of the* —, una persona fuori del comune; *a woman above the* —, una donna straordinaria ‖ *physician in* — (*to the king*), medico del re ‖ *ship in* —, (*mar.*) nave in disarmo 2. magistrato che giudica nella propria giurisdizione; (*eccl.*) vescovo di una diocesi, arcivescovo di una provincia; (*dir. scoz.*) giudice 3. (*eccl.*) ordinale (della messa) 4. pranzo ad ore e prezzi fissi (in trattoria) 5. biciclo 6. (*arald.*) comune emblema.

ordinate ['ɔ:dnit], *s.* (*geom.*) ordinata.

ordination [,ɔ:di'neiʃən], *s.* 1. classificazione 2. (*eccl.*) ordinazione, consacrazione 3. ordine; decreto.

ordinee [,ɔ:di'ni:], *s.* diacono ordinato di recente.

ordnance ['ɔ:dnəns], *s.* 1. artiglieria: *piece of* —, cannone 2. (*mil.*) ufficio approvvigionamento; sussistenza ☆ — *office*, deposito di materiali d'artiglieria; — (*survey*) *map*, carta topografica militare.

ordure ['ɔ:djuə*], *s.* 1. escremento; concime; immondizia 2. (*fam.*) linguaggio osceno.

ore [ɔ:*], *s.* 1. minerale 2. (*poet.*) metallo (specialmente prezioso) ☆ — *-body*, giacimento di minerale; — *-hearth*, forno di fusione per minerali; — *-pocket*, silo sotterraneo per minerale; — *-pulp*, (*miner.*) torbida.

oread ['ɔ:riæd], *s.* (*mit.*) oreade.

orectic [ə'rektik], *ag.* (*rar. fil.*) appetitivo.

Orestes [ə'resti:z], *no.pr.m.* (*mit.*) Oreste.

orfe [ɔ:f], *s.* (*ittiol.*) leucisco.

organ ['ɔ:gən], *s.* 1. (*mus. anat.*) organo: *the organs of respiration*, gli organi della respirazione; *to set to the* —, comporre musica per organo 2. organo, giornale, bollettino (di partito politico, ecc.) 3. voce: *he has a strong* —, ha una voce forte, sonora ☆ — *-builder*, fabbricante di organi; — *-grinder*, suonatore d'organetto; — *-loft*, tribuna per organo; — *-pipe*, canna d'organo ‖ *barrel-* — (o *hand-* o *street-* —), organetto di Barberia; *electric-* —, organo elettro-acustico, di tipo Hammond; *mouth-* —, armonica.

organdy, organdie ['ɔ:gəndi], *s.* organdi.

organic(al) [ɔ:'gænik(əl)], *ag.* 1. (*fisiol. patol. chim.*) organico: — *remains*, rifiuti organici 2. organico, organizzato; armonico: *an* — *whole*, un insieme armonico 3. costituzionale, fondamentale, strutturale ☆ — *chemistry*, chimica organica.

organically [ɔ:'gænikəli], *av.* organicamente.

organism ['ɔ:gənizəm], *s.* organismo.

organist ['ɔ:gənist], *s.c.* organista.

organizable ['ɔ:gənaizəbl], *ag.* organizzabile.

organization [,ɔ:gənai'zeiʃən], *s.* organizzazione; organismo ☆ *charity* —, opera assistenziale.

to organize ['ɔ:gənaiz], *v.t.i.* organizzare, organizzarsi: *to* — *a race*, organizzare una corsa.

organizer ['ɔ:gənaizə*], *s.c.* organizzatore, organizzatrice.

organogeny [,ɔ:gə'nɔdʒini], *s.* (*biol.*) organogenesi, organogenia.

organon ['ɔ:gənon], *s.* 1. (*fil.*) metodo logico 2. (*fil.*) « organon » (scritti di logica di Aristotele).

organoplasty [,ɔ:gənə'plæsti], *s.* (*chir.*) organoplastia.

organotherapy [,ɔ:gənə'θerəpi], *s.* (*med.*) opoterapia.

organum ['ɔ:gənəm], *s.* 1. *V.* **organon** 2. (*mus.*) antica forma di accompagnamento vocale.

organza [ɔ:'gænzə], *s.* organza.

organzine [,ɔ:gənzi:n], *s.* organzino.

orgasm ['ɔ:gæzəm], *s.* eccitazione; parossismo.

orgastic [ɔ:'gæstik], *ag.* orgastico.

orgeat ['ɔ:dʒiət], *s.* orzata.

orgiastic [,ɔ:dʒi'æstik], *ag.* orgiastico.

orgy ['ɔ:dʒi], *s.* 1. *gener. pl.* (*st.*) orge, baccanali 2. orgia, gozzoviglia 3. *fig.* tripudio.

Oriana [,ɔri'ɑ:nə], *no.pr.f.* Oriana.

oriel ['ɔ:riəl], *s.* (*arch.*) bovindo, balcone chiuso a vetrata.

orient ['ɔ:riənt], *ag.* 1. (*poet.*) orientale 2. prezioso, lucente (di perle, ecc.): — *pearl*, perla orientale, preziosa, di bella luce 3. nascente, levante (di sole, ecc.) ‖ *s.* 1. *Orient*, (*poet.*) levante, est 2. *Orient*, (*geog.*) l'Oriente 3. perla orientale 4. lucentezza (di perla).

to orient, *v.t.i.* 1. orientare; volgere, volgersi verso oriente: *to* — (*oneself*), orientarsi (anche *fig.*) 2. costruire (una chiesa) con l'altare rivolto ad oriente.

Oriental [,ɔri'entl], *ag.* s. orientale.

orientalism [,ɔ:ri'entəlizəm], *s.* orientalismo.

orientalist [,ɔ:ri'entəlist], *s.c.* orientalista.

to orientalize [,ɔ:ri'entəlaiz], *v.t.i.* rendere, diventare orientale.

orientalization [,ɔ:ri,entəlai'zeiʃən], *s.* il rendere orientale; il divenire come gli orientali.

orientally [,ɔri'entli], *av.* orientalmente.

to orientate ['ɔ:rienteit], *V.* **to orient**.

orientation [,ɔ:rien'teiʃən], *s.* orientamento.

orifice ['ɔrifis], *s.* orifizio; foro; bocca.

oriflamme ['ɔriflæm], *s.* orifiamma.

origan ['ɔrigən], **origanum** [ə'rigənəm], *s.*(*bot.*)origano.

origin ['ɔridʒin], *s.* 1. origine, principio: *the* — *of civilization*, l'origine della civiltà; *the* — *of a quarrel*, l'origine di una lite 2. origine, nascita, lignaggio: *a man of humble* —, un uomo di umili natali.

original [ə'ridʒənl], *ag.* 1. originale; originario; primitivo: *the* — *inhabitants of a country*, i primi abitanti di un paese; *the* — *plan*, il progetto originale; *the* — *sin*, il peccato originale 2. autentico, genuino: *that's an* — *picture*, quello è un quadro autentico 3. nuovo: — *ideas*, idee nuove; *an* — *writer*, scrittore originale 4. strano, stravagante: *he made an* — *remark*, fece una strana osservazione ‖ *s.* 1. originale: *this is not the* —, *it's only a copy*, questo non è l'originale, è solo una copia 2. lingua originale: *he reads Homer in the* —, egli legge Omero nell'originale 3. originale, persona eccentrica: *he is an* —, è un originale 4. (*arc.*) origine, principio.

originality [ə,ridʒi'næliti], *s.* originalità.

originally [ə'ridʒnəli], *av.* 1. originariamente, in origine 2. originalmente.

to originate [ə'ridʒineit], *v.t.i.* dare origine a; iniziare; produrre; aver origine, derivare, provenire: *the quarrel originated in a misunderstanding*, la lite derivò da un malinteso; *to* — *from a common ancestor*, discendere da un comune antenato; *to* — *a new style*, creare, iniziare un nuovo stile.

origination [ə,ridʒi'neiʃən], *s.* origine, fonte; creazione, invenzione; abbozzo (di progetto); derivazione.

originative [ə'ridʒineitiv], *ag.* creativo; inventivo.

originator [ə'ridʒineitə*], *s.c.* creatore, creatrice; autore, autrice; iniziatore, iniziatrice.

orinasal [,ɔ:ri'neizəl], *ag.* pronunciato tra bocca e naso; nasale ‖ *s.* vocale nasale.

Orinoco [,ɔri'noukou], *no.pr.* (*geog.*) Orinoco.

oriole ['ɔ:rioul], *s.* (*ornit.*) rigogolo.

Orion [ə'raiən], *no.pr.m.* (*mit.*) Orione ‖ *s.* (*astr.*) Orione.

orison ['ɔrizən], *s.gener. pl.* (*poet.*) orazione, preghiera.

Orkney Islands (the) ['ɔ:kni'ailəndz], *no.pr.* (*geog.*) le Isole Orcadi.

Orlando [ɔ:'lændou], *no.pr.m.* Orlando.

Orleans [ɔːˈliənz], *no.pr.* (*geog.*) Orléans ‖ *s.* **1.** orléans (tessuto di lana e cotone) **2.** qualità di prugna.
orlon [ˈɔːlɔn], *s.* orlon (fibra tessile).
orlop [ˈɔːlɔp], *s.* (*mar.*) corridoio.
ormolu [ˈɔːməluː], *s.* bronzo dorato per decorazioni di mobili; similoro.
ornament [ˈɔːnəmənt], *s.* **1.** ornamento, decorazione; guarnizione (di abito): *by way of —,* per ornamento; *a gown rich in ornaments,* un abito ricco di guarnizioni **2.** *fig.* ornamento, lustro: *a man who is an — to his profession,* un uomo che onora la sua professione **3.** ninnolo: *the mantelpiece was crowded with ornaments,* la mensola del camino era carica di ninnoli **4.** *gener. pl.* (*eccl.*) paramenti **5.** *pl.* (*mus.*) abbellimenti.
to **ornament** [ˈɔːnəment], *v.t.* adornare, ornare, decorare.
ornamental [ˌɔːnəˈmentl], *ag.* ornamentale, decorativo.
ornamentalist [ˌɔːnəˈmentəlist], *s.* decoratore.
ornamentally [ˌɔːnəˈmentəli], *av.* in modo ornamentale, decorativo; per ornamento.
ornamentation [ˌɔːnəmenˈteiʃən], *s.* **1.** ornamentazione, decorazione **2.** ornamenti; abbellimenti, decorazioni.
ornamentist [ˈɔːnəmentist], *s.* decoratore.
ornate [ɔːˈneit], *ag.* eccessivamente, riccamente adorno, decorato; elaborato: *an — style,* uno stile elaborato, ricco.
ornately [ɔːˈneitli], *av.* con sovrabbondanza di ornamenti; in stile troppo elaborato.
ornateness [ɔːˈneitnis], *s.* decorazione esagerata; eccessiva elaboratezza (di stile).
ornithological [ˌɔːniθəˈlɔdʒikəl], *ag.* ornitologico.
ornithologist [ˌɔːniˈθɔlədʒist], *s.* ornitologo.
ornithology [ˌɔːniˈθɔlədʒi], *s.* ornitologia.
ornithomancy [ˈɔːniθou,mænsi], *s.* ornitomanzia.
ornithorhynchus [ˌɔːniθouˈriŋkəs], *s.* (*zool.*) ornitorinco.
orographic(al) [ˌɔrouˈgræfik(əl)], *ag.* orografico.
orography [ɔˈrɔgrəfi], *s.* orografia.
oroide [ˈɔːrouid], *s.* lega di rame e zinco avente l'aspetto dell'oro.
orology [ɔˈrɔlədʒi], *s.* orografia.
orotund [ˈɔroutʌnd], *ag.* pomposo; magniloquente, altisonante, pretenzioso.
orphan [ˈɔːfən], *ag.* orfano ‖ *s.c.* orfano, orfana: *to be left an —,* restare orfano ☆ *— -boy,* orfanello; *— -girl,* orfanella; *— home* (o *— -asylum*), orfanotrofio *| war —,* orfano di guerra.
to **orphan**, *v.t.* rendere orfano: *he was orphaned,* rimase orfano.
orphanage [ˈɔːfənidʒ], *s.* **1.** la condizione di orfano **2.** orfanotrofio.
orphanhood [ˈɔːfənhud], **orphanism** [ˈɔːfənizəm], *s.* l'essere orfano.
Orphean [ɔːˈfi(ː)ən], *ag.* orfico, di Orfeo; *fig.* melodioso, affascinante.
Orpheus [ˈɔːfjuːs], *no.pr.m.* (*mit.*) Orfeo.
Orphic [ˈɔːfik], *ag.* **1.** orfico, di Orfeo **2.** *fig.* mistico, occulto (di oracoli); melodioso, affascinante (di musica).
Orphism [ˈɔːfizəm], *s.* orfismo, religione orfica.
orphray, orphrey [ˈɔːfrei], *s.* (*eccl.*) fregio dorato, ricamo di piviale, pianeta.
orpiment [ˈɔːpimənt], *s.* (*chim.*) orpimento; trisolfuro d'arsenico.
orrery [ˈɔrəri], *s.* planetario.
orris[1] [ˈɔris], *s.* (*bot.*) iris, giaggiuolo.
orris[2], *s.* pizzo, ricamo in oro, argento; passamaneria.
ort [ɔːt], *s. gener. pl.* briciole, avanzi ‖ *to make orts of sthg.,* (*fam.*) attribuire poca importanza a ql.co.
orthicon [ˈɔːθikən], *s.* (*tv.*) orticonoscopio.
orthochromatic [ˈɔːθoukrouˈmætik], *ag.* (*foto.*) ortocromatico.

orthochromatism [ˈɔːθouˈkroumətizəm], *s.* (*foto.*) ortocromatismo.
orthodox [ˈɔːθədɔks], *ag.* **1.** ortodosso (dogma, ecc.)‖ *the Orthodox Church,* la Chiesa Ortodossa **2.** ben pensante (di persona); ortodosso, classico (di metodo, opinione, ecc.).
orthodoxly [ˈɔːθədɔksli], *av.* in modo ortodosso.
orthodoxness [ˈɔːθədɔksnis], *s.* ortodossia.
orthodoxy [ˈɔːθədɔksi], *s.* ortodossia; *fig.* conformismo (di dottrina, ecc.).
orthoepic(al) [ˌɔːθouˈepik(əl)], *ag.* ortoepico.
orthoepically [ˌɔːθouˈepikəli], *av.* in modo ortoepico, con corretta pronuncia.
orthoepy [ˈɔːθouepi], *s.* ortoepia.
orthogenesis [ˌɔːθouˈdʒenisis], *s.* (*biol.*) ortogenesi.
orthogonal [ɔːˈθɔgənl], *ag.* (*geom.*) ortogonale.
orthogonally [ɔːˈθɔgənəli], *av.* (*geom.*) ortogonalmente.
orthographical [ˌɔːθəˈgræfikəl], *ag.* **1.** (*gram.*) ortografico **2.** (*geom.*) ortogonale.
orthographically [ˌɔːθəˈgræfikəli], *av.* **1.** (*gram.*) ortograficamente **2.** (*geom.*) ortogonalmente.
orthography [ɔːˈθɔgrəfi], *s.* **1.** (*gram.*) ortografia **2.** (*geom.*) proiezione ortogonale.
orthopaedic(al) [ˌɔːθouˈpiːdik(əl)], *ag.* ortopedico.
orthopaedics [ˌɔːθouˈpiːdiks], *s.* ortopedia.
orthopaedist [ˌɔːθouˈpiːdist], *s.* ortopedico.
orthopaedy [ˈɔːθoupiːdi], *s.* ortopedia.
Orthoptera [ɔːˈθɔptərə], *s.pl.* (*entom.*) ortotteri.
orthoptics [ɔːˈθɔptiks], *s.* (*med.*) ortottica.
ortolan [ˈɔːtələn], *s.* (*ornit.*) ortolano.
oryx [ˈɔriks], *s.* (*zool.*) orice.
Oscar [ˈɔskə*], *no.pr.m.* Oscar ‖ *s.* Oscar (premio cinematografico assegnato negli Stati Uniti).
to **oscillate** [ˈɔsileit], *v.t.i.* (far) oscillare (anche *fig.*): *to — between two opinions,* oscillare fra due opinioni.
oscillation [ˌɔsiˈleiʃən], *s.* oscillazione; *fig.* esitazione.
oscillator [ˈɔsileitə*], *s.* (*elett. mec.*) oscillatore.
oscillatory [ˈɔsilətəri], *ag.* oscillatorio.
oscillogram [ɔˈsiləgræm], *s.* registrazione fatta con l'oscillografo.
oscillograph [ɔˈsiləgrɑːf], *s.* (*elett.*) oscillografo.
oscitancy [ˈɔsitənsi], *s.* (*rar.*) **1.** indolenza, trascuratezza **2.** lo sbadigliare; sonnolenza, torpore.
oscitation [ˌɔsiˈteiʃən], *s.* (*rar.*) **1.** lo sbadigliare; sonnolenza **2.** trascuratezza, negligenza.
osculant [ˈɔskjulənt], *ag.* **1.** (*zool.*) di carattere affine, comune **2.** in stretto contatto; che bacia.
oscular [ˈɔskjulə*], *ag.* **1.** (*scherz.*) relativo alla bocca, al baciare **2.** (*geom.*) osculatore, combaciante.
to **osculate** [ˈɔskjuleit], *v.t.i.* **1.** (*scherz.*) baciare **2.** (*geom.*) combaciare.
osculation [ˌɔskjuˈleiʃən], *s.* **1.** (*scherz.*) bacio **2.** (*geom.*) osculazione, tangenza.
osculatory [ˈɔskjulətəri], *ag.* **1.** che bacia, che abbraccia **2.** (*geom.*) osculatore, combaciante ☆ *— point,* (*geom.*) punto di osculazione.
osier [ˈouʒə*], *s.* (*bot.*) vimine ☆ *— -bed,* terreno per la coltivazione del vimine.
osiery [ˈouʒəri], *s.* lavoro in vimini.
Osiris [ouˈsaiəris], *no.pr.m.* (*mit.*) Osiride.
osmium [ˈɔzmiəm], *s.* (*chim.*) osmio.
osmose [ˈɔzmous], **osmosis** [ɔzˈmousis], *s.* (*fis.*) osmosi.
osmotic [ɔzˈmɔtik], *ag.* (*fis.*) osmotico.
osmund[1] [ˈɔzmənd], *s.* (*bot.*) osmunda.
osmund[2], *s.* (*arc.*) qualità pregiata di ferro.
osprey [ˈɔspri], *s.* **1.** (*ornit.*) ossifraga, procellaria **2.** egretta (piuma per cappello da signora).
osseous [ˈɔsiəs], *ag.* (*anat.*) osseo.
Ossian [ˈɔsiən], *no.pr.m.* (*lett.*) Ossian.
Ossianic [ˌɔsiˈænik], *ag.* (*lett.*) ossianico, di Ossian.
ossicle [ˈɔsikl], *s.* (*anat.*) ossicino.
ossification [ˌɔsifiˈkeiʃən], *s.* ossificazione.
ossifrage [ˈɔsifridʒ], *s.* (*ornit.*) ossifraga, procellaria.

to **ossify** ['ɔsifai], *v.t.i.* ossificare, ossificarsi; indurire, indurirsi.

ossuary ['ɔsjuəri], *s.* ossario; urna funebre.

Ostend [ɔs'tend], *no.pr.* (*geog.*) Ostenda.

ostensibility [ɔs,tensi'biliti], *s.* ostensibilità; apparenza.

ostensible [ɔs'tensəbl], *ag.* apparente; simulato, finto: *he came in with the — aim of,* egli entrò con il pretesto di.

ostensibly [ɔs'tensəbli], *av.* apparentemente, con il pretesto di.

ostension [ɔs'tenʃən], *s.* (*eccl.*) ostensione.

ostensive [ɔs'tensiv], *ag.* visibile, manifesto.

ostensively [ɔs'tensivli], *av.* in modo manifesto, dimostrabile.

ostensory [ɔs'tensəri], *s.* (*eccl.*) ostensorio.

ostentation [,ɔsten'teiʃən], *s.* ostentazione; pompa.

ostentatious [,ɔsten'teiʃəs], *ag.* ostentato; pomposo.

ostentatiously [,ɔsten'teiʃəsli], *av.* ostentatamente.

ostentatiousness [,ɔsten'teiʃəsnis], *s.* ostentazione.

osteogenesis [,ɔstiə'dʒenisis], *s.* (*fisiol.*) osteogenesi.

osteography [,ɔsti'ɔgrəfi], *s.* (*med.*) trattato di osteologia.

osteoid ['ɔstiɔid], *ag.* osteoide, simile ad osso.

osteological [,ɔstiə'lɔdʒikəl], *ag.* (*med.*) osteologico.

osteology [,ɔsti'ɔlədʒi], *s.* (*med.*) osteologia.

osteopathy [,ɔsti'ɔpəθi], *s.* osteopatia.

osteotomy [,ɔsti'ɔtəmi], *s.* (*chir.*) osteotomia.

ostiary ['ɔstiəri], *s.* (*eccl.*) ostiario.

ostler ['ɔslə*], *s.* mozzo di stalla.

ostracism ['ɔstrəsizəm], *s.* ostracismo.

to **ostracize** ['ɔstrəsaiz], *v.t.* dare l'ostracismo a; bandire, mettere al bando.

ostreiculture ['ɔstrii,kʌltʃə*], *s.* ostricoltura.

ostrich ['ɔstritʃ], *s.* struzzo ‖ *to have the digestion of an —,* (*fam.*) avere uno stomaco da struzzo ‖ *to pursue an — policy,* (*fam.*) fare lo struzzo, rifiutarsi di riconoscere i fatti, un pericolo imminente ☆ *— farm,* allevamento di struzzi; *— -feather,* piuma di struzzo; *— -plume,* pennacchio di piume, piuma di struzzo.

Ostrogoth ['ɔstrəgɔθ], *s.* (*st.*) ostrogoto.

Ostrogothic [,ɔstrə'gɔθik], *ag.* (*st.*) ostrogoto; ostrogotico.

Oswald ['ɔzwəld], *no.pr.m.* Osvaldo.

otalgia [ou'tældʒiə], *s.* (*patol.*) otalgia.

otalgic [ou'tældʒik], *ag.* (*patol.*) otalgico; di otalgia.

otalgy [ou'tældʒi], *s.* (*patol.*) otalgia.

otary ['outəri], *s.* (*zool.*) otaria.

Othello [ou'θelou], *no.pr.m.* (*lett.*) Otello.

other ['ʌðə*], *ag.* altro; diverso: *every — day,* un giorno sì e uno no; *on the — hand,* d'altra parte; *people have seen it,* altri l'hanno visto; *they came the — day,* vennero l'altro giorno; *they don't wish him — than he is,* non lo vorrebbero diverso da com'è ‖ *pron.*; *pl.* **others** ['ʌðəz], altro, altri: *the others,* gli altri; *each —,* l'un l'altro (fra due); *he and no — told me so,* egli e nessun altro me lo disse; *it was no — than your cousin,* non era altri che tuo cugino; *let others talk, I act,* parlino pure gli altri, io agisco; *this hat is too big, have you any others?,* questo cappello mi è troppo grande, ne avete altri?; *why choose this day of all others?,* perchè scegliere proprio questo giorno? ‖ *av.* altrimenti.

otherness ['ʌðənis], *s.* (*rar.*) l'essere un altro; differenza, diversità.

otherwhere ['ʌðəwɛə*], *av.* (*arc.*) altrove.

otherwhile ['ʌðəwail], *av.* (*arc.*) un'altra volta.

otherwise ['ʌðəwaiz], *ag.* diverso: *his answer could not be —,* la sua risposta non poteva essere differente ‖ *av.* **1.** altrimenti, diversamente: *she could not do — than follow him,* non potè fare a meno di seguirlo ‖ *C. L. Dodgson, — Lewis Carrol,* C. L. Dodgson, alias Lewis Carrol **2.** altrimenti, in caso contrario: *obey him, — you may repent of it,* ubbidiscigli, altrimenti te ne potresti pentire **3.** sotto gli altri aspetti, per il resto.

otherworld ['ʌðəwə:ld], *s.* mondo ultraterreno.

otherworldliness [,ʌðə'wə:ldlinis], *s.* distacco da mondo terreno; spiritualità intensa.

otherworldly ['ʌðə,wə:ldli], *ag.* staccato dal mondo.

Otho ['ouθou], *no.pr.m.* (*st.*) Ottone.

otiose ['ouʃious], *ag.* **1.** (*rar.*) ozioso, indolente **2.** futile; inutile; superfluo; ozioso.

otioseness ['ouʃiousnis], *s.* **1.** oziosità **2.** inutilità.

otitis [ou'taitis], *s.* (*patol.*) otite.

otology [ou'tɔlədʒi], *s.* (*med.*) otologia.

otoscope ['outəskoup], *s.* (*med.*) otoscopio.

otter ['ɔtə*], *s.* lontra; pelle di lontra ☆ *— dog* (o *— -hound*), cane per la caccia alla lontra.

otto ['ɔtou], *s.* essenza.

Ottoman[1] ['ɔtəmən], *ag.s.* ottomano, turco.

ottoman[2], *s.* ottomana, divano alla turca.

oubliette [,u:bli'et], *s.* prigione con apertura a botola.

ouch [autʃ], *s.* (*arc.*) **1.** castone **2.** spilla; fermaglio.

ought[1] [ɔ:t], *V.* **aught**[2].

ought[2], *s.* zero.

ought[3], *v. difettivo*; (2ª *persona sing.* (*arc.*) **oughtest** ['ɔ:tist], **oughtst** [ɔ:tst]; *forma negativa* **ought not** [ɔ:t nɔt]; *forma contratta* **oughtn't** ['ɔ:tnt]) **1.** dovere, essere necessario (*al condiz. per indicare consiglio, rimprovero, dovere*): *they — to respect their parents,* dovrebbero rispettare i loro genitori; *you — to have eaten less,* avresti dovuto mangiare meno **2.** dovere (*al condiz. per indicare probabilità*): *your horse — to win,* il tuo cavallo ha buone probabilità di vincere.

ounce[1] [auns], *s.* (*abbr. oz.*) (*avoirdupois*) —, oncia (misura di peso avoirdupois = g. 28); (*troy*) —, oncia (misura di peso troy = g. 31,104); *fig.* oncia.

ounce[2], *s.* (*zool.*) irbis; (*arc. poet.*) lince.

our ['auə*], *ag.poss.* 1ª *persona pl.* **nostro, nostra, nostri, nostre:** *— family,* la nostra famiglia; *— house and garden,* la nostra casa e il nostro giardino.

ours ['auəz], *pron.poss.* 1ª *persona. pl.* **il nostro, la nostra, i nostri, le nostre:** *— is a large family,* la nostra è una famiglia numerosa; *her house is in town and — is in the country,* la sua casa è in città e la nostra in campagna; *I like — better,* il nostro mi piace di più ‖ *he is a friend of —,* è (un) nostro amico ‖ *Mr. Jones of —,* (*comm.*) il nostro Signor Jones (appartenente alla nostra ditta).

ourself [,auə'self], *pron.* 1ª *persona pl.* (*di maestà*) **1.** *r.* noi stessi, ci: *by —,* da soli **2.** (*enfatico*) **noi stessi.**

ourselves [,auə'selvz], *pron.* 1ª *persona pl.* **1.** *r.* **noi stessi, ci:** *we should only do harm to —,* faremmo soltanto del male a noi stessi ‖ (*all*) *by —,* da soli **2.** (*enfatico*) **noi stessi:** *it was good for others if not for —,* andò bene per gli altri se non per noi; *we — will see to it,* ce ne occuperemo noi; *we shall go —,* andremo noi stessi ‖ *s.* **noi stessi:** *we are not — to-day,* non siamo in forma oggi; *we have now come to —,* ci siamo finalmente resi conto.

ousel ['u:zl], *s.* (*ornit.*) merlo.

to **oust** [aust], *v.t.* espellere; soppiantare; privare: *the captain was ousted from his command,* il capitano fu privato del comando; *he ousted his brother of...,* (*dir.*) egli privò suo fratello di....

ouster ['austə*], *s.* (*dir.*) evizione; spoglio illegale.

out [aut], *av.* **1.** fuori, al di fuori, all'esterno, fuori di casa, via: *my master is —,* il padrone è fuori di casa; *the secret came —,* il segreto venne svelato; *she leant —,* si sporse in fuori; *to go —,* andare fuori, uscire ‖ *— and —,* completamente ‖ *— and away,* di gran lunga ‖ *— at elbow,* coi gomiti fuori, stracciato ‖ *— at sea,* in mare, al largo ‖ *— there,* laggiù ‖ *— with him!,* caccialo fuori! ‖ *— with it!,* dillo! ‖ *all —,* a tutta velocità ‖ *all sails —,* a vele spiegate ‖ *day —,* giorno di libera uscita ‖ *voyage —,* andata ‖ *hear me —!,* stammi bene a sentire! ‖ *speak —!,* parlate pure!; *speak — loud!,* parlate ad alta voce! **2.** (*particolari significati con* to be): *before the week is —,* prima della fine della settimana; *the book is — at last,* il libro è stato finalmente pubblicato; *the dockers are* —, gli scaricatori sono in sciopero; *the flowers are* —, i fiori sono sbocciati; *he is all* — *to achieve sthg. good*, (*sl.*) egli lotta per raggiungere qualche buon risultato; *he was* — *after a rich wife*, (*sl.*) andava alla caccia di una moglie ricca; *I'm* — *with Mary*, io e Maria siamo in disaccordo; *large hats are* —, i cappelli grandi non si usano più; *the light is* —, la luce è spenta; *the moon is* —, la luna splende; *that girl is not yet* —, quella ragazza non va ancora in società; *we were £. 30* —, avevamo speso 30 sterline più del previsto; *your ankle is* —, hai la caviglia slogata ‖ *you will be* — *and about in four weeks*, tra quattro settimane sarai guarito e in grado di uscire ‖ *prep.* (*amer.*) fuori di: — *the window*, fuori della finestra ‖ **out of**, *prep.* **1. fuori, fuori di, fuori da:** *I walked two miles* — *town*, camminai per due miglia fuori di città; *she went* — *the house*, uscì di casa; *to throw sthg.* — *the window*, gettare ql.co. dalla finestra ‖ *I like to drink tea* — *good china cups*, mi piace bere il tè in tazze di porcellana ‖ *she didn't succeed in getting money* — *her aunt*, non riuscì a farsi dare del denaro da sua zia ‖ *we were* — *provisions*, eravamo a corto di provviste ‖ — *sight*, — *mind*, *prov.* lontan dagli occhi, lontan dal cuore **2. tra, fra:** *you must choose* — *these*, devi scegliere fra questi **3. per; a causa di:** — *kindness*, per gentilezza; *I just asked* — *curiosity*, chiedevo così per curiosità **4. (Fraseologia):** — *action*, fuori combattimento; — *breath*, senza fiato; — *favour*, in disgrazia; — *mind*, dimenticato; — *one's mind*, pazzo; — *order*, guasto; — *print*, esaurito, fuori stampa; — *sight*, fuori del campo visivo; — *tune*, stonato ‖ *I feel* — *it with such people*, non mi sento a mio agio con gente simile.

out, *ag. attributivo* **1.** esterno, all'esterno: *an* — *match*, (*spor.*) una partita in trasferta; *the* — *parts of the diocese*, la zona limitrofa della diocesi **2.** insolito: — *size*, misura fuori dell'ordinario ‖ *s.* **1.** (*tip.*) pesce **2.** (*fam.*) gita **3.** (*amer.*) inconveniente **4.** (*amer.*) permesso di uscire; uscita **5.** *pl.* ambulatorio (di ospedale); (*pol.*) partito, membri del partito non al potere **6.** *at outs*, (*amer.*) in disaccordo: *to be at outs with s.o.*, essere in disaccordo con qlcu.

to out, *v.t.i.* **1.** uscire, venir fuori, essere svelato: *truth will* —, la verità verrà a galla ‖ *murder will* —, *prov.* ogni nodo viene al pettine **2.** mandar fuori; (*boxe*) metter fuori combattimento.

out, (*nei composti*): — *-building*, dipendenza (di casa, ecc.); — *-clearing*, (*comm.*) invio di assegni, effetti, ecc. alla stanza di compensazione ‖ — *-lier*, parte isolata (di ql.co.); animale isolato; persona non residente; (*geol.*) parte di giacimento staccato; — *-date*, fuori moda, antiquato; — *-of-door(s)*, all'aperto, fuori di casa; — *-of-hand*, immediatamente; fuori controllo; — *-of-the-way*, remoto, recluso; insolito; — *-of-work*, disoccupato; — *-post*, (*mil.*) avamposto; — *-runner*, lacchè, battistrada.

to outact [aut'ækt], *v.t.* superare nella recitazione (sulla scena).

to out-argue [aut'ɑːgjuː], *v.t.* vincere discutendo.

to out-ask [aut'ɑːsk], *v.t.* chiedere, proclamare per l'ultima volta (di pubblicazione di matrimonio in chiesa).

outback ['autbæk], *ag. attributivo* (*austral.*) dell'interno ‖ *s.* paesi dell'interno ‖ *av.* nell'interno.

outbade [aut'beid], *pass.* di to **outbid**.

to outbalance [aut'bæləns], *v.t.* eccedere, superare (di peso, valore).

to out-bargain [aut'bɑːgin], *v.t.* avere la meglio su (in affari, contratti, ecc.).

to outbid [aut'bid], *pass.* **outbade** [aut'beid], *p.p.* **outbidden** [aut'bidn], *v.t.* **1.** rincarare su; rilanciare (all'asta, alle carte) **2.** sorpassare.

    outbidder [aut'bidə*], *s.* maggiore offerente.

    outbidding [aut'bidiŋ], *s.* rilancio (ad un'asta).

    outboard ['autbɔːd], *ag.av.* fuoribordo ☆ — *motor*, fuoribordo.

outbound ['autbaund], *ag.* (*mar.*) uscente; diretto ad un porto lontano.

    outbounds ['autbaundz], *s.pl.* (*poet.*) estremi confini.

to outbrag [aut'bræg], *pass.p.p.* **outbragged** [aut'brægd], *v.t.* sorpassare in vanterie, spacconate.

to outbrave [aut'breiv], *v.t.* **1.** sfidare **2.** sorpassare (in ardire, ecc.).

outbreak ['autbreik], *s.* **1.** esplosione, scoppio, eruzione; *fig.* scoppio, impeto **2.** sommossa, insurrezione **3.** (*geol.*) affioramento superficiale.

to outbreak [aut'breik], *pass.* **outbroke** [aut'brouk], *p.p.* **outbroken** [aut'broukən], *v.i.* esplodere, scoppiare.

to outbreathe [aut'briːð], *v.t.i.* (*poet.*) esalare; spirare.

to outbreed [aut'briːd], *pass.p.p.* **outbred** [aut'bred], *v.t.i.* accoppiare, accoppiarsi con soggetti non consanguinei.

outbroke [aut'brouk], *pass.* **outbroken** [aut'broukən], *p.p.* di to **outbreak**.

to outburn [aut'bəːn], *pass.p.p.* **outburnt** [aut'bəːnt], *v.t.i.* bruciare più a lungo di; bruciare completamente.

outburst ['autbəːst], *s.* **1.** eruzione, esplosione **2.** *fig.* scoppio, accesso; slancio **3.** (*geol.*) affioramento.

outby ['autbai], *av.* (*scoz.*) all'aria aperta; all'esterno.

outcast ['autkɑːst], *ag.* (*rar.*) espulso, bandito, proscritto, esiliato ‖ *s.* proscritto, esiliato.

outcaste ['autkɑːst], *ag.* che non appartiene ad alcuna casta (in India) ‖ *s.* paria (in India).

to outcaste, *v.t.* espellere da una casta (in India).

to outclass [aut'klɑːs], *v.t.* superare di gran lunga.

outcome ['autkʌm], *s.* risultato; conseguenza.

outcrop ['autkrɔp], *s.* (*geol.*) affioramento.

to outcrop, *pass.p.p.* **outcropped** ['autkrɔpt], *v.i.* (*geol.*) affiorare.

outcry ['autkrai], *s.* grido; chiasso; scalpore: *a serious* — *was raised against him*, si levò un grave scalpore contro di lui.

to outcry [aut'krai], *v.t.* urlare, gridar più forte di.

to outdare [aut'dɛə*], *v.t.* **1.** sorpassare in ardimento **2.** sfidare.

to outdistance [aut'distəns], *v.t.* distanziare; sorpassare.

to outdo [aut'duː], *pass.* **outdid** [aut'did], *p. p.* **outdone** [aut'dʌn], *v.t.* sorpassare, superare: *he outdid himself*, egli superò se stesso.

outdoor ['autdɔː*], *ag.* esterno; all'aperto ☆ — *games*, giuochi, sports all'aria aperta; — *scenes*, (*cine.*) esterni.

outdoors [aut'dɔːz], *av.* all'aperto; fuori di casa.

outedge ['autedʒ], *s.* limite estremo.

outer[1] ['autə*], *ag.* esteriore; esterno: *the* — *garments*, gli abiti; *the* — *man*, l'aspetto esteriore dell'uomo ‖ *s.* parte del bersaglio lontana dal centro; palla fuori centro.

outer[2], *s.* (*boxe*) colpo che mette l'avversario k.o.

outerly ['autəli], *av.* esternamente.

outermost ['autəmoust], *ag.* (*superl.* di **outer**) esterno; il più in fuori; estremo; il più remoto; il più lontano.

to outface [aut'feis], *v.t.* tener testa a; sfidare; far abbassare gli occhi a.

outfall ['autfɔːl], *s.* **1.** foce; capo (di valle) **2.** bocca di scarico.

outfield ['autfiːld], *s.* **1.** terreno lontano dalla fattoria **2.** (*cricket baseball*) parte del campo più lontana dai battitori.

to outfight [aut'fait], *pass.p.p.* **outfought** [aut'fɔːt], *v.t.* superare in battaglia, nella lotta, per tattica: *they were outfought*, essi si dimostrarono inferiori.

outfit ['autfit], *s.* **1.** corredo, equipaggiamento; l'occorrente (per ql.co.): *carpenter's* —, gli arnesi del falegname **2.** (*mil. amer.*) compagnia, gruppo ☆ — *allowance*, (*mil.*) indennità di equipaggiamento ‖ *first aid* —, cassetta di pronto soccorso.

to outfit, *pass.p.p.* **outfitted** ['aut,fitid], *v.t.i.* rifornire, rifornirsi di equipaggiamento.

outfitter ['aut,fitə*], *s.c.* fornitore, fornitrice; chi vende, confeziona (articoli di abbigliamento).

outfitting ['aut͟ˌfitiŋ], *s.* **1.** equipaggiamento, armamento (di nave) ☆ — *department*, (*comm.*) reparto confezioni.

to **outflank** [aut'flæŋk], *v.t.* **1.** (*mil.*) aggirare (il nemico) **2.** *fig.* raggirare, circuire.

to **outflash** [aut'flæʃ], *v.t.* vincere in splendore.

outflow ['autflou] *s.* uscita, efflusso; colata.

to **outflow** [aut'flou], *v.i.* defluire.

outflush ['autflʌʃ], *s.* improvviso rossore, vampata.

to **outflush** [aut'flʌʃ], *v.t.* arrossire più violentemente di.

to **outfly** [aut'flai], *pass.* **outflew** [aut'flu:], *p.p.* **outflown** [aut'floun], *v.t.* sorpassare nel volo.

outfought [aut'fo:t], *pass.p.p.* di to **outfight**.

to **outfrown** [aut'fraun], *v.t.* (*poet.*) reprimere con cipiglio severo.

to **outgeneral** [aut'dʒenərəl], *pass.p.p.* **outgeneralled** [aut'dʒenərəld], *v.t.* superare in capacità, in tattica.

to **outgive** [aut'giv], *pass.* **outgave** [aut'geiv], *p.p.* **outgiven** [aut'givn], *v.t.* superare in liberalità.

outgiving ['aut͟ˌgiviŋ], *s.* (*amer.*) dichiarazione politica.

outgo ['autgou], *pl.* **outgoes** ['autgouz], *s.* uscita; spesa.

to **outgo** [aut'gou], *pass.* **outwent** [aut'went], *p.p.* **outgone** [aut'gon], *v.t.i.* sorpassare; oltrepassare; eccellere.

outgoer ['aut͟ˌgouə*], *s.c.* chi lascia (una carica, ecc.).

outgoing ['aut͟ˌgouiŋ], *ag.* **1.** che sorpassa, eccelle **2.** uscente, dimissionario; in partenza; d'uscita: — *letters*, lettere in partenza ‖ *s.* **1.** uscita **2.** *pl.* spese: *the outgoings exceed the incomings*, le uscite superano le entrate.

outgone [aut'gon], *p.p.* di to **outgo**.

to **outgrow** [aut'grou], *pass.* **outgrew** [aut'gru:], *p.p.* **outgrown** [aut'groun], *v.t.* **1.** diventare troppo grande per: *I have outgrown my dress*, il vestito non mi va più bene, è stretto **2.** sorpassare (in statura): *he outgrew his elder brother*, sorpassò in altezza suo fratello maggiore **3.** perdere, disfarsi di: *he outgrew his bad habits*, egli perse le sue cattive abitudini.

outgrowth ['autgrou͟θ], *s.* **1.** escrescenza; apofisi **2.** risultato, conseguenza.

to **out-Herod** [aut'herəd], *v.t.* superare in crudeltà: *to — Herod*, essere più crudele di Erode.

outhouse ['authaus], *s.* rimessa, tettoia; dipendenza; fabbricato annesso.

▶ **outing** ['autiŋ], *s.* passeggiata; gita (di piacere); scampagnata ☆ — *-suits*, abiti sportivi.

outland ['autlənd], (*arc. poet.*) *ag.* straniero ‖ *s.* paese straniero.

outlander ['aut͟ˌlændə*], *ag.s.* (*poet.*) straniero.

outlandish [aut'lændiʃ], *ag.* **1.** (*arc.*) straniero **2.** strano, bizzarro **3.** remoto, lontano: *to live in an — place*, abitare in capo al mondo.

to **outlast** [aut'la:st], *v.t.* sopravvivere a; durare più a lungo di.

outlaw ['aut-lo:], *s.* fuorilegge, criminale, bandito.

to **outlaw**, *v.t.* proscrivere, bandire.

outlawing ['aut-lo:iŋ], **outlawry** ['aut-lo:ri], *s.* condizione di proscritto; proscrizione.

outlay ['aut-lei], *s.* spesa; aggravio ☆ *capital —*, spese di impianto.

to **outlearn** [aut'lə:n], *pass.p.p.* **outlearnt** [aut-'lə:nt], *v.t.* superare in sapere.

outlet ['aut-let], *s.* **1.** sbocco, sfogo, via d'uscita (anche *fig.*): *his energy wants an —*, la sua energia ha bisogno di uno sfogo **2.** cortile, spazio cintato **3.** (*rad. tv.*) attacco ☆ — *angle*, (*mec.*) angolo d'uscita; — *box*, (*elett.*) scatola di connessione; — *end*, lato di uscita; — *plug*, tappo di scarico.

outline ['aut-lain], *s.* **1.** contorno, profilo **2.** abbozzo, schema, schizzo **3.** *fig. gener. pl.* elementi: "*An Outline of English Literature*", «Lineamenti di Letteratura Inglese».

to **outline**, *v.t.* **1.** tracciare i contorni di: *the house was outlined against the sky*, la casa si stagliava sul cielo **2.** abbozzare schizzare **3.** *fig.* delineare.

to **outlive** [aut'liv], *v.t.* sopravvivere a; vivere, durare più a lungo di: *he has outlived his day*, egli è sopravvissuto ai suoi bei giorni.

outlook ['aut-luk], *s.* **1.** vista: *from my window I have a pleasant — over the river*, dalla mia finestra godo una bella vista sul fiume **2.** prospettiva: *this — is none too promising*, questa prospettiva non è delle più rassicuranti **3.** *fig.* veduta, modo di vedere: *a narrow —*, vedute limitate **4.** osservatorio; punto di osservazione: *the sea viewed from a distant —*, il mare visto da un punto lontano.

to **outlook** [aut'luk], *v.t.* **1.** fissare fino a fare abbassare gli occhi **2.** affrontare con coraggio.

outlying ['aut͟ˌlaiiŋ], *ag.* esterno, isolato; periferico; fuori mano: *an — district*, una zona periferica.

to **outmanoeuvre** [ˌautmə'nu:və*], *v.t.* aver la meglio su (nemico) per superiorità strategica.

to **outmarch** ['aut'ma:tʃ], *v.t.* marciare più in fretta di; superare nella marcia.

outmoded [aut'moudid], *ag.* antiquato, fuori moda.

outmost ['autmoust], *V.* **outermost**.

to **outname** [aut'neim], *v.t.* superare in fama, importanza.

outness ['autnis], *s.* esteriorità.

to **outnumber** [aut'nʌmbə*], *v.t.* superare in numero.

to **outpace** [aut'peis], *v.t.* sorpassare; camminare più in fretta di.

outparish ['aut͟ˌpæriʃ], *s.* parrocchia fuori le mura, fuori mano.

outpart ['autpa:t], *s.* parte esterna.

outpatient ['aut͟ˌpeiʃənt], *s.* malato esterno (che non è ricoverato nell'ospedale che lo ha in cura).

to **outplay** [aut'plei], *v.t.* superare in un giuoco; battere ‖ *to be outplayed*, *fig.* trovare un osso duro, un avversario temibile.

outport ['autpo:t], *s.* (*dir. comm.*) porto franco.

outpost ['autpoust], *s.* (*mil.*) avamposto.

outpour ['autpo:*], *s.* **1.** scroscio di pioggia **2.** *fig.* sfogo.

to **outpour** [aut'po:*], *v.t.i.* **1.** versare a torrenti; scrosciare **2.** *fig.* sfogare.

outpouring ['aut͟ˌpo:riŋ], *s.* sfogo, effusione.

output ['autput], *s.* **1.** produzione; rendimento; (*mec.*) potenza sviluppata **2.** (*fisiol.*) prodotti residuati del metabolismo ☆ — *stage*, (*rad.*) stadio di uscita, finale; *sound —*, (*cine.*) emissione del suono.

outrage ['aut-reidʒ], *s.* oltraggio, offesa: *an — upon decency*, un oltraggio al pudore.

to **outrage**, *v.t.* oltraggiare, insultare; maltrattare; violare (legge, ecc.).

outrageous [aut'reidʒəs], *ag.* **1.** eccessivo; furioso, violento **2.** oltraggioso; atroce; immorale, indegno.

outrageously [aut'reidʒəsli], *av.* **1.** in modo eccessivo, eccessivamente **2.** oltraggiosamente.

outrageousness [aut'reidʒəsnis], *s.* **1.** enormità: *I was appalled at the — of the price*, fui inorridito dall'enormità del prezzo **2.** oltraggio; comportamento oltraggioso; indegnità.

outrance ['autrəns], *s.* oltranza.

to **outrange** [aut'reindʒ], *v.t.* **1.** avere una portata maggiore di (di cannone, missile) **2.** superare, sorpassare.

to **outreach** [aut'ri:tʃ], *v.t.* estendersi oltre, sorpassare; eccedere.

to **outreign** [aut'rein], *v.t.* regnare più a lungo di.

to **outride** [aut'raid], *pass.* **outrode** [aut'roud], *p.p.* **outridden** [aut'ridn], *v.t.* **1.** superare (a cavallo); cavalcare più velocemente di **2.** (*mar.*) riuscire a superare (una tempesta).

outrider ['aut͟ˌraidə*], *s.* battistrada, lacchè.

outrigger ['aut͟ˌrigə*], *s.* **1.** (*mec.*) sporgenza esterna **2.** (*mar.*) buttafuori; scalmiera **3.** (*aer.*) intelaiatura di sostegno.

outright ['aut-rait], *ag. attributivo* **1.** diretto, franco **2.** completo, intero: — *sale*, vendita in blocco.

outright [aut'rait], *av.* **1.** apertamente, francamente:

he laughed at us —, ci scoppiò a ridere in faccia **2.** completamente; tutto in una volta: *to buy* —, comprare in blocco **3.** al primo colpo; sul colpo.

outrightness [aut'raitnis], *s.* immediatezza; franchezza.

to **outrival** [aut'raivəl], *pass.p.p.* **outrivalled** [aut-'raivəld], *v.t.* vincere, superare, aver la meglio su.

outroar ['autro:*], *s.* baccano, fracasso.

outrode [aut'roud], *pass.* di to **outride**.

to **outroot** [aut'ru:t], *v.t.* sradicare.

to **outrun** [aut'rʌn], *pass.* **outran** [aut'ræn], *p.p.* **outrun**, *v.t.* **1.** correre più presto di; vincere alla corsa; oltrepassare **2.** *fig.* superare: *his fancy outruns the facts*, la sua fantasia supera i fatti.

outrunner ['aut,rʌnə*], *s.* battistrada.

outrush ['aut-rʌʃ], *s.* fuga (di gas, acqua, ecc.).

to **outsail** [aut'seil], *v.t.* **1.** (*mar.*) oltrepassare **2.** *fig.* distanziare.

outsat [aut'sæt], *pass.p.p.* di to **outsit**.

to **outsell** [aut'sell], *pass.p.p.* **outsold** [aut'sould], *v.t.* **1.** vendere a prezzo superiore **2.** vendere in quantità superiore.

outset ['aut-set], *s.* principio, inizio; avviamento, esordio: *at the* —, al principio; *from the* —, dal principio.

to **outshine** [aut'ʃain], *pass.p.p.* **outshone** [aut'ʃon], *v.t.* sorpassare in splendore, eclissare (anche *fig.*).

to **outshoot** [aut'ʃu:t], *pass.p.p.* **outshot** [aut'ʃot], *v.t.i.* **1.** superare nel lancio **2.** sporgere.

outside [aut'said], *ag. attributivo* **1.** esterno; esteriore; *fig.* superficiale: — *worker*, operaio a domicilio; *to sell to* — *parties*, vendere a terzi; *to talk of* — *subjects*, parlare di argomenti che esulano dal previsto **2.** estremo, massimo: — *price*, prezzo massimo || *s.* **1.** l'esterno, la parte esterna: *the* — *of my house is green*, l'esterno della mia casa è verde **2.** apparenza, aspetto esteriore: *don't judge from the* —, non giudicare dall'aspetto esteriore **3.** il (limite) massimo: *at the very* — *there were only forty people*, c'erano quaranta persone al massimo **4.** imperiale, cassetta; passeggiere che viaggia a cassetta **5.** *pl.* (*tip.*) fogli esterni (di una risma).

outside, *av.* **1.** fuori; all'aperto; a cassetta, sull'imperiale: *let us sit* —, sediamoci fuori; *to ride* —, viaggiare a cassetta **2.** all'esterno; superficialmente: *to paint a boat* —, verniciare l'esterno di una barca || *to get* — *of a good dinner*, (*sl.*) far fuori un buon pranzo || *prep.* **1.** fuori di, all'esterno di: *don't let him stand* — *the door*, non lasciarlo fuori dalla porta **2.** al di fuori di: *that's* — *the main question*, ciò esula dal problema centrale **3.** (*fam.*) eccetto, all'infuori di: *no one knows* — *the members of my own family*, nessuno lo sa all'infuori dei miei familiari.

outsider ['aut'saidə*], *s.* **1.** persona non competente, profana **2.** estraneo: *she is an* — *for us*, è estranea al nostro mondo, al nostro modo di pensare **3.** (*ippica*) cavallo non favorito **4.** (*calcio*) ala.

outsight ['autsait], *s.* spirito di osservazione.

to **outsit** [aut'sit], *pass.p.p.* **outsat** [aut'sæt], *v.t.* rimanere, trattenersi in visita più a lungo di.

outsize ['aut-saiz], *ag.* fuori taglia (di abiti); fuori misura (di scarpe, ecc.) || *s.* taglia fuori misura (di abiti); misura fuori dell'ordinario (di scarpe, ecc.) ☆ — *department*, reparto vendita di abiti di taglia grande.

outskirts ['aut-skə:ts], *s. pl.* sobborghi; periferia; dintorni.

to **outsleep** [aut'sli:p], *pass.p.p.* **outslept** [aut'slept], *v.t.* dormire più a lungo di; dormire per, oltre (un determinato tempo).

outsold [aut'sould], *pass.p.p.* di to **outsell**.

to **outspan** [aut'spæn], *pass.p.p.* **outspanned** [aut-'spænd], **1.** *v.t.i.* (*sudafricano*) staccare (cavalli, buoi) **2.** accamparsi.

to **outspeak** [aut'spi:k], *pass.* **outspoke** [aut'spouk], *p.p.* **outspoken** [aut'spoukən], *v.t.i.* **1.** superare nella conversazione **2.** parlare schiettamente; dichiarare.

outspent ['autspent], *ag.* esausto.

outspoke [aut'spouk], *pass.* di to **outspeak**.

outspoken [aut'spoukən], *p.p.* di to **outspeak** || *ag.* franco, schietto; esplicito: *to be* —, parlar franco: *he is an* — *man*, è un uomo che ama parlare a cuore aperto.

outspokenly [aut'spoukənli], *av.* francamente.

outspokenness [aut'spoukənnis], *s.* franchezza, schiettezza.

outspread ['aut'spred], *ag.* disteso, spiegato: *with* — *sails*, a vele spiegate; *with* — *wings*, ad ali distese || *s.* distesa; mostra; spiegamento.

to **outspread** [aut'spred], *pass.p.p.* **outspread**, *v.t.i.* estendere, estendersi; spiegare, spiegarsi.

to **outstand** [aut'stænd], *pass.p.p.* **outstood** [aut-'stud], *v.t.i.* **1.** sporgere **2.** (*mar.*) salpare **3.** rimanere indietro (nel tempo) **4.** (*dial.*) resistere a, sostenere.

outstanding [aut'stændiŋ], *ag.* **1.** sporgente; prominente; *fig.* saliente; rilevante; fuori del comune; eminente: *an* — *personality*, una personalità di rilievo **2.** in sospeso, arretrato, non pagato **3.** che oppone resistenza.

outstation ['aut,steiʃən], *s.* stazione decentrata, nei sobborghi, in aperta campagna.

to **outstay** [aut'stei], *v.t.* trattenersi più a lungo di: *to* — *one's welcome*, prolungare troppo una visita.

to **outstep** [aut'step], *pass.p.p.* **outstepped** [aut-'stept], *v.t.* sorpassare, superare il limite di.

outstood [aut'stud], *pass.p.p.* di to **outstand**.

outstretched ['aut-stretʃt], *ag.* disteso; spiegato: *with* — *arms*, a braccia aperte.

to **outstrip** [aut'strip], *pass.p.p.* **outstripped** [aut-'stript], *v.t.* **1.** superare in corsa, in velocità **2.** *fig.* eccellere, superare.

to **outvalue** [aut'vælju:], *v.t.* superare in valore.

to **outvie** [aut'vai], *v.t.* superare, sorpassare, vincere.

to **outvoice** [aut'vois], *v.t.* gridare più forte di.

to **outvote** [aut'vout], *v.t.* avere più voti di.

outvoter ['aut,voutə*], *s.* elettore che può votare in una circoscrizione pur non avendovi la residenza.

to **outwalk** [aut'wo:k], *v.t.* camminare più lesto di; andare più lontano di.

outward ['autwəd], *ag.* **1.** esterno: *for* — *application*, (*farm.*) uso esterno **2.** apparente; esteriore: — *man*, (*teol.*) il corpo; (*scherz.*) le vesti **3.** verso l'esterno, d'andata || *s.* aspetto esteriore || *av.* al di fuori; esternamente; (*arc.*) verso l'esterno ☆ — *-bound*, (*mar.*) destinato a un porto straniero; — *mail*, posta in partenza.

outwardly ['autwədli], *av.* **1.** esternamente **2.** apparentemente.

outwardness ['autwədnis], *s.* **1.** apparenza esteriore **2.** obiettività.

outwards ['autwədz], *av.* al di fuori; esternamente; (*arc.*) verso l'esterno.

to **outwatch** [aut'wotʃ], *v.t.* **1.** vegliare più a lungo di **2.** osservare (un oggetto) finchè non scompare.

to **outwear** [aut'wɛə*], *pass.* **outwore** [aut'wo:*], *p.p.* **outworn** [aut'wo:n], *v.t.* **1.** sciupare, usare (indumenti) fino a sciuparli **2.** trascorrere, passare (tempo) **3.** durare più a lungo di.

to **outweigh** [aut'wei], *v.t.* **1.** pesare più di; sorpassare in peso **2.** superare in valore, importanza.

to **outwing** [aut'wiŋ], *v.t.* superare volando.

to **outwit** [aut'wit], *pass.p.p.* **outwitted** [aut'witid], *v.t.* **1.** superare in astuzia **2.** (*fam.*) mettere nel sacco.

outwore [aut'wo:*], *pass.* di to **outwear**.

outwork ['aut-wə:k], *s.* **1.** (*mil.*) fortificazione esterna **2.** lavoro a domicilio, esterno.

to **outwork** [aut'wə:k], *v.t.* **1.** lavorare meglio, più in fretta di **2.** portare a termine, finire.

outworker ['aut,wə:kə*], *s.* lavorante a domicilio.

outworn ['aut-wo:n], *p.p.* di to **outwear** || *ag.* logoro; trito; vecchio, sorpassato; fuori tempo, moda.

ouzel ['u:zl], *s.* (*ornit.*) merlo.

oval ['ouvəl], *ag.s.* ovale || *the Oval*, « the Oval » (campo sportivo londinese).

ovariotomy [ou,vɛəri'otəmi], *s.* (*chir.*) ovariatomia.

ovary ['ouvəri], *s.* (*anat.*) ovaia; (*bot.*) ovario.

ovate ['ouveit], *ag.* ovato.

ovation [ou'veiʃən], *s.* ovazione: *to receive an —,* ottenere un'ovazione.

oven ['ʌvn], *s.* forno: *in a quick —,* a forno caldo; *to cook sthg. in a gentle, slow —,* cuocere ql.co. a forno moderato ‖ *Dutch —,* forno da campagna con brace intorno e sopra ☆ — *-bird,* (*ornit.*) fornaio; — *-man,* fornaio.

over ['ouvə*], *av.* **1.** di sopra, al di sopra; al di là, dall'altra parte: *the ball went — into the road,* la palla passò al di sopra (del muro) e cadde in strada; *take this — to his office,* porta questo nel suo ufficio; *to jump —,* saltare al di là; *to lean —,* sporgersi ‖ — *here,* qui; — *there,* là, laggiù ‖ *he is — from France,* viene dalla Francia **2. interamente, dappertutto; dal principio alla fine:** *to be all — dust,* essere tutto coperto di polvere; *to paint —,* verniciare completamente; *to read a letter —,* leggere tutta una lettera **3. in più, in eccesso:** *children of fourteen and —,* i bambini di quattordici anni e più; *I have a card —,* ho una carta in più **4.** (*unito ad ag. av.*) **troppo, eccessivamente:** — *confident,* troppo sicuro di sè; *to act — cautiously,* agire con troppa prudenza **5.** (*con to be*): *it's — with us,* è finita per noi; *the storm is —,* il temporale è passato **6.** (*indica ripetizione*): *six times —,* sei volte di seguito; *read —!,* rileggete!; *to think sthg. —,* riflettere su ql.co. ‖ — *and —* (*again*), più e più volte.

over, *prep.* **1. su, sopra, al di sopra, per di sopra:** *with his hat — his eyes,* col cappello sugli occhi; *she fell asleep — her work,* si addormentò sul suo lavoro; *the sky was — our heads,* il cielo era sopra di noi ‖ *his has no command — himself,* egli non sa controllarsi; *he laughed — the absurdity of it,* l'assurdità della cosa lo fece ridere; *to do sthg. — s.o.'s head,* fare ql.co. all'insaputa di qlcu.; *to have power — s.o.,* avere influenza su qlcu.; *to watch — a person,* vegliare su una persona **2. per, attraverso; da una parte all'altra:** — *the way,* dall'altra parte; *all — the world,* per tutto il mondo; *there was a bridge — the river,* un ponte attraversava il fiume **3. più di, oltre:** *her mother cannot be — fifty,* sua madre non deve avere più di cinquant'anni; *there were — two hundred people,* c'erano più di duecento persone ‖ — *and above,* di più, inoltre; oltre a tutto ciò, per soprammercato **4. durante:** — *Christmas,* durante l'intero periodo natalizio; *to keep sthg. — the season,* tenere ql.co. durante tutta la stagione.

over, *s.* **1.** (*comm.*) eccedenza **2.** (*cricket*) serie di palle (sei o otto) **3.** (*maglieria*) aumento **4.** (*artigl.*) colpo lungo.

over, *ag.* (*unito a s.*) troppo, eccessivo: — *anxiety,* ansietà eccessiva; — *-confidence,* eccessiva sicurezza di sè; — *-development,* sviluppo eccessivo.

to overabound ['ouvə*baund], *v.i.* sovrabbondare.

to overact ['ouvər'ækt], *v.t.i.* (*teat.*) esagerare (una parte); caricare (un'interpretazione); eccedere; strafare.

overall ['ouvərɔ:l], *ag.* completo, globale, in tutta la sua lunghezza ‖ *s.* **1.** camice da lavoro; grembiule **2.** *pl.* tuta da lavoro ☆ — *attenuation,* (*rad.*) attenuazione globale; — *dimensions,* dimensioni di ingombro; — *gain,* (*rad.*) amplificazione totale; — *length,* (*mar.*) lunghezza fuori tutto.

to overarch ['ouvər'ɑ:tʃ], *v.t.* coprire con una volta.

overate ['ouvər'et], *pass.* di to overeat.

to overawe [,ouvər'ɔ:], *v.t.* impaurire; intimidire.

overbalance [,ouvə'bæləns], *s.* **1.** eccedenza; soprappiù **2.** *fig.* preponderanza.

to overbalance, *v.t.i.* **1.** pesare più di, superare in peso; preponderare su **2.** sbilanciare, rovesciare **3.** perdere l'equilibrio, far perdere l'equilibrio, rovesciarsi.

to overbear [,ouvə'bɛə*], *pass.* **overbore** [,ouvə'bɔ:*], *p.p.* **overborne** [,ouvə'bɔ:n], *v.t.* **1.** dominare, domare **2.** soverchiare; angariare; sopraffare.

overbearing [,ouvə'bɛəriŋ], *ag.* arrogante; imperioso; autoritario.

overbearingly [,ouvə'bɛəriŋli], *av.* arrogantemente; imperiosamente.

overbearingness [,ouvə'bɛəriŋnis], *s.* arroganza; imperiosità.

to overbid ['ouvə'bid], *pass.* **overbid,** *p.p.* **overbidden** ['ouvə'bidn], *v.t.i.* **1.** offrire un prezzo maggiore del valore di; rilanciare su (all'asta) **2.** (*carte*) fare una dichiarazione superiore a (un altro).

to overblow ['ouvə'blou], *pass.* **overblew** ['ouvə'blu:], *p.p.* **overblown** ['ouvə'bloun], *v.t.i.* **1.** coprire (di neve, polvere, ecc.) **2.** spazzar via, soffiar via (di vento) **3.** passare, diminuire di violenza (di tempesta).

overblown ['ouvə'bloun], *p.p.* di to overblow ‖ *ag.* completamente, troppo sbocciato (di fiore).

overboard ['ouvəbɔ:d], *av.* (*mar.*) fuori bordo, in mare: *to throw —,* gettare a mare; *to throw a scheme —, fig.* abbandonare un progetto ‖ *man —!,* (*mar.*) un uomo in mare!.

to overboil ['ouvə'bɔil], *v.t.i.* (far) bollire troppo.

overbold ['ouvə'bould], *ag.* sfacciato, presuntuoso.

overboldly ['ouvə'bouldli], *av.* sfacciatamente; impudentemente.

overborne [,ouvə'bɔ:n], *p.p.* di to overbear.

overbought ['ouvə'bɔ:t], *pass.p.p.* di to overbuy.

overbridge ['ouvə'bridʒ], *s.* soprapassaggio, cavalcavia.

to overbrim ['ouvə'brim], *pass.p.p.* **overbrimmed** ['ouvə'brimd], *v.t.i.* traboccare (da): *the milk overbrimmed the cup,* il latte traboccò dalla tazza.

to overbrood ['ouvə'bru:d], *v.t.* **1.** covare (anche *fig.*) **2.** incombere su.

to overbrow ['ouvə'brau], *v.t.* incombere; sovrastare su.

to overbuild ['ouvə'bild], *pass.p.p.* **overbuilt** ['ouvə'bilt], *v.t.* sovraccaricare di costruzioni (una zona).

overbuilt ['ouvə'bilt], *pass.p.p.* di to overbuild ‖ *ag.* sovraccarico di costruzioni.

overburden [,ouvə'bə:dn], *s.* **1.** sovraccarico **2.** (*min.*) terreno di copertura, copertura.

to overburden, *v.t.* sovraccaricare: *don't — him with work,* non sovraccaricarlo di lavoro.

to overburn ['ouvə'bə:n], *pass.p.p.* **overburnt** ['ouvə'bə:nt], *v.t.i.* **1.** bruciare troppo **2.** ardere di zelo.

overbusy ['ouvə'bizi], *ag.* **1.** occupatissimo **2.** troppo zelante; che si dà troppo da fare.

to overbuy ['ouvə'bai], *pass.p.p.* **overbought** ['ouvə'bɔ:t], *v.t.* (*comm.*) comprare in quantità eccessiva; comprare oltre le proprie possibilità.

overcame [,ouvə'keim], *pass.* di to overcome.

to overcapitalize ['ouvəkə'pitəlaiz], *v.t.* sopravvalutare il capitale nominale di (una società per azioni).

overcare ['ouvə'kɛə*], *s.* cura, premura eccessiva.

overcareful ['ouvə'kɛəful], *ag.* **1.** troppo accurato **2.** troppo prudente.

to overcarry ['ouvə'kæri], *v.t.* **1.** portare troppo lontano **2.** *fig.* portare oltre il giusto limite.

overcast ['ouvə-kɑ:st], *pass.p.p.* di to overcast ‖ *ag.* scuro, coperto di nubi; *fig.* offuscato, velato ‖ *s.* **1.** cortina di nubi **2.** sopraggitto.

to overcast, *pass.p.p.* **overcast,** *v.t.i.* **1.** offuscare, offuscarsi; oscurare, oscurarsi: *her eyes were — with tears,* i suoi occhi erano velati di lacrime **2.** cucire a sopraggitto.

overcasting ['ouvə-kɑ:stiŋ], *s.* **1.** offuscamento **2.** sopraggitto **3.** intonacatura.

overcautious ['ouvə'kɔ:ʃəs], *ag.* eccessivamente cauto, troppo prudente.

overcautiously ['ouvə'kɔ:ʃəsli], *av.* troppo cautamente, troppo prudentemente.

over-charge ['ouvə'tʃɑ:dʒ], *s.* **1.** sovraccarico **2.** prezzo eccessivo; sovrapprezzo ‖ *fraudulent —,* estorsione.

to overcharge, *v.t.* **1.** sovraccaricare: *to — a book with quotations,* sovraccaricare un libro di citazioni **2.** far pagare troppo caro: *they overcharged him one pound,* gli fecero pagare una sterlina in più del giusto prezzo.

to **overcloud** [,ouvə'klaud], *v.t.i.* rannuvolare, rannuvolarsi (anche *fig.*).

to **overcloy** ['ouvə'kloi], *v.t.* satollare; rimpinzare.

overcoat ['ouvəkout], *s.* soprabito; cappotto.

overcoating ['ouvə,koutiŋ], *s.* stoffa per soprabiti.

to **overcolour** ['ouvə'kʌlə*], *v.t.* colorire eccessivamente (anche *fig.*).

to **overcome** [,ouvə'kʌm], *pass.* **overcame** [,ouvə-'keim], *p.p.* **overcome**, *v.t.i.* vincere; sopraffare; prevalere; domare: *he was — with liquor*, era ubriaco fradicio; *she is — by emotion*, è sopraffatta dall'emozione; *to — an obstacle*, vincere, superare un ostacolo.

overconfident ['ouvə'konfidənt], *ag.* troppo sicuro di sè; presuntuoso.

overcooked ['ouvə'kukt], *ag.* troppo cotto.

to **overcount** ['ouvə'kaunt], *v.t.* 1. sopravvalutare 2. superare nel numero.

to **overcover** ['ouvə'kʌvə*],*v.t.*coprire completamente.

overcredulity ['ouvəkri'dju:liti], *s.* credulità eccessiva.

overcredulous ['ouvə'kredjuləs], *ag.* troppo credulo.

to **overcrop** ['ouvə'krɔp], *pass.p.p.* **overcropped** ['ouvə'krɔpt], *v.t.* esaurire (un terreno) con coltivazioni intensive.

to **overcrow** ['ouvə'krou], *v.t.* trionfare su.

to **overcrowd** [,ouvə'kraud], *v.t.i.* affollare, affollarsi eccessivamente: *an overcrowded beach*, una spiaggia sovraffollata.

overcrowding [,ouvə'kraudiŋ], *s.* 1. affollamento eccessivo 2. sovrapopolamento.

overcunning ['ouvə'kʌniŋ], *ag.* troppo astuto.

to **overdare** ['ouvə'dɛə*], *v.t.i.* 1. osare troppo 2. avere più ardimento di.

to **over-develop** ['ouvədi'veləp], [*v.t.* 1. sviluppare troppo 2. (*foto.*) sovrasviluppare.

to **overdo** [,ouvə'du:], *pass.* **overdid** [,ouvə'did], *p.p.* **overdone** [,ouvə'dʌn], *v.t.i.* 1. esagerare; eccedere; strafare: *she overdid her apology*, si scusò esageratamente 2. stancare, affaticare; esaurire: *he overdid himself and now he has a nervous breakdown*, si è affaticato troppo e ora ha l'esaurimento nervoso.

overdone [,ouvə'dʌn], *p.p.* di to **overdo** ‖ *ag.* stracotto, cotto troppo: *this meat is —* questa carne è stracotta.

overdose ['ouvədous], *s.* dose eccessiva.

to **overdose** ['ouvə'dous], *v.t.* somministrare rimedi in dosi eccessive a.

overdraft ['ouvədrɑ:ft], *s.* 1. (*comm.*) ammontare dovuto dal correntista alla banca in conto corrente 2. corrente d'aria che passa sopra il fuoco di una fornace.

overdrank ['ouvə'dræŋk], *pass.* di to **overdrink**.

to **overdraw** ['ouvə'drɔ:], *pass.* **overdrew** ['ouvə-'dru:], *p.p.* **overdrawn** ['ouvə'drɔ:n], *v.t.* 1. esagerare (una descrizione, un racconto) 2. (*comm.*) eccedere, oltrepassare; scoprire (il proprio conto in banca) ☆ *overdrawn account*, (*comm.*) conto scoperto.

to **overdress** ['ouvə'dres], *v.t.i.* vestire, vestirsi con eccessivo lusso, ricercatezza; portare troppi ornamenti.

overdrew ['ouvə'dru:], *pass.* di to **overdraw**.

to **overdrink** ['ouvə'driŋk], *pass.* **overdrank** ['ouvə-'dræŋk], *p.p.* **overdrunk** ['ouvə'drʌŋk], *v.i.r.* bere troppo: *to — (oneself)*, ubriacarsi.

to **overdrive** ['ouvə'draiv], *pass.* **overdrove** ['ouvə-'drouv], *p.p.* **overdriven** ['ouvə'drivn], *v.t.* 1. affaticare; esaurire 2. sfruttare troppo.

overdrunk ['ouvə'drʌŋk], *p.p.* di to **overdrink**.

overdue ['ouvə'dju:], *ag.* 1. (*comm.*) in sofferenza, scaduto 2. in ritardo.

to **overeat** ['ouvər'i:t], *pass.* **overate** ['ouvər'et], *p.p.* **overeaten** ['ouvər'i:tn], *v.i.r.* mangiare troppo: *to — (oneself)*, fare indigestione.

to **overestimate** ['ouvər'estimeit], *v.t.* sopravvalutare; stimare eccessivamente.

overexcitable ['ouvərik'saitəbl], *ag.* sovraeccitabile.

to **overexcite** ['ouvərik'sait], *v.t.* sovraeccitare.

overexcited ['ouvərik'saitid], *ag.* sovraeccitato.

overexcitement ['ouvərik'saitmənt], *s.* sovraeccitazione.

to **overexert** ['ouvərig'zə:t], *v.t.* stancare; sfruttare: *to — oneself*, abusare delle proprie forze.

to **over-expose** ['ouvəriks'pouz], *v.t.* (*foto.*) sovraesporre.

overexposure ['ouvəriks'pouʒə*], *s.* (*foto.*) sovraesposizione.

overfall ['ouvə'fɔ:l], *s.* 1. tratto di mare agitato per marea, correnti 2. (*ing. idraulica*) stramazzo 3. (*arc.*) cascata.

over-fatigue ['ouvəfə'ti:g], *s.* fatica eccessiva.

to **over-fatigue** ['ouvəfə'ti:g], *v.t.* affaticare eccessivamente.

to **overfeed** ['ouvə'fi:d], *pass.p.p.* **overfed** ['ouvə'fed], *v.t.i.* nutrire eccessivamente; mangiare troppo.

overfeeding ['ouvə'fi:diŋ], *s.* superalimentazione.

to **overfill** ['ouvə'fil], *v.t.i.* riempire, riempirsi troppo.

to **overfilm** ['ouvə'film], *v.t.* offuscare.

to **overfish** ['ouvə'fiʃ], *v.t.* esaurire le risorse ittiche di.

overflew ['ouvə'flu:], *pass.* di to **overfly**.

overflow ['ouvə-flou], *s.* 1. inondazione; straripamento 2. *fig.* sovrabbondanza; profusione.

to **overflow** [,ouvə'flou], *v.t.i.* inondare; far straripare; traboccare.

overflowing [,ouvə'flouiŋ], *ag.* 1. traboccante; straripante 2. sovrabbondante ‖ *s.* 1. inondazione; straripamento 2. sovrabbondanza; esuberanza.

to **overfly** ['ouvə'flai], *pass.* **overflew** ['ouvə'flu:], *p.p.* **overflown** ['ouvə'floun], *v.t.* 1. sorvolare 2. volare più alto, più a lungo di; superare in volo.

overfond ['ouvə'fond], *ag.* troppo appassionato; troppo innamorato.

overfull ['ouvə'ful], *ag.* troppo pieno; sazio.

to **overgrow** ['ouvə'grou], *pass.* **overgrew** ['ouvə-'gru:], *p.p.* **overgrown** ['ouvə'groun], *v.t.i.* 1. crescere troppo in fretta; diventare troppo grande per: *he has overgrown all his clothes*, è cresciuto tanto che tutti gli abiti gli son divenuti stretti; *to — oneself*, crescere troppo in fretta 2. coprire, coprirsi: *to — with leaves*, coprire, coprirsi di foglie.

overgrown ['ouvə'groun], *p.p.* di to **overgrow** ‖ *ag.* 1. cresciuto troppo 2. coperto: *to be all — with*, essere tutto coperto di.

overgrowth ['ouvəgrouθ], *s.* 1. crescita eccessiva 2. vegetazione sovrabbondante.

overhand ['ouvəhænd], *ag. attributivo* 1.: *— stroke*, (*nuoto*) bracciata all'indiana; *— service*, (*tennis*) servizio alto 2. cucito a sopraggitto ☆ *— knot*, (*mar.*) nodo semplice.

overhang ['ouvəhæŋ], *s.* (*arch.*) sporgenza, aggetto.

to **overhang** ['ouvə'hæŋ], *pass.p.p.* **overhung** ['ouvə-'hʌŋ], *v.t.i.* 1. pendere; essere sospeso; sovrastare; aggettare: *a slight mist overhung the forest*, una nebbia leggera sovrastava la foresta 2. adornare con tendaggi 3. *fig.* minacciare.

overhanging ['ouvə'hæŋiŋ], *ag.* sovrastante; sospeso; (*arch.*) aggettante, sporgente, a sbalzo.

overhastily ['ouvə'heistili], *av.* troppo precipitosamente.

overhasty ['ouvə'heisti], *ag.* troppo precipitoso.

overhaul ['ouvəhɔ:l], *s.* revisione, esame minuzioso; riparazione.

to **overhaul** [,ouvə'hɔ:l], *v.t.* 1. smontare per verificare; revisionare; riparare 2. (*mar.*) raggiungere, sorpassare.

overhead ['ouvəhed], *ag.* 1. alto; sopra la testa; aereo: *— wires*, fili aerei 2. (*comm.*) generale, globale ☆ *— charges*, spese generali; *— valves*, (*mec.*) valvole in testa.

overhead ['ouvə'hed], *av.* in alto, al di sopra: *the people in the room —*, la gente nella stanza di sopra.

to **overhear** [,ouvə'hiə*], *pass.p.p.* **overheard** [,ouvə-'hə:d], *v.t.* 1. udire per caso; sorprendere (una conversazione): *he overheard a few words*, colse alcune parole 2. origliare.

overheat ['ouvə'hi:t], *s.* surriscaldamento.

to **overheat**, *v.t.i.* **1.** surriscaldare; surriscaldarsi **2.** *fig.* eccitarsi.

overhung ['ouvə'hʌŋ], *pass.p.p.* di to **overhang**.

overindulgence ['ouvərin'dʌldʒəns], *s.* **1.** eccessiva bontà, indulgenza **2.** abuso, eccesso (nel bere, ecc.). **overindulgent** ['ouvərin'dʌldʒənt], *ag.* eccessivamente indulgente.

overissue ['ouvər'isju:], *s.* emissione eccessiva.

to **overissue** ['ouvər'isju:], *v.t.* emettere in eccesso (banconote, ecc.).

overjoy [,ouvə'dʒɔi], *s.* gioia smisurata.

overjoyed [,ouvə'dʒɔid], *ag.* felicissimo, pazzo di gioia: *he was — at her consenting*, era felicissimo che ella acconsentisse.

to **overjump** ['ouvə'dʒʌmp], *v.t.* saltare al di là di, trascurare.

overkind ['ouvə'kaind], *ag.* troppo gentile.

overkindness ['ouvə'kaindnis], *s.* gentilezza eccessiva.

to **overlabour** ['ouvə'leibə*], *v.t.* **1.** elaborare troppo; sviscerare (un argomento) **2.** stancare; far lavorare troppo.

to **overlade** ['ouvə'leid], *pass.* **overladed** ['ouvə'leidid], *p.p.* **overladen** ['ouvə'leidn], *v.t.* sovraccaricare.

overladen ['ouvə'leidn], *p.p.* di to **overlade** || *ag.* stracarico, sovraccarico.

overlaid [,ouvə'leid], *pass.p.p.* di to **overlay**.

overlain [,ouvə'lein], *p.p.* di to **overlie**.

overland [,ouvə'lænd], *av.* via terra.

overlap ['ouvəlæp]. *s.* sovrapposizione.

to **overlap** [,ouvə'læp], *pass.p.p.* **overlapped** [,ouvə'læpt], *v.t.i.* **1.** coprire; sovrapporre, sovrapporsi **2.** *fig.* coincidere.

overlay ['ouvəlei], **overlaying** [,ouvə'leiiŋ], *s.* copertura (*p.e.* copriletto, tovaglietta).

to **overlay** [,ouvə'lei], *pass.p.p.* **overlaid** [,ouvə'leid], *v.t.* **1.** gettare, porre su; ricoprire **2.** *fig.* gravare, opprimere.

overlay [,ouvə'lei], *pass.* di to **overlie**.

overleaf ['ouvə'li:f], *av.* sul verso, retro della pagina.

to **overleap** [,ouvə'li:p], *pass.p.p.* **overleaped**, **overleapt** [,ouvə'lept], *v.t.* **1.** saltare al di là di, oltrepassare **2.** omettere.

to **overlie** [,ouvə'lai], *pass.* **overlay** [,ouvə'lei], *p.p.* **overlain** [,ouvə'lein], *v.t.* **1.** coprire **2.** soffocare coricandosi sopra **3.** *fig.* opprimere; soffocare.

to **overlive** ['ouvə'liv], *V.* to **outlive**.

overliver ['ouvə'livə*], *s.* superstite.

overload ['ouvəloud], *s.* carico eccessivo, superfluo; sovraccarico; zavorra; aggravio.

to **overload** ['ouvə'loud], *v.t.* caricare troppo; aggravare.

to **overlook** [,ouvə'luk], *v.t.* **1.** guardare dall'alto; dominare dall'alto: *to — the town from the hill*, guardare la città dalla collina **2.** trascurare; lasciarsi sfuggire: *I overlooked the fact*, questo fatto m'è sfuggito **3.** tollerare, chiudere gli occhi su **4.** ispezionare; sorvegliare **5.** stregare; gettare il malocchio su.

overlooker ['ouvə'lukə*], *s.* **1.** ispettore; sovrintendente; sorvegliante **2.** spia.

overlord ['ouvələ:d], *s.* signore feudale; signore supremo, sovrano.

overlordship ['ouvələ:dʃip], *s.* impero, sovranità.

overly ['ouvəli], *av.* (*scoz. amer.*) eccessivamente troppo.

overlying ['ouvə'laiiŋ], *ag.* sovrapposto.

overman ['ouvəmæn], *pl.* **overmen** ['ouvəmen], *s.* **1.** sorvegliante; capo minatore **2.** (*fil.*) superuomo.

overmasted ['ouvə'ma:stid], *ag.* (*mar.*) munito di alberi troppo alti e pesanti.

to **overmaster** [,ouvə'ma:stə*], *v.t.* spadroneggiare su; dominare; soggiogare.

overmatch ['ouvəmætʃ], *s.* avversario di forze superiori.

to **overmatch** [,ouvə'mætʃ], *v.t.* essere più forte di; vincere, superare.

overmeasure ['ouvə'meʒə*], *s.* eccesso; soprappiù.

overmodest ['ouvə'mɔdist], *ag.* ultramodesto.

to **overmount** ['ouvə'maunt], *v.t.i.* sormontare; salire troppo.

overmuch ['ouvə'mʌtʃ], *ag.* eccessivo; soverchio || *s.* eccesso.

overmuch, *av.* troppo, eccessivamente.

overnice ['ouvə'nais], *ag.* troppo delicato; esigente; incontentabile; cavilloso, pedante.

overnicely ['ouvə'naisli], *av.* incontentabilmente.

overnight ['ouvə'nait], *ag.* **1.** compiuto durante la notte: *an — solution*, una soluzione trovata durante la notte **2.** per una notte: *an — case*, valigia per l'occorrente di una notte || *s.* (*amer.*) la notte precedente.

overnight, *av.* **1.** durante la notte: *stay — and go away early tomorrow*, rimani stanotte e vai via domattina presto **2.** ieri sera.

overpaid ['ouvə'peid], *pass.p.p.* di to **overpay**.

to **overpass** [,ouvə'pa:s], *v.t.i.* **1.** attraversare; passare oltre **2.** sorpassare; eccedere; eccellere **3.** trasgredire; trascurare, ignorare.

overpast ['ouvə'pa:st], *ag.* passato, finito: *the time was — to do that*, era ormai troppo tardi per fare ciò.

to **overpay** ['ouvə'pei], *pass.p.p.* **overpaid** ['ouvə'peid], *v.t.* pagare più del dovuto; ricompensare largamente.

overpayment ['ouvə'peimənt], *s.* pagamento eccessivo, retribuzione eccessiva.

to **overpeople** ['ouvə'pi:pl], *v.t.* sovrapopolare.

overpeopled ['ouvə'pi:pld], *ag.* sovrapopolato.

to **overpersuade** ['ouvəpə'sweid], *v.t.* costringere a persuadersi.

to **overpicture** ['ouvə'piktʃə*], *v.t.* esagerare nel dipingere.

to **overpitch** ['ouvə'pitʃ], *v.t.* **1.** (*cricket*) lanciare (la palla) troppo lontano **2.** *fig.* esagerare: *to — one's praise of s.o.*, lodare qlcu. smoderatamente.

to **overplay** ['ouvə'plei], *v.t.i.* **1.** (*teat.*) esagerare (una parte); strafare **2.** (*carte*) dichiarare troppo alto **3.** (*golf*) fare un tiro troppo lungo.

overplus ['ouvə-plʌs], *s.* soprappiù, sovrabbondanza; eccesso; eccedenza.

to **overpoise** ['ouvə'pɔiz], *V.* to **outweigh**.

overpopulated ['ouvə'pɔpjuleitid], *ag.* sovrapopolato.

overpopulation ['ouvə,pɔpju'leiʃən], *s.* sovrapopolazione.

to **overpot** ['ouvə'pɔt], *pass.p.p.* **overpotted** ['ouvə'pɔtid], *v.t.* (*agr.*) piantare in vaso troppo grande.

to **overpower** [,ouvə'pauə*], *v.t.* sopraffare, soverchiare; opprimere; vincere; dominare; soggiogare, schiacciare: *he was overpowered with sorrow*, egli fu sopraffatto dal dolore; *your kindness overpowers me*, la vostra gentilezza mi confonde.

overpowering [,ouvə'pauəriŋ], *ag.* **1.** opprimente, schiacciante: — *forces*, forze schiaccianti; — *heat*, caldo opprimente; — *smell*, odore soffocante **2.** prepotente, irresistibile (di desiderio, ecc.).

overpoweringly [,ouvə'pauəriŋli], *av.* irresistibilmente, prepotentemente.

to **overpraise** [,ouvə'preiz], *v.t.* lodare oltremodo.

to **overpress** ['ouvə'pres], *v.t.* **1.** opprimere al di là di ogni sopportazione **2.** insistere eccessivamente su (un argomento).

overpressure ['ouvə'preʃə*], *s.* (*fis.*) sovrapressione.

to **overprint** ['ouvə'print], *v.t.* (*foto.*) sovrastampare.

to **overprize** ['ouvə'praiz], *v.t.* sopravvalutare.

to **overproduce** ['ouvə-prə'dju:s], *v.t.* produrre in eccesso.

overproduction ['ouvə-prə'dʌkʃən], *s.* sovraproduzione.

overproud ['ouvə'praud], *ag.* troppo orgoglioso.

overran [,ouvə'ræn], *pass.* di to **overrun**.

to **overrate** ['ouvə'reit], *v.t.* **1.** sopravvalutare: *don't — your possibilities,* non sopravvalutare le tue possibilità **2.** tassare eccessivamente.

to **overreach** [,ouvə'ri:tʃ], *v.t.i.* **1.** oltrepassare; andare, spingersi al di là di, al di sopra di ‖ *to — oneself,* sopravvalutare le proprie forze; fare il passo più lungo della gamba; *(fam.)* darsi la zappa sui piedi **2.** ferirsi le zampe anteriori con le posteriori (di cavalli) **3.** imbrogliare, abbindolare, mettere nel sacco.

overread ['ouvə'red], *pass.p.p.* di to **overread** ‖ *ag.* che ha letto troppo.

to **overread** ['ouvə'ri:d], *pass.p.p.* **overread** ['ouvə-red], *v.i.* leggere troppo.

to **overrefine** ['ouvə-ri'fain], *v.i.* sottilizzare.

overrefinement ['ouvə-ri'fainmənt], *s.* eccessiva raffinatezza.

to **overrent** ['ouvə'rent], *v.t.* imporre un canone d'affitto troppo alto a.

to **override** [,ouvə'raid], *pass.* **overrode** [,ouvə'roud], *p.p.* **overridden** ['ouvə'ridn], *v.t.i.* **1.** far scorrere in (territorio nemico) con truppe a cavallo **2.** passare a cavallo sul corpo di **3.** *fig.* calpestare; infrangere (legge); annullare: *decision that overrides a former decision,* decisione che annulla la precedente **4.** passar sopra a, non tener conto di: *to — another person's claims,* non tener conto dei diritti altrui ‖ *to — one's commission,* commettere un abuso di potere **5.** stancare (un cavallo) **6.** sovrapporsi (delle parti di un osso fratturato).

overripe ['ouvə'raip], *ag.* troppo maturo.

overrode [,ouvə'roud], *pass.* di to **override**.

to **overrule** [,ouvə'ru:l], *v.t.* **1.** governare, dirigere (di autorità superiore): *the Ministry of Education overrules all decisions,* tutte le decisioni devono essere vagliate dal Ministero dell'Istruzione **2.** scartare, respingere, annullare (di autorità): *the major overruled the captain's order,* il maggiore annullò l'ordine del capitano **3.** *(dir.)* cassare, annullare (sentenza): *the judge overruled the previous sentence,* il giudice annullò la sentenza precedente **4.** dominare, essere più forte di: *fate overruled him,* il destino fu più forte di lui.

overruler [,ouvə'ru:lə*], *s.* chi governa, dirige, domina.

overruling [,ouvə'ru:liŋ], *ag.* che governa, dirige, domina.

to **overrun** [,ouvə'rʌn], *pass.* **overran** [,ouvə'ræn], *p.p.* **overrun**, *v.t.i.* **1.** invadere; infestare; depredare; devastare: *the district was — with bandits,* la regione era infestata dai banditi; *garden — with weeds,* giardino infestato da erbacce; *house — with cockroaches,* casa infestata dagli scarafaggi; *the whole country was —,* tutto il paese fu invaso **2.** inondare; traboccare, straripare; *fig.* diffondersi (di idee): *the flood overran the field,* la piena straripò nel campo **3.** oltrepassare: *his speech overran the time allowed,* il suo discorso si protrasse oltre il limite di tempo concesso ‖ *to — oneself, fig.* lasciarsi trasportare **4.** *(tip.)* superare la giustezza, l'altezza; trasportare (caratteri): *line that overruns into the margin,* riga che supera la giustezza **5.** *(mec.)* sorpassare la velocità limite **6.** *(aut.)* imballare il motore.

overrunner ['ouvə'rʌnə*], *s.* invasore.

overrunning [,ouvə'rʌniŋ], *s.* **1.** invasione; devastazione; incursione **2.** inondazione **3.** *(tip.)* trasposizione di caratteri.

to **oversail** ['ouvə'seil], *v.i.* *(arch.)* proiettarsi, sporgersi.

oversailing ['ouvə'seiliŋ], *ag.* *(arch.)* sporgente.

oversaw ['ouvə'sɔ:], *pass.* di to **oversee**.

to **overscore** ['ouvə'skɔ:*], *v.t.* cancellare (parole) con linea, trattino.

oversea ['ouvə'si:], *ag.* straniero; d'oltremare ‖ *av.* oltremare, d'oltremare.

overseas ['ouvə'si:z], *av.* oltremare, d'oltremare.

to **oversee** ['ouvə'si:], *pass.* **oversaw** ['ouvə'sɔ:], *p.p.* **overseen** ['ouvə'si:n], *v.t.* ispezionare, sopraintendere, dirigere, sorvegliare (lavori in corso, operai, ecc.).

overseen ['ouvə'si:n], *p.p.* di to **oversee** ‖ *ag.* errato, in errore.

overseer ['ouvəsiə*], *s.* **1.** ispettore, soprintendente; incaricato responsabile; capo squadra **2.** *(tip.)* proto.

overseership ['ouvə,siəʃip], *s.* ispettorato, soprintendenza.

to **oversell** ['ouvə'sell], *pass.p.p.* **oversold** ['ouvə-'sould], *v.t.* vendere più (merce) di quello che si ha in magazzino.

to **overset** ['ouvə'set], *pass.p.p.* **overset**, *v.t.i.* **1.** rovesciare, rovesciarsi; far ribaltare (vettura); far capovolgere, capovolgersi (di battello) **2.** scompigliare, mettere sottosopra, sconvolgere (anche *fig.*); far fallire (piani, ecc.).

to **oversew** ['ouvə'sou], *pass.* **oversewed** ['ouvə-'sould], *p.p.* **oversewn** ['ouvə'soun], *v.t.* fare il sopraggitto a; unire con sopraggitto.

oversewn ['ouvə'soun], *p.p.* di to **oversew**.

to **overshade** ['ouvə'feid], *v.t.* adombrare; oscurare.

to **overshadow** [,ouvə'ʃædou], *v.t.* **1.** ombreggiare, proiettare ombra su; *fig.* adombrare; oscurare, eclissare: *clouds that — the sky,* nuvole che oscurano il cielo **2.** proteggere.

to **overshine** ['ouvə'ʃain], *pass.p.p.* **overshone** ['ouvə'ʃon], *v.t.* **1.** illuminare **2.** superare in splendore; eclissare.

overshoe ['ouvə'ʃu:], *s.* **1.** soprascarpa **2.** *pl.* *(aer.)* dispositivo meccanico antighiaccio.

overshone ['ouvə'ʃon], *pass.p.p.* di to **overshine**.

overshoot ['ouvə'ʃu:t], *s.* *(aer.)* atterraggio lungo.

to **overshoot**, *pass.p.p.* **overshot** ['ouvə'ʃot], *v.t.i.* **1.** tirare al di là del bersaglio; lanciare lungo, troppo alto; sbagliare la mira; passare il segno (anche *fig.*): *to — the mark,* passare i limiti ‖ *to — oneself,* fare il passo più lungo della gamba **2.** *(aer.)* atterrare lungo e richiamare.

overshot ['ouvə'ʃot], *pass.p.p.* di to **overshoot** ‖ *ag.* sporgente (di mascella di cane) ☆ *— wheel,* ruota idraulica a pale.

overside ['ouvə'said], *av.* lungo il fianco ‖ *to load, unload, a vessel —,* *(mar.)* caricare, scaricare una nave per mezzo di chiatte.

oversight ['ouvəsait], *s.* **1.** svista, sbaglio, sbadataggine, trascuratezza ‖ *through (o by) an —,* per distrazione; per inadempienza **2.** sorveglianza; tutela: *rights of — of a commission,* diritti di tutela di una commissione; *to be under the — of,* essere sotto la tutela di.

oversize ['ouvəsaiz], *s.* misura, taglia superiore al normale.

to **overskip** ['ouvə'skip], *pass.p.p.* **overskipped** ['ouvə'skipt], *v.t.* **1.** saltare, passare sopra a **2.** omettere.

overskirt ['ouvə'skə:t], *s.* sopragonna.

overslaugh ['ouvə-slɔ-], *s.(mil.)* esenzione da un ufficio in considerazione di altro più importante.

to **overslaugh,** *v.t.* **1.** *(mil.)* esentare da un ufficio in considerazione di altro più importante **2.** *(amer.)* escludere da una nomina per favorire altri **3.** ostacolare.

to **oversleep** ['ouvə'sli:p], *pass.p.p.* **overslept** ['ouvə'slept], *v.t.i.* dormire troppo a lungo, dormire oltre (l'ora fissata).

oversleeve ['ouvəsli:v], *s.* soprammanica.

overslept ['ouvə'slept], *pass.p.p.* di to **oversleep**.

overslip ['ouvə'slip], *pass.p.p.* **overslipped** ['ouvə-'slipt], *v.t.* **1.** omettere **2.** sfuggire l'attenzione di.

to **oversmoke** ['ouvə'smouk], *v.i.* fumare troppo; rovinarsi la salute fumando troppo.

oversold ['ouvə'sould], *pass.p.p.* di to **oversell**.

oversoul ['ouvəsoul], *s.* *(fil.)* superanima (dei trascendentalisti americani).

oversped ['ouvə'sped], *pass.p.p.* di to **overspeed**.

overspeed ['ouvə'spi:d], *s.* (*mec.*) velocità di fuga, velocità superiore alla massima normale ☆ — *test*, prova di centrifugazione.

to **overspeed**, *pass.p.p.* **overspeeded** ['ouvə'spi:-did], **oversped** ['ouvə'sped], *v.i.* raggiungere una velocità eccessiva.

to **overspend** ['ouvə'spend], *pass. p.p.* **overspent** ['ouvə'spent], *v.t.i.* spendere troppo: *to* — (*oneself*), spendere oltre le proprie possibilità.

overspent ['ouvə'spent], *pass.p.p.* di to **overspend** || *ag.* esausto, sfinito.

to **overspread** [,ouvə'spred], *pass.p.p.* **overspread** *v.t.i.* **1.** coprire, ricoprire: *contempt* — *with blandness*, *fig.* disprezzo celato dall'affabilità; *the sky was* — *with clouds*, il cielo era coperto di nubi; *the snow overspreads the plain*, la neve ricopre la pianura **2.** spargere, spargersi, diffondersi: *a flush* — *her face*, un rossore le si diffuse sul volto; *a mist* — *the forest*, una nebbia avvolgeva la foresta **3.** inondare (di acqua, luce).

to **overstand** ['ouvə'stænd], *pass.p.p.* **overstood** ['ouvə'stud], *v.t.* resistere più a lungo di.

to **overstate** ['ouvə'steit], *v.t.* esagerare: *I am neither overstating nor understating the case*, non esagero nè in un senso nè nell'altro.

overstatement ['ouvə'steitment], *s.* esagerazione.

to **overstay** ['ouvə'stei], *v.t.* trattenersi più a lungo di.

to **overstep** ['ouvə'step], *pass.p.p.* **overstepped** ['ouvə'stept], *v.t.* oltrepassare; trasgredire; eccedere: *don't* — *the mark*, non eccedete; *to* — *the truth*, oltrepassare i confini della verità.

overstimulation ['ouvə,stimju'leifən], *s.* sovraeccitazione.

overstock ['ouvə'stɔk], *s.* sovrabbondanza; sovraccarico.

to **overstock**, *v.t.* ingombrare; riempire esageratamente.

overstrain ['ouvə-strein], *s.* tensione eccessiva.

to **overstrain** ['ouvə'strein], *v.t.i.* **1.** spingere all'eccesso; sforzare, sforzarsi; strapazzarsi: *to* — *oneself with working*, strapazzarsi eccessivamente per il lavoro **2.** (*mec.*) sollecitare oltre il limite elastico.

overstress ['ouvəstres], *s.* (*mec.*) sovrasollecitazione, sollecitazione eccessiva.

to **overstress** [,ouvə'stres], *v.t.* **1.** (*mec.*) sollecitare eccessivamente **2.** insistere troppo su (un dettaglio, ecc.).

to **overstretch** ['ouvə'stretf], *v.t.* estendere, allargare eccessivamente; esagerare.

to **overstride** ['ouvə'straid], *pass.* **overstrode** ['ouvə'stroud], *p.p.* **ovestridden** ['ouvə'stridn], *v.t.* **1.** scavalcare **2.** stare a cavalcioni su **3.** superare, sorpassare.

overstrung ['ouvə'strʌŋ], *ag.* esaurito; spossato, sfinito; sovraeccitato ☆ — *piano*, pianoforte obliquo.

to **overstudy** ['ouvə'stʌdi], *v.t.i.* studiare troppo intensamente.

to **overstuff** ['ouvə'stʌf], *v.t.* **1.** rimpinzare **2.** ricoprire, imbottire (mobili).

to **oversubscribe** ['ouvəsəb'skraib], *v.t.* raccogliere più del necessario per (una sottoscrizione).

oversupply ['ouvəsə'plai], *s.* fornitura superiore (in quantità) alla richiesta.

to **oversupply**, *v.t.* fornire in quantità superiore alla richiesta.

to **overswarm** ['ouvə'swɔ:m], *v.t.i.* **1.** dilagare su; invadere **2.** sciamare (delle api).

to **oversway** ['ouvə'swei], *v.t.* **1.** fare inclinare, ribaltare **2.** (*arc.*) influire su; convincere.

to **overswell** ['ouvə'swel], *v.t.i.* **1.** gonfiare, gonfiarsi troppo **2.** straripare.

overt ['ouvə:t], *ag.* chiaro, evidente, manifesto; pubblico ☆ — *market*, mercato pubblico.

to **overtake** [,ouvə'teik], *pass.* **overtook** [,ouvə'tuk], *p.p.* **overtaken** [,ouvə'teikən], *v.t.* **1.** cogliere; sorpren-

dere: *he was overtaken by the blizzard*, fu colto dalla tormenta; *overtaken in fault*, sorpreso in fallo || *overtaken in drink*, ubriaco **2.** raggiungere; superare, sorpassare: *to* — *another car on the road*, sorpassare un'altra automobile sulla strada; *to step out in order to* — *s.o.*, allungare il passo per raggiungere qlcu.

overtaken [,ouvə'teikən], *p.p.* di to **overtake** || *ag.* brillo, ubriaco.

overtaking [,ouvə'teikiŋ], *s.* (*aut.*) sorpasso || *no* —, divieto di sorpasso.

to **overtask** ['ouvə'tɑ:sk], *v.t.* imporre un compito troppo grave a; sovraccaricare || *to* — *one's strength*, abusare delle proprie forze.

to **overtax** ['ouvə'tæks], *v.t.* **1.** pretendere troppo da, abusare di: *to* — *s.o.'s patience*, abusare della pazienza di qlcu. **2.** tassare eccessivamente.

overthrew [,ouvə'θru:], *pass.* di to **overthrow**.

overthrow ['ouvə-θrou], *s.* **1.** rovesciamento; *fig.* disfatta; rovina **2.** (*cricket*) palla che rimbalza indietro.

to **overthrow** [,ouvə'θrou], *pass.* **overthrew** [,ouvə'θru:], *p.p.* **overthrown** [,ouvə'θroun], *v.t.* **1.** rovesciare, capovolgere **2.** *fig.* rovinare; demolire; sconfiggere; abbattere: *they overthrew the government*, rovesciarono il governo.

overthrust ['ouvə-θrʌst], *s.* (*geol.*) faglia di carreggiamento ☆ — *sheet*, coltre di carreggiamento.

overthwart ['ouvə-θwɔ:t], *ag.* **1.** in posizione trasversale **2.** avverso, sfavorevole; contrario || *s.* **1.** posizione trasversale; passaggio collaterale, trasversale **2.** contraddizione **3.** esperienza negativa.

to **overthwart** [.ouvə'θwɔ:t], *v.t.* **1.** traversare **2.** fare opposizione a, ostacolare.

overtime ['ouvətaim], *av.* oltre l'ora fissata: *to work* —, fare dello straordinario || *s.* (lavoro) straordinario: *all* — *will be paid*, tutti gli straordinari saranno pagati.

to **overtime** ['ouvə'taim], *v.t.* **1.** dedicare troppo tempo a **2.** (*foto.*) sovraesporre.

to **overtire** ['ouvə'taiə*], *v.t.* stancare troppo; strapazzare: *to* — *oneself*, stancarsi troppo, strapazzarsi.

overtly ['ouvə:tli], *av.* chiaramente, manifestamente; pubblicamente.

to **overtoil** ['ouvə'tɔil], *V.* to **overwork 1**.

overtone ['ouvətoun], *s.* (*mus.*) ipertono.

overtook [,ouvə'tuk], *pass.* di to **overtake**.

to **overtop** ['ouvə'tɔp], *pass.p.p.* **overtopped** ['ouvə'tɔpt], *v.t.* **1.** elevarsi al disopra di; sovrastare; superare: *mountain that overtops the range*, montagna che domina la catena; *Tom will soon have overtopped his father*, |Tommaso presto supererà in statura suo padre **2.** *fig.* eclissare, offuscare **3.** eccellere su.

to **overtower** ['ouvə'tauə*], *v.t.i.* dominare, troneggiare su.

to **overtrade** ['ouvə'treid], *v.t.i.* commerciare al di là delle proprie possibilità finanziarie; acquistare (merci) in eccedenza.

to **overtrain** ['ouvə'trein], *v.t.i.* allenare, allenarsi in modo eccessivo.

to **overtrip** ['ouvə'trip], *pass.p.p.* **overtripped** ['ouvə'tript], *v.t.* passare agilmente sopra; sfiorare.

to **overtrump** ['ouvə-trʌmp], *v.i.* (*carte*) buttare una carta che vale di più.

overture ['ouvətjuə*], *s.* **1.** *gener.pl.* (*comm.*) proposta, offerta **2.** (*mus.*) preludio.

overturn ['ouvətə:n], *s.* rovesciamento; capovolgimento.

to **overturn** [,ouvə'tə:n], *v.t.i.* **1.** capovolgere; rovesciare, rovesciarsi; *fig.* sconvolgere: *the boat overturned*, la barca si rovesciò **2.** (*mar.*) sommergersi **3.** conquistare; sconfiggere.

overuse ['ouvərju:s], *s.* uso eccessivo (di ql.co.); abuso.

to **overuse** [,ouvər'ju:z], *v.t.* usare troppo; abusare di.

overvaluation ['ouvə,vælju'eiʃən], *s.* sopravvalutazione.

to **overvalue** ['ouvə'vælju:], *v.t.* sopravvalutare.

to **overveil** ['ouvə'veil], *v.t.* velare, coprire.

overvoltage ['ouvə'voultidʒ], *s.* sovratensione.

to **overwalk** ['ouvə'wɔ:k], *v.t.i.* far stancare camminando; stancarsi camminando troppo.

to **overwatch** ['ouvə'wɔtʃ], *v.t.i.* **1.** stancarsi per lunga veglia **2.** vigilare su, curarsi di.

to **overwear** ['ouvə'wɛə*], *pass* **overwore** ['ouvə'wɔ:*], *p.p.* **overworn** ['ouvə'wɔ:n], *v.t.* **1.** consumare con l'uso **2.** crescere tanto da non riuscire più ad indossare (i propri indumenti).

overweary ['ouvə'wiəri], *ag.* stremato, esausto.

to **overween** ['ouvə'wi:n], *v.i.* (*arc.*) farsi illusioni essere presuntuoso, arrogante.

overweening [,ouvə'wi:niŋ], *ag.* arrogante; presuntuoso || *s.* (*rar.*) presunzione.

overweeningly [,ouvə'wi:niŋli], *av.* arrogantemente; presuntuosamente.

to **overweigh** ['ouvə'wei], *v.t.* **1.** superare in peso **2.** *fig.* opprimere.

overweight ['ouvə'weit], *ag.* che supera il peso || *s.* **1.** sovraccarico **2.** preponderanza ☆ — *luggage*, bagaglio in eccedenza.

to **overwhelm** [,ouvə'welm], *v.t.* **1.** seppellire, sommergere **2.** distruggere, schiacciare **3.** *fig.* sopraffare, opprimere: *he was overwhelmed with remorse*, era oppresso dal rimorso.

overwhelming [,ouvə'welmiŋ], *ag.* opprimente, schiacciante: — *worry*, gravissima preoccupazione.

overwhelmingly [,ouvə'welmiŋli], *av.* in modo opprimente, schiacciante.

to **overwind** ['ouvə'waind], *pass. p.p.* **overwound** ['ouvə'waund], *v.t.i.* **1.** caricare troppo (*p.e.* un orologio) **2.** (*elett.*) fare un avvolgimento sovradimensionato.

overwore ['ouvə'wɔ:*], *pass.* di to **overwear**.

overwork ['ouvə'wə:k], *nel senso* **2.** ['ouvəwə:k], *s.* **1.** lavoro eccessivo **2.** lavoro straordinario.

to **overwork**, *v.t.i.* **1.** lavorare, far lavorare eccessivamente: *he didn't* — *himself!*, (*fam.*) non prese troppo a cuore quel lavoro! **2.** fare uso eccessivo di: *he overworks that excuse*, si serve un po' troppo di quella scusa.

overworld ['ouvə'wə:ld], *s.* mondo superiore; mondo degli dei.

overworn ['ouvə'wɔ:n], *p.p.* di to **overwear** || *ag.* logoro, trito, antiquato.

overwound ['ouvə'waund], *pass.p.p.* di to **overwind**.

to **overwrite** ['ouvə'rait], *pass.* **overwrote** ['ouvə'rout], *p.p.* **overwritten** ['ouvə'ritn], *v.t.i.* **1.** scrivere troppo || *to* — *oneself*, guastare la propria fama con produzione troppo copiosa **2.** coprire con altro scritto (come in un palinsesto) **3.** riscrivere.

overwrought ['ouvə'rɔ:t], *ag.* **1.** esausto **2.** ricercato, troppo ornato, tormentato (di stile).

Ovid ['ɔvid], *no.pr.m.* (*st. lett.*) Ovidio.

Ovidian [ɔ'vidiən], *ag.* (*lett.*) ovidiano.

oviduct ['ouvidʌkt], *s.* (*anat.*) ovidotto.

oviferous [ou'vifərəs], *ag.* che fa uova.

oviform ['ouvifɔ:m], *ag.* oviforme, ovoide.

ovine ['ouvain], *ag.* ovino.

oviparous [ou'vipərəs], *ag.* oviparo.

ovipositor [,ouvi'pozitə*], *s.* (*entom.*) ovopositore.

ovoid ['ouvɔid], *ag.* ovoide.

ovoviviparous [,ouvouvi'vipərəs], *ag.* (*zool.*) ovoviviparo.

ovule ['ouvju:l], *s.* (*bot. zool. fisiol.*) ovulo.

ovum ['ouvəm], *pl.* **ova** ['ouvə], *s.* **1.** (*biol.*) ovulo; uovo **2.** (*arch.*) ovolo.

to **owe** [ou], *v.t.i.* **1.** dovere, essere debitore (di): *to* — *s.o. sthg.* (o *sthg. to s.o.*), dover ql.co. a qlcu.: *they* — *me* (*back*) *a hundred pounds*, mi devono cento sterline; *you still* — *me for the book*, mi devi ancora

pagare il libro **2.** essere obbligato, essere riconoscente per: *I* — *everything to you*, io ti devo tutto.

owing ['ouiŋ], *ag. predicativo* **1.** dovuto; causato; imputabile: *this was* — *to his ill-luck*, ne fu causa la sfortuna che lo perseguitava **2.** (*comm.*) dovuto: *you must pay what is* —, dovete pagare il vostro debito.

owing to ['ouiŋtu], *prep.* a causa di, a motivo di; in seguito a: — *the drought the crop is short*, a causa della siccità il raccolto è scarso.

owl [aul], *s.* (*ornit.*) gufo, allocco, barbagianni; civetta ☆ — *-eyed*, dagli occhi di gufo; — *-light*, l'imbrunire.

owlery ['auləri], *s.* nido di civetta, di gufo.

owlet ['aulit], *s.* gufo giovane.

owlish ['auliʃ], *ag.* simile a gufo.

own [oun], *ag.* (*spec. rafforzativo dopo un poss.*) **proprio:** *my* — *little child*, bimbo mio caro; *I wrote it with my* — *hand*, l'ho proprio scritto di mio pugno; *she cooks her* — *meals*, si fa la cucina da sè || *s.: an idea of her* —, una sua idea personale; *Louise has a taste of her* —, Luisa ha un gusto tutto suo; *on his* —, di sua propria iniziativa; *on one's* —, da solo; *they came into their* —, entrarono in possesso di ciò che loro spettava || *to hold one's* —, *fig.* mantenere le proprie posizioni; mantenersi in forza.

to **own**, *v.t.i.* **1.** possedere; avere in proprietà: *she owns a lovely cottage*, possiede una bella villetta **2.** ammettere, riconoscere: *he owned the dog as his own*, riconobbe che il cane era suo; *they won't* — *their weakness*, non vogliono riconoscere la loro debolezza; *this you must* —, devi ammettere ciò; *you shall* — *she behaved badly*, devi riconoscere che si è comportata male **3.** *to* — *to* (*sthg.*), confessare: *she owned to a sense of shame*, confessò un senso di vergogna.

owner ['ounə*], *s.* **1.** proprietario; padrone (di ditta) **2.** (*sl. mar.*) capitano ☆ *part-* —, comproprietario; *ship-* —, armatore.

ownership ['ounəʃip], *s.* proprietà, possesso.

ox [ɔks], *pl.* **oxen** ['ɔksən], *s.* bue, bove; *pl.* i bovini (in genere) || *the black* — *has trod on his foot*, *fig.* la sfortuna si è abbattuta su di lui; non è più giovane ☆ — *bow*, collare del giogo per i buoi; (*amer.*) ansa di fiume; — *eyed*, dall'occhio bovino; — *-fly*, (*entom.*) tafano; — *-hide*, cuoio, pelle di bue; — *-tail soup*, minestra con brodo di codino.

oxalate ['ɔksəleit], *s.* (*chim.*) ossalato.

oxalic [ɔk'sælik], *ag.* (*chim.*) ossalico.

oxalis ['ɔksəlis], *s.* (*bot.*) acetosella.

oxalite ['ɔksəlait], *s.* (*chim.*) ossalite.

Oxbridge ['ɔksbridʒ], *s.* (*contr. di Oxford e Cambridge*) le università inglesi tradizionali.

oxen ['ɔksən], *pl.* di **ox**.

oxeye ['ɔksai], *s.* **1.** (*ornit.*) cinciallegra **2.** (*bot.*) occhio di bove, falsa camomilla.

Oxford ['ɔksfəd], *no.pr.* (*geog.*) Oxford (famoso centro universitario inglese).

oxidable ['ɔksidəbl], *ag.* (*chim.*) ossidabile.

to **oxidate** ['ɔksideit], *v.t.i.* (*rar.*) ossidare, ossidarsi.

oxidation [,ɔksi'deiʃən], *s.* (*chim.*) ossidazione.

oxide ['ɔksaid], *s.* (*chim.*) ossido.

oxidization [,ɔksidai'zeiʃən], *s.* (*chim.*) ossidazione.

to **oxidize** ['ɔksidaiz], *v.t.i.* (*chim.*) ossidare, ossidarsi ☆ *oxidized silver*, argento brunito.

oxlip ['ɔkslip], *s.* (*bot.*) primula.

Oxonian [ɔk'sounjən], *ag.* ossoniense, ossoniano (dell'università di Oxford) || *s.* membro dell'università di Oxford.

oxygen ['ɔksidʒən], *s.* ossigeno ☆ — *mask*, (*neol.*) maschera ad ossigeno; — *tent*, (*neol. med.*) tenda ad ossigeno.

to **oxygenate** [ɔk'sidʒineit], *v.t.* ossigenare.

oxygenation [,ɔksidʒi'neiʃən], *s.* ossigenazione.

to **oxygenize** [ɔk'sidʒinaiz], *v.t.* ossigenare.

oxygenous [ɔk'sidʒinəs], *ag.* appartenente all'ossigeno, estratto da esso.

oxyhydrogen [ˈɔksiˈhaidridʒən], *ag.* ossidrico ☆ — *blowpipe*, cannello ossidrico, becco ossidrico.

oxymel [ˈɔksimel], *s.* ossimele (sciroppo).

oxymoron [ˌɔksiˈmɔːrɔn], *pl.* **oxymora** [ˌɔksiˈmɔːrə], *s.* (*ret.*) ossimoro.

oxytone [ˈɔksitoun], *ag.* (*gram.*) ossitono.

oyer [ˈɔiə*], *s.* (*dir.*) udienza, processo.

oyes, oyez [ouˈjes], *inter.* udite! (usato per imporre silenzio nelle aule giudiziarie, ecc.).

oyster [ˈɔistə*], *s.* **1.** ostrica **2.** (*sl.*) persona taciturna ☆ — *-bank* (o — *-bed*), banco di ostriche; — *-catcher*, (*ornit.*) ostricaio; uccello marino; — *-farm* (o — *-field*), allevamento di ostriche; — *-knife*, coltello da ostriche; — *-man*, — *-woman*, ostricaio, ostricaia; — *-plant*, (*bot.*) scorzonera.

oz [auns], *s.* (*abbr.*) di **ounce, ounces.**

ozaena [ouˈziːnə], *s.* (*patol.*) ozena.

ozocerite [ouˈzɔsərait], **ozokerit(e)** [ouˈzoukərit], *s.* (*chim. min.*) ozocerite, cera minerale.

ozone [ˈouzoun], *s.* (*chim.*) ozono.

ozonic [ouˈzɔnik], *ag.* (*chim.*) ozonico.

ozonization [ˌouzouniˈzeifən], *s.* (*chim.*) ozonizzazione.

to ozonize [ˈouzounaiz], *v.t.* (*chim.*) ozonizzare.

P

p [pi:], *pl.* **ps, p's** [pi:z], *s.* (*sedicesima lettera dell'alfabeto inglese*) p ‖ — *for Peter*, (*tel.*) p come Palermo ‖ *to mind one's p's and q's*, controllare il proprio modo di parlare e di agire; aprire gli occhi; fare molta attenzione.

pa [pu:], *s.* (*abbr. fam.* di *papa*) papà, babbo.

pabulum ['pæbjuləm], *s.* cibo, nutrimento (anche *fig.*): *mental* —, nutrimento dello spirito.

paca ['pækə], *s.* (*zool.*) paca.

pace [peis], *s.* **1.** passo: *ten paces off*, a dieci passi di distanza; *in few paces he joined the others*, in pochi passi egli raggiunse gli altri **2.** andatura, passo, velocità: *paces of a horse*, andatura di un cavallo; *at a good, quick* —, di buon passo, a tutta velocità; *at a walking* — (o *at foot* —), al passo: *to force the* —, forzare il passo, l'andatura; *to gather* —, acquistare velocità; *to keep* — *with s.o.*, tenere il passo, procedere di pari passo con qlcu.; *to keep* — *with sthg.*, tenersi al corrente di ql.co.; *to quicken* (o *to hasten*) *one's* —, affrettare il passo; *to set* (o *to make the* — *for s.o.*, dare il passo, l'andatura a qlcu.; *to slacken one's* —, rallentare il passo, l'andatura ‖ *to go the* —, andare a tutta velocità; *fig.* far vita allegra, correre la cavallina ‖ *to put a horse through its paces*, far bella mostra di un cavallo ‖ *to put s.o. through his paces*, (*fam.*) mettere qlcu. alla prova **3.** ambio (passo del cavallo) ☆ — -*maker*, (*spor.*) chi fa l'andatura; battistrada.

to pace, *v.t.i.* **1.** andare al passo; camminare, marciare **2.** percorrere, misurare (a passi): *he paced the room slowly*, misurò la stanza a lenti passi ‖ *to* — (*out* o *off*) *a distance of thirty yards*, misurare (a passi) una distanza di trenta iarde ‖ *to* — *up and down*, passeggiare su e giù **3.** dare l'andatura a (corridori, cavalli, ecc.) **4.** addestrare (cavalli) a un determinato passo **5.** ambiare (di cavalli).

paced [peist], *ag.* **1.** misurato (a passi) **2.** a una determinata andatura (nelle corse dei cavalli) ☆ *even*- —, a passi uguali; *slow*- —, a passi lenti; *dal passo lento*.

pacer ['peisə*], *s.* **1.** cavallo addestrato (al passo dell'ambio **2.** (*spor.*) chi fa l'andatura, battistrada.

pachyderm ['pækidə:m] *s.* (*zool.*) pachiderma (anche *fig.*).

pachydermatous [,pæki'də:mətəs], **pachydermous** [,pæki'də:məs], *ag.* **1.** relativo ai pachidermi **2.** *fig.* insensibile, che ha la pelle dura.

pacifiable ['pæsifaiəbl], *ag.* pacificabile.

pacific [pə'sifik], *ag.* pacifico, quieto, calmo, tranquillo ‖ *the Pacific Coast*, la costa del Pacifico; *the Pacific Ocean*, l'Oceano Pacifico ‖ **Pacific**, *no.pr.* (*geog.*) Pacifico.

pacifically [pə'sifikəli], *av.* pacificamente, tranquillamente.

to pacificate [pə'sifikeit], *v.t.* pacificare.

pacification [,pæsifi'keiʃən], *s.* pacificazione.

pacificator [pə'sifikeitə*], *s.* pacificatore.

pacificatory [pə'sifikətəri], *ag.* conciliativo, conciliante.

pacifier ['pæsifaiə*], *s.c.* pacificatore, pacificatrice.

pacifism ['pæsifizəm], *s.* pacifismo.

pacifist ['pæsifist], *s.* pacifista.

to pacify ['pæsifai], *v.t.* pacificare; calmare, sedare, placare, quietare.

pack[1] [pæk], *s.* **1.** pacco, involto, fagotto; balla ‖ *a* — *of lies*, (*fam.*) un mucchio di bugie **2.** carico; basto; (*mil.*) zaino: *put on packs!*, zaini in spalla! **3.** imballaggio **4.** quantità di prodotto, di raccolto imballato in un anno **5.** muta (di cani, ecc.); *fig.* banda, masnada **6.** mazzo di carte **7.** (*med.*) impacco; impiastro **8.** banchisa polare **9.** muro, pilastro di sostegno **10.** (*metal.*) pacchetto **11.** custodia (di paracadute) ☆ — -*animal*, bestia da soma; — -*cloth*, tela da imballaggio; — -*horse*, cavallo da carico; — -*ice*, ghiaccio di banchisa; — -*load*, soma; — -*road*, mulattiera; — -*saddle*, basto: *to put on, to take off the* — -*saddle*, mettere, togliere il basto; — -*wool*, lana in balle.

to pack[1], *v.t.i.* **1.** imballare; impacchettare; incassare; inscatolare; fare i bagagli: *have you packed* (*up*) *your things?*, avete fatto i bagagli? ‖ *to send s.o. packing*, (*fam.*) mandar via qlcu. **2.** stipare, stiparsi; raggruppare, raggrupparsi: *the students packed round their teacher*, gli studenti si stringevano intorno al loro maestro; *they were packed like sardines*, erano stipati come sardine **3.** mettere la soma a (una bestia) **4.** radunare, radunarsi in una muta **5.** raccogliere (le carte) in mazzo **6.** (*med.*) fare un impacco a; applicare un impiastro a **7.** (*mec.*) guarnire, montare una guarnizione **8.** *to* — **off**, spedire, mandar via: — *these books off*, spedite questi libri; *the child was packed off to bed*, il bambino fu spedito a letto **9.** *to* — **up**, fare i bagagli; *fig.* far fagotto.

pack[2], *s.* (*arc.*) complotto, congiura.

to pack[2], *v.t.i.* (*arc.*) complottare; attirare a far parte di una congiura, far parte di una congiura.

package ['pækidʒ], *s.* **1.** imballaggio **2.** pacco, pacchetto, involto; balla; collo; cassa **3.** (*amer.*) prodotto finito e pronto per l'uso; (*tv. rad.*) programma già organizzato e ceduto come è; viaggio organizzato ☆ — *library*, (*amer.*) biblioteca circolante.

to package, *v.t.* **1.** imballare **2.** impacchettare, involtare.

packer[1] ['pækə*], *s.* **1.** imballatore; impaccatore **2.** macchina per impacchettare.

packer[2], *s.* cospiratore, congiurato.

packet ['pækit], *s.* **1.** pacco, pacchetto: *a* — *of cigarettes*, un pacchetto di sigarette; *a* — *of needles*, una cartina d'aghi **2.** (*mar.*) postale ☆ — -*boat* (o — -*ship*), (*mar.*) postale ‖ — *postal* —, pacco postale.

to packet, *v.t.* impacchettare, involtare.

packing ['pækin], *s.* **1.** imballaggio; l'imbarilare (di aringhe, ecc.); confezione (di derrate per la conservazione) ‖ *to do one's* —, fare i bauli **2.** (*mar.*) baderna, guarnizione **4.** (*med.*) impacco ☆ — -*case*, cassa da imballaggio; — -*expenses*, spese d'imballaggio; — -*free*, franco d'imballaggio; — -*gland*, (*mec.*) premistoppa; — -*list*, distinta di imballaggio; — -*paper*, carta da imballaggio; — -*press*, torchio per imballare; — -*strip*, guarnizione; — -*thread*, spago per imballaggio ‖ *hemp*- —, *leather*- —, guarnizione di canapa, di cuoio.

packman, *pl.* **packmen** ['pækmən], *s.* venditore ambulante.

pact [pækt], *s.* patto; convenzione; contratto: *to make a* — *with s.o.*, stringere, firmare un patto con qlcu. ☆ *four-power* —, patto, convenzione a quattro.

pad[1] [pæd], *s.* **1.** imbottitura; cuscinetto imbottito; sella imbottita **2.** zampa di animale (cane, lepre, lupo, volpe); l'impronta di tali zampe; cuscinetto carnoso (nelle zampe di alcuni animali); qualsiasi parte carnosa nel corpo di animali **3.** (*mec.*) flangia di attacco; cuscino ammortizzatore **4.** gambale da cricket **5.** (*med.*) tampone; cuscinetto ☆ — *saw*, (*strum. artig.*) saracco ‖ *blotting-* —, tampone di carta assorbente; *drawing-* —, blocco di carta da disegno; *kidney - —*, cuscinetto per rene mobile; *note-* —, notes, taccuino, agenda; *shoulder-* —, imbottitura per spalle; *stamp-* —, tampone per timbri; *writing-* —, cartella per scrivere.

to **pad**[1], *pass.p.p.* **padded** ['pædid], *v.t.* **1.** imbottire; tamponare; ovattare **2.** *fig.* infarcire (un discorso) di pleonasmi **3.** (*tec.*) impermeabilizzare **4.** (*mec.*) applicare pattini a.

pad[2], *s.* **1.** (*dial.*) strada; sentiero **2.** (*dial.*) brigantaggio **3.** — (*-nag*), ronzino.

to **pad**[2], *v.t.i.* **1.** percorrere (una strada) a piedi **2.** camminare con passi dal suono soffocato (di quadrupedi) **3.** (*dial.*) tracciare, spianare (un sentiero) a forza di passarci **4.** rubare su una strada maestra.

pad[3], *s.* **1.** rumore sordo di passi, di bastone sul terreno **2.** passo dal suono soffocato.

pad[4], *s.* **1.** paniere, cesta (generalmente di vimini) **2.** paniere usato come misura (per pesci, frutta, ecc.).

padding ['pædiŋ], *s.* **1.** imbottitura; ovatta; borra **2.** *fig.* verbosità (di discorso, opera letteraria).

paddle[1] ['pædl], *s.* **1.** (*ind.*) spatola **2.** (*mar.*) pagaia **3.** (*mar.*) pala (di elica, di ruota a pale) **4.** natatoria (di cetaceo, tartaruga, ecc.); pinna; aletta; zampa palmata ☆ — *-board*, (*mar.*) pala di ruota; — *boat* (o — *steamer*), piroscafo con ruota a pale; — *-box*, (*mar.*) tamburo; — *-shaft*, (*mar.*) albero di ruota; — *-wheel*, (*mar.*) elica, ruota a pale.

to **paddle**[1], *v.t.i.* **1.** remare con la pagaia; remare lentamente ‖ *to* — *one's own canoe*, (*fam.*) provvedere a se stessi senza aiuto altrui **2.** (*mar.*) procedere a mezzo di pale (di navi a vapore) **3.** nuotare (di palmipedi).

to **paddle**[2], *v.i.* **1.** sguazzare nell'acqua; camminare nell'acqua a piedi nudi: *children love paddling in water*, ai bambini piace sguazzare nell'acqua **2.** giocherellare con le dita.

paddock[1] ['pædək], *s.* **1.** recinto per i cavalli da corsa **2.** pastura; prato chiuso **3.** (*miner.*) deposito per il minerale.

to **paddock**[1], *v.t.* **1.** chiudere in un recinto **2.** (*miner.*) immagazzinare (il minerale).

paddock[2], *s.* rospo.

paddy[1] ['pædi], *s.* riso vestito ☆ — *-field*, risaia.

Paddy[2], *no.pr.m. dim.* di **Patrick** ‖ **paddy**, *s.***1.** (*scherz.*) irlandese **2.** garzone di muratore **3.** accesso di collera, ira.

padishah ['pɑːdiʃɑː], *s.* padiscià.

padlock ['pædlɔk], *s.* lucchetto.

to **padlock**, *v.t.* chiudere con lucchetto.

padre ['pɑːdri], *s.* **1.** (*eccl.*) padre **2.** (*sl. mil.*) cappellano militare.

Padua ['pædjuə], *no.pr.* (*geog.*) Padova.

Paduan ['pædjuən], *ag.* padovano ‖ *s.c.* padovano, padovana.

paduasoy ['pædjuəsɔi], *s.* (*arc.*) seta di Padova.

paean ['piːən], *s.* (*poes.*) peana.

paederast ['pedəræst], *s.* pederasta.

paederasty ['pedəræsti], *s.* pederastia.

paediatric [ˌpiːdiˈætrik], *ag.* pediatrico.

paediatrician [ˌpiːdiəˈtriʃən], *s.c.* pediatra.

paediatrics [ˌpiːdiˈætriks], *s.* pediatria.

paediatrist [ˌpiːdiˈætrist], *s.c.* pediatra.

paeony ['piːəni], *s.* (*bot.*) peonia.

pagan ['peigən], *ag.* pagano ‖ *s.c.* idolatra.

pagandom ['peigəndəm], *s.* il mondo dei pagani.

paganish ['peigəniʃ], *ag.* da pagano; paganeggiante.

paganism ['peigənizəm], *s.* paganesimo.

to **paganize** ['peigənaiz], *v.t.i.* **1.** paganizzare **2.** divenire pagano **3.** paganeggiare, vivere da pagano.

page[1] [peidʒ], *s.* **1.** paggio **2.** ragazzo, fattorino d'albergo (in livrea) ☆ — *-boy*, fattorino d'albergo (in livrea).

to **page**[1], *v.t.* far cercare, chiamare da un fattorino.

page[2], *s.* **1.** pagina: *at the foot* (o *bottom*) *of a* —, a piede di pagina; *at the top of a* —, in testa di pagina; *on* — *3*, a pagina 3; *to double down the* —, piegare l'angolo della pagina come segno; *to turn the* — *over*, voltar pagina **2.** *fig.* episodio della vita, della storia **3.** (*tip.*) composizione ☆ *left-hand* —, verso; — *proof*, bozza impaginata; *right-hand* —, recto.

to **page**[2], *v.t.* **1.** numerare le pagine di (un libro) **2.** (*tip.*) impaginare.

pageant ['pædʒənt], *s.* **1.** (*teat.*) scena di una sacra rappresentazione medievale (mistero) **2.** parata, corteo, processione; cavalcata storica; spettacolo teatrale all'aperto (generalmente storico) **3.** pompa, fasto; ostentazione.

pageantry ['pædʒəntri], *s.* pompa, fasto; ostentazione.

pagehood ['peidʒhud], *s.* condizione di paggio.

paginal ['pædʒinl], **paginary** ['pædʒinəri], *ag.* **1.** di pagina **2.** pagina per pagina: — *reproduction*, riproduzione pagina per pagina.

to **paginate** ['pædʒineit], *v.t.* **1.** numerare le pagine di (un libro) **2.** (*tip.*) impaginare.

pagination [ˌpædʒiˈneiʃən], *s.* **1.** paginatura, numerazione delle pagine di un libro **2.** impaginazione.

pagoda [pəˈgoudə], *s.* **1.** pagoda **2.** moneta d'oro indiana ☆ — *-tree*, (*bot.*) sofora del Giappone: *to shake the* — *-tree*, (*fam.*) fare fortuna con poca fatica (in Oriente).

pah [pɑː], *inter.* puh! (per esprimere disgusto, disprezzo).

paid [peid], *pass.p.p.* di to **pay**.

pail [peil], *s.* secchia, secchio.

pailful ['peilful], *s.* secchiata, il contenuto di una secchia: *a* — *of water*, un secchio pieno d'acqua.

paillasse [pælˈjæs], *s.* pagliericcio.

pain [pein], *s.* **1.** dolore, sofferenza, male (fisico, morale); inquietudine; tormento: *the pains of hell*, le pene dell'inferno; *a shooting* —, un dolore lancinante; *to be out of* —, aver finito di soffrire; *to give s.o.* —, far soffrire qlcu., far pena a qlcu.; *to put a wounded animal out of its* —, dare il colpo di grazia a un animale ‖ *she is a* — *in the neck*, (*fam.*) è una scocciatrice **2.** pena, castigo, punizione: *on* (o *under*) — *of death*, sotto pena di morte **3.** *pl.* doglie (del parto) **4.** *pl.* fatica, pena; cura: *to be at great pains to do sthg.*, sforzarsi di fare qlco.; *to have one's labour for one's pains*, darsi da fare; *to have one's pains for nothing* (o *to have nothing for one's pains*), darsi pena per niente; *to take pains over sthg.*, fare ql.co. con molta cura ☆ — *-killer*, calmante, antinevralgico.

to **pain**, *v.t.i.* causare dolore a; fare male, far soffrire: *it pains me to say so*, mi è penoso dirlo; *my arm pains me* (o *my arm is paining*), mi fa male il braccio.

painful ['peinful], *ag.* doloroso, penoso; gravoso; arduo: — *to behold*, penoso a vedersi; *I find walking* —, mi fa male camminare, soffro a camminare; *it is a* — *work*, è un lavoro gravoso; *my knee was getting* —, cominciava a farmi male il ginocchio.

painfully ['peinfuli], *av.* dolorosamente, penosamente; gravosamente.

painfulness ['peinfulnis], *s.* dolore, pena; afflizione.

painless ['peinlis], *ag.* indolore: — *childbirth*, parto indolore.

painlessly ['peinlisli], *av.* senza dolore.

painstaking ['peinzˌteikiŋ], *ag.* diligente, coscienzioso ‖ *s.* cura, diligenza: *with a little* —, con un po' di cura.

paint [peint], *s.* **1.** pittura, vernice; colore: *a coat of* —, una mano di vernice **2.** verniciatura **3.** belletto, rossetto ☆ — *-box*, scatola di colori; — *-sprayer*, aerografo ‖ *antifire* —, vernice ignifuga; *filler* —, vernice di fondo; *ground* —, colore in polvere; *lead* —, minio; *spray* —, vernice, verniciatura a spruzzo.

to **paint**, *v.t.i.* **1.** dipingere (anche *fig.*); pitturare; verniciare: *they painted the door green*, verniciarono la porta di verde ‖ *to — everything in rosy colours*, vedere tutto rosa ‖ *to — the town red*, (*sl.*) fare baldoria; fare del chiasso in pubblico ‖ *the devil is not so black as he is painted*, il diavolo non è poi brutto come lo si dipinge **2.** dipingersi, imbellettarsi **3.** *to — out*, cancellare passando sopra una mano di vernice.

painted ['peintid], *ag.* **1.** adorno di pitture **2.** imbellettato **3.** fittizio, simulato.

painter[1] ['peintə*], *s.* **1.** pittore **2.** decoratore; imbianchino; verniciatore ☆ —'s colic, (*patol.*) colica saturnina ‖ *landscape —*, paesaggista; *ornamental —*, decoratore; *portrait —*, ritrattista.

painter[2], *s.* (*mar.*) barbetta, cima da ormeggio.

painter[3], *s.* (*zool.*) coguaro.

painting ['peintiŋ], *s.* **1.** pittura; verniciatura, tinteggiatura: *to study —*, studiare pittura **2.** dipinto, quadro: *his best paintings are water-colours*, i suoi migliori quadri sono acquerelli.

paintress ['peintris], *s.* pittrice; decoratrice.

painty ['peinti], *ag.* **1.** imbrattato di colore **2.** sovraccarico di colore.

pair [pɛə*], *s.* paio; coppia: *a — of horses*, una pariglia di cavalli; *a — of rabbits*, una coppia di conigli; *a — of shoes*, un paio di scarpe; *carriage and —*, carrozza a due cavalli; *a nice —*, una coppia simpatica ☆ — *-oar*, imbarcazione a due remi; — *-royal*, tris (a carte, dadi).

to **pair**, *v.t.i.* **1.** appaiare, appaiarsi; accoppiare, accoppiarsi; far paio **2.** *to — off*, mettere, mettersi due per due; (*fam.*) sposarsi: *he paired off with my cousin*, ha sposato mia cugina.

paired [pɛəd], *ag.* accoppiati; appaiati.

pajamas [pə'dʒɑːməz], *s.pl.* (*amer.*) pigiama.

Pakistan [ˌpɑːkis'tɑːn], *no.pr.* (*geog.*) Pakistan.

Pakistani [ˌpɑːkis'tɑːni], *ag.* pachistano ‖ *s.c.* pachistano, pachistana.

pal [pæl], *s.* (*fam.*) compagno, camerata; amico.

to **pal**, *pass.p.p.* **palled** [pæld], *v.i.* (*fam.*) fare amicizia: *to — (up) with s.o.*, fare amicizia con qlcu.

palace ['pælis], *s.* palazzo ☆ — *-car*, (*ferr. amer.*) vettura salone; — *guard*, guardia di protezione a un palazzo, ai suoi abitanti; (*spreg.*) gli intimi di un monarca, presidente, ecc.; guardia del corpo.

paladin ['pælədin], *s.* paladino; cavaliere errante.

palaestra [pə'lestrə], *s.* palestra.

palafitte ['pæləfit], *s.* palafitta.

Palamedes [ˌpælə'miːdiːz], *no.pr.m.* (*lett.*) Palamede.

Palamon ['pæləmən], *no.pr.m.* (*lett.*) Palamone.

palankeen, **palanquin** [ˌpælən'kiːn], *s.* palanchino; lettiga.

palatable ['pælətəbl], *ag.* **1.** gustoso, saporito **2.** *fig.* gradevole; accettabile: *truth is seldom — to kings*, raramente la verità piace ai re.

palatableness ['pælətəblnis], *s.* gustosità.

palatably ['pælətəbli], *av.* gustosamente; gradevolmente.

palatal ['pælətl], *ag.* (*anat. gram.*) palatale: — *sound*, suono palatale ‖ *s.* (*gram.*) consonante palatale.

palatalization ['pælətəlai'zeiʃən], *s.* (*gram.*) palatalizzazione.

palate ['pælit], *s.* **1.** (*anat.*) palato **2.** *fig.* (senso del) gusto.

to **palate**, *v.t.* assaggiare, gustare (cibi).

palatial [pə'leiʃəl], *ag.* da palazzo; sontuoso, magnifico.

palatinate [pə'lætinit], *s.* palatinato ‖ **Palatinate**, *no.pr.* (*geog.*) Palatinato ☆ — *purple*, porpora degli abiti accademici, delle insegne sportive dell'università di Durham.

palatine[1] ['pælətain], *ag.* palatino; di palazzo ‖ *s.* **1.** palatino; conte palatino **2.** suddito di un palatinato ‖ **Palatine**, *no.pr.* (*geog.*) Palatino.

palatine[2], *ag.* (*anat.*) palatale ‖ *s.* osso palatale.

palaver [pə'lɑːvə*], *s.* **1.** discussione, abboccamento (tra europei e indigeni dell'Africa) **2.** chiacchiere **3.** adulazione, blandizie.

to **palaver**, *v.t.i.* **1.** discutere **2.** chiacchierare **3.** adulare; blandire.

pale[1] [peil], *ag.* pallido; scialbo; squallido; *fig.* debole: *to grow (o to turn) —*, impallidire ☆ — *-face*, viso pallido (nome dato ai bianchi dai pellirosse).

to **pale**[1], *v.t.i.* impallidire, far impallidire.

pale[2], *s.* **1.** palo **2.** palizzata; spazio chiuso, recinto ‖ *he had done something which put him out of (o beyond) the —*, *fig.* aveva commesso ql.co. che lo escludeva dalla società **3.** territorio, distretto ‖ *the (English) Pale*, (*st.*) la zona dell'Irlanda sottoposta alla giurisdizione inglese; *the English Pale in France*, (*st.*) il territorio di Calais **4.** (*arald.*) riga, fascia verticale (nel centro di uno scudo).

to **pale**[2], *v.t.* circondare con palizzata; rinchiudere.

paled [peild], *ag.* circondato da palizzata, cintato.

palely ['peilli], *av.* pallidamente.

paleness ['peilnis], *s.* pallore.

paleographer [ˌpæli'ɔgrəfə*], *s.* paleografo.

paleographic [ˌpæliou'græfik], *ag.* paleografico.

paleography [ˌpæli'ɔgrəfi], *s.* paleografia.

paleolithic [ˌpæliou'liθik], *ag.* paleolitico.

paleologist [ˌpæli'ɔlədʒist], *s.* paleologo.

paleology [ˌpæli'ɔlədʒi], *s.* paleologia.

paleontological ['pæliəntə'lɔdʒikəl], *ag.* paleontologico.

paleontologist [ˌpæliɔn'tɔlədʒist], *s.* paleontologo.

paleontology [ˌpæliɔn'tɔlədʒi], *s.* paleontologia.

paleozoic [ˌpæliou'zouik], *ag.* (*geol.*) paleozoico.

Palestine ['pælistain], *no.pr.* (*geog.*) Palestina.

Palestinian [ˌpæles'tinian], *ag.s.c.* palestinese.

palestra [pə'lestrə], *s.* palestra.

paletot ['pæltou], *s.* cappotto.

palette ['pælit], *s.* (*pitt.*) tavolozza ☆ — *-knife*, spatola.

palfrey ['pɔːlfri], *s.* (*arc. poet.*) palafreno.

Pali ['pɑːli], *s.* pali (antica lingua indiana).

palimpsest ['pælimpsest], *s.* palinsesto.

palindrome ['pælindroum], *ag.s.* palindromo.

paling ['peiliŋ], *s.* **1.** palizzata, steccato, stecconata.

palingenesis [ˌpælin'dʒenisis], *s.* palingenesi.

palinode ['pælinoud], *s.* (*poes.*) palinodia.

Palinurus [ˌpæli'njuərəs], *no.pr.m.* (*lett.*) Palinuro.

palisade [ˌpæli'seid], *s.* stecconata, palizzata.

to **palisade**, *v.t.* stecconare, cintare, rinchiudere con palizzata.

palisander [ˌpæli'sændə*], *s.* palissandro (legno).

palish ['peiliʃ], *ag.* palliduccio.

pall[1] [pɔːl], *s.* **1.** drappo funebre **2.** (*arc.*) drappo, mantello **3.** (*eccl.*) pallio; palla (d'altare) **4.** *fig.* manto, velo: *the — of darkness*, il manto dell'oscurità ☆ — *-bearer*, chi regge un lembo del drappo funebre, i cordoni (a un funerale); (*amer.*) chi porta la bara.

to **pall**[1], *v.t.* coprire con un drappo, un pallio.

to **pall**[2], *v.t.i.* saziare, saziarsi; nauseare, nausearsi; stancare, stancarsi: *food, literature that palls*, cibo, letteratura di cui ci si stanca presto; *happiness that never palls on me*, la felicità di cui non sono mai sazio.

Palladian[1] [pə'leidjən], *ag.* palladio, di Pallade.

Palladian[2], *ag.* (*arch.*) palladiano.

palladium[1] [pə'leidjəm], *s.* **1.** palladio (simulacro della dea Pallade) **2.** *fig.* palladio, difesa, protezione.

palladium[2], *s.* (*chim.*) palladio.

Pallas ['pæləs], *no.pr.f.* (*mit.*) Pallade: — *Athena*, Pallade Atena.

pallet[1] ['pælit], *s.* giaciglio; pagliericcio.

pallet[2], *s.* **1.** paletta (da vasaio); spatola **2.** (*pitt.*) tavolozza **3.** (*mar.*) bocchetta (dell'ancora) **4.** (*mec.*) nottolino (di comando, regolazione di una ruota dentata) **5.** (*ind.*) paletta, piattaforma portatile.

pallet[3], *s.* (*arald.*) verghetta.

palliasse [pæl'jæs], *s.* pagliericcio.

to **palliate** ['pælieit], *v.t.* **1.** attenuare, mitigare, sminuire **2.** scusare.

palliation [,pæli'eiʃən], *s.* mitigazione, attenuazione.

palliative ['pæliətiv], *ag. s.* palliativo.

palliatory ['pæliətəri], *ag.* palliativo.

pallid ['pælid], *ag.* pallido; smunto.

pallidity [pə'liditi], *s.* pallidezza.

pallidly ['pælidli], *av.* pallidamente.

pallidness ['pælidnis], *s.* pallore.

pallium ['pæliəm], *pl.* **pallia** ['pæliə], *s.* **1.** (*st. antica, eccl.*) pallio **2.** mantello (di mollusco brachiopodo).

pall-mall ['pel'mel], *s.* (*giuoco*) pallamaglio ‖ *Pall-Mall*, via di Londra dove hanno sede famosi club.

pallor ['pælə*], *s.* pallore.

palm[1] [pɑ:m], *s.* **1.** (*bot.*) palma; palmizio **2.** ramo di palma; palma pasquale ‖ *Palm-Sunday*, Domenica delle Palme **3.** *fig.* vittoria; trionfo: *to bear the —*, portar la palma, essere vincitore; *to yield the — to s.o.*, cedere la palma a qlcu. ☆ *— -house*, serra per palme; *— -oil*, olio di palma; *— -tree*, palmizio; *— -wine*, vino di palma.

palm[2], *s.* **1.** (*anat.*) palmo ‖ *to grease* (o *to oil* o *to tickle*) *s.o.'s —*, (*sl.*) corrompere qlcu. con denaro, unger le ruote ‖ *to hold s.o. in the — of one's hand*, (*fam.*) tener qlcu. in proprio potere **2.** palmo (misura di lunghezza = cm. 7,62 o cm. 10,16) **3.** (*mar.*) patta dell'ancora **4.** spatola, parte piatta e larga al fondo (di strumento); pala di un remo **5.** forcature (dei palchi delle corna di un cervo) ☆ *— -oil*, *fig.* (*scherz.*) mancia.

to **palm**[2], *v.t.* **1.** toccare con la mano; maneggiare **2.** nascondere in mano (come fanno i bari con le carte, i dadi) **3.** (*sl.*) corrompere (con denaro) **4.** *to — off*, imporre con l'inganno; appioppare.

palmaceous [pæl'meiʃəs], *ag.* (*bot.*) di palma.

palmar ['pælmə*], *ag.* palmare.

palmary ['pælməri], *ag.* che merita la palma; eccellente.

palmate ['pælmit], **palmated** ['pælmeitid], *ag.* palmato.

palmer ['pɑ:mə*], *s.* **1.** palmiere (pellegrino che torna dalla Terra Santa con rami di palma) **2.** monaco cercatore **3.** *— (worm)*, (*entom.*) bruco peloso (di varie specie).

palmetto [pæl'metou], *s.* (*bot.*) palma nana.

palmiferous [pæl'mifərəs], *ag.* (*bot.*) palmifero.

palmiped ['pælmiped], **palmipede** ['pælmipi:d], *ag.s.* (*ornit.*) palmipede.

palmist ['pɑ:mist], *s.c.* chiromante.

palmistry ['pɑ:mistri], *s.* chiromanzia.

palmitic [pæl'mitik], *ag.* (*chim.*) palmitico.

palmitin(e) ['pælmitin], *s.* (*chim.*) palmitina.

palmy ['pɑ:mi], *ag.* **1.** coperto, ricco di palme **2.** vittorioso, glorioso **3.** prosperoso.

palmyra [pæl'maiərə], *s.* (*bot.*) borasso.

palp [pælp], *s.* (*entom.*) palpo (appendice dell'apparato boccale).

palpability [,pælpə'biliti], *s.* **1.** palpabilità **2.** *fig.* evidenza.

palpable ['pælpəbl], *ag.* **1.** palpabile **2.** *fig.* evidente.

palpableness ['pælpəblnis], *V.* **palpability**.

palpably ['pælpəbli], *av.* **1.** palpabilmente **2.** *fig.* evidentemente; chiaramente.

to **palpate** ['pælpeit], *v.t.* (*med.*) palpare, toccare.

palpation [pæl'peiʃən], *s.* (*med.*) palpazione.

palpebral ['pælpibrəl], *ag.* (*anat.*) palpebrale.

palpitant ['pælpitənt], *ag.* palpitante.

to **palpitate** ['pælpiteit], *v.i.* palpitare.

palpitation [,pælpi'teiʃən], *s.* palpitazione.

palpus ['pælpəs], *pl.* **palpi** ['pælpai], *V.* **palp**.

palsgrave ['po:lzgreiv], *s.* (*st.*) conte palatino.

palsied ['po:lzid], *ag.* **1.** paralizzato; paralitico **2.** *fig.* tremante.

palsy ['po:lzi], *s.* paralisi (anche *fig.*).

to **palsy**, *v.t. gener. fig.* paralizzare.

to **palter** ['po:ltə*], *v.i.* **1.** tergiversare; ricorrere a sotterfugi; equivocare: *to — with s.o.*, tergiversare con qlcu. **2.** mercanteggiare.

paltriness ['po:ltrinis], *s.* meschinità; grettezza.

paltry ['po:ltri], *ag.* meschino; gretto; miserabile: *— excuses*, scuse meschine; *a — price*, un prezzo irrisorio.

paludal [pə'lju:dl], *ag.* (*med.*) paludoso; malarico.

paludament [pə'lju:dəmənt], *s.* paludamento.

paludism ['pæljudizəm], *s.* (*patol.*) paludismo, malaria.

paly[1] ['peili], *ag.* (*poet.*) pallido; piuttosto pallido.

paly[2], *ag.* (*arald.*) a strisce verticali (di scudo).

pam [pæm], *s.* **1.** fante di fiori **2.** giuoco a carte (simile al napoleone, in cui il fante di fiori è la carta più alta).

Pamela ['pæmilə], *no.pr.f.* Pamela.

pampa ['pæmpə], *s. gener. pl.* pampa.

to **pamper** ['pæmpə*], *v.t.* **1.** coccolare, viziare **2.** (*ar.*) rimpinzare di leccornie.

pamphlet ['pæmflit], *s.* **1.** opuscolo; trattato **2.** libello.

pamphleteer [,pæmfli'tiə*], *s.* **1.** autore di opuscoli, trattati **2.** libellista.

to **pamphleteer**, *v.i.* scrivere opuscoli, trattati, libelli.

pan[1] [pæn], *s.* **1.** padella, tegame; casseruola ‖ *pots and pans*, batteria di cucina ‖ *to fall from the frying — into the fire*, cadere dalla padella nella brace **2.** vaschetta, bacinella **3.** piatto (di bilancia) **4.** (*geol.*) strato, depressione, bacino **5.** scodellino (di antica arma da fuoco) ‖ *flash in the —*, (*fam.*) fuoco di paglia **6.** (*mec.*) « carter », coppa dell'olio **7.** (*cine. tv.*) panoramica ☆ *— -handle*, manico di padella; lingua di territorio che si insinua tra i confini di altri stati; *— -handler*, (*sl. amer.*) mendicante ‖ *baking- —*, teglia, tortiera; *brain- —*, (*fam.*) cranio; *frying- —*, padella; *hard- —*, (*geol.*) strato secco di terreno; *perfume- —*, brucia-profumi; *preserving- —*, pentola per cuocere marmellate; *salt- —*, salina.

to **pan**[1], *pass.p.p.* **panned** [pænd], *v.t.i.* **1.** sottoporre a lavaggio (sabbie aurifere) **2.** estrarre oro **3.** *fig.* riuscire, risultare **4.** (*rar.*) cuocere in padella **5.** essiccarsi e indurirsi (di terreno) **6.** *to — out*, produrre oro.

Pan[2], *no.pr.m.* (*mit.*) Pan, Pane (il dio dei pastori) ‖ *s.* paganesimo ☆ *— -pipes* (*mus.*) fistula.

pan[3], *s.* (*arch.*) pannello quadrato di mattoni o intonaco (nelle case a travature di legno).

pan[4], *ag.* (*nei composti*) tutto unito: *— -Americanism*, panamericanismo; *— -Germanism*, pangermanesimo; *— -Hellenism*, panellenismo; *— -Slavism*, panslavismo.

panacea [,pænə'siə], *s.* panacea.

panache [pə'næʃ], *s.* **1.** pennacchio **2.** *fig.* ostentazione; boria.

panada [pə'nɑ:də], *s.* panata, pancotto.

Panama [,pænə'mɑ:], *no.pr.* (*geog.*) Panama ☆ *— hat*, (cappello di) panama.

Panathenaea [,pænæθi'ni:ə], *s.pl.* (*st. greca*) Panatenee.

pancake ['pænkeik], *s.* **1.** frittella ‖ *as flat as a —*, completamente piatto **2.** (*aer.*) atterraggio in picchiata.

to **pancake**, *v.i.* (*aer.*) scendere in picchiata: *the aeroplane pancaked on the roof*, l'aeroplano scese in picchiata sul tetto.

panchromatic ['pænkrou'mætik], *ag.* (*foto.*) pancromatico.

Pancras ['pæŋkrəs], *no.pr.m.* Pancrazio.

pancratium [pæn'kreiʃəm], *s.* (*st. greca*) pancrazio.

pancreas ['pæŋkriəs], *s.* (*anat.*) pancreas.

pancreatic [,pæŋkri'ætik], *ag.* (*anat.*) pancreatico.

pancreatin ['pæŋkriətin], *s.* (*fisiol.*) pancreatina.

panda ['pændə], *s.* (*zool.*) panda.

Pandean [pæn'di:ən], *ag.* (*mit.*) del dio Pan.

pandects ['pændekts], *s.pl.* (*dir.*) pandette.

pandemia [pæn'di:miə], *s.* pandemia, epidemia.

pandemic [pæn'demik], *ag.* pandemico, epidemico ‖ *s.* pandemia, epidemia.

pandemonium [,pændi'mounjəm], *s.* pandemonio.

pander ['pændə*], *s.* mezzano, ruffiano.

to **pander**, *v.t.i.* fare il mezzano (a).

panderess ['pændəris], s. ruffiana.
panderism ['pændərizəm], s. ruffianesimo.
panderly ['pændəli], av. da ruffiano.
Pandora[1] [pæn'dɔːrə], no.pr.f. (mit.) Pandora || —'s box, il vaso di Pandora.
pandora[2], **pandore** [pæn'dɔː:*], s. (mus.) pandora.
pandour ['pænduə*], s. 1. pl. (st.) panduri (milizia serbo-croata) 2. soldataccio; soldato brutale.
pane[1] [pein], s. 1. vetro, lastra di vetro 2. faccia, faccetta (di brillante, ecc.) 3. (edil.) pannello 4. scacco (di tessuto a quadretti) ☆ window- —, vetro di finestra.
to pane, v.t. 1. confezionare (abiti) con strisce di diverso colore 2. mettere i vetri a (una finestra).
pane[2], s. penna (di martello).
paned [peind], ag. 1. a scacchi, a strisce (di abito, stoffa) 2. fornito di lastre di vetro.
panegyric(al) [,pæni'dʒirik(əl)], ag. laudativo.
panegyric [,pæni'dʒirik], s. panegirico: — upon, panegirico di.
panegyrically [,pæni'dʒirikəli],av. in modo laudativo.
panegyrist [,pæni'dʒirist], s. panegirista.
to panegyrize ['pænidʒiraiz], v.t. fare il panegirico di.
panel ['pænl], s. 1. panno sottosella; panno usato al posto della sella 2. (dir.) lista dei giurati 3. (scoz. dir.) accusato; coll. gli accusati 4. lista dei dottori della mutua 5. (neol.) gruppo di esperti; comitato, commissione: a — of examiners, commissione esaminatrice; a — of telecasters, un gruppo di tecnici della televisione 6. pannello 7. (miner.) sezione ☆ — doctor, dottore della mutua; — heating, riscaldamento a pannelli; — patient, malato mutuato; — work, (edil.) lavori a pannelli || instrument —, (aer. aut.) cruscotto.
to panel, pass.p.p. **panelled** ['pænld], v.t. 1. sellare 2. convocare (una giuria) 3. rivestire di pannelli (pareti, ecc.); ornare di pannello (un abito) 4. (miner.) sezionare.
panelling ['pæniɳ], s. (lavoro ornamentale a) pannelli, rivestimento a pannelli.
panful ['pæn-ful], s. padellata.
pang [pæɳ], s. dolore fortissimo; fitta acuta; fig. stretta al cuore: a sudden —, una fitta subitanea.
to pang, v.t. torturare, tormentare (anche fig.).
pangolin [pæɳ'goulin], s. (zool.) pangolino.
panic[1] ['pænik], ag. panico: — terror, timor panico || s. panico; terrore; — -monger, allarmista; — -stricken (o — -struck), colto da panico.
to panic[1], pass.p.p. **panicked** ['pænikt], v.t.i. 1. allarmare; allarmarsi; creare panico tra; essere in preda al panico 2. (sl. teat.) entusiasmare (il pubblico); provocare gli applausi di.
panic[2], s. (bot.) panico.
panicky ['pæniki], ag. in preda a panico; allarmato.
panicle ['pænikl], s. pannocchia.
panicled ['pænikld], **paniculate** [pə'nikjulit], **paniculated** [pə'nikjuleitid], ag. a pannocchia.
panification [,pænifi'keiʃən], s. panificazione.
panjandrum [pən'dʒændrəm], s. (fam. scherz.) padrone del vapore; pezzo grosso.
panne [pæn], s. felpa soffice e pelosa.
pannier ['pæniə*], s. 1. paniere (da basto); gerla; cesto coperto (per trasportare strumenti chirurgici e medicine nelle autoambulanze) 2. « panier », crinolina.
pannikin ['pænikin], s. 1. piccolo boccale di metallo 2. tegamino.
panoplied ['pænəplid], ag. armato da capo a piedi.
panoply ['pænəpli], s. panoplia, armatura completa.
panorama [,pænə'rɑːmə], s. panorama.
panoramic [,pænə'ræmik], ag. panoramico.
panoramically [,pænə'ræmikəli], av. panoramicamente.
pansy ['pænzi], s. 1. viola del pensiero 2. — (boy), (fam.) giovane effeminato; omosessuale.
pant [pænt], s. 1. palpitazione; palpito; ansito, respiro affannoso 2. sbuffo (di locomotiva).
to pant, v.t.i. 1. ansimare, ansare; battere violente-

mente; palpitare 2. aver voglia: to — for sthg., agognare ql.co.; to — to do sthg., desiderare ardentemente di fare ql.co. 3. to — out, dire ansimando, con voce rotta: she panted out a few words, pronunciò con voce rotta alcune parole.
pantagruelian [,pæntəgruː'eljən], ag. pantagruelico.
Pantaloon [,pæntə'luːn], no.pr.m. (st. teat.) Pantalone || **pantaloons** [,pæntə'luːnz], s.pl. 1. (st.) pantaloni (con calza unita) 2. (amer.) pantaloni.
pantechnicon [pæn'teknikən], s. — (-van), furgone da trasporto (per mobili, masserizie, ecc.).
pantheism ['pænθiː(ː)izəm], s. (fil.) panteismo.
pantheist ['pænθiː(ː)ist], s. (fil.) panteista.
pantheistic(al) [,pænθiː(ː)'istik(əl)], ag. (fil.) panteistico.
pantheon [pæn'θiːən], s. panteon.
panther ['pænθə*], s. pantera (maschio) ☆ American —, puma, coguaro.
pantheress ['pænθəris], s. pantera (femmina).
panties ['pæntiz], s.pl. (fam.) mutandine da bambino; calzoncini da donna.
pantile ['pæntail], s. (edil.) tegola alla fiamminga.
panting ['pæntiɳ], ag. ansante, ansimante || s. palpitazione, ansito; fig. ansia, bramosia.
pantingly ['pæntiɳli], av. ansimando, palpitando; fig. ansiosamente.
Pantisocracy [,pænti'sɔkrəsi], s. Pantisocrazia (comunità utopistica ideata dal Coleridge).
pantograph ['pæntəgrɑːf], s. pantografo.
pantography [pæn'tɔgrəfi], s. pantografia.
pantometer [pæn'tɔmitə*], s. pantometro.
pantomime ['pæntəmaim], s. 1. (teat. romano) mimo (attore, rappresentazione) 2. (teat. inglese) pantomima.
pantomimic(al) [,pæntə'mimik(əl)], ag. pantomimico.
pantomimist [,pæntə'maimist], s. (teat.) pantomima.
pantry ['pæntri], s. 1. dispensa 2. (butler's) —, « office » (stanza in cui si conserva il vasellame e la cristalleria).
pants [pænts], s.pl. 1. mutande 2. (abbr. di pantaloons) pantaloni, calzoni.
pap[1] [pæp], s. 1. (arc.) capezzolo 2. pl. due o più colline a forma conica, una vicino all'altra.
pap[2], s. 1. pappa (per neonati, infermi, ecc.) 2. polpa di frutta.
papa[1] [pə'pɑː], s. (spec. nel linguaggio infantile) papà, babbo.
papa[2] ['pɑːpə], s. (relig. ortodossa) pope.
papacy ['peipəsi], s. papato, pontificato.
papal ['peipəl], ag. papale, pontificio.
papalism ['peipəlizəm], s. papismo.
papalist ['peipəlist], s. papista.
to papalize ['peipəlaiz], v.t.i. convertire, convertirsi al cattolicesimo.
papaveraceous [pə,peivə'reiʃəs], ag. (bot.) papaveraceo.
papaverine [pə'peivərain], s. (chim.) papaverina.
papaverous [pə'peivərəs], ag. 1. papaverico 2. fig. soporifero.
papaw [pə'pɔː], **papaya** [pə'paiə], s. (bot.) papaia.
paper ['peipə*], s. 1. carta: on —, secondo le statistiche, in teoria, sulla carta || to commit sthg. to —, mettere ql.co. per scritto; to put pen to —, cominciare a scrivere; to waste —, scribacchiare 2. certificato, documento; pl. incartamenti, documenti, carte || to send in one's papers, dare le dimissioni 3. prova (d'esame), composizione: to set a —, scegliere un soggetto 4. studio, saggio: to read a — (at a congress), fare un discorso (a un congresso) 5. giornale, gazzetta, periodico: to write in the papers, fare del giornalismo 6. cambiale, assegno; banconota ☆ — -back, « brochure »; — -bag, sacchetto di carta; — board, cartone; — -bound (o — -backed o — -covered), in « brochure », non rilegato; — -case, portacarte; — -chase, giuoco simile al rimpiattino; — -file, registratore (di documenti, carte, ecc.); — -hanger, tappezziere; — -hanging, tappezzeria;

— -knife (o — -cutter), tagliacarte; — -maker, fabbricante di carta; — -making, fabbricazione della carta; — -mill (o — -factory), cartiera; — -money (o — currency), carta moneta; — -nautilus, (zool.) argonaura; — -office, archivio; — war, controversia giornalistica; — -weight, fermacarte || blotting- —, carta assorbente; carbon —, carta carbone; crinkled —, carta crespata; emery- —, carta smerigliata; family papers, carte di famiglia; hair — (o curl —), bigodino; history —, prova scritta di storia; India — (o Bible —), carta India; note- —, carta da lettera; packing- —(o wrapping — o brown —), carta da imballaggio; tissue- —, carta velina; velina detergente; voting —, scheda elettorale; wall- —, carta da parato; waste- —, carta straccia.

to **paper**, v.t. **1.** incartare **2.** tappezzare **3.** fissare sulla carta; descrivere **4.** (sl.) riempire (un teatro) distribuendo biglietti gratuiti.

papering ['peipərin], s. tappezzeria di carta.

papery ['peipəri], ag. cartaceo; simile a carta.

papeterie [,pæpi'tri:], s. cartella con l'occorrente per scrivere.

Paphlagonia [,pæflə'gounjə], no.pr. (geog.) Paflagonia.

papier mâché ['pæpjei'ma:ʃei], s. cartapesta.

papilionaceous [pə,pilio'neiʃəs], ag. (bot.) papilionaceo.

papilla [pə'pilə], pl. **papillae** [pə'pili:], s. (anat. bot.) papilla.

papillary [pə'piləri], ag. (anat. bot.) papillare.

papillate [pə'pilit], ag. (anat. bot.) a forma di papilla; coperto di papille.

papilloma [,pæpi'loumə], s. (patol.) papilloma.

papillose ['pæpilous], ag. (anat. bot.) papilloso.

papillote ['pæpilout], s. bigodino, diavoletto.

papism ['peipizəm], s. papismo.

papist ['peipist], s. papista.

papistic(al) [pə'pistik(əl)], ag. papistico.

papistry ['peipistri], s. papismo.

papoose [pə'pu:s], s.c. bimbo, bimba pellirossa.

pappose [pæ'pous], **pappous** ['pæpəs], ag. (bot.) papposo.

pappus ['pæpəs], pl. **pappi** ['pæpai], s. (bot.) pappo.

pappy ['pæpi], ag. simile a pappa; molle.

paprica, paprika ['pæprikə], s. (bot. cuc.) paprica.

Papua ['pæpjuə], no.pr. (geog.) Papuasia.

Papuan ['pæpjuən], ag.s.c. (abitante) della Papuasia.

papula ['pæpjulə], **papule** ['pæpju:l], pl. **papulae** ['pæpjuli:], **papules** ['pæpju:lz], s. papula, pustola.

papyraceous [,pæpi'reiʃəs], ag. papiraceo.

papyrology [,pæpi'roulədʒi], s. papirologia.

papyrus [pə'paiərəs], pl. **papyri** [pə'paiərai], s. papiro.

par¹ [pa:], s. **1.** (spec. comm.) pari, parità: exchange above, at, below —, cambio sopra la, alla, sotto la pari; on a — with, alla pari con || to be below —, (fam.) non essere in forma **2.** (golf) norma.

par², abbr. di **paragraph**.

par³, V. **parr**.

parabasis [pə'ræbəsis], pl. **parabases** [pə'ræbəsi:z], s. (teat. greco) parabasi.

parable ['pærəbl], s. (ret.) parabola || to take up one's —, (arc.) cominciare un sermone.

to **parable**, v.t.i. (rar.) rappresentare, esprimere con parabole; parlare per parabole.

parabola [pə'ræbələ], s. (geom.) parabola.

parabolic(al) [,pærə'bolik(əl)], ag. **1.** (geom.) parabolico **2.** (ret.) di parabola.

parabolically [,pærə'bolikəli], av. (ret.) con parabole.

to **parabolize** [pə'ræbəlaiz], v.t. **1.** (ret.) esporre in forma di parabola **2.** (geom.) rendere parabolico.

paraboloid [pə'ræbəloid], s. (geom.) paraboloide.

Paracelsus [,pærə'selsəs], no.pr.m. (st. med.) Paracelso.

parachute ['pærəʃu:t], s. paracadute.

to **parachute**, v.t.i. paracadutare; scendere col paracadute.

parachutist ['pærəʃu:tist], s.c. paracadutista.

Paraclete ['pærəkli:t], s. Paracleto.

parade [pə'reid], s. **1.** parata, mostra, sfoggio: to

make a — of sthg., fare sfoggio di ql.co. **2.** corteo, processione **3.** (mil.) parata; piazza d'armi **4.** (scherma) parata **5.** passeggio, viale, passeggiata ☆ — -ground, campo di manovre; — -order, ordine di parata || beauty —, sfilata delle partecipanti a un concorso di bellezza; fashion —, sfilata di modelli.

to **parade**, v.t.i. **1.** fare sfoggio di, ostentare **2.** marciare, sfilare **3.** disporre in parata **4.** passare in rivista.

paradigm ['pærədaim], s. (gram.) paradigma, esempio.

paradisaic(al) [,pærədi'seiik(əl)], ag. paradisiaco.

paradise ['pærədais], s. **1.** paradiso; fig. luogo di delizie: the earthly —, il paradiso terrestre || bird of —, uccello del paradiso **2.** (arch.) cortile davanti (o presso) al portico di una chiesa **3.** (teat. sl.) loggione.

paradisiac [,pærə'disiæk], **paradisiacal** [,pærədi'saiəkəl], ag. paradisiaco.

parados ['pærədos], s. (edil. mil.) spalletta.

paradox ['pærədoks], s. paradosso.

paradoxer ['pærədoksə*], s. chi fa paradossi.

paradoxical [,pærə'doksikəl], ag. paradossale.

paradoxically [,pærə'doksikəli], av. in modo paradossale.

paraffin ['pærəfin], s. (chim.) paraffina ☆ — -oil, olio di paraffina.

to **paraffin**, v.t. trattare con, cospargere di paraffina.

paragoge [,pærə'goudʒi], s. (gram.) paragoge.

paragogic(al) [,pærə'godʒik(əl)], ag. paragogico.

paragon ['pærəgən], s. **1.** modello (di perfezione, di virtù, ecc.); esemplare **2.** brillante perfetto di 100 o più carati **3.** (tip.) corpo 19 o 20.

to **paragon**, v.t. **1.** (poet.) paragonare; citare come paragone **2.** (rar.) superare: to — description, superare ogni descrizione.

paragraph ['pærəgrɑ:f], s. **1.** paragrafo **2.** capoverso || new —, a capo **3.** trafiletto (di giornale).

to **paragraph**, v.t. **1.** dividere in paragrafi **2.** scrivere un trafiletto (di giornale) su.

paragrapher ['pærə,grɑ:fə*], **paragraphist** ['pærə,grɑ:fist], s. cronista (di giornale).

paragraphy ['pærəgrəfi], s. (patol.) paragrafia.

Paraguay ['pærəgwai], no.pr. (geog.) Paraguai.

Paraguayan [,pærə'gwaiən], ag. paraguaiano || s.c. paraguaiano, paraguaiana.

parakeet ['pærəki:t], s. (ornit.) parrocchetto.

parakite ['pærəkait], s. aquilone usato a scopi scientifici.

paralipomena [,pærəlai'pomənə], s.pl. paralipomeni.

parallax ['pærəlæks], s. (astr.ott.) parallasse.

parallel ['pærəlel], ag. parallelo: — lines, linee parallele; to be, to run — with (o to) sthg., essere, correre parallelo a ql.co. || s. **1.** (geom.) parallela **2.** (geog.) parallelo: a — of latitude, un parallelo di latitudine **3.** fig. parallelo, paragone, confronto: without —, senza pari, che non ha eguale; to draw a — between two things, fare un paragone tra due cose **4.** (mil.) trincea parallela **5.** (elett.) parallelo: working in —, (elett.) marcia in parallelo **6.** pl. (tip.) barre ☆ — bars, parallele (attrezzo da ginnastica); — connection, (elett. rad.) collegamento in parallelo, in derivazione.

to **parallel**, pass.p.p. **paralleled** ['pærəleld], v.t. **1.** fare un parallelo, paragonare: to — with, paragonare a **2.** essere parallelo a **3.** (elett.) mettere in parallelo.

parallelepiped [,pærələ'lepiped], s. (geom.) parallelepipedo.

parallelism ['pærələlizəm], s. parallelismo.

parallelogram [,pærə'leləgræm], s. (geom.) parallelogramma.

paralogism [pə'rælədʒizəm], s. (log.) paralogismo.

paralysation [,pærəlai'zeiʃən], s. paralisi.

to **paralyse** ['pærəlaiz], v.t. paralizzare; fig. paralizzare, agghiacciare: paralysed with fear, paralizzato dalla paura.

paralysis [pə'rælisis], s. **1.** (patol.) paralisi **2.** inattività, paralisi ☆ infantile —, (patol.) paralisi infantile.

paralytic [,pærə'litik], ag.s. paralitico.

to **paralyze**, *V.* to **paralyse**.

paramagnetic [,pærəmæg'netik], *ag.* (*elett.*) paramagnetico.

paramagnetism [,pærə'mægnitizəm], *s.* (*elett.*) paramagnetismo.

paramatta [,pærə'mætə], *s.* tessuto misto di lana e cotone, o lana e seta.

paramecium [,pærə'mi:ʃjəm], *s.* (*zool.*) paramecio.

parameter [pə'ræmitə*], *s.* (*mat.*) parametro.

paramount ['pærəmaunt], *ag.* dominante; sovrano; supremo: *of — importance*, di somma importanza || *s.* capo supremo, signore assoluto.

paramountcy ['pærəmauntsi], *s.* supremazia, eminenza.

paramour ['pærəmuə*], *s.* amante.

parang ['pɑːræŋ], *s.* pesante coltello malese.

paranoia [,pærə'nɔjə], *s.* (*patol.*) paranoia.

paranoiac [,pærə'nɔjæk], *ag.s.* (*patol.*) paranoico.

paranymph ['pærənimf], *s.* paraninfo.

parapet ['pærəpit], *s.* **1.** parapetto **2.** (*mil.*) bastione, trincea.

parapeted ['pærəpitid], *ag.* munito di parapetto.

paraphernalia [,pærəfə'neiljə], *s.pl.* **1.** arnesi, armamentaria, accessori **2.** (*dir.*) paraferna; sopraddote.

paraphrase ['pærəfreiz], *s.* parafrasi.

to **paraphrase**, *v.t.i.* parafrasare, fare una parafrasi.

paraphrastic [,pærə'fræstik], *ag.* parafrastico.

paraphrastically [,pærə'fræstikəli], *av.* parafrasticamente.

paraplegia [,pærə'pli:dʒiə], *s.* (*patol.*) paraplegia.

paraplegic [,pærə'pli:dʒik], *ag.* (*patol.*) paraplegico.

parapsychologic(al) ['pærə,saikə'lɔdʒik(əl)], *ag.* metapsichico.

parapsychology ['pærəsai'kɔlədʒi], *s.* metapsichica.

parasang ['pærəsæŋ], *s.* (*st.*) parasanga (misura itineraria persiana di km. 6,4).

paraselene [,pærəsi'li:ni], *pl.* **paraselenae** [,pærəsi'li:ni:], *s.* (*astr.*) paraselene.

parasite ['pærəsait], *s.* parassita (anche *fig.*).

parasitic(al) [,pærə'sitik(əl)], *ag.* parassitico.

parisitically [,pærə'sitikəli], *av.* da parassità.

parasiticide [,pærə'sitisaid], *s.* insetticida.

parasitism ['pærəsai,tizəm], *s.* parassitismo.

parasitology [,pærəsai'tɔlədʒi], *s.* parassitologia.

parasol [,pærə'sɔl], *s.* parasole, ombrellino.

paratactic [,pærə'tæktik], *ag.* (*gram.*) paratattico.

parataxis [,pærə'tæksis], *s.* (*gram.*) paratassi.

parathyroid [,pærə'θairoid], *s.* (*anat.*) paratiroide.

paratrooper ['pærə,tru:pə*], *s.* (*mil.*) paracadutista.

paratroops ['pærətru:ps], *s.pl.* (*mil.*) truppe paracadutate.

paratyphoid ['pærə'taifoid], *ag.* (*patol.*) paratifoideo || *s.* paratifo.

paravane ['pærəvein], *s.* (*mar.*) paramine.

to **parboil** ['pɑːbɔil], *v.t.* bollire parzialmente; *fig.* surriscaldare.

parbuckle ['pɑːbʌkl], *s.* (*mar.*) lentia.

to **parbuckle**, *v.t.* sollevare per mezzo di una lentia.

Parcae ['pɑːsi:], *s.pl.* (*mit.*) Parche.

parcel ['pɑːsl], *s.* **1.** pacco, pacchetto: *make up this — for me*, preparami questo pacco || *— of lies*, *fig.* un sacco di bugie **2.** appezzamento di terreno, lotto **3.** (*comm.*) partita **4.** *fig.* gruppo, branco: *they are a — of scoundrels*, sono un branco di mascalzoni **5.** (*arc.*) porzione ☆ *— delivery*, consegna pacchi || *— post*, ufficio spedizione pacchi.

to **parcel**, *pass p.p.* **parcelled** ['pɑːsld], *v.t.* **1.** dividere in più parti; spartire: *to — (out) sthg.*, distribuire, spartire ql.co. **2.** (*mar.*) bendare **3.** *to — up*, impaccare.

parcel, *av.* (*arc.*) parzialmente: *— blind*, mezzo cieco; *— gilt*, parzialmente dorato.

parcelling ['pɑːsliŋ], *s.* **1.** spartizione; distribuzione **2.** (*mar.*) benda.

parcenary ['pɑːsənəri], *s.* (*dir.*) coeredità.

parcener ['pɑːsənə*], *s.* (*dir.*) coerede.

to **parch** [pɑːtʃ], *v.t.i.* **1.** arrostire; disseccare, disseccarsi (di cereali, ecc.) **2.** bruciare, bruciarsi; inaridire: *the earth was parched*, la terra era riarsa; *to be parched with thirst*, morire di sete, avere la gola riarsa.

parching ['pɑːtʃiŋ], *ag.* bruciante; divorante: *a — heat*, un calore bruciante.

parchment ['pɑːtʃmənt], *s.* pergamena, cartapecora ☆ *— paper*, carta uso pergamena || *undressed —*, pergamena grezza.

pard[1] [pɑːd], *s.* (*arc. poet.*) leopardo; pantera.

pard[2], *s.* (*sl. amer.*) socio.

pardon ['pɑːdn], *s.* **1.** perdono; grazia; scusa: *to beg s.o.'s —*, chiedere scusa a ql.co. || *I beg your —?*, come ha detto?; prego? **2.** (*eccl.*) indulgenza **3.** (*dir.*) amnistia: *general —*, amnistia generale.

to **pardon**, *v.t.* perdonare, accordare il perdono, la grazia a: *— me!*, perdonatemi!; *to — s.o. sthg.*, perdonare ql.co. a qlcu.

pardonable ['pɑːdnəbl], *ag.* perdonabile, scusabile.

pardonably ['pɑːdnəbli], *av.* scusabilmente.

pardoner ['pɑːdnə*], *s.* **1.** chi perdona **2.** (*eccl.*) venditore di indulgenze.

to **pare** [pɛə*], *v.t.* **1.** pareggiare; tagliare; ritagliare: *to — one's nails to the quick*, tagliarsi le unghie fin al vivo **2.** sbucciare (frutta, ecc.); mondare; radere **3.** *to — away*, **down**, ridurre gradualmente: *to — down expenditures*, ridurre le spese.

parent ['pɛərənt], *s.c.* **1.** genitore, genitrice; padre, madre: *parents and relations*, ascendenti e collaterali; *our first parents*, i nostri progenitori, Adamo ed Eva **2.** *fig.* causa, origine: *that was the — of every evil*, ciò fu l'origine di ogni male.

parentage ['pɛərəntidʒ], *s.* genitori; famiglia; nascita; lignaggio, stirpe: *— unknown*, di ignoti.

parental [pə'rentl], *ag.* paterno, materno; di genitori.

parenthesis [pə'renθisis], *pl.* **parentheses** [pə'renθisi:z], *s.* parentesi; *fig.* intervallo, pausa: *in parentheses*, tra parentesi.

to **parenthesize** [pə'renθisaiz], *v.t.* mettere tra parentesi.

parenthetic [,pærən'θetik], *ag.* parentetico.

parenthetically [,pærən'θetikəli], *av.* tra parentesi.

parenthood ['pɛərənthud], *s.* paternità, maternità.

parentless ['pɛərəntlis], *ag.* orfano (di entrambi i genitori).

paresis ['pærisis], *s.* (*patol.*) paresi.

par excellence [pɑːr'eksəlɑːns], *l. av.* per eccellenza, per antonomasia.

parfait [pɑː'fei], *s.* gelato al caffè.

parget ['pɑːdʒit], *s.* bianco di calce, intonaco, gesso, scagliola.

to **parget**, *pass.p.p.* **pargetted** ['pɑːdʒitid], *v.t.* intonacare, dare il bianco a, decorare con gesso, dare il gesso a.

parhelion [pɑː'hiːljən], *pl.* **parhelia** [pɑː'hiːljə], *s.* (*astr.*) parelio.

pariah ['pæriə], *s.* paria (anche *fig.*) ☆ *—-dog*, cane randagio.

Parian ['pɛəriən], *ag.* di Paro || *s.c.* abitante di Paro || *s.* porcellana di Paro ☆ *— marble*, (marmo) pario.

parietal [pə'raiitl], *ag.* (*anat.*) parietale ☆ *— bone*, osso parietale.

paring ['pɛəriŋ], *s.* **1.** buccia; truciolo; raffilatura **2.** rifilatura; tosatura; mondatura; levigatura; ripulitura (di terreno da erbacce).

Paris[1] ['pæris], *no.pr.m.* (*mit.*) Paride.

Paris[2], *no.pr.* (*geog.*) Parigi ☆ *— doll*, manichino (da sarta); *— green*, arsenito di rame (sostanza insetticida); *— white*, bianco di Parigi.

parish ['pæriʃ], *s.* **1.** parrocchia; i parrocchiani || *to go on the —*, vivere della carità della parrocchia **2.** piccolo comune rurale; municipio; distretto ☆ *— child*, orfano, trovatello allevato a spese della parrocchia; *— church*, chiesa parrocchiale; *— clerk*, laico addetto alla parrocchia; *— council*, consiglio municipale; *— lantern*, (*fam.*) luna; — *priest*, parroco; — *register*, registro parrocchiale; — *road*, strada vicinale; — *school*, scuola comunale ‖ *civil* —, piccolo comune rurale; municipio.

parishioner [pə'riʃənə*], *s.c.* parrocchiano, parrocchiana.

Parisian [pə'rizjən], *ag.* parigino ‖ *s.c.* parigino, parigina.

parisyllabic ['pærisi'læbik], *ag.* parisillabo.

paritor ['pæritə*], (*arc.*) apparitore, cursore.

parity[1] ['pæriti], *s.* 1. parità; uguaglianza (di rango, ecc.) ‖ *exchange at* —, (*comm.*) cambio alla pari 2. analogia (di ragionamento, ecc.).

parity[2], *s.* (*med.*) parità.

park [pɑ:k], *s.* 1. parco: *public* —, giardino pubblico 2. riserva di caccia 3. (*mil.*) parco 4. (*aut.*) (*car*) —, posteggio ☆ *artillery-* —, parco d'artiglieria; *deer-* —, riserva di caccia per cervi; *national* —, parco nazionale; *oyster-* —, vivaio d'ostriche.

to **park**, *v.t.* 1. coltivare a parco, adibire a parco 2. rinchiudere (animali) in parco, riserva 3. (*mil.*) parcare ‖ *to* — *oneself*, (*amer. pop.*) piantar le tende 4. (*aut.*) posteggiare, parcheggiare: *can I* — *my car here?*, posso parcheggiare qui la mia macchina?.

parking ['pɑ:kiŋ], *s.* 1. (*aut.*) parcheggio, posteggio ‖ — *free*, posteggio gratuito; *no* —, divieto di sosta, di parcheggio 2. (*amer.*) aiuola spartitraffico ☆ — *meter*, contatore per parcheggio; — *-place* (o — *-lot*), area per parcheggio; — *-ticket*, multa per sosta vietata.

parkway ['pɑ:kwei], *s.* (*amer.*) viale, strada alberata.

parky ['pɑ:ki], *ag.* (*sl.*) fresco (di tempo, aria, ecc.).

parlance ['pɑ:ləns], *s.* linguaggio; parlata; gergo: *in legal* —, in termini legali; *military* —, gergo militare.

parle [pɑ:l], *s.* (*arc. dial.*) 1. discorso, colloquio 2. abboccamento; discussione, dibattito.

to **parle**, *v.i.* (*arc. dial.*) 1. parlare 2. discutere; parlamentare.

parley ['pɑ:li], *s.* (*spec. mil.*) colloquio, abboccamento ‖ *to beat* (o *to sound*) *a* —, chiamare a parlamento.

to **parley**, *v.t.i.* 1. (*spec. mil.*) parlamentare, conferire 2. (*scherz.*) parlare (una lingua straniera).

parleyvoo [ˌpɑ:li'vu:], *s.* (*scherz.*) 1. francese 2. lingua francese.

to **parleyvoo**, *v.i.* (*scherz.*) parlare il francese.

parliament ['pɑ:ləmənt], *s.* parlamento: *in open* —, in pieno parlamento; *to summon, to open, to dissolve Parliament*, convocare, aprire, sciogliere il Parlamento ‖ *Act of Parliament*, legge ‖ *the Houses of Parliament*, il palazzo del Parlamento (a Londra) ‖ *Member of Parliament*, deputato, membro del Parlamento (*abbr.* M. P.) ☆ — *-cake*, focaccia croccante allo zenzero; — *-house*, Parlamento; — *-man*, parlamentare.

parliamentarian [ˌpɑ:ləmən'tɛəriən], *ag.* parlamentare ‖ *s.* 1. parlamentare, membro del Parlamento 2. (*st. inglese*) partigiano del Parlamento nella guerra civile.

parliamentarianism [ˌpɑ:ləmen'tɛəriənizəm], *s.* (*st. pol.*) parlamentarismo.

parliamentary [ˌpɑ:lə'mentəri], *ag.* parlamentare ☆ — *agent*, persona incaricata da privati o società di sostenere presso i deputati determinati progetti di legge; — *election*, elezioni politiche.

parlour ['pɑ:lə*], *s.* salotto (in casa privata); sala privata (di locali pubblici); parlatorio (di collegio) ☆ — *-boarder*, allievo di un collegio che vive presso la famiglia del direttore; — *car*, (*amer. ferr.*) vettura salone; — *-maid*, cameriera (per il servizio di tavola) ‖ *bar-* —, (*amer.*) saletta interna di un bar; *beauty* —, istituto di bellezza.

parlous ['pɑ:ləs], *ag.* (*arc. scherz.*) 1. pericoloso 2. astuto.

parlous, *av.* (*arc. scherz.*) estremamente.

Parmesan [ˌpɑ:mi'zæn], *ag.* parmigiano ☆ — *cheese*, formaggio parmigiano.

Parnassian [pɑ:'næsiən], *ag.s.* (*st. lett.*) parnassiano.

Parnassus [pɑ:'næsəs], *no.pr.* (*geog.*) Parnaso ‖ *s. fig.* la poesia.

Parnellism ['pɑ:nelizəm], *s.* (*st.*) movimento politico per l'autonomia dell'Irlanda.

parochial [pə'roukjəl], *ag.* 1. parrocchiale 2. *fig.* ristretto, limitato.

parochialism [pə'roukjəlizəm], *s.* 1. *fig.* ristrettezza (di vedute) 2. campanilismo.

to **parochialize** [pə'roukjəlaiz], *v.t.i.* 1. rendere parrocchiale; dividere in parrocchie 2. reggere una parrocchia.

parodist ['pærədist], *s.* parodista.

parody ['pærədi], *s.* parodia.

to **parody**, *v.t.* parodiare.

parol ['pærəl], *ag.* orale, verbale: — *contract*, contratto verbale ‖ *s.* (*dir.*) parola: *by* —, verbalmente.

parole [pə'roul], *s.* 1. parola d'onore: *on* —, sulla parola 2. (*mil.*) parola d'ordine ☆ — *violator*, chi infrange la parola data.

to **parole**, *v.t.* liberare (un prigioniero) sulla parola.

parolee [ˌpərou'li:], *s.* prigioniero liberato sulla parola.

paronomasia [ˌpərɔnou'meiʒiə], *s.* (*ret.*) paronomasia.

paroquet ['pærəkit], *s.* (*ornit.*) parrocchetto.

parosmia [pæ'rɔsmiə], *s.* (*patol.*) parosmia.

parotid [pə'rotid], *ag.* (*anat.*) parotideo ‖ *s.* (*anat.*) parotide.

parotitis [ˌpærou'taitis], *s.* (*patol.*) parotite.

paroxysm ['pærəksizəm], *s.* parossismo.

paroxysmal [ˌpærək'sizməl], *ag.* parossistico.

paroxytone [pə'roksitoun], *ag. s.* (*gram.*) parossitono.

parquet ['pɑ:kei], *s.* «parquet», pavimento in legno a tasselli ☆ — *circle*, (*amer.*) le ultime file di posti in platea.

to **parquet**, *v.t.* pavimentare in legno: *a parqueted room*, una stanza con pavimento in legno.

parquetry ['pɑ:kitri], *s.* pavimentazione in legno.

parr [pɑ:*], *s.* (*ittiol.*) salmone giovane.

parricidal [ˌpæri'saidl], *ag.* parricida.

parricide ['pærisaid], *s.* 1. parricida 2. parricidio.

parrot ['pærət], *s.* (*ornit.*) pappagallo (anche *fig.*) ☆ — *-beak nail*, unghia adunca; — *-disease* (o — *fever*), (*patol.*) psittacosi; — *-fish*, (*ittiol.*) scaro.

to **parrot**, *v.t.* ripetere pappagallescamente.

parrotry ['pærətri], *s.* imitazione pappagallesca.

parry ['pæri], *s.* parata (anche *fig.*).

to **parry**, *v.t.* parare; schivare (colpi, pugni, ecc.), *to* — *a question*, *fig.* eludere una domanda.

to **parse** [pɑ:z], *v.t.* (*gram.*) analizzare, fare l'analisi di.

Parsee [pɑ:'si:], *s.* 1. Parso (seguace di Zoroastro) 2. lingua dei Parsi.

Parseeism [pɑ:'si:izəm], *s.* (*relig.*) parsismo.

parsimonious [ˌpɑ:si'mounjəs], *ag.* 1. parsimonioso; economo 2. meschino.

parsimoniously [ˌpɑ:si'mounjəsli], *av.* 1. con parsimonia 2. con meschinità.

parsimoniousness [ˌpɑ:si'mounjəsnis], **parsimony** ['pɑ:siməni], *s.* 1. parsimonia, economia 2. meschinità.

parsing ['pɑ:siŋ], *s.* (*gram.*) analisi.

parsley ['pɑ:sli], *s.* prezzemolo.

parsnip ['pɑ:snip], *s.* (*bot.*) pastinaca.

parson ['pɑ:sn], *s.* parroco (anglicano); (*fam.*) pastore ‖ —*'s nose*, (*fam.*) bocconcino del prete.

parsonage ['pɑ:snidʒ], *s.* (*eccl.*) canonica, parrocchia, rettorato.

parsonie(al) [pɑ:'sɔnik(əl)], *ag.* di, da parroco (anglicano), di, da pastore.

part [pɑ:t], *s.* 1. parte, porzione: *an adverb is a* — *of speech*, un avverbio è una parte del discorso; *it was not my* — *to interfere*, non toccava a me interferire; *the three parts of English verbs are...*, le tre voci dei verbi inglesi sono...; *you have done your* —, avete fatto la vostra parte; *to take* — *in sthg.*, partecipare a ql.co. ‖ *for the most* —, per massima parte ‖ *for my* —, quanto a me ‖ *in* —, parzialmente ‖ *on our* —, da parte nostra ‖ *to be* — *and parcel of sthg.*, essere parte integrante di ql.co. ‖ *to take sthg. in ill* —, aversene a male per ql.co. **2.** (*teat.*) parte, personaggio (anche *fig.*): *please stop playing a — and be natural*, finiscila di fingere e sii naturale **3.** (*tip.*) dispensa: *this book is to be issued in fortnightly parts*, questo libro sarà pubblicato a dispense quindicinali **4.** (*dir.*) parte (in una disputa, ecc.): *to take s.o.'s — (o lo take — with s.o.)*, prendere le parti di qlcu., parteggiare per qlcu. **5.** (*mus.*) parte, voce: *to sing in parts*, cantare a più voci **6.** (*mec.*) pezzo **7.** *pl.* regione, luogo: *I am a stranger in these parts*, non conosco questi luoghi **8.** *pl.* (*arc.*) abilità, doti naturali: *a man of (good) parts*, un uomo di talento ☆ — *- owner*, comproprietario; — *-song*, canto a più voci; — *-time job*, impiego a mezza giornata || *spare parts*, accessori, pezzi di ricambio.

to **part**, *v.t.i.* **1.** dividere, dividersi; separare, disgiungere; divergere: *the crowd parted to let them pass*, la folla si divise per lasciarli passare; *now our roads —*, ora le nostre strade divergono || *to — one's hair*, farsi la scriminatura **2.** lasciarsi, separarsi: *it is time to —*, è ora di lasciarci; *to — friends*, separarsi da amici; *to — from s.o.*, lasciare qlcu., separarsi da qlcu.; *to — with sthg.*, rinunciare a qlcu.; cedere ql.co.; *to — (with one's money)*, (*fam.*) pagare **3.** (*chim.*) isolare **4.** (*mar.*) rompere **5.** (*arc.*) distribuire, spartire **6.** (*arc.*) andarsene, partire || *the parting day*, (*poet.*) il giorno che muore.

part, *av.* parzialmente, in parte: *our ladder is made — of iron and — of wood*, la nostra scala a pioli è fatta parte in ferro e parte in legno.

to **partake** [pɑːˈteik], *pass.* **partook** [pɑːˈtuk], *p.p.* **partaken** [pɑːˈteikən], *v.t.i.* **1.** partecipare, prendere parte: *they partook of the same games*, essi partecipavano agli stessi giuochi; *we partook in the same feelings*, condividevamo gli stessi sentimenti **2.** prendere una porzione (di cibo): *he partook of our supper*, partecipò alla nostra cena; *she partook of the cake*, (*fam.*) si prese buona parte della focaccia.

partaker [pɑːˈteikə*], *s.* partecipante.

parted [ˈpɑːtid], *ag.* **1.** separato, diviso **2.** (*arc.*) morto ☆ *four- —, three- —*, quadripartito, tripartito.

parterre [pɑːˈtɛə*], *s.* **1.** aiuola **2.** (*teat.*) « parterre », platea.

parthenogenesis [ˈpɑːθinouˈdʒenisis], *s.* (*biol.*) partenogenesi.

Parthenon [ˈpɑːθinən], *s.* Partenone.

Parthenope [pɑːˈθenəpi], *no.pr.f.* (*mit.*) Partenope.

Parthian [ˈpɑːθjən], *ag.s.* (*st. romana*) Parto || — *shot* (o — *shaft*), freccia del Parto.

parti [ˈpɑːti], *s.* partito: *she is a desirable —*, è un partito desiderabile.

partial [ˈpɑːʃəl], *ag.* **1.** parziale; propenso, favorevole: — *to*, propenso verso **2.** parziale, non totale: — *eclipse*, eclisse parziale.

partiality [ˌpɑːʃiˈæliti], *s.* **1.** parzialità; favoritismo **2.** predilezione: — *for sthg.*, predilezione per ql.co.

partially [ˈpɑːʃəli], *av.* **1.** parzialmente, in parte **2.** parzialmente, con parzialità.

partibility [ˌpɑːtiˈbiliti], *s.* divisibilità.

partible [ˈpɑːtibl], *ag.* divisibile.

participance [pɑːˈtisipəns], *s.* (*amer.*) partecipazione.

participant [pɑːˈtisipənt], *ag.* partecipe || *s.c.* partecipante.

to **participate** [pɑːˈtisipeit], *v.t.i.* **1.** partecipare; prendere parte a; condividere: *he did not — in the conversation*, egli non prese parte alla conversazione; *I — in your joy*, prendo parte alla vostra gioia **2.** partecipare: *he participates of the intelligence of his mother*, ha qualche cosa dell'intelligenza della madre || *to — sthg. with s.o.*, dividere ql.co. con qlcu.

participation [pɑːˌtisiˈpeiʃən], *s* partecipazione.

participator [pɑːˈtisipeitə*], *s.c.* partecipante.

participial [ˌpɑːtiˈsipiəl], *ag.* (*gram.*) participiale.

participle [ˈpɑːtisipl], *s.* (*gram.*) participio.

particle [ˈpɑːtikl], *s.* **1.** particella: *there is not a — of truth in this story*, non c'è ombra di verità in questa storia **2.** (*gram.*) particella **3.** (*eccl.*) particola.

particoloured [ˈpɑːtiˌkʌləd], *ag.* multicolore; variegato.

particular [pəˈtikjulə*], *ag.* **1.** particolare, speciale; individuale, personale: *for no — reason*, per nessuna ragione speciale; *he took — trouble*, si prese un grande disturbo; *whatever his — hobby may be*, qualunque sia il suo particolare passatempo || *in —*, in particolare, specialmente: *they mentioned one case in —*, citarono un caso in particolare **2.** accurato; dettagliato; esatto: *a full and — account*, un minuzioso resoconto **3.** esigente; meticoloso; puntiglioso: *he's very — about his suits*, è molto esigente per quanto riguarda i suoi abiti || *I am not — about it*, non ho preferenze || *s.* **1.** particolare, dettaglio: *the particulars of a business*, le circostanze particolari di un affare **2.** informazione, ragguaglio: *for further particulars*, per ulteriori informazioni; *he was asked every — about himself*, gli furono richiesti tutti i suoi dati personali.

particularism [pəˈtikjulərizəm], *s.* (*pol. teol.*) particolarismo.

particularist [pəˈtikjulərist], *s.* (*pol. teol.*) particolarista.

particularity [pəˌtikjuˈlæriti], *s.* **1.** particolarità, singolarità, peculiarità **2.** meticolosità **3.** (*arc.*) cura assidua; attenzione particolare: *particularities to s.o.*, cure particolari verso qlcu.

particularization [pəˌtikjuləraiˈzeiʃən], *s.* particolarizzazione.

to **particularize** [pəˈtikjuləraiz], *v.t.i.* particolareggiare; dettagliare; specificare.

particularly [pəˈtikjuləli], *av.* particolarmente; dettagliatamente; specificatamente.

parting [ˈpɑːtiŋ], *s.* **1.** congedo; partenza; separazione: *to be at the — of the ways*, trovarsi al bivio (anche *fig.*) **2.** divisione, scriminatura **3.** (*geol.*) fessura **4.** (*mar.*) rottura di una gomena ☆ — *directions*, ultime raccomandazioni prima della partenza; — *look*, uno sguardo d'addio; — *visit*, una visita di congedo.

partisan[1] [ˌpɑːtiˈzæn], *ag.* partigiano (anche *mil.*) || *s.* **1.** partigiano **2.** (*mil.*) partigiano; guerrigliero.

partisan[2] [ˈpɑːtizən], *s.* (*st.*) **1.** partigiana **2.** soldato armato di partigiana.

partisanship [ˌpɑːtiˈzænʃip] *s.* partigianeria; settarismo.

partite [ˈpɑːtait], *ag.* (*bot. enom.*) partito.

partition [pɑːˈtiʃən], *s.* **1.** divisione, separazione; (*dir.*) divisione; spartizione **2.** (*mat.*) scomposizione **3.** divisorio, tramezzo **4.** sezione compartimento.

to **partition**, *v.t.* dividere, separare; spartire; smembrare || *to — (off) a room*, dividere una stanza con un tramezzo, con un divisorio.

partitioned [pɑːˈtiʃənd], *ag.* diviso da tramezzo.

partitive [ˈpɑːtitiv], *ag.s.* (*gram.*) partitivo.

partizan, *V.* **partisan**[1].

partly [ˈpɑːtli], *av.* in parte.

partner [ˈpɑːtnə*], *s.c.* **1.** (*comm.*) socio, socia: *let's be partners*, associamoci **2.** « partner » (dama, cavaliere al ballo): *he was my — in the last dance*, fu il mio cavaliere nell'ultimo ballo **3.** marito, moglie || *s.pl.* (*mar.*) mastre ☆ *active* (o *managing-*) —, (*comm.*) socio gerente; *general* —, (*comm.*) socio accomandatario; *limited* (o *sleeping-*) —, (*comm.*) socio accomandante; *nominal* —, socio nominale; *secret* —, (*comm.*) socio occulto.

to **partner**, *v.t.* **1.** essere socio di; associare, associarsi a: *to — s.o. with s.o.*, associare una persona a un'altra **2.** essere il « partner » di (nei giuochi, ecc.) **3.** guidare (una dama in un ballo).

partnership [ˈpɑːtnəʃip], *s.* **1.** associazione: *I was charged with — in the crime*, fui accusato di complicità nel delitto **2.** (*comm.*) società, associazione: *deed* (o *articles*) *of —*, contratto di associazione; *to dissolve a —*, sciogliere una società; *to enter* (o *to go*) *into —*, entrare a far parte di una società, associarsi; *to give s.o. a — in the business*, interessare qlcu. nella propria azienda ☆ *general* — (o *unlimited* —), società in nome collettivo; *limited* —, società in accomandita semplice.

partook [pɑ:'tuk], *pass.* di to **partake**.

partridge ['pɑ:tridʒ], *s* pernice: *a brace of partridges*, una coppia di pernici ☆ — *-berry*, (*bot.*) gaultheria del Canada; — *-net*, bucine per pernici; — *-poult* (o *young* —), perniciotto; — *-wood*, legno pernice.

parturient [pɑ:'tjuəriənt], *ag.* 1. partoriente 2. *fig.* che sta per generare (un'idea, ecc.).

parturition [,pɑ:tjuə'rifən], *s.* parto.

party¹ ['pɑ:ti], *s.* 1. parte, partito politico, fazione 2. brigata, comitiva; riunione, trattenimento: *they were a big* —, erano una comitiva numerosa; *will you join our* —?, vuoi essere dei nostri?; *to give a* —, dare una festa 3. (*mil.*) pattuglia, plotone 4. (*dir. comm.*) parte, parte in causa, parte interessata: *for account of a third* —, per conto terzi; *to become* — *to an action*, costituirsi parte in un processo; *to become a* — *to an agreement*, firmare un contratto; *to be* (o *to become*) *a* — *to a crime*, rendersi complice in un delitto; *to make s.o. a* — *to an undertaking*, associare qlcu. a un'impresa 5. (*fam.*) individuo, persona: *the* — *in a white hat*, l'individuo dal cappello bianco ☆ — *-dress* (o — *-frock*), abito da sera; — *-leader*, capo di partito; — *-line*, politica di un partito; — *-man*, partigiano, uomo di partito; — *-politics*, politica di partito; — *-spirit*, spirito di parte; — *-wall*, (*arch.*) muro comune divisorio (tra due proprietà) ‖ *advance* —, avanguardia; *contracting* —, (*comm.*) parte contraente; *dinner* —, pranzo; *fatigue* —, squadra di corvè; *firing* —, plotone d'esecuzione; *garden* —, ricevimento all'aperto; *injured* —, parte lesa; *landing* —, pattuglia da sbarco; *rescue* — (o *search* —), squadra di soccorso; *shooting* —, partita di caccia; *storming* —, truppe d'assalto.

party², *ag.* (*arald.*) diviso in parti di diverso colore.

partyism ['pɑ:tiizəm], *s.* spirito di parte.

parvenu ['pɑ:vənju:], *ag.s.* (da) nuovo ricco.

parvis ['pɑ:vis], *s.* sagrato.

pas [pɑ:], *s.* 1. passo, precedenza 2. passo di danza.

paschal ['pɑ:skəl], *ag.* pasquale: — *lamb*, agnello pasquale.

pascual ['pæskjuəl], *ag.* di pascolo.

pasha ['pɑ:fə], *s.* pascià.

pashalic ['pɑ:fəlik], *s.* pascialato, giurisdizione di un pascià.

Pasiphae [pə'sifii:], *no.pr.f.* (*mit.*) Pasifae, Pasife.

pasque-flower ['pɑ:sk,flauə*], *s.* (*bot.*) anemone.

Pasquin¹ ['pæskwin], *no.pr.m.* Pasquino.

to **pasquin²**, *v.t.i.* satireggiare.

pasquinade [,pæskwi'neid], *s.* pasquinata, satira.

to **pasquinade**, *v.t.* satireggiare.

pass¹ [pɑ:s], *s.* passo; passaggio; valico; gola, strettoia; (*rar.*) guado ‖ *to sell the* —, tradire il proprio paese, il proprio partito ☆ *fish*- —, passaggio per i pesci (sopra, in una diga).

pass², *s.* 1. passaggio ‖ *to bring to* —, portare a compimento; *to come to* —, capitare, aver luogo 2. trapasso, decesso 3. promozione 4. posizione, situazione: *things came to such a* — *that...*, le cose giunsero a tal punto che... 5. lasciapassare; permesso; (*mil.*) certificato di licenza: *soldier on* —, soldato in permesso 6. (*free*) —, biglietto di viaggio gratuito; biglietto (di teatro, ecc.) di favore 7. (*metal.*) canale; (*miner.*) fornello di gettito. trucco (di prestigiatore) 9. (*scherma*) botta, stoccata, passata, assalto 10. (*calcio*) passaggio 11. (*carte*) astensione temporanea dal giuoco ☆ — *-book*, libretto di banca; (*aut.*) trittico; — *-key*, « passe-partout » ‖ *custom-house* —, lasciapassare della dogana; *international travelling* —, (*aut.*) permesso internazionale di circolazione.

to **pass²**, *pass.p.p.* **passed** [pɑ:st], *v.t.i.* 1. passare, oltrepassare; superare, sorpassare: *to* — *an examination*, passare un esame; *to* — *from one place to another*, passare da un luogo a un altro; *to* — *a headland*, oltrepassare, doppiare un capo ‖ *he had already passed the*

Chair, era già stato presidente ‖ *to* — *by the name of*, essere conosciuto sotto il nome di ‖ *to* — *for (as)*, passare per ‖ *to* — *from s.o., sthg.*, allontanarsi da qlcu., ql.co. ‖ *to* — *in review*, (*mil.*) passare in rivista 2. trascorrere: *a fortnight passed*, passarono quindici giorni; *how time passes!*, come passa il tempo! 3. accadere: *I know what has passed*, so quello che è accaduto 4. (*comm.*) aver corso: *coin that passes in England*, moneta corrente in Inghilterra 5. accettare, approvare, essere approvato; ammettere: *the bill won't* —, il progetto di legge non sarà approvato; *to* — *a candidate*, promuovere un candidato (ad un esame); *to* — *a dividend*, (*comm.*) approvare un dividendo 6. dare, passare: — *me the water please*, passami l'acqua, per favore; *to* — *one's word*, dare la propria parola ‖ *to* — *a sentence*, (*dir.*) emettere una sentenza 7. passare, rinunciare (a carte) 8. *to* — *across* (*sthg.*) attraversare 9. *to* — *along* (*sthg.*), passare per (la strada, ecc.) 10. *to* — *between* (*s.o.*), intercorrere fra 11. *to* — *by* (*s.o., sthg.*), passare per; passare a fianco di; non curarsi di 12. *to* — *into* (*sthg.*), trasformarsi, diventare: *that sentence has passed into a proverb*, quella frase è divenuta proverbiale; *water passes into steam*, l'acqua si trasforma in vapore 13. *to* — *over* (*sthg.*), oltrepassare; attraversare; tralasciare; omettere; sorvolare su: *let us* — *over these things*, non parliamo di queste cose; *to* — *over an obstacle*, superare un ostacolo 14. *to* — *round* (*s.o., sthg.*), circondare, aggirare 15. *to* — *through*, attraversare, passare attraverso: *traveller passing through Paris*, viaggiatore di passaggio a Parigi; *to* — *through a crisis*, attraversare una crisi 16. *to* — *along*, passare oltre, circolare; far passare di mano in mano 17. *to* — *away*, sparire, dissiparsi, morire: *his anger soon passed away*, la sua ira si dissipò presto; *she passed away in the night*, morì durante la notte 18. *to* — *by*, sfilare; passare oltre: *the procession passed by slowly*, il corteo sfilò lentamente; *to* — *by on the other side*, passare sull'altro lato (di strada, ecc.) 19. *to* — *in*, entrare ‖ *to* — *in one's checks*, (*sl. amer.*) morire 20. *to* — *off*, passare, svanire; far passare per: *the novelty will soon* — *off*, la novità passerà presto; *to* — *off one's goods as those of another brand*, far passare i propri prodotti per quelli di un'altra marca ‖ *to* — *sthg. off as a joke*, prendere ql.co. in ridere 21. *to* — *on*, far circolare; trasmettere; passar oltre; morire; circolare: — *on please!*, circolate! ‖ *to* — *on to a new subject*, passare a un nuovo argomento 22. *to* — *out*, uscire; (*fam.*) svenire; morire ‖ *to* — *sthg. out of one's hands*, cedere ql.co.; *to* — *sthg. out of the window*, far uscire ql.co. dalla finestra 23. *to* — *over*, passare; morire; dissiparsi (di tempesta): *to* — *over to the enemy*, passare al nemico 24. *to* — *round*, (far) circolare: *to* — *round the wine*, far passare il vino.

passable ['pɑ:səbl], *ag.* 1. praticabile; guadabile, navigabile 2. passabile, discreto; adeguato 3. corrente (di moneta) 4. che può entrare in vigore (di legge).

passably ['pɑ:səbli], *av.* passabilmente, abbastanza.

passage¹ ['pæsidʒ], *s.* 1. passaggio; migrazione; transito: — *of birds*, passaggio di uccelli; — *of a ray of light*, passaggio di un raggio di luce; *bird of* —, uccello migratore 2. tragitto; traversata; viaggio su nave: *to have a bad, fine* —, avere, fare una cattiva, buona traversata; *to get free* — *in a steamer*, ottenere un passaggio gratuito in battello 3. passaggio, varco: *to force one's* —, aprirsi a forza un varco 4. corridoio, andito 5. diritto, permesso di passaggio: *to pay for one's* —, pagare il proprio passaggio; *to work one's* —, guadagnarsi la traversata lavorando 6. adozione, approvazione (di legge) 7. (*lett. mus.*) brano, passo: *selected passages from*, passi scelti da; *this* — *is extremely difficult*, questo brano è estremamente difficile 8. rapporto, scambio: — *of arms*, conflitto 9. scambio (di parole, colpi, gentilezze, ecc.) fra due persone 10. (*anat.*) condotto, canale; (*fisiol.*) escrezione ☆ — *-boat*, (*mar.*) postale; — *-money*, pedaggio; — *-way*, vicolo; (*amer.*) corridoio to **passage**[1], *v.i.* **1.** viaggiare; compiere una traversata **2.** prendere parte a un combattimento, una lite.

to **passage**[2], *v.t.i.* avanzare di fianco (di cavallo); far avanzare (il cavallo) di fianco.

passant ['pæsənt], *ag.* (*arald.*) passante (di animali).

passé ['pɑːsei], *ag.* passato; antiquato; sfiorito.

passementerie [pæs'mentri], *s.* passamaneria.

passenger ['pæsindʒə*], *s.c.* viaggiatore, viaggiatrice; passeggiero, passeggiera ☆ — *-service*, servizio passeggieri; — *-train*, treno viaggiatori.

passer ['pɑːsə*], *s.c.* passante ☆ — *-by*, passante.

Passeres ['pæsəriːz], *s.pl.* (*ornit.*) passeracei.

passerine ['pæsərain], *ag.* di, simile a passero.

passibility [,pæsi'biliti], *s.* passibilità.

passible ['pæsibl], *ag.* passibile.

passim ['pæsim], *av.* (*lat.*) passim, qua e là.

passimeter [pæ'simitə*], *s.* distributore automatico di biglietti ferroviari.

passing ['pɑːsiŋ], *ag.* **1.** passante **2.** effimero, passeggiero; rapido; fuggevole **3.** casuale; incidentale ‖ *s.* **1.** passaggio; transito; superamento; *fig.* morte, trapasso ‖ *the* — *in and out,* (*comm.*) le entrate e le uscite ‖ *in* —, incidentalmente; tra parentesi **2.** adozione, entrata in vigore, approvazione (di legge) **3.** ammissione (di candidato) **4.** pronunciazione (di sentenza, giudizio) **5.** (*calcio*) passaggio ‖ *av.* assai; eccessivamente; in sommo grado: *he is* — *rich*, è straricco ☆ — *away*, morte; — *-bell*, campana a morto; — *-note*, (*mus.*) nota di passaggio; — *on*, trasmissione (di ordine, ecc.); — *through*, traversata.

passion ['pæʃən], *s.* **1.** passione, ardore, zelo: *they always work with* —, lavorano sempre con passione **2.** passione, collera, sdegno: *to give way* (o *to yield*) *to one's passions*, abbandonarsi alle proprie passioni; *to put s.o. into a* —, far andare qlcu. su tutte le furie **3.** passione, amore: *he conceived a short but violent* — *for her*, concepì per lei un amore breve ma violento **4.** *the Passion*, (*relig.*) la Passione ‖ *Passion-play*, (*st. lett.*) Mistero della Passione ‖ *Passion-Sunday*, Domenica di Passione; *Passion-tide*, periodo pasquale; *Passion-week*, Settimana di Passione ‖ *Saint Mathew Passion*, (*mus.*) Passione secondo San Matteo ☆ — *-flower*, (*bot.*) passiflora.

to **passion**, *v.t.i.* (*poet.*) permeare di passione; esprimere passione.

passional ['pæʃənl], *ag.* passionale ‖ *s.* (*eccl.*) passionale.

passionate ['pæʃənit], *ag.* **1.** appassionato; passionale **2.** irascibile **3.** forte, veemente (di emozione, sentimento).

passionately ['pæʃənitli], *av.* **1.** appassionatamente; perdutamente **2.** con ira **3.** veementemente.

passionateness ['pæʃənitnis], *s.* **1.** passione **2.** passionalità **3.** veemenza.

passioned ['pæʃənd], *ag.* appassionato.

Passionist ['pæʃənist], *s.* (*eccl.*) passionista.

passionless ['pæʃənlis], *ag.* impassibile; calmo.

passive ['pæsiv], *ag.* passivo (anche *gram.*) ‖ *s.* (*gram.*) passivo ☆ — *debts*, debiti sui quali non si paga interesse; — *resistance*, resistenza passiva.

passively ['pæsivli], *av.* passivamente.

passiveness ['pæsivnis], *s.* passività, inerzia.

passivism ['pæsivizəm], *s.* (*amer.*) attitudine alla passività, all'inerzia.

passivity [pæ'siviti], *s.* passività, inerzia.

passkey ['pɑːs-kiː], *s.* « passe-partout » (chiave universale).

passman ['pɑːs-mæn], *pl.* **passmen** ['pɑːs-men], *s.* studente di Oxford che si laurea col minimo dei voti.

passover ['pɑːs,ouvə*], *s.* (*arc.*) agnello pasquale; *fig.* Cristo: *to eat the* —, mangiar l'agnello pasquale ‖ *Passover*, Pasqua ebraica.

passport ['pɑːs-pɔːt], *s.* passaporto; lasciapassare; salvacondotto.

password ['pɑːs-wəːd], *s.* (*mil.*) parola d'ordine.

past [pɑːst], *ag.* **1.** passato, trascorso; compiuto, consumato, finito: *the* — *week*, la settimana scorsa; *her prime is* —, la sua bellezza è sfiorita **2.** (*gram.*) passato ‖ *s.* **1.** passato: *a city with a* —, una metropoli con una storia; *a woman with a* —, una donna di dubbia reputazione; *to undo the* —, distruggere il passato **2.** (*gram.*) tempo passato.

past, *av.* vicino, presso; oltre: *he ran* —, passò oltre di corsa ‖ *prep.* dopo; al di là di; fuori di, senza: *an old man* — *eighty*, un vecchio di oltre ottant'anni; *it is* — *hope*, è al di là di ogni speranza; *they stayed till* — *three o'clock*, si fermarono fin dopo le tre ‖ *half* — *three*, le tre e mezzo ‖ *he 's* — *praying for*, (*fam.*) è un caso disperato.

paste [peist], *s.* **1.** pasta; impasto **2.** (*amer.*) colla (di farina): colla forte da pittore **3.** impasto per gemme false; gemme false **4.** (*elett.*) massa attiva ☆ *anchovy* —, pasta d'acciughe; *puff* —, pasta sfoglia; *starch* —, colla d'amido; *tooth-* —, pasta dentrifica.

to **paste**, *v.t.* **1.** impastare **2.** incollare, appiccicare **3.** (*sl. aer.*) martellare, distruggere bombardando.

paste-board ['peistbɔːd], *ag.* di cartone; *fig.* inconsistente; fittizio ‖ *s.* **1.** cartone **2.** (*sl.*) carta da visita **3.** (*sl.*) carta da giuoco **4.** (*sl.*) biglietto ferroviario **5.** (*cuc.*) asse per la pasta.

pastel[1] ['pæs'tel], *s.* **1.** pastello **2.** quadro a pastello; l'arte di dipingere a pastello ☆ — *crayon*, matita a pastello.

pastel[2] ['pæstel], *s.* **1.** (*bot.*) guado **2.** tintura azzurra ricavata dal guado.

pastellist [pæs'telist], *s.* (*pitt.*) pastellista.

pastern ['pæstən], *s.* pasturale (di cavallo).

pasteurism ['pæstərizəm], *s.* (*med.*) metodo Pasteur (per la cura dell'idrofobia).

pasteurization [,pæstərai'zeiʃən], *s.* pastorizzazione.

to **pasteurize** ['pæstəraiz], *v.t.* pastorizzare.

pastiche [pæs'tiːʃ], *s.* (*lett. mus. pitt.*) «pastiche» (accozzaglia di elementi eterogenei a carattere satirico).

pastil(le) ['pæsti:l], *s.* **1.** pastiglia, pasticca **2.** pastiglia di resina da bruciare per profumare, deodorare un ambiente.

pastime ['pɑːs-taim], *s.* passatempo.

pastor ['pɑːstə*], *s.* **1.** (*eccl.*) pastore **2.** (*rar.*) pastore, guardiano di greggi.

pastoral ['pɑːstərəl], *ag.* pastorale: — *symphony*, sinfonia pastorale ‖ *s.* **1.** (*poes.*) pastorale, idillio; (*mus.*) pastorale **2.** (*eccl.*) lettera pastorale **3.** pastorale (bastone vescovile).

pastorale [,pæstə'rɑːli], *s.* componimento musicale a soggetto pastorale.

pastorally ['pɑːstərəli], *av.* in modo pastorale; semplicemente.

pastorate ['pɑːstərit], *s.* (*eccl.*) **1.** ufficio di pastore **2.** i pastori (collettivamente).

pastry ['peistri], *s.* **1.** dolci, pasticceria **2.** pasta (da dolci, pasticci) ☆ — *-board*, asse per la pasta.

pastrycook ['peistrikuk], *s.* pasticciere.

pasturable ['pɑːstjurəbl], *ag.* pascolativo.

pasturage ['pɑːstjuridʒ], *s.* pastura, pascolo.

pasture ['pɑːstʃə*], *s.* pascolo, pastura ☆ — *land*, (terreno da) pascolo.

to **pasture**, *v.t.i.* **1.** condurre al pascolo **2.** pascolare.

pasty ['peisti] *come s.* ['pæsti], *ag.* di pasta, pastoso (anche di colore); molle; scialbo ‖ *s.* (*cuc.*) pasticcio ☆ — *-faced*, dal viso pallido.

pat[1] [pæt], *ag.* opportuno, adatto; proprio; giusto; felice (di espressione, ecc.): *he always had an excuse* —, avere sempre una scusa pronta ‖ *av.* a proposito; esattamente: *his story came* — *to the purpose*, la sua storia servì appuntino allo scopo; *to know sthg. off* —, sapere ql.co. esattamente, a memoria ‖ *to stand* —, (*amer. sl.*) rimaner saldo sulla propria posizione ‖ *s.* **1.** buffetto, colpetto: *a* — *on the back*, un colpetto sulla spalla; *fig.* elogio, incoraggiamento **2.** pallina (di sostanza malleabile); pane di burro **3.** scalpiccio, ticchettio ☆ — -a-cake, giuoco di bambini (del tipo « batti-batti le manine »); — hand, carte servite (al poker).

to **pat**[1], pass.p.p. **patted** ['pætid], v.t.i. **1.** carezzare; dare un buffetto a; battere affettuosamente (sulla spalla, ecc.): he patted his pupil on the back, incoraggiò il suo allievo battendogli affettuosamente sulla spalla **2.** tamburellare (con le dita).

Pat[2], no.pr.m. dim. di **Patrick** || no.pr.f. dim. di **Patricia** || s. (scherz.) irlandese (da St. Patrick, patrono d'Irlanda).

patch [pætʃ], s. **1.** pezza, toppa || it is not a — on this one, (fam.) è molto inferiore rispetto a questo **2.** benda (su un occhio ferito); cerotto **3.** neo posticcio **4.** macchia; chiazza || to strike a bad —, attraversare un periodo sfortunato **5.** appezzamento: a — of potatoes, un pezzo di terra coltivato a patate ☆ — -box, scatolino porta nèi; — pocket, tasca applicata.

to **patch**, v.t. **1.** aggiustare; mettere una pezza a: I must try to — the pieces of this vase together, debbo cercare di mettere assieme i pezzi di questo vaso **2.** applicare nèi posticci a **3.** to — up, accomodare, rappezzare: they will — up the roof, accomoderanno il tetto; this business is to be patched up at any cost, bisogna accomodare la faccenda a tutti costi; you have got to — up your blouse, devi rammendarti la camicetta.

patched [pætʃt], ag. rappezzato, rattoppato; fatto in tutta fretta.

patcher ['pætʃə*], s.c. rappezzatore, rappezzatrice.

patchery ['pætʃəri], s. rappezzamento.

patchiness ['pætʃinis], s. **1.** rappezzatura **2.** disposizione a macchie, chiazze.

patchwork ['pætʃwə:k], s. **1.** mescolanza di cose eterogenee, confuse, irregolari **2.** lavoro di cucito formato da pezze di diversi colori **3.** fig. raffazzonamento, mosaico.

patchy ['pætʃi], ag. **1.** rappezzato, rattoppato **2.** a macchie, a chiazze **3.** fig. irregolare; vario; non uniforme: — knowledge, istruzione eclettica.

pate [peit], s. (fam.) **1.** capo, zucca: bald —, testa pelata **2.** cervello.

pâté [pɑ:'tei], s. (cuc.) pâté, pasticcio.

patella [pə'telə], pl. **patellae** [pə'teli:], s. **1.** (anat.) rotula **2.** (zool.) patella **3.** (archeol.) piccola padella.

paten ['pætən], s. **1.** (eccl.) patena **2.** piattino di metallo.

patency ['peitənsi], s. **1.** evidenza, chiarezza **2.** (med.) pervietà.

patent ['peitənt, spec. amer. 'pætənt], ag. **1.** manifesto, evidente, ovvio; piano, chiaro: a — absurdity, un'evidente assurdità **2.** privilegiato, che ha diritto, privilegio riconosciuto **3.** brevettato, patentato **4.** (fam.) originale, ingegnoso: he has a — device for avoiding seasickness, ha un modo suo proprio per evitare il mal di mare || s. **1.** brevetto; cosa brevettata: to apply for a —, chiedere un brevetto; to grant s.o. a —, concedere un brevetto a qlcu.; to take out a —, brevettare **2.** privilegio ufficiale: a — of nobility, una patente di nobiltà ☆ — food, specialità alimentare; — -leather, cuoio verniciato; — medicine, specialità farmaceutica; Patent Office, ufficio brevetti; — -right, diritto di brevetto || letters- —, ordinanze, decreti sovrani.

to **patent**, v.t. brevettare.

patentable ['peitəntəbl], ag. brevettabile.

patented ['peitəntid], ag. brevettato.

patentee [,peintən'ti:], s. **1.** detentore di brevetto **2.** concessionario di brevetto.

pater ['peitə*], s. (fam.) padre, papà.

paterfamilias ['peitəfə'miliæs], s. (st. scherz.) padre di famiglia, genitore; capo famiglia.

paternal [pə'tə:nl], ag. **1.** paterno **2.** paternalistico: — government, governo paternalistico.

paternalism [pə'tə:nəlizm], s. paternalismo.

paternally [pə'tə:nəli], av. paternamente.

paternity [pə'tə:niti], s. paternità (anche fig.).

paternoster ['pætə'nɔstə*], s. **1.** padrenostro (pre-

ghiera) **2.** grano del padrenostro in un rosario; rosario **3.** preghiera borbottata || devil's —, imprecazione borbottata a mezza voce ☆ — line, (pesca) dirlindana.

path [pɑ:θ], pl. **paths** [pɑ:ðz], s. **1.** sentiero, viottolo, stradicciuola: a trodden —, un sentiero battuto **2.** sentiero riservato a pedoni **3.** orbita (di un pianeta), traiettoria **4.** (spor.) pista **5.** fig. linea di condotta.

pathetic [pə'θetik], ag. patetico; commovente: a — sight, uno spettacolo commovente ☆ — muscle, (anat.) muscolo grande obliquo dell'occhio.

pathetically [pə'θetikəli], av. pateticamente, in modo commovente.

pathetics [pə'θetiks], s.pl. **1.** studio del patetico **2.** sensibilità eccessiva.

pathfinder ['pɑ:θ,faində*], s. **1.** esploratore; pioniere **2.** (aer.) ricognitore.

pathless ['pɑ:θlis], ag. **1.** privo di sentieri **2.** inesplorato; impenetrabile.

pathogen ['pæθoudʒen], s. microbo patogeno.

pathogenesis [,pæθou'dʒenisis], s. patogenesi.

pathogenetic [,pæθoudʒi'netik], **pathogenic** [,pæθou'dʒenik], **pathogenous** [pə'θɔdʒinəs], ag. patogeno.

pathogeny [pə'θɔdʒini], s. patogenesi.

pathologic(al) [,pæθə'lɔdʒik(əl)], ag. patologico.

pathologically [,pæθə'lɔdʒikəli], av. patologicamente.

pathologist [pə'θɔlədʒist], s. patologo.

pathology [pə'θɔlədʒi], s. patologia.

pathos ['peiθɔs], s. pathos, commozione.

pathway ['pɑ:θ-wei], s. sentiero.

patience ['peiʃəns], s. **1.** pazienza, calma, sopportazione: he wore out my —, mi fece perdere le staffe; to be out of — with s.o., non poter più sopportare qlcu.; to drive s.o. past —, far perdere la pazienza a qlcu.; to have no — with, non aver pazienza alcuna con: to try s.o.'s —, mettere alla prova la pazienza di qlcu. **2.** perseveranza, costanza **3.** (carte) solitario ☆ — -dock, (bot.) romice, pazienza.

patient ['peiʃənt], ag. **1.** paziente; tollerante: — of sthg., che sopporta ql.co. **2.** diligente, perseverante **3.** passibile, suscettibile: his words are — of two interpretations, le sue parole si prestano a due interpretazioni || s. paziente, ammalato.

patiently ['peiʃəntli], av. pazientemente, con pazienza.

patina ['pætinə], s. patina.

patinated ['pætineitid], ag. patinato.

patination [,pæti'neiʃən], s. patinatura.

patois ['pætwɑ:], s. dialetto, gergo.

Patras [pə'træs], no.pr. (geog.) Patrasso.

patriarch ['peitriɑ:k], s. patriarca.

patriarchal [,peitri'ɑ:kəl], ag. patriarcale.

patriarchate ['peitriɑ:kit], s. (eccl.) patriarcato.

patriarchy ['peitriɑ:ki], s. patriarcato (sistema sociale di governo).

Patricia [pə'triʃə], no.pr.f. Patrizia.

patrician[1] [pə'triʃən], ag. s. patrizio.

patrician[2], s. (st. eccl.) patriciano.

patriciate [pə'triʃiit], s. patriziato.

patricidal [,pætri'saidl], ag. (rar.) parricida.

patricide ['pætrisaid], s. **1.** parricidio **2.** parricida.

Patrick ['pætrik], no.pr.m. Patrizio.

patrimonial [,pætri'mounjəl], ag. patrimoniale, ereditario.

patrimony ['pætriməni], s. **1.** patrimonio, beni ereditari **2.** patrimonio (di una chiesa, di un'istituzione).

patriot ['peitriət], s. patriota.

patriotic [,pætri'ɔtik], ag. patriottico.

patriotically [,pætri'ɔtikəli], av. patriotticamente.

patriotism ['pætriətizəm], s. patriottismo.

patristic [pə'tristik], ag. patristico, dei Padri della Chiesa.

patristics [pə'tristiks], s.pl. (teol.) patristica.

Patroclus [pə'trɔkləs], no.pr.m. (lett.) Patroclo.

patrol [pə'troul], s. **1.** pattuglia; ronda: on —, di guardia **2.** (aer.) volo di ricognizione ☆ — -wagon, (amer.) carrozzone cellulare.

to **patrol**, *pass.p.p.* **patrolled** [pə'trould], *v.t.i.* (*mil.*) pattugliare; fare la ronda; perlustrare.

patrolman [pə'troulmæn], *pl.* **patrolmen** [pə'troulmen], *s.* (*mil.*) chi è di pattuglia; (*amer.*) poliziotto.

patron ['peitrən], *s.* **1.** patrono; benefattore, mecenate; protettore: *a — of the arts*, un mecenate dello arti || *Patron Saint's Day*, festa del Santo Patrono **2.** (*fam.*) cliente abituale (di negozio).

patronage ['pætrənidʒ], *s.* **1.** patronato, mecenatismo, patrocinio **2.** facoltà di assegnare certi uffici (ecclesiastici) od onori (politici) **3.** (*fam.*) clientela abituale (di negozio).

patronal [pə'trounl], *ag.* patronale; protettivo.

patroness ['peitrənis], *s.* patronessa.

to **patronize** ['pætrənaiz], *v.t.* **1.** patrocinare; proteggere; favorire; incoraggiare **2.** trattare con condiscendenza **3.** essere cliente abituale di (negozio).

patronizer ['pætrənaizə*], *s.c.* patrocinatore, patrocinatrice; protettore, protettrice.

patronizing ['pætrənaiziŋ], *ag.* **1.** protettivo; protettore **2.** condiscendente.

patronizingly ['pætrənaiziŋli], *av.* **1.** con aria di protezione **2.** in modo condiscendente.

patronless ['peitrənlis], *ag.* senza patrono; senza protettore.

patronymic [,pætrə'nimik], *ag. s.* patronimico.

patroon [pə'tru:n], *s.* (*st. amer.*) possidente terriero sotto l'antica amministrazione olandese di New York e del New Jersey.

patten ['pætn], *s.* **1.** sorta di soprascarpa con suola lignea per tenere il piede sollevato dal fango **2.** (*arch.*) zoccolo.

patter[1] ['pætə*], *s.* **1.** gergo, linguaggio particolare **2.** discorso rapido e meccanico (da imbonitori, ciarlatani, ecc.) **3.** parole di una canzone, commedia, ecc.

to **patter**[1], *v.t.i.* **1.** recitare (preghiere) meccanicamente **2.** parlare in fretta e meccanicamente (a mo' di imbonitori, ciarlatani, ecc.).

patter[2], *s.* picchiettio; ticchettio (di pioggia); successione di piccoli colpi.

to **patter**[2], *v.t.i.* **1.** picchiettare; far picchiettare: *the rain was pattering against the roof*, la pioggia picchiettava sul tetto **2.** camminare a passi corti e veloci; sgambettare (detto di bambini, ecc.).

pattern ['pætən], *s.* **1.** modello, esempio; campione; tipo; ideale: *a bicycle of an old —*, una bicicletta di vecchio tipo: *she cut her dress out on a paper —*, si tagliò il vestito su un modello di carta **2.** disegno (di stoffa, tappezzerie, ecc.): *what a nice —!*, che bel disegno! ☆ *— book*, campionario (di stoffe, ecc.); *— designer*, disegnatore di modelli; *— -moulder*, fabbricante di modelli; *— wife*, moglie ideale.

to **pattern**, *v.t.* **1.** eseguire sulla base di un modello: *to — sthg. after* (o *upon*) *a design*, eseguire ql.co. sulla base di un disegno **2.** decorare (stoffe, tappezzerie, ecc.) con disegni.

patty ['pæti], *s.* « vol-au-vent » (sorta di pasticcio) ☆ *— pan*, teglia per cuocere tale pasticcio.

patulous ['pætjuləs], *ag.* aperto, largo, disteso.

paucity [po:siti], *s.* scarsità; insufficienza.

Paul [po:l], *no.pr.m.* Paolo.

Paula ['po:lə], *no.pr.f.* Paola.

Paulina [po:'lainə], **Pauline** [po:'li:n], *no.pr.f. dim.* di Paula.

Pauline ['po:lain], *ag.* paolino, di S. Paolo || *the — Epistles*, le lettere di S. Paolo || *s.* allievo della Scuola di S. Paolo a Londra.

Paulinus [po:'lainəs], *no.pr.m.* Paolino.

Paulus ['po:ləs], *no.pr.m.* Paolo.

paunch[1] [po:ntʃ], *s.* **1.** pancia; ventre **2.** (*anat.*) rumine.

to **paunch**[1], *v.t.* sventrare; sbudellare.

paunch[2], *s.* (*mar.*) paglietto.

paunchy ['po:ntʃi], *ag.* panciuto.

pauper ['po:pə*], *s.* povero, indigente; mendicante.

pauperism ['po:pərizəm], *s.* **1.** povertà, indigenza **2.** le classi povere.

pauperization [,po:pərai'zeiʃən], *s.* impoverimento.

to **pauperize** ['po:pəraiz], *v.t.* impoverire.

Pausanias [po:'seiniæs], *no.pr.m.* (*st.*) Pausania.

pause [po:z], *s.* **1.** pausa, interruzione **2.** esitazione, indugio **3.** (*mus.*) pausa **4.** (*poes.*) cesura ☆ *— dots*, puntini di sospensione.

to **pause**, *v.i.* **1.** fare una pausa **2.** esitare, indugiare.

pauseless ['po:zlis], *ag.* incessante.

pauselessly ['po:zlisli], *av.* incessantemente.

pavage ['peividʒ], *s.* **1.** pavimentazione **2.** tassa per la pavimentazione delle strade.

pavan(e) ['pævən], *s.* (*mus.*) pavana.

to **pave** [peiv], *v.t.* **1.** pavimentare; lastricare (anche *fig.*): *the road to hell is paved with good intentions*, la strada dell'inferno è lastricata di buone intenzioni; *her path was paved with flowers*, il suo cammino era cosparso di fiori **2.** *fig.* aprire la via, preparare il terreno: *they'll — the way for you*, essi ti apriranno la via.

pavement ['peivmənt], *s.* **1.** pavimentazione, selciato, lastricato **2.** marciapiede ☆ *— artist*, chi disegna figure sul marciapiede per ottenere denaro dai passanti; *— glass* (o *— light*), lucernario; *— roadway* (o *— street*), (*amer.*) strada selciata.

paver ['peivə*], *s.* **1.** selciatore, lastricatore **2.** pietra da selciato ☆ *— road —*, pavimentatrice stradale.

pavid ['pævid], *ag.* pavido.

pavilion [pə'viljən], *s.* **1.** tenda, padiglione **2.** (*arch.*) padiglione (di ospedale, mostra, ecc.): *the French — at the exhibition*, il padiglione francese alla mostra **3.** (*anat.*) padiglione **4.** padiglione (di diamante).

to **pavilion**, *v.t.* coprire con tende; erigere padiglioni su; rinchiudere in padiglioni.

paving ['peiviŋ], *s.* pavimentazione; selciato ☆ *— -stone*, pietra da selciato.

paviour ['peivjə*], *s.* **1.** selciatore, lastricatore **2.** pietra da selciato **3.** mattone da selciato.

pavis ['pævis], *s.* pavese.

paw [po:], *s.* **1.** zampa (anche *fig.*) **2.** (*sl.*) mano **3.** (*sl.*) scrittura.

to **paw**, *v.t.i.* **1.** toccare, battere con la zampa; scalpitare (di cavalli): *the dog pawed at the door*, il cane toccò la porta con la zampa **2.** (*sl.*) toccare, maneggiare goffamente.

pawkily ['po:kili], *av.* (*scoz.*) astutamente; malignamente.

pawkiness ['po:kinis], *s.* (*scoz.*) astuzia; malignità.

pawky ['po:ki], *ag.* (*scoz.*) astuto, furbo.

pawl [po:l], *s.* (*mec.*) dente d'arresto (di argano); nottolino d'arresto.

to **pawl**, *v.t.* (*mec.*) fermare con dente di arresto.

pawn[1] [po:n], *s.* pegno, garanzia: *at —* (o *in —*), in pegno, in garanzia ☆ *— -ticket*, ricevuta di pegno.

to **pawn**[1], *v.t.* **1.** impegnare; dare in pegno, garanzia **2.** *fig.* rischiare (vita, onore, ecc.).

pawn[2], *s.* pedina (negli scacchi); *fig.* pedina.

pawnbroker ['po:n,broukə*], *s.* prestatore su pegno.

pawnbroking ['po:n,broukiŋ], *s.* il prestare denaro su pegno.

pawnee [po:'ni:], *s.* prestatore su pegno.

pawner ['po:nə*], *s.* chi prende a prestito denaro contro pegno.

pawnshop ['po:n-ʃop], *s.* agenzia di prestiti su pegno.

pax [pæks], *s.* **1.** pace (anche *eccl.*) **2.** (*sl. scolastico*) silenzio!.

pay[1] [pei], *s.* **1.** paga; salario: *she drew her — every fortnight*, ella era pagata a quindicina || *in the — of*, al servizio di; (*spreg.*) al soldo di: *he is in the — of Mr. Smith*, è al servizio del signor Smith; *he is in the — of the enemy*, è al soldo del nemico **2.** *fig.* compenso, indennità, ricompensa **3.** prodotto (di miniere) ☆ *— -day*, giorno di paga; *— -load*, (*aer.*) carico pagante; *— -office*, ufficio paga || *— back*, arretrati di paga, salario; *extra- —*, paga supplementare; gratifica; *flying*

—, indennità di volo; *full-* —, paga intera; *half-* —, mezza paga.

to **pay**[1], *pass.p.p.* **paid** [peid], *v.t.i.* **1.** pagare: *a well paid job*, un lavoro ben retribuito; *to* — *a bill*, pagare, regolare un conto; *to* — *in advance*, pagare in anticipo; *to* — *money into an account*, versare denaro su un conto; *to* — *ready money* (o *cash down*), pagare in contanti; *to* — *s.o. for a thing*, pagare una cosa a qlcu.; *to* — *s.o. to do sthg.*, pagare qlcu. per fare ql.co.: *I paid him ten pounds to hold his tongue*, ho comprato il suo silenzio con dieci sterline; *to* — *sthg. for s.o.*, offrire ql.co. a qlcu. (al ristorante, teatro, ecc.); *to* — *to the order of...*, pagare all'ordine di... ‖ — *as you earn* (o *amer.* — *as you go*), trattenuta di ricchezza mobile sugli stipendi ‖ *a promise to* —, un impegno di pagamento ‖ *to* — *attention*, fare attenzione ‖ *to* — *honour to s.o.*, fare onore a qlcu. ‖ *to* — *s.o. in his own coin*, rendere pane per focaccia ‖ *to* — *one's addresses to*, fare la corte a qlcu. ‖ *to* — *one's respects to s.o.*, presentare i propri ossequi a qlcu. ‖ *to* — *one's way*, sbarcare il lunario, non fare debiti ‖ *to* — *the piper*, (*sl.*) pagare le spese (per gli altri) ‖ *to* — *s.o. a visit*, fare una visita a qlcu. ‖ *to* — *through the nose*, (*fam.*) pagare prezzi esorbitanti ‖ *who breaks pays*, *prov.* chi rompe paga **2.** rendere, fruttare; compensare: *business that does not* —, affare che non rende niente; *it will* — *you better in the end*, ti renderà maggiormente alla fine; *it would not* — *me to go*, non mi varrebbe la pena di andare **3.** *to* — *for* (*s.o.*, *sthg.*), pagare, espiare: *he will* — *for his insolence*, pagherà cara la sua insolenza; *to* — *for one's folly*, pagare caro i propri capricci, essere vittima della propria follia **4.** *to* — *away*, pagare (denaro) **5.** *to* — *back*, rimborsare, restituire **6.** *to* — *down*, pagare in contanti ‖ *to* — *sthg. down*, (*comm.*) versare ql.co. in conto provvigione **7.** *to* — *in*, pagare, versare: *to* — *in a cheque*, versare un assegno **8.** *to* — *off*, saldare, liquidare; licenziare, congedare; ripagare in pieno, dare risultato pieno (sia in bene che in male) **9.** *to* — *out*, pagare; versare; sborsare; (*mar.*) mollare, filare (una gomena): *to* — *out the wages*, distribuire le paghe ‖ *to* — *s.o. out*, (*fam.*) vendicarsi di qlcu., rendere a qlcu. la pariglia **10.** *to* — *over*, pagare, versare (denaro) **11.** *to* — *up*, saldare (conti), pagare (arretrati).

to **pay**[2], *pass.p.p.* **payed, paid** [peid], *v.t.* (*mar.*) catramare, impeciare.

payable ['peiəbl], *ag.* **1.** pagabile; dovuto: *to make a cheque* — *to bearer*, fare un assegno pagabile al portatore **2.** redditizio (di miniere, ecc.).

payee [pei'i:], *s.c.* (*comm.*) creditore, creditrice; beneficiario, beneficiaria ‖ *s.* portatore (di un effetto).

payer ['peiə*], *s.c.* pagatore, pagatrice.

paying ['peiiŋ], *s.* pagamento.

paymaster ['pei,mɑ:stə*], *s.* (*mil.*) ufficiale pagatore.

payment ['peimənt], *s.* **1.** pagamento; versamento: *to cease payments*, cessare i pagamenti; *to demand* —, fare domanda di pagamento; *to meet payments*, fare fronte ai pagamenti **2.** *fig.* ricompensa ☆ *cash* —, (*comm.*) pagamento in contanti.

paynim ['peinim], *s.c.* (*arc.*) pagano, pagana; musulmano, musulmana.

payoff ['peiɔːf], *s.* **1.** giorno di paga **2.** liquidazione; *fig.* resa dei conti; conclusione.

payola [pei'oulə], *s.* (*neol. amer.*) bustarella (corruzione mediante una segreta e sapiente distribuzione di denaro).

payroll ['peiroul], **pay-sheet** ['pei-ʃi:t], *s.* libro paga: *to be on the* —, essere sul libro paga; far parte di una impresa.

pea[1] [pi:], *pl.* **peas** [pi:z], *pl.coll.* **pease** [pi:z], *s.* **1.** (*bot.*) pisello **2.** cosa simile a pisello ☆ — *-blossom*, fiore di pisello; — *-green*, verde pisello; — *-husk*, guscio di pisello; — *-shooter*, cerbottana; — *-soup*, passato di piselli; — *-souper*, (*sl.*) nebbione ‖ *chick* —, cece; *green -peas*, piselli freschi.

pea[2], *s.* (*mar.*) unghia.

pea[3], *s.* **1.** romano (della stadera) **2.** valvola di sicurezza.

peace [pi:s], *s.* **1.** pace, concordia; calma: — *of mind*, pace dello spirito; — *to his ashes*, pace alle sue ceneri!; — *be with you!*, la pace sia con voi!; *to be at* —, essere, stare in pace, essere d'accordo; *to make* —, fare la pace, riconciliarsi ‖ *to hold one's* —, mantenere il silenzio, non protestare **2.** ordine pubblico: *to break the* —, violare l'ordine pubblico (di notte), schiamazzare; *to keep the* —, mantenere l'ordine pubblico ‖ *the King's* (*the Queen's*) —, l'ordine pubblico ‖ *to be sworn of the* —, essere nominato giudice di pace ☆ — *breaker*, perturbatore dell'ordine pubblico; — *-offering*, dono propiziatorio; — *party*, (*pol.*) partito pacifista; — *pipe*, pipa della pace.

peaceable ['pi:səbl], *ag.* pacifico, tranquillo.

peaceableness ['pi:səblnis], *s.* disposizione alla pace; pacatezza, tranquillità; pace, calma.

peaceably ['pi:səbli], *av.* pacificamente, tranquillamente.

peaceful ['pi:sful], *ag.* pacifico, tranquillo, quieto, calmo; sereno.

peacefully ['pi:sfuli], *av.* pacificamente, tranquillamente; serenamente.

peacefulness ['pi:sfulnis], *s.* pace, calma; serenità.

peaceless ['pi:slis], *ag.* agitato, inquieto.

peacelessness ['pi:slisnis], *s.* inquietudine.

peacemaker ['pi:s,meikə*], *s.c.* pacificatore, pacificatrice ‖ *s.* **1.** (*scherz.*) revolver **2.** (*scherz.*) nave da guerra.

peach[1] [pi:tʃ], *s.* **1.** (*bot.*) pesca: *the down of a* —, la peluria di una pesca ‖ — *Melba*, gelato con pesca sciroppata **2.** — (*-tree*); pesco **3.** (*sl.*) tesoro, amore ‖ (*fam.*) *it's a* —!, è un poema! ☆ — *-blossom*, fiore di pesco; — *-coloured*, che ha il colore della pesca; — *-wood*, legno di fernambuco ‖ *clingstone* —, pesca duracina.

to **peach**[2], *v.t.i.* (*sl.*) denunciare (i propri complici), parlare.

peacher ['pi:tʃə*], *s.* (*sl.*) accusatore (dei propri complici).

pea-chick ['pi:-tʃik], *s.* giovane pavone.

peachy ['pi:tʃi], *ag.* simile a pesca; soffice, vellutato.

peacock ['pi:kɔk], *s.* **1.** pavone **2.** *fig.* persona vanitosa ☆ — *-blue*, blu pavone; — *-butterfly*, (*entom.*) pavonia.

to **peacock**, *v.t.i.* ostentare; pavoneggiarsi.

peacockery ['pi:,kɔkəri], *s.* vanità; fatuità.

peacockish ['pi:,kɔkiʃ], *ag.* vanitoso.

peafowl ['pi:-faul], *s.* pavone; femmina del pavone.

peahen ['pi:-hen], *s.* femmina del pavone.

pea-jacket ['pi:,dʒækit], *s.* giaccotto da marinaio.

peak[1] [pi:k], *s.* **1.** picco, cima, sommità (di monte, ecc.) **2.** punta (della barba, ecc.) **3.** visiera (di cappello) **4.** massimo, punta: *the* — *of efficiency*, il massimo del rendimento **5.** (*mar.*) angolo di penna **6.** (*mar.*) gavone ☆ — *-load*, (*mec. elett.*) carico massimo; — *period*, periodo di massima attività (consumo, produzione, ecc.); — *season*, alta stagione.

to **peak**[1], *v.t.i.* sporgere, innalzarsi a picco **2.** spingere al massimo; accentuare.

to **peak**[2], *v.t.i.* **1.** (*mar.*) alzare (il pennone) verticalmente **2.** disporre (i remi) a picco **3.** drizzare (la coda) nell'immergersi a picco (di cetacei).

to **peak**[3], *v.i.* (*arc.*) **1.** deperire; languire; consumarsi ‖ *to* — *and pine*, (*fam.*) languire, struggersi **2.** avere l'aria malaticcia.

Peak[4], *no.pr.* (*geog.*) Peak (distretto collinoso del Derbyshire).

peaked [pi:kt], *ag.* **1.** aguzzo, appuntito; a punta, a forma di picco **2.** affilato (di lineamenti) scarno, emaciato ☆ *two-* — *mountain*, montagna a due picchi.

peakish ['pi:kiʃ], *ag. V.* **peaky**[2].

peaky[1] ['pi:ki], *ag.* **1.** dai (molti) picchi **2.** appuntito, a forma di picco.

peaky[2], *ag.* (*dial. fam.*) mingherlino; malaticcio; palliduccio.

peal [pi:l], *s.* **1.** scampanio; suono (di campane, d'organo); concerto di campane ‖ *at full* —, a distesa **2.** salva d'artiglieria: *a — of ordnance*, una salva d'artiglieria **3.** scoppio; scroscio (di risa, applausi, ecc.); fragore; rimbombo.

to peal, *v.t.i.* **1.** scampanare; suonare a distesa **2.** (*far*) rimbombare, tuonare; rumoreggiare; echeggiare ‖ *he pealed out the news*, annunciò la notizia a gran voce.

peanut ['pi:nʌt], *s.* **1.** (*bot.*) arachide **2.** *pl. fig.* (*sl. amer.*) persona insignificante, da poco ☆ — *butter*, pasta d'arachidi; — *oil*, olio di arachidi.

pear [pɛə*], *s.* **1.** pera **2.** — (*-tree*), pero ☆ — *-shaped*, a forma di pera; — *-switch*, interruttore a pera.

Pearl¹ [pəl], *no.pr.f.* Perla.

pearl², *s.* **1.** perla (anche *fig.*): *a string of pearls*, un filo di perle; *she is a — of girl*, è una perla di ragazza ‖ *to cast pearls before swine*, gettare le perle ai porci **2.** (*tip.*) corpo 5 **3.** — (*-eye*), (*rar. patol.*) cataratta **4.** (*arald.*) argento ☆ — *-ash*, (*chim.*) carbonato di potassio; — *-barley*, orzo perlato; — *button*, bottone di madreperla; — *-diver* (o — *-fisher*), pescatore di perle; — *-drop*, orecchino con perla a goccia; — *-fishery*, pesca delle perle; — *grey*, grigio perla; — *-oyster*, ostrica perlifera; — *-powder* (o — *white*), cosmetico per rendere bianca la pelle; — *-shell*, madreperla greggia; — *-stone*, pietra perlata, specie di quarzo; — *-studded*, tempestato di perle ‖ *culture pearls*, perle coltivate; *mother-of-* —, madreperla; *seed-* —, perlina.

to pearl², *v.t.i.* **1.** pescare perle **2.** imperlare; ornare di perle **3.** rendere perlaceo **4.** perlare (riso, orzo, ecc.).

pearl³, *s.* «picot» (puntina di pizzo, bordura).

pearled [pəld], *ag.* **1.** adorno di perle **2.** perlato (di orzo, ecc.).

pearlies ['pəliz], *s.pl.* abito di venditore ambulante guarnito di molti bottoni di madreperla.

pearliness ['pəlinis], *s.* trasparenza di perla; color perla.

pearling ['pəliŋ], *s.* **1.** pesca delle perle **2.** perlatura (d'orzo, ecc.).

pearly ['pəli], *ag.* **1.** perlaceo **2.** ricco di perle.

peasant ['pezənt], *s.c.* contadino, contadina ☆ — *boy*, contadinello; — *-like*, contadinesco.

peasantry ['pezəntri], *s.* **1.** contadiname, gente di campagna **2.** contadinanza, stato, condizione di contadino.

peas(e)cod ['pi:zkɔd], *s.* baccello di pisello.

peat [pi:t], *s.* (*min.*) torba: *to dig* (o *to cut*) —, estrarre la torba ☆ — *-bed* (o — *-bog* o — *-moss*), (*miner.*) torbiera.

peatery ['pi:təri], *s.* (*miner.*) torbiera.

peaty ['pi:ti], *ag.* torboso.

pebble ['pebl], *s.* **1.** ciottolo **2.** cristallo di rocca ☆ — *-leather*, zigrino (tipo di cuoio); — *-paving*, acciottolato; — *-powder*, polvere da sparo a grana grossa; — *-stone*, ciottolo ‖ *Scotch* —, (*min.*) agata.

to pebble, *v.t.* **1.** lapidare **2.** zigrinare.

pebbled ['pebld], *ag.* **1.** sassoso, ghiaioso **2.** zigrinato.

pebbling ['pebliŋ], *s.* **1.** lapidazione **2.** zigrinatura.

pebbly ['pebli], *ag.* **1.** ciottoloso **2.** zigrinato.

pecan [pi'kæn], *s.* **1.** noce americano **2.** noce americana.

peccability [,pekə'biliti], *s.* peccabilità.

peccable ['pekəbl], *ag.* peccabile.

peccadillo [,pekə'dilou], *s.* peccatuccio.

peccancy ['pekənsi], *s.* colpevolezza; peccato.

peccant ['pekənt], *ag.* **1.** peccaminoso; colpevole **2.** insalubre, che causa malattie.

peccantly ['pekəntli], *av.* in modo peccaminoso.

peccary ['pekəri], *s.* (*zool.*) pecari.

peck¹ [pek], *s.* **1.** «peck» (misura di capacità per cereali = l. 9,092) **2.** (*fam.*) sacco; mucchio; quantità: *she was in a — of troubles*, era in un mare di guai.

peck², *s.* **1.** beccata; (*scherz.*) bacetto **2.** (*sl.*) cibo.

to peck², *v.t.i.* **1.** beccare; (*scherz.*) dare un bacetto a **2.** (*sl.*) mangiare (di persone): *to — (at) food*, mangiucchiare, piluccare.

to peck³, *v.t.i.* **1.** (*arc. dial.*) scagliare **2.** inciampare.

pecked [pekt], *ag.* beccato ☆ *hen-* — *husband*, (*fam.*) marito dominato dalla moglie.

pecker ['pekə*], *s.* **1.** (*ornit.*)picchio **2.** piccone **3.** (*sl.*) naso; becco **4.** coraggio: *keep your—up!*, fatti coraggio!.

peckish ['pekiʃ], *ag.* (*fam.*) affamato.

pecten ['pekten], *pl.* **pectines** ['pektini:z], *s.* (*zool.*) pettine.

pectin ['pektin], *s.* (*chim.*) pectina.

pectoral ['pektərəl], *ag.* pettorale: — *cross*, croce pettorale ‖ *s.* pettorale.

to peculate ['pekjuleit], *v.t.i.* (*dir.*) appropriarsi di (fondi pubblici avuti in custodia); far del peculato.

peculation [,pekju'leiʃn], *s.* (*dir.*) peculato.

peculator ['pekjuleitə*], *s.* reo di peculato.

peculiar [pi'kju:ljə*], *ag.* **1.** peculiare, particolare; speciale; personale, individuale: *a — flavour*, un odore speciale; *his — charm*, il suo fascino particolare; *my own — property*, la mia proprietà personale **2.** strano, bizzarro, originale: *well, that's — !*, questo è strano davvero! ‖ *s.* **1.** proprietà, privilegio particolare **2.** parrocchia, chiesa extragiurisdizionale.

peculiarity [pi,kju:li'æriti], *s.* particolarità, caratteristica, singolarità ‖ *special peculiarities*, segni particolari (su documenti) **2.** bizzarria, eccentricità.

to peculiarize [pi'kju:ljəraiz], *v.t.* rendere peculiare.

peculiarly [pi'kju:ljəli], *av.* **1.** particolarmente, peculiarmente **2.** in modo strano.

peculium [pi'kju:ljəm], *s.* peculio.

pecuniary [pi'kju:njəri], *ag.* pecuniario.

pecunious [pi'kju:niəs], *ag.* ricco.

pedagogic(al) [,pedə'gɔdʒik(əl)], *ag.* pedagogico.

pedagogics [,pedə'gɔdʒiks], *s.* pedagogia.

pedagogism ['pedəgɔgizəm], *s.* pedagogismo.

pedagogue ['pedəgɔg], *s.* pedagogo.

pedagoguism ['pedəgɔgizəm], *s.* pedagogismo.

pedagogy ['pedəgɔgi], *s.* pedagogia.

pedal ['pedl], *ag.* di piede ‖ *s.* (*mus. mec.*) pedale ☆ — *pushers*, (*amer.*) calzoni da donna (a mezza gamba).

to pedal, *pass.p.p.* **pedalled** ['pedld], *v.t.i.* **1.** pedalare; condurre (una bicicletta) pedalando **2.** (*mus.*) usare i pedali dell'organo.

pedant ['pedənt], *s.* pedante.

pedantic [pi'dæntik], *ag.* pedantesco, pedante.

pedantically [pi'dæntikəli], *av.* in modo pedantesco.

pedantry ['pedəntri], *s.* pedanteria.

to peddle ['pedl], *v.t.i.* **1.** fare il venditore ambulante **2.** vendere al minuto: *to — goods*, vendere merci al minuto ‖ *to — jobs*, (*fig. pol.*) vendere incarichi, posti **3.** *to — away*, gingillarsi, perdere tempo.

peddler, *V.* pedlar.

peddling ['pedliŋ], *ag.* futile; insignificante.

pederasty ['pedəræsti], *s.* pederastia.

pedestal ['pedistl], *s.* piedistallo, basamento.

to pedestal, *pass.p.p.* **pedestalled** ['pedistld], *v.t.* mettere su un piedistallo.

pedestrian [pi'destriən], *ag.* **1.** che va a piedi **2.** *fig.* pedestre, piatto ‖ *s.* **1.** pedone **2.** podista.

pedestrianism [pi'destriənizəm], *s.* podismo.

to pedestrianize [pi'destriənaiz], *v.i.* **1.** passeggiare **2.** fare del podismo.

pediatric [,pi:di'ætrik], *ag.* (*med.*) pediatrico.

pediatrician [,pi:diə'triʃən], *s.* (*med.*) pediatra.

pediatrics [,pi:di'ætriks], *s.* (*med.*) pediatria.

pediatrist [,pi:di'ætrist], *s.* (*med.*) pediatra.

pedicel ['pedisəl], *s.* (*bot. zool.*) pedicello.

pedicellate ['pedisəleit], *ag.* pedicellato.

pedicle ['pedikl], *s.* (*bot. zool.*) pedicello.

pedicular [pi'dikjulə*], *ag.* pidocchioso.

pediculate [pi'dikjulit], *ag.* pedicellato.

pediculous [pi'dikjuləs], *ag.* pidocchioso.

pedicure [ˌ'pedikjuə¹], *s.* **1.** pedicure, callista **2.** cura dei piedi.

pedigree ['pedigri:], *s.* **1.** albero genealogico **2.** lignaggio, ascendenza **3.** origine, etimologia (di parola) **4.** « pedigree » (documento d'origine di un cane).

pedigreed ['pedigri:d], *ag.* che ha una genealogia; di stirpe nobile.

pediment ['pedimənt], *s.* (*arch.*) frontone, timpano.

pedimental [ˌpedi'mentl], **pedimented** ['pedimentid], *ag.* (*arch.*) ornato di frontone; simile a frontone.

pedlar ['pedlə¹], *s.* venditore ambulante ‖ — 's *French*, gergo dei ladri ‖ — *of gossip*, *fig.* chiacchierone.

pedlary ['pedləri], *s.* **1.** commercio di venditore ambulante **2.** mercanzia (di venditore ambulante).

pedometer [pi'dɔmitə¹], *s.* (*strum.*) pedometro.

peduncle [pi'dʌŋkl], *s.* (*bot. zool.*) peduncolo.

peduncular [pi'dʌŋkjulə¹], *ag.* (*bot. zool.*) peduncolare.

pedunculate [pi'dʌŋkjulit], *ag.* (*bot. zool.*) peduncolato, sostenuto da peduncolo.

peek [pi:k], *s.* sbirciata, sguardo furtivo.

to peek, *v.i.* **1.** gettare un colpo d'occhio, sbirciare: *to* — *at s.o.*, *sthg.*, guardare furtivamente, sbirciare qlcu., ql.co.; *to* — *inside* (o *into a room*), dare un'occhiata all'interno di una stanza **2.** mostrarsi, far capolino: *her curls peeked* (*out*) *from under her hat*, le spuntavano i riccioli dal cappello.

peekabo(o) ['ˌpi:kə,bu:], *s.* (*amer.*) giuoco del cucù.

peel¹ [pi:l], *s.* buccia, corteccia.

to peel¹, *v.t.i.* **1.** sbucciare, sbucciarsi; scortecciare; scorticarsi; squamarsi; spellarsi **2.** (*sl.*) spogliarsi **3.** *to* — **off**, (*aer. mar.*) staccarsi (da una formazione).

peel², *s.* (*mil.*) torre fortificata (sul confine scozzese).

peel³, *s.* **1.** pala (generalmente di fornaio) **2.** (*tip.*) gruccia.

peeled [pi:ld], *ag.* **1.** saccheggiato **2.** nudo ‖ *to keep one's eyes* —, (*amer.*) tenere gli occhi ben aperti **3.** logoro **4.** pelato, sbucciato; mondato.

peeler ['pi:lə¹], *s.* (*sl.*) poliziotto.

peeling ['pi:liŋ], *s.* buccia ☆ *potato peelings*, bucce di patate.

peen [pi:n], *s.* penna (del martello).

to peen, *v.t.* battere, piegare con la penna del martello.

peep¹ [pi:p], *s.* **1.** sguardo, occhiata furtiva: *to get a* — *at sthg.*, intravvedere ql.co.; *to have* (o *to take*) *a* — *at sthg.*, gettare uno sguardo furtivo su ql.co. **2.** — (*of dawn*), l'alba, lo spuntare del giorno: *at the* — *of day*, all'alba ☆ — *-hole*, spiraglio; — *-show*, apparecchio contenente diapositive di vario soggetto visibili attraverso una lente; — *-sight*, mirino.

to peep¹, *v.i.* **1.** guardare furtivamente; guardare attraverso un buco; lanciare occhiate: *to* — *at sthg.*, *at s.o.*, guardare furtivamente ql.co., qlcu.; *the cat was peeping at the chicken*, il gatto stava adocchiando il pollo; *to* — *in* (o *into*), dare un'occhiata all'interno; *he peeped into the room*, gettò uno sguardo furtivo nella stanza; *to* — *through the keyhole*, guardare dal buco della serratura **2.** far capolino; mostrarsi; nascere, spuntare (del giorno, di fiore, di oggetto lontano): *they peeped through the foliage*, fecero capolino tra le foglie.

peep², *s.* pigolio; squittio.

to peep², *v.i.* pigolare; squittire.

peep³, *s.* (*sl. amer. mil.*) « jeep », camionetta.

peeper¹ ['pi:pə¹], *s.* **1.** persona curiosa, indiscreta **2.** specchio **3.** cannocchiale **4.** (*sl. spec. pl.*) occhio **5.** *pl.* paio d'occhiali.

peeper², *s.* pollastro; piccioncino.

peeping ['pi:piŋ], *ag.* indiscreto ☆ — *Tom*, individuo indiscreto.

peer¹ [piə¹], *s.* **1.** pari, persona dello stesso grado, rango: *without* —, senza pari; *where could you find his* —?, dove potreste trovare un suo pari? **2.** Pari, membro della Camera dei Lords ‖ *the House of Peers*, la Camera dei Pari ‖ *spiritual Peers*, vescovi appartenenti alla Camera Alta.

to peer¹, *v.t.i.* **1.** uguagliare: *to* — *with s.o.*, *sthg.*, essere alla pari di qlcu., ql.co. **2.** (*fam.*) creare Pari.

to peer², *v.i.* **1.** far capolino, spuntare, apparire: *the sun peered through the clouds*, il sole si affacciò tra le nubi **2.** *to* — *at* (*s.o.*, *sthg.*), guardare attentamente, scrutare: *he peered at her*, la guardò attentamente.

peerage ['piəridʒ], *s.* **1.** i pari **2.** nobiltà, aristocrazia **3.** almanacco nobiliare inglese.

peeress ['piəris], *s.* **1.** nobildonna **2.** paressa, consorte di un pari.

peering ['piəriŋ], *ag.* penetrante, acuto (di sguardo).

peerless ['piəlis], *ag.* senza pari, impareggiabile.

peerlessly ['piəlisli], *av.* in modo impareggiabile.

peery ['piəri], *ag.* curioso, ficcanaso; furbo.

to peeve [pi:v], *v.t.i.* irritare, irritarsi.

peeved [pi:vd], *ag.* (*fam.*) irritato.

peevish ['pi:viʃ], *ag.* irritabile, stizzoso, fastidioso.

peevishly ['pi:viʃli], *av.* irritabilmente, stizzosamente.

peevishness ['pi:viʃnis], *s.* irritabilità, stizza; cattivo umore.

peewee ['pi:wi:], *s.* (*fam. amer.*) persona, cosa molto piccola.

peewit ['pi:wit], *s.* (*ornit.*) pavoncella.

peg¹ [peg], *s.* **1.** piuolo, caviglia, picchetto; attaccapanni ‖ *she is a square* — *in a round hole*, (*fam.*) non è al suo posto ‖ *to buy a dress* (o *a suit*) *off the* —, (*fam.*) comprare un abito bello e fatto ‖ *to take s.o. down a* — *or two*, rimettere qlcu. al proprio posto, fargli abbassare la cresta **2.** zipolo (di botte) **3.** (*mus.*) bischero, spina **4.** *fig.* scusa, pretesto: — *to hang a grievance on*, pretesto di lamentela **5.** bevanda alcoolica: *a* — *of whisky*, (*ang.-in.*) whisky con seltz ☆ — *-ladder*, scala a piuoli ‖ *clothes-* —, gruccia per abiti.

to peg¹, *pass.p.p.* **pegged** [pegd], *v.t.i.* **1.** incavigliare, picchettare, mettere un piuolo a **2.** fissare, stabilizzare i prezzi di **3.** *to* — *at* (*s.o.*,¦ *sthg.*), (*sl.*) gettare pietre contro **4.** *to* — **away** (*at sthg.*), perseverare (in ql.co.) **5.** *to* — **down**, fissare con caviglie, picchetti, ecc. ‖ *to* — *s.o. down to his promise*, *fig.* obbligare qlcu. a mantenere la promessa **6.** *to* — **out**, segnare il limite (di terreno, ecc.); (*sl.*) morire; (*sl.*) essere rovinato.

Peg², *no.pr.f. dim.* di **Margaret**.

pegamoid ['pegəmɔid], *s.* pegamoide.

Pegasus ['pegəsəs], *no.pr.m.* (*mit. astr.*) Pegaso ‖ *s. fig.* ispirazione poetica.

pegged [pegd],¦ *ag.* **1.** munito di cavicchi; segnato da piuoli **2.** fissato, stabilizzato (di prezzi, ecc.): — *market*, mercato stabilizzato; — *rent*, affitto bloccato.

Peggy ['pegi], *no.pr.f. dim.* di **Margaret**.

peignoir ['peinwɑ:*], *s.* **1.** accappatoio **2.** mantellina per pettinarsi.

pejorative ['pi:dʒərətiv], *ag. s.* peggiorativo.

pekan ['pekən], *s.* (*zool.*) martora canadese.

peke [pi:k], *s.* (*abbr. di Pekin(g)ese*) cane pechinese.

pekin [pi:'kin], *s.* seta di Pechino.

Pekinese [ˌpi:ki'ni:z], **Pekingese** [ˌpi:kiŋ'i:z], *ag.* pechinese ‖ *s.* **1.** pechinese **2.** cane pechinese.

Peking [pi:'kiŋ], *no.pr.* (*geog.*) Pechino.

pekoe ['pi:kou], *s.* « pekoe » (tè nero pregiato).

pelage [ˌ'pelidʒ], *s.* pelame (di mammifero).

pelagic [pe'lædʒik], *ag.* oceanico.

pelargonium [ˌpelə'gounjəm], *s.* (*bot.*) pelargonio.

Pelasgian [pe'læzgiən], *ag.* pelasgico.

Pelasgians [pe'læzgiənz], *s.pl.* (*st.*) Pelasgi.

Pelasgic [pe'læzgik], *ag.* pelasgico.

pelerine ['peləri:n], *s.* mantellina, pellegrina.

Peleus ['pi:lju:s], *no.pr.m.* (*mit.*) Peleo.

pelf [pelf], *s.* (*spreg.*) denaro, ricchezza.

pelican ['pelikən], *s.* (*ornit.*) pellicano.

Pelion ['pi:liən], *no.pr.* (*geog. st.*) Pelio.

pelisse [pe'li:s], *s.* **1.** mantello per signora **2.** soprabito per bambino **3.** giacca guarnita di pelliccia.

pellagra [pe'leigrə], *s.* (*patol.*) pellagra.

pellagrous [pe'leigrəs], *ag.* (*patol.*) pellagroso.

pellet ['pelit], *s.* **1.** pallottolina (di carta, pane, ecc.) **2.** (*mil.*) pallottola **3.** pillola **4.** (*chim.*) tavoletta usata come unità di misura nell'industria delle materie plastiche.

to **pellet**, *pass.p.p.* **pelletted** ['pelitid], *v.t.* **1.** (*arc.*) appallottolare **2.** colpire con pallottole.

pellicle ['pelikl], *s.* pellicola, membrana.

pellicular [pe'likjulə*], *ag.* di pellicola, di membrana.

pell-mell ['pel'mel], *ag.* confuso ‖ *s.* confusione.

pell-mell, *av.* confusamente, alla rinfusa.

pellucid [pe'lju:sid], *ag.* chiaro, limpido, traslucido; trasparente (anche *fig.*).

pellucidity [,pelju:'siditi], **pellucidness** [pe'lju:sidnis], *s.* limpidezza, traslucidità; trasparenza.

pelmet ['pelmit], *s.* mantovana (di tendaggio).

Peloponnesian [,peləpə'ni:ʃən], *ag.* del Peloponneso ‖ *s.c.* abitante del Peloponneso.

pelota [pi'loutə], *s.* (*spor.*) pelota.

pelt[1] [pelt], *s.* **1.** colpo (di proiettile, sasso, ecc.); *fig.* frecciata ‖ *at full* —, a tutta velocità **2.** crepitio (di pioggia, ecc.) **3.** (*dial.*) attacco d'ira.

to **pelt**[1], *v.t.i.* **1.** colpire (con proiettili, sassi, ecc.); tirare, lanciare continuamente (proiettili, pietre, ecc.); *fig.* colpire (con rimproveri, ecc.) **2.** affrettarsi.

pelt[2], *s.* pelle (di pecora, capra, animale da pelliccia, ecc.); pelle greggia; (*scherz.*) pelle umana.

pelta ['peltə], *pl.* **peltae** ['pelti:], *s.* **1.** pelta (antico scudo) **2.** (*bot.*) foglia a forma di scudo.

peltast ['peltæst], *s.* (*st. greca*) peltasta.

peltate ['pelteit], *ag.* (*bot.*) peltato, a forma di scudo.

peltmonger ['pelt,mʌngə*], *s.* commerciante in pellami.

peltry ['peltri], *s. coll.* pelli grezze.

pelvic ['pelvik], *ag.* (*anat.*) pelvico.

pelvis ['pelvis], *s.* (*anat.*) pelvi, bacino.

pe(m)mican ['pemikən], *s.* **1.** «pemmican» (carne seccata e compressa) **2.** *fig.* pensiero, argomento estremamente sintetico.

pen[1] [pen], *s.* **1.** penna (di uccello); calamo; aculeo di porcospino **2.** penna (per scrivere): *a stroke of the* —, una riga, un tratto di penna ‖ *he lives by his* —, vive della sua professione di letterato ‖ *to put one's* — (o *to set* —) *to paper* (o *to take* — *in hand*), prendere la penna in mano **3.** (*rar. fig.*) scrittore; letterato: *the best pens of the day*, i maggiori scrittori del giorno ☆ — *-and ink*, occorrente per scrivere; disegno a penna; — *-case*, portapenne; — *feather*, penna dell'ala di uccello; — *-friend*, (*neol.*) corrispondente; — *-name*, pseudonimo di letterato; — *-nib*, pennino; — *-wiper*, nettapenne ‖ *ball point* —, penna a sfera; *fountain-* —, penna stilografica.

to **pen**[1], *pass. p.p.* **penned** [pend], *v.t.* scrivere, comporre: *she penned down a letter*, scrisse una lettera.

pen[2], *s.* **1.** recinto per animali **2.** animali nel recinto ☆ *play* —, recinto per bambini; *submarine* —, rifugio per sommergibili.

to **pen**[2], *v.t.* rinchiudere (animali) in un recinto ‖ *they penned up the pigs and the fowls*, chiusero in un recinto maiali e polli.

pen[3], *s.* (*ornit.*) femmina del cigno.

penal ['pi:nl], *ag.* penale ☆ — *code*, codice penale; — *servitude*, lavori forzati.

to **penalize** ['pi:nəlaiz], *v.t.* (*dir. spor.*) penalizzare.

penally ['pi:nəli], *av.* penalmente.

penalty ['penlti], *s.* (*dir. spor.*) penalità; ammenda; multa; punizione ☆ — *area*, (*calcio*) area di rigore; — *kick*, (*calcio*) calcio di rigore; — *stroke*, (*golf*) colpo di ammenda.

penance ['penəns], *s.* (*eccl.*) penitenza: *to do* —, far penitenza.

to **penance**, *v.t.* dare una penitenza a.

Penates [pe'neiti:z], *s.pl.* (*relig. romana*) Penati.

pence [pens], *pl. di* **penny**.

pencel ['pensl], *s.* (*arc.*) pennoncello.

penchant ['pɑ:ŋʃɑ:ŋ], *s.* inclinazione, simpatia.

pencil ['pensl], *s.* **1.** (*arc.*) pennello (anche *fig.*): *coarse* —, pennello ruvido **2.** matita **3.** (*ott.*) pennello (gruppo di raggi convergenti) **4.** (*geom.*) raggiera ☆ — *-cap*, salvapunte; — *-case*, portamatite; — *-shaped*, a forma di matita ‖ *drawing* —, matita da disegno; *indelible* — matita copiativa; *propelling* —, matita automatica.

to **pencil**, *pass.p.p.* **pencilled** ['pensld], *v.t.* **1.** scribacchiare a matita **2.** disegnare, abbozzare (anche *fig.*).

pencilled, *ag.* disegnato a matita; segnato a matita: — *eyebrows*, sopracciglia segnate a matita.

penciller ['pensə*], *s.* (*sl.*) allibratore.

pendant ['pendənt], *ag.* **1.** pendente, pendulo **2.** sospeso, indeciso ‖ *s.* **1.** pendente, ciondolo **2.** (*mar.*) pennone **3.** « pendant » (oggetto che fa paio con un altro).

pendency ['pendənsi], *s.* pendenza.

pendent, *V.* **pendant**.

pendentive [pen'dentiv], *s.* (*arch.*) pennacchio.

pending ['pendiŋ], *ag.* pendente, vertente, non deciso; in sospeso.

pending, *prep.* **1.** durante: — *these discussions*, durante queste discussioni **2.** fino a: — *his return*, fino al suo ritorno.

pendragon [pen'drægən], *s.* (*st.*) capo, re (degli antichi Britanni e Gallesi).

pendular ['pendjulə*], *ag.* pendolare.

to **pendulate** ['pendjuleit], *v.i.* oscillare; *fig.* essere indeciso.

penduline ['pendjulain], *ag.* sospeso, pendulo (di nido); pendolino (di uccello).

pendulous ['pendjuləs], *ag.* sospeso, pendulo; oscillante.

pendulously ['pendjuləsli], *av.* in modo oscillante.

pendulum ['pendjuləm], *pl.* **pendulums** ['pendjuləmz], (*rar.*) **pendula** ['pendjulə], *s.* **1.** pendolo **2.** persona, cosa oscillante (anche *fig.*) ☆ — *motion*, moto pendolare.

Penelope [pi'neləpi], *no.pr.f.* (*lett.*) Penelope ‖ —*'s web*, tela di Penelope ‖ *s. fig.* moglie fedele.

peneplain ['pi:ni,plein], *s.* (*geol.*) regione quasi piana.

penetrability [,penitrə'biliti], *s.* penetrabilità.

penetrable ['penitrəbl], *ag.* penetrabile.

penetrableness ['penitrəblnis], *s.* penetrabilità.

penetralia [,peni'treiljə], *s.pl.* penetrali.

penetrant ['penitrənt], *ag.* penetrante, acuto (anche *fig.*).

to **penetrate** ['penitreit], *v.t.i.* **1.** penetrare, entrare in: *the mist penetrated the room*, la nebbia entrò nella stanza **2.** *fig.* capire, afferrare: *we soon penetrated the mystery*, scoprimmo presto il mistero **3.** diffondersi, spargersi: *the ideals of the French Revolution soon penetrated through Europe*, gli ideali della Rivoluzione Francese si diffusero ben presto in Europa **4.** *fig.* permeare: *his soul was penetrated with pity*, il suo animo era commosso.

penetrating ['penitreitiŋ], *ag.* penetrante, acuto (anche *fig.*).

penetratingly ['penitreitiŋli], *av.* in modo penetrante, acuto.

penetration [,peni'treiʃən], *s.* **1.** penetrazione **2.** discernimento, perspicacia, acutezza.

penetrative ['penitrətiv], *ag.* penetrante.

penetratively ['penitrətivli], *av.* in modo penetrante.

penguin ['peŋgwin], *s.* pinguino.

penial ['pi:niəl], *ag.* (*anat.*) del pene.

penicillate ['penisilit], *ag.* (*bot. zool.*) che termina a pennello.

penicillin [,peni'silin], *s.* (*farm.*) penicillina.

penicillium [,peni'siliəm], *s.* (*bot.*) penicillio.

peninsula [pi'ninsjulə], *s.* penisola.

peninsular [pi'ninsjulə*], *ag.* peninsulare.

penis ['pi:nis], *pl.* **penes** ['pi:niz], **penises** ['pi:nisiz], *s.* (*anat.*) pene.

penitence ['penitəns], *s.* penitenza.

penitent ['penitənt], *ag. s.c.* penitente.

penitential [,peni'tenʃəl], ag. penitenziale ‖ s. (eccl.) manuale delle penitenze.

penitentially [,peni'tenʃəli], av. da penitente.

penitentiary [,peni'tenʃəri], ag. penitenziale ‖ s. 1. (eccl.) penintenziere; penitenziera 2. riformatorio; casa di redenzione per prostitute; (amer.) penitenziario.

penitently ['penitəntli], av. da penitente.

penknife ['pennaif], pl. **penknives** ['pennaivz], s. temperino.

penman, pl. **penmen** ['penmən], s. 1. scrivano; calligrafo 2. autore, scrittore.

penmanship ['penmənʃip], s. 1. calligrafia; scrittura 2. arte dello scrivere.

pennant ['penənt], s. (mar.) 1. penzolo 2. fiamma 3. bandiera da segnalazione.

pennate ['penit], ag. pennuto.

penner ['penə*], s. (arc. dial.) custodia per penne.

penniform ['penifo:m], ag. penniforme.

penniless ['penilis], ag. senza un centesimo, al verde, poverissimo.

pennon ['penən], s. 1. pennone, pennoncello 2. (mar.) fiamma 3. bandiera, vessillo 4. sommolo (di ala di uccello).

penny ['peni], pl. **pennies** ['peniz], (per indicare il numero di monete), **pence** [pens] (per indicarne il valore) s. 1. penny (dodicesima parte di uno scellino abbr. d.) 2. soldo, denaro ‖ that's a pretty —, è una bella sommetta ‖ to earn (o to turn) an honest —, guadagnarsi onestamente da vivere ‖ a — for your thoughts, pagherei per sapere a che cosa pensi ‖ to take care of the pence, badare al centesimo ‖ in for a —, in for a pound, prov. chi è in ballo deve ballare ☆ — -a-liner, giornalista da strapazzo; — ante, (poker) apertura al buio di un « cent »; — -dreadful, libro giallo da pochi centesimi; rivista contenente storie orribili; — -farthing, (fam.) biciclo; — in-the-slot machine, distributrice automatica in cui si inseriscono monete da un « penny »; — -post, (arc.) organizzazione del servizio postale (istituita nel 1840); — -postage, affrancatura da un « penny »; — -weight, « penny-weight » (misura di peso = gr. 1,555); — -wise, attento alle più piccole spese: — -wise and pound foolish, taccagno nelle piccole, prodigo nelle grandi spese; — -worth, (fam.) un soldo, inezia: a — -worth of sweets, un soldo di dolci; a good — -worth, un buon affare.

pennyroyal ['peni'roiəl], s. (bot.) menta romana.

pennywort ['peniwə:t], s. (bot.) (erba) miseria.

penology [pi:'nolədʒi], s. (dir.) criminologia.

pensile ['pensail], ag. 1. pensile 2. (ornit.) di pendolino.

pension ['penʃən], nel senso 2. ['pa:ŋsio:ŋ], s. 1. pensione; vitalizio: to live on a —, vivere di una pensione 2. pensione: to live in —, vivere in pensione ☆ war —, pensione di guerra.

to pension, v.t. 1. pensionare; assegnare una pensione a 2. to — off, collocare a riposo, mettere in pensione.

pensionable ['penʃənəbl], ag. 1. avente diritto a pensione 2. che dà diritto a pensione.

pensionary ['penʃənəri], ag. 1. di pensione 2. pensionato ‖ s.c. 1. pensionato, pensionata 2. mercenario, mercenaria.

pensioner ['penʃənə*], s.c. 1. pensionato, pensionata 2. (rar.) mercenario, mercenaria ‖ 3. studente pagante alle università di Cambridge, Dublino.

pensive ['pensiv], ag. pensoso; triste.

pensively ['pensivli], av. pensosamente; mestamente.

pensiveness ['pensivnis], s. pensosità; malinconia.

penstock ['penstok], s. chiusa, diga.

pent [pent], ag. rinchiuso, chiuso ‖ — up emotion, emozione contenuta ☆ — -roof, tetto ad una falda.

pentachord ['pentəko:d], s. (mus.) pentacordo.

pentacle ['pentəkl], s. pentacolo.

pentad ['pentæd], s. 1. numero, gruppo di cinque; periodo di cinque anni 2. (chim.) elemento pentavalente.

pentagon ['pentəgən], s. 1. (geom.) pentagono 2. the Pentagon, il Pentagono (Ministero della Difesa negli U.S.A.).

pentagonal [pen'tægən], ag. (geom.) pentagonale.

pentagram ['pentəgræm], s. 1. pentacolo 2. (geom.) pentagono.

pentahedron [,pentə'hi:drən], s. (geom.) pentaedro.

pentameter [pen'tæmitə*], s. (poes.) pentametro.

pentane ['pentein], s. (chim.) pentano.

pentapody [pen'tæpədi], s. (poes.) pentapodia.

pentarchy ['pentə:ki], s. pentarchia.

pentasyllabic [,pentəsi'læbik], ag. (poes.) pentasillabico.

Pentateuch ['pentətju:k], s. (Bibbia) Pentateuco.

pentathlon [pen'tæθlon], s. (spor.) pentatlon.

Pentecost ['pentikost], s. (eccl.) Pentecoste.

Pentecostal [,penti'kostl], ag. (eccl.) di Pentecoste.

Penthesilea [,penθesi'li(:)ə], no.pr.f. (mit.) Pentesilea.

penthouse ['penthaus], s. 1. tettoia 2. piccolo fabbricato annesso 3. (amer.) appartamento sito sulla copertura di un edificio.

pentose ['pentous], s. (chim.) pentosio.

pentothal ['pentəθæl], s. pentotal, siero della verità.

penult(imate) [pi'nʌlt(imit)], ag. penultimo ‖ s. penultima sillaba.

penumbra [pi'nʌmbrə], s. penombra.

penumbral [pi'nʌmbrəl], ag. in penombra.

penurious [pi'njuəriəs], ag. 1. magro, sterile (di terreno) 2. miserabile, povero, indigente 3. economo, parsimonioso; avaro 4. meschino.

penuriously [pi'njuərəsli], av. 1. poveramente, miserabilmente 2. parsimoniosamente; avaramente 3. meschinamente.

penuriousness [pi'njuəriəsnis], s. 1. penuria; insufficienza 2. parsimonia; avarizia 3. meschinità.

penury ['penjuri], s. povertà (anche fig.), penuria, indigenza, miseria: — of ideas, povertà di idee; the — of their language, la povertà del loro linguaggio; they lived in —, vivevano nell'indigenza.

penwoman ['pen,wumən], pl. **penwomen** ['pen,wimin], s. scrittrice.

peon [pju:n], nel senso 2. ['pi:ən], s. 1. soldato di fanteria; poliziotto indigeno; attendente (in India) 2. peone, lavoratore a giornata (nell'America Latina) 3. chi è costretto a lavorare per risarcire un debito (nel Messico).

peonage ['pi:ənidʒ], **peonism** ['pi:ənizəm], s. peonaggio (sistema di lavoro forzato nel Messico).

peony ['piəni], s. (bot.) peonia ‖ to blush like a —, diventar rosso come un papavero.

people ['pi:pl], s. 1. popolo: the peoples of Asia, i popoli asiatici; English-speaking peoples, popoli di lingua inglese; government by the —, governo popolare; measures directed against the —, misure antipopolari; the peace-loving peoples, le nazioni amanti della pace; rising of the —, insurrezione popolare; the warlike peoples, i popoli guerrieri; the will of the —, la volontà del popolo, della nazione 2. coll. (con costruzione pl.) gente, persone: an employer and his —, un padrone e i suoi impiegati; the king and his —, il re e i suoi sudditi; most —, la maggior parte della gente; nice —, gente simpatica; old —, young —, i vecchi, i giovani; — are not always ready to help one another, la gente non è sempre pronta ad aiutarsi reciprocamente; — say, la gente dice, si dice; some hundred — were gathered there, erano circa cento le persone radunate là; young — prefer young company, i giovani preferiscono la compagnia dei giovani 3. coll. (con costruzione pl.) genitori, famiglia.

to people, v.t. popolare: densely peopled country, paese molto popolato; woods peopled with birds, boschi popolati di uccelli.

pep [pep], s. (sl. amer.) vigore, forza; iniziativa: full of —, pieno di iniziativa ☆ — talk, discorsino di incoraggiamento; ramanzina.

to **pep**, *pass. p.p.* **pepped** [pept], *v.t. (sl. amer.)* stimolare; rinvigorire ‖ *you need sthg. to — you up,* hai bisogno di ql.co. che ti tiri su il morale.

Pepin ['pepin], *no.pr.m. (st.)* Pipino ‖ *— the Short,* Pipino il Breve.

peplos ['peplɔs], **peplum** ['pepləm], **peplus** ['pepləs], *s.* peplo.

pepper ['pepə*], *s.* pepe: *black, white —,* pepe nero, pepe bianco; *ground —, whole —,* pepe in polvere, pepe in grani ‖ *to be as hot as —,* essere irritabile ☆ *-box* (o *-pot*) pepaiola; *— -caster* (o *— -castor),* pepaiola a spolvero; *— -mill,* macinapepe; *— -and-salt,* color pepe e sale.

to **pepper**, *v.t.* **1.** cospargere di pepe; condire con pepe **2.** *(mil.)* colpire: *to — the enemy with machine-gun fire,* mitragliare il nemico **3.** punire severamente.

peppercorn ['pepəkɔ:n], *s.* grano di pepe ☆ *— rent, (dir.)* affitto nominale per enfiteusi.

pepperiness ['pepərinis], *s.* l'essere pepato (anche *fig.*).

peppermint ['pepəmint], *s.* **1.** *(bot.)* menta peperita **2.** olio di menta peperita **3.** caramella di menta.

pepper-wort ['pepəwə:t], *s. (bot.)* crescione.

peppery ['pepəri], *ag.* **1.** pepato **2.** *fig.* pungente **3.** collerico, irascibile.

peppiness ['pepinis], *s. (sl. amer.)* energia, vigore, slancio.

peppy ['pepi], *ag. (sl. amer.)* pieno di energia.

pepsin ['pepsin], *s. (chim. biol.)* pepsina.

peptic ['peptik], *ag. (med.)* peptico, gastrico; digestivo ‖ *s.* **1.** digestivo **2.** *pl. (scherz.)* apparato digerente.

peptone ['peptoun], *s. (chim.)* peptone.

to **peptonize** ['peptənaiz], *v.t. (chim.)* peptonizzare.

per [pə*], *prep.* **1. per:** *— annum,* per anno; ogni anno; *— caput* (o *— head),* per ciascuno, a testa; *— cent,* per cento: *a five — cent discount,* uno sconto del cinque per cento; *— se,* per se stesso, per natura; *— yard,* alla iarda ‖ *as — enclosed account,* secondo l'acconto qui incluso; *as — sample,* secondo il campione; *as — usual, (fam.)* come al solito **2.** per, attraverso, per mezzo: *— post,* per posta; *— procurationem* (abbr. p. proc.), per procura; *— rail,* per ferrovia.

peracute [pərə'kju:t], *ag. (med.)* peracuto.

peradventure [pərəd'ventʃə*], **1.** *av. (arc.)* per caso **2.** forse ‖ *s. (arc.)* dubbio, incertezza: *without* (o *beyond) (all) —,* senza alcun dubbio.

to **perambulate** [pə'ræmbjuleit], *v.t.i.* **1.** passeggiare **2.** portare a spasso (un bambino) nella carrozzella **3.** visitare ufficialmente; ispezionare (un territorio) **4.** stabilire i confini (di parrocchia, ecc.).

perambulation [pə,ræmbju'leiʃən], *s.* **1.** passeggiata; giro **2.** visita ufficiale; ispezione (di un territorio percorrendone l'ambito) **3.** determinazione dei confini (di parrocchia, ecc. compiuta percorrendone l'ambito).

perambulator ['præmbjuleitə*], *s.* carrozzella per bambini.

perambulatory ['præmbjuleitəri], *ag.* **1.** vagante, mobile **2.** ispettivo; di, da ispezionare.

percale [pə'keil], *s.* percalle (tessuto).

percaline [,pə'kə'li:n], *s.* percallina (tessuto).

perceivable [pə'si:vəbl], *ag.* percettibile (con la mente e coi sensi): *no — difference,* nessuna sensibile differenza, nessuna differenza notevole.

perceivably [pə'si:vəbli], *av.* in modo percettibile.

to **perceive** [pə'si:v], *v.t.* **1.** percepire (con la mente e coi sensi): *to — the futility of sthg.,* rendersi conto della futilità di ql.co. **2.** accorgersi: *he perceived that he was being watched,* s'accorse che lo stavano osservando **3.** (I, V) scorgere: *I perceived him coming,* lo vidi arrivare.

percentage [pə'sentidʒ], *s.* percentuale: *only a small — of books are worth reading,* solo una piccola percentuale di libri è degna di essere letta; *to allow a — on all transactions, (comm.)* concedere un tanto per cento su tutte le operazioni.

percept ['pə:sept], *s. (fil.)* oggetto di percezione.

perceptibility [pə,septə'biliti], *s.* percettibilità.

perceptible [pə'septəbl], *ag.* percettibile (con la mente e coi sensi): *— to the eye,* visibile.

perceptibly [pə'septəbli], *av.* in modo percettibile.

perception [pə'sepʃən], *s.* **1.** percezione; intuizione: *the — of truth,* l'intuizione della verità **2.** *(dir.)* riscossione (di imposte, rendite).

perceptive [pə'septiv], *ag.* percettivo.

perceptiveness [pə'septivnis], **perceptivity** [,pə:sep-'tiviti], *s.* percettività.

perch[1] [pə:tʃ], *s.* **1.** gruccia; posatoio (per uccelli): *the bird takes its —,* l'uccello si posa ‖ *come off your —, (fam.)* scendi dal piedistallo, non darti tante arie ‖ *to hop the —, (fam.)* morire ‖ *to knock s.o. off his —,* spodestare qlcu. **2.** *(arc.)* pertica, bastone **3.** pertica (misura di lunghezza = m. 5,0292) **4.** timone (di vettura a quattro ruote) ☆ *square —, (agr.)* pertica (misura di superficie = m.² 25,292).

to **perch**[1], *v.t.i.* appollaiarsi, stare appollaiato; collocare su sostegno, posatoio: *the town was perched on a hill,* la città era appollaiata su di una collina; *to — on a stool,* appollaiarsi su di uno sgabello.

perch[2], *s. (ittiol.)* pesce persico.

perchance [pə'tʃɑ:ns], *av. (arc.)* **1.** forse: *to sleep, — to dream,* dormire, forse sognare **2.** per caso, per avventura.

perching [pə'tʃiŋ], *s. (ind. tessile)* esame dei difetti di un tessuto.

perchlorate [pə'klɔ:rit], *s. (chim.)* perclorato.

Perceval ['pə:sivəl], *no.pr.m. (lett.)* Parsifal.

percipience [pə(:)'sipiəns], **percipiency** [pə(:)'sipiənsi], *s.* (facoltà di) percezione.

percipient [pə(:)'sipiənt], *ag.* capace di percezione ‖ *s.* individuo che ha facoltà telepatiche.

to **percolate** ['pə:kəleit], *v.t.i.* filtrare; infiltrarsi, penetrare (anche *fig.*): *rain percolates through sand,* la pioggia penetra nella sabbia; *theories percolating through the people,* dottrine che s'infiltrano tra il popolo; *to — the coffee,* filtrare, passare il caffè.

percolation [,pə:kə'leiʃən], *s.* filtrazione; infiltrazione (anche *fig.*).

percolator ['pə:kəleitə*], *s.* **1.** filtro **2.** macchinetta per il caffè.

to **percuss** [pə'kʌs], *v.t.* **1.** *(med.)* battere (a scopo di diagnosi), sottoporre a percussione **2.** percuotere.

percussion [pə'kʌʃən], *s.* percussione (anche *med.*) ☆ *— band,* orchestrina di strumenti a percussione; *— -cap,* capsula a percussione; *— -gun,* fucile a percussione; *— -pin,* percussore (di arma da fuoco).

percussive [pə'kʌsiv], *ag.* che percuote; di percussione.

percutaneous [,pə:kju(:)'teinjəs], *ag.* sottocutaneo.

perdition [pə'diʃən], *s.* **1.** perdizione **2.** *(teol.)* pena, castigo eterno; dannazione.

perdu(e) [pə'dju:], *ag.* **1.** nascosto **2.** *(mil.)* in posizione avanzata e pericolosa; in agguato: *to lie —,* essere in posizione avanzata e pericolosa; tendere un'imboscata ‖ *s. (arc.)* soldato, soldati in missione pericolosa, disperata.

perdurability [pə,djurə'biliti], *s.* perdurabilità.

perdurable [pə'djuərəbl], *ag.* **1.** durevole (di amicizia, ecc.); stabile, permanente (di pace, ecc.); resistente (di granito, ecc.) **2.** *(teol.)* eterno (di vita, ecc.).

perdurably [pə'djuərəbli], *av.* durevolmente; stabilmente, permanentemente.

perdurance [pə'djurəns], *s.* permanenza.

to **peregrinate** ['perigrineit], *v.i.* vagare; peregrinare.

peregrination [,perigri'neiʃən], *s.* peregrinazione.

peregrinator ['perigrineitə*], *s.c.* viaggiatore, viaggiatrice; pellegrino, pellegrina.

peregrin(e) ['perigrin], *ag.* **1.** *(arc.)* forestiero; peregrino, strano, esotico **2.** migratorio (di uccello) ‖ *s. (ornit.)* falcone pellegrino.

peremptorily [pə'remptərili], *av.* perentoriamente; imperiosamente.

peremptoriness [pə'remptərinis], s. perentorietà; imperiosità.

peremptory [pə'remptəri], ag. 1. (dir.) perentorio 2. imperioso, autoritario; dogmatico, cattedratico ☆ — -writ, mandato di comparizione.

perennial [pə'renjəl], ag. perenne: — source, fonte perenne ‖ s. (bot.) pianta perenne.

perenniality [pə,reni'æliti], s. perennità.

perennially [pə'renjəli], av. perennemente.

perfect ['pə:fikt], ag. 1. perfetto; eccellente; compiuto, completo, intero; puro, vero: he is a — fool, è un perfetto idiota; he is a — stranger to me, mi è completamente sconosciuto; there is no such thing as — bliss, non esiste una felicità assoluta; to be —, avere tutte le perfezioni; to have a — knowledge of sthg., conoscere ql.co. a fondo 2. (mat.) perfetto, esatto: — number, — square, numero, quadrato perfetto 3. (bot. zool.) tipico, caratteristico 4. (gram.) perfetto 5. (mus.) giusto ‖ s. (gram.) il perfetto ☆ past —, (gram.) trapassato prossimo; present —, (gram.) passato prossimo.

to **perfect** [pə'fekt], v.t. perfezionare, migliorare; rendere perfetto; completare, terminare, dare l'ultimo tocco a: to — an invention, perfezionare un'invenzione; to — oneself in a foreign language, perfezionarsi in una lingua straniera.

perfectibility [pə,fekti'biliti], s. perfettibilità.

perfectible [pə'fektəbl], ag. perfettibile.

perfection [pə'fekʃən], s. 1. perfezione: to attain —, raggiungere la perfezione; to do sthg. to —, fare ql.co. alla perfezione; to succeed to —, riuscire a perfezione 2. perfezionamento; compimento: the — of the machine took many months, il perfezionamento della macchina richiese molti mesi 3. personificazione (di qualità): to be the — of beauty, essere la bellezza personificata 4. (bot. zool.) sviluppo completo; maturità.

perfectionism [pə'fekʃənizəm], s. (fil. teol.) perfezionismo.

perfectionist [pə'fekʃənist], s.c. perfezionista.

perfectiveness [pə'fektivnis], s. l'essere perfettivo.

perfective [pə'fektiv], ag. perfettivo (di verbo).

perfectly ['pə:fiktli], av. perfettamente: it is — ridiculous, è assolutamente, completamente ridicolo; she is — right, ha perfettamente ragione; to do sthg. —, fare ql.co. alla perfezione.

perfectness ['pə:fiktnis], s. perfezione.

perfervid [pə:'fə:vid], ag. fervidissimo; molto ardente; intenso.

perfidious [pə:'fidiəs], ag. perfido, sleale, infido.

perfidiously [pə:'fidiəsli], av. perfidamente, slealmente.

perfidiousness [pə:'fidiəsnis], **perfidy** ['pə:fidi], s. perfidia, slealtà: an act of —, una perfidia.

perfoliate [pə:'fouliit], ag. (bot.) perfogliato.

perforable ['pə:fərəbl], ag. perforabile.

to **perforate** ['pə:fəreit], v.t.i. 1. (mec.) perforare; forare 2. penetrare.

perforated ['pə:fəreitid], ag. 1. perforato 2. poroso.

perforating ['pə:fəreitiŋ], ag. (patol.) perforante: — ulcer, ulcera perforante.

perforation [,pə:fə'reiʃən], s. 1. perforazione 2. foro; serie di fori.

perforative ['pə:fərətiv], ag. perforante.

perforator ['pə:fəreitə*], s. 1. perforatore 2. (mec.) perforatrice.

perforce [pə'fɔ:s], av. per forza.

to **perform** [pə'fɔ:m], v.t.i. 1. operare, compiere, adempiere: he performed without speaking what he had been told, eseguì senza parlare ciò che gli avevano detto; to — one's duties, adempiere i propri doveri; to — an operation on s.o., (chir.) operare qlcu. 2. (mus.) eseguire 3. (teat.) rappresentare; recitare, interpretare una parte: what play did they —?, che commedia recitarono? 4. dare spettacolo (di animali ammaestrati).

performable [pə'fɔ:məbl], ag. 1. eseguibile; fattibile; celebrabile 2. (teat.) rappresentabile.

performance [pə'fɔ:məns], s. 1. adempimento, esecuzione, atto: his — was worthy of praise, il suo fu un atto degno di lode 2. rappresentazione, spettacolo teatrale: at the afternoon —, alla rappresentazione del pomeriggio; there are two performances a day, ci sono due rappresentazioni al giorno ☆ — rights, diritti di esecuzione, di rappresentazione.

performer [pə'fɔ:mə*], s.c. 1. esecutore, esecutrice 2. attore, attrice.

performing [pə'fɔ:miŋ], ag. ammaestrato ☆ — dog, cane ammaestrato.

perfume ['pə:fju:m], s. profumo.

to **perfume** [pə'fju:m], v.t. profumare.

perfumeless ['pə:fju:mlis], ag. senza profumo.

perfumer [pə'fju:mə*], s.c. profumiere, profumiera.

perfumery [pə'fju:məri], s. 1. profumeria 2. profumi.

perfunctorily [pə'fʌŋktərili], av. superficialmente; con negligenza.

perfunctoriness [pə'fʌŋktərinis], s. noncuranza, negligenza.

perfunctory [pə'fʌŋktəri], ag. 1. meccanico, superficiale: a — examination, un esame superficiale 2. negligente, noncurante: a — lecturer, un oratore svogliato.

to **perfuse** [pə'fju:z], v.t. aspergere; cospargere: to — a bunch of flowers with water, aspergere d'acqua un mazzo di fiori.

perfusion [pə'fju:ʒən], s. aspersione; (med.) perfusione.

perfusive [pə'fju:siv], ag. che effonde, sparge, versa.

pergameneous [,pə:gə'mi:niəs], ag. pergamenaceo.

pergola ['pə:gələ], s. pergola, pergolato.

perhaps [pə'hæps], av. forse, probabilmente: — we shall return tomorrow, forse ritorneremo domani ‖ — so, — not, forse sì, forse no.

peri ['piəri], s. (mit. persiana) peri (genio benefico).

periagua [,peri'ægwə], s. piroga.

perianth ['periænθ], s. (bot.) perianzio.

periapt ['periæpt], s. amuleto, talismano.

pericarditis [,perika:'daitis], s. (patol.) pericardite.

pericardium [,peri'ka:djəm], s. (anat.) pericardio.

pericarp ['perika:p], s. (bot.) pericarpo.

Pericles ['perikli:z], no.pr.m. (st. greca) Pericle.

pericranium [,peri'kreinjəm], s. 1. (anat.) pericranio 2. (scherz.) cervello, intelligenza.

periderm ['peridə:m], s. (bot.) epidermide.

peridot ['peridət], s. (min.) crisolito.

perigastric [,peri'gæstrik], ag. (anat.) perigastrico.

perigee ['peridʒi:], s. (astr.) perigeo.

perihelion [,peri'hi:ljən], s. (astr.) perielio.

peril ['peril], s. pericolo, rischio: at the — of, col rischio di; at your —, a vostro rischio.

to **peril**, pass. p.p. **perilled** ['perild], v.t. porre in pericolo, a repentaglio; rischiare.

perilous ['periləs], ag. pericoloso.

perilously ['periləsli], av. pericolosamente.

perilousness ['periləsnis], s. pericolo, rischio.

perimeter [pə'rimitə*], s. (geom.) perimetro.

perimetric(al) [,peri'metrik(əl)], ag. perimetrico.

perineal [,peri'ni:əl], ag. (anat.) perineale, del perineo.

perineum [,peri'ni:əm], s. (anat.) perineo.

period ['piəriəd], ag. relativo ad un periodo; caratteristico di un'epoca ‖ s. 1. periodo, spazio di tempo: a — of three months, un periodo di tre mesi; in the difficult periods of our lives, nei momenti difficili della nostra vita ‖ the —, oggigiorno: the girl of the —, il tipo di ragazza d'oggi 2. (astr. fis. geol.) periodo, ciclo 3. (med.) stadio, fase di una malattia; pl. (fisiol.) mestruazioni 4. (mus.) periodo 5. (gram.) frase, periodo; punto (segno ortografico): a long —, un periodo lungo 6. (spor.) fase, tempo di una partita ☆ — furniture, mobili antichi; — pieces, mobili di antiquariato; — play, commedia di costume.

periodic[1] [,piəri'ɔdik], ag. periodico: — paper, periodico ☆ — table, (chim.) tavola dei periodici.

periodic[2], ag. (chim.) periodico: — acid, acido periodico.

periodical [ˌpiəri'odikəl], *ag.s.* periodico.
periodically [ˌpiəri'odikəli], *av.* periodicamente.
periodicity [ˌpiəriə'disiti], *s.* periodicità.
periosteal [ˌperi'ostiəl], *ag.* (*anat.*) del periostio.
periosteum [ˌperi'ostiəm], *s.* (*anat.*) periostio.
periostitis [ˌperios'taitis], *s.* (*patol.*) periostite.
peripatetic [ˌperipə'tetik], *ag.* peripatetico ‖ *s.* **1.** (*fil.*) peripatetico **2.** (*scherz.*) venditore ambulante.
peripatetically [ˌperipə'tetikəli], *av.* da peripatetico.
peripateticism [ˌperipə'tetisizəm], *s.* peripateticismo.
peripet(e)ia [ˌperipi'taiə], *s.* peripezia, vicissitudine; improvviso cambiamento di fortuna.
peripheral [pə'rifərəl], *ag.* periferico.
peripherally [pə'rifərəli], *av.* perifericamente.
periphery [pə'rifəri], *s.* **1.** periferia; circonferenza; perimetro **2.** superficie.
periphrase ['perifreiz], **periphrasis** [pə'rifrəsis], *s.* perifrasi.
periphrastic [ˌperi'fræstik], *ag.* perifrastico.
periphrastically [ˌperi'fræstikəli], *av.* in modo perifrastico.
periplus ['peripləs], *s.* periplo, circumnavigazione.
perique [pə'ri:k], *s.* tabacco della Luisiana.
periscope ['periskoup], *s.* (*mar. ott.*) periscopio.
periscopic [ˌperi'skopik], *ag.* (*mar. ott.*) periscopico.
to **perish** ['periʃ], *v.t.i.* **1.** perire, morire (anche *fig.*): *he perished by the sword*, morì in un combattimento all'arma bianca; *to — with cold, starvation*, morire di freddo, di fame: *she was perishing with cold, fig.* moriva di freddo **2.** distruggere, rovinare: *the frost had perished all the flowers in the garden*, il gelo aveva rovinato tutti i fiori del giardino.
perishable ['periʃəbl], *ag.* **1.** mortale **2.** deperibile; deteriorabile: *— goods*, merci soggette a deterioramento.
perishableness ['periʃəblnis], *s.* deperibilità; deteriorabilità.
perishables ['periʃəblz], *s.pl.* merci, cibi deteriorabili.
perisperm ['perispə:m], *s.* (*bot.*) perisperma.
perispomenon [ˌperi'spouminən], *ag.* (*gram. greca*) perispomeno ‖ *s.* (*gram. greca*) vocabolo perispomeno.
perissodactyl(e) [pəˌrisou'dæktil], *ags.* (*zool.*) perissodattilo.
peristalsis [ˌperi'stælsis], *s.* (*fisiol.*) peristalsi.
peristaltic [ˌperi'stæltik], *ag.* (*fisiol.*) peristaltico.
peristoma [pi'ristoumə], **peristome** ['peristoum], *s.* (*bot. zool.*) peristoma.
peristyle ['peristail], *s.* (*arch.*) peristilio.
peritoneum [ˌperitou'ni:əm], *s.* (*anat.*) peritoneo.
peritonitis [ˌperitə'naitis], *s.* (*patol.*) peritonite.
periwig ['periwig], *s.* parrucca.
periwinkle[1] ['peri,wiŋkl], *s.* (*bot.*) pervinca.
periwinkle[2], *s.* (*zool.*) litorina.
to **perjure** ['pə:dʒə*], *v.t.*: *to — oneself*, spergiurare, rendersi spergiuro.
perjured ['pə:dʒəd], *ag.* spergiuro.
perjurer ['pə:dʒərə*], *s.c.* spergiuro, spergiura.
perjurious [pə'dʒuəriəs], *ag.* spergiuro.
perjuriously [pə'dʒuəriəsli], *av.* da spergiuro.
perjury ['pə:dʒəri], *s.* spergiuro, giuramento falso.
perk[1] [pə:k], *s.* (*sl.*) *abbr.* di **perquisite**.
to **perk**[2], *v.t.i.* **1.** rizzare, drizzare: *the dog perked up its ears*, il cane drizzò le orecchie **2.** avere un portamento fiero, altezzoso **3.** rianimare; infondere fiducia a: *the news perked me up no end*, (*fam.*) la notizia mi rallegrò infinitamente.
perky ['pə:ki], *ag.* disinvolto; birichino; impertinente.
perlite ['pə:lait], *s.* (*min.*) perlite.
perm [pə:m], *s.* (*fam.*) ondulazione permanente ☆ *home —*, permanente fatta in casa.
permanence ['pə:mənəns], **permanency** ['pə:mənənsi], *s.* **1.** permanenza **2.** cosa che rimane: *I can't offer you a —*, non posso offrirvi un'occupazione fissa.
permanent ['pə:mənənt], *ag.* permanente, fisso: *— address*, indirizzo permanente; *— situation*, occupazione fissa; *— wave*, ondulazione permanente.

permanently ['pə:mənəntli], *av.* permanentemente.
permanganate [pə:'mæŋgənit], *s.* (*chim.*) permanganato.
permeability [ˌpə:mjə'biliti], *s.* permeabilità.
permeable ['pə:mjəbl], *ag.* permeabile.
permeance ['pə:miəns], *s.* (*elett.*) permeanza.
permeant ['pə:miənt], *ag.* permeante.
to **permeate** ['pə:mieit], *v.t.i.* permeare, penetrare: *ideas that have permeated (through o into o among) the people*, idee che si sono diffuse tra il popolo.
permeation [ˌpə:mi'eiʃən], *s.* (*fis.*) permeazione.
permed [pə:md], *ag.* ondulato con la permanente.
permissibility [pəˌmisi'biliti], *s.* ammissibilità.
permissible [pə'misəbl], *ag.* ammissibile, tollerabile.
permissibly [pə'misəbli], *av.* in modo ammissibile, tollerabile.
permission [pə'miʃən], *s.* permesso, autorizzazione: *you have my — to do it*, hai la mia autorizzazione a farlo.
permissive [pə'misiv], *ag.* **1.** che permette **2.** permesso, lecito **3.** facoltativo.
permissively [pə'misivli], *av.* lecitamente.
permit ['pə:mit], *s.* permesso, autorizzazione ☆ *driving —*, patente di guida; *international driving —*, patentino internazionale.
to **permit** [pə'mit], *pass.p.p.* **permitted** [pə'mitid], *v.t.i.* (III, IV) permettere, concedere, tollerare, autorizzare: *— me to introduce my friend to you*, permettetemi di presentarvi il mio amico; *he permits his name to be mentioned*, egli permette che si faccia il suo nome; *she was not permitted to go*, non la autorizzarono ad andare; *the situation permits of no delay*, la situazione non ammette indugio; *to be permitted to sit for an examination*, essere ammesso ad un esame ‖ *weather permitting*, tempo permettendo.
permittee [ˌpə:mi'ti:], *s.c.* chi ha un permesso.
permitter [pə'mitə*], *s.c.* chi permette, chi autorizza.
permutable [pə'mju:təbl], *ag.* permutabile.
permutableness [pə'mju:təblnis], *s.* permutabilità.
permutably [pə'mju:təbli], *av.* in modo permutabile.
permutation [ˌpə:mju(:)'teiʃən], *s.* **1.** (*mat.*) permutazione **2.** (*rar.*) cambiamento.
to **permute** [pə'mju:t], *v.t.* permutare, alterare, cambiare.
pernicious [pə:'niʃəs], *ag.* pericoloso, nocivo; fatale ☆ *— anaemia*, (*patol.*) anemia perniciosa.
perniciously [pə:'niʃəsli], *av.* in modo pernicioso, nocivo.
perniciousness [pə:'niʃəsnis], *s.* perniciosità.
pernickety [pə'nikiti], *ag.* (*fam.*) **1.** meticoloso; pedante, noioso **2.** delicato, ipersensibile.
pernoctation [ˌpə:nɔk'teiʃən], *s.* veglia notturna; (*eccl.*) notte passata in preghiere.
peronospora [ˌperou'nospərə], *s.* (*bot.*) peronospora.
to **perorate** ['perəreit], *v.i.* **1.** perorare **2.** pronunciare un'arringa.
peroration [ˌperə'reiʃən], *s.* **1.** perorazione **2.** arringa.
peroxide [pə'roksaid], *s.* (*chim.*) perossido: *— of hydrogen*, acqua ossigenata.
to **peroxide**, *v.t.* ossigenare.
to **perpend** [pə:'pend], *v.t.i.* (*arc. scherz.*) riflettere (su); ponderare (su).
perpendicular [ˌpə:pən'dikjulə*], *ag.* perpendicolare ‖ *s.* **1.** (*geom.*) perpendicolare **2.** archipenzolo, filo a piombo **3.** (*sl.*) pasto consumato in piedi ☆ *— style*, (*arch.*) gotico fiammeggiante.
perpendicularity ['pə:pən,dikju'læriti], *s.* perpendicolarità.
perpendicularly [ˌpə:pən'dikjuləli], *av.* perpendicolarmente.
perpetrable ['pə:pitrəbl], *ag.* perpetrabile.
to **perpetrate** ['pə:pitreit], *v.t.* perpetrare, consumare, commettere.
perpetration [ˌpə:pi'treiʃən], *s.* perpetrazione.
perpetrator ['pə:pitreitə*], *s.* perpetratore.
perpetual [pə'petjuəl], *ag.* **1.** perpetuo, perenne, eter-

no 2. continuo; costante: — *nagging*, continuo lagnarsi (specialmente di donna) ☆ — *motion*, moto perpetuo.

perpetually [pə'petjuəli], *av.* 1. perpetuamente, eternamente 2. continuamente.

perpetuance [pə'petjuəns], *s.* perpetuazione.

to perpetuate [pə'petjueit], *v.t.* perpetuare, rendere perpetuo.

perpetuation [pə,petju'eiʃən], *s.* perpetuazione.

perpetuator [pə'petjueitə*], *s.* perpetuatore.

perpetuity [,pə:pi'tju(:)iti], *s.* 1. perpetuità, eternità; continuità: *in* (o *for* o *to*) —, in perpetuo, per sempre 2. proprietà a vita 3. (*dir.*) rendita vitalizia.

to perplex [pə'pleks], *v.t.* 1. rendere perplesso; mettere in imbarazzo: *to — s.o.*, render perplesso qlcu. 2. complicare, imbrogliare: *to — a matter*, imbrogliare una faccenda.

perplexed [pə'plekst], *ag.* perplesso, confuso, imbarazzato.

perplexedly [pə'pleksidli], *av.* con perplessità; con aria imbarazzata.

perplexing [pə'pleksiŋ], *ag.* che rende perplesso; imbarazzante.

perplexingly [pə'pleksiŋli], *av.* in modo da rendere perplesso, in modo imbarazzante.

perplexity [pə'pleksiti], *s.* 1. perplessità; imbarazzo 2. complicazione, confusione.

perquisite ['pə:kwizit], *s.* 1. vantaggio; guadagno occasionale; profitto eventuale 2. mancia abituale 3. (*dir.*) prerogativa, diritto.

perquisition [,pə:kwi'ziʃən], *s.* perquisizione (di domicilio).

perron ['perən], *s.* (*arch.*) gradinata esterna (di chiesa, ecc.).

perry ['peri], *s.* sidro di pere.

perse [pə:s], *ag.s.* (*arc.*) 1. (color) grigio azzurro 2. (color) perso.

per se [pə:'sei], *l.av.* in sè, da sè.

to persecute ['pə:sikju:t], *v.t.* 1. perseguitare 2. importunare; tormentare, molestare.

persecution [,pə:si'kju:ʃən], *s.* persecuzione ☆ — *mania*, mania di persecuzione.

persecutor ['pə:sikju:tə*], *s.* persecutore.

persecutory ['pə:sikju:təri], *ag.* persecutore.

Persephone [pə:'sefəni], *no.pr.f.* (*mit.*) Persefone.

Perseus ['pə:sju:s], *no.pr.m.* (*mit.*) Perseo.

perseverance [,pə:si'viərəns], *s.* perseveranza, costanza.

perseverant [,pə:si'viərənt], *ag.* (*rar.*) perseverante.

to persevere [,pə:si'viə*], *v.i.* perseverare, persistere.

persevering [,pə:si'viəriŋ], *ag.* perseverante.

perseveringly [,pə:si'viəriŋli], *av.* con perseveranza.

Persia ['pə:ʃə], *no.pr.* (*geog.*) Persia.

Persian ['pə:ʃən], *ag.* persiano, della Persia ‖ *s.c.* persiano, persiana ‖ *s.* lingua persiana ☆ — *blinds*, persiane; — *carpet*, tappeto persiano; — *lamb*, agnellino di Persia.

persiennes [,pə:si'enz], *s.pl.* persiane incanalate.

persiflage [,pəəsi'fla:ʒ], *s.* canzonatura, presa in giro.

persimmon [pə:'simən], *s.* 1. (*bot.*) ebano, diospiro 2. kaki (pianta, frutto).

to persist [pə'sist], *v.i.* 1. persistere; continuare, durare: *the fever persists*, la febbre persiste 2. ostinarsi; perseverare: *to — in sthg.*, ostinarsi in ql.co.; *to — in doing sthg.*, ostinarsi a fare ql.co.

persistence [pə'sistəns], **persistency** [pə'sistənsi], *s.* 1. persistenza, durata 2. perseveranza; ostinazione, tenacia.

persistent [pə'sistənt], *ag.* 1. persistente, duraturo; continuo 2. ostinato; tenace 3. (*bot. zool.*) permanente.

persistently [pə'sistəntli], *av.* 1. costantemente; in modo permanente 2. con ostinazione.

person ['pə:sn], *s.* 1. persona, individuo; *pl.* persone, gente: *in —*, *in one's own —*, di persona, personalmente; *the Queen's sacred —*, la sacra persona della regina; *who is that —?*, (anche *spreg.*) chi è quel

tizio, quell'individuo? ‖ *young persons*, i giovani 2. corpo, figura: *she has a fine —*, ha una bella figura 3. (*gram.*) persona: *verb in the first —*, verbo alla prima persona 4. (*dir.*) persona 5. (*teol.*) persona: *the three persons of the Godhead*, le tre persone della Trinità 6. (*arc. teat.*) carattere, personaggio.

persona [pə:'sounə], *pl.* **personae** [pə:'souni:], *s.* 1. (*psicologia*) persona, individuo 2. (*lett.*) personaggio.

personable ['pə:snəbl], *ag.* bello, ben fatto, di bell'aspetto.

personage ['pə:snidʒ], *s.* 1. personaggio, persona importante: *a high —*, una personalità 2. personaggio (di commedia, romanzo, ecc.).

personal ['pə:snl], *ag.* 1. personale, individuale; privato: — *acquaintance*, conoscenza personale; — *business* (o — *matter*), affare privato; — *effects*, effetti personali 2. (*gram.*) personale: — *pronoun*, pronome personale ‖ *s.* (*gener. pl. amer.*) cronaca mondana ☆ — *column*, avvisi personali nella piccola pubblicità; — *estate* (o — *goods*), beni mobili.

personality [,pə:sə'næliti], *s.* 1. personalità: *to be lacking in —*, mancare di personalità 2. *pl.* critica malevola: *to indulge in personalities*, abbandonarsi a critiche malevole ☆ — *cult*, (*neol.*) culto della personalità.

personalization [,pə:sənəlai'zeiʃən], *s.* personificazione.

to personalize ['pə:sənəlaiz], *v.t.* personificare.

personally ['pə:snəli], *av.* personalmente; di persona.

personalty ['pə:snlti], *s.* (*dir.*) beni mobili.

to personate ['pə:səneit], *v.t.* 1. (*teat.*) impersonare; fare la parte di, rappresentare 2. (*dir.*) farsi passare per (con scopo disonesto).

personation [,pə:sə'neiʃən], *s.* 1. (*teat.*) rappresentazione (d'un personaggio) 2. sostituzione di persona (per frode) 3. personificazione (di qualità, ecc.).

personator ['pə:səneitə*], *s.* 1. attore; caratterista 2. chi si fa passare per un altro.

personification [pə:,sonifi'keiʃən], *s.* personificazione.

to personify [pə:'sonifai], *v.t.* personificare.

personnel [,pə:sə'nel], *s.* personale ☆ *managing —*, personale direttivo.

perspective [pə'spektiv], *ag.* prospettico; di, in prospettiva ‖ *s.* 1. (*geom.*) prospettiva 2. disegno in prospettiva 3. vista, veduta; *fig.* prospettiva: *a fine — opened out before his eyes*, una bella vista si apriva davanti ai suoi occhi; *with a long — of happy days before us*, una lunga prospettiva di giorni felici davanti a noi.

perspectively [pə'spektivli], *av.* prospettivamente.

perspicacious [,pə:spi'keiʃəs], *ag.* perspicace, penetrante, sagace.

perspicaciously [,pə:spi'keiʃəsli], *av.* perspicacemente.

perspicacity [,pə:spi'kæsiti], *s.* perspicacia, sagacità.

perspicuity [,pə:spi'kju(:)iti], *s.* perspicuità, chiarezza.

perspicuous [pə'spikjuəs], *ag.* perspicuo, chiaro, evidente.

perspicuously [pə'spikjuəsli], *av.* in modo chiaro, chiaramente.

perspicuousness [pə'spikjuəsnis], *s.* perspicuità, chiarezza.

perspirable [pəs'paiərəbl], *ag.* 1. che permette la traspirazione 2. traspirabile, che può essere eliminato con la traspirazione.

perspiration [,pə:spə'reiʃən], *s.* traspirazione, sudore.

perspiratory [pəs'paiərətəri], *ag.* sudorifero.

to perspire [pəs'paiə*], *v.t.i.* traspirare, sudare.

persuadable [pə'sweidəbl], *ag.* persuadibile.

to persuade [pə'sweid], *v.t.* (IV) persuadere, convincere: *I'm not persuaded of that fact*, non sono persuaso di quel fatto; *she persuaded him into leaving at once*, lo persuase a partire subito; *they will — him to do it*, lo persuaderanno a farlo; *to — oneself*, persuadersi.

persuader [pə'sweidə*], *s.c.* chi persuade ‖ *s.pl.* (*sl.*) speroni.

persuasibility [pə‚sweisi′biliti], *s.* disposizione a essere persuaso.

persuasible [pə′sweisibl], *ag.* persuasibile.

persuasion [pə′sweiʒən], *s.* **1.** persuasione, convinzione **2.** credenza, fede **3.** (*scherz.*) razza, genere: *a man of German* —, un uomo di nazionalità tedesca.

persuasive [pə′sweisiv], *ag.* persuasivo ‖ *s.* cosa che persuade; motivo.

persuasively [pə′sweisivli], *av* persuasivamente.

persuasiveness [pə′sweisivnis], *s.* capacità persuasiva; forza di persuasione.

persuasory [pə′sweisəri], *ag.* persuasivo.

pert [pə:t], *ag.* **1.** impudente, impertinente **2.** lesto, vivo, sveglio **3.** (*rar.*) abile, esperto.

to **pertain** [pə:′tein], *v.i.* appartenere; riferirsi: *the enthusiasm pertaining to youth*, l'entusiasmo proprio della gioventù; *subjects pertaining to religion*, soggetti che concernono, riguardano la religione.

pertinacious [‚pə:ti′neiʃəs], *ag.* pertinace; ostinato, testardo; persistente.

pertinaciously [‚pə:ti′neiʃəsli], *av.* pertinacemente; ostinatamente; persistentemente.

pertinaciousness [‚pə:ti′neiʃəsnis], **pertinacity** [‚pə:ti′næsiti], *s.* pertinacia; ostinatezza, ostinazione.

pertinence [′pə:tinəns], **pertinency** [′pə:tinənsi], *s.* pertinenza; convenienza; opportunità.

pertinent [′pə:tinənt], *ag.* pertinente; conveniente; adatto, appropriato.

pertinently [′pə:tinəntli], *av.* in modo pertinente, appropriato.

pertly [′pə:tli], *av.* **1.** insolentemente **2.** vivacemente.

pertness [′pə:tnis], *s.* **1.** insolenza; petulanza **2.** vivacità.

to **perturb** [pə′tə:b], *v.t.* perturbare; sconvolgere; allarmare.

perturbation [‚pə:tə:′beiʃən], *s.* perturbamento; perturbazione.

perturbative [pə′tə:bɔtiv], *ag.* perturbativo.

perturbator [′pə:tə‚beitə*], **perturber** [pə′tə:bə*], *s.* perturbatore.

pertussis [pə′tʌsis], *s.* (*patol.*) pertosse.

Peru [pə′ru:], *no.pr.* (*geog.*) Perù.

peruke [pə′ru:k], *s.* parrucca.

perusal [pə′ru:zəl], *s.* **1.** lettura (attenta) **2.** *fig.* esame attento (di persona, ecc.).

to **peruse** [pə′ru:z], *v.t.* **1.** leggere (attentamente) **2.** *fig.* studiare, esaminare (persone, ecc.).

peruser [pə′ru:zə*], *s.* lettore; esaminatore.

Peruvian [pə′ru:vjən], *ag.* peruviano ‖ *s.c.* peruviano, peruviana.

to **pervade** [pə:′veid], *v.t.* pervadere; permeare; saturare, riempire: *to become pervaded with*, compenetrarsi di, saturarsi di.

pervasion [pə:′veiʒən], *s.* penetrazione; diffusione.

pervasive [pə:′veisiv], *ag.* penetrante (di profumo, ecc.); invadente.

pervasively [pə:′veisivli], *av.* in modo penetrante.

pervasiveness [pə:′veisivnis], *s.* penetrazione.

perverse [pə′və:s], *ag.* **1**.perverso; cattivo; corrotto; pervertito **2.** capriccioso; intrattabile **3.** errato; ingiusto (di verdetto).

perversely [pə′və:sli], *av.* perversamente; corrottamente.

perverseness [pə′və:snis], *s.* perversità; cattiveria.

perversion [pə:′və:ʃən], *s.* perversione; pervertimento.

perversity [pə′və:siti], *s.* perversità; cattiveria.

perversive [pə′və:siv], *ag.* tendente a pervertire.

pervert [′pə:və:t], *s.* **1.** persona pervertita; pervertito (sessuale) **2.** apostata.

to **pervert** [pə′və:t], *v.t.* pervertire; corrompere; snaturare, falsare (discorsi, fatti, ecc.).

perverted [pə′və:tid], *ag.* pervertito; perverso: *a — mind*, uno spirito perverso, corrotto, snaturato.

pervertedly [pə′və:tidli], *av.* con perversione, da pervertito.

perverter [pə′və:tə*], *s.c.* pervertitore, pervertitrice; corruttore, corruttrice.

pervertible [pə′və:tibl], *ag.* che può essere pervertito.

pervicacious [‚pə:vi′keiʃəs], *ag.* pervicace, caparbio.

pervicaciousness [‚pə:vi′keiʃəsnis], *s.* pervicacia.

pervious [′pə:vjəs], *ag.* **1.** penetrabile; permeabile **2.** *fig.* accessibile: *heart — to love*, cuore sensibile all'amore.

perviousness [′pə:vjəsnis], *s.* **1.** penetrabilità; permeabilità **2.** *fig.* accessibilità.

Pesa(e)h [′peisɑ:k], *s.* Pasqua ebraica.

peseta [pə′setə], *s.* peseta (moneta).

pesky [′peski], *ag.* (*sl. amer.*) noioso, scocciante: *what — weather!*, che tempo uggioso!.

peso [′peisou], *pl.* **pesos** [′peisouz], *s.* peso (moneta).

pessary [′pesəri], *s.* (*med.*) pessario.

pessimism [′pesimizəm], *s.* pessimismo.

pessimist [′pesimist], *s.c.* pessimista.

pessimistic [‚pesi′mistik], *ag.* pessimistico.

pessimistically [‚pesi′mistikəli], *av.* in modo pessimistico.

pest [pest], *s.* **1.** *fig.* peste, flagello (di persona, animale, cosa noiosa): *that child is a perfect* —, quel bambino è proprio una peste; *those rabbits are a* —, quei conigli sono un flagello **2.** (*rar.*) peste, pestilenza ☆ — *-house*, lazzaretto.

to **pester** [′pestə*], *v.t.* **1.** importunare, seccare, tormentare **2.** infestare (un luogo).

pesterer [′pestərə*], *s.c.* seccatore, seccatrice.

pesticide [′pestisaid], *s.* insetticida.

pestiferous [pes′tifərəs], *ag.* **1.** pestifero, pestilenziale **2.** *fig.* pernicioso, malefico **3.** (*fam.*) noioso.

pestiferously [pes′tifərəsli], *av.* in modo pestifero, pernicioso.

pestilence [′pestiləns], *s.* pestilenza.

pestilent [′pestilənt], *ag.* **1.** pestilente; nocivo; esiziale **2.** pernicioso, corruttore **3.** noioso, molesto.

pestilential [‚pesti′lenʃəl], *ag.* **1.** pestilenziale **2.** pernicioso, dannoso **3.** detestabile.

pestilentially [‚pesti′lenʃəli], **pestilently** [′pestiləntli], *av.* pestilenzialmente.

pestle [′pesl], *s.* pestello.

to **pestle**, *v.t.i.* pestare, polverizzare (con pestello); usare il pestello.

pet[1] [pet], *ag.* favorito, prediletto; vezzeggiato, viziato ‖ *s.* **1.** animale (generalmente domestico) favorito, prediletto **2.** favorito, beniamino, coccolo ☆ — *name*, vezzeggiativo; — *-shop*, negozio in cui si vendono animali domestici.

to **pet**[1], *pass.p.p.* **petted** [′petid], *v.t.i.* **1.** vezzeggiare, coccolare; (*fam.*) allevare nella bambagia **2.** (*amer.*) abbandonarsi a effusioni amorose.

pet[2], *s.* collera; cattivo umore: *to be in a* —, tenere il broncio.

petal [′petl], *s.* (*bot.*) petalo.

petal(l)ed [′petld], *ag.* con petali ☆ *long-* —, dai lunghi petali.

petard [pe′tɑ:d], *s.* petardo.

petasos [′petəsos], **petasus** [′petəsəs], *s.* petaso (cappello greco a larghe falde).

petaurist [pi′tɔ:rist], *s.* (*zool.*) petauro.

Peter[1] [′pitə*], *no.pr.m.* Pietro ‖ *blue* —, (*mar.*) segnale di partenza ‖ *to rob* — *to pay Paul*, fare un debito nuovo per pagarne uno vecchio ☆ — *-penny* (o —*'s-penny* o —*'s pence*), obolo di S. Pietro; tributo volontario pagato al Papa.

to **peter**[2], *v.i.* **1.** (*sl.*) esaurirsi (di filone aurifero, impresa, corrente d'acqua, ecc.) **2.** *to* — *out*, spegnersi lentamente; finire gradatamente; esaurirsi.

petersham [′pi:təʃəm], *s.* « gros grain » (stoffa, nastro).

petiolar [′petioulə*], *ag.* di picciuolo.

petiole [′petioul], *s.* picciuolo.

petiolule [′petiəlju:l], *s.* piccolo picciuolo.

petit ['petit], *ag.* piccolo, insignificante ☆ — *-maître*, damerino; — *-verre*, bicchiere da liquore.

petite [pə'tiːt], *ag.* piccola, piccina, minuta, graziosa (di donna, ragazza).

petition [pi'tiʃən], *s.* petizione, supplica, istanza, domanda; ricorso: *to draw up a* —, stendere una petizione ‖ *Petition of Right*, (*st.*) Petizione dei Diritti (1628).

to **petition**, *v.t.i.* **1.** fare, presentare una supplica, una petizione a: *he petitioned the sovereign for his son*, presentò una supplica al sovrano per suo figlio **2.** supplicare, chiedere umilmente: *to — for sthg.*, *to do sthg.*, chiedere ql.co., di fare ql.co.

petitionary [pi'tiʃnəri], *ag.* **1.** di petizione **2.** (*rar.*) supplicante.

petitioner [pi'tiʃnə*], *s.c.* supplicante, postulante.

Petrarch ['petrɑːk], *no.pr.* (*st. lett.*) Petrarca.

petrel ['petrəl], *s.* (*ornit.*) procellaria.

petrifaction [ˌpetri'fækʃən], *s.* pietrificazione.

petrifactive [ˌpetri'fæktiv], *ag.* pietrificativo.

petrification [ˌpetrifi'keiʃən], *s.* pietrificazione.

to **petrify** ['petrifai], *v.t.i.* **1.** pietrificare, pietrificarsi; diventare di pietra **2.** *fig.* impietrire.

petrography [pi'trɒgrəfi], *s.* petrografia.

petrol ['petrəl], *s.* benzina (per automobili) ☆ — *lorry*, autocisterna; — *tank*, serbatoio di benzina.

petroleum [pi'trouljəm], *s.* petrolio grezzo.

petroleur [ˌpɔitrə'lɔː*], *s.* petroliere; incendiario.

petroliferous [ˌpetrə'lifərəs], *ag.* petrolifero.

petronel ['petrənəl], *s.* (*mil. st.*) pettrinale.

Petronilla [ˌpetrə'nilə], *no.pr.f.* Petronilla.

Petronius [pi'trouniəs], *no.pr.m.* (*lett. lat.*) Petronio.

petrous ['petrəs], *ag.* pietroso.

petticoat ['petikout], *s.* **1.** sottoveste, sottana; sottogonna **2.** (*fam.*) donna, gonnella: *wherever a — may be found*, ovunque si trovi una donna ‖ — *government*, (*scherz.*) matriarcato.

to **pettifog** ['petifɒg], *pass.* *p.p.* **pettifogged** ['petifɒgd], *v.i.* occuparsi di cavilli legali, di cause poco oneste; cavillare; fare l'azzeccagarbugli.

pettifogger ['petifɒgə*], *s.* azzeccagarbugli, leguleio.

pettifoggery ['petifɒgəri], *s.* cavillosità; garbuglio; causa legale di poca importanza.

pettifogging ['petifɒgiŋ], *ag.* meschino; litigioso.

pettily ['petili], *av.* meschinamente.

pettiness ['petinis], *s.* piccolezza; meschinità.

petting ['petiŋ], *s.* (*amer.*) carezze amorose.

pettish ['petiʃ], *ag.* dispettoso; lunatico; stizzoso.

pettishly ['petiʃli], *av.* dispettosamente.

pettishness ['petiʃnis], *s.* stizza, cattivo umore.

pettitoes ['petitouz], *s.pl.* **1.** (*cuc.*) piedini di maiale **2.** (*fam.*) piedi umani (specialmente di bambini).

petty ['peti], *ag.* **1.** piccolo; trascurabile; insignificante: — *farmers*, piccoli proprietari terrieri; *a — king*, un re travicello; *a — prince*, un principe da operetta; *a — quarrel*, una lite per cose futili **2.** meschino; gretto **3.** subalterno, subordinato ☆ — *cash*, (*comm.*) piccola cassa; — *officer*, (*mar.*) sottufficiale.

petulance ['petjuləns], **petulancy** ['petjulənsi], *s.* petulanza; insolenza.

petulant ['petjulənt], *ag.* petulante; insolente.

petulantly ['petjuləntli], *av.* con petulanza.

petunia [pi'tjuːnjə], *s.* (*bot.*) petunia.

pew [pjuː], *s.* banco (di chiesa) ‖ *take a* —, (*fam.*) siediti pure ☆ *family* —, banco di famiglia.

pewit ['piːwit], *s.* (*ornit.*) pavoncella.

pewter ['pjuːtə*], *s.* **1.** peltro **2.** oggetti di peltro **3.** (*sl.*) premio in denaro.

Phaedra ['fiːdrə], *no.pr.f.* (*mit.*) Fedra.

pewterer ['pjuːtərə*], *s.* fabbricante di oggetti di peltro.

Phaedra ['fiːdrə], *no.pr.f.* (*mit.*) Fedra.

Phaethon ['feiəθən], *no.pr.m.* (*mit.*) Fetonte.

phaeton ['feitn], *s.* « phaeton » (carrozza scoperta a quattro ruote tirata da due cavalli).

phagocyte ['fægəsait], *s.* (*biol.*) fagocita.

phagocytosis [ˌfægəsai'tousis], *s.* (*biol.*) fagocitosi.

phalangal [fə'læŋgəl], *ag.* (*anat.*) di falange.

phalange ['fælændʒ], *V.* **phalanx.**

phalangeal [fə'lændʒiəl], *ag.* (*anat.*) di falange.

phalanger [fə'lændʒə*], *s.* (*zool.*) falangista.

phalanstery ['fælənstəri], *s.* **1.** (*st.*) falansterio **2.** (*st.*) sede di falansterio.

phalanx ['fælæŋks], *pl.* **phalanxes** ['fælæŋksiz], *s.* **1.** (*st. greca*) falange **2.** falange, gruppo di persone unite da uno scopo comune; falansterio **3.** (*anat.*) falange.

phallic ['fælik], *ag.* fallico.

phallus ['fæləs], *pl.* **phalli** ['fælai], *s.* fallo (simbolo della forza generatrice della natura).

phanerogam ['fænərougæm], *s.* (*bot.*) fanerogama.

phanerogamic [ˌfænərou'gæmik], **phanerogamous** [ˌfænə'rogəməs], *ag.* (*bot.*) di fanerogama.

phantasm ['fæntæzəm], *s.* **1.** fantasma **2.** *fig.* illusione; illusione ottica.

phantasma [fæn'tæzmə], *pl.* **phantasmata** [fæn-'tæzmətə], *s.* (*arc.*) fantasma.

phantasmagoria [ˌfæntæzmə'gɔriə], *s.* fantasmagoria.

phantasmagorial [ˌfæntæzmə'gɔriəl], **phantasmagorie** [ˌfæntæzmə'gɔrik], *ag.* fantasmagorico.

phantasmagory [fæn'tæzməgɔri], *s.* fantasmagoria.

phantasmal [fæn'tæzməl], *ag.* di fantasma; spettrale.

phantasmally [fæn'tæzməli], *av.* da fantasma; in modo spettrale.

phantasmie [fæn'tæzmik], *ag.* di fantasma; spettrale.

phantasy, *V.* **fantasy.**

phantom ['fæntəm], *s.* **1.** fantasma, spettro **2.** *fig.* illusione; apparizione ☆ — *ship*, vascello fantasma.

Pharamond ['færəmənd], *no.pr.m.* (*lett.*) Faramondo.

Pharaoh ['fɛərou], *s.* (*st.*) faraone.

pharaonie [ˌfɛərə'ɔnik], *ag.* faraonico.

pharisaie(al) [ˌfæri'seiik(əl)], *ag.* farisaico (anche *fig.*).

pharisaically [ˌfæri'seiikəli], *av.* farisaicamente.

pharisaicalness [ˌfæri'seiikəlnis], *s.* *fig.* fariseismo.

Pharisaism ['færiseiizəm], *s.* fariseismo.

Pharisee ['færisiː], *s.* (*Bibbia*) fariseo.

Phariseeism ['færisiːizəm], *s.* fariseismo.

pharmaceutic(al) [ˌfɑːmə'sjuːtik(əl)], *ag.* farmaceutico.

pharmaceutically [ˌfɑːmə'sjuːtikəli], *av.* secondo la farmaceutica.

pharmaceuties [ˌfɑːmə'sjuːtiks], *s.* farmaceutica.

pharmacist ['fɑːməsist], *s.* farmacista.

pharmacodynamics [ˌfɑːməkədai'næmiks], *s.* farmacodinamica.

pharmacologist [ˌfɑːmə'kɔlədʒist], *s.* farmacologo.

pharmacology [ˌfɑːmə'kɔlədʒi], *s.* farmacologia.

pharmacopoeia [ˌfɑːməkə'piːə], *s.* farmacopea.

pharmacy ['fɑːməsi], *s.* farmacia.

pharos ['fɛərɔs], *s.* faro.

Pharsalia [fɑː'seiljə], *no.pr.* (*geog. st.*) Farsaglia.

pharyngal [fə'riŋgəl], **pharyngeal** [ˌfærin'dʒiːəl], *ag.* (*anat.*) faringeo.

pharyngeal [ˌfærin'dʒiːəl], *V.* **pharingal.**

pharingitis [ˌfærin'dʒaitis], *s.* (*patol.*) faringite.

pharyngotomy [ˌfærin'gɔtəmi], *s.* (*chir.*) faringotomia.

pharynx ['færiŋks], *s.* (*anat.*) faringe.

phase [feiz], *s.* **1.** fase, periodo: *phases of an illness*, fasi di una malattia **2.** (*fis.*) fase ☆ — *-angle*, (*elett.*) angolo di sfasamento; (*astr.*) angolo di fase; — *-convertor*, (*elett.*) convertitore di fase; — *-diagram*, (*metal.*) diagramma di stato; — *-modulation*, (*rad.*) modulazione di fase; — *transformer*, (*elett.*) trasformatore ‖ *single - — current*, corrente monofase.

phasis ['feisis], *pl.* **phases** ['feisiːz], *s.* (*astr.*) fase.

pheasant ['feznt], *s.* (*ornit.*) fagiano.

pheasantry ['fezntri], *s.* recinto per fagiani.

phenacetin [fi'næsitin], *s.* (*chim.*) fenacetina.

phenic ['fiːnik], *ag.* fenico.

phenix, Phenix, *V.* **phoenix, Phoenix.**

phenol ['fiːnɔl], *s.* (*chim.*) fenolo.

phenology [fi'nɔlədʒi] s. (biol.) fenologia.
phenomenal [fi'nɔminl], ag. **1.** (fil. scient.) fenomenico **2.** fenomenale; straordinario.
phenomenalism [fi'nɔminəlizəm], s.(fil.)fenomenismo.
to **phenomenalize** [fi'nɔminəlaiz], v.t. rendere, rappresentare fenomenicamente.
phenomenism [fi'nɔminizəm], s. (fil.) fenomenismo.
phenomenology [fi,nɔmi'nɔlədʒi], s. fenomenologia.
phenomenon [fi'nɔminən], pl. **phenomena** [fi'nɔminə], s. fenomeno (anche fil.).
phew [fju:], inter. puah!.
phial ['faiəl], s. fiala; ampolla; provetta ☆ Leyden —, bottiglia di Leida.
Phidias ['fidiæs], no.pr.m. (st. art.) Fidia.
Philadelphia [,filə'delfjə], no.pr. (geog.) Filadelfia.
to **philander** [fi'lændə*], v.i. fare il cascamorto.
philanderer [fi'lændərə*], s. cascamorto.
philanthrope ['filənθroup], s. filantropo.
philanthropic(al) [,filən'θrɔpik(əl)], ag. filantropico.
philanthropically [,filən'θrɔpikəli], av. filantropicamente.
philanthropism [fi'lænθrəpizəm], s. filantropia.
philanthropist [fi'lænθrəpist], s. filantropo.
to **philanthropize** [fi'lænθrəpaiz], v.t.i. fare il filantropo; beneficare; rendere filantropo.
philanthropy [fi'lænθrəpi], s. filantropia.
philatelic(al) [,filə'telik(əl)], ag. filatelico.
philatelically [,filə'telikəli], av. da filatelico.
philatelist [fi'lætəlist], s. filatelico.
philately [fi'lætəli], s. filatelia.
Philemon [fi'li:mɔn], no.pr.m. (mit.) Filemone.
philharmonic [,filɑ:'mɔnik], ag.s. filarmonico.
philhellene ['fil,heli:n], ag. s. filelleno.
philhellenic [,filhe'li:nik], ag. filelleno, filellenico.
philhellenism [fil'helinizəm], s. filellenismo.
philhellenist [fil'helinist], s. filelleno.
philibeg ['filibeg], s. «kilt» (gonnellino del costume tradizionale scozzese).
Philip ['filip], no.pr.m. Filippo.
Philippa ['filipə], no.pr.f. Filippa.
Philippi [fi'lipai], no.pr. (geog. st.) Filippi.
philippic [fi'lipik], s. filippica; invettiva.
philippina [,fili'pi:nə], **philippine**[1] ['filipi:n], s. **1.** mandorla, noce con doppio ghiriglio **2.** convenzione scherzosa fra due commensali che si dividono un frutto siffatto: nell'occasione di un successivo incontro il primo che pronuncerà la formula « Good Morning Philippine » (nell'uso italiano « Bonjour Philippine ») riceverà dall'altro un dono.
Philippine[2] ['filipi:n], ag. filippino ‖ the — Islands (o the Philippines), le Isole Filippine.
Philistine ['filistain], ag. filisteo (anche fig.); volgare; ignorante ‖ s. **1.** (st.) filisteo ‖ to fall among Philistines, (scherz.) cadere in mani nemiche **2.** filisteo, individuo grossolano.
philistinism ['filistinizəm], s. filisteismo.
philogynist [fi'lɔdʒinist], s. filogino.
philogyny [fi'lɔdʒini], s. filoginia.
philologer [fi'lɔlədʒə*], **philologian** [,filə'loudʒiən], s. filologo.
philologic(al) [,filə'lɔdʒik(əl)], ag. filologico.
philologically [,filə'lɔdʒikəli], av. filologicamente.
philologist [fi'lɔlədʒist], s. filologo.
to **philologize** [fi'lɔlədʒaiz], v.i. occuparsi di filologia.
philology [fi'lɔlədʒi], s. filologia.
Philomel ['filomel], **Philomela** [,filou'mi:lə], no.pr.f. (mit.) Filomela ‖ s. (poet.) usignolo.
philoprogenitive [,filəprou'dʒenitiv], ag. prolifico.
philosopher [fi'lɔsəfə*], s. filosofo ☆ —'s stone, pietra filosofale ‖ moral —, moralista; natural —, scienziato.
philosophic(al) [,filə'sɔfik(əl)], ag. filosofico.
philosophically [,filə'sɔfikəli], av. filosoficamente.
philosophism [fi'lɔsəfizəm], s. filosofismo.
philosophist [fi'lɔsəfist], s. pseudofilosofo.
to **philosophize** [fi'lɔsəfaiz], v.i. filosofare.

philosophy [fi'lɔsəfi], s. filosofia ☆ moral —, etica; natural —, fisica.
Philostratus [fi'lɔstrətəs], no.pr.m. (lett.) Filostrato.
philter, philtre ['filtə*], s. filtro (d'amore).
phiz [fiz], **phizog** [fi'zɔg], s. (sl.abbr. di physiognomy) faccia; fisionomia.
phlebitic [fli'bitik], ag. (patol.) flebitico.
phlebitis [fli'baitis], s. (patol.) flebite.
phlebotomist [fli'bɔtəmist], s. flebotomo.
to **phlebotomize** [fli'bɔtəmaiz], v.t. (med.) salassare.
phlebotomy [fli'bɔtəmi], s. (med.) flebotomia, salasso.
Phlegeton ['flegiθɔn], no.pr. (geog. mit.) Flegetonte.
phlegm [flem], s. **1.** (fisiol.) flemma **2.** flemma, lentezza; apatia.
phlegmatic(al) [fleg'mætik(əl)] ag. flemmatico; apatico, indifferente.
phlegmatically [fleg'mætikəli], av. flemmaticamente.
phlegmon ['flegmən], s. (patol.) flemmone.
phlegmonic [fleg'mɔnik], **phlegmonous** ['flegmənəs], ag. (patol.) flemmonoso.
phlegmy ['flemi], ag. (med.) flemmatico.
phloem ['flouem], s. (bot.) floema.
phlogistic [flɔ'dʒistik], ag. (patol.) flogistico, infiammatorio.
phlogiston [flɔ'dʒistən], s. (chim.) flogisto.
phlogosis [flɔ'gousis], s. (patol.) flogosi; erisipela.
phlox [flɔks], s. (bot.) flogo.
phobia ['foubjə], s. fobia.
phoca ['foukə], pl. **phocae** ['fousi:], **phocas** ['foukəz], s. (zool.) foca.
phocine ['fousain], ag.s. (di) foca.
Phoebe[1] ['fi:bi], no.pr.f. (mit.) Artemide ‖ s. (poet.) luna.
phoebe[2], s. (ornit.) pavoncella.
Phoebus ['fi:bəs], no.pr.m. (mit.) Febo ‖ s. (poet.) sole.
Phoenicia [fi'nifjə], no.pr. (geog. st.) Fenicia.
Phoenician [fi'nifiən], ag. s. fenicio.
phoenix ['fi:niks], s. (mit.) fenice ‖ **Phoenix**, no.pr. (astr.) Fenice.
pholas ['foulæs], pl. **pholades** ['foulədi:z], s. (zool.) folade.
phon [fɔn], s. (acu.) fon.
to **phonate** [fou'neit], v.i. produrre suoni vocalici.
phonation [fou'neifən], s. fonazione.
phone[1] [foun], s. suono (di vocale, consonante).
(to) **phone**[2], (abbr. fam.) di (to) **telephone**.
phoneme ['founi:m], s. (fonet.) fonema.
phonetic(al) [fou'netik(əl)], ag. fonetico.
phonetically [fou'netikəli], av. foneticamente.
phonetician [,founi'tifən], s. studioso di fonetica.
to **phoneticize** [fou'netisaiz], v.t. rendere fonetico.
phonetics [fou'netiks], s. fonetica.
phonetist ['founitist], s. **1.** studioso di fonetica **2.** sostenitore della scrittura fonetica.
phoney ['founi], ag. (sl.) falso; contraffatto; fittizio: a — five-dollar note, biglietto falso da cinque dollari; he is specializing in — divorce cases, egli si sta specializzando in casi di divorzio per cause fittizie; he thinks the suicide is —, crede che il suicidio sia falso ‖ that — war, (fam.) quella guerra strampalata (detto dei primi mesi della seconda guerra mondiale) ‖ s. (sl. amer.) **1.** falsità: he loathed phonies, aborriva dalle falsità **2.** impostore: he is a —, è un impostore, un ipocrita.
phonic ['founik], ag. fonico.
phonics ['founiks], s. scienza dei suoni.
phonogram ['founəgræm], s. fonogramma.
phonograph ['founəgrɑ:f], s. fonografo ☆ light —, fotofonografo, apparecchio per la riproduzione acustica.
phonographic [,founə'græfik], ag. **1.** fonografico **2.** stenografico (sistema Pitman).
phonographically [,founə'græfikəli], av. **1.** fonograficamente **2.** stenograficamente.
phonographist [fou'nɔgrəfist], s. stenografo.
phonography [fou'nɔgrəfi], s. **1.** fonografia **2.** stenografia (sistema Pitman).

phonolite ['founəlait], s. (min.) fonolite.
phonologic(al) [‚founə'lɔdʒik(əl)], ag. fonologico.
phonologically [‚founə'lɔdʒikəli], av. fonologicamente.
phonologist [fou'nɔlədʒist], s. studioso di fonologia.
phonology [fou'nɔlədʒi], s. fonologia.
phonometer [fə'nomitə*], s. (fis.) fonometro.
phonoscope ['founəskoup], s. (fis.) fonoscopio.
phonotype ['founoutaip], s. fonotipo.
phonotypic(al) [‚founə'tipik(əl)], ag. fonotipico.
phonotypist ['founoutaipist], s. fonotipista.
phonotypy ['founoutaipi], s. fonotipia.
phony, V. **phoney**.
phormium ['fɔ:miəm], s. (bot.) formio.
phosgene ['fɔzdʒi:n], s. (chim.) fosgene.
phosphate ['fɔsfeit], s. (chim.) fosfato ☆ alkaliphosphates, fosfati alcalini; calcium —, fosfato di calcio.
phosphatic [fɔs'fætik], ag. (chim.) fosfatico: — fertilizers, concimi fosfatici.
phosphatization [‚fɔsfəti'zeiʃən], s. (chim.) fosfatizzazione.
to **phosphatize** ['fɔsfətaiz], v.t. (chim.) fosfatizzare.
phosphaturia [‚fɔsfə'tjuəriə], s. (patol.) fosfaturia.
phosphene ['fɔsfi:n], s. (fisiol.) fosfeno.
phosphid(e) ['fɔsfid], s. (chim.) fosfuro.
phosphin(e) ['fɔsfi(:)n], s. (chim.) fosfina.
phosphite ['fɔsfait], s. (chim.) fosfito.
Phosphor ['fɔsfə*], no.pr. (astr. poet.) Fosforo, Venere, Lucifero ‖ **phosphor** s. (chim.) fosforo.
to **phosphorate** ['fɔsfəreit], v.t. combinare con, impregnare di fosforo.
to **phosphoresce** [‚fɔsfə'res], v.i. fosforeggiare.
phosphorescence [‚fɔsfə'resns], s. fosforescenza; luce fosforica.
phosphorescent [‚fɔsfə'resnt], ag. fosforescente.
phosphoret(t)ed ['fɔsfəretid], ag. (chim.) fosforato.
phosphoric [fɔs'fɔrik], ag. 1. (chim.) fosforico 2. fosforescente ☆ — acid, acido fosforico; — bronze, metallo fosforato.
phosphorism ['fɔsfərizəm], s. (patol.) fosforismo.
phosphorite ['fɔsfərait], s. (min.) fosforite.
phosphorous ['fɔsfərəs], ag. (chim.) 1. fosforoso 2. fosforescente ☆ — acid, acido fosforoso; — pentoxide, anidride fosforosa.
Phosphorus ['fɔsfərəs], no.pr. (astr. poet.) Fosforo, Venere, Lucifero ‖ **phosphorus**, s. (chim.) fosforo ☆ — necrosis, (patol.) necrosi mascellare.
phosphuret(t)ed ['fɔsfəretid], ag. (chim.) fosforato ☆ — hydrogen, idrogeno fosforato.
phossy ['fɔsi], ag.: — jaw, (patol. pop.) necrosi fosforica della mascella.
photo ['foutou], pl. **photos** ['foutouz], s. (fam.) fotografia.
to **photo**, v.t. (fam.) fotografare.
photocatalysis [‚foutəkə'tælisis], s. (fis. chim.) fotocatalisi.
photo-cathode [‚foutə'kæθoud], s. (tv.) fotocatodo.
photocell ['foutəsel], s. (fis.) cellula fotoelettrica.
photochemical [‚foutə'kemikəl], ag. fotochimico: — reaction, reazione fotochimica.
photochemistry [‚foutə'kemistri], s. fotochimica.
photochromatic [‚foutəkrou'mætik], ag. fotocromatico.
photochrome ['foutəkroum], s. fotografia a colori.
photochromy ['foutə‚kroumi], s. (foto.) fotocromia.
photochronograph [‚foutə'krɔnəgra:f], s. (fis.) fotocronografo.
photocomposition [‚foutə‚kɔmpə'ziʃən], s. (tip.) fotocalcografia.
photoconductivity [‚foutə‚kɔndʌk'tiviti], s. (elett.) fotoconduttività.
photodisintegration [‚foutədis‚inti'greiʃən], s. (fis. atomica) fotodisintegrazione.
photodynamic(al) [‚foutədai'næmik(əl)], ag. (fis.) fotodinamico.

photodynamics [‚foutədai'næmiks], s. (fis.) fotodinamica.
photoelectric(al) [‚foutəi'lektrik(əl)], ag. (elett. fis.) fotoelettrico ☆ — cell, cellula fotoelettrica.
photoelectron [‚foutəi'lektrɔn], s. (fis. atomica chim.) fotoelettrone.
photoelectricity [‚foutəi‚lek'trisiti], s. (elett.) fotoelettricità.
to **photoengrave** [‚foutəin'greiv], v.t. (foto.) fotoincidere.
photoengraver [‚foutəin'greivə*], s. (foto.) fotoincisore.
photoengraving [‚foutəin'greiviŋ], s. (foto.) fotoincisione.
photofinish [‚foutə'finiʃ], s. (spor.) ordine d'arrivo determinato con fotografia.
photoflash [‚foutə'flæʃ], s. fotografia al lampo di magnesio ☆ — lamp, lampada per fotografie al lampo di magnesio.
photogen ['foutədʒen], **photogene** ['foutədʒi:n], s. (chim.) fotogene.
photogenic [‚foutə'dʒenik], ag. 1. (biol.) fosforescente, fotogenetico 2. fotogenico.
photogenically [‚foutə'dʒenikəli], av. in modo fotogenico.
photogrammetry [‚foutə'græmitri], s. (topografia) fotogrammetria.
photograph ['foutəgra:f], s. fotografia: to take a — (of s.o., sthg.), fotografare (qlcu., ql.co.).
to **photograph**, v.t.i. 1. fotografare 2. esercitare l'arte fotografica, fare il fotografo (di professione) 3. riuscire (bene, male) in fotografia: I always — badly, well, riesco sempre male, bene in fotografia.
photographer [fə'tɔgrəfə*], s.c. fotografo, fotografa.
photographic(al) [‚foutə'græfik(əl)], ag. fotografico ☆ — reproduction, riproduzione fotografica.
photographically [‚foutə'græfikəli], av. fotograficamente.
photography [fət'ɔgrəfi], s. fotografia (arte fotografica) ☆ colour —, fotografia a colori; still —, posa fotografica; trick —, fotografia truccata.
photogravure [‚foutəgrə'vjuə*], s. (foto.) fotoincisione.
to **photogravure**, v.t. fotoincidere.
photolithograph [‚foutə'liθəgra:f], s. fotolitografia (riproduzione).
to **photolithograph**, v.t. fotolitografare.
photolithography [‚foutəli'θɔgrəfi], s. (tip.) fotolitografia (procedimento, arte).
photomap ['foutə‚mæp], s. 1. (topografia) carta fotogrammetrica 2. (astr.) carta del cielo.
photomagnetic [‚foutəmæg'netik], ag. (fis.) fotomagnetico.
photomagnetism [‚foutə'mægnitizəm], s. (fis.) fotomagnetismo.
photomechanical [‚foutəmi'kænikəl], ag. fotomeccanico.
photometer [fə'tɔmitə*], s. (ott.) fotometro.
photometrical [‚foutə'metrikəl], ag. (fis.) fotometrico.
photometry [fə'tɔmitri], s. (fis.) fotometria.
photomicrograph [‚foutə'maikrəgra:f], s. (amer. foto.) microfotografia.
photomicrography [‚foutəmai'krɔgrəfi], s. (amer. foto.) microfotografia (procedimento).
photomontage [‚foutoumɔn'ta:ʒ], s. fotomontaggio.
photon ['foutɔn], s. (fis.) fotone.
photoneutron [‚foutə'nju:trɔn], s. (fis. atomica) fotoneutrone.
photophily [fə'tɔfili], s. (biol.) fotofilismo.
photophobia [‚foutə'foubjə], s. (patol.) fotofobia.
photoplay ['foutəplei], s. versione cinematografica di un lavoro teatrale.
photoprint ['foutəprint], s. fotostampa, fotocopia.
photoradio [‚foutə'reidiou], s. (foto.) radiofototelegrafia.
photosculpture [‚foutə'skʌlptʃə*], s. fotoscultura.
photosphere ['foutousfiə*], s. (astr.) fotosfera.

photostat ['foutoustæt], *s.* **1.** apparecchio fotostatico **2.** riproduzione, copia fotostatica.

photosynthesis [,foutə'sinθisis], *s.* (*bot.*) fotosintesi.

phototechnie [,foutə'teknik], *ag.* fototecnico: — *lithography*, litografia fototecnica.

phototelegraph [,fontə'teligrɑːf], *s.* fototelegrafo.

phototelegraphy [,foutəti'legrəfi], *s.* (*foto. tel.*) fototelegrafia.

phototelephony [,foutəti'lefəni], *s.* (*foto. tel.*) fototelefonia.

phototelescope [,foutə'teliskoup], *s.* (*astr.*) fototelescopio.

phototherapeutics [,foutə,θerə'pjuːtiks], **phototherapy** [,foutə'θerəpi], *s.* (*med.*) fototerapia.

phototopography [,foutətə'pogrəfi], *s.* fotogrammetria.

phototropism [fou'tɔtrəpizəm], *s.* (*bot.*) fototropismo.

phototube ['foutətjuːb], *s.* fotovalvola, valvola fotoelettrica.

phototype ['foutətaip], *s.* (*tip.*) fototipo.

phototypography [,foutətai'pogrəfi], *s.* fototipografia.

phototypy ['foutətaipi], *s.* (*tip.*) fototipia.

photovoltaic [,foutəvol'teiik], *ag.* (*elett. fis.*) fotoelettrico.

photoxilography [,foutəzai'logrəfi], *s.* fotoxilografia.

photozincography [,foutəziŋ'kɔgrəfi], *s.* (*tip.*) fotozincotipia.

phrasal ['freizəl], *ag.* di frase: — *felicity*, felicità di espressione.

phrase [freiz], *s.* **1.** locuzione; espressione idiomatica; modo di dire; frase fatta; aforisma: *an adverbial* —, una locuzione avverbiale; *graceful* —, espressione elegante; *technical* —, locuzione tecnica; *to talk in set phrases*, parlare con frasi fatte ‖ *as the* — *goes*, come si suol dire, secondo l'espressione consacrata dall'uso; *in the* — *of*, per usare la frase di **2.** stile: *felicity of* —, felicità di espressione; *in simple* —, in uno stile semplice **3.** (*mus.*) frase **4.** *pl.* (*spreg.*) chiacchiere; parole inutili: *we have had enough of phrases*, ne abbiamo avuto abbastanza di belle frasi ☆ — *-book*, libro di fraseologia, raccolta di frasi idiomatiche; — *-monger*, fraseggiatore.

to phrase, *v.t.* **1.** esprimere: *that is how he phrased it*, ecco come si è espresso, ecco l'espressione da lui usata **2.** (*mus.*) fraseggiare.

phraseogram ['freiziəgræm], *s.* simbolo (specialmente stenografico) che rappresenta una espressione.

phraseological [,freiziə'lodʒikəl], *ag.* fraseologico.

phraseology [,freizi'olədʒi], *s.* fraseologia, frasario.

phrasing ['freiziŋ], *s.* **1.** fraseologia, frasario **2.** (*mus.*) fraseggio.

phratry ['freitri], *s.* (*st. greca*) fratria.

phrenesis [fri'niːsis], *s.* (*patol.*) frenite; frenesia, delirio.

phrenetic(al) [fri'netik(əl)], *ag.* frenetico, delirante; folle; fanatico.

phrenic ['frenik], *ag.* (*anat.*) frenico.

phrenitis [fri'naitis], *s.* (*patol.*) frenite.

phrenologic(al) [,frenə'lodʒik(əl)], *ag.* frenologico.

phrenologically [,frenə'lodʒikəli], *av.* frenologicamente.

phrenologist [fri'nɔlədʒist], *s.* frenologo.

phrenology [fri'nɔlədʒi], *s.* frenologia.

phrensy, *V.* **frenzy**.

Phrygia ['fridʒiə], *no.pr.* (*st. geog.*) Frigia.

Phrygian ['fridʒiən], *ag.* frigio ‖ — *cap*, (*st.*) berretto frigio ‖ *s.c.* abitante della Frigia.

Phryne ['fraini(ː)], *no.pr.f.* (*st.*) Frine.

phthalein ['fθæliin], *s.* (*chim.*) ftaleina.

phthalic ['fθælik], *ag.* (*chim.*) ftalico.

phthisic(al) ['θaisik(əl)], *ag.* (*patol.*) tisico.

phthisis ['θaisis], *s.* (*patol.*) tisi, etisia.

phut [fʌt], *s.* (*sl.*) fischio, sibilo (di pallottola, vescica che si sgonfia, ecc.) ‖ *to go* —, andare in rovina; andare in fumo (di progetto, ecc.); andare in pezzi (di macchina, ecc.); bruciare (di lampadina, ecc.).

phylactery [fi'læktəri], *s.* **1.** filatterio ‖ *to make broad one's* —, (*fam.*) ostentare la propria religiosità, rettitudine **2.** amuleto, talismano.

Phyllis ['filis], *no.pr.f.* (*poet.*) Fillide ‖ *s.* (*poet.*) **1.** campagnola, villanella **2.** ragazza del cuore.

phylloxera [,filok'siərə], *s.* (*entom.*) fillossera.

physic ['fizik], *s.* **1.** medicina (arte, scienza medica) **2.** (*fam.*) medicina, farmaco; lassativo, purgante **3.** (*arc. fig.*) rimedio.

to physic, *v.t.* pass. p.p. **physicked** ['fizikt], *v.t.* **1.** (*fam.*) somministrare (una medicina, specialmente un lassativo); purgare **2.** curare; *fig.* alleviare.

physical ['fizikəl], *ag.* **1.** fisico: — *beauty*, bellezza fisica; — *education*, educazione fisica; — *exercises* (o *drill* o *sl. jerks*), esercizi di ginnastica; — *strength*, forza fisica **2.** (*fis. scient.*) fisico, naturale: — *laws*, leggi fisiche; *the force of gravitation is a* — *fact*, la forza di gravitazione è un fenomeno fisico **3.** sensuale: — *love*, amore sensuale **4.** materiale: — *force*, forza materiale; — *impossibility*, impossibilità materiale ☆ — *chemistry*, chimica fisica; — *geography*, geografia fisica.

physically ['fizikəli], *av.* fisicamente; materialmente: *it is* — *impossible*, è materialmente impossibile.

physician [fi'ziʃən], *s.* medico.

physicist ['fizisist], *s.* **1.** fisico **2.** (*fil.*) fisicista.

physics ['fiziks], *s.* **1.** fisica: — *is difficult*, la fisica è difficile **2.** (*arc.*) scienza, filosofia della natura: *Aristotle's* —, la fisica di Aristotele ☆ *applied* —, fisica applicata; *general* —, fisica generale.

physiocracy [,fizi'okrəsi], *s.* (*st. econ.*) fisiocrazia.

physiocrat ['fizioukræt], *s.* (*st. econ.*) fisiocratico.

physiocratic [,fiziou'krætik], *ag.* (*st. econ.*) fisiocratico.

physiognomic(al) [,fiziə'nomik(əl)], *ag.* fisiognomico, fisionomico.

physiognomist [,fizi'onəmist], *s.c.* fisonomista.

physiognomy [,fizi'onəmi], *s.* **1.** fisiognomia **2.** fisionomia; *fig.* aspetto caratteristico (di un paese, ecc.) **3.** (*volg.*) viso.

physiographer [,fizi'ogrəfə*], *s.* fisiografo.

physiographic(al) [,fiziə'græfik(əl)], *ag.* fisiografico.

physiography [,fizi'ogrəfi], *s.* fisiografia.

physiologic(al) [,fiziə'lodʒik(əl)], *ag.* fisiologico.

physiologically [,fiziə'lodʒikəli], *av.* fisiologicamente.

physiologist [,fizi'olədʒist], *s.* fisiologo.

physiology [,fizi'olədʒi], *s.* fisiologia.

physiotherapy [,fiziou'θerəpi], *s.* (*med.*) fisioterapia.

physique [fi'ziːk], *s.* costituzione fisica, fisico.

phytogenesis [,faitou'dʒenisis], **phytogeny** [fai'tɔdʒini], *s.* fitogenesi.

phytography [fai'togrəfi], *s.* fitografia.

phytology [fai'tolədʒi], *s.* fitologia.

phytophagous [fai'tofəgəs], *ag.* (*entom.*) fitofago.

phytotomy [fai'totəmi], *s.* fitotomia.

Phytozoa [,faitou'zouə], *s.pl.* (*zool.*) fitozoi.

pi[1] [pai], *ag.* (*sl. scolastico*) pio; virtuoso ☆ — *-jaw*, predica.

pi[2], *s.* (*geom.*) p greca (π).

piacular [pai'ækjulə*], *ag.* **1.** espiatorio **2.** che richiede espiazione; peccaminoso; malvagio.

to piaffe [pi'æf], *v.i.* andare al trotto moderato.

piaffer [pi'æfə*], *s.* trotto moderato.

pia mater ['paiə'meitə*], *s.* (*anat.*) pia madre.

pianette [,piə'net], *s.* piccolo pianoforte.

pianissimo [,piæ'nisimou], *s.* (*mus.*) pianissimo.

pianist ['pjænist], *s.c.* pianista.

piano ['pjɑːnou], *s.* (*mus.*) piano.

piano ['pjænou], *pl.* **pianos** ['pjænouz], **pianoforte** [,pjænou'fɔːti], *s.* (*mus.*) piano, pianoforte: *to play* (*on*) *the* —, suonare il pianoforte; *to set for the* —, comporre per piano ☆ — *organ*, organino; — *-player*, pianola; *pianista*; — *stool*, sgabello per piano; — *tuner*, accordatore; — *-wire*, (*mec.*) filo armonico, corda ‖ *baby grand* —, piano a mezza coda; *cottage* —, piccolo piano verticale; *grand* —, piano a coda; *upright* —, piano verticale.

pianola [pjæ'noulə], s. (mus.) pianola.

piaster, piastre [pi'æstə*], s. piastra (moneta).

piazza [pi'ædzə], s. 1. piazza (in Italia) 2. (amer.) veranda.

pibroch ['pi:brɔk], s. variazioni per cornamusa generalmente su temi marziali.

pica[1] ['paikə], s. (tip.) corpo 12: small —, corpo 11.

pica[2], s. (patol.) picacismo.

picador ['pikədɔ:*], s. « picador » (uomo a cavallo che, nelle corride, ha il compito di aizzare il toro mediante una picca).

Picardy ['pikədi], no.pr. (geog.) Piccardia.

picaresque [,pikə'resk], ag. (lett.) picaresco.

picaroon [,pikə'ru:n], s. 1. picaro; brigante; furfante; pirata 2. nave corsara.

picayune [,pikə'ju:n], ag. (amer.) meschino, spregevole ‖ s. (amer.) 1. monetina da cinque centesimi 2. (fam.) cosa di poco valore; persona insignificante.

Piccadilly [,pikə'dili], s. Piccadilly (strada del centro di Londra): — Circus, Piccadilly Circus (piazza all'estremità orientale di Piccadilly).

piccalilli ['pikəlili], s. (cuc.) sottaceti drogati.

piccaninny ['pikənini], ag. piccino, neonato ‖ s. piccolo bimbo (specie negretto, moretto).

piccolo ['pikəlou], pl. **piccolos** ['pikəlouz], s. (mus.) ottavino.

piccoloist ['pikələist], s. (mus.) suonatore di ottavino.

pice [pais], s. « pice » (moneta anglo-indiana del valore di ¼ di anna).

piceous ['pisiəs], ag. 1. piceo, color pece 2. infiammabile, combustibile.

pick[1] [pik], s. 1. strumento appuntito; piccone 2. (dial.) quadri (nei giuochi di carte) ☆ tooth- —, stuzzicadenti.

to pick[1], v.t.i. 1. scavare, perforare; rompere col piccone: to — a hole in sthg., fare un buco in ql.co. ‖ to — holes in sthg., fig. trovare da ridire su ql.co. 2. pulire, mondare; spennare: to — a bone, spolpare un osso; to — a fowl, spennare un pollo; to — one's nose, teeth, mettersi le dita nel naso, stuzzicare i denti ‖ to — one's brains, spremersi il cervello; to — to pieces, separare; fig. analizzare, criticare con malevolenza ‖ to have a bone to — with s.o., avere ql.co. da rimproverare a qlcu. 3. cogliere, raccogliere (fiori, frutti) 4. mangiucchiare, piluccare, sbocconcellare; beccare (di uccelli): he picked (at) his food, mangiava di malavoglia 5. scegliere con cura: she always picks the best, scegliere sempre il meglio ‖ to — and choose, scegliere meticolosamente, fare il difficile ‖ to — a quarrel, attaccar briga 6. rubare; rubacchiare; aprire una serratura (per rubare): they picked his pocket, lo borseggiarono; to — a lock, forzare una serratura (per rubare) 7. to — off, cogliere, togliere (foglie, fiori, frutti da una pianta); bersagliare, abbattere (i nemici) uno dopo l'altro: he picked off some grapes from the bunch, piluccò alcuni acini dal grappolo; they picked off the enemy soldiers on the horizon, bersagliarono i nemici all'orizzonte 8. to — out, scegliere; distinguere; scoprire il significato di; accennare un motivo (al pianoforte); mettere in evidenza (con un colore vivace): to — out a figure in red, campire una figura in rosso; to — out the good from the bad, scegliere il buono dal cattivo; to — out the meaning of a passage, cogliere il significato di un brano; to — out a person in the twilight, distinguere una persona nel crepuscolo 9. to — up, prendere, raccogliere; rialzare, rialzarsi; far salire; far conoscenza; imparare; riacquistare forza; trovare, scovare; (rad.) captare; I can't understand where he could — up this information, non riesco a capire dove egli abbia raccolto queste informazioni; she picked me up with the car at the crossroad, mi fece salire sulla automobile al crocicchio; she picked up a little German, imparò un po' di tedesco; that is a nice clock, where did you — it up?, che bella pendola, dove l'hai scovata?; to — oneself up, rialzarsi; to — up one's path, ritrovare la propria strada.

pick[2], s. 1. zappata 2. raccolta di frutta 3. scelta il meglio (di ql.co.), il fior fiore 4. (tip.) macchia.

pick[3], s. (ind. tessile) filo della trama.

pick-a-back ['pikəbæk], av. sul dorso; sulle spalle: to ride — on s.o., montare sulle spalle di qlcu. ‖ s.: to give s.o. a —, portare qlcu. sul dorso.

pickaninny, V. **piccaninny.**

pickax(e) ['pikæks], s. gravina, piccone.

to pickax(e), v.t.i. picconare, lavorare, rimuovere con la gravina, col piccone.

picked[1] [pikt], ag. (arc.) acuminato, appuntito.

picked[2], ag. scelto: — men, uomini scelti.

picker[1] ['pikə*], s. 1. zappatore, foratore; cernitore; battitore; raccoglitore ‖ — of pockets, borsaiolo ‖ — of quarrels, attaccabrighe 2. piccone, zappa, gravina 3. grimaldello ☆ corn —, cotton —, raccoglitore di grano, di cotone.

picker[2], s. (ind. tessile) lancianavetta.

pickerel ['pikərəl], s. (ittiol.) piccolo luccio.

picket ['pikit], s. 1. piolo; palo; palo a cui si legano i cavalli 2. (mil.) picchetto; sentinella: to be on —, essere di picchetto 3. gener. pl. picchetti (di scioperanti).

to picket, v.t.i. 1. circondare, proteggere con palizzata 2. legare (cavalli) a un palo 3. (mil.) mettere di picchetto; essere di picchetto 4. organizzare picchetti (di scioperanti).

picking ['pikiŋ], ag. 1. che scava, perfora 2. che pulisce 3. che raccoglie (fiori, frutti, ecc.) 4. che mangiucchia; becca 5. che sceglie con cura 6. che ruba; saccheggia ‖ s. 1. lo scavare, il perforare 2. pulitura, mondatura 3. raccolta, raccolto 4. rosicchiatura; beccatura 5. cernita 6. furto; saccheggio 7. (ind. tessile) inserzione (della trama) 8. pl. rimanenze, avanzi.

pickle[1] ['pikl], s. 1. salamoia 2. pl. sottaceti 3. (metal.) soluzione acida per decapare; bagno di decapaggio 4. (sl.) situazione spiacevole: sad —, un bel pasticcio 5. (fam.) diavoletto (di bimbo).

to pickle[1], v.t. 1. conservare in salamoia; mettere sotto aceto; salare 2. (metal.) decapare 3. (st.) strofinare sale e aceto sul dorso di un marinaio staffilato.

pickle[2], s. (scoz.) granello; piccola quantità.

pickling ['pikliŋ], s. (metal.) decapaggio.

picklock ['piklɔk], s. 1. scassinatore, ladro 2. grimaldello.

pick-me-up ['pikmi(:)ʌp], s. (fam.) cordiale, bevanda stimolante.

pickpocket ['pik,pɔkit], **pickpurse** ['pikpə:s], s. ladro, borsaiolo.

picksome ['piksəm], ag. pignolo, noioso.

pickthank ['pikθæŋk], s. (arc.) 1. adulatore 2. delatore.

pick-up ['pikʌp], s. 1. il raccogliere, il prendere; la cosa raccolta 2. (mec.) accelerazione, ripresa 3. (elett.) riproduttore acustico, fonorivelatore 4. (tv.) dispositivo di presa (di telecamera); conversione dell'immagine in energia elettrica ☆ — truck, furgoncino.

picnic ['piknik], s. 1. pic-nic, scampagnata 2. (sl.) cosa facile, piacevole: it is no —, non è facile, piacevole.

to picnic, pass.p.p. **picnicked** ['piknikt], v.i. fare un pic-nic, prendere parte a una scampagnata: we are going picnicking, stiamo andando a fare una scampagnata.

picnicker ['piknikə*], s.c. gitante.

picot ['pi:kou], s. festoncino.

picotee [,pikə'ti:], s. (bot.) garofano screziato.

picquet, V. **picket.**

picrate ['pikreit], s. (chim.) picrato.

picric ['pikrik], ag. (chim.) picrico ☆ — acid, acido picrico.

Piet [pikt], s. (st.) appartenente alla tribù dei Pitti.

pictograph ['piktəgra:f], s. (archeol.) ideogramma.

pictorial [pik'tɔ:riəl], ag. 1. illustrato 2. pittorico 3. pittoresco ‖ s. giornale illustrato.

pictorially [pik'tɔ:riəli], av. 1. con illustrazioni 2. pittoricamente 3. pittorescamente.

picture ['piktʃə*], s. **1.** quadro, dipinto, pittura; immagine; disegno, vignetta, illustrazione; fotografia; fotogramma; *(tv.)* immagine: *to paint a —,* fare un quadro **2.** bella persona, oggetto, scena: *she's like a —,* è molto bella **3.** ritratto (anche *fig.*): *he is the — of his father,* è il vero ritratto di suo padre; *he looks the — of health,* è il ritratto della salute **4.** descrizione; *fig.* quadro: *he gave us a very bright — of the whole thing,* ci descrisse tutto quanto a tinte vivaci; *to draw a mental — of sthg.,* immaginarsi ql.co.; *to draw a — of human misery,* fare un quadro delle miserie umane; *to draw a rapid — of sthg.,* descrivere ql.co. a grandi linee **5.** *pl.* *(abbr. fam.* di *moving* o *motion pictures)* cinematografo, cinema ☆ — *-book,* libro illustrato; — *-card, (carte)* figura; — *-frame,* cornice (di un quadro); — *-gallery,* pinacoteca; — *-goer,* assiduo frequentatore di cinema; — *-hat,* ampio cappello da signora (sec. XIX); — *-house* (o — *-place* o — *-theatre*), cinematografo; — *play* (o — *show*), film; — *postcard,* cartolina illustrata; — *-restorer,* restauratore di quadri; — *size, (foto.)* formato; — *window,* finestra panoramica; — *-writing,* scrittura ideografica ‖ *silent pictures,* film muto; *sound pictures,* film sonoro; *talking pictures,* film parlato.

to picture, *v.t.* **1.** fare un quadro di, dipingere; disegnare; illustrare; rappresentare: *several painters have pictured this event,* parecchi pittori hanno rappresentato questo avvenimento **2.** *to — to oneself,* figurarsi, immaginarsi: *— to yourself how I felt,* immaginati come mi sentivo.

picturesque [,piktʃə'resk], *ag.* pittoresco.
picturesquely [,piktʃə'reskli], *av.* pittorescamente.
picturesqueness [,piktʃə'resknis], *s.* l'essere pittoresco.

to piddle ['pidl], *v.i.* **1.** *(fam.)* fare pipì (di bambini) **2.** *(arc.)* gingillarsi, perdere il tempo in cose di nessuna importanza **3.** *(arc.)* mangiucchiare.
piddling ['pidliŋ], *ag.* futile, di scarsa importanza ‖ *a — little man,* *(sl.)* un ometto.
piddock ['pidək], *s.* *(zool.)* folade.
pidgin ['pidʒin], *ag.* *(corruzione cinese* di *business)*: — *English,* inglese corrotto (usato tra cinesi e europei) ‖ *s.* *(sl.)* affare: *that's my —,* ciò è affare mio.
pie¹ [pai], *s.* *(ornit.)* pica, gazza.
pie², *s.* torta; pasticcio ‖ *to eat humble —,* fare penitenza ‖ *to have a finger in the —,* avere le mani in pasta, essere addentro in una faccenda ☆ — *-plant, (amer. bot.)* rabarbaro ‖ *cherry- —,* torta di ciliege; *meat- —,* pasticcio di carne; *mud- —,* formina di terra (fatta dai bambini).
pie³, *s.* **1.** *(tip.)* refuso **2.** *fig.* confusione, disordine.
to pie³, *v.t.* **1.** *(tip.)* refusare **2.** *fig.* far confusione.
pie⁴, *s.* « pie » (la più piccola moneta di rame anglo-indiana).
piebald ['paibɔːld], *ag.* **1.** pezzato, pomellato (di cavallo) **2.** *fig.* eterogeneo, misto ‖ *s.* cavallo pezzato.
piece [piːs], *s.* **1.** pezzo, frammento, parte: *a — of land,* un appezzamento di terreno; *a — of paper,* un pezzo di carta; *to break to pieces,* fare a pezzi; *to come* (o *to fall* o *to go*) *to pieces,* andare in pezzi, andare in rovina (anche *fig.*); *to pull* (o *to tear*) *to pieces,* stracciare, lacerare, ridurre in pezzi, demolire (anche *fig.*); *to tear an argument to pieces,* demolire una tesi; *to take to pieces,* smontare, disfare (macchine, abiti) ‖ *a —,* cadauno, ciascuno; — *by —,* pezzo per pezzo, un pezzo per volta; *all of a —,* tutto d'un pezzo, uniforme, omogeneo; coerente **2.** *a — of,* (solo con sostantivi che *non possono essere preceduti da articolo indeterminato nè formare il plurale)* un, uno, una; singola manifestazione, atto di: *a — of advice,* un consiglio; *a — of bravery,* un atto di coraggio; *a — of furniture,* un mobile; *a — of kindness,* un atto di gentilezza; *a — of luck,* una fortuna; *a — of music,* un brano musicale; *a — of news,* una notizia; *a — of nonsense,* una sciocchezza; *a — of wit,* un tratto di spirito; *a — of work,* un la-

voro **3.** *(scacchi, dama, ecc.)* pedina; pezzo **4.** pezza (di tessuto); barile (di vino); rotolo (di carta da tappezzeria) ‖ *by the —, (comm.)* a cottimo: *to work by the —,* lavorare a cottimo **5.** moneta: *a — of silver,* una moneta d'argento **6.** *(mil.)* pezzo d'artiglieria; fucile: *to load one's —,* caricare il proprio fucile **7.** *(sl.)* tipo: *he is a bossy —,* è un tipo autoritario; *she is a pretty —,* è un bel pezzo di ragazza ☆ — *-dyed,* tinto in pezza; — *-goods,* tessuti in pezza; — *-list, (comm.)* distinta, elenco dei prezzi; — *-test,* provino, saggio ‖ *distance —, (mec.)* distanziatore; *pole —, (mec.)* espansione polare; *two- —,* a due pezzi: *two- — dress,* abito a due pezzi.

to piece, *v.t.* **1.** rappezzare, rattoppare, raggiustare, rammendare **2.** unire, connettere **3.** *to — on,* unire, unirsi; collegarsi **4.** *to — out,* mettere insieme (una storia, ecc.) **5.** *to — up,* raccomodare; rabberciare.
piecemeal ['piːsmiːl], *ag.* frammentario; fatto pezzo per pezzo: — *information* (o *news*), notizie frammentarie; *to work on a — plan,* lavorare senza metodo, senza organizzazione ‖ *av.* a pezzi, pezzo per pezzo; a poco a poco.
piecer ['piːsə*], *s.c.* rappezzatore, rappezzatrice; giuntatore, giuntatrice.
piecework ['piːswəːk], *s.* *(comm.)* (lavoro a) cottimo ☆ — *price,* prezzo di cottimo.
pieceworker ['piːswəːkə*], *s.* cottimista.
pied [paid], *ag.* variegato, variopinto; macchiettato, screziato, pezzato (di cavallo).
Piedmont ['piːdmənt], *no.pr.* *(geog.)* Piemonte.
Piedmontese [,piːdmən'tiːz], *ag.* *s.c.* piemontese.
pieman, *pl.* **piemen** ['paimən], *s.* venditore di pasticcini.
pier [piə*], *s.* **1.** frangiflutti **2.** diga; molo; banchina, pontile, imbarcadero **3.** *(arch.)* stipite, piedritto, pilastro; pila, pilone (di ponte) ☆ — *dues, (comm.)* diritti di banchina; — *-glass,* specchiera; — *-head,* testa, punta di molo; antibecco, sprone di pila; — *-light,* faro (di molo); — *-shaft,* fusto verticale di un pilastro; — *-table,* mensola.
pierage ['piəridʒ], *s.* *(comm.)* diritti di banchina.
to pierce [piəs], *v.t.i.* **1.** forare; penetrare; *(min.)* perforare; *(mil.)* sfondare: *to — a hole in a wall,* fare un buco in un muro; *flashes of lightning pierced the night,* lampi squarciavano la notte; *to — (into o through) the enemy's lines,* incunearsi nelle linee nemiche **2.** *fig.* trafiggere, commuovere, toccare: *his words pierced her to the heart,* le sue parole la commossero profondamente.
pierceable ['piəsəbl], *ag.* forabile, perforabile; penetrabile.
pierced [piəst], *ag.* forato, perforato, traforato; *fig.* trafitto.
piercer ['piəsə*], *s.c.* punzonatore, punzonatrice ‖ *s.* *(strum.)* foratoio, succhiello; punzone.
piercing ['piəsiŋ], *ag.* penetrante, pungente; perforante: *a — look,* uno sguardo penetrante; *a — sound,* un suono lacerante ‖ *s.* **1.** perforamento; perforazione; traforo **2.** punzonatura.
piercingly ['piəsiŋli], *av.* acutamente, in modo penetrante.
piercingness ['piəsiŋnis], *s.* acutezza (di freddo, suono, ecc.); penetrazione.
Pierian [pai'eriən], *ag.* pierio, delle Pieridi, delle Muse ‖ — *spring, fig.* ispirazione.
Pierides [pai'eridiːz], *no.pr.f.pl.* *(mit.)* Pieridi, Muse.
pierrette [piə'ret], *s.* « pierrette » (maschera carnevalesca femminile).
pierrot ['piərou], *s.* « pierrot », (maschera carnevalesca maschile).
piet ['paiət], *s.* *(ornit.)* gazza.
pietism ['paiətizəm], *s.* **1.** *(st. relig.)* pietismo **2.** pietismo, bigottismo.
pietist ['paiətist], *s.* **1.** *(st. relig.)* pietista **2.** bigotto.
pietistic(al) [,paiə'tistik(əl)], *ag.* pietista.

piety ['paiəti], *s.* pietà, religiosità, devozione; reverenza, rispetto.

piezoelectric [pai,i:zoui'lektrik], *ag.* (*elett. min.*) piezoelettrico.

piezoelectricity [pai,i:zoui,lek'trisiti], *s.* (*elett. min.*) piezoelettricità.

piezometer [,pai'zomitə*], *s.* (*fis.*) piezometro.

piffle ['pifl], *s.* (*sl.*) futilità, sciocchezze; chiacchiere incoerenti: *to talk* —, dire delle sciocchezze.

to **piffle**, *v.i.* (*sl.*) 1. dire delle sciocchezze; agire da sciocco 2. gingillarsi.

piffler ['piflə*], *s.* (*sl.*) 1. chiacchierone 2. gingillone.

piffling ['piflin], *ag.* (*sl.*) futile, vano.

pig[1] [pig], *s.* 1. maiale, porco; maialino: *he is as fat as a* —, è grasso come un maialino, un porcellino || *when pigs fly*, quando gli asini voleranno, il giorno di San mai || *to bring one's pigs to a pretty* (o *to the wrong*) *market*, fare un cattivo affare || *to buy a* — *in a poke*, comprare la gatta nel sacco, alla cieca || *to make a* — *of oneself*, mangiare ingordamente || *to sleep like a* —, dormire come un ghiro 2. (*cuc.*) carne di maiale, maialino da latte 3. *fig.* persona ghiotta, sudicia, grossolana, testarda: *don't be a* —, *let me see your photos*, (*sl.*) non essere cattivo, ostinato, fammi vedere le tue fotografie; *he is an obstinate* —, è testardo come un mulo; *you are a dirty little* —, sei un porcellino 4. (*metal.*) lingotto, pane 5. (*metal.*) fossa, canale di colata per lingotti ☆ — *-bed*, letto di colata per lingotti; — *boat*, (*sl. mar. mil.*) « maiale »; — *-deer*, (*zool.*) babirussa; — *-driver*, guardiano di porci; — *-eyed*, dagli occhi porcini; — *-iron*, ghisa di prima fusione, grezza, d'alto forno; — *-lead*, piombo in pani; — *-meat*, salumi; — *-nut*, (*bot.*) bulbocastano, castagna di terra; — *-sticker*, cacciatore di cinghiali; cavallo per la caccia al cinghiale; (*fam.*) coltellaccio; — *-sticking*, caccia al cinghiale con la lancia; — *'s-wash*, risciacquatura, avanzi di cucina || *guinea-* —, porcellino d'India; *roast* —, (*cuc.*) porchetta; *wild* —, cinghiale.

to **pig**[1], *pass.p.p.* **pigged** [pigd], *v.t.i.* 1. figliare (dei maiali) 2. vivere come porci 3. (*metal.*) colare (la ghisa) in pani.

pig[2], *s.* (*scoz.*) 1. vaso, brocca 2. scaldaletto di terracotta.

pigeon[1] ['pidʒin], *s.* 1. piccione, colombo: *young* —, piccioncino || *—'s milk*, (*scherz.*) pesce d'Aprile || *that's my* —, (*fam.*) è affar mio 2. *fig.* sempliciotto, sciocco ☆ — *-berry*, (*bot. amer.*) fitolacca; — *-breast*, sterno sporgente, torace carenato; — *-gram*, messaggio portato da un piccione viaggiatore; — *-hearted*, timido, timoroso; — *-house*, colombaia, piccionaia; — *-livered*, (*arc.*) timido; — *-match*, tiro al piccione; — *-post*, l'inviare lettere per mezzo di piccioni; — *-toed*, dal piede varo || *carrier-* — (o *homing* —), piccione viaggiatore; *clay* —, (*spor.*) piattello; *cock-* —, piccione maschio; *hen-* —, piccione femmina; *wood-* —, piccione selvatico.

to **pigeon**[1], *v.t.* ingannare: *to* — *s.o. of sthg.*, imbrogliare qlcu. in ql.co.

pigeon[2], *V.* **pidgin**.

pigeon-hole ['pidʒinhoul], *s.* 1. nicchia di colombaia 2. casella ☆ *pigeon-holes case*, casellario.

to **pigeon-hole**, *v.t.* 1. incasellare, archiviare: *my request has been pigeon-holed*, la mia domanda è stata archiviata, si è arenata 2. classificare.

pigeonry ['pidʒənri], *s.* piccionaia, colombaia.

piggery ['pigəri], *s.* 1. porcile (anche *fig.*) 2. sudiciume; grossolanità; golosità; testardaggine.

piggin ['pigin], *s.* (*dial.*) secchiello di legno con una doga lunga per manico; secchio da latte; piccola votazza.

piggish ['pigiʃ], *ag.* 1. porcino 2. *fig.* sudicio; grossolano; goloso; testardo.

piggishness ['pigiʃnis], *s.* sudiciume; grossolanità; golosità; testardaggine.

piggy ['pigi], **piggywig(gy)** ['pigiwig(i)], *s.* (*nel linguaggio infantile*) maialino, porcellino (anche *fig.*).

pigheaded ['pig'hedid], *ag.* ostinato, testardo.

pigheadedly ['pig'hedidli], *av.* ostinatamente, con testardaggine.

pigheadedness ['pig'hedidnis], *s.* ostinazione, testardaggine.

piglet ['piglit], **pigling** ['piglin], *s.* maialino, porcellino.

pigment ['pigmənt], *s.* pigmento; colore.

to **pigment**, *v.t.* colorare.

pigmental [pig'mentl], **pigmentary** ['pigmentəri], *ag.* pigmentario.

pigmentation [,pigmən'teiʃən], *s.* pigmentazione.

pigmy ['pigmi], *ag.s.* pigmeo.

to **pignorate** ['pignəreit], *v.t.* pignorare.

pignoration [,pignə'reiʃən], *s.* pignoramento.

pigskin ['pigskin], *s.* pelle di cinghiale ☆ — *-gloves*, guanti di cinghiale.

pigsty ['pigstai], *s.* porcile.

pigtail ['pigteil], *s.* 1. codino di maiale 2. treccia; codino (dei cinesi) 3. treccia di tabacco.

pike[1] [paik], *s.* 1. piccone; gravina 2. (*agr.*) forcone, forca 3. punta (di bastone ferrato, ecc.) 4. spina; aculeo 5. corno (di incudine).

pike[2], *s.* 1. picco 2. (*agr.*) covone; bica 3. torre, faro, ecc. su sommità.

pike[3], *pl.* **pike**, *s.* (*ittiol.*) luccio.

pike[4], *s.* picca, asta ☆ — *-man*, picchiere; *-staff*, bastone con punta di metallo.

to **pike**[4], *v.t.* trafiggere, uccidere con la picca.

pike[5], *s.* (*dial. amer.*) barriera; pedaggio (che si pagava ad una barriera); strada sottoposta a pedaggio.

piked [paikt], *ag.* appuntito; munito di punta.

pilaff ['pilæf], *V.* **pilau**.

pilaster [pi'læstə*], *s.* (*arch.*) pilastro.

Pilate ['pailət], *no.pr.m.* (*st.*) Pilato.

pilau, pilaw [pi'lau], *s.* «pilaf» (piatto orientale di riso con carne e droghe varie).

pilch [piltʃ], *s.* triangolo di flanella per neonati.

pilchard ['piltʃəd], **pilcher** ['piltʃə*], **pilcherd** ['piltʃəd], *s.* (*ittiol.*) sardella.

pile[1] [pail], *s.* 1. mucchio, ammasso, massa; catasta (di legna); fascio (d'armi): *a* — *of gold*, un mucchio di denaro || *to make a* —, far fortuna, far molto denaro 2. fabbricato, edificio 3. rogo, pira 4. (*elett.*) pila: *atomic* —, pila atomica; *galvanic* —, pila galvanica; *voltaic* —, pila di Volta 5. (*metal.*) pacchetto (di ferro).

to **pile**[1], *v.t.i.* 1. ammucchiare, ammucchiarsi; ammassare; ammonticchiare, ammonticchiarsi; accatastare; stiparsi; mettere (armi) in fascio: *the crowd piled on to him*, la folla si accalcava attorno a lui; *to* — *books on each other*, ammucchiare i libri uno sull'altro; *to* — *on* (o *up*) *the expenses*, far salire le spese; *to* — *up money*, ammassare denaro || *to* — *it on*, esagerare 2. (*metal.*) formare un pacchetto.

pile[2], *s.* 1. (*edil.*) palo di fondazione, palafitta 2. (*arald.*) pila ☆ — *-bridge*, ponte su palafitte; — *-drawer*, leva; — *-driving*, conficcamento del palo; — *-engine* (o *-driver*), (*mec.*) berta, battipalo; — *-pier*, molo costruito su palafitte; — *-work*, palafitta || *foundation-* —, palo di fondazione.

to **pile**[2], *v.t.* conficcare pali in; fare palizzate.

pile[3], *s.* pelo umano, animale; pelo (di tessuto, ecc.).

pile[4], *s.gener.pl.* (*patol.*) nodulo emorroidario.

pile[5], *s.* (*arc.*) rovescio di moneta || *cross or* —, testa o croce.

piles [pailz], *s.pl.* (*patol.*) emorroidi.

pileus ['pailiəs], *pl.* **pilei** ['pailiai], *s.* pileo.

to **pilfer** ['pilfə*], *v.t.i.* rubacchiare.

pilferage ['pilfəridʒ], *s.* piccolo furto.

pilferer ['pilfərə*], *s.* ladruncolo.

pilfering ['pilfərin], *s.* il rubacchiare; furterello.

pilgarlic [pil'gɑ:lik], *s.* (*arc.*) 1. uomo calvo 2. povero diavolo.

pilgrim ['pilgrim], *s.* pellegrino || *Pilgrim Fathers*, (*st. amer.*) Padri Pellegrini.

pilgrimage ['pilgrimidʒ], *s.* pellegrinaggio; *fig.* viaggio della vita: *to go on* (*a*) —, andare in pellegrinaggio ☆ *love* —, pellegrinaggio d'amore.

to **pilgrimage**, *v.i.* andare in pellegrinaggio.

piliferous [pai'lifərəs], *ag.* pilifero.

piling[1] ['pailiŋ], *s.* **1.** ammucchiamento **2.** (*metal.*) il formare un pacchetto ☆ — *up*, accatastamento.

piling[2], *s.* (*edil.*) palificazione di sostegno.

pill[1] [pil], *s.* **1.** pillola; *fig.* cosa noiosa, spiacevole: *it was a bitter — for him to swallow*, dovette ingoiare una pillola ben amara; *to gild the* —, indorare la pillola **2.** proiettile **3.** (*sl.*) palla; *pl.* biliardo **4.** (anche *pl.*) (*scherz.*) medico ☆ — *-box*, scatoletta per pillole; (*sl. mil.*) casamatta; (*scherz.*) piccola vettura; piccola costruzione.

to **pill**[1], *v.t.* **1.** somministrare pillole a **2.** (*sl.*) bocciare; dare voto contrario a.

to **pill**[2], *v.t.* **1.** (*arc.*) saccheggiare; depredare **2.** (*arc. dial.*) privare dei capelli; spellare; scorticare.

pillage ['pilidʒ], *s.* **1.** saccheggio; rapina; devastazione **2.** bottino.

to **pillage**, *v.t.* saccheggiare, devastare, depredare.

pillager ['pilidʒə*], *s.* saccheggiatore, predone.

pillar ['pilə*], *s.* **1.** pilastro; sostegno; colonna ‖ *the Pillars of Hercules*, (*mit.*) le colonne d'Ercole ‖ *to drive s.o. from — to post*, mandare qlcu. da Erode a Pilato **2.** *fig.* colonna, persona il cui aiuto è valido: *he was a — of the Academy*, fu una colonna dell'Accademia ☆ — *-box*, cassetta per (imbucare) le lettere; — *-saint*, (*sl. relig.*) stilita.

to **pillar**, *v.t.* sostenere, rinforzare con pilastri.

pillarist ['pilərist], *s.* (*st. relig.*) stilita.

pillion ['piljən], *s.* **1.** sella da donna **2.** sellino posteriore (di motocicletta, ecc.).

pilliwinks ['piliwiŋks], *s.* (*st.*) strumento scozzese di tortura per schiacciare le dita.

pillory ['piləri], *s.* berlina, gogna (anche *fig.*): *to be in the* —, *fig.* essere alla berlina.

to **pillory**, *v.t.* mettere alla berlina (anche *fig.*); esporre al ridicolo.

pillow ['pilou], *s.* **1.** guanciale, cuscino; capezzale ‖ *take counsel of your* —, dormici sopra, ripensaci bene **2.** (*mec.*) cuscinetto; cuscino di supporto **3.** (*mar.*) cuscino (dell'albero di bompresso) ☆ — *-case* (o — *-slip*), federa; — *-fight*, battaglia coi cuscini.

to **pillow**, *v.t.i.* posare, posarsi, riposare su un guanciale; servire di guanciale a ‖ *to — one's head on one's arms*, reclinare la testa sulle braccia.

pillowed ['piloud], *ag.* munito di cuscino.

pillowy ['piloui], *ag.* simile a cuscino; soffice.

pillworm ['pilwə:m], *s.* (*entom.*) millepiedi.

pilose ['pailous], *ag.* peloso.

pilosity [pai'lositi], *s.* pelosità.

pilot ['pailət], *s.* **1.** (*mar.*) pilota, timoniere, nocchiero **2.** (*aer.*) pilota **3.** *fig.* consigliere; guida ‖ *to drop the* —, non badare a chi dà buoni consigli ☆ — *-balloon*, pallone di prova; — *-bar*, barra di guida; — *-boat*, battello pilota; — *-cloth*, stoffa di lana blu per soprabiti; — *-engine*, rimorchiatore; — *-fish*, pesce pilota; — *-lamp*, lampada spia; — *-light*, lampada spia; accenditoio; — *-program*, (*amer.*) programma pilota ‖ *air-line* —, (*aer.*) pilota di linea; *deep-sea* —, pilota d'altomare; *dock-* —, pilota di porto.

to **pilot**, *v.t.* (*fig. letter.*) pilotare.

pilotage ['pailətidʒ], *s.* **1.** pilotaggio **2.** compenso dato al pilota.

pilotless ['pailətlis], *ag.* senza pilota ☆ — *bombs*, bombe radiocomandate, missili.

pilous ['pailəs], *ag.* peloso.

pilular ['piljulə*], *ag.* (*farm.*) pillolare.

pilule ['pilju:l], *s.* piccola pillola.

pilum ['pailəm], *pl.* **pila** ['pailə], *s.* (*st.*) pilo, giavellotto.

pimento [pi'mentou], *s.* (*bot. cuc.*) pimento.

pimp [pimp], *s.* mezzano.

to **pimp**, *v.i.* fare il mezzano.

pimpernel ['pimpənel], *s.* (*bot.*) anagallide, mordigallina ☆ *scarlet* —, primula rossa.

pimpinella [,pimpi'nelə], *s.* (*bot.*) pimpinella.

pimping ['pimpiŋ], *ag.* **1.** meschino; insignificante **2.** malaticcio.

pimple ['pimpl], *s.* foruncolo; bollicina; pustoletta.

pimpled ['pimpld], *ag.* foruncoloso.

pin [pin], *s.* **1.** spillo ‖ *pins and needles*, formicolio: *to have pins and needles in one's foot*, sentirsi il formicolio a un piede; *to be on pins and needles*, essere sulle spine ‖ *he doesn't care a — for it*, non gliene importa un bel niente ‖ *you might have heard a — fall*, si sarebbe sentito volare una mosca **2.** cavicchio; piolo; perno **3.** « pin » (misura di capacità = l. 20,46) **4.** bischero (di strumento musicale) **5.** *pl.* (*sl.*) gambe ☆ — *-case*, astuccio per spilli; — *-feather*, penna nascente; — *head*, capocchia di spillo; — *-maker*, fabbricante di spilli; — *-money*, (*dir.*) spillatico; — *-prick*, puntura di spillo, *fig.* leggera irritazione; — *table*, biliardino; — *-up* (*girl*), fotografia (da appendere) di donna procace; modella per tali fotografie; — *-wheel*, (*mec.*) ruota a pioli ‖ *crank* —, (*mec.*) perno di manovella; *drawing* - —, puntina da disegno; *fig.* osservazione sarcastica; *hair* —, forcina; *knitting* —, ferro da calza; *percussion* —, (*mec.*) percussore; *piston* —, (*mec.*) perno stantuffo, spinotto; *rolling-* —, (*cuc.*) mattarello; *safety-* —, spilla da balia; *thumb* —, puntina da disegno.

to **pin**, *pass.p.p.* **pinned** [pind], *v.t.* **1.** puntare, appuntare, fermare, attaccare (con spilli): *to — together*, attaccare insieme ‖ *to — one's faith to sthg.*, riporre la propria fiducia in ql.co. **2.** *fig.* inchiodare; fissare: *they pinned him to the wall*, lo inchiodarono al muro; *to — s.o.* (*down*) *to a bargain*, costringere qlcu. a concludere un affare **3.** *to — on*, puntare, attaccare con uno spillo: *she pinned on her hat*, si appuntò il cappello con uno spillone **4.** *to — up*, puntare, attaccare, fissare (*p. e.* alla parete con uno spillo).

pinaceous [pai'neiʃəs], *ag.* di pino.

pinafore ['pinəfɔ:*], *s.* grembiulino per bambini.

pinaster [pai'næstə*], *s.* (*bot.*) pinastro.

pince-nez ['pænsnei], *s.* pince-nez, occhiali a molla.

pincers ['pinsəz], *s.pl.* **1.** tenaglie; pinze: *a pair of* —, un paio di tenaglie **2.** (*zool.*) chele ☆ — *movement*, (*mil.*) movimento a tenaglia.

pinch [pintʃ], *s.* **1.** pizzico, pizzicotto; *fig.* morso: *to give s.o. a* —, dare un pizzicotto a qlcu.; *the — of hunger*, il morso della fame **2.** presa (di tabacco, ecc.): *he offered him a — of tobacco*, gli offrì una presa di tabacco **3.** *fig.* angustia, miseria, pena, dolore; crisi: *to be at a* —, essere in angustia.

to **pinch**, *v.t.i.* **1.** pizzicare; stringere; serrare: *I've pinched my finger in the door*, mi sono schiacciato un dito nella porta; *she pinched his ear*, ella gli tirò un orecchio **2.** stringere troppo, premere: *she used to — her waist*, ella si stringeva troppo alla vita ‖ *that is where the shoe pinches*, questo è il punto difficile, doloroso **3.** causare dolore: *the cold pinches*, il freddo punge **4.** tenere a stecchetto, privare, lesinare: *to — for food*, lesinare il cibo; *to — oneself*, tirare la cinghia, privarsi del necessario; vivere stentatamente ‖ *to — pennies*, fare economia **5.** estorcere: *to — sthg. from* (o *out of*) *s.o.*, estorcere ql.co. a qlcu. **6.** deperire: *she pinched for want of food*, deperì per mancanza di cibo **7.** incalzare (un cavallo) **8.** essere avaro **9.** (*sl.*) rubare, derubare **10.** (*sl.*) arrestare, prendere in custodia.

pinchbeck ['pintʃbek], *ag.* **1.** di princisbecco, di similoro **2.** falso, di poco prezzo ‖ *s.* princisbecco, similoro.

pinched [pintʃt], *ag.* **1.** costretto, serrato; schiacciato **2.** tormentato.

pinchers ['pintʃəz], *s.pl.* (*dial.*) tenaglie.

pinchfist ['pintʃfist], *s.* spilorcio, taccagno.

pinching ['pintʃiŋ], *ag.* **1.** pungente (di freddo) **2.** *fig.* urgente **3.** parsimonioso ‖ *s.* **1.** puntura **2.** parsimonia.

pincushion ['pin,kuʃin], *s.* puntaspilli.

Pindar ['pində*], *no.pr.m.* (*st. lett.*) Pindaro.

Pindaric [pin'dærik], *ag.* (*poes.*) pindarico ‖ *s.* ode pindarica.

pine[1] [pain], *s.* **1.** — (*-tree*), pino **2.** — (*-timber*), legno (di pino, di conifera) ☆ — *-apple*, ananasso (frutto); (*sl. amer. mil.*) granata a mano; — *clad*, rivestito, coperto di pini; — *-cone*, pigna; — *-forest* (o — *-grove*), pineta; — *-house*, serra per ananassi; — *-kernel*, pignolo; — *-needle*, ago di pino; — *-plantation*, pineta; — *-stove*, serra per ananassi; — *-thistle*, (*bot.*) cardo azzurro; — *-wood*, pineta; legname, legno di pino, abete ‖ *parasol* — (o *umbrella* —), pino a ombrello; *pitch* —, « pitchpine » (legno duro d'America).

to **pine**[2], *v.i.* **1.** struggersi, languire ‖ *to* — *for s.o.*, struggersi per qlcu.; *to* — *with hunger*, languire dalla fame **2.** desiderare ardentemente, anelare: *to* — *after* (o *for*) *s.o.*, desiderare ardentemente qlcu.; *to* — *o do sthg.*, struggersi, desiderare ardentemente di fare ql.co. **3.** *to* — **away**, struggersi, consumarsi di dolore.

pineal ['piniəl], *ag.* (*anat.*) pineale ☆ — *gland*, (*anat.*) ghiandola pineale, epifisi.

pinery ['painəri], *s.* **1.** piantagione di ananassi **2.** pineta.

pinetum [pai'ni:təm], *pl.* **pineta** [pai'ni:tə], *s.* pineto.

pinfold ['pinfould], *s.* recinto per animali.

to **pinfold**, *v.t.* rinchiudere (animali).

ping [piŋ], *s.* sibilo, fischio (come di pallottola) ☆ — *-pong*, ping pong, tennis da tavolo.

to **ping**, *v.t.i.* sibilare, fischiare; far fischiare.

pinguid ['piŋgwid], *ag.* **1.** pingue; grasso **2.** fertile (di suolo).

pinguidity [piŋ'gwiditi], *s.* **1.** pinguedine **2.** fertilità (di suolo).

pinguin ['piŋgwin], *s.* bromelia (pianta e frutto).

pinhole ['pinhoul], *s.* foro di spillo; foro per perno ☆ — *camera*, (*foto.*) stenoscopio.

pinion[1] ['pinjən], *s.* **1.** sommolo; (*poet.*) ala **2.** penna remigante.

to **pinion**[1], *v.t.* tagliare le ali a; legare ali, braccia a; *fig.* vincolare; immobilizzare; paralizzare.

pinion[2], *s.* (*mec.*) pignone ☆ *bevel* —, pignone conico; *satellite* —, pignone satellite.

pinioned ['pinjənd], *ag.* alato.

pink[1] [piŋk], *ag.* rosa: — *cheeks*, guance rosee ‖ — *socialism*, socialismo moderato ‖ *s.* **1.** colore rosa **2.** (*bot.*) garofano: *variegated* —, garofano screziato **3.** *fig.* fiore, modello, quintessenza: *the* — *of perfection*, il modello della perfezione, la perfezione stessa; *in the* — *of condition*, in condizioni eccellenti; *she is in the* —, (*fam.*) è in perfetta forma **4.** giacca rossa, scarlatta (usata per partite di caccia): *to hunt in* —, cacciare con la giacca rossa ☆ — *-eye*, (*patol. vet.*) congiuntivite batterica.

to **pink**[1], *v.t.i.* tingere, tingersi di rosa.

pink[2], *s.* (*ittiol.*) salmone giovane.

pink[3], *s.* (*mar.*) pinco.

pink[4], *s.* pigmento giallo.

to **pink**[5], *v.t.i.* **1.** traforare; decorare con trafori e smerli **2.** *fig.* trafiggere, pugnalare.

to **pink**[6], *v.i.* battere in testa, detonare (di motore).

to **pink**[7], *v.i.* (*dial.*) **1.** guardare furtivamente; sbattere le palpebre; ammiccare **2.** ridursi, diminuire (di luce).

pinkish ['piŋkiʃ], *ag.* roseo, rosato.

Pinkster ['piŋkstə*], *s.* (*amer. dial.*) Pentecoste.

pinky ['piŋki], *ag.* roseo, rosato.

pinna[1] ['pinə], *s.* pinna (mollusco bivalve).

pinna[2], *pl.* **pinnae** ['pini:], **pinnas** ['pinəz], *s.***1.** (*anat.*) pinna **2.** pinna (di pesce) **3.** (*bot.*) lobo di foglia pennata.

pinnace ['pinis], *s.* (*mar.*) scialuppa, imbarcazione di bordo.

pinnacle ['pinəkl], *s.* **1.** (*arch.*) pinnacolo **2.** cima (di montagna) **3.** *fig.* culmine: *the* — *of glory*, il sommo della gloria.

to **pinnacle**, *v.t.* sormontare, ornare con pinnacolo.

pinnate ['pinit], **pinnated** ['pineitid], *ag.* **1.** (*bot.*) pennato **2.** fornito di pinne, di ali.

pinner ['pinə*], *s.* **1.** cappuccio da donna con lembi laterali (secc. XVII-XVIII) **2.** grembiule con pettorina.

pinniped ['piniped], *ag.s.* (*zool.*) pinnipede.

pinnule ['pinju:l], *s.* **1.** pinnula (di alidada) **2.** (*bot.*) fogliolina di foglia pennata **3.** piccola pinna; aletta.

pinny ['pini], *s.* (*nel linguaggio infantile*) grembiulino.

pinpoint ['pin-point], *s.* **1.** capocchia di spillo **2.** *fig.* inezia **3.** (*aer.*) punto di riferimento al suolo ☆ — *bombing*, bombardamento di precisione.

to **pinpoint**, *v.t.* **1.** localizzare con precisione; fissare, determinare con esattezza **2.** bombardare (un bersaglio preciso).

pint [paint], *s.* pinta (misura di capacità = l. 0,568 in Gran Bretagna; = l. 0,473 negli Stati Uniti).

pintle ['pintl], *s.* **1.** perno **2.** (*mar.*) agugliotto.

pinto ['pintou], *pl.* **pintos** ['pintouz], *ag.s.* (*amer.*) (cavallo) pezzato.

Pinxter ['piŋkstə*], *s.* (*amer. dial.*) Pentecoste.

piny ['paini], *ag.* **1.** ricco di pini **2.** simile a pino.

piolet [,pi:ə'lei], *s.* piccozza (degli alpinisti).

pioneer [,paiə'niə*], *s.* soldato esploratore; pioniere ‖ *to do* — *work in a field*, lavorare sperimentalmente, fare un lavoro sperimentale in un campo ☆ — *stage*, stadio sperimentale.

to **pioneer**, *v.t.i.* aprire la strada (a); fare da pioniere (a): *to* — *a cause*, farsi pioniere di una causa.

pious ['paiəs], *ag.* **1.** pio, religioso, devoto: *he is a* — *man*, è un uomo pio **2.** pietoso, a fin di bene: *a* — *fraud*, un pietoso inganno **3.** (*arc.*) rispettoso, pieno di pietà filiale.

piously ['paiəsli], *av.* piamente, religiosamente, devotamente.

piousness ['paiəsnis], *s.* pietà, devozione; religiosità.

pip[1] [pip], *s.* **1.** (*vet.*) pipita **2.** (*sl.*) malessere, indisposizione; cattivo umore: *to have the* —, essere di cattivo umore.

to **pip**[1], *pass.p.p.* **pipped** [pipt], *v.t.i.* **1.** pigolare **2.** rompere (il guscio).

pip[2], *s.* **1.** puntino, macchia (sul domino, sui dadi, ecc.) **2.** (*fam.*) stelletta (di ufficiale) **3.** (*bot.*) fiore (di infiorescenza a grappolo) **4.** segmento romboidale di ananasso.

to **pip**[2], *v.t.* (*sl.*) **1.** votare contro **2.** sconfiggere, battere **3.** colpire con una fucilata.

pip[3] *s.* **1.** seme di mela, pera **2.** mela ranetta.

pip[4], *s.* **1.** suono breve (generalmente meccanico): *the pips*, segnale orario **2.** (*tel. mil.*) la lettera p nelle segnalazioni: *five* — *emma* (5 *p. m.*), le cinque del pomeriggio.

pipage ['paipidʒ], *s.* **1.** tubature **2.** trasporto per tubatura; canalizzazione **3.** costo di tale trasporto.

pipe[1] [paip], *s.* **1.** condotto, tubo; canna; cannuccia: — *of a stove*, tubo di una stufa; *to convey by means of pipes*, distribuire, convogliare a mezzo di tubazioni **2.** (*mus.*) strumento a fiato (piffero, flauto, zampogna, ecc.) **3.** pipa: *to smoke a* —, fumare la pipa **4.** (*geol. miner.*) camino di vulcano; vena di minerale **5.** *fig.* voce; cinguettio **6.** fischietto di marinaio (per chiamare la ciurma) ☆ — *-dream*, illusione, sogno; — *fish*, pesce signato; — *-fitting*, pezzo sagomato (dei tubi); — *-lagging*, rivestimento di tubo; — *-laying*, montaggio dei tubi; — *-line*, oleodotto; — *-line walker*, (*amer.*) sorvegliante di oleodotti; — *-major*, capobanda (di suonatori); — *-organ*, organo a canne; — *-rack*, rastrelliera per pipe; — *-stem*, cannuccia di pipa; — *-still*, distillatore tubolare; — *-tree*, (*bot.*) lilla ‖ *coil*— —, tubo serpentino; *cross*— —, tubo a croce; *drain*- —, tubo di scarico; *elbow*- —, tubo a gomito; *exhaust* —, tubo di scappamento; *gas* — *line*, conduttura a gas; *oil* — *line*, oleodotto.

to **pipe**[1], *v.t.i.* **1.** suonare (piffero, flauto, zampogna, ecc.) **2.** (*rad. tv.*) trasmettere per filo (o cavo coassiale) **3.** emettere suoni acuti; cinguettare (di uccelli);

cantare lamentosamente ‖ *to — one's eye(s)*, (*fam.*) piangere, singhiozzare **4.** (*mar.*) richiamare con fischio (la ciurma) **5.** posare tubature, fornire di tubature; convogliare per mezzo di tubazioni **6.** (*agr.*) riprodurre per talea **7.** adornare, profilare (abiti) con bordino, cordoncino **8.** (*cuc.*) ornare (dolci) **9.** *to — away*, (*mar.*) dare il segnale della partenza **10.** *to — down*, (*sl.*) far meno rumore: *— down!*, calmati!, frenati! **11.** *to — in*, (*scoz.*) suonare la cornamusa in segno di benvenuto **12.** *to — up*, intonare (un canto, una melodia).

pipe[2], *s.* grosso barile.

pipeclay ['paipklei], *s.* terra da pipa.

to pipeclay, *v.t.* **1.** imbiancare con terra da pipa **2.** *fig.* sistemare con cura.

pipeful ['paipful], *s.* pipata, contenuto di una pipa.

piper ['paipə*], *s.* pifferaio, suonatore di piffero ‖ *he who pays the — calls the tune*, chi fa le spese, ha diritto di scelta.

piperidine [pi'peridain], *s.* (*chim.*) piperidina.

piperine ['pipərain], *s.* (*chim.*) piperina.

pipet(te) [pi'pet], *s.* (*chim.*) pipetta.

piping ['paipiŋ], *ag.* **1.** che suona il piffero, la zampogna, ecc. **2.** arcadico: *the — times of peace*, i giorni sereni della pace **3.** acuto, alto, penetrante (di suono, voce) ‖ *— hot*, caldo bollente.

piping, *s.* **1.** il suonare la zampogna **2.** suono di piffero, zampogna, ecc. **3.** suono acuto, alto, penetrante **4.** (*sl.*) pianto, lamento **5.** tubature, tubazioni **6.** (*bot.*) talea **7.** cordoncino, profilo (per abiti) **8.** (*cuc.*) decorazione di zucchero filato su torte, ecc.

pipistrel(le) [,pipis'trel], *s.* piccolo pipistrello.

pipit ['pipit], *s.* (*ornit.*) calandro, pispola.

pipkin ['pipkin], *s.* vaso, tegame di terracotta.

pipless ['piplis], *ag.* senza semi.

pippin ['pipin], *s.* mela ranetta.

pip-pip ['pip'pip], *inter.* **1.** (*sl.*) ciao! **2.** (*aut.*) pot-pot! (suono del clacson).

pippy ['pipi], *ag.* pieno di semi.

pip-squeak ['pip-skwi:k], *s.* **1.** proiettile dal sibilo acuto **2.** (*sl.*) persona, cosa insignificante.

pipy ['paipi], *ag.* **1.** tubolare, a tubo **2.** flautato (di suono).

piquancy ['pi:kənsi], *s.* gusto piccante.

piquant ['pi:kənt], *ag.* piccante; *fig.* frizzante, arguto.

piquantly ['pi:kəntli], *av.* in modo piccante; *fig.* in modo frizzante, argutamente.

pique[1] [pi:k], *s.* picca, ripicco; animosità, risentimento ‖ *in a fit of —*, per ripicco; *out of —*, per puntiglio.

to pique[1], *v.t.* **1.** ferire l'orgoglio di; irritare **2.** stimolare (curiosità, interesse, ecc.) **3.** *to — oneself on*, piccarsi di.

pique[2], *s.* vincita di trenta punti al picchetto.

to pique[2], *v.t.i.* segnare trenta punti al picchetto (contro).

piqué ['pi:kei], *s.* picchè.

piquet [pi'ket], *s.* (*giuoco*) picchetto.

piracy ['paiərəsi], *s.* **1.** pirateria **2.** plagio.

piragua [pi'rægwə], *s.* piroga.

pirate ['paiərit], *s.* **1.** pirata, corsaro **2.** plagiario **3.** nave pirata.

to pirate, *v.t.i.* **1.** pirateggiare **2.** plagiare.

piratic(al) [pai'rætik(ə)l], *ag.* pirata, piratico.

piratically [pai'rætikəli], *av.* da pirata, piraticamente.

pirn [pə:n], *s.* (*ind. tessile*) cannetta.

pirogue [pi'roug], *s.* piroga.

pirouette [,piru'et], *s.* piroetta: *to perform a —*, fare una piroetta.

to pirouette, *v.i.* piroettare.

piscary ['piskəri], *s.* **1.** (*dir.*) diritto di pesca ‖ *common of —*, diritto di pesca pubblica **2.** luogo di pesca.

piscatorial [,piskə'tɔ:riəl], **piscatory** ['piskətəri], *ag.* peschereccio; pescatorio.

Pisces ['pisi:z], *no.pr.pl.* (*astr.*) Pesci.

piscicultural [,pisi'kʌltʃərəl], *ag.* relativo alla piscicoltura.

pisciculture ['pisikʌltʃə*], *s.* piscicoltura.

pisciculturist [,pisi'kʌltʃərist], *s.* piscicoltore.

pisciform ['pisifɔ:m], *ag.* a forma di pesce.

piscina [pi'si:nə], *pl.* **piscinae** [pi'si:ni:], **piscinas** [pi'si:nəz], *s.* **1.** (*st. romana*) piscina **2.** peschiera, piscina.

piscine[1] ['pisain], *ag.* di pesce.

piscine[2] [pi'si:n], *s.* **1.** (*st. romana*) piscina **2.** peschiera, piscina.

piscivorous [pi'sivərəs], *ag.* ittiofago.

pish [piʃ], *inter.* puah!, puh!.

to pish, *v.i.* dire puah; esprimere impazienza, disgusto.

pishogue [pi'ʃoug], *s.* (*irl.*) incantesimo, magia, stregoneria.

pisiform ['paisifɔ:m], *ag.* a forma di pisello ☆ *— bone*, (*anat.*) osso pisiforme.

Pisistratus [pai'sistrətəs], *no.pr.m.* (*st.*) Pisistrato.

pismire ['pismaiə*], *s.* formica.

piss [pis], *s.* (*volg.*) orina.

to piss, *v.t.i.* (*volg.*) **1.** orinare **2.** bagnare di orina.

pistachio [pis'ta:ʃiou], *pl.* **pistachios** [pis'ta:ʃiouz], *s.* **1.** (*bot.*) pistacchio **2.** color pistacchio.

pistil ['pistil], *s.* (*bot.*) pistillo.

pistillate ['pistilit], **pistilliferous** [,pisti'lifərəs], *ag.* (*bot.*) pistillifero.

pistol ['pistl], *s.* pistola ☆ *— -case*, fondina (per pistola); *— -shot*, tiro di pistola.

to pistol, *pass.p.p.* **pistolled** ['pistld], *v.t.* colpire con colpi di pistola.

pistole [pis'toul], *s.* pistola (antica moneta d'oro spagnola).

pistoleer, pistolier [,pistou'liə*], *s.* soldato armato di pistola.

piston ['pistən], *s.* pistone, stantuffo ☆ *— -engine aircraft*, aereo con motore a pistoni; *— -pin*, spinotto, perno di stantuffo; *— -rod*, biella ‖ *curved head —*, pistone a testa bombata; *full —*, pistone pieno; *hollow — (o perforate —)*, pistone forato.

pit[1] [pit], *s.* **1.** voragine, abisso, burrone: *a bottomless —*, un abisso senza fondo ‖ *the —*, (*scherz.*) l'inferno **2.** fossa, fosso; buca (per riparazioni di autoveicoli); trappola ‖ *to dig a — for s.o.*, *fig.* tendere un tranello a qlcu. **3.** arena (per combattimento di galli) **4.** (*miner.*) cava, pozzo **5.** cavo, cavità: *— of the stomach*, bocca dello stomaco **6.** fossetta (di guancia); buttero (del vaiolo) **7.** (*teat.*) platea; pubblico di platea **8.** (*amer.*) mercato di borsa **9.** (*metal.*) alveolo, puntinatura ☆ *— -coal*, carbon fossile; *— -pony*, cavallino usato nelle miniere; *— -saw*, sega a mano per tronchi; *— -stall*, poltrona di platea; *— -village*, villaggio di minatori ‖ *casting- —*, (*metal.*) fossa di colata; *clay- —*, cava d'argilla; *gravel- —*, cava di ghiaia; *sand- —*, cava di sabbia; *saw- —*, pozzo di segheria; *surface- —*, cava a cielo aperto; *wheat —*, mercato del grano.

to pit[1], *pass.p.p.* **pitted** ['pitid], *v.t.* **1.** mettere, riporre in un buco, in una fossa **2.** fare buchi in; butterare: *he is pitted with small-pox*, è butterato dal vaiolo **3.** mettere in gara: *to — a person against another*, opporre una persona ad un'altra **4.** (*metal.*) mordere, forare (di acidi).

pit[2], *s.* (*amer.*) nocciolo; seme.

pit-a-pat ['pitə'pæt], *s.* **1.** palpitazione, batticuore **2.** scalpiccio; ticchettio ‖ *av.* palpitando, con scalpiccio ‖ *to go —*, picchierellare (di pioggia); scalpicciare (di piedi); palpitare, fare tic-tac (del cuore).

Pitcairn Island ['pitkɛən'ailənd], *no.pr.* (*geog.*) Isola Pitcairn.

pitch[1] [pitʃ], *s.* **1.** lancio, tiro (anche *spor.*) **2.** (*aer. mar.*) beccheggio; passo **3.** (*mec. elett.*) passo; distanza **4.** (*spor.*) campo (tra le due porte) **5.** posteggio (di venditore ambulante) **6.** punto, grado di elevazione;

altezza (anche *fig.*): *to a right* —, ad un punto ragionevole; *to bring to a high* — *of excellence*, portare ad un alto grado di perfezione **7.** (*mus.*) tono fondamentale, intonazione, tonalità; diapason (di strumento); altezza (di suono); timbro (di voce): *her voice has a very high* —, la sua voce è molto acuta; *it must be taken on a lower* —, deve essere preso su un tono più basso; *to give the orchestra the* —, dare il tono all'orchestra **8.** (*arch.*) altezza di arco, volta **9.** inclinazione, pendenza; declivio; falda (di tetto) ☆ — *-circle* (o — *-line*), (*mec.*) circonferenza primitiva; — *-pipe*, (*mus.*) diapason a fiato; — *-setting*, (*aer.*) calottamento, passo di riferimento ‖ *propeller* —, (*aer.*) passo dell'elica; *screw* —, (*mar.*) passo dell'elica.

to pitch[1], *v.t.i.* **1.** gettare, scagliare, lanciare: *to be pitched off one's horse*, essere disarcionato **2.** (*aer. mar.*) beccheggiare: *the ship pitched awfully*, la nave beccheggiava da far paura **3.** (*cricket, baseball*) servire **4.** esporre (in vendita); disporre in ordine **5.** cadere, precipitare, abbattersi; tuffare, tuffarsi; (*aer.*) impennarsi, picchiare: *he pitched on his head and died*, cadde a capofitto e morì **6.** (*mus.*) intonare, dare il tono a (anche *fig.*) **7.** ficcare, piantare, conficcare (nella terra); piantare una tenda, attendarsi, accamparsi: *a cottage pitched on the top of a hill*, una casetta piantata sulla cima di una collina; *where will they* — *their camp?*, dove metteranno le tende? **8.** (*mec.*) ingranare, innestare **9.** pavimentare **10.** *to* — *into* (*s.o.*), (*fam.*) dare addosso a, assalire (anche *fig.*) **11.** *to* — (*up*)*on* (*sthg.*), trovare per caso: *I pitched upon sthg. I liked*, trovai per caso ql.co. che mi piaceva **12.** *to* — *in*, (*pop.*) darci dentro, lavorare con energia **13.** *to* — *over*, cadere supino.

pitch[2], *s.* pece, resina, bitume: *dregs of* — *and tar*, feccia di pece e catrame ☆ — *-black* (o — *-dark*), nero come la pece; — *-darkness*, *fig.* buio pesto; — *pine*, (*bot.*) abete resinoso, pino rosso americano ‖ *Burgundy* —, pece bianca di Borgogna.

to pitch[2], *v.t.* impeciare, incatramare.

pitchblende ['pitʃblend], *s.* (*min.*) pechblenda.

pitched[1] [pìtʃt], *ag.* **1.** (*cricket, baseball*) servito (di palla) **2.** disposto in ordine di battaglia; accampato; stabilito, regolare **3.** esposto (in vendita) **4.** immerso, tuffato **5.** conficcato, fisso **6.** pavimentato **7.** avente un particolare tono musicale ☆ — *battle*, battaglia campale ‖ *high-* —, *low-* —, acuto, grave (di suono).

pitched[2], *ag.* impeciato, incatramato.

pitcher[1] ['pitʃə*], *s.* **1.** (*spec. baseball*) lanciatore **2.** posteggiatore **3.** ciottolo (per selciato).

pitcher[2], *s.* **1.** brocca (di terracotta); (*amer.*) recipiente a larga imboccatura ‖ *little pitchers have long ears*, i bambini hanno le orecchie lunghe ‖ *the* — *goes so often to the well that at last it breaks*, *prov.* tanto va la gatta al lardo che ci lascia lo zampino **2.** (*bot.*) ascidio ☆ — *-plant*, (*bot.*) nepente.

pitchfork[1] ['pitʃfɔ:k], *s.* forcone (per il fieno).

to pitchfork[1], *v.t.* **1.** rimuovere (fieno, ecc.) con il forcone **2.** *fig.* spingere, forzare a raggiungere: *he was pitchforked into office*, fu costretto volente o nolente ad accettare la carica **3.** attaccare, colpire con il forcone.

pitchfork[2], *s.* (*mus.*) diapason.

pitching ['pitʃin], *ag.* beccheggiante: — *ship*, nave che beccheggia ‖ *s.* **1.** lancio **2.** (*mar.*) beccheggio **3.** esposizione (di merce) **4.** pavimentazione, selciato.

pitchy ['pitʃi], *ag.* **1.** impeciato; pecioso **2.** *fig.* nero, scuro come la pece.

piteous ['pitiəs], *ag.* **1.** pietoso **2.** miserando; deplorevole.

piteously ['pitiəsli], *av.* **1.** pietosamente **2.** deplorevolmente.

piteousness ['pitiəsnis], *s.* stato compassionevole.

pitfall ['pitfɔ:l], *s.* **1.** trappola; trappola coperta per animali **2.** *fig.* inganno, tranello.

pith [piθ], *s.* **1.** midollo **2.** *fig.* essenza, quintessenza: *the* — *and marrow of sthg.*, la quintessenza di

ql.co. **3.** forza, vigore, nerbo ‖ *of great* — *and moment*, (*letter.*) di grande importanza e significato.

pithead ['pit-hed], *s.* **1.** terreno che circonda la bocca di un pozzo minerario **2.** insieme dei macchinari disposti in prossimità della bocca di un pozzo minerario.

pithecanthrope [,piθi'kænθroup], *s.* (*paleont.*) pitecantropo.

pithily ['piθili], *av.* **1.** concisamente **2.** vigorosamente; efficacemente.

pithiness ['piθinis], *s.* **1.** abbondanza di midollo **2.** *fig.* intima essenza **3.** vigoria.

pithless ['piθlis], *ag.* **1.** senza midollo **2.** *fig.* senza forza.

pithy ['piθi], *ag.* **1.** pieno di midollo; simile a midollo **2.** conciso, succinto; vigoroso (di stile, ecc.).

pitiable ['pitiəbl], *ag.* pietoso, misero, deplorevole.

pitiableness ['pitiəblnis], *s.* stato compassionevole, pietoso.

pitiably ['pitiəbli], *av.* pietosamente.

pitiful ['pitiful], *ag.* **1.** compassionevole, pietoso **2.** miserando, meschino.

pitifully ['pitifuli], *av.* compassionevolmente; pietosamente.

pitifulness ['pitifulnis], *s.* **1.** pietà, compassione **2.** stato pietoso, compassionevole.

pitiless ['pitilis], *ag.* spietato, crudele.

pitilessly ['pitilisli], *av.* spietatamente, crudelmente.

pitilessness ['pitilisnis], *s.* crudeltà.

pitman, *pl.* **pitmen** ['pitmən], *s.* minatore (di pozzo carbonifero).

pitpan ['pitpæn], *s.* (*amer.*) canoa, piroga.

pittance ['pitəns], *s.* **1.** elemosina **2.** quantità esigua di denaro **3.** magro salario **4.** (*st.*) lascito a comunità religiose per razioni supplementari di cibo in speciali ricorrenze.

pitted ['pitid], *ag.* butterato.

to pitter ['pitə*], *v.i.* (*onomatopeico*) far cri-cri.

pitter-patter ['pitə'pætə*], *s.* picchiettio leggero ‖ *av.* con leggero picchiettio.

pittite[1] ['pitait], *s.c.* (*fam.*) spettatore, spettatrice di platea.

Pittite[2], *s.* (*st.*) seguace della politica di W. Pitt.

pituitary [pi'tju(:)itəri], *ag.* (*anat.*) pituitario, mucoso ☆ — *gland*, glandola pituitaria; — *membrane*, pituitaria.

pituite ['pitjuait], *s.* (*anat.*) pituita.

pituitous [pi'tju(:)itəs], *ag.* (*anat.*) pituitoso.

pituitrin [pi'tju(:)itrin], *s.* (*fisiol.*) pituitrina.

pity ['piti], *s.* **1.** compassione, pietà: *to feel* — *for s.o.*, provar pietà per qlcu.; *to have* (o *to take*) — *on s.o.*, aver compassione di qlcu.; *to move s.o. to* —, destare la compassione di qlcu. ‖ *for pity's sake*, per pietà, di grazia **2.** peccato (espressione di rimpianto): *such a* — *you didn't come*, è proprio un peccato che tu non sia venuto; *what a* —!, che peccato!.

to pity, *v.t.* compatire; provare pietà per; avere pietà di: *he's to be pitied*, bisogna avere pietà di lui.

pitying ['pitiin], *ag.* compassionevole, pietoso.

pityingly ['pitiinli], *av.* pietosamente, compassionevolmente.

pityriasis [,piti'raiəsis], *s.* (*patol.*) pitiriasi.

Pius ['paiəs], *no.pr.m.* Pio.

pivot ['pivət], *s.* **1.** cardine, perno (anche *fig.*): *to set on a* —, (*mec.*) imperniare; *to turn upon a* —, girare su un perno **2.** (*mil.*) soldato che funge da perno in manovre di rotazione.

to pivot, *v.t.i.* imperniare; girare su di un perno.

pixie ['piksi], *s.* fata; folletto.

pixilated ['piksileitid], *ag.* **1.** (*dial. amer.*) visionario, svitato, picchiatello **2.** (*sl. amer.*) ubriaco.

pixy ['piksi], *s.* fata; folletto.

pizzicato [,pitsi'kɑ:tou], *ag. s.* (*mus.*) pizzicato.

placeability [,plækə'biliti], *s.* placabilità.

placable ['plækəbl], *ag.* placabile.

placableness ['plækəblnis], *s.* placabilità.

placably ['plækəbli], *av.* placabilmente.

placard ['plækɑ:d], *s.* manifesto, cartellone, affisso.

to **placard**, *v.t.* **1.** affiggere, attaccare cartelli, ma-
'esti su **2.** annunciare con manifesti, su affissi.
to **placate** [plə'keit], *v.t.* **1.** placare; pacificare; coniare **2.** (*amer.*) comperare la connivenza (degli av-
rsari).
placation [plə'keiʃən], *s.* placamento; conciliazione.
placatory ['plækətəri], *ag.* placatore; conciliante.
place [pleis], *s.* **1.** luogo, posto: *a — of amusement,*
luogo di divertimento; — *of birth,* luogo di nascita;
of business, luogo di affari; — *of residence,* (luogo
) residenza; — *of worship,* luogo di culto; *to change
e's* —, cambiare di posto ‖ *in — of,* invece di **2.** pun-
. zona: *a sore — on the arm,* una zona dolente sul
accio **3.** (*fam.*) casa, dimora; villa di campa-
a **4.** piazza (anche *comm.*): *a trading* —, una piazza
mmerciale **5.** passo, brano; segno: *I've lost my* —,
. perso il segno **6.** spazio, posto: *six places were laid
that table,* c'erano sei coperti su quella tavola ‖
give — to, dar luogo a, cedere a: *the drama is giving
. to the cinema,* il teatro sta cedendo il passo al cima; *his anger gave — to a feeling of pity,* la sua ira
dette a un senso di pietà ‖ *to go places,* (*amer.*) aver
ccesso ‖ *to take* —, aver luogo, accadere: *the marge will not take* —, il matrimonio non avrà luogo;
ease, take your places,* prego, accomodatevi **7.** posi-
one, carica, impiego: *he gave up his* —, diede le
missioni; *she cannot find a* —, non riesce a trovare
. impiego **8.** posizione sociale, rango, condizione:
keep s.o. in his —, tenere qlcu. al suo posto; *to
now one's* —, saper stare al proprio posto ‖ *high
aces,* alte sfere, posti d'onore ‖ *in high* —, alto-
cato **9.** compito, dovere **10.** (*spor.*) piazzamento:
back a horse for a —, giocare un cavallo piazzato
. — *kick,* (*rugby*) calcio piazzato.
to **place,** *v.t.* **1.** collocare, situare, mettere, posare:
. *this book on the table,* metti questo libro sul tavolo;
. *placed a big order with...,* (*comm.*) egli collocò un
osso ordine presso...; *to — oneself,* mettersi: *he placed
mself at my disposal,* si mise a mia disposizione **2.** pro-
rare un posto, impiego a: *he was placed in command
. the regiment,* fu posto al comando del reggimen-
3. dare un grado, una posizione a, classificare; identifi-
re: *to — a person,* (*fam.*) ricordarsi chi sia una per-
na, dove la si sia conosciuta **4.** riporre (fede, fiducia
. qlcu., ql.co.): *to — confidence in s.o.,* riporre fiducia
. qlcu.; *to — one's hopes on sthg.,* riporre le proprie
eranze in ql.co. **5.** investire, depositare (denaro):
n you tell me where I could — my money?, sapete
rmi dove potrei investire il mio denaro? **6.** (*mil.*)
ostare (artiglierie) **7.** (*spor.*) piazzare.
placeman, *pl.* **placemen** ['pleismən], *s.* **1.** (*spreg.*)
npiegato governativo **2.** arrivista.
placement ['pleismənt], *s.* collocamento ☆ — *bureau,*
zenzia di collocamento.
placenta [plə'sentə], *pl.* **placentae** [plə'senti:], **pla-
entas** [plə'sentəz], *s.* (*anat.*) placenta.
placental [plə'sentl], *ag.* (*fisiol.*) placentale.
placer[1] ['pleisə*], *s.* collocatore.
placer[2], *s.* (*miner. geol.*) giacimento alluvionale.
placet ['pleiset], *s.* beneplacito.
placid ['plæsid], *ag.* placido, calmo; sereno.
placidity [plæ'siditi], *s.* placidità, calma; sere-
ità.
placidly ['plæsidli], *av.* placidamente.
placidness ['plæsidnis], *s.* placidità.
plack [plæk], *s.* **1.** (*arc.*) « plack » (monetina scozze-
e) **2.** *fig.* cosa di poco valore.
placket ['plækit], *s.* **1.** apertura (in una gonna) **2.** ta-
ca (specialmente di una gonna) **3.** (*arc.*) sottoveste.
plafond [plɑ'fɔn], *s.* soffitto (dipinto, affrescato).
plagal ['pleigəl], *ag.* (*mus.*) plagale.
plagiarism ['pleidʒərizəm], *s.* plagio.
plagiarist ['pleidʒərist], *s.* plagiario.
plagiaristic [,pleidʒə'ristik], *ag.* plagiario, di plagio.
to **plagiarize** ['pleidʒəraiz], *v.t.* plagiare.

plagiary ['pleidʒəri], *s.* **1.** plagio **2.** plagiario.
plague [pleig], *s.* **1.** peste, pestilenza **2.** *fig.* piaga,
flagello, afflizione; castigo divino ‖ — *on it!,* accidenti!
☆ — *spot,* segno sulla pelle (caratteristico della peste);
località dove infuria la peste; *fig.* fonte, sintomo di corruzione ‖ *bubonic* —, peste bubbonica.
to **plague,** *v.t.* **1.** (*rar.*) appestare, infestare **2.** affliggere, tormentare: *plagued with,* afflitto da; *to — s.o.
with questions,* tormentare qlcu. con domande.
plaguer ['pleigə*], *s.* tormentatore; seccatore.
plaguesome ['pleigsəm], *ag.* seccante, noioso.
plaguey ['pleigi], *ag.* **1.** (*rar.*) pestifero, pestilenziale **2.** seccante, scocciante **3.** (*fam.*) notevole; cospicuo:
a — nuisance, una tremenda seccatura ‖ *av.* **1.** in modo
seccante **2.** (*fam.*) estremamente; in modo notevole:
I'm — glad to be here, sono estremamente contento di
essere qui.
plaguily ['pleigili], *av.* fastidiosamente.
plaguy, *V.* **plaguey.**
plaice [pleis], *s.* (*ittiol.*) passerino, pianuzza.
plaid [plæd], *s.* **1.** sciarpone di lana generalmente
a scacchi che si porta sul costume scozzese **2.** stoffa
spesso a quadri usata per confezionare il costume
scozzese.
plaided ['plædid], *ag.* **1.** che indossa una sciarpa
scozzese **2.** fatto di stoffa scozzese; stampato, tessuto
a quadri scozzesi.
plain[1] [plein], *ag.* **1.** piano, liscio: — *ground,* terreno
piano **2.** chiaro, evidente: *the meaning is quite* —, il
significato è del tutto chiaro ‖ *as — as can be* (o *as
— as daylight*), chiaro come il sole; *it is as — as a pikestaff* (o *as the nose on your face*), salta agli occhi **3.** semplice: — *cooking,* cucina semplice; — *living,* abitudini
semplici **4.** facile: — *sewing,* facile lavoro di cucito ‖
it is all — sailing, corre tutto liscio **5.** ordinario, comune; insignificante, scialbo: *a — face,* un viso comune,
non bello; *the — man,* l'uomo medio, di media intelligenza **6.** sincero, schietto, franco: — *dealing,* sincerità, candore; — *truth,* pura verità; *to be — with s.o.,*
essere schietti con qlcu. ‖ *to use — language,* per dirla
francamente ‖ *s.* pianura; piano: *in the open* —, in
aperta pianura ☆ — *-chant* (o — *-song*), (*mus.*) canto
fermo, gregoriano; — *-clothes,* abiti borghesi: — *-clothes
man,* poliziotto in borghese; — *-spoken,* che non ha
peli sulla lingua.
plain[1], *av.* **1.** chiaramente **2.** semplicemente **3.** francamente.
to **plain**[2], *v.i.* (*arc.*) lamentarsi.
plainly ['pleinli], *av.* **1.** chiaramente **2.** semplicemente: — *dressed,* vestito alla buona **3.** francamente.
plainness ['pleinnis], *s.* **1.** chiarezza, evidenza **2.** semplicità **3.** franchezza, schiettezza **4.** aspetto insignificante, scialbo.
plainsman, *pl.* **plainsmen** ['pleinzmən], *s.* abitante
della pianura.
plaint [pleint], *s.* **1.** (*poet.*) compianto, lamento **2.** (*dir.*) querela, accusa.
plaintful ['pleintful], *ag.* lamentevole.
plaintiff ['pleintif], *s.* (*dir.*) querelante, attore.
plaintive ['pleintiv], *ag.* lamentoso; triste.
plaintively ['pleintivli], *av.* lamentosamente; tristemente ‖
plaintiveness ['pleintivnis], *s.* tono lamentoso; tristezza.
plaintless ['pleintlis], *ag.* senza lamenti.
plait [plæt], *s.* **1.** piega **2.** treccia (di paglia, nastri,
capelli).
to **plait,** *v.t.* **1.** pieghettare (abiti, biancheria) **2.** intrecciare (paglia, nastri, capelli).
plaited ['plætid], *ag.* **1.** pieghettato, a pieghe (di
abiti, biancheria) **2.** intrecciato; attorcigliato (di paglia,
nastri, capelli).
plaiting ['plætin], *s.* pieghettatura ☆ *accordion-* —
(o *sunburst* —), pieghettatura a fisarmonica, a soleil.
plan [plæn], *s.* **1.** piano, progetto, disegno, schema:

it would not be a bad — to do this, non sarebbe una cattiva idea fare questo; *what are your plans for the future?*, quali sono i tuoi progetti per l'avvenire? ‖ *according to —*, secondo il previsto 2. pianta, disegno.

to **plan**, *pass.p.p.* **planned** [plænd], *v.t.* 1. progettare: *to — a trip to Bournemouth*, progettare una gita a Bournemouth 2. fare la pianta, il piano di; disegnare ☆ *planned economy*, economia pianificata.

planch(e) [plɑːnʃ], *s.* 1. (*dial.*) asse 2. lastra di metallo, di pietra, di argilla.

planchet ['plɑːnʃit], *s.* plancia, disco di metallo su cui si imprime il conio.

planchette [plɑːnʃet], *s.* tavoletta per sedute spiritiche.

plane[1] [plein], *ag.* piano, piatto; uguale; livellato ‖ *s.* 1. piano, superficie piana 2. *fig.* livello, stadio di sviluppo: *the discussion proceeded on a lofty —*, la discussione procedeva a un livello elevato 3. (*mec.*) piano di riscontro 4. (*aer.*) piano alare, ala; (*fam.*) aereo ☆ *— geometry*, geometria piana; *— surface*, (*geom.*) superficie piana ‖ *cargo —*, aereo da carico; *combat —*, aereo da combattimento; *focal —*, (*ott.*) piano focale; *four-engined —*, quadrimotore; *inclined —*, (*geom.*) piano inclinato; *land —*, aeroplano terrestre; *passenger —*, aereo passeggeri; *pursuit —*, (*aer.*) caccia; *training —*, aereo per addestramento; *transport —*, aereo da trasporto.

to **plane**[1], *v.i.* 1. planare, volare (di uccelli, ecc.) 2. (*fam.*) viaggiare in aereo.

plane[2], *s.* (*strum.*) pialla ☆ *— iron*, ferro da pialla; *compasso —*, pialla rotonda, sponderuola a barca; *dovetail —*, pialla a linguette; *jack- —*, sbozzino, pialla per sgrossare; *jointing- —* (o *shooting- —*), piallone; *moulding- —*, pialla da modanatura; *toothing- —*, pialla a denti.

to **plane**[2], *v.t.* piallare, livellare ☆ *planing machine*, piallatrice.

plane[3], *s.* — (*tree*), (*bot.*) platano.

planer ['pleinə*], *s.* 1. piallatore 2. (*mec.*) piallatrice 3. (*tip.*) battitoio.

planet[1] ['plænit], *s.* (*astr.*) pianeta.

planet[2], *s.* (*eccl.*) pianeta (veste sacerdotale).

planetarium [ˌplæniˈtɛəriəm], *s.* planetario.

planetary ['plænitəri], *ag.* 1. planetario: *— influence*, influenza dei pianeti; *— system*, sistema planetario 2. terrestre 3. (*arc.*) errante; vagabondo.

planetoid ['plænitoid], *s.* (*astr.*) asteroide, pianeta minore.

plangency ['plændʒənsi], *s.* 1. risonanza 2. suono am entoso.

plangent ['plændʒənt], *ag.* 1. risonante, rumoroso 2. lamentoso.

plangently ['plændʒəntli], *av.* 1. con risonanza 2. lamentosamente.

planimeter [plæˈnimitə*], *s.* (*geom.*) planimetro.

planimetry [plæˈnimitri], *s.* (*geom.*) planimetria.

to **planish** ['plæniʃ], *v.t.* 1. martellare 2. (*mec.*) spianare.

planisher ['plæniʃə*], *s.* 1. spianatore 2. arnese per spianare.

planisphere ['plænisfiə*], *s.* (*astr.*) planisfero.

plank [plæŋk], *s.* 1. tavola, tavolone; asse 2. *fig.* uno degli elementi alla base di un programma politico: *a — in the Tory platform*, un caposaldo del programma politico dei conservatori 3. (*mar.*) bordatura ‖ *to walk the —*, (*arc.*) camminare ad occhi bendati lungo un'asse sporgente in mare, fino a cadervi (di chi è prigioniero di pirati) ☆ *— bed*, tavolaccio (di prigione).

to **plank**, *v.t.* 1. coprire, pavimentare, rivestire di tavole 2. *to — down*, (*sl.*) buttare denaro sul tavolo con energia e senza indugio: *— down!*, fuori i soldi!.

planking ['plæŋkiŋ], *s.* 1. impalcatura; tavolato, assito 2. (*mar.*) fasciame ☆ *bottom —*, fasciame della carena; *deck —*, (*mar.*) tavolato del ponte.

plankton ['plæŋktən], *s.* (*biol.*) plancton.

planless ['plænlis], *ag.* senza piani, progetti.

planner ['plænə*], *s.* progettista ☆ *town —*, urbanista.

planning ['plæniŋ], *s.* 1. progettazione 2. pianificazione urbanistica ☆ *— chief*, capo progettazione, capo ufficio studi.

plant [plɑːnt], *s.* 1. pianta: *in —*, ancora in pianta, che sta crescendo; *a — bearing fruit*, una pianta fruttifera; *take this — out of its pot*, togli questa pianta dal vaso ‖ *to miss —*, non germogliare 2. apparato; macchinario; impianto; fabbrica, stabilimento: *chemical —*, stabilimento chimico 3. atteggiamento; posa 4. (*sl.*) merce rubata, refurtiva 5. (*sl.*) trappola, inganno 6. (*sl.*) agente della polizia segreta 7. (*amer.*) ostrica d'allevamento ☆ *— -life*, vita vegetale; *— -louse*, (*entom.*) afidio ‖ *electric power —*, centrale elettrica; *heating —*, impianto di riscaldamento; *pilot —*, impianto pilota.

to **plant**, *v.t.* 1. piantare, seminare: *to — a field with corn*, seminare un campo a grano; *to — oysters*, seminare ostriche (per vivaio) 2. fissare, conficcare, infiggere (nel terreno); fondare; colonizzare: *to — an idea in s.o.'s mind*, *fig.* ficcare un'idea nella mente di qlcu.; *to — a monastery in a heathen land*, fondare un monastero in terra pagana 3. *fig.* piantare; appostare (come spia): *to — oneself in front of s.o.*, piantarsi di fronte a qlcu. 4. rifornire (un vivaio, un bosco 5. (*sl. spor.*) affibbiare (un colpo): *a well-planted blow*, un colpo ben dato 6. (*sl.*) nascondere (refurtiva); architettare (un imbroglio) 7. (*rar.*) piantare in asso: *there I was, fairly planted*, così mi trovai piantato in asso.

Plantagenet ['plænˈtædʒinit], *ag. s.* (*st.*) Plantageneto.

plantain[1] ['plæntin], *s.* (*bot.*) piantaggine.

plantain[2], *s.* (*bot.*) varietà di banano e frutto che esso produce.

plantain[3], *s.* (*bot. rar.*) platano.

plantar ['plæntə*], *ag.* (*anat.*) plantare.

plantation [plænˈteiʃən], *s.* 1. piantagione (di alberi, cotone, ecc.) ‖ *to send s.o. to the plantations*, (*st.*) mandare qlcu. in una colonia penale 2. (*st.*) colonia; colonizzazione ☆ *— song*, canzone dei negri (delle piantagioni).

planter ['plɑːntə*], *s.* 1. piantatore; agricoltore 2. colonizzatore; pioniere 3. proprietario, conduttore di piantagione 4. macchina piantatrice ☆ *coffee- —*, piantatore di caffè.

plantigrade ['plæntigreid], *ag.s.* (*zool.*) plantigrado.

planting ['plɑːntiŋ], *s.* (*scoz.*) piantagione; atto del piantare.

plantless ['plɑːntlis], *ag.* senza piante.

plantlet ['plɑːntlit], *s.* pianticella.

plantlike ['plɑːntlaik], *ag.* simile a pianta.

plantocracy [plænˈtɔkrəsi], *s.* (*st.*) classe dominante di proprietari terrieri nelle Indie Occidentali.

planxty ['plæŋksti], *s.* (*mus.*) vivace canto irlandese con accompagnamento d'arpa.

to **plap** [plæp], *pass.p.p.* **plapped** [plæpt], *v.i.* cadere (col rumore di un oggetto che finisca in acqua).

plaque [plɑːk], *s.* 1. placca, piastra (di bronzo, marmo, ecc.) 2. placca (d'un ordine di cavalleria, ecc.); decorazione 3. (*patol.*) placca.

plaquette [plæˈket], *s.* piccola placca, piastrina.

plash[1] [plæʃ], *s.* pozzanghera.

plash[2], *s.* rumore di cosa che cade nell'acqua; rumore dell'acqua che cade sopra ql.co.

to **plash**[2], *v.t.i.* colpire la superficie di (acqua) frangendola; spruzzare; sollevare spruzzi; sguazzare; sciaguattare (di acqua).

to **plash**[3], *v.t.* tagliare, intrecciare (rami, ecc.) per formare siepi; accomodare, fare (siepi) intrecciando rami.

plashy[1] ['plæʃi], *ag.* fangoso; acquitrinoso.

plashy[2], *ag.* che spruzza.

plasm ['plæzəm], *s.* (*biol. fisiol.*) protoplasma.

plasma ['plæzmə], *s.* 1. (*biol. fisiol.*) plasma 2. (*min.*

plasma, varietà di quarzo di colore verde **3**. (*neol.*
fis.) plasma (gas ionizzato) ☆ *blood* —, plasma sanguigno.

plasmatic [plæz'mætik], **plasmic** ['plæzmik], *ag.*
(*biol. fisiol.*) plasmatico.

plasmodium [plæz'moudiəm], *pl.* **plasmodia** [plæz-
'moudiə], *s.* (*biol. zool.*) plasmodio.

plaster ['plɑ:stə*], *s.* **1**. cerotto; impiastro ‖ *a* —
for all sores, fig. un rimedio per tutti i mali **2**. gesso;
stucco; calcina; intonaco: *coat of* —, intonacatura
☆ — *cast*, calco, modello in gesso; — *kiln*, forno
per gesso; — *of Paris*, solfato di calcio; — *-quarry*,
cava di gesso; — *-work*, intonaco ‖ *sticking-* —, cerotto
adesivo.

to **plaster**, *v.t.* **1**. applicare un cerotto a **2**. (*med.*)
ingessare **3**. intonacare **4**. ricoprire (anche *fig.*); affiggere, incollare: *wall plastered with advertisements*, muro
ricoperto di avvisi; *to* — *s.o. with praises*, ricoprire
di lodi qlcu. **5**. trattare (il vino) con solfato di calcio
(per neutralizzarne l'acidità) **6**. *to* — **down**, impomatare:
hair plastered down over the forehead, capelli impomatati sulla fronte **7**. *to* — **up**, rappezzare in qualche
modo.

plasterer ['plɑ:stərə*], *s.* **1**. imbianchino **2**. modellatore di figure in gesso.

plastering ['plɑ:stəriŋ], *s.* **1**. (*med.*) ingessatura **2**. intonacatura ☆ — *trowel*, cazzuola per intonaco.

plastic ['plæstik], *ag.* **1**. plastico: — *clay*, argilla
plastica; — *material*, materia plastica **2**. *fig.* plasmabile, malleabile: *he has a* — *character*, ha un carattere malleabile ☆ — *arts*, arti plastiche; — *model*,
(*arch.*) plastico; — *surgery*, chirurgia plastica.

plastically ['plæstikəli], *av.* plasticamente.

plasticine ['plæstisi:n], *s.* (*scult.*) plastilina.

plasticity [plæs'tisiti], *s.* **1**. plasticità **2**. (*cine.*) rilievo (di immagine); effetto plastico.

plasticization [,plæstisai'zeiʃən], *s.* (*ind.*) plastifica-
zione, masticazione.

to **plasticize** ['plæstisaiz], *v.t.i.* rendere plastico, diventare plastico.

plasticizer ['plæstisaizə*], *s.* (*ind.*) plastificante,
masticatore.

plastics ['plæstiks], *s.pl.* (*ind.*) materie plastiche.

plastron ['plæstrən], *s.* **1**. (*scherma*) piastrone; piastra (di corazza) **2**. piastrone (di tartaruga) **3**. pettorina (d'abito femminile); sparato inamidato (di camicia da uomo).

plat[1] [plæt], *s.* piano, superficie piana; bassopiano.

plat[2], *s.* **1**. piccolo appezzamento (di terreno) **2**. (*amer.*) pianta, mappa.

to **plat**[2], *pass.p.p.* **platted** ['plætid], *v.t.* (*amer.*) fare
la pianta di.

plat[3], *s.* **1**. treccia, intreccio **2**. *pl.* (*mar.*) treccia (di
corde).

to **plat**[3], *v.t.* intrecciare (capelli, paglia, ecc.).

plat[4] [plɑ:], *s.* piatto: *a* — *of fruit*, un piatto di
frutta; — *fruit* —, piatto da frutta.

platan ['plætən], *s.* platano.

plate [pleit], *s.* **1**. foglio, lamina; lamiera; lastra;
piastra **2**. (*elett.*) placca, piastra **3**. (*ferr.*) piastrina,
disco **4**. targa **5**. (*rad.*) placca, armatura **6**. incisione,
impronta **7**. tavola fuori testo (di libro) **8**. (*edil.*)
piano di posa; trave orizzontale **9**. piatto (contenente
e contenuto); coperto: *dinner at three dollars a* —,
pranzo a tre dollari (a testa) **10**. piattino per elemosina **11**. vasellame (di metallo, generalmente oro, argento) **12**. coppa (data in premio alle corse) **13**. (*anat.*)
rotula **14**. (*zool.*) squama **15**. (*med.*) placca di resina
cui si applicano i denti artificiali; dentiera **16**. (*baseball*)
piatto ☆ — *-armour*, piastra di armatura; — *-glass*,
cristallo, vetro per specchi; — *-iron*, foglio di lamiera;
— *-layer*, operaio addetto alle rotaie; — *-leather*, pelle
per pulire l'argenteria; — *-paper*, carta da stampa;
— *-pewter*, lega di peltro per vasellami; — *-powder*,
polvere per pulire l'argenteria; — *-rack*, scolapiatti;

— *-roller*, laminatoio; — *-warmer*, scaldapiatti ‖
armour- —, corazza (di carro armato, ecc.); *bearing*
— (o *tie* —), (*ferr.*) piastrina di appoggio; *dessert-* —,
piatto da frutta; *dinner-* —, piatto; *fish* —, ganascia;
licence —, targa di registrazione (di autoveicoli, ecc.);
press —, piastra da pressa; *soup-* —, fondina.

to **plate**, *v.t.* **1**. rivestire di piastre metalliche; placcare (dorare, inargentare, ecc.); incamiciare (vasellame, ecc.); trattare galvanicamente **2**. (*tip.*) preparare
le matrici di ☆ *to lead-* —, piombare; *to platinum-* —,
platinare; *to zinc-* —, zincare.

plateau ['plætou], *pl.* **plateaux**, **plateaus** ['plætouz],
s. **1**. altipiano **2**. vassoio, piatto di portata decorato **3**. placca **4**. (*econ.*) punto fermo, stabilizzazione.

plated ['pleitid], *ag.* placcato ☆ *armour-* —, corazzato; *gold-* —, placcato oro.

plateful ['pleitful], *s.* piatto, la quantità contenuta
in un piatto: *a* — *of soup*, un piatto di minestra.

platen ['plætən], *s.* **1**. (*mec.*) piastra metallica; tavola **2**. rullo di macchina da scrivere **3**. (*tip.*) platina
☆ — *press*, macchina (da stampa) a platina.

plater ['pleitə*], *s.* **1**. placcatore **2**. mediocre cavallo da corsa.

platform ['plætfɔ:m], *s.* **1**. piattaforma; terrazza **2**. (*ferr.*) marciapiede, banchina **3**. impalcatura;
palco; tribuna **4**. (*amer.*) programma politico: *if this*
— *has been voted I would like to know by whose authority*, se questo programma politico è stato approvato
vorrei sapere con l'autorizzazione di chi ☆ — *car*,
(*ferr.*) pianale; — *roofing*, pensilina, tettoia per marciapiedi; — *truck*, carrello senza sponde ‖ *loading* —,
piattaforma di caricamento; *revolving* —, piattaforma
girevole; *swinging* —, piattaforma mobile.

plating ['pleitiŋ], *s.* **1**. (*ind. metal.*) placcatura **2**. (*ind.*)
preparazione delle lamiere **3**. (*aer.*) rivestimento; (*mar.*)
fasciame metallico **4**. corsa (di cavalli) a premi ☆ —
bath, bagno di placcaggio; bagno galvanico.

platinic [plə'tinik], *ag.* (*chim.*) platinico.

platiniferous [,plæti'nifərəs], *ag.* (*miner.*) platinifero.

platiniridium [,plætinai'ridiəm], *s.* (*min.*) platini-
ridio.

to **platinize** ['plætinaiz], *v.t.* platinare.

platinoid ['plætinɔid], *s.* (*metal.*) platinoide.

platinotype ['plætinoutaip], *s.* (*foto.*) platinotipia.

platinous ['plætinəs], *ag.* **1**. (*chim.*) platinico, di
platino **2**. (*miner.*) platinifero.

platinum ['plætinəm], *s.* (*chim.*) platino ☆ — *black*,
nero di platino; — *blonde*, (*fam.*) bionda platinata; —
metals, platinoidi; — *plating*, platinatura; — *sponge*,
spugna di platino.

platitude ['plætitju:d], *s.* banalità, luogo comune,
osservazione sciocca.

platitudinarian ['plæti,tju:di'nɛəriən], *s.* individuo
che si compiace di banalità.

to **platitudinize** [,plæti'tju:dinaiz], *v.i.* dire banalità.

platitudinous [,plæti'tju:dinəs], *ag.* banale, piatto,
comune.

Plato ['pleitou], *no.pr.m.* (*st.fil.*) Platone.

Platonic [plə'tonik], *ag.* platonico ‖ — *love*, amore
platonico.

Platonically [plə'tonikəli], *av.* platonicamente.

Platonism ['pleitənizəm], *s.* (*fil.*) platonismo.

Platonist ['pleitənist], *s.* (*fil.*) platonico.

to **Platonize** ['pleitənaiz], *v.t.i.* **1**. rendere platonico,
idealizzare **2**. seguire la filosofia platonica.

platoon [plə'tu:n], *s.* **1**. (*mil. arc.*) plotone, squadra **2**. cricca, banda.

platter ['plætə*], *s.* **1**. (*amer.*) piatto grande **2**. (*sl.*)
disco fonografico ☆ *cold cuts* —, piatto di carne fred-
da assortita.

platting ['plætiŋ], *s.* treccia, lavoro di intreccio.

platypus ['plætipəs], *s.* (*zool.*) ornitorinco.

plaudit ['plɔ:dit], *s. gener.* *pl.* applauso, acclamazione.

plausibility [,plɔ:zə'biliti], *s.* plausibilità.

plausible ['plɔ:zəbl], *ag.* plausibile, credibile.
plausibleness ['plɔ:zəblnis], *s.* plausibilità.
plausibly ['plɔ:zəbli], *av.* plausibilmente.
plausive ['plɔ:siv], *ag.* plaudente.
Plautus ['plɔ:təs], *no.pr.m.* (*st. lett.*) Plauto.

play [plei], *s.* **1.** giuoco; divertimento, trastullo, spasso: — *of light*, scintillio, giuoco di luce: — *on words*, giuoco di parole; *in* —, per giuoco, per scherzo; *he made* — *with his gloves*, giocherellava con i guanti; *it is child's* —, è facile, è un giuoco da bambini **2.** giuoco d'azzardo: *the* — *was high*, si giocava forte **3.** (*teat.*) spettacolo, rappresentazione; dramma, produzione teatrale: *Oscar Wilde's plays*, il teatro di O. Wilde; *to give a* —, dare uno spettacolo **4.** (*mus.*) esecuzione **5.** corso, sfogo: *he gave full* — *to his fancy*, diede libero sfogo alla sua fantasia **6.** condotta, azione: *fair* —, lealtà; *foul* —, condotta criminosa **7.** *fig.* attività, azione: *to be in full* —, essere in azione: *to come into* —, entrare in azione ☆ — *-actor*, (*spreg.*) attore di prosa; — *-bill*, cartellone, affisso teatrale; — *-day*, vacanza scolastica; giorno di recita; — *-debt*, debito d'onore; — *-goer*, frequentatore di teatro; — *-mate*, compagno di giuochi; — *-pen*, recinto per bambini; — *-time*, ricreazione; — *-world*, mondo immaginario dei bambini; — *-writer*, drammaturgo.

to play, *v.t.i.* **1.** giocare; divertirsi: *to* — (*at*) *billiards*, *cards*, giocare al biliardo, a carte; *to* — (*at*) *robbers*, *soldiers*, giocare ai banditi, ai soldati ‖ *to* — *fast and loose*, comportarsi da irresponsabile ‖ *to* — *into s.o.'s hands*, fare il giuoco di qlcu. ‖ *to* — *one's cards well*, *fig.* giocare bene le proprie carte ‖ *to* — *a trick on s.o.*, giocare un brutto tiro a qlcu.; beffarsi di qlcu. ‖ *to* — (*up*)*on s.o.'s credulity*, approfittare della credulità di qlcu. ‖ *to* — (*up*)*on words*, giocare sulle parole, equivocare ‖ *to* — *with fire*, scherzare col fuoco; *to* — *with s.o.*, *fig.* divertirsi con qlcu., trattare qlcu. con leggerezza **2.** giocare d'azzardo **3.** (*teat.*) interpretare un ruolo; recitare: *she plays well*, recita bene; *to* — *in a film*, interpretare un film; *to* — *a part*, interpretare un ruolo **4.** agire, comportarsi: *to* — *foul*, agire in modo disonesto; *to* — *the game*, agire correttamente, lealmente; *to* — *havoc*, cagionare rovina; *to* — *the man*, comportarsi da uomo ‖ *to* — *the deuce* (o *the devil*), fare il diavolo a quattro ‖ *to* — *it low* (*down*) *on*, (*sl.*) agire in modo sleale verso ‖ *to* — *s.o. fair*, agire lealmente verso qlcu.; *to* — *s.o. false*, tradire qlcu. **5.** suonare (uno strumento musicale): *to* — (*on*) *the flute*, *the piano*, suonare il flauto, il piano ‖ *to* — *first fiddle*, *fig.* avere la parte più importante, dominare; *to* — *second fiddle to s.o.*, venire dopo qlcu., avere una parte secondaria **6.** dirigere, indirizzare: *to* — *the guns on sthg.*, dirigere il fuoco su ql.co.; *to* — *a searchlight upon an object*, dirigere un riflettore su un oggetto; *to* — *water on the fire*, dirigere getti d'acqua sull'incendio **7.** muoversi velocemente (di acqua, luce, ecc.); ondeggiare, fluttuare: *her hair played on her shoulders*, i capelli le ondeggiavano sulle spalle; *the sun plays on the water*, il sole giuoca sull'acqua **8.** (*mec.*) mettere in moto; funzionare: *the machine is already playing*, la macchina è già in funzione **9.** (*pesca*) *to* — *a fish*, stancare un pesce (dandogli corda) **10.** *to* — *away*, perdere al giuoco **11.** *to* — *down*, dare poca importanza a, minimizzare ‖ *to* — *down to the crowd*, adeguarsi al gusto del grosso pubblico **12.** *to* — *off* (*s.o. against s.o.*), opporre (una persona ad un'altra); *to* — *sthg. off on sthg. else*, far passare una cosa per un'altra; (*spor.*) rigiocare un incontro nullo **13.** *to* — *out*, (*teat.*) interpretare una parte fino in fondo ‖ *to be played out*, *fig.* essere finito, esaurito **14.** *to* — *up*, spendere tutte le proprie energie, fare del proprio meglio.

playable ['pleiəbl], *ag.* **1.** recitabile **2.** messo a punto (di strumento).
playbook ['pleibuk], *s.* raccolta di opere teatrali.
playboy ['pleiboi], *s.* **1.** giovane attore **2.** (*irl.*) buffone, furfantello **3.** (*amer. fam.*) giovane gaudente.

player ['pleiə*], *s.c.* **1.** giocatore, giocatrice **2.** suonatore, suonatrice **3.** attore, attrice ‖ *s.* giocatore di professione (specialmente di cricket) ☆ — *-piano*, pianola ‖ *strolling* —, attore girovago.
playfellow ['plei,felou], *s.c.* compagno, compagna di giuoco.
playful ['pleiful], *ag.* giocoso, scherzoso, gaio.
playfully ['pleifuli], *av.* scherzosamente, gaiamente.
playfulness ['pleifulnis], *s.* allegria, gaiezza.
playgame ['pleigeim], *s.* inezia, bazzecola: *it's a* — *in comparison*, al confronto è una bazzecola.
playground ['plei-graund], *s.* **1.** terreno annesso a una scuola usato per la ricreazione **2.** luogo di svago, di villeggiatura: *Miami Beach is a famous* —, Miami Beach è un famoso luogo di villeggiatura.
playhouse ['pleihaus], *s.* **1.** teatro **2.** (*amer.*) luogo di ricreazione per bambini **3.** (*amer.*) casa delle bambole.
playing ['pleiiɲ], *s.* **1.** giuoco; il giocare; il modo di giocare **2.** (*teat.*) rappresentazione **3.** (*teat.*) interpretazione **4.** (*mus.*) esecuzione ☆ — *-cards*, carte da giuoco; — *-field*, campo da giuoco.
playlet ['pleilit], *s.* commediola.
playsome ['pleisom], *ag.* giocoso, scherzoso.
plaything ['plei-θiɲ], *s.* giocattolo, balocco (anche *fig.*).
playwright ['pleirait], *s.* commediografo; drammaturgo.
plea [pli:], *s.* **1.** scusa, giustificazione: *on the* — *of*, con la scusa di **2.** (*dir.*) difesa, argomento di difesa; eccezione: *dilatory* —, eccezione dilatoria; *incidental* —, eccezione incidentale.
to pleach [pli:tʃ], *v.t.* (*poet.*) intrecciare.
to plead [pli:d], *v.t.i.* **1.** (*dir.*) patrocinare, perorare, difendere (una causa); difendersi, far valere le proprie ragioni in giudizio: *to* — *the cause of the unemployed*, perorare la causa dei disoccupati; *to* — *for mercy*, implorare pietà; *to* — *for s.o.*, perorare a favore di qlcu.; *to* — *with s.o. for sthg.*, *s.o.*, intercedere presso qlcu. per, a favore di ql.co., qlcu. **2.** (*dir.*) confessarsi, protestarsi: *to* — *guilty*, confessarsi reo, ammettere la propria colpa; *to* — *not guilty*, dichiararsi innocente, protestare la propria innocenza **3.** addurre a pretesto: *he pleaded ignorance*, addusse a pretesto l'ignoranza.
pleadable ['pli:dəbl], *ag.* allegabile, adducibile.
pleader ['pli:də*], *s.* patrocinatore, difensore, avvocato difensore ☆ *special* —, consulente legale.
pleading ['pli:diɲ], *ag.* supplichevole, implorante ‖ *s.* (*dir.*) **1.** difesa, patrocinio (di causa) **2.** arringa, discussione; conclusionale **3.** *pl.* dichiarazioni (delle due parti in un processo).
pleadingly ['pli:diɲli], *av.* in tono supplichevole, implorante.
pleasance ['plezəns], *s.* (*arc.*) **1.** piacevolezza, gaiezza **2.** giardino (di fastosa dimora).
pleasant ['pleznt], *ag.* **1.** piacevole, amabile, gradevole, simpatico **2.** gaio, allegro **3.** (*arc.*) ameno, faceto.
pleasantly ['plezntli], *av.* **1.** piacevolmente **2.** gaiamente; affabilmente.
pleasantness ['plezntnis], *s.* **1.** piacevolezza, amenità **2.** allegria, giocondità; affabilità.
pleasantry ['plezntri], *s.* facezia, scherzo, arguzia, frizzo.
to please [pli:z], *v.t.i.* **1.** piacere a, far piacere a; soddisfare: *it is difficult to* — *everybody*, è difficile soddisfare tutti; *to* — *oneself*, compiacersi, fare piacere a se stesso, (*fam.*) fare il proprio comodo ‖ — *God*, a Dio piacendo ‖ — *the pigs*, (*sl.*) se il destino lo permette **2.** desiderare; volere, aver voglia: *it pleased him to do so*, volle fare così ‖ (*if you*) —, per favore; se permette (anche *iron.*).
pleased [pli:zd], *ag.* lieto, soddisfatto: *be* — *to accept these flowers*, La prego di accettare questi fiori; *very* — *to meet you*, molto lieto di fare la Sua conoscenza; *to be* — *to do sthg.*, far ql.co. volentieri, con gran piacere; *to be* — *with s.o.*, essere soddisfatto di qlcu.;

to be anything but —, essere tutt'altro che soddisfatto ‖ *as — as Punch*, contento come una pasqua.

pleasing ['pli:ziŋ], *ag.* piacevole; amabile; ridente; ameno; leggiadro.

pleasingly ['pli:ziŋli], *av.* piacevolmente.

pleasurable ['pleʒərəbl], *ag.* piacevole; divertente.

pleasurableness ['pleʒərəblnis], *s.* piacevolezza.

pleasurably ['pleʒərəbli], *av.* piacevolmente.

pleasure ['pleʒə*], *s.* **1.** piacere; compiacimento: *I have had the — of knowing him for many years,* ho il piacere di conoscerlo da molti anni; *I have much — in informing you that,* ho il piacere di informarLa che; *it is a — to have you,* è un piacere averti con noi; *to find* (o *to take*) *— in doing sthg.,* fare ql.co. volentieri **2.** diletto, divertimento: *to travel for —,* viaggiare per diporto **3.** desiderio, volontà; *at —,* a volontà, a piacere; *it is our — that...,* desideriamo graziosamente che... **4.** voluttà, piacere sensuale ‖ *a man of —,* un dissoluto ☆ *— -boat,* battello da diporto; *— -ground,* giardino, parco; *— -house,* casino; *— -resort,* luogo di divertimento.

to pleasure, *v.t.i.* compiacere, far piacere a, piacere a; prendere piacere, dilettarsi: *John pleasured in fishing,* John si dilettava di pesca.

pleat [pli:t], *s.* piega.

to pleat, *v.t.* **1.** pieghettare **2.** (*arc.*) intrecciare (ghirlande, capelli).

pleb [pleb], *s.* (*sl.*) plebeo.

plebe [pli:b], *s.* (*amer. fam.*) allievo di primo corso (nell'Accademia militare di West Point e nell'Accademia navale di Annapolis).

plebeian [pli'bi(:)ən], *ag. s.* plebeo.

to plebeianize [pli'bi(:)ənaiz], *v.t.* rendere plebeo.

plebiscitary [pli'bisitəri], *ag.* plebiscitario.

plebiscite ['plebisit], *s.* plebiscito.

plebs [plebz], *pl.* **plebes** ['pli:bi:z], *s.* (*st. romana*) (la) plebe.

plectrum ['plektrəm], *pl.* **plectra** ['plektrə], **plectrums** ['plektrəmz], *s.* (*mus.*) plettro.

pledge [pledʒ], *s.* **1.** pegno, garanzia: *to put sthg. in —,* impegnare ql.co.; *to take sthg. as a —,* prendere ql.co. in pegno **2.** promessa, impegno, voto: *under — of secrecy,* con impegno di segretezza ‖ *to take the —,* promettere di astenersi dall'alcool **3.** brindisi.

to pledge, *v.t.* **1.** impegnare, dare in pegno; garantire: *he pledged his watch,* impegnò l'orologio; *to — s.o. to do sthg.,* impegnare qlcu. a fare ql.co. **2.** brindare alla salute di.

pledgee [ple'dʒi:], *s.c.* chi riceve in pegno.

pledgeless ['pledʒlis], *ag.* senza pegno.

pledger ['pledʒə*]. *s.c.* chi dà in pegno.

pledget ['pledʒit], *s.* tampone d'ovatta.

Pleiad ['plaiəd], *pl.* **Pleiades** ['plaiədi:z], *no.pr.f.* (*mit.*) Pleiade ‖ *no.pr.pl.* (*astr.*) Pleiadi ‖ *the Pleiad,* (*lett. francese*) la «Plèiade».

pleistocene ['plaistousi:n], *s.* (*geol.*) pleistocene.

plenarily ['pli:nərili], *av.* plenariamente, interamente, pienamente.

plenariness ['pli:nərinis], *s.* plenarietà, pienezza.

plenary ['pli:nəri], *ag.* plenario, completo, intero ☆ *— indulgence,* indulgenza plenaria; *— meeting,* seduta plenaria.

plenipotentiary [,plenipə'tenʃəri], *ag. s.* plenipoenziario.

to plenish ['pleniʃ], *v.t.* **1.** (*arc.*) riempire **2.** (*scoz.*) mmobiliare, arredare (una stanza).

plenitude ['plenitju:d], *s.* pienezza, completezza, bbondanza.

plenteous ['plentjəs], *ag.* (*poet.*) abbondante, cooioso.

plenteously ['plentjəsli], *av.* (*poet.*) abbondantente, copiosamente.

plenteousness ['plentjəsnis], *s.* (*poet.*) abbondanza, opiosità.

plentiful ['plentiful], *ag.* abbondante, copioso.

plentifully ['plentifuli], *av.* abbondantemente, copiosamente.

plentifulness ['plentifulnis], *s.* abbondanza, copia.

plenty ['plenti], *ag.* (*amer. gener. predicativo*) abbondante, copioso: *harvest was — last year,* l'anno scorso il raccolto fu abbondante ‖ *s.* abbondanza: *there are — of things you don't know,* ci sono moltissime cose che non sai; *there is — of time,* c'è ancora moltissimo tempo ‖ *horn of —,* cornucopia ‖ *land of —,* paese di cuccagna.

plenty, *av.* (*fam.*) abbondantemente; copiosamente: *he enjoyed himself —,* si divertì un mondo ‖ *it's — large enough,* è proprio abbastanza grande.

plenum ['pli:nəm], *s.* **1.** (*fis.*) pieno **2.** assemblea plenaria ☆ *— -system,* (*mec.*) sistema a sovrapposizione.

pleomorphism [,pli:ou'mo:fizəm], *s.* (*biol.*) pleomorfismo, polimorfismo.

pleonasm ['pli(:)ənæzəm], *s.* (*gram.*) pleonasmo.

pleonastic [pliə'næstik], *ag.* (*gram.*) pleonastico.

pleonastically [pliə'næstikəli], *av.* (*gram.*) pleonasticamente.

plesiosaurus ['pli:siə'so:rəs], *s.* (*paleont.*) plesiosauro.

plethora ['pleθərə], *s.* **1.** pletora, sovrabbondanza, eccesso **2.** (*med.*) pletora.

plethoric [ple'θorik], *ag.* **1.** pletorico, sovrabbondante, eccessivo **2.** (*med.*) pletorico, congesto.

plethorically [ple'θorikəli], *av.* in sovrabbondanza.

pleura ['pluərə], *pl.* **pleurae** ['pluəri:], *s.* (*anat.*) pleura.

pleural ['pluərəl], *ag.* (*anat.*) pleurico.

pleurisy ['pluərisi], *s.* (*patol.*) pleurite.

pleuritic [pluə'ritik], *ag.* (*patol.*) pleuritico.

pleuropneumonia ['pluərounju(:)'mounjə], *s.* (*patol.*) pleuropolmonite.

pleurotomy [pluə'rotəmi], *s.* (*chir.*) pleurotomia.

pleximeter [plek'simitə*], *s.* (*med.*) plessimetro.

plexus ['pleksəs], *s.* (*anat.*) plesso ☆ *solar —,* plesso solare.

pliability [,plaiə'biliti], *s.* **1.** pieghevolezza, flessibilità **2.** *fig.* docilità, arrendevolezza, sottomissione.

pliable ['plaiəbl], *ag.* **1.** pieghevole, flessibile **2.** *fig.* docile, arrendevole, conciliante.

pliableness ['plaiəblnis], *V.* **pliability.**

pliably ['plaiəbli], *av.* **1.** pieghevolmente, flessibilmente **2.** *fig.* arrendevolmente, docilmente.

pliancy ['plaiənsi], *s.* **1.** pieghevolezza, flessibilità **2.** *fig.* adattabilità, arrendevolezza.

pliant ['plaiənt], *ag.* **1.** pieghevole, flessibile **2.** *fig.* adattabile; compiacente; influenzabile.

pliantly ['plaiəntli], *av.* **1.** pieghevolmente, flessibilmente **2.** *fig.* docilmente; compiacentemente.

pliantness ['plaiəntnis], *V.* **pliancy.**

plica ['plaikə], *pl.* **plicae** ['plaisi:], *s.* (*anat.*) plica.

plicate ['plaikit], **plicated** ['plaikeitid], *ag.* (*bot. zool. geol.*) pieghettato; piegato.

plication [plai'keiʃən], **plicature** ['plikətʃə*], *s.* **1.** piegatura; piega **2.** (*geol.*) sistema di pieghe.

pliers ['plaiəz], *s.pl.* pinze ☆ *cutting —,* pinze universali; *flat* (*nose*) *—,* pinze piane.

plight[1] [plait], *s.* stato, condizione, situazione (specialmente sociale e finanziaria): *to be in an evil —,* essere in una brutta situazione.

plight[2], *s.* impegno; promessa.

to plight[2], *v.t.* impegnare; promettere: *to — one's faith,* impegnare la propria parola.

plighted ['plaitid], *ag.* impegnato, promesso ☆ *— faith,* fede giurata; *— lovers,* fidanzati.

Plimsoll ['plimsəl], (*nei composti*): *— line* (o *— mark*), (*mar.*) linea Plimsoll, di carico.

plimsolls ['plimsəlz], *s.pl.* scarpe di tela con suola di gomma.

plinth [plinθ], *s.* (*arch.*) plinto, zoccolo; basamento.

Pliny ['plini], *no.pr.m.* (*st. lett.*) Plinio: *— the Elder,* Plinio il Vecchio; *— the Younger,* Plinio il Giovane.

pliocene ['plaiəsi:n], *ag.* (*geol.*) pliocenico ‖ *s.* (*geol.*) pliocene.

plod [plɔd], *s.* **1.** il camminare faticoso **2.** passo pesante **3.** lavoro faticoso.

to plod, *pass.p.p.* **plodded** ['plɔdid], *v.t.i.* **1.** camminare lentamente e faticosamente: *to — one's way,* percorrere faticosamente il proprio cammino **2.** *to — along,* avanzare a fatica; (*fam.*) tirare avanti: *to — along through life,* tirare avanti faticosamente nella vita **3.** *tc — away,* lavorare assiduamente e pazientemente: *to — away at one's lessons,* sgobbare sulle proprie lezioni **4.** *to — on,* continuare coraggiosamente il proprio cammino; *fig.* perseverare; *to — on in the rain,* proseguire sotto la pioggia.

plodder ['plɔdə*], *s.* **1.** chi cammina lentamente e faticosamente **2.** sgobbone.

ploddingly ['plɔdiŋli], *av.* a fatica.

plop [plɔp], *s.* (*onomatopeico*) tonfo.

to plop, *pass.p.p.* **plopped** [plɔpt], *v.t.i.* gettare nell'acqua, cadere con un tonfo.

plop, *av.* con un tonfo sordo.

plosion ['plouʒən], *s.* (*fonetica*) esplosione.

plosive ['plousiv], *ag. s.* (*fonetica*) esplosiva.

plot [plɔt], *s.* **1.** appezzamento **2.** (*lett.*) trama, intreccio: *unravelling of the —,* scioglimento dell'intreccio; *the — thickens,* l'intreccio si complica **3.** trama, complotto, congiura, cospirazione: *to hatch* (o *to lay*) *a —,* ordire una congiura **4.** (*amer.*) carta, diagramma, mappa ☆ *building —,* terreno da costruzione.

to plot, *pass.p.p.* **plotted** ['plɔtid], *v.t.i.* **1.** fare la pianta di; fare il rilievo di (un terreno, ecc.) **2.** tracciare: *to — a diagram,* tracciare un diagramma; *to — the graph of an equation,* tracciare il grafico di un'equazione **3.** tramare, complottare, cospirare, macchinare: *they plotted his ruin,* concertarono la sua rovina; *what mischief are you plotting between you?,* cosa state complottando tra di voi?.

Plotinus [plə'tainəs], *no.pr.m.* (*st. fil.*) Plotino.

plotless ['plɔtlis], *ag.* senza trama, senza intreccio (di romanzo, ecc.).

plottage ['plɔtidʒ], *s.* (*amer.*) area di terreno.

plotter ['plɔtə*], *s.c.* cospiratore, cospiratrice; congiuratore, congiuratrice; chi ordisce intrighi.

plotting ['plɔtiŋ], *s.* **1.** il progettare **2.** tracciato, grafico **3.** complotto, trama ☆ — *paper,* carta millimetrata.

plough[1] [plau], *s.* **1.** aratro ‖ *Plough,* (*astr.*) Orsa Maggiore ‖ *to put* (o *to lay* o *to set*) *one's hand to the —, fig.* por mano all'opera **2.** terreno arato **3.** (*legatoria*) blocco per la rifilatura ☆ — *-iron,* coltro; — *-Monday,* lunedì dopo l'Epifania; — *-staff,* nettatoio (di aratro); — *-tree,* manico (di aratro) ‖ *breaking- —,* (*agr.*) dissodatrice; *disk —,* aratro a dischi; *snow- —,* spartineve; *subsoil —,* aratro talpa.

to plough[1], *v.t.i.* **1.** arare; solcare; fendere; attraversare; usare un aratro: *the ship was slowly ploughing the waves,* la nave solcava lentamente le onde ‖ *to — one's way,* procedere faticosamente ‖ *to — the sands,* (*fam.*) fare un lavoro inutile **2.** rifilare (libri, nella rilegatura) **3.** *to — through* (*sthg.*), aprirsi faticosamente un varco attraverso: *he is ploughing through a very difficult problem,* cerca affannosamente una risposta a un problema molto difficile.

plough[2], *s.* (*sl.*) bocciatura di un candidato all'esame.

to plough[2], *v.t.* (*sl.*) bocciare un candidato all'esame.

ploughable ['plau-əbl], *ag.* arabile.

ploughboy ['plaubɔi], *s.* **1.** ragazzo che aiuta l'aratore **2.** contadinello.

plougher ['plau-ə*], *s.* aratore; bifolco.

ploughing ['plauiŋ], *s.* aratura ☆ — *-land,* terreno arabile.

ploughland ['plaulænd], *s.* **1.** (*st. medioevale*) unità di misura di terreno corrispondente all'area che otto buoi possono arare in un anno **2.** terreno arabile.

ploughman, *pl.* **ploughmen** ['plaumən], *s.* **1.** aratore **2.** contadino; agricoltore.

ploughshare ['plau-ʃɛə*], *s.* **1.** vomere; coltro **2.** (*anat.*) vomere.

plover ['plʌvə*], *s.* (*ornit.*) **1.** piviere; pivieressa **2.** (*pop.*) vanello.

plow, (*amer.*) per **plough.**

to plow, (*amer.*) per **to plough.**

ploy [plɔi], *s.* (*scoz.*) **1.** spedizione, impresa **2.** occupazione, impiego **3.** passatempo **4.** scappatella.

to ploy, *v.i.* (*mil.*) **1.** ridurre il fronto **2.** incolonnarsi.

pluck [plʌk], *s.* **1.** strappo, lo strappare; lo spennare; il tirare: *he gave my sleeve a —,* mi tirò la manica **2.** (*sl.*) bocciatura (a un esame) **3.** frattaglie **4.** *fig.* coraggio, fegato: *he lacks —,* manca di coraggio, manca di fegato.

to pluck, *v.t.i.* **1.** strappare (capelli, peli); spennare: *to — at one's hair,* strapparsi i capelli; *to — the eyebrows,* depilare le sopracciglia; *to — a goose,* spennare un'oca ‖ *to — a pigeon, fig.* spennare un pollo **2.** tirare: *to — (at) s.o.'s sleeve* (o *to — s.o. by the sleeve*), tirare qlcu. per la manica **3.** (*mus.*) pizzicare (strumento a corde) **4.** cogliere: *to — flowers,* cogliere fiori **5.** (*sl.*) bocciare (a un esame) **6.** *to — up,* sradicare: *to — up a tree,* sradicare un albero ‖ *to — up one's heart* (o *spirits* o *courage*), *fig.* farsi coraggio, prendere il coraggio a due mani.

plucker ['plʌkə*], *s.c.* **1.** chi strappa **2.** raccoglitore, raccoglitrice ‖ *s.* (*ind. tessile*) sfeltratrice, macchina per sfeltrare.

pluckily ['plʌkili], *av.* coraggiosamente.

pluckiness ['plʌkinis], *s.* coraggio, ardimento.

plucky ['plʌki], *ag.* **1.** coraggioso **2.** (*foto.*) chiaro, ben definito.

plug [plʌg], *s.* **1.** tappo (di lavandino, ecc.) **2.** (*med.*) tampone; otturazione (dentaria) **3.** (*elett. tel.*) spina **4.** tassello **5.** tavoletta di tabacco compresso; pezzo di tabacco da masticare **6.** (*sl.*) vecchio ronzino; omuncolo; oggetto di nessun valore **7.** (*sl.*) pugno, ceffone **8.** (*fam.*) pubblicità insistente; pubblicità radiofonica ☆ — *basin,* lavandino; — *-cock,* rubinetto a maschio; — *-cord,* (*elett.*) cordone a spina; — *-fuse,* (*elett.*) fusibile a tappo; — *-gauge,* (*mec.*) calibro a tampone; — *-hat,* (*sl. amer.*) cappello a cilindro; — *-tap,* (*mec.*) maschio finitore; — *-ugly,* (*sl. amer.*) attaccabrighe, teppista; — *-valve,* valvola a maschio ‖ *fire- —,* idrante antincendi; *spark* (o *sparking*) *—,* (*mec.*) candela; *water- —,* presa d'acqua; idrante.

to plug, *pass.p.p.* **plugged** [plʌgd], *v.t.i.* **1.** tappare, turare; tamponare: *to — (up) an opening,* tappare, tamponare un'apertura **2.** (*sl.*) sparare: *to — a cop,* sparare contro un poliziotto **3.** (*sl.*) colpire con pugni: *to — s.o.* (o *s.o.'s plans*), mettere i bastoni tra le ruote a qlcu. **4.** (*fam.*) cercare di rendere popolare (una canzone, teoria, ecc.) ripetendola senza sosta **5.** — *in,* inserire corrente (con una spina): — *the iron in,* attacca il ferro da stiro; *power lines plugged into a building,* linee elettriche installate in un edificio; *they — their loudspeakers into the circuit,* innestano i loro altoparlanti nel circuito con una spina **6.** *to — away at work,* (*fam.*) sgobbare.

plugger ['plʌgə*], *s.* **1.** installatore **2.** (*odontoiatria*) otturatore **3.** (*fam.*) sgobbone (specialmente studente) **4.** sostenitore entusiasta; propagandista.

plum [plʌm], *s.* **1.** (*bot.*) prugna; susina **2.** — (*-tree*) prugno, susino **3.** uva secca, uva passa **4.** *fig.* il meglio di ql.co.: *you've got the —,* ti è toccato il pezzo migliore **5.** (*sl.*) centomila sterline ☆ — *-cake,* plum-cake, panfrutto; — *-duff,* budino con uva passa; — *-pudding,* budino natalizio tradizionale in Inghilterra; — *-pudding stone,* (*geol.*) conglomerato, puddinga.

plumage ['plu:midʒ], *s.* piume, penne.

plumb [plʌm], *ag.* **1.** a piombo, verticale, perpendicolare **2.** *fig.* completo, assoluto: *a — nonsense,* una vera sciocchezza ‖ *s.* **1.** filo a piombo; piombino: *out of —,* non verticale **2.** (*mar.*) scandaglio ☆ — *-line,* filo a piombo; — *-rule,* (*edil.*) archipendolo.

to plumb, *v.t.i.* **1.** misurare la profondità di; scandagliare (anche *fig.*); verificare la verticalità di **2.** rendere verticale **3.** lavorare col piombo (*spec.* di idraulico) **4.** impiombare, sigillare con piombini.

plumb, *av.* **1.** a piombo, verticalmente, perpendicolarmente: *it hangs —*, cade a piombo **2.** *fig.* esattamente: *— in face of*, esattamente di faccia a **3.** (*sl. amer.*) completamente, assolutamente: *he was — crazy*, era proprio pazzo.

plumbaginous [plʌmˈbædʒinəs], *ag.* di piombaggine.

plumbago [plʌmˈbeigou], *s.* (*min.*) piombaggine, grafite.

plumbeous [ˈplʌmbjəs], *ag.* plumbeo.

plumber [ˈplʌmə*], *s.* idraulico.

plumbery [ˈplʌməri], *s.* negozio, lavoro di idraulico.

plumbic [ˈplʌmbik], *ag.* (*chim.*) piombico.

plumbiferous [plʌmˈbifərəs], *ag.* (*miner.*) piombifero.

plumbing [ˈplʌmiŋ], *s.* **1.** piombatura **2.** lavori idraulici.

plumbism [ˈplʌmbizəm], *s.* (*patol.*) saturnismo.

plumbous [ˈplʌmbəs], *ag.* (*chim.*) piombico.

plumbum [ˈplʌmbəm], *s.* (*min.*) piombo.

plume [plu:m], *s.* **1.** piuma, penna; piumaggio ‖ *borrowed plumes*, *fig.* penne di pavone (il vantarsi di cose compiute da altri) **2.** (*mil.*) pennacchio **3.** palma, trofeo ☆ *-plucked*, spennacchiato; umile.

to **plume,** *v.t.* **1.** guarnire di penne **2.** ripulirsi le penne (di uccelli) **3.** vantarsi: *to — oneself on sthg.*, vantarsi di ql.co.

plumed [plu:md], *ag.* piumato.

plumeless [ˈplu:mlis], *ag.* senza penne.

plumelet [ˈplu:mlit], *s.* piccola piuma.

plumelike [ˈplu:mlaik], *ag.* simile a, come una piuma.

plummet [ˈplʌmit], *s.* **1.** piombino, piombo; filo a piombo; scandaglio **2.** *fig.* peso opprimente.

to **plummet,** *pass. p.p.* **plummetted** [ˈplʌmitid], *v.i.* cadere, gettarsi a capofitto.

plummy [ˈplʌmi], *ag.* (*fam.*) buono; desiderabile.

plumose [pluˈmous], *ag.* piumoso.

plumosity [pluˈmɔsiti], *s.* piumosità.

plump[1] [plʌmp], *ag.* paffuto, pienotto, grassottello: *— cheeks*, guance paffute; *a — partridge*, una pernice grassa.

to **plump**[1], *v.t.i.* ingrassare; fare ingrassare: *she has plumped up*, è ingrassata.

plump[2], *ag.* diretto, netto; brusco; chiaro: *a — refusal*, un netto rifiuto ‖ *s.* **1.** (*fam.*) tonfo, caduta pesante **2.** (*scoz.*) scroscio improvviso di pioggia.

to **plump**[2], *v.t.i.* **1.** cadere, far cadere pesantemente, improvvisamente: *she plumped down panting in a chair*, ansando, ella si lasciò cadere su una sedia **2.** dare il voto ad un solo candidato: *they all plumped for him*, tutti votarono solo per lui.

plump[2], *av.* **1.** improvvisamente: *they came — on the enemy*, assalirono improvvisamente il nemico **2.** direttamente; bruscamente; chiaramente.

plumper[1] [ˈplʌmpə*], *s.* gonfiatura; pallottola tenuta in bocca per gonfiare le guance.

plumper[2], *s.* **1.** caduta improvvisa, pesante **2.** voto dato ad un solo candidato; chi vota per un solo candidato **3.** (*sl.*) bugia sfacciata.

plumply [ˈplʌmpli], *av.* largamente, senza riserve.

plumpness [ˈplʌmpnis], *s.* rotondità, paffutezza.

plumpy [ˈplʌmpi], *ag.* (*rar.*) paffuto, grassottello.

plumule [ˈplu:mju:l], *s.* **1.** (*bot.*) piumetta **2.** piuma piccola e soffice.

plumy [ˈplu:mi], *ag.* piumoso.

plunder [ˈplʌndə*], *s.* **1.** saccheggio **2.** bottino; (*sl.*) profitto, guadagno.

to **plunder,** *v.t.* saccheggiare, depredare; rapinare.

plunderage [ˈplʌndəridʒ], *s.* **1.** saccheggio; (*mar.*) appropriazione indebita di merce a bordo **2.** bottino.

plunderer [ˈplʌndərə*], *s.* saccheggiatore, predone; rapinatore.

plunge [plʌndʒ], *s.* **1.** tuffo; immersione **2.** *fig.* passo, decisione difficile ‖ *to take the —*, *fig.* saltare il fosso ☆ *— bath*, piscina, vasca da bagno.

to **plunge,** *v.t.i.* **1.** tuffare, tuffarsi; immergere, immergersi (anche *fig.*): *the city plunged into darkness*, la città piombò nell'oscurità; *I plunged my hands into the cold water*, immersi le mani nell'acqua fredda; *to — the country into war, misery*, trascinare il paese nella guerra, nella miseria; *to — into business*, tuffarsi negli affari; *to — a sword*, immergere una spada; *to — pots*, interrare vasi di fiori **2.** gettarsi, precipitarsi (anche *fig.*): *to — downstairs*, precipitarsi giù dalle scale **3.** slanciarsi in avanti (di cavallo) **4.** beccheggiare (di nave) **5.** (*sl.*) giocare d'azzardo; indebitarsi.

plunger [ˈplʌndʒə*], *s.c.* tuffatore, tuffatrice ‖ *s.* **1.** (*mec.*) stantuffo, pistone **2.** (*sl.*) soldato di cavalleria **3.** (*sl.*) giocatore d'azzardo; speculatore.

plunging [ˈplʌndʒiŋ], *s.* tuffo; immersione (anche *fig.*) ☆ *— fire*, (*mil.*) fuoco dall'alto.

plunk [plʌŋk], *s.* **1.** suono metallico; pizzicato (di strumento a corde) **2.** (*fam.*) colpo forte **3.** (*sl.*) dollaro.

to **plunk,** *v.t.i.* **1.** gettare, scagliare violentemente **2.** (*far*) cadere pesantemente.

plunk, *av.* **1.** con suono metallico, sordo **2.** esattamente: *— in the middle*, esattamente nel mezzo.

pluperfect [ˈplu:ˈpə:fikt], *ag. s.* (*gram.*) piuccheperfetto, trapassato.

plural [ˈpluərəl], *ag.s.* (*gram.*) plurale ☆ *— offices*, uffici, benefici tenuti da una sola persona.

pluralism [ˈpluərəlizəm], *s.* (*eccl. fil.*) pluralismo.

pluralist [ˈpluərəlist], *s.* **1.** (*eccl.*) chi possiede più di un beneficio **2.** (*fil.*) pluralista.

pluralistic [ˌpluərəˈlistik], *ag.* pluralistico.

plurality [pluəˈræliti], *s.* **1.** pluralità; molteplicità **2.** (*pol.*) maggioranza relativa **3.** (*eccl.*) pluralismo.

to **pluralize** [ˈpluərəlaiz], *v.t.* **1.** pluralizzare **2.** (*eccl.*) detenere più di un beneficio.

plus [plʌs], *ag.* **1.** addizionale, in più **2.** (*elett. mat.*) positivo ‖ *s.* (*pl.* **plusses** [ˈplʌsiz]) **1.** più (segno dell'addizione) **2.** quantità addizionale **3.** quantità positiva ☆ *— electric charge*, carica elettrica positiva; *— -fours*, (*sl.*) calzoni alla zuava; *— quantity*, quantità addizionale.

plus, *prep.* più: *courage — sense*, coraggio più buon senso.

plush [plʌʃ], *ag.* (*sl. amer.*) elegante, raffinato (di ambiente, arredamento) ‖ *s.* **1.** « peluche », felpa **2.** *pl.* pantaloni della livrea di un valletto.

Plutarch [ˈplu:ta:k], *no.pr.m.* (*st. lett.*) Plutarco.

plutarchy [ˈplu:ta:ki], *s.* plutocrazia.

Pluto [ˈplu:tou], *no.pr.m.* (*mit.*) Plutone ‖ *no.pr.* (*astr.*) Plutone.

plutocracy [plu:ˈtɔkrəsi], *s.* plutocrazia.

plutocrat [ˈplu:təkræt], *s.* plutocrate.

plutocratic [ˌplu:təˈkrætik], *ag.* plutocratico.

Plutonian [plu:ˈtounjən], **Plutonic** [plu:ˈtɔnik], *ag.* **1.** plutonio, infernale; sotterraneo **2.** (*geol.*) plutonico ☆ *— rock*, roccia plutonica.

Plutonism [ˈplu:tənizəm], *s.* (*geol.*) plutonismo.

plutonium [plu:ˈtounjəm], *s.* (*chim.*) plutonio.

Plutus [ˈplu:təs], *no.pr.m.* (*mit.*) Pluto.

pluvial [ˈplu:vjəl], *ag.* **1.** pluviale **2.** (*geol.*) alluvionale ‖ *s.* (*eccl.*) piviale.

pluviometer [ˌplu:viˈɔmitə*], *s.* pluviometro.

pluviometric(al) [ˌplu:vjəˈmetrik(əl)], *ag.* pluviometrico.

pluviose [ˈplu:vjous], **pluvious** [ˈplu:vjəs], *ag.* piovoso.

Pluviòse [ˈplu:vious], *s.* (*st. francese*) piovoso.

ply [plai], *s.* **1.** piega **2.** *fig.* piega, tendenza **3.** capo, filo (di tela, lana); trefolo (di corda) **4.** strato (in legno compensato, cartone) ☆ *three- —*, *four- — wool*, lana a tre, quattro capi.

to **ply,** *pass.p.p.* **plied** [plaid], *v.t.i.* **1.** maneggiare, fare uso di, impiegare: *to — the oars*, remare **2.** lavorare assiduamente, attendere a (un compito): *to — a trade*, esercitare un mestiere **3.** assediare, importunare (con richieste, domande, offerte): *they plied the doctor with questions*, assediarono di domande il dottore; *to — s.o. with drinks*, offrire insistentemente da bere a qlcu. **4.** fare la spola da un luogo all'altro (di veicoli); traghettare (di navi) **5.** (*mar.*) orzare; bordeggiare **6.** frequentare un luogo in attesa di clienti (detto di barcaiolo, tassista, facchino): *car plying for hire*, automobile di piazza.

plyer ['plaiə*], *s.* **1.** lavoratore **2.** (*mar.*) battello che va all'orza.

plying ['plaiiŋ], *s.* **1.** impiego, utilizzazione **2.** esercizio, esecuzione (di un lavoro, un compito) **3.** insistenza (nel chiedere, nell'offrire) **4.** (*mar.*) l'andare all'orza; il bordeggiare **5.** (*tec.*) applicazione delle tele (nella fabbricazione dei pneumatici).

Plymouth ['pliməθ], *no.pr.* (*geog.*) Plymouth || — *Brethren*, confraternita di Plymouth (setta religiosa); — *Colony*, colonia fondata dai Padri Pellegrini sulla costa del Massachusetts; — *Rock*, la roccia di Plymouth nel Massachusetts dove approdarono i Padri Pellegrini.

plywood ['plaiwud], *s.* legno compensato.

pneuma ['nju:mə], *s.* anima, spirito.

pneumatic [nju(:)'mætik], *ag.s.* pneumatico ☆ — *brake*, freno pneumatico; — *digger*, scavatrice pneumatica; — *dispatch*, posta pneumatica; — *hammer*, martello pneumatico; — *tire*, pneumatico.

pneumatically [nju(:)'mætikəli], *av.* ad aria compressa ☆ — *controlled*, con freno pneumatico; — *operated*, funzionante ad aria compressa.

pneumatics [nju(:)'mætiks], *s.* (*fis.*) pneumatica.

pneumatology [,nju:mə'tɔlədʒi], *s.* **1.** (*fil.*) pneumatologia **2.** (*fis.*) pneumatica.

pneumatometer [,nju:mə'tɔmitə*], *s.* (*med.*) pneumometro.

pneumococcus [,nju:mə'kɔkəs], *pl.* **pneumococci** [,nju:mə'kɔksai], *s.* (*biol.*) pneumococco.

pneumogastric [,nju:mə'gæstrik], *ag.* (*anat.*) pneumogastrico ☆ — *nerve*, vago, nervo pneumogastrico.

pneumograph ['nju:məgrɑ:f], *ag.* (*med.*) pneumografo.

pneumonia [nju(:)'mounjə], *s.* (*patol.*) polmonite ☆ *broncho-* —, broncopolmonite; *double* —, polmonite doppia.

pneumonic [nju(:)'mɔnik], *ag.* (*med.*) pneumonico; polmonare.

pneumonitis [,nju:mə'naitis], *s.* (*patol.*) polmonite.

pneumothorax [,nju:mə'θɔ:ræks], *s.* (*med.*) pneumotorace.

to **poach¹** [poutʃ], *v.t.* cuocere (uova senza guscio) in acqua bollente ☆ *poached eggs*, uova affogate, in camicia.

to **poach²**, *v.t.i.* **1.** calpestare; sbriciolare (la terra con gli zoccoli) **2.** diventare soffice, fangoso (di terra); rendere soffice, fangoso; mescolare con acqua per ridurre a consistenza uniforme (*p.e.* creta) **3.** cacciare, pescare di frodo; fare il bracconiere: *to — on s.o.'s preserves*, cacciare di frodo nelle riserve di qlcu. (anche *fig.*) **4.** (*spor.*) avvantaggiarsi con mezzi scorretti.

poacher ['poutʃə*], *s.* **1.** bracconiere; cacciatore, pescatore di frodo **2.** *fig.* chi slealmente porta via affari ad altri.

poaching ['poutʃiŋ], *s.* caccia, pesca di frodo.

poachy ['poutʃi], *ag.* fangoso, acquitrinoso.

pochard ['poutʃəd], *s.* (*ornit.*) moretta.

pock [pɔk], *s.* (*patol.*) pustola vaiolosa; buttero.

pocket ['pɔkit], *s.* **1.** tasca (anche *fig.*); taschino: *he paid out of his* —, ha pagato di tasca sua || *I am out of* — *by it*, ci ho rimesso di tasca mia || *to be in* —, aver guadagnato || *to have a deep* —, essere ricco; *to have an empty* —, essere al verde || *to be always in s.o.'s* —, star sempre appiccicato a qlcu. || *to have a person in one's* —, poter disporre liberamente di una persona || *to keep one's hands in one's* —, stare con le mani in mano || *to line one's pockets*, farsi il gruzzolo || *to put one's pride in one's* —, soffocare il proprio orgoglio **2.** bu-

ca (di biliardo) **3.** (*anat.*) sacco, sacca || *she had pockets under her eyes*, aveva le borse sotto gli occhi **4.** sacco (misura di peso per aridi = kg. 76,2) **5.** (*geol. miner.*) sacca, cavità **6.** (*mil.*) sacca, zona isolata ☆ — *-book*, taccuino: portafogli; libro formato tascabile; — *-comb*, pettine da tasca; — *-edition*, edizione tascabile; — *-handkerchief*, fazzoletto da tasca; — *-knife*, temperino; — *-money*, denaro per le piccole spese; — *-picking*, borseggio; — *-piece*, moneta portafortuna; — *-pistol*, rivoltella da tasca, (*scherz.*) fiaschetta tascabile per liquori; — *-sized*, tascabile || *air-* —, (*aer.*) vuoto d'aria; *water-* —, sacca d'acqua.

to **pocket**, *v.t.* **1.** intascare, mettere in tasca; appropriarsi di: *he received the money for expenses, but he pocketed most of it*, ricevette del denaro in conto spese, ma ne intascò la maggior parte **2.** *fig.* incassare, sopportare (insulti, offese, ecc.) **3.** nascondere, soffocare (sentimenti, ecc.): *I — my pride*, soffoco il mio orgoglio **4.** tagliar la strada a (concorrenti, in una corsa) **5.** (*biliardo*) mettere (la palla) in buca.

pocketful ['pɔkitful], *s.* tascata.

pockety ['pɔkiti], *ag.* **1.** (*miner.*) a sacche (di depositi di minerale) **2.** (*aer.*) a vuoti d'aria.

pockmark ['pɔkmɑ:k], *s.* buttero.

pockmarked ['pɔkmɑ:kt], **pocky** ['pɔki], *ag.* butterato.

poco-curante ['poukoukjuə'rænti], *ag. s.* (persona) noncurante.

poco-curant(e)ism ['poukoukjuə'rænt(i)izəm], *s.* noncuranza.

pod¹ [pɔd], *s.* **1.** baccello; guscio; capsula; bozzolo **2.** (*mar.*) nassa (per la pesca delle anguille).

to **pod¹**, *pass p.p.* **podded** ['pɔdid], *v.t.i.* **1.** produrre baccelli (di piante) **2.** sgusciare (piselli).

pod², *s.* (*mec.*) portapunta.

pod³, *s.* piccolo gruppo (di foche, balene); piccolo stormo (di uccelli, ecc.).

to **pod³**, *v.t.* far riunire (foche, balene, uccelli) in un gruppo.

podagra [pə'dægrə], *s.* (*patol.*) podagra.

podagral [pə'dægrəl], **podagric** [pə'dægrik], **podagrous** ['pɔdəgrəs], *ag.* (*patol.*) gottoso.

podded ['pɔdid], *ag.* **1.** che produce baccelli **2.** *fig.* benestante; comodo.

podge [pɔdʒ], *s.* (*fam.*) persona tozza.

podginess ['pɔdʒinis], *s.* (*fam.*) l'essere piccolo e tozzo.

podgy ['pɔdʒi], *ag.* (*fam.*) tozzo, piccolo e grasso.

podium ['poudjəm], *pl.* **podia** ['poudjə], *s.* podio.

poem ['pouim], *s.* **1.** poesia, composizione poetica: *a short* —, una poesia breve **2.** poema ☆ *prose* —, poema in prosa, prosa poetica.

poesy ['pouizi], *s.* (*arc.*) poesia.

poet ['pouit], *s.* poeta || *Poet Laureate*, poeta laureato || *Poets' Corner*, Angolo dei Poeti (transetto meridionale dell'Abbazia di Westminster a Londra, dove sono sepolti celebri poeti e scrittori); (*scherz.*) parte di giornale riservata a componimenti in versi.

poetaster [,pouі'tæstə*], *s.* poetastro.

poetess ['pouitis], *s.* poetessa.

poetic [pou'etik], *s.* poetica.

poetic(al) [pou'etik(əl)], *ag.* poetico: — *diction*, dizione poetica; — *inspiration*, ispirazione poetica; — *licence*, licenza poetica; *the — works of Walter Scott*, le opere in versi di Walter Scott.

poetically [pou'etikəli], *av.* poeticamente.

to **poeticize** [pou'etisaiz], *v.t.i.* rendere poetico; scrivere, parlare come un poeta.

poetics [pou'etiks], *s.* poetica.

to **poetize** ['pouitaiz], *v.t.i.* **1.** poetare **2.** poetizzare **3.** fare il, darsi le arie di poeta.

poetry ['pouitri], *s.* poesia: — *and prose*, poesia e prosa || *Horace's "Art of Poetry"*, l'« Arte poetica » di Orazio.

pogo ['pougou], *pl.* **pogos** ['pougouz], *s.* — (*-stick*) « pogo » (sorta di trampolo con molla, in uso come giocattolo infantile).

pogrom ['pɔgrəm], *s.* «pogrom» (massacro organizzato, specialmente di ebrei in Russia).

poignancy ['poinənsi], *s.* **1.** amarezza; acutezza (del dolore) **2.** mordacità.

poignant ['poinənt], *ag.* **1.** acuto, vivo, cocente: — *tears*, lacrime cocenti; *they were deeply moved by his — words*, furono profondamente commossi dai suoi accenti di dolore **2.** piccante: — *sauce*, salsa piccante **3.** sarcastico, mordace: — *wit*, spirito sarcastico.

poignantly ['poinəntli], *av.* acutamente; pungentemente.

poilu [pwɑːˈluː], *s.* (*sl.*) «poilu» (soldato francese).

poinsettia [poin'setiə], *s.* (*bot.*) poinsettio.

point [point], *s.* **1.** punto (nello spazio): *the — of intersection of two lines*, il punto di intersezione di due linee **2.** (*ortografia, tip. mus.*) punto: — *of interrogation*, punto interrogativo || *three — five* (*3.5*), tre virgola cinque (3,5) **3.** punto, grado: *the thermometer went up three points*, il termometro salì di tre gradi **4.** (*spor. comm. giuoco*) punto: *to beat s.o. on points*, (*boxe*) battere qlcu. ai punti; *to give points to s.o.*, dare dei punti a qlcu. (anche *fig.*); *to score so many points*, fare tanti punti **5.** punto (nel tempo), momento, istante: *at the — of death*, in punto di morte; *to be on the — of doing sthg.*, essere sul punto di fare ql.co. **6.** argomento, questione; rapporto; opinione: *a — of conscience*, una questione di coscienza; *a — of law*, una questione di diritto || *at all points*, completamente || *beside the* (o *off the*) —, fuori questione || *from all points of view* (o *in every* —), sotto tutti gli aspetti, sotto ogni rapporto || *in* (o *to the*) —, in questione || *in — of fact*, in realtà || *to carry one's* —, sostenere, far prevalere la propria opinione **7.** caratteristica, singolarità, qualità essenziale: *his strong* —, la sua caratteristica || *the — of a joke*, l'arguzia di una storiella || *to come to the* —, venire al punto essenziale || *to miss the* —, non cogliere l'essenziale || *to make a — of doing sthg.*, farsi un dovere di fare ql.co. || *to stick to the* —, (*fam.*) non divagare **8.** scopo: *what would be the — of doing that?*, quale sarebbe lo scopo di fare questo? **9.** punta, estremità; punta delle corna (di un cervo): *the — of a knife*, la punta di un coltello; *at the — of the sword*, sulla punta della spada; *fig.* a mano armata; *to give a — to a pencil*, fare la punta a una matita **10.** capo, promontorio: *to round a* —, (*mar.*) doppiare un promontorio **11.** (*mar.*) punto (della rosa dei venti); quarta **12.** *pl.* zampe (di cavallo) **13.** il puntare (di cane) **14.** (*strum. artig.*) bulino **15.** (*elett.*) puntina, presa di corrente **16.** (*ferr.*) scambio deviatorio **17.** (*mar.*) matafione **18.** — (*lace*), merletto a punto ago ☆ — *duty*, servizio (di poliziotto addetto alla circolazione); — *-paper*, (*tec.*) spolvero; — *rail*, (*ferr.*) ago || *boiling-* —, punto di ebollizione; *brittle-* —, punto di fragilità; *burning-* —, punto di accensione; *cardinal* —, punto cardinale; *cloud-* —, (*chim.*) punto di intorbidimento; *decimal* —, virgola decimale; *freezing-* —, punto di congelamento; *spark plug* —, (*mec.*) puntina di candela; *stage-* —, capolinea (di tram, ecc.); *turning-* —, svolta decisiva.

to point, *v.t.i.* **1.** indicare; mostrare, provare: *all evidence points to his guilt*, ogni testimonianza prova la sua colpa; *it is rude to* —, non è educato indicare col dito; *this points a moral*, questo è di lezione **2.** puntare; orientare: *they will — the gun in this direction*, punteranno il cannone in questa direzione; *to — a telescope*, orientare un telescopio **3.** mettere una punta; fare la punta, aguzzare: *to — a pencil*, fare la punta a una matita **4.** puntare (di cane) **5.** riempire di calce e cemento (lo spazio fra i mattoni) **6.** (*rar.*) punteggiare (uno scritto, ecc.) **7.** suppurare **8.** *to — at* (*s.o.*), indicare, segnare a dito: *she was pointed at by everybody*, era segnata a dito da tutti **9.** *to — to a direction*, indicare il cammino da prendere (di persone); guardare verso (di cose): *the house points to the east*, la casa è rivolta verso est **10.** *to — out*, indicare, porre in ri-

lievo; far notare, far rilevare: *he pointed out to me where his house was*, mi indicò dove era la sua casa; *they pointed him out the risks*, gli fecero rilevare i pericoli che correva.

point-blank ['point'blæŋk], *ag.* diretto; orizzontale: — *fire* (o — *shot*), fuoco diretto || *av.* direttamente; senza esitazione; ad un tratto; a bruciapelo: *he said — he would not do it*, disse chiaro e tondo che non lo voleva fare.

pointed ['pointid], *ag.* **1.** appuntito, acuto, aguzzo **2.** *fig.* arguto, piccante, frizzante: *a — epigram*, un epigramma mordace **3.** chiaro, evidente, intenzionale: *a — allusion*, una allusione evidente **4.** (*arch.*) ogivale ☆ — *arch*, arco a sesto acuto.

pointedly ['pointidli], *av.* **1.** in modo arguto **2.** chiaramente, esplicitamente, con intenzione.

pointedness ['pointidnis], *s.* **1.** acutezza; *fig.* arguzia, spirito **2.** evidenza; carattere esplicito (di un'allusione).

pointel ['pointl], *s.* stilo.

pointer ['pointə*], *s.* **1.** indicatore; indice **2.** lancetta (di orologio, bilancia, ecc.) **3.** «pointer» (cane da ferma) **4.** (*amer.*) indicazione, suggerimento **5.** *pl.* le due stelle dell'Orsa Maggiore la cui retta di congiunzione indica la stella polare **6.** (*mil.*) puntatore (di cannone).

pointing ['pointiŋ], *s.* **1.** (*gram.*) punteggiatura **2.** indicazione, suggerimento **3.** il cementare i mattoni in una costruzione.

pointless ['point-lis], *ag.* **1.** senza punta, spuntato; smussato **2.** *fig.* ottuso **3.** inutile, senza scopo **4.** (*spor.*) che non ha segnato punti.

pointlessly ['point-lisli], *av.* inutilmente, senza scopo.

pointlessness ['point-lisnis], *s.* inutilità; mancanza di significato.

pointsman, *pl.* **pointsmen** ['pointsmən], *s.* **1.** (*ferr.*) deviatore addetto agli scambi **2.** poliziotto che regola il traffico.

poise [poiz], *s.* **1.** equilibrio, stabilità; *fig.* ponderatezza **2.** portamento **3.** indecisione, irresoluzione.

to poise, *v.t.i.* **1.** bilanciare, equilibrare; essere in equilibrio **2.** pesare, soppesare; *fig.* ponderare **3.** essere sospeso; volteggiare, planare (di uccelli, specialmente da preda): *to — in the air* (o *in mid air*), volteggiare a mezz'aria.

poison ['poizn], *s.* veleno (anche *fig.*) ☆ — *-fang*, dente avvelenato (di serpente); — *-gas*, gas tossico, asfissiante; — *-gland*, ghiandola secernente veleno; — *-tree*, albero velenoso.

to poison, *v.t.* **1.** avvelenare; intossicare **2.** *fig.* corrompere; rovinare: *to — a person's mind against s.o.*, istillare nella mente di una persona odio e sospetto verso qlcu.

poisoner ['poiznə*], *s.c.* avvelenatore, avvelenatrice.

poisoning ['poizniŋ], *s.* avvelenamento ☆ *blood* —, (*patol.*) setticemia.

poisonous ['poiznəs], *ag.* **1.** velenoso **2.** *fig.* pernicioso, dannoso **3.** disgustoso.

poisonously ['poiznəsli], *av.* velenosamente.

poisonousness ['poiznəsnis], *s.* velenosità.

poke[1] [pouk], *s.* **1.** (*dial.*) borsa, sacco || *to buy a pig in a* —, comperare a occhi chiusi **2.** (*vet.*) gonfiore sul collo di pecore ☆ — *-pudding*, (*scoz.*) persona corpulenta e ghiotta; inglese.

poke[2], *s.* ala, visiera di cappello da donna || — *-bonnet*, cuffia a visiera, legata sotto il mento.

poke[3], *s.* **1.** spinta; gomitata; urto; colpo **2.** giogo applicato agli animali perchè non fuggano dai recinti **3.** (*amer. fam.*) persona pigra, bighellone.

to poke[3], *v.t.i.* **1.** spingere, cacciare innanzi; urtare: *to — fun at s.o.*, mettere in ridicolo qlcu., beffarsi di qlcu. || *to — s.o. in the ribs*, dare una gomitata amichevole a qlcu. **2.** mettere il giogo **3.** *fig.* incitare; eccitare; irritare **4.** frugare: *to — (about) in every corner*, frugare in ogni angolo; *to — into other people's business*, ficcare il naso, intromettersi negli affari altrui || *to — and* *pry*, indagare **5.** attizzare (il fuoco) **6.** sporgere, chinare: *to — (the head)*, sporgere la testa: *to — one's head out of the window*, sporgere la testa dalla finestra **7.** rinchiudere, confinare: *to — oneself up in a tiny house*, rinchiudersi in una casetta **8.** bighellonare, oziare.

poke[4], *s.* **1.** (*bot.*) fitolacca, uvina americana **2.** (*bot.*) elleboro.

poker[1] ['poukə*], *s.* **1.** attizzatoio **2.** *fig.* persona rigida, severa: *as stiff as a —*, rigido come se avesse ingerito un bastone **3.** mazza, verga (di mazziere, ecc.) **4.** mazziere (all'università di Oxford, Cambridge) **5.** (*pirografia*) punta metallica ☆ — *-work*, pirografia (su legno).

to **poker**[1], *v.t.* **1.** attizzare **2.** pirografare.

poker[2], *s.* (*carte*) «poker» ☆ — *-face*, (*sl. amer.*) viso inscrutabile, impassibile.

poker[3], *s.* (*fam. amer.*) uomo nero, lupo mannaro || *Old Poker*, il diavolo.

poker[4], *V.* **pochard.**

poking ['poukiŋ], *ag.* **1.** sporgente **2.** *V.* **poky** || *s.* **1.** attizzamento **2.** intromissione (negli affari altrui).

poky ['pouki], *ag.* **1.** piccolo e stretto: *a — little room*, una stanzuccia **2.** modesto, meschino, noioso (di occupazione) **3.** logoro, sdrucito.

polacca [pou'lækə], **polacre** [pou'lɑ:kə*], *s.* (*mar.*) polacca.

Poland ['poulənd], *no.pr.* (*geog.*) Polonia.

polar ['poulə*], *ag.* **1.** polare **2.** (*elett.*) magnetico, di polo magnetico **3.** *fig.* antitetico: — *characters*, caratteri opposti ☆ — *bear*, orso polare; — *circle*, circolo polare; — *hare*, lepre polare; — *lights*, aurora boreale, australe; — *seas*, mari artici.

polarimeter [,poulə'rimitə*], *s.* (*fis.*) polarimetro.

polariscope [pou'læriskoup], *s.* (*fis.*) polariscopio.

polarity [pou'læriti], *s.* polarità.

polarization [,poulərai'zeiʃən], *s.* (*fis.*) polarizzazione.

to **polarize** ['pouləraiz], *v.t.i.* (*fis.*) polarizzare, polarizzarsi.

polarizer ['pouləraizə*], *s.* (*fis.*) polarizzatore.

polatouche [polə'tu:ʃ], *s.* (*zool.*) scoiattolo volante.

polder ['poldə*], *s.* «polder», terreno bonificato (nei Paesi Bassi).

pole[1] [poul], *s.* **1.** palo, asta: *to set a —*, piantare un palo **2.** pertica (misura di lunghezza = m. 5,0292) **3.** timone (di carro trainato da buoi) **4.** (*mar.*) albero: *bare poles*, alberi senza vele ☆ — *-jumping* (o — *vaulting*), (*spor.*) salto con l'asta || *square —*, (*agr.*) pertica (misura di superficie = m.[2] 25,292); *telegraph —*, palo telegrafico, telefonico.

to **pole**[1], *v.t.* **1.** mettere pali a, sostenere con pali **2.** spingere (veicolo) con pali **3.** attaccare (animale) al carro.

pole[2], *s.* polo; *fig.* antipode || *North —*, *South —*, Polo Nord, Polo Sud || *to be as far apart as the Poles*, essere agli antipodi ☆ — *face*, (*elett.*) superficie polare; — *piece*, espansione polare; — *star*, (*astr.*) stella polare; *fig.* guida || *asunder poles*, (*elett.*) poli opposti; *celestial —*, (*astr.*) polo celeste; *magnetic —*, (*fis. elett.*) polo magnetico; *negative —*, *positive —*, (*fis.*) catodo, anodo.

Pole[3], *s.c.* polacco, polacca.

pole-ax(e) ['poulæks], *s.* **1.** ascia; scure **2.** alabarda.

to **pole-ax(e)**, *v.t.* macellare con scure.

polecat ['poulkæt], *s.* (*zool.*) puzzola.

polemarch ['polimɑ:k], *s.* (*st.*) polemarco.

polemic [po'lemik], *ag.* polemico || *s.* **1.** polemica **2.** *pl.* (*teol.*) controversia **3.** polemista; (*teol.*) controversista.

polemical [po'lemikəl], *ag.* polemico.

polemically [po'lemikəli], *av.* polemicamente.

polemicist [po'lemisist], **polemist** ['polimist], *s.* polemista.

to **polemize** ['polimaiz], *v.i.* polemizzare.

polenta [pou'lentə], *s.* polenta.

police [pə'li:s], *s.* **1.** polizia; ordine pubblico: *the — of that city is very efficient*, la polizia di quella città è molto efficiente **2.** polizia; *coll.* (*con costruzione pl.*) i poliziotti: *the — are on his tracks*, la polizia è sulle sue tracce ☆ — *-court*, tribunale di polizia; — *-dog*, cane poliziotto; — *-force*, corpo di polizia; — *-magistrate*, magistrato di polizia; — *-station*, posto di polizia; —*-van*, furgone cellulare.

to **police**, *v.t.* **1.** mantenere l'ordine pubblico (per mezzo di agenti di polizia) in; fornire di agenti di polizia **2.** *fig.* controllare, vigilare.

policeman, *pl.* **policemen** [pə'li:smən], *s.* poliziotto, agente.

policewoman [pə'li:s,wumən], *pl.* **policewomen** [pə'li:s,wimin], *s.* donna poliziotto.

policlinic [,poli'klinik], *s.* **1.** clinica privata **2.** ambulatorio.

policy[1] ['polisi], *s.* **1.** indirizzo, sistema, linea di condotta: *our — is to satisfy our customers*, il nostro sistema è di soddisfare i clienti **2.** politica; arte del governo; diplomazia (anche *spreg.*) || *wait-and-see —*, politica temporeggiatrice **3.** *fig.* accortezza, sagacia **4.** *pl.* (*scoz.*) terre, proprietà, parco (intorno a un castello) ☆ *domestic —* (o *home —*), politica interna; *foreign —*, politica estera.

policy[2], *s.* polizza ☆ — *-holder*, persona assicurata || *insurance —*, polizza di assicurazione; *open —*, (*comm. mar.*) polizza aperta d'abbonamento.

polio ['pouliou], *s.* (*patol.*) (*abbr. di poliomyelitis*) poliomielite ☆ — *invalid*, poliomielitico.

poliomyelitis ['poulioumaiə'laitis], *s.* (*patol.*) poliomielite.

Polish[1] ['pouliʃ], *ag.* polacco || *s.* lingua polacca.

polish[2] ['poliʃ], *s.* **1.** lucentezza, brillantezza (ottenuta strofinando) **2.** lucidatura **3.** lucido; vernice; smalto **4.** *fig.* raffinatezza, grazia, eleganza; belle maniere: *a writer of great —*, uno scrittore dallo stile raffinato ☆ *floor —*, cera da pavimenti; *nail- —*, smalto per unghie; *shoe —*, lucido da scarpe.

to **polish**[2], *v.t.i.* **1.** lucidare; lustrare; lisciare; divenire lucido; (*mec.*) brillantare; ravvivare (colori) **2.** rendere elegante; ingentilire, ingentilirsi; dirozzare, dirozzarsi; civilizzare, civilizzarsi **3.** *to — off*, finire; consumare; sbrigare: *to — off the enemy*, sbaragliare il nemico; *to — off a job*, portare a termine un lavoro in fretta; *to — off a plateful of meat*, mangiarsi un intero piatto di carne **4.** *to — up*, pulire, rendere lindo; *fig.* abbellire; perfezionare; raffinare.

polishable ['poliʃəbl], *ag.* **1.** lucidabile **2.** che può essere raffinato.

polished ['poliʃt], *ag.* **1.** ripulito; lucente, lucido **2.** *fig.* raffinato, distinto: — *manners*, modi distinti; — *style*, stile raffinato.

polisher ['poliʃə*], *s.* **1.** lucidatore **2.** lucido; liquido, pasta per lucidare ☆ *bell-* —, (*sl.*) visitatore che nel congedarsi indugia a lungo sulla soglia; *floor —*, lucidatore di pavimenti; *furniture —*, lucidatore di mobili.

polishing ['poliʃiŋ], *s.* lucidatura, lustratura; (*mec.*) brillantatura ☆ — *-machine*, lucidatrice; — *-paste* (o — *cream*), pasta, crema per lucidare.

polishment ['poliʃmənt], *s.* lucidatura.

polite [pə'lait], *ag.* **1.** educato, gentile, cortese, garbato: *a — answer*, una risposta garbata **2.** raffinato, colto, elegante ☆ — *learning* (o — *letters*), le belle lettere; — *living*, bel vivere; — *society*, il bel mondo, la gente colta.

politely [pə'laitli], *av.* gentilmente, cortesemente.

politeness [pə'laitnis], **politesse** [,poli'tes], *s.* gentilezza, cortesia, belle maniere, garbo.

Politian [pə'liʃən], *no.pr.* (*st. lett.*) Poliziano.

politic ['politik], *ag.* **1.** prudente; abile, accorto; (*spreg.*) astuto **2.** (*rar.*) politico || *the body —*, lo Stato.

political [pə'litikəl], *ag.* politico, relativo alla politica, allo Stato, al governo: — *agent*, agente politico || *s.* agente politico ☆ — *economy*, economia politica; — *geography*, geografia politica; — *resident*, (*st.*) ufficiale britannico consigliere di governatore indiano; — *science*, scienze politiche.

politically [pə'litikəli], *av.* politicamente.

politicaster [pou'litikæstə*], *s.* (*spreg.*) politicastro.
politician [,poli'tiʃən], *s.* **1.** uomo politico, statista **2.** politicante.
to **politicize** [pou'litisaiz], *v.t.i.* **1.** far l'uomo politico; fare della politica **2.** dare carattere politico a.
politicly ['politikli], *av.* **1.** accortamente; astutamente **2.** (*rar.*) politicamente.
politics ['politiks], *s.* **1.** politica: — *is the one career*, la politica è l'unica vera carriera; *to dabble in* —, fare della politica; *to go into* —, gettarsi nella politica; *to talk* —, parlare di politica **2.** *pl.* politica, idee politiche: — *are my favourite subject*, la politica è il mio argomento preferito; *what are your* —?, quali sono le vostre idee politiche?.
polity ['politi], *s.* **1.** forma, sistema, organizzazione di governo **2.** stato.
to **polk** [pouk], *v.i.* (*arc.*) ballare la polca.
polka ['polkə], *s.* **1.** (*mus.*) polca **2.** giacca da donna (generalmente lavorata a maglia) ☆ — *-dot pattern*, disegno a pallini (di stoffe): *a blue* — *-dot dress*, un abito blu a pallini.
poll[1] [poul], *s.* **1.** (*dial. scherz.*) testa; cuoio capelluto; nuca ‖ *per* —, a testa **2.** votazione; scrutinio; lista elettorale; voti: *the day before the* —, il giorno precedente le elezioni; *heavy, small* —, alta, bassa percentuale di votanti; *to declare the* —, proclamare i risultati della votazione; *to head the* —, riscuotere il maggior numero di voti ‖ *to go to the poll(s)*, andare alle urne ☆ — *book*, registro elettorale; — *-man* (o — *watcher*), scrutatore; — *-tax*, testatico ‖ *public-opinion* —, inchiesta sull'opinione pubblica.
to **poll**[1], *v.t.i.* **1.** radere; tosare **2.** svettare, cimare (alberi) **3.** tagliare le corna **4.** votare: *Brighton polls next Wednesday*, Brighton voterà mercoledì prossimo **5.** raccogliere voti, registrare voti **6.** condurre alle urne **7.** fare un'inchiesta.
poll[2] [pol], *s.* (*sl. universitario*) laureato con votazione legale: *to go out in the* —, prendere la laurea con i voti legali.
poll[3] [poul], *ag.* **1.** senza cima (di albero) **2.** senza corna ☆ — *-beast*, — *-ox*, animale, bue senza corna.
Poll [pol], *no.pr.f. dim.* di **Mary** ‖ *no.pr.* Loreto (nome dato ai pappagalli).
pollack ['polək], *s.* (*ittiol.*) gado.
pollard ['poləd], *ag.* senza cima ‖ *s.* **1.** (*agr.*) capitozza **2.** animale senza corna, dalle corna spezzate **3.** miscuglio di farina e crusca.
to **pollard**, *v.t.* (*agr.*) capitozzare, cimare.
polled [pould], *ag.* **1.** cimato **2.** senza corna.
pollen ['polin], *s.* (*bot.*) polline.
poller ['poulə*], *s.c.* **1.** chi cima alberi **2.** votante **3.** impiegato, impiegata di ufficio elettorale.
pollex ['poleks], *pl.* **pollices** ['polisi:z], *s.* pollice.
pollicitation [po,lisi'teiʃən], *s.* (*dir.*) pollicitazione.
to **pollinate** ['polineit], *v.t.* (*bot.*) impollinare.
pollination [,poli'neiʃən], *s.* (*bot.*) impollinazione.
polling ['poulin], *ag.* votante ‖ *s.* **1.** il cimare (alberi) **2.** votazione elettorale ☆ — *-booth*, cabina elettorale; — *-clerk*, scrutatore; — *-district* (o — *-station*), sezione elettorale; — *-machine*, apparecchio automatico per votazione.
pollinic [pə'linik], *ag.* (*bot.*) pollinico.
polliniferous [,poli'nifərəs], *ag.* (*bot.*) pollinifero.
polliwog ['poliwog], *s.* (*zool.*) girino.
pollock ['polək], *s.* (*ittiol.*) gado.
pollster ['poulstə*], *s.* (*amer.*) raccoglitore di dati statistici.
to **pollute** [pə'lu:t], *v.t.* **1.** contaminare, profanare, violare **2.** sporcare, inquinare: **3.** *fig.* corrompere.
polluted [pə'lu:tid], *ag.* **1.** profanato **2.** sudicio, sporco.
pollutedly [pə'lu:tidli], *av.* impuramente.
pollutedness [pə'lu:tidnis], *s.* **1.** profanazione **2.** impurità.
polluter [pə'lu:tə*], *s.c.* **1.** contaminatore, contaminatrice; profanatore, profanatrice **2.** corruttore, corruttrice.

pollution [pə'lu:ʃən], *s.* **1.** contaminazione; profanazione **2.** inquinamento **3.** *fig.* corruzione **4.** (*fisiol.*) polluzione.
Pollux ['poləks], *no.pr.m.* (*mit.*) Polluce ‖ *no.pr.* (*astr.*) Polluce.
Polly ['poli], *V.* **Poll**.
polo ['poulou], *s.* (*spor.*) polo ☆ — *coat*, soprabito di pelo di cammello; — *shirt*, camiciotto sportivo con maniche corte ‖ *water* —, polo giocato in acqua.
poloist ['pouləist], *s.* (*spor.*) giocatore di polo.
polonaise [,polə'neiz], *s.* **1.** (*mus.*) polacca **2.** polacca (abito per signora).
polonium [pə'lounjəm], *s.* (*chim.*) polonio.
Polonius [pə'lounjəs], *no.pr.m.* (*lett.*) Polonio.
polony [pə'louni], *s.* mortadella.
poltergeist ['poltəgaist], *s.* (*spiritismo*) spirito che si annunzia battendo alcuni colpi.
poltroon [pol'tru:n], *s.* codardo, vigliacco.
poltroonery [pol'tru:nəri], *s.* codardia, vigliaccheria.
polyamid(e) [,poli'æmid], *s.* (*chim.*) poliamide.
polyandria [,poli'ændriə], *s.* poliandria.
polyandrist [,poli'ændrist], *s.* donna con più mariti.
polyandrous [,poli'ændrəs], *ag.* **1.** che ha più mariti **2.** (*bot.*) con parecchi stami.
polyandry ['poliændri], *s.* poliandria.
polyanthus [,poli'ænθəs], *s.* (*bot.*) polianto.
polyarchy ['polia:ki], *s.* poliarchia.
polyatomic [,poliə'tomik], *ag.* poliatomico.
polyautography [,polio:'togrəfi], *s.* litografia.
polybasic [,poli'beisik], *ag.* (*chim.*) polibasico.
Polybius [po'libiəs], *no.pr.m.* (*st. lett.*) Polibio.
Polycarp ['polika:p], *no.pr.m.* Policarpo.
polycarpous [,poli'ka:pəs], *ag.* (*bot.*) policarpico.
Polychaeta [,poli'ki:tə], *s. pl.* (*zool.*) i policheti.
polychord ['poliko:d], *s.* (*mus.*) policordo.
polychromatic [,polikrə'mætik], *ag.* policromatico.
polychrome ['polikroum], *ag.* policromo ‖ *s.* **1.** opera d'arte policroma **2.** policromia.
polychromic [,poli'kroumik], **polychromous** [,poli'krouməs], *ag.* policromo
polychromy ['poli,kroumi], *s.* policromia.
polyclinic [,poli'klinik], *s.* policlinico.
Polycrates [po'likrəti:z], *no.pr.m.* (*st.*) Policrate.
polydactyl [,poli'dæktil], *ag.* polidattilo.
polydactylism [,poli'dæktilizm], *s.* polidattilia.
polydaemonism [,poli'di:mənizm], *s.* polidemonismo.
Polydorus [,poli'do:rəs], *no.pr.m.* (*st.*) Polidoro.
polyethylene [,poli'eθili:n], *s.* (*chim.*) polietilene.
polygala [pə'ligələ], *s.* (*bot.*) poligala.
polygamian [,poli'geimiən], *ag.* (*bot.*) poligamo.
polygamist [po'ligəmist], *s.* poligamo.
polygamous [po'ligəməs], *ag.* poligamo (anche *zool. bot.*).
polygamy [po'ligəmi], *s.* poligamia (anche *zool. bot.*).
polygenesis [,poli'dʒenisis], *s.* poligenesi.
polygenism [po'lidʒinizm], *s.* (*fil.*) poligenismo.
polygeny [pə'lidʒini], *s.* poligenesi.
polyglot ['poliglot], *s.c.* poliglotta.
poliglottie(al) [,poli'glotik(əl)], *ag.* poliglotta.
polyglottism ['poli,glotizəm], *s.* poliglottismo.
polygon ['poligən], *s.* (*geom.*) poligono.
polygonal [po'ligənl], *ag.* (*geom.*) poligonale.
polygram ['poligræm], *s.* poligramma.
polygraph ['poligra:f], *s.* poligrafo.
polygraphic [,poli'græfik], *ag.* poligrafico.
polygraphy [pə'ligrəfi], *s.* poligrafia.
Polygynia [,poli'dʒiniə], *s. pl.* (*bot.*) le poliginie.
polygyny [pə'lidʒini], *s.* poliginia (anche *zool.*).
polyhedral ['poli'hedrəl], *ag.* (*geom.*) poliedrico.
polyhedron ['poli'hedrən], *s.* (*geom.*) poliedro.
polyhistor [,poli'histə*], **polyhistorian** [,polihis'to:riən], *s.* dotto, erudito.
Polyhymnia [,poli'himnjə], *no.pr.f.* (*mit.*) Polinnia.
polymath ['polimæθ], *s.* dotto, erudito, enciclopedico.

polymer ['pɔlimə*], s. (chim.) polimero.
polymeric [,pɔli'merik], ag. (chim.) polimerico.
polymerism [pɔ'limərizəm], s. (chim.) polimeria.
polymerization [pɔ,limərai'zeifən], s. (chim.) polime-
rizzazione.
to **polymerize** ['pɔliməraiz], v.t. (chim.) polimerizzare.
polymerous [pə'limərəs], ag. (chim.) polimero.
polymorph ['pɔlimɔːf], s. (biol. min.) polimorfo.
polymorphic [,pɔli'mɔːfik], ag. (biol. min.) polimorfo.
polymorphism [,pɔli'mɔːfizəm], s. (biol. min.) polimorfismo.
polymorphous [,pɔli'mɔːfəs], ag. (biol. min.) polimorfo.
Polynesia [,pɔli'niːzjə], no.pr. (geog.) Polinesia.
Polynesian [,pɔli'niːzjən], ag. polinesiano ‖ s.c.
polinesiano, polinesiana.
polynomial [,pɔli'noumjəl], ag. s. (mat.) (di) polinomio.
polyp ['pɔlip], s. (zool.) polipo.
polypary ['pɔlipəri], s. (zool.) polipaio.
polype ['pɔlip], s. (zool.) polipo.
polyphagia [,pɔli'feidʒiə], **polyphagy** [pə'lifədʒi], s.
polifagia.
polyphase ['pɔlifeiz], ag. (elett.) polifase.
Polypheme ['pɔlifiːm], **Polyphemus** [,pɔli'fiːməs],
no.pr.m. (lett.) Polifemo.
polyphonic [,pɔli'fɔnik], **polyphonous** [pə'lifənəs],
ag. (mus.) polifonico.
polyphony [pə'lifəni], s. (mus.) polifonia.
polypidom [pə'lipidəm], s. (zool.) polipaio.
polypod[1] ['pɔlipɔd], ag. che ha molti piedi ‖ s. (entom.)
millepiedi.
polypod[2], **polypody** ['pɔlipədi], s. (bot.) polipodio.
polypoid ['pɔlipɔid], **polypous** ['pɔlipəs], ag. (zool.)
di, da polipo.
polyptyc(h) ['pɔliptik], s. (pitt.) polittico.
polypus ['pɔlipəs], pl. **polypuses** ['pɔlipəsiz], **polypi**
['pɔlipai], s. (patol.) polipo.
polyrhythm ['pɔliriðəm], s. (mus.) poliritmo.
polyrhythmic [,pɔli'riðmik], ag. (mus.) poliritmico.
polysaccharid(e) [,pɔli'sækərid], s. (chim.) polisac-
caride.
polystyrene [,pɔli'stairiːn], s. (chim.) polistirene.
polysyllabic(al) ['pɔlisi'læbik(əl)], ag. polisillabo,
polisillabico.
polysyllable ['pɔ li,siləbl], s. polisillabo.
polysyndeton [,pɔli'sinditən], s. (ret.) polisindeto.
polysynthesis [,pɔli'sinθisis], s. polisintesi.
polysynthetic [,pɔlisin'θetik], ag. polisintetico ☆ —
languages, lingue agglutinanti.
polytechnic [,pɔli'teknik], ag. s. politecnico.
polytheism ['pɔliθi(:)izəm], s. politeismo.
polytheist ['pɔliθi(:)ist], s.c. politeista.
polytheistic(al) [,pɔliθi(:)'istik(əl)], ag. politeistico.
polytonality [,pɔlitə'næliti], s. (mus.) politonalità.
polyuria [,pɔli'juəriə], s. (patol.) poliuria.
polyuric [,pɔli'juərik], ag. (patol.) poliurico.
polyvalence [,pɔli'veiləns], s. (chim.) polivalenza.
polyvalent [,pɔli'veilənt], ag. (chim.) polivalente.
polyvinyl [,pɔli'vainil], ag. (chim.) polivinilico ‖ s.
(chim.) polivinile.
polyzoic [,pɔli'zouik], ag. (zool.) polizoico.
Polyxena [pɔ'liksinə], no.pr.f. (lett.) Polissena.
pom [pɔm], s. (abbr. di Pomeranian) pomero, cane
di Pomerania.
pomace ['pʌmis], s. 1. polpa (di mele, nella preparazione del sidro; di altri frutti) 2. residui, scorie (di
pesci, semi dopo l'estrazione dell'olio) usati come fertilizzanti.
pomaceous [pou'meifəs], ag. di mela.
pomade [pə'mɑːd], s. pomata.
to **pomade**, v.t. impomatare.
pomander [pou'mændə*], s. (st.) sfera d'oro, d'argento, d'avorio contenente sostanze aromatiche che si
riteneva preservassero dalle infezioni.

pomatum [pə'meitəm], s. pomata.
to **pomatum**, v.t. impomatare.
pome [poum], s. 1. (bot.) pomo 2. (poet.) mela 3. globo
(simbolo della potenza regale).
pomegranate ['pɔm,grænit], s. (bot.) 1. melagra-
na 2. — (-tree), melograno.
pomelo ['pɔmilou], pl. **pomelos** ['pɔmilouz], s. varietà di pompelmo.
Pomeranian [,pɔmə'reinjən], ag. s.c. (abitante) della
Pomerania ‖ s. pomero, cane della Pomerania.
pomiculture ['poumi,kʌltfə*], s. pomicoltura, frutti-
coltura.
pomiferous [pou'mifərəs], ag. pomifero,
pommel ['pʌml], s. pomo (della spada, della sella);
pomello.
to **pommel**, pass.p.p. **pommelled** ['pʌmld], v.t.
battere; picchiare con pugni.
pomological [,poumə'lɔdʒikəl], ag. (agr.) pomo-
logico.
pomologist [pou'mɔlədʒist], s. frutticoltore.
pomology [pou'mɔlədʒi], s. (agr.) pomologia.
Pomona [pə'mounə], no.pr.f. (mit.) Pomona.
pomp [pɔmp], s. pompa, fasto, sfoggio.
Pompeian [pɔm'pi(:)ən], ag. (geog.) pompeiano.
Pompeii [pɔm'piːai], no.pr. (geog.) Pompei.
Pompey ['pɔmpi], no.pr.m. (st.) Pompeo.
pompier ['pɔmpiə*], s. pompiere.
pom-pom ['pɔmpɔm], s. (sl.) mitragliatrice Maxim a
tiro lungo.
pompon ['pɔ:mpɔːŋ], s. pompon, fiocco, nappa.
pomposity [pɔm'pɔziti] s. pomposità; enfasi; pompa;
ampollosità (di stile).
pompous ['pɔmpəs], ag. pomposo; enfatico; ampolloso (di stile).
pompously ['pɔmpəsli], av. pomposamente; ampollosamente.
pompousness ['pɔmpəsnis], V. **pomposity**.
poncho ['pɔntfou], pl. **ponchos** ['pɔntfouz], s. poncio
(mantello di lana usato nel Sud America).
pond [pɔnd], s. stagno; peschiera, vivaio ☆ — lily,
(bot.) ninfea; — weed, vegetazione d'acqua stagnante.
to **pond**, v.t.i. stagnare; far stagnare.
pondage ['pɔndidʒ], s. 1. riserva d'acqua 2. capacità
(di stagno, ecc.).
to **ponder** ['pɔndə*], v.t.i. ponderare, considerare;
meditare, riflettere.
ponderability [,pɔndərə'biliti], s. ponderabilità.
ponderable ['pɔndərəbl], ag. ponderabile.
ponderableness ['pɔndərəblnis], s. ponderabilità.
ponderation [,pɔndə'reifən], s. ponderazione.
ponderer ['pɔndərə*], s.c. chi pondera.
ponderingly ['pɔndəriŋli], av. ponderatamente.
ponderosity [,pɔndə'rɔsiti], s. ponderosità.
ponderous ['pɔndərəs], ag. 1. ponderoso; pesante,
massiccio 2. fig. grave; pesante, ampolloso (di stile).
ponderously ['pɔndərəsli], av. 1. pesantemente 2. fig.
gravemente; ampollosamente.
ponderousness ['pɔndərəsnis], s. 1. ponderosità 2. fig.
gravità; ampollosità (di stile).
pongee [pɔn'dʒiː], s. varietà di seta cinese.
pongo ['pɔŋgou], s. (sl.) orang-outang.
poniard ['pɔnjəd] s. pugnale.
to **poniard**, v.t. (arc.) pugnalare.
pons[pɔnz], pl. **pontes** ['pɔntiːz], s. (anat. zool.) ponte.
pontage ['pɔntidʒ], s. (st. dir.) pedaggio (da pagarsi
per poter percorrere un ponte).
Pontic ['pɔntik], ag. (geog. st.) pontico ‖ the — Sea, il
Ponto Eusino.
pontifex ['pɔntifeks], pl. **pontifices** [pɔn'tifisiːz], s.
(st. romana) pontefice.
pontiff ['pɔntif], s. 1. pontefice; papa 2. alto prelato;
vescovo.
pontifical [pɔn'tifikəl], ag. pontificio; pontificale ‖
‖ s. 1. pontificale (libro contenente il rituale dei vescovi) 2. pl. vestimenti e insegne episcopali.

pontificalia [pon͵tifiˈkeiliə], *s.pl.* vestimenti e insegne dei vescovi.

pontifically [ponˈtifikəli], *av.* 1. pontificalmente; 2. *fig.* pomposamente, solennemente.

pontificate [ponˈtifikit], *s.* pontificato.

to **pontificate** [ponˈtifikeit], to **pontify** [ˈpontifai], *v.i.* pontificare (anche *fig.*).

pontil [ˈpontil], *s.* (*ind. vetro*) pontello.

Pontine [ˈpontain], *ag.* (*geog.*) pontino ‖ the — Marshes, le Paludi Pontine.

Pontius Pilate [ˈpontjəsˈpailət], *no.pr.m.* (*st.*) Ponzio Pilato.

pontlevis [pontˈlevis], *s.* ponte levatoio.

ponton [ˈpontən], *s.* (*amer. mil.*) pontone.

pontoneer, pontonier [͵pontouˈniə*], *s.* (*mil.*) pontiere.

pontoon[1] [ponˈtuːn], *s.* 1. (*mil.*) pontone; ponte di barche, ponte galleggiante 2. (*mar.*) pontone; chiatta; barca da ponte ☆ — -bridge, ponte di barche.

to **pontoon**[1], *v.t.* attraversare (un fiume) su un ponte di barche.

pontoon[2], *s.* (*carte*) tressette.

Pontus [ˈpontəs], *no.pr.* (*geog. st.*) Ponto.

ponty [ˈponti], *s.* canna di ferro per soffiare il vetro.

pony [ˈpouni], *s.* 1. « pony », piccolo cavallo ‖ *Jerusalem* —, buricco, ronzino 2. (*sl.*) venticinque sterline 3. (*amer. fam.*) bigino 4. (*fam.*) bicchierino di, da liquore ☆ — edition, edizione in formato ridotto; — tail, (pettinatura a) coda di cavallo.

to **pony**, *v.t.i.* (*sl. amer.*) 1. pagare; saldare un conto 2. tradurre (con bigino).

pooch [puːtʃ], *s.* (*sl.*) cane bastardo.

pood [puːd], *s.* « pood » (misura di peso russa = kg. 16,38).

poodle [ˈpuːdl], *s.* barboncino, cagnolino da compagnia ☆ — -cut hair, capelli (tagliati) alla tifo; — -faker, (*sl.*) donnaiolo.

pooh [puː], *inter.* (*spreg.*) puah!, poh!.

Pooh-Bah [ˈpuːˈbɑː], *s.* (*spreg.*) chi copre parecchie cariche allo stesso tempo.

to **pooh-pooh** [puːˈpuː], *v.t.i.* mettere in ridicolo; esprimere disprezzo per: *they pooh-poohed my suggestion*, disdegnarono il mio consiglio.

pooka [ˈpuːkə], *s.* folletto, diavoletto.

pool[1] [puːl], *s.* 1. specchio d'acqua; stagno; pozza; pozzanghera 2. punto dove un fiume è molto profondo ‖ *The London Pool*, il Tamigi a valle della City di Londra ☆ — swimming —, (o bathing —), piscina.

to **pool**[1], *v.t.* fare (buchi) per inserire cunei in lavori di scavo, in miniere.

pool[2], *s.* 1. l'insieme delle poste nei giuochi di carte e nelle scommesse 2. giuoco di biliardo in cui il vincitore si prende tutte le poste 3. (*comm.*) fondo comune 4. (*comm.*) « pool » (accordo tra concorrenti per unificare attività e prezzi); sindacato ☆ betting — (o foot-ball — o soccer —), totocalcio; steel —, cartello dell'acciaio.

to **pool**[2], *v.t.i.* 1. mettere in un fondo comune; associare 2. formare un sindacato.

poop [puːp], *s.* (*mar.*) poppa; cassero di poppa ☆ — lantern, fanale di poppa; — -rail, parapetto.

to **poop**, *v.t.* rompersi contro la poppa di (una nave) (di onde) 2. ricevere (onde) da poppa (di nave).

poor [puə*], *ag.* 1. povero, misero; indigente, bisognoso ‖ the —, i poveri: *the rich ought to help the —*, i ricchi dovrebbero aiutare i poveri; *the poorer classes*, il proletariato ‖ *to be as — as a church-mouse*, essere povero in canna; *to be as — as Job* o (*amer.*) as Job's cat, essere povero come Giobbe 2. insufficiente, mediocre; inferiore; umile: *a — crop*, un magro raccolto; — quality, qualità scadente; — soil, terreno povero; *in my — opinion*, (*iron.*) secondo il mio modesto parere; *she is a — driver*, è una guidatrice mediocre; *she is very — at geography*, è molto debole in geografia ‖ *there was a — house*, (*teat.*) la sala era quasi vuota ‖ *to cut*

a — figure, fare una magra figura 3. disprezzabile, miserabile, gretto 4. degno di pietà; sfortunato: — fellow!, poveretto!, povero diavolo!; — me!, povero me!; *he is a — creature*, è una povera creatura, degna di compassione ☆ — -box, cassetta per l'elemosina; — -law, legge per l'assistenza ai poveri; — -rate, tassa per opere assistenziali; — -spirited, pusillanime.

poorhouse [ˈpuəhaus], *s.* ospizio per i poveri.

poorly [ˈpuəli], *av.* male, scarsamente ‖ *he is very — off*, è povero in canna ‖ *ag.predicativo* (*fam.*) malaticcio, indisposto: *he feels rather — today*, oggi non si sente tanto bene.

poorness [ˈpuənis], *s.* 1. povertà; scarsità; miseria: — of the soil, sterilità del suolo 2. meschinità; mediocrità; povertà (di contenuto): *the — of his ideas*, la povertà delle sue idee.

pop[1] [pop], *s.* 1. schiocco; scoppio, esplosione 2. (*sl.*) pistola 3. bevanda effervescente 4. macchia, segno 5. (*sl.*) l'impegnare: *to be in —*, avere impegnato ql.co. (al Monte di Pietà) ☆ — -corn, granoturco soffiato; — eyes, occhi grossi e sporgenti, di bove; — -gun pistola (giocattolo); — -shop, monte pegni; — -weed, (*bot.*) otricolaria.

to **pop**[1], *pass.p.p.* **popped** [popt], *v.t.i.* 1. schioccare, far schioccare; scoppiare, far scoppiare; saltare (di tappo): *to — (out) like a cork*, saltar via come un turacciolo 2. (*fam.*) scaricare (una pistola); sparare: *to — at a bird*, sparare a un uccello; *to — a gun*, tirare una fucilata 3. (*fam.*) andare; venire; capitare all'improvviso 4. (*fam.*) ficcare, mettere: *to — one's head out of the window*, sporgere la testa dalla finestra; *to — sthg. into a drawer*, ficcare ql.co. in un cassetto ‖ *to — down one's ideas on paper*, mettere le proprie idee per iscritto 5. (*fam.*) impegnare, portare al monte pegni 6. *to — the question*, (*fam.*) chiedere in sposa, fare la dichiarazione 7. *to — back*, (*aut.*) avere un ritorno di fiamma 8. *to — in*, entrare all'improvviso; fare una visitina 9. *to — off*, (*fam.*) scappare; (*sl.*) morire di un colpo 10. *to — out*, uscire: *to — out of the water*, emergere bruscamente dall'acqua 11. *to — up*, alzarsi d'improvviso, fare un balzo.

pop[1], *av.* improvvisamente, ad un tratto ‖ *to go —*, saltare, esplodere.

pop[1], *inter.* crac!, pum!.

pop[2], *s.* (*abbr. fam. di popular concert*) concerto popolare ☆ Sunday —, concerto domenicale.

pop[3], *s.* associazione universitaria (a Eton).

pop[4], *s.* (*amer. sl.*) papà.

pope[1] [poup], *s.* 1. (*eccl.*) papa ‖ —'s eye, (*cuc.*) noce (di vitello, ecc.) ‖ —'s nose, (*cuc.*) boccone del prete ‖ —'s head, spazzola, scopa con manico lungo; (*bot.*) melocatto ‖ *Pope Joan*, Papessa Giovanna; giuoco di carte 2. *fig.* persona di grande autorità 3. (*ittiol.*) acerina.

pope[2], *s.* pope (sacerdote ortodosso).

popedom [ˈpoupdəm], **popehood** [ˈpouphud], *s.* papato, pontificato.

popery [ˈpoupəri], *s.* (*spreg.*) papismo.

popinjay [ˈpopindʒei], *s.* 1. (*arc.*) pappagallo 2. (*arc.*) bersaglio di legno raffigurante un pappagallo 3. zerbinotto, damerino 4. (*ornit.*) picchio verde.

popish [ˈpoupiʃ], *ag.* (*spreg.*) di tendenze papiste; cattolico romano.

popishly [ˈpoupiʃli], *av.* (*spreg.*) da cattolico.

poplar [ˈpoplə*], *s.* — (tree), pioppo ☆ trembling —, pioppo tremulo; white — (o silver —), gattice, pioppo bianco.

poplin [ˈpoplin], *s.* « popeline » (tessuto).

popliteal [popˈlitiəl], *ag.* (*anat.*) popliteo.

poppa [ˈpopə], *s.* (*amer. fam.*) papà.

poppet [ˈpopit], *s.c.* (*sl.*) piccino; piccina, pupattola: *she is a —*, è una bimba graziosissima ‖ *s.* 1. (*mec.*): — (-head), testa di tornio; — (-valve), valvola verticale 2. (*mar.*) scalmiera.

poppied [ˈpopid], *ag.* 1. coperto di papaveri 2. (*poet.*) sonnolento; drogato.

popple ['pɔpl], *s.* ondeggiamento, flusso (d'acqua).

to popple, *v.i.* ondeggiare, fluttuare (d'acqua).

poppy ['pɔpi], *s.* papavero ☆ — -*head*, capsula dei semi di papavero; (*scult.*) fiore crociforme in legno (specialmente negli stalli delle chiese gotiche); — *red* (o — -*coloured*), rosso papavero.

poppycock ['pɔpikɔk], *s.* (*amer. fam.*) chiacchiere senza senso, sciocchezze, inezie.

popsy (-wopsy) ['pɔpsi ('wɔpsi)], *s.* (*fam.*) bambolina.

populace ['pɔpjuləs], *s.* plebaglia; popolaccio; volgo.

popular ['pɔpjulə*], *ag.* **1.** popolare, del popolo: — *election*, elezione popolare; — *front*, fronte popolare **2.** accessibile a tutti: — *prices*, prezzi popolari **3.** universalmente ammirato; in voga: — *preacher*, predicatore ben conosciuto; — *song*, canzone in voga; *he is* — *with his men*, è ben conosciuto (e apprezzato) dai suoi uomini; *this girl is very* —, questa ragazza è molto corteggiata; *to make oneself* —, farsi benvolere.

popularity [,pɔpju'læriti], *s.* popolarità; favore popolare; l'essere ammirato, apprezzato.

popularization [,pɔpjulərai'zeiʃən], *s.* popolarizzazione; divulgazione.

to popularize ['pɔpjuləraiz], *v.t.* popolarizzare, rendere popolare; divulgare.

popularizer ['pɔpjuləraizə*], *s.c.* divulgatore, divulgatrice; volgarizzatore, volgarizzatrice.

popularly ['pɔpjuləli], *av.* popolarmente.

to populate ['pɔpjuleit], *v.t.* popolare: *that district is densely populated*, quella regione è densamente popolata.

population [,pɔpju'leiʃən], *s.* popolazione: *increase in* —, aumento demografico.

Populism ['pɔpjulizəm], *s.* (*pol. amer.*) populismo.

Populist ['pɔpjulist], *s.* (*pol. amer.*) populista.

populous ['pɔpjuləs], *ag.* **1.** popoloso; densamente popolato **2.** produttivo, fecondo (di tempo, stagione).

populousness ['pɔpjuləsnis], *s.* densità di popolazione.

porbeagle ['pɔ:,bi:gl], *s.* (*ittiol.*) specie di squalo.

porcelain ['pɔ:slin], *s.* porcellana.

to porcelainize ['pɔ:slinaiz], *v.t.* porcellanare.

porcel(l)aneous [,pɔ:sə'leinjəs], *ag.* di porcellana.

porch [pɔ:tʃ], *s.* **1.** portico, porticato **2.** (*amer.*) veranda.

porcine ['pɔ:sain], *ag.* porcino, di porco.

porcupine ['pɔ:kjupain], *s.* (*zool.*) porcospino, riccio.

pore[1] [pɔ:*], *s.* poro: *enlarged pores*, pori dilatati.

to pore[2], *v.i.* guardare fisso; studiare, esaminare pazientemente: *I found him poring at a problem*, lo trovai intento a esaminare un problema; *to* — *on the mysteries of the universe*, meditare sui misteri dell'universo; *to* — *one's eyes out*, rovinarsi gli occhi leggendo; *to* — *over a book*, essere immerso nella lettura di un libro.

to porge [pɔ:dʒ], *v.t.* (*relig. ebraica*) purificare (carne di animale).

porgy ['pɔ:dʒi], *s.* (*amer. ittiol.*) pagro.

porism ['pɔ:rizəm], *s.* (*mat.*) corollario.

pork [pɔ:k], *s.* **1.** carne di maiale **2.** (*arc.*) porco, maiale **3.** (*sl. amer.*) denaro, posizione, ecc. che si ottengono dal governo attraverso intrighi politici ☆ — -*butcher*, salumiere; — -*chop*, braciola di maiale; — -*pie*, pasticcio di carne di maiale; — -*pie-hat*, cappello con cupola bassa e ala rialzata; — -*rind*, cotenna.

porker ['pɔ:kə*] **porket** ['pɔ:kit], **porkling** ['pɔ:-kliŋ], *s.* maialino da latte; porchetta.

porky ['pɔ:ki], *ag.* di, simile a porco.

pornographic [,pɔ:nə'græfik], *ag.* pornografico.

pornography [pɔ:'nɔgrəfi], *s.* pornografia.

porosity [pɔ:'rɔsiti], *s.* (*fis.*) porosità.

porous ['pɔ:rəs], *ag.* (*fis.*) poroso; permeabile.

porousness ['pɔ:rəsnis], *s.* (*fis.*) porosità.

porphyrite ['pɔ:firait], *s.* (*min.*) porfirite.

porphyritic [,pɔ:fi'ritik], *ag.* (*min.*) porfirico.

Porphyrius [pɔ:'firiəs], *no.pr.m.* (*st. fil.*) Porfirio.

porphyry ['pɔ:firi], *s.* (*min.*) porfido.

porpoise ['pɔ:pəs], *s.* (*zool.*) porco marino, marsovino, focena.

porraceous [pɔ'reifəs], *ag.* porraceo, verde porro.

porrect [pɔ'rekt], *ag.* proteso.

to porrect, *v.t.* **1.** stendere orizzontalmente (parte del corpo) **2.** (*dir. eccl.*) presentare (un documento).

porridge ['pɔridʒ], *s.* « porridge » (pappa di fiocchi d'avena, o preparata con farina di altri cereali) ‖ *keep your breath to cool your* —, impicciati degli affari tuoi, non so che farmene dei tuoi consigli.

porringer ['pɔrindʒə*], *s.* scodella, ciotola per « porridge ».

Porsena ['pɔ:sinə], *no.pr.m.* (*st.*) Porsenna.

port[1] [pɔ:t], *s.* porto (anche *fig.*); scalo: — *of call*, approdo, scalo; — *of loading, discharge*, porto di carico, scarico; — *of registry*, porto di immatricolazione ☆ — -*admiral*, comandante di porto; — -*captain*, capitano di porto; — -*charges* (o — -*dues*), tasse portuali ‖ *free* —, porto franco; *naval* —, porto militare.

port[2], *s.* **1.** (*scoz.*) porta (di città) fortificata **2.** (*mec.*) apertura, foro **3.** (*mar.*) — (-*hole*), portello, oblò ☆ — -*side*, (*mar.*) babordo.

to port[2], *v.t.i.* (*mar.*) girare (il timone) a babordo, poggiare a sinistra.

port[3], *s.* **1.** portamento; andatura **2.** (*mil.*) posizione che si assume nel portare le armi ad armacollo.

to port[3], *v.t.* (*mil.*) portare (le armi) ad armacollo ‖ *port arms!*, portat'arm!.

port[4], *s.* porto (vino rosso del Portogallo) ☆ — -*wine mark*, voglia di vino (macchia congenita).

portability [,pɔ:tə'biliti], *s.* l'essere portatile.

portable ['pɔ:təbl], *ag.* **1.** portatile: — *radio*, radio portatile; — *typewriter*, macchina per scrivere portatile **2.** (*arc.*) sopportabile.

portage ['pɔ:tidʒ], *s.* **1.** trasporto ‖ *mariner's* —, spazio concesso a bordo a un marinaio (che poteva darlo a nolo) in luogo di salario non corrisposto **2.** trasporto a via terra di imbarcazioni, merci da un corso navigabile ad un altro **3.** spese di trasporto, porto.

to portage, *v.t.* trasportare (barche, merci) via terra da un corso navigabile ad un altro.

portal ['pɔ:tl], *ag.* (*anat.*) relativo alla vena porta ‖ *s.* portale; entrata ☆ — *vein*, vena porta.

portamento [,pɔ:tə'mentou], *s.* (*mus.*) portamento.

portative ['pɔ:tətiv], *ag.* atto a portare, sostenere.

portcullis [pɔ:t'kʌlis], *s.* saracinesca (di fortezza, castello).

to portcullis, *v.t.* sbarrare, chiudere con saracinesca.

Porte [pɔ:t], *s.* (*st.*) *the* (*Sublime* o *Ottoman*) —, la Sublime Porta (corte e governo del Sultano turco).

to portend [pɔ:'tend], *v.t.* **1.** presagire, preannunciare: *wind that portends a storm*, vento che preannuncia una tempesta **2.** (*rar.*) predire, pronosticare (di persona).

portent ['pɔ:tent], *s.* **1.** presagio, pronostico (specialmente cattivo) **2.** portento, prodigio.

portentous [pɔ:'tentəs], *ag.* **1.** funesto; sinistro **2.** portentoso, prodigioso **3.** (*scherz.*) solenne: — *silence*, silenzio solenne, pieno di attesa.

portentously [pɔ:'tentəsli], *av.* **1.** sinistramente **2.** portentosamente, prodigiosamente.

porter[1] ['pɔ:tə*], *s.* **1.** facchino **2.** (*metal.*) agitatore, mescolatore **3.** (*amer.*) inserviente di vagone letto ☆ — *'s knot*, cinghia da facchino.

porter[2], *s.* custode, portiere, portinaio ‖ — *'s lodge*, alloggio del custode, portineria.

porter[3], *s.* — (*'s ale*), birra scura ☆ — -*house*, (*amer.*) birreria; osteria; — -*house steak*, bistecca di manzo.

porterage ['pɔ:təridʒ], *s.* **1.** facchinaggio **2.** spese di facchinaggio.

portfire ['pɔ:t,faiə*], *s.* miccia.

portfolio [pɔ:t'fouljou], *pl.* **portfolios** [pɔ:t'fouljouz], *s.* **1.** cartella, busta (per carte, disegni, ecc.) **2.** (*amer.*) portafoglio (lista dei titoli in possesso di un istituto finanziario) **3.** portafoglio, dicastero: *Minister without* —, ministro senza portafoglio.

porthole ['pɔ:thoul], s. 1. (mar.) oblò; portello 2. (arch.) feritoia.

Portia ['pɔ:ʃjə], no.pr.f. Porzia.

portico ['pɔ:tikou], pl. **porticos, porticoes** ['pɔ:tikouz], s. portico; colonnato.

portiere [pɔ:'tjɛə*], s. portiera, tenda pesante.

portion ['pɔ:ʃən], s. 1. parte; porzione; razione 2. dote; parte di eredità 3. destino, fato: suffering is our — here below, il nostro destino quaggiù è di soffrire.

to **portion**, v.t. 1. to — (out), dividere, ripartire, distribuire 2. assegnare: to — land to s.o., assegnare della terra a qlcu.

portionless ['pɔ:ʃənlis], ag. senza dote.

portliness ['pɔ:tlinis], s. 1. corpulenza 2. maestosità; prestanza.

portly ['pɔ:tli], ag. 1. corpulento; grosso 2. dignitoso; maestoso; imponente.

portmanteau [pɔ:t'mæntou], **portmanteaux** [pɔ:t'mæntouz], s. baule armadio ☆ — word, parola macedonia (parola che riunisce il senso di due vocaboli; p. e. brunch, composta da breakfast e lunch, colazione del mattino consumata a mezzogiorno; smog, composta da smoke e fog, nebbia mista a fumo di città industriale).

portolano [ˌpɔ:tou'la:nou], s. (mar.) portolano.

portrait ['pɔ:trit], s. 1. ritratto: to sit for one's —, posare per un ritratto 2. fig. descrizione, ritratto ☆ — -gallery, galleria di ritratti; — -painter, ritrattista ‖ full-length —, ritratto a figura intera; half-length —, ritratto a mezzo busto.

portraitist ['pɔ:tritist], s. ritrattista.

portraiture ['pɔ:tritʃə*], s. 1. ritrattistica 2. ritratto; pittura; rappresentazione 3. fig. descrizione 4. coll. pitture, ritratti.

to **portray** [pɔ:'trei], v.t. 1. dipingere, ritrarre, fare il ritratto di 2. fig. descrivere; rappresentare: to — characters, rappresentare i caratteri.

portrayal [pɔ:'treiəl], s. 1. ritratto 2. fig. descrizione, rappresentazione.

portrayer [pɔ:'treiə*], s. 1. ritrattista, pittore 2. fig. descrittore: a faithful — of the manners of his time, un fedele descrittore dei costumi dei suoi tempi.

portreeve ['pɔ:t-ri:v], s. 1. (st. inglese) primo magistrato (di una città, distretto) 2. funzionario con carica inferiore al sindaco (in alcune città).

portress ['pɔ:tris], s. (rar.) portinaia; suora portinaia.

Portugal ['pɔ:tjugəl], no.pr. (geog.) Portogallo.

Portuguese [ˌpɔ:tju'gi:z], ag.s.c. portoghese ‖ s. lingua portoghese.

posaune [pə'zɔ:n], s. (mus.) trombone.

pose [pouz], s. 1. posa, atteggiamento (del corpo) 2. pose, affettazione: without —, senza pose, semplicemente 3. (domino) posa.

to **pose**[1], v.t.i. 1. esprimere (un'opinione); proporre (quesito, problema) 2. mettere in posa (modella, ecc.); posare, mettersi in posa (per ritratto); (fam.) atteggiarsi a: he posed as tired of amusements, si atteggiava a uomo sazio di divertimenti 3. (domino) porre il primo pezzo.

to **pose**[2], v.t. imbarazzare con quesito, problema.

Poseidon [pɔ'saidən], no.pr.m. (mit.) Poseidone.

poser ['pouzə*], s. quesito, domanda imbarazzante.

poseur [pou'zə:*], s. posatore, persona affettata.

posh [pɔʃ], ag. (fam.) elegante, di lusso.

posingly ['pouziŋli], av. con domande imbarazzanti.

to **posit** ['pɔzit], v.t. 1. enunciare un postulato; premettere 2. mettere, collocare in un posto.

position [pə'ziʃən], s. 1. posizione, posa (del corpo): to sit in a comfortable —, sedere in una posizione comoda 2. atteggiamento, punto di vista; asserzione: the senator's — on international affairs, l'atteggiamento del senatore verso le questioni internazionali 3. posto, posizione; condizione: in —, a posto; out of —, fuori posto; he is in a — to explain that, è in grado di spiegarlo; to determine a ship's —, (mar.) stabilire la po-

sizione di una nave 4. condizione, rango sociale: he is a person of —, è una persona altolocata 5. posizione, impiego, ufficio: he has a — in the Civil Service, ha un impiego statale 6. (mil.) posizione: the — was attacked, la posizione fu attaccata.

to **position**, v.t. 1. mettere in posizione 2. (mil.) piazzare 3. determinare la posizione di ‖ to — a plane on its arrival, far atterrare un aereo nel punto prestabilito.

positional [pə'ziʃənl], ag. di posizione.

positive ['pɔzətiv], ag. 1. preciso, definitivo, assoluto: he has — ideas, ha idee precise 2. convinto, certo; sicuro di sè: I am — of this, sono sicuro di quel che dico 3. (gram. arit. elett. foto.) positivo 4. (fam.) effettivo, reale: he is a — nuisance, è proprio un seccatore ‖ s. 1. realtà; cosa positiva 2. (gram.) (grado) positivo 3. (foto.) positiva.

positively ['pɔzətivli], av. 1. positivamente; con sicurezza; certamente 2. effettivamente, realmente.

positiveness ['pɔzətivnis], s. 1. positività 2. sicurezza, certezza 3. tono deciso, perentorio.

positivism ['pɔzitivizəm], s. (st. fil.) positivismo.

positivist ['pɔzitivist], s. (st. fil.) positivista.

positivistic [ˌpɔziti'vistik], ag. positivistico.

positron ['pɔzitron], s. (fis.) positrone.

posology [pou'sɔlədʒi], s. (med.) posologia.

posse ['pɔsi], s. corpo di uomini con autorità legale ☆ — comitatus, (dir.) gruppo di persone convocabili dallo sceriffo per far rispettare la legge in caso di disordini.

to **possess** [pə'zes], v.t. 1. possedere, essere possessore di, avere: that's all I —, questo è tutto quello che ho; to be possessed of a quality, a property, avere, possedere una qualità, una proprietà; to — oneself, dominarsi, esser padrone di se stesso 2. impadronirsi, appropriarsi: to — oneself of sthg., impadronirsi di qualcosa 3. ossessionare; dominare: possessed by (o with) an idea, ossessionato da un'idea; what possesses you?, che cosa ti prende?.

possessed [pə'zest], ag. indemoniato; invasato dal demonio.

possession [pə'zeʃən], s. 1. possesso: in — of, in possesso di; to come (o to enter) into — of, entrare in possesso di; to remain in — of the field, fig. rimanere padrone del campo; to take (o to get) — of, prender possesso di ‖ writ of —, (dir.) decreto di immissione in possesso ‖ — is nine points (o tenths) of the law, possedere una cosa è già quasi averla per diritto 2. pl. beni, possedimenti, ricchezze: my personal possessions, i miei beni personali.

possessive [pə'zesiv], ag. 1. (gram.) possessivo 2. possessivo, tendente al possesso: don't be so — with your husband, non essere tanto soffocante con tuo marito; this mother is very —, questa madre è molto gelosa ‖ s. (gram.) aggettivo, pronome, caso possessivo.

possessively [pə'zesivli], av. possessivamente.

possessiveness [pə'zesivnis], s. senso di possesso.

possessor [pə'zesə*], s. 1. possessore 2. (comm.) portatore (di cambiale).

possessory [pə'zesəri], ag. possessorio.

posset ['pɔsit], s. (st.) bevanda calda di latte cagliato con vino.

possibility [ˌpɔsə'biliti], s. 1. possibilità, eventualità: — of selling, possibilità di vendere; the — he may come is remote, l'eventualità che egli possa venire, è remota; to foresee all possibilities, prevedere tutte le eventualità 2. pl. possibilità di successo: the plan has possibilities, il progetto offre possibilità di successo.

possible ['pɔsəbl], ag. 1. possibile, eventuale: is it — that he knows nothing?, possibile che non sappia nulla?; she did her — to avoid it, fece tutto il possibile per evitarlo; that's quite —, ciò è certamente possibile; to insure against — accidetns, assicurare contro eventuali incidenti 2. (fam.) sopportabile, frequentabile (di persona): *they are quite — people*, sono persone frequentabili.

possibly ['posəbli], *av*. **1.** possibilmente: — *it is as you say*, forse è come dite; *if I can — do it*, se mi è possibile farlo **2.** (*in frasi negative*) assolutamente: *he cannot — do it*, non può assolutamente farlo.

possum ['posəm], *s*. (*aferesi di opossum*) opossum ‖ *to play* (o *to act*) —, (*fam.*) fingersi ammalato, morto.

post[1] [poust], *prep*. (*lat.*) dopo: — *bellum*, dopo la guerra civile negli Stati Uniti; — *meridiem* (*abbr.* p.m.), dopo pranzo; — *mortem*, dopo la morte ☆ — *-mortem examination*, autopsia; *fig*. riesame degli avvenimenti.

post[2], *s*. **1.** (*st.*) corriere, procaccia **2.** vettura postale **3.** posta, corrispondenza; servizio postale: *has the — come?*, è arrivata la posta? ‖ *return of —*, a giro di posta ‖ *today is no — day*, oggi la posta non arriva ‖ *when is the next — due?*, quando avrà luogo la prossima distribuzione della posta? **4.** posta, ufficio postale ☆ — *-bag*, sacco della corrispondenza; — *-boat*, battello postale; — *-box*, cassetta postale; — *-card*, (*abbr.* P. C.) cartolina postale; — *-chaise*, diligenza; — *-free* (o — *-paid*), (*comm.*) franco di porto; — *-horses*, cavalli da posta; — *-man*, postino, portalettere; — *-mark*, timbro postale; — *-master*, — *-mistress*, direttore, direttrice di ufficio postale; — *-office*, ufficio postale; — *-office box*, casella postale; — *office order*, vaglia postale; — *-office savings-bank*, cassa di risparmio postale; — *-parcel*, pacco postale.

to post[2], *v.t.i.* **1.** (*arc.*) viaggiare in diligenza, con cavalli da posta **2.** affrettarsi **3.** imbucare, impostare; inviare per posta: *will you — this letter for me, please?*, mi imbuchi questa lettera, per favore? **4.** (*comm.*) trascrivere, registrare sul libro mastro; aggiornare (i libri di contabilità) **5.** mettere al corrente: *he posted me* (*up*) *with the latest news*, mi mise al corrente delle ultime novità; *to keep s.o. posted* (*up*), tenere qlcu. al corrente **6.** *to — off*, **over**, ritardare, posporre.

post[2], *av*. **1.** (*st.*) con cavalli da posta **2.** velocemente, in fretta.

post[3], *s*. **1.** palo, pilastro; sostegno; puntello; montante; stipite ‖ *between you and me and the* (*door-*) —, (*fam.*) detto in gran segreto ‖ *she is as deaf as a —*, è sorda come una campana ‖ *to be tossed from pillar to —*, essere mandato da Erode a Pilato **2.** (*mar.*) dritto di poppa **3.** (*miner.*) gamba **4.** (*metal.*) carica di minerale ☆ *door-* —, stipite di porta; *lamp-* —, lampione; *railing —*, colonnetta della ringhiera; *sign-* —, indicatore stradale; *starting-* —, (*spor.*) punto di partenza; *winning-* —, (*spor.*) traguardo.

to post[3], *v.t.* **1.** affiggere, affissare: *to — a wall*, coprire un muro con affissi; *to — up a notice on the board*, esporre un avviso sull'albo ‖ — *no bills*, divieto d'affissione **2.** pubblicare, annunciare (mediante affissi) **3.** scrivere il nome di (un candidato) nella lista dei respinti (nelle università inglesi); (*mar.*) iscrivere il nome di (una nave) come dispersa.

post[4], *s*. **1.** (*mil.*) posto; postazione: *to be on —*, essere di sentinella **2.** *fig*. posto del dovere: *to remain at one's —*, rimanere al proprio posto **3.** ufficio, carica: *to take up a — as a secretary*, assumere la carica di segretario **4.** (*mar.*) carica di capitano ☆ *trading- —*, stazione commerciale.

to post[4], *v.t.* (*mil.*) postare; mettere al comando di: *to — a sentinel at the gate*, mettere una sentinella al cancello; *to be posted to a command*, essere nominato ad un comando.

postage ['poustidʒ], *s*. spese postali, tariffa postale ☆ — *paid*, porto pagato; — *stamp*, francobollo ‖ *additional —*, soprattassa postale.

postal ['poustəl], *ag*. postale ‖ *s*. (*fam. amer.*) cartolina postale ☆ — *order*, vaglia postale; — *union*, unione postale.

post-classical ['poust'klæsikəl], *ag*. post-classico.

post-communion ['poustkə'mju:njən], *s*. (*eccl.*) post-communio.

postdate ['poust'deit], *s*. data posteriore alla data effettiva.

to postdate, *v.t.* posdatare, datare con data posteriore: *to — a cheque, a letter*, posdatare un assegno, una lettera.

post-diluvian ['poustdai'lu:vjən], *ag*. postdiluviano.

poster[1] ['poustə*], *s*. cavallo (da posta).

poster[2], *s*. **1.** affisso, cartellone, manifesto **2.** attacchino.

poste-restante ['poust'resta:nt], *s*. fermo posta.

posterior [pos'tiəriə*], *ag*. posteriore ‖ *s. gener. pl.* **1.** posteri **2.** deretano.

posteriority [pos,tiəri'oriti], *s*. posteriorità.

posteriorly [pos'tiəriəli], *av*. posteriormente.

posterity [pos'teriti], *s*. posterità.

postern ['poustə:n], *s*. posterla; porta posteriore, segreta ☆ — *gate*, cancello posteriore.

postfix ['poustfiks], *s*. (*gram.*) suffisso.

to postfix [poust'fiks], *v.t.* (*gram.*) porre come suffisso.

post-glacial ['poust'gleisjəl], *ag*. (*geol.*) postglaciale.

post-graduate ['poust'grædjuit], *ag*. dopo il diploma, la laurea ‖ *s*. diplomato, laureato che frequenta corsi di perfezionamento ☆ — *courses*, corsi di perfezionamento per laureati, diplomati.

post-haste ['poust'heist], *av*. in gran fretta.

posthumous ['postjuməs], *ag*. postumo.

posthumously ['postjuməsli], *av*. dopo la morte: *the book was published —*, il libro fu pubblicato postumo.

postiche [pos'ti:ʃ], *ag*. posticcio, falso, artificiale ‖ *s*. **1.** aggiunta posticcia; capelli, baffi posticci **2.** ornamento superfluo o inadatto.

postignition ['poustig'niʃən], (*mec.*) postaccensione.

postil ['postil], *s*. postilla, glossa.

to postil, *pass.p.p.* **postilled** ['postild], *v.t.* postillare.

postil(l)ion [pos'tiljən], *s*. postiglione.

post-impressionism ['poust-im'preʃnizəm], *s*. (*pitt.*) post-impressionismo.

post-impressionist ['poust-im'preʃnist], *s*. (*pitt.*) post-impressionista.

posting[1] ['poustin], *s*. **1.** il viaggiare in diligenza, con cavalli da posta **2.** spedizione per posta **3.** (*comm.*) trascrizione sul libro mastro; aggiornamento (dei libri di contabilità).

posting[2], *s*. **1.** affissione **2.** pubblicazione, iscrizione.

postliminium ['poustli'minjəm], **postliminy** ['poust-'limini], *s*. (*st. dir.*) posliminio.

postlude ['poustlju:d], *s*. (*mus.*) postludio.

post-meridian ['poustmə'ridiən], *ag*. pomeridiano.

post-natal ['poust'neitl], *ag*. posteriore alla nascita.

post-nuptial ['poust'nʌpʃəl], *ag*. posteriore alle nozze.

post-obit ['poust'obit], *s*. (*dir.*) impegno formale preso da un futuro erede di pagare una somma al creditore dopo la morte del testatore.

postponable ['poust'pounəbl], *ag*. posponibile.

to postpone [poust'poun], *v.t.i.* **1.** (I) posporre, rimandare, differire, procrastinare **2.** tardare (di febbre periodica) **3.** subordinare, trattare da inferiore.

postponement [poust'pounmənt], *s*. rinvio, posposizione, differimento.

postponer [poust'pounə*], *s*. procrastinatore.

postposition ['poustpə'ziʃən], *s*. **1.** posposizione **2.** (*gram.*) particella enclitica.

postpositive [poust'pozitiv], *ag*. (*gram.*) enclitico ‖ *s*. (*gram.*) particella enclitica.

post-prandial ['poust'prændiəl], *ag*. (*spec. scherz.*) dopo un pranzo, un banchetto.

postscript ['pousskript], *s*. poscritto.

postulant ['postjulənt], *s.c.* (*spec. eccl.*) postulante.

postulate ['postjulit], *s*. postulato (anche *geom.*).

to postulate ['postjuleit], *v.t.i.* **1.** (*log. geom.*) porre come postulato 2. (*eccl.*) postulare 3. *to* — (*for*) *sthg.*, postulare, domandare, reclamare ql.co.

postulation [ˌpɔstjuˈleiʃən], *s.* **1.** (*log.*) postulato **2.** postulazione (anche *eccl.*).

postulator [ˈpɔstjuleitə*], *s.* **1.** postulante, sollecitatore **2.** (*eccl.*) postulatore.

posture [ˈpɔstʃə*], *s.* **1.** posizione, atteggiamento (di corpo); attitudine (di mente) **2.** posa (di modello) **3.** condizione, situazione (di affari, ecc.): *the present* — *of affairs*, l'attuale stato degli affari.

to **posture**, *v.t.i.* **1.** assumere una posizione; *fig.* assumere un atteggiamento, posare: *to* — *as a buffoon*, fare il buffone **2.** mettere (il modello) in posa.

post-war [ˈpoustˈwɔː*], *ag. attributivo* del dopoguerra: *the* — *period was tough on some people*, il dopoguerra fu duro per certe persone.

posy [ˈpouzi], *s.* **1.** mazzolino di fiori **2.** (*arc.*) motto inciso (su anello, coltello, ecc.).

pot[1] [pɔt], *s.* **1.** vaso; recipiente; barattolo; pentola; boccale ‖ *pots and pans*, batteria da cucina ‖ *the* — *calls the kettle black*, da che pulpito viene la predica ‖ *to go to* — —, (*pop.*) andare in rovina ‖ *to make the* — *boil*, lavorare per procurarsi il denaro necessario per vivere **2.** contenuto di pentola, recipiente, ecc. **3.** (*metal.*) crogiuolo metallico **4.** (*spor. fam.*) coppa; premio **5.** piccolo elmo (usato in cavalleria) **6.** (*fam.*) persona importante: *a big* —, un pezzo grosso **7.** (*fam.*) grossa somma di denaro: *a* — *of money*, un mucchio di soldi **8.** cavallo favorito (alle corse) ☆ — *-bellied*, panciuto; — *-belly*, pancione, persona obesa; — *-boiler*, lavoro intellettuale eseguito solo per denaro; chi fa tale lavoro: *that novel of mine was only a* — *-boiler*, scrissi quel romanzo solo per fare quattrini; — *-bound*, soffocato in vaso piccolo (di pianta); — *-boy*, — *-girl*, barista; — *-hat*, (*fam.*) cappello duro; — *-herbs*, ortaggi; — *-hole*, (*geol.*) marmitta; — *holer*, (*fam.*) speleologo; — *-hunter*, chi partecipa a gare sportive solo per collezionare coppe; cacciatore che spara senza scegliere la preda; — *-luck*, pasto alla buona: *come and take* — *-luck with us*, (*fam.*) vieni a mangiare un boccone con noi; — *-shot*, colpo sparato solo per procurarsi cibo: *to take a* — *-shot at sthg.*, *s.o.*, (*fam.*) tirare a vanvera contro ql.co., qlcu.; — *-still*, alambicco riscaldato su fiamma diretta; — *-valiant*, coraggioso perchè brillo ‖ *chamber-* —, vaso da notte; *chimney-* —, comignolo; *coffee-* —, caffettiera; *ink-* —, calamaio; *melting* —, (*metal.*) crogiuolo; *porous-* —, (*elett.*) vaso poroso; *tea-* —, teiera.

to **pot**[1], *pass.p.p.* **potted** [ˈpɔtid], *v.t.i.* **1.** conservare (in vaso, scatola) **2.** piantare (in vaso) **3.** uccidere (selvaggina) per procurarsi cibo; sparare **4.** (*biliardo*) far biglia.

pot[2], *s.* (*scoz.*) profonda cavità.

potable [ˈpoutəbl], *ag.* potabile; bevibile.

potables [ˈpoutəblz], *s.pl.* bibite.

potash [ˈpɔtæʃ], **potass** [pouˈtæs], *s.* (*chim.*) potassa.

potassic [pouˈtæsik], *ag.* (*chim.*) potassico.

potassium [pəˈtæsjəm], *s.* (*chim.*) potassio ☆ — *chlorate*, *nitrate*, clorato, nitrato di potassio.

potation [pouˈteiʃən], *s.* **1.** bevuta; sorso **2.** bevanda alcoolica.

potato [pəˈteitou], *pl.* **potatoes** [pəˈteitouz], *s.* patata ☆ — *-box* (o — *-trap*), (*sl.*) bocca; — *-chips*, patatine fritte; — *-flour*, fecola di patate ‖ *mashed potatoes*, purè di patate; *sweet potatoes*, patate americane.

poteen [poˈtiːn], *s.* whisky (irlandese) di contrabbando.

potence [ˈpoutəns], *s.* potenza, forza; abilità.

potency [ˈpoutənsi], *s.* **1.** potenza; autorità **2.** efficacia **3.** potenzialità.

potent[1] [ˈpoutənt], *ag.* **1.** (*poet.*) potente, forte; autorevole (di persona) **2.** efficace: *a* — *argument*, un argomento efficace; *a* — *drug*, una droga potente.

potent[2], *s.* (*arald.*) potenza.

potentate [ˈpoutənteit], *s.* potentato, sovrano, dominatore.

potential [pəˈtenʃəl], *ag.* **1.** potenziale, latente: — *criminals*, criminali in potenza; *a* — *danger*, un pericolo latente **2.** (*gram. elett.*) potenziale ‖ *s.* **1.** (*gram.*) modo potenziale **2.** (*elett.*) potenziale **3.** rendimento: *it reached its highest* —, raggiunse il suo massimo rendimento ☆ — *curve*, (*elett.*) curva del potenziale; — *drop*, (*elett.*) caduta di potenziale.

potentiality [pəˌtenʃiˈæliti], *s.* potenzialità.

to **potentialize** [pəˈtenʃəlaiz], *v.t.* convertire in energia potenziale.

potentially [pəˈtenʃəli], *av.* potenzialmente.

to **potentiate** [pouˈtenʃieit], *v.t.* **1.** potenziare **2.** rendere possibile.

potentilla [ˌpoutənˈtilə], *s.* (*bot.*) rosacea.

potentiometer [pouˌtenʃiˈomitə*], *s.* (*elett.*) potenziometro.

potently [ˈpoutəntli], *av.* potentemente.

potheen [poˈθiːn], *V.* **poteen.**

pother [ˈpɔðə*], *s.* **1.** polverone; fumo soffocante; nube di polvere **2.** chiasso, rumore, tumulto, agitazione: *all this* — *about nothing*, tante storie per niente; *to be in a* —, essere in agitazione; *to make* (o *to raise*) *a* —, fare un gran chiasso, far storie.

to **pother**, *v.t.i.* **1.** infastidire, dar noia **2.** far baccano, far confusione; far storie.

pothouse [ˈpɔthaus], *s.* birreria ‖ — *manners*, modi volgari.

potion [ˈpouʃən], *s.* (*med.*) pozione.

Potiphar [ˈpotifə*], *no.pr.m.* (*Bibbia*) Putifarre.

pot-pourri [pouˈpuri(ː)], *s.* (*mus. lett.*) «pot-pourri», mescolanza; scelta, selezione.

pottage [ˈpotidʒ], *s.* (*arc.*) minestra: *Esau sold his right of primogeniture for a mess of* —, Esaù vendette la sua primogenitura per un piatto di lenticchie.

potted [ˈpotid], *ag.* conservato (di cibo) ☆ — *foods*, derrate in conserva; — *meat*, carne conservata.

potter[1] [ˈpotə*], *s.* vasaio ☆ — *'s wheel*, tornio da vasaio.

potter[2], *s.* **1.** azione senza importanza **2.** (*scoz.*) chiacchiere.

to **potter**[2], *v.t.i.* **1.** lavoricchiare; gingillarsi **2.** *to* — *about*, gironzolare, girellare **3.** *to* — *away* (*one's time*), perdere (il proprio tempo) ciondolando, bighellonare.

pottery [ˈpotəri], *s.* **1.** terraglie, stoviglie **2.** arte della ceramica **3.** luogo dove si fabbricano terraglie ‖ *the Potteries*, distretto dello Staffordshire (dove si fabbricano ceramiche).

potting [ˈpotiŋ], *s.* il mettere in vasi (conserve, piante).

pottle [ˈpotl], *s.* (*arc.*) **1.** «pottle» (misura di capacità = l. 2,272) **2.** cestino per fragole.

potty [ˈpoti], *ag.* (*sl.*) **1.** insignificante; poco importante **2.** facile, semplice **3.** mezzo pazzo; svanito; fissato.

pouch [pautʃ], *s.* **1.** tasca, borsa **2.** (*arc.*) borsellino **3.** (*mil.*) tascapane, giberna **4.** (*zool.*) marsupio **5.** (*bot.*) baccello ☆ *tobacco-* —, borsa da tabacco.

to **pouch**, *v.t.i.* **1.** intascare, mettere in tasca **2.** gonfiare: *the monkey pouched its cheeks*, la scimmia gonfiò le gote **3.** drappeggiare (vestito); formare un drappeggio (di vestito) **4.** (*sl.*) dare la mancia a.

pouched [pautʃt], *ag.* che ha borse.

pouchy [ˈpautʃi], *ag.* a forma di borsa, di tasca.

pouf(fe) [puːf], *s.* **1.** sgabello imbottito (da salotto) **2.** acconciatura di capelli **3.** cuscinetto per dar rilievo ai fianchi.

poulp(e) [puːlp], *s.* (*zool.*) polipo.

poult [poult], *s.* giovane gallinaceo (fagianotto, pollastrello, ecc.).

poult-de-soie [ˌpuːdəˈswɑː], *s.* «poult-de-soie» (tipo di seta pesante).

poulterer [ˈpoultərə*], *s.* pollivendolo.

poultice [ˈpoultis], *s.* impiastro, cataplasma.

to **poultice**, *v.t.* applicare un impiastro a.

poultry [ˈpoultri], *s.* pollame; gallinacei domestici ☆ — *-farm*, allevamento di polli; — *-pen*, pollaio; — *-yard*, cortile di pollaio.

pounce[1] [pauns], *s.* artiglio (anche *fig.*).

pounce², *s.* balzo; lo scagliarsi (su preda, vittima, ecc.) ‖ *on the —,* in agguato.

to pounce², *v.t.i.* **1.** avventarsi per afferrare **2.** assalire, piombare improvvisamente: *he pounced upon his prey,* piombò sulla sua preda ‖ *to — upon a mistake,* cogliere al volo un errore **3.** entrare improvvisamente: *they pounced into the room,* piombarono nella stanza.

pounce³, *s.* polvere di sandracca, di pomice, ecc.

to pounce³, *v.t.* **1.** lisciare con polvere di pomice, ecc. **2.** trasportare, ricalcare (un disegno) con polvere di sandracca, ecc. **3.** *(arc.)* spruzzare, cospargere di piccole macchie.

pound¹ [paund], *s.* **1.** *(abbr. sing.* lb., *pl.* lb., lbs.) *(avoirdupois)* —, libbra (misura di peso avoirdupois = g. 453,6); *(troy)* —, libbra (misura di peso troy = g. 373,248) **2.** — *(sterling) (abbr.* £), lira sterlina (equivalente a 20 scellini): *five pounds,* cinque sterline ‖ *penny wise and — -foolish,* taccagno nelle piccole spese e prodigo nelle grandi **3.** lira turca ed egiziana ☆ — *-cake,* dolce contenente quantità uguali dei principali ingredienti.

to pound¹, *v.i.* controllare il peso delle monete pesandone quante ne occorrono per formare una libbra.

pound², *s.* **1.** chiuso, recinto per animali dispersi **2.** *fig.* recinto; prigione **3.** camera della morte (ultimo scomparto della rete da pesca) **4.** bacino, serbatoio **5.** *(caccia)* posizione difficile ☆ — *-lock, (idraulica)* chiusa.

to pound², *v.t.* **1.** chiudere in un recinto (animali) **2.** *fig.* imprigionare, rinchiudere **3.** *to get pounded, (caccia)* mettersi in una posizione difficile.

pound³, *s.* **1.** torchio da sidro **2.** botta, colpo; tonfo.

to pound³, *v.t.i.* **1.** fare a pezzi, polverizzare **2.** colpire, battere, pestare: *who is pounding (on) the piano?,* chi sta pestando sul piano? **3.** rollare (di nave, ecc.) **4.** correre, camminare pesantemente, a stento; aprirsi faticosamente una strada ‖ *they pounded along,* continuarono il loro difficile cammino **5.** *to — at, away, on (sthg.),* colpire duramente.

poundage¹ ['paundidʒ], *s.* **1.** *(st.)* tassa devoluta alla Corona su ogni sterlina per transazione in denaro **2.** commissione, percentuale **3.** dividendo **4.** prezzo per libbra **5.** scommesse eccessivamente alte.

poundage², *s.* **1.** il tenere il bestiame in un recinto **2.** tassa per tenere il bestiame in un recinto.

pounder¹ ['paundə*], *s.* oggetto che pesa una libbra ☆ *thirty- —, (artigl.)* pezzo da trenta (che lancia proiettili da trenta libbre); *thousand- —,* persona con mille sterline di entrata; banconota da mille sterline.

pounder², *s.* **1.** pestello, mortaio **2.** persona che pesta.

pour [po:*], *s.* **1.** acquazzone, scroscio d'acqua, diluvio **2.** *(metal.)* colata (di metallo fuso).

to pour, *v.t.i.* **1.** versare; riversare: *— the tea,* versa il tè; *the sunlight pours through the window,* il sole entra a fiotti dalla finestra; *this river pours itself into the sea,* questo fiume si versa nel mare ‖ *people poured into the hall,* la folla si riversò nella sala ‖ *to — cold water, fig.* scoraggiare ‖ *to — oil upon troubled waters, fig.* placare le acque **2.** scrosciare (della pioggia) ‖ *it never rains but it pours,* o troppo o niente; le disgrazie non vengono mai sole **3.** *(metal.)* colare: *to — the metal,* colare il metallo **4.** *to — down,* diluviare: *the rain poured down,* pioveva a dirotto **5.** *to — forth,* riversare, esprimere: *— forth your wishes, (fam.)* esprimi i tuoi desideri **6.** *to — in,* entrare a fiotti, arrivare in massa: *letters poured in from everywhere,* giungevano lettere in gran numero da ogni parte **7.** *to — out,* versare; elargire; scorrere, riversarsi fuori: *— me one more glass,* versami un altro bicchiere; *people poured out,* la gente si riversò fuori; *she poured out gifts,* elargì doni.

pourboire ['puəbwa:*], *s.* « pourboire », mancia.

pourparler [puə'pɑ:lei], *s.* « pourparler », trattative, accordi preliminari.

pourpoint ['puəpoint], *s. (st.)* farsetto imbottito.

poussette [pu:'set], *s.* danza rustica (a girotondo).

pout¹ [paut], *s.* broncio ‖ *in the pouts,* col broncio.

to pout¹, *v.t.i.* sporgere le labbra; fare il broncio.

pout², *s.* nome di vari tipi di pesci (gado, merlango, anguilla, ecc.).

pouter ['pautə*], *s.* **1.** musone; chi fa, tiene il broncio **2.** *(ornit.)* piccione gozzuto.

pouting ['pautiŋ], *s.* broncio, il fare il broncio.

poutingly ['pautiŋli], *av.* col broncio.

poverty ['povəti], *s.* **1.** povertà; miseria **2.** meschinità, inferiorità: *the — of his style, of his spirit,* la meschinità del suo stile, del suo spirito ☆ — *-stricken,* caduto in miseria; d'aspetto miserabile.

powder¹ ['paudə*], *s.* **1.** polvere: *to reduce sthg. to —,* ridurre ql.co. in polvere; *fig.* annientare ‖ *it is not worth — and shot, (fam.)* non ne vale la pena ‖ *to keep one's — dry,* essere pronto ad ogni emergenza **2.** *(farm.)* polvere, polverina ☆ — *-box,* scatola per cipria; — *-flask,* fiasca contenente polvere da sparo; — *-magazine,* polveriera; santabarbara; — *-mill,* polverificio; — *-monkey, (st.)* ragazzo incaricato di portare la polvere da sparo dalla santabarbara al cannone; — *-puff,* piumino per la cipria; — *-room, (mar.)* santabarbara ‖ *baking- —,* lievito artificiale; *face- —,* cipria; *tooth- —,* dentifricio in polvere.

to powder¹, *v.t.i.* **1.** polverizzare, polverizzarsi; ridurre, andare in polvere: *some salts — easily,* alcuni sali si polverizzano facilmente **2.** incipriare, incipriarsi: *a powdered face,* un viso incipriato; *to — one's nose* (o *oneself),* incipriarsi **3.** spolverizzare, cospargere di polvere **4.** adornare (una superfice) con disegni, macchioline.

powder², *s. (rar. dial.)* impeto, forza: *with* (o *in) a —,* con impeto, con violenza.

powdered ['paudəd], *ag.* **1.** in polvere **2.** cosparso di polvere **3.** incipriato ☆ — *sugar,* zucchero in polvere.

powdery ['paudəri], *ag.* **1.** polverizzabile, friabile **2.** polveroso, coperto di polvere.

power ['pauə*], *s.* **1.** potenza, capacità, facoltà: *he is losing his powers,* sta perdendo le sue facoltà intellettive; *it is not within my — to help you,* non è in mio potere aiutarti **2.** forza, vigore: *the — of a blow,* il vigore di un colpo ‖ *more — to your elbow!,* forza!, buona fortuna! **3.** potere, autorità: — *of attorney,* procura; *have you no — over him?,* non hai ascendente su di lui?; *to do everything in one's —,* fare quanto sta in proprio potere **4.** *(pol.)* potere, governo ‖ *the powers above,* gli dei ‖ *with full powers,* con pieni poteri ‖ *the powers that be,* l'autorità costituita ‖ *to come into —,* giungere al potere **5.** *(pop.)* gran numero, gran quantità: *he does a — of work,* fa una gran quantità di lavoro; *it will do you a — of good,* ti farà un gran bene **6.** *(mec. elett.)* energia **7.** potenza, effetto, rendimento: *a machine of high —,* una macchina ad alto rendimento **8.** *(mat.)* potenza: *4 is the second — of 2,* 4 è 2 alla seconda potenza **9.** potere di ingrandimento (di lenti) ☆ — *-house,* centrale elettrica; — *-line,* linea elettrica; — *-loom,* telaio meccanico; — *-plant,* impianto di energia elettrica; — *-press,* torchio; — *-station,* centrale elettrica ‖ *candle- —,* intensità luminosa; *electric —,* energia elettrica; *heating —,* potenza calorifica; *horse- —, (abbr.* H. P.) cavallo vapore; *motive —* (o *moving —* o *propelling —),* forza motrice; *staying —,* resistenza; *water —,* energia idraulica.

to power, *v.t.* motorizzare, fornire di motore: *to — a boat,* motorizzare una barca.

powered ['pauəd], *ag.* che ha potenza ☆ *high- — engine,* motore di grande potenza.

powerful ['pauəful], *ag.* potente, poderoso, efficace.

powerfully ['pauəfuli], *av.* potentemente.

powerfulness ['pauəfulnis], *s.* potenza; efficacia.

powerless ['pauəlis], *ag.* impotente, fiacco; inefficace.

powerlessly ['pauəlisli], *av.* fiaccamente, debolmente; in modo inefficace.

powerlessness ['pauəlisnis], *s.* impotenza; inefficacia.

pow-wow ['pauwau], *s.* **1.** stregone (presso i pellirosse) **2.** cerimonia dei pellirosse (con riti magici),

riunione (presso i pellirosse) **3.** (*mil.*) riunione di ufficiali durante le manovre militari **4.** (*amer.*) conferenza,
discussione.

to pow-wow, *v.t.i.* **1.** esercitare la medicina, la magia
(presso i pellirosse) **2.** tenere una cerimonia sacra (presso
i pellirosse) **3.** curare con arti magiche **4.** (*amer.*) tenere una discussione, riunione.

pox [pɔks], *s.* (*patol.*) sifilide ☆ *chickon-* —, varicella; *small-* —, vaiuolo.

pozzolana [ˌpɔtsouˈlɑːnə], **pozzuolana** [ˌpɔtswouˈ
ˈlɑːnə], *s.* (*min.*) pozzolana.

praam [prɑːm], *s.* (*mar.*) prania.

practic [ˈpræktik], *ag.* (*arc.*) pratico ‖ *s.* (*dir.*) pratica.

practicability [ˌpræktikəˈbiliti], *s.* praticabilità.

practicable [ˈpræktikəbl], *ag.* praticabile; fattibile.

practicableness [ˈpræktikəblnis], *s.* praticabilità.

practicably [ˈpræktikəbli], *av.* in modo praticabile, fattibile.

practical [ˈpræktikəl], *ag.* **1.** pratico; fattibile; positivo: *useless for — purposes*, inutilizzabile in pratica;
he overcame the — difficulties of a scheme, superò le
difficoltà pratiche di un progetto **2.** reale; virtuale:
the — owner, il vero proprietario **3.** pratico, esperto,
abile ‖ — *joke*, tiro birbone.

practically [ˈpræktikəli], *av.* **1.** praticamente **2.** virtualmente; quasi: *we are — there*, siamo quasi arrivati.

practicalness [ˈpræktikəlnis], *s.* praticità; senso pratico.

practice [ˈpræktis], *s.* **1.** pratica: *in* —, in pratica;
to put into —, mettere in pratica **2.** abitudine, regola,
norma: *the — of closing at 2 p.m.*, l'abitudine di chiudere alle 14; *to make a — of sthg.*, fare una regola di
ql.co. **3.** esercizio; (*spor.*) allenamento; (*mil.*) esercizio
di tiro; (*mus.*) esercizio, studio: — *makes perfect*, con
l'esercizio si raggiunge la perfezione; *in*, *out of* —,
in, fuori esercizio; *this is good* —, questo è un buon
esercizio **4.** esercizio di una professione: *Dr. Brown has
retired from* —, il Dr. Brown si è ritirato dalla professione; **5.** *coll.* clienti, clientela (di medico, avvocato):
has he got a large —?, ha una vasta clientela? **6.** (*pl.
arc.*) intrighi, raggiri, trucchi.

practician [prækˈtiʃən], *s.* **1.** *V.* **practitioner 2.** persona pratica, esperta (in un lavoro).

to practise [ˈpræktis], *v.t.i.* **1.** praticare, mettere in
pratica: — *what you preach*, metti in pratica ciò che
predichi: *they — the same method*, usano lo stesso metodo **2.** (I) esercitare, esercitarsi: *she must — English an
hour a day*, deve esercitarsi in inglese un'ora al
giorno **3.** professare, esercitare (una professione): *to —
medicine*, fare il medico **4.** (*arc.*) ordire, complottare:
to — to deceive s.o., cospirare allo scopo di ingannare
qlcu. **5.** — *upon* (*s.o.*, *sthg.*), approfittare di: *to —
upon s.o.'s inexperience*, approfittare dell'inesperienza
di qlcu.

practised [ˈpræktist], *ag.* esperto; abile; perito.

practiser [ˈpræktisə*], *s.* praticante: *he is a — of
what he preaches*, mette in pratica quello che predica.

practising [ˈpræktisiŋ], *ag.* **1.** che esercita la professione **2.** (*relig.*) praticante ☆ — *barrister*, avvocato
che esercita la professione.

practitioner [prækˈtiʃnə*], *s.* professionista (specialmente medico) ☆ *general* —, medico generico.

praenomen [priːˈnoumen], *s.* (*st. romana*) prenome.

praepostor [priːˈpɔstə*], *s.* prefetto, monitore (nei
collegi).

praetor [ˈpriːtə*], *s.* (*st. romana*) pretore.

praetorial [priː(ː)ˈtɔːriəl], *ag.* (*st. romana*) pretoriale.

praetorian [priː(ː)ˈtɔːriən], *ag.s.* (*st.romana*) pretoriano.

pragmatic [prægˈmætik], *ag.* **1.** (*st.*) prammatico ‖
the Pragmatic Sanction, (*st.*) la Prammatica Sanzio-
ne **2.** (*fil.*) prammatico **3.** attivo, pratico **4.** impiccione,
importuno **5.** presuntuoso **6.** dogmatico ‖ *s.* **1.** prammatica sanzione **2.** persona attiva **3.** persona importuna, piena di sè.

pragmatical [prægˈmætikəl], *ag.* **1.** (*fil.*) pramma-

tico **2.** (*rar.*) esperto; astuto **3.** impiccione, importuno **4.** presuntuoso **5.** intransigente, dogmatico.

pragmatically [prægˈmætikəli], *av.* **1.** (*fil.*) in modo
prammatico **2.** importunamente **3.** dogmaticamente.

pragmaticalness [prægˈmætikəlnis], *s.* **1.** praticità **2.** presunzione.

pragmatism [ˈprægmətizəm], *s.* **1.** (*fil.*) pragma-
tismo **2.** pedanteria **3.** inopportunità **4.** praticità.

pragmatist [ˈprægmətist], *s.* (*fil.*) pragmatista.

pragmatistic [ˌprægməˈtistik], *ag.* prammatistico.

to pragmatize [ˈprægmətaiz], *v.t.* rappresentare come
reale (miti, ecc.).

Prairial [ˌpreiriˈɑːl], *s.* (*st. francese*) pratile.

prairie [ˈprɛəri], *s.* prateria (specialmente nel Nord
America) ☆ — *-chicken* (o — *-hen*), (*ornit.*) tetraone;
— *-dog*, (*zool.*) cinomio, cane delle praterie; — *-oyster*,
(*fam.*) uovo all'ostrica; — *-schooner*, (*amer.*) carro dei
pionieri.

praise [preiz], *s.* lode; elogio; encomio; approvazione; glorificazione: *I'll sing a song in thy* —, (*poet.*)
canterò un inno in tua lode; *this is beyond all* —, ciò
supera ogni elogio ‖ — *be to God!*, Dio sia lodato!.

to praise, *v.t.* **1.** lodare; elogiare: *they love being
praised*, sono molto sensibili alle lodi; *to — oneself*, lo-
darsi **2.** portare alle stelle; glorificare.

praiseful [ˈpreizful], *ag.* **1.** laudativo **2.** laudatore.

praiser [ˈpreizə*], *s.c.* laudatore, laudatrice ‖ *s.* panegirista.

praiseworthily [ˈpreizˌwəːðili], *av.* lodevolmente.

praiseworthiness [ˈpreizˌwəːðinis], *s.* lodevolezza.

praiseworthy [ˈpreizˌwəːði], *ag.* lodevole.

praline [ˈprɑːliːn], *s.* mandorla caramellata.

pram[1] [præm], *s.* **1.** (*fam. abbr.* di *perambulator*) carrozzina per bambini **2.** (*sl.*) carretto del lattaio.

pram[2] [prɑːm], *s.* (*mar.*) prania.

to pram-push [ˈpræm-puʃ], *v.i.* (*fam.*) spingere la
carrozzina di un bambino.

prance [prɑːns], *s.* impennata; salto; balzo.

to prance, *v.t.i.* **1.** impennarsi (dei cavalli) **2.** far impennare (un cavallo) **3.** *fig.* camminare pavoneggiandosi.

prancing [ˈprɑːnsiŋ], *ag.* che si impenna ‖ *s.* impennata.

prandial [ˈprændiəl], *ag.* (*scherz.*) di, del pranzo.

prang [præŋ], *s.* (*sl. aer.*) bombardamento aereo.

to prang, *v.t.* (*sl. aer.*) distruggere un obiettivo,
bombardare pesantemente.

prank[1] [præŋk], *s.* **1.** monelleria, birichinata; tiro,
scherzo, burla: *he played one of his pranks*, ne ha fatta
una delle sue; *to play a — on s.o.*, fare uno scherzo,
un tiro a qlcu.; *to play all sorts of pranks*, farne di
tutti i colori **2.** movimento strano, impennata (di animale) **3.** funzionamento irregolare (di macchina).

to prank[1], *v.t.i.* **1.** ornare, ornarsi; vestire in modo
vistoso **2.** fare pompa di sè; mettersi in mostra.

to prank[2], (*dial.*) *V.* **to prance.**

prankish [ˈpræŋkiʃ] *ag.* birichino, burlone.

prankishness [ˈpræŋkiʃnis], *s.* maliziosità.

prankster [ˈpræŋkstə*], *s.* burlone.

praseodymium [ˌpreiziəˈdimjəm], *s.* (*chim.*) praseodimio.

prate [preit], *s.* chiacchiera, ciancia; discorso inutile, ozioso.

to prate, *v.t.i.* chiacchierare, cianciare, pettegolare;
fare discorsi inutili, oziosi.

prater [ˈpreitə*], *s.c.* chiacchierone, chiacchierona.

prating [ˈpreitiŋ], *ag.* loquace, chiacchierone ‖ *s.*
chiacchierio.

pratique [ˈprætik], *s.* (*mar.*) pratica (permesso di
sbarco dopo la quarantena).

prattle [ˈprætl], *s.* **1.** balbettio, cinguettio (di bambini, ecc.) **2.** chiacchiera, ciancia.

to prattle, *v.t.i.* **1.** balbettare, cinguettare, cian-
gottare (di bambini, ecc.); mormorare (di acque) **2.** *fig.*
chiacchierare, cianciare; parlare in modo infantile.

prattler [ˈprætlə*], *s.c.* chiacchierone, chiacchierona.

prattling ['prætliŋ], *ag.* loquace ‖ *s.* **1.** balbettio, cinguettio (di bambini); mormorio (di acque) **2.** chiacchierio, ciarle (di donne).

prattlingly ['prætliŋli], *av.* loquacemente.

pravity ['præviti], *s.* **1.** (*rar.*) pravità, perversità **2.** deteriorazione (di cibo).

prawn [prɔːn], *s.* (*zool.*) palemone, gambero.

to prawn, *v.i.* pescare gamberi.

praxis ['præksis], *s.* **1.** prassi; pratica consueta **2.** (*gram.*) raccolta di esempi.

Praxiteles [præk'sitəliːz], *no.pr.m.* (*st.scult.*) Prassitele.

to pray [prei], *v.t.i.* **1.** pregare; supplicare, implorare: *let us —* (*to*) *God that He may help us*, preghiamo Dio, affinchè ci aiuti; *they prayed him for a boon*, gli chiesero un favore; *to — in aid of*, (*arc.*) in aiuto **2.** (*I*) *— (you)*, di grazia, per favore: *what is the use of that —?*, scusa, ma a [cosa serve?].

prayer[1] [preə*], *s.* **1.** preghiera: *to say one's prayers*, dir le preghiere ‖ *The Book of Common Prayer*, il rituale della Chiesa Anglicana ‖ *the Lord's-Prayer*, il Paternostro **2.** desiderio; petizione, supplica: *her — has been granted*, il suo desiderio è stato esaudito ☆ *-book*, libro di preghiere; *— -carpet* (o *— mat* o *— rug*), preghiera (tappeto) ‖ *evening —, morning —*, preghiera della sera, del mattino.

prayer[2] ['preiə*], *s.c.* **1.** fedele **2.** chi prega, chiede.

prayerful ['preəful], *ag.* pio, devoto.

prayerfulness ['preəfulnis], *s.* devozione.

prayerless ['preəlis], *ag.* **1.** senza preghiere **2.** non abituato a pregare.

preach [priːtʃ], *s.* (*fam.*) sermone, predica.

to preach, *v.t.i.* **1.** predicare; pronunciare un sermone; tenere un discorso: *to — the Gospel*, predicare il Vangelo; *to — a sermon*, fare una predica **2.** *fig.* ammonire, fare la predica: *don't — to him*, (*fam.*) non fargli la predica **3.** *to — down*, denigrare **4.** *to — up*, lodare, esaltare.

preacher ['priːtʃə*], *s.c.* predicatore, predicatrice ‖ *s.* (*eccl.*) pastore.

preachership ['priːtʃəʃip], *s.* ufficio di predicatore.

to preachify ['priːtʃifai], *v.i.* **1.** predicare in modo noioso **2.** fare la morale, tenere predicozzi.

preaching ['priːtʃiŋ], *s.* predicazione; predica, sermone.

preachingly ['priːtʃiŋli], *av.* in tono sentenzioso; da predicatore.

preachment ['priːtʃmənt], *s.* predica, sermone; (*fam.*) ramanzina.

preachy ['priːtʃi], *ag.* (*fam.*) incline a far prediche.

to preacquaint ['priːə'kweint], *v.t.* informare in precedenza, preavvisare.

pre-acquaintance ['priːə'kweintəns], *s.* informazione preventiva.

pre-adamic ['priːə'dæmik], *ag.* preadamitico.

pre-adamite ['priːæ'dæmait], *s.* preadamita.

to pre-admonish ['priːəd'mɔniʃ], *v.t.* preavvisare; preammonire.

pre-admonition ['priːˌædmə'niʃən], *s.* preavviso.

preamble [priː'æmbl], *s.* preambolo, preliminare.

to preamble, *v.i.* fare un preambolo.

to pre-announce ['priːə'nauns], *v.t.* preannunziare.

preannouncement ['priːə'naunsmənt], *s.* preannunzio.

to prearrange ['priːə'reindʒ], *v.t.* predisporre.

prearrangement ['priːə'reindʒmənt], *s.* predisposizione: *according to a —*, secondo quanto disposto in precedenza.

preassurance ['priːə'ʃuərəns], *s.* preassicurazione.

preaudience [priː'ɔːdjəns], *s.* (*dir.*) diritto di precedenza di parola (tra avvocati).

prebend ['prebənd], *s.* (*eccl.*) prebenda.

prebendal [pri'bendl], *ag.* (*eccl.*) di, relativo a prebenda ☆ *— stalls*, stalli dei canonici.

prebendary ['prebəndəri], *s.* (*eccl.*) prebendario (chi gode di una prebenda).

precarious [pri'kɛəriəs], *ag.* precario; incerto; rischioso: *the — life of a fisherman*, la vita rischiosa di un pescatore.

precariously [pri'kɛəriəsli], *av.* precariamente; rischiosamente.

precariousness [pri'kɛəriəsnis], *s.* precarietà.

precative ['prekətiv], *V.* **precatory.**

precatorily ['prekətərili], *av.* in forma di richiesta.

precatory ['prekətəri], *ag.* esprimente preghiera.

precaution [pri'kɔːʃən], *s.* precauzione: *to take precautions against sthg.*, *s.o.*, prendere precauzioni contro ql.co., qlcu. ☆ *air-raid precautions* (*A.R.P.*), misure di protezione antiaerea.

to precaution, *v.t.* (*arc.*) preavvertire; mettere in guardia.

precautional [pri'kɔːʃənl], *ag.* precauzionale.

precautionary [pri'kɔːʃnəri], *ag.* cautelativo, preventivo.

precautious [pri'kɔːʃəs], *ag.* che usa precauzioni, cautela.

to precede [pri(ː)'siːd], *v.t.i.* precedere; venire prima: *they will — forgiveness with punishment*, faranno precedere la punizione al perdono; *we went on, preceded by our guide*, andammo avanti preceduti dalla nostra guida.

precedence [pri(ː)'siːdəns], **precedency** [pri(ː)'siːdənsi], *s.* precedenza, priorità: *she yielded — to her sister*, ella cedette il passo a sua sorella; *they quarrelled about —*, litigarono per la precedenza; *to have, to take the — of s.o.*, avere, prendere la precedenza su qlcu.

precedent [pri'siːdənt], *ag.* (*rar.*) precedente ☆ *condition —*, condizione prima.

precedent ['presidənt], *s.* precedente: *without —*, senza precedenti; *to set a —*, creare un precedente.

precedented ['presidəntid], *ag.* che ha precedenti.

precedential [ˌpresi'denʃəl], *ag.* **1.** che costituisce precedente **2.** preliminare, antecedente.

precedently [pri'siːdəntli], *av.* precedentemente.

preceding [pri(ː)'siːdiŋ], *ag.* precedente: *the year preceding his election*, l'anno prima della sua elezione.

to precent [pri(ː)'sent], *v.t.i.* (*eccl.*) dirigere (il coro); fare da maestro del coro.

precentor [pri(ː)'sentə*], *s.* (*eccl.*) maestro del coro.

precept ['priːsept], *s.* **1.** precetto, massima: *no arts are without their precepts*, nessun'arte manca dei suoi precetti **2.** (*dir.*) mandato.

preceptive [pri'septiv], *ag.* istruttivo, didattico.

preceptor [pri'septə*], *s.* precettore; istitutore.

preceptorial [ˌpriːsep'tɔːriəl], *ag.* di precettore.

preceptorship [pri'septəʃip], *s.* ufficio di precettore.

preceptory [pri'septəri], *s.* **1.** comunità di Cavalieri Templari **2.** beni appartenenti ai Cavalieri Templari.

preceptress [pri'septris], *s.* governante; istitutrice.

precession [pri'seʃən], *s.* (*astr.*) precessione: *— of the equinoxes*, precessione degli equinozi.

prechristian [priː'kristjən], *ag.* precristiano.

precinct ['priːsiŋkt], *s.* **1.** luogo recinto: *the sacred —*, il sacro recinto **2.** *pl.* vicinanze **3.** confine, limite **4.** (*amer.*) suddivisione di città per scopi elettorali, per servizio di polizia.

preciosity [ˌpreʃi'ositi], *s.* preziosità, ricercatezza (di linguaggio).

precious ['preʃəs], *ag.* **1.** prezioso (anche *fig.*); costoso; ricercato: *a — opportunity*, un'occasione preziosa; *— words*, parole ricercate **2.** (*fam.*) perfetto, completo: *a — friend you've been!*, bell'amico che sei stato!; *you made a — mess of everything*, di tutta la faccenda ne faceste proprio un bel pasticcio ☆ *— metals*, metalli preziosi; *— stones*, pietre preziose.

precious, *av.* (*fam.*) molto, eccezionalmente: *it is — cold*, fa eccezionalmente freddo; *there is — little left of it*, ce n'è rimasto ben poco.

preciously ['preʃəsli], *av.* **1.** preziosamente **2.** con affettazione, ricercatezza **3.** (*fam.*) estremamente.

preciousness ['preʃəsnis], *s.* **1.** preziosità, pregio, valore **2.** ricercatezza, preziosismo.

precipice ['presipis], *s.* precipizio (anche *fig.*): *to fall over a —*, cadere in un precipizio.

precipitability [pri,sipitə'biliti], *s.* (*chim. fis.*) precipitabilità.

precipitable [pri'sipitəbl], *ag.* (*chim. fis.*) precipitabile.

precipitance [pri'sipitəns], **precipitancy** [pri'sipitənsi], *s.* **1.** precipitazione, fretta, premura **2.** avventatezza.

precipitant [pri'sipitənt], *ag.* (*arc.*) *V.* **precipitate** ‖ *s.* (*chim.*) precipitante.

precipitate [pri'sipitit], *ag.* **1.** precipitoso; affrettato **2.** sconsiderato, avventato ‖ *s.* (*chim.*) precipitato.

to **precipitate** [pri'sipiteit], *v.t.i.* **1.** precipitare, spingere (anche *fig.*): *to — a country into a conflict*, spingere un paese in un conflitto; *to — s.o. into despair*, (far) precipitare qlcu. nella disperazione **2.** precipitare, affrettare, accelerare: *to — s.o.'s ruin*, accelerare, precipitare la rovina di qlcu. **3.** (*chim. fis. metereologia*) precipitare.

precipitately [pri'sipititli], *av.* **1.** precipitosamente, a precipizio **2.** precipitatamente, avventatamente.

precipitation [pri,sipi'teiʃən], *s.* **1.** precipitazione **2.** avventatezza **3.** (*chim. fis. metereologia*) precipitazione.

precipitous [pri'sipitəs], *ag.* **1.** ripido, a picco, erto **2.** (*rar.*) precipitoso.

precipitously [pri'sipitəsli], *av.* **1.** a picco **2.** (*rar.*) precipitosamente, a precipizio.

precipitousness [pri'sipitəsnis], *s.* **1.** ripidezza, forte pendenza **2.** (*rar.*) precipitazione.

précis ['preisi:], *pl.* **precis** ['preisi:z], *s.* riassunto, sommario.

to **précis**, *v.t.* fare un riassunto, un sommario di.

precise [pri'sais], *ag.* **1.** preciso, esatto **2.** meticoloso, scrupoloso; pignolo.

precisely [pri'saisli], *av.* precisamente, esattamente ‖ *— (so)!*, proprio così!.

preciseness [pri'saisnis], *s.* **1.** precisione, esattezza **2.** meticolosità, scrupolosità.

precisian [pri'siʒən], *s.* rigorista (specialmente in materia religiosa); pedante.

precisianism [pri'siʒənizəm], *s.* rigorismo (specialmente in materia religiosa).

precision [pri'siʒən], *s.* **1.** precisione, esattezza **2.** meticolosità, scrupolosità ☆ *— instruments*, apparecchi di precisione.

precisionist [pri'siʒənist], *s.* purista, rigorista.

preclassical [pri:'klæsikəl], *ag.* preclassico.

to **preclude** [pri'klu:d], *v.t.* precludere, impedire; escludere; rendere impossibile: *it will — his career*, gli precluderà la carriera; *to — any doubt, I'm bound to say...*, per evitare ogni possibile dubbio, devo dire...; *to be precluded from doing sthg.*, essere nell'impossibilità di fare ql.co.; *to be precluded from an opportunity*, essere privati di un'occasione.

preclusion [pri'klu:ʒən], *s.* (*rar.*) ostacolo, impedimento.

preclusive [pri'klu:siv], *ag.* che preclude, impedisce, esclude.

precocious [pri'kouʃəs], *ag.* precoce.

precociousness [pri'kouʃəsnis], **precocity** [pri'kɔsiti], *s.* precocità.

precognition ['pri:kɔg'niʃən], *s.* **1.** precognizione, preconoscenza, prescienza **2.** (*scoz. dir.*) istruttoria (di un processo); interrogatorio preliminare (dei testimoni); deposizione (di un testimonio in istruttoria).

to **preconceive** ['pri:kən'si:v], *v.t.* **1.** pensare, concepire anticipatamente **2.** avere preconcetti su.

preconception ['pri:kən'sepʃən], *s.* preconcetto; pregiudizio.

to **preconcert** ['pri:kən'sə:t], *v.t.* predisporre, preordinare, prestabilire.

to **precondemn** ['pri:kən'dem], *v.t.* condannare anticipatamente.

preconization ['pri:kənai'zeiʃən], *s.* (*eccl.*) preconizzazione.

to **preconize** ['pri:kənaiz], *v.t.* **1.** preconizzare; proclamare, lodare pubblicamente **2.** (*eccl.*) preconizzare **3.** convocare.

preconsideration ['pri:kən,sidə'reiʃən], *s.* considerazione antecedente, preliminare.

pre-contract [pri:'kɔntrækt], *s.* contratto preesistente.

precursive [pri(:)'kə:siv], *ag.* precursore.

precursor [pri(:)'kə:sə*], *s.* precursore; predecessore.

precursory [pri(:)'kə:səri], *ag.* **1.** precursore **2.** introduttivo, preliminare.

predaceous, predacious [pri'deiʃəs], *ag.* rapace, predace.

predaceousness, predaciousness [pri'deiʃəsnis], **predacity** [pri'dæsiti], *s.* rapacità; istinto di rapina.

to **predate** [pri:'deit], *v.t.* **1.** predatare (lettera, assegno, ecc.) **2.** precedere (nel tempo).

predator ['predətə*], *s.* predatore; predone.

predatorily ['predətərili], *av.* in modo predatorio; rapacemente.

predatoriness ['predətərinis], *s.* rapacità.

predatory ['predətəri], *ag.* predatorio; rapace ☆ *a — animal*, un rapace; *— raid*, una razzia.

to **predecease** ['pri:di'si:s], *v.t.* premorire.

predecessor ['pri:disesə*], *s.* predecessore.

predella [pri'delə], *s.* predella.

predesignate [pri:'dezignit], *ag.* designato prima.

to **predesignate** [pri:'dezigneit], *v.t.* designare prima.

predesignation ['pri:,dezig'neiʃən], *s.* designazione fatta in precedenza.

predestinarian ['pri:(:),desti'nɛəriən], *ag.* (*teol.*) che riguarda la predestinazione ‖ *s.* **1.** (*st. relig.*) predestinaziano **2.** fatalista.

predestinarianism ['pri:(:),desti'nɛəriənizəm], *s.* (*teol.*) dottrina della predestinazione.

predestinate [pri:(:)'destinit], *ag.* predestinato.

to **predestinate** [pri:(:)'destineit], *v.t.* (*teol.*) predestinare.

predestination [pri:(:),desti'neiʃən], *s.* (*teol.*) predestinazione.

to **predestine** [pri:(:)'destin], *v.t.* preordinare; predestinare.

predetermination ['pri:di,tə:mi'neiʃən], *s.* **1.** predeterminazione **2.** (*teol.*) predestinazione.

to **predetermine** ['pri:di'tə:min], *v.t.* predeterminare, preordinare.

predial ['pri:diəl], *ag.* (*dir.*) prediale ‖ *s.* (*arc.*) servo della gleba.

predicability [,predikə'biliti], *s.* (*fil.*) l'essere predicabile.

predicable ['predikəbl], *ag.s.* (*fil.*) predicabile.

predicament [pri'dikəmənt], *s.* **1.** *gener. pl.* (*fil.*) predicamento, categoria (aristotelica) **2.** stato, condizione, situazione (generalmente difficile): *he was in a fine —!*, (*iron.*) era in un bell'impiccio!.

predicant ['predikənt], *ag.* predicante ‖ *s.* predicatore.

predicate ['predikit], *ag.s.* (*log. gram.*) predicato.

to **predicate** ['predikeit], *v.t.* **1.** (*fil.*) predicare **2.** affermare, asserire: *to — the goodness of sthg.* (o *that sthg. is good*), affermare che ql.co. è buono.

predication [,predi'keiʃən], *s.* **1.** (*arc.*) predicazione **2.** (*log.*) affermazione.

predicative [pri'dikətiv], *ag.* **1.** (*log. gram.*) predicativo **2.** affermativo.

predicatory ['predikeitəri], *ag.* predicatorio.

to **predict** [pri'dikt], *v.t.* predire; profetizzare.

predictable [pri'diktəbl], *ag.* che si può predire.

prediction [pri'dikʃən], *s.* predizione; profezia.

predictive [pri'diktiv], *ag.* che predice; profetico.

predictively [pri'diktivli], *av.* profeticamente.

predictor [pri'diktə*], *s.* **1.** indovino; profeta **2.** (*aer.*) calcolatore, previsore.

to **predigest** ['pri:di'dʒest], *v.t.* (*med.*) predigerire.

predigestion ['pri:di'dʒestʃən], *s.* (*med.*) predigestione.
predilection [ˌpri:di'lekʃən], *s.* predilezione.
to **predispose** ['pri:dis'pouz], *v.t.* predisporre.
predisposition ['pri:ˌdispə'ziʃən], *s.* predisposizione.
predominance [pri'dominəns], **predominancy** [pri'dominənsi], *s.* predominanza, predominio; preponderanza.
predominant [pri'dominənt], *ag.* predominante.
predominantly [pri'dominəntli], *av.* in modo predominante; con preponderanza.
to **predominate** [pri'domineit], *v.i.* predominare; preponderare: *to — over s.o.*, avere predominio su qlcu.
predomination [priˌdomi'neiʃən], *s.* predominio.
to **pree** [pri:], *v.t.* (*scoz.*) assaggiare, provare ‖ *to — the mouth of s.o.*, baciare qlcu.
pre-election ['pri:i'lekʃən], *ag.attributivo* antecedente alle elezioni: — *promises*, promesse di candidatura.
pre-eminence [pri(:)'eminəns], *s.* preminenza.
pre-eminent [pri(:)'eminənt], *ag.* preminente.
pre-eminently [pri(:)'eminəntli], *av.* preminentemente.
to **pre-empt** [pri(:)'empt], *v.t.i.* 1. (*dir.*) acquistare per diritto di prelazione; (*amer.*) stabilirsi su (terreno) per acquistare diritto di prelazione 2. appropriarsi di 3. (*bridge*) fare un'apertura preventiva.
pre-emption [pri(:)'empʃən], *s.* 1. (*dir.*) prelazione, priorità 2. (*fam.*) appropriazione ☆ — *right*, diritto di prelazione.
pre-emptive [pri(:)'emptiv], *ag.* (*dir.*) di prelazione ☆ — *bid*, (*bridge*) apertura preventiva.
preen[1] [pri:n], *s.* (*scoz. dial.*) 1. spillo; spilla 2. cosa di poco valore.
to **preen**[1], *v.t.* (*scoz. dial.*) appuntare con uno spillo.
to **preen**[2], *v.t.* lisciarsi (le penne) col becco ‖ *to — oneself*, agghindarsi, azzimarsi; *fig.* pavoneggiarsi.
to **pre-engage** ['pri:in'geidʒ], *v.t.* impegnare in anticipo.
pre-engagement ['pri:in'geidʒmənt], *s.* impegno precedente.
to **pre-establish** ['pri:is'tæbliʃ], *v.t.* prestabilire.
pre-examination ['pri:igˌzæmi'neiʃən], *s.* esame preliminare.
to **pre-examine** ['pri:ig'zæmin], *v.t.* fare un esame preliminare.
to **pre-exist** ['pri:ig'zist], *v.i.* preesistere.
pre-existence ['pri:ig'zistəns], *s.* preesistenza.
prefab ['pri:'fæb], *s.* (*fam.*) casa prefabbricata.
to **prefabricate** ['pri:'fæbrikeit], *v.t.* prefabbricare: *prefabricated house*, casa prefabbricata.
prefabrication ['pri:ˌfæbri'keiʃən], *s.* prefabbricazione.
preface ['prefis], *s.* 1. prefazione, introduzione 2. (*eccl.*) prefazio.
to **preface**, *v.t.i.* 1. fare una prefazione a: *to — a book*, scrivere la prefazione di un libro 2. preludere a (di eventi): *the events that prefaced the crisis*, gli eventi che preludevano alla crisi 3. iniziare: *the headmaster prefaced his remarks with a sharp rap on the table*, il direttore iniziò le sue osservazioni con un secco colpo sul tavolo 4. fare osservazioni preliminari.
prefatorial [ˌprefə'tɔ:riəl], *ag.* introduttivo, preliminare.
prefatorily ['prefətərili], *av.* preliminarmente; come prefazione.
prefatory ['prefətəri], *ag.* introduttivo, preliminare.
prefect ['pri:fekt], *s.* 1. prefetto 2. prefetto (studente anziano con funzioni disciplinari).
prefectorial [ˌpri:fek'tɔ:riəl], *ag.* di prefetto.
prefectship ['pri:fektʃip], *s.* dignità, giurisdizione di prefetto.
prefectural [pri'fektjurəl], *ag.* di prefettura.
prefecture ['pri:fektjuə*], *s.* prefettura.
to **prefer** [pri'fə:*], *pass.p.p.* **preferred** [pri'fə:d], *v.t.* 1. (II, IV) preferire: *I — working to doing nothing*, preferisco lavorare che far niente; *they — to die rather*

than submit, preferiscono morire piuttosto che sottomettersi 2. promuovere, elevare: *he was preferred to the rank of admiral*, egli fu promosso, elevato al rango di ammiraglio 3. (*dir. amm.*) presentare: *a charge was preferred against her*, ella venne citata in giudizio; *to — a complaint*, presentare un reclamo.
preferability [ˌprefərə'biliti], *s.* preferibilità.
preferable ['prefərəbl], *ag.* preferibile.
preferableness ['prefərəblnis], *s.* preferibilità.
preferably ['prefərəbli], *av.* preferibilmente, a preferenza.
preference ['prefərəns], *s.* preferenza ☆ — *shares*, (*comm.*) azioni privilegiate.
preferential [ˌprefə'renʃəl], *ag.* preferenziale; di favore: — *treatment*, trattamento di favore ☆ — *voting*, voto preferenziale.
preferentially [ˌprefə'renʃəli], *av.* con preferenza, con carattere preferenziale.
preferment [pri'fə:mənt], *s.* avanzamento, promozione.
preferred [pri'fə:d], *ag.* privilegiato ☆ — *stock*, (*comm.*) titolo privilegiato.
prefiguration ['pri:ˌfigju'reiʃən], *s.* prefigurazione.
prefigurative [pri'figjurətiv], *ag.* che prefigura, simbolico.
to **prefigure** [pri'figə*], *v.t.* prefigurare.
prefix ['pri:fiks], *s.* 1. (*gram.*) prefisso 2. titolo (che precede un nome proprio): *now you have full right to the — of Dr.*, ora hai pieno diritto al titolo di dottore.
to **prefix** [pri:'fiks], *v.t.* 1. premettere; far precedere: *to — a paragraph to Chapter IX*, premettere un passo al Capitolo IX 2. mettere come prefisso: *to — a particle to a word*, mettere un prefisso a una parola.
to **preform** ['pri:'fɔ:m], *v.t.i.* preformare.
preformation ['pri:fɔ:'meiʃən], *s.* preformazione ‖ *theory of —*, (*biol.*) teoria della preformazione.
pregnable ['pregnəbl], *ag.* espugnabile, prendibile.
pregnancy ['pregnənsi], *s.* 1. gestazione, gravidanza 2. *fig.* significato; importanza: *the political — of a deed*, il significato politico di un'azione.
pregnant ['pregnənt], *ag.* 1. incinta, gravida: *a woman three months —*, una donna incinta di tre mesi 2. ricco di idee 3. significativo, importante: — *events*, avvenimenti di grande importanza 4. ricco, pieno: — *with consequences*, gravido di conseguenze.
pregnantly ['pregnəntli], *av.* fecondamente, fruttuosamente.
prehensile [pri'hensail], *ag.* prensile.
prehensility [ˌpri:hen'siliti], *s.* l'essere prensile.
prehension [pri'henʃən], *s.* 1. prensione 2. apprendimento.
prehistoric ['pri:his'tɔrik], *ag.* preistorico.
prehistorically ['pri:his'tɔrikəli], *av.* in epoca preistorica: *these islands were — inhabited by...*, queste isole in epoca preistorica erano abitate da....
prehistory ['pri:'histəri], *s.* preistoria.
pre-human ['pri:'hju:mən], *ag.* anteriore alla comparsa dell'uomo.
to **pre-instruct** ['pri:in'strʌkt], *v.t.* istruire in precedenza.
to **prejudge** ['pri:'dʒʌdʒ], *v.t.* 1. giudicare prima del tempo 2. avere un pregiudizio contro.
prejudgement ['pri:'dʒʌdʒmənt], *s.* giudizio prematuro.
prejudice ['predʒudis], *s.* pregiudizio, preconcetto, prevenzione: *pride and —*, orgoglio e pregiudizio; *without —*, senza pregiudizio.
to **prejudice**, *v.t.* 1. pregiudicare, danneggiare 2. ispirare pregiudizi a.
prejudicial[1] [ˌpredʒu'diʃəl], *ag.* pregiudizievole, dannoso: *to be — to s.o.'s interests*, nuocere agli interessi di qlcu.
pre-judicial[2], *ag.* (*dir. romano*) pregiudiziale: — *action*, azione pregiudiziale.

prejudicially [ˌpredʒu'diʃəli], *av.* in modo pregiudizievole; dannosamente.

preknowledge ['priː'nɒlidʒ], *s.* prescienza.

prelacy ['preləsi], *s.* **1.** prelatura **2.** governo prelatizio.

prelate ['prelit], *s.* prelato.

prelatess ['prelitis], *s.* badessa, madre superiora.

prelatic(al) [prɪ'lætɪk(əl)], *ag.* prelatizio.

prelatically [prɪ'lætikəli], *av.* da prelato.

prelatism ['prelətizəm], *s.* governo prelatizio.

prelatist ['prelətist], *s.* fautor del governo prelatizio.

to **prelatize** ['prelətaiz], *v.t.* porre (la Chiesa) sotto il governo dei prelati.

prelature ['prelətjuə*], *s.* prelatura.

to **preleet** [pri'lekt], *v.i.* tenere una conferenza, una lezione universitaria.

prelection [pri'lekʃən], *s.* conferenza; lezione universitaria.

prelector [pri'lektə*], *s.* conferenziere; lettore.

prelibation [ˌpriːlai'beiʃən], *s. gener. fig.* pregustazione.

preliminarily [pri'liminərili], *av.* preliminarmente.

preliminary [pri'liminəri], *ag.* preliminare ∥ *s. gener. pl.* introduzione, premessa, preliminari: *the preliminaries to peace*, i preliminari della pace.

prelude ['prelju:d], *s.* **1.** introduzione, proemio **2.** (*mus.*) preludio.

to **prelude**, *v.t.i.* **1.** servire da preludio; preludere **2.** (*mus.*) preludiare.

preludial [pri'lju:diəl], *ag.* (*rar. mus.*) di preludio.

prelusion [pri'lju:ʒən], *s.* preludio, introduzione.

prelusive [pri'lju:siv], **prelusory** [pri'lju:səri], *ag.* preliminare, introduttivo.

premature [ˌpremə'tjuə*], *ag.* prematuro ☆ *a — baby*, un neonato prematuro.

prematurely [ˌpremə'tjuəli], *av.* prematuramente.

prematureness [ˌpremə'tjuənis], **prematurity** [ˌpremə'tjuəriti], *s.* l'essere prematuro.

premedical [priː'medikəl], *ag.* (*amer.*) propedeutico allo studio della medicina: — *course*, corso propedeutico allo studio della medicina.

to **premeditate** [pri(ː)'mediteit], *v.t.* premeditare.

premeditated [pri(ː)'mediteitid], *ag.* premeditato.

premeditatedly [pri(ː)'mediteitidli], *av.* con premeditazione.

premeditation [pri(ː)ˌmedi'teiʃən], *s.* premeditazione.

premier ['premjə*], *ag.* (*spec. sl.*) primo (in ordine di importanza, tempo, ecc.) ∥ *s.* (*pol.*) primo ministro.

premiership ['premjəʃip], *s.* ufficio, dignità di primo ministro.

premise ['premis], *s.* **1.** (*log.*) premessa **2.** *pl.* (*dir.*) premesse; l'oggetto di queste premesse **3.** *pl.* immobile; edificio; stabile con terreni annessi: *off the premises*, fuori dallo stabile, dall'edificio ∥ *to be drunk on the premises*, da bersi sul posto ☆ *major —*, (*log.*) premessa maggiore; *minor —*, (*log.*) premessa minore.

to **premise** [pri'maiz], *v.t.i.* premettere; far precedere; fare delle premesse: *to — a book with a few general remarks*, premettere alcune osservazioni generali a un libro.

premiss ['premis], *s.* (*log.*) premessa.

premium ['priːmjəm], *s.* **1.** premio, ricompensa **2.** premio (d'assicurazione) **3.** somma addizionale; interesse ∥ *to sell shares at a —*, vendere azioni a premio, sopra la pari **4.** aggio.

premolar [priː'moulə*], *ag. s.* (*anat.*) premolare.

to **premonish** [pri'mɒniʃ], *v.t.* premonire.

premonition [ˌpriːmə'niʃən], *s.* premonizione, presentimento.

premonitorily [pri'mɒnitərili], *av.* in modo premonitorio.

premonitory [pri'mɒnitəri], *ag.* premonitorio.

prenatal ['priː'neitl], *ag.* prenatale.

prenotion ['priː'nouʃən], *s.* prenozione.

prentice ['prentis] *s.* (*arc.*) apprendista.

preoccupation [pri(ː)ˌɒkju'peiʃən], *s.* **1.** precedente occupazione **2.** preoccupazione: — *with sthg.*, preoccupazione per ql.co. **3.** prevenzione, pregiudizio.

preoccupied [pri(ː)'ɒkjupaid], *ag.* preoccupato; assorto.

preoccupiedly [pri(ː)'ɒkjupaidli], *av.* con aria preoccupata, assorta.

to **preoccupy** [pri(ː)'ɒkjupai], *v.t.* **1.** occupare in precedenza **2.** preoccupare: *to be preoccupied with sthg.*, preoccuparsi di ql.co.

to **preordain** ['priːɔː'dein], *v.t.* preordinare; predeterminare.

preordination ['priːɔːdi'neiʃən], *s.* preordinazione.

prep [prep], (*sl. scolastico abbr.*) di **preparatory, preparation 1.**

prepaid ['priː'peid], *pass.p.p.* di to **prepay** ∥ *ag.* (*comm.*) franco di porto; pagato anticipatamente ∥ *answer prepaid*, risposta pagata (di lettere, telegrammi).

preparation [ˌprepə'reiʃən], *s.* **1.** preparazione; preparativo: *to make preparations for a trip*, fare i preparativi per un viaggio **2.** (*med.*) preparato.

preparative [pri'pærətiv], *ag.* preparatorio ∥ *s.* primo segnale, segnale preparatorio.

preparatively [pri'pærətivli], *av.* in modo preparatorio; come preparazione.

preparatory [pri'pærətəri], *ag.* preparatorio ☆ — *school*, scuola di preparazione a scuola superiore.

to **prepare** [pri'pɛə*], *v.t.i.* preparare; prepararsi; allestire: *I must — a cake for dinner*, devo preparare un dolce per il pranzo; *to — for an examination*, prepararsi a un esame; *to — s.o. for a piece of bad news*, preparare ql.cu. ad una cattiva notizia.

prepared [pri'pɛəd], *ag.* preparato.

preparedness [pri'pɛədnis], *s.* l'esser pronto, preparato: *everything was in a state of —*, tutto era predisposto.

preparer [pri'pɛərə*], *s.c.* preparatore, preparatrice.

to **prepay** ['priː'pei], *pass. p.p.* **prepaid** ['priː'peid], *v.t.* pagare anticipatamente.

prepayment ['priː'peimɒnt], *s.* pagamento anticipato.

prepense [pri'pens], *ag.* (*dir.*) deliberato, premeditato, intenzionale: *through malice —*, con premeditazione.

prepensely [pri'pensli], *av.* deliberatamente, premeditatamente.

preponderance [pri'pɒndərəns], **preponderancy** [pri'pɒndərənsi], *s.* preponderanza.

preponderant [pri'pɒndərənt], *ag.* preponderante.

preponderantly [pri'pɒndərəntli], *av.* in modo preponderante.

to **preponderate** [pri'pɒndəreit], *v.i.* **1.** predominare, prevalere: *to — in the voting*, aver la prevalenza nelle votazioni **2.** (*arc.*) essere più pesante.

preponderating [pri'pɒndəreitiŋ], *ag.* preponderante.

preponderation [pri,pɒndə'reiʃən], *s.* preponderanza.

to **prepose** [priː'pouz], *v.t.* (*gram.*) preporre.

preposition [ˌprepə'ziʃən], *s.* (*gram.*) preposizione.

prepositional [ˌprepə'ziʃənl], *ag.* (*gram.*) di preposizione.

prepositive [pri'pozitiv], *ag.* (*gram.*) prepositivo ∥ *s.* particella prepositiva.

prepositor [pri'pozitə*], *V.* **prepostor.**

to **prepossess** [ˌpriːpə'zes], *v.t.* **1.** (*rar.*) occupare in precedenza **2.** influire; predisporre;

prepossessing [ˌpriːpə'zesiŋ], *ag.* simpatico; attraente, che predispone favorevolmente: *he has a — face*, il suo viso ispira simpatia, ha un viso aperto; *his looks are not particularly —*, il suo aspetto non è particolarmente attraente.

prepossessingly [ˌpriːpə'zesiŋli], *av.* in modo simpatico; in modo attraente.

prepossession [ˌpriːpə'zeʃən], *s.* **1.** (*arc.*) occupazione precedente **2.** buona predisposizione **3.** prevenzione, pregiudizio.

preposterous [pri'pɒstərəs], *ag.* **1.** contrario alla natura, al buon senso; assurdo, irrazionale **2.** sciocco, ridicolo: *what a — idea!*, che idea strampalata!.

preposterously [pri'pɔstərəsli], *av.* **1.** assurdamente, irrazionalmente **2.** scioccamente, ridicolmente.

preposterousness [pri'pɔstərəsnis], *s.* **1.** assurdità. **2.** scioccaggine, ridicolaggine.

prepostor [pri'pɔstə*], *s.* prefetto, monitore (nei collegi).

prepotence [pri'poutəns], **prepotency** [pri'poutənsi], *s.* **1.** predominio, prevalenza; strapotenza **2.** (*biol.*) predominanza dei caratteri genetici.

prepotent [pri'poutənt], *ag.* predominante; strapotente.

prepuce ['pri:pju:s], *s.* (*anat.*) prepuzio.

preputial [pri'pju:ʃəl], *ag.* (*anat.*) prepuziale.

Pre-Raphaelite ['pri:'ræfəlait], *ag. s.* (*lett. pitt.*) preraffaellita.

Pre-Raphaelitism ['pri:'ræfəlaitizəm], *s.* (*lett. pitt.*) preraffaellismo.

prerequisite ['pri:'rekwizit], *ag.* presupposto ‖ *s.* presupposto, requisito primo.

prerogative [pri'rɔgətiv], *ag.* **1.** privilegiato; concesso in privilegio **2.** (*st. romana*) avente il diritto di votare per primo ‖ *s.* **1.** prerogativa, privilegio, facoltà: *the — of mercy*, il diritto di grazia; *the royal —*, il privilegio reale; *it is our — to do it*, è nostra prerogativa il farlo **2.** (*rar.*) diritto di dare il primo voto e così influenzare i seguenti ☆ *— court*, (*st. inglese*) corte arcivescovile per la verifica dei testamenti.

prerogatively [pri'rɔgətivli], *av.* con privilegio; per prerogativa.

presage ['presidʒ], *s.* presagio, pronostico; auspicio; presentimento: *evil —*, cattivo presagio.

to presage, *v.t.i.* presagire, avere un presentimento; predire, far presagi; augurare: *this sign presages well for the future*, questo segno è di buon augurio per il futuro.

presageful ['presidʒful], *ag.* pieno di presagi.

presager ['presidʒə*], *s.* chi fa presagi.

presbyope ['prezbioup], *s.* (*med.*) presbite.

presbyopia [,prezbi'oupjə], *s.* (*med.*) presbiopia.

presbyopic [,prezbi'ɔpik], *ag.* (*med.*) presbite.

presbyter ['prezbitə*], *s.* (*eccl.*) **1.** anziano che dirige e amministra la chiesa locale (nella Chiesa Cristiana primitiva) **2.** sacerdote (nella Chiesa Anglicana) **3.** anziano (nella Chiesa Presbiteriana).

presbyteral [prez'bitərəl], *ag.* (*eccl.*) presbiterale.

presbyterate [prez'bitərit], *s.* (*eccl.*) presbiterato.

presbyterial [,prezbi'tiəriəl], *ag.* (*eccl.*) presbiterale.

Presbyterian [,prezbi'tiəriən], *ag. s.* (*relig.*) presbiteriano ‖ *the — Church*, la Chiesa Presbiteriana (scozzese).

Presbyterianism [,prezbi'tiəriənizəm], *s.* (*relig.*) presbiterianismo.

presbytery ['prezbitəri], *s.* presbiterio.

preschool ['pri:'sku:l], *s.* (*amer.*) asilo ☆ *— age*, età prescolastica.

prescience ['presiəns], *s.* prescienza, previsione.

prescient ['presiənt], *ag.* presciente, prevedente.

presciently ['presiəntli], *av.* prescientemente.

to prescind [pri'sind], *v.t.i.* prescindere, fare astrazione: *— from sthg.*, prescindere da ql.co.

to prescribe [pri'skraib], *v.t.i.* **1.** prescrivere, ordinare: *prescribed textbooks*, libri di testo adottati; *to — a line of action*, prescrivere, indicare una linea di azione **2.** (*med.*) prescrivere; fare prescrizioni, ricette **3.** (*dir.*) comandare, pretendere in forza di prescrizione: *to — to* (o *for*) *a right*, pretendere un diritto in forza di prescrizione.

prescript ['pri:skript], *s.* ordinanza, legge.

prescriptibility [pris,kripti'biliti], *s.* prescrittibilità.

prescriptible [pris'kriptibl], *ag.* prescrittibile.

prescription [pris'kripʃən], *s.* **1.** ordine, prescrizione, istruzione **2.** (*med.*) ricetta **3.** (*dir.*) prescrizione.

prescriptive [pris'kriptiv], *ag.* prescrittivo.

presence ['prezns], *s.* **1.** presenza: *in the — of*, alla presenza di; *an invisible —*, una presenza invisibile; *your — is requested at*, Ella è invitata ad assistere

a ‖ *— of mind*, presenza di spirito, sangue freddo ‖ *to be admitted to the Presence*, essere ammesso alla Augusta Presenza **2.** aspetto, sembianza; prestanza: *a man of noble —*, un uomo di nobile aspetto **3.** (*arc.*) adunanza, assemblea ☆ *— -chamber*, sala di adunanze.

present[1] ['preznt], *ag.* **1.** presente: *all the people —*, tutti i presenti; *to be — at*, essere presente, assistere a **2.** presente, questo: *in the — case*, in questo caso; *the — volume*, questo volume **3.** (*gram.*) presente: *— participle*, participio presente **4.** attuale: *his — address*, il suo indirizzo attuale; *in the — fashion*, alla moda del giorno; *its — value*, (*comm.*) il suo valore attuale; *up to the — day*, fino ad oggi **5.** corrente, in corso: *the — month*, il corrente mese; *the — year*, l'anno in corso **6.** (*rar.*) attento; presente a se stesso **7.** (*rar.*) immediato; efficace ☆ *— -day*, contemporaneo: *— -day novelist*, romanziere contemporaneo.

present[1], *s.* **1.** presente, tempo presente: *at — he is abroad*, attualmente egli è all'estero; *I don't want any more lessons at —*, per ora non voglio più lezioni; *this will do for the —*, questo basterà per il momento; *until the —*, *up to the —*, sino ad ora, fino ad oggi **2.** (*gram.*) tempo presente: *historical —*, presente storico **3.** *gener. pl.* documento: *these presents*, (*dir.*) questo documento.

present[2], *s.* dono, regalo: *as a — to*, in dono a; *to make s.o. a — of sthg.*, far dono a ql.cu. di ql.co. ☆ *Christmas presents*, regali di Natale, strenne natalizie.

to present[2] [pri'zent], *v.t.* **1.** regalare, donare, offrire, fare omaggio a: *to — s.o. with sthg.*, regalare ql.co. a ql.cu. ‖ *to — one's apologies to s.o.*, offrire le proprie scuse a ql.cu. **2.** presentare: *he presented himself at* (o *for*) *an examination*, si presentò ad un esame; *to — an actor in a play*, presentare un attore in una commedia; *to — arms*, (*mil.*) presentare le armi, rendere onore a ql.cu.; *to — a cheque for payment*, presentare un assegno all'incasso; *to — a plea*, (*dir.*) presentare una istanza; *to — s.o. to the Bishop*, raccomandare ql.cu. al vescovo (per fargli ottenere un beneficio ecclesiastico) **3.** presentare, mostrare, rivelare: *the case presented some difficulties*, il caso presentava delle difficoltà; *it presents several vulnerable points*, rivela parecchi punti deboli.

present[3], *s.* puntamento (di arma); presentat-arm.

presentability [pri,zentə'biliti], *s.* presentabilità.

presentable [pri'zentəbl], *ag.* presentabile.

presentably [pri'zentəbli], *av.* presentabilmente.

presentation [,prezen'teiʃən], *s.* **1.** presentazione **2.** (*fil. teat.*) rappresentazione **3.** dono: *to make a — to s.o.*, fare un dono a ql.cu. **4.** (*comm.*) presentazione: *payable on — of the coupon*, pagabile contro presentazione del tagliando **5.** (*eccl.*) collazione (di beneficio) ☆ *— -copy*, libro offerto in omaggio dall'autore; specimen.

presentee [,prezən'ti:], *s.* **1.** persona raccomandata (per ottenere un incarico) **2.** debuttante (a Corte) **3.** chi riceve un dono **4.** (*eccl.*) beneficiario.

presenter [pri'zentə*], *s.c.* **1.** presentatore, presentatrice: *— of a debutante*, madrina di debuttante (a Corte) **2.** donatore, donatrice.

presentient [pri'senʃiənt], *ag.* che presagisce, che prevede.

presentiment [pri'zentimənt], *s.* presentimento.

presently ['prezntli], *av.* **1.** tra poco, a momenti, presto, quanto prima: *I'm coming —*, vengo subito **2.** (*rar. dial.*) al presente; subito.

presentment [pri'zentmənt], *s.* **1.** (*fil. pitt. teat.*) rappresentazione **2.** presentazione, esposizione, descrizione **3.** (*dir.*) dichiarazione emessa dai giurati sotto giuramento **4.** (*eccl.*) esposto al vescovo **5.** (*comm.*) presentazione (di tratta, ecc.).

preservable [pri'zə:vəbl], *ag.* conservabile; che può essere preservato.

preservation [,prezə(:)'veiʃən], *s.* preservazione, conservazione: *— of peace*, mantenimento della pace;

— *of public health*, difesa della salute pubblica; *these paintings are in an excellent state of* —, questi quadri sono in ottimo stato di conservazione.

preservative [pri'zɛ:vətiv], *ag. s.* preservativo.

preserve [pri'zɛ:v], *s.* **1.** marmellata; *pl.* conserva di frutta **2.** riserva (di caccia, pesca) **3.** *pl.* occhiali protettivi.

to preserve, *v.t.i.* **1.** preservare, proteggere: *may God — you from evil!*, che Dio ti protegga dal male!; *Saints — us!*, che i Santi ci proteggano! **2.** conservare: mantenere; riservare: *a well preserved old man*, un vecchio ben portante; *bodies which — heat*, corpi che mantengono il calore ‖ *to — a river*, riservare il diritto di pesca in un fiume **3.** fare conserve (di); sciroppare: *I'm going to — apricots and peaches*, ho intenzione di mettere in conserva albicocche e pesche.

preserver [pri'zɛ:və*], *s.c.* preservatore, preservatrice.

to preside [pri'zaid], *v.i.* presiedere: *to — over sthg.*, presiedere a ql.co., essere a capo di ql.co (anche *fig.*) ‖ *to — at the organ*, *piano*, suonare l'organo, il piano (in pubblico).

presidency ['prezidənsi], *s.* presidenza.

president ['prezidənt], *s.* **1.** presidente: *President Wilson*, il Presidente Wilson ‖ *President of the Board of Trade*, ministro del Commercio (in Inghilterra) ‖ *— of a trade-union*, segretario generale di un sindacato operaio **2.** rettore (di università).

presidentess ['prezidəntis], *s.* presidentessa; moglie di presidente.

presidential [,prezi'denʃəl], *ag.* presidenziale ☆ — *year*, *(amer.)* anno delle elezioni presidenziali.

presidentially [,prezi'denʃəli], *av.* da presidente.

presidentship ['prezidəntʃip], *s.* presidenza.

presidial [pri'sidiəl], *ag.* presidiale; presidiato: *a — castle*, un castello presidiato.

presidiary [pri'sidjəri], *ag.* presidiario ☆ — *troops*, milizie presidiarie.

presiding [pri'zaidiŋ], *ag.* che presiede.

to presignify [pri'signifai], *v.t.* **1.** notificare in precedenza **2.** presagire.

press[1] [pres], *s.* **1.** pressione, stretta: *a — of the hand*, una stretta di mano **2.** pressa, strettoio, torchio **3.** macchina per stampare; stamperia; *fig.* stampa: *it is in the —*, è in corso di stampa; *to correct the —*, correggere le bozze; *to have a good —*, avere una buona stampa; *to sign for —*, dare il nulla osta per la stampa; *to uphold the freedom of the —*, sostenere la libertà di stampa **4.** fretta, urgenza, pressione: *the — of events*, l'incalzare degli avvenimenti; *the — of modern life*, l'attività febbrile della vita moderna **5.** ressa, calca, folla, mischia, pigia pigia: *he threw himself into the — of the battle*, egli si lanciò nel folto della mischia; *he was surrounded by a great — of people*, era circondato da una gran ressa **6.** armadio a muro ☆ — *-advertising*, pubblicità a mezzo stampa; — *-agent*, agente pubblicitario; — *-bed*, letto pieghevole; — *-box*, *(spor.)* tribuna della stampa; — *campaign*, campagna giornalistica; — *conference*, conferenza stampa: *to give a — conference*, tenere una conferenza stampa; — *corrector*, correttore di bozze; — *-cutting* (o — *-clipping*), ritaglio di giornale; — *-gallery*, galleria della stampa; — *-mark*, segnatura (di libri in biblioteca); — *-proof*, bozza finale (pronta per la stampa); — *-room*, sala stampa; — *-warrant*, permesso di stampa; — *work*, *(tip.)* tiratura ‖ *clothes-* —, armadio a muro per abiti, biancheria; *cold-* —, *hot-* —, cilindratore a freddo, a caldo; *engine-* —, pressa meccanica; *hydraulic* —, pressa, torchio idraulico; *kitchen-* —, armadio di cucina; *mass-circulation* —, stampa a grande tiratura; *printing-* —, macchina da stampa; *proof-* —, tirabozze, tirapròve; *punching-* —, punzonatrice; *racket* —, *(spor.)* pressa per racchetta da tennis; *wine-* —, torchio da vino.

to press[1], *v.t.i.* **1.** premere, schiacciare, comprimere; stringere; spremere: *he pressed his face against*

the *window-pane*, appoggiò il viso contro il vetro della finestra; *she pressed her child to her breast*, strinse al seno il suo bambino; *to — the button*, premere un bottone, mettere in moto un meccanismo; *fig.* fare un passo decisivo; *to — the juice out of sthg.*, spremere il succo da ql.co. ‖ *to — a record*, stampare un disco (da una matrice) **2.** esercitare pressione; imporre, costringere; mettere alle strette; incalzare: *he pressed fifty thousand lire upon her*, la costrinse ad accettare cinquantamila lire; *time presses*, il tempo stringe; *who pressed him to that crime?*, chi lo spinse a commettere quel delitto?; *to — the enemy*, incalzare il nemico; *to — a gift*, *advice on s.o.*, offrire con insistenza un dono, un consiglio a qlcu.; *to — s.o. hard*, mettere qlcu. alle strette **3.** affollare, affollarsi; accalcarsi: *his friends pressed close against him*, i suoi amici gli si affollarono intorno **4.** tormentare, opprimere, importunare: *these preoccupations pressed upon his mind*, queste preoccupazioni lo tormentavano **5.** *to — back*, ricacciare, respingere **6.** *to — down*, appoggiare; comprimere: *to — the pedal down*, *(aut.)* schiacciare il pedale **7.** *to — forward* (o *— on*), spingere innanzi, avanzare; affrettarsi: *you must — on with your work*, devi affrettarti nel tuo lavoro **8.** *to — out*, esprimere: *to — out a few words*, spiccicare poche parole **9.** *to — up*, ammassare, affollarsi.

press[2], *s.* *(mil. spec. mar.)* arruolamento forzato ☆ — *gang*, marinai autorizzati ad arruolare forzatamente; — *money*, premio per l'arruolamento forzato; — *warrant*, *(st. mar.)* permesso d'arruolamento forzato.

to press[2], *v.t.* *(mil. spec. mar.)* arruolare forzatamente: *to — men for the army*, procedere ad un arruolamento forzato per l'esercito.

pressed [prest], *ag.* **1.** schiacciato, compresso, pressato, pigiato **2.** oppresso; a corto (di): *to be hard —*, essere in difficoltà; *to be — for money*, essere a corto di denaro **3.** stampato alla pressa ☆ — *beef*, manzo in scatola.

presser ['presə*], *s.* premistoffa (di macchina da cucire).

pressing[1] ['presiŋ], *ag.* **1.** insistente, pressante; incalzante: *since you are so —*, poiché sei così insistente **2.** pressante, urgente: *to have nothing more — to do than*, non avere niente di più urgente da fare che ‖ *s.* **1.** insistenza, sollecitazione: *he wanted no —*, non si fece pregare **2.** pressione **3.** *gener. pl.* succo spremuto ☆ *metal sheet* —, *(mec.)* stampaggio mediante pressa.

pressing[2], *s.* *(mil.)* arruolamento forzato.

pressingly ['presiŋli], *av.* urgentemente; insistentemente.

pression ['preʃən], *s.* pressione.

pressman, *pl.* **pressmen** ['presmən], *s.* **1.** giornalista, cronista **2.** *(tip.)* stampatore.

pressure ['preʃə*], *s.* **1.** *(fis. med.)* pressione **2.** *(elett.)* forza elettromotrice **3.** *fig.* pressione: *to be under —*, essere sotto pressione; *you're under too much —*, voi lavorate troppo. **4.** oppressione, afflizione ☆ — *-cabin*, *(neol. aer.)* cabina pressurizzata; — *-cooker*, pentola a pressione; — *-gauge*, manometro ‖ *atmospheric* —, pressione atmosferica; *blood-* —, pressione sanguigna; *high-* —, alta pressione.

to pressurize ['preʃəraiz], *v.t.* *(aer.)* pressurizzare.

Prester John ['prestə'dʒɔn], *no.pr.m.* Prete Gianni (figura leggendaria di re abissino favolosamente ricco).

prestidigitation ['presti,didʒi'teiʃən], *s.* prestidigitazione.

prestidigitator [,presti'didʒiteitə*], *s.* prestidigitatore, prestigiatore.

prestige [pres'ti:ʒ], *s.* prestigio: *man of —*, uomo di prestigio.

prestissimo [pres'tisimou], *s.* *(mus.)* prestissimo.

presto[1] ['prestou], *s.* *(mus.)* presto.

presto[2], *ag.* rapido, svelto ‖ *av.* rapidamente: *hey —*, ecco.

presumable [pri'zju:məbl], *ag.* presumibile.

presumably [pri'zju:məbli], *av.* presumibilmente.

to presume [pri'zju:m], *v.t.i.* **1.** presumere; supporre, ritenere: *let us — that*, supponiamo che; *no one, I —, denies it*, nessuno, ritengo, può negarlo **2.** permettersi, avere la presunzione di: *he presumed to compare himself with you*, si è permesso di paragonarsi a lei **3.** *to — (up)on (s.o., sthg.)*, abusare, approfittare: *to — upon s.o.*, abusare di qlcu.; *to — on sthg.*, approfittare di ql.co.

presumedly [pri'zju:midli], *av.* presumibilmente.

presumer [pri'zju:mə*], *s.c.* presuntuoso, presuntuosa.

presuming [pri'zju:miŋ], *ag.* presuntuoso; arrogante.

presumingly [pri'zju:miŋli], *av.* presuntuosamente.

presumption [pri'zʌmpʃən], *s.* **1.** presunzione **2.** supposizione, congettura.

presumptive [pri'zʌmptiv], *ag.* presunto, presuntivo ☆ *— death*, morte presunta || *heir- —*, erede presunto.

presumptively [pri'zʌmptivli], *av.* presuntivamente.

presumptuous [pri'zʌmptjuəs], *ag.* presuntuoso; arrogante.

presumptuously [pri'zʌmptjuəsli], *av.* presuntuosamente; arrogantemente.

presumptuousness [pri'zʌmptjuəsnis], *s.* presunzione; arroganza.

to presuppose [,pri:sə'pouz], *v.t.* presupporre.

presupposition [,pri:sʌpə'ziʃən], *s.* **1.** presupposizione **2.** presupposto, congettura.

pretence [pri'tens], *s.* **1.** pretesa: *free from pretences*, senza pretese; *I make no — to style*, non ho pretese di stile; *this bibliography has no — at completeness*, questa bibliografia non ha alcuna pretesa di essere completa **2.** simulazione; pretesto, falsa apparenza: *under the — of religion*, con il pretesto della religione; *he makes — of protecting you*, egli finge di proteggerti; *he obtained money under false —*, (*dir.*) egli si fece dare denaro con frode **3.** ostentazione.

to pretend [pri'tend], *v.t.i.* **1.** fingere, simulare: *he pretends to be very tired*, finge di essere stanchissimo; *let us — we are kings and queens*, facciamo finta di essere re e regine; *to — friendship, illness*, fingere amicizia, una malattia **2.** pretendere; vantarsi: *he does not — to be artistic*, non pretende d'intendersi d'arte **3.** *to — to sthg.*, aspirare a; rivendicare: *the prince pretended to the throne*, il principe rivendicò un preteso diritto al trono.

pretended [pri'tendid], *ag.* preteso, falso, simulato: *a — illness*, una finta malattia; *her — virtue*, la sua falsa virtù ☆ *— father*, padre putativo.

pretendedly [pri'tendidli], *av.* falsamente.

pretender [pri'tendə*], *s.c.* simulatore, simulatrice || *s.* pretendente (al trono, alla mano di qlcu.).

pretension [pri'tenʃən], *s.* **1.** pretensione; pretesa: *she has pretensions to taste*, pretende di aver buon gusto **2.** diritto **3.** presunzione, arroganza.

pretentious [pri'tenʃəs], *ag.* pretenzioso.

pretentiously [pri'tenʃəsli], *av.* pretenziosamente.

pretentiousness [pri'tenʃəsnis], *s.* l'essere pretenzioso.

preterhuman [,pri:tə'hju:mən], *ag.* sovrumano.

preterit(e) ['pretərit], *ag.* **1.** (*gram.*) preterito: *— tense*, tempo passato **2.** (*scherz.*) passato, d'altri tempi || *s.* (*gram.*) preterito.

preterition [,pri:tə'riʃən], *s.* preterizione, omissione.

pretermission [,pri:tə'miʃən], *s.* **1.** pretermissione, omissione **2.** interruzione, sospensione: *without —*, senza requie.

to pretermit [,pri:tə'mit], *pass. p.p.* **pretermitted** [,pri:tə'mitid], *v.t.* **1.** omettere **2.** interrompere, sospendere.

preternatural [,pri:tə'nætʃrəl], *ag.* preternaturale, soprannaturale.

preternaturalism [,pri:tə'nætʃrəlizəm], *s.* dottrina che concerne il preternaturale.

preternaturally [,pri:tə'nætʃrəli], *av.* in modo soprannaturale.

pretext ['pri:tekst], *s.* pretesto, scusa: *on* (o *under*) *the — of*, col pretesto di; *to give sthg. as a —*, addurre ql.co. a pretesto.

to pretext [pri'tekst], *v.t.* addurre come pretesto.

to prettify ['pritifai], *v.t.* (*fam.*) rendere grazioso; illeggiadrire.

prettily ['pritili], *av.* graziosamente, gentilmente, leggiadramente.

prettiness ['pritinis], *s.* **1.** grazia, leggiadria **2.** (*lett.*) affettazione (di stile, ecc.).

pretty ['priti], *ag.* **1.** grazioso, attraente, carino, leggiadro: *a — face*, un visino grazioso **2.** abile, intelligente: *he has a — wit*, ha uno spirito acuto **3.** (*iron.*) bello: *a — mess*, un bel pasticcio; *I have heard some — tales about him*, ne ho sentite di belle sul suo conto **4.** (*arc.*) bello, robusto: *a — fellow*, un bel pezzo d'uomo **5.** (*arc.*) considerevole (in estensione, valore): *he earns a — sum*, guadagna una discreta cifra || *s.* **1.** persona, cosa bella, graziosa **2.** ninnolo, gingillo **3.** scanalatura, bordo lavorato (di coppa, bicchiere): *fill it up to the —!*, riempilo fino al bordo **4.** (*golf*) percorso libero **5.** *pl.* (*fam.*) biancheria intima || *av.* abbastanza, moderatamente: *— good*, piuttosto bene; *I am — well*, sto abbastanza bene; *you had better do it — quick*, sarebbe meglio che tu lo facessi piuttosto in fretta.

prettyish ['pritiiʃ], *ag.* piuttosto grazioso.

pretty-pretty ['priti,priti], *ag.* (*fam.*) molto carino, molto grazioso || *s.* ninnolo.

pretzel ['pretsəl], *s.* ciambellina salata ☆ *— bowl*, bicchiere da birra.

to prevail [pri'veil], *v.i.* **1.** prevalere, essere in maggioranza: *German names — here*, i nomi tedeschi prevalgono qui; *these customs still —*, queste usanze persistono ancora; *to — against* (o *over*) *s.o.*, trionfare su qlcu. || *to — (up)on s.o. to do sthg.*, persuadere qlcu. a fare ql.co. **2.** predominare, regnare: *the parties then prevailing in the country*, i partiti che allora predominavano nel paese.

prevailing [pri'veiliŋ], *ag.* **1.** prevalente, dominante, predominante: *the — custom of the country*, l'abitudine generale del paese **2.** potente, efficace, influente.

prevailingly [pri'veiliŋli], *av.* prevalentemente.

prevalence ['prevələns], **prevalency** ['prevələnsi], *s.* prevalenza.

prevalent ['prevələnt], *ag.* prevalente, predominante: *— practice*, uso prevalente.

prevalently ['prevələntli], *av.* prevalentemente.

to prevaricate [pri'værikeit], *v.i.* **1.** tergiversare; equivocare **2.** mentire.

prevarication [pri,væri'keiʃən], *s.* **1.** tergiversazione **2.** menzogna.

prevaricator [pri'værikeitə*], *s.c.* **1.** chi tergiversa **2.** chi mente.

prevenient [pri'vi:njənt], *ag.* **1.** preliminare, antecedente **2.** (*spec. med.*) preventivo ☆ *— grace*, (*teol.*) grazia preveniente.

to prevent [pri'vent], *v.t.* **1.** impedire; ostacolare: *he was prevented from leaving*, gli si impedì di partire; *snow prevented her coming* (o *her from coming*), la neve le impedì di venire **2.** evitare: *to — war*, evitare la guerra **3.** (*arc.*) anticipare, prevenire (desiderio, domanda, ecc.) **4.** (*teol.*) guidare: *God prevents us with His grace*, Iddio ci guida con la sua grazia.

preventable [pri'ventəbl], *ag.* prevenibile, evitabile; impedibile.

preventative [pri'ventətiv], *V.* **preventive**.

preventer [pri'ventə*], *s.c.* chi previene, impedisce || *s.* **1.** impedimento, ostacolo **2.** (*mar.*) elemento (cavo, ecc.) ausiliario provvisorio.

preventible, *V.* **preventable**.

prevention [pri'venʃən], *s.* **1.** impedimento, ostacolo **2.** prevenzione; misura preventiva: *— of crime*, prevenzione del delitto; *— of disease*, difesa preventiva contro le malattie, profilassi || *Society for Prevention of Cruelty to Animals*, Società protettrice degli animali ||

— is better than cure, prov. è meglio prevenire che curare.

preventive [pri'ventiv], *ag.* preventivo; profilattico: *—measures*, misure preventive ‖ *Preventive Service*, servizio guardacoste ‖ *s.* 1. misura preventiva 2. medicina profilattica ☆ *rust —*, antiruggine.

preventively [pri'ventivli], *av.* preventivamente.

preview ['pri:'vju:], *s.* 1. (*neol. cine. teat.*) anteprima 2. (*amer.*) prossimamente (di film).

to preview, *v.t.* vedere in anteprima, presentare in anteprima (film, spettacolo teatrale).

previous ['pri:vjəs], *ag.* 1. previo, preliminare; precedente, antecedente, anteriore: *a — appointment*, un precedente appuntamento; *according to a letter — to this one...*, secondo una lettera antecedente a questa... 2. (*sl.*) precipitoso: *you are too —*, sei troppo impulsivo ‖ *av. — to*, prima di: *— to calling I wrote to him*, gli scrissi prima di passare da lui ☆ *— question*, questione pregiudiziale (in parlamento).

previously ['pri:vjəsli], *av.* precedentemente, antecedentemente, anteriormente; preliminarmente.

previousness ['pri:vjəsnis], *s.* 1. precedenza, priorità, antecedenza, anteriorità 2. (*sl.*) precipitazione.

to previse [pri(:)'vaiz], *v.t.* 1. (*rar.*) prevedere 2. preavvisare, prevenire.

prevision [pri(:)'viʒən], *s.* 1. previsione 2. profezia; pronostico.

previsional [pri(:)'viʒənl], *ag.* 1. previsto 2. profetico.

prevue ['pri:'vju:], *s.* (*amer.*) prossimamente (di film).

pre-war ['pri:'wo:*], *ag. attributivo* prebellico, di anteguerra ‖ *av.* prima della guerra.

prex [preks], **prexy** ['preksi], *s.* (*sl. scolastico amer.*) preside; rettore.

prey [prei], *s.* 1. preda, rapina: *beasts of —*, animali da preda; *bird of —*, uccello di rapina, rapace 2. *fig.* preda, vittima: *to be a — to sthg.*, essere in preda a ql.co.; *to fall a — to* (*enemy, fear, etc.*), cadere in preda a (nemico, timore, ecc.) 3. (*arc.*) bottino.

to prey, *v.i.*: *to — (up)on* (*s.o., sthg.*), depredare, saccheggiare; derubare; vivere alle spalle di; predare, cacciare (di animali); *fig.* devastare, consumare; tormentare: *cats — upon mice*, i gatti cacciano i topi; *grief was preying on her mind*, il dolore la distruggeva; *he lives by preying on his relations*, vive alle spalle dei suoi conoscenti ‖ *the strong — upon the weak, prov.* i pesci grossi mangiano i piccoli.

preyer ['preiə*], *s.* predatore, saccheggiatore; distruttore; ladro.

Priam ['praiəm], *no.pr.m.* (*lett.*) Priamo.

priapism ['praiəpizəm], *s.* 1. lascivia, libidine 2. (*patol.*) priapismo.

Priapus [prai'eipəs], *no.pr.m.* (*mit.*) Priapo.

price [prais], *s.* 1. prezzo: *above* (*o beyond o without*) *—*, inestimabile, senza prezzo; *fair —*, prezzo equo; *the — is on the fall*, il prezzo tende al ribasso; *the — keeps up*, il prezzo è sostenuto; *I bought it under —*, lo comperai sottocosto; *there was a rise in the prices*, c'è stato un rialzo dei prezzi; *to advance* (*o to rise*) *in —*, rincarare; *to cut prices close*, ridurre i prezzi al minimo; *to quote* (*o to name*) *a —*, fare un prezzo; *to set a — on an article*, valutare un articolo; *to set a high — on sthg.*, *fig.* attribuire grande valore, importanza a ql.co. ‖ *all at one —*, *one shilling*, a scelta, uno scellino ‖ *every man has his price*, ogni uomo ha il suo prezzo 2. *fig.* costo: *not at any —*, per nulla al mondo; *it must be done at any —*, deve essere fatto a qualunque costo 3. premio, ricompensa; taglia: *to set a — on a person's head*, mettere una taglia sulla testa di una persona 4. (*ippica*) quotazione ‖ *what —...?*, (*sl.*) che probabilità ci sono...?: *what — a holiday next Friday?*, che probabilità ci sono che venerdì sia vacanza? ‖ *what — my new car?*, cosa ne pensi della mia nuova macchina? ☆ *-current*, listino prezzi correnti; *— estimate*, preventivo; *—list*, catalogo, listino prezzi; *listino di borsa; — of money*, tasso di sconto ‖ *additional —*,

supplemento di prezzo; *all-round —*, prezzo globale; *average —*, prezzo medio; *cash —*, prezzo in contanti; *close —*, prezzo ristretto; *closing —*, prezzo di chiusura; *cost —*, prezzo di costo; *current —*, prezzo corrente; *factory* (*o manufacturer's —*), prezzo di fabbrica; *fixed —* (*o set —*), prezzo fisso; *gross —*, prezzo lordo; *invoice —*, prezzo di fattura; *market —* (*o trade —*), prezzo di mercato; *net —*, prezzo netto; *piecework —*, prezzo di cottimo; *purchase —*, prezzo di acquisto; *retail —*, prezzo al minuto; *sale —* (*o selling —*), prezzo di vendita; *store —*, prezzo di magazzino, all'ingrosso; *supply —*, prezzo dell'offerta; *top —*, prezzo massimo; *wholesale —*, prezzo di partita, all'ingrosso.

to price, *v.t.* 1. stabilire i prezzi di: *this book is priced at five shillings net*, questo libro si vende al prezzo netto di cinque scellini 2. valutare: *to — sthg. high, low*, attribuire un valore alto, basso a ql.co. 3. (*fam.*) chiedere il prezzo di.

priced [praist], *ag.* che ha il prezzo segnato; prezzato: *everything in the window is —*, ogni cosa in vetrina ha il suo prezzo ☆ *— catalogue*, listino prezzi ‖ *high- —*, dal prezzo elevato.

priceless ['praislis], *ag.* 1. inestimabile; senza prezzo 2. (*sl.*) impagabile, divertente; assurdo: *that is a — story!*, è una storiella divertentissima!.

pricelessness ['praislisnis], *s.* valore inestimabile.

prick [prik], *s.* 1. puntura 2. punta, puntina; aculeo; pungiglione 3. *fig.* pungolo; rimorso: *pricks of conscience*, rimorsi di coscienza ☆ *-bar*, (*mec.*) attizzatoio; riavolo; *— -eared*, con orecchie appuntite (di cane); con gli orecchi tesi (di persona): *— -eared rascal*, (*st. fam.*) puritano; *— -punch*, punzone, punteruolo; *— -song*, (*mus.*) discanto, contrappunto; *— -wood*, (*bot.*) fusaggine.

to prick, *v.t.i.* 1. pungere, pungersi; dolorare: *my finger is pricking*, mi fa male un dito 2. conficcare, fissare 3. segnare, contrassegnare (*arc.*) designare: *to — (off) names on a list*, segnare dei nomi su una lista ‖ *to — music*, (*arc.*) punteggiare, copiare della musica 4. aguzzare, rizzare: *to — (up) one's ears*, rizzare gli orecchi 5. (*arc.*) spronare (un cavallo) 6. inacetire; inasprirsi (di vino, ecc.) 7. pizzicare, formicolare (di parti del corpo) 8. *to — in, off, out*, (*agr.*) trapiantare 9. *to — off*, (*mar.*) tracciare la rotta 10. *to — out*, apparire qua e là (di stelle).

pricker ['prikə*], *s.* 1. oggetto appuntito; ago, spillo; punteruolo; punzone 2. bracchiere a cavallo.

pricket ['prikit], *s.* 1. giovane daino; cerbiatto 2. punta di candeliere su cui si infila la candela.

pricking ['prikin], *s.* puntura, punzecchiatura; foratura.

prickle ['prikl], *s.* 1. spina 2. pungiglione, aculeo 3. *fig.* pungolo ☆ *-back*, (*ittiol.*) spinarello.

to prickle, *v.t.i.* 1. pungere; punzecchiare; solleticare 2. formicolare (di parti del corpo).

prickliness ['priklinis], *s.* spinosità.

prickly ['prikli], *ag.* spinoso, pungente ☆ *— heat*, (*patol.*) lichen dei tropici; *— pear*, fico d'India.

pride[1] [praid], *s.* 1. orgoglio, fierezza; amor proprio; superbia; insolenza: *puffed up* (*o blown up*) *with —*, gonfio d'orgoglio; *it is but false — on his side*, non è che vanità da parte sua; *Mary is her parents' —*, Maria è l'orgoglio dei suoi genitori; *to take a — in* (*doing sthg.*), gloriarsi di (fare ql.co.); *to wound s.o.'s —*, ferire l'amor proprio di qlcu. ‖ *in its, their —*, (*arald.*) roteante, roteanti (di pavone) 2. (*poet.*) splendore, fasto, pompa 3. colmo, apogeo: *in the — of years*, nel fiore dell'età 4. foga, ardore (di cavallo).

to pride[1], *v.t.*: *to — oneself (up)on* (*sthg., doing sthg.*), essere orgoglioso di, vantarsi di (ql.co.), fare ql.co.).

pride[2], *s.* (*ittiol.*) lampreda.

prideful ['praidful], *ag.* (*scoz.*) orgoglioso, altezzoso, sprezzante.

pridefully ['praidfuli], *av.* orgogliosamente.

pridefulness ['praidfulnis], *s.* (*scoz.*) orgoglio, alterigia, arroganza.

prideless ['praidlis], *ag.* senza orgoglio.

prier ['praiə*], *s.c.* ficcanaso; curiosone, curiosona.

priest ['pri:st], *s.* **1.** prete, sacerdote: *the priests*, il clero; *to become a* —, farsi prete **2.** mazza, maglio per uccidere pesci ☆ — *-king*, re sacerdote; — *-like*, sacerdotale; — *-ridden*, oppresso da preti; — *-vicar* (o *assistant* —), vicario.

priestcraft ['pri:stkrɑ:ft], *s.* (*spreg.*) clericalismo

priestess ['pri:stis], *s.* sacerdotessa.

priesthood ['pri:sthud], *s.* **1.** clero **2.** sacerdozio: *to enter the* —, farsi prete.

priestling ['pri:stliŋ], *s.* pretino; (*spreg.*) pretucolo.

priestly ['pri:stli], *ag.* di prete, sacerdotale.

prig [prig], *s.* **1.** saputello; presuntuoso; vanesio **2.** pedante **3.** (*sl.*) ladruncolo.

to prig, *pass.p.p.* **prigged** [prigd], *v.t.* (*sl.*) rubare, rubacchiare.

priggery ['prigəri], *s.* **1.** presunzione **2.** pedanteria.

priggish ['prigiʃ], *ag.* **1.** borioso, presuntuoso **2.** pedante, meticoloso; piccino.

priggishly ['prigiʃli], *av.* **1.** presuntuosamente **2.** pedantescamente.

priggishness ['prigiʃnis], **priggism** ['prigizəm], *s.* **1.** boria, presuntuosità **2.** pedanteria.

prim [prim], *ag.* affettato, smorfioso; compassato; cerimonioso.

to prim, *pass.p.p.* **primmed** [primd], *v.t.i.* **1.** assumere un'aria altezzosa, di disgusto; atteggiare (viso, labbra) a disgusto **2.** rassettare; agghindare: *to* — *oneself* (*up*), agghindarsi; *to* — (*up*) *one's home*, rassettare, mettere in ordine la casa.

primacy ['praiməsi], *s.* **1.** primato, supremazia **2.** (*eccl.*) carica del primate; suprema autorità del Papa (nella Chiesa Cattolica).

primage[1] ['praimidʒ], *s.* (*mar. comm.*) percentuale sul nolo a beneficio del proprietario.

primage[2], *s.* (*mec.*) acqua di adescamento.

primal ['praiməl], *ag.* **1.** originale; primitivo, primiero **2.** primario, principale.

primally ['praiməli], *av.* **1.** primitivamente, originariamente **2.** fondamentalmente.

primarily ['praimərili], *av.* **1.** in primo luogo; originalmente **2.** essenzialmente; fondamentalmente.

primariness ['praimərinis], *s.* preminenza.

primary ['praiməri], *ag.* **1.** primo; primario; primitivo; originale; originario: — *meaning of a word*, significato originario di una parola **2.** principale, fondamentale: *of* — *importance*, di importanza fondamentale ‖ *s.* **1.** fondamento, principio **2.** (*astr.*) pianeta primario **3.** penna maestra (di uccello) **4.** (*amer.*) riunione di elettori di un partito per eleggere delegati, proporre candidati ☆ — *-battery*, (*elett.*) pila; — *education*, istruzione elementare; — *rocks*, (*geol.*) rocce primarie; — *vowels*, vocali fondamentali.

primate ['praimit], *s.* (*eccl.*) primate.

primates [prai'meiti:z], *s.pl.* (*zool.*) primati (ordine superiore dei mammiferi).

primateship]'praimitʃip], *s.* (*eccl.*) dignità e ufficio di primate.

prime[1] [praim], *ag.* **1.** primo, primario, primitivo, originale, fondamentale **2.** eccellente, di prima qualità: — *cut of meat*, pezzo di carne di prima scelta **3.** primo, insigne, eccellente ☆ — *cost*, prezzo di costo, costo di fabbricazione; *Prime Minister*, primo ministro.

prime[1], *s.* **1.** principio, primordio; *fig.* primavera **2.** fiore; forza; rigoglio; splendore; perfezione: — *of perfection*, colmo della perfezione; — *of youth*, fiore della giovinezza; *fruit in its* —, frutta di piena stagione; *in the* — *of life* (o *in one's* —), nel fiore degli anni **3.** scelta, merci scelte **4.** (*liturgia*) ora di prima **5.** minuto primo; il segno (apice) che denota il minuto primo (') **6.**

(*arit.*) numero primo **7.** (*mus.*) suono fondamentale **8.** (*scherma*) prima **9.** (*pitt.*) mestica **10.** *V.* **inch 1.**

to prime[1], *v.i.* susseguirsi ad intervalli minori (di marea).

to prime[2], *v.t.i.* **1.** caricare, innescare (arma da fuoco, mina); adescare (pompa) **2.** *fig.* dare l'imbeccata; mettere al corrente; preparare, istruire: *he must be well primed with the particulars beforehand*, deve essere messo prima al corrente dei particolari; *to* — *s.o. with a speech*, preparare qlcu. a fare un discorso ‖ — *s.o. with liquor*, (*sl.*) far bere qlcu. **3.** (*pitt.*) mesticare.

to prime[3], *v.i.* saltare (di pesci).

primely ['praimli], *av.* eccellentemente; perfettamente.

primeness [p'raimnis], *s.* eccellenza; perfezione.

primer[1] ['praimə*], *s.* **1.** libro di preghiere (usato prima della Riforma) **2.** sillabario; piccolo manuale, testo elementare ☆ *Latin* —, testo elementare di latino.

primer[2], *s.* **1.** (*artigl.*) innesco, fulminante **2.** (*mec.*) iniettore ☆ — *case*, capsula ‖ *electrical* —, (*artigl.*) innesco elettrico.

primeval [prai'mi:vəl], *ag.* primevo, primordiale.

primevally [prai'mi:vəli], *av.* primitivamente.

primigenial [,praimi'dʒi:njəl], *ag.* primigenio; (*arc.*) primitivo.

priming[1] ['praimiŋ], *s.* acceleramento nel succedersi delle maree.

priming[2], *s.* **1.** adescamento (di arma da fuoco, caldaia, mina, ecc.) **2.** polvere da sparo, innesco **3.** (*pitt.*) mestica; mano di fondo; prima mano **4.** insegnamento frettoloso.

primipara [prai'mipərə], *s.* (*med.*) primipara.

primitive [,primitiv], *ag.* **1.** primitivo ‖ *the Primitive Church*, la Chiesa primitiva **2.** semplice, rozzo ‖ *s.* (*st. pitt.*) primitivo.

primitively ['primitivli], *av.* primitivamente.

primitiveness ['primitivnis], *s.* **1.** stato, carattere primitivo **2.** rozzezza (di un popolo).

primitivism ['primitivizəm], *s.* primitivismo.

primly ['primli], *av.* compitamente; cerimoniosamente; affettatamente.

primness ['primnis], *s.* compitezza; affettazione.

primogenitor [,praimou'dʒenitə*], *s.* progenitore

primogeniture [,praimou'dʒenitʃə*], *s.* primogenitura.

primordial [prai'mo:djəl], *ag.* primordiale.

primordially [prai'mo:djəli], *av.* primordialmente.

primp [primp], *ag.* (*amer.*) elegante, ricercato.

to primp, *v.t.i.* (*amer.*) vestire, vestirsi in modo ricercato: *to* — *oneself* (*up*), adornarsi, farsi elegante.

primrose ['primrouz], *ag.* giallo pallido, color primula ‖ *s.* (*bot.*) primula, primaverina ‖ *the* — *path of dalliance*, il sentiero fiorito del piacere.

primula ['primjulə], *s.* (*bot.*) primula.

primum mobile ['praiməm'moubili:], *s.* (*fil.*) primo mobile.

primus[1] ['praiməs], *ag.* primo (in ordine di età, anzianità; usato nelle scuole inglesi per distinguere un allievo da un omonimo) ‖ *s.* vescovo che presiede la Chiesa Episcopale Scozzese.

primus[2], *s.* stufa a petrolio.

prince [prins], *s.* **1.** principe ‖ *Prince of the Church*, principe della Chiesa, cardinale; *Prince of Darkness* (o *of this World*), il demonio, Satana; *Prince of Peace*, Gesù; *Prince of Wales*, Principe di Galles (titolo dell'erede al trono britannico) **2.** *fig.* principe, esponente sovrano: *he is the* — *of liars*, è il principe dei bugiardi ☆ *Prince Albert* (*coat*), (*amer.*) finanziera, « redingote »; *Prince Consort*, principe consorte; —'s *feather*, (*bot.*) amaranto; —'s *metal*, (*chim.*) ottone.

princedom ['prinsdəm], *s.* principato.

princekin ['prinskin], *s.* (*scherz.*) principino.

princelet ['prinslit], *s.* (*spreg.*) principotto.

princelike ['prinslaik], *ag.* principesco.

princeliness ['prinslinis], *s.* dignità di principe.

princeling ['prinsliŋ], *s.* (*spreg.*) principotto.

princely ['prinsli], *ag.* principesco; sontuoso ‖ *av.* (*rar.*) principescamente.

princess [prin'ses], *s.* principessa ☆ — *dress*, « princesse », abito intero da donna; — *royal*, principessa reale (primogenita del sovrano di Gran Bretagna).

Princeton ['prinstən], *no.pr.* (*geog.*) Princeton ‖ — (*University*), (Università di) Princeton (fondata nel 1746).

principal ['prinsəpəl], *ag.* principale, essenziale, fondamentale: — *part of a verb*, radice di un verbo; *the* — *town in Tuscany*, la città principale della Toscana ‖ *s.* **1.** capo, principale, direttore (di fabbrica, scuola, ecc.) **2.** (*dir.*) principale responsabile di un delitto **3.** duellante (in quanto distinto dal suo padrino o secondo) **4.** (*edil.*) trave maestra **5.** (*comm.*) capitale **6.** (*comm.*) mandante **7.** (*mus.*) registro d'organo **8.** (*teat.*) primo attore, ruolo principale ☆ — *boy*, protagonista (generalmente un'attrice in vesti maschili) di una pantomima ‖ *lady* —, direttrice (di scuola).

principality [,prinsi'pæliti], *s.* **1.** principato: *the Principality of Monaco*, il Principato di Monaco ‖ *the Principality*, il Galles **2.** sovranità; autorità suprema **3.** *pl.* (*teol.*) principati (ordine angelico).

principally ['prinsəpli], *av.* principalmente.

principalship ['prinsəpəlʃip], *s.* rettorato; carica di principale, di capo.

principate ['prinsipit], *s.* (*rar.*) principato.

principle ['prinsəpl], *s.* **1.** principio; teoria: *the — of natural selection*, la teoria della selezione naturale; *the principles of political economy*, i principi di economia politica; *first principles of geometry*, principi fondamentali di geometria **2.** principio, legge morale: *man of no principles*, uomo senza principi; *on* —, per principio ☆ *active* —, (*chim.*) principio attivo.

principled ['prinsəpld], *ag.* avente principi morali ☆ *high-* —, moralissimo, retto; *loose-* —, di dubbia moralità.

to prink [priŋk], *v.t.i.* rendere elegante, adornare; vestirsi con eleganza: *to* — *oneself* (*up*), (*fam.*) adornarsi, farsi elegante; lisciarsi le penne (di uccello).

print [print], *s.* **1.** impronta; impressione; orma; segno; traccia: *the — of a naked foot*, l'orma di un piede nudo **2.** *fig.* segno, marchio: *the — of age*, il segno dell'età **3.** (*tip.*) stampa, carattere: *in good* —, con una bella stampa; *small, large, clear print*, caratteri piccoli, grandi, chiari ‖ *that book is in* —, quel libro è stampato e pubblicato; *that book is out of* —, quel libro è esaurito **4.** (*spec. amer.*) giornale, periodico, pubblicazione **5.** stampa, riproduzione: *an old — of London Bridge*, una vecchia stampa del Ponte di Londra **6.** (*foto.*) copia **7.** caratteri a stampatello: *write the address in* —, scrivi l'indirizzo a stampatello **8.** tessuto di cotone stampato **9.** stampo, forma ☆ — *seller*, venditore di stampe; — *shop*, negozio di stampe; — *-works*, stamperia (di stoffe).

to print, *v.t.i.* **1.** (*tip.*) stampare; pubblicare; stamparsi: *the book is printing*, il libro è in corso di stampa; *printed for the author*, stampato a spese dell'autore **2.** imprimere (anche *fig.*): *that event is still printed on my mind*, quel fatto mi è ancora impresso nella mente **3.** stampare (stoffe, ecc.) **4.** scrivere a stampatello **5.** fare lo stampatore **6.** *to* — *off*, *out a negative*, (*foto.*) stampare una copia da una negativa ☆ *printed matter*, stampe, stampati: *printed matter rate*, tariffa postale per le stampe.

printable ['printəbl], *ag.* stampabile; imprimibile.

printer ['printə*], *s.* **1.** tipografo; stampatore ‖ —*'s devil*, apprendista tipografo, fattorino di tipografia **2.** (*mec.*) stampatrice ☆ —*'s error*, errore di stampa; —*'s reader*, correttore di bozze.

printery ['printəri], *s.* (*amer.*) tipografia; stamperia.

printing ['printiŋ], *s.* **1.** stampa **2.** tiratura **3.** tipografia ☆ — *-ink*, inchiostro da stampa; — *-press*, pressa tipografica; — *-types*, caratteri da stampa.

prior ['praiə*], *ag.* precedente, anteriore, antecedente ‖ *s.* (*eccl. st.*) priore.

prior, *av.* anteriormente: — *to*, prima di: *it happened* — *to my arrival*, accadde prima del mio arrivo.

priorate ['praiərit], *s.* **1.** priorato **2.** *V.* **priory**.

prioress ['praiəris], *s.* (*eccl.*) priora, superiora.

priority [prai'oriti], *s.* priorità, anteriorità, precedenza; ordine di precedenza: *according to* —, secondo l'ordine di precedenza.

priorship ['praiəʃip], *s.* (*eccl.*) priorato.

priory ['praiəri], *s.* monastero retto da priore, priora.

Priscian ['priʃiən], *no.pr.m.* (*st.*) Prisciano.

Priscilla [pri'silə], *no.pr.f.* Priscilla.

to prise [praiz], *v.t.* far leva su.

prism ['prizəm], *s.* (*geom. min.*) prisma.

prismatic(al) [priz'mætik(əl)], *ag.* (*geom. min.*) prismatico.

prismy ['prizmi], *ag.* (*rar.*) a, di colori prismatici.

prison ['prizn], *s.* **1.** prigione, carcere **2.** reclusione ☆ *State* —, carcere politico; (*amer.*) prigione di Stato.

to prison, *v.t.* (*poet.*) imprigionare, incarcerare.

prisoner ['priznə*], *s.* prigioniero (anche *fig.*); detenuto: — *at the bar*, (*dir.*) accusato; — *of State*, detenuto politico; — *of war*, (*abbr.*) P.O.W.) prigioniero di guerra; *to take s.o.* —, far prigioniero, catturare qlcu.

pristine ['pristain], *ag.* antico; primitivo; intatto.

prithee ['priði(:)], *inter.* (*arc. contr. di I pray thee*) ti prego, di grazia.

prittle-prattle ['pritl,prætl], *s.* chiacchiere.

privacy ['praivəsi], *s.* **1.** intimità: *there is no* — *in this house*, in questa casa non si può star mai da soli **2.** riserbo, segretezza: *he achieved his object with great privacy*, ha raggiunto il suo scopo in gran segretezza.

private ['praivit], *ag.* **1.** privato: — *house*, casa privata ‖ *in* —, in privato **2.** particolare **3.** isolato, appartato: *here we are quite* —, qui siamo completamente appartati **4.** riservato, segreto; personale: *this letter was marked* —, su questa lettera c'era scritto confidenziale; *to keep the news* —, tener segreta la notizia **5.** semplice (di soldato) **6.** civile, borghese (di abito, ecc.): *in* — *clothes*, in abiti borghesi ‖ *s.* **1.** (*mil.*) soldato semplice **2.** *pl.* organi sessuali ☆ — *bill*, progetto di legge concernente un interesse particolare; — *party*, riunione privata; — *property*, proprietà privata; — *school*, scuola privata.

privateer [,praivə'tiə*], *s.* **1.** nave corsara **2.** capitano di nave corsara **3.** *pl.* ciurma di nave corsara.

to privateer, *v.i.* fare il corsaro.

privateering [,praivə'tiəriŋ], *s.* pirateria: *to go* —, far la guerra di corsa, darsi alla pirateria.

privately ['praivitli], *av.* **1.** privatamente **2.** segretamente.

privateness ['praivitnis], *s.* (*rar.*) **1.** segretezza **2.** riservatezza.

privation [prai'veiʃən], *s.* privazione: *to live in* —, condurre una vita di stenti.

privative ['privətiv], *ag.* privativo (anche *gram.*).

privatively ['privətivli], *av.* privativamente.

privet ['privit], *s.* (*bot.*) ligustro.

privilege ['privilidʒ], *s.* privilegio; prerogativa; diritto esclusivo: *breach of* —, infrazione di privilegio parlamentare; *by way of* —, per privilegio; *writ of* —, (*dir.*) mandato di libertà per persona di rango, arrestata per cause civili; *to grant s.o. a* —, accordare un privilegio a qlcu. ‖ *it's a* — *for me to be with you*, (*fam.*) è un piacere per me stare con Lei.

to privilege, *v.t.* privilegiare, accordare privilegi a ‖ *to* — *from*, esentare da.

privileged ['privilidʒd], *ag.* privilegiato: *the* — *classes*, le classi privilegiate.

privily ['privili], *av.* privatamente; segretamente.

privity ['priviti], *s.* **1.** conoscenza segreta: *without my* —, a mia insaputa; *to have* — *to sthg.*, essere a conoscenza di ql.co. **2.** (*dir.*) vincolo (di sangue, ecc.) **3.** (*dir.*) rapporto contrattuale.

privy ['privi], *ag*. **1.** nascosto; segreto; appartato; privato ‖ *Privy Council*, consiglio privato (di sovrano); *Privy Purse*, appannaggio reale; *Privy Seal*, sigillo privato **2.** al corrente di un segreto: *to be — to sthg.*, essere a conoscenza, consapevole di ql.co. ‖ *s*. **1.** (*dir*.) parte interessata **2.** (*arc*.) latrina.

prize[1] [praiz], *s*. **1.** premio; trofeo; ricompensa: *who carried off the —?*, chi ha vinto il premio? **2.** meta, scopo; l'oggetto per il cui possesso si combatte ☆ — *-fellow*, studente premiato agli esami; — *-fellowship*, premio assegnato a chi eccelle negli esami; — *-fight*, gara di pugilato a premio; — *-fighter*, pugile professionista che combatte per il premio; — *-giving*, distribuzione dei premi; — *-ring* spazio destinato alle gare di pugilato a premio.

to **prize**[1], *v.t.* valutare; apprezzare, stimare.

prize[2], *s*. (*mar*.) preda (di guerra), bottino: *to make — of a ship*, catturare una nave ‖ *Prize Court*, dipartimento dell'Ammiragliato sopraintendente alle catture sul mare (per diritto di guerra) ☆ — *-crew*, equipaggio a bordo della nave catturata (per condurla in porto); — *-money*, denaro ricavato da una preda e diviso fra l'equipaggio della nave che l'ha catturata.

to **prize**[2], *v.t.* (*mar*.) catturare (nave, carico).

prize[3], *s*. **1.** leva **2.** azione della leva.

to **prize**[3], *v.t.* far leva su: *to — a box open*, aprire una scatola (facendo leva).

pro[1] [prou], *prep*. (*lat*.) pro; per; in favore di ‖ *s*. (*pl*. **pros** [prouz]) **1.** persona che vota in favore **2.** pro: *— and con*, il pro e il contro, le ragioni in favore e in sfavore ☆ — *-communist*, filo-comunista; — *-fascist*, filo-fascista.

pro[2], *pl*. **pros** [prouz], *s*. (*abbr. sl*. di *professional man*) professionista.

proa ['prouə], *s*. (*mar*.) canotto malese a vela.

probabilism ['probəbilizəm], *s*. (*fil*.) probabilismo.

probabilist ['probəbilist], *s*. (*fil*.) probabilista.

probability [,probə'biliti], *s*. probabilità: *in all —*, con tutta probabilità; *there is no — of his coming*, non c'è nessuna probabilità che venga ‖ *calculus of —*, (*mat*.) calcolo delle probabilità.

probable ['probəbl], *ag*. probabile, verosimile ‖ *s*. un candidato, una scelta, ecc., probabile.

probably ['probəbli], *av*. probabilmente.

probang ['proubæŋ], *s*. (*med*.) sonda, specillo.

probate ['proubit], *s*. **1.** (*dir*.) omologazione: *to take — of a will*, fare omologare un testamento ‖ *The Probate, Divorce and Admiralty Division*, la sezione dell'Alta Corte di Giustizia competente in materia di testamenti, divorzi e diritto marittimo **2.** copia autenticata di testamento ☆ — *duty*, tassa di successione.

probation [prə'beiʃən], *s*. **1.** esame, prova, esperimento: *on —*, in prova, in esperimento **2.** (*eccl*.) probazione; tirocinio, noviziato **3.** (*dir*.) libertà condizionata ☆ — *officer*, sorvegliante di condannati in libertà condizionata.

probational [prə'beiʃənl], **probationary** [prə'beiʃnəri], *ag*. probatorio.

probationer [prə'beiʃnə*], *s*. **1.** tirocinante, apprendista; (*eccl*.) novizio **2.** (*dir*.) chi beneficia di libertà condizionata.

probationership [prə'beiʃnəʃip], *s*. tirocinio, apprendistato; (*eccl*.) noviziato.

probative ['proubətiv], *ag*. probativo, atto a provare.

probatory ['proubətəri], *ag*. probatorio, provante, di prova.

probe [proub], *s*. **1.** (*med*.) sonda, specillo **2.** (*amer. fig*.) investigazione.

to **probe**, *v.t.i.* **1.** (*med*.) sondare, specillare; usare lo specillo **2.** *fig*. sondare; esplorare; scandagliare.

probity ['proubiti], *s*. probità.

problem ['probləm], *s*. problema (anche *fig*.): *the — of unemployment*, il problema della disoccupazione ☆ — *child*, bambino difficile; — *play*, lavoro teatrale a tesi.

problematic(al) [,probli'mætik(əl)], *ag*. problematico.

problematically [,probli'mætikəli], *av*. problematicamente.

proboscidean [,probo'sidiən], *ag*. proboscidato.

proboscis [prə'bosis], *s*. proboscide.

procacious [prə'keiʃəs], *ag*. petulante; impertinente.

procacity [prou'kæsiti], *s*. petulanza; impertinenza.

procedural [prə'si:dʒərəl], *ag*. (*dir*.) procedurale.

procedure [prə'si:dʒə*], *s*. **1.** procedimento **2.** (*dir*.) procedura.

to **proceed** [prə'si:d], *v.i.* **1.** procedere, avanzare; proseguire; continuare: *— with what you were doing*, continua a fare ciò che stavi facendo; *negotiations are now proceeding*, i negoziati sono ora in corso; *the play proceeded without further interruption*, la rappresentazione continuò senza ulteriore interruzione; *we proceeded to the next town*, proseguimmo fino alla città seguente **2.** agire: *to — cautiously*, agire con prudenza ‖ *to — to action*, venire a vie di fatto ‖ *to — to violence*, ricorrere alla violenza **3.** derivare, provenire: *sounds proceeding from a room*, suoni provenienti da una stanza **4.** (*dir*.) procedere, agire: *to — against s.o.*, intentare causa contro qlcu.

proceeding [prə'si:diŋ], *s*. **1.** procedimento, corso; comportamento; azione **2.** *pl*. riunione, seduta; dibattiti; deliberazioni **3.** *pl*. azione legale: *to institute legal proceedings*, dar inizio a una causa, procedere per vie legali.

proceeds ['prousi:dz], *s.pl*. profitto, provento, ricavo, ricavato: *the — will be devoted to charity*, il ricavato sarà devoluto ad opere di beneficenza ☆ *net —*, ricavo netto.

process[1] ['prouses], *s*. **1.** andamento, corso, svolgimento; progresso (di tempo): *in — of time*, col passare del tempo; *changes are in —*, sono in corso cambiamenti **2.** metodo, processo, operazione, procedimento: *it is made by a new —*, è fatto con un nuovo procedimento **3.** processo, sviluppo; (serie di) mutamenti: *the — of growth*, il processo della crescita **4.** (*anat*.) apofisi **5.** (*bot. zool*.) appendice **6.** (*dir*.) processo; vie, atti legali; citazione **7.** (*tip*.) procedimento meccanico (di stampa) ☆ — *-block*, «cliché»; — *engraving*, zincografia.

to **process**[1], *v. t*. **1.** (*dir*.) istruire un processo; intentare giudizio contro **2.** (*ind. chim*.) sottoporre a processo, procedimento; trattare: *to — sulphur*, raffinare lo zolfo.

to **process**[2] [prə'ses], *v.i.* (*fam. scherz*.) andare, camminare in processione.

processed ['prousest], *ag*. (*ind. chim*.) trattato ☆ — *rubber*, gomma artificiale.

processing ['prousesiŋ], *s*. (*ind*.) lavorazione; trattamento: *the — of metals*, la lavorazione dei metalli ☆ — *tax*, tassa di lavorazione.

procession [prə'seʃən], *s*. **1.** processione, corteo **2.** (*teol*.) emanazione dello Spirito Santo ☆ — *caterpillar* (o — *moth*), (*entom*.) processionaria.

to **procession**, *v.t.i.* andare in processione; camminare in processione per (una strada, ecc.).

processional [prə'seʃənl], *ag*. di, per processione ‖ *s*. (*eccl*.) innario per processioni.

processionally [prə'seʃnəli], *av*. in processione, in corteo.

proclaim [prə'kleim], *s*. proclama.

to **proclaim**, *v.t.* **1.** proclamare, promulgare, dichiarare, bandire: *peace was proclaimed in 1918*, la pace fu proclamata nel 1918 **2.** rivelare: *his manners proclaimed him a gentleman*, i suoi modi rivelavano in lui l'aristocratico **3.** proibire (comizi, ecc.) **4.** mettere sotto interdetto: *the whole county is proclaimed*, tutta la contea è sotto interdetto.

proclamation [,proklə'meiʃən], *s*. **1.** proclamazione **2.** proclama, editto, bando.

proclitic [prou'klitik], *ag*. (*gram*.) proclitico ‖ *s*. (*gram*.) particella proclitica.

proclive [prə'klaiv], *ag*. (*arc*.) proclive, incline.

proclivity [prə'kliviti], *s*. proclività, propensione,

tendenza naturale, inclinazione: — *to vice*, inclinazione al vizio.

proconsul [prou'konsəl], *s.* **1.** (*st. romana*) proconsole **2.** governatore di una colonia moderna.

proconsular [prou'konsjulə*], *ag.* proconsolare.

proconsulate [prou'konsjulit], **proconsulship** [prou'konsəlʃip], *s.* proconsolato.

Procopius [prə'koupjəs], *no.pr.m.* (*lett.*) Procopio.

to **procrastinate** [prou'kræstineit], *v.t.i.* procrastinare.

procrastination [prou,kræsti'neiʃən], *s.* procrastinazione.

procrastinator [prou'kræstineitə*], *s.c.* chi procrastina, indugia, temporeggia.

procreant ['proukriənt], *ag.* fecondo ‖ *s.c.* procreatore, procreatrice.

to **procreate** ['proukrieit], *v.t.i.* procreare, generare.

procreation [,proukri'eiʃən], *s.* procreazione.

procreative ['proukrieitiv], *ag.* generativo, produttivo.

procreator ['proukrieitə*], *s.c.* chi procrea.

Procrustean [prou'krʌstiən], *ag.* **1.** di Procuste **2.** *fig.* ferreo, drastico.

proctor ['proktə*], *s.* **1.** censore, prefetto (nelle università, collegi inglesi, incaricato di sorvegliare la disciplina e la condotta morale degli studenti dentro e fuori dell'istituto) ‖ *proctors'* (*bull*)*dogs*, sorveglianti che accompagnano i prefetti nell'ispezione notturna **2.** (*dir. eccl.*) procuratore ‖ *King's Proctor*, Procuratore Generale (nelle cause di divorzio).

to **proctorize** ['proktəraiz], *v.t.* esercitare l'autorità di « proctor » verso (gli studenti); punire, ammonire.

proctorship ['proktəʃip], *s.* **1.** ufficio di « proctor », censore **2.** (*dir. eccl.*) ufficio di procuratore.

procumbent [prou'kʌmbənt], *ag.* **1.** giacente, prono, bocconi **2.** (*bot.*) procombente, rasente terra.

procurable [prə'kjuərəbl], *ag.* procurabile.

procuration [,prokjuə'reiʃən], *s.* **1.** (*dir.*) procura: *to sign by* — (o *per* —), firmare per procura **2.** (*eccl.*) procurazione **3.** lenocinio ☆ — *holder*, procuratore.

procurator ['prokjuəreitə*], *s.* (*dir.*) procuratore ☆ — *-fiscal*, (*dir. scoz.*) Pubblico Ministero.

procuratorial [,prokjuərə'tɔ:riəl], *ag.* (*dir.*) procuratorio.

procuratorship ['prokjuəreitəʃip], *s.* (*dir.*) procuratorato.

procuratory ['prokjuərətəri], *s.* (*dir.*) procura: *letter of* —, lettera di procura.

procuratrix [,prokjuə'reitriks], *s.* (*eccl.*) economa.

to **procure** [prə'kjuə*], *v.t.i.* **1.** procurare, procurarsi; ottenere; (*arc.*) causare (la morte di qlcu.) **2.** adescare (ragazze) a scopo di prostituzione.

procurement [prə'kjuəmənt], *s.* **1.** conseguimento; ottenimento **2.** (*amer.*) raccolta di viveri, ecc. da parte dello Stato **3.** lenocinio.

procurer [prə'kjuərə*], *s.* lenone, mezzano.

procuress [prə'kjuəris], *s.* mezzana.

Procyon ['prousjən], *no.pr.* (*astr.*) Procione.

prod [prod], *s.* **1.** pungolo **2.** *fig.* stimolo, incitamento: *let's give him a* —, punzecchiamolo un po'.

to **prod**, *pass.p.p.* **prodded** ['prodid], *v.t.* **1.** *to* — (*at*), pungolare, spingere con un pungolo **2.** *fig.* stimolare, incitare: *to* — *s.o. on*, stimolare qlcu.

prodelision [,proudi'liʒən], *s.* elisione di vocale iniziale (*p.e. I'm* invece di *I am*).

prodigal ['prodigəl], *ag.* prodigo, dissipatore: *a* — *administration*, una amministrazione dissipatrice ‖ *the* — *son*, il figliol prodigo ‖ *s.c.* chi dissipa.

prodigality [,prodi'gæliti], *s.* prodigalità.

to **prodigalize** ['prodigəlaiz], *v.t.* scialacquare.

prodigally ['prodigəli], *av.* prodigalmente.

prodigious [prə'didʒəs], *ag.* prodigioso, meraviglioso; enorme; sorprendente: *a* — *sum of money*, un'enorme quantità di denaro.

prodigiously [prə'didʒəsli], *av.* prodigiosamente, meravigliosamente; sorprendentemente.

prodigiousness [prə'didʒəsnis], *s.* prodigiosità.

prodigy ['prodidʒi], *s.* prodigio; fenomeno: *prodigies of valour*, prodigi di valore ☆ *infant* —, (*fam.*) bambino prodigio.

prodromal ['prodrəməl], *ag.* **1.** (*med.*) prodromico **2.** preliminare.

prodrome ['prodrəm], *s.* prodromo (anche *med.*); prefazione; preambolo.

produce ['prodju:s], *s.* **1.** prodotto; rendimento, risultato: *the* — *of much work*, il risultato di molto lavoro **2.** *coll.* prodotti grezzi; derrate ☆ *farm* —, prodotti agricoli; *home* —, prodotto locale, nostrano; *raw* —, materie prime.

to **produce** [prə'dju:s], *v.t.i.* **1.** presentare, esibire; estrarre; (*dir.*) produrre: *he produced a book from a drawer*, tirò fuori un libro da un cassetto; *to* — *witnesses*, produrre testimoni **2.** generare, produrre (di terra, piante); figliare **3.** produrre, fabbricare; fruttare, rendere **4.** presentare (sulla scena, sullo schermo): *when will they* — *the new comedy?*, quando presenteranno la nuova commedia? ‖ *produced by*, regia di **5.** (*geom.*) prolungare (una linea).

producer [prə'dju:sə*], *s.c.* produttore, produttrice ‖ *s.* produttore cinematografico; impresario teatrale ☆ *gas-* —, gasogeno.

producible [prə'dju:səbl], *ag.* producibile.

product ['prodʌkt], *s.* prodotto; *fig.* frutto; effetto ☆ *secondary* —, sottoprodotto.

production [prə'dʌkʃən], *s.* **1.** esibizione (di documenti, ecc.); (*dir.*) produzione (di testimoni, ecc.) **2.** produzione, fabbricazione; elaborazione; prodotto: *cost of* —, costo di fabbrica **3.** rendimento **4.** produzione letteraria **5.** rappresentazione di lavoro teatrale **6.** (*geom.*) prolungamento (di una linea) ☆ *belt* —, produzione a catena, in serie.

productive [prə'dʌktiv], *ag.* produttivo; fecondo, fertile.

productively [prə'dʌktivli], *av.* in modo produttivo; profittevolmente.

productiveness [prə'dʌktivnis], **productivity** [,prodʌk'tiviti], *s.* produttività; rendimento.

proem ['prouem], *s.* proemio, esordio, prefazione.

profanation [,profə'neiʃən], *s.* profanazione, atto profano.

profane [prə'fein], *ag.* **1.** profano: — *history*, storia profana; — *literature*, letteratura profana **2.** pagano (di rito, ecc.): — *practices*, cerimonie pagane **3.** blasfemo, empio: — *language*, lingua sacrilega.

to **profane**, *v.t.* profanare, violare.

profanely [prə'feinli], *av.* profanamente.

profaneness [prə'feinnis], *s.* profanità; irriverenza.

profaner [prə'feinə*], *s.c.* profanatore, profanatrice.

profanity [prə'fæniti], *s.* profanità; irriverenza.

to **profess** [prə'fes], *v.t.i.* **1.** professare; dichiarare, esprimere; fare professione: *he professed his deep regret*, espresse il suo profondo rammarico **2.** dichiarare, manifestare (falsamente); pretendere: *he doesn't* — *to be a scholar*, non pretende di essere un letterato; *he professes great interest in your future*, egli manifesta un grande interesse per il tuo avvenire **3.** professare, esercitare: *to* — *medicine*, esercitare la professione di medico **4.** (*eccl.*) professare **5.** insegnare: *to* — *history*, insegnare storia.

professed [prə'fest], *ag.* **1.** dichiarato: *a* — *atheist*, un ateo dichiarato; *a* — *enemy*, un nemico dichiarato **2.** preteso, sedicente: *a* — *friend*, un sedicente amico **3.** (*eccl.*) professo: *a* — *nun*, una suora professa.

professedly [prə'fesidli], *av.* apertamente, pubblicamente: *he is* — *an agnostic*, egli dichiara di essere un libero pensatore.

profession [prə'feʃən], *s.* **1.** professione ‖ *the learned professions*, le professioni liberali (teologia, legge e medicina) **2.** dichiarazione: *insincere* —, dichiarazione poco sincera **3.** (*eccl.*) il pronunciare voti; i voti.

professional [prəˈfeʃənl], *ag.* di professione, professionale: — *footballer*, calciatore di professione; *conduct which is not* —, condotta non conforme agli usi della professione ‖ *s.* professionista (anche *spor.*) ‖ *the professionals*, gli esperti ☆ — *classes*, i professionisti; — *man*, professionista; — *woman*, donna che esercita una professione.

professionalism [prəˈfeʃnəlizəm], *s.* professionismo (anche *spor.*).

to **professionalize** [prəˈfeʃnəlaiz], *v.t.* trasformare in professione.

professionally [prəˈfeʃnəli], *av.* professionalmente.

professor [prəˈfesə*], *s.* **1.** professore (universitario): — *in charge*, incaricato (universitario) **2.** adepto (di una dottrina, ecc.).

professorate [prəˈfesərit], *s.* professorato.

professorial [ˌprofeˈsoːriəl], *ag.* di professore, professorale.

professorially [ˌprofeˈsoːriəli], *av.* in modo professorale.

professorship [prəˈfesəʃip], *s.* professorato.

proffer [ˈprofə*], *s.* (*letter.*) proposta; offerta, profferta.

to **proffer**, *v.t.* (*letter.*) offrire, profferire.

proficiency [prəˈfiʃənsi], *s.* abilità, perizia, competenza; conoscenza: — *in English*, buona conoscenza dell'inglese; *to attain* (o *to reach*) —, arrivare a una buona competenza ☆ — *pay*, (*mil.*) premio di specialità.

proficient [prəˈfiʃənt], *ag.* abile, esperto, competente: — *at* (o *in*) *sthg.*, esperto in ql.co.: *he is* — *in teaching*, egli è esperto nell'insegnamento ‖ *s.* esperto, conoscitore.

proficiently [prəˈfiʃəntli], *av.* abilmente, con competenza.

profile [ˈproufiːl], *s.* **1.** profilo (anche *letter.*); contorno: — *of an author*, profilo d'un autore; *the* — *of a distant hill*, il profilo di una collina lontana; *drawn in* —, disegnato di profilo **2.** (*arch.*) sezione **3.** (*teat.*) quinta ☆ — *cutter*, (*ind.*) fresa sagomata.

to **profile**, *v.t.* **1.** profilare; ritrarre in profilo; scrivere il profilo di **2.** (*tec.*) sagomare, profilare.

profit [ˈprofit], *s.* **1.** profitto; guadagno; vantaggio; beneficio: *I have read it to my great* —, l'ho letto con grande profitto; *here is no* — *in recrimination*, è inutile recriminare; *to turn sthg. to* —, trarre profitto da ql.co. **2.** (*comm.*) guadagno, reddito, utile: *gross* —, ricavo lordo; *net* —, utile netto ‖ — *and loss account*, conto profitti e perdite ☆ — *-sharing*, compartecipazione agli utili.

to **profit**, *v.t.i.* **1.** approfittare, trarre vantaggio (da), guadagnare: *he profited by their confusion to run away*, approfittò della loro confusione per scappar via; *I shall* — *by your experience*, trarrò profitto dalla tua esperienza **2.** essere di vantaggio, giovare: *it profits little to read too much*, non giova gran che leggere troppo; *it will not* — *him*, non gli gioverà.

profitable [ˈprofitəbl], *ag.* vantaggioso, utile, lucroso: *it is more* — *to us to sell it*, è più vantaggioso per noi venderlo.

profitableness [ˈprofitəblnis], *s.* vantaggio, profitto, utilità, beneficio.

profitably [ˈprofitəbli], *av.* vantaggiosamente, con profitto, utilmente.

profiteer [ˌprofiˈtiə*], *s.c.* profittatore, profittatrice ☆ *war* —, pescecane, arricchito di guerra.

to **profiteer**, *v.i.* guadagnare illecitamente (specialmente in tempo di guerra, di difficoltà economiche).

profiteering [ˌprofiˈtiəriŋ], *s.* il guadagnare illecitamente.

profitless [ˈprofitlis], *ag.* senza profitto, inutile.

profitlessly [ˈprofitlisli], *av.* inutilmente.

profitlessness [ˈprofitlisnis], *s.* inutilità.

profligacy [ˈprofligəsi], *s.* **1.** sregolatezza; libertinag-

gio; depravazione **2.** sperpero **3.** (*fam.*) profusione: *a real* — *of pictures*, quadri a profusione.

profligate [ˈprofligit], *ag.* sregolato; dissoluto; depravato ‖ *s.c.* **1.** libertino, donna dissoluta **2.** scialacquatore, scialacquatrice.

profligately [ˈprofligitli], *av.* **1.** dissolutamente **2.** con sperpero.

profligateness [ˈprofligitnis], *V.* **profligacy**.

profound [prəˈfaund], *ag.* **1.** profondo: — *bow*, inchino profondo; *the* — *depths of the ocean*, le profondità dell'oceano; *a* — *sigh*, un sospiro profondo **2.** profondo, approfondito; intenso: *a* — *study*, uno studio profondo; *to listen to s.o. with* — *interest*, ascoltare qlcu. con profondo interesse ‖ *s.* (*poet.*) profondità.

profoundly [prəˈfaundli], *av.* profondamente: — *grateful*, profondamente grato.

profoundness [prəˈfaundnis], **profundity** [prəˈfʌnditi], *s.* profondità (di abisso, scienza, ecc.).

profuse [prəˈfjuːs], *ag.* **1.** abbondante: — *perspiration*, sudore abbondante **2.** generoso, prodigo: *to be* — *in one's apologies*, sprofondarsi in scuse; *to be* — *of praise*, essere prodigo di lodi.

profusely [prəˈfjuːsli], *av.* **1.** abbondantemente, a profusione **2.** con prodigalità.

profuseness [prəˈfjuːsnis], *s.* **1.** profusione, esuberanza **2.** prodigalità.

profusion [prəˈfjuːʒən], *s.* **1.** abbondanza, profusione: *there were flowers in* —, c'erano fiori a profusione **2.** prodigalità; spreco.

prog[1] [prog], *s.* **1.** (*dial.*) provviste (generalmente per viaggio); cibo **2.** *fig.* nutrimento della mente.

to **prog**[1], *pass.p.p.* **progged** [progd], *v.i.* (*fam.*) andare in cerca di ql.co. (specialmente cibo); chiedere l'elemosina.

prog[2], (*sl.*) per **proctor 1.**

to **prog**[2], (*sl.*) per **proctorize**.

prog[3], *s.* strumento pungente; spada; stiletto.

to **prog**[3], *v.t.* (*dial.*) pungere; pugnalare.

progenitor [prouˈdʒenitə*], *s.* **1.** progenitore, antenato **2.** *fig.* predecessore politico, intellettuale **3.** *fig.* originale (di manoscritto, ecc.).

progenitress [prouˈdʒenitris], *s.* progenitrice.

progeniture [prouˈdʒenitʃə*], *s.* **1.** generazione, il generare **2.** progenie, discendenza.

progeny [ˈprodʒini], *s.* **1.** progenie, prole, discendenza **2.** *fig.* conseguenza: *the* — *of war*, la conseguenza della guerra.

proglottis [prəˈglotis], *pl.* **proglottides** [prəˈglotidiːz], *s.* (*zool.*) proglottide.

prognathism [ˈpgronəθizəm], *s.* (*antropologia*) prognatismo.

prognathous [progˈneiθəs], *ag.* prognato.

prognosis [progˈnousis], *pl.* **prognoses** *ag.* [progˈnousiːz], *s.* (*med.*) prognosi.

prognostic [progˈnostik], *ag.* profetico; rivelatore: — *symptoms*, sintomi rivelatori ‖ *s.* **1.** pronostico; presagio **2.** (*med.*) sintomo.

prognosticable [progˈnostikəbl], *ag.* che può essere pronosticato.

to **prognosticate** [progˈnostikeit], *v.t.* pronosticare.

prognostication [progˌnostiˈkeiʃən], *s.* pronostico, predizione.

prognosticator [progˈnostikeitə*], *s.c.* pronosticatore, pronosticatrice.

program(me) [ˈprougræm], *s.* **1.** programma: *a political* —, un programma politico; *what is the* — *for to-morrow?*, qual è il programma per domani? **2.** (*teat.*) programma; rappresentazione; (*cine.*) fuoriprogramma: *the* — *was a huge success*, lo spettacolo fu un enorme successo ☆ — *-music*, musica descrittiva ‖ *ball* —, « carnet » di ballo.

to **program(me)**, *v.t.* **1.** progettare, fare il programma di **2.** (*cine.*) programmare.

programming [ˈprougræmiŋ], *s.* (*cine.*) programmazione.

progress ['prougres], *s.* (*solo sing.*) **1.** avanzata; avanzamento; carriera: *the — of the enemy was violently checked*, l'avanzata nemica fu bruscamente arrestata; *as an employee he made slow —*, come impiegato progredì lentamente **2.** andamento, corso: *the — of events*, il corso degli avvenimenti; *works in —*, lavori in corso; *an inquiry is now in —*, è in corso un'inchiesta; *preparations are in —*, continuano i preparativi **3.** sviluppo; progresso, miglioramento: *the — of civilization*, il progresso della civiltà; *— of thought*, sviluppo del pensiero; *to make —*, fare progressi **4.** (*arc.*) viaggio (di un sovrano, ufficiale ecc.); cammino ‖ " *The Pilgrim's Progress* ", (*lett.*) « Il viaggio del Pellegrino ».

to **progress** [prə'gres], *v.i.* avanzare, progredire; migliorare; svilupparsi: *the patient is progressing satisfactorily*, il malato fa progressi soddisfacenti; *science progresses*, la scienza è in progresso; *to — with one's work*, avanzare nel proprio lavoro.

progression [prə'greʃən], *s.* **1.** avanzamento; successione; progressione **2.** (*mat. mus.*) progressione: *arithmetical, geometrical —*, progressione aritmetica, geometrica.

progressional [prə'greʃənl], *ag.* progressivo.

progressionist [prə'greʃnist], **progressist** [prə'gresist], *s.c.* (*pol.*) progressista.

progressive [prə'gresiv], *ag.* **1.** progressivo: *— age*, età di progresso; *— disease*, malattia progressiva **2.** (*pol.*) progressista: *the — parties*, i partiti progressisti ‖ *s.c.* (*pol.*) progressista.

progressively [prə'gresivli], *av.* **1.** progressivamente **2.** (*pol.*) da, in modo progressista.

progressiveness [prə'gresivnis], *s.* progressione; il progredire.

to **prohibit** [prə'hibit], *v.t.* proibire, vietare, impedire: *the sale of liquors is prohibited*, è proibita la vendita degli alcoolici; *they prohibited him from coming*, gli proibirono di venire.

prohibition [,proui'biʃən], *s.* **1.** proibizione, veto **2.** proibizionismo (l'insieme dei provvedimenti adottati negli Stati Uniti per reprimere la vendita degli alcoolici) **3.** (*dir.*) dichiarazione di incompetenza.

prohibitionism [,proui'biʃnizəm], *s.* (*pol.*) proibizionismo.

prohibitionist [,proui'biʃnist], *s.c.* (*pol.*) proibizionista.

prohibitive [prə'hibitiv], *ag.* proibitivo: *— prices*, prezzi proibitivi.

prohibitively [prə'hibitivli], *av.* in modo proibitivo.

prohibitory [prə'h bitəri], *ag.* (*dir.*) proibitivo: *— laws*, leggi coercitive.

project ['prodʒekt], *s.* progetto, disegno; schema, piano.

to **project** [prə'dʒekt], *v.t.i.* **1.** progettare: *to — a new waterworks*, progettare un nuovo impianto idraulico; *to — a plan*, progettare un piano **2.** proiettare (anche *fig.*): *to — an image on a screen*, (*cine.*) proiettare un'immagine su uno schermo; *to — a line*, (*geom.*) proiettare una linea; *to — a missile*, lanciare un missile; *to — one's thoughts into the future*, proiettare i propri pensieri nel futuro ‖ *to — oneself into a person's feelings*, *fig.* mettersi nei panni di qlcu. **3.** sporgere, aggettare: *these stones — from the wall*, queste pietre sporgono dal muro.

projectile [prə'dʒektail], *come s.* ['prodʒiktail], *ag.* che proietta, può essere proiettato con violenza ‖ *s.* proiettile; missile ☆ *— force*, forza di proiezione.

projection [prə'dʒekʃən], *s.* **1.** proiezione **2.** progetto **3.** (*arch.*) aggetto, sporto ☆ *— machine*, macchina per proiezioni; *— room*, cabina di proiezione.

projective [prə'dʒektiv], *ag.* proiettivo ☆ *— geometry*, geometria proiettiva.

projector [prə'dʒektə*], *s.c.* **1.** progettista **2.** promotore, promotrice; fondatore, fondatrice (di una compagnia) ‖ *s.* (*mec. elett.*) proiettore.

prolapse ['proulæps], *s.* (*patol.*) prolasso.

to **prolapse**, *v.i.* (*patol.*) prolassare.

prolapsus [prou'læpsəs], *s.* (*patol.*) prolasso.

prolate ['prouleit], *ag.* allungato; esteso.

prolegomena [,proule'gominə], *s.pl.* prolegomeni.

prolepsis [prou'lepsis], *pl.* **prolepses** [prou'lepsi:z], *s.* (*ret.*) prolessi.

proleptic [prou'leptik], *ag.* (*ret.*) prolettico.

proleptically [prou'leptikəli], *av.* **1.** (*ret.*) con prolessi **2.** antecedentemente, precedentemente.

proletarian [,proule'tɛəriən], *ag. s.* proletario.

proletarianism [,proule'tɛəriənizəm], *s.* proletariato (condizione e classe dei proletari).

proletariat [,proule'tɛəriət], **proletariate** [,proule-'tɛəriit], *s.* **1.** (*pol. econ.*) proletariato: *dictatorship of the —*, dittatura del proletariato **2.** (*st. romana*) le classi inferiori.

proletary ['prouletəri], *ag.s.* proletario.

to **proliferate** [prou'lifəreit], *v.t.i.* (*biol.*) prolificare; proliferare; moltiplicarsi.

proliferation [prou,lifə'reiʃən], *s.* (*biol.*) proliferazione.

proliferous [prou'lifərəs], *ag.* (*biol.*) prolifero.

prolific [prə'lifik], *ag.* prolifico; fecondo; fertile; produttivo: *a — writer*, uno scrittore fecondo; *a measure — of much misery*, un provvedimento generatore di grande miseria.

prolificacy [prou'lifikəsi], *s.* (*biol.*) prolificità.

prolifically [prə'lifikəli], *av.* abbondantemente; in modo prolifico.

prolificity [,prouli'fisiti], **prolificness** [prə'lifiknis], *s.* prolificità.

proligerous [prou'lidʒirəs], *ag.* prolifero.

prolix ['prouliks], *ag.* prolisso: *a — speech*, un discorso prolisso.

prolixity [prou'liksiti], *s.* prolissità.

prolixly [prou'liksli], *av.* prolissamente.

prolixness [prou'liksnis], *s.* prolissità.

prolocutor [prou'lokjutə*], *s.* presidente (di congregazione anglicana).

to **prologize** ['proulədʒaiz], *v.i.* comporre, pronunciare un prologo.

prologue ['proulog], *s.* **1.** prologo; introduzione; prefazione **2.** (*arc.*) chi recita il prologo.

to **prologue**, *v.t.* introdurre con un prologo.

to **prologuize** ['proulegaiz], *V.* to **prologize**.

to **prolong** [prə'loŋ], *v.t.* **1.** prolungare: *a prolonged visit*, una lunghissima visita **2.** (*comm.*) prorogare: *to — a bill*, prorogare la scadenza di una cambiale.

prolongable [prə'loŋəbl], *ag.* prolungabile.

to **prolongate** ['proulongeit], *v.t.* prolungare.

prolongation [,proulon'geiʃən], *s.* **1.** prolungamento **2.** (*comm.*) proroga.

prolonge [prə'londʒ], *s.* (*mil.*) prolunga.

prolusion [prou'lju:ʒən], *s.* prolusione; saggio introduttivo.

prolusory [prou'lju:səri], *ag.* preliminare; introduttivo.

prom [prom], *s.* **1.** (*fam. abbr. di promenade concert*) concerto a cui il pubblico può assistere stando in piedi o passeggiando **2.** (*amer. fam.*) ballo studentesco.

promenade [,promi'na:d], *s.* **1.** passeggiata **2.** passeggiata; passeggio pubblico; lungomare ☆ *— concert*, concerto popolare a cui molti assistono stando in piedi o passeggiando; *— deck*, (*mar.*) ponte di passeggio.

to **promenade**, *v.t.i.* passeggiare; condurre a passeggio attraverso (un posto).

Promethean [prə'mi:θjən], *ag.* **1.** di, simile a Prometeo **2.** *fig.* creativo; ardito.

Prometheus [prə'mi:θju:s], *no.pr.m.* (*mit.*) Prometeo.

promethium [prə'mi:θjəm], *s.* (*chim.*) prometeo.

prominence ['prominəns], **prominency** ['prominənsi], *s.* **1.** prominenza; sporgenza; risalto **2.** *fig.* cospicuità; importanza.

prominent ['prominənt], *ag.* **1.** prominente; sporgente **2.** *fig.* cospicuo; importante, notevole.

prominently ['prɔminəntli], *av.* **1.** in modo prominente **2.** *fig.* cospicuamente; notevolmente.

promiscuity [ˌprɔmis'kju(:)iti], *s.* promiscuità; confusione.

promiscuous [prə'miskjuəs], *ag.* **1.** promiscuo; confuso; indiscriminato **2.** (*fam.*) casuale, accidentale.

promiscuously [prə'miskjuəsli], *av.* **1.** promiscuamente **2.** (*fam.*) casualmente, accidentalmente.

promiscuousness [prə'miskjuəsnis], *s.* **1.** promiscuità **2.** confusione.

promise ['prɔmis], *s.* promessa (anche *fig.*): *a — of help* (o *to help*), una promessa d'aiuto; *the land of —*, la terra promessa; *writer of great —*, scrittore di grandi speranze; *he surrendered on the — that his life would be spared*, si arrese dietro la promessa d'aver salva la vita; *to break one's —*, mancare alla propria promessa; *to keep one's —*, mantenere una promessa; *to make a —*, fare una promessa ☆ *— -breach,* (*arc.*) violazione di promessa; *— -crammed,* (*letter.*) pieno di vane speranze.

to promise, *v.t.i.* **1.** promettere; fare una promessa: *the clouds — rain,* le nubi promettono pioggia; *to — s.o. sthg.* (o *sthg. to s.o.*), promettere ql.co. a qlcu. || *to — no end of wonders,* promettere mari e monti **2.** (*fam.*) assicurare: *I — you, it will not be so easy,* ti assicuro che non sarà così facile || *to — oneself sthg.,* ripromettersi ql.co.; sperare in ql.co

promised ['prɔmist], *ag.* promesso || *the Promised Land,* la Terra Promessa.

promisee [ˌprɔmi'si:], *s.* (*dir.*) promissario.

promising ['prɔmisiŋ], *ag.* promettente.

promisingly ['prɔmisiŋli], *av.* in modo promettente.

promisor ['prɔmisə*], *s.* (*dir.*) promettitore; persona che fa una promessa.

promissory ['prɔmisəri], *ag.* implicante una promessa; promettente ☆ *— note,* (*comm.*) pagherò cambiario.

promontory ['prɔməntri], *s.* (*geog. anat.*) promontorio.

to promote [prə'mout], *v.t.* **1.** promuovere: *he was promoted sergeant,* fu promosso sergente **2.** promuovere, incoraggiare, favorire, sostenere: *to — a bill in Parliament,* promuovere un progetto di legge in Parlamento; *to — learning,* dare impulso alla cultura **3.** (*scacchi*) scambiare (un pezzo) con uno di importanza maggiore.

promoter [prə'moutə*], *s.* promotore; fondatore (di società commerciali).

promotion [prə'mouʃən], *s.* **1.** promozione **2.** incoraggiamento; impulso.

promotive [prə'moutiv], *ag.* promotore.

prompt [prɔmpt], *ag.* **1.** pronto, lesto, sollecito: *a — assistant,* un assistente sollecito; *a — reply,* una risposta sollecita, a giro di posta **2.** (*comm.*) in contanti || *s.* **1.** (*comm.*) termine di pagamento **2.** (*teat.*) suggerimento ☆ *— -book,* (*teat.*) testo del suggeritore; *— -box,* (*teat.*) buca del suggeritore; *— -note,* pro-memo del termine di pagamento; *— payment,* pagamento in contanti; pronta consegna e pronta cassa.

to prompt, *v.t.* **1.** spingere, incitare: *to — to action,* spingere all'azione **2.** suggerire, dettare, consigliare: *envy prompted her words,* l'invidia le dettò quelle parole **3.** (*teat.*) suggerire.

prompter ['prɔmptə*], *s.* (*teat.*) suggeritore.

promptitude ['prɔmptitju:d], *s.* prontezza, sollecitudine.

promptly ['prɔmptli], *av.* **1.** prontamente, sollecitamente **2.** (*comm.*) in contanti; a pronta cassa.

promptness ['prɔmptnis], *s.* prontezza; sollecitudine.

to promulgate ['prɔmɔlgeit], *v.t.* **1.** promulgare, proclamare (legge, dogma, ecc.) **2.** diffondere, propagare: *to — a new belief,* propagare un nuovo credo.

promulgation [ˌprɔmɔl'geiʃən], *s.* **1.** promulgazione, proclamazione **2.** propagazione, diffusione.

promulgator ['prɔmɔlgeitə*], *s.* promulgatore.

pronaos [prou'neiɔs], *pl.* **pronaoi** [prou'neiɔi], *s.* (*arch.*) pronao.

to pronate ['prouneit], *v.t.* (*fisiol.*) mettere (mano, avambraccio) in posizione prona.

pronation [prou'neiʃən], *s.* (*fisiol.*) pronazione.

pronator [prou'neitə*], *s.* (*anat.*) (muscolo) pronatore.

prone [proun], *ag.* **1.** prono, bocconi (di persona): *he fell — on the floor,* cadde bocconi sul pavimento **2.** inclinato, ripido (di terreno) **3.** *fig.* incline, propenso, proclive: *he is — to error,* è proclive all'errore.

pronely ['prounli], *av.* bocconi; in posizione prona.

proneness ['prounnis], *s.* *fig.* inclinazione, propensione, disposizione.

prong [prɔŋ], *s.* **1.** forca **2.** rebbio, dente (di forcone, forchetta).

to prong, *v.t.* **1.** sollevare, infilzare con la forca **2.** munire di rebbi.

pronged [prɔŋd], *ag.* munito di punte, di rebbi ☆ *three- — fork,* tridente.

pronominal [prə'nɔminl], *ag.* (*gram.*) pronominale.

pronominally [prə'nɔminəli], *av.* pronominalmente.

pronoun ['prounaun], *s.* (*gram.*) pronome.

to pronounce [prə'nauns], *v.t.i.* **1.** dire, pronunciare: *the child can't — my name,* il bimbo non sa dire il mio nome **2.** proferire; enunciare; dichiarare: *he was pronounced dead,* fu dichiarato morto; *the judge pronounced the sentence,* il giudice proferì la sentenza **3.** pronunciarsi, dichiararsi: *I — in his favour,* mi dichiaro favorevole a lui.

pronounceable [prə'naunsəbl], *ag.* pronunciabile.

pronounced [prə'naunst], *ag.* **1.** pronunciato, detto **2.** pronunciato, forte, marcato: *a — tendency,* una tendenza marcata.

pronouncedly [prə'naunstli], *av.* in modo pronunciato, marcato.

pronouncement [prə'naunsmənt], *s.* dichiarazione solenne.

pronouncing [prə'naunsiŋ], *s.* pronuncia ☆ *English — dictionary,* dizionario della pronuncia inglese.

pronto ['prɔntou], *av.* (*sl. amer.*) subito, immediatamente, in fretta.

pronunciamento [prəˌnʌnsiə'mentou], *s.* dichiarazione, manifesto (di rivoluzione).

pronunciation [prəˌnʌnsi'eiʃən], *s.* pronuncia: *his — is perfect, mine is often faulty,* la sua pronuncia è perfetta, la mia è spesso errata.

proof [pru:f], *ag.* a prova di, resistente a, inaccessibile a: *— against temptation,* resistente alle tentazioni || *s.* **1.** prova (anche *dir. mat.*); evidenza: *in* (o *as a*) *— of,* a prova di; *the police have strong grounds for suspicion, but no proofs,* la polizia ha seri motivi di sospetto, ma nessuna prova; *to give — of one's gratitude to s.o.,* dare prova della propria gratitudine a qlcu.; *to have — of sthg.,* avere la prova di ql.co.; *to put s.o., sthg., to the —,* mettere qlcu., ql.co., alla prova || *the — of the pudding is in the eating,* *prov.* alla prova si scortica l'asino **2.** (*chim.*) provetta **3.** (*sheet*), (*tip.*) bozza di stampa **4.** (*incisione*) prova **5.** misura base della gradazione alcoolica ☆ *— -charge,* carica di prova (di fucile); *— -press,* (*tip.*) torchio per bozze; *— -puller,* (*tip.*) tirabozze; *— -reader,* correttore di bozze; *— -spirit,* alcool a gradazione regolamentare || *bomb- —,* a prova di bomba; *burglar - —,* a prova di scasso; *clean —,* (*tip.*) seconda bozza; *foul —,* (*tip.*) prima bozza; *galley- —,* (*tip.*) prima bozza (non impaginata); *press- —,* (*tip.*) ultima bozza; *water- —,* impermeabile.

to proof, *v.t.* **1.** rendere impermeabile, resistente **2.** (*tip.*) tirare una bozza, una prova di.

prop¹ [prɔp], *s.* **1.** puntello **2.** *fig.* sostegno, appoggio: *he is the — and stay of the home,* è il sostegno e l'appoggio della casa.

to prop¹, *pass.p.p.* **propped** [prɔpt], *v.t.i.* **1.** appoggiare: *to — a ladder against the wall,* appoggiare una scala contro il muro **2.** puntellare; sostenere (anche *fig.*): *to — a patient* (*up*) *against his pillows,* sostenere un malato con guanciali; *to — up a piece of fur-*

niture, sostenere un mobile con zeppe ‖ *to — one's eyelids*, combattere contro il sonno 3. (*miner.*) puntellare 4. arrestarsi improvvisamente (di cavallo).

prop[2], *s.* (*sl.*) spilla per cravatta.

prop, (*sl. scolastico abbr.*) di **proposition**.

propaedeutic(al) [ˌproupiːˈdjuːtik(əl)], *ag.* propedeutico.

propaedeutics [ˌproupiːˈdjuːtiks], *s.* propedeutica.

propagable [ˈprɔpəgəbl], *ag.* propagabile.

propaganda [ˌprɔpəˈgændə], *s.* propaganda: *for — purposes*, a scopo di propaganda, per propaganda.

propagandism [ˌprɔpəˈgændizəm], *s.* divulgazione.

propagandist [ˌprɔpəˈgændist], *s.c.* propagandista.

propagandistic [ˌprɔpəgænˈdistik], *ag.* propagandistico.

to **propagandize** [ˌprɔpəˈgændaiz], *v.t.* propagandare, fare propaganda di, a.

to **propagate** [ˈprɔpəgeit], *v.t.i.* 1. (*bot. zool.*) riprodurre, riprodursi: *to — plants by cuttings*, far riprodurre le piante per talea 2. trasmettere, trasmettersi; propagare, propagarsi; diffondere, diffondersi (anche *fig.*): *a disease propagated from generation to generation*, una malattia trasmessa di generazione in generazione; *light is propagated in a straight line*, la luce si propaga in linea retta; *to — news*, diffondere notizie.

propagation [ˌprɔpəˈgeiʃən], *s.* 1. (*bot. zool.*) riproduzione 2. propagazione, trasmissione, diffusione (anche *fig.*).

propagative [ˈprɔpəgeitiv], *ag.* atto a propagare.

propagator [ˈprɔpəgeitə*], *s.c.* propagatore, propagatrice.

propane [ˈproupein], *s.* (*chim.*) propano.

proparoxytone [ˌproupəˈrɔksitoun], *ag.* proparossitono ‖ *s.* parola proparossitona.

to **propel** [prəˈpel], *pass.p.p.* **propelled** [prəˈpeld], *v.t.* spingere innanzi, propulsare; muovere (anche *fig.*): *propelled by steam*, azionato a vapore ☆ *jet-propelled plane*, aviogetto.

propellant [prəˈpelənt], *s.* propulsore.

propellent [prəˈpelənt], *ag. s.* propulsore.

propeller [prəˈpelə*], *s.* 1. propulsore 2. (*screw*) —, (*aer. mar.*) elica 3. (*mar.*) piroscafo ad elica ☆ *— blades*, pale dell'elica; *— noise*, rombo dell'elica; *— shaft*, (*aut.*) albero di trasmissione; *— turbine engine*, motore a turboelica.

propelment [prəˈpelmənt], *s.* propulsione.

to **propend** [prəˈpend], *v.i.* (*rar.*) propendere.

propense [prəˈpens], *ag.* (*rar.*) incline, propenso.

propensely [prəˈpensli], *av.* (*rar.*) in modo propenso.

propension [prəˈpenʃən], **propensity** [prəˈpensiti], *s.* propensione; tendenza, inclinazione: *— to* (o *towards*) *sthg.*, *— for doing sthg.*, inclinazione verso ql.co., a fare ql.co.

proper [ˈprɔpə*], *ag.* 1. proprio, particolare: *— name*, nome proprio; *the — sense of this sentence*, il senso particolare di questa frase; *this heat is — to certain countries*, questo caldo è proprio, tipico di alcuni paesi 2. adatto, appropriato, conveniente, confacente: *a — behaviour*, un contegno decoroso; *— tool*, arnese adatto; *it must be done in the — way*, bisogna farlo in modo appropriato 3. giusto, corretto, esatto: *I do not think it — for him to say...*, non ritengo giusto da parte sua dire... 4. propriamente detto: *Italy —*, l'Italia propriamente detta (escluse le isole) 5. (*fam.*) vero e proprio: *a — scoundrel*, un vero e proprio mascalzone; *she was in a — rage*, era veramente infuriata 6. (*arc.*) bello, grazioso 7. (*mat.*) proprio: *a — fraction*, una frazione propria 8. (*arc.*) proprio, personale: *at my — cost*, a mie spese 9. (*arald.*) al naturale: *tiger —*, tigre al naturale.

properispomenon [ˈprouˌperiˈspouminən], *ag.* properispomeno ‖ *s.* parola properispomena.

properly [ˈprɔpəli], *av.* 1. a modo, bene, correttamente: *to behave —*, comportarsi bene 2. propriamente, realmente: *he is not, — speaking, a doctor*, non è, per

essere esatti, dottore 3. (*fam.*) completamente: *he was — drunk*, era completamente ubriaco.

propertied [ˈprɔpətid], *ag.* possidente.

Propertius [prəˈpɔːʃəs], *no.pr.m.* (*st. lett.*) Properzio

property [ˈprɔpəti], *s.* 1. proprietà, diritto di proprietà 2. proprietà, fondi, averi, beni mobili e immobili: *acquisition of —*, acquisto della proprietà; *a man of —*, un possidente; *title to —*, titolo alla proprietà 3. proprietà, qualità, caratteristica: *hardness is a — of diamonds*, la durezza è una caratteristica dei diamanti 4. *pl.* (*teat.*) costumi, oggetti per la scena, ecc. ☆ *— -man*, (*teat.*) trovarobe; *— -room*, (*teat.*) ripostiglio per costumi, ecc.; *— -tax*, imposta sul patrimonio ‖ *literary —*, proprietà letteraria; *personal —*, beni mobili; *private —*, proprietà privata; *public —*, proprietà pubblica; *real —*, beni immobili.

propertyless [ˈprɔpətilis], *s.* nullatenente.

prophecy [ˈprɔfisi], *s.* profezia, predizione.

prophesier [ˈprɔfisaiə*], *s.c.* profeta, profetessa.

to **prophesy** [ˈprɔfisai], *v.t.i.* 1. profetizzare, predire; essere profeta 2. (*arc.*) interpretare le Sacre Scritture.

prophet [ˈprɔfit], *s.* 1. indovino; profeta: *— of evil*, profeta di sventura ‖ *the Prophet*, il Profeta, Maometto 2. (*sl.*) informatore segreto (alle corse di cavalli).

prophetess [ˈprɔfitis], *s.* profetessa.

prophetic(al) [prəˈfetik(əl)], *ag.* profetico.

prophetically [prəˈfetikəli], *av.* profeticamente.

prophylactic [ˌprɔfiˈlæktik], *ag.* (*med.*) profilattico ‖ *s.* medicina, misura profilattica.

prophylactically [ˌprɔfiˈlæktikəli], *av.* in modo profilattico.

prophylaxis [ˌprɔfiˈlæksis], *s.* (*med.*) profilassi.

propinquity [prəˈpiŋkwiti], *s.* 1. vicinanza; prossimità (di tempo, spazio) 2. affinità; somiglianza.

propitiable [prəˈpiʃiəbl], *ag.* propiziabile.

to **propitiate** [prəˈpiʃieit], *v.t.* 1. propiziare, render propizio: *to — the gods*, propiziarsi gli dei 2. calmare, rabbonire.

propitiation [prəˌpiʃiˈeiʃən], *s.* 1. propiziazione 2. espiazione 3. (*arc.*) dono, sacrificio propiziatorio.

propitiator [prəˈpiʃieitə*], *s.c.* propiziatore, propiziatrice.

propitiatory [prəˈpiʃiətəri], *ag.* propiziatorio ‖ *s.* propiziatorio (tavola nell'Arca della Santa Alleanza, per la preghiera).

propitious [prəˈpiʃəs], *ag.* propizio, favorevole: *— omens*, presagi favorevoli; *the weather was —*, il tempo era propizio.

propitiously [prəˈpiʃəsli], *av.* favorevolmente.

propitiousness [prəˈpiʃəsnis], *s.* natura propizia, favorevole.

propolis [ˈprɔpəlis], *s.* propoli.

proponent [prəˈpounənt], *ag. s.* proponente.

proportion [prəˈpɔːʃən], *s.* 1. proporzione: *in — to*, in proporzione a; *in fair —*, in giusta proporzione; *out of — to*, sproporzionato a; *the proportions of the building are faulty*, le proporzioni dell'edificio sono sbagliate 2. *pl.* misure, dimensioni: *a ship of majestic proportions*, una nave di dimensioni imponenti 3. parte: *to divide profits in equal proportions*, dividere i profitti in parti uguali 4. (*mat.*) proporzione.

to **proportion**, *v.t.* 1. proporzionare 2. dividere in parti proporzionate.

proportionable [prəˈpɔːʃnəbl], *ag.* proporzionabile.

proportionableness [prəˈpɔːʃnəblnis], *s.* proporzionabilità.

proportionably [prəˈpɔːʃnəbli], *av.* in proporzione.

proportional [prəˈpɔːʃənl], *ag.* proporzionale ☆ *— representation*, (*pol.*) rappresentanza proporzionale.

proportionality [prəˌpɔːʃəˈnæliti], *s.* proporzionalità.

proportionally [prəˈpɔːʃnəli], *av.* proporzionalmente.

proportionate [prəˈpɔːʃnit], *ag.* proporzionato.

proportionately [prəˈpɔːʃnitli], *av.* proporzionatamente.

proportionateness [prə'pɔ:ʃnitnis], *s.* proporzionalità; buone proporzioni.

proportionless [prə'pɔ:ʃənlis], *ag.* sproporzionato, senza proporzioni.

proportionment [prə'pɔ:ʃənmənt], *s.* proporzionamento.

proposal [prə'pouzəl], *s.* **1.** proposta; progetto: *the — was never carried out*, la proposta non fu mai realizzata; *to make a —*, fare una proposta **2.** proposta, offerta di matrimonio: *she had a —*, ebbe una domanda di matrimonio.

to **propose** [prə'pouz], *v.t.i.* **1.** proporre: *the object I — to myself*, lo scopo che mi propongo; *we — Mr. Smith as chairman*, proponiamo il signor Smith come presidente ‖ *man proposes, God disposes*, *prov.* l'uomo propone e Dio dispone **2.** fare richiesta di matrimonio: *he proposed to her*, le chiese di sposarlo **3.** fare un brindisi a: *to — the health of s.o.*, bere alla salute di qlcu. **4.** (II) intendere, prefiggersi: *I — to finish my work by tomorrow*, mi prefiggo di finire il lavoro per domani; *we — leaving at noon*, intendiamo partire a mezzogiorno.

proposer [prə'pouzə*], *s.c.* proponente.

proposition [,prɒpə'ziʃən], *s.* **1.** asserzione: *an absurd —*, un'asserzione infondata **2.** proposta, progetto, affare: *this is an expensive —*, è un progetto un po' caro **3.** (*gram. log.*) proposizione **4.** (*mat.*) teorema, problema.

propositional [,prɒpə'ziʃənl], *ag.* **1.** di proposizione **2.** di proposta.

to **propound** [prə'paund], *v.t.* **1.** proporre; offrire **2.** (*dir.*) far omologare (un testamento).

proprietary [prə'praiətəri], *ag.* di proprietà, di proprietario ‖ **1.** stato, diritto di proprietario **2.** classe dei proprietari ☆ *— medicines*, specialità medicinali; *— rights*, diritti di proprietà.

proprietor [prə'praiətə*], *s.c.* proprietario, proprietaria ☆ *joint —*, comproprietario.

proprietorial [prə,praiə'tɔ:riəl], *ag.* di proprietario.

proprietorship [prə'praiətəʃip], *s.* **1.** condizione di proprietario **2.** proprietà.

proprietress [prə'praiətris], *s.* proprietaria.

propriety [prə'praiəti], *s.* **1.** proprietà: *I doubt of the — of the term*, dubito della proprietà della parola **2.** decoro, decenza: *his behaviour was a real breach of —*, la sua condotta era un vero strappo alla morale **3.** opportunità: *I doubt of the — of calling on them*, non mi sembra opportuno far loro visita **4.** *pl.* convenienze: *proprieties must be observed*, le regole di buona creanza devono esser osservate.

props [props], (*sl. teat. abbr.*) di **property** **4.**

proptosed ['proptoust], *ag.* (*med.*) protuberante.

proptosis [prop'tousis], *s.* (*med.*) proptosi, esoftalmo.

propulsion [prə'pʌlʃən], *s.* **1.** propulsione **2.** *fig.* spinta ☆ *jet —*, propulsione a reazione.

propulsive [prə'pʌlsiv], **propulsory** [prə'pʌlsəri], *ag.* propulsivo.

propylaeum [,prɒpi'li(:)əm], *pl.* **propylaea** [,prɒpi'li(:)ə], *s.* (*arch.*) propileo.

propylon ['prɒpilon], *V.* **propylaeum.**

to **prorate** [prou'reit], *v.t.i.* (*amer.*) dividere, distribuire proporzionalmente.

prorogation [,prourə'geiʃən], *s.* proroga; prolungamento; (*dir.*) rinvio.

to **prorogue** [prə'roug], *v.t.i.* **1.** prorogare (una legislatura) **2.** ritardare, rimandare; sospendere **3.** essere differito.

prosaic [prou'zeiik], *ag.* prosaico, prosastico; comune, banale.

prosaically [prou'zeiikəli], *av.* prosaicamente.

prosaicism [prou'zeiisizəm], *s.* **1.** prosaicismo **2.** espressione prosaica.

prosaicness [prou'zeiiknis], *s.* prosaicità.

prosaist ['prouzeist], *s.* **1.** prosatore **2.** individuo prosaico.

proscenium [prou'si:njəm], *pl.* **proscenia** [prou'si:njə], *s.* (*teat.*) proscenio; (*teat. antico*) palcoscenico, scena.

to **proscribe** [prous'kraib], *v.t.* **1.** proscrivere; esiliare; bandire (anche *fig.*) **2.** condannare; vietare.

proscribed [prous'kraibd], *ag.* proscritto.

proscriber [prous'kraibə*], *s.* proscrittore, chi proscrive.

proscription [prous'kripʃən], *s.* **1.** proscrizione **2.** proibizione.

proscriptive [prous'kriptiv], *ag.* che proscrive; di proscrizione.

prose [prouz], *s.* **1.** prosa **2.** prosaicità: *the — of existence*, la prosaicità della vita **3.** (*eccl.*) sequenza **4.** discorso noioso ☆ *— poem*, poema in prosa; *— works*, opere in prosa; *— writer*, prosatore.

to **prose**, *v.t.i.* **1.** scrivere in prosa **2.** volgere dalla poesia in prosa **3.** parlare prosaicamente.

prosector [prou'sektə*], *s.* (*med.*) prosettore.

to **prosecute** ['prɒsikju:t], *v.t.i.* **1.** proseguire; continuare: *— your studies*, continuate i vostri studi; *to — an inquiry*, condurre un'inchiesta **2.** (*dir.*) perseguire (un'azione legale), intentare giudizio: *trespassers will be prosecuted*, i contravventori verranno processati a termine di legge; *to — the charge*, sostenere l'accusa **3.** esercitare (un mestiere, ecc.).

prosecuting ['prɒsikju:tiŋ], *ag.* che persegue un'azione legale ☆ *— attorney*, (*dir.*) pubblico ministero.

prosecution [,prɒsi'kju:ʃən], *s.* **1.** proseguimento; prosecuzione **2.** (*dir.*) accusa, processo: *to start a — against*, intentare un processo contro **3.** parte agente, querelante: *witness for the —*, testimone d'accusa **4.** esercizio (di un mestiere, ecc.).

prosecutor ['prɒsikju:tə*], *s.* **1.** prosecutore; continuatore **2.** (*dir.*) accusatore, querelante, attore ☆ *public — (o — for the Crown)*, pubblico accusatore, pubblico ministero.

prosecutrix ['prɒsi,kju:triks], *pl.* **prosecutrices** [,prɒsi'kju:trisi:z], *s.* (*dir.*) accusatrice; querelante.

proselyte ['prɒsilait], *s.* proselito ‖ *— of the gate*, convertito all'ebraismo senza sottomettersi alla circoncisione.

to **proselyte**, *v.t.i.* fare proseliti; convertire.

proselytism ['prɒsilitizəm], *s.* proselitismo.

to **proselytize** ['prɒsilitaiz], *v.t.i.* fare proseliti; convertire.

proselytizer ['prɒsilitaizə*], *s.c.* chi fa proseliti.

prosenchyma [prɒs'eŋkimə], *s.* (*bot.*) prosenchima.

proser ['prouzə*], *s.* **1.** prosatore **2.** narratore tedioso; chiacchierone noioso.

Proserpine ['prɒsəpain], *no.pr.f.* (*mit.*) Proserpina.

to **prosify** ['prouzifai], *v.t.i.* **1.** volgere in prosa, scrivere in prosa **2.** parlare, scrivere in modo prosaico.

prosily ['prouzili], *av.* **1.** prosaicamente **2.** tediosamente.

prosiness ['prouzinis], *s.* **1.** prosaicità **2.** banalità.

prosit ['prousit], *inter.* prosit!, salute!

prosodiac [prə'soudiæk], **prosodiacal** [,prɒsou'daiəkəl], **prosodial** [prə'soudiəl], **prosodic(al)** [prə'sodik(əl)], *ag.* prosodico.

prosodically [prə'sɔdikəli], *av.* prosodicamente.

prosodist ['prɒsədist], *s.* studioso di prosodia.

prosody ['prɒsədi], *s.* prosodia, metrica.

prosopopoeia [prə,soupə'pi:jə], *s.* (*ret.*) prosopopea.

prospect ['prospekt], *s.* **1.** panorama, vista: *after the storm the country offered a sad —*, dopo l'uragano la campagna aveva un aspetto triste; *from my window I see a fine —*, dalla mia finestra vedo un bel panorama **2.** prospettiva: *travelling opens new prospects to a man's mind*, il viaggiare apre nuove prospettive alla mente dell'uomo **3.** *gener. pl.* speranza, aspettativa; avvenire: *the prospects of the harvest are excellent*, si prevede un eccellente raccolto; *his prospects are brilliant*, ha un brillante avvenire; *there is no — of success in staging this comedy*, non vi è speranza di successo mettendo in scena questa commedia **4.** (*miner.*) luogo di assaggio per minerali; campione di prova **5.** (*amer.*) possibile cliente, candidato.

tò prospect [prəs'pekt], *v.t.i.* **1.** esplorare (in cerca di oro, ecc.): *they prospected (the district) for silver*, esplorarono la regione in cerca di giacimenti d'argento **2.** promettere: *that mine prospects well*, si spera che quella miniera sia ricca **3.** cercare, esplorare.

prospecting [prəs'pektiŋ], *s.* ricerca; (*miner.*) esplorazione.

prospection [prəs'pekʃən], *s.* (*rar.*) **1.** aspettativa **2.** previsione; previdenza.

prospective [prəs'pektiv], *ag.* **1.** concernente il futuro: *the law was exclusively —*, la legge riguardava esclusivamente il futuro **2.** probabile, eventuale: *a — customer*, un eventuale cliente; *the — bridegroom*, il futuro sposo.

prospectively [prəs'pektivli], *av.* riguardo al futuro, in previsione.

prospectiveness [prəs'pektivnis], *s.* previsione.

prospectless ['prɔspektlis], *ag.* senza avvenire; senza prospettive.

prospector [prəs'pektə*], *s.* cercatore (d'oro, petrolio, ecc.).

prospectus [prəs'pektəs], *pl.* **prospectuses** [prəs'pektəsiz], *s.* prospetto, programma: *a — of the courses*, prospetto dei corsi (di una scuola).

to prosper ['prɔspə*], *v.t.i.* prosperare; far prosperare; rendere prospero.

prosperity [prɔs'periti], *s.* prosperità.

Prospero ['prɔsperou], *no.pr.m.* (*lett.*) Prospero.

prosperous ['prɔsperəs], *ag.* **1.** prospero; florente; benestante **2.** favorevole, propizio.

prosperously ['prɔsperəsli], *av.* prosperamente; con successo.

prosperousness ['prɔsperəsnis], *s.* prosperità.

prostate ['prɔsteit], *s.* (*anat.*) prostata.

prostatic [prɔs'tætik], *ag.* (*anat.*) prostatico.

prosthesis ['prɔsθisis], *s.* **1.** (*gram.*) prostesi **2.** (*chir.*) protesi.

prosthetic [prɔs'θetik], *ag.* **1.** (*gram.*) prostetico **2.** (*chir.*) protetico.

prostitute ['prɔstitju:t], *ag.* (*rar.*) prostituito; corrotto ‖ *s.* **1.** prostituta, meretrice, cortigiana **2.** *fig.* vile mercenario; politicante corrotto.

to prostitute, *v.t.* prostituire (anche *fig.*): *to — one's talents*, vendere il proprio talento

prostitution [ˌprɔsti'tju:ʃən], *s.* prostituzione (anche *fig.*).

prostitutor ['prɔstitju:tə*], *s.* prostitutore.

prostrate ['prɔstreit], *ag.* **1.** prosternato, bocconi **2.** *fig.* prostrato, abbattuto; sopraffatto **3.** (*bot.*) procombente.

to prostrate [prɔs'treit], *v.t.i.* **1.** prosternare, prosternarsi; distendere, distendersi per terra: *to — oneself before s.o.*, prosternarsi davanti a qlcu. **2.** *fig.* prostrare, abbattere; sopraffare: *prostrated by the heat*, prostrato dal caldo.

prostration [prɔs'treiʃən], *s.* **1.** prosternazione **2.** *fig.* prostrazione, abbattimento, avvilimento; sopraffazione.

prostyle ['proustail], *ag. s.* (*arch.*) prostilo.

prosy ['prouzi], *ag.* **1.** prosaico **2.** noioso, monotono; banale.

protagonist [prou'tægənist], *s.c.* protagonista.

Protagoras [prou'tægəræs], *no.pr.m.* (*st. fil.*) Protagora.

protasis ['prɔtəsis], *pl.* **protases** ['prɔtəsi:z], *s.* (*gram.*) protasi.

protatic [prou'tætik], *ag.* (*gram.*) protatico.

protean [prou'ti:ən], *ag.* proteiforme; versatile.

to protect [prə'tekt], *v.t.* **1.** proteggere, tutelare, salvaguardare (anche *econ.*): *to — s.o. from* (o *against*) *sthg.*, proteggere qlcu. da ql.co. **2.** (*comm.*) onorare: *to — a bill*, onorare una cambiale.

protecting [prə'tektiŋ], *ag.* protettivo.

protectingly [prə'tektiŋli], *av.* con aria di protezione.

protection [prə'tekʃən], *s.* **1.** protezio e, difesa, salvaguardia, tutela; (*econ.*) protezionismo: *he was under the — of the law*, egli era sotto la tutela della legge; *she wore a scarf as — against the cold*, indossava una sciarpa per difendersi dal freddo **2.** protettore **3.** salvacondotto **4.** (*mar.*) certificato di nazionalità americana.

protectionism [prə'tekʃənizəm], *s.* (*econ.*) protezionismo.

protectionist [prə'tekʃənist], *s.* (*econ.*) protezionista.

protective [prə'tektiv], *ag.* protettivo, difensivo ☆ *— custody*, carcere preventivo; *— tariff*, (*econ.*) tariffa protettiva.

protectively [prə'tektivli], *av.* in modo protettivo.

protectiveness [prə'tektivnis], *s.* protezione, difesa; (*st. econ.*) protezionismo.

protector [prə'tektə*], *s.* **1.** protettore; mecenate **2.** reggente ‖ *Lord Protector of the Commonwealth*, (*st.*) Lord Protettore della Repubblica (titolo di Oliver e Richard Cromwell) **3.** (*mec.*) dispositivo di protezione.

protectoral [prə'tektərəl], *ag.* di protettore.

protectorate [prə'tektərit], *s.* protettorato.

protectorless [prə'tektəlis], *ag.* senza protettore.

protectorship [prə'tektəʃip], *s.* protettorato.

protectory [prə'tektəri], *s.* patronato (specialmente per poveri e fanciulli da rieducare).

protectress [prə'tektris], *s.* protettrice; patrona; patronessa.

protégé ['prouteʒei], *s.* protetto.

protégée ['prouteʒei], *s.* protetta.

proteid(e) ['prouti:d], *s.* (*chim. fisiol.*) protide.

proteiform ['prouti:fɔ:m], *ag.* proteiforme; variabile.

protein ['prouti:n], *s.* (*chim. fisiol.*) proteina.

proteinaceous [ˌprouti'neiʃəs], **proteinic** [ˌprouti'inik], **proteinous** [prou'ti:inəs], *ag.* (*chim. fisiol.*) proteico.

proteolysis [ˌprouti'ɔlisis], *s.* (*biol.*) proteolisi.

protest ['proutest], *s.* **1.** protesta: *to make* (o *to set up*) *a — against sthg.*, protestare contro ql.co.; *to raise a —*, elevare protesta **2.** (*dir.*) riserva: *— in writing*, riserva; *under —*, sotto riserva **3.** (*comm.*) protesto (di cambiale) ☆ *ship's —*, (*mar.*) dichiarazione d'avaria.

to protest [prə'test], *v.t.i.* **1.** protestare, affermare, dichiarare: *to — one's innocence, one's good faith*, protestare la propria innocenza, la propria buona fede **2.** protestare, elevare protesta **3.** (*comm.*) protestare, mandare in protesto (una cambiale).

protestant ['prɔtistənt], *ag.* **1.** che protesta **2.** *Protestant*, (*relig.*) protestante ‖ *s.c.* **1.** chi protesta **2.** *Protestant*, (*relig.*) protestante.

Protestantism ['prɔtistəntizəm], *s.* (*relig.*) protestantesimo.

to protestantize ['prɔtistəntaiz], *v.t.i.* (*relig.*) **1.** rendere protestante **2.** diventare protestante.

protestation [ˌproutes'teiʃən], *s.* **1.** protesta **2.** affermazione solenne, dichiarazione: *solemn — of friendship*, solenne dichiarazione di amicizia.

protestingly [prə'testiŋli], *av.* per protesta; in tono di protesta.

protestor [prə'testə*], *s.c.* chi protesta.

Proteus ['proutju:s], *no.pr.m.* (*mit.*) Proteo ‖ **proteus**, *s.* **1.** persona volubile, che cambia sovente atteggiamento e modi **2.** (*zool.*) proteo.

prothalamion [ˌprouθə'leimiən], **prothalamium** [ˌprouθə'leimiəm], *pl.* **prothalamia** [ˌprouθə'leimiə], *s.* (*poes.*) epitalamio.

prothallium [prə'θæliəm], *pl.* **prothallia** [prə'θæliə], *s.* (*bot.*) protallo.

prothesis ['prɔθisis], *s.* (*gram. eccl.*) protesi.

prothonotary [ˌprouθə'noutəri], *s.* **1.** (*st.*) protonotario **2.** (*dir.*) cancelliere capo (negli Stati Uniti).

prothorax [prou'θɔ:ræks], *s.* (*entom.*) protorace.

Protista [prou'tistə], *s.pl.* (*biol.*) i protisti.

protocol ['proutəkɔl], *s.* protocollo.

to **protocol**, *pass.p.p.* **protocolled** ['proutəkɔld], *v.t.i.* **1.** protocollare **2.** redigere protocolli.

protocolist ['proutəkɔlist], *s.* protocollista.

protogine ['proutədʒin], *s.* (*min.*) protogino.

protomartyr ['proutə,mɑ:tə*], *s.* protomartire.

proton ['proutɔn], *s.* (*fis.*) protone.

protonotary [,proutə'noutəri], *V.* **prothonotary**.

protoplasm ['proutəplæzəm], *s.* (*biol.*) protoplasma.

protoplasmatic [,proutəplæz'mætik], **protoplasmic** ,proutə'plæzmik], *ag.* (*biol.*) di protoplasma.

protoplast ['proutəplæst], *s.* **1.** protoplasto, archetipo **2.** (*biol.*) unità, massa di protoplasma.

protoplastic [,proutə'plæstik], *ag.* protoplastico.

prototypal ['proutətaipl], *ag.* prototipo.

prototype ['proutətaip], *s.* prototipo, archetipo.

prototypic(al) [,proutə'tipik(əl)], *ag.* prototipo.

protoxide [prou'tɔksaid], *s.* (*chim.*) protossido.

Protozoa [,proutə'zouə], *s.pl.* (*biol.*) i protozoi.

to **protract** [prə'trækt], *v.t.* **1.** protrarre, prolungare: *to — a visit*, protrarre una visita **2.** differire, dilazionare **3.** rilevare; riprodurre in scala (un terreno).

protracted [prə'træktid], *ag.* **1.** protratto, prolungato **2.** differito, dilazionato.

protractedly [prə'træktidli], *av.* **1.** prolungatamente; in modo prolisso **2.** con ritardo.

protractile [prə'træktail], *ag.* protrattile (di organo di animale).

protraction [prə'trækʃən], *s.* **1.** protrazione, prolungazione **2.** rilievo; disegno in scala (di un terreno).

protractive [prə'træktiv], *ag.* dilatorio.

protractor [prə'træktə*], *s.* **1.** (*geom.*) goniometro **2.** muscolo estensore **3.** (*chir.*) estrattore.

to **protrude** [prə'tru:d], *v.t.i.* **1.** sporgere, sporgersi, tirar fuori: *to — one's tongue*, metter fuori la lingua **2.** *fig.* intromettersi; imporre, imporsi: *to — one's opinions on the public*, imporre le proprie opinioni al pubblico.

protrusible [prə'tru:səbl], *ag.* estensibile; che si può spingere fuori.

protrusile [prou'tru:sil], *ag.* pratrattile (di arto, ecc.).

protrusion [prə'tru:ʒən], *s.* **1.** l'avanzare, lo sporgere, il far sporgere in fuori **2.** (*patol.*) protrusione.

protrusive [prə'tru:siv], *ag.* **1.** sporgente **2.** (*patol.*) protundente.

protrusively [prə'tru:sivli], *av.* in modo da sporgere.

protuberance [prə'tju:bərəns], **protuberancy** [prə'tju:bərənsi], *s.* protuberanza, prominenza.

protuberant [prə'tju:bərənt], *ag.* protuberante, prominente.

protuberantly [prə'tju:bərəntli], *av.* in modo protuberante, prominente.

to **protuberate** [prə'tju:bəreit], *v.i.* essere prominente, sporgere in fuori; formare protuberanza.

proud [praud], *ag.* **1.** fiero, orgoglioso; superbo, altero; presuntuoso: *too — to complain*, troppo fiero per lamentarsi; *to be — of sthg.*, gloriarsi di ql.co.: *to be — to do sthg.*, considerare un onore fare ql.co. ‖ *you do me —*, (*fam.*) Lei mi onora grandemente ‖ *to do oneself —*, (*fam.*) non privarsi di niente **2.** imponente, magnifico, superbo (di paesaggio, città, ecc.): *a — sight*, una veduta splendida **3.** in piena (di acque): *— waters*, acque ingrossate ☆ *— -flesh*, (*med.*) granulazione esuberante.

proudish ['praudiʃ], *ag.* orgoglioselto.

proudly ['praudli], *av.* orgogliosamente; superbamente.

proudness ['praudnis], *s.* orgoglio; superbia.

provable ['pru:vəbl], *ag.* provabile; dimostrabile.

provableness ['pru:vəblnis], *s.* dimostrabilità.

provably ['pru:vəbli], *av.* in modo provabile, dimostrabile.

provand ['prɔvənd], *s.* (*arc.*) provenda, vettovaglia, rifornimento di derrate (specialmente per l'esercito).

to **prove** [pru:v], *v.t.i.* **1.** provare, mettere alla prova, verificare: *to — gold*, saggiare l'oro; *to — the*

patience of s.o., mettere alla prova la pazienza di qlcu. **2.** provare; dimostrare: *he proved his innocence*, dimostrò la sua innocenza ‖ *the exception proves the rule*, *prov.* l'eccezione conferma la regola **3.** (*arit.*) verificare, fare la prova di: *to — a sum*, verificare una somma **4.** risultare; dimostrarsi: *the manuscript proved to be a forgery*, il manoscritto si rivelò una contraffazione; *the news proved false*, le notizie risultarono false **5.** omologare, convalidare: *to — a will*, omologare un testamento.

proveditor [prou'veditə*], **provedore** [,prɔvi'dɔː*], *s.* **1.** (*st.*) provveditore (della Repubblica Veneta) **2.** chi è addetto agli approvvigionamenti.

proven ['pru:vən], *ag.* (*dir. scoz.*) provato: *not — verdict*, assoluzione per mancanza di prove.

provenance ['prɔvinəns], *s.* provenienza, origine.

Provençal [,prɔvɑ:n'sɑ:l], *ag.s.c.* provenzale ‖ *s.* lingua provenzale.

provender ['prɔvində*], *s.* **1.** foraggio, biada **2.** (*scherz.*) provvigioni, cibo.

to **provender**, *v.t.* foraggiare, nutrire con foraggio.

provenience [prə'vi:njəns], *s.* provenienza, origine.

proverb ['prɔvəb], *s.* proverbio, detto, massima ‖ *the Book of Proverbs*, i Proverbi (libro biblico).

proverbial [prə'və:bjəl], *ag.* proverbiale.

proverbiality [prə,və:bi'æliti], *s.* carattere proverbiale.

proverbially [prə'və:bjəli], *av.* proverbialmente.

proviant ['prɔviant], *s.* provenda, vettovaglia.

to **provide** [prə'vaid], *v.t.i.* **1.** provvedere, fornire; procurare: *the Lord will —*, Dio provvederà; *to — for one's children's education*, provvedere all'educazione dei figli; *to — an opportunity for s.o. to do sthg.*, procurare a qlcu. l'occasione di fare ql.co. **2.** prendere provvedimenti, premunirsi: *to — against sthg.*, premunirsi contro ql.co. ‖ *to — for a bill*, (*comm.*) provvedere per una cambiale **3.** rifornire: *to — s.o. with sthg.*, provvedere, munire qlcu. di ql.co. **4.** stipulare (in un atto): *the contract provides that cases of dispute shall go to arbitration*, il contratto stabilisce che in caso di contese si ricorrerà ad arbitraggio.

provided [prə'vaidid], *ag.* **1.** provvisto, munito: *— with sthg.*, provvisto di ql.co. **2.** preparato: *— for all eventualities*, preparato ad ogni eventualità ☆ *— school*, scuola comunale.

provided, *cong.* — (*that*), purchè, a patto che: *you may stay here — you keep your ideas for yourself*, puoi star qui purchè tu ti tenga per te le tue idee.

providence ['prɔvidəns], *s.* previdenza; economia; provvidenza ‖ *Providence*, la Provvidenza.

provident ['prɔvidənt], *ag.* previdente; economo; provvido, provvidente.

providential [,prɔvi'denʃəl], *ag.* provvidenziale; opportuno.

providentially [,prɔvi'denʃəli], *av.* provvidenzialmente.

providently ['prɔvidəntli], *av.* provvidamente; previdentemente; con senso di economia.

provider [prə'vaidə*], *s.* chi provvede; fornitore, fornitrice ☆ *lion's —*, sciacallo (anche *fig.*); *universal —*, commerciante in tutti gli articoli.

providing [prə'vaidiŋ], *cong.* — (*that*), purchè, a patto che.

province ['prɔvins], *s.* **1.** provincia: *in the provinces*, in provincia **2.** (*dir.*) giurisdizione **3.** (*eccl.*) diocesi **4.** *fig.* sfera, campo d'attività: *this is not (within) our —*, questo non è di nostra competenza.

provincial [prə'vinʃəl], *ag.* provinciale ‖ *s.c.* provinciale ‖ *s.* (*eccl.*) padre provinciale.

provincialism [prə'vinʃəlizəm], *s.* provincialismo.

provincialist [prə'vinʃəlist], *s.* provinciale.

provinciality [prə,vinʃi'æliti], *s.* provincialismo.

to **provincialize** [prə'vinʃəlaiz], *v.t.i.* rendere provinciale, divenire provinciale.

provincially [prə'vinʃəli], *av.* provincialmente, da provinciale.

provision [prə'viʒən], *s.* **1.** provvedimento; preparativo: *to make — against sthg.*, premunirsi contro ql.co.; *to make — for one's family*, provvedere ai bisogni della propria famiglia; *to make — for sthg., to secure sthg.*, prendere le necessarie disposizioni per ql.co., per assicurarsi ql.co. **2.** *pl.* provviste, viveri, provvigioni **3.** (*dir.*) clausola, articolo, condizione: *the provisions of military law*, le vigenti leggi militari **4.** (*eccl.*) nomina sub condicione ☆ — *dealer*, commerciante in commestibili; — *room*, (*mar.*) cambusa.

to **provision**, *v.t.* approvvigionare.

provisional [prə'viʒənl], *ag.* **1.** provvisorio, temporaneo **2.** (*dir.*) provvisionale **3.** (*eccl.*) sub condicione.

provisionality [prə͵viʒə'næliti], *s.* provvisorietà.

provisionally [prə'viʒnəli], *av.* provvisoriamente; (*eccl.*) sub condicione.

provisionary [prə'viʒənəri], *ag.* provvisorio; (*eccl.*) sub condicione.

provisioner [prə'viʒənə*], *s.* approvvigionatore.

proviso [prə'vaizou], *pl.* **provisoes** [prə'vaizouz], *s.* (*dir.*) clausola condizionale.

provisor [prə'vaizə*], *s.* **1.** (*eccl.*) detentore di nomina sub condicione **2.** (*eccl.*) vicario generale (della Chiesa Cattolica).

provisorily [prə'vaizərili], *av.* provvisoriamente; (*dir.*) condizionalmente.

provisory [prə'vaizəri], *ag.* provvisorio; (*dir.*) condizionale.

provocation [͵prɔvə'keiʃən], *s.* provocazione; stimolo.

provocative [prə'vɔkətiv], *ag.* provocativo, provocante; eccitante, stimolante ‖ *s.* stimolante.

provocatively [prə'vɔkətivli], *av.* provocantemente.

provokable [prə'vɔkəbl], *ag.* provocabile.

to **provoke** [prə'vouk], *v.t.* **1.** provocare; incitare: *to — laughter*, provocare il riso **2.** irritare, contrariare, esasperare: *don't — me!*, non mi esasperare!.

provoker [prə'voukə*], *s.c.* provocatore, provocatrice.

provoking [prə'voukiŋ], *ag.* provocante, irritante; esasperante: *a — child*, un bambino esasperante, insopportabile.

provokingly [prə'voukiŋli], *av.* in modo provocatorio.

provost ['prɔvəst], *s.* **1.** (*eccl.*) prevosto (nella Chiesa Protestante) **2.** rettore (di collegio) **3.** (*scoz.*) sindaco ‖ *The Lord Provost of Glasgow*, il Sindaco di Glasgow ☆ — *marshal* [ma'ʃæl], (*mar.*) capo della polizia militare.

provostship ['prɔvəst-ʃip], *s.* **1.** prepositura **2.** rettorato **3.** ufficio del sindaco (in Scozia).

prow[1] [prau], *s.* **1.** (*mar.*) prua, prora **2.** tagliamare **3.** (*zool.*) proiezione simile a prora.

prow[2], *ag.* (*arc.*) prode, degno, valoroso.

prowess ['prauis], *s.* prodezza, valore.

prowl [praul], *s.* l'andare in giro in cerca di preda: *on the —*, in cerca di preda (anche *scherz. fig.*).

to **prowl**, *v.t.i.* **1.** andare in cerca di bottino; cercar la preda (di fiere) **2.** attraversare furtivamente (luoghi) **3.** *to — about*, vagare.

prowler ['praulə*], *s.* **1.** chi vaga in cerca di preda **2.** parassita.

prowling ['prauliŋ], *ag.* che vaga in cerca di preda ‖ *s.* vagabondaggio in cerca di preda.

proximal ['prɔksiməl], *ag.* (*anat.*) prossimale.

proximate ['prɔksimit], *ag.* **1.** vicino; immediato: — *cause*, causa prossima **2.** approssimativo.

proximately ['prɔksimitli], *av.* **1.** immediatamente **2.** approssimativamente.

proximity [prɔk'simiti], *s.* prossimità: — *of blood*, consanguineità.

proximo ['prɔksimou], *av.* (*gener. abbr. in prox.*) del mese prossimo, venturo: *I shall ship the goods on the 10th prox.*, spedirò la merce il 10 del mese prossimo.

proxy ['prɔksi], *s.* **1.** procuratore **2.** procura: *married by —*, sposato per procura.

to **proxy**, *v.i.* votare, agire per procura.

prude [pru:d], *s.c.* persona (specialmente donna) eccessivamente pudica, affettatamente modesta.

prudence[1] ['pru:dəns], *s.* prudenza; giudizio; avvedutezza.

Prudence[2], *no.pr.f.* Prudenza.

prudent ['pru:dənt], *ag.* prudente, cauto; avveduto; circospetto; giudizioso.

prudential [pru(:)'denʃəl], *ag.* prudenziale: *for — motives*, per ragioni prudenziali ☆ — *insurance*, assicurazione industriale.

prudentially [pru(:)'denʃəli], *av.* prudenzialmente, precauzionalmente.

prudentials [pru(:)'denʃəlz], *s.pl.* provvedimenti, considerazioni precauzionali.

prudently ['pru:dəntli], *av.* prudentemente, con prudenza; con cautela.

prudery ['pru:dəri], *s.* ritrosia; eccessiva pudicizia.

prudish ['pru:diʃ], *ag.* ritrosetto; pudibondo; austero.

prudishly ['pru:diʃli], *av.* pudicamente; in modo ritroso, schizzinoso, austero.

prudishness ['pru:diʃnis], *s.* ritrosia; affettazione di pudicizia.

pruinose ['pru:inous], *ag.* (*bot.*) pruinoso.

prune[1] [pru:n], *s.* **1.** prugna secca ‖ *prunes and prisms*, (*fam.*) modo di parlare affettato **2.** color prugna **3.** (*sl. amer.*) sciocco.

to **prune**[2], *v.t.* **1.** potare, scapezzare; mondare **2.** *fig.* sfrondare: *to — a speech*, sfrondare un discorso.

to **prune**[3], *V.* to **preen**[2].

prunella[1] [pru(:)'nelə], *s.* prunella (stoffa per calzature).

prunella[2], *s.* **1.** (*bot.*) prunella **2.** (*arc. patol.*) malattia della gola curata con prunella.

prunello [pru(:)'nelou], *pl.* **prunellos** [pru(:)'nelouz], *s.* prugna secca di qualità pregiata.

pruner ['pru:nə*], *s.* potatore.

pruning ['pru:niŋ], *s.* potatura ☆ — *hook* (o — *bill*), falcetto, potatoio.

prunt [prʌnt], *s.* ornamento in rilievo su vetro.

prurience ['pruəriəns], **pruriency** ['pruəriənsi], *s.* **1.** (*arc.*) prurito, pizzicore (anche *fig.*) **2.** libidine.

prurient ['pruəriənt], *ag.* **1.** (*arc.*) che pizzica; pruriginoso **2.** lubrico, lascivo.

pruriently ['pruəriəntli], *av.* lascivamente.

pruriginous [pru'ridʒinəs], *ag.* (*patol.*) pruriginoso.

prurigo [pru'raigou], *s.* (*patol.*) prurigine.

pruritus [pru'raitəs], *s.* (*med.*) prurito.

Prussia ['prʌʃə], *no.pr.* (*geog.*) Prussia.

Prussian ['prʌʃən], *ag.* prussiano ‖ *s.c.* prussiano, prussiana ☆ — *blue*, (*chim.*) blu di Prussia, ferrocianuro di potassio.

prussiate ['prʌʃiit], *s.* (*chim.*) prussiato.

prussic ['prʌsik], *ag.* (*chim.*) prussico ☆ — *acid*, acido prussico.

pry[1] [prai], *s.* **1.** lo scrutare, l'indagare; lo spiare **2.** individuo indiscreto, curioso.

to **pry**[1], *v.i.* **1.** scrutare, indagare; spiare ‖ *to — into sthg.*, impicciarsi di ql.co.; ficcare il naso in ql.co. **2.** *to — out*, indagare fino in fondo.

pry[2], *s.* (*mec.*) leva.

to **pry**[2], *v.t.* (*mec.*) forzare con una leva; far leva su.

prying ['praiiŋ], *ag.* **1.** curioso; ficcanaso indiscreto **2.** scrutatore.

pryingly ['praiiŋli], *av.* curiosamente; indiscretamente.

Prytaneum [͵pritə'ni:əm], *s.* (*st. greca*) Pritaneo.

psalm [sa:m], *s.* salmo.

psalmist ['sa:mist], *s.* salmista ‖ *The Psalmist*, (*Bibbia*) Re Davide il Salmista.

psalmodie [sæl'mɔdik], *ag.* salmodico.

psalmodist ['sælmədist], *s.* salmodiante, salmista.

to **psalmodize** ['sælmədaiz], *v.i.* cantare salmi, salmodiare.

psalmody ['sælmədi], *s.* salmodia.

Psalter ['sɔ:ltə*], *s.* (*Bibbia*) Salterio, libro dei salmi.

psalterer ['sɔ:ltərə*], *s.* suonatore di salterio.

psaltery ['sɔ:ltəri], *s.* (*mus.*) salterio.

psaltress ['sɔ:ltris], *s.* sonatrice di salterio.

pseudepigrapha [,psju:di'pigrəfə], *s.pl.* libri apocrifi; scritture spurie (specialmente ebraiche).

pseudo ['psju:dou], *ag.* pseudo, falso.

pseudograph ['psju:dougrɑ:f], *s.* opera letteraria spuria; scritto spurio, falso.

pseudologer [psju:'dɔlədʒə*], **pseudologist** [psju:'dɔlədʒist], *s.c.* (*iron.*) mentitore; mentitrice.

pseudomorph ['psju:doumɔ:f], *s.* (*min.*) cristallo pseudomorfo.

pseudomorphic ['psju:də'mɔ:fik], *ag.* pseudomorfo.

pseudomorphosis ['psju:doumɔ'fousis], *s.* (*min.*) pseudomorfosi.

pseudomorphous ['psju:də'mɔ:fəs], *ag.* (*min.*) pseudomorfo.

pseudonym ['psju:dənim], *s.* pseudonimo.

pseudonymous [psju:'dɔniməs], *ag.* pseudonimo.

pseudonymously [psju:'dɔniməsli], *av.* sotto pseudonimo.

pseudoscope ['psju:douskoup], *s.* (*ott.*) pseudoscopio.

pshaw [pʃɔ:], *inter.* puah; uff (esprimente disprezzo, impazienza).

to **pshaw**, *v.t.i.* esclamare puah, uff: *to — (at) sthg.*, esprimere disprezzo, impazienza per ql.co.

psilanthropism [psai'lænθrəpizəm], *s.* dottrina che nega la divinità di Cristo.

psittacosis [,psitə'kousis], *s.* (*patol.*) psittacosi.

psoas ['psouəs], *s.* muscoli psoas, lombari ☆ — *magnus, parvus*, grande, piccolo psoas.

psora ['psɔ:rə], *s.* (*patol.*) scabbia; psoriasi.

psoriasis [psɔ'raiəsis], *s.* (*patol.*) psoriasi.

psychasthenia [,psaikæs'θi:njə], *s.* (*patol.*) psicastenia; nevrosi.

Psyche ['saiki(:)], *no.pr.f.* (*mit.*) Psiche ‖ **psyche**, *s.* **1.** psiche, anima, spirito, mente **2.** (*entom.*) psiche **3.** psiche, specchiera girevole.

psychiater [sai'kaiətə*], *s.* psichiatra.

psychiatric(al) [,saiki'ætrik(əl)], *ag.* psichiatrico.

psychiatrist [sai'kaiətrist], *s.* psichiatra.

psychiatry [sai'kaiətri], *s.* psichiatria.

psychic ['saikik], *ag.* **1.** psichico **2.** medianico ‖ *s.* **1.** medium **2.** *pl.* psicologia.

psychical ['saikikəl], *ag.* psichico, della mente, dell'animo.

psychically ['saikikəli], *av.* psichicamente.

psychism ['saikizəm], *s.* (*fil.*) psichismo.

psychist ['saikist], *s.* (*fil.*) studioso di psichismo.

psychoanalysis [,saikouə'næləsis], *s.* psicanalisi.

psychoanalyst [,saikou'ænəlist], *s.* psicanalista.

psychoanalytic(al) ['saikou,ænə'litik(əl)], *ag.* psicanalitico.

to **psychoanalyze** [,saikou'ænəlaiz],*v.t.* psicanalizzare.

psychodynamics [,saikoudai'næmiks], *s.* psicodinamica.

psychogenesis [,saikou'dʒenisis], *s.* psicogenesi.

psychograph ['saikougrɑ:f], *s.* (*psicologia*) psicografo.

psychokinesis [,saikouki'ni:sis], *s.* (*psicologia*) psicocinesi.

psychologic(al) [,saikə'lɔdʒik(əl)], *ag.* psicologico ☆ — *warfare*, (*neol. pol.*) guerra psicologica.

psychologically [,saikə'lɔdʒikəli], *av.* psicologicamente.

psychologist [sai'kɔlədʒist], *s.c.* psicologo, psicologa.

to **psychologize** [sai'kɔlədʒaiz], *v.i.* fare della psicologia.

psychology [sai'kɔlədʒi], *s.* psicologia.

psychometry [sai'kɔmitri], *s.* (*psicologia*) psicometria.

psychoneurosis [,saikounju'rousis], *s.* (*patol.*) psiconeurosi.

psychopath ['saikoupæθ], *s.* (*patol.*) psicopatico.

psychopathic [,saikou'pæθik], *ag.* (*patol.*) psicopatico.

psychopathist [sai'kɔpəθist], *s.* alienista.

psychopathologist [,saikoupə'θɔlədʒist], *s.* psicopatologo.

psychopathology [,saikoupə'θɔlədʒi], *s.* psicopatologia.

psychopathy [sai'kɔpəθi], *s.* (*patol.*) psicopatia.

psychophysics [,saikou'fiziks], *s.* psicofisica.

psychosis [sai'kousis], *s.* psicosi.

psychosomatic [,saikousə'mætik], *ag.* psicosomatico.

psychosomatics [,saikousə'mætiks], *s.* psicosomatica.

psychotechnology [,saikoutek'nɔlədʒi], *s.* psicotecnica.

psychotherapy ['saikou'θerəpi], *s.* psicoterapia.

psychotic [sai'kɔtik], *ag.s.* (*patol.*) psicopatico.

psychrometer [sai'krɔmitə*], *s.* (*meteorologia*) psicrometro.

ptarmigan ['tɑ:migən], *s.* (*ornit.*) pernice bianca, roncaso.

pteridology [,pteri'dɔlədʒi], *s.* (*bot.*) studio delle felci.

pteris ['pteris], *s.* (*bot.*) pteride.

pterodactyl [,pterou'dæktil], *s.* (*paleont.*) pterodattilo.

pteropod ['pterəpod], *s.* (*zool.*) pteropodo.

pteropus ['pterəpəs], *s.* (*zool.*) pteropo, rossetta.

pterosaur ['pterəsɔ:*], *s.* (*paleont.*) pterosauro.

pterygoid ['pterigoid], *ag.* (*anat.*) pterigoideo ☆ — *process*, apofisi pterigoidea.

ptisan [ti'zæn], *s.* tisana, decotto d'orzo.

Ptolemaic [,tɔli'meiik], *ag.* **1.** (*st.*) tolemaico **2.** — *system*, (*astr.*) sistema tolemaico.

Ptolemy ['tɔlimi], *no.pr.m.* (*st.*) Tolomeo.

ptomaine ['toumein], *s.* (*chim.*) ptomaina.

ptosis ['ptousis], *s.* (*patol.*) ptosi.

ptyalin ['ptaiəlin], *s.* (*fisiol.*) ptialina.

ptyalism ['ptaiəlizəm], *s.* (*patol.*) ptialismo.

pub [pʌb], *s.* (*sl. abbr.* di *public house*) bar (di tipo inglese).

puberty ['pju:bəti], *s.* pubertà.

pubes ['pju:bi:z], *s.* (*anat.*) pube.

pubescence [pju:(')besns], *s.* (*anat. bot.*) pubescenza.

pubescent [pju:(')besnt], *ag.* (*anat. bot.*) pubescente.

pubic ['pju:bik], *ag.* (*anat.*) pubico.

pubis ['pju:bis], *s.* (*anat.*) pube (osso della pelvi).

public ['pʌblik], *ag.* **1.** pubblico **2.** noto, pubblico: *to make sthg.* —, rendere noto ql.co.; pubblicare ‖ *s.* pubblico ☆ — *house*, bar (di tipo inglese); — *library*, biblioteca pubblica; — *school*, collegio e scuola privata di tipo liceale (in Inghilterra); scuola governativa (in America e altrove); — *-spirited*, dotato di senso civico; — *-spiritedness*, civismo; — *utility undertaking*, (*amer.*) impresa di servizi pubblici ‖ *the reading* —, il pubblico che legge, i lettori.

publican ['pʌblikən], *s.* **1.** oste; proprietario di birreria, locanda **2.** (*st.*) pubblicano.

publication [,pʌbli'keifən], *s.* pubblicazione.

publicist ['pʌblisist], *s.* **1.** pubblicista **2.** pubblicitario.

publicity [pʌb'lisiti], *s.* pubblicità.

to **publicize** ['pʌblisaiz], *v.t.* fare la pubblicità a.

publicly ['pʌblikli], *av.* pubblicamente.

publicness ['pʌbliknis], *s.* pubblicità, notorietà.

to **publish** ['pʌblif], *v.t.* **1.** render noto, divulgare: *to — the news*, divulgare la notizia **2.** promulgare; pubblicare (libri, riviste, ecc.): *the book is now publishing*, il libro è in corso di pubblicazione ‖ *to — counterfeit paper*, (*amer.*) mettere in circolazione moneta falsa.

publishable ['pʌblifəbl], *ag.* pubblicabile.

published ['pʌblift], *ag.* pubblicato: *just* —, appena pubblicato, uscito (di libro).

publisher ['pʌblifə*], *s.* **1.** editore **2.** (*amer.*) proprietario di giornale.

Publius ['pʌbliəs], *no.pr.m.* (*st.*) Publio.

puccoon [pʌ'ku:n], *s.* (*bot.*) idraste canadese.

puce [pju:s], *ag. s.* (di) color pulce.

pucelle [pju'sel], *s.* pulzella; vergine.

puck[1] [pʌk], *s.* **1.** folletto, diavoletto ‖ *Puck*, « Puck » (nome di uno spiritello maligno) **2.** *fig.* bimbo vivace, demonietto.

puck[2], *s.* **1.** (*ornit.*) caprimulgo **2.** malattia del bestiame.

puck[3], *s.* (*spor.*) disco di gomma usato per il giuoco dell'hockey su ghiaccio.

pucka ['pʌkə], *ag.* (*ang.-in.*) **1.** dal peso esatto **2.** buono, genuino; completo **3.** permanente.

pucker ['pʌkə*], *s.* **1.** ruga; grinza **2.** piega (delle vesti) **3.** (*fam.*) agitazione, confusione.

to pucker, *v.t.i.* **1.** corrugare; raggrinzare, raggrinzirsi **2.** pieghettare; drappeggiare.

puckery ['pʌkəri], *ag.* **1.** che tende a raggrinzirsi; ripiegato; raggrinzito **2.** che fa allegare i denti.

puckish ['pʌkiʃ], **pucklike** ['pʌklaik], *ag.* da folletto; malizioso.

pud [pʌd], *s.* (*linguaggio infantile*) **1.** mano (di bimbo) **2.** zampa anteriore (di alcuni animali).

pudding ['pudiŋ], *s.* **1.** budino; pasticcio, sformato ‖ *more praise than* —, più lodi che ricompense **2.** tipo di salsiccia **3.** (*mar.*) fasciatura di protezione ☆ — *-face*, viso largo e grasso; — *-head*, stupido, ottuso; — *-heart*, vile, codardo; — *-pie*, pasticcio di carne, frutta; — *-stone*, (*geol.*) puddinga, conglomerato ‖ *black* —, sanguinaccio; *Christmas* —, budino di Natale; *milk* —, budino al latte (con riso, tapioca, ecc.).

puddle ['pʌdl], *s.* **1.** pozzanghera **2.** *fig.* ammasso confuso, disordine **3.** malta.

to puddle, *v.t.i.* **1.** sguazzare nel fango **2.** rendere fangoso; infangare, imbrattare (anche *fig.*) **3.** fare la malta **4.** (*metal.*) puddellare, sottomettere alla puddellatura **5.** rendere impermeabile spalmando di malta.

puddler ['pʌdlə*], *s.* (*metal.*) **1.** rimestatore, puddellatore **2.** forno di puddellatura.

puddling ['pʌdliŋ], *s.* (*metal.*) puddellatura ☆ — *furnace*, (*metal.*) forno di puddellatura.

puddly ['pʌdli], *ag.* fangoso, melmoso; sudicio, disgustoso.

pudency ['pju:dənsi], *s.* pudicizia, modestia.

pudenda [pju:'dendə], *s. pl.* parti genitali.

pudge [pʌdʒ], *s.* (*fam.*) individuo, animale grasso e tozzo.

pudginess ['pʌdʒinis], *s.* l'essere grasso e tozzo.

pudgy ['pʌdʒi], *ag.* grasso e tozzo.

pudic ['pju:dik], *ag.* (*rar.*) pudico.

pudicity [pju:'disiti], *s.* (*rar.*) pudicizia, modestia.

pudsy ['pʌdzi], *ag.* (*fam.*) grassotto, paffuto, pienotto.

pueblo [pu'eblou], *pl.* **pueblos** [pu'eblouz], *s.* **1.** cittadina, villaggio in Spagna, nell'America Latina) **2.** (*amer.*) villaggio (di indiani negli Stati del sud-ovest).

puerile ['pjuərail], *ag.* puerile.

puerilely ['pjuərailli], *av.* puerilmente.

puerilism ['pjuərilizəm], *s.* (*patol.*) infantilismo.

puerility [pjuə'riliti], *s.* puerilità.

puerperal [pju:'əːpərəl], *ag.* puerperale.

Puerto Rican ['pwəːtou'riːkən], *ag.* portoricano ‖ *o.c.* portoricano, portoricana.

Puerto Rico ['pwəːtou'riːkou], *no.pr.* (*geog.*) Portorico.

puff [pʌf], *s.* **1.** soffio, sbuffo, buffata: *puffs of smoke from a pipe*, sbuffi di fumo da un pipa **2.** (*fam.*) respiro; *fig.* nonnulla: *the least* — *would knock it over*, il più leggero soffio lo abbatterebbe **3.** puff! (esclamazione onomatopeica) **4.** ciuffo (di capelli) **5.** sboffo (di manica, veste) **6.** sfogliatella **7.** réclame, gonfiatura, montatura ☆ — *-*, (*linguaggio infantile*) ciuf ciuf, il treno; — *-adder*, vipera del Sud Africa; — *-ball*, (*bot.*) vescia di lupo; — *-box*, scatola con cipria e piumino; — *-paste*, pasta sfoglia: — *-paste cake*, sfogliata ‖ *powder* —, piumino della cipria.

to puff, *v.t.i.* **1.** soffiare, sbuffare; ansare: *to* — *and blow*, ansimare **2.** emettere, tirare buffate: *he was puffing at his pipe*, tirava boccate di fumo dalla pipa **3.** fare pubblicità esagerata a, esaltare: *the quack-doctor was puffing his cures*, il ciarlatano esaltava le sue cure **4.** far salire i prezzi (ad un'asta) **5.** *to* — *away*, sbuffare: *the engine puffed away*, la locomotiva si mosse sbuffando **6.** *to* — *out*, gonfiare, gonfiarsi: *to* — *out one's skirt*, far gonfiare la gonna **7.** *to* — *up*, gon-

nare; *fig.* insuperbire, far insuperbire: *very much puffed up by his success*, molto insuperbito dal suo successo.

puffed [pʌft], *ag.* gonfio, gonfiato ☆ — *rice*, — *wheat*, riso, grano duro gonfiato.

puffer ['pʌfə*], *s.* **1.** compare (specialmente alle aste) **2.** (*linguaggio infantile*) ciuf ciuf, il treno.

puffery ['pʌfəri], *s.* **1.** lode sperticata **2.** pubblicità eccessiva **3.** sboffi, falpalà.

puffin ['pʌfin], *s.* (*ornit.*) puffino.

puffiness ['pʌfinis], *s.* **1.** gonfiezza **2.** ampollosità.

puffing ['pʌfiŋ], *s.* **1.** il soffiare, lo sbuffare **2.** lode esagerata; il prodigare lodi esagerate.

puffingly ['pʌfiŋli], *av.* **1.** ampollosamente **2.** con lodi esagerate **3.** ciarlatanescamente.

puffy ['pʌfi], *ag.* **1.** gonfio: *eyes* — *with sleep*, occhi gonfi di sonno **2.** paffuto, grasso, obeso **3.** ansimante, dal fiato corto.

pug[1] [pʌg], *s.* **1.** carlino (specie di cane) **2.** piccolo animale domestico; cagnetto; scimmietta; volpe **3.** folletto, spiritello **4.** (*sl.*) capocameriere **5.** (*sl.*) locomotiva di manovra ☆ — *-faced*, dal viso rincagnato; — *-nose*, naso rincagnato; — *-nosed*, dal naso rincagnato.

pug[2], *s.* impasto di creta, argilla usato come materiale edilizio ☆ — *-mill*, impastatoio per argilla.

to pug[2], *pass.p.p.* **pugged** [pʌgd], *v.t.* **1.** impastare creta, argilla come materiale edilizio **2.** riempire (interstizi, ecc.) con argilla.

pug[3], *s.* (*ang.-in.*) orma di belva.

to pug[3], *v.t.* (*ang.-in.*) seguire per mezzo delle orme.

pug, *s.* (*sl. abbr.* di *pugilist*), pugile.

pugg(a)ree ['pʌg(ə)ri], *s.* (*ang.-in.*) **1.** leggero turbante **2.** sciarpa di seta avvolta attorno al casco e pendente sul dietro.

pugilism ['pju:dʒilizəm], *s.* pugilato.

pugilist ['pju:dʒilist], *s.* pugile.

pugilistic [,pju:dʒi'listik], *ag.* pugilistico, del pugilato.

pugnacious [pʌg'neiʃəs], *ag.* pugnace, combattivo; litigioso.

pugnaciously [pʌg'neiʃəsli], *av.* pugnacemente; litigiosamente.

pugnaciousness [pʌg'neiʃəsnis], **pugnacity** [pʌg'næsiti], *s.* combattività, indole battagliera; litigiosità.

puisne ['pju:ni], *ag.* (*dir.*) più recente; più giovane (in carica) ‖ *s.* giudice subalterno (in Inghilterra).

puissance ['pju:(:)isns], *s.* (*letter.*) potenza, possanza.

puissant ['pju:(:)isnt], *ag.* (*letter.*) potente, poderoso.

puissantly ['pju:(:)isntli], *av.* (*letter.*) potentemente, poderosamente.

puke [pju:k], *s.* **1.** vomito **2.** emetico.

to puke, *v.t.i.* vomitare.

pukka, *V.* **pucka**.

pulchritude ['pʌlkritju:d], *s.* (*letter.*) bellezza.

to pule [pju:l], *v.i.* gemere; piagnucolare.

puler ['pju:lə*], *s.* piagnucolone.

puling ['pju:liŋ], *ag.* piagnucoloso ‖ *s.* piagnucolamento.

pulingly ['pju:liŋli], *av.* piagnucolosamente.

pull [pul], *s.* **1.** tirata, strappo, strappata: *to give a* — *at a rope*, tirare una fune **2.** forza di attrazione **3.** vantaggio: *he had a* — *over his brother*, era in vantaggio rispetto a suo fratello **4.** *fig.* influenza, ascendente: *he has a strong* — *with the manager*, ha una grande influenza sul direttore **5.** sorsata; boccata (di fumo): *he took only a* — *of beer*, bevve solo un sorso di birra **6.** (*mec.*) tensione, trazione **7.** sforzo: *it was really a* — *to the top of the mountains!*, fu davvero uno sforzo scalare la montagna! **8.** maniglia (di cassetto); cordone (di campanello) **9.** vogata: *we went for a* — *on the lake*, andammo a fare una vogata sul lago **10.** (*tip.*) prima bozza ☆ — *-back*, (*fam.*) impedimento, ostacolo.

to pull, *v.t.i.* **1.** tirare, stirare: *I'll* — *this boy's ears*, tirerò le orecchie a questo ragazzo; *she pulled a muscle in the game*, si stirò un muscolo durante la partita ‖ *to* — *a* (*wry*) *face*, fare una smorfia ‖ *to* — *s.o.'s leg*, (*sl.*) fare una burla a qlcu.; prendere in giro qlcu. **2.** strappare, estrarre: *he had two teeth pulled,* si fece togliere due denti; *the policeman pulled his revolver,* il poliziotto estrasse la pistola; *she pulled several roses,* divelse molte rose ‖ *to — to pieces,* fare a pezzi; *fig.* criticare aspramente **3.** bere un sorso, tirare una boccata (di fumo) **4.** trascinare, trascinarsi, procedere con sforzo: *they pulled up the hill,* si trascinarono a fatica su per la collina **5.** (*spor.*) trattenere (un cavallo per fargli perdere la corsa) **6.** (*cricket, golf*) battere (la palla) mandandola a sinistra **7.** (*tip.*) tirare, stampare: *the proofs were neatly pulled,* le bozze furono accuratamente tirate **8.** (*mar.*) remare, vogare ‖ *to — for,* remare in direzione di **9.** (*sl.*) arrestare: *the police pulled the thief,* la polizia arrestò il ladro **10.** (*sl.*) aver successo, influire: *these are ideas that — with the general public,* queste sono idee che hanno successo presso la massa; *to — for a candidate,* esercitare la propria influenza a favore di un candidato **11.** *to be pulled,* essere depresso: *he is quite pulled,* è assai depresso **12.** *to —* **about,** stiracchiare; trascinare qua e là; maltrattare **13.** **— apart,** separare, dividere **14.** *to —* **away,** strappare; tirar via; trascinare; (*mar.*) vogare lontano: *he pulled away from shore,* remò al largo **15.** *to —* **back,** tirare indietro; trattenere; ritardare **16.** *to —* **down,** calare; abbattere; *fig.* demolire, criticare: *that book was pulled down by everybody,* quel libro fu aspramente criticato da tutti; *to — down one's hat over one's eyes,* calarsi il cappello sugli occhi **17.** *to —* **in,** far entrare; (*ferr.*) entrare in stazione; ridurre (spese) **18.** *to —* **off,** levare, levarsi; strappare, togliere; (*spor.*) vincere ‖ *the lid pulls off,* il coperchio si può levare **19.** *to —* **on,** calzare, infilare: *— on your gloves,* infilati i guanti **20.** *to —* **out,** strappare; far uscire; (*ferr.*) uscire dalla stazione; dilungare (un racconto) ‖ *to — out from behind a vehicle,* uscire dalla fila per sorpassare (di automobile) ‖ *to — out of the fire, fig.* salvare da una situazione disperata **21.** *to —* **round,** riaversi, rimettersi; rianimare, rianimarsi **22.** *to —* **through,** (far) uscire da una difficoltà; rimettersi in salute: *he succeeded in pulling the business through,* riuscì a portare a buon fine l'affare; *she is very ill, but she may — through,* è molto malata, ma può ristabilirsi **23.** *to —* **together,** agire, operare in armonia ‖ *to — oneself together,* riprendere animo **24.** *to —* **up,** sollevare; sradicare, strappare; arrestare, fermare bruscamente; fermarsi; (*fam.*) rimproverare, riprendere; riprendersi, controllarsi: *— yourself up!,* controllati!; *the car pulled up in front of the door,* l'automobile si fermò davanti alla porta.

puller ['pulə*], *s.* **1.** (*mec.*) estrattore **2.** cavallo da tiro.

pullet ['pulit], *s.* pollastrella.

pulley ['puli], *s.* (*mec.*) puleggia; carrucola.

pullman(car) ['pulmən(kɑ:)*], *s.* (*ferr.*) « pullman », carrozza di lusso.

pullover ['pul,ouvə*], *s.* « pullover » (corpetto a maglia di lana che si infila dalla testa).

pullulant ['pʌljulənt], *ag.* pullulante, in piena germogliazione.

to pullulate ['pʌljuleit], *v.i.* pullulare, germogliare; moltiplicarsi.

pullulation [,pʌlju'leifən], *s.* pullulazione, germogliazione.

to pully-haul ['puli,hɔ:l], *v.t.i.* (*fam.*) tirare a forza di braccia.

pully-hauly ['puli'hɔ:li], *s.* (*fam.*) il tirare a forza di braccia.

pulmonary ['pʌlmənəri], *ag.* **1.** polmonare **2.** affetto da, soggetto a malattie polmonari.

pulmonate ['pʌlmənit], *ag.* (*zool.*) fornito di polmoni.

pulmonic [pʌl'mɔnik], *ag.* polmonare ‖ *s.* affetto da malattia polmonare.

pulp [pʌlp], *s.* **1.** polpa **2.** pasta (di stracci, legno per fare la carta) **3.** minerale macinato misto con acqua **4.** *pl.* (*sl. amer.*) rivista che si stampa su carta ruvida di legno (onde il nome) e generalmente contie-

ne materiale letterario di scarso valore ☆ *— -fiction,* romanzetto da quattro soldi ‖ *dental —,* polpa dentale; *fruit —,* polpa di frutto.

to pulp, *v.t.i.* **1.** ridurre in polpa, in pasta **2.** diventare polposo.

pulper ['pʌlpə*], *s.* (*mec.*) raffinatrice.

to pulpify ['pʌlpifai], *v.t.* ridurre in polpa.

pulpiness ['pʌlpinis], *s.* polposità.

pulpit ['pulpit], *s.* pulpito, pergamo; cattedra; tribuna.

pulpiteer [,pulpi'tiə*], *s.* (*spreg.*) predicatore.

to pulpiteer, *v.i.* (*spreg.*) predicare.

pulpless ['pʌlplis], *ag.* senza polpa; spolpato.

pulpous ['pʌlpəs], *ag.* **1.** polposo **2.** molle.

pulpousness ['pʌlpəsnis], *s.* polposità.

pulpwood ['pʌlp,wud], *s.* **1.** (*ind. cartaria*) pasta di legno **2.** qualità di legname usato per pasta da carta.

pulpy ['pʌlpi], *ag.* **1.** polposo **2.** molle.

pulque ['pu:lkei], *s.* « pulque » (bevanda messicana).

to pulsate [pʌl'seit], *v.i.* pulsare; battere; vibrare.

pulsatile ['pʌlsətail], *ag.* **1.** pulsatile **2.** (*mus.*) di percussione.

pulsatilla [,pʌlsə'tilə], *s.* (*bot. farm.*) pulsatilla.

pulsation [pʌl'seifən], *s.* pulsazione; vibrazione; (*mat. fis. elett.*) pulsazione, frequenza angolare.

pulsator [pʌl'seitə*], *s.* **1.** pulsometro **2.** setaccio, griglia mobile (per separare diamanti).

pulsatory ['pʌlsətəri], *ag.* pulsante; pulsatile.

pulse[1] [pʌls], *s.* **1.** polso, pulsazione, battito; vibrazione: *febrile —,* battito febbrile; *quick —,* polso frequente; *weak —,* polso debole; *to feel s.o.'s —,* sentire il polso a qlcu. (anche *fig.*) **2.** *fig.* polso, energia, vitalità **3.** (*rad.*) impulso **4.** (*poes. mus.*) ritmo, cadenza **5.** *pl.* emozione: *to stir s.o.'s pulses,* eccitare le emozione di qlcu. ☆ *— curve,* (*med.*) sfigmogramma; *— generator,* (*rad.*) generatore d'impulsi.

to pulse[1], *v.t.i.* pulsare; battere: *the life pulsing through a great city,* la vita che anima una grande città ‖ *to — out, to — in the blood,* far uscire, far entrare il sangue mediante pulsazioni.

pulse[2], *s.* *coll.* legumi.

pulseless ['pʌlslis], *ag.* senza battiti (di polso).

pulselessness ['pʌlslisnis], *s.* assenza di battiti.

pulser ['pʌlsə*], *s.* (*rad.*) generatore d'impulsi.

pulsimeter [pʌl'simitə*], *s.* (*med.*) pulsimetro.

pulsometer [pʌl'sɔmitə*], *s.* (*mec.*) pulsometro.

pultaceous [pʌl'teifəs], *ag.* pultaceo; molle, polposo.

pulverable ['pʌlvərəbl], *ag.* polverizzabile.

pulverizable ['pʌlvəraizəbl], *ag.* polverizzabile.

pulverization [,pʌlvərai'zeifən], *s.* polverizzazione.

to pulverize ['pʌlvəraiz], *v.t.i.* **1.** polverizzare, polverizzarsi; vaporizzare, vaporizzarsi **2.** *fig.* abbattere, demolire: *to — an argument,* demolire un argomento.

pulverizer ['pʌlvəraizə*], *s.* polverizzatore; vaporizzatore.

pulverous ['pʌlvərəs], *ag.* polveroso.

pulverulent [pʌl'verjulənt], *ag.* **1.** pulverulento; polveroso **2.** friabile (di roccia).

pulvinate ['pʌlvinit], **pulvinated** ['pʌlvineitid], *ag.* **1.** (*arch.*) a faccia convessa **2.** (*bot.*) simile a cuscinetto.

puma ['pju:mə], *s.* (*zool.*) puma.

pumice ['pʌmis], *s.* *— (-stone),* pietra pomice.

to pumice, *v.t. to — (-stone),* impomiciare.

pumiceous [pju'mifəs], *ag.* pomicioso.

to pummel ['pʌml], *pass. p.p.* **pummelled** ['pʌmld], *v.t.* prendere a pugni; picchiare di santa ragione.

pump[1] [pʌmp], *s.* **1.** pompa; (*aut.*) distributore: *to prime a —,* caricare, adescare una pompa **2.** *fig.* tentativo di strappare informazioni con abile interrogatorio ☆ *— feed,* alimentazione a pompa; *— handle,* maniglia di pompa; *— shot,* colpo di pompa ‖ *bicycle —,* pompa da bicicletta; *feed —* (o *fuel —*), pompa d'alimentazione; *force —,* pompa premente; *hand —,* pompa a mano; (*sl.*) vigorosa stretta di mano; *lubri-*

cation —, pompa oliatrice; *motor-drive* —, elettropompa; *oil* —, pompa dell'olio; *petrol* —, distributore di benzina; *primer* —, pompa di adescamento; *suction* —, pompa aspirante; *tyre* —, pompa per pneumatici.

to **pump**[1], *v.t.i.* **1.** azionare una pompa; pompare: *to — a well dry*, asciugare un pozzo ‖ *to — bullets, shots into s.o.*, sparare ripetutamente su qlcu. ‖ *to — a person's hand*, stringere la mano a qlcu. con effusione **2.** (*mar.*) delfinare (di sottomarino) **3.** *fig.* estrarre, strappare (notizie, informazioni, ecc.) a forza: *to — news out of s.o.*, strappare notizie a qlcu. **4.** *to — up*, gonfiare: *to — up a tyre*, gonfiare un pneumatico.

pump[2], *s.* scarpa da ballo; scarpa scollata.

pumper ['pʌmpə*], *s.* **1.** chi pompa **2.** (*amer.*) pozzo di petrolio **3.** (*fam.*) chi riesce a strappare notizie, segreti, ecc.

pumpernickel ['pumpənikl], *s.* pane di segala.

pumpkin ['pʌmpkin], *s.* **1.** (*bot.*) zucca **2.** *fig.* persona sciocca e presuntuosa **3.** *pl.* (*sl. amer.*) persona, luogo, evento importante.

pun[1] [pʌn], *s.* giuoco di parole.

to **pun**[1], *pass.p.p.* **punned** [pʌnd], *v.i.* fare giuochi di parole.

to **pun**[2], *v.t.* rendere solido (terreno, ecc.) battendo, premendo col compressore.

puna ['pu:nə], *s.* **1.** altipiano (nelle Ande peruviane) **2.** mal di montagna.

punch[1] [pʌntʃ], *s.* punzone; stampo; cacciatoia; strumento per perforare il cuoio, metalli, carta ☆ — *card*, (*neol.*) scheda perforata; — *press*, pressa ‖ *center* —, punzone a guida; *nail* —, punzone per chiodi; *shearing* —, tagliolo.

to **punch**[1], *v.t.* **1.** perforare; punzonare: *to — tickets*, forare i biglietti **2.** dare un pugno a; picchiare **3.** spingere (bestiame).

punch[2], *s.* **1.** pugno **2.** (*fam.*) energia, forza; *fig.* mordacità: *joke with — in it*, barzelletta mordace; *style with — in it*, stile incisivo ☆ — *drunk*, tramortito; stordito (anche *fig.*).

punch[3], *s.* **1.** ponce **2.** ricevimento durante il quale si beve ponce: *to give a — in honour of s.o.*, offrire un ponce in onore di qlcu. ☆ — *bowl*, bicchiere da ponce.

punch[4], *s.* **1.** (*Suffolk*) —, piccolo cavallo da traino, con zampe corte **2.** (*sl.*) uomo basso e tarchiato.

Punch, *no.pr.m.* (*abbr.* di *Punchinello*) **1.** Pulcinella ‖ *— and Judy (show)*, (teatrino di) burattini ‖ *I am as pleased as —*, sono contento come una pasqua **2.** «Punch» (settimanale umoristico inglese, il cui simbolo è Pulcinella che ride) ‖ *s. fig.* tontoccio, burattino.

puncheon ['pʌntʃən], *s.* **1.** (*rar.*) punteruolo; stampo **2.** bietta; regolo d'appoggio; palo di sostegno.

puncher ['pʌntʃə*], *s.* **1.** punzone **2.** (*amer.*) chi spinge il bestiame.

Punchinello [,pʌntʃi'neləu], *no.pr.m.* (*teat.*) Pulcinella ‖ *s.* (*fam.*) persona tozza.

punchy ['pʌntʃi], *ag.* grosso, tarchiato, tozzo.

punctate ['pʌŋkteit], **punctated** ['pʌŋkteitid], *ag.* (*bot. zool.*) maculato.

punctation [pʌŋk'teiʃən], *s.* maculazione.

punctilio [pʌŋk'tiliou], *pl.* **punctilios** [pʌŋk'tiliouz], *s.* **1.** correttezza di modi; formalismo **2.** meticolosità; puntiglio.

punctilious [pʌŋk'tiliəs], *ag.* **1.** cerimonioso **2.** scrupoloso; puntiglioso; minuzioso.

punctiliously [pʌŋk'tiliəsli], *av.* **1.** cerimoniosamente **2.** in modo puntiglioso; minuziosamente.

punctiliousness [pʌŋk'tiliəsnis], *s.* **1.** formalismo **2.** puntigliosità; minuziosità.

punctual ['pʌŋktjuəl], *ag.* puntuale; esatto.

punctuality [,pʌŋktju'æliti], *s.* puntualità; esattezza.

punctually ['pʌŋktjuəli], *av.* puntualmente; esattamente.

punctualness ['pʌŋktjuəlnis], *s.* puntualità; esattezza.

to **punctuate** ['pʌŋktjueit], *v.t.i.* **1.** punteggiare; usare la punteggiatura **2.** dare enfasi a.

punctuation [,pʌŋktju'eiʃən], *s.* punteggiatura, interpunzione ☆ — *marks*, segni d'interpunzione.

punctuative ['pʌŋktjueitiv], *ag.* di punteggiatura, d'interpunzione.

punctum ['pʌŋktəm], *pl.* **puncta** ['pʌŋktə], *s.* **1.** (*anat. zool.*) punto, macchia **2.** (*mus. medioevale*) nota quadrata ☆ — *luteum*, (*anat.*) macula lutea ‖ *lachrymal* —, (*anat.*) punto lacrimale.

puncture ['pʌŋktʃə*], *s.* puntura, iniezione; trafittura, perforazione; foratura (di pneumatico) ☆ *lumbar* —, (*med.*) puntura lombare.

to **puncture**, *v.t.i.* **1.** pungere; perforare **2.** bucare, forare; bucarsi, forarsi (di pneumatico) **3.** tatuare.

punctured ['pʌŋktʃəd], *ag.* perforato.

pundit ['pʌndit], *s.* **1.** «pandit» (indù molto colto) **2.** (*scherz.*) insegnante dotto; sapientone.

pungency ['pʌndʒənsi], *s.* **1.** gusto piccante; odore forte, acuto **2.** *fig.* acutezza (di dolore); asprezza, acrimonia.

pungent ['pʌndʒənt], *ag.* **1.** (*bot.*) pungente, spinoso **2.** cocente, acuto: *a — sorrow*, un dolore acuto **3.** mordace, caustico: *a — style*, uno stile mordace **4.** piccante: *— mustard*, mostarda piccante.

pungently ['pʌndʒəntli], *av.* in modo piccante.

Punic ['pju:nik], *ag.* punico ‖ *s.* punico (lingua).

puniness ['pju:ninis], *s.* piccolezza, sparutezza.

to **punish** ['pʌniʃ], *v.t.* **1.** punire: *to — s.o. for sthg.*, punire qlcu. per ql.co. **2.** (*fam.*) battere, malmenare.

punishability [,pʌniʃə'biliti], *s.* punibilità.

punishable ['pʌniʃəbl], *ag.* punibile.

punisher ['pʌniʃə*], *s.c.* punitore, punitrice ‖ *s.* pugilatore che colpisce forte.

punishment ['pʌniʃmənt], *s.* **1.** punizione; correzione **2.** (*fam.*) batosta, sconfitta ☆ *capital* —, pena capitale.

punitive ['pju:nitiv], **punitory** ['pju:nitəri], *ag.* punitivo.

punk[1] [pʌŋk], *ag.* **1.** marcio, fradicio (di frutta, legno, ecc.) **2.** (*sl.*) miserabile; male in arnese ‖ *s.* (*spec. amer.*) **1.** legno marcio, fungo che cresce sul legno usati come esca; esca (per fuochi d'artificio) **2.** incenso cinese **3.** sciocchezza: *to talk a lot of —*, dire un mucchio di sciocchezze.

punk[2], *s.* **1.** (*arc.*) prostituta **2.** giovane vagabondo **3.** (*sl. amer. cine.*) aiuto-operatore.

punka(h) ['pʌŋkə], *s.* (*ang.-in.*) ventola appesa al soffitto e azionata a mano; scacciamosche.

punner ['pʌnə*], *s.* compressore, mazzeranga.

punnet ['pʌnit], *s.* canestro (per frutta).

punningly ['pʌniŋli], *av.* con giuochi di parole.

punster ['pʌnstə*], *s.* chi si compiace di bisticci, giuochi di parole; freddurista.

punt[1] [pʌnt], *s.* barchino; chiatta, pontone ☆ — *-fisher*, chi pesca con un barchino; — *-fishing*, pesca fatta da un barchino; — *-gun*, spingarda; — *-pole*, pertica (usata per spingere un barchino); — *-shooting*, caccia da un barchino.

to **punt**[1], *v.t.i.* **1.** spingere (chiatta, altra imbarcazione) con una pertica; andare con una chiatta **2.** trasportare con chiatta, pontone.

punt[2], *s.* (*spor.*) calcio dato al pallone prima che abbia toccato terra.

to **punt**[2], *v.t.* **1.** (*spor.*) esercitarsi a colpire (il pallone) prima che tocchi terra **2.** (*rar.*) colpire, battere.

punt[3], *s.* pontello (usato nella fabbricazione del vetro).

to **punt**[4], *v.i.* puntare contro il banco (in alcuni giuochi di carte); (*fam.*) puntare su un cavallo.

punter[1] ['pʌntə*], *s.* chiattaiolo, chi usa imbarcazioni spinte da pertiche.

punter[2], *s.* puntatore (al giuoco, alle corse di cavalli).

puntist ['pʌntist], *V.* **punter**[1].

punty ['pʌnti], *s.* pontello.

puny ['pju:ni], *ag.* piccino; sparuto; malaticcio.

pup[1] [pʌp], *s.* cucciolo: *to be in* (o *with*) —, essere pregna (di cagna) ‖ *a conceited* —, ragazzo, giovanotto pieno di boria ‖ *to sell a person a* —, raggirare una persona; vendere ql.co. che non vale il prezzo.

to **pup**[1], *pass.p.p.* **pupped** [pʌpt], *v.t.i.* figliare, partorire (di cagna).

pup[2], (*sl. scolastico abbr.*) di **pupil**.

pupa ['pju:pə], *pl.* **pupae** ['pju:pi:], *s.* (*entom.*) pupa, crisalide.

pupal ['pju:pəl], *ag.* (*entom.*) di crisalide.

to **pupate** ['pju:peit], *v.i.* diventare una crisalide.

pupil[1] ['pju:pl], *s.c.* **1.** allievo, allieva; scolaro, scolara **2.** (*dir.*) pupillo, pupilla ☆ — *teacher*, allievo maestro.

pupil[2], *s.* (*anat.*) pupilla.

pupil(l)age ['pju:pilidʒ], *s.* **1.** condizione di discente; periodo in cui si riceve la propria educazione **2.** (*dir.*) minorità: *child in* —, bambino sotto tutela.

pupil(l)ar[1] ['pju:pilə*], *ag.* **1.** di allievo **2.** (*dir.*) pupillare, di pupillo.

pupil(l)ar[2], *ag.* (*anat.*) pupillare.

pupil(l)arity [.pju:pi'læriti], *s.* **1.** (*dir.*) condizione di pupillo **2.** periodo della prima pubertà.

pupil(l)ary[1] ['pju:piləri], *ag.* **1.** di allievo **2.** (*dir.*) pupillare, di pupillo.

pupil(l)ary[2], *ag.* (*anat.*) pupillare (della pupilla).

to **pupil(l)ize** ['pju:pilaiz], *v.t.i.* **1.** prendere allievi **2.** insegnare, dare lezioni private a.

pupilship ['pju:plʃip], *s.* (*dir.*) minorità.

Pupipara [pju'pipərə], *s.pl.* (*entom.*) i pupipari.

puppet ['pʌpit], *s.* burattino, fantoccio, marionetta (anche *fig.*) ☆ — *-player*, burattinaio; — *government*, governo fantoccio; — *-show*, rappresentazione di marionette; — *-valve*, (*mec.*) valvola a fungo.

puppetry ['pʌpitri], *s.* **1.** burattinata; mascherata **2.** rappresentazione di burattini **3.** personaggi falsi (di romanzo).

puppy ['pʌpi], *s.* **1.** cucciolo; cagnolino **2.** *fig.* damerino, giovane vanesio ☆ — *-dog*, cagnolino; — *love*, i primi amori.

puppyhood ['pʌpihud], *s.* **1.** condizione di cucciolo **2.** *fig.* anni verdi, la gioventù.

puppyish ['pʌpiiʃ], *ag.* fatuo, vanesio.

puppyism ['pʌpiizəm], *s.* affettazione; vanità maschile.

purblind ['pə:blaind], *ag.* **1.** miope, mezzo cieco **2.** *fig.* cieco; ottuso.

purblindness ['pə:blaindnis], *s.* (*rar.*) semicecità.

purchasable ['pə:tʃəsəbl], *ag.* acquistabile.

purchase ['pə:tʃəs], *s.* **1.** acquisto; compera: — *on credit*, acquisto a credito; *he filled the car with his purchases*, riempì l'automobile con le compere fatte **2.** valore (specialmente rendita annua di proprietà): *this land is sold at twenty years'* —, questo terreno è in vendita al prezzo equivalente al reddito di venti anni ‖ *life is not worth an hour's* —, (*fam.*) la vita è legata a un filo **3.** (*mec.*) morsa, presa, punto d'appoggio **4.** (*mar.*) paranco; calorna **5.** (*dir.*) acquisizione ☆ — *-bill*, (*comm.*) fattura d'acquisto; — *block*, (*mar.*) bozzello di calorna; — *-deed*, (*comm.*) atto, contratto d'acquisto; — *department*, ufficio acquisti; — *money* (o — *price*), prezzo d'acquisto; — *order*, ordine d'acquisto ‖ *hire* —, acquisto rateale; *twofold* —, (*mar.*) paranco doppio.

to **purchase**, *v.t.* **1.** comperare; acquistare (anche *fig.*): *to* — *freedom with one's blood*, acquistare la libertà a prezzo del proprio sangue **2.** (*dir.*) rilevare **3.** (*mar.*) sollevare (l'àncora) con argano.

purchaser ['pə:tʃəsə*], *s.c.* acquirente, compratore, compratrice.

purchasing ['pə:tʃəsiŋ], *s.* acquisto ☆ — *power*, potere di acquisto.

purdah ['pə:da:], *s.* **1.** tenda che ripara le donne indiane dalla vista di estranei **2.** sistema indiano di tener recluse le donne di un certo rango **3.** stoffa a righe per tende.

pure [piuə*], *ag.* **1.** puro; schietto: — *alcohol*, alcole puro; — *water*, acqua pura **2.** puro, casto: *a* — *woman*, una donna casta **3.** chiaro, distinto: — *note*, nota pura **4.** mero, semplice, puro: — *mischief*,

pura cattiveria ☆ — *-blood*, puro sangue; — *mathematics*, matematica pura.

to **pure**, *v.t.* (*rar.*) purificare.

purée ['pjuərei], *s.* (*cuc.*) purè, passato.

purely ['pjuəli], *av.* **1.** puramente, semplicemente, unicamente, esclusivamente: *done* — *by accident*, fatto solamente per sbaglio **2.** (*rar.*) con purezza.

pureness ['pjuənis], *s.* purezza.

purfle ['pə:fl], *s.* (*arc.*) bordo ricamato (di vestito).

to **purfle**, *v.t.* (*arc.*) **1.** adornare di un bordo ricamato **2.** abbellire; fregiare.

purfling ['pə:fliŋ], *s.* **1.** (*arch.*) fregio **2.** profilatura di violino.

purgation [pə:'geiʃən], *s.* **1.** (*med.*) purga **2.** (*st. dir.*) purgazione **3.** *fig.* purificazione **4.** (*relig.*) purgazione.

purgative ['pə:gətiv], *ag.* purgativo ‖ *s.* purgante.

purgatorial [.pə:gə'to:riəl], *ag.* del purgatorio.

purgatory ['pə:gətəri], *ag.* purgatorio ‖ *s.* purgatorio.

purge [pə:dʒ], *s.* **1.** (*med.*) purga, purgante **2.** (*pol.*) epurazione.

to **purge**, *v.t.i.* **1.** purgare; purificare; chiarificare **2.** (*med.*) purgare; purgarsi **3.** (*dir.*) prosciogliere **4.** espiare **5.** (*pol.*) epurare: *five reactionary members have been purged*, cinque membri reazionari sono stati epurati **6.** (*chim.*) depurare.

purging ['pə:dʒiŋ], *ag.* purgativo; epurante ‖ *s.* **1.** purga **2.** purificazione **3.** (*pol.*) epurazione **4.** (*chim.*) depurazione.

purification [.pjuərifi'keiʃən], *s.* **1.** purificazione **2.** (*chim.*) depurazione.

purificator ['pjuərifikeitə*], *s.* (*eccl.*) purificatoio.

purificatory ['pjuərifikeitəri], *ag.* purificatore.

purifier ['pjuərifaiə*], *s.* **1.** purificatore **2.** depuratore.

to **purify** ['pjuərifai], *v.t.i.* **1.** purificare, purificarsi **2.** (*chim.*) depurare, depurarsi.

purifying ['pjuərifaiiŋ], *ag.* purificante ‖ *s.* **1.** purificazione **2.** (*chim.*) depurazione.

Purim ['pjuərim], *s.* (*relig.*) Purim (festa ebraica).

purism ['pjuərizəm], *s.* purismo.

purist ['pjuərist], *s.c.* purista.

puristic(al) [pjuə'ristik(əl)], *ag.* di, da purista.

Puritan ['pjuəritən], *ag.* puritano ‖ *s.c.* (*st.*) puritano, puritana ‖ *s. fig.* puritano; persona di rigidi principi morali.

puritanic(al) [.pjuəri'tænik(əl)], *ag.* di, da puritano; rigido, severo.

puritanically [.pjuəri'tænikəli], *av.* da puritano; in modo puritano.

Puritanism ['pjuəritənizəm], *s.* **1.** (*st.*) puritanismo **2.** *fig.* puritanismo, rigidezza, severità di costumi.

to **puritanize** ['pjuəritənaiz], *v.t.i.* predicare il puritanismo; comportarsi da puritano; fingersi puritano; convertire al puritanismo.

purity ['pjuəriti], *s.* purezza, purità.

purl[1] [pə:l], *s.* **1.** smerlo; bordatura fatta con fili d'oro e argento intrecciati **2.** punto rovescio (a maglia).

to **purl**[1], *v.t.i.* **1.** orlare con bordure d'oro e argento, con smerli, ecc. **2.** lavorare a maglia a punto rovescio.

purl[2], *s.* mormorio, gorgoglio (di ruscello).

to **purl**[2], *v.i.* **1.** scorrere mormorando, gorgogliare (di acqua) **2.** incresparsi; scorrere in vortici (di acqua).

purl[3], *s.* (*fam.*) caduta a capofitto, ruzzolone.

to **purl**[3], *v.t.i.* **1.** (*fam.*) mettere sottosopra **2.** cadere, far cadere (con una spinta) **3.** roteare; far mulinello.

purl[4], *s.* (*arc.*) birra calda con droghe.

purler ['pə:lə*], *s.* (*fam.*) colpo, forte spinta che fa cadere a capofitto.

purlieu ['pə:lju:], *s.* **1.** tratto di terra al limite di una foresta (in parte soggetto alle leggi forestali) **2.** *pl.* dintorni, vicinanze; quartieri periferici.

purlin ['pə:lin], *s.* (*edil.*) arcareccio, trave.

purling[1] ['pə:liŋ], *s.* il fare la maglia a rovescio.

purling[2], *ag.* mormorante ‖ *s.* mormorio (di acqua).

to **purloin** [pə:'loin], *v.t.* sottrarre, rubare.

purloiner [pə:'lɔinə*], *s.c.* frodatore, frodatrice, ladro, ladra.

purloining [pə:'lɔiniŋ], *s.* sottrazione, furto.

purple ['pə:pl], *ag.* **1.** porporino, purpureo; violaceo **2.** imperiale, regale **3.** paonazzo: *to become — with rage*, diventar paonazzo dalla rabbia **4.** ornato, elaborato, fiorito: *— passages* (o *patches*), passi (di un libro) elaborati ‖ *s.* **1.** porpora (colore) **2.** *fig.* porpora (emblema), veste regale, cardinalizia: *to be raised to the —,* essere innalzato alla porpora.

to purple, *v.t.i.* **1.** tingere color porpora **2.** *fig.* imporporare; imporporarsi.

purples ['pə:plz], *s.pl.* (*patol.*) porpora.

purplish ['pə:pliʃ], *ag.* porporino, purpureo; violaceo.

purport ['pə:pət], *s.* **1.** tenore; senso, significato, valore (di un discorso, ecc.) **2.** (*rar.*) mira; scopo; intento; proposito.

to purport, *v.t.* **1.** significare; mostrare; far apparire; implicare: *his words — that he understood nothing,* le sue parole mostrano che non capì nulla **2.** aver la pretesa di, tendere a: *to — to be sthg.,* avere la pretesa d'essere ql.co.

purpose ['pə:pəs], *s.* **1.** mira, scopo, fine; intenzione: *the — of my life,* la ragione della mia vita; *he did it on —,* l'ha fatto apposta; *he wrote a novel with a —,* scrisse un romanzo a tesi; *it will not answer your —,* non servirà al vostro scopo; *not to the —,* inutile, non a proposito; *to no —,* con nessun risultato; *to what —?,* a che scopo? **2.** fermezza, proposito: *he is weak, he is always wanting in —,* egli è debole, manca sempre di fermezza; *infirm of —,* irresoluto, senza carattere.

to purpose, *v.t.* (II) proporre, proporsi (di); avere intenzione di; avere in animo di: *I did not know what he purposed to do,* non sapevo che cosa avesse in animo di fare.

purposed ['pə:pəst], *ag.* proposto, progettato.

purposedly ['pə:pəstli], *av.* a bella posta.

purposeful ['pə:pəsful], *ag.* **1.** fatto di proposito, intenzionalmente; premeditato **2.** pieno di significato **3.** avveduto **4.** tenace.

purposefully ['pə:pəsfuli], *av.* espressamente, intenzionalmente, deliberatamente.

purposefulness ['pə:pəsfulnis], *s.* **1.** intenzione **2.** tenacia **3.** avvedutezza.

purposeless ['pə:pəslis], *ag.* **1.** inutile; senza scopo **2.** senza intenzione.

purposelessly ['pə:pəslisli], *av.* **1.** inutilmente; senza scopo **2** senza intenzione.

purposelessness ['pə:pəslisnis], *s.* **1.** inutilità, mancanza di scopo **2.** mancanza di intenzione.

purposely ['pə:pəsli], *av.* di proposito, volutamente, intenzionalmente.

purposive ['pə:pəsiv], *ag.* **1.** premeditato, intenzionale **2.** utile **3.** risoluto.

purpura ['pə:pjurə], *s.* **1.** (*patol.*) porpora **2.** (*zool.*) murice, porpora.

purpure ['pə:pjuə*], *s.* (*arald.*) porpora.

purpuric [pʌ'pjuərik], *ag.* di porpora, purpureo ☆ *— acid,* acido purpurico; *— fever,* febbre porporina.

purpurin ['pə:pjurin], *s.* (*chim.*) porporina.

purr [pə:*], *s.* fusa.

to purr, *v.t.i.* **1.** fare le fusa **2.** *fig.* esprimere (soddisfazione, ecc.) facendo le fusa.

purree ['pʌri], *s.* materia colorante gialla dell'India.

purring ['pə:riŋ], *s.* il far le fusa.

purse [pə:s], *s.* **1.** borsellino, borsa **2.** (*spor.*) premio in denaro: *to give a —* (o *to put up a —*), stabilire una borsa (per una manifestazione sportiva) **3.** (*st.*) *— of silver, gold,* una somma di 500, 10.000 piastre (nell'impero ottomano) ☆ *-bearer,* tesoriere; *— -net,* rete per conigli; *—-proud,* orgoglioso delle proprie ricchezze; *— -seine,* sciabica; *— -strings,* cordoni della borsa: *to hold the — -strings,* controllare le spese; *to loosen the — -strings,* essere generoso; *to tighten the — -strings,* essere avaro ‖ *heavy —* (o *long —*), (*fam.*)

ricchezza; *light —,* povertà; *public —,* tesoro pubblico.

to purse, *v.t.i.* **1.** contrarre (le labbra); corrugare (la fronte); increspare, incresparsi; raggrinzirsi **2.** (*rar.*) mettere in borsa.

purser ['pə:sə*], *s.* (*mar.*) commissario di bordo.

pursership ['pə:səʃip], *s.* commissariato di bordo.

pursiness ['pə:sinis], *s.* **1.** obesità **2.** asma.

purslane ['pə:slin], *s.* (*bot.*) porcellana.

pursuable [pə'sju:əbl], *ag.* **1.** che può essere inseguito, perseguito **2.** che può essere continuato.

pursuance [pə'sju:(:)əns], *s.* **1.** continuazione, proseguimento **2.** esecuzione; perseguimento.

pursuant [pə'sju:(:)ənt], *ag.* che persegue ‖ *— to,* conforme a, in seguito a.

pursuantly [pə'sju:(:)əntli], *av.* conformemente.

to pursue [pə'sju:], *v.t.i.* **1.** seguire (per catturare, uccidere), inseguire; perseguitare: *the remorse of his sin pursues him,* il rimorso del suo peccato lo tormenta continuamente: *to — (after) s.o., sthg.,* inseguire qlcu., ql.co. **2.** ricercare, aspirare a, perseguire: *they — their aims,* essi perseguono i loro scopi; *we — happiness,* aspiriamo alla felicità **3.** continuare: *I want to — my profession,* voglio continuare a esercitare la mia professione **4.** (*dir. scoz.*) perseguire per legge; intentare un giudizio a.

pursuer [pə'sju:(:)ə*], *s.c.* **1.** inseguitore, inseguitrice **2.** continuatore, continuatrice **3.** (*dir. scoz.*) attore.

pursuit [pə'sju:t], *s.* **1.** inseguimento; caccia; ricerca **2.** occupazione, impiego; carriera **3.** (*dir. scoz.*) procedimento legale **4.** *pl.* studi.

pursuivant ['pə:sivənt], *s.* **1.** (*st.*) attendente dell'araldo **2.** (*poet.*) seguace.

pursy[1] ['pə:si], *ag.* **1.** ansante **2.** grasso, corpulento.

pursy[2], *ag.* **1.** increspato, arricciato **2.** gonfio **3.** *fig.* ricco; orgoglioso delle proprie ricchezze.

purtenance ['pə:tinəns], *s.* (*arc.*) frattaglie.

purulence ['pjuəruləns], **purulency** ['pjuərulənsi], *s.* purulenza, suppurazione.

purulent ['pjuərulənt], *ag.* purulento, marcio.

purulently ['pjuəruləntli], *av.* in modo purulento.

to purvey [pə:'vei], *v.t.i.* provvedere, approvvigionare; far provvigioni.

purveyance [pə:'veiəns], *s.* approvvigionamento; provvigioni.

purveyor [pə:'veiə*], *s.c.* approvvigionatore, approvvigionatrice.

purview ['pə:vju:], *s.* **1.** (*dir.*) testo, dispositivo **2.** limite; scopo; intenzione: *questions outside the — of our enquiry,* domande al di fuori dei limiti della nostra inchiesta **3.** vista; *fig.* campo, sfera: *to come within the — of s.o.,* giungere a portata di vista di qlcu.; *fig.* rientrare nella competenza di qlcu.

pus [pʌs], *s.* pus.

Puseyism ['pju:ziizəm], *s.* (*spreg.*) puseismo (dottrina religiosa predicata da E. B. Pusey, 1830-40).

Puseyite ['pju:ziait], *s.c.* puseista.

push [puʃ], *s.* **1.** spinta; cozzo, urto; botta; colpo ‖ *to get the —,* (*sl.*) essere licenziato; *to give the —,* (*sl.*) licenziare **2.** influenza; pressione **3.** sforzo: *make a — to get it done,* fai uno sforzo per finirlo **4.** operosità, energia; iniziativa **5.** bisogno, momento critico: *at a —,* in caso di emergenza; *when it came to the —,* quando arrivò il momento critico **6.** (*elett.*) pulsante, bottone **7.** (*sl.*) arrivismo: *he has plenty of —,* egli è un vero arrivista **8.** (*sl.*) banda di ladri, di deportati, ecc.

to push, *v.t.i.* **1.** spingere: *please, — that book nearer to me,* per favore, avvicina a me quel libro; *to — s.o. into the room,* far entrare qlcu. a forza nella stanza **2.** spingersi, avanzare; farsi strada (anche *fig.*): *to — one's way,* introdursi a forza; *to — (one's way) through the crowd,* aprirsi un varco tra la folla **3.** *fig.* incalzare, spingere, fare pressioni: *don't — me for payment,* non fate pressioni su di me per il pagamento ‖ *he was pushed for time,* gli mancava il tempo ‖ *to be pushed for money,* essere a corto di denaro **4.** rivendicare: *to — one's claims*, rivendicare i propri diritti **5.** perseguire: *to — one's advantage*, perseguire il proprio vantaggio **6.** lanciare (moda, articolo, ecc.); attivare (commercio): *to — one's wares*, propagandare il proprio articolo **7.** (*biblico*) colpire, dar di corna **8.** *to — aside*, scostare, mettere da parte **9.** *to — away*, allontanare, respingere **10.** *to — back*, respingere, spingere indietro; indietreggiare **11.** *to — down*, far cadere; spingere giù **12.** *to — forth*, mettere (foglie, rami, ecc.) **13.** *to — forward*, aprirsi una strada, spingersi avanti; (far) avanzare **14.** *to — in*, spingere, spingersi dentro **15.** *to — off*, (*mar.*) spingersi al largo **16.** *to — on*, spingersi avanti; (far) avanzare; spronare, incitare; accelerare; affrettarsi: *to — s.o. on to do sthg.*, incitare qlcu. a fare ql.co. **17.** *to — out*, spinger(si) fuori; cacciare, espellere: *the cape pushed out into the sea*, il promontorio si protendeva nel mare; *plants — out new roots*, le piante mettono nuove radici; *to — a boat out*, mettere in acqua un'imbarcazione **18.** *to — over*, far cadere **19.** *to — through*, (far) passare attraverso; condurre a termine; far accettare (progetto di legge, ecc.) **20.** *to — to*, chiudere, accostare con una spinta (porta, imposte) **21.** *to — up*, far salire || *he was pushed up*, (*fam.*) è arrivato a furia di spinte, è stato ben raccomandato.

push, (*nei composti*): *— -ball*, pallone di cuoio; giuoco del pallone; *— -bike*, (*fam.*) bicicletta; *— -button*, pulsante: *— -button civilization*, la civiltà delle macchine; *— -button switch*, interruttore; *— -over*, (*neol.*) oppositore, nemico facilmente debellabile; facile vittima; problema senza difficoltà; *— rod*, (*mec.*) puntale.

pushcart ['puʃkɑːt], *s.* carretto a mano; passeggino (tipo di carrozzella per bambini).

pusher ['puʃə*], *s.c.* **1.** chi spinge **2.** *fig.* chi fa strada nel mondo; arrivista **3.** chi lancia (moda, articolo, ecc.) || *s.* **1.** aeroplano ad elica propulsiva **2.** (*mec.*) spingitoio ☆ *— -screw*, (*aer.*) elica propulsiva || *share — —*, chi cerca di collocare titoli poco stabili (in Borsa).

pushful ['puʃful], *ag.* **1.** energico; intraprendente **2.** aggressivo.

pushfulness ['puʃfulnis], *s.* **1.** energia; intraprendenza **2.** aggressività.

pushing ['puʃiŋ], *ag.* **1.** operoso, energico **2.** intraprendente; che si fa strada nel mondo **3.** indiscreto || *s.* **1.** spinta || *— of oneself*, arrivismo || *— of oneself forward*, indiscrezione, intrusione **2.** attività commerciale.

pushingly ['puʃiŋli], *av.* **1.** vigorosamente **2.** con intraprendenza.

pusillanimity [,pju:silæ'nimiti], *s.* pusillanimità.

pusillanimous [,pju:si'læniməs], *ag.* pusillanime.

pusillanimously [,pju:si'læniməsli], *av.* da pusillanime.

pusillanimousness [,pju:si'læniməsnis], *s.* pusillanimità.

puss [pus], *s.* **1.** micio, micino || *Puss in Boots*, il Gatto con gli stivali || *— in the corner*, (*giuoco*) i quattro cantoni || *you naughty —!*, ah birichina! **2.** lepre.

pussy ['pusi], *s.* micino ☆ *— -wants-a-corner*, (*amer.*) (*giuoco*) i quattro cantoni.

pussyfoot ['pusifut], *s.* **1.** acqua cheta; gattamorta **2.** (*amer.*) proibizionista.

pustular ['pʌstjulə*], **pustulate** ['pʌstjulit], *ag.* pustoloso.

to **pustulate** ['pʌstjuleit], *v.t.i.* coprire, coprirsi di pustole.

pustulation [,pʌstju'leiʃən], *s.* formazione di pustole.

pustule ['pʌstjuːl], *s.* **1.** pustola: *malignant —*, pustola maligna **2.** (*bot.*) escrescenza **3.** (*zool.*) porretta, porro.

pustulous ['pʌstjuləs], *ag.* pustoloso.

put[1] [put], *s.* **1.** spinta; (*spor.*) lancio **2.** diritto di opzione, opzione || *— and call*, opzione doppia (per acquisto, vendita, a scelta) ☆ *— option*, opzione di vendita.

to **put**[1], *pass.p.p.* put, *v.t.i.* **1.** mettere, porre, posare: *— the money in your pocket*, mettiti il denaro in

tasca; *the child was — to bed*, il bambino fu messo a letto; *have you — milk in my tea?*, mi hai già messo il latte nel tè? **2.** mettere (in una determinata condizione): *— yourself at ease*, mettiti a tuo agio, fai pure i tuoi comodi; *— yourself in his place*, mettiti nei suoi panni; *to — an end* (*o a stop*) *to sthg.*, por fine a ql.co.; *to — a field under* (*o to*) *wheat*, mettere un campo a grano; *to — a matter right*, sistemare per bene una faccenda; *to — a play on the stage*, mettere in scena un dramma; *to — s.o. through an examination*, sottoporre qlcu. ad un esame; *to — s.o. to the test*, mettere qlcu. alla prova; *to — sthg. into s.o.'s hands*, affidare ql.co. a qlcu.; *to — sthg. to the vote*, mettere ql.co. ai voti || *I must — him through Milton's works*, devo fargli conoscere le opere di Milton || *she — a check to his words*, non gli permise di parlare || *to — s.o. in a hole*, mettere qlcu. in una situazione imbarazzante || *to — s.o. in the wrong*, far apparire qlcu. in torto || *to — s.o. out of temper*, far perdere la pazienza a qlcu. || *to — s.o. right*, correggere qlcu. || *to — s.o.'s nose out of joint*, lasciare qlcu. con un palmo di naso || *to — sthg. in(to) s.o.'s hands*, affidare ql.co. a qlcu. || *to — sthg. out of one's head*, togliersi dalla testa ql.co. || *to — to death*, mandare a morte || *to — to flight*, mettere in fuga || *to — (a dog) to sleep*, far abbattere (un cane) || *to be hard — to it*, essere messo in imbarazzo **3.** apporre (firma), fare (segno) **4.** sottoporre, esporre: *to — a case before s.o.*, sottoporre un caso a qlcu.; *to — a question to s.o.* (*o to — s.o. a question*), rivolgere una domanda a qlcu. || *I — it to you whether...*, io vi chiedo se... **5.** esprimere, esporre; tradurre: *he — his thought into harsh words*, espresse il suo pensiero con parole aspre; *she knows how to — a case with clearness*, sa esporre un caso con chiarezza; *she must — this letter into French*, deve tradurre in francese questa lettera **6.** stimare, valutare: *you can — her net income at £. 5,000 a year*, puoi calcolare che abbia un reddito netto di £. 5.000 sterline all'anno **7.** indurre; obbligare: *he can do anything you like once he is — to it*, può fare qualsiasi cosa tu voglia una volta che vi sia stato costretto; *what has — him to get into that business?*, che cosa lo ha spinto ad immischiarsi in quell'affare? **8.** dirigere, dirigersi; (*mar.*) far rotta: *he — his horse to the fence*, portò il cavallo all'ostacolo; *the river puts into the lake*, il fiume sfocia nel lago; *the ship — to the nearest harbour*, la nave si diresse verso il porto più vicino; *to — to sea*, prendere il mare **9.** indirizzare (a una professione): *to — a boy to shoe-making*, indirizzare un ragazzo al mestiere del calzolaio **10.** investire (denaro); puntare, scommettere: *he — a large sum into that property*, investì una grossa somma in quella proprietà; *to — money on a horse*, puntare su un cavallo **11.** conficcare: *he — a bullet through his brains*, si fece saltare le cervella **12.** (*spor.*) lanciare: *to — the weight*, lanciare il peso **13.** (*miner.*) spingere (carrelli) **14.** *to — about*, (*mar.*) far circolare (notizie, ecc.); invertire la direzione di marcia di, voltare; (*spec. al passivo*) darsi pensiero, inquietarsi; (*mar.*) virare di bordo **15.** *to — across*, eseguire con successo: *you can't — that across me*, non riesci a farmela **16.** *to — aside*, mettere da parte, accantonare **17.** *to — away*, mettere a posto; mettere da parte (idea, ecc.); mettere in serbo; (*fam.*) togliere di mezzo, uccidere; (*fam.*) imprigionare, segregare; (*fam.*) far fuori; consumare (cibi, bevande); (*mar.*) partire; (*arc.*) ripudiare **18.** *to — back*, rimettere a posto; ostacolare, rallentare; mettere indietro (le lancette di un orologio); (*mar.*) rientrare in porto **19.** *to — by*, eludere (domande), stornare (discorso); serbare, mettere da parte **20.** *to — down*, deporre, posare; reprimere, abbattere; sopprimere; ridurre al silenzio; umiliare; mettere per iscritto; ridurre (spese, ecc.); considerare: *I — down few words*, scrissi poche parole; *I — him down as* (*o for*) *a good boy*, lo considero un bravo ragazzo; *I should — her down as thirty-five*, le darei trentacinque anni || *to — down sthg. to s.o., to sthg.*, metter ql.co. in conto a qlcu.; attribuire ql.co. a qlcu., a ql.co. **21.** to — **forth**, metter fuori; buttare (di piante, ecc.); mettere in circolazione (libro, ecc.) **22.** to — **forward**, proporre, avanzare (teorie, ecc.); mettere avanti: to — oneself forward, mettersi in evidenza **23.** to — **in**, immettere; introdurre; interporre (parola); installare, collocare; inoltrare (reclamo, richiesta); produrre, esibire (documento); fare; (fam.) passare il tempo; (mar.) fare scalo ‖ to — in for, presentare la propria candidatura per **24.** to — **off**, (I) rimandare, rinviare, differire, aggiornare; togliere (abiti, ecc.); sbarazzarsi di; sconcertare, sviare; dissuadere, scoraggiare: to — off (from the shore), partire; lasciare la riva **25.** to — **on**, indossare; assumere (carattere, aspetto); fingere; aumentare (di peso, velocità, ecc.); accendere (luce, fuoco); puntare (al giuoco); segnare (punti); mettere avanti (orologio); spronare, incitare; mettere in scena; mettere in servizio (treni); mettere in comunicazione (telefonica): — on your coat !, mettiti il soprabito!; to — on airs, darsi delle arie; to — on the invalid, fare il malato: to — on weight, crescere, aumentare di peso; to be — on to s.o., essere messo in comunicazione con qlcu. **26.** to — **out**, stendere, allungare (mani, braccia); esporre; tirare, metter fuori; espellere, cacciare; slogarsi, lussarsi; spegnere (luce, fuoco, ecc.); (boxe) mettere k. o.; pubblicare (un libro); mettere in imbarazzo, confondere, sconcertare; seccare, scomodare, infastidire; produrre (merci); dare fuori (lavoro da eseguire); prestare (denaro) a interesse; (mar.) salpare: to — out one's washing, dar fuori la biancheria a lavare ‖ to — a baby out to nurse, mettere un bimbo a balia ‖ to — oneself out for s.o., farsi in quattro per qlcu. **27.** to — **over**, (amer.) assicurare il successo a (commedie, film); imporsi a (un auditorio) **28.** to — **through**, portare a termine (affare, ecc.); mettere in comunicazione telefonica: — me through to the police, datemi la polizia **29.** to — **to**, attaccare (i cavalli) **30.** to — **together**, mettere insieme, unire, riunire; montare (macchina) ‖ to — two and two together, arrivare ad una conclusione (previo esame dei fatti) **31.** to — **up**, alzare, sollevare, issare; innalzare, offrire (una preghiera); mettere in scena, rappresentare (una commedia); alzare (i prezzi); presentare, presentarsi (come candidato); attaccare, affiggere (avviso); fare le pubblicazioni (matrimoniali); mettere (in vendita, all'asta, ecc.); riporre, metter via; impacchettare; mettere in fuga (animali); fabbricare, costruire, montare (tenda); alloggiare, offrire alloggio (temporaneo); far crescere i prezzi; fornire (il denaro necessario); assumere; (sl.) macchinare, concertare ‖ to — s.o. up to sthg., to do sthg., incitare, istigare qlcu. a ql.co., a fare ql.co. ‖ to — s.o. up to a thing, mettere al corrente qlcu. di ql.co. ‖ to — up with sthg., accontentarsi di, sopportare, rassegnarsi a **32.** to — **upon** (s.o.), (fam.) prendersi giuoco di, ingannare, maltrattare (qlcu.): don't be — upon by him, non lasciarti mettere sotto i piedi da lui; I will not be — upon, non voglio che mi si prenda in giro.

(to) **put²**, V. (to) **putt**.

put³ [pʌt], s. napoleone (giuoco a carte).

put⁴, s. (sl. arc.) zuccone, zoticone.

putative ['pju:tətiv], ag. putativo, apparente.

putatively ['pju:tətivli], ag. putativamente, apparentemente.

puteal ['pju:tiəl], s. (archeol.) puteale.

Puteoli [pju:'tiəli], no.pr. (geog.) Pozzuoli.

putlock ['pʌtlɔk], **putlog** ['pʌtlɔg], s. (edil.) putrella, longarina (di legno).

put-off ['put'ɔ:f], s. **1.** ritardo **2.** pretesto, scusa; scappatoia.

put-on ['put'ɔn], ag. affettato; ricercato.

putrefaction [,pju:tri'fækʃən], s. **1.** putrefazione **2.** fig. corruzione morale.

to **putrefy** ['pju:trifai], v.t.i. **1.** putrefare, putrefarsi **2.** fig. corrompere, corrompersi.

putrescence [pju:'tresns], s. **1.** putrescenza; marciume **2.** fig. corruzione, decadenza morale.

putrescent [pju:'tresnt], ag. **1.** putrescente **2.** fig. corrotto.

putrescible [pju:'tresibl], ag. putrescibile ‖ s. sostanza putrescibile.

putrid ['pju:trid], ag. **1.** putrido **2.** fig. corrotto **3.** (sl.) di cattiva qualità ☆ — fever, (patol.) tifo; — sore throat, (patol.) faringite cancrenosa.

putridity [pju:'triditi], **putridness** ['pju:tridnis], s. **1.** putridità **2.** fig. corruzione.

putsch [putʃ], s. (neol.) colpo di mano, tentativo rivoluzionario.

putt [pʌt], s. (golf) « put(t) » (leggero colpo dato alla palla per farla entrare in buca).

to **putt**, v.t.i. (golf) battere leggermente (la palla per farla entrare nella buca).

puttee ['pʌti], s. mollettiera, fascia.

putter ['pʌtə*], s. (golf) **1.** « putter » (una delle mazze per il golf) **2.** giocatore che da alla palla il colpo che deve portarla alla buca.

putting ['pʌtiŋ], s. (golf) pratica del « put(t) » ☆ — green, spazio erboso intorno alla buca.

putty ['pʌti], s. mastice; stucco; intonachino a gesso.

to **putty**, v.t. stuccare.

put-up ['put'ʌp], ag. attributivo: a — bed, un letto di fortuna; a — job, una macchinazione.

puy [pwi:], s. (geol.) collina conica di natura vulcanica (specialmente in Alvernia).

puzzle ['pʌzl], s. **1.** imbarazzo; confusione; perplessità **2.** problema; intrigo; enigma: your sister is a real — to me, tua sorella è per me un vero enigma **3.** giuoco di pazienza; enigma ☆ — -headed, che ha le idee confuse ‖ crossword —, parole incrociate; jig-saw —, giuoco di pazienza a incastro; pictorial —, rebus.

to **puzzle**, v.t.i. **1.** imbarazzare, confondere, imbrogliare; rendere perplesso: he puzzled me with a question, mi pose una domanda imbarazzante **2.** to — about, over (sthg.), rompersi la testa per capire.

puzzledom ['pʌzldəm], **puzzlement** ['pʌzlmənt], s. perplessità; imbarazzo.

puzzler ['pʌzlə*], s. **1.** chi, ciò che rende perplessi **2.** chi si interessa di giuochi di pazienza.

puzzling ['pʌzliŋ], ag. imbarazzante.

puzzlingly ['pʌzliŋli], av. in modo imbarazzante.

puzzolana [,pʌtsou'la:nə], s. (min.) pozzolana.

pyaemia [pai'i:mjə], s. (patol.) piemia.

pyelitis [,paii'laitis], s. (patol.) pielite.

pyemia [pai'i:mjə], s. (patol.) piemia.

Pygmalion [pig'meiljən], no.pr.m. (mit.) Pigmalione.

pygmean [pig'mi:ən], ag. pigmeo.

pygmy ['pigmi], ag. s. pigmeo.

pyjamas [pə'dʒɑ:məz], s.pl. pigiama.

Pylades ['pilədi:z], no.pr.m. (mit.) Pilade.

pylon ['pailən], s. **1.** pilone (nei templi egizi) **2.** (aer. elett.) pilone.

pyloric [pai'lɔrik], ag. (anat.) pilorico.

pylorus [pai'lɔ:rəs], pl. **pylori** [pai'lɔ:rai], s. (anat.) piloro.

pyorrh(o)ea [,paiə'riə], s. (patol.) piorrea.

pyralidid [pi'rælidid], s. (entom.) piralide.

pyramid ['pirəmid], s. **1.** (arch. geom.) piramide **2.** mucchio, albero, ecc. a forma di piramide.

pyramidal [pi'ræmidl], ag. piramidale.

pyramidally [pi'ræmidəli], av. a piramide.

pyramidic(al) [,pirə'midik(əl)], ag. (rar.) piramidale.

pyramidwise ['pirəmid,waiz], av. a piramide.

Pyramus ['pirəməs], no.pr.m. (mit.) Piramo.

pyre ['paiə*], s. pira, rogo.

pyrene [pai'ri:ni], s. (chim.) pirene.

Pyrenean [,pirə'ni:ən], ag. dei Pirenei.

Pyrenees (the) [,pirə'ni:z], no.pr.pl. (geog.) Pirenei.

pyrethrum [pai'ri:θrəm], s. (bot.) piretro.

pyretic [pai'retik], ag. piretico, febbrile.

pyrexia [pai'reksiə], *s.* (*patol.*) piressia.
pyrheliometer [pə:‚hi:li'omitə*], *s.* pireliometro.
pyridin(e) ['pairidin], *s.* (*chim.*) piridina.
pyriform ['pirifo:m], *ag.* a forma di pera.
pyrite ['pairait], *s.* (*min.*) pirite.
pyritic(al) [pai'ritik(əl)], *ag.* (*min.*) piritico.
to **pyritize** ['pairitaiz], *v.t.* (*min.*) trasformare in pirite.
pyritous ['pairitəs], *ag.* (*min.*) piritico.
pyroelectricity [‚pairoui‚lek'trisiti], *s.* (*fis. min.*) piroelettricità.
pyrogallic [‚pairou'gælik], *ag.* (*chim.*) pirogallico.
pyrogenetic [‚pairoudʒi'netik], **pyrogenic** [‚pairou'dʒenik], *ag.* (*fis.*) pirogeno.
pyrogenous [pai'rodʒinəs], *ag.* **1.** (*chim.*) pirogenato **2.** (*geol.*) igneo.
pyrography [pai'rogrəfi], *s.* pirografia.
pyrolusite [‚pairou'lju:sait], *s.* (*min.*) pirolusite.
pyromancy ['pairou‚mænsi], *s.* piromanzia.
pyrometer [pai'romitə*], *s.* pirometro.
pyrope ['pairoup], *s.* (*min.*) piropo.
pyrosis [pai'rousis], *s.* (*patol.*) pirosi.
pyrotechnic(al) [‚pairou'teknik(əl)], *ag.* pirotecnico.
pyrotechnics [‚pairou'tekniks], *s.* pirotecnica.
pyrotechnist [‚pairou'teknist], *s.* pirotecnico.
pyrotechny ['pairətekni], *s.* pirotecnica.

pyroxene ['pairoksi:n], *s.* (*min.*) pirosseno.
pyroxylin(e) [pai'roksilin], *s.* (*chim.*) pirossilina.
Pyrrhic ['pirik], *ag.* (*st.*) pirrico, di Pirro ‖ — *victory*, *fig.* vittoria di Pirro.
pyrrhic[2], *ag.* pirrico ‖ *s.* (danza) pirrica.
pyrrhic[3], *ag.s.* (*poes.*) pirricchio.
pyrrhonic [pi'ronik], *ag.* (*fil.*) pirronico.
pyrrhonism ['pirənizəm], *s.* (*fil.*) pirronismo, scetticismo.
pyrrhonist ['pirənist], *s.* (*fil.*) pirronista, scettico.
Pyrrhus ['pirəs], *no.pr.m.* (*st.*) Pirro.
Pythagoras [pai'θægəræs], *no.pr.m.* (*st. fil.*) Pitagora.
Pythagorean [pai‚θægə'ri(:)ən], *ag.s.* (*fil.*) pitagorico.
Pythagorism [pai'θægərizəm], *s.* (*fil.*) pitagorismo.
Pythian ['piθiən], *ag.* (*st. greca*) pitico ‖ *s.* **1.** abitante di Delfi **2.** Pizia, sacerdotessa di Apollo **3.** Apollo.
python[1] ['paiθən], *s.* (*mit. zool.*) pitone.
python[2], *s.* **1.** demone **2.** ossesso.
pythoness ['paiθənes], *s.* (*st. greca*) pitonessa.
pythonic [pai'θonik], *ag.* pitonico, divinatore.
pyx [piks], *s.* **1.** coppella (per monete di metalli preziosi) **2.** (*eccl.*) pisside.
pyxidium [pik'sidiəm], *pl.* **pyxidia** [pik'sidiə], *s.* (*bot.*) pisside.
pyxis ['piksis], *pl.* **pyxides** ['piksidi:z], *s.* **1.** piccola scatola, cofano, **2.** (*bot.*) pisside.

Q

q [kju:], *pl.* **qs, q's** [kju:z], *s.* (*diciassettesima lettera dell'alfabeto inglese*) q ‖ — *for Queenie*, (*tel.*) q come Quarto ☆ *Q-boat* (o *Q-ship*), (*mar.*) nave civetta (per combattere i sommergibili).

qua [kwei], *cong.* (*lat.*) come; in quanto.

quack¹ [kwæk], *s.* ciarlatano: *a — doctor*, un medicastro.

to quack¹, *v.i.* fare il ciarlatano; parlare da ciarlatano.

quack², *s.* lo schiamazzare dell'anitra; il gracchiare del corvo, ecc. ☆ — - —, (*sl. infantile*) anitra, papera.

to quack², *v.i.* schiamazzare (di anitra); gracchiare (di corvo, ecc.).

quackery ['kwækəri], *s.* ciarlataneria; empirismo.

quackish ['kwækiʃ], *ag.* ciarlatanesco; empirico.

quacksalver ['kwæksælvə*], *s.* ciarlatano.

quad¹ [kwɔd], *abbr.* di **quadrangle**.

quad², *abbr.* di **quadrat**.

to quad², *pass.p.p.* **quadded** ['kwɔdid], *v.t.* (*tip.*) inserire quadrati in; riempire con quadrati.

quad³, *ag. abbr.* di **quadruple**.

quadrable ['kwɔdrəbl], *ag.* (*mat.*) quadrabile.

quadragenarian [,kwɔdrədʒi'nɛərjən], *ag.* quadragenario ‖ *s.c.* quadragenario, quadragenaria.

Quadragesima [,kwɔdrə'dʒesimə], *s.* (*eccl.*) quadragesima.

quadragesimal [,kwɔdrə'dʒesiməl], *ag.* (*eccl.*) quadragesimale.

quadrangle ['kwɔ,dræŋgl], *s.* **1.** (*geom.*) quadrangolo **2.** corte quadrangolare interna (di palazzo, scuola).

quadrangular [kwɔ'dræŋgjulə*], *ag.* quadrangolare.

quadrant ['kwɔdrənt], *s.* **1.** (*geom. astr.*) quadrante **2.** (*mec.*) settore, quadrante ☆ *tooth —*, (*mec.*) set tore dentato.

quadrantal [kwɔ'dræntl], *ag.* di, a forma di quadrante.

quadrat ['kwɔdrət], *s.* (*tip.*) quadratino.

quadrate ['kwɔdrit], *ag.* (*spec. anat.*) quadrato ‖ *s.* **1.** quadrato **2.** (*anat.*) muscolo quadrato.

to quadrate [kwɔ'dreit], *v.t.i.* **1.** (*mat.*) quadrare, squadrare **2.** quadrare, adattarsi.

quadratic [kwɔ'drætik], *ag.* (*alg.*) quadratico ‖ *s.* equazione quadratica.

quadrature ['kwɔdrətʃə*], *s.* (*geom. astr.*) quadratura: *the — of the circle*, la quadratura del circolo.

quadrennial [kwɔ'drenjəl], *ag.* quadriennale.

quadrennially [kwɔ'drenjəli], *av.* ogni quattro anni.

quadriceps ['kwɔdriseps], *s.* (*anat.*) quadricipite.

quadriennium [,kwɔdri'eniəm], *pl.* **quadriennia** [,kwɔdri'eniə], *s.* quadriennio.

quadrifoliate [,kwɔdri'fouliit], *ag.* (*bot.*) quadrifoglio.

quadriga [kwə'dri:gə], *pl.* **quadrigas** [kwə'dri:gəz], **quadrigae** [kwə'dri:gi:], *s.* quadriga.

quadrilateral [,kwɔdri'lætərəl], *ag.s.* (*geom.*) quadrilatero.

quadrille¹ [kwə'dril], *s.* quadriglia (danza e musica).

quadrille², *s.* quadriglio (giuoco di carte).

quadrillion [kwɔ'driljən], *s.* quadrilione.

quadrinomial [,kwɔdri'noumiəl], *ag.* (*alg.*) quadrinomiale.

quadripartite [,kwɔdri'pɑ:tait], *ag.* quadripartito.

quadripartition [,kwɔdripɑ:'tiʃən], *s.* quadripartizione.

quadrireme ['kwɔdriri:m], *s.* (*st. mar.*) quadrireme.

quadrisyllabic ['kwɔdrisi'læbik], *ag.* quadrisillabo.

quadrisyllable ['kwɔdri'siləbl], *s.* quadrisillabo.

quadrivium [kwɔ'driviəm], *s.* (*st.*) quadrivio (delle arti medievali).

quadroon [kwɔ'dru:n], *s.* incrocio di bianco e mulatto; persona che ha un quarto di sangue negro.

quadrumane ['kwɔdrumein], *s.* (*zool.*) quadrumane.

quadrumanous [kwɔ'dru:mənəs], *ag.* (*zool.*) quadrumane.

quadruped ['kwɔdruped], *ag.s.* quadrupede.

quadruple ['kwɔdrupl], *ag.* quadruplo; quadruplice ‖ *s.* quadruplo.

to quadruple, *v.t.i.* quadruplicare, quadruplicarsi.

quadruplet ['kwɔdruplit], *s.* **1.** ogni combinazione di quattro cose unite, operanti insieme **2.** bicicletta a quattro posti **3.** *pl.* quattro nati in un solo parto.

quadruplicate [kwɔ'dru:plikit], *ag.* quadruplice, quadruplo ‖ *s.* **1.** *in —*, in quattro copie **2.** *pl.* quattro esemplari.

to quadruplicate [kwɔ'dru:plikeit], *v.t.* **1.** quadruplicare **2.** fare quattro copie di.

quadruplication [kwɔ,dru:pli'keiʃən], *s.* quadruplicazione.

quadruplicity [,kwɔdru'plisiti], *s.* quadruplicità.

quaere ['kwiəri], *s.* domanda, quesito.

quaere, *v.t. imperat.* (*lat.*) di', dimmi un po' (con valore interrogativo); (*in margine a documenti*) prego informarsi, assicurarsi: —, *is this true?*, prego verificare se questo è esatto; *but —, was the money ever paid?*, ma dimmi, è stato mai versato il denaro?.

quaestor ['kwi:stə*], *s.* (*st. romana*) questore.

quaestorial [kwi:'stɔ:riəl], *ag.* (*st. romana*) di, da questore.

quaestorship ['kwi:stəʃip], *s.* (*st. romana*) questura (funzione, ufficio, carica di questore).

quaff [kwɑ:f], *s.* lungo sorso.

to quaff, *v.t.i.* tracannare; bere a lunghi sorsi.

quaffer ['kwɑ:fə*], *s.* beone.

quag [kwæg], *s.* luogo fangoso, paludoso.

quagga ['kwægə], *s.* (*zool.*) quagga.

quaggy ['kwægi], *ag.* fangoso, paludoso.

quagmire ['kwægmaiə*], *s.* pantano, palude ‖ *to be in a —*, essere nei pasticci.

quail¹ [kweil], *s.* (*ornit.*) quaglia ☆ — *-pipe*, quagliere.

to quail², *v.t.i.* **1.** sgomentarsi, avvilirsi: *his heart quailed*, il suo cuore tremò **2.** (*rar.*) sottomettere; intimidire.

quaint [kweint], *ag.* bizzarro, curioso, strano; antiquato: *a — saying*, un detto curioso, strano; *she wears — little hats*, porta dei buffi cappellini antiquati.

quaintly ['kweintli], *av.* bizzarramente; originalmente; pittorescamente.

quaintness ['kweintnis], *s.* bizzarria, singolarità.

quake [kweik], *s.* tremito; scossa; (*fam.*) terremoto.

to quake, *v.i.* **1.** avere i brividi; tremare: *to — for* (o *with*) *fear*, tremare di paura **2.** tremare (di terra).

Quaker ['kweikə*], *s.* (*st. relig.*) quacchero (membro della « Società degli Amici », setta fondata da George Fox verso la metà del sec. XVII, che si distingue per la semplicità del culto e dei costumi e prescrive una vita fraterna).

Quakerdom ['kweikədəm], *s.* quaccherismo.

Quakeress ['kweikəris|, *s.* quacchera.
Quakerish ['kweikəriʃʃ, *ag.* alla quacchera.
Quakerism ['kweikərizəm], *s.* (*relig.*) quaccherismo.
Quakerly ['kweikəli], *ag.* (*relig.*) di, simile a quacchero ‖ *av.* (*relig.*) da quacchero.
quaking ['kweikiŋ], *s.* tremito.
quakingly ['kweikiŋli], *av.* con tremito.
quaky ['kweiki], *ag.* tremante.
qualifiable ['kwɔlifaiəbl], *ag.* qualificabile.
qualification [,kwɔlifi'keiʃən], *s.* **1.** condizione, riserva, restrizione: *he accepted my offer without —*, accettò la mia offerta senza riserva, incondizionatamente **2.** qualificazione; capacità; requisito; titolo: *he showed he had the necessary qualifications for that post*, mostrò di avere i requisiti necessari a quell'impiego; *send in all the qualifications you have*, presenta tutti i titoli che hai **3.** qualifica: *the — of one's opponent as a fool is dangerous*, è pericoloso qualificare pazzo il proprio avversario ☆ *property —* (*to vote*), (*amm.*) censo (elettorale).
qualificatory ['kwɔlifikətəri], *ag.* qualificativo.
qualified ['kwɔlifaid], *ag.* **1.** qualificato; competente; atto, idoneo: *he is fully — to do this*, egli ha tutte le qualità necessarie per far questo **2.** modificato; limitato ☆ *— acceptance*, (*comm.*) accettazione con riserva.
qualifier ['kwɔlifaiə*], *s.* (*gram.*) parola che modifica (aggettivo, avverbio).
to qualify ['kwɔlifai], *v.t.i.* **1.** qualificare (anche *gram.*); definire: *to — documents as heretical*, qualificare dei testi come eretici **2.** qualificare; render(si) adatto; abilitare, abilitarsi; diplomare, diplomarsi; prepararsi: *he qualified as a dentist last year*, prese la specializzazione in odontoiatria l'anno scorso; *I want to — for that office*, voglio rendermi adatto a quell'incarico; *my nephew wants to — as a pilot*, mio nipote vuole prendere il brevetto di pilota; *to — s.o. for doing sthg.* (*o to do sthg.*), rendere qlcu. adatto a fare ql.co. **3.** (*dir.*) autorizzare **4.** avanzare riserve; modificare; limitare **5.** miscelare, correggere (bevande): *to — a cup of tea with brandy*, correggere una tazza di tè con acquavite.
qualitative ['kwɔlitətiv], *ag.* qualitativo.
quality ['kwɔliti], *s.* **1.** qualità; grado di eccellenza: *of good, high, poor —*, di qualità buona, superiore, inferiore; *to have —*, essere di qualità ‖ *she has — in every movement*, tutti i suoi movimenti sono pieni di distinzione **2.** qualità, caratteristica: *the qualities of a dictator*, le caratteristiche di un dittatore **3.** (*arc.*) posizione sociale; classe elevata: *the people of —*, la gente d'alto rango ‖ *the —*, la nobiltà **4.** qualità (di suono, voce, ecc.) ☆ *first —*, di prima qualità; *heating —*, potere calorifico: *heating — of a combustible*, potere calorifico di un combustibile.
qualm [kwɔːm], *s.* **1.** nausea; malessere **2.** rimorso, scrupolo **3.** preoccupazione: *to feel some qualms about the future*, avere delle inquietudini per l'avvenire.
qualmish ['kwɔːmiʃ], *ag.* **1.** che ha la nausea; soggetto a nausee **2.** nauseante, nauseabondo **3.** scrupoloso **4.** inquieto; che si sente a disagio.
qualmishly ['kwɔːmiʃli], *av.* a disagio; con inquietudine.
qualmishness ['kwɔːmiʃnis], *s.* **1.** nausea **2.** scrupolo, rimorso **3.** disagio.
quandary ['kwɔndəri], *s.* perplessità, imbarazzo.
quant [kwænt], *s.* pertica per spingere una barca (con un disco a una estremità per impedire che affondi nel fango).
to quant, *v.t.i.* spingere (barca) con pertica.
quantitative ['kwɔntitətiv], *ag.* quantitativo.
quantitavely ['kwɔntitətivli], *av.* quantitativamente.
quantity ['kwɔntiti], *s.* **1.** quantità; abbondanza: *the — of shares depends on the subscriptions*, la quantità di azioni dipende dalle sottoscrizioni; *he generally buys goods in great quantities*, egli di solito compra grandi quantitativi di merci **2.** (*mat. fis. elett.*) quantità, grandezza: *— of electricity*, quantità di elettricità;

negligible —, quantità trascurabile (anche *fig.*): *he is a negligible —*, è una nullità **3.** (*mus.*) quantità; durata: *when he plays he never keeps the —*, quando suona non tiene mai il tempo **4.** (*prosodia*) quantità, lunghezza: *you must study better the — of those lines*, devi studiare meglio la quantità di quei versi ☆ *— mark*, segno di quantità (posto su vocali per indicarne la lunghezza) ‖ *unknown —*, (*mat.*) incognita.
quantivalence [kwɔn'tivələns], *s.* (*chim.*) valenza.
quantum ['kwɔntəm], *pl.* **quanta** ['kwɔntə], *s.* **1.** (*fis.*) quantum di energia **2.** quantità sufficiente; quantità richiesta, desiderata **3.** (*med.*) quantità; quanto ☆ *— theory*, (*fis.*) teoria dei quanti.
quaquaversal [,kweikwə'vɔ:səl], *ag.* (*geol.*) inclinato, rivolto in tutte le direzioni.
quarantine ['kwɔrənti:n], *s.* quarantena.
to quarantine, *v.t.* mettere in quarantena (anche *fig.*).
quarrel[1] ['kwɔrəl], *s.* lite, controversia, disputa, contesa: *to make up a —*, appianare le divergenze; *to pick a — with s.o.*, attaccar briga con qlcu. ‖ *to find quarrels in a straw*, trovare ovunque motivo di litigio.
to quarrel[1], *pass.p.p.* **quarrelled** ['kwɔrəld], *v.i.* litigare; attaccar briga; venire a contesa; azzuffarsi: *to — with s.o.*, litigare con qlcu. ‖ *to — with one's bread and butter*, *fig.* agire contro il proprio interesse.
quarrel[2], *s.* **1.** quadrello (tipo di freccia) **2.** vetro quadrato, romboidale per finestra **3.** (*artig.*) diamante (da vetraio) **4.** (*tec.*) bulino a quattro lati.
quarreller ['kwɔrələ*], *s.c.* attaccabrighe; contendente.
quarrelling ['kwɔrəliŋ], *s.* disputa, lite, contesa.
quarrelsome ['kwɔrəlsəm], *ag.* attaccabrighe, litigioso, rissoso; irascibile.
quarrelsomely ['kwɔrəlsəmli], *av.* litigiosamente.
quarrelsomeness ['kwɔrəlsəmnis], *s.* umore litigioso; irascibilità.
quarrier ['kwɔriə*], *s.* cavapietre.
quarry[1] ['kwɔri], *s.* **1.** cava **2.** *fig.* fonte (di informazione): *family papers are often a — of information for historians*, le carte di famiglia sono spesso fonti di informazione per gli storiografi ☆ *marble —*, cava di marmo; *stone —*, cava di pietra.
to quarry[1], *v.t.* **1.** cavare (marmo, pietre, ecc.) **2.** *fig.* ricavare informazioni da.
quarry[2], *s.* selvaggina; preda (anche *fig.*).
to quarry[2], *v.t.* inseguire (la selvaggina, una preda).
quarry[3], *s.* quadretto, losanga di vetro piombato.
quarryman, *pl.* **quarrymen** ['kwɔrimən], *s.* cavatore.
quart[1] [kwɔ:t], *s.* **1.** « quart » (misura di capacità = l. 1,136) **2.** boccale di due pinte di capacità.
quart[2] [kɑ:t], *s.* **1.** (*scherma*) quarta **2.** (*carte*) sequenza di quattro carte.
to quart[2], *v.t.i.* (*scherma*) essere, mettersi in quarta; tirare indietro (la testa) nella posizione di quarta.
quartan ['kwɔ:tn], *ag.* di (febbre) quartana ‖ *s.* (febbre) quartana.
quartation [kwɔ'teiʃən], *s.* (*metal.*) inquartazione.
quarter ['kwɔ:tə*], *s.* **1.** quarto, quarta parte: *a — of an apple*, un quarto di mela; *a — of a century*, un quarto di secolo; *a — of an hour*, un quarto d'ora: *he had a bad — of an hour*, *fig.* passò un brutto quarto d'ora; *he isn't a — as clever as his brother*, non ha nemmeno un quarto dell'intelligenza di suo fratello; *it is a — to five*, sono le cinque meno un quarto; *this clock strikes the quarters*, questo orologio batte i quarti **2.** quarto (di animale macellato) **3.** (*mar.*) (quartiere di) poppa: *wind on the —*, vento al largo (di poppa) **4.** (*arald.*) quarto, quartiere **5.** (*abbr.* qr) « quarter » (misura di peso = kg. 12,7); « quarter » (misura di capacità per cereali = hl. 2,908) **6.** quarto di Luna: *the moon is in its last —*, la Luna è all'ultimo quarto **7.** quarto di dollaro (corrispondente a 25 cents) **8.** direzione, parte, regione (anche *fig.*): *the four quarters of the globe*, le quattro parti del mondo; *the news spread in all quarters*, la notizia si sparse

ai quattro venti; *this is told in high quarters*, questo si dice nelle alte sfere; *what — is the wind in?*, in che direzione soffia il vento?; *fig.* come vanno le cose?; *the wind blows from all quarters at once*, il vento soffia da tutte le parti **9.** quartiere, rione: *he lives in the industrial —*, egli abita nel rione industriale; *a new residential — is now building*, un nuovo quartiere residenziale è in costruzione **10.** *pl.* alloggio, quartiere, appartamentino; stanze d'abitazione; (*mil.*) acquartieramento; posto di combattimento: *officers and men at once took up their quarters*, ufficiali e uomini andarono subito ai loro posti di combattimento; *these are our living quarters*, queste sono le stanze dove abitiamo normalmente; *the troops put up in the winter quarters*, le truppe si acquartierarono negli alloggiamenti invernali **11.** grazia (concessa al nemico che si arrende): *to cry —*, chiedere grazia **12.** (*spor.*) (gara di corsa di) ¼ di miglio ☆ *— -bell*, campana che batte i quarti; *— -binding*, rilegatura con dorso in pelle; *— -bound*, rilegato con dorso in pelle; *— -butt*, stecca corta da biliardo; *— -day*, giorno convenzionale di pagamenti, affitti trimestrali; *— -deck*, (*mar.*) cassero; *— -face portrait*, ritratto di profilo; *— -gallery*, (*mar.*) balconata di poppa; *— -ill*, (*vet.*) antrace sintomatico; *— -left*, *— right*, quarto d'angolo a sinistra, a destra; *— -plate*, (*foto.*) lastra fotografica di cm. 10,8 × 8,2; *— -sessions*, (*dir.*) tribunale di giurisdizione civile e penale limitata che si riunisce trimestralmente; *— -staff*, randello (usato anticamente dai contadini come arma); *— -tone*, (*mus.*) quarto di tono; *— -wind*, (*mar.*) vento di poppa || *for— —*, *hind— —*, quarto anteriore, quarto posteriore (di animale macellato).

to **quarter**, *v.t.i.* **1.** dividere in quattro parti: *to — an apple*, dividere una mela in quattro **2.** smembrare, squartare: *the traitor's body was quartered*, il corpo del traditore fu squartato **3.** alloggiare; (*mil.*) acquartierare, acquartierarsi **4.** (*arald.*) inquartare **5.** battere un terreno (di cani) **6.** (*mec.*) mettere ad angolo retto.

quarterage ['kwɔ:təridʒ], *s.* **1.** pagamento, affitto, pensione trimestrale **2** (*mil.*) acquartieramento.

quartering ['kwɔ:təriŋ], *s.* **1.** il dividere in quattro parti **2.** squartamento **3.** (*mil.*) acquartieramento, alloggiamento **4.** (*arald.*) inquartamento.

quarterly ['kwɔ:təli], *ag.* trimestrale || *s.* pubblicazione trimestrale || *av.* **1.** trimestralmente **2.** (*arald.*) a quartieri alternati.

quartermaster ['kwɔ:tə,ma:stə*], *s.* **1.** (*mil.*) commissario; furiere; (*st.*) quartiermastro || *Quartermaster General (Q.M.G.)*, (*mil.*) capo del dipartimento amministrazione e alloggi **2.** (*mar.*) secondo capo timoniere.

quartern ['kwɔ:tən], *s.* **1.** « quartern » (misura di capacità = l. 0,142) **2.** — (*-loaf*), pane, pagnotta di 4 libbre (= kg. 1,800 circa).

quartet [kwɔ:'tet], *s.* (*mus.*) quartetto ☆ *string —*, quartetto d'archi.

quarto ['kwɔ:tou], *pl.* **quartos** ['kwɔ:touz], *ag.s.* (*tip.*) (volume) in quarto.

quartz [kwɔ:ts], *s.* (*min.*) quarzo.

quartziferous [kwɔ:'siferəs], *ag.* (*min.*) quarzifero.

quartzite ['kwɔ:tsait], *s.* (*min.*) quarzite.

quartzose ['kwɔ:tsous], **quartzous** ['kwɔ:tsəs], **quartzy** ['kwɔ:tsi], *ag.* (*min.*) quarzoso.

to **quash** [kwɔʃ], *v.t.* **1.** schiacciare, sopprimere **2.** (*dir.*) annullare, invalidare.

quashee ['kwɔʃi], *s.* (*fam.*) negro.

quasi ['kwa:zi], *cong.* quasi, cioè, come se fosse || *prefisso*, (*spec.* di *s. ag.*) quasi, semi: *a — -official position*, una posizione semiufficiale.

Quasimodo [,kweisai'moudou], *s.* (*eccl.*) domenica in Albis.

quassia ['kwɔʃə], *s.* (*bot. farm.*) quassia.

quatercentenary [,kwætəsən'ti:nəri], *s.* quarto centenario.

quaternary [kwə'tə:nəri], *ag.* (*chim. mat. geol.*) quaternario || *the Quaternary period*, (*geol.*) il periodo quaternario || *s.* **1.** gruppo di quattro **2.** il numero quattro **3.** (*geol.*) periodo quaternario.

quatorzain [kə'tɔ:zein], *s.* (*poes.*) sonetto irregolare.

quatrain ['kwɔtrein], *s.* (*poes.*) quartina.

quatrefoil ['kætrəfoil], *s.* (*arch. bot.*) quadrifoglio.

quattrocentist [,kwa:trou'tʃentist], *s.* quattrocentista (artista del Quattrocento italiano).

quattrocento [,kwa:trou'tʃentou], *s.* (*art. lett. italiana*) quattrocento.

quaver ['kweivə*], *s.* **1.** trillo, vibrazione **2.** tremolio; voce tremula **3.** (*mus.*) croma.

to **quaver**, *v.t.i.* **1.** trillare, tremare (di voce) **2.** gorgheggiare, trillare; cantare con voce tremula: *to — (out) an air*, cantare un'aria con voce tremolante.

quaveringly ['kweivəriŋli], *av.* **1.** con trilli, vibrazioni **2.** con voce malsicura.

quavery ['kweivəri], *ag.* **1.** trillante; vibrante **2.** tremolante.

quay [ki:], *s.* banchina, molo.

quayage ['ki:idʒ], *s.* tassa, diritto di banchina.

quean [kwi:n], *s.* **1.** ragazza impudente, sfrontata; sgualdrina **2.** (*scoz.*) ragazza.

queasiness ['kwi:zinis], *s.* **1.** delicatezza (di stomaco); facilità alla nausea **2.** scrupolosità.

queasy ['kwi:zi], *ag.* **1.** nauseabondo, stomachevole **2.** delicato (di stomaco) **3.** scrupoloso.

queen [kwi:n], *s.* **1.** regina || *Queen Anne's Bounty*, lascito a beneficio dei sacerdoti poveri (della Chiesa d'Inghilterra) || *Queen Anne's dead*, (*scherz.*) è una notizia vecchia || *Queen Anne style*, (*arch.*) stile regina Anna || *Queen's Counsel (Q.C.)*, consigliere della regina (titolo onorifico dato ad avvocati) || *Queen of Scots*, Maria Stuarda || *to take the —'s shilling*, arruolarsi **2.** *fig.* regina: *the — of beauty*, la reginetta di bellezza; *Queen of Grace*, Regina delle Grazie; *the — of the seas*, la Gran Bretagna; *Venice, the — of the Adriatic*, Venezia, la regina dell'Adriatico **3.** regina (a carte, scacchi): *— of hearts*, regina di cuori (anche *fig.*); *to go to —*, andare a regina, chiedere regina ☆ *— -bee*, (*entom.*) ape regina; *— -consort*, regina consorte; *— -dowager*, regina (vedova di re); *— -mother*, regina madre; *— -of-the-meadows*, (*bot.*) spirea; *—'s-pincushion*, (*bot.*) palla di neve; *— -post*, (*edil.*) monaco; *— -regent*, reggente; *— -regnant*, regina regnante.

to **queen**, *v.t.i.* **1.** fare regina, incoronare regina **2.** essere regina, regnare **3.** (*scacchi*) andare a, chiedere regina.

queendom ['kwi:ndəm], *s.* dignità, ufficio di regina.

queenhood ['kwi:nhud], *s.* regalità; l'essere regina.

queening ['kwi:niŋ], *s.* mela calvilla.

queenlike ['kwi:nlaik], *V.* **queenly**.

queenliness ['kwi:nlinis], *s.* regalità.

queenly ['kwi:nli], *ag.* regale; degno di una regina.

queenship ['kwi:nʃip], *s.* dignità, condizione di regina.

queer[1] [kwiə*], *ag.* **1.** strano, bizzarro, eccentrico; capriccioso || *he is a — fish*, (*fam.*) è un individuo eccentrico || *to be — in the attic*, (*sl.*) avere una rotella di meno || *to be in Queer Street*, (*sl.*) essere in difficoltà finanziaria **2.** dubbio, sospetto **3.** debole, indisposto: *I feel —*, sento un malessere **4.** (*sl.*) ubriaco **5.** (*sl. amer.*) falso: *— money*, denaro falso.

to **queer**[1], *v.t.* (*sl.*) **1.** mettere in ridicolo **2.** ingannare; rovinare || *to — the pitch for s.o.*, (*sl.*) rompere le uova nel paniere a qlcu.

queer[2], *ag.* (*sl.*) cattivo; spregevole (nello *sl.* dei ladri).

queerish ['kwiəriʃ], *ag.* alquanto strano, piuttosto bizzarro.

queerly ['kwiəli], *av.* bizzarramente, stranamente.

queerness ['kwiənis], *s.* **1.** stranezza, bizzarria, stravaganza **2.** indisposizione.

to **quell** [kwel], *v.t.* **1.** (*poet.*) reprimere; soffocare; schiacciare; domare: *to — a rebellion*, soffocare una rivolta **2.** calmare: *to — grief*, calmare il dolore.

queller ['kwelə*], *s.c.* **1.** chi reprime, soffoca **2.** chi calma.

to quench [kwentʃ], *v.t.* **1.** spegnere, estinguere: *to — a fire*, spegnere un fuoco; *to — s.o.'s thirst*, dissetare qlcu. **2.** *fig.* calmare; spegnere: *to — passions*, calmare le passioni **3.** raffreddare; temperare (metalli) **4.** (*sl.*) ridurre al silenzio (un avversario).

quenchable ['kwentʃəbl], *ag.* estinguibile, domabile.

quencher ['kwentʃə*], *s.* **1.** estintore, spegnitore **2.** (*sl.*) bibita dissetante; bevanda.

quenchless ['kwentʃlis], *ag.* inestinguibile.

quenelle [kə'nel], *s.* polpettina di carne, pesce.

querist ['kwiərist], *s.c.* chi chiede, investiga.

quern [kwə:n], *s.* **1.** macina a mano **2.** macinapepe.

querulous ['kweruləs], *ag.* querulo, lamentevole, gemebondo.

querulously ['kweruləsli], *av.* in modo querulo, lamentevolmente.

querulousness ['kweruləsnis], *s.* querimonia; tono dolente, lamento.

query ['kwiəri], *s.* **1.** domanda, quesito: *to raise a —*, porre un quesito **2.** *gener. abbr.* qy. (per introdurre una domanda): *—, was he really tried?*, scusate, fu veramente processato? **3.** (*abbr.* qu.) punto interrogativo.

to query, *v.t.i.* **1.** chiedere; indagare **2.** metter in dubbio; esprimere dubbio: *I — very much whether it is wise to act so hastily*, mi chiedo proprio se è saggio agire così affrettatamente **3.** mettere un punto interrogativo (per esprimere dubbio).

quest [kwest], *s.* **1.** ricerca: *the dogs go in — of their prey*, i cani seguono le tracce della preda; *to go in — of s.o.*, andare alla ricerca di qlcu. **2.** (*dir. arc. dial.*) inchiesta: *the coroner —*, l'inchiesta del «coroner» **3.** (*eccl.*) questua.

to quest, *v.t.i.* **1.** cercare (di un cane) **2.** (*rar.*) questuare.

question ['kwestʃən], *s.* **1.** domanda, interrogazione: *— and answer*, botta e risposta; *direct, indirect* (o *oblique*) *—*, interrogazione diretta, indiretta; *rhetorical —*, interrogazione retorica; *to ask s.o. a —* (o *to put a — to s.o.*) fare una domanda a qlcu. **2.** dubbio, obiezione: *he called in — her leaving tomorrow*, egli sollevò obiezioni sulla sua partenza per domani; *his going is beyond all* (o *out of* o *past* o *without*) *—*, la sua andata è indubbia, fuori questione; *they made no — about* (o *of*) *the result of the game*, non fecero obiezioni al risultato del giuoco **3.** problema, questione; discussione; soggetto di discussione: *the Eastern —*, la questione d'Oriente; *his career will be only a — of time*, la sua carriera sarà solo questione di tempo; *it is a — of limits*, è questione di limiti; *our staying here came into —*, sorse il problema della nostra permanenza qui; *that is the —*, ecco il problema; *what he said is not the —*, quel che disse è trascurabile, senza importanza; *to open a —*, aprire una discussione; *to put the —*, sollevare una discussione ‖ *—!*, all'argomento! (per richiamare al punto della discussione) ‖ *it is a — whether*, rimane da sapere se ‖ *this is out of the —*, ciò è fuori discussione, è impossibile **4.** (*arc.*) tortura (per strappare una confessione): *he was put to the —*, fu sottoposto alla tortura ☆ *— -answer show*, (*rad.*) programma «botta e risposta»; *— mark*, punto interrogativo.

to question, *v.t.* **1.** interrogare, fare domande a: *he was questioned by the police*, fu interrogato dalla polizia **2.** contestare, dubitare di, mettere in dubbio: *it cannot be questioned*, non c'è dubbio; *to — the accuracy of sthg.*, mettere in dubbio l'esattezza di ql.co. **3.** interrogare, consultare (libri, fenomeni, ecc.): *to — the Scriptures*, consultare le Scritture.

questionable ['kwestʃənəbl], *ag.* **1.** dubbio, incerto **2.** contestabile, discutibile **3.** ambiguo, equivoco.

questionableness ['kwestʃənəblnis], *s.* **1.** contestabilità **2.** incertezza **3.** ambiguità.

questionably ['kwestʃənəbli], *av.* discutibilmente, in modo dubbio.

questionary ['kwestʃənəri], *s.* questionario.

questioner ['kwestʃənə*], *s.c.* interrogatore, interrogatrice; esaminatore, esaminatrice.

questioning ['kwestʃəniŋ], *ag.* interrogativo, dubbioso ‖ *s.* inchiesta, domanda.

questioningly ['kwestʃəniŋli], *av.* interrogativamente.

questionless ['kwestʃənlis], *ag.* incontestabile, fuori di ogni dubbio.

questionnaire [,kwestʃə'nɛə*], *s.* questionario.

questor ['kwestə*], *s.* (*st. romana*) questore.

quetzal [ket'sa:l], *s.* **1.** (*ornit.*) trogone splendido **2.** «quetzal» (unità di moneta del Guatemala).

queue [kju:], *s.* **1.** coda, codino **2.** coda (fila di persone): *to stand in a —*, fare la coda.

to queue, *v.t.i.* **1.** mettere in coda; fare la coda **2.** *to — up*, mettersi in coda.

quezal [ke'sa:l], *V.* quetzal.

quibble ['kwibl], *s.* **1.** giuoco di parole, bisticcio, doppio senso **2.** scappatoia, sotterfugio; cavillo.

to quibble, *v.i.* **1.** fare giuochi di parole **2.** cavillare, sofisticare: *I won't — if you are a few minutes late*, non farò storie se arrivi un po' in ritardo.

quibbler ['kwiblə*], *s.c.* **1.** chi fa giuochi di parole **2.** cavillatore, cavillatrice.

quibbling ['kwibliŋ], *ag.* **1.** a doppio senso **2.** elusivo ‖ *s.* **1.** equivocazione **2.** sofisticheria, cavillo.

quibblingly ['kwibliŋli], *av.* **1.** elusivamente **2.** cavillosamente.

quick [kwik], *ag.* **1.** rapido, veloce, svelto: *a — train*, un treno veloce; *be —!*, sbrigatevi!; *he has a very — way of doing things*, ha un modo lesto, sbrigativo di fare le cose ‖ *he is — to take offence*, è facile ad offendersi **2.** vivace; pronto; acuto; intelligente, perspicace: *that child is not very —*, quel bambino non è molto sveglio **3.** (*arc.*) vivo ‖ *the — and the dead*, i vivi ed i morti ‖ *s.* **1.** carne viva: *the cut was deep to the —*, il taglio arrivava alla carne viva **2.** *fig.* punto vivo: *he is a Tory to the —*, è conservatore fino al midollo; *those sharp words stung him to the —*, quelle dure parole lo colpirono sul vivo.

quick, *av.* presto, rapidamente: *—!*, presto!; *don't talk too —*, non parlare troppo svelto.

quick, (*nei composti*): *— -change actor*, trasformista; *— -eyed*, dagli occhi vivaci, penetranti; *— -eared*, dall'orecchio fino; *— -firer*, fucile a ripetizione; *— -lime*, calce viva; *— -lunch counter*, tavola calda; *— -scented*, dal naso fino; *— -sighted*, dalla vista acuta; *— -sightedness*, vista acuta; *fig.* perspicacia; *— -tempered*, irascibile, collerico; *— -wittedness*, intelligenza viva.

to quicken ['kwikən], *v.t.i.* **1.** affrettare, affrettarsi; (*mus.*) accelerare: *to — the step*, affrettare il passo **2.** animare, animarsi; ravvivare; vivificare, vivificarsi; stimolare; eccitare: *good literature quickens the imagination*, la buona letteratura stimola l'immaginazione **3.** avvertire i primi movimenti fetali (di donna gravida).

quickener ['kwikənə*], *s.c.* animatore, animatrice ‖ *s.* stimolante, eccitante.

quickening ['kwikəniŋ], *ag.* vivificante, stimolante ‖ *s.* **1.** rianimazione, rinascita **2.** accelerazione: *a — of the pulse*, accelerazione del polso.

to quick-freeze ['kwikfri:z], *pass.* **quick-froze** ['kwikfrouz], *p.p.* **quick-frozen** ['kwik,frouzən], *v.t.* congelare rapidamente, surgelare (cibi, per conservarne il sapore, vitamine, ecc.).

quickly ['kwikli], *av.* presto, rapidamente, senza indugio, prontamente.

quickness ['kwiknis], *s.* rapidità, celerità; *fig.* prontezza; vivacità; acutezza; penetrazione.

quicksand ['kwiksænd], *s.* sabbia mobile.

quickset ['kwikset], *ag.* (*bot.*) di sempreverdi ‖ *s.* siepe di sempreverdi.

quicksilver ['kwik,silvə*], *s.* mercurio; argento vivo (anche *fig.*).

to **quicksilver**, *v.t.* trattare col mercurio; rivestire di mercurio.

quicksilvered ['kwik,silvəd], *ag.* rivestito di mercurio; *fig.* che ha l'argento vivo addosso.

quickstep ['kwikstep], *s.* 1. (*mil.*) passo cadenzato 2. (*danza*) « quickstep » (« foxtrot » veloce).

quickthorn ['kwikθɔ:n], *s.* biancospino.

quid[1] [kwid], *s.* quid, elemento caratteristico.

quid[2], *s.* (*invariato al pl.*) (*sl.*) sovrana, sterlina: *he works for four — a week*, lavora per quattro sterline alla settimana.

quid[3], *s.* cicca (di tabacco da masticare).

to **quid**[3], *pass.p.p.* **quidded** ['kwidid], *v.t.i.* 1. ciccare, masticare tabacco 2. lasciar cadere dalla bocca (il cibo) mezzo masticato (di cavallo).

quiddity ['kwiditi], *s.* 1. quiddità, essenza 2. cavillo, sottigliezza.

to **quiddle** ['kwidl], *v.i.* 1. (*dial.*) perdere il tempo in inezie 2. parlare a vanvera.

quiddler ['kwidlə*], *s.* perdigiorno, fannullone.

quidnunc ['kwidnʌŋk], *s.c.* pettegolo, pettegola; chiacchierone, chiacchierona.

quid pro quo ['kwidprou'kwou], *s.* 1. (*rar.*) qui pro quo, equivoco, sbaglio 2. compenso, contraccambio.

quiescence [kwai'esns], **quiescency** [kwai'esnsi], *s.* quiescenza; quiete.

quiescent [kwai'esnt], *ag.* quiescente, tranquillo.

quiescently [kwai'esntli], *av.* tranquillamente.

quiet ['kwaiət], *ag.* 1. quieto, tranquillo, pacifico, calmo: *to live in a — way*, vivere in modo tranquillo ‖ *all — on the western front*, niente di nuovo sul fronte occidentale 2. dolce, docile: *a — disposition*, un carattere dolce 3. semplice, sobrio: *a — style*, uno stile sobrio 4. tenue, pallido, pastello (di colore) 5. intimo, segreto: *to keep sthg. —*, tenere ql.co. segreto ‖ *s.* 1. quiete, tranquillità: *the — of the evening*, la quiete della sera 2. riposo 3. calma, pace, serenità 4. *on the —*, di nascosto: *to do sthg. on the —*, (*fam.*) fare ql.co. di nascosto; *to tell sthg. on the —*, (*fam.*) dire ql.co. a quattr'occhi.

to **quiet**, *v.t.i.* 1. acquietare, calmare; (*rar.*) calmarsi; pacificare 2. *to — down*, acquietarsi, calmarsi.

to **quieten** ['kwaiətn], *v.t.i.* acquietare, acquietarsi.

quieter ['kwaiətə*], *s.* 1. paciere; pacificatore 2. calmante.

quietism ['kwaiitizəm], *s.* (*st. relig.*) quietismo.

quietist ['kwaiitist], *ag.* (*st. relig.*) quietistico ‖ *s.* (*st. relig.*) quietista.

quietly ['kwaiətli], *av.* con calma, tranquillamente; *fig.* pazientemente, dolcemente.

quietness ['kwaiətnis], **quietude** ['kwaiitju:d], *s.* quiete, tranquillità; *fig.* calma; riposo; pace.

quietus [kwai'i:təs], *s.* 1. (*rar.*) quietanza 2. morte; liberazione finale: *to give s.o. his —*, (*fam.*) regolare i conti con qlcu.; mandare qlcu. all'altro mondo.

quill [kwil], *s.* 1. penna; calamo; aculeo (di riccio) 2. (*ind. tessile*) fuso, bobina 3. penna d'oca, cannuccia (per scrivere) 4. sugherino, piccolo galleggiante (per canna da pesca) 5. (*mus.*) penna, plettro ☆ *— -driver*, (*spreg.*) scrittorucolo, imbrattacarte.

to **quill**, *v.t.* 1. pieghettare; increspare 2. (*ind. tessile*) avvolgere sui fusi.

quilled [kwild], *ag.* a forma di penna; fornito di penne.

quillet ['kwilit], *s.* (*arc.*) quisquilia, sottigliezza; giuoco di parole.

quilling ['kwiliŋ], *s.* increspatura.

quilt[1] [kwilt], *s.* trapunta, coperta imbottita.

to **quilt**[1], *v.t.* 1. coprire con tessuto trapuntato 2. trapuntare, imbottire 3. comporre (un'opera letteraria) con frammenti e idee di altri autori.

to **quilt**[2], *v.t.* (*sl.*) percuotere, battere.

quilting ['kwiltiŋ], *s.* imbottitura a trapunta; tessuto imitante una trapunta.

quinary ['kwainəri], *ag.* quinario.

quinate ['kwainit], *ag.* (*bot.*) composto di cinque foglioline.

quince [kwins], *s.* (*bot.*) 1. cotogna 2. — (*-tree*), cotogno ☆ — *jam*, marmellata di cotogne.

quincentenary [,kwinsen'ti:nəri], *ag.* relativo al quinto centenario ‖ *s.* quinto centenario.

quincuncial [kwin'kʌnʃəl], *ag.* (*bot.*) quinconciale.

quincuncially [kwin'kʌnʃəli], *av.* (*bot.*) a quinconce.

quincunx ['kwinkʌŋks], *s.* (*bot.*) quinconce; disposizione a quinconce.

quindecagon [kwin'dekəgən], *s.* (*geom.*) poligono a quindici angoli.

quinine [kwi'ni:n], *s.* (*farm.*) chinino.

quinquagenarian [,kwiŋkwədʒi'nɛəriən], **quinquagenary** [kwiŋ'kwædʒinəri], *ag.* quinquagenario ‖ *s.c.* quinquagenario, quinquagenaria.

Quinquagesima [,kwiŋkwə'dʒesimə], *s.* (*eccl.*) Quinquagesima ‖ — *Sunday*, (*eccl.*) domenica di quinquagesima.

quinquennial [kwiŋ'kweniəl], *ag.* quinquennale.

quinquennially [kwiŋ'kweniəli], *av.* ogni quinquennio.

quinquennium [kwiŋ'kweniəm], *s.* quinquennio.

quinquereme ['kwiŋkwiri:m], *s.* quinquereme.

quinquina [kwiŋ'kwainə], *s.* (*bot.*) chinchina.

quinsied ['kwinzid], *ag.* (*patol.*) affetto da tonsillite, da angina.

quinsy ['kwinzi], *s.* (*patol.*) tonsillite; angina.

quint[1] [kwint], *s.* 1. (*mus.*) quinta 2. tassa di un quinto.

quint[2], *s.* quinta (al picchetto, giuoco delle carte).

quintain ['kwintin], *s.* (*st.*) quintana: *to tilt at the —*, correr la quintana.

quintal ['kwintl], *s.* quintale (misura di peso = 220.46 lb.).

quintan ['kwintən], *ag.* (*patol.*) di, relativo a quintana ‖ *s.* (*patol.*) quintana.

quinte [kænt], *s.* (*scherma*) quinta.

quintessence [kwin'tesns], *s.* quintessenza.

quintessential [,kwinti'senʃəl], *ag.* purissimo; concentrato.

quintet [kwin'tet], *s.* (*mus.*) quintetto.

Quintilian [kwin'tiljən], *no.pr.m.* (*st. lett.*) Quintiliano.

quintillion [kwin'tiljən], *s.* quintilione; (*amer.*) un milione elevato al cubo.

Quintin ['kwintin], *no.pr.m.* Quintino.

quintuple ['kwintjupl], *ag.s.* quintuplo.

to **quintuple**, *v.t.i.* quintuplicare, quintuplicarsi.

quintuplet ['kwintjuplit], *s.* 1. serie di cinque 2. *pl.* cinque nati da un medesimo parto.

quintuplicate [kwin'tju:plikit], *ag.* quintuplice ‖ *s.* uno di cinque esemplari uguali: *in —*, in cinque copie.

to **quintuplicate** [kwin'tju:plikeit], *v.t.* quintuplicare.

Quintus ['kwintəs], *no.pr.m.* Quinto.

quip [kwip], *s.* 1. frizzo, canzonatura, sarcasmo 2. giuoco di parole 3. cavillo, arzigogolo.

to **quip**, *pass.p.p.* **quipped** [kwipt], *v.t.i.* (*rar.*) 1. canzonare, motteggiare; far giuochi di parole 2. cavillare, arzigogolare.

quipu ['kwipu:], *s.* quipu (antica scrittura peruviana).

quire[1] ['kwaiə*], *s.* gruppo di quattro fogli; ventiquattro fogli di carta da lettera.

to **quire**[1], *v.t.* sistemare in quinterni.

quire[2], *V.* **choir**.

to **quire**[2], *V.* to **choir**.

Quirinal ['kwirinəl], *no.pr.* (*geog.*) Quirinale.

Quirinus [kwi'rainəs], *no.pr.m.* Quirino.

quirk [kwə:k], *s.* 1. arguzia 2. cavillo; sotterfugio; scappatoia 3. svolazzo (di penna) 4. (*mus.*) variazione improvvisa 5. (*arch.*) scanalatura.

to **quirk**, *v.t.i.* 1. cavillare; motteggiare; sferzare 2. parlare, muoversi a scatti.

quirky ['kwə:ki], *ag.* 1. che ama i motti arguti, le facezie 2. sinuoso (di strada).

quirt [kwə:t], *s.* frustino (di cavaliere).

to quirt, *v.t.* colpire col frustino.

quisling ['kwizliŋ], *s.* (*neol.*) collaborazionista; (*pop.*) traditore.

quit [kwit], *ag.* **1.** liberato; libero **2.** disobbligato; sdebitato: *to get — of sthg.*, sdebitarsi di ql.co.

to quit, *pass.p.p.* **quitted** ['kwitid], *v.t.i.* **1.** abbandonare, lasciare; andarsene: *to — a place*, abbandonare un luogo; *to — office*, dimettersi; *to — one's job*, dare le dimissioni, lasciare il proprio lavoro **2.** (*amer.*) cessare, smettere: *— grumbling*, smettila di borbottare; *when will you — smoking?*, quando smetterai di fumare? **3.** lasciar andare: *to — hold of sthg.*, lasciar andar ql.co. **4.** quietanzare; pagare; saldare **5.** sloggiare ‖ *to give notice to —*, dare la disdetta (ad un inquilino) **6.** (*poet.*) ripagare: *to — love with hate*, ricambiare l'amore con odio **7.** (*arc.*) comportarsi: — *yourselves like men*, comportatevi da uomini **8.** (*arc.*) liberarsi di, sbarazzarsi di.

quitch [kwitʃ], *s.* — (*-grass*), (*bot.*) gramigna.

quite [kwait], *av.* **1.** completamente, interamente, del tutto; affatto; proprio, veramente: *— otherwise*, ben diversamente; *— so!*, proprio così!; — *young*, giovanissimo; *he was — mistaken in*, si sbagliava proprio a; *I am — well*, sto proprio bene; *I can — believe that*, credo bene che; *it is — late!*, è ben tardi!; *it is — right*, è giustissimo; *this banana is not — ripe*, questa banana non è del tutto matura; *you are — wrong*, hai torto marcio **2.** piuttosto, abbastanza: *it's — cold this morning*, fa piuttosto freddo stamattina.

quits [kwits], *ag. predicativo* pari: *to be —*, essere pari ‖ *to cry —*, rinunciare a competere.

quittance ['kwitəns], *s.* (*arc. poet.*) **1.** ricevuta, quietanza ‖ *omittance is no —*, il fatto di non richiedere un pagamento non significa che il debito abbia cessato di esistere **2.** ricompensa **3.** rappresaglia.

to quittance, *v.t.* (*arc.*) ripagare.

quitter ['kwitə*], *s.* (*amer. fam.*) chi tralascia, rinunzia facilmente; codardo, disertore, vile.

quiver[1] ['kwivə*], *s.* faretra ‖ *— full of children*, *fig.* famiglia numerosa ‖ *to have an arrow left in one's —*, *fig.* avere ancora qualche risorsa.

quiver[2], *ag.* attivo; agile; vivace ‖ *s.* fremito, brivido; tremito.

to quiver[2], *v.t.i.* **1.** tremare, fremere, palpitare, avere brividi: *he quivered with cold*, tremava di freddo; *her voice quivered*, le tremò la voce **2.** agitare: *the skylark quivered its wings*, l'allodola scosse le ali.

quivering ['kwivəriŋ], *ag.* fremente, tremolante, tremante ‖ *s.* brivido, tremito, tremolio.

quiveringly ['kwivəriŋli], *av.* in modo tremolante, con brividi.

quiverish ['kwivəriʃ], *ag.* tremante.

qui vive [ki:'vi:v], *s.* chi va là ‖ *to be on the —*, stare sul chi va là, stare all'erta.

Quixote ['kwiksət], *no.pr.m.* (*lett.*) Chisciotte ‖ **quixote,** *s.* visionario entusiasta.

quixotic [kwik'sɔtik], *ag.* **1.** donchisciottesco **2.** *fig.* idealista, stravagante.

quixotically [kwik'sɔtikəli], *av.* donchisciottescamente; stravagantemente.

quixoties [kwik'sɔtiks], *s.pl.* sentimenti donchisciotteschi.

quixotism ['kwiksətizəm], **quixotry** ['kwiksətri], *s.* atteggiamento donchisciottesco, stravagante.

quiz[1] [kwiz], *pl.* **quizzes** ['kwiziz], *s.* **1.** burlone **2.** scherzo, burla **3.** (*arc.*) persona strana, eccentrica.

to quiz[1], *pass.p.p.* **quizzed** [kwizd], *v.t.* burlare, canzonare.

quiz[2], *pl.* **quizzes,** *s.* **1.** indovinello; quesito; questionario **2.** (*amer.*) interrogazione scolastica; prova orale d'esame ☆ *— master*, presentatore di « quiz »; — *show*, programma di « quiz ».

to quiz[2], *pass.p.p.* **quizzed,** *v.t.* **1.** porre quesiti, indovinelli a **2.** (*amer.*) interrogare, esaminare (studenti).

quizzical ['kwizikəl], *ag.* **1.** scherzoso, canzonatorio, faceto **2.** curioso, eccentrico, strambo.

quizzically ['kwizikəli], *av.* scherzosamente.

quizziness ['kwizinis], *s.* stranezza; eccentricità.

quizzing ['kwiziŋ], *s.* burla; beffa ☆ — *glass*, monocolo.

quod [kwɔd], *s.* (*sl.*) prigione.

to quod, *pass.p.p.* **quodded** ['kwɔdid], *v.t.* (*sl.*) imprigionare.

quoin [kɔin], *s.* **1.** cantone **2.** pietra, mattone formante angolo **3.** zeppa, bietta **4.** (*arch.*) concio d'angolo **5.** (*tip.*) serraforme.

to quoin, *v.t.* **1.** (*arch.*) rafforzare, innalzare con ganci **2.** (*tip.*) serrare a cunei **3.** fissare con zaffe.

quoit [kɔit], *s.* **1.** anello di corda, di metallo piatto usato per giocare **2.** *pl.* giuoco in cui si deve infilare un anello in un piolo nel terreno.

to quoit, *v.t.i.* (*rar.*) giocare a « quoits »; lanciare a guisa di disco.

quondam ['kwɔndæm], *ag.* (*lat.*) di un tempo: *a — acquaintance*, una conoscenza del passato.

quorum ['kwɔ:rəm], *s.* (*lat.*) **1.** « quorum » (numero legale per deliberare in assemblea) **2.** (*arc.*) adunanza di conciliatori.

quota ['kwoutə], *s.* **1.** quota, rata; tassa **2.** (*comm.*) contingentamento ☆ — *immigrant*, (*amer.*) quota di immigrazione (secondo la legge 1924).

quotation [kwou'teiʃən], *s.* **1.** citazione **2.** (*comm.*) quotazione **3.** (*tip.*) quadrato (pezzetto di metallo per regolare gli spazi fra le parole) ☆ — *marks*, virgolette.

quote [kwout], *s.* (*fam.*) **1.** citazione **2.** *pl.* virgolette: *end of quotes*, chiuse le virgolette.

to quote, *v.t.* **1.** citare, addurre: *to — an instance*, citare un esempio; *to — from an author, from a book*, citare da un autore, da un libro; *to — Milton*, citare Milton **2.** (*comm.*) quotare (in borsa) **3.** (*tip.*) virgolettare.

quoth [kwouθ], *v.t.* (*arc.*): — *I*, — *he*, dissi, disse.

quotha ['kwouθə], *inter.* (*arc.*) davvero!.

quotidian [kwɔ'tidiən], *ag.* quotidiano ‖ *s.* malaria quotidiana.

quotient ['kwouʃənt], *s.* (*arit.*) quoziente.

R

r [ɑ:*], *pl.* **rs**, **r's** [ɑ:z], *s.* (*diciottesima lettera dell'alfabeto inglese*) r: *to roll one's r's*, parlare con l'erre || — *for Robert*, (*tel.*) r come Roma || *the — months*, i mesi con l'erre (da settembre a aprile) indicati per il consumo di ostriche e crostacei || *the three R's* (*reading*, (*w*)*riting*, (*a*)*rithmetic*), le tre erre (leggere, scrivere e far di conto, come base della istruzione elementare).

rabbet ['ræbit], *s.* 1. (*mec.*) scanalatura, gola, sede 2. incastro ☆ — *-joint*, giunto a maschio e femmina; — *plane*, pialletto a scanalare.

to rabbet, *v.t.* 1. scanalare 2. incastrare; congiungere con un incastro.

rabbi ['ræbai], *s.* rabbino || *Chief Rabbi*, Gran Rabbino.

rabbinate ['ræbinit], *s.* 1. carica di rabbino 2. l'insieme dei rabbini.

rabbinic(al) [ræ'binik(əl)], *ag.* rabbinico, di rabbino.

rabbinically [ræ'binikəli], *av.* da rabbino, come un rabbino.

rabbinism ['ræbinizəm], *s.* rabbinismo.

rabbinist ['ræbinist], *s.* rabbinista.

rabbit[1] ['ræbit], *s.* 1. coniglio 2. (*fam.*) schiappa (nel giuoco) ☆ — *-fish*, (*ittiol.*) pesce gatto; — *-hutch*, conigliera; — *-warren*, garenna, conigliera || *buck* —, coniglio maschio; *doe* —, coniglia.

to rabbit[1], *v.i.* andare a caccia di conigli.

to rabbit[2], *v.t.*: *odd* — *it!*, (*volg.*) il diavolo se lo porti!.

rabbitry ['ræbitri], *s.* allevamento di conigli; conigliera.

rabbity ['ræbiti], *ag.* ricco di conigli; simile a coniglio.

rabble[1] ['ræbl], *s.* folla, calca || *the* —, la plebaglia, la feccia.

to rabble[1], *v.t.i.* 1. attaccare, assalire tumultuando (di plebe); linciare 2. trasformarsi in plebaglia.

rabble[2], *s.* (*metal.*) raschiatoio; agitatore, mescolatore.

to rabble[2], *v.t.* (*metal.*) raschiare; rimescolare rapidamente.

to rabble[3], *v.t.i.* parlare indistintamente, farfugliare.

Rabelaisian [ˌræbə'leizjən], *ag.* rabelasiano, nello stile di Rabelais || *s.* ammiratore, studioso, imitatore di Rabelais.

rabid ['ræbid], *ag.* 1. rabbioso, furioso, violento: — *enemy*, nemico feroce 2. ostinato, irragionevole; fanatico: *a* — *comunist*, un comunista arrabbiato 3. (*patol.*) idrofobo ☆ — *dog*, cane idrofobo.

rabidity [rə'biditi], *s.* 1. rabbia, furia, furore 2. ostinazione; fanatismo.

rabidly ['ræbidli], *av.* 1. rabbiosamente, furiosamente, violentemente 2. ostinatamente, irragionevolmente; fanaticamente.

rabidness ['ræbidnis], *V.* **rabidity**.

rabies ['reibi:z], *s.* (*patol.*) idrofobia, rabbia.

raccoon [rə'ku:n], *s.* (*zool.*) procione lavatore.

race[1] [reis], *s.* 1. corso (della vita, del Sole, della Luna): *his* — *is nearly run*, è quasi giunto alla fine dei suoi giorni 2. (*spor.*) corsa (di cavalli, ecc.); gara di velocità 3. *pl.* corse, concorso ippico 4. corrente (di mare, fiume, ecc.) 5. canale di adduzione, di condotta (dell'acqua) 6. (*aer. amer.*) flusso 7. (*mec.*) gola di scorrimento; sede di rotolamento; pista 8. (*tec.*) corsa (della spola) ☆ — *-ball*, ballo dato in occasione di un concorso ippico; — *-card*, programma delle corse; —

-*cup*, (*spor.*) coppa; — *-meeting*, concorso ippico; — *-path* (o — *-track*), campo delle corse, ippodromo; — *-way*, (*idraulica*) canale di condotta d'acqua; (*elett.*) canalizzazione || *horse-* —, corsa di cavalli; *road-* —, corsa su strada.

to race[1], *v.t.i.* 1. correre, far correre a grande velocità 2. prender parte a una corsa; correre, gareggiare: *I raced with him and won by a length*, gareggiai con lui e vinsi per una lunghezza 3. allevare cavalli da corsa; far correre (i propri cavalli): *he races his horses at all the big meetings*, fa correre i suoi cavalli in tutte le corse più importanti 4. (*mec.*) imballarsi (di motore) 5. *to* — *away a fortune*, scialacquare un patrimonio alle corse dei cavalli.

race[2], *s.* 1. razza, schiatta, stirpe: *the white races*, le razze bianche; *he was a man of ancient and noble* —, era un uomo di antica e nobile schiatta 2. razza, stirpe, gruppo di persone con caratteristiche simili: *the* — *of poets*, la stirpe dei poeti 3. (*rar.*) fragranza, gusto del vino 4. *fig.* caratteristica (di stile letterario, ecc.) ☆ — *-hatred*, odio di razza.

race[3], *s.* radice (di zenzero).

racecourse ['reis-ko:s], *s.* ippodromo, campo delle corse.

racehorse ['reisho:s], *s.* cavallo da corsa.

raceme [rə'si:m], *s.* (*bot.*) racemo.

racemose ['ræsimous], *ag.* (*bot.*) racemoso.

racer ['reisə*], *s.* 1. corridore 2. cavallo da corsa 3. (*aer. aut. mar.*) mezzo da corsa 4. serpente (specialmente serpente nero americano) 5. (*mil.*) piattaforma girevole.

Rachel ['reitʃəl], *no.pr.f.* Rachele.

rachis ['reikis], *pl.* **rachides** ['reikidi:z], *s.* 1. rachide (di foglie, piume) 2. (*anat.*) rachide, colonna vertebrale.

rachitic [ræ'kitik], *ag.* (*patol.*) rachitico: *a* — *child*, un bimbo rachitico.

rachitis [ræ'kaitis], *s.* (*patol.*) rachitismo.

racial ['reiʃəl], *ag.* razziale.

racialism ['reiʃəlizəm], *s.* razzismo.

racialist ['reiʃəlist], *s.c.* razzista.

racially ['reiʃəli], *av.* dal punto di vista razziale; per razza.

racily ['reisili], *av.* 1. in modo piccante, arguto 2. vivacemente; vigorosamente.

raciness ['reisinis], *s.* 1. forza, vigore; brio 2. arguzia.

racing ['reisiŋ], *ag.* da corsa || *the* — *world*, il mondo dell'ippica || *s.* 1. corsa, corse 2. (*mec.*) fuga ☆ — *car*, automobile da corsa; — *craft*, aereo da competizione; imbarcazione da competizione; — *stud*, scuderia di cavalli da corsa || *horse* —, le corse, l'ippica; *road* —, corse su strada; *track* —, corsa su pista.

racism ['reisizəm], *s.* (*neol.*) razzismo.

racist ['reisist], *s.c.* razzista.

rack[1] [ræk], *s.* 1. rastrelliera (per foraggio) 2. rastrelliera, scolapiatti 3. reticella portabagagli 4. (*mec.*) cremagliera ☆ — *-rail*, (*mec.*) rotaia a cremagliera; — *-railway*, ferrovia a cremagliera; — *-wheel*, ruota dentata || *pipe-* —, portapipe; *plate-* —, scolapiatti.

to rack[1], *v.t.i.*: — *up*, riempire di foraggio la rastrelliera; mettere del foraggio nella rastrelliera per (un cavallo); legare (un cavallo) alla rastrelliera.

rack[2], *s.* ruota (strumento di tortura); tortura: *to be on the* —, essere alla tortura; *fig.* essere sulle spine.

to **rack**[2], *v.t.* **1.** mettere alla tortura, torturare (anche *fig.*): *he was racked with fever*, era tormentato dalla febbre **2.** sforzare; sfruttare || *to — one's brains*, spremersi il cervello ☆ — *-rent*, affitto esorbitante; — *-renter*, chi esige, paga un affitto esorbitante.

rack[3], *s.* nembo, nuvole minacciose, nuvolaglia.

to **rack**[3], *v.i.* fuggire, correre (di nubi).

rack[4], *s.* ambio (andatura di cavallo, tra il trotto e il galoppo).

to **rack**[4], *v.i.* ambiare, correre all'ambio.

rack[5], *s.* rovina, distruzione || *to go to — and ruin*, andare in malora.

rack[6], *s.* « arrack » (liquore orientale).

to **rack**[7], *v.t.* travasare (vino).

to **rack**[8], *v.t.* (*mar.*) legare alla portoghese.

racket[1] ['rækit], *s.* **1.** racchetta **2.** racchetta da neve **3.** largo zoccolo (per uomini e cavalli) con il quale procedere su terreno paludoso **4.** *pl.* « rackets » (giuoco con racchette praticato al chiuso).

racket[2], *s.* **1.** fracasso, chiasso, schiamazzo; tumulto: *to kick up* (o *to make*) *a —*, far schiamazzo **2.** baldoria; vita movimentata e dissipata: *he went on the —*, si abbandonò ai piaceri **3.** (*sl. amer.*) attività illegale (di gangster, ecc.); affare, organizzazione losca: *do you want to be in on this —?*, vuoi far parte della banda? || *the rum —*, organizzazione clandestina per la vendita di alcoolici **4.** (*sl. amer.*) ricatto organizzato; piano per ottenere denaro o altro con mezzi illegali e spesso violenti **5.** dura esperienza: *to stand the —*, superare con successo la prova; affrontare le conseguenze di un'azione.

to **racket**[2], *v.i.* **1.** far baldoria; condurre vita allegra **2.** fare chiasso, fracasso; muoversi rumorosamente.

racketeer [,ræki'tiə*], *s.* chi ottiene denaro con mezzi illegali, con ricatti; ricattatore.

to **racketeer**, *v.i.* ottenere guadagni con mezzi illeciti.

racketeering [,ræki'tiəriŋ], *s.* metodi illeciti per ottenere denaro; ricatto organizzato.

racketing ['rækitiŋ], *ag. V.* **rackety** || *s.* chiasso, schiamazzo; allegria rumorosa.

rackety ['rækiti], *ag.* **1.** chiassoso, rumoroso **2.** amante della bella vita.

racking[1] ['rækiŋ], *ag.* torturante; doloroso.

racking[1], *s. fig.* tormento.

racking[2], *s.* ambio.

racking[3], *s.* travaso, tramutamento (di liquidi).

raconteur [,ræknˈtə:*], *s.* chi racconta aneddoti, favole.

racoon [rəˈku:n], *s.* (*zool.*) procione lavatore.

racy ['reisi], *ag.* **1.** caratteristico: *a — flavour*, un aroma caratteristico **2.** di razza (di animale): *a — dog*, un cane di razza **3.** vivido; penetrante; pungente: *a — humour*, un umorismo pungente **4.** genuino; fragrante; fresco: *— wine*, vino genuino.

rad [ræd], *abbr.* di **radical**.

radar ['reidə*], *s.* **1.** (acrostico di *Radio Detection And Ranging*) radar: *ship equipped with —*, nave fornita di radar **2.** apparecchiatura usata per il radar ☆ *— beacon*, radarfaro; — *-man*, addetto al radar.

raddle[1] ['rædl], *s.* ocra rossa.

to **raddle**[1], *v.t.* **1.** dipingere con ocra rossa **2.** imbellettare: *raddled face*, viso imbellettato.

raddle[2], *s.* **1.** canniccio, vimini (per recinti, ecc.) **2.** recinto, porta, ecc. fatti di canniccio, vimini intrecciati.

to **raddle**[2], *v.t.* intrecciare, legare insieme.

radial ['reidjəl], *ag.* **1.** (*anat.*) radiale **2.** radiale, di raggio, attinente a raggio ☆ *— axle*, asse radiale; — *flow turbine*, turbina radiale; — *nerve*, (*anat.*) nervo radiale; — *rotor*, rotore a pale radiali (di elicottero).

radially ['reidjəli], *av.* a raggiera.

radian ['reidjən], *s.* (*geom.*) radiante.

radiance ['reidjəns], **radiancy** ['reidjənsi], *s.* radiosità, splendore, fulgore.

radiant ['reidjənt], *ag.* **1.** raggiante, che emana raggi:

— sun, sole raggiante **2.** *fig.* radioso, raggiante; gioioso: *— eyes*, occhi raggianti; *a face — with smiles*, un volto sorridente e radioso **3.** (*fis.*) radiante: — *heat*, calore radiante || *s.* (*fis. astr.*) (punto) radiante ☆ — *heating*, riscaldamento a pannelli radianti.

radiantly ['reidjəntli], *av.* radiosamente.

radiate ['reidiit], *ag.* radiato, a raggi.

to **radiate** ['reidieit], *v.t.i.* **1.** raggiare; emettere raggi, irradiare, irradiarsi: *heat radiates from fire*, il calore emana dal fuoco **2.** brillare, sfavillare: *happiness radiates from her eyes*, la gioia brilla nei suoi occhi.

radiated ['reidieitid], *ag.* radiato, raggiato.

radiately ['reidiitli], *av.* a raggiera.

radiation [,reidi'eiʃən], *s.* radiazione, irradiazione, irraggiamento ☆ *homogeneous —*, (*med.*) radiazione omogenea; *infrared —*, (*fis.*) radiazione infrarossa; *ultraviolet —*, (*fis.*) radiazione ultravioletta.

radiative ['reidiitiv], *ag.* radiante.

radiator ['reidieitə*], *s.* **1.** radiatore, termosifone **2.** (*mec.*) radiatore **3.** (*rad.*) antenna trasmittente ☆ *honeycomb —*, radiatore a nido d'api; *hot water —*, radiatore ad acqua calda; *panel —*, radiatore a pannelli.

radical ['rædikəl], *ag.* radicale: *a — change*, un mutamento radicale; *a — number*, un numero radicale; *the — party*, il partito radicale || *s.* (*mat. chim. pol.*) radicale.

radicalism ['rædikəlizəm], *s.* (*pol.*) radicalismo.

radically ['rædikəli], *av.* radicalmente.

to **radicate** ['rædikeit], *v.t.* (*arc. spec. fig.*) far mettere radici a.

radicel ['rædisel], *s.* (*bot.*) radicetta.

radicle ['rædikl], *s.* **1.** (*bot.*) radicetta **2.** (*anat.*) radicicola **3.** (*chim.*) radicale.

radio ['reidiou], *pl.* **radios** ['reidouz], *s.* **1.** radio (radiotelegrafia) radiotelefonia **2.** radiotelegramma **3.** — (*set*), apparecchio radiofonico: *— set with pick-up and gramophone*, radiogrammofono ☆ *— amateur*, (*neol.*) radioamatore; *— -beacon*, radiofaro; — *engineer*, ingegnere specializzato in radiofonia; *— equipment*, (*aer.*) impianto radio; — *flying*, (*aer.*) volo radioguidato; — *frequency*, radiofrequenza; *— -guided missiles*, missili radiocomandati; *— -gramophone*, radiogrammofono; — *licence*, abbonamento alle radioaudizioni; — *link*, collegamento radiofonico; *— -operator*, radiotelegrafista; — *receiver*, radioricevitore; — *static*, disturbi atmosferici; — *tower*, antenna di trasmissione; — *transmitter*, radiotrasmettitore; — *transmitting valve*, valvola trasmittente; — *wave*, radioonda.

to **radio**, *v.t.i.* radiotelegrafare; diramare per radio: *radioed instructions*, istruzioni diramate via radio; *he radioed me*, mi comunicò per radio.

radioactive ['reidiou'æktiv], *ag.* radioattivo.

radioactivity ['reidiouæk'tiviti], *s.* radioattività.

radiobiology ['reidioubai'olədʒi], *s.* radiobiologia.

radioconductor ['reidioukən'dʌktə*], *s.* radioconduttore.

radioelement ['reidiou'elimənt], *s.* elemento radioattivo.

radiogoniometer ['reidiou,gouni'omitə*], *s.* radiogoniometro.

radiogram ['reidiougræm], *s.* **1.** radiogramma, marconigramma **2.** (*abbr.* di *radio-gramophone*) radiogrammofono.

radiograph ['reidiougrɑ:f], *s.* **1.** radiografia **2.** radiografo.

to **radiograph**, *v.t.* fare la radiografia di.

radiographer [,reidi'ogrəfə*], *s.* radiologo.

radiographic(al) [,reidiou'græfik(əl)], *ag.* radiografico.

radiographically [,reidiou'græfikəli], *av.* per mezzo di radiografia.

radiography [,reidi'ogrəfi], *s.* radiografia.

radioisotope ['reidiou'aisoutoup], (*chim. fis.*) isotopo radioattivo.

radiolocation ['reidioulou'keiʃən], *s.* radiolocalizzazione, localizzazione a mezzo radar.

radiolocator [ˈreidiouˌlouˈkeitə*], *s.* radiolocalizzatore, radar.

radiologie(al) [ˌreidiouˈlɔdʒik(əl)], *ag.* radiologico.

radiologist [ˌreidiˈɔlədʒist], *s.* radiologo.

radiology [ˌreidiˈɔlədʒi], *s.* radiologia.

radiometer [ˌreidiˈɔmitə*], *s.* radiometro.

radiophone [ˈreidioufoun], *s.* **1.** (*fis.*) radiofono **2.** (*rad.*) radiotelefono.

radiophonie [ˌreidiouˈfɔnik], *ag.* radiofonico.

radiophony [ˌreidiˈɔfəni], *s.* radiofonia.

radiophotography [ˈreidioufətˈɔgrəfi], *s.* radiofotografia.

radioscopic(al) [ˌreidiouˈskɔpik(əl)], *ag.* radioscopico.

radioscopy [ˌreidiˈɔskəpi], *s.* radioscopia.

radiosensitive [ˌreidiouˈsensitiv], *ag.* (*med.*) sensibile al radio: — *tumours*, tumori sensibili al radio.

radiotelegram [ˈreidiouˈteligræm], *s.* radiotelegramma, marconigramma.

radiotelegraphy [ˈreidioutiˈlegrəfi], *s.* radiotelegrafia.

radiotelephony [ˈreidioutiˈlefəni], *s.* radiotelefonia.

radioteleprinter [ˈreidiouˈteliˌprintə*], *s.* radiotelescrivente.

radiotherapeutic [ˈreidiouˌθerəˈpjuːtik], *ag.* radioterapico.

radiotherapeutics [ˈreidiouˌθerəˈpjuːtiks], **radiotherapy** [ˈreidiouˈθerəpi], *s.* radioterapia.

radiovision [ˈreidiouˈviʒən], *s.* radiovisione, televisione.

radish [ˈrædiʃ], *s.* (*bot.*) rafano, ravanello.

radium [ˈreidjəm], *s.* (*chim.*) radio ☆ — *-therapy*, radioterapia.

radius [ˈreidjəs], *pl.* **radii** [ˈreidiai], *s.* **1.** raggio (anche *geom.*): — *of action of an aeroplane*, raggio di azione di un aereo; *I know everybody within a* — *of five miles*, conosco tutti nel raggio di cinque miglia ‖ *the (four-mile)* —, area londinese che si estende per un raggio di quattro miglia da Charing Cross **2.** (*anat.*) radio ☆ — *vector*, (*mat. astr.*) raggio vettore.

radix [ˈreidiks], *pl.* **radixes** [ˈreidiksiz], **radices** [ˈreidiˈsiːz], *s.* **1.** (*mat.*) radice **2.** (*bot.*) radice **3.** radice, origine (di un male, ecc.).

radon [ˈreidɔn], *s.* (*chim.*) radon.

raff [ræf], *V.* **riff-raff**.

raffia [ˈræfiə], *s.* (*bot.*) rafia ☆ — *goods*, oggetti in rafia.

raffish [ˈræfiʃ], *ag.* **1.** dissipato; spregevole; basso **2.** vistoso, appariscente.

raffishly [ˈræfiʃli], *av.* **1.** in modo dissipato; bassamente **2.** in modo vistoso.

raffishness [ˈræfiʃnis], *s.* **1.** dissipatezza; bassezza **2.** vistosità.

raffle[1] [ˈræfl], *s.* riffa, lotteria.

to raffle[1], *v.t.i.* **1.** vendere per mezzo di una lotteria **2.** prendere i biglietti di una lotteria.

raffle[2], *s.* rifiuti, detriti.

raft [rɑːft], *s.* **1.** zattera; chiatta **2.** (*edil.*) trave **3.** (*amer.*) grosso stormo di uccelli sull'acqua ☆ — *-bridge*, ponte di barche.

to raft, *v.t.i.* trasportare con zattera; usare una zattera come mezzo di trasporto; attraversare (un corso d'acqua) su una zattera.

rafter[1] [ˈrɑːftə*], *s.* (*edil.*) travetto inclinato del tetto.

to rafter[1], *v.t.* **1.** fornire di travi; sostenere con travi **2.** arare a mezza aratura.

rafter[2], *s.* chi si occupa del trasporto di legname sull'acqua; zattiere.

raftsman, *pl.* **raftsmen** [ˈrɑːftsmən], *s.* chi lavora su zattere; zattiere.

rag[1] [ræg], *s.* **1.** cencio, brandello, straccio; avanzo di stoffa: *in rags*, a brandelli; *he has not a* — *to cover him*, non ha uno straccio con cui coprirsi ‖ *cooked to rags*, cotto e stracotto ‖ *she reduced him to a* —, lo ridusse a uno straccio ‖ *there was not a* — *of evidence*, non c'era la minima prova **2.** *gener. pl.* abito vecchio; vestito a brandelli ☆ — *-baby* (o — *-doll*), bambola di stracci; — *-bag*, sacco per gli stracci; — *-bolt*, (*mec.*) bullone di fondazione; — *-fair*, mercato di abiti usati; — *-man*, straccivendolo; — *-money*, (*fam.*) moneta cartacea; — *-paper*, carta fatta di stracci; — *-tag* (*and bob-tail*), (*sl.*) plebaglia, feccia.

rag[2], *s.* **1.** (*arc. dial.*) pietra dura **2.** lastra di ardesia per copertura di tetto **3.** (*geol.*) varietà di roccia friabile.

to rag[2], *pass.p.p.* **ragged** [rægd], *v.t.* frantumare (un minerale) con un martello.

rag[3], *s.* (*sl. universitario*) baldoria, baccano.

to rag[3], *v.t.i.* **1.** (*sl.*) rimproverare, sgridare severamente **2.** stuzzicare, tormentare, fare scherzi grossolani a **3.** mettere in disordine (una stanza) **4.** essere rumoroso, attaccabrighe.

ragamuffin [ˈrægəˌmʌfin], *s.* pezzente, straccione; monello di strada.

ragamuffinly [ˈrægəˌmʌfinli], *av.* da pezzente.

rage [reidʒ], *s.* **1.** (*arc.*) follia **2.** rabbia, collera, furore; ardore, furore bellico: *in the* — *of the battle*, nell'ardore della battaglia; *to be in a* — *with s.o.*, essere in collera con qlcu.; *to fly* (o *to get*) *into a* —, andare in collera **3.** furia (degli elementi): *the* — *of the wind*, la furia del vento **4.** furore, ispirazione poetica; ispirazione profetica; frenesia musicale **5.** mania, passione: *the* — *for money*, la passione del denaro; *she had a* — *for old stamps*, aveva la mania dei francobolli antichi ‖ *to be* (*all*) *the* —, essere di gran moda, essere in voga, furoreggiare, far furore.

to rage, *v.i.* **1.** andare in collera, infuriarsi: *to* — *against* (o *at*) *s.o.*, essere furioso con qlcu. **2.** infierire; scatenarsi; infuriare (degli elementi): *the plague raged*, la peste infieriva **3.** *to* — *oneself out*, placarsi, calmarsi: *the storm raged itself out*, la tempesta si placò.

ragee [ˈrægi], *s.* (*ang.-in.*) sorta di miglio.

ragged [ˈrægid], *ag.* **1.** logoro, lacero, stracciato, cencioso, pezzente: *a* — *beggar*, un mendicante cencioso; *a* — *coat*, una giacca a brandelli **2.** scabro, aspro; frastagliato: *a* — *edge*, un orlo frastagliato **3.** ispido, irsuto; spettinato: — *hair*, capelli spettinati **4.** rozzo; imperfetto; non uniforme: — *rhymes*, rime imperfette **5.** stridente, aspro: — *voice*, voce stridente ☆ — *-lady*, (*bot.*) fanciullaccia; — *-Robert*, (*bot.*) geranio roberziano; — *Robin*, (*bot.*) fior di cuculo; — *-school*, (*st.*) scuola gratuita per bambini poveri.

raggedly [ˈrægidli], *av.* **1.** a brandelli; da cencioso **2.** ispidamente **3.** in modo non uniforme **4.** aspramente.

raggedness [ˈrægidnis], *s.* **1.** cenciosità **2.** ineguaglianza, mancanza di uniformità **3.** imperfezione.

raggee [ˈrægi], *s.* (*ang.-in.*) sorta di miglio.

raging [ˈreidʒiŋ], *ag.* furioso; infuriato, impetuoso; violento: *the* — *ocean*, l'oceano tempestoso; *s.* furia, furore; violenza; impeto ☆ — *fever*, febbre da cavallo; — *mad*, pazzo da legare.

ragingly [ˈreidʒiŋli], *av.* furiosamente; violentemente; impetuosamente.

raglan [ˈræglən], *s.* « raglan » (tipo di cappotto) ☆ — *sleeves*, maniche alla « raglan ».

ragout [ˈræguː], *s.* (*cuc.*) ragú.

ragtime [ˈrægtaim], *s.* (*mus.*) « ragtime » (ritmo sincopato) ☆ — *army*, un esercito da farsa; — *music*, musica fortemente sincopata.

ragwheel [ˈrægwiːl], *s.* (*mec.*) ruota dentata.

ragwort [ˈrægwɔːt], *s.* (*bot.*) erba colderina.

raid [reid], *s.* irruzione; scorreria; incursione aerea; irruzione della polizia in ambienti sospetti ☆ — *air-* —, incursione aerea: *air-* — *precautions*, misure antiaeree; *air-* — *shelter*, rifugio antiaereo; *air-* — *warning*, allarme aereo; *pirate* —, razzia di pirati.

to raid, *v.t.i.* fare una scorreria, un'incursione; invadere; assalire; attaccare.

raider [ˈreidə*], *s.* invasore; razziatore; predone.

rail[1] [reil], *s.* **1.** sbarra **2.** *pl.* inferriata, cancello, stecconata **3.** parapetto; sponda; ringhiera; balaustra **4.** (*mar.*) battagliola, orlo di murata **5.** (*ferr.*)

rotaia, binario ‖ *by* —, per ferrovia, a mezzo di ferrovia: *I have travelled by* —, ho viaggiato in treno; *to send sthg. by* —, inviare ql.co. per ferrovia ‖ *to run off the rails*, deragliare, *fig.* sviarsi **6.** *pl.* (*Borsa*) titoli ferroviari ☆ — *-car*, automotrice; — *cross-section*, sezione della rotaia; — *gauge*, scartamento; — *-motor* (o — *-motor -car*), littorina; — *post*, (*edil.*) colonnino di ringhiera ‖ *central contact* —, rotaia centrale; *check* —, controrotaia; *hand-* —, (*edil.*) corrimano.

to rail[1], *v.t.i.* **1.** fornire di cancelli; provvedere di sbarre **2.** viaggiare in ferrovia **3.** trasportare per ferrovia **4.** posare le rotaie **5.** *to* — *in*, delimitare, rinchiudere con inferriate, ecc. **6.** *to* — *off*, separare con inferriate, ecc. **7.** *to* — *round*, circondare con inferriate.

rail[2], *s.* (*ornit.*) rallo.

rail[3], *s.* (*rar.*) insulto; offesa.

to rail[3], *v.i.*: *to* — *against, at* (*s.o., sthg.*), burlarsi di; prendersela con.

railed [reild], *ag.* **1.** a rotaie **2.** chiuso da cancellata ☆ *double-* —, a due binari; *single-* —, a un solo binario.

railer ['reilə*], *s.* canzonatore; ingiuriatore.

railhead ['reilhed], *s.* **1.** (*mil.*) stazione ferroviaria in cui termina il trasporto per ferrovia **2.** estremità di linea ferroviaria in costruzione.

railing[1] ['reiliŋ], *ag.* ingiurioso ‖ *s.* canzonatura; ingiuria.

railing[2], *s.* **1.** inferriata; grata; cancellata **2.** parapetto; ringhiera; balaustra **3.** rotaie **4.** il posare le rotaie (su strada).

railingly ['reiliŋli], *av.* in modo canzonatorio; ingiuriosamente.

raillery ['reiləri], *s.* canzonatura; motteggio.

railless ['reillis], *ag.* **1.** sprovvisto di rotaie **2.** sprovvisto di parapetto, balaustra.

railroad ['reilroud], *s.* (*amer.*) ferrovia, strada ferrata ☆ — *-car*, vagone ferroviario.

to railroad, *v.t.i.* (*amer.*) **1.** trasportare per ferrovia **2.** fornire di ferrovie **3.** far funzionare una ferrovia **4.** viaggiare per ferrovia **5.** *to* — *a bill*, (*sl.*) far approvare in fretta un progetto di legge.

railroader ['reil‚roudə*], *s.* (*amer.*) ferroviere.

railroading ['reil‚roudiŋ], *s.* (*amer.*) il costruire, il mantenere in azione le strade ferrate.

railway ['reilwei], *s.* ferrovia, strada ferrata ‖ *at* — *speed*, a tutta velocità ☆ — *cabin*, casello ferroviario; — *-carriage*, vagone ferroviario; — *-chair*, ganascia delle rotaie; — *company*, compagnia ferroviaria; — *-crossing*, incrocio ferroviario; — *network*, rete ferroviaria; — *rates*, tariffe ferroviarie; — *section*, tronco ferroviario; — *-sleepers*, traversine di strada ferrata; — *station*, stazione ferroviaria; — *-switch*, deviatore; — *tariff*, tariffa ferroviaria; — *-terminus*, capolinea; — *-turnplate*, piattaforma girevole ‖ *branch* —, diramazione ferroviaria; *cable* —, funicolare; *light* —, binario a scartamento ridotto; *underground* —, ferrovia sotterranea, metropolitana.

railwayless ['reilweilis], *ag.* senza strada ferrata.

railwayman, *pl.* **railwaymen** ['reilweimən], *s.* ferroviere.

raiment ['reimənt], *s.* (*poet. arc.*) vestito; abbigliamento; equipaggiamento.

rain [rein], *s.* **1.** pioggia (anche *fig.*): *a* — *of fire, of kisses, of sparks, fig.* una pioggia di fuoco, di baci, di scintille; *driving* (o *pelling*) —, pioggia scrosciante; *in the* —, sotto la pioggia ‖ — *or shine*, con il brutto o con il bel tempo ‖ *it looks like* —, vuol piovere ‖ *to be as right as* —, (*fam.*) sentirsi, trovarsi benissimo ‖ *to be caught in the* —, essere sorpreso dalla pioggia ‖ *to be drenched with* —, essere inzuppato di pioggia ‖ *to go out in the* —, uscire sotto la pioggia **2.** *pl.* piogge; stagione delle piogge ‖ *the Rains*, zone piovose dell'Atlantico ☆ — *-bird*, picchio verde; cuculo della Giamaica; — *-box*, (*teat.*) macchina per imitare la pioggia; — *-doctor*, mago della pioggia; — *-forest*, foresta tropicale; — *-gauge*, pluviometro; — *-glass*,

barometro; — *-water*, acqua piovana; — *-worm*, lombrico.

to rain, *v.t.i.* **1.** *imp.* piovere ‖ *it has rained itself out*, ha cessato di piovere ‖ *it is raining cats and dogs*, (*fam.*) piove a catinelle ‖ *it rains in torrents*, piove a dirotto ‖ *it never rains but it pours*, *prov.* le disgrazie non vengono mai sole; o troppo o niente! **2.** *fig.* piovere, far piovere; scorrere; cadere, far cadere, riversare: *invitations rained upon her*, le piovvero inviti; *tears rained down her cheeks*, lacrime scorrevano copiose sulle sue guance; *they rained praises on him*, riversarono lodi su di lui; *to* — *benefits upon*, far piovere benefici su.

rainbow ['reinbou], *s.* arcobaleno; iride.

raincoat ['reinkout], *s.* impermeabile.

raindrop ['rein-drɔp], *s.* goccia di pioggia.

rainfall ['reinfɔ:l], *s.* **1.** scroscio di pioggia **2.** piovosità ☆ *annual* —, piovosità annuale.

rainily ['reinili], *av.* con pioggia.

raininess ['reininis], *s.* piovosità.

rainless ['reinlis], *ag.* senza pioggia, secco.

rainproof ['reinpru:f], *ag.* impermeabile ☆ — *material*, tessuto impermeabile.

to rainproof, *v.t.* impermeabilizzare.

rainy ['reini], *ag.* piovoso, di pioggia: — *day*, giorno piovoso; *fig.* tempo duro, avversità: *to provide against a* — *day*, assicurarsi il necessario per i momenti di bisogno; — *season*, stagione piovosa; stagione delle piogge; — *weather*, tempo piovoso.

raise[1] [reiz], *s.* **1.** strada sopraelevata **2.** aumento; (*fam.*) aumento di salario.

to raise[1], *v.t.* **1.** alzare, levare; elevare, innalzare; sollevare, tirar su, rialzare: *he raised a great weight*, sollevò un grave peso; *he raised me from my knees*, mi aiutò a rialzarmi; *she raised her voice*, alzò la voce; *to* — *bread*, far lievitare il pane; *to* — *hymns*, innalzare inni; *to* — *one's eyes*, alzare gli occhi; *to* — *one's eyebrows*, aggrottare le sopracciglia; *to* — *one's glass to*, brindare alla salute di; *to* — *one's hat*, levarsi il cappello per salutare; *to* — *to the throne*, elevare al trono ‖ *to* — *one's head*, apparire ‖ *to* — *s.o. from the dead*, fare risuscitare qlcu. **2.** *fig.* levare, sollevare; proporre; suscitare; causare, provocare; evocare: *to* — *a claim*, avanzare una pretesa; *to* — *a country against the enemy*, sollevare un paese contro il nemico; *to* — *a ghost*, evocare uno spirito; *to* — *a laugh*, suscitare una risata; *to* — *an objection*, sollevare una obiezione; *to* — *a question*, fare una domanda; *to* — *a shout*, levare un grido; *to* — *s.o.'s spirits*, sollevare il morale a qlcu. ‖ *to* — *a dust*, eccitarsi; suscitare gran confusione; *to* — *hell*, scatenare un pandemonio **3.** costruire; erigere: *they raised a palace*, costruirono un palazzo **4.** allevare; coltivare; produrre: *she raised a large family*, allevò ed educò una numerosa famiglia; *to* — *cattle*, allevare bestiame; *to* — *corn*, coltivare grano **5.** procurarsi (denaro); riscuotere (tasse): *to* — *capital*, procurarsi, raccogliere capitali ‖ *to* — *the wind*, (*sl.*) procurarsi del denaro **6.** far salire, aumentare (prezzo, valore, ecc.): *they raised the price of goods*, aumentarono il prezzo della merce **7.** (*mil.*) togliere, levare (un assedio): *to* — *a siege, a blockade*, togliere l'assedio, il blocco **8.** (*mil.*) raccogliere (nuove leve), arruolare **9.** *to* — *the land*, (*mar.*) scorgere la terra.

raise[2], *s.* cumulo di pietre (per indicare una tomba, un confine, ecc.).

raised [reizd], *ag.* **1.** sollevato, alzato **2.** in rilievo: — *embroidery*, ricamo in rilievo **3.** (*cuc.*) lievitato.

raiser ['reizə*], *s.* **1.** chi solleva, innalza **2.** allevatore (di bestiame); coltivatore **3.** ricevitore (di tasse).

raisin ['reizn], *s.* uva passa.

raising ['reiziŋ], *s.* **1.** innalzamento, sollevamento; aumento (di prezzi) **2.** allevamento (di bestiame); coltivazione **3.** riscossione (di tasse) **4.** educazione (di bambini) **5.** (*mil.*) il togliere un assedio **6.** raccolta (di truppe) **7.** evocazione (di spiriti) **8.** (*ind. tessile*) garzatura.

raison d'être ['reizɔ:n'deitə*], s. scopo; giustificazione.

to rait [reit], V. to ret.

raj [rɑ:dʒ], s. (ang.-in.) sovranità; dominio; regno.

raja(h) ['rɑ:dʒə], s. «rajah», ragià.

Rajpoot, Rajput ['rɑ:dʒput], s. «Rajpoot» (membro di casta militare indù).

rake[1] [reik], s. 1. rastrello || as lean as a —, magro come un chiodo 2. persona molto magra.

to rake[1], v.t.i. 1. rastrellare; raccogliere (anche fig.): to — the leaves (up together), ammassare le foglie con il rastrello 2. cercare a fondo; scandagliare; passare in rassegna; indagare, scrutare: he raked Roman history for examples, passò in rassegna l'intera storia romana per trovare esempi || to — among (o in), frugare tra 3. (mil.) colpire, battere d'infilata 4. percorrere rapidamente con lo sguardo; fig. dominare: from her window she raked the valley, dalla sua finestra dominava la vallata 5. raschiare, grattare 6. to — away, off, liberare da, togliere (foglie, ecc.) con il rastrello 7. to — up, attizzare (fuoco, ecc.); riesumare; ammassare con il rastrello: to — up an old quarrel, risuscitare un vecchio rancore.

rake[2], s. 1. (mar.) slancio: — of the stem, slancio del dritto di prua 2. (mar.) inclinazione 3. (mec.) angolo di inclinazione, di spoglia 4. inclinazione, pendenza; declivio.

to rake[2], v.t.i. 1. (mar.) avere un'inclinazione 2. inclinare, dare una inclinazione a.

rake[3], s. individuo scapestrato; libertino || " The Rake's Progress ", (mus.) « La carriera del libertino ».

to rake[3], v.i. essere un libertino; condurre una vita dissipata.

rake[4], s. (scoz.) 1. sentiero, cammino 2. sentiero praticato dagli armenti che vanno al pascolo; tratturo 3. pascolo 4. (miner.) filone obliquo 5. solco.

to rake[5], v.i. 1. procedere, avanzare; camminare; vagabondare 2. inseguire a volo la preda (di falco).

rakehell ['reikhel], s. (arc.) individuo scostumato; libertino.

rakehelly ['reik,helil], ag. dissoluto; scostumato; libertino.

rakish[1] ['reikiʃ], ag. scostumato, dissoluto, libertino.

rakish[2], ag. slanciato, dalla forma snella (di nave); di tipo corsaro (di nave).

rakishly ['reikiʃli], av. scostumatamente, dissolutamente.

rakishness ['reikiʃnis], s. scostumatezza, dissolutezza.

râle [rɑ:l], s. (med.) rantolo.

rallentando [,rælen'tændou], s. (mus.) rallentando.

rally[1] ['ræli], s. 1. raccolta; riunione; adunata 2. ricupero di forza 3. colpi scambiati velocemente (al tennis).

to rally[1], v.t.i. 1. raccogliere, chiamare a raccolta; riunirsi; radunarsi 2. ricuperare i sensi; riprendere coraggio; rianimare, rianimarsi; rimettersi in forze.

rally[2], s. canzonatura; motteggio.

to rally[2], v.t. canzonare, motteggiare.

rallying ['ræliiŋ], ag. canzonatorio.

rallyingly ['ræliiŋli], av. in tono scherzoso; motteggiando.

Ralph [reif], no.pr.m. Rodolfo.

ram[1] [ræm], s. 1. ariete, montone || the Ram, (astr.) l'Ariete 2. (mil.) ariete 3. (mar.) sperone (di nave); nave munita di sperone 4. (mec.) slittone; pistone di pompa idrostatica ☆ — jet, (mec.) colpo di pistone.

to ram[1], pass.p.p. **rammed** [ræmd], v.t. 1. conficcare con forza: he rammed his hat down on his head, si ficcò il cappello in testa; to — one's clothes into a bag, ficcare a forza i propri indumenti in una valigia 2. spianare (il terreno) con mazza di legno 3. (mar.) speronare 4. urtare, sbattere.

ram[2], s. (mar.) lunghezza completa di un veliero.

Ramadan [,ræmə'dɑ:n], s. Ramadan (nono mese del calendario arabo, epoca di digiuno religioso).

ramal ['reiməl], ag. (bot.) di ramo, appartenente a ramo.

ramble[1] ['ræmbl], s. 1. passeggiata (senza metà); gita; escursione 2. fig. divagazione.

to ramble[1], v.i. 1. gironzolare; vagare: to — through the streets, vagare per le strade 2. fig. divagare; vaneggiare 3. estendersi senza ordine (di vegetazione).

ramble[2], s. (geol.) leggero strato di scisto argilloso.

rambler ['ræmblə*], s. 1. vagabondo; chi passeggia senza meta 2. fig. divagatore 3. (bot.) rosa rampicante.

rambling ['ræmbliŋ], ag. 1. errante, errabondo, girovago, vagante || — thoughts, divagazioni 2. sconnesso; incoerente; inconseguente 3. (bot.) rampicante.

ramblingly ['ræmbliŋli], av. 1. errando qua e là 2. fig. sconnessamente; incoerentemente.

rambunctious [ræm'bʌŋkʃəs], ag. (sl. amer.) rumoroso; turbolento; sfrenato.

ramekin, ramequin ['ræmkin], s. (cuc.) pasticcio di formaggio con pane grattugiato e uova, cotto al forno.

ramie ['ræmi], s. (ind. tessile) ramié.

ramification [,ræmifi'keiʃən], s. ramificazione.

to ramify ['ræmifai], v.t.i. ramificare, ramificarsi.

rammer ['ræmə*], s. 1. (art.) pillo; pestello 2. (mec.) battipalo 3. (artigl.) calcatoio.

rammish ['ræmiʃ], ag. puzzolente; rancido.

ramose [rə'mous], **ramous** ['reiməs], ag. ramoso.

ramp[1] [ræmp], s. arrampicata, scalata.

ramp[2], s. (sl.) imposizione di prezzi esorbitanti; truffa, inganno.

to ramp[2], v.t. (sl.) imporre prezzi esorbitanti a; truffare.

ramp[3], s. 1. rampa; pendio; piano inclinato: the — of a plane, la scaletta di un aereo 2. differenza di livello.

to ramp[3], v.t.i. 1. (arald.) rampare 2. (scherz.) infuriare, tempestare 3. gesticolare in modo minaccioso 4. elevarsi (di muro) 5. (arch. mil.) costruire a rampa 6. (dial.) arrampicarsi, scalare.

rampage [ræm'peidʒ], s. azione, contegno violento, sfrenato: to be on the —, (fam.) prendersela con tutti; comportarsi da matto.

to rampage, v.i. (fam.) comportarsi in modo violento, sfrenato; infuriare; smaniare.

rampageous [ræm'peidʒəs], ag. violento; furioso; sfrenato.

rampageously [ræm'peidʒəsli], av. violentemente; furiosamente.

rampageousness [ræm'peidʒəsnis], s. violenza, furia; ira; aggressività.

rampancy ['ræmpənsi], s. 1. violenza; aggressività; sfrenatezza 2. rigoglio; esuberanza.

rampant ['ræmpənt], ag. 1. violento; aggressivo; sfrenato 2. predominante: superstition was —, la superstizione imperversava 3. esuberante, lussureggiante (di piante, ecc.) 4. (arald. arch.) rampante.

rampantly ['ræmpəntli], av. 1. violentemente; sfrenatamente 2. in modo esuberante.

rampart ['ræmpɑ:t], s. 1. bastione 2. fig. difesa.

to rampart, v.t. circondare di bastioni, fortificare.

rampion ['ræmpjən], s. (bot.) raperonzolo.

rampire ['ræmpaiə*], s. 1. bastione 2. fig. difesa.

to rampire, v.t. circondare di bastioni, fortificare.

ramrod ['ræmrod], s. bacchetta (di fucile); (artigl.) scovolo.

ramshackle ['ræm,ʃækl], ag. che cade in rovina, instabile, sganacherato (di costruzione, veicolo): — old house, vecchia casa cadente.

ramson ['ræmsən], s. (bot.) aglio orsino.

ramulose ['ræmjulous], ag. avente molti piccoli rami.

ran[1] [ræn], s. matassa di spago della lunghezza di circa 20 iarde.

ran[2], pass. di to run.

rancee[1] [rɑ:ns], s. marmo rosso del Belgio.

rance[2] [ræns], *s.* barra; bastone; supporto.

ranch [ra:nʃʃ], *s.* « ranch », grande fattoria con allevamento di bestiame (negli Stati Uniti).

to ranch, *v.i.* (*amer.*) dirigere un « ranch ».

rancher ['ra:ntʃə*], *s.* (*amer.*) chi possiede, dirige un « ranch ».

ranchman, *pl.* **ranchmen** ['ra:ntʃmən], *V.* **rancher.**

rancid [rænsid], *ag.* rancido; stantio.

rancidity [ræn'siditi], *s.* rancidità.

rancidly ['rænsidli], *av.* rancidamente.

rancidness ['rænsidnis], *s.* rancidume.

rancorous ['ræŋkərəs], *ag.* acrimonioso.

rancorously ['ræŋkərəsli], *av.* con rancore.

rancour ['ræŋkə*], *s.* rancore, acrimonia.

rand [rænd], *s.* **1.** soletta (di scarpa) **2.** altopiano sui fianchi della valle di un fiume (in Sud Africa) || *the Rand*, distretto aurifero vicino a Johannesburg **3.** «rand» (unità monetaria adottata nel Sud Africa dal 14-2-1961) **4.** (*arc. dial.*) orlo, margine.

randan[1] ['rændæn], *s.* **1.** vita disordinata; baldoria: *to be on the* —, fare baldoria **2.** (*rar.*) persona rissosa.

randan[2], *s.* imbarcazione da regata a tre.

randem ['rændəm], *s.* tiro a tre.

randem, *av.* con tre cavalli attaccati l'uno dietro l'altro.

Randolph ['rændolf], *no.pr.m.* Rodolfo.

random ['rændəm], *ag.* **1.** fatto a caso, a casaccio: *a* — *shot*, un tiro a casaccio **2.** irregolare, con pietre di diversa forma (di costruzione) || *s.* (*rar.*) caso || *at* —, a caso, a casaccio; sbadatamente.

randomly ['rændəmli], *av.* (*rar.*) **1.** a caso, a casaccio, sbadatamente **2.** irregolarmente.

randy ['rændi], *ag.* (*scozz.*) **1.** vociante, rumoroso **2.** selvatico (di animale) **3.** lascivo (di persona).

ranee [ra:'ni:], *s.* moglie di ragià.

rang [ræŋ], *pass.* di **to ring.**

range [reindʒ], *s.* **1.** serie; fila; catena (di montagne): *two ranges of cottages*, due file di casette; *the whole* — *of events*, la serie completa degli avvenimenti **2.** spazio, distesa; habitat (di animali, piante); (*amer.*) pascolo aperto: *a wide* — *of meadows*, una vasta distesa di prati **3.** campo, sfera; (*mus.*) estensione; gamma: — *of action*, campo di attività; — *of visibility*, campo di visibilità; *a wide* — *of colours*, una vasta gamma di colori; *within, beyond my* —, alla, fuori della mia portata; *the* — *of her reading was astonishing* (o *her reading was of very wide*—), le sue letture abbracciavano un campo molto vasto **4.** direzione; posizione; distanza; tiro, portata; poligono, campo di tiro: *within the* — *of twenty miles*, nel raggio di venti miglia; *the enemy were out of* —, il nemico era fuori tiro; *he kept his boat in* — *with the lighthouse*, tenne la barca in direzione del faro; *rifle that has a* — *of*..., fucile che ha una portata di...; *to correct the* —, rettificare il tiro **5.** variazione, oscillazione (di barometro, ecc.) **6.** (*mar. aer.*) autonomia **7.** fornello, cucina economica ☆ — *clock*, cronoindicatore; — *indication*, (*radar*) indicazione della distanza || *audio* —, gamma delle audiofrequenze; gamma musicale; *mountain* —, catena di montagne; *operating* —, raggio d'azione.

to range, *v.t.i.* **1.** allineare, disporre, ordinare: *they ranged the troops*, allinearono le truppe; *to* — *oneself, with, against s.o.*, schierarsi con, contro qlcu. || *to* — *oneself*, (*fam.*) sistemarsi **2.** classificare, annoverare: *he is ranged among the best novelists*, è annoverato tra i migliori romanzieri **3.** estendersi, allungarsi: *to* — *along the sea*, estendersi lungo il mare **4.** errare, vagare; (*mar.*) costeggiare: *to* — *over the country*, errare per il paese **5.** (*artigl.*) avere una gittata, portata di; puntare per il tiro; dare l'alzo: *this gun ranges over a mile*, questo fucile ha la portata di oltre un miglio **6.** variare, oscillare: *temperatures ranging from ten to thirty degrees*, temperature che oscillano tra i dieci e i trenta gradi.

rangefinder ['reindʒ,faində*], *s.* telemetro.

ranger ['reindʒə*], *s.* **1.** (*rar.*) chi ordina, dispone **2.** guardia forestale **3.** vagabondo **4.** bracco, seguizio **5.** *pl.* corpo di truppe a cavallo **6.** *Ranger*, scolta (delle « Girl Guides »).

rangership ['reindʒəʃip], *s.* impiego di guardia forestale.

Rangoon [ræŋ'gu:n], *no.pr.* (*geog.*) Rangoon.

rangy ['reindʒi], *ag.* **1.** capace di coprire lunghe distanze; dalle gambe lunghe, slanciato, sottile (di male) **2.** spazioso (di luogo) **3.** (*austral.*) montuoso.

rank[1] [ræŋk], *ag.* **1.** lussureggiante, rigoglioso; (troppo) fertile, grasso: — *vegetation*, vegetazione lussureggiante; — *weeds*, erbacce rigogliose; *land too* — *to grow corn*, terreno troppo grasso per la coltivazione del grano **2.** rozzo, volgare; indecente; corrotto **3.** puzzolente; rancido; forte (di odore) **4.** inconfondibile; evidente; eccessivo: — *nonsense*, idiozia estrema.

rank[2], *s.* **1.** (*mil.*) fila, rango; schiera; *pl.* soldati semplici, truppa: *to break, to close the ranks*, rompere, serrare le file; *to rise from the* —, diventare ufficiale (da soldato semplice); *fig.* venire dalla gavetta; *to serve in the ranks*, essere soldato semplice || *the* — *and file*, la truppa; *fig.* la gran massa || *reduction to the ranks*, degradazione **2.** rango; classe sociale; ordine, grado: *the* — *of admiral*, il grado di ammiraglio; *a writer of the first* —, uno scrittore di primo piano; *he is a person of (high)* —, è una persona di alto rango; *to hold the* — *of*..., avere il grado di... **3.** fila; linea **4.** posteggio (per automobili, ecc.) ☆ *front* —, (*mil.*) prima fila; *rear* —, (*mil.*) ultima fila.

to rank[2], *v.t.i.* **1.** schierare, schierarsi; mettere in fila || *to* — *past*, (*mil.*) sfilare **2.** classificare, essere classificato; assegnare un posto a, collocare; essere nel rango, nel numero: *he ranks next to the president*, il suo grado è inferiore solo a quello del presidente; *she ranks among the great artists*, ella è nel numero dei grandi artisti; *to* — *above the average*, classificare, essere al di sopra della media **3.** (*amer.*) avere il grado massimo; essere eminente; (*mil.*) avere la precedenza su.

ranker ['ræŋkə*], *s.* (*mil.*) soldato semplice; ufficiale proveniente dalla gavetta.

to rankle ['ræŋkl], *v.t.i.* **1.** infiammarsi; suppurare (di ferita) **2.** inasprire, inasprirsi; bruciare; far male; (anche *fig.*): *her words rankled in his bosom*, le parole di lei lo ferirono profondamente.

rankly ['ræŋkli], *av.* **1.** rigogliosamente **2.** rozzamente; in modo offensivo **3.** fetidamente, puzzolentemente.

rankness ['ræŋknis], *s.* **1.** rigoglio; esuberanza **2.** grossolanità; indecenza; oscenità **3.** rancidità; odore forte; puzza.

to ransack ['rænsæk], *v.t.* **1.** frugare, rovistare **2.** saccheggiare: *to* — *a city*, saccheggiare una città.

ransacker ['rænsækə*], *s.* saccheggiatore; predone.

ransom ['rænsəm], *s.* **1.** riscatto; prezzo del riscatto: *to hold s.o. to* —, tenere qlcu. prigioniero fino al pagamento del riscatto; *to obtain sthg. at a* — *price*, ottenere ql.co. a prezzo d'oro; *to pay* —, pagare il riscatto || *to be worth a king's* —, (*fam.*) essere di grande valore **2.** estorsione, ricatto ☆ — *-bill* (o — *-bond*), (*st.*) impegno (da parte di nave catturata) di pagare il riscatto.

to ransom, *v.t.* **1.** riscattare: *to* — *a prisoner*, riscattare un prigioniero **2.** (*teol.*) redimere; salvare.

ransomless ['rænsəmlis], *ag.* esente da riscatto.

rant [rænt], *s.* declamazione; linguaggio ampolloso.

to rant, *v.t.i.* parlare in modo ampolloso, declamare; predicare in modo esaltato.

ranter ['ræntə*], *s.* declamatore ampolloso; predicatore esaltato.

ranting ['ræntiŋ], *ag.* declamatorio; ampolloso; altisonante; esaltato.

rantingly ['ræntiŋli], *av.* ampollosamente; in tono declamatorio; da esaltato.

ranunculus [rə'nʌŋkjuləs], *pl.* **ranunculuses** [rə'nʌŋkjuləsiz], **ranunculi** [rə'nʌŋkjulai], *s.* (*bot.*) ranuncolo.

rap¹ [ræp], *s.* **1.** colpo, colpetto: *a — on the knuckles*, un colpo sulle nocche delle dita (punizione inflitta ai bambini) **2.** colpo (di battente sulla porta); colpo (durante una seduta spiritica).

to rap¹, *pass.p.p.* **rapped** [ræpt], *v.t.i.* **1.** picchiare, battere: *he rapped at the door*, egli bussò alla porta **2.** usare un linguaggio forte **3.** *to — out*, esclamare, lasciarsi sfuggire (un'esclamazione, ecc.): *he rapped out an oath*, si lasciò scappare una bestemmia ‖ *to — out a message*, comunicare un messaggio per mezzo di colpi (nelle sedute spiritiche).

rap², *s.* matassa di 120 yarde (= m. 103).

rap³, *s.* **1.** (*st. irl.*) moneta da un «halfpenny» contraffatta **2.** atomo; minimo ‖ *I don't care a —*, non me ne importa affatto.

to rap⁴, *pass.p.p.* **rapped, rapt** [ræpt], *v.t.* trasportare; rapire.

rapacious [rə'peiʃəs], *ag.* rapace; ingordo.

rapaciously [rə'peiʃəsli], *av.* rapacemente.

rapaciousness [rə'peiʃəsnis], **rapacity** [rə'pæsiti], *s.* rapacità; voracità; avarizia.

rape¹ [reip], *s.* **1.** (*poet.*) ratto, rapimento ‖ *the Rape of Lucrece*, il ratto di Lucrezia **2.** violentamento (di donna).

to rape¹, *v.t.* **1.** (*poet.*) prendere per forza; rapire **2.** violare, violentare (una donna) **3.** (*rar.*) rubare, saccheggiare.

rape², *s.* ciascuna delle sei divisioni amministrative del Sussex.

rape³, *s.* (*bot.*) **1.** rapa **2.** ravizzone ☆ *— -cake*, concime di semi di ravizzone; *— -oil*, olio di ravizzone ‖ *wild —*, senape di campo.

rape⁴, *s.* **1.** raspo **2.** recipiente in cui si forma l'aceto.

Raphael ['ræfeiəl], *no.pr.m.* **1.** (*Bibbia*) Raffaele **2.** (*st. pitt.*) Raffaello (Sanzio).

Raphaelesque [ˌræfeiə'lesk], *ag.* raffaellesco.

raphia ['reifiə], *s.* (*bot.*) rafia.

rapid ['ræpid], *ag.* **1.** rapido, celere **2.** erto, ripido ‖ *s. gener. pl.* rapida (di fiume).

rapidity [rə'piditi], *s.* **1.** rapidità, celerità **2.** ripidezza.

rapidly ['ræpidli], *av.* **1.** rapidamente, celermente **2.** in modo erto, ripidamente.

rapier ['reipjə*], *s.* stocco; spadino ☆ *— -thrust*, stoccata (anche *fig.*).

rapine ['ræpain], *s.* rapina, saccheggio.

rapparee [ˌræpə'ri:], *s.* (*st. irl.*) soldato irregolare, avventuriero del XVII secolo; vagabondo.

rappee [ræ'pi:], *s.* rapè (tabacco da fiuto).

rappel [ra:'pel], *s.* rullo di tamburo (che chiama a raccolta i soldati).

rapper ['ræpə*], *s.c.* chi batte, picchia ‖ *s.* **1.** battente (di porta) **2.** (*arc.*) bugia; cattiva scusa ☆ *spirit - —*, medium.

rapping ['ræpiŋ], *s.* colpo (all'uscio).

rapport [ræ'pɔ:*], *s.* rapporto, comunicazione, relazione: *to be in — with*, essere in intimità con.

rapscallion [ræp'skæljən], *s.* (*arc.*) mascalzone, birbante.

rapt [ræpt], *ag.* rapito, estatico; assorto: *he listened with — attention*, ascoltava con attenzione rapita.

raptorial [ræp'tɔ:riəl], *ag.* (*zool.*) rapace, da preda ‖ *s.* uccello da preda.

rapture ['ræptʃə*], *s.* estasi, rapimento; trasporto: *to be in raptures*, essere in estasi; *to go into raptures*, andare in estasi.

raptured ['ræptʃəd], *ag.* rapito, estasiato.

rapturous ['ræptʃərəs], *ag.* estatico; rapito; entusiastico: *— applause*, applauso frenetico.

rapturously ['ræptʃərəsli], *av.* estaticamente; entusiasticamente.

rapturousness ['ræptʃərəsnis], *s.* estasi; entusiasmo.

rare¹ [reə*], *ag.* **1.** raro; non comune; insolito, eccezionale: *a — occurrence*, un avvenimento insolito; *it is — for a person to be so unselfish*, è raro che una persona sia così altruista **2.** rarefatto: *— atmosphere*, atmosfera

rarefatta **3.** meraviglioso; incomparabile; prelibato: *we had — fun*, ci divertimmo immensamente ☆ *— earths*, (*chim.*) terra rara.

rare², *ag.* (*amer.*) poco cotto (specialmente di carne): *I want my steak —*, voglio la mia bistecca al sangue.

rare³, *ag.* (*rar.dial.*) mattiniero ‖ *av.* (*rar. dial.*) presto, di buon'ora.

rarebit ['reəbit], *s.* crostino di formaggio fuso (specialità del Galles).

raree-show ['reəriːʃou], *s.* apparecchio contenente diapositive di soggetto vario visibili attraverso una lente.

rarefaction [ˌreəri'fækʃən], *s.* rarefazione.

rarefactive [ˌreəri'fæktiv], *ag.* rarefattivo.

to rarefy ['reərifai], *v.t.i.* **1.** rarefare; rarefarsi **2.** raffinare (il gusto) **3.** rendere sottile, acuto (idea, ecc.).

rarely ['reəli], *av.* **1.** di rado; raramente; insolitamente **2.** ottimamente; in modo eccellente.

rareness ['reənis], **rarity** ['reəriti], *s.* **1.** rarità, rarezza; eccezionalità: *here a fine day is a —*, qui le belle giornate sono rare **2.** rarefazione **3.** eccellenza.

rascal ['ra:skəl], *ag.* (*arc.*) plebeo, volgare ‖ *the — rout*, il popolino ‖ *s.* **1.** briccone, furfante, mascalzone: *he is a fine —*, (*iron.*) è una buona lana **2.** (*scherz.*) birbantello, monello.

rascaldom ['ra:skəldəm], *s.* **1.** l'insieme dei furfanti **2.** condotta, azione furfantesca.

rascalism ['ra:skəlizəm], *s.* **rascality** [ra:s'kæliti], *s.* canagliata; furfanteria, bricconata.

rascally ['ra:skəli], *ag.* bricconesco, furfantesco; ignobile, disonesto: *a — trick*, un tiro birbone.

to rase, *V.* to raze.

rash¹ [ræʃ], *ag.* avventato, sconsiderato; imprudente; temerario: *— act*, colpo di testa; *— words*, parole sconsiderate.

rash², *s.* (*patol.*) esantema.

rasher ['ræʃə*], *s.* fetta sottile di prosciutto, pancetta.

rashly ['ræʃli], *av.* avventatamente sconsideratamente; imprudentemente; temerariamente.

rashness ['ræʃnis], *s.* avventatezza; precipitazione; imprudenza; temerarietà.

rasp¹ [ra:sp], *s.* **1.** raspa **2.** stridore, stridio.

to rasp¹, *v.t.* **1.** raspare; raschiare; grattare **2.** *fig.* irritare, innervosire: *to — s.o.'s feelings*, produrre una impressione sgradevole su qlcu.; irritare qlcu. **3.** stridere; far stridere.

rasp², *V.* raspberry.

raspatory ['ra:spətəri], *s.* (*chir.*) raschia-periostio.

raspberry ['ra:zbəri], *s.* **1.** lampone **2.** (*sl.*) segno, gesto di disapprovazione, derisione **3.** (*sl.*) congedo ☆ *— -bush*, lampone (pianta); *— -jam*, marmellata di lamponi; *— -wine*, sciroppo di lampone.

rasper ['ra:spə*], *s.* **1.** raschiatore **2.** ostacolo alto e difficile (a caccia) **3.** (*sl.*) persona, cosa irritante.

rasping ['ra:spiŋ], *ag.* stridente; rauco: *a — voice*, una voce rauca.

raspy ['ra:spi], *ag.* **1.** stridente; aspro **2.** irritabile.

rasse [ræs], *s.* (*zool.*) viverricola, rasse.

rat [ræt], *s.* **1.** topo, ratto: *to clear a house of rats*, derattizzare una casa ‖ *rats!*, (*sl.*) sciocchezze!, non ci credo! ‖ *he looked like a drowned —*, sembrava un pulcino bagnato ‖ *to be caught like a — in a trap*, essere preso come un topo in trappola ‖ *to die like a — in a hole*, morire come un cane ‖ *to see rats* (o *to have got the rats*), vaneggiare, avere allucinazioni (come chi è affetto da «delirium tremens») **2.** essere pazzo da legare ‖ *to smell a —*, nutrire un sospetto, subodorare un inganno **2.** (*pol.*) disertore, traditore **3.** crumiro ☆ *— -catcher*, acchiappatopi; *— -poison*, veleno per topi; *— -snake*, (*zool.*) serpente che si nutre di topi; *— 's-tail* (o *— -tail*), coda di topo; ql.co. a forma di coda di topo; (*vet.*) ugnella; *— -trap*, trappola per topi; (*mec.*) pedale di bicicletta dentato ‖ *musk- —*, topo muschiato; *water- —*, topo di fogna; (*fam.*) marinaio; pirata.

to **rat,** *pass.p.p.* **ratted** ['rætid], *v.i.* **1.** andare a caccia di topi; uccidere topi **2.** (*pol.*) cambiar bandiera; defezionare **3.** fare il crumiro.

rata ['reitə], *s.* rata (grande albero della Nuova Zelanda).

ratability [ˌreitə'biliti], *s.* imponibilità, tassabilità.

ratable ['reitəbl], *ag.* **1.** imponibile, tassabile **2.** (*arc.*) proporzionale ☆ — *value,* (*amm.*) valore imponibile.

ratably ['reitəbli], *av.* in modo imponibile, tassabile.

ratafee [ˌrætə'fi:], **ratafia** [ˌrætə'fiə], *s.* **1.** ratafia **2.** biscotto simile all'amaretto **3.** ciliegia visciola.

ratal ['reitl], *s.* (*amm.*) imponibile.

ratan, *V.* **rattan.**

rataplan [ˌrætə'plæn], *s.* rataplan, rullo di tamburo.

to **rataplan,** *pass.p.p.* **rataplanned** [ˌrætə'plænd], *v.t.i.* suonare il tamburo; suonare sul tamburo.

(to) **ratch** [rætʃ], *V.* (to) **ratchet.**

ratchet ['rætʃit], *s.* (*mec.*) dente di arresto, nottolino di arresto, fermo ☆ — *-gear,* arpionismo; — *-wheel,* ruota a cricco.

to **ratchet,** *v.t.* (*mec.*) munire di denti, dentare.

rate[1] [reit], *s.* **1.** corso, saggio, tasso: — *of exchange,* corso di cambio; *at the* — *of...,* al tasso di... **2.** prezzo; quota; tariffa; aliquota: — *fixed by authorities,* calmiere; — *of the tax,* aliquota dell'imposta; *alternations in the rates,* varianti alle tariffe; *at a high, low* —, ad un prezzo alto, basso; *to increase* (o *to raise*), *to lower* (o *to reduce*) *the rates,* aumentare, diminuire le tariffe ‖ *at any* —, a qualunque costo, in ogni caso; *at that* —, se è così; così, in tal modo: *I can't go on at that* —, non posso andare avanti così **3.** imposta, tassa; contributo: *rates and taxes,* imposte e tasse **4.** stima, valutazione: *to value sthg. at a low* —, stimare poco qualcosa **5.** percentuale, proporzione **6.** andamento, passo, ritmo; velocità: *at the* — *of sixty miles an hour,* alla velocità di sessanta miglia all'ora; *juvenile delinquency is increasing at a fearful* —, la delinquenza minorile cresce ad un ritmo impressionante **7.** (*arc.*) classe, rango **8.** (*amer.*) classifica (di alunno) ☆ — *-book,* prontuario delle tariffe; — *-collector,* ricevitore delle imposte ‖ *bank* —, tasso di sconto ufficiale; *birth-* —, *death* - —, natalità, mortalità; *first-* —, *second-* —, di primo, second'ordine; *going rates,* tariffe correnti; *house rates,* tasse sul valore locativo; *insurance rates,* tasse d'assicurazione; *ordinary rates,* tariffe ordinarie; *pulse* —, frequenza del polso; *railway rates,* tariffe ferroviarie; *renewal* —, saggio di rinnovo; *subscription rates,* quote di abbonamento.

to **rate**[1], *v.t.i.* **1.** stimare, valutare (anche *fig.*) **2.** tassare: *we are highly rated,* siamo fortemente tassati **3.** annoverare; considerare: *he rated me among his benefactors,* mi annoverava tra i suoi benefattori **4.** classificare; essere classificato: *to* — *a student second,* (*amer.*) classificare un allievo al secondo posto **5.** regolare, verificare (cronometro).

rate[2], *s.* sgridata ad un cane.

to **rate**[2], *v.t.i.* sgridare, rimproverare vivacemente; pronunciare forti rimproveri: *to* — *s.o. soundly,* dare una lavata di capo a qlcu.

to **rate**[3], (*dial.*) per to **ret.**

rateable, *V.* **ratable.**

ratel ['reitel], *s.* (*zool.*) ratele.

ratepayer ['reitˌpeiə*], *s.* contribuente.

rater ['reitə*], *s.* **1.** chi stima, valuta **2.** panfilo da corsa (di un dato tonnellaggio) **3.** persona di una data classe, di un dato grado ☆ *first-* —, (*fam.*) asso, campione; *second-* —, (*fam.*) mediocrità, persona mediocre; *ten-* —, panfilo da corsa di dieci tonnellate.

rathe [reið], *ag.* (*poet.*) primaticcio; precoce; prematuro.

rather ['rɑ:ðə*], *av.* **1.** piuttosto: *he is clever* — *than intelligent,* è abile piuttosto che intelligente; *I* — *think that...,* sono indotto a credere che..., sono di avviso, dell'idea che...; *orderliness is not the result of law,* — *it is the cause of it,* l'ordine non è il risultato della legge, ma piuttosto la causa di essa ‖ *the* — *that,*

tanto più che ‖ *or* —, o piuttosto, o per meglio dire: *she was an intimate friend, or* — *she was a sister to me,* era per me un'intima amica, o meglio una sorella **2.** abbastanza; alquanto; un poco: *Albert was* — *out of sorts,* Alberto era un po' indisposto; *he came* — *early,* venne alquanto presto; *she is* — *silly,* ella è piuttosto sciocca **3.** di preferenza, piuttosto che: *he would* — *starve than accept such an offer,* preferirebbe morire di fame piuttosto che accettare una simile offerta ‖ *I had* — *not, I would* — *not,* preferirei di no, non ci tengo **4.** (*fam. nelle risposte*) certamente, eccome: *did you enjoy yourself?* — *!,* ti sei divertito? altro che!.

ratheripe ['reiðˌraip], *ag.* precoce; primaticcio ‖ *s.* frutto primaticcio, verdura primaticcia.

ratherish ['rɑ:ðəriʃ], *av.* (*fam. amer.*) un tantino, un pochino.

rathripe ['rɑ:θˌraip], *V.* **ratheripe.**

rathskeller ['rɑ:tskelə*], *s.* (*amer.*) taverna, birreria sotterranea.

ratification [ˌrætifi'keiʃən], *s.* ratifica, sanzione.

ratifier ['rætifaiə*], *s.c.* ratificatore, ratificatrice.

to **ratify** ['rætifai], *v.t.* ratificare, sanzionare.

ratine [ræ'ti:n], *s.* rattina (tessuto).

rating[1] ['reitin], *s.* **1.** stima, valutazione **2.** grado, ordine; classifica: *the ratings of certain radio programs were checked by poll,* (*amer.*) attraverso un'inchiesta si controllò la popolarità di certi programmi radio **3.** tassa; contributo fissato da un municipio **4.** posizione, classe di marinaio sul libro di bordo; *pl.* marinai semplici **5.** classe, categoria (di panfili da corsa) **6.** (*fam.*) categoria, classe sociale **7.** (*amer.*) classificazione (di allievo).

rating[2], *s.* sgridata.

ratio ['reiʃiou], *pl.* **ratios** ['reiʃiouz], *s.* (*mat.*) rapporto, proporzione: — *of 1 to 11,* rapporto di 1 a 11.

to **ratiocinate** [ˌræti'ɔsineit], *v.i.* raziocinare, ragionare.

ratiocination [ˌrætiɔsi'neiʃən], *s.* raziocinio, ragionamento.

ratiocinative [ˌræti'ɔsinitiv], *ag.* raziocinante, ragionante.

ratiocinator [ˌræti'ɔsineitə*], *s.* ragionatore.

ration ['ræʃən], *s.* **1.** razione, porzione **2.** *pl.* (*mil.*) provvigioni ☆ — *-book* (o — *-card*), tessera di razionamento ‖ *iron* —, (*fam.*) viveri di riserva.

to **ration,** *v.t.* razionare.

rational[1] ['ræʃənl], *ag.* **1.** ragionevole **2.** razionale (anche *mat.*).

rational[2], *s.* (*eccl.*) razionale.

rationale [ˌræʃiə'nɑ:li], *s.* **1.** base, fondamento logico; ragione effettiva **2.** (*rar.*) analisi ragionata, spiegazione.

rationalism ['ræʃnəlizəm], *s.* (*fil.*) razionalismo.

rationalist ['ræʃnəlist], *s.c.* (*fil.*) razionalista.

rationalistic [ˌræʃnə'listik], *ag.* (*fil.*) razionalistico.

rationalistically [ˌræʃnə'listikəli], *av.* (*fil.*) in modo razionalistico; da razionalista.

rationality [ˌræʃə'næliti], *s.* razionalità.

rationalization [ˌræʃnəlai'zeiʃən], *s.* **1.** razionalizzazione **2.** (*econ.*) organizzazione razionale (del lavoro).

to **rationalize** ['ræʃnəlaiz], *v.t.i.* **1.** razionalizzare; rendere razionale (anche *mat.*) **2.** spiegare, interpretare su basi razionali **3.** (*econ.*) organizzare (un'industria, ecc.) **4.** essere, agire da razionalista.

rationally ['ræʃnəli], *av.* razionalmente; ragionevolmente.

rationals ['ræʃənlz], *s.pl.* (*st.*) gonna pantalone.

ratlin(e)s ['rætlinz], **ratlings** ['rætlinz], *s.pl.* (*mar.*) griselle.

ratoon [rə'tu:n], *s.* germoglio di canna da zucchero.

to **ratoon,** *v.i.* produrre germogli nuovi (di canna da zucchero).

ratsbane ['rætsbein], *s.* veleno per topi.

rattan [rə'tæn], *s.* **1.** malacca (canna d'India per bastoni, manichi d'ombrello, ecc.). **2.** bastone di malacca.

to **ratten** ['rætn], *v.t.* sabotare.

rattener ['rætənə*], s. sabotatore.

ratter ['rætə*], s. **1.** chi caccia topi; cane che caccia i topi **2.** (pol.) traditore **3.** crumiro.

rattery ['rætəri], s. **1.** (pol.) l'abbandonare il proprio partito nei momenti difficili **2.** crumiraggio **3.** topaia.

rattle[1] ['rætl], s. **1.** sonaglio, sonaglino; raganella (strumento) **2.** rantolo **3.** rumore (di carrozza); tintinnio (di catene, ecc.) **4.** fracasso, frastuono; baldoria **5.** chiaccherio vuoto, insignificante, inconsistente **6.** chiacchierone; chi parla a vuoto, a vanvera **7.** (bot.) cresta di gallo **8.** pl. (patol. fam.) crup ☆ — -box, giocattolo a sonaglio per bambini; — -brain(ed), — -head(ed), scervellato, testa vuota; chiacchierone.

to **rattle**[1], v.t.i. **1.** risuonare; far tintinnare; scuotere, scuotersi rumorosamente: *the ghost rattled his chains,* lo spettro fece risuonare le sue catene **2.** (sl.) confondere, sconcertare; innervosire; spaventare: *to get rattled,* innervosirsi **3.** to — off, cianciare, parlare rapidamente: *the girl rattled off her poem,* la ragazza snocciolò la sua poesia in gran fretta **4.** to — on, continuare a chiacchierare: *the woman rattled on for hours,* la donna continuò a chiacchierare per ore.

to **rattle**[2], v.t. (mar.) fornire di griselle.

rattler ['rætlə*], s. **1.** chi, ciò che produce un rumore, un tintinnio **2.** (amer.) serpente a sonagli **3.** (sl.) persona, cosa eccezionale.

rattlesnake ['rætlsneik], s. (zool.) crotalo.

rattletrap ['rætltræp], s. **1.** veicolo traballante e sconnesso **2.** pl. cianfrusaglie; curiosità **3.** (sl.) bocca.

rattling ['rætliŋ], ag. **1.** (fam.) vivace; vigoroso: *a — wind,* un vento impetuoso **2.** tintinnante, risuonante **3.** di prima qualità, splendido.

rattling, av. (fam.) molto: — good, molto buono.

ratty ['ræti], ag. **1.** infestato da topi **2.** (sl.) bisbetico; irritato **3.** (sl.) disgraziato, vile, basso; miserabile.

raucity ['rɔːsiti], s. raucedine; afonia.

raucous ['rɔːkəs], ag. rauco, aspro (di suono).

raucously ['rɔːkəsli], av. raucamente.

raucousness ['rɔːkəsnis], s. raucedine.

raughty, V. **rorty.**

rauque [rouk], ag. (rar.) rauco.

ravage ['rævidʒ], s. **1.** strage; rovina; devastazione **2.** pl. danni: *the ravages of time,* i danni prodotti dal tempo.

to **ravage,** v.t.i. devastare, compiere devastazioni; saccheggiare: *his face was ravaged by grief,* il suo volto era devastato dall'angoscia; *the whole peninsula was ravaged in the war,* l'intera penisola fu saccheggiata durante la guerra.

ravager ['rævidʒə*], s. devastatore, distruttore.

rave[1] [reiv], s. **1.** sponda di carro **2.** pl. sponde a rastrello di carro.

rave[2], s. **1.** delirio, vaneggiamento **2.** (sl. amer.) infatuazione; lode smisurata.

to **rave**[2], v.t.i. **1.** delirare, vaneggiare; gridare in delirio **2.** declamare con passione **3.** andare pazzo, andare in estasi: *to — about sthg.,* andare pazzo per ql.co. **4.** infuriare (di mare, vento, ecc.).

ravel ['rævəl], s. **1.** groviglio, nodo, complicazione **2.** lembo sfilacciato.

to **ravel,** pass.p.p. **ravelled** ['rævəld], v.t.i. **1.** ingarbugliare; intralciare; confondere; complicare; imbrogliarsi **2.** sfilacciarsi, sfrangiarsi (di stoffa) **3.** to — out, dipanare; sbrogliare; srotolare (anche fig.).

ravelin ['rævlin], s. (edil. mil.) rivellino.

raven[1] ['reivn], ag. corvino, nero: — hair, capelli corvini ‖ s. corvo.

to **raven**[2] ['rævn], v.t.i. **1.** saccheggiare, far preda, andare in cerca di preda **2.** divorare, mangiare con avidità, avere un appetito formidabile.

ravenous ['rævinəs], ag. **1.** vorace; ingordo **2.** (rar.) rapace.

ravenously ['rævinəsli], av. **1.** ingordamente; voracemente **2.** (rar.) in modo rapace.

ravenousness ['rævinəsnis], s. **1.** ingordigia; voracità **2.** fame divorante.

ravin ['rævin], s. (poet.) rapina; furto: *beast of —,* animale da preda.

ravine [rə'viːn], s. burrone; gola.

ravined [rə'viːnd], ag. pieno di burroni.

raving ['reiviŋ], ag. **1.** delirante, frenetico; furioso **2.** che suscita ammirazione, notevole ‖ s. delirio, vaneggiamento ☆ — mad, pazzo furioso, matto da legare.

ravingly ['reiviŋli], av. con delirio, freneticamente; furiosamente.

ravioli [,rævi'ouli], s.pl. (cuc.) ravioli.

to **ravish** ['ræviʃ], v.t. **1.** rapire, strappare con violenza **2.** violentare (donna) **3.** fig. estasiare, incantare.

ravisher ['ræviʃə*], s. **1.** rapitore; predone **2.** violentatore, stupratore.

ravishing ['ræviʃiŋ], ag. **1.** che rapisce **2.** affascinante, incantevole: — sight, spettacolo affascinante.

ravishingly ['ræviʃiŋli], av. in modo affascinante.

ravishment ['ræviʃmənt], s. **1.** ratto, rapimento **2.** stupro, violazione **3.** fig. estasi, incanto.

raw [rɔː], ag. **1.** crudo: — meat, carne cruda **2.** greggio; naturale: — whisky, whisky liscio **3.** fig. inesperto; immaturo; alle prime armi: *he is a — lad,* è un ragazzo inesperto **4.** scorticato; a nudo; inflammato: *a — sore,* una piaga scoperta ‖ — head and bloody bones, spauracchio **5.** umido, freddo (di vento, clima, ecc.): *a — wind,* un vento umido, freddo ‖ s. punto sensibile, parte viva ‖ *to touch (a person) on the —,* toccare (una persona) sul vivo ☆ — cotton, cotone greggio; — silk, seta cruda, greggia.

to **raw,** v.t. (rar.) lisciare contropelo (spec. cavalli).

rawboned ['rɔːbound],ag. ossuto, scarno, sparuto.

rawish ['rɔːiʃ], ag. **1.** alquanto crudo **2.** piuttosto inesperto **3.** escoriato **4.** freddo e umidiccio.

rawly ['rɔːli], av. (rar.) **1.** crudamente **2.** fig. da inesperto; rozzamente.

rawness ['rɔːnis], s. **1.** crudezza **2.** fig. inesperienza; rozzezza **3.** escoriazione; irritazione **4.** umidità.

ray[1] [rei], s. **1.** raggio: — of light, raggio luminoso **2.** fig. lampo; filo: *a — of courage,* un filo di coraggio; *a — of genius,* un lampo di genio; *a — of hope,* (fam.) un filo di speranza ☆ — -fungus, (biol.) fungo ifomiceta ‖ heat-rays, raggi termici; ultraviolet rays, raggi ultravioletti; X rays, raggi X.

to **ray**[1], v.t.i. irradiare; irradiarsi.

ray[2], s. (ittiol.) razza, raia.

Ray[3], no.pr.m. dim. di **Raymond.**

rayah ['raiə], s. (st.) suddito turco non maomettano.

rayed [reid], ag. raggiato, a raggi.

rayless ['reilis], ag. **1.** senza raggi **2.** senza luce, oscuro, triste.

Raymond ['reimənd], no.pr.m. Raimondo.

Rayner ['reinə*], no.pr.m. Raniero.

rayon ['reion], s. raion, seta artificiale ☆ — fabrics, tessuti di raion.

to **raze** [reiz], v.t. **1.** radere al suolo, distruggere completamente: *the town was razed to the ground,* la città fu rasa al suolo **2.** (rar.) scalfire, ferire leggermente; sfiorare **3.** (rar. fig.) cancellare: to — s.o.'s name from remembrance, cancellare dalla memoria il nome di qlcu.

razee [rə'ziː], s. nave rasa (a cui è stato tolto il ponte superiore).

to **razee,** v.t. togliere il ponte superiore (a una nave).

razor ['reizə*], s. rasoio ‖ as sharp as a —, tagliente come un rasoio ‖ to be on a —'s edge, trovarsi in una situazione difficile; camminare sul filo del rasoio ☆ — -back, (zool.) pecari; fisalo; — -bill, (ornit.) smergo minore; gazza marina; — -blade, lametta da rasoio; — -edge, filo del rasoio; linea di demarcazione; — -strop, coramella, cuoio per affilare il rasoio ‖ safety- —, rasoio di sicurezza.

to **razor** v.t. (rar.) radere, rasare.

to **razz** [ræz], *v.t.i.* (*sl. amer.*) prendersi giuoco, deridere.

razzia ['ræzjə], *s.* razzia, incursione, saccheggio.

razzle-dazzle ['ræzl,dæzl], *s.* **1.** (*sl.*) eccitazione, confusione, baldoria: *to go on the* —, far baldoria **2.** giostra a moto ondulatorio.

re[1] [ri:], *s.* (*mus.*) re.

re[2], *prep.* (*comm. dir.*) con riferimento a, riguardo a, circa, in merito a: — *your letter of the 1st inst.*, con riferimento alla vostra lettera del 1° corr.

're, *contr.* di *are: they're*, essi sono.

to **reabsorb** ['ri:əb'sɔ:b], *v.t.* riassorbire.

reabsorption ['ri:əb'sɔ:pʃən], *s.* riassorbimento.

reach[1] [ri:tʃ], *s.* **1.** portata, estensione; potere, capacità, possibilità; limite, sfera: *it is above* (o *beyond* o *out of*) *my* —, va oltre le mie possibilità, non ci arrivo; *it is within my* —, rientra nelle mie possibilità; *it was within easy* — (*of*), era a breve distanza (da); *to be out of* — (*of*), essere distanti (da) **2.** tratto diritto di corso d'acqua (specialmente di fiume tra due curve, di canale fra due chiuse) **3.** (*mil.*) tiro: *the town was within* — *of the guns*, la città era sotto il tiro dei cannoni **4.** *fig.* penetrazione: — *of thought*, penetrazione di pensiero **5.** (*arc.*) promontorio ☆ — *-me-down*, (abito) già confezionato.

to **reach**[1], *v.t.i.* **1.** giungere a, pervenire a, raggiungere, arrivare a: *some places can be reached only by plane*, si possono raggiungere alcuni luoghi solo per via aerea; *we reached home a few minutes later*, giungemmo a casa alcuni minuti dopo; *your cheque has reached us*, ci è pervenuto il vostro assegno **2.** passare, porgere: — *me that book*, porgimi quel libro **3.** stendere, stendersi; estendere, estendersi; allungare, allungarsi: *a desert reaching* (*out*) *from east to west*, un deserto che si estende da oriente ad occidente; *he reached out his hand for his gloves*, stese la mano per prendersi i guanti; *she reached her hand across the table*, allungò la mano al di sopra del tavolo || *as far as eye can* —, sin dove l'occhio può spaziare **4.** raggiungere, colpire (obiettivo): *to* — *the mark*, colpire nel segno **5.** toccare: *to* — *land*, toccare terra **6.** tendere: *the mind reaches forward to an ideal*, la mente tende verso un ideale.

to **reach**[2], *v.i.* avere conati di vomito; vomitare.

reachable ['ri:tʃəbl], *ag.* raggiungibile; alla portata.

to **react**[1] [ri(:)'ækt], *v.i.* **1.** reagire: *how did she* —?, come reagì?; *to* — *against*, reagire contro **2.** (*chim.*) reagire: *some substances* — *upon each other*, alcune sostanze reagiscono reciprocamente **3.** ripercuotersi: *tyranny reacts upon the tyrant*, la tirannia si ripercuote sul tiranno **4.** (*mil.*) contrattaccare.

to **re-act**[2] ['ri:'ækt], *v.t.* **1.** (*teat.*) recitare, rappresentare di nuovo; replicare **2.** fare di nuovo, rifare.

reaction [ri(:)'ækʃən], *s.* **1.** reazione: *action and* —, azione e reazione; *what was her* — *to the news?*, quale fu la sua reazione alla notizia? **2.** (*pol.*) reazione: *we must fight the forces of* —, dobbiamo combattere le forze della reazione, i reazionari **3.** (*chim.*) reazione ☆ —*-time*, (*psicologia*) tempo di reazione || *chain-* —, (*fis.*) reazione a catena.

reactionary [ri(:)'ækʃnəri], **reactionist** [ri(:)-'ækʃənist], *ag.s.* (*pol.*) reazionario.

reactive [ri(:)'æktiv], *ag.* reattivo, reagente.

reactively [ri(:)'æktivli], *av.* per, con reazione.

reactiveness [ri(:)'æktivnis], **reactivity** [,ri(:)æk'tiviti], *s.* (*fis. atomica*) reattività.

reactor [ri(:)'æktə*], *s.* **1.** reattore **2.** (*elett.*) reattanza ☆ *nuclear* —, reattore nucleare.

read [red], *ag.* colto, istruito: *well* — *in philosophy*, versato in filosofia; *to be deeply* — *in sthg.*, conoscere a fondo ql.co.

read [ri:d], *s.* lettura; tempo impiegato nella lettura.

to **read**, *pass.p.p.* **read** [red], *v.t.i.* **1.** leggere: *he reads well*, egli legge bene; *I can* — *German*, so leggere il tedesco; *to* — (*aloud*) *to s.o.*, leggere a qlcu.

(ad alta voce) || *to* — *oneself hoarse*, leggere fino a diventare rauco || *to* — *s.o. a lesson*, fare la predica a qlcu. || *to* — *s.o. to sleep*, leggere fino a far addormentare qlcu. || *to* — *to oneself*, leggere in silenzio **2.** studiare: *to* — *for a degree, for the bar*, studiare per prendere una laurea, per diventare avvocato **3.** leggere; interpretare, decifrare: *my silence is not to be* — *as consent*, il mio silenzio non deve essere interpretato come consenso; *to* — (*music*) *at sight*, leggere (la musica) a prima vista; *to* — *dreams*, interpretare i sogni; *to* — *hieroglyphs*, decifrare i geroglifici; *to* — *a riddle*, risolvere un indovinello; *to* — *the sky*, leggere gli astri; *to* — *s.o.'s face, heart, thoughts*, leggere in viso, nel cuore, nei pensieri di qlcu. || *to* — *between the lines*, leggere tra le righe || *to* — *too much into sthg.*, leggere in ql.co. quello che non c'è **4.** segnare (di strumenti): *the thermometer reads thirty-five degrees*, il termometro segna trentacinque gradi **5.** essere concepito; leggersi: *this letter reads like a threat*, questa lettera suona come una minaccia; *this play reads better than it acts*, questa commedia è più adatta alla lettura che alle scene; *we received your wire reading: "goods sent"*, abbiamo ricevuto il vostro telegramma così concepito: « merce spedita » **6.** *to* — *in: to* — *oneself in*, (*eccl.*) prendere possesso di un ufficio (di pastore protestante) **7.** *to* — **out**, leggere ad alta voce; leggere fino alla fine **8.** *to* — **over**, rileggere **9.** *to* — **through**, prendere visione di; leggere fino alla fine **10.** *to* — **up**, documentarsi su: *to* — *up a subject*, documentarsi su un argomento.

readability [,ri:də'biliti], *s.* leggibilità.

readable ['ri:dəbl], *ag.* **1.** interessante, piacevole a leggersi: *is it* —?, si può leggere?, è interessante? **2.** (*rar.*) leggibile: *her handwriting is very* —, la sua scrittura è molto chiara.

readableness ['ri:dəblnis], *s.* leggibilità.

readably ['ri:dəbli], *av.* leggibilmente.

to **readdress** ['ri:ə'dres], *v.t.* **1.** cambiare l'indirizzo (su una busta, un pacco); scrivere un nuovo indirizzo su **2.** rispedire.

reader ['ri:də*], *s.c.* **1.** lettore, lettrice **2.** lettore, lettrice (in una università) **3.** (*tip.*) correttore, correttrice di bozze; lettore, lettrice di manoscritti || *s.* libro di lettura (per scuole): *an Anglo-Saxon* —, antologia di passi in anglosassone || *the first* —, il sillabario.

readership ['ri:dəʃip], *s.* lettorato.

readily ['redili], *av.* **1.** prontamente, sollecitamente **2.** volentieri; senza difficoltà: *the facts were* — *ascertained*, i fatti furono facilmente accertati.

readiness ['redinis], *s.* **1.** prontezza, speditezza: — *to believe evil*, prontezza a prestar fede al male **2.** buona volontà; buona disposizione **3.** facilità; vivacità (di spirito): — *of speech*, facilità di parola; — *of wit*, prontezza di spirito **4.** *in* —: *all is in* —, tutto è pronto; *everything was put in* — *for the attack*, ogni cosa fu preparata per l'attacco.

reading[1] ['ri:diŋ], *ag.* **1.** che legge || *the* — *public*, i lettori, il pubblico che legge **2.** studioso ☆ — *student*, (*fam.*) sgobbone.

reading[1], *s.* **1.** lettura: — *and writing are taught to children*, aibambini viene insegnato a leggere e scrivere **2.** conoscenza letteraria: *he is a man of vast* —, è un uomo di vasta conoscenza letteraria **3.** lezione, versione (di manoscritto, testo): *there are various readings, but this seems to be the best* —, vi sono parecchie versioni, ma questa sembra essere la migliore **4.** interpretazione: *there are numberless readings of Hamlet*, vi sono infinite interpretazioni di Amleto; *what is your* — *of the facts?*, qual è la tua interpretazione dei fatti? **5.** — *of a bill*, lettura di un progetto di legge in Parlamento ☆ —*-book*, libro di lettura; —*-desk*, leggio; — *-lamp*, lampada da scrittoio, comodino; — *-room*, sala di lettura.

Reading[2] ['rediŋ], *no.pr.* (*geog.*) Reading || — *University College*, Collegio Universitario di Reading (fondato nel 1892); (adesso) Università di Reading.

to **readjourn** ['ri:ə'dʒə:n], *v.t.* prorogare nuovamente.

readjournment ['ri:ə'dʒə:nmənt], *s.* nuova proroga.

to **readjust** ['ri:ə'dʒʌst], *v.t.* riaggiustare; riassettare: *to — oneself*, riassettarsi, rimettersi in ordine.

readjustment ['ri:ə'dʒʌstmənt], *s.* riordinamento; riassestamento: *a period of —*, un periodo di riassestamento.

readmission ['ri:əd'miʃən], *s.* riammissione.

to **readmit** ['ri:əd'mit], *pass.p.p.* **readmitted** ['ri:əd'mitid], *v.t.* riammettere.

readmittance ['ri:əd'mitəns], *s.* riammissione.

ready ['redi], *ag.* **1.** pronto, preparato; a portata di mano; *fig.* pronto, disposto, incline: *— to act*, pronto ad agire; *are you —?, go!*, pronti?, via!; *breakfast is —*, la colazione è pronta; *get — for the party*, preparati per la festa; *he is — for death*, è preparato a morire; *make* (o *get*) *everything —*, prepara ogni cosa; *to find an instrument — to hand*, trovare un arnese a portata di mano **2.** pronto, svelto, lesto; abile: *a — answer*, una pronta risposta; *a — sale*, un rapido smercio; *a — worker*, un abile operaio; *this boy is — at excuses*, questo ragazzo ha la scusa sempre pronta ‖ *s.* **1.** (*sl.*) denaro contante: *he planked down the —*, egli buttò giù il denaro **2.** (*mil.*) posizione di puntamento (del fucile) ‖ *av.* **1.** completamente **2.** prontamente ☆ *— -built*, prefabbricato; *— -made*, confezionato: *— -made shop*, negozio di confezioni; *— money*, denaro in contanti, cassa: *to pay in — money*, pagare in contanti; *— reckoner*, libro dei conti; *— -to-serve*, pronto da servire; *— -to-wear*, confezionato, fatto; *— -witted*, dallo spirito pronto, dall'ingegno vivace.

to **ready**, *v.t.* **1.** preparare **2.** (*sl. ippica*) assicurare un buon « handicap » a (un cavallo).

to **reaffirm** ['ri:ə'fə:m], *v.t.* riaffermare.

reaffirmation ['ri:æfə'meiʃən], *s.* riaffermazione.

to **reafforest** ['ri:æ'fɔrist], *v.t.* rimboschire.

reafforestation ['ri:æˌfɔris'teiʃən], *s.* rimboschimento.

reagency [ri(:)'eidʒənsi], *s.* (*chim.*) (capacità di) reazione.

reagent [ri(:)'eidʒənt], *s.* (*chim.*) reagente.

real[1] [riəl], *ag.* **1.** reale; vero, effettivo; genuino, autentico; sincero, schietto: *— flowers and paper ones*, fiori veri e di carta; *— friend*, amico sincero; *— value*, valore effettivo; *this is the — ring*, questo è l'anello autentico **2.** (*dir.*) immobile ‖ *s.* (*fil.*) (il) reale: *the — and the ideal*, il reale e l'ideale ☆ *— estate* (o *property*), beni immobili; *— -estate man*, agente per la compravendita di immobili.

real[2] [rei'ɑ:l], *s.* reale (antica moneta spagnola).

realgar [ri(:)'ælgə*], *s.* (*min.*) realgar.

realism ['riəlizəm], *s.* realismo.

realist ['riəlist], *s.c.* realista.

realistic [riə'listik], *ag.* realistico.

realistically [riə'listikəli], *av.* realisticamente.

reality [ri(:)'æliti], *s.* **1.** realtà: *in —*, in realtà; *we are face to face with realities*, ci troviamo di fronte a delle realtà **2.** realismo; verosimiglianza: *reproduced with surprising —*, riprodotto con sorprendente realismo.

realizable ['riəlaizəbl], *ag.* realizzabile.

realization [ˌriəlai'zeiʃən], *s.* **1.** percezione: *I had the sudden — that I couldn't do it alone*, ebbi l'improvvisa percezione di non poterlo fare da solo **2.** realizzazione; attuazione, compimento: *the — of one's hopes*, il compimento delle proprie speranze **3.** (*comm.*) realizzo.

to **realize** ['riəlaiz], *v.t.* **1.** capire; accorgersi di, rendersi conto di: *don't you — that you're wrong?*, non ti rendi conto di avere torto?; *he didn't — his position*, non si rendeva conto della sua posizione; *I — I am old now*, capisco di essere ormai vecchio; *when he realized what he had done he felt sorry*, quando si accorse di ciò che aveva fatto ne provò dispiacere **2.** realizzare, effettuare, attuare: *to — one's hopes*, attuare le proprie speranze; *to — a project*, realizzare un progetto **3.** (*comm.*) realizzare: *to — large profits*, realiz-

zare dei forti guadagni ‖ *to — securities*, convertire titoli in denaro contante.

really ['riəli], *av.* realmente, in realtà; veramente; davvero: *do you — think so?*, lo pensi davvero?; *I am — sorry*, sono veramente dispiaciuto; *what do you — think about it?*, cosa ne pensi, in realtà?.

realm [relm], *s.* **1.** (*poet. letter.*) reame, regno: *the realms of heaven*, il regno dei cieli **2.** *fig.* regno, dominio: *the — of fancy*, il regno della fantasia.

realtor ['riəltə*], *s.* (*amer.*) agente per la compravendita di immobili.

realty ['riəlti], *s.* (*dir.*) proprietà immobiliare; beni immobili.

ream[1] [ri:m], *s.* **1.** risma (circa 500 fogli di carta) **2.** *pl.* enorme quantità (di versi, scritti, carta stampata): *he wrote reams and reams to you last week*, ti ha scritto pagine e pagine la settimana scorsa.

ream[2], *s.* (*dial.*) panna; schiuma di un liquido.

to **ream**[3], *v.t.* **1.** (*mec.*) allargare (un foro) con alesatoio; alesare **2.** (*mar.*) aprire (le commessure) per calafatare.

reamer ['ri:mə*], *s.* (*mec.*) alesatore.

to **reanimate** ['ri:'ænimeit], *v.t.* rianimare; rincuorare.

reanimation ['ri:ˌæni'meiʃən], *s.* rianimazione.

to **reannex** ['ri:ə'neks], *v.t.* riannettere.

reannexation ['ri:ˌænek'seiʃən], *s.* riannessione.

to **reap** [ri:p], *v.t.i.* **1.** mietere (il grano, ecc.): *to — a field*, mietere un campo ‖ *to — laurels*, *fig.* mietere allori **2.** fare il raccolto, raccogliere (anche *fig.*): *to — the fruits of sthg.*, raccogliere i frutti di ql.co. ‖ *to — where one has not sown*, approfittare della fatica altrui ‖ *he who sows the wind, shall — the whirlwind*, *prov.* chi semina vento raccoglie tempesta ‖ *we — as we sow*, *prov.* quel che si semina si raccoglie.

reaper ['ri:pə*], *s.c.* mietitore, mietitrice ‖ *s.* (*mec.*) mietitrice.

reaping ['ri:piŋ], *s.* mietitura; messe, raccolto ☆ *— -hook*, falce; *— -machine*, (*mec.*) mietitrice; *— -time*, epoca della mietitura.

to **reapparel** ['ri:ə'pærəl], *v.t.* vestire, equipaggiare di nuovo.

to **reappear** ['ri:ə'piə*], *v.i.* riapparire, ricomparire; ripresentarsi.

reappearance ['ri:ə'piərəns], *s.* riapparizione, ricomparsa.

to **reapply** ['ri:ə'plai], *v.t.* riapplicare.

to **reappoint** ['ri:ə'pɔint], *v.t.* nominare di nuovo; reintegrare nelle proprie funzioni.

reappointment ['ri:ə'pɔintmənt], *s.* reintegrazione.

rear[1] [riə*], *ag.* posteriore; ultimo: *— rank*, ultima fila ‖ *s.* **1.** (*mil.*) retroguardia, retrovia; coda: *he was sent to the — because of his age*, fu inviato alle retrovie a causa dell'età; *to bring up the —*, formare la retroguardia, venire per ultimo, essere in coda **2.** parte posteriore, retro: *the — of the buildings*, il retro degli edifici; *at the — of*, dietro a **3.** (*fam.*) latrina, gabinetto ☆ *— -admiral*, contrammiraglio; *— -arch*, arco interno; *— -guard*, retroguardia; *— sight*, alzo (di arma da fuoco).

rear[2], *ag.* cotto male, poco cotto.

to **rear**[3], *v.t.i.* **1.** innalzare, levare, erigere: *to — a cathedral*, innalzare una cattedrale **2.** alzare, sollevare: *to — one's head, one's voice*, alzare il capo, la voce **3.** allevare (bestiame); coltivare (piante); educare (prole) **4.** impennarsi (di cavallo).

rearer ['riərə*], *s.c.* allevatore, allevatrice; educatore, educatrice ‖ *s.* cavallo che si impenna.

rearhorse ['riəhɔ:s], *s.* (*entom.*) mantide religiosa.

to **rearm** ['ri:'ɑ:m], *v.t.* riarmare.

rearmament ['ri:'ɑ:məmənt], *s.* riarmo; riarmamento.

rearmost ['riəmoust], *ag.* il più arretrato, l'ultimo.

to **rearrange** ['ri:ə'reindʒ], *v.t.* riordinare.

rearrangement ['ri:ə'reindʒmənt], *s.* riordinamento.

rearward ['riəwəd], *ag.* **1.** posteriore **2.** che appartiene alla retroguardia ‖ *s.* (*mil.*) retroguardia.

rearward(s) ['riəwəd(z)], *av.* verso la retroguardia; indietro.

to reascend ['ri:ə'send], *v.t.i.* riascendere; risalire: *to — the throne*, riascendere al trono.

reason ['ri:zn], *s.* **1.** causa, motivo, ragione: *by — of*, a causa di; *I shall never understand — why she decided so*, non capirò mai il motivo della sua decisione; *there is no — for shouting like that*, non c'è motivo di gridare in quel modo; *we have (every) — to believe him guilty*, abbiamo (ogni) motivo per ritenerlo colpevole; *we have no — to complain*, non abbiamo motivo di lamentarci; *to give reasons for*, addurre ragioni per, motivare ‖ *— of State*, ragion di Stato ‖ *a woman's —*, (*scherz.*) logica femminile: *she gave only a woman's —: it was right, because it was right*, addusse un motivo illogico: era giusto, perchè era giusto **2.** ragione; raziocinio: *the use of —*, l'uso della ragione; *to be restored to —*, rinsavire; *to bring s.o. to —*, indurre qlcu. alla ragione; *to listen to —*, lasciarsi persuadere; *to lose one's —*, perdere la ragione **3.** ragionevolezza; buon senso ‖ *within —*, ragionevole: *I will do anything within — for him*, farò per lui tutto quanto è ragionevole che io faccia ‖ *it stands to — that*, è evidente che ‖ *without rhyme or —*, senza capo nè coda **4.** (*log.*) premessa minore (di un sillogismo).

to reason, *v.t.i.* **1.** ragionare; discorrere: *to — about*, (o *of* o *upon*) *a subject*, ragionare, discutere di, su un argomento; *to — with s.o.*, discorrere con qlcu. **2.** esaminare: *we reasoned the matter together*, esaminammo insieme la cosa **3.** persuadere (col ragionamento): *I reasoned him into accepting my proposal*, lo persuasi ad accettare la mia proposta.

reasonable ['ri:znəbl], *ag.* **1.** ragionevole; logico **2.** moderato (di prezzo).

reasonableness ['ri:znəblnis], *s.* **1.** ragionevolezza **2.** moderazione (di prezzi).

reasonably ['ri:znəbli], *av.* ragionevolmente.

reasoner ['ri:znə*], *s.c.* ragionatore, ragionatrice.

reasoning ['ri:zniŋ], *s.* ragionamento; modo di ragionare: *your — is quite good*, il vostro modo di ragionare è ottimo.

reasonless ['ri:znlis], *ag.* **1.** senza ragione, senza motivo **2.** irragionevole.

to reassemble ['ri:ə'sembl], *v.t.i.* **1.** adunare, adunarsi di nuovo; riunire, riunirsi **2.** (*mec.*) rimontare.

to reassert ['ri:ə'sə:t], *v.t.* riaffermare, riasserire.

reassertion ['ri:ə'sə:ʃən], *s.* riasserzione.

to reassess ['ri:ə'ses], *v.t.* **1.** tassare di nuovo **2.** valutare di nuovo (un danno, una proprietà).

reassessment ['ri:ə'sesmənt], *s.* **1.** il tassare di nuovo **2.** il valutare di nuovo (un danno, una proprietà).

to reassign ['ri:ə'sain], *v.t.* riassegnare.

reassurance [,ri:ə'ʃuərəns], *s.* **1.** rassicurazione **2.** (*dir.*) riassicurazione.

to reassure [,ri:ə'ʃuə*], *v.t.* **1.** rassicurare; tranquillizzare **2.** (*dir.*) riassicurare.

reassuring [,ri:ə'ʃuəriŋ], *ag.* rassicurante.

reassuringly [,ri:ə'ʃuəriŋli], *av.* in modo rassicurante.

to reave[1] [ri:v], *pass.p.p.* **reft** [reft], *v.t.i.* (*arc.*) rapire; rapinare; saccheggiare, fare razzie.

to reave[2], *pass.p.p.* **reft**, *v.t.* (*arc.*) rompere; fendere; spaccare.

reaver ['ri:və*], *s.* (*arc.*) rapinatore; saccheggiatore.

to reawaken ['ri:ə'weikən], *v.t.i.* risvegliare, risvegliarsi; riattizzare: *to — s.o.'s interest*, risvegliare l'interesse di qlcu.

rebaptism ['ri:'bæptizəm], *s.* ribattezzamento.

to rebaptize ['ri:bæp'taiz], *v.t.* ribattezzare.

rebate[1] ['ri:beit], *s.* (*comm.*) **1.** riduzione, sconto; abbuono **2.** rimborso.

to rebate[1] [ri'beit], *v.t.* **1.** (*rar.*) diminuire, ridurre (l'effetto, la forza di) **2.** spuntare, ottundere, rintuzzare (un'arma).

(to) rebate[2], *V.* (to) **rabbet**.

rebec ['ri:bek], *s.* (*mus.*) ribeca.

Rebecca [ri'bekə], *no.pr.f.* Rebecca.

rebeck ['ri:bek], *s.* (*mus.*) ribeca.

rebel ['rebl], *ag.s.c.* ribelle.

to rebel [ri'bel], *pass.p.p.* **rebelled** [ri'beld], *v.i.* **1.** ribellarsi: *his mind rebels at the prospect of such drudgery*, la sua mente si ribella all'idea di una simile fatica **2.** sollevarsi, sorgere in armi: *the crowd rebelled against the tyrant*, la folla si sollevò contro il tiranno.

rebellion [ri'beljən], *s.* ribellione.

rebellious [ri'beljəs], *ag.* ribelle; refrattario.

rebelliously [ri'beljəsli], *av.* in maniera ribelle.

rebelliousness [ri'beljəsnis], *s.* spirito, carattere ribelle; atteggiamento ribelle.

to rebellow ['ri:'belou], *v.t.i.* (*poet.*) riecheggiare.

to rebind ['ri:'baind], *pass.p.p.* **rebound** ['ri:'baund], *v.t.* rilegare (un libro).

rebirth ['ri:'bə:θ], *s.* rinascita: *— of learning*, rinascita della cultura.

reboant ['rebouənt], *ag.* (*poet.*) rimbombante, risonante, riecheggiante.

reborn ['ri:'bɔ:n], *ag.* rinato.

rebound[1] ['ri:'baund], *pass.p.p.* di to **rebind**.

rebound[2] [ri'baund], *s.* rimbalzo; ripercussione ‖ *to take s.o. on the —*, approfittare della reazione di qlcu.

to rebound[2], *v.i.* **1.** rimbalzare; ricadere; ripercuotersi: *your evil actions will — upon yourself*, le tue cattive azioni ricadranno su di te **2.** riecheggiare.

to rebroadcast ['ri:'brɔ:dka:st], *v.t.* ritrasmettere.

rebuff [ri'bʌf], *s.* rifiuto, diniego; mortificazione.

to rebuff, *v.t.* respingere, rifiutare; mortificare.

to rebuild ['ri:'bild], *pass.p.p.* **rebuilt** ['ri:'bilt], *v.t.* ricostruire, riedificare.

rebuke [ri'bju:k], *s.* **1.** sgridata, rimprovero: *to administer a —*, fare un rimprovero **2.** biasimo: *without —*, senza biasimo.

to rebuke, *v.t.* **1.** sgridare, rimproverare **2.** biasimare.

rebukingly [ri'bju:kiŋli], *av.* con tono di rimprovero.

rebus ['ri:bəs], *s.* rebus.

to rebut [ri'bʌt], *pass.p.p.* **rebutted** [ri'bʌtid], *v.t.* **1.** respingere; rifiutare: *to — a person's offers*, rifiutare le offerte di una persona **2.** (*dir.*) confutare, ribattere.

rebutment [ri'bʌtmənt], **rebuttal** [ri'bʌtl], *s.* **1.** rifiuto **2.** (*dir.*) confutazione.

rebutter [ri'bʌtə*], *s.* **1.** (*dir.*) difesa **2.** confutazione.

recalcitrance [ri'kælsitrəns], **recalcitrancy** [ri'kælsitrənsi], *s.* recalcitramento; *fig.* ostinata opposizione.

recalcitrant [ri'kælsitrənt], *ag.* ricalcitrante; *fig.* restio.

to recalcitrate [ri'kælsitreit], *v.i.* ricalcitrare; *fig.* essere refrattario; essere restio.

recalcitration [ri,kælsi'treiʃən], *s.* resistenza, opposizione; contrasto.

to recalesce ['ri:kə'les], *v.i.* (*metal.*) recalescere.

recalescence ['ri:kə'lesns], *s.* (*metal.*) recalescenza.

recall [ri'kɔ:l], *s.* **1.** richiamo **2.** revoca: *it is beyond* (o *past*) *—*, è irrevocabile, non può essere annullato **3.** (*mil.*) segnale di ritirata: *to sound the —*, suonare la ritirata.

to recall, *v.t.* **1.** richiamare, far ritornare: *he was recalled to his duty*, fu richiamato al dovere; *to — an ambassador*, fare rimpatriare un ambasciatore **2.** richiamare alla mente; far ricordare: *the photograph recalled memories of his youth*, la fotografia gli ricordò la sua giovinezza **3.** ricordarsi: *to — sthg.* (*to mind*), ricordarsi di ql.co.: *I don't — his words*, non mi ricordo le sue parole **4.** (*poet.*) far rivivere **5.** annullare (un giudizio); revocare (un decreto); ritrattare (una promessa).

recallable [ri'kɔ:ləbl], *ag.* **1.** richiamabile **2.** revocabile.

to recant [ri'kænt], *v.t.i.* **1.** ritrattare, revocare, ripudiare (idea, opinione) **2.** abiurare; fare una pubblica sconfessione.

recantation [ˌriːkænˈteiʃən], s. 1. ritrattazione 2. abiura.

recanter [riˈkæntə*], s.c. 1. chi ritratta 2. chi abiura.

to **recapitulate** [ˌriːkəˈpitjuleit], v.t.i. ricapitolare; riepilogare.

recapitulation [ˈriː-kəˌpitjuˈleiʃən], s. ricapitolazione; riepilogo.

recapitulative [ˌriː-kəˈpitjuleitiv],] **recapitulatory** [ˌriː-kəˈpitjulətəri], ag. riassuntivo.

recapture [ˈriːˈkæptʃə*], s. riconquista.

to **recapture**, v.t. riconquistare; riprendere; fig. richiamare alla memoria.

recast [ˈriːˈkɑːst], s. 1. (metal.) nuova forma 2. nuova disposizione; nuova stesura (di opera letteraria).

to **recast**, pass.p.p. **recast**, v.t. 1. (metal.) rifondere 2. rimaneggiare, ricomporre (cose, opere letterarie, ecc.) 3. (teat.) allestire con nuovi attori: the play has been entirely —, la commedia è stata allestita con nuovi attori.

to **recede**[1] [riˈ(ː)ˈsiːd], v.i. 1. recedere, indietreggiare; allontanarsi: as the ship headed for the open sea, the coast gradually receded, mentre la nave si dirigeva verso l'alto mare la costa si allontanava ‖ to — into the background, fig. perdere influenza 2. diminuire, rimpicciolire; restringersi; declinare: to — in importance, perdere importanza 3. ritirarsi: to — from sthg., ritirarsi da, rinunciare a ql.co.

to **recede**[2], v.t. restituire (territori, ecc.).

receding [riˈ(ː)ˈsiːdiŋ], ag. rientrante; sfuggente: — chin, mento sfuggente.

receipt [riˈsiːt], s. 1. (comm.) ricezione, ricevimento: on — (of goods), al ricevimento (della merce); we are in — of your letter, abbiamo ricevuto la vostra (lettera); to acknowledge — of, accusare ricevuta di 2. ricevuta, quietanza: to sign a —, firmare una ricevuta 3. gener. pl. introiti: the gross receipts, gli introiti lordi 4. V. **recipe** 5. (arc.) ricevitoria ☆ — -book, (cuc.) ricettario; (comm.) registro delle ricevute ‖ clean — (o trust —), (comm.) ricevuta di fiducia, ricevuta senza riserve; consignment —, ricevuta di spedizione, consegna.

to **receipt**, v.t. (comm.) quietanzare.

receivable [riˈsiːvəbl], ag. 1. ricevibile; accettabile: — certificates, certificati accettabili 2. (comm.) esigibile: bills —, (comm.) cambiali esigibili.

to **receive** [riˈsiːv], v.t.i. 1. ricevere: she received a good education, ricevette una buona educazione; she received a wonderful gift, ricevette un dono meraviglioso; to — the Sacrament, ricevere i Sacramenti, comunicarsi; to — s.o.'s confessions, ricevere le confessioni, le confidenze di qlcu. ‖ to — stolen goods, ricettare merci rubate 2. ricevere, dare ricevimenti; accogliere: he received us with open arms, ci accolse a braccia aperte; Mrs. X receives on Mondays, la signora X riceve il lunedì 3. contenere; servire da recipiente per: this boat is large enough to — ten men, questa barca è abbastanza grossa per portare dieci uomini 4. sostenere, sopportare: the arch receives the weight of the roof, l'arco sostiene il peso del tetto 5. dar credito a, accettare come vero: it is an axiom universally received, è un assioma universalmente accettato 6. subire; soffrire: they received but insults, non subirono che insulti; to — a heavy blow, subire un duro colpo ‖ to — thirty days, essere condannati a un mese di prigione.

received [riˈsiːvd], ag. accettato.

receiver [riˈsiːvə*], s.c. chi riceve; (comm.) destinatario, destinataria ‖ s. 1. (tec.) ricevitore: to lift the —, alzare il ricevitore 2. (dir.) ricettatore (di merci rubate) 3. (dir.) curatore fallimentare 4. (rad.) apparecchio radioricevente 5. (chim.) recipiente.

receivership [riˈsiːvəʃip], s. (dir.) ufficio di curatore fallimentare.

receiving [riˈsiːviŋ], ag. ricevente ‖ s. 1. ricezione 2. (dir.) ricettazione ☆ — -order, (dir.) ordinanza

con cui si nomina un curatore fallimentare; — -set, (rad. tv.) apparecchio ricevente.

recency [ˈriːsnsi], s. carattere, data recente.

recension [riˈsenʃən], s. 1. recensione, revisione (di testo) 2. testo riveduto.

recensionist [riˈsenʃənist], s. revisore, censore.

recent [ˈriːsnt], ag. recente; fresco; moderno: — news, notizia fresca; it is a — event, è un avvenimento recente.

recently [ˈriːsntli], av. recentemente, di recente.

recentness [ˈriːsntnis], s. attualità; novità.

receptacle [riˈseptəkl], s. ricettacolo.

reception [riˈsepʃən], s. 1. il ricevere: the rooms were prepared for his —, i locali furono preparati per riceverlo 2. ricevimento: after the ceremony there will be a —, dopo la cerimonia ci sarà un ricevimento; to give a —, dare un ricevimento 3. ricezione: he has a great faculty of —, ha una grande capacità di ricezione 4. accoglienza: a cold, a warm —, un'accoglienza fredda, cordiale; the book had a favourable —, il libro ebbe una accoglienza favorevole; these ideas have a general —, queste idee sono largamente accettate 5. (rad.) ricettività, ricezione ☆ — office, ufficio ricevimento (di albergo); — -order, ordine di internamento (in ospedale, manicomio); — -room, sala di ricevimento.

receptionist [riˈsepʃənist], s. impiegato che ha l'incarico di ricevere i clienti (in un albergo, ufficio, ecc.).

receptive [riˈseptiv], ag. ricettivo.

receptively [riˈseptivli], av. ricettivamente.

receptiveness [riˈseptivnis], **receptivity** [risepˈtiviti], s. ricettività.

receptor [riˈseptə*], s. 1. persona, cosa che riceve 2. (fisiol.) ricettore sensitivo.

recess [riˈses], s. 1. intervallo; vacanza ‖ parliamentary —, tregua parlamentare 2. rientranza; nicchia; alcova 3. recesso, luogo ritirato, appartato: the inmost recesses of the heart, fig. gli intimi recessi del cuore 4. retrocessione (di ghiacciaio, terra, ecc.); decrescenza (di acque).

to **recess**, v.t.i. 1. recludere, segregare, nascondere 2. aprire una nicchia, una rientranza in: to — a wall, aprire una nicchia in un muro 3. prendersi le vacanze (di Parlamento, Corte, Università); aggiornarsi (di Parlamento).

recession [riˈseʃən], s. 1. ritiro; arretramento, retrocessione: the — of the sea from the coast-line, l'arretramento del mare dalla costa 2. (comm. amer.) diminuzione (di prezzi, ecc.).

recessional [riˈseʃənl], ag. 1. (eccl.) dell'inno (cantato all'uscita del clero e del coro) 2. fatto in un intervallo (di seduta parlamentare) ‖ s. — (hymn), (eccl.) inno (cantato all'uscita del clero e del coro dopo il servizio).

recessive [riˈsesiv], ag. 1. retrocedente, regressivo: — accent, (fonet.) accento che si sposta dall'ultima alla prima sillaba (di una parola) 2. (biol.) recessivo (carattere delle leggi di Mendel) ‖ s. (biol.) carattere recessivo (delle leggi di Mendel).

Rechabite [ˈrekəbait], s.c. 1. recabita (appartenente a una setta votata all'astinenza; da Recab, personaggio biblico) 2. astemio, astemia.

recharge [ˈriːˈtʃɑːdʒ], s. ricarica.

to **recharge**, v.t.i. 1. caricare di nuovo 2. (mil.) tornare alla carica 3. (dir.) accusare di nuovo.

réchauffé [reiˈʃoufei], s. 1. piatto riscaldato 2. fig. rimaneggiamento letterario.

recherché [rəˈʃɛəʃei], ag. ricercato, raffinato.

to **rechristen** [ˈriːˈkrisn], v.t. ribattezzare; dare un nuovo nome a.

recidivism [riˈsidivizəm], s. recidività.

recidivist [riˈsidivist], s.c. recidivo, recidiva.

recipe [ˈresipi], s. 1. (cuc.) ricetta: the — for the cake, la ricetta per la torta 2. (arc. med.) prescrizione, ricetta (medica) (farm.) formula ‖ the — for happiness, la chiave della felicità.

recipiency [riˈsipiənsi], s. ricettività; capacità di ricevere.

recipient [riˈsipiənt], ag. ricevente; ricettivo ‖

s.c. chi riceve, ricevente; destinatario, destinataria; beneficiario, beneficiaria ‖ *s.* (*chim.*) recipiente.

reciprocal [ri'siprəkəl], *ag.* reciproco, scambievole: — *affection*, affetto reciproco; — *aggreement*, accordo bilaterale; *we made the — mistake of taking each other for Mr. Jones*, abbiamo fatto il reciproco errore di scambiarci per il sig. Jones ‖ *s.* (*mat.*) numero reciproco ☆ — *pole*, (*geom.*) antipolo; — *pronoun*, (*gram.*) pronome reciproco; — *ratio*, (*mat.*) rapporto inverso.

reciprocality [ri,siprə'kæliti], *V.* **reciprocity.**

reciprocally [ri'siprəkəli], *av.* reciprocamente, scambievolmente, vicendevolmente.

to **reciprocate** [ri'siprəkeit], *v.t.i.* 1. (*mec.*) muovere, muoversi alternativamente 2. contraccambiare, ricambiare; scambiare: *George reciprocates her affection*, Giorgio contraccambia il suo affetto; *he reciprocated by wishing her a pleasant journey*, ricambiò augurandole buon viaggio; *he reciprocated with a birthday present*, (*fam.*) egli ricambiò con un regalo per il suo compleanno.

reciprocating [ri'siprəkeitiŋ], *ag.* (*mec.*) alternativo ☆ — *compressor*, compressore a stantuffo; — *-engine*, motore alternativo; — *motion*, moto alternativo; — *saw*, sega alternativa.

reciprocation [ri,siprə'keiʃən], *s.* 1. (*mec.*) moto alterno 2. ricambio, contraccambio; scambio: — *of kindnesses*, scambio di gentilezze.

reciprocity [,resi'prɔsiti], *s.* reciprocità, scambievolezza: — *of displacements*, (*mec.*) reciprocità degli spostamenti.

recision [ri'siʒən], *s.* (*rar.*) potatura.

recital [ri'saitl], *s.* 1. racconto; relazione 2. (*dir.*) esposto; fatto 3. « recital » (esibizione di un solista, di un attore) ☆ *piano —*, « recital » di pianoforte.

recitation [,resi'teiʃən], *s.* 1. recitazione; recita 2. narrazione.

recitative [,resitə'ti:v], *ag.* recitativo; narrativo ‖ *s.* (*mus.*) recitativo.

to **recite** [ri'sait], *v.t.i.* 1. recitare, declamare: *will you — to us?*, volete recitare ql.co. per noi?; *to — a lesson*, recitare, dire la lezione; *to — a poem*, declamare una poesia 2. (*dir.*) fare una relazione; esporre (i fatti) per iscritto.

reciter [ri'saitə*], *s.c.* recitatore, recitatrice; dicitore, dicitrice ‖ *s.* libro di recitazione; raccolta di monologhi.

recivilization ['ri:,sivilai'zeiʃən], *s.* rincivilimento.

to **recivilize** ['ri:'sivilaiz], *v.t.* rincivilire.

to **reck** [rek], *v.t.i.* (*ret. poet. solo in frasi interrogative, negative*) preoccuparsi: *I — not my life*, non mi preoccupo molto della mia vita; *what recks it (me) that?*, che (m')importa?; *to — but little of sthg.*, far poco conto di ql.co.

reckless ['reklis], *ag.* noncurante; incauto; avventato: — *of danger*, incurante del pericolo, temerario.

recklessly ['reklisli], *av.* incautamente, avventatamente; temerariamente.

recklessness ['reklisnis], *s.* noncuranza, avventatezza; temerarietà.

to **reckon** ['rekən], *v.t.i.* 1. contare, calcolare, computare, enumerare: *I reckoned ten of them*, ne contai dieci ‖ *to — without one's host*, fare i conti senza l'oste 2. considerare, reputare, stimare: *he was reckoned a clever boy*, era considerato un ragazzo sveglio 3. (*fam.*) credere, supporre: *they will be here before long, I —*, saranno qui tra breve, penso 4. *to — (up)on* (*s.o., sthg.*), contare, fare assegnamento su: *I — on your coming*, conto sulla vostra venuta.

reckoner ['reknə*], *s.c.* calcolatore, calcolatrice; contabile; computista ‖ *s.* (*ready*) —, prontuario dei conti fatti.

reckoning ['rekniŋ], *s.* 1. conto, computo, calcolo: *to be out in one's —*, ingannarsi nei propri calcoli ‖ *we made no — of it*, non ne tenemmo conto, non vi facemmo caso 2. *short reckonings make long friends*, prov. patti chiari amicizia lunga 2. conto (da pagare), nota; *fig.* scotto, fio: *sooner or later you will have to pay the*

— *for your present misdeeds*, presto o tardi dovrai pagare il fio dei tuoi misfatti di oggi ‖ *day of —*, giorno della resa dei conti, del Giudizio Universale 3. (*mar. aer.*) determinazione della posizione.

reclaim [ri'kleim], *s.* (*rar.*) 1. revoca: *beyond (o past) —*, irrevocabile, irrimediabile 2. rivendicazione (di terre).

to **reclaim**, *v.t.i.* 1. richiamare al dovere, correggere, redimere: *to — a confirmed criminal*, redimere un criminale incallito; *to — s.o. from vice*, redimere qlcu. dal vizio 2. bonificare: *to — land*, bonificare la terra 3. (*ind.*) ricuperare (un sottoprodotto); rigenerare (la gomma) 4. rivendicare, reclamare: *to — colonies*, rivendicare le colonie 5. (*rar.*) reclamare, protestare.

reclaimable [ri'kleiməbl], *ag.* 1. correggibile 2. civilizzabile 3. bonificabile 4. (*ind.*) ricuperabile (di sottoprodotto) 5. rivendicabile.

reclamation [,reklə'meiʃən], *s.* 1. correzione; redenzione 2. civilizzazione 3. bonifica 4. rivendicazione, richiesta 5. reclamo; protesta.

reclinate ['reklineit], *ag.* (*bot.*) reclinato.

to **recline** [ri'klain], *v.t.i.* 1. inclinare, inclinarsi; appoggiare, appoggiarsi; chinare, chinarsi; posare; giacere 2. *to — upon (s.o.)*, *fig.* fidarsi di.

reclined [ri'klaind], *ag.* inclinato; chinato; posato.

reclining [ri'klainiŋ], *ag.* reclinato, inclinato; chinato; coricato.

to **reclothe** ['ri:'klouð], *v.t.* rivestire.

recluse [ri'klu:s], *ag.* recluso; separato; appartato ‖ *s.* anacoreta, eremita.

reclusion [ri'klu:ʒən], *s.* 1. reclusione 2. eremo.

reclusive [ri'klu:siv], *ag.* di reclusione.

recognition [,rekəg'niʃən], *s.* riconoscimento (anche *fig.*); identificazione: *she has altered past —*, è diventata irriconoscibile.

recognitory [ri'kɔgnitəri], *ag.* (*rar.*) di riconoscimento.

recognizability [,rekəg,naizə'biliti], *s.* riconoscibilità.

recognizable ['rekəgnaizəbl], *ag.* riconoscibile.

recognizably ['rekəgnaizəbli], *av.* in modo riconoscibile.

recognizance [ri'kɔgnizəns], *s.* 1. (*dir.*) impegno assunto di fronte ad un magistrato di osservare delle condizioni 2. (*dir.*) cauzione 3. (*rar.*) riconoscimento (di persone) 4. (*arc.*) simbolo, segno, indizio.

recognizant [ri'kɔgnizənt], *ag.* riconoscente, memore: — *of past favours*, memore di passati favori.

to **recognize** ['rekəgnaiz], *v.t.* 1. riconoscere, ravvisare (cosa, persona nota): *I hardly — you*, ti riconosco a malapena; *to — s.o. by his walk*, riconoscere qlcu. dall'andatura 2. riconoscere, ammettere; accettare: *I — his superiority*, riconosco la sua superiorità; *to — s.o. as king*, riconoscere qlcu. come sovrano; *to — a government, a country*, riconoscere un governo, un paese 3. conoscere, discernere: *I — a good picture, when I see one*, riconosco un buon quadro, quando ne vedo uno 4. (*amer.*) dare la parola a (in parlamento, in una riunione).

recoil [ri'kɔil], *s.* 1. movimento di ripugnanza, di orrore 2. (*artigl.*) rimbalzo, rinculo 3. (*ar. mil.*) ritirata.

to **recoil**, *v.i.* 1. indietreggiare, retrocedere (inorridito): *I — from doing evil*, mi ripugna fare il male 2. *fig.* ricadere, ritornare: *the evil will — on the evil-doer*, il male ricadrà su chi lo ha fatto 3. (*artigl.*) rinculare.

to **recollect**[1], to **re-collect** ['ri:-kə'lekt], *v.t.i.* raccogliere, radunare, radunarsi (di nuovo) ‖ *to — one's thoughts*, riprendersi ‖ *to — oneself*, riaversi, riprendersi, rimettersi.

to **recollect**[2] [,rekə'lekt], *v.t.i.* 1. (II) ricordare; ricordarsi: *as far as I —*, se ricordo bene; *I — saying...*, ricordo d'aver detto... 2. concentrarsi in contemplazione 3. (*rar.*) ricomporsi.

recollection[1] ['ri:kə'lekʃən], *s.* 1. il raccogliersi; il radunarsi (di nuovo) 2. ricapitolazione.

recollection[2] [,rekə'lekʃən], *s.* 1. memoria; reminiscenza; ricordo: *he has a dim — of his illness*, ha un confuso ricordo della sua malattia; *it is in my —*

that this happened in 1927, ricordo che questo avvenne nel 1927; *it has never happened within my* —, non è mai accaduto, per quanto io ricordi 2. concentrazione (religiosa) di pensiero; raccoglimento.

recollective [ˌrekəˈlektiv], *ag.* 1. che fa ricordare 2. dedito ai ricordi.

to **recolour** [ˈriːˈkʌlə*], *v.t.* ricolorire; ritingere.

to **recombine** [ˈriːˈkəmˈbain], *v.t.* ricombinare; ricomporre.

to **recomfort** [ˈriːˈkʌmfət], *v.t.* (*arc.*) riconfortare, consolare; rinvigorire.

to **recommence** [ˈriːkəˈmens], *v.t.i.* ricominciare, far ricominciare: *it recommenced to rain*, si rimise a piovere.

recommencement [ˈriːkəˈmensmənt], *s.* ricominciamento.

to **recommend** [ˌrekəˈmend], *v.t.* raccomandare: *his manners* — *him to us*, i suoi modi ce lo raccomandano; *I* — *him as fit for this post*, lo raccomando come persona adatta a questo posto; *I* — *you to do it*, ti raccomando di farlo; *to* — *oneself to God*, raccomandarsi a Dio.

recommendable [ˌrekəˈmendəbl], *ag.* raccomandabile.

recommendation [ˌrekəmenˈdeiʃən], *s.* raccomandazione: *letter of* —, lettera di raccomandazione.

recommendatory [ˌrekəˈmendətəri], *ag.* raccomandatorio; commendatizio.

recommender [ˌrekəˈmendə*], *s.c.* raccomandatore, raccomandatrice.

to **recommit** [ˈriːkəˈmit], *pass.p.p.* **recommitted** [ˈriːkəˈmitid], *v.t.* 1. rinviare ad una commissione: *to* — *a bill to a committee*, rinviare un progetto di legge a un comitato 2. affidare di nuovo, riaffidare: *to* — *a criminal to prison*, incarcerare nuovamente un criminale 3. commettere di nuovo.

recommitment [ˈriːkəˈmitmənt], **recommittal** [ˈriːkəˈmitl], *s.* 1. rinvio (di un progetto di legge) ad una commissione 2. nuova incarcerazione.

recompense [ˈrekəmpens], *s.* 1. ricompensa, compenso; rimunerazione 2. risarcimento.

to **recompense**, *v.t.* 1. ricompensare, compensare; rimunerare 2. risarcire.

to **recompose** [ˈriːkəmˈpouz], *v.t.* 1. ricomporre, riordinare 2. rasserenare 3. (*tip.*) ricomporre.

recomposition [ˈriːˌkəmpəˈziʃən], *s.* ricomposizione.

to **recompound** [ˈriːkəmˈpaund], *v.t.* ricomporre.

reconcilability [ˌrekənˌsailəˈbiliti], *s.* riconciliabilità.

reconcilable [ˈrekənsailəbl], *ag.* riconciliabile.

reconcilableness [ˈrekənsailəblnis], *s.* riconciliamento.

to **reconcile** [ˈrekənsail], *v.t.* 1. riconciliare: *to* — *a person to* (o *with*) *another*, riconciliare due persone 2. conciliare, comporre: *to* — *differences*, comporre dissidi; *to* — *two points of view*, conciliare due punti di vista 3. rassegnarsi: *to* — *oneself to doing sthg.*, rassegnarsi a fare ql.co. 4. riconsacrare (un luogo sacro profanato).

reconcilement [ˈrekənsailmənt], **reconciliation** [ˌrekənsiliˈeiʃən], *s.* 1. riconciliazione, riavvicinamento 2. conciliazione, composizione 3. rassegnazione 4. riconsacrazione (di luogo sacro).

recondite [riˈkəndait], *ag.* 1. recondito 2. oscuro; astruso: *a* — *author*, un autore oscuro; — *studies*, studi astrusi.

reconditely [riˈkəndaitli], *av.* 1. in modo recondito, di nascosto 2. oscuramente; astrusamente.

reconditeness [riˈkəndaitnis], *s.* (*rar.*) 1. occultamento 2. astrusità; oscurità.

to **recondition** [ˈriːkənˈdiʃən], *v.t.* ripristinare; rimettere in efficienza; revisionare.

reconditioned [ˈriːkənˈdiʃənd], *ag.* ripristinato; revisionato: — *car*, automobile revisionata.

to **reconduct** [ˈriːkənˈdʌkt], *v.t.* ricondurre.

reconnaissance [riˈkənisəns], *s.* 1. (*mil.*) ricognizione, esplorazione: — *in force*, ricognizione in mas-

sa; *to go on a* —, andare in ricognizione 2. (*mil.*) pattuglia di ricognizione 3. esame preliminare, sopraluogo.

to **reconnect** [ˈriːkəˈnekt], *v.t.* (*elett.*) riallacciare.

to **reconnoitre** [ˌrekəˈnɔitə*], *v.t.i.* fare una ricognizione, essere in ricognizione; perlustrare; esplorare; fare una indagine.

reconnoitrer [ˌrekəˈnɔitrə*], *s.* ricognitore; esploratore.

reconnoitring [ˌrekəˈnɔitriŋ], *ag.* esplorativo ‖ *s.* ricognizione; perlustrazione.

to **reconquer** [ˈriːˈkəŋkə*], *v.t.* riconquistare.

reconquest [ˈriːˈkəŋkwest], *s.* riconquista.

to **reconsecrate** [ˈriːˈkənsikreit], *v.t.* riconsacrare.

to **reconsider** [ˈriːkənˈsidə*], *v.t.* riconsiderare; riesaminare.

reconsideration [ˈriːkənˌsidəˈreiʃən], *s.* nuovo esame, revisione.

reconstituent [ˈriːkənˈstitjuənt], *ag.s.* (*farm.*) ricostituente.

to **reconstitute** [ˈriːˈkənstitjuːt], *v.t.* ricostituire.

reconstitution [ˈriːˌkənstiˈtjuːʃən], *s.* ricostituzione.

to **reconstruct** [ˈriːkənsˈtrʌkt], *v.t.* ricostruire.

reconstruction [ˈriːkənsˈtrʌkʃən], *s.* ricostruzione.

reconstructive [ˈriːkənsˈtrʌktiv], *ag.* ricostruttivo.

reconversion [ˈriːkənˈvəːʃən], *s.* riconversione.

to **reconvert** [ˈriːkənˈvəːt], *v.t.* riconvertire.

record [ˈrekɔːd], *s.* 1. nota, registrazione; documento; documentazione; testimonianza: — *of attendances*, registro delle presenze; — *of a deed*, registrazione di un atto; *failing of* —, mancata produzione di documenti; *matter of* —, fatto, cosa da registrarsi, degno di nota; *he can bear* — *to*, può testimoniare che; *keep a* — *of all your expenses*, prendi nota di tutte le spese; *we can find no* — *of it*, non vi è alcuna documentazione in merito; *to keep a detailed* — *of sthg.*, tenere una documentazione particolareggiata di ql.co.; *to keep to the* —, (*dir.*) attenersi ai fatti, alle cose più importanti ‖ *off the* —, ufficioso, non ufficiale ‖ *to be on* —, essere registrato ‖ *to put oneself on* —, (*amer.*) assicurarsi un posto nella storia ‖ *to travel out of the* —, (*dir.*) perdersi nei particolari 2. documento, atto pubblico; *pl.* annali, archivi: *the earliest records extant*, i più antichi documenti che ci siano pervenuti 3. curriculum vitae; fedina penale; passato: *he has a good* —, il suo stato di servizio è buono; *your* — *is against you*, il tuo passato ti è sfavorevole; *to have* (o *to show*) *a clean* —, avere la fedina pulita 4. (*spor.*) primato: *to beat* (o *to break* o *to cut*) *a* —, battere un primato; *to lower a* —, abbassare un primato 5. (*mus.*) disco ☆ — *changer*, cambiadischi automatico; — *-holder*, detentore di un primato; — *library*, discoteca; *Record Office*, Archivio di Stato; — *output*, produzione che costituisce un primato; — *player*, giradischi, grammofono; — *prices*, prezzi imbattibili ‖ *long-playing* —, disco microsolco; *service* —, stato di servizio; *speed* —, primato di velocità; *world* —, record mondiale.

to **record** [riˈkɔːd], *v.t.* 1. registrare; prendere atto di; mettere a verbale; mettere per iscritto: *he already has several convictions recorded against him*, ha già diverse condanne al suo attivo; *the result is worth recording*, il risultato merita di essere segnalato; *to have a deed recorded*, protocollare un atto 2. ricordare, perpetuare; narrare, riportare: *Livy records how...*, Tito Livio racconta, ci dice che...; *this stone records a famous battle*, questa pietra ricorda una celebre battaglia 3. indicare, marcare: *the temperature recorded was 5° C below zero*, la temperatura registrata era di 5° C sotto zero 4. incidere, registrare: *to* — *an opera*, incidere un'opera; *to* — *on tape*, registrare su nastro 5. (*poet.*) cantare sommessamente (di uccelli) ☆ *recorded music*, musica riprodotta.

recordable [riˈkɔːdəbl], *ag.* 1. registrabile; degno di essere ricordato 2. che può essere inciso.

recordation [ˌrekəˈdeiʃən], *s.* (*poet.*) ricordo; commemorazione.

recorder[1] [ri'kɔ:də*], s. **1.** (*dir.*) consigliere civile e giudiziario (di una città) **2.** cancelliere; archivista **3.** registratore; apparecchio registratore ☆ *altitude* —, (*aer.*) registratore di quota, altimetro registratore; *flight path* —, (*aer.*) registratore di rotta; *tape* — (o *wire* —), magnetofono a nastro.

recorder[2], s. (*arc. mus.*) flauto.

recording [ri'kɔ:diŋ], *ag.* registrante, registratore ‖ *s.* registrazione; incisione fonografica; *a new* — *of Beethoven's quartets*, una nuova incisione fonografica dei quartetti di Beethoven ☆ — *angel*, angelo che registra le buone e cattive azioni degli uomini; — *apparatus*, apparecchio registratore; — *room*, cabina di registrazione; — *speed*, velocità d'incisione ‖ *tape* —, registrazione su nastro.

to **recount**[1] [ri'kaunt], *v.t.* raccontare dettagliatamente; fare una relazione dettagliata di.

to **re-count**[2] ['ri:'kaunt], *v.t.* contare di nuovo.

to **recoup** [ri'ku:p], *v.t.i.* **1.** risarcire, indennizzare: *to* — *a person for a loss*, risarcire una persona per una perdita **2.** (*dir.*) dedurre, trattenere (parte di una somma); fare una deduzione.

recoupment [ri'ku:pmənt], s. **1.** indennizzo, rimborso, risarcimento **2.** (*dir.*) trattenuta.

recourse [ri'kɔ:s], s. **1.** ricorso: — *to liquor is worse than* — *to smoke*, ricorrere agli alcoolici è peggio che ricorrere al fumo; *to have* — *to*, far ricorso a, ricorrere a: *to have* — *to legal proceedings*, ricorrere alle vie legali, adire il tribunale ‖ *without* —, (*comm.*) senza rivalsa (di cambiale) **2.** risorsa, espediente: *his usual* — *is wit*, l'umorismo è la sua solita risorsa.

recover[1] [ri'kʌvə*], s. (*scherma*) ripresa di attacco.

to **recover**[1], *v.t.i.* **1.** ricuperare; riacquistare; riguadagnare; riprendere; riavere: *the child recovered his appetite*, il bambino ritrovò il suo appetito; *she recovered his affection*, riguadagnò il suo affetto; *to* — *lost time*, ricuperare il tempo perduto ‖ *to* — *one's legs*, rimettersi in piedi (dopo una caduta) ‖ *to be recovered to life*, essere restituito alla vita **2.** ritrovare, riscoprire: *he managed to* — *the umbrella he had lost*, riuscì a trovare l'ombrello che aveva perduto **3.** ristabilirsi, rimettersi, guarire; riaversi; riprendersi: *he recovered (his health)*, riacquistò la salute; *to* — *(oneself)*, riprendere i sensi, riaversi; *to* — *from agitation, from fears*, riaversi da agitazioni, da timori; *to be recovered from an illness*, essere guarito da una malattia **4.** (*arc.*) raggiungere; far ritorno **5.** (*dir.*) ottenere (risarcimenti, riparazioni); ottenere un giudizio a proprio favore; vincere una causa: *to* — *damages*, ottenere il risarcimento dei danni.

to **re-cover**[2] ['ri:'kʌvə*], *v.t.* ricoprire, coprire di nuovo.

recoverable [ri'kʌvərəbl], *ag.* **1.** ricuperabile; ritrovabile **2.** guaribile.

recovery [ri'kʌvəri], s. **1.** ricupero, ritrovamento **2.** guarigione: *a prompt* —, una pronta guarigione ‖ *past* —, incurabile **3.** (*comm. dir.*) ricupero; miglioramento; ripresa economica: — *of a credit*, ricupero di un credito; *liable to* —, suscettibile di miglioramento ‖ *European Recovery Program*, Programma di Ricostruzione Europea **4.** (*scherma*) ripresa d'attacco.

recreance[1] ['rekriəns], s. ricreazione, ristoro.

recreance[2], **recreancy** ['rekriənsi], s. **1.** viltà, codardia **2.** apostasia.

recreant ['rekriənt], *ag.s.* (*poet.*) **1.** vile, codardo **2.** rinnegato.

recreantly ['rekriəntli], *av.* **1.** vilmente, codardamente **2.** proditoriamente.

to **recreate**[1] ['rekrieit], *v.t.i.* divertire, divertirsi; rianimare: *to* — *(oneself) with sthg., with doing sthg.*, divertirsi con ql.co., facendo ql.co.

to **re-create**[2] ['ri:-kri'eit], *v.t.* ricreare, creare di nuovo.

recreation[1] [,rekri'eiʃən], s. ricreazione, divertimento, svago: *some people look upon gardening as a* —, alcuni considerano il giardinaggio come uno svago.

re-creation[2] ['ri:-kri'eiʃən], s. nuova creazione.

recreational [,rekri'eiʃənl], *ag.* ricreativo: — *activities*, attività ricreative.

recreative[1] ['rekrieitiv], *ag.* ricreativo; divertente.

recreative[2] ['ri:-kri'eitiv], *ag.* che crea di nuovo.

recrement ['rekrimənt], s. **1.** (*rar.*) rifiuto; scoria **2.** (*fisiol.*) secrezione riassorbita nel sangue.

recrementitious [,rekrimen'tiʃəs], *ag.* **1.** di rifiuto **2.** (*fisiol.*) di secrezione riassorbita nel sangue.

to **recriminate** [ri'krimineit], *v.i.* recriminare.

recrimination [ri,krimi'neiʃən], s. recriminazione.

recriminative [ri'kriminətiv], **recriminatory** [ri'kriminətəri], *ag.* recriminatorio.

to **recross** [ri'krɔs], *v.t.* riattraversare.

to **recrudesce** [,ri:-kru'des], *v.i.* rincrudire; essere in stato di recrudescenza.

recrudescence [,ri:-kru'desns], **recrudescency** [,ri:-kru'desnsi], s. recrudescenza.

recrudescent [,ri:-kru'desnt], *ag.* che rincrudisce.

recruit [ri'kru:t], s. **1.** (*mil.*) recluta **2.** proselito **3.** principiante, novizio ‖ *raw* —, novellino.

to **recruit**, *v.t.i.* **1.** (*mil.*) reclutare **2.** fare proseliti **3.** rinforzare; rinvigorire; ovviare a deficienze in **4.** ristabilirsi, riacquistare la salute.

recruital [ri'kru:tl], s. ricupero, riacquisto (di forza, salute, ecc.).

recruitment [ri'kru:tmənt], s. **1.** reclutamento **2.** rinvigorimento.

rectal ['rektəl], *ag.* (*anat.*) rettale.

rectangle ['rek,tæŋgl], s. (*geom.*) rettangolo.

rectangular [rek'tæŋgjulə*], *ag.* rettangolare.

rectangularity [rek,tæŋgju'læriti], s. l'essere rettangolare.

rectangularly [rek'tæŋgjuləli], *av.* in forma rettangolare; ad angolo retto.

rectifiable ['rektifaiəbl], *ag.* rettificabile.

rectification [,rektifi'keiʃən], s. rettificazione.

rectifier ['rektifaiə*], *s.c.* rettificatore, rettificatrice ‖ *s.* **1.** (*elett.*) raddrizzatore **2.** (*rad.*) rivelatore.

to **rectify** ['rektifai], *v.t.* **1.** rettificare, correggere **2.** (*chim. geom.*) rettificare **3.** (*mec.*) rettificare **4.** (*elett. rad.*) raddrizzare.

rectilineal [,rekti'liniəl], **rectilinear** [,rekti'liniə*], *ag.* rettilineo.

rectilinearity [,rekti,lini'æriti], s. l'essere rettilineo.

rectilinearly [,rekti'liniəli], *av.* in linea retta.

rectitude ['rektitju:d], s. **1.** rettitudine, dirittura **2.** (*rar.*) correttezza, giustezza.

recto ['rektou], s. (*tip.*) recto, pagina anteriore.

rector ['rektə*], s. **1.** rettore di parrocchia anglicana; superiore (di istituto religioso) **2.** rettore (di università); direttore, preside (di scuola, collegio).

rectorate ['rektərit], s. rettorato.

rectorial [rek'tɔ:riəl], *ag.* di rettore.

rectorship ['rektəʃip], s. rettorato.

rectory ['rektəri], s. **1.** presbiterio; rettoria; canonica **2.** beneficio, prebenda.

rectress ['rektris], s. **1.** direttrice, preside (di scuola) **2.** (*fam.*) moglie di rettore.

rectum ['rektəm], s. (*anat.*) retto.

recumbency [ri'kʌmbənsi], s. **1.** l'essere appoggiato, sdraiato, coricato **2.** (*rar.*) fiducia.

recumbent [ri'kʌmbənt], *ag.* **1.** appoggiato; supino, adagiato, sdraiato **2.** (*amer.*) in riposo; inoperoso.

recumbently [ri'kʌmbəntli], *av.* in posizione supina.

to **recuperate** [ri'kju:pəreit], *v.t.i.* **1.** ristabilire, ristabilirsi; ricuperare (le forze); guarire: *to* — *one's health*, ristabilirsi in salute **2.** riguadagnare, rifarsi.

recuperation [ri,kju:pə'reiʃən], s. ricupero; ripresa; guarigione.

recuperative [ri'kju:pərətiv], *ag.* **1.** ricuperatore, rigeneratore **2.** (*mec.*) di ricupero ‖ *s.* sostanza fertilizzante.

recuperator [ri'kju:pəreitə*], s. (*mec. mil.*) ricuperatore ☆ *spring* —, (*mec.*) ricuperatore a molla.

to **recur** [ri'kə:*], *pass.p.p.* **recurred** [ri'kə:d], *v.i.* **1.** ricorrere; riaccadere; ripresentarsi: *a problem* *which recurs periodically*, un problema che ricorre periodicamente; *to — to the mind*, ripresentarsi alla mente (di idea) **2.** ritornare: *to — to our former subject*, per ritornare al nostro precedente argomento.

recurrence [ri'kʌrəns], *s.* ricorso; ricorrenza; ritorno (periodico); ripresa.

recurrent [ri'kʌrənt], *ag.* **1.** ricorrente; periodico **2.** (*anat. bot.*) ricorrente ☆ — *artery, nerve*, arteria, nervo ricorrente; — *fever*, febbre periodica.

recurrently [ri'kʌrəntli], *av.* con ricorrenza; periodicamente.

recurring [ri'kə:riŋ], *ag.* ricorrente; periodico ☆ — *decimals*, frazioni decimali periodiche.

recurvate [ri:'kə:vit], *ag.* ricurvo.

recurvature [ri:'kə:vətʃə*], *s.* curva, curvatura all'indietro.

to **recurve** [ri:'kə:v], *v.t.i.* curvare, curvarsi all'indietro.

recusance ['rekjuzəns], **recusancy** ['rekjuzənsi], *s.* **1.** ricusa; rifiuto **2.** (*st. inglese*) rifiuto dei cattolici di assistere alle funzioni religiose della Chiesa Anglicana.

recusant ['rekjuzənt], *ag.* dissidente, dissenziente || *s. c.* **1.** (*st.inglese*) cattolico, cattolica che si rifiutava di assistere alle funzioni religiose della Chiesa Anglicana **2.** chi rifiuta di sottomettersi ad un'autorità; dissenziente.

to **recuse** [ri'kju:z], *v.t.* (*rar.*) ricusare; opporsi a.

red [red], *comp.* **redder** ['redə*], *superl.* **reddest** ['redist], *ag.* **1.** rosso: — *with anger*, rosso di collera; *to turn* (o *to go*) —, arrossire (di persona); arrossare, diventar rosso (di cosa); imporporarsi (di cielo) || *Red Cross*, Croce Rossa || *Red Ensign*, bandiera della Marina mercantile Britannica || *The Red Sea*, il Mar Rosso || *it is a — rag to him*, ciò lo rende furioso, gli fa vedere rosso || *to paint the town —*, (*sl.*) fare schiamazzi, far baldoria || — *-currant*, (*bot.*) ribes **2.** (*letter.*) insanguinato; cruento: — *battle*, battaglia cruenta; — *hands*, mani insanguinate **3.** (*pol.*) anarchico; « rosso »; comunista; sovietico: — *ideas*, idee comuniste || *the Red Army*, l'esercito sovietico || *s.* **1.** color rosso: *to be* (*dressed*) *in* —, essere vestito di rosso || *the —, white and blue*, (*fam.*) la Marina Britannica || *to be in the* —, (*amer.*) avere il conto scoperto, essere passivo || *to see* —, *fig.* veder rosso **2.** palla rossa (del biliardo) **3.** (*pol.*) anarchico; comunista, sovietico || *the Reds*, i comunisti ☆ — *admiral*, (*entom.*) vanessa atalanta; — *-blooded*, vigoroso; — *-book*, libro rosso (almanacco della nobiltà inglese); — *-brick*, (*neol. sl.*) università di recente fondazione; — *-cap*, (*sl. mil.*) soldato della polizia militare; — *cent*, (*amer. fam.*) centesimo: *I don't care a — cent*, non me ne importa un bel niente; — *flag*, bandiera rossa; — *-haired*, dai capelli rossi; — *-handed*, con le mani insanguinate: *to catch a person — -handed*, (*fam.*) cogliere una persona in flagrante, con le mani nel sacco; — *-hat*, cappello cardinalizio; (*sl.*) ufficiale di stato maggiore; — *-head*, persona rossa di capelli; — *herring*, aringa affumicata: *to draw a — herring across the track*, *fig.* sviare la conversazione; — *-hot*, rovente; *fig.* entusiastico, ardente; *Indian* (o — *-man*), pellerossa; — *-lead*, minio; — *-letter day*, giorno festivo; *fig.* giorno memorabile; — *-light*, segnale rosso di pericolo; (*aut.*) luci rosse: *to see the — light*, *fig.* rendersi conto di un pericolo imminente; — *meat*, carne al sangue; manzo; — *mullet*, (*ittiol.*) triglia; — *pepper*, pepe di Caienna; — *ribbon*, (*st.*) nastro rosso (insegna dell'Ordine del Bagno); — *-tape*, nastro rosso (usato negli uffici statali); *fig.* burocrazia; — *-tapery* (o — *-tapism*), burocrazia; — *-tapist*, burocrate || *blood-* —, rosso sangue; *cherry* —, rosso ciliegia; *fire* — (o *flame* —), rosso fiamma.

to **redact** [ri'dækt], *v.t.* redigere; sistemare per la pubblicazione.

redaction [ri'dækʃən], *s.* **1.** redazione; revisione **2.** nuova edizione.

redactor [ri'dæktə*], *s.* redattore; revisore.

redan [ri'dæn], *s.* (*mil.*) saliente.

redbreast ['redbrest], *s.* (*ornit.*) pettirosso.

redcoat ['redkout], *s.* (*st.*) soldato inglese.

to **redd** [red] *v.t.* (*scoz.*) pulire; ordinare; sistemare.

to **redden** ['redn], *v.t.i.* **1.** arrossare; rendere rosso **2.** arrossire; fare arrossare.

reddish ['rediʃ], *ag.* rossiccio, rossastro.

reddle ['redl], *s.* ocra rossa.

to **reddle**, *v.t.* colorare con ocra rossa.

rede [ri:d], *s.* (*arc.*) **1.** consiglio **2.** piano, progetto **3.** racconto.

to **rede**, *v.t.* (*arc.*) **1.** consigliare **2.** interpretare (sogni); spiegare (indovinelli).

to **redeem** [ri'di:m], *v.t.* **1.** riscattare, svincolare: *to — a debt*, liberarsi da un debito; *to — a mortgage*, estinguere un'ipoteca; *to — one's watch from pawn*, riscattare il proprio orologio **2.** mantenere (una promessa) **3.** liberare; redimere; salvare: *Christ redeemed us*, Cristo ci ha redenti; *he has one redeeming feature*, ha un particolare che lo salva **4.** ricuperare; compensare; controbilanciare: *to — the time*, ricuperare il tempo perduto.

redeemable [ri'di:məbl], *ag.* **1.** redimibile, riscattabile **2.** rimborsabile **3.** ricuperabile.

redeemer [ri'di:mə*], *s.* redentore; liberatore || *the Redeemer*, il Redentore.

redemption [ri'dempʃən], *s.* **1.** (*relig.*) redenzione: *Christ was the — of human kind*, Cristo fu la salvezza dell'umanità || *in the 500th year of our —*, nell'anno di grazia 500 **2.** liberazione; riscatto; salvezza || *it is beyond* (o *past* o *without*) —, non vi è scampo **3.** (*comm.*) rimborso; estinzione; ammortamento: — *before due date*, rimborso anticipato.

redemptive [ri'demptiv], *ag.* che redime.

redemptor [ri'demptə*], *s.* redentore.

to **redescend** ['ri:-di'send], *v.i.* ridiscendere.

redingote ['rediŋgout], *s.* **1.** « redingote » (sorta di soprabito da signora) **2.** prefettizia, finanziera.

to **redintegrate** [re'dintigreit], *v.t.* reintegrare; ristabilire: *to — s.o. in his possessions*, reintegrare qlcu. nei suoi possedimenti.

redintegration [re,dinti'greiʃən], *s.* reintegrazione.

to **redirect** ['ri:-di'rekt], *v.t.* indirizzare di nuovo.

redirection ['ri:-di'rekʃən], *s.* nuovo indirizzo.

to **rediscover** ['ri:-dis'kʌvə*], *v.t.* riscoprire; ritrovare.

rediscovery ['ri:-dis'kʌvəri], *s.* nuova scoperta.

redness ['rednis], *s.* rossore; color rosso.

redolence ['redouləns], *s.* profumo, fragranza.

redolent ['redoulənt], *ag.* **1.** profumato, fragrante: — *of Spring*, fragrante di primavera **2.** *fig.* suggestivo.

to **redouble** [ri'dʌbl], *v.t.i.* **1.** raddoppiare, aumentare, intensificare **2.** (*bridge*) surcontrare.

redoubt [ri'daut], *s.* (*mil.*) ridotto; fortino.

redoubtable [ri'dautəbl], *ag.* formidabile; temibile.

redoubted [ri'dautid], *ag.* (*arc.*) formidabile; temuto.

to **redound** [ri'daund], *v.i.* **1.** contribuire; tornare (a vantaggio); risultare: *it will — to your advantage, to your credit*, tornerà a vostro vantaggio, a vostro credito **2.** ricadere.

redox ['redoks], *s.* (*chim.*) ossiriduzione.

redress[1] [ri'dres], *s.* riparazione (di un torto); soddisfazione: *injury beyond —*, torto irreparabile.

to **redress**[1], *v.t.* **1.** riparare; rettificare; rimediare: *to — wrongs*, riparare torti || *a fault confessed is half redressed*, prov. peccato confessato è mezzo perdonato **2.** correggere; raddrizzare.

to **redress**[2] ['ri:'dres], *v.t.i.* rivestire; rivestirsi.

redskin ['red-skin], *s.* pellerossa.

to **reduce** [ri'dju:s], *v.t.i.* **1.** ridurre (di formato, di numero, ecc.): *the new governor will — taxes*, il nuovo governatore ridurrà le imposte **2.** (*fam.*) dimagrire: *if you want to — you have to go on a diet*, se vuoi dimagrire devi metterti a dieta **3.** ridurre (in una determinata condizione): *the revolted towns were reduced to submission*, le città ribelli furono ridotte alla sottomissione **4.** (*chir. mat. chim.*) ridurre: *to — a broken bone*, ridurre una frattura; *to — an equation*, ridurre un'equazione **5.** (*mil.*) degradare; retrocedere di rango: *to — a sergeant to the ranks*, degradare un sergente a soldato semplice **6.** costringere: *he was reduced to borrow clothes,* fu costretto a prendere vestiti a prestito; *to — to discipline,* ridurre alla disciplina.

reduced [ri'dju:st], *ag.* ridotto: *— prices,* prezzi ridotti; *— scale,* scala ridotta ‖ *in — circumstances,* in povertà; in strettezze.

reducer [ri'dju:sə*], *s.* **1.** riduttore, dispositivo di riduzione **2.** (*idraulica*) giunto di riduzione **3.** (*chim.*) agente riducente, deossidante.

reducibility [ri,dju:sə'biliti], *s.* riducibilità.

reducible [ri'dju:səbl], *ag.* riducibile.

reducibly [ri'dju:səbli], *av.* riducibilmente.

reduction [ri'dʌkʃən], *s.* **1.** riduzione; ribasso: *great reductions in prices,* grandi ribassi dei prezzi **2.** riduzione su piccola scala (di disegno, carta geografica) **3.** dimagrimento **4.** (*mat. chir. chim.*) riduzione **5.** (*mil.*) degradazione.

reductional [ri'dʌkʃənl], *ag.* (*amer.*) di riduzione.

reductive [ri'dʌktiv], *ag.* che serve a ridurre; tendente a ridurre.

reduit [rə'dwi:], *s.* (*mil.*) fortino.

redundance [ri'dʌndəns], **redundancy** [ri'dʌndənsi], *s.* sovrabbondanza; ridonanza: *the — of labour,* la sovrabbondanza di mano d'opera.

redundant [ri'dʌndənt], *ag.* sovrabbondante, ridondante: *— style, words,* stile, parole ridondanti.

redundantly [ri'dʌndəntli], *av.* sovrabbondantemente; ridondantemente.

reduplicate [ri'dju:plikit], *ag.* doppio; raddoppiato.

to **reduplicate** [ri'dju:plikeit], *v.t.* raddoppiare; ripetere.

reduplication [ri,dju:pli'keiʃən], *s.* raddoppiamento; ripetizione.

reduplicative [ri'dju:plikətiv], *ag.* tendente al raddoppiamento, alla ripetizione.

redwing ['redwiŋ], *s.* (*ornit.*) tordo.

redwood ['redwud], *s.* **1.** sequoia **2.** legno rosato (di sandalo, ecc.).

to **re-dye** ['ri:'dai], *v.t.* ritingere.

reebok ['ri:bok], *s.* (*zool.*) pelea (specie di antilope).

to **re-echo** [ri(:)'ekou], *v.t.i.* (far) riecheggiare.

reed [ri:d], *s.* **1.** canna, giunco ‖ *to lean on a —,* *fig.* fare assegnamento su cosa, persona molto debole ‖ *broken —,* persona, cosa infida **2.** cannicci, canne per formare tetti **3.** (*poet.*) dardo, strale **4.** (*poet.*) zampogna; *fig.* poesia pastorale **5.** (*mus.*) linguetta, ancia (di strumenti a fiato) **6.** (*ind. tessile*) pettine (di telaio) ☆ *— -mace,* (*bot.*) coda di gatto; *— -organ,* armonium; *— -pheasant,* (*ornit.*) cincia barbuta; *— -pipe,* zampogna; canna d'organo; *— -sparrow,* (*ornit.*) passero dei canneti.

to **reed,** *v.t.* **1.** ricoprire (un tetto) con cannicci, decorare con giunchi **2.** fornire (uno strumento musicale) di linguetta, di ancia.

reeded ['ri:did], *ag.* **1.** coperto di canne **2.** fornito di ancia (di strumento musicale).

re-edification ['ri:,edifi'keiʃən], *s.* riedificazione, ricostruzione.

to **re-edify** ['ri:'edifai], *v.t.* riedificare.

reediness ['ri:dinis], *s.* **1.** abbondanza di canne **2.** *fig.* esilità; debolezza **3.** acutezza (di voce).

to **re-edit** ['ri:'edit], *v.t.* ripubblicare, apprestare una nuova edizione di.

re-edition ['ri:i'diʃən], *s.* riedizione, nuova edizione.

reedling ['ri:dliŋ], *s.* (*ornit.*) cincia barbuta.

to **re-educate** ['ri:'edju(:)keit], *v.t.* rieducare.

re-education ['ri:,edju(:)'keiʃən], *s.* rieducazione.

reedy ['ri:di], *ag.* **1.** folto di canne **2.** fatto di canne: *a — couch,* un giaciglio di canne **3.** esile; debole **4.** acuto (di voce).

reef[1] [ri:f], *pl.* **reefs** [ri:fs], *s.* (*mar.*) terzaruolo ‖ *to take in a —,* *fig.* agire con cautela; ridurre il tenore di vita ☆ *— -knot,* nodo piano; *— -point,* matafione di terzaruolo.

to **reef**[1], *v.t.* **1.** (*mar.*) terzarolare **2.** accorciare.

reef[2], *s.* **1.** scoglio, scogliera, frangente; secca; ban-

co **2.** (*miner.*) filone di quarzo aurifero ☆ *coral- —* banco di coralli ‖ *lagoon- —,* atollo.

reefer ['ri:fə*], *s.* **1.** chi fa terzaruolo; (*sl.*) guardiamarina **2.** giacchetta a doppio petto **3.** nodo di terzaruolo **4.** (*sl. amer.*) sigaretta alla marijuana.

reefy ['ri:fi], *ag.* pieno di scogli.

reek [ri:k], *s.* **1.** (*scoz. letter.*) fumo; vapore; esalazione **2.** puzzo, fetore.

to **reek,** *v.i.* **1.** fumare, emettere fumo **2.** evaporare; esalare vapore; trasudare **3.** puzzare: *he reeks of whisky,* puzza di whisky ‖ *this story reeks of murder,* questo affare puzza di assassinio.

reekie, reeky ['ri:ki], *ag.* (*scoz. letter.*) affumicato; fumoso ‖ *Auld Reekie,* (*scoz. fam.*) la Vecchia Fumosa (Edimburgo).

reel[1] [ri:l], *s.* **1.** rocchetto, bobina ‖ *off the —,* rapidamente, tutto d'un fiato **2.** mulinello (di canna da pesca) **3.** (*cine.*) rotolo, bobina (di pellicola).

to **reel**[1], *v.t.i.* **1.** innaspare; avvolgere **2.** frinire (di cavallette, grilli) **3.** *to — off,* sdipanare ‖ *to — off a list of names,* snocciolare una lista di nomi.

reel[2], *s.* giro vorticoso; barcollamento; vacillamento; oscillazione; ondeggiamento.

to **reel**[2], *v.i.* **1.** girare, roteare, turbinare; barcollare, vacillare; oscillare: *he went reeling down the path,* si avviò barcollando giù per il sentiero **2.** *fig.* girare; vacillare: *I feel so ill that my eyes are reeling,* mi sento così male che vedo girare tutto intorno a me; *my head reels,* mi gira la testa.

reel[3], *s.* « reel » (vivace danza scozzese).

to **reel**[3], *v.i.* ballare un « reel ».

to **re-elect** ['ri:i'lekt], *v.t.* rieleggere.

re-election ['ri:i'lekʃən], *s.* rielezione.

reeler ['ri:lə*], *s.* pellicola cinematografica ☆ *two- —, three- —, four- —,* film composto di due, tre, quattro rotoli di pellicola.

re-eligible ['ri:'elidʒəbl], *ag.* rieleggibile.

reeling ['ri:liŋ], *ag.* barcollante; roteante ‖ *s.* barcollamento; passo vacillante.

reelingly ['ri:liŋli], *av.* vacillando; barcollando.

to **re-emerge** ['ri:i'mə:dʒ], *v.i.* riemergere.

to **re-enable** ['ri:i'neibl], *v.t.* rimettere in grado.

to **re-enact** ['ri:i'nækt], *v.t.* **1.** rimettere in vigore (una legge) **2.** riprodurre (una scena).

to **re-enforce** ['ri:in'fo:s], *v.t.* **1.** (*amer.*) per to **reinforce 2.** rimettere in vigore (una legge).

re-enforcement ['ri:in'fo:smənt], (*amer.*) per **reinforcement.**

to **re-enter** ['ri:'entə*], *v.t.i.* **1.** rientrare; presentarsi di nuovo: *to — for an examination,* presentarsi di nuovo ad un esame **2.** registrare di nuovo.

re-entrance ['ri:'entrəns], *s.* rientrata; rientramento.

re-entrant ['ri:'entrənt], *ag.* rientrante ‖ *s.* angolo rientrante.

re-entry ['ri:'entri], *s.* **1.** rientro (anche al giuoco del bridge) **2.** nuova registrazione.

to **re-establish** ['ri:is'tæbliʃ], *v.t.* ristabilire; restaurare: *to — the king's authority,* restaurare l'autorità del re; *to — s.o. in public esteem,* riabilitare qlcu. nella pubblica opinione ‖ *to — one's health,* ristabilirsi.

re-establishment ['ri:is'tæbliʃmənt], *s.* ristabilimento; restaurazione.

reeve[1] [ri:v], *s.* **1.** (*st.*) alto magistrato (di città, provincia) **2.** presidente del consiglio municipale in zone rurali (in Canada) **3.** (*eccl.*) piccolo funzionario.

reeve[2], *s.* (*ornit.*) pavoncella pugnace.

to **reeve**[3], *pass.p.p.* **rove** [rouv], **reeved** [ri:vd], *v.t.* (*mar.*) **1.** assicurare, passare una corda attraverso a **2.** superare (secca, banchisa di ghiacci).

re-examination ['ri:ig,zæmi'neiʃən], *s.* **1.** nuovo esame **2.** (*dir.*) nuovo interrogatorio.

to **re-examine** ['ri:ig'zæmin], *v.t.* **1.** riesaminare **2.** (*dir.*) interrogare di nuovo (un testimonio).

re-export ['ri:'ekspo:t], *s.* riesportazione.

to **re-export** ['ri:eks'po:t], *v.t.* riesportare.

re-exportation [ˈriːˌekspɔːˈteiʃən], *s.* riesportazione.

to **reface** [riːˈfeis], *v.t.* rinnovare la facciata di (un edificio); ripararare (un muro).

to **refashion** [riːˈfæʃən], *v.t.* 1. rifoggiare, rimodellare 2. rimodernare.

re-fashionment [riːˈfæʃnmənt], *s.* rimodernamento, rifacimento.

refection [riˈfekʃən], *s.* refezione; ristoro, rinfresco.

refectory [riˈfektəri], *s.* refettorio.

to **refer** [riˈfəː*], *pass.p.p.* **referred** [riˈfəːd], *v. t.i.* 1. attribuire; assegnare: *I — my ill temper to indigestion*, attribuisco il mio malumore a cattiva digestione; *to — the origins of sculpture to Egypt*, attribuire le origini della scultura all'Egitto 2. riferire, riferirsi, alludere; ricorrere, appellarsi, rivolgersi: *he referred to his sister*, si rivolse a sua sorella; *he referred to his watch for the exact time*, consultò il suo orologio per sapere l'ora esatta; *is this the place you referred to?*, è questo il luogo a cui alludeste?; *it does not — to my subject*; ciò non ha alcun rapporto col mio argomento ‖ *referring to your letter*, con riferimento alla vostra lettera 3. rimettere, affidare: *I — myself to your generosity*, mi affido alla vostra generosità; *he will — the matter to a tribunal*, sottoporrà il fatto a un tribunale; *to — to an authority*, consultare un'autorità; *to — to drawer*, (*comm.*) rivolgersi al traente 4. rimandare (per informazioni): *I — you to Messrs. Smith*, per informazioni vogliate rivolgervi alla Ditta Smith; *to — the reader to a foot-note*, rimandare il lettore a una nota in calce.

referable [riˈfərəbl], *ag.* riferibile; attribuibile; assegnabile.

referee [ˌrefəˈriː], *s.* 1. (*spor.*) arbitro 2. (*dir.*) giudice; arbitro 3. (*comm.*) garante.

to **referee**, *pass.p.p.* **refereed** [ˌrefəˈriːd], *v.t.i.* (*spor.*) fare da arbitro, arbitrare.

reference [ˈrefrəns], *s.* 1. (*dir.*) il deferire, il sottomettere (una questione) ad autorità per la decisione; ricorso ad arbitrato: *measures were taken without — to the king*, si presero provvedimenti senza rimetterne la decisione al re 2. riferimento; relazione, rapporto: *in* (o *with*) *— to*, con riferimento a 3. allusione, menzione, accenno; riferimento; richiamo: *— was made to your new book*, si accennò al tuo nuovo libro; *this writer loads his books with references*, questo scrittore appesantisce i suoi libri con frequenti citazioni 4. consultazione: *— to a dictionary is necessary when you translate*, è necessario consultare un dizionario quando si traduce 5. raccomandazione; benservito; referenza; informazione: *I allowed him to use my name as —*, gli permisi di usare il mio nome come referenza; *to take up s.o.'s references*, prendere informazioni su qlcu. ‖ *these gentlemen are my references*, questi signori sono miei garanti 6. competenza, potere: *this is outside the — of our committee*, ciò esula dalla competenza della nostra commissione ☆ *— book* (o *-work*), libro di consultazione; *— library*, biblioteca di consultazione; *— -mark*, segno di rimando; *— sample*, (*comm.*) campione di riferimento ‖ *cross- —*, rimando ad altra pagina, a passo della stessa opera.

referendary [ˌrefəˈrendəri], *s.* (*rar.*) 1. referendario 2. arbitro.

referendum [ˌrefəˈrendəm], *s.* referendum: *to call a —*, indire un referendum.

referential [ˌrefəˈrenʃəl], *ag.* di riferimento; di referenza.

refill [ˈriːˌfil], *s.* ricambio ☆ *ball-point pen —*, ricambio di penna a sfera.

to **refill** [ˈriːˈfil], *v.t.i.* riempire, riempirsi di nuovo; rifornire; ricaricare.

to **refine** [riˈfain], *v.t.i.* 1. raffinare, purificare: *to — sugar*, raffinare lo zucchero 2. *fig.* raffinare, raffinarsi; perfezionare, perfezionarsi: *to — one's mind, one's style, one's taste*, raffinare la propria mente, il proprio stile, il proprio gusto 3. sottilizzare: *to — (up)on a question*, sottilizzare su una questione.

refined [riˈfaind], *ag.* 1. raffinato, purificato 2. *fig.* raffinato, perfezionato; fine; forbito; ricercato: *— cruelty*, crudeltà raffinata; *— manners*, modi ricercati ☆ *— sugar*, zucchero raffinato.

refinedly [riˈfainidli], *av.* raffinatamente, elegantemente; ricercatamente.

refinedness [riˈfainidnis], *s.* raffinatezza.

refinement [riˈfainmənt], *s.* 1. (*ind.*) raffinamento, raffinazione 2. *fig.* raffinatezza, finezza; perfezionamento; ricercatezza: *the refinements of luxury*, le raffinatezze del lusso; *a person of —*, una persona raffinata 3. sottigliezza (di ragionamento).

refiner [riˈfainə*], *s.c.* 1. raffinatore, raffinatrice 2. purificatore, purificatrice.

refinery [riˈfainəri], *s.* raffineria.

refit [ˈriːˈfit], *s.* (*spec. mar.*) raddobbo.

to **refit**, *pass.p.p.* **refitted** [ˈriːˈfitid], *v.t.i.* 1. riparare, riattare 2. (*mar.*) subire riparazioni; raddobbare.

refitment [ˈriːˈfitmənt], *s.* (*spec. mar.*) raddobbo, riparazione.

reflation [riː(ˈ)ˈfleiʃən], *s.* (*econ.*) nuova inflazione (dopo una deflazione).

to **reflect** [riˈflekt], *v.t.i.* 1. riflettere, riflettersi; rispecchiare: *the mirror reflected the girl*, lo specchio rifletteva la ragazza; *to shine with reflected light*, brillare di luce riflessa 2. *fig.* riflettere, riflettersi; rispecchiare; ripercuotersi, ricadere: *his rudeness reflects only on himself*, la sua villania nuoce solo a lui stesso; *the play reflects the ideas of the century*, il dramma rispecchia le idee del secolo; *this reflects credit on you*, questo torna a tuo credito; *this will — upon you*, questo ricadrà su di voi 3. riflettere, meditare, pensare: *I — that my efforts have been useless*, penso che i miei sforzi siano stati vani; *I reflected (up)on the matter*, ho riflettuto sulla questione; *to — how, whether, why*, domandarsi come, se, perchè 4. (*rar.*) ripiegare: *to — the corner of the paper*, ripiegare l'angolo del foglio 5. gettare biasimo; dubitare: *he reflects (up)on our new method*, critica il nostro nuovo metodo; *to — (up)on s.o.'s honour*, fare insinuazioni sull'onore di qlcu.

reflectingly [riˈflektiŋli], *av.* riflessivamente.

reflection [riˈflekʃən], *s.* 1. riflessione; riflesso, riverbero; immagine riflessa: *angle of —*, angolo di riflessione; *to see one's — in a mirror*, vedere la propria immagine riflessa in uno specchio 2. (*fisiol.*) riflesso 3. riflessione, meditazione: *on —*, riflettendovi 4. censura, biasimo, critica: *to cast reflections on s.o.*, criticare, biasimare qlcu. 5. *pl.* pensieri, considerazioni: *reflections (up)on history*, considerazioni sulla storia.

reflective [riˈflektiv], *ag.* 1. riflessivo, meditativo 2. (*fis.*) riflettente 3. (*rar.*) riflesso 4. (*gram.*) riflessivo.

reflectively [riˈflektivli], *av.* riflessivamente.

reflectiveness [riˈflektivnis], *s.* capacità di riflessione.

reflector [riˈflektə*], *s.* 1. (*fis.*) riflettore 2. (*aut.*) catarifrangente 3. *fig.* specchio: *literature is a — of the age*, la letteratura è lo specchio di un'epoca ☆ *parabolic —*, riflettore parabolico.

reflex [ˈriːˈfleks], *ag.* 1. riflesso, indiretto (anche *fig.*): *— influence*, influenza riflessa; *— light*, luce riflessa 2. (*fisiol.*) riflesso 3. introspettivo 4. (*gram. rar.*) riflessivo 5. (*rar.*) ricurvo ‖ *s.* 1. riflesso (anche *fig.*): *his fame is but a pale — of that of his father*, la sua fama è solo un pallido riflesso di quella di suo padre 2. (*pitt.*) riflesso 3. (*fisiol.*) riflesso: *the doctor tested his patient's reflexes*, il dottore provò i riflessi del suo paziente ☆ *— camera*, (*foto.*) macchina fotografica reflex; *— movement*, movimento riflesso.

to **reflex** [riˈfleks], *v.t.* 1. riflettere 2. flettere all'indietro.

reflexed [riˈflekst], *ag.* (*bot.*) ricurvo.

reflexibility [riˌfleksiˈbiliti], *s.* riflessibilità.

reflexible [riˈfleksibl], *ag.* riflessibile.

reflexion, *V.* reflection.

reflexive [riˈfleksiv], *ag.s.* (*gram.*) riflessivo.

reflexively [riˈfleksivli], *av.* riflessivamente.

to **refloat** [ˈriːˈflout], *v.t.* rimettere a galla.

reflorescence [ˈriːfloˈresns], *s.* rifioritura.

to **reflow** [ˈriːˈflou], *v.i.* rifluire.

refluence [ˈrefluəns], *s.* riflusso.

refluent [ˈrefluənt], *ag.* rifluente ☆ — *tide*, (*mar.*) riflusso.

reflux [ˈriːflʌks], *s.* riflusso: *the flux and — of the tide*, il flusso e il riflusso della marea.

to **refoot** [ˈriːˈfut], *v.t.* rifare il piede a (una calza).

to **reforest** [ˈriːˈfɔrist], *v.t.* rimboschire, ricoprire di bosco.

reforestation [ˈriːfɔrisˈteiʃən], *s.* rimboschimento.

reform[1] [riˈfɔːm], *s.* riforma ‖ *the Reforms of 1831*, (*st.*) le riforme parlamentari del 1831 ☆ — *school*, riformatorio.

to **reform**[1], *v.t.i.* riformare; correggere, correggersi; emendare, emendarsi: *to — oneself*, correggersi.

to **reform**[2] [ˈriːˈfɔːm], *v.t.i.* formare di nuovo, formarsi di nuovo.

reformable [riˈfɔːməbl], *ag.* riformabile; correggibile.

reformation[1] [ˌrefəˈmeiʃən], *s.* riforma; emendamento ‖ *the Reformation*, (*st. relig.*) la Riforma.

reformation[2] [ˈriːfɔːˈmeiʃən], *s.* nuova formazione.

reformational [ˌrefəˈmeiʃənl], *ag.* relativo a riforma.

reformative [riˈfɔːmətiv], *ag.* riformativo; riformatore.

reformatory [riˈfɔːmətəri], *ag.* riformativo; riformatore ‖ *s.* riformatorio, casa di correzione.

reformed [riˈfɔːmd], *ag.* riformato; corretto; emendato ‖ *Reformed Churches*, Chiese riformate.

reformer [riˈfɔːmə*], *s.* riformatore.

reformist [riˈfɔːmist], *s.* (*pol.*) riformista.

to **refract** [riˈfrækt], *v.t.* 1. (*fis.*) rifrangere 2. (*chim.*) analizzare (il nitro) per determinare la percentuale di impurità.

refraction [riˈfrækʃən], *s.* (*fis.*) rifrazione.

refractional [riˈfrækʃənl], *ag.* (*fis.*) relativo a rifrazione.

refractive [riˈfræktiv], *ag.* (*fis.*) rifrattivo, rifrangente.

refractometer [ˌriːfrækˈtɔmitə*], *s.* (*fis.*) rifrattometro.

refractor [riˈfræktə*], *s.* (*fis.*) rifrattore.

refractorily [riˈfræktərili], *av.* 1. ostinatamente, caparbiamente 2. (*chim. min. med.*) refrattariamente.

refractoriness [riˈfræktərinis], *s.* 1. ostinazione; caparbietà 2. (*chim. min. med.*) refrattarietà.

refractory [riˈfræktəri], *ag.* 1. ostinato, caparbio 2. (*chim. min. med.*) refrattario ‖ *s.* sostanza refrattaria.

refrain[1] [riˈfrein], *s.* ritornello.

to **refrain**[2], *v.t.i.* 1. trattenersi, fermarsi; astenersi: *to — from doing sthg.*, trattenersi dal fare ql.co. 2. frenare, trattenere: *she refrained her tears*, ella trattenne le lacrime; *to — oneself*, frenarsi.

refrangibility [riˌfrændʒiˈbiliti], *s.* (*fis.*) rifrangibilità.

refrangible [riˈfrændʒibl], *ag.* (*fis.*) rifrangibile.

to **refresh** [riˈfreʃ], *v.t.i.* 1. rinvigorire, rinvigorirsi; rianimare, rianimarsi; ristorare, ristorarsi: *to — the eye, the mind*, riposare lo sguardo, la mente; *to — oneself*, ristorarsi 2. rinfrescare, ravvivare (la memoria); rinfrescare (di aria, ecc.): *to — one's memory*, rinfrescarsi la memoria 3. ricaricare (una batteria elettrica, ecc.).

refresher [riˈfreʃə*], *s.* 1. chi, cosa che rinfresca 2. onorario supplementare (di avvocato, per prolungamento di causa) 3. (*fam.*) rinfresco, bibita: *let's have a —*, andiamo a bere ql.co. ☆ — *course*, corso di aggiornamento.

refreshing [riˈfreʃiŋ], *ag.* rinfrescante; ristorante; ricreante: *a — breeze*, una brezza rinfrescante; *a — sleep*, un sonno ristoratore; *it was quite — to hear him*, faceva bene ascoltarlo.

refreshingly [riˈfreʃiŋli], *av.* in modo riposante, rinfrescante.

refreshment [riˈfreʃmənt], *s.* 1. ristoro; riposo; ricreazione; sollievo: *to have some —*, rifocillarsi 2. *gener.*

pl. rinfresco (bibite, dolci, ecc.) ☆ — *car*, vagone-ristorante; — *room*, buffet di stazione ferroviaria.

refrigerant [riˈfridʒərənt], *ag.s.* refrigerante.

to **refrigerate** [riˈfridʒəreit], *v.t.i.* 1. refrigerare; raffreddare: *to — food*, refrigerare cibo 2. (*rar.*) raffreddarsi, diventar freddo.

refrigeration [riˌfridʒəˈreiʃən], *s.* refrigerazione.

refrigerative [riˈfridʒərətiv], *ag.* refrigerativo.

refrigerator [riˈfridʒəreitə*], *s.* refrigerante; frigorifero; cella frigorifera ☆ — *van* (o — *car*), vagone frigorifero.

refrigeratory [riˈfridʒərətəri], *ag.s.* refrigerante.

reft [reft], *pass. p.p.* di to **reave**[1], to **reave**[2].

to **refuel** [ˈriːˈfjuːəl], *pass.p.p.* **refuelled** [ˈriːˈfjuːəld], *v.t.i.* (*aer. mar.*) rifornire, rifornirsi di carburante.

refuge [ˈrefjuːdʒ], *s.* 1. rifugio (anche *fig.*); asilo, riparo: *he is the — of the distressed*, egli è il rifugio degli afflitti; *to seek —*, cercare rifugio; *to take — in*, rifugiarsi in: *to take — in silence*, *fig.* rifugiarsi nel silenzio ‖ *house of —*, asilo per i senza tetto, ospizio 2. salvagente (stradale); spartitraffico.

to **refuge**, *v.t.i.* (*rar.*) 1. dare rifugio a 2. rifugiarsi.

refugee [ˌrefju(ː)ˈdʒiː], *s.* rifugiato, profugo ☆ — *government*, governo in esilio.

refulgence [riˈfʌldʒəns], **refulgency** [riˈfʌldʒənsi], *s.* fulgidezza, fulgore, splendore.

refulgent [riˈfʌldʒənt], *ag.* rifulgente, fulgido, risplendente.

refulgently [riˈfʌldʒəntli], *av.* fulgidamente, risplendentemente.

refund[1] [ˈriːfʌnd], *s.* rimborso.

to **refund**[1] [riːˈfʌnd], *v.t.i.* rifondere; rimborsare; restituire (denaro); effettuare un rimborso.

to **refund**[2], *v.t.* (*econ.*) ricostituire (un fondo); riconvertire (un prestito); investire nuovamente.

refundment [riːˈfʌndmənt], *s.* rimborso.

to **refurnish** [ˈriːˈfəːniʃ], *v.t.* 1. riammobiliare 2. rifornire.

refusable [riˈfjuːzəbl], *ag.* rifiutabile.

refusal [riˈfjuːzəl], *s.* 1. rifiuto: — *of payment*, (*comm.*) rifiuto di pagamento; *he will take no —*, non ammette rifiuti; *to give a flat —*, dare un netto rifiuto; *to meet a —*, ottenere un rifiuto 2. diritto di opzione: *to have the — of sthg.*, avere il diritto di opzione su ql.co.

refuse[1] [ˈrefjuːs], *ag.* di rifiuto, di scarto ‖ *s.* rifiuto, scarto.

to **refuse**[1] [riˈfjuːz], *v.t.i.* 1. rifiutare, rifiutarsi: *he refused to go there*, si rifiutò di andarvi; *the horse refused the fence*, il cavallo rifiutò di saltare l'ostacolo; *to — an invitation, a present*, rifiutare un invito, un regalo; *to — obedience*, rifiutarsi di obbedire; *to — s.o.*, rifiutare di sposare qlcu. 2. (*carte*) passare 3. (*mil.*) ritirare (truppe) dalla prima linea.

to **refuse**[2] [ˈriːˈfjuːz], *v.t.* fondere di nuovo.

refuser [riˈfjuːzə*], *s.c.* ricusante ‖ *s.* cavallo che rifiuta l'ostacolo.

refutability [ˌrefjutəˈbiliti], *s.* (*rar.*) confutabilità.

refutable [ˈrefjutəbl], *ag.* confutabile.

refutal [riˈfjuːtəl], **refutation** [ˌrefju(ː)ˈteiʃən], *s.* confutazione.

to **refute** [riˈfjuːt], *v.t.* confutare.

refuter [riˈfjuːtə*], *s.c.* confutatore, confutatrice.

Reg [redʒ], *no.pr.m.dim.* di **Reginald**.

to **regain** [riˈgein], *v.t.* 1. riguadagnare, ricuperare: *to — consciousness*, riprendere conoscenza; *to — one's footing*, riprendere l'equilibrio; *fig.* riguadagnare la propria posizione ‖ " *Paradise Regained* ", (*lett.*) « Il Paradiso riconquistato » 2. raggiungere di nuovo (un luogo); ricongiungersi con.

regal[1] [ˈriːgəl], *ag.* regale; reale, regio ‖ *s.* 1. (*rar.*) principe, governante 2. calice eucaristico usato durante l'incoronazione dei sovrani inglesi.

regal[2], *s. gener. pl.* (*mus.*) regale, ninfale.

regale[1] [riˈgeiliː], *s.* (*eccl. st.*) regalia.

regale[2] [riˈgeil], *s.* 1. banchetto 2. leccornia.

to **regale**[2], *v.t.i.* **1.** intrattenere piacevolmente (anche *iron.*): *he regaled us with his wit*, ci intrattenne con la sua brillante conversazione **2.** rallegrare; deliziare: *flowers to — our eyes*, fiori per rallegrare i nostri occhi; *to — oneself with a cigar*, concedersi il piacere di un sigaro **3.** cibarsi prelibatamente: *he regaled (himself) with caviar*, si gustò del caviale.

regalement [ri'geilmənt], *s.* **1.** festino **2.** l'intrattenere piacevolmente; il rallegrare **3.** leccornia.

regalia[1] [ri'geiljə], *s.pl.* **1.** insegne reali **2.** insegne di ordine, classe **3.** (*rar.*) prerogative regie.

regalia[2], *s.* sigaro di qualità superiore.

regalism ['ri:gəlizəm], *s.* supremazia del sovrano (specialmente in materie ecclesiastiche).

regality [ri'gæliti], *s.* regalità, sovranità.

regally ['ri:gəli], *av.* regalmente, da re.

Regan ['ri:gən], *no.pr.f.* (*lett.*) Regana.

regard [ri'gɑ:d], *s.* **1.** considerazione, rispetto, riguardo, cura: *he has no — for the feelings of others*, egli non ha alcun riguardo per i sentimenti altrui **2.** stima; affetto: *to hold a person in high, low —*, avere grande, poca stima di una persona **3.** *pl.* saluti, complimenti, ossequi: *my best regards to your parents*, i miei migliori saluti ai tuoi genitori; *with kind regards*, con cordiali saluti **4.** relazione, rispetto, punto di vista: *in* (o *with*) *— to*, riguardo a, in merito a; *in this —*, a questo proposito **5.** (*arc. letter.*) sguardo, occhiata.

to **regard**, *v.t.i.* **1.** considerare, stimare, tener conto di: *he didn't — my advice*, non prese in considerazione i miei consigli; *I — him as a dangerous fellow*, lo considero un individuo pericoloso; *I — the offer as absurd*, considero l'offerta assurda; *we — the matter with horror*, consideriamo con orrore la faccenda **2.** riguardare, concernere: *as regards* (o *regarding*) *money, your offer...*, per quanto riguarda il denaro, la vostra offerta...; *the matter does not — you*, la faccenda non vi riguarda **3.** guardare, guardare fissamente, con sguardo intento: osservare: *she regarded him with curiosity*, lo osservò con curiosità.

regardant [ri'gɑ:dənt], *ag.* **1.** che osserva con occhio intento, fissamente **2.** (*arald.*) che guarda indietro.

regardful [ri'gɑ:dful], *ag.* riguardoso; rispettoso; attento: *— of expenses*, attento alle spese.

regardfully [ri'gɑ:dfuli], *av.* riguardosamente; rispettosamente; attentamente, con cura.

regardfulness [ri'gɑ:dfulnis], *s.* (*rar.*) riguardo; rispetto; cura, attenzione.

regardless [ri'gɑ:dlis], *ag.* incurante, noncurante, senza riguardo, indifferente: *— of expenses*, che non bada a spese.

regardless, *av.* **1.** senza riguardo: *he did it — of what I said*, lo fece senza badare a quanto io ne dicevo **2.** (*sl.*) senza badare a spese: *he was got up —*, non aveva badato a spese per vestirsi.

regardlessly [ri'gɑ:dlisli], *av.* senza riguardo; con indifferenza; con negligenza: *to act — of...*, agire senza considerazione, per.

regardlessness [ri'gɑ:dlisnis], *s.* noncuranza, negligenza, trascuratezza; mancanza di riguardo.

regatta [ri'gætə], *s.* regata ☆ *Henley —*, la regata di Henley; *yachting —*, regata di panfili.

to **regelate** ['ri:dʒileit], *v.i.* (*fis.*) ricongelarsi.

regelation [,ri:dʒi'leiʃən], *s.* (*fis.*) ricongelamento.

regency ['ri:dʒənsi], *s.* reggenza || *the Regency*, (*st. inglese*) la Reggenza (di Giorgio, principe di Galles, 1810-1820): *Regency style*, stile Reggenza.

to **regenerate** [ri'dʒenəreit], *v.t.i.* **1.** rigenerare, rigenerarsi; migliorare **2.** ricrescere, formarsi nuovamente: *polypus regenerates after extraction*, il polipo (tumore) si riforma dopo l'estrazione **3.** (*teol.*) redimere **4.** (*ind.*) recuperare; rigenerare **5.** (*rad.*) amplificare, rigenerare.

regeneration [ri,dʒenə'reiʃən], *s.* **1.** rigenerazione **2.** (*ind.*) ricupero **3.** (*rad.*) amplificazione, rigenerazione.

regenerative [ri'dʒenərətiv], *ag.* **1.** rigeneratore; tendente alla rigenerazione **2.** (*ind.*) a ricupero ☆ — *air heater*, riscaldatore d'aria a ricupero; — *brake*, (*mec.*) freno a ricupero; — *furnace*, forno a ricupero.

regenerator [ri'dʒenəreitə*], *s.c.* rigeneratore, rigeneratrice || *s.* (*ind.*) preriscaldatore a ricupero.

regent ['ri:dʒənt], *ag.* reggente || *s.* **1.** reggente || *Prince Regent*, principe reggente **2.** (*amer.*) membro di consiglio amministrativo (di università di stato).

regentship ['ri:dʒənt-ʃip], *s.* reggenza.

to **regerminate** ['ri:dʒə:mineit], *v.i.* rigerminare.

regermination ['ri:,dʒə:mi'neiʃən], *s.* rigerminazione.

Reggie ['redʒi], *no.pr.m. dim.* di **Reginald**.

regicidal [,redʒi'saidl], *ag.* regicida.

regicide[1] ['redʒisaid], *s.* regicida.

regicide[2], *s.* regicidio.

regime, régime [rei'ʒi:m], *s.* regime, forma di governo; sistema sociale, amministrativo.

regimen ['redʒimen], *s.* **1.** (*rar.*) regime, sistema di governo **2.** (*med.*) regime, dieta **3.** (*gram.*) reggenza.

regiment ['redʒimənt], *s.* **1.** (*mil.*) reggimento **2.** *pl.* gran numero, moltitudine **3.** (*arc.*) governo.

to **regiment** ['redʒiment], *v.t.* **1.** (*mil.*) irreggimentare; (*amer.*) assegnare ad un reggimento **2.** disciplinare, organizzare a gruppi.

regimental [,redʒi'mentl], *ag.* di reggimento.

regimentals [,redʒi'mentlz], *s.pl.* divisa di un particolare reggimento; uniforme || *in full —*, in alta uniforme.

Regina[1] [ri'dʒainə], *s.* (*abbr. R.*) regina regnante: — *v. Jones*, (*dir.*) la Regina contro Jones (formula usata in atti legali); *E.R., V.R.*, Regina Elisabetta, Vittoria Regina (firma in proclami, ecc.).

Regina[2], *no.pr.f.* Regina.

Reginald ['redʒinld], *no.pr.m.* Reginaldo.

region ['ri:dʒən], *s.* **1.** regione, zona: *the — between the Elbe and the Rhine*, la regione tra l'Elba e il Reno; *the Arctic Regions*, le regioni artiche; *a desert, fertile —*, una regione deserta, fertile || *the lower regions*, l'inferno, il regno dei morti; *the upper regions*, il paradiso, il cielo **2.** sfera, regno, campo: *the — of metaphysics*, la sfera della metafisica **3.** (*anat.*) regione: *the lumbar —*, la regione lombare.

regional ['ri:dʒənl], *ag.* regionale.

register[1] ['redʒistə*], *s.* **1.** registro: *the registers of births, marriages, deaths*, i registri di stato civile || *Register House*, (*scoz.*) gli Archivi || *Commercial* (o *Trade*) *Register*, Registro del Commercio; *Companies Register*, Registro delle Società Anonime || *Federal Register*, (*amer.*) Gazzetta Ufficiale || *Lloyd's Register*, Registro del Lloyd **2.** registratore, valvola di regolazione **3.** (*mus. tip.*) registro: *in —, out of —*, (*tip.*) in registro, fuori registro **4.** (*amer. pol.*) lista elettorale ☆ — *office*, ufficio di stato civile; anagrafe; ufficio collocamento || *cash- —*, registratore di cassa; calcolatrice; *counterpart- —*, registro a matrice; *discount —*, giornale di portafoglio; *draft —*, registro dei conti, di corrispondenza; *gas —, air —*, regolatore, valvola del gas, dell'aria.

to **register**[1], *v.t.i.* **1.** registrare, protocollare; iscrivere, iscriversi; immatricolare: *to — a birth*, registrare una nascita; *to — a car*, immatricolare un'automobile; *to — a deed*, (*dir.*) registrare un atto; *to — a fact*, registrare un fatto; *to — a name*, iscrivere un nome; *to — a trade-mark*, depositare un marchio di fabbrica **2.** *fig.* scolpire (nella mente) **3.** esprimere: *his face registered fear*, la paura era dipinta sul suo viso **4.** raccomandare (lettere); assicurare (bagaglio) **5.** indicare: *the thermometer registered 38° C*, il termometro segnava 38° C **6.** (*pol. amer.*) farsi iscrivere nella lista elettorale.

register[2], (*amer.*) per **registrar**.

registered ['redʒistəd], *ag.* **1.** registrato, iscritto, immatricolato **2.** raccomandato, assicurato ☆ — *letter*, (lettera) raccomandata; *Registered Nurse* (*abbr. R.N.*), infermiera diplomata; — *stock*, titolo nominativo; — *trade-mark*, marchio di fabbrica depositato.

registrable ['redʒistrəbl], *ag.* registrabile.

registrant ['redʒistrənt], *s.c.* chi registra.

registrar [,redʒis'trɑ:*], *s.* **1.** segretario; cancelliere; archivista **2.** ufficiale di stato civile.

registrarship ['redʒistrɑ:ʃip], *s.* ufficio, funzioni di segretario, cancelliere, archivista, ufficiale di stato civile.

registration [,redʒis'treiʃən], *s.* **1.** registrazione; iscrizione **2.** raccomandazione (di lettera); assicurazione (di bagaglio) **3.** (*dir.*) tassa di registro ☆ — *day*, giorno di iscrizione (a scuola); — *duty*, tassa di iscrizione.

registry ['redʒistri], *s.* **1.** registrazione: *certificate of* —, (*mar.*) certificato d'immatricolazione delle navi **2.** — (*office*), (ufficio del) registro; ufficio di stato civile: *they got married at a* — (*office*), si sposarono civilmente ☆ *servant's* — (*office*), ufficio di collocamento per personale di servizio.

Regius ['ri:dʒəs], *ag.* titolare (di professore universitario): — *professor of Latin*, professore titolare di latino.

regnal ['regnl], *ag.* di regno ☆ — *day*, anniversario dell'assunzione al trono di un re; — *year*, anno che ha inizio con l'assunzione al trono di un re.

regnant ['regnənt], *ag.* **1.** regnante: *King* —, re regnante **2.** *fig.* predominante, prevalente.

to **regorge** ['ri:'gɔ:dʒ], *v.t.i.* **1.** vomitare; rigurgitare (anche *fig.*) **2.** rifluire (di fiume) **3.** inghiottire di nuovo.

to **regrate** [ri'greit], *v.t.* (*st.*) incettare; vendere al minuto.

regrater, regrator [ri'greitə*], *s.* incettatore.

regress ['ri:gres], *s.* **1.** retrocessione; regresso **2.** (*astr.*) retrogradazione.

to **regress** [ri'gres], *v.i.* **1.** retrocedere; regredire **2.** (*astr.*) retrogradare.

regression [ri'greʃən], *s.* regresso, regressione.

regressive [ri'gresiv], *ag.* regressivo.

regressively [ri'gresivli], *av.* regressivamente.

regressiveness [ri'gresivnis], *s.* regressività.

regret [ri'gret], *s.* rimpianto, rammarico, rincrescimento; dispiacere: *the — for the loss of a relative*, il dispiacere per la perdita di un parente: *much to my —*, con mio grande dispiacere; *he expressed his — at not being able to come*, espresse il suo rammarico di non poter venire; *please accept my regrets*, vi prego di accettare le mie scuse.

to **regret**, *pass. p.p.* **regretted** [ri'gretid], *v.t.* **1.** rimpiangere: *he was regretted by all of us*, fu rimpianto da tutti noi **2.** rammaricarsi di; dolersi di; pentirsi di: *he regretted he had spoken so rudely*, si pentì di aver parlato in modo così villano; *I — having deceived him*, mi duole di averlo ingannato.

regretful [ri'gretful], *ag.* pieno di rimpianto, di rincrescimento.

regretfully [ri'gretfuli], *av.* con rimpianto, con rincrescimento.

regrettable [ri'gretəbl], *ag.* spiacevole, deplorevole, increscioso.

regrettably [ri'gretəbli], *av.* spiacevolmente, deplorevolmente, incresciosamente.

regrettingly [ri'gretiŋli], *av.* con dispiacere, con rammarico.

to **regroup** [ri:'gru:p], *v.t.* raggruppare di nuovo.

regulable ['regjuləbl], *ag.* regolabile.

regular ['regjulə*], *ag.* **1.** regolare (anche *gram. geom.*); normale; regolato: — *habits*, abitudini regolate; — *people*, persone normali; *he has no — work*, non ha un lavoro regolare; *to live a — life*, condurre un'esistenza regolata ‖ *as — as a clockwork*, (*fam.*) preciso come un orologio **2.** regolare; armonioso: — *features*, lineamenti regolari **3.** regolare; formale: *a — introduction*, una presentazione formale **4.** regolare; qualificato: — *army*, esercito regolare; — *clergy*, clero regolare **5.** (*fam.*) vero e proprio, completo; perfetto: *he is a — rascal*, è un briccone matricolato; *she is a — cook*, è una perfetta cuoca ‖ *s.* **1.** soldato regolare **2.** membro del clero regolare **3.** (*fam.*) cliente abituale **4.** (*fam.*) impiegato fisso.

regular, *av.* (*volg.*) molto: *he is — angry*, egli è arrabbiatissimo.

regularity [,regju'læriti], *s.* regolarità.

regularization [,regjulərai'zeiʃən], *s.* regolarizzazione.

to **regularize** ['regjuləraiz], *v.t.* regolarizzare.

regularly ['regjuləli], *av.* regolarmente.

to **regulate** ['regjuleit], *v.t.* regolare: *to — one's conduct*, regolare la propria condotta; *to — the traffic*, regolare il traffico; *to — a watch*, regolare un orologio.

regulation [,regju'leiʃən], *s.* **1.** regolamento; regola; ordine **2.** (*mec. elett. rad.*) regolazione ☆ — *speed*, velocità regolamentare: *to exceed the — speed*, superare la velocità regolamentare.

regulative ['regjulətiv], *ag.* regolatore.

regulator ['regjuleitə*], *s.c.* regolatore, regolatrice ‖ *s.* (*mec. elett.*) regolatore; bilanciere; registro (di orologio) ☆ *voltage* —, regolatore di tensione.

regulus ['regjuləs], *pl.* **reguli** ['regjulai], *s.* (*chim. ornit.*) regolo ‖ *Regulus*, (*astr.*) Regolo (stella della costellazione del Leone).

to **regurgitate** [ri'gə:dʒiteit], *v.t.i.* rigurgitare; rigettare, gettare fuori.

regurgitation [ri,gə:dʒi'teiʃən], *s.* rigurgito.

to **rehabilitate** [,ri:ə'biliteit], *v.t.* **1.** riabilitare **2.** ripristinare.

rehabilitation ['ri:ə,bili'teiʃən], *s.* **1.** riabilitazione **2.** ripristino: *the — of the railroad net*, il ripristino della rete ferroviaria.

to **rehandle** [ri:'hændl], *v.t.* rimaneggiare.

rehash [ri:'hæʃ], *s.* rimaneggiamento; rifacimento.

to **rehash**, *v.t.* rimaneggiare; rifare.

to **rehear** [ri:'hiə*], *pass.p.p.* **reheard** [ri:'hə:d], *v.t.* (*dir.*) riesaminare.

rehearing [ri:'hiəriŋ], *s.* (*dir.*) nuova udienza.

rehearsal [ri'hə:səl], *s.* **1.** ripetizione; narrazione; enumerazione; recitazione **2.** (*teat.*) prova ☆ *dress* —, prova generale.

to **rehearse** [ri'hə:s], *v.t.* **1.** ripetere; raccontare; enumerare; recitare (preghiere, ecc.) **2.** (*teat.*) provare; fare le prove di: *to — a play*, fare le prove di una commedia.

rehearser [ri'hə:sə*], *s.c.* **1.** recitatore, recitatrice; ripetitore, ripetitrice **2.** (*teat.*) chi prova.

reification [,ri:ifi'keiʃən], *s.* materializzazione, conversione in cosa reale.

to **reify** ['ri:ifai], *v.t.* materializzare, convertire in cosa reale.

reign [rein], *s.* **1.** regno (anche *fig.*): *in the — of*, sotto il regno di ‖ *the Reign of Terror*, (*st. francese*), il regno del Terrore **2.** dominio, influenza: *the — of fashion*, l'influenza della moda ☆ *mineral, vegetal —)* regno minerale, vegetale.

to **reign**, *v.i.* **1.** regnare: *to — over France*, regnare sulla Francia **2.** *fig.* regnare, dominare; prevalere: *silence reigned*, regnava il silenzio.

reigning ['reiniŋ], *ag.* regnante, dominante: *his was the — mind*, la sua era la mente dominante.

reimbursable [,ri:im'bə:səbl], *ag.* rimborsabile.

to **reimburse** [,ri:im'bə:s], *v.t.* rimborsare.

reimbursement [,ri:im'bə:smənt], *s.* rimborso.

reimport ['ri:im'pɔ:t], *s.* **1.** l'importare di nuovo **2.** articolo importato di nuovo.

to **reimport**, *v.t.* importare di nuovo.

reimportation ['ri:,impɔ:'teiʃən], *s.* **1.** l'importare di nuovo **2.** merce importata di nuovo.

rein[1] [rein], *s. gener. pl.* redine, briglia (anche *fig.*): *to assume, to drop the reins of government*, assumere, abbandonare le redini del governo; *to draw —*, tirare le redini; *fig.* ridurre le spese; *to give — (o the reins) to one's imagination*, dare libero corso alla propria immaginazione; *to give a horse free — (o the reins)*, dare briglia sciolta al cavallo.

to **rein**[1], *v.t.i.* **1.** guidare con le redini; *fig.* governare, controllare, guidare **2.** frenare, trattenere; fermare, fermarsi; rallentare **3.** *to — back*, far rinculare (un cavallo) **4.** *to* — **in**, rimettere al passo (un cavallo) **5.** *to* — **up**, arrestare (un cavallo) tirando le redini.

rein[2], *s.* (*zool.*) renna.

to **reincarnate** [riːˈinkɑːneit], *v.t.* reincarnare.

reincarnation [ˈriːinkɑːˈneiʃən], *s.* reincarnazione, metempsicosi.

to **reincorporate** [ˈriːinˈkɔːpəreit], *v.t.* incorporare di nuovo.

reindeer [ˈreindiə*], *s.* (*invariato al pl.*) renna: *buck* —, *doe* —, maschio, femmina di renna.

reinforce [ˌriːinˈfɔːs], *s.* rinforzo; (*mil.*) pezzo di rinforzo.

to **reinforce**, *v.t.* **1.** rinforzare, rafforzare, consolidare; ristabilire (la salute) **2.** *fig.* avvalorare (un argomento).

reinforcement [ˌriːinˈfɔːsmənt], *s.* **1.** rinforzo **2.** *pl.* (*mil.*) rinforzi ☆ — *-bars*, ferri dell'armatura; —- *ring*, (*mec.*) cerchiatura di rinforzo.

reinless [ˈreinlis], *ag.* **1.** senza redini (di cavallo) **2.** *fig.* (*fam.*) sfrenato (di passioni).

reins [reinz], *s.pl.* (*arc.*) reni; lombi **2.** (*Bibbia*) centro dei sentimenti, degli affetti.

to **reinstate** [ˈriːinˈsteit], *v.t.* ristabilire; ripristinare; reintegrare.

reinstatement [ˈriːinˈsteitmənt], *s.* ristabilimento; ripristino; reintegrazione.

reinsurance [ˈriːinˈʃuərəns], *s.* riassicurazione.

to **reinsure** [ˈriːinˈʃuə*], *v.t.* riassicurare, assicurare di nuovo.

to **reintegrate** [riːˈintigreit], *v.t.* reintegrare.

reintegration [ˈriːˌintiˈgreiʃən], *s.* reintegrazione.

reintegrative [riːˈintigreitiv], *ag.* reintegrativo.

to **reinter** [ˈriːinˈtəː*], *v.t.* riseppellire, seppellire di nuovo.

to **reinvest** [ˈriːinˈvest], *v.t.* **1.** rinvestire, investire di nuovo **2.** impiegare, convertire di nuovo (denaro, ecc.).

reinvestiture [ˈriːinˈvestitʃə*], *s.* nuova investitura.

reinvestment [ˈriːinˈvestmənt], *s.* nuovo investimento.

to **reinvigorate** [ˈriːinˈvigəreit], *v.t.* rinvigorire.

reinvigoration [ˈriːinˌvigəˈreiʃən], *s.* rinvigorimento.

to **reiterate** [riːˈitəreit], *v.t.* ripetere, reiterare.

reiteratedly [riːˈitəreitidli], *av.* ripetutamente, reiteratamente.

reiteration [riːˌitəˈreiʃən], *s.* ripetizione insistente; reiterazione.

reiterative [riːˈitərətiv], *ag.* ripetuto insistentemente; reiterato.

to **reive**, *V.* to **reave**.

reiver [ˈriːvə*], *s.* (*arc.*) rapinatore; saccheggiatore.

reject [ˈriːdʒekt], *s.* **1.** persona, cosa rifiutata, scartata **2.** (*mil.*) persona riformata: *there were ten rejects in the last batch of conscripts*, dieci giovani furono dichiarati inabili nell'ultimo gruppo di coscritti ☆ *export* —, articolo difettoso, non adatto per l'esportazione.

to **reject** [riˈdʒekt], *v.t.* **1.** rigettare; rifiutare; respingere: *to* — *a suitor*, respingere un corteggiatore **2.** (*mil.*) riformare **3.** vomitare; evacuare.

rejectable [riˈdʒektəbl], *ag.* rigettabile, rifiutabile.

rejectamenta [riˌdʒektəˈmentə], *s. pl.* **1.** rifiuti, materiale di scarto; detriti portati a galla dal mare **2.** escrementi.

rejecter [riˈdʒektə*], *s.c.* chi rigetta, respinge.

rejection [riˈdʒekʃən], *s.* **1.** rigetto, rifiuto, scarto **2.** (*pl.*) escrementi.

rejector [riˈdʒektə*], *s.c.* chi rigetta, respinge.

to **rejoice** [riˈdʒɔis], *v.t.i.* **1.** rallegrare, rallegrarsi; allietare; gioire, godere: *he was rejoiced at* (o *by*) *it*, egli ne fu rallegrato; *I* — *that the matter has been settled*, sono lieto che la faccenda sia stata sistemata; *it rejoices his heart to hear his son*, l'udire suo figlio lo rallegra assai; *the news rejoiced me*, la notizia mi rallegrò **2.** far festa, celebrare un evento **3.** *to* — *in* (*sthg.*), (*scherz.*) avere, possedere: *he rejoices in a Morris Minor*, egli è ben contento di possedere una Morris Minor.

rejoicing [riˈdʒɔisiŋ], *s.* **1.** allegria, gioia, giubilo, esultanza **2.** *gener. pl.* feste pubbliche, festeggiamenti.

rejoicingly [riˈdʒɔisiŋli], *av.* allegramente, gioiosamente.

to **rejoin**[1] [riˈdʒɔin], *v.t.i.* (*dir.*) replicare, rispondere (ad un'accusa).

to **rejoin**[2] [ˈriːdʒɔin], *v.t.i.* ricongiungere, ricongiungersi; raggiungere (un compagno, ecc.).

rejoinder [riˈdʒɔində*], *s.* (*dir.*) risposta, replica (ad accusa).

to **rejuvenate** [riˈdʒuːvineit], *v.t.i.* ringiovanire.

rejuvenation [riˌdʒuːviˈneiʃən], *s.* ringiovanimento.

to **rejuvenesce** [ˌriːdʒuːviˈnes], *v.t.i.* **1.** ringiovanire **2.** (*biol.*) acquistare nuova vitalità, dare nuova vitalità a.

rejuvenescence [ˌriːdʒuːviˈnesns], *s.* ringiovanimento.

rejuvenescent [ˌriːdʒuːviˈnesnt], *ag.* che ringiovanisce.

to **rejuvenize** [riˈdʒuːvinaiz], *v.t.i.* ringiovanire.

to **rekindle** [ˈriːˈkindl], *v.t.i.* riaccendere, riaccendersi (anche *fig.*): *our hopes rekindled*, le nostre speranze si riaccesero.

relaid, re-laid [ˈriːˈleid], *pass.p.p.* di to **relay**[2], to **re-lay**.

relapse[1] [riˈlæps], *s.* **1.** ricaduta **2.** (*med.*) ricaduta, recidiva.

to **relapse**[1], *v.i.* **1.** ricadere: *to* — *into error*, ricadere nell'errore **2.** (*med.*) avere una ricaduta.

relapse[2], *s.* (*rar.*) recidivo.

to **relate** [riˈleit], *v.t.i.* **1.** narrare, raccontare; riferire **2.** mettere in relazione: *I cannot* — *it to* (o *with*) *what happened last year*, non posso metterlo in relazione con quanto avvenne l'anno scorso **3.** avere rapporto, avere attinenza: *she is interested in nothing but what relates to herself*, si interessa esclusivamente di ciò che la riguarda **4.** *to be related*, essere imparentato: *I am not related to him in any way*, non sono imparentato con lui in nessun modo; *to be closely related to*, essere parente prossimo di.

relatedness [riˈleitidnis], *s.* **1.** relazione **2.** parentela.

relater [riˈleitə*], *s.c.* chi narra, racconta.

relating [riˈleitiŋ], *ag.* relativo, concernente: *information* — *to a given subject*, informazioni relative a un dato argomento.

relation [riˈleiʃən], *s.* **1.** narrazione, racconto: *the* — *of his adventures*, il racconto delle sue avventure **2.** relazione, rapporto, connessione, attinenza: *the relations between husband and wife*, i rapporti fra marito e moglie; *strained commercial relations*, (*comm.*) relazioni commerciali tese; *there is no* — *between them*, non c'è alcuna attinenza fra di loro ‖ *in* — *to*, in relazione a **3.** parente, congiunto, consanguineo: *a* — *of ours*, un nostro parente; *is he any* — *to you?*, è imparentato con voi? **4.** (*rar.*) parentela **5.** (*dir.*) esposto (del querelante) **6.** retrodatazione (di atto, documento).

relational [riˈleiʃənl], *ag.* relativo, affine.

relationship [riˈleiʃənʃip], *s.* **1.** relazione, rapporto **2.** parentela.

relatival [ˌreləˈtaivəl], *ag.* (*gram.*) relativo.

relative [ˈrelətiv], *ag.* **1.** (*gram.*) relativo: — *pronoun*, pronome relativo **2.** relativo; in relazione; in rapporto; pertinente: *everything is* —, tutto è relativo; *with* — *coolness*, con relativo sangue freddo ‖ — *to*, in relazione a: *I wrote to him* — *to that matter*, gli scrissi in relazione a quell'affare; *supply is* — *to demand*, l'offerta è in relazione alla domanda ‖ *s.* (*gram.*) (pronome) relativo ‖ *s.c.* parente.

relatively [ˈrelətivli], *av.* relativamente.

relativeness [ˈrelətivnis], *s.* relatività.

relativism [ˈrelətivizəm], *s.* (*fil.*) relativismo.

relativist [ˈrelətivist], *s.c.* (*fil.*) relativista.

relativity [ˌreləˈtiviti], *s.* relatività ‖ *theory of* —, (*fil.*) teoria della relatività.

relator [riˈleitə*], *s.* **1.** (*dir.*) relatore **2.** (*rar.*) narratore.

to **relax** [riˈlæks], *v.t.i.* **1.** rilassare, rilassarsi; riposare, riposarsi: *try to* — *now*, cerca di rilassarti ora;

to — *the muscles*, rilassare i muscoli **2.** allentare; mitigare, moderare; ridurre: *he relaxed his grasp*, allentò la stretta; *to* — *discipline*, rendere meno severa la disciplina; *to* — *in one's efforts*, diminuire i propri sforzi.

relaxation [ˌriːlækˈseiʃən], *s.* **1.** rilassamento, distensione (di muscoli, nervi, ecc.) **2.** riposo, distensione; divertimento: *television is the only* — *left to us*, la televisione è l'unico svago che ci sia rimasto; *you need a period of* —, hai bisogno di un periodo di riposo **3.** mitigazione; moderazione; diminuzione (di pena, ecc.).

relaxing [riˈlæksiŋ], *ag.* rilassante, distensivo.

relay[1] [riˈlei], *s.* **1.** cavalli di ricambio **2.** muta di ricambio di cani da caccia **3.** squadra di operai che dà il cambio: *to work by* (o *in*) *relays*, lavorare a turni **4.** materiale di ricambio **5.** (*elett.*) relè, soccorritore **6.** (*rad.*) collegamento ☆ -*race*, corsa a staffetta.

to relay[1], *v.t.i.* **1.** fornire, fornirsi di cavalli, uomini, materiale di ricambio **2.** (*elett.*) controllare a mezzo di soccorritore, di relè **3.** (*rad.*) collegare.

to relay[2], **to re-lay** [ˈriːˈlei], *pass.p.p.* **relay, re-laid** [ˈriːˈleid], *v.t.* porre di nuovo.

release [riˈliːs], *s.* **1.** liberazione, scarcerazione: — *on bail*, libertà provvisoria; *order of* —, ordine di scarcerazione **2.** quietanza; remissione (di debito, ecc.); esenzione (da tasse) **3.** (*dir.*) cessione (di proprietà, diritto) **4.** distribuzione; autorizzazione: — *of a film*; distribuzione di un film; — *of a speech*, autorizzazione di pubblicare un discorso **5.** (*mec.*) scarico, scappamento (di gas, liquido) **6.** (*foto. mec.*) scatto.

to release, *v.t.* **1.** liberare, rilasciare, scarcerare: *to* — *a prisoner*, rilasciare un prigioniero **2.** rimettere (debiti); esentare (da tasse) **3.** (*dir.*) cedere (proprietà, diritto) **4.** autorizzare: *to* — *a film*, autorizzare a mettere in commercio un film; *to* — *an article*, autorizzare la pubblicazione di un articolo **5.** (*mec.*) sganciare; liberare (gas, ecc.): *to* — *the brake*, allentare il freno; *to* — *a spring*, scaricare una molla **6.** (*foto.*) far scattare: *to* — *the shutter*, far scattare l'otturatore.

releasee [riˌliːˈsiː], *s.* cessionario, persona a cui si è fatto cessione (di proprietà, diritto).

releasement [riˈliːsmənt], *V.* **release.**

releaser [riˈliːsə*], *s.* **1.** distributore di film **2.** (*mec.*) dispositivo di scatto.

releasor [riˈliːsə*], *s.c.* (*dir.*) **1.** esoneratore, chi rimette un debito **2.** chi cede una proprietà, un diritto.

relegable [ˈreligəbl], *ag.* **1.** che si può rimandare **2.** trasferibile.

to relegate [ˈreligeit], *v.t.* **1.** relegare; esiliare, bandire: *she was relegated to a convent*, fu relegata in convento ‖ *to* — *a team*, (*calcio*) far passare una squadra in una categoria inferiore **2.** rimettere, rimandare: *to* — *a matter to s.o.*, affidare un affare a qlcu.

relegation [ˌreliˈgeiʃən], *s.* **1.** (*dir.*) relegazione, esilio **2.** rinvio.

to relent [riˈlent], *v.i.* addolcirsi; diventare meno severo; intenerirsi.

relentingly [riˈlentiŋli], *av.* con minor severità.

relentless [riˈlentlis], *ag.* inflessibile; inesorabile, implacabile; spietato.

relentlessly [riˈlentlisli], *av.* inflessibilmente; inesorabilmente, implacabilmente; spietatamente.

relentlessness [riˈlentlisnis], *s.* inflessibilità; inesorabilità, implacabilità; spietatezza.

relevance [ˈrelivəns], **relevancy** [ˈrelivənsi], *s.* relazione, rapporto; pertinenza; attinenza.

relevant [ˈrelivənt], *ag.* relativo; pertinente; attinente: *the* — *documents*, i documenti relativi; — *to*, relativo a.

relevantly [ˈrelivəntli], *av.* con attinenza.

reliability [riˌlaiəˈbiliti], *s.* **1.** attendibilità; fidatezza **2.** regolarità (di funzionamento, ecc.) ☆ — *trials*, (*aut.*) prove di collaudo; prove di resistenza.

reliable [riˈlaiəbl], *ag.* fidato, degno di fiducia; attendibile: *I had it from a* — *source*, l'ho saputo da una fonte attendibile.

reliableness [riˈlaiəblnis], *V.* **reliability.**

reliably [riˈlaiəbli], *av.* in modo degno di fiducia; in modo attendibile.

reliance [riˈlaiəns], *s.* **1.** fiducia, fede: — (*up*)*on* (o *in*), fede in: *to have, to place* — *upon s.o.*, avere, riporre la propria fiducia in qlcu. **2.** cosa in cui si ripone fiducia; sostegno, appoggio.

reliant [riˈlaiənt], *ag.* fiducioso; fidente; che fa assegnamento.

relic [ˈrelik], *s.* reliquia (anche *eccl.*); resto, vestigio: *relics of the past*, vestigia del passato.

relict [ˈrelikt], *s.* (*arc.*) vedova.

relief[1] [riˈliːf], *s.* **1.** sollievo, conforto, ristoro: *the doctor's treatment brought him some* —, la cura del medico gli fu di un certo sollievo; *he gave a sigh of* —, egli ebbe un sospiro di sollievo; *to my great* — *all difficulties are overcome*, con mio gran sollievo ogni difficoltà è sormontata; *to find* — *in work*, trovar sollievo nel lavoro **2.** soccorso, aiuto; sussidio: — *of old people*, assistenza ai vecchi; *to go to s.o.'s* —, portar soccorso a qlcu.; *to live on public* —, essere a carico dell'assistenza pubblica **3.** (*mil.*) liberazione: soccorso **4.** (*dir.*) riparazione di un torto **5.** esenzione: — *from income tax*, esenzione dalla imposta sul reddito **6.** cambio; persona che dà il cambio: *the* — *of a sentry*, il cambio della sentinella **7.** diversivo, cambiamento: *a comic scene followed by way of* —, come diversivo seguì una scena comica ☆ — *fund*, fondo di soccorso; — *man*, sentinella; — *train*, treno sussidiario; — *troops*, truppe di soccorso; — *valve*, (*mec.*) valvola di sicurezza; — *works*, lavori pubblici organizzati per dar lavoro ai disoccupati ‖ *indoor* —, assistenza in sede; assistenza dei poveri in ospedale; *outdoor* —, soccorso a domicilio.

relief[2], *s.* **1.** rilievo (anche *scult.*): *it stands out in* —, spicca, ha rilievo; *to give* — *to one's style*, *fig.* dar rilievo al proprio stile **2.** (*pitt.*) prospettiva ☆ — *map*, (*geog.*) plastico; carta fisica ‖ *high* —, altorilievo; *low* —, bassorilievo.

relier [riˈlaiə*], *s.* (*rar.*) chi ripone fiducia, chi fa assegnamento.

relievable [riˈliːvəbl], *ag.* soccorribile; rimediabile; che si può aiutare; sostituibile; riparabile.

to relieve [riˈliːv], *v.t.* **1.** alleviare, mitigare, sollevare: *he was much relieved to hear it*, fu molto sollevato nell'udir ciò; *to* — *pain*, alleviare il dolore ‖ *to* — *one's feelings*, sfogarsi **2.** aiutare, soccorrere: *to* — *the distressed*, soccorrere gli afflitti **3.** liberare: *it relieves me of all responsibility*, mi libera da ogni responsabilità; *the town will be relieved*, la città sarà liberata; *to* — *s.o. from an obligation*, (*dir.*) liberare qlcu. da un obbligo **4.** alleggerire: *he was relieved of his purse*, (*scherz.*) è stato alleggerito del portafoglio; *to* — *s.o. of a burden*, alleggerire qlcu. di un peso ‖ *to* — *nature*, (*fisiol.*) evacuare **5.** rendere meno monotono, noioso, spiacevole: *to* — *the tedium of the journey*, ingannare la noia del viaggio **6.** (*mil.*) dare il cambio a: *to* — *the watch*, cambiare il quarto di guardia **7.** dare rilievo a, dare spicco a: *a tall figure relieved against the blue sky*, un'alta figura stagliata nell'azzurro del cielo.

reliever [riˈliːvə*], [*s.* **1.** chi conforta; soccorritore **2.** liberatore.

relieving [riˈliːviŋ], *ag.* **1.** che allevia, soccorre **2.** (*mil.*) che dà il cambio ☆ — *arch*, (*arch.*) arco di sostegno; — *officer*, incaricato di opere assistenziali.

relievo [riˈliːvou], *s.* (*scult.*) rilievo.

religion [riˈlidʒən], *s.* **1.** religione, confessione religiosa ‖ *to get* —, (*amer. pop.*) convertirsi alla fede **2.** vita monastica: *to enter into* —, farsi religioso, farsi monaco **3.** dovere; passione: *she makes a* — *of relieving the poor*, si fa un dovere di aiutare i poveri ☆ *established* —, religione di stato.

religioner [riˈlidʒənə*], *s.c.* **1.** membro di un ordine monastico **2.** bigotto, bigotta.

religionism [riˈlidʒənizəm], *s.* bigotteria.

religionist [ri'lidʒənist], *s.c.* bigotto, bigotta; fanatico, fanatica (nel culto religioso).

to **religionize** [ri'lidʒənaiz], *v.t.i.* **1.** convertire alla religione; imbevere di dottrine religiose **2.** fare mostra di zelo religioso, ostentare fede religiosa.

religionless [ri'lidʒənlis], *ag.* senza religione.

religiose [ri,lidʒi'ous], *ag.* morbosamente religioso, esaltato, fanatico.

religiosity [ri,lidʒi'ɔsiti], *s.* **1.** religiosità **2.** fanatismo religioso.

religious [ri'lidʒəs], *ag.* **1.** religioso, pio, devoto **2.** scrupoloso ‖ *s.* (*invariato al pl.*) appartenente ad un ordine religioso, monaco ☆ — *book*, libro di devozione; — *exercises*, esercizi spirituali; — *wars*, guerre di religione.

religiously [ri'lidʒəsli], *av.* religiosamente.

religiousness [ri'lidʒəsnis], *s.* religiosità.

to **reline** ['ri:'lain], *v.t.* rinnovare la fodera di.

to **relinquish** [ri'liŋkwiʃ], *v.t.* **1.** abbandonare, lasciare; cedere, rinunziare a, desistere da: *to — hopes*, abbandonare ogni speranza; *to — a plan*, rinunziare ad un progetto; *to — a right*, rinunziare a un diritto **2.** allentare la presa su.

relinquishment [ri'liŋkwiʃmənt], *s.* abbandono; rinuncia.

reliquary ['relikwəri], *s.* reliquiario.

reliques [ri'li:ks], *s.pl.* resti, reliquie.

reliquiae [ri'likwiæ], *s. pl.* **1.** reliquie, resti **2.** (*geol.*) fossili (di animali, piante) **3.** (*bot.*) foglie avvizzite su una pianta.

relish ['reliʃ], *s.* **1.** gusto; piacere; attrattiva: *the — of novelty*, l'attrattiva della novità; *this boy has no — for poetry*, questo ragazzo non ha il gusto della poesia; *to eat, to read with great —*, mangiare, leggere con gran piacere **2.** sapore; profumo, aroma, fragranza: *food has no more — for him*, il cibo non ha più sapore per lui **3.** condimento, salsa, spezia ‖ *with hunger for a —*, (*fam.*) con l'appetito per condimento **4.** piccola dose, pizzico: *there was a — of malice in his action*, c'era un pizzico di malizia nella sua azione.

to **relish**, *v.t.i.* **1.** gustare, godere, apprezzare: *he relished this simple family life*, egli apprezzava questa semplice vita di famiglia **2.** mangiare con appetito, assaporare **3.** dar sapore a, rendere saporito **4.** aver sapore: *to — of sthg.*, avere un leggero sapore di ql.co.

relishable ['reliʃəbl], *ag.* appetitoso, saporito, ghiotto.

to **relive** ['ri:'liv], *v.t.i.* rivivere.

to **reload** ['ri:'loud], *v.t.* caricare di nuovo, ricaricare.

relucent [ri'lu:snt], *ag.* (*rar.*) rilucente, brillante.

to **reluct** [ri'lʌkt], *v.i.* (*rar.*) essere riluttante, mostrare riluttanza; fare opposizione: *to — at* (*o against*) *sthg.*, mostrarsi riluttante verso ql.co.

reluctance [ri'lʌktəns], **reluctancy** [ri'lʌktənsi], *s.* riluttanza; ripugnanza: *to affect —*, fare lo smorfioso; *to show — to do sthg.*, mostrarsi poco disposto a fare qualche cosa.

reluctant [ri'lʌktənt], *ag.* **1.** riluttante; che agisce a malincuore, di malavoglia, forzatamente: *to be — to do sthg.*, essere riluttante, mal disposto a fare ql.co. **2.** difficile da trattare.

reluctantly [ri'lʌktəntli], *av.* con riluttanza; con ripugnanza; a malincuore, di mala voglia.

to **reluctate** [ri'lʌkteit], *V.* to **reluct**.

reluctation [,relʌk'teiʃən], *s.* riluttanza; ripugnanza.

to **relume** [ri'lju:m], *v.t.* (*poet.*) riaccendere, ridar splendore a.

to **rely** [ri'lai], *v.i.* fare assegnamento; fidarsi, aver fiducia: *to — (up)on s.o., sthg.*, fare assegnamento su qlcu., su ql.co.: *don't — on him*, non fidarti di lui; *you can — upon me to do it*, potete contare su di me per fare ciò ‖ *— on yourself only*, *prov.* chi fa da sè fa per tre.

remain [ri'mein], *s.* **1.** *gener. pl.* resto, avanzo; vestigia: *the remains of a Greek temple*, gli avanzi di un tempio greco **2.** *pl.* reliquie; spoglie mortali, cadavere **3.** *pl.* opere postume.

to **remain**, *v.i.* rimanere, restare; avanzare: *at least one thing remains certain*, almeno una cosa resta certa; *nothing remains but to sign the agreement*, non resta che da firmare il contratto ‖ *I — yours truly*, sono il vostro devotissimo (formula di chiusura di una lettera).

remainder [ri'meində*], *ag.* (*arc.*) restante, rimanente ‖ *s.* **1.** resto, residuo, avanzo; rimanenza (di libri invenduti e offerti a prezzi ridotti): *the — of his life*, il resto della sua vita **2.** persone rimanenti: *twenty people came in and the — stayed outside*, entrarono venti persone e le rimanenti rimasero fuori **3.** (*dir.*) riversione: *the estate is left to A with — to B*, la successione passa ad A con riversione su B **4.** (*arit.*) resto: *division with no —*, divisione senza resto.

to **remainder**, *v.t.* liquidare (un'edizione).

remaining [ri'meiniŋ], *ag.* restante, che resta: *his — days*, il resto dei suoi giorni.

to **remake** ['ri:'meik], *pass.p.p.* **remade** ['ri:'meid], *v.t.* rifare.

to **reman** ['ri:'mæn], *pass.p.p.* **remanned** ['ri:'mænd], *v.t.* **1.** (*mar.*) riequipaggiare, fornire di nuovi uomini **2.** ridare coraggio a.

remand [ri'mɑ:nd], *s.* (*dir.*) rinvio (di imputato) in carcere (per un supplemento d'istruttoria): *to be on —*, essere trattenuto a disposizione della legge ☆ *— home*, carcere preventivo.

to **remand**, *v.t.* **1.** (*dir.*) rinviare (imputato) in carcere per un supplemento d'istruttoria **2.** (*rar.*) restituire.

remanent ['remənənt], *ag.* (*rar.*) rimanente, residuo: *— magnetism*, (*fis.*) rimanenza magnetica.

remanet ['remənet], *s.* **1.** parte rimanente, residuo **2.** (*dir.*) causa, progetto di legge rinviato ad altra sessione.

remark [ri'mɑ:k], *s.* **1.** nota, attenzione: *worthy of —*, degno di nota; *to let the matter pass without —*, lascia passare la cosa inosservata **2.** osservazione, appunto; commento: *his remarks are often interesting*, le sue osservazioni sono spesso interessanti; *to make remarks about* (o *to pass remarks upon*) *s.o.*, fare delle osservazioni su qlcu.

to **remark**, *v.t.i.* **1.** osservare; considerare con attenzione; notare; far notare; far rimarcare **2.** fare osservazioni, fare commenti: *don't — (up)on it*, non fare commenti su ciò.

remarkable [ri'mɑ:kəbl], *ag.* notevole; ragguardevole; eccezionale, straordinario; sorprendente: *— event*, avvenimento eccezionale; *a man — for his courage*, un uomo notevole per il suo coraggio.

remarkableness [ri'mɑ:kəblnis], *s.* ragguardevolezza; rilievo; eccezionalità.

remarkably [ri'mɑ:kəbli], *av.* notevolmente; ragguardevolmente; eccezionalmente; particolarmente.

remarker [ri'mɑ:kə*], *s.c.* **1.** osservatore, osservatrice **2.** commentatore, commentatrice.

remarriage ['ri:'mæridʒ], *s.* nuovo matrimonio; seconde nozze.

to **remarry** ['ri:'mæri], *v.t.i.* unire, unirsi di nuovo in matrimonio; risposarsi.

to **remast** ['ri:'mɑ:st], *v.t.* (*mar.*) rifornire di albero, di alberi (una nave).

remblai [,rɑ:n'blei], *s.* (*mil.*) terra usata per fare fortificazioni; terrapieni.

Rembrandtesque [,rembræn'tesk], *ag.* nello stile di Rembrandt.

remeant ['ri:miənt], *ag.* (*rar.*) che ritorna.

remediable [ri'mi:djəbl], *ag.* rimediabile.

remediableness [ri'mi:djəblnis], *s.* rimediabilità.

remediably [ri'mi:djəbli], *av.* in modo rimediabile.

remedial [ri'mi:djəl], *ag.* atto a rimediare; riparatore.

remedially [ri'mi:djəli], *av.* in modo da rimediare; come rimedio.

remediless ['remidilis], *ag.* irrimediabile, irreparabile; incurabile.

remedilessly ['remidilisli], *av.* irrimediabilmente, irreparabilmente.

remedilessness ['remidilisnis], *s.* irrimediabilità.

remedy ['remidi], *s.* **1.** rimedio, riparo; medicina; cura: *a good — for a cold*, una buona medicina per il raffreddore ‖ *past —*, irrimediabile, irreparabile; incurabile **2.** (*dir.*) ricorso **3.** tolleranza di peso concessa alla moneta di nuovo conio.

to **remedy**, *v.t.* **1.** rimediare, porre rimedio a; correggere **2.** (*rar.*) guarire; curare.

to **remember** [ri'membə*], *v.t.i.* **1.** ricordare, ricordarsi; rammentare, rammentarsi: *— me to your parents*, ricordami ai tuoi genitori, salutali da parte mia; *— to tell him*, ricordati di dirglielo; *do you — me?*, mi riconosci?, ti ricordi di me?; *he remembered me in his will*, si ricordò di me nel suo testamento; *I — telling him about it*, ricordo di avergliene parlato; *I shall ever — you*, ti ricorderò sempre ‖ *— the porter*, non dimenticare la mancia al facchino **2.** ricordare, sapere a memoria: *I — every date in English history*, so a memoria tutte le date della storia inglese.

remembrance [ri'membrəns], *s.* **1.** ricordo, memoria: *in — of*, in ricordo di, alla memoria di; *within my —*, per quanto io ricordi; *I have no — of it*, non lo ricordo affatto; *it escapes my —*, sfugge alla mia memoria; *to call to —*, richiamare alla memoria; *to have in —*, avere in mente; *to put in —*, far ricordare ‖ *Remembrance Day*, 11 novembre (anniversario dell'armistizio del 1918) **2.** *pl.* ossequi, saluti (inviati a mezzo di terza persona): *give my best remembrances to him*, porgigli i miei migliori saluti.

remembrancer [ri'membrənsə*], *s.* **1.** « souvenir », ricordo, ricordino **2.** promemoria **3.** *City Remembrancer*, rappresentante della City di Londra presso il Parlamento; *King's, Queen's Remembrancer*, segretario del tesoro reale.

remex ['ri:meks], *pl.* **remiges** ['remidʒi:z], *s.* (penna) remigante (degli uccelli).

to **remigrate** ['ri:'maigreit], *v.i.* rimpatriare.

remigration ['ri:mai'greiʃən], *s.* rimpatrio.

remilitarization ['ri:'militərai'zeiʃən], *s.* nuova militarizzazione.

to **remilitarize** ['ri:'militəraiz], *v.t.* militarizzare di nuovo.

to **remind** [ri'maind], *v.t.* ricordare a, far ricordare a, rammentare a: *— everybody that we are leaving in a few minutes*, ricorda a tutti che fra pochi minuti si parte; *— him of his promise*, ricordagli la sua promessa; *— me to settle this account to-day*, ricordami di saldare questo conto oggi; *that reminds me of a joke I once heard*, ciò mi fa venire in mente una barzelletta che udii una volta; *you — me of your father*, mi ricordi tuo padre.

reminder [ri'maində*], *s.* **1.** ricordo, promemoria **2.** (*comm.*) lettera di sollecitazione.

remindful [ri'maindful], *ag.* **1.** che fa ricordare, che ravviva la memoria **2.** memore.

to **reminisce** [,remi'nis], *v.i.* (*fam. scherz.*) raccontare i propri ricordi; abbandonarsi ai propri ricordi.

reminiscence [,remi'nisns], *s.* **1.** reminiscenza; rimembranza; ricordo: *the scene awakens réminiscences of my youth*, la scena risveglia i ricordi della mia giovinezza **2.** *pl.* memorie: *to write one's reminiscences*, scrivere le proprie memorie.

reminiscent [,remi'nisnt], *ag.* **1.** che richiama alla mente: *a landscape — of Turner's paintings*, paesaggio che rammenta i quadri di Turner **2.** che si abbandona ai ricordi: *the old man became —*, il vecchio si lasciò trasportare dai ricordi.

reminiscential [,remini'senʃəl], *ag.* relativo a reminiscenza.

remise[1] [rə'mi:z], *s.* **1.** (*scherma*) rimessa **2.** (*arc.*) rimessa (per vettura); carrozza presa a nolo.

to **remise**[1], *v.i.* (*scherma*) fare una rimessa.

to **remise**[2] [ri'maiz], *v.t.* (*dir.*) rinunciare a, cedere (diritti, proprietà).

remiss [ri'mis], · *ag.* negligente, trascurato; lento; fiacco, svogliato.

remissible [ri'misibl], *ag.* remissibile; perdonabile.

remission [ri'miʃən], *s.* **1.** remissione, perdono; (*dir.*) condono: *to grant s.o. — of his sins*, assolvere qlcu. dai suoi peccati **2.** rinuncia (a rivendicazione, diritto); annullamento (di tassa, debito); esonero (da tasse, ecc.) **3.** abbassamento, diminuzione **4.** (*med.*) remittenza.

remissive [ri'misiv], *ag.* **1.** remissivo, che perdona **2.** caratterizzato da abbassamento, diminuzione.

remissly [ri'misli], *av.* negligentemente, trascuratamente; lentamente; svogliatamente.

remissness [ri'misnis], *s.* negligenza, trascuratezza; lentezza, svogliatezza.

to **remit** [ri'mit], *pass.p.p.* **remitted** [ri'mitid], *v.t.i.* **1.** rimettere, perdonare; (*dir.*) condonare: *God will — your sins*, Dio perdonerà i vostri peccati **2.** diminuire; mitigare, mitigarsi; rallentare: *his anger began to —*, la sua collera cominciò a sbollire **3.** rimettere, sottomettere (ad una autorità); (*dir.*) rinviare (a giudizio in altra sede) **4.** mettere di nuovo, ristabilire: *to — a tribe into slavery*, rendere una tribù nuovamente schiava **5.** (*comm.*) rimettere; effettuare un pagamento: *kindly — by cheque*, favorite effettuare il pagamento con assegno **6.** rimandare; differire; rinviare.

remittal [ri'mitl], *s.* **1.** remissione, perdono; (*dir.*) condono **2.** (*dir.*) rinvio di processo (ad altro tribunale).

remittance [ri'mitəns], *s.* (*comm.*) rimessa: *— of balance*, invio del saldo; *to send s.o. a —*, fare una rimessa a qlcu. ☆ *-man*, persona che vive delle rimesse inviategli da casa.

remitee [ri,mi'ti:], *s.* (*comm.*) destinatario (di rimessa).

remittent [ri'mitənt], *ag.* (*med.*) remittente (di febbre).

remitter[1] [ri'mitə*], *s.c.* **1.** (*rar.*) chi rimette; chi assolve, chi perdona **2.** (*comm.*) chi effettua una rimessa.

remitter[2], *s.* (*dir.*) rinvio a giudizio in altra sede.

remittor [ri'mitə*], *s.* (*comm. amer.*) chi effettua una rimessa.

remnant ['remnənt], *ag.* rimanente, rimasto ‖ *s.* **1.** avanzo, resto, residuo: *the remnants of an ancient church*, i resti di un'antica chiesa **2.** scampolo; frammento; rimanenza ☆ *— sale*, liquidazione, saldo.

to **remodel** ['ri:'mɔdl], *pass.p.p.* **remodelled** ['ri:'mɔdld], *v.t.* rimodellare; ricomporre, rimaneggiare.

to **remonetize** [ri:'mʌnitaiz], *v.t.* ridare corso legale a (una moneta).

remonstrance [ri'mɔnstrəns], *s.* rimostranza.

remonstrant [ri'mɔnstrənt], *ag.s.c.* rimostrante.

remonstrantly [ri'mɔnstrəntli], *av.* con rimostranze.

to **remonstrate** [ri'mɔnstreit], *v.t.i.* fare rimostranze; obiettare; protestare: *to — against sthg.*, protestare contro ql.co.; *to — with s.o. upon sthg.*, protestare con qlcu. per ql.co.

remonstratingly [ri'mɔnstreitiŋli], *av.* con rimostranze; con proteste.

remonstration [,remən'streiʃən], *V.* **remonstrance**.

remonstrative [ri'mɔnstrətiv], *ag.* rimostrante; di rimostranza, di protesta.

remonstrator [ri'mɔnstreitə*], *s.c.* rimostrante.

remontant [ri'mɔntənt], *ag.* rifiorente (specialmente di rosa) ‖ *s.* pianta che fiorisce più volte (specialmente rosa).

remora ['remərə], *s.* **1.** (*ittiol.*) remora **2.** (*rar.*) remora, indugio; impedimento, ostacolo.

to **remord** [ri'mɔ:d], *v.t.* (*arc.*) rimordere, tormentare.

remorse [ri'mɔ:s], *s.* rimorso.

remorseful [ri'mɔ:sful], *ag.* tormentato dal rimorso.

remorsefully [ri'mɔ:sfuli], *av.* con rimorso.

remorsefulness [ri'mɔ:sfulnis], *s.* forte rimorso.

remorseless [ri'mɔ:slis], *ag.* senza rimorsi; spietato, crudele.

remorselessly [ri'mɔ:slisli], *av.* senza rimorsi; spietatamente, crudelmente.

remorselessness [ri'mɔ:slisnis], *s.* assenza di rimorso; mancanza di pietà; crudeltà.

remote [ri'mout], *ag.* **1.** remoto; distante; lontano: *he is a — kinsman of mine,* è un mio lontano parente; *he lives — from the town,* abita lontano dalla città **2.** *fig.* estraneo, alieno: *sciences — from each other,* scienze estranee l'una all'altra **3.** appartato: *a — house,* una casa appartata **4.** leggero, vago: *a — resemblance,* una vaga rassomiglianza; *he had not the remotest idea of what I meant,* non aveva la più pallida idea di ciò che volessi dire.

remotely [ri'moutli], *av.* **1.** remotamente; lontanamente; alla lontana **2.** leggermente; vagamente.

remoteness [ri'moutnis], *s.* distanza; lontananza.

remotion [ri'mouʃən], *s.* rimozione, allontanamento; eliminazione.

to remould ['ri:'mould], *v.t.* riplasmare; rimodellare.

remount ['ri:maunt], *s.* (*mil.*) **1.** rimonta **2.** cavallo fresco.

to remount [ri:'maunt], *v.t.i.* **1.** rimontare (a cavallo, in bicicletta, ecc.) **2.** risalire (una collina, ecc.) **3.** (*mil.*) rifornire di cavalli freschi **4.** risalire (a una data).

removability [ri,mu:və'biliti], *s.* (*amm.*) amovibilità.

removable [ri'mu:vəbl], *ag.* **1.** (*amm.*) amovibile **2.** rimovibile; trasportabile ∥ *s.* magistrato amovibile (in Irlanda).

removal [ri'mu:vəl], *s.* **1.** rimozione; allontanamento; (*chir.*) ablazione **2.** destituzione **3.** trasferimento; trasloco ☆ *— expenses,* spese di trasferta.

remove [ri'mu:v], *s.* **1.** portata che viene dopo un'altra (a tavola) **2.** promozione (a scuola): *he did not get his —,* non ottenne la promozione **3.** grado (di parentela, ecc.): *all my cousins even to the fourth — remember me,* tutti i miei cugini sino al quarto grado si ricordano di me **4.** (*rar.*) rimozione; trasferimento.

to remove, *v.t.i.* **1.** rimuovere, spostare; togliere; levare: *this will — all traces of blood,* ciò eliminerà ogni traccia di sangue; *will you — your son from school?,* ritirerete vostro figlio da scuola?; *to — all doubts,* togliere ogni dubbio **2.** destituire, congedare (da ufficio, impiego); dare il cambio a: *to — a sentry,* dare il cambio a una sentinella **3.** traslocare, trasferirsi; allontanarsi: *to — from one place to another,* trasferirsi da un posto all'altro ∥ *to — furniture,* fare traslochi (per mestiere) **4.** sopprimere, togliere di mezzo, assassinare: *he was removed by poison,* fu soppresso col veleno.

removed [ri'mu:vd], *ag.* lontano; estraneo: *his feeling was not far — from pity,* il suo sentimento era molto simile alla pietà ∥ *first cousin once, twice —,* cugino di secondo, terzo grado.

removedness [ri'mu:vidnis], *s.* lontananza; isolamento.

remover [ri'mu:və*], *s.* **1.** chi, cosa che rimuove, allontana, toglie **2.** chi per mestiere effettua traslochi ☆ *stain- —,* smacchiatore; *superfluous hair —,* depilatorio; *varnish —,* acqua ragia, solvente per vernice.

to remunerate [ri'mju:nəreit], *v.t.* rimunerare, ricompensare.

remuneration [ri,mju:nə'reiʃən], *s.* rimunerazione, ricompensa.

remunerative [ri'mju:nərətiv], *ag.* rimunerativo.

remuneratively [ri'mju:nərətivli], *av.* in modo rimunerativo.

remunerator [ri'mju:nəreitə*], *s.* rimuneratore.

Remus ['ri:məs], *no.pr.m.* Remo.

renaissance [rə'neisəns], *s.* rinascimento ∥ *the Renaissance,* il Rinascimento: *Renaissance painter,* pittore del Rinascimento.

renal ['ri:nəl], *ag.* (*anat.*) renale.

to rename ['ri:'neim], *v.t.* rinominare; dare un nome nuovo a.

renascence [ri'næsns], *s.* rinascita, rinascenza; rinascimento; rinnovamento ∥ *the Renascence,* il Rinascimento.

renascent [ri'næsnt], *ag.* rinascente.

rencontre [ren'kɔntə*], **rencounter** [ren'kauntə*], *s.* (*rar.*) **1.** scontro; scaramuccia; battaglia; duello **2.** incontro casuale.

to rencounter, *v.t.i.* **1.** incontrare per caso, incontrarsi per caso **2.** (*rar.*) scontrarsi.

to rend [rend], *pass.p.p.* **rent** [rent], *v.t.i.* strappare, strapparsi; lacerare, lacerarsi; squarciare, squarciarsi; dividere (anche *fig.*): *anarchy will — the country,* l'anarchia dividerà il paese; *the clouds rent,* le nubi si squarciarono; *my heart is rent,* il mio cuore è a pezzi; *a province rent from the empire,* una provincia strappata all'impero; *the shouts rent the air,* le urla squarciavano l'aria; *to — one's garments, one's hair,* strapparsi le vesti, i capelli ∥ *to — sthg. apart* (o *asunder*), strappare in due ql.co. ∥ *to — sthg. off* (o *away*), strappar via ql.co.

render[1] ['rendə*], *s.c.* chi squarcia, lacera.

render[2], *s.* **1.** restituzione **2.** pagamento (di tributo) **3.** (*edil.*) rinzaffo, prima mano di intonaco.

to render[2], *v.t.* **1.** rendere, restituire: *to — good for evil,* rendere bene per male ∥ *— (un)to Caesar the things that are Caesar's,* date a Cesare quello che è di Cesare **2.** rendere, pagare (tributo, ecc.); mostrare (obbedienza, ecc.): *to — homage,* rendere omaggio; *to — service,* rendere servizio **3.** rendere, far diventare: *my work renders me nervous,* il mio lavoro mi rende nervoso **4.** rendere, rappresentare: *he rendered Hamlet very well,* rappresentò Amleto molto bene; *the resemblance was perfectly rendered by the painter,* la rassomiglianza fu perfettamente resa dal pittore **5.** rendere, tradurre: *poetry cannot be adequately rendered in another language,* non si può adeguatamente tradurre la poesia in un'altra lingua **6.** sciogliere (grasso); raffinare (olio) **7.** (*edil.*) inzaffare, dare la prima mano di intonaco a.

rendering ['rendəriŋ], *s.* **1.** restituzione; resa **2.** traduzione; interpretazione **3.** fusione (di grasso); raffinazione (di olio) **4.** (*edil.*) rinzaffo; rinzaffatura.

render-set ['rendəset], *ag.* intonacato (con due strati d'intonaco) ∥ *s.* intonaco (formato da due strati).

to render-set, *pass.p.p.* **render-set,** *v.t.* intonacare (con un doppio strato di intonaco).

rendezvous ['rɔndivu:], *pl.* **rendezvous** ['rɔndivu:z], *s.* **1.** (*mar. mil.*) luogo di raduno **2.** luogo di convegno **3.** appuntamento; convegno.

to rendezvous, *v.i.* riunirsi; incontrarsi.

rending ['rendiŋ], *s.* **1.** strappo; lacerazione **2.** spaccatura.

rendition [ren'diʃən], *s.* **1.** traduzione **2.** interpretazione (teatrale, musicale) **3.** (*rar.*) resa (di fortezza, ecc.).

René [rə'nei], *no.pr.m.* Renato.

renegade ['renigeid], *s.* **1.** (*relig.*) rinnegato, apostata **2.** traditore; disertore.

to renegade, *v.i.* **1.** (*relig.*) abiurare, apostatare **2.** agire da rinnegato, disertare: *he renegaded from his party,* abbandonò il suo partito.

renegado [,reni'geidou], (*arc.*) per **renegade.**

renegation [,reni'geiʃən], *s.* **1.** (*relig.*) abiura, apostasia **2.** rinnegamento; diserzione.

to reneg(u)e [ri'ni:g], *v.t.i.* **1.** (*carte*) passare **2.** (*arc.*) rinnegare; rifiutare; abbandonare; rinunciare a.

to renew [ri'nju:], *v.t.i.* **1.** rinnovare, rinnovarsi; rinvigorire, rinforzare: *to — the air,* ventilare un locale; *to — a bill,* rinnovare una cambiale; *to — a lease,* rinnovare un contratto d'affitto; *to — one's attention,* raddoppiare l'attenzione; *to — one's complaints,* rinnovare le proprie lagnanze; *to — one's strength,* rinvigorire le proprie forze; *— a promise,* rinnovare una promessa; *to — a request* (o *an attempt*), (*fam.*) ritornare alla carica; *to — the water in the bowls,* rinnovare l'acqua nei vasi **2.** sostituire (pezzo di macchina, ecc.).

renewable [ri'nju(:)əbl], *ag.* rinnovabile.

renewal [ri'nju(:)əl], *s.* **1.** rinnovo; rinnovamento: — *of a bill*, rinnovo di una cambiale **2.** ripresa: — *of negotiations*, ripresa dei negoziati **3.** sostituzione (di pneumatico, ecc.) ☆ — *bill*, (*comm.*) rivalsa cambiaria.

renewedly [ri'nju:idli], *av.* di nuovo; ripetutamente.

renewer [ri'nju:ə*], *s.c.* rinnovatore, rinnovatrice.

reniform ['renifɔ:m], *ag.* reniforme.

renitency [ri'naitənsi], *s.* renitenza, riluttanza.

renitent [ri'naitənt], *ag.* renitente, restio riluttante.

rennet[1] ['renit], *s.* presame, caglio.

rennet[2], *s.* mela ranetta.

to **renominate** ['ri:'nɔmineit], *v.t.* **1.** nominare di nuovo **2.** riproporre come candidato.

renounce [ri'nauns], *s.* (*carte*) rifiuto.

to **renounce**, *v.t.i.* **1.** rinunciare a: *to — a right*, (*dir.*) rinunciare a un diritto; *to — the throne*, rinunciare al trono; *to — the world*, rinunciare alla vita mondana **2.** rinnegare, ripudiare: *to — old friends*, ripudiare i vecchi amici; *to — one's faith*, rinnegare la propria fede **3.** (*carte*) rifiutare.

renouncement [ri'naunsmənt], *s.* rinuncia.

renouncer [ri'naunsə*], *s.c.* **1.** rinunciatore, rinunciatrice **2.** (*dir.*) rinunciatario, rinunciataria.

to **renovate** ['renouveit], *v.t.* **1.** rinnovare, ripristinare **2.** rinvigorire.

renovation [,renou'veiʃən], *s.* rinnovazione, rinnovamento.

renovator ['renouveitə*], *s.c.* rinnovatore, rinnovatrice.

renown [ri'naun], *s.* rinomanza, celebrità, fama: *man of great —*, uomo di chiara fama.

to **renown**, *v.t.* (*rar.*) dar rinomanza a.

renowned [ri'naund], *ag.* rinomato, celebre, famoso.

rent[1] [rent], *s.* **1.** pigione, affitto; nolo: *we pay a high —*, paghiamo un affitto alto ‖ *for —*, (*amer.*) affittasi **2.** reddito, entrata; rendita ☆ — *free*, esente da affitto; — *-restriction*, blocco degli affitti; — *-roll*, censimento delle entrate da beni immobili.

to **rent**[1], *v.t.i.* **1.** affittare, prendere in affitto; dare in affitto: *to — a house*, affittare una casa; *to — one's tenants low*, far pagare un affitto basso ai propri inquilini **2.** essere affittato: *this room rents for little money*, questa camera viene affittata a basso prezzo.

rent[2], *s.* **1.** strappo; laceramento, squarcio **2.** spaccatura, fessura; scoscendimento **3.** *fig.* (*rar.*) rottura, scisma.

rent[2], *pass.p.p.* di to **rend** ‖ *ag.* strappato.

to **rent**[2], (*arc.*) per to **rend**.

rentable ['rentəbl], *ag.* affittabile.

rental ['rentl], *s.* **1.** introito derivante da affitti **2.** (somma pagata, ricevuta come) affitto ☆ — *library*, (*amer.*) biblioteca circolante.

rente [rɑ:ɳt], *s.* rendita.

renter ['rentə*], *s.* **1.** fittavolo **2.** distributore di film ‖ *s.c.* **1.** affittuario, affittuaria **2.** locatore, locatrice.

rentier ['rontiei], *s.* chi vive di rendita.

to **renumber** ['ri:'nʌmbə*], *v.t.* **1.** contare di nuovo **2.** rinumerare, rifare la numerazione di.

renunciant [ri'nʌnʃiənt], *ag.s.* rinunziante; rinunciatario.

renunciation [ri,nʌnsi'eiʃən], *s.* **1.** rinuncia; abbandono: — *of property*, (*dir.*) cessione di proprietà **2.** ripudio, rinnegamento: — *on oath*, abiura.

renunciative [ri'nʌnʃiətiv], **renunciatory** [ri'nʌnʃiətəri], *ag.* rinunciante, rinunciatorio.

reoccupation ['ri:,ɔkju'peiʃən], *s.* rioccupazione.

to **reoccupy** ['ri:'ɔkjupai], *v.t.* rioccupare.

to **reopen** ['ri:'oupən], *v.t.i.* riaprire, riaprirsi.

reopening ['ri:'oupniŋ], *s.* riapertura.

reorganization ['ri:,ɔ:gənai'zeiʃən], *s.* riorganizzazione, riassetto.

to **reorganize** ['ri:'ɔ:gənaiz], *v.t.i.* riorganizzare, riorganizzarsi.

rep[1] [rep], *s.* « reps », tessuto a coste.

rep[2], *s.c.* (*abbr.* di *reprobate*) (*teol.*) reprobo, reproba; dannato, dannata.

rep, *s.* (*abbr.* di *repetition*) (*sl. scolastico*) lezione imparata a memoria.

to **repaint** ['ri:'peint], *v.t.* ridipingere.

repair[1] [ri'peə*], *s.* **1.** (*arc.*) riparo, rifugio, ritiro: *place of safe —*, rifugio sicuro **2.** (*rar.*) affluenza (di persone): *place of great —*, luogo molto frequentato.

to **repair**[1], *v.i.* riparare; rifugiarsi: *to — to a place*, riparare, trovare rifugio in un luogo.

repair[2], *s.* **1.** riparazione, restauro: *beyond —*, irreparabile: *broken beyond —*, irrimediabilmente rotto; *our telephone is out of —*, il nostro telefono è guasto; *the road is under —*, la strada è in riparazione; *this house needs a lot of repairs*, questa casa ha bisogno di molti restauri ‖ *repairs done while you wait*, riparazioni rapide **2.** stato: *in bad —*, in cattivo stato; *in good —*, in buono stato **3.** (*mar.*) raddobbo.

to **repair**[2], *v.t.* **1.** riparare; restaurare; fare riparazioni a: *to — a house*, restaurare una casa **2.** *fig.* riparare; rimediare: *he repaired his past misdeeds*, ha rimediato alle malefatte del passato.

repairable [ri'peərəbl], *ag.* riparabile.

repairer [ri'peərə*], *s.c.* riparatore, riparatrice.

repairing [ri'peəriŋ], *s.* riparazione.

repand [ri'pænd], *ag.* ondulato.

to **repaper** ['ri:'peipə*], *v.t.* ritappezzare.

reparable ['repərəbl], *ag.* riparabile.

reparably ['repərəbli], *av.* in modo riparabile.

reparation [,repə'reiʃən], *s.* **1.** riparazione **2.** risarcimento: *reparations for war damages*, risarcimento dei danni di guerra.

reparative [ri'pærətiv], *ag.* **1.** di riparazione; che ripara **2.** che risarcisce.

repartee [,repɑ:'ti:], *s.* **1.** risposta pronta e spiritosa; replica arguta **2.** abilità nel dare risposte spiritose.

to **repartee**, *v.i.* (*rar.*) replicare, rispondere in modo spiritoso, argutamente.

repartition [,repɑ:'tiʃən], *s.* ripartizione; suddivisione.

to **repartition**, *v.t.* ripartire; suddividere.

to **repass** ['ri:'pɑ:s], *v.t.i.* ripassare (per un luogo); riattraversare.

repassage ['ri:'pæsidʒ], *s.* successivo passaggio.

repast [ri'pɑ:st], *s.* pasto: *a rich —*, un ricco pasto.

repatriate [ri:'pætrieit], *s.c.* rimpatriato, rimpatriata.

to **repatriate**, *v.t.i.* rimpatriare.

repatriation ['ri:pætri'eiʃən], *s.* rimpatrio.

to **repay** [ri:'pei], *pass.p.p.* **repaid** [ri:'peid], *v.t.i.* **1.** pagare; restituire: *this money will soon be repaid to you*, questo denaro ti sarà presto restituito; *to — a visit*, restituire una visita **2.** ricompensare; risarcire: *it will — you for your trouble*, ciò ti ricompenserà per il tuo disturbo.

repayable [ri:'peiəbl], *ag.* **1.** rimborsabile, restituibile **2.** ricompensabile.

repayment [ri:'peimənt], *s.* **1.** rimborso, restituzione **2.** ricompensa.

repeal [ri'pi:l], *s.* revoca, abrogazione; annullamento.

to **repeal**, *v.t.* revocare, abrogare; abolire, annullare: *to — a law*, abrogare una legge; *to — a will*, annullare un testamento.

repealable [ri'pi:ləbl], *ag.* revocabile, abrogabile.

repealer [ri'pi:lə*], *s.* **1.** abrogatore; abolitore **2.** (*st. irl.*) oppositore all'unione con la Gran Bretagna.

repeat [ri'pi:t], *s.* **1.** ripetizione **2.** (*mus.*) ripresa ☆ — *order*, (*comm.*) ordine successivo (di merce dello stesso genere).

to **repeat**, *v.t.i.* **1.** ripetere; studiare, recitare a memoria: *to — oneself*, ripetersi **2.** ricorrere; ritornare **3.** suonare a ripetizione (di orologio) **4.** (*mat.*) ripetersi all'infinito **5.** tornare alla gola (di cibo) **6.** (*amer.*) votare più volte in una stessa elezione.

repeatable [ri'pi:təbl], *ag.* ripetibile.

repeated [ri'pi:tid], *ag.* ripetuto.

repeatedly [ri'pi:tidli], *av.* ripetutamente.

repeater [ri'pi:tə*], *s.c.* **1.** ripetitore, ripetitrice **2.** ripetente (a scuola) ‖ *s.* **1.** (*amer.*) elettore fraudolento (che vota due volte) **2.** delinquente recidivo **3.** arma da fuoco a ripetizione **4.** orologio a ripetizione; bussola ripetitrice; (*tel.*) ripetitore **5.** (*mat.*) numero periodico.

repeating [ri'pi:tiŋ], *ag.* a ripetizione ☆ — *decimal*, decimale periodico; — *rifle*, fucile a ripetizione; — *watch*, orologio a ripetizione ‖ *s.* ripetizione.

to **repel** [ri'pel], *pass.p.p.* **repelled** [ri'peld], *v.t.* **1.** respingere: *to — the enemy*, respingere il nemico: *to — a suitor*, respingere un corteggiatore **2.** (*fis. chim.*) respingere; essere incapace a combinarsi con: *water repels oil*, l'acqua non si combina con l'olio **3.** ripugnare a; ispirare ripugnanza a: *such things — me*, queste cose mi ripugnano.

repellent [ri'pelənt], *ag.* repellente, ripulsivo, ripugnante: *to be — to s.o.*, essere ripugnante a qlcu.

repellently [ri'peləntli], *av.* in modo repellente, repulsivo, ripugnante.

repent[1] [ri'pənt], *ag.* (*zool.*) strisciante; (*bot.*) rampicante.

to **repent**[2] [ri'pent], *v.t.i.* (I) pentirsi; pentirsi di: *he had nothing to — of*, non aveva nulla di cui pentirsi; *I — being so unfair to you*, mi pento di essere stato così ingiusto verso di voi; *I will not — this* (o *of this*), non me ne pentirò.

repentance [ri'pentəns], *s.* pentimento, resipiscenza.

repentant [ri'pentənt], *ag.* pentito; contrito.

repentantly [ri'pentəntli], *av.* con pentimento; con compunzione, contritamente.

repenter [ri'pentə*], *s.c.* penitente.

to **repeople** [ri:'pi:pl], *v.t.* ripopolare.

repercussion [,ri:pə:'kʌʃən], *s.* ripercussione.

repercussive [,ri:pə:'kʌsiv], *ag.* ripercussivo.

repertoire ['repətwɑ:*], *s.* (*teat.*) repertorio.

repertory ['repətəri], *s.* **1.** repertorio; lista, catalogo **2.** (*teat.*) repertorio.

repetend [ri'petend], *s.* **1.** (*mat.*) periodo (di frazione periodica) **2.** ritornello; motivo ricorrente.

repetition [,repi'tiʃən], *s.* **1.** ripetizione; copia; replica **2.** lezione da impararsi a memoria.

repetitious [,repi'tiʃəs], *ag.* che (si) ripete; noioso.

repetitive [ri'petitiv], *ag.* che ripete, caratterizzato da una ripetizione.

to **rephrase** ['ri:'freiz], *v.t.* esprimere, formulare di nuovo.

to **repiece** ['ri:'pi:s], *v.t.* ricomporre; ricostruire; rimettere insieme.

to **repine** [ri'pain], *v.i.* dolersi; lamentarsi; lagnarsi; affliggersi: *to — against s.o.*, mormorare contro qlcu.; *to — at one's fate*, dolersi del proprio destino.

repiningly [ri'painiŋli], *av.* lamentosamente, con tono scontento, insoddisfatto.

repique ['ri:'pi:k], *s.* il segnare 30 punti di vantaggio o più al picchetto prima di iniziare il giuoco.

to **repique**, *v.t.i.* (*giuoco del picchetto*) segnare 30 punti o più di vantaggio contro (l'avversario); segnare 30 punti o più di vantaggio.

to **replace** [ri'pleis], *v.t.* **1.** ricollocare, rimettere a posto; restituire **2.** rimpiazzare; sostituire; prendere il posto di; succedere a: *to — a lost book with a new one*, sostituire un libro perso con uno nuovo; *to be replaced by s.o.*, essere sostituito da qlcu.

replaceable [ri'pleisəbl], *ag.* sostituibile.

replacement [ri'pleismənt], *s.* **1.** ricollocamento **2.** sostituzione.

to **replant** ['ri:'plɑ:nt], *v.t.* ripiantare; trapiantare.

replantation ['ri:plæn'teiʃən], *s.* nuova piantagione; trapianto.

replay ['ri:-plei], *s.* partita ripetuta, di spareggio.

to **replay** ['ri:'plei], *v.t.* rigiocare (una partita).

to **replenish** [ri'pleniʃ], *v.t.* **1.** riempire: *to — with water*, riempire di acqua **2.** (*arc.*) ripopolare.

replenishment [ri'pleniʃmənt], *s.* riempimento, rifornimento.

replete [ri'pli:t], *ag.* **1.** pieno, ripieno, zeppo, colmo: — *with*, pieno di **2.** sazio, satollo.

repleteness [ri'pli:tnis], *s.* **1.** pienezza **2.** sazietà.

repletion [ri'pli:ʃən], *s.* **1.** pienezza; sazietà: *full to —*, satollo **2.** (*patol.*) pletora.

replevin [ri'plevin], *s.* (*dir.*) **1.** restituzione sotto cauzione **2.** decreto concedente tale restituzione **3.** azione derivante da tale restituzione.

to **replevy** [ri'plevi], *v.t.* (*dir.*) ricuperare sotto cauzione.

replica ['replikə], *s.* **1.** (*art.*) copia (di quadro, statua eseguita dall'artista stesso) **2.** fac-simile, copia, riproduzione esatta; duplicato.

replicate ['replikit], *ag.* (*bot.*) ripiegato su se stesso.

replicate, *s.* (*mus.*) motivo ripetuto in ottava più alta, più bassa.

to **replicate** ['replikeit], *v.t.* (*rar.*) **1.** replicare, ripetere **2.** piegare all'indietro.

replication [,repli'keiʃən], *s.* **1.** risposta; (*dir.*) replica **2.** ripercussione, eco **3.** riproduzione, copia **4.** (*rar.*) piega, ripiegatura.

replier [ri'plaiə*], *s.* chi replica, risponde.

reply [ri'plai], *s.* **1.** risposta: *what did she say in —?*, che cosa disse in risposta? **2.** (*dir.*) replica **3.** (*comm.*) riscontro: *in — to your letter*, facendo riscontro alla vostra lettera ☆ — *card*, cartolina con risposta pagata; — *-paid*, risposta pagata (di telegramma).

to **reply**, *v.t.i.* rispondere, replicare: *replying to your letter*, in risposta alla vostra lettera; *to — in the affirmative*, rispondere di sì.

to **repopulate** ['ri:'pɔpjuleit], *v.t.* ripopolare.

repopulation ['ri:,pɔpju'leiʃən], *s.* ripopolamento.

report [ri'pɔ:t], *s.* **1.** voce (pubblica), rumore, notizia, diceria: *idle reports*, chiacchiere inutili ‖ *the — goes*, si dice **2.** reputazione, fama: *a woman of good —*, una donna di buona reputazione **3.** rapporto, relazione; servizio (giornalistico) **4.** rumore; scoppio, rimbombo, detonazione: *a loud —*, una forte detonazione ☆ *law reports*, cronaca giudiziaria; (*dir.*) raccolta di giurisprudenza; *weather- —*, bollettino meteorologico.

to **report**, *v.t.i.* **1.** riportare, riferire, raccontare: *he is badly reported of*, si dice male di lui; *it is reported that*, si dice che; *you must — everything to us*, ci dovete riferire ogni cosa ‖ *reported speech*, (*gram.*) discorso indiretto **2.** fare la relazione di; render conto di; presentare, stendere rapporto: *they — weekly on the situation*, fanno rapporto ogni settimana sulla situazione; *to — a trial*, fare la cronaca di un processo **3.** essere corrispondente, cronista: *he reports for " The Times "*, è corrispondente del « Times » **4.** presentarsi: *you must — on Monday*, dovete presentarvi lunedì **5.** riportare, denunciare.

reportable [ri'pɔ:təbl], *ag.* riferibile.

reportage [,repɔ:'tɑ:ʒ], *s.* **1.** « reportage », servizio giornalistico **2.** stile giornalistico.

reporter [ri'pɔ:tə*], *s.* **1.** cronista, corrispondente (di giornale) ‖ *the Reporters' Gallery*, tribuna della stampa (in Parlamento) **2.** stenografo (al Parlamento) ☆ *crime —*, cronista di cronaca nera; *sports —*, cronista sportivo.

reposal [ri'pouzəl], *s.*: — *of trust* (o *confidence*) *in s.o.*, fiducia in qlcu.

repose[1] [ri'pouz], *s.* **1.** riposo; quiete, tranquillità **2.** armonia; serenità (in opere d'arte).

to **repose**[1], *v.t.i.* **1.** posare; riposare, riposarsi; dare riposo: *his body reposes under this stone*, il suo corpo riposa sotto questa pietra; *to — one's head on a pillow*, riposare il capo su un guanciale; *to — oneself*, riposarsi **2.** basarsi: *to — on sthg.*, basarsi su ql.co.

to **repose**[2], *v.t.* **1.** porre, riporre (fiducia, ecc.): *to — one's trust in s.o.*, riporre la propria fiducia in qlcu. **2.** (*rar.*) porre, riporre, depositare.

reposeful [ri'pouzful], *ag.* riposante; tranquillo.

reposefully [ri'pouzfuli], *av.* in modo riposante, tranquillamente.

repository [ri'pɔzitəri], *s.* **1.** deposito; magazzino; ripostiglio **2.** museo, collezione **3.** *fig.* miniera (d'informazioni, ecc.) **4.** tomba **5.** *fig.* confidente.

to **repossess** ['ri:pə'zes], *v.t.* rientrare in possesso di.

to **repost**, *V.* to **ripost(e)**.

to **repot** ['ri:'pɔt], *pass.p.p.* **repotted** ['ri:'pɔtid], *v.t.* rinvasare.

repoussé [rə'puːsei], *ag.* sbalzato, a sbalzo, martellato ‖ *s.* metallo lavorato a sbalzo.

repp [rep], *s.* « reps », tessuto a coste.

to **reprehend** [,repri'hend], *v.t.* riprendere, rimproverare, biasimare, censurare.

reprehensible [,repri'hensəbl], *ag.* riprensibile, biasimevole.

reprehensibly [,repri'hensəbli], *av.* riprensibilmente, biasimevolmente.

reprehension [,repri'henʃən], *s.* biasimo, critica; rimprovero.

to **represent** [,repri'zent], *v.t.* **1.** spiegare: *nobody can — the mysteries of religion*, nessuno sa spiegare i misteri della religione **2.** rappresentare, descrivere: *exactly as represented*, conforme alla descrizione; *picture representing a hunting scene*, quadro raffigurante una scena di caccia **3.** far notare, far presente; dichiarare: *they must — their urgent need to the government*, devono far presente al governo le loro urgenti necessità **4.** *fig.* raffigurare, dipingere: *he represents himself as a model of virtue*, pretende di essere un modello di virtù **5.** significare, avere valore di: *these words — nothing*, queste parole non significano nulla **6.** rappresentare (una commedia); recitare (una parte) **7.** simboleggiare; rappresentare, sostituire, fare le veci di: *the Queen was represented by the Duke of Edinburgh*, la regina era rappresentata dal Duca di Edimburgo.

representable [,repri'zentəbl], *ag.* rappresentabile.

representation [,reprizen'teiʃən], *s.* **1.** rappresentazione, raffigurazione; immagine **2.** rappresentanza **3.** *(teat.)* rappresentazione; interpretazione **4.** istanza; esposto; rimostranza, protesta ☆ *proportional —*, *(pol.)* rappresentanza proporzionale (in Parlamento, ecc.).

representational [,reprizen'teiʃənl], *ag.* relativo a rappresentanza, rappresentazione.

representative [,repri'zentətiv], *ag.* **1.** rappresentativo: *— government*, governo rappresentativo; *— men*, uomini rappresentativi **2.** che rappresenta, che simbolizza: *allegory — of charity*, allegoria che rappresenta la carità **3.** *(comm.)* tipo; tipico, caratteristico: *a — modern play*, una tipica commedia moderna ‖ *s.* **1.** esempio tipico, campione **2.** delegato; rappresentante (anche *comm.*) **3.** deputato.

representatively [,repri'zentətivli], *av.* in modo rappresentativo.

representativeness [,repri'zentətivnis], *s.* carattere rappresentativo.

to **repress** [ri'pres], *v.t.* reprimere; frenare: *to — a rising*, reprimere una rivolta.

repressed [ri'prest], *ag.* represso, contenuto.

repressible [ri'presəbl], *ag.* reprimibile.

repression [ri'preʃən], *s.* repressione.

repressive [ri'presiv], *ag.* repressivo.

repressively [ri'presivli], *av.* in modo repressivo.

repressiveness [ri'presivnis], *s.* carattere repressivo.

reprieve [ri'priːv], *s.* **1.** dilazione **2.** sospensione, commutazione di pena capitale.

to **reprieve**, *v.t.* **1.** accordare una dilazione a; concedere una tregua a **2.** sospendere l'esecuzione di; commutare la pena capitale a (un condannato).

reprimand ['reprimɑːnd], *s.* rimprovero, sgridata.

to **reprimand**, *v.t.* rimproverare, riprendere, sgridare.

reprint ['riː'print], *s.* ristampa; nuova tiratura.

to **reprint**, *v.t.* ristampare.

reprisal [ri'praizəl], *s.* **1.** rappresaglia: *to make reprisals*, compiere rappresaglie **2.** *gener. pl.* compenso.

reprise [ri'praiz], *s.* **1.** *(dir.)* detrazione annua **2.** *(rar.)* rappresaglia **3.** *(mus.)* ripresa, ritornello.

reproach [ri'proutʃ], *s.* **1.** rimprovero, biasimo: *to abstain from —*, astenersi dai rimproveri; *to heap reproaches on s.o.*, coprire qlcu. di improperi ‖ *the Reproaches*, *(eccl.)* gli Improperi **2.** vituperio, obbrobrio; vergogna, disonore: *a — to civilization*, una vergogna per la civiltà.

to **reproach**, *v.t.* **1.** rimproverare, biasimare, censurare: *to — s.o. with sthg.*, rimproverare qlcu. di ql. co. **2.** *(rar.)* esporre ai rimproveri, al biasimo.

reproachable [ri'proutʃəbl], *ag.* riprovevole.

reproachably [ri'proutʃəbli], *av.* *(rar.)* in modo riprovevole.

reproachful [ri'proutʃful], *ag.* **1.** di rimprovero **2.** riprovevole; vergognoso.

reproachfully [ri'proutʃfuli], *av.* **1.** con rimprovero **2.** *(arc.)* in modo riprovevole.

reproachfulness [ri'proutʃfulnis], *s.* **1.** aria, tono di rimprovero **2.** *(arc.)* carattere riprovevole.

reproachingly [ri'proutʃiŋli], *av.* *(rar.)* con rimprovero.

reproachless [ri'proutʃlis], *ag.* irreprensibile.

reprobate ['reproubeit], *ag.* empio, reprobo, dannato ‖ *s.c.* *(teol.)* reprobo, reproba; dannato, dannata.

to **reprobate**, *v.t.* **1.** riprovare; biasimare; censurare **2.** *(teol.)* dannare.

reprobation [,reprou'beiʃən], *s.* **1.** riprovazione; biasimo: *the fear of public —*, il timore del biasimo pubblico **2.** *(teol.)* condanna, dannazione.

to **reproduce** [,riːprə'djuːs], *v.t.i.* riprodurre, riprodursi: *design that will — well*, disegno che ben si presta alla riproduzione; *some creatures can — a lost limb*, alcuni animali possono riprodurre un arto perduto; *to — one's kind*, riprodurre la propria specie.

reproduceable [,riːprə'djuːsəbl], *ag.* riproducibile.

reproducer [,riːprə'djuːsə*], *s.c.* chi riproduce.

reproducible [,riːprə'djuːsibl], *ag.* riproducibile.

reproduction [,riːprə'dʌkʃən], *s.* **1.** riproduzione, generazione **2.** copia, imitazione; riproduzione.

reproductive [,riːprə'dʌktiv], *ag.* riproduttivo; riproduttore.

reproductively [,riːprə'dʌktivli], *av.* riproduttivamente.

reproductiveness [,riːprə'dʌktivnis], *s.* riproduttività, fertilità.

reproof[1] [ri'pruːf], *s.* rimprovero; biasimo.

to **reproof**[2] ['riː'pruːf], *v.t.* rendere nuovamente impermeabile.

to **reprove** [ri'pruːv], *v.t.* rimproverare; biasimare: *to — s.o. for his faults*, riprendere qlcu. per le sue colpe.

reprovingly [ri'pruːviŋli], *av.* in tono di rimprovero.

reps [reps], *s.* « reps », tessuto a coste.

reptant ['reptənt], *ag.* **1.** *(zool.)* strisciante **2.** *(bot.)* rampicante.

reptile ['reptail], *ag.* **1.** *(zool.)* strisciante **2.** *fig.* servile ‖ *the — press*, la stampa prezzolata ‖ *s.* rettile.

Reptilia [rep'tiliə], *s.pl.* i rettili.

reptilian [rep'tiliən], *ag.* **1.** di, simile a rettile **2.** *fig.* servile, strisciante ‖ *s.* rettile.

reptiliferous [,repti'lifərəs], *ag.* *(geol.)* contenente rettili fossilizzati.

reptiliform [rep'tilifɔːm], *ag.* a forma di rettile.

republic [ri'pʌblik], *s.* repubblica ‖ *the — of letters*, la repubblica delle lettere.

republican [ri'pʌblikən], *ag.s.* repubblicano.

republicanism [ri'pʌblikənizəm], *s.* repubblicanesimo.

to **republicanize** [ri'pʌblikənaiz], *v.t.* **1.** trasformare in repubblica **2.** rendere repubblicano.

republication ['riː,pʌbli'keiʃən], *s.* **1.** nuova edizione **2.** *(dir.)* nuova pubblicazione (di legge, decreto); nuova stesura (di testamento).

to **republish** ['riː'pʌbliʃ], *v.t.* **1.** ripubblicare, preparare una nuova edizione di (libro, ecc.) **2.** emanare nuovamente (una legge); cambiare (un testamento).

to **repudiate** [ri'pju:dieit], *v.t.* **1.** ripudiare **2.** disconoscere, rinnegare **3.** ribellarsi; rifiutarsi di.

repudiation [ri,pju:di'eiʃən], *s.* **1.** ripudio **2.** disconoscimento, rinnegazione **3.** rifiuto.

repudiator [ri'pju:dieitə*], *s.c.* chi ripudia, rinnega.

to **repugn** [ri'pju:n], *v.t.i.* **1.** ripugnare, essere ripugnante **2.** (*poet.*) opporsi a, resistere a, lottare (contro).

repugnance [ri'pʌgnəns], *s.* **1.** ripugnanza, antipatia; avversione: — *against* (o *to*) *sthg.*, ripugnanza per ql.co. **2.** incompatibilità: — *of sthg. to* (o *with*) *sthg.*, incompatibilità di ql.co. con ql.co.; — *of* (o *between*) *tempers*, incompatibilità di caratteri.

repugnant [ri'pʌgnənt], *ag.* **1.** ripugnante: *it is — to me*, mi ripugna **2.** incompatibile, contrario: *this clause is — to the terms of the contract*, questa clausola è incompatibile con le condizioni del contratto **3.** opposto, antagonistico: — *forces*, forze antagonistiche.

to **repullulate** [ri'pʌljuleit], *v.i.* **1.** riprodursi; rigenerarsi **2.** ripetersi (di malattia) **3.** rigermogliare.

repulse [ri'pʌls], *s.* **1.** ripulsa; rifiuto: *to meet with a —*, ricevere un rifiuto **2.** sconfitta; scacco (anche *fig.*).

to **repulse**, *v.t.* **1.** respingere, ricusare: *to — a suitor*, respingere un corteggiatore **2.** respingere; sconfiggere (anche *fig.*).

repulsion [ri'pʌlʃən], *s.* **1.** repulsione, ripugnanza, avversione **2.** (*fis.*) repulsione.

repulsive [ri'pʌlsiv], *ag.* **1.** ripulsivo, repellente, ributtante **2.** (*arc.*) respingente, distante (di persona, atteggiamento, ecc.) **3.** (*fis.*) repulsivo.

repulsively [ri'pʌlsivli], *av.* in modo ripulsivo, ripugnante, repellente, ributtante.

repulsiveness [ri'pʌlsivnis], *s.* **1.** l'essere ripulsivo, repellente, ributtante **2.** (*fis.*) forza di ripulsione.

repurchase ['ri:'pə:tʃəs], *s.* riacquisto, riscatto.

to **repurchase**, *v.t.* riacquistare, riscattare.

reputability [,repjutə'biliti], *s.* (*amer.*) onorabilità, rispettabilità.

reputable ['repjutəbl], *ag.* rispettabile, onorato, onorevole: — *employment*, un impiego onorevole.

reputably ['repjutəbli], *av.* rispettabilmente, onoratamente, onorevolmente.

reputation [,repju(:)'teiʃən], *s.* reputazione; rispettabilità; fama: *person of —*, persona onorata; *I know him only by —*, lo conosco solo di fama; *she enjoys a high —*, gode di una grande considerazione; *to acquire* (o *to make*) *a —* (*for oneself*), farsi un gran nome; *to have a — for integrity, for generosity*, goder fama di essere integro, generoso; *to have the — of being stingy*, aver fama di essere tirchio; *to lose one's —*, perdere la propria reputazione.

repute [ri'pju:t], *s.* reputazione; fama: *a place of ill —*, un luogo malfamato; *he is a doctor of —*, è un medico di fama; *these wines are held in high —*, questi vini sono molto rinomati; *to know s.o. by —*, conoscere qlcu. di fama.

to **repute**, *v.t.* (*gener. al passivo*) reputare, stimare, giudicare: *she is reputed the most beautiful of the sisters*, è ritenuta, passa per la più bella delle sorelle; *to be reputed wealthy*, aver fama di essere ricco.

reputed [ri'pju:tid], *ag.* **1.** supposto, presunto, ipotetico: *a — Turner*, un quadro attribuito a Turner; *his — clemency*, la sua supposta clemenza **2.** (*dir.*) putativo: — *father*, padre putativo.

reputedly [ri'pju:tidli], *av.* **1.** presumibilmente; secondo l'opinione generale **2.** (*dir.*) putativamente.

request [ri'kwest], *s.* **1.** domanda, richiesta; petizione; preghiera: *at the — of s.o.*, su richiesta, domanda di qlcu.; *by —*, su richiesta, a richiesta; *to grant a —*, accogliere una preghiera, una richiesta; *to make — for sthg.*, sollecitare ql.co. **2.** (*dir.*) istanza **3.** richiesto: *article in great —*, (*comm.*) articolo molto richiesto ‖ *to be in —*, essere richiesto; essere di moda.

to **request**, *v.t.* (IV) richiedere; domandare; sollecitare; pregare: *your presence is requested*, si richiede la vostra presenza; *to — s.o. to do sthg.*, chiedere a, pregare qlcu.

di fare ql.co.; *to — sthg. of s.o.*, chiedere ql.co. a qlcu.; *to — (permission) to do sthg.*, chiedere di poter fare ql.co.

to **requicken** ['ri:'kwikən], *v.t.i.* ravvivare; rianimare, rianimarsi.

requiem ['rekwiem], *s.* (*eccl. mus.*) messa di requiem.

requirable [ri'kwaiərəbl], *ag.* **1.** esigibile **2.** occorrente, necessario.

to **require** [ri'kwaiə*], *v.t.i.* **1.** richiedere; esigere; pretendere: *an oath is required when giving evidence*, si richiede un giuramento per testimoniare; *a passport is required to travel abroad*, si esige il passaporto per viaggiare all'estero **2.** (IV) ordinare, costringere, obbligare; domandare, chiedere: *I was required to go to the chemist's*, mi si chiese di andare dal farmacista; *they required him to go*, gli ordinarono di andarsene **3.** aver bisogno di, essere necessario; occorrere: *children — to be fed*, i bambini hanno bisogno di essere nutriti; *the development of industry requires the construction of new factories*, lo sviluppo dell'industria rende necessaria la costruzione di nuove fabbriche; *it required all my courage to tell her*, ci volle tutto il mio coraggio per dirglielo; *it requires a lot of work to do it*, ci vuole molto lavoro per farlo; *this machine requires little care*, questa macchina non ha bisogno di molta manutenzione; *twenty workers are required to do this*, occorrono venti operai per fare ciò **4.** (*gram.*) reggere: *this verb requires the preposition "to"*, questo verbo regge la preposizione « to ».

required [ri'kwaiəd], *ag.* richiesto, domandato; necessario: — *courses*, (*amer.*) corsi obbligatori (in scuole); *acids — for industry*, acidi necessari all'industria.

requirement [ri'kwaiəmənt], *s.* **1.** richiesta, esigenza; bisogno, necessità: *this sum will meet my requirements*, questa somma soddisferà alle mie necessità; *to meet all requirements*, (*comm.*) rispondere a tutte le esigenze **2.** fabbisogno **3.** requisito: *the requirements for university entrance*, i requisiti per l'ammissione all'università ☆ *coal —*, fabbisogno di carbone.

requisite ['rekwizit], *ag.* richiesto; necessario; indispensabile ‖ *s.* requisito; oggetto, cosa necessaria.

requisiteness ['rekwizitnis], *s.* necessità; qualità indispensabile.

requisition [,rekwi'ziʃən], *s.* **1.** richiesta, istanza, domanda; ordine: — *for materials, for supplies*, richiesta di materiali, di rifornimenti **2.** (*mil.*) requisizione: *to call into* (o *to put in*) —, requisire; ricorrere a **3.** requisito **4.** domanda di estradizione.

to **requisition**, *v.t.* requisire (specialmente per scopi militari): *to — horses*, requisire cavalli.

requital [ri'kwaitl], *s.* **1.** ricambio, contraccambio: *as a — for*, in contraccambio di **2.** ricompensa: *a poor — for his sacrifices*, una misera ricompensa per i suoi sacrifici **3.** vendetta, rappresaglia: *in — for this act of perfidy*, per vendicarmi di questa perfida azione.

to **requite** [ri'kwait], *v.t.* **1.** ricompensare: *to — s.o. for sthg.*, ricompensare qlcu. per ql.co. **2.** contraccambiare: *to — evil with good*, contraccambiare il male col bene **3.** vendicare ‖ *to — like for like*, (*fam.*) rendere pan per focaccia.

to **reread** ['ri:'ri:d], *pass.p.p.* **reread** ['ri:'red], *v.t.* rileggere.

reredos ['riədɔs], *s.* (*arch.*) **1.** dossale (in una chiesa dietro l'altare) **2.** muro di fondo di camino.

rerun ['ri:'rʌn], *s.* presentazione di film in seconda visione.

resalable ['ri:'seiləbl], *ag.* rivendibile.

to **rescind** [ri'sind], *v.t.* rescindere, abrogare, annullare; revocare.

rescission [ri'siʒən], *s.* rescissione; abrogazione; revoca; annullamento.

rescript ['ri:skript], *s.* **1.** rescritto **2.** (*archeol.*) palinsesto **3.** nuova trascrizione.

rescuable ['reskju:əbl], *ag.* salvabile.

rescue ['reskju:], *s.* **1.** liberazione; salvezza; scampo; salvataggio, soccorso: *to come to the —*, venire in soccorso 2. (*dir.*) liberazione illegale (di prigioniero) 3. il recuperare (beni) con la violenza ☆ — *corps*, squadra di salvataggio.

to **rescue**, *v.t.* 1. liberare; salvare: *to — from danger*, *from ill*, liberare dal pericolo, dal male 2. (*dir.*) liberare illegalmente (un prigioniero) 3. ricuperare (beni) con la violenza.

rescuer ['reskjuə*], *s.* liberatore; salvatore; soccorritore.

research [ri'sə:tʃ], *s.* ricerca; indagine: — *after* (o *for*) *sthg.*, ricerca di ql.co.; *scientific researches*, ricerche scientifiche; *to be engaged in research*, essere impegnato in ricerche ☆ — *department*, ufficio, servizio ricerche; — *work*, lavori di ricerca; ricerche, investigazioni.

to **research**, *v.i.* fare ricerche.

researcher [ri'sə:tʃə*], *s.* ricercatore; investigatore.

to **reseat** ['ri:'si:t], *v.t.* 1. fornire di nuove sedie, poltrone (una chiesa, un teatro) 2. rimettere a sedere.

to **resect** [ri:'sekt], *v.t.* (*chir.*) resecare.

resection [ri:'sekʃən], *s.* (*chir.*) resezione.

reseda ['residə], *s.* 1. (*bot.*) reseda 2. color verde pallido.

to **resell** ['ri:'sel], *pass.p.p.* **resold** ['ri:'sould], *v.t.* rivendere.

resemblance [ri'zembləns], *s.* rassomiglianza, somiglianza: *the — between them is striking*, la somiglianza tra di loro è sorprendente; *to bear a strong — to*, avere una forte rassomiglianza con.

resemblant [ri'zemblənt], *ag.* (*rar.*) rassomigliante.

to **resemble** [ri'zembl], *v.t.* 1. assomigliare a: *the two brothers — each other*, i due fratelli si assomigliano 2. (*arc.*) paragonare.

to **resent** [ri'zent], *v.t.* 1. risentirsi di; offendersi per: *to — s.o.'s behaviour*, offendersi per il comportamento di qlcu. 2. irritarsi per: *you — my being here*, la mia presenza ti irrita.

resentful [ri'zentful], *ag.* 1. pieno di risentimento, risentito; offeso; sdegnato 2. permaloso.

resentfully [ri'zentfuli], *av.* con risentimento.

resentment [ri'zentmənt], *s.* risentimento; rancore: *I bear no — against him*, non gli serbo alcun rancore; *to cherish a secret — against s.o.*, nutrire un segreto rancore per qlcu.

reservation [,rezə'veiʃən], *s.* 1. riserva; restrizione: *with reservations*, con riserve, con beneficio d'inventario 2. (*dir. eccl.*) riserva 3. prenotazione: — *of a seat in a train, of a room in a hotel*, prenotazione di un posto in treno, di una camera in albergo 4. (*amer.*) riserva, terreno riservato ☆ *Indian —*, riserva di indiani pellirosse; *mental —*, riserva mentale.

reserve [ri'zə:v], *s.* 1. riserva: — *of energy*, riserva d'energie; *in —*, di scorta 2. riserva, limitazione, restrizione: *without —*, senza riserve 3. riserbo, riservatezza; discrezione: *to maintain an attitude of —*, tenere un atteggiamento riservato 4. (*comm.*) riserva: *with all proper reserves*, con tutte le debite riserve; *under —*, salvo buon fine 5. (*mil. spor.*) riserva: *the reserves*, le riserve 6. terreno riservato, riserva ☆ — *capital*, capitale autorizzato ma non emesso; — *fund*, fondo di riserva; — *price*, prezzo di riserva; — *troops*, truppe di riserva ‖ *bank —*, riserva bancaria; *cash —*, riserva di cassa; *gold —*, riserva aurea.

to **reserve**, *v.t.* 1. riservare: *I — the right to decide later*, mi riservo il diritto di decidere più tardi; *to — for* (o *to*) *oneself*, riservare per sè 2. prenotare: *to — a seat for s.o.*, prenotare un posto per qlcu. 3. serbare, mettere da parte; destinare ‖ *to — oneself for...*, riservarsi per....

reserved [ri'zə:vd], *ag.* 1. riservato: — *seats*, posti riservati 2. *fig.* riservato; contegnoso.

reservedly [ri'zə:vidli], *av.* con riservatezza.

reservedness [ri'zə:vidnis], *s.* riservatezza.

reservist [ri'zə:vist], *s.* (*mil.*) riservista.

reservoir ['rezəvwɑ:*], *s.* 1. serbatoio, cisterna; ba-

cino di riserva 2. (*anat.*) cavità; sacco 3. *fig.* riserva, raccolta: *a great — of facts*, una miniera di fatti ☆ — *pen*, penna stilografica ‖ *bile —*, sacco biliare.

reset[1] [ri'set], *s.* (*dir.*) ricettazione; il dar ricetto (a ladri, ecc.).

to **reset**[1], *pass.p.p.* **resetted** [ri'setid], *v.t.* (*scoz. dir.*) ricettare; dare ricetto a.

reset[2] ['ri:'set], *s.* 1. riordinamento, risistemazione 2. messa a punto, a zero; (*tip.*) ricomposizione, rifacimento.

to **reset**[2], *pass.p.p.* **reset**, *v.t.* 1. incastonare di nuovo (pietre, ecc.) 2. regolare: *I must — my watch*, devo regolare il mio orologio 3. ripreparare, ripiantare: *to — a rosebush*, ripiantare un rosaio 4. rimettere a posto, aggiustare: *to — a limb*, (*med.*) aggiustare, ingessare un arto 5. (*tip.*) ricomporre.

resetter [ri'setə*], *s.c.* (*scoz.*) ricettatore, ricettatrice.

to **resettle** ['ri:'setl], *v.t.i.* 1. risistemare, risistemarsi 2. colonizzare di nuovo (un paese) 3. depositarsi di nuovo (di liquidi).

resettlement ['ri:'setlmənt], *s.* 1. risistemazione; ristabilimento 2. nuova colonizzazione 3. nuovo deposito (di liquidi).

to **reshape** ['ri:'ʃeip], *v.t.* dare nuova forma a, rifoggiare.

to **reship** ['ri:'ʃip], *pass.p.p.* **reshipped** ['ri:'ʃipt], *v.t.i.* 1. rimbarcare, rimbarcarsi 2. trasportare su altra nave.

reshipment ['ri:'ʃipmənt], *s.* rimbarco; nuova spedizione.

reshuffle ['ri:'ʃʌfl], *s.* 1. il mescolare di nuovo (carte) 2. (*pol. fam.*) rimaneggiamento.

to **reshuffle**, *v.t.* 1. rimescolare (le carte) 2. (*pol. fam.*) rimaneggiare.

to **reside** [ri'zaid], *v.i.* 1. risiedere, dimorare, abitare: *permission to —*, permesso di soggiorno 2. trovarsi, essere presente: *all powers — in the Emperor*, tutti i poteri sono nelle mani dell'imperatore.

residence ['rezidəns], *s.* 1. residenza, soggiorno: *in —*, in residenza; — *is required*, obbligo di residenza; *to take up one's —*, prendere residenza 2. dimora, abitazione, casa signorile: — *for sale*, casa signorile in vendita ☆ — *permit*, permesso di soggiorno.

residency ['rezidənsi], *s.* residenza ufficiale di rappresentante del governo inglese nelle colonie.

resident ['rezidənt], *ag.* 1. residente: *to be — in a place*, risiedere in un luogo 2. non migratorio (di uccello) 3. interno (insegnante, medico, ecc.) 4. inerente; localizzato: *powers of sensation — in the nerves*, poteri di sensazione localizzati nei nervi; *privileges — in a class*, privilegi pertinenti ad una classe ‖ *s.* 1. residente, abitante 2. membro interno (di collegio, ecc.) 3. (*pol.*) residente (specialmente in India).

residential [,rezi'denʃəl], *ag.* 1. adatto per, occupato da abitazioni, residenziale 2. relativo a residenza ☆ — *quarter*, quartiere residenziale, signorile.

residentiary [,rezi'denʃəri], *ag.* residente; obbligato alla residenza: *canon —*, canonico residente ‖ *s.* ecclesiastico che ha obbligo di residenza.

residual [ri'zidjuəl] *ag.* residuo; restante ‖ *s.* 1. (*chim.*) residuo, sostanza residua 2. (*elett.*) residuo 3. (*arit.*) resto, differenza ☆ — *magnetism*, (*elett.*) magnetismo residuo; — *oil*, olio pesante, nafta.

residuary [ri'zidjuəri], *ag.* rimanente, restante residuo ☆ — *legatee*, legatario universale.

residue ['rezidju:], *s.* 1. residuo, resto 2. (*chim.*) sostanza residua 3. (*dir.*) residuo, attivo netto (di patrimonio dopo aver pagato debiti, spese e legati).

residuum [ri'zidjuəm], *pl.* **residua** [ri'zidjuə], *s.* 1. residuo, avanzo; errore residuo (nei calcoli) 2. (*chim.*) residuo, sostanza residua.

to **resign**[1] [ri'zain], *v.t.i.* 1. dimettersi, rassegnare le dimissioni; rinunciare a: *he resigned from the cabinet*, si dimise dalla carica di ministro; *I will not — m* *rights!*, non rinuncerò ai miei diritti!; *the president resigned*, il presidente diede le dimissioni 2. consegnare, affidare: *I — my son to your care*, affido mio figlio alle tue cure; *I — myself into your hands*, mi metto nelle vostre mani 3. *to — oneself*, rassegnarsi; sottomettersi: *I — myself to my fate, to living alone*, mi rassegno al mio destino, a vivere solo.

to **resign**[2], to **re-sign** ['ri:'sain], *v.t.i.* firmare di nuovo.

resignation [,rezig'neiʃən], *s.* 1. dimissioni: *to send in (o to give) one's —*, dare le dimissioni 2. abbandono, rinuncia 3. rassegnazione: *to accept one's fate with —*, accettare il proprio destino con rassegnazione.

resigned [ri'zaind], *ag.* 1. rassegnato 2. dimissionario.

resignedly [ri'zainidli], *av.* rassegnatamente.

to **resile** [ri'zail], *v.i.* 1. rimbalzare (di corpi elastici) 2. riassumere forma, misura primitiva (dopo dilatazione, compressione) 3. avere, mostrare elasticità, potere di ricupero 4. ritirarsi: *to — from a contract*, rescindere un contratto.

resilience [ri'ziliəns], **resiliency** [ri'ziliənsi], *s.* 1. rimbalzo; elasticità 2. resilienza 3. capacità di ricupero: *to have —*, avere capacità di ripresa.

resilient [ri'ziliənt], *ag.* 1. rimbalzante; elastico 2. resiliente 3. che ha capacità di ricupero.

resin ['rezin], *s.* resina.

to **resin**, *v.t.* trattare con resina; applicare resina a.

resinate ['rezinət], *s.* (*chim.*) resinato.

to **resinate** ['rezineit], *v.t.* impregnare di resina.

resiniferous [,rezi'nifərəs], *ag.* resinifero.

to **resinify** ['rezinifai], *v.t.i.* resinificare, resinificarsi.

resinous ['rezinəs], *ag.* resinoso.

resipiscence [,resi'pisəns], *s.* resipiscenza, ravvedimento.

resipiscent [,resi'pisənt], *ag.* resipiscente, che si ravvede.

resist [ri'zist], *s.* sostanza che impedisce l'azione di agenti chimici.

to **resist**, *v.t.i.* 1. resistere (anche *fig.*); opporsi a: *nobody can — his will*, nessuno può opporsi alla sua volontà; *to — cold*, resistere al freddo; *to — the enemy*, opporsi al nemico; *to — temptation*, resistere alla tentazione 2. (I) trattenersi dal; fare a meno di: *I could not — telling him my secret*, non potei trattenermi dal dirgli il mio segreto.

resistance [ri'zistəns], *s.* 1. resistenza ‖ *to take the line of least —*, *fig.* prendere la via più facile 2. — (*movement*), movimento della resistenza (al nemico occupante) 3. (*elett. mec.*) resistenza: *the — is in*, la resistenza è inserita ☆ *— -box*, (*rad.*) cassetta di resistenza; *— -coil*, (*elett.*) bobina di resistenza ‖ *high- —*, (*metal.*) ad alta resistenza.

resistant, resistent [ri'zistənt], *ag.* resistente.

resister [ri'zistə*], *s.* chi resiste; oppositore; elemento, forza resistente ☆ *passive —*, chi oppone resistenza passiva.

resistibility [ri,zisti'biliti], *s.* capacità di opporre resistenza; resistenza.

resistible [ri'zistibl], *ag.* a cui si può resistere.

resistive [ri'zistiv], *ag.* che tende a resistere; resistente.

resistless [ri'zistlis], *ag.* 1. irresistibile; inevitabile 2. incapace di, senza resistenza.

to **resole** [ri:'soul], *v.t.* risolare.

resolubility [ri,zolju'biliti], *s.* risolvibilità.

resoluble [ri'zoljubl], *ag.* 1. risolubile, risolvibile: *— problem*, problema risolvibile 2. scomponibile, analizzabile: *body — into its elements*, corpo che può scomporsi nei suoi elementi.

resolute ['rezəlu:t], *ag.* risoluto, deciso: *a — man*, un uomo deciso.

resolutely ['rezəlu:tli], *av.* risolutamente, con decisione.

resoluteness ['rezəlu:tnis], *s.* risolutezza, fermezza, decisione.

resolution [,rezə'lu:ʃən], *s.* 1. risolutezza, fermezza, decisione: *lack of —*, mancanza di fermezza; *to show great —*, mostrare grande risolutezza 2. risoluzione, decisione: *to make a —*, prendere una decisione 3. deliberazione, ordine del giorno: *to pass (o to carry) a —*, approvare un ordine del giorno, una deliberazione 4. soluzione, risposta: *the — of the problem*, la soluzione del problema 5. scomposizione, analisi 6. (*chim.*) scissione 7. (*foto.*) definizione (di immagine) 8. (*mus.*) risoluzione.

resolutive ['rezəlu:tiv], *ag.* risolutivo.

resolvability [ri,zolvə'biliti], *s.* risolvibilità.

resolvable [ri'zolvəbl], *ag.* risolvibile.

resolve [ri'zolv], *s.* risoluzione; decisione: *he kept his —*, mantenne la sua decisione.

to **resolve**, *v.t.i.* 1. risolvere; decidere; deliberare (in un Parlamento, comitato): *he resolved that he would go (o upon going)*, risolse di andare; *to — oneself*, risolversi; decidersi; *to — to do sthg.*, risolversi a fare ql.co.; *to — upon sthg.*, decidersi per ql.co. 2. indurre, persuadere: *that resolves me to study (o on studying)*, ciò mi induce a studiare 3. risolvere; spiegare, chiarire: *to — a doubt, a riddle*, risolvere un dubbio, un indovinello 4. risolvere, risolversi: *the inflammation resolved*, l'inflammazione si risolse 5. scomporre; analizzare: *to — sthg. into its elements*, scomporre ql.co. nei suoi elementi 6. (*chim.*) scindere, scindersi 7. (*foto.*) definire 8. (*mus.*) risolvere.

resolved [ri'zolvd], *ag.* risoluto, deciso.

resolvedly [ri'zolvidli], *av.* risolutamente.

resolvedness [ri'zolvidnis], *s.* risolutezza.

resolvent [ri'zolvənt], *ag.s.* 1. (*med.*) solvente, risolvente 2. (*chim.*) solvente.

resonance ['rezənəns], *s.* risonanza ☆ *— curve*, (*acu.*) curva di risonanza; *— factor*, (*rad.*) coefficiente di risonanza.

resonant ['rezənənt], *ag.* risonante: *a — voice*, una voce risonante; *a place — with laughter*, un luogo risonante di risa ☆ *— circuit*, (*rad.*) circuito di risonanza.

resonantly ['rezənəntli], *av.* con risonanza.

resonator ['rezəneitə*], *s.* (*elett. acu.*) risonatore; (*rad.*) circuito di risonanza.

to **resorb** [ri'so:b], *v.t.* ria sorbire.

resorbence [ri'so:bəns], *s.* riassorbimento.

resorbent [ri'so:bənt], *ag.* riassorbente.

resorcin [re'zo:sin], *s.* (*chim.*) resorcina.

resorption [ri'so:pʃən], *s.* riassorbimento.

resort[1] [ri'zo:t], *s.* 1. ricorso: *to have — to force*, ricorrere alla forza 2. risorsa: *the last —*, l'ultima risorsa 3. afflusso; ritrovo, convegno: *a place of great —*, un luogo molto frequentato; *this is the — of the richest people in town*, questo è il ritrovo delle persone più ricche della città 4. luogo di soggiorno, stazione climatica ☆ *boating —*, centro di canottaggio; *fishing —*, luogo di pesca; *health —*, stazione climatica, luogo di cura; *holiday —*, luogo di villeggiatura; *mountain —*, luogo di soggiorno in montagna; *seaside —*, stazione balneare; *summer —*, stazione balneare; *winter —*, stazione invernale.

to **resort**[1], *v.i.* 1. ricorrere, far ricorso: *to — to an experiment*, ricorrere a un esperimento 2. recarsi, andare; affluire: *they found him where he was known to — to*, lo trovarono in un luogo che sapevano era solito frequentare.

to **resort**[2] ['ri:'so:t], *v.t.* scegliere di nuovo, selezionare di nuovo.

to **resound** [ri'zaund], *v.t.i.* 1. risonare; echeggiare (di voce, suono, strumento); riecheggiare: *the whole country resounded with his praises*, *fig.* l'intero paese risonava delle sue lodi 2. *fig.* essere celebrato, famoso: *his fame resounded through the world*, la sua fama era celebrata universalmente 3. far risonare, proclamare: *to — the virtues of s.o.*, proclamare le virtù di qlcu.

resoundingly [riˈzaundiŋli], *av.* con risonanza, rimbombo, fracasso.

resource [riˈsɔːs], *s.* **1.** *gener. pl.* risorse; mezzi: *at the end of one's resources*, alla fine delle proprie risorse; *a nation's resources*, i mezzi finanziari di una nazione **2.** espediente, ripiego, rimedio **3.** passatempo, distrazione: *playing an instrument is a wonderful —*, suonare uno strumento è un piacevole passatempo **4.** *fig.* risorsa; ingegnosità; abilità; *a person full of —*, una persona piena di risorse.

resourceful [riˈsɔːsful], *ag.* pieno di risorse; ingegnoso; disinvolto, intraprendente.

resourcefully [riˈsɔːsfuli], *av.* con molte risorse.

resourcefulness [riˈsɔːsfulnis], *s.* abbondanza di risorse; ingegnosità.

resourceless [riˈsɔːslis], *ag.* senza risorse.

resourcelessness [riˈsɔːslisnis], *s.* mancanza di risorse.

respect [risˈpekt], *s.* **1.** rispetto, stima, riguardo: *I did it out of — for her*, lo feci per riguardo verso di lei; *with all — for his learning, I think he is wrong*, con tutta la stima per la sua cultura, credo che abbia torto; *to have — for s.o., sthg.*, aver stima per qlcu., ql.co.; *to hold s.o. in —*, tenere qlcu. in considerazione; *to win the respect of s.o.*, guadagnarsi la stima di qlcu. **2.** *pl.* saluti; ossequi: *give your parents my respects*, porgete i miei ossequi ai vostri genitori; *to pay one's respects to*, ossequiare, rendere omaggio a; *to send one's respects to*, inviare i propri saluti a **3.** attenzione; considerazione: *— of persons*, eccessivo riguardo, parzialità verso i potenti; *we must have* (o *pay*) *— to the needs of the general reader*, dobbiamo fare attenzione alle esigenze del lettore comune **4.** relazione, riferimento: *in — of* (o *to*), riguardo a; *with — to*, in riferimento a, in merito a **5.** punto di vista; punto; aspetto; rapporto: *in all respects*, da tutti i punti di vista; *in every —*, sotto ogni aspetto; *in one — he is wrong*, in un solo punto ha torto; *in that — he is right*, da quel punto di vista, egli ha ragione; *they are like each other in many respects*, sotto molti aspetti si rassomigliano ☆ *self- —*, dignità; rispetto per la propria persona.

to respect, *v.t.* **1.** rispettare, considerare, avere riguardo per: *to — the law, s.o.'s sorrow*, rispettare la legge, il dolore di qlcu. ‖ *to — oneself*, comportarsi in modo degno; mostrare dignità **2.** (*rar.*) riguardare, concernere, riferirsi a: *a treaty respecting international relations*, un trattato riguardante le relazioni internazionali **3.** (*arc.*) considerare, giudicare, stimare ‖ *to — persons*, mostrare parzialità verso persone ricche e potenti.

respectability [risˌpektəˈbiliti], *s.* **1.** rispettabilità **2.** *pl.* convenzioni sociali: *to observe the respectabilities*, osservare le convenienze sociali **3.** persona rispettabile: *the respectabilities of the town*, i pezzi grossi della città.

respectable [risˈpektəbl], *ag.* **1.** rispettabile: *poor but —*, povero ma degno di rispetto; *to act from — motives*, agire per motivi rispettabili **2.** discreto: *a — number of people*, un discreto numero di persone; *a — painter*, un pittore abbastanza buono; *— weather*, tempo passabile **3.** ragguardevole, considerevole **4.** onesto, decoroso (di intenti, abiti, ecc.).

respectably [risˈpektəbli], *av.* **1.** rispettabilmente **2.** discretamente **3.** onestamente, decentemente.

respecter [risˈpektə*], *s.* chi, che rispetta: *death is no — of persons*, la morte non rispetta nessuno; *to be no — of*, non tener conto di; non aver parzialità per.

respectful [risˈpektful], *ag.* rispettoso; deferente; sottomesso.

respectfully [risˈpektfuli], *av.* rispettosamente; con deferenza.

respectfulness [risˈpektfulnis], *s.* **1.** carattere rispettoso **2.** deferenza, rispetto.

respecting [risˈpektiŋ], *prep.* rispetto a, riguardo a, relativamente a: *legislation — property*, legislazione

relativa alla proprietà; *we could not agree — the price*, non ci siamo potuti mettere d'accordo sul prezzo.

respective [risˈpektiv], *ag.* rispettivo, relativo: *put them in their — places*, mettili ai loro rispettivi posti.

respectively [risˈpektivli], *av.* rispettivamente.

respectless [risˈpektlis], *ag.* (*rar.*) senza rispetto, senza riguardo: *— of*, senza riguardo per.

to respell [ˈriːˈspel], *pass.p.p.* **respelled** [ˈriːˈspeld], **respelt** [ˈriːˈspelt], *v.t.* **1.** sillabare, compitare di nuovo **2.** modificare l'ortografia di (una parola).

respirability [resˌpiərəˈbiliti], *s.* respirabilità.

respirable [ˈrespirəbl], *ag.* respirabile.

respiration [ˌrespəˈreiʃən], *s.* **1.** respirazione **2.** respiro.

respirator [ˈrespəreitə*], *s.* **1.** (*med.*) respiratore; maschera respiratoria **2.** (*mil.*) maschera antigas.

respiratory [risˈpaiərətəri], *ag.* (*fisiol.*) respiratorio ☆ *— centre*, centro della respirazione; *— tract*, (*anat.*) vie aeree.

to respire [risˈpaiə*], *v.t.i.* respirare; *fig.* (ri)prender fiato.

respite [ˈrespait], *s.* **1.** dilazione, proroga, rinvio: *we cannot grant you a further —*, (*comm.*) non possiamo concedervi un'ulteriore dilazione **2.** tregua, pausa, respiro, sollievo.

to respite, *v.t.* **1.** concedere una dilazione, un rinvio, una tregua a **2.** apportare sollievo a; dar respiro a.

resplendence [risˈplendəns], **resplendency** [risˈplendənsi], *s.* splendore, fulgore.

resplendent [risˈplendənt], *ag.* splendente, risplendente, brillante; smagliante.

resplendently [risˈplendəntli], *av.* splendentemente, brillantemente.

respond [risˈpɔnd], *s.* **1.** (*eccl.*) responsorio **2.** (*arch.*) colonnino appaiato.

to respond, *v.i.* **1.** rispondere, replicare: *to — to a toast*, rispondere a un brindisi **2.** (*eccl.*) recitare, cantare il responsorio **3.** rispondere; essere sensibile; obbedire: *my reflexes don't —*, i miei riflessi non rispondono; *to — to music*, essere sensibile alla musica **4.** (*amer. dir.*) rispondere, essere responsabile **5.** (*rar.*) corrispondere, essere analogo.

respondence [risˈpɔndəns], **respondency** [risˈpɔndənsi], *s.* rispondenza, corrispondenza.

respondent [risˈpɔndənt], *ag.* **1.** che risponde **2.** rispondente; sensibile; che reagisce ‖ *s.* **1.** chi sostiene una tesi **2.** (*dir.*) convenuto, imputato.

response [risˈpɔns], *s.* **1.** risposta, replica, responso: *a letter which brought no —*, una lettera senza risposta; *the responses of the oracles*, i responsi degli oracoli **2.** reazione; corrispondenza: *her kindness called forth no — in his breast*, la sua cortesia non suscitò in lui alcuna reazione **3.** (*eccl.*) responsorio: *to make the response at mass*, rispondere alla Messa.

responsibility [risˌpɔnsəˈbiliti], *s.* responsabilità: *on one's own —*, sotto la propria responsabilità; *nobody will take the — of doing it*, nessuno si assumerà la responsabilità di fare ciò; *without — on our part*, senza impegno nè responsabilità da parte nostra.

responsible [risˈpɔnsəbl], *ag.* **1.** responsabile: *he is not — for his actions*, egli non è responsabile delle sue azioni **2.** di, che comporta responsabilità: *a — position*, una posizione di responsabilità **3.** competente; capace; degno di fiducia.

responsibly [risˈpɔnsəbli], *av.* responsabilmente.

responsions [risˈpɔnʃənz], *s.pl.* il primo di tre esami per ottenere a Oxford il titolo di « Bachelor of Arts ».

responsive [risˈpɔnsiv], *ag.* **1.** rispondente **2.** sensibile; impressionabile, facile alle emozioni: *they are — to affection*, sono sensibili all'affetto **3.** (*eccl.*) con, caratterizzato da responsorio.

responsively [risˈpɔnsivli], *av.* in maniera rispondente; con simpatia: *she glanced at him and he smiled —*, lei gli lanciò uno sguardo al quale lui rispose con un sorriso.

responsiveness [ris'ponsivnis], *s.* **1.** rispondenza **2.** sensibilità; prontezza a simpatizzare.

responsory [ris'ponsəri], *s.* (*eccl.*) responsorio.

rest[1] [rest], *s.* **1.** riposo: sonno: — *is necessary after work*, il riposo è necessario dopo il lavoro; *to give s.o.*, *sthg. a* —, far riposare qlcu., ql.co.; *to have* (o *to take*) *a* —, riposare, riposarsi ‖ *at* —, in stato di riposo; in pace; morto: *the poor woman is now at* —, la povera donna ora riposa in pace; *to set a question at* —, definire, sistemare una questione; *to set s.o.'s mind at* —, tranquillizzare qlcu. ‖ *to lay to* —, seppellire **2.** alloggio, ricovero (per marinai, vetturini, ecc.) **3.** supporto, appoggio **4.** (*mus. ret.*) pausa; (*poes.*) cesura ☆ — *-cure*, cura del riposo; — *-day*, giorno di riposo; — *-gown*, vestaglia; — *-house*, ospizio; (*arc.*) albergo in una stazione di posta.

to **rest**[1], *v.t.i.* **1.** riposare, riposarsi; far riposare, lasciar riposare: *God* — *his soul*, che Dio dia pace alla sua anima; *let him* — *in peace*, lasciatelo riposare in pace; *lie down and* —, sdraiati e riposa; *she rests in the churchyard*, riposa al camposanto; *this colour rests my eyes*, questo colore mi riposa gli occhi; *to* — *from one's labours*, riposarsi dalle proprie fatiche ‖ *to* — *on one's laurels*, riposarsi sugli allori ‖ *to* — *upon one's oars*, smettere di remare; *fig.* prendersi un periodo di riposo **2.** appoggiare, appoggiarsi; posare, posarsi; basare, basarsi; confidare: *he rested his elbow on the table*, appoggiò il gomito sul tavolo; *I* — *in his promises*, confido nelle sue promesse; *to* — *in God*, confidare in Dio.

rest[2], *s.* **1.** resto, residuo: *take what you want and throw the* — *away*, prendine quanto vuoi e getta il resto ‖ *and* (*all*) *the* — (*of it*), eccetera, e così via ‖ *for the* —, quanto al resto **2.** costruzione *pl.* i rimanenti, gli altri: *the* — *were busy*, gli altri erano occupati **3.** (*comm.*) saldo, chiusura **4.** fondo di riserva bancario **5.** (*tennis*) serie di ribattute.

to **rest**[2], *v.t.i.* **1.** restare, rimanere: *the affair rests a mystery*, la faccenda rimane un mistero; *I* — *your faithful friend*, (*arc.*) mi dico il vostro fedele amico; *to* — *assured*, essere sicuro; *to* — *satisfied*, rimanere soddisfatto **2.** *to* — *with* (*s.o.*), toccare a, dipendere da, esser lasciato nelle mani di: *it rests with you to settle the question*, tocca a te sistemare la questione; *the maintenance of peace rests with us*, il mantenimento della pace è nelle nostre mani.

rest[3], *s.* resta: *lance in* —, lancia in resta.

restage ['ri:'steidʒ], *s.* (*teat.*) ripresa teatrale.

to **restamp** ['ri:'stæmp], *v.t.* timbrare di nuovo; affrancare di nuovo.

restart ['ri:'stɑ:t], *s.* **1.** nuovo inizio; ripresa **2.** rimessa in moto (di motore).

to **restart**, *v.t.i.* **1.** ricominciare; riprendere **2.** rimettere in moto (un motore).

to **restate** ['ri:'steit], *v.t.* riesporre, enunciare di nuovo; esprimere in altra forma: *the question needs to be restated*, il problema ha bisogno di essere messo a punto.

restatement ['ri:'steitmənt], *s.* riaffermazione.

restaurant ['restərɔnt], *s.* ristorante ☆ — *-car*, (*ferr.*) vagone ristorante.

restaurateur [,restɔ(:)rə'tə:*], *s.* chi gestisce un ristorante.

restful ['restful], *ag.* riposante; tranquillo, quieto.

restfully ['restfuli], *av.* in modo riposante; tranquillamente.

restfulness ['restfulnis], *s.* riposo, tranquillità, quiete, pace.

restharrow ['rest,hærou], *s.* (*bot.*) ononide, bonaga.

restiff ['restif], (*rar.*) per **restive**.

resting ['restiŋ], *ag.* in riposo; *the silence of the* — *household*, il silenzio della casa addormentata ‖ *s.* riposo ☆ — *-place*, luogo di riposo, rifugio: *the last* — *-place*, la tomba.

to **restitute** ['restitju:t], *v.t.* (*rar.*) **1.** restituire, rifondere **2.** restaurare; riabilitare.

restitution [,resti'tju:ʃən], *s.* restituzione; risarcimento: *to make* —, fare ammenda ‖ — *of conjugal rights*, (*dir.*) reintegrazione dei diritti coniugali.

restive ['restiv], *ag.* **1.** restio, ricalcitrante; caparbio, ostinato, indocile: *a* — *horse*, un cavallo recalcitrante **2.** irrequieto; intrattabile.

restively ['restivli], *av.* **1.** in modo restio, ricalcitrante; caparbiamente, ostinatamente **2.** intrattabilmente.

restiveness ['restivnis], *s.* **1.** caparbietà, ostinazione **2.** irrequietezza; nervosismo.

restless ['restlis], *ag.* **1.** irrequieto; inquieto, agitato: *a* — *boy*, un ragazzo irrequieto; *a* — *night*, una notte agitata **2.** incessante, senza riposo: — *activity*, attività incessante **3.** (*amer.*) insoddisfatto, scontento: *for some time the masses had been* —, da qualche tempo le masse erano scontente.

restlessly ['restlisli], *av.* **1.** irrequietamente; inquietamente, nervosamente, febbrilmente **2.** incessantemente, senza riposo.

restlessness ['restlisnis], *s.* irrequietezza, inquietudine, agitazione; nervosismo; insonnia.

to **restock** ['ri:'stɔk], *v.t.i.* **1.** rifornire, rifornirsi **2.** ripopolare (vivaio, stagno).

restorable [ris'tɔ:rəbl], *ag.* **1.** restituibile **2.** restaurabile; ripristinabile.

restoration [,restə'reiʃən], *s.* **1.** restituzione **2.** restauro (di edificio, quadro, ecc.) **3.** ricostruzione **4.** ripristino, reintegrazione; restaurazione (di dinastia, forma di governo) ‖ *the Restoration*, (*st. inglese*) la Restaurazione (degli Stuart, nel 1660) **5.** ristabilimento (di salute).

restorationism [,restə'reiʃənizəm], *s.* dottrina del riscatto universale.

restorationist [,restə'reiʃənist], *s.* seguace della dottrina del riscatto universale.

restorative [ris'tɔrətiv], *ag.* ristorativo, corroborante ‖ *s.* ricostituente, tonico; cordiale.

restoratively [ris'tɔrətivli], *av.* in modo ristorativo, corroborante.

to **restore** [ris'tɔ:*], *v.t.* **1.** restituire, rendere **2.** restaurare, riparare, ripristinare: *to* — *a church, a picture*, restaurare una chiesa, un quadro **3.** ricostruire: *to* — *an extint animal*, ricostruire un fossile **4.** reintegrare; ristabilire; rimettere al proprio posto; restaurare (una dinastia, una forma di governo): *to* — *friendship between two people*, ristabilire l'amicizia tra due persone; *to* — *a king* (*to the throne*), rimettere un re sul trono; *to* — *an officer to his command*, reintegrare un ufficiale nel suo grado; *to* — *a statue to its pedestal*, rimettere una statua sul suo piedestallo **5.** ristorare, rinvigorire.

restorer [ris'tɔ:rə*], *s.* restauratore; ripristinatore ☆ *hair-* —, lozione per rinvigorire i capelli.

to **restrain**[1] [ris'trein], *v.t.i.* **1.** reprimere, frenare, trattenere, trattenersi: *I could hardly* — *from laughing*, potevo appena trattenermi dal ridere ‖ *restrained style*, stile misurato **2.** limitare, restringere: *to* — *trade*, limitare il commercio **3.** confinare; imprigionare: *to* — *the insane*, confinare gli alienati.

to **restrain**[2] ['ri:'strein], *v.t.* **1.** forzare di nuovo **2.** filtrare di nuovo.

restrainable [ris'treinəbl], *ag.* reprimibile, frenabile.

restrainedly [ris'treinidli], *av.* con ritegno.

restraint [ris'treint], *s.* **1.** freno; controllo; misura; ritegno: *to put a* — *on s.o.*, mettere un freno a qlcu. **2.** limitazione, restrizione: *without* —, senza limitazione, liberamente **3.** relegamento; detenzione: *to be under* —, essere sotto controllo (generalmente di alienati).

to **restrict** [ris'trikt], *v.t.* restringere, limitare: *to* — *within narrow limits*, limitare entro ristretti confini; *to be restricted to doing sthg.*, limitarsi a fare ql.co.

restrictedly [ris'triktidli], *av.* limitatamente.

restriction [ris'trikʃən], *s.* restrizione, limitazione: *to place restrictions on trade*, imporre restrizioni al commercio ☆ *mental* —, restrizione mentale.

restrictive [ris'triktiv], *ag.* restrittivo.

restrictively [ris'triktivli], *av.* in modo restrittivo.

to **restuff** ['ri:'stʌf], *v.t.* imbottire di nuovo (materasso, ecc.); rimpinzare di nuovo.

result [ri'zʌlt], *s.* **1.** risultato, esito: *as a — (of)*, come risultato (di); *without —*, senza risultato, inutilmente; *to give out the results*, (spor.) dare i risultati **2.** conseguenza: *that's the — of the way he was brought up*, quella è la conseguenza della sua educazione ☆ *— clause*, (gram.) proposizione consecutiva.

to **result**, *v.i.* **1.** derivare, risultare: *much harm resulted from this*, ne è derivato un gran male **2.** risolversi, concludersi: *the accident resulted in his death*, l'incidente si concluse con la sua morte; *it may — in a large profit*, potrebbe risolversi in un gran guadagno.

resultant [ri'zʌltənt], *ag.s.* risultante.

resultful [ri'zʌltful], *ag.* **1.** fruttuoso; che dà buoni risultati **2.** pieno di conseguenze.

resultless [ri'zʌltlis], *ag.* **1.** senza risultato **2.** senza consequenze.

resumable [ri'zju:məbl], *ag.* recuperabile.

to **resume** [ri'zju:m], *v.t.i.* **1.** riprendere, ricuperare: *to — one's courage*, riprendere coraggio; *to — the thread of one's discourse*, riprendere il filo del discorso **2.** riprendere, ricominciare: *the House resumed (work) yesterday*, la Camera ha ripreso i lavori ieri **3.** ricuperare (posto, territorio, ecc.) **4.** riassumere, ricapitolare.

résumé ['rezju(:)mei], *s.* riassunto, sunto, sommario.

to **resummon** ['ri:'sʌmən], *v.t.* (dir. arc.) **1.** citare di nuovo **2.** riconvocare (assemblea, ecc.).

resummons ['ri:'sʌmənz], *s.* (dir. arc.) **1.** nuova citazione **2.** nuova convocazione.

resumption [ri'zʌmpʃən], *s.* ripresa: *— of production*, ripresa di produzione; *— of residence*, (dir.) reintegrazione di domicilio.

resumptive [ri'zʌmptiv], *ag.* di ripresa.

resupinate [ri'sju:pineit], *ag.* (bot.) invertito, capovolto.

resupination [ri,sju:pi'neiʃən], *s.* (bot.) inversione, capovolgimento.

resupine [,ri:sju'pain], *ag.* supino.

to **resurge** ['ri:'sə:dʒ], *v.i.* (rar. scherz.) risorgere; rivivere.

resurgence [ri:'sə:dʒəns], *s.* risurrezione; rinascita.

resurgent ['ri:'sə:dʒənt], *ag.* risorgente.

to **resurrect** [,rezə'rekt], *v.t.i.* (fam.) risuscitare; far risorgere, far rivivere; esumare: *to — an old use*, far rivivere una vecchia usanza.

resurrection [,rezə'rekʃən], *s.* **1.** risurrezione ‖ *the Resurrection*, (relig.) la Resurrezione **2.** fig. rinascita, ripresa (di moda, abitudine, ecc.) **3.** esumazione ☆ *— man*, chi esumava cadaveri per venderli agli anatomisti.

resurrectional [,rezə'rekʃən], *ag.* di risurrezione.

resurrectionist [,rezə'rekʃənist], *s.c.* chi fa rivivere (moda, abitudini, ecc.) ‖ *s.* chi disseppelliva clandestinamente cadaveri per venderli agli anatomisti.

resurvey ['ri:'sə:vei], *s.* riesame, nuova valutazione.

to **resurvey** ['ri:sə:'vei], *v.t.* riesaminare, valutare di nuovo.

to **resuscitate** [ri'sʌsiteit], *v.t.i.* risuscitare.

resuscitation [ri,sʌsi'teiʃən], *s.* risuscitamento, richiamo in vita.

resuscitative [ri'sʌsiteitiv], *ag.* che richiama in vita.

resuscitator [ri'sʌsiteitə*], *s.c.* risuscitatore, risuscitatrice.

to **ret** [ret], *pass.p.p.* **retted** ['retid], *v.t.i.* **1.** macerare (canapa, ecc.) **2.** guastarsi (di fieno, ecc. per umidità).

retable [ri'teibl], *s.* (eccl.) predella, pala d'altare.

retail ['ri:teil], *s.* vendita al minuto, al dettaglio: *by —*, al minuto; *did you buy this wholesale or —?*, l'hai comperato all'ingrosso o al minuto?; *to sell —*, vendere al dettaglio ☆ *— dealer*, dettagliante; *— price*, prezzo al minuto; *— trade*, commercio al minuto.

to **retail** [ri:'teil], *v.t.i.* **1.** vendere al minuto, al dettaglio; essere venduto al minuto: *this article retails at five pounds*, quest'articolo si vende al dettaglio acinque sterline **2.** raccontare dettagliatamente.

retailer [ri:'teilə*], *s.* **1.** dettagliante **2.** (fam.) chiacchierone; divulgatore di notizie.

to **retain** [ri'tein], *v.t.* **1.** ritenere, trattenere, mantenere; conservare, serbare: *the waters are retained by a dyke*, le acque sono trattenute da una diga; *to — all one's faculties*, conservare tutte le proprie facoltà; *to — a clear memory of sthg.*, conservare un chiaro ricordo di ql.co. **2.** prendere, fissare: *to — a barrister, a counsel*, scegliere un avvocato, un consulente legale; *to — s.o.'s services*, assicurarsi i servigi di qlcu.

retainable [ri'teinəbl], *ag.* che si può ritenere, serbare, ricordare.

retainer[1] [ri'teinə*], *s.* (rar. dir.) **1.** diritto di ritenzione **2.** onorario versato ad un avvocato all'atto in cui gli si affida la causa **3.** (mec.) fermo; gabbia.

retainer[2], *s.* **1.** chi, che conserva, trattiene: *a brick is a — of heat*, un mattone conserva il calore **2.** (st.) dipendente, seguace di un signore.

retaining [ri'teiniŋ], *ag.* che ritiene ☆ *— fee*, (dir.) onorario anticipato ad un avvocato; *— wall*, muro di sostegno.

retake ['ri:'teik], *s.* (cine.) replica di una ripresa.

to **retake**, *pass.* **retook** ['ri:'tuk], *p.p.* **retaken** ['ri:'teikən], *v.t.* **1.** riprendere, riconquistare: *to — a town from the enemy*, riconquistare una città al nemico **2.** (cine.) ripetere la ripresa di (una scena).

to **retaliate** [ri'tælieit], *v.t.i.* **1.** ricambiare (insulto, offesa): *to — an accusation upon s.o.*, ritorcere un'accusa su qlcu. **2.** rendere la pariglia; far rappresaglie; (econ. pol.) imporre dazi di rappresaglia su merci importate.

retaliation [ri,tæli'eiʃən], *s.* pariglia; rappresaglia; (dir.) ritorsione ‖ *law of —*, legge del taglione.

retaliative [ri'tæliətiv], **retaliatory** [ri'tæliətəri], *ag.* di rappresaglia; vendicativo; (dir.) di ritorsione.

retard [ri'ta:d], *s.* ritardo, indugio: *— of the tide*, ritardo della marea.

to **retard**, *v.t.i.* ritardare; rallentare; tardare; indugiare.

retardation [,ri:ta:'deiʃən], *s.* **1.** ritardo; rallentamento; indugio **2.** (mus.) ritardo.

retardative [ri'ta:dətiv], **retardatory** [ri'ta:dətəri], *ag.* che causa ritardo, rallentamento.

retardment [ri'ta:dmənt], *s.* ritardo; rallentamento.

to **retaste** ['ri:'teist], *v.t.* assaggiare di nuovo.

retch [ri:tʃ], *s.* conato di vomito.

to **retch**, *v.i.* avere conati di vomito.

to **retell** ['ri:'tel], *pass.p.p.* **retold** ['ri:'tould], *v.t.* ripetere; raccontare di nuovo.

retention [ri'tenʃən], *s.* **1.** (spec. med.) ritenzione **2.** conservazione (di un uso, un'autorità, ecc.) **3.** facoltà di ritenere; memoria.

retentive [ri'tentiv], *ag.* **1.** ritentivo, ten ce (di memoria) **2.** che trattiene, che conserva: *a — soil*, terreno che trattiene l'acqua **3.** ritenitivo (di fasciatura, ecc.).

retentively [ri'tentivli], *av.* **1.** in modo da ritenere **2.** in modo da ricordare.

retentiveness [ri'tentivnis], *s.* **1.** capacità di ritenere; tenacità (di memoria) **2.** capacità di trattenere.

retentivity [,ri:ten'tiviti], *s.* (fis.) capacità di trattenere la magnetizzazione.

retenue [rət'nju:], *s.* riserbo; autocontrollo.

retiarius [,ri:ti'ɛəriəs], *s.* (st. romana) reziario.

retiary ['ri:ʃəri], *s.* ragno orbitelio.

reticence ['retisns], **reticency** ['retisnsi], *s.* reticenza; riservatezza; taciturnità.

reticent ['retisnt], *ag.* reticente; riservato; taciturno.

reticently ['retisntli], *av.* con reticenza; con riservatezza.

reticle ['retikl], *s.* (ott.) reticolo.

reticular [ri'tikjulə*], *ag.* reticolare.

reticulate [ri'tikjulit], *ag.* reticolato; retiforme.

to **reticulate** [ri'tikjuleit], *v.t.i.* reticolare, dare

l'aspetto di rete; diventare reticolare, assumere aspetto di rete.

reticulately [ri'tikjulitli], *av.* a rete.

reticulation [ri,tikju'leiʃən], *s.* reticolazione; struttura, forma reticolata; (*foto. pitt.*) retinatura.

reticule ['retikju:l], *s.* **1.** (*ott.*) reticolo **2.** borsetta a rete.

reticulum [ri'tikjuləm], *pl.* **reticula** [ri'tikjulə], *s.* (*anat. zool.*) reticolo.

retiform ['ri:tifo:m], *ag.* retiforme, a guisa di rete.

retina ['retinə], *pl.* **retinas** ['retinəz], **retinae** ['retini:], *s.* (*anat.*) retina.

retinite ['retinait], *s.* (*min.*) retinite.

retinitis [,reti'naitis], *s.* (*patol.*) retinite.

retinue ['retinju:], *s.* seguito; corteo; scorta.

retire [ri'taiə*], *s.* (*mil.*) ritirata.

to **retire**, *v.t.i.* **1.** ritirarsi: *he retired (to bed) before ten*, si ritirò (andò a letto) prima delle dieci; *to — from the world*, ritirarsi dal mondo ‖ *to — into oneself*, rinchiudersi in se stesso **2.** ritirarsi, far ritirare (ufficiali del servizio attivo); dare le dimissioni, andare in pensione: *he will soon — on a pension*, andrà presto in pensione; *to — from business*, ritirarsi dagli affari **3.** (*mil.*) battere in ritirata; far ritirare (truppe, ecc.): *our army retired in good order*, il nostro esercito si ritirò in buon ordine **4.** (*comm.*) ritirare, togliere dalla circolazione: *to — a bill*, togliere dalla circolazione una cambiale.

retired [ri'taiəd], *ag.* **1.** ritirato; appartato, solitario; nascosto: *a — life*, una vita ritirata; *a — valley*, una valle solitaria **2.** a riposo, in pensione: *a — general*, un generale a riposo ☆ *— list*, lista degli ufficiali in pensione; *— pay*, pensione; *— person*, pensionato.

retiredly [ri'taiədli], *av.* ritiratamente, appartatamente, privatamente.

retiredness [ri'taiədnis], *s.* ritiro; solitudine.

retirement [ri'taiəmənt], *s.* **1.** ritiro: *— from the world*, ritiro dal mondo **3.** collocamento a riposo **3.** (*mil.*) ritirata **4.** (*comm.*) ritiro dalla circolazione (di cambiale) **5.** isolamento; solitudine **6.** luogo appartato; dimora solitaria ☆ *old age — account*, fondo pensione di vecchiaia.

retiring [ri'taiəriŋ], *ag.* **1.** riservato; discreto; schivo; timido **2.** che si ritira, uscente; (*mil.*) che batte in ritirata ☆ *— pension*, pensione; *— room*, ritirata.

retiringly [ri'taiəriŋli], *av.* riservatamente, modestamente.

retiringness [ri'taiəriŋnis], *s.* riservatezza, modestia.

retorsion [ri'to:ʃən], *s.* (*dir.*) ritorsione; rappresaglia.

retort[1] [ri'to:t], *s.* **1.** ritorsione **2.** risposta per le rime.

to **retort**[1], *v.t.i.* **1.** ritorcere (accusa); ribattere (argomento); ricambiare (insulto); replicare; rispondere **2.** far indietreggiare, indietreggiare **3.** riflettere (luce, suono).

retort[2], *s.* (*chim.*) storta.

to **retort**[2], *v.t.* (*chim.*) distillare in una storta.

retortion [ri'to:ʃən], *s.* **1.** ripiegamento, indietreggiamento **2.** (*dir.*) ritorsione; rappresaglia.

retouch ['ri:'tʌtʃ], *s.* ritocco (a quadro, ecc.).

to **retouch**, *v.t.* ritoccare (quadro, fotografia, ecc.).

retoucher ['ri:'tʌtʃə*], *s.* ritoccatore, ritoccatrice.

to **retrace**[1] [ri'treis], *v.t.* **1.** rintracciare; analizzare minuziosamente **2.** ripercorrere, rifare il cammino di (anche *fig.*): *to — one's steps*, ritornare sui propri passi; *to — one's way*, ripercorrere all'indietro la strada percorsa **3.** rievocare, risalire alle origini di.

to **re-trace**[2] [ri'treis], *v.t.* tracciare di nuovo.

retraceable [ri'treisəbl], *ag.* rintracciabile.

to **retract**[1] [ri'trækt], *v.t.i.* ritrarre, ritrarsi, tirare indietro, far rientrare: *a cat can — its claws*, un gatto può ritrare le unghie.

to **retract**[2], *v.t.i.* ritrattare, ritrattarsi; revocare; riconoscere l'errore, la falsità di; disdirsi; ritirarsi.

retractable[1] [ri'træktəbl], *ag.* retrattile.

retractable[2], *ag.* ritrattile.

retractation [,ri:træk'teiʃən], *s.* ritrattazione.

retractile [ri'træktail], *ag.* retrattile.

retractility [,ri:træk'tiliti], *s.* retrattilità.

retraction [ri'trækʃən], *s.* **1.** ritiro, azione del ritrarre **2.** ritrazione, contrazione **3.** ritrattazione, revoca.

retractive [ri'træktiv], *ag.* ritrattivo; retrattile.

retractor [ri'træktə*], *s.* **1.** (*med.*) divaricatore, spatola **2.** *— (muscle)*, (*anat.*) muscolo retrattore.

retral ['ri:trəl], *ag.* posteriore.

to **retread**[1] ['ri:'tred], *pass.* **retrod** ['ri:'trod], *p.p.* **retrodden** ['ri:'trodn], *v.t.* ripercorrere, calpestare di nuovo.

to **re-tread**[2], *v.t.* (*aut.*) ricostruire (un copertone).

retreat [ri'tri:t], *s.* **1.** (*mil.*) ritirata: *our army intercepted the — of the enemy*, il nostro esercito tagliò la ritirata al nemico; *to be in full —*, essere in rotta; *to beat a —*, battere in ritirata; *to sound the —*, suonare la ritirata **2.** ritiro, luogo appartato; nascondiglio; eremo; asilo; casa di cura **3.** ritiro (di acque, ghiacciaio, ecc.) **4.** (*eccl.*) ritiro **5.** (*arch.*) rientro.

to **retreat**, *v.t.i.* **1.** ritirarsi, indietreggiare (anche *fig.*) **2.** (*mil.*) battere in ritirata **3.** (*scacchi*) ritirare.

retreating [ri'tri:tiŋ], *ag.* **1.** che si ritira, si allontana, indietreggia; (*mil.*) in ritirata **2.** sfuggente, rientrante: *a — chin*, un mento sfuggente ‖ *s.* (*mil.*) ritirata.

to **retrench**[1] [ri'trenʃ], *v.t.i.* **1.** togliere; tagliar via; sopprimere **2.** restringere; diminuire; ridurre le spese.

to **retrench**[2], *v.t.* (*mil.*) trincerare (la seconda linea di difesa).

retrenchment[1] [ri'trenʃmənt], *s.* **1.** soppressione **2.** limitazione, diminuzione, restrizione; riduzione (di spese).

retrenchment[2], *s.* (*mil.*) trinceramento, trincea interna.

retrial ['ri:'traiəl], *s.* (*dir.*) giudizio di seconda istanza.

retribution [,retri'bju:ʃən], *s.* **1.** castigo, punizione ‖ *the Day of Retribution*, il Giorno del Giudizio **2.** ricompensa.

retributive [ri'tribjutiv], *ag.* **1.** punitivo **2.** retributivo.

retributively [ri'tribjutivli], *av.* **1.** per punizione **2.** per ricompensa.

retributory [ri'tribjutəri], *V.* retributive.

retrievable [ri'tri:vəbl], *ag.* **1.** ricuperabile **2.** riparabile, rimediabile.

retrieval [ri'tri:vəl], *s.* **1.** ricupero (di beni) **2.** riparazione, rimedio (a errore, ecc.).

retrieve [ri'tri:v], *s.* (possibilità di) ricupero, riparazione ‖ *beyond —*, irricuperabile, irreparabile.

to **retrieve**, *v.t.i.* **1.** rintracciare e riportare la selvaggina (di cani da caccia) **2.** ricuperare; ripristinare: *to — freedom*, ricuperare la libertà **3.** riparare, rimediare a: *he retrieved his errors*, riparò le sue colpe **4.** richiamare alla mente **5.** salvare: *she retrieved him from ruin*, lo salvò dalla rovina*.

retriever [ri'tri:və*], *s.* cane da presa.

to **retrim** ['ri:'trim], *pass.p.p.* **retrimmed** ['ri:'trimd], *v.t.* riordinare, riassettare.

to **retroact** [,retrou'ækt], *v.i.* **1.** reagire; operare in senso contrario **2.** (*dir.*) avere effetto retroattivo.

retroaction [,retrou'ækʃən], *s.* **1.** reazione **2.** (*dir.*) azione retroattiva.

retroactive [,retrou'æktiv], *ag.* (*dir.*) retroattivo.

retroactively [,retrou'æktivli], *av.* retroattivamente.

retroactivity [,retrouæk'tiviti], *s.* retroattività.

to **retrocede**[1] [,retrou'si:d], *v.t.i.* **1.** retrocedere, tornare indietro **2.** colpire le parti interne (di gotta).

to **retrocede**[2], *v.t.* restituire (territorio).

retrocession[1] [,retrou'seʃən], *s.* **1.** indietreggiamento **2.** (*patol.*) retrocessione (di eruzione, gotta, ecc.)

retrocession[2], *s.* restituzione (di territorio); recessione (di diritti).

retrochoir ['ri:troukwaiə*], *s.* coro (luogo dietro l'altare maggiore).

retroflection [,retrou'flekʃən], *s.* (*med.*) retroflessione.

retroflex ['retroufleks], *ag.* retroflesso.

retroflexion [,retrou'flekʃən], *s.* (*med.*) retroflessione.

retrogradation ['retrougrə'deiʃən], *s.* **1.** regressione, retrocessione, ritorno, movimento all'indietro **2.** retrogressione, regresso; declino, decadimento; degenerazione **3.** (*astr.*) retrogradazione.

retrograde ['retrougreid], *ag.* **1.** retrogrado (anche *fig.*): — *policy*, politica retrograda **2.** inverso; contrario: *in* — *order*, in ordine inverso ‖ *s.* **1.** (*rar.*) persona degenerata **2.** tendenza retrograda ☆ — *amnesia*, (*patol.*) amnesia retrograda; — *movement*, (*astr.*) movimento retrogrado.

to **retrograde**, *v.i.* **1.** retrocedere **2.** (*astr.*) retrogradare **3.** degenerare; declinare.

to **retrogress** [,retrou'gres], *v.i.* **1.** regredire; retrocedere **2.** deteriorarsi.

retrogression [,retrou'greʃən], *s.* **1.** *V.* **retrogradation 2.** (*med.*) retrocessione.

retrogressive [,retrou'gresiv], *ag.* regressivo; retrogrado ☆ — *erosion*, (*geol.*) erosione regressiva.

retrogressively [,retrou'gresivli], *av.* regressivamente.

retropulsion [,retrou'pʌlʃən], *s.* **1.** spinta all'indietro **2.** (*patol.*) retropulsione.

retrorse [ri'trɔːs], *ag.* volto all'indietro.

retrorsely [ri'trɔːsli], *av.* all'indietro.

retrospect ['retrouspekt], 's. esame, sguardo retrospettivo; visione retrospettiva.

retrospection [,retrou'spekʃən], *s.* retrospezione; esame, sguardo retrospettivo.

retrospective [,retrou'spektiv], *ag.* **1.** retrospettivo **2.** (*dir.*) retroattivo.

retrospectively [,retrou'spektivli], *av.* **1.** retrospettivamente **2.** (*dir.*) retroattivamente.

retroversion [,retrou'vəːʃən], *s.* (*spec. med.*) retroversione.

to **retrovert** [,retrou'vəːt], *v.t.* (*spec. med.*) retrovertere, rovesciare, voltare all'indietro.

to **retry** ['riː'trai], *v.t.* **1.** ritentare; rifare (una esperienza) **2.** (*dir.*) rifare (un processo).

rettery ['retəri], *s.* maceratoio (per canapa, ecc.).

return [ri'təːn], *s.* **1.** ritorno: *on my* —, al mio ritorno ‖ *by* — (*of post*), (*comm.*) a giro di posta ‖ *many happy returns of the day!*, cento di questi giorni! **2.** restituzione; rinvio; ricompensa: *in* — *for*, in cambio di; *ask for the* — *of the book*, chiedi la restituzione del libro **3.** *gener. pl.* provento, profitto, guadagno **4.** relazione, rapporto, rendiconto (ufficiale) ‖ *returns*, prospetti statistici **5.** (*spor.*) risposta, rimando **6.** *pl.* tabacco dolce da pipa **7.** — (*ticket*), biglietto di andata e ritorno ☆ — *journey*, viaggio di ritorno; — *match*, (*spor.*) rivincita; — *wall*, muro di risvolto, d'accompagnamento ‖ *election returns*, risultati elettorali.

to **return**, *v.t.i.* **1.** ritornare: *to* — *home*, ritornare a casa; *to* — *to London*, ritornare a Londra **2.** replicare, rispondere: *to* — *a denial*, rispondere con un rifiuto **3.** ritornare, restituire, rendere; rimettere, rimandare: *to* — *a book*, *a sum*, restituire un libro, una somma **4.** ricambiare, contraccambiare; ripagare: *to* — *a compliment*, *a visit*, ricambiare un complimento, una visita; *to* — *s.o.'s love*, contraccambiare l'amore di qlcu. ‖ *to* — *like for like*, rendere pan per focaccia **5.** produrre, rendere, dare: *this estate returns little profit*, questa proprietà rende poco **6.** riportare, riferire, comunicare ufficialmente: *they returned the list of the wounded*, comunicarono la lista dei feriti **7.** (*spor.*) rinviare, rimandare (palla, ecc.) **8.** (*dir.*) dichiarare: *to be returned guilty, unfit for work*, essere dichiarato colpevole, inabile al lavoro **9.** (*pol.*) eleggere: *to* — *members to Parliament*, eleggere deputati al parlamento **10.** rinfoderare (un'arma) ☆ *returned emigrant*, emigrante rimpatriato; *returned soldier*, reduce; *returning officer*, membro di seggio elettorale.

returnable [ri'təːnəbl], *ag.* **1.** restituibile **2.** da restituirsi **3.** (*pol.*) eligibile **4.** (*dir.*) (di mandato) di rinvio.

returnless [ri'təːnlis], *ag.* senza ritorno.

Réunion (Island) [ri'juːniən('ailənd)], *no.pr.* (*geog.*) Isola Riunione.

reunion ['riː'juːnjən], *s.* **1.** riunione: *a* — *of old friends*, una riunione di vecchi amici **2.** nuova unione; nuovo patto.

reunionism ['riː'juːnjənizəm], *s.* dottrina mirante a riunire la Chiesa Anglicana a quella Cattolica.

reunionist ['riː'juːnjənist], *s.* fautore dell'unione delle Chiese Anglicana e Cattolica.

to **reunite** ['riː'juː'nait], *v.t.i.* **1.** riunire, riunirsi **2.** riconciliarsi.

to **reurge** ['riː'əːdʒ], *v.t.* **1.** premere, incalzare di nuovo **2.** risollecitare **3.** soffermarsi, insistere, indugiare di nuovo su (un argomento, ecc.).

to **rev** [rev], *pass.p.p.* **revved** [revd], *v.t.i.*: *to* — **up**, (*fam.*) fare imballare, imballarsi: *to* — *up the engine*, (*aut.*) far imballare il motore.

to **revaccinate** ['riː'væksineit], *v.t.* rivaccinare.

revaccination ['riː,væksi'neiʃən], *s.* rivaccinazione.

revalenta [,revə'lentə], *s.* cibo preparato con farina di lenticchie e orzo.

revalorization ['riː,vælərai'zeiʃən], *s.* rivalorizzazione, rivalutazione.

revaluation ['riː,vælju'eiʃən], *s.* rivalutazione.

to **revalue** ['riː'væljuː], *v.t.* rivalutare.

reveal[1] [ri'viːl], *s.* (*rar.*) rivelazione.

to **reveal**[1], *v.t.* rivelare: *the work reveals the author*, l'opera rivela l'autore; *to* — *oneself*, rivelarsi; *to* — *a secret*, rivelare un segreto ‖ *revealed religion*, religione rivelata.

reveal[2], *s.* (*edil.*) stipite; strombatura.

revealable [ri'viːləbl], *ag.* rivelabile.

reveille [ri'væli], *s.* (*mil.*) sveglia, diana.

revel ['revl], *s.* **1.** festa (chiassosa); baldoria, orgia, gozzoviglia **2.** *gener. pl.* festeggiamenti ☆ — *-rout*, gruppo di persone che gozzovigliano; orgia.

to **revel**, *pass.p.p.* **revelled** ['revld], *v.t.i.* **1.** divertirsi (con chiasso); far baldoria, fare delle orge; gozzovigliare **2.** festeggiare; banchettare **3.** trovare diletto, piacere: *to* — *in sports*, trovare diletto negli sport **4.** *to* — **away**, sperperare, sprecare: *he revelled his money away*, egli sprecò il suo denaro in divertimenti.

revelation [,revi'leiʃən], *s.* rivelazione (anche *teol.*): *what a* —*!*, che rivelazione! ‖ *the Revelation*, l'Apocalisse.

revelational [,revi'leiʃən], *ag.* di rivelazione.

revelationist [,revi'leiʃənist], *s.* credente nella rivelazione divina ‖ *the Revelationist*, l'autore dell'Apocalisse.

reveller ['revlə*], *s.* chi si dà a orge, piaceri.

revelling ['reviln], *s.* baldoria, orgia, gozzoviglia.

revelry ['revlri], *s.* baldoria, orgia, gozzoviglia.

revenant ['revənənt], *s.c.* chi ritorna dopo lunga assenza ‖ *s.* spettro, fantasma, ombra.

revendication [ri,vendi'keiʃən], *s.* rivendicazione.

revenge [ri'vendʒ], *s.* **1.** vendetta, spirito di vendetta: *out of* —, per vendetta; *he was still harbouring thoughts of* —, aveva sempre la vendetta nel cuore; *to take* — *for sthg. on s.o.*, vendicarsi di ql.co. su qlcu. **2.** rivincita (al giuoco): *to give s.o. his* —, dare la rivincita a qlcu.

to **revenge**, *v.t.i.* **1.** vendicare: *to* — *oneself (up)on s.o.*, vendicarsi su qlcu. **2.** vendicarsi, trarre vendetta.

revengeful [ri'vendʒful], *ag.* **1.** vendicativo **2.** vendicatore.

revengefully [ri'vendʒfuli], *av.* vendicativamente; per vendetta.

revengefulness [ri'vendʒfulnis], *s.* animo vendicativo; spirito di vendetta.

revenger [ri'vendʒə*], *s.c.* vendicatore, vendicatrice.

revengingly [ri'vendʒiŋli], *av.* in modo vendicativo; per spirito di vendetta.

revenue ['revinjuː], *s.* **1.** entrata, entrate; reddito ‖ — *and expenditure*, (*comm.*) entrate e spese in bilancio **2.** *gener. pl.* entrate dello Stato **3.** fisco; erario ☆ — *-cutter*, lancia della Guardia di finanza; — *officer*, funzionario doganale; — *stamp*, marca da bollo; — *tax*, imposta sull'entrata.

reverberant [ri'və:bərənt], *ag.* (*poet.*) che riverbera; che risuona, risonante, sonoro.

to **reverberate** [ri'və:bəreit], *v.t.i.* riverberare; risuonare, riecheggiare ☆ *reverberating furnace*, forno a riverbero.

reverberation [ri,və:bə'reiʃən], *s.* **1.** (*fis.*) riverbero **2.** (*acu.*) riverberazione; coda sonora.

reverberative [ri'və:bəreitiv], *ag.* che riverbera.

reverberator [ri'və:bəreitə*], *s.* **1.** riflettore; lampada a riverbero **2.** (*fis.*) superficie di riverbero.

reverberatory [ri'və:bərətəri], *ag.* a, di riverbero ‖ *s.* forno a riverbero ☆ — *furnace*, forno a riverbero.

to **revere** [ri'viə*], *v.t.* riverire; venerare.

reverence ['revərəns], *s.* **1.** riverenza; venerazione; rispetto: *to be held in* —, essere rispettato; *to pay* — *to,* rendere onore a; *to regard with* —, considerare con rispetto ‖ *saving your* —, (*arc.*) con rispetto parlando ‖ *your* —, (*irl.*) reverendo **2.** (*arc.*) riverenza, inchino.

to **reverence**, *v.t.* riverire, considerare con riverenza.

reverend ['revərənd], *ag.* **1.** venerando **2.** (*eccl.*) reverendo ‖ *Reverend* (*abbr. Rev.*), reverendo: *Very Reverend,* molto reverendo (riferito a decano); *Right Reverend,* reverendissimo (riferito a vescovo) ‖ *s.* ecclesiastico, prete.

reverent ['revərənt], *ag.* riverente; pieno di venerazione; rispettoso.

reverential [,revə'renʃəl], *ag.* riverente; reverenziale.

reverentially [,revə'renʃəli], *av.* con rispetto, con timore riverenziale.

reverently ['revərəntli], *av.* con riverenza; con venerazione; con rispetto.

reverer [ri'viərə*], *s.* veneratore.

reverie ['revəri], *s.* sogno a occhi aperti; fantasticheria: *she was lost in* (a) —, sognava ad occhi aperti.

revers [ri'viə*], *pl.* **revers** [ri'viəz], *s.* risvolto (di abito).

reversal [ri'və:səl], *s.* **1.** rovesciamento; inversione **2.** (*dir.*) annullamento, revoca.

reverse [ri'və:s], *ag.* rovescio, inverso; opposto, contrario ‖ *s.* **1.** il rovescio, l'inverso; l'opposto, il contrario: *the* — *of a coin,* il rovescio di una moneta **2.** disgrazia; rovescio finanziario; disfatta militare: *to suffer a* —, subire un rovescio finanziario **3.** (*aut.*) retromarcia; (*mec.*) invertitore di marcia: *on the* —, a marcia indietro.

to **reverse**, *v.t.i.* **1.** rovesciare, ribaltare, capovolgere **2.** far agire in senso contrario; (*elett.*) invertire (corrente); (*aut.*) innestare la retromarcia **3.** girare in senso inverso (nella danza) **4.** (*dir.*) revocare.

reversely [ri'və:sli], *av.* in senso inverso, contrario.

reversi [ri'və:si], *s.* **1.** reversino (giuoco di carte) **2.** giuoco praticato sulla scacchiera della dama con pezzi diversamente colorati sulle due facce.

reversibility [ri,və:sə'biliti], *s.* reversibilità.

reversible [ri'və:səbl], *ag.* **1.** reversibile; rovesciabile; ribaltabile **2.** (*dir.*) revocabile **3.** a due diritti (di stoffa) **4.** (*mec.*) a inversione di marcia.

reversion [ri'və:ʃən], *s.* **1.** reversione, ritorno (a stato precedente) **2.** (*dir.*) riversione; diritto di riversione **3.** (*biol.*) reversione, regressione.

reversional [ri'və:ʃənl], *ag.* **1.** di, da reversione **2.** (*dir.*) riversibile; di reversione.

reversionally [ri'və:ʃnəli], *av.* **1.** per reversione **2.** (*dir.*) per riversione.

reversionary [ri'və:ʃnəri], *ag.* **1.** reversibile (a stato precedente) **2.** (*dir.*) riversibile; di riversione **3.** atavico.

to **revert** [ri'və:t], *v.t.i.* **1.** volgere indietro (occhi, passi) **2.** (*dir.*) spettare (per riversione) **3.** (*rar.*) ritornare: *to* — *to a topic,* ritornare su un argomento.

reverter [ri'və:tə*], *s.* (*dir.*) riversione.

revertible [ri'və:təbl], *ag.* (*dir.*) riversibile.

to **revet** [ri'vet], *pass.p.p.* **revetted** [ri'vetid], *v.t.* rivestire (di cemento, pietra).

revetment [ri'vetmənt], *s.* **1.** rivestimento (di cemento, pietra) **2.** contrafforte.

review [ri'vju:], *s.* **1.** esame, analisi; revisione; sguardo retrospettivo; ripasso (di lezioni) **2.** recensione, critica, rassegna **3.** rivista, periodico: *a quarterly* —, una rivista trimestrale **4.** (*mil.*) rivista: *to pass in* —, passare in rivista **5.** (*dir.*) revisione **6.** (*teat.*) rivista ☆ — *order,* (*mil.*) alta uniforme.

to **review**, *v.t.i.* **1.** rivedere; riesaminare; dare uno sguardo retrospettivo a **2.** recensire, fare la rassegna di; fare recensioni: *to* — *a novel,* recensire un romanzo **3.** (*mil.*) passare in rivista **4.** (*dir.*) sottoporre a revisione.

reviewable [ri'vju:əbl], *ag.* **1.** rivedibile; riesaminabile **2.** recensibile **3.** (*mil.*) da passare in rivista **4.** (*dir.*) da sottoporre a revisione.

reviewal [ri'vju(:)əl], *s.* esame; recensione, critica.

reviewer [ri'vju(:)ə*], *s.* recensore, critico letterario.

to **revile** [ri'vail], *v.t.i.* **1.** ingiuriare, insultare **2.** servirsi di linguaggio oltraggioso.

reviler [ri'vailə*], *s.* oltraggiatore, offensore.

reviling [ri'vailiŋ], *s.* ingiuria.

revilingly [ri'vailiŋli], *av.* ingiuriosamente; oltraggiosamente.

revisable [ri'vaizəbl], *ag.* rivedibile.

revisal [ri'vaizəl], *s.* revisione; correzione.

revise [ri'vaiz], *s.* **1.** (*tip.*) seconda bozza **2.** (*rar.*) revisione.

to **revise**, *v.t.* **1.** rivedere; riesaminare ‖ *the Revised Version of the Bible,* la versione riveduta (1870-84) della Bibbia Anglicana **2.** (*tip.*) correggere (bozze).

reviser [ri'vaizə*], *s.* **1.** revisore **2.** (*tip.*) correttore (di bozze).

revision [ri'viʒən], *s.* **1.** revisione **2.** (*tip.*) correzione (di bozze).

revisional [ri'viʒənl], *ag.* di revisione.

revisory [ri'vaizəri], *ag.* che rivede, corregge, emenda.

to **revitalize** ['ri:'vaitəlaiz], *v.t.* dare nuova vita a.

revivable [ri'vaivəbl], *ag.* che si può rianimare, resuscitare, far rivivere.

revival [ri'vaivəl], *s.* **1.** ripristino; riesumazione; ripresa; risveglio; rifiorimento: *the* — *of a custom,* il ripristino di un'usanza; *the* — *of a play,* la ripresa di un lavoro teatrale; *the* — *of trade,* il rifiorire del commercio **2.** rinascita, rinascimento: *the* — *of letters,* la rinascita delle lettere ‖ *the Revival of Learning,* il Rinascimento **3.** risveglio (religioso); ritorno (alla religione) **4.** ritorno alla vita; ripresa dei sensi, delle forze.

revivalism [ri'vaivəlizəm], *s.* revivalismo, ‖ movimento promotore di un risveglio religioso.

revivalist [ri'vaivəlist], *s.* esponente del revivalismo; promotore di un risveglio religioso.

to **revive** [ri'vaiv], *v.t.i.* **1.** resuscitare, far rinascere; rivivere, ritornare in vita: *water revives flowers,* l'acqua fa rivivere i fiori **2.** ravvivare, ravvivarsi; rianimarsi; rinvigorirsi: *his hopes revived,* le sue speranze si ravvivarono **3.** rimettere in uso: *an old custom was revived,* una vecchia consuetudine fu rimessa in uso; *to* — *a dead phrase,* rimettere in uso un'espressione morta **4.** (*chim.*) riportare (un metallo, specialmente il mercurio) allo stato naturale.

reviver [ri'vaivə*], *s.c.* chi fa rivivere, rianima, rinnova, rimette in voga ‖ *s.* **1.** preparato per ravvivare colori sbiaditi **2.** (*sl.*) cicchetto (sorsata di liquore).

revivification [ri(:),vivifi'keiʃən], *s.* **1.** ritorno in vita; richiamo in vita **2.** (*chim.*) riduzione.

to **revivify** [ri(:)'vivifai], *v.t.* **1.** ravvivare; rianimare; rinvigorire **2.** (*chim.*) riportare (un metallo, specialmente il mercurio) allo stato naturale.

reviviscence [,revi'visns], *s.* reviviscenza; ritorno alla vita.

reviviscent [,revi'visnt], *ag.* revivisciente; che torna in vita, in forze.

revivor [ri'vaivə*], *s.* (*dir.*) ripresa di causa, lite (dopo la morte di una delle parti).

revocability [,revəkə'biliti], *s.* revocabilità.

revocable ['revəkəbl], *ag.* revocabile.

revocably ['revəkəbli], *av.* in modo revocabile.

revocation [,revə'keiʃən], *s.* revoca, abrogazione; annullamento; ritiro: — *of driving licence*, (*aut.*) ritiro di patente.

revocatory ['revəkətəri], *ag.* revocatorio.

revoke [ri'vouk], *s.* **1.** (*rar.*) revoca ‖ *beyond* —, irrevocabile; irrevocabilmente **2.** (*carte*) rifiuto.

to revoke, *v.t.i.* **1.** revocare; abrogare; annullare; ritirare (una promessa) **2.** (*carte*) rifiutare.

revolt [ri'voult], *s.* **1.** rivolta; ribellione: *in* —, in rivolta **2.** disgusto, ripugnanza.

to revolt, *v.t.i.* **1.** rivoltarsi, ribellarsi: *to — against s.o.*, ribellarsi a qlcu. **2.** rifuggire, provare orrore: *common sense revolts at* (o *against* o *from*) *such a supposition*, il buon senso rifugge da una tale supposizione **3.** rivoltare, disgustare: *the scene revolted him*, la scena lo disgustò.

revolted [ri'voultid], *ag.* in rivolta, ribelle: — *subjects*, sudditi ribelli.

revolter [ri'voultə*], *s.* rivoltoso; ribelle, insorto.

revolting [ri'voultiŋ], *ag.* **1.** rivoltante, disgustoso, ributtante **2.** in rivolta.

revoltingly [ri'voultiŋli], *av.* in modo rivoltante, disgustoso, ributtante.

revolute ['revəlju:t], *ag.* (*bot.*) accartocciato, rivolto all'indietro.

revolution [,revə'lu:ʃən], *s.* **1.** rivoluzione; ribellione ‖ *the French Revolution*, la Rivoluzione Francese **2.** trasformazione; rivolgimento **3.** giro, rotazione: *that wheel makes three revolutions a second*, quella ruota compie tre giri al secondo **4.** (*astr.*) rivoluzione.

revolutionary [,revə'lu:ʃnəri], *ag.* **1.** rivoluzionario **2.** (*mec.*) rotatorio ‖ *s.* rivoluzionario.

revolutionism [,revə'lu:ʃnizəm], *s.* rivoluzionarismo.

revolutionist [,revə'lu:ʃnist], *s.* rivoluzionario.

to revolutionize [,revə'lu:ʃnaiz], *v.t.* rivoluzionare; mutare radicalmente.

to revolve [ri'volv], *v.t.i.* **1.** rivolgere; meditare, ponderare: *to — a problem* (*in one's mind*), esaminare un problema **2.** rotare, girare, muoversi in giro: *the planets — round the sun*, i pianeti ruotano intorno al Sole; *to — on a spindle*, girare su un asse **3.** ricorrere, ritornare: *seasons — incessantly*, le stagioni si avvicendano senza posa.

revolver [ri'volvə*], *s.* rivoltella.

revolving [ri'volviŋ], *ag.* **1.** rotante; che gira intorno **2.** ricorrente (di stagioni, ecc.) **3.** (*tec.*) girevole; rotativo **4.** (*comm.*) rotativo ☆ — *credit*, (*comm.*) credito rotativo; — *door*, porta girevole.

revue [ri'vju:], *s.* (*teat.*) rivista ☆ *variety show* —, rivista di varietà.

revulsion [ri'vʌlʃən], *s.* **1.** mutamento improvviso (di circostanze, atteggiamento); reazione **2.** (*rar.*) ritiro: *the — of capital from trade*, il ritiro del capitale dagli affari **3.** (*med.*) revulsione.

revulsive [ri'vʌlsiv], *ag.s.* (*med.*) revulsivo.

reward [ri'wo:d], *s.* ricompensa; rimunerazione; compenso.

to reward, *v.t.* ricompensare; rimunerare; compensare.

rewardable [ri'wo:dəbl], *ag.* ricompensabile.

rewarder [ri'wo:də*], *s.c.* rimuneratore, rimuneratrice.

rewarding [ri'wo:diŋ], *ag.* rimunerativo ‖ *s.* rimunerazione; ricompensa.

rewardless [ri'wo:dlis], *ag.* senza compenso, senza rimunerazione.

to reword [ri:'wə:d], *v.t.* **1.** formulare con nuove parole **2.** ripetere con le stesse parole.

to rewrite ['ri:'rait], *pass.* **rewrote** ['ri:'rout], *p.p.* **rewritten** ['ri:'ritn], *v.i.* riscrivere; rimaneggiare (uno scritto).

Reynard ['renəd], *no.pr.m.* (*lett.*) «Reynard», la Volpe.

Reynold ['renld], *no.pr.m.* Rinaldo.

rhabdomancy ['ræbdou,mænsi], *s.* rabdomanzia.

rhabdomantist ['ræbdou,mæntist], *s.* rabdomante.

Rhadamanthus [,rædə'mænθəs], *no.pr.m.* (*mit.*) Radamanto.

Rhaetia ['ri:ʃjə], (*geog. st.*) Rezia.

Rhaetian ['ri:ʃjən], *ag.* retico ‖ *s.c.* abitante della Rezia.

Rhaetic ['ri:tik], *ag.* retico.

rhapsode ['ræpsoud], *s.* rapsodo.

rhapsodic(al) [ræp'sodik(əl)], *ag.* **1.** rapsodico **2.** (*fam.*) entusiastico.

rhapsodically [ræp'sodikəli], *av.* **1.** rapsodicamente **2.** (*fam.*) entusiasticamente.

rhapsodist ['ræpsədist], *s.* rapsodo.

to rhapsodize ['ræpsədaiz], *v.t.i.* **1.** recitare come un rapsodo **2.** (*mus.*) scrivere rapsodie **3.** *to — about, over* (*sthg.*), (*fam.*) andare in estasi per.

rhapsody ['ræpsədi], *s.* **1.** (*lett. mus.*) rapsodia **2.** (*fam.*) entusiasmo.

Rhenish ['ri:niʃ], *ag.* renano ‖ *s.* vino del Reno.

rhenium ['ri:njəm], *s.* (*chim.*) renio.

rheometer [ri'omitə*], *s.* (*elett.*) reometro.

rheophore ['ri:oufo:*], *s.* (*elett.*) reoforo.

rheoscope ['ri:əskoup], *s.* (*elett.*) reoscopio, galvanoscopio.

rheostat ['ri:əstæt], *s.* (*elett.*) reostato.

rhetor ['ri:tə*], *s.* retore.

rhetoric ['retərik], *s.* **1.** retorica **2.** trattato di retorica.

rhetorical [ri'torikəl], *ag.* retorico.

rhetorically [ri'torikəli], *av.* retoricamente.

rhetorician [,retə'riʃən], *s.* retore.

rheum[1] [ru:m], *s.* **1.** (*arc.*) catarro; muco **2.** (*poet.*) lacrime **3.** *gener. pl.* reumatismi.

rheum[2], *s.* (*bot.*) rabarbaro.

rheumatic [ru(:)'mætik], *ag.* reumatico ‖ *s.* **1.** reumatico **2.** *pl.* (*fam.*) reumatismi.

rheumatically [ru(:)'mætikəli], *av.* da reumatico; di reumatismo.

rheumaticky [ru(:)'mætiki], *ag.* (*fam.*) reumatico.

rheumatism ['ru:mətizəm], *s.* reumatismo.

rheumy ['ru:mi], *ag.* **1.** (*arc.*) catarrale; catarroso **2.** umido (specialmente dell'aria).

rhinal ['rainl], *ag.* delle narici, del naso.

Rhine [rain], *no.pr.* (*geog.*) Reno ☆ — *-stone*, varietà di cristallo di rocca; «strass» (diamante artificiale).

Rhineland ['rainlænd], *no.pr.* (*geog.*) Renania.

rhinitis [rai'naitis], *s.* (*patol.*) rinite.

rhino[1] ['rainou], *s.* (*sl.*) denaro.

rhino[2], *s.* **1.** (*abbr. di rhinoceros*) rinoceronte **2.** (*amer. mec.*) pontone da sbarco con motore fuoribordo.

rhinoceros [rai'nosərəs], *pl.* **rhinoceroses** [rai'nosərəsiz], *s.* rinoceronte.

rhinology [rai'nolədʒi], *s.* (*med.*) rinologia.

rhinopharyngeal [,rainoufə'rindʒiəl],*ag.* rinofaringeo.

rhinoplasty ['rainəplæsti], *s.* (*chir.*) rinoplastica.

rhinorrhea [,rainə'ri:ə], *s.* (*patol.*) rinorrea.

rhinoscope ['rainəskoup], *s.* (*med.*) rinoscopio.

rhinoscopy [rai'noskəpi], *s.* (*med.*) rinoscopia.

rhizome ['raizoum], *s.* (*bot.*) rizoma.

Rhodes [roudz], *no.pr.* (*geog.*) Rodi.

Rhodesia [rou'di:zjə], *no. pr.* (*geog.*) Rhodesia.

Rhodesian [rou'di:zjən], *ag.* di Rhodesia ‖ *s.c.* abitante della Rhodesia.

Rhodian ['roudjən], *ag.* rodio ‖ *s.c.* rodiota.

rhodic ['roudik], *ag.* (*chim.*) rodico.

rhodium[1] ['roudjəm], *s.* — (*-wood*), legno di Rodi.

rhodium[2], *s.* (*chim.*) rodio.

rhododendron [,roudə'dendrən], *s.* (*bot.*) rododendro.

rhodonite ['roudənait], *s.* (*min.*) rodonite.

rhomb [rom], *s.* **1.** (*geom.*) rombo **2.** romboedro.

rhombic ['rombik], *ag.* **1.** (*geom.*) rombico **2.** romboedrico.

rhombohedral [,rombou'hi:drəl], *ag.* (*min.*) romboedrico.

rhombohedron [ˌrɔmbouˈhi:drən], pl. **rhombohedra** [ˌrɔmbouˈhi:drə], s. (geom.) romboedro.

rhomboid [ˈrɔmbɔid], ag.s. (geom.) romboide ☆ — muscle, (anat.) muscolo romboide.

rhomboidal [rɔmˈbɔidl], ag. romboidale; (di muscolo) romboide.

rhombus [ˈrɔmbəs], pl. **rhombuses** [ˈrɔmbəsiz], **rhombi** [ˈrɔmbai], s. 1. (ittiol.) rombo 2. (geom.) rombo.

Rhone [roun], no.pr. (geog.) Rodano.

rhotacism [ˈroutəsizəm], s. rotacismo, rotacizzazione.

to **rhotacize** [ˈroutəsaiz], v.i. rotacizzare.

rhubarb [ˈru:bɑ:b], s. rabarbaro.

rhubarby [ˈru:bɑ:bi], ag. di rabarbaro.

rhumb [rʌm], s. (mar.) 1. rombo 2. — (line), (mar.) rotta lossodromica: to sail by the —, navigare seguendo la linea lossodromica.

rhyme [raim], s. 1. rima: imperfect —, rima imperfetta; I prefer blank verse to —, preferisco il verso sciolto al verso rimato ‖ without — or reason, senza senso, assurdo 2. verso, versi; poesia: here are some rhymes of mine, ecco alcuni miei versi; this is an old English —, questa è una vecchia poesia inglese; to put in —, mettere in rima ☆ nursery —, poesia per bambini.

to **rhyme**, v.t.i. 1. metter in rima: to — one word with another, far rimare una parola con un'altra 2. comporre versi, rime 3. rimare, far rima.

rhymeless [ˈraimlis], ag. senza rima, non rimato.

rhymelessness [ˈraimlisnis], s. assenza di rima.

rhymer [ˈraimə*], s. 1. rimatore; verseggiatore 2. (mec.) alesatore.

rhymester [ˈraimstə*], s. poetastro.

rhythm [ˈriðəm], s. ritmo.

rhythmic(al) [ˈriðmik(əl)], ag. ritmico.

rhythmically [ˈriðmikəli], av. ritmicamente.

rhythmist [ˈriðmist], s. compositore di ritmi.

rhythmless [ˈriðəmlis], ag. senza ritmo; aritmico.

riant [ˈraiənt], ag. ridente, allegro.

rib [rib], s. 1. (anat.) costola; (scherz.) moglie: in that accident he fractured his ribs, in quell'incidente riportò una frattura alle costole; to poke s.o. in the ribs, dar di gomito ‖ Adam's —, fig. la costola di Adamo, Eva 2. costa (di tessuto, lavoro a maglia); costola, dorso (di libro); costa (di lama) 3. stecca (di ombrello, di violino) 4. cresta (di monte) 5. (aer.) centina (alare); ordinata 6. (arch.) costolone, nervatura; centina 7. (mar.) costa, corba 8. (geol.) vena, strato 9. (bot.) costa, nervatura 10. (agr.) porca 11. (mec.) nervatura ☆ — fabric, tessuto a coste; — -work, ossatura (di nave).

to **rib**, pass.p.p. **ribbed** [ribd], v.t. 1. munire di, rinforzare con coste, costoloni 2. scanalare.

ribald [ˈribəld], ag. osceno, licenzioso ‖ s. individuo sboccato, che si compiace di scherzi volgari.

ribaldry [ˈribəldri], s. oscenità; linguaggio sboccato; scherzo volgare.

riband [ˈribənd], V. ribbon.

ribband [ˈribənd], s. (mar.) longherina.

ribbed [ribd], ag. 1. rigato, scanalato 2. a coste (di tessuto) 3. (arch.) a nervature, a costoloni 4. (bot.) nervato (di foglie) 5. (mec.) nervato; alettato.

ribbing [ˈribiŋ], s. 1. (arch.) armatura (di volta) 2. (bot.) nervature 3. coste, rigature (di tessuto) 4. (mec.) nervature.

ribbon [ˈribən], s. 1. nastro; fettuccia: to tie up one's hair with a —, annodarsi i capelli con un nastro 2. nastrino, cordone (di decorazione) ‖ Ribbon Society, (st.) società segreta irlandese fomentatrice di disordini agrari ‖ blue —, insegna dell'Ordine della Giarrettiera; red —, insegna dell'Ordine del Bagno 3. pl. brandelli: to hang in ribbons, essere a brandelli; to tear to ribbons, ridurre a brandelli 4. pl. redini (di cavallo): to handle (o to take) the ribbons, prendere le redini, guidare ☆ — -building (o — -development), allineamento di case lungo le principali vie di comunicazione; — -grass, (bot.) canaria; — -saw, sega a nastro ‖ typewriter- —, nastro per macchina da scrivere.

ribes [ˈraibi:z], s. (bot.) ribes.

Ribston pippin [ˈribstənˈpipin], s. varietà di mele coltivate a Ribston, nello Yorkshire.

ribwork [ˈribwə:k], s. (mec.) struttura nervata.

rice [rais], s. (bot.) riso: — is one of the most important produce of Northern Italy, il riso è uno dei prodotti più importanti dell'Italia settentrionale ☆ — -bird, passero di Giava; — -field (o — -swamp), risaia; — -milk, riso e latte; — mill, pileria di riso; — -paper, varietà di carta usata dai cinesi per dipingere; — -pudding, budino di riso ‖ husked —, riso brillato.

rich [ritʃ], ag. 1. ricco: — in hope, ricco di speranze; — in ideas, ricco di idee; a — man, un uomo ricco; a town — in monuments, una città ricca di monumenti; this invention made him —, questa invenzione lo arricchì ‖ the vulgar —, gli arricchiti 2. costoso; sontuoso: — clothes, vesti sontuose; — presents, ricchi doni 3. abbondante; fertile: — crop, raccolto abbondante; — soil, terreno fertile 4. nutriente, sostanzioso, molto condito (di cibo); generoso (di vino): — cream, crema grassa; — foods, cibi nutrienti; this dish is too — for me, questo piatto è troppo pesante per me 5. vivido, smagliante, intenso (di colore); pieno (di voce); molto forte (di profumo) 6. (sl.) divertente, comico: this is a — idea, questa è un'idea divertente.

Richard [ˈritʃəd], no.pr.m. Riccardo.

riches [ˈritʃiz], s. gener. pl. ricchezza, ricchezze (anche fig.): he had great —, era molto ricco; to heap up —, accumulare ricchezze.

richly [ˈritʃli], av. 1. riccamente, sontuosamente 2. abbondantemente; ampiamente; grandemente: he — deserves punishment, merita bene una punizione.

richness [ˈritʃnis], s. 1. ricchezza 2. sontuosità, magnificenza; lusso: the quiet — of her dress, la sobria eleganza del suo abito 3. abbondanza; fertilità (di terreno) 4. ricchezza nutritiva (di alimenti); generosità (di vino) 5. vivacità (di colore) 6. ampiezza (di voce).

ricin [ˈraisin], s. (farm.) ricina.

ricinine [ˈrisini:n], s. (farm.) ricinina.

ricinoleic [ˌrisinəˈliːik], ag. ricinoleico.

ricinus [ˈrisinəs], s. (bot.) ricino.

rick[1] [rik], s. mucchio (di grano, fieno, ecc.); bica ☆ — -barton, pagliaio; fienile; granaio.

to **rick**[1], v.t. formare mucchi di (grano, fieno, ecc.); accatastare.

rick[2], s. storta, distorsione: I have a — in the neck, ho il torcicollo.

to **rick**[2], v.t. storcere; stortare; lussare.

ricket(s) [ˈrikit(s)], s. (patol.) rachitismo, rachitide.

rickety [ˈrikiti], ag. 1. (patol.) rachitico 2. fragile, traballante, malsicuro (di persone, mobili, ecc.).

ricksha(w) [ˈrikʃɔ:], s. « risciò ».

ricochet [ˈrikəʃet], s. rimbalzo (di proiettile).

to **ricochet**, v.t.i. 1. rimbalzare: the bullet ricocheted upwards, la pallottola rimbalzò verso l'alto; the echo ricocheted off the cliffs, l'eco rimbalzò giù per le scogliere 2. (artigl.) colpire di rimbalzo.

to **rid** [rid], pass. **rid**, **ridded** [ˈridid], p.p. **rid**, v.t. 1. liberare, sbarazzare: I — him of his fears, lo liberai dai suoi timori; to get — of, liberarsi da, sbarazzarsi di; (mat.) eliminare 2. (arc.) abolire.

ridable [ˈraidəbl], ag. cavalcabile: — horse, cavallo cavalcabile ☆ — road, strada cavalcabile.

riddance [ˈridəns], s. liberazione ‖ a good —!, che liberazione!.

riddel [ˈridl], s. (eccl.) cortina d'altare.

ridden [ˈridn], p.p. di to ride.

riddle[1] [ˈridl], s. 1. indovinello; enigma 2. fig. enigma, persona, cosa, fatto enigmatico.

to **riddle**[1], v.t.i. 1. parlare per indovinelli; proporre indovinelli 2. risolvere (un indovinello, un enigma): to — (out) a dream, spiegare un sogno.

riddle[2], s. vaglio; crivello.

to **riddle**[2], v.t. 1. vagliare, setacciare (anche fig.):

to — an argument, vagliare, sviscerare un argomento **2.** crivellare, perforare (con pallottole, ecc.).

riddler ['ridlə*], *s.c.* chi compone enigmi; chi parla per enigmi.

riddlingly ['ridliŋli], *av.* con indovinelli; enigmaticamente.

ride [raid], *s.* **1.** cavalcata, passeggiata (a cavallo); scarrozzata, corsa (su un veicolo): *we had a — in the new car,* abbiamo fatto un giro con l'automobile nuova; *to go for* (o *to take*) *a —,* fare una passeggiata a cavallo ‖ *to take s.o. for a —,* (*arc. sl.*) prendere in giro, ingannare qlcu.; prelevare qlcu. col proposito di ucciderlo **2.** tragitto, percorso (a cavallo, su un veicolo): *it is only a quarter of an hour's —,* non è che un percorso di un quarto d'ora; *to steal a — (on a lorry, on a train),* farsi trainare abusivamente, viaggiare senza biglietto **3.** pista, sentiero (tra i boschi) per cavalcare **4.** (*mil.*) gruppo di reclute a cavallo.

to ride, *pass.* **rode** [roud], (*arc.*) **rid** [rid], *p.p.* **ridden** ['ridn], (*arc.*) **rid,** *v.t.i.* **1.** cavalcare; montare (cavallo, bicicletta, ecc.); andare, passeggiare, percorrere (a cavallo): *he rides astride and she rides side-saddle,* egli monta a cavalcioni ed ella all'amazzone; *he used to — when he was younger,* andava a cavallo quando era più giovane; *she was riding full speed,* cavalcava a tutta velocità; *we rode 80 miles,* percorremmo 80 miglia (a cavallo); *witches — (on) broomsticks,* le streghe vanno a cavallo di una scopa; *to — a child on one's back,* portare un bambino in groppa; *to — a ford,* passare un guado a cavallo; *to — a horse, (on) a bicycle,* andare a cavallo, in bicicletta; *to — one's horse at a fence,* dirigere il cavallo su un ostacolo; *to — on s.o.'s knee, shoulders,* stare a cavalcioni sulle ginocchia, sulle spalle di qlcu.; *to — a prairie,* percorrere una prateria a cavallo; *to — a race,* competere in una corsa (a cavallo) ‖ *the moon is riding high,* la luna è alta nel cielo ‖ *to — a-cock-horse,* montare a cavalcioni ‖ *to — bodkin,* viaggiare schiacciato tra due persone ‖ *to — the high horse,* darsi delle arie ‖ *to — a horse to death,* sfiancare un cavallo ‖*to — a story to death, fig.* ripetere una storia fino alla noia ‖ *to — to hounds,* andare alla caccia della volpe **2.** andare, correre (su veicoli, ecc.); andare, correre (di veicoli): *they will — back in my car,* torneranno indietro con la mia automobile; *this car rides smoothly, hard,* questa automobile è ben molleggiata, arranca **3.** pesare (di fantino): *he rides 9 stone,* pesa 57 chili **4.** (*mar.*) fluttuare, galleggiare; essere all'ancora: *the ship rides at anchor,* la nave è ancorata; *the ship rides on the waves,* la nave fende i flutti ‖ *to — out the storm,* uscire illesi da una burrasca (anche *fig.*) ‖ *to — the whirlwind,* sostenere la tempesta **5.** accavallarsi, sovrapporsi (di ossa, funi, ecc.) **6.** *fig.* opprimere, dominare: *he is ridden by prejudices,* è dominato da pregiudizi; *the nightmare rode the sick man,* l'incubo opprimeva il malato; *to be ridden by fear,* essere oppresso, dominato dalla paura **7.** essere praticabile, cavalcabile (di terreno) **8.** (*amer. jazz*) improvvisare liberamente su un tema **9.** *to — down,* travolgere; calpestare; caricare (la folla): *the squadron rode them down,* lo squadrone passò sui loro corpi **10.** *to — off,* partire, allontanarsi (a cavallo); (*fam.*) fare una digressione; (*spor.*) urtare (un avversario, al polo) **11.** *to — over,* compiere un tragitto (a cavallo): *I often — over to see them,* vado spesso a trovarli (a cavallo) **12.** *to — up,* arrivare (a cavallo).

rider ['raidə*], *s.c.* cavallerizzo, cavallerizza; viaggiatore, viaggiatrice (in veicolo); ciclista; motociclista: *to be a good —,* cavalcare bene ‖ *s.* **1.** cavaliere; fantino: (*arc.*) viaggiatore di commercio **2.** codicillo; clausola addizionale (d'un progetto di legge); correttivo (di una formula) **3.** (*mat.*) esercizio di applicazione (di un teorema) **4.** *pl.* (*mar.*) rinforzi per ordinate; ordinate supplementari **5.** (*geol.*) vena, giacimento secondario **6.** cavaliere (di bilancia) ☆ *gentleman —, «*gentleman

rider» (cavallerizzo dilettante); *lady —,* cavallerizza.

riderless ['raidəlis], *ag.* senza cavaliere.

ridge [ridʒ], *s.* **1.** spigolo (tra due superfici inclinate) **2.** (*edil.*) colmo (del tetto) **3.** cresta (di monti), vetta; crinale, spartiacque; catena di montagne, giogaia; linea di scogli affioranti **4.** (*agr.*) porca ☆ — *-beam,* trave di colmo; — *-bone,* spina dorsale.

to ridge, *v.t.i.* **1.** (*agr.*) formare porche in (un campo) **2.** corrugare, corrugarsi; incresparsi (specialmente del mare).

ridgy ['ridʒi], *ag.* **1.** (*agr.*) solcato **2.** increspato.

ridicule ['ridikju:l], *s.* ridicolo; scherno.

to ridicule, *v.t.* rendere ridicolo; mettere in ridicolo; beffare, canzonare, schernire.

ridiculous [ri'dikjuləs], *ag.* ridicolo; assurdo: *a — price,* un prezzo irrisorio.

ridiculously [ri'dikjuləsli], *av.* ridicolamente; in modo assurdo.

ridiculousness [ri'dikjuləsnis], *s.* ridicolaggine; assurdità.

riding[1] ['raidiŋ], *s.* **1.** corsa (su un veicolo); cavalcata **2.** maneggio; equitazione: *to go in for —,* montare a cavallo **3.** sentiero percorribile a cavallo **4.** rada, ancoraggio ☆ — *-boots,* stivali da equitazione; — *-breeches,* calzoni da cavallerizzo, cavallerizza; — *-ground,* galoppatoio; — *-habit,* abito da amazzone; — *-lamp,* — *-light,* lampada, lanterna di naviglio all'ancora; — *-school,* scuola d'equitazione; — *-whip,* frustino.

riding[2], *s.* divisione amministrativa nello Yorkshire, nel «Commonwealth»: *East —,* divisione di Levante.

rifacimento [ri,faːtʃi'mentou], *s.* rifacimento (di opere letterarie).

rife [raif], *ag. predicativo* **1.** dominante; comune; corrente; diffuso: *superstition is still — in the country,* la superstizione è ancora diffusa nelle campagne **2.** abbondante, ricco: *to be — with sthg.,* abbondare di ql.co.

rifely ['raifli], *av.* **1.** comunemente; correntemente **2.** abbondantemente.

rifeness ['raifnis], *s.* abbondanza, prevalenza.

riff-raff ['rifræf], *s.* **1.** canaglia; plebaglia **2.** scarto, robaccia; immondizia.

rifle[1] ['raifl], *s.* (*dial. amer.*) **1.** legnetto per affilare la falce **2.** parte ricurva del manico della falce.

rifle[2], *s.* **1.** rigatura (nell'anima delle bocche da fuoco) **2.** fucile a palla, carabina **3.** *pl.* fucilieri ☆ — *-corps,* corpo di fucilieri volontari; — *-pit,* trincea per fucilieri; — *-range,* portata di un fucile; campo di tiro a segno, poligono; — *-shot,* portata, colpo di fucile; tiratore (di fucile).

to rifle[2], *v.t.i.* **1.** (*artigl.*) scanalare **2.** sparare col fucile; fucilare.

to rifle[3], *v.t.i.* svaligiare; saccheggiare; rapinare; commettere rapine.

rifleman, *pl.* **riflemen** ['raiflmən], *s.* fuciliere.

rifler ['raiflə*], *s.* predone, ladrone; saccheggiatore.

rifling ['raifliŋ], *s.* rigatura (di fucile, ecc.).

rift[1] [rift], *s.* **1.** crepa; crepaccio; spaccatura; fessura; fenditura: *a little — within the lute,* una incrinatura nel liuto (per cui diventa stonato); *fig.* incrinatura in un'amicizia, nell'armonia, nella felicità **2.** schiarita: *a — in the fog,* una schiarita nella nebbia ☆ — *-valley,* vallata a pendii scoscesi.

to rift[1], *v.t.* spaccare, fendere.

rift[2], *s.* **1.** cateratta; rapida **2.** lo sbattere del frangente sulla spiaggia.

to rift[3], *v.t.i.* (*rar. scoz.*) **1.** ruttare **2.** eruttare.

rig[1] [rig], *s.* (*dial.*) bufera; tempesta; forte vento.

rig[2], *s.* (*fam.*) **1.** tiro; scherzo; imbroglio; inganno **2.** (*comm.*) accaparramento; ribasso, rialzo dei prezzi procurato con artificio.

to rig[2], *pass.p.p.* **rigged** [rigd], *v.t.* (*sl.*) **1.** ingannare; fare tiri scherzosi a **2.** trattare con disonestà ‖ *to — the market,* provocare rialzi, ribassi artificiosi sul mercato.

rig[3], *s.* **1.** (*mar.*) attrezzatura, impianto **2.** (*-up* o *-up*), (*sl.*) modo di vestire; tenuta, abbigliamento: *to be in full* —, essere in gran tenuta, in ghinghieri **3.** (*amer. miner.*) impianto di sondaggio; (*mec.*) installazione meccanica **4.** vettura a cavalli.

to **rig**[3], *v.t.i.* **1.** (*mar.*) attrezzare; attrezzarsi **2.** (*sl.*) vestire; equipaggiare ‖ *to — oneself out*, abbigliarsi in modo inconsueto **3.** arrangiare; sistemare.

to **rig**[4], *v.i.* (*dial.*) giocare rumorosamente, disordinatamente.

rigadoon [,rigə'du:n], *s.* rigodone (musica, danza).

rigescence [ri'dʒesəns], *s.* (*bot.*) l'irrigidirsi; notevole rigidità.

rigescent [ri'dʒesənt], *ag.* (*bot.*) che si irrigidisce; piuttosto rigido.

rigged [rigd], *ag.* (*mar.*) attrezzato, con velatura, vela.

rigger[1] ['rigə*], *s.* **1.** (*aer.*) montatore **2.** attrezzatore (di navi) **3.** (*mec.*) puleggia a cinghia **4.** *V.* **outrigger 2.** ☆ *square* —, nave a vela quadra.

rigger[2], *s.* **1.** individuo disonesto **2.** (*comm.*) incettatore, trafficante.

rigging ['rigiŋ], *s.* **1.** (*mar.*) attrezzatura, attrezzi; sartiame, incappellaggio; manovre **2.** (*aer.*) montaggio, regolazione; sartiame, cavi portanti **3.** tenuta, abbigliamento ☆ — *-loft*, (*mar.*) impalcatura degli arsenali per l'attrezzatura delle navi; (*teat.*) galleria sopra il palcoscenico per la manovra degli scenari.

right[1] [rait], *ag.* **1.** retto; giusto; onesto: *always do what is* —, fate sempre ciò che è giusto; *it is — of s.o. to do sthg.*, è giusto da parte di qlcu. fare qualcosa **2.** corretto, esatto: *the — answer*, la risposta esatta; *the — time*, l'ora esatta; *which is the — way to the zoo?*, qual è la strada giusta per il giardino zoologico?; *to put* (o *to set*) —, mettere a posto, sistemare ‖ *all* —!, benissimo!; *quite* —!, perfettamente!; *that's* —, va bene, d'accordo ‖ *to be* (*quite*) —, avere (assolutamente) ragione **3.** adatto, appropriato, conveniente: — *price*, prezzo giusto; *he is the — man in the — place*, è proprio l'uomo che ci vuole; *this is the — time to do it*, questo è il momento adatto per farlo; *to do sthg. in the — way*, fare ql.co. nel modo appropriato, come si deve ‖ *the — side of a fabric*, il diritto di un tessuto ‖ *to be on the — side of forty*, essere al di sotto della quarantina ‖ *to get on the — side of s.o.*, insinuarsi nelle buone grazie di qlcu. **4.** (*geom.*) retto; rettangolo; (*rar.*) diritto; perpendicolare: *a — angle*, un angolo retto; *a — line*, una linea retta; *a — triangle*, un triangolo rettangolo **5.** destro: *take it with your — hand, not with your left*, prendilo con la mano destra, non con la sinistra **6.** sano, in buone condizioni (fisiche, mentali): *he is not — in his head*, non ha la testa a posto; *she is not in her — mind* (o *senses*), non è in possesso delle sue facoltà mentali; *this medicine will put you — again*, questa medicina vi rimetterà in forze ‖ *as — as a trivet, as — as rain*, (*fam.*) in perfetto stato, in ottime condizioni **7.** (*pol.*) conservatore **8.** (*arc.*) vero, genuino.

right[1], *s.* **1.** il giusto, il bene: — *and wrong*, il giusto e l'ingiusto, il bene e il male; *to be in the* —, essere dalla parte della ragione; *to do* —, fare il bene ‖ *to do a person* —, rendere giustizia ad una persona **2.** (*dir.*) diritto: *rights and duties*, i diritti e i doveri; — *and might*, il diritto e la forza; *woman's rights*, i diritti della donna; *I have the — to do it* (o *of doing it*), ho il diritto di farlo ‖ — *of way*, servitù di passaggio ‖ *by* (o *of*) —, di, per diritto: *by — he should be king*, di diritto dovrebbe essere re; *the house belongs to him by* —, la casa gli appartiene di diritto **3.** destra; mano destra; lato destro: *from left to* —, da sinistra a destra; *on your* —, alla vostra destra; *to the* —, a destra **4.** dritto (di tessuto, ecc.) **5.** (*pol.*) la destra; i conservatori ‖ *the Right and the Left*, la destra e la sinistra **6.** *to put* (o *to set*) *to rights*, mettere in ordine.

to **right**[1], *v.t.i.* **1.** drizzare, drizzarsi; raddrizzare, raddrizzarsi; (*mar.*) disincagliare (una nave) *the ship*

righted herself, la nave si raddrizzò; *to — oneself*, raddrizzarsi, ricuperare l'equilibrio **2.** rendere giustizia; riparare; vendicare: *your wrongs will be righted*, vi sarà fatta giustizia **3.** correggere (un errore) **4.** mettere in ordine.

right[1], *av.* **1.** rettamente, giustamente, bene; correttamente, esattamente: —!, bene!; *if I remember* —, se ben ricordo; *it serves him* —!, gli sta bene!, se lo merita!; *to act* —, agire rettamente **2.** appropriatamente, convenientemente: *hold your pen* —, tieni la penna come si deve **3.** in linea retta; direttamente: *go — on*, proseguite diritto; *he went — at him*, si diresse direttamente verso di lui; *she was — behind us*, ella era proprio alle nostre spalle **4.** precisamente, proprio; completamente: — *here and now*, proprio qui ed ora; — *in the middle*, proprio nel mezzo; — *round the house*, tutt'intorno alla casa **5.** a destra: *turn — when you reach the main road*, voltate a destra quando raggiungete la strada maestra **6.** (*gener. amer.*) immediatamente, senza indugio: — *away*, immediatamente **7.** (*rar.*) molto, completamente ‖ *the Right Reverend*, il molto Reverendo.

right[1], (*nei composti*): — *-about* (*face o turn*)!, (*mil.*) dietro front!: *to send a person to the — -about*, mandar via, licenziare una persona; — *-and-left*, bilaterale; bilateralmente; — *-angled*, (*geom.*) che ha un angolo retto; — *-down*, completo, assoluto; molto, veramente; — *-hand*, situato a destra; di assoluta fiducia: *his — -hand man*, il suo uomo di fiducia, il suo braccio destro; *on the — -hand side of the street*, sul lato destro della strada; — *-handed*, che usa di preferenza la destra; di destra: *a — -handed blow*, un colpo sferrato con la destra; — *-hander*, chi usa di preferenza la destra; colpo sferrato con la destra; — *-lined*, rettilineo; — *-mind*, onesto, retto; (*fam.*) sano di mente; — *-mindedness*, onestà, rettitudine; — *-thinking*, saggio, giudizioso; — *-wing*, (*calcio*) di ala destra; (*pol.*) di estrema destra; — *-winger*, (*calcio*) ala destra; (*pol.*) appartenente all'estrema destra.

right[2], *V.* **rite.**

rightable ['raitəbl], *ag.* correggibile; emendabile.

to **righten** ['raitn], *v.t.* drizzare, raddrizzare.

righteous ['raitʃəs], *ag.* **1.** retto; virtuoso; giusto **2.** giusto, giustificato: *a — anger*, una collera giusta.

righteously ['raitʃəsli], *av.* rettamente; giustamente; bene; virtuosamente.

righteousness ['raitʃəsnis], *s.* **1.** rettitudine; giustizia; integrità; virtù, meriti **2.** legittimità.

righter ['raitə*], *s.c.* chi fa giustizia; riparatore, riparatrice (di torti).

rightful ['raitful], *ag.* **1.** legittimo; vero **2.** giusto; retto, equo; virtuoso.

rightfully ['raitfuli], *av.* **1.** legittimamente; con diritto **2.** giustamente; equamente; rettamente.

rightfulness ['raitfulnis], *s.* **1.** legittimità **2.** giustizia; equità.

rightist ['raitist], *ag.* (*pol.*) conservatore ‖ *s.* conservatore; membro della destra.

rightless ['raitlis], *ag.* senza diritto.

rightly ['raitli], *av.* **1.** rettamente, giustamente **2.** esattamente, correttamente: *I don't — know*, non so esattamente.

rightness ['raitnis], *s.* **1.** dirittura, rettitudine **2.** correttezza, esattezza; giustezza.

rightward ['raitwəd], *ag.* di destra.

rightward, rightwards ['raitwədz], *av.* verso destra.

rigid ['ridʒid], *ag.* **1.** rigido: *a — winter*, un inverno rigido; *she held her arm* —, teneva il braccio teso, rigido **2.** severo, rigido, inflessibile, intransigente; rigoroso: *he adopted a — attitude*, prese un atteggiamento severo.

rigidity [ri'dʒiditi], *s.* **1.** rigidità **2.** inflessibilità; severità, intransigenza; rigore.

rigidly ['ridʒidli], *av.* **1.** rigidamente **2.** inflessibilmente, severamente; rigorosamente.

rigidness ['ridʒidnis], *V.* **rigidity**.

rigmarole ['rigməroul], *s.* (*fam.*) lungagnata, tiritera; discorso senza capo nè coda: *he told me a long — as an excuse*, per scusarsi mi fece una lungagnata.

rigol ['rigəl], *s.* (*arc. dial.*) grondaia; canalino.

rigor ['raigo:*], *s.* **1.** (*patol.*) brivido **2.** rigidità: *— mortis*, rigidità, irrigidimento cadaverico.

rigorism ['rigərizəm], *s.* rigorismo; austerità.

rigorist ['rigərist], *s.c.* rigorista; persona austera.

rigorous [rigərəs], *ag.* **1.** rigoroso, rigido, severo, intransigente **2.** rigoroso, preciso, esatto, scrupoloso **3.** rigido, inclemente (di tempo): *a — winter*, un inverno rigido.

rigorously ['rigərəsli], *av.* rigorosamente.

rigorousness ['rigərəsnis], *s.* rigorosità.

rigour ['rigə*], *s.* **1.** rigore, severità; intransigenza; austerità (di vita, ecc.); rigorismo ‖ *rigours*, atti di rigore **2.** esattezza, precisione **3.** difficoltà; carestia **4.** rigore, inclemenza (di tempo).

Rigveda [rig'veidə], *s.* (*relig. indù*) Rigveda.

to rile [rail], *v.t.i.* (*sl.amer.*) **1.** annoiare, irritare **2.** intorbidire **3.** *to* — **up,** arrabbiarsi.

rill [ril], *s.* **1.** rigagnolo, ruscello **2.** *V.* **rille**.

to rill, *v.t.i.* **1.** scorrere come un ruscello **2.** *fig.* fluire (di note, di canto).

rille [ril], *s.* (*astr.*) stretta valle lunare.

rillet ['rilit], *s.* ruscelletto.

rim[1] [rim], *s.* **1.** bordo, orlo, margine **2.** cerchio; cerchione (di ruota); (*mec.*) corona **4.** (*poet.*) cerchio, oggetto circolare **3.** (*mec.*) corona **4.** (*poet.*) linea dell'orizzonte ☆ *golden —*, (*poet.*) corona; *spectacle rims*, montatura di occhiali.

to rim[1], *pass.p.p.* **rimmed** [rimd], *v.t.* bordare, orlare; cerchiare.

rim[2], *s.* (*arc. anat.*) peritoneo.

(to) rime[1], *V.* (to) **rhyme.**

rime[2] [raim], *s.* (*poet.*) brina.

to rime[2], *v.t.* (*poet.*) ricoprire di brina.

rimless ['rimlis], *ag.* **1.** senza bordo, orlo; senza montatura (di occhiali) **2.** senza cerchio.

rimmed [rimd], *ag.* **1.** bordato, orlato **2.** cerchiato ☆ *gold- — spectacles*, occhiali montati in oro.

rimose ['raimous], **rimous** ['raiməs], *ag.* (*bot.*) screpolato, pieno di fessure.

rimy ['raimi], *ag.* brinato.

rind [raind], *s.* **1.** corteccia; scorza; buccia; crosta (di formaggio, di pane); cotenna (di lardo) **2.** aspetto esteriore, apparenza.

to rind, *v.t.* scortecciare; sbucciare; pelare; togliere la crosta da.

rinded ['raindid], *ag.* dalla buccia ☆ *gold- —*, dalla buccia dorata; *hard- —*, dalla crosta dura.

rinderpest ['rindəpest], *s.* (*vet.*) peste bovina.

ring[1] [riŋ], *s.* **1.** anello: *fingers covered with rings*, dita coperte di anelli **2.** anello; cerchio; bordo, orlo, cerchio (di monete, ruote, ecc.); catena chiusa (di atomi); disco, rotella (di racchetta da sci); alone (di macchia); aureola (della Luna); metamero (di verme, ecc.); collare (di uccelli): *rings of smoke*, anelli di fumo; *the falling stone made rings on the water surface*, la pietra nel cadere fece cerchi sull'acqua; *to have rings round the eyes*, avere gli occhi cerchiati **3.** circolo; movimento circolare: *the children danced in a —*, i bambini danzavano in cerchio **4.** (*spor.*) pista; recinto degli allibratori; (*boxe*) « ring », quadrato; (*ippica*) recinto del peso; recinto per esposizione di bestiame ‖ *the Ring*, borsa, mercato ufficiale; il peso; gli allibratori **5.** (*comm.*) sindacato **6.** (*mec.*) ghiera; anello ☆ *— -finger*, anulare; *— -fence*, siepe di cinta; *— -gauge*, (*mec.*) calibro ad anello; *— -man*, allibratore; *— -master*, direttore di circo equestre; *— -necked*, dal collo a strisce colorate; *— -tailed*, dalla coda a strisce colorate ‖ *annual —*, anello di crescita annuale (di albero); *arm- —*, braccialetto; *engagement —*, anello di fidanzamento; *key- —*, portachiavi; *lock —*, (*mec.*) anello di sicurezza; *oil —*, anello di lubrificazione;

snap- —, (*mec.*) anello elastico; *wedding- —*, anello nuziale.

to ring[1], *v.t.i.* **1.** accerchiare, circondare ‖ *to — about* (o *in* o *round*), fare cerchio intorno a **2.** ornare di anello; mettere un anello a: *to — a bull*, mettere l'anello al naso di un toro **3.** levarsi in volo a spirale (di falchi); correre in cerchio (di volpi, lepri braccate) **4.** accerchiare a cavallo (bestiame, selvaggina, per radunarla) **5.** tagliare a fette rotonde (frutta, ecc.).

ring[2], *s.* **1.** scampanio **2.** scampanellata; squillo: *a loud — at the door*, una forte scampanellata alla porta **3.** timbro (di voce); *fig.* accento: *there was a — of sincerity in his promise*, vi era un accento di sincerità nella sua promessa **4.** tintinnio (di vetri, monete, ecc.) **5.** (*fam.*) telefonata; squillo del telefono: *give me a —*, dammi un colpo di telefono.

to ring[2], *pass.* **rang** [ræŋ], *p.p.* **rung** [rʌŋ], *v.t.i.* **1.** suonare, squillare: *the bells rang*, suonarono le campane; *the cyclist didn't —*, il ciclista non suonò il campanello; *I rang for the maid*, suonai per chiamare la cameriera; *to — the alarm*, suonare l'allarme; *to — the bell*, suonare il campanello; (*fam.*) raggiungere il successo ‖ *to — the changes on sthg.*, cantarla su tutti i toni ‖ *to — the death of sthg.*, segnare la fine di ql.co. **2.** tintinnare; risuonare; riecheggiare; vibrare: *the air rang with their cries*, l'aria risuonava delle loro grida; *his voice rings in my ears*, la sua voce mi risuona nelle orecchie; *his words — with emotion*, le sue parole vibrano di emozione; *to — false, true*, risuonare falsa, vera (di moneta, di affermazione, ecc.) **3.** *to* — **down,** (*teat.*) far calare (il sipario) **4.** *to* — **in,** celebrare al suono di campane l'entrata di **5.** *to* — **off,** togliere la comunicazione telefonica **6.** *to* — **out,** celebrare al suono di campane l'uscita di **7.** *to* — **up,** (*teat.*) far alzare il sipario; (*fam.*) dare un colpo di telefono a: *— up your wife*, telefona a tua moglie.

ringed [riŋd], *ag.* inanellato (di dita); cerchiato (di occhi); dal collare (di uccello); ad anelli; circondato da anello; a forma di anello.

ringent ['rindʒənt], *ag.* (*bot.*) lobato (di corolle).

ringer[1] ['riŋə*], *s.* **1.** anello di ferro (nel giuoco dei « quoits ») **2.** (*miner.*) palanchino **3.** animale che corre in cerchio quando è cacciato.

ringer[2], *s.* **1.** chi suona; campanaro **2.** (*mec.*) suoneria **3.** (*amer.*) imbroglione.

ringing ['riŋiŋ], *ag.* risonante; sonoro: *a — laugh*, un riso sonoro ‖ *s.* suono, tintinnio; scampanio.

ringleader ['riŋˌliːdə*], *s.* capo di rivoltosi; capobanda.

ringless ['riŋlis], *ag.* senza anello.

ringlet ['riŋlit], *s.* **1.** anellino; cerchietto **2.** ricciolo.

ringleted ['riŋlitid], *ag.* ricciuto, inanellato.

ringster ['riŋstə*], *s.* (*sl.amer.*) membro di cricca politica.

ringworm ['riŋwə:m], *s.* (*patol.*) tricofizia.

rink [riŋk], *s.* **1.** (*ice-skating*) —, pista solo per pattinaggio sul ghiaccio **2.** (*roller-skating*) —, pista solo di schettinaggio **3.** campo di ghiaccio (per il giuoco del « curling ») **4.** squadra di giocatori di « curling ».

to rink, *v.i.* pattinare (generalmente con pattini a rotelle).

rinker ['riŋkə*], *s.* pattinatore (generalmente con pattini a rotelle).

rinse [rins], *s.* risciacquata.

to rinse, *v.t.* **1.** risciacquare, sciacquare: *to — one's hands*, sciacquarsi le mani ‖ *to — away* (o *out*), pulire risciacquando **2.** *to* — **down,** (*sl.*) annaffiare (cibo, con vino, birra).

rinsing ['rinsiŋ], *s.* risciacquatura.

riot ['raiət], *s.* **1.** rivolta, sommossa; disordine; tumulto ‖ *Riot Act*, (*st.*) legge contro gli assembramenti: *to read the Riot Act*, ammonire severamente qlcu. (prima di ricorrere alla forza); *to read the Riot Act to s.o.*, (*scherz.*) fare una paternale a qlcu. **2.** stravizio, orgia, gozzoviglia; intemperanza, licenza, sregolatezza: *to run*

—, abbandonarsi ad eccessi; perdere ogni freno (anche *fig.*) **3.** profusione; abbondanza (di vegetazione, colori): *the fields were a — of colour*, i campi erano una profusione di colori ☆ — *squad*, (polizia) volante.

to **riot**, *v.t.i.* **1.** fare chiasso; tumultuare **2.** gozzovigliare; darsi ai piaceri: *they were rioting all night after the boat race*, dopo la regata essi passarono tutta la notte in gozzoviglie **3.** perdere ogni freno: *the tyrant rioted in cruelty*, il tiranno perse ogni freno nella sua crudeltà **4.** *to —* **away**, sprecare (tempo, denaro) in gozzoviglie.

rioter ['raiətə*], *s.* **1.** rivoltoso **2.** (*arc.*) chi si dà a orge e piaceri.

riotous ['raiətəs], *ag.* **1.** tumultuante, sedizioso **2.** sregolato, intemperante, dissoluto, licenzioso, sfrenato.

riotously ['raiətəsli], *av.* **1.** sediziosamente **2.** sregolatamente, dissolutamente.

riotousness ['raiətəsnis], *s.* (*rar.*) **1.** tumulto, disordine **2.** sregolatezza, intemperanza, dissolutezza.

riotry ['raiətri], *s.* disordine, tumulto.

rip[1] [rip], *s.* (*dial.*) cestino di vimini per pesci.

rip[2], *s.* lacerazione; strappo; scucitura ☆ — *-saw*, segaccio (per segare il legno lungo le fibre).

to **rip**[2], *pass.p.p.* **ripped** [ript], *v.t.i.* **1.** strappare, strapparsi; lacerare, lacerarsi; scucire, scucirsi; squarciare, squarciarsi: *to — along the seams*, scucirsi (di abito); *to — a parcel open*, aprire un pacco lacerandolo **2.** segare per il lungo **3.** scoperchiare (un tetto) **4.** (*fam.*) correre a tutta velocità: *let her —!*, lasciate che vada a tutta velocità! (di automobile, ecc.) **5.** *to —* **off**, strappar via **6.** *to —* **out**, strappar via; (*fam.*) pronunciare: *to — out an oath*, prorompere in una bestemmia **7.** *to —* **up**, strappare; sventrare; (*fam.*) rinnovare (un dolore), riaprire (una ferita).

rip[3], *s.* **1.** maretta **2.** il ribollire delle acque (nei fiumi).

rip[4], *s.* **1.** vecchio ronzino **2.** persona dissoluta; libertino **3.** (*rar.*) prostituta **4.** persona di poco valore.

riparian [rai'pεəriən], *ag.s.* rivierasco.

ripe [raip], *ag.* **1.** maturo: — *age*, età matura; — *beauty*, bellezza matura; — *lips*, labbra piene, turgide ‖ *soon — soon rotten*, prov. rosso di fuoco dura poco **2.** stagionato: — *cheese*, formaggio stagionato **3.** *fig.* pronto: — *for mischief*, pronto a fare del male **4.** (*med.*) maturo: *growth — for operation*, tumore maturo per essere operato.

to **ripe**, *v.t.i.* (*poet.*) maturare.

ripely ['raipli], *av.* maturamente, a tempo debito.

to **ripen** ['raipən], *v.t.i.* **1.** maturare; far maturare **2.** far stagionare.

ripeness ['raipnis], *s.* **1.** maturità **2.** (*fig.*) perfezione.

ripening ['raipniŋ], *s.* maturazione: — *of a plan*, maturazione d'un progetto.

ripost(e) [ri'poust], *s.* (*spor.*) replica; *fig.* risposta incisiva; replica.

to **ripost(e)**, *v.i.* **1.** (*spor.*) rispondere, eseguire una risposta **2.** *fig.* dare una risposta incisiva; fare una ritorsione.

ripper ['ripə*], *s.* **1.** chi strappa, lacera, squarcia, scuce ‖ *Jack the Ripper*, Jack lo Sventratore **2.** (*mec.*) estrattore per chiodi; (*agr.*) scarificatore; (*strum. artig.*) saracco **3.** (*sl.*) persona, cosa bella, straordinaria, divertente.

ripping ['ripiŋ], *ag.* (*sl.*) bello, splendido, straordinario, divertente.

ripping, *av.* (*sl.*) straordinariamente, splendidamente: *I had a — good time*, mi divertii immensamente.

ripple[1] ['ripl], *s.* (*strum. artig.*) gramola (per canapa, lino, ecc.).

to **ripple**[1], *v.t.* gramolare (canapa, lino, ecc.).

ripple[2], *s.* **1.** increspamento, increspatura **2.** ondulazione (dei capelli, ecc.) **3.** gorgoglio, mormorio **4.** (*amer.*) piccola rapida (di fiume) ☆ — *-cloth*, crespo di lana; — *-mark*, solco ondulato (in sabbia, fango, roccia,

prodotto dall'acqua, da vento); — *-silk*, crespo di seta.

to **ripple**[2], *v.t.i.* **1.** increspare; ondulare; incresparsi (di acqua, capelli, ecc.) **2.** gorgogliare, mormorare.

ripplet ['riplit], *s.* leggera increspatura.

ripply ['ripli], *ag.* **1.** increspato; crespo **2.** gorgogliante, mormorante.

riprap ['ripræp], *s.* (*edil.*) pietrame per fondazioni subacquee; fondazioni in pietrame alla rinfusa.

Ripuarian [ˌripju(:)'εəriən], *ag.* (*st.*) ripuario.

rise [raiz], *s.* **1.** levata, sorgere (del sole, ecc.); alzata; (*aer.*) ascensione: *the — of the curtain*, l'alzarsi del sipario; *the — of day*, alba ‖ *to be on the —*, abboccare (di pesce) ‖ *to get* (o *to take*) *a — out of s.o.*, canzonare qlcu.; far uscire qlcu. dai gangheri **2.** salita; rampa: *a steep —*, una salita ripida **3.** altura: *the villa stood on a —*, la villa era situata su un'altura **4.** ascesa; progresso; promozione, avanzamento, miglioramento sociale: *the — and fall of an empire*, l'ascesa e la caduta di un impero; *the — to power*, l'ascesa al potere; *he had a — in life*, migliorò le sue condizioni **5.** aumento, rialzo, rincaro: *the — of stock*, il rialzo delle azioni; *ask for a —*, chiedi un aumento (di stipendio); *prices are on the —*, i prezzi sono in rialzo **6.** crescita, innalzamento di livello (di acque); flusso (di marea); aumento (di temperatura, pressione): *the — and fall of the sea*, il flusso e il riflusso del mare; *the — of the tide*, il flusso della marea; *a sudden — of temperature*, un improvviso aumento di temperatura **7.** sorgente; origine; principio: *the — of a stream*, la sorgente di un corso d'acqua; *the river has* (o *takes*) *its — in...*, il fiume ha origine a...; *to give — to*, dare origine a **8.** (*arch.*) freccia, monta (di arco); freccia di (ponte); alzata (di gradino) **9.** (*miner.*) fornello **10.** uscita (di minatori dopo il lavoro).

to **rise**, *pass.* **rose** [rouz], *p.p.* **risen** ['rizn], *v.t.i.* **1.** sorgere, levarsi, alzarsi; *fig.* risorgere: *all rose to meet him*, tutti si alzarono per andargli incontro; *Christ is risen*, Cristo è risorto; *the audience rose at the actress*, gli spettatori si alzarono per applaudire l'attrice; *the sun rises*, sorge il sole; *the wind rose*, si levò il vento; *to — from one's seat*, alzarsi dal proprio posto; *to — from table*, alzarsi da tavola; *to — to one's feet*, alzarsi in piedi; *to — with the lark*, alzarsi al canto del gallo, prestissimo ‖ *the House rose just before Christmas*, la Camera sospese i suoi lavori poco prima di Natale **2.** salire; crescere, aumentare: *the rising generation*, la nuova generazione; *the interest of this novel rises with every page*, l'interesse di questo romanzo aumenta a ogni pagina; *the Po is rising*, il Po è in piena, *prices are rising*, i prezzi aumentano; *the tide, the barometer is rising*, la marea, il barometro sale **3.** elevarsi, ergersi (anche *fig.*): — *above this nonsense*, siate superiori a queste sciocchezze; *our spirits rose*, il nostro spirito si risollevò, *these trees — to over 18 feet*, questi alberi superano i sei metri; *this boy does not — above mediocrity*, questo ragazzo non è al disopra della mediocrità; *a tower rises behind the church*, una torre si erge dietro la chiesa; ‖ *to — in the world*, farsi strada nel mondo; *to — to greatness*, assurgere a grandezza ‖ *to — to the occasion*, mostrarsi all'altezza della situazione **4.** gonfiarsi; lievitare: *blisters rose on his hands*, le sue mani si coprirono di vesciche; *the dough will not — la pasta non lievita; *the sea is rising*, il mare si alza, s'ingrossa **5.** sollevarsi, insorgere: *to — in arms*, sollevarsi in armi ‖ *my stomach rises*, mi si rivolta lo stomaco **6.** aver origine, nascere, provenire: *the dispute rose from a misunderstanding*, la disputa nacque per un malinteso; *where does the Thames —?*, dove nasce il Tamigi? **7.** (*pesca*) prendere, pescare: *I did not — a single fish last week*, non ho pescato neanche un pesce la settimana scorsa.

riser ['raizə*], *s.c.* chi si alza (da letto): *I'm an early —*, sono mattiniero ‖ *s.* **1.** ribelle, rivoltoso **2.** alzata (di gradino) **3.** (*ind.*) montante **4.** (*miner.*) fornello.

risibility [ˌrizi'biliti], *s.* risibilità.

risible ['rizibl], *ag.* **1.** incline, facile al riso **2.** risibile, ridicolo.

rising ['raiziŋ], *ag.* **1.** sorgente, nascente: *the — sun*, il sole nascente ‖ *the — generation*, la nuova generazione **2.** ascendente; in salita: *— ground*, terreno in salita **3.** crescente, in aumento: *— price*, prezzo in aumento; *— tide*, marea crescente; *the — waters*, le acque in aumento **4.** che avanza, che progredisce; che migliora **5.** (*amer.*) che si avvicina: *— twenty*, vicino ai vent'anni; *— twenty thousand*, circa ventimila ‖ *— of ten thousand*, più di diecimila ‖ *s.* **1.** il sorgere; il levarsi; l'alzarsi: *the — of the moon*, il sorgere della luna; *he doesn't like early —*, non gli piace alzarsi presto ‖ *the — of Parliament was discussed at length*, si discusse lungamente circa la sospensione dei lavori in Parlamento **2.** salita; ascesa **3.** crescita; aumento; progresso; miglioramento **4.** elevazione (di astro, terreno); innalzamento di livello (di acque) **5.** sollevamento, insurrezione, rivolta: *— of the people*, sommossa popolare **6.** (*patol.*) foruncolo.

risk [risk], *s.* rischio, pericolo imprevisto: *at the — of failure, of punishment, of one's life*, a rischio di fallire, di essere punito, della propria vita; *the goods travel at customer's own —*, la merce viaggia a rischio e pericolo del cliente; *insurance covering all risks*, assicurazione comprendente tutti i rischi; *to run* (o *to incur*) *the — of losing sthg.*, correre il rischio di perdere ql.co.; *to take risks*, correre dei rischi.

to risk, *v.t.* (I) rischiare; arrischiare; mettere a repentaglio: *I dare not — it, it is too dangerous*, non oso arrischiare, è troppo pericoloso; *let's — it!*, tentiamo!; *to — a battle*, rischiare una battaglia; *to — one's reputation*, porre a repentaglio la propria reputazione.

riskily ['riskili], *av.* arrischiatamente.

riskiness ['riskinis], *s.* natura rischiosa; rischi e pericoli.

riskless ['risklis], *ag.* senza rischi, senza pericolo.

risky ['riski], *ag.* **1.** rischioso, arrischiato **2.** scabroso: *a — story*, una storia scabrosa.

risqué [,ri:s'kei], *ag.* (*gener. fig.*) azzardato, audace, ardito.

rissole ['risoul], *s.* (*cuc.*) polpetta, crocchetta (di carne, pesce).

Rita ['ri:tə], *no.pr.f.* (*dim.* di *Margaret*) Rita.

rite [rait], *s.* rito; cerimonia: *the Anglican —*, il rito anglicano; *burial rites*, riti funebri.

riteless ['raitlis], *ag.* senza riti; senza cerimonia.

ritual ['ritjuəl], *ag.* secondo il rito, rituale ‖ *s.* **1.** rituale; cerimoniale **2.** riti, cerimonie.

ritualism ['ritjuəlizəm], *s.* ritualismo.

ritualist ['ritjuəlist], *s.* ritualista.

ritualistic [,ritjuə'listik], *ag.* relativo, conforme al rituale.

ritualistically [,ritjuə'listikəli], *av.* conformemente al rituale.

to ritualize ['ritjuəlaiz], *v.t.i.* rendere rituale; divenire rituale.

ritually ['ritjuəli], *av.* ritualmente.

rivage ['raividʒ], *s.* (*poet.*) riva, sponda.

rival ['raivəl], *ag.* rivale; che compete ‖ *s. c.* rivale; competitore, competitrice ‖ *without a —*, senza pari.

to rival, *pass.p.p.* **rivalled** ['raivəld], *v.t.i.* **1.** rivaleggiare (con), gareggiare (con); emulare **2.** (*rar.*) essere rivale.

rivality [rai'væliti], **rivalry** ['raivəlri], **rivalship** ['raivəlfip], *s.* rivalità; concorrenza; emulazione.

to rive [raiv], *pass.* **rived** [raivd], *p.p.* **rived, riven** ['rivən], *v.t.i.* **1.** spaccare, spaccarsi; lacerare; strappare: *to — sthg. from s.o.*, strappare ql.co. a qlcu. ‖ *to — off a branch*, strappare un ramo **2.** *fig.* spezzare; strappare: *it rives my heart*, mi spezza il cuore.

to rivel ['rivəl], *pass.p.p.* **rivelled** ['rivəld], *v.t.i.* (*arc.*) raggrinzire, raggrinzirsi.

riven ['rivən], *p.p.* di to **rive.**

river[1] ['rivə*], *s.* **1.** fiume (anche *fig.*): *the River*

Thames, il fiume Tamigi; *the Hudson River*, il fiume Hudson; *rivers of blood, of tears, fig.* fiumi di sangue, di lacrime ‖ *down* (*the*) *—*, a valle; *up* (*the*) *—*, a monte **2.** acqua (di diamante) ☆ *— -bank*, riva, sponda di fiume; *— -bed*, alveo di fiume; *— -god*, divinità fluviale; *— -head*, sorgente di fiume; *— -horse*, ippopotamo; *— -man*, battelliere; *— novel*, romanzo fiume.

river[2] ['raivə*], *s.* chi spacca (legna, pietre).

riverain ['rivərein], *ag.s.* rivierasco.

riverine ['rivərain], *ag.* fluviale: *— plants*, piante fluviali.

riverless ['rivəlis], *ag.* senza fiume.

riverside ['rivəsaid], *ag.* lungo il fiume, rivierasco ‖ *s.* lungofiume; sponda, riva (di fiume).

rivet ['rivit], *s.* chiodo, rivetto, ribattino; bullone. ☆ *mushroom-head —*, chiodo a testa tonda larga; *snap-head —*, chiodo a testa tonda.

to rivet, *pass.p.p.* **rivet(t)ed** ['rivitid], *v.t.* **1.** inchiodare, ribadire (anche *fig.*): *to — an error*, ribadire un errore **2.** fissare, concentrare: *everybody's attention will be riveted on you*, l'attenzione di tutti sarà concentrata su di voi.

riveter ['rivitə*], *s.c.* chi inchioda, ribadisce ‖ *s.* (*mec.*) chiodatrice, ribaditrice.

rivet(t)ing ['rivitiŋ], *s.* chiodatura; ribaditura ☆ *— -hammer*, martello per ribadire; *— -machine*, (*mec.*) chiodatrice.

riviere [ri:'vjɛə*], *s.* collana di gemme (generalmente a più giri).

rivulet ['rivjulit], *s.* fiumicello, ruscelletto.

rix-dollar ['riks'dolə*], *s.* tallero (antica moneta).

roach[1] [routʃ], *s.* (*ittiol.*) lasca ‖ *to be as sound as a —*, essere sano come un pesce.

roach[2], *s.* lunata (di vela).

to roach[2], *v.t.* **1.** fornire (una vela) di lunate **2.** tagliare (capelli, criniera) a spazzola.

roach[3], *s.* (*entom. abbr.* di *cockroach*) scarafaggio.

road [roud], *s.* **1.** strada; via: *across the —*, dall'altra parte della strada; *on the —*, per strada; *car that holds the — well*, automobile che tiene bene la strada ‖ *the rule of the —*, il regolamento del traffico **2.** cammino, percorso; strada, via (anche *fig.*): *the — to London*, la strada per Londra; *on the —*, in cammino; *I am not certain of our —*, non sono sicura che questa sia la strada giusta; *to be on the right —* (anche *fig.*) essere sulla buona strada; *to get in s.o.'s —*, *fig.* impedire, ostacolare il cammino a qlcu. ‖ *the — to success*, la via del successo ‖ *the royal — to*, la strada più facile per ‖ *get out of my —!*, (*fam.*) togliti di mezzo! **3.** *gener. pl.* (*mar.*) rada: *in the roads*, nella rada; *to leave the roads*, andare al largo **4.** (*amer.*) strada ferrata **5.** (*miner.*) galleria ☆ *— -book*, guida stradale; *— -crossing*, crocevia; *— -fork*, bivio stradale; *— -hog*, automobilista, ciclista incosciente; *— -making*, costruzione di strada; *— -roller*, compressore stradale; *— -sense*, attitudine alla guida; *— -sign*, cartello stradale ‖ *carriage —*, rotabile; *country —*, strada di campagna; *main —*, strada principale.

roadhouse ['roudhaus], *s.* albergo, locanda, trattoria (frequentata da automobilisti).

roadless ['roudlis], *ag.* senza strade.

roadman, *pl.* **roadmen** ['roudmən], *s.* stradino.

roadside ['roudsaid], *ag.* sul bordo della strada ‖ *s.* bordo della strada.

roadstead ['roudsted], *s.* (*mar.*) rada.

roadster ['roudstə*], *s.* **1.** (*mar.*) nave in rada **2.** cavallo da tiro **3.** bicicletta, auto da turismo **4.** viaggiatore esperto.

roadway ['roudwei], *s.* carreggiata, piano stradale.

roam [roum], *s.* vagabondaggio; cammino senza meta: *a half-hour's —*, una passeggiatina di mezz'ora.

to roam, *v.t.i.* percorrere; errare, vagabondare, vagare per: *to — about the world*, vagabondare per il mondo; *to — the seas*, solcare i mari.

roamer ['roumə*], *s.* vagabondo, nomade.

roan[1] [roun], *ag.s.* roano.

roan[2], *s.* pelle di pecora uso marocchino.

roar [rɔ:*], *s.* **1.** ruggito; muggito **2.** urlo (di dolore, di rabbia) **3.** scoppio; scroscio: *roars of laughter*, scoppi di risa **4.** rombo (di cannone, di tuono); rimbombo, boato; frastuono; strepito; il mugghiare (del vento, del mare).

to roar, *v.t.i.* **1.** ruggire; muggire: *the lion roars*, il leone ruggisce **2.** urlare, gridare a squarciagola; vociare; strepitare: *to — (out) an order*, gridare un ordine; *to — with pain*, urlare di dolore || *to — oneself hoarse*, diventare rauco a furia di urlare || *to — s.o. down*, soverchiare, urlando, le grida di qlcu. || *to — with laughter*, scoppiare dalle risa **3.** tuonare; rumoreggiare, mugghiare (di vento, di mare); rimbombare **4.** respirare rumorosamente (di cavallo bolso).

roarer ['rɔ:rə*], *s.* **1.** sbraitone **2.** cavallo bolso.

roaring ['rɔ:riŋ], *ag.* **1.** rugghiante; mugghiante (anche *fig.*) **2.** urlante **3.** rumoroso, fragoroso; scrosciante; tumultuoso: *a — applause*, un applauso scrosciante; *a — fire*, un fuoco crepitante; *a — night*, una notte tempestosa, una notte di baldoria **4.** (*fam.*) prospero: *we did — business*, abbiamo fatto affari d'oro; *to be in — health*, scoppiare di salute || *what a — time I had!*, quanto mi sono divertito!|| *s.* **1.** *V.* **roar 2.** (*vet.*) bolsaggine.

roast [roust], *ag.* arrosto, arrostito || *s.* **1.** arrosto: *a — of veal*, un arrosto di vitello || *to rule the —*, *fig.* dettar legge, fare il bello e il cattivo tempo **2.** arrostitura; arrostimento (di metalli); tostatura (di caffè) **3.** (*sl.*) burla, beffa ☆ *— -beef*, arrosto di manzo, di bue; *— chicken*, pollo arrosto.

to roast, *v.t.i.* **1.** arrostire, arrostirsi: *to — in the sun*, *fig.* arrostirsi al sole; *to — on a spit*, arrostire allo spiedo **2.** cuocere, cuocersi al forno **3.** tostare (caffè, ecc.) **4.** (*metal.*) arrostire, calcinare **5.** (*fam.*) deridere, burlarsi di, farsi beffe di.

roaster ['roustə*], *s.* **1.** rosticciere **2.** girarrosto; casseruola, forno per arrostire **3.** tostino, macchina per tostare il caffè **4.** pollame, selvaggina da arrosto **5.** (*metal.*) arrostitore **6.** (*fam.*) giornata torrida.

roasting ['roustiŋ], *ag.* rovente, cocente; torrido || *s.* **1.** arrostimento; arrostitura **2.** torrefazione **3.** (*metal.*) arrostimento **4.** beffa, canzonatura; lavata di capo, ramanzina ☆ *— -jack*, girarrosto.

Rob [rɔb], *no.pr.m.* dim. di **Robert**.

to rob, *pass.p.p.* **robbed** [rɔbd], *v.t.i.* **1.** derubare: *to — s.o. (of sthg.)*, rubare (ql.co.) a qlcu., derubare qlcu. (di ql.co.) || *to — Peter to pay Paul*, *fig.* fare un buco per tapparne un altro **2.** svaligiare, saccheggiare: *to — a bank, a shop*, svaligiare una banca, un negozio **3.** privare; spogliare: *to — a tree of its fruit*, spogliare un albero dei suoi frutti **4.** rubare, commettere furti, rapine.

robber ['rɔbə*], *s.* **1.** ladro; rapinatore **2.** ladrone, predone, brigante ☆ *— -fly*, (*entom.*) assillo.

robbery ['rɔbəri], *s.* furto; rapina; estorsione || *to charge so much for it is — !*, è un furto farlo pagar tanto! ☆ *armed —*, rapina a mano armata; *highway —*, brigantaggio.

Robbie ['rɔbi], *no.pr.m.* dim. di **Robert**.

robe [roub], *s.* **1.** abito lungo e sciolto **2.** toga; abito (indicante carica, professione, ecc.): *magistrates in their robes*, magistrati in toga || *the Coronation robes*, gli abiti e le insegne usati per l'incoronazione || *gentlemen of the —*, i giuristi **3.** *pl.* vestiti **4.** mantello ☆ *— -de-chambre*, vestaglia || *baby's —*, vestito lungo da neonato; *bath- —*, accappatoio; *priest's —*, abito talare.

to robe, *v.t.i.* vestire, vestirsi; rivestire, rivestirsi (anche *fig.*): *hills robed in verdure*, colline rivestite di verde.

Robert ['rɔbət], *no.pr.m.* Roberto.

Roberta [rou'bə:tə], *no.pr.f.* Roberta.

Robin ['rɔbin], *no.pr.m.* dim. di **Robert** || *— Goodfellow*, « Robin Goodfellow » (nome di uno spiritello maligno) || **robin**, *s. — (redbreast)*, pettirosso.

robinia [rou'biniə], *s.* (*bot.*) robinia.

robomb ['roubɔm], *s.* bomba volante (con spinta) a reazione e giroguidata.

roborant ['roubərənt], *ag.s.* (*farm.*) corroborante.

robot ['roubɔt], *s.* **1.** « robot », automa (anche *fig.*) **2.** semaforo automatico **3.** dispositivo automatico ☆ *— bomb*, bomba volante; *— pilot*, pilota automatico.

robotism ['roubətizəm], *s.* automazione.

roburite ['roubərait], *s.* (*chim.*) roburite.

robust [rə'bʌst], *ag.* **1.** robusto; sano; gagliardo; vigoroso: *a — young fellow*, un giovane gagliardo **2.** faticoso, pesante: *— work*, lavoro pesante **3.** retto, equilibrato (di intelletto): *a — mind*, una mente assennata **4.** (*rar.*) rozzo, grossolano.

robustious [rou'bʌstjəs], *ag.* **1.** turbolento, rumoroso; millantatore, presuntuoso **2.** violento (di vento, ecc.); rigido (di clima) **3.** (*arc.*) robusto; vigoroso.

robustly [rə'bʌstli], *av.* robustamente; vigorosamente.

robustness [rə'bʌstnis], *s.* robustezza.

roc [rɔk], *s.* gigantesco uccello dei racconti orientali.

rocambole ['rɔkəmboul], *s.* (*bot.*) aglio di Spagna.

rochet[1] ['rɔtʃit], *s.* (*eccl.*) rocchetto.

rochet[2], *s.* (*ittiol.*) capone rosso.

rock[1] [rɔk], *s.* **1.** roccia: *as hard as —*, duro come la roccia; *built on the —*, costruito sulla roccia, *fig.* sicuro; *they climbed up among the rocks*, si arrampicarono su per le rocce **2.** rupe, scoglio: *the ship struck a — and sank*, la nave urtò contro uno scoglio e affondò; *to run upon the rocks*, naufragare (anche *fig.*) || *on the rocks*, (*sl.*) al verde: *to go on the rocks*, andare in malora **3.** rocca || *the Rock (of Gibraltar)*, (la Rocca di) Gibilterra; *Rock English*, dialetto anglo-arabo-spagnolo di Gibilterra || *the Rock of Ages*, Gesù Cristo || *the Lord is my —*, il Signore è la mia difesa **4.** macigno, masso: *we sat down on a flat —*, sedemmo su un macigno piatto **5.** croccante; zucchero candito **6.** (*sl. amer.*) diamante; moneta ☆ *— -bed*, fondo roccioso; *— bottom*, (*fam.*) bassissimo, minimo (di prezzo); *— -crystal*, cristallo di rocca; *— -dove*, colombo selvatico; *— -fish*, pesce di scoglio; *— -goat*, stambecco; *— -oil*, petrolio grezzo, nafta; *— -rabbit*, (*zool.*) irace; *— -rose*, (*bot.*) eliantemo; *— -salt*, salgemma; *— -tar*, petrolio grezzo || *almond —*, croccante di mandorle.

rock[2], *s.* dondolio; oscillazione ☆ *— -and-roll*, (*neol.*) « rock-and-roll » (danza moderna americana).

to rock[2], *v.t.i.* **1.** dondolare, dondolarsi; cullare, cullarsi: *the boat was rocked by the waves*, la barca era cullata dalle onde; *he sat rocking (himself) in his chair*, si dondolava sulla sedia || *to — a baby to sleep (o asleep)*, cullare un bimbo finchè si addormenta || *to be rocked in hopes*, cullarsi nell'illusione **2.** vibrare, far vibrare; scuotere: *the buildings rocked during the earthquake*, gli edifici tremarono durante il terremoto; *the explosion rocked the house*, l'esplosione fece oscillare la casa **3.** (*dial.*) vacillare, barcollare **4.** (*miner.*) vagliare.

rock[3], *s.* (*arc.*) rocca; conocchia.

rockaway ['rɔkəwei], *s.* (*amer.*) « rockaway » (carrozza a quattro ruote, aperta sui fianchi).

rocker ['rɔkə*], *s.* **1.** chi dondola, culla **2.** dondolo (di sedia, cavallo, ecc.) || *to be off one's —*, (*sl.*) essere un po' tocco **3.** cavallo a dondolo; (*amer.*) sedia a dondolo **4.** (*miner.*) vaglio per sabbie aurifere **5.** (*mec.*) bilanciere **6.** pattino con lama ricurva.

rockery ['rɔkəri], *s.* giardino roccioso.

rocket[1] ['rɔkit], *s.* (*bot.*) **1.** ruca, ruchetta **2.** violacciocca svizzera.

rocket[2] *s.* (*neol.*) razzo; missile; motore a razzo ☆ *— -bomb*, bomba volante, missile a razzo; *— engine* (o *— motor*), motore a razzo; *— launcher*, lanciarazzi; *— missile*, missile a razzo; *— plane*, avioplano a razzo, aeroplano a razzo; *— propulsion*, propulsione a razzo || *nuclear-power —*, razzo atomico.

to rocket[2], *v.t.i.* **1.** bombardare con razzi **2.** dare un balzo in aria (di cavallo); elevarsi come un razzo (di uccelli), salire vertiginosamente (di prezzi); (aer.) salire in candela.

rocketer ['rɔkitə*], s. uccello (fagiano, ecc.) che si leva a mo' di razzo.

rocketry [,rɔkitri], s. (neol.) missilistica.

rockiness ['rɔkinis], s. rocciosità.

rocking ['rɔkin], ag. 1. a dondolo 2. vacillante, barcollante, traballante: a — gait, un'andatura traballante 3. (mec.) oscillante || s. dondolio; oscillazione; scosse ☆ — -chair, sedia a dondolo; — -horse, cavallo a dondolo.

rockless ['rɔklis], ag. senza rocce.

rocklike ['rɔklaik], ag. simile a roccia.

rocky[1] ['rɔki], ag. 1. roccioso: a — coast, una costa rocciosa || the Rocky Mountains (o the Rockies), (geog.) le Montagne Rocciose 2. saldo come roccia, sicuro 3. duro come roccia (anche fig.).

rocky[2], ag. (rar.) 1. malfermo, traballante 2. (sl. amer.) ubriaco.

rococo [rə'koukou], ag.s. (st. art.) rococò.

rod [rɔd], s. 1. bastone; mazza; verga, bacchetta; fig. punizione, castigo || Black Rod, usciere della Camera dei Pari, del Lord Ciambellano || to have a — in pickle for s.o., avere in serbo una punizione per qlcu. || to kiss the —, sottomettersi a una punizione senza protestare || to make a — for one's own back, scavarsi la fossa sotto i piedi || spare the — and spoil the child, prov. il medico pietoso fa la piaga cancrenosa 2. (fishing-) —, canna da pesca 3. (mec. metal.) verga, asta; barra 4. (Bibbia) razza, tribù: the — of Jesse, la discendenza di Jesse 5. pertica (misura di lunghezza = m. 5,0292) 6. (anat.) bastoncino della retina 7. (sl. amer.) pistola ☆ divining- —, bacchetta divinatoria, di rabdomante; piston —, biella; square —, (agr.) pertica (misura di superficie = m.[2] 25,292).

rode [roud], pass. di to ride.

rodent ['roudənt], ag.s. (zool.) roditore.

rodeo [rou'deiou], s. 1. « rodeo » (spettacolo di abilità dei « cow-boys ») 2. «rodeo» (riunione del bestiame per la marcatura) 3. recinto per « rodeo » 4. gara motociclistica di abilità.

Roderic(k) ['rɔdərik], no.pr.m. Rodrigo.

rodless ['rɔdlis], ag. senza bacchetta, verga, asta.

rodlike ['rɔdlaik], ag. simile a bacchetta, asta, ecc.

rodomontade [,rɔdəmɔn'teid], ag. rodomontesco || s. rodomontata, smargiassata.

to **rodomontade**, v.i. agire, parlare da rodomonte; vantarsi.

rodomontader [,rɔdəmɔn'teidə*], s. rodomonte, smargiasso.

roe[1] [rou], s. — (-deer), capriolo ☆ — -buck, capriolo maschio.

roe[2], s. (hard) —, (complesso di) uova (nelle ovaie) dei pesci ☆ — -corn, uovo (di aringa, salmone); — -stone, (geol.) oolite || soft —, sperma di pesce.

roed [roud], ag. pieno di uova (di pesce).

rogation [rou'geiʃən], s. 1. (st. romana) rogazione 2. gener. pl. (eccl.) rogazione.

rogatory ['rɔgətəri], ag. (dir.) rogatorio.

Roger ['rɔdʒə*], no.pr.m. Ruggero || (Jolly) —, bandiera nera dei pirati || (Sir) — de Coverley, danza campestre inglese ||'inter. 1. (rad. tel.) ricevuto! 2. bene!.

rogue [roug], s. 1. (arc.) vagabondo 2. briccone, mariuolo, furfante; (scherz.) bricconcello, birbante: they formed a real —'s gallery, (fam.) avevano tutti una faccia patibolare 3. elefante, bufalo solitario 4. (bot.) mala erba 5. cavallo restio, che rifiuta l'ostacolo.

to **rogue**, v.t.i. 1. (arc.) vagabondare 2. ingannare, truffare 3. mondare, togliere le male erbe da.

roguery ['rougəri], s. 1. bricconeria, furfanteria; birbonata, bricconata 2. birichinata, marachella.

roguish ['rougiʃ], ag. 1. bricconesco, furfantesco 2. (scherz.) furbo, smaliziato: — eyes, occhi furbi.

roguishly ['rougiʃli], av. 1. da briccone, da furfante 2. (scherz.) furbescamente, maliziosamente.

roguishness ['rougiʃnis], s. 1. bricconeria, furfanteria 2. (scherz.) malizia, furberia.

to **roil** [rɔil], v.t. (amer.) 1. intorbidire 2. irritare; fare arrabbiare.

roily ['rɔili], ag. torbido.

roinek ['rɔinek], s. 1. nuovo venuto, immigrante (in Sud Africa) 2. soldato inglese (durante la guerra boera).

to **roister** ['rɔistə*], v.i. fare il diavolo a quattro; far baldoria.

roisterer ['rɔistərə*], s. chiassone; buontempone.

roistering ['rɔistəriŋ], ag. chiassoso, rumoroso || s. chiasso; baldoria.

Roland ['roulənd], no.pr.m. Rolando, Orlando || to give a — for an Oliver, rendere pan per focaccia.

role [roul], s. 1. (teat.) ruolo 2. funzione, ufficio.

roll[1] [roul], s. 1. rotolo: a — of bread, un panino; a — of butter, un rotolino di burro; a — of cloth, of paper, un rotolo di tela, di carta; a — of film, un rotolo di pellicola || she has rolls of fat on her, ha degli strati di grasso 2. (arch.) cartoccio, voluta (di capitello ionico) 3. ruolo, registro, lista, elenco || — of honour, elenco dei caduti in guerra || the Rolls, (st.) l'Archivio di Stato a Londra || the Roll(s), elenco ufficiale degli avvocati: to strike s.o. off the Rolls, radiare qlcu. dall'albo degli avvocati 4. rullo; cilindro ☆ — -call, appello (militare, scolastico, ecc.) || nip —, (mec.) rullo di compressione; printing —, cilindro per stampa.

roll[2], s. 1. rotolamento 2. (mar. aer.) rollio: angle of —, angolo di rollio 3. ondeggiamento (di andatura, ecc.) 4. (aer.) frullo orizzontale 5. rullo (di tamburo); rombo (di cannone, tuono) 6. ondulazione (di terreno) 7. cadenza (di versi, nel modo di recitare).

to **roll**[2], v.t.i. 1. rotolare, far rotolare, rotolarsi: the ball rolled under the bed, la palla rotolò sotto il letto; he rolled a barrel along the road, fece rotolare un barile lungo la via 2. correre, andare (di veicolo a ruote, di chi vi è trasportato) 3. arrotolare; avvolgere, avvolgersi: — the drawing in a piece of paper, avvolgi il disegno in un pezzo di carta; to — a cigarette, arrotolare una sigaretta 4. appallottolare, appallottolarsi: to — snow into a ball (o — a snow ball), fare una palla di neve; to — wool into a ball, fare un gomitolo di lana 5. roteare, ruotare: the earth rolls round the sun, la Terra ruota intorno al Sole; his eyes rolled with amazement, i suoi occhi roteavano con stupore 6. (mar. aer.) rollare: the ship rolled and pitched, la nave rollava e beccheggiava 7. dondolare (nell'andatura) 8. rullare, spianare: to — a lawn, spianare un prato; to — (out) paste, (cuc.) stendere la pasta; to — a road, rullare, cilindrare una strada 9. rullare (di tamburi); rimbombare (di tuono, voce, ecc.) 10. parlare con enfasi: to — one's r's, arrotare la erre 11. ondulare, ondularsi (di paesaggio, onde, ecc.) 12. (mec.) rullare; (tip.) inchiostrare a rullo; (metal.) laminare 13. (fam.) guazzare (anche fig.): the child rolled in the bath, il bambino guazzava nella vasca da bagno; to — in money, guazzare nell'oro 14. to — by, passare; scorrere (di tempo): the rich — by in their cars, i ricchi passano nelle loro automobili; the years — by, gli anni passano 15. to — down, ruzzolare; (far) rotolare: the tears rolled down her face, le lacrime le rigavano il volto; to — down a slope, ruzzolare giù per il pendio 16. to — in, entrare, far entrare; (mec.) mandrinare: the money began to — in, i soldi cominciarono a entrare abbondantemente: to — in the ball, (spor.) rimettere la palla in giuoco 17. to — on, scorrere (di tempo); stendere (inchiostro, ecc.) con rullo 18. to — over, rivoltare; rovesciare; rotolare, rotolarsi 19. to — up, arrotolare; accumulare; (fam.) arrivare (in automobile, ecc.).

rollback ['roulbæk], s. (amer.) riduzione dei prezzi (per intervento governativo).

roller[1] ['roulə*], s. 1. rullo; rullo compressore 2. cilindro, rotella 3. maroso, cavallone 4. piccione acrobata ☆ — -bandage, benda, rotolo di garza; — -bearing, (mec.) cuscinetto a rulli; — -skates, pattini a

rotelle; — -towel, bandinella ǁ road —, compressore stradale; steam —, rullo compressore stradale a vapore.
roller[2], s. (ornit.) ghiandaia marina.
to rollick, v.i. essere gioviale, allegro oltre misura; far baldoria.
rollick ['rɔlik], s. allegria sfrenata; baldoria.
rollicking ['rɔlikiŋ], **rollicksome** ['rɔliksəm], ag. gioviale, allegro oltre misura.
rolling ['rouliŋ], ag. 1. rotolante: a — stone, un sasso che rotola ǁ a — stone gathers no moss, (prov.) pietra che rotola non raccoglie muschio 2. ondulato: a — plain, una pianura ondulata 3. oscillante, barcollante: a — gait, un'andatura traballante 4. ruotante, roteante; — eyes, occhi roteanti 5. ricorrente: the — seasons, le stagioni ricorrenti ǁ s. 1. rotolamento 2. arrotolamento ☆ — -mill, laminatoio; — -pin, (cuc.) matterello; — -press, (ind.) calandra; — stock, (ferr.) materiale rotabile.
roly-poly ['rouli'pouli], ag. grassoccio, pienotto (di bambino) ǁ s. — (pudding), sfoglia arrotolata con marmellata.
Romaic [rou'meiik], ag.s. (il) romaico (lingua greca moderna).
Roman ['roumən], ag. romano ǁ — Catholic, cattolico romano; — Catholic Church, Chiesa Cattolica Apostolica Romana ǁ the Holy — Empire, (st.) il Sacro Romano Impero ǁ s.c. romano, romana ☆ — calendar, calendario romano; — fever, malaria; — nose, naso aquilino; — numerals, numeri romani.
Romance [rə'mæns], ag. romanzo, neolatino: — languages, lingue romanze ǁ s. romanzo, lingua romanza.
romance, s. 1. romanzo cavalleresco; racconto fantastico, sentimentale 2. avventura romanzesca, episodio romanzesco: our meeting was quite a —, il nostro incontro fu romanzesco; to travel in search of —, viaggiare in cerca d'avventura 3. romanticheria; idillio: — between two young people, idillio tra due giovani; a girl full of —, una ragazza piena di romanticherie 4. esagerazione fantasiosa 5. poesia; atmosfera fantasiosa: the — of history, la poesia della storia 6. (mus.) romanza.
to romance, v.i. romanzare, esagerare, alterare la verità.
romancer [rə'mænsə*], s.c. 1. autore, autrice di racconti cavallereschi, di opere romanzesche 2. chi abbellisce, inventa i fatti nel raccontarli.
Romanesque [,roumə'nesk], ag. 1. (arch.) romanico 2. romanzo (di lingua) ǁ s. 1. (arch.) stile romanico 2. lingua romanza.
Romania [rou'meinjə], no.pr. (geog.) Romania.
Romanic [rou'mænik], ag. romanico, romanzo (di lingua) ǁ s. lingua romanica, romanza.
Romanish ['rouməniʃ], ag. 1. cattolico 2. ladino.
Romanism ['roumənizəm], s. 1. romanismo 2. cattolicesimo.
Romanist ['roumənist], s. 1. romanista 2. cattolico romano.
Romanity [rou'mæniti], s. (rar.) romanità.
Romanization [,roumənai'zeifən], s. 1. (st. eccl.) romanizzazione 2. (tip.) trascrizione in caratteri latini.
to Romanize ['roumənaiz], v.t.i. 1. latinizzare; atteggiarsi ad antico romano 2. convertire, convertirsi alla religione cattolica romana; atteggiarsi a cattolico romano 3. trascrivere in caratteri latini.
Romansh [rou'mænʃ], ag.s. (il) ladino.
romantic [rə'mæntik], ag. 1. romantico; sentimentale: a — girl, una ragazza romantica 2. romanzesco; fantastico; irreale: a — situation, una situazione irreale; a — tale, un racconto fantastico 3. (art. lett. mus.) romantico: Shelley was a — poet, Shelley era un poeta romantico ǁ s. 1. persona romantica 2. pl. idee, espressioni romantiche.
romantically [rə'mæntikəli], av. 1. romanticamente 2. romanzescamente.

romanticism [rə'mæntisizəm], s. (lett. mus.) romanticismo.
romanticist [rə'mæntisist], s.c. (lett. mus.) romantico, romantica.
to romanticize [rə'mæntisaiz], v.t.i. 1. romanzare 2. assumere atteggiamenti romantici.
Romany ['romǝni], ag. zingaresco ǁ s.c. zingaro, zingara ǁ s. dialetto degli zingari ☆ — rye, chi simpatizza per gli zingari.
romaunt [rə'mɔ:nt], s. (arc. lett.) racconto cavalleresco (generalmente in versi) ǁ "The Romaunt of the Rose", « Il Romanzo della Rosa ».
Rome [roum], no.pr. (geog.) Roma ǁ all roads lead to —, tutte le strade conducono a Roma ǁ when in —, do as Romans do, prov. paese che vai usanze che trovi ☆ — penny, obolo di San Pietro.
Romeo ['roumiou], no.pr.m. Romeo ǁ s.fig. innamorato.
Romewards ['roumwədz], av. 1. verso Roma 2. verso la Chiesa Cattolica Romana.
Romish ['roumiʃ], ag. (gener. spreg.) cattolico romano; papista.
Romishly ['roumiʃli], av. (gener. spreg.) da cattolico romano, da papista.
Romishness ['roumiʃnis], s. (gener. spreg.) cattolicesimo romano; papismo.
Rommany, V. Romany.
Romola ['roməlǝ], no.pr.f. Romola.
romp [romp], s. 1. bambino chiassoso 2. ragazza rumorosa, maschiaccio 3. giuoco violento, rumoroso 4. (sl. ippica) andatura veloce ǁ to win in a —, vincere con facilità.
to romp, v.i. 1. giocare in modo rumoroso, violento 2. (sl. ippica) correre velocemente ǁ to — in (o home), vincere facilmente ǁ to — through an examination, passare un esame senza il minimo sforzo.
romper ['rompə*], s. 1. grembiule da bambino 2. pl. pagliaccetto.
rompish ['rompiʃ], ag. chiassoso; turbolento.
rompishness ['rompiʃnis], s. chiasso, baccano.
rompy ['rompi], ag. chiassoso, rumoroso.
Romulus ['romjuləs], no.pr.m. Romolo.
Ronald ['ronld], no.pr.m. Ronaldo.
ronde [rond], s. (tip.) tondo.
rondeau ['rondou], pl. **rondeaus**, **rondeaux** ['rondouz], s. (poes.) rondò.
rondel ['rondl], s. (poes.) rondello, rondò.
rondo ['rondou], pl. **rondos** ['rondouz], s. (mus.) rondò.
rondure ['rondʒə*], s. (poet.) 1. rotondità 2. oggetto rotondo; cerchio; globo.
rood [ru:d], s. 1. croce; crocifisso ǁ the Holy Rood, la Santa Croce 2. (agr.) « rood » (misura di superficie = dam.[2] 10,1168); fig. piccola estensione di terreno: not even a — was left to him, non gli restò neppure un palmo di terra ☆ — -beam, putrella di sostegno del crocifisso; — -cloth, velo per ricoprire la croce durante la quaresima; — -loft, (arch.) galleria (sovrastante il — -screen); — -screen, (arch.) parete divisoria tra la navata e il coro.
roof [ru:f], s. 1. tetto, volta (anche fig.): — of heaven, volta celeste ǁ — of the mouth, palato duro ǁ the — of the world, il « tetto del mondo », il Pamir ǁ to be under s.o.'s —, essere sotto il tetto di qlcu., essere ospite di qlcu. ǁ to lift the —, fig. applaudire fragorosamente 2. imperiale (di autobus, diligenza) ☆ — -garden, giardino pensile; — -gutter, grondaia; — -lamp, plafoniera ǁ flat —, tetto a terrazza; lantern —, tetto a lucernaio; mansard —, tetto a mansarda; slate —, tetto di ardesia; sliding —, (aut.) « capote ».
to roof, v.t. 1. ricoprire con tetto 2. ospitare; alloggiare.
roofer ['ru:fə*], s. 1. conciatetti 2. (fam.) lettera di ringraziamento per ospitalità ricevuta.
roofing ['ru:fiŋ], ag. da tetto ǁ s. 1. copertura con tetto 2. costruzione di tetto 3. materiale da costru-

zione per tetti **4.** tetto; *fig.* rifugio ☆ — *slate*, ardesia; — *tile*, tegola.

roofless ['ruːflis], *ag.* senza tetto.

rook[1] [ruk], *s.* **1.** (*ornit.*) cornacchia **2.** baro (al giuoco).

to rook[1], *v.t.i.* **1.** (*arc.*) barare **2.** (*fam.*) truffare; far pagare prezzi esorbitanti: *to* — *s.o. of his money*, truffare qlcu.

rook[2], *s.* (*scacchi*) torre.

rookery ['rukəri], *s.* **1.** gruppo d'alberi su cui vive una colonia di cornacchie **2.** colonia di cornacchie, di altri uccelli; colonia di pinguini, foche **3.** gruppo di case malandate, malfamate, sovrappopolate.

rookie ['ruki], *s.* (*sl. mil.*) recluta.

rooklet ['ruklit], *s.* (*ornit.*) piccola cornacchia.

rooky ['ruki], *ag.* abitato da cornacchie.

room [ruːm], *s.* **1.** spazio, posto, luogo: *plenty of* —, spazio in abbondanza; *is there* — *for two more?* c'è ancora posto per due?; *to leave* (o *to make*) — *for*, far posto a; *to take up little, much* —, prendere poco, molto posto ‖ *I would rather have his* — *than his company*, mi è cordialmente antipatico ‖ *there is no* — *to swing a cat*, (*sl.*) non c'è spazio per girarsi **2.** camera, stanza, locale; *pl.* appartamento: *I have rooms in town*, ho un appartamento in città **3.** occasione, possibilità: *there is no* — *for doubt*, non c'è possibilità di dubbio ‖ *there is plenty of* — *for improvement in your work*, hai molto da imparare **4.** (*arc.*) posizione, rango ☆ — *-mate* (o — *-fellow*), compagno di stanza; — *-temperature*, temperatura ambientale ‖ *breakfast-* —, tinello; *class-* —, aula scolastica; *dining-* —, sala da pranzo; *drawing-* — (o *sitting-* —), salotto; *living-* —, soggiorno; *mess-* —, mensa; *smoking-* —, salotto per fumatori; *spare* —, stanza disponibile; *standing-* —, (*teat.*) ingressi, posti in piedi; *waiting-* —, sala d'aspetto.

to room, *v.i.* (*amer.*) alloggiare: *he is rooming with my friend*, egli alloggia con il mio amico.

roomer ['ruːmə*], *s.* (*amer.*) inquilino, affittuario.

roomette [ruː'met], *s.* (*amer. ferr.*) piccolo scompartimento separato (con letto ribaltabile).

roomful ['rumful], *s.* **1.** camera piena: *a* — *of children*, una stanza piena di bambini **2.** gente, oggetti in una camera.

roomily ['rumili], *av.* spaziosamente.

roominess ['ruminis], *s.* spaziosità.

roomy ['rumi], *ag.* spazioso, ampio.

to roose [ruːz], *v.t.* (*dial.*) lodare.

roost [ruːst], *s.* **1.** posatoio (di uccelli, polli) ‖ *at* —, appollaiato **2.** pollaio ‖ *curses come home to* —, *fig.* le maledizioni ricadono su chi le ha lanciate **3.** *fig.* giaciglio, letto: *at* —, (*fam.*) a letto; *to go to* —, (*fam.*) andare a riposare.

to roost, *v.t.i.* **1.** appollaiarsi **2.** (*fam.*) andare a dormire; alloggiare, dare da dormire a.

rooster ['ruːstə*], *s.* gallo domestico.

root[1] [ruːt], *s.* **1.** radice: *the* — *of the tongue*, la radice della lingua; *the* — *of a tooth*, la radice di un dente; *to lay axe to* — *of*, cominciare ad abbattere (anche *fig.*); *to pull up by the roots*, sradicare (anche *fig.*); *to take* (o *to strike*) —, prender radice (anche *fig.*) ‖ — *-and-branch*, completamente **2.** *fig.* causa; origine; fondamento, base; sorgente: *the* — *of all evil*, la causa, l'origine di tutti i mali; *to get at the roots of things*, andare a fondo nelle cose **3.** (*mat.*) radice **4.** (*mus.*) nota fondamentale **5.** (*filologia*) radice: *the* — *of a word*, la radice di una parola ☆ — *-bound*, (*amer.*) bevanda frizzante estratta da radici; — *-bound*, fissato alla terra da radici; — *-cap*, (*bot.*) cuffia; — *-cause*, causa prima; — *-circle* (o — *line*), (*mec.*) cerchio interno, cerchio di fondo; — *-climber*, (*bot.*) rampicante; — *-eater*, (*zool.*) rizofago; — *-fast*, radicato saldamente; — *idea*, idea base; — *-parasite*, pianta parassita delle radici; — *-sign*, (*mat.*) radicale; — *-stock*, (*bot.*) rizoma; *fig.* radice, origine; — *-syllable*, (*gram.*) sillaba radicale ‖ *cube-* — (o *third* —), radice cubica; *square-* — (o *second* —), radice quadrata.

to root[1], *v.t.i.* **1.** piantare; mettere radice, attecchire: *some plants* — *freely*, alcune piante attecchiscono facilmente **2.** *fig.* radicarsi, allignare; stabilire, stabilirsi; fissare, fissarsi: *fear rooted him to the ground*, il timore lo inchiodò al suolo; *her affection is deeply rooted*, il suo affetto è profondamente radicato **3.** *to* — **away, out, up**, sradicare, svellere, estirpare (anche *fig.*).

to root[2], *v.t.i.* **1.** grufolare, razzolare ‖ —, *hog, or die*, (*amer.*) lotta o muori **2.** *fig.* grufolare, frugare: *to* — *among papers*, frugare tra le carte **3.** *to* — *for* (*s.o.*), (*sl. amer.*) sostenere, fare il tifo per: *to* — *for a candidate*, sostenere un candidato **4.** *to* — **out, up**, snidare, trovare.

rootage ['ruːtidʒ], *s.* **1.** radicamento **2.** l'insieme delle radici (di piante).

rootedly ['ruːtidli], *av.* radicatamente.

rootedness ['ruːtidnis], *s.* radicamento: *her affection* —, ...

rooter[1] ['ruːtə*], *s.* sradicatore, estirpatore.

rooter[2], *s.* (*sl. amer.*) tifoso.

rootless ['ruːtlis], *ag.* senza radice.

rootlet ['ruːtlit], *s.* radichetta.

rooty ['ruːti], *ag.* pieno di radici; simile a radice ‖ *s.* (*sl. mil.*) pane.

rope[1] [roup], *s.* **1.** fune, canapo; capestro; (*mar.*) cavo: *throw him a* —, gettagli una fune ‖ — *of sand*, *fig.* legame tenue, debole ‖ *on the* —, (*spor.*) in cordata ‖ *on the high ropes*, (*fam. fig.*) sdegnato, adirato; superbo ‖ *to come to the end of one's* —, *fig.* vedere frustrati i propri piani criminosi ‖ *to give s.o.* —, (*fam. fig.*) dar corda a qlcu., lasciarlo fare ‖ *to know the ropes*, (*fam. fig.*) saperla lunga ‖ *to put s.o. up to the ropes*, mettere qlcu. al corrente ‖ *to give a fool* — *enough and he'll hang himself*, *prov.* dà la corda a uno sciocco e quello si impicca **2.** *pl.* (*spor.*) corde (che limitano « ring », ecc.) **3.** resta (di cipolle, ecc.); filza, filo (di perle) **4.** filamento (di liquido viscoso) **5.** (*amer.*) « lazo » **6.** (*neol.*) cordata ☆ — *-dancer* (o — *-walker*), funambolo; — *-dancing* (o — *-walking*), funambolismo; — *'s end*, sferza; — *-ladder*, scala di corda; — *-yarn*, filaccia, sfilaccio; *fig.* cosa da nulla ‖ — *tight-* —, fune tesa (per funamboli); *tow-* —, fune per rimorchio.

to rope[1], *v.t.i.* **1.** legare con fune: *to* — *s.o. to a tree*, legare qlcu. a un albero **2.** (*spor.*) mettere, mettersi in cordata **3.** rimorchiare con fune **4.** (*spor.*) frenare un cavallo (per impedirgli di vincere); perdere una corsa intenzionalmente **5.** diventar viscoso, viscido **6.** (*amer.*) prendere al « lazo » **7.** *to* — **in**, cintare (un terreno) con corde; *fig.* associare (qlcu.) con la forza (ad un progetto, ecc.).

rope[2], *s.* (*dial. gener. pl.*) intestino, budella.

roper ['roupə*], *s.* **1.** funaio, cordaio **2.** chi frena un cavallo per impedirgli di vincere una corsa; chi intenzionalmente perde una corsa **3.** (*sl. amer.*) chi lancia il « lazo » **4.** (*sl. amer.*) chi attrae clientela con raggiri (in case da giuoco).

ropery ['roupəri], *s.* **1.** corderia **2.** (*arc.*) mascalzonata.

ropeway ['roupwei], *s.* teleferica.

ropiness ['roupinis], *s.* viscosità (di liquido, sciroppo).

ropy ['roupi], *ag.* viscoso, fibroso.

roquelaure ['rokələ:*], *s.* (*st.*) « roquelaure » (mantello da uomo fino al ginocchio, del XVIII secolo).

roquet ['rouki], *s.* (*croquet*) « roquet » (colpo dato alla palla di un avversario con la propria).

to roquet, *v.t.i.* (*croquet*) colpire (la palla dell'avversario) con la propria; colpire la palla dell'avversario.

rorqual ['rɔːkwəl], *s.* (*zool.*) balenottera.

rorty ['rɔːti], *ag.* (*sl.*) **1.** divertente: *to have a* — *time*, divertirsi molto **2.** amante dei divertimenti.

rosace ['rouzeis], *s.* (*arch.*) rosone.

rosaceous [rou'zeiʃəs], *ag.* (*bot.*) rosaceo.

Rosalba [rou'zælbə], *no.pr.f.* Rosalba.

Rosalie ['rɔzəli], *no.pr.f.* Rosalia.

Rosalind ['rozəlind], *no.pr.f.* Rosalinda.
Rosaline ['rozəlain], *no.pr.f.* Rosalina.
Rosamond ['rozəmənd], *no.pr.f.* Rosmunda.
rosaniline [rouz'æniliːn], *s.* (*chim.*) rosanilina.
rosarian [rou'zɛəriən], *s.c.* chi ama, coltiva rose ‖ **Rosarian**, *s.* membro della confraternita del Rosario.
rosarium [rou'zɛəriəm], *s.* roseto.
rosary ['rouzəri], *s.* **1.** roseto **2.** (*eccl.*) rosario.
rose[1] [rouz], *ag.* rosa, di color rosa ‖ *s.* **1.** rosa: *bed of roses*, roseto: *life is not a bed of roses*, fig. la vita non è tutta rose e fiori; *a path strewn with roses*, un sentiero cosparso di rose ‖ *Rose of Jericho*, rosa di Gerico ‖ *under the —*, in segreto, confidenzialmente ‖ *the War of the Roses*, (*st.*) la guerra delle due Rose ‖ *to gather roses*, fig. ricercare il piacere ‖ *no — without a thorn*, prov. non c'è rosa senza spine **2.** color rosa: *she has lost her roses*, ha perso il suo incarnato **3.** rosetta (diamante) **4.** rosetta (di inaffiatoio) **5.** (*patol.*) erisipela ☆ *— -bay*, oleandro; rododendro; *— -bud*, bocciolo di rosa; fig. ragazza graziosa; (*amer.*) giovane debuttante; *— -bush*, rosaio; cespuglio di rose; *— -chafer*, (*entom.*) cetonia dorata; *— -colour*, color di rosa; fig. situazione rosea; *— -coloured*, di color rosa; fig. roseo, ottimista; *— -cut*, tagliato a rosetta; *— -diamond*, rosetta; *— -gall*, galla di rosa; *— -laurel*, oleandro; *— -leaf*, foglia di rosa; petalo di rosa; *— -lipped*, dalle labbra rosa; *— -rash*, (*patol.*) rosolia; *— -water*, acqua di rose (anche fig.); *— -window*, (*arch.*) rosone ‖ *brier- —* (o *dog- —*), rosa canina; *compass- —*, rosa della bussola; *damask- —*, rosa damascena; *guelder- —*, (*bot.*) viburno; *moss- —*, rosa muschiata; *musk- —*, rosa muschiata; *tea- —*, rosa tea.
to **rose**[1], *v.t.* rendere rosa, colorire di rosa.
Rose[2], *no.pr.f.*
rose[3], *pass.* di to **rise**.
roseate ['rouziit], *ag.* roseo, rosato.
roseately ['rouziitli], *av.* in modo roseo.
roseless ['rouzlis], *ag.* senza rose.
roselike ['rouzlaik], *ag.* come una rosa, simile a rosa.
rosella [rou'zelə], *s.* (*ornit.*) rosella.
roselle [rou'zel], *s.* (*bot.*) ibisco indiano.
rosemary[1] ['rouzməri], *s.* (*bot.*) rosmarino.
Rosemary[2], *no.pr.f.* Rosamaria.
Rosencrantz ['rouzənkrænts], *no.pr.m.* (*lett.*) Rosencrantz.
roseola [rou'ziːələ], *s.* (*patol.*) rosolia.
rosery ['rouzəri], *s.* roseto.
Rosetta [rou'zetə], *no.pr.* (*geog.*) Rosetta ‖ *the — Stone*, (*archeol.*) la stele di Rosetta.
rosette [rou'zet], *s.* **1.** rosetta, coccarda **2.** (*arch.*) rosone **3.** rosetta (diamante) **4.** (*metal.*) rosetta.
rosewood ['rouzwud], *s.* palissandro.
Rosicrucian [ˌrouzi'kruːʃən], *ag.s.* (di) Rosacroce (membro di una società fondata nel XV secolo, o di una associazione a carattere massonico).
rosily ['rouzili], *av.* in modo roseo.
rosin ['rozin], *s.* resina; colofonia, pece greca.
to **rosin**, *v.t.* cospargere di resina, pece greca (specialmente l'archetto del violino, ecc.).
Rosinante [ˌrozi'nænti], *no.pr.m.* (*lett.*) Ronzinante ‖ *s.* ronzino.
rosiness ['rouzinis], *s.* color roseo.
rosiny ['rozini], *ag.* resinoso.
rosolio [rou'zouliou], *s.* rosolio.
roster ['roustə*], *s.* **1.** (*mil. mar.*) ruolino, turno di servizio **2.** (*amm.*) lista, elenco, ruolo ☆ *duty —*, ruolino di servizio; *promotion —*, ruolo di promozione (di personale).
rostral ['rostrəl], *ag.* relativo a rostro; adorno di rostro ☆ *— column*, (*st. romana*) colonna rostrata.
rostrate(d) ['rostreit(id)], *ag.* rostrato.
rostrum ['rostrəm], *pl.* **rostra** ['rostrə], **rostrums** ['rostrəmz], *s.* **1.** rostro, becco **2.** (*st. romana*) rostro (di nave) **3.** gener. pl. rostri, tribuna **4.** leggìo per conferenziere (a Oxford).

rosy ['rouzi], *ag.* **1.** roseo, rosato, di color rosa (anche fig.): *a — future*, un roseo futuro; *to paint everything in — colours*, (fam.) vedere tutto rosa; *to turn —*, diventar roseo **2.** fatto, cosparso di rose; (*arc.*) profumato di rosa.
rot [rot], *s.* **1.** putrefazione; marciume **2.** carie dentaria **3.** malattia al fegato (di pecore) **4.** successione di sbagli **5.** (*sl.*) stupidaggine: *to talk (tommy) —*, dire delle stupidaggini ☆ *— -gut*, liquore cattivo; (*sl.*) liquore forte, whisky liscio ‖ *dry- —*, carie secca del legno.
to **rot**, *pass.p.p.* **rotted** ['rotid], *v.t.i.* **1.** imputridire, far imputridire, marcire, far marcire; putrefarsi, corrompersi (anche fig.) **2.** essere affetto da malattia al fegato (di pecore) **3.** (*sl.*) dire sciocchezze **4.** (*sl.*) parlare ironicamente di; farsi beffe di.
rota ['routə], *s.* **1.** orario dei turni (di lavoro, studio) **2.** lista; ruolo **3.** *the Rota*, (*dir. eccl.*) la Rota.
Rotarian [rou'tɛəriən], *ag.* rotariano ‖ *s.* rotariano, membro del « Rotary Club ».
rotary ['routəri], *ag.* rotante, rotatorio; a rotazione ‖ *s.* **1.** *— (machine* o *— press)*, (*tip.*) rotativa **2.** *Rotary (Club)*, « Rotary Club » (società internazionale fondata nel 1911 in Gran Bretagna ☆ *— drill*, (*miner.*) sonda a rotazione; *— engine*, (*mec.*) macchina rotativa; *— motion*, movimento rotatorio; *— table*, (*mec.*) tavola rotante, girevole; *— traffic*, traffico rotatorio; *— valve*, (*mec.*) valvola rotativa.
rotate ['routit], *ag.* (*bot.*) a forma di ruota.
to **rotate** [rou'teit], *v.t.i.* **1.** rotare, far rotare **2.** coltivare a rotazione.
rotation [rou'teiʃən], *s.* rotazione; successione (periodica e regolare): *— of crops*, rotazione delle colture; *the — of seasons*, la successione delle stagioni; *by* (o *in) —*, a rotazione ☆ *clockwise —*, rotazione a destra.
rotational [rou'teiʃənl], *ag.* rotatorio.
rotative ['routətiv], *ag.* rotatorio.
rotator [rou'teitə*], *s.* **1.** (*anat.*) muscolo rotatorio **2.** motorino elettrico ad elevato numero di giri.
rotatory ['routətəri], *ag.* rotatorio.
rote [rout], *s.* abitudine meccanica; memoria meccanica: *to do sthg. by —*, fare ql.co. meccanicamente; *to learn sthg. by —*, imparare ql.co. a memoria, pappagallescamente.
to **rote**, *v.t.* ripetere meccanicamente.
Rotifera [rou'tifərə], *s.pl.* (*zool.*) i rotiferi.
rotor ['routə*], *s.* **1.** (*mec.*) girante, ruota **2.** (*elett.*) rotore, indotto **3.** (*aer.*) rotore ☆ *— plane*, velivolo ad ala rotante; *— ship*, rotonave ‖ *lifting —*, elica di quota, rotore principale (di elicottero).
rotten ['rotn], *ag.* **1.**' marcio, putrido, putrefatto; fig. corrotto: *the politics of that country are —*, la politica di quel paese è corrotta ‖ *— boroughs*, (*st. inglese*) sezioni elettorali con pochissimi votanti (abolite nel 1832) **2.** (*sl.*) sgradevole, disgustoso; abominevole ‖ *what — luck!*, che scalogna! **3.** affetto da malattia di fegato (di pecora) ☆ *— -stone*, tripolo, farina fossile.
rottenly ['rotnli], *av.* (*sl.*) malissimo; in modo pietoso: *my watch is working —*, il mio orologio va malissimo.
rottenness ['rotnnis], *s.* marciume, putrefazione; fig. corruzione.
rotter ['rotə*], *s.* (*sl.*) farabutto, mascalzone: *don't be a —*, non far la carogna; *he behaved like a —*, si comportò da mascalzone.
rotula ['rotjulə], *s.* (*anat.*) rotula.
rotund [rou'tʌnd], *ag.* **1.** paffuto, rotondetto **2.** profondo (di voce) **3.** enfatico, magniloquente (di discorso).
rotunda [rou'tʌndə], *s.* (*arch.*) rotonda.
rotundate [rou'tʌndit], *ag.* arrotondato.
rotundity [rou'tʌnditi], *s.* rotondità.
rotundly [rou'tʌndli], *av.* rotondamente.
rouble ['ruːbl], *s.* rublo.
roué [ruː'ei], *s.* libertino.

rouge[1] [ru:ʒ], *ag.* rosso ‖ *s.* **1.** belletto; rossetto **2.** (*chim.*) rossetto inglese, di Parigi **3.** rivoluzionario **4.** — *-et-noir*, (*carte*) trenta e quaranta.

to rouge[1], *v.t.i.* dare il belletto, il rossetto a, imbellettarsi, mettersi il rossetto.

rouge[2], *s.* (*rugby*) mischia.

rough [rʌf], *ag.* **1.** irregolare, disuguale; ruvido, scabro: — *hands*, mani ruvide; — *road*, strada accidentata **2.** tempestoso, burrascoso; violento, impetuoso: *a* — *passage*, una traversata burrascosa; — *sea*, mare grosso; — *weather*, tempo burrascoso **3.** rudimentale, approssimativo: *a* — *translation*, una traduzione approssimativa **4.** rude, sgarbato; rozzo, zotico: — *handling*, trattamento rude; — *manners*, modi bruschi; — *words*, parole sgarbate **5.** aspro, acre: *a* — *wine*, un vino aspro **6.** disagevole, scomodo; difficile: *a* — *life*, una vita difficile ‖ *what* — *luck!*, che scalogna! ‖ *to have a* — *time*, passarne di tutti i colori ‖ *s.* **1.** terreno accidentato; (*golf*) erba lunga **2.** giovinastro, teppista **3.** stato grezzo ‖ *in the* —, allo stato grezzo: *he explained his ideas in the* —, espose le sue idee per sommi capi **4.** lato spiacevole delle cose ‖ *to take the* — *with the smooth*, prendere le cose come vengono.

to rough, *v.t.* **1.** rendere ruvido; increspare; arruffare: *to* — (*up*) *the hair*, arruffare i capelli ‖ *to* — *it*, (*fam.*) vivere primitivamente ‖ *to* — *s.o. up the wrong way*, irritare qlcu. **2.** ferrare a ramponi (cavalli) **3.** *to* — *in*, *out*, abbozzare; schizzare **4.** *to* — *up*, accordare malamente (un pianoforte).

rough, *av.* **1.** rudemente: *they treated him* —, lo trattarono rudemente **2.** grossolanamente.

rough, (*nei composti*): — *-and-ready*, non elaborato, improvvisato; — *diamond*, diamante grezzo; *fig.* persona di grande valore, ma di modi rozzi; — *-hewn*, grossolano; appena sbozzato; — *-house*, (*sl.*) rissa; — *-neck*, (*sl. amer.*) zoticone; attaccabrighe; — *-shod*, ferrato a ramponi; — *-rider*, domatore di cavalli; (*mil.*) soldato irregolare di cavalleria; — *-spoken*, aspro nel parlare; — *-wrought*, lavorato grossolanamente.

roughage [ˈrʌfidʒ], *s.* crusca di cereali.

rough-and-tumble [ˈrʌfənˈtʌmbl], *ag.* irregolare, disordinato ‖ *s.* zuffa, mischia.

rough-cast [ˈrʌfkɑːst], *s.* intonaco.

to rough-cast, *pass. p.p.* **rough-cast**, *v.t.* intonacare.

to rough-draft [ˈrʌfˈdrɑːft], *v.t.* abbozzare.

to roughen [ˈrʌfən], *v.t.i.* **1.** irruvidire, irruvidirsi **2.** rendere, diventare grossolano.

to rough-grind [ˈrʌfgraind], *pass.p.p.* **rough-ground** [ˈrʌfgraund], *v.t.* arrotare senza cura.

roughish [ˈrʌfiʃ], *ag.* **1.** piuttosto ruvido **2.** piuttosto grossolano.

roughly [ˈrʌfli], *av.* **1.** rudemente, bruscamente **2.** grossolanamente **3.** approssimativamente.

roughness [ˈrʌfnis], *s.* **1.** ruvidezza; anfrattuosità, scabrosità (di terreno) **2.** violenza, agitazione; inclemenza, rigidità (di tempo) **3.** rudezza, sgarbatezza.

roulade [ruːˈlɑːd], *s.* trillo, gorgheggio.

rouleau [ruːˈlou], *pl.* **rouleaux, rouleaus** [ruːˈlouz], *s.* rotolo di monete d'oro.

roulette [ruːˈlet], *s.* **1.** roulette (giuoco) **2.** (*mec.*) brunitoio a rotella **3.** bigodino **4.** (*geom.*) cicloide.

Roumania [ruːˈmeinjə], *no.pr.* (*geog.*) Romania.

round [raund], *ag.* **1.** rotondo; circolare; sferico; cilindrico: *a* — *face*, un viso tondo, paffuto; *as* — *as a ball*, tondo come una palla ‖ *the Round Table*, (*st. lett.*) la Tavola Rotonda **2.** intero, completo: — *dozen*, una buona dozzina; *in* — *figures*, in cifre tonde **3.** franco, sincero: — *unvarnished tale*, racconto schietto; verità sacrosanta; *to be* — *with s.o.*, (*arc.*) parlare chiaro a qlcu. **4.** scorrevole (di stile) **5.** sonoro, pieno (di voce) **6.** vigoroso, agile (di passo): *to go at a good* — *pace*, camminare di buon passo **7.** considerevole (di somma): *that is a good* — *sum*, è una bella somma **8.** pronunciata arrotondando le labbra (di vocale).

round, *s.* **1.** cerchio; sfera, globo: *to dance in a* —. ballare in cerchio; *to draw a* —, disegnare un cerchio ‖ *the* — *of heaven*, la volta celeste **2.** piuolo (di sedia, scala): *rounds of a ladder*, piuoli di una scala **3.** corso, ciclo, serie: — *of daily labours*, ciclo di lavori quotidiani; *the* — *of the seasons*, il ciclo delle stagioni **4.** giro; (*mil.*) ronda: *to go for a good* —, andare a fare una bella passeggiata; *to go the rounds*, (*mil.*) fare la ronda; *to make* (*o to go*) *one's rounds*, fare il solito giro di visite, di ispezione (di dottore, poliziotto) **5.** *fig.* ambito, cerchia: *in the* — *of my friends*, nell'ambito delle mie amicizie **6.** (*scult.*) tutto tondo, tutto rilievo: *statue in the* —, statua a tutto rilievo **7.** (*carte*) mano, giro; (*boxe*) « round », ripresa; (*golf*) giro **8.** (*mus.*) canone **9.** scoppio, scroscio (di risa, applausi) **10.** (*mil.*) carica, colpo, salva, scarica: *101 rounds were shot in his honour*, risuonarono 101 salve in suo onore **11.** (*miner.*) volata **12.** (*cuc.*) girello.

to round, *v.t.i.* **1.** arrotondare, arrotondarsi: *stones and pebbles rounded by the action of water*, pietre e ciottoli arrotondati dall'azione dell'acqua ‖ *to* — *a dog's ears*, mozzare le orecchie a un cane **2.** girare, ruotare; (*mar.*) doppiare: *the ship rounded the Cape*, la nave doppiò il Capo **3.** completare; perfezionare: *he rounded* (*off*) *his sentence with...*, finì la frase con...; *he rounded off the negotiations*, completò i negoziati **4.** svilupparsi, crescere: *the boy had rounded into a man*, il ragazzo era diventato uomo **5.** *to* — *on* (*s.o.*), (*fam.*) rivoltarsi irosamente contro; informare **6.** *to* — *in*, (*mar.*) alare **7.** *to* — *to*, (*mar.*) orzare, venire al vento **8.** *to* — *up*, (*mar.*) alare dall'alto al basso.

round, *av.* intorno, attorno; in giro, all'intorno: *the children gathered* —, i bambini si radunarono all'intorno; *he knew everybody for five miles* —, conosceva tutti nel raggio di cinque miglia; *her wrist is only five inches* —, il suo polso misura soltanto cinque pollici; *a sitting-room hung* — *with pictures*, un salotto con quadri tutt'intorno; *tea was served* —, il tè fu servito a tutti; *they didn't have enough cake to go* —, non avevano abbastanza torta per tutti; *the wheel goes* —, la ruota gira; *to hand* —, distribuire, dare in giro; *to turn* — *and* —, continuare a girare, girare su se stessi ‖ *all the year* —, tutto l'anno ‖ *taken all* —, (*fam.*) nell'insieme ‖ *come* — *and see us this evening*, vieni a trovarci questa sera ‖ *he brought us a long way* —, ci fece fare un lungo giro, un giro vizioso ‖ *let's go in the other way* —, entriamo dalla parte opposta ‖ *read the other way* —, leggi in senso inverso ‖ *Summer comes* — *again*, l'estate è di nuovo alle porte ‖ *to show a person* —, portare in giro, fare da guida a una persona ‖ *to sleep the clock* —, dormire per dodici o ventiquattro ore.

round, *prep.* intorno a, tutto intorno a: — *the corner*, dietro l'angolo; — *the neck*, attorno al collo; *the earth turns* — *its centre of gravity*, la Terra gira intorno al suo centro di gravità; *he wrote a novel* — *this subject*, scrisse un romanzo intorno a questo argomento; *it must be* — *one o'clock*, dev'essere circa l'una; *snow was falling all* — *me*, la neve mi cadeva tutt'intorno; *the swallows were turning* — *and* — *the tower*, le rondini volteggiavano intorno alla torre; *try to go* — *this obstacle*, cerca di aggirare questo ostacolo; *to argue* — *and* — *a subject*, girare intorno a un argomento; *to travel* — *the world*, fare il giro del mondo ‖ *to go* — *the bend*, (*sl.*) comportarsi in modo stravagante.

round, (*nei composti*): — *angle*, (*geom.*) angolo giro; — *-arch*, arco a tutto sesto; — *-fish*, (*ittiol.*) carpa; — *-game*, giuoco in circolo; — *-house*, (*amer.*) rimessa per locomotive; (*mar.*) tuga; — *-shouldered*, dalla schiena curva; — *-towel*, bandinella, asciugamano a rullo; — *-trip*, viaggio di andata e ritorno; — *-up*, (*amer.*) battuta a cavallo per radunare il bestiame; (*sl.*) retata.

roundabout [ˈraundəbaut], *ag.* **1.** indiretto; obliquo; tortuoso: *she told him in a* — *way*, ella glielo disse in modo involuto, indiretto **2.** (*arc.*) grassoccio ‖ *s.* **1.** gio-

stra 2. via traversa 3. rondò 4. — (phrase), circonlocuzione 5. (amer.) giacca corta, attillata da uomo
☆ — traffic system, sistema di traffico a senso unico.
rounded ['raundid], ag. 1. arrotondato; levigato 2. limato (di stile).
roundel ['raundl], s. 1. tondo, medaglione decorativo 2. (mus. poes.) rondò.
roundelay ['raundilei], s. 1. (mus. poes.) rondò 2. canzonetta con ritornello 3. canto d'uccello.
rounder ['raundə*], s. 1. (fam. amer.) recidivo; fannullone; pilastro di bettola 2. pl. giuoco simile al
« baseball » 3. strumento per arrotondare.
roundhand ['raundhænd], s. calligrafia rotonda.
Roundhead ['raundhed], s. (st.) testa tonda, puritano (specialmente detto dei soldati di Cromwell).
rounding ['raundin], ag. 1. rotondo; rotondeg-
giante 2. arrotondante || s. (mar.) fasciatura.
roundish ['raundiʃ], ag. quasi rotondo; tondeggiante.
roundlet ['raundlit], s. cerchietto; disco.
roundly ['raundli], av. 1. in tondo; in giro, circolarmente 2. vigorosamente; severamente 3. francamente;
esplicitamente 4. fluentemente.
roundness ['raundnis], s. 1. rotondità, sfericità 2. scorrevolezza; tornitura (di stile) 3. franchezza.
roundsman, pl. **roundsmen** ['raundzmən], s. 1. fattorino 2. (amer.) poliziotto con funzioni di ispettore.
roup [raup], s. (scoz.) asta (vendita).
to **roup**, v.t. (scoz.) vendere all'asta.
rouse[1] [rauz], s. 1. (mil.) sveglia 2. scossone violento.
to **rouse**[1], v.t.i. 1. svegliare, destare; alzarsi; svegliarsi (anche fig.): he roused (up) at seven, si svegliò
alle sette; he wants rousing, fig. egli è indolente; I was
roused by the ringing of a bell, fui svegliato dal suono di
un campanello; to — s.o. from indolence, scuotere qlcu.
dall'indolenza 2. stanare (selvaggina, ecc.) 3. risvegliare (sentimenti, ecc.) 4. sollevare, agitare, provocare: when roused he is dangerous, provocato diventa
pericoloso 5. agitare, mescolare (liquidi) 6. (mar.) alare
con forza.
rouse[2], s. (arc.) 1. sorso, bicchiere di liquore 2. brindisi; gozzoviglia: to give a —, proporre un brindisi,
fare un brindisi || to take one's —, gozzovigliare.
to **rouse**[3], v.t. mettere sotto sale (aringhe).
rouser ['rauzə*], s.c. 1. chi stimola 2. chi ridesta ||
s. 1. (fam.) bugia oltraggiosa 2. arnese per rimestare
la birra 3. forte rumore; persona rumorosa.
rousing ['rauzin], ag. 1.eccitante, stimolante 2. (fam.)
notevole, stupefacente.
roustabout ['raustəbaut], s. 1. (amer.) scaricatore di
porto; uomo adatto a lavori saltuari e di fatica 2. (austral.) galoppino.
rout[1] [raut], s. 1.folla tumultuante; plebaglia 2. (dir.)
associazione a delinquere 3. tumulto, sommossa 4. (rar.)
branco, mandria 5. riunione.
rout[2], s. (mil.) 1. sconfitta, disfatta; rotta: to put
to —, mettere in rotta 2. esercito sconfitto in fuga.
to **rout**[2], v.t. mettere in rotta, sconfiggere.
to **rout**[3], V. to **root**[2].
route [ru:t], s. 1. via, rotta, itinerario; cammino,
strada: en —, in cammino, per strada 2. (mil.) ordini
di marcia: to get, to give the —, ricevere, dare gli ordini
di marcia ☆ — -map, carta stradale; — -march, (mil.)
marcia di addestramento; — -step, (mil.) passo di
strada || air —, (aer.) rotta aerea.
to **route**, v.t. spedire, instradare: the troops will be
routed to Venice via Milan, le truppe saranno instra-
date per Venezia via Milano; to — goods, spedire merci.
routine [ru:'ti:n], s. « routine »; pratica, abitudine
meccanica: to do sthg. as a matter of —, fare ql.co.
d'abitudine ☆ — treatment, (med.) terapia comune;
— work, lavoro quotidiano.
routinism [ru:'ti:nizəm], s. regolarità meccanica.
routinist [ru:'ti:nist], s.c. abitudinario, abitudinaria.

rove[1] [rouv], s. (mar.) rondella (di rame).
rove[2], s. 1. vagabondaggio: to be on the —, (fam.)
vagabondare 2. (dial.) metodo per arare in superficie.
to **rove**[2], v.t.i. errare, vagare (anche fig.); vagabondare, percorrere, attraversare: his eyes roved from the
one to the other, i suoi occhi erravano dall'uno all'altro;
his mind roved back to his youth, il suo pensiero ritornò
alla giovinezza; that drunkard roved the streets all night,
quell'ubriaco vagò tutta la notte per le strade || to —
over sea and land, vagare per mare e per terra.
rove[3], s. (ind. tessile) stoppino, lucignolo.
to **rove**[3], v.t. torcere lana per filare.
rover[1] ['rouvə*], s. 1. vagabondo, giramondo 2. (scoutismo) « rover » 3. (tiro all'arco) bersaglio lontano ed
indeterminato || to shoot at rovers, (fam.) tirare a ca-
saccio.
rover[2], s. 1. pirata 2. nave corsara.
rover[3], s. (ind. tessile) banco per lucignolo.
rovery ['rouvəri], s. (arc.) vagabondaggio; pirateria.
roving[1] ['rouvin], s. 1. viaggio senza meta; vagabondaggio 2. il tiro a un bersaglio casuale.
roving[2], s. (ind. tessile) torcitura di lana, ecc.
rovingly ['rouvinli], av. in modo vagabondo; in vagabondaggio.
row[1] [rou], s. fila, linea (di persone, cose, ecc.); filare:
a — of plants, un filare di piante; in the first —, in
prima fila (a teatro, ecc.); sitting in a — (o in rows),
seduti in fila || a hard — to hoe, (amer. fig.) un osso
duro, cosa difficile da eseguire.
row[2] [rau], s. (sl.) 1. baruffa, rissa, zuffa, tafferuglio;
schiamazzo: to make (o to kick up) a —, far baccano;
protestare 2. rimprovero: she got into a —, si buscò
un rimprovero coi fiocchi.
to **row**[2], v.t.i. (sl.) 1. sgridare, rimproverare 2. azzuffarsi.
row[3] [rou], s. giro in barca; remata ☆ — barge, canotto, barca a remi.
to **row**[3], v.t.i. 1. remare, vogare; trasportare a forza
di remi; essere spinto da remi: shall I — you across the
river?, vuoi che ti porti colla barca all'altra sponda
del fiume? || to — a fast stroke, remare a ritmo acce-
lerato 2. essere canottiere: he rows No. 2. in our crew,
è il secondo vogatore del nostro equipaggio 3. essere
attrezzato con un certo numero di remi (di imbarcazione) 4. to — down, raggiungere remando (specialmente durante le gare) 5. to — out, esaurirsi per il
troppo remare: they were completely rowed out, i vogato-
ri erano spossati per un lungo remare.
rowan ['rauən], s. (scoz.) 1. — -(tree), sorbo selvatico 2. — -(berry), sorba selvatica.
rowdiness ['raudinis], s. turbolenza.
rowdy ['raudi], ag. turbolento; chiassoso; tumultuoso ☆ s. attaccabrighe; persona turbolenta.
rowdyish ['raudiiʃ], ag. turbolento; chiassoso.
rowdyism ['raudiizəm], s. turbolenza; baccano.
rowel ['rauəl], s. 1. stella di sperone 2. (vet.) setone.
to **rowel**, pass.p.p. **rowelled** ['rauəld], v.t. 1. speronare
(un cavallo) 2.(vet.) applicare un setone a (un cavallo).
rowen ['rauən], s. (amer. dial.) guaime; secondo
taglio (di erba, fieno, ecc.).
rower ['rouə*], s.c. rematore, rematrice || s. canot-
tiere, vogatore.
Rowland ['roulənd], no.pr.m. (lett.) Rolando, Orlando.
rowlock ['rɔlək], s. (mar.) scalmo, scalmiera.
Roxana [rɔks'ænə], no.pr.f. Rossana.
royal ['rɔiəl], ag. 1. reale, regale; regio: the — family, la famiglia reale; a — princess, una principessa
di sangue reale || Royal Air Force (R.A.F.), Aviazione
militare britannica || the Royal Navy, la Marina bri-
tannica || His Royal Highness, Sua Altezza Reale ||
Princess Royal, principessa (primogenita di sovrano) 2. degno di re; splendido, maestoso: a — magnanimity, una splendida magnanimità; a — welcome una
accoglienza splendida || it is no — road, non è un si-
stema facile, ci sono degli ostacoli || to be in — spirits,

essere di ottimo umore ‖ *s.* **1.** (*fam.*) membro di famiglia reale **2.** cervo reale **3.** *the Royals*, primo reggimento di fanteria britannica **4.** (*mar.*) controvelaccio ☆ — *blue*, blu savoia; — *fern*, (*bot.*) osmunda; — *jelly*, pappa reale; — *paper*, carta reale; — *sail*, (*mar.*) controvelaccio ‖ *blood* —, la famiglia reale.

royalism ['rɔiəlizm], *s.* attaccamento alla monarchia.

royalist ['rɔiəlist], *s.* realista, monarchico.

royalistic [,rɔiə'listik], *ag.* monarchico.

royally ['rɔiəli], *av.* regalmente, da re; (*fam.*) splendidamente.

royalty ['rɔiəlti], *s.* **1.** dignità di re, regalità, sovranità **2.** membro di famiglia reale; i reali: *the play was performed in the presence of* —, la commedia fu rappresentata alla presenza dei reali **3.** *pl.* prerogative, privilegi reali **4.** «*royalty*» (pagamento di una percentuale sugli utili a chi concede lo sfruttamento di miniere, pozzi petroliferi, foreste, ecc.) **5.** diritto d'autore.

Ruanda-Urundi [ru:'ɑ:ndɑ:-u:'ru:ndi], *no.pr.* (*geog.*) Ruanda-Urundi.

rub[1] [rʌb], *s.* **1.** fregata; grattata; frizione: *give that silver bowl a good* —, pulisci bene quella coppa d'argento **2.** ineguaglianza (del terreno, specialmente in un campo di bocce) **3.** impedimento; ostacolo, difficoltà; esperienza irritante: *the rubs and worries of life*, le difficoltà e le preoccupazioni della vita; *there's the* —, ecco l'ostacolo **4.** (*dial.*) cote ☆ *pleural* —, (*patol.*), sfregamento pleurico.

to **rub**[1], *pass.p.p.* **rubbed** [rʌbd], *v.t.i.* **1.** fregare, fregarsi; frizionare; strofinare: *this shoe rubs my foot*, questa scarpa mi scortica il piede; *you must have rubbed your dress against some wet paint*, devi esserti strofinato il vestito contro la vernice fresca ‖ *to* — *one's hands*, fregarsi le mani (per la soddisfazione) ‖ *to* — *shoulders with s.o.*, *fig.* entrare in contatto con qlcu. ‖ *to* — *the wrong way*, *fig.* prendere per il verso sbagliato, irritante **2.** pulire, asciugare, lustrare, lucidare fregando: *to* — *the surface dry*, asciugare una superficie strofinandola **3.** riprodurre (incisione) **4.** (*bocce*) incontrare un ostacolo che ritarda e devia il percorso della boccia **5.** scorticare, logorare (fregando) **6.** *to* — **along**, (*fam.*) arrangiarsi, cavarsela **7.** *to* — **away**, togliere fregando; cancellare **8.** *to* — **down**, strofinare, pulire fregando; massaggiare; strigliare (un cavallo) **9.** *to* — **in**, far penetrare frizionando; *fig.* imprimere bene (nella mente una lezione, ecc.): *don't* — *it in!*, (*fam.*) non insistere, ho capito! **10.** *to* — **off**, togliere fregando; cancellare **11.** *to* — **out**, togliere, cancellare con la gomma; (*sl. amer.*) uccidere **12.** *to* — **through**, (*fam.*) cavarsela con difficoltà **13.** *to* — **up**, fregare, levigare; lucidare; *fig.* rinfrescare (una nozione nella memoria): *my Latin needs to be rubbed up*, il mio latino ha bisogno di una buona rinfrescata.

rub[2], *abbr.* di **rubber**[2].

rub-a-dub ['rʌbə,dʌb], *s.* rataplan (di tamburo).

rubber[1] ['rʌbə*], *s.c.* massaggiatore, massaggiatrice ‖ *s.* **1.** strofinaccio; cancellino; gomma da cancellare **2.** (*India*) —, caucciù **3.** *pl.* (*amer.*) soprascarpe di gomma ☆ — *-cored*, (*golf*) palla con l'interno di caucciù: — *gloves*, guanti di gomma; — *neck*, (*amer.*) ficcanaso; turista: — *-neck bus*, torpedone per turisti; — *-plant*, albero della gomma; — *-solution*, mastice; — *-stamp*, timbro di gomma; — *-tyre*, pneumatico ‖ *sheet* —, gomma in fogli; *sponge* —, gomma spugna.

rubber[2], *s.* **1.** (*bridge*, ecc.) «rubber» (insieme di tre partite successive): *to have a* —, fare una partita **2.** *the* —, la bella, la partita decisiva.

to **rubberize** ['rʌbəraiz], *v.t.* gommare.

to **rubber-stamp** [,rʌbə'stæmp], *v.t.* **1.** timbrare **2.** *fig.* approvare (un progetto, ecc. senza riflettere).

rubbish ['rʌbiʃ], *s.* (*solo sing.*) **1.** rottami; macerie, calcinacci **2.** immondizie, rifiuti, scarti ‖ *a good riddance of bad* —!, Grazie a Dio ce ne siamo liberati! **3.** roba di poco conto; robaccia; *fig.* idee assurde, sciocchezze: —!, sciocchezze!; *to talk* —, dire delle

stupidaggini ☆ — *-bin*, pattumiera; — *-heap*, mucchio di spazzatura.

rubbishing ['rʌbiʃiŋ], **rubbishy** ['rʌbiʃi], *ag.* **1.** di scarto; senza valore **2.** senza senso.

rubble ['rʌbl], *s.* **1.** pietrisco; frantumi di pietra grezza; macerie **2.** pietra da sbozzare **3.** (*geol.*) breccia.

rubbly ['rʌbli], *ag.* frantumato, spezzato.

rubdown ['rʌbdaun], *s.* massaggio (dopo il bagno).

rube [ru:b], *s.* (*sl. amer.*) contadino, campagnolo, persona rozza.

rubella [ru:'belə], **rubeola** [ru:'bi:ələ], *s.* (*patol.*) rosolia.

Rubicon ['ru:bikən], *no.pr.* (*geog. st.*) Rubicone ‖ *to cross* (o. *to pass*) *the* —, *fig.* passare il Rubicone.

rubicund ['ru:bikənd], *ag.* rubicondo.

rubicundity [,ru:bi'kʌnditi], *s.* aspetto rubicondo.

rubidium [ru:(:)'bidiəm], *s.* (*chim.*) rubidio.

rubied ['ru:bid], *ag.* di color rubino.

rubiginous [ru:'bidʒinəs], *ag.* di color ruggine.

rubious ['ru:biəs], *ag.* (*poet.*) di color rubino.

rubric ['ru:brik], *s.* **1.** rubrica (anche *eccl.*) **2.** (*arc.*) rubrica, ocra rossa.

rubrical ['ru:brikəl], *ag.* di rubrica (anche *eccl.*).

to **rubricate** ['ru:brikeit], *v.t.* **1.** (*eccl.*) rubricare **2.** rubricare, provvedere di titoli in rosso.

rubrication [,ru:bri'keiʃən], *s.* **1.** (*eccl.*) rubricazione **2.** rubricazione, il provvedere di titoli in rosso.

ruby ['ru:bi], *ag.* di color rubino, rosso rubino: — *nose*, naso da avvinazzato; — *wine*, vino d'un bel rosso rubino ‖ *s.* **1.** (*min.*) rubino **2.** color rubino **3.** bitorzolo rosso **4.** (*boxe*) sangue ☆ *balas* —, rubino balascio; *spinel* —, rubino spinello.

to **ruby**, *v.t.* tingere in color rubino.

ruck[1] [rʌk], *s.* **1.** mucchio (di combustibile, cereali, ecc.) **2.** moltitudine, folla; *fig.* massa **3.** *the* —, (*ippica*) il gruppo (lasciato indietro dai vincenti).

to **ruck**[1], *v.i.* appollaiarsi; raggomitolarsi.

ruck[2], *s.* piega; arricciatura; increspatura.

to **ruck**[2], *v.t.i.*: *to* — (*up*), arricciare, arricciarsi; increspare, incresparsi; spiegazzare, spiegazzarsi.

ruckle[1] ['rʌkl], *s.* piega; arricciatura; increspatura.

to **ruckle**[1], *v.t.i.*: *to* — (*up*), arricciare, arricciarsi; increspare, incresparsi.

ruckle[2], *s.* rantolo.

to **ruckle**[2], *v.i.* rantolare.

rucksack ['ruksæk], *s.* sacco da montagna.

ruction ['rʌkʃən], *s.* (*sl.*) tumulto, disordine; lite: *there will be ructions*, vi saranno dei disordini.

rudd [rʌd], *s.* (*ittiol.*) scardola.

rudder ['rʌdə*], *s.* **1.** (*mar. aer.*) timone **2.** *fig.* guida **3.** agitatore (nella fabbricazione della birra) **4.** *pl.* penne timoniere (di uccello) ☆ — *-band*, freno del timone; — *-fish*, pesce pilota; — *-hole*, (*mar.*) losca.

rudderless ['rʌdəlis], *ag.* senza timone; senza guida; alla deriva (anche *fig.*).

ruddily ['rʌdili], *av.* con aria rubiconda; con colorito rosso.

ruddiness ['rʌdinis], *s.* aspetto rubicondo; colorito rosso.

ruddle ['rʌdl], *s.* sinopia, argilla rossa, ocra rossa.

to **ruddle**, *v.t.* marcare, colorare con ocra rossa.

ruddock ['rʌdək], *s.* (*dial.*) pettirosso.

ruddy ['rʌdi], *ag.* **1.** rubicondo; rosso **2.** rosato; roseo **3.** (*sl. volg.*) maledetto, odioso.

to **ruddy**, *v.t.i.* rendere, diventare rubicondo.

rude [ru:d], *ag.* **1.** rude, grossolano, rustico; primitivo, incolto; incivile, ineducato: — *people*, gente rozza, senza educazione **2.** grezzo, rudimentale: *a* — *tool*, un utensile rudimentale **3.** violento, aspro, brusco: *a* — *awakening*, un brusco risveglio; *a* — *passion*, una passione violenta **4.** sgarbato; impertinente; offensivo: *don't be* —, non essere scortese; *he said some* — *words*, disse delle parole insolenti; *to be* — *to s.o.*, insultare qlcu. **5.** vigoroso, florido: — *health*, salute ottima ☆ — *ore*, minerale grezzo.

rudely ['ru:dli], *av.* **1.** rozzamente, grossolanamente **2.** violentemente **3.** scortesemente; insolentemente; offensivamente.

rudeness ['ru:dnis], *s.* **1.** rozzezza; ineducazione **2.** violenza **3.** scortesia; intrattabilità, asprezza, insolenza, impertinenza.

rudiment ['ru:dimənt], *s.* **1.** *pl.* rudimenti, elementi fondamentali (di arti, scienze, ecc.) **2.** (*biol.*) rudimento (di arto, ecc.): *that animal reveals a — of a thumb*, quell'animale ha un rudimento di pollice.

rudimental [,ru:di'mentl], *ag.* (*rar.*) rudimentale.

rudimentarily [,ru:di'mentərili], *av.* rudimentalmente.

rudimentariness [,ru:di'mentərinis], *s.* carattere rudimentale.

rudimentary [,ru:di'mentəri], *ag.* (*rar.*) rudimentale.

rudish ['ru:diʃ], *ag.* alquanto rozzo, violento, scortese, insolente.

Rudolf, Rudolph ['ru:dɔlf], *no.pr.m.* Rodolfo || *Lake Rudolf*, Lago Rodolfo.

rue[1] [ru:], *s.* **1.** (*arc.*) dolore, pentimento; rammarico **2.** pietà, compassione.

to rue[1], *v.t.* pentirsi di; rammaricarsi di; rimpiangere; lamentare, deplorare.

rue[2], *s.* (*bot.*) ruta.

rueful ['ru:ful], *ag.* lamentevole, miserando, doloroso, pietoso.

ruefully ['ru:fuli], *av.* lamentevolmente; tristemente, pietosamente.

ruefulness ['ru:fulnis], *s.* tono lamentevole; tristezza; pietà.

ruff[1] [rʌf], *s.* **1.** gorgiera, lattuga **2.** collare (di uccello) **3.** (*ornit.*) piccione dal collare.

to ruff[1], *v.t.* (*rar.*) fornire di collare, gorgiera.

ruff[2], *s.* piccolo pesce persico.

ruff[3], *s.* (*carte*) il tagliare con un « atout ».

ruff[4], *s.* (*ornit.*) pavoncella pugnace.

ruff[5], *s.* (*mil.*) leggero rullo di tamburo.

to ruff[6], *v.t.i.* (*scoz.*) **1.** rullare (di tamburo); battere (il tamburo) **2.** battere i piedi in segno di applauso.

ruffian ['rʌfjən], *ag.* brutale, crudele || *s.* ribaldo.

ruffianism ['rʌfjənizəm], *s.* scelleratezza; brutalità.

ruffianly ['rʌfjənli], *ag.* scellerato, brutale.

ruffle[1] ['rʌfl], *s.* **1.** colletto, davantino, polso, guarnizione pieghettata, increspata **2.** collare (di uccello) **3.** increspatura (di acqua, superficie) **4.** sconvolgimento, turbamento; esperienza sconvolgente **5.** l'azione di fare scorrere fra le dita carte da giuoco.

to ruffle[1], *v.t.i.* **1.** increspare, incresparsi; pieghettare **2.** ornare di pieghettature, increspature **3.** sbucciarsi (la pelle) **4.** arruffare, arruffarsi (di penne); scompigliare, disordinare (capelli); drizzare le penne (di un uccello in segno d'ira) **5.** agitare, irritare; conturbare; travagliare **6.** sfogliare affrettatamente (le pagine di un libro); far scorrere velocemente (le carte da giuoco) fra le dita.

ruffle[2], *s.* **1.** tumulto, rissa; schermaglia; contesa, disputa **2.** avvenimento che turba.

to ruffle[2], *v.i.* **1.** scatenarsi, infuriare (di venti) **2.** (*arc.*) combattere, lottare, contendere **3.** (*arc.*) darsi delle arie, essere borioso.

ruffle[3], *s.* (*mil.*) leggero rullo di tamburo.

ruffler ['rʌflə*], *s.* (*arc.*) vanaglorioso; borioso, arrogante.

rufous ['ru:fəs], *ag.* rossastro; rosso bruno.

rug [rʌg], *s.* **1.** coperta (specialmente da viaggio) **2.** tappetino, pedana ☆ *bedside —*, scendiletto; *hearth —*, tappetino da camino.

Rugby ['rʌgbi], *s.* (*spor.*) « rugby », pallaovale.

rugged ['rʌgid], *ag.* **1.** ruvido, scabro, irregolare: *— features*, lineamenti irregolari **2.** ispido, irsuto; ruvido **3.** austero, inflessibile; scontroso **4.** rozzo, rude, incivile, sgarbato **5.** (*amer.*) robusto; vigoroso; ardito.

ruggedly ['rʌgidli], *av.* **1.** ruvidamente, scabrosamente, irregolarmente **2.** ispidamente **3.** austeramente; duramente **4.** rozzamente, rudemente.

ruggedness ['rʌgidnis], *s.* **1.** ruvidezza, scabrosità, irregolarità **2.** austerità **3.** durezza; asprezza; rudezza.

rugger ['rʌgə*], *s.* (*spor. fam.*) « rugby », pallaovale.

rugose ['ru:gous], *ag.* (*spec. bot.*) rugoso.

rugosely ['ru:gousli], *av.* rugosamente.

rugosity [ru:'gositi], *s.* rugosità.

rugous ['ru:gəs], *ag.* rugoso.

ruin [ruin], *s.* rovina (anche *fig.*): *the ruins of Rome*, le rovine di Roma; *this will be the — of us*, questo sarà la nostra rovina; *to bring to —*, portare alla rovina; *to go to —*, andare in rovina; *to lay a town in ruins*, distruggere completamente una città.

to ruin, *v.t.* **1.** rovinare; distruggere: *he ruined himself*, si rovinò; *to — a competitor*, far fallire un concorrente; *to — a girl*, sedurre una ragazza **2.** (*poet.*) cadere, andare in rovina.

ruinate ['ru:ineit], *ag.* (*arc.*) rovinato; in rovina.

to ruinate, *v.t.i.* (*arc.*) rovinare; distruggere.

ruination [rui'neiʃən], *s.* rovina; perdita completa.

ruined [ruind], *ag.* rovinato; in rovina.

ruiner ['ruinə*], *s.* distruttore.

ruinous ['ruinəs], *ag.* **1.** rovinoso, dannoso: *— expenses*, spese che portano in rovina; *a — flood*, un'inondazione rovinosa **2.** in rovina, in stato di rovina.

ruinously ['ruinəsli], *av.* rovinosamente.

ruinousness ['ruinəsnis], *s.* rovina; stato rovinoso.

rule [ru:l], *s.* **1.** regola, regolamento, norma, precetto: *the — of the road*, il codice della strada; *— of three*, regola del tre; *by —*, secondo le regole; *the rules of a school*, il regolamento di una scuola; *to break, to keep the rules*, infrangere, attenersi alle regole; *to make it a — to do sthg.*, farsi un dovere di fare ql.co. || *— of thumb*, regola empirica approssimativa || *hard and fast —*, regola fissa || *the exception proves the —*, (*prov.*) l'eccezione conferma la regola **2.** regola, abitudine: *as a —*, di regola, generalmente; *my rule is to have breakfast at seven o' clock*, d'abitudine faccio la prima colazione alle sette **3.** governo, regime, dominio, autorità: *many countries were under the — of Rome*, molti paesi erano sotto il dominio di Roma **4.** (*dir.*) ordinanza **5.** (*eccl.*) regola: *the — of St. Dominic*, la regola di S. Domenico **6.** riga graduata **7.** (*tip.*) filetto ☆ *foot —*, riga di circa trenta centimetri; *slide —*, regolo calcolatore *wave —*, (*tip.*) filetto ondulato.

to rule, *v.t.i.* **1.** governare, reggere; dominare: *he ruled (over) England several years*, governò sull'Inghilterra parecchi anni; *to — a country, a people*, governare una nazione, un popolo **2.** predominare: *humour rules the book*, l'umorismo predomina nel libro **3.** guidare, consigliare: *he is ruled by his brother*, è consigliato da suo fratello **4.** controllare, dirigere; regolare: *to — one's passions*, controllare le proprie passioni **5.** (*dir.*) decidere, decretare **6.** rigare, fare righe: *to — a sheet of paper*, rigare un foglio di carta **7.** (*comm.*) mantenersi a un certo livello: *prices are ruling high*, i prezzi restano elevati **8.** *to — off*, (*comm.*) chiudere, regolare (un conto) **9.** *to — out*, scartare, escludere: *possibility that cannot be ruled out*, possibilità che non si può escludere.

ruleless ['ru:llis], *ag.* senza regola, senza legge.

ruler ['ru:lə*], *s.* **1.** governatore; dominatore; sovrano; signore, padrone **2.** regolo; riga.

rulership ['ru:ləʃip], *s.* governo, dominio, sovranità.

ruling ['ru:liŋ], *ag.* dominante, dirigente; predominante: *— passion*, passione dominante; *— prices*, prezzi correnti || *s.* **1.** governo, dominio, dominazione **2.** (*dir.*) decisione, ordinanza: *the — of the chairman*, la decisione del presidente ☆ *-pen*, tiralinee.

rum[1] [rʌm], *s.* **1.** rum **2.** (*amer.*) qualsiasi liquore molto forte ☆ *-runner*, (*fam.*) contrabbandiere di alcoolici; *-running*, (*fam.*) contrabbando di alcoolici; *-shrub*, cordiale al rum.

rum[2], *ag.* (*sl.*) strano, strambo, originale; curioso: *a — customer*, un'individuo, un tipo bizzarro; *— joke*, scherzo di cattivo gusto; *a — start*, un fatto sorprendente.

Rumania [ru(:)'meinjə], *no.pr.* (*geog.*) Romania.

Rumanian [ru(:)'meinjən], *ag.* romeno ‖ *s.c.* romeno, romena ‖ *s.* lingua romena.

rumble[1] ['rʌmbl], *s.* **1.** rombo (di tuono); brontolio, rumore sordo **2.** sedile posteriore (in carrozze, ecc.).

to rumble[1], *v.t.i.* **1.** rombare; rumoreggiare **2.** brontolare (sordamente); borbottare.

to rumble[2], *v.t.* (*sl.*) scoprire; scandagliare.

rumbling ['rʌmbliŋ], *ag.* rumoreggiante; brontolante ‖ *s.* rumoreggiamento; brontolio.

rumbustious [rʌm'bʌstʃəs], *ag.* (*fam.*) turbolento.

rumen ['ru:men], *s.* rumine.

ruminant ['ru:minənt], *ag.* **1.** ruminante **2.** meditativo ‖ *s.* ruminante.

Ruminantia [ˌru:mi'nænʃiə], *s.pl.* (*zool.*) i ruminanti.

to ruminate ['ru:mineit], *v.t.i.* **1.** ruminare **2.** *fig.* ruminare, riconsiderare; meditare, ponderare.

rumination [ˌru:mi'neiʃən], *s.* **1.** ruminazione **2.** *fig.* meditazione.

ruminative ['ru:minətiv], *ag.* **1.** ruminante **2.** *fig.* meditativo.

ruminator ['ru:mineitə*], *s.* ruminante.

rummage ['rʌmidʒ], *s.* **1.** perquisizione doganale (a una nave) **2.** ricerca, rovistio **3.** (*rar.*) confusione **4.** insieme di oggetti, cianfrusaglie ☆ — *sale*, vendita di merce non ritirata (da magazzino, porto, ecc.); vendita di cianfrusaglie per beneficenza.

to rummage, *v.t.i.* **1.** frugare; rovistare; cercare buttando all'aria **2.** perquisire.

rummager ['rʌmidʒə*], *s.* perquisitore.

rummer ['rʌmə*], *s.* grosso bicchiere.

rummily ['rʌmili], *av.* (*sl.*) stranamente.

rumminess ['rʌminis], *s.* (*sl.*) stranezza.

rummy[1] ['rʌmi], *ag.* (*sl.*) strano, strambo, originale.

rummy[2], *s.* ramino (giuoco di carte).

rumness ['rʌmnis], *s.* (*sl.*) stranezza.

rumour ['ru:mə*], *s.* **1.** chiacchiera, diceria, voce: *public* —, voce pubblica **2.** (*arc.*) rumore.

to rumour, *v.t.* (*generalmente al passivo*) far correre voce, spargere la voce (su), vociferare: *it is rumoured that...*, corre voce che...; *they are rumoured to be*, si dice che essi siano, corre voce che siano.

rump [rʌmp], *s.* **1.** groppone, groppa, posteriore; estremità di coda **2.** gruppo superstite di un partito o parlamento dopo la scissione di esso ‖ *the Rump* (*Parliament*), (*st.*) i membri del « Long Parliament » che rimasero dopo l'espulsione dei Presbiteriani (1648). ☆ —*bone*, (*anat.*) coccige; — *steak*, bistecca di filetto.

rumple ['rʌmpl], *s.* **1.** piega; ruga **2.** disordine (di capelli, ecc.).

to rumple, *v.t.* **1.** spiegazzare; sciupare; sgualcire **2.** arruffare, scompigliare (capelli).

rumpless ['rʌmplis], *ag.* senza coda.

rumpus ['rʌmpəs], *s.* (*sl.*) chiasso; scompiglio; tumulto; rissa.

run [rʌn], *s.* **1.** il correre; corsa: *I went for a* —, feci una corsa ‖ *at a* —, di corsa ‖ *on the* —, in fuga; in attività: *the enemy is on the* —, il nemico batte in ritirata; *she is always on the* —, è sempre indaffarata ‖ *everything went with a* —, (*fam.*) andò tutto a gonfie vele ‖ *to break into a* —, mettersi a correre ‖ *to give s.o. a* — *for his money*, dare del filo da torcere a qlcu. ‖ *to have a* — *for one's money*, spendere bene il proprio denaro ‖ *to make a* — *at s.o.*, slanciarsi su qlcu. ‖ *to take a* — *over sthg.*, abbracciare ql.co. con uno sguardo ‖ *to take a short* —, prendere una piccola rincorsa **2.** gita, breve viaggio; giro; traversata; tragitto, percorso: *a good* —, un buon viaggio, una buona traversata; *it is a quick* — *from Edinburgh to Glasgow*, il tragitto è breve tra Edimburgo e Glasgow; *the milkman has finished his* —, il lattaio ha finito il suo giro; *they have left London for a* — *on the Continent*, sono partiti da Londra per un breve viaggio in Europa **3.** crollo (di edificio, prezzi, temperature): *prices have come down with a* —, i prezzi hanno avuto un crollo **4.** corso,

andamento; ritmo, cadenza (di versi): *the* — *of events was unusual*, gli avvenimenti si susseguirono in modo insolito; *how is the* — *of the market?*, com'è l'andamento del mercato? **5.** serie, sequela; periodo: *a* — *of bad weather*, un periodo di brutto tempo; *a* — *of five*, una sequenza di cinque (alle carte); *a* — *of luck*, una serie di eventi fortunati; un colpo di fortuna (al giuoco); *a long* — *of a play*, (*teat.*) un prolungato periodo di rappresentazione; *that play had a* — *of ninety nights*, quella commedia tenne il cartellone per novanta sere ‖ *in the long* —, a lungo andare ‖ *to have a* — *of luck*, (*fam.*) essere in vena **6.** richiesta: *a great* — *on a book*, una forte richiesta di un libro; *there was a* — *on the bank*, ci fu un forte afflusso agli sportelli della banca (per prelevare denaro) **7.** orientamento, direzione: *the* — *of a curve*, l'andamento di una curva; *the* — *of a lode*, (*miner.*) la direzione di un filone; *the* — *of the mountains*, l'orientamento delle montagne **8.** categoria, classe: *above the common* —, al di sopra della media; *the common* — *of men*, la media degli uomini **9.** recinto; pascolo; pista (di animali) **10.** branco, gregge **11.** (*fam.*) libero accesso: *he allowed me the* — *of his books*, mise i suoi libri a mia disposizione; *I had the* (*free*) — *of their house*, avevo libero accesso in casa loro ‖ *to have the* — *of one's teeth* (o *of one's knife*), mangiare gratis e a volontà **12.** rampa (di scale) **13.** conduttura (per acqua) **14.** (*cricket*) corsa (del battitore); punto **15.** (*mus.*) volata **16.** (*mec. aut.*) marcia; marcia a vuoto; percorso, corsa; deviazione: *the* — *of the rudder*, la corsa del timone **17.** (*tip.*) tiratura **18.** (*mar.*) stellato di poppa sotto la linea d'acqua **19.** (*aer.*) volo di bombardamento **20.** (*arch.*) distanza tra due alzate successive **21.** (*min.*) calcopirite **22.** (*amer.*) corso d'acqua, ruscello **23.** (*amer.*) smagliatura (di calza) ☆ — -*down*, scarico (di orologio); esaurito, debilitato (di persona); — -*off*, (*spor.*) corsa decisiva; — -*on*, (*poes.*) con « enjambement », di seguito ‖ *chicken*- —, recinto per polli; *circular* —, (*spor.*) circuito; *first* —, (*cine.*) prima; *landing* —, corsa di atterraggio; *sheep* - —, pascolo per pecore; *take-off* —, (*aer.*) corsa di decollo; *trial* —, giro di prova.

to run, *pass.* **ran** [ræn], *p.p.* **run**, *v.t.i.* **1.** correre; affrettarsi; far correre: *the child ran to meet his mother*, il bambino corse incontro a sua madre; *he ran to help him*, si precipitò in suo aiuto; *his horse ran in the Derby*, il suo cavallo partecipò al Derby; *my horse ran first*, il mio cavallo arrivò primo; *will you* — *your horse?*, farai correre il tuo cavallo?; *to* — *past s.o.*, sorpassare qlcu. correndo ‖ *the story runs that...*, si dice che... ‖ *to* — *a blockade*, forzare il blocco ‖ *to* — *a candidate*, appoggiare un candidato ‖ *to* — *a chance*, avere buone probabilità ‖ *to* — *cigarettes*, far contrabbando di sigarette ‖ *to* — *errands*, fare commissioni ‖ *to* — *foul of sthg.*, (*mar.*) entrare in collisione con ql.co.; *to* — *foul of s.o.*, avere uno scontro vivace con qlcu. ‖ *to* — *for Parliament*, presentarsi come candidato al Parlamento ‖ *to* — *a high temperature*, avere la febbre alta ‖ *to* — *in the blood* (o *in the family*), essere una caratteristica ereditaria ‖ *to* — *like a hare* (o *like blazes* o *like wild-fire* o *like the devil*), correre a gambe levate ‖ *to* — *a risk*, correre un rischio ‖ *to* — *the streets*, vivere sulla strada (di monelli) **2.** fuggire, scappare: *as soon as we fired the enemy ran*, appena aprimmo il fuoco il nemico fuggì ‖ *now let's* — *for it*, (*fam.*) ed ora battiamocela **3.** correre, andare; passare, partire; far servizio (di veicoli): *buses* — *every two, three minutes*, gli autobus passano ogni due, tre minuti; *sledges* — *on snow*, le slitte corrono sulla neve; *trains* — *at forty miles an hour*, i treni corrono a quaranta miglia all'ora; *trains running between Rome and Milan*, treni che fanno servizio tra Roma e Milano **4.** (*far*) scorrere; fluire; spandersi; versarsi; colare, gocciolare; liquefarsi; fondere; piangere (di occhi); fluire, trascorrere (di tempo): *his nose was running*, gli gocciolava il naso; *the river ran quickly*, il fiume scorreva rapidamente; *rivers running into the sea*, fiumi che sfociano nel mare; *several weeks ran smoothly*, varie settimane passarono tranquillamente; *these lines do not — well*, questi versi non sono molto scorrevoli; *this teapot runs*, questa teiera perde; *with the heat the ice began to —*, con il caldo il ghiaccio cominciò a fondersi ‖ *money runs through his fingers like water through a sieve*, (*fam.*) ha le mani bucate **5.** diventare, trasformarsi in: *my blood ran cold*, mi si agghiacciò il sangue; *the river is running dry*, il fiume sta asciugandosi; *to — high*, aumentare (di prezzo, ecc.); ingrossarsi (di mare); accendersi (di sentimento, ecc.): *words ran high*, si accese una disputa; *to — low*, diminuire, venire a mancare; *to — riot*, scatenarsi, dare in eccessi; imboschire (di piante); *to — short (of sthg.)*, finire (ql.co.): *I ran short of money*, finii il denaro **6.** estendersi; diffondersi (di notizie); spandersi (di colore); stingere: *the coast runs north and south*, la costa si estende da nord a sud; *a hedge runs round the villa*, una siepe circonda la villa; *the news ran in a few seconds*, la notizia si diffuse in pochi secondi **7.** (*mec.*) (far) funzionare: *car that can be — at small cost*, automobile economica; *the lift is running*, l'ascensore funziona **8.** far muovere; guidare; dirigere; mettere in servizio; (*mar.*) far rotta, dirigersi, veleggiare: *he ran his car into the garage*, portò l'automobile in garage; *the ship ran into the port*, la nave si diresse in porto ‖ *to — aground*, incagliare, incagliarsi **9.** gestire, dirigere, amministrare: *to — a business*, dirigere un'azienda; *to — a country*, governare un paese; *to — a school*, dirigere una scuola ‖ *to — the show*, (*sl.*) essere il capo, tenere le fila **10.** seguire; inseguire: *things must — their course*, le cose devono seguire il loro corso; *to — a fox*, cacciare la volpe; *to — to earth*, inseguire (un animale) fino alla tana; *fig.* scoprire dopo lunghe ricerche; *to — a scent*, seguire una pista; *to — s.o. close (o hard)*, incalzare, inseguire qlcu. da vicino; essere quasi alla pari con qlcu. **11.** entrare, essere in vigore; durare: *the contract will — for two more years*, il contratto sarà valido per altri due anni; *his play will — (for) several weeks*, la sua commedia terrà il cartellone per molte settimane; *the interest will — from next month*, gli interessi decorreranno dal prossimo mese **12.** passare, far passare: *he ran his fingers through his hair*, si passò le dita fra i capelli; *her eyes were running over the objects in the room*, i suoi occhi vagavano dall'uno all'altro oggetto nella stanza; *his fingers ran over the keys of the piano*, le sue dita scorrevano velocemente sui tasti del piano ‖ *to — a sword through s.o.*, trafiggere qlcu. con la spada ‖ *this tune keeps running in my head*, ho sempre in mente questo motivo; *various thoughts ran through his head*, vari pensieri attraversavano la sua mente **13.** risalire (i fiumi) (di trote, salmoni, ecc.) **14.** smagliarsi (di calze) **15.** cucire con piccoli punti **16.** suppurare (di ferita) ‖ **Seguito da prep. 17.** *to — across*, imbattersi in, incontrarsi con **18.** *to — after*, correre dietro, far la corte a **19.** *to — against*, andar contro, urtare; imbattersi in: *he ran his head against the wall*, battè il capo contro il muro (anche *fig.*) **20.** *to — at*, precipitarsi contro, assalire **21.** *to — by*, passar vicino, davanti correndo; sorpassare (un concorrente) **22.** *to — into*, incorrere; fondersi; entrare in collisione con, raggiungere: *to — into absurdity*, cadere nell'assurdo; *to — into debts*, indebitarsi, incorrere in debiti; *to — into five editions*, toccare, raggiungere la quinta edizione **23.** *to — on*, concernere, riguardare: *the talk ran on philosophy*, parlavano di filosofia **24.** *to — over*, dare una scorsa; ripassare; ricapitolare; investire; suonare rapidamente (sul pianoforte): *he was — over by a car*, fu investito da un'automobile **25.** *to — through*, sperperare (sostanze, ecc.); esaminare rapidamente; sfogliare (libro): *he ran through his notes*, diede una scorsa ai suoi appunti **26.** *to — to*, raggiungere (somma, cifra, ecc.); aver abbastanza denaro, abilità per; tendere a: *we cannot — to a winter holiday*,

non possiamo permetterci una vacanza invernale; *to — to coarseness*, aver tendenza alla volgarità; *to — to extremes*, tendere agli estremi; *to — to ruin*, andare in rovina; *to — to seed*, andare in seme (di piante) **27.** *to — upon*, imbattersi in (di persona); soffermarsi su (pensieri) ‖ **Seguito da av. 28.** *to — about*, correre qua e là **29.** *to — away*, fuggire; prender la mano (di cavallo); (*spor.*) distaccare i concorrenti ‖ *to — away with*, fuggire con la refurtiva, la persona rapita; mettersi in testa (un'idea); sperperare (denaro, ecc.); prender la mano: *he ran away with the idea that he was the best*, si era messo in testa di essere il migliore; *his imagination runs away with him*, la sua immaginazione gli prende la mano **30.** *to — by*, passare correndo; passare rapidamente (di tempo) **31.** *to — down*, (*mec.*) scaricarsi; indebolirsi; scoprire; catturare; gettare il discredito su; investire: *I am — down*, mi sento esaurito; *the police ran him down*, la polizia lo catturò; *they ran down the quotation*, trovarono infine la citazione; *to — down a ship*, colare a picco una nave; *to — down s.o. in the papers*, stroncare qlcu. attraverso i giornali **32.** *to — in*, fare una breve visita; combattere a corpo a corpo; (*fam.*) arrestare; (*fam.*) assicurare l'elezione di un candidato; (*mec.*) rodare: *to — in to see s.o.*, fare una breve visita a qlcu. **33.** *to — off*, fuggire; (far) scorrere; scrivere di getto; recitare tutto di un fiato; fare digressioni; (*tip.*) tirare (copie); (*spor.*) disputare (gare, corse, competizioni, ecc.); (*metal.*) colare: *the race will be — off on Monday*, la finale sarà disputata lunedì; *to — off a letter on a typewriter*, battere a macchina velocemente una lettera **34.** *to — on*, parlare continuamente; passare (di tempo); (*tip.*) stampare, essere stampato di seguito (senza gli a capo, ecc.); seguire il proprio corso (di malattia, ecc.); continuare a salire (di debiti) **35.** *to — out*, esaurire, esaurirsi; venire a mandare; scadere, terminare (di tempo); colare, spandersi (di liquido); perdere (di recipiente); filare (cavo, gomena); sporgere, protendersi: *to — oneself out*, esaurirsi (a forza di correre) ‖ *to — out of sthg.*, rimanere senza ql.co. **36.** *to — over*, traboccare; esaminare rapidamente; ricapitolare **37.** *to — through*, trapassare (con la spada, ecc.); cancellare (con una riga) **38.** *to — up*, (lasciar) crescere rapidamente; salire, aumentare (di prezzo); (lasciar) accumulare rapidamente (soldi, debiti, ecc.); issare, innalzare; costruire, erigere rapidamente; addizionare (cifre); rilanciare (alle aste): *the price of meat has — up a lot*, il prezzo della carne è aumentato molto ‖ *to — up against*, incontrare, imbattersi in.

runabout ['rʌnəbaut], *s.* **1.** vagabondo **2.** «spider» (vettura a due posti); motoscafo **3.** *gener. pl.* (*austral.*) bestiame allo stato brado.

runagate ['rʌnəgeit], *s.* (*arc.*) vagabondo; fuggiasco.

runaway ['rʌnəwei], *ag.* (*attributivo*) **1.** fuggiasco, fuggitivo; che prende la mano (di cavallo) **2.** fatto fuggendo; di corsa: *— knock, — ring*, bussata, scampanellata data per scherzo da persona che poi fugge; *they made a — match (o marriage)*, dopo essere fuggiti si sposarono **3.** decisivo: *— victory*, vittoria decisiva **4.** (*comm. amer.*) in rapido rialzo: *— market*, mercato in rapido rialzo ‖ *s.* **1.** fuggitivo, disertore **2.** cavallo che ha preso la mano **3.** fuga ☆ *— speed*, velocità di fuga.

runcinate ['rʌnsinit], *ag.* (*bot.*) roncinato.

rundle ['rʌndl], *s.* **1.** piuolo **2.** ruota, rotella.

rundlet ['rʌndlit], *s.* (*arc.*) barilotto.

rune [ru:n], *s.* **1.** runa, carattere runico **2.** simbolo misterioso, magico **3.** antica poesia finnica, scandinava ☆ *-staff*, bacchetta magica con iscrizioni runiche; calendario runico.

rung[1] [rʌŋ], *s.* piuolo; raggio (di ruota).

rung[2], *p.p.* di *to* **ring**.

runic ['ru:nik], *ag.* runico ‖ *s.* iscrizione runica.

run-in ['rʌnin], *ag.* inserito ‖ *s.* **1.** inserzione **2.** (*sl. amer.*) alterco, lite.

runlet[1] ['rʌnlit], *s.* (*arc.*) barilotto.

runlet², s. ruscelletto, torrentello.

runnel ['rʌnl], s. 1. ruscello, ruscelletto, rigagnolo 2. scolatoio, canaletto.

runner ['rʌnə*], s. 1. corridore 2. fattorino; messo; (mil.) staffetta; (comm.) collettore; procuratore ‖ (Bow -Street) —, (st.) ufficiale di polizia 3. (blockade-) —, forzatore di blocco, contrabbandiere 4. passatoia; striscia ornamentale (su un tavolo, ecc.) 5. smagliatura 6. (bot.) stolone, rampollo; viticcio 7. (ornit.) rallo acquatico 8. pattino di slitta; lama di pattino; (aer.) pattino 9. (mec.) guida di scorrimento; carrello; ruota 10. (metal.) canale di colata 11. (mar.) bozzello mobile 12. macina, mola 13. (amer.) macchinista di treno ☆ — -bean, fagiuolo rampicante; — -up, (spor.) finalista; buon secondo; chi è incaricato di rilanciare (ad un'asta).

running ['rʌniŋ], ag. 1. che corre, in corsa; da corsa 2. corrente (di acqua, ecc.); fluente, scorrevole (di stile) 3. continuo; regolare; consecutivo: he won three times —, vinse per tre volte consecutive 4. (mec.) in marcia, funzionante 5. purulento: — sore, ferita purulenta ‖ s. 1. il correre; corsa ‖ the — of a film, la durata di un film 2. to be in, out of the —, avere, non avere probabilità di vittoria ‖ to make the —, dare l'andatura (anche fig.) ‖ to take up the —, condurre la corsa: the father has died, and the son is taking up the —, fig. il padre è morto, e il figlio ne prenderà il posto 2. esercizio, direzione amministrativa (di albergo, ferrovia, ecc.) 3. scolo, flusso, scorrimento (d'acqua, ecc.) 4. (mec.) marcia, funzionamento 5. suppurazione 6. contrabbando ☆ — -board, (aut.) pedana; — cable, fune portante; — channel, (metal.) canale di colata; — commentary, (spor.) radiocronaca; — -cost, (ind.) costo di esercizio; — -gear, parti mobili (di una macchina); — -hand, scrittura rapida, corsiva; — horse, cavallo da corsa; — -in, (mec.) rodaggio; — -knot, nodo scorsoio; — -mate, (amer.) compagno di corsa; (fig. pol.) candidato alla meno importante di due cariche abbinate; — -on, (mec.) funzionamento ad accensione tolta; — -out, (mec.) funzionamento per inerzia; — -powers, (ferr.) diritti di passaggio; — shed, tettoia (di stazione); — -speed, velocità di funzionamento; — -track, (spor.) pista ‖ ahead, astern —, marcia avanti, indietro (di macchine, ecc.); slow —, (mec.) minimo.

Runnymede ['rʌnimid], no.pr. (geog.) Runnymede (luogo dove fu firmata la Magna Charta nel 1215).

runt [rʌnt], s. 1. razza di mucche più piccole del normale 2. animale più piccolo del normale 3. nano 4. varietà di piccione domestico 5. tronco d'albero morto.

runway ['rʌnwei], s. 1. pista, sentiero (per cui passano animali diretti ai pascoli, agli abbeveratoi) 2. pendio (lungo il quale vengono fatti scivolare i tronchi) 3. passerella (per lancio, tuffo, ecc.) 4. (mec.) rotaia, piano di scorrimento; guida di finestra 5. (aer.) pista di decollo, di atterraggio; scivolo (per idrovolanti) 6. canale.

rupee [ru:'pi:], s. rupia (moneta d'argento indiana).

rupestral [ru:'pestrəl], **rupestrine** [ru:'pestrin], ag. (bot.) rupestre, di rupe.

rupia ['ru:piə], s. (patol.) rupia.

rupicola [ru:'pikələ], s. (ornit.) rupicola.

rupture ['rʌptʃə*], s. 1. rottura (anche fig.) 2. (patol.) ernia; rottura.

to **rupture**, v.t.i. 1. rompere (relazione, matrimonio), rompersi; spezzarsi; scoppiare 2. rompere, far scoppiare (membrana, vena); provocare ernia: to — a ligament, strappare un legamento, un tendine.

rural ['ruərəl], ag. rurale, campestre, rustico: — manners, modi rustici, grossolani; — occupations, lavori campestri.

rurality [ruə'ræliti], s. rusticità.

ruralization [ˌruərəli'zeiʃən], s. ruralizzazione.

to **ruralize** ['ruərəlaiz], v.t.i. ruralizzare, ruralizzarsi.

rurally ['ruərəli], av. rusticamente.

rusa ['ru:sə], s. cervo dell'India Orientale.

ruscus ['rʌskəs], s. (bot.) rusco, pungitopo.

ruse [ru:z], s. 1. « ruse », stratagemma, astuzia, trucco 2. frode.

rush¹ [rʌʃ], s. 1. giunco, festuca; (fam.) paglia (per sedie) 2. fig. inezia; cosa di poco o nessun valore: I don't care a —, non m'importa assolutamente nulla; it is not worth a —, non vale proprio un bel niente ☆ — -bearing, festa dei giunchi (in occasione della quale si offrono giunchi e ghirlande per decorare le chiese); — candle, candela di midollo di giunco; — -like, simile a giunco; flessibile; — -ring, anello di giunco (usato come anello nuziale improvvisato).

to **rush**¹, v.t. impagliare (sedie); ricoprire di giunchi (pavimento, ecc.).

rush², s. 1. attacco, assalto; corsa precipitosa; impeto: the — of the waves, l'impeto delle onde 2. afflusso, flusso: — of blood to the head, flusso di sangue alla testa; — of people, afflusso di gente 3. (calcio, ecc.) attacco violento 4. (comm.) grande richiesta: a — for straw hats, una grande richiesta di cappelli di paglia ☆ — -hours, ore di punta ‖ gold- —, la febbre dell'oro.

to **rush**², v.t.i. 1. balzare; precipitarsi; avventarsi; scagliarsi: the soldiers rushed forward, i soldati si precipitarono innanzi; they rushed out of the room, si precipitarono fuori dalla stanza; to — to a conclusion, fig. giungere a una conclusione affrettata 2. far muovere, spostare velocemente ‖ fresh troops were rushed up to the front, truppe di rinforzo furono mandate subito in prima linea 3. scorrere impetuosamente, irrompere, affluire: the blood flushed to his face, il sangue gli affluì al viso; tears rushed to his eyes, gli salirono le lacrime agli occhi 4. forzare, trascinare: I refuse to be rushed, I must think it over, non voglio essere forzato, devo rifletterci sopra; to — s.o. into danger, trascinare qlcu. nel pericolo 5. (mil.) occupare con improvvisa irruzione: to — the enemy's trenches, irrompere nelle trincee nemiche 6. (sl.) chiedere prezzi esorbitanti: how much did they — you for this?, quanto ti hanno chiesto per questo? 7. to — up, costruire in fretta (una casa).

rushen ['rʌʃən], ag. di giunco.

rushlight ['rʌʃlait], s. 1. luce debole (come di candela di giunco) 2. fig. barlume d'intelligenza.

rushy ['rʌʃi], ag. 1. fatto di giunchi 2. folto di giunchi 3. simile a giunchi.

rusk [rʌsk], s. (fetta di) pane dolce biscottato.

Ruskinian [rʌs'kinjən], ag. di, alla maniera di John Ruskin ‖ s.c. seguace di John Ruskin.

Russ [rʌs], pl. **Russ**, **Russes** ['rʌsiz], V. **Russian**.

russet ['rʌsit], ag. 1. ruggine; rosso bruno 2. (rar.) rustico, casalingo, semplice ‖ s. 1. (st.) veste da contadino 2. color ruggine 3. mela ruggine.

russety ['rʌsiti], ag. tendente al ruggine (di colore).

Russia ['rʌʃə], no.pr. (geog.) Russia ☆ — leather, cuoio di Russia.

Russian ['rʌʃən], ag. russo ‖ s.c. russo, russa ‖ s. lingua russa ☆ White —, russo bianco.

to **Russianize** ['rʌʃənaiz], **Russify** ['rʌsifai], v.t. rendere russo.

Russophil ['rʌsoufil], **Russophile** ['rʌsoufail], ag.s. russofilo.

Russophilism [rʌ'sofilizəm], s. russofilismo.

Russophobe ['rʌsoufoub], ag.s. russofobo.

Russophobia [ˌrʌsou'foubiə], s. russofobia.

rust [rʌst], s. 1. ruggine: to get covered with —, coprirsi di ruggine 2. fig. ruggine, torpore della mente (causato da inattività) ‖ to rub the — off, togliere la ruggine; fig. rimettersi al corrente, aggiornarsi 3. ruggine (malattia delle piante) ☆ — -coloured, color ruggine; — -eaten, roso dalla ruggine; — -preventer, antiruggine; — -proof (o — -resistant), inossidabile; — red, color ruggine.

to **rust**, *v.t.i.* **1.** arrugginire, arrugginirsi; corrodere, corrodersi **2.** deteriorare, deteriorarsi; diventare inattivo: *idleness rusts the mind*, l'ozio arrugginisce la mente ‖ *better wear out than — out*, *prov.* è meglio esaurirsi lavorando che languire oziando **3.** diventare color ruggine **4.** (*bot.*) essere affetto da ruggine.

rustle ['rʌstlk], *ag.* **1.** rustico, campestre **2.** semplice; rozzo, grossolano: *— mind*, mente semplice; *— speech, manners*, linguaggio, modi rozzi **3.** grezzo, non rifinito ‖ *s.c.* campagnuolo, campagnuola; zotico, zotica.

rustically ['rʌstikəli], *av.* rusticamente; rozzamente.

to **rusticate** ['rʌstikeit], *v.t.i.* **1.** vivere in campagna; condurre una vita rustica; ritirarsi in campagna **2.** relegare, mandare in campagna **3.** rendere rustico **4.** sospendere temporaneamente (studente universitario) **5.** (*arch.*) costruire al rustico; bugnare.

rustication [ˌrʌsti'keiʃən], *s.* **1.** vita rustica, campestre **2.** espulsione temporanea (dall'università) **3.** (*arch.*) rustico; bugnato.

rusticity [rʌs'tisiti], *s.* **1.** rusticità; semplicità **2.** rozzezza, rustichezza.

rustily ['rʌstili], *av.* **1.** rugginosamente **2.** in modo antiquato.

rustiness ['rʌstinis], *s.* rugginosità, ruggine (anche *fig.*).

rustle[1] ['rʌsl], *s.* fruscio (di carta, seta, ecc.); stormire (di foglie); picchiettìo (di pioggia); mormorìo (di vento, ecc.).

to **rustle**[2], *v.t.i.* (far) frusciare (carta); (far) stormire (foglie); picchiettare (di pioggia); mormorare (di vento, ecc.).

to **rustle**[2], *v.t.i.* (*sl. amer.*) **1.** darsi da fare; affrettarsi; sbrigarsi **2.** ammassare dandosi da fare (*p. e.* quattrini) **3.** rubare (bestiame).

rustler ['rʌslə*], *s.* (*sl. amer.*) **1.** persona attiva, energica **2.** ladro di bestiame.

rustless ['rʌstlis], *ag.* **1.** senza ruggine **2.** inossidabile.

rustling ['rʌsliŋ], *ag.* frusciante; mormorante ‖ *s.* fruscìo; mormorìo.

rusty[1] ['rʌsti], *ag.* **1.** rugginoso, arrugginito (anche *fig.*): *to get —*, arrugginirsi (anche *fig.*) **2.** antiquato; vecchio (di abiti) **3.** rauco (di voce) **4.** di color ruggine, rugginoso; scolorito (di tessuti neri) **5.** (*bot.*) affetto da ruggine.

rusty[2], *ag.* (*dial.*) rancido (generalmente di lardo).

rusty[3], *ag.* **1.** ombroso (di cavallo) **2.** intrattabile, arrabbiato, offeso (di persona): *to turn* (o *to cut up*) *—*, arrabbiarsi, fare l'offeso.

rut[1] [rʌt], *s.* fregola (di animali).

to **rut**[1], *pass.p.p.* **rutted** ['rʌtid], *v.i.* essere in fregola (di animali).

rut[2], *s.* **1.** rotaia, carreggiata, solco **2.** *fig.* abitudine inveterata ‖ *to settle* (o *to sink*) *into a —*, fossilizzarsi.

to **rut**[2], *pass.p.p.* **rutted**, *v.t.* solcare.

rut[3], *s.* (*dial. amer.*) mugghio (del mare).

Ruth[1] [ru:θ], *no.pr.f.* (*Bibbia*) Ruth.

ruth[2], *s.* **1.** (*arc.*) pietà, compassione **2.** (*rar.*) pentimento; rimorso **3.** dolore, sofferenza, angoscia.

Ruthenian [ru(:)'θi:njən], *ag.* rutenico, dei ruteni ‖ *s.c.* ruteno, rutena ‖ *s.* lingua rutenica.

ruthenium [ru(:)'θi:njəm], *s.* (*chim.*) rutenio.

rutherford ['rʌðəfəd], *s.* (*fis.*) rutherford (unità di misura della forza radioattiva).

ruthless ['ru:θlis], *ag.* spietato, crudele, duro, inumano.

ruthlessly ['ru:θlisli], *av.* spietatamente, crudelmente.

ruthlessness ['ru:θlisnis], *s.* crudeltà.

rutty ['rʌti], *ag.* pieno di solchi (di strada).

rye [rai], *s.* **1.** (*bot.*) segale **2.** *— -(whisky)*, (*fam.*) whisky ottenuto dalla segale ☆ *— -bread*, pane di segale; *— -grass*, (*bot.*) loglio.

ryot ['raiət], *s.* (*ang.-in.*) contadino, coltivatore della terra.

Ryukyu Islands [ri'u:kju:'ailəndz], *no.pr.* (*geog.*) isole Ryukyu.

S

s [es], *pl.* ss, s's ['esiz], *s.* 1. (*diciannovesima lettera dell'alfabeto inglese*) s ‖ — *for sugar*, (*tel.*) s come Savona 2. (*usato come att.*) s: *an — sofa*, un divano a forma di s.
s., *abbr.* di shilling(s), second(s).
S., *abbr.* di south.
's, 1. (*usato per formare il caso poss. dei s. sing. e pl. irregolari*): *boy's*, del ragazzo; *men's* degli uomini; *St. James's Park*, il parco di St. James 2. (*usato per indicare il pl. di numeri, lettere, nomi propri*): *5's, t's, the Mary's*, i 5, le t, le Marie 3. (*fam.*) *abbr.* di *is, has, us*: *he's here*, egli è qui; *he's written*, egli ha scritto; *let's go*, andiamocene; *what's your name?*, come vi chiamate?.
Saar [za:*], *no.pr.* (*geog.*) Saar.
sabadilla [ˌsæbə'dilə], *s.* (*bot.*) sabadiglia.
Sabaean [sə'bi(:)ən], *ag.s.* (*st.*) sabeo.
Sabaism ['seibiizəm], *s.* (*st. relig.*) sabeismo.
Sabaoth [sæ'beiɔθ], *s.* (*Bibbia*) Sabaot(h), esercito: *the Lord of* —, il Dio Sabaoth, degli eserciti.
Sabbatarian [ˌsæbə'tɛəriən], (*teol. Bibbia*) *ag.* sabatino ‖ *s.* sabatario.
Sabbatarianism [ˌsæbə'tɛəriənizəm], *s.* (*teol. Bibbia*) pratica, dottrina dei sabatari.
Sabbath ['sæbəθ], *s.* 1. il settimo giorno della settimana dedicato al riposo (sabato per gli ebrei, domenica per i cristiani): *to keep, to break the* —, osservare, non osservare il sabato 2. *fig.* periodo di riposo 3. (*witches'*) —, sabba ☆ — *-day's journey*, (*relig. ebraica*) viaggio permesso il sabato; *fig.* viaggio breve; — *-school*, oratorio festivo.
sabbatic(al) [sə'bætik(əl)], *ag.* sabatico: — *year*, (*biblico*) anno sabatico (nelle scuole) ‖ — *leave*, congedo concesso ogni sette anni ai professori delle università di alcuni paesi anglosassoni per studi, ricerche di aggiornamento.
Sabean [sə'bi(:)ən], *ag.s.* (*st.*) sabeo.
Sabellian¹ [sə'beliən], *ag.s.* (*st.*) sabellico.
Sabellian², *ag.s.* (*teol.*) sabelliano.
saber, (*amer.*) per sabre.
Sabian ['seibiən], *ag.s.* (*st. relig.*) sabeo.
Sabina [sə'bainə], Sabine¹ ['sæbin], *no.pr.f.* Sabina, Savina.
Sabine² ['sæbain], *ag.* (*st.*) sabino ‖ *s.c.* sabino, sabina.
sable ['seibl], *ag.* 1. di zibellino 2. (*poet. ret.*) oscuro, fosco, nero ‖ *s.* 1. zibellino; pelliccia di zibellino 2. (*art.*) pennello (di martora) 3. (*arald.*) colore nero 4. *pl.* abiti da lutto ☆ — *antelope*, antilope nera; — *-coloured*, dai colori scuri, foschi.
to sable, *v.t.* (*arc.*) 1. oscurare, offuscare 2. vestire a lutto.
sabot ['sæbou], *s.* zoccolo.
sabotage ['sæbətɑ:ʒ], *s.* sabotaggio.
to sabotage, *v.t.i.* sabotare; compiere atti di sabotaggio (anche *fig.*).
saboteur [ˌsæbə'tə:*], *s.c.* sabotatore, sabotatrice.
Sabra ['seibrə], *s.c.* (*neol.*) nativo, nativa del nuovo Stato di Israele.
sabre ['seibə*], *s.* 1. sciabola 2. *pl.* unità di cavalleria ☆ — *-cut*, sciabolata; cicatrice da sciabolata; — *-rattling*, spacconate; minacce di guerra.
to sabre, *v.t.* sciabolare, colpire, ferire con la sciabola.
sabretache ['sæbətæʃ], *s.* (*mil.*) giberna (di ufficiale di cavalleria).
sabulous ['sæbjuləs], *ag.* 1. sabbioso; arenoso 2. (*med.*) sabbioso, granuloso.

saburra [sə'bə:rə], *s.* (*patol.*) saburra.
saburration [ˌsæbə'reiʃən], *s.* (*med.*) sabbiatura.
sac [sæk], *s.* (*anat. bot. zool.*) sacco.
saccate ['sækeit], *ag.* (*bot.*) a forma di sacco; contenuto in un sacco.
sacchariferous [ˌsækə'rifərəs], *ag.* saccarifero.
saccharification [sə,kærifi'keiʃən], *s.* saccarificazione.
saccharin(e) ['sækərin], *s.* saccarina.
saccharine ['sækərain], *ag.* saccarino, zuccherino.
saccharoid ['sækərɔid], *ag. s.* saccaroide.
saccharometer [ˌsækə'rɔmitə*], *s.* saccarometro.
saccharose ['sækərous], *s.* saccarosio.
saccharous ['sækərəs], *ag.* saccarifero, che contiene zucchero.
sacciform ['sæksifɔ:m], *ag.* sacciforme, a forma di sacco, di sacca.
saccular ['sækjulə*], *ag.* (*anat.*) sacciforme ☆ — *gland*, ghiandola acinosa.
saccule ['sækju:l], *s.* (*anat.*) sacculo, piccolo sacco.
sacerdocy ['sæsə,dousi], *s.* (*rar.*) sacerdozio.
sacerdotage ['sæsə,doutidʒ], *s.* (*scherz.*) condizione sacerdotale, sacerdozio.
sacerdotal [ˌsæsə'doutl], *ag.* sacerdotale.
sacerdotalism [ˌsæsə'doutəlizəm], *s.* 1. sacerdozio 2. dottrina, credenza che il sacerdozio assicuri speciali diritti e poteri.
sacerdotally [ˌsæsə'doutəli], *av.* sacerdotalmente.
sachem ['seitʃəm], *s.* 1. capo pellirossa 2. *fig.* personaggio importante.
sachet ['sæʃei], *s.* sacchetto profumato (per biancheria).
sack¹ [sæk], *s.* 1. sacco 2. « sack » (misura di capacità variabile) 3. (*sl.*) congedo, licenziamento: *to get the* —, essere licenziato, congedato; *to give s.o. the* —, licenziare qlcu. 4. (*sl. amer.*) sacco a pelo; letto 5. (*baseball*) base ☆ — *duty* (o — *time*), (*sl. amer.*) ore di riposo; — *-race*, corsa nei sacchi.
to sack¹, *v.t.* 1. insaccare 2. (*sl.*) licenziare, congedare 3. (*sl.*) sconfiggere in una gara.
sack², *s.* (*mil.*) sacco, saccheggio: *to put to* —, saccheggiare.
to sack², *v.t.* 1. (*mil.*) saccheggiare, mettere a sacco 2. spogliare dei beni.
sack³, *s.* vino bianco delle Canarie, della Spagna.
sack⁴, *s.* soprabito a sacco; (*neol.*) vestito a sacco.
sackbut ['sækbʌt], *s.* (*arc.*) trombone.
sackcloth ['sæk-klɔθ], *s.* tela da sacco; panno ruvido ‖ *in* — *and ashes*, vestito di sacco e col capo cosparso di cenere.
sacker¹ ['sækə*], *s.c.* 1. chi fabbrica sacchi 2. chi riempie sacchi.
sacker², *s.* saccheggiatore.
sackful ['sækful], *s.* saccata, il contenuto di un sacco.
sacking¹ ['sækiŋ], *s.* 1. insaccamento 2. tela da sacco, iuta.
sacking², *s.* saccheggio.
sackless ['sæklis], *ag.* (*arc. scoz.*) innocente; innocuo; sciocco.
sacral¹ ['seikrəl], *ag.* (*anat.*) sacro.
sacral², *ag.* rituale.
sacrament ['sækrəmənt], *s.* 1. sacramento: *to administer the last Sacraments to s.o.*, somministrare gli ultimi Sacramenti a qlcu.; *to receive the Sacrament*, ri-

cevere i Sacramenti **2.** cosa misteriosa di significato sacro; simbolo sacro **3.** giuramento.

to sacrament ['sækrəmənt], *v.t.* vincolare con giuramento.

sacramental [,sækrə'mentl], *ag.* sacramentale ‖ *s.pl.* sacramentali.

sacramentally [,sækrə'mentəli], *av.* sacramentalmente.

sacramentarian [,sækrəmən'tɛəriən], *ag. s.* (*st. relig.*) sacramentario.

sacramentarianism [,sækrəmən'tɛəriənizəm], *s.* (*st. relig.*) dottrina dei sacramentari.

sacrarium [sə'krɛəriəm], *pl.* **sacraria** [sə'krɛəriə], *s.* (*st. romana, eccl.*) sacrario.

sacred ['seikrid], *ag.* **1.** sacro; religioso: — *book*, libro sacro; — *music*, musica sacra ‖ *the — orders*, gli ordini sacri **2.** inviolabile; sacrosanto: *a — duty*, un dovere sacro **3.** consacrato, dedicato: — *to the memory of*, dedicato alla memoria di.

sacredly ['seikridli], *av.* **1.** in modo sacro **2.** inviolabilmente.

sacredness ['seikridnis], *s.* **1.** santità; carattere sacro (di luogo, ecc.) **2.** inviolabilità (di giuramento).

sacrifice ['sækrifais], *s.* **1.** sacrificio, olocausto: *a sheep was offered (up) as a —*, una pecora venne offerta in sacrificio ‖ *the Sacrifice of the Mass*, il sacrificio della Messa **2.** sacrificio; rinuncia, abnegazione: *she showed a spirit of —*, ella mostrò spirito di abnegazione ‖ *the last —*, il sacrificio della vita **3.** (*comm.*) perdita, svendita: *to sell sthg. at a —*, svendere ql.co.

to sacrifice, *v.t.i.* **1.** sacrificare, immolare: *he sacrificed an ox to the god*, egli immolò un bue al dio **2.** sacrificare; rinunziare a: *he sacrificed himself for his country*, egli si sacrificò per il suo paese; *he sacrificed his life to save the drowning child*, egli sacrificò la sua vita per salvare il bambino che annegava **3.** (*comm.*) svendere.

sacrificer ['sækrifaisə*], *s.* sacrificatore (generalmente sacerdote).

sacrificial [,sækri'fiʃəl], *ag.* **1.** propiziatorio; espiatorio **2.** (*comm.*) sottocosto.

sacrificially [,sækri'fiʃəli], *av.* in modo espiatorio.

sacrilege ['sækrilidʒ], *s.* sacrilegio.

sacrilegious [,sækri'lidʒəs], *ag.* sacrilego.

sacrilegiously [,sækri'lidʒəsli], *av.* sacrilegamente.

sacrilegist [sækri'lidʒist], *s.* (*rar.*) sacrilego.

sacring ['seikriŋ], *s.* (*eccl.*) consacrazione (durante la Messa; di vescovi, ecc.) ☆ — *-bell*, campanello della elevazione.

sacrist ['seikrist], **sacristan** ['sækristən], *s.* (*eccl.*) sagrestano.

sacristy ['sækristi], *s.* (*eccl.*) sagrestia.

sacrosanct ['sækrousæŋkt], *ag.* sacrosanto, inviolabile.

sacrosanctity [,sækrou'sæŋktiti], *s.* inviolabilità; santità.

sacrosanctly ['sækrousæŋktli], *av.* sacrosantamente.

sacrum ['seikrəm], *pl.* **sacra** ['seikrə], *s.* (*anat.*) osso sacro.

sad [sæd], *ag.* **1.** triste, mesto; lugubre, fosco, grave: *to become* (o *to grow*) —, rattristarsi; *to make s.o.* —, rattristare qlcu. ‖ *a sadder and a wiser man*, un uomo disilluso ‖ *in — earnest*, assai seriamente **2.** opaco, smorto, neutro (di colore) **3.** deplorevole, brutto, incorreggibile: *a — fellow*, un povero diavolo, un tristo; *his last book is — stuff*, il suo ultimo libro fa pietà; *to make a — mistake*, commettere un errore deplorevole ‖ *a — dog*, uno scapestrato **4.** (*dial.*) mal lievitato (di pane, pasta) ☆ — *-eyed*, dallo sguardo triste; — *-iron*, pesante ferro da stiro.

to sadden ['sædn], *v.t.i.* **1.** rattristare, rattristarsi **2.** scolorire.

saddish ['sædiʃ], *ag.* alquanto triste; piuttosto fosco, grave, lugubre.

saddle ['sædl], *s.* **1.** sella; sellino (di bicicletta,

ecc.): *to be in the —*, essere in sella; *to get into the — again*, rimettersi in sella (anche *fig. fam.*); *to vault into the —*, balzare in sella ‖ *to put the — on the right* (*wrong*) *horse*, criticare o biasimare una persona giustamente (ingiustamente) **2.** (*geog.*) giogaia, sella (di monte) **3.** (*geol.*) anticlinale **4.** (*cuc.*) sella (di montone, ecc.) **5.** (*mec.*) cannello; bilanciere; bietta a forma di U; testa mobile ☆ — *-bag*, bisaccia da sella; « moquette »; — *-cloth*, gualdrappa; — *-horse*, cavallo da sella; — *-joint*, (*anat.*) articolazione a sella; — *-nose*, naso a sella; — *-roof*, tetto a due falde; — *-room*, selleria (locale della scuderia in cui si ripongono i finimenti); — *-sore*, malandato dalla sella ‖ *hunting —*, sella all'inglese; *side —* (o *lady's —*), sella da donna: *to ride side —*, cavalcare all'amazzone.

to saddle, *v.t.* **1.** sellare; mettere la sella a **2.** *fig.* gravare, caricare: *to — s.o. with sthg.*, *to — sthg. on s.o.*, addossare ql.co. a qlcu., gravare qlcu. di ql.co.

saddleback ['sædlbæk], *s.* **1.** (*edil.*) tetto a schiena d'asino **2.** (*geog.*) sella **3.** (*geol.*) sella anticlinale **4.** (*zool.*) animale, insetto dal dorso ricurvo **5.** (*patol.*) lordosi.

saddlebacked ['sædlbækt], *ag.* a schiena d'asino.

saddler ['sædlə*], *s.* **1.** sellaio **2.** (*amer.*) cavallo da sella.

saddlery ['sædləri], *s.* **1.** selleria **2.** (*fam.*) oggetti di selleria **3.** arte del sellaio.

saddling ['sædliŋ], *s.* sellatura.

Sadducean [,sædju'si:ən],. *ag. s.* (*st.*) sadduceo.

Sadducee ['sædjusi:], *s.c* (*st.*) sadduceo, sadducea.

sadism ['sædizəm], *s.* sadismo.

sadistic [sæ'distik], *ag.* sadico.

sadly ['sædli], *av.* **1.** tristemente, mestamente **2.** deplorevolmente; miseramente, meschinamente **3.** gravemente; eccessivamente; molto: *I need it —*, ne ho un grande bisogno; *to be — afraid*, aver gran timore.

sadness ['sædnis], *s.* tristezza, mestizia, melanconia: *in —*, seriamente.

safari [sə'fɑ:ri], *s.* partita di caccia (in Africa).

safe [seif], *ag.* **1.** sicuro, al riparo: *at last we are —*, infine siamo al sicuro; *the money is — in your hands*, il denaro è al sicuro in mano tua ‖ *— as the Bank of England* (o *— as houses*), (*fam.*) sicurissimo **2.** salvo; intatto: *his honour is —*, il suo onore è salvo; *I saw her — home*, la riaccompagnai a casa sana e salva; *the parcel came —*, il pacco arrivò intatto ‖ *— and sound*, sano e salvo **3.** innocuo: *a murderer is only — when he is in prison*, un omicida è innocuo solo quando è in prigione **4.** cauto, prudente: *he is a — judge of man*, egli è cauto nel giudicare gli uomini; *is it — to leave him alone?*, è prudente lasciarlo solo?; *she kept at a — distance from the dog*, ella si tenne a una rispettosa distanza dal cane ‖ *to be on the — side*, mantenersi cauto, tenere un margine di sicurezza **5.** fido, fidato: *a — friend is better than a clever one*, un amico fidato è meglio di un amico intelligente **6.** certo: *she is — to get that job*, è certa che avrà quel lavoro.

safe, *s.* **1.** cassaforte; scrigno **2.** credenza; ghiacciaia **3.** (*armi*) sicura: *rifle* (*set*) *at —*, carabina in posizione di sicura, di sicurezza.

safe, (*nei composti*): — *-conduct*, salvacondotto; — *-deposit*, cassetta di sicurezza; — *-keeping*, buona guardia, custodia.

safeguard ['seifgɑ:d], *s.* salvaguardia; scorta.

to safeguard, *v.t.* salvaguardare, difendere, proteggere: *to be safeguarded against*, essere al riparo da.

safely ['seifli], *av.* **1.** sicuramente, senza pericolo, senza incidenti **2.** in salvo, in luogo sicuro.

safeness ['seifnis], *s.* **1.** sicurezza, certezza **2.** solidità (anche *fig.*).

safety ['seifti], *s.* sicurezza; salvezza; scampo: *for —'s sake*, per maggior sicurezza; *in —*, in salvo; *to seek — in flight*, cercar scampo nella fuga; — *first!*, prudenza innanzitutto! ‖ *Committee of Public Safety*, (*stor.*) Comitato di Salute Pubblica ☆ — *-appliance*, dispositivo di sicurezza; — *-belt*, cintura di sicurezza, di salvataggio; — *-bolt*, sicura (di arma da fuoco);

— -*catch*, arresto di sicurezza; — *device*, dispositivo di sicurezza; — *factor*, coefficiente di sicurezza; — -*glass*, vetro di sicurezza; — -*hook*, moschettone; — -*island*, salvagente (stradale); — -*lamp*, lampada di sicurezza; — -*lock*, serratura di sicurezza; — -*match*, fiammifero svedese; — -*pin*, spilla di sicurezza, da balia; — -*stop*, dispositivo di arresto, arresto di sicurezza; — -*valve*, valvola di sicurezza (anche *fig.*).

saffian ['sæfiən], *s.* pelle di pecora, di capra conciata col sommacco e colorata vivacemente.

safflower ['sæflauə*], *s.* **1.** (*bot.*) cartamo **2.** (*chim.*) cartamina.

saffron ['sæfrən], *ag.* di color zafferano || *s.* zafferano.

to **saffron**, *v.t.* colorire, cospargere di zafferano.

saffrony ['sæfrəni], *ag.* (*rar.*) dal colore di zafferano.

safranin, safranine ['sæfrənin], *s.* **1.** (*chim.*) safranina **2.** colore rosso-giallastro.

sag [sæg], *s.* **1.** abbassamento; ripiegamento **2.** (*comm.*) diminuzione, flessione dei prezzi **3.** (*ing.*) cedimento; cunetta (nella strada) **4.** (*mar.*) scarroccio **5.** (*aer.*) insellamento (cedimento centrale dell'asse longitudinale).

to **sag**, *pass. p.p.* **sagged** [sægd], *v.t.i.* **1.** piegarsi; chinarsi; curvarsi; abbassarsi; cedere sotto il peso **2.** (*amer.*) indebolirsi **3.** (*comm.*) cedere (di prezzi) **4.** far curvare, curvarsi al centro **5.** *to* — *to leeward*, (*mar.*) andare alla deriva, a scarroccio.

saga ['sɑːgə], *s.* **1.** saga; epica medievale **2.** serie di libri che trattano di una stessa famiglia; romanzo fiume.

sagacious [sə'geiʃəs], *ag.* acuto, perspicace; sagace.

sagaciously [sə'geiʃəsli], *av.* acutamente, perspicacemente; sottilmente; sagacemente.

sagaciousness [sə'geiʃəsnis], **sagacity** [sə'gæsiti], *s.* sagacia, perspicacia.

sagamore ['sægəmɔ:*], *s.* capo di tribù pellirosse.

sagapenum [,sægə'pi:nəm], *s.* (*bot.*) sagapeno.

sage[1] [seidʒ], *s.* (*bot.*) salvia ☆ — -*cheese*, formaggio inglese aromatizzato con salvia; — -*cock* (o -*grouse*), gallinaceo del Nord America; — -*green*, color grigioverde; — -*rabbit*, leprotto del Nord America; — -*tea*, decotto di foglie di salvia (usato come tonico).

sage[2], *ag.* saggio; sapiente, colto, esperto || *s.* saggio, dotto, sapiente dell'antichità: *one of the seven sages*, uno dei sette savi.

sagely ['seidʒli], *av.* saggiamente.

sageness ['seidʒnis], *s.* **1.** saggezza **2.** prudenza; discrezione.

saggar ['sægə*], *s.* **1.** recipiente di argilla (usato nella cottura della porcellana) **2.** (*metal.*) cassetta di cementazione.

sagging ['sægiŋ], *s.* **1.** cedimento; abbassamento; curvatura; inclinazione **2.** diminuzione (di prezzi) **3.** (*mar.*) scarroccio.

saggy ['sægi], *ag.* curvato; avvallato; piegato.

Sagitta [sə'ɡitə], *no.pr.* (*astr.*) Sagitta (piccola costellazione nordica).

Sagittarius [,sædʒi'tɛəriəs], *no.pr.* (*astr.*) Sagittario.

sagittary ['sædʒitəri], *ag.* (*arc.*) sagittario, simile a freccia || *s.* **1.** (*mit.*) centauro **2.** arciere.

sagittate ['sædʒiteit], *ag.* (*bot.*) sagittario, a forma di freccia.

sago ['seigou], *s.* sago, sagù (fecola estratta dal midollo di palme delle Indie Orientali).

sagum ['seigəm], *pl.* **saga** ['seigə], *s.* (*st. romana*) mantello dei soldati romani.

sagy ['seidʒi], *ag.* aromatizzato con salvia.

Sahara [sə'hɑːrə], *no.pr.* (*geog.*) Sahara.

Sahib ['sɑːhib], *s.* (*ang.-in.*) signore (titolo per indicare un europeo).

sai ['sɑːi], *s.* scimmia cappuccina.

saic, saick [sɑː'iːk], *s.* (*mar.*) saica.

said [sed], *pass.p.p.* di to *say*.

saiga ['saigə], *s.* (*zool.*) saiga.

sail[1] [seil], *s.* **1.** (*mar.*) vela; *coll.* velatura: *full* —, a vele spiegate; *to crowd all sails*, far forza di vele; *to*

hoist, to lower a —, issare, abbassare una vela; *to make more* —, aumentare la velatura; *to set* —, spiegare le vele, salpare; *to strike* —, ammainare le vele, *fig.* abbassare le pretese **2.** qualsiasi tipo d'imbarcazione a vela; *coll.* velieri: *a fleet of thirty* —, una flotta di trenta velieri || — *ho!*, nave in vista! **3.** ala, pala (di mulino) **4.** larga pinna dorsale (di pesce) ☆ — -*axle*, asse d'ala; — -*boat*, (*amer.*) barca a vela; — -*cloth*, tela di olona, tela per vele; — -*flying*, (*aer.*) volo a vela; — -*loft*, veleria; — -*maker*, velaio; — -*match*, regata; — -*room*, magazzino, deposito vele || *fore-and-aft* —, vela aurica, di taglio; *fore royal studding-* —, coltellaccio di controvelaccino; *fore-top gallant* —, velaccino; *fore-topmast studding* —, coltellaccio di parrocchetto; *main* —, vela di maestra; *main-royal studding-* —, coltellaccio di controvelaccio; *main-topgallant* —, velaccio; *main-topmast studding-* —, coltellaccio di gabbia; *mizzen-* —, mezzana; *mizzen-topgallant* —, belvedere; *square-* —, vela quadra; *studding-* —, coltellaccio.

to **sail**[1], *v.t.i.* **1.** veleggiare; navigare; costeggiare; muovere, muoversi sull'acqua: *to* — *against the wind*, andar contro corrente (anche *fig.*); *to* — *along a headland*, costeggiare un promontorio; *to* — *before the wind*, navigare col vento in poppa; *to* — *close* (o *near*) *to the wind*, navigare controvento, orzare; *fig.* rasentare il precipizio **2.** salpare, far vela; iniziare un viaggio: *we* — *next week*, salpiamo la settimana prossima **3.** volare; veleggiare (di uccelli, nubi, ecc.) **4.** incedere (specialmente di donna) **5.** sorvolare: *the plane sailed over the city*, l'aereo sorvolò la città; *to* — *the Pacific Ocean*, sorvolare l'Oceano Pacifico **6.** controllare la navigazione di **7.** *to* — *into* (*s.o.*, *sthg.*), (*sl.*) rimproverare, inveire contro **8.** *to* — *in*, *fig.* iniziare (ql.co.) con energia.

sail[2], *s.* **1.** gita, escursione su imbarcazione a vela: *to go for a* —, fare una gita in barca a vela **2.** durata di traversata (per mare): *it's an hour's* — *from Dover to Calais*, la traversata da Dover a Calais dura un'ora.

sailable ['seiləbl], *ag.* navigabile.

sailer ['seilə*], *s.* veliero; nave.

sailing ['seiliŋ], *s.* **1.** navigazione, traversata: *fast* —, navigazione veloce || *it's all plain* —, (*fam.*) la cosa va da sè, la faccenda non fa una grinza **2.** partenza (di navi): *list of sailings*, elenco delle partenze ☆ — *master*, ufficiale di rotta; — *orders*, istruzioni per le partenze.

sailless ['seillis], *ag.* senza vele.

sailor ['seilə*], *s.* marinaio, navigatore || —*'s home*, casa del marinaio || —*'s knot*, nodo da marinaio || *are you a good or a bad* —?, soffri o no il mal di mare? ☆ — -*blouse*, blusa alla marinara; — -*hat*, cappello alla marinara.

sailorly ['seiləli], *ag.* da marinaio, alla marinara.

sailplane ['seil-plein], *s.* (*aer.*) aliante, veleggiatore.

to **sain** [sein], *v.t.* **1.** (*arc.*) fare il segno della Croce, benedire **2.** guarire, risanare.

sainfoin ['sæn-foin], *s.* (*bot.*) trifoglio; lupinella.

saint [seint (*forma forte*), sənt, snt (*forme deboli*)], *ag.* **1.** (*abbr.* St.) San, Santo: *St. Michael*, San Michele; *St. Paul's*, la cattedrale di S. Paolo a Londra || *St. Anthony's fire*, (*patol.*) il fuoco di Sant'Antonio, erisipela || *St. Bernard*, cane San Bernardo || *St. Elmo's fire*, (*mar.*) fuoco di Sant'Elmo || *St. Vitus's dance*, (*patol.*) ballo di San Vito || *to keep St. Monday*, celebrare il lunedì del barbiere, prendersi vacanza **2.** santo; sacro; benedetto || *s.* santo (canonizzato): *to live like a* —, vivere da santo; *to provoke* (o *to try*) *the patience of a* —, (*fam.*) far scappare la pazienza ad un santo || *All Saints' day*, Ognissanti || *patron* —, santo patrono || *young saints old devils*, *prov.* chi non fa pazzie in gioventù le fa in vecchiaia.

to **saint**, *v.t.* canonizzare, santificare || *to* — *it*, fare il santo.

saintdom ['seintdəm], *s.* santità.

sainted ['seintid], *ag.* **1.** santo; canonizzato, santificato **2.** consacrato; sacro (di luogo).

sainthood ['seinthud], *s.* santità ‖ *the* —, i santi.

saintlike ['seintlaik], *ag.* da, simile a santo.

saintliness ['seintlinis], *s.* santità.

saintling ['seintliŋ], *s.c.* (*iron.*) bacchettone; santarellina; beghina.

saintly ['seintli], *ag.* santo; di, da santo: *he lived a* — *life*, visse da santo; *she puts on such a* — *air!*, (*iron.*) prende certe arie da santarellina!.

saith [seθ], (*arc.*) 3ª *persona sing. pres.* di to **say.**

Saitic [sei'itik], *ag.* saitico, di Sais.

sajou [sə'dʒu:], *s.* scimmia cappuccina.

sake [seik], *s.* amore; interesse; beneficio; causa; riguardo; rispetto: *for his own* —, nel suo interesse; *he didn't do it for her* —, non lo fece per riguardo verso di lei; *she saved money for the* — *of her family*, risparmiò del denaro per il bene della sua famiglia ‖ *art for art's* —, l'arte per l'arte; *for any* —, (*arc.*) a tutti i costi; *for God's* (o *for goodness*) —, per l'amor di Dio; *for old times'* — (o *for old* —'s —), in ricordo del passato.

saké ['sɑ:ki], *s.* sakè (bevanda alcoolica giapponese tratta dal riso).

saker ['seikə*], *s.* **1.** (*ornit.*) sagro (specialmente femmina) **2.** (*artigl.*) sagro, falconetto.

sakeret ['seikərit], *s.* (*ornit.*) sagro maschio.

saki ['sɑ:ki], *s.* (*zool.*) pitecia.

sal¹ [sɑ:l], *s.* **1.** albero dell'India da cui si ricava un legno pregiato («shorea robusta») **2.** legno del medesimo.

sal² [sæl], *s.* (*arc. chim. farm.*) sale ☆ — *ammoniaca*, cloruro d'ammonio; — *soda*, carbonato di sodio.

Sal, *no.pr.f. dim.* di **Sarah.**

salaam [sə'lɑ:m], *s.* riverenza, salamelecco, inchino (saluto orientale).

to salaam, *v.t.i.* fare salamelecchi; far riverenze.

salability [ˌseilə'biliti], *s.* facilità di smercio.

salable ['seiləbl], *ag.* vendibile, che si vende, commerciabile.

salacious [sə'leiʃəs], *ag.* salace; lascivo, lussurioso, sensuale.

salaciously [sə'leiʃəsli], *av.* salacemente.

salaciousness [sə'leiʃəsnis], **salacity** [sə'læsiti], *s.* salacità; lubricità; lascivia, dissolutezza.

salad ['sæləd], *s.* insalata ☆ — *-bowl*, insalatiera; — *days*, (*fam.*) inesperienza giovanile; — *-dressing*, salsa per condire l'insalata; — *-oil*, olio da tavola ‖ *fruit* —, macedonia di frutta.

salamander ['sæləˌmændə*], *s.* **1.** (*zool.*) salamandra **2.** chi sopporta ed ama il calore **3.** graticola, piastra.

salamandrian [ˌsælə'mændriən], **salamandrine** [ˌsælə'mændrin], *ag.* **1.** simile a salamandra **2.** *fig.* insensibile al fuoco.

salangane ['sæləŋgein], *s.* (*ornit.*) salangana.

salariat [sə'lɛəriət], *s.* classi stipendiate.

salaried ['sælərid], *ag.* stipendiato; retribuito ☆ *high* —, ben retribuito: *a high-* — *official*, un funzionario ben retribuito.

salary ['sæləri], *s.* stipendio; mensile.

to salary, *v.t.* stipendiare.

sale [seil], *s.* **1.** vendita: *bill of* — (o *of sales*), fattura; *conditions of* —, (*comm.*) condizioni di vendita; *sales are up, down this year*, si vendono più, meno merci quest'anno; *will there be any* — *for these tiger skins?*, vi sarà qualche possibilità di vendere queste pelli di tigre? *on* (o *for*) —, in vendita: *to set* (o *to put*) *up thg. for* —, mettere ql.co. in vendita **2.** asta, vendita all'incanto: — *by auction*, vendita all'asta; *there will be a* — *of all the furniture in this house*, tutto il mobilio di questa casa sarà venduto all'asta; *to put up for* —, offrire all'asta **3.** liquidazione, svendita, saldo ☆ *sales-clerk*, (*amer.*) commesso; — *-goods*, merci in liquidazione; — *price*, prezzo di liquidazione; — *-ring*, il cerchio dei compratori intorno al

banditore; — *-room*, sala di vendite all'asta ‖ *bargain* —, fiera del bianco.

salep ['sæləp], *s.* (*farm.*) salep.

salesgirl ['seilzgə:l], *s.* commessa.

salesman, *pl.* **salesmen** ['seilzmən], *s.* **1.** venditore, commesso **2.** (*amer.*) commesso viaggiatore, propagandista.

salesmanship ['seilzmənʃip], *s.* l'arte del vendere; l'abilità nel vendere.

saleswoman ['seilzˌwumən], *pl.* **saleswomen** ['seilzˌwimin], *s.* commessa, venditrice.

Salic ['sælik], *ag.* (*st.*) salico ‖ *the* — *law*, la legge salica.

salicin ['sælisin], *s.* (*chim.*) salicina.

salicylate [sæ'lisileit], *s.* (*chim.*) salicilato.

salicylic [ˌsæli'silik], *ag.* (*chim.*) salicilico.

salience ['seiliəns], **saliency** ['seiliənsi], *s.* **1.** prominenza **2.** superiorità; cospicuità, importanza.

salient ['seiliənt], *ag.* **1.** sporgente, prominente: — *eyes*, occhi sporgenti **2.** saliente, notevole; principale; cospicuo, considerevole: *the* — *features of his work*, le caratteristiche più notevoli della sua opera **3.** (*poet.*) saltellante; zampillante: *a* — *fountain*, una fontana zampillante **4.** (*arald.*) saliente ‖ *s.* (*mil.*) saliente.

saliently ['seiliəntli], *av.* in modo saliente, notevole.

saliferous [sə'lifərəs], *ag.* (*geol.*) salifero.

salifiable ['sælifaiəbl], *ag.* (*chim.*) salificabile.

salification [ˌsælifi'keiʃən], *s.* (*chim.*) salificazione.

to salify ['sælifai], *v.t.i.* (*chim.*) salificare.

salimeter [sə'limitə*], *s.* salimetro.

saline ['seilain], *come s.* [sə'lain], *ag.* salino, salso; salato: *a* — *taste*, un sapore salato ‖ *s.* **1.** sorgente salina; salina **2.** sale purgativo.

salinity [sə'liniti], *s.* salsedine, salinità.

salinometer [ˌsæli'nomitə*], *s.* salinometro.

saliva [sə'laivə], *s.* saliva.

salival [sə'laivəl], *ag.* salivare.

salivant ['sælivənt], *ag.* salivatorio ‖ *s.* sostanza salivatoria.

salivary ['sælivəri], *ag.* salivare.

to salivate ['sæliveit], *v.t.i.* (far) salivare.

salivation [ˌsæli'veiʃən], *s.* salivazione.

sallet ['sælit], *s.* celata.

sallow¹ ['sælou], *ag.* giallastro; olivastro; terreo.

to sallow¹, *v.t.i.* rendere, diventare giallastro, olivastro, pallido.

sallow², *s.* (*bot.*) **1.** salice **2.** legno di salice.

sallowness ['sælounis], *s.* colorito giallastro, olivastro, pallido.

sallowy ['sæloui], *ag.* coperto di salici.

Sallust ['sæləst], *no.pr.m.* (*st. lett.*) Sallustio.

sally¹ ['sæli], *s.* **1.** (*mil.*) sortita **2.** escursione, gita **3.** slancio, impeto; scoppio (di passioni) **4.** *fig.* motto di spirito, facezia **5.** (*arch.*) aggetto.

to sally¹, *v.i.* **1.** (*mil.*) fare una sortita **2.** *to* — **out**, **forth**, uscire; balzare fuori; mettersi in viaggio: *they put their lunch into baskets and sallied out into the country*, messa la colazione nei cestini, andarono a fare una gita in campagna.

sally², *s.* **1.** movimento iniziale di campana **2.** impugnatura di corda di campana ☆ — *-hole*, foro per cui passa la corda di una campana.

Sally, *no.pr.f. dim.* di **Sarah.**

Sally Lunn ['sæli'lʌn], *s.* «Sally Lunn» (panino dolce da tè).

salmagundi [ˌsælmə'gʌndi], *s.* **1.** piatto di carne, uova, cipolle e acciughe **2.** *fig.* guazzabuglio.

salmi ['sælmi(:)], *s.* (*cuc.*) salmì.

salmon ['sæmən], *ag.* di color salmone ‖ *s.* (*invariato al pl.*) **1.** salmone **2.** color salmone ☆ — *-trout*, trota salmonata.

Salome [sə'loumi], **Salomé** [ˌsɑ:lou'mei], *no.pr.f.* (*Bibbia*) Salomè.

salon ['sælɔ:ŋ], *s.* **1.** salone (da ricevimento, esposizione) **2.** salotto; ricevimento (letterario, mondano, ecc.) **3.** galleria d'arte || *the Salon*, il « Salon» (mostra di artisti francesi viventi tenuta annualmente a Parigi).

Salonica [*st. moderna* sǝ'lɔnikǝ, *st. greca* ˌsælǝ'naikǝ], *no.pr.* (*geog.*) Salonicco.

saloon [sǝ'lu:n], *s.* **1.** salone, sala da ricevimento (specialmente di luogo pubblico) **2.** (*mar.*) cabina di lusso; ritrovo per passeggeri **3.** (*amer.*) bar ☆ — *-bar*, bar di prim'ordine; — *-car* (o — *-carriage*), (*ferr.*) vettura salone; (*aut.*) berlina; — *-deck*, ponte di prima classe; — *-keeper*, (*amer.*) gestore di bar || *dancing* —, sala da ballo; *dining* —, (*ferr.*) vettura ristorante; *hairdressing* —, (*amer.*) negozio di parrucchiere per signora; istituto di bellezza; *shaving* —, (*amer.*) bottega di barbiere; *sleeping* —, (*ferr.*) vettura letto.

saloop [sǝ'lu:p], *s.* **1.** salep **2.** infuso caldo di *salep*, sassafrasso.

Salopian [sǝ'loupjǝn], *ag.s.c.* (abitante) dello Shropshire.

salpingitis [ˌsælpin'dʒaitis], *s.* (*patol.*) salpingite.

salpinx ['sælpiŋks], *pl.* **salpinges** [sæl'pindʒi:z], *s.* **1.** (*mus.*) salpinge (antica tromba greca) **2.** (*anat.*) salpinge uterina, tromba di Falloppio **3.** (*anat.*) salpinge uditiva, tromba di Eustachio.

salsify ['sælsifi], *s.* (*bot.*) sassefrica ☆ *black* —, scorzonera.

salsuginous [sæl'sju:dʒinǝs], *ag.* salmastro; che cresce in terreno impregnato di sale (di piante).

salt [sɔ:lt], *ag.* **1.** salato: — *provision*, viveri salati; *too* —, troppo salato **2.** conservato, sotto sale: — *beef*, carne di manzo salata **3.** *fig.* amaro; piccante; mordace: — *stories*, storielle piccanti; — *wit*, spirito mordace; *she wept* — *tears*, ella versò lacrime salate, amare **4.** che cresce nel mare, in acqua salata (di piante): — *plant*, pianta marina || *s.* **1.** sale: *in* —, sotto sale; *a pinch of* —, un pizzico di sale (anche *fig.*) || *I eat my salad just with* —, mangio l'insalata con un po' di sale soltanto || *you are the* — *of the earth*, (Bibbia) voi siete il sale della terra || *you are not worth your* —, non vali nulla, nemmeno il pane che mangi || *to eat* — *with s.o.*, essere ospite di qlcu. || *to sit above the* —, sedere tra i convitati di riguardo; *to sit below the* —, sedere in fondo alla tavola, tra servi e famigli || *to rub* — *into a wound*, *fig.* rincrudire una ferita || *to take sthg. with a grain* (o *a pinch*) *of* —, accettare ql.co. con riserve **2.** *fig.* sale, frizzo, spirito: *talk full of* —, discorso arguto || *Attic* —, spirito attico **3.** *pl.* (*farm. med.*) sali: *a dose of salts*, una dose di sali, un purgante **4.** (*chim.*) cloruro sodico: — *of lemon*, ossalato di potassa **5.** (*fam.*) lupo di mare: *he is an old* —, egli è un vecchio lupo di mare **6.** salina (naturale, artificiale).

to salt, *v.t.* **1.** salare; cospargere, impregnare di sale: *to* — (*down*) *butter*, *meat*, salare burro, carne **2.** condire, rendere piccante (anche *fig.*) **3.** (*comm.*) alterare (conti); calcare sui prezzi: *it is a salted bill!*, è un conto salato! **4.** (*vet. med.*) immunizzare alle fatiche: *he has salted his horse*, ha abituato il suo cavallo alle fatiche; *to be salted against disease*, essere immunizzato contro le malattie **5.** (*sl.*) dar falsa apparenza di ricchezza a: *to* — *a mine*, far apparire una miniera più ricca (apportandovi minerale greggio) **6.** *to* — **away**, **down**, conservare sotto sale || *to* — *down money*, *stock*, *etc.* (*fam. amer.*) economizzare, mettere da parte denaro, titoli, ecc. **7.** *to* — **out**, (*chim.*) far precipitare una soluzione.

salt, (*nei composti*): — *-box*, recipiente per il sale; — *-cat*, mangime per piccioni; — *-cellar*, (anche *anat. fam.*) saliera; — *dome*, cupola salina; — *-free diet*, (*med.*) dieta aclorurata; — *-glaze*, smalto di ceramica (ottenuto con sale); — *-junk*, (*sl. mar.*) carne di manzo salata; — *-horse*, (*sl.*) manzo salato; — *-lick*, (*amer.*) terreno salato (per il bestiame); — *-marsh*, palude salata (coperta dall'alta marea); — *-meadow*, prato salato; — *-mine*, salina, miniera di sale; — *-pan*, bacino di salina; — *-pit*, salina; — *-rising*, (*amer.*) lievito; — *solution*, soluzione isotonica salina; — *-spoon*,

cucchiaino per il sale; — *-water*, acqua di mare, acqua salsa: — *-water fish*, pesce di mare, d'acqua salata; — *-works*, raffineria di sale; — *-wort*, (*bot.*) salicornia || *basic* —, sale basico; *common* — (o *kitchen* —), sale grosso, da cucina; *Epsom* —, (*farm.*) sale inglese; *rock* —, salgemma; *sea-* —, sale marino; *table* —, sale da tavola; *white* —, sale bianco, sale fino.

saltant ['sæltǝnt], *ag.* (*arald.*) saliente (generalmente scoiattolo, gatto).

saltarello [ˌsæltǝ'relou], *s.* saltarello (danza, musica).

saltation [sæl'teifǝn], *s.* **1.** il saltare; salto **2.** (*biol.*) mutazione **3.** movimento brusco improvviso.

saltatorial [ˌsæltǝ'tɔ:riǝl], **saltatory** ['sæltǝtǝri], *ag.* saltatore.

salter ['sɔ:ltǝ*], *s.c.* salatore, salatrice || *s.* **1.** produttore, venditore di sale **2.** salinaio.

saltern ['sɔ:ltǝn], *s.* **1.** raffineria di sale **2.** salina.

saltier ['sæltiǝ*], *s.* (*arald.*) croce di Sant'Andrea.

saltigrade ['sæltigreid], *ag.s.* (*entom.*) saltigrado.

salting ['sɔ:ltiŋ], *s.* **1.** insalatura, salatura **2.** *pl.* palude costiera salata.

saltire ['sæltaiǝ*], *s.* (*arald.*) croce di Sant'Andrea.

saltirewise ['sæltaiǝwaiz], *av.* a forma di croce, a guisa di croce.

saltish ['sɔ:ltiʃ], *ag.* salmastro, salaticcio.

saltishly ['sɔ:ltiʃli], *av.* in modo piuttosto salato.

saltishness ['sɔ:ltiʃnis], *s.* gusto salmastro.

saltless ['sɔ:ltlis], *ag.* senza sale; *fig.* insipido, scipito.

saltlessness ['sɔ:ltlisnis], *s.* insipidezza (anche *fig.*).

saltly ['sɔ:ltli], *av.* in modo salato.

saltness ['sɔ:ltnis], *s.* salsedine.

saltpetre ['sɔ:ltˌpi:tǝ*], *s.* salnitro ☆ — *bed*, deposito di salnitro; — *rot*, muffa su muri umidi che ne disintegra la malta.

saltpetrous [ˌsɔ:lt'pi:trǝs], *ag.* salnitroso.

salty ['sɔ:lti], *ag.* **1.** salato; salmastro, incrostato di sale: *there is a* — *deposit in this bottle*, questa bottiglia è incrostata di sale **2.** piccante (anche *fig.*): *a* — *tale*, un racconto piccante.

salubrious [sǝ'lu:briǝs], *ag.* salubre, sano.

salubriously [sǝ'lu:briǝsli], *av.* salubremente.

salubriousness [sǝ'lu:briǝsnis], **salubrity** [sǝ'lu:briti], *s.* salubrità.

salutarily ['sæljutǝrili], *av.* in modo salutare.

salutary ['sæljutǝri], *ag.* salutare.

salutation [ˌsælju(:)'teifǝn], *s.* saluto: — *of a letter*, inizio di lettera || *the Angelic Salutation*, (*eccl.*) l'Ave Maria.

salutatory [sǝ'lu:tǝtǝri], *ag.* di saluto || *s.* (*amer.*) orazione letta da uno studente all'inizio del corso.

salute [sǝ'lu:t], *s.* **1.** saluto; gesto di saluto **2.** (*mar. mil.*) saluto; salva: — *with cheers*, saluto alla voce; *to fire a* —, tirare una salva, rendere saluto con le artiglierie; *to stand at* (*the*) —, (*mil.*) fare il saluto; *to take the* —, rispondere al saluto; *royal* —, saluto a salve (con 21 colpi di cannone) **3.** (*scherma*) saluto **4.** (*scherz.*) bacio.

to salute, *v.t.* **1.** salutare; dare il benvenuto a **2.** (*mar. mil.*) salutare; fare il saluto militare: *to* — *with 10 guns*, sparare 10 colpi a salve **3.** colpire (l'orecchio); offrirsi (allo sguardo): *the first object that salutes the eye*, il primo oggetto che si offre allo sguardo.

saluter [sǝ'lu:tǝ*], *s.c.* salutatore, salutatrice.

salvable ['sælvǝbl], *ag.* salvabile; ricuperabile.

salvage ['sælvidʒ], *s.* **1.** indennità di ricupero **2.** salvataggio, ricupero (di merci danneggiate in naufragio, incendio, ecc.): *to make* — *of goods*, salvare della merce **3.** merci ricuperate ☆ — *operation*, operazione di ricupero.

to salvage, *v.t.* ricuperare, salvare (da naufragio, incendio, ecc.).

salvation [sæl'veifǝn], *s.* **1.** salvezza **2.** (*teol.*) salvezza, salute eterna; redenzione: *to work out one's* —, assicurarsi la salvezza eterna || *Salvation Army*, Esercito della Salvezza.

Salvationist [sæl'veifʃnist], *s.c.* membro dell'Esercito della Salvezza.

salve[1] [sɑːv], *s.* **1.** (*farm.*) unguento, balsamo; pomata (specialmente per le labbra) **2.** *fig.* rimedio, balsamo: *her kind words were a — for him*, le sue gentili parole furono un balsamo per lui.

to salve[1], *v.t.* **1.** (*rar.*) ungere con balsamo, ecc. **2.** *fig.* guarire, sanare, lenire.

salve[2], *s.* **1.** salve! (forma di saluto) **2.** (*eccl.*) Salve Regina.

to salve[3] [sælv], *v.t.* salvare (da un naufragio, un incendio, ecc.).

salver ['sælvə*], *s.* vassoio, piatto (per lettere, carte, ecc.).

salvo[1] ['sælvou], *pl.* **salvoes** ['sælvouz], *s.* **1.** riserva: *with an express — of all my rights*, riservandomi tutti i miei diritti **2.** scappatoia; pretesto, scusa **3.** espediente (per salvare la reputazione, per tranquillizzare la coscienza).

salvo[2], *s.* **1.** (*mil.*) salva **2.** scroscio: *— of applause*, scroscio di applausi.

salvolatile [,sælvə'lætəli], *s.* **1.** (*chim.*) sali di carbonato di ammonio **2.** (*fam.*) sali odorosi.

salvor ['sælvə*], *s.* (*mar.*) **1.** chi salva (da naufragio) nave, merci **2.** nave usata per ricuperi.

Sam [sæm], *no.pr.m. abbr.* di **Samuel** ‖ *— Browne* (*belt*), cinturone da ufficiale ‖ *Uncle —*, (*fam.*) gli Stati Uniti ‖ *upon my —!*, (*sl.*) parola d'onore! ‖ *to stand —*, (*sl.*) sostenere le spese (di un trattenimento, ecc.).

samara ['sæmərə], *s.* (*bot.*) samara.

Samaritan [sə'mæritn], *ag.* samaritano ‖ *s.c.* samaritano, samaritana ‖ *the good —*, il buon Samaritano.

samarium [sə'mɛəriəm], *s.* (*chim.*) samario.

samba ['sæmbə], *s.* samba (danza).

sambo ['sæmbou] *pl.* **sambos, samboes** ['sæmbouz], *s.* meticcio (specialmente di sangue negro e indiano o negro ed europeo) ‖ *Sambo*, (*sl. scherz.*) « Sambo » (nomignolo dato ad un negro).

same [seim], *ag.* **1.** medesimo, stesso, uguale: *he is of the — age as myself*, ha la mia stessa età; *she is the — girl we saw yesterday*, è la stessa ragazza che vedemmo ieri; *these barrels are exactly the — width*, queste botti sono della medesima larghezza ‖ *at the — time*, nello stesso tempo; tuttavia: *at the — time you must remember that she behaved badly*, nondimeno devi ricordarti che si comportò male; *don't speak all at the — time*, non parlate tutti insieme ‖ *the very — thing* (o *one and the — thing*), proprio la stessa cosa ‖ *it comes to the — thing*, fa lo stesso **2.** medesimo, invariato: *the — old daily round*, sempre la stessa routine, il solito trantran; *he i the — odd chap he used to be*, è sempre il solito originale.

same, *pron.* **1.** lo stesso, il medesimo: *"Merry Christmas to you!", "The — to you!"*, « Buon Natale a te! », « Altrettanto! »; *he is much the — as yesterday*, sta proprio come ieri; *we found her just the — as before*, la trovammo immutata; *whatever he did, I did the —*, qualunque cosa facesse, io lo imitavo; *you must be sure to say the —*, devi essere sicuro di dire la stessa cosa **2.** (*comm. senza art.*): *please return — by return of post*, si prega di rimandare a giro di posta; *to soling strings of —, 2/3*, (*nelle fatture*) per la risuolatura delle scarpe, 10 scellini e due « pence »; per *stringhe alle medesime, 2 scellini e tre « pence »*.

same, *av.* **nello stesso modo**: *I think the — as him*, la penso come lui ‖ *all the —*, non di meno, malgrado tutto: *it is nice of you all the —*, è carino da parte tua, nonostante tutto.

samel ['sæməl], *ag.* mal cotto (di mattoni, tegole, ecc.).

samely ['seimli], *ag.* monotono, uniforme.

sameness ['seimnis], *s.* **1.** identità; somiglianza **2.** uniformità, monotonia.

Samian ['seimjən], *ag.* samio ‖ *s.c.* abitante di Samo.

samite ['sæmait], *s.* sciamito (stoffa).

samlet ['sæmlit], *s.* (*ittiol.*) salmone giovane.

Sammy ['sæmi], *no.pr.m. dim.* di **Samuel** ‖ **sammy**, *s.* (*sl.*) « sammy », soprannome dato ai soldati americani (nella guerra 1915-18).

Samnites ['sæmnaits], *s.* (*st.*) Sanniti.

Samoa [sə'mouə], *no.pr.* (*geog.*) Samoa.

Samoan [sə'mouən], *ag.* samoano ‖ *s.c.* abitante delle isole Samoa ‖ *s.* lingua di Samoa.

Samos ['seimɔs], *no.pr.* (*geog.*) Samo.

Samothrace ['sæmouθreis], *no.pr.* (*geog.*) Samotracia.

Samothracian [,sæmou'θreiʃjən], *ag.s.c.* (abitante) di Samotracia.

samovar [,sæmou'vɑː*], *s.* samovar.

Samoyed(e) [,sæmɔi'ed], *ag.s.* samoiedo.

Samoyedic [,sæmɔi'edik], *ag.* samoiedo.

samp [sæmp], *s.* (*amer.*) granoturco macinato grossolanamente e fatto bollire nel latte.

sampan ['sæmpæn], *s.* « sampan » (imbarcazione cinese).

samphire ['sæmfaiə*], *s.* (*bot.*) salicornia.

sample ['sɑːmpl], *s.* campione, modello; saggio, esemplare: *up to —*, conforme a campione; *to buy sthg. from —*, comprare su campione; *to give a — of one's knowledge*, *fig.* dare un saggio della propria sapienza ‖ *by — post*, come campione senza valore ‖ *— book*, campionario; *— room*, locale per mostra campionaria.

to sample, *v.t.* **1.** campionare **2.** saggiare, provare (un vino, un cibo, ecc.).

sampler[1] ['sɑːmplə*], *s.* **1.** imparaticcio (saggio, modello di ricamo) **2.** albero tipo.

sampler[2], *s.c.* chi prepara, esamina campioni ‖ *s.* (*soil*) —, (*mec.*) sonda campionatrice (per terreno).

sampling ['sɑːmpliŋ], *s.* campionatura.

Sam(p)son ['sæmpsn], *no.pr.m.* (*Bibbia*) Sansone ☆ *—'s post*, (*mar.*) puntale.

Samuel ['sæmjuəl], *no.pr.m.* Samuele.

sanative ['sænətiv], *ag.* salutare, curativo.

sanatorium [,sænə'tɔːriəm], *pl.* **sanatoria** [,sænə'tɔːriə], *s.* **1.** sanatorio **2.** stazione climatica montana **3.** infermeria (nei collegi).

sanatory ['sænətəri], *ag.* sanativo, curativo.

sanbenito [,sænbə'niːtou], *s.* (*st.*) « sanbenito » (sacco che si metteva ai condannati dall'Inquisizione).

sanctification [,sæŋktifi'keiʃən], *s.* santificazione; canonizzazione.

sanctified ['sæŋktifaid], *ag.* **1.** santificato; santo, sacro; consacrato **2.** che affetta devozione.

sanctifier ['sæŋkti,faiə*], *s.c.* santificatore, santificatrice.

to sanctify ['sæŋktifai], *v.t.* santificare, consacrare, purificare.

sanctimonious [,sæŋkti'mounjəs], *ag.* santarello, che affetta devozione; ipocrita.

sanctimoniously [,sæŋkti'mounjəsli], *av.* ipocritamente, con falsa aria di santità.

sanctimoniousness [,sæŋkti'mounjəsnis], *s.* santocchieria, aria di santità.

sanction ['sæŋkʃən], *s.* **1.** autorizzazione, approvazione, permesso: *with the — of the author*, con l'autorizzazione dell'autore **2.** (*dir.*) ratifica, decreto ‖ *the pragmatic —*, (*st.*) la prammatica sanzione **3.** (*dir.*) sanzione, pena: *punitive —*, sanzione punitiva; *remuneratory —*, provvedimento remuneratorio.

to sanction, *v.t.* **1.** autorizzare, approvare **2.** ratificare, decretare **3.** aggiungere delle sanzioni penali a (una legge).

sanctionary ['sæŋkʃnəri], *ag.* sanzionario.

sanctionless ['sæŋkʃnlis], *ag.* non sanzionato.

sanctity ['sæŋktiti], *s.* **1.** santità, religiosità ‖ *in (the) odour of —*, in odore di santità **2.** carattere sacro (d'un terreno, d'un giuramento, ecc.); inviolabilità (di terreno, della vita privata, ecc.).

sanctuary ['sæŋktjuəri], *s.* **1.** santuario, tempio, chiesa **2.** asilo, rifugio: *right of —*, diritto d'asilo; *to take —*, cercare asilo in un santuario **3.** riserva (di uccelli e animali selvatici).

sanctum ['sæŋktəm], *s.* **1.** luogo sacro, santuario ‖

Sanctum Sanctorum, (*eccl.*) Tabernacolo; *fig.* rifugio intimo 2. (*fam.*) studio privato; ritiro, rifugio ‖ *lady's* —, spogliatoio per signora.

Sanctus ['sæŋktəs], *s.* (*eccl. mus.*) sanctus.

sand [sænd], *s.* 1. sabbia, rena; *pl.* granelli di sabbia ‖ *to build on* —, *to plough the* —, *fig.* costruire sulla sabbia 2. *pl.* spiaggia; banco di sabbia: *children playing on the sands*, bambini che giuocano sulla spiaggia 3. (*sl. amer.*) coraggio, fegato: *a fellow with plenty of* —, un individuo che ha del fegato 4. (*patol.*) sabbia 5. *pl. fig.* scadenza di tempo (nella clessidra) ☆ — -*bank*, banco di sabbia; — -*bath*, (*chim.*) bagnosabbia; — -*blast*, (*mec. metal.*) sabbiatura; — -*box*, (*ferr.*) sabbiera; — -*crack*, screpolature dei talloni; (*vet.*) malattia dello zoccolo dei cavalli; fessure nei mattoni; — -*fly*, (*entom.*) simulia; — -*glass*, clessidra; — -*hill*, duna; — -*hopper*, (*entom.*) pulce di mare; — -*martin*, (*ornit.*) rondine di mare; — -*pit*, cava di sabbia; — -*shoes*, scarpe da spiaggia; — -*spout*, tromba di sabbia; — -*storm*, bufera di sabbia; — -*table*, (*mil.*) tavola per plastici.

to sand, *v.t.* 1. coprire, cospargere di sabbia 2. mescolare, alterare con sabbia 3. insabbiare, arenare 4. smerigliare; (*tec.*) carteggiare.

sandal[1] ['sændl], *s.* 1. sandalo 2. cinghietta (di calzature).

to sandal[1], *pass.p.p.* **sandalled** ['sændld], *v.t.* calzare sandali a.

sandal[2], *s.* legno di sandalo.

sandalled ['sændld], *ag.* calzato di sandali.

sandalwood ['sændlwud], *s.* legno di sandalo.

sandarae ['sændəræk], *s.* (*min. bot.*) sandracca.

sandbag ['sændbæg], *s.* 1. sacchetto di sabbia (per zavorra, fortificazioni, ecc.) 2. sacchetto di sabbia usato come arma.

to sandbag, *pass.p.p.* **sandbagged** ['sændbægd], *v.t.* 1. munire, zavorrare con sacchetti di sabbia 2. colpire con un sacchetto di sabbia.

sanderling ['sændəliŋ], *s.* (*ornit.*) piovanello tridattilo.

sanders ['sɑːndəz], *s.* legno di sandalo.

Sandhurst ['sændhəːst], *no.pr.* (*geog.*) Sandhurst (sede di un famoso Collegio Militare).

sandiness ['sændinis], *s.* arenosità.

sandiver ['sændivə*], *s.* scoria del vetro fuso.

sandman ['sændmæn], *pl.* **sandmen** ['sændmen], *s.* (*linguaggio infantile*) l'uomo nero.

sandpaper ['sænd,peipə*], *s.* cartavetrata.

sandstone ['sændstoun], *s.* (*min.*) arenaria.

sandwich ['sænwidʒ], *s.* « sandwich », tramezzino ‖ *to sit* —, essere seduto fra due persone ☆ —*man* (*o* — -*boy*), uomo-sandwich.

to sandwich, *v.t.* serrare; intercalare; inserire: *to* — *a dangerous clause between harmless ones in a proposal*, inserire una clausola pericolosa fra due innocue in uno schema di contratto.

sandy ['sændi], *ag.* 1. sabbioso, arenoso 2. biondo rosso (di capelli).

Sandy, *no.pr.m. dim.* di **Alexander** ‖ *s.* (*fam.*) uno scozzese.

sane [sein], *ag.* sano di mente; sensato; equilibrato.

sanely ['seinli], *av.* sensatamente; ragionevolmente.

saneness ['seinnis], **sanity** ['sæniti], *s.* sanità (di mente); equilibrio.

sanforized ['sænfəraizd], *ag.* irrestringibile.

sang [sæŋ], *pass.* di to **sing**.

sangaree [,sæŋgə'riː], *s.* bevanda di vino e spezie.

sang-froid ['sɑːŋ'frwɑː], *s.* sangue freddo.

Sangrail, Sangreal [sæŋ'greil], *s.* (*lett.*) Santo Graal.

sanguiferous [sæŋ'gwifərəs], *ag.* sanguifero.

sanguification [,sæŋgwifi'keiʃən], *s.* (*med.*) sanguificazione.

sanguinaria [,sæŋgwi'nɛəriə], *s.* (*bot.*) sanguinaria.

sanguinarily ['sæŋgwinərili], *av.* in modo sanguinario.

sanguinariness ['sæŋgwinərinis], *s.* carattere sanguinario.

sanguinary ['sæŋgwinəri], *ag.* sanguinario, crudele ‖ — *language*, linguaggio scurrile.

sanguine ['sæŋgwin], *ag.* 1. sanguigno 2. ottimistico, fiducioso: *to be of a* — *disposition*, essere portato all'ottimismo; *to feel* (*o to be*) — *about the future*, aver fiducia nell'avvenire 3. (*rar.*) sanguinario; assetato di sangue ‖ *s.* (*art. min.*) sanguigna.

sanguinely ['sæŋgwinli], *av.* con ottimismo, con fiducia.

sanguineness ['sæŋgwinnis], *s.* 1. ottimismo, fiducia, speranza 2. (*rar.*) temperamento sanguigno.

sanguineous [sæŋ'gwiniəs], *ag.* 1. del sangue, sanguigno 2. (*spec. bot.*) sanguigno, rosso sangue 3. (*med.*) pletorico, sanguigno.

sanguinivorous [,sæŋgwi'nivərəs], *ag.* sanguivoro.

sanguinolent [sæŋ'gwinələnt], *ag.* sanguinolento.

sanguisorba [sæŋgwi'sɔːbə], *s.* (*bot.*) sanguisorba.

sanguivorous [sæŋ'gwivərəs], *ag.* sanguivoro.

Sanhedrim ['sænidrim], **Sanhedrin** ['sænidrin], *s.* (*st. ebraica*) Sinedrio.

sanicle ['sænikl], *s.* (*bot.*) sanicola.

sanidine ['sænidiːn], *s.* (*min.*) sanidina.

sanies ['seiniiːz], *s.* (*patol.*) sanie.

to sanify ['sænifai], *v.t.* rendere salubre, migliorare le condizioni sanitarie di.

sanious ['seiniəs], *ag.* (*patol.*) purulento.

sanitarian [,sæni'tɛəriən], *ag.* igienico; sanitario ‖ *s.* igienista.

sanitarily ['sænitərili], *av.* igienicamente.

sanitarist ['sænitərist], *s.* igienista.

sanitarium [,sæni'tɛəriəm], *pl.* **sanitariums** [,sæni-'tɛəriəmz], **sanitaria** [,sæni'tɛəriə], *s.* sanatorio, casa di cura.

sanitary ['sænitəri], *ag.* igienico; sanitario ☆ — *engineering*, tecnica sanitaria; costruzioni e materiale sanitari; — *inspector*, ufficiale sanitario.

to sanitate ['sæniteit], *v.t.* 1. rendere igienico 2. fornire di materiale sanitario.

sanitation [,sæni'teiʃən], *s.* miglioramento delle condizioni igieniche.

sanity ['sæniti], *s.* sanità di mente; equilibrio, ragionevolezza, buon senso.

sanjak ['sændʒæk], *s.* sangiaccato.

sank [sæŋk], *pass.* di to **sink**.

sans [sænz], *prep.* (*arc. poet.*) senza.

Sanserit, Sanskrit ['sænskrit], *ag.s.* sanscrito.

Santa Claus [,sæntə'klɔːz], *no.pr.m.* « Santa Claus » (personaggio di fiaba corrispondente a Babbo Natale).

santal ['sæntəl], *s.* (*bot.*) legno di sandalo.

santalin ['sæntəlin], *s.* (*chim.*) santalina.

santon ['sæntən], *s.* santone; asceta mussulmano.

santonin(e) ['sæntənin], *s.* (*farm.*) santonina.

Saorstat Eireann ['sɛəstɔː'tɛərən], *no.pr.* (*pol.*) Stato Libero d'Irlanda (in gaelico).

Sao Tomé e Principe Islands [,sauntu'mɛəi'priːnsipə'ailəndz], *no.pr.* (*geog.*) isole di San Tomaso e Principe.

sap[1] [sæp], *s.* 1. (*bot.*) linfa; succo 2. *fig.* vigore, energia ☆ — -*wood*, alburno.

to sap[1], *pass.p.p.* **sapped** [sæpt], *v.t.* 1. essiccare (legno, ecc.) 2. *fig.* sfiaccare, svigorire.

sap[2], *s.* 1. (*mil.*) trincea sotterranea 2. *fig.* subdolo processo di indebolimento.

to sap[2], *v.t.i.* 1. scavare una trincea sotterranea; avvicinare, avvicinarsi attraverso una trincea sotterranea 2. minare le fondamenta di, distruggere; *fig.* insidiare, minare: *his health is sapped by the damp climate*, la sua salute è insidiata dal clima umido.

sap[3], *s.* (*sl. scolastico*) secchione, sgobbone.

to sap[3], *v.i.* (*sl. scolastico*) sgobbare sui libri.

sap[4], *s.* (*sl.*) scimunito.

sapajou ['sæpədʒuː], *s.* cappuccina.

sapan ['sæpən], **sapan-wood** ['sæpən-wud], *s.* (*bot.*) brasiletto, verzino.

sapful ['sæpful], *ag.* 1. succoso 2. vigoroso.

saphead[1] ['sæphed], *s.* (*fam.*) citrullo.
saphead[2], *s.* bocca di trincea.
saphena [sə'fi:nə], *s.* (*anat.*) safena.
sapid ['sæpid], *ag.* sapido, gustoso (anche *fig.*).
sapidity [sə'piditi], **sapidness** ['sæpidnis], *s.* sapidità; gustosità (anche *fig.*).
sapience ['seipjəns], *s.* 1. (*iron.*) pedanteria 2. (*arc.*) sapienza, saggezza.
sapient ['seipjənt], *ag.* 1. (*iron.*) pedante 2. (*arc.*) sapiente, savio.
sapiential [,seipj'enʃəl], *ag.* sapienziale.
sapiently ['seipjəntli], *av.* con aria sapiente.
sapindus [sə'pindəs], *s.* (*bot.*) sapindo.
sapless ['sæplis], *ag.* 1. secco, avvizzito 2. fiacco, senza vigore 3. scialbo, insipido.
sapling ['sæpliŋ], *s.* 1. alberello 2. *fig.* giovane inesperto 3. cucciolo del levriero.
sapodilla [,sæpou'dilə], *s.* (*bot.*) sapotiglia.
saponaceous [,sæpou'neiʃəs], *ag.* 1. saponoso 2. *fig.* elusivo; mellifluo.
saponaria [,sæpou'neiriə], *s.* (*bot.*) saponaria.
saponifiable [sə'pɔnifaiəbl], *ag.* (*chim.*) saponificabile.
saponification [sə,pɔnifi'keiʃən], *s.* (*chim.*) saponificazione.
to saponify [sə'pɔnifai], *v.t.i.* (*chim.*) saponificare, saponificarsi.
saponin(e) ['sæpənin], *s.* (*chim.*) saponina.
sapor ['seipə*], *s.* (*rar.*) sapore, gusto.
saporous ['seipərəs], *ag.* (*rar.*) saporito, gustoso.
sapour ['seipə*], *s.* (*rar.*) sapore, gusto.
sapper ['sæpə*], *s.* 1. zappatore 2. (*mil.*) geniere.
Sapphic ['sæfik], *ag.* (*poes.*) saffico || *s.* (*poes.*) verso saffico.
sapphire ['sæfaiə*], *ag.* di colore blu zaffiro || *s.* 1. (*min.*) zaffiro 2. colore blu zaffiro.
sapphirine ['sæfirain], *ag.* zaffirino, simile a zaffiro.
Sapphism ['sæfizəm], *s.* saffismo.
Sappho ['sæfou], *no.pr.f.* (*st. lett.*) Saffo.
sappiness ['sæpinis], *s.* succosità.
sappy ['sæpi], *ag.* 1. (*bot.*) pieno di linfa 2. *fig.* energico; vigoroso 3. (*fam.*) sciocco, fatuo.
saprophyte ['sæproufait], *s.* (*bot.*) saprofito.
saprophytic [,sæprou'fitik], *ag.* (*bot.*) saprofitico.
Sara ['sɛərə], *no.pr.f.* Sara.
saraband ['særəbænd], *s.* sarabanda (musica, danza spagnola).
Saracen ['særəsn], *ag.s.* saraceno.
Saracenic [,særə'senik], *ag.* saraceno.
Sarah ['sɛərə], *no.pr.f.* Sara.
sarcasm ['sɑ:kæzəm], *s.* sarcasmo; ironia.
sarcastic [sɑ:'kæstik], *ag.* sarcastico; ironico.
sarcastically [sɑ:'kæstikəli], *av.* sarcasticamente; ironicamente.
sarcenet, *V.* **sarsenet**.
sarcocele ['sɑ:kousi:l], *s.* (*patol.*) sarcocele.
sarcocolla [,sɑ:kə'kɔlə], *s.* sarcocolla.
sarcode ['sɑ:koud] *s.* (*biol.*) sarcode.
sarcology [sɑ:'kɔlədʒi], *s.* (*med.*) sarcologia.
sarcoma [sɑ:'koumə], *pl.* **sarcomata** [sɑ:'koumətə], *s.* (*patol.*) sarcoma.
sarcomatous [sɑ:'koumətəs], *ag.* (*patol.*) sarcomatoso.
sarcophagus [sɑ:'kɔfəgəs], *pl.* **sarcophagi** [sɑ:'kɔfəgai], *s.* sarcofago.
sard [sɑ:d], *s.* (*min.*) sardonice.
Sardanapalus [,sɑ:də'næpələs], *no.pr.m.* (*st.*) Sardanapalo.
sardelle [sɑ:'del], *s.* (*ittiol.*) sardella.
sardine [sɑ:'di:n], *s.* (*ittiol.*) sardina.
Sardinia [sɑ:'dinjə], *no.pr.* (*geog.*) Sardegna.
Sardinian [sɑ:'dinjən], *ag.* sardo || *s.c.* sardo, sarda.
sardonic [sɑ:'dɔnik], *ag.* sardonico.
sardonically [sɑ:'dɔnikəli], *av.* sardonicamente.
sardonyx ['sɑ:dəniks], *s.* (*min.*) sardonice.

sargasso [sɑ:'gæsou], *s.* (*bot.*) sargasso || *Sargasso Sea*, Mar dei Sargassi.
sari ['sɑ:ri(:)], *s.* sari (indumento femminile indiano).
Sarmatian [sɑ:'meiʃjən], *ag.* sarmatico || *s.c.* sarmata.
sarmentose [,sɑ:mən'tous], **sarmentous** [sɑ:'mentəs], *ag.* (*bot.*) sarmentoso.
sarong [sə'rɔŋ], *s.* «sarong» (indumento malese).
sarrusophone [sæ'rʌsəfoun], *s.* (*mus.*) salsapariglia.
sarsaparilla [,sɑ:səpə'rilə], *s.* (*bot. farm.*) salsapariglia.
sarsenet ['sɑ:snit], *s.* tessuto sottile di seta (usato specialmente per fodere).
sartorial [sɑ:'tɔ:riəl], *ag.* 1. di, da sarto; di sartoria 2. (*anat.*) del muscolo sartorio.
sartorius [sɑ:'tɔ:riəs], *s.* (*anat.*) (muscolo) sartorio.
Sarum ['sɛərəm], *no.pr.* (*geog. st.*) Salisbury.
sash[1] [sæʃ], *s.* fascia, cintura, sciarpa, fusciacca (specialmente come parte di uniforme).
sash[2], *s.* telaio scorrevole (di finestra) ☆ — *-cord* (o — *-line*), corda del contrappeso (nelle finestre a ghigliottina); — *-pulley*, puleggia su cui scorre la corda del contrappeso (nelle finestre a ghigliottina); — *-weight*, contrappeso (nelle finestre a ghigliottina); — *-window*, finestra a ghigliottina.
to sash[2], *v.t.* montare il telaio scorrevole su (una finestra).
sassafras ['sæsəfræs], *s.* (*bot. farm.*) sassafrasso.
Sassanian [sæ'seinjən], **Sassanid** ['sæsənid], *ag.s.* (*st.*) sassanide.
Sassenach ['sæsənæk], *ag.s.c.* (*scoz. irl.*) inglese, scozzese della Scozia meridionale.
sassolite ['sæsəlait], *s.* (*min.*) sassolite.
sat [sæt], *pass.p.p.* di to **sit**.
Satan ['seitən], *no.pr.m.* Satana.
Satanas ['sætənəs], *no.pr.m.* (*arc.*) Satanasso.
satanic(al) [sə'tænik(əl)], *ag.* satanico.
satanically [sə'tænikəli], *av.* satanicamente.
satanism ['seitənizm], *s.* satanismo.
to satanize ['seitənaiz], *v.t.* invasare.
satchel ['sætʃəl], *s.* cartella (da scolaro).
to sate [seit], *v.t.* saziare, satollare; soddisfare.
sateen [sæ'ti:n], *s.* rasatello, tessuto di cotone satinato.
sateless ['seitlis], *ag.* insaziabile.
satellite ['sætəlait], *s.* 1. (*astr.*) satellite 2. *fig.* seguace, satellite ☆ — *town*, città satellite.
satellitic [,sætə'litik], *ag.* di satellite.
satiable ['seiʃjəbl], *ag.* saziabile, appagabile.
satiate ['seiʃieit], *ag.* sazio, satollo.
to satiate, *v.t.* saziare, satollare.
satiation [,seiʃi'eiʃən], **satiety** [sə'taiəti], *s.* sazietà.
satin ['sætin], *ag.* di raso, simile a raso || *s.* 1. raso 2. (*sl.*) gin ☆ — *beauty* (o — *carpet*), (*entom.*) varietà di tignola «Boarmia abietaria»; — *-finish*, (*metal.*) finitura satinata; — *flower*, (*bot.*) lunaria; — *-paper*, carta satinata; — *-stitch*, punto raso.
satinet ['sætinit], *s.* rasetto.
satining ['sætiniŋ], *s.* (*tec.*) cilindratura, levigazione.
satiny ['sætini], *ag.* satinato.
satire ['sætaiə*], *s.* 1. (*lett.*) satira: *he wrote a — on his critics*, scrisse una satira contro i suoi critici 2. canzonatura; sarcasmo.
satiric(al) [sə'tirik(əl)], *ag.* satirico.
satirically [sə'tirikəli], *av.* satiricamente.
satirist ['sætərist], *s.* autore di satire.
to satirize ['sætəraiz], *v.t.* satireggiare.
satisfaction [,sætis'fækʃən], *s.* 1. soddisfazione, appagamento: *it is a great — for me that...*, è motivo di grande gioia per me che...; *the work will be done to your —*, il lavoro sarà fatto in modo da accontentarvi; *to have the — of doing sthg.*, provare la soddisfazione di fare ql.co. 2. riparazione: *to demand — for an insult*, domandare riparazione per un insulto; *to make full — to s.o.*, concedere piena riparazione a qlcu. 3. (*dir.*) pagamento: *to enter —*, registrare l'avvenuto pagamento.

satisfactorily [ˌsætisˈfæktərili], *av.* soddisfacentemente; esaurientemente.

satisfactoriness [ˌsætisˈfæktərinis], *s.* carattere soddisfacente.

satisfactory [ˌsætisˈfæktəri], *ag.* **1.** soddisfacente; esauriente: *your excuse is not* —, la tua scusa lascia a desiderare **2.** (*teol.*) espiatorio.

satisfiable [ˈsætisfaiəbl], *ag.* che può essere soddisfatto.

to satisfy [ˈsætisfai], *v.t.i.* **1.** soddisfare, appagare, accontentare: *nobody is satisfied with his own condition*, nessuno è soddisfatto della propria condizione ‖ *to* — *the examiners*, superare un esame (universitario) con votazione minima **2.** convincere, persuadere; assicurare: *to* — *s.o. of a fact*, convincere qlcu. di un fatto **3.** (*dir.*) pagare, compensare **4.** fare ammenda a; (*eccl. teol.*) riparare.

satisfying [ˈsætisfaiiŋ], *ag.* soddisfacente.

satisfyingly [ˈsætisfaiiŋli], *av.* soddisfacentemente.

satrap [ˈsætrəp], *s.* (*st.*) satrapo.

satrapal [ˈsætrəpəl], **satrapical** [səˈtræpikəl], *ag.* di, da satrapo.

saturable [ˈsætʃərəbl], *ag.* saturabile.

saturate [ˈsætʃərit], *ag.* **1.** saturo **2.** intenso (di colore).

to saturate [ˈsætʃəreit], *v.t.* saturare, imbeverare, impregnare (anche *chim. fis.*): *to become saturated with sthg.*, saturarsi, impregnarsi di ql.co.

saturation [ˌsætʃəˈreiʃən], *s.* saturazione (anche *chim. fis.*)

Saturday [ˈsætədi], *s.* sabato: *he arrived last* —, arrivò sabato scorso ‖ — *to Monday*, fine settimana; — *week*, sabato a otto ‖ *Holy* —, Sabato Santo.

Saturn [ˈsætən], *no.pr.m.* (*mit.*) Saturno ‖ *no.pr.* (*astr.*) Saturno.

Saturnalia [ˌsætəˈneiljə], *s.pl.* **1.** (*st.*) Saturnali **2.** orgia, trattenimento improntato a licenziosità.

saturnalian [ˌsætəˈneiljən], *ag.* **1.** (*st.*) saturnale **2.** licenzioso.

Saturnian [sæˈtəːnjən], *ag.* (*astr. mit.*) di Saturno, saturnio ‖ *s.* abitante di Saturno.

saturnic [səˈtəːnik], *ag.* (*patol.*) affetto da saturnismo.

saturnine [ˈsætənain], *ag.* **1.** triste, mesto **2.** (*patol.*) saturnino.

saturnism [ˈsætənizəm], *s.* (*patol.*) saturnismo.

satyr [ˈsætə*], *s.* **1.** (*mit.*) satiro (anche *fig.*) **2.** (*entom.*) satiro **3.** (*zool. rar.*) orango.

satyriasis [ˌsætiˈraiəsis], *s.* (*patol.*) satiriasi.

satyric [səˈtirik], *ag.* di, da satiro, satiresco.

satyrion [səˈtiriən], *s.* (*bot.*) satirio.

sauce [sɔːs], *s.* **1.** salsa; intingolo; condimento (anche *fig.*) ‖ *hunger is the best* —, *prov.* la fame è il miglior condimento ‖ *to serve with the same* —, *prov.* rendere pan per focaccia **2.** (*fam.*) impertinenza, impudenza: *none of your* —!, niente impertinenze! ☆ — *-boat*, salsiera; — *-box*, (*fam.*) sfacciato, impertinente.

to sauce, *v.t.* **1.** condire; rendere piccante (anche *fig.*) **2.** (*fam.*) dire impertinenze a.

sauceless [ˈsɔːslis], *ag.* senza condimento.

saucepan [ˈsɔːspən], *s.* casseruola, pentolino.

saucer [ˈsɔːsə*], *s.* piattino, sottocoppa ☆ — *-eyes*, occhi spalancati e rotondi ‖ *flying* —, disco volante.

saucerful [ˈsɔːsəful], *s.* il contenuto di un piattino.

saucerless [ˈsɔːsəlis], *ag.* senza piattino.

saucily [ˈsɔːsili], *av.* sfacciatamente, insolentemente; in modo impertinente.

sauciness [ˈsɔːsinis], *s.* sfacciataggine, insolenza; impertinenza.

saucy [ˈsɔːsi], *ag.* **1.** sfacciato, insolente; impertinente **2.** (*sl.*) vivace, arguto.

Saudi [səˈuːdi], *ag.* saudita: — *Arabia*, Arabia Saudita.

sauerkraut [ˈsauəkraut], *s.* (*cuc.*) crauti.

saul [sɔːl], *V.* **sal**[1].

saunter [ˈsɔːntə*], *s.* passeggiatina, giretto.

to saunter, *v.i.* bighellonare; andare a zonzo.

saunterer [ˈsɔːntərə*], *s.c.* bighellone, bighellona; girandolone, girandolona.

saunteringly [ˈsɔːntəriŋli], *av.* bighellonando.

Sauria [ˈsɔːriə], *s.pl.* (*zool.*) i sauri.

saurian [ˈsɔːriən], *ag.s.* (*zool.*) appartenente all'ordine dei sauri.

saury [ˈsɔːri], *s.* (*ittiol.*) costardella.

sausage [ˈsɔsidʒ], *s.* **1.** salsiccia, salame **2.** (*sl. mil.*) pallone frenato ☆ — *-meat*, carne trita per ripieni, salsicce; — *-roll*, salatino di pasta arrotolata, ripiena di carne ‖ *Bologna* —, mortadella di Bologna.

sauté [ˈsoutei], *ag.* (*cuc.*) saltato, fritto in padella.

savable [ˈseivəbl], *ag.* salvabile.

savage [ˈsævidʒ], *ag.* **1.** selvaggio, barbaro **2.** feroce, crudele: *a* — *dog*, un cane feroce **3.** (*fam.*) furioso, arrabbiato ‖ *s.* **1.** selvaggio, barbaro **2.** persona crudele, brutale.

to savage, *v.t.* **1.** attaccare, mordere, calpestare selvaggiamente (di cavallo): *he was savaged by his horse*, fu selvaggiamente calpestato dal suo cavallo **2.** *fig.* assalire.

savagedom [ˈsævidʒdəm], *s.* **1.** stato selvaggio **2.** *coll.* selvaggi.

savagely [ˈsævidʒli], *av.* selvaggiamente, barbaramente, ferocemente.

savageness [ˈsævidʒnis], **savagery** [ˈsævidʒəri], **savagism** [ˈsævidʒizəm], *s.* **1.** ‖stato selvaggio; selvatichezza **2.** ferocia, crudeltà.

savannah [səˈvænə], *s.* savana.

savant [ˈsævənt], *s.* dotto, erudito.

save [seiv], *s.* **1.** (*spor.*) azione che impedisce all'avversario di segnare un punto **2.** (*carte*) condotta di giuoco per evitare gravi perdite.

to save, *v.t.i.* **1.** salvare, difendere, proteggere (anche *fig.*): *Christ alone has power to* — *sinners*, solo Cristo può salvare i peccatori; *he saved me from being killed*, egli impedì che venissi ucciso; *to* — *appearances*, salvare le apparenze; *to* — *one's face*, salvare la faccia; *to* — *one's skin* (o *neck* o *bacon*), (*fam.*) salvare la pelle; *to* — *a person's life*, salvare la vita a una persona ‖ — *us!*, poveri noi! ‖ — *your reverence*, con rispetto parlando ‖ *God* — *me from my friends!*, dagli amici mi guardi Iddio! ‖ *God* — *the Queen!*, Dio salvi la Regina! **2.** conservare, mettere in serbo, risparmiare; fare risparmi, economie; evitare perdite di (tempo, denaro, ecc.): *he saved* (*up*) *a lot of money*, mise da parte un sacco di soldi; *his secretary saved him a lot of time*, la sua segretaria gli faceva risparmiare molto tempo; *you had better* — *me the trouble of telling you...*, faresti meglio a risparmiarmi la noia di dirti... ‖ *shall we* — *the tide?*, arriveremo in tempo per la marea? ‖ *a penny saved is a penny gained*, *prov.* quattrino risparmiato due volte guadagnato ‖ *a stitch in time saves nine*, *prov.* un punto in tempo ne salva cento **3.** (*spor.*) impedire che l'avversario segni punti.

save, *prep.* salvo, eccetto, fuorché, ad eccezione di: *all the crew were drowned* — *one man*, tutto l'equipaggio perì tranne un uomo ‖ *cong.* (*arc. letter.*) eccetto che, tranne che: *he was a good man* — *that he had one great fault*, era un brav'uomo, però aveva un gran difetto.

save-all [ˈseivɔːl], *s.* **1.** reggimoccolo **2.** (*mec. mar.*) raccoglitore **3.** (*mar.*) vela posta sotto vela.

saveloy [ˈsæviloi], *s.* (*cuc.*) cervellata.

saver [ˈseivə*], *s.c.* salvatore, salvatrice; liberatore, liberatrice ‖ *s.* **1.** risparmiatore, economizzatore **2.** apparecchio economizzatore.

savin, savine [ˈsævin], *s.* **1.** (*bot.*) sabina, savina **2.** (*farm.*) essenza di sabina.

saving [ˈseiviŋ], *ag.* **1.** che salva, che redime **2.** economo **3.** economico **4.** (*dir.*) restrittivo: — *clause*, clausola restrittiva ‖ *s.* **1.** liberazione; salvezza **2.** *gener.* *pl.* risparmio, economia **3.** (*dir.*) riserva, eccezione

☆ **savings-bank**, Cassa di Risparmio ‖ *labour* —, che risparmia fatica; pratico.

savingly ['seiviŋli], *av.* economicamente.

savingness ['seiviŋnis], *s.* (*rar.*) economia.

saviour ['seivjə*], *s.* salvatore, redentore.

savory ['seivəri], *s.* (*bot. cuc.*) santoreggia.

savour ['seivə*], *s.* sapore, gusto, aroma (anche *fig.*).

to **savour**, *v.t.i.* **1.** sapere, avere sapore (anche *fig.*): *this fact savours of rebellion*, questo fatto sa di ribellione **2.** (*rar.*) gustare, assaporare, sentire il sapore di.

savouriness ['seivərinis], *s.* sapidità; gustosità.

savourless ['seivəlis], *ag.* insipido, scipito.

savoury ['seivəri], *ag.* **1.** saporito, piccante **2.** delizioso, squisito ‖ *s.* **1.** salatino **2.** pietanza appetitosa ☆ — *herbs*, piante aromatiche.

Savoy [sə'vɔi], *no.pr.* (*geog.*) Savoia ‖ *the* —, l'albergo Savoia, il teatro Savoia (a Londra) ‖ *s.* **1.** cavolo cappuccino, verza **2.** (biscotto) savoiardo.

Savoyard [sə'vɔiɑ:d], *ag.* savoiardo ‖ *s.c.* savoiardo, savoiarda.

savvy ['sævi], *s.* (*sl.*) senso pratico; buon senso; intelligenza ‖ —?, capisci? ‖ *no* —, non so.

saw[1] [sɔ:], *s.* sega ☆ — *-blade*, lama della sega; — *-fish*, (*ittiol.*) pesce sega; — *-fly*, (*entom.*) tentredine; — *-frame*, telaio di sega; — *-horse*, cavalletto per segare la legna; — *-mill*, segheria; — *-toothed*, dentellato; — *-wort*, (*bot.*) serratula ‖ *band-* —, sega a nastro; *butcher's* —, sega da macellaio; *circular* —, sega circolare; *compass-* —, (*mec.*) gattuccio; *cross cut* - —, sega a mano per tronchi; *fret-* —, seghetta per traforo; *hand-* —, seghetto.

to **saw**[1], *pass.* **sawed** [sɔ:d], *p.p.* **sawn** [sɔ:n], (*rar.*) **sawed**, *v.t.i.* **1.** segare: *he has been sawing three hours*, sta segando da tre ore; *wood that saws well*, legna facile da segare; *to* — *up timber*, segare il legname ‖ *to* — *the air*, (*fam.*) gesticolare **2.** fare movimenti avanti e indietro.

saw[2], *s.* massima; detto; proverbio: *an old* —, una massima antica.

saw, *pass.* di to **see**.

sawbones ['sɔ:bounz], *s.* (*sl.*) aggiustaossa, chirurgo.

sawder ['sɔ:də*], *s.*: (*soft*) —, adulazioni, parole lusinghiere.

sawdust ['sɔ:dʌst], *s.* segatura.

sawing ['sɔ:iŋ], *s.* il segare ☆ — *machine*, segatrice.

sawn [sɔ:n], *p.p.* di to **saw**.

Sawney ['sɔ:ni], *s.* **1.** (*scherz.*) scozzese **2.** semplicione.

sawyer ['sɔ:jə*], *s.* **1.** segatore, segantino **2.** (*amer.*) albero galleggiante su un fiume.

saxatile ['sæksətail], *ag.* (*bot. zool.*) che cresce, vive tra le rocce.

saxe [sæks], *ag.s.* blu di Sassonia.

saxhorn ['sækshɔ:n], *s.* (*mus.*) basso tuba.

saxicoline [sæk'sikəlain], **saxicolous** [sæk'sikələs], *ag.* (*zool.*) che cresce, vive tra le rocce.

saxifrage ['sæksifridʒ], *s.* (*bot.*) sassifraga.

Saxon ['sæksn], *ag.s.c.* sassone ‖ *s.* lingua sassone ☆ — *blue*, blu di Sassonia.

Saxonism ['sæksənizəm], *s.* modo, forma sassone.

Saxonist ['sæksənist], *s.* studioso della lingua e della cultura sassone.

Saxony ['sæksni], *no.pr.* (*geog.*) Sassonia ‖ *s.* lana di Sassonia; stoffa di lana di Sassonia.

saxophone ['sæksəfoun], *s.* (*mus.*) sassofono.

saxtuba ['sæks,tju:bə], *s.* (*mus.*) basso tuba.

say[1] [sei], *s.* il dire; detto, parola: *he said his* —, egli disse la sua; *let him have his* —, lasciatelo parlare; *to have no* — *in the matter*, non avere voce in capitolo.

to **say**[1], *pass.p.p.* **said** [sed], *v.t.i.* (*3ª persona sing. pres. indic.* **says** [sez], (*arc.*) **saith** [seθ]) **1.** dire, affermare; esprimere un'opinione: *he has only to* — *one word to me*, basta che mi dica una parola; *I have heard* — *that*, ho sentito dire che; *in her letter she said she would come*, nella lettera annunciava la sua venuta; *so you* —?, dici?; *you may well* — *so*, hai ben ragione

di dirlo; *what have you to* — *for yourself?*, che cosa hai da dire in tua difesa?; *"What about a cup of tea?"*, *"Yes, please"*, *said he*, « Che ne diresti di una tazza di tè? », « Sì, grazie », rispose ‖ *I* —!, senti!, scusa!, davvero? ‖ *I dare* —, direi ‖ *it goes without saying*, è ovvio, è evidente ‖ *send me some books*, — *five*, mandami alcuni libri, facciamo cinque ‖ *so to* —, per così dire ‖ *that is to* —, vale a dire; cioè ‖ *you don't* — *so?*, davvero? mi sembra impossibile **2.** pronunciare, recitare: *he said his lesson*, ripeté la lezione; *Mass will be said at 9 a. m.*, alle 9 si celebrerà la Messa **3.** credere, ritenere: *I should* — *not*, non lo credo, direi di no; *nobody would* — *he is so old*, nessuno lo crederebbe così vecchio; *you might as well* —, avresti ragione di credere; *and so* — *all of us*, la pensiamo anche noi così **4.** (*rar.*) parlare **5.** *to* — **out**, esprimere il proprio parere senza reticenze, dire chiaro e tondo: *he said out what he thought about her*, disse apertamente ciò che pensava di lei.

say[2], *s.* saia (tessuto pregiato di lana, seta).

sayer ['seiə*], *s.* dicitore.

saying ['seiiŋ], *s.* proverbio, detto, massima: *as the* — *goes*, come dice il proverbio ‖ *doings and sayings*, vita, morte e miracoli.

scab [skæb], *s.* **1.** crosta (di piaga, ecc.) **2.** (*vet.*) rogna, scabbia **3.** rogna (delle piante) **4.** (*sl.*) poco di buono; pitocco **5.** crumiro **6.** (*metal.*) aderenza.

to **scab**, *pass.p.p.* **scabbed** [skæbd], *v.i.* **1.** ricoprirsi di croste, di scabbia **2.** fare il crumiro.

scabbard ['skæbəd], *s.* fodero, guaina (di spada, ecc.) ‖ *to throw away the* —, (*fam.*) dichiarare guerra a oltranza.

to **scabbard**, *v.t.* mettere nel fodero, nella guaina.

scabbed [skæbd], *ag.* **1.** coperto di croste **2.** (*vet.*) scabbioso, rognoso **3.** (*sl.*) meschino; inutile; basso.

scabbedness ['skæbidnis], **scabbiness** ['skæbinis], *s.* **1.** l'essere coperto di croste **2.** (*vet.*) l'essere scabbioso, rognoso **3.** (*sl.*) meschinità, bassezza.

to **scabble** ['skæbl], *v.t.* sbozzare (pietre, ecc.).

scabby ['skæbi], *V.* **scabbed**.

scabies ['skeibii:z], *s.* (*patol.*) scabbia.

scabious ['skeibjəs], *ag.* scabbioso, rognoso ‖ *s.* (*bot.*) scabbiosa.

scabrous ['skeibrəs], *ag.* **1.** scabro **2.** scabroso.

scabrousness ['skeibrəsnis], *s.* scabrosità.

scad [skæd], *s.* (*ittiol.*) sgombro.

scaffold ['skæfld], *s.* **1.** (*edil.*) ponte; ponteggio, impalcatura; tribuna **2.** patibolo, forca.

to **scaffold**, *v.t.* (*edil.*) erigere impalcature, ponteggi.

scaffolding ['skæfəldiŋ], *s.* (*edil.*) impalcatura, incastellatura, ponteggio.

scagliola [skæl'joulə], *s.* stucco, scagliola (imitazione di marmo).

scalable ['skeiləbl], *ag.* scalabile.

scalade [skə'lɑ:d], **scalado** [skə'lɑ:dou], *s.* (*mil. arc.*) scalata.

scalar ['skeilə*], *ag.* (*mat.*) numerico, scalare.

scalariform [skə'lærifɔ:m], *ag.* (*bot. zool.*) scalariforme.

scalawag ['skæləwæg], *s.* **1.** animale più piccolo del normale, mal nutrito **2.** (*sl.*) buono a nulla, fannullone; birbante, scavezzacollo **3.** (*amer.*) sudista passato al servizio del governo dopo la guerra civile.

scald[1] [skɔ:ld], *s.* (*st. lett.*) scaldo, bardo.

scald[2], *s.* scottatura.

to **scald**[2], *v.t.i.* **1.** scottare, scottarsi; sentirsi scottare (anche *fig.*); ustionare; bruciare, bruciarsi **2.** portare a un grado di calore di poco inferiore alla ebollizione **3.** sterilizzare con acqua bollente.

scald[3], *ag.* (*dial.*) **1.** tignoso **2.** meschino, spregevole.

scaldhead ['skɔ:ldhed], *s.* **1.** tigna **2.** forfora.

scalding ['skɔ:ldiŋ], *ag.* bollente; bruciante, scottante (anche *fig.*) ‖ *s.* **1.** scottatura **2.** (*ind. tessile*) cottura, lisciviatura.

scale[1] [skeil], *s.* piatto (di bilancia); *gener. pl.* bilancia (anche *fig.*): *the — of justice*, la bilancia della giustizia; (*pair of*) *scales*, bilancia, bascula; *to go* (o *to ride*) *to —*, (*ippica*) andare al peso; *to turn the —*, fare pendere la bilancia (anche *fig.*) ‖ *the Scales*, (*astr.*) la Libra, la Bilancia ‖ *victory was long in the —*, la vittoria fu a lungo incerta ‖ *to hold the scales even*, mantenere l'equilibrio; essere imparziali ☆ *— -maker*, fabbricatore di bilance; *— -pan*, piatto della bilancia ‖ *baby- —*, bilancia per bambini; *platform- —*, stadera a ponte.

to scale¹, *v.t.i.* **1.** pesare; soppesare; bilanciare **2.** (*ippica*) venir pesato.

scale², *s.* **1.** scaglia, squama, lamella **2.** scoria, incrostazione, ossido (sui metalli) **3.** (*med.*) tartaro dei denti **4.** *fig.* velo: *to remove the scales from s.o.'s eyes*, togliere il velo dagli occhi di qlcu., mostrare la verità a qlcu. ☆ *— -armour*, armatura a squame; *— -board*, legno in foglio (per impiallacciare); *— -fern*, (*bot.*) asplenio; *— -insects*, (*entom.*) coccidi; *— -wing*, (*entom.*) lepidottero; *— -work*, ornamentazione, lavorazione a squame.

to scale², *v.t.i.* **1.** squamare, squamarsi; sfaldare, sfaldarsi; sfogliarsi: *to — a fish*, squamare un pesce **2.** incrostarsi, incrostarsi (di pentole, caldaie, ecc.): *London smoke has scaled the stones of its churches*, il fumo di Londra ha incrostato la pietra delle sue chiese **3.** pulire (i denti) dal tartaro **4.** pulire (la canna di un fucile) sparando un colpo **5.** *to — off*, scrostare, scrostarsi: *the paint scaled off*, la vernice si è scrostata.

scale³, *s.* **1.** scala, misura, gradazione: *in —*, in gradazione; *to —*, secondo le proporzioni **2.** (*fis. geog. mat. mus.*) scala: *to practise scales on the piano*, fare esercizi di scale al pianoforte **3.** gamma: *a — of colours*, una gamma di colori **4.** ordine; scala; graduatoria: *high, low in the social —*, alto, basso nella scala sociale ☆ *— sliding —*, (*econ.*) scala mobile.

to scale³, *v.t.i.* **1.** assalire con scale, dare la scalata a **2.** raggiungere il sommo di (un monte, di un muro) **3.** graduare, regolare; ridurre a data scala; ridurre a scala comune **4.** *to — down*, diminuire (i prezzi) **5.** *to — up*, aumentare i prezzi.

sealed [skeild], *ag.* **1.** scaglioso, squamoso **2.** coperto di tegole disposte a scala.

scaleless ['skeillis], *ag.* senza squame, senza scaglie.

scalene ['skeili:n], *ag.s.* (*geom. anat.*) scaleno.

sealer ['skeilǝ*], *s.* chi, ciò che squama; chi, ciò che scrosta; raschietto.

scaliness ['skeilinis], *s.* squamosità.

scaling¹ ['skeiliŋ], *s.* **1.** incrostazione **2.** scrostamento; desquamazione.

scaling² , *s.* **1.** scalata **2.** graduazione ☆ *— -ladder*, scala d'assedio.

scall [sko:l], *ag.* **1.** rognoso **2.** *fig.* gretto, meschino ‖ *s.* tigna; scabbia, rogna.

scallawag, *V.* scalawag.

scallion ['skæljǝn], *s.* (*bot.*) scalogna, scalogno.

scallop ['skolǝp], *s.* **1.** (*zool.*) pettine; conchiglia **2.** conchiglia, recipiente per cuocere ostriche, ecc. **3.** dentellatura; festone, smerlo (su stoffa).

to scallop, *v.t.* **1.** tagliare a festone **2.** (*cuc.*) cuocere (pesce) in conchiglia.

scallywag ['skæliwæg], *V.* scalawag.

scalp¹ [skælp], *s.* **1.** (*anat.*) cranio; cuoio capelluto **2.** scalpo; *fig.* trofeo ‖ *to be out for scalps*, (*fam. amer.*) essere in giro per far la festa a qlcu. **3.** parrucca **4.** cima nuda, tondeggiante (di montagna) **5.** (*sl. amer.*) piccolo guadagno realizzato con rapida operazione (di Borsa) ☆ *— -hunter*, cacciatore di teste; *— -lock*, (*amer.*) ciuffo sulla testa dei pellirosse, segno di sfida.

to scalp¹, *v.t.* **1.** scalpare **2.** criticare aspramente, demolire **3.** (*sl. amer.*) fare il bagarino; realizzare piccoli guadagni con rapide operazioni (di Borsa).

scalp² , *s.* (*scoz.*) colonia di ostriche, molluschi.

scalpel ['skælpǝl], *s.* (*chir.*) scalpello, bisturi.

scalper ['skælpǝ*], *s.* **1.** chi scalpa **2.** buratto, cri-

vello **3.** scalpello (di incisore) **4.** (*sl. amer.*) bagarino; chi profitta di rapide operazioni (di Borsa).

scalping ['skælpiŋ], *ag.* aspro, caustico, corrosivo ‖ *s.* raschiamento; scotennamento ☆ *— -iron*, (*chir.*) raschietto, bisturi; *— -knife*, coltello per scalpare (i nemici).

scalpless ['skælplis], *ag.* senza cuoio capelluto.

scalpriform ['skælprifo:m], *ag.* a forma di scalpello (di denti incisivi).

sealy ['skeili], *ag.* **1.** squamoso; fatto a squame **2.** (*sl.*) meschino; gretto.

to scamble ['skæmbl], *v.t.i.* **1.** camminare, muoversi goffamente **2.** spandere; raccogliere alla rinfusa.

scammony ['skæmǝni], *s.* (*bot. farm.*) scamonea.

scamp¹ [skæmp], *s.* **1.** farabutto, furfante, mascalzone **2.** birichino, furfantello (di bimbo).

to scamp¹, *v.i.* (*scoz.*) vagabondare oziosamente.

to scamp², *v.t.i.* **1.** abborracciare, fare in modo inadeguato, superficiale **2.** (*amer.*) essere spilorcio, eccessivamente economo.

scamper ['skæmpǝ*], *s.* **1.** corsa rapida **2.** galoppata.

to scamper, *v.i.* **1.** correre, sgambettare, scorrazzare **2.** svignarsela ‖ *to — away*, darsela a gambe.

scampish ['skæmpiʃ], *ag.* da furfante, da birbante.

to scan [skæn], *pass.p.p.* scanned [skænd], *v.t.i.* **1.** misurare, scandire (versi); essere metricamente esatto: *this line won't —*, questo verso non si può scandire **2.** esaminare, scrutare, sondare: *to — the horizon*, scrutare l'orizzonte; *to — s.o.'s face*, scrutare il viso di qlcu. **3.** (*fam.*) scorrere in fretta con gli occhi: *to — the newspaper*, scorrere velocemente il giornale **4.** (*tv.*) analizzare, esplorare (l'immagine).

scandal ['skændl], *s.* **1.** scandalo; onta, vergogna: *he was the — of his family*, era la vergogna della famiglia; *to create* (o *to give rise to*) *a —*, provocare uno scandalo **2.** maldicenza: *to talk —*, fare della maldicenza; *to talk — about s.o.*, sparlare di qlcu. ‖ *"The School for Scandal"*, (*lett.*) «La scuola della maldicenza» **3.** (*dir.*) diffamazione; mancanza di rispetto ☆ *— -monger*, maldicente, mala lingua.

to scandalize¹ ['skændǝlaiz], *v.t.* **1.** scandalizzare, disgustare: *to be scandalized*, scandalizzarsi **2.** (*rar.*) diffamare, sparlare di.

to scandalize², *v.t.* ridurre il volume di (una vela).

scandalous ['skændǝlǝs], *ag.* **1.** scandaloso, vergognoso **2.** (*dir.*) diffamatorio, calunnioso.

scandalously ['skændǝlǝsli], *av.* **1.** scandalosamente **2.** (*dir.*) calunniosamente.

scandalousness ['skændǝlǝsnis], *s.* carattere scandaloso, infamante.

scandent ['skændǝnt], *ag.* (*bot. ornit.*) rampicante.

Scandinavia [,skændi'neivjǝ], *no.pr.* (*geog.*) Scandinavia.

Scandinavian [,skændi'neivjǝn], *ag.* scandinavo ‖ *s.c.* scandinavo, scandinava ‖ *s.* scandinavo (lingua).

scandium ['skændjǝm], *s.* (*chim.*) scandio.

scanner ['skænǝ*], *s.* (*tv.*) analizzatore, dispositivo di esplorazione ☆ *— belt- —*, analizzatore a nastro.

scanning ['skæniŋ], *s.* **1.** scansione (di versi) **2.** (*tv.*) analisi, esplorazione, scansione ☆ *— -beam*, (*tv.*) fascio esploratore; *— -line*, (*tv.*) linea di scansione.

scansion ['skænʃǝn], *s.* scansione.

seansorial [skæn'so:riǝl], *ag.* (*ornit.*) rampicante.

scant [skænt], *ag.* **1.** (*arc. poet.*) scarso, insufficiente; magro, povero: *— vegetation*, vegetazione povera; *in — attire*, in tenuta piuttosto succinta **2.** avaro, parco: *to be — of speech*, essere avaro di parole.

to scant, *v.t.* (*arc.*) restringere, limitare; togliere.

scant, *av.* (*dial.*) appena, scarsamente.

scantily ['skæntili], *av.* debolmente, scarsamente; sommariamente.

scantiness ['skæntinis], *s.* insufficienza, scarsezza; ristrettezza.

scantling ['skæntliŋ], *s.* **1.** misura (per pietra, legname) **2.** assicella (per costruzioni) **3.** piccola quantità **4.** (*arc.*) campione.

scantly ['skæntli], *av.* scarsamente.

scanty ['skænti], *ag.* scarso, insufficiente; angusto, esiguo, ristretto: — *hair*, capelli radi; — *meal*, pasto frugale; *in* — *attire*, in tenuta succinta.

Scapa Flow ['skæpə'flou], *no.pr. (geog.)* Scapa Flow.

scape[1] [skeip], *s.* **1.** *(bot.)* scapo **2.** basi di antenna (in insetto); cannello di penna (in uccello) **3.** *(arch.)* scapo (di colonna).

scape[2], *s.* panorama, veduta ☆ *sea*-—, marina.

scape[3], *s. (arc.)* fuga.

to scape[3], *V.* **to escape**[1].

scapegallows ['skeip,gælouz], *s.* avanzo di galera.

scapegoat ['skeipgout], *s.* capro espiatorio.

scapegrace ['skeipgreis], *s. (scherz.)* **1.** scapestrato, cattivo soggetto **2.** monello, bambino incorreggibile.

scaphoid ['skæfoid], *ag.s. (anat.)* scafoide.

scapula ['skæpjulə], *pl.* **scapulae** ['skæpjuli:], *s. (anat.)* scapola.

scapular ['skæpjulə*], **scapulary** ['skæpjuləri], *ag. (anat.)* scapolare ‖ *s. (eccl.)* scapolare.

scar[1] [skɑ:*], *s.* cicatrice (anche *fig.*); sfregio; segno di bruciatura.

to scar[1], *pass.p.p.* **scarred** [skɑ:d], *v.t.i.* **1.** cicatrizzare, cicatrizzarsi **2.** sfregiare; butterare.

scar[2], *s.* rupe; scogliera ☆ — *-limestone*, roccia carbonifera.

scar[3], *s. (ittiol.)* scaro.

scarab ['skærəb], **scarabaeus** [,skærə'bi(:)əs], *s. (entom. archeol.)* scarabeo.

Scaramouch ['skærəmautʃ], *no.pr.m. (teat.)* Scaramuccia ‖ **scaramouch**, *s.* smargiasso.

scarce [skɛəs], *ag.* scarso, insufficiente; raro ‖ *to make oneself* —, *(fam.)* tagliare la corda ‖ *av. (arc. poet.)* appena, a fatica.

scarcely ['skɛəsli], *av.* appena; a fatica, a mala pena: — *anyone*, quasi nessuno; — *ever*, raramente, quasi mai; *he could* — *speak*, poteva a mala pena parlare; *he is* — *fifteen years old*, non ha più di quindici anni.

scarcement ['skɛəsmənt], *s.* aggetto, sporgenza (di muro, roccia).

scarceness ['skɛəsnis], **scarcity** ['skɛəsiti], *s.* scarsezza, penuria, carestia; rarità.

scare [skɛə*], *s.* terrore, sgomento, spavento, panico: *to raise a* —, provocare panico ‖ *he did give me a* —!, *(fam.)* che spaghetto mi ha fatto prendere! ☆ — *-head(ing)* (o — *-line*), *(giornalismo)* titolo allarmante.

to scare, *v.t.* spaventare, sgomentare; far fuggire (per lo spavento): *the sight of the supposed ghost scared him away and out the room*, la vista di quel che credeva uno spettro lo fece scappare dalla stanza ‖ *to be scared to death*, avere una paura da morire ‖ *to be scared stiff of sthg.*, *(sl.)* avere una paura matta di ql.co.

scarecrow ['skɛə-krou], *s.* **1.** spaventapasseri **2.** persona malvestita; spauracchio.

scaremonger ['skɛə,mʌŋgə*], *s.c.* chi diffonde notizie allarmanti, allarmista.

scarf[1] [skɑ:f], *pl.* **scarfs** [skɑ:fs], **scarves** [skɑ:vz], *s.* **1.** sciarpa; fascia; cravattone; banda; striscia **2.** *(eccl.)* stola ☆ — *-pin*, spilla da cravatta.

to scarf[1], *v.t.* **1.** drappeggiare, mettere a mo' di sciarpa **2.** *fig.* coprire; velare.

scarf[2], *s.* **1.** *(tec.)* ammorsatura **2.** *(tec. mar.)* parella, ammorsatura. ☆ — *-joint*, *(tec.)* giunto ad ammorsatura.

to scarf[2], *v.t.i.* **1.** *(mec.)* rastremare **2.** *(tec.)* fare un giunto, congiungere ad ammorsatura.

scarf[3], *s. (dial. ornit.)* cormorano.

scarf[4], *s.* incisione longitudinale fatta nel corpo di una balena.

to scarf[4], *v.t.* fare una incisione nel (grasso di una balena).

scarfskin ['skɑ:fskin], *s.* epidermide; cute.

scarfwise ['skɑ:fwaiz], *av.* a tracolla.

scarification [,skɛərifi'keiʃən], *s. (chir. agr.)* scarificazione.

scarificator ['skɛərifi,keitə*], **scarifier** ['skɛəri,faiə*], *s. (agr. chir.)* scarificatore.

to scarify ['skɛərifai], *v.t.* **1.** *(chir.)* scarificare **2.** *(agr.)* smuovere (terreno) **3.** *fig.* criticare severamente.

scarious ['skɛəriəs], *ag. (bot.)* sottile; secco; membranoso.

scarlatina [,skɑ:lə'ti:nə], *s. (patol.)* scarlattina.

scarlet ['skɑ:lit], *ag.* scarlatto, porporino: *to blush* —, arrossire ‖ *s.* **1.** color scarlatto **2.** stoffa, abiti scarlatti ☆ — *-fever*, *(patol.)* scarlattina; — *-hat*, cappello cardinalizio; — *-rash*, rosolia; — *-runner*, fagiuolo di Spagna; — *woman*, prostituta; *(spreg.)* la Chiesa di Roma.

scarp(e)[1] [skɑ:p], *(arald.)* traversa.

scarp(e)[2], *s.* scarpata; declivio.

to scarp(e)[2], *v.t.* rendere scosceso; costruire a scarpata.

scarred [skɑ:d], *ag.* **1.** sfregiato, segnato di cicatrici **2.** eroso.

scarry ['skɑ:ri], *ag.* precipite; roccioso.

scarus ['skɛərəs], *s. (ittiol.)* scaro.

scary ['skɛəri], *ag.* **1.** *(amer. fam.)* allarmante, pauroso **2.** timido, pauroso.

scat[1] [skæt], *s.* imposta fondiaria (nelle isole Shetland e Orkney); *(st.)* tassa, tributo.

scat[2], *inter. (fam.)* vattene!, va' via!.

scathe [skeið], *s. (arc. dial.)* guasto, danno: *without* —, sano e salvo.

to scathe, *v.t.* **1.** danneggiare; distruggere; guastare **2.** fulminare **3.** *fig.* nuocere con satira a.

scatheless ['skeiðlis], *ag.* indenne, illeso, sano e salvo: *he did not get away* —, vi ha lasciato le penne.

scathing ['skeiðiŋ], *ag.* sarcastico, mordace, caustico: — *irony*, ironia mordace; *he can be very* —, egli sa essere molto caustico; *to write a* — *criticism of a play*, sottoporre una commedia ad una critica pungente.

scathingly ['skeiðiŋli], *av.* sarcasticamente; in modo mordace, caustico.

scatology [skə'tɔlədʒi], *s.* scatologia.

to scatter ['skætə*], *v.t.i.* **1.** spargere, spargersi; sparpagliare; disseminare: *do not* — *bits of paper on the floor!*, ┃non sparpagliare pezzi di carta sul pavimento!; *I always* — *my table with books*, ho sempre i libri sparsi sul tavolo; *to* — *seeds*, seminare **2.** mettere in fuga; disperdere, disperdersi; dissipare: *the police scattered the crowd*, la polizia disperse la folla; *the shot scattered the birds*, lo sparo mise in fuga gli uccelli **3.** diffondere, diffondersi (anche *fig.*); spandere, spandersi: *the news scattered*, la notizia si diffuse.

scatter-brain ['skætəbrein], *s.c. (fam.)* persona scervellata, sventata, stordita.

scatterbrained ['skætəbreind], *ag.* scervellato, sventato, stordito.

scattered ['skætəd], *ag.* sparso, disseminato; disperso; sparpagliato: — *light*, luce diffusa; — *news*, notizie sparse; *the villas lie* — *on the slopes*, le ville sono disseminate per i pendii.

scattering ['skætəriŋ], *s.* **1.** sparpagliamento; dispersione; *(fis.)* diffusione, dispersione **2.** quantità, numero ridotto e sparso: *he has a mere* — *of supporters*, i suoi sostenitori sono pochi e senza coesione.

scatteringly ['skætəriŋli], *av.* alla rinfusa, alla spicciolata.

scatterling ['skætəliŋ], *s. (arc.)* vagabondo.

scatty ['skæti], *ag. (sl.)* svitato, scervellato.

scaup(-duck) ['skɔ:p(dʌk)], *s. (ornit.)* germano maggiore.

scauper ['skɔ:pə*], *V.* **scalper**.

scaur [skɔ:], *s.* rupe; scogliera.

to scavenge ['skævindʒ], *v.t.i.* **1.** spazzare; raccogliere spazzatura **2.** *(mec.)* lavare, evacuare **3.** *(chim.)* purificare, deossidare.

scavenger ['skævindʒə*], *s.* **1.** spazzino **2.** animale, insetto che si ciba di rifiuti **3.** *fig.* chi si compiace di argomenti osceni **4.** *(chim.)* antipiombo **5.** *(fis.)* spazzatore (di sostanze radioattive).

to **scavenger**, *v.t.i.* **1.** fare lo spazzino **2.** cibarsi di rifiuti (detto di animali) **3.** *fig.* trattare argomenti osceni.

scavenging ['skævindʒiŋ], *s.* **1.** pulitura (di strade, ecc.) **2.** (*mec.*) lavaggio **3.** (*fis.*) spazzamento, espulsione.

scazon ['skeizɔn], *s.* (*poes.*) scazonte; coliambo.

scena ['ʃeinə], *s.* (*mus.*) scena di opera lirica.

scenario [si'nɑːriou], *pl.* **scenarios** [si'nɑːriouz], *s.* (*cine.*) sceneggiatura; scenario.

scenarist ['siːnərist], *s.* (*cine.*) sceneggiatore.

(to) **scend**, *V.* (to) **send**[2].

scene [siːn], *s.* **1.** scena: *the — of operations*, il teatro delle operazioni; *the — is laid in Milan*, la scena è ambientata a Milano **2.** scena, episodio: *a distressing —*, un episodio spiacevole; *the ghost — in "Hamlet"*, la scena dello spettro nell'«Amleto» **3.** (*arc.*) palcoscenico: *to appear on the —*, entrare in scena (anche *fig.*) || *to quit the —*, *fig.* andarsene, morire **4.** scenario, quinta: *to be behind the scenes*, essere, agire dietro le quinte (anche *fig.*) **5.** vista, veduta, panorama, spettacolo, colpo d'occhio: *I need a change of —*, ho bisogno di un cambiamento d'ambiente; *the sunset from my window was a fine —*, il tramonto dalla mia finestra era un bello spettacolo **6.** scenata, colloquio agitato: *don't make a —!*, non fare una scenata! ☆ *— -dock*, magazzino di scenari; *— -painter*, scenografo; *— -shifter*, macchinista di scena.

scenery ['siːnəri], *s.* **1.** scena, scenario **2.** prospettiva, veduta; panorama: *he has a passion for mountain —*, ha la passione dei paesaggi di montagna.

scenic ['siːnik], *ag.* scenico, teatrale; drammatico ☆ *— railway*, ferrovia in miniatura (in un parco di divertimenti).

scenically ['siːnikəli], *av.* scenicamente.

scenographer [si'nɔgrəfə*], *s.* scenografo.

scenographic [ˌsiːnə'græfik], *ag.* scenografico.

scenographically [ˌsiːnə'græfikəli], *av.* scenograficamente.

scenography [si'nɔgrəfi], *s.* scenografia.

scent [sent], *s.* **1.** odore, profumo (di fiori, ecc.): *the — of roses*, il profumo delle rose **2.** essenza, profumo: *she put some — on her handkerchief*, mise del profumo sul fazzoletto **3.** traccia, pista (anche *fig.*): *to get — of sthg.*, aver sentore di ql.co.; *to throw off the —*, far perdere la traccia, deviare i sospetti **4.** odorato, fiuto (anche *fig.*): *to have a good —*, (*fam.*) aver buon fiuto ☆ *— -bag*, sacchetto profumato; *— -bottle*, flacone da profumo.

to **scent**, *v.t.* **1.** fiutare, annusare; seguire la traccia di; sospettare; subodorare **2.** profumare **3.** *to — out*, scoprire.

scented ['sentid], *ag.* profumato, odorante.

scentless ['sentlis], *ag.* inodoro.

sepsis ['sepsis], *s.* scepsi; dubbio filosofico.

sceptic ['skeptik], *s.* scettico (anche *fil.*).

sceptical ['skeptikəl], *ag.* scettico (anche *fil.*).

sceptically ['skeptikəli], *av.* scetticamente.

scepticism ['skeptisizəm], *s.* scetticismo.

sceptre ['septə*], *s.* **1.** scettro **2.** *fig.* autorità sovrana.

to **sceptre**, *v.t.* **1.** armare, fornire di scettro **2.** conferire sovranità a **3.** toccare con lo scettro (in segno di assenso).

sceptreless ['septəlis], *ag.* **1.** senza scettro **2.** non soggetto a sovranità.

schedule ['ʃedjuːl], (*amer.*) 'skedjuːl], *s.* **1.** catalogo, distinta, elenco, lista, tabella; scheda **2.** (*amer.*) orario; programma (di lavoro, viaggio, ecc.): *according to —*, secondo il previsto, all'ora prevista **3.** appendice, allegato a legge o documento legale.

to **schedule**, *v.t.* **1.** comporre una lista, un catalogo di **2.** (*amer.*) mettere in lista, in orario: *to — a new train*, istituire un nuovo treno **3.** inserire (un allegato) a legge o documento legale.

Scheherazade [ʃiˌhiərə'zɑːdə], *no.pr.f.* (*lett.*) Shahrazade.

Scheldt [skelt], *no.pr.* (*geog*) Schelda.

schema ['skiːmə], *pl.* **schemata** ['skiːmətə], *s.* schema.

schematic(al) [ski'mætik(əl)], *ag.* schematico.

schematically [ski'mætikəli], *av.* in modo schematico

schematism ['skiːmətizəm], *s.* schematismo.

to **schematize** ['skiːmətaiz], *v.t.* schematizzare, esporre in modo schematico.

scheme[1] [skiːm], *s.* **1.** schema || *— of composition*, (*dir.*) concordato preventivo **2.** piano, progetto, disegno, sistema: *he drew up a — of work*, tracciò un piano di lavoro **3.** macchinazione, intrigo, complotto: *to lay a —*, ordire un intrigo ☆ *colour —*, (*pitt.*) combinazione di colore.

to **scheme**[1], *v.t.i.* **1.** progettare, fare il piano di **2.** macchinare, tramare.

scheme[2], *s.* *— -(arch)*, arcata a raggio maggiore nel mezzo di un arco a tre centri.

schemer ['skiːmə*], *s.c.* **1.** chi fa piani, calcoli, progetti **2.** affarista, intrigante.

scheming ['skiːmiŋ], *ag.* **1.** che progetta **2.** intrigante. astuto, scaltro || *s.* **1.** progetti **2.** macchinazioni; imbrogli.

Schiedam [ski:'dæm], *s.* gin olandese.

schism ['sizəm], *s.* (*relig.*) scisma.

schismatic [siz'mætik], *ag. s.* (*relig.*) scismatico.

schismatical [siz'mætikəl], *ag.* (*relig.*) scismatico.

schismatically [siz'mætikəli], *av.* da scismatico.

to **schismatize** ['sizmətaiz], *v.i.* **1.** agire da scismatico **2.** produrre uno scisma.

schist [ʃist], *s.* (*geol.*) schisto.

schistose ['ʃistous], **schistous** ['ʃistəs], *ag.* (*geol.*) schistoso.

schizoid ['skizoid], *ag. s.* (*patol.*) schizoide.

schizophrenia [ˌskitsou'friːnjə], *s.* (*patol.*) schizofrenia.

schizophrenic [ˌskitsou'frenik], *ag.s.* (*patol.*) schizofrenico.

schnapper ['ʃnæpə*], *s.* (*ittiol.*) pagro.

schnap(ps) [ʃnæp(s)], *s.* «schnaps» (gin forte simile all'olandese); grappa.

scholar ['skɔlə*], *s.* **1.** (*arc. volg.*) scolaro **2.** discepolo, discente **3.** studioso, letterato **4.** vincitore di una borsa di studio.

scholarly ['skɔləli], *ag.* dotto; istruito; studioso.

scholarship ['skɔləʃp], *s.* **1.** dottrina, sapere, scienza **2.** borsa di studio.

scholastic [skə'læstik], *ag.***1.** scolastico; pedante **2.** (*fil. teol.*) scolastico, appartenente, relativo alla scolastica || *s.* **1.** scolastico; pedante; formalista **2.** (*fil. teol.*) seguace della dottrina scolastica ☆ *— agency*, agenzia di collocamento per insegnanti.

scholastically [skə'læstikəli], *av.* scolasticamente; secondo la scolastica.

scholasticism [skə'læstisizəm], *s.* **1.** scolasticheria **2.** (*fil. teol.*) scolastica.

scholiast ['skouliæst], *s.* scoliaste, chiosatore.

scholium ['skouljəm], *pl.* **scholia** ['skouljə], *s.* (*lett. gram.*) scolio; nota esplicativa.

school[1] [skuːl], *s.* **1.** scuola; classe; allievi: *all the — welcomed the new headmaster*, tutti gli allievi diedero il benvenuto al nuovo preside; *experience is the best —*, l'esperienza è la scuola migliore; *he is at the bottom of the —*, è l'ultimo della classe; *he is at the head of the —*, è il primo della classe || *old — tie*, la cravatta coi colori della propria scuola; *fig.* legami persistenti tra ex-compagni di scuola **2.** scuola; lezione; ora di lezione: *yesterday we had no —*, ieri non avemmo lezione; *to go to —*, andare a lezione, a scuola; *to leave —*, lasciare la scuola **3.** istituto, accademia || *"The School for Wives"*, (*lett.*) «La scuola delle mogli» **4.** scuola; indirizzo, corrente, gruppo: *the Aristotelian —*, (*fil.*) la scuola aristotelica; *the Venetian —*, (*pitt.*) la scuola veneta; *he has left no — behind him*, non ha lasciato discepoli || *of the old —*, di vecchio stampo **5.** *pl.* università medioevali ☆ *— -bag*, cartella per i libri; *— -bell*, campana che annuncia l'inizio delle lezioni; *—*

-board, comitato scolastico; — *-book*, libro di testo; — *-child*, scolaro; — *-dame*, *(arc.)* maestra di scuola; — *-day*, giorno di scuola; — *-divine*, teologo scolastico; — *-divinity*, teologia scolastica; — *-doctor*, dottore della scuola; — *-friend*, amico di scuola; — *-friendship*, amicizia di scuola; — *-going*, che va a scuola; — *-house*, scuola (edificio); — *-inspector*, ispettore scolastico; — *-ma'am*, *(amer.)* maestra; — *-maid*, scolara; — *-mastership*, insegnamento (professione); — *-mate*, compagno di scuola; — *-miss*, *(fam.)* educanda; — *report*, pagella; — *-ship*, nave scuola; — *-taught*, che ha istruzione scolastica; — *-teacher*, insegnante; — *-teaching*, insegnamento; — *-term*, trimestre; — *-time*, ora delle lezioni; periodo scolastico; — *-trained*, istruito a scuola; — *-work*, compito in classe ‖ *boarding-* —, collegio; convitto; *day-* —, scuola diurna (opposta a scuola serale e a convitto); *elementary* — (o *primary* —), scuola elementare; *grammar-* —, ginnasio; *high* —, scuola media superiore, liceo; *infant* —, asilo (dai 5 ai 7 anni); *junior-* —, scuola (dai 7 agli 11 anni); *night-* —, scuola serale; *nursery-* —, asilo (dai 2 ai 5 anni); *open-air-* —, scuola all'aperto; *parish-* —, scuola parrocchiale; *preparatory-* —, scuola che prepara alla *public-school* (in Gran Bretagna), al *college* (negli Stati Uniti); *public-* —, scuola statale; scuola privata, collegio per l'insegnamento secondario (in Gran Bretagna); *secondary grammar-* —, *secondary modern-* —, *secondary technical-* —, ginnasio, liceo moderno, istituto tecnico (i tre tipi di scuola secondaria statale in Gran Bretagna); *Sunday-* —, oratorio festivo; *vocational-* —, scuola d'arte e mestieri.

to **school**[1], *v.t.* 1. *(rar.)* mandare a scuola 2. istruire; addestrare, ammaestrare; controllare; riprendere: *he doesn't want to be schooled*, non vuole essere ripreso; *he must — his temper*, deve controllare la sua ira; *I schooled him to patience*, gli insegnai a esser paziente.

school[2], *s.* banco (di pesci).

to **school**[2], *v.i.* raggrupparsi in banchi (di pesci).

schoolable ['sku:ləbl], *ag.* in età, condizione da ricevere istruzione.

schoolboy ['sku:lbɔi], *s.* scolaro; collegiale.

schoolcraft['sku:lkrɑ:ft],*s.*(*arc.*)istruzione scolastica.

schoolfellow ['sku:l,felou], *s.* compagno di scuola.

schoolgirl ['sku:lgə:l], *s.* scolara; collegiale.

schooling ['sku:liŋ], *s.* 1. istruzione, educazione, disciplina scolastica 2. tasse scolastiche; retta (di convitto) 3. *(arc.)* castigo, rimprovero.

schoolman, *pl.* **schoolmen** ['sku:lmən], *s.* 1. *(fil.)* scolastico 2. *(amer.)* insegnante.

schoolmaster ['sku:l,mɑ:stə*], *s.* 1. maestro, insegnante 2. direttore 3. *(arc.)* precettore, istitutore.

schoolmistress ['sku:l,mistris],*s.*maestra,insegnante.

schoolroom ['sku:lrum], *s.* aula scolastica.

schooner[1] ['sku:nə*], *s.* *(mar.)* goletta ☆ *prairie - —*, carrozzone tipico dei pionieri americani.

schooner[2], *s.* *(amer.)* alto boccale da birra.

schorl [ʃɔ:l], *s.* *(min.)* tormalina nera.

schottische [ʃɔ'ti:ʃ], *s.* danza, musica scozzese simile alla polca.

sciagram ['saiəgræm], **sciagraph** ['saiəgrɑ:f], *s.* *(arch. astr.)* sciografia.

sciagraphic [,saiə'græfik], *ag.* *(arch. astr.)* sciografico.

sciagraphically [,saiə'græfikəli], *av.* *(arch. astr.)* sciograficamente.

sciagraphy [sai'ægrəfi], *s.* 1. arte di disegnare in prospettiva, a chiaroscuro 2. *(med.)* radiografia 3. *(arch. astr.)* sciografia.

sciamachy [sai'æməki], *s.* finto combattimento (per esercitazione); *fig.* lotta con le ombre.

sciametry [sai'æmitri], *s.* *(fis.)* misurazione del potere di penetrazione dei raggi Roentgen.

sciascopy [sai'æskəpi], *s.* *(med.)* schiascopia.

sciatic(al) [sai'ætik(əl)], *ag.* *(anat. patol.)* sciatico.

sciatica [sai'ætikə], *s.* *(patol.)* sciatica.

science ['saiəns], *s.* 1. scienza ‖ *the dismal —*, *(fam.)*

economia politica ‖ *man of —*, scienziato 2. tecnica, abilità (in uno sport): *boxer who lacks —*, pugile che manca di tecnica 3. *(arc.)* conoscenza ☆ *— fiction*, *(neol.)* letteratura di fantascienza ‖ *exact —*, scienza esatta; *natural —*, scienze naturali; *social —*, scienze sociali.

scienter [sai'entə*], *av.* *(dir.)* scientemente, intenzionalmente.

sciential [sai'enʃəl], *ag.* 1. relativo alla conoscenza, alla scienza 2. che sa.

scientific [,saiən'tifik], *ag.* scientifico; sistematico; accurato: *— game*, giuoco scientifico; *to have — training*, avere esperienza nel campo scientifico.

scientifically [,saiən'tifikəli], *av.* scientificamente; sistematicamente; accuratamente.

scientism ['saiəntizəm], *s.* *(relig.)* scientismo.

scientist ['saiəntist], *s.c.* 1. scienziato: scienzista 2. *(relig.)* seguace dello scientismo.

scilicet ['sailiset], *av.* cioè, vale a dire.

scilla ['silə], *s.* *(bot.)* scilla.

scimitar ['simitə*], *s.* scimitarra.

scintilla [sin'tilə], *s.* scintilla; minimo; barlume: *a — of evidence*, un minimo di evidenza; *a — of genius*, una scintilla di genio.

scintillant ['sintilənt], *ag.* scintillante.

to **scintillate** ['sintileit], *v.i.* scintillare, brillare.

scintillation [,sinti'leiʃən], *s.* scintillio; sfavillio.

sciography [sai'ogrəfi], *V.* **sciagraphy**.

sciolism ['saiəlizəm], *s.* conoscenza superficiale; infarinatura.

sciolist ['saiəlist], *s.* saccente, saputello.

sciolistic [,saiə'listik], **sciolous** ['saiələs], *ag.* saccente, saputello.

sciomachy [sai'oməki], *V.* **sciamachy**.

sciomancy [saiə'mænsi], *s.* sciomanzia, negromanzia.

sciomantic [,saiə'mæntik], *ag.* negromantico.

scion ['saiən], *s.* 1. *(bot.)* pollone; *(agr.)* innesto 2. rampollo; discendente.

sciopticon [sai'optikən], *s.* *(foto.)* lanterna magica.

Sciot(e) ['saiot], *ag. s.c.* (abitante) di Scio.

scire facias ['saiəri'feiʃiæs], *s.* *(dir.)* mandato di comparizione.

scirocco [si'rokou], *s.* scirocco.

scirrhous ['sirəs], *ag.* *(patol.)* scirroso.

scirrhus ['sirəs], *s.* *(patol.)* scirro.

scissel ['sisəl], *s.* sbavatura, ritagli (di metallo).

scissile ['sisail], *ag.* scissile; atto a essere scisso.

scission ['siʒən], *s.* scissione, divisione.

to **scissor** ['sizə*], *v.t.* tagliare con le forbici ‖ *to — (out)*, ritagliare (da giornali, ecc.).

scissoring ['sizəriŋ], *s.* taglio con forbici, forbiciata.

scissors ['sizəz], *s.pl.* (*a pair of*) —, forbici; cesoie ☆ *-and-paste*, lavoro di mera compilazione con ritagli di altri scritti; — *-bill*, *(ornit.)* rincope nero; — *-bird* (o *— -tail*), *(ornit.)* milvulo; — *-cut*, forbiciata; *—(s)-grinder*, arrotino ‖ *nail- —*, forbicine da unghie.

scissorwise ['sizəwaiz], *av.* a forbice.

scissure ['siʃə*], *s.* taglio longitudinale; fessura.

sciurine ['saijurin], *ag.* di scoiattolo, di sciuridi; da scoiattolo ‖ *s.* scoiattolo.

Sclav [sklɑ:v], *V.* **Slav**.

sclerenchyma [skliə'reŋkimə], *s.* *(zool. bot.)* sclerenchima.

scleroma [skliə'roumə], *pl.* **scleromata** [skliə'roumətə], *s.* *(patol.)* sclerosi.

sclerosis [skliə'rousis], *s.* *(patol.)* sclerosi.

sclerotic [skliə'rotik], *ag.* sclerotico ‖ *s.* *(anat.)* sclerotica.

sclerotitis [,skliərou'taitis], *s.* *(patol.)* sclerite.

sclerotomy [skliə'rotəmi], *s.* *(chir.)* sclerotomia.

scobs [skɔbz], *s. pl.* 1. segatura; limatura 2. scorie; ritagli.

scoff[1] [skɔf], *s.* 1. beffa; derisione; scherno 2. zimbello; oggetto di scherno: *to be the — of the town*, essere lo zimbello della città.

to **scoff**[1], *v.t.i.* beffare; deridere, schernire: *to — a* *sthg.*, *at s.o.*, farsi beffe di ql.co., di qlcu.; *to be scoffed at*, essere deriso.

scoff², *s.* (*sl.*) cibo; pasto.

to **scoff²**, *v.t.* (*sl.*) mangiare avidamente.

scoffer ['skɔfə*], *s.c.* chi deride, schernitore.

scoffing ['skɔfiŋ], *ag.* derisorio; beffardo ‖ *s.* derisione; scherno.

scoffingly ['skɔfiŋli], *av.* beffardamente, derisivamente.

scold [skould], *s.* donna bisbetica, brontolona; megera.

to **scold**, *v.t.i.* **1.** sgridare; rimproverare: *the boy was scolded for being late*, il ragazzo fu rimproverato per il suo ritardo **2.** parlare in tono adirato.

scolder ['skouldə*], *s.c.* chi rimprovera; chi brontola.

scolding ['skouldiŋ], *ag.* che rimprovera; brontolone ‖ *s.* sgridata; rimprovero: *to give s.o. a good* —, dare una bella sgridata, dare una lavata di testa a qlcu.

scoldingly ['skouldiŋli], *av.* con sgridate, con rimproveri.

scoliosis [ˌskɔli'ousis], *s.* (*patol.*) scoliosi.

(to) **scollop**, *V.* (to) **scallop**.

scolopender [ˌskɔlə'pendə*], **scolopendra** [ˌskɔlə-'pendrə], *s.* (*entom.*) scolopendra, millepiedi.

scolopendriform [ˌskɔlə'pendrifɔːm], **scolopendrine** [ˌskɔlə'pendrin], *ag.* a forma di, simile a scolopendra.

scolopendrium [ˌskɔlə'pendriəm], *s.* (*bot.*) scolopendro, lingua cervina.

scomber ['skɔmbə*], *s.* (*ittiol.*) scombro, maccarello.

sconce¹ [skɔns], *s.* **1.** candeliere con manico; candelabro a muro **2.** bocciolo del candeliere.

sconce², *s.* (*scherz.*) testa, zucca ‖ *he has a crack on the* —, gli manca un venerdì.

sconce³, *s.* **1.** contrafforte, baluardo **2.** riparo, protezione **3.** (*dial.*) sedile fisso accanto al focolare.

sconce⁴, *s.* penalità di un boccale di birra imposta agli studenti di Oxford per infrazione alle regole d'etichetta a tavola.

to **sconce⁴**, *v.t.* multare di un boccale di birra (chi, a Oxford, non osserva le regole d'etichetta a tavola): *to be sconced*, essere multato, essere costretto a pagare da bere.

scon(e) [skɔn], *s.* pasticcino di farina d'orzo, di grano.

scoop¹ [skuːp], *s.* **1.** pala; paletta **2.** ramaiuolo, mestolo **3.** (*mar.*) sessola, gottazza **4.** (*mec.*) tazza.

to **scoop¹**, *v.t.* **1.** (*rar.*) levar acqua da (con paletta, ramaiuolo, cucchiaio); vuotare: *to* — *a boat dry*, togliere l'acqua da una barca **2.** scavare: *to* — (*out*) *a hole in the sand*, scavare una buca nella sabbia **3.** (*sl. giornalistico*) procacciarsi una notizia in esclusiva **4.** *to* — **in**, (*sl.*) realizzare (guadagni) **5.** *to* — **up**, raccogliere (carbone, farina, ecc.) con la pala.

scoop², *s.* **1.** palettata; mestolata ‖ *at one* (o *with a*) —, d'un sol colpo: *they earned one thousand dollars in one* —, guadagnarono mille dollari in un colpo solo **2.** bacino; cavità **3.** (*sl. giornalistico*) servizio, notizia in esclusiva **4.** (*sl.*) forte e subitaneo guadagno.

scooper ['skuːpə*], *s.* **1.** scalpello da intagliatore **2.** (*ornit.*) avosetta.

scoopful ['skuːpful], *s.* palettata; mestolata.

scoot [skuːt], *s.* fuga precipitosa: *to make a* — *for shelter*, correre verso un riparo.

to **scoot**, *v.i.* (*fam.*) correre, precipitarsi; andarsene rapidamente, guizzar via.

scooter ['skuːtə*], *s.* **1.** monopattino **2.** (*amer.*) imbarcazione a vela **3.** « scooter », motoretta.

scop [skɔp], *s.* (*st. lett.*) bardo (anglosassone).

scope [skoup], *s.* **1.** portata; possibilità, opportunità: *undertaking of wide* —, impresa di vasta portata; *this gives ample* — *to individual ability*, ciò dà grandi opportunità all'abilità individuale; *this is beyond the* — *of a child's mind*, questo esula dalla possibilità di una mente infantile **2.** prospettiva; sfera, campo (d'azione): *to extend the* — *of one's activities*, allargare il proprio campo d'azione; *to give free* (o *full*) —, dare piena li-

bertà d'azione **3.** (*mar.*) tratto non immerso del cavo dell'ancora **4.** (*arc.*) scopo, proposito, intenzione.

scorbutic [skɔːˈbjuːtik], *ag.s.* (*patol.*) scorbutico.

scorbutus [skɔːˈbjuːtəs], *s.* (*patol.*) scorbuto.

scorch [skɔːtʃ], *s.* **1.** bruciatura, scottatura superficiale **2.** (*fam.*) volata (in automobile, bicicletta).

to **scorch**, *v.t.i.* **1.** bruciacchiare, bruciacchiarsi **2.** riardere, inaridire (di sole, gelo, ecc.) **3.** *fig.* scottare; ferire i sentimenti di **4.** (*mil.*) mettere a ferro e fuoco (un territorio) prima di abbandonarlo al nemico **5.** (*fam.*) andare a forte velocità (di automobilista, ciclista).

scorcher ['skɔːtʃə*], *s.* **1.** chi, che brucia **2.** (*sl.*) giornata caldissima: *today is a* —, oggi si va arrosto **3.** (*sl.*) aspro rimprovero **4.** (*sl.*) automobilista, ciclista che va a forte velocità **5.** (*sl.*) bell'esemplare.

scorching ['skɔːtʃiŋ], *ag.* **1.** bruciante; ardente **2.** *fig.* caustico; mordace, pungente: — *criticism*, critica pungente.

scorchingly ['skɔːtʃiŋli], *av.* in modo bruciante, caustico.

score [skɔː*], *s.* **1.** tacca; scanalatura; sfregio: *the rock was covered with scores*, la roccia era coperta di scanalature **2.** linea; segno: *the scores of the whip showed on the boy's chest*, i segni della frusta erano visibili sul petto del ragazzo; *he made a* — *through my name with a pencil*, cancellò il mio nome con la matita **3.** linea di partenza, limite (in giuochi, corse) ‖ *to go off at* —, iniziare con foga; intavolare con entusiasmo un discorso **4.** conto, debito: *death pays all scores*, *fig.* la morte salda tutti i conti; *he paid his* —, egli pagò il suo debito; *he paid off* (o *settled*) *old scores*, *fig.* egli regolò vecchi conti ‖ *to quit scores with s.o.*, *fig.* rendere la pariglia a qlcu. **5.** ragione, causa, motivo: *on that* —, per questa ragione; a questo riguardo: *he may be easy on that* —, può star tranquillo in quanto a questo; *on what* —?, per quale motivo?; *he was excused on the* — *of illness*, fu scusato a causa della sua malattia **6.** (*invariato al pl.*) venti, ventina: *half a* —, una decina; *two* — *of handkerchiefs*, quaranta fazzoletti ‖ *three* — (*years*) *and ten*, settant'anni ‖ *scores of*, una gran quantità di **7.** (*spor.*) punti, punteggio: *what's the* —?, qual è il punteggio?; *to keep* (*the*) —, segnare il punteggio **8.** (*mus.*) spartito, partitura **9.** (*sl.*) bel colpo: *what a* —!, che fortuna! ☆ *full* —, partitura d'orchestra.

to **score**, *v.t.i.* **1.** intaccare; intagliare; incidere: *face scored with scars*, volto segnato da cicatrici **2.** marcare; segnare: *the translation was scored with corrections and crossings-out*, la traduzione era piena di correzioni e cancellature **3.** (*spor.*) segnare il punteggio; fare i punti: *they failed to* —, non fecero neanche un punto; *we scored five points*, facemmo cinque punti; *will you* —, *please?*, vuoi segnare il punteggio, per favore?; *to* — *a goal*, segnare un goal **4.** (*mus.*) orchestrare; arrangiare **5.** assicurarsi un vantaggio; aver fortuna: *to* — (*a success*), riportare un successo **6.** (*amer.*) rimproverare, sgridare **7.** *to* — **off**, (*sl.*) avere la meglio su; umiliare **8.** *to* — **out**, tirare una riga su (parole) **9.** *to* — **under**, sottolineare **10.** *to* — **up**, mettere in conto: *to* — *up sthg. to* (o *against*) *a customer*, mettere in conto ql.co. a un cliente.

scorer ['skɔːrə*], *s.* (*spor.*) chi segna il punteggio; marcatore.

scoria ['skɔːriə], *pl.* **scoriae** ['skɔːriiː], *s.* scoria.

scoriaceous [ˌskɔːriˈeiʃəs], *ag.* di scoria.

scorification [ˌskɔːrifiˈkeiʃən], *s.* (*metal.*) scorificazione.

scorifier ['skɔːrifaiə*], *s.* (*metal.*) scorificatoio.

to **scorify** ['skɔːrifai], *v.t.* ridurre in scorie; (*metal.*) scorificare.

scoring ['skɔːriŋ], *s.* (*mus.*) orchestrazione; trascrizione; arrangiamento.

scorn [skɔːn], *s.* **1.** disprezzo, disdegno; scherno: *eyes full of* —, occhi pieni di disprezzo; *to laugh to* —, deridere, schernire; *to think — of s.o.*, disprezzare qlcu.; *to think it — to do sthg.*, pensare di abbassarsi facendo ql.co. **2.** oggetto di disprezzo; zimbello.

to **scorn**, *v.t.* **1.** disprezzare; disdegnare: *he scorns a lie*, egli disdegna la menzogna; *to — to do* (o *doing*) *sthg.*, disdegnare di fare ql.co. **2.** (*arc.*) schernire; farsi beffe di.

scorner ['skɔːnə*], *s.c.* sprezzatore, sprezzatrice; schernitore, schernitrice.

scornful ['skɔːnful], *ag.* sprezzante; sdegnoso: *to be — of sthg.*, disdegnare, disprezzare ql.co.

scornfully ['skɔːnfuli], *av.* sprezzantemente; sdegnosamente.

scornfulness ['skɔːnfulnis], *s.* sdegnosità; disdegno; disprezzo.

Scorpio ['skɔːpiou], *no.pr.* (*astr.*) Scorpione.

scorpion ['skɔːpjən], *s.* **1.** (*zool.*) scorpione **2.** (*mil.*) scorpione, balestra **3.** (*biblico*) gatto a nove code ☆ *— -broom* (o *— -thorn*), (*bot.*) ginestra; *— -fish*, (*ittiol.*) scorfano; *— -grass*, (*bot.*) non-ti-scordar-di-me.

scorzonera [ˌskɔːzou'niərə], *s.* (*bot.*) scorzonera.

Scot[1] [skɔt], *s.* scozzese; (*st.*) scoto: *Mary, Queen of Scots*, Maria (Stuarda), regina di Scozia; *the Picts and the Scots*, i Pitti e gli Scoti;| *a native of Scotland likes to call himself a — or a Scotsman and not a Scotchman*, uno scozzese ama autodefinirsi « Scot » o « Scotsman » e non « Scotchman ».

scot[2], *s.* (*st.*) pagamento; scotto; tassa || *— and lot*, (*st.*) tassa proporzionale richiesta da una corporazione ai suoi membri; *to pay — and lot*, pagare le tasse (al Comune, ecc.); *fig.* regolare i conti ☆ *— -free*, sicuro, impunito; (*rar.*) esente da pagamento: *to go — -free*, cavarsela bene, passarla liscia.

Scotch[1] [skɔtʃ], *ag.* scozzese || *the —*, gli Scozzesi || *s.* **1.** scozzese (abitante, lingua) **2.** *— (whisky)*, whisky scozzese: *— and soda*, whisky e soda; *give me a drop of —*, dammi un goccio di whisky ☆ *— broth*, zuppa di orzo e verdura; *— collops*, bistecche con cipolle; *— egg*, uovo sodo con salsiccia; *— elm*, (*bot.*) olmo montano; *— fir*, pino silvestre; *— mist*, pioggerella; *— pebble*, (*min.*) agata, calcedonio; *— rose*, rosa spinosa; *— thistle*, cardo di Scozia || *broad —*, (dialetto) scozzese genuino.

scotch[2], *s.* tacca, incisione, taglio.

to **scotch**[2], *v.t.* **1.** (*rar.*) intaccare **2.** graffiare; ferire; rendere innocuo.

scotch[3], *s.* cuneo, arresto, zeppa.

to **scotch**[3], *v.t.i.* **1.** arrestare con cuneo, zeppa (ruote, ecc.) **2.** (*rar. dial.*) esitare.

Scotchman, *pl.* **Scotchmen** ['skɔtʃmən], *s.* (uomo) scozzese.

Scotchwoman ['skɔtʃˌwumən], *pl.* **Scotchwomen** ['skɔtʃˌwimin], *s.* (donna) scozzese.

scoter ['skoutə*], *s.* (*ornit.*) orco marino.

scotia ['skouʃə], *s.* (*arch.*) scozia.

Scoticism, *V.* **Scotticism**.

to **Scoticize**, *V.* to **Scotticize**.

Scotism ['skoutizəm], *s.* (*fil.*) scotismo.

Scotland ['skɔtlənd], *no.pr.* (*geog.*) Scozia || *— Yard*, « Scotland Yard » (la polizia metropolitana di Londra).

scotoma [skou'toumə], *pl.* **scotomata** [skou'toumətə], *s.* (*patol.*) scotoma.

Scots [skɔts], *ag.* (*rar.*) scozzese: *— law*, legge scozzese || *s.* (dialetto) scozzese ☆ *pound —*, (*st.*) sterlina scozzese.

Scotsman, *pl.* **Scotsmen** ['skɔtsmən], *s.* (uomo) scozzese || *the Flying Scotsman*, (*ferr.*) la Freccia della Scozia.

Scotswoman ['skɔtsˌwumən], *pl.* **Scotswomen** ['skɔtsˌwimin], *s.* (donna) scozzese.

Scottice ['skɔtisi(ː)], *av.* in scozzese.

Scotticism ['skɔtisizəm], *s.* parola, frase idiomatica scozzese.

to **Scotticize** ['skɔtisaiz], *v.t.i.* **1.** imitare la parlata, le abitudini scozzesi **2.** rendere scozzese.

Scottish ['skɔtiʃ], *ag.* scozzese: *— dance, literature,*

danza, letteratura scozzese; *— rite*, rito scozzese (nella Massoneria) || *s.* dialetto scozzese.

scoundrel ['skaundrəl], *s.* furfante, farabutto; mascalzone; ribaldo.

scoundrelism ['skaundrəlizəm], *s.* furfanteria; ribalderia.

scoundrelly ['skaundrəli], *ag.* furfante; ribaldo; infame.

scour[1] [skauə*], *s.* **1.** pulizia; lavaggio **2.** sostanza detergente; detersivo **3.** *gener. pl.* diarrea; dissenteria (del bestiame).

to **scour**[1], *v.t.i.* **1.** fregare; sfregare; stropicciare; strofinare; lucidare; pulire: *she scoured the pot till it shone*, lucidò la pentola sino a farla brillare; *to — the floor*, fregare il pavimento **2.** spazzar via: *the fleet scoured the seas of enemy ships*, la flotta spazzò via le navi nemiche dai mari; *to — invaders from one's country*, liberare la patria dagli invasori **3.** sgrassare, lavare (lana) **4.** purgare energicamente: *to — a horse*, purgare un cavallo.

to **scour**[2], *v.t.i.* **1.** correre velocemente; muoversi rapidamente (in un posto, all'inseguimento di qlcu., ql.co.) **2.** percorrere, perlustrare: *to — a town for a thief*, perlustrare una città in cerca di un ladro; *to — the woods*, perlustrare i boschi **3.** scorrazzare di notte (molestando, rompendo vetri, ecc.).

scoured ['skauəd], *ag.* lavato; sgrassato: *'— wool*, lana lavata.

scourer[1] ['skauərə*], *s.* **1.** smacchiatore; lucidatore **2.** purgante energico.

scourer[2], *s.* nottambulo; vagabondo; disturbatore notturno.

scourge [skəːdʒ], *s.* **1.** (*arc.*) sferza, staffile, frusta **2.** *fig.* flagello; castigo; punizione: *the — of God*, il flagello di Dio; *the — of war*, il flagello della guerra || *the white —*, la tisi.

to **scourge**, *v.t.* **1.** (*arc.*) sferzare, fustigare, flagellare **2.** castigare, punire (severamente).

scourger ['skəːdʒə*], *s.* **1.** (*st.*) fustigatore (anche *fig.*) **2.** (*st. relig.*) flagellante.

scout[1] [skaut], *s.* chiatta, battello fluviale olandese da trasporto.

scout[2], *s.* **1.** esploratore; ricognitore (anche *mil.*) || *boy —*, giovane esploratore; *girl —*, (*amer.* per *girl guide*) giovane esploratrice **2.** (*fam.*) individuo, tipo: (*amer.*) buon uomo **3.** (*mar.*) nave da ricognizione; (*aer.*) aereo ricognitore **4.** (*mil.*) esplorazione; ricognizione: *on the —*, in ricognizione.

to **scout**[2], *v.t.i.* **1.** andare in esplorazione, in ricognizione; perlustrare: *to be out scouting*, essere in esplorazione, ricognizione **2.** *to — about*, andare in cerca di informazioni, ecc.

scout[3], *s.* nome comune di alcuni uccelli marini dell'Inghilterra.

scout[4], *s.* inserviente (nelle università di Oxford, Yale, Harvard).

to **scout**[5], *v.t.* respingere con disprezzo; considerare ridicolo: *to — a suggestion*, respingere sdegnosamente un suggerimento.

scouter ['skautə*], *s.* **1.** (*aer.*) ricognitore **2.** membro adulto (di organizzazione di giovani esploratori).

scouting ['skautiŋ], *s.* **1.** esplorazione; ricognizione **2.** scoutismo ☆ *— -plane*, ricognitore.

scow [skau], *s.* zattera, chiatta.

scowl [skaul], *s.* cipiglio; sguardo torvo; viso arcigno; aspetto minaccioso.

to **scowl**, *v.t.i.* **1.** aggrottare le ciglia, lanciare occhiate torve, minacciose: *the thief scowled at* (o *on*) *the policeman*, il ladro guardò torvamente il poliziotto **2.** *to — down*, intimidire, zittire con fiero cipiglio.

scowling ['skauliŋ], *ag.* torvo, accigliato.

scowlingly ['skauliŋli], *av.* torvamente, con viso accigliato.

scrabble ['skræbl], *s.* scarabocchio, sgorbio.

to **scrabble**, *v.t.i.* **1.** scarabocchiare; scribacchiare **2.** cardare (lana) **3.** cercare a tentoni.

scrag[1] [skræg], *s.* **1.** persona, animale scheletrico **2.** collottola di montone, vitello **3.** (*sl.*) collo di persona.

to **scrag**[1], *pass.p.p.* **scragged** [skrægd], *v.t.* **1.** (*sl.*) torcere il collo a, strangolare; impiccare **2.** (*rugby*) afferrare per il collo **3.** (*sl. scolastico*) stringere il collo di (un ragazzo) sotto il braccio (per picchiarlo).

scrag[2], *s.* **1.** (*dial.*) tronco, ceppo d'albero **2.** prominenza, sporgenza (di roccia, albero, ecc.) **3.** terreno roccioso e sterile.

scraggily[1] ['skrægili], *av.* magramente, in modo scheletrico.

scraggily[2], *av.* ruvidamente, scabrosamente.

scragginess[1] ['skrægīnis], *s.* magrezza scheletrica.

scragginess[2], *s.* ruvidezza, scabrosità.

scraggy[1] ['skrægi], *ag.* **1.** ossuto; scarno; scheletrico **2.** magro (di carne).

scraggy[2], *ag.* ruvido, scabroso.

to **scram** [skræm], *v.i.* (*sl. amer. gener. all'imperat.*) andarsene, battersela, levar le tende: —!, togliti dai piedi!.

scramble ['skræmbl], *s.* **1.** arrampicata; scalata **2.** contesa, gara, lotta; tafferuglio, parapiglia: *the — for a living*, la lotta per l'esistenza; *to fling oneself into the —*, gettarsi nella mischia.

to **scramble**, *v.t.i.* **1.** arrampicarsi con mani e piedi, inerpicarsi; avanzare a tentoni; strisciare: *he scrambled up the hill*, si arrampicò su per la collina **2.** arraffare ‖ *to — up wealth*, ammucchiare ricchezze **3.** rimescolare, mescolare alla rinfusa: *to — cards*, rimescolare le carte **4.** (*cuc.*) strapazzare (uova) **5.** *to — for (sthg.)*, affannarsi per; battersi per: *he scrambles for a living*, lotta per guadagnarsi da vivere: *the players scrambled for the ball*, i giocatori si contendevano la palla.

scrambling ['skræmbliŋ], *ag.* irregolare: *to do sthg. in a — fashion*, fare ql.co. in modo disordinato, senza metodo.

scramblingly ['skræmbliŋli], *av.* irregolarmente; alla meglio; con fatica.

scran [skræn], *s.* (*sl.*) cibo, commestibili.

scrannel ['skræn], *ag.* **1.** (*arc.*) leggero; sottile, debole (di suono) **2.** aspro: *a — voice*, una voce aspra.

scranny ['skræni], *ag.* (*dial.*) magro; scarno; povero.

scrap[1] [skræp], *s.* pezzetto: *a — of paper*, un pezzo di carta: *it is only a — of paper*, non è che un pezzo di carta; *fig.* una promessa, un patto che si può infrangere ‖ *not a —*, niente affatto **2.** frammento; brano; estratto: *I read scraps of the essay*, lessi alcuni brani del saggio **3.** *pl.* rimasugli, avanzi (di cibo); ritagli (di giornali, ecc.) **4.** *coll.* scarti; rottame ☆ — *-book*, album (per ritagli di giornali, ecc.); — *-heap*, mucchio di rifiuti; — *-iron*, rottame di ferro; — *lunch*, una colazione con cibo avanzato.

to **scrap**[1], *pass.p.p.* **scrapped** [skræpt], *v.t.* scartare; mettere fuori servizio; smantellare: *to — old machinery*, scartare vecchio macchinario.

scrap[2], *s.* (*sl.*) contesa, litigio; discussione violenta.

to **scrap**[2], *v.i.* (*sl.*) litigare; discutere violentemente.

scrape [skreip], *s.* **1.** graffio, scalfittura: *a — on the elbow*, un graffio al gomito ‖ *a — of the pen*, un tratto di penna ‖ *bread and —*, (*sl.*) pane leggermente imburrato **2.** suono prodotto da una raschiatura **3.** *fig.* impiccio, imbroglio, difficoltà: *he is always getting into scrapes*, si mette sempre nei guai; *to get out of a —*, togliersi da un impiccio ☆ — *-good* (o — *-penny*), avaro, tirchio; — *-gut*, violinista da strapazzo.

to **scrape**, *v.t.i.* **1.** raschiare; scrostare; grattare: *to — paint from a door*, grattare la vernice da una porta‖ *to — one's chin*, radersi ‖ *to — one's plate*, (*scherz.*) leccare il piatto ‖ *to — a ship's bottom*, raschiare la carena di una nave **2.** levigare **3.** sfregare; strisciare: *the boat scraped her side against a rock*, la barca strisciò il fianco contro una roccia; *the boy scraped his knee*,

il ragazzo si sbucciò il ginocchio ‖ *to bow and —*, fare salamelecchi **4.** racimolare, raggranellare: *he scraped a few pounds together*, raggranellò alcune sterline ‖ *to — acquaintance with s.o.*, riuscire ad introdursi presso qlcu. ‖ *to — a living*, sbarcare il lunario **5.** strimpellare: *to — a violin*, strimpellare il violino **6.** *to — along*, vivacchiare ‖ *they — along together*, vanno abbastanza d'accordo **7.** *to — down*, zittire (un oratore) pestando i piedi **8.** *to — out*, scavare **9.** *to — up*, raccogliere; racimolare: *to — up the dirt from the road*, raccogliere la spazzatura dalla strada **10.** *to — through*, cavarsela: *to — through an examination*, passare (al un esame) per il buco della serratura.

scraper ['skreipə*], *s.* **1.** raschiatoio; raschietto **2.** (*agr.*) ruspa **3.** strimpellatore **4.** (*rar.*) spilorcio **5.** (*spreg.*) barbiere ☆ — *ring*, (*aut.*) anello raschiaolio ‖ *shoe —*, zerbino, stoino.

scraping ['skreipiŋ], *s.* **1.** raschiatura; scrostatura **2.** *pl.* risparmi.

scrapper ['skræpə*], *s.* (*sl.*) **1.** attaccabrighe **2.** pugile che ha del fegato.

scrappily ['skræpili], *av.* in modo frammentario.

scrappiness ['skræpinis], *s.* frammentarietà.

scrappy ['skræpi], *ag.* frammentario.

scratch[1] [skrætʃ], *ag.* messo insieme in fretta, a caso: *a — dinner*, una cena improvvisata; *— team*, squadra mista, eterogenea.

scratch[1], *s.* **1.** graffiatura; graffio; leggera ferita, scalfittura: *she survived the terrible accident with a mere —*, in quello spaventoso incidente se la cavò con una leggera ferita **2.** (*fam.*) scarabocchio; sgorbio: *a — of the pen*, un tratto di penna; una firma **3.** grattata, grattatina: *my pussy enjoys a good —*, al mio gattino piace farsi grattare **4.** linea di partenza; *fig.* zero: *to start from —*, cominciare dal nulla; partire da zero ‖ *to come up to (the) —*, comparire al momento giusto; *fig.* far fronte ai propri impegni; mostrarsi all'altezza della situazione **5.** colpo fortunato al biliardo **6.** *gener. pl.* (*vet.*) rappa ☆ — *-brush*, (*tec.*) grattapugia; — *-cat*, (*fam.*) bambino stizzoso; donna dispettosa; — *man*, concorrente che concede un certo vantaggio al suo avversario; — *race*, corsa in cui tutti i concorrenti hanno condizioni pari; — *-wig*, parrucchino; — *-work*, decorazione a graffito.

to **scratch**[1], *v.t.i.* **1.** graffiare: *the cat scratched the child*, il gatto graffiò il bambino; *he scratched himself on the thorns*, si graffiò con le spine **2.** *fig.* scalfire; sfiorare: *the speaker only scratched the surface of the problem*, il conferenziere sfiorò appena l'argomento **3.** grattare, grattarsi: *to — one's head*, grattarsi la testa (anche *fig.*) ‖ *my back and I'll — yours*, (*amer.*) aiutami che ti aiuterò **4.** (*fam.*) scribacchiare, buttar giù: *to — a few words*, buttar giù due righe **5.** ritirare da una gara (cavallo, concorrente); ritirarsi: *the horse was scratched*, il cavallo fu ritirato; *she scratched on the morning of the game*, si ritirò la mattina dalla gara **6.** razzolare: *the hen scratched for food for her chicks*, la gallina razzolava in cerca di cibo per i suoi pulcini **7.** stridere: *this pen scratches*, questa penna stride **8.** *to — along*, vivacchiare **9.** *to — out, through*, cancellare: *— my name out*, cancella il mio nome (dalla lista) **10.** *to — up*, raggranellare, racimolare: *he managed to — up enough money*, riuscì a racimolare abbastanza denaro.

scratch[2], *s.* (*old*) —, il diavolo, Satana.

scratchy ['skrætʃi], *ag.* **1.** graffiato; scalfito **2.** scarabocchiato; irregolare: *a — drawing*, un disegno mal fatto; *a — writing*, scrittura a zampe di gallina **3.** stridente: *a — pen*, una penna stridente **4.** (*mus.*) ineguale; discordante: *a — performance*, un'esecuzione ineguale **5.** ruvido; rozzo (di stoffa, ecc.).

scrawl [skrɔ:l], *s.* **1.** scarabocchio, sgorbio **2.** lettera, biglietto scarabocchiato in fretta.

to **scrawl**, *v.t.i.* **1.** scarabocchiare; imbrattare: *to — (all) over a piece of paper*, scarabocchiare, imbrattare un foglio **2.** scribacchiare; scrivere malamente, in modo illeggibile.

scrawler ['skrɔːlə*], *s.c.* chi scarabocchia, imbratta; scribacchino, scribacchina.

scrawly ['skrɔːli], *ag.* scarabocchiato; tutto sgorbi ‖ — *writing*, (*fam.*) scritto a zampe di gallina.

scrawny ['skrɔːni], *ag.* (*dial.*) magro; scarno.

scray, scraye [skrei], *s.* (*ornit.*) rondine di mare.

screak [skriːk], *s.* stridore; scricchiolio, cigolio.

to screak, *v.i.* stridere; scricchiolare, cigolare.

scream [skriːm], *s.* **1.** grido acuto, strillo, urlo: *a — of pain*, un urlo di dolore **2.** (*sl.*) persona, cosa ridicola: *she is a perfect —*, è terribilmente ridicola.

to scream, *v.t.i.* **1.** gridare, strillare, urlare: *the baby screamed all night*, il neonato strillò tutta la notte; *to — (out) an order*, urlare un ordine **2.** fischiare (di locomotiva, ecc.) **3.** ridere senza ritegno: *to — (with laughter)*, ridere a crepapelle.

screamer ['skriːmə*], *s.c.* strillone, strillona ‖ *s.* (*sl.*) **1.** scritto che fa scoppiare dalle risa **2.** esemplare straordinario (di qualsiasi cosa) **3.** (*amer.*) titolo sensazionale **4.** (*ornit.*) palamedea.

screaming ['skriːmiŋ], *ag.* **1.** strillante, urlante **2.** sguaiato; chiassoso: — *colours*, colori chiassosi **3.** (*fam.*) che fa scoppiare dalle risa, spassoso: *a — farce*, una farsa molto spassosa ‖ *s.* grida, strilli, urla.

screamingly ['skriːmiŋli], *av.* (*fam.*) da far scoppiare dalle risa: *the farce was — funny*, la farsa era terribilmente buffa.

scree [skriː], *s. gener. pl.* **1.** (*geol.*) ghiaione **2.** ghiaia.

screech [skriːtʃ], *s.* **1.** grido; strillo acuto **2.** stridio, stridore ☆ — *-owl*, (*ornit.*) barbagianni; strige.

to screech, *v.t.i.* **1.** gridare; strillare **2.** stridere: *the brakes screeched*, i freni stridettero.

screecher ['skriːtʃə*], *s.c.* chi strilla, chi grida.

screechy ['skriːtʃi], *ag.* stridulo; acuto; stridente.

screed [skriːd], *s.* **1.** lunga filastrocca **2.** geremiade **3.** (*edil.*) guida (per intonaco).

screen [skriːn], *s.* **1.** paravento **2.** (*arch.*) transenna; parete divisoria **3.** cartellone per affisso murale **4.** (*mec.*) vaglio, crivello **5.** riparo, protezione, cortina, schermo (anche *fig.*): *the — of indifference*, la maschera dell'indifferenza; *under the — of night*, col favore della notte **6.** (*mil.*) truppe di copertura **7.** (*mar.*) scorta (di convoglio) **8.** (*cine. tv.*) schermo ‖ *the —*, l'industria cinematografica ☆ — *-play*, soggetto cinematografico; — *-star*, divo, diva dello schermo ‖ *folding- —*, paravento pieghevole; *smoke —*, (*mil. aer.*) cortina di fumo.

to screen, *v.t.i.* **1.** riparare, proteggere; fornire di schermo; mettere al coperto; nascondere: *to — s.o. from the crowd*, proteggere qlcu. dalla folla **2.** selezionare; vagliare **3.** (*elett.*) schermare; *to — a valve*, schermare una valvola **4.** (*cine.*) proiettare; adattare, ridurre per lo schermo (romanzo, dramma, ecc.); essere adatto per lo schermo (di storia, ecc.): *this story screens well but that one screens badly*, questa storia è adatta per lo schermo, quella non lo è **5.** *to — off*, separare (con paravento, ecc.).

screenings ['skriːniŋz], *s.pl.* **1.** materiale vagliato **2.** residui, scarti di vagliatura.

screw [skruː], *s.* **1.** vite; cavo della vite; giro di vite (anche *fig.*): *to give another (turn of) —*, dare un altro giro di vite ‖ *to have a — loose*, (*fam.*) avere una rotella fuori posto, essere svitato ‖ *to put the — on*, *fig.* esercitare pressione su **2.** succhiello; cavatappi **3.** — *(-propeller)*, elica **4.** — *(-steamer)*, vapore ad elica **5.** (*biliardo*) effetto **6.** cartoccio; piccola quantità **7.** (*sl.*) taccagno, spilorcio **8.** (*sl.*) ronzino **9.** (*sl.*) paga **10.** (*sl.*) chiave falsa; furto con chiavi false **11.** (*sl. amer.*) secondino ☆ — *-cutting machine*, filettatrice; — *-eye*, occhiello a vite; — *-nut*, dado della vite; — *-pile*, palo a vite; — *-pine*, (*bot.*) pandano; — *-pitch gauge*, calibro per filettatura; — *-press*, bilanciere; — *-ship*, nave a elica; — *-stair*, scala a chiocciola; — *-thread*, filettatura; — *-wheel*, ruota ad elica; — *-wrench*, chiave

inglese a rullino ‖ *differential —*, vite differenziale; *female —*, vite femmina; *Hindley's —*, vite globoidale; *jack- —*, banda a vite; (*med.*) vite regolatrice dell'arco di contenzione delle protesi dentarie; *left-handed —*, vite sinistrorsa; *male —*, vite maschia; *perpetual —* (o *endless —*), vite perpetua; *worm- —*, vite senza fine.

to screw, *v.t.i.* **1.** avvitare; stringere, serrare: *to — tight*, avvitare ben stretto; *to — two pieces of wood together*, avvitare insieme due pezzi di legno ‖ *to have one's head screwed on the right way*, (*fam.*) avere la testa a posto **2.** torcere, torcersi; contorcere, contorcersi: *to — one's head (round) to see sthg.*, torcere la testa per vedere ql.co. **3.** *fig.* spremere, estorcere; vessare: *to — sthg. of s.o.*, estorcere ql.co. a qlcu. **4.** (*sl.*) essere tirchio, spilorcio **5.** *to — back*, rimbalzare all'indietro (di palla) **6.** *to — in*, avvitare, fare entrare a forza **7.** *to — off, out*, svitare **8.** *to — up*, serrare con vite; tendere le corde (di violino); torcere, contorcere; chiudere rapidamente: *she screwed up her eyes on going out into the sunshine*, strizzò gli occhi uscendo fuori alla luce del sole ‖ *to — up one's courage*, *fig.* prendere il coraggio a due mani.

screwball ['skruːbɔːl], *s.* (*sl.*) svitato, testa matta.

screwdriver ['skruːˌdraivə*], *s.* cacciavite.

screwed [skruːd], *ag.* **1.** a vite; avvitato **2.** contorto **3.** (*sl.*) ubriaco.

screwer ['skruːə*], *s.* **1.** (*mec.*) avvitatrice **2.** (*mar.*) nave ad elica.

screwy ['skruːi], *ag.* **1.** brillo **2.** tirchio, spilorcio **3.** bizzoso (di cavallo).

scribal ['skraibəl], *ag.* di copista: *a — error*, un errore del copista.

scribble[1] ['skribl], *s.* sgorbio; scarabocchio (anche *fig.*).

to scribble[1], *v.t.i.* sgorbiare; scarabocchiare; scribacchiare.

to scribble[2], *v.t.* (*ind. tessile*) cardare in grosso.

scribbler[1] ['skriblə*], *s.* chi scarabocchia; scribacchino, imbrattacarte.

scribbler[2], *s.* (*ind. tessile*) **1.** cardatore in grosso **2.** (*mec.*) carda in grosso.

scribe [skraib], *s.* **1.** copista, amanuense **2.** (*rar.*) scrittore: *I am no great —*, non so scrivere bene **3.** (*Bibbia*) scriba **4.** (*st.*) scrivano pubblico; segretario **5.** (*scherz. spreg.*) scrittore di politica; giornalista **6.** (*mec.*) punta a tracciare.

to scribe, *v.t.i.* **1.** fare il copista, scrivere **2.** (*mec.*) tracciare, incidere (legno, metalli, ecc.).

scriber ['skraibə*], *s.* punta a tracciare ☆ *timber —*, graffietto da falegnami.

Scriblerus [skrib'liərəs], *no.pr.* (*st.lett.*) Scriblerus.

scrim [skrim], *s.* tela; canovaccio (da ricamo); tessuto a rete (per tende).

scrimmage ['skrimidʒ], *s.* **1.** baruffa; schermaglia **2.** (*spor.*) mischia.

to scrimp [skrimp], *V.* to skimp.

scrimpy ['skrimpi], *ag.* **1.** scarso **2.** tirchio, meschino.

to scrimshank ['skrimʃæŋk], *v.i.* (*sl. mil.*) sottrarsi al proprio dovere, scansare fatiche.

scrimshanker ['skrimˌʃæŋkə*], *s.* (*sl.mil.*) scansafatiche.

scrimshaw ['skrimʃɔː], *s.* **1.** decorazione, incisione, intaglio (di conchiglie, avorio, ecc.) **2.** oggetto (di avorio, ecc.) intagliato, decorato.

to scrimshaw, *v.t.i.* intagliare; decorare con intagli.

scrip[1] [skrip], *s.* (*arc.*) bisaccia (di pellegrino, ecc.).

scrip[2], *s.* **1.** pezzo di carta **2.** frammento di uno scritto **3.** (*amer.*) moneta cartacea di piccolo taglio.

scrip[3], *s.* **1.** certificato provvisorio; cedola; polizza **2.** *gener. coll.* azioni; obbligazioni; titoli.

script [skript], *s.* **1.** (*dir.*) documento originale **2.** scrittura a mano; (*tip.*) corsivo **3.** (*teat.*) manoscritto; testo; copione **4.** compito scritto (di esaminando).

scriptorium [skrip'tɔːriəm], *pl.* **scriptoria** [skrip'tɔːriə], *s.* **1.** sala di scrittura (in monastero) **2.** sala di redazione (di dizionario, ecc.).

scriptural [ˈskriptʃərəl], *ag.* basato su, concernente la Sacra Scrittura; biblico.

scripturalist [ˈskriptʃərəlist], *s.* interprete letterale delle Sacre Scritture.

scripture [ˈskriptʃə*], *s.* **1.** la Sacra Scrittura ‖ *Holy Scriptures*, le Sacre Scritture, la Bibbia **2.** (*arc.*) scritto, documento; iscrizione **3.** (*rar.*) citazione biblica **4.** libro, scritto sacro ☆ — *-reader*, lettore della Bibbia (in casa dei poveri).

scrivener [ˈskrivnə*], *s.* scrivano pubblico; notaio; agente d'affari ☆ — *'s palsy*, crampo dello scrittore.

scrobiculate [skrouˈbikjulit], **scrobiculated** [skrou-ˈbikjuleitid], *ag.* (*bot. zool.*) pieno di fossette.

scrod [skrɔd], *s.* (*amer. cuc.*) piccolo merluzzo.

scrofula [ˈskrɔfjuls], *s.* (*patol.*) scrofola.

scrofulous [ˈskrɔfjuləs], *ag.* (*patol.*) scrofoloso.

scroll [skroul], *s.* **1.** rotolo (di pergamena, carta) **2.** (*arch.*) decorazione a spirale, voluta, cartoccio; cartiglio **3.** svolazzo (nella firma) **4.** chiocciola (del violino) **5.** (*mec.*) chiocciola, coclea **6.** (*ind. tessile*) lumaca **7.** (*arc.*) scritto; lista ☆ — *-head*, voluta alla prua della nave; — *-lathe*, tornio a spirale; — *-saw*, sega a svolgere; — *-wheel*, ruota a spirale; — *-work*, voluta, spira ornamentale.

to scroll, *v.t.i.* **1.** avvolgere, avvolgersi a rotolo **2.** decorare, adornare di svolazzi.

scrolled [skrould], *ag.* **1.** decorato con volute; a forma di spirale, voluta **2.** a svolazzi (di firma, ecc.).

scroop [skru:p], *s.* stridore; scricchiolio; cigolio.

to scroop, *v.i.* stridere; scricchiolare; cigolare.

scrophularia [ˌskrɔfjuˈlɛəriə], *s.* (*bot.*) scrofularia.

scrotal [ˈskroutl], *ag.* (*anat.*) scrotale.

scrotum [ˈskroutəm], *pl.* **scrota** [ˈskroutə], *s.* (*anat.*) scroto.

to scrounge [skraundʒ], *v.t.i.* (*sl.*) rubacchiare; scroccare; elemosinare ‖ *to — around for sthg.*, andare alla ricerca di ql.co.

scrounger [ˈskraundʒə*], *s.c.* ladruncolo, ladruncola; scroccone, scroccona.

scrub[1] [skrʌb], *s.* **1.** pianta stentata **2.** sottobosco; boscaglia; macchia **3.** « scrub » (tipo di steppa australiana con vegetazione di cespugli spinosi) **4.** bovino di razza piccola **5.** *fig.* individuo scialbo, povero diavolo.

scrub[2], *s.c.* **1.** donna, uomo di fatica ‖ pezzente ‖ *s.* **1.** spazzolata; lavata; pulitura a fondo **2.** spazzola (a setole corte); scopa **3.** (*fam. amer.*) giocatore di riserva; partita ridotta (di baseball).

to scrub[2], *pass.p.p.* **scrubbed** [skrʌbd], *v.t.i.* **1.** pulire fregando forte, fregare: *to — a floor*, pulire, fregare un pavimento **2.** (*chim.*) lavare.

scrubber [ˈskrʌbə*], *s.c.* chi pulisce, spazzola ‖ *s.* (*chim.*) gorgogliatore di lavaggio.

scrubbing [ˈskrʌbiŋ], *s.* fregamento, lavaggio energico: *the child's knees needed a good* —, le ginocchia del bambino avevano bisogno di una buona lavata ☆ — *brush*, spazzola dura, bruschino.

scrubby[1] [ˈskrʌbi], *ag.* **1.** esile, debole; macilento; stentato, intristito (di piante) **2.** coperto di boscaglia **3.** *fig.* insignificante, meschino.

scrubby[2], *ag.* irsuto, spinoso.

scruff[1] [skrʌf], *s.* **1.** crosta, strato, rivestimento sottile **2.** rifiuto, scarto.

scruff[2], *s.* nuca; collottola: *to take s.o. by the — of the neck*, prendere qlcu. per la collottola.

scrummage [ˈskrʌmidʒ], *V.* **scrimmage**.

scrumptious [ˈskrʌmpʃəs], *ag.* (*sl.*) delizioso, di primo ordine, eccezionale.

scrunch [skrʌntʃ], *s.* **1.** lo stritolare rumorosamente (con denti, piedi, ruote) **2.** scricchiolio, il cricchiare (di cibo sotto i denti, ghiaia sotto i piedi, ecc.).

to scrunch, *v.t.i.* **1.** schiacciare rumorosamente **2.** scricchiolare, far scricchiolare: *the frozen snow scrunched under the wheels*, la neve gelata scricchiolava sotto le ruote.

scruple[1] [ˈskru:pl], *s.* scrupolo; dubbio, incertezza,

esitazione: *man of no scruples*, uomo senza scrupoli; *to have scruples about* (o *in*) *doing sthg.* (o *to* |*make* — *to do sthg.*), farsi scrupolo di fare ql.co.; *to have* (o *to make*) *no* — *about doing sthg.*, non farsi scrupolo di fare ql.co.

to scruple[1], *v.t.i.* **1.** avere scrupoli; farsi scrupolo (generalmente in frase negativa): *she would not* — *to tell lies*, non si farebbe scrupolo di dire bugie **2.** (*arc.*) esitare davanti a (ql.co.).

scruple[2], *s.* **1.** scrupolo (misura di peso = g. 1,29) **2.** un sessantesimo di grado, di ora **3.** (*arc.*) quantità minima.

scrupler [ˈskru:plə*], *s.c.* persona scrupolosa.

scrupulosity [ˌskru:pjuˈlɔsiti], *s.* **1.** scrupolosità **2.** meticolosità, pedanteria.

scrupulous [ˈskru:pjuləs], *ag.* **1.** scrupoloso **2.** meticoloso, pignolo.

scrupulously [ˈskru:pjuləsli], *av.* **1.** scrupolosamente **2.** meticolosamente.

scrupulousness [ˈskru:pjuləsnis], *s.* **1.** scrupolosità **2.** meticolosità, pedanteria.

scrutator [skru:ˈteitə*], *s.c.* investigatore, investigatrice.

scrutineer [ˌskru:tiˈniə*], *s.c.* scrutatore, scrutatrice (alle urne elettorali).

to scrutinize [ˈskru:tinaiz], *v.t.* scrutinare; esaminare minuziosamente: *to — a proposal*, esaminare a fondo una proposta; *to — s.o.'s face*, scrutare qlcu. con sguardo penetrante.

scrutinizer [ˈskru:tinaizə*], *s.c.* scrutatore, scrutatrice.

scrutinizing [ˈskru:tinaiziŋ], *ag.* scrutinatore; inquisitivo ‖ *s.* **1.** esame minuzioso **2.** (*pol.*) verifica di uno scrutinio.

scrutinous [ˈskru:tinəs], *ag.* scrutinatore; inquisitivo.

scrutiny [ˈskru:tini], *s.* **1.** esame minuzioso; esame critico: *his record does not bear* —, il suo passato non è ineccepibile **2.** (*pol.*) verifica di uno scrutinio: — *of an electoral list*, scrutinio di una lista elettorale.

scud [skʌd], *s.* **1.** rapida corsa; fuga **2.** nuvolaglia.

to scud, *pass.p.p.* **scudded** [ˈskʌdid], *v.t.i.* correre velocemente; guizzar via, fuggir via ‖ *to — along* (o *before the wind*), (*mar.*) navigare in direzione del vento.

scudo [ˈsku:dou], *pl.* **scudi** [ˈsku:di:], *s.* scudo (moneta).

scuff[1] [skʌf], *V.* **scruff**[2].

to scuff[2], *v.t.i.* **1.** strascicare (i piedi); camminare strascicando i piedi **2.** sfiorare **3.** (*mec.*) pregrippare.

scuffle[1] [ˈskʌfl], *s.* **1.** zuffa; tafferuglio; rissa; mischia **2.** strascichio (di piedi).

to scuffle[1], *v.t.i.* **1.** azzuffarsi; picchiarsi **2.** agire affrettatamente, superficialmente: *to — through a task*, portare a termine un compito in fretta e furia **3.** strascicare i piedi.

scuffle[2], *s.* (*agr.*) sarchio.

to scuffle[2], *v.t.* (*agr.*) sarchiare.

scuffler [ˈskʌflə*], *s.* (*agr.*) sarchio.

scuffy [ˈskʌfi], *ag.* (*scoz.*) logoro, consumato.

to sculk, *V.* **to skulk**.

scull [skʌl], *s.* (*mar.*) **1.** palella; bratto: *a pair of sculls*, un paio di palelle **2.** remata.

to scull, *v.t.i.* spingere (un'imbarcazione) con palelle, col bratto; vogare di coda.

sculler [ˈskʌlə*], *s.* **1.** chi rema con palelle **2.** sandolino.

scullery [ˈskʌləri], *s.* retrocucina; acquaio ☆ — *-boy*, sguattero; — *-maid*, sguattera.

scullion [ˈskʌljən], *s.* (*arc.*) sguattero.

to sculp [skʌlp], (*fam.*) *abbr.* di **to sculpture**.

sculpin [ˈskʌlpin], *s.* **1.** (*ittiol.*) scorpena, scorfano **2.** (*fam.*) buono a nulla.

sculptor [ˈskʌlptə*], *s.* scultore.

sculptress [ˈskʌlptris], *s.* scultrice.

sculptural [ˈskʌlptʃərəl], *ag.* scultorio, statuario; di scultura: — *beauty*, bellezza scultorea.

sculpturally [ˈskʌlptʃərəli], *av.* in modo scultoreo: *she is* — *beautiful*, è bella come una statua.

sculpture [ˈskʌlptʃə*], *s.* **1.** scultura **2.** (*bot. zool.*) solchi; rilievi.

to **sculpture**, *v.t.i.* **1.** scolpire **2.** adornare di, con sculture **3.** (*bot. zool.*) avere solchi, rilievi.

sculpturesque [ˌskʌlptʃəˈresk],*ag.*scultoreo;statuario.

scum [skʌm], *s.* **1.** schiuma; spuma **2.** feccia (anche *fig.*): *the — of society*, la feccia della società **3.** (*metal.*) scoria.

to **scum**, *pass.p.p.* **scummed** [skʌmd], *v.t.i.* **1.** schiumare; togliere la schiuma da; far schiuma, ricoprirsi di schiuma **2.** produrre feccia, scorie.

scumble [ˈskʌmbl], *s.* (*pitt.*) smorzatura di tinte; sfumatura di contorni.

to **scumble**, *v.t.* (*pitt.*) smorzare (le tinte); sfumare (i contorni).

scummer [ˈskʌmə*], *s.* schiumaiuola.

scumming [ˈskʌmiŋ], *s.* **1.** lo schiumare **2.** *pl.* scorie, feccia.

scummy [ˈskʌmi], *ag.* **1.** schiumoso; di, simile a schiuma **2.** disprezzabile; basso; meschino.

scunner [ˈskʌnə*], *s.* (*scoz.*) avversione; ripugnanza: *to take a — at* (o *against*) *s.o.*, avere una forte antipatia per qlcu.

to **scunner**, *v.t.i.* (*scoz.*) disgustare, nauseare; sentir nausea; provare disgusto.

scupper[1] [ˈskʌpə*], *s.* (*arch.*) sbocco di scarico dell'acqua piovana; (*mar.*) ombrinale.

to **scupper**[2], *v.t.* **1.** (*sl. mil.*) attaccare di sorpresa e massacrare (ciurma); sorprendere e affondare (nave) **2.** *fig.* mettere, lasciare in difficoltà.

scuppernong [ˈskʌpənɒŋ], *s.* (*amer.*) **1.** varietà di uva americana **2.** vino ottenuto da tale uva.

scurf[1] [skə:f], *s.* **1.** squama, forfora **2.** incrostazioni, pellicole (sulle foglie di alcune piante) **3.** crosta (di piaga) **4.** incrostazione (in caldaia).

to **scurf**[1], *v.t.* grattar via (squame), togliere (incrostazioni).

scurf[2], *s.* (*ittiol.*) trota di mare.

scurfiness [ˈskə:finis], *s.* **1.** tendenza alla formazione di forfora, croste, squame **2.** squamosità.

scurfy [ˈskə:fi], *ag.* **1.** squamoso, forforoso **2.** incrostato.

scurril(e) [ˈskʌril], *ag.* (*arc.*) scurrile, sboccato, triviale.

scurrility [skʌˈriliti], *s.* scurrilità, volgarità, trivialità.

scurrilous [ˈskʌriləs], *ag.* scurrile, osceno, triviale.

scurrilously [ˈskʌriləsli], *av.* scurrilmente, trivialmente.

scurrilousness [ˈskʌriləsnis], *s.* scurrilità, oscenità, trivialità.

scurry [ˈskʌri], *s.* **1.** movimento affrettato; fretta, precipitazione **2.** breve corsa, gara a cavallo **3.** turbine, turbinio.

to **scurry**, *v.i.* affrettarsi a piccoli passi; sgambettare.

scurvily [ˈskə:vili], *av.* spregevolmente, meschinamente, disonorevolmente.

scurviness [ˈskə:vinis], *s.* bassezza, meschinità, piccineria.

scurvy [ˈskə:vi], *ag.* spregevole, meschino, basso, vile: *a — action*, una vile azione ‖ *s.* (*patol.*) scorbuto ☆ *— -grass*, (*bot.*) coclearia.

scut [skʌt], *s.* **1.** coda corta (generalmente di lepre, coniglio) **2.** lepre **3.** (*sl.*) individuo spregevole.

scutage [ˈskju:tidʒ], *s.* (*st.*) « scutagium » (somma pagata dal vassallo invece di prestazioni personali).

scutch[1] [skʌtʃ], *s.* (*tec.*) gramola, maciulla, scotola.

to **scutch**[1], *v.t.* **1.** (*ind.*) gramolare, maciullare, scotolare (canapa, lino) **2.** battere, trebbiare, macinare (grano).

scutch[2], *s.* (*bot.*) gramigna.

to **scutch**[3], *v.t.* (*dial.*) colpire con un bastone; sferzare.

scutcheon [ˈskʌtʃən], *V.* **escutcheon**.

scute [skju:t], *V.* **scutum**.

scutellar [ˈskju:(ː)teləˈ*], **scutellate** [ˈskju:təleit], *ag.* (*zool.*) a forma di scudo.

scutellum [skju:(ː)ˈteləm], *pl.* **scutella** [skju:(ː)ˈtelə], *s.* (*zool.*)scaglia, piastra(specie di armatura in insetti, ecc.).

scutiform [ˈskju:tifo:m], *ag.* scudiforme.

to **seutter** [ˈskʌtə*], *V.* to **scurry**.

scuttle[1] [ˈskʌtl], *s.* (*coal-*) —, recipiente per carbone.

scuttle[2], *s.* **1.** (*mar.*) portellino, boccaportella **2.** botola, sportello **3.** (*aut.*) cappottatura del cruscotto.

to **scuttle**[2], *v.t.* **1.** produrre falle in (una nave per affondarla) **2.** forare (il ponte di una nave) per salvarne il carico.

scuttle[3], *s.* (*ittiol.*) seppia.

scuttle[4], *s.* corsa affrettata; fuga precipitosa.

to **scuttle**[4], *v.t.i.* **1.** (*pol. sl.*) abbandonare improvvisamente ed in modo indecoroso la propria carica **2.** *to — away, off*, correre velocemente, fuggire; (*sl.*) eclissarsi.

scutum [ˈskju:təm], *pl.* **seuta** [ˈskju:tə], **scutums** [ˈskju:təmz], *s.* **1.** (*st. romana*) scudo **2.** (*anat.*) rotula **3.** (*zool.*) scaglia.

Scylla [ˈsilə], *no.pr.* (*mit. geog.*) Scilla ‖ *between — and Charybdis*, tra Scilla e Cariddi.

scyphus [ˈsaifəs], *pl.* **scyphi** [ˈsaifai], *s.* **1.** (*archeol.*) tazza, cratere **2.** corona (di fiore).

scythe [saið], *s.* falce.

to **scythe**, *v.t.* falciare.

scythed [saiðd], *ag.* **1.** armato di falce **2.** falciato ☆ *— chariot*, (*st.*) carro falcato.

scytheman, *pl.* **scythemen** [ˈsaiðmən], *s.* falciatore.

Scythia [ˈsiðiə], *no.pr.* (*geog.*) Scizia.

Scythian [ˈsiðiən], *ag.* scitico ‖ *s.c.* scita.

'sdeath [zdeθ], *inter.* (*arc. abbr.* di *God's death*) perdinci!, maledizione!.

sea [si:], *s.* **1.** mare, oceano: *arm of the —*, braccio di mare; *at the bottom of the —*, in fondo al mare ‖ *at —*, in mare, *fig.* smarrito: *he was buried at —*, fu sepolto in mare; *to be all at —*, essere disorientato, perdere la bussola, non sapere che pesci pigliare; *to be out at —*, essere in alto mare (anche *fig.*) ‖ *beyond* (o *over* o *across*) *the —*, oltremare, all'estero: *he has lived beyond the — for many years*, vive da molti anni oltremare ‖ *by —*, per mare: *by land and —*, per terra e per mare; *to travel by —*, viaggiare per mare ‖ *by the —*, (vicino) al mare: *he lives by the —*, vive (vicino) al mare ‖ *mistress of the —*, signora dei mari, potenza navale ‖ *on the —*, sul mare; a bordo: *the boat is on the —*, la barca è in mare; *Bournemouth is on the —*, Bournemouth è sul mare; *my son is on the —*, mio figlio è in mare, a bordo ‖ *when the — gives up its dead*, il giorno della resurrezione ‖ *to be between the devil and the deep blue —*, essere fra l'incudine e il martello ‖ *to follow the —*, fare il marinaio ‖ *to go* (o *to put*) *out to —*, prendere il largo ‖ *to go to —*, diventar marinaio ‖ *to keep the —*, tenere il mare (di nave durante la tempesta) ‖ *to stand out to —*, dirigersi al largo; partire **2.** *Sea*, (*geog.*) Mare: *the Black Sea*, il Mar Nero; *the Caspian Sea*, il Mar Caspio; *the Dead Sea*, il Mar Morto; *the Mediterranean Sea*, Mare Mediterraneo; *the North Sea*, il Mare del Nord ‖ *within the four Seas*, in Gran Bretagna **3.** mare (condizione, moto); onda, ondata, maroso, cavallone: *heavy* (o *strong*) *—*, mare grosso; *long —*, mare lungo; *the — is calm, short, stormy, very rough, smooth*, il mare è calmo, corto, tempestoso, molto agitato, piatto; *the — was like a looking-glass* (o *sheet of glass*), il mare era come uno specchio, liscio come l'olio ‖ *half seas over*, alquanto brillo ‖ *to ship a* (*green*) *—*, essere investito da un'ondata **4.** *fig.* mare, grande quantità: *seas of blood*, fiumi di sangue; *a — of faces*, un mare di facce; *a — of troubles*, un mare di guai ☆ *— -acorn*, (*zool.*) balano; *— -air*, aria di mare; *— -anchor*, ancora galleggiante; *— -anemone*, (*zool.*) attinia, anemone di mare; *— -bathing*, bagni di mare; *— -bear*, orso polare; *— -bird*, uccello marino; *— -biscuit*, galletta; *— -born*, nato, sorto dal mare; *— -breeze*, brezza marina; *— -calf*, (*zool.*) foca; *— -canary*, (*zool.*) balena bianca; *— -captain*, capitano di marina; capitano di lungo corso; *— -chestnut*, (*zool.*) echino, riccio di mare; *— -cob*, (*ornit.*) gabbiano; *— -cow*, (*zool.*) sirenide; ippopotamo; *— -crow*, (*ornit.*)

nome riferito a vari uccelli come il cormorano, ecc.; — -cucumber, (zool.) oloturia; — -devil, (ittiol.) raia, razza; rana pescatrice; diavolo di mare, ecc.; — -dog, (zool.) foca; piccolo pescecane; fig. lupo di mare; — -eagle, (ornit.) aquila marina; falco pescatore; — ear, (zool.) orecchia marina; — -elephant, (zool.) macrorrino; — -fan, (zool.) gorgonia a ventaglio; — -fennel, (bot.) critmo, finocchio marino; — -fight, battaglia navale; — -fire, fosforescenza del mare; — -flower, (zool.) anemone marino; — -foam, schiuma di mare; — -food, (amer.) frutti di mare, pesce; — -fowl, uccello marino; — -front, lungomare; — -gauge, pescaggio (di nave); scandaglio; — -girt, circondato dal mare; — -god, — -goddess, divinità marina; — -going, che veleggia in alto mare; adatto per le grandi traversate; — -green, verde mare; — -gull, (ornit.) gabbiano; — -hedgehog, (zool.) riccio di mare; — -hog, (zool. rar.) marsovino; — -jelly, (zool.) medusa; — -kale, (bot.) cavolo di mare; — -king, (st.) capo vichingo; (mit.) dio del mare; — -lawyer, squalo; (sl.) marinaio attaccabrighe; — -legs, capacità di tenersi in equilibrio (propria dei marinai): to find (o to get) one's — -legs, acquistare la capacità di mantenersi in equilibrio (su una nave); — -lemon, (zool.) doride; — -letter (o — -pass), (mar.) permesso di navigazione (per nave neutrale in tempo di guerra); — -level, livello del mare; — -lily, (zool.) crinoide; — -line, linea d'orizzonte sul mare; — -lion, (zool.) otaria, leone marino; Sea Lord, membro dell'Ammiragliato; — -maid, sirena; — -mark, boa, gavitello; faro; — -mew, gabbiano; — -mile, (mar.) miglio marittimo; — -monster, mostro marino; — -mouse, (zool.) afridite; — -nettle, (zool.) medusa; — -ox, (zool.) tricheco; — -pad, (zool.) stella di mare; — -pay, (zool.) paga dei marinai; — -perch, (ittiol.) pesce persico; — -pie, (cuc. mar.) pasticcio (di carne salata, legumi, ecc.); (ornit.) ghiandaia, gazza marina; — -piece, (pitt.) marina; — -pig, (zool.) delfino; marsovino; — -pike, (ittiol.) luccio di mare; — -power, potenza navale; — -quake, maremoto; — -room, (mar.) spazio per manovrare; — -rover, pirata; — -scape, panorama marino; (pitt.) marina; — -scout, giovane esploratore di mare; — -shell, conchiglia; — -snipe, (ornit.) beccaccia marina; — -squirt, (zool.) ascidia; — -star, (zool.) stella di mare; — -stock, provviste di bordo; — -storm, mareggiata; — -tangle, (bot.) laminaria; — -toad, (ittiol.) rana pescatrice; — -trout, (ittiol.) trota salmonata; — -urchin, (zool.) riccio di mare; — -wall, diga marittima; — -ware, alghe (come concime); — -washed, bagnato dal mare; — -water, acqua di mare; — -way, rotta; il mare (come mezzo di comunicazione); — -wolf, (ittiol.) pesce lupo, lupo di mare; (arc.) pirata; — -worm, logorato dal mare || closed —, mare chiuso; the high seas, the open —, l'alto mare, il mare aperto; inland —, mare interno, mediterraneo.

seaboard ['si:bɔ:d], ag. (rar.) marittimo; costiero || s. costa, litorale, spiaggia.

seacoast ['si:'koust], s. costa, riva del mare; spiaggia.

seadrome ['si:droum], s. (aer.) aeroporto galleggiante.

seafarer ['si:ˌfɛərə*], s. navigante; navigatore; uomo di mare.

seafaring ['si:ˌfɛəriŋ], ag. di mare, marinaro || s. viaggi per mare.

seahorse ['si:hɔ:s], s. 1. (ittiol.) ippocampo, cavalluccio marino 2. (zool.) tricheco 3. (arc.) ippopotamo.

seal¹ [si:l], s. 1. foca 2. pelle di foca; pelliccia di foca ☆ — -fishery, caccia di foche; zona di caccia di foche || eared — (o furred —), otaria; hooded —, foca monaca.

to **seal¹**, v.i. andare a caccia di foche.

seal², s. 1. sigillo; timbro: removal of the seals, rimozione dei sigilli; to affix (o to put) the —, apporre il sigillo || Fisher's Seal, anello piscatorio (con S. Pietro in veste di pescatore); Great Seal of England, Gran Sigillo d'Inghilterra; Keeper of the Seals, Guardasigilli;

Privy Seal, Sigillo Reale || given under my hand and —, da me sottoscritto e sigillato || to set one's — on sthg. (fam.) autorizzare, dare la propria approvazione a ql.co. 2. fig. sigillo, suggello; vincolo; marchio: the — of love, il suggello dell'amore; he spoke under the — of secrecy, parlò sotto il vincolo del segreto; she had the — of death in her face, aveva sul volto il segno della morte 3. (mec.) sifone a tenuta idraulica; (amer.) guarnizione di tenuta ☆ — -ring, anello con sigillo || lead —, piombino, sigillo di piombo.

to **seal²**, v.t. 1. sigillare; chiudere ermeticamente; bollare: the drawers are sealed (up), sono stati apposti i sigilli ai cassetti; to — (up) un'envelope, sigillare una busta || my lips are sealed up, fig. le mie labbra sono suggellate 2. suggellare; autenticare; ratificare: to — a bargain, suggellare un patto 3. fig. segnare; destinare; determinare: I am sealed for (o to) damnation, sono destinato alla dannazione; to — one's fate, decidere la propria sorte 4. bloccare: the vessel was sealed in ice, la nave era bloccata dal ghiaccio 5. (mec.) fissare (con cemento, ecc.); piombare 6. (elett.) stabilire un buon contatto.

seal³, s. (dial.) salice.

sealed [si:ld], ag. 1. sigillato 2. ermetico, misterioso: algebra is a — book to many people, l'algebra è un mistero per molta gente ☆ — -pattern, (mil.) modello (di arma) accettato ufficialmente (anche fig.).

sealer¹ ['si:lə*], s. 1. cacciatore di foche 2. imbarcazione per la caccia alla foca.

sealer², s. 1. chi appone un sigillo ad un documento 2. ispettore di pesi e misure 3. (pitt.) mano di fondo, mano isolante.

sealery ['si:ləri], s. caccia, luogo di caccia alla foca.

sealing¹ ['si:liŋ], s. caccia alla foca.

sealing², s. suggellamento, impronta del sigillo, piombatura ☆ — -tape, nastro di carta gommata; — -wax, ceralacca.

sealskin ['si:l-skin], s. pelle di foca; pelliccia di foca.

seam¹ [si:m], s. 1. cucitura, costura; giuntura, linea di giunzione 2. sutura; cicatrice 3. (geol. miner.) strato; vena; banco, filone: — of coal, giacimento di carbone 4. (mar.) comento; commessura 5. (metal.) paglia 6. (fonderia) bava, riccio ☆ — -folding machine, (mec.) aggraffatrice.

to **seam¹**, v.t. 1. unire con cucitura; segnare con cucitura 2. rigare, segnare: her face was seamed with sorrow, il suo viso era segnato dal dolore 3. lavorare a punto costa (nei lavori a maglia).

seam², s. (dial.) soma.

seaman, pl. **seamen** ['si:mən], s. marinaio, uomo di mare ☆ able —, marinaio scelto.

seamanlike ['si:mənlaik], ag. marinaresco; proprio di marinaio.

seamanship ['si:mənʃip], s. arte della navigazione; nautica: it was a fine piece of —, fu una bella manovra.

seamless ['si:mlis], ag. senza giunzioni, senza cuciture ☆ — stockings, calze senza cucitura.

seamstress ['semstris], s. cucitrice.

seamy ['si:mi], ag. provvisto di cuciture; simile a cucitura || the — side, il rovescio; fig. il lato meno attraente, il rovescio della medaglia: the — side of town life, il lato spiacevole della vita cittadina.

Seanad Eireann ['sænɑ:d'ɛəriŋ], s. (pol.) Senato dello Stato Libero d'Irlanda (in gaelico).

séance ['seiɑ:ns], s. 1. seduta 2. seduta spiritica.

seaplane ['si:-plein], s. idroplano, idrovolante.

seaport ['si:-pɔ:t], s. porto marittimo.

sear¹ [siə*], ag. (poet.) disseccato; inaridito; appassito; avvizzito (anche fig.).

to **sear¹**, v.t. 1. disseccare; inaridire; far appassire 2. bruciare; cauterizzare; marcare a fuoco 3. fig. inaridire; rendere insensibile.

sear², s. dente d'arresto del cane (del fucile).

search [sə:tʃ], s. 1. ricerca; indagine; investigazione;

inchiesta; esame: *the — for the missing student was successful*, la ricerca dello studente scomparso fu coronata da successo; *to be in — of sthg.*, *s.o.*, essere in cerca di ql.co., qlcu.; *to make — for sthg.*, fare ricerca di ql.co. **2.** perquisizione; visita doganale ‖ *right of —*, diritto di perquisizione (del belligerante nei riguardi delle navi neutrali) ☆ *— -warrant*, mandato di perquisizione.

to search, *v.t.i.* **1.** perlustrare, perquisire; frugare: *they searched the prisoner*, perquisirono il prigioniero; *they searched the town for the murderer*, perlustrarono la città in cerca dell'assassino; *to — a house*, perquisire una casa **2.** *fig.* ricercare; esaminare; esplorare; investigare, indagare; frugare: *I have searched my memory, but I can't remember that date*, ho frugato nella mia memoria ma non riesco a ricordare quella data; *to — into the cause of sthg.*, ricercare la causa di ql.co. ‖ *— me!*, *(amer.)* chi lo sa! **3.** *(chir.)* sondare, scandagliare (anche *fig.*): *to — one's heart, men's hearts*, sondare il proprio cuore, il cuore degli uomini **4.** penetrare in: *the wind searched every corner of the village*, il vento penetrava in ogni angolo del paese **5.** *to — after (sthg.)*, andare in cerca di; ricercare: *to — after truth*, ricercare la verità **6.** *to — for (s.o., sthg.)*, cercare **7.** *to — out*, cercare; scoprire, scovare.

searchable ['sə:tʃəbl], *ag.* investigabile; indagabile.

searcher ['sə:tʃə*], *s.c.* ricercatore, ricercatrice: *a — after truth*, un ricercatore della verità ‖ *s.* **1.** investigatore **2.** doganiere perquisitore **3.** *(chir.)* sonda.

searching ['sə:tʃiŋ], *ag.* **1.** indagatore, inquisitorio, scrutatore: *a — glance*, uno sguardo indagatore **2.** perspicace; penetrante; acuto: *a — smell*, un odore penetrante **3.** approfondito; minuzioso; rigoroso; completo: *a — examination*, un esame minuzioso ‖ *s.* **1.** ricerca; esame; investigazione, indagine, inchiesta **2.** perlustrazione; perquisizione **3.** *(chir.)* sondaggio (anche *fig.*) ‖ *searchings of heart* (o *heart-searchings*), apprensioni, scrupoli, esami di coscienza.

searchingly ['sə:tʃiŋli], *av.* in modo inquisitorio, in modo penetrante, con perspicacia; minuziosamente.

searchingness ['sə:tʃiŋnis], *s.* penetrazione; minuziosità.

searchlight ['sə:tʃ-lait], *s.* **1.** riflettore **2.** fascio di luce (proiettata da riflettore).

seared [siəd], *ag.* **1.** appassito, avvizzito **2.** cauterizzato **3.** indurito: *a — soul*, un animo inaridito.

searedness ['siəridnis], *s.* **1.** secchezza; **2.** insensibilità.

searing-iron ['siəriŋ‚aiən], *s.* cauterio.

seashore ['si:'ʃɔ:*], *s.* spiaggia; lido; litorale.

seasickness ['si:-siknis], *s.* mal di mare, nausea.

seaside ['si:'said], *s.* spiaggia; riva del mare; marina: *to go to the* |—, andare al mare (in villeggiatura) ☆ *— resort*, stazione balneare.

season ['si:zn], *s.* **1.** stagione: *the coming —*, la stagione ventura; *the four seasons*, le quattro stagioni **2.** epoca, stagione (caratterizzata da particolare attività): *in —*, di stagione: *peaches are now in —*, ora è la stagione delle pesche; *in — and out of —*, in tutte le stagioni, sempre; *fig.* a proposito ed a sproposito; *out of —*, fuori stagione; *fig.* a sproposito, intempestivo ‖ *Lenten —*, Quaresima; *London —*, stagione di manifestazioni mondane a Londra **3.** periodo di tempo: *a — of inaction*, un periodo di inattività; *you should rest for a —*, dovreste riposarvi per un po' di tempo **4.** tempo opportuno, momento opportuno: *in due —*, a tempo debito; *a word in —*, *fig.* una parola opportuna, un consiglio dato al momento opportuno; *this is the — for rest*, questo è il tempo adatto per riposarvi **5.** *(sl.)* abbonamento (ferroviario, a spettacoli, ecc.) ☆ *— ticket*, biglietto in abbonamento ‖ *dead —* (o *off —*), stagione morta; *foot-ball —*, stagione calcistica; *holiday —*, stagione di villeggiatura; *strawberry —*, stagione delle fragole.

to season, *v.t.i.* **1.** stagionare, stagionarsi; maturarsi, invecchiarsi (di vino): *this wood is well seasoned*,

questo legno è ben stagionato; *timber seasons well in the open air*, il legname stagiona bene all'aria aperta **2.** abituare; acclimatare; allenare: *to — s.o. to a climate*, abituare qlcu. a un clima **3.** condire; rendere più saporito, più gustoso; rendere piccante: *highly seasoned food*, cibo assai piccante, saporito; *speech seasoned with irony*, *fig.* discorso condito d'ironia **4.** *(arc.)* temperare: *mercy should — justice*, la misericordia dovrebbe temperare la giustizia.

seasonable ['si:znəbl], *ag.* **1.** di stagione: *— weather*, clima di stagione **2.** opportuno; tempestivo; a proposito: *— advice*, consigli opportuni.

seasonableness ['si:znəblnis], *s.* opportunità; tempestività (di consiglio, obiezione, ecc.).

seasonably ['si:znəbli], *av.* opportunamente; tempestivamente; a proposito.

seasonal ['si:zənl], *ag.* stagionale, di stagione: *— rates*, tariffe di stagione; *fruit picking is a — occupation*, la raccolta della frutta è un'occupazione stagionale.

seasonally ['si:zənəli], *av.* secondo la stagione; periodicamente.

seasoned ['si:znd], *ag.* **1.** stagionato: *— wine*, vino vecchio **2.** condito; piccante (anche *fig.*): *highly — anecdote*, un aneddoto gustoso **3.** allenato; abituato: *a — traveller*, un viaggiatore esperto.

seasoner ['si:znə*], *s.c.* stagionatore, stagionatrice ‖ *s.* marinaio, pescatore assunto per la stagione; avventizio.

seasoning ['si:zniŋ], *s.* **1.** condimento (anche *fig.*) **2.** stagionatura (di legno, ecc.); invecchiamento (di vino, ecc.) **3.** *fig.* moderazione.

seat [si:t], *s.* **1.** sedile; posto (a sedere); sedia; sgabello; trono: *a car with six seats*, un'automobile a sei posti; *keep your seats*, rimanete seduti, state al vostro posto; *these seats are uncomfortable*, questi posti sono scomodi; *won't you take a —?*, non volete accomodarvi? ‖ *take your seats!*, *(ferr.)* in vettura! **2.** sedere, deretano; fondo di sedia, di pantaloni **3.** seggio; diritto a un seggio: *to give up* (o *to resign*) *one's —*, dare le dimissioni; *to have a — in Parliament*, avere un seggio in Parlamento; *to win* (*to lose*) *a —*, vincere (perdere) un seggio **4.** *(mec.)* centro; sede (di una valvola) **5.** residenza di campagna; villa; castello: *my friend has a — in Essex*, il mio amico ha una villa nell'Essex **6.** modo di stare in sella (a cavallo, in bicicletta, ecc.): *she has a graceful —*, ella sta in sella con grazia **7.** sede, centro: *the lungs are the — of many diseases*, i polmoni sono la sede di molte malattie; *news from the — of war*, notizie dal teatro di guerra ☆ *— -holder*, abbonato; *— -rent*, pagamento della sedia (in chiesa) ‖ *corner —*, posto d'angolo; *country - —*, residenza di campagna; *emergency —* (o *folding —*), strapuntino; *first-class —*, posto di prima classe; *flat —*, *(mec.)* sede piana; *front, back —*, sedile anteriore, posteriore; *rail —*, *(ferr.)* sede per la rotaia.

to seat, *v.t.* **1.** mettere a sedere; far sedere: *please be seated*, accomodatevi, prego; *she seated the child on a chair*, |ella mise il bambino a sedere su una seggiola; *to — oneself*, mettersi a sedere, accomodarsi; *to — one's guests*, fare accomodare i propri ospiti **2.** insediare, collocare; installare; fissare: *to — a candidate*, insediare un candidato in Parlamento: *to — machinery*, installare macchinario; *to — oneself in a country*, stabilirsi in un paese **3.** fornire, essere fornito di posti a sedere: *this cinema can — two thousand people*, questo cinema è fornito di duemila posti a sedere; *to — a hall*, fornire una sala di posti a sedere **4.** riparare il fondo (di sedie, pantaloni, ecc.): *to — a chair*, rifare il fondo di una sedia.

seated ['si:tid], *(nei composti)*: *double —*, a due posti; *single —*, a un posto.

seater ['si:tə*], *s.* chi fa accomodare i clienti ☆ *four - —*, *(aut.)* automobile a quattro posti; *single- —*, *(aer. aut.)* automobile, aeroplano monoposto; *two- —*, *(aer. aut.)* aeroplano, automobile a due posti.

seating ['si:tiŋ], *s.* **1.** il provvedere, l'essere provveduto di sedie, posti **2.** l'atto di sedere; far sedere: *the — of the guests took a long time*, ci volle molto tempo per far sedere gli ospiti **3.** stoffa per ricoprire sedili **4.** (*mec.*) sede ☆ *— accomodation* (o *— capacity*), numero di posti a sedere.

seaward ['si:wəd], *ag.* che va verso il mare ‖ *s.* (*to*) —, in direzione del mare: *five leagues to —*, cinque leghe nella direzione del mare.

seaward(s) ['si:wəd(z)], *av.* verso il mare.

seaweed ['si:wi:d], *s.* alga marina.

seaworthiness ['si:ˌwə:ðinis], *s.* (*mar.*) capacità di tenere il mare.

seaworthy ['si:ˌwə:ði], *ag.* atto a tenere il mare.

sebaceous [si'beiʃəs], *ag.* sebaceo ☆ *— glands*, glandole sebacee.

sebacic [si'bæsik], *ag.* (*chim.*) sebacico.

Sebastian [si'bæstjən], *no.pr.m.* Sebastiano.

seborrh(o)ea [ˌsebou'ri:ə], *s.* (*med.*) seborrea.

sebum ['si:bəm], *s.* (*fisiol.*) sebo.

sec [sek], *ag.* secco (di vino).

secant ['si:kənt], *ag.s.* (*geom.*) secante.

secco ['sekkou], *s. — (painting)*, pittura a secco.

to secede [si'si:d], *v.i.* separarsi, ritirarsi (da associazione politica, religiosa): *he seceded from his party*, si ritirò dal suo partito.

seceder [si'si:də*], *s.c.* secessionista, separatista; dissenziente.

seceding [si'si:diŋ], *ag.* secessionista, separatista.

to secern [si'sə:n], *v.t.* **1.** separare; discriminare **2.** (*fisiol.*) secernere.

secernent [si'sə:nənt], *ag.* secretorio ‖ *s.* **1.** organo secretorio **2.** sostanza che stimola la secrezione.

secernment [si'sə:nmənt], *s.* secrezione.

secession [si'seʃən], *s.* secessione; scissione, separazione ‖ *War of Secession*, (*amer.*) Guerra di Secessione (1861-65).

secessionism [si'seʃnizəm], *s.* separatismo.

secessionist [si'seʃnist], *s.c.* secessionista; separatista.

seekel ['sekəl], *s.* (*amer.*) varietà di pera.

to seclude [si'klu:d], *v.t.* appartare; isolare; rinchiudere: *Moslems — their wives in the harem*, i musulmani rinchiudono le loro mogli nell'harem; *to — oneself from society*, appartarsi dalla società.

secluded [si'klu:did], *ag.* appartato; isolato; ritirato; solitario: *a — life*, una vita ritirata; *a — valley*, una valle isolata, solitaria ☆ *— monks*, monaci di clausura.

secludedly [si'klu:didli], *av.* appartatamente, in disparte.

seclusion [si'klu:ʒən], *s.* **1.** isolamento: *the — of prisoners in cells*, l'isolamento dei prigionieri in celle **2.** solitudine; stato appartato: *to live in —*, vivere in solitudine; *to live in the — of one's own home*, vivere nella solitudine della propria casa **3.** ritiro; clausura.

seclusive [si'klu:siv], *ag.* che tende, serve ad isolare.

second¹ ['sekənd], *s.* (minuto) secondo; *fig.* istante: *I will be ready in a —*, sarò pronto in un istante ☆ *seconds-hand*, lancetta dei secondi; *seconds-mark*, segno ('') che indica i secondi.

second², *ag. num. ord.* **1.** secondo: *— class*, seconda classe; *— floor*, secondo piano; *the — (day) of the month*, il due del mese; *the — largest town in Italy*, la seconda città (per grandezza) d'Italia; *Charles the Second*, Carlo II; *Norah is her — daughter*, Norah è la sua seconda figlia ‖ *— cousin*, secondo cugino ‖ *at — hand*, per sentito dire ‖ *in the — place*, in secondo luogo ‖ *on — thoughts*, ripensandoci meglio **2.** secondo, inferiore, secondario: *to be — to s.o.*, essere inferiore a qlcu. ‖ *to play — fiddle (to s.o.)*, essere in condizioni d'inferiorità (rispetto a qlcu.) **3.** secondo, altro, nuovo: *— ballot*, seconda votazione; *he was a — father*, fu un secondo padre; *I need a — pair of trousers*, ho bisogno di un secondo paio di pantaloni ‖ *— Advent*, Secondo Avvento (di Cristo) ☆ *— chamber*, (*pol.*) camera alta;

— childhood, seconda infanzia; *— nature*, seconda natura; *— self*, « alter ego »; *— speed*, (*aut.*) la seconda marcia; *— violin*, (*mus.*) secondo violino.

second², *s.* **1.** secondo: *— to none*, non secondo a nessuno; *a good —*, (*spor.*) un buon secondo; *you are the — to ask me that*, sei il secondo a domandarmi ciò ‖ *— in command*, (*mil.*) vicecomandante; (*mar.*) ufficiale in seconda **2.** secondo, padrino (in un duello) **3.** (*mus.*) seconda, intervallo di seconda **4.** *pl.* merce di seconda scelta **5.** dodicesima parte di un pollice (misura di lunghezza = cm. 0,21).

second², *av.* **1.** secondariamente **2.** al secondo posto: *to come (in) —*, arrivare secondo.

second², (*nei composti*): *— -best*, secondo per qualità; mediocre: *to come off — -best*, avere la peggio; *— -class*, di seconda classe; di qualità inferiore: *a — -class ticket*, un biglietto (ferroviario) di seconda classe; *— -day*, lunedì; *— -degree*, (*alg.*) di secondo grado (equazione); *— -hand*, di seconda mano; *— -rate*, di seconda categoria (alberghi, ecc.).

to second², *v.t.* **1.** assecondare, favorire, incoraggiare, appoggiare, spalleggiare: *to — a motion*, appoggiare una mozione **2.** fare da secondo a (in un duello).

to second³ [si'kɔnd], *v.t.* (*mil.*) distaccare (ufficiali) dal reggimento (per funzioni speciali).

secondarily ['sekəndərili], *av.* secondariamente.

secondariness ['sekəndərinis], *s.* secondarietà.

secondary ['sekəndəri], *ag.* **1.** secondario: *— accent*, accento secondario; *— cause*, causa secondaria **2.** (*geol.*) secondario; mesozoico ‖ *s.* **1.** subalterno; delegato; (*eccl.*) membro secondario del capitolo **2.** (*astr.*) pianeta minore, satellite **3.** (*ornit.*) remigante secondaria **4.** ala posteriore (di insetti) **5.** (*geol.*) formazione secondaria ☆ *— education*, istruzione post-elementare; *— school*, scuola media.

seconde [si'kɔnd], *s.* (*scherma*) seconda.

seconder ['sekəndə*], *s.c.* chi asseconda; sostenitore, sostenitrice: *to be the — of a proposal*, appoggiare una proposta.

secondly ['sekəndli], *av.* in secondo luogo; secondariamente.

secrecy ['si:krisi], *s.* **1.** segretezza: *in —*, in segreto; *there is no — about it*, non ci sono misteri in tutto ciò **2.** riserbo; discrezione: *you can rely on his —*, puoi contare sulla sua discrezione; *to bind s.o. to —*, impegnare qlcu. al segreto; *to tell s.o. sthg. under pledge of —*, dire ql.co. a qlcu. in segreto.

secret ['si:krit], *ag.* **1.** segreto: *a — treaty*, trattato segreto; *— marriage*, matrimonio segreto ‖ *the Secret Service*, servizio segreto britannico (di spionaggio) **2.** nascosto; intimo ‖ *the — parts*, parti intime del corpo **3.** discreto; riservato; personale **4.** isolato, appartato (di luogo) ‖ *s.* **1.** segreto (anche *fig.*): *the — of happiness, of success*, il segreto della felicità, del successo; *to keep a —*, mantenere un segreto; *to let s.o. into the —*, mettere qlcu. a parte del segreto ‖ *an open —*, un segreto di Pulcinella **2.** mistero: *the secrets of Nature*, i misteri della natura **3.** (*eccl.*) segreta **4.** *pl.* organi genitali ☆ *— agent*, agente segreto; *— door*, porta segreta ‖ *top —*, (*pol. mil.*) riservatissimo.

secretaire [ˌsekrə'tɛə*], *s.* scrittoio; scrivania.

secretarial [ˌsekrə'tɛəriəl], *ag.* segretariale.

secretariat(e) [ˌsekrə'tɛəriət], *s.* **1.** segretariato **2.** segreteria.

secretary ['sekrətri], *s.c.* segretario, segretaria: *— of embassy, of legation*, segretario di ambasciata, di legazione; *honorary —*, segretario onorario; *private —* segretaria privata ‖ *s.* **1.** ministro preposto a un dicastero ‖ *Secretary of State*, Ministro Segretario di Stato (in Gran Bretagna); Ministro degli Esteri (negli Stati Uniti) ‖ *Home Secretary*, Ministro degli Interni (in Gran Bretagna) **2.** scrivania, scrittoio **3.** (*tip.*) corsivo **4.** *— (-bird)*, (*ornit.*) serpentario.

secretaryship ['sekrətriʃip], *s.* segretariato.

to **secrete**[1] [si'kri:t], *v.t.* (*fisiol.*) secernere.

to **secrete**[2], *v.t.* **1.** occultare, nascondere **2.** sottrarre.

secreting [si'kri:tiŋ] *V.* **secretory**.

secretion[1] [si'kri:ʃən], *s.* (*fisiol.*) secrezione.

secretion[2], *s.* **1.** occultamento **2.** sottrazione.

secretive [si'kri:tiv], *ag.* riservato, taciturno, poco comunicativo; reticente.

secretively [si'kri:tivli], *av.* riservatamente.

secretiveness [si'kri:tivnis], *s.* riservatezza; reticenza.

secretly ['si:kritli], *av.* segretamente, in segreto; in modo reticente.

secretness ['si:kritnis], *s.* segretezza.

secretory [si'kri:təri], *ag.* (*fisiol.*) secretore; secretorio || *s.* organo secretore.

sect [sekt], *s.* setta.

sectarial [sek'tɛəriəl], *ag.* settario.

sectarian [sek'tɛəriən], *ag.* settario, di setta || *s.* settario.

sectarianism [sek'tɛəriənizəm], *s.* spirito di setta.

to **sectarianize** [sek'tɛəriənaiz], *v.t.* imbevere di spirito di setta.

sectary ['sektəri], *s.* settario; affiliato a una setta.

sectator [sek'teitə*], *s.* (*rar.*) seguace; discepolo.

sectile ['sektil], *ag.* (*min.*) tagliabile, segabile.

section ['sekʃən], *s.* **1.** (*chir.*) sezione; (*rar.*) taglio, divisione, separazione **2.** parte; sezione; pezzo; porzione; fetta; tratto: — *of an orange,* fetta d'arancia; *microscopic* —, porzione microscopica; *machine built in sections,* macchina costruita in pezzi **3.** paragrafo **4.** parte (di popolazione); regione, quartiere, distretto **5.** (*geom.*) sezione, spaccato **6.** (*bot. zool.*) suddivisione (di gruppo, famiglia, ecc.) **7.** (*mil.*) plotone **8.** (*ferr.*) tronco di linea; scompartimento (di vagone letto) **9.** (*metal.*) profilato ☆ — *mark,* segno di paragrafo (§) || *conic* —, sezione conica; *cross* — (o *transverse* —), sezione trasversale; *vertical* —, sezione verticale, spaccato.

to **section**, *v.t.* sezionare; suddividere; fare la sezione di.

sectional ['sekʃən]], *ag.* **1.** parziale; di classe, di partito: — *interests,* interessi di classe **2.** a sezioni.

sectionalism ['sekʃnəlizəm], *s.* spirito di parte; campanilismo.

to **sectionalize** ['sekʃnəlaiz], *v.t.* dividere in sezioni.

sectionally ['sekʃnəli], *av.* a sezioni.

sectioning ['sekʃəniŋ], *s.* **1.** (*elett.*) sezionamento **2.** (*disegno*) tratteggio.

to **sectionize** ['sekʃənaiz], *v.t.* ripartire in sezioni.

sector ['sektə*], *s.* settore.

to **sector**, *v.t.* dividere in settori.

secular ['sekjulə*], *ag.* **1.** secolare: *a* — *tree,* una pianta secolare **2.** secolare, laico **3.** mondano, profano: — *music,* musica profana || *s.* secolare, laico ☆ — *clergy,* clero secolare; — *school,* scuola laica.

secularism ['sekjulərizəm], *s.* secolarismo; laicismo.

secularist ['sekjulərist], *ag.s.* laico; fautore del laicismo.

secularity [,sekju'læriti], *s.* laicità.

secularization ['sekjulərai'zeiʃən], *s.* secolarizzazione.

to **secularize** ['sekjuləraiz], *v.t.* secolarizzare; laicizzare.

secularly ['sekjuləli], *av.* in modo secolare; laicamente.

secund [si'kʌnd], *ag.* (*bot. zool.*) unilaterale.

secundine ['sekʌndain], *s.* (*fisiol.*) secondina.

secundogeniture [si,kʌndə'dʒenitʃə*], *s.* secondogenitura.

securable [si'kjuərəbl], *ag.* assicurabile.

secure [si'kjuə*], *ag.* **1.** sicuro, certo, assicurato: *a* — *future,* un avvenire sicuro; *a* — *victory,* una vittoria sicura **2.** sicuro, salvo: — *against assaults,* sicuro da assalti; — *from foes,* salvo da nemici; *have you got her*

—?, l'hai messa al sicuro? || — *retreat,* asilo sicuro **3.** sicuro, ben saldo: *this ladder is* —, questa scala è sicura **4.** (*arc.*) sicuro, fiducioso: — *of a welcome,* sicuro di una buona accoglienza.

to **secure**, *v.t.* **1.** assicurare, salvaguardare; proteggere; rafforzare; (*mil.*) fortificare: *to* — *a town against* (o *from*) *floods,* proteggere una città dalle inondazioni **2.** (*dir. comm.*) garantire: *secured by mortgage,* garantito da ipoteca **3.** mettere al sicuro: *to* — *a prisoner, valuables,* mettere al sicuro un prigioniero, oggetti di valore **4.** chiudere saldamente (porte, finestre, fibbie) **5.** assicurarsi; procurarsi: *to* — *information, a prize, seats at a theatre,* assicurarsi informazioni, un premio, dei posti a teatro; *to* — *substantial orders,* assicurarsi ordini importanti.

securely [si'kjuəli], *av.* **1.** al sicuro, in salvo **2.** saldamente **3.** fiduciosamente.

secureness [si'kjuənis], *s.* **1.** sicurezza **2.** saldezza **3.** fiducia.

securiform [si'kjuərifɔ:m], *ag.* a forma di scure.

security [si'kjuəriti], *s.* **1.** sicurezza; protezione; senso di sicurezza: *Italy's* — *depends on her frontiers,* la sicurezza dell'Italia dipende dalle sue frontiere || *the Security Council,* il Consiglio di Sicurezza (dell'O. N.U.) **2.** certezza **3.** garanzia, cauzione: *in* — *for,* a garanzia di; *to give* —, versare cauzione **4.** *pl.* (*comm.*) titoli, valori: *securities listed on the Stock Exchange,* titoli ammessi alla quotazione ufficiale in borsa; *securities of large, small denomination,* titoli di grosso, piccolo taglio ☆ — *device,* dispositivo di sicurezza || *gilt-edged securities,* (*comm.*) titoli di sicuro affidamento; *government securities,* (*comm.*) titoli di stato; *social* —, previdenza sociale.

sedan [si'dæn], *s.* **1.** — (-*chair*), portantina **2.** (*aut.*) guida interna; berlina a guida interna.

sedate [si'deit], *ag.* **1.** posato; composto; pacato; tranquillo; sereno: *a* — *judgement,* un giudizio sereno **2.** grave, serio; maturo: *she is too* — *for her years,* è troppo seria per la sua età.

sedately [si'deitli], *av.* **1.** posatamente; tranquillamente **2.** gravemente; seriamente.

sedateness [si'deitnis], *s.* **1.** posatezza; pacatezza; tranquillità; calma **2.** gravità; serietà.

sedative ['sedətiv], *ag.* sedativo, calmante || *s.* — (*draught*), pozione calmante, sedativo.

sedent ['si:dənt], *ag.* seduto (specialmente di statua).

sedentarily ['sedntərili], *av.* da sedentario, in modo sedentario.

sedentariness ['sedntərinis], *s.* stato sedentario; vita sedentaria; abitudini sedentarie.

sedentary ['sedntəri], *ag.* **1.** sedentario: — *life,* vita sedentaria **2.** non migratore (di uccello) || *s.* sedentario.

sederunt [si'diərənt], *s.* (*scoz. dir.*) seduta, assemblea.

sedge [sedʒ], *s.* (*bot.*) carice.

sedged [sedʒd], **sedgy** ['sedʒi], *ag.* pieno di carici.

sedilia [se'dailjə], *s.pl.* (*eccl.*) stalli di pietra (per gli officianti).

sediment ['sedimənt], *s.* sedimento, deposito; (*chim.*) residuo.

sedimentary [,sedi'mentəri], *ag.* sedimentario.

sedimentation [,sedimən'teiʃən], *s.* sedimentazione.

sedition [si'diʃən], *s.* sedizione.

seditionary [si'diʃnəri], *s.* sedizioso.

seditionist [si'diʃnist], *s.* sedizioso.

seditious [si'diʃəs], *ag.* sedizioso.

seditiously [si'diʃəsli], *av.* sediziosamente.

seditiousness [si'diʃəsnis], *s.* spirito sedizioso.

to **seduce** [si'dju:s], *v.t.* sedurre; corrompere; tentare: *to* — *a woman,* sedurre una donna; *to* — *s.o. from his duty,* distogliere qlcu. dal proprio dovere.

seducement [si'dju:smənt], *s.* seduzione.

seducer [si'dju:sə*], *s.c.* seduttore, seduttrice.

seducible [si'dju:sibl], *ag.* seducibile.

seducing [si'dju:siŋ], *ag.* seducente.

seducingly [si'dju:siŋli], *av.* in modo seducente.

seduction [si'dʌkʃən], *s.* seduzione, tentazione; attrattiva.

seductive [si'dʌktiv], *ag.* seducente; allettante.

seductively [si'dʌktivli], *av.* in modo seducente.

seductiveness [si'dʌktivnis], *s.* seduzione; attrattiva; attrazione.

sedulity [si'dju:liti], *s.* assiduità, perseveranza; diligenza.

sedulous ['sedjuləs], *ag.* assiduo, perseverante; diligente.

sedulously ['sedjuləsli], *av.* assiduamente; diligentemente.

sedulousness ['sedjuləsnis], *s.* assiduità; diligenza.

to **see**[1] [si:], *pass.* **saw** [so:], *p.p.* **seen** [si:n], *v.t.i.* 1. (I, V, VI) vedere, scorgere, osservare: *as all can —*, come tutti possono vedere; *as far as the eye can —*, a perdita d'occhio; *he could — the house from there*, poteva scorgere la casa di là; *he was seen to go*, fu visto partire; *he will — the house being built*, vedrà la casa in costruzione; *I saw him go*, l'ho visto partire; *I saw him running*, lo vidi correre; *she has seen a good deal in her short life*, ha visto molto nella sua breve vita; *they wonder what he sees in her*, si domandano cosa veda in lei ‖ *I'll — you far (o further) first*, (*sl.*) ti sbagli di grosso (se credi che faccia questo) ‖ *she is not fit to be seen*, non è presentabile, è conciata da far paura ‖ *she will never — thirty again*, ha trent'anni suonati ‖ *to — the back (o the last) of s.o.*, vedere per l'ultima volta qlcu.; liberarsi di qlcu. ‖ *to — everything black*, *fig.* veder tutto nero ‖ *to — stars*, vedere le stelle ‖ *to — things*, avere allucinazioni, avere le traveggole 2. capire, afferrare; rendersi conto di; accorgersi di; notare: *as far as I can —*, per quanto possa capire; *I — what you mean*, capisco quello che vuoi dire; *I can — no fault in her*, non noto in lei alcun difetto; *I saw that he didn't understand me*, mi resi conto che non mi capiva ‖ *—?*, (*fam.*) vedi?, capisci?; *I —*, capisco ‖ *to — daylight*, cominciare a capire, a vederci chiaro; essere quasi al termine di un lavoro ‖ *to — one's way to doing sthg.*, riuscire a fare ql.co. 3. considerare, osservare; considerare; giudicare; pensare, riflettere: *I must — what I can do*, devo vedere quello che posso fare; *we shall — who is right!*, si vedrà chi ha ragione!; *you can — for yourself*, puoi vedere da te; *to — differently*, non essere della stessa opinione, pensare diversamente ‖ *to — eye to eye*, essere della stessa opinione, considerare le cose allo stesso modo ‖ *to — fit to do sthg.*, ritenere adatto a, giusto, opportuno fare ql.co.: *I do not — you fit for this work*, non ti ritengo adatto per questo lavoro 4. fare in modo che, assicurarsi che: *— that the child has some food*, assicurati che il bambino abbia da mangiare; *— that he comes in time*, fate in modo che arrivi in tempo 5. visitare, frequentare, vedere: *he sees a great deal of the Browns*, frequenta molto i Brown; *I'll — you on Friday (o fam. — you on Friday)*, a venerdì; *I'll go to — the doctor tomorrow*, domani andrò dal dottore; *she will come and — me next week*, verrà a trovarmi la settimana ventura 6. accompagnare: *to — s.o. home, to the station*, accompagnare qlcu. a casa, alla stazione 7. (I, V, VI) stare a vedere, permettere: *I cannot — him offending my father*, non posso permettere che egli offenda mio padre 8. *to — about (sthg.)*, occuparsi, assumersi l'incarico di: *I'll — about it*, me ne occuperò; ne riparleremo; ci penserò; *will you — about it?*, te ne occupi tu? 9. *to — after (sthg.)*, occuparsi di, badare a 10. *to — into (s.o., sthg.)*, penetrare (coll'intelletto, col pensiero); esaminare; studiare: *I could — into him*, gli leggevo dentro; *I want to — into the matter*, voglio esaminare la faccenda 11. *to — through (s.o., sthg.)*, vedere attraverso; *fig.* penetrare, indovinare: *the fog was so thick you couldn't — through*, la nebbia era così fitta che non si vedeva nulla; *I can — through him, through his game*, ho capito che tipo è, ho capito il suo giuoco 12. *to — to (sthg.)*, badare a,

aver cura di, occuparsi di: *will you — to the luggage?*, vuoi occuparti dei bagagli? 13. *to — in*, veder arrivare: *to — the New Year in*, aspettare l'anno nuovo 14. *to — off*, accompagnare (alla partenza): *she ordered the butler to — him off*, ordinò al maggiordomo di accompagnarlo alla porta; *won't you — me off?*, non verrai a salutarmi alla partenza? 15. *to — out*, accompagnare (all'uscita, alla porta); vedere fino alla fine, vedere la fine di; portare a buon fine; sopravvivere a: *he is very old but he may — us all out*, è molto vecchio, ma ci metterà tutti nella tomba; *I want to — the show out*, voglio rimanere fino alla fine dello spettacolo; *to — a matter out*, portare una faccenda a buon fine 16. *to — over*, ispezionare, esaminare 17. *to — through*, sostenere, aiutare fino in fondo; vedere la conclusione di (avvenimento, ecc.); portare a buon fine; andare fino in fondo a: *don't worry, I'll — you through*, non darti pensiero, ti aiuterò io; *he saw it through*, andò fino in fondo.

see[2], *s.* (*eccl.*) sede; diocesi, vescovato; arcivescovato ‖ *the Holy See* (o *the See of Rome* o *the Apostolic See*), la Santa Sede.

seed [si:d], *s.* 1. seme; semenza, semente: *seeds of a grape*, vinacciuoli; *to keep potatoes for —*, riservare le patate per la semina ‖ *to run (o to go) to —*, sementire (di pianta); inselvatichirsi (di terreno); *fig.* sciuparsi, logorarsi 2. *fig.* seme, principio, germe: *to plant the seeds of virtue*, inculcare i principi della virtù; *to sow the — of rebellion*, seminare il germe della rivolta 3. stirpe, discendenza: *the — of Abraham*, la stirpe di Abramo; *all those of his —*, tutti i suoi discendenti ☆ *— -ball*, (*bot.*) capsula; *— -corn*, grano da semina; *— -drill*, (*mec.*) seminatrice; *— -fish*, pesce pronto a deporre le uova; *— -leaf* (o *— -lobe*), (*bot.*) cotiledone; *— -oyster*, giovane ostrica; *— -pearl*, perla scaramazza; *— -plant*, piante da semi; *— -plough*, aratro con seminatrice automatica; *— -time*, tempo della semina; *— -vessel*, (*bot.*) pericarpo.

to **seed**, *v.t.i.* 1. sementire, produrre semi; tallire 2. seminare 3. togliere i semi da, sgranare 4. (*spor.*) selezionare.

seedbed ['si:d'bed], *s.* semenzaio, vivaio.

seedcake ['si:d'keik], *s.* (*cuc.*) dolce con semi di carvi.

seedcoat ['si:d'kout], *s.* guscio del seme.

seeder ['si:də*], *s.* 1. (*mec.*) seminatrice 2. (*mec.*) sgranatrice 3. pesce che depone le uova.

seediness ['si:dinis], *s.* 1. abbondanza di semi 2. (*fam.*) logoramento (di abiti); trascuratezza (di persona) 3. malessere; debolezza; atonia.

seeding ['si:diŋ], *s.* seminagione, semina.

seedless ['si:dlis], *ag.* senza semi.

seedling ['si:dliŋ], *s.* (*bot.*) pianticella; alberello ☆ *— nursery*, vivaio forestale.

seedsman, *pl.* **seedsmen** ['si:dzmən], *s.* venditore di semi.

seedy ['si:di], *ag.* 1. pieno di semi 2. tallito; germogliato 3. (*fam.*) frusto, logoro (di abiti) 4. (*fam.*) sofferente, indisposto: *I feel —*, non mi sento in forma.

to **seek** [si:k], *pass.p.p.* **sought** [so:t], *v.t.i.* 1. cercare; andare alla ricerca di; investigare: *he sought peace, shelter*, cercava pace, rifugio; *to — death*, cercare la morte; *to — employment*, cercare un impiego; *to — the solution of a problem, of a mystery*, cercare la soluzione di un problema, di un mistero ‖ *to — one's bed*, andare a dormire ‖ *politeness is much to — among them*, la loro gentilezza lascia molto a desiderare ‖ *the reason is not far to —*, il motivo è facile da scoprire 2. cercare di ottenere; aspirare a; perseguire: *he is going to — his fortune in America*, va a cercar fortuna in America 3. chiedere, domandare; ricorrere a: *he sought his father's advice*, chiese consiglio a suo padre; *to — an explanation of a person's conduct*, domandare spiegazioni sulla condotta di qlcu.; *to — satisfaction from s.o.*, chiedere soddisfazione a qlcu. 4. tentare; cercare di: *he sought to draw his sword*, tentò di estrarre la spada; *I sought to help him*, cercavo di aiutarlo **5.** *to* — *after* (*s.o.*, *sthg.*), inseguire; aspirare a: *she is much sought after*, è molto corteggiata **6.** *to* — *for* (*sthg.*), ricercare: *to* — *for glory*, ricercare la gloria **7.** *to* — *out*, trovare, scovare.

seeker ['si:kə*], *s.c.* cercatore, cercatrice; investigatore, investigatrice.

seeking ['si:kiŋ], *s.* ricerca.

to seel [si:l], *v.t.* **1.** (*arc.*) accecare (un falco) cucendo le palpebre **2.** *fig.* accecare, ingannare.

to seem [si:m], *v.i.* **1.** (costruzione *pers.*) sembrare; apparire, mostrarsi; aver l'aria di: *he seemed very old to us*, ci sembrò molto vecchio; *he seems to be happy*, sembra felice; *how does it — to you?*, che ve ne sembra?; *I — to know him*, mi sembra di conoscerlo; *you — tired*, hai l'aria stanca **2.** *imp.* sembrare: *it seemed as though* (o *as if*) *he didn't understand*, sembrava che non capisse; *it would — not*, sembrerebbe di no; *it would — so*, sembrerebbe così.

seeming ['si:miŋ], *ag.* apparente; esteriore ‖ *s.* apparenza; esteriorità.

seemingly ['si:miŋli], *av.* apparentemente: *he was — happy*, apparentemente era felice.

seemless ['si:mlis], *ag.* indecoroso; sconveniente.

seemliness ['si:mlinis], *s.* decenza, decoro; convenienza: *she spoke with fitting —*, ella parlava con il dovuto decoro.

seemly ['si:mli], *ag.* decoroso, decente; che si addice ‖ *av.* (*rar.*) decorosamente.

seen [si:n], *p.p.* di to **see**.

to seep [si:p], *v.i.* **1.** gocciolare; colare; filtrare: *water was seeping through the roof*, l'acqua filtrava attraverso il tetto **2.** asciugarsi.

seepage ['si:pidʒ], *s.* gocciolamento; infiltrazione.

seer[1] ['si(:)ə*], *s.* **1.** (*rar.*) chi vede, veggente **2.** profeta.

seer[2] [siə*], *s.* « seer » (misura di peso indiana = kg. 0,93).

seersucker ['siə,sʌkə*], *s.* tessuto indiano di lino, cotone a righe bianche o blu

seesaw ['si:-sɔ:], *ag.* **1.** fluttuante, ondeggiante **2.** (*mec.*) che si muove con moto alternativo ‖ *s.* altalena ☆ — *motion*, (*mec.*) moto alternativo.

to seesaw, *v.i.* **1.** giocare all'altalena **2.** andare su e giù; *fig.* vacillare, esitare **3.** (*mec.*) muoversi con moto alternativo.

seesaw, *av.* **1.** a guisa di altalena; in modo fluttuante **2.** (*mec.*) a moto alternativo.

to seethe [si:ð], *pass.p.p.* **seethed** [si:ðd], (*arc.*) *pass.* **sod** [sɔd], *p.p.* **sodden** ['sɔdn], *v.t.i.* **1.** bollire, far bollire; lessare **2.** *fig.* ribollire; fermentare; agitarsi; essere in subbuglio: *I could see he was seething with excitement*, mi accorgevo che era sovreccitato; *the whole country was seething with discontent*, l'intero paese era in subbuglio, in fermento.

seething ['si:ðiŋ], *ag.* **1.** in ebollizione **2.** *fig.* in agitazione, in fermento: *she has a — brain*, ha il cervello in ebollizione ‖ *s.* ebollizione, agitazione, fermento.

segar [si'gɑ:*], *s.* (*arc.*) sigaro.

segment ['segmənt], *s.* **1.** segmento, sezione (anche *geom.*); fetta, spicchio: — *of a line*, segmento di una linea; *the — of an orange*, lo spicchio di un'arancia **2.** segmento, anello, metamero (di insetti, ecc.): *the — of a worm*, il segmento di un verme ☆ — *cores*, (*tec.*) anime a sezioni; — *gear*, settore dentato.

to segment, *v.t.i.* **1.** dividere, dividersi in segmenti **2.** (*fisiol.*) riprodursi per gemmazione.

segmental [seg'mentl], **segmentary** [seg'mentəri], *ag.* a segmenti; segmentale ☆ — *wheel*, (*mec.*) mola a settori.

segmentation [,segmən'teiʃən], *s.* **1.** (*geom. zool.*) segmentazione **2.** (*fisiol.*) riproduzione per scissione.

segregable ['segrigəbl], *ag.* segregabile.

segregate ['segrigeit], *ag.* **1.** (*arc.*) segregato, separato **2.** (*bot. zool.*) semplice, non composto.

to segregate, *v.t.i.* segregare; separare, separarsi; allontanare, allontanarsi; scindere, scindersi (di cristalli).

segregation [,segri'geiʃən], *s.* segregazione; separazione; scissione.

segregationist [,segri'geiʃnist], *s.* (*amer.*) segregazionista.

segregative ['segrigeitiv], *ag.* **1.** tendente a segregare, a dividere **2.** insocievole.

Seidlitz powder ['sedlits'paudə*], *s.* (*chim.*) polvere di Seidlitz.

seigneur [sei'njə:*], *s.* (*st.*) feudatario, signore.

seigneurial [sei'njə:riəl], *ag.* (*st.*) signorile, di, da signore, da feudatario.

seignior ['seinjə*], *s.* (*st.*) feudatario, signore.

seigniorage ['seinjəridʒ], *s.* (*st.*) diritto feudale, sovrano (specialmente il diritto della corona di prelevare una parte del metallo portato alla zecca per il conio).

seigniorial ['seinjəriəl], *ag.* (*st.*) signorile, di, da signore.

seigniory ['seinjəri], *s.* (*st.*) signoria, diritto feudale.

seine[1] [sein], *s.* scorticaria (grande rete da pesca).

to seine[1], *v.t.* pescare con la scorticaria.

Seine[2], *no.pr.* (*geog.*) Senna.

to seise, *V.* to **seize 3.**

seisin ['si:zin], *s.* (*dir.*) presa di possesso; possesso.

seismal ['saizməl], **seismic(al)** ['saizmik(əl)], *ag.* sismico.

seismogram ['saizməgræm], *s.* sismogramma.

seismograph ['saizməgrɑ:f], *s.* sismografo.

seismographic [,saizmə'græfik], *ag.* sismografico.

seismography [saiz'mɔgrəfi], *s.* sismografia.

seismologic(al) [,saizmə'lɔdʒik(əl)], *ag.* sismologico.

seismologist [saiz'mɔlədʒist], *s.* sismologo.

seismology [saiz'mɔlədʒi], *s.* sismologia.

seismometer [saiz'mɔmitə*], *s.* sismometro.

seismoscope ['saizməskoup], *s.* sismoscopio.

seismoscopic [,saizmə'skɔpik], *ag.* sismoscopico.

seizable ['si:zəbl], *ag.* **1.** afferrabile **2.** (*dir.*) sequestrabile, confiscabile.

to seize [si:z], *v.t.i.* **1.** afferrare, prendere, impadronirsi di (anche *fig.*): *he seized a knife on the table*, afferrò un coltello sulla tavola; *she seized all she could get hold of*, arraffò tutto ciò che poteva prendere; *to — an opportunity*, afferrare un'opportunità, un'occasione; *to — the throne*, impadronirsi del trono; *to be seized with amazement, terror, wonder*, essere preso da stupore, terrore, meraviglia; *to be seized with fever, a desire to do sthg.*, essere preso dalla febbre, dal desiderio di fare ql.co. ‖ *to — (up)on an excuse, a pretext*, prendere una scusa, un pretesto **2.** afferrare, capire, comprendere: *to — the meaning of sthg.*, afferrare il significato di ql.co. **3.** (*dir.*) mettere in possesso; *fig.* informare: *to — s.o. with sthg.*, concedere a qlcu. il possesso di ql.co.; *to be* (o *to stand*) *seized of a property*, essere investito di una proprietà; *to be seized of some facts*, essere reso edotto di alcuni fatti **4.** (*dir.*) confiscare, pignorare, sequestrare: *all the goods were seized*, tutta la merce fu confiscata **5.** (*tec. mec.*) grippare, bloccarsi: *the bearings, the brakes are seizing*, i cuscinetti, i freni si grippano, si bloccano **6.** (*mar.*) legare.

seizin ['si:zin], *s.* (*dir.*) presa di possesso; possesso.

seizing ['si:ziŋ], *s.* **1.** atto dell'afferrare, del ghermire, del prendere **2.** conquista; cattura **3.** (*dir.*) sequestro, confisca **4.** — (*up*), (*tec. mec.*) grippaggio, bloccaggio, ingranamento **5.** (*mar.*) legatura ☆ *round* —, (*mar.*) legatura piana per gassa.

seizure ['si:ʒə*], *s.* **1.** (*dir.*) confisca, sequestro; presa di possesso **2.** conquista, cattura **3.** (*patol.*) attacco, colpo (apoplettico) **4.** (*tec. mec.*) bloccaggio, grippaggio, ingranamento.

sejant ['si:dʒənt], *ag.* (*arald.*) sedente.

Sejanus [si'dʒeinəs], *no.pr.m.* (*st.*) Seiano.

sekos ['si:kɔs], *s.* (*archeol.*) adito (nei templi antichi).

selachian [si'leikjən], *ag.* (*ittiol.*) appartenente ai selaci ‖ *s.* pesce dei selaci.

seldom ['seldəm], *av.* raramente: *I am — out, I — go out*, sono di rado fuori, esco di rado ‖ *— seen, soon forgotten, prov.* lontan dagli occhi, lontan dal cuore.

select [si'lekt], *ag.* 1. scelto, selezionato; eccellente 2. schizzinoso: *Mrs. Jones is very — in the people she invites*, la signora Jones sceglie i suoi invitati con la massima cura ☆ *— committee*, commissione d'inchiesta (in Parlamento); *— -man*, (*amer.*) consigliere municipale (nella Nuova Inghilterra).

to select, *v.t.* scegliere, eleggere.

selection [si'lekʃən], *s.* 1. selezione, scelta: *natural —*, (*biol.*) selezione naturale 2. *pl.* brani scelti: *selections from...*, brani scelti da...-

selective [si'lektiv], *ag.* selettivo.

selectively [si'lektivli], *av.* selettivamente.

selectivity [silek'tiviti], *s.* (*rad.*) selettività.

selectness [si'lektnis], *s.* eccellenza; distinzione, raffinatezza.

selector [si'lektə*], *s.c.* sceglitore, sceglitrice; selettore, selettrice ‖ *s.* (*tel. rad. tv.*) selettore ☆ «*omnibearing*» *—*, (*aer.*) selettore di rotta.

selenate ['selinit], *s.* (*chim.*) seleniato.

Selene [si'li:ni:], *no.pr.f.* (*mit.*) Selene.

selenic [si'lenik], *ag.* (*chim.*) selenico.

selenious [si'li:njos], *ag.* (*chim.*) selenioso.

selenite¹ ['selinait], *s.* (*min.*) selenite.

selenite² [si'li:nait], *s.* selenita.

selenitic [,seli'nitik], *ag.* (*chim.*) selenitico.

selenium [si'li:njəm], *s.* (*chim.*) selenio.

selenographer [,seli'nogrəfə*], *s.* selenografo.

selenographic [si,li:nou'græfik], *ag.* selenografico.

selenography [,seli'nogrəfi], *s.* selenografia.

selenology [,seli'nolədʒi], *s.* selenologia.

Seleucid [si'lju:sid], *pl.* Seleucids [si'lju:sidz], Seleucidae [si'lju:sidi:], *no.pr.* (*st.*) Seleucide.

self [self], *pl.* selves [selvz], *pron.* (*comm. fam.* per *oneself, myself, himself, etc.*): *— and wife*, (*fam.*) io e mia moglie; *payable to —*, (*comm.*) pagabile al firmatario ‖ *s.* 1. l'io, la personalità, l'individuo: *— is his god*, fa di se stesso un dio; *— is often a bad adviser*, l'io è spesso un cattivo consigliere 2. (*preceduto da ag.*): *the higher, lower —*, i sentimenti più elevati, più bassi della nostra natura; *his second —*, il suo «alter ego», il suo amico più caro; *my better —*, la parte migliore di me stesso; *for my own — I think he is wrong*, per conto mio penso che abbia torto; *it was his very —*, era proprio lui in persona; *now I feel my old — again*, ora ho ritrovato me stesso; ora mi sento bene come prima, ho ritrovato l'energia di un tempo 3. pianta, animale di un solo colore.

self, *ag.* 1. della stessa materia, sostanza: *a straw hat with — trimming*, un cappello di paglia con guarnizioni della stessa paglia 2. uniforme, dello stesso colore: *a — flower*, un fiore monocolore 3. puro: *— whisky*, whisky puro.

-self, *suffisso* per la formazione dei *pron. r.*: oneself, myself, himself, herself, itself, ourself, ourselves, yourself, yourselves, themselves.

self-, (*nei composti*): *— -abasement*, autoumiliazione; autoannientamento; *— -absorbed*, assorto; *— -acting*, automatico; *— -adjusting*, ad autoregolarizzazione; *— -admiration*, ammirazione di se stesso, narcisismo; *— -applause*, lode, compiacimento di se stesso; *— -appointed*, autonominatosi; *— -assertive*, autoritario; perentorio; arrogante, borioso; *— -assurance*, sicurezza di sè; (*fam.*) faccia tosta; *— -bias*, (*elett.*) autopolarizzazione; *— -binder*, (*agr.*) mietitrice legatrice; *— -centred*, egocentrico; *— -closing*, che si chiude automaticamente; *— -collected*, calmo, sereno; di sangue freddo; *— -coloured*, monocolore; *— -command*, sangue freddo; padronanza di sè; *— -communion*, introspezione, meditazione; *— -complacence* (o *— -complacency*), autocompiacimento; fatuità; *— -conceit*, presunzione; vanità; fatuità: *he is full of* (o *he is eaten up with*) *— -conceit*, è pieno di sè; *— -conceited*, presuntuoso;

vanitoso; *— -condemned*, che si condanna da sè; *— -confidence*, fiducia in sè; *— -confident*, sicuro di sè, che ha fiducia in sè; *— -conscious*, impacciato; vergognoso; affettato, manierato; (*fil.*) autocosciente; *— -consciousness*, imbarazzo; posa; (*fil.*) autocoscienza; *— -contained*, riservato, circospetto (di persona); autonomo, indipendente (di casa, macchina, ecc.); *— -contradiction*, contraddizione di sè; incoerenza; contraddizione in termini; *— -contradictory*, che si contraddice, che è in contraddizione; *— -control*, autocontrollo, padronanza di sè; sangue freddo; *— -cooled*, a raffreddamento automatico; *— -defence*, autodifesa: *the art of — -defence*, la boxe, (*arc.*) la scherma; *in — -defence*, per legittima difesa; *— -delusion*, illusione; *— -denial*, abnegazione, rinuncia a se stesso; frugalità; *— -denying*, che accetta, si impone rinunce; frugale, parco; *— -destruction*, autodistruzione; suicidio; *— -determination*, autodeterminazione, autodecisione: *right of — -determination*, (*pol.*) diritto (di un popolo) di scegliere il proprio ordinamento; *— -educated*, autodidatta; *— -effacing*, che rinuncia ai propri diritti; che si mette in disparte; *— -elected*, autoelettosi; scelto spontaneamente: *he set to work at his — -elected task*, si mise a fare il lavoro che si era scelto; *— -elective*, che ha il diritto di eleggere i propri membri (di assemblea, ecc.); che si autoelegge (di persona); *— -energizing*, (*elett.*) autoeccitante; *— -esteem*, stima di sè; amor proprio; *— -evident*, evidente, lampante; *— -evident truth*, verità lapalissiana; *— -examination*, esame di coscienza; introspezione; *— -existent*, autoesistente; *— -explanatory*, autoesplicativo; ovvio; *— -expression*, autoespressione; *— -feeding*, ad alimentazione automatica continua; *— -fertilization*, (*biol. bot.*) autoimpollinazione, autofecondazione; *— -forgetful*, dimentico di sè; disinteressato; *— -governing*, indipendente, autonomo; *— -government*, indipendenza, autonomia; *— -hardening*, (*metal.*) autotemprante; *— -heal*, (*bot.*) brunella; *— -help* il fare da sè; *— -importance*, presunzione, prosopopea; *— -important*, presuntuoso, arrogante; *— -induction*, (*elett.*) autoinduzione; *— -inductive*, (*elett.*) autoinduttivo; *— -indulgence*, mollezza, intemperanza; *— -inflicted*, causato da sè; *— -inflicted wound*, (*mil.*) autolesione; *— -instructed*, autodidatta; *— -instructor*, manuale, guida (per autodidatti); *— -interest*, interesse personale; *— -interested*, interessato; *— -limited*, che ha un decorso stabilito (di malattia); *— -loading*, (*mec.*) a caricamento automatico; *— -locking*, (*mec.*) a chiusura automatica; a bloccaggio automatico; *— -love*, egoismo; *— -lubricated*, autolubrificato; *— -made*, che si è fatto da sè; *— -mastery*, padronanza, dominio di sè, autocontrollo; *— -murder*, suicidio; *— -oiling*, lubrificazione automatica; *— -opening*, (*mec.*) ad apertura automatica; *— -opinionated* (o *— -opinioned*), caparbio, ostinato; *— -pity*, autocommiserazione; *— -portrait*, autoritratto; *— -possessed*, padrone di sè; calmo; flemmatico; *— -possession*, padronanza di sè; calma; flemma; *— -preservation*, autoconservazione: *instinct, spirit of — -preservation*, istinto, spirito di conservazione; *— -priming*, autoadescante (di pompa); *— -propelled*, a propulsione autonoma, semovente; *— -raising*, che contiene una certa percentuale di lievito (di farina); *— -recording* (o *— -registering*), autoregistratore; *— -regard*, rispetto di sè; amor proprio; *— -regulating*, (*mec.*) autoregolatore; *— -reliance*, fiducia in se stesso; *— -reliant*, fiducioso in sè; *— -reproach*, autoaccusa; rimorso; *— -respect*, rispetto di sè; amor proprio; *— -righteous*, che si considera più giusto e virtuoso degli altri; farisaico, ipocrita; *— -righting* che non si può capovolgere (di barca, ecc.); *— -sacrificing*, che si sacrifica per gli altri; *— -same*, assolutamente lo stesso; *— -satisfaction*, autocompiacimento fatuità; *— -satisfied*, contento di sè; vanesio; *— -seeking*, egoista; *— -service*, il servirsi da sè (in ristoranti, ecc.); (*fam.*) locale in cui ci si serve da sè; *— -sown* spontaneo (di pianta); *— -starter*, avviatore automa tico, motorino di avviamento; — *-styled*, sedicente; — *-sufficiency*, autosufficienza; vanità, presunzione: *national* — *-sufficiency*, autarchia; — *-sufficient*, autosufficiente; presuntuoso; — *-suggestion*, autosuggestione; — *-supporting*, che si mantiene da sè; indipendente; — *-surrender*, abnegazione; — *-taught*, autodidatta; per autodidatti; — *-timer*, (*foto.*) autoscatto; — *-tipping*, (*ferr. aut.*) a ribaltamento automatico; — *-willed*, ostinato, caparbio; — *-winding*, a carica automatica (di orologio).

selfhood ['selfhud], *s.* (*rar.*) **1.** personalità; individualità **2.** egoismo, egocentrismo.

selfish ['selfiʃ], *ag.* egoistico; interessato.

selfishly ['selfiʃli], *av.* egoisticamente.

selfishness ['selfiʃnis], *s.* egoismo.

selfless ['selflis], *ag.* disinteressato, altruistico.

selflessly ['selflisli], *av.* disinteressatamente, altruisticamente.

selflessness ['selflisnis], *s.* altruismo.

selfness ['selfnis], *s.* egoismo, egocentrismo.

sell [sel], *s.* (*fam.*) delusione, disappunto; seccatura: *what a* —*!*, che seccatura! ☆ — *-out*, (*sl. amer.*) svendita; esaurimento di merce.

to **sell**, *pass.p.p.* **sold** [sould], *v.t.i.* **1.** vendere; promuovere la vendita di; smerciare; avere smercio: *he sold his car easily*, vendette la macchina con facilità; *it is not their low price, but their quality which sells our goods*, non è il prezzo basso, ma la qualità della nostra merce che la fa vendere; *this book sells well*, questo libro si vende bene; *what are strawberries selling at?*, a quanto si vendono le fragole?; *to — at a loss*, svendere, vendere in perdita; *to — by auction*, vendere all'asta, all'incanto; *to — by instalments*, vendere a rate; *to — cheap, dear*, vendere a buon mercato, vendere caro; *to — for cash*, vendere a pronta cassa; *to — on commission*, vendere a provvigione; *to — on credit*, vendere a credito; *to — short* (o *to — a bear*, (*comm.*) vendere allo scoperto (in Borsa); *to — wholesale*, vendere all'ingrosso ‖ *flat to —* (o *to be sold*), appartamento da vendere ‖ *to — like hot cakes*, andare a ruba **2.** *fig.* vendere; tradire: *the judge sold justice*, il giudice si lasciò corrompere; *to — one's country*, tradire il proprio paese; *to — one's life dearly*, vendere a caro prezzo la propria vita; *to — one's soul*, vendere la propria anima ‖ *to — the pass*, tradire una causa **3.** (*sl.*) ingannare; dar(la) a bere a: *you can't — me that*, non me la dai ad intendere ‖ *sold again!*, me l'hanno fatta ancora! ‖ *to — s.o. a pup*, (*sl.*) raggirare qlcu. **4.** (*fam. amer.*) essere accettato: *do you think the idea will —?*, credete che l'idea avrà successo? **5.** *to —* **off**, (*comm.*) liquidare **6.** *to —* **out**, (*comm.*) svendere; (*st. mil.*) cedere il proprio grado di ufficiale **7.** *to —* **up**, (*dir.*) vendere (per sanare un fallimento).

seller ['selə*], *s.c.* venditore, venditrice ‖ *s.* articolo che si vende: *a good, bad —*, articolo che si vende bene, male ☆ *best- —*, libro, autore di successo: *this novel is the best- — of the year*, questo è il romanzo più venduto dell'anno; *book- —*, libraio.

selling ['seliŋ], *s.* vendita, smercio ☆ — *-agent*, agente di vendita; — *off* (o — *out*), liquidazione; — *-price*, prezzo di vendita.

seltzer (-water) ['seltsə*('wɔ:tə*)], *s.* (acqua di) seltz: *a bottle of —*, un sifone di acqua di seltz.

seltzogene ['seltsədʒi:n], *s.* (*aut.*) gassogeno.

selvage ['selvidʒ], *s.* **1.** (*ind. tessile*) cimosa; bordo; vivagno **2.** bocchetta (di serratura) **3.** (*geol.*) salbanda.

selvagee ['selvədʒi:], *s.* (*mar.*) sbirro di commando.

selvedge, *V.* selvage.

selves [selvz], *pl.* di self.

semantic [si'mæntik], *ag.* semantico.

semantics [si'mæntiks], *s.* semantica.

semaphore ['seməfɔ:*], *s.* semaforo ☆ — *arm* (o *amer. — blade*), (*ferr.*) braccio del semaforo; — *-signal*, (*ferr.*) semaforo, segnalatore a braccio mobile.

to **semaphore**, *v.t.i.* segnalare, trasmettere (una comunicazione) per mezzo di semaforo.

semaphoric(al) [,semə'fɔrik(əl)], *ag.* semaforico.

semasiology [si,meisi'ɔlədʒi], **sematology** [,semə'tɔlədʒi], *s.* semantica.

semblable ['sembləbl], *ag.* (*arc.*) simile, assomigliante; apparente.

semblance ['sembləns], *s.* **1.** aspetto, apparenza, parvenza: *in —*, apparentemente; *a mere — of friendship*, una falsa apparenza di amicizia; *he went away without the — of an excuse*, se ne andò senza un gesto di scusa **2.** somiglianza; immagine: *to bear the — of sthg.*, rassomigliare a ql.co.

semblant ['semblənt], *ag.* **1.** somigliante **2.** apparente.

semé(e) ['semei], *ag.* (*arald.*) seminato, punteggiato: *shield — of* (o *with*) *stars*, scudo punteggiato, seminato di stelle.

semeiologist [,si:mai'ɔlədʒist], *s.* (*med.*) semiologo.

semeiology [,si:mai'ɔlədʒi], *s.* (*med.*) semiologia.

semeiotic [,si:mai'ɔtik], *ag.* (*med.*) semeiotico, sintomatico.

semeiotics [,si:mai'ɔtiks], *s.* (*med.*) semeiotica, sintomatologia.

Semele ['semili], *no.pr.f.* (*mit.*) Semele.

semen ['si:men], *pl.* **semina** ['seminə], *s.* sperma.

semester [si'mestə*], *s.* semestre (scolastico, accademico).

semi ['semi], *prefisso* **1.** semi, mezzo, metà **2.** semi, in parte, non completamente, in modo imperfetto, quasi **3.** due volte (in un periodo determinato) ☆ — *-annual*, semestrale; — *-annually* (o — *-yearly*), semestralmente, ogni sei mesi; — *-automatic*, semiautomatico; — *-barbarian*, semibarbaro; — *-beam*, (*mec. edil.*) trave a sbalzo; — *-circumference*, semicirconferenza; — *conscius*, semicosciente, che sta per perdere, riprendere conoscenza; — *-darkness*, penombra, semioscurità; — *detached*, appaiate (di case); — *-grand*, a mezza coda (pianoforte); — *-literate*, semidotto, che ha cultura superficiale; — *-lunar*, (*bot. zool. anat.*) semilunare; — *manufactured*, (*ind.*) semilavorato; — *-military*, paramilitare (di associazione, corpo, ecc.); — *-monthly*, bimensile, quindicinale (di pubblicazione); — *-nude*, seminudo; — *-official*, semiufficiale, ufficioso; — *-profile*, a tre quarti (di ritratto); — *-rigid*, semirigido; — *-skilled*, semiqualificato; — *-smile*, tenue sorriso, mezzo sorriso; — *-sparkling*, frizzantino (di vino); — *-steel*, ghisa acciaiosa; — *-transparent*, semitrasparente, translucido; — *-tropical*, (*rar.*) subtropicale; — *-weekly*, (*amer.*) bisettimanale.

semibreve ['semibri:v], *s.* (*mus.*) semibreve.

semicircle ['semi,sə:kl], *s.* (*geom.*) semicerchio.

semicircular ['semi'sə:kjulə*], *ag.* (*geom.*) semicircolare ☆ — *arch*, (*arch.*) arco a tutto sesto; — *canals*, canali semicircolari (dell'orecchio).

semicolon ['semi'koulən], *s.* punto e virgola.

semifinal ['semi'fainl], *ag. s.* semifinale.

semifinalist ['semi'fainəlist], *s.c.* semifinalista.

semifinished ['semi'finiʃt], *ag.* (*mec. ind.*) semilavorato ☆ — *products*, (*ind.*) semilavorati; — *steel*, (*metal.*) acciaio in barre, billette, lamiere, ecc.

seminal ['si:minl], *ag.* **1.** seminale; che contiene seme, sperma; riproduttivo **2.** simile a seme; germinale, originario, embrionale: *in the — state*, allo stato embrionale, latente ☆ — *power*, forza riproduttrice.

seminar ['semina:*], *s.* seminario (di università): *the — for Italian teachers of English*, il seminario per gli insegnanti italiani di inglese.

seminarist ['seminərist], *s.* (*eccl.*) seminarista.

seminary ['seminəri], *s.* **1.** (*eccl.*) seminario **2.** *fig.* vivaio: *slums are seminaries of crime*, i bassifondi sono i vivai del crimine **3.** (*arc.*) scuola privata, collegio (specialmente per giovinette).

semination [,semi'neiʃən], *s.* (*bot.*) seminatura; propagazione, spargimento di seme.

seminiferous [‚semi'nifərəs], *ag.* seminifero, portante semi; che trasporta semi.

semiology [‚simai'olədʒi], *s.* (*med.*) semiologia.

semiped ['semiped], *s.* (*poes.*) semipiede.

semiprivate ['semi'praivit], *ag.* (*amer.*) semiprivato (specificatamente di camera d'ospedale a due, tre, quattro letti).

semiquaver ['semi‚kweivə*], *s.* (*mus.*) semicroma.

Semiramis [se'mirəmis], *no.pr.f.* (*st.*) Semiramide.

Semite ['si:mait], *ag.* semitico || *s.* semita.

Semitic [si'mitik], *ag.* semitico.

Semitics [si'mitiks], *s.* studio della lingua, letteratura, civiltà dei semiti.

Semitism ['semitizəm], *s.* lingua, caratteristica, modo di pensare semitico.

semitone ['semitoun], *s.* (*mus.*) semitono.

semitonic ['semi'tɔnik], *ag.* (*mus.*) semitonico ☆ — *scale*, (*mus.*) scala cromatica.

semitrailer ['semi'treilə*], *s.* (*amer.*) « semitrailer », semirimorchio.

semivowel ['semi'vauəl], *s.* (*fonet.*) semivocale.

semolina [‚semə'li:nə], *s.* semolino ☆ — *pudding*, budino di semolino.

sempiternal [‚sempi'tə:n]], *ag.* (*rar.*) sempiterno, eterno, perpetuo.

sempiternally [‚sempi'tə:nəli], *av.* (*rar.*) eternamente.

sempiternity [‚sempi'tə:niti], *s.* (*rar.*) eternità.

sempstress ['sempstris], *s.* cucitrice.

sen [sen], *s.* « sen » (moneta giapponese corrispondente a 1/100 di yen).

senarius [si'nɛəriəs], *pl.* **senarii** [si'nɛəriai], *s.* (*poes.*) senario.

senary ['si:nəri], *ag.* senario.

senate ['senit], *s.* 1. senato 2. senato, consiglio accademico (nelle università) || *Senate house*, Palazzo del Senato (anche nelle università).

senator ['senətə*], *s.* senatore.

senatorial [‚senə'tɔ:riəl], *ag.* senatoriale (di senatore); senatorio ☆ — *dignity*, dignità senatoriale; — *district*, (*amer.*) regione qualificata ad eleggere un senatore.

senatorship ['senətəʃip], *s.* carica, ufficio, dignità senatoria.

senatus consult(um) [se'neitəskən'sʌlt(əm)], *pl.* **senatus consulta** [kən'sʌltə], *s.* senatoconsulto.

to send[1] [send], *pass.p.p.* **sent** [sent], *v.t.i.* 1. mandare, inviare, spedire: *to — a child to school*, mandare un bambino a scuola; *to — a member to Parliament*, delegare un deputato alla Camera; *to — s.o. as ambassador to London*, mandare qlcu. in veste di ambasciatore a Londra || *the blow sent him sprawling*, il colpo gli fece fare un ruzzolone || *this record sends me*, (*fam.*) questo disco mi rende frenetico (specialmente di mùsica jazz) || *your question has sent me to the dictionary*, la tua domanda mi ha costretto a consultare il dizionario || *to — coals to Newcastle*, portare vasi a Samo, mandare acqua al mare || *to — s.o. about his business*, (*fam.*) mandare qlcu. al diavolo, a quel paese || *to — s.o. crazy*, far impazzire qlcu. || *to — s.o. flying*, mandar via, licenziare qlcu. sui due piedi; *to — sthg. flying*, scaraventare via ql.co. || *to — into a fit* (o *into fits*), far andare qlcu. fuori dai gangheri || *to — s.o. packing*, far fare fagotto a qlcu. || *to — s.o. to sleep*, mandare a letto, fare addormentare qlcu. || *to — to the bottom*, (*mar.*) colare a picco || *to — word to s.o.*, mandare un messaggio a qlcu. || *to be sent into the world*, essere messo al mondo 2. inviare un messaggio, un messaggiero: *to — me tomorrow morning*, mandami a dire ql.co. domattina; *Mary has sent to ask, to see if...*, Maria ha mandato a chiedere, a vedere se... 3. accordare; permettere: *God — him victorious*, Dio gli conceda la vittoria; *God — that I may arrive in time*, Dio voglia che io possa giungere in tempo 4. *to — for* (*s.o., sthg.*), mandare a chiamare, a prendere: *the doctor was sent for*, si   mandato a chiamare il

dottore; *we ought to send for further stock of wool*, dovremmo farci arrivare altre provviste di lana 5. *to — along*, inviare (da qlcu.): — *him along*, mandamelo, digli di venire da me 6. *to — away*, congedare; mandar via 7. *to — back*, rinviare, mandare indietro; riflettere (luce, ecc.): *have you sent back his umbrella?*, gli hai restituito l'ombrello?; *I sent her back home*, la rimandai a casa 8. *to — down*, far scendere: inviare dalla città (specialmente Londra) in provincia; sospendere, espellere (dall'università) 9. *to — forth*, esalare, spandere (odore, ecc.); lanciare, gettare, emettere (scintille, raggi, ecc.); germogliare 10. *to — in*, introdurre, far entrare; far pervenire: *applications should be sent in before the end of the month*, le domande dovranno pervenire entro la fine del mese; *he has already sent in his bill*, ha già mandato il conto; *he sent in his card*, si fece precedere dal suo biglietto da visita; *she always sends in her name*, si fa sempre annunciare; *to — in one's papers* (o *resignation*), inviare le proprie dimissioni, dimettersi 11. *to — off*, inviare (in missione, ecc.); spedire (lettera, ecc.) 12. *to — on*, inoltrare (lettere, ecc.); trasmettere (un ordine) 13. *to — out*, mandar fuori, far uscire; mettere alla porta; emettere (luce, fumo, ecc.): *to — out circulars*, mandare delle circolari; *to — out leaves*, germogliare 14. *to — round*, divulgare; far passare, far circolare; (*fam.*) inviare: *is the parcel ready? I'll — round tomorrow*, è pronto il pacco? lo manderò a prendere domani; *please, — round the wine bottle*, per favore fai passare la bottiglia del vino 15. *to — through*, trasmettere (telegramma, ecc.) 16. *to — up*, far salire; lanciare; inviare dalla provincia in città (specialmente Londra); (*fam. amer.*) condannare alla prigione: *the crisis sent up the prices*, la crisi fece salire i prezzi; *to — up a rocket*, lanciare un razzo || *to — up a bill to the Upper House*, presentare un progetto di legge alla Camera Alta (in Parlamento).

send[2], *s.* 1. impeto (di onda discendente) 2. (*mar.*) beccheggio.

to send[2], *pass.p.p.* **sended** ['sendid], *v.i.* beccheggiare.

sendal ['sendl], *s.* zendale, zendado.

sender ['sendə*], *s.* 1. mandante, mittente || *returned to —*, respinto al mittente 2. (*tel. rad.*) chi segnala, segnalatore; apparecchio trasmettitore, emettitore 3. (*comm.*) speditore, spedizioniere; rimettitore (di denaro) ☆ *Morse —*, trasmettitore Morse.

sending ['sendiŋ], *s.* 1. invio; (*comm.*) spedizione; rimessa (di denaro) 2. (*tel. rad.*) trasmissione ☆ — *station*, stazione trasmittente.

send-off ['send'ɔ:f], *s.* (*fam.*) 1. festa d'addio; espressioni cordiali, amichevoli (per qlcu. che parte, inizia una carriera) 2. soffietto, recensione favorevole di libro.

Seneca ['senikə], *no.pr.m.* (*st. lett.*) Seneca.

senecio [si'ni:ʃiou], *s.*(*bot.*) senecio, senecione, cineraria.

Senegal [‚seni'go:l], *no.pr.* (*geog.*) Senegal.

Senegalese ['senigə'li:z], *ag.s.c.* senegalese || *s.* lingua senegalese.

senescence [si'nesns], *s.* senescenza.

senescent [si'nesnt], *ag.* senescente.

seneschal ['seniʃəl], *s.* (*st.*) siniscalco, maggiordomo.

sengreen ['sengri:n], *s.* (*bot.*) semprevivo.

senile ['si:nail], *ag.* senile ☆ — *decay*, decadimento senile.

senility [si'niliti], *s.* senilità.

senior ['si:njə*], *ag.* 1. più vecchio, più anziano: *she is three years — to me*, ha tre anni più di me 2. (*abbr. sen.*, amer. *sr.*): seniore, padre, fratello maggiore: *John Smith —*, John Smith seniore 3. superiore, più ragguardevole; che ha più anzianità (di ufficio) || *the — master*, il maestro più anziano; *the — Italian master*, il titolare della prima cattedra d'Italiano; *the — officer* (*mil.*) il decano degli ufficiali; *my — officer*, il mio ufficiale superiore || *the Senior Service*, la Marina || *s.* 1. decano, anziano: *he is my — by two years*, ha due anni più di me || *the seniors*, gli allievi più anziani; (*amer.*) studenti licenziandi (di scuola superiore) 2. il supe riore, il più ragguardevole ☆ — *clerk*, capocommesso; capoufficio; — *partner*, socio dirigente; — *technician*, tecnico specializzato.

seniority [ˌsiːniˈɔriti], *s.* anzianità (d'anni, di grado); superiorità (di grado, posizione): *right of* —, diritto di anzianità; *he was promoted by* —, fu promosso per anzianità ☆ — *list*, ordine d'anzianità.

senna [ˈsenə], *s.* (*farm.*) senna ☆ — *tea*, infuso di senna.

Sennacherib [seˈnækərib], *no.pr.m.* (*st.*) Sennacherib.

sennet [ˈsenit], *s.* (*arc. teat.*) fanfara, suono di tromba (per annunciare l'entrata in scena di personaggi importanti).

sennight [ˈsenait], *s.* (*arc.*) settimana; otto giorni: *this day* —, oggi a otto.

sennit [ˈsenit], *s.* (*mar.*) garzetta, gaschetta, treccia (di corda, paglia, ecc.).

sensation [senˈseiʃən], *s.* **1.** senso, sensazione, impressione: *he had a* — *of falling*, gli sembrava di cadere; *to have a* — *of cold*, provare un senso di freddo **2.** sensazione, effetto sensazionale, colpo, impressione: *to create* (o *to make* o *to cause*) *a* —, far colpo, impressionare, creare un effetto ☆ — *drama*, dramma a sensazione.

sensational [senˈseiʃənl], *ag.* **1.** che dipende dai sensi **2.** sensazionale, di grande effetto, impressionante: *a* — *happening*, un avvenimento sensazionale; *a* — *piece of news*, una notizia che fa colpo ☆ — *writer*, autore di opere a sensazione.

sensationalism [senˈseiʃənəlizəm], *s.* **1.** ricerca del sensazionale **2.** (*st. fil.*) sensismo.

sensationalist [senˈseiʃənəlist], *s.* **1.** chi cerca di far colpo, sensazione **2.** (*st. fil.*) sensista.

sensationally [senˈseiʃənəli], *av.* in modo da creare sensazione.

sense [sens], *s.* **1.** senso: *the five senses*, i cinque sensi; *the sixth* —, il sesto senso; (*scherz.*) l'intuizione; *to be with senses all alert*, stare all'erta, essere ben sveglio; *to have a keen* — *of hearing*, avere l'udito fine; *to kindle the senses of s.o.*, eccitare i sensi di qlcu. **2.** *pl.* comprensione, facoltà mentali: *are you in your right senses?*, sei nelle tue piene facoltà mentali?; *have you taken leave of your senses?*, hai perso la testa?; *to bring s.o. to his senses*, far rinsavire qlcu.; *to drive s.o. out of his senses*, fare impazzire qlcu. **3.** conoscenza: *to come to one's senses*, rinvenire, riprendere conoscenza; *to lose one's senses*, perdere la conoscenza **4.** senso, sensazione, impressione: — *of colour*, senso del colore; *he has no stage* —, non ha temperamento drammatico; *to have a high* — *of duty*, avere un alto senso del dovere; *to have a high* — *of one's importance*, avere un'alta opinione di se stessi; *to have no* — *of the proprieties*, non avere la minima idea delle convenienze ‖ *to take the* — *of the meeting*, consultare l'assemblea, sentire l'opinione dell'assemblea **5.** buon senso, saggezza; intelligenza: *there is no* — *in that!*, non vi è senso comune!; *what is the* — *of talking like that?*, che ragione c'è di parlare a quel modo?; *to act against all* —, agire scioccamente; *to talk* —, parlare con saggezza ‖ *he has more* — *than to do that*, è troppo avveduto per fare ciò **6.** senso, significato: *figurative* —, senso figurato; *in a* —, in un certo senso; *in the full* — *of the word*, nel vero senso della parola; *I can't make* — *out of this passage*, non riesco a capire il significato di questo brano ‖ *to make* — *out of nonsense*, trovare per forza un senso dove non c'è ☆ — *organs*, organi dei sensi ‖ *common* —, buon senso: *to take a common* — *view of things*, vedere il lato pratico delle cose.

to sense, *v.t.* **1.** intuire, avere la sensazione di; capire, rendersi conto ‖ *to* — *the audience*, (*fam.*) tastare il pubblico **2.** (*fil.*) percepire attraverso i sensi.

senseful [ˈsensful], *ag.* pieno di significato; significativo.

senseless [ˈsenslis], *ag.* **1.** inanimato, senza conoscenza (di persone): *to fall* —, cadere privo di sensi;

to knock s.o. —, tramortire, atterrare qlcu. **2.** insensato; senza senno; stupido, insulso; assurdo (di persone e cose): *a* — *custom*, un'abitudine stupida; *a* — *remark*, una osservazione sciocca **3.** insensibile, privo di facoltà sensorie.

senselessly [ˈsenslisli], *av.* insensatamente, scioccamente, stupidamente, irragionevolmente.

senselessness [ˈsenslisnis], *s.* **1.** stupidità; mancanza di buon senso **2.** insensibilità.

sensibility [ˌsensiˈbiliti], *s.* **1.** sensibilità, sensitività: *tactile* —, sensibilità tattile **2.** sensibilità, emotività, impressionabilità: *this painter has a great* —, questo pittore ha una grande sensibilità; *" Sense and Sensibility " by Jane Austen*, « Buon senso e sensibilità » di Jane Austen **3.** *spec. pl.* suscettibilità: *to outrage s.o.'s sensibilities*, ferire la suscettibilità di qlcu.

sensible [ˈsensəbl], *ag.* **1.** sensato, giudizioso, assennato, saggio; razionale, pratico: — *clothing*, indumenti pratici; — *furniture*, mobili razionali; *a* — *person*, una persona giudiziosa, piena di buon senso; *be* —, sii ragionevole ‖ — *people*, i saggi **2.** sensibile, percettibile, che può essere percepito attraverso i sensi: — *heat*, calore sensibile; — *horizon*, orizzonte visibile **3.** notevole, considerevole, rilevante: *a* — *fall in temperature*, un notevole abbassamento di temperatura **4.** consapevole, conscio: *she is very* — *of her good looks*, si rende perfettamente conto della sua avvenenza; *to be* — *of the fact that*, apprezzare il fatto che; *to be* — *of one's danger*, essere cosciente del pericolo, rendersi conto del pericolo; *to be* — *of s.o.'s sympathy*, apprezzare, essere commosso dalla comprensione di qlcu. ‖ *I am* — *of your grief*, partecipo al vostro dolore **5.** (*rar.*) sensibile: *he was* — *to her influence*, si lasciava molto influenzare da lei **6.** cosciente: *he was still* — *despite his fall*, non aveva perso i sensi malgrado la caduta.

sensibleness [ˈsensəblnis], *s.* buon senso; giudizio; intelligenza: *the* — *of their choice*, la loro saggia scelta.

sensibly [ˈsensəbli], *av.* **1.** assennatamente; giudiziosamente; razionalmente: *she was* — *dressed*, era vestita in modo pratico **2.** sensibilmente; percettibilmente; intensamente (di sentimenti).

sensism [ˈsensizəm], *s.* (*st. fil.*) sensismo.

sensist [ˈsensist], *s.* (*st. fil.*) sensista.

sensitive [ˈsensitiv], *ag.* **1.** sensitivo, sensibile; delicato; sensorio: — *skin*, pelle delicata; — *tooth*, dente sensibile; *he is* — *to cold*, è freddoloso, sente molto il freddo; *to be* — *to* (o *of*) *sthg.*, essere sensibile a qualcosa **2.** sensibile, suscettibile, impressionabile: *don't be so* —, non essere così suscettibile; *she is too* — *to what people say about her*, è troppo suscettibile a ciò che la gente dice di lei ‖ — *market*, (*comm.*) mercato, piazza instabile ‖ *s.c.* persona sensibile alle influenze psichiche; soggetto sensibile ☆ — *nerves*, nervi sensori; — *plant*, (*bot.*) sensitiva, mimosa; — *plate*, (*chim. foto.*) lastra sensibile, impressionabile; — *scales*, bilancia sensibile ‖ *colour-* —, (*foto.*) ortocromatico.

sensitively [ˈsensitivli], *av.* sensibilmente; delicatamente.

sensitiveness [ˈsensitivnis], **sensitivity** [ˌsensiˈtiviti], *s.* **1.** sensibilità; delicatezza: *lack of* —, mancanza di sensibilità **2.** suscettibilità, emotività **3.** (*foto.*) sensibilità: — *of an emulsion*, impressionabilità di un'emulsione.

sensitizable [ˈsensitaizəbl], *ag.* (*foto.*) sensibilizzabile (di carta).

sensitization [ˌsensitaiˈzeiʃən], *s.* (*foto.*) sensibilizzazione.

to sensitize [ˈsensitaiz], *v.t.* sensibilizzare, rendere sensibile; acuire la sensibilità.

sensitizer [ˈsensitaizə*], *s.* (*foto.*) sensibilizzatore.

sensitizing [ˈsensitaiziŋ], *ag.* sensibilizzatore ‖ *s.* sensibilizzazione ☆ — *bath*, (*foto.*) bagno sensibilizzatore.

sensitometer [ˌsensiˈtɔmitə*], *s.* (*foto.*) sensitometro.

sensorial [senˈsɔːriəl], *ag.* sensorio.

sensorium [sen'sɔ:riəm], *pl.* **sensoria** [sen'sɔ:-riə], **sensoriums** [sen'sɔ:riəmz], *s.* (*fisiol. biol.*) sensorio.

sensory ['sensəri], *ag.* sensoriale ☆ — *deafness*, (*med.*) sordità psichica; — *-motor*, (*anat.*) nervo sensorio-motore.

sensual ['sensjuəl], *ag.* **1.** sensorio **2.** sensuale; animale voluttuoso; carnale; libidinoso: — *enjoyment*, voluttà; — *expression*, espressione voluttuosa, sensuale ☆ — *instinct*, istinto animale.

sensualism ['sensjuəlizəm], *s.* **1.** (*st. fil.*) sensualismo; edonismo **2.** sensualità.

sensualist ['sensjuəlist], *s.c.* **1.** (*st. fil.*) sensualista; edonista **2.** persona sensuale.

sensualistic [,sensjuə'listik], *ag.* **1.** (*st. fil.*) sensualistico; edonistico **2.** sensuale.

sensuality [,sensju'æliti], *s.* **1.** sensualità, animalità **2.** sensualità, lascivia.

to **sensualize** ['sensjuəlaiz], *v.t.* rendere sensuale.

sensually ['sensjuəli], *av.* **1.** sensualmente, in modo animale **2.** sensualmente, in modo lascivo.

sensuous ['sensjuəs], *ag.* dei sensi; voluttuoso, inebriante: — *life*, vita sibaritica, raffinata; *soft*, — *music*, musica dolce, inebriante.

sensuously ['sensjuəsli], *av.* sensualmente; voluttuosamente.

sensuousness ['sensjuəsnis], *s.* sensualità; voluttà.

sent [sent], *pass. p.p.* di to **send**.

sentence ['sentəns], *s.* **1.** giudizio, sentenza; condanna; pena: — *of death*, condanna a morte; *commutation of —*, commutazione di pena; *to pass* (*a*) —, pronunciare una sentenza, una condanna: *the judge passed — of three months' emprisonment on the burglar*, il giudice condannò lo scassinatore a tre mesi di prigione; *to undergo a —*, scontare una condanna **2.** (*gram.*) frase: *well constructed —*, frase ben costruita **3.** massima, detto **4.** (*arc.*) opinione ☆ *complex —*, periodo; *compound —*, frase composta; *life —*, ergastolo.

to **sentence**, *v.t.* giudicare, pronunciare una sentenza, una condanna contro; condannare: *he shall be sentenced to a term of 5 years*, sarà condannato a 5 anni di reclusione; *to — s.o. to two months' imprisonment, to death*, condannare qlcu. a due mesi di carcere, a morte.

sententious [sen'tenʃəs], *ag.* sentenzioso; aforistico: *a — man*, un uomo sentenzioso, (*iron.*) uno sputasentenze; — *speech*, discorso sentenzioso; *to have a gift for — phrases*, avere il dono di esprimersi per aforismi.

sententiously [sen'tenʃəsli], *av.* sentenziosamente, aforisticamente: *to talk —*, parlare per aforismi, (*iron.*) sputar sentenze.

sententiousness [sen'tenʃəsnis], *s.* sentenziosità, carattere, tono sentenzioso.

sentience ['senʃəns], *s.* sensibilità, facoltà di sentire.

sentient ['senʃənt], *ag.* senziente, sensibile, cosciente: — *experience*, esperienza sensibile.

sentiently ['senʃəntli], *av.* in modo sensibile; coscientemente.

sentiment ['sentimənt], *s.* **1.** sentimento: — *of pity*, sentimento di pietà; *noble, base sentiments*, sentimenti nobili, volgari; — *should be controlled by reason*, il sentimento dovrebbe essere controllato dalla ragione; *have you ever shown any — towards her?*, hai mai tradito qualche sentimento nei confronti di lei? **2.** opinione, parere, idea: *these are my sentiments* (o *volg. them's my sentiments*), ecco la mia opinione, ecco come la penso; *to change one's sentiments*, cambiare parere **3.** (*spreg.*) sentimentalità, sentimentalismo: *there's no room for — in business*, non c'è posto per i sentimentalismi negli affari **4.** (*art.*) sentimento artistico **5.** augurio; brindisi: *he concluded his speech with a —*, concluse il suo discorso con un brindisi.

sentimental [,senti'mentl], *ag.* **1.** sentimentale, tenero, patetico, romantico: *a — girl*, una ragazza sentimentale; — *poetry*, poesia sentimentale, romantica; — *reasons*, ragioni sentimentali **2.** (*spreg.*) sentimentale, lacrimoso: *the — comedy*, (*lett.*) la commedia sen-timentale; *a trashy — novel*, un romanzo lacrimoso da quattro soldi.

sentimentalism [,senti'mentəlizəm], *s.* sentimentalismo.

sentimentalist [,senti'mentəlist], *s.c.* persona sentimentale, romantica.

sentimentality [,sentimen'tæliti], *s.* sentimentalità.

to **sentimentalize** [,senti'mentəlaiz], *v.t.i.* fare del sentimentalismo, affettare sensibilità; rendere sentimentale.

sentimentally [,senti'mentəli], *av.* sentimentalmente.

sentinel ['sentinl], *s.* **1.** sentinella, guardia, vedetta: *to stand —*, montare la guardia, stare di sentinella, essere di vedetta **2.** — (*crab*), granchio dell'Oceano Indiano.

to **sentinel**, *pass.p.p.* **sentinelled** ['sentinld], *v.t.* **1.** collocare, disporre sentinelle a; mettere di sentinella **2.** vigilare, vegliare su.

sentry ['sentri], *s.* **1.** (*mil. mar.*) sentinella, guardia, scolta, vedetta, gabbiere: *to relieve a —*, dare il cambio a una sentinella **2.** fazione, guardia: *to come off —*, smontare di guardia; *to force a —*, forzare la consegna; *to stand* (o *to be on*) —, montare la sentinella, essere di vedetta ☆ — *box*, garitta; — *-go*, guardia: *to be on — -go*, essere di guardia; (*sl.*) prendere un granchio ‖ *advanced —* (o *outlying —*), sentinella avanzata.

sepal ['sepəl], *s.* (*bot.*) sepalo.

separability [,sepərə'biliti], *s.* separabilità.

separable ['sepərəbl], *ag.* separabile.

separableness ['sepərəblnis], *s.* separabilità.

separably ['sepərəbli], *av.* separabilmente, in modo separabile.

separate ['seprit], *ag.* separato, staccato; isolato, appartato; individuale, distinto: — *volumes are not sold*, i volumi non si vendono separati; *entered in a — column*, registrato in una colonna a parte, distinta; *everyone has a — tooth-brush*, ognuno ha uno spazzolino da denti personale; *he stood — from the others*, se ne stava appartato dagli altri; *my room has a — entrance*, la mia camera ha un'entrata indipendente; *they wanted — rooms, beds*, volevano camere, letti separati; *this matter is quite — from the previous one*, questa questione è ben distinta dalla precedente ‖ *s.* (*tip.*) pubblicazione a parte ☆ — *estate*, (*dir.*) beni della moglie (su cui il marito non ha diritti); — *maintenance*, (*dir.*) alimonia, alimenti.

to **separate** ['separeit], *v.t.i.* separare, separarsi; dividere, dividersi; disunire; lasciarsi; spartire: *the Channel separates France from England*, la Manica separa la Francia dall'Inghilterra; *cream separates from milk*, la panna si separa dal latte; *he separated from the party*, si staccò dalla compagnia; *she separated from her best friend last year*, l'anno passato ruppe ogni rapporto con la sua migliore amica; *to — a layer*, (*agr.*) distaccare un margotto, piantare per talea; *to — the milk*, scremare, centrifugare il latte; *to — two quarrellers*, dividere due litiganti.

separately ['sepritli], *av.* separatamente, a parte; singolarmente.

separateness ['sepritnis], *s.* separazione; isolamento.

separation [,sepə'reiʃən], *s.* separazione; divisione; rottura (anche *fig.*) ☆ — *-deed*, (*dir.*) atto di separazione ‖ *judicial —*, separazione legale.

separationist [,sepə'reiʃənist], *s.* (*st. pol.*) separatista; (*relig.*) scismatico.

separatism ['sepərətizəm], *s.* (*st. pol.*) separatismo; (*relig.*) tendenza scismatica.

separatist ['sepərətist], *ag.s.* (*st. pol.*) separatista; (*relig.*) scismatico.

separative ['sepərətiv], *ag.* separativo, separatore.

separator ['sepəreitə*], *s.* **1.** separatore, divisore **2.** (*cream*) —, scrematrice ☆ *baffle —*, (*ind.*) separatore ad urto; *centrifugal —*, (*mec.*) separatore centrifugo; *magnetic —*, (*elett.*) separatore (elettro)magnetico.

sepia ['si:pjə], *s.* **1.** seppia **2.** inchiostro di seppia **3.** (*pitt.*) nero di seppia **4.** color seppia ☆ — *-drawing*, disegno a nero di seppia.

sepoy ['si:pɔi], *s.* « sepoy » (soldato indigeno dell'esercito anglo-indiano).

seps [seps], *s.* (*zool.*) sepa.

sepsine ['sepsin], *s.* (*chim.*) sepsina.

sepsis ['sepsis], *s.* (*patol.*) sepsi.

sept [sept], *s.* 1. (*spec. irl.*) « clan », tribù 2. recinto 3. (*edil.*) tramezzo.

septal ['septl], *ag.* (*anat.*) del setto, relativo al setto.

septangular [sep'tæŋgjulə*], *ag.* ettagonale.

septate ['septeit], *ag.* (*anat.*) con setti; diviso a setti; ripartito.

septation [sep'teiʃən], *s.* divisione a setti.

September [səp'tembə*], *s.* settembre.

Septembrist [səp'tembrist], *s.* (*st.*) settembrista.

septemvir [sep'temvə*], *pl.* **septemviri** [sep'temvirai], *s.* (*st. romana*) settenviro.

septemvirate [sep'temvirit], *s.* (*st. romana*) settenvirato.

septenary ['septinəri], *ag.s.* (*poes.*) settenario.

septennate [sep'tenit], *s.* settennato, settennio.

septennial [sep'tenjəl], *ag.* settennale.

septennially [sep'tenjəli], *av.* ogni sette anni.

septentrional [sep'tentriən], *ag.* settentrionale.

septet [sep'tet], *s.* 1. (*mus.*) settimino 2. gruppo di sette persone.

septfoil ['setfɔil], *s.* 1. (*arch.*) figura divisa in sette cuspidi 2. (*bot.*) tormentilla.

septic ['septik], *ag.* (*med.*) settico ‖ *s.* (*med.*) sostanza settica ☆ — *tank*, (*edil.*) fossa settica.

septicaemia [ˌsepti'si:miə], *s.* (*patol.*) setticemia.

septicaemic [ˌsepti'si:mik], *ag.* (*patol.*) setticemico.

septicidal [ˌsepti'saidl], *ag.* (*bot.*) setticida.

septicity [sep'tisiti], *s.* (*med.*) tendenza ad infezione settica.

septimal ['septiməl], *ag.* del numero sette.

septime ['septi:m], *s.* (*scherma*) settima posizione.

septuagenarian [ˌseptjuədʒi'nɛəriən], *ag.* settuagenario ‖ *s.c.* settuagenario, settuagenaria.

septuagenary [ˌseptjuə'dʒi:nəri], *ag.* settuagenario.

Septuagesima [ˌseptjuə'dʒesimə], *s.* (*eccl.*) Settuagesima.

septuagint ['septjuədʒint], *s.* versione dei settanta (versione greca del Vecchio Testamento, III sec. a. C.).

septum ['septəm], *pl.* **septa** ['septə], **septums** ['septəmz], *s.* (*anat. bot. zool.*) setto, diaframma.

septuple ['septjupl], *ag.* settuplo.

to septuple, *v.t.* moltiplicare per sette.

sepulchral [si'pʌlkrəl], *ag.* sepolcrale (anche *fig.*): — *look*, *fig.* aspetto funereo: — *monuments*, monumenti sepolcrali; — *voice*, *fig.* voce sepolcrale.

sepulchre ['sepəlkə*], *s.* sepolcro ‖ *the Holy Sepulchre*, il Santo Sepolcro ‖ *whited* —, *fig.* sepolcro imbiancato, persona ipocrita.

to sepulchre, *v.t.* seppellire.

sepulture ['sepəltʃə*], *s.* sepoltura.

sequacious [si'kweiʃəs], *ag.* 1. poco originale; influenzabile; servile 2. coerente (di ragionamento, pensiero).

sequel ['si:kwəl], *s.* 1. conseguenza: *that action had an unfortunate* —, quell'azione ebbe una triste conseguenza ‖ *by way of* —, in conseguenza 2. seguito, continuazione: *the* — *of the novel*, la continuazione del romanzo.

sequela [si'kwi:lə], *pl.* **sequelae** [si'kwi:li:], *s.* (*med.*) postumo (di malattia).

sequence ['si:kwəns], *s.* 1. successione, sequela; (*carte*) sequenza: *the historical* — *of events*, la successione storica degli eventi 2. (*gram.*) sintassi (dei tempi) 3. (*eccl. mus. cine.*) sequenza.

sequent ['si:kwənt], **sequential** [si'kwenʃəl], *ag.* seguente, successivo; conseguente.

sequentially [si'kwenʃəli], *av.* successivamente.

to sequester [si'kwestə*], *v.t.i.* 1. isolare, appartare: *she sequestered herself from the world*, si appartò dal mondo; *to live a sequestered life*, vivere una vita appartata 2. (*dir.*) sequestrare, confiscare 3. (*dir.*) rinunciare ai diritti sulle proprietà del defunto marito.

sequestrable [si'kwestrəbl], *ag.* sequestrabile.

to sequestrate [si'kwestreit], *v.t.i.* 1. (*dir.*) sequestrare, confiscare 2. (*dir.*) rinunciare ai diritti sulla proprietà del marito defunto.

sequestration [ˌsi:kwes'treiʃən], *s.* 1. (*dir.*) sequestro, confisca 2. (*rar.*) isolamento.

sequestrator ['si:kwestreitə*], *s.* (*dir.*) sequestratario.

sequin ['si:kwin], *s.* 1. lustrino 2. zecchino (moneta).

sequoia [si'kwɔiə], *s.* (*bot.*) sequoia.

serac ['seræk], *s.* seracco, ghiaccione.

seraglio [se'rɑ:liou], *pl.* **seraglios** [se'rɑ:liouz], *s.* serraglio; harem.

serai [se'rai], *s.* caravanserraglio.

seraph ['serəf], *pl.* **seraphim** ['serəfim], **seraphs** ['serəfs], *s.* (*relig.*) serafino.

seraphic(al) [se'ræfik(əl)], *ag.* 1. serafico ‖ *the Seraphic Doctor*, dottor serafico, San Bonaventura 2. *fig.* dolce; angelico; celestiale: — *smile*, sorriso angelico.

seraphically [se'ræfikəli], *av.* in modo serafico.

seraphine ['serəfi:n], *s.* (*mus.*) antico armonium.

Serapis ['serəpis], *no.pr.m.* (*mit.*) Serapide.

seraskier [ˌserə'skiə*], *s.* (*st. turca*) serraschiere.

Serb [sə:b], *V.* **Serbian**.

Serbia ['sə:bjə], *no.pr.* (*geog.*) Serbia.

Serbian ['sə:bjən], *ag.* serbo ‖ *s.c.* serbo, serba ‖ *s.* lingua serba.

Serbo-Croat ['sə:bə'krouət], **Serbo-Croatian** ['sə:bə krou'eifjən], *ag.* serbo-croato ‖ *s.c.* serbo-croato, serbo-croata ‖ *s.* lingua serbo-croata.

Serbonian bog [sə'bounjən,bɔg], *no.pr.* (*geog.*) palude Serbonide (nel delta del Nilo) ‖ *s. fig.* situazione difficile.

sere [siə*], *ag.* (*poet.*) dissecato; avvizzito, appassito.

serenade [ˌseri'neid], *s.* (*mus.*) serenata.

to serenade, *v.i.* (*mus.*) fare una serenata.

serenader [ˌseri'neidə*], *s.* chi fa una serenata.

serene [si'ri:n], *ag.* 1. sereno, senza nubi: *the sky is* —, il cielo è sereno 2. calmo, tranquillo: *a* — *old age*, una vecchiaia tranquilla; *the* — *waters of the Mediterranean*, le acque calme del Mediterraneo ‖ *all* — !, (*sl.*) tutto va bene! 3. *Serene*, Serenissimo: *His* (o *Her*) *Serene Highness*, Sua Altezza Serenissima ‖ *s.* 1. serenità (del cielo) 2. calma (del mare).

to serene, *v.t.* (*poet.*) rasserenare.

serenely [si'ri:nli], *av.* serenamente, tranquillamente.

serenity [si'reniti], *s.* 1. serenità, limpidezza (di cielo) 2. tranquillità, calma 3. *Serenity*, Serenità: *Your Serenity*, la Serenità Vostra.

serf [sə:f], *s.* (*st.*) servo della gleba; *fig.* servo.

serfage ['sə:fidʒ], **serfdom** ['sə:fdəm], *s.* (*st.*) servitù della gleba; *fig.* servaggio, schiavitù.

serge [sə:dʒ], *s.* « serge », saia ☆ *silk* —, saia di seta.

sergeancy ['sɑ:dʒənsi], *s.* funzione, grado di sergente.

sergeant ['sɑ:dʒənt], *s.* 1. (*mil.*) sergente 2. (*polizia*) brigadiere ☆ — (o *serjeant*) - *at - arms*, funzionario addetto alle cerimonie della Corte, del Parlamento, della Camera dei Pari; — -*drummer*, (*mil.*) tamburo maggiore; — -*major*, sergente maggiore ‖ *lance*- —, caporale che fa le veci di sergente; *quartermaster*- —, sergente di fureria.

sergeantship ['sɑ:dʒəntʃip], *s.* grado, funzione di sergente.

sergette [sə:'dʒet], *s.* saia sottile.

serial ['siəriəl], *ag.* 1. di serie, d'ordine 2. periodico; a puntate; a dispense ‖ *s.* romanzo a puntate; pubblicazione periodica ☆ — *rights*, diritti di riproduzione in giornali, ecc., di un romanzo a puntate; — *story*, romanzo a puntate.

serially ['siəriəli], *av.* 1. in serie 2. periodicamente; a puntate.

seriate ['siəriit], *ag.* in serie, in successione.

to seriate ['siərieit], *v.t.* disporre in serie.

seriated ['siərieitid], *ag.* in serie, in successione.

seriately ['siəriitli], *av.* in serie.

seriatim [ˌsiəri'eitim], *av.* successivamente, in ordine regolare.

Seric ['serik], *ag.* (*letter.*) **1.** cinese **2.** serico.
sericeous [si'riʃiəs], *ag.* (*bot. zool.*) sericeo.
sericultural [,seri'kʌltʃərəl], *ag.* sericolo.
sericulture ['seri,kʌltʃə*], *s.* sericoltura.
sericulturist [,seri'kʌltʃərist], *s.* sericoltore.
seriema [,seri'i:mə], *s.* (*ornit.*) seriema.
series, *pl.* **series** ['siəri:z], *s.* **1.** serie, sequela, successione: *a — of misfortunes*, una serie di disgrazie; *a — of stamps*, una serie di francobolli **2.** (*geol. chim. mat. elett.*) serie.
serin ['serin], *s.* (*ornit.*) verzellino.
seringa [si'ringə], *s.* (*bot.*) **1.** siringa **2.** evea brasiliana.
serio-comic ['siəriou'kɔmik], *ag.* semiserio.
serious ['siəriəs], *ag.* **1.** serio; sincero: *a — worker*, un lavoratore serio; *are you — when you say you won't come?*, dici sul serio che non verrai?; *you look very — to-day*, hai un'aria molto seria oggi **2.** grave, serio, importante: *a — alteration*, una modifica importante; *a — illness*, una malattia grave; *a — offence*, un'offesa grave ☆ *— -minded*, riflessivo, serio.
seriously ['siəriəsli], *av.* **1.** sul serio, seriamente: *but —, what will you do?*, ma scherzi a parte, cosa vuoi fare? **2.** gravemente.
seriousness ['siəriəsnis], *s.* **1.** serietà (di aspetto, comportamento, ecc.) || *in all —*, in tutta serietà, seriamente **2.** gravità: *the — of the news*, la gravità della notizia.
serjeant ['sa:dʒənt], *s.* **1.** — (*-at-law*), (*st.*) avvocato di ordine superiore **2.** *V.* **sergeant.**
sermon ['sə:mən], *s.* **1.** sermone, predica: *at —*, durante la predica; *to preach a —*, fare una predica || *the Sermon on the Mount*, (*Bibbia*) il Discorso della Montagna **2.** (*fam.*) predicozzo, ramanzina.
to sermonize ['sə:mənaiz], *v.t.i.* **1.** predicare; tenere un sermone **2.** (*fam.*) fare un predicozzo a.
sermonizer ['sə:mənaizə*], *s.c.* predicatore, predicatrice.
seron ['siərən], *s.* balla, collo avvolto in pelli (contenente prodotti esotici).
serosity [si'rɔsiti], *s.* sierosità.
serotherapy [,siərou'θerəpi], *s.* (*med.*) sieroterapia.
serotine ['serətain], *s.* (*zool.*) vespertilio.
serous ['siərəs], *ag.* (*anat. patol.*) sieroso.
serpent ['sə:pənt], *s.* **1.** serpente (anche *fig.*) || *Serpent*, (*astr.*) Serpente || *the Old Serpent*, l'antico serpente, il diavolo **2.** (*mus.*) serpentone ☆ *—-charmer*, incantatore di serpenti; *— -eater*, (*ornit.*) serpentario; *—-grass*, (*bot.*) serpentina; *— -lizard*, (*zool.*) sepa; *—'s tongue*, (*bot.*) ofioglossa, lingua di serpente || *Pharaoh's —*, (*chim.*) serpente di Faraone.
to serpent, *v.i.* (*rar.*) serpeggiare.
serpentaria [,sə:pən'tɛəriə], *s.* (*bot.*) serpentaria.
Serpentarius [,sə:pən'tɛəriəs], *no.pr.* (*astr.*) Serpentario.
serpentiform [sə'pentifɔ:m], *ag.* serpentiforme.
serpentine ['sə:pəntain], *ag.* **1.** serpentino **2.** serpeggiante, sinuoso, tortuoso: *the — turnings of the road*, le curve tortuose della strada; *— windings*, sinuosità (di fiume, lago, sentiero) **3.** *fig.* subdolo; infido || *s.* (*min. chim.*) serpentino.
to serpentine, *v.i.* serpeggiare, muoversi tortuosamente.
serpentlike ['sə:pəntlaik], *ag.* serpentino.
serpiginous [sə'pidʒinəs], *ag.* (*patol.*) serpiginoso.
serpigo [sə'paigou], *s.* (*patol.*) serpigine.
serpula ['sə:pjulə], *pl.* **serpulae** ['sə:pjuli:], *s.* (*zool.*) serpula.
serrate ['serit], **serrated** [se'reitid], *ag.* (*anat. bot. zool.*) dentellato, seghettato.
serration [se'reiʃən], **serrature** ['serətjuə*], *s.* (*anat. bot. zool.*) dentellatura, seghettatura.
serrefile ['serəfail], *s.* (*gener. pl. mil.*) serrafila.
serried ['serid], *ag.* serrato, compatto; fitto.
serrulate(d) ['serjuleit(id)], *ag.* (*anat. bot. zool.*) finemente dentellato, seghettato.

serum ['siərəm], *pl.* **sera** ['siərə], **serums** ['siərəmz], *s.* (*fisiol. med.*) siero ☆ *— sickness*, malattia da siero; *— -therapy*, sieroterapia.
servable ['sə:vəbl], *ag.* che si può servire.
serval ['sə:vəl], *s.* (*zool.*) gatto servalino.
servant ['sə:vənt], *s.c.* **1.** servo, servitore, serva, domestico, domestica: *a large staff of servants*, una servitù numerosa || *your humble —*, (*arc.*) servitor vostro umilissimo; *your obedient —*, vostro devotissimo (a chiusura di lettere ufficiali) || *money is a good —, but a bad master*, il denaro è buon servitore, ma cattivo padrone **2.** *fig.* seguace: *a humble — of God*, un umile servitore di Dio ☆ *civil —*, impiegato statale; *railway —*, impiegato delle ferrovie.
serve [sə:v], *s.* (*spor.*) servizio || *—!*, palla!; *it's your —!*, a te la palla!.
to serve, *v.t.i.* **1.** servire (in un negozio, ristorante, ecc.); prestar servizio, essere al servizio di; lavorare; (*arc.*) essere schiavo: *are you being served?*, la stanno servendo?; *he first served her with a pound of meat*, per prima cosa le servì una libbra di carne; *he has served as a waiter in this restaurant for two years*, fa il cameriere in questo ristorante da due anni; *she has always served her husband hand and foot*, ha sempre servito suo marito di tutto punto || *she served on the jury*, (*dir.*) faceva parte della giuria || *to — God*, condurre vita virtuosa || *to — one's apprenticeship*, far tirocinio || *to — mass*, servir messa **2.** servire, essere utile: *how can I — you?*, posso esserti utile? || *if my memory serves me right*, se la memoria non mi inganna **3.** servire, essere sufficiente: *one hospital serves the entire city*, un ospedale serve per tutta la città **4.** scontare, espiare: *to — a sentence*, scontare una pena || *to — time*, essere in prigione **5.** servire, presentare (una vivanda, ecc.): *dinner is served, Madam*, Signora, il pranzo è servito; *she served cocktails to us*, ci preparò dei cocktails; *to — at table*, servire a tavola; *to — a dish*, servire un piatto in tavola; *to — s.o. with soup*, servire la minestra a qlcu. **6.** essere sotto le armi, combattere: *he has served five years in the navy*, è in marina da cinque anni; *they served under Napoleon*, militarono sotto Napoleone; *to — in the army*, prestar servizio nell'esercito **7.** servire (di linee ferroviarie, ecc.): *many localities in this country are badly served by the railways*, molte località in questo paese hanno un cattivo servizio ferroviario **8.** trattare, comportarsi con: *see how I am served!*, guarda come mi trattano!; *she was cruelly served*, fu trattata in modo crudele || *she serves him with the same sauce*, lo ripaga della stessa moneta || *they served him a dirty trick*, gli giocarono un brutto tiro **9.** (*dir.*) notificare: *to — a summons on s.o.*, notificare una citazione a qlcu. **10.** montare, fecondare (di bestiame) **11.** (*mar.*) fasciare, proteggere con fasciatura: *to — a rope*, fasciare una gomena, un cavo **12.** servire, fungere: *this table will — me as a desk*, questo tavolo mi servirà da scrittoio; *to — as a guidance*, servire da norma; *to — as a pretext*, servire da pretesto **13.** (*mil.*) servire, caricare, far funzionare (un pezzo di artiglieria) **14.** (*tennis*) servire **15.** *to — out*, distribuire: *they served out the rations*, distribuirono le razioni || *to — s.o. out*, (*fam.*) servire qlcu., dirgli il fatto suo: *I'll — him out*, gliela farò pagare **16.** *to — up*, servire, mettere in tavola: *this dish should be served up hot*, questo piatto dovrebbe essere servito caldo.
server ['sə:və*], *s.c.* chi serve || *s.* **1.** vassoio **2.** (*eccl.*) chierico **3.** (*spor.*) chi ha il servizio ☆ *fish-servers, salad-servers*, posate per il pesce, per l'insalata.
Servia ['sə:vjə], *no.pr.* (*geog.*) Serbia.
Servian[1] ['sə:vjən], *V.* **Serbian.**
Servian[2], *ag.* di Servio Tullio.
service[1] ['sə:vis], *s.* **1.** servizio (anche *mil.*): *he is on* (o *in*) *active —*, è in servizio attivo; *the meals are good, but the — is very bad*, si mangia bene, ma il servizio è pessimo; *that girl went out to — when she was fourteen*,

quella ragazza andò a servizio quando aveva quattordici anni; *they are in the civil*—, sono funzionari statali; *which branch of the — do you expect to enter?*, in quale arma pensi di arruolarti? ‖ *On His (Her) Majesty's Service* (*abbr. O.H.M.S.*), Servizio di Stato (detto di corrispondenza proveniente da uffici governativi che usufruisce di franchigia postale) ‖ *to have seen* —, essere veterano (specialmente di soldato, marinaio) **2.** servigio, favore; utilità: *can I be of — to you?*, posso essere utile?; *his services to the cause of learning deserve recognition*, i suoi servigi in favore della scienza meritano un riconoscimento; *will you do me a* —?, mi vuoi fare un piacere? **3.** ufficio divino, funzione religiosa: *are you going to the* —?, vai alla funzione? **4.** servizio di stoviglie, posate **5.** *pl.* forze armate **6.** (*tennis*) servizio: *whose — is it?*, a chi tocca servire? **7.** (*dir.*) notificazione **8.** (*comm.*) assistenza **9.** (*mar.*) fasciatura ☆ — *area*, (*tv.*) zona utile; — *-book*, rituale, libro di preghiere; — *call*, (*tel.*) chiamata di servizio, chiamata di controllo; — *dress*, uniforme d'ordinanza; — *engineer*, capo del servizio di manutenzione; — *hatch*, passavivande; — *-man*, militare; — *pipe*, tubo di alimentazione; — *-reservoir*, serbatoio di alimentazione; — *rifle*, fucile d'ordinanza; — *station*, (*neol. aut.*) stazione di servizio ‖ *burial* —, servizio funebre; *civil* —, pubblica amministrazione; *fighting services*, forze armate; *flight information* —, servizio informazioni di volo; *merchant* —, (*mar.*) marina mercantile; *public* —, servizi pubblici; *tea* —, servizio da tè; *telephone* —, servizio telefonico; *train* —, servizio ferroviario.

to service[1], *v.t.* **1.** servire, fornire, provvedere di **2.** mettere, mantenere in buone condizioni **3.** controllare (automobile, ecc.); revisionare (apparecchio radio, ecc.).

service[2], *s.* — (*-tree*), (*bot.*) sorbo.

serviceable ['sə:visəbl], *ag.* **1.** utile, pratico (di cosa); durevole **2.** (*rar.*) servizievole (di persona).

serviceableness ['sə:visəblnis], *s.* **1.** praticità; durata (di cosa) **2.** l'essere servizievole (di persona).

serviceably ['sə:visəbli], *av.* **1.** utilmente; durevolmente **2.** in modo servizievole.

serviette [,sə:vi'et], *s.* tovagliolo.

servile ['sə:vail], *ag.* **1.** servile, di servo: *of — birth*, di nascita servile ‖ — *works*, (*eccl.*) opere servili **2.** abbietto, meschino: — *feelings*, sentimenti abbietti.

servilely ['sə:vaili], *av.* **1.** servilmente **2.** vilmente, meschinamente.

servilism ['sə:vilizəm], *s.* servilismo.

servility [sə:'viliti], *s.* servilità, avvilimento, bassezza.

serving ['sə:viŋ], *ag.* **1.** che serve, che è al servizio di **2.** (*mil.*) che è in servizio.

serving, *s.* **1.** servizio, il servire (padroni, ecc.) **2.** servizio (di tavola): *the maid's — at table left much to be desired*, il servizio di tavola della cameriera lasciò molto a desiderare **3.** (*tennis*) servizio: *a turn at* —, turno di servizio **4.** (*dir.*) notifica: *the — of a writ*, la notifica di un decreto **5.** (*mar.*) fasciatura.

serving, (*nei composti*): — *-mallet*, (*mar.*) maglietto per fasciare (corde); — *-man*, (*arc.*) domestico; — *-woman*, (*arc.*) domestica.

servitor ['sə:vitə*], *s.* **1.** (*arc. poet.*) servitore, servo **2.** (*arc.*) apprendista **3.** (*st.*) borsista (all'Università di Oxford) **4.** partigiano, seguace.

servitorship ['sə:vitəʃip], *s.* condizione, stato di borsista (all'Università di Oxford).

servitude ['sə:vitju:d], *s.* **1.** servitù, servaggio; schiavitù, asservimento: *to deliver a country from* —, liberare un popolo dalla schiavitù **2.** (*dir.*) servitù ‖ *penal- — for life*, lavori forzati a vita ☆ *praedial* —, (*dir.*) servitù prediale.

servo-brake ['sə:və'breik], *s.* (*aut.*) servofreno.

servo-control ['sə:vəkən'troul], *s.* (*mec.*) servocomando.

Servo-Croat ['sə:və'krouət], **Servo-Croatian** ['sə:vəkrou'eiʃən], *V.* **Serbo-Croat**, **Serbo-Croatian**.

servo-motor ['sə:və'moutə*], *s.* (*mec.*) servomotore

sesame ['sesəmi], *s.* (*bot.*) sesamo ‖ *open- — !* apriti, sesamo!: *money is a good open-* —, il denaro apre molte porte.

sesamoid ['sesəmɔid], *ag.* sesamoide, a forma di sesamo ‖ *s.* (*anat.*) sesamoide.

sesamum ['sesəməm], *V.* **sesame**.

seseli ['sesili], *s.* (*bot.*) seseli, seselio.

sesquipedal [ses'kwipidl], **sesquipedalian** ['seskwipi'deiljən], *ag.* sesquipedale; molto lungo; ingombrante; pedantesco.

sessile ['sesil], *ag.* (*bot. zool.*) sessile.

session ['seʃən], *s.* **1.** sessione; seduta, assemblea, riunione: *sessions of a committee*, riunioni di una commissione; *at the opening of the* —, all'apertura della seduta; *the House is in* —, (*pol.*) la Camera sta deliberando, è in seduta; *to go into secret* —, convocare una seduta segreta **2.** *pl.* (*dir.*) udienza ‖ *the Court of Session*, (*scoz.*) l'Alta Corte, la Corte Suprema **3.** trimestre; sessione universitaria (negli Stati Uniti); anno accademico (in Scozia e negli Stati Uniti) ☆ *general sessions*, udienze per reati penali; *kirk-* —, (*scoz.*) tribunale ecclesiastico; *petty sessions*, udienze dei giudici di pace per reati minori; *special sessions*, udienze per reati speciali.

sessional ['seʃənl], *ag.* di sessione.

sesterce ['sestə:s], *s.* sesterzio (moneta romana).

sestertium [ses'tə:tjəm], *pl.* **sestertia** [ses'tə:tjə], *s.* (*st. romana*) mille sesterzi.

sestertius [ses'tə:tjəs], *pl.* **sestertii** [ses'tə:tjai], *s.* sesterzio (moneta romana).

sestet(te) [ses'tet], *s.* **1.** (*mus.*) sestetto **2.** (*poes.*) le due terzine di un sonetto.

set[1] [set], *ag.* **1.** fermo, fisso, immobile; rigido: — *stare*, sguardo fisso ‖ *of — purpose*, di saldi principi **2.** stabilito; prestabilito; prescritto: — *task*, compito assegnato; *at a — time*, ad un'ora fissata **3.** studiato, preparato; formale, convenzionale: *a — speech*, un discorso preparato; *in — phrases*, con frasi fatte **4.** ostinato; deciso, risoluto: *a man of — opinions*, un uomo ostinato ‖ *s.* **1.** il porre, il collocare **2.** posizione, atteggiamento: *I knew her by the — of her head*, la riconobbi dall'atteggiamento del capo **3.** direzione; *fig.* tendenza: *the — of the current*, la direzione della corrente; *the — of popular opinion*, *fig.* l'orientamento dell'opinione popolare **4.** il solidificarsi; presa (di cemento) **5.** allicciatura (della sega) **6.** puntata (di cane da caccia) ‖ *to make a dead — at*, *fig.* fare guerra sorda a; cercare di cattivarsi la stima, l'amicizia di **7.** velo, terza mano (d'intonaco) **8.** tana del tasso **9.** (*tip.*) spessore (della lettera); fusione (di carattere) **10.** (*bot.*) talea **11.** (*tennis*) « set », partita **12.** (*teat. cine. tv.*) « set », scena, scenario **13.** (*poet.*) tramonto.

to set[1], *pass.p.p.* **set**, *v.t.i.* **1.** mettere, porre, collocare: *she — the flowers in water*, mise i fiori nell'acqua; *she — her hand on his shoulder*, gli mise la mano sulla spalla; *to — a glass to one's lips*, accostare un bicchiere alle labbra; *to — one's hand* (o *name* o *signature*) *to a document*, apporre la propria firma ad un documento; *to — s.o. amongst the great writers*, collocare qlcu. fra i grandi scrittori; *to be* —, essere situato ‖ *to — at naught*, deridere, trascurare ‖ *to — the axe to*, accingersi a tagliare, distruggere ‖ *to — eyes on*, vedere: *I had never — eyes on him before*, non l'avevo mai visto prima ‖ *to — foot in*, mettere piede in, andare a ‖ *to — free*, liberare ‖ *to — going*, mettere in moto ‖ *to — a hen*, far covare una gallina ‖ *to — on fire*, appiccare fuoco a, incendiare ‖ *to — one's foot on sthg.*, calpestare ql.co. ‖ *to — one's hand to the plough*, mettersi all'opera, incominciare ‖ *to — one's life on a chance* (o *on a throw of the dice*), rischiare la vita ‖ *to — one's mind at rest*, togliersi una preoccupazione ‖ *to — one's mind* (o *one's heart*) *on sthg.*, rivolgere i propri desideri a ql.co. ‖ *to — pen to paper*, scrivere ‖ *to — s.o. at ease,* mettere qlcu. a proprio agio ‖ *to — s.o. on his way*, indicare la via a qlcu. ‖ *to — s.o. on one's feet*, *fig.* aiutare qlcu. a sistemarsi, ristabilirsi ‖ *to — s.o. right*, correggere qlcu. ‖ *to — s.o.'s doubts at rest*, risolvere i dubbi di qlcu. ‖ *to — s.o.'s teeth on edge*, fare allegare i denti a qlcu.; dare sui nervi a qlcu. ‖ *to — (much) store by*, tenere in gran conto ‖ *to — straight* (o *right*), mettere a posto ‖ *to — the table*, apparecchiare la tavola ‖ *to — the Thames on fire*, *fig.* fare ql.co. di inusitato ‖ *to — type*, (*tip.*) comporre ‖ *to — words to music*, musicare parole **2.** sistemare; mettere a punto, regolare: *to — an alarm clock*, regolare una sveglia; *to — a fracture, a leg*, (*med.*) mettere a posto una frattura, una gamba rotta; *to — a razor*, affilare un rasoio; *to — the sails*, (*mar.*) spiegare le vele; *to — a saw*, allicciare una sega; *to — a scene*, (*teat.*) montare una scena; *to — a trap*, tendere una trappola; *to — a watch*, regolare un orologio ‖ *to — one's hair*, mettersi in piega i capelli **3.** tramontare (anche *fig.*): *his star has —*, *fig.* la sua stella è tramontata; *the sun is setting*, il sole tramonta **4.** assegnare: *the teacher — them a difficult exercise* l'insegnante assegnò loro un esercizio difficile **5.** mettere, mettersi: *to — a man to saw wood*, mettere un uomo a segar legna; *to — (oneself) to work*, cominciare a lavorare **6.** presentare; dare: *to — s.o. an example*, dare a qlcu. un esempio ‖ *to — the fashion*, lanciare la moda ‖ *to — the pace*, segnare il passo, *fig.* essere all'avanguardia, servire da modello **7.** fissare, stabilire: *to — a date*, fissare una data; *to — limits*, fissare dei limiti ‖ *to — the course*, (*mar.*) tracciare la rotta **8.** solidificare, solidificarsi; coagularsi: *cold sets jellies*, il freddo fa rapprendere la gelatina **9.** irrigidire, contrarre: *to — one's lips*, serrare le labbra **10.** rendere fisso, fissare, assicurare: *to — a diamond*, incastonare un diamante; *to — the glass in a window*, fissare il vetro ad una finestra **11.** sviluppare, svilupparsi; assumere forma definitiva; formarsi (di mente): *excessive exercise — his muscles prematurely*, l'eccessivo esercizio fisico sviluppò prematuramente i suoi muscoli **12.** dirigere, dirigersi; muovere, muoversi: *the river sets southwards*, il fiume scorre verso sud; *the wind sets from the south*, il vento soffia dal sud ‖ *the tide has — in his favour*, (*fam.*) va a gonfie vele **13.** adattarsi (di abito, ecc.): *her new dress sets very well*, l'abito nuovo le sta benissimo **14.** puntare (di cane da caccia) **15.** fissare il numero dei punti (al giuoco) **16.** *to — about* (*s.o., sthg.*), accingersi a, cominciare; (*fam.*) assalire **17.** *to — upon* (*s.o., sthg.*), assalire, attaccare; intraprendere **18.** *to — about*, diffondere, far circolare **19.** *to — apart*, separare; mettere da parte **20.** *to — aside*, mettere da parte; respingere; (*dir.*) annullare **21.** *to — back*, mettere indietro; impedire; ritardare; (*sl. amer.*) costare: *my new coat sets me back quite a bit*, il mio nuovo cappotto mi costò un bel po' **22.** *to — by*, mettere da parte (denaro, ecc.) **23.** *to — down*, metter giù; far scendere; mettere per iscritto; considerare; attribuire; fissare; (*fam.*) riprendere, umiliare: *me down as a subscriber*, mettimi fra i sottoscrittori; *the bus will — you down at the station*, l'autobus ti porterà alla stazione; *to — s.o. down for an actor*, prendere qlcu. per attore **24.** *to — forth*, dichiarare; esporre; avviarsi, partire **25.** *to — forward*, favorire, sostenere; dichiarare, enunciare; (*arc.*) avviarsi, partire **26.** *to — in*, incominciare; stabilirsi; muoversi, dirigersi; montare (pietre, vetri, maniche a un vestito): *this fashion is setting in*, questa moda attacca; *the tide is setting in*, la marea sale; *the weather is setting in fine*, il tempo si mette al bello **27.** *to — off*, avviarsi, partire; far esplodere; scaricare (fucile, ecc.); far cominciare; mettere in risalto, sottolineare; controbilanciare: *that answer — him off on a long disquisition*, quella risposta gli fece cominciare una lunga disquisizione; *to — off a gain against a loss*, compensare una perdita con un guadagno **28.** *to — on*, incitare, istigare

(ad assalire, a fare, ecc.); avanzare **29.** *to — out*, esporre, spiegare; adornare, valorizzare; avviarsi, partire **30.** *to — to*, incominciare, accingersi a; (*fam.*) venire alle mani, discutere **31.** *to — up*, fissare, installare; innalzare; fondare, costituire; avviare, avviarsi (a una carriera, ecc.); proporre; fornire; emettere (grido, ecc.); sviluppare (il corpo con esercizi fisici); ristabilire; causare; (*tip.*) comporre: *he — up his son in business*, avviò suo figlio negli affari; *a holiday will soon — him up again*, una vacanza lo rimetterà in sesto; *to — up a defence*, fornire una difesa; *to — up the standard of revolt*, iniziare una rivolta ‖ *to — up for* (o *to — oneself up as*), farsi passare per ‖ *to — up for oneself*, mettersi a lavorare per conto proprio.

set[1], (*nei composti*): *— -back*, contrattempo; regresso; ricaduta (di malattia); arretramento (di muri perimetrali); *— -down*, rimprovero, lavata di capo; *— -in*, inizio; *— -off*, contrasto; compenso; ornamento; partenza; (*arch.*) aggetto, sporto; *— -out*, mostra, esposizione (specialmente di merci); inizio; *— -square*, squadra (da disegno); *— -to*, incontro pugilistico; zuffa; disputa; *— -up*, portamento; sistemazione, messa a punto; (*amer.*) incontro di boxe truccato.

set[2], *s.* **1.** serie completa, insieme; collezione; servizio; batteria (da cucina); « parure » (di biancheria, ecc.): *a — of ash-trays*, una serie di portacenere; *a — of books*, una collezione di libri; *a — of diamonds*, una « parure » di diamanti; *— of furniture*, mobilia **2.** gruppo (di persone); circolo; classe: *a — of actors*, un gruppo di attori; *— of thieves*, banda di ladri; *I don't belong to their —*, non appartengo al loro ambiente ‖ *the smart —*, *fig.* il bel mondo **3.** covata **4.** (*rad.*) apparecchio ricevente **5.** (*miner.*) quadro ☆ *china —*, servizio di porcellana; *crystal —*, radio a galena; *receiving —*, apparecchio radioricevente; *smoker's —*, servizio da fumo; *tea —*, servizio da tè; *telegraph —*, apparecchio telegrafico; *telephone —*, apparecchio telefonico; *television —*, televisore; *wireless —*, apparecchio radio.

setaceous [si'teiʃəs], *ag.* **1.** setoloso **2.** a forma di setola.

setiferous [si'tifərəs], *ag.* setoloso.

setiform ['sitifo:m], *ag.* a forma di setola.

setigerous [si'tidʒərəs], *ag.* setoloso.

seton ['si:tn], *s.* (*vet.*) setone.

setose ['si:tous], *ag.* setoloso.

sett [set], *s.* **1.** V. **set**[1], **set**[2] **2.** (*tec.*) pietra rettangolare per lastricati.

settee[1] [se'ti:], *s.* divano.

settee[2], *s.* (*mar.*) saettia.

setter ['setə*], *s.c.* **1.** chi pone; chi mette in opera **2.** informatore, spia della polizia ‖ *s.* « setter », cane da ferma.

setterwort ['setəwə:t], *s.* (*bot.*) elleboro fetido.

setting ['setiŋ], *s.* **1.** messa in opera, montaggio; adattamento (*mec.*) messa a punto; (*mus.*) messa in musica **2.** ambiente; (*teat.*) messa in scena, scenario **3.** montatura, incastonatura (di gioiello) **4.** (*tip.*) composizione **5.** (*med.*) riduzione **6.** tramonto **7.** (*mus.*) arrangiamento: *— for piano*, arrangiamento per piano **8.** presa (di cemento); (*chim.*) coagulazione (di albumine) **9.** covata ☆ *— -angle*, (*aer.*) angolo di calettamento; *— -board*, bacheca (per farfalle, ecc.); *— coat*, velo, terza mano di intonaco; *— -free*, liberazione *— -lotion*, liquido per messa in piega; *— -point*, (*chim.*) punto di congelamento; (*amer. chim.*) punto di fusione *— -rule*, (*tip.*) compositoio ‖ *hair- —*, messa in piega; *page- —*, (*tip.*) impaginazione; *quick —*, presa rapida (di cemento).

settle ['setl], *s.* panca (con alta spalliera e bracciuoli); cassapanca.

to **settle**, *v.t.i.* **1.** fissare; decidere, determinare, risolvere: *everything* (o *the matter*) *is settled*, l'affare è fatto; *the terms were settled*, si stabilirono le condizioni; *there is nothing settled yet*, non c'è ancora null di stabilito; *what have you settled (on)?*, che cosa avete deciso?; *to — the day*, fissare la data; *to — the succession*, stabilire la successione; *to — to do sthg.*, risolvere di fare ql.co. **2.** saldare, regolare, liquidare (conti, questioni, ecc.): *to — a bill*, saldare un conto; *to — a question*, sistemare una questione; *to — with creditors*, saldare i creditori || *to — (up) accounts with s.o.*, *(fam.)* saldare i conti con qlcu. || *to — s.o.'s hash*, *(sl.)* dare una bella lezione a qlcu. **3.** sistemare, sistemarsi; mettere a posto, mettersi a posto; accomodare, accomodarsi: *the bird settled on a branch*, l'uccello si posò su un ramo; *to — a gun*, mettere in assetto un fucile; *to — one's affairs*, sistemare i propri affari; *to — one's feet in the stirrups*, sistemare i piedi nelle staffe; *to — oneself in an armchair*, accomodarsi in una poltrona; *to — to work*, mettersi al lavoro || *the matters will soon — into shape*, le cose si aggiusteranno presto || *to — one's daughter*, accasare una figlia **4.** stabilire, stabilirsi (in un luogo); stabilirsi in colonia, colonizzare: *I shall — in London*, mi stabilirò a Londra; *the British settled in Burma*, gli inglesi colonizzarono la Birmania **5.** calmare, calmarsi; ricomporre, ricomporsi; stabilizzare, stabilizzarsi (di tempo): *give me sthg. to — my stomach*, datemi ql.co. per calmarmi lo stomaco; *a good thunder-storm would — the weather*, un bel temporale potrebbe stabilizzare il tempo; *let the excitement — (down)*, lasciate calmare l'eccitazione; *to — one's nerves*, calmare i propri nervi **6.** depositare, depositarsi (di polvere, sedimenti, ecc.): *the dust settled on everything*, la polvere si depositò su ogni cosa; *to let sthg. —*, lasciar depositare ql.co. **7.** schiarire, schiarirsi; diventare limpido (di liquidi): *to — coffee with milk*, schiarire il caffè col latte || *to take a liqueur to — one's dinner*, *(fam.)* bere ql.co. di forte per digerire il pranzo **8.** abbassare, abbassarsi; *(mar.)* affondare; cedere per assestamento (di terreno): *the foundations of the house settled*, le fondamenta della casa si assestarono; *the ship was settling*, la nave affondava; *to — a sail*, abbassare una vela **9.** *(dir.)* legare, lasciare per legge: *to — an annuity on a person*, fissare a una persona una rendita annua; *to — one's property on one's son*, legare i propri beni al proprio figlio **10.** *to — upon (s.o., sthg.)*, decidersi per; riversarsi (di affetti) **11.** *to — down*, stabilirsi (in un luogo); disporsi a, dedicarsi a; sistemarsi; stabilizzarsi: *as soon as the market settles down*, non appena il mercato si stabilizza; *he settled down in the country*, si stabilì in campagna; *they are now married and settled down*, ora sono sposati e sistemati; *to — down for life*, sposarsi; *to — down to dinner*, mettersi a tavola; *to — down to sthg.*, dedicarsi a ql.co. con impegno **12.** *to — in*, stabilirsi (in una nuova casa): *are you settled in yet?*, vi siete già sistemati?

settled ['setld], *ag.* **1.** fissato, stabilito: *a man of — habits*, un uomo abitudinario **2.** permanente; stabile (di tempo): — *melancholy*, malinconia permanente; — *rain*, pioggia persistente; — *weather*, tempo stabile **3.** saldato (di conto).

settlement ['setlmənt], *s.* **1.** determinazione; risoluzione, decisione **2.** saldo, liquidazione || *in (full) —*, *(comm.)* a saldo **3.** sistemazione; *(dir.)* transazione, accordo: *they hope for a — of all these troubles*, essi confidano in un accomodamento di tutte queste controversie; *to make a — with s.o.*, venire ad un accordo con qlcu. || *Act of Settlement*, *(st.)* Atto di Successione **4.** lo stabilirsi (in un luogo); colonizzazione **5.** colonia, distretto **6.** gruppo di persone che si stabiliscono nei quartieri poveri per promuovere riforme sociali **7.** *(edil.)* cedimento di assestamento; *pl.* rottura di assestamento **8.** lo schiarire (un liquido) **9.** disposizione legale: — *of an annuity on*, costituzione di un vitalizio a beneficio di ☆ *legal —*, concordato; *marriage —*, dote; *penal —*, colonia penale; *yearly —*, *(comm.)* liquidazione di fine d'anno.

settler ['setlə*], *s.c.* **1.** chi stabilisce, decide **2.** chi

si stabilisce in colonia || *s.* *(fam.)* colpo, argomento decisivo; *this was a — for him*, questo gli ha chiuso il becco, lo ha messo a tacere.

settling ['setliŋ], *s.* **1.** decisione **2.** stabilizzazione **3.** saldo, liquidazione, pagamento **4.** *(edil.)* cedimento; sedimentazione, deposito ☆ — *-day*, *(comm.)* giorno di liquidazione; — *pits*, pozzi filtranti; — *tank*, vasca di sedimentazione.

setwall ['setwɔ:l], *s.* *(bot. farm.)* valeriana.

Sevastopol [si'væstəpəl], *no.pr.* *(geog.)* Sebastopoli.

seven ['sevn], *ag.num.card.s.* sette: *in sevens*, a sette a sette, in gruppi di sette || *the Seven Stars*, *(astr.)* le Pleiadi || *at sixes and sevens*, in gran confusione ☆ — *gills*, *(zool.)* notidanide (specie di squalo); — *-hilled*, dai sette colli; — *-league (boots)*, (stivali) dalle sette leghe; — *-score*, sette ventine, centoquaranta.

sevenfold ['sevnfould], *ag.* settuplo || *av.* sette volte tanto.

seventeen ['sevn'ti:n], *ag.num.card.s.* diciassette || *sweet —*, *(fam.)* la bella età dei diciassette anni (di fanciulla).

seventeenth ['sevn'ti:nθ], *ag.num.ord.s.* diciassettesimo.

seventh ['sevnθ], *ag.num.ord.* settimo || *the Seventh Day*, il Sabato degli Ebrei || *in the — heaven*, al settimo cielo, estremamente felice || *s.* **1.** settima parte **2.** *(mus.)* settima: *dominant —*, settima dominante.

seventhly ['sevnθli], *av.num.* in settimo luogo.

seventieth ['sevntiiθ], *ag.num.ord.s.* settantesimo.

seventy ['sevnti], *ag.num.card.s.* settanta || *in the seventies*, tra i 70 e gli 80 anni di età; tra il '70 e l'80 ☆ — *-four*, *(st.)* nave da guerra con settantaquattro cannoni.

to sever ['sevə*], *v.t.i.* staccare, staccarsi; dividere, dividersi; separare, separarsi (anche *fig.*): *he cannot — the good from the bad*, non sa separare il bene dal male; *to — the head from the body*, staccare la testa dal corpo; *to — one's connections with s.o.*, cessare ogni relazione con qlcu.; *to — a rope with a knife*, recidere una corda con un coltello.

severable ['sevərəbl], *ag.* staccabile; separabile, divisibile.

several ['sevrəl], *ag.* **1.** parecchi, diversi: *I have — friends*, ho parecchi amici; *it seems to have been built at — times*, sembra che sia stato costruito a parecchie riprese **2.** separato, distinto, differente; rispettivo: *three — pillars*, tre differenti colonne; *each has his — ideal*, ciascuno ha il suo ideale; *they went their — ways*, se ne andarono ognuno per la sua strada || *in —*, separatamente **3.** *(dir.)* individuale: — *estate*, proprietà individuale || *joint and — bond*, *(dir.)* obbligazione solidale || *pron.* parecchi, diversi: — *(of them) saw me*, parecchi (di loro) mi videro; *I already have —*, ne ho già parecchi.

severally ['sevrəli], *av.* separatamente, distintamente; individualmente; rispettivamente.

severalty ['sevrəlti], *s.* **1.** spartizione; separazione **2.** *(dir.)* bene personale; proprietà individuale: *estate held in —*, proprietà posseduta per diritto individuale.

severance ['sevərəns], *s.* separazione, disgiunzione; distacco; rottura (di relazioni, ecc.): *our — from the British Empire*, il nostro distacco dall'Impero Britannico.

severe [si'viə*], *ag.* **1.** severo, austero; duro, rigoroso: *a — discipline*, disciplina rigorosa; *a — look*, uno sguardo severo; *to be — with one's children*, essere severo coi propri figliuoli **2.** violento, forte; grave; rigido (di clima): *a — cold*, un forte raffreddore; *a — illness*, una malattia grave; *a — pain*, un dolore violento; *a — storm*, una tempesta violenta; — *winter*, inverno rigido **3.** difficile, arduo: *a — competition*, una gara difficile **4.** severo; sobrio, disadorno: — *architecture*, architettura severa; — *style*, stile sobrio **5.** sarcastico: — *remarks*, commenti sarcastici.

severely [si'viəli], *av.* **1.** severamente **2.** violentemente; gravemente || *to leave sthg. — alone*, ignorare, trascurare completamente ql.co.

severeness [si'viənis], *s.* severità.

severity [si'veriti], *s.* **1.** severità; durezza, rigore **2.** *pl.* critiche, giudizi severi **3.** violenza; intensità, gravità **4.** difficoltà **5.** sobrietà.

Seville ['sevil], *no.pr.* (*geog.*) Siviglia ☆ — *orange*, arancio amaro.

Sèvres ['seivr], *no.pr.* (*geog.*) Sèvres || *s.* porcellana di Sèvres.

to sew[1] [sou], *pass.* **sewed** [soud], *p.p.* **sewn** [soun], *v.t.i.* **1.** cucire **2.** *to* — *on*, attaccare (bottoni, ecc.) **3.** *to* — *up*, cucire, ricucire; (*sl.*) sfinire, metter fuori combattimento; fare ubriacare.

to sew[2] [sju:], *v.t.i.* **1.** (*mar.*) rimanere in secca **2.** (*dial.*) far scolare; stillare.

sewage ['sju(:)idʒ], *s.* acque di scolatura.

to sewage, *v.t.* concimare (con le acque di fognatura).

sewen ['sju:en], *s.* trota salmonata del Galles.

sewer[1] ['souə*], *s.c.* cucitore, cucitrice.

sewer[2] ['sju:ə*], *s.* **1.** canale artificiale di drenaggio **2.** fogna, cloaca ☆ — *gas*, (*chim.*) gas mefitico; — *-rat*, topo di chiavica.

to sewer[2], *v.t.* fornire di fogne.

sewer[3], *s.* (*st.*) valletto (per il servizio di tavola).

sewerage ['sjuəridʒ], *s.* **1.** drenaggio **2.** scarico, fognatura.

sewin ['sju:in], *s.* trota salmonata del Galles.

sewing ['souiŋ], *s.* **1.** il cucire **2.** cucito; lavoro di cucito: *I have got my* — *to do*, devo fare il mio lavoro di cucito ☆ — *-machine*, macchina da cucire; — *-press*, (*tip.*) cucitrice; — *-thread*, (*ind. tessile*) cucirino.

sewn [soun], *p.p.* di to **sew**[1].

sex [seks], *s.* sesso || *the fair* (o *gentle*) —, il bel sesso; *the sterner* —, il sesso forte; *the weaker* (o *softer*) —, il sesso debole || *the* —, (*scherz.*) le donne ☆ — *-appeal*, attrazione del sesso: *she has* — *-appeal*, è seducente, conturbante; — *-cell*, (*biol.*) sperma; *pl.* (*bot.*) gameti; — *-reversal*, cambiamento di sesso.

sexagenarian [,seksədʒi'neəriən], *ag.* sessagenario || *s.c.* chi è nella sessantina.

sexagenary [sek'sædʒinəri], *ag.* **1.** sessagenario **2.** (*mat.*) relativo al 60; sessagesimale || *s.* (*mat.*) frazione sessagesimale.

Sexagesima [,seksə'dʒesimə], *s.* (*eccl.*) sessagesima.

sexagesimal [,seksə'dʒesiməl], *ag.* sessagesimale || *s.* (*mat.*) frazione sessagesimale.

sexangle ['seksæŋgl], *s.* (*geom.*) esagono.

sexangular [seks'æŋgjulə*], *ag.* (*geom.*) esagonale.

sexennial [seks'eniəl], *ag.* sessennale.

sexennially [seks'eniəli], *av.* ogni sei anni; per sei anni.

sexfid ['seksfid], *ag.* (*bot.*) diviso in sei.

sexfoil ['seksfoil], *s.* **1.** (*arch.*) figura, decorazione a sei lobi **2.** (*bot.*) pianta con foglie a gruppi di sei.

sexillion [sek'siljən], *V.* **sextillion**.

sexless ['sekslis], *ag.* asessuale.

sexlessness ['sekslisnis], *s.* asessualità.

sext [sekst], *s.* (*eccl.*) sesta.

sextain ['sekstein], *s.* (*poes.*) sestina.

sextan ['sekstən], *ag.* (*med.*) sestano (di febbre, ecc.).

sextant ['sekstənt], *s.* **1.** (*astr.*) sestante **2.** (*rar. geom.*) sesta parte del cerchio.

sextet(te) [seks'tet], *s.* **1.** (*mus.*) sestetto **2.** gruppo di sei (persone, cose).

sextic ['sekstik], *ag.* (*mat.*) di sesto grado || *s.* (*mat.*) equazione di sesto grado.

sextile ['sekstail], *ag.* (*astr.*) sestile || *s.* (*astr.*) aspetto, posizione sestile.

sextillion [seks'tiljən], *s.* **1.** sesta potenza di un milione **2.** (*amer.*) settima potenza di mille.

sexto ['sekstou], *s.* (*tip.*) (libro in) sesto.

sextodecimo ['sekstou'desimou], *s.* (*tip.*) in sedicesimo.

sexton ['sekstən], *s.* **1.** sagrestano **2.** becchino ☆ — *-beetle*, (*entom.*) becchino.

sextuple ['sekstjupl], *ag.s.* sestuplo.

to sextuple, *v.t.i.* moltiplicare per sei.

Sextus ['sekstəs], *no.pr.m.* (*st. romana*) Sesto.

sexual ['seksjuəl], *ag.* sessuale ☆ — *organs*, organi genitali.

sexualism ['seksjuəlizəm], *s.* erotismo.

sexuality [,seksju'æliti], *s.* sessualità.

sexualization [,seksjuəli'zeiʃən], *s.* attribuzione del sesso.

to sexualize ['seksjuəlaiz], *v.t.* attribuire un sesso a (cose).

sexually ['seksjuəli], *av.* sessualmente.

sexy ['seksi], *ag.* (*sl.*) **1.** erotico **2.** eroticamente conturbante.

Seychelles [sei'ʃelz], *no.pr.* (*geog.*) le isole Seychelles.

sforzando [sfo:t'sændou], *s.* (*mus.*) sforzando.

shabbily ['ʃæbili], *av.* **1.** poveramente **2.** spregevolmente; meschinamente.

shabbiness ['ʃæbinis], *s.* **1.** l'esser male in arnese; straccioneria **2.** piccineria, meschinità; grettezza.

shabby ['ʃæbi], *ag.* **1.** male in arnese, cencioso, stracciato; logoro: — *clothes*, vestiti frusti; — *room*, stanza squallida **2.** *fig.* spregevole; meschino, gretto: *it is very* — *of him*, è molto meschino da parte sua || *to play s.o. a* — *trick*, giocare a qlcu. un brutto tiro ☆ — *-genteel*, che ha visto tempi migliori, che tenta di salvare le apparenze.

shabbyish ['ʃæbiiʃ], *ag.* **1.** piuttosto logoro, frusto **2.** gretto, meschino.

shabrack ['ʃæbræk], *s.* (*mil.*) gualdrappa.

shack [ʃæk], *s.* **1.** grano (nelle secce); ghiande (nei boschi): *to go* (o *to run*) *at* —, andare al pascolo nella seccia, nei boschi (di maiali, polli, ecc.) **2.** diritto di pascolo.

to shack, *v.t.i.* pascolare; mandare (maiali, ecc.) al pascolo nella seccia.

shackle ['ʃækl], *s.* **1.** *pl.* manette; ceppi **2.** *pl. fig.* impedimenti; restrizioni: *the shackles of habit*, i legami della consuetudine; *the shackles of rhyme*, le restrizioni imposte dalla rima **3.** catena (di manette) **4.** gambo (di lucchetto) **5.** (*mec.*) anello di trazione (ad U, chiuso da perno) **6.** (*mar.*) lunghezza (di catena) **7.** (*mar.*) maniglia (di catena di ancora) **8.** (*tel.*) isolatore d'arresto ☆ — *-bolt*, stanghetta (che chiude un anello ad U); — *-bone*, (*scoz. dial.*) polso. ·

to shackle, *v.t.* **1.** mettere in catene, in ceppi; ammanettare **2.** *fig.* ostacolare, impedire: *shackled by convention*, soffocato dalle convenzioni **3.** (*mar.*) ammanigliare.

shad [ʃæd], *s.* (*ittiol.*) alosa.

shaddock ['ʃædək], *s.* (*bot.*) (varietà di) pompelmo.

shade [ʃeid], *s.* **1.** ombra (anche *fig.*): *not a* — *of doubt*, non un'ombra di dubbio; *the pleasant* — *of those trees*, la piacevole ombra di quegli alberi; *without light or* —, senza luce nè ombra; *fig.* monotono, uniforme || *he is a* — *better*, sta un pochino meglio || *to throw* (o *put*) *s.o. into the* —, *fig.* mettere in ombra qlcu.; eclissare qlcu. **2.** sfumatura (di colore, significato, ecc.): *delicate shades of meaning*, delicate sfumature di significato; *she wants the same colour in a lighter* —, vuole lo stesso colore in una sfumatura più chiara **3.** spirito, ombra: *the* — *of Anchises*, l'ombra di Anchise; *he went down to the shades*, (*poet.*) morì, visitò gli Inferi **4.** schermo, riparo **5.** *pl.* (*poet.*) oscurità, tenebre: *the shades of night*, le ombre della notte **6.** *pl.* (*poet.*) luogo fresco e riparato; ritiro **7.** tendina (per finestra) ☆ — *-deck*, (*mar.*) ponte a tenda; — *-plant*, pianta che cresce all'ombra; — *-tree*, albero ombrifero || *eye-* —, visiera, paralume; *lamp-* —, paralume; *sun-* —, parasole; *window-* —, tendina (di finestra).

to shade, *v.t.i.* **1.** ombreggiare; proteggere, riparare (da luce, calore): *he shaded his eyes from the sun*, si riparò gli occhi dal sole; *a huge oak shaded the house*, una grande quercia ombreggiava la casa **2.** velare, oscurare (anche *fig.*): *a gloomy look shaded her face*, *fig.* un'espressione melanconica le offuscava il viso; *to*

— *the light,* velare la luce **3.** (*pitt.*) ombreggiare **4.** (*mus.*) modulare il tono di **5.** (*comm. amer.*) ridurre leggermente (i prezzi) **6.** *to* — **off,** sfumare: *red shading off into pink,* rosso che sfuma nel rosa.

shaded ['ʃeidid], *ag.* **1.** ombreggiato, ombroso **2.** (*pitt.*) ombreggiato; sfumato.

shadeless ['ʃeidlis], *ag.* **1.** senza ombra **2.** (*pitt.*) senza ombreggiatura, senza sfumatura.

shadily ['ʃeidili], *av.* ombrosamente.

shadiness ['ʃeidinis], *s.* **1.** ombrosità **2.** dubbia reputazione; aspetto losco.

shading ['ʃeidiŋ], *s.* **1.** l'ombreggiare, il dare ombra **2.** ombreggiatura; sfumatura, gradazione (di colori) **3.** (*mus.*) modulazione di tono.

shadoof [ʃə'duːf], *s.* mazzacavallo (per attingere acqua).

shadow ['ʃædou], *s.* **1.** ombra (anche *fig.*): *the* — *of death is on his face, fig.* l'ombra della morte è sul suo viso; *his face is in deep* —, il suo viso è completamente nell'ombra; *this cast a* — *over the festivities, fig.* questo gettò un'ombra di tristezza sui festeggiamenti ‖ *may your* — *never grow less!,* auguri per la vostra salute! ‖ *to be afraid of one's own* —, aver timore della propria ombra **2.** *gener. pl.* oscurità: *the shadows of evening,* l'oscurità della sera **3.** ombra, immagine; spettro: *he is only a* — *of his former self,* è solo l'ombra di se stesso; *he was only the* — *of his father,* non era che l'immagine di suo padre; *what shadows we are!,* non siamo che ombre! ‖ *worn to a* —, esausto **4.** segno, traccia: *not a* — *of doubt,* non un'ombra di dubbio **5.** compagno inseparabile **6.** spia **7.** protezione; (*rar.*) rifugio: *under the* — *of the Almighty,* sotto la protezione dell'Onnipotente.

to shadow, *v.t.* **1.** pedinare; seguire come un'ombra: *the detective shadowed the suspect,* l'investigatore seguì il sospetto **2.** (*poet.*) oscurare, far ombra a **3.** (*rar.*) ombreggiare, sfumare (un disegno) **4.** *to* — **forth,** (*letter.*) rappresentare allegoricamente, simboleggiare.

shadowiness ['ʃædouinis], *s.* ombrosità; oscurità.

shadowing ['ʃædouiŋ], *s.* **1.** ombreggiamento **2.** simbolo, immagine.

shadowless ['ʃædoulis], *ag.* senz'ombra.

shadowy ['ʃædoui], *ag.* **1.** ombroso, ombreggiato: — *woods,* boschi ombrosi **2.** indistinto, vago: *a* — *form,* una forma indistinta **3.** chimerico, irreale: *a* — *hope,* una speranza illusoria.

shady ['ʃeidi], *ag.* **1.** ombreggiato, all'ombra: *the* — *side of the street,* il lato ombreggiato della strada ‖ *on the* — *side of forty,* che ha superato la quarantina **2.** (*fam.*) disonesto, infido, losco: *a* — *person,* una persona infida.

shaft¹ [ʃɑːft], *s.* **1.** lancia, giavellotto, freccia, dardo, strale (anche *fig.*): *the shafts of Cupid,* gli strali di Cupido; *the shafts of satire,* gli strali della satira; *the air was darkened by the shafts of the archers,* l'aria fu oscurata dai dardi degli arcieri **2.** fulmine; raggio (di luce) **3.** gambo, stelo; fusto: *the* — *of a candlestick,* lo stelo di un candeliere; *the* — *of a column,* lo scapo di una colonna **4.** comignolo; fumaiolo **5.** asta, bastone; pertica; palo; manico; *pl.* stanghe (di carri, ecc.): *the* — *of an axe,* il manico di un'ascia; *pair of shafts,* stanghe di una carrozza **6.** (*arch.*) colonnina; (*amer.*) colonna commemorativa; obelisco **7.** (*mec.*) albero; (*ind. tessile*) liccio ☆ — *-horse,* cavallo da tiro; — *horsepower,* (*mec.*) potenza sull'asse, potenza al freno; — *passage,* (*mar.*) galleria dell'albero ‖ *accessory drive-* —, (*mec.*) albero comando accessori; *axle* —, (*aut.*) semiasse; *cam-* —, (*aut.*) albero a camme; *drive* - —, (*mec.*) albero motore; (*aut.*) semiasse; *driven-* —, (*aut.*) albero secondario; *feed* —, (*mec.*) albero (di comando) dell'avanzamento; *gear* —, (*aut.*) albero del cambio; *hollow* —, (*mec.*) albero cavo; *intermediate* —, (*mar.*) asse intermedio; *lay* —, (*mec.*) albero di rinvio; *propeller-* —, (*aut.*) albero di trasmissione; (*mec.*) albero di propulsione; (*mar.*) albero dell'elica; (*aer.*) al-

bero portaelica; *standard* —, (*mec.*) albero base; *tai* —, (*mar.*) albero dell'elica.

to shaft¹, *v.t.* **1.** munire di asta **2.** far avanzare (chiatte, ecc.) a mezzo di una pertica.

shaft², *s.* sfiatatoio; condotto; (*miner.*) pozzo ☆ — *top,* accesso del pozzo ‖ *air-* —, pozzo d'aerazione; *downcast-* —, pozzo di ventilazione discendente; *hauling* —, pozzo di estrazione; *upcast-* —, pozzo di ventilazione ascendente; *ventilating* —, condotto di ventilazione; *vertical-* —, pozzo verticale.

shafted ['ʃɑːftid], *ag.* **1.** munito di asta, di manico, di stanga **2.** (*mec.*) munito di albero di trasmissione **3.** (*arch.*) ornato di colonnine.

shafting¹ ['ʃɑːftiŋ], *s.* **1.** (*mec.*) sistema di trasmissione ad alberi **2.** (*arch.*) colonnine ornamentali.

shafting², *s.* sistema di sfiatatoi; (*miner.*) sistema di pozzi.

shag¹ [ʃæg], *s.* **1.** pelo ispido **2.** tessuto peloso ruvido **3.** tabacco forte (trinciato) ☆ — *-bark,* (*bot.*) noce bianco americano; — *-haired,* (*arc.*) dai capelli ispidi.

to shag¹, *pass.p.p.* **shagged** [ʃægd], *v.t.* rendere peloso, rendere ispido.

shag², *s.* (*ornit.*) cormorano crestato.

shagged [ʃægd], *V.* **shaggy.**

shaggedness ['ʃægidnis], **shagginess** ['ʃæginis], *s.* **1.** ispidezza; villosità; ruvidezza **2.** scabrosità.

shaggy ['ʃægi], *ag.* **1.** di pelo lungo, ispido, irsuto; incolto, arruffato (di capelli) **2.** peloso, ruvido (di tessuto) **3.** incolto, coperto di sterpi (di terreno); folto, intonso (di alberi) **4.** (*bot.*) vellutato, peloso.

shagreen [ʃæ'griːn], *s.* zigrino.

to shagreen, *v.t.* zigrinare.

Shah [ʃɑː], *s.* scià (di Persia).

shake [ʃeik], *s.* **1.** scossa, scuotimento (anche *fig.*); urto: *to give a person a good* —, urtare violentemente una persona ‖ *a* — *of the hand,* una stretta di mano; *a* — *of the head,* una scrollata di capo ‖ *he is no great shakes,* è un uomo di poco conto ‖ *to give s.o. a fair* —, (*amer.*) agire lealmente verso qlcu. **2.** tremore, tremito, tremolio; (*fam.*) terremoto: *with a* — *in his voice,* con voce tremula ‖ *to be all of a* —, (*fam.*) tremare in tutte le membra ‖ *to have the shakes,* avere la tremarella **3.** (*amer.*) frullato **4.** (*mus.*) trillo **5.** (*fam.*) istante, tempo brevissimo: *in a* — (o *in a brace of shakes* o *in two shakes of a lamb's tail*), in un batter d'occhio **6.** fenditura, fessura (di legno) **7.** *pl.* (*med.*) febbre malarica.

to shake, *pass.* **shook** [ʃuk], *p.p.* **shaken** ['ʃeikən], *v.t.i.* **1.** scuotere; scrollare; agitare (liquidi): — *the bottle,* agitare il flacone; *he shook his head at my question,* scrollò il capo alla mia domanda; *to* — *a carpet,* sbattere un tappeto ‖ —*!,* (*amer.*) felicitazioni! ‖ *to* — *hands over a bargain,* concludere un affare; *to* — *hands with s.o.* (o *s.o. by the hand*), stringere la mano a qualcuno (in segno di saluto, di accordo) ‖ *to* — *one's finger, one's fist at s.o.,* minacciare qlcu. col dito, col pugno ‖ *to* — *one's sides with laughter,* sbellicarsi dalle risa **2.** tremare, far tremare; vacillare, far vacillare (anche *fig.*): *the earth shook,* la terra tremò; *threats cannot* — *my purpose,* le minacce non possono far vacillare il mio proposito; *to* — *the table,* far vacillare la tavola; *to* — *with fear,* tremare di paura ‖ *to* — *in one's shoes,* tremare di apprensione **3.** turbare, turbarsi; impressionare: *he was badly shaken by the news,* fu molto turbato dalla notizia **4.** indebolire, infirmare: *the firm's credit was badly shaken,* il credito della ditta ricevette una brusca scossa; *his faith in Providence was greatly shaken,* la sua fede nella Provvidenza fu molto indebolita; *the ranks were shaken but not broken,* (*mil.*) le linee furono indebolite ma non spezzate; *this fact shook the witness's evidence,* questo fatto infirmò la deposizione testimoniale **5.** (*mus.*) trillare **6.** *to* — **down,** scuoter, far cadere scuotendo; installarsi; assuefarsi: *to* — *down fruit from a tree,* scuotere i frutti di un albero; *to — down to a routine, into a job*, abituarsi a un sistema di vita, a un lavoro 7. *to — off*, scuotere da, scuotersi da; districarsi; liberarsi di (anche *fig.*); *to — off a cold*, liberarsi da un raffreddore; *to — off the yoke*, liberarsi dal giogo; *to — s.o. off*, liberarsi dalle mani di qlcu. ‖ *to — off the dust from one's feet*, (*fam.*) allontanarsi con sdegno da un luogo 8. *to — out*, far uscire scuotendo; vuotare; svegliare bruscamente; (*mar.*) spiegare (vele, bandiere, ecc.); (*mec.*) distaffare 9. *to — up*, sprimacciare; mescolare scuotendo (liquidi, ecc.); scuotere (dall'indolenza, ecc.): *the ingredients are shaken up together in a bottle*, si mescolano insieme gli ingredienti agitandoli in una bottiglia.

shake, (*nei composti*): *— -out*, (Borsa) crisi, svendita; (*metal.*) distaffatura, sformatura: *— -out sand*, (*metal.*) terra di sformatura; *— -rag*, (*arc.*) straccione, pezzente; *— -up*, (*amer.*) rimaneggiamento, riorganizzazione ‖ *egg- —*, zabaglione; *milk- —*, frappè, frullato al latte.

shakedown ['ʃeik'daun], *s.* **1.** letto di fortuna **2.** (*amer.*) esazione, estorsione di denaro.

shaken ['ʃeikən], *p.p.* di **to shake.**

shaker ['ʃeikə*], *s.c.* scuotitore, scuotitrice ‖ *s.* **1.** «shaker» per cocktail **2.** (*ind.*) trasportatore a scosse **3.** (*mec.*) lupo battitore **4.** (*agr.*) scuotipaglia **5.** *Shaker*, (*amer.*) membro di una setta che sostiene che Cristo è già apparso una seconda volta sulla Terra ☆ *— pins*, (*mec.*) aste a scosse.

shakerism ['ʃeikərizəm], *s.* (*amer.*) dottrina che sostiene il secondo avvento di Cristo.

Shak(e)spearian [ʃeiks'piəriən], *ag.* (*st. lett.*) shakespeariano.

shakily ['ʃeikili], *av.* **1.** instabilmente; in modo vacillante; in modo tremulo **2.** debolmente.

shakiness ['ʃeikinis], *s.* **1.** instabilità, vacillamento, tremore **2.** debolezza.

shaking ['ʃeikiŋ], *ag.* tremante; vacillante; tremulo: *a — voice*, una voce tremula ‖ *s.* **1.** scossa; scuotimento; sballottamento: *to get a —*, essere scosso, essere sballottato **2.** tremore; tremolio **3.** (*ind. tessile*) scuotimento **4.** *pl.* (*mar.*) scarti di cavi vecchi ☆ *— machine*, (*chim.*) agitatore.

shako ['ʃeikou], *pl.* **shakos** ['ʃækouz], *s.* chepì.

shaky ['ʃeiki], *ag.* **1.** instabile, tremolante, vacillante; precario (di salute): *a — hand*, una mano tremolante; *a — table*, una tavola vacillante; *I feel — to-day*, oggi non mi sento in forze ‖ *to be — on one's legs*, (*fam.*) tremare sulle gambe **2.** malsicuro, incerto (di conoscenza); debole (di carattere): *his English is —*, il suo inglese è traballante **3.** screpolato, pieno di fessure.

shale[1] [ʃeil], *s.* (*min.*) schisto ☆ *— -oil*, olio distillato da schisto bituminoso.

to shale[2], *v.i.* (*dial.*) cadere (di seme, grano da spiga).

shall [ʃæl (*forma forte*), ʃəl (*forma debole*)], *v.* difettivo (V); (2ª *persona sing. pres.* (*arc.*) **shalt** [ʃælt (*forma forte*), ʃəlt (*forma debole*)]; *forma negativa* **shall not** [ʃæl nɔt]; *forma contratta* **shan't** [ʃɑːnt]; *per il pass.* **should** *V.* a questa voce) **1.** (*ausiliare per la* 1ª *persona sing. pl. del futuro predicente*): *— we arrive in time to catch our train?*, arriveremo in tempo a prendere il treno?; *I — go to England next summer*, andrò, prevedo di andare in Inghilterra l'estate prossima **2.** (*ausiliare per la* 2ª, 3ª *persona sing. pl. del futuro volitivo*): *you — go to bed at once*, andrai a letto immediatamente **3.** (*nel senso di* dovere *nella* 2ª, 3ª *persona sing. pl. pres. indic.*): *children — do what their parents tell them*, i bambini devono fare quello che i genitori dicono loro di fare; *tell him that he — read that book*, digli che deve leggere quel libro ‖ *thou shalt not kill*, (*Bibbia*) non uccidere **4.** (*in forme interrogative, nelle espressioni di cortesia per la* 1ª *persona sing. pl.*): *— I mail your letters?*, vuoi che ti imbuchi le lettere?.

shalloon [ʃæ'luːn], *s.* saia, raso di lana.

shallop ['ʃæləp], *s.* scialuppa.

shallot [ʃə'lɔt], *s.* (*bot.*) scalogno.

shallow ['ʃælou], *ag.* **1.** poco profondo; basso: *— water*, acqua poco profonda **2.** *fig.* leggero, superficiale ‖ *s. gener. pl.* (*mar.*) bassofondo, secca ☆ *— -brained*, di poco cervello, sciocco, frivolo; *— -minded*, superficiale, leggero.

to shallow, *v.t.i.* **1.** rendere, divenire meno profondo **2.** *fig.* divenire superficiale.

shallowly ['ʃælouli], *av.* **1.** poco profondamente **2.** *fig.* superficialmente.

shallowness ['ʃælounis], *s.* **1.** poca profondità (di acqua, ecc.) **2.** *fig.* superficialità; futilità.

shalot [ʃə'lɔt], *s.* (*bot.*) scalogno.

shalt [ʃælt (*forma forte*), ʃəlt (*forma debole*)], (2ª *persona sing. pres.* (*arc.*) di **shall**): *thou — not steal*, (*Bibbia*) non rubare, tu non ruberai.

shaly ['ʃeili], *ag.* schistoso.

sham [ʃæm], *ag.* finto, falso, simulato; fittizio: *— fight*, finto combattimento; *— pearls*, perle false; *— plea*, (*dir.*) pretesto (per guadagnar tempo) ‖ *s.* **1.** finta; inganno; impostura; mistificazione; imitazione: *are those real diamonds or only shams?*, sono diamanti veri quelli o solo imitazioni?; *his love was a mere —*, il suo amore era tutta una finta; *it's all —, he is only afraid*, è tutta una mistificazione, ha soltanto paura **2.** ipocrita: *he is a —*, è un ipocrita ☆ *sheet - —*, sopracoperta.

to sham, *pass.p.p.* **shammed** [ʃæmd], *v.t.i.* **1.** fingere, simulare: *to — illness*, simulare una malattia; *to — sleep*, fingere di dormire **2.** far finta di essere: *to — dead*, far finta di essere morto ‖ *to — Abraham*, (*sl. mar.*) far finta di essere ammalato.

sham, *s. abbr.* di **champagne.**

shaman ['ʃæmən], *s.* sciamano (stregone dei pel lirosse; sacerdote medico nelle tribù asiatiche).

shamanism ['ʃæmənizəm], *s.* (*st. relig.*) sciamanismo.

shamanistic [,ʃæmə'nistik], *ag.* sciamanistico.

shamble ['ʃæmbl], *s.* passo strascicato; andatura dinoccolata.

to shamble, *v.i.* camminare con passo strascicato, con andatura dinoccolata.

shambles ['ʃæmblz], *s.pl.* (*gener. costruzione sing.*) **1.** mattatoio; *fig.* carneficina; scena di sangue: *the room was a regular —*, *fig.* la stanza era un vero macello, si nuotava nel sangue **2.** (*sl.*) confusione, disordine; *the children left the house a —*, i bambini lasciarono la casa in un gran disordine.

shambling ['ʃæmbliŋ], *ag.* **1.** dinoccolato, strascicato: *a — gait*, un'andatura dinoccolata **2.** zoppicante (di verso, stile).

shame [ʃeim], *s.* **1.** vergogna; pudore: *he is quite without —*, *he is lost to —*), è uno svergognato ‖ *— on you!*, vergognati!; *for —!*, vergogna! ‖ *to cry — upon s.o.*, redarguire aspramente qlcu. **2.** disonore; infamia: *child of —*, figlio del disonore; *he brings — upon his name*, infama il proprio nome ‖ *to cry —*, gridare allo scandalo ‖ *to put s.o. to —*, svergognare qlcu., *fig.* eclissare qlcu. **3.** (*fam.*) peccato, vergogna: *it's a — that they were cheated*, è una vergogna che siano stati ingannati; *it is a — to laugh at him*, non è giusto prendersi giuoco di lui ‖ *what a —!*, che peccato!.

to shame, *v.t.i.* **1.** svergognare; far arrossire di vergogna; (*arc.*) vergognarsi **2.** disonorare **3.** indurre, costringere (per vergogna, rimprovero): *he shamed her into apologizing*, la indusse a chiedere scusa; *he was shamed out of his bad habits*, fu costretto ad abbandonare le sue cattive abitudini.

shamefaced ['ʃeimfeist], *ag.* vergognoso; confuso; (*poet.*) timido, modesto.

shamefacedly ['ʃeimfeistli], *av.* in modo imbarazzato; timidamente.

shamefacedness ['ʃeimfeistnis], *s.* confusione; timidezza, modestia.

shameful ['ʃeimful], *ag.* vergognoso; disonorevole.

shamefully ['ʃeimfuli], av. vergognosamente; disonorevolmente.

shamefulness ['ʃeimfulnis], s. vergogna; indegnità.

shameless ['ʃeimlis], ag. 1. svergognato; sfacciato, sfrontato; impudico 2. vergognoso, indecente.

shamelessly ['ʃeimlisli], av. sfacciatamente, impudentemente; senza vergogna.

shamelessness ['ʃeimlisnis], s. impudenza, sfacciataggine; immodestia.

shammer ['ʃæmə*], s.c. simulatore, simulatrice.

shammy (-leather) ['ʃæmi('leðə*)], s. pelle di camoscio.

shamoy ['ʃæmɔi], s. (zool.) camoscio.

shamoying ['ʃæmɔiŋ], s. camosciatura.

shampoo [ʃæm'pu:], s. 1. lavatura dei capelli 2. «shampoo » (preparato per lavare i capelli) ☆ — powder, shampoo in polvere ‖ dry —, shampoo secco.

to shampoo, v.t. lavare (i capelli): to — one's hair, lavarsi i capelli.

shampooer [ʃæm'pu:ə*], s.c. chi lava i capelli.

shampooing [ʃæm'pu:iŋ], s. lavatura dei capelli.

shamrock ['ʃæmrɔk], s. trifoglio d'Irlanda.

shandrydan ['ʃændridæn], s. 1. calesse 2. vecchio veicolo sgangherato.

shandy(gaff) ['ʃændi(gæf)], s. bevanda composta di birra e zenzero.

Shanghai [ʃæn'hai], no.pr. (geog.) Sciangai.

to shanghai, v.t. (sl. mar.) drogare e portare inconscio (qlcu.) a bordo come marinaio.

shank [ʃæŋk], s. 1. gamba; tibia, stinco ‖ to go on Shanks's pony (o mare), (scherz.) andare a piedi, andare col cavallo di San Francesco 2. gambo, stelo 3. fusto (di colonna) 4. manico (di cucchiaio, ecc.); gambo, stelo, codolo (di utensile) 5. canna, fusto (di chiave) 6. (mar.) fuso (di ancora) ☆ — -bone, stinco, tibia; — -cutter, fresa frontale a codolo; — -painter, (mar.) serrabozze ‖ rivet- —, gambo del chiodo.

to shank, v.t.i. 1. (golf) colpire di tacco (la palla) 2. to — off, (bot.) avvizzire, cadere per malattia dello stelo.

shanked [ʃæŋkt], ag. provvisto di gambo, stelo, fusto ☆ short- —, dalle gambe corte; con canna corta (di chiave).

shan't [ʃɑ:nt], contr. di shall not.

shantung [ʃæn'tʌŋ], s. «shantung» (tessuto di seta).

shanty ['ʃænti], s. 1. (amer.) capanna, baracca 2. (sl.) bettola, osteria.

to shanty, v.i. 1. vivere in una capanna 2. (sl.) frequentare osterie.

shapable ['ʃeipəbl], ag. formabile, plasmabile.

shape [ʃeip], s. 1. forma; figura; struttura; modello (di abito): clouds of different shapes, nuvole di varie forme; a devil in human —, un diavolo sotto sembianza umana; in the — of, sotto forma di; in any or form, di qualsiasi tipo; sthg. in the — of..., ql.co. con l'apparenza di...; to get out of (o to lose) —, perdere la forma, sformarsi ‖ to put an article into —, (giornalismo) mettere a punto un articolo 2. forma, concretezza: ideas that take — in action, idee che si concretizzano nell'azione 3. ombra, apparizione, spettro: two shapes loomed up in the darkness, due ombre si profilarono nell'oscurità 4. stampo 5. (fam. amer.) condizione, stato (di salute): to be in good (o first class) —, essere in gran forma 6. (metal.) profilato speciale ☆ — cutting machine, (mec.) macchina per eseguire tagli sagomati ‖ hat —, stampo per cappelli; jelly —, stampo per gelatina.

to shape, v.t.i. 1. creare; dar forma a; prender forma; modellare, modellarsi: before I had time to shape my answer, prima che avessi tempo di formulare la mia risposta; to — s.o.'s character, formare il carattere di qlcu. ‖ to — well, promettere bene: he is shaping well at Latin, promette bene in latino; our plans are shaping well, i nostri piani promettono bene 2. adattare: — your plans to your abilities, adatta i tuoi piani

alle tue capacità 3. dirigere, regolare (vita, condotta, ecc.): to — the destiny of a man, regolare, dirigere il destino di un uomo ‖ to — a course, (mar.) far rotta 4. (mec.) limare; sagomare.

shaped [ʃeipt], ag. formato, modellato, sagomato, a forma di ☆ queer- —, di forma bizzarra; well- —, benfatto.

shapeless ['ʃeiplis], ag. informe; confuso.

shapelessly ['ʃeiplisli], av. in modo confuso; informemente.

shapelessness ['ʃeiplisnis], s. mancanza di forma; deformità; fig. goffaggine.

shapeliness ['ʃeiplinis], s. bellezza; simmetria; proporzione di forme.

shapely ['ʃeipli], ag. ben fatto; di bell'aspetto e proporzione.

shaper ['ʃeipə*], s.c. modellatore, modellatrice ‖ s. (mec.) limatrice.

shaping ['ʃeipiŋ], s. conformazione, formazione; sagomatura.

shard[1] [ʃɑ:d], s. coccio: to break into shards, ridurre in frammenti.

shard[2], s. elitra.

share[1] [ʃeə*], s. 1. parte, porzione, quota: a fair —, una parte equa; I took more than my — of the burden, ho preso più della mia parte di onere ‖ — and — alike, in parti uguali ‖ lion's —, la parte del leone ‖ to go shares, dividere equamente 2. (comm.) azione, titolo: to hold shares in a company, avere delle azioni di una società.

to share[1], v.t.i. 1. dividere, spartire: he shares his frugal meal with those he loves, spartisce il suo pasto frugale con coloro che ama; we shared 500 pounds among five men, dividemmo 500 sterline tra cinque uomini; to — in (sthg.), partecipare a ql.co. 2. condividere; partecipare, prender parte: to — s.o.'s opinion, condividere l'opinione di qlcu. ‖ to — and — alike, partecipare in egual misura 3. to — out, distribuire: to — out food to the poor, distribuire cibo ai poveri.

share[1], (nei composti): — -capital, capitale azionario; — -certificate, certificato azionario; — -list, listino valori; — -out, distribuzione (di cibo, ecc. fatta da un istituto di beneficenza); — -pusher, (fam. spreg.) venditore di azioni (generalmente di poco valore) a domicilio del cliente ‖ deferred —, azione differita; ordinary —, azione ordinaria; paid-up —, azione interamente versata; preference (o preferred) —, azione preferenziale; transferable —, azione al portatore.

share[2], s. (agr.) vomere.

sharecropper ['ʃeə,krɔpə*], s. mezzadro.

sharecropping ['ʃeə,krɔpiŋ], s. mezzadria.

shareholder ['ʃeə,houldə*], s.c. azionista.

sharer ['ʃeərə*], s.c. partecipante, compartecipe.

sharing ['ʃeəriŋ], s. 1. divisione, distribuzione; spartizione 2. partecipazione, compartecipazione.

shark [ʃɑ:k], s. 1. squalo; pescecane 2. fig. profittatore; truffatore 3. (sl. amer.) persona in gamba; studente brillante ☆ — -oil, olio di fegato di pescecane.

to shark, v.t.i. 1. truffare; scroccare ‖ he sharks for a living, vive di espedienti, di truffe 2. ingoiare avidamente.

sharker ['ʃɑ:kə*], s.c. truffatore, truffatrice.

sharkskin ['ʃɑ:k-skin], s. zigrino, sagrì.

sharp [ʃɑ:p], ag. 1. tagliente, affilato: a — knife, coltello affilato 2. aguzzo; ad angolo acuto: — edge, spigolo acuto; — features, lineamenti angolosi; — summit, cima aguzza; a — turn, curva brusca 3. scosceso, ripido: a — ascent, una salita ripida; a — descent, una discesa scoscesa 4. netto, chiaro, distinto: a — difference, una netta differenza; a — outline, un profilo netto 5. acuto, penetrante; acre (di odori): a — appetite, un appetito robusto; a — cry, un grido penetrante; — flavour, sapore aspro; — frost, gelo pungente; a — pain, un dolore acuto; — sight, vista acuta 6. fig. severo; tagliente, mordace: — criticism, critica severa; — *temper*, temperamento irascibile; — *tongue*, lingua caustica **7.** intelligente, acuto, vivace, sveglio: *a — child*, un bambino vivace, intelligente; *to be — at arithmetic*, essere bravo in aritmetica || *he is as — as a needle*, è molto sveglio, molto acuto || *to keep a — look-out*, star bene in guardia **8.** scaltro; disonesto; poco scrupoloso: — *practice*, procedimenti poco onesti; *he was too — for me*, mi ha raggirato **9.** rapido, lesto; impetuoso: *a — struggle*, una lotta accanita; *a — walk*, una rapida passeggiata **10.** (*mus.*) diesis **11.** (*fonet.*) sordo || *s.* **1.** (*mus.*) diesis **2.** (*fonet.*) consonante sorda **3.** *gener. pl.* sottile ago per cucire **4.** (*fam.*) truffatore; baro **5.** (*sl. amer.*) esperto, conoscitore **6.** *pl.* cruschello.

to **sharp**, *v.t.i.* **1.** (*mus.*) diesare **2.** imbrogliare, truffare: *he sharps at cards*, bara al giuoco.

sharp, *av.* **1.** puntualmente, in punto: *at ten o'clock —*, alle dieci in punto **2.** presto, rapidamente; bruscamente: *the road turns — right*, la strada svolta bruscamente a destra || *look —!*, svelto!, fate presto! **3.** (*mus.*) con un tono troppo acuto.

sharp, (*nei composti*): — *-cut*, chiaro, netto; — *-edged*, tagliente; — *-set*, famelico; — *-shod*, ferrato a ghiaccio (di cavallo); — *-shooter*, tiratore scelto; — *-sighted*, — *-witted*, dalla vista, dall'intelligenza acuta.

to **sharpen** ['ʃɑ:pən], *v.t.i.* **1.** affilare; aguzzare: *to — a pencil*, far la punta a una matita **2.** *fig.* rendere più acuto; affinare, affinarsi; inasprire, inasprirsi: *an injury sharpened by an insult*, un torto inasprito da un insulto; *to — one's wits*, aguzzare l'ingegno **3.** (*mus.*) diesare.

sharpener ['ʃɑ:pnə*], *s.* **1.** arrotino **2.** (*mec.*) affilatoio; affilatrice ☆ *blade —*, (*mec.*) affilatrice per lame; *pencil- —*, temperino.

sharper ['ʃɑ:pə*], *s.* imbroglione; baro.

sharply ['ʃɑ:pli], *av.* **1.** acutamente **2.** nettamente, chiaramente **3.** vivamente; attentamente.

sharpness ['ʃɑ:pnis], *s.* **1.** filo, affilatura; punta **2.** acutezza; asprezza **3.** vivacità, intelligenza; mordacità **4.** (*mus.*) suono acuto, discordante.

shatter ['ʃætə*], *s.* frammento, frantume: *to break into shatters*, mandare in frantumi ☆ *-brain(ed)* (o — *-pate(d)* o — *-wit(ted)*), scervellato, pazzo.

to **shatter**, *v.t.i.* **1.** frantumare, frantumarsi; fracassare, fracassarsi: *the glass was shattered*, il bicchiere andò in frantumi **2.** *fig.* distruggere; infrangere: *shattered hopes*, speranze infrante **3.** rovinare (la salute); sconvolgere (i nervi): *shattered nerves*, nervi in pezzi, scossi.

shattery ['ʃætəri], *ag.* friabile.

shave[1] [ʃeiv], *s.* **1.** rasatura || *— and hair-cut*, barba e capelli **2.** sfioramento, massimo avvicinamento || *to have a close* (o *narrow*) —, (*fam.*) cavarsela per un pelo **3.** truffa, imbroglio **4.** (*comm.*) tasso d'interesse ☆ — *-grass*, (*bot.*) equiseto.

to **shave**[1], *v.t.i.* **1.** radere, radersi: *he shaves every morning*, si rade ogni mattina **2.** tagliar via: *to — a slice off a piece of meat*, tagliare una fetta da un pezzo di carne **3.** rasentare, sfiorare: *the wheel of the car shaved the kerb*, la ruota dell'automobile sfiorò l'orlo del marciapiede **4.** piallare **5.** (*eccl.*) tonsurare **6.** (*sl. amer.*) truffare **7.** (*comm.*) acquistare (un titolo, una cambiale, ecc.) con forte tasso di sconto.

shave[2], *s.* pialla.

shaveling ['ʃeivliŋ], *s.* **1.** sbarbatello **2.** (*arc.*) frate, monaco.

shaven ['ʃeivn], *ag.* **1.** rasato **2.** (*eccl.*) tonsurato.

shaver ['ʃeivə*], *s.* **1.** barbiere **2.** commerciante avido di guadagni **3.** (*fam.*) ragazzo, giovinetto.

Shavian ['ʃeivjən], *ag.* di, come, alla Shaw || *s.* seguace, ammiratore di Shaw.

shaving ['ʃeiviŋ], *s.***1.** il radersi, il farsi la barba **2.** truciolo; ritaglio ☆ — *-basin*, bacinella per barba; — *-brush*, pennello da barba; — *-case*, « nécessaire » per barba; — *-soap*, sapone da barba; — *-stick*, bastoncino di sapone da barba.

shaw [ʃɔ:], *s.* (*arc. poet.*) boschetto.

shawl [ʃɔ:l], *s.* scialle.

to **shawl**, *v.t.* coprire con, avvolgere in uno scialle.

shawm [ʃɔ:m], *s.* (*mus.*) cennamella.

shay [ʃei], *s.* calesse, biroccino; carrozza da nolo.

she [ʃi:], *pron. pers.* **3ª** *persona f.* **1.** ella, lei, colei: *do you see that ship over there? — sails tomorrow*, vedi quella nave laggiù? salpa domani; *here — comes*, eccola che viene; *it's —*, è lei; *you are as tall as — is*, tu sei alto quanto lei **2.** (*antecedente di pron. rel.*): — *who sings*, colei che canta; — *whom you think of*, colei a cui pensi || *att.* indicante il *sesso* (di animali): *a — -bear*, un'orsa || *a — -devil*, una diavolessa, un demonio di donna, una indemoniata || *s.* femmina: *the not impossible —*, la donna che si potrebbe amare || *it is a —!*, è una femmina! (di animale).

shea [ʃiə], *s.* (*bot.*) bassia ☆ — *-butter*, burro di Galam.

sheaf [ʃi:f], *pl.* **sheaves** [ʃi:vz], *s.* **1.** fascio; covone: *a — of flowers*, un fascio di fiori **2.** (*geom.*) fascio (di rette, ecc.) ☆ — *-binder*, chi raccoglie covoni; (*agr.*) macchina per legare i covoni.

to **sheaf**, *v.t.* legare in fasci, raccogliere in covoni.

sheafy ['ʃi:fi], *ag.* di fasci, di covoni; simile a covone.

shealing, *V.* **shieling**.

shear[1] [ʃiə*], *s.* **1.** *pl.* cesoie, forbici: *a pair of shears*, un paio di cesoie **2.** (*dial.*) recisione, taglio; tosatura; falciatura (di fieno) **3.** (*mar.*) biga, capra **4.** (*fis. mec.*) deformazione di taglio, forza elastica trasversale ☆ — *-grass*, erba dalle foglie acuminate; — *-hulk*, (*mar.*) pontone a biga; — *-legs*, (*mar.*) biga, capra; — *steel*, (*metall.*) acciaio affinato; — *tail*, (*ornit.*) rondine di mare; colibrì || *garden shears*, forbici da giardino; *hedge shears*, cesoie per le siepi; *pruning shears*, cesoie per potatura.

to **shear**[1], *pass.* **sheared** [ʃiəd], (*arc.*) **shore** [ʃɔ:*], *p.p.* (*rar.*) **sheared**, **shorn** [ʃɔ:n], *v.t.* **1.** cesoiare, tranciare **2.** recidere; tosare; tagliare (capelli); falciare (erba); cimare (lana) **3.** *fig.* spennare: *he came home shorn*, tornò a casa senza soldi **4.** (*mec.*) sottoporre a deformazione di taglio.

shear[2], *s.* sbarra del banco del tornio.

shearer ['ʃiərə*], *s.c.* tosatore, tosatrice || *s.* tranciatrice meccanica.

shearing ['ʃiəriŋ], *s.* **1.** recisione, taglio **2.** *pl.* i resti della tosatura, della cimatura **3.** (*dial.*) pecora tosata una sola volta ☆ — *machine*, (*mec.*) tranciatrice; — *strength*, (*fis. mec.*) resistenza al taglio; — *stress*, (*mec.*) sollecitazione di taglio.

shearling ['ʃiəliŋ], *s.* pecora tosata una sola volta.

shearman, *pl.* **shearmen** ['ʃiəmən], *s.* (*artig.*) cimatore.

shearwater ['ʃiə,wɔːtə*], *s.* (*ornit.*) berta.

sheath [ʃi:θ], *s.* **1.** guaina, fodero (di ombrelli, ecc.); astuccio **2.** (*anat. bot.*) guaina; (*entom.*) elitra **3.** (*edil.*) argine di pietre (per impedire lo straripamento di un fiume) **4.** (*elett.*) guaina ☆ — *-knife*, coltello a lama fissa con fodero; — *-winged*, (*entom.*) coleottero.

to **sheathe** [ʃi:ð], *v.t.* **1.** inguainare; mettere nel fodero || *to — the sword*, *fig.* fare la pace **2.** (*bot.*) inguainare: *the leaves — the stem*, le foglie inguainano lo stelo **3.** rivestire, ricoprire di: *they sheathed the ship's bottom with copper*, rivestirono di rame il fondo della nave.

sheathing ['ʃi:ðiŋ], *s.* **1.** inguainamento **2.** rivestimento, copertura; (*mec.*) guaina di protezione; (*mar.*) fasciame; fodera ☆ — *-leaves*, (*bot.*) foglie con lo stelo nella guaina; — *-paper*, (*elett.*) carta per rivestimenti isolanti || *cable —*, (*elett.*) protezione per cavi.

sheathless ['ʃi:θlis], *ag.* privo di guaina, privo di fodero.

sheave [ʃi:v], *s.* (*mec.*) carrucola.

sheaves [ʃi:vz], *pl.* di **sheaf**.

Sheba ['ʃi:bə], *no.pr.geog.* (*arc.*) Saba.

shed[1] [ʃed], *s.* **1.** (*ind. tessile*) passo **2.** (*dial.*) scriminatura **3.** (*amer.*) spartiacque.

to **shed**[1], *pass.p.p.* **shed**, *v.t.* **1.** versare, spandere, spargere; diffondere: *roses — their fragrance*, le rose diffondono la loro fragranza; *they — their brothers' blood*, sparsero il sangue dei loro fratelli; *to — tears*, versare lacrime ‖ *to — (a) light on a matter, fig.* far luce su una questione 2. lasciar cadere, disfarsi di, perdere: *he sheds his bad reputation as a snake its skin, fig.* si libera dalla sua cattiva reputazione come un serpente della pelle; *oilskin sheds water*, la tela cerata non lascia penetrare l'acqua; *those trees — their leaves*, quegli alberi perdono le foglie.

shed², *s.* tettoia; capannone; « hangar »; ripostiglio (d'arnesi, ecc.); riparo (per il bestiame).

to shed², *v.t. pass.p.p.* **shedded** [ˈʃedid], *v.t.* riparare sotto una tettoia; mettere in rimessa; riporre.

shedder [ˈʃedə*], *s.* 1. spargitore: *a — of blood*, un assassino 2. (*zool.*) crostaceo che si sta liberando del guscio 3. salmone che ha deposto le uova.

shedding [ˈʃediŋ], *s.* 1. spargimento, versamento 2. perdita; caduta (di foglie, ecc.); muda (di animali) 3. (*ind. tessile*) formazione del passo.

sheeling, *V.* **shieling**.

sheen [ʃiːn], *s.* splendore, lucentezza: *— on the hair*, lucentezza dei capelli.

sheeny [ˈʃiːni], *ag.* splendente, rilucente.

sheep [ʃiːp], *s.* (*invariato al pl.*) 1. pecora, ovino ‖ *the black — of the family, fig.* la pecora nera della famiglia ‖ *lost* (o *stray*) —, *fig.* pecorella smarrita ‖ *a wolf in —'s clothing*, un lupo in veste di agnello ‖ *that have no shepherd, fig.* folla smarrita, senza guida ‖ *one may as well be hanged for a — as a lamb*, tanto vale commettere un crimine grave che uno lieve (se la punizione è la stessa) ‖ *to cast —'s eyes at s.o.*, fare l'occhio di triglia a qlcu. ‖ *to follow like —*, seguire come pecore ‖ *to separate the — from the goats*, separare i buoni dai cattivi 2. *fig.* persona debole e timida 3. *fig.* membro di una comunità religiosa 4. cartapecora; bazzana ☆ — *-bot*, (*entom.*) estro della pecora; — *-dog*, cane da pastore; — *-faced*, timido, impacciato; — *-farmer*, allevatore di pecore; — *-fold* (o — *-cote*), ovile, chiuso; — *-like*, a mo' di pecora; — *-louse* (o — *-tick*), pidocchio della pecora; — *-run*, pascolo; — *'s head*, (*cuc.*) testicciola; *fig.* persona stupida; — *-shearing*, tosatura; — *-station*, azienda per l'allevamento degli ovini (in Australia).

sheepish [ˈʃiːpiʃ] *ag.* 1. timido, vergognoso; impacciato 2. sbigottito, confuso, sconcertato 3. sciocco.

sheepishly [ˈʃiːpiʃli], *av.* 1. timidamente, goffamente 2. con aria sbigottita 3. scioccamente.

sheepishness [ˈʃiːpiʃnis], *s.* 1. timidezza, goffaggine 2. aria sbigottita.

sheepskin [ˈʃiːp-skin], *s.* 1. pelle di pecora 2. indumento, tappeto di pelle di pecora 3. pergamena, cartapecora. 4. documento; diploma.

sheepwalk [ˈʃiːp-wɔːk], *s.* pascolo.

sheer¹ [ʃiə*], *ag.* 1. puro, semplice; assoluto: *a — waste of time*, una semplice perdita di tempo; *by — accident*, per mero caso; *it is a — madness*, è una pura follia 2. puro, liscio, non diluito (di bevande) 3. sottile, leggero, trasparente (di tessuti): *stockings of — silk*, calze di seta sottile 4. perpendicolare, a piombo, a picco (di muro, rocce, ecc.): *a — cliff*, una falesia.

to sheer¹, *v.i.* innalzarsi verticalmente (di rocce).

sheer¹, *av.* 1. del tutto, assolutamente, completamente 2. a piombo, perpendicolarmente, a picco.

sheer², *s.* (*mar.*) 1. virata, cambio di rotta 2. posizione di nave ormeggiata a ruota.

to sheer², *v.t.i.* 1. (*mar.*) deviare, far deviare; cambiar rotta 2. *to — off*, (*mar.*) scostarsi, allargarsi; *fig.* svignarsela, fuggire, prendere il largo.

sheer³, *s.* (*mar.*) insellatura, curvatura del ponte (della nave) ☆ — *-hulk*, (*mar.*) pontone a biga; — *-legs*, (*mar.*) biga, capra.

sheers [ʃiəz], *s.* — *-(legs)*, (*mar.*) biga, capra.

sheet¹ [ʃiːt], *s.* 1. lenzuolo ‖ *to get between the sheets*,

andare a letto ‖ *to stand in a white —*, pentirsi apertamente 2. foglio, pagina: *a — of paper*, un foglio di carta ‖ *a book in sheets*, un libro non rilegato 3. giornale, quotidiano 4. lamina, lamiera: *a — of iron*, una lamina di ferro 5. lastra, distesa (di ghiaccio, di neve); specchio (d'acqua) 6. (*arc. poet.*) vela 7. (*geol.*) filone ☆ — *bar*, (*metal.*) bidone; — *gauge*, (*mec.*) calibro per lamiere; — *glass*, lastra di vetro; — *-lightning*, baleno diffuso, lampeggio; — *metal worker*, (*ind.*) battilastra, lattoniere; — *piling*, (*edil.*) palizzata; — *-rubber*, (*ind.*) gomma in fogli ‖ *balance —*, (*comm.*) bilancio; *cone —*, (*geol.*) filone conico; *grid —*, carta quadrettata; *labor engagement —*, (*amer.*) modulo di assunzione; *tank —*, (*ind.*) lamiera per serbatoi; *winding - —*, sudario.

to sheet¹, *v.t.* 1. coprire con, avvolgere in un lenzuolo 2. foderare, rivestire: *to — a gallery*, (*miner.*) rivestire una galleria 3. coprire (con lastra, strato): *river sheeted with ice*, fiume ricoperto di ghiaccio.

sheet², *s.* (*mar.*) scotta: *to let a — fly*, mollare una scotta ‖ *three sheets in the wind*, (*fam.*) ubriaco ☆ — *-anchor*, (*mar.*) ancora di tonneggio; *fig.* ancora di salvezza; — *bend*, nodo di scotta, nodo di bandiera.

to sheet², *v.t.* (*mar.*) bordare; legare al bordo le scotte ‖ *to — home*, stringere il vento alando le scotte.

sheeted [ˈʃiːtid], *ag.* 1. avvolto in un lenzuolo 2. come, a somiglianza di un foglio 3. foderato; laminato.

sheetful [ˈʃiːtful], *s.* foglio pieno (di figure, numeri, ecc.).

sheeting [ˈʃiːtiŋ], *s.* 1. tela per lenzuola 2. rivestimento, copertura con fogli e lamiere 3. (*ind.*) materiale in fogli 4. (*geol.*) struttura lamellare ☆ — *mill*, (*ind.*) mescolatore per foglie.

sheik(h) [ʃeik], *s.* 1. sceicco 2. (*sl.*) rubacuori.

shekel [ˈʃekl], *s.* 1. siclo (moneta, peso ebraico) 2. *pl.* (*iron.*) denaro.

sheldrake [ˈʃel-dreik], *s.* (*ornit.*) volpoca (maschio).

shelduck [ˈʃeldʌk], *s.* (*ornit.*) volpoca (femmina).

shelf¹ [ʃelf], *pl.* **shelves** [ʃelvz], *s.* 1. palchetto, ripiano; mensola; scaffale, scansia ‖ *to be on the —*, essere messo in disparte; non aver prospettive matrimoniali (di donna) 2. sporgenza (di roccia) 3. (*mar.*) dormiente 4. (*geol.*) piattaforma ☆ — *-catalogue*, catalogo di biblioteca ordinato per ripiani; — *-mark*, segnatura (dei libri di una biblioteca).

shelf², *s.* secca, bassofondo (di mare, di fiume).

shelfy [ˈʃelfi], *ag.* pieno di secche, cosparso di scogli.

shell [ʃel], *s.* 1. conchiglia; guscio; scorza; crosta; squama, scaglia: *they used to gather shells on the seashore*, erano soliti raccogliere conchiglie sulla spiaggia ‖ *in the —*, nel guscio, non ancora nato; *fig.* in embrione ‖ *to come out of one's —*, uscire dal proprio guscio (anche *fig.*); *to retire into one's —*, ritirarsi nel proprio guscio (anche *fig.*) 2. involucro; carcassa; ossatura (di nave, edificio): *the — of a boiler*, l'involucro, il corpo di una caldaia; *after the fire only the — of the house was left*, dopo l'incendio era rimasta solo l'ossatura della casa 3. apparenza, parvenza: *a mere — of religion*, (*fam.*) una mera parvenza di religione 4. schema (di progetto, ecc.) 5. bossolo (di cartuccia); (*amer.*) cartuccia 6. (*artigl.*) proiettile; bomba; granata 7. bara interna; bara provvisoria 8. leggera imbarcazione da corsa, schifo 9. guardamano (di spada) 10. classe intermedia (di scuola) 11. (*poet. mus.*) lira 12. (*fis. atomica*) strato elettronico ☆ — *-less*, senza guscio, senza conchiglia; — *-like*, simile a conchiglia; — *-limestone*, calcare fossilifero; — *-mould*, (*metal.*) forma a guscio; — *plating*, (*mar.*) fasciame; — *-sand*, sabbia calcarea; — *transformer*, (*elett. mec.*) trasformatore a mantello, corazzato; — *-work*, decorazione a conchiglie ‖ *radiator —*, (*aut.*) intelaiatura esterna del radiatore.

to shell, *v.t.i.* 1. sgusciare, sgranare; uscir dal guscio: *to — peas*, sgranare piselli 2. (*artigl.*) bombardare **3.** ricoprire, ornare di conchiglie **4.** *to — out*, (*sl.*) pagare, tirar fuori del denaro.

she'll [ʃiːl], *contr.* di *she will, she shall*.

shellac [ʃə'læk], *s.* (*chim.*) gomma lacca.

to **shellac**, *pass. p.p.* **shellacked** [ʃə'lækt], *v.t.* verniciare con gomma lacca.

sheller ['ʃelə*], *s.c.* chi sbuccia, sguscia, sgrana ‖ *s.* sgranatoio; sgranellatoio.

shellfire ['ʃel,faiə*], *s.* bombardamento.

shellfish ['ʃel-fiʃ], *s.* crostaceo.

shelling ['ʃeliŋ], *s.* **1.** sbucciatura, sgranamento **2.** bombardamento, cannoneggiamento.

shellproof ['ʃel-pruːf], *ag.* a prova di bomba.

shellshock ['ʃel-ʃɔk], *s.* (*patol.*) psicosi traumatica (dovuta a bombardamento).

shelly ['ʃeli], *ag.* **1.** ricoperto di conchiglie; pieno di conchiglie **2.** a forma di conchiglia.

shelter ['ʃeltə*], *s.* riparo, tettoia; rifugio; *fig.* difesa, protezione: *under —*, al riparo; *to find —*, trovar rifugio, trovar asilo; *to take —*, ripararsi, rifugiarsi; *to take s.o. under one's —*, (*fam.*) prendere qlcu. sotto la propria protezione ☆ *air-raid —*, rifugio antiaereo; *Anderson —*, ricovero antiaereo trasportabile in lamiera ondulata.

to **shelter**, *v.t.i.* riparare, ripararsi; mettere al coperto; dar asilo a; proteggere: *he sheltered the escaping prisoner*, diede asilo al prigioniero fuggiasco; *the trenches sheltered the soldiers from the enemy's fire*, le trincee ripararono i soldati dal fuoco del nemico ‖ *sheltered trade*, commercio protetto contro la concorrenza straniera.

shelterer ['ʃeltərə*], *s.c.* **1.** chi offre un asilo; protettore, protettrice **2.** chi cerca rifugio.

shelterless ['ʃeltəlis], *ag.* senza riparo, senza asilo; senza difesa.

sheltie, shelty ['ʃelti], *s.* (*scoz.*) pony delle isole Shetland.

to **shelve**[1] [ʃelv], *v.t.* **1.** provvedere di scaffali **2.** mettere negli scaffali **3.** *fig.* differire, rinviare (soluzione, decisione, ecc.) **4.** licenziare.

to **shelve**[2], *v.i.* digradare (di declivio).

shelves [ʃelvz], *pl.* di **shelf**.

shelving[1] ['ʃelviŋ], *s.* **1.** scaffalatura, sistemazione a ripiani **2.** disposizione negli scaffali **3.** *fig.* differimento, rinvio **4.** licenziamento.

shelving[2], *ag.* degradante, in pendio ‖ *s.* pendio, pendenza.

Shem [ʃem], *no.pr.m.* (*Bibbia*) Sem.

to **shend** [ʃend], *pass.p.p.* **shent** [ʃent], *v.t.* **1.** (*arc.*) infamare, esporre al disprezzo **2.** biasimare, riprendere **3.** danneggiare, oltraggiare.

shepherd ['ʃepəd], *s.* **1.** pastore, pecoraio **2.** *fig.* ministro del culto; prete ‖ *the Good Shepherd*, il Buon Pastore ☆ *—'s club*, (*bot.*) verbasco; *—'s crook*, bastone da pastore; *—'s plaid*, stoffa di lana a quadretti bianchi e neri; *—'s purse*, (*bot.*) borsa di pastore.

to **shepherd**, *v.t.* **1.** guardare, custodire (pecore) **2.** *fig.* guidare; aver cura di: *to — one's own interests*, curarsi dei propri interessi; *to — school-children through the town*, (*fam.*) guidare gli scolari per la città.

shepherdess ['ʃepədis], *s.* pastora, pecoraia: *young —*, pastorella.

sherbet ['ʃəːbət], *s.* succo di frutta.

sherd [ʃəːd], *s.* coccio.

shereef [ʃə'riːf], *s.* **1.** sceriffo, discendente di Maometto **2.** primo magistrato della Mecca.

sheriff ['ʃerif], *s.* sceriffo ☆ *— -clerk*, (*scoz.*) cancelliere di tribunale; *— -officer*, (*scoz.*) ufficiale giudiziario.

sheriffalty ['ʃerifəlti], **sheriffdom** ['ʃerifdəm], **sheriffhood** ['ʃerifhud], **sheriffship** ['ʃerifʃip], *s.* ufficio, carica di sceriffo.

sherry ['ʃeri], *s.* « sherry » (vino di Xeres).

she's [ʃiːz], *contr.* di *she is, she has*.

to **shew**, *V.* to **show**.

Shiah ['ʃiːə], *s.* (*st. relig.*) sciita.

shibboleth ['ʃibəleθ], *s.* **1.** parola, attitudine (comprovanti l'appartenenza a una particolare classe, par-

tito, setta) **2.** formula, parola d'ordine **3.** dottrina antiquata e screditata.

shield [ʃiːld], *s.* **1.** scudo ‖ *the other side of the —*, (*fam.*) il rovescio della medaglia **2.** *fig.* protezione, difesa: *the Lord is our help and our —*, il Signore è il nostro aiuto e protezione **3.** (*mec.*) schermo protettivo **4.** (*arald.*) stemma; scudo **5.** guscio (di animale) ☆ *— -hand*, (*arc.*) mano sinistra; *— -maid* (o *— -maiden*), (*rar*) amazzone.

to **shield**, *v.t.* **1.** proteggere, difendere: *her youth and innocence shielded her from danger*, la sua giovinezza e la sua innocenza la protessero dal pericolo; *to — s.o. with one's own body*, fare scudo del proprio corpo a qlcu. **2.** salvare, proteggere (da punizione): *I told a lie to — my friend*, ho detto una bugia per salvare il mio amico **3.** (*mec.*) schermare.

shieldless ['ʃiːldlis], *ag.* senza scudo; *fig.* indifeso.

shieling ['ʃiːliŋ], *s.* (*scoz.*) **1.** pascolo **2.** riparo (per pastori, cacciatori) **3.** ovile.

shift [ʃift], *s.* **1.** cambiamento; sostituzione; avvicendamento; (*agr.*) rotazione: *— of crops*, rotazione di colture; *— of wind*, cambiamento di vento **2.** risorsa; espediente; sotterfugio: *to live on shifts*, vivere di espedienti ‖ *to be at one's last —*, essere all'estremo delle proprie risorse ‖ *to make (a) —*, arrangiarsi ‖ *to make — with*, accontentarsi di **3.** turno; squadra (di lavoro): *to work in shifts*, lavorare a squadre **4.** (*arc.*) camicia (da donna) **5.** (*dial.*) trasloco ☆ *— -key*, tasto maiuscole (di macchina per scrivere); *— lock*, (*tasto*) fissa maiuscole (di macchina per scrivere); *— -work*, lavoro a turni ‖ *day- —*, turno di giorno; *night- —*, turno di notte.

to **shift**, *v.t.i.* **1.** spostare, spostarsi; trasferire, trasferirsi; cambiare; sostituire: *he shifted the rifle from his right to his left shoulder*, spostò il fucile dalla spalla destra alla sinistra; *the scene shifted*, la scena cambiò; *they — their lodgings*, cambiano casa, traslocano; *they went to — their clothes*, (*dial.*) andarono a cambiarsi gli abiti; *to — responsibility on to s.o. else*, riversare la responsabilità su qlcu. altro ‖ *to — the helm*, (*mar.*) spostare la barra ‖ *to — one's ground*, *fig.* prendere un nuovo atteggiamento (in una discussione, ecc.) **2.** arrangiarsi, ingegnarsi, ricorrere ad espedienti: *they had to — for themselves*, dovettero cavarsela da soli **3.** (*aut.*) cambiare la marcia **4.** *to — about*, cambiare continuamente di posto **5.** *to — off*, liberarsi, sbarazzarsi di: *to — off a load*, liberarsi di un peso.

shiftable ['ʃiftəbl], *ag.* movibile; sostituibile.

shifter ['ʃiftə*], *s.c.* **1.** chi cambia, sposta (scene, ecc.) **2.** persona malfida; imbroglione, imbrogliona ‖ *s.* (*mec.*) dispositivo spostatore ‖ *belt —*, (*mec.*) spostacinghia; *scene- —*, (*teat.*) macchinista.

shiftily ['ʃiftili], *av.* **1.** volubilmente **2.** astutamente, scaltramente; ambiguamente.

shiftiness ['ʃiftinis], *s.* **1.** volubilità **2.** astuzia, scaltrezza; ambiguità.

shifting ['ʃiftiŋ], *ag.* **1.** mutevole; mobile **2.** astuto, scaltro; ambiguo ‖ *s.* cambiamento, spostamento ☆ *— sands*, sabbie mobili.

shiftingly ['ʃiftiŋli], *av.* **1.** mutevolmente **2.** astutamente, con espedienti, con raggiri.

shiftless ['ʃiftlis], *ag.* **1.** senza risorse, incapace, inabile **2.** insufficiente, inefficace.

shiftlessly ['ʃiftlisli], *av.* **1.** inettamente **2.** inefficacemente.

shiftlessness ['ʃiftlisnis], *s.* **1.** inettitudine, incapacità **2.** inefficacia, insufficienza.

shifty ['ʃifti], *ag.* **1.** volubile; mutevole **2.** malfido, ambiguo; astuto: *— glance*, sguardo sfuggente; *that fellow is too — to be trusted*, quell'individuo è troppo ambiguo perchè se ne possa avere fiducia.

Shiite ['ʃiːait], *s.* (*st. relig.*) sciita.

shilling ['ʃiliŋ], *s.* scellino ‖ *to cut s.o. off with a —*, diseredare qlcu. ‖ *to take the King's* (o *Queen's*) *—*, (*st.*) arruolarsi nell'esercito.

shillingsworth ['ʃiliŋzwə:θ], s. valore di uno scellino.

shilly-shally ['ʃili,ʃæli], ag. esitante, indeciso, tentennante ‖ s. esitazione, indecisione.

to shilly-shally, v.i. esitare, tentennare.

shim [ʃim], s. (mec.) zeppa, spessore.

to shim, pass.p.p. **shimmed** [ʃimd], v.t. (mec.) inserire spessori, zeppe in.

shimmer ['ʃimə*], s. luccichio, bagliore; scintillio.

to shimmer, v.i. luccicare, mandare bagliori, riflessi.

shimmy[1] ['ʃimi], s. (fam.) camicia (da donna).

shimmy[2], s. **1.** « shimmy » (danza) **2.** (aut.) « shimmy ».

to shimmy[2], v.i. ballare lo « shimmy ».

shin [ʃin], s. **1.** (anat.) cresta tibiale **2.** garretto di bue ☆ — -bone, (anat.) tibia; — -guard, parastinchi; — -plaster, (fam. amer.) banconota di piccolo taglio.

to shin, pass.p.p. **shinned** [ʃind], v.t.i. **1.** dare un calcio negli stinchi a **2.** to — around, (amer.) correre qua e là **3.** to — down, discendere precipitosamente **4.** to — off, battersela, svignarsela **5.** to — up, arrampicarsi a forza di braccia e gambe: to — up a tree, arrampicarsi su un albero.

shindy ['ʃindi], s. (fam.) chiasso, baccano ‖ to kick up a —, fare un gran baccano, fare il diavolo a quattro.

shine[1] [ʃain], s. **1.** splendore; luminosità, lucentezza: dazzled by the — of gold, abbagliato dallo splendore dell'oro ‖ to take the — out of, togliere la lucentezza a; fig. eclissare, diminuire lo splendore di **2.** luce del sole, bel tempo ‖ rain or —, qualunque sia il tempo **3.** lucidatura, lucidata (di scarpe): to give one's shoes a good —, (fam.) dare una buona lucidata alle proprie scarpe.

to shine[1], pass.p.p. **shone**[ʃon], nei sensi **3.** e **4.** **shined** [ʃaind], v.t.i. **1.** splendere, brillare (anche fig.); emettere, riflettere luce: a cat's eyes — in the dark, gli occhi del gatto brillano nella oscurità; his face shone with gratitude, il suo viso brillava di gratitudine; the sun is shining, il sole brilla **2.** essere brillante, eccellere: he does not — in conversation, non è brillante nella conversazione **3.** (amer.) lucidare: he has shined your boots, ti ha lucidato gli stivali **4.** to — up, (fam.) pulire, lucidare, lustrare ‖ to — up to s.o., (pop. amer.) cercare di cattivarsi la simpatia di qlcu.

shine[2], s. **1.** festa, riunione conviviale **2.** rissa; baccano, rumore **3.** pl. scherzi, burle **4.** to take a — to, (pop. amer.) invaghirsi di.

shiner ['ʃainə*], s. **1.** cosa che splende, che brilla **2.** lustrascarpe **3.** (fam.) moneta d'oro; pl. denaro **4.** (amer. ittiol.) lasca; sgombro **5.** (sl. amer.) un occhio nero, pesto.

shingle[1] ['ʃiŋgl], s. **1.** (edil.) assicella di copertura **2.** (fam. amer.) targa, insegna **3.** taglio dei capelli « à la garçonne ».

to shingle[1], v.t. **1.** (edil.) coprire con assicelle **2.** tagliare (i capelli) « à la garçonne ».

shingle[2], s. **1.** ciottoli **2.** greto ciottoloso.

to shingle[3], v.t. (metal.) disincrostare al maglio, eliminare le scorie da.

shingles ['ʃiŋglz], s.pl. (patol.) fuoco di Sant'Antonio.

shingly ['ʃiŋgli], ag. **1.** ciottoloso **2.** simile a ciottolo.

shining ['ʃainiŋ], ag. risplendente, brillante; luminoso.

Shinto ['ʃintou], **Shintoism** ['ʃintouizəm], s. (relig.) scintoismo.

Shintoist ['ʃintouist], s.c. (relig.) scintoista.

shiny ['ʃaini], ag. rilucente, splendente; scintillante; lustro, lucido: a — day, un giorno radioso; clothes made — by long wear, abiti lucidi per l'uso ‖ s. oggetto lucente ‖ the —, (sl.) denaro.

ship [ʃip], s. **1.** nave; bastimento; vascello: — lying at anchor, nave alla fonda; launch of a —, varo di una nave ‖ — of the desert, cammello ‖ when his — comes home, fig. quando farà fortuna ‖ to take —, imbarcarsi **2.** (sl.) barca (specialmente da regata) **3.** (amer.) aeroplano; dirigibile ☆ — -biscuit, galletta (per marinai); — -boy, (mar.) mozzo; — -breaker, chi smantella vecchie navi; — -broker, agente di navigazione; agente di assicurazione marittima; — -canal, canale navigabile;

— ('s)-carpenter, carpentiere navale; — -chandler, fornitore navale; — -fever, (patol.) tifo; — -holder, (ittiol.) remora; — -load, carico completo di una nave; — -master, capitano di nave; — -money, (st.) tassa imposta alle città di mare; — -of-the-line, (st.) vascello di linea; — -owner, armatore; —'s articles, (mar.) contratto d'ingaggio; —'s company, (mar.) equipaggio (esclusi gli ufficiali); —'s husband, (mar.) raccomandatario; —'s papers, documenti di bordo; — -way, (mar.) scalo (di varo, ecc.); canale navigabile; — -worm, (zool.) bruma; cargo- —, nave da carico; coast- — (o defence- —), nave guardacoste; convoy- —, nave scorta; flag- —, nave ammiraglia; hospital- —, nave ospedale; landing - —, mezzo da sbarco; merchant- —, nave mercantile; oil —, petroliera; repair- —, nave officina; sailing- —, veliero; seagoing- —, nave di lungo corso; sister- —, nave gemella.

to ship, v.t.i. **1.** imbarcare, imbarcarsi; caricare; prendere a bordo; ingaggiare: he shipped as a cook, si imbarcò come cuoco; to — a crew for a voyage, ingaggiare un equipaggio per un viaggio ‖ to — water, imbarcare acqua **2.** (comm.) spedire: to — goods to America, spedire delle merci in America **3.** partire (per nave): we — from Marseilles tomorrow, partiamo da Marsiglia domani **4.** (mar.) montare, mettere in posizione ‖ to — the oars, disarmare i remi **5.** to — off, mandar via: to — a young man off to the colonies, mandare, spedire un giovane nelle colonie.

shipboard ['ʃipbo:d], s. (mar.) bordo: on —, a bordo.

shipbuilder ['ʃip,bildə*], s. costruttore navale; ingegnere navale.

shipman, pl. **shipmen** ['ʃipmən], s. (arc.) **1.** marinaio **2.** capitano; pilota.

shipmate ['ʃipmeit], s. compagno di bordo, di navigazione.

shipment ['ʃipmənt], s. **1.** imbarco, spedizione (di merci) **2.** carico.

shippen ['ʃipən], s. (spec. dial.) stalla.

shipper ['ʃipə*], s. (comm.) spedizioniere marittimo.

shipping ['ʃipiŋ], s. **1.** forze navali; marina mercantile **2.** imbarco; spedizione ☆ — -agent, agente di navigazione; (comm.) spedizioniere; — -articles, (mar.) contratto di ingaggio; — -bill, (comm.) dichiarazione di sortita, bolletta di uscita (per merci soggette a dazio); — -company, compagnia di navigazione; — -documents, documenti di imbarco; — -master, commissario di bordo; — -office, agenzia di navigazione; — -trade, commercio marittimo.

shippon ['ʃipən], s. (spec. dial.) stalla.

shipshape, [,ʃipʃeip], ag. ordinato; pulito ‖ av. in perfetto ordine.

shipwreck ['ʃip-rek], s. **1.** naufragio: to suffer —, far naufragio **2.** relitto di nave naufragata **3.** fig. rovina, distruzione: the — of one's hopes, il crollo delle proprie speranze ‖ to make — of, rovinare, distruggere.

to shipwreck, v.t.i. naufragare; far naufragare (anche fig.): he was shipwrecked, fece naufragio.

shipwright ['ʃip-rait], s. (mar.) maestro d'ascia.

shipyard ['ʃip-ja:d], s. arsenale, cantiere navale.

shire ['ʃaiə*, come suffisso ʃiə*, ʃə*], s. contea ‖ the Shires, le contee dell'Inghilterra centrale ☆ — -bred horse (o — -horse), grosso cavallo da tiro; — -moot, (arc.) tribunale di contea; — -reeve, (arc.) sceriffo.

shirk [ʃə:k], s.c. scansafatiche.

to shirk, v.t. schivare, evitare; eludere; sottrarsi a: to — the question, eludere la domanda; to — responsibility, sottrarsi alla responsabilità.

shirker ['ʃə:kə*], s.c. scansafatiche.

shirt [ʃə:t], s. **1.** camicia (da uomo) ‖ to get s.o.'s — off, (sl.) far arrabbiare qlcu.; to have one's — out, (sl.) adirarsi ‖ to keep one's — on, mantenersi calmo ‖ to put one's — on (o upon), (sl.) scommettere fino all'ultimo soldo su **2.** camicetta di foggia maschile ☆ — -collar, colletto di camicia; — -front, sparato di camicia; — -sleeves, maniche di camicia.

to **shirt**, *v.t.* far indossare la camicia a.

shirting ['ʃə:tiŋ], *s.* tela per camicie.

shirtless ['ʃə:tlis], *ag.* senza camicia.

shirtwaist ['ʃə:tweist], *s.* (*amer.*) camicetta.

shirty ['ʃə:ti], *ag.* (*sl.*) irascibile, irritabile; incollerito.

shit [ʃit], *s.* merda.

shive [ʃaiv], *s.* (*dial.*) **1.** fetta (di pane) **2.** turacciolo piatto e sottile.

shiver[1] ['ʃivə*], *s.* **1.** scheggia, frammento: *the glass fell and broke into shivers*, il bicchiere cadde ed andò in frantumi **2.** pietra schistosa **3.** (*mec.*) puleggia.

to **shiver**[1], *v.t.i.* frantumare, frantumarsi; fracassare, mandare in pezzi ‖ *— my timbers!*, (*sl. mar.*) alla malora!.

shiver[2], *s.* brivido, fremito: *a — went down his back*, un brivido gli corse per la schiena ‖ *the shivers*, febbre malarica; (*fam.*) brivido di raccapriccio.

to **shiver**[2], *v.t.i.* **1.** rabbrividire; tremare: *to — with cold, with fear*, rabbrividire dal freddo, dalla paura **2.** (*mar.*) fileggiare; ralingare.

shivering ['ʃivəriŋ], *ag.* tremante; tremolante ‖ *s.* brivido; tremore.

shiveringly ['ʃivəriŋli], *av.* tremando, rabbrividendo.

shivery[1] ['ʃivəri], *ag.* fragile, facile a rompersi.

shivery[2], *ag.* tremante; in preda ai brividi: *to feel —*, avere i brividi; aver freddo; sentirsi febbricitante.

shoal[1] [ʃoul], *ag.* poco profondo ‖ *s.* **1.** secca, bassofondo **2.** *gener. pl. fig.* insidie, pericoli nascosti ☆ *—-mark*, indicazione di secca.

to **shoal**[1], *v.i.* diminuire di profondità (di fondo marino).

shoal[2], *s.* moltitudine, gran quantità; banco (di pesci) ‖ *in shoals*, in gran quantità.

to **shoal**[2], *v.i.* affollarsi, riunirsi in banchi (di pesci).

shoaliness ['ʃoulinis], *s.* (*rar.*) scarsa profondità; frequenza di secche.

shoaly ['ʃouli], *ag.* poco profondo; pieno di secche.

shock[1] [ʃok], *s.* **1.** collisione, cozzo; colpo: *the — of a fall*, il colpo di una caduta **2.** «shock», forte impressione, colpo, violenta emozione: *it gave me a dreadful —*, mi diede una forte emozione **3.** (*patol.*) collasso; colpo; sindrome: *he died of —*, morì per un collasso **4.** (*geol.*) sismo **5.** (*elett.*) scossa **6.** (*mil.*) scontro, assalto ☆ *—-absorber*, (*mec.*) ammortizzatore; *— excitation*, (*rad.*) eccitazione ad impulso; *— tactics*, tattica d'urto; *—-troops*, truppe d'assalto; *— wave*, (*aer.*) onda d'urto ‖ *apoplectic —*, (*patol.*) colpo apoplettico; *earthquake —*, scossa di terremoto.

to **shock**[1], *v.t.i.* **1.** colpire; disgustare; scandalizzare: *a book that is shocking the public*, un libro che scandalizza il pubblico; *he is easily shocked*, si scandalizza con facilità; *he was shocked at* (o *by*) *the news of his friend's death*, fu colpito dalla notizia della morte del suo amico **2.** provocare uno shock, un collasso **3.** dare una scossa elettrica **4.** collidere, scontrarsi.

shock[2], *s.* bica, mucchio di covoni di grano.

to **shock**[2], *v.t.* far biche, ammucchiare covoni di grano.

shock[3], *s.* folta chioma ☆ *—-head*, testa, capelli arruffati; *—-headed*, dai capelli arruffati.

shocker[1] ['ʃokə*], *s.c.* chi colpisce ‖ *s.* **1.** cosa che colpisce **2.** romanzo scandalistico.

shocker[2], *s.c.* persona che ammucchia covoni ‖ *s.* macchina per ammucchiare covoni.

shocking ['ʃokiŋ], *ag.* **1.** che colpisce; disgustoso, sconveniente: *a — behaviour*, un comportamento disgustoso **2.** (*fam.*) pessimo, abominevole: *a — lunch*, una colazione orribile; *— weather*, un tempo infame ‖ *av.* terribilmente, molto: *— bad*, (*fam.*) terribilmente cattivo.

shockingly ['ʃokiŋli], *av.* **1.** terribilmente, disgustosamente **2.** estremamente, eccessivamente.

shockingness ['ʃokiŋnis], *s.* ciò che colpisce, disgusta.

shod [ʃod], *pass.p.p.* di to **shoe** ‖ *ag.* **1.** calzato **2.** ferrato **3.** rivestito, ricoperto.

shoddy ['ʃodi], *ag.* **1.** scadente e pretenzioso (di

cosa) **2.** pretenzioso, falso (di persona) ‖ *s.* **1.** lana rigenerata; cascame **2.** roba scadente e appariscente.

shoe [ʃu:], *s.* **1.** scarpa, calzatura: *shoes down at heel*, scarpe scalcagnate; *she buys her shoes at Smith's*, si compera le scarpe da Smith ‖ *dead men's shoes*, proprietà, posizione a cui aspira il presunto erede ‖ *that's another pair of shoes*, questo è un'altro paio di maniche ‖ *that's where the — pinches!*, ecco le difficoltà!, ecco gli svantaggi! ‖ *to be in s.o.'s shoes*, essere nei panni di qlcu. ‖ *to die in one's shoes*, morire di morte violenta ‖ *to put the — on the right foot*, biasimare con ragione ‖ *to shake in one's shoes*, tremare di paura **2.** ferro di cavallo **3.** puntale **4.** (*elett. ferr.*) pattino **5.** (*mec.*) ceppo ☆ *— brake*, (*mec.*) freno a ceppi; *—-brush*, spazzola per scarpe; *—-buckle*, fibbia di scarpa; *—-cream*, lucido da scarpe; *—-lace* (o *—-string*), stringa; *—-leather*, cuoio per calzature: *as good a man as ever trod —-leather*, il miglior uomo del mondo.

to **shoe**, *pass.p.p.* **shod** [ʃod], (*rar.*) **shoeed** [ʃu:d], *v.t.* **1.** calzare, mettere le scarpe a **2.** ferrare (cavalli) **3.** coprire, rivestire.

shoeblack ['ʃu:blæk], *s.* lustrascarpe.

shoehorn ['ʃu:ho:n], *s.* corno da scarpa.

shoeless ['ʃu:lis], *ag.* senza scarpe, scalzo.

shoemaker ['ʃu:,meikə*], *s.* calzolaio, ciabattino.

shoemaking ['ʃu:,meikiŋ], *s.* calzoleria, arte del calzolaio.

shoer ['ʃu:ə*], *s.* maniscalco.

shone [ʃon], *pass.p.p.* di to **shine**.

shoo [ʃu:], *inter.* sciò (suono emesso per spaventare gli uccelli).

to **shoo**, *v.t.i.* far sciò-sciò (per spaventare gli uccelli).

shook[1] [ʃuk], *s.* **1.** (*spec. amer.*) fascio di doghe e fondi (per la costruzione di botti, ecc.) **2.** bica di covoni.

to **shook**[1], *v.t.* (*spec. amer.*) raccogliere in fasci.

shook[2], *pass.* di to **shake**.

shoot [ʃu:t], *s.* **1.** partita, spedizione di caccia **2.** riserva di caccia **3.** germoglio, virgulto **4.** rapida (di fiume) **5.** puntura, fitta **6.** getto d'acqua, zampillo **7.** (*tec.*) condotto inclinato, scivolo **8.** (*geol.*) giacimento (di minerali) **9.** (*edil.*) spinta (di arco).

to **shoot**, *pass.p.p.* **shot** [ʃot], *v.t.i.* **1.** lanciare, lanciarsi; gettare, gettarsi: *we were shot out of the carriage*, fummo gettati fuori dalla carrozza; *to — an arrow*, scoccare una freccia; *to — dice*, gettare i dadi; *to — a glance*, lanciare un'occhiata **2.** scaricare (un fucile); sparare, tirare: *he shoots well*, tira bene; *to — at s.o.*, far fuoco su qlcu.; *to — straight*, mirar bene ‖ *to — one's bolt*, sparare le proprie cartucce ‖ *to — wide of the mark*, mirar male **3.** uccidere sparando; fucilare: *to — s.o. with a revolver*, uccidere qlcu. con un revolver ‖ *to — s.o. dead*, colpire a morte qlcu. **4.** cacciare: *to — sparrows*, cacciar passeri ‖ *to — a match*, partecipare a una gara di tiro **5.** muoversi, passare rapidamente: *the dog shot past us*, il cane passò come un lampo accanto a noi; *I have shooting pains in my legs*, ho dolori lancinanti alle gambe ‖ *to — ahead of s.o.*, superare qlcu. ‖ *to — the moon*, (*sl.*) far trasloco di notte per non pagare l'affitto **6.** versare: *to — coal into the cellar*, rovesciare carbone in cantina ‖ *to — the cat*, (*sl.*) vomitare **7.** fotografare, fare una istantanea a: *to — a film*, girare un film ‖ *—!*, (*cine.*) si gira! **8.** (*bot.*) germogliare **9.** (*calcio*) sparare in rete **10.** scendere, precipitare (di rapide) **11.** (*astr.*) determinare l'altezza di (una stella) **12.** (*mec.*) azionare **13.** (*artig.*) piallare **14.** *to — away*, abbattere (con arma da fuoco); continuare a sparare; esaurire le munizioni **15.** *to — off*, sfrecciar via; (*spor.*) fare un'eliminatoria (per gara di tiro) **16.** *to — out*, (far) uscire; protendersi: *that cape shoots out into the sea*, quel capo si protende nel mare ‖ *to — out one's tongue*, tirar fuori la lingua **17.** *to — up*, salire (di prezzi); guizzare (di fiamme); germogliare (di piante); crescere (di bimbi); (*amer.*) terrorizzare (con colpi di fucile).

shooter ['ʃu:tə*], *s.c.* cacciatore, cacciatrice; tiratore, tiratrice ‖ *s.* **1.** cannoniere; arciere **2.** rivoltella ☆ *six-* —, rivoltella a sei colpi.

shooting ['ʃu:tiŋ], *s.* **1.** tiro, sparo; scarica (di fucile) **2.** caccia **3.** riserva di caccia **4.** spasimo, fitta; dolore lancinante **5.** il fotografare; il girare un film **6.** germoglio ☆ — *-box* (o — *-lodge*), casino di caccia; — *-coat* (o — *-jacket*), giacca da cacciatore; — *-gallery*, sala di tiro al bersaglio; — *-licence*, licenza di caccia; — *-party*, partita di caccia; — *-pocket*, carniere; — *-range*, tiro a segno; — *-star*, stella cadente, meteora.

shop [ʃɔp], *s.* **1.** bottega, negozio, magazzino, fondaco: *chemist's* —, farmacia; *to go from* — *to* —, fare il giro dei negozi; *to keep a* —, tenere un negozio ‖ *all over the* —, dappertutto; in disordine ‖ *you have come to the wrong* —, (*fam.*) sei capitato male **2.** officina, laboratorio, fucina ‖ *to go through the shops*, seguire un corso di apprendistato **3.** professione, mestiere; affari ‖ *to shut up* —, ritirarsi dagli affari, dal lavoro ‖ *to sink* —, evitare di parlare d'affari; *to talk* —, parlare di affari, del proprio mestiere **4.** (*sl.*) istituzione; edificio (dove si svolge un'attività) ‖ *the Shop*, (*sl. mil.*) l'accademia militare reale di Woolwich ☆ — *-assistant*, commesso di negozio; — *-book*, libro dei conti; — *-boy*, commesso, fattorino; — *-equipment*, (*mec.*) attrezzatura di officina; — *front*, facciata di negozio; — *-girl*, commessa; — *hours*, orario di negozio; — *-lifter*, taccheggiatore; — *-lifting*, taccheggio; — *like*, comune, grossolano; — *-steward*, rappresentante sindacale di officina; — *-window*, vetrina; — *-woman*, bottegaia, commessa di negozio ‖ *assembling* —, (*mec.*) officina di montaggio; *body* —, (*aut. mec.*) reparto lastratura (della scocca); *pattern* —, (*metal.*) reparto modellisti.

to **shop**, *pass.p.p.* **shopped** [ʃɔpt], *v.t.i.* **1.** far compere, fare acquisti: *to go shopping*, andare a far spese **2.** (*sl.*) chiudere in gattabuia; far imprigionare.

shopboard ['ʃɔpbo:d], *s.* banco (di negozio).

shopkeeper ['ʃɔp,ki:pə*], *s.c.* negoziante.

shopkeeping ['ʃɔp,ki:piŋ], *s.* commercio al minuto.

shopman, *pl.* **shopmen** ['ʃɔpmən], *s.* **1.** commesso di negozio **2.** (*rar.*) bottegaio **3.** (*amer.*) operaio d'officina.

shopper ['ʃɔpə*], *s.c.* chi gira per i negozi, chi fa compere.

shopping ['ʃɔpiŋ], *s.* compere, acquisti; visita ai negozi: *to go* —, fare acquisti ☆ — *'-bag*, borsa per la spesa; — *centre*, zona degli acquisti.

shoppy ['ʃɔpi], *ag.* **1.** da bottega, da bottegaio: — *manners*, modi da bottegaio **2.** pieno di negozi: *a* — *neighbourhood*, quartiere pieno di negozi.

shopworn ['ʃɔpwɔ:n], *ag.* sciupato, scolorito (per essere stato esposto in vetrina).

shore[1] [ʃo:*], *s.* **1.** spiaggia, lido; riva, sponda; (*mar.*) terra: *on the* —, sulla spiaggia ‖ *in* —, vicino alla costa; *off* —, al largo; *on* —, a terra: *to set foot on* —, (*mar.*) sbarcare, scendere a terra ‖ *to hug the* —, costeggiare **2.** (*poet.*) paese **3.** (*dir.*) tratto di spiaggia delimitato dai segni di alta e bassa marea ☆ — *-boat*, battello costiero; — *-crab*, (*zool.*) granchio riparo; — *fast*, (*mar.*) cavo d'ormeggio; — *-leave*, congedo, permesso di scendere a terra; — *-line*, linea costiera.

to **shore**[1], *v.t.i.* (*mar.*) **1.** (far) sbarcare, scendere a terra **2.** costeggiare.

shore[2], *s.* (*edil.*) puntello, sostegno ☆ *bilge* —, (*mar.*) puntello di sentina.

to **shore**[2], *v.t.* (*edil.*) puntellare: *to* — (*up*) *a wall*, puntellare un muro.

shore[3], *s.* (*arc.*) per **sewer**[2].

shore[4], *pass.* di to **shear**[1].

shoreless ['ʃo:lis], *ag.* senza sponda, illimitato.

shoreward ['ʃo:wəd], *ag.* diretto verso la spiaggia.

shoreward(s) ['ʃo:wəd(z)], *av.* verso la spiaggia.

shoring ['ʃo:riŋ], *s.* (*edil.*) puntellamento.

shorl [ʃo:l], *s.* (*min.*) tormalina nera.

shorn [ʃo:n], *p.p.* di to **shear** ‖ *ag.* tosato, rasato.

short [ʃo:t], *ag.* **1.** corto; breve: — *hair*, capelli corti; — *steps*, piccoli passi; *a* — *syllable*, (fonet.) una sillaba breve; *a* — *winter*, un inverno breve; *the string is* —, lo spago è corto ‖ *a* — *time ago*, poco tempo fa ‖ *a* — *way off*, poco lontano ‖ *at* — *notice*, con breve preavviso **2.** basso, piccolo (di statura): *a* — *man*, un uomo basso; — *stature*, di statura piccola **3.** conciso, breve, serrato: *in speaking one should be* —, nel parlare si dovrebbe essere concisi ‖ *in* —, in breve ‖ *he is called Bob for* —, il suo diminutivo è Bob ‖ *to cut* —, tagliar corto: *to cut a long story* —, a farla breve **4.** brusco, rude, sgarbato: *he was very* — *with me*, è stato molto brusco nei miei riguardi **5.** scarso, insufficiente; mancante: — *of money*, a corto di denaro; *a* — *ten miles*, dieci miglia scarse; *he never gives* — *weight*, non fa mai peso scarso; *we are three collars* —, ci mancano tre colletti ‖ *he is* — *of breath*, è senza fiato ‖ *to fall* —, essere insufficiente ‖ *to fall* (o *to come*) — *of*, mancare, fallire, non raggiungere pienamente ‖ *to run* —, scarseggiare: *our tea is running* —, il nostro tè sta finendo ‖ *to run* — *of*, essere a corto di **6.** friabile, fragile **7.** (*comm.*) a breve scadenza (di tratta) **8.** non disponibile (di azioni, merce, ecc. vendute allo scoperto): *copper is* — *today*, il rame non è disponibile oggi **9.** (*fam.*) non diluito, forte: *she wanted sthg.* —, aveva bisogno di ql.co. di forte.

short,¦ *s.* **1.** vocabolo, sillaba breve: *longs and shorts*, le lunghe e le brevi **2.** (*neol. cine.*) cortometraggio **3.** *pl.* calzoncini corti.

short, *av.* **1.** bruscamente; improvvisamente: *he pulled up* —, si fermò di botto; *she took him up* —, lo interruppe; *to stop* —, fermarsi bruscamente **2.** (*comm.*) allo scoperto: *to sell* —, vendere allo scoperto (azioni, merci, ecc.) **3.** — *of*, eccetto, fuorchè: — *of what is dishonourable, I will do anything to help you*, per aiutarti farò tutto, tranne ciò che è disonorevole.

short, (*nei composti*): — *-cut*, scorciatoia; — *-dated*, (*comm.*) a breve scadenza; — *-fall*, deficienza di produzione; — *-handed*, scarso di mano d'opera; — *-horn*, bue dalle corna corte; — *-lived*, di breve durata, di breve vita; — *-sight*, miopia; — *-sighted*, miope; — *-spoken*, secco, brusco nel parlare; — *-staple*, dalla fibra corta; — *-sword*, spada dalla lama corta; — *-tempered*, irascibile; — *-waisted*, dalla vita alta; — *waves*, (*rad.*) onde corte; — *-winded*, dal fiato corto.

shortage ['ʃo:tidʒ], *s.* deficienza, mancanza, carenza: — *of food*, carenza di cibo; — *of staff*, mancanza di personale ‖ *to make up the* —, (*comm.*) colmare il deficit.

shortbread ['ʃo:tbred], **shorteake** ['ʃo:tkeik], *s.* torta, biscotti di pasta frolla.

short-eircuit ['ʃo:t'sə:kit], *s.* (*elett.*) corto circuito.

to **short-eircuit**, *v.t.i.* provocare un corto circuito: *to* — *the motor*, (elett.) chiudere il motore in corto circuito.

shortcoming ['ʃo:t'kʌmiŋ], *s.* **1.** mancanza, insufficienza, deficit: *a* — *in money*, una mancanza di denaro **2.** *pl.* difetti, imperfezioni.

to **shorten** ['ʃo:tn], *v.t.i.* **1.** accorciare, accorciarsi; diminuire, abbreviare: *to* — *a price*, (*comm.*) ridurre, diminuire un prezzo ‖ *to* — *sails*, (*mar.*) ridurre le vele ‖ *to* — *step*, (*mil.*) accorciare il passo **2.** rendere friabile.

shortener ['ʃo:tnə*], *s.c.* chi abbrevia ‖ *s.* ciò che abbrevia.

shortening ['ʃo:tniŋ], *ag.* che diminuisce; che si accorcia ‖ *s.* **1.** accorciamento, abbreviazione; diminuzione **2.** grasso usato in pasticceria.

shorthand ['ʃo:thænd], *s.* stenografia: *to take down in* —, stenografare ☆ — *typist*, stenodattilografo; — *writer*, stenografo.

shortly ['ʃo:tli], *av.* **1.** presto, fra breve **2.** concisamente; brevemente **3.** seccamente, bruscamente.

shortness ['ʃo:tnis], *s.* **1.** brevità, cortezza: — *of sight*, miopia **2.** asprezza (di carattere) **3.** mancanza, insufficienza **4.** friabilità; fragilità.

shot[1] [ʃot], *s.* **1.** sparo, colpo; scarica: *without firing a* —, senza colpo ferire; *to fire a* —, sparare un colpo ‖

it's a — at you, fig. è una frecciata diretta contro di te **2.** tiro, portata (d'arma da fuoco e *fig.*) **3.** proiettile, granata, pallottola; mina; (*arc.*) palla di cannone: *to fire a —*, far brillare una mina ‖ *a big —*, (*sl. fig.*) un pezzo grosso ‖ *without a — in the locker, fig.* senza un soldo in tasca, senza risorse ‖ *it is not worth powder and —, fig.* il giuoco non vale la candela ‖ *to be off like a —, fig.* partire come una palla di schioppo ‖ *to waste powder and —*, sprecare il ranno e il sapone, sprecare tempo e fatica **4.** (*gener.* invariato al *pl.*) pallini di piombo; graniglia (di metallo): *to take a (flying) — at a bird*, sparare ad un uccello **5.** colpo, mossa (al giuoco e *fig.*): *at the first —*, alla prima mossa; *good —!*, bel colpo!; *I'll have a — (at it)*, tenterò il colpo; *it is your —*, tocca a te (giocare); *to make a bad —*, fallire, mancare il colpo **6.** tiratore **7.** (*cine. foto.*) ripresa; sequenza; inquadratura; piano; (*foto.*) istantanea **8.** (*pesca*) retata **9.** (*fonderia*) iniezione **10.** (*ind. tessile*) lunghezza del filo di trama; trama che attraversa l'ordito **11.** (*spor.*) tiro; lancio; colpo; (*spor.*) tiro in porta; (*atletica*) peso **12.** (*sl.*) presa, dose di cocaina; iniezione di morfina; cicchetto, sorso (di liquore) ☆ *—-belt*, giberna; *— blasting*, (*mec.*) pallinatura, granigliatura; *— -cartridge*, cartuccia a pallini; *— -hole*, foro di proiettile; (*arc.*) feritoia; *— -peening*, (*mec.*) pallinatura ‖ *angle —*, (*cine.*) ripresa inclinata; *angolazione* (di presa); *blank —*, colpo a salve, in bianco; *close —*, (*cine.*) mezzo primopiano; *exterior —*, (*cine.*) esterno; *high —*, colpo in aria; *long —*, (*cine.*) campo lungo; *panning —*, (*cine.*) panoramica; *pistol- —*, colpo di pistola; *within pistol- —*, a tiro (di pistola); *ricocheting —*, colpo di rimbalzo; *running — (o travel —)*, (*cine.*) carrellata; presa mobile; *snap —*, (*foto.*) istantanea.

to **shot**[1], *pass.p.p.* **shotted** ['ʃɔtid], *v.t.* **1.** caricare (un'arma da fuoco) **2.** (*foto.*) fare un'istantanea a **3.** applicare piombini a (una rete da pesca, ecc.) **4.** (*metal.*) granulare.

shot[2], *s.* conto; quota: *to pay one's —*, pagare la propria parte.

shot[3], *pass.p.p.* di to **shoot**.

shotgun ['ʃɔtgʌn], *s.* fucile da caccia.

shotproof ['ʃɔtpruːf], *ag.* a prova di proiettile.

shotten ['ʃɔtn], *ag.* che ha deposto le uova (generalmente di aringa) ‖ *lean as a — herring*, (*fam.*) magro come un'acciuga.

should [ʃud (*forma forte*); ʃəd (*forma debole*)], *v.* difettivo (V), *pass.* di **shall**; (2ª *persona sing. pass.* (*arc.*) **shouldst** [ʃudst]; *forma negativa* **should not** [ʃud nɔt]; *forma contratta* **shouldn't** ['ʃudnt] **1.** (*ausiliare per la* 1ª *persona sing. pl. del condiz.*): *I — be very happy to see you*, sarei felicissimo di vederti; *we — buy it if we had enough money*, lo compreremmo se avessimo denaro sufficiente ‖ *I — think so*, penso, penserei di sì **2.** (*nel senso di* dovere, *in tutte le persone sing. pl. del condiz.*): *he — arrive any moment*, dovrebbe arrivare da un momento all'altro; *it — be so*, dovrebbe essere così; *they — have been in by this time*, avrebbero dovuto essere a casa a quest'ora; *they — have studied English better*, avrebbero dovuto studiare meglio l'inglese; *you — not deal with such business*, non dovresti trattare questi affari **3.** (*ausiliare per tutte le persone sing. pl. del congiunt.*): *he ordered that they — be helped immediately*, ordinò che fossero aiutati immediatamente; *I gave him my history-book so that he — read it*, gli diedi il mio libro di storia perchè lo leggesse; *it is better you — know it*, è meglio che tu lo sappia **4.** (*nel senso di* dovere, *in tutte le persone sing. pl. dell'imperfetto congiunt.*): *— it rain, I shall stay in*, se dovesse piovere rimarrò in casa; *if he — come, tell him I am in the living-room*, se dovesse venire digli che sono nella stanza di soggiorno; *if you — see him, give him my regards*, se tu lo dovessi vedere porgigli i miei saluti.

shoulder ['ʃouldə*], *s.* **1.** spalla: *— to —*, spalla a spalla; *fig.* in stretta collaborazione; *across* (o *over*) *the*

—, *a tracolla; he has round shoulders*, ha le spalle curve; *to bring the gun to the —*, portare il fucile a spalla ‖ *old head on young shoulders*, giovane assennato ‖ *he shifted all the responsibility on to my shoulders*, gettò tutta la responsabilità sulle mie spalle ‖ *to give one the cold —*, trattare qlcu. con freddezza, dall'alto in basso ‖ *to have broad shoulders, fig.* avere le spalle larghe ‖ *to have a head on one's shoulders*, avere la testa sulle spalle ‖ *to hit out straight from the —*, colpire in pieno; *to tell s.o. sthg. straight from the —*, dire chiaramente ql.co. a qlcu. ‖ *to lay the blame on s.o.'s shoulders*, incolpare qlcu. altro ‖ *to put one's — to the wheel*, mettersi all'opera, darci dentro **2.** bordo, margine (di strada); spalla (di collina, bastione, ecc.) **3.** attaccapanni **4.** (*cuc.*) spalla **5.** (*tip.*) occhio **6.** (*mec.*) spallamento ☆ *—-belt*, tracolla; *—-blade*, (*anat.*) scapola; *—-of-mutton sail*, (*mar.*) vela triangolare; *—-knot*, cordone (sulla livrea di un domestico); *—-strap*, spallina.

to **shoulder**, *v.t.i.* **1.** spingere con le spalle ‖ *to — one's way*, farsi largo con le spalle **2.** portare sulle spalle, caricarsi di; *fig.* sobbarcarsi, addossarsi: *he shouldered his son's debts*, si sobbarcò i debiti di suo figlio ‖ *— arms!*, (*mil.*) spall'arm!.

shout [ʃaut], *s.* grido; grida, chiasso; clamore ‖ *it's my —*, (*sl.*) questa volta pago io.

to **shout**, *v.t.i.* **1.** gridare; urlare; schiamazzare; strepitare: *he shouted with pain*, gridò di dolore **2.** chiamare ad alta voce **3.** *to — at* (*s.o.*), aggredire con urla **4.** *to — down*, far tacere a forza di grida; fischiare (oratore, ecc.).

shouter ['ʃautə*], *s. c.* chi grida.

shouting ['ʃautiŋ], *s.* grido; acclamazione; vocio.

shove [ʃʌv], *s.* spinta; urto; colpo: *to give a — off*, dare una spinta in avanti.

to **shove**, *v.t.i.* **1.** spingere; spingersi; far avanzare **2.** (*fam.*) ficcare: *to — one's nose into s.o.'s business*, ficcare il naso negli affari altrui; *to — sthg. into a drawer*, ficcare ql.co. in un cassetto **3.** *to — along*, avanzare a spintoni, a fatica **4.** *to — away*, allontanare; respingere **5.** *to — down*, far scendere a spintoni **6.** *to — off*, (*mar.*) spingere (una barca) al largo; (*fam.*) allontanarsi, partire.

shovel ['ʃʌvl], *s.* pala ☆ *—-hat*, cappello a larghe tese (portato dal clero anglicano).

to **shovel**, *pass.p.p.* **shovelled** ['ʃʌvld], *v.t.* spalare ‖ *to — food into one's mouth*, mangiare a quattro palmenti.

shovel-board ['ʃʌvlbɔːd], *s.* giuoco' delle piastrelle, murielle.

shovelful ['ʃʌvlful], *s.* palata, palettata.

shoveller ['ʃʌvlə*], *s.* **1.** chi lavora con pala; spalatore **2.** (*ornit.*) mestolone.

show [ʃou], *s.* **1.** mostra, esibizione; esposizione: *the — is open in the afternoon*, la mostra è aperta al pomeriggio ‖ *Lord Mayor's Show*, processione solenne del sindaco di Londra ‖ *to vote by — of hands*, votare per alzata di mano **2.** apparenza, sembiante: *— of resistance*, apparenza di resistenza; *he made a — of going out*, fece finta di uscire; *to make — of friendship* ‖ *— arms!*, fingere amicizia **3.** parata, pompa, ostentazione: *for —*, per figura; *to be fond of —*, amare le esteriorità; *to make a — of courage*, ostentare coraggio; *to make a fine —*, fare un bell'effetto **4.** parvenza, segno, traccia: *there is no — of common sense in his speech*, non c'è traccia di buon senso nel suo discorso; *you can see a — of oil on the floor*, puoi vedere una traccia di petrolio sul pavimento **5.** (*fam.*) spettacolo teatrale: *they put up a good —*, essi recitarono abbastanza bene **6.** (*sl.*) affare: *to boss the —*, assumere il controllo di un affare ‖ *to give the whole — away*, rivelare tutti i difetti, le manchevolezze (di ql.co.) ☆ *—-bill*, cartellone, manifesto; *—-boat*, (*amer.*) battello su cui si danno spettacoli teatrali; *—-box*, vetrinetta; *—-card*, manifesto, cartello (in vetrina); *—-case*, bacheca; vetrina di museo; *—-down*, chiarificazione, spiegazione; carte in tavola; — -girl, (amer. teat.) generica di varietà; — -off, esibizionismo, posa; — -place, monumento; luogo di interesse turistico; — -ring, arena di vendita (di bestiame, ecc.); — -room, salone per esposizioni; — -window, vetrina ‖ cattle- —, mostra di bestiame; dumb- —, pantomima; first- —, prima visione; flower- —, mostra di fiori; motor- —, salone dell'automobile; puppet- —, spettacolo di burattini; samples- —, esposizione di campioni; shadow- —, ombre cinesi.

to **show**, pass. **showed** [ʃoud], p.p. **shown** [ʃoun], v.t.i. **1.** mostrare, far vedere; esporre: just — me your drawings, mostrami i tuoi disegni; what can I — you, madam?, la signora desidera? (nei negozi); to — the goods on sale, esporre la merce in vendita; to — oneself, mostrarsi (in pubblico); to — one's ticket, esibire il proprio biglietto; to — a picture on the screen, proiettare un film ‖ to — a clean pair of heels, darsela a gambe ‖ to — daylight, (fam.) essere bucherellato (di vestito) ‖ to — the cloven hoof, mostrare cattive disposizioni ‖ to — fight, mostrarsi bellicoso, non cedere facilmente ‖ to — a leg, (sl. mar.) alzarsi dal letto ‖ to — one's cards, one's hand, mettere le carte in tavola; fig. giocare a carte scoperte ‖ to — one's teeth, mostrare i denti (anche fig.) ‖ to — the white feather, mostrarsi codardo **2.** rappresentare, figurare, indicare: as shown above, come sopra indicato; this picture shows an imaginary island, questa illustrazione rappresenta un'isola immaginaria; to — the time, indicare l'ora (di orologio) ‖ to — s.o. the door, mettere qualcuno alla porta **3.** dimostrare, provare; rivelare: it only shows the falsity of his tale, questo non dimostra che la falsità del suo racconto; she shows her age, dimostra la sua età; to — one's right, (dir.) far valere i propri diritti; to — reason, addurre delle ragioni valide ‖ time will —, prov. chi vivrà vedrà **4.** apparire, farsi vedere: buds are showing, cominciano ad apparire i boccioli **5.** condurre, accompagnare: to — s.o. downstairs, upstairs, far scendere, far salire qlcu.; to — s.o. round, accompagnare qlcu. in giro **6.** (teat.) dare una rappresentazione **7.** to — down, mettere le carte in tavola (anche fig.) **8.** to — in, fare entrare **9.** to — off, mettere in valore; darsi delle arie, posare, mettersi in mostra: to — off before s.o., cercare di meravigliare qlcu. **10.** to — out, far uscire, accompagnare alla porta **11.** to — up, svelare, smascherare; disegnarsi (su uno sfondo), stagliarsi; (fam.) fare atto di presenza.

shower[1] [ʃauə*], s. **1.** acquazzone, rovescio; scroscio; fig. tempesta passeggera: a heavy —, un diluvio **2.** fig. pioggia, grande quantità: a — of blows, una grandine di colpi **3.** — (party), (amer.) ricevimento in cui ognuno porta un dono all'ospite d'onore ☆ — -bath, doccia ‖ April —, acquazzone d'aprile.

to **shower**[1], v.t.i. **1.** versare, far cadere (acqua) **2.** fig. far piovere; coprire: to — blows on s.o., (fam.) far grandinare colpi su qlcu.; to — s.o. with honours, coprire qlcu. di onori **3.** piovere a dirotto, diluviare.

shower[2] [ʃouə*], s. chi mostra, espositore.

showerless [ʃaulis], ag. senza pioggia.

showery [ʃauəri], ag. piovoso.

showily [ʃouili], av. fastosamente, pomposamente; vistosamente.

showiness [ʃouinis], s. fasto, splendore; vistosità.

showing [ʃouiŋ], s. **1.** esposizione, rappresentazione ‖ on his (your, etc.) own —, a sentir lui (voi, ecc.); on this —, se si considerano così le cose **2.** manifestazione (di sentimenti) **3.** prova (di un fatto) ☆ — -off, esibizionismo, posa.

showman, pl. **showmen** [ʃoumən], s. **1.** imbonitore (nelle fiere) **2.** direttore, capocomico (di spettacoli di varietà).

showmanship [ʃoumənʃip], s. arte di presentare, capacità di interessare il pubblico.

shown [ʃoun], p.p. di to **show**.

showy [ʃoui], ag. fastoso; appariscente; vistoso.

shrank [ʃræŋk], pass. di to **shrink**.

shrapnel [ʃræpnl], s. «shrapnel» (granata a tempo).

shred [ʃred], s. ritaglio; striscia; frammento; brandello; rimasuglio: her dress was all in shreds, il suo abito era a brandelli; to cut sthg. into shreds, tagliare ql.co. a strisce ‖ to tear s.o.'s reputation to shreds, tagliare i panni addosso a qlcu.

to **shred**, pass.p.p. **shredded** [ʃredid], v.t. stracciare, lacerare, fare a brandelli; tagliuzzare.

shrew [ʃru:], s. **1.** donna brontolona, pettegola, bisbetica ‖ "The Taming of the Shrew", (lett.) «La bisbetica domata» **2.** (zool.) toporagno.

shrewd [ʃru:d], ag. **1.** sagace, accorto, astuto, perspicace **2.** pungente, tagliente.

shrewdly [ʃru:dli], av. sagacemente, accortamente, astutamente; argutamente.

shrewdness [ʃru:dnis], s. accortezza, perspicacia, sagacia, sottigliezza, astuzia.

shrewish [ʃru:iʃ], ag. brontolone; petulante; bisbetico.

shrewishly [ʃru:iʃli], av. stizzosamente, con petulanza.

shrewishness [ʃru:iʃnis], s. acrimonia, petulanza.

shriek [ʃri:k], s. grido; strillo; fischio; suono lacerante: a — of anguish, un grido di angoscia; the — of a locomotive, il fischio di una locomotiva.

to **shriek**, v.t.i. gridare; strillare; stridere ‖ to — with laughter, ridere in modo isterico.

shrieker [ʃri:kə*], s.c. chi grida, chi strilla.

shrieking [ʃri:kiŋ], s. grida, urla; stridore.

shrievalty [ʃri:vəlti], s. **1.** giurisdizione di uno sceriffo **2.** carica di sceriffo.

shrift [ʃrift], s. (relig.) confessione e assoluzione ‖ short —, breve periodo di tempo concesso al condannato a morte per confessarsi.

shrike [ʃraik], s. (ornit.) averla.

shrill [ʃril], ag. **1.** stridulo; acuto; penetrante **2.** fig. importuno; insistente.

to **shrill**, v.t.i. strillare, stridere; emettere suono stridulo, acuto; cantare con voce stridula.

shrillness [ʃrilnis], s. **1.** acutezza di suono; stridore **2.** inopportunità; insistenza.

shrilly [ʃrili], av. acutamente; in modo stridulo.

shrimp [ʃrimp], s. **1.** (zool.) gamberetto (di mare); granchiolino **2.** fig. omiciattolo, nano, pigmeo ☆ — -girl, venditrice di gamberetti; — -net, gamberana.

to **shrimp**, v.i. pescare gamberetti (di mare).

shrimper [ʃrimpə*], s. pescatore di gamberetti (di mare).

shrine [ʃrain], s. **1.** reliquiario; tomba (di santo) **2.** altare; tempio; santuario (anche fig.): — of knowledge, culla del sapere.

to **shrine**, v.t. **1.** racchiudere in un reliquiario **2.** considerare come sacro.

shrink [ʃriŋk], s. **1.** restringimento; contrazione **2.** (metal. ind. tessile) ritiro ☆ — -fitting, (mec.) montaggio a caldo, sottozero; — proof, irrestringibile.

to **shrink**, pass. **shrank** [ʃræŋk], p.p. **shrunk** [ʃrʌŋk], (arc.) **shrunken** [ʃrʌŋkən], v.t.i. **1.** (far) restringere, restringersi; contrarre, contrarsi; ritirarsi; accorciare, accorciarsi: ordinary soap will — your jumpers, il sapone comune farà infeltrire i tuoi golfini; this cloth does not —, questa stoffa è irrestringibile ‖ to — with cold, essere rattrappito per il freddo; to — with pain, contorcersi dal dolore **2.** indietreggiare, allontanarsi; fig. rifuggire, evitare: he never shrank from danger, non indietreggiò mai di fronte al pericolo; a shy man shrinks from meeting strangers, una persona timida rifugge dai contatti con estranei; you didn't — from telling me, non ti sei trattenuto dal dirmi **3.** to — on, (mec.) calettare a caldo, sottozero: to — on a tyre, calettare un cerchione.

shrinkable [ʃriŋkəbl], ag. restringibile.

shrinkage [ʃriŋkidʒ], s. **1.** diminuzione; restringimento; rimpicciolimento; contrazione **2.** (comm.) deprezzamento; calo, contrazione ☆ — *porosity*, (*metal.*) porosità di ritiro.

shrinker ['ʃriŋkə*], *s.* (*mec.*) **1.** macchina per calettare **2.** operaio addetto alla calettatura.

shrinking ['ʃriŋkiŋ], *ag.* **1.** che si restringe, che si contrae **2.** timido; riluttante || *s.* contrazione; diminuzione; ritiro.

shrinkingly ['ʃriŋkiŋli], *av.* **1.** timidamente, con diffidenza **2.** con contrazione.

to **shrive** [ʃraiv], *pass.* **shrove** [ʃrouv], *p.p.* **shriven** ['ʃrivn], *v.t.* (*arc.*) confessare e assolvere: *to — oneself*, confessarsi.

to **shrivel** ['ʃrivl], *pass.p.p.* **shrivelled** ['ʃrivld], *v.t.i.* accartocciare, accartocciarsi; aggrinzare, aggrinzarsi; corrugare, corrugarsi; far avvizzire: *the heat shrivelled (up) the flowers*, il caldo fece avvizzire i fiori.

shriver ['ʃraivə*], *s.* confessore.

shriving ['ʃraiviŋ], *s.* confessione e assoluzione.

shroff [ʃrof], *s.* **1.** banchiere; cambiavalute (in Oriente) **2.** esperto nel distinguere monete false.

to **shroff**, *v.t.* esaminare (monete, per separare le correnti dalle false).

shroffage ['ʃrofidʒ], *s.* esame e cernita delle monete.

shroud[1] [ʃraud], *s.* **1.** sudario, lenzuolo funebre: *to wrap a corpse in a —*, avvolgere un morto nel sudario **2.** *fig.* velo; schermo, riparo: *— of mist*, velo di nebbia; *in a — of mystery*, in un velo di mistero **3.** (*aut.*) pannello di separazione tra motore e abitacolo.

to **shroud**[1], *v.t.i.* **1.** avvolgere nel sudario **2.** nascondere, velare: *the country was shrouded in mist*, la campagna era avvolta nella nebbia; *a fact shrouded in mystery*, un fatto avvolto nel mistero **3.** (*arc.*) proteggere, riparare, ripararsi.

shroud[2], *s. gener. pl.* (*mar.*) sartia.

shrouded ['ʃraudid], *ag.* **1.** velato, nascosto; avvolto nel sudario **2.** riparato, protetto.

shroudless ['ʃraudlis], *ag.* **1.** senza sudario; senza velo **2.** *fig.* esposto, evidente.

shroudy ['ʃraudi], *ag.* che copre; che dà rifugio.

shrove [ʃrouv], *pass.* di to **shrive**.

Shrove Sunday ['ʃrouv'sʌndi], *s.* domenica di Quinquagesima.

Shrovetide ['ʃrouvtaid]. *s.* ¹ gli ultimi tre giorni di carnevale.

Shrove Tuesday ['ʃrouv'tjuːzdi], *s.* martedì grasso.

shroving ['ʃrouviŋ], *s.* (*dial.*) feste carnevalesche; baldoria.

shrub[1] [ʃrʌb], *s.* arbusto, cespuglio.

shrub[2], *s.* **1.** cordiale fatto di succo di agrumi e liquore **2.** (*amer.*) bibita di succo di frutta con aceto.

shrubbery ['ʃrʌbəri], *s.* macchia, boscaglia d'arbusti.

shrubby ['ʃrʌbi], *ag.* cespuglioso, coperto di arbusti.

shrug [ʃrʌg], *s.* spallucciata.

to **shrug**, *pass.p.p.* **shrugged** [ʃrʌgd], *v.t.i.* scrollare (le spalle); alzare le spalle; stringersi nelle spalle: *she shrugged her shoulders*, fece spallucce; *to — one's shoulders at sthg.*, infischiarsi di ql.co.

shrugging ['ʃrʌgiŋ], *s.* scrollata, alzata di spalle.

shrunk [ʃrʌŋk], **shrunken** ['ʃrʌŋkən], *p.p.* di to **shrink** || *ag.* raggrinzito; dimagrito; contratto.

shuck [ʃʌk], *s.* (*amer.*) **1.** baccello; guscio; valva **2.** oggetto di scarsissimo valore: *this is not worth shucks*, questo non vale niente.

to **shuck**, *v.t.* (*amer.*) sgusciare, sgranare.

shucker ['ʃʌkə*], *s.c.* chi sgrana, sguscia, apre valve, gusci.

shudder ['ʃʌdə*], *s.* brivido; tremito.

to **shudder**, *v.i.* rabbrividire, avere i brividi; fremere, tremare; provare disgusto: *to — at the thought of*, rabbrividire al pensiero di.

shuddering ['ʃʌdəriŋ], *ag.* tremante, rabbrividente || *s.* brivido; tremito; fremito.

shudderingly ['ʃʌdəriŋli], *av.* fremendo, tremando.

shuffle ['ʃʌfl], *s.* **1.** passo strascicato; passo di danza **2.** scompiglio, confusione; tramestio **3.** il mesco-

lare (le carte da giuoco): *it's your —*, tocca a te mescolare le carte **4.** sotterfugio, artificio, inganno; equivoco ☆ — *-board*, giuoco della morella, muriella; tavola, moneta per il giuoco della morella || *double- —*, passo doppio (di danza).

to **shuffle**, *v.t.i.* **1.** trascinare, trascinarsi, muoversi a fatica: *the old woman shuffled along*, la vecchia si trascinava a fatica; *to — one's feet*, strascicare i piedi **2.** mescolare; confondere; scompigliare: *to — cards*, mescolare le carte **3.** tergiversare; agire in modo equivoco **4.** *to — into* (*a place*), introdursi, insinuarsi in **5.** *to — in*, introdursi; insinuarsi **6.** *to — off*, liberarsi di, sottrarsi a || *to — off responsibility on others*, riversare la responsabilità sugli altri **7.** *to — out*, uscire furtivamente, sgattaiolare **8.** *to — up*, affastellare.

shuffler ['ʃʌflə*], *s.c.* **1.** chi mescola le carte **2.** truffatore, truffatrice; ingannatore, ingannatrice.

shuffling ['ʃʌfliŋ], *ag.* **1.** strascicante **2.** evasivo, che tergiversa || *s.* **1.** passo strascicato **2.** confusione **3.** tergiversazione.

shufflingly ['ʃʌfliŋli], *av.* **1.** con sotterfugi; evasivamente **2.** trascinando i piedi.

to **shun** [ʃʌn], *pass.p.p.* **shunned** [ʃʌnd], *v.t.* sfuggire, scansare, evitare, schivare: *she shuns society*, evita la compagnia; *to — s.o. like the plague*, sfuggire qlcu. come la peste.

'shun, *inter.* (*abbr. mil.* di *attention!*) attenti!.

shunt [ʃʌnt], *s.* **1.** (*elett.*) derivazione **2.** (*ferr.*) scambio ☆ — *circuit*, (*elett.*) circuito derivato; — *connection*, (*elett.*) collegamento in derivazione; — *terminal*, (*elett.*) morsetto di derivazione; — *wire*, (*elett.*) filo di derivazione.

to **shunt**, *v.t.i.* **1.** (*elett.*) inserire in derivazione; derivare **2.** (*ferr.*) smistare; smistarsi **3.** posporre, mettere da parte.

shunter ['ʃʌntə*], *s.* (*ferr.*) **1.** deviatore, manovratore di scambi **2.** piccola locomotiva da smistamento.

shunting ['ʃʌntiŋ], *s.* **1.** (*elett.*) derivazione **2.** (*ferr.*) smistamento; instradamento ☆ — *engine*, (*ferr.*) locomotiva di manovra; — *lines*, (*ferr.*) binari di smistamento; — *official*, (*ferr.*) capomanovratore || *field* —, (*elett.*) derivazione di campo.

shut [ʃʌt], *ag.* **1.** ben chiuso: *a — door*, una porta chiusa **2.** (*fonet.*) occlusivo || *s.* **1.** portello, sportello **2.** momento di chiusura **3.** atto del chiudere **4.** (*mec.*) linea di saldatura **5.** (*metal.*) sovrapposizione, piega, sovraddosso.

to **shut**, *pass.p.p.* **shut**, *v.t.i.* **1.** chiudere, chiudersi; serrare, serrarsi (anche *fig.*): *please — the door*, per favore chiudi la porta; *the shops are —*, i negozi sono chiusi; *to — a book, a fan, an umbrella*, chiudere un libro, un ventaglio, un ombrello; *to — one's dress in the door*, chiudersi il vestito nella porta; *to — one's eyes*, chiudere gli occhi; *fig.* non arrendersi all'evidenza; *to — one's heart to pity*, essere inaccessibile alla pietà; *to — one's mouth*, tacere || *to — the door on proposals*, rifiutare delle proposte **2.** *to — down*, abbassare, abbassarsi; sospendere l'attività (in una fabbrica); (*aer.*) fermare il motore **3.** *to — in*, rinchiudere, circondare (di colline, case, mare, ecc.) **4.** *to — off*, separare, escludere, isolare (dalla società, ecc.); chiudere (l'acqua, il gas); (*fam.*) interrompere una telefonata **5.** *to — out*, chiudere, escludere: *to — out a view, air, light*, escludere una veduta, l'aria, la luce **6.** *to — up*, sbarrare; rinchiudere (in prigione) || *to — up shop*, chiudere bottega, ritirarsi dagli affari || — *up!*, (*fam.*) taci!, smettila!.

shutdown ['ʃʌtdaun], *s.* interruzione, sospensione; chiusura temporanea (di fabbrica).

shutter ['ʃʌtə*], *s.* **1.** imposta; persiana; saracinesca: *to put up the —* (*of shop*), abbassare la saracinesca; *fig.* chiudere bottega **2.** (*foto.*) otturatore: *to wind up the —*, caricare l'otturatore ☆ *folding- —*, persiana pieghevole; *rolling- —*, serranda avvolgibile; *sliding- —*, persiana scorrevole.

to **shutter**, *v.t.* **1.** provvedere di imposte **2.** chiudere le imposte di.

shutting ['ʃʌtiŋ], s. il chiudere; chiusura.

shuttle[1] ['ʃʌtl], s. spola, navetta ☆ — *mechanism*, meccanismo alternativo; — *movement*, (mec.) movimento alternativo; — *picking*, (ind. tessile) lancio della navetta; — *service*, servizo di spola; — *train*, treno di collegamento (tra luoghi vicini); — *winding*, (elett.) avvolgimento a doppia T.

to shuttle[1], *v.t.i.* muovere alternativamente; fare la spola; andare avanti e indietro.

shuttle[2], *s.* chiusa idraulica.

shuttlecock ['ʃʌtlkɔk], s. **1.** volano; giuoco del volano **2.** fig. persona volubile.

shuttling ['ʃʌtliŋ], s. spola, navetta.

shy[1] [ʃai], comp. **shyer**, (arc.) **shier** ['ʃai-ə*], superl. **shyest**, (arc.) **shiest** ['ʃaiist], ag. **1.** riservato, timido, schivo; timoroso: *a — child*, un bimbo scontroso; *a — person*, una persona timida, schiva; *he makes me —*, mi intimidisce; *she is — of crowds*, la folla la intimidisce; *they are — of asking*, esitano a chiedere **2.** ombroso: *a — horse*, un cavallo ombroso **3.** diffidente: *to fight — of s.o., sthg.*, tenersi alla larga da qlcu., ql.co. **4.** poco produttivo, sterile (di piante): *a — tree*, un albero che produce poco **5.** *he is — of* (o *on*) *money*, (sl. amer.) è a corto di denaro ☆ — *-looking*, d'aspetto timido.

shy[1], *s.* scarto (di cavallo).

to shy[1], *pass.p.p.* **shied** [ʃaid], *v.t.i.* **1.** spaventare, spaventarsi; esitare a fare qualche cosa **2.** fare uno scarto; impennarsi (di cavallo): *the horse shied at the car*, il cavallo fece uno scarto davanti all'automobile **3.** *to — off*, schivare; fig. trovare un mezzo di evasione.

shy[2], *s.* (fam.) getto, lancio || *to have a — at*, tentare di ottenere.

to shy[2], *v.t.i.* (fam.) gettare, lanciare (pietra, palla).

shyly ['ʃai-li], *av.* **1.** timidamente **2.** sospettosamente; con diffidenza.

shyness ['ʃai-nis], *s.* **1.** timidezza, riservatezza **2.** ritrosia, scontrosità; diffidenza.

si [si:], *s.* (mus.) si.

Siamese [ˌsaiə'mi:z], *ag.s.c.* siamese || *s.* lingua siamese ☆ — *cat*, gatto siamese; — *twins*, fratelli siamesi; fig. amici inseparabili.

Siberia [sai'biəriə], *no.pr.* (geog.) Siberia.

Siberian [sai'biəriən], *ag.* siberiano || *s.c.* siberiano, siberiana.

sibil ['sibil], *s.* **1.** (st.) sibilla **2.** fattucchiera; strega.

sibilant ['sibilənt], *ag.s.* (spec. gram.) sibilante.

to sibilate ['sibileit], *v.t.i.* sibilare; pronunciare sibilando.

sibilation [ˌsibi'leiʃən], *s.* sibilo; fischio.

sibilance ['sibiləns], **sibilancy** ['sibilənsi], *s.* sibilo.

sibling ['sibliŋ], *s.c. spec. pl.* **1.** fratello; sorella **2.** fratellastro; sorellastra.

Sibyl ['sibil], *no.pr.f.* Sibilla || **sibyl**, *s.* **1.** (st.) sibilla **2.** fattucchiera; strega.

sibylline ['sibilain], *ag.* sibillino || *the — books*, (st.) i libri sibillini.

siccative ['sikətiv], *ag.* essiccante || *s.* sostanza essiccante.

sice [sais], *s.* sei (ai dadi).

Sicilian [si'siljən], *ag.* siciliano || *s.c.* siciliano, siciliana.

Sicily ['sisili], *no.pr.* (geog.) Sicilia.

sick [sik], *ag.* **1.** (spec. attributivo) malato; ammalato; indisposto, sofferente || *the —*, i malati || *to fall —*, ammalarsi || *to report —*, (mil.) darsi ammalato **2.** (predicativo) nauseato; fig. disgustato; stanco; depresso: *I am — of it*, non ne posso più; *it makes me —*, mi dà la nausea || *to be — at heart*, essere abbattuto || *to be — for home*, aver nostalgia di casa ☆ — *-bay*, infermeria di bordo; — *-bed*, letto di un ammalato; fig. letto di dolore; — *-benefit*, indennità di malattia; — *-call*, (mil.) segnale di visita medica; — *-flag*, bandiera gialla di quarantena; — *-fund*, fondo di soccorso per malattie; — *-house*, ospedale; — *-leave*, licenza per

malattia; — *-list*, (mil.) lista dei malati; — *-tired*, (fam.) stanco fino alla nausea.

to sicken ['sikn], *v.t.i.* **1.** far ammalare, ammalarsi **2.** sfiorire, ingiallire (di piante) **3.** sentir nausea; fig. disgustare, disgustarsi: *to — at the sight of blood*, sentir nausea alla vista del sangue **4.** essere sazio, stanco; annoiarsi: *he soon sickened of his wife*, si stancò presto di sua moglie.

sickener ['siknə*], *s.* cosa che nausea, disgusta; esperienza spiacevole || *s. c.* (sl. scolastico) persona sgradevole, noiosa.

sickening ['sikniŋ], *ag.* nauseabondo, stomachevole; rivoltante; sgradevole.

sickeningly ['sikniŋli], *av.* in modo nauseabondo, stomachevole, sgradevole.

sickish ['sikiʃ], *ag.* **1.** malaticcio; indisposto **2.** nauseante; ributtante.

sickle ['sikl], *s.* falcetto.

sickleman, *pl.* **sicklemen** ['siklmən], *s.* mietitore.

sickliness ['siklinis], *s.* **1.** salute delicata **2.** pallore **3.** scipitezza **4.** nausea (anche fig.).

sickly ['sikli], *ag.* **1.** malaticcio; debole **2.** pallido, delicato: *a — pink*, un rosa pallido **3.** nauseante; insalubre: *a — season*, una stagione insalubre; *a — smell*, un odore nauseante.

sickness ['siknis], *s.* **1.** malattia **2.** nausea ☆ *falling- —*, (patol.) epilessia; *home- —*, nostalgia; *sea- —*, mal di mare; *sleeping- —*, malattia del sonno; *sleepy- —*, (patol.) encefalite letargica.

sicknurse ['siknə:s], *s.* infermiera.

sickroom ['sik-rum], *s.* camera per ammalati.

side[1] [said], *s.* **1.** lato, fianco: — *by —*, fianco a fianco; *the — of a ship*, il fianco di una nave; *right, left —*, lato destro, sinistro; *I have a pain in my right —*, ho un dolore al fianco destro || *to shake one's sides, to split one's sides with laughing*, ridere a crepapelle **2.** versante; sponda, riva; margine: *by the — of the river*, sulla sponda del fiume; *by the — of the road*, sul margine della strada || *the other —*, (amer.) l'altra sponda dell'Atlantico || *this —*, (amer.) questa sponda dell'Atlantico **3.** lato, parte; fig. aspetto: *on either —*, dalle due parti; da una parte e dall'altra; *on the other —*, d'altra parte; *the other — of the picture*, il rovescio della medaglia; *the right, wrong —*, il lato buono, cattivo; il diritto, rovescio (di stoffe) || *on the wrong — of the blanket*, di nascita illegittima || *on the wrong — of the door*, chiuso fuori (di casa) || *to be on the right, wrong — of forty*, essere al di sotto, al di sopra dei quarant'anni **4.** partito, parte, fazione: *he is on our —*, è dei nostri, del nostro partito; *to change sides*, cambiare partito; *to hear both sides*, sentire le due parti; *to join the winning —*, accodarsi al partito vincente; *to take sides (with)*, prender partito (per) **5.** discendenza, lato, parte: *on his mother's —*, da parte di madre ☆ — *-band*, (rad.) banda laterale; — *-box*, palco laterale; — *-chain*, (chim.) catena laterale (di atomi); — *-comb*, pettine laterale; — *-cutting*, (tec.) cava di prestito; — *-dish*, portata extra; — *-door*, porta laterale, di servizio; — *-face*, profilo; — *-glance* (o *-look*), occhiata in tralice; — *-issue*, questione secondaria; — *-line*, (comm.) articolo secondario; (ferr.) linea secondaria; — *-lines*, (spor.) linee laterali; — *-note*, nota marginale; — *-on*, laterale; — *-path*, sentiero laterale; — *-post*, stipite; — *-saddle*, sella da amazzone; — *-saddle flower*, varietà di pianta di palude («Sarracenia»); — *-show*, mostra secondaria; — *-slip*, slittamento; fig. figlio illegittimo; (aer.) scivolata d'ala; (aut.) sbandata; — *-splitting*, che fa ridere a crepapelle; — *-stroke*, colpo laterale; nuoto alla marinara; — *-table*, tavolino spostabile, di servizio; — *-track*, (ferr.) binario di raccordo; — *view*, veduta di fianco (disegno); — *-wheeler*, (mar.) battello a pale; — *-whiskers*, favoriti, basette; — *-wind*, (mar.) vento di traverso; fig. fonte indiretta.

to side[1], *v.t.i.* **1.** essere dalla parte di; parteggiare:

we found out he sided with the opposite party, scoprimmo che parteggiava per il partito avversario **2.** camminare a lato di **3.** digrossare, squadrare (legno).

side², *s.* (*fam.*) boria, arroganza: *he was putting on too much — for my liking, and I told him so,* si dava troppe arie per i miei gusti, e glielo dissi.

sidearms ['saidɑ:mz], *s. pl.* armi bianche.

sideboard ['saidbɔ:d], *s.* credenza.

sideburns ['saidbə:nz], *s. pl.* basette.

sidecar ['saidkɑ:*], *s.* «side-car», motocarrozzetta.

sided ['saidid], *ag.* a lati, a facce ☆ *twelve- — polyhedron,* dodecaedro.

sidedly ['saididli], *av.* parzialmente, unilateralmente.

sidelight ['saidlait], *s.* **1.** luce laterale; riflesso; *fig.* spiegazione, informazione fortuita: *to throw a — on a subject,* chiarire fortuitamente un argomento **2.** (*mar.*) fanale di posizione **3.** *pl.* (*aer. mar.*) fanali di via.

sideling ['saidliŋ], *ag.* **1.** obliquo; inclinato **2.** *fig.* indiretto (di discorso, ecc.) || *av.* obliquamente; di fianco.

sidelock ['saidlɔk], *s.* tirabaci.

sidelong ['saidlɔŋ], *ag.* laterale; obliquo: *to cast a — glance at s.o.,* guardare qlcu. con la coda dell'occhio.

sidelong, *av.* lateralmente; obliquamente; con la coda dell'occhio.

sider ['saidə*], *s.* partigiano.

sidereal [sai'diəriəl], *ag.* sidereo, siderale: *— day,* giorno siderale.

siderite ['saidərait], *s.* (*min.*) siderite.

siderography [,saidə'rɔgrəfi], *s.* siderografia.

sidesman, *pl.* **sidesmen** ['saidzmən], *s.* (*eccl.*) fabbriciere aggiunto.

sidewalk ['said-wɔ:k], *s.* (*amer.*) marciapiede.

sideward ['saidwəd], *ag.* laterale.

sidewards ['saidwədz], *av.* lateralmente.

sideways ['said-weiz], **sidewise** ['said-waiz], *av.* lateralmente; obliquamente; a sghembo.

siding ['saidiŋ], *s.* (*ferr.*) binario di raccordo.

to **sidle** ['saidl], *v.i.* **1.** camminare di fianco; andare a sghembo: *to — along the wall,* camminare rasente il muro **2.** *to — up: to — up to s.o.,* accostarsi con esitazione a qlcu.

siege [si:dʒ], *s.* assedio: *state of —,* stato d'assedio; *to lay — to a town,* assediare, cingere d'assedio una città; *to raise the —,* togliere l'assedio; *to stand a —,* sostenere un assedio ☆ *— -train,* (*mil.*) equipaggio d'assedio; *— -works,* (*artigl.*) opere d'assedio.

Siegfried ['si:gfri:d], *no.pr.m.* (*lett.*) Sigfrido.

Sienna [si'enə], *no.pr.* (*geog.*) Siena || **sienna,** *s.* (*pitt.*) terra di Siena.

Siennese [,sie'ni:z], *ag. s.c.* senese.

sierra ['siərə], *s.* sierra.

Sierra Leone ['siərəli'oun], *no.pr.* (*geog.*) Sierra Leone.

siesta [si'estə], *s.* siesta: *to take a —,* fare la siesta.

sieve [siv], *s.* setaccio, crivello, vaglio: *to pass sthg. through a —,* passare ql.co. al setaccio.

to **sieve**, *v.t.* setacciare, crivellare.

to **sift** [sift], *v.t.i.* **1.** setacciare, vagliare; *fig.* esaminare minuziosamente: *to — (out) the true from the false,* distinguere, separare il vero dal falso **2.** filtrare (di luce, polvere, ecc.).

sifter ['siftə*], *s.c.* chi setaccia, chi vaglia; *fig.* chi esamina minuziosamente || *s.* setaccio; buratto.

sifting ['siftiŋ], *s.* **1.** setacciatura, vagliatura; *fig.* esame minuzioso **2.** *pl.* residui, mondiglia.

sigh [sai], *s.* sospiro: *sighs and sobs,* sospiri e singulti; *deep —,* sospiro profondo.

to **sigh**, *v.t.i.* **1.** sospirare; esprimere sospirando: *to — out* (o *forth*) *a prayer,* pronunciare una preghiera sospirando; *to — with relief, for grief,* respirare di sollievo, sospirare per il dolore **2.** sospirare, soffiare: *the wind sighs through the trees,* il vento sibila tra le piante **3.** *to — after, for* (*sthg.*), desiderare, bramare: *to — for home,* avere nostalgia del focolare.

sigher ['saiə*], *s.c.* chi sospira.

sighful ['saiful], *ag.* sospiroso.

sighing ['saiiŋ], *s.* il sospirare; sospiri.

sighingly ['saiiŋli], *av.* sospirosamente.

sight [sait], *s.* **1.** vista; visione: *at first —,* a prima vista; *out of —,* fuori di vista; *payable at —,* (*comm.*) pagabile a vista; *to be within —,* essere in vista; *to catch — of sthg.,* intravedere ql.co.; *to come in — of s.o., sthg.,* arrivare in vista di qlcu., ql.co.; *to have good —,* avere una buona vista; *to keep in —,* mantenersi in vista; *to know s.o. by —,* conoscere qlcu. di vista; *to lose — of s.o.,* perdere di vista qlcu. || *out of — out of mind, prov.* lontano dagli occhi, lontano dal cuore **2.** veduta, panorama; spettacolo: *a fine —,* una bella vista; *what a —!,* che spettacolo! || *to make a — of oneself,* rendersi ridicolo **3.** occhiata; sguardo: *to take a — at,* dare un'occhiata a; (*fam.*) fare un gesto di scherno a **4.** mira: *to take a — before shooting,* prendere la mira prima di sparare **5.** mirino **6.** *pl.* cose notevoli (da vedere): *to see the sights,* visitare i monumenti, le cose interessanti (di un luogo) **7.** (*fam.*) grande quantità: *it costs a — of money,* costa un sacco di soldi ☆ *— -finder,* (*arc.*) mirino; *— -reader,* chi legge musica a prima vista; *— -seeing,* visita turistica; *— -seer,* turista; *— -worthy,* degno di essere veduto || *long- —,* presbiopia; *fig.* previdenza; *short- —,* miopia; *fig.* imprevidenza.

to **sight**, *v.t.i.* **1.** avvistare: *to — land,* avvistare terra **2.** osservare: *to — a star,* osservare una stella **3.** prendere la mira **4.** fornire di mirino.

sighted ['saitid], *ag.* **1.** fornito di vista **2.** fornito di mirino (di arma da fuoco) ☆ *long- —* (o *far -*), presbite; *fig.* previdente; *quick- —,* oculato; *short- —,* miope; *fig.* imprevidente.

sightless ['saitlis], *ag.* **1.** che non vede, cieco **2.** (*poet.*) invisibile.

sightlessly ['saitlisli], *av.* cecamente.

sightlessness ['saitlisnis], *s.* cecità.

sightliness ['saitlinis], *s.* bellezza, avvenenza; grazia.

sightly ['saitli], *ag.* **1.** avvenente; seducente; di bella presenza **2.** (*amer.*) che offre una bella vista.

sigil ['sidʒil], *s.* **1.** suggello; sigillo **2.** segno occulto.

sigillaria [,sidʒi'lɛəriə], *s.* (*paleont. bot.*) sigillaria.

sigillate ['sidʒilit], *ag.* **1.** a disegni stampati (di ceramica) **2.** (*bot.*) con segni a forma di sigillo.

Sigismond, Sigismund ['sigismənd], *no.pr.m.* Sigismondo.

sigma ['sigmə], *s.* sigma (lettera dell'alfabeto greco).

sigmate ['sigmit], *ag.* a forma di sigma, sigmatico.

to **sigmate** ['sigmeit], *v.t.* aggiungere un sigma a.

sigmatic [sig'mætik], *ag.* sigmatico.

sigmatism ['sigmətizəm], *s.* sigmatismo.

sigmoid ['sigmɔid], *ag.* (*anat.*) sigmoideo || *s.* (*anat.*) sigma.

sign [sain], *s.* **1.** segno, cenno: *to make signs to s.o.,* far cenni a qlcu. || *to make the — of the cross,* fare il segno della croce **2.** indicazione; indizio; traccia; presagio: *a — of the times,* un segno dei tempi **3.** insegna (di albergo, ecc.): *to put up at the — of the Golden Lion,* alloggiare all'insegna del Leon d'Oro **4.** simbolo: *negative, positive —,* (*mat.*) segno negativo, positivo ☆ *— -board,* insegna (di bottega, taverna, ecc.); *— -language,* mimica; *— -painter,* pittore di insegne; *— -post,* palo indicatore || *radical —,* (*mat.*) segno di radice.

to **sign**, *v.t.i.* **1.** segnare; firmare; sottoscrivere: *to — one's name,* fare la propria firma **2.** *to — away,* cedere (diritti) per iscritto **3.** *to — on,* assumere (un operaio, ecc.); ingaggiare (un marinaio); impegnarsi (per un lavoro); firmare il registro delle presenze **4.** *to — up,* (*amer.*) arruolarsi; iscriversi.

signal ['signl], *ag.* notevole; cospicuo; esemplare || *s.* segnale, segno ☆ *— -box,* cabina di segnalazione; *— -gun,* colpo di cannone sparato per segnalazione; *— -light,* fanale; *— -mast* (o *— -post*), palo segnavia; *— -rocket,* razzo di segnalazione || *distress —,* segnale di soccorso.

to **signal**, *pass.p.p.* **signalled** ['signld], *v.t.i.* far segnali; segnalare.

to **signalize** ['signəlaiz], *v.t.* segnalare: *to — oneself*, distinguersi.

signaller ['signələ*], *s.* segnalatore.

signally ['signəli], *av.* segnalatamente, notevolmente.

signalman, *pl.* **signalmen** ['signlmən], *s.* segnalatore.

signatory ['signətəri], *s.* firmatario.

signature ['signitʃə*], *s.* **1.** firma, autografo; sigla **2.** (*tip.*) segnatura **3.** (*mus.*) indicazione (del tono, del tempo) **4.** (*arc.*) marchio, segno ☆ — *-tune*, (*rad.*) sigla musicale (di una trasmissione, di un complesso) ǁ *key —*, (*mus.*) segno di chiave.

signer ['sainə*], *s.c.* firmatario, firmataria.

signet ['signit], *s.* sigillo ǁ *Writer to the Signet*, (scoz.) procuratore ☆ — *-ring*, anello con sigillo.

significance [sig'nifikəns], **significancy** [sig'nifikənsi], *s.* **1.** espressione: *there is no — in his eyes*, non c'è espressione nei suoi occhi **2.** significato, senso: *the real — of his words was not grasped*, il vero significato delle sue parole non fu afferrato **3.** importanza: *incident of no —*, incidente di nessuna importanza.

significant [sig'nifikənt], *ag.* **1.** espressivo, significativo: — *look*, sguardo significativo **2.** importante.

significantly [sig'nifikəntli], *av.* in modo significativo.

signification [,signifi'keiʃən], *s.* significato, senso.

significative [sig'nifikətiv], *ag.* significativo.

significatively [sig'nifikətivli], *av.* in modo significativo.

significatory [sig'nifikətəri], *ag.* significativo.

to **signify** ['signifai], *v.t.i.* **1.** significare, voler dire; avere un significato: *what does this word —?*, cosa significa questa parola? **2.** denotare, indicare; preannunziare, presagire: *a broad forehead signifies intelligence*, una fronte ampia è segno di intelligenza; *a halo round the moon signifies rain*, un alone intorno alla luna preannunzia la pioggia **3.** far conoscere, far sapere: *he signified that he could not consent*, fece sapere che non poteva acconsentire **4.** importare, essere importante: *it does not —*, non ha importanza.

signing ['sainiŋ], *s.* firma, sottoscrizione.

Signior, Signor ['si:njo:*], *s.* signore ǁ *The Grand —*, (*st.*) il Sultano di Turchia.

Sikh [si:k], *s.* « sik » (membro di una comunità indù).

silage ['sailidʒ], *s.* **1.** conservazione di foraggio in silos **2.** foraggio conservato in silos.

to **silage**, *v.t.* riporre in silos.

silence ['sailəns], *s.* silenzio: *the — of the night*, il silenzio della notte; *a dead —*, un silenzio di tomba; *they listened in —*, ascoltarono in silenzio; *to break, to keep —*, rompere, mantenere il silenzio; *to pass over sthg. in —*, passare ql.co. sotto silenzio; *to put to —*, ridurre al silenzio, imporre il silenzio ǁ *— gives consent*, *prov.* chi tace acconsente ǁ *— is golden*, *prov.* il silenzio è d'oro.

to **silence**, *v.t.* far tacere, imporre il silenzio a; far cessare, far tacere (il fuoco del nemico): *to — one's conscience*, far tacere la propria coscienza.

silencer ['sailənsə*], *s.* silenziatore.

silent ['sailənt], *ag.* **1.** silenzioso, taciturno; quieto, tranquillo: *he kept —*, rimase zitto **2.** muto (anche *gram.*): *a — l*, una l muta; *history is — on these things*, la storia tace questi fatti ☆ — *film*, film muto ǁ *-partner*, (*amer.*) socio inattivo.

silently ['sailəntli], *av.* in silenzio, silenziosamente.

silentness ['sailəntnis], *s.* silenzio, taciturnità.

Silenus [sai'li:nəs], *no.pr.m.* (*mit.*) Sileno.

Silesia [sai'li:zjə], *no.pr.* (*geog.*) Slesia ǁ **silesia**, *s.* sottile tessuto per fodere.

Silesian [sai'li:zjən], *ag.s.c.* (abitante) della Slesia.

silex ['saileks], *s.* (*min.*) silice.

silhouette [,silu(:)'et], *s.* silhouetta; profilo; contorno: *in —*, di profilo.

to **silhouette**, *v.t.* fare la silhouetta di; ritrarre di profilo.

silica ['silikə], *s.* (*min.*) silice.

silicate ['silikit], *s.* (*min. chim.*) silicato.

silicated ['silikeitid], *ag.* impregnato di silicato.

siliceous [si'liʃəs], *ag.* siliceo.

silicic [si'lisik], *ag.* silicico.

silicification [si,lisifi'keiʃən], *s.* silicificazione.

to **silicify** [si'lisifai], *v.t.i.* silicizzare, silicizzarsi.

silicious [si'liʃəs], *ag.* siliceo.

silicon ['silikən], *s.* (*chim.*) silicio.

silicosis [,sili'kousis], *s.* (*patol.*) silicosi.

siliqua ['silikwə], **silique** [si'li:k], *s.* (*bot.*) siliqua.

silk [silk], *ag.* di seta, serico ǁ *s.* **1.** seta, tessuto di seta ǁ *to take the —*, essere nominato consigliere del re **2.** *pl.* articoli di seta ☆ — *-hat*, cilindro; — *-mill*, filanda; — *-shag*, felpa di seta; — *-thrower*, tessitore di seta ǁ *artificial, natural —*, seta artificiale, naturale; *raw —*, seta grezza.

silken ['silkən], *ag.* **1.** serico, di seta; vestito di seta **2.** morbido; lucente **3.** *fig.* dolce; gentile; insinuante.

to **silken**, *v.t.* render morbido come seta.

silkgrower ['silk,grouə*], *s.* sericoltore.

silkiness ['silkinis], *s.* **1.** natura serica **2.** morbidezza; lucentezza **3.** *fig.* dolcezza, delicatezza.

silkworm ['silk-wə:m], *s.* baco da seta ☆ — *breeder*, sericoltore; — *-breeding*, sericoltura; — *-nursery*, bachicoltura; — *-rot*, calcino (malattia del baco da seta).

silky ['silki], *ag.* **1.** di seta, serico **2.** morbido, lucente **3.** *fig.* delicato; insinuante.

sill [sil], *s.* **1.** (*edil.*) soglia; davanzale **2.** (*miner.*) soletta (di galleria) **3.** (*geol.*) « sill », filone-strato.

sillabub ['siləbab], *s.* quagliata con zucchero e vino.

siller ['silə*], *s.* (scoz.) argento; denaro.

sillily ['silili], *av.* scioccamente.

silliness ['silinis], *s.* stupidità, sciocchezza.

silly ['sili], *ag.* sciocco, stupido: *don't be —*, non fare lo stupido ǁ *a — Billy*, uno sciocchino ǁ *s.c.* persona sciocca.

silo ['sailou], *pl.* **silos** ['sailouz], *s.* silos.

to **silo**, *v.t.* conservare, mettere in silos.

silt [silt], *s.* fango; melma.

to **silt**, *v.t.i.: to — (up)*, ostruire (con melma, fango); ostruirsi (per melma, fango).

silty ['silti], *ag.* melmoso; fangoso.

Silurian [sai'ljuəriən], *ag. s.* (*geol.*) siluriano, silurico.

silurus [si'ljuərəs], *s.* (*ittiol.*) siluro.

silvan ['silvən], *ag.* silvano.

silver ['silvə*], *ag.* d'argento; argenteo; argentino: — *inkstand*, calamaio d'argento; — *spoon*, cucchiaio d'argento ǁ *to be born with a — spoon in one's mouth*, essere nato con la camicia ǁ *to have a — tongue*, essere molto eloquente ǁ *every cloud has a — lining*, *prov.* dopo il brutto viene il bello ǁ *speech is — but silence is golden*, *prov.* la parola è d'argento, ma il silenzio è d'oro ǁ *s.* argento; argenteria; moneta d'argento ☆ — *-fox*, volpe argentata; — *-gilt*, argento dorato; — *-grey*, grigio argento; — *-haired*, dai capelli d'argento; — *-plate*, argenteria; — *plating*, argentatura; — *-stick*, ufficiale della guardia a palazzo reale; — *-thaw*, nevischio; — *wedding*, nozze d'argento ǁ *flat —*, posate d'argento; *German —*, argentone; *quick —*, mercurio.

to **silver**, *v.t.i.* inargentare, inargentarsi; diventare argenteo.

silvered ['silvəd], *ag.* argentato.

silvering ['silvəriŋ], *s.* argentatura.

silvern ['silvən], *ag.* (*arc.*) d'argento, argenteo.

silversmith ['silvə-smiθ], *s.* argentiere.

silverware ['silvəwɛə*], *s.* argenteria.

silvery ['silvəri], *ag.* d'argento; argenteo; argentino.

simian ['simiən], *ag.* scimmiesco ǁ *s.* scimmia.

similar ['similə*], *ag.* simile; somigliante; analogo: — *triangles*, triangoli simili ǁ *s.* cosa simile, analoga.

similarity [,simi'læriti], *s.* somiglianza, rassomiglianza.

simile ['simili], *s.* (*ret.*) similitudine, paragone.

similitude [si'militju:d], *s.* **1.** (*ret.*) similitudine, paragone **2.** immagine, somiglianza: *God made man in his own —,* Dio creò l'uomo a propria immagine.

to similize ['similaiz], *v.t.i.* usare similitudini; illustrare per mezzo di similitudini.

similor ['similo:*], *s.* similoro.

simious ['simiəs], *ag.* scimmiesco.

simmer ['simə*], *s.* stato di lenta ebollizione: *at a* (*o on the*) *—,* al punto di ebollizione.

to simmer, *v.t.i.* **1.** incominciare a bollire; far bollire lentamente **2.** *fig.* essere sul punto di scoppiare; contenere, reprimere (ira, indignazione, ecc.): *to — with rage,* ribollire d'ira.

simnel-cake ['simnl-keik], *s.* (*cuc.*) « simnel-cake » (tipo di pan di Spagna).

Simon ['saimən], *no.pr.m.* Simone.

simoniac [sai'mouniək], *ag.s.* simoniaco.

simoniacal [,saimə'naiəkəl], *ag.* simoniaco.

simoniacally [,saimə'naiəkəli], *av.* con simonia.

simony ['saiməni], *s.* simonia.

simoom [si'mu:m], *s.* « simun » (vento del deserto).

simper ['simpə*], *s.* sorriso affettato; smorfia.

to simper, *v.t.i.* sorridere, parlare in modo affettato; esprimere sorridendo.

simperer ['simpərə*], *s.c.* persona leziosa, affettata.

simpering ['simpəriŋ], *s.* affettazione; smorfie.

simperingly ['simpəriŋli], *av.* affettatamente; smorfiosamente.

simple ['simpl], *ag.* **1.** semplice, elementare, facile: *it was a very — problem,* era un problema di assai facile soluzione **2.** semplice; sincero; naturale, non sofisticato: *she has — tastes,* ha dei gusti semplici **3.** autentico: *such an act was — madness,* un tale atto fu vera e propria pazzia **4.** ignorante, senza esperienza; ingenuo; credulone: *he is not as — as you believe,* non è ingenuo come credi **5.** umile; di basso rango: *a — peasant,* un umile contadino ‖ *s. gener. pl.* semplici (erbe medicinali) ☆ *— -hearted* (*o — -minded*), semplice, ingenuo; *— -mindedness,* semplicità, ingenuità.

simpleness ['simplnis], *V.* simplicity.

simpleton ['simpltən], *s.c.* sempliciotto, sempliciotta.

simpliciter [sim'plisitə*], *av.* assolutamente; incondizionatamente; senza limiti.

simplicity [sim'plisiti], *s.* **1.** semplicità; candore, ingenuità **2.** chiarezza; facilità.

simplification [,simplifi'keiʃən], *s.* semplificazione.

to simplify ['simplifai], *v.t.* semplificare.

simplism ['simplizəm], *s.* affettazione di semplicità.

simply ['simpli], *av.* **1.** semplicemente; solamente: *he is — a workman,* egli è solamente un operaio; *to dress —,* vestirsi semplicemente **2.** facilmente; chiaramente.

simulacrum [,simju'leikrəm], *pl.* simulacra [,simju-'leikrə], *s.* simulacro.

simulant ['simjulənt], *ag.* che simula.

to simulate ['simjuleit], *v.t.* **1.** simulare, fingere **2.** imitare l'apparenza di, prendere l'aspetto di, imitare.

simulation [,simju'leiʃən], *s.* simulazione, finzione.

simulator ['simjuleitə*], *s.c.* simulatore, simulatrice.

simultaneity [,siməltə'nieti], *s.* simultaneità.

simultaneous [,siməl'teinjəs], *ag.* simultaneo.

simultaneously [,siməl'teinjəsli], *av.* simultaneamente.

simultaneousness [,siməl'teinjəsnis], *s.* simultaneità.

sin [sin], *s.* **1.** peccato, colpa: *to fall into, to live in —,* cadere in, vivere nel peccato ‖ *deadly, capital —,* peccato mortale, capitale; *the forgiveness of sins,* la remissione dei peccati; *original —,* peccato originale; *the seven deadly sins,* i sette peccati capitali ‖ *as ugly as —,* brutto come il peccato ‖ *like —,* (*sl.*) violentemente: *it is raining like —,* piove a dirotto **2.** offesa: *it is a — against good taste,* è un'offesa al buon gusto ☆ *— -offering,* (*st.*) sacrificio espiatorio.

to sin, *pass.p.p.* sinned [sind], *v.t.i.* peccare; macchiare col peccato: *wherein have I sinned?,* in cosa ho peccato?; *to — one's soul,* macchiare la propria anima ‖ *to — against propriety,* trasgredire le convenienze.

Sinai ['sainiai], *no.pr.* (*geog.*) Sinai.

Sinanthropus [,sainæn'θroupəs], *s.* (*antropologia*) sinantropo.

sinapism ['sinəpizəm], *s.* (*farm.*) senapismo.

since [sins], *av.* da allora, da allora in poi: *I last spoke to her five days ago, I haven't heard from her —,* le ho parlato per l'ultima volta cinque giorni fa, da allora non ne ho più saputo nulla; *she went to Australia soon after the war, and has lived there ever —,* si trasferì in Australia subito dopo la guerra e da allora vive là; *the town was heavily bombed and has — been entirely rebuilt,* la città subì forti bombardamenti e da allora è stata interamente ricostruita ‖ *long —,* molto tempo fa: *that was long —,* accadde molto tempo fa; molto tempo è passato da allora ‖ *many years —,* molti anni fa ‖ *cong.* **1.** da quando, dal tempo in cui: *— I have known them,* da quando li conosco; *it is long — I last met her,* è trascorso molto tempo da quando la vidi per l'ultima volta **2.** poiché, dal momento che: *— we cannot go, you'd better stay with us,* dal momento che non possiamo andare, fareste meglio a trattenervi con noi.

since, *prep.* da: *— that time* (*o — then*), da allora; *— when have you been waiting for us?,* da quando ci aspetti?; *I have not seen her — last Sunday,* non la vedo da domenica scorsa; *nobody has heard from him — his going to Australia,* nessuno ha avuto sue notizie da quando si è recato in Australia.

sincere [sin'siə*], *ag.* sincero, schietto, franco.

sincerely [sin'siəli], *av.* sinceramente ‖ *yours —,* cordialmente vostro (nelle lettere).

sincerity [sin'seriti], *s.* sincerità, buona fede: *in all —,* con tutta sincerità; con assoluta buona fede.

sinciput ['sinsipʌt], *s.* (*anat.*) sincipite.

sine [sain], *s.* (*trigonometria*) seno.

sinecure ['sainikjuə*], *s.* (*dir. eccl.*) sinecura.

sinecurism ['sainikjurizəm], *s.* (*dir. eccl.*) concessione, godimento di sinecure.

sinecurist ['saini,kju:rist], *s.* (*eccl.*) chi ha una sinecura.

sine-die ['saini'daii(:)], *av.* (*lat.*) sine die, a tempo indeterminato.

sinew ['sinju:], *s.* **1.** tendine, nervo **2.** *pl. fig.* nerbo, forza, vigore; sostegno, colonna ‖ *the sinews of war,* il nerbo della guerra (il denaro).

to sinew, *v.t.* (*poet.*) sostenere, servire da sostegno a.

sinewiness ['sinju(:)inis], *s.* muscolosità; vigore, forza.

sinewless ['sinju(:)lis], *ag.* **1.** senza tendini, nervi **2.** *fig.* senza nerbo, senza vigore.

sinewy ['sinju(:)i], *ag.* **1.** tendinoso, fibroso **2.** *fig.* nerboruto, muscoloso; vigoroso, energico; terso (di stile).

sinfonia [,sinfə'ni:ə], *s.* (*mus.*) sinfonia.

sinful ['sinful], *ag.* peccaminoso; colpevole; corrotto.

sinfully ['sinfuli], *av.* peccaminosamente.

sinfulness ['sinfulnis], *s.* iniquità; colpevolezza.

sing [siŋ], *s.* (*fam. amer.*) **1.** canto (corale) **2.** sibilo.

to sing, *pass.* sang [sæŋ], *p.p.* sung [sʌŋ], *v.t.i.* **1.** cantare; intonare (una canzone): *to — in tune, out of tune,* cantare intonato, stonato; *to — s.o. to sleep,* fare addormentare qlcu. cantando; *to learn to —,* imparare a cantare ‖ *to — another song, fig.* cambiar modo d'agire ‖ *to — for one's supper, fig.* guadagnarsi la cena ‖ *to — small,* abbassare il tono di voce; *fig.* diventare umile **2.** lodare, celebrare le lodi di: *to — s.o.'s praises,* decantare i meriti di qlcu. **3.** poetare, celebrare in versi: *arms and the man I —...,* (*letter.*) canto le armi e l'eroe... **4.** accompagnare con canti: *to — a bride to her new house,* accompagnare una sposa con canti alla sua nuova casa; *to — the harvest home,* trasportare al chiuso il raccolto cantando; *to — the old year out, the new year in,* salutare l'anno vecchio con canti, inneggiare all'anno nuovo **5.** fischiare (di vento, ecc.);

ronzare; borbottare: *the kettle sings on the fire*, la pentola borbotta sul focolare; *the mosquitoes — round my head*, le zanzare ronzano attorno al mio capo; *my ears are singing*, mi ronzano le orecchie **6.** *to* — **out**, cantare a voce spiegata, gridare; (*sl.*) fare la spia, denunziare i propri complici.

singable ['siŋəbl], *ag.* cantabile; facile da cantare.

Singapore [,siŋɡo'pɔː*], *no.pr.* (*geog.*) Singapore.

singe [sindʒ], *s.* (*rar.*) bruciacchiatura; strinatura.

to singe, *v.t.i.* bruciacchiare, bruciacchiarsi, strinare (anche *fig.*): *his reputation is a little singed*, la sua reputazione è intaccata; *to* — *one's wings* (o *feathers*), bruciarsi le ali.

singer ['siŋə*], *s.c.* cantante, cantatrice || *s.* cantore, poeta.

singing ['siŋiŋ], *ag.* che canta, canoro || *s.* **1.** canto **2.** fischio (di vento, ecc.); ronzio ☆ — *-bird*, uccello canoro; — *lesson*, lezione di canto; — *-man*, cantante; — *-master*, maestro di canto.

single ['siŋgl], *ag.* **1.** solo, unico; semplice: *he did not know a* — *soul*, non conosceva anima viva; *the nation spoke with a* — *voice*, la nazione si espresse unanime || *every* — *day*, tutti i giorni **2.** individuale, particolare: *a* — *room*, una stanza singola **3.** celibe, nubile: *are you married or* —*?*, sei sposato o celibe? **4.** sincero, semplice, onesto: *a* — *heart*, un cuore sincero || *s.* (*tennis*) singolo ☆ *the* — *blessedness*, l'essere scapolo, nubile; — *-breasted*, a un petto (di giacca); — *-eyed*, con un solo occhio; *fig.* onesto, sincero; — *-handed*, con una mano sola; *fig.* solo, senza aiuto; — *-hearted* (o — *-minded*), semplice, sincero; — *-seater*, monoposto; — *-spindle*, (*mec.*) monomandrino; — *ticket*, (*ferr.*) biglietto semplice.

to single, *v.t.* separare; distinguere; scegliere: *to* — (*out*) *sthg.*, scegliere ql.co.

singleness ['siŋglnis], *s.* **1.** unicità **2.** sincerità; onestà.

singlestick ['siŋgl-stik], *s.* **1.** bastone simile a spada **2.** (*spor.*) scherma praticata con tale bastone.

singlet ['siŋglit], *s.* camiciola, maglia.

singleton ['siŋgltən], *s.* **1.** (*carte*) carta unica di una serie **2.** unico nato.

singly ['siŋgli], *av.* **1.** separatamente, ad uno ad uno **2.** da solo; senza aiuto **3.** (*rar.*) solamente, unicamente **4.** sinceramente.

singsong ['siŋ-sɔŋ], *ag.* monotono, noioso || *s.* **1.** canto monotono; cantilena **2.** (*fam.*) riunione tenuta per cantare; concerto improvvisato.

to singsong, *v.t.i.* parlare, recitare con ritmo monotono.

singular ['siŋgjulə*], *ag.* **1.** singolare; solo **2.** sorprendente; eccezionale **3.** singolare; bizzarro, strano; eccentrico **4.** (*gram.*) singolare || *s.* (*gram.*) singolare.

singularity [,siŋgju'læriti], *s.* **1.** singolarità; rarità **2.** particolarità **3.** stranezza; eccentricità.

singularization [,siŋgjuləri'zeifən], *s.* singolarizzazione.

to singularize ['siŋgjuləraiz], *v.t.* distinguere, particolarizzare.

singularly ['siŋgjuləli], *av.* **1.** singolarmente **2.** (*gram.*) al singolare.

sinister ['sinistə*], *ag.* **1.** sinistro, funesto; di cattivo augurio **2.** disonesto **3.** (*arald.*) sinistro.

sinisterly ['sinistəli], *av.* **1.** sinistramente, funestamente **2.** disonestamente.

sinistral ['sinistrəl], *ag.* **1.** (*rar.*) sinistro **2.** che gira a sinistra (di spirale).

sinistrorse ['sinistrɔːs], *ag.* (*bot.*) sinistrorso.

sinistrous ['sinistrəs], *ag.* sinistro; di cattivo augurio.

sinistrously ['sinistrəsli], *av.* minacciosamente.

sink [siŋk], *s.* **1.** lavandino, acquaio **2.** scolo; fogna, sentina (anche *fig.*) **3.** (*geol.*) foiba, voragine **4.** (*teat.*) botola ☆ — *-hole*, pozzo di scolo; (*amer.*) foiba.

to sink, *pass.* **sank** [sæŋk], (*rar.*) **sunk** [sʌŋk], *p.p.*, **sunk**, *v.t.i.* **1.** affondare, andare a fondo; mandare a fondo: *the ship sank*, la nave affondò; *to* — *like a stone*,

colare a picco **2.** sprofondare; penetrare; immergersi; conficcare, conficcarsi: *the car sank into the mud*, l'automobile sprofondò nel fango; *her words sank into my mind*, le sue parole mi si impressero nella mente; *let the dye* — *in*, lascia assorbire la tintura; *to* — *into decay*, andare in rovina; *to* — *into a deep sleep*, sprofondare in un sonno profondo; *to* — *into vice*, sprofondare nel vizio **3.** discendere; abbassare, abbassarsi; calare; diminuire: *the ground sinks abruptly*, il terreno scende di colpo, s'affossa; *his voice sank*, la sua voce si abbassò; *prices are sinking*, i prezzi calano; *the river has sunk*, il fiume si è abbassato; *the sun is sinking*, il sole sta calando, tramonta **4.** cadere; cedere (di muro, terreno); crollare, abbattersi: *his legs sank under him*, gli cedettero le gambe; *my heart sank at the news*, a quella notizia il mio cuore mancò; *to* — *into one's chair*, lasciarsi cadere su una sedia; *to* — *on one's knees*, cadere in ginocchio **5.** scavare (pozzo, ecc.) **6.** *fig.* ignorare, trascurare; passar sotto silenzio; lasciar cadere: *they sank their differences*, dimenticarono le loro divergenze **7.** investire denaro a fondo perduto.

sinkable ['siŋkəbl], *ag.* affondabile.

sinker ['siŋkə*], *s.* **1.** scavatore (di pozzi, ecc.) **2.** piombo, peso (per lenza) **3.** (*sl. amer.*) frittella malcotta.

sinking ['siŋkiŋ], *s.* **1.** affondamento **2.** cedimento, abbassamento; abbattimento; indebolimento (anche *fig.*) **3.** scavo, sterro **4.** ammortamento; investimento a fondo perduto ☆ — *-fund*, fondo di ammortamento.

sinless ['sinlis], *ag.* senza peccato, innocente, puro.

sinlessly ['sinlisli], *av.* senza peccato, innocentemente.

sinlessness ['sinlisnis], *s.* innocenza, purezza.

sinner ['sinə*], *s.c.* peccatore, peccatrice.

sinnet ['sinit], *V.* **sennit**.

Sinn Fein ['ʃin'fein], *s.* (*irl.*) « Sinn Fein » (movimento separatista irlandese, fondato nel 1905).

sinologue ['sinələg], *s.* sinologo.

sinology [si'nɔlədʒi], *s.* sinologia.

sinter ['sintə*], *s.* **1.** (*geol.*) geyserite **2.** (*amer. metal.*) scoria.

sinuate ['sinjuit], *ag.* **1.** sinuoso, serpeggiante **2.** (*bot.*) dentellato, frastagliato.

to sinuate ['sinjueit], *v.i.* (*rar.*) serpeggiare; essere sinuoso, serpeggiare.

sinuately ['sinjuitli], *av.* sinuosamente.

sinuation [,sinju'eifən], *s.* sinuosità.

sinuous ['sinjuəs], *ag.* sinuoso, tortuoso.

sinuosity [,sinju'ositi], *s.* sinuosità.

sinuously ['sinjuəsli], *av.* sinuosamente.

sinus ['sainəs], *pl.* **sinuses** ['sainəsiz], *s.* **1.** (*bot.*) sinuosità (tra due lobi di foglie) **2.** (*anat.*) seno, cavità **3.** (*patol.*) fistola.

sinusitis [,sainə'saitis], *s.* (*patol.*) sinusite.

sinusoid ['sainəsɔid], *s.* (*geom.*) sinusoide.

Sion ['saiən], *no.pr.* (*geog. st.*) Sionne.

sip [sip], *s.* sorso.

to sip, *pass.p.p.* **sipped** [sipt], *v.t.i.* sorseggiare, centellinare.

sipahee [si'pɔːi], *V.* **sepoy**.

siphon ['saifən], *s.* **1.** (*fis. zool.*) sifone **2.** — (*-bottle*), sifone da seltz.

to siphon, *v.t.i.* travasare con un sifone; fluire attraverso un sifone.

siphonage ['saifənidʒ], *s.* il travasare con un sifone.

siphonal ['saifənl], **siphonic** [sai'fɔnik], *ag.* di, simile a sifone.

sipper ['sipə*], *s.c.* chi sorseggia.

sippet ['sipit], *s.* crostino di pane.

sir [sə*], *s.* **1.** (*vocativo*) signore: *thank you* —, grazie, signore || *Dear Sir, Dear Sirs*, Egregio Signore, Spettabile Ditta **2.** *Sir*, « Sir » (titolo premesso al nome di battesimo di un cavaliere, di un baronetto).

to sir, *v.t.* rivolgersi a (qlcu.) col titolo di « sir ».

sircar ['sə:ka:*], *s.* (*ang.-in.*) **1.** governo **2.** provincia **3.** maggiordomo **4.** impiegato, contabile.

sirdar ['sǝ:dɑ:*], s. **1.** capo indigeno (in India) **2.** (st.) comandante in capo dell'esercito anglo-egiziano.

sire ['saiǝ*], s. **1.** genitore (di animali); stallone **2.** (poet.) padre; antenato **3.** Sire, (vocativo arc.) Sire, Maestà.

to **sire**, v.t. generare (specialmente di stalloni).

siren ['saiǝrin], s. **1.** (mit.) sirena; fig. donna affascinante, incantatrice **2.** (mec.) sirena.

sirenian [sai'ri:njǝn], ag. (zool.) dei sirenidi ‖ s. (zool.) sirenide.

siriasis [si'raiǝsis], s. (patol.) siriasi.

Sirius ['siriǝs], no.pr. (astr.) Sirio.

sirkar, V. **sircar**.

sirloin ['sǝ:lǝin], s. lombo di manzo.

siroe ['sirɔk], **sirocco** [si'rɔkou], s. scirocco.

sirrah ['sirǝ], s. (vocativo arc. spreg.) messere.

sirup ['sirǝp], s. sciroppo.

sirupy ['sirǝpi], ag. sciropposo.

sirvente [,si:'vɑ:ŋt], s. (poes.) serventese.

sisal ['saisǝl], s. (bot.) agave sisaliana ☆ — grass (o — hemp), « sisal », fibra d'agave.

siskin ['siskin], s. (ornit.) lucherino.

sissy ['sisi], s. (sl.) ragazzo, uomo effeminato.

sist [sist], s. (scoz. dir.) sospensione di atti giudiziari.

to **sist**, v.t. (scoz. dir.) **1.** sospendere (atti giudiziari) **2.** chiamare in tribunale, citare.

sister ['sistǝ*], s. **1.** sorella ‖ the Fatal Sisters (o the three Sisters), le Parche **2.** amica intima **3.** suora ‖ — of mercy, suora di carità **4.** infermiera capo-reparto ☆ — block, (mar.) bozzello a vergine; — element, (chim.) elemento affine; — -hook, femmina di gancio; — -in-law, cognata; — ships, navi gemelle ‖ half —, sorellastra.

sisterhood ['sistǝhud], s. sorellanza; congregazione religiosa; comunità di donne.

sisterless ['sistǝlis], ag. senza sorelle.

sisterliness ['sistǝlinis], s. qualità, affetto di sorella.

sisterly ['sistǝli], ag. di sorella; amorevole ‖ av. da sorella; amorevolmente.

Sistine Chapel ['sistain'tʃæpǝl], s. Cappella Sistina.

sistrum ['sistrǝm], pl. **sistra** ['sistrǝ], s. (mus.) sistro.

Sisyphean [,sisi'fi(:)ǝn], ag. di Sisifo.

Sisyphus ['sisifǝs], no.pr.m. (mit.) Sisifo.

to **sit** [sit], pass.p.p. **sat** [sæt], v.t.i. **1.** sedere, essere seduto, stare seduto; mettere a sedere, far sedere: he was sitting on a chair, era seduto su una sedia; they sat looking at each other, rimasero (seduti) a guardarsi; we were sitting at tea, stavamo prendendo il tè; would you rather — here?, preferisci sedere qui?; to — at table, essere, stare a tavola; to — oneself (down), sedersi; to — still, starsene (seduti) immobili ‖ to — at home, rimanere a casa; essere disoccupato ‖ to — for a constituency, rappresentare un collegio elettorale ‖ to — for an examination, dare un esame ‖ to — for a portrait, posare per un ritratto ‖ to — in Parliament, sedere in Parlamento ‖ to — loose to sthg., (fam. amer.) essere indifferente a ql.co. ‖ to — tight, tenersi saldo (specialmente in sella); fig. non lasciarsi smuovere, tener duro **2.** essere in seduta; tener seduta, riunirsi in seduta: the court sits on Mondays, il tribunale tiene seduta il lunedì; Parliament is sitting, il Parlamento è in seduta **3.** appollaiarsi, posare, stare appollaiato (di uccelli); accovacciarsi (di animali) **4.** covare: hens — in summer, le galline covano d'estate **5.** stare, cadere (bene, male, di abiti): this skirt sits well, questa gonna cade bene, sta bene **6.** to — (a horse) well, badly, stare bene, male in sella; cavalcare bene, male **7.** (arc. poet.) spirare (di vento): how sits the wind?, da dove spira il vento?; (fam.) che vento tira? **8.** to — over (s.o., sthg.), (bridge) essere alla sinistra di (chi giuoca), essere in posizione di vantaggio su ‖ to — over a book, immergersi nella lettura di un libro ‖ to — over a pipe, starsene seduto a gustare la pipa **9.** to — under (s.o.), ascoltare (regolarmente) le prediche di; seguire le lezioni di **10.** to — (up)on (s.o., sthg.), con-

durre un'inchiesta su, esaminare (di comitato, giuria); gravare, pesare (anche fig.); addirsi, confarsi; (sl.) trattare dall'alto in basso, dare una buona lezione a: his losses — lightly upon him, le sue perdite non gli pesano molto; his new dignities — rather awkwardly upon him, si adatta piuttosto goffamente alle sue nuove cariche; this cake sits heavy on my stomach, questo dolce mi pesa sullo stomaco; to — on a case, esaminare un caso giudiziario ‖ we sat on him because he was getting too big for his boots, l'abbiamo messo a posto perchè si dava troppe arie ‖ to — on the fence, non prendere partito ‖ to — on a jury, far parte di una giuria **11.** to — down, mettersi a sedere; prendere posto; (mil.) accampare, accamparsi (per assediare una città): to — down to table, mettersi a tavola ‖ to — down hard on a plan, (fam.) bocciare un progetto ‖ to — down under an insult, incassare un insulto **12.** to — out, sedere all'aperto; non prender parte a (danza, ecc.); rimanere fino alla fine: he sat the lecture out, ascoltò la conferenza fino alla fine; they sat him out, rimasero finchè egli non se ne andò **13.** to — up, stare eretto; mettersi in posizione eretta; rizzarsi (sul letto); vegliare, rimanere alzato: — up boys!, state dritti ragazzi!; I sat up late for him last night, l'ho aspettato alzata fino a tardi la notte scorsa; to — up with a sick person, vegliare un malato ‖ to make s.o. — up, sorprendere, spaventare qlcu., far sussultare qlcu.: the news made him — up, la notizia lo colse di sorpresa, lo fece sussultare; you ought to make your employees — up a bit, dovresti svegliare un po' i tuoi impiegati ‖ to — up and take notice, (fam.) drizzare le orecchie.

sitdown ['sitdaun], ag. attributivo a sedere: I prefer — lunches to buffet lunches, preferisco far colazione al tavolo piuttosto che in piedi ‖ — strike, sciopero bianco ‖ s. il sedersi (per un po'): let's have a —, sediamoci un momento.

site [sait], s. **1.** sito, luogo; posizione **2.** area fabbricabile.

to **site**, v.t.i. porre; situare, essere situato; trovarsi.

sith [siθ], (arc.) per **since**.

sitology [sai'tolǝdʒi], s. dietetica.

sitter ['sitǝ*], s.c. **1.** chi sta seduto **2.** persona che prende parte ad una seduta **3.** (pitt. scult., ecc.) modello, modella ‖ s. **1.** chioccia **2.** (spor.) occasione fortunata per segnare un punto; (caccia) colpo facile ☆ — -in, « baby-sitter » (chi custodisce i bimbi durante l'assenza dei genitori).

sitting ['sitiŋ], ag. **1.** seduto **2.** presente ad una seduta ‖ s. **1.** posa; seduta; breve periodo di tempo: he finished my portrait in three sittings, finì il mio ritratto in tre pose; to finish a job at one —, finire un lavoro in una volta sola **2.** adunanza, riunione ‖ the sittings, le sessioni dell'anno giudiziario **3.** covata **4.** posto, banco riservato (in una chiesa) ☆ — -room, stanza di soggiorno.

situate ['sitjueit], ag. (arc.) situato, posto, collocato.

situated ['sitjueitid], ag. **1.** situato, collocato, posto (di luogo): a badly — town, una città situata male **2.** in una certa posizione, situazione (di persona): this is how I am —, questa è la situazione in cui mi trovo.

situation [,sitju'eiʃǝn], s. **1.** situazione, posizione, ubicazione **2.** stato, situazione, circostanza: the political — seems calm, la situazione politica appare tranquilla **3.** posto, impiego: he found a — as a gardener, trovò un posto di giardiniere; to apply for a —, fare una domanda d'impiego; to be out of a —, essere disoccupato; to get a —, ottenere un impiego ‖ situations wanted, richieste di impiego.

Siva ['sivǝ], no.pr.m. (relig. indù) Siva.

six [siks], ag.num.card.s. sei ‖ — of one and half a dozen of the other, se non è zuppa è pan bagnato ‖ to be at — and seven (o sixes and sevens), essere in disordine ☆ — -foot, che misura sei piedi: — -foot way, (ferr.) interbinario; — -footer, persona alta sei piedi; — -shooter, rivoltella a sei colpi.

sixain ['siksein], *s.* (*poes.*) sestina.
sixer ['siksə*], *s.* (*cricket*) colpo che vale per sei.
sixfold ['siksfould], *ag.* sestuplo ‖ *av.* sei volte tanto.
sixpence ['sikspəns], *s.* moneta da sei « pennies », mezzo scellino.
sixpenny ['sikspəni], *ag.* che vale mezzo scellino ‖ *s.* **1.** moneta da sei « pennies » **2.** pubblicazione da due soldi, a buon mercato ☆ — *piece*, moneta da sei « pennies »; — *stamp*, francobollo da sei « pennies ».
sixte [sikst], *s.* (*scherma*) posizione di sesta.
sixteen ['siks'ti:n], *ag.num.card.s.* sedici.
sixteenmo [siks'ti:nmou], *ag.s.* (*tip.*) (formato, volume) in sedicesimo.
sixteenth ['siks'ti:nθ], *ag. num. ord. s.* sedicesimo.
sixth [siksθ], *ag.num.ord.* sesto ‖ *s.* **1.** sesta parte **2.** (*mus.*) sesta.
sixthly ['siksθli], *av.num.* in sesto luogo.
sixtieth ['sikstiiθ], *ag.num.ord.s.* sessantesimo.
sixty ['siksti], *ag.num.card.s.* sessanta: *he is not far off —*, egli non è lontano dalla sessantina ‖ *the sixties*, gli anni fra il '60 e il '70: *it happened in the sixties of the eighteenth century*, accadde fra il 1760 e il 1770.
sizable ['saizəbl], *ag.* piuttosto grande.
sizar ['saizə*], *s.* studente universitario che usufruisce di una « sizarship ».
sizarship ['saizəʃip], *s.* borsa di studio (a Cambridge, Dublino).
size[1] [saiz], *s.* **1.** grandezza, misura, dimensione, taglia; statura: *all of a —*, tutti della stessa grandezza; *out of —*, fuori misura; *these shoes are a — too big*, queste scarpe sono di una misura più grande; *what is your —?*, che taglia avete? **2.** formato: *the — of that book is too big*, il formato di quel libro è troppo grande **3.** (*sl. universitario*) razione di cibo, bevanda **4.** calibro.
to **size**[1], *v.t.i.* **1.** misurare, graduare, classificare secondo la misura ‖ *to — down*, graduare in ordine decrescente **2.** (*sl. universitario*) chiedere una razione di cibo, di bevanda **3.** *to — up*, misurare la capacità; valutare (una persona).
size[2], *s.* (*ind.*) turapori; (*ind. tessile*) bozzima.
to **size**[2], *v.t.* (*ind. tessile*) imbozzimare.
sizeable ['saizəbl], *ag.* piuttosto grande.
sized [saizd], *ag.* **1.** di una certa statura, grandezza, dimensione **2.** classificato in ordine di grandezza, statura, dimensione ☆ *large- —*, grande, di grandi dimensioni.
sizer ['saizə*], *s.* calibro.
sizing[1] ['saiziŋ], *s.* **1.** (*sl. universitario*) richiesta di razione supplementare (di cibo) **2.** (*mec.*) controllo delle dimensioni.
sizing[2], *s.* incollatura; (*ind. tessile*) imbozzimatura.
sizy ['saizi], *ag.* viscoso, attaccaticcio.
sizzle ['sizl], *s.* (*fam.*) sfrigolio.
to **sizzle**, *v.i.* (*fam.*) sfrigolare.
skald, *V.* **scald**[1].
skate[1] [skeit], *s.* pattino ☆ *roller- —*, pattino a rotelle.
to **skate**[1], *v.i.* pattinare ‖ *to — over thin ice*, *fig.* camminare sul filo del rasoio.
skate[2], *s.* (*ittiol.*) razza.
skater ['skeitə*], *s.c.* pattinatore, pattinatrice.
skating ['skeitiŋ], *s.* pattinaggio ☆ — *-rink*, pista per pattinaggio.
skean, *V.* **skene**.
skedaddle [ski'dædl], *s.* (*fam.*) corsa sfrenata; fuga precipitosa: *there was a general —*, ci fu un fuggi-fuggi generale.
to **skedaddle**, *v.i.* (*fam.*) scappare; svignarsela.
skeel [ski:l], *s.* (*sl.*) secchia; mastello.
skeet [ski:t], *s.* (*mar.*) gottazza, sessola.
skeeter ['ski:tə*], (*amer.*) *abbr.* di **mosquito**.
skeg[1] [skeg], *s.* (*mar.*) calcagnuolo.
skeg[2], *s.* (*bot.*) prugnolo.
skegger ['skegə*], *s.* (*ittiol.*) salmoncino.
skein [skein], *s.* **1.** matassa **2.** *fig.* confusione, scompiglio **3.** stormo (di oche selvatiche).

to **skelder** ['skeldə*], *v.t.i.* (*arc.*) **1.** mendicare **2.** ingannare; truffare.
skeletal ['skelitl], *ag.* scheletrico.
skeleton ['skelitn], *s.* **1.** scheletro (anche *fig.*): *he is a living —*, egli è uno scheletro vivente; *she is reduced to a —*, ella è ridotta uno scheletro ‖ *a — at a feast*, un guastafeste ‖ *a — in the cupboard* (o *the family —*), un fatto che si vuol celare per vergogna **2.** (*arch. mar.*) ossatura; intelaiatura **3.** (*bot.*) venatura **4.** canovaccio; schema; abbozzo ☆ — *construction*, (*arch.*) struttura a telai; — *crew*, (*mil.*) equipaggio ridotto; — *drill*, (*mil.*) esercizio di quadri; — *essay*, canovaccio di composizione; — *key*, chiave madre ‖ *building —*, ossatura muraria.
to **skeletonize** ['skelitənaiz], *v.t.* **1.** scheletrire; ridurre all'essenziale (anche *fig.*) **2.** schematizzare.
to **skelly** ['skeli], *v.i.* (*scoz.*) essere strabico.
skelp [skelp], *s.* (*scoz.*) **1.** ceffone, schiaffo **2.** rumore (di schiaffo).
to **skelp**, *v.t.i.* (*scoz.*) **1.** schiaffeggiare; picchiare **2.** muoversi in fretta.
to **skelter** ['skeltə*], *v.i.* affrettarsi; precipitarsi; sfrecciare.
skene [ski:n], *s.* (*st.*) pugnale scozzese ☆ — *-dhu*, pugnale (elemento del costume scozzese).
skep [skep], *s.* **1.** canestro; paniere **2.** alveare (di paglia, vimini).
skepsis ['skepsis], *s.* scetticismo; dubbio filosofico.
skeptic ['skeptik], *ag. s.* scettico (anche *fil.*).
skeptical ['skeptikəl], *ag.* scettico (anche *fil.*).
skeptically ['skeptikəli], *av.* scetticamente.
skepticism ['skeptisizəm], *s.* scetticismo (anche *fil.*).
skerry ['skeri], *s.* (*scoz.*) scoglio.
sketch [sketʃ], *s.* **1.** (*pitt.*) schizzo; abbozzo: *to take* (o *to make*) *a — of a scene*, fare lo schizzo di una scena **2.** (*rar.*) descrizione sommaria; profilo generale **3.** (*teat.*) « sketch », scenetta; (*lett.*) bozzetto; (*mus.*) breve composizione (per pianoforte) ☆ — *-block* (o *-book*), album per schizzi; — *plate*, (*metal.*) lamiera sagomata ‖ *first —*, primo getto.
to **sketch**, *v.t.i.* **1.** abbozzare; schizzare; fare uno schizzo **2.** *to — in*, disegnare sommariamente (dettagli) **3.** *to — out*, impostare il canovaccio di (un romanzo); delineare (un progetto).
sketchable ['sketʃəbl], *ag.* degno di essere disegnato; degno di essere rappresentato.
sketcher ['sketʃə*], *s.c.* disegnatore, disegnatrice.
sketchily ['sketʃili], *av.* in modo impreciso, in modo incompleto; per sommi capi.
sketchiness ['sketʃinis], *s.* mancanza di finitura, di dettagli: *the — of his knowledge*, la superficialità della sua cultura.
sketching ['sketʃiŋ], *s.* l'abbozzare; lo schizzare.
sketchy ['sketʃi], *ag.* abbozzato, non rifinito; impreciso; incompleto.
skew [skju:], *ag.* obliquo; sbieco; sghembo ‖ *s.* spiovente ☆ — *-back*, (*arch.*) imposta (di un arco); — *-chisel*, (*strum. artig.*) scalpello a taglio obliquo; — *curve*, (*mat.*) curva dissimmetrica; — *eyes*, occhi strabici; — *gear*, (*mec.*) ingranaggio conico a denti sghembi; — *wall*, (*arch.*) parete a sbieco.
to **skew**, *v.t.i.* **1.** mettere, mettersi di traverso **2.** guardare di traverso: *to — at s.o.*, guardare qlcu. di traverso **3.** deviare; far deviare.
skewer ['skju:ə*], *s.* **1.** spiedo **2.** (*scherz.*) spada.
to **skewer**, *v.t.* infilare sullo spiedo.
ski [ski:], *s.* sci ☆ — *-boots*, scarponi da sci; — *-jump*, salto (con gli sci); — *-lift*, sciovia; — *-troops*, (*mil.*) reparti sciatori.
to **ski**, *v.i.* sciare.
skiagram ['skaiəgræm], *s.* (*med.*) radiografia.
skiagraph ['skaiəgra:f], *s.* (*med.*) radiografia.
skid [skid], *s.* **1.** slittamento (di ruota) **2.** (*tec.*) scivolo **3.** (*mec.*) pattino **4.** (*aer.*) pattino di coda ☆ — *chain*, (*aut.*) catena antisdrucciolevole ‖ *side —*, (*aut. aer.*) sbandamento.

to **skid**, *pass.p.p.* **skidded** ['skidid], *v.t.i.* **1.** scivolare, far scivolare **2.** (*aut.*) slittare **3.** (*aer.*) derapare.

to **skidoo** [ski'du:], *v.i.* (*sl. amer.*) andarsene.

skier ['ski:ə*], *s.c.* sciatore, sciatrice.

skiff [skif], *s.* (*mar.*) schifo, palischermo; scialuppa.

skilful ['skilful], *ag.* abile, esperto, destro: *to be —
in doing sthg.*, essere abile nel fare ql.co.

skilfully ['skilfuli], *av.* abilmente, destramente.

skilfulness ['skilfulnis], *s.* abilità, destrezza.

skill [skil], *s.* abilità, destrezza, capacità.

skilled [skild], *ag.* esperto, versato, abile ☆ — *labour*, mano d'opera specializzata; — *witness*, (*dir.*) perito; — *worker*, operaio specializzato.

skillet ['skilit], *s.* casseruola con lungo manico e tre piedi.

skill-less ['skillis], *ag.* (*rar.*) inabile, maldestro.

skilly ['skili], *s.* brodaglia; zuppa di avena.

skim [skim], *ag.* schiumato; scremato ‖ *s.* **1.** schiuma **2.** coltello superiore dell'aratro ☆ — *-coulter*, (*agr.*) avanvomere; — *-milk*, latte scremato.

to **skim**, *pass.p.p.* **skimmed** [skimd], *v.t.i.* **1.** schiumare; scremare: *to — the cream off*, scremare; *fig.* prendere il meglio di **2.** sfiorare, rasentare: *the birds were skimming (over) the ground*, gli uccelli volavano raso terra; *a plane skimmed (along) the grass*, un aeroplano sfiorava l'erba; *she skimmed the subject*, trattò l'argomento con superficialità **3.** scorrere, sfogliare; leggere superficialmente: *to — (over, through) a novel*, scorrere un romanzo.

skimble-skamble ['skimbl,skæmbl], *ag.* (*sl.*) stravagante, strampalato, incoerente.

skimmer ['skimə*], *s.* **1.** schiumaiuola, schiumarola, schiumatoio **2.** lancia (imbarcazione) **3.** (*ornit.*) rincope nero.

skimming ['skimiŋ], *s.* **1.** scrematura **2.** *gener. pl.* (*metal.*) scorie levate dal metallo fuso ☆ — *-dish*, (*sl.*) panfilo da corsa a fondo piatto.

skimmington ['skimiŋtən], *s.* (*st.*) **1.** corteo farsesco (anticamente in uso nelle campagne inglesi per svergognare adulteri) **2.** marito tradito.

to **skimp** [skimp], *v.t.i.* **1.** lesinare; limitare; tenere a corto, a stecchetto; razionare il cibo: *to — one's children in money*, tenere i propri figli a corto di quattrini **2.** risparmiare, essere parsimonioso; essere tirchio: *my dressmaker is very good at skimping materials*, la mia sarta è abilissima nel far economia di stoffa.

skimpiness ['skimpinis], *s.* **1.** ristrettezza; razionamento **2.** spilorceria.

skimpingly ['skimpiŋli], *av.* **1.** parsimoniosamente **2.** spilorciamente.

skimpy ['skimpi], *ag.* **1.** scarso **2.** tirchio, meschino.

skin [skin], *s.* **1.** pelle, cute: *to have a fair, dark —*, avere una carnagione chiara, scura ‖ *wet to the —*, bagnato fino alle ossa ‖ *I would not be in his —*, non vorrei essere nei suoi panni ‖ *to be only — and bone*, essere pelle e ossa ‖ *to come off with a whole —*, uscirne sano e salvo ‖ *to escape by the — of one's teeth*, cavarsela per il rotto della cuffia ‖ *to fear for one's —*, temere per la propria pelle ‖ *to have a thin, thick —*, essere sensibile, insensibile ‖ *to jump out of one's — for joy*, non star più nella pelle dalla gioia ‖ *to save one's —*, salvare la pelle **2.** pelle (di animale); pellame: *raw skins*, pelli grezze; *tanned skins*, pelli conciate, cuoio **3.** otre **4.** buccia, scorza; pelle **5.** involucro; pellicola (del latte, ecc.) **6.** (*sl.*) persona, tipo: *he isn't a bad —*, è un brav'uomo **7.** (*mar.*) fasciame ☆ — *-deep*, a fior di pelle, superficiale; — *-disease*, dermatosi, malattia della pelle; — *-dresser*, conciatore di pelli; — *-effect*, (*elett.*) effetto pelle; — *-game*, (*sl.*) truffa; — *-grafting*, (*chir.*) innesto epidermico; — *-tight*, aderente alla pelle ‖ *inner —* (o *true —*), derma; *outer —*, epidermide.

to **skin**, *pass.p.p.* **skinned** [skind], *v.t.i.* **1.** scuoiare, scorticare, spellare; sbucciare: *my foot was skinned in several places*, avevo il piede scorticato in parec-

chi punti; *they skinned the tiger*, scuoiarono la tigre; *to — alive*, scorticare vivo ‖ *to — a flint*, (*fam.*) essere spilorcio ‖ *to keep ones's eyes skinned*, (*sl.*) tenere gli occhi bene aperti **2.** (*sl.*) truffare, frodare, pelare **3.** *to — over*, (*med.*) cicatrizzare, cicatrizzarsi, rimarginarsi.

skinflint ['skin-flint], *s.* taccagno, spilorcio.

skink [skiŋk], *s.* (*zool.*) scinco.

skinless ['skinlis], *ag.* senza pelle.

skinned [skind], *ag.* **1.** rivestito di pelle **2.** (*arc.*) scorticato.

skinner ['skinə*], *s.* **1.** conciapelli, cuoiaio **2.** (*arc.*) scorticatore; scuoiatore.

skinniness ['skininis], *s.* magrezza; macilenza.

skinny ['skini], *ag.* **1.** magro; scarno; macilento **2.** avaro, taccagno.

skip[1] [skip], *s.* **1.** salto, balzo **2.** omissione **3.** servitore di collegio (specialmente a Dublino).

to **skip**[1], *pass.p.p.* **skipped** [skipt], *v.t.i.* **1.** saltare: *to — rope*, (*giuoco*) saltare la corda **2.** avanzare, muoversi a balzi **3.** omettere, saltare: *to — a few lines*, saltare qualche riga **4.** (*sl.*) svignarsela: *to — school*, marinare la scuola **5.** *to — over* (*sthg.*), scavalcare.

skip[2], *s.* **1.** (*miner.*) gabbia **2.** benna.

skipper[1] ['skipə*], *s.* **1.** saltatore **2.** chi omette ql.co. leggendo **3.** (*entom.*) esperia **4.** (*ittiol.*) luccio sauro.

skipper[2], *s.* **1.** capitano, comandante di nave mercantile ‖ —*'s daughters*, onde altissime con la cresta bianca **2.** (*spor.*) capitano di squadra **3.** (*aer. amer.*) comandante.

skippet ['skipit], *s.* (*st.*) custodia per sigilli.

skipping ['skipiŋ], *s.* **1.** salti **2.** omissione **3.** (*tip.*) salto di uno spazio ☆ — *-rope*, corda per saltare.

skippingly ['skipiŋli], *av.* saltellando, a balzi.

to **skirl** [skə:l], *v.i.* (*scoz.*) strillare, stridere; suonare come di cornamusa.

skirmish ['skə:miʃ], *s.* scaramuccia; schermaglia.

to **skirmish**, *v.i.* scaramucciare.

skirmisher ['skə:miʃə*], *s.* scaramucciatore.

skirmishing ['skə:miʃiŋ], *s.* scaramuccia.

skirret ['skirit], *s.* (*bot.*) sisaro.

skirt [skə:t], *s.* **1.** sottana; gonna **2.** orlo, lembo; falda (di vestito) **3.** *pl.* estremità; confini: *the skirts of London*, i sobborghi, la periferia di Londra.

to **skirt**, *v.t.i.* **1.** orlare; circondare **2.** confinare **3.** costeggiare: *the path skirts the wood*, il sentiero costeggia il bosco.

skirting ['skə:tiŋ], *s.* **1.** orlo, bordo; fascia **2.** stoffa per gonne **3.** zoccolatura, bordatura ☆ — *-board*, (*edil.*) zoccolo di legno.

skirtless ['skə:tlis], *ag.* **1.** senza gonna **2.** senza orlo.

skit[1] [skit], *s.* scherzo, burla.

to **skit**[1], *pass.p.p.* **skitted** ['skitid], *v.t.i.* **1.** motteggiare; satireggiare **2.** saltare, balzellare.

skit[2], *s.* (*sl.*) **1.** gran numero, folla **2.** *pl.* mucchi.

to **skitter** ['skitə*], *v.i.* **1.** far schizzare l'acqua nell'alzarsi, nel posarsi (di uccelli acquatici) **2.** pescare tenendo l'esca sul pelo dell'acqua.

skittish ['skitiʃ], *ag.* **1.** capriccioso; frivolo; volubile, incostante **2.** ombroso (di cavallo).

skittishly ['skitiʃli], *av.* **1.** capricciosamente; volubilmente **2.** ombrosamente.

skittishness ['skitiʃnis], *s.* **1.** volubilità; frivolezza **2.** ombrosità (di cavallo).

skittle ['skitl], *s.* birillo; *pl.* giuoco dei birilli ‖ *skittles!*, (*sl.*) sciocchezze! ‖ *life is not all beer and skittles*, la vita non è tutta rose e fiori ☆ — *-alley* (o — *-ground*), luogo destinato al giuoco dei birilli; — *-ball*, palla per il giuoco dei birilli.

skive[1] [skaiv], *s.* ruota per pulire i diamanti.

to **skive**[2], *v.t.* **1.** tagliare a strisce (pelli, gomma, ecc.) **2.** raschiare (pelli).

skiver ['skaivə*], *s.* **1.** coltello per tagliare pelli **2.** sottile striscia di pelle.

skivvy ['skivi], *s.* (*fam.*) serva, sguattera.

skua ['skju:ə], *s.* (*ornit.*) stercorario.

skulk [skʌlk], s. imboscato; codardo.

to skulk, v.i. 1. stare nascosti; imboscarsi; fig. sottrarsi al proprio dovere 2. muoversi furtivamente.

skulker ['skʌlkə*], s. imboscato; codardo.

skulkingly ['skʌlkiŋli], av. 1. vilmente 2. furtivamente.

skull [skʌl], s. cranio, teschio ‖ — and crossbones, teschio e tibie incrociate (simbolo della morte) ☆ — -cap, papalina; (bot.) scutellaria.

skunk [skʌŋk], s. 1. (zool.) moffetta; pelliccia di moffetta 2. (fam.) persona ignobile; farabutto.

sky [skai], s. cielo (anche fig.); volta celeste, firmamento: clear —, cielo sereno; overcast —, cielo coperto ‖ in the skies, in estasi ‖ out of a clear —, inaspettatamente ‖ to praise s.o. to the skies, portare qlcu. alle stelle ‖ to sleep under the open —, dormire all'addiaccio ☆ — -blue, azzurro cielo; — -born, (poet.) di nascita divina; — -high, altissimo; — -pilot, (sl.) prete; — -rocket, razzo; — -scraper, grattacielo; (mar.) pappafico; — -truck, aereo per trasporto merci; — -wave, (rad.) onda indiretta, raggio riflesso; — -winder, (sl. amer. aer.) pilota; — -writing, scrittura aerea (per pubblicità).

skyclad ['skaiklæd], ag. (fam.) nudo.

skye(terrier) [skai('teriə*)], s. terrier di Skye.

skylark ['skailɑ:k], s. allodola.

to skylark, v.t.i. 1. gabbare, prendersi giuoco di 2. far chiasso, baldoria.

skylight ['skailait], s. 1. lucernario; lanterna di lucernario 2. (mar.) osteriggio, spiraglio.

skyline ['skailain], s. 1. linea, profilo (di monti, colline, ecc.) contro il cielo 2. orizzonte.

skyliner ['skai,lainə*], s. aeroplano gigante per trasporto passeggeri.

skysail ['skaiseil], s. (mar.) decontrovelaccio, decontrovelaccino, decontrobelvedere.

skyward ['skaiwəd], ag.av. verso il cielo.

skywards ['skaiwədz], av. verso il cielo.

skyway ['skaiwei], s. rotta (di aereo).

slab¹ [slæb], s. 1. lastra, piastra 2. fetta, pezzo: a — of plum-cake, una fetta di panfrutto 3. sciavero; (metal.) slebo ☆ — -sided, (fam. amer.) spilungone ‖ concrete —, (edil.) piastra di calcestruzzo.

to slab¹, pass.p.p. slabbed [slæbd], v.t. 1. ridurre in lastre 2. lastricare 3. segare gli sciaveri da (un tronco).

slab², ag. (arc.) semi-solido; viscido ‖ s. fanghiglia.

(to) slabber ['slæbə*], e derivati, V. (to) slobber, e derivati.

slack¹ [slæk], ag. 1. molle, allentato: the rope was too —, la fune era troppo lenta 2. debole, fiacco; indolente; negligente; inerte: to be — at sthg., prendere ql.co. con indolenza ‖ to keep a — hand, fig. governare fiaccamente 3. (comm.) debole, fiacco; morto; calmo; stagnante: business is —, gli affari languono; the market is —, il mercato è fiacco; summer is a — season for antique dealers, l'estate è una stagione morta per gli antiquari ‖ s. 1. (mar.) imbando 2. inattività; (fam.) riposo 3. (comm.) stagione morta 4. (dial.) impertinenza 5. (mec.) giuoco 6. pl. calzoni sportivi o da donna ☆ — lime, calce spenta; — -jaw, (fam.) discorso impertinente; — -rope, corda da funambolo; — silk, seta floscia; — -water, bassa marea; distesa di acqua stagnante.

to slack¹, v.t.i. 1. allentare, allentarsi; rallentare 2. trascurare 3. (fam.) rilassarsi, riposarsi 4. (comm.) ristagnare; languire 5. spegnere, spegnersi (di calce) 6. to — off, allentare; rilassare, rilassarsi 7. to — up, rallentare (di treno).

slack¹, av. debolmente, fiaccamente; indolentemente; trascuratamente.

slack², s. polvere di carbone.

to slacken ['slækən], v.t.i. 1. allentare; mollare: to — the reins, allentare le briglie 2. diminuire; moderare; smorzarsi: business is slackening, gli affari ristagnano; to — speed, diminuire la velocità 3. spegnersi (di calce).

slackening ['slækniŋ], s. 1. allentamento 2. rilassamento 3. rallentamento; ristagno; diminuzione.

slacker ['slækə*], s.c. fannullone, fannullona; scansafatiche.

slackly ['slækli], av. 1. fiaccamente, debolmente 2. negligentemente, trascuratamente 3. insufficientemente.

slackness ['slæknis], s. 1. flaccidezza, rilassamento 2. trascuratezza, negligenza 3. (comm.) ristagno.

slag [slæg], s. (metal.) scoria, loppa ☆ — cement, cemento di scoria; — -wool, lana di scoria; cotone silicato ‖ basic —, (metal.) scoria basica.

to slag, pass.p.p. slagged [slægd], v.i. (metal.) scorificare.

slagging ['slægiŋ], s. (metal.) scorificazione.

slaggy ['slægi], ag. simile a scoria.

slain [slein], p.p. di to slay.

to slake [sleik], v.t.i. 1. estinguere, estinguersi; smorzare; spegnersi: to — one's thirst, estinguere la propria sete 2. fig. appagare, soddisfare 3. spegnere, spegnersi (di calce).

slakeless ['sleiklis], ag. inestinguibile; insaziabile.

slalom ['sleiləm], s. (spor.) slalom.

slam¹ [slæm], s. sbatacchiamento: the door closed with a —, la porta si chiuse sbatacchiando.

to slam¹, pass.p.p. slammed [slæmd], v.t.i. sbattere, sbatacchiare; chiudere, chiudersi violentemente: he slammed the book (down) on the table, sbatté il libro sul tavolo.

slam², s. (bridge) « slam »: grand —, grande « slam », cappotto; little —, piccolo « slam », stramazzo.

to slam², v.t.i. (bridge) fare uno « slam »; vincere con uno « slam ».

slander ['slɑ:ndə*], s. calunnia, maldicenza; (dir.) diffamazione: action for —, querela per diffamazione.

to slander, v.t. calunniare; (dir.) diffamare.

slanderer ['slɑ:ndərə*], s.c. calunniatore, calunniatrice; maldicente; (dir.) diffamatore, diffamatrice.

slanderous ['slɑ:ndərəs], ag. calunnioso, maldicente; (dir.) diffamatorio.

slanderously ['slɑ:ndərəsli], av. calunniosamente.

slanderousness ['slɑ:ndərəsnis], s. carattere diffamatorio, calunnioso.

slang¹ [slæŋ], s. gergo: he likes using —, gli piace parlare in gergo ☆ Newgate —, gergo da ladri; schoolboy —, gergo scolastico.

to slang¹, v.t. vituperare, ingiurare; sgridare.

slang², s. (sl.) 1. catena 2. pl. ceppi.

slangily ['slæŋili], av. in gergo.

slangy ['slæŋi], ag. 1. di gergo 2. che usa gergo.

slank [slæŋk], pass. (rar.) di to slink.

slant [slɑ:nt], ag. sghembo; inclinato ‖ s. 1. inclinazione, pendenza; china 2. (sl.) opportunità, occasione 3. (amer.) punto di vista 4. (cine.) prospettiva.

to slant, v.t.i. essere in pendenza; inclinare, inclinarsi; deviare, far deviare obliquamente.

slanting ['slɑ:ntiŋ], ag. inclinato; obliquo; sghembo: ☆ — eyes, occhi a mandorla.

slantingly ['slɑ:ntiŋli], av. in pendenza; obliquamente; di traverso.

slantwise ['slɑ:nt-waiz], ag. obliquo, trasversale ‖ av. obliquamente; di traverso.

slap [slæp], s. 1. pacca; schiaffo, ceffone 2. fig. affronto; rabbuffo; rimprovero ‖ a — in the eye (o in the face), (fam.) uno schiaffo in pieno viso; un insulto.

to slap, pass.p.p. slapped [slæpt], v.t. 1. schiaffeggiare; colpire; dare una pacca a: to — s.o. on the back, dare pacche sulle spalle a qlcu. 2. sbattere, chiudere violentemente (porta, ecc.) 3. to — down, buttar giù con forza: she slapped the dictionary down on the table, sbatté il dizionario sul tavolo.

slap, av. 1. violentemente; improvvisamente 2. in pieno.

slap, (nei composti): — -bang, (fam.) violentemente; rumorosamente; — -up, (sl.) di prim'ordine; all'ultima moda.

slapdash ['slæpdæʃ], ag. impetuoso, avventato; affrettato; noncurante ‖ *s.* cosa fatta a casaccio; lavoro affrettato.

to slapdash, *v.i.* fare, agire precipitosamente; abborracciare ql.co.

slapdash, *av.* precipitosamente; a casaccio.

slapjack ['slæpdʒæk], *s.* (*amer.*) frittella.

slapping ['slæpiŋ], *ag.* vigoroso; robusto; gagliardo, ben piantato.

slapstick ['slæpstik], *s.* **1.** spatola d'Arlecchino **2.** *fig.* farsa grossolana.

slash [slæʃ], *s.* **1.** taglio, apertura **2.** frustata, sferzata, scudisciata **3.** resti (di alberi tagliati).

to slash, *v.t.i.* **1.** tagliare; fendere; fare un'apertura; sfregiare **2.** frustare, sferzare **3.** criticare aspramente **4.** *to — at* (*s.o.*), colpire violentemente.

slashed [slæʃt], *ag.* sfregiato; a, con fenditure ☆ *— sleeves,* maniche con aperture (per lasciare trasparire una fodera di altro colore).

slashing ['slæʃiŋ], *ag.* mordace, spietato: *a — criticism,* una stroncatura ‖ *s.* frustata, taglio, apertura.

slat[1] [slæt], *s.* assicella (di legno); stecca (di persiana).

to slat[1], *pass.p.p.* **slatted** ['slætid], *v.t.* fornire di, fare con assicelle.

slat[2], *s.* improvviso colpo di vento.

to slat[2], *v.t.i.* (*dial.*) battere, colpire; sbatacchiare.

slate[1] [sleit], *s.* **1.** ardesia **2.** tegola d'ardesia ‖ *to have a — loose* (o *off*), (*sl.*) essere un po' tocco **3.** lavagna ‖ *to clean the —,* *fig.* cominciare una nuova vita **4.** color ardesia **5.** lista provvisoria di candidati ☆ *— -black,* nero ardesia; *— -coloured,* del colore dell'ardesia; *— -grey,* grigio ardesia; *— -pencil,* matita d'ardesia; *— -quarry,* cava d'ardesia.

to slate[1], *v.t.* **1.** coprire con tegole d'ardesia **2.** mettere in lista **3.** disegnare.

to slate[2], *v.t.* (*fam.*) **1.** sgridare; punire **2.** criticare severamente (specialmente libri, autori).

slater ['sleitə*], *s.* operaio che copre i tetti con tegole di ardesia, conciatetti.

slather ['slæðə*], *s.* (*sl. amer. spec. pl.*) grande quantità: *slathers of money,* un mucchio di denaro.

slating[1] ['sleitiŋ], *s.* **1.** tegole d'ardesia **2.** copertura con tegole d'ardesia.

slating[2], *s.* **1.** rimbrotto: *he gave him a good —,* egli gli ha dato una buona lavata di testa **2.** critica severa; stroncatura.

slatted ['slætid], *ag.* a stecche.

slattern ['slætə(:)n], *s.* sudiciona, sciattona.

to slattern, *v.t.i.* **1.** essere sciatto, trascurato **2.** *to — away,* buttar via, sprecare (tempo, occasioni).

slatternliness ['slætə(:)nlinis], *s.* sporcizia; sciatteria.

slatternly ['slætə(:)nli], *ag.* sudicio; sciatto ‖ *av.* sudiciamente; sciattamente.

slaty ['sleiti], *ag.* **1.** di ardesia **2.** color ardesia **3.** schistoso.

slaughter ['slɔːtə*], *s.* **1.** macello **2.** carneficina, massacro, strage ‖ *the — of the innocents,* la strage degli innocenti.

to slaughter, *v.t.* **1.** macellare **2.** massacrare; far strage di (anche *fig.*): *to — candidates wholesale,* (*fam.*) fare un'ecatombe di candidati.

slaughterer ['slɔːtərə*], *s.* **1.** macellatore **2.** uccisore; massacratore.

slaughterhouse ['slɔːtəhaus], *s.* mattatoio.

slaughterous ['slɔːtərəs], *ag.* (*letter.*) sanguinario; micidiale.

slaughterously ['slɔːtərəsli], *av.* in modo sanguinario; in modo micidiale.

Slav [slɑːv], *ag.* slavo ‖ *s.c.* slavo, slava ‖ *s.* lingua slava.

slave [sleiv], *s.c.* **1.** schiavo, schiava (anche *fig.*): *a — of prejudices,* schiavo di pregiudizi; *to be the — of* (o *to*) *a passion,* essere schiavo di una passione; *to become a — to duty,* diventare schiavo del dovere ‖ *— States,* Stati schiavisti **2.** persona meschina, abietta ☆ *— -born,* nato in schiavitù; *— -driver,* negriero

(anche *fig.*); *— -grown,* prodotto dal lavoro di schiavi; *— -holder* (o *— owner*), proprietario di schiavi; *— -labour,* lavoro di schiavi; *— -ship,* nave negriera; *— -trade,* tratta degli schiavi; *— -trader,* commerciante di schiavi ‖ *white — trade,* tratta delle bianche.

to slave, *v.t.i.* **1.** rendere schiavo; trattare da schiavo **2.** lavorare come uno schiavo; sgobbare: *I have been slaving at this work four years,* mi logoro per questo lavoro da quattro anni.

slaver[1] ['sleivə*], *s.* **1.** saliva; bava **2.** *fig.* adulazione servile.

to slaver[1], *v.t.i.* **1.** imbavare **2.** far bava, sbavare.

slaver[2], *s.* **1.** schiavista; negriero **2.** nave negriera.

slaverer ['sleivərə*], *s.c.* **1.** chi emette bava **2.** *fig.* adulatore, adulatrice servile.

slavery[1] ['sleivəri], *ag.* bavoso.

slavery[2], *s.* **1.** schiavitù (anche *fig.*) **2.** lavoro faticoso.

Slavic ['slævik], *ag.* slavo ‖ *s.* lingua slava.

slavish ['sleiviʃ], *ag.* **1.** di schiavo; servile: *a — imitation,* una imitazione servile **2.** abietto.

slavishly ['sleiviʃli], *av.* **1.** da schiavo; servilmente **2.** bassamente.

slavishness ['sleiviʃnis], *s.* **1.** servilismo **2.** bassezza.

Slavism ['slævizəm], *s.* slavismo.

Slavonian [slə'vouniən], *ag.* slavo ‖ *s.c.* slavo, slava ‖ *s.* lingua slava.

Slavonic [slə'vɔnik], *ag.* slavo ‖ *s.c.* slavo, slava ‖ *s.* lingua slava.

Slavophil ['slævoufil], **Slavophile** ['slævoufail], *ag.* slavofilo ‖ *s.c.* slavofilo, slavofila.

Slavophobe ['slævoufoub], *ag.* slavofobo ‖ *s.c.* slavofobo, slavofoba.

to slay [slei], *pass.* **slew** [sluː], *p.p.* **slain** [slein], *v.t.* **1.** (*letter.*) ammazzare; trucidare **2.** (*amer.*) assassinare.

slayer ['sleiə*], *s.* **1.** uccisore **2.** (*amer.*) assassino.

slaying ['sleiiŋ], *s.* **1.** uccisione; massacro **2.** (*amer.*) assassinio.

sleaziness ['sliːzinis], *s.* sottigliezza; tenuità; inconsistenza (di stoffe).

sleazy ['sliːzi], *ag.* inconsistente; leggero (di stoffe).

sled [sled], *s.* (*dial. amer.*) slitta.

to sled, *pass.p.p.* **sledded** ['sledid], *v.t.i.* **1.** (*amer.*) trasportare su slitta **2.** andare su slitta.

sledding ['slediŋ], *s.* **1.** (*amer.*) trasporto (su slitta); corsa (su slitta) ‖ *hard —,* *fig.* impresa difficile **2.** terreno adatto al passaggio di slitte.

sledge[1] [sledʒ], *s.* slitta.

to sledge[1], *v.t.i.* **1.** trasportare su slitta **2.** andare su slitta.

sledge[2], *s.* martello da fabbro; maglio.

sleek [sliːk], *ag.* **1.** liscio; levigato; lustro **2.** soffice, morbido (di capelli, ecc.) **3.** *fig.* sdolcinato; mellifluo.

to sleek, *v.t.* lisciare; lustrare.

sleeker ['sliːkə*], *s.* utensile per lisciare; (*metal.*) lisciatoio; (*strum. artig.*) bussetto.

sleekly ['sliːkli], *av.* **1.** con un aspetto liscio, lustro **2.** mellifluamente; sdolcinatamente.

sleekness ['sliːknis], *s.* **1.** lucentezza; levigatezza **2.** *fig.* untuosità.

sleekstone ['sliːk-stoun], *s.* (*metal.*) lisciatoio; (*strum. artig.*) brunitoio.

sleeky ['sliːki], *ag.* **1.** liscio; lustro **2.** soffice, morbido.

sleep [sliːp], *s.* **1.** sonno; *fig.* quiete, riposo: *broken —,* sonno interrotto; *a restless —,* sonno inquieto; *she put her child to —,* fece addormentare il bambino; *to fall into a deep* (o *into a sound*) *—,* cadere in un sonno profondo; *to go to —,* addormentarsi; *fig.* morire; *to lose one's —,* perdere il sonno; *to rouse s.o. from his —,* svegliare qlcu.; *to walk in one's —,* essere sonnambulo ‖ *the — that knows no breaking,* *fig.* il sonno della morte **2.** dormita; periodo di riposo: *to have a good —,* fare una buona dormita ☆ *— walker,* sonnambulo; *— walking,* sonnambulismo ‖ *beauty —,* primo sonno.

to **sleep**, *pass.p.p.* **slept** [slept], *v.t.i.* **1.** dormire, riposare (anche *fig.*) ‖ — *on it*, dormici sopra ‖ *I did not* — *a wink all night*, non ho chiuso occhio tutta la notte ‖ *to* — *the clock round*, dormire dodici ore filate; *to* — *like a log* (o *a top*), dormire come un ghiro ‖ *to* — *on a matter*, rimandare la soluzione di un problema ‖ *to* — *one's last sleep*, essere morto ‖ *to* — *oneself sober*, smaltire la sbornia dormendo ‖ *to* — *the sleep of the just*, dormire il sonno del giusto ‖ *to* — *the winter away*, trascorrere l'inverno dormendo ‖ *to* — *with one eye open*, dormire con un occhio solo; *fig.* stare in guardia ‖ *let sleeping dogs lie*, *prov.* non svegliare il can che dorme **2.** passare la notte: *I shall* — *in London to-night*, passerò la notte a Londra; *to* — *out*, dormire fuori di casa **3.** (*fam.*) dare da dormire a: *this hotel sleeps 100 people*, questo albergo ha 100 letti.

sleeper ['sli:pə*], *s.c.* dormiente; dormiglione, dormigliona; *fig* persona indolente: *a light, sound* —, chi ha il sonno leggero, pesante ‖ *s.* **1.** travetto; (*ferr.*) traversina **2.** (*aer.*) poltrona letto; (*amer. ferr.*) vagone letto.

sleepily ['sli:pili], *av.* con aria assonnata.

sleepiness ['sli:pinis], *s.* **1.** sopore, sonnolenza **2.** pesantezza; languore; apatia.

sleeping ['sli:piŋ], *ag.* dormiente; addormentato; assopito ‖ *s.* sonno; riposo ☆ — -*bag*, sacco a pelo; — -*berth*, cuccetta; — -*car*, vagone letto; — *draught*, narcotico; sonnifero; — *partner*, (*comm.*) socio accomandante; — -*quarters*, dormitorio; camerata; — *sickness*, (*patol.*) malattia del sonno; encefalite letargica; — -*suit*, pigiama.

sleepless ['sli:p-lis], *ag.* insonne; agitato; tormentato: *a* — *night*, una notte bianca; *the* — *ocean*, l'oceano che non ha riposo.

sleeplessly ['sli:p-lisli], *av.* senza riposo; *fig.* senza pace.

sleeplessness ['sli:p-lisnis], *s.* insonnia.

sleepy ['sli:pi], *ag.* **1.** assonnato, sonnolento: *a* — *look*, un'aria addormentata; *to be* —, aver sonno **2.** apatico; indolente; molle ☆ — -*head*, dormiglione; pigro.

sleet [sli:t], *s.* nevischio.

to **sleet**, *v. imp.* nevischiare: *it sleets*, vien giù nevischio.

sleety ['sli:ti], *ag.* di nevischio; simile a nevischio.

sleeve [sli:v], *s.* **1.** manica: *to pluck s.o.'s* —, tirare qlcu. per la manica; *to turn* (o *to roll*) *up one's sleeves*, rimboccarsi le maniche ‖ *to have a card* (o *a plan*) *up one's* —, *fig.* avere un asso nella manica ‖ *to laugh in one's* —, ridere sotto i baffi ‖ *to wear one's heart on one's* —, avere il cuore in mano **2.** busta (di un disco) **3.** (*mec.*) manicotto; (*elett. mec.*) lanterna, bussola **4.** (*aer.*) manica a vento ☆ — -*board*, stiramaniche; — -*collar*, (*mec.*) fascetta; — -*link*, gemelli; — -*valve*, (*mec.*) valvola a fodero.

to **sleeve**, *v.t.* mettere le maniche a.

sleeved [sli:vd], *ag.* con maniche.

sleeveless ['sli:vlis], *ag.* senza maniche.

sleigh [slei], *s.* slitta.

to **sleigh**, *v.t.i.* **1.** andare in slitta **2.** trasportare con slitta.

sleight [slait], *s.* abilità, destrezza; giuoco di abilità; furberia ☆ — -*of-hand*, giuoco di prestigio.

slender ['slendə*], *ag.* **1.** magro; snello, esile, sottile: *a* — *girl*, una ragazza esile, snella; *she has a very* — *waist*, ha la vita molto sottile **2.** debole, fiacco; esiguo, scarso: — *hopes*, deboli speranze; — *income*, rendita esigua; — *means*, mezzi insufficienti.

slenderly ['slendəli], *av.* **1.** sottilmente **2.** modestamente; modicamente.

slenderness ['slendənis], *s.* **1.** magrezza; snellezza; delicatezza **2.** esiguità; modicità.

slept [slept], *pass.p.p.* di to **sleep**.

to **sleuth** [slu:θ], *v.t.i.* pedinare; fare l'investigatore.

sleuth-hound ['slu:θˈhaund], *s.* **1.** (*arc.*) segugio; cane poliziotto **2.** (*amer.*) agente investigativo.

slew[1] [slu:], *s.* deviazione; giro.

to **slew**[1], *v.t.i.* girare, far girare; rotare; volgere, volgersi.

slew[2], *pass.* di to **slay**.

sley [slei], *s.* (*ind. tessile*) battente (di telaio).

slice [slais], *s.* **1.** pezzo, parte; fetta, porzione; spicchio **2.** spatola, paletta.

to **slice**, *v.t.* affettare, tagliare, dividere in parti.

slicer ['slaisə*], *s.* affettatrice.

slick [slik], *ag.* (*fam. amer.*) **1.** liscio, levigato; scorrevole **2.** abile, svelto **3.** eccellente, ottimo.

to **slick**, *v.t.* lisciare, levigare; lucidare.

slick, *av.* **1.** abilmente, destramente **2.** direttamente, in pieno **3.** velocemente.

slide [slaid], *s.* **1.** scivolata **2.** (*mec.*) scorrimento; piano, superficie di scorrimento **3.** scivolo, sdrucciolo; piano inclinato; pista in discesa **4.** (*mec.*) pattino; slitta; carrello; cursore **5.** vetrino (per microscopio) **6.** (*foto.*) diapositiva, lastra **7.** (*mus.*) note scivolate ☆ — -*bar*, (*mec.*) asta di guida; — -*depth gauge*, calibro a corsoio per profondità; — -*fastener*, (*amer.*) cerniera lampo; — -*gauge*, compasso graduato; — -*rest*, (*mec.*) lunetta mobile; — -*rule*, regolo calcolatore; — -*valve*, cassetto di distribuzione; saracinesca; — -*way*, guida di scorrimento.

to **slide**, *pass.p.p.* **slid** [slid], *v.t.i.* **1.** scivolare, far scivolare (anche *fig.*); sdrucciolare; scorrere, far scorrere: *the book slid off my knee*, il libro mi scivolò dalle ginocchia; *he slid into vice*, scivolò nel vizio; *the sword slides into its scabbard*, la spada scorre nel fodero; *to* — *over a delicate subject*, sorvolare su un argomento delicato; *to let things* —, lasciar correre (le cose) **2.** allontanarsi, sfuggire; entrare, uscire furtivamente: *to* — *out of a room*, uscire da una stanza alla chetichella.

slider ['slaidə*], *s.c.* chi sdrucciola, scivola ‖ *s.* **1.** (*mec.*) corsoio, cursore **2.** (*amer.*) (varietà di) tartaruga acquatica **3.** mattonella (gelato tra due cialde).

sliding ['slaidiŋ], *ag.* scorrevole; mobile ☆ — -*door*, porta scorrevole; — -*panel*, pannello scorrevole; — -*roof*, (*aut.*) soffietto, « capote »; — -*rule*, regolo calcolatore; — -*scale*, scala mobile (di salari); — -*seat*, sedile scorrevole.

slight [slait], *ag.* **1.** magro; minuto; esile; smilzo: *a* — *girl*, una ragazza esile **2.** leggero; scarso; inadeguato: *we had a* — *lunch*, facemmo una colazione leggera **3.** superficiale ‖ *s.* disprezzo; affronto; trascuratezza; mancanza di riguardo: *to put a* — *on s.o.*, trattare qlcu. con disprezzo, con ostentata indifferenza.

to **slight**, *v.t.* disprezzare; guardare dall'alto in basso; mancare di riguardo a, verso; trascurare.

slighter ['slaitə*], *s.c.* chi disprezza; chi trascura.

slightingly ['slaitiŋli], *av.* sprezzatamente, sdegnosamente; con noncuranza; negligentemente.

slightish ['slaitiʃ], *ag.* **1.** piuttosto magro, esile, snello **2.** piuttosto leggero.

slightly ['slaitli], *av.* leggermente, lievemente; scarsamente; in modo insignificante; un poco.

slightness ['slaitnis], *s.* **1.** magrezza **2.** leggerezza; debolezza; tenuità.

slily, *V.* **slyly**.

slim [slim], *ag.* **1.** magro, sottile, esile; snello; smilzo; affusolato (di dita) **2.** furbo; astuto; scaltro **3.** debole; leggero; scarso.

to **slim**, *pass.p.p.* **slimmed** [slimd], *v.t.i.* dimagrire, fare dimagrire (con dieta e ginnastica).

slime [slaim], *s.* **1.** melma, limo; fanghiglia **2.** bava; umore viscoso **3.** bitume.

to **slime**, *v.t.i.* **1.** ricoprire di melma, bava **2.** *to* — *out of* (o *through*) *a difficulty*, togliersi da un pasticcio con mezzi illeciti.

sliminess ['slaiminis], *s.* **1.** viscosità; melmosità **2.** *fig.* servilità, ossequiosità.

slimly ['slimli], *av.* **1.** esilmente **2.** astutamente.

slimness ['slimnis], *s.* **1.** sottigliezza; snellezza; gracilità **2.** astuzia, scaltrezza.

slimsy ['slimsi], *ag.* (*amer.*) sottile, tenue, esile.

slimy ['slaimi], *ag.* **1.** limaccioso; fangoso **2.** viscoso; sdrucciolevole **3.** *fig.* servile, ossequioso.

sling[1] [sliŋ], *s.* **1.** fionda, frombola **2.** (*st.*) balista ☆ — *-shot*, (*amer.*) fionda; catapulta: — *-shot pilot*, (*sl. amer.*) pilota catapultato.

to sling[1], *pass.p.p.* **slung** [slʌŋ], *v.t.* scagliare con la fionda; gettare, lanciare: *to* — *mud at*, *fig.* lanciare fango su; *to* — *a stone*, lanciare un sasso con la fionda ‖ *to* — *the bat*, parlare la lingua locale ‖ *to* — *ink*, (*sl.*) scribacchiare, scrivere (per giornali, ecc.) ‖ *to* — *one's hook*, borseggiare ‖ *to* — *words*, parlare, perorare.

sling[2], *s.* **1.** cinghia; imbracatura **2.** (*med.*) bendaggio a fionda: *he had his arm in a* —, portava il braccio al collo **3.** *pl.* (*mar.*) ghia, braca ☆ — *-cart*, (*mil.*) affusto; — *-hoop*, cappio.

to sling[2], *v.t.* **1.** sospendere; appendere: *to* — *a hammock*, sospendere un'amaca; *to* — *over one's shoulder*, portare ad armacollo **2.** (*mar.*) imbracare **3.** tirar su, issare: *to* — (*up*) *a load with a crane*, issare un peso con la gru.

slinger ['sliŋə*], *s.* fromboliere; lanciatore di pietre.

slink [sliŋk], *ag.* nato prematuramente (di animale); (*dial.*) magro, esile ‖ *s.* **1.** aborto (di animale); vitello nato prematuramente **2.** (*fam.*) codardo.

to slink, *pass.* **slunk** [slʌŋk], (*rar.*) **slank** [slæŋk], *p.p.* **slunk**, *v.t.i.* **1.** sgattaiolare, svignarsela; muoversi furtivamente **2.** partorire prematuramente (di animali).

slip[1] [slip], *s.* **1.** (*amer.*) latte coagulato **2.** (*ind. ceramica*) argilla semiliquida.

slip[2], *s.* **1.** innesto **2.** persona giovane e snella **3.** striscia (di terra, ecc.) **4.** (*tip.*) bozza in colonna **5.** (*ittiol.*) piccola sogliola.

to slip[2], *v.i.* tagliare rami per innesto.

slip[3], *s.* **1.** (*mar.*) scalo, molo, ponte d'approdo, imbarcadero **2.** guinzaglio **3.** sottoveste **4.** federa **5.** *pl.* (*teat.*) quinte **6.** scivolata, scivolone: *to give s.o. the* —, evitare qlcu. ‖ *there's many a* —' *twixt the cup and the lip*, *prov.* tra il dire e il fare c'è di mezzo il mare **7.** errore; svista; passo falso: *to make a* —, commettere un errore **8.** scontrino **9.** *pl.* calzoncini da bagno ☆ — *coach*, (*ferr.*) vagone sganciabile in corsa; — *-galley*, (*tip.*) vantaggio per colonne; — *-hook*, scatto; — *-knot*, nodo scorsoio; — *-over*, indumento che si indossa facilmente; — *-proof*, (*tip.*) prima bozza; — *-ring*, (*elett.*) anello di contatto.

to slip[3], *pass.p.p.* **slipped** [slipt], *v.t.i.* **1.** scivolare, far scivolare; inciampare, perdere l'equilibrio; scorrere, far scorrere: *he slipped into the water*, scivolò in acqua; *my foot slipped*, inciampai; *to* — *the film*, (*cine.*) far scorrere la pellicola; *to* — *one's hand into a pocket*, far scivolare la mano in tasca ‖ *it slips my memory*, (*fam.*) mi sfugge ‖ *to* — *into bed*, infilarsi a letto ‖ *to* — *one's shoes off*, togliersi le scarpe **2.** entrare, uscire furtivamente **3.** sguisciare, liberarsi: *the dog slipped his chain*, il cane si liberò dalla catena **4.** (*mar.*) filare, infilare: *to* — *an anchor*, filare l'ancora **5.** abortire (di animali) **6.** *to* — *away*, scorrere (di tempo); eclissarsi: *life is slipping away and we get very little done*, la vita passa rapidamente e riusciamo a fare ben poco; *you had better* — *away while the hymn is being sung*, faresti meglio ad eclissarti mentre si canta l'inno **7.** *to* — **down**, scivolar giù; cadere **8.** *to* — **over**, infilarsi per la testa (di abito) **9.** *to* — **up**, (*amer.*) sbagliare, fare una gaffe; fallire, far fiasco (di progetto).

slipper ['slipə*], *s.* **1.** pantofola; pianella; ciabatta **2.** (*mec.*) pattino; (*ferr.*) freno sulla rotaia.

slippered ['slipəd], *ag.* in pantofole.

slipperily ['slipərili], *av.* **1.** sdrucciolevolmente **2.** volubilmente **3.** ingannevolmente; astutamente.

slipperiness ['slipərinis], *s.* **1.** sdrucciolevolezza **2.** scaltrezza, astuzia.

slippery ['slipəri], *ag.* **1.** sdrucciolevole; viscido (anche *fig.*): *a* — *deck*, un ponte sdrucciolevole: *as* —

as an eel, viscido come un'anguilla **2.** incerto, instabile **3.** *fig.* evasivo; non scrupoloso; infido.

slippy ['slipi], *ag.* veloce, attivo, rapido: *to look* —, muoversi rapidamente, essere vivace, svelto.

slipshod ['slipʃɔd], *ag.* **1.** in ciabatte **2.** disordinato; trasandato; trascurato (di stile); scorretto.

slipslop ['slipslɔp], *ag.* **1.** insipido **2.** incoerente ‖ *s.* **1.** brodo, brodaglia; bevanda analcolica **2.** risciacquatura di piatti **3.** discorso incoerente; chiacchiera; scritto sdolcinato **4.** (*letter.*) sproposito.

slipway ['slipwei], *s.* (*mar.*) invasatura.

slit [slit], *s.* fessura; crepa, fenditura; incisione: — *of a letter-box*, fessura di una buca delle lettere ☆ — *-eyed*, dagli occhi a mandorla; — *-pocket*, finta tasca (di soprabito, impermeabile, ecc., che permette d'introdurre la mano nella tasca del vestito).

to slit, *pass.p.p.* **slit**, *v.t.i.* fendere, fendersi; spaccare, spaccarsi; tagliare a strisce; incidere.

to slither ['sliðə*], *v.t.i.* **1.** (*fam.*) scivolare, far scivolare, sdrucciolare **2.** (*sl.*) affrettarsi.

sliver ['slivə*], *s.* scheggia; frammento.

to sliver, *v.t.i.* scheggiare, scheggiarsi.

slobber ['slɔbə*], *s.* **1.** bava **2.** sdolcinatura.

to slobber, *v.t.i.* **1.** sbavare **2.** comportarsi in modo sdolcinato: *to* — *over s.o.*, soffocare qlcu. di tenerezze **3.** pasticciare, eseguire disordinatamente.

slobberer ['slɔbərə*], *s.c.* chi sbava.

slobberiness ['slɔbərinis], *s.* bavosità.

slobbery ['slɔbəri], *ag.* bavoso.

sloe [slou], *s.* (*bot.*) prugnolo; prugnola ☆ — *-gin*, liquore di prugnole.

slog [slɔg], *s.* (*fam.*) **1.** colpo violento **2.** lavoro faticoso.

to slog, *pass.p.p.* **slogged** [slɔgd], *v.t.i.* **1.** colpire fortemente (specialmente nella boxe, nel cricket) **2.** lavorare tenacemente **3.** camminare faticosamente **4.** *to* — **along**, avanzare a fatica, con passo pesante.

slogan ['slougən], *s.* **1.** (*st.*) grido di guerra (scozzese) **2.** parola d'ordine; motto **3.** « slogan », motto pubblicitario.

sloid, *V.* **sloyd**.

sloop [slu:p], *s.* (*mar.*) corvetta.

slop[1] [slɔp], *s.* **1.** *pl.* brodo, brodaglia; bevande analcoliche **2.** *pl.* liquidi sporchi; risciacquatura di piatti ☆ — *-basin*, scodella per i fondi del tè lasciati nelle tazze; — *-pail*, secchio per l'acqua sporca.

to slop[1], *pass.p.p.* **slopped** [slɔpt], *v.t.i.* **1.** versare, rovesciare liquidi **2.** spruzzare, schizzare **3.** camminare nella fanghiglia **4.** (*fig. amer.*) prodigarsi in effusioni; essere sdolcinato.

slop[2], *s.* **1.** *pl.* abiti confezionati **2.** *pl.* corredo completo (per marinai) ☆ — *-room*, (*mar.*) magazzino degli indumenti; — *-seller*, venditore di abiti confezionati; — *-shop*, negozio di abiti confezionati.

slop[3], *s.* (*sl.*) poliziotto, sbirro.

slope [sloup], *s.* **1.** pendenza; pendio, declivio: *steep* —, pendio ripido **2.** (*ferr.*) scarpata.

to slope, *v.t.i.* **1.** essere in pendenza, pendere, inclinarsi; declinare: *the garden slopes down to the river*, il giardino declina verso il fiume **2.** inclinare, dare pendenza a **3.** (*sl.*) sparire; svignarsela.

slopewise ['sloupwaiz], *av.* in pendenza; obliquamente.

sloping ['sloupiŋ], *ag.* inclinato; obliquo; in pendenza: — *writing*, calligrafia inclinata.

slopingly ['sloupiŋli], *av.* in pendenza; obliquamente.

sloppily ['slɔpili], *av.* **1.** disordinatamente; trascuratamente **2.** sdolcinatamente.

sloppiness ['slɔpinis], *s.* **1.** fangosità (di strada ecc.) **2.** l'essere bagnato (di tavolo, ecc.) **3.** trascuratezza, sciatteria **4.** sdolcinatura; sentimentalismo.

sloppy ['slɔpi], *ag.* **1.** bagnato di pioggia; fangoso; pieno di pozzanghere **2.** bagnato (di tavolo, pavimento ecc.) **3.** disordinato; trascurato, sciatto **4.** sdolcinato: — *sentimentality*, sentimentalismo sdolcinato.

slosh [slɔʃ], s. **1.** fango, poltiglia **2.** brodaglia.

to slosh, v.t.i. **1.** scuotere, agitare (liquidi) **2.** diguazzare, sguazzare **3.** (sl.) battere, sconfiggere **4.** (amer.) passare il tempo oziando.

sloshy ['slɔʃi], ag. **1.** fangoso, motoso **2.** brodoso.

slot[1] [slɔt], s. sbarra; chiavistello.

slot[2], s. fessura; scanalatura ☆ — -machine, distributore automatico a gettoni; — -meter, contatore a gettoni.

to slot[2], pass.p.p. **slotted** ['slɔtid], v.t. **1.** fare una fessura in; scanalare **2.** introdurre (una moneta) in un distributore automatico.

slot[3], s. traccia, pista, orme (di animali, specialmente cervi) ☆ — -hound, segugio.

sloth [slouθ], s. **1.** pigrizia, indolenza; infingardaggine **2.** (zool.) bradipo.

slothful ['slouθful], ag. pigro, indolente; infingardo.

slothfully ['slouθfuli], av. pigramente, indolentemente.

slothfulness ['slouθfulnis], s. infingardaggine; pigrizia, indolenza.

slouch [slautʃ], s. **1.** andatura dinoccolata, goffa **2.** pigrone; (sl. amer.) persona inefficiente ☆ — -hat, cappello a cencio.

to slouch, v.t.i. **1.** muoversi, camminare goffamente **2.** abbassare la tesa di (cappello).

slouching ['slautʃiŋ], ag. goffo, dinoccolato.

slouchingly ['slautʃiŋli], av. goffamente.

slough[1] [slau], s. pozzanghera; pantano.

slough[2] [slʌf], s. **1.** spoglia (di serpe); parte del corpo che un animale perde, muta **2.** crosta, escara **3.** fig. abitudine, vizio di cui ci si libera.

to slough[2], v.t.i. **1.** cambiare pelle; squamarsi; spogliarsi **2.** staccarsi (di croste) **3.** fig. liberarsi di (abitudini, vizi, ecc.).

sloughy[1] ['slaui], ag. pantanoso, fangoso.

sloughy[2] ['slʌfi], ag. **1.** che si sfalda, si squama **2.** pieno di croste, di squame.

Slovak ['slouvæk], ag. slovacco || s.c. slovacco, slovacca || s. lingua slovacca.

Slovakia [slou'væklə], no.pr. (geog.) Slovacchia.

sloven ['slʌvn], s. sudicione; sciattone; pigrone.

Slovene ['slouvi:n], ag. sloveno || s.c. sloveno, slovena.

Slovenia [slou'vi:njə], no.pr. (geog.) Slovenia.

Slovenian [slou'vi:njən], ag. sloveno || s.c. sloveno, slovena || s. lingua slovena.

slovenliness ['slʌvnlinis], s. sciatteria; trascuratezza; negligenza; sporcizia.

slovenly ['slʌvnli], ag. sciatto; sudicio; negligente.

slovenry ['slʌvnri], (arc.) per **slovenliness**.

slow [slou], ag. **1.** lento: at a — pace, a passo lento; goods of — sale, merci che si vendono poco; plants of — growth, piante tardive; to cook in a — oven, cuocere a fuoco lento; he was — to answer (o in answering), non aveva la risposta pronta; she is — to anger, non si arrabbia facilmente || — and steady wins the race, prov. chi va piano va sano e va lontano **2.** tardo, ottuso: — child, bambino tardivo **3.** noioso: the party was —, il ricevimento fu noioso **4.** in ritardo, indietro: the guests were — in arriving, gli ospiti erano in ritardo; my watch is always ten minutes —, il mio orologio è sempre indietro dieci minuti **5.** pesante (di terreno, ecc.) **6.** (foto.) lento (di pellicola).

to slow, v.t.i.: to — (up o down), rallentare, ritardare: the train was slowing down, il treno rallentava.

slow, av. lentamente, adagio: go —, va' piano; fig. sii cauto.

slow, (nei composti): — -down, rallentamento; — -foot, (dal passo) lento; — -match, miccia; — -motion, (cine.) al rallentatore; — -moving, lento, che si muove lentamente; tardigrado.

slowcoach ['slou-koutʃ], s.c. (fam.) **1.** posapiano, trottapiano **2.** persona ottusa, tarda di mente **3.** persona retrograda.

slowly ['slouli], av. lentamente; adagio.

slowness ['slou-nis], s. **1.** lentezza; pigrizia, indo-

lenza, ignavia **2.** ottusità mentale **3.** ritardo (d'orologio).

slow-worm ['slouwə:m], s. (zool.) orbettino.

sloyd [sloid], s. metodo pedagogico svedese che consiglia il lavoro manuale, specialmente su legno.

slub [slʌb], s. (ind. tessile) ringrosso.

to slub, pass p.p. **slubbed** [slʌbd], v.t. (ind. tessile) torcere leggermente (filo).

to slubber ['slʌbə*], V. **to slobber**.

slubbing ['slʌbiŋ], s. (ind. tessile) torcitura leggera (di filati).

sludge [slʌdʒ], s. **1.** fango, melma **2.** acque sudice, di scolo **3.** (mar.) ghiaccio galleggiante **4.** morchia.

sludgy ['slʌdʒi], ag. fangoso, melmoso.

(to) slue, V. **(to) slew**[1].

slug[1] [slʌg], s. lumaca || s.c. persona pigra; fannullone, fannullona.

to slug[1], pass.p.p. **slugged** [slʌgd], v.i. (rar.) **1.** muoversi lentamente; indugiare **2.** poltrire.

slug[2], s. **1.** pallottola, proiettile (di forma irregolare) **2.** pepita; gettone **3.** (tip.) lingotto.

to slug[2], v.t.i. **1.** caricare (arma da fuoco) **2.** adattarsi alla canna del fucile (di proiettile).

(to) slug[3], V. **(to) slog**.

sluggard ['slʌgəd], ag. indolente, fannullone, pigro || s.c. persona indolente; fannullone, fannullona.

sluggish ['slʌgiʃ], ag. pigro, tardo, indolente; lento (nei movimenti): a — digestion, una digestione lenta, difficile; a — fellow, un individuo pigro, indolente; a — river, un fiume dal corso lento.

sluggishly ['slʌgiʃli], av. pigramente, indolentemente; lentamente.

sluggishness ['slʌgiʃnis], s. pigrizia, indolenza; lentezza.

sluice [slu:s], s. chiusa, cateratta; canale con chiusa ☆ — -gate, saracinesca, paratoia; — head, testa di chiusa || inlet —, paratoia di presa.

to sluice, v.t.i. **1.** munire di chiusa, chiuse **2.** inondare, allagare (per mezzo di chiuse) **3.** bagnare abbondantemente; risciacquare **4.** scorrere violentemente, riversarsi (come da una chiusa).

sluicy ['slu:si], ag. a fiotti; a torrenti.

slum [slʌm], s. **1.** viuzza, vicolo **2.** pl. bassifondi.

to slum, pass.p.p. **slummed** [slʌmd], v.i. visitare i quartieri poveri di una città.

slumber ['slʌmbə*], s. **1.** dormiveglia, assopimento **2.** fig. stato di inattività.

to slumber, v.t.i. **1.** dormire, sonnecchiare **2.** essere in uno stato di inattività **3.** to — away, perdere tempo dormendo.

slumberer ['slʌmbərə*], s.c. chi dorme, sonnecchia.

slumbering ['slʌmbəriŋ], ag. addormentato, sonnecchiante, assopito || s. dormiveglia.

slumberingly ['slʌmbəriŋli], av. sonnecchiando.

slumberless ['slʌmbəlis], ag. senza sonno.

slumberous ['slʌmbərəs], ag. **1.** che dorme; assopito **2.** calmo, tranquillo **3.** soporifero.

slumberously ['slʌmbərəsli], av. sonnecchiosamente, torpidamente.

slummer ['slʌmə*], s.c. chi bazzica, abita i bassifondi di una città.

slump[1] [slʌmp], s. grande quantità: by (o in) (the) —, in blocco.

to slump[1], v.t. ammucchiare.

slump[2], s. (comm.) crollo, caduta (dei prezzi); crisi economica.

to slump[2], v.i. **1.** (comm.) crollare (di prezzi) **2.** cadere (nel fango, nell'acqua).

slung [slʌŋ], pass.p.p. di **to sling**.

slunk [slʌŋk], pass.p.p. di **to slink**.

slur [slə:*], s. **1.** insulto, affronto, accusa; macchia: to cast a — on s.o.'s reputation, macchiare la reputazione di qlcu. **2.** (mus.) legatura **3.** pronuncia, dizione difettosa (di una parola) **4.** (tip.) doppieggiatura.

to slur, pass.p.p. **slurred** [slə:d], v.t. **1.** calunniare, denigrare, macchiare **2.** sorvolare; passar sopra a: to —

over details, sorvolare sui particolari 3. (*mus.*) legare due note 4. pronunciare difettosamente, in maniera confusa 5. (*tip.*) fare una doppieggiatura a.

slurring ['slə:rin], *s.* 1. calunnia, maldicenza 2. (*mus.*) legatura 3. pronuncia, espressione difettosa 4. (*tip.*) doppieggiatura.

slush [slʌʃ], *s.* 1. poltiglia, fango, melma; neve sciolta 2. *fig.* sdolcinatezza 3. (*mec.*) antiruggine; grasso lubrificante 4. (*sl. amer.*) concussione; corruzione; carta-moneta falsa.

to **slush**, *v.t.* 1. schizzare di fango 2. (*mar.*) lubrificare 3. lavare (con molta acqua).

slushy ['slʌʃi], *ag.* 1. fangoso, melmoso 2. *fig.* sentimentale, sdolcinato.

slut [slʌt], *s.* 1. sudiciona, sciattona 2. cagna 3. (*arc.*) sgualdrina 4. (*arc. scherz.*) birba, birbetta.

sluttery ['slʌtəri], *s.* sporcizia, sudiciume; disordine.

sluttish ['slʌtiʃ], *ag.* sporco, sudicio; trascurato.

sluttishly ['slʌtiʃli], *av.* sudiciamente; trascuratamente.

sluttishness ['slʌtiʃnis], *s.* sporcizia, sudiciume; disordine.

sly [slai], *ag.* 1. astuto, accorto, malizioso ‖ *a — dog*, un sornione, un furbacchione 2. infido, insincero, sleale 3. segreto; furtivo ‖ *on the—*, furtivamente, in sordina.

slyboots ['slaibu:ts], *s.* (*scherz.*) sornione; furbacchione.

slyly ['slai-li], *av.* 1. scaltramente, astutamente 2. slealmente 3. furtivamente.

slyness ['slai²nis], *s.* 1. astuzia, furberia, malizia, scaltrezza 2. ipocrisia, slealtà.

smack¹ [smæk], *s.* sapore; aroma, fragranza; sentore; traccia: *there is the — of the old days in it*, v'è il profumo dei tempi andati in ciò.

to **smack¹**, *v.i.: to — of* (*sthg.*) sapere di, avere il gusto di; *fig.* far pensare a, ricordare: *this wine smacks of cork*, questo vino sa di tappo.

smack², *s.* 1. schiocco (di labbra, frusta) 2. bacio con lo schiocco 3. schiaffo, colpo (dato con la mano aperta): *a — in the face*, uno schiaffo in faccia; *fig.* un severo rimprovero ‖ *a — in the eye*, una delusione inaspettata.

to **smack²**, *v.t.i.* 1. schioccare, far schioccare (labbra, frusta) 2. schioccare baci; baciare 3. schiaffeggiare, colpire (con la mano aperta) 4. andare a sbattere.

smack², *av.* improvvisamente; in pieno; direttamente; con un tonfo: *he fell — into the puddle*, cadde in pieno nella pozzanghera.

smack³, *s.* peschereccio.

smacker ['smæke*], *s.* 1. schiaffo sonoro 2. bacio con lo schiocco 3. esemplare grande, notevole 4. (*sl. amer.*) dollaro.

smacking ['smækin], *ag.* schioccante ‖ *s.* 1. schiocco 2. schiaffo.

smacksman, *pl.* **smacksmen** ['smæksmən], *s.* marinaio di un peschereccio; proprietario di un peschereccio.

small [smɔ:l], *ag.* 1. piccolo, minuto: *it is a — room*, è una camera piccola 2. leggero; debole: *the beer is rather —*, la birra è piuttosto leggera; *she has a — voice*, ha la voce debole ‖ *the still — voice*, la coscienza 3. poco, scarso; limitato, ristretto: *he showed — interest in that film*, mostrò poco interesse per quel film; *they have — Latin*, sanno poco di latino 4. di poca importanza; insignificante: *a — tradesman*, un piccolo commerciante; *— worries*, preoccupazioni di poca importanza 5. umile, oscuro; povero: *— people love to talk of the great*, gli umili amano parlare dei potenti; *to feel, to look —*, sentirsi umiliato, aver l'aspetto dimesso; *to live in a — way*, vivere modestamente ‖ *great and —*, tutti i ceti sociali 6. meschino; gretto: *he is a — man*, è un uomo meschino; *that is very — of you*, questo non è generoso da parte tua ‖ *s.* 1. oggetto piccolo 2. la parte più piccola: *— of the back*, le reni 3. *pl.* esame di matricola (primo dei tre esami del «Bachelor of Arts», a Oxford) 4. carbone minuto 5. *pl.* (*fam.*) biancheria intima.

small, *av.* 1. poco; in piccola quantità 2. a bassa voce: *to sing —*, cantare a bassa voce; *fig.* divenir umile; abbassare la cresta.

small, (*nei composti*): *— -and-early*, (*fam.*) piccola riunione fra amici; *— -arms*, armi portatili; *— -beer*, birra leggera: *he thinks no — -beer of himself*, (*fam.*) è presuntuoso, pieno di sè; *— -craft*, naviglio di piccola portata; *— -hours*, ore piccole; *— -minded*, dalla mentalità ristretta; *— -shot*, pallini da caccia; *— -talk*, conversazione futile; *— -wares*, mercerie; chincaglieria.

smallage ['smɔ:lidʒ], *s.* (*bot.*) appio, sedano.

smallholder ['smɔ:l'houldə*], *s.* proprietario di una piccola fattoria.

smallholding ['smɔ:l'houldin], *s.* piccola fattoria di campagna.

smallish ['smɔ:liʃ], *ag.* piuttosto piccolo.

smallness ['smɔ:lnis], *s.* 1. piccolezza, esiguità, scarsità 2. meschinità: *the — of his mind*, la sua piccineria.

smallpox ['smɔ:l-pɔks], *s.* (*patol.*) vaiolo.

smalt [smɔ:lt], *s.* smalto.

smaragd ['smærægd], *s.* (*arc.*) smeraldo.

smaragdine [smə'rægdin], *ag.* color verde smeraldo.

to **smarm** [smɑ:m], *v.t.* (*fam.*) 1. impiastrare: *to — one's hair down*, impomatarsi i capelli 2. *fig.* adulare: *to — over s.o.*, adulare, lisciare qlcu.

smarmy ['smɑ:mi], *ag.* (*fam. fig.*) untuoso, strisciante.

smart [smɑ:t], *ag.* 1. acuto, pungente; aspro; forte; severo, mordace; doloroso: *a — pain*, un dolore lancinante; *a — saying*, una battuta mordace; *— words*, parole dure, severe 2. vivace; sveglio, intelligente, abile; attivo; brillante, spiritoso: *a — pace*, un'andatura veloce; *a — pupil*, un allievo sveglio; *a — talker*, un oratore brillante ‖ *— -aleck*, (*fam.*) saccente 3. elegante, attillato, alla moda ‖ *the — set*, il bel mondo 4. (*fam.*) grande, considerevole ‖ *s.* dolore acuto; bruciore; sofferenza (fisica, morale) ☆ *— money*, risarcimento, indennizzo; *— -ticket*, certificato d'indennizzo.

to **smart**, *v.i.* 1. dolere, far male; bruciare: *his wound smarts*, gli fa male la ferita; *my finger smarts from a burn*, mi sono scottato un dito e mi fa male 2. soffrire: *to — under an insult*, soffrire per un insulto ‖ *to — for sthg.*, subire le conseguenze di ql.co.: *you shall — for this!*, questa me la pagherai.

to **smarten** ['smɑ:tn], *v.t.i.* abbellire; riordinare ‖ *to — up*, rianimarsi.

smarting ['smɑ:tin], *ag.* doloroso; cocente; pungente; acuto ‖ *s.* dolore acuto; bruciore.

smartish ['smɑ:tiʃ], *ag.* abbastanza elegante.

smartly ['smɑ:tli], *av.* 1. acutamente; aspramente; severamente; mordacemente 2. vivacemente; prontamente; attivamente; brillantemente, argutamente 3. elegantemente; alla moda.

smartness ['smɑ:tnis], *s.* 1. acutezza; abilità; vivacità, brio; spirito, arguzia 2. eleganza.

smartweed ['smɑ:t-wi:d], *s.* (*bot.*) persicaria.

smash¹ [smæʃ], *s.* 1. forte colpo; urto; scontro, collisione (accompagnata da forte rumore) 2. rovina; bancarotta, fallimento: *to go to —*, andare in rovina 3. (*amer.*) bevanda alcoolica a base di menta.

to **smash¹**, *v.t.i.* 1. frantumare; fracassare, sfasciare; colpire violentemente; sbattere; urtare ‖ *to — a door open*, sfondare una porta 2. sconfiggere, annientare 3. andare a sbattere, fracassarsi: *the car smashed into a wall*, l'automobile si sfasciò contro un muro 4. (*fam.*) fallire, far bancarotta 5. *to — in*, fare irruzione fracassando tutto 6. *to — up*, fracassare.

smash¹, (*nei composti*): *— -and-grab*, furto compiuto infrangendo una vetrina; *— -up*, rovina completa.

smash², *s.* moneta falsa.

to **smash²**, *v.t.* spacciare (moneta falsa).

smasher¹ ['smæʃə*], *s.c.* chi frantuma, fracassa *s.* 1. (*fam.*) caso eccezionale, straordinario 2. (*fam.* risposta mordace; articolo severo, che stronca 3. (*mec.* pressatoio per rilegatore.

smasher², *s.* spacciatore di moneta falsa.

smashing ['smæʃiŋ], *ag.* **1.** che fracassa, che rompe tutto **2.** (*fam.*) straordinario, formidabile.

smatter ['smætə*], *s.* infarinatura, conoscenza superficiale.

to smatter, *v.t.i.* **1.** avere un'infarinatura: *to — a language,* avere una vaga conoscenza di una lingua **2.** parlare senza competenza su (un argomento).

smatterer ['smætərə*], *s.c.* persona che ha cultura superficiale; saccente.

smattering ['smætəriŋ], *V.* **smatter.**

smaze [smeiz], *s.* (*amer. contr.* di *smoke* e *haze*) aria afosa e fumosa.

smear [smiə*], *s.* **1.** macchia (generalmente di unto); imbrattatura **2.** *fig.* calunnia.

to smear, *v.t.i.* **1.** macchiare (con sostanza grassa); insudiciare, insudiciarsi; imbrattare, imbrattarsi **2.** *fig.* calunniare.

smeary ['smiəri], *ag.* **1.** grasso, untuoso, vischioso **2.** macchiato, imbrattato.

smectite ['smektait], *s.* (*ind. tessile*) argilla smettica.

smell [smel], *s.* **1.** odorato, olfatto; fiuto: *dogs have a quick —,* i cani hanno un buon fiuto; *to have a keen —,* avere l'odorato fine **2.** odore; cattivo odore: *bad* (o *nasty*) —, puzzo; *a sweet —,* un buon profumo **3.** atto dell'annusare, del fiutare: *to take a — at,* annusare, fiutare **4.** (*amer.*) traccia, sfumatura.

to smell, *pass.p.p.* **smelt** [smelt], *v.t.i.* **1.** (I) fiutare, annusare; sentire l'odore, il profumo di; avere il senso dell'odorato: *the dog smelt the meat from far off,* il cane sentì l'odore della carne da lontano; *I can — sthg. burning,* sento odore di bruciato; *I can't — anything,* non sento alcun odore; *not all animals can —,* non tutti gli animali hanno l'odorato; *to — a flower,* sentire il profumo di un fiore ‖ *to — a rat, fig.* sospettare, fiutare un imbroglio **2.** odorare, avere odore di: *the milk smelt sour,* il latte aveva odore di acido; *these flowers don't —,* questi fiori non hanno profumo ‖ *to — of,* sapere da; *fig.* far pensare a: *it smells of the lamp,* sa di tavolino, « lucernam olet » (di opera letteraria); *this room smells of smoke,* in questa stanza c'è odore di fumo **3.** *to — out,* scovare; *fig.* scoprire (segreto, ecc.) **4.** *to — round, about,* fiutare di qua e di là; (*fam.*) cercare di ottenere informazioni.

smellable ['smeləbl], *ag.* odorabile.

smeller ['smelə*], *s.c.* chi fiuta ‖ *s.* **1.** (*sl.*) naso **2.** forte colpo (specialmente sul naso).

smelling ['smeliŋ], *ag.* odorifero; odoroso ‖ *s.* atto dell'odorare, del fiutare ☆ *— -bottle,* boccetta dei sali; *— -salts,* sali odorosi (da fiuto).

smelly ['smeli], *ag.* (*fam.*) che manda cattivo odore; puzzolente.

smelt¹ [smelt], *s.* (*ittiol.*) eperlano.

to smelt², *v.t.* (*metal.*) **1.** fondere (minerale) **2.** estrarre (il metallo) per fusione.

smelt³, *pass.p.p.* di to **smell.**

smelter ['smeltə*], *s.* fonditore.

smeltery ['smeltəri], *s.* (*metal.*) fonderia.

smelting ['smeltiŋ], *s.* fusione ☆ *— -furnace,* forno di fusione; *— -house,* fonderia.

smew [smju:], *s.* (*ornit.*) smergo.

smilax ['smailæks], *s.* (*bot.*) salsapariglia, smilace.

smile [smail], *s.* **1.** sorriso: *a scornful —,* un sorriso di derisione; *to keep down a —,* trattenere un sorriso **2.** *pl.* favori, disposizione favorevole: *the smiles of fortune,* i favori della fortuna.

to smile, *v.t.i.* **1.** sorridere, esprimere con un sorriso: *he smiled an affected smile,* sorrise con affettazione; *to — at sthg.,* sorridere di ql.co. ‖ *to — consent,* approvare con un sorriso ‖ *to — bad thoughts away,* scacciare i cattivi pensieri con un sorriso **2.** favorire, essere favorevole: *the occasion smiles on us,* l'occasione ci è favorevole.

smileless ['smaillis], *ag.* **1.** senza sorriso, serio **2.** scuro, triste.

smiler ['smailə], *s.c.* chi sorride.

smiling ['smailiŋ], *ag.* **1.** sorridente; sereno: *a — face,* un viso sorridente **2.** favorevole ‖ *s.* sorriso.

smilingly ['smailiŋli], *av.* con aria sorridente.

smilingness ['smailiŋnis], *s.* aria sorridente.

smirch [sme:tʃ], *s.* macchia (anche *fig.*).

to smirch, *v.t.* macchiare (anche *fig.*).

smirk [sme:k], *s.* sorriso affettato, sciocco.

to smirk, *v.i.* sorridere affettatamente, scioccamente.

smirking ['sme:kiŋ], *ag.* lezioso, affettato; sciocco.

smite [smait], *s.* (*fam.*) **1.** colpo; percossa **2.** tentativo.

to smite, *pass.* **smote** [smout], *p.p.* **smitten** ['smitn], *v.t.i.* **1.** colpire; percuotere; battere con violenza (anche *fig.*): *he was smitten with a serious disease,* fu colpito da una grave malattia; *the idea smote him,* gli venne un lampo di genio; *a queer sound smote upon my ear,* uno strano suono mi ferì l'orecchio; *to — one's hands together,* battere le mani ‖ *to be smitten with s.o.,* (*fam.*) essere innamorato di ql.cu. **2.** sconfiggere, sgominare; distruggere: *to — the enemy hip and thigh,* sconfiggere definitivamente il nemico **3.** affliggere, castigare: *God smites the bad,* Dio punisce i cattivi; *his conscience smites him,* gli rimorde la coscienza **4.** (*mus. poet.*) pizzicare (uno strumento): *to — a harp,* pizzicare, suonare l'arpa **5.** *to — down,* abbattere; colpire a morte **6.** *to — off,* decapitare.

smiter ['smaitə*], *s.c.* chi colpisce, batte.

smith [smiθ], *s.* fabbro.

to smith, *v.t.i.* **1.** battere il ferro o altro metallo **2.** fare il fabbro.

smithereens ['smiðə'ri:nz], *s.pl.* frammenti, pezzetti: *to smash sthg.* (*in*)*to —,* ridurre ql.co. in briciole.

smithery ['smiθəri], **smithy** ['smiði], *s.* forgia, fucina.

smitten ['smitn], *p.p.* di to **smite.**

smock [smɔk], *s.* **1.** (*arc.*) camicia (da donna) **2.** grembiule da bambino ☆ *— -frock,* camiciotto, blusa da contadino.

smocking ['smɔkiŋ], *s.* (*ricamo*) punto smock.

smog [smɔg], *s.* (*contr.* di *smoke* e *fog*) smog (miscela di fumo e nebbia).

smokable ['smoukəbl], *ag.* fumabile.

smokables ['smoukəblz], *s.pl.* tabacco; qualsiasi cosa che si può fumare.

smoke [smouk], *s.* **1.** fumo: *there were clouds of — in that room,* quella stanza era piena di fumo ‖ *from — into smother,* dalla padella nella brace ‖ *like —,* (*sl.*) facilmente, rapidamente, senza difficoltà ‖ *to go up in — (o to end in —),* finire in fumo, sfumare ‖ *to sell —,* imbrogliare ‖ *there is no — without fire, prov.* dove c'è fumo c'è fuoco ‖ *there is no fire without —, prov.* non c'è rosa senza spine **2.** fumata; (*fam.*) sigaro, sigaretta: *let's have a —,* facciamoci una fumatina ☆ *— -ball* (o *— -bomb*), (*mil.*) bomba fumogena; *— -bell,* parafumo; *— -black,* nerofumo; *— -box,* (*mec.*) camera a fumo; *— -bush,* (*bot.*) sommacco; *— -curing,* affumicatura; *— -dried,* affumicato; *— -hole,* (*geol.*) fumarola; *— -house,* affumicatoio; *— -jack,* girarrosto a corrente d'aria calda; (*sl.*) confusionario; *— -room,* sala per fumatori; *— -room story,* storiella per soli uomini; *— -screen,* (*mar. mil.*) cortina di fumo; *— -stack,* fumaiolo; ciminiera; *— -stone,* quarzo giallo, bruno.

to smoke, *v.t.i.* **1.** fumare, emettere fumo, vapore: *the lamp is still smoking,* la lampada fumiga ancora **2.** fumare: *do you —?,* fumi? ‖ *he has smoked himself sick,* ha fumato tanto da sentirsi male ‖ *put it in your pipe and — it,* (*fam.*) prendi e metti in tasca **3.** affumicare; annerire di fumo: *the lamp has smoked the ceiling,* la lampada ha annerito il soffitto; *there was smoked haddock for breakfast,* c'era merluzzo affumicato per colazione **4.** (*rar.*) sospettare; aver sentore di: *he smoked the plot,* ebbe sentore della congiura **5.** *to — out,* cacciare, distruggere col fumo: *masses of ants were smoked out,* caterve di formiche furono distrutte col fumo.

smokeless ['smouk-lis], *ag.* senza fumo.

smokeproof ['smouk-pru:f], *ag.* a prova di fumo.

smoker ['smoukə*], *s.c.* fumatore, fumatrice ‖ *s.* (*ferr.*) carrozza, scompartimento per fumatori.

smokiness ['smoukinis], *s.* fumosità.

smoking ['smoukiŋ], *ag.* fumante, che fuma ‖ *s.* fumo; il fumare ‖ — *forbidden* (o *no* — *allowed*), vietato fumare ☆ — *-car(riage)* (o — *-compartment*), carrozza, scompartimento per fumatori; — *-concert*, concerto durante il quale è permesso fumare; — *-jacket*, giacca da casa; — *-mixture*, miscela di tabacco da pipa.

smoky ['smouki], *ag.* **1.** fumoso, che fa fumo **2.** affumicato, annerito dal fumo; pieno di fumo **3.** che sa di fumo.

to **smooch** [smu:tʃ], *v.t.* (*amer.*) imbrattare.

smooth [smu:ð], *ag.* **1.** liscio, levigato; piano: — *skin*, pelle liscia **2.** ben amalgamato, omogeneo: — *paste*, pasta ben amalgamata **3.** armonioso (di suono, ecc.); gradevole, dolce (di sapore): *a* — *line*, un verso scorrevole; *a* — *wine*, un vino gradevole **4.** dolce, affabile; mellifluo: — *manners*, modi melliflui **5.** calmo, tranquillo: *the sea is* — *today*, il mare è calmo oggi; *we had a* — *crossing*, abbiamo avuto una traversata tranquilla ‖ *to be in* — *waters*, *fig.* essere tranquillo, al sicuro ‖ *s.* **1.** lisciata: *she gave her hair a* —, si ravviò i capelli **2.** parte liscia; terreno uniforme ‖ *to take the rough with the* —, far buon viso a cattiva sorte ☆ — *-bore*, (fucile) a canna liscia; — *-faced*, imberbe; *fig.* dall'espressione mellifluа; — *-tempered*, di carattere dolce; — *-tongued*, dalle parole adulatrici, mellifluе.

to **smooth(e)**, *v.t.i.* **1.** lisciare; spianare; levigare; *fig.* facilitare; appianare: *to* — *away* (o *over*) *differences*, attenuare le differenze; *to* — *the way for s.o.*, *fig.* appianare la strada a qlcu. **2.** *to* — **down**, calmarsi: *the sea is smoothing down*, il mare si sta calmando **3.** *to* — *off*, smussare (un angolo).

smoothing ['smu:ðiŋ], *s.* lisciatura; spianatura; levigatura ☆ — *-iron*, ferro da stiro; — *-plane*, pialla.

smoothly ['smu:ðli], *av.* **1.** pianamente; facilmente **2.** soavemente, armonicamente **3.** in modo conciliante; in modo mellifluo.

smoothness ['smu:ðnis], *s.* **1.** levigatezza; regolarità **2.** scorrevolezza, armonia (di verso, suono) **3.** dolcezza, affabilità **4.** calma, tranquillità.

smote [smout], *pass.* di to **smite**.

smother ['smʌðə*], *s.* **1.** fumo soffocante; nuvola (di fumo, polvere, ecc.) **2.** (*arc.*) brace.

to **smother**, *v.t.i.* **1.** soffocare; opprimere; sopprimere; reprimere (anche *fig.*): *he smothered the fire with sand*, soffocò il fuoco con la sabbia; *the scandal was smothered up*, lo scandalo fu soffocato; *this sultry weather smothers me*, questa afa mi soffoca; *to* — *s.o. with kisses*, soffocare uno di baci; *to* — *a yawn*, reprimere uno sbadiglio **2.** ricoprire: *biscuits smothered in* (o *with*) *cream*, biscotti ricoperti di crema **3.** (*rar.*) morire soffocato.

smothering ['smʌðəriŋ], *ag.* soffocante, asfissiante, opprimente (anche *fig.*) ‖ *s.* soffocamento; oppressione; soppressione; repressione.

smotheringly ['smʌðəriŋli], *av.* in modo soffocante.

smothery ['smʌðəri], *ag.* soffocante, opprimente.

smoulder ['smouldə*], *s.* **1.** fumo denso **2.** brace **3.** combustione lenta.

to **smoulder**, *v.i.* bruciare sotto la cenere (anche *fig.*); bruciare senza fiamma: *for a long time hatred smouldered in her heart*, l'odio covò a lungo nel suo cuore.

smouldering ['smouldəriŋ], *s.* combustione lenta.

smudge[1] [smʌdʒ], *s.* **1.** macchia; imbrattatura; sgorbio **2.** massa confusa.

to **smudge**[1], *v.t.i.* macchiare, insudiciare; scarabocchiare; spandersi (di inchiostro, disegno).

smudge[2], *s.* (*amer.*) **1.** fumo denso **2.** fuoco all'aperto che produce molto fumo (per allontanare gli insetti).

to **smudge**[2], *v.t.i.* (*amer.*) accendere un fuoco producendo fumo denso.

smudginess ['smʌdʒinis], *s.* sporcizia; imbrattatura.

smudgy ['smʌdʒi], *ag.* macchiato, imbrattato.

smug [smʌg], *ag.* **1.** (*arc.*) dall'aspetto rispettabile **2.** soddisfatto di sè; presuntuoso ‖ *s.* **1.** (*arc.*) persona soddisfatta di sè **2.** (*sl. universitario*) sgobbone.

to **smuggle** ['smʌgl], *v.t.i.* contrabbandare; esercitare, fare il contrabbando: *to* — *sth. into, out of a country*, introdurre, far uscire da un paese merce di contrabbando.

smuggler ['smʌglə*], *s.* **1.** contrabbandiere **2.** nave usata da contrabbandieri.

smuggling ['smʌgliŋ], *s.* contrabbando.

smugly ['smʌgli], *av.* con aria di sufficienza; con piena soddisfazione di sè.

smugness ['smʌgnis], *s.* mediocrità compiaciuta di sè.

smut [smʌt], *s.* **1.** macchia prodotta da fuliggine **2.** linguaggio, discorso osceno **3.** (*agr.*) golpe.

to **smut**, *pass.p.p.* **smutted** ['smʌtid], *v.t.i.* **1.** annerire con sostanza scura, sudicia; imbrattare **2.** (*agr.*) ammalarsi di golpe.

smuttily ['smʌtili], *av.* indecentemente, oscenamente, sconciamente.

smuttiness ['smʌtinis], *s.* **1.** sporcizia; nerume **2.** oscenità, sconcezza.

smutty ['smʌti], *ag.* **1.** annerito; sporco; fuligginoso **2.** sboccato, osceno, sconcio **3.** (*agr.*) che ha la golpe.

Smyrna ['smə:nə], *no.pr.* (*geog.*) Smirne.

snack [snæk], *s.* **1.** boccone; porzione; parte ‖ *to go snacks*, dividere ‖ *snacks!*, dammi la mia parte! **2.** merenda, spuntino: *to take a* —, fare uno spuntino ☆ — *-bar*, tavola calda; — *-basket*, cestino per pic-nic.

snaffle ['snæfl], *s.* morso snodato (del cavallo): *to ride s.o. on* (o *with*) *the* —, *fig.* guidare qlcu. con delicatezza, con facilità.

snag [snæg], *s.* **1.** sporgenza; protuberanza; parte di un ramo tagliato sporgente dal tronco **2.** tronco, grosso ramo conficcatosi nel fondo di un fiume e che ostacola la navigazione **3.** *fig.* intoppo; difficoltà imprevista **4.** dente rotto, irregolare.

to **snag**, *pass.p.p.* **snagged** [snægd], *v.t.* **1.** far urtare (una nave) contro un ostacolo nascosto: *to be snagged*, urtare contro un ostacolo nascosto, uno scoglio **2.** ripulire un fiume da ostacoli nascosti **3.** tagliare in modo imperfetto lasciando sporgenze.

snagged [snægd], **snaggy** ['snægi], *ag.* **1.** nodoso, pieno di protuberanze (di ramo, albero) **2.** pieno di ostacoli imprevisti (di fiume, ecc.).

snail [sneil], *s.* chiocciola; lumaca (anche *fig.*) ‖ *to go at a* —'s *gallop* (o *pace*), andare, avanzare a passo di lumaca ☆ — *clover* (o — *trefoil*), varietà di erba medica; — *-fish*, nicchio marino, conchiglia; — *-slow*, lento come una lumaca; — *wheel*, lumaca; spirale (d'orologio) ‖ *Roman* —, chiocciola romana.

to **snail**, *v.t.i.* **1.** liberare (un luogo) dalle lumache **2.** andare in cerca di lumache **3.** slumacare.

snailery ['sneiləri], *s.* luogo ove si allevano lumache.

snake [sneik], *s.* **1.** serpente; serpe; biscia ‖ *snakes!*, maledizione! ‖ *a* — *in the grass*, *fig.* il serpente fra l'erbe; pericolo, nemico nascosto ‖ *to cherish* (o *to warm*) *a* — *in one's bosom*, allevare una serpe in seno ‖ *to raise* (o *to wake*) *snakes*, fare, provocare una rissa ‖ *to see snakes*, (*sl. amer.*) avere il delirium tremens **2.** *fig.* persona cattiva, sleale ☆ — *-charmer*, incantatore di serpenti; — *-dance*, danza del serpente; — *-fence*, (*amer.*) graticcio a zig-zag; —'s *head*, (*bot.*) fritillaria; — *-root*, (*bot.*) serpentaria; — *-weed*, (*bot.*) bistorta ‖ *hooded* —, cobra; *rattle* —, serpente a sonagli; *water* —, serpente d'acqua.

snakelike ['sneiklaik], *ag.* simile a serpente; lungo e snello, anguiforme.

snakestone ['sneik-stoun], *s.* (*paleont.*) ammonite.

snakily ['sneikili], *av.* tortuosamente, come un serpente; *fig.* slealmente.

snakiness ['sneikinis], *s.* tortuosità, sinuosità.

snaky ['sneiki], *ag.* **1.** serpentino **2.** serpeggiante; sinuoso, tortuoso (di strada).

snap [snæp], *s.* **1.** colpo secco di denti; morso, morsicata; schiocco: *to make a — at sthg.*, cercare di afferrare, addentare ql.co. ‖ *I don't care a —*, (*fam.*) non me ne importa un fico secco ‖ *to speak with a —*, parlare con tono tagliente **2.** rottura improvvisa, rumorosa **3.** fermaglio, fibbia; bottone automatico **4.** (*fam.*) energia, vigore; vivacità: *his style is full of —*, il suo stile è pieno di brio **5.** giuoco di carte infantile **6.** biscotto croccante **7.** (*teat.*) breve scrittura **8.** *V.* **snapshot** ☆ — *debate*, dibattito inatteso; — *vote*, votazione improvvisa; — *-hook* (o — *-link*), moschettone; — *-lock*, serratura a scatto; — *-switch*, (*elett.*) interruttore a scatto ‖ *cold —*, ondata di freddo intenso; *soft —*, lavoro facile.

to snap, *pass.p.p.* **snapped** [snæpt], *v.t.i.* **1.** schioccare, far schioccare; aprirsi di colpo; spezzare, spezzarsi con un colpo secco: *he snapped the stick over his knee*, spezzò il bastone sul ginocchio ‖ *to — one's fingers at s.o., sthg.*, infischiarsi di qlcu., ql.co.: *to — one's fingers at a threat*, infischiarsene di una minaccia **2.** (*foto.*) scattare una istantanea a **3.** *to — at* (*s.o., sthg.*), azzannare; tentar di mordere, ghermire; *fig.* investire, parlare aspramente a: *the dog snapped (at) the meat*, il cane azzannò la carne; *he snapped at the boy*, parlò aspramente al ragazzo **4.** *to — out of (sthg.*), liberarsi bruscamente di: *he managed to — out of smoking*, riuscì a liberarsi subito del vizio del fumo ‖ *— out of it!*, sbrigati! **5.** *to — off*, portar via con un morso; *fig.* interrompere bruscamente ‖ *to — off s.o.'s head* (o *nose*), dare un rabbuffo a qlcu.; parlare irosamente a qlcu. **6.** *to — up*, afferrare: *to — up a bargain*, afferrare un'occasione.

snapdragon ['snæp,drægən], *s.* **1.** (*bot.*) bocca di leone **2.** consuetudine natalizia consistente nell'immergere uvetta nel cognac ardente e nel mangiarla calda.

snapper ['snæpə*], *s.c.* persona stizzosa; persona che dà risposte mordaci, caustiche ‖ *s.* **1.** osservazione, battuta caustica **2.** fotografo che scatta istantanee.

snappish ['snæpiʃ], *ag.* **1.** stizzoso; ringhioso; mordace, caustico **2.** che scatta facilmente.

snappishly ['snæpiʃli], *av.* stizzosamente; bruscamente.

snappishness ['snæpiʃnis], *s.* asprezza, tono stizzoso; viso arcigno.

snappy ['snæpi], *ag.* **1.** stizzoso, irritabile, iroso; aspro, brusco **2.** vivace, brillante (di stile) **3.** (*fam.*) elegante.

snapshot ['snæpʃot], *s.* **1.** (*foto.*) istantanea: *to take a —*, scattare una istantanea **2.** colpo frettoloso tirato senza mira.

to snapshot, *pass.p.p.* **snapshotted** ['snæp,ʃotid], *v.t.i.* fare, prendere istantanee.

snare [snɛə*], *s.* **1.** trappola; rete; laccio; tagliuola: *to lay* (o *to set*) *a —*, tendere una trappola **2.** *fig.* trappola, insidia; tentazione: *popularity is a —*, la popolarità è un'insidia **3.** (*chir.*) ansa metallica (per l'escisione di polipi, ecc.).

to snare, *v.t.* prendere al laccio, in trappola (anche *fig.*).

snarer ['snɛərə*], *s.c.* chi tende trappole; chi insidia.

snark [snɑːk], *s.* (*lett.*) drago, mostro immaginario.

snarl¹ [snɑːl], *s.* **1.** intrico, viluppo, ginepraio; groviglio **2.** arruffatura, nodo; (*tessitura*) arricciatura.

to snarl¹, *v.t.i.* **1.** aggrovigliare, aggrovigliarsi; annodarsi, arruffarsi **2.** *fig.* prendere in trappola.

snarl², *s.* **1.** ringhio **2.** voce irosa; (*fam.*) brontolamento.

to snarl², *v.i.* ringhiare; parlare con acredine; pronunciare parole dure, irose; (*fam.*) brontolare.

snarler ['snɑːlə*], *s.c.* brontolone, brontolona ‖ *s.* cane ringhioso.

snarling ['snɑːliŋ], *s.* metodo per sbalzare il metallo ☆ — *iron*, strumento per sbalzare metallo.

snarlingly ['snɑːliŋli], *av.* **1.** ringhiosamente **2.** stizzosamente.

snarly ['snɑːli], *ag.* **1.** ringhioso **2.** stizzoso.

snatch [snætʃ], *s.* **1.** strappo, strattone, presa: *to make a — at sthg.*, ghermire ql.co. **2.** brano, frammento: *short snatches of songs*, brevi brani di canzoni **3.** breve periodo (di tempo): *to work in* (o *by*) *snatches*, lavorare saltuariamente **4.** pasto affrettato; spuntino.

to snatch, *v.t.i.* **1.** afferrare, afferrarsi, ghermire, agguantare, acchiappare: *a fish may — a worm from the hook*, un pesce può strappare il verme dall'amo; *he snatched the opportunity*, afferrò l'occasione; *to — a half-hour's rest*, prendersi mezz'ora di riposo **2.** *to — at* (*sthg.*), cercare di prendere **3.** *to — away*, rapire, portar via: *all hope of happiness has been snatched away*, ogni speranza di felicità svanì **4.** *to — off*, strappare, portar via: *the wind snatched his hat off*, il vento gli portò via il cappello **5.** *to — up*, tirar su, raccogliere in fretta: *he snatched his basket up from the ground*, raccolse il suo paniere da terra.

snatcher ['snætʃə*], *s.* ladro; rapinatore ☆ *body - —*, dissotterratore di cadaveri.

snatchily ['snætʃili], *av.* improvvisamente; bruscamente; avidamente; in fretta.

snatchy ['snætʃi], *ag.* frammentario, irregolare.

sneak [sniːk], *s.c.* **1.** persona vile, abietta, codarda **2.** (*sl. scolastico*) spia ‖ *s.* (*cricket*) palla lanciata raso terra ‖ *to take a —*, svignarsela ☆ *—-raid*, (*sl. amer.*) bombardamento improvviso; *—-thief*, (*amer.*) ladruncolo.

to sneak, *v.t.i.* **1.** insinuarsi; introdursi furtivamente; strisciare **2.** (*sl. scolastico*) fare la spia **3.** (*sl.*) rubare; (*amer.*) contrabbandare: *my watch was sneaked in the crowd*, nella ressa mi fu rubato l'orologio **4.** *to — away*, andar via di soppiatto **5.** *to — in*, entrare furtivamente.

sneaker ['sniːkə*], *s.* (*cricket*) palla lanciata raso terra.

sneakers ['sniːkəz], *s.pl.* (*amer. sl.*) scarpette per ginnastica (in tela, con suole di gomma).

sneaking ['sniːkiŋ], *ag.* **1.** servile; vile; abietto **2.** furtivo; nascosto; celato: *a — idea*, un'idea vaga, un sospetto; *to have a — affection for s.o.*, nutrire un affetto inconfessato per qlcu.

sneakingly ['sniːkiŋli], *av.* **1.** servilmente; vilmente **2.** dissimulatamente; furtivamente.

sneaky ['sniːki], *ag.* **1.** basso, servile **2.** (*sl. scolastico*) che ha la tendenza a fare la spia.

sneck [snek], *s.* (*spec. scoz.*) chiavistello; saliscendi.

to sneck, *v.t.i.* chiudere a chiavistello (una porta); chiudersi col chiavistello (di porta).

sneer [sniə*], *s.* **1.** sogghigno beffardo; tono canzonatorio **2.** motteggio, canzonatura.

to sneer, *v.t.i.* **1.** sorridere beffardamente, sogghignare **2.** *to — at* (*s.o.*), schernire, canzonare, burlarsi di.

sneerer ['sniərə*], *s.c.* schernitore, schernitrice; motteggiatore, motteggiatrice.

sneering ['sniəriŋ], *ag.* beffardo; canzonatorio; sarcastico ‖ *s.* sarcasmo; beffa.

sneeringly ['sniəriŋli], *av.* beffardamente, in modo canzonatorio.

sneeze [sniːz], *s.* starnuto.

to sneeze, *v.i.* **1.** starnutire ‖ *to — into a basket*, *fig.* essere ghigliottinato **2.** *to — at* (*s.o.*), disprezzare: *a thing not to be sneezed at*, una cosa non disprezzabile.

sneezing ['sniːziŋ], *s.* lo starnutire.

snell [snel], *s.* (*amer.*) pezzetto di crine, di budello che unisce l'amo alla lenza.

snick [snik], *s.* **1.** taglietto, piccola incisione; tacca **2.** (*cricket*) colpo che fa deviare la palla.

to snick, *v.t.* **1.** incidere; fare piccole intaccature in **2.** (*cricket*) far deviare leggermente (la palla) con la mazza.

snicker ['snikə*], *s.* **1.** nitrito **2.** risata repressa.

to snicker, *v.i.* **1.** nitrire **2.** reprimere il riso.

snide [snaid], *ag.* (*sl.*) falso, contraffatto ‖ *s.* gioielli, monete false ‖ *—'s man*, spacciatore di monete false.

sniff [snif], *s.* **1.** l'annusare, il fiutare **2.** annusata, fiutata.

to sniff, *v.t.i.* **1.** aspirare rumorosamente col naso; fiutare **2.** *fig.* presagire, prevedere: *to — danger*, prevedere un disastro **3.** *to — at* (*s.o.*, *sthg.*), annusare; *fig.* dimostrare disapprovazione, disprezzo per ‖ *to — at s.o.'s calves*, tentare di mordere i polpacci di qlcu. (di cani) **4.** *to — up*, fiutare; inspirare.

sniffy ['snifi], *ag.* **1.** (*fam.*) sprezzante, sdegnoso **2.** maleodorante.

snifting-valve ['sniftiŋ-vælv], *s.* (*mec.*) valvola di scappamento.

snigger ['snigə*], *s.* risolino malizioso, cinico.

to snigger, *v.i.* ridere sotto i baffi; ridacchiare.

sniggering ['snigəriŋ], *s.* il ridere maliziosamente, cinicamente.

to sniggle ['snigl], *v.i.* pescare anguille (introducendo l'amo nella loro tana).

snip [snip], *s.* **1.** ritaglio; scampolo **2.** forbiciata **3.** (*fam.*) sarto **4.** *pl.* forbici da lattoniere **5.** (*sl. ippico*) certezza; vincitore sicuro ☆ *— -snap*, colpo di forbici; dialogo vivace, spiritoso.

to snip, *pass.p.p.* **snipped** [snipt], *v.t.i.* tagliuzzare, fare dei tagli (con forbici, cesoie, ecc.): *to — a hole*, fare un buco; *to — at a cloth*, fare dei tagli in una stoffa ‖ *to — off the ends of s.o.'s hair*, spuntare i capelli a qlcu.

snipe [snaip], *s.* **1.** (*ornit.*) beccaccino **2.** *fig.* sciocco, stupido **3.** (*amer.*) mozzicone (di sigaretta) **4.** colpo sparato da luogo nascosto ☆ *— -fish*, (*ittiol.*) pesce trombetta.

to snipe, *v.t.i.* **1.** andare a caccia di beccaccini **2.** (*mil.*) sparare da luogo nascosto: *to be sniped*, essere ferito, essere ucciso in un'imboscata; *to — at the enemy*, tendere un'imboscata al nemico.

sniper ['snaipə*], *s.* **1.** chi caccia beccaccini **2.** (*mil.*) chi spara di soppiatto; franco tiratore.

snipper ['snipə*], *s.* **1.** sarto **2.** *pl.* forbici.

snippet ['snipit], *s.* **1.** pezzetto; ritaglio **2.** *pl.* frammenti (di notizie, di opere letterarie, ecc.).

snippetiness ['snipitinis], *s.* frammentarietà.

snippety ['snipiti], *ag.* frammentario; scucito (di stile).

snipy ['snaipi], *ag.* **1.** simile a beccaccino; dal becco lungo **2.** ricco di beccaccini (di località, ecc.).

snitch [snitʃ], *s.* (*pop.*) **1.** naso **2.** informatore; spia.

snivel ['snivl], *s.* **1.** moccio **2.** piagnucolamento **3.** finta commozione.

to snivel, *pass.p.p.* **snivelled** ['snivld], *v.i.* **1.** moccicare, avere il moccio **2.** piagnucolare, frignare **3.** simulare commozione.

sniveller ['snivlə*], *s.c.* **1.** piagnucolone, piagnucolona **2.** chi finge di essere commosso.

snivelling ['snivliŋ], *ag.* **1.** moccioso **2.** piagnucoloso ‖ *s.* **1.** piagnucolio **2.** lacrime finte.

snively ['snivli], *ag.* **1.** moccioso **2.** piagnucoloso.

snob [snob], *s.c.* « snob » ‖ *s.* **1.** (*arc.*) persona di umile origine; persona di bassa condizione sociale; (*fam.*) ciabattino **2.** (*sl. universitario arc.*) cittadino, uomo di città.

snobbery ['snobəri], *s.* snobismo; sussiego.

snobbish ['snobiʃ], *ag.* snobistico; affettato.

snobbishly ['snobiʃli], *av.* snobisticamente; affettatamente.

snobbishness ['snobiʃnis], **snobbism** ['snobizəm], *s.* snobismo; sussiego.

snobling ['snobliŋ], *s.* piccolo snob; vanerello.

snood [snud], *s.* **1.** nastro per i capelli (usato dalle ragazze scozzesi) **2.** reticella da tuppè **3.** lenza.

snook[1] [snuk], *s.* (*ittiol.*) luccio di mare.

snook[2], *s.* (*sl.*) maramao: *to cock* (o *to cut* o *to make*) *a —*, fare maramao.

to snoop [snu:p], *v.t.i.* (*amer. fam.*) **1.** interessarsi dei fatti altrui, ficcare il naso **2.** spiare (qlcu.) per coglierlo in flagrante **3.** rubare.

snooze [snu:z], *s.* pisolino, sonnellino, siesta.

to snooze, *v.t.i.* **1.** sonnecchiare, fare un pisoli-

no **2.** *to — time away*, passare il tempo oziando.

snoozer ['snu:zə*], *s.* **1.** dormiglione **2.** fannullone.

snore [sno:*], *s.* il russare.

to snore, *v.t.i.* russare ‖ *he snored away* (o *out*) *the morning*, ha passato tutta la mattina a dormire come un ghiro.

snorer ['sno:rə*], *s.c.* chi russa.

snoring ['sno:riŋ], *s.* il russare.

snorkel ['sno:kəl], *s.* « snorkel » (presa d'aria per sommergibili).

snort [sno:t], *s.* **1.** sbuffo; sbuffata; rumore sbuffante (di locomotiva, motore, ecc.) **2.** (*sl. amer.*) sorsata di liquore.

to snort, *v.t.i.* **1.** sbuffare **2.** esprimere sbuffando (ira, disprezzo, ecc.): *to — out one's opinion*, esprimere la propria opinione sbuffando.

snorter ['sno:tə*], *s.* **1.** chi sbuffa **2.** (*sl.*) forte vento **3.** (*sl.*) cosa strabiliante, eccezionale, violenta: *— of an answer*, risposta mordente.

snot [snot], *s.* (*volg.*) **1.** muco, moccio **2.** individuo spregevole ☆ *— -rag*, fazzoletto.

snotty[1] ['snoti], *ag.* **1.** moccioso **2.** (*sl.*) arrogante; di cattivo umore, sdegnoso ☆ *— -nosed*, moccioso; *fig.* spregevole.

snotty[2], *s.* (*sl.*) aspirante di marina.

snout [snaut], *s.* **1.** muso; grugno; ceffo; grifo **2.** (*spreg.*) naso **3.** (*mec.*) becco; cannello.

snouted ['snautid], **snouty** ['snauti], *ag.* **1.** a forma di grugno; dal muso prominente **2.** a becco.

snow [snou], *s.* **1.** neve; tempesta, bufera di neve; nevicata: *eternal —*, nevi perenni; *a fall of —*, una nevicata **2.** *fig.* bianchezza, candore: *her hands are as white as —*, le sue mani sono bianche come la neve ‖ *the snows of seventy years*, i capelli bianchi **3.** (*sl.*) cocaina; (*amer.*) eroina ☆ *— -bird*, (*ornit.*) fringuello bianco; *— -blindness*, (*patol.*) ambliopia (causata dal riflesso della neve); *— -blink*, riflesso della neve; *— -boot*, soprascarpa per neve; *— -bound*, bloccato dalla neve; seppellito sotto la neve; *— -capped*, nevoso, incappucciato di neve; *— -field*, nevaio; *— -goggles*, occhiali da neve; *— -goose*, oca polare; *— -leopard*, (*zool.*) lince; *— -like*, niveo, come la neve; *— -man*, pupazzo di neve; l'uomo delle nevi; *— -plant*, alga (contenente eritrina); *— -plough*, spazzaneve; *— -report*, bollettino della neve; *— -shoe*, racchetta per la neve; *— -shovel*, pala da neve; *— -slide* (o *— -slip*), valanga; *— -storm*, bufera di neve; *— -white*, niveo.

to snow, *v.t.i.* **1.** *imp.* nevicare: *it is snowing*, nevica ‖ *to be snowed in* (o *up*), essere bloccato dalla neve; *fig.* essere sopraffatto **2.** *fig.* cospargere, spruzzare di neve: *the years had snowed his hair*, gli anni gli avevano imbiancato i capelli.

snowball ['snoubo:l], *s.* palla di neve ☆ *— -tree*, (*bot.*) viburno, pallone di neve.

to snowball, *v.t.i.* lanciare palle di neve a; fare a palle di neve: *to — s.o.*, tirare palle di neve a qlcu.

snowdrift ['snou-drift], *s.* **1.** cumulo di neve **2.** raffica di neve.

snowdrop ['snoudrop], *s.* (*bot.*) bucaneve.

snowfall ['snou-fo:l], *s.* nevicata.

snowflake ['snou-fleik], *s.* **1.** fiocco di neve **2.** (*bot.*) niveola.

snowily ['snouili], *av.* nevosamente.

snowiness ['snouinis], *s.* nevosità.

snowless ['snoulis], *ag.* senza neve.

snowline ['snoulain], *s.* limite delle nevi perenni.

snowy ['snoui], *ag.* **1.** nevoso, di neve, coperto di neve: *the — season*, la stagione delle nevi **2.** niveo: *— hair*, capelli candidi **3.** *fig.* puro, candido.

snub[1] [snʌb], *ag.* camuso, rincagnato ‖ *s.* *—* (*-nose*), naso camuso ☆ *— -nosed*, dal naso rincagnato.

snub[2], *s.* **1.** rimprovero, rabbuffo umiliante; mortificazione; affronto: *to suffer a —*, subire un rimprovero, un affronto **2.** (*mar.*) arresto improvviso.

to snub[2], *pass.p.p.* **snubbed** [snʌbd], *v.t.* **1.** rim-

proverare, umiliare, riprendere; trattare con disprezzo **2.** mozzar la parola a **3.** (*mar.*) arrestare improvvisamente.

snubbing ['snʌbiŋ], *s.* **1.** il rimproverare, il riprendere; l'umiliare **2.** (*mar.*) arresto improvviso ☆ — -*post*,
(*mar.*) bitta.

snubbingly ['snʌbiŋli], *av.* con aria di rimprovero; in
modo umiliante.

snuff[1] [snʌf], *s.* **1.** aspirazione, l'aspirare col naso **2.** tabacco da fiuto: *a pinch of* —, una presa di
tabacco; *to take* —, fiutare il tabacco ‖ *to be up to* —,
(*sl.*) essere accorto ‖ *to give s.o. a* —, dare una lavata
di capo a qlcu. ☆ — -*and-butter*, giallo scuro; — -*box*,
tabacchiera; — -*brown*, marrone scuro; — -*coloured*,
color tabacco; — -*taker*, chi fiuta tabacco, chi ta-
bacca.

to snuff[1], *v.t.i.* **1.** annusare, aspirare col naso **2.** fiutare tabacco.

snuff[2], *s.* moccolaia, lucignolo (di candela); smoccolatura.

to snuff[2], *v.t.i.* **1.** smoccolare (una candela) **2.** *to* —
out, spegnere (una candela) con le dita; (*fam.*) spegnere,
soffocare (una speranza, un progetto); (*sl.*) morire, spegnersi: *his dreams were snuffed out*, i suoi sogni furono
soffocati.

snuffer[1] ['snʌfə*], *s.c.* chi fiuta tabacco, chi ta-
bacca.

snuffer[2], *s.c.* chi smoccola ‖ **snuffers** ['snʌfəz], *s.pl.*
smoccolatoio ☆ *snuffer(s)-stand* (o — -*tray*), piatto
dello smoccolatoio.

snuffing[1] ['snʌfiŋ], *s.* **1.** l'annusare, il fiutare, l'aspirare col naso **2.** abitudine di fiutare tabacco.

snuffing[2], *s.* smoccolatura.

snuffle ['snʌfl], *s.* **1.** lo sbuffare, l'annusare, il respirare rumorosamente col naso **2.** catarro nasale ‖ *to
have the snuffles*, avere il naso chiuso, essere raffreddato **3.** (tono di) voce nasale ‖ *hypocritical* —, modo
di fare ipocrita.

to snuffle, *v.t.i.* **1.** fiutare, annusare: *to* — *at sthg.*,
fiutare, annusare ql.co. **2.** pronunciare con tono nasale:
to — *out a prayer*, dire con tono nasale una preghiera.

snuffler ['snʌflə*], *s.c.* **1.** chi parla col naso **2.** (*fam.*)
ipocrita.

snuffling ['snʌfliŋ], *ag.* **1.** che fiuta, annusa **2.** raffreddato **3.** ipocrita ‖ *s.* **1.** il fiutare; il respirare rumorosamente col naso **2.** il parlare col naso **3.** (*fam.*)
ipocrisia.

snufflingly ['snʌfliŋli], *av.* con suono, voce nasale.

snuffy ['snʌfi], *ag.* **1.** tabaccoso; che ha odor di tabacco **2.** sporco, in disordine.

snug [snʌg], *ag.* **1.** comodo; caldo; tranquillo: *I am
longing to be* — *at home*, non vedo l'ora di essere a
casa tranquillo; *it is very* — *in here*, si sta bene qui;
to lie — *in bed*, stare al calduccio sotto le coperte;
to make oneself —, mettersi comodo, a proprio agio ‖
as — *as a bug in a rug*, (*sl.*) tranquillo, pacifico e
beato **2.** ordinato; adatto, ben fatto (di abito): *she was
wearing a* — *dress*, indossava un abito che le stava a
pennello **3.** non esposto; nascosto: *to lie* —, rimanere
nascosto **4.** discreto, abbastanza buono: *a* — *little
income*, una discreta rendita **5.** (*mar.*) preparato a
ogni evenienza (di nave).

to snug, *pass.p.p.* **snugged** [snʌgd], *v.t.i.* **1.** ripararsi; rannicchiarsi; mettersi al coperto **2.** mettere in
ordine **3.** (*mar.*) preparare (una nave ad affrontare il
cattivo tempo).

snuggery ['snʌgəri], *s.* cameretta, luogo, cantuccio
comodo e tranquillo (specialmente in un bar).

to snuggle ['snʌgl], *v.t.i.* **1.** rannicchiarsi, accomo-
darsi, accovacciarsi, mettersi in posizione rilassante **2.** abbracciare, stringere, coccolare: *the poor mother
snuggled her child close to her heart*, la povera madre
si strinse al seno il bambino.

snugly ['snʌgli], *av.* comodamente; tranquillamente;
a bell'agio.

snugness ['snʌgnis], *s.* comodità; comodo; agio.

so [sou], *av.* così, tanto; in tal modo; nello stesso
modo: — *good a dinner*, un pranzo così buono; *I'm
not* — *bad as you think*, non sono tanto cattivo quanto
credi; *I told him to do* —, gli dissi di fare così; *it is* —
kind of you, è molto gentile da parte tua; *she is going to
England and* — *is he*, ella va in Inghilterra ed egli pure;
she was — *poorly prepared that she failed in her examinations*, era così poco preparata che fu bocciata
agli esami; *they are* — *good*, sono talmente buoni ‖
— *as to...*, così da...: *he speaks* — *as to be understood*,
parla in modo da essere compreso; *would you be* —
kind as to give me that book?, vorresti per gentilezza
darmi quel libro? ‖ — *far*, fino ad ora, fino ad oggi:
far I have not seen him, fino ad ora non l'ho visto; *in* —
far as, per quanto: *in* — *far as it concerns me*, per quanto
mi riguarda ‖ — *long as*, a condizione, a patto che:
I'll give you the money — *long as you give it back to me*,
ti do il denaro a patto che tu me lo restituisca ‖ —
much, tanto; altrettanto: *he has been studying* — *much*,
ha studiato tanto; — *much* — *that*, a tal punto che;
— *many*, altrettanti: — *many men*, — *many minds*,
tante teste, tanti pareri ‖ — *that* (*amer.* —), affinchè;
cosicchè: *he gave me a good dictionary* — *that* (*amer.*
—) *I might translate properly*, mi diede un buon dizionario affinchè traducessi esattamente; —... *that*,
così... da, che: *he spoke* — *low that I could not understand him*, parlava così sottovoce che non riuscivo a
comprenderlo; *I spoke French and* — *it was that we
understood each other*, parlai francese e fu così che ci
capimmo ‖ — *to say* (o — *to speak*), per così dire ‖
and — *on* (o *and* — *forth*), eccetera, e così via ‖ *how*
—?, come mai?; *why* —?, perchè mai? ‖ *if* —, in tal
caso ‖ *or* —, circa: *he was away ten days or* —, si as-
sentò per circa dieci giorni ‖ *I believe* (o *I think* o *I
suppose* o *I fancy*) —, credo di sì; *I fear* —, temo di
sì; *I hope* —, lo spero ‖ *is he really ill?*, — *it seems*,
è davvero ammalato?, così sembra ‖ *is that* —?, davvero? ‖ *that being* —, stando così le cose ‖ *cong.* perciò:
it was a beautiful day, — *we went for a walk*, era una
bella giornata, perciò andammo a passeggio.

soak [souk], *s.* **1.** immersione, bagnatura; inzuppamento, imbevimento: *to be* (o *to lie*) *in* —, essere a
bagno (di biancheria, ecc.); *to put sthg. in* —, mettere
ql.co. a bagno; (*sl. amer.*) impegnare ql.co. **2.** (*sl.*)
bevuta, sbornia **3.** (*sl.*) ubriacone **4.** (*austral.*) terreno
paludoso.

to soak, *v.t.i.* **1.** immergere, immergersi; bagnare,
bagnarsi; imbevere, imbeversi; inzuppare, inzupparsi;
macerare; (*fis.*) saturare, saturarsi: *the cook soaked the
sponge-cake in cherry-brandy*, il cuoco imbevve il pan di
Spagna di cerasella; *the rain soaked me to the skin*,
la pioggia mi ha bagnato fino alle ossa ‖ *to* — *oneself in
the classics*, *fig.* imbeversi di letteratura classica **2.** (*sl.*)
tassare fortemente; estorcere denaro a: *to* — *the rich*,
tassare fortemente i ricchi **3.** (*sl.*) ubriacarsi; bere come
una spugna **4.** *to* — *away*, sparire per infiltrazione (di
liquidi) **5.** *to* — *in*, penetrare (di liquidi); imbeversi;
assorbire **6.** *to* — *out*, estrarre per macerazione; smacchiare mediante immersione **7.** *to* — *through*, penetrare: *I was soaked through*, ero tutto inzuppato **8.** *to*
— *up*, assorbire, bere, impregnarsi di: *the earth soaked
up all the water*, la terra assorbì tutta l'acqua.

soakage ['soukidʒ], *s.* **1.** inzuppatura; macerazione;
saturazione **2.** liquido assorbito; acqua d'infiltrazione **3.** infiltrazione.

soaked [soukt], *ag.* inzuppato, imbevuto, impregnato: — *ground*, terreno fradicio; — *to the skin*,
bagnato fino alle ossa ☆ *oil*- —, impregnato d'olio.

soaker ['soukə*], *s.c.* **1.** chi bagna, immerge **2.** chi
assorbe **3.** ubriacone, ubriacona ‖ *s.* acquazzone, diluvio.

soaking ['soukiŋ], *ag.* **1.** che bagna, inzuppa **2.** bagnato, inzuppato: — *wet*, bagnato fradicio ‖ *s.* **1.** immersione, bagnatura **2.** assorbimento **3.** *pl.* acqua d'in-

filtrazione ☆ — *in*, imbevimento, infiltrazione; — *up*, imbevimento; — *vat*, vasca di macerazione.

so-and-so ['souənsou], *s.* persona, cosa non specificata: *he tells me to do* —, (*fam.*) egli mi dice di fare così e cosà ‖ *Mr. So-and-so*, il Signor Tal dei Tali.

soap [soup], *s.* **1.** sapone: *cake of* —, pezzo di sapone, saponetta; — *house shiny with* — *and water*, casa riluciente di pulizia **2.** (*sl.*) adulazione **3.** (*sl. amer.*) denaro (specialmente usato per corrompere) ☆ — *-ball*, saponetta; — *-bubble*, bolla di sapone; — *-dish* (o — *-tray*), portasapone; — *-flakes*, sapone in scaglie; — *-opera*, (*sl. amer.*) trasmissione radiofonica, televisiva a puntate; — *-stone*, (*min.*) steatite, talco; — *-suds*, saponata; — *-works*, saponificio ‖ *shaving-* —, sapone da barba; *soft* —, sapone liquido; *fig.* adulazione.

to **soap**, *v.t.i.* **1.** insaponare, insaponarsi **2.** (*sl.*) adulare, lodare.

soapbox ['soupbɔks], *s.* **1.** cassa per sapone **2.** (*fam.*) palco improvvisato per un oratore (da strada).

soapboxer ['soup‚bɔksə*], *s.* (*fam.*) oratore improvvisato (da strada).

soapily ['soupili], *av.* **1.** in modo saponoso **2.** (*sl.*) in tono adulatorio.

soapiness ['soupinis], *s.* **1.** saponosità **2.** *fig.* adulazione, untuosità.

soaping ['soupiŋ], *s.* insaponatura ☆ — *-machine*, macchina per insaponare.

soapless ['souplis], *ag.* senza sapone.

soapwort ['soupwɔ:t], *s.* (*bot.*) saponaria.

soapy ['soupi], *ag.* **1.** saponoso; impregnato di sapone **2.** che sa di sapone **3.** (*bot.*) saponaceo **4.** *fig.* adulatore, insinuante, untuoso.

to **soar** [sɔ:*], *v.i.* **1.** librarsi in aria; spiccare il volo; elevarsi (anche *fig.*) **2.** (*aer.*) veleggiare.

soarer ['sɔ:rə*], *s.* (*aer.*) veleggiatore.

soaring ['sɔ:riŋ], *ag.* **1.** che spicca il volo; innalzantesi; librantesi: — *spire*, guglia slanciata **2.** che aumenta incessantemente (di prezzi, ecc.) **3.** ambizioso ‖ *s.* **1.** volo **2.** *fig.* volo, slancio **3.** aumento, rialzo (di prezzi) **4.** elevazione; (*aer.*) volo a vela, volo planato ☆ — *flight*, volo planato (di uccelli); — *society*, società di volo a vela.

soaringly ['sɔ:riŋli], *av.* elevatamente.

sob [sɔb], *s.* singhiozzo: *he choked down a* —, soffocò un singhiozzo ☆ — *-stuff*, (*amer.*) scritto, film, ecc. lagrimoso, sentimentale.

to **sob**, *pass.p.p.* **sobbed** [sɔbd], *v.t.i.* **1.** singhiozzare **2.** *to* — *out*, dire singhiozzando: *the girl sobbed out her sad story*, la fanciulla raccontò tra i singhiozzi la sua triste storia.

sobbing ['sɔbiŋ], *ag.* singhiozzante ‖ *s.* il singhiozzare; singhiozzi.

sobbingly ['sɔbiŋli], *av.* singhiozzando, con voce rotta dai singhiozzi.

sober ['soubə*], *ag.* **1.** sobrio; temperante nel bere: *he is a* — *man*, è un uomo moderato nel bere ‖ *he slept himself* —, smaltì la sbornia dormendo **2.** equilibrato, assennato; calmo, composto; misurato: *a* — *judgement*, un giudizio assennato ‖ *in* — *fact*, in realtà, stando ai fatti **3.** sobrio, discreto (di colore) ☆ — *-looking*, dall'aria grave; — *-minded*, saggio, serio; — *-paced*, a passi misurati; — *-suited*, (*poet.*) vestito sobriamente.

to **sober**, *v.t.i. to* — (*down*) **1.** rendere sobrio; smaltire la sbornia **2.** calmare, calmarsi; far rinsavire.

soberly ['soubəli], *av.* **1.** sobriamente, moderatamente **2.** con calma; equilibratamente, assennatamente.

soberness ['soubənis], **sobriety** [sou'braiəti], *s.* **1.** sobrietà, moderazione, temperanza **2.** calma; assennatezza, equilibrio.

sobriquet ['soubrikei], *s.* soprannome, nomignolo.

soc [sɔk], *s.* (*st. dir.*) giurisdizione.

so-called ['sou'kɔ:ld], *ag.* cosiddetto, così chiamato.

soc(c)age ['sɔkidʒ], *s.* sistema feudale di affitto della terra.

soccer ['sɔkə*], *s.* (*fam. contr.* di *association football*) « football », calcio.

sociability [‚souʃə'biliti], *s.* socievolezza.

sociable ['souʃəbl], *ag.* socievole; comunicativo; amichevole: — *animals*, animali socievoli; — *evening*, serata animata; *he has* — *manners*, ha modi affabili ‖ *s.* **1.** carrozza scoperta (con sedili faccia a faccia) **2.** divano a due posti **3.** (*amer.*) riunione sociale.

sociableness ['souʃəblnis], *s.* socievolezza.

sociably ['souʃəbli], *av.* socievolmente; amichevolmente.

social ['souʃəl], *ag.* **1.** sociale, della società: — *problems*, problemi di ordine sociale; — *reform*, riforma sociale **2.** socievole, che vive in gruppi: *man is an essentially* — *animal*, l'uomo è essenzialmente un animale socievole **3.** sociale, mondano ‖ *to reach the top of the* — *ladder*, raggiungere la cima della scala sociale **4.** (*st. romana, greca*) sociale ‖ *the Social Wars*, le guerre sociali **5.** riunione sociale ☆ — *club*, circolo sociale; — *evening*, serata mondana; *the* — *evil*, prostituzione; *the* — *good*, il bene comune; — *science*, sociologia; *the* — *system*, la società.

socialism ['souʃəlizəm], *s.* socialismo.

socialist ['souʃəlist], *ag.s.c.* socialista.

socialistic [‚souʃə'listik], *ag.* socialistico, socialista.

socialistically [‚souʃə'listikəli], *av.* conformemente al socialismo.

socialite ['souʃəlait], *s.c.* (*fam. amer.*) persona con posizione sociale preminente.

sociality [‚souʃi'æliti], *s.* **1.** sociabilità; socievolezza **2.** *pl.* relazioni sociali.

socialization [‚souʃəlai'zeiʃən], *s.* socializzazione.

to **socialize** ['souʃəlaiz], *v.t.* socializzare.

socially ['souʃəli], *av.* socialmente.

society [sə'saiəti], *s.* **1.** società, compagnia: *he avoids the* — *of his schoolfellows*, evita la compagnia dei suoi compagni di scuola; *to be fond of* —, amare la compagnia **2.** società, bel mondo: *he is embarrassed in* —, non si sente a suo agio in società; *they live on the fringe of* —, vivono ai margini della società **3.** società, compagnia, associazione, confraternita: *he was a member of several charitable societies*, dava la sua opera a diverse società di beneficenza ‖ *Society of Friends*, associazione dei quacqueri; *Society of Jesus*, Compagnia di Gesù ‖ *the Royal Society*, accademia fondata nel 1668 in Inghilterra per l'incremento degli studi scientifici e delle arti ☆ — *gossip*, — *news*, pettegolezzi, notizie mondane; — *people*, gente di mondo; — *verse*, versi da salotto ‖ *affluent* —, (*neol.*) società ad alto tenore di vita; *fashionable* —, il bel mondo; *high* —, alta società.

Socinian [sou'siniən], *ag.s.* (*st. relig.*) sociniano.

Socinianism [sou'siniənizəm], *s.* (*st. relig.*) socinianismo.

Socinus [sou'sainəs], *no.pr.m.* (*st. relig.*) Socino.

sociological [‚sousjə'lɔdʒikəl], *ag.* sociologico.

sociologically [‚sousjə'lɔdʒikəli], *av.* sociologicamente.

sociologist [‚sousi'ɔlədʒist], *s.* sociologo.

sociology [‚sousi'ɔlədʒi], *s.* sociologia.

sock[1] [sɔk], *s.* **1.** calza corta, calzino ‖ *you'll have to pull up your socks to succeed in your exams*, (*fam.*) dovrai darti da fare se vuoi riuscire agli esami **2.** soletta **3.** socco; *fig.* commedia ‖ — *and buskin*, socco e coturno, commedia e tragedia ☆ — *-suspender*, giarrettiera.

sock[2], *s.* (*sl.*) colpo, pugno (anche *fig.*): *to give s.o. socks*, prendere a pugni qlcu.: *he tried to convince me but I gave him socks!*, cercava di convincermi, ma gli ho dato scacco matto!.

to **sock**[2], *v.t.* (*sl.*) **1.** colpire violentemente; percuotere: *to* — (*into*) *s.o.*, picchiare qlcu., sonarle a qlcu. **2.** scagliare, lanciare: *to* — *a stone at s.o.*, scagliare un sasso contro qlcu.

sock², av. (sl.) con un colpo, con un pugno: *to hit s.o. — on the nose*, colpire qlcu. con un pugno sul naso.

sock³, s. (sl. *studentesco*) pasticcini, dolciumi.

to **sock³**, v.t.i. (sl. *studentesco*) dare dolci a, mangiare molti dolci.

sockdolager, sockdologer [ɐɔk'dɔlədʒə*], s. (sl. amer.) 1. colpo di grazia 2. argomento decisivo 3. cosa enorme, eccezionale.

socker ['sɔkə*], s. (fam. contr. di *association football*) « football », calcio.

socket ['sɔkit], s. 1. cavità 2. (elett.) portalampada; bocciuolo (di candeliere); presa di corrente: *there is no bulb in the — of this lamp*, manca la lampadina in questo portalampada 3. (anat.) orbita; cavità ☆ — -joint, (anat.) enartrosi; (tec.) manicotto, giunto ad incastri; — wrench, chiave a tubo ‖ bayonet —, (elett.) portalampada con attacco a baionetta; eye —, orbita (dell'occhio); flush —, (elett.) presa di corrente incassata; tooth —, alveolo dentario.

to **socket**, v.t. 1. porre in una cavità; praticare un incavo in 2. (golf) colpire (la palla) con l'estremità della mazza.

sockeye ['sɔkai], s. (ittiol.) salmone dal dorso azzurro.

sockless ['sɔklis], ag. senza calze.

socle ['sɔkl], s. (arch.) zoccolo, piedistallo.

Socotra [sə'koutrə], no.pr. (geog.) Socotra.

Socrates ['sɔkrəti:z], no.pr.m. (st. fil.) Socrate.

Socratic [sə'krætik], ag.s. socratico.

Socratical [sə'krætikəl], ag. socratico.

socratically [sə'krætikəli], av. socraticamente.

sod¹ [sɔd], s. piota; zolla erbosa; tappeto erboso ‖ under the —, (fam.) sepolto: *to put s.o. under the —*, mandare qlcu. all'altro mondo.

to **sod¹**, pass.p.p. **sodded** ['sɔdid], v.t. coprire di zolle.

sod², s. (volg. abbr. di *sodomite*) sodomita.

soda ['soudə], s. 1. (chim.) soda, carbonato di sodio 2. (acqua di) soda ☆ — biscuits, (amer.) gallette sottili; — cake, torta lievitata con bicarbonato di sodio; — -fountain, sifone (per acqua di seltz); (amer.) mescita di bibite; — -water, acqua di seltz: — -water -counter, mescita di bibite al seltz ‖ baking — (o cooking —), bicarbonato di sodio; caustic —, (chim.) soda caustica; washing —, (ind. chim.) soda per lavare.

sodality [sou'dæliti], s. congregazione, confraternita; sodalizio.

sodden ['sɔdn], ag. 1. inzuppato d'acqua; fradicio (di terreno) 2. mal cotto; molle; pesante (di cibo): *the bread is — to-day*, oggi il pane è mal cotto 3. fig. istupidito (per il troppo bere): *he is — with drink*, è abbrutito dall'alcool.

to **sodden**, v.t.i. bagnare, bagnarsi; inzuppare, inzupparsi (d'acqua, ecc.).

soddenness ['sɔdnnis], s. 1. umidità; l'essere inzuppato, impregnato 2. fig. stupidità, ottusità (specialmente causata da ubriachezza).

soddy ['sɔdi], ag. erboso, coperto di zolle ‖ s. (amer.) capanna di terriccio e sterpi.

sodic ['soudik], ag. (chim.) sodico.

sodium ['soudjəm], s. (chim.) sodio ☆ — carbonate, carbonato di sodio; — chloride, cloruro di sodio; salgemma.

Sodom ['sɔdəm], no.pr. (st. geog.) Sodoma.

sodomite ['sɔdəmait], s. sodomita.

sodomitical [,sɔdə'mitikəl], ag. sodomitico.

sodomy ['sɔdəmi], s. sodomia.

sofa ['soufə], s. divano, sofà ☆ — bed, divano-letto.

soffit ['sɔfit], s. (arch.) intradosso.

sofi ['soufi], s. (relig. musulmana) chi pratica il sufismo.

Sofia ['soufjə], no.pr. (geog.) Sofia.

sofism ['soufizəm], s. (relig. musulmana) sufismo.

soft [sɔft], ag. 1. molle; tenero; malleabile: — pencil, matita morbida; as — as butter, tenero come il burro 2. liscio; morbido; soffice: — hair, capelli soffici; — skin, pelle liscia; — wool, lana morbida 3. dolce; mite; quieto, tranquillo: — breeze, dolce brezza; —

claret, vino dolce; — slumbers, sonno tranquillo; — winter, inverno mite 4. delicato; amabile; gentile: — answer, risposta gentile; — manners, modi gentili 5. tenue, attenuato (di colore, suono, ecc.): — light, luce tenue; — music, musica in sordina; — rain, pioggia fine, leggera; — voice, voce tenue, sommessa; g is — in gin, (fonet.) la g è dolce in gin 6. debole; effeminato; rammollito: — muscles, muscoli deboli 7. semplice, sciocco 8. (sl.) facile, agevole: he has a — job, ha un lavoro facile 9. (chim.) dolce, privo di sali (di acqua) ‖ s.c. persona debole, sciocca.

soft, av. dolcemente, delicatamente; tranquillamente.

soft, inter. (arc.) piano!, adagio!.

soft, (nei composti): — -boiled, « à la coque » (di uovo); — coal, carbone bituminoso; — -eyed, dagli occhi dolci; — -footed, dal passo felpato; — -hearted, dal cuore tenero; sensibile; — -palate, (anat.) palato molle; — -pedal, sordina (di pianoforte); — -sawder, (fam.) lusinga; adulazione; — -soap, sapone molle; fig. adulazione; — soldered, (mec.) saldato a dolce; — steel, (metal.) acciaio dolce.

to **soften** ['sɔfn], v.t.i. 1. ammollire, ammorbidire, ammorbidirsi 2. calmare, calmarsi; raddolcire, raddolcirsi; intenerire, intenerirsi; attenuare: the weather was softening, la stagione migliorava; to — at the sight of sthg., commuoversi alla vista di ql.co.; to — a contrast, attenuare un contrasto; to — s.o.'s pain, calmare il dolore di qlcu.

softener ['sɔfnə*], s. 1. emolliente 2. pennello morbido 3. (chim.) depuratore ☆ water- —, (chim.) depuratore, addolcitore d'acqua.

softening ['sɔfniŋ], ag. che rende molle, dolce; emolliente ‖ s. 1. mollificazione, ammorbidimento; rammollimento ‖ — of the brain, (patol.) rammollimento cerebrale 2. intenerimento, addolcimento 3. attenuazione.

softhead ['sɔfthed], s.c. persona stupida, sciocca.

softish ['sɔftiʃ], ag. 1. piuttosto molle, tenero 2. (sl.) piuttosto facile: — job, lavoro piuttosto facile.

softly ['sɔftli], av. 1. teneramente; dolcemente, delicatamente 2. sommessamente 3. pian piano; adagio.

softness ['sɔftnis], s. 1. morbidezza, delicatezza 2. dolcezza, mitezza; — of manner, affabilità 3. stupidità 4. debolezza, effeminatezza.

softwood ['sɔftwud], s. legno dolce.

softy ['sɔfti], s.c. (sl.) persona debole, sciocca.

sogginess ['sɔginis], s. umidità; pesantezza (dell'atmosfera).

soggy ['sɔgi], ag. 1. umido; bagnato; pesante, saturo d'umidità (di atmosfera) 2. mal cotto (di pane).

Soho¹ [sou'hou], no.pr. Soho (quartiere di Londra).

soho², inter. ohi là!, suvvia!, ecco!, buono! (per calmare i cavalli, ecc.).

soil¹ [sɔil], s. suolo, terra, terreno: good, poor, rich —, terreno buono, povero, ricco ☆ — -bound, attaccato, legato al suolo, alla terra ‖ native —, terra, paese natio.

soil², s. 1. macchia (anche fig.) 2. letame, sterco 3. luogo paludoso ☆ — -pipe, tubo di scarico (di gabinetto, ecc.).

to **soil²**, v.t.i. 1. macchiare, macchiarsi; sporcare, sporcarsi (anche fig.): give me a new collar, I have soiled mine, dammi un colletto pulito, il mio è sudicio; I would never — my hands with his money, non vorrei mai e poi mai sporcarmi le mani col suo denaro; it soils easily, si sporca facilmente 2. concimare.

to **soil³**, v.t. nutrire (il bestiame) con foraggio fresco.

soiled [sɔild], ag. sporco, macchiato: — linen, biancheria sporca.

soilless ['sɔillis], ag. senza macchia.

soirée ['swɑːrei], s. « soirée », serata, veglia mondana.

sojourn ['sɔdʒə:n], s. soggiorno.

to **sojourn**, v.i. soggiornare.

sojourner ['sɔdʒə:nə*], s.c. ospite di passaggio.

sojourning ['sɔdʒə:niŋ], s. soggiorno; dimora temporanea.

soke [souk], *s.* (*dir.*) giurisdizione.

sol[1] [sɔl], *s.* (*mus.*) sol.

Sol[2], *s.* (*scherz.*) sole.

sol, *abbr.* di **solution**.

solace ['sɔləs], *s.* sollievo, conforto, consolazione.

to solace, *v.t.* consolare; confortare; alleviare.

solacement ['sɔləsmənt], *V.* **solace**.

solan ['soulən], *s.* — (-*goose*), (*ornit.*) sula.

solano [sou'lɑ:nou], *s.* solano (vento della Spagna).

solanum [sou'leinəm], *s.* (*bot.*) solano.

solar ['soulə*], *ag.* solare; di, del sole ☆ — *myth*, mito del Sole; — *plexus*, (*anat.*) plesso solare; — *system*, sistema solare; — *year*, anno solare.

solarism ['soulərizəm], *s.* (*st. relig.*) elioteismo.

solarist ['soulərist], *s.c.* (*st. relig.*) elioteista.

solarium [sou'lɛəriəm], *s.* solario, stabilimento elioterapico.

solarization [,soulərai'zeiʃən], *s.* (*foto.*) sovraesposizione.

to solarize ['souləraiz], *v.t.i.* (*foto.*) rovinare, rovinarsi per sovraesposizione.

solatium [sou'leiʃjəm], *pl.* **solatia** [sou'leiʃjə], *s.* **1.** compenso, risarcimento **2.** consolazione, conforto.

sold [sould], *pass.p.p.* di to **sell**.

soldan ['sɔldən], *s.* soldano, sultano.

soldanella [,sɔldə'nelə], *s.* (*bot.*) soldanella.

solder ['sɔldə*], *s.* **1.** (*mec.*) lega per saldatura **2.** *fig.* unione; congiungimento ☆ *hard* —, (*mec.*) lega per saldatura a forte; *soft* —, (*mec.*) lega per saldatura a dolce.

to solder, *v.t.* **1.** (*mec.*) saldare **2.** *fig.* unire, congiungere.

soldering ['sɔldəriŋ], *s.* (*mec.*) saldatura ☆ — -*iron*, saldatore di rame; saldatoio.

soldier ['souldʒə*], *s.* **1.** soldato, militare: *to go for a* —, andare soldato; *to play at soldiers*, giocare alla guerra ‖ — *of fortune*, soldato di fortuna ‖ *every inch a* —, soldato da capo a piedi ‖ *the Unknown Soldier*, il Milite Ignoto **2.** stratega: *he is not a great* —, non è un grande stratega **3.** (*entom.*) formica, termite soldato **4.** (*sl. mar.*) scansafatiche **5.** (*sl.*) aringa rossa ☆ — -*crab*, (*zool.*) bernardo eremita ‖ *common* —, soldato semplice; *fellow*- —, commilitone; *foot*- —, soldato di fanteria; *horse*- —, soldato di cavalleria; *old* —, veterano; *fig.* uomo di molte risorse; (*fam.*) bottiglia vuota; *tin* — (o *toy* —), soldatino di piombo.

to soldier, *v.i.* **1.** fare il soldato **2.** (*sl. mar.*) scansare le fatiche.

soldierlike ['souldʒəlaik], **soldierly** ['souldʒəli], *ag.* marziale, militare; militaresco: — *bearing*, portamento marziale; *he has a* — *character*, ha una tempra militaresca.

soldiership ['souldʒəʃip], *s.* **1.** l'essere soldato **2.** qualità militari; abilità militare.

soldiery ['souldʒəri], *s.coll.* soldati, truppa; soldatesca.

sole[1] ['soul], *ag.* **1.** solo; unico; esclusivo: *he is the* — *heir*, è l'unico erede **2.** (*arc.*) solo, non accompagnato ☆ — *agent*, agente esclusivo ‖ *femme* —, (*dir.*) nubile.

sole[2], *s.* **1.** pianta (del piede) **2.** suola: *shoe with a double* —, scarpa con doppia suola **3.** fondo, base: *the* — *of a golf-club*, la base di una mazza da golf **4.** (*mar.*) suola ☆ — *leather*, cuoio per risolatura ‖ *inner* —, soletta (di scarpe, ecc.).

to sole[2], *v.t.* risolare: *to* — *and heel*, rifar suola e tacchi.

sole[3], *s.* (*ittiol.*) sogliola.

solecism ['sɔlisizəm], *s.* **1.** (*gram.*) solecismo **2.** comportamento scorretto; sconvenienza ‖ *he would have been a* — *in this company*, in questa compagnia egli sarebbe stato fuori posto.

to solecize ['sɔlisaiz], *v.i.* **1.** (*gram.*) solecizzare **2.** comportarsi in modo scorretto.

soled [sould], *ag.* dalla suola ☆ *thick*- —, con suole grosse; *thin*- —, con suole sottili.

solely ['soulli], *av.* solamente, unicamente; interamente, esclusivamente.

solemn ['sɔləm], *ag.* **1.** solenne; grave: — *question*, domanda grave, che fa riflettere; — *silence*, silenzio solenne **2.** grave, serio, solenne (di persona): *to put on a* — *face*, mettersi in sussiego.

solemness ['sɔləmnis], **solemnity** [sə'lemniti], *s.* **1.** solennità, gravità **2.** rito solenne; festa solenne.

solemnization ['sɔləmnai'zeiʃən], *s.* celebrazione.

to solemnize ['sɔləmnaiz], *v.t.* **1.** solennizzare, celebrare con solennità **2.** rendere solenne.

solemnly ['sɔləmli], *av.* **1.** solennemente **2.** gravemente.

solen ['soulən], *s.* (*zool.*) cannello, cannolicchio.

solenoid ['soulinɔid], *s.* (*elett.*) solenoide ☆ — *operated control*, comando azionato a solenoide.

sol-fa [sɔl'fɑ:], *s.* (*mus.*) solfeggio.

to sol-fa, *v.t.i.* (*mus.*) solfeggiare.

solfeggio [sɔl'fedʒiou], *s.* (*mus.*) solfeggio.

to solicit [sə'lisit], *v.t.i.* **1.** sollecitare, fare una sollecitazione; richiedere (con insistenza): *to* — *favours of s.o.*, sollecitare favori da qlcu.; *to* — *s.o. for sthg.* (o *sthg. from s.o.*), sollecitare ql.co. da qlcu. **2.** importunare, adescare.

solicitant [sə'lisitənt], *s.c.* postulante, richiedente.

solicitation [sə,lisi'teiʃən], *s.* **1.** sollecitazione, richiesta, insistenza: *to do sthg. at s.o.'s* —, fare ql.co. per l'insistenza di qlcu. **2.** invito, adescamento.

solicitor [sə'lisitə*], *s.* **1.** sollecitatore **2.** (*dir.*) avvocato (con facoltà di discutere cause presso le corti di grado inferiore) ‖ *Solicitor General*, avvocato erariale **3.** (*amer.*) piazzista; galoppino elettorale.

solicitorship [sə'lisitəʃip], *s.* carica, mansioni di avvocato (avente facoltà di discutere cause presso le corti di grado inferiore).

solicitous [sə'lisitəs], *ag.* **1.** sollecito, premuroso: *to be* — *for s.o.'s comfort*, avere a cuore il benessere di qlcu. **2.** desideroso, ansioso: — *of sthg.*, desideroso di ql.co.; — *to please*, ansioso di piacere **3.** preoccupato: *to be* — *about sthg.*, essere preoccupato per ql.co.

solicitously [sə'lisitəsli], *av.* **1.** sollecitamente; premurosamente **2.** ansiosamente **3.** con preoccupazione.

solicitousness [sə'lisitəsnis], **solicitude** [sə'lisitju:d], *s.* **1.** sollecitudine; premura **2.** ansia **3.** preoccupazione.

solid ['sɔlid], *ag.* **1.** solido; consistente, compatto, omogeneo: — *colour*, tinta solida; *water can become* —, l'acqua può solidificarsi **2.** solido; reale; fondato; serio, posato: — *argument*, argomento fondato; *a* — *man*, un uomo solido, posato, serio **3.** solidale; unanime: *a* — *vote*, un voto unanime; *to go* (o *to be*) — *for*, essere solidale con, parteggiare per **4.** (*comm.*) solvibile **5.** (*mat.*) intero **6.** pieno, massiccio: — *wall*, muro pieno ‖ *s.* corpo solido, tutto d'un pezzo; (*geom.*) solido ☆ — *number*, (*mat.*) numero intero.

solidarity [,sɔli'dæriti], *s.* solidarietà.

solidary ['sɔlidəri], *ag.* solidale.

solidifiable [sə'lidifaiəbl], *ag.* solidificabile.

solidification [sə,lidifi'keiʃən], *s.* solidificazione; condensazione.

to solidify [sə'lidifai], *v.t.i.* solidificare, solidificarsi; congelare, congelarsi; coagulare, coagularsi (di sangue).

solidity [sə'liditi], *s.* **1.** solidità **2.** (*comm.*) solvenza.

solidly ['sɔlidli], *av.* **1.** solidamente, saldamente **2.** all'unanimità.

solidness ['sɔlidnis], *s.* **1.** solidità **2.** compattezza, unanimità.

solidus ['sɔlidəs], *pl.* **solidi** ['sɔlidai], *s.* **1.** «solidus» (antica moneta aurea romana) **2.** (*tip.*) barra trasversale che separa gli scellini dai pence: *2/6*, due scellini e mezzo.

soliloquist [sə'liləkwist], *s.c.* chi fa soliloqui, chi parla con se stesso.

to soliloquize [sə'liləkwaiz], *v.i.* fare un soliloquio, recitare monologhi; parlare con se stesso.

soliloquy [sə'liləkwi], *s.* soliloquio, monologo.

soling ['souliŋ], *s.* solatura, risolatura.

soliped ['sɔliped], **solipede** [sɔlipi:d], *ag.s.* (*zool.*) solipede.

solitaire [ˌsɔli'tɛɚ*], s. 1. solitario (pietra preziosa) 2. solitario (giuoco di carte) 3. (rar.) solitario, anacoreta, eremita.

solitarily ['sɔlitərili], av. da solo, tutto solo, solitariamente.

solitariness ['sɔlitərinis], s. solitudine, isolamento.

solitary ['sɔlitəri], ag. 1. solo, unico ‖ not a — one, nemmeno uno 2. solitario, solingo: a — walk, una passeggiata solitaria 3. isolato, romito, deserto, non frequentato (di luogo): a — house, una casa isolata ‖ s. solitario; anacoreta, eremita.

solitude ['sɔlitju:d], s. 1. solitudine, isolamento: to live in —, vivere in solitudine 2. luogo solitario, deserto, isolato.

to **solmizate** ['sɔlmizeit], v.i. (mus.) solfeggiare.

solmization [ˌsɔlmi'zeiʃən], s. (mus.) solfeggio.

solo ['soulou], ag. solo, non accompagnato, suonato come assolo ‖ s. (pl. **solos** ['soulouz]) 1. (mus.) a solo: to play —, suonare un a solo, un assolo 2. giuoco di carte: to go —, giocare a «solo» 3. (aer.) volo solitario.

solo, av. da solo.

soloist ['soulouist], s.c. (mus.) solista.

Solomon ['sɔləmən], no.pr.m. (Bibbia) Salomone ‖ s. persona saggia ☆ —'s seal, (bot.) ginocchietto, sigillo di Salomone.

Solomonian [ˌsɔlə'mouniən], **Solomonic** [ˌsɔlə'mɔnik], ag. salomonico.

Solomon Islands ['sɔləmən'ailəndz], no.pr. pl. (geog.) Isole Salomone.

Solon ['soulən], no.pr.m. (st.) Solone ‖ s. saggio legislatore.

so-long ['sou'lɔŋ], inter. (fam.) ciao, addio, arrivederci, a presto.

solstice ['sɔlstis], s. (astr.) solstizio ☆ summer, winter —, solstizio d'estate, d'inverno.

solstitial [sɔl'stiʃəl], ag. (astr.) solstiziale, solstiziario ☆ — points, punti solstiziali.

solubility [ˌsɔlju'biliti], s. 1. (chim.) solubilità 2. risolubilità (di un problema, ecc.).

soluble ['sɔljubl], ag. 1. (chim.) solubile: — in alcohol, solubile in alcool; — when heated, solubile al caldo; to make —, rendere solubile 2. scomponibile 3. solubile, risolvibile (di problema, ecc.) ☆ — glass, (chim.) vetro solubile, silicato di sodio.

solubleness ['sɔljublnis], s. solubilità.

solus ['souləs], ag. (teat.) solo, da solo (specialmente nelle didascalie sceniche): enter King —, entra il Re solo.

solute [sə'lju:t], ag. (chim.) soluto ‖ s. (chim.) sostanza sciolta.

solution [sə'lu:ʃən], s. 1. (chim.) soluzione 2. processo di dissolvimento; interruzione 3. risoluzione; spiegazione 4. (med.) risoluzione, crisi risolutiva: — of a disease, crisi risolutiva di una malattia ‖ — of continuity, soluzione di continuità ☆ chemical —, soluzione chimica; inapplicable —, (mat.) soluzione impossibile; rubber —, soluzione di gomma, mastice; standard —, (chim.) soluzione titolata.

to **solution**, v.t. 1. risolvere 2. (ind. gomma) fare aderire con soluzione di gomma.

solutionist [sə'lu:ʃənist], s. risolutore d'enigmistica.

solutive [sə'lju:tiv], ag. (med.) solutivo, lassativo.

solvability [ˌsɔlvə'biliti], s. 1. (comm.) solvibilità 2. (chim.) risolubilità 3. risolvibilità (di problema).

solvable ['sɔlvəbl], ag. 1. (comm.) solvibile 2. (chim.) solubile 3. risolvibile (di problema).

solvate ['sɔlveit], s. (chim. fis.) solvato.

solvation [sɔl'veiʃən], s. (chim.) solvatazione.

to **solve** [sɔlv], v.t. 1. risolvere; chiarire; spiegare: to — an equation, risolvere un'equazione; to — many doubts, chiarire molti dubbi; to — a problem, risolvere un problema 2. (arc.) saldare, liquidare (un debito) 3. (arc.) sciogliere.

solvency ['sɔlvənsi], s. 1. (comm.) solvibilità 2. (chim.) capacità solvente.

solvent ['sɔlvənt], ag. 1. (comm.) solvibile 2. (chim.)

solvente, dissolvente ‖ s. (chim.) solvente, dissolvente.

solver ['sɔlvə*], s.c. chi risolve, risolutore, risolutrice.

solving ['sɔlviŋ], s. soluzione (di problemi, ecc.).

Somali [sou'mɑ:li], pl. **Somalis** [sou'mɑ:liz], **Somali**, s. somalo (abitante, lingua).

Somaliland [sou'mɑ:llænd], no.pr. (geog.) Somalia.

somatic(al) [sou'mætik(əl)], ag. somatico: — characteristics, caratteristiche somatiche.

somatologic(al) [ˌsoumətə'lɔdʒik(əl)], ag. somatologico.

somatology [ˌsoumə'tɔlədʒi], s. somatologia.

sombre ['sɔmbə*], ag. fosco, scuro; fig. tetro, triste: a — sky, un cielo scuro; a man of — character, un uomo di carattere tetro, triste.

sombrely ['sɔmbəli], av. oscuramente, tenebrosamente; fig. tetramente, tristemente.

sombreness ['sɔmbənis], s. oscurità, tenebra; fig. tetraggine, tristezza.

sombrero [sɔm'brɛərou], pl. **sombreros** [sɔm'brɛərouz], s. sombrero.

sombrous ['sɔmbrəs], ag. (poet.) cupo, fosco, oscuro, tetro, tenebroso.

some [sʌm (forma forte), səm (forma debole)], ag. 1. qualche, alcuni, certi: — miles away, ad alcune miglia di distanza; — days she is better, — days she is worse, alcuni giorni sta meglio, alcuni peggio 2. qualche, un certo, qualsiasi: at — distance, a una certa distanza; — friend or other will take me there, o l'uno o l'altro amico mi accompagnerà là; come and see me — day, vieni a trovarmi qualche giorno, un giorno o l'altro; he will arrive — day, arriverà uno di questi giorni; I read it in — paper, l'ho letto in un giornale; she has been waiting (for) — time, attende già da un po'; they will come — time, verranno una volta o l'altra ‖ — way or (an)other, in un modo o nell'altro 3. (partitivo) del, della, dei, degli, delle; un po' di: I ate — fruit, mangiai della frutta; they asked me for — water, mi chiesero dell'acqua 4. (sl. amer. rafforzativo): this is — battle!, questa è una battaglia! ‖ pron. 1. alcuni, alcune: — of his friends saw him, alcuni dei suoi amici lo videro; — of them were wrong, alcuni di essi erano in errore ‖ — ... — ..., alcuni ... altri ...; gli uni ... gli altri ...; chi ... chi ...: — agree with him and — don't, gli uni sono del suo avviso, gli altri no; — stayed there and — went away, alcuni rimasero là, altri se ne andarono 2. un po', una parte, una porzione; ne: give me — of that paper, dammi un po' di quella carta; I have —, ne ho (alcuni); I have — more, ne ho ancora; I shall be away all May and — of June, sarò assente tutto maggio e una parte di giugno; take —!, prendine! ‖ av. 1. circa: he waited for him — quarter of an hour, lo aspettò per circa un quarto d'ora 2. (sl. amer. rafforzativo) piuttosto, abbastanza: he seemed annoyed —, egli sembrava piuttosto seccato.

somebody ['sʌmbədi], pron. indef. qualcuno: — else, qualcun altro; — came to see you, qualcuno venne a trovarti ‖ s. (pl. **somebodies** ['sʌmbədi:z]) qualcuno, una persona famosa: nobodies posing as somebodies, delle nullità che posano da persone famose.

somehow ['sʌmhau], av. in qualche modo, in un modo o nell'altro; in certo qual modo: — or other I have never been able to see him, per una ragione o per l'altra non ho mai potuto vederlo; he — left the company, in certo qual modo egli lasciò la compagnia; this must be done —, in un modo o nell'altro questo deve essere fatto.

someone ['sʌmwʌn], pron.indef. qualcuno: — else, qualcun altro; — will come today, qualcuno verrà oggi; you should follow —'s example, dovresti seguire l'esempio di qualcuno.

somersault ['sʌməsɔ:lt], **somerset**[1] ['sʌməsit], s. 1. salto mortale; capitombolo; capriola: double —, doppio salto mortale; to turn a —, fare un salto mortale, fare una capriola 2. (aer.) capottamento; (aut.) ribaltamento.

to **somersault**, to **somerset**[1], *v.i.* **1.** far salti mortali, capitomboli, capriole **2.** (*aer.*) capottare; (*aut.*) ribaltare.

somerset[2] ['sʌməsit], *s.* sella speciale per mutilati di una gamba.

something ['sʌmθiŋ], *pron.indef.* **qualche cosa**: — *or other*, una cosa o l'altra; *I must get — to eat*, devo prendere qualche cosa da mangiare; *she lost —*, perse qualche cosa; *there is — queer in him*, c'è qualcosa di strano in lui; *we have — else to do*, abbiamo altro da fare ‖ *he has seen — of the world*, egli ha visto un po' di mondo ‖ *he is — of a worker*, è in un certo senso un lavoratore ‖ *he was made a manager or —*, fu nominato direttore o qualcosa di simile ‖ *there is — in what he says*, c'è qualcosa di vero in quel che dice ‖ *there was — of an improvement*, ci fu un certo miglioramento ‖ *av.* **1.** **un poco**: *I found him — impatient*, lo trovai un po' impaziente **2.** **circa, pressappoco**: *he left — like a million*, lasciò circa un milione; *it must be — like six o'clock*, devono essere circa le sei **3.** (*intensivo*): *that's — like!*, è magnifico!; *this is — like a book!*, questo è veramente un buon libro!.

sometime ['sʌmtaim], *ag.* attributivo di un tempo, precedente: *my — teacher*, il mio antico insegnante.

sometime, *av.* **1.** un tempo, già, altre volte: *he was — mayor of his town*, fu nel passato sindaco della sua città **2.** presto o tardi, un giorno o l'altro, una qualche volta: *— soon*, uno di questi giorni; *I am sure to see him —*, sono certo di vederlo un giorno o l'altro.

sometimes ['sʌmtaimz], *av.* qualche volta, alcune volte, di quando in quando, talvolta: *I have met him —*, l'ho incontrato qualche volta, di quando in quando; *it is — good, — bad*, è ora buono, ora cattivo.

someway ['sʌmwei], *av.* in un modo o nell'altro, in qualche modo.

somewhat ['sʌmwɔt], *pron.indef.* **1.** un poco: *he is — of a miser*, è piuttosto avaro **2.** (*arc.*) qualche cosa: *he found — he didn't expect*, trovò qualcosa che non s'aspettava ‖ *av.* alquanto, un po', piuttosto: *I did it — hastily*, lo feci alquanto in fretta; *the translation was — difficult*, la traduzione era piuttosto difficile; *you are — rash in making such promises*, sei un po' precipitoso nel fare tali promesse.

somewhere ['sʌmwεə*], *av.* in qualche luogo: *— else*, in qualche altro luogo, altrove; *he lives — in the neighbourhood*, abita, vive in qualche posto nelle vicinanze; *I shall meet him —*, lo incontrerò in qualche posto.

somite ['soumait], *s.* metamero (di animali).

somnambulant [som'næmbjulənt], *ag.s.* (*rar.*) sonnambulo.

to **somnambulate** [som'næmbjuleit], *v.i.* (*rar.*) essere sonnambulo.

somnambulism [som'næmbjulizəm], *s.* sonnambulismo ‖ *artificial —*, ipnotismo.

somnambulist [som'næmbjulist], *s.c.* sonnambulo, sonnambula.

somnambulistic [som,næmbju'listik], *ag.* di sonnambulo.

somniferous [som'nifərəs], **somnific** [som'nifik], *ag.* soporifero, sonnifero.

somniloquent [som'niləkwənt], *ag.* di, da sonniloquo.

somniloquist [som'niləkwist], *s.* sonniloquo.

somniloquous [som'niləkwəs], *ag.* di, da sonniloquo.

somniloquy [som'niləkwi], *s.* sonniloquio.

somnipathy [som'nipəθi], *s.* sonno ipnotico.

somnolence ['somnələns], **somnolency** ['somnələnsi], *s.* sonnolenza, sopore.

somnolent ['somnələnt], *ag.* sonnolento, sonnacchioso; assopito.

somnolently ['somnələntli], *av.* in modo sonnolento, sonnacchiosamente.

somnolism ['somnəlizəm], *s.* sonno ipnotico.

son [sʌn], *s.* **1.** figlio, figliolo: *he is his father's —*, è degno di suo padre, è come suo padre ‖ *— of a gun*, (*gener. scherz.*) briccone ‖ *the Son (of Man, of God)*, il Figlio (dell'Uomo, di Dio) ‖ *the Son of Heaven*, il Figlio del Cielo, l'Imperatore della Cina ‖ *— of Mars*, soldato, guerriero ‖ *the sons of Abraham*, i discendenti di Abramo ‖ *the sons of men*, l'umanità **2.** indigeno, nativo: *England's sons*, gli inglesi ☆ *—-in-law*, genero.

sonancy ['sounənsi], *s.* risonanza, sonorità.

sonant ['sounənt], *ag.* risonante, sonoro ‖ *s.* (*fonet.*) consonante sonora.

sonar ['souna:*], *s.* (*mar.*) ecogoniometro.

sonata [sə'na:tə], *s.* (*mus.*) sonata.

sonatina [,sonə'ti:nə], *s.* (*mus.*) sonatina.

song [soŋ], *s.* **1.** canto: *the — of the birds*, il canto degli uccelli; *to burst into —*, mettersi a cantare **2.** canzone (anche *poes.*); aria ‖ *The Song of Roland*, (*lett.*) «La canzone di Rolando» ‖ *to buy, to sell sthg. for a —*, (*fam.*) comperare, vendere ql.co. per una sciocchezza ‖ *nothing to make a — about*, (*fam.*) niente d'importante **3.** (*poes.*) poesia, componimento poetico **4.** (*eccl.*) cantico: *the Song of Songs* (o *the Song of Solomon*), il Cantico dei Cantici ☆ *-school*, scuola di canto; *—-thrush*, (*ornit.*) tordo; *— -writer*, compositore, autore di canzoni ‖ *action —*, canzone mimata; *love- —*, romanza.

songbird ['soŋbə:d], *s.* uccello canterino.

songbook ['soŋbuk], *s.* canzoniere.

songful ['soŋful], *ag.* **1.** melodioso, armonioso **2.** canterino, che ama cantare.

songless ['soŋlis], *ag.* che non canta; senza voce, muto.

songster ['soŋs-tə*], *s.* **1.** cantante **2.** poeta **3.** uccello canterino.

songstress ['soŋs-tris], *s.* **1.** cantante **2.** poetessa.

sonic ['sonik], *ag.* sonico ☆ *— bang* (o *- -boom*), (*aer.*) scoppio sonico, esplosione sonica; *— -wall*), barriera, muro del suono; *— depth-finder*, (*mar.*) scandaglio acustico; *— mine*, (*mar.*) mina acustica.

soniferous [sou'nifərəs], *ag.* sonoro, risonante.

sonnet ['sonit], *s.* (*poes.*) sonetto: *Elizabethan —*, sonetto elisabettiano; *Italian —*, sonetto all'italiana; *Shakespearian —*, sonetto shakespeariano.

to **sonnet**, *v.t.i.* comporre sonetti; celebrare con sonetti.

sonneteer [,soni'tiə*], *s.* (*gener. spreg.*) scrittore, compositore di sonetti.

to **sonneteer**, *v.t.i.* (*gener. spreg.*) comporre sonetti; celebrare con sonetti.

sonny ['sʌni], *s.* (*fam. vezzeggiativo*) figliolino, piccino mio.

sonometer [sou'nomitə*], *s.* (*fis.*) sonometro.

sonorific [,sonə'rifik], *ag.* sonoro, risonante.

sonority [sə'noriti], *s.* sonorità, risonanza.

sonorous [sə'no:rəs], *ag.* **1.** sonoro, risonante **2.** *fig.* altisonante: *— titles*, titoli altisonanti.

sonorously [sə'no:rəsli], *av.* sonoramente, in modo risonante.

sonorousness [sə'no:rəsnis], *s.* sonorità, risonanza.

sonship ['sʌn-ʃip], *s.* stato, condizione di figlio.

sonsy ['sonsi], *ag.* (*scoz.*) **1.** lieto, gaio **2.** prosperoso, fiorente: *she is a — lass*, è una ragazza prosperosa.

soon [su:n], *av.* **1.** presto, tosto, tra poco: *— after*, non molto dopo, poco dopo, subito dopo; *too —*, troppo presto; in anticipo: *he arrived an hour too —*, arrivò con un'ora d'anticipo; *very —*, ben presto, quanto prima; *how — can you be ready?*, tra quanto tempo sarai pronto?; *it will — be three years since...*, saranno presto tre anni che...; *see you again — !*, a tra poco!, a presto! ‖ *as — as*, (non) appena che, tosto che: *as — as possible*, il più presto possibile ‖ *the sooner the better*, prima è meglio è ‖ *sooner or later*, presto o tardi, prima o poi ‖ *no sooner than...*, non appena che...: *he had no sooner seen us than he fled away*, non appena ci vide scappò via; *no sooner said than done*, detto fatto **2.** piuttosto; volentieri: *he would as — die as live in poverty*, morirebbe piuttosto che vivere in miseria; *I would as — stay here*, starei qui volentieri ‖ *I had sooner stop,* preferirei fermarmi; *I would sooner give it up than see him*, preferirei rinunciarvi piuttosto che vederlo.

soot [sut], *s.* fuliggine ☆ — *-cancer* (o — *-wart*), cancro degli spazzacamini.

to soot, *v.t.* **1.** macchiare, sporcare di fuliggine **2.** fertilizzare (il terreno) con cenere.

sooth [su:θ], *s.* (*arc.*) verità; realtà: *in* —, in verità, veramente; *to speak* (o *to say*) —, dire la verità.

to soothe [su:ð], *v.t.* **1.** calmare, placare; blandire, lenire, addolcire: *to* — *s.o.'s anger*, calmare la collera di qlcu. **2.** adulare, lusingare.

soother ['su:ðə*], *s.c.* **1.** chi calma, chi rasserena **2.** adulatore, adulatrice ‖ *s.* tettarella di gomma.

soothfast ['su:θfɑ:st], *ag.* (*arc.*) vero, veritiero; leale, onesto.

soothing ['su:ðiŋ], *ag.* lenitivo, calmante ☆ — *draught*, (*farm.*) calmante.

soothingly ['su:ðiŋli], *av.* dolcemente, con dolcezza.

to soothsay ['su:θsei], *v.i.* (*rar.*) predire.

soothsayer ['su:θˌseiə*], *s.c.* divinatore, divinatrice; indovino, indovina.

soothsaying ['su:θˌseiiŋ], *s.* divinazione, predizione.

sootiness ['sutinis], *s.* l'essere fuligginoso.

sootish ['sutiʃ], *ag.* fuligginoso, coperto di fuliggine.

sootless ['sutlis], *ag.* senza fuliggine.

sooty ['suti], *ag.* fuligginoso, coperto di fuliggine: *a — atmosphere*, un'atmosfera fuligginosa.

sop [sɔp], *s.* **1.** pezzo di pane, biscotto inzuppato **2.** *fig.* offa, dono propiziatorio.

to sop, *pass.p.p.* **sopped** [sɔpt], *v.t.i.* intingere; inzuppare, inzupparsi.

soph [sɔf], *abbr.* di **sophomore, sophister**.

Sophia [sə'faiə], *no.pr.f.* Sofia.

sophism ['sɔfizəm], *s.* sofisma; cavillo.

sophist ['sɔfist], *s.c.* **1.** (*fil.*) sofista **2.** sofista, cavillatore, cavillatrice.

sophister ['sɔfistə*], *s.* **1.** studente del terzo o quarto anno a Dublino **2.** (*arc.*) studente del secondo o terzo anno a Cambridge.

sophistic(al) [sə'fistik(əl)], *ag.* sofistico; pedante, capzioso.

sophistically [sə'fistikəli], *av.* sofisticamente.

to sophisticate [sə'fistikeit], *v.t.i.* **1.** sofisticare; privare della semplicità; fare il sofistico **2.** alterare (un testo, ecc.) **3.** adulterare (sostanze, cibi).

sophisticated [sə'fistikeitid], *ag.* **1.** sofisticato; raffinato: — *taste*, gusto eccessivamente raffinato **2.** sofisticato, adulterato (di vini, cibi).

sophistication [səˌfisti'keiʃən], *s.* **1.** ragionamento sofistico, sofisma **2.** gusti complicati, raffinati **3.** sofisticazione, adulterazione.

sophisticator [sə'fistikeitə*], *s.c.* falsificatore, falsificatrice.

sophistry ['sɔfistri], *s.* sofisma, sofisticheria; cavillo.

Sophoclean [ˌsɔfə'kli(:)ən], *ag.* (*poes.*) sofocleo.

Sophocles ['sɔfəkli:z], *no.pr.m.* (*st. lett.*) Sofocle.

sophomore ['sɔfəmɔ:*], *s.* (*amer.*) studente del secondo anno di università; (*gergo studentesco*) fagiolo.

soporiferous [ˌsoupə'rifərəs], *ag.* soporifero.

soporiferousness [ˌsoupə'rifərəsnis], *s.* qualità soporifera.

soporific [ˌsoupə'rifik], *ag.* soporifico, soporifero ‖ *s.* sonnifero, narcotico.

soporose ['soupərous], **soporous** ['soupərəs], *ag.* soporoso.

soppy ['sɔpi], *ag.* **1.** inzuppato **2.** (*fam.*) sentimentale, svenevole.

sopranist [sə'prɑ:nist], *s.* (*mus.*) sopranista.

soprano [sə'prɑ:nou], *pl.* **sopranos** [sə'prɑ:nouz], **soprani** [sə'prɑ:ni(:)], *s.* (*mus.*) soprano.

sorb [sɔ:b], *s.* (*bot.*) **1.** — (*-apple*), sorba **2.** — (*-apple -tree*), sorbo.

sorbefacient [ˌsɔ:bi'feiʃənt], *ag.* (*farm.*) che favorisce l'assorbimento ‖ *s.* (*farm.*) rimedio che favorisce l'assorbimento.

sorbet ['sɔ:bət], *s.* sorbetto.

sorbic ['sɔ:bik], *ag.* (*chim.*) sorbico ☆ — *acid*, acido sorbico.

sorbite ['sɔ:bait], *s.* (*chim.*) sorbite.

sorcerer ['sɔ:sərə*], *s.* stregone, mago, incantatore.

sorceress ['sɔ:səris], *s.* strega, maga, incantatrice, fattucchiera.

sorcerous ['sɔ:sərəs], *ag.* incantato, stregato.

sorcery ['sɔ:səri], *s.* stregoneria, sortilegio, malia, fattura, incantesimo.

sordid ['sɔ:did], *ag.* **1.** sordido, avaro, taccagno, spilorcio; vile, ignobile, meschino **2.** (*di piante, animali*) opaco, scuro **3.** infetto **4.** (*arc.*) squallido, miserabile; sudicio, sozzo.

sordidly ['sɔ:didli], *av.* **1.** sordidamente, grettamente, spilorciamente; vilmente, meschinamente **2.** (*arc.*) in modo sporco, sozzamente.

sordidness ['sɔ:didnis], *s.* **1.** sordidezza, spilorceria; viltà, meschinità **2.** (*arc.*) sporcizia, sudiciume.

sordine [sɔ:'di:n], **sordino** [sɔ:'di:nou], *s.* (*mus.*) sordina.

sore [sɔ:*], *ag.* **1.** doloroso; dolorante; infiammato, irritato; ulcerato: *to be* — *all over*, essere tutto indolenzito; *to have a* — *arm*, aver male a un braccio ‖ *like a bear with a* — *head*, di umore nero ‖ *that's her* — *spot*, (*fam.*) è il suo punto debole ‖ *you are a sight for* — *eyes*, vederti è un vero piacere ‖ *to put one's finger on the* — *place*, mettere il dito sulla piaga **2.** addolorato, triste, afflitto, desolato; depresso: *my heart is* — *for them*, mi dispiace sinceramente per loro; *to be, to feel* — *about sthg.*, essere, sentirsi addolorato per ql.co.; *to be* — *at heart*, essere desolato; *to get* —, (*fam. amer.*) cominciare a seccarsi **3.** estremo, intenso, grave, grande: *a* — *defeat*, una grave sconfitta; *I was in* — *need of money*, mi trovavo in estrema necessità di danaro ‖ *s.* piaga, ulcera; ferita (anche *fig.*): *it reopened my old sores*, ciò riaprì le mie vecchie ferite ☆ — *-throat*, mal di gola; faringite ‖ *heart* —, crepacuore.

sore, *av.* **1.** dolorosamente; amaramente; crudelmente **2.** gravemente, grandemente.

soredium [sə'ri:diəm], *pl.* **soredia** [sə'ri:diə], *s. gener. pl.* (*bot.*) soredio.

sorel, *V.* **sorrel**².

sorely ['sɔ:li], *av.* **1.** dolorosamente; amaramente; crudelmente **2.** gravemente, grandemente.

soreness ['sɔ:nis], *s.* **1.** dolore, male **2.** pena; dispiacere **3.** rancore; irritazione.

sorgho ['sɔ:gou], **sorghum** ['sɔ:gəm], *s.* (*bot.*) sorgo.

sorites [sə'raiti:z], *s.* (*log.*) sorite, serie di sillogismi.

sorner ['sɔ:nə*], *s.c.* (*scoz.*) scroccone, scroccona.

sorority [sə'rɔriti], *s.* **1.** comunità religiosa femminile **2.** (*amer.*) associazione femminile universitaria.

sorrel¹ ['sɔrəl], *s.* (*bot.*) acetosa ☆ *wood-* —, acetosella.

sorrel², *ag.* di color sauro ‖ *s.* sauro, cavallo sauro.

sorrily ['sɔrili], *av.* **1.** tristemente; dolorosamente **2.** meschinamente.

sorriness ['sɔrinis], *s.* **1.** afflizione **2.** povertà, meschinità.

sorrow ['sɔrou], *s.* **1.** dispiacere, dolore, pena; tristezza: *to my great* —, con mio grande dolore; *I left him with* —, lo lasciai con dolore **2.** rincrescimento; pentimento **3.** *gener. pl.* sventura: *her sorrows turned her hair white*, le sventure la fecero incanutire.

to sorrow, *v.i.* affliggersi, addolorarsi; lamentarsi: *to* — *at* (o *about* o *over*) *sthg.*, affliggersi di, per ql.co.; *to* — *for* (o *after*) *s.o.*, *sthg.*, rimpiangere qlcu., ql.co.; piangere qlcu., ql.co.

sorrower ['sɔrouə*], *s.c.* chi soffre; persona addolorata, afflitta.

sorrowful ['sɔrəful], *ag.* **1.** triste, infelice; addolorato, afflitto: *a* — *look*, uno sguardo melanconico, triste **2.** penoso, doloroso (di notizie, ecc.).

sorrowfulness ['sɔrəfulnis], *s.* tristezza, dolore, afflizione.

sorrowing ['sɔrouiŋ], *ag.* afflitto, addolorato ‖ *s.* afflizione, dolore.

sorrowless ['sɔroulis], *ag.* senza dolore, libero da dolore.

sorry ['sɔri], *ag.* **1.** dispiacente, dolente, addolorato; triste: *he was — for me*, gli dispiacque per me; *I am — to say that...*, mi rincresce dire che...; *I am very — for that*, me ne dispiace tanto; *to be — about sthg.*, essere spiacente per ql.co. ‖ *—!*, scusate! **2.** meschino, miserabile, povero; pietoso: *a — excuse*, una scusa meschina; *a — man*, un uomo miserabile ‖ *to cut a — figure*, fare una magra figura.

sort [sɔːt], *s.* **1.** sorta, genere, specie; ordine; classe: *all sorts of men*, uomini di tutti i generi; *nothing of the —*, niente di simile; *this — of thing*, questo genere di cose; *what — of people?*, che sorta di gente?; *he didn't say anything of the —*, non disse niente del genere ‖ *he is an awfully good —*, (*fam.*) è proprio una brava persona ‖ *to be out of sorts*, essere in cattive condizioni di salute; essere di malumore **2.** (*arc.*) modo, maniera ‖ *in some —*, in un certo modo, fino ad un certo punto.

to sort, *v.t.i.* **1.** raggruppare, classificare; scegliere, selezionare; distribuire: *to — the letters*, smistare le lettere; *to — out sthg. from sthg.*, separare una cosa dall'altra: *I sorted out the small from the large ones*, separai i piccoli dai grandi **2.** (*arc.*) accordarsi; adattarsi; frequentare: *to — with s.o.*, andar d'accordo con qlcu.; frequentare qlcu.

sortable ['sɔːtəbl], *ag.* **1.** classificabile, selezionabile **2.** conveniente, adatto, acconcio.

sortably ['sɔːtəbli], *av.* convenientemente, in modo acconcio.

sorter ['sɔːtə*], *s.* selezionatore, classificatore.

sortie ['sɔːti(ː)], *s.* (*mil.*) sortita.

sortilege ['sɔːtilidʒ], *s.* **1.** divinazione **2.** sortilegio, magia.

sorting ['sɔːtiŋ], *s.* classificazione; selezione.

sorus ['sourəs], *pl.* **sori** ['sourai], *s.* (*bot.*) soro.

S. O. S. [ˌes,ou'es], *s.* **1.** (*mar. aer.*) S. O. S.: *to send out an —*, lanciare l' S.O.S. **2.** *fig.* appello urgente.

so-so ['sousou], *ag. predicativo* mediocre, passabile ‖ *av.* così così: " *How does he feel this morning?* ", "—", « Come sta questa mattina? », « Così così. »

sostenuto [ˌsɔstə'nuːtou], *s.* (*mus.*) sostenuto.

sot [sɔt], *s.c.* ubriacone, ubriacona; persona abbrutita dall'alcool.

to sot, *pass.p.p.* **sotted** ['sɔtid], *v.i.* ubriacarsi; istupidirsi, abbrutirsi (per il troppo bere).

sottish ['sɔtiʃ], *ag.* istupidito, abbrutito dall'alcool; da ubriacone.

sottishly ['sɔtiʃli], *av.* da ubriacone.

sottishness ['sɔtiʃnis], *s.* ubriachezza; alcoolismo, abbrutimento (da alcool).

sotto voce ['sɔtou'voutʃi], *av.* sotto voce.

sou [suː], *s.* soldo: *he hasn't a —*, (*fam.*) non ha il becco d'un quattrino.

soubriquet ['suːbrikei], *s.* soprannome, nomignolo.

Soudan [suː'dɑːn], *no.pr.* (*geog.*) Sudan.

Soudanese [ˌsuːdə'niːz], *ag.s.c.* sudanese.

souffle ['suːfl], *s.* (*med.*) soffio.

soufflé ['suːflei], *ag.* soufflé, montato ‖ *s.* (*cuc.*) soufflé, sformato ☆ *— pan*, stampo per sformato.

sough¹ [sau], *s.* **1.** mormorio, sussurro (di vento, ecc.) **2.** sospiro profondo **3.** diceria, voce.

to sough¹, *v.t.i.* **1.** mormorare, sussurrare (di vento, ecc.) **2.** sospirare profondamente **3.** canterellare.

sough² [saf], *s.* **1.** pozzanghera **2.** fogna **3.** entrata (di miniera).

to sough², *v.t.i.* costruire (canali, argini).

sought [sɔːt], *pass.p.p.* di **to seek**.

soul [soul], *s.* **1.** anima, animo, spirito: *body and —*, anima e corpo; *he was the — of the company*, era l'anima della compagnia; *his pictures have no —*, i suoi quadri mancano d'anima; *his whole — was against it*, tutta la sua anima si ribellava a ciò; *to pray for s.o.'s —*, pre-

gare per l'anima di qlcu. ‖ *upon my —!*, parola mia! ‖ *the departed souls*, le anime dei trapassati **2.** anima, essere; creatura, persona: *the great souls of ancient times*, i grandi spiriti dei tempi antichi; *population of two thousand souls*, popolazione di duemila anime; *many souls were lost in that war*, in quella guerra caddero molti uomini; *the poor — didn't know where to go*, la povera creatura non sapeva dove andare; *there was not a —*, non c'era anima viva **3.** personificazione, essenza: *she is the — of charity*, è la carità in persona **4.** coraggio; forza spirituale ☆ *-bell*, campana a morto; *— -destroying*, che abbrutisce; estremamente monotono, scoraggiante; *— -felt*, sentito, sincero, caloroso; *— -searching*, che va in fondo all'anima; *— -stirring*, commovente, emozionante.

soulful ['soulful], *ag.* pieno di sentimento; sentimentale.

soulfully ['soulfuli], *av.* con molto sentimento; sentimentalmente.

soulfulness ['soulfulnis], *s.* sentimento, espressione.

soulless ['soullis], *ag.* senz'anima; inespressivo; prosaico.

soullessly ['soullisli], *av.* senz'anima; in modo inespressivo; prosaicamente.

soullessness ['soullisnis], *s.* mancanza d'anima; inespressività; prosaicità.

sound¹ [saund], *ag.* **1.** sano; intero; in buono stato: *— fruit*, frutta sana ‖ *a — mind in a — body*, mente sana in corpo sano ‖ *as — as a bell*, sano come un pesce **2.** buono; solido; valido, legittimo; giudizioso: *a — financial situation*, una situazione finanziaria solida; *a — title*, (*comm.*) un titolo solido; *— views*, vedute equilibrate **3.** profondo; totale, completo: *a — sleep*, un sonno profondo **4.** sincero, leale, onesto: *a — behaviour*, un comportamento leale.

sound¹, *av.* profondamente: *she was — asleep*, dormiva profondamente.

sound¹, (*nei composti*): *— -headed*, equilibrato; *— -hearted*, di cuore sincero; *— -judging*, che giudica lealmente; *— -minded*, di buon senso.

sound², *s.* **1.** suono, rumore; rimbombo; tocco, rintocco: *musical —*, suono musicale; *to hear a —*, udire un suono **2.** tono, intonazione: *he didn't like the — of it*, non gli piacque il tono di ciò ☆ *— -absorption*, assorbimento acustico; *— barrier*, barriera del suono; *— -body* (o *— -box*), cassa di risonanza; *— -deadener*, antisuono; *— -effects*, (*cine.*) effetti sonori; *— -film* (o *— -picture*), film sonoro; *— -hole*, esse (di violino); *— -post*, anima (di violino); *— -projector*, (*cine.*) proiettore sonoro; *— -proof*, impenetrabile al suono; *— -shift*, (*fonet.*) rotazione consonantica; *— -track*, (*cine.*) colonna sonora; *— -truck*, (*cine.*) carro sonoro; *— -wave*, onda sonora.

to sound², *v.t.i.* **1.** suonare, risuonare; rimbombare; echeggiare: *the cries sounded dreadful in the night*, le grida echeggiarono spaventose nella notte **2.** sembrare, dare l'impressione di, aver l'aria di: *it sounds to me like s.o. crying*, ho l'impressione che qlcu. stia piangendo; *that sounds true*, sembra vero; *this may — very strange to you*, ciò può sembrarti molto strano **3.** suonare, far suonare, far risuonare; far sentire; far risapere: *to — an alarm*, dare l'allarme; *to — the retreat*, suonare la ritirata; *to — the horns*, suonare i corni ‖ *to — s.o.'s praises*, cantare le lodi di qlcu. **4.** (*med.*) auscultare: *the doctor sounded my chest*, il dottore mi auscultò il torace.

sound³, *s.* **1.** (*mar.*) sondaggio **2.** (*chir.*) sonda.

to sound³, *v.t.i.* **1.** (*mar.*) sondare, scandagliare; fare dei sondaggi **2.** (*chir.*) sondare ‖ *to — s.o. about sthg.*, (*fam.*) sondare qlcu. a proposito di ql.co.

sound⁴, *s.* **1.** braccio di mare; stretto **2.** vescica natatoria (di pesci) **3.** (*ittiol.*) seppia.

soundable ['saundəbl], *ag.* sondabile.

sounder ['saundə*], *s.* **1.** ricevitore telegrafico acustico **2.** (*tel.*) manipolatore fonico ☆ *echo* —, (*mar.*) scandaglio acustico.

sounding[1] ['saundiŋ], *ag.* sonoro, sonante, risonante; *fig.* pomposo, ridondante (di stile, ecc.) ‖ *s.* **1.** suono, risonanza; sonorità; rimbombo **2.** segnale (di tromba, ecc.) **3.** (*med.*) auscultazione ☆ — *-board*, (*mus.*) tavola armonica ‖ *sharp-* —, dal suono acuto.

sounding[2], *s.* **1.** (*mar.*) scandaglio: *to take soundings*, fare scandagli **2.** *pl.* (*mar.*) fondali scandagliabili: *to be in soundings*, essere in acque poco profonde; *to strike soundings*, toccare il fondo **3.** (*chir.*) sondaggio ☆ — *balloon*, (*aer.*) pallone sonda; — *-machine*, (*mar.*) scandaglio.

soundless[1] ['saundlis], *ag.* muto, senza suono, senza rumore.

soundless[2], *ag.* (*mar.*) insondabile, non scandagliabile; senza fondo.

soundly ['saundli], *av.* **1.** sanamente; solidamente; giudiziosamente **2.** fortemente, profondamente: *to sleep* —, dormire profondamente.

soundness ['saundnis], *s.* **1.** stato sano, buona condizione (di salute); buono stato **2.** (*comm.*) solidità, solvibilità **3.** solidità (di argomento, ecc.), vigore; sicurezza; rettitudine, ortodossia (di dottrine, ecc.): *the* — *of her judgement*, la sua sicurezza di giudizio.

soup [su:p], *s.* zuppa, minestra; brodo ‖ *to be in the* —, (*fam.*) trovarsi nei pasticci ☆ — *-kitchen*, mensa gratuita per i poveri; — *-ladle*, cucchiaione, mestolo; — *-plate*, fondina, scodella; — *-tureen*, zuppiera ‖ *clear* —, « consommè »; *pea-* —, passato di piselli.

soupy ['su:pi], *ag.* **1.** simile a zuppa, come zuppa **2.** spesso, denso.

sour ['sauə*], *ag.* **1.** agro, aspro; acerbo: — *apples*, mele acerbe; *to taste* —, aver sapore aspro **2.** acido, fermentato: — *milk*, latte acido; *to turn* —, inacidire: *to turn sthg.* —, fare inacidire ql.co. **3.** bisbetico, arcigno, amaro: *a* — *temper*, un carattere acido, bisbetico; *failure made him* —, l'insuccesso lo rese amaro **4.** umido, fangoso; poco fecondo (di terreno) ‖ *s.* sostanza, soluzione acida; acqua acidulata; (*amer.*) bevanda acida ☆ — *-dock*, (*bot.*) acetosa; — *eyed*, dallo sguardo cupo; — *-sweet*, agro-dolce.

to **sour**, *v.t.i.* **1.** rendere agro; inacidire, inacidirsi; acidificare **2.** *fig.* esacerbare, inasprire: *soured by poverty*, inasprito dalla povertà; *to* — *s.o.'s life*, avvelenare l'esistenza a qlcu.

source [so:s], *s.* **1.** fonte, sorgente (di fiume, ecc.): *the Po takes its* — *in the Alps*, il Po nasce nelle Alpi **2.** fonte, origine; principio; causa: — *of heat*, fonte di calore; — *of infection*, fonte d'infezione; *his presence is a* — *of great joy to his family*, la sua presenza è causa di grande gioia per la sua famiglia; *I learnt it from a good* —, lo seppi da fonte sicura ‖ *idleness is the* — *of all evil*, *prov.* l'ozio è il padre dei vizi **3.** documenti, libri, materiale di consultazione ☆ — *-book*, raccolta di documenti.

sourdine [suə'di:n], *s.* (*mus.*) sordina.

souring ['sauəriŋ], *s.* inasprimento; inacidimento.

sourish ['sauəriʃ], *ag.* acidulo; asprigno.

sourly ['sauəli], *av.* acidamente, acerbamente; aspramente (anche *fig.*).

sourness ['sauənis], *s.* **1.** acidità; acerbità; asprezza **2.** *fig.* acrimonia; asprezza.

souse[1] [saus], *s.* **1.** (*dial. amer.*) vivande marinate, in salamoia (specialmente piedini ed orecchie di maiale) **2.** orecchio **3.** salamoia.

to **souse**[1], *v.t.i.* **1.** (*cuc.*) marinare, mettere in salamoia **2.** immergere, tuffare (nell'acqua); inzuppare, inzupparsi **3.** rovesciare **4.** (*sl.*) ubriacarsi.

souse[1], *av.* con un tuffo repentino e profondo.

souse[2], *s.* **1.** tuffo, immersione; (*dial.*) bagno **2.** (*sl.*) ubriacatura **3.** sciabordio.

souse[3], *s.* (*sl.*) botta, colpo forte; caduta pesante.

to **souse**[3], *v.t.i.* (*sl.*) **1.** colpire, picchiare con forza **2.** cadere pesantemente.

souse[4], *av.* **1.** all'improvviso **2.** a capofitto **3.** d'un colpo.

soused [saust], *ag.* (*sl. amer.*) ubriaco.

sousing ['sausiŋ], *ag.* **1.** marinato **2.** immerso (nell'acqua); inzuppato ‖ *s.* **1.** (*cuc.*) marinatura, il mettere in salamoia **2.** immersione (nell'acqua).

soutane [su:'tɑ:n], *s.* (*eccl.*) tonaca, sottana dei preti.

south [sauθ], *ag.* del sud, del mezzogiorno, meridionale ‖ *South Sea*, (*st.*) il Pacifico ‖ *s.* sud, mezzogiorno, mezzodì: *in the* —, al sud: *they lived in the* — *of Italy*, vivevano nell'Italia meridionale ☆ — *coast*, costa meridionale; — *countryman*, abitante del sud, meridionale; — *wind*, vento del sud.

to **south**, *v.i.* **1.** (*astr.*) passare il meridiano (di stella) **2.** (*mar.*) andare verso il sud, dirigersi a sud; fare rotta per il sud.

south, *av.* a sud, verso sud: *to travel* —, viaggiare verso il sud.

South Africa (Union of) ['sauθ'æfrikə], *no.pr.* (*geog.*) (Unione del) Sud Africa.

southdown ['sauθdaun], *ag.* delle regioni del sud (Hampshire, Sussex) ‖ *s.* razza di pecore del sud.

south-east ['sauθ'i:st], *ag.* di sud-est ‖ *s.* sud-est ‖ *av.* verso sud-est.

south-easter [sauθ'i:stə*], *s.* vento di sud-est, scirocco.

south-easterly [sauθ'i:stəli], *ag.* di sud-est ‖ *av.* verso sud-est.

south-eastern [sauθ'i:stən], *ag.* di sud-est.

south-eastward [sauθ'i:stwəd], *ag.* a, di sud-est.

south-eastward(s) [sauθ'i:stwəd(z)], *av.* verso sud-est.

souther ['sʌðə*], *V.* **south-easter.**

southerliness ['sʌðəlinis], *s.* natura, carattere meridionale.

southerly ['sʌðəli], *ag.* del sud, che viene dal sud (di vento); meridionale, australe: — *latitude*, latitudine australe ‖ *av.* verso sud; dal sud (di vento).

southern ['sʌðən], *ag.* **1.** del sud, del mezzogiorno, meridionale, australe: *the* — *countries*, i paesi del sud ‖ *Southern Cross*, (*astr.*) Croce del Sud **2.** (*st. amer.*) sudista ‖ *s.c.* abitante del sud, meridionale ‖ *s.* (*st. amer.*) sudista ☆ — *lights*, aurora australe.

southerner ['sʌðənə*], *s.c.* abitante del sud, meridionale ‖ *s.* (*st. amer.*) sudista.

southernly ['sʌðənli], *av.* a sud; verso sud.

southernmost ['sʌðənmoust], *ag.* il più a sud, il più meridionale.

southernwood ['sʌðənwud], *s.* (*bot.*) artemisia.

southing ['sauðiŋ], *s.* **1.** rotta verso sud **2.** (*mar.*) differenza di latitudine (nella navigazione al sud) **3.** (*astr.*) culminazione.

Southland ['sauθlənd], *s.* (il) Sud.

southmost ['sauθmoust], *ag.* il più a sud; il più meridionale.

southron ['sʌðrən], *ag.s.c.* **1.** (abitante) del sud **2.** (*arc. scoz. spreg.*) inglese.

southward ['sauθwəd], *ag.* verso sud ‖ *s.* sud: *to the* —, verso sud.

southward(s) ['sauθwəd(z)], *av.* verso sud.

Southwark ['sʌðək], *no.pr.* « Southwark » (quartiere di Londra).

south-west ['sauθ'west], *ag.* di sud-ovest: — *wind*, vento di sud-ovest ‖ *s.* sud-ovest ‖ *av.* verso sud-ovest.

south-wester [sauθ'westə*], *s.* **1.** vento di sud-ovest; libeccio, garbino **2.** cappellaccio a gronda.

south-westerly [sauθ'westəli], *ag.* a sud-ovest, di sud-ovest, verso sud-ovest ‖ *av.* verso sud-ovest.

south-westward [sauθ'westwəd], *ag.* verso sud-ovest ‖ *s.* sud-ovest.

souvenir ['su:vəniə*], *s.* « souvenir », ricordo.

sovereign ['sɔvrin], *ag.* sovrano, supremo, superiore; estremo, sommo: *the* — *good*, il sommo bene; — *remedy*, (*fam.*) rimedio sovrano, infallibile ‖ *s. c.* sovrano, sovrana; re, regina ‖ *s.* **1.** monarca; principe (regnante) **2.** sovrana, sterlina (d'oro).

sovereignly ['sɔvrinli], *av.* sovranamente.

sovereignty ['sɔvrənti], *s.* sovranità.

soviet ['souviet], *s.* « soviet », consiglio ‖ *the Union of Socialist Soviet Republics (U.S.S.R.)*, l'Unione delle Repubbliche Socialiste Sovietiche (U.R.S.S.).

sovietic ['souvietik], *ag.* sovietico.

sovran ['sɔvrən], *V.* **sovereign.**

sovranty ['sɔvrənti], *s.* sovranità.

sow¹ [sau], *s.* **1.** scrofa ‖ *to be as drunk as a —*, essere ubriaco fradicio ‖ *to get the wrong — by the ear*, prendere un granchio **2.** donna sudicia, pigra **3.** (*metal.*) canale di colata per lingotti; metallo solidificato nei canali di colata **4.** (*st. mil.*) testuggine, vigna ☆ *— -bread*, (*bot.*) pan porcino, ciclamino; *— -bug*, (*zool.*) onisco.

to **sow²** [sou], *pass.* **sowed** [soud], *p.p.* **sowed, sown** [soun], *v.t.* seminare (anche *fig.*); spargere, disseminare; spargere: *he sowed the seeds of discord between the families*, seminò la zizzania fra le famiglie; *to — land with corn*, seminare un terreno a grano.

sower ['souə*], *s.c.* seminatore, seminatrice.

sowing ['souiŋ], *s.* seminagione ☆ *— -machine*, macchina seminatrice; *— -seed*, semenza; *— -time*, tempo, stagione della seminagione.

sown [soun], *p.p.* di to **sow.**

soy [soi], **soya** ['soiə], *s.* (*cuc.*) « soi » (salsa piccante cinese e giapponese fatta con la soia) ☆ *— bean*, (*bot.*) soia.

spa [spɑː], *s.* **1.** sorgente d'acqua minerale (da Spa in Belgio) **2.** stazione termale: *to go to a —*, andare in una stazione termale, andare a passare le acque.

space [speis], *s.* **1.** spazio, intervallo (di tempo); momento, istante: *after a short —*, dopo breve tempo; *in the — of a month*, nello spazio di un mese; *let him rest a —*, lascialo riposare un momento **2.** spazio; posto; distesa; superficie; estensione: *the building occupies a large —*, l'edificio occupa una vasta superficie; *it would take up too much — to write all that*, ci vorrebbe troppo spazio per scrivere tutto ciò; *to leave — for sthg.*, lasciare il posto per ql.co. **3.** spazio libero, intervallo, distanza; (*tip.*) spazio (tra due parole): *— between two things*, spazio tra due cose; *blank —*, spazio in bianco: *the blank spaces of a paper*, gli spazi in bianco di un giornale **4.** (*mus.*) spazio, intervallo ☆ *— achievement*, conquista spaziale; *— -bar*, barra spaziatrice (di macchina per scrivere); *— capsule*, capsula spaziale; *— -line*, (*tip.*) interlinea; *— -pilot*, pilota spaziale; *— probe*, sonda spaziale; *— -ship*, astronave; *— -time*, (*fil.*) spazio tempo; *— -travel*, astronautica; *— -traveller*, astronauta; *— -writer*, giornalista pagato un tanto per riga ‖ *air- —*, spazio aereo.

to **space**, *v.t.* **1.** spaziare; scaglionare, disporre ad intervalli: *to — the lines*, (*tip.*) spaziare le righe **2.** *to — off* (*a line*), dividere, suddividere (una riga) **3.** *to — out* (*the type*), (*tip.*) allargare gli spazi (fra le lettere).

spaceless ['speislis], *ag.* senza confini, illimitato.

spaceman, *pl.* **spacemen** ['speismən], *s.* (*neol.*) astronauta.

spacer ['speisə*], *s.* spaziatore (di macchina per scrivere).

spacial ['speiʃəl], *ag.* spaziale.

spacing ['speisiŋ], *s.* **1.** (*tip.*) spaziatura, interlineatura **2.** scaglionamento; suddivisione.

spacious ['speiʃəs], *ag.* spazioso, ampio, vasto.

spaciously ['speiʃəsli], *av.* spaziosamente, ampiamente, vastamente.

spaciousness ['speiʃəsnis], *s.* spaziosità, vastità.

spade¹ [speid], *s.* vanga, badile ‖ *to call a — a —*, (*fam.*) dire pane al pane (e vino al vino) ☆ *— -bone*, (*anat.*) scapola; *— -husbandry*, vangatura in profondità; *— -work*, vangatura; *fig.* lavoro preliminare, lavoro di sondaggio; lavoro arduo.

to **spade¹**, *v.t.* **1.** vangare **2.** estrarre grasso da (una balena).

spade², *s.* picche (seme delle carte): *ace of spades* asso di picche.

spadeful ['speidful], *s.* palata, vangata.

spadger ['spædʒə*], *s.* (*sl.*) passero.

spadille [spə'dil], *s.* asso di picche (nei giuochi ombra e quadriglio).

spadix ['speidiks], *pl.* **spadices** [spei'daisi:z], *s.* (*bot.*) spadice.

spado ['spɑːdou], *s.* (*dir.*) persona sterile.

spaghetti [spə'geti], *s.* (*cuc.*) spaghetti.

spahee, spahi ['spɑːhiː], *s.* spahi (soldato turco).

Spain [spein], *no.pr.* (*geog.*) Spagna.

spake [speik], *pass.* (*arc.*) di to **speak.**

spall [spɔːl], *s.* (*ind.*) scheggia, frammento.

to **spall**, *v.t.i.* **1.** (*ind.*) fendere, fendersi; scheggiare, scheggiarsi **2.** preparare (il minerale grezzo) per la scelta.

spam [spæm], *s.* (*amer. contr.* di *spiced ham*) carne suina in scatola.

span¹ [spæn], *s.* **1.** spanna, palmo **2.** breve spazio di tempo: *our life is but a —*, la vita non è che un breve lasso di tempo **3.** larghezza, apertura **4.** (*arch.*) luce; campata ☆ *— -counter* (o *— -farthing*), piastrella (giuoco); *— -long*, lungo una spanna; *— -new*, nuovo di zecca; *— -roof*, tetto a due spioventi ‖ *single- — bridge*, ponte ad una sola arcata; *wing- —*, apertura d'ala.

to **span¹**, *pass.p.p.* **spanned** [spænd], *v.t.* **1.** misurare a spanne **2.** circondare; abbracciare **3.** formare un arco con, estendersi attraverso, attraversare (di arcobaleno, ponte, ecc.) **4.** gettare un ponte attraverso.

span², *s.* **1.** (*mar.*) penzolo **2.** pariglia (di cavalli); coppia di buoi.

to **span²**, *v.t.i.* **1.** attaccare, aggiogare (buoi, cavalli) **2.** (*mar.*) fissare, assicurare (col penzolo) **3.** (*amer.*) formare una pariglia.

spandrel ['spændrəl], *s.* (*arch.*) **1.** pennacchio (di un arco) **2.** altezza dei portali (di finestre).

spangle ['spæŋgl], *s.* lustrino, « paillette »; piccolo oggetto scintillante ☆ *oak- —*, escrescenza spugnosa (sulle foglie della quercia).

to **spangle**, *v.t.i.* **1.** coprire, ornare di lustrini, di « paillettes » **2.** brillare, risplendere.

spangly ['spæŋgli], *ag.* ricoperto di lustrini.

Spaniard ['spænjəd], *s.c.* spagnolo, spagnola.

spaniel ['spænjəl], *s.* **1.** « spaniel », cane spagnolo **2.** *fig.* persona strisciante, servile; leccapiedi.

Spanish ['spæniʃ], *ag.* di Spagna, spagnolo ‖ *s.* lingua spagnola ☆ *— -black*, (*pitt.*) nero di Spagna; *— fly*, (*entom.*) cantaride; *— influenza*, (*patol.*) spagnola; *— leather*, cuoio di Cordova; *— liquorice*, liquirizia.

spank¹ [spæŋk], *s.* (*fam.*) sculacciata.

to **spank¹**, *v.t.i.* (*fam.*) **1.** sculacciare; schiaffeggiare **2.** mandare avanti a forza di sculaccioni, frustare **3.** cadere con un tonfo.

to **spank²**, *v.i.* (*fam.*) **1.** muoversi agilmente, velocemente **2.** trottare serrato (di cavalli) **3.** (*mar.*) filare.

spanker ['spæŋkə*], *s.* **1.** (*mar.*) randa **2.** cavallo veloce **3.** (*fam.*) persona, cosa eccezionale.

spanking ['spæŋkiŋ], *ag.* (*fam.*) di prim'ordine, eccellente; gagliardo, vigoroso: *— breeze*, forte brezza; *to spend a — holiday*, fare una vacanza straordinaria.

spanless ['spænlis], *ag.* (*poet.*) smisurato, sconfinato, incommensurabile.

spanner ['spænə*], *s.* (*mec.*) chiave ☆ *monkey- —* (o *screw- —* o *shifting —*), chiave inglese.

spar¹ [spɑː*], *s.* (*dial.*) trave, palo, pertica, bastone; (*mar.*) alberatura.

to **spar¹**, *pass.p.p.* **sparred** [spɑːd], *v.t.* munire di pali; (*mar.*) fornire di alberatura ‖ *to — in a field*, recingere un campo.

spar², *s.* (*min.*) spato ☆ *diamond —*, corindone.

spar³, *s.* **1.** combattimento di galli **2.** incontro di pugilato **3.** (*fam.*) scaramuccia, battibecco.

to **spar³**, *v.i.* **1.** combattersi, battersi (di galli) **2.** esercitarsi al pugilato: *to — at s.o.* (o *to — up to s.o.*), mettersi in posizione di combattimento contro qlcu. **3.** (*fam.*) venire a parole.

sparable ['spærəbl], *s.* chiodo senza testa (per suole).

spare [spɛə*], *ag.* **1.** parco, frugale, sobrio: *a — meal,* un pasto frugale **2.** magro, smilzo, sparuto: *a — man,* un uomo sparuto **3.** d'avanzo, disponibile, superfluo, in più **4.** di riserva, di ricambio (di pezzi, accessori, ecc.) ‖ *s.* pezzo di ricambio.

to **spare**, *v.t.i.* **1.** essere frugale, economo; risparmiare, risparmiarsi; economizzare, far economia: *to — no expense,* non badare a spese; *to — no pains,* non risparmiare fatica ‖ *— the rod and spoil the child,* il medico pietoso fa la piaga cancrenosa **2.** privarsi, fare a meno di; risparmiare (tempo): *they couldn't — her,* non potevano fare a meno di lei; *to have enough and to —,* avere più del necessario; *to have nothing to —,* non aver niente da buttar via, avere lo stretto necessario **3.** fare grazia di, evitare: *I want to — you all the suffering I can,* voglio risparmiarti tutta la sofferenza che posso; *to — s.o.'s life,* far grazia della vita a qlcu. ‖ *to — oneself,* risparmiare le proprie energie, evitare le fatiche.

spare, (*nei composti*): *— room,* camera in più (per gli ospiti); *— time,* tempo disponibile: *I did it as a — -time occupation,* l'ho fatto per occupare il mio tempo libero; *— parts,* pezzi di ricambio; *— wheel,* (*aut.*) ruota di scorta.

sparely ['spɛəli], *av.* **1.** parcamente, frugalmente **2.** stentatamente.

spareness ['spɛənis], *s.* magrezza, sparutezza.

sparer ['spɛərə*], *s.c.* persona economa; risparmiatore, risparmiatrice.

sparerib ['spɛərib], *s.* costoletta di maiale.

sparger ['spɑ:dʒə*], *s.* spruzzatore; innaffiatoio.

sparing ['spɛəriŋ], *ag.* **1.** parco, frugale; sobrio; economo, parsimonioso: *he is — of words,* è sobrio di parole, è di poche parole; *to be — with sthg.,* risparmiare ql.co. **2.** limitato, moderato, ristretto: *— use of sthg.,* uso moderato, limitato di ql.co. ‖ *s.* risparmio, economia.

sparingly ['spɛəriŋli], *av.* **1.** frugalmente; sobriamente; economicamente **2.** moderatamente, limitatamente.

sparingness ['spɛəriŋnis], *s.* frugalità; sobrietà; parsimonia, economia.

spark[1] [spɑ:k], *s.* **1.** scintilla, favilla: *the sparks were flying upward,* le faville volavano verso l'alto **2.** *fig.* lampo, barlume: *not even a — of hope,* neppure un barlume di speranza **3.** battuta, motto di spirito: *his conversation is full of sparks,* la sua conversazione è piena di battute di spirito **4.** (*elett.*) scintilla **5.** *pl.* (*sl. mar. aer.*) radiotelegrafista ☆ *— -arrester,* parascintille; *— -plug,* (*aut.*) candela.

to **spark**[1], *v.t.i.* **1.** emettere scintille, scintillare **2.** (*elett.*) fare esplodere, accendere (con scintille).

spark[2], *s.* uomo galante, damerino.

to **spark**[2], *v.i.* fare il damerino, fare il galante.

sparking ['spɑ:kiŋ], *s.* (*elett.*) **1.** emissione di scintille **2.** accensione mediante scintilla elettrica ☆ *— -plug,* (*aut.*) candela (d'accensione).

sparkish ['spɑ:kiʃ], *ag.* **1.** brillante, vivace; galante (di persona) **2.** elegante (di cosa).

sparkle ['spɑ:kl], *s.* **1.** scintilla, favilla **2.** scintillio; splendore **3.** vivacità di spirito.

to **sparkle**, *v.i.* **1.** emettere scintille (di fuoco) **2.** scintillare, sfavillare, brillare, risplendere (anche *fig.*): *her eyes sparkled with joy,* gli occhi le brillavano di gioia; *her wit sparkles,* ha uno spirito brillante **3.** spumeggiare, mussare (di vino).

sparkler ['spɑ:klə*], *s.* **1.** persona, cosa brillante **2.** *spec. pl.* diamante.

sparkless ['spɑ:klis], *ag.* senza scintille.

sparklet ['spɑ:klit], *s.* piccola scintilla.

sparkling ['spɑ:kliŋ], *ag.* **1.** scintillante, brillante

(anche *fig.*): *— conversation,* conversazione brillante **2.** spumante (di vino): *— wine,* vino spumante.

sparklingly ['spɑ:kliŋli], *av.* in modo scintillante, brillantemente (anche *fig.*).

sparklingness ['spɑ:kliŋnis], *s.* (*rar.*) splendore, scintillio (anche *fig.*).

sparling ['spɑ:liŋ], *s.* (*ittiol.*) eperlano.

sparrow ['spærou], *s.* (*ornit.*) passero ☆ *— -bill,* chiodo senza capocchia; *— -grass,* (*dial.*) asparago; *— -hawk,* sparviero.

sparry ['spɑ:ri], *ag.* (*min.*) spatico.

sparse [spɑ:s], *ag.* **1.** rado, poco denso **2.** che si trova, che avviene ad intervalli irregolari.

sparsely ['spɑ:sli], *av.* **1.** scarsamente, poco: *— populated,* poco popolato **2.** ad intervalli irregolari.

sparseness ['spɑ:snis], *s.* radezza, scarsità.

Sparta ['spɑ:tə], *no.pr.* (*geog. st.*) Sparta.

Spartan ['spɑ:tən], *ag.* spartano ‖ *s.c.* spartano, spartana.

Spartanly ['spɑ:tənli], *av.* spartanamente.

spasm ['spæzəm], *s.* **1.** spasmo; crampo **2.** accesso, attacco: *a — of coughing, of temper,* un attacco di tosse, di collera ‖ *to work in spasms,* (*fam.*) lavorare affannosamente.

spasmodic(al) [spæz'mɔdik(əl)], *ag.* **1.** spasmodico **2.** intermittente, discontinuo.

spasmodically [spæz'mɔdikəli], *av.* **1.** spasmodicamente **2.** in modo intermittente, in modo discontinuo.

spasmology [spæz'mɔlədʒi], *s.* spasmologia.

spastic ['spæstik], *ag.* spasmodico, spastico.

spat[1] [spæt], *s.* uova di mollusco.

to **spat**[1], *pass.p.p.* **spatted** ['spætid], *v.t.i.* deporre uova (di molluschi).

spat[2], *s.* (*abbr.* di *spatterdash*) ghettina.

spat[3], *s.* **1.** colpo secco, schiocco **2.** (*fam. amer.*) battibecco.

to **spat**[3], *v.t.i.* **1.** schioccare; battere seccamente **2.** (*fam. amer.*) avere un battibecco, litigare.

spat[4], *pass.p.p.* di to **spit**.

spatchcock ['spætʃkɔk], *s.* (*cuc.*) pollo, uccello alla griglia.

to **spatchcock**, *v.t.* **1.** (*cuc.*) cuocere (un volatile) alla griglia **2.** (*fam.*) inserire frettolosamente (parole) in un telegramma, in un messaggio, ecc.

spate [speit], *s.* piena; inondazione: *the river was in —,* il fiume era in piena.

spathaceous [spə'θeiʃəs], *ag.* (*bot.*) a forma di spata.

spathe [speið], *s.* (*bot.*) spata.

spathic ['spæθik], *ag.* (*min.*) spatico.

spathiform ['spæθifɔ:m], *ag.* (*min.*) spatiforme.

spathose [spæ'θous], *ag.* (*min.*) spatico.

spathous ['spæθəs], *ag.* (*bot.*) provvisto di spate; spatiforme.

spatial ['speiʃəl], *ag.* spaziale.

spatiality [,speiʃi'æliti], *s.* spazialità.

spatially ['speiʃəli], *av.* spazialmente, nello spazio.

spattee [spæ'ti:], *s.* ghetta di lana (da donna, bambino).

spatter ['spætə*], *s.* **1.** schizzo, spruzzatura; macchia **2.** gocciolio.

to **spatter**, *v.t.i.* **1.** schizzare, inzaccherare; macchiare: *to — s.o. with sthg.,* schizzare qlcu. con ql.co. **2.** gocciolare.

spatterdash ['spætə,dæʃ], *s. gener. pl.* uose, ghette.

spatula ['spætjulə], *s.* spatola.

spatular ['spætjulə*], **spatulate** ['spætjulit], *ag.* a forma di spatola.

spatule ['spætju:l], *s.* (*zool.*) organo a forma di spatola.

spatuliform ['spætjulifɔ:m], *ag.* a forma di spatola.

spavin ['spævin], *s.* (*vet.*) spavenio.

spavined ['spævind], *ag.* (*vet.*) affetto da spavenio.

to **spawl** [spɔ:l], *v.t.i.* sputare (anche *fig.*).

spawn [spɔ:n], *s.* **1.** uova (di pesce, mollusco, ecc.); (*spreg.*) razza, progenie **2.** (*bot.*) micelio.

to **spawn**, *v.t.i.* **1.** deporre uova (di pesci, molluschi, ecc.); (*spreg.*) generare, produrre **2.** moltiplicarsi,

spawner ['spɔ:nə*], *s.* pesce, mollusco che depone uova.
spawning ['spɔ:niŋ], *s.* fecondazione (di pesci, molluschi, ecc.).
to **spay** [spei], *v.t.* (*vet.*) castrare; asportare le ovaie a.
to **speak** [spi:k], *pass.* **spoke** [spouk], (*arc.*) **spake** [speik], *p.p.* **spoken** ['spoukən], *v.t.i.* **1.** parlare: *I will — to him*, gli parlerò; *Mr. X will — at the meeting*, il signor X parlerà alla riunione; *whom did you — with?*, con chi parlasti?; *to — well, ill of s.o., sthg.*, parlare bene, male di qlcu., ql.co. ‖ *honestly speaking*, (per parlare) francamente ‖ *roughly speaking*, approssimativamente ‖ *so to —*, per così dire ‖ *to —* (o *speaking*) *for myself*, per quel che mi riguarda **2.** parlare, usare una lingua: *do you — English?*, parlate l'inglese?; *he can — several languages*, sa parlare diverse lingue **3.** esprimere; rivelare, far conoscere, manifestare: *her conduct spoke her small mind*, la sua condotta rivelò una mente ristretta; *that speaks a generous heart*, ciò indica un cuore generoso ‖ *to — daggers*, dire cose dure, offensive ‖ *to — one's mind*, parlare liberamente, dire la propria opinione ‖ *to — s.o.'s praises*, fare l'elogio di qlcu. ‖ *to — well for*, parlare in favore di; mettere in buona luce **4.** scambiare saluti ed informazioni (di navi) **5.** produrre suoni: *the trumpets spoke*, le trombe suonarono **6.** to *— at* (*s.o.*), alludere a, fare dell'ironia su: *is he speaking at you?*, sta alludendo a te? **7.** *to — for* (*s.o.*), parlare per, essere il portavoce di; testimoniare per ‖ *that speaks volumes for his goodness*, ciò testimonia ampiamente della sua bontà **8.** *to — of* (*s.o., sthg.*), parlare di ‖ *nothing to — of*, niente d'importante ‖ *speaking of...*, a proposito di... **9.** to *— to* (*sthg.*), garantire, testimoniare: *he can — to my not having said that*, egli può testimoniare che non ho detto questo **10.** to *— out*, parlare ad alta voce; parlare francamente: *— out your mind!*, di' francamente come la pensi! **11.** to *— up*, parlare più forte, alzare la voce: *— up!*, alza la voce! ‖ *to — up for s.o.*, parlare a favore di qlcu.
speakable ['spi:kəbl], *ag.* **1.** esprimibile, dicibile **2.** pronunciabile.
speak-easy ['spi:k‚i:zi], *s.* (*sl. amer.*) bar clandestino.
speaker ['spi:kə*], *s.c.* parlatore, parlatrice; interlocutore, interlocutrice ‖ *s.* **1.** oratore **2.** annunciatore **3.** *the Speaker*, il presidente (di una seduta): *the Speaker of the House of Commons*, il presidente della Camera dei Comuni ☆ *loud- —*, altoparlante; *moving coil* (*loud*) *—*, (*rad.*) altoparlante magnetodinamico.
speakership ['spi:kəʃip], *s.* carica di presidente, presidenza.
speaking ['spi:kiŋ], *ag.* parlante, che parla; espressivo, eloquente: *— eyes*, occhi espressivi; *— likeness*, somiglianza parlante ‖ *s.* **1.** il parlare; discorso; parola: *to be on — terms*, conoscersi abbastanza da rivolgersi la parola: *they were no longer on — terms*, non si rivolgevano più la parola **2.** eloquenza, declamazione, arte oratoria.
speaking, (*nei composti*): *-trumpet*, portavoce; *—-tube*, tubo acustico, portavoce a tubo ‖ *evil- —*, maldicente.
speakingly ['spi:kiŋli], *av.* con espressione; con tono eloquente.
spear[1] [spiə*], *s.* **1.** lancia; alabarda; asta; giavellotto **2.** lanciere **3.** fiocina **4.** *pl.* spine (di piante); pinne appuntite (di pesce); aculei (di porcospino) ☆ *—-grass*, (*bot.*) gramigna; *—-shaft* (o *—-side*), discendenza maschile; *—-wood*, (*bot.*) acacia; eucalipto australiano.
to **spear**[1], *v.t.i.* **1.** pungere, trafiggere con lancia **2.** *to — up*, rizzarsi.
spear[2], *s.* germoglio; filo d'erba.
to **spear**[2], *v.i.* germogliare, germinare: *the grass is spearing* (*out*), l'erba sta germogliando.
spearhead ['spiəhed], *s.* ferro di lancia; punta di lancia ☆ *atomic —*, testata atomica.
spearman, *pl.* **spearmen** ['spiəmən], *s.* lanciere.

spearmint ['spiəmint], *s.* menta da giardino.
spec [spek], *abbr.* di **speculation**.
special ['speʃəl], *ag.* **1.** speciale, particolare; apposito: *— command*, ordine speciale; *— examination*, esame speciale; *— nothing —*, niente di particolare; *this word is used in a very — sense*, questa parola è usata con significato del tutto particolare; *what is your — work?*, quale è il vostro vero lavoro?; *to make a — study of German*, specializzarsi in tedesco ‖ *— peculiarities*, segni particolari **2.** eccezionale, straordinario; eccessivo: *— mission*, missione straordinaria; *he holds her in — honour*, egli le usa speciali onori; *to take — care over sthg.*, occuparsi in modo eccessivo di ql.co. **3.** intimo, preferito, amato: *my — friend*, il mio amico intimo ‖ *s.* **1.** chi sotto giuramento in speciali occasioni assume funzioni e prerogative di agente di polizia **2.** inviato speciale **3.** edizione straordinaria (di giornale) **4.** esame speciale (sostenuto prima della discussione della tesi di laurea) **5.** treno speciale.
special, (*nei composti*): *— constable*, chi sotto giuramento in speciali occasioni assume funzioni e prerogative di agente di polizia; *— correspondent*, inviato speciale; *— crossing*, (*comm.*) sbarramento speciale (di assegno); *— delivery*, (*amer.*) spedizione per espresso: *by — delivery*, per espresso; *— edition*, edizione straordinaria (di giornale); *— examination*, esame speciale (sostenuto prima della discussione della tesi di laurea); *— partner*, (*comm.*) socio vincolato da responsabilità limitata; *— pleader*, consulente legale; *— train*, treno speciale.
specialism ['speʃəlizəm], *s.* specializzazione.
specialist ['speʃəlist], *s.c.* specialista (anche *med.*): *to become a — in sthg.*, specializzarsi in ql.co.; *to consult a —*, consultare uno specialista.
specialistic [‚speʃə'listik], *ag.* specializzato.
speciality [‚speʃi'æliti], *s.* specialità; particolarità; caratteristica: *knitting is my —*, il lavoro a maglia è il mio forte.
specialization [‚speʃəlai'zeiʃən], *s.* specializzazione.
to **specialize** ['speʃəlaiz], *v.t.i.* **1.** specializzare, specializzarsi: *to — in sthg.*, specializzarsi in ql.co. **2.** limitare; modificare **3.** (*biol.*) differenziare.
specializing ['speʃəlaiziŋ], *s.* specializzazione.
specially ['speʃəli], *av.* specialmente, particolarmente; soprattutto.
specialty ['speʃəlti], *s.* **1.** (*comm.*) specialità, articolo speciale: *dealer in medical specialties*, commerciante in specialità medicinali **2.** (*dir.*) contratto sigillato; documento legale sotto sigillo.
specie ['spi:ʃi:], *s.* (*solo sing.*) numerario, denaro contante.
species, *pl.* **species** ['spi:ʃi:z], *s.* **1.** (*bot. zool.*) specie, classe: *the human —*, la specie umana, l'umanità **2.** sorta, genere, tipo: *books of various —*, libri di vario genere **3.** (*fil. teol.*) specie, apparenza; immagine, forma: *Eucharistic —*, specie Eucaristica.
specifiable ['spesifaiəbl], *ag.* specificabile, determinabile; distinguibile.
specific(al) [spi'sifik(əl)], *ag.* **1.** specifico; particolare: *— cause*, causa specifica **2.** preciso, determinato: *— aim*, scopo preciso ‖ *s.* (*farm.*) (rimedio) specifico ☆ *—-weight* (o *— gravity*), (*fis.*) peso specifico.
specifically [spi'sifikəli], *av.* specificatamente; particolarmente; precisamente.
specification [‚spesifi'keiʃən], *s.* **1.** specificazione ‖ *— of charge*, (*dir.*) capo d'accusa **2.** descrizione dettagliata: *— of a car*, descrizione dettagliata di una automobile.
specificity [‚spesi'fisiti], **specificness** [spi'sifiknis], *s.* specificità (di medicamento, ecc.).
to **specify** ['spesifai], *v.t.* specificare, precisare; determinare: *it is specified in the agreement*, ciò è specificato nel contratto ‖ *unless otherwise specified*, salvo indicazione contraria.
specimen ['spesimin], *s.* **1.** modello, esemplare, sag-

gio, campione: *a fine — of mosaic work*, un bell'esemplare di mosaico; *it was a — of what he could do*, era un saggio di ciò che era capace di fare; *to take a — of s.o.'s blood*, prelevare un campione di sangue a qlcu. **2.** (*fam.*) tipo, individuo; campione: *what a —!*, che tipo! ☆ — *copy*, libro in esame.

speciosity [,spi:ʃiˈositi], *s.* speciosità, apparenza ingannevole.

specious [ˈspi:ʃəs], *ag.* specioso; capzioso.

speciously [ˈspi:ʃəsli], *av.* speciosamente.

speciousness [ˈspi:ʃəsnis], *s.* speciosità.

speck¹ [spek], *s.* **1.** macchiolina, punto; chiazza **2.** granello, atomo (di polvere, ecc.) **3.** briciola, filo (di speranza, ecc.): *not a — of hope*, non un filo di speranza **4.** difetto, macchia.

to **speck¹**, *v.t.* macchiare; chiazzare.

speck², *s.* (*amer.* e *sudafricano*) **1.** carne grassa; lardo **2.** grasso, lardo (di balena, ecc.).

speckle [ˈspekl], *s.* macchiolina (specialmente sulla pelle).

to **speckle**, *v.t.* macchiare; screziare.

speckled [ˈspekld], *ag.* macchiato; screziato.

· **speckless** [ˈspeklis], *ag.* senza macchia (anche *fig.*).

specksioneer [,spekʃəˈniə*], *s.* capo ramponiere.

specs [speks], *s.pl.* (*abbr.* di *spectacles*) occhiali.

spectacle [ˈspektəkl], *s.* **1.** spettacolo; vista: *a charming —*, uno spettacolo incantevole; *to make a — of oneself*, (*fam.*) dare spettacolo di sè **2.** *pl.* occhiali: *to put on one's spectacles*, mettersi gli occhiali ‖ *she sees life through rose-coloured spectacles*, *fig.* vede la vita in rosa ☆ — *-case*, astuccio per occhiali; — *-frame*, montatura per occhiali; — *-glass*, vetro per occhiali; — *-maker*, occhialaio, ottico.

spectacled [ˈspektəkld], *ag.* **1.** che porta gli occhiali, occhialuto **2.** (*zool.*) avente macchie a forma di occhiali ☆ — *snake*, serpente con gli occhiali.

spectacular [spekˈtækjulə*], *ag.* spettacolare, grandioso; teatrale.

spectacularly [spekˈtækjuləli], *av.* spettacolosamente; in modo spettacolare.

spectator [spekˈteitə*], *s.* spettatore.

spectatress [spekˈteitris], **spectatrix** [spekˈteitriks], *s.* spettatrice.

spectral [ˈspektrəl], *ag.* **1.** spettrale, fantomatico: — *ship*, nave fantasma **2.** (*fis.*) spettrale: *the — colours*, i colori dello spettro.

spectrally [ˈspektrəli], *av.* spettralmente.

spectre [ˈspektə*], *s.* spettro, fantasma; apparizione ☆ — *-bat*, (*zool.*) vampiro; — *-lemur*, (*zool.*) tarsio.

spectrograph [ˈspektrougra:f], *s.* (*fis.*) spettrografo.

spectrographic [,spektrouˈgræfik], *ag.* (*fis.*) spettrografico.

spectrography [spekˈtrogrəfi], *s.* (*fis.*) spettrografia.

spectroheliograph [,spektrouˈhi:liougra:f], *s.* (*astr.*) spettroeliografo.

spectrometer [spekˈtromitə*], *s.* (*fis.*) spettrometro.

spectrometric [,spektrəˈmetrik], *ag.* (*fis.*) spettrometrico.

spectroscope [ˈspektrəskoup], *s.* (*fis.*) spettroscopio.

spectroscopic(al) [,spektrəsˈkɔpik(əl)], *ag.* (*fis.*) spettroscopico.

spectroscopically [,spektrəsˈkɔpikəli], *av.* (*fis.*) spettroscopicamente.

spectroscopist [spekˈtroskəpist], *s.* spettroscopista.

spectroscopy [spekˈtroskəpi], *s.* (*fis.*) spettroscopia.

spectrum [ˈspektrəm], *pl.* **spectra** [ˈspektrə], **spectrums** [ˈspektrəmz], *s.* (*fis.*) spettro ☆ — *-analysis*, analisi spettroscopica ‖ *absorption —*, spettro di assorbimento; *diffraction —*, spettro di diffrazione; *magnetic —*, spettro magnetico; *solar —*, spettro solare.

specular [ˈspekjulə*], *ag.* speculare: — *surface*, superficie speculare.

to **speculate** [ˈspekjuleit], *v.t.i.* **1.** speculare, meditare, considerare; congetturare: *to — on* (o *upon* o *about*) *sthg.*, meditare su ql.co. **2.** (*comm.*) speculare.

speculation [,spekjuˈleiʃən], *s.* **1.** speculazione, contemplazione, meditazione; congettura: *he is much given to —*, è molto portato alla meditazione **2.** (*comm.*) speculazione.

speculative [ˈspekjulətiv], *ag.* **1.** speculativo, contemplativo, meditativo; congetturale: — *philosophy*, filosofia speculativa **2.** (*comm.*) speculativo.

speculatively [ˈspekjulətivli], *av.* **1.** speculativamente; congetturalmente **2.** (*comm.*) in modo speculativo.

speculativeness [ˈspekjulətivnis], *s.* qualità speculativa, carattere speculativo.

speculator [ˈspekjuleitə*], *s.* **1.** spirito speculativo, pensatore; osservatore **2.** (*comm.*) speculatore.

speculum [ˈspekjuləm], *pl.* **specula** [ˈspekjulə], *s.* **1.** (*med.*) specolo **2.** specchio (di telescopio, ecc.) **3.** ocello (di uccello).

sped [sped], *pass.p.p.* di to **speed**.

speech [spi:tʃ], *s.* **1.** parola, favella; modo di parlare: *he is slow of —*, egli è lento nel parlare; *to lose the power* (o *the faculty*) *of —*, perdere l'uso della parola **2.** discorso, ragionamento; osservazione: *after this — he left the room*, dopo queste parole lasciò la stanza **3.** lingua, linguaggio **4.** discorso; arringa: *to make* (o *to deliver*) *a —*, fare, pronunciare un discorso ‖ *King's, Queen's —* (o — *from the throne*), discorso della Corona (all'apertura del Parlamento) ‖ *maiden —*, (*pol.*) primo discorso (di un membro del Parlamento) **5.** (*gram.*) discorso: *direct, indirect —*, discorso diretto, indiretto; *parts of —*, parti del discorso ☆ — *-day*, giorno della premiazione (nelle scuole); — *-maker*, oratore; — *-reading*, interpretazione, comprensione della parola dal movimento delle labbra.

speechification [,spi:tʃifiˈkeiʃən], *s.* (*spreg.*) l'arringare; il fare discorsi.

speechifier [ˈspi:tʃifaiə*], *s.* oratore da strapazzo.

to **speechify** [ˈspi:tʃifai], *v.i.* (*spreg.*) fare discorsi; arringare.

speechless [ˈspi:tʃlis], *ag.* **1.** senza parole, muto (anche *fig.*): — *grief*, doloro muto; *he was — with surprise*, rimase muto per la sorpresa **2.** (*sl.*) ubriaco fradicio.

speechlessly [ˈspi:tʃlisli], *av.* mutamente, senza parola.

speechlessness [ˈspi:tʃlisnis], *s.* **1.** mutismo **2.** afonia.

speed [spi:d], *s.* **1.** velocità, rapidità, celerità; fretta; passo rapido: *at full —*, a tutta velocità; *a briglia sciolta; a gambe levate*; *to do sthg. with all —*, fare ql.co. in tutta fretta ‖ *at the top of one's —*, alla massima velocità, a rotta di collo ‖ *more haste less —*, *prov.* chi ha fretta vada adagio **2.** (*arc.*) successo; prosperità: *God send you good —*, Dio ti mandi buona fortuna; *to wish s.o. good —*, augurare buona fortuna a qlcu. ☆ — *-indicator*, (*aut.*) tachimetro; — *-limit*, limite di velocità; — *-trial*, (*mar.*) prova di velocità; — *-well*, (*bot.*) veronica ‖ *top —*, velocità massima.

to **speed**, *pass.p.p.* **sped** [sped], *nel senso* **5. speeded** [ˈspi:did], *v.t.i.* **1.** affrettarsi, andare in fretta ‖ *we must — down*, dobbiamo affrettarci a scendere ‖ *to — off*, partire a grande velocità **2.** (*arc. letter.*) prosperare, aver successo; far prosperare, aiutare: *God — you!*, che Dio ti aiuti! **3.** (*arc.*) accomiatare, salutare: *to — the parting guest*, salutare l'ospite in partenza **4.** (*arc.*) far partire: *to — an arrow from the bow*, scoccare una freccia **5.** regolare la velocità di: *to — an engine*, regolare la velocità di una macchina **6.** *to — up*, accelerare, affrettare: *to — up the work*, affrettare i lavori.

speedboat [ˈspi:dbout], *s.* (*mar.*) fuoribordo.

speedcop [ˈspi:dkɔp], *s.* (*sl. amer.*) agente della Polizia Stradale.

speeder [ˈspi:də*], *s.* (*tec.*) regolatore di velocità.

speedily [ˈspi:dili], *av.* rapidamente, prontamente, affrettatamente, presto.

speediness [ˈspi:dinis], *s.* celerità, rapidità, velocità; prontezza; sollecitudine.

speedometer [spiˈdɔmitə*], *s.* (*aut.*) tachimetro, indicatore di velocità.

speedster ['spi:dstə*], *s.c.* chi guida ad alta velocità ‖ *s.* imbarcazione a motore; automobile veloce.

speedway ['spi:d-wei], *s.* **1.** pista, circuito (di autodromo) **2.** (*amer.*) autostrada.

speedy ['spi:di], *ag.* rapido, pronto, spedito, veloce, celere: *a — answer*, una risposta pronta.

speiss [spais], *s.* (*metal.*) miscela di arseniuri metallici.

spelaean [spi'li:ən], *ag.* **1.** cavernicolo **2.** a forma di caverna.

spelaeologist [,spi:li'ɔlədʒist], *s.* speleologo.

spelaeology [,spi:li'ɔlədʒi], *s.* speleologia.

spelean, *V.* **spelaean.**

spelicans ['spelikənz], *V.* **spillikin 2.**

spell[1] [spel], *s.* formula magica; incanto, incantesimo, malia; fascino, attrattiva, seduzione: *this music wields a mysterious —*, questa musica esercita un fascino misterioso; *to be under a —*, essere sotto un incantesimo; *fig.* essere ammaliato; *to be under the — of s.o.*, subire il fascino di qlcu.; *to break the —*, rompere l'incantesimo; *to cast a — over s.o.* (o *to put a — on s.o.*), gettare un incantesimo su qlcu.; *fig.* affascinare qlcu.

to spell[1], *v.t.* **1.** affascinare, incantare **2.** investire di poteri magici.

spell[2], *s.* **1.** turno (di lavoro); cambio (di sentinella, cavalli, ecc.): *to do a — of duty*, fare un turno di servizio **2.** spazio di tempo; breve periodo, momento: *he was for a — at the hospital*, fu all'ospedale per un breve periodo di tempo; *stay here for a —*, stai qui per un momento **3.** (*fam.*) breve distanza.

to spell[2], *v.t.* (*rar.*) **1.** dare il turno a, prendere il posto di, sostituire **2.** (*austral.*) lasciar riposare (un cavallo, ecc.); prendersi (un momento di riposo).

to spell[3], *pass.p.p.* **spelt** [spelt], **spelled** [speld], *v.t.i.* **1.** compitare, sillabare, scrivere le lettere di una parola: *how do you — it, please?*, come si scrive, per piacere?; *she couldn't —*, ella non sapeva l'ortografia; *to — badly*, fare errori d'ortografia ‖ *to — out* (o *over*), compitare, scrivere a stento **2.** *fig.* significare, implicare: *that change spells ruin to him*, quel cambiamento significa la rovina per lui **3.** formare parole (con lettere): *what does b.u.t. —?*, che parola formano b.u.t.?.

to spellbind ['spelbaind], *pass.p.p.* **spellbound** ['spelbaund], *v.t.* affascinare, incantare.

spellbinder ['spel,baində*], *s.* (*fam. amer.*) oratore affascinante.

spellbindery ['spel,baindəri], *s.* capacità di affascinare.

spellbound ['spelbaund], *pass.p.p.* di **to spellbind** ‖ *ag.* affascinato, incantato, ammaliato; sotto l'influenza di un incantesimo.

speller ['spelə*], *s.c.* chi compita, pronunzia; chi scrive: *to be a good, bad —*, conoscere bene, male l'ortografia ‖ *s.* sillabario.

spelling ['speliŋ], *s.* **1.** compitazione **2.** ortografia: *he is very good at —*, è molto forte in ortografia ☆ — -*bee*, gara di ortografia; — -*book*, abbecedario.

spelt[1] [spelt], *s.* (*bot.*) spelta, grano farro.

spelt[2], *pass.p.p.* di **to spell.**

spelter ['speltə*], *s.* zinco commerciale.

spelunker [spi'lʌŋkə*], *s.* (*amer.*) speleologo dilettante.

spence [spens], *s.* (*arc.*) dispensa.

spencer[1] ['spensə*], *s.* «spencer» (corta giubba di lana).

spencer[2], *s.* (*mar.*) vela di cappa.

Spencerian [spen'siəriən], *ag.* (*fil.*) spenseriano.

Spencerianism [spen'siəriənizəm], **Spencerism** ['spensərizəm], *s.* (*fil.*) dottrina di Spencer.

to spend [spend], *pass.p.p.* **spent** [spent], *v.t.i.* **1.** spendere, sborsare: *to — money on s.o., on stgh.*, spendere danaro per qlcu., per ql.co. **2.** dedicare, impiegare: *he spent a whole chapter on unimportant details*, ha dedicato un intero capitolo a dettagli senza importanza; *to — time on stgh., in doing stgh.*, dedicare il tempo a ql.co, a fare ql.co. **3.** consumare, consumarsi; esaurire,

esaurirsi: *the fire spent fast*, l'incendio si esaurì in fretta **4.** passare, trascorrere: *I spent my holidays in France*, ho trascorso le vacanze in Francia.

spendable ['spendəbl], *ag.* spendibile.

spender ['spendə*], *s.c.* chi spende ☆ — -*thrift*, dissipatore, prodigo.

spending ['spendiŋ], *s.* lo spendere; spesa.

Spenserian [spen'siəriən], *ag.* (*lett.*) spenseriano: — *stanza*, stanza spenseriana.

spent [spent], *pass.p.p.* di **to spend** ‖ *ag.* consumato; esausto, esaurito: — *cartridge*, cartuccia vuota; — *volcano*, vulcano spento.

sperm [spə:m], *s.* (*biol.*) **1.** sperma **2.** spermatozoo ☆ — -*oil*, olio di balena; — -*whale*, (*zool.*) capidoglio.

spermaceti [,spə:mə'seti], *s.* spermaceti, bianco di balena.

spermary ['spə:məri], *s.* (*anat.*) ghiandola spermatica; testicolo.

spermatic [spə'mætik], *ag.* spermatico.

spermatism ['spə:mətizəm], *s.* spermatismo.

spermatocele ['spə:mətousi:l], *s.* (*patol.*) spermatocele.

spermatorrhea [,spə:mətou'ri:ə], *s.* spermatorrea.

spermatozoon [,spə:mətou'zouən], *pl.* **spermatozoa** [,spə:mətou'zouə], *s.* (*biol.*) spermatozoo.

spew [spju:], *s.* vomito.

to spew, *v.t.i.* **1.** vomitare **2.** abbassarsi (di arma, per fuoco troppo rapido).

spewing ['spju:iŋ], *s.* vomito.

to sphacelate ['sfæsileit], *v.t.i.* incancrenire, incancrenirsi.

sphacelation [,sfæsi'leiʃən], *s.* (*patol.*) sfacelo, cancrena.

sphagnum ['sfægnəm], *s.* (*bot.*) sfagno.

sphene [sfi:n], *s.* (*min.*) sfeno, titanite.

sphenoid ['sfi:nɔid], *ag.s.* (*anat.*) sfenoide.

sphenoidal [sfi'nɔidl], *ag.* (*anat.*) sfenoidale.

sphere [sfiə*], *s.* **1.** sfera, globo; (*poet.*) cieli: *the celestial —*, la sfera celeste **2.** *fig.* ambiente; sfera: — *of action*, sfera, campo d'azione; *I belong to another —*, appartengo ad un altro ambiente.

to sphere, *v.t.* **1.** racchiudere (in una sfera); rendere sferico **2.** (*poet.*) portare alle stelle.

spheric(al) ['sferik(əl)], *ag.* sferico: — *geometry*, geometria sferica.

spherically ['sferikəli], *av.* sfericamente.

sphericity [sfi'risiti], *s.* sfericità.

spheries ['sferiks], *s.* geometria, trigonometria sferica.

spheriform ['sferifo:m], *ag.* a forma di sfera.

spheroid ['sfiərɔid], *s.* (*geom.*) sferoide.

spheroidal [sfiə'rɔidl], *ag.* (*geom.*) sferoidale.

spheroidally [sfiə'rɔidəli], *av.* (*geom.*) in modo sferoidale.

spheroidic(al) [sfiə'rɔidik(əl)], *ag.* (*geom.*) sferoidale.

spheroidicity [,sfiərɔi'disiti], *s.* (*geom.*) sferoidicità.

spherometer [sfiə'rɔmitə*], *s.* (*fis.*) sferometro.

spherular ['sferjulə*], *ag.* a forma di piccola sfera.

spherule ['sferju:l], *s.* piccola sfera, sferetta.

sphincter ['sfiŋktə*], *s.* (*anat.*) sfintere.

sphincteral ['sfiŋktərəl], **sphincterial** [sfiŋk'tiəriəl], **sphincteric** [sfiŋk'terik], *ag.* (*anat.*) sfinterico.

Sphinx [sfiŋks], *no.pr.f.* (*mit.*) Sfinge ‖ **sphinx**, *pl.* **sphinges** ['sfindʒi:z], **sphinxes** ['sfiŋksiz], **1.** (*arch.*) sfinge ‖ *the Sphinx*, la Sfinge (in Egitto) **2.** *fig.* sfinge, persona enigmatica **3.** — (-*moth*), (*entom.*) sfinge **4.** — (-*baboon*), (*zool.*) babbuino ☆ — *like*, simile a sfinge, enigmatico.

sphragistics [sfrə'dʒistiks], *s.* (*archeol.*) sfragistica.

sphygmograph ['sfigmougra:f], *s.* (*med.*) sfigmografo.

sphygmus ['sfigməs], *s.* (*fisiol.*) pulsazione, polso.

spica ['spaikə], *s.* **1.** spiga **2.** (*med.*) bendaggio a spiga.

spicate ['spaikit], *ag.* spigato; a forma di spiga.

spice [spais], *s.* **1.** spezie, aroma **2.** *fig.* sapore, gusto; sfumatura: *there was a — of malice in his speech*, vi era una sfumatura di malizia nel suo discorso; *to give — to a story*, rendere gustosa, salace una storiella ☆ *— -bush*, (*bot.*) benzoino.

to **spice**, *v.t.* **1.** condire con spezie, aromatizzare **2.** *fig.* dar sapore, gusto a; rendere interessante (racconto, ecc.)

spiced [spaist], *ag.* **1.** condito con spezie, aromatizzato **2.** *fig.* gustoso, saporoso.

spicery ['spaisəri], *s. coll.* spezie, aromi.

spicily ['spaisili], *av.* **1.** aromaticamente, profumatamente **2.** *fig.* gustosamente.

spiciness ['spaisinis], *s.* **1.** gusto aromatico; aroma, profumo **2.** (*fam. fig.*) pepe, arguzia, salacità.

spick(-)and(-)span ['spikən'spæn], *ag.* (*fam.*) lindo; accurato; fresco; lucente: *her flat is always —*, la sua casa è sempre lucida come uno specchio ‖ *s.* cosa nuova, linda.

spicular ['spikjulə*], *ag.* a punta, acuminato.

spiculate ['spikjulit], *ag.* composto, coperto di piccole punte.

spicule ['spaikju:l], *s.* **1.** piccolo corpo appuntito; punta **2.** (*zool.*) spicola (delle spugne) **3.** (*bot.*) spiga piccola, secondaria.

spicy ['spaisi], *ag.* **1.** aromatico; piccante; pepato **2.** *fig.* arguto, mordace, caustico **3.** (*fam.*) vistoso, sgargiante.

spider ['spaidə*], *s.* **1.** ragno **2.** (*amer.*) treppiedi, trespolo **3.** (*mec.*) crociera **4.** (*elett.*) sistema di bracci **5.** (*metal.*) armatura ☆ *— -catcher*, (*ornit.*) rampichino; *— -crab*, (*zool.*) maia, ragno di mare; *— -gears*, (*aut.*) satelliti; *— -line*, (*ott.*) reticolo; *— -monkey*, (*zool.*) atele; *— -web*, ragnatela.

spiderlike ['spaidəlaik], *ag.* simile a ragno.

spiderwort ['spidəwə:t], *s.* (*bot.*) tradescanzia, erba miseria.

spidery ['spaidəri], *ag.* **1.** simile a ragno **2.** infestato da ragni.

spiegeleisen ['spi:gəl,aizən], *s.* (*metal.*) ghisa speculare.

spiel [spi:l], *s.* (*sl. amer.*) discorso, allocuzione; storiella.

to **spiel**, *v.t.i.* (*sl. amer.*) pronunciare (un discorso); raccontare (una storiella); discorrere.

spieler ['spi:lə*], *s.* (*sl. amer.*) conferenziere verboso; chiacchierone; imbonitore.

spier ['spaiə*], *s.c.* spia.

spiff [spif], *ag.* (*sl.*) meraviglioso, splendido; elegante.

spiffing ['spifin], *ag.* (*sl.*) meraviglioso, splendido.

to **spifflicate** ['spiflikeit], *v.t.* (*sl.*) **1.** malmenare, maltrattare **2.** demolire; annientare.

spifflication [,spifli'keiʃən], *s.* (*sl.*) **1.** bastonata **2.** annientamento; distruzione.

spiffy ['spifi], *ag.* (*sl.*) meraviglioso, splendido; eccellente.

spigot ['spigət], *s.* **1.** zipolo, cavicchio, piuolo **2.** (*amer.*) rubinetto ☆ *— -and-socket-joint*, (*tec.*) giunto a manicotto; *tank —*, (*amer.*) rubinetto del serbatoio.

spike[1] [spaik], *s.* **1.** punta, aculeo **2.** (*tec.*) grosso chiodo a becco ☆ *— -drawer*, (*mec.*) leva a piede di capra; *— -nail*, (*ferr.*) arpione; *— -tongs*, pinza per arpioni di rotaie.

to **spike**[1], *v.t.* **1.** inchiodare; fermare con punte; munire di aculei **2.** (*mil.*) rendere inservibile (un cannone) ‖ *— s.o.'s guns*, (*fig.*) guastare i piani di qlcu.

spike[2], *s.* **1.** spiga **2.** inflorescenza a spiga ☆ *— -lavender*, spigo, lavanda; *— -oil*, essenza di làvanda.

spiked [spaikt], *ag.* fornito di punte, aculei.

spikelet ['spaiklit], *s.* (*bot.*) spighetta, špiga secondaria.

spikenard ['spaikna:d], *s.* (*bot.*) spiganardo.

spiky ['spaiki], *ag.* **1.** aguzzo, irto; munito di punte **2.** (*fam.*) intransigente: *— Anglican*, anglicano intransigente.

spile[1] [spail], *s.* **1.** piuolo, caviglia, cavicchio **2.** piccolo tappo; zipolo **3.** (*amer.*) piccolo tubo per estrarre la linfa dall'acero da zucchero.

to **spile**[1], *v.t.* **1.** tappare per mezzo di zipolo **2.** (*dial.*) spillare **3.** (*amer.*) fornire di zipolo.

spile[2], *s.* palafitta, palo di fondazione.

spiling ['spailin], *s.* **1.** *coll.* palafitte, pali **2.** *pl.* (*mar.*) (dimensioni della) curva delle assi nello scafo di una nave.

spill[1] [spil], *s.* **1.** rovesciamento **2.** caduta, capitombolo: *I had a nasty —*, ho fatto una brutta caduta.

to **spill**[1], *pass.p.p.* **spilt** [spilt], **spilled** [spild], *v.t.i.* **1.** versare, versarsi; spandere, spandersi; rovesciare, rovesciarsi; traboccare: *without spilling a drop*, senza versare una goccia ‖ *to — blood*, *fig.* versare sangue, uccidere ‖ *to — money*, (*sl.*) perdere denaro in scommesse ‖ *it is no use crying over spilt milk*, *prov.* è inutile piangere sul latte versato **2.** disarcionare; far cadere: *we were all spilled into the ditch*, fummo tutti rovesciati nel fosso **3.** (*mar.*) sventare **4.** (*sl. amer.*) divulgare ‖ *to — the beans*, svelare le magagne; fare delle indiscrezioni.

spill[2], *s.* **1.** scheggia (di legno, osso, ecc.) **2.** legnetto, carta arrotolata per accendere candele, pipe **3.** zipolo.

spill[3], *s.* **1.** bacchetta; verga **2.** perno.

spiller ['spilə*], *s.* rete da pesca a strascico.

spillikin ['spilikin], *s.* **1.** stecco di legno, d'osso **2.** *pl.* « Shangai » (giuoco fatto con stecchi).

spillway ['spilwei], *s.* sfioratore (di diga).

spilt [spilt], *pass.p.p.* di to **spill**.

spilth [spilθ], *s.* (*arc.*) **1.** ciò che è sparso **2.** eccesso, soprappiù.

spin [spin], *s.* **1.** movimento rotatorio, rotazione ‖ *to get into a —*, fare la trottola **2.** (*aer.*) avvitamento **3.** breve corsa (in bicicletta, auto, barca): *to go for a —*, andare a fare una passeggiata (in auto, ecc.).

to **spin**, *pass.* **span** [spæn], **spun** [spʌn], *p.p.* **spun**, *v.t.i.* **1.** filare: *the spider spins its web*, il ragno fila la sua ragnatela; *to — cotton*, filare il cotone **2.** (*mec.*) imbutire, lavorare al tornio **3.** *fig.* produrre, comporre, stendere (un articolo, un racconto) ‖ *to — a yarn*, (*fam.*) raccontare una storia **4.** girare, far girare; ruotare, far ruotare: *my head was spinning*, mi girava la testa; *to — a top*, far girare una trottola **5.** pescare (con l'amo) **6.** (*sl.*) bocciare, respingere agli esami **7.** (*fam.*) muoversi, girarsi rapidamente **8.** *to — along*, andare a tutta velocità (di automobile, ecc.) **9.** *to — out*, prolungare, tirare in lungo (un discorso, una discussione); passare, consumare (la vita, il tempo): *— out one's life in travelling*, passare la vita viaggiando.

spinaceous [spi'neiʃəs], *ag.* di, simile a spinace.

spinach, spinage ['spinidʒ], *s.* spinace, spinacio.

spinal ['spainl], *ag.* (*anat.*) spinale, vertebrale ☆ *— column*, colonna vertebrale; *— cord*, midollo spinale.

spindle ['spindl], *s.* **1.** fuso, fusello **2.** (*mec.*) perno, asse; mandrino **3.** (*metal.*) lanterna **4.** (*aer.*) aerometro **5.** (*mar.*) asse, albero **6.** persona, cosa sottile ☆ *— -shanks*, persona dalle gambe lunghe, affusolate; *— -shaped*, fusiforme; *— -side*, ramo femminile di una famiglia.

to **spindle**, *v.t.i.* **1.** crescere in forma lunga, affusolata; crescere in altezza (di piante) **2.** (*mec.*) dar forma fusiforme a.

spindly ['spindli], *ag.* sottile, affusolato.

spindrift ['spin-drift], *s.* spruzzaglia delle onde del mare ☆ *— clouds*, nuvole leggere, trasparenti; cirri.

spine [spain], *s.* **1.** spino, spina; lisca **2.** spina dorsale, colonna vertebrale **3.** dorso (di libro).

spined [spaind], *ag.* **1.** spinato, spinoso **2.** (*zool.*) vertebrato.

spinel [spi'nel], *s.* (*min.*) spinello.

spineless ['spainlis], *ag.* **1.** senza spine, lische **2.** senza spina dorsale **3.** (*fam.*) debole, molle, senza carattere (di persona).

spinet [spi'net], *s.* (*mus.*) spinetta.

spiniferous [spai'nifərəs], *ag.* spinoso.

spiniform ['spainifo:m], *ag.* a forma di spina.

spininess ['spaininis], *s.* spinosità.

spink [spiŋk], *s.* fringuello.

spinnaker ['spinəkə*], *s.* larga vela triangolare dei panfili da corsa.

spinner ['spinə*], *s.* **1.** ragno filatore **2.** (*ind. tessile*) macchina filatrice ‖ *s.c.* **1.** filatore, filatrice **2.** (*fam.*) narratore, narratrice; chiacchierone, chiacchierona.

spinneret ['spinəret], *s.* **1.** (*ind. tessile*) filiera **2.** filiera (di ragno); ghiandole salivari (di baco da seta).

spinnery ['spinəri], *s.* filanda.

spinney ['spini], *s.* boschetto, sottobosco.

spinning ['spiniŋ], *s.* **1.** (*ind. tessile*) filatura; filato **2.** movimento rotatorio, rotazione ☆ — -*frame*, (*ind. tessile*) filatoio; — -*jenny*, (*ind. tessile*) gianetta; — -*mill* (o — *factory*), stabilimento di filatura, filanda; — -*wheel*, filatoio.

spinose ['spainous], *ag.* spinoso.

spinosity [spai'nositi], *s.* **1.** problema, argomento spinoso **2.** (*arc.*) spinosità.

spinous ['spainəs], *ag.* spinoso.

Spinozism [spi'nouzizəm], *s.* (*fil.*) spinozismo.

Spinozist [spi'nouzist], *ag.s.* (*fil.*) spinoziano.

spinster ['spinstə*], *s.* **1.** filatrice **2.** (*dir.*) donna nubile; (*fam.*) zitella.

spinsterhood ['spinstəhud], *s.* **1.** l'essere nubile; condizione di zitella **2.** *coll.* (*fam.*) zitelle.

spinstress ['spinstris], *s.* filatrice.

spinthariscope [spin'θæriskoup], *s.* spinteriscopio.

spinule ['spainju:l], *s.* spinola; lischetta.

spinuliferous [,spainju'lifərəs], **spinulose** ['spainjulous], **spinulous** ['spainjuləs], *ag.* pieno di spine, spinoso.

spiny ['spaini], *ag.* **1.** pieno di spine, spinoso **2.** *fig.* spinoso, difficile; imbarazzante.

spiracle ['spairəkl], *s.* orifizio per respirare; sfiatatoio (dei cetacei); stimma (degli insetti).

spiracular [spai'rækjulə*], *ag.* (*zool.*) di, che serve da orifizio, stimma, sfiatatoio.

spiraculate [spai'rækjulit], *ag.* (*zool.*) fornito di orifizio, stimma, sfiatatoio.

spiraea [spai'riə], *s.* (*bot.*) spirea.

spiral ['spaiərəl], *ag.* spirale, a spirale, elicoidale ‖ *s.* **1.** (*geom.*) spirale, elica **2.** *fig.* movimento graduale di ascesa, discesa.

to **spiral**, *pass.p.p.* **spiralled** ['spaiərəld], *v.t.i.* **1.** formare una spirale; girare a spirale **2.** dar forma spirale a **3.** *to* — **down**, (*aer.*) discendere a spirale **4.** *to* — **up**, (*aer.*) salire a spirale.

spirality [spaiə'ræliti], *s.* forma di spirale.

spirally ['spaiərəli], *av.* spiralmente, a spirale.

spirant ['spaiərənt], *ag.s.* (*fonet.*) spirante.

spire[1] ['spaiə*], *s.* **1.** guglia; cuspide **2.** (*rar.*) stelo (d'erba); vetta (di albero).

to **spire**[1], *v.t.i.* **1.** innalzarsi a guglia; fornire di guglie **2.** spuntare, germogliare.

spire[2], *s.* spira; spirale.

spired ['spaiəd], *ag.* a punta; a guglia.

spirit ['spirit], *s.* **1.** spirito, anima: *God is pure* —, Dio è puro spirito; *he is vexed in* —, ha l'animo tormentato; *we were with you in* —, eravamo con te in spirito ‖ *the* — *of the times*, lo spirito del tempo **2.** spirito; folletto; fantasma; essere incorporeo: *are these phenomena really the work of spirits?*, sono veramente opera di spiriti questi fenomeni?; *to raise a* —, evocare uno spirito **3.** spirito, genio, intelletto: *he is a noble* —, è un nobile intelletto; *he is recognized as one of the greatest spirits of his day*, è riconosciuto come uno dei più grandi ingegni del suo tempo **4.** coraggio; vigore; vivacità, brio: *a young man of* —, un giovane pieno di energia; *the king faced his accusers with* —, il re affrontò i suoi accusatori con coraggio **5.** *pl.* umore, disposizione, stato d'animo: *to be in high spirits*, avere il morale alto; *to be out of spirits* (o *in low spirits*), essere depresso; *to break s.o.'s spirits*, deprimere il morale di qlcu.; *to keep up one's spirits*, tenersi su di morale **6.** intendimento, significato: *he obeyed the true* — *of the law*, si attenne al vero spirito della legge ‖

to enter into the — *of sthg.*, entrare nello spirito di ql.co. ‖ *to take sthg. in a* (o *the*) *wrong* —, prendere ql.co. in mala parte **7.** spirito, alcool **8.** *pl.* bevande fortemente alcooliche ☆ — -*blue*, blu anilina; — -*lamp*, lampada a spirito; — -*level*, livella a bolla d'aria; — -*rapper*, medium; — -*rapping*, spiritismo; — -*trade*, commercio di liquori.

to **spirit**, *v.t.* **1.** *to* — (**away**), rapire, portar via **2.** *to* — **up**, animare; rallegrare; incoraggiare.

spirited ['spiritid], *ag.* brioso, vivace; animoso; ardente, focoso ☆ *high-* —, fiero, ardente; *mean-* —, meschino; *poor-* —, fiacco; vile; *public-* —, dotato di senso di civismo.

spiritedly ['spiritidli], *av.* coraggiosamente, animosamente; ardentemente; con foga, con vigore.

spiritedness ['spiritidnis], *s.* coraggio; slancio; vigoria, energia; brio, vivacità.

spiritism ['spiritizəm], *s.* spiritismo.

spiritist ['spiritist], *s.c.* spiritista.

spiritistic [,spiri'tistik], *ag.* spiritico.

spiritless ['spiritlis], *ag.* **1.** inanimato, esanime **2.** monotono; insulso **3.** pusillanime **4.** abbattuto, avvilito; fiacco, apatico.

spiritlessly ['spiritlisli], *av.* **1.** senz'anima, senza vita **2.** da pusillanime **3.** mollemente, fiaccamente, apaticamente.

spiritlessness ['spiritlisnis], *s.* **1.** apatia **2.** monotonia **3.** pusillanimità **4.** abbattimento, avvilimento.

spiritous ['spiritəs], *ag.* (*arc.*) **1.** spiritoso **2.** alcoolico.

spiritual ['spiritjuəl], *ag.* spirituale, dello spirito: — *life*, vita spirituale ‖ — *gifts*, (*teol.*) i doni dello Spirito Santo ‖ *Lords Spiritual*, vescovi membri del Parlamento inglese.

spiritual, *s.* (*amer.*) canto religioso negro.

spiritualism ['spiritjuəlizəm], *s.* **1.** (*fil.*) spiritualismo **2.** spiritismo.

spiritualist ['spiritjuəlist], *s.c.* **1.** spiritualista **2.** spiritista.

spiritualistic [,spiritjuə'listik], *ag.* **1.** spiritualistico **2.** spiritistico.

spirituality [,spiritju'æliti], *s.* **1.** spiritualità **2.** *pl.* (*st.*) beni ecclesiastici.

spiritualization [,spiritjuəlai'zeifən], *s.* spiritualizzazione.

to **spiritualize** ['spiritjuəlaiz], *v.t.* spiritualizzare.

spiritually ['spiritjuəli], *av.* spiritualmente.

spiritualness ['spiritjuəlnis], *s.* spiritualità.

spirituel(le) [,spi:ri:,tju:'el], *ag.* raffinato; delicato, sensibile; grazioso (generalmente di donna).

spirituous ['spiritjuəs], *ag.* alcoolico, spiritoso.

spirituousness ['spiritjuəsnis], *s.* alcoolicità.

spiritus ['spiritəs], *s.* (*gram. greca*) spirito: — *asper*, *lenis*, spirito aspro, dolce.

spirivalve ['spairivælv], *ag.* con guscio a spirale.

spirket(t)ing ['spə:kitiŋ], *s.* (*mar.*) serretta di trincarino.

spirometer [,spaiə'romitə*], *s.* spirometro.

spirt [spə:t], *s.* zampillo, getto improvviso.

to **spirt**, *v.t.i.* **1.** schizzare, far schizzare; sprizzare, zampillare **2.** *to* — **out**, sprizzar fuori.

spiry[1] ['spaiəri], *ag.* **1.** a punta; simile a guglia; slanciato **2.** ricco di guglie (di città).

spiry[2], *ag.* a spire, a spirale; avviticchiato.

spit[1] [spit], *s.* **1.** (*cuc.*) spiedo, schidione **2.** (*geog.*) lingua di terra; banco lungo e stretto **3.** (*spreg.*) spada.

to **spit**[1], *pass.p.p.* **spitted** ['spitid], *v.t.* **1.** mettere allo spiedo, schidionare **2.** trafiggere.

spit[2], *s.* sputo; saliva ‖ *the very* — *of*, (*fam.*) il ritratto (parlante) di ☆ — *box*, sputacchiera.

to **spit**[2], *pass.p.p.* **spat** [spæt], (*arc. amer.*) **spit**, *v.t.i.* **1.** sputare (saliva, sangue, ecc.) **2.** fare rumore come di chi sputa (in segno di rabbia, disprezzo) **3.** cadere lievemente (di pioggia) **4.** mandar faville (di fuoco, candela, ecc.) **5.** spruzzare inchiostro (di penna) **6.** *to* — *at*, *upon* (*s.o.*, *sthg.*), trattare con disprezzo **7.** *to* — **out**, *fig.* dire, pronunciare con violenza, sputar fuori: — *it out!*, (*sl.*) sputa fuori!, di' quello che devi dire!.

spit[3], *s.* 1. vangata 2. profondità raggiunta con una vangata.

spitchcock ['spitʃkɔk], *s.* (*cuc.*) anguilla aperta e arrostita (sulla graticola).

to spitchcock, *v.t.* (*cuc.*) aprire ed arrostire sulla graticola (anguille, pesci, ecc.).

spite [spait], *s.* dispetto, ripicco; rancore, malevolenza: *out of* — (o *from* —), per dispetto, per picca; *to have a* — *against s.o.*, portare rancore a qlcu. || *in* — *of*, nonostante, malgrado, a dispetto di.

to spite, *v.t.* far dispetto a, importunare, vessare, contrariare.

spiteful ['spaitful], *ag.* dispettoso; vendicativo; malevolo; malintenzionato.

spitefully ['spaitfuli], *av.* per dispetto; con rancore; in modo vendicativo.

spitefulness ['spaitfulnis], *s.* rancore, malevolenza.

spitfire ['spitfaiə*], *s.* 1. persona collerica, violenta, irascibile 2. « spitfire » (aereo da caccia).

spitted ['spitid], *ag.* (*cuc.*) allo spiedo.

spitter ['spitə*], *s.* chi sputa.

spitting ['spitiŋ], *s.* sputo; espettorazione; lo sputare ☆ — *-box*, sputacchiera.

spittle ['spitl], *s.* sputo; saliva, bava.

spittoon [spi'tu:n], *s.* sputacchiera.

spitz [spits], *s.* (*zool.*) pomero.

spiv [spiv], *s.* (*sl.*) persona che vive di espedienti.

splanchnic ['splæŋknik], *ag.* splancnico, viscerale ☆ — *nerves*, (*anat.*) grande e piccolo splancnico.

splanchnology [splæŋk'nɔlədʒi], *s.* (*anat.*) splancnologia.

splanchnotomy [splæŋk'nɔtəmi], *s.* (*chir.*) splancnotomia.

splash [splæʃ], *s.* 1. schizzo, spruzzo; (*fam.*) spruzzo d'acqua di seltz: *whisky and a* —, whisky al seltz || *to make a* —, *fig.* far colpo, attrarre l'attenzione 2. tonfo: *to fall with a* —, cadere con un tonfo 3. pillacchera; macchia, chiazza: *a* — *of colour*, una macchia di colore; *splashes of rain on the ground*, gocce di pioggia sul terreno; *you have a* —| *on your dress*, hai una macchia sul vestito 4. (*fam.*) cipria: *to put on the* —, mettersi la cipria ☆ — *-board*, parafango; paraurti; — *headline*, titolo sensazionale.

to splash, *v.t.i.* 1. schizzare, spruzzare; cadere, far cadere: *to* — *gravy over the table*, versare sugo sulla tavola; *to* — *water about*, spruzzare acqua tutt'intorno || *to* — *one's money about*, *fig.* scialacquare il proprio denaro 2. inzaccherare, infangare; impantanarsi: *to* — *s.o. with mud* (o *to* — *mud over s.o.*), inzaccherare, infangare qlcu. 3. cadere con un tonfo (in acqua): *he splashed into the water*, cadde nell'acqua con un tonfo 4. diguazzare: *to* — (*one's way*) *through the river*, attraversare il fiume diguazzando 5. macchiare: *to* — *ink on sthg.*, macchiare ql.co. d'inchiostro.

splasher ['splæʃə*], *s.* 1. schizzatore, spruzzatore 2. parafango 3. racchetta| per camminare su terreno melmoso.

splashing ['splæʃiŋ], *s.* schizzata, spruzzata; spruzzamento.

splashy ['splæʃi], *ag.* 1. bagnato; fangoso, melmoso, limaccioso 2. pieno di pozzanghere.

to splatter ['splætə*], *v.t.i.* 1. schizzare, spruzzare; sciabordare 2. barbugliare (una lingua).

splatterdash ['splætədæʃ], *s.* 1. chiasso, clamore 2. *pl.* uose, ghette.

splay [splei], *ag.* 1. largo e piatto 2. obliquo; storto; volto verso l'esterno 3. (*edil.*) strombato || *s.* (*edil.*) sguancio, strombo; svasatura ☆ — *-foot*, piede piatto volto all'infuori; — *mouth*, bocca larga; smorfia.

to splay, *v.t.i.* 1. (*arch.*) svasare; strombare, sguanciare (una finestra, ecc.) 2. essere in posizione obliqua 3. slogare; spallare: *to* — *a horse*, spallare un cavallo.

spleen [spli:n], *s.* 1. (*anat.*) milza 2. *fig.* malumore, umore nero; bile, collera: *in a fit of* —, in un momento di malumore; *to have the* —, essere di cattivo umore; *to vent one's* — (*up*)*on s.o.*, scaricare la propria collera su qlcu., sfogare la propria stizza su qlcu. ☆ — *pulp*, polpa splenica.

spleenful ['spli:nful], **spleenish** ['spli:niʃ], *ag.* 1. ipocondriaco, bilioso 2. malinconico; di cattivo umore.

spleenfully ['spli:nfuli], **spleenishly** ['spli:niʃli], *av.* 1. malinconicamente 2. stizzosamente.

spleenless ['spli:nlis], *ag.* di buon umore.

spleenwort ['spli:nwə:t], *s.* (*bot.*) asplenio.

spleeny ['spli:ni], *V.* **spleenful**.

splenalgia [spli'nældʒiə], *s.* (*patol.*) splenalgia.

splendent ['splendənt], *ag.* rilucente, lucente, brillante.

splendid ['splendid], *ag.* 1. splendido, magnifico, stupendo; sfarzoso: *a* — *victory*, una splendida vittoria; — *weather*, tempo splendido; *she was simply* —!, era semplicemente meravigliosa! 2. (*fam.*) eccellente, ottimo: |*a* — *friend*, un ottimo amico; *a* — *idea*, un'idea eccellente; *that's* —!, fantastico!.

splendidly ['splendidli], *av.* splendidamente, magnificamente, superbamente.

splendidness ['splendidnis], *s.* splendidezza, magnificenza.

splendiferous [splen'difərəs], *ag.* (*fam.*) splendido, magnifico, stupendo.

splendour ['splendə*], *s.* splendore, lustro, magnificenza; pompa; imponenza, grandezza.

splenectomy [spli'nektəmi], *s.* (*chir.*) splenotomia.

splenetic [spli'netik], *ag.s.* 1. (*patol.*) splenetico, bilioso 2. collerico, irritabile; stizzoso.

splenetically [spli'netikəli], *av.* biliosamente; stizzosamente.

splenial ['spli:niəl], *ag.* (*anat.*) dello splenio.

splenic ['splenik], *ag.* (*anat.*) splenico ☆ — *fever*, (*patol.*) carbonchio.

splenitis [spli'naitis], *s.* (*patol.*) splenite.

splenius ['spli:niəs], *pl.* **splenii** ['spli:niai], *s.* (*anat.*) splenio.

splenization [,spleni'zeiʃən], *s.* (*patol.*) splenificazione.

splenotomy [spli'nɔtəmi], *s.* (*chir.*) splenotomia.

splice [splais], *s.* 1. (*mar.*) impiombatura 2. (*carpenteria mec.*) giunto a ganasce, giunto assiale ☆ *eye-* —, (*mar.*) impiombatura di gassa.

to splice, *v.t.* 1. (*mar.*) impiombare 2. (*carpenteria mec.*) calettare 3. (*cine.*) montare (un film) 4. (*fam.*) unire in matrimonio: *to get spliced*, sposarsi 5. *to* — *the main-brace*, (*mar.*) distribuire una razione supplementare di rum.

splicing ['splaisiŋ], *s.* 1. (*mar.*) impiombatura 2. (*carpenteria mec.*) calettatura, giuntura 3. (*cine.*) montaggio.

spline [splain], *s.* 1. (*mec.*) chiavetta, linguetta (per fissare la ruota sull'asse) 2. striscia di legno flessibile (per disegnare curve) 3. scanalatura.

to spline, *v.t.* 1. (*mec.*) fornire di chiavetta, linguetta 2. scanalare.

splint [splint], *s.* 1. (*med.*) assicella, stecca 2. scheggia 3. (*vet.*) sopprosso, tumore duro (sulle gambe di un cavallo) ☆ — *-armour*, armatura a scaglie.

to splint, *v.t.* (*med.*) steccare, fissare con assicelle (un arto fratturato).

splinter ['splintə*], *s.* 1. scheggia, frantume 2. (*med.*) stecca 3. (*vet.*) sopprosso ☆ — *-bar*, bilancino; — *-bone*, (*anat.*) fibula; — *-proof*, antischegge (specialmente schegge di proiettile, ecc.).

to splinter, *v.t.i.* 1. scheggiare, scheggiarsi; frantumare, frantumarsi; fendere, fendersi 2. (*med.*) sostenere con stecche.

splintery ['splintəri], *ag.* 1. pieno di schegge 2. simile a scheggia 3. scheggioso, scheggiabile.

split [split], *ag.* spaccato, diviso || *s.* 1. fessura; spaccatura; crepaccio; strappo (di tessuto) 2. divisione, separazione; rottura; scissione 3. giunco (per canestri) **4.** (*sl.*) mezza bottiglia, quarto di bottiglia (di bibita, acqua minerale); mezzo bicchierino (di liquore) **5.** *pl.* (*ginnastica*) spaccata: *to do the splits*, fare la spaccata.

to **split**, *pass.p.p.* **split**, *v.t.i.* **1.** fendere, fendersi; spaccare, spaccarsi; scheggiare, scheggiarsi ‖ *my head is splitting*, mi scoppia la testa ‖ *to* — *hairs*, *fig.* spaccare un capello in quattro ‖ *to* — *on a rock*, *fig.* trovare difficoltà insuperabili ‖ *to* — *one's sides* (*with laughing*), ridere a crepapelle **2.** strappare, strapparsi; stracciare, stracciarsi: *he* — *his shirt*, si strappò la camicia **3.** dividere, dividersi; ripartire; frazionare, frazionarsi; scindere, scindersi: *the Church is* — *by parties*, la Chiesa è divisa dalle fazioni; *to* — *an apple*, dividere una mela in due; *to* — *the atom*, (*fis.*) scindere l'atomo; *to* — *the profits*, dividere i profitti **4.** *to* — *on* (*s.o.*), (*sl.*) denunciare, tradire **5.** *to* — *off*, distaccare, distaccarsi; separare, separarsi **6.** *to* — **up**, frazionare, frazionarsi; suddividere, suddividersi (anche *fig.*).

split, (*nei composti*): — -*flap*, (*aer.*) ipersostentatore a spacco; — -*grid*, mezza griglia; — -*image*, (*tv.*) immagine divisa; — -*mind*, (*patol.*) schizofrenia; — -*peas*, piselli secchi sgusciati e divisi a metà; — -*personality*, tendenza alla schizofrenia; — -*pin*, chiavetta; — -*pulley*, puleggia divisa; — -*ring*, anello doppio; — -*second*, frazione di secondo.

splitter ['splitə*], *s.c.* **1.** chi fende; spaccalegna **2.** *fig.* (*hair-*) —, cavillatore, cavillatrice ☆ *side-* —, barzelletta; persona assai divertente.

splitting ['splitiŋ], *ag.* **1.** che si fende **2.** che fende; *fig.* acuto: *a* — *headache*, un acuto mal di testa ‖ *s.* **1.** fessura, spaccatura; scheggiamento: — *of the atom*, (*fis.*) disintegrazione dell'atomo **2.** divisione; separazione.

splodge [splɔdʒ], *s.* macchia, chiazza.

splosh [splɔʃ], *s.* **1.** (*fam.*) getto d'acqua **2.** (*sl.*) denaro.

splotch [splɔtʃ], *s.* macchia, chiazza.

to **splotch**, *v.t.* macchiare, chiazzare.

splotchy ['splɔtʃi], *ag.* macchiato, chiazzato.

splurge [splə:dʒ], *s.* (*fam.*) ostentazione, esibizionismo.

to **splurge**, *v.i.* (*fam.*) darsi arie.

to **splutter** ['splʌtə*], *v.t.i.* **1.** barbugliare, parlare in modo confuso **2.** sputacchiare (nel parlare); spruzzare (di penna) **3.** crepitare.

splutterer ['splʌtərə*], *s.* barbuglione.

spoffish ['spɔfiʃ], *ag.* (*sl.*) rumoroso, chiassoso.

spoil [spɔil], *s. gener. pl.* **1.** spoglia, preda; bottino; *fig.* profitto, vantaggio **2.** spoglia (di serpenti); carcame **3.** (*miner.*) detrito ☆ *spoils-system*, (*amer.*) sistema di favorire i fautori del partito al potere attribuendo loro cariche, uffici, ecc.

to **spoil**, *pass.p.p.* **spoiled** [spɔild], **spoilt** [spɔilt], *v.t.i.* **1.** rovinare, danneggiare; alterare; sciupare, deturpare; viziare: *he spoils his child*, egli vizia suo figlio; *that news spoilt my holiday*, quella notizia mi rovinò le vacanze; *to* — *the beauty of sthg.*, *s.o.*, deturpare la bellezza di ql.co., qlcu. **2.** saccheggiare, predare; rubare **3.** guastarsi, avariarsi, alterarsi (di cibi): *this fruit will* — *before to morrow*, questa frutta si guasterà prima di domani.

spoiler ['spɔilə*], *s.c.* saccheggiatore, saccheggiatrice; predatore, predatrice.

spoiling ['spɔiliŋ], *s.* **1.** deterioramento, avaria **2.** (*arc.*) saccheggio, ruberia.

spoilt [spɔilt], *ag.* guasto, avariato, rovinato; viziato: *a* — *child*, un bimbo viziato.

spoke¹ [spɔuk], *s.* **1.** (*mec.*) razza, raggio (di ruota) **2.** piuolo (di scala) **3.** (*mar.*) impugnatura del timone; maniglia **4.** bastone per arrestare le ruote di un carro ‖ *to put a* — *in s.o.'s wheel*, mettere i bastoni fra le ruote a qlcu.

to **spoke¹**, *v.t.* **1.** mettere i raggi a (una ruota) **2.** arrestare (le ruote) di un carro **3.** *fig.* impedire, ostacolare.

spoke², *pass.* di to **speak**.

spoken ['spɔukən], *p.p.* di to **speak**.

spokesman, *pl.* **spokesmen** ['spɔuksmən], *s.* portavoce.

spokeswoman ['spɔuks,wumən], *pl.* **spokeswomen** ['spɔuks,wimin], *s.* portavoce.

to **spoliate** ['spɔulieit], *v.t.i.* saccheggiare, commettere saccheggi.

spoliation [,spɔuli'eiʃən], *s.* **1.** ruberia, saccheggio **2.** (*dir.*) distruzione, alterazione (di documenti).

spoliator ['spɔulieitə*], *s.* saccheggiatore.

spoliatory ['spɔuliətəri], *ag.* che saccheggia; predace.

spondaic(al) [spɔn'deiik(əl)], *ag.* (*poes.*) spondaico.

spondee ['spɔndi:], *s.* (*poes.*) spondeo.

spondyle ['spɔndil], *s.* (*anat.*) spondilo.

sponge [spʌndʒ], *s.* **1.** spugna ‖ *to pass the* — *over an offence*, (*fam.*) passare la spugna su un'offesa ‖ *to throw up the* —, (*boxe*) gettare la spugna, abbandonare il combattimento **2.** colpo di spugna; spugnatura **3.** (*med.*) compressa, batuffolo **4.** (*cuc.*) pasta morbida; dolce spugnoso **5.** (*artigl.*) scovolo **6.** *fig.* spugna, scroccone, parassita **7.** parassitismo ☆ — -*bath*, (*med.*) spugnatura; — -*cloth*, (*ind. tessile*) spugna; — -*fisher*, pescatore di spugne; — -*iron*, (*metal.*) ferro spugnoso.

to **sponge**, *v.t.i.* **1.** pulire, lavare (con la spugna); (*ind. tessile*) decatizzare **2.** (*med.*) fare spugnature a **3.** pescare spugne **4.** *fig.* scroccare: *to* — *a dinner*, scroccare un pranzo **5.** *to* — *on* (*s.o.*), vivere alle spalle di (qlcu.): *to* — *on s.o. for drinks*, scroccare da bere a qlcu. **6.** *to* — **down**, (*med.*) passare con la spugna il corpo di **7.** *to* — **out**, cancellare (anche *fig.*): — *that out of your memory!*, dimenticalo! **8.** — **up**, assorbire con spugna (acqua, ecc.).

spongecake ['spʌndʒ'keik], *s.* pan di Spagna; savoiardo.

spongeous ['spʌndʒəs], *ag.* spugnoso.

sponger ['spʌndʒə*], *s.* **1.** pescatore di spugne **2.** parassita, scroccone.

spongiform ['spʌndʒifɔ:m], *ag.* spongiforme.

sponginess ['spʌndʒinis], *s.* spugnosità.

sponging ['spʌndʒiŋ], *s.* **1.** lavatura con la spugna; (*ind. tessile*) decatizzazione **2.** parassitismo **3.** pesca delle spugne ☆ — -*house*, prigione provvisoria per debitori.

spongiopiline [,spʌndʒiou'pailain], *s.* (*med.*) tessuto spugnoso impermeabilizzato su una delle superfici che, imbevuto di acqua calda, viene usato come impiastro.

spongious ['spʌndʒiəs], *ag.* (*arc.*) spugnoso.

spongy ['spʌndʒi], *ag.* spugnoso, poroso; elastico; assorbente ☆ — *platinum*, (*chim.*) spugna di platino.

sponsal ['spɔnsəl], *ag.* sponsale.

sponsion ['spɔnʃən], *s.* (*dir.*) malleveria, garanzia.

sponson ['spɔnsn], *s.* **1.** (*mar.*) piattaforma sporgente per cannoni **2.** (*aer. mar.*) cassa d'aria (laterale) stabilizzatrice.

sponsor ['spɔnsə*], *s.c.* (*eccl.*) padrino, madrina: *to stand* — *to a child*, tenere a battesimo un bambino ‖ *s.* **1.** (*dir.*) garante, mallevadore **2.** chi offre un programma radiofonico (a scopo pubblicitario): *to be* — *to a programme*, offrire un programma ☆ *fellow* —, compare, comare.

to **sponsor**, *v.t.* **1.** rendersi responsabile di; essere garante di **2.** offrire (un programma radiofonico): *this concert is sponsored by the X Company*, questo concerto è offerto dalla ditta X.

sponsorial [spɔn'sɔ:riəl], *ag.* **1.** di garanzia, di malleveria **2.** di padrino, di madrina.

sponsorship ['spɔnsəʃip], *s.* **1.** garanzia **2.** condizione, qualità di padrino, di madrina **3.** pubblicità radiofonica: *radio programs depend on* (*commercial*) —, i programmi radiofonici dipendono dalla pubblicità (commerciale).

spontaneity [,spɔntə'ni:iti], *s.* spontaneità.

spontaneous [spɔn'teinjəs], *ag.* spontaneo; involontario; automatico.

spontaneously [spɔn'teinjəsli], *av.* spontaneamente; involontariamente; automaticamente.

spontaneousness [spɔn'teinjəsnis], *s.* spontaneità.

spontoon [spɔn'tu:n], *s.* spuntone (specie di alabarda).

spoof [spu:f], *s.* (*sl.*) truffa, imbroglio, frode.

to **spoof**, *v.t.* (*sl.*) truffare, imbrogliare, frodare.

spook [spu:k], *s.* (*fam.*) spettro, apparizione.

to **spook**, *v.t.* frequentare (di spettro).

spool [spu:l], *s.* rocchetto, bobina: — *of cotton*, rocchetto di cotone ☆ *delivery* (o *feed*) —, bobina svolgitrice; *take-up* —, (*cine.*) bobina ricevitrice.

to **spool**, *v.t.* (*ind. tessile*) 1. avvolgere su rocchetto, incannare (filo, seta, ecc.) 2. *to* — *off*, svolgere.

to **spoom** [spu:m], *v.i.* (*mar.*) navigare velocemente.

spoon [spu:n], *s.* 1. cucchiaio || *to be born with a silver* — *in one's mouth*, essere nato con la camicia 2. (*chir.*) cucchiaio 3. (*golf*) mazza 4. esca metallica 5. (*st.*) l'ultimo nell'elenco dei laureati in matematica (a Cambridge) 6. (*sl.*) sempliciotto 7. (*sl.*) cascamorto || *to be spoons on*, essere innamorato cotto di ☆ — *-bill*, (*ornit.*) spatola; — *-wort*, (*bot.*) coclearia || *dessert-* —, cucchiaino da dessert; *table-* —, cucchiaio da tavola.

to **spoon**, *v.t.i.* 1. prendere con un cucchiaio: *to* — (*out*) *the cream*, servire la crema (con cucchiaio); *to* — (*up*) *one's soup*, mangiare la minestra 2. pescare con esca metallica 3. (*croquet*) accompagnare la palla con la mazza; (*cricket*) battere (la palla) debolmente 4. combaciare, far combaciare 5. scavare 6. (*sl.*) fare la corte a, fare il cascamorto a.

spoondrift ['spu:n-drift], *V.* **spindrift**.

to **spoon-feed** ['spu:n-fi:d], *pass.p.p.* **spoon-fed** ['spu:n-fed], *v.t.* 1. nutrire (un bambino) col cucchiaio 2. (*fam. fig.*) far la pappa a, coccolare.

spoonful ['spu:nful], *s.* cucchiaiata: *two spoonfuls of sugar*, due cucchiai di zucchero.

spoonily ['spu:nili], *av.* (*sl.*) 1. scioccamente 2. svenevolmente.

spooniness ['spu:ninis], *s.* (*sl.*) 1. stupidaggine, credulità 2. svenevolezza.

spoonmeat ['spu:n-mi:t], *s.* cibo liquido.

spoony ['spu:ni], *ag.* (*sl.*) 1. stupido 2. svenevole: — *eyes*, occhi di triglia || *s.* (*sl.*) cascamorto, spasimante.

spoor [spuə*], *s.* traccia, odore, pista (di animale).

to **spoor**, *v.t.i.* seguire una pista, una traccia di (animale).

spoorer ['spuərə*], *s.* chi segue piste, tracce di animali.

sporadic(al) [spə'rædik(əl)], *ag.* sporadico (anche *med.*); isolato, raro: *it is a* — *fact*, è un fatto sporadico ☆ — *cholera*, (*med.*) dissenteria colerisimile.

sporadically [spə'rædikəli], *av.* sporadicamente.

sporadicalness [spə'rædikəlnis], *s.* sporadicità.

sporangium [spə'rændʒiəm], *pl.* **sporangia** [spə'rændʒiə], *s.* (*bot.*) sporangio.

sporation [spə'reiʃən], *s.* (*bot.*) sporulazione.

spore [spɔ:*], *s.* (*biol. bot.*) spora ☆ — *-case*, sporangio.

sporran ['spɔrən], *s.* borsa coperta di pelo (accessorio del costume scozzese).

sport [spɔ:t], *s.* 1. giuoco; divertimento; passatempo || *to be the* — *of fortune*, *fig.* essere lo zimbello della fortuna || *to spoil the* —, guastare la festa 2. scherzo, burla: *in* —, per burla || *to make* — *of s.o.*, farsi giuoco di qlcu. 3. sport: *to go in for sports*, darsi agli sport 4. *pl.* gare, incontri 5. (*biol.*) specie anomala (di piante, animali) 6. (*sl.*) persona sportiva; *fig.* persona di spirito: *he is a* (*real*) —, è un buon giocatore; *fig.* è un tipo chic; *come, be a* —*!*, orsù, sii sportivo!, prendila con spirito! 7. (*amer.*) giocatore d'azzardo ☆ *sports-edition*, edizione sportiva; *sports-ground*, terreno da giuoco; *stadio*; *sports-model* (*car*), automobile da corsa; *sports-suit*, tenuta sportiva || *aquatic*, *athletic sports*, sport acquatici, atletici; *field-sports*, sport all'aperto.

to **sport**, *v.t.i.* 1. giocare, divertirsi; praticare sport (caccia, ecc.) 2. scherzare, burlarsi: *to* — *at* (o over o upon) *s.o.*, burlarsi di qlcu. 3. trastullarsi; baloccarsi 4. (*biol.*) produrre una specie anomala (di animali, piante) 5. ostentare (lusso, ricchezze, ecc.); mettere in mostra; pavoneggiarsi: *he was sporting a new coat*, si pavoneggiava con una giacca nuova || *to* — *one's oak*, (*sl. universitario*) tenere la porta chiusa per non essere disturbato.

sporter ['spɔ:tə*], *s.c.* chi si diverte || *s.* 1. sportivo 2. (*fam.*) chi si pavoneggia, chi ostenta.

sportful ['spɔ:tful], *ag.* scherzoso; gaio, giocoso.

sportfully ['spɔ:tfuli], *av.* giocosamente; scherzosamente.

sportfulness ['spɔ:tfulnis], *s.* giovialità, festevolezza.

sporting ['spɔ:tiŋ], *ag.* sportivo: — *spirit*, spirito sportivo || *s.* 1. sport, esercizio fisico 2. (*biol.*) produzione di specie anomala (di animali, piante) ☆ — *daily*, quotidiano sportivo; — *-dog*, cane da caccia; — *-gun*, fucile da caccia.

sportingly ['spɔ:tiŋli], *av.* sportivamente.

sportive ['spɔ:tiv], *ag.* 1. gioviale 2. sportivo.

sportively ['spɔ:tivli], *av.* 1. giovialmente 2. sportivamente.

sportiveness ['spɔ:tivnis], *s.* giovialità, gaiezza, umore allegro.

sportless ['spɔ:tlis], *ag.* privo di brio; triste.

sportsman, *pl.* **sportsmen** ['spɔ:tsmən], *s.* 1. sportivo (specialmente cacciatore, pescatore) 2. uomo animato da spirito sportivo; uomo leale, semplice, cavalleresco: *he is a real* —, è un giocatore leale 3. (*amer.*) giocatore d'azzardo.

sportsmanlike ['spɔ:tsmənlaik], *ag.* caratteristico, proprio di uno sportivo; leale.

sportsmanship ['spɔ:tsmənʃip], *s.* 1. abilità sportiva 2. spirito sportivo; lealtà.

sportswear ['spɔ:tswɛə*], *s. coll.* abiti sportivi.

sportswoman ['spɔ:ts,wumən], *pl.* **sportswomen** ['spɔ:ts,wimin], *s.* donna sportiva, amante degli sport.

sporular ['spɔrjulə*], *ag.* (*biol.*) simile a spora.

sporule ['spɔrju:l], *s.* (*biol.*) spora, sporula.

spot [spɔt], *s.* 1. luogo, località, posto: *a pretty* —, un bel posticino; *I was on the* — *within five minutes*, arrivai sul posto entro cinque minuti; *the manager should always be on the* —, il direttore dovrebbe sempre essere sul posto || *on the* —, sul colpo; immediatamente; sveglio, all'altezza della situazione: *he is always on the* — *in an emergency*, è sempre all'altezza della situazione in un momento critico; *they were killed on the* —, furono uccisi sul colpo; *to do sthg. on the* —, fare ql.co. immediatamente || *this is his weak* —, questo è il suo punto debole || *to put s.o. on the* —, (*sl.*) mettere in imbarazzo qlcu.; (decidere di) assassinare qlcu. 2. macchia (anche *fig.*); « pois »; chiazza della pelle: *a red dress with white spots*, un vestito rosso a pallini bianchi; *his reputation has many spots*, la sua reputazione ha molte macchie 3. goccia; (*fam.*) goccio: *a* — *of whisky*, un goccio di whisky ☆ — *cash*, (*comm.*) denaro contante; — *market*, (*comm.*) mercato del disponibile; — *remover*, smacchiatore.

to **spot**, *pass.p.p.* **spotted** ['spɔtid], *v.t.i.* 1. macchiare, macchiarsi; punteggiare: *this material spots easily*, questa stoffa si macchia facilmente 2. *fig.* macchiare, macchiarsi; infamare; tacciare 3. (*fam.*) individuare, distinguere, riconoscere; scoprire; indovinare: *I spotted her right away among the crowd*, la individuai subito tra la folla; *I spotted him as a German*, lo riconobbi per tedesco; *they always* — *the winner*, indovinano sempre chi sarà il vincitore 4. (*mil.*) localizzare, individuare.

spotless ['spɔtlis], *ag.* senza macchia; immacolato; puro (anche *fig.*): — *snow*, neve immacolata; — *conscience*, coscienza pulita.

spotlessly ['spɔtlisli], *av.* senza macchia; puramente.

spotlessness ['spɔtlisnis], *s.* candore; pulizia.

spotlight ['spɔt-lait], *s.* (*teat. cine.*) luce della ribalta;

proiettore, riflettore: *to hold the —*, essere al centro della scena; *(fam.)* attirare l'attenzione.

to spotlight, *v.t. (teat. cine.)* puntare i riflettori su; mettere in evidenza, illuminare.

spotted ['spotid], *ag.* macchiato, chiazzato, picchiettato; maculato; a pallini ☆ — *fever, (patol.)* meningite cerebro-spinale; febbre tifoidea; tifo petecchiale.

spottedness ['spotidnis], *s.* l'essere macchiato.

spotter ['spotə*], *s.* **1.** persona, cosa che macchia **2.** *(aer.)* ricognitore **3.** *(fam. amer.)* investigatore privato.

spottiness ['spotinis], *s.* l'essere macchiato, non uniforme.

spotty ['spoti], *ag.* **1.** chiazzato, macchiato **2.** foruncoloso **3.** irregolare, ineguale, non uniforme.

spousal ['spauzl], *ag.:* nuziale, matrimoniale.

spousals ['spauzlz], *s.pl. (arc.)* sponsali, sposalizio.

spouse [spauz], *s.c. (arc.)* sposo, sposa; coniuge.

spouseless ['spauzlis], *ag.* senza coniuge.

spout [spaut], *s.* **1.** tubo di scarico; grondaia; beccuccio (di teiera, ecc.) **2.** getto, colonna (di acqua, vapore, ecc.); cascata **3.** montacarichi (al monte di pietà); monte di pietà || *to be up the —, (sl.)* essere in pegno (al monte di pietà) ☆ *sand- —*, turbine di sabbia; *water- —*, tromba marina.

to spout, *v.t.i.* **1.** scaricare; gettare; zampillare, far zampillare; scaturire, sgorgare: *blood spouted from his wound,* il sangue gli zampillò dalla ferita **2.** *(sl.)* declamare; parlare a getto continuo **3.** *(sl.)* impegnare al monte di pietà.

spouter ['spautə*], *s.* declamatore: *a Hyde Park —,* un oratore da Hyde Park, da comizio.

spouting ['spautiŋ], *s.* **1.** zampillo, getto **2.** *fig.* declamazione.

spoutless ['spautlis], *ag.* sprovvisto di beccuccio.

sprag [spræg], *s.* **1.** *(aut.)* puntone di arresto **2.** *(miner.)* puntello.

to sprag, *pass.p.p.* **spragged** [sprægd], *v.t. (miner.)* puntellare; inserire un puntello in.

sprain [sprein], *s.* distorsione; strappo muscolare.

to sprain, *v.t.* distorcere; storcere: *he has sprained his wrist,* si è slogato il polso.

sprang [spræŋ], *pass.* di to **spring.**

sprat [spræt], *s. (ittiol.)* spratto (piccola aringa) || *to throw a — to catch a whale,* dare poco per aver molto **2.** *(scherz.)* bimbo mingherlino.

to sprat, *pass.p.p.* **spratted** ['sprætid], *v.i.* pescare spratti.

spratter ['sprætə*], *s.* pescatore di spratti.

spratting ['sprætiŋ], *s.* pesca dello spratto.

sprawl [spro:l], *s.* stiracchiamento; lo sdraiarsi, l'essere sdraiato.

to sprawl, *v.t.i.* **1.** adagiarsi in modo scomposto: *to — on the bed,* sdraiarsi sul letto; *to send s.o. sprawling,* mandar qlcu. a gambe all'aria **2.** disporre (truppe) irregolarmente **3.** strisciare; allargarsi, estendersi (di piante, di scrittura, ecc.): *the name sprawled over the whole page,* il nome copriva tutta la pagina.

spray¹ [sprei], *s.* rametto, frasca.

spray², *s.* **1.** spruzzo, schiuma **2.** getto vaporizzato (di acqua, profumo, ecc.); liquido per vaporizzazioni **3.** vaporizzatore, polverizzatore, spruzzatore ☆ — *-cooling, (mec.)* raffreddamento mediante vaporizzazione; — *-painting,* verniciatura a spruzzo || *scent- —,* vaporizzatore di profumo.

to spray², *v.t.* **1.** polverizzare, vaporizzare, atomizzare (un liquido) **2.** aspergere, spruzzare; innaffiare.

sprayer ['spreiə*], *s.* spruzzatore, vaporizzatore; *(agr.)* irroratrice.

sprayey¹ ['spreii], *ag.* a forma di ramoscello; con ramoscelli.

sprayey², *ag.* vaporizzato.

spraying ['spreiiŋ], *s.* **1.** polverizzazione, vaporizzazione (di un liquido) **2.** irrorazione, annaffiamento ☆ — *machine,* macchinetta vaporizzatrice.

spread [spred], *ag.* steso; aperto; spiegato: — *wings,* ali spiegate || — *table,* tavola apparecchiata || *s.* **1.** crescita; espansione **2.** estensione; apertura (di compasso, ecc.): — *of wings,* apertura d'ali **3.** diffusione, divulgazione, propagazione: *the — of that disease,* la diffusione di quella malattia **4.** coperta; tappeto (da tavola) **5.** *(fam.)* festino, banchetto: *cold —,* cena fredda **6.** *(amer.)* differenza tra il prezzo di produzione e quello di vendita ☆ — *-eagle, (arald.)* aquila spiegata; figura del pattinaggio artistico; *(cuc.)* pollo alla diavola, ai ferri.

to spread, *pass.p.p.* **spread,** *v.t.i.* **1.** stendere, stendersi; spargere, spargersi; spiegare, spiegarsi; spalmare; coprire: *a corn field — out before us,* un campo di grano si stendeva davanti a noi; *the meadows are now — with flowers,* i prati sono ora cosparsi di fiori; *she — the newspaper,* ella spiegò il giornale; *a sudden flush — over her face,* un improvviso rossore si diffuse sul suo viso; *to — a carpet on the floor,* stendere un tappeto sul pavimento; *to — jam on bread,* spalmare la marmellata sul pane || *to — the table,* apparecchiare la tavola **2.** *fig.* spargere; diffondere, diffondersi; propagare, propagarsi; disseminare: *flies — disease,* le mosche propagano le malattie; *he — the news that...,* egli sparse la notizia che...; *the news — over the country,* la notizia si diffuse nel paese || *to — oneself, (fam.)* farsi in quattro; avere mille attività; darsi delle arie, pavoneggiarsi **3.** tendere, protendere: *he — his hands to the fire,* egli tese le mani verso il fuoco **4.** estendersi (nel tempo), svolgersi: *a course of study spreading over two years,* un corso di studi che si svolge in due anni.

spreader ['spredə*], *s.c.* chi propaga, divulga (idee, notizie, ecc.) || *s.* **1.** spruzzatore **2.** *(agr.)* concimatrice.

spreading ['sprediŋ], *ag.* **1.** che si propaga; che si estende **2.** folto, frondoso: *a — tree,* un albero frondoso || *s.* **1.** estensione, sviluppo **2.** *fig.* propagazione, diffusione ☆ — *-machine, (ind.)* macchina spalmatrice.

spree [spri:], *s.* baldoria; bisboccia: *to be on the —,* far baldoria, bisboccia.

to spree, *v.i.* far baldoria, gozzovigliare.

sprig¹ [sprig], *s.* **1.** ramoscello, rametto **2.** disegno, lavoro a fiorami, a foglie **3.** *(spreg.)* rampollo; *(arc.)* giovincello.

to sprig¹, *pass.p.p.* **sprigged** [sprigd], *v.t.* ornare a fiorami, a foglie.

sprig², *s.* puntina; chiodino.

sprigged [sprigd], *ag.* a fiori, a ramoscelli ☆ — *muslin,* mussola a fiorami.

spriggy ['sprigi], *ag.* ornato di ramoscelli.

spright [sprait], *s.* folletto, elfo, spiritello.

sprightliness ['spraitlinis], *s.* allegria, brio, vivacità.

sprightly ['spraitli], *ag.* allegro, brioso, gaio, vivace.

spring [spriŋ], *s.* **1.** sorgente, fonte; *pl.* terme **2.** *gener. pl. fig.* principio, origine; causa: *the springs of his behaviour,* l'origine, le cause del suo comportamento **3.** primavera: *in —,* in primavera **4.** salto, balzo, slancio: *to make a — at s.o.,* slanciarsi su qlcu.; *to take a —,* fare un salto **5.** elasticità: *my step has lost its —,* il mio passo ha perso elasticità **6.** molla: *the coil of a —,* la spira di una molla; *to put a — under tension* (o *to stretch a —*), tendere una molla **7.** *(mar.)* falla, spaccatura (di albero maestro); traversino **8.** *(arch.)* linea, piano d'imposta ☆ — *-balance,* bilancia a molla — *-bed,* letto a molle; — *-board,* trampolino; — *-cart,* carro su molle; — *-cleaning,* pulizia di primavera; — *-clip, (aut.)* staffa della balestra; — *-day,* giorno di primavera; — *-flower,* fiore primaverile; — *-frame, (mec.* telaio molleggiato; — *-gauge,* calibro a molla; — *-halt, (vet.)* spavenio; — *-head,* fontana, sorgente; — *-loaded,* caricato a molla; — *-lock,* serratura a scatto; — *-mattress,* materasso a molle; — *-pawl,* arresto a molla; — *-water,* acqua di sorgente, acqua viva || *hot springs,* fonti d'acqua calda; *leaf —, (mec.)* balestra; *spiral —*

(*mec.*) molla a elica cilindrica; *thermal springs*, sorgente, stazione termale.

to **spring**, *pass.* **sprang** [spræŋ], *p.p.* **sprung** [sprʌŋ], *v.t.i.* **1.** nascere, discendere, derivare, procedere; scaturire (di acqua); spuntare (di germogli): *a maid sprung from a noble race*, una fanciulla di nobile lignaggio; *his action springs from fear*, la sua azione deriva dal timore; *water sprang from the ground*, l'acqua scaturì dal suolo ‖ *to — into existence*, nascere **2.** saltare, far saltare; spiccare, far spiccare (un salto): *to — (over) a ditch*, saltare un fosso; *to — forward*, slanciarsi in avanti; *to — into the saddle*, balzare in sella; *to — to s.o.'s help*, precipitarsi in aiuto di qlcu. ‖ *to — to one's feet*, balzare in piedi **3.** levare (la selvaggina) **4.** scattare, far scattare (sotto l'azione di una molla): *the door sprang open*, la porta si spalancò di scatto **5.** munire di sospensioni (una vettura) **6.** (*mar.*) fendere, fendersi; incrinare, incrinarsi: *to — a leak*, aprire una falla **7.** far brillare (una mina) **8.** (*fam.*) proporre, mettere sul tappeto; produrre: *he has sprung a new theory*, ha proposto una nuova teoria ‖ *to — a surprise on s.o.*, fare una sorpresa a qlcu., prendere qlcu. alla sprovvista **9.** *to — at* (*s.o.*), gettarsi su: *to — at the enemy*, balzare sul nemico **10.** *to — up*, saltare su; spuntare, crescere (di piante): *to — up into the air*, fare un balzo in aria.

springal(d) ['spriŋəl(d)], *s.* (*arc.*) giovanotto, garzone.

springbok ['spriŋbok], *s.* (*zool.*) antidorcade (antilope del Sud-Africa) ‖ *the Springboks*, i sud-africani; la squadra di calcio sud-africana.

springe [sprindʒ], *s.* laccio, calappio, lacciuolo.

to **springe**, *v.t.* prendere al laccio, accalappiare.

springer ['spriŋə*], *s.c.* saltatore, saltatrice ‖ *s.* **1.** (*zool.*) antilope sud-africana **2.** varietà di cane « spaniel » **3.** (*zool.*) grampo **4.** (*arch.*) chiave dell'arco; nervatura **5.** chi fa brillare le mine.

springiness ['spriŋinis], *s.* elasticità, forza elastica.

springing ['spriŋiŋ], *s.* **1.** principio, origine, sorgente; nascita; zampillamento **2.** il balzare, il saltare **3.** (*aut.*) sospensione **4.** (*arch.*) linea di imposta.

springless ['spriŋlis], *ag.* senza molla.

springlet ['spriŋlit], *s.* **1.** piccola sorgente, fontana **2.** piccola molla.

springlike ['spriŋlaik], *ag.* primaverile, di primavera.

springtide ['spriŋ-taid], *s.* **1.** tempo di primavera **2.** marea equinoziale.

springtime ['spriŋ-taim], *s.* tempo di primavera.

springy ['spriŋi], *ag.* **1.** pieno di sorgenti **2.** elastico; svelto, agile.

sprinkle ['spriŋkl], *s.* **1.** aspersione, spruzzatina: *a — of rain*, una spruzzatina di pioggia **2.** pizzico: *a — of pepper*, un pizzico di pepe.

to **sprinkle**, *v.t.i.* **1.** spargere; spruzzare, aspergere, irrorare: *the meadow was sprinkled with dew*, il prato era irrorato di rugiada **2.** *imp.* piovigginare.

sprinkler ['spriŋklə*], *s.* **1.** spruzzatore; innaffiatoio **2.** (*eccl.*) aspersorio.

sprinkling ['spriŋkliŋ], *s.* **1.** spruzzamento, aspersione, spruzzo **2.** *gener.* pizzico; infarinatura: *to have a — of history*, avere un'infarinatura di storia.

sprint [sprint], *s.* (*spor.*) « sprint », scatto finale.

to **sprint**, *v.t.i.* percorrere (una distanza) alla massima velocità; correre a tutta velocità.

sprinter ['sprintə*], *s.* (*spor.*) velocista.

sprit [sprit], *s.* (*mar.*) pennoncino ☆ — *-sail*, (*mar.*) tarchia.

sprite [sprait], *s.* folletto, elfo, spirito.

sprocket ['sprokit], *s.* (*mec. cine.*) rocchetto, rullo dentato ☆ — *-chain*, catena articolata ; — *-hole*, perforazione (di pellicola cinematografica) ; — *-hum*, (*cine.*) ronzio; — *-wheel*, (*mec.*) ruota dentata.

sprout [spraut], *s.* **1.** germoglio; tallo **2.** *pl.* (*Brussels*) *sprouts*, cavolini di Bruxelles.

to **sprout**, *v.t.i.* germogliare, far germogliare; spun-

tare; crescere, far crescere: *to — a moustache*, farsi crescere i baffi.

sprouting ['sprautiŋ], *s.* il germogliare, il crescere.

spruce[1] [spru:s], *ag.* attillato; azzimato; lindo; elegante.

to **spruce**[1], *v.t.* adornare, agghindare: *to — oneself up*, azzimarsi, agghindarsi.

spruce[2], *s.* (*bot.*) abete rosso ☆ — *-beer*, birra (fatta con foglie e ramoscelli di abete).

sprucely ['spru:sli], *av.* lindamente; in modo azzimato.

spruceness ['spru:snis], *s.* lindezza; ricercatezza; eleganza.

sprue[1] [spru:], *s.* (*metal.*) **1.** canale di colata **2.** colame.

sprue[2], *s.* (*patol.*) psilosi.

sprung [sprʌŋ], *p.p.* di to **spring** ‖ *ag.* **1.** a sospensione, a molla **2.** spaccato, rotto **3.** (*sl.*) alticcio, sbronzo.

spry [sprai], *ag.* (*sl.*) attivo, vivace, agile.

spud [spʌd], *s.* **1.** (*agr.*) sarchio **2.** persona, oggetto corto e tozzo **3.** (*fam.*) patata.

to **spud**, *pass.p.p.* **spudded** ['spʌdid], *v.t.* sarchiare, rimuovere (erbacce) col sarchio.

to **spuddle** ['spʌdl], *v.i.* (*dial.*) vangare leggermente (di chi si dedica al giardinaggio per diletto).

spuddy ['spʌdi], *ag.* piccolo, tarchiato.

to **spue**, *V.* to **spew**.

spume [spju:m], *s.* spuma, schiuma.

to **spume**, *v.i.* spumare, schiumare.

spumescence [spju'mesəns], *s.* spumosità.

spumescent [spju'mesənt], *ag.* spumoso.

spuminess ['spju:minis], *s.* spumosità.

spumous ['spju:məs], **spumy** ['spju:mi], *ag.* spumoso.

spun [spʌn], *pass. p.p.* di to **spin**.

spunge, *V.* **sponge**.

spunk [spʌŋk], *s.* **1.** coraggio, audacia, fegato **2.** ira, collera **3.** esca (per accendere il fuoco) **4.** (*scoz.*) favilla; fiammifero.

spunky ['spʌŋki], *ag.* **1.** audace, coraggioso **2.** irato.

spur [spə:*], *s.* **1.** sperone: *to put* (o *to set*) *the spurs to a horse*, dar di sprone a un cavallo ‖ *to win one's spurs*, (*st.*) essere investito cavaliere; *fig.* distinguersi, farsi un nome **2.** *fig.* sprone, stimolo, impulso: *on the — of the moment*, di impulso; lì per lì **3.** sperone (di gallo) **4.** contrafforte (di montagna) **5.** (*bot. edil.*) sperone ☆ — *-clad*, armato di speroni; — *-gear*, (*mec.*) ingranaggio a ruota; — *-rowel*, spronella; — *track*, raccordo ferroviario; — *-wheel*, (*mec.*) ruota dentata: — *-wheel reversing gear*, (*mec.*) invertitore di marcia ad ingranaggi cilindrici.

to **spur**, *pass.p.p.* **spurred** [spə:d], *v.t.i.* **1.** spronare; *fig.* stimolare, incitare **2.** fornire di speroni **3.** *to — on*, cavalcare a spron battuto, affrettarsi.

spurge [spə:dʒ], *s.* (*bot.*) euforbia.

spurious ['spjuəriəs], *ag.* **1.** spurio, falso; apocrifo: — *coin*, moneta falsa **2.** illegittimo, bastardo (di persona).

spuriously ['spjuəriəsli], *av.* **1.** spuriamente, falsamente **2.** illegittimamente.

spuriousness ['spjuəriəsnis], *s.* **1.** falsità, contraffazione; carattere apocrifo (di un testo) **2.** illegittimità.

spurless ['spə:lis], *ag.* senza speroni.

spurling-line ['spə:liŋ-lain], *s.* (*mar.*) sagola dell'assiometro.

spurn [spə:n], *s.* **1.** disprezzo, disdegno; rifiuto sdegnoso **2.** calcio.

to **spurn**, *v.t.i.* **1.** disprezzare, disdegnare; rifiutare sdegnosamente **2.** dare un calcio (a), respingere.

spurner ['spə:nə*], *s.c.* sprezzatore, sprezzatrice.

spurred [spə:d], *ag.* fornito di speroni.

spurring ['spə:riŋ], *s.* speronata; *fig.* incitamento, stimolo.

spurry ['spə:ri], *s.* (*bot.*) spergula.

spurt[1] [spə:t], *s.* breve sforzo improvviso; scatto (di velocità).

to **spurt**[1], *v.i.* **1.** fare un breve sforzo improvviso **2.** scattare (in velocità).

(to) **spurt**[2], *V.* (to) **spirt**.

sputnik ['sputnik], *s.* (*neol.*) (*astronautica*) sputnik.

sputter ['spʌtə*], *s.* **1.** barbugliamento; discorso rapido e confuso **2.** spruzzo (di penna) **3.** crepitio, scoppiettio (di candela, legno, ecc.).

to **sputter**, *v.t.i.* **1.** barbugliare, parlare in modo confuso **2.** sputacchiare (nel parlare); spruzzare (di penna) **3.** crepitare.

sputterer ['spʌtərə*], *s.* barbuglione.

sputtering ['spʌtəriŋ], *V.* **sputter**.

sputteringly ['spʌtəriŋli], *av.* barbugliando.

sputum ['spju:təm], *pl.* **sputa** ['spju:tə], *s.* sputo; espettorato.

spy [spai], *s.* spia, spione, delatore: *he plays the — on me,* spia i miei movimenti ☆ *— -glass,* (*ott.*) cannocchiale; *— -hole,* (*mec.*) spia, foro di vista; *— -system,* spionaggio.

to **spy**, *v.t.i.* **1.** spiare; fare la spia: *he was spying upon us,* spiava i nostri movimenti; *she spied into his secrets,* cercò di scoprire i suoi segreti **2.** notare; osservare, scrutare: *she is very quick at spying everybody's faults,* nota subito i difetti di tutti **3.** *to — out,* indagare segretamente; scoprire.

spying ['spaiiŋ], *s.* spionaggio.

squab [skwɔb], *ag.* **1.** tozzo; tarchiato; grassoccio **2.** implume **3.** timido ‖ *s.* **1.** persona tozza **2.** piccione implume **3.** cuscino ben imbottito **4.** sofà, divano ☆ *— -chick,* pulcino implume; *— -pie,* pasticcio di piccione.

to **squab**, *pass. p.p.* **squabbed** [skwɔbd], *v.t.i.* **1.** imbottire **2.** cadere pesantemente.

squab, *av.* pesantemente: *to come down — on the floor,* cadere pesantemente sul pavimento.

squabble ['skwɔbl], *s.* battibecco; lite; alterco; zuffa: *we had a good — about it,* abbiamo avuto un vivace battibecco su ciò.

to **squabble**, *v.t.i.* **1.** venire a parole; accapigliarsi; altercare: *they keep on squabbling,* non fanno altro che litigare **2.** (*tip.*) far sovrapporre (i caratteri).

squabbler ['skwɔblə*], *s.c.* attaccabrighe.

squabby ['skwɔbi], *ag.* tozzo; tarchiato; grassoccio.

squacco ['skwækou], *s.* (*ornit.*) sgarza ciuffetto.

squad [skwɔd], *s.* **1.** (*mil.*) squadra; plotone; drappello ‖ *the Flying Squad,* la (Squadra) Volante **2.** (*fam.*) banda, cricca: *he and his —,* lui e la sua banda **3.** (*spor. amer.*) squadra ☆ *awkward —,* squadra di coscritti.

squadron ['skwɔdrən], *s.* **1.** (*mar. aer.*) squadra, squadriglia **2.** (*mil.*) squadrone (di cavalleria); battaglione (di fanteria) **3.** gruppo organizzato (di persone) ☆ *— -leader,* comandante di squadriglia ‖ *bombing —,* (*aer.*) squadra da bombardamento; *rear —,* (*mil.*) retroguardia; *van —,* (*mil.*) avanguardia.

to **squadron**, *v.t.* (*mil.*) disporre in squadre; dividere in squadriglie.

squailer ['skweilə*], *s.* pertica; bacchio.

squails [skweilz], *s.pl.* birilli.

squalid ['skwɔlid], *ag.* squallido, miserabile; sordido.

squalidity [skwɔ'liditi], *s.* squallore, miseria; sordidezza, sudiciume.

squalidly ['skwɔlidli], *av.* squallidamente, miseramente; sordidamente.

squalidness ['skwɔlidnis], *s.* squallore, miseria; sudiciume.

squall[1] [skwɔ:l], *s.* urlo; schiamazzo; strepito.

to **squall**[1], *v.t.i.* urlare; vociare; schiamazzare; strepitare.

squall[2], *s.* **1.** turbine; bufera ‖ *look out for squalls,* sta' all'erta **2.** *fig.* burrasca; litigio: *they are always having squalls at home,* c'è sempre burrasca a casa loro.

squaller ['skwɔ:lə*], *s.* schiamazzatore, strillone.

squalling ['skwɔ:liŋ], *ag.* schiamazzante ‖ *s.* grido; schiamazzo.

squally ['skwɔ:li], *ag.* tempestoso, burrascoso (anche *fig.*).

squaloid ['skweilɔid], *ag.* simile a squalo.

squalor ['skwɔlə*], *s.* squallore, miseria; sudiciume.

squalus ['skweiləs], *pl.* **squali** ['skweilai], *s.* squalo, pesecane.

squama ['skweimə], *pl.* **squamae** ['skweimi:], *s.* squama.

squamate ['skweimit], *ag.* coperto di squame.

squamose ['skweimous], **squamous** ['skweiməs], *ag.* squamoso; scaglioso.

to **squander** ['skwɔndə*], *v.t.* sciupare, sprecare; sperperare, scialacquare: *it's so much money squandered,* sono soldi sprecati.

squanderer ['skwɔndərə*], *s.c.* sciupone, sciupona; sperperatore, sperperatrice.

squandering ['skwɔndəriŋ], *s.* sciupio; spreco; sperperamento.

squanderingly ['skwɔndəriŋli], *av.* da sprecone; da sperperatore.

squandermania ['skwɔndə'meinjə], *s.* mania di sperperare.

square [skwɛə*], *ag.* **1.** quadro, quadrato: *— chin,* mento quadrato; *dress with a — neck,* abito con scollo quadrato ‖ *to be a — peg in a round hole, fig.* non essere adatto ad un lavoro, posto, ecc. **2.** robusto, massiccio, tozzo **3.** ad angolo retto, perpendicolare **4.** *fig.* sistemato, pareggiato; ordinato: *I must get things —,* devo sistemare le cose; *to be — with s.o.,* sdebitarsi con qlcu. **5.** esatto; netto, deciso: *give me a — answer,* dammi una risposta precisa **6.** giusto, leale, onesto: *his behaviour was not quite —,* il suo comportamento non fu del tutto onesto **7.** (*arit.*) quadrato, al quadrato **8.** (*golf*) pari **9.** (*fam.*) completo, sostanzioso (di pasto); abbondante (di bevanda): *we made a — meal,* facemmo un pasto sostanzioso **10.** (*sl. della « beat generation »*) conformista.

square, *s.* **1.** quadrato, oggetto di forma quadrata; (*mil.*) quadrato, disposizione a quadrato **2.** piazza ‖ *Russell Square,* piazza Russell **3.** blocco, isolato (di case) **4.** squadra (per disegno) ‖ *by the —,* esattamente ‖ *on the —,* (*fam.*) onestamente: *to act on the —,* agire onestamente ‖ *out of —,* fuori di squadra (anche *fig.*) **5.** (*arit.*) quadrato: *the — of a number,* il quadrato di un numero **6.** scacco (quadretto della scacchiera) **7.** (*metal.*) barra quadra **8.** (*sl. della « beat generation »*) conformista.

to **square**, *v.t.i.* **1.** quadrare, squadrare, riquadrare ‖ *to — the circle,* trovare la quadratura del circolo; *fig.* compiere cose impossibili **2.** pareggiare, sistemare (un conto) ‖ *to — accounts with s.o., fig.* fare i conti con qlcu. ‖ *to — matters,* sistemare le cose, mettere tutti d'accordo **3.** conformare; accordare, accordarsi; adattare, adattarsi: *her practice does not — with her principles,* le sue azioni non si accordano con i suoi principî **4.** (*arit.*) elevare al quadrato **5.** (*fam.*) corrompere: *he was squared to hold his tongue,* il suo silenzio fu comprato **6.** (*mec.*) regolare, mettere a punto **7.** (*golf*) essere pari **8.** (*mar.*) bracciare **9.** *to — off,* quadrettare (un foglio), ecc.) **10.** *to — up,* squadrare ‖ *to — up to s.o.,* assumere un atteggiamento bellicoso verso qlcu. ‖ *to — up with s.o., fig.* regolare i conti con qlcu.

square, *av.* **1.** ad angolo retto; in forma quadrata; in squadra **2.** direttamente; esattamente: *he was hit — on the face,* fu colpito proprio in faccia **3.** (*fam.*) onestamente, con lealtà: *play —, please,* agisci con lealtà, per piacere.

square, (*nei composti*): *— -built,* tarchiato; *— -face,* (*sl.*) gin; *— -head,* (*sl. amer.*) testa quadra (scandinavo immigrato negli Stati Uniti, nel Canada); *— -jawed,* dalla mascella quadrata; *— measure,* misura di superficie; *— -necked,* dallo scollo quadrato (di abito, ecc.); *— number,* numero al quadrato; *— -root,* radice quadrata; *— -shouldered,* dalle spalle larghe e diritte; *— -toed,* dalla punta quadrata (di scarpe); *fig.* conservatore, formale; pedante; — *-toes*, persona formalista; conservatore; pedante.

.squared [skwæəd], *ag.* **1.** squadrato, quadrato **2.** (*arit.*) elevato al quadrato **3.** quadrettato (di foglio, ecc.).

squarely ['skwæəli], *av.* **1.** a forma di quadrato **2.** direttamente: *to face sthg.* —, affrontare ql.co. con coraggio **3.** lealmente, onestamente.

squareness ['skwæənis], *s.* **1.** forma quadrata **2.** onestà, lealtà, franchezza.

squarer ['skwæərə*], *s.* **1.** squadratore (di marmo, legno, ecc.) **2.** (*arc.*) attaccabrighe.

squarish ['skwæəriʃ], *ag.* piuttosto quadrato.

squarrose ['skwærous], **squarrous** ['skwærəs], *ag.* **1.** (*bot. zool.*) squamoso, scaglioso **2.** coperto di croste, squame.

squash[1] [skwoʃ], *s.* **1.** cosa schiacciata **2.** schiacciamento; spremitura; spremuta (di frutta) **3.** ressa, calca, pigia pigia; (*fam.*) ricevimento affollato **4.** caduta di corpo molle; rumore prodotto da tale caduta ‖ *to fall — on sthg.*, appiattirsi, schiacciarsi su ql.co.; schiacciare ql.co. cadendoci sopra ☆ — *-hat*, cappello floscio; — *rackets*, « squash » (giuoco praticato con racchette e palla in un campo cintato) ‖ *lemon-* —, spremuta di limone; *orange-* —, spremuta di arancia.

to squash[1], *v.t.i.* **1.** schiacciare, spiacciare; spremere: *to — an orange*, spremere [un'arancia **2.** accalcarsi, pigiarsi, schiacciarsi: *to — into a room*, entrare a forza in una stanza; *to — through the gate*, pigiarsi nell'uscire da un cancello **3.** cadere spiacciandosi; cadere con un suono sordo **4.** (*fam.*) sopprimere, stroncare: *to — a revolt*, soffocare una rivolta **5.** *fig.* ridurre al silenzio; sconcertare: *to — a presumptuous person*, confondere un presuntuoso.

squash[2], *s.* (*bot.*) melopopone.

squashiness ['skwoʃinis], *s.* mollezza.

squashy ['skwoʃi], *ag.* **1.** molle, molliccio; tenero: *this apple is too — for my liking*, questa mela è troppo tenera per il mio gusto **2.** acquitrinoso; pantanoso: *after so much rain the ground is very —*, dopo tutta la pioggia che è caduta, il terreno è ridotto un pantano.

squat [skwot], *ag.* **1.** rannicchiato, accoccolato, seduto sui calcagni: — *like a toad*, accoccolato come un rospo **2.** tozzo, corto; tarchiato; schiacciato (di oggetto, ecc.): *a — building*, un edificio tozzo; — *letters*, lettere schiacciate ‖ *s.* **1.** posizione accoccolata, accucciata **2.** persona tozza.

to squat, *pass.p.p.* **squatted** ['skwotid], *v.t.i.* **1.** accovacciarsi, accoccolarsi: *the savages squatted about the fire*, i selvaggi si accovacciarono attorno al fuoco **2.** acquattarsi (di animali in pericolo) **3.** (*fam.*) sedersi, far sedere **4.** impossessarsi abusivamente di un terreno pubblico, di uno stabile vuoto; occupare un terreno pubblico per farne pascolo (in Australia).

squatter ['skwotə*], *s.* **1.** persona che si accovaccia; animale accovacciato, acquattato **2.** chi occupa abusivamente uno stabile, un terreno; chi occupa un terreno per ottenere dal governo il diritto di tenerlo (negli Stati Uniti) **3.** grande allevatore di bestiame (specialmente di ovini) (in Australia).

to squatter, *v.i.* avanzare a fatica in terreno pantanoso.

squatting ['skwotiŋ], *ag.* **1.** rannicchiato, accovacciato **2.** che si impossessa abusivamente di un terreno pubblico; che occupa un terreno pubblico per farne pascolo (in Australia) ‖ *s.* **1.** il rannicchiarsi, l'accovacciarsi, l'accoccolarsi **2.** l'impossessarsi abusivamente di un terreno pubblico; occupazione di un terreno pubblico per farne pascolo (in Australia).

squaw [skwo:], *s.* **1.** « squaw » (moglie, donna dei pellirosse) **2.** (*amer. scherz.*) donna **3.** persona debole, effeminata.

squawk [skwo:k], *s.* grido rauco e aspro; richiamo (specialmente di uccelli).

to squawk, *v.t.i.* **1.** emettere un grido rauco, spezzato; gridare raucamente (di uccelli) **2.** (*fam.*) lamen-

tare, lamentarsi con voce piagnucolosa di: *he squawked his troubles all over the town*, si lamentò dei suoi affanni per tutta la città.

squawker ['skwo:kə*], *s.* **1.** chi grida raucamente, aspramente **2.** chi si lamenta, chi protesta con voce aspra e rauca.

squawman, *pl.* **squawmen** ['skwo:mən], *s.* bianco sposato ad una indiana.

squeak [skwi:k], *s.* **1.** grido acuto, strillo **2.** grido, pigolio, squittio, guaito (di animali); cigolio, scricchiolio, suono acuto (di cose): — *of a hinge*, cigolio di un cardine **3.** *to have a (narrow)* —, (*sl.*) scamparla bella, scamparla per un filo.

to squeak, *v.t.i.* **1.** strillare in tono acuto; dire con voce stridula **2.** squittire, guaire (di animali); stridere, cigolare, scricchiolare (di cose): *pen that squeaks in writing*, penna che scricchiola scrivendo **3.** (*sl.*) fare la spia, cantare, confessare.

squeaker ['skwi:kə*], *s.* **1.** chi, ciò che emette un grido, un suono acuto, uno strillo, uno squittio, uno scricchiolio **2.** lattonzolo; maialino da latte; uccello implume **3.** (*sl.*) informatore, traditore, delatore, spia.

squeakily ['skwi:kili], *av.* in modo stridente, scricchiolante.

squeaky ['skwi:ki], *ag.* **1.** che grida, strilla con voce acuta (di persona) **2.** che guaisce, squittisce (di animale); cigolante, scricchiolante, stridente (di cosa): — *door*, porta cigolante; — *sound*, suono stridente.

squeal [skwi:l], *s.* grido forte ed acuto, strillo.

to squeal, *v.t.i.* **1.** strillare, gridare: *to — (out) sthg.*, gridare ql.co. con voce stridente, acuta **2.** (*sl.*) protestare vivacemente (contro le tasse, ecc.) **3.** (*sl.*) fare la spia, tradire **4.** *to make s.o.* —, (*sl.*) ricattare qlcu.

squealer ['skwi:lə*], *s.c.* **1.** chi strilla, grida **2.** (*sl.*) chi si lamenta e protesta **3.** (*sl.*) chi fa la spia, tradisce ‖ *s.* uccello implume (generalmente piccione).

squealing ['skwi:liŋ], *ag.* che strilla, che grida ‖ *s.* grido forte ed acuto, strillo.

squeamish ['skwi:miʃ], *ag.* **1.** soggetto a nausee: — *stomach*, stomaco delicato **2.** schizzinoso, schifiltoso, di gusti difficili: *don't be so* —, non essere così difficile **3.** scrupoloso; timido, riservato.

squeamishly ['skwi:miʃli], *av.* **1.** con nausea **2.** svogliatamente, con riluttanza.

squeamishness ['skwi:miʃnis], *s.* **1.** disposizione alle nausee, delicatezza di stomaco **2.** l'essere schizzinoso, di gusti difficili.

squeegee ['skwi:'ʒi:], *s.* (*mar. foto.*) seccatoio.

to squeegee, *v.t.* (*mar. foto.*) asciugare, pulire col seccatoio.

squeezability [,skwi:zə'biliti], *s.* compressibilità.

squeezable ['skwi:zəbl], *ag.* **1.** schiacciabile, comprimibile **2.** spremibile ‖ *their industry becomes more — for taxes*, (*fam.*) la loro industria diventa maggiormente tassabile.

squeeze [skwi:z], *s.* **1.** compressione, pressione, schiacciamento **2.** spremitura; poche gocce (ottenute mediante spremitura): *a — of lemon*, poche gocce di limone **3.** stretta; abbraccio; pizzicotto: *to give s.o. a* —, abbracciare qlcu.; *to give s.o. a — of the hand*, stringere la mano a qlcu. **4.** calca, affollamento: *it was a tight* —, si era pigiati come sardine **5.** estorsione di denaro; appropriazione indebita (da parte di funzionari, di domestici in Oriente) **6.** (*spec. archeol.*) calco, impronta **7.** (*miner.*) graduale chiusura di galleria (per avvenuto sfruttamento di strati) **8.** (*bridge*) «squeeze» (il fare in modo che l'avversario giuochi una carta importante) ☆ — *roller*, (*ind. tessile*) cilindro spremitore; apparecchio a cilindri spremitori; (*foto.*) rullo asciugatore.

to squeeze, *v.t.i.* **1.** spremere, spremersi: *lemon that squeezes well*, limone sugoso, che si spreme bene; *to — the juice out of an orange*, spremere il succo da un'arancia; *to — a lemon dry*, spremere un limone fino all'ultima goccia; *to — out a tear*, (*fam.*) spremere una lagrimuccia ‖ *squeezed orange*, arancia spremuta;

fig. uomo finito, sfinito **2.** stringere; abbracciare **3.** accalcarsi; spingere, spingersi; stringersi; farsi strada spingendo: *the crowd squeezed up*, la folla si strinse; *he squeezed his way into the room*, entrò con difficoltà nella stanza; *he was squeezed into a car*, fu fatto entrare a forza in un'automobile; *please — up a little*, per favore stringetevi un pochino **4.** estorcere (denaro); opprimere (con tasse): *they squeezed the last penny out of him*, gli estorsero fino all'ultimo centesimo **5.** (*spec. archeol.*) fare calchi, copie **6.** (*bridge*) far giocare carte importanti.

squeezer ['skwi:zə*], *s.* **1.** chi, ciò che preme, spreme, strizza, schiaccia **2.** (*fam.*) oppressore, tiranno **3.** (*mec.*) strettoio, torchio **4.** *pl.* carte da giuoco col valore segnato in alto a destra ☆ *lemon —*, spremilimone.

squeezing ['skwi:ziŋ], *s.* **1.** compressione, pressione **2.** estorsione (di denaro).

squelch [skweltʃ], *s.* **1.** colpo; tonfo: *I heard a heavy —*, udii un gran tonfo **2.** rumore di chi sguazza nel fango **3.** cosa, massa schiacciata **4.** rabbuffo.

to squelch, *v.t.i.* **1.** schiacciare, spiacciare **2.** *fig.* sopprimere; soffocare; ridurre al silenzio: *to — a revolt*, soffocare una sommossa **3.** fare cic ciac: *the water squelched in his shoes*, l'acqua gli faceva cic ciac nelle scarpe.

squib [skwib], *s.* **1.** petardo; razzo; miccia: *to let off a —*, far partire un petardo ‖ *a damp —*, *fig.* un affare mancato, un fiasco **2.** pasquinata, satira.

to squib, *pass.p.p.* **squibbed** [skwibd], *v.t.i.* **1.** sparare petardi **2.** satireggiare.

squid [skwid], *s.* **1.** (*zool.*) calamaro, seppia **2.** seppia usata come esca; esca artificiale **3.** (*aer.*) calotta a distensione parziale.

to squid, *pass.p.p.* **squidded** ['skwidid], *v.i.* pescare con una seppia come esca.

squiffer ['skwifə*], *s.* (*mus.*) concertina.

squiffy ['skwifi], *ag.* (*sl.*) brillo, alticcio.

squilgee ['skwil'dʒi:], *s.* (*mar. foto.*) seccatoio.

squill [skwil], *s.* **1.** (*bot.*) scilla, cipolla marittima **2.** (*zool.*) squilla, cannocchia.

squint [skwint], *ag.* strabico ‖ *s.* **1.** strabismo: *he has a fearful —*, è tremendamente strabico **2.** sguardo furtivo; occhiata furtiva: *I had a — at his letter*, gettai uno sguardo furtivo alla sua lettera **3.** inclinazione, tendenza: *a — towards radicalism*, una tendenza radicale **4.** (*arch.*) apertura, finestrella obliqua ☆ *— -eyed*, strabico; *fig.* maligno.

to squint, *v.t.i.* **1.** essere strabico **2.** *fig.* guardar obliquamente, furtivamente, di traverso: *to — at slhg.*, lanciare un'occhiata furtiva a ql.co. **3.** aver inclinazione, tendenza: *to — towards anarchy*, avere una tendenza all'anarchia **4.** chiudere rapidamente (gli occhi); tenere (gli occhi) socchiusi (come per miopia).

squinter ['skwintə*], *s.c.* strabico, strabica.

squinting ['skwintiŋ], *s.* strabismo.

squintingly ['skwintiŋli], *av.* **1.** da strabico, obliquamente **2.** furtivamente, di traverso.

squirage ['skwaiəridʒ], *s.* **1.** *coll.* proprietari terrieri, piccola nobiltà **2.** almanacco araldico dei proprietari terrieri.

squirarchy, *V.* **squirearchy**.

squire ['skwaiə*], *s.* **1.** gentiluomo, nobiluomo di campagna, castellano ‖ *the —*, il principale possidente della contea, il signore del villaggio **2.** (*st.*) scudiero **3.** cavalier servente: *— of dames*, cicisbeo **4.** (*amer.*) giudice di pace, magistrato.

to squire, *v.t.i.* **1.** accompagnare, scortare; fare da scorta a (una donna) **2.** dominare, governare.

squirearchy ['skwaiəra:ki], *s.* **1.** *coll.* i proprietari terrieri, i gentiluomini di campagna **2.** (*st. inglese*) governo dei proprietari terrieri.

squireen [ˌskwaiə'ri:n], *s.* piccolo signorotto di campagna (specialmente in Irlanda).

squirehood ['skwaiəhud], *s.* **1.** condizione di gentiluomo, di signorotto, di scudiero **2.** *coll.* i signorotti, i nobili di campagna.

squirely ['skwaiəli], *ag.* da gentiluomo di campagna; da scudiero.

squireship ['skwaiəʃip], *V.* **squirehood 1.**

squirm [skwə:m], *s.* contorsione, contorcimento; attorcigliamento

to squirm, *v.i.* **1.** contorcersi; dimenarsi; attorcigliarsi **2.** *fig.* mostrare imbarazzo, umiliazione; essere sulle spine: *to — under a reproach*, aversela a male, impazientirsi per un rimprovero.

squirrel ['skwirəl], *s.* scoiattolo ☆ *-cage*, gabbia di scoiattolo (anche *elett.*); *— -monkey*, (*zool.*) crisotrice; *— -tail*, (*bot.*) orzo selvatico.

squirt [skwə:t], *s.* **1.** siringa **2.** estintore d'incendi **3.** zampillo, schizzo, piccolo getto d'acqua **.** (*dial. amer.*) saputello, presuntuoso **5.** (*dial.*) diarrea ☆ *— -gun*, pistola ad acqua.

to squirt, *v.t.i.* schizzare (liquido); zampillare; siringare; iniettare: *the radiator squirts*, il radiatore perde; *to — soda water into a glass*, spruzzare il seltz in un bicchiere.

squish [skwiʃ], *s.* (*sl.*) **1.** marmellata d'arance **2.** sciocchezza, stupidaggine.

squit [skwit], *s.* (*sl.*) persona insignificante, nullità.

stab [stæb], *s.* **1.** coltellata, pugnalata (anche *fig.*): *a — in the back*, una pugnalata nella schiena; *fig.* colpo sleale, a tradimento **2.** fitta, dolore acuto.

to stab, *pass.p.p.* **stabbed** [stæbd], *v.t.i.* **1.** pugnalare, accoltellare; ferire (anche *fig.*): *to — at s.o.*, dare una pugnalata a qlcu.; *to — at s.o.'s reputation*, danneggiare la reputazione di qlcu.; *to — s.o. to the heart*, trafiggere il cuore di qlcu., offendere gravemente qlcu. **2.** martellare, dar colpi con la martellina a: *to — a wall*, martellare una parete.

stabber ['stæbə*], *s.c.* accoltellatore, accoltellatrice; assassino, assassina; omicida.

stabbing ['stæbiŋ], *s.* il colpire con pugnale, l'accoltellare.

stability [stə'biliti], *s.* stabilità, fermezza; equilibrio (anche *fig.*): *the — of a country, of a government*, la solidità di un paese, di un governo; *man of no —*, uomo incostante ☆ *directional —*, (*aer.*) stabilità di rotta.

stabilization [ˌsteibilai'zeiʃən], *s.* stabilizzazione.

to stabilize ['steibilaiz], *v.t.* stabilizzare, dare stabilità a.

stabilizer ['steibilaizə*], *s.* (*chim. aer.*) stabilizzatore.

stable¹ ['steibl], *ag.* stabile, fermo, saldo; permanente; equilibrato (anche *fig.*): *the government is becoming —*, il governo si consolida; *he is a — man*, egli è una persona costante; *I want a — job*, desidero un'occupazione permanente ☆ *— oscillation*, (*fis.*) oscillazione costante.

stable², *s.* **1.** scuderia, stalla ‖ *to shut the — after the horse is stolen*, *prov.* chiudere la stalla quando i buoi sono fuggiti **2.** *coll.* scuderia, allevamento di cavalli da corsa; personale di scuderia **3.** *pl.* (*mil.*) servizio di stalla ☆ *— -boy*, mozzo di stalla; *— -companion*, cavallo della stessa scuderia; (*fam.*) membro dello stesso circolo; compagno di scuola ‖ *livery- —*, stallaggio con noleggio di cavalli; *racing- —*, scuderia (di cavalli da corsa).

to stable², *v.t.i.* **1.** mettere, tenere in stalla, scuderia **2.** alloggiare, prendere alloggio: *he must — where he can*, deve alloggiare dove può.

stableness ['steiblnis], *s.* (*rar.*) stabilità, fermezza; equilibrio (anche *fig.*).

stabling ['steibliŋ], *s.* **1.** stallaggio **2.** *coll.* stalle, scuderie.

to stablish ['stæbliʃ], *v.t.* (*arc.*) fissare solidamente; stabilire.

stably ['steibli], *av.* stabilmente; costantemente.

staccato [stə'kɑ:tou], *s.* (*mus.*) staccato.

stack [stæk], *s.* **1.** mucchio, cumulo, ammasso, catasta; bica; pagliaio; fascio (di fucili) **2.** (*fam.*) mucchio, grande quantità: *I have stacks (o a whole —) of work*

to get through, ho un mucchio di lavoro da fare; *to make stacks of money,* fare un sacco di soldi, fare soldi a palate **3.** gruppo di camini **4.** *(smoke-)* —, fumaiolo **5.** ‹ stack › (misura per combustibili = m.³ 3,06) **6.** faraglione (specialmente al largo delle coste della Scozia e delle Orcadi) ☆ — *-funnel,* sfiatatoio, bocchetta per l'aria; — *-furnace,* ciminiera di fabbrica; — *-guard,* copertura (di pagliaio); — *-stand,* base rialzata (di pagliaio); — *-yard,* cortile, aia (di cascinale).
 to **stack,** *v.t.* ammucchiare, accatastare, fare un mucchio di; abbicare: *the cyclists stacked their machines,* i corridori accatastarono le biciclette; *to — arms,* ammucchiare armi (a piramide) ‖ *to — the cards,* barare.
 stacte ['stækti:], *s.* storace, benzoino.
 stactometer [stæk'tɔmitə*], *s.* contagocce.
 staddle ['stædl], *s.* **1.** alberello superstite (di bosco ceduo) **2.** troncone (di albero) **3.** palo di sostegno (specialmente di pagliaio).
 stadium ['steidjəm], *pl.* **stadia** ['steidjə], *s.* **1.** *(st.)* stadio (misura itineraria greca variabile) **2.** stadio, campo sportivo **3.** stadio (di malattia).
 stadtholder ['stæt,houldə*], *s.* *(st.)* statolder (vicerè, governatore dei Paesi Bassi).
 stadtholdership ['stæt,houldəʃip], *s.* *(st.)* carica di statolder.
 staff[1] [stɑ:f], *pl.* **staffs** [stɑ:fs], *nel senso* **8. staves** [steivz], *s.* **1.** *gener. fig.* bastone; sostegno: *bread is the — of life,* il pane è il sostegno della vita; *to have the — of s.o.'s old age,* essere il bastone della vecchiaia di qlcu. ‖ — *and staple,* ingredienti principali ‖ *to have the — in one's own hand,* avere il coltello per il manico ‖ *to set (o to put up o to put down)* one's —, stabilirsi in un luogo **2.** bastone (insegna di comando) **3.** sostegno, asta (di bandiera, ecc.); *(mar.)* albero, alberetto **4.** *(mil.)* stato maggiore **5.** personale (di servizio, ufficio, ecc.): *to dismiss one's —,* licenziare il personale **6.** *(agrimensura)* paletto graduato; biffa **7.** *(med. chir.)* catetere; sonda scannellata **8.** *(mus.)* rigo musicale ☆ — *-angle,* *(edil.)* paraspigolo; — *cards,* schede del personale; — *-college,* scuola militare: — *-college officer,* ufficiale proveniente da una scuola militare: — *-corps,* *(mil.)* personale di assistenza; — *-head,* manico di bastone (generalmente lavorato); — *-officer,* ufficiale di stato maggiore; — *patterns,* *(amer.)* quadri del personale dirigente; — *-room,* camera di servizio ‖ *diplomatic* —, corpo diplomatico; *domestic* —, personale di servizio; *editorial* —, corpo redazionale: *the editorial — of a newspaper,* i redattori di un giornale; *medical* —, personale sanitario; *nursing* —, corpo infermiere; *pastoral* —, *(eccl.)* pastorale; *pilgrim's* —, bordone; *teaching* —, corpo insegnante; *white* —, bastone (carica) di gran tesoriere.
 to **staff**[1], *v.t.* fornire di personale: *army staffed with war-hardened officers,* esercito che dispone di ufficiali provati alla guerra; *to — an office with women,* assumere personale femminile per un ufficio ☆ *over-staffed,* con eccedenza di personale; *well-staffed,* ben fornito di personale: *well-staffed house,* casa ben fornita di servitù.
 staff[2], *s.* *(edil.)* specie di gesso misto a fibre per decorazioni.
 stag [stæg], *ag. attributivo* maschio, maschile ‖ **1.** cervo **2.** castrato **3.** giovane gallo da combattimento **4.** *(sl. comm.)* speculatore di Borsa; agente di cambio irregolare **5.** *(sl. amer.)* uomo che va a riunioni, feste senza essere accompagnato da una signora **6.** *(sl.)* informatore, spione: *to turn* —, fare il delatore ☆ — *-beetle,* *(entom.)* cervo volante; — *-hound,* rosso cane da caccia; — *-hunt(ing),* caccia al cervo; — *-party,* *(sl. amer.)* riunione per soli uomini.
 to **stag,** *pass.p.p.* **stagged** [stægd], *v.t.i.* *(sl.)* **1.** spiare, osservare furtivamente **2.** *(amer.)* andare a una riunione senza essere accompagnato da una signora.
 stage [steidʒ], *s.* **1.** piattaforma; impalcatura **2.** palcoscenico; teatro: *front of the —,* proscenio; *the English —,* il teatro inglese; *to come on the —,* entrare in scena;

to go on (o to take to) the —, diventare attore, calcare le scene; *to keep the —,* tenere il cartellone; *to leave (o to retire from) the —,* abbandonare le scene; *to put a play on the —,* mettere in scena un'opera teatrale **3.** *fig.* campo d'azione, scena, teatro: *he quitted the — of politics,* abbandonò la scena politica; *a larger — opened to him,* gli si aprì davanti un campo d'azione più vasto **4.** grado, stadio, momento, periodo (di sviluppo): *the early stages of existence,* i primi stadi dell'esistenza; *at that — an interruption occurred,* in quel momento ci fu un'interruzione; *he reached a critical —,* raggiunse un momento critico; *to be in the last —,* essere all'ultimo stadio **5.** tappa; distanza tra due tappe: *to travel by easy stages,* viaggiare a piccole tappe **6.** *(geol.)* strato **7.** *(microscopia)* piatto portaoggetti ☆ — *-box,* *(teat.)* palco di proscenio; — *-coach,* diligenza: — *-coach-man,* postiglione; — *-craft,* scenotecnica; — *-direction,* *(teat.)* didascalie; — *-door,* porta di servizio (di teatro); — *-effect,* effetto scenico; — *-flood,* riflettore per palcoscenico; — *-folk,* artisti; — *-fright,* *(sl. teat.)* timore panico prima del debutto; — *-hand,* *(teat.)* macchinista; — *-manager,* *(teat.)* regista; — *-name,* nome d'arte; — *-setting,* allestimento scenico; — *-slang,* gergo teatrale; — *-whisper,* *(teat.)* a parte: *to speak in a — -whisper,* *fig.* mormorare in modo da essere intesi ‖ *back-* —, dietro le quinte; *floating* —, *(mar.)* pontone; *fore-* —, ribalta; *hanging* —, *(edil.)* ponte volante; *landing-* —, *(mar.)* pontile, imbarcatoio, molo di sbarco; *revolving* —, palcoscenico girevole.
 to **stage,** *v.t.i.* **1.** mettere in scena, rappresentare; essere adatto alla rappresentazione: *this play does not — well,* questa commedia non si presta ad essere rappresentata **2.** inscenare (una dimostrazione, ecc.): *their indignation was staged,* la loro indignazione era tutta una messa in scena **3.** viaggiare a tappe; andare in diligenza: *staging to London,* andando a Londra in diligenza.
 stager ['steidʒə*], *s.* persona esperta, scaltrita: *an old* —, una vecchia volpe.
 staggard ['stægəd], *s.* cervo di quattro anni.
 stagger ['stægə*], *s.* **1.** barcollamento, ondeggiamento, andatura a zig-zag: *the — of a drunken man,* il barcollare di un ubriaco **2.** *pl.* vertigini: *to have the staggers,* avere le vertigini **3.** *pl.* *(vet.)* capogatto (degli ovini, dei cavalli) **4.** *(mec.)* sfalsamento **5.** *(aer.)* scalamento.
 to **stagger,** *v.t.i.* **1.** vacillare, far vacillare; barcollare, far barcollare; brancolare; ondeggiare; far ondeggiare: *the bearers staggered under the heavy burden,* i portatori vacillarono sotto il pesante carico; *he was staggered by the blow,* barcollò sotto il colpo; *she staggered out of the room,* uscì barcollando dalla stanza ‖ *to — forward,* avanzare barcollando **2.** dubitare, esitare; sconcertare, sconcertarsi; scuotere; impressionare, impressionarsi: *I was staggered by the news,* fui scosso dalla notizia **3.** distribuire in turni; scaglionare: *to — the working hours of the staff,* stabilire dei turni di lavoro per il personale **4.** *(mec.)* sfalsare **5.** *(aer.)* scalare.
 staggerer ['stægərə*], *s.c.* chi cammina barcollando, vacillando ‖ *s.* avvenimento, argomento, obiezione sconcertante.
 staggering ['stægəriŋ], *s.* **1.** barcollamento, vacillamento **2.** esitazione; stupore **3.** *(mec.)* lo sfalsare **4.** *(aer.)* lo scalare.
 staggeringly ['stægəriŋli], *av.* **1.** barcollando, vacillando **2.** con esitazione; con stupore; in maniera sconcertante.
 staginess ['steidʒinis], *s.* teatralità; artificiosità.
 staging ['steidʒiŋ], *s.* **1.** *(teat.)* messa in scena, allestimento scenico: *the — of a play is in itself a work of art,* l'allestimento di uno spettacolo è un lavoro artistico di per se stesso **2.** *(edil.)* impalcatura, ponteggio **3.** viaggio in diligenza; guida di una diligenza.
 Stagirite ['stædʒirait], *ag.* di Stagira ‖ *s.* stagirita ‖ *the* —, lo Stagirita, Aristotele.

stagnancy ['stægnənsi], *s.* ristagno, stasi.

stagnant ['stægnənt], *ag.* stagnante, fermo (anche *fig.*): — *water*, acqua stagnante, acqua morta; *business is* —, c'è un ristagno negli affari.

stagnantly ['stægnəntli], *av.* in modo stagnante (anche *fig.*).

to stagnate ['stægneit], *v.i.* 1. ristagnare, fermarsi, cessare di scorrere (di liquido) 2. ristagnare; intorpidirsi; essere inattivo, fermo.

stagnation [stæg'neifən], *s.* 1. ristagno: — *of blood*, ristagno di sangue 2. stasi, inattività; torpore: *the dullness and* — *of a country town*, la noia e il torpore di una città di provincia ☆ — *point*, (*fis.*) punto di ristagno.

stagnicolous [stæg'nikələs], *ag.* palustre.

stagy ['steidʒi], *ag.* (*spreg.*) teatrale, istrionico; artificioso.

staid [steid], *ag.* posato, serio, equilibrato; sobrio.

staidly ['steidli], *av.* seriamente, con equilibrio; posatamente.

staidness ['steidnis], *s.* compostezza, serietà; saggezza, ponderazione.

stain [stein], *s.* 1. macchia; scolorimento: *to remove a* —, togliere una macchia 2. *fig.* taccia, macchia, onta, vergogna: *the* — *of sin*, la macchia del peccato; *reputation without a* —, reputazione immacolata; *he came out of it without a* — *on his character*, ne uscì senza onta; *to cast a* — *on s.o.'s honour*, macchiare l'onore di qlcu. 3. colore, tinta 4. (*chim.*) colorante (usato per ricerche istologiche) ☆ — *-remover*, smacchiatore ‖ *wood-* —, tinta per legno.

to stain, *v.t.i.* 1. macchiare, macchiarsi; sporcare, sporcarsi (anche *fig.*): *hands stained with blood*, mani macchiate di sangue 2. stingere: *this cloth will not* —, questa stoffa non stinge 3. colorare (legno, vetro, ecc.); tingere 4. (*istologia*) colorare 5. stampare a colori (stoffa, carta da parati).

stainable ['steinəbl], *ag.* 1. macchiabile; sporcabile 2. colorabile, tingibile 3. (*chim.*) che prende la colorazione di Gram (in istologia).

stained [steind], *ag.* 1. macchiato, sporco (anche *fig.*); scolorito 2. colorato, tinto 3. (*chim.*) colorato (in istologia) ☆ — *glass*, vetro colorato (per finestre, vetrate, ecc.): — *glass window*, vetrata colorata, istoriata (di chiesa); — *paper*, carta da parato ‖ *guilt* —, *fig.* macchiato di colpa.

stainer ['steinə*], *s.* 1. tintore 2. (*chim.*) colorante.

staining ['steiniŋ], *s.* 1. tintura; colorazione 2. (*chim.*) colorazione (in istologia) ☆ — *agent*, (*chim.*) agente rivelatore; — *test*, (*chim.*) prova con rivelatore.

stainless ['steinlis], *ag.* 1. senza macchia, immacolato (anche *fig.*): — *reputation*, reputazione senza macchia; *the* — *mirror of the lake*, (*poet.*) lo specchio terso del lago 2. che non scolorisce, non stinge 3. che non arrugginisce, inossidabile ☆ — *steel*, acciaio inossidabile.

stainlessly ['steinlisli], *av.* immacolato, senza macchia (anche *fig.*).

stair [stɛə*], *s.* 1. scalino, gradino 2. *gener. pl.* scale: *I passed her on the stairs*, le passai accanto sulle scale; *to run up, down the stairs*, salire, scendere correndo le scale ‖ *below stairs*, nel seminterrato, nelle stanze della servitù ☆ — *-carpet*, passatoia; — *-rail*, ringhiera delle scale; — *-rod*, bacchetta metallica per fissare il tappeto alla scala; — *-well*, pozzo delle scale ‖ *flight of stairs*, rampa di scale; gradinata; *top* —, ultimo gradino (in alto).

staircase ['stɛəkeis], *s.* 1. scala; scalone 2. tromba delle scale ☆ *moving* —, scala mobile; *winding* — (o *corkscrew* — o *spiral* —), scala a chiocciola.

stairhead ['stɛəhed], *s.* pianerottolo.

stairway ['stɛəwei], *s.* scala, scalone.

staith(e) [steið], *s.* molo, scalo per il carbone.

stake¹ [steik], *s.* 1. palo (di sostegno, di steccato, ecc.); piuolo, picchetto; paletto 2. (palo del) rogo: *she was condemned to the* —, fu condannata al rogo 3. pic-

cola incudine, tassetto (da stagnaio, zincaio); piuolo (da falegname); (*conciatura*) orbello 4. (*topografia*) palina, picchetto; biffa ☆ — *-net*, (*pesca*) gradella.

to stake¹, *v.t.* 1. sostenere con pali, piuoli; palare; infrascare 2. attaccare, legare a piuolo, palo 3. trafiggere; (*st.*) impalare: *his horse got staked in trying to jump the fence*, il suo cavallo si sventrò nel tentativo di saltare lo steccato 4. (*conciatura*) passare all'orbello 5. *to* — *off, out*, cintare, chiudere con una palizzata; circoscrivere, delimitare con picchetti, biffe, ecc.; (*topografia*) palinare, picchettare; biffare: *to* — *out a telegraph line*, tracciare una linea telegrafica ‖ *to* — *out a claim*, *fig.* reclamare, pretendere, rivendicare.

stake², *s.* 1. posta, scommessa, puntata: *the stakes are five shillings*, la posta è di cinque scellini; *put down your stakes!*, fate il vostro giuoco!; *to lay the stakes*, giocare, puntare; *to play one's last* —, giocare l'ultima carta, pedina; *to sweep the stakes*, vincere tutte le poste, far piazza pulita ‖ *at* —, in giuoco: *he has large sums at* — *in that business*, ha impegnate, ha in giuoco forti somme di denaro in quell'affare; *his life is at* —, è in giuoco la sua vita ‖ *to have a* — *in sthg.*, avere degli interessi in ql.co. 2. *pl.* (*ippica*) premio; corsa ☆ — *-holder*, chi tiene le scommesse; — *-money*, posta, scommessa ‖ *consolation* —, premio di consolazione.

to stake², *v.t.* mettere in giuoco, scommettere, giocare, rischiare: — *your money!*, fate il vostro giuoco!; *I'd* — *my life on it*, ci scommetterei l'osso del collo; *to* — *heavily*, giocar forte, rischiare molto; *to* — *one's all*, mettere tutto in giuoco, rischiare il tutto per tutto, giocare l'ultima carta.

stalactic [stə'læktik], *ag.* stalattitico.

stalactiform [stə'læktifo:m], *ag.* stalattiforme.

stalactite ['stæləktait], *s.* stalattite.

stalactitic [,stælək'titik], *ag.* stalattitico.

stalagmite ['stæləgmait], *s.* stalagmite ☆ — *marble*, onice.

stalagmitic [,stæləg'mitik], *ag.* stalagmitico.

stale¹ [steil], *ag.* 1. vecchio, stantio: — *air*, aria viziata; — *beer*, birra vecchia; — *bead*, pane raffermo; *to smell* —, sapere di vecchio, di stantio, di rinchiuso 2. *fig.* vecchio, trito: — *joke*, barzelletta vecchia 3. esaurito, spossato: *an athlete becomes* — *through overtraining*, un atleta si esaurisce con l'allenamento eccessivo; *his talent has gone* —, il suo talento si è esaurito 4. (*comm.*) fermo (di mercato) 5. (*dir.*) caduto in prescrizione; scaduto (di assegno).

to stale¹, *v.t.i.* 1. rendere, diventare stantio, vecchio; prendere aria (di birra, ecc.) 2. *fig.* togliere, perdere sapore, interesse.

stale², *s.* orina (di bestiame).

to stale², *v.i.* (*arc. dial.*) orinare (di bestiame).

stale³, *s.* uccello da richiamo.

stalely ['steilli], *av.* (*rar.*) in modo trito.

stalemate ['steil'meit], *s.* 1. (*scacchi*) stallo 2. *fig.* punto morto, situazione senza via di uscita: *the war reached a* —, la guerra raggiunse una fase di stasi.

to stalemate, *v.t.* 1. (*scacchi*) fare stallo a, tenere in scacco 2. *fig.* portare a un punto morto, a una situazione senza via d'uscita.

staleness ['steilnis], *s.* 1. l'essere rafferno (di pane) 2. l'odorar di stantio, di chiuso 3. scipitezza, banalità.

stalk¹ [sto:k], *s.* 1. (*bot.*) stelo, gambo; (*bot. anat.*) peduncolo 2. stelo (di bicchiere, vaso): *old drinking -glasses with tall stalks*, vecchi bicchieri a calice 3. (*arch.*) ornamento a forma di stelo 4. alta ciminiera (di fabbrica) ☆ — *-borer*, larva di insetto che si nutre di peduncoli; — *-eyed*, (*zool.*) con gli occhi in cima alle antenne ‖ *abdominal* —, cordone ombelicale.

stalk², *s.* 1. andatura rigida e maestosa; passo altero 2. caccia furtiva alla preda; pedinamento silenzioso

to stalk², *v.t.i.* 1. camminare con andatura rigida e maestosa; camminare a passi misurati 2. inseguire furtivamente (la selvaggina).

stalked [stɔ:kt], *ag.* (*bot.*) fornito di gambo, di peduncolo.

stalker ['stɔ:kə*], *s.* **1.** persona che incede maestosamente **2.** cacciatore; cacciatore in agguato.

stalking-horse ['stɔ:kiŋhɔ:s], *s.* **1.** cavallo dietro a cui si apposta il cacciatore **2.** *fig.* pretesto, maschera: *hypocrisy is the devil's* —, l'ipocrisia è la maschera del diavolo.

stalkless ['stɔ:klis], *ag.* senza gambo; senza picciuolo; senza peduncolo.

stalklet ['stɔ:klit], *s.* (*bot.*) piccolo gambo, picciuolo, stelo secondario.

stalky ['stɔ:ki], *ag.* (*bot.*) **1.** a forma di picciuolo **2.** fornito di picciuolo; con lungo gambo.

stall[1] [stɔ:l], *s.* **1.** stalla; « box » di stalla **2.** banco di vendita; bancarella; chiosco: *I picked up this dictionary in* (o *on*) *a book* —, ho trovato questo dizionario su una bancarella; *to have a* —, avere una bancarella (al mercato) **3.** reparto, « stand » **4.** (*eccl.*) stallo, scanno; *fig.* dignità di canonico: *a canon's* —, stallo canonico; *fig.* canonicato **5.** (*teat.*) poltrona (di platea): *I should like a seat in the stalls*, vorrei un posto in poltrona **6.** reparto, recesso per un minatore (in una miniera di carbone) **7.** (*aer.*) stallo ☆ — -*rent*, tassa d'esercizio per venditori ambulanti.

to stall[1], *v.t.i.* **1.** mettere, tenere (bestiame) in stalla (per l'ingrasso): *stalled oxen*, buoi tenuti in stalla per l'ingrasso **2.** fornire (una stalla) di « boxes » **3.** impantanarsi, affondare (nella neve, ecc.) **4.** (*mec.*) fermarsi **5.** (*aer.*) stallare **6.** fornire di scanni (un coro, ecc.).

stall[2], *s.* **1.** complice di borsaiolo, palo **2.** (*sl. amer.*) espediente, pretesto elusivo.

to stall[2], *v.t.i.* (*amer.*) parlare, agire evasivamente (per eludere, ritardare un'azione): *stop stalling!*, smettila di menare il can per l'aia! **2.** ritardare (una azione) con espedienti elusivi **3.** *to* — *off*, tenere a bada: *he could no longer* — *off his creditors*, egli non potè più tenere a bada i creditori.

stallage ['stɔ:lidʒ], *s.* **1.** posteggio (di bancarella) **2.** diritto di posteggio, di esercizio **3.** tassa di posteggio.

stalling ['stɔ:liŋ], *s.* **1.** il mettere, il tenere in stalla (il bestiame) **2.** (*mec.*) il fermarsi bruscamente **3.** (*aer.*) lo stallare ☆ —*speed velocity*, velocità di atterraggio.

stallion ['stæljən], *s.* stallone.

stallman, *pl.* **stallmen** ['stɔ:lmən], *s.* **1.** venditore di bancarella **2.** minatore.

stalwart ['stɔ:lwət], *ag.* **1.** robusto, forte, gagliardo **2.** prode, valente, coraggioso; risoluto || *s.* **1.** persona coraggiosa **2.** (*pol.*) sostenitore, uomo di parte: *one of the old stalwarts*, uno della vecchia guardia.

stalwartness ['stɔ:lwətnis], *s.* **1.** vigoria, robustezza **2.** risolutezza, coraggio.

stamen ['steimen], *s.* (*bot.*) stame.

stamened ['steimənd], *ag.* fornito di stami.

stamina ['stæminə], *s.* capacità di resistenza, forza vitale, vigore: *man of great* —, uomo di fibra robusta; *man who lacks* —, uomo senza spina dorsale; *to lose one's* —, impigrirsi.

staminal ['stæminəl], *ag.* **1.** staminale, degli stami **2.** (*med.*) fortificante.

staminate ['stæminit], *ag.* (*bot.*) avente stami; maschio (di fiore).

stamineous, [stə'minjəs], *V.* **staminal**.

staminiferous [,stæmi'nifərəs], *ag.* staminifero.

stammer ['stæmə*], *s.* balbettamento; balbuzie.

to stammer, *v.t.i.* **1.** balbettare, tartagliare **2.** farfugliare, parlare confusamente (per eccitazione, impaccio).

stammerer ['stæmərə*], *s.c.* balbuziente.

stammering ['stæməriŋ], *ag.* balbuziente, balbettante || *s.* balbuzie; balbettio.

stammeringly ['stæməriŋli], *av.* balbettando; farfugliando.

stamp [stæmp], *s.* **1.** impronta, segno (anche *fig.*): *he stamps of his heavy boots*, le impronte dei suoi pesanti stivali; *he bears the* — *of genius*, porta in sè l'im-

pronta del genio **2.** bollo, francobollo; marchio; stampigliatura; timbro: *official* —, marchio officiale || *Stamp Act*, (*st. amer.*) legge sul bollo **3.** (*mec.*) mazza battente **4.** (*metal.*) stampo **5.** *fig.* tipo, sorta, stampo, genere: *man of that* —, uomo di tal tempra; *of the right* —, del tipo adatto; *of the same* —, dello stesso stampo, della stessa stoffa **6.** colpo (di piede): *with a* — *of the foot*, battendo il piede ☆ — -*album*, album per francobolli; — -*battery*, (*miner.*) macchina a maglio per sgretolare minerale; — -*collector*, filatelico; — -*duty*, tassa di bollo; — -*mill*, (*mec.*) molino a pestello; — -*office*, ufficio del bollo; — -*paper*, carta da bollo || *ad valorem* —, bollo proporzionale; *date-* —, timbro a data; *postage-* —, affrancatura postale; *revenue-* —, (*comm.*) marca da bollo; *twopenny* —, francobollo da due penny.

to stamp, *v.t.i.* **1.** imprimere, incidere, stampare; lasciare una impronta di; *fig.* imprimersi, incidersi (nella mente, ecc.): *to* — *one's foot on the snow*, lasciare le proprie impronte sulla neve; *to* — *sthg. on the mind*, imprimersi ql.co. nella mente; *to have one's initials stamped on sthg.*, far incidere, stampare le proprie iniziali su ql.co. **2.** marcare, dare l'impronta a; caratterizzare: *face stamped with melancholy*, viso improntato alla malinconia; *cruelty was stamped on his face*, la sua faccia portava il marchio della crudeltà; *that alone stamps the story as an invention*, basta questo a dimostrare che è tutta una frottola; *that stamps him*, da questo si può capire che tipo è **3.** timbrare; apporre un visto a; stampigliare; bollare; affrancare: *stamped paper*, carta bollata; documento vistato; *that letter is insufficiently stamped*, quella lettera non è affrancata sufficientemente; *we made another attempt to get the deed stamped*, tentammo ancora una volta di far autenticare il documento **4.** pestare, battere i piedi: *stamped earth*, terra battuta; *she stamped along the corridor*, i suoi passi riecheggiarono nel corridoio; *she stamped the snow from her feet*, si scrollò la neve dalle scarpe; *they stamped upstairs*, salirono le scale rumorosamente; *to* — *with rage*, pestare i piedi per la rabbia **5.** (*miner.*) frantumare; sgretolare, sbriciolare, polverizzare **6.** (*metal.*) stampare, punzonare **7.** *to* — *out*, soffocare, domare; annientare: *the rebellion was stamped out*, la ribellione fu soffocata.

stampede [stæm'pi:d], *s.* **1.** fuga disordinata e precipitosa (di massa di animali) **2.** fuggi-fuggi, serra-serra (anche *fig.*): *during the crisis there was a* — *to sell shares*, durante la crisi ci fu una corsa pazza a vendere azioni; *there was a* — *for the door*, si precipitarono tutti terrorizzati verso la porta.

to stampede, *v.t.i.* fuggire, far fuggire in disordine; causare panico, essere presi dal panico: *they are not easily stampeded*, non perdono la testa facilmente.

stamper ['stæmpə*], *s.c.* timbratore, timbratrice; punzonatore, punzonatrice || *s.* (*mec.*) stampo; timbratrice; punzone; frantumatrice.

stamping ['stæmpiŋ], *s.* **1.** scalpitio, il battere i piedi **2.** timbratura; bollatura; affrancatura **3.** (*mec.*) stampaggio **4.** (*miner.*) polverizzazione, sbriciolamento; frantumatura ☆ — -*ground*, (*sl.*) luogo di ritrovo molto frequentato; — -*machine*, affrancatrice postale; — -*mill*, (*miner.*) reparto frantumatura.

stance [stæns], *s.* (*golf, cricket*) posizione che si assume per dare un colpo alla palla: *to take up one's* —, mettersi in posizione di giuoco.

(to) stanch [sta:ntʃ], *V.* (to) **staunch**.

stanchion ['sta:nʃən], *s.* **1.** sostegno, puntello **2.** (*mec.*) montante **3.** stanghe (per attaccare il bestiame nelle stalle).

to stanchion, *v.t.* **1.** puntellare, rinforzare con sostegni, puntelli **2.** attaccare alle stanghe (bestiame).

stand [stænd], *s.* **1.** pausa, fermata, arresto; ristagno; (*teat.*) tappa (di compagnia): *a one-day* —, tappa di un giorno; *to come* (o *to be brought*) *to a* —, fermarsi, doversi fermare **2.** presa di posizione; resistenza: *to make* *a — against an abuse*, insorgere contro un'ingiustizia; *to make a — against the enemy*, opporre resistenza al nemico **3.** posizione, posto: *to take one's — near the door*, mettersi vicino alla porta **4.** luogo d'appostamento, d'imboscata; posto di guardia: *to take a — to shoot a deer*, appostarsi per sparare a un cervo **5.** palco, tribuna, piattaforma; (*amer.*) posto riservato ai testimoni in tribunale: *grand —*, tribuna d'onore; *to take the —*, (*amer.*) deporre in tribunale; *fig.* dire la propria opinione **6.** posteggio **7.** banco di vendita, bancarella; chiosco **8.** piedistallo, sostegno; scaffale, leggio; (*mec.*) supporto **9.** (*amer.*) pezzo di terreno coltivato; crescita di seminato: *a good — of corn*, un rigoglioso campo di grano **10.** (*mil.*) dotazione: *— of arms*, armamento (di un soldato) ‖ *— of colours*, insegne di un reggimento.

‘ **to stand**, *pass.p.p.* **stood** [stud], *v.t.i.* **1.** essere, stare in piedi: *I am too weak to —*, sono troppo debole per reggermi in piedi; *I could hardly —*, mi reggevo a stento; *I left her standing in the middle of the room*, la lasciai in piedi in mezzo alla stanza ‖ *— at ease!*, (*mil.*) riposo!; *— to attention!*, (*mil.*) attenti! ‖ *to — on one's own legs*, far da sè, essere indipendenti; *that boy hasn't a leg to — on*, quel ragazzo non ha proprio nessuna scusa **2.** stare, trovarsi: *the car is standing at the door*, l'automobile è alla porta; *here once stood a wonderful old castle*, qui sorgeva una volta un meraviglioso vecchio castello; *to — fast* (*o firm*), tener duro ‖ *to buy sthg. as it stands*, comperare ql.co. così com'è **3.** fermarsi, trattenersi, indugiare: *don't — on the platform*, non fermatevi sul marciapiede; *I stood and I looked at him*, mi fermai a guardarlo; *they were commanded to —*, ebbero l'ordine di fermarsi ‖ *— and deliver!*, o la borsa o la vita! **4.** durare, rimaner valido; conservarsi; sopravvivere: *the same remark stands good*, vale la stessa osservazione; *this building will — another century*, questo edificio si conserverà ancora cent'anni; *we — or fall together*, insieme per la vita e per la morte; *will this colour — or not?*, è solido questo colore o sbiadirà? **5.** essere (in determinate condizioni): *the balance of the account stands at £ 10*, il saldo del conto è di 10 sterline; *the Company does not — in his name*, la ditta non è intestata al suo nome; *gold stands higher than ever*, il prezzo dell'oro è più alto che mai; *how do you — for money?*, come stanno le tue finanze?; *how do you — with him?*, in che rapporti sei con lui?; *the thermometer stands at 80°*, il termometro segna 80°; *to — aloof*, isolarsi, rimanersene in disparte; *to — as a candidate*, (*pol.*) presentarsi come candidato; *to — as a guarantee*, farsi mallevadore; *to — convicted of sthg.*, essere colpevole, essere dichiarato colpevole di ql.co.; *to — in danger of*, rischiare di, essere esposto al pericolo di; *to — under heavy obligations*, aver grossi debiti, avere forti impegni; *to — well with s.o.*, essere stimato da, essere in buoni rapporti con qlcu. ‖ *he made my hair — on end*, mi fece rizzare i capelli dalla paura ‖ *to — at bay*, mettersi sulla difensiva in un momento di pericolo ‖ *to — in s.o.'s light*, ostacolare la riuscita di qlcu. ‖ *to — in a white sheet*, confessare umilmente i propri errori **6.** ristagnare; depositare; depositarsi (di liquidi): *the water appears to — here*, l'acqua sembra ristagnare in questo punto; *to allow a liquid to —*, lasciar depositare un liquido; *to let tea —*, lasciare il tè in infusione **7.** mettere in piedi; porre, collocare in posizione eretta: *I will — you in a corner, if you are naughty again*, se fai ancora il cattivo, ti metterò nel cantuccio; *— that chair against the wall*, appoggia quella sedia contro il muro **8.** sopportare, resistere: *it would be more than nature can —*, è al di là della capacità di sopportazione della natura umana; *she can't — him*, non lo può soffrire; *to — any amount of wear*, essere molto resistente; *to — one's ground*, mantenere le proprie posizioni, tener duro **9.** (*fam.*) pagare, sostenere le spese; offrire: *he promised to — us a good lunch*, ha promesso di offrirci un buon pranzetto; *William stood a round*, Guglielmo offrì da bere a

tutti **10.** *to — by* (*s.o.*, *sthg.*), stare accanto a; aiutare, sostenere; restare fedele a (promesse, impegni): *all I could do was to — by him*, non potei far altro che stargli accanto; *to — by the anchor*, (*mar.*) essere pronti a gettare l'ancora **11.** *to — for* (*sthg.*), voler dire, significare; implicare; sostenere (una causa); (*pol.*) essere candidato a; (*amer.*) sopportare, tollerare: *I am not going to — for that*, non ho nessuna intenzione di sopportare questo; *U. S. stands for United States*, U. S. significa Stati Uniti; *to — for nothing*, non contar niente **12.** *to — on* (*sthg.*), insistere, osservare scrupolosamente: *don't — on ceremony*, non far complimenti **13.** *to — to* (*sthg.*), aderire a, essere fedele a, mantenere; (*mar.*) dirigersi verso: *he stood to his promise*, mantenne la promessa ‖ *to — to* (*one's arms*), (*mil.*) stare all'erta **14.** *to — away*, allontanarsi: *to — away from shore*, (*mar.*) prendere il largo **15.** *to — by*, assistere, essere spettatore; tenersi pronto: *— by!*, (*tel.*) attenda all'apparecchio **16.** *to — down*, lasciare la barra (di testimoni); (*mil.*) smontare di guardia **17.** *to — in*, costare; associarsi: *this hat stood me in £ 10*, questo cappello mi è costato la bellezza di 10 sterline; *to — in with others*, associarsi, far lega con altri ‖ *to — s.o. in good stead*, essere utile a qlcu. **18.** *to — off*, allontanarsi; mantenersi distante; sospendere temporaneamente dal lavoro **19.** *to — on*, (*mar.*) tenere la rotta **20.** *to — out*, resistere, tener duro; spiccare, predominare; far contrasto: *the enemy stood out bravely*, il nemico resistè con coraggio; *those green velvet curtains will — out in your drawing-room*, quelle tende di velluto verde spiccheranno nel tuo salotto; *work that stands out from all the others*, lavoro che si distingue da tutti gli altri **21.** *to — over*, essere differito; restare in sospeso: *accounts standing over*, (*comm.*) conti in sospeso **22.** *to — up*, alzarsi in piedi ‖ *to — up for s.o.*, prendere le difese di qlcu. ‖ *to — up to s.o.*, affrontare coraggiosamente qlcu.

stand, (*nei composti*): *—-by*, partigiano, sostenitore; riserva; *— -in*, accordo, intesa; (*cine.*) controfigura; *—-offish*, riservato, altero; *— -offishness*, riserbo, alterigia; *— -patter*, (*fam. amer.*) uomo politico conservatore; *— -to*, (*mil.*) allarme, parata militare del mattino; *— -up*, rialzato, montante, eretto; in piedi; in regola, perfetto: *a — -up collar*, un colletto montante; *a — -up fight*, un combattimento in perfetta regola; *a — -up lunch*, una colazione in piedi ‖ *band- —*, palco per la banda; *music- —*, leggio; *testing —*, (*mec.*) banco di prova, di collaudo; *threelegged —*, treppiedi.

standard ['stændǝd], *s.* **1.** stendardo, bandiera, insegna: *the eagle was the — of the Roman legion*, l'aquila era l'insegna della legione romana ‖ *to march under the — of s.o.*, *fig.* essere seguace di qlcu. ‖ *to raise the — of revolt*, *fig.* iniziare una rivolta, una sommossa **2.** modello, campione, tipo; misura; norma: *do not judge all men by the same —*, non giudicare tutti gli uomini con lo stesso metro; *to make others conform to one's —*, fare che gli altri si adattino al proprio punto di vista; *to sin against accepted standards*, peccare contro norme di vita prestabilite ‖ *up to —*, (*comm.*) secondo campione **3.** grado di eccellenza; livello, qualità, tenore: *the — of living*, il tenore di vita; *the — of wages* il livello dei salari; *to reach a high — of efficiency*, raggiungere un alto livello di efficienza **4.** supporto, base piedistallo **5.** (*bot.*) arbusto tagliato ad alberello ☆ *—-bearer*, alfiere; capo di partito; *— car*, automobile di serie; *— edition*, edizione normale; *— English*, l'inglese corrente; *— gauge*, (*ferr.*) scartamento normale; (*cine.*) passo normale; *— lamp*, lampada a stelo; *— measure*, misura standard; *— metre*, metro campione; *— pound*, libbra regolamentare; *— sample*, campione unificato *— time*, ora legale.

standardization [,stændǝdai'zeiʃǝn], *s.* standardizzazione, uniformità, livellamento: *— of tariffs*, perequazione delle tariffe.

to **standardize** ['stændədaiz], *v.t.* standardizzare, uniformare, normalizzare ☆ *standardized production*, produzione in serie.

standee [stæn'di:], *s.* (*fam. amer.*) chi sta in piedi (in coda, a teatro, ecc.).

stander ['stændə*], *s.* chi sta in piedi ☆ —*-by*, spettatore, astante, testimone.

standing ['stændiŋ], *ag.* **1.** che sta in piedi, eretto; verticale: — *spectator*, spettatore in piedi ‖ *all* —, (*mar.*) tutto in buono stato; senza disarmare: *to turn into bed all* —, (*fam.*) coricarsi senza nemmeno spogliarsi ‖ *to be left* —, essere abbandonato sul posto **2.** fermo; inattivo, inoperoso: — *cabs*, autopubbliche in posteggio; — *engine*, macchina in riposo, inattiva **3.** fisso, immutabile, invariabile, permanente: — *colour*, colore solido; — *custom*, abitudine radicata; *a* — *invitation to dinner*, invito permanente a pranzo.

standing, *s.* **1.** posizione eretta, lo stare in piedi **2.** luogo di fermata, arresto (di auto, tram, ecc.) **3.** posizione, situazione; rango, importanza; reputazione: *the* — *of a firm*, l'importanza di una ditta; *the financial* — *of a company*, la situazione finanziaria di una società; *man of good* —, persona stimata; *man of no* —, persona che non gode di stima; *paper of good* —, giornale attendibile, serio **4.** durata, periodo di tempo: *officer of six months* —, ufficiale in servizio da sei mesi; *servant of old* —, vecchio servitore.

standing, (*nei composti*): — *-army*, esercito permanente; — *-bowl*, coppa a calice; — *-camp*, campo permanente, fisso; — *crop*, messi non mietute; — *-cup*, coppa a calice; — *dish*, piatto del giorno; — *-easy*, (*mil.*) posizione di riposo; — *-expenses*, spese generali, spese di casa; — *-ground*, punto d'appoggio; — *joke*, scherzo abituale, tradizionale, classico; — *-jump*, salto da fermo, senza rincorsa; — *orders*, regole permanenti di condotta, di procedura; — *price*, prezzo fisso; — *rigging*, (*mar.*) manovra fissa; — *room*, posti in piedi; — *rule*, regola fissa; — *-stone*, (*archeol.*) menhir; — *time*, durata della fermata; — *water*, acqua stagnante ‖ *hard* —, (*aer.*) piazzuola per il parcheggio di aerei pesanti; *long* —, di vecchia data.

standish ['stændiʃ], *s.* (*arc.*) calamaio e portapenna.

standpoint ['stændpoint], *s.* **1.** posizione, luogo di osservazione **2.** punto di vista.

standstill ['stændstil], *ag.* in riposo, fermo, immobile; che immobilizza ☆ — *order*, ordine di immobilizzazione completa: proibizione di trasportare del bestiame in una zona colpita da afta epizootica.

standstill, *s.* **1.** arresto, fermata, pausa: *many mills are at a* —, molte fabbriche sono inattive; *trade is at a* —, gli affari sono stagnanti; *to come to a* —, fermarsi; (*aut.*) restare in panne: *the conference has come to a* —, la conferenza è giunta ad un punto morto **2.** incapacità di movimento per esaurimento di forze.

stang [stæŋ], *s.* palo, pertica.

stanhope ['stænəp], *s.* calessino, biroccino (generalmente ad un posto solo).

staniel ['stænjəl], *s.* (*ornit.*) gheppio.

Stanislas ['stænisləs], **Stanislaus** ['stænislɔ:s], *no.pr. n.* Stanislao.

stank [stæŋk], *s.* **1.** stagno; pozza **2.** (*scoz. dial.*) diga, sbarramento.

to **stank**, *v.t.* (*scoz. dial.*) fare una diga; incanalare.

stannary ['stænəri], *s.* miniera di stagno ‖ *the Stanaries*, regione delle miniere di stagno della Cornovaglia e del Devon.

stannic ['stænik], *ag.* (*chim.*) stannico ☆ — *acid*, acido stannico.

stannite ['stænait], *s.* (*min.*) stagno pirifero; (*chim.*) stannito.

stannous ['stænəs], *ag.* (*chim.*) stannoso ☆ — *xyde*, ossido stannoso.

stanza ['stænzə], *pl.* **stanzas** ['stænzəz], *s.* (*poes.*) stanza, strofa.

staple[1] ['steipl], *ag.* principale: — *commodities*, prin-

cipali generi di consumo ‖ *s.* **1.** prodotto, articolo principale (di un paese, ecc.); industria, commercio principale: *coffee is the* — *of Brazil*, il caffè è il prodotto principale del Brasile; *the manufacture of cotton has long been the* — *of this country*, l'industria cotoniera è da tempo l'industria principale di questa nazione **2.** *fig.* oggetto, argomento principale di una conversazione: *to form the* — *of s.o.'s conversation*, formare l'argomento principale della conversazione di qlcu. **3.** materia prima, materiale grezzo **4.** (*st.*) fondaco **5.** (*arc.*) mercato principale, centro commerciale.

to **staple**[1], *v.t.* (*st.*) **1.** ricevere (merci per esportazione) in un fondaco **2.** controllare, selezionare (merci) secondo le regole del fondaco.

staple[2], *s.* **1.** (*artig.*) cavallottino, cambretta **2.** (*mec.*) ponticello, forcella; supporto di formatura **3.** serratura **4.** (*tip.*) graffetta, punto metallico.

to **staple**[2], *v.t.* **1.** fissare, unire con graffetta, chiodo, gancio **2.** (*tip.*) cucire a macchina.

staple[3], *s.* **1.** (*ind. tessile*) fibra; fiocco: *cotton of fine* —, cotone di fibra sottile; *highly curled* —, fiocco molto arricciato **2.** deposito, strato di vegetazione decomposta su una roccia ☆ — *thread*, (*ind. tessile*) filo di fibra selezionata.

to **staple**[3], *v.t.* cernere, classificare i fiocchi di (lana, cotone, ecc.).

staple[4], *s.* (*miner.*) piccolo cunicolo di comunicazione.

stapler[1] ['steiplə*], *s.* (*st.*) mercante di fondaco; membro dell'associazione dei mercanti di fondaco.

stapler[2], *s.* (*tip.*) macchina cucitrice.

stapler[3], *s.* classificatore, cernitore di lana.

stapling ['steipliŋ], *s.* cucitura con punti metallici ☆ — *-machine*, macchina cucitrice.

star [sta:*], *s.* **1.** stella, astro ‖ *to see stars*, *fig.* vedere le stelle ‖ *to sleep under the stars*, dormire all'addiaccio **2.** *fig.* stella, fortuna, destino: *you may thank your star you were not there!*, ringrazia il cielo che non c'eri!; *to be born under a lucky, evil* —, nascere sotto una buona, cattiva stella ‖ *my stars!*, caspita!, perbacco! **3.** stella (di stemma); decorazione, medaglia; (*mil.*) stelletta ‖ *the Stars and Stripes*, la bandiera degli Stati Uniti d'America **4.** (*tip.*) asterisco **5.** stella, diva, divo, celebrità: *literary* —, celebrità letteraria ☆ — *-beam*, raggio di stella; — *bit*, (*geol.*) trapano a croce; — *-bright*, lucente come una stella; risplendente; — *-chart*, mappa del sistema siderale; — *-cluster*, gruppo di stelle; — *connection*, (*elett.*) collegamento a stella; — *drift*, movimento proprio delle stelle; — *-dust*, polvere di stelle; — *-fort*, forte a pianta stellata; — *-gazer*, (*scherz.*) astronomo; — *-of-Bethlehem*, (*bot.*) stella di Betlemme; — *-shell*, (*mil.*) bengala, razzo illuminante; — *-shower*, pioggia di stelle cadenti, di meteore; — *-spangled*, stellato (specialmente della bandiera americana); — *-stone*, zaffiro; — *turn*, (*teat.*) numero principale; — *-wheel*, (*mec.*) ruota di arpionismo ‖ *evening* —, stella della sera, Espero; *fixed* —, stella fissa; *morning* —, stella del mattino, Lucifero; *north-* — (*o pole* —), stella polare; *shooting-* — (*o falling* —), stella filante; meteora.

to **star**, *pass.p.p.* **starred** [sta:d], *v.t.i.* **1.** adornare di stelle; costellare; tempestare di stelle: *grass starred with daisies*, prato cosparso di margheritine; *mantle starred with jewels*, mantello costellato di pietre preziose **2.** (*tip.*) segnare con asterisco, mettere un asterisco **3.** incrinarsi a raggiera (di vetro) **4.** (*cine. teat.*) primeggiare; avere il ruolo di protagonista: *to* — *in a film*, avere un ruolo importante in un film.

starboard ['sta:bəd], *ag.* (*mar.*) di tribordo ‖ *s.* (*mar.*) tribordo, dritta, destra: *to alter course to* —, dirigere la rotta verso destra.

to **starboard**, *v.t.* girare, mettere (il timone) a tribordo.

starch [sta:tʃ], *s.* **1.** amido ‖ *to take the* — *out of s.o.*, smontare qlcu. **2.** *fig.* rigidezza, formalismo; affettazione, ricercatezza **3.** (*fam. amer.*) energia, vigore ☆ — *-bandage*, fasciatura con bende inamidate; — *finish*, (*tec.*)

appretto a base d'amido; — *gum, (chim.)* destrina; — *paste,* colla d'amido; — *-splitting,* idrolisi dell'amido; — *sugar,* glucosio ‖ *potato-* —, fecola di patate.

to starch, *v.t.* **1.** inamidare, incollare (con colla d'amido) **2.** *fig.* rendere formale, affettato.

starched [stɑːtʃt], *ag.* **1.** inamidato **2.** *fig.* sostenuto (di comportamento); affettato: — *manners,* maniere affettate, ricercate.

starchedness [ˈstɑːtʃidnis], *s.* **1.** inamidatura **2.** *fig.* rigidità, sostenutezza; formalismo.

starcher [ˈstɑːtʃə*], *s.* **1.** operaio addetto all'inamidatura, alla carica di tessuti **2.** macchina per appretto, per caricare i tessuti **3.** *(fam.)* colletto inamidato.

starchiness [ˈstɑːtʃinis], *V.* **starchedness.**

starching [ˈstɑːtʃiŋ], *s.* inamidatura, apprettatura: — *of fabrics,* apprettatura di tessuti; — *of shirts,* inamidatura delle camicie ☆ — *machine, (ind. tessile)* macchina per ingommare.

starchy [ˈstɑːtʃi], *ag.* **1.** *(chim.)* amidaceo: — *foods,* cibi ricchi d'amido **2.** amidoso; inamidato **3.** *fig.* sostenuto, rigido; formale; affettato.

stardom [ˈstɑː-dəm], *s. (teat. cine.)* divismo, celebrità: *to rise to* —, diventare un divo, una diva; raggiungere la celebrità; *(fam.)* sfondare.

stare [stɛə*], *s.* sguardo fisso: *glassy* —, sguardo vitreo; *stormy* —, sguardo bieco; *with a — of astonishment,* con occhi spalancati per la meraviglia; *to give s.o. a* —, fissare qlcu. con occhio inquisitore.

to stare, *v.t.i.* fissare, lanciare sguardi; squadrare; sgranare gli occhi: *he stared into the room,* lanciò uno sguardo inquisitore nella stanza; *she is not accustomed to be stared at,* non è abituata ad essere squadrata; *they were staring rudely at each other,* si guardavano in cagnesco; *to — in s.o.'s face,* fissare qlcu. in viso; *to — into the distance,* guardare lontano; *to — s.o. into silence,* imporre silenzio a qlcu. con uno sguardo; *to — s.o. out of countenance,* fissare qlcu. fino a confonderlo; *to — s.o. up and down,* squadrare qlcu. da capo a piedi ‖ *it's staring you in the face,* salta agli occhi, è evidente.

starer [ˈstɛərə*], *s.c.* chi fissa intensamente ‖ *s. pl.* occhialino.

starfish [ˈstɑː-fiʃ], *s.* stella di mare.

staring [ˈstɛəriŋ], *ag.* **1.** fisso; stupefatto; sbalordito (di sguardo); spalancato, sbarrato (di occhio) **2.** chiassoso, sgargiante, vistoso: *a — dress,* un abito chiassoso; *a — tie,* una cravatta sgargiante ‖ *stark — mad,* pazzo da legare ‖ *s.* sguardo fisso; sguardo sfrontato.

staringly [ˈstɛəriŋli], *av.* fissamente; con occhi sbarrati; con tanto d'occhi.

stark [stɑːk], *ag.* **1.** rigido, duro: *he lay — in death,* giaceva nella rigidità della morte **2.** completo, vero e proprio: *the — desolation of the district,* la completa desolazione della zona; — *madness,* pura follia; *it is a — nonsense,* è una vera sciocchezza; *they stripped him* —, lo denudarono completamente **3.** *(poet.)* vigoroso; inflessibile.

stark, *av.* completamente, interamente: — *mad,* matto da legare; — *naked,* completamente nudo.

starkness [ˈstɑːknis], *s.* **1.** rigidità, durezza **2.** nudità.

starless [ˈstɑː-lis], *ag.* senza stelle.

starlet [ˈstɑːlit], *s.* **1.** piccola stella, stellina **2.** *(cine.)* stellina.

starlight [ˈstɑː-lait], *ag.* stellato; stellare: *a — evening,* una sera stellata ‖ *s.* luce, chiarore stellare: *by* (o *in the*) —, al chiarore delle stelle.

starlike [ˈstɑːlaik], *ag.* simile a stella; lucente.

starling[1] [ˈstɑːliŋ], *s. (ornit.)* storno, stornello.

starling[2], *s. (edil.)* palizzata di protezione e di sostegno.

starlit [ˈstɑː-lit], *ag.* illuminato dalle stelle; stellato.

starred [stɑːd], *ag.* **1.** stellato, adorno di stelle **2.** stellato, a stella **3.** influenzato dalle stelle **4.** *(tip.)* segnato con asterisco **5.** incrinato a raggiera (di vetro) ☆ *ill -* —, nato sotto una cattiva stella, sfortunato.

starring [ˈstɑːriŋ], *s. (teat. cine.)* ruolo principale ‖ *to make a — tour,* fare una « tournée » in qualità di primo attore.

starry [ˈstɑːri], *ag.* **1.** stellato, trapunto di stelle: — *night,* notte stellata **2.** brillante, lucente come stella: — *eyes,* occhi splendenti.

start [stɑːt], *s.* **1.** inizio, partenza; luogo di partenza: *at the* —, all'inizio: *business muddled at the* —, affari imbrogliati fin dall'inizio; *for a* —, *the report is wrong,* tanto per cominciare, il resoconto è errato; *for a — you will work here,* tanto per cominciare lavorerete qui; *from — to finish,* dall'inizio alla fine; *he got a good — in his career,* cominciò la sua carriera felicemente ‖ *to give an artist a good* —, lanciare un artista ‖ *to make an early* —, cominciare di buon'ora ‖ *to make a fresh — in life,* ricominciare, rifarsi una vita **2.** sobbalzo, soprassalto: *he gave a* —, sobbalzò; *to give a — of surprise,* fare un gesto di sorpresa; *to give s.o. a* —, far trasalire qlcu.; *to wake with a* —, svegliarsi di soprassalto ‖ *by fits and starts,* irregolarmente; a sprazzi **3.** posizione vantaggiosa; vantaggio dato all'inizio di una corsa: *they had a — of 10 yards,* avevano un vantaggio di 10 yarde ‖ *to give s.o. a* —, lasciare, far partire qlcu. per primo; *to get the — of s.o.,* mettere qlcu. in svantaggio; *to have the — of s.o.,* avere del vantaggio su qlcu. **4.** *(mec.)* avviamento **5.** situazione (imbarazzante): *rum* —, *(fam.)* fatto strano, avvenimento strano ☆ *cold* —, *(mec.)* avviamento a freddo; *kick* —, *(mec.)* avviamento a pedale.

to start, *v.t.i.* **1.** partire, mettersi in viaggio: *the train starts at noon,* il treno parte a mezzogiorno; *you'll — for London to-morrow,* partirai domani per Londra; *to — (off), (aut.)* partire; *(aer.)* decollare; *(mar.)* levare le ancore; *to — on a flight, (aer.)* decollare ‖ *I started back the next day,* il giorno dopo ripresi la via del ritorno **2.** *(II)* cominciare, iniziare, aver inizio: *negotiations have started well,* le trattative sono cominciate bene; *you started as a doctor,* cominciasti come medico *to — afresh* (o *again*), ricominciare; *fig.* rifarsi una vita; *to — at the beginning,* cominciare dall'inizio; *to — at £ 2 a week,* cominciare a lavorare con un salario di due sterline alla settimana; *to — by doing sthg.* cominciare col far qualcosa; *to — in life,* debuttare *to — (off* o *out) on a journey,* cominciare un viaggio *to — (up)on sthg.,* mettersi a fare ql.co.; *to — with toma — soup,* cominciare con una crema di pomodori *starting from...,* prendendo spunto da... ‖ *to — with you should go home,* tanto per cominciare, dovresti andare a casa **3.** dare inizio, dare l'avvio a; far partire; *(mec.)* mettere in moto; far funzionare: *he started a conversation with me,* intavolò una conversazione con me; *to — (off) a horse at a gallop,* far partire un cavallo al galoppo; *to — (up) a machine,* far funzionare, mettere in moto una macchina; *to — a race,* dare inizio a una corsa; *to — s.o. in business,* lanciare qlcu. negli affari; *to — s.o. on a career,* lanciare qlcu. in una carriera; *to — a topic,* introdurre un argomento di conversazione ‖ *to — a fire,* provocare un incendio **4.** trasalire; far trasalire; sobbalzare, far sobbalzare; sussultare: *he started at the sound of my voice,* trasalendo la mia voce; *he started from his chair,* si alzò bruscamente dalla sedia; *he started with surprise,* ebbe un moto di sorpresa ‖ *his eyes were starting out of his head,* aveva gli occhi fuori dell'orbita ‖ *to — to one's feet,* balzare in piedi **5.** stanare (selvaggina) **6.** disgiungersi, far disgiungere; staccarsi, far staccare (di legname); *(med.)* slogarsi **7.** *(mar.)* scaricare; svuotare **8.** *to — in, (fam.)* cominciare: *to — in to do sthg.,* cominciare a fare ql.co. **9.** *to — out, (fam.)* cominciare, avere intenzione di: *to — out to do sthg.,* avere intenzione di far qualcosa **10.** *to — up,* alzarsi bruscamente; crescere, spuntare (di piante); *fig.* nascere, sorgere: *mushroom villages were starting up everywhere,* villaggi sorgevano dappertutto come funghi ‖ *to — up from* (o *out of) one's sleep,* svegliarsi di colpo, di soprassalto.

starter ['stɑ:tə*], *s.c.* iniziatore, iniziatrice; autore, autrice (di progetto, ecc.); fondatore, fondatrice (di giornale, ecc.) || *s.* **1.** (*spor.*) (cavallo) partente **2.** (*spor.*) « starter », mossiere **3.** cane che stana la selvaggina **4.** (*aut.*) motorino d'avviamento ☆ — *battery*, (*elett.*) batteria d'avviamento || *self-* —, (*aut.*) avviamento automatico.

starting ['stɑ:tiŋ], *s.* **1.** inizio, partenza **2.** debutto; lancio: *the — of a new company*, il lancio di una nuova società **3.** (*mec.*) messa in moto; avviamento **4.** sussulto; sobbalzo; soprassalto ☆ — *handle*, (*mec.*) manovella di avviamento; — *-line*, (*spor.*) linea di partenza; — *-point*, punto di partenza; — *-post*, palo di partenza (di corse); — *-price*, prezzo iniziale; (*spor.*) ultima puntata (su un cavallo) prima della partenza.

startle ['stɑ:tl], *s.* trasalimento, sussulto improvviso.

to startle, *v.t.i.* spaventare, spaventarsi; far trasalire; allarmare: *he was startled to see her so pale*, si allarmò vedendola così pallida || *to — s.o. out of his sleep*, svegliare qlcu. di soprassalto.

startled ['stɑ:tld], *ag.* spaventato, allarmato: *a — cry*, un grido di spavento, d'allarme.

startler ['stɑ:tlə*], *s.* **1.** cosa, notizia allarmante **2.** cosa, notizia sensazionale, sorprendente.

startling ['stɑ:tliŋ], *ag.* **1.** allarmante, impressionante **2.** sensazionale; sorprendente: — *events*, eventi, fatti sensazionali; — *resemblance*, somiglianza sorprendente.

startlingly ['stɑ:tliŋli], *av.* **1.** in modo allarmante **2.** in modo sensazionale.

startlish ['stɑ:tliʃ], *ag.* eccitabile, impressionabile, pauroso; ombroso (di cavallo).

starvation [stɑ:'veiʃən], *s.* **1.** inedia, fame: *to die of —*, morire di fame; *to surrender from —*, arrendersi per fame **2.** estrema povertà ☆ — *wages*, salario da fame.

to starve [stɑ:v], *v.t.i.* **1.** morire di fame, far morire di fame; soffrire la fame, far soffrire la fame: *he starved to death*, morì di fame; *we would rather —*, preferiremmo morire di fame || *I am simply starving*, (*fam.*) muoio di fame || *to — a fever*, stare a dieta quando si ha la febbre || *to — the garrison into surrender*, costringere la guarnigione ad arrendersi per fame **2.** (*rar.*) morire di freddo, far morire di freddo: *to be starving with cold*, essere congelato **3.** deperire, intristire (di piante) **4.** (*amer. mec.*) mancare di carburante: *to — at high speed*, mancare di carburante a regime alto, avere alimentazione povera a regime elevato **5.** *to — for (sthg.)*, bramare: *they are starving for social life*, desiderano vivamente far vita mondana **6.** *to — out*, rendere per fame: *to — out a town*, prendere una città per fame; *to — s.o. out*, tagliare i viveri a qlcu.

starveling ['stɑ:vliŋ], *ag.* affamato, famelico, denutrito: *a little — kitten*, un gattino affamato || *s.* affamato; persona, animale mezzo morto di fame.

stash [stæʃ], *s.* (*contr.* di *store* e *cache*) (*sl. amer.*) cosa messa in serbo.

to stash, *v.t.* (*sl. amer.*) mettere in serbo.

stasis ['steisis], *pl.* **stases** ['steisi:z], *s.* **1.** (*patol.*) stasi; ristagno **2.** interruzione nello sviluppo.

statable ['steitəbl], *ag.* affermabile; che può essere chiarato, stabilito, specificato.

state [steit], *s.* **1.** stato, condizione, situazione, posizione: *the — of the case*, i fatti e le circostanze relative al caso; — *of mind*, disposizione d'animo; *people in a savage —*, gente allo stato selvaggio; *just look what — I am in*, guarda in che stato mi trovo || *here's a nice (o pretty) — of things!*, è un bel rebus!, è un bel pasticcio! **2.** *State*, (*pol.*) stato, nazione; governo: *affairs of State*, affari di stato; *Church and State*, Chiesa e Stato; *secretary of State*, (*amer.*) segretario di stato, ministro degli Esteri; *the States of the Church* (o *the Papal States*), gli Stati Pontifici || *the States*, gli Stati Uniti **3.** rango, dignità; pompa, parata; splendore, magnificenza: *he lived in a style befitting his —*, aveva un tenore di vita adatto al suo rango; *he wore his robes of —*, por-

tava l'uniforme di gala; *to bear great —*, avere una carica importante; essere importante (di cose); *to dine in —*, partecipare a un pranzo di gala; *to escort s.o. in —*, scortare qlcu. con grande pompa; *to live in —*, vivere in gran pompa **4.** (*arch.*) trono, baldacchino sul trono ☆ — *-aided*, sovvenzionato dallo stato; — *-apartments*, appartamento di rappresentanza; — *-ball*, ballo ufficiale, di corte; — *-cabin*, (*mar.*) cabina di lusso; — *-carriage* (o *-coach*), carrozza di gala; — *-control*, (*econ.*) controllo di stato, statalizzazione; — *-documents*, documenti ufficiali; — *-forest*, foresta demaniale; — *-house*, palazzo del governo; — *-prisoner*, prigioniero politico; — *-reception*, ricevimento ufficiale; — *-trial*, processo politico.

to state, *v.t.* **1.** affermare, asserire; dichiarare, enunciare; specificare: *as stated above*, come espresso sopra; *I have seen it stated*, l'ho visto citato; *it is stated in orders that...*, (*mil.*) è stabilito (negli ordini) che...; *it should also be stated that...*, si deve aggiungere che...; *please — below*, pregasi annotare qui sotto; *you must — full particulars*, si devono dichiarare tutte le circostanze, i particolari; *to — an account*, (*comm.*) fare un estratto conto; *to — one's case*, (*dir.*) esporre i fatti; *to — sthg. definitely*, specificare ql.co. **2.** fissare, stabilire **3.** (*mat.*) enunciare, esprimere con formule.

statecraft ['steitkrɑ:ft], *V.* **statesmanship**.

stated ['steitid], *ag.* **1.** dichiarato: *above —*, sopracitato **2.** stabilito; fisso: *at — intervals*, a intervalli fissi; *on — days*, a giorni fissi.

statedly ['steitidli], *av.* a intervalli regolari; nel modo stabilito.

stateless ['steitlis], *ag.* **1.** senza patria; senza nazionalità; apolide **2.** senza cerimoniale, senza pompa.

stateliness ['steitlinis], *s.* aspetto imponente; grandiosità, imponenza, magnificenza, maestosità.

stately ['steitli], *ag.* nobile, signorile; maestoso, magnifico, sontuoso; altero; elevato (di stile): — *bearing*, portamento maestoso; — *grace*, bellezza altera; *the — homes of England*, le sontuose dimore d'Inghilterra.

statement ['steitmənt], *s.* **1.** esposto; esposizione (di fatti, situazioni, ecc.); rapporto, relazione: *certified —*, dichiarazione controllata, verificata; *official —*, comunicato ufficiale; *the — made by the witness*, la deposizione fatta dal testimone; — *of conclusions arrived at*, esposto sulle decisioni prese; *to draw up a —*, redigere un esposto; *to make* (o *to publish*) *a —*, fare un rapporto **2.** asserzione, affermazione, dichiarazione: *a — appeared in the press to the effect that...*, una dichiarazione di stampa diceva che...; *his — was unfounded*, la sua asserzione era infondata; *to contradict a —*, ritirare, smentire una dichiarazione **3.** (*comm. amm.*) denunzia, dichiarazione: — *as to income*, dichiarazione del reddito; — *of expenses*, conto spese; *account —*, estratto conto; *monthly —*, bilancio mensile.

stater ['steitə*], *s.* statere (antica moneta greca).

stateroom ['steit-rum], *s.* **1.** sala di rappresentanza **2.** (*mar.*) cabina del capitano, di alto ufficiale **3.** cabina di lusso per passeggeri (su nave da trasporto); scompartimento privato (su un treno).

statesman, *pl.* **statesmen** ['steitsmən], *s.* **1.** uomo di stato; statista **2.** (*dial.*) piccolo proprietario terriero.

statesmanlike ['steitsmənlaik], **statesmanly** ['steitsmənli], *ag.* da uomo di stato, da statista.

statesmanship ['steitsmənʃip], *s.* arte di governo; arte, scienza politica.

static(al) ['stætik(əl)], *ag.* statico ☆ — *balance*, equilibrio statico; — *electricity*, elettricità statica; — *friction*, attrito di primo distacco; — *transformer*, trasformatore statico.

statically ['stætikəli], *av.* staticamente.

statics ['stætiks], *s.* **1.** (*fis.*) statica **2.** (*rad.*) disturbi atmosferici; perturbazioni atmosferiche **3.** (*cine.*) effluvi.

station ['steiʃən], *s.* **1.** posto, luogo; posto assegnato: *take your stations!*, (*mar.*) ai vostri posti!; *to be in —*, *out of —*, essere, non essere al proprio posto; *to take* *up a* —, prender posto, stabilirsi 2. stazione; base; posto di operazione: *a* — *near the Pole*, una stazione vicino al Polo; *naval* —, porto militare; *to be on* — *in India*, (*mil.*) essere di guarnigione in India 3. (*ferr. mar. aer. rad.*) stazione; (*miner.*) recetta: *to reach the* —, arrivare in stazione; entrare in stazione (di treni) 4. posizione, condizione sociale, rango: *the duties of his high* —, i doveri derivanti dalla sua posizione elevata; *what is her* — *in life?*, a che classe sociale appartiene?; *to marry below one's* —, sposarsi con qlcu. di condizione inferiore 5. (*eccl.*) stazione della Via Crucis 6. (*bot. zool.*) «habitat» ☆ — *-bill*, (*mil.*) ruolo delle destinazioni; — *-bus*, vettura d'albergo di servizio alla stazione; — *-house*, guardina; (*amer.*) posto di polizia; (*ferr.*) stazione secondaria; — *-hotel*, albergo della stazione; — *-log*, (*rad.*) giornale, registro della stazione; — *-master*, capostazione; — *-price*, (*comm.*) prezzo alla stazione di partenza; — *-rod*, (*topografia*) stadia; — *-roof*, pensilina ferroviaria; — *-wagon*, (*aut.*) giardinetta || *action* —, (*mar.*) posto di combattimento; *airplane-* —, scalo aereo; *broadcasting* —, (*rad.*) stazione emittente; *central* —, (*amer.*) centrale elettrica; *coaling-* —, stazione di carbonamento; *control-* —, stazione di controllo; *goods-* —, scalo merci; *illicit* —, (*rad.*) stazione clandestina; *military-* —, guarnigione; *petrol* — (o *filling* —), stazione di rifornimento; *police-* —, commissariato di polizia; *polling-* —, sezione elettorale; *reversing* —, stazione di testa; *sheep* — (o *cattle* —), (*austral.*) allevamento di ovini, bovini; *shunting* —, (*ferr.*) stazione di smistamento; *terminal* —, (*ferr.*) stazione di testa; *through-* —, stazione di transito; *weather-* —, stazione meteorologica.

to **station**, *v.t.* assegnare un posto a, collocare, piazzare: *to* — *oneself behind a tree*, appostarsi dietro un albero; *to* — *troops*, (*mil.*) postare truppe; *to be stationed at...*, (*mil.*) essere di guarnigione a...; (*mar.*) essere ormeggiato a....

stationary ['steiʃnəri], *ag.* stazionario, fermo, immoto; permanente, fisso; (*mil.*) sedentario: — *temperature*, (*med.*) temperatura stazionaria; *to remain* —, restare immobile ☆ — *car*, automobile in sosta; — *troops*, truppe sedentarie.

stationer ['steiʃnə*], *s.* cartolaio: — *'s* (*shop*), cartoleria || *Stationers' Hall*, «Stationers' Hall» (sede londinese della «Company of Stationers», che regolò sino al 1842 l'attività editoriale).

stationery ['steiʃnəri], *s.* cartoleria; articoli di cancelleria || *H. M. Stationery Office*, Istituto Poligrafico dello Stato.

statist ['steitist], *s.* 1. statista, uomo di stato 2. esperto in statistica.

statistic(al) [stə'tistik(əl)], *ag.* statistico.

statistically [stə'tistikəli], *av.* statisticamente.

statistician [ˌstætis'tiʃən], *s.* esperto, studioso di statistica.

statistics [stə'tistiks], *s.* 1. (scienza della) statistica: — *is very interesting*, la statistica è una scienza molto interessante 2. *pl.* statistiche: — *show a fair decrease in birth rate*, le statistiche mettono in evidenza una certa diminuzione delle nascite.

statistology [ˌstætis'tɔlədʒi], *s.* la statistica.

statoscope ['stætəskoup], *s.* (*fis.*) statoscopio.

statuary ['stætjuəri], *ag.* 1. statuario, scultorio 2. scolpito || *s.* 1. scultura 2. scultore ☆ — *art*, arte statuaria; — *marble*, marmo da scultura.

statue ['stætju:], *s.* statua: *he stands like a* —, sta fermo e impalato come una statua.

statued ['stætju:d], *ag.* 1. adorno di statue: *vased and* — *terraces*, terrazze adorne di vasi e statue 2. scolpito: *raffigurato in statua: the* — *satyrs*, i satiri di pietra.

statuesque [ˌstætju'esk], *ag.* statuario, scultoreo; plastico: *a* — *beauty*, una bellezza statuaria.

statuesquely [ˌstætju'eskəli], *av.* scultoriamente.

statuette [ˌstætju'et], *s.* statuetta, statuina.

stature ['stætʃə*], *s.* statura: *to be short of* —, esser di bassa statura; *to increase in* —, crescere di statura.

status ['steitəs], *s.* 1. stato (anche *dir.*); condizione sociale, rango || *without any official* —, senza titolo ufficiale 2. situazione, stato, condizione: *the present* — *of broadcasting*, la situazione odierna delle trasmissioni radio || — *quo*, status quo ☆ *civil* —, stato civile; *legal—*, condizione giuridica; *social* —, posizione sociale.

statutable ['stætjutəbl], *V.* **statutory**.

statutably ['stætjutəbli], *av.* in conformità con la legge, con lo statuto.

statute ['stætju:t], *s.* 1. statuto, regolamento, ordinamento 2. (*Bibbia*) tavole della legge: *the statutes of God*, i comandamenti di Dio ☆ — *-book*, raccolta di leggi approvate dal Parlamento; — *-law*, legge statutaria; *University statutes*, regolamenti universitari.

statutory ['stætjutəri], *ag.* 1. statutario, imposto dalla legge 2. regolamentare, conforme alla legge 3. riconosciuto dalla legge (di delitto) ☆ — *declaration*, dichiarazione statutaria.

staunch [stɔ:ntʃ], *ag.* 1. fedele, leale; sicuro: — *faith*, fede incrollabile; — *friend*, amico fedele 2. impermeabile all'aria e all'acqua 3. solido, saldo; massiccio: *a* — *wall*, un muro solido || *s.* 1. emostatico 2. chiusa, diga.

to **staunch**, *v.t.* 1. arrestare, fermare l'uscita di (generalmente sangue); arrestare l'emorragia di 2. alleviare (il dolore); arrestare (il corso di malattia).

staunchly ['stɔ:ntʃli], *av.* 1. fedelmente, lealmente 2. fermamente, con fermezza.

staunchness ['stɔ:ntʃnis], *s.* 1. fedeltà, lealtà 2. impermeabilità 3. solidità, stabilità.

stave [steiv], *s.* 1. doga (di botte) 2. piuolo (di scala) 3. (*poes.*) stanza, strofa; verso 4. (*mus.*) pentagramma ☆ — *-rhyme*, allitterazione.

to **stave**, *pass.p.p.* **staved** [steivd], **stove** [stouv], *v.t.* 1. cambiare le doghe a (un barile) 2. *to* — **in** fare un foro in (un barile, una barca, ecc.); sfondare (una scatola, ecc.); sformare (un cappello, ecc.). 3. *to* — **off**, stornare, allontanare; ritardare, differire: *they staved off bankruptcy*, evitarono la bancarotta; *to* — (*off*) *s.o from doing sthg.*, trattenere qlcu. dal fare ql.co.

staves [steivz], *pl.* di **stave** e di **staff** 8.

stavesacre ['steivz,eikə*], *s.* (*bot.*) stafisagria.

stay[1] [stei], *s.* 1. soggiorno, periodo di permanenza: *a fortnight's* —, un soggiorno di due settimane 2. pausa, fermata; (*dir.*) sospensione: — *of execution*, sospensione dell'esecuzione di una sentenza; — *of proceedings*, procedura sospesa 3. (*letter.*) resistenza 4. (*letter.*) controllo, freno.

to **stay**[1], *v.t.i.* 1. fermarsi, sostare, trattenersi; soggiornare: —!, *you have forgotten sthg.*, (*arc.*) un momento!, hai dimenticato ql.co.; *get him to* — *a minute*, fallo fermare un minuto; *he has come to* —, è venuto per passare qualche giorno con noi; *I stayed in town last winter*, passai lo scorso inverno in città; *shall I* — *with you?*, mi volete con voi?; *to* — *at a hotel*, alloggiare in un albergo; *to* — *in bed*, restare a letto || — *put*, fermati dove sei! 2. fermare, arrestare; trattenere: — *the progress of an epidemic*, arrestare il corso di un'epidemia; *to* — *s.o.'s arm*, trattenere qlcu. per braccio 3. resistere; sopportare: *that horse cannot* — *three miles*, quel cavallo non può sostenere una corsa sulla distanza di tre miglia 4. (*dir.*) differire, posporre, sospendere: *to* — *a judgement*, soprassedere un giudizio 5. controllare, frenare; calmare: *to* — *one hunger*, calmare l'appetito 6. *to* — **away**, essere assente, non partecipare 7. *to* — **in**, non uscire, stare in casa; (*mil.*) essere consegnato 8. *to* — **up**, vegliare, stare alzato: *to* — *up late*, coricarsi tardi.

stay[2], *s.* 1. sostegno (anche *fig.*); supporto; piedestallo: *the* — *of his old age*, il bastone della sua vecchiaia 2. (*mec.*) puntello; supporto di lunetta; tubo montante 3. *pl.* corsetto, busto ☆ — *-bolt*, (*mec.*) chiodo di collegamento, tirante; — *-lace* (o — *-tape* laccio, stringa per busto; — -maker, bustaia; — -rod, (mec.) tirante; — -tube, (mec.) tirante (di una caldaia).

to **stay**², v.t. (mec. ing.) puntellare, armare di puntelli: to — a roof, (miner.) rafforzare il soffitto (d'una galleria); to — (up) a wall, puntellare un muro.

stay³, s. **1.** (mar.) straglio ‖ slack in stays, lento a virare (di bordo); to miss (o to lose) stays, non riuscire a virare (di bordo) **2.** fune (di asta, di bandiera, ecc.) ☆ — -tackle, (mar.) paranco di straglio ‖ funnel- —, (mar.) straglio del fumaiuolo.

to **stay**³, v.t. (mar.) **1.** sostenere (gli alberi) di una nave con gli stragli **2.** far virare di bordo (una nave).

stay-at-home ['steiəthoum], ag. casalingo ‖ s. persona casalinga: she is a —, ella sta sempre in casa.

stayer ['steiə*], s.c. chi resta, chi rimane ‖ s. (spor.) atleta fondista; cavallo di fondo.

staying ['steiiŋ], s. **1.** soggiorno, visita **2.** resistenza **3.** arresto; interruzione **4.** (dir.) aggiornamento, rinvio ☆ — power, capacità di resistenza.

stayless¹ ['steilis], ag. senza sosta, senza interruzione; incessante.

stayless², ag. senza sostegno.

staysail ['stei-seil], s. (mar.) vela di straglio.

stead [sted], s. (letter.) vece, posto, luogo: to act in s.o.'s —, fare le veci di qlcu. ‖ to stand s.o. in good —, essere di vantaggio, di aiuto a qlcu.

to **stead**, v.t. aiutare; essere di aiuto, di vantaggio a.

steadfast ['stedfəst], ag. fermo; risoluto; costante: — in adversity, incrollabile di fronte alle avversità; — in love, costante in amore; — policy, linea d'azione costante.

steadfastly ['stedfəstli], av. stabilmente, fermamente; risolutamente; con costanza.

steadfastness ['stedfəstnis], s. fermezza; tenacia; costanza: man who lacks —, uomo senza (forza di) carattere.

steadily ['stedili], av. **1.** saldamente; fermamente: tables that do not stand —, tavoli traballanti; to refuse — to do sthg., rifiutarsi fermamente di fare ql.co. **2.** regolarmente, costantemente; assiduamente, diligentemente: to work — at sthg., lavorare assiduamente a ql.co.

steadiness ['stedinis], s. **1.** fermezza, sicurezza; fissità: — of gaze, fissità dello sguardo; — of hand, fermezza della mano **2.** assiduità, perseveranza, diligenza, applicazione: — in doing sthg., perseveranza nel fare ql.co. **3.** regolarità, stabilità: — of prices, stabilità di prezzi **4.** condotta equilibrata, posata; saggezza.

steading ['stediŋ], s. **1.** tenuta agricola, fattoria **2.** (amer.) lotto di terreno per costruzioni edili.

steady ['stedi], ag. **1.** fermo, saldo, fisso, rigido: as — s a rock, saldo come una roccia; to be — on one's legs, stare saldo sulle gambe **2.** calmo, equilibrato; disciplinato, controllato: — horse, cavallo calmo; — nerves, nervi calmi; — troops, truppe disciplinate; — ship in any sea, nave che tiene bene il mare **3.** continuo, regolare, costante, persistente: — breeze, brezza persistente, forte; — demand, (comm.) richiesta costante; — market, mercato sostenuto; — pace, andatura regolare; — pulse, (med.) polso regolare; — trot, trotto sostenuto; — weather, tempo stabile; — worker, lavoratore assiduo ‖ to grow —, stabilizzarsi; the market is growing —, (comm.) il mercato si va stabilizzando **4.** fedele, assiduo; serio: to be — in one's principles, restare fedele ai propri principi **5.** attento!, fermo!, calmo!: — (the helm)!, (mar.) barra dritta! ☆ — current, (elett.) corrente costante; — -going, regolare, ponderato; metodico.

steady, s. (mec.) supporto, lunetta fissa ‖ s.c. (sl. amer.) amico, amica del cuore.

to **steady**, v.t.i. **1.** rafforzare rinforzare, rinforzarsi; rendere fermo, equilibrato; consolidare; ritrovare l'equilibrio: to — the nerves, rafforzare, calmare, distendere i nervi; to — the running of a machine, stabilizzare, regolarizzare la corsa di una macchina **2.** (mar.) riprendere l'equilibrio: the boat steadied, la nave si rimise in

rotta **3.** to — down, mettere giudizio: that girl has steadied down, quella ragazza ha messo giudizio.

steak [steik], s. fetta (di carne, di pesce) ☆ beef —, bistecca di manzo; fillet —, bistecca di filetto.

steal¹ [sti:l], s. **1.** (dial. bot.) picciuolo **2.** manico (di utensile, ecc.).

steal², s. **1.** furto; affare disonesto **2.** refurtiva **3.** (golf) colpo lungo che va in buca.

to **steal**², pass. **stole** [stoul], p.p. **stolen** ['stoulən], v.t.i. **1.** rubare, sottrarre: thou shalt not —, (Bibbia) non rubare; to — a few hours from one's sleep, rubare qualche ora al sonno; to — a glance at s.o., lanciare uno sguardo furtivo a qlcu.; to — a kiss, rubare un bacio; to — a march on s.o., prevenire qlcu., prendere vantaggio su qlcu.; to — (away) s.o.'s heart, sedurre il cuore di qlcu. **2.** to — into (a place), entrare di nascosto, furtivamente **3.** to — over (s.o., sthg.), impossessarsi: their emotion had stolen over me, la loro emozione si era impossessata di me **4.** to — upon (s.o.), avvicinarsi pian piano a: he felt sleep stealing upon him, sentì che il sonno si impossessava di lui **5.** to — along, camminare furtivamente, in punta di piedi **6.** to — away, svignarsela quatto quatto **7.** to — in, out, entrare, uscire di soppiatto.

stealer ['sti:lə*], s.c. ladro, ladra.

stealing ['sti:liŋ], s. furto; ruberia ‖ — by finding, appropriazione indebita di cosa trovata.

stealth [stelθ], s. procedimento segreto; segretezza ‖ by —, segretamente, furtivamente: to do sthg. by —, fare ql.co. di nascosto.

stealthily ['stelθili], av. furtivamente, di soppiatto: to creep in —, entrare di soppiatto.

stealthiness ['stelθinis], s. carattere furtivo (di azione, movimento).

stealthy ['stelθi], ag. furtivo: — glance, sguardo furtivo, di soppiatto.

steam [sti:m], s. **1.** vapore: at full —, (mar.) a tutto vapore; full — ahead!, (mar.) avanti a tutto vapore!; to get up —, aumentare la pressione, alzare il vapore; to keep up —, restare sotto pressione; to let off —, lasciare andare il vapore; to proceed under one's own —, (mar.) avanzare coi propri mezzi (anche fig.) **2.** (fam.) energia; spirito: to get up —, raccogliere le proprie forze; to let off —, sfogarsi ☆ -boiler, caldaia a vapore; — -box (o -chest), camera (di distribuzione) del vapore; — -brake, freno a vapore; — -coal, carbone a fiamma corta; — -colour, colore fissato a vapore; — -crane, gru a vapore; — -cylinder, cilindro a vapore; — -dome, duomo, cupola di presa del vapore; — -engine, macchina a vapore; — -gas, vapore surriscaldato; — -gauge, manometro; — -generator, generatore di vapore; — -hammer, maglio a vapore; — -heating, riscaldamento a vapore; — -jackrt, camicia di vapore; — -jet, getto di vapore; — navigation, navigazione a vapore; — -navvy, draga a vapore; — -piston, stantuffo a vapore; — -power, forza a vapore; — -press, pressa a vapore; — -pump, pompa a vapore; — -roller, compressore stradale (a vapore); — -trap, scaricatore di condensa a vapore; — -tug, rimorchiatore a vapore; — -whistle, fischio a vapore ‖ dry —, vapore secco; super-heated —, vapore surriscaldato.

to **steam**, v.t.i. **1.** esporre al vapore; trattare con vapore (legno); passare al vapore (stoffa): to — open an envelope, aprire una busta al vapore **2.** cuocere a vapore: to — a sole, cuocere una sogliola a vapore **3.** emettere, esalare vapore; fumare: horses steaming with sweat, cavalli fumanti di sudore; soup steaming in the bowls, minestra fumante nelle scodelle **4.** funzionare, andare a vapore (di treni, navi, ecc.): how fast are we steaming?, a che velocità andiamo? ‖ to — ahead, avanzare (di macchine a vapore); (fam.) fare grandi progressi, lavorare sodo **5.** to — away, partire; evaporare: the train steamed away, il treno partì **6.** to — up, aumentare la pressione del vapore; (fam.) darci dentro.

steamboat ['sti:mbout], *s*. battello a vapore.
steamer ['sti:mə*], *s*. **1**. battello, vaporetto **2**. macchina a vapore **3**. pentola a pressione.
steaminess ['sti:minis], *s*. **1**. esalazione di vapore; vaporosità **2**. appannamento.
steamship ['sti:m-ʃip], *s*. piroscafo, nave a vapore, vapore.
steamtight ['sti:m-tait], *ag*. a tenuta di vapore.
steamy ['sti:mi], *ag*. **1**. che esala vapore (di cibi, ecc.), fumante; pieno di vapore, vaporoso **2**. appannato; umido: — *windows*, finestre appannate.
stearate ['stiəreit], *s*. (*chim*.) stearato.
stearic [sti'ærik], *ag*. (*chim*.) stearico.
stearin ['stiərin], *s*. (*chim*.) stearina ☆ — *candle*, candela di stearina.
stearinery ['stiərinəri], *s*. stearineria.
steatite ['stiətait]. *s*. (*min*.) steatite.
steed [sti:d], *s*. (*letter. scherz*.) corsiero, destriero.
steel [sti:l], *s*. **1**. acciaio ‖ *grip of —*, *fig*. pugno d'acciaio **2**. arma, spada, lama, arma bianca: *to fight with cold —*, battersi all'arma bianca **3**. acciarino; cote **4**. (*farm*.) ferro: *tincture of —*, tintura di percloruro di ferro ☆ — *cap*, elmetto; — *casting*, (*metal*.) getto d'acciaio; — *-clad*, rivestito d'acciaio; — *company*, acciaieria; — *-grey*, grigio acciaio; — *-hearted*, *fig*. dal cuore duro come l'acciaio; — *-pen*, pennino d'acciaio; — *-plate*, lastra, piastra d'acciaio; — *-plated*, corazzato; — *-road*, (*amer*.) ferrovia; — *-wool*, lana d'acciaio; (*fam*.) paglietta ‖ *bar- —*, acciaio in barre; *blister- —*, acciaio di cementazione; acciaio cementato; *cold-drawn —*, acciaio tirato a freddo; *cold-rolled —*, acciaio laminato a freddo; *electroplated —*, acciaio argentato; *hard —*, acciaio duro; *hardened —*, acciaio temprato; *hot-rolled —*, acciaio laminato a caldo; *mild —* (o *soft —*), acciaio dolce; *nickel- —*, acciaio al nickel; *stainless —*, acciaio inossidabile.
to steel, *v.t*. **1**. coprire d'acciaio, armare con acciaio: *to — a copper plate*, coprire d'acciaio una piastra di rame **2**. *fig*. rendere duro come l'acciaio; indurire: *selfishness had steeled his heart*, l'egoismo gli aveva indurito il cuore; *we must — our hearts against compassion*, dobbiamo farci un cuore di pietra e non aver compassione; *to — oneself against sthg.*, corazzarsi contro ql.co.; *to — oneself* (o *one's heart*) *to sthg.*, *to do sthg.*, armarsi di coraggio per ql.co., per fare ql.co.
steeliness ['sti:linis], *s*. durezza; inflessibilità; insensibilità.
steelwork ['sti:lwə:k], *s*. **1**. lavoro in acciaio; struttura di acciaio **2**. *pl*. acciaierie.
steely ['sti:li], *ag*. **1**. di acciaio; simile ad acciaio **2**. *fig*. insensibile; severissimo; inflessibile: *his — wrist*, il suo polso di ferro.
steelyard ['stiljɑ:d], *s*. **1**. stadera **2**. valvola, leva di sicurezza (di caldaia).
steenbok ['sti:nbɔk], *s*. (*zool*.) raficero.
steening ['sti:niŋ], *s*. rivestimento in pietra (di pozzo).
steep¹ [sti:p], *ag*. **1**. ripido, scosceso, erto: *a — hill*, una collina erta **2**. (*fig. fam*.) esorbitante, irragionevole; incredibile: — *price*, prezzo esorbitante; *a — story*, una storiella strabiliante **3**. *fig*. arduo, ambizioso; *you are aiming at a very — task*, aspiri a una mansione assai ardua ‖ *s*. luogo erto, scosceso, a picco; pendio ripido; erta; precipizio ☆ — *-to*, (*mar*.) a picco: — *-to shore*, costa a picco.
steep², *s*. **1**. macerazione; l'inzuppare, l'impregnare (ql.co. con un liquido) **2**. liquido impregnante, bagno di macerazione; infusione.
to steep², *v.t*. immergere (anche *fig*.); impregnare, inzuppare; macerare: *he is steeped in mathematics*, è immerso nella matematica; *steeped in ignorance, in prejudice*, imbevuto di ignoranza, di pregiudizi; *terrace steeped in the glare*, terrazza immersa di sole; *to — gherkins in vinegar*, conservare cetrioli sott'aceto; *to — oneself in drink*, annegare i dispiaceri nell'alcool.

to steepen ['sti:pən], *v.t.i*. **1**. rendere, diventare scosceso, erto **2**. *fig*. aumentare, crescere.
steeper ['sti:pə*], *s*. **1**. addetto alla macerazione **2**. macero, maceratoio; recipiente per macerazione, per infusione.
steeping ['sti:piŋ], *s*. immersione prolungata; macerazione; infusione.
steeple ['sti:pl], *s*. guglia; campanile ☆ — *-head*, (*mec*.) chiodo a testa conica; — *-jack*, chi compie riparazioni su campanili, camini.
steeplechase ['sti:pltʃeis], *s*. (*ippica*) «steeplechase», corsa ad ostacoli.
to steeplechase, *v.i*. (*ippica*) partecipare a corse ad ostacoli.
steeplechaser ['sti:pl,tʃeisə*], *s*. (*ippica*) **1**. chi partecipa alle corse ad ostacoli **2**. cavallo addestrato per corse ad ostacoli.
steepled ['sti:pld], *ag*. fornito di campanile.
steeply ['sti:pli], *av*. a picco, ripidamente: *cliffs that fall — into the sea*, scogliera a picco sul mare; — *inclined road*, strada a forte pendio.
steepness ['sti:pnis], *s*. pendenza, ripidezza; inclinazione: — *of a curve*, (*geom*.) grado d'inclinazione d'una curva.
steepy ['sti:pi], *ag*. (*arc*.) erto, ripido, scosceso; inclinato.
steer¹ [stiə*], *s*. bue giovane, manzo.
to steer², *v.t.i*. **1**. guidare, governare; manovrare: *his car steers hard*, lo sterzo della sua macchina è duro; *the ship refuses to —*, la nave non governa; *to — by the wind*, governare secondo il vento **2**. dirigere, dirigersi: *to — north*, fare rotta verso nord **3**. *to — clear of sthg.*, *s.o.*, evitare ql.co., qlcu.
steerable ['stiərəbl], *ag*. governabile, manovrabile.
steerage ['stiəridʒ], *s*. (*mar*.) **1**. governo del timone **2**. alloggio dei passeggeri di 3ª classe: *to go* (*to travel*) —, fare la traversata in terza classe; *viaggiare sul ponte* ☆ — *-way*, abbrivo.
steerer ['stiərə*], *s*. (*mar*.) timoniere; pilota.
steering ['stiəriŋ], *s*. direzione; guida; governo del timone, dei timone (di navi, automobili, ecc.): *good —*, buona, cattiva manovra; *to lose — control*, perdere il controllo della guida ☆ — *-angle*, angolo di sterzata; — *-box*, scatola dello sterzo; — *-column*, albero di sterzo; piantone di guida; — *-gear*, dispositivo comando di sterzo, di timone; — *-wheel*, (*aut*.) volante; (*mar*.) ruota del timone.
steersman, *pl*. **steersmen** ['stiəzmən], *s*. timoniere, pilota.
steersmanship ['stiəzmənʃip], *s*. (*mar*.) abilità, mestiere di timoniere, di pilota.
steeve¹ [sti:v], *s*. (*mar*.) angolo del bompresso con l'orizzonte.
to steeve¹, *v.t.i*. (*mar*.) inclinare (il bompresso) a angolo con l'orizzonte; fare angolo con l'orizzonte (il bompresso).
steeve², *s*. (*mar*.) barra di stivaggio.
to steeve², *v.t.i*. (*mar*.) stivare (il carico).
stein [stain], *s*. boccale da birra in ceramica.
steinbock ['stainbɔk], *s*. (*zool*.) stambecco.
stele ['sti:li(:)], *pl*. **stelae** ['sti:li:], **steles** ['sti:li], *s*. (*archeol*.) stele.
Stella ['stelə], *no.pr.f*. Stella.
stellar ['stelə*], *ag*. stellare, astrale.
stellate ['stelit], **stellated** ['steleitid], *ag*. (*poet*.) stellato; a forma di stella; disposto a stella ☆ — *leav-*, foglie radiate.
stelliferous [ste'lifərəs], *ag*. stellato.
stelliform ['stelifɔ:m], *ag*. stelliforme.
stellion ['steliən], *s*. (*zool*.) stellione.
stellular ['steljulə*], **stellulate** ['steljulit], *ag*. forma di piccola stella; cosparso di piccole stelle.
stem¹ [stem], *s*. **1**. (*bot*.) tronco; gambo; picciolo **2**. stelo (di bicchiere); cannello (di pipa); gamba (di nota musicale) **3**. ceppo, ramo (di famiglia,

descended from a collateral —, discendente da un ramo collaterale **4.** (*gram.*) radice (di parola) ☆ *underground* —, (*bot.*) rizoma.

to **stem**[1], *pass.p.p.* **stemmed** [stemd], *v.t.i.* **1.** togliere il gambo (a fiori, foglie, ecc.) **2.** (*amer.*) discendere.

stem[2], *s.* (*mar.*) prua: *from — to stern*, da prua a poppa.

to **stem**[2], *v.t.i.* (*mar.*) **1.** dirigere (la prua, la nave) verso **2.** andare contro corrente **3.** mantenere una rotta.

to **stem**[3], *v.t.i.* **1.** arrestare; controllare; arginare, contenere (anche *fig.*): *to — the tide of popular indignation*, arrestare l'ondata di sdegno popolare **2.** poggiare saldamente (un arto) **3.** (*miner.*) tappare, otturare, tamponare.

stemless ['stemlis], *ag.* senza gambo; senza picciuolo.

stemlet ['stemlit], *s.* piccolo stelo, piccolo gambo.

stemma ['stemə], *pl.* **stemmata** ['stemətə], *s.* **1.** albero genealogico **2.** (*entom.*) occhio semplice; faccetta di occhio composto.

stemple ['stempl], *s.* **1.** (*miner.*) sbarra, puntello di sostegno in una galleria **2.** scalino di legno.

stench [stentʃ], *s.* puzzo, tanfo: *what a —!*, che puzzo! ☆ *- -trap*, pozzetto, sifone intercettatore.

stenchy ['stentʃi], *ag.* fetido, puzzolente.

stencil ['stensl], *s.* **1.** stampino **2.** decorazione, riproduzione fatta con stampino **3.** marchio ☆ *— copy*, codia a ciclostile; *— -plate*, lastra di stampaggio.

to **stencil**, *pass.p.p.* **stencilled** ['stensld], *v.t.* stampinare; riprodurre mediante stampini; (*fam.*) ciclostilare.

sten-gun ['stengʌn], *s.* (*mil.*) « sten » (fucile mitragliatore).

stenochromy ['stenəkroumi], *s.* stampa a colori.

stenograph ['stenəgrɑːf], *s.* **1.** segno stenografico **2.** macchina per stenografare.

to **stenograph**, *v.t.* stenografare.

stenographer [ste'nogrəfə*], *s.c.* stenografo, stenografa.

stenographic [ˌstenə'græfik], *ag.* stenografico.

stenographically [ˌstenə'græfikəli], *av.* stenograficamente.

stenography [ste'nogrəfi], *s.* stenografia.

stenosis [sti'nousis], *pl.* **stenoses** [sti'nousiːz], *s.* (*patol.*) stenosi.

stenotypist ['stenəˌtaipist], *s.c.* stenotipista.

stenotypy ['stenəˌtaipi], *s.* stenotipia.

Stentor ['stentoː*], *no.pr.m.* (*lett. greca*) Stentore ‖ **stentor**, *s.* persona dalla voce stentorea.

stentorian [sten'toːriən], *ag.* stentoreo (di voce).

stentorphone ['stentəfoun], *s.* altoparlante.

step [step], *s.* **1.** passo (anche *fig.*); andatura; cadenza: *a — back, forward*, un passo indietro, avanti; *within a — from his house*, a due passi da casa sua; *do not move a —*, non ti muovere assolutamente; *do you know her —?*, conosci la sua andatura?; *there is but a — from life to death*, c'è solo un breve passo dalla vita alla morte; *there is a good* (o *long*) —, c'è un buon tratto di strada; *watch your —!*, fa' attenzione, guarda dove metti i piedi!; *to be in — with s.o.*, tenere il passo con qlcu.; *to break —*, rompere il passo; *to fall into, out of —*, mettersi al, perdere il passo; *to keep —*, tenere il tempo, stare al passo; *to retrace one's steps*, tornare sui propri passi, tornare indietro; *to take a —*, dirigersi verso... ‖ *— by —*, gradualmente, un poco alla volta ‖ *in —*, (*elett.*) in fase: *alternators in —*, alternatori sincronizzati **2.** orma, impronta: *steps in the soil*, impronte sul terreno; *in his steps*, sulle sue orme; *fig.* seguendo il suo esempio; *I have found his steps*, ho trovato le sue tracce **3.** misura, provvedimento: *a rash, prudent —*, un provvedimento affrettato, una misura prudente; *to take the necessary steps to prevent sthg.*, prendere le misure necessarie per impedire ql.co.; *to take no steps until...*, trattenersi dal fare ql.co. fino a che... **4.** gradino, piolo (di scala); cengia (di monte); *pl.* scaletta ‖ *flight of steps*, scalinata **5.** grado: *avan-*

zamento: a — in army rank, un grado nell'esercito; *when did you get your —?*, quando ti hanno promosso? **6.** (*med.*) fase, momento **7.** (*mus.*) intervallo **8.** (*mar.*) scassa ☆ *— -bearing*, (*mec.*) supporto di base, ralla di estremità; *— -pulley*, (*mec.*) puleggia multipla a gradini ‖ *angular- —*, gradino d'angolo; *folding steps*, (*mar.*) scala pieghevole; *hanging- —*, gradino a sbalzo; *landing- —*, (*mar.*) scaletta di sbarco, di imbarco; *waltz- —*, passo di valzer.

to **step**, *pass.p.p.* **stepped** [stept], *v.t.i.* **1.** camminare, andare, venire: *— here* (o *this way*), vieni qua ‖ *— lively!*, (*amer.*) sbrigatevi!, spicciatevi! ‖ *to — high*, andar di buon trotto (di cavallo) ‖ *to — short*, accorciare il passo **2.** misurare a passi: *to — (off) a distance*, misurare a passi una distanza **3.** danzare: *— it with him*, balla con lui **4.** scalinare, disporre a scala **5.** (*mar.*) fissare (l'albero) nella scassa **6.** *to — into* (*sthg.*), entrare in; *fig.* ottenere: *to — into a boat*, salire a bordo; *fig. — into a fortune*, ereditare un patrimonio **7.** *to — on* (*sthg.*), camminare su: *don't — on the grass*, non camminate sull'erba; *to — on board*, salire a bordo ‖ *— on it!*, *I am in a hurry*, spicciati che ho fretta! ‖ *to — on the gas*, (*amer. sl. aut.*) accelerare **8.** *to — across*, attraversare; (*fam.*) fare una visitina **9.** *to — aside*, farsi da parte; fare una digressione **10.** *to — back*, indietreggiare **11.** *to — down*, discendere; (*elett.*) ridurre, diminuire (tensione) **12.** *to — forward*, avanzare **13.** *to — in*, entrare; montare, salire su (un veicolo); *fig.* intervenire, frapporsi, intromettersi **14.** *to — off*, partire; iniziare; scendere (da vettura, ecc.): *to — off with the right foot*, partire col piede destro; *fig.* cominciare bene ‖ *we'll soon tell him where he steps off*, (*amer.*) non esiteremo a dirgli il fatto suo **15.** *to — out*, uscire; scendere (da vettura); affrettare il passo; (*fam. amer.*) andare a spassarsela **16.** *to — over*, saltare ‖ *to — over to s.o.'s house*, fare un salto in casa di qlcu. **17.** *to — up*, salire; aumentare: (*elett.*) aumentare (tensione): *to — up the standard of education in the schools*, (*amer.*) elevare il livello culturale nelle scuole.

stepbrother ['stepˌbrʌðə*], *s.* fratellastro.

stepchild ['steptʃaild], *pl.* **stepchildren** ['stepˌtʃildrən], *s.c.* figliastro, figliastra.

stepdaughter ['stepˌdoːtə*], *s.* figliastra.

stepfather ['stepˌfɑːðə*], *s.* patrigno.

Stephen ['stiːvn], *no.pr.m.* Stefano.

stepmother ['stepˌmʌðə*], *s.* matrigna.

stepney ['stepni], *s.* (*aut.*) ruota di ricambio.

steppe [step], *s.* steppa.

stepping ['stepiŋ], *s.* andatura ☆ *— -stone*, pietra per guadare; *fig.* gradino, trampolino: *this position is a — -stone to success*, questa posizione è un trampolino di lancio verso il successo.

stepsister ['stepˌsistə*], *s.* sorellastra.

stepson ['stepsʌn], *s.* figliastro.

stercoraceous [ˌstəːkə'reiʃəs], *ag.* stercoraceo.

stercorary ['stəːkərəri], *ag.* stercorario.

stercoration [ˌstəːkə'reiʃən], *s.* concimazione.

stere [stiə*], *s.* stero (unità di volume = 1.308 cu. yd.).

stereo ['stiəriou], *pl.* **stereos** ['stiəriouz], *ag.* (*abbr.* di *stereoscopic*) stereoscopico ‖ *s.* **1.** (*abbr.* di *stereotype*) stereotipo **2.** (*abbr.* di *stereoscope*) stereoscopio.

stereograph ['stiəriəgrɑːf], *s.* stereografo.

stereographic [ˌstiəriə'græfik], *ag.* (*geom.*) stereografico.

stereography [ˌstiəri'ogrəfi], *s.* (*geom.*) stereografia.

stereometer [ˌstiəri'omitə*], *s.* (*geom.*) stereometro.

stereometry [ˌstiəri'omitri], *s.* (*geom.*) stereometria.

stereophonic [ˌstiəriə'fonik], *ag.* stereofonico.

stereoscope ['stiəriəskoup], *s.* (*ott.*) stereoscopio.

stereoscopic(al) [ˌstiəriəs'kopik(əl)], *ag.* stereoscopico.

stereoscopy [ˌstiəri'oskəpi], *s.* stereoscopia.

stereotype ['stiəriətaip], *s.* (*tip.*) stereotipo, « cliché » (anche *fig.*).

to **stereotype**, *v.t.* (*tip.*) stereotipare, stampare per mezzo di stereotipie.

stereotyper ['stɪərɪəˌtaɪpə*], **stereotypist** ['stɪərɪəˌtaɪpɪst], *s.* (*tip.*) stereotipista.

stereotypy ['stɪərɪəˌtaɪpɪ], *s.* (*tip.*) stereotipia.

sterile ['sterail], *ag.* sterile: *a — discussion*, una discussione senza alcun risultato; *a — land*, una terra sterile.

sterility [ste'rɪlɪti], *s.* sterilità.

sterilization [ˌsterɪlaɪ'zeɪʃən], *s.* sterilizzazione.

to **sterilize** ['sterɪlaɪz], *v.t.* rendere sterile, infecondo, isterilire; sterilizzare: *to — water*, sterilizzare l'acqua ☆ *sterilized milk*, latte pastorizzato.

sterilzer ['sterɪlaɪzə*], *s.* sterilizzatore; autoclave.

sterlet ['stə:lit], *s.* (*ittiol.*) sterleto.

sterling ['stə:lɪŋ], *ag.* **1.** di buona lega, genuino (di monete, metalli preziosi): *— silver*, argento puro; *10 pounds —*, 10 lire sterline **2.** schietto, sincero; solido; puro: *a — character*, carattere schietto ‖ *s.* moneta legale inglese.

stern[1] [stə:n], *ag.* severo, austero; rigido, rigoroso: *a — manager*, un direttore severo ‖ *the sterner sex*, il sesso forte.

stern[2], *s.* **1.** (*mar.*) poppa: *from stem to —*, da prua a poppa **2.** deretano; coda (di animale) ☆ *— -board*, (*mar.*) manovra a ritroso; *— -fast*, (*mar.*) codetta, cima per ormeggio di poppa; *— -post*, (*aer. mar.*) dritto di poppa; *— -wheeler*, (*mar.*) battello a ruota posteriore.

sternly ['stə:nli], *av.* severamente, rigidamente, austeramente.

sternness ['stə:nnis], *s.* severità, austerità, rigidezza.

sternsheets ['stə:nʃi:ts], *s.pl.* (*mar.*) poppa.

sternum ['stə:nəm], *pl.* **sternums** ['stə:nəmz], **sterna** ['stə:nə], *s.* (*anat.*) sterno.

sternutation [ˌstə:nju'teɪʃən], *s.* starnuto.

sternutative [stə'nju:tətiv], **sternutatory** [stə'nju:tətəri], *ag.s.* starnutatorio.

sternway ['stə:nwei], *s.* (*mar.*) abbrivo indietro.

stertorous ['stə:tərəs], *ag.* (*patol.*) stertoroso: *— respiration*, respiro stertoroso.

stertorousness ['stə:tərəsnis], *s.* (*patol.*) stertore.

stet [stet], *s.* (*nella correzione di bozze*) vive.

to **stet**, *pass.p.p.* **stetted** ['stetid], *v.t.* (*nella correzione di bozze*) approvare la versione originale di.

stethoscope ['steθəskoup], *s.* (*med.*) stetoscopio.

to **stethoscope**, *v.t.* auscultare con lo stetoscopio.

stethoscopic [ˌsteθəs'kɔpik], *ag.* (*med.*) stetoscopico.

stethoscopy [ste'θɔskəpi], *s.* (*med.*) stetoscopia.

stevedore ['sti:vidɔ:*], *s.* stivatore.

stew[1] [stju:], *s.* **1.** vivaio di pesci, peschiera **2.** vivaio di ostriche.

stew[2], *s.* **1.** umido, stufato **2.** *fig.* ansietà, agitazione; preoccupazione: *to be in a —*, (*fam.*) essere sui carboni ardenti, sulle spine; essere in grande agitazione **3.** (*arc.*) terme, bagni **4.** *pl.* bordello, lupanare ☆ *Irish —*, spezzatino di montone.

to **stew**, *v.t.i.* **1.** cuocere, far cuocere in umido, stufare ‖ *to let s.o. — in his own juice* (o *grease*), (*fam.*) lasciar cuocere qlcu. nel proprio brodo **2.** *fig.* soffocare, mancar d'aria **3.** (*sl.*) sgobbare (negli studi).

steward [stjuəd], *s.* **1.** amministratore, intendente, castaldo: *the estate —*, l'amministratore della tenuta **2.** dispensiere; (*mil.*) capo furiere **3.** (*aer. mar.*) cameriere di bordo **4.** sovrintendente incaricato; commissario di gara, ecc. ‖ *Lord Steward of the Household*, Siniscalco di Corte (in Inghilterra) ‖ *Lord High Steward of England*, cerimoniere per l'incoronazione di un re; giudice del tribunale che deve giudicare i Pari (in Inghilterra) ☆ *—'s mate*, (*mar.*) cambusiere; *—'s room*, (*mar.*) cambusa ‖ *megaphone- —*, annunciatore; *shop- —*, membro della commissione interna (di uno stabilimento).

stewardess ['stjuədis], *s.* **1.** dispensiera **2.** (*mar. aer.*) cameriera di bordo.

stewardship ['stjuədʃip], *s.* **1.** amministrazione, gestione: *he gave a detailed account of his —*, diede un resoconto minuzioso della sua amministrazione **2.** carica di gerente, di amministratore.

stewing ['stju:iŋ], *s.* stufato, umido ☆ *— beef*, carne di manzo per stufato; *— plums*, prugne da cuocere.

stewpan ['stju:-pæn], *s.* tegame.

St. Gotthard [snt'gɔtəd], *no.pr.* (*geog.*) (passo del) San Gottardo.

St. Helena [ˌsenti'li:nə], *no.pr.* (*geog.*) Sant'Elena.

sthenic ['sθenik], *ag.* (*med.*) stenico, attivo, forte: *— type*, tipo stenico.

stibium ['stibiəm], *s.* (*chim.*) antimonio.

stick [stik], *s.* **1.** bastone, bastone da passeggio; manico (di ombrello, ecc.): *he walks with a —*, cammina col bastone; *he wants the —*, ha bisogno di un po' di vergate; *to get the —*, ricevere delle bastonate ‖ *any — is good to beat a dog*, ogni mezzo è buono per colpire il nemico ‖ *to be as cross as two sticks*, essere di umor nero, arrabbiato ‖ *to be in a cleft —*, (*fam.*) essere tra due fuochi, non saper che pesci prendere ‖ *to cut one's —*, tagliare la corda ‖ *to use big — methods*, fare ricorso alla forza **2.** bastoncino, legnetto: *the house was pulled down and not a — was left standing*, la casa fu rasa al suolo completamente; *to collect dry sticks for the fire*, raccogliere legnetti secchi per il fuoco; *to put a — in the ground to mark a point*, ficcare un bastoncino nel terreno per indicare un punto ‖ *to go to sticks and staves*, andare in rovina **3.** barra, stecca: *a — of shaving-soap*, un bastoncino di sapone da barba; *a — of sugar candy, of chocolate*, una stecca di zucchero filato, di cioccolato **4.** *fig.* allocco, barbogio, persona non intelligente **5.** bacchetta (di direttore d'orchestra) **6.** (*mar. sl.*) albero maestro: *the sticks*, l'alberatura **7.** (*mil.*) grappolo di bombe **8.** (*cuc.*) gambo, stelo, foglia: *a — of asparagus*, un asparago; *a — of celery*, un gambo di sedano ☆ *broom- —*, manico di scopa: *a witch riding on a broom- —*, una strega a cavallo di un manico di scopa; *cocktail- sticks*, bastoncini salati; *drum- —*, bacchetta per tamburo; *golf- —*, mazza da golf; *hockey- —*, bastone da hockey; *lip- —*, rossetto; *loaded- —*, sfollagente; *orange- —*, bastoncino in legno d'arancio (per le unghie); *shooting- —*, bastone sedile (per assistere a gare di golf, ecc.); *sword - —*, bastone animato; *vine- —*, paletto per sostenere le viti; *walking- —*, bastone da passeggio.

to **stick**, *pass.p.p.* **stuck** [stʌk], *v.t.i.* **1.** ficcare, ficcarsi; conficcare, conficcarsi; introdurre, introdursi: *cake stuck* (*over*) *with almonds*, torta decorata con mandorle; *to — a pin into sthg.*, conficcare uno spillo in ql.co.; *to — a stake in the ground*, conficcare un picchetto nel terreno ‖ *it sticks in my throat*, (*sl.*) non posso mandarla giù ‖ *to — s.o.*, (*sl.*) pugnalare qlcu. **2.** infilare, porre: *don't — your hands in your pockets*, non mettere le mani in tasca; *he stuck a flower in his buttonhole*, infilò un fiore all'occhiello; *she stuck a candle in a bottle*, infilò una candela nel collo di una bottiglia **3.** incollare, incollarsi; appiccicare, appiccicarsi; attaccare, attaccarsi (anche *fig.*): *the meat has stuck to the pan*, la carne si è attaccata al tegame; *money sticks to his fingers*, il denaro gli resta attaccato alle dita; *the nickname will — to him*, il soprannome gli resterà per sempre; *this envelope will not —*, questa busta non si incolla; *to — like a leech* (o *like glue* o *like a burr*) *to s.o.*, appiccicarsi a qlcu. come una mignatta; *to — to one's opinions*, rimanere della stessa idea, difendere le proprie convinzioni; *to — to one's word*, mantenere la parola; *to — to the text*, mantenersi fedeli al testo; *to — a wound*, (*med.*) fare aderire i labbri di una ferita; *to — to it!*, (*fam.*) non mollare! persevera! ‖ *I'm going to — indoors all day*, (*fam.*) resterò tappato in casa tutto il giorno ‖ *to be stuck*: *here I am stuck in this bed*, eccomi inchiodato a letto; *I am stuck*, sono nell'imbarazzo; *to get* (o *to become*) *stuck*, insabbiarsi; *I got stuck in alge-*

bra, (*sl. scolastico*) sono caduto in algebra; *this problem sticks me*, non riesco a risolvere questo problema **4.** (*fam.*) sopportare: *I cannot — him*, non lo sopporto, mi dà fastidio **5.** (*orticoltura*) mettere dei sostegni a (piante) **6.** *to — at* (*sthg.*), arrestarsi, fermarsi: *to — at nothing*, non avere scrupoli, essere capace di tutto || *to — at a task*, fare il proprio lavoro indefessamente **7.** *to — down*, (*fam.*) buttare giù, gettar giù; posare: — *it down anywhere you like*, mettilo dove ti pare; *to — sthg. down in a diary*, fare delle note in un diario **8.** *to — on*, incollare; (*fam.*) darsi delle grandi arie || *to — it on*, (*sl.*) esagerare, fare delle frange **9.** *to — out*, sporgere; tirar fuori, fare uscire; (*fam.*) persistere: *he stuck out his tongue*, tirò fuori la lingua; *to — out for sthg.*, non cedere nelle proprie richieste per ql.co.; *to — out from the background*, risaltare sullo sfondo; *to — out one's arm before turning*, (*aut.*) sporgere la mano dal finestrino per indicare che si svolta || *to — it out*, resistere fino alla fine **10.** *to — up*, alzare, alzarsi; innalzare, innalzarsi || *to — s.o. up*, (*sl.*) mettere qlcu. nell'imbarazzo || *to — up a bank*, (*sl. amer.*) assaltare una banca || *to — up to s.o.*, tener testa a qlcu. || *— 'em up!*, (*sl.*) mani in alto!.

sticker ['stikə*], *s*. **1.** attacchino **2.** pugnale; coltellaccio da macellaio **3.** (*pesca*) gaffa, arpione **4.** persona noiosa, scocciatore **5.** (*amer.*) etichetta gommata **6.** (*fam.*) partigiano, seguace (di un partito).

stickily ['stikili], *av*. viscosamente; tenacemente.

stickiness ['stikinis], *s*. viscosità, adesività; tenacità.

sticking ['stikin], *ag*. appiccicoso, adesivo; colloso|| *s*. **1.** aderenza, adesività; incollatura **2.** (*mec.*) arresto; bloccaggio; grippaggio ☆ *— -plaster*, cerotto; *— -point*, punto d'arresto (di una vite).

stick-in-the-mud ['stikin∂əmʌd], *ag*. lento, tardo; senza iniziativa || *s*. persona lenta, senza iniziativa: *hurry up, old — !*, sbrigati, vecchia lumaca! || *Mr., Mrs. Stick-in-the-mud*, (*sl.*) il signor, la signora Tal dei Tali.

stickjaw ['stikdʒɔ:], *s*. caramelle, dolci gommosi.

to stickle ['stikl], *v.t.i*. **1.** (*arc.*) interporsi, intervenire **2.** sollevare obiezioni; esitare **3.** *to — for* (*sthg.*), combattere (per un'idea, ecc.).

stickleback ['stiklbæk], *s*. (*ittiol.*) spinarello.

stickler ['stiklə*], *s*. **1.** accanito sostenitore: *I'm no great — for authority*, non sono un accanito sostenitore dell'autorità **2.** pignolo; intransigente.

sticky ['stiki], *ag*. **1.** appiccicaticcio; adesivo; viscoso; viscido: — *road*, strada viscida; *to have — fingers*, avere le dita appiccicose; *fig.* avere le mani lunghe **2.** poco accomodante; sgradevole: *the bank was very — about an overdraft*, la banca fu molto rigida circa un assegno scoperto; *he had a — ten minutes*, ha passato un brutto quarto d'ora; *he will come to a — end*, finirà male.

stiff [stif], *ag*. **1.** rigido, duro; *fig.* inflessibile, ostinato: *he lies — in death*, giace irrigidito nella morte; *he met the charge with a — denial*, negò recisamente ogni addebito || *to keep a — upper lip*, mostrare fermezza di carattere **2.** indolenzito, intorpidito; irrigidito: *to be quite —*, essere tutto indolenzito **3.** freddo; riservato, contenuto; affettato: — *bow*, saluto freddo; — *style*, stile affettato; *he has — manners*, ha modi alteri, affettati **4.** che funziona male: *a — door*, una porta non scorrevole **5.** difficile, duro, faticoso: *a — climb*, una salita erta; *a — examination*, un esame difficile; *I had a — job to get it*, ho avuto un bel da fare per ottenere ciò **6.** (*fam.*) alto, salato (di prezzo); forte (di bevanda): *a — bill*, un conto salato; *a — glass of rum*, un bicchiere di rum forte ☆ *— collar*, colletto duro; — *market*, (*comm.*) mercato stazionario; *— -neck*, torcicollo; *— -necked*, ostinato; — *joint*, (*patol.*) anchilosi || *bored —*, (*fam.*) annoiato a morte; *frozen —*, (*fam.*) rigido come un pezzo di ghiaccio; *scared —*, (*fam.*) morto di paura.

stiff, *s*. (*sl.*) **1.** cambiale **2.** cadavere **3.** un buono a nulla **4.** denaro.

to stiffen ['stifn], *v.t.i*. **1.** indurire, indurirsi; irrigidire, irrigidirsi (anche *fig.*); inamidare, apprettare (stoffe, ecc.): *to — a shirt-front*, inamidare uno sparato **2.** indolenzire; intorpidire, intorpidirsi: *age has stiffened his joints*, la vecchiaia gli ha intorpidito le membra **3.** rassodare, rassodarsi; prendere consistenza: *to — the paste*, rassodare la pasta **4.** rinforzare; *fig.* rincuorare: *the general tried to — his battalion*, il generale cercò di rincuorare il suo battaglione; *to — a drink*, rinforzare, correggere una bibita **5.** rendere più difficile, diventare più difficile: *to — an examination*, rendere un esame più difficile.

stiffener ['stifnə*], *s*. **1.** (*mec.*) elemento di rinforzo **2.** (*sl.*) tonico, stimolante.

stiffening ['stifnin], *s*. **1.** indurimento; rafforzamento; consolidamento **2.** (*ind. tessile*) appretto, inamidatura ☆ *— piece* (o *— plate*), (*mec.*) lamiera di rinforzo.

stiffly ['stifli], *av*. **1.** rigidamente; inflessibilmente; ostinatamente **2.** affettatamente.

stiffness ['stifnis], *s*. **1.** durezza; rigidezza; *fig.* ostinazione; sostenutezza **2.** intorpidimento; indolenzimento (di membra) **3.** consistenza; solidità: *the — of this pudding*, la consistenza di questo budino **4.** affettazione: *— of speech*, discorso affettato **5.** difficoltà, asperità.

stifle¹ ['staifl], *s*. **1.** grasciuola, grassella (di cavallo) **2.** (*vet.*) malattia della grasciuola ☆ *— -bone*, rotula (di cavallo).

to stifle², *v.t.i*. **1.** soffocare, sentirsi soffocare: *I was stifled by the smoke*, fui soffocato dal fumo **2.** *fig.* soffocare; reprimere; trattenere: *to — a rumour*, soffocare una diceria; *to — a sneeze*, trattenere uno starnuto; *to — a yawn*, reprimere uno sbadiglio.

stifling ['staiflin], *ag*. soffocante: *it's — here!*, qui si soffoca! || *s*. soffocamento.

stiflingly ['staiflinli], *av*. in modo soffocante.

stigma ['stigmə], *pl*. **stigmas** ['stigməz] (*nei sensi* **1. 2. 3. 6.**), **stigmata** ['stigmətə] (*nei sensi* **4. 5.**), *s*. **1.** (*arc.*) marchio, segno (di schiavo, ecc.) **2.** *fig.* bollo, marchio d'infamia **3.** (*patol.*) stigmata emorragica **4.** macchia cutanea **5.** *pl.* stimmate **6.** (*bot.*) stimma.

stigmatic [stig'mætik], *ag*. **1.** marchiato; bollato (anche *fig.*) **2.** (*ott.*) anastigmatico **3.** *fig.* diffamante **4.** (*patol.*) stigmatico **5.** (*med.*) macchiato, chiazzato **6.** segnato da stimmate **7.** (*bot.*) di stimma.

stigmatist ['stigmətist], *s.c*. persona che porta le stimmate.

stigmatization [,stigmətai'zeiʃən], *s*. **1.** lo stigmatizzare; il marchiare d'infamia **2.** infamia **3.** il prodursi delle stimmate; il segnare con stimmate.

to stigmatize ['stigmətaiz], *v.t*. **1.** marchiare **2.** stigmatizzare; bollare, disonorare: *since then he has been stigmatized as a coward*, da allora egli è bollato come codardo **3.** produrre stimmate su (per suggestione ipnotica).

stile¹ [stail], *s*. scaletta (per scavalcare un muro).

stile², *s*. (*artig.*) montante verticale.

stiletto [sti'letou], *pl*. **stilettos**, **stilettoes** [sti'letouz], *s*. **1.** stiletto, piccolo pugnale **2.** (*artig.*) punteruolo ☆ *— heels*, tacchi a spillo.

still¹ [stil], *ag*. **1.** tranquillo, calmo; immobile; silenzioso: — *evening*, una sera tranquilla; *a — lake*, un lago calmo; *how — everything is!*, come è tutto tranquillo!; *stand —*, non muoverti || *— as the grave*, silenzioso come la morte || *— small voice*, la voce della coscienza || *to keep a — tongue in one's head*, tacere || *— waters run deep*, *prov.* le acque chete rovinano i ponti **2.** non spumante, non frizzante (di vino).

still¹, *s*. **1.** (*poet.*) silenzio, quiete, calma: *in the — of night*, nel silenzio della notte **2.** (*foto.*) posa.

to still¹, *v.t.i*. acquietare, acquietarsi; calmare, calmarsi; placare, placarsi: *the tempest stilled*, la tempesta si placò: *to — s.o.'s apprehensions*, calmare le preoccupazioni di qlcu. ‖ *that great pen is stilled for ever*, quel grande scrittore tace per sempre.

still[1], *av*. **I. ancora, tuttora:** *he — has ten pounds*, egli ha ancora dieci sterline; *he — has to thank me*, mi deve ancora ringraziare; *is the train — in the station?*, è ancora in stazione il treno?; *the second problem was — more difficult*, il secondo problema era ancor più difficile ‖ *— less*, ancor meno; *— more*, ancor più **2. tuttavia, nondimeno; pure:** *— the problem is that...*, tuttavia il problema è che...; *but —, if she does not go*, (*fam*.) ma alla fine, se non se ne andasse...; *she is not beautiful, — I love her*, non è bella, ma io l'amo.

still[1], (*nei composti*): *— -birth*, mortinatalità, nascita di una creatura morta; *— -born*, nato-morto; *— -life*, (*pitt*.) natura morta.

still[2], *s*. alambicco ☆ *— -house*, (*amer*.) distilleria; *— -room*, laboratorio di distilleria; dispensa.

to **still**[2], *v.t*. (*arc*.) distillare; stillare.

stillage ['stilidʒ], *s*. supporto, sostegno; banco; piattaforma.

stilling ['stiliŋ], **stillion** ['stiliən], *s*. cavalletto per botte.

stillness ['stilnis], *s*. calma, quiete, tranquillità; silenzio.

stilly ['stili], *ag*. (*poet*.) calmo, tranquillo; silenzioso ‖ *av*. (*poet*) tranquillamente, quietamente; silenziosamente.

stilt [stilt], *s*. **1.** trampolo: *on stilts*, sui trampoli; *fig*. ampolloso **2.** (*dial*.) manico dell'aratro ☆ *— -bird* (o *— -plover* o *— -walker*), (*ornit*.) trampoliere.

to **stilt**, *v.t*. sollevare sui trampoli.

stilted ['stiltid], *ag*. **1.** montato sui trampoli **2.** pomposo, roboante, ampolloso (di stile) **3.** sopraelevato (di arco).

stiltedly ['stiltidli], *av*. ampollosamente, pomposamente.

stiltedness ['stiltidnis], *s*. ampollosità, pomposità, magniloquenza.

Stilton ['stiltn], *no.pr*. (*geog*.) Stilton ‖ *s*. «stilton» (formaggio piccante prodotto nella zona di Stilton).

stimulant ['stimjulənt], *ag.s*. stimolante, eccitante‖ *he never takes stimulants*, (*fam*.) non prende mai alcoolici.

to **stimulate** ['stimjuleit], *v.t*. stimolare; incitare, spronare: *to — s.o. to do sthg.*, incoraggiare, spronare qlcu. a fare ql.co.

stimulating ['stimjuleitiŋ],‖ *ag*. stimolante, eccitante.

stimulation [,stimju'leiʃən], *s*. stimolo.

stimulative ['stimjulətiv], *ag*. stimolativo, eccitante.

stimulator ['stimjuleitə*], *s*. **1.** stimolatore **2.** stimolante, eccitante.

stimulatress ['stimjuleitris], *s*. stimolatrice.

stimulose ['stimjulous], *ag*. (*bot*.) spinoso; coperto di peli pungenti.

stimulus ['stimjuləs], *pl*. **stimuli** ['stimjulai], *s*. **1.** stimolo (anche *fisiol*.); pungolo, incentivo; impulso: *ambition is her only —*, l'ambizione è l'unico incentivo per lei; *to apply a — to a muscle*, stimolare un muscolo; *bo give — to commerce*, dare impulso al commercio **2.** (*bot*.) spino, aculeo; pelo pungente.

to **stimy**, *V*. to **stymie**.

sting [stiŋ], *s*. **1.** pungiglione, aculeo: *the — of a wasp*, il pungiglione di una vespa **2.** puntura d'insetto: *his face was covered with stings*, aveva il volto pieno di punzecchiature **3.** dolore acuto (anche *fig*.) **4.** pungolo, stimolo, morso: *the — of hunger*, il morso della fame; *the — of remorse*, il pungolo del rimorso **5.** frizzo, frecciata: *a jest with a — in it*, uno scherzo maligno ☆ *— -bull*, (*ittiol*.) ragana, dragone marino; *— -nettle*, (*bot*.) ortica; *— -winkle*, (*zool*.) murice.

to **sting**, *pass.p.p*. **stung** [stʌŋ], *v.t.i*. **1.** pungere: *a mosquito stung his finger*, una zanzara gli punse il dito; *some bees do not —*, alcune api non pungono **2.** colpire; ferire (anche *fig*.): *those reproaches stung him to the quick*, quei rimproveri lo punsero sul vivo **3.** bruciare; sentire delle fitte (di parti del corpo) **4.** (*sl*.)

truffare; derubare: *we were stung for four dollars*, ci truffarono di quattro dollari.

stinger ['stiŋə*], *s.c*. chi punge, ferisce ‖ *s*. colpo violento.

stingily ['stindʒili], *av*. avaramente, tirchiamente; meschinamente.

stinginess ['stindʒinis], *s*. avarizia, spilorceria; meschinità; grettezza.

stinging ['stiŋiŋ], *ag*. pungente; *fig*. mordace ‖ *s*. puntura.

stingingly ['stiŋiŋli], *av*. pungentemente; *fig*. mordacemente.

stingless ['stiŋlis], *ag*. senza aculeo, senza pungiglione; *fig*. innocuo, innocente.

stingo ['stiŋgou], *s*. (*arc*.) **1.** birra forte **2.** *fig*. vivacità, brio ‖ *to give s.o. —*, dare una lavata di capo a qlcu.; mortificare qlcu.

stingy ['stindʒi], *ag*. avaro, taccagno, spilorcio.

stink [stiŋk], *s*. **1.** puzzo, fetore **2.** *pl*. (*sl*.) chimica ☆ *— -bomb*, bomba puzzolente; (*sl. mil*.) bomba asfissiante; *— -brand*, ruggine delle graminacee; *— -trap*, (*mec*.) sifone.

to **stink**, *pass*. **stank** [stæŋk], *p.p*. **stunk** [stʌŋk], *v.t.i*. **1.** puzzare; riempire di puzzo; (*sl*.) sentire l'odore di: *this meat stinks*, questa carne puzza ‖ *I can — it a mile off*, (*sl*.) me ne accorgo a un chilometro di distanza ‖ *they — of money miles off*, (*sl*.) puzzano di denaro a mille miglia di distanza ‖ *to — s.o. out of the room*, costringere qlcu. a lasciare la stanza per il cattivo odore **2.** *fig*. essere ripugnante, odioso; (*sl. amer*.) essere scadente.

stinkard ['stiŋkəd], *s*. persona, animale che puzza.

stinker ['stiŋkə*], *s*. **1.** persona, animale che emana cattivo odore **2.** (*ornit*.) ossifraga, procellaria gigante **3.** (*sl*.) cosa irritante, offensiva: *I wrote him a real —*, gliene ho scritto proprio di tutti i colori **4.** (*spreg*.) fetente.

stinking ['stiŋkiŋ], *ag*. puzzolente, fetido.

stinkingly ['stiŋkiŋli], *av*. puzzolentemente, fetidamente.

stint[1] [stint], *s*. **1.** limite, restrizione: *to work without —*, lavorare indefessamente **2.** porzione, quantità di lavoro assegnato, compito: *to do one's daily —*, eseguire il proprio lavoro quotidiano.

to **stint**[1], *v.t.i*. **1.** limitare, limitarsi; imporre, imporsi delle restrizioni; razionare: *to — oneself for one's children*, sottoporsi a privazioni per i propri figli; *to — one's horses of hay*, razionare il fieno ai cavalli; *to — the servants in* (o *of*) *food*, far stare la servitù a stecchetto, misurare il pane alla servitù **2.** (*dial*.) assegnare un compito, una quantità di lavoro.

stint[2], *s*. (*ornit*.) piovanello.

stinted ['stintid], *ag*. limitato, scarso; ristretto; misurato.

stintedly ['stintidli], *av*. scarsamente; con parsimonia.

stintedness ['stintidnis], *s*. limitatezza; ristrettezza; scarsezza.

stinting ['stintiŋ], *s*. restrizione, limitazione; risparmio.

stintingly ['stintiŋli], *av*. scarsamente; con parsimonia.

stintless ['stintlis], *ag*. senza limitazioni, restrizioni; abbondante, prodigo.

stipe [staip], *s*. (*bot*.) gambo; stipite; picciuolo.

stipel ['staipəl], *s*. (*bot*.) stipula.

stipend ['staipend], *s*. stipendio, salario; rendita ufficiale (specialmente di ecclesiastici).

stipendiary [stai'pendjəri], *ag.s*. stipendiato, salariato.

stipes ['staipi:z], *pl*. **stipites** ['stipiti:z], *V*. **stipe**.

stipitate ['stipiteit], *ag*. fornito di gambo, stipite, picciuolo.

stipple ['stipl], *s*. **1.** (*st. pitt*.) puntinismo; (*tip*.) tec nica dell'incisione a retino 2. (*pitt.*) disegno a puntini; (*tip.*) incisione a retino.

to stipple, *v.t.* (*pitt.*) punteggiare; (*tip.*) incidere a retino.

stippler ['stiplə*], *s.* (*tip.*) incisore a retino.

to stipulate ['stipjuleit], *v.t.i.* stipulare, pattuire; convenire; accordarsi; stabilire: *to — for sthg.*, accordarsi su ql.co.; *to — (in writing) that...*, accordarsi (per iscritto) che....

stipulation [ˌstipju'leiʃən], *s.* (*dir.*) stipulazione, convenzione, patto, accordo: *on the — that...*, a patto, a condizione che....

stipulator ['stipjuleitə*], *s.* (*dir.*) stipulante.

stipule ['stipjuːl], *s.* (*bot.*) stipula.

stir[1] [stə:*], *s.* **1.** il rimescolare; l'attizzare: *to give the fire a —*, attizzare il fuoco; *to give one's coffee a —*, dare una rimescolata al caffè **2.** moto, movimento; animazione: *full of — and movement*, pieno di vita e movimento; *there is no — in the air*, non vi è un alito di vento **3.** tumulto, subbuglio; commozione; sensazione: *the crowd was in a —*, la folla era in tumulto; *the event caused a — in the village*, l'avvenimento mise il villaggio in subbuglio; *to create little —*, aver scarsa risonanza; *to make a —*, far sensazione **4.** (*comm.*) movimento nei prezzi, nelle quotazioni.

to stir[1], *pass.p.p.* **stirred** [stə:d], *v.t.i.* **1.** muovere; muoversi; agitare, agitarsi: *don't —!*, non ti muovere!; *if you —, I shoot!*, se ti muovi, sparo!; *not a breath stirred the leaves*, non un soffio di vento agitava le foglie; *she did not — from the library for the whole afternoon*, ella non si mosse dalla biblioteca per tutto il pomeriggio; *she was not stirring yet*, non si era ancora alzata ‖ *— your stumps!*, muoviti!, spicciati! ‖ *to — heaven and earth*, (*fam.*) muovere mari e monti ‖ *not to — a finger to help s.o.*, non muovere un dito per aiutare qlcu. **2.** rimescolare; agitare: *to — a cream*, rimescolare una crema; *to — glass*, (*ind.*) agitare il vetro fuso **3.** commuovere, appassionare; eccitare: *stirring music*, una musica che commuove; *he stirred my wrath*, egli mi fece andar su tutte le furie; *to be stirred*, essere emozionato ‖ *to — the blood*, entusiasmare, eccitare **4.** *to — about*, circolare: *there is no news stirring about*, non ci sono notizie in circolazione **5.** *to — up*, stimolare; eccitare; fomentare; attizzare: *she wants stirring up*, ha bisogno di essere stimolata, incitata; *to — up curiosity*, eccitare la curiosità; *to — up hatred*, fomentare odio; *to — up s.o.'s courage*, stimolare il coraggio di qlcu.; *to — up the fire*, attizzare il fuoco.

stir[2], *s.* (*sl.*) prigione.

stirabout ['stə:rəbaut], *ag.* indaffarato, affaccendato ‖ *s.c.* persona indaffarata ‖ *s.* « porridge » (zuppa d'avena).

stirless ['stə:lis], *ag.* immobile; calmo.

stirpiculture ['stə:piˌkʌltʃə*], *s.* allevamento di razze speciali (di bestiame, ecc.).

stirps [stə:ps], *pl.* **stirpes** ['stə:piːz], *s.* **1.** (*dir.*) progenitore, capostipite **2.** (*zool.*) famiglia.

stirrer ['stə:rə*], *s.c.* **1.** incitatore, incitatrice; istigatore, istigatrice **2.** chi si muove: *to be an early —*, essere in piedi di buon mattino; *to be a late —*, essere un dormiglione ‖ *s.* (*ind. chim.*) apparecchio agitatore.

stirringly ['stə:riŋli], *av.* in modo emozionante, commovente.

stirrup ['stirəp], *s.* **1.** staffa ‖ *to lose one's stirrups*, *fig.* perdere le staffe **2.** (*mar.*) corda a staffa ☆ *— -bone*, (*anat.*) staffa; *— -cup*, *fig.* bicchiere della staffa; *— -leather*, staffile; *— -pump*, estintore portatile.

stitch [stitʃ], *s.* **1.** punto (anche *chir.*): *what long stitches!*, che punti lunghi!; *I am learning a new —*, sto imparando un nuovo punto; *to put stitches in a wound*, (*chir.*) suturare una ferita ‖ *he has not a dry — on him*, (*fam.*) è bagnato fradicio ‖ *a — in time saves nine*, *prov.* un punto a tempo ne risparmia cento **2.** maglia: *to drop a —*, saltare, lasciar cadere una maglia;

to take up a —, riprendere una maglia **3.** fitta, trafitta ☆ *— -wheel*, (*strum. artig.*) rullino marca-punti sul cuoio; *— -work*, ricamo ‖ *cross- —*, punto a croce; *darning —*, punto rammendo.

to stitch, *v.t.i.* **1.** cucire; (*chir.*) suturare **2.** *to — down*, ribattere una cucitura **3.** *to — on*, applicare con cuciture: *to — on a pocket*, applicare una tasca **4.** *to — up*, rammendare; (*chir.*) suturare.

stitcher ['stitʃə*], *s.c.* cucitore, cucitrice.

stitchery ['stitʃəri], *s.* lavoro di cucito.

stitching ['stitʃiŋ], *s.* cucitura; impuntura; (*chir.*) sutura ☆ *back —*, punto indietro; *ornamental —*, ricamo.

stitchwort ['stitʃwə:t], *s.* (*bot.*) stellaria, centocchio.

stiver ['staivə*], *s.* soldo, quattrino ‖ *I don't care a —*, non me ne importa proprio nulla; *he has not a —*, è povero in canna.

St. Lucia [snt'luːʃə], *no.pr.* (*geog.*) Santa Lucia.

stoa ['stouə], *pl.* **stoae** ['stouiː], **stoas** ['stouəz], *s.* (*arch. greca*) stoa, portico.

stoat[1] [stout], *s.* ermellino (specialmente nella stagione estiva, quando ha il pelo scuro).

to stoat[2], *v.t.* rammendare con punti invisibili.

stock [stɔk], *s.* **1.** tronco, ceppo; fusto da innesto; *fig.* razza, famiglia, stirpe: *he comes of a good —*, viene da una buona famiglia; *person of the good old —*, (*fam.*) persona di stampo antico ‖ *stocks and stones*, cose inanimate; *fig.* persone apatiche e stupide **2.** base, sostegno; calcio (di fucile); ceppo (di aratro, ancora, incudine) **3.** rifornimento, approvvigionamento, provvista; (*comm.*) riserva, scorta (di merci): *— of tea*, scorta di tè; *in —*, in magazzino; *old (o dead) —*, fondi, avanzi di magazzino; *to be out of —*, essere sprovvisto; *to lay in a — of sthg.*, far provvista di ql.co.; *to sell the whole — (of a firm)*, vendere in blocco; *to take —*, far l'inventario *— in hand*, merce in magazzino ‖ *— of plays*, repertorio teatrale **4.** (*finanza*) titoli, azioni, obbligazioni: *the stocks*, titoli di stato; *stocks and shares*, valori di borsa, titoli; *to buy —*, comprare azioni ‖ *his — is going up*, (*fam.*) le sue azioni sono in rialzo ‖ *to take — in s.o., sthg.*, (*amer.*) far caso a qlcu., ql.co. **5.** materia prima **6.** brodo da minestra **7.** *pl.* (*st.*) gogna, berlina: *to be in the stocks*, essere alla berlina (anche *fig.*); *to put s.o. in the stocks*, mettere in ceppi qlcu. **8.** *pl.* (*mar.*) taccate: *ship on the stocks*, nave in cantiere ‖ *to have a piece of work on the stocks*, avere qualcosa in lavorazione **9.** (*st.*) collare rigido **10.** (*bot.*) violaciocca.

to stock, *v.t.* **1.** approvvigionare, fornire, rifornire (merce, bestiame); seminare erba in; rimboscare, piantare alberi in; ripopolare (stagni di pesci, ecc.): *the books that — my library*, i libri che formano la mia biblioteca; *to — a warehouse with goods*, rifornire un magazzino **2.** tenere in magazzino (merci): *I do not — this article*, non tengo quest'articolo **3.** montare un fucile **4.** (*mar.*) inceppare (un'ancora) **5.** (*st.*) mettere alla gogna, alla berlina.

stock, (*nei composti*): *— -book*, (*comm.*) libro magazzino; *— -car*, automobile di serie; (*amer.*) carro bestiame; *— -company*, (*comm.*) società per azioni; (*teat.*) compagnia stabile; *— -dove*, (*ornit.*) palombella; *— -duck*, (*ornit.*) germano reale; *— -exchange*, (*comm.*) borsa valori; *— -farm*, fattoria per l'allevamento del bestiame; *— -in-trade*, tutti gli strumenti di un commercio, professione; *fig.* risorse mentali; *— -jobber*, speculatore di Borsa; *— -list*, (*comm.*) listino di Borsa; *— -market*, (*comm.*) mercato finanziario; Borsa valori; *— -play*, (*teat.*) lavoro di repertorio; *— -pot*, pentola per il brodo; *— -raising*, allevamento di bestiame; *— -size*, taglia corrente; *— -solution*, (*foto.*) soluzione concentrata; *— -still*, completamente immobile ‖ *chicken —*, brodo di pollo; *common —*, (*comm.*) azioni ordinarie; *fat —*, bestiame da macello; *joint- — company*, (*comm.*) società anonima; *laughing —*, zimbello; *live- —*, bestiame; *paper- —*, stracci per la carta; *preference- —*, (*comm.*) azioni preferenziali; *surplus —*, residui.

stockade [stɔ'keid], *s.* stecconata, palizzata.

to **stockade,** *v.t.* cingere con palizzata, stecconata.

stockbroker ['stɔk,broukə*], *s.* (*comm.*) agente di cambio.

stockbroking ['stɔk,broukiŋ], *s.* professione dell'agente di cambio: *he has taken up* —, è agente di cambio.

stocker ['stɔkə*], *s.* **1.** montatore (d'armi da fuoco) **2.** (*amer.*) animale da macello.

stockfish ['stɔkfiʃ], *s.* stoccafisso.

stockholder ['stɔk,houldə*], *s.c.* (*comm.*) azionista.

Stockholm ['stɔkhoum], *no.pr.*(*geog.*) Stoccolma.

stockinet [,stɔki'net], *s.* tessuto a maglia elastico per biancheria.

stocking ['stɔkiŋ], *s.* **1.** calza (lunga): *a pair of stockings,* un paio di calze || *blue* —, (*fig. spreg.*) donna intellettuale **2.** balza (di cavallo) ☆ — *-foot,* piede della calza: *in one's* — *-feet,* senza scarpe; — *-frame* (o — *-loom* o — *-machine*), telaio per calze; — *-stitch,* punto calza || *elastic* —, calza elastica.

stockist ['stɔkist], *s.* (*comm.*) grossista.

stockman, *pl.* **stockmen** ['stɔkmən], *s.* guardiano di bestiame.

stockpile ['stɔkpail], *s.* riserva di materiali, armi, viveri, ecc. ☆ *atomic* —, riserva di armi atomiche.

to **stockpile,** *v.t.* far riserve di (materiali, armi, viveri, ecc.).

stocktaking ['stɔk,teikiŋ], *s.* (*comm.*) inventario.

stocky ['stɔki], *ag.* tarchiato, tracagnotto.

stodge [stɔdʒ], *s.* **1.** (*sl.*) cibo pesante; *fig.* libro indigesto, mattone **2.** scorpacciata **3.** mangione.

to **stodge,** *v.t.i.* (*sl.*) ingozzare, ingozzarsi; rimpinzare, rimpinzarsi: *to* — *oneself with sthg.,* rimpinzarsi di ql.co.

stodger ['stɔdʒə*], *s.* individuo noioso, privo di spirito.

stodginess ['stɔdʒinis], *s.* **1.** (*fam.*) pesantezza (di cibo, libro, ecc.) **2.** l'essere stipato.

stodgy ['stɔdʒi], *ag.* **1.** (*fam.*) pesante, indigesto (di cibo, stile) **2.** pieno zeppo; stipato (di recipiente).

stoic ['stouik], *ag.s.* (*st. fil.*) stoico.

stoical ['stouikəl], *ag.* (*st. fil.*) stoico.

stoically ['stouikəli], *av.* stoicamente.

stoicalness ['stouikəlnis], **stoicism** ['stouisizəm], *s.* (*st. fil.*) stoicismo.

to **stoke** [stouk], *v.t.i.* **1.** attizzare (il fuoco); caricare, alimentare (fornello di caldaia, ecc.) **2.** fare il fuochista; sorvegliare le caldaie **3.** (*fam.*) trangugiare il cibo.

stokehold ['stoukhould], *s.* (*mar.*) sala caldaie.

stoke-hole ['stoukhoul], *s.* **1.** bocca del forno **2.** sala caldaie.

stoker ['stoukə*], *s.* fuochista ☆ *mechanical* —, (*mec.*) alimentatore automatico.

stoking ['stoukiŋ], *s.* sorveglianza, cura, alimentazione di forni, caldaie.

stole[1] [stoul], *s.* stola, sciarpa, scialle.

stole[2], *s.* (*bot.*) stolone.

stole[3], *pass.* di to **steal.**

stolen ['stoulən], *p.p.* di to **steal.**

stolid ['stɔlid], *ag.* imperturbabile; flemmatico; calmo, non precipitoso.

stolidity [stɔ'liditi], **stolidness** ['stɔlidnis], *s.* flemma, lentezza.

stolon ['stoulən], *s.* (*bot.*) stolone.

stoma['stoumə], *pl.* **stomata**['stɔmətə], *s.*(*bot.*) stoma.

stomach ['stʌmək], *s.* **1.** stomaco: *on a full, empty,* —, a stomaco pieno, vuoto; *pain in the* —, mal di stomaco; *such a thing turns my* —, *fig.* una tal cosa mi rivolta lo stomaco || *to be of a proud* (o *of a high*) —, (*fam.*) essere altezzoso || *to stay one's* —, calmare i morsi della fame **2.** ventre: *to crawl on one's* —, strisciare sul ventre **3.** desiderio, inclinazione; coraggio: *he had no* — *for a fight,* non si sentiva in vena di combattere; *this will put some* — *into him,* questo gli metterà un po' di sangue nelle vene ☆ — *-ache,* mal di stomaco,

mal di pancia; — *-cough,* (*patol.*) tosse gastrica; — *-pump,* sonda per lavaggio gastrico; — *-tooth,* canino inferiore (della prima dentizione); — *-tube,* sonda per drenaggio gastrico; sonda per l'alimentazione artificiale; — *-worm,* ascaride lombricoide.

to **stomach,** *v.t.* ingoiare, inghiottire; digerire; sopportare: *he can hardly* — *that!,* non può proprio ingoiarla!, la cosa non gli va giù!; *he cannot* — *such an insult,* non può digerire un simile insulto; *I cannot* — *Latin,* non posso soffrire il Latino.

stomachal ['stʌməkəl], *ag.* gastrico.

stomacher ['stʌməkə*], *s.* (*st.*) pettorina di vestito femminile (XV-XVII sec.).

stomachful ['stʌməkful], *s.* rimpinzata, scorpacciata: *he had a* — *of cakes,* si è rimpinzato di dolci.

stomachic [stə'mækik], *ag.* (*farm.*) stomatico *s.* **1.** (*farm.*) stomatico **2.** (*fam.*) aperitivo.

stomatitis [,stɔmə'taitis], *s.* (*patol.*) stomatite.

stomatology [,stɔmə'tolədʒi], *s.* stomatologia.

stomatoscope [stə'mætəskoup], *s.* (*med.*) stomatoscopio.

stone [stoun], *ag. attributivo* **1.** di pietra, in pietra; di grès, in grès **2.** dell'età della pietra || *s.* (*nel senso* **6.** *pl.* **stone**) **1.** pietra, ⌐roccia; cote, pietra da taglio: *his heart is as hard as a* —, il suo cuore è duro come una pietra || *not to leave a* — *standing,* non lasciare pietra su pietra || *to leave no* — *unturned,* tentare ogni mezzo || *the Stone Age,* l'età della pietra **2.** ciottolo, sasso: *shower* (o *fall*) *of stones,* caduta di sassi; *to cast* (o *to throw*) *stones at s.o.,* lanciare sassi contro qlcu. lapidare qlcu. || *at a stone's throw,* a un tiro di schioppo || *those who live in glass houses should not throw stones,* chi è senza peccato scagli la prima pietra || *to kill two birds with one* —, prendere due piccioni con una fava **3.** pietra preziosa **4.** nocciolo (di frutta): *remove the stones from plums,* togli il nocciolo alle prugne **5.** (*patol.*) calcolo; litiasi: *he underwent an operation for* —, è stato operato di calcoli **6.** «stone» (misura di peso = kg. 6,350): *it weighs two* —, pesa 28 libbre || *to give a* — *and a beating to s.o.,* superare facilmente qlcu. ☆ — *-blind,* completamente cieco; — *-borer,* (*zool.*) mollusco litofago; — *-break,* (*bot.*) sassifraga; — *-breaker,* spaccapietre, tagliapietre; (*mec.*) frantoio; — *-coal,* antracite; — *-cold,* freddo come la pietra, gelido; — *-coloured,* del colore della pietra; — *-curlew* (o — *-plover*), (*ornit.*) gran piviere; — *-cutter,* tagliapietre; — *-cutting,* taglio della pietra; — *-dead,* morto stecchito; — *-deaf,* sordo come una campana, completamente sordo; — *-falcon* (o — *hawk*), (*ornit.*) smeriglio; — *-fruit,* frutto con nocciolo; — *hammer,* (*mec.*) mazzetta; — *mason,* scalpellino, tagliapietre; — *mason's disease,* (*patol.*) silicosi; — *-pit* (o — *-quarry*), cava di pietra; — *-snipe,* (*ornit.*) piviere americano; — *-work,* lavoro in muratura; scultura, lavoro di scultura || *alum* —, (*min.*) allume di rocca; *Bristol* —, (*min.*) cristallo di rocca; *cornish* —, (*min.*) caolino; *meteoric* —, meteorite.

to **stone,** *v.t.* **1.** lapidare; colpire a sassate **2.** rivestire di pietra; pavimentare con pietre, ciottoli (strada, ecc.) **3.** snocciolare, togliere il nocciolo a (frutta) **4.** affilare, molare, arrotare: *to* — (*down*) *a knife,* affilare un coltello.

stonechat ['stoun-tʃæt], *s.* (*ornit.*) saltimpalo.

stonehorse ['stoun-hɔ:s], *s.* (*dial.*) stallone.

stoneless ['stounlis], *ag.* **1.** senza pietre, senza sassi **2.** senza nocciolo (di frutta).

stonen ['stounən], *ag.* (*arc.*) di pietra.

stoner ['stounə*], *s.* **1.** lapidatore **2.** (*amer.*) tagliapietre **3.** (*amer.*) snocciolatoio, strumento per togliere noccioli.

stonewall ['stoun-wɔ:l], *s.* **1.** (*cricket*) giuoco di difesa **2.** (*austral. pol.*) ostruzionismo parlamentare **3.** muro di pietra; muro a secco.

to **stonewall,** *v.t.i.* **1.** (*cricket*) giocare in difesa, fare un giuoco prudente **2.** (*pol.*) fare dell'ostruzionismo parlamentare; ostacolare.

stonewaller ['stoun'wɔ:lə*], *s.* **1.** (*cricket*) giuocatore prudente, che non rischia **2.** (*austral. pol.*) ostruzionista.

stoneware ['stoun-wɛə*], *s.* grès, ceramica.

stonily ['stounili], *av.* freddamente, duramente; impassibilmente.

stoniness ['stouninis], *s.* **1.** natura pietrosa (di suolo, ecc.) **2.** *fig.* insensibilità, durezza (di cuore).

stony ['stouni], *ag.* **1.** pietroso, sassoso; di pietra: — *path*, sentiero sassoso **2.** *fig.* duro, freddo, insensibile: *a* — *heart*, un cuore di pietra; *a* — *stare*, uno sguardo gelido ☆ — *-broke*, in bolletta, al verde; — *-hearted*, dal cuore di pietra.

stood [stud], *pass.p.p.* di to **stand**.

stool [stu:l], *s.* **1.** sgabello; seggiolino; panchetto; scanno ‖ *to fall between two stools*, lasciarsi sfuggire ambedue le occasioni per indecisione **2.** (*arch.*) davanzale di finestra **3.** (*fisiol.*) feci ‖ *to go to* —, andar di corpo **4.** (*night-* o *close-*) —, seggetta **5.** (*bot.*) radice, tronco da cui spuntano polloni **6.** (*caccia*) legno su cui è attaccato l'uccello di richiamo ☆ — *-pigeon*, piccione da richiamo; *fig.* persona che fa da esca ‖ *folding* — (o *camp* —), seggiolino pieghevole; *foot* —, posapiedi.

to stool, *v.i.* **1.** (*bot.*) mettere polloni; germogliare: *this corn stools well*, questo grano germoglia bene **2.** (*arc.*) andare di corpo.

stoop[1] [stu:p], *s.* **1.** curvatura, inclinazione del corpo in avanti; inchino: *to walk with a* —, camminare curvo, a schiena curva **2.** *fig.* condiscendenza; atto di umiltà, di sottomissione **3.** (*arc.*) lo scendere in picchiata (del falco).

to stoop[1], *v.t.i.* **1.** curvare, curvarsi, chinarsi, piegarsi; inclinare: *I had to* — *to get into the car*, mi dovetti chinare per entrare nell'automobile; *she begins to* —, comincia ad incurvarsi; *to* — *in walking*, camminare ricurvo **2.** *fig.* accondiscendere; abbassarsi; umiliarsi, degradarsi: *did he* — *to that?*, si abbassò proprio fino a quel punto?; *she would* — *to anything*, è disposta ad ogni bassezza; *to* — *to conquer*, umiliarsi per conquistare **3.** (*poet.*) abbattersi in picchiata sulla preda.

stoop[2], *s.* (*amer. canadese*) terrazza sopraelevata sul fronte della casa; veranda.

stop [stɔp], *s.* **1.** sosta, arresto, interruzione; fermata; (*mar. aer.*) scalo: *a five minutes'* —, una pausa, una fermata di cinque minuti; *do you get off at this* —?, scende a questa fermata?; *to bring sthg. to a* —, fermare, arrestare ql.co.; *to make* (o *to come to*) *a sudden* —, fermarsi bruscamente; *to put a* — *to sthg.*, porre termine a ql.co. **2.** segno di punteggiatura: *to put in the stops*, mettere la punteggiatura **3.** cambiamento di tono (anche *fig.*) **4.** (*mus.*) registro musicale (d'organo) **5.** (*mec.*) dispositivo di bloccaggio, d'arresto **6.** (*ott. foto.*) diaframma dell'obbiettivo ☆ — *-cock*, (*mec.*) rubinetto di arresto; — *-dowel*, (*mec.*) grano di arresto; — *-gap*, rimedio temporaneo; (*fam.*) tappa buchi; — *-motion*, (*cine.*) variatore della velocità di presa; — *-press*, (*giornalismo*) ultimissime; — *-watch*, cronometro a scatto ‖ *full* —, punto.

to stop, *pass.p.p.* **stopped** [stɔpt], *v.t.i.* **1.** turare, tamponare; otturare; chiudere: *the dentist will* — *your tooth*, il dentista ti otturerà il dente; *you must* — (*up*) *that hole in the roof*, devi chiudere quel buco nel tetto; *to* — *one's ears*, turarsi le orecchie; *to* — *a wound*, tamponare una ferita ‖ *to* — *a gap*, *fig.* tappare un buco; colmare una lacuna ‖ *to* — *s.o.'s mouth*, (*fam.*) tappare la bocca a qlcu. **2.** (I) fermare, fermarsi; arrestare, arrestarsi; cessare, far cessare; (*mec.*) bloccare: — *that bus!*, ferma quell'autobus!; — *that noise!*, basta con questo rumore!; *the car stopped dead at the kerb*, l'automobile si fermò di colpo vicino al marciapiede; *frost has stopped the growth of plants*, il gelo ha arrestato la crescita delle piante; *I'll* — *it!*, metterò fine a ciò!; *they stopped to look at the view*, si fermarono per ammirare il paesaggio; *to* — *at a port, an airport*, (*mar. aer.*) fare scalo; *to* — *the game*, porre fine al

giuoco; *to* — *talking*, smettere di parlare; *to* - *the traffic*, arrestare il traffico **3.** impedire, trattenere: *nothing will* — *his interfering*, niente lo tratterrà dall'interferire; *what is to* — *me from coming?*, cosa mi impedirà di venire? **4.** (*fam.*) trattenersi, fermarsi, dimorare: *are you going to* — *at this hotel long?*, vi tratterrete a lungo in questo albergo?; *don't* — *with your friends too long*, non fermarti troppo a lungo coi tuoi amici **5.** (*comm.*) cessare (i pagamenti); (*fam.*) tagliare: *they stopped his water supply*, gli tagliarono le condutture dell'acqua; *to* — *the leave of all soldiers*, (*mil.*) consegnare tutti i soldati; *to* — *s.o.'s wages*, cessare di pagare il salario a qlcu.; *to* — *sthg. out of s.o.'s salary*, trattenere una certa somma dal salario di qlcu. **6.** (*mus.*) cambiare il tono (di uno strumento): *to* — *a flute*, tappare i buchi di un flauto (con le dita); *to* — *a string*, premere una corda con le dita (per mutare le vibrazioni), cambiare le vibrazioni di una corda **7.** (*gram.*) punteggiare: *the composition was badly stopped*, la punteggiatura del tema era scorretta **8.** (*mar.*) abbozzare **9.** *to* — *by* (*s.o.*), (*fam. amer.*) fare un salto da, fare una breve visita a **10.** *to* — *down*, (*foto.*) diaframmare (l'obiettivo); ridurre l'esposizione **11.** *to* — *off*, (*fonderia*) riempire di sabbia (uno stampo) **12.** *to* — *out*, stuccare (incisioni).

stoppage ['stɔpidʒ], *s.* **1.** fermata; sosta, pausa; arresto; interruzione; sospensione; cessazione: — *of business*, arresto degli affari; — *of leave*, (*mil.*) consegna; — *of payment*, cessazione, sospensione di pagamento; — *of traffic*, interruzione del traffico **2.** ostruzione, ingombro; intasatura: — *of a pipe*, ostruzione di un tubo **3.** (*comm.*) giacenza; diritti di giacenza.

stopper ['stɔpə*], *s.c.* chi arresta, ferma ‖ *s.* **1.** tappo, turacciolo; otturatore; zaffo **2.** (*ind. chim.*) agente stabilizzante **3.** (*amer.*) stucco **4.** (*mar.*) bozza ☆ *glass* —, tappo di vetro; *screw* —, tappo a vite; *tobacco-* —, pressatabacco (per pipa).

to stopper, *v.t.* **1.** tappare, turare; tamponare **2.** (*amer.*) stuccare.

stopping ['stɔpiŋ], *s.* **1.** otturazione, tamponamento: — *of a road*, sbarramento di una strada; — *of a tooth*, otturazione di un dente **2.** il fermare, l'arrestare **3.** (*comm.*) cessazione, sospensione (di pagamenti, ecc.) **4.** (*gram.*) punteggiatura **5.** stucco; stuccatura **6.** (*min.*) sbarramento per ventilazione ☆ — *brake*, (*mec.*) freno d'arresto; — *knife*, spatola (per stucco); — *power*, (*fis.*) potere d'arresto; — *time*, tempo d'arresto.

stopple ['stɔpl], *s.* tappo, turacciolo.

to stopple, *v.t.* turare, tappare.

storage ['stɔ:ridʒ], *s.* **1.** immagazzinamento **2.** deposito, magazzino **3.** (*comm.*) magazzinaggio **4.** (*elett.*) carica (di energia) ☆ — *battery*, (*elett.*) batteria di accumulatori; — *bin*, (*agr.*) silos; — *capacity*, capacità d'immagazzinamento; — *cell*, (*elett.*) elemento di accumulatore ‖ *cold* —, conservazione in frigorifero.

storax ['stɔ:ræks], *s.* (*bot.*) storace.

store [stɔ:*], *s.* **1.** provvista, riserva; quantità, abbondanza: *that was in* — *for me!*, *fig.* questo mi era riservato dalla sorte!; *to have a good* — *of courage*, *fig.* avere una buona dose di coraggio; *to have a good* — *of wines*, avere una buona scorta di vini; *to hold* (o *to keep*) *sthg. in* —, tenere ql.co. in serbo, di riserva; *to lay in a* — *of sthg.*, fare una provvista di ql.co. ‖ *to set great* — *by s.o.*, tenere in gran conto, valutare molto qlcu. **2.** magazzino, deposito; (*amer.*) negozio **3.** *pl.* depositi di magazzino, scorte di materie prime; rifornimenti; munizioni; (*mar.*) provviste di bordo **4.** *pl.* grandi magazzini, cooperativa ☆ — *-cattle*, bestiame da ingrasso; — *-keeper*, magazziniere; (*amer.*) negoziante; — *-ship*, nave da carico.

to store, *v.t.* **1.** fornire, rifornire: — *your mind with knowledge*, coltiva la mente **2.** immagazzinare, accumulare; mettere da parte (anche *fig.*): *to* — (*up*) *sthg.*, accantonare, immagazzinare ql.co.: *the crop was stored*, il raccolto fu riposto nel granaio; *he stored up what* *he had learnt, fig.* accantonò ciò che aveva imparato; *to — up electricity,* immagazzinare elettricità **3.** depositare: *I have stored my furniture,* ho depositato il mobilio in magazzino **4.** contenere: *this room can — twenty cars,* questo locale può contenere venti automobili ☆ *well-stored,* ben fornito: *he has a well-stored mind,* ha un ingegno fecondo.

storehouse ['stɔːhaus], *s.* magazzino, deposito: *she is a — of erudition, fig.* è una miniera di erudizione.

storeroom ['stɔːrum], *s.* magazzino.

storey ['stɔːri], *s.* piano (di edificio): *on the first —,* al primo piano; *upper, lower storeys,* piani superiori, inferiori; *this house has six storeys,* questa casa ha sei piani ‖ *the upper —, (fam.)* il cervello.

storeyed ['stɔːrid], *ag. (edil.)* a piani.

storiated ['stɔːrieitid], *ag. (tip.)* istoriato, decorato.

storied[1] ['stɔːrid], *ag.* **1.** istoriato, ornato con figure, decorato: *— windows,* vetrate, finestre a vetri istoriati **2.** celebrato in storie, leggende.

storied[2], *ag. (edil.)* a piani ☆ *two- —,* a due piani.

storiette [,stɔːri'et], *s.* novellina, raccontino.

stork [stɔːk], *s.* cicogna: *a visit from the —, fig.* l'arrivo della cicogna ☆ *—'s-bill, (bot.)* geranio, pelargonio.

storm [stɔːm], *s.* **1.** tempesta; temporale; bufera, burrasca; fortunale; uragano (anche *fig.*): *a — of applause, fig.* uno scroscio di applausi; *the — is raging,* la tempesta infuria; *a sudden — frightened the crew,* un improvviso fortunale atterrì la ciurma; *to take the audience by —, fig.* trascinare l'uditorio ‖ *a — in a teacup,* una tempesta in un bicchier d'acqua ‖ *after a — comes a calm, prov.* dopo la tempesta viene il sereno **2.** tumulto, agitazione; guerra; disputa: *period of — and stress,* periodo di disordine ed agitazione; *a political —,* un tumulto politico **3.** *(mil.)* assalto: *to take by —,* prendere d'assalto ☆ *— -belt,* zona delle tempeste; *— -centre,* centro dell'uragano; *fig.* focolaio d'agitazione; *— -cloud,* nube tempestosa; *— -damage,* danno causato dalla tempesta; *— -door, (amer.)* porta doppia; *— -sail, (mar.)* vela di fortuna; *— -tossed,* sballottato dalla tempesta; *— -troops,* truppe d'assalto; *— -window,* controfinestra ‖ *hail- —,* grandinata; *snow - —,* tempesta di neve, tormenta.

o **storm,** *v.t.i.* **1.** infuriare, scatenarsi: *it is storming outside,* fuori infuria la tempesta **2.** *(fam.)* adirarsi; rimproverare: *to — at s.o.,* fare una scenata a qlcu. **3.** *(mil.)* prendere d'assalto.

stormbound ['stɔːmbaund], *ag.* trattenuto, immobilizzato dalla tempesta.

stormer ['stɔːmə*], *s. (mil.)* assalitore.

stormily ['stɔːmili], *av.* tempestosamente.

storminess ['stɔːminis], *s.* natura burrascosa, tempestosa.

storming ['stɔːmin], *s.* **1.** violenza, furia **2.** *(mil.)* assalto ☆ *— -party,* truppe d'assalto.

stormless ['stɔːmlis], *ag.* senza tempeste, calmo.

stormproof ['stɔːmpruːf], *ag.* **1.** resistente alla tempesta **2.** *(mil.)* inespugnabile.

stormy ['stɔːmi], *ag.* burrascoso, tempestoso, procelloso: *a — discussion, fig.* una discussione violenta; *a — meeting, fig.* una riunione tumultuosa; *— sea,* mare in burrasca; *— sunset,* un tramonto che promette tempesta; *— wind,* vento di tempesta; *it is —,* fa tempo di burrasca ☆ *— -petrel, (ornit.)* procellaria.

story[1] ['stɔːri], *s.* **1.** storia, racconto: *according to her —,* stando a quel che dice; *good, funny —,* storiella, aneddoto: *idle —,* storia campata in aria; *I read the — of his life,* ho letto la sua biografia; *it is quite another — now, (fam.)* è un altro paio di maniche; *it is the same old —, (fam.)* è sempre la stessa storia; *to know the — of printing,* conoscere la storia dell'arte della stampa; *to tell a —,* raccontare una storia ‖ *the — goes...,* si dice che... ‖ *to make a long — short,* per farla breve **2.** novella; favola **3.** storia, intreccio **4.** *(fam.)* menzogna, bugia: *to tell stories,* contar frottole **5.** *(amer.)* articolo (di giornale); spunto interessante per un ser-

vizio giornalistico ☆ *— -book,* libro di storie, di novelle; *— -teller,* novelliere, narratore; cantastorie; *(fam.)* bugiardo ‖ *film —,* fotoromanzo; *short —,* novella.

story[2], *V.* **storey.**

stoup [stuːp], *s.* **1.** acquasantiera **2.** *(arc.)* boccale; brocca.

stout[1] [staut], *ag.* **1.** forte, robusto, vigoroso **2.** fermo, risoluto; coraggioso, intrepido: *a — heart,* un cuore intrepido; *he is a — fellow,* è un uomo coraggioso; *to make (o to put up) a — resistance,* resistere risolutamente **3.** solido, resistente (di cose): *— ship,* nave solida **4.** grosso; tozzo, corpulento: *to grow (o to get) —,* ingrassare ☆ *— -hearted,* intrepido, valoroso, coraggioso; *— -heartedness,* coraggio, intrepidezza, ardimento.

stout[2], *s.* birra scura fortissima.

stoutish ['stautiʃ], *ag.* **1.** tarchiatello, piuttosto grasso **2.** piuttosto solido (di cose).

stoutly ['stautli], *av.* **1.** fortemente, vigorosamente **2.** fermamente, risolutamente: *to deny sthg. —,* negare fermamente ql.co. **3.** solidamente; robustamente.

stoutness ['stautnis], *s.* **1.** corpulenza, pinguedine **2.** fermezza, risolutezza **3.** durezza, resistenza.

stove[1] [stouv], *s.* **1.** stufa (per riscaldamento) **2.** *(cooking-) —,* stufa, cucina economica **3.** *(agr.)* serra riscaldata **4.** scaldapiedi **5.** *(ind.)* vernice a fuoco ☆ *— -plants,* piante di serra; *— -setter,* fumista ‖ *gas- —,* stufa, cucina a gas; *slow-combustion —,* stufa a fuoco continuo.

to **stove**[1], *v.t.* **1.** mettere in forno, stufa; riscaldare, far asciugare in forno, stufa **2.** far crescere, coltivare (delle piante) in serra **3.** disinfettare, sterilizzare (indumenti, ecc.).

stove[2], *pass.p.p.* di to **stave.**

stovepipe ['stouvpaip], *s.* tubo da stufa ☆ *— hat, (amer.)* cappello a cilindro.

stover ['stouvə*], *s. (sl.)* foraggio (di paglia).

to **stow** [stou], *v.t.* **1.** mettere a posto, ordinare, collocare accuratamente in un luogo: *to — sthg. away,* mettere via, nascondere ql.co.; *(fam.)* mangiare ql.co. ‖ *to — the anchor, (mar.)* traversare l'ancora ‖ *to — the sails, (mar.)* ammainare le vele **2.** *(mar.)* stivare, mettere nella stiva: *to — tea-boxes,* stivare casse di tè **3.** riempire: *to — a waggon with coal,* riempire un vagone di carbone **4.** *(sl.)* smettere, cessare di: *— that nonsense,* smettila di dire sciocchezze **5.** *(miner.)* rinterrare, chiudere (gallerie) con detriti.

stowage ['stouidʒ], *s.* **1.** *(mar.)* stivaggio: *— in bulk,* stivaggio alla rinfusa; *— in riders,* stivaggio in ranghi; *broken (o negligent) —,* stivaggio difettoso; *certificate of —, (mar. comm.)* certificato di stivaggio **2.** *(mar. comm.)* spese di stivaggio **3.** *(mec.)* sistemazione.

stowaway ['stouəwei], *s.c.* passeggero clandestino (specialmente su una nave) ‖ *s.* nascondiglio.

to **stowaway,** *v.i.* imbarcarsi clandestinamente: *to — on board a liner,* imbarcarsi clandestinamente su un transatlantico.

strabism ['streibizəm], *s.* strabismo ☆ *convergent — (o internal — o cross-eye —),* strabismo convergente; *divergent — (o external —),* strabismo divergente.

strabismal [strə'bizməl], **strabismic** [strə'bismik], *ag.* strabico.

strabismus [strə'bizməs], *V.* **strabism.**

Strabo ['streibou], *no.pr.m. (lett. greca)* Strabone.

strabotomy [strə'botəmi], *s. (chir.)* strabotomia.

straddle ['strædl], *s.* **1.** lo stare, il mettersi a cavalcioni; posizione a gambe divaricate **2.** *(sl. Borsa)* opzione **3.** *fig.* incertezza, indecisione sulla scelta fra due linee di condotta ☆ *— -legged,* che sta a cavalcioni.

to **straddle,** *v.t.i.* **1.** cavalcare, stare a cavalcioni di; divaricare; stare a gambe divaricate: *to — (out) one's legs,* divaricare le gambe **2.** *(artigl.)* fare forcella **3.** *fig.* esitare, vacillare (fra due linee di condotta).

Stradivarius [,strædi'vɑːriəs], *no.pr. (st. mus.)* Stradivari ‖ **stradivarius,** *s. (mus.)* stradivario (violino di pregio).

strafe [strɑːf], *s.* (*sl.*) **1.** (*mil.*) bombardamento; assalto furioso **2.** bastonata; punizione; sgridata.

to strafe, *v.t.* (*sl.*) **1.** (*mil.*) bombardare (con artiglieria di grosso calibro) **2.** bastonare di santa ragione; sgridare, punire.

to straggle ['strægl], *v.i.* disperdersi, sparpagliarsi; sbandarsi, muoversi disordinatamente; andare alla spicciolata; *fig.* divagare: *houses that* — *round the lake*, case sparpagliate attorno al lago ‖ *the crowd straggled slowly away*, la folla si disperse lentamente. ‖ *the workers* — *off*, gli operai se ne vanno a piccoli gruppi.

straggler ['stræglə*], *s.* **1.** chi rimane indietro, ritardatario; (*mil.*) soldato sbandato **2.** (*arc.*) vagabondo **3.** (*bot.*) succhione.

straggling ['stræglíŋ], *ag.* sparso, disperso; isolato: — *beard*, barba rada; — *houses*, case sparse ☆ — *plants*, (*bot.*) piante rampicanti.

straggling, *s.* andatura, marcia sbandata; vagabondaggio (anche *fig.*).

stragglingly ['stræglíŋli], *av.* sparpagliatamente, qua e là, in ordine sparso; a casaccio.

straggly ['strægli], *ag.* sparso, sparpagliato.

straight [streit], *ag.* **1.** diritto, rettilineo: *a* — *back*, una schiena diritta; — *hair*, capelli lisci; — *line*, linea retta; *with a* — *knee*, col ginocchio teso ‖ — *as a die*, diritto come un fuso ‖ *to fly as* — *as an arrow*, volare dritto come una freccia ‖ *to stand as* — *as a post*, star dritto come un palo **2.** onesto, retto; leale, franco: — *answer*, risposta franca; — *dealings*, affari onesti; *a* — *girl*, una ragazza sincera; — *speaking*, il parlar franco; *he is perfectly* — *in all his dealings*, egli è sempre onesto e leale in tutti i suoi affari; *to be* — *with s.o.*, agire lealmente verso qlcu. ‖ *to keep* —, *fig.* rigare diritto **3.** netto; ordinato; accurato, lindo: — *definition*, definizione chiara; *accounts are* —, i conti sono in ordine; *to put everything* —, riordinare ogni cosa **4.** diritto, perpendicolare; simmetrico: *are the pictures* —?, sono diritti i quadri?; *your tie is not* —, hai la cravatta storta ‖ *he needs a hundred pounds to get* —, *fig.* ha bisogno di un centinaio di sterline per rimettersi in sesto **5.** autorevole, attendibile: — *tip*, informazione esatta, attendibile **6.** (*amer.*) non diluito, non mescolato: *a* — *whisky*, un whisky liscio.

straight, *s.* **1.** posizione diritta, a piombo: *to cut a cloth on the* —, tagliare della stoffa in dritto filo **2.** *fig.* condotta onesta, leale: *he is out of the* —, è fuori dalla retta via; *to act on the* —, agire lealmente **3.** rettilineo: *they were even when they reached the* —, (*spor.*) erano alla pari quando raggiunsero il rettilineo (d'arrivo).

straight, *av.* **1.** diritto, in linea retta: *the smoke rises* — *upwards*, il fumo si leva diritto verso l'alto; *to go* —, andare diritto; *to look* — *ahead*, guardare dritto in avanti; *to shoot* —, mirare dritto ‖ *to go* — *on*, proseguire diritto ‖ *to read a book* — *through*, leggere un libro dal principio alla fine **2.** bene, correttamente: *he does not see* —, non vede bene ‖ *to run* —, *fig.* vivere onestamente **3.** direttamente; senza interruzione, senza deviazione: *I shall go* — *to Paris without stopping at Dover*, andrò direttamente a Parigi senza fermarmi a Dover; *she came* — *from school*, venne direttamente da scuola ‖ — *out*, chiaro e tondo: *I told him* — *out what I thought of it*, gli dissi chiaro e tondo che cosa ne pensavo ‖ *to come* — *to the point*, venire direttamente al punto ‖ *to drink* — *from the bottle*, bere dalla bottiglia **4.** in modo eretto: *to stand* —, stare eretto **5.** (*arc.*) subito, immantinente ‖ — *off*, senza esitazione, immediatamente.

straight, (*nei composti*): — *angle*, (*geom.*) angolo piatto; — *arch*, (*arch.*) piattabanda; — *-cut*, tabacco trinciato; — *-edge*, riga, regolo; — *fiber*, (*ind. tessile*) fibra diritta; — *fight*, (*pol.*) competizione fra due candidati alle elezioni; — *joint*, (*edil.*) giunto retto; — *lined*, rettilineo; — *motor*, (*mec.*) motore a cilindri in linea; — *right*, — *left*, (*boxe*) diretto destro, sinistro;

— *ticket*, (*amer. pol.*) lista definitiva dei candidati di un partito.

straightaway ['streitəwei], *V.* **straightway.**

to straighten ['streitn], *v.t.i.* **1.** drizzare, drizzarsi; raddrizzare, raddrizzarsi: *to* — (*out*) *an iron bar*, raddrizzare una sbarra di ferro **2.** mettere in ordine, rassettare: *to* — (*out*) *a business*, regolare un affare; *to* — (*out*) *one's accounts*, regolare i propri conti; *to* — *a room*, riassettare una stanza **3.** (*mec.*) spianare; lisciare **4.** *to* — **out**, (*aer.*) raddrizzarsi, riprendere il volo orizzontale **5.** *to* — **up**, raddrizzarsi (di persona); (*sl.*) diventare onesto; (*aer.*) raddrizzarsi, riprendere il volo orizzontale.

straightener ['streitnə*], *s.c.* raddrizzatore, raddrizzatrice ‖ *s.* (*aer. mec.*) raddrizzatore.

straightforth ['streitfɔːθ], *av.* immediatamente, direttamente.

straightforward [streit'fɔːwəd], *ag.* **1.** diritto; diretto **2.** schietto, franco, leale: *a* — *man*, un uomo leale; *to give a* — *answer*, dare una risposta franca **3.** semplice, chiaro: — *language*, linguaggio semplice, chiaro.

straightforwardly [streit'fɔːwədli], *av.* **1.** in linea retta **2.** francamente, schiettamente, onestamente, sinceramente **3.** semplicemente, chiaramente.

straightforwardness [streit'fɔːwədnis], *s.* **1.** onestà; schiettezza, franchezza; dirittura morale **2.** semplicità, chiarezza.

straightness ['streitnis], *s.* **1.** l'esser rettilineo **2.** onestà, lealtà, rettitudine.

straightway ['streit-wei], *av.* (*arc.*) immediatamente, subito.

strain[1] [strein], *s.* **1.** tensione (anche *fig.*): *the* — *of modern life*, la tensione della vita moderna; *the* — *on the cable*, la tensione sul filo **2.** sforzo, fatica: *the* — *of business*, la stanchezza causata dagli affari; *it was a great* — *on his resources*, fu un grave sforzo per le sue risorse; *to write, to speak a foreign language without* —, scrivere, parlare una lingua straniera con naturalezza **3.** distorsione, strappo muscolare **4.** (*mec. fis.*) tensione; deformazione; sollecitazione **5.** tono; stile: *he spoke in a dismal* —, parlò in tono cupo **6.** disposizione mentale, tendenza: *a* — *of melancholy*, una tendenza alla melanconia **7.** (*poet.*) poesia, canto **8.** *gener. pl.* melodia, aria musicale.

to strain[1], *v.t.i.* **1.** sottoporre a tensione, tendere fino al limite: *to* — *a rope to breaking-point*, tirare una corda al massimo **2.** sforzare, sforzarsi; affaticare, affaticarsi: *this light strains my eyes*, questa luce mi affatica gli occhi ‖ *to* — *oneself*, affaticarsi ‖ *to* — *one's ear*, tendere l'orecchio **3.** esigere troppo da (persone, cose, facoltà): *she strained his friendship*, ella pretese troppo dalla sua amicizia; *to* — *one's authority*, oltrepassare i limiti della propria autorità **4.** forzare il significato di (una parola): *to* — *s.o.'s words*, forzare il significato delle parole di qlcu. **5.** danneggiare, deformare (per eccessiva tensione); slogarsi (arto, ecc.): *he strained his ankle*, si slogò una caviglia; *to* — *the springs*, rovinare, danneggiare le molle **6.** filtrare, colare: *water is straining through the soil*, l'acqua filtra attraverso il terreno; *to* — *wine*, filtrare il vino **7.** (*arc.*) stringere forte, abbracciare: *to* — *s.o. to one's bosom*, stringersi qlcu. al petto **8.** *to* — *after* (*sthg.*), cercare di raggiungere, fare grandi sforzi: *that writer strains after effect*, quello scrittore cerca di fare effetto **9.** *to* — *at* (*sthg.*), tirare forte, essere eccessivamente scrupoloso: *she strained at her work*, si dava molto da fare col suo lavoro **10.** *to* — *off*, scolare: *to* — *off salad*, scolare l'insalata.

strain[2], *s.* **1.** razza (di animali): *cow of a good* —, vacca di buona razza **2.** stirpe, lignaggio; famiglia; origini: *he is of noble* —, è di nobile famiglia **3.** carattere ereditario; costituzione: *he has a* — *of American blood in his veins*, ha tracce di sangue americano nelle vene.

strained [streind], *ag.* **1.** teso: — *nerves*, nervi tesi; — *relations*, rapporti tesi **2.** danneggiato, indebolito:

— *heart*, cuore debole **3.** forzato, non spontaneo, artificiale: — *cordiality*, cordialità affettata; *the quality of mercy is not* —, la misericordia deve essere spontanea **4.** filtrato, colato.

strainer ['streinə*], *s.* **1.** colino, filtro **2.** depuratore **3.** (*ind.*) trafila ☆ *air-* —, purificatore d'aria; *centrifugal* —, (*ind.*) depuratore centrifugo; *tea-* —, colino da tè.

straining ['streiniŋ], *s.* **1.** ipertensione, sforzo, fatica **2.** interpretazione forzata, esagerazione **3.** filtratura.

strait [streit], *ag.* (*arc.*) **1.** stretto, angusto: *a* — *gate*, una porta stretta **2.** rigoroso; pieno di scrupoli: *the straitest group of a religious sect*, il gruppo più rigoroso di una setta religiosa ‖ *s.* **1.** *gener. pl.* (*geog.*) stretto ‖ *the Straits of Dover, of Gibraltar*, lo stretto di Dover, di Gibilterra **2.** *pl.* posizione difficile, critica; ristrettezze: *to be in great straits*, essere in grande difficoltà ☆ — *-jacket* (o — *-waistcoat*), camicia di forza; — *-laced*, pieno di scrupoli, rigoroso; puritano.

to straiten ['streitn], *v.t.i.* **1.** mettere in difficoltà (specialmente finanziarie): *he found himself straitened by excessive expenses*, si trovò in difficoltà a causa delle spese eccessive ‖ *he was straitened for bread*, gli mancava il pane **2.** (*rar.*) serrare, stringere, restringere, restringersi; *fig.* stringere (un legame affettivo, ecc.): *they straitened their friendship*, rafforzarono la loro amicizia.

straitened ['streitnd], *ag.* difficile; precario; misero, povero: — *circumstances*, precarie situazioni economiche; — *household*, famiglia povera, misera.

straitly ['streitli], *av.* (*arc.*) **1.** strettamente; intimamente **2.** rigorosamente, rigidamente.

straitness ['streitnis], *s.* (*arc.*) **1.** strettezza, ristrettezza **2.** inflessibilità, rigore, severità **3.** difficoltà; imbarazzo; angustia.

strake[1] [streik], *s.* **1.** (*mar.*) corso di fasciame **2.** sezione del cerchione (di ruota di carro) **3.** striscia di colore diverso dal resto della superficie.

strake[2], *s.* pozzo poco profondo per il lavaggio di minerali (in Cornovaglia).

stramineous [strə'miniəs], *ag.* (*arc.*) **1.** di, simile a paglia **2.** *fig.* senza valore.

stramonium [strə'mouniəm], *s.*(*bot. chim.*)stramonio.

strand[1] [strænd], *s.* **1.** trefolo **2.** filo; giro (di una collana) **3.** fune, cavo **4.** treccia **5.** (*mar.*) legnolo.

to strand[1], *v.t.* **1.** scomporre (una corda) in trefoli **2.** formare (una corda) intrecciandone i vari fili **3.** (*poet.*) inserire; intrecciare: *age stranded her beautiful hair with white*, il tempo disseminava di fili bianchi i suoi bei capelli.

strand[2], *s.* (*poet.*) sponda; spiaggia, lido ‖ *the Strand*, lo Strand (famosa strada di Londra).

to strand[2], *v.t.i.* (*spec. mar.*) arenare; arenarsi; far arenare; incagliarsi.

stranded ['strændid], *ag.* **1.** (*mar.*) arenato, incagliato, insabbiato **2.** *fig.* in difficoltà; (*fam.*) rimasto al verde.

stranding ['strændiŋ], *s.* incaglio, arenamento.

strange [streindʒ], *ag.* **1.** strano, bizzarro, singolare, insolito; straordinario: *I heard a* — *story about him the other day*, ho sentito una strana storia sul suo conto l'altro giorno; *she wore rather* — *clothes*, era vestita in modo eccentrico **2.** estraneo, sconosciuto; nuovo: *in a* — *land*, in terra straniera; *I heard a* — *voice*, udii una voce che non conoscevo; *the team cannot play on a* — *ground*, la squadra non può giocare su un campo nuovo **3.** perplesso, confuso **4.** senza esperienza; non abituato: *I am* — *to this job*, sono nuovo a questo lavoro.

strangely ['streindʒli], *av.* stranamente, bizzarramente; in modo insolito, inusitato.

strangeness ['streindʒnis], *s.* **1.** stranezza; singolarità; bizzarria **2.** novità.

stranger ['streindʒə*], *s.c.* estraneo, estranea; sco-

nosciuto, sconosciuta; forestiero, forestiera: *he is no* — *to me*, lo conosco bene; *she made a* — *of him*, lo trattò come un estraneo; *she was a* — *to their intrigues*, era estranea ai loro intrighi; *they were strangers*, non erano pratici del luogo; *you are a* — *now*, non ti si vede più dalle nostre parti ‖ *the little* —, il neonato ‖ *I spy strangers*, formula usata alla Camera dei Comuni per richiedere che la discussione avvenga a porte chiusi.

to strangle ['stræŋgl], *v.t.* strangolare; soffocare; *fig.* reprimere, sopprimere: *to* — *a laugh*, soffocare una risata; *to* — *a sneeze*, reprimere uno starnuto.

stranglehold ['stræŋglhould], *s.* **1.** stretta mortale **2.** *fig.* (*pol. comm.*) controllo paralizzante.

strangler ['stræŋglə*], *s.c.* strangolatore, strangolatrice.

strangles ['stræŋglz], *s.pl.* (*vet.*) stranguglioni.

strangling ['stræŋgliŋ], *s.* strangolamento.

to strangulate ['stræŋgjuleit], *v.t.* **1.** (*patol. chir.*) strozzare; fermare la circolazione a **2.** (*rar.*) strangolare ☆ *strangulated hernia*, ernia strozzata.

strangulation [,stræŋgju'leiʃən], *s.* **1.** strangolamento **2.** (*patol. chir.*) strozzatura.

strangurious [stræŋ'gjuəriəs], *ag.* (*patol.*) **1.** relativo a stranguria **2.** affetto da stranguria.

strangury ['stræŋgjuri], *s.* (*patol.*) stranguria.

strap [stræp], *s.* **1.** cinghia, correggia ‖ *the* —, sferzata (per punizione) **2.** maniglia a pendaglio (su tram, autobus, ecc.) **3.** staffa (di pantaloni) **4.** (*mec.*) nastro; cinghia; moietta **5.** (*mar.*) stroppo **6.** (*bot.*) ligula, linguetta **7.** (*rar.*) coramella (per rasoio) ☆ — *-bolt*, (*mec.*) bullone a staffa; — *-hanger*, (*sl.*) passeggero che si regge alla maniglia (in tram, autobus, ecc.); — *-oil*, (*sl.*) percosse (inflitte con cinghia) ‖ *shoulder-* —, spallina (anche *mil.*); *watch* —, cinturino da orologio.

to strap, *pass.p.p.* **strapped** [stræpt], *v.t.* **1.** assicurare, legare con cinghie **2.** percuotere con una cinghia, frustare **3.** affilare **4.** mettere un cerotto a; coprire (una ferita) con un cerotto **5.** (*mar.*) stroppare.

to strap-hang ['stræphæŋ], *pass.p.p.* **strap-hung** ['stræphʌŋ], *v.i.* viaggiare in piedi (in treno, autobus, ecc.) sostenendosi a una maniglia.

strappado [strə'peidou], *pl.* **strappados** [strə'peidouz], *s.* **1.** strappata (supplizio della corda) **2.** strappata di fune.

to strappado, *v.t.* torturare, punire con la strappata.

strapped [stræpt], *ag.* **1.** attaccato, legato con una cinghia **2.** (*sartoria*) guarnito, decorato con bande **3.** (*sl. amer.*) al verde.

strapper ['stræpə*], *s. c.* persona gagliarda, vigorosa, ben piantata.

strapping ['stræpiŋ], *ag.* vigoroso, gagliardo, robusto, ben piantato: *a* — *peasant girl*, una contadinotta.

strapping, *s.* **1.** chiusura per mezzo di cinghie **2.** colpo di cinghia, staffilata **3.** *coll.* bande, nastri; bretelle, spalline **4.** cerotto **5.** (*mec.*) moietta, reggetta.

strass [stræs], *s.* « strass » (brillante artificiale).

stratagem ['strætidʒəm], *s.* stratagemma.

strategie(al) [strə'ti:dʒik(əl)], *ag.* strategico.

strategically [strə'ti:dʒikəli], *av.* strategicamente.

strategies [strə'ti:dʒiks], *s.* strategia.

strategist ['strætidʒist], *s.* strategia.

strategus [strə'ti:gəs], *pl.* **strategi** [strə'ti:dʒai], *s.* (*st. greca*) stratega.

strategy ['strætidʒi], *s.* strategia.

Stratford(-on-Avon) ['strætfəd(ən'eivən)], *no.pr.* (*geog.*) Stratford-on-Avon.

strath [stræθ], *s.* (*scoz.*) larga vallata.

strathspey [stræθ'spei], *s.* « strathspey » (vivace danza, musica scozzese).

stratification [,strætifi'keiʃən],*s.*(*geol.*) stratificazione.

stratiform ['strætifɔ:m], *ag.* (*geol.*) stratiforme.

to stratify ['strætifai], *v.t.i.* disporre a strati, stratificare, stratificarsi.

stratigraphic [,stræti'græfik], *ag.* (*geol.*) stratigrafico.

stratigraphically [ˌstræti'græfikəli], *av.* (*geol.*) in modo stratigrafico.

stratigraphy [strə'tigrəfi], *s.* (*geol.*) stratigrafia.

stratocracy [strə'tɔkrəsi], *s.* dittatura militare.

stratocruiser ['strætou,kru:zə*], *s.* (*aer.*) stratoplano.

stratosphere ['strætousfiə*], *s.* stratosfera.

stratospheric [ˌstrætou'sferik], *ag.* stratosferico.

stratum ['stra:təm], *pl.* **strata** ['stra:tə], *s.* **1.** (*geol.*) strato; giacimento **2.** strato sociale, classe: *the highest and lowest strata of society*, le classi più abbienti e le più povere della società.

stratus ['streitəs], *pl.* **strati** ['streitai], *s.* (*meteorologia*) strato.

straw[1] [strɔ:], *ag.* di paglia ‖ *s.* **1.** paglia: *stuffed with* —, imbottito di paglia ‖ *man of* —, *fig.* uomo di paglia **2.** fuscello, festuca, cannuccia; *fig.* cosa da nulla: *to drink sthg. through a* —, bere ql.co. con una cannuccia ‖ *I don't care a* —, non me ne importa nulla ‖ *it is not worth a* —, non vale un fico secco ‖ *to catch at a* —, *fig.* attaccarsi ad una pagliuzza ‖ *it is the last — that breaks the camel's back*, *prov.* è l'ultima goccia che fa traboccare il vaso **3.** — (*-hat*), paglietta ☆ — *-colour*, giallo paglierino; — *-cutter*, (*agr.*) trinciapaglia; — *vote*, votazione esplorativa; — *-yard*, pagliaio.

to **straw**[2], (*arc.*) per to **strew**.

strawberry ['strɔ:bəri], *s.* fragola ☆ — *-leaves*, (*arald.*) dignità, corona ducale; — *-mark*, (*patol.*) neo angiomatoso; — *-shrub*, (*bot.*) calicantus; — *-tree*, corbezzolo.

strawy ['strɔ:i], *ag.* di, simile a paglia; contenente paglia.

stray [strei], *ag.* **1.** smarrito; sviato; randagio; errante: *a — dog*, un cane randagio **2.** casuale, fortuito, accidentale: *a few — visitors*, alcuni visitatori casuali **3.** isolato, staccato: — *thoughts*, pensieri isolati; *a few — houses*, qualche casa isolata.

stray, *s.* **1.** animale domestico smarritosi **2.** fanciullo abbandonato ‖ *waifs and strays*, fanciulli abbandonati; derelitti **3.** (*dir.*) proprietà che passa allo stato per mancanza di eredi **4.** (*elett.*) dispersione **5.** *pl.* radiodisturbi ☆ — *field*, (*elett.*) campo di dispersione; — *lines*, (*elett.*) linee di dispersione.

to **stray**, *v.i.* **1.** vagare, vagabondare (anche *fig.*): *to let one's mind* —, lasciar vagare la mente **2.** deviare; perdersi, smarrirsi (anche *fig.*): *to — from the right path*, deviare dalla retta via **3.** (*elett.*) disperdersi.

streak [stri:k], *s.* **1.** linea, riga, striscia, striatura; banda: *a — of light*, un raggio di luce; *a — of lightning*, un lampo ‖ *white with black streaks*, bianco a righe nere ‖ *like a — of lightning*, in un attimo; come un lampo ‖ *the silver* —, la Manica **2.** vena (anche *fig.*): *a — of eccentricity*, un tocco, una punta d'eccentricità; *a — of gold*, una vena d'oro; *a — of luck*, (*fam.*) un momento di fortuna; *he has a — of humour*, *fig.* ha una vena di umorismo ‖ *there was a yellow — in him*, c'era un che di vile in lui.

to **streak**, *v.t.i.* **1.** striare; rigare: *blood streaked his face*, il sangue gli rigava il viso **2.** venare: *white marble streaked with red*, marmo bianco venato di rosso **3.** muoversi velocemente, andare svelto come un lampo ‖ *they streaked off*, se ne andarono a gran velocità.

streaked [stri:kt], *ag.* a strisce, striato, screziato.

streakiness ['stri:kinis], *s.* striatura, screziatura; venatura.

streaky ['stri:ki], *ag.* **1.** striato, screziato; lardellato (di carne) **2.** (*fam.*) vario, disuguale.

stream [stri:m], *s.* **1.** corso d'acqua, ruscello; fiume; torrente **2.** flusso, fiotto, getto continuo; fiumana, colata (di lava): *a — of blood*, un fiotto di sangue; *a — of people was* (o *were*) *coming out from the church*, una fiumana di gente usciva di chiesa; *she shed streams of tears*, versò fiumi di lacrime **3.** corrente, corso (anche *fig.*): *against* (o *up*) *the* —, controcorrente: *to go up* —, risalire un fiume, andar contro corrente; *to move down* —, scendere un fiume, seguire la corrente ‖ — *of con-*

sciousness, (*lett. psicologia*) flusso di coscienza ‖ *the Gulf Stream*, la Corrente del Golfo ‖ *in the main — of English tradition*, secondo la migliore tradizione inglese ‖ *to go with the* —, seguir la corrente, essere facilmente influenzabile **4.** (*ind. petrolifera*) produzione: *to be on* —, produrre (distillato, ecc.); *to put on* —, avviare la produzione ☆ — *-anchor*, (*mar.*) ancora di media grandezza; ancoretto da tonneggio; — *-cable*, (*mar.*) cavo di imbozzamento; — *-gold*, — *-tin*, (*miner.*) oro, stagno in depositi alluvionali; — *novel*, romanzo fiume; — *time*, periodo di produzione (di petrolio).

to **stream**, *v.t.i.* **1.** (*far*) scorrere; (*far*) fluire; (*far*) sgorgare; (*far*) scaturire; colare: *the rain streamed down the windows*, la pioggia scorreva a torrenti sui vetri delle finestre **2.** ondeggiare, fluttuare: *hair, flags streaming in the wind*, capelli, bandiere ondeggianti al vento **3.** (*miner.*) lavare il minerale **4.** *to — the buoy*, (*mar.*) gettare il gavitello **5.** *to — forth*, uscire a fiotti: *blood streamed forth from his wound*, il sangue usciva a fiotti dalla sua ferita **6.** *to — in*, penetrare, entrare: *all the crowd streamed in through the gates*, la fiumana di gente penetrò attraverso i cancelli **7.** *to — out*, effondersi, riversarsi (fuori): *when the film finished the people streamed out*, quando il film terminò, gli spettatori si riversarono all'aperto.

streamer ['stri:mə*], *s.* **1.** pennone; (*mar.*) fiamma, banderuola **2.** nastro **3.** *pl.* aurora boreale **4.** (*amer.*) titolo su tutta la larghezza della pagina.

streamless ['stri:mlis], *ag.* **1.** senza corrente **2.** senz'acqua; senza corsi d'acqua.

streamlet ['stri:mlit], *s.* ruscelletto; rivolo d'acqua.

streamline ['stri:mlain], *s.* **1.** (*idraulica*) linea di flusso; linea di corrente **2.** (*aut. aer.*) linea aerodinamica, affusolata.

to **streamline**, *v.t.* (*aut. aer.*) dare forma, linea aerodinamica, affusolata a: *a streamlined car*, una automobile dalla carrozzeria aerodinamica.

streamy ['stri:mi], *ag.* **1.** simile a corrente **2.** uscente a fiotti **3.** ricco di corsi d'acqua **4.** fluente (di capigliatura).

street [stri:t], *s.* via, strada: *the main streets of the town*, le principali vie della città; *to go across the* —, attraversare la strada ‖ *Fleet Street*, Fleet Street (strada in cui si trovano le redazioni dei giornali a Londra); *fig.* la stampa ‖ *Wall Street*, Wall Street (strada in cui si trova la Borsa a New York); *fig.* la Borsa americana ‖ *the man in the* —, l'uomo della strada ‖ *manners of the* —, maniere di strada ‖ *not in the same — with s.o.*, (*fam.*) di molto inferiore a qlcu. ‖ *he is streets ahead of you*, (*fam.*) è di gran lunga superiore a te ‖ *to be in Queer Street*, essere in cattive acque ‖ *to be* (o *to live*) *on the streets*, vivere di prostituzione ‖ *to deal in the* —, stipulare contratti in strada (dopo la chiusura della Borsa) ‖ *to turn s.o. into the streets*, buttare qlcu. sul lastrico ‖ *to walk the streets*, vivere una vita randagia; battere il marciapiede ☆ — *-boy*, ragazzo di strada; — *-car*, (*amer.*) tram; — *-door*, portone; — *-level*, pianterreno; — *-orderly*, spazzino; — *-plate*, targa stradale; — *-railway*, tram; — *-walker*, prostituta ‖ *by* —, via secondaria; *main* —, strada principale; *one-way* —, strada a senso unico; *side* —, via laterale.

strength [streŋθ], *s.* **1.** forza, vigore, energia (anche *fig.*): *the — of evidence*, la forza dell'evidenza; *the — of a man*, la forza di un uomo; — *of mind*, forza di volontà; *it is too much for my* —, è al di sopra delle mie forze; *that is beyond human* —, ciò va oltre il limite delle forze umane ‖ *by sheer* —, a viva forza ‖ *on the — of*, basandosi, contando su: *I did it on the — of your promise*, lo feci basandomi sulla tua promessa ‖ *to have the — of a horse*, essere forte come un toro **2.** solidità, rigidezza, tenacia; (*fis.*) resistenza: *the — of a rope*, la resistenza di una corda; *the — of a wall*, la solidità di una parete **3.** efficacia; intensità (anche *fis.*); (*chim.*) densità: — *of a current*, (*elett.*) intensità di una corrente; — *of a wine*, grado alcoolico di un vino **4.** sostegno spirituale: *God is our* —, Dio è la nostra forza **5.** quantità, numero: *to be present in great* —, esser presenti in gran numero **6.** (*mil.*) truppe, forze effettive: *fighting* —, effettivi mobilitabili; *to be on the* —, figurare nei ruoli; *to bring a regiment up to* —, completare i ranghi di un reggimento; *to strike s.o. off the* —, radiare qlcu. dai ranghi ☆ *breaking* —, resistenza alla rottura; *elastic* —, resistenza elastica; *strain* —, resistenza alla deformazione.

to **strengthen** ['streŋθən], *v.t.i.* **1.** dar forza a; fortificare; rafforzare, rafforzarsi; irrobustire, irrobustirsi; consolidare, consolidarsi: *her words strengthened my point of view*, le sue parole rinforzarono il mio punto di vista; *to — a government*, consolidare un governo **2.** (*chim.*) aumentare la concentrazione di (soluzione, ecc.) **3.** (*mil.*) potenziare.

strengthener ['streŋθənə*], *s.* **1.** cosa che dà forza **2.** (*med.*) corroborante.

strengthening ['streŋθəniŋ], *ag.* fortificante; rafforzante ‖ *s.* rafforzamento, irrobustimento, consolidamento ☆ — *piece*, (*mec.*) rinforzo; — *band*, (*mar.*) banda di rinforzo d'una tela.

strengthful ['streŋθful], *ag.* pieno di forza.

strengthless ['streŋθlis], *ag.* debole, privo di forza.

strenuous ['strenjuəs], *ag.* **1.** strenuo, energico; attivo; accanito: — *game*, giuoco accanito, molto combattuto; — *opposition*, opposizione accanita; — *worker*, lavoratore zelante **2.** arduo; duro: — *life*, vita dura.

strenuously ['strenjuəsli], *av.* strenuamente; accanitamente; vigorosamente.

strenuousness ['strenjuəsnis], *s.* vigore, energia; ardore, zelo; accanimento.

streptococcus [,streptou'kɔkəs], *pl.* **streptococci** [,streptou'kɔkai], *s.* streptococco.

streptomycin [,streptou'maisin], *s.* (*farm.*) streptomicina.

stress [stres], *s.* **1.** spinta; pressione; costrizione; tensione: *in times of* —, in periodi di difficoltà; *times of tranquillity and times of* —, periodi di tranquillità e periodi di intenso lavoro; *under the — of anger*, sotto l'impulso dell'ira; *under the — of hardship*, costretto, spinto dalle difficoltà **2.** enfasi, importanza; insistenza: *to lay special — on sthg.*, porre in rilievo qualcosa **3.** (*gram.*) accento tonico: *the — is on the first syllable*, l'accento cade sulla prima sillaba **4.** (*scienza delle costruzioni*) sollecitazione, sforzo, tensione: *this beam is under* —, questa trave è soggetta a sforzo ☆ *breaking* —, resistenza alla rottura; *maximum* —, carico di rottura; *torsional* —, sollecitazione di torsione.

to **stress**, *v.t.* **1.** forzare, sottoporre a tensione **2.** (*gram.*) accentuare: *to — a syllable*, mettere l'accento su una sillaba **3.** porre in rilievo, dare enfasi a, sottolineare, accentuare: *he stressed the fact that...*, mise in risalto il fatto che...; *to — a melody*, (*mus.*) mettere in rilievo un tema.

stressing ['stresiŋ], *s.* **1.** enfasi, insistenza **2.** accentazione **3.** (*scienza delle costruzioni*) sforzo, tensione.

stressless ['streslis], *ag.* **1.** (*gram.*) senza accento tonico **2.** senza rilievo, senza enfasi **3.** (*scienza delle costruzioni*) senza sforzo, senza tensione.

stretch [stretʃ], *s.* **1.** stiramento, tensione; sforzo; *fig.* abuso: *by a — of authority, he got it*, l'ha ottenuto abusando della propria autorità; *by a — of the imagination*, (*fam.*) facendo uno sforzo d'immaginazione; *every faculty under* —, ogni facoltà sotto tensione; *with a — and a yawn he went to bed*, stirandosi e sbadigliando se ne andò a letto **2.** periodo, spazio di tempo: *for a short — of time*, per un breve periodo di tempo ‖ *at a* (o *at one*) —, tutto d'un fiato, tutto di seguito: *he slept ten hours at a* —, dormì per dieci ore di seguito **3.** distesa, estensione di spazio: *a — of road*, un bel tratto di strada; *a wide — of water*, un'ampia distesa d'acqua **4.** (*sl.*) periodo di detenzione, di lavori forzati: *they are doing their* —, stanno scon-

tando la pena **5.** (*amer.*) rettilineo d'ippodromo **6.** (*mar.*) bordata **7.** (*miner.*) orientamento (di filone).

to **stretch**, *v.t.i.* **1.** tirare; tendere, tendersi; stendere: *don't yawn and — like that!*, non sbadigliare e non stirarti a quel modo!; *the eagle stretched its wings*, l'aquila allargò le ali; *he stretched his legs in front of the fire*, allungò le gambe verso il caminetto; *rubber stretches easily*, la gomma si tende facilmente; *to — a wire across a room*, tirare una corda attraverso una stanza ‖ *my means don't — to it*, (*fam.*) le mie finanze non arrivano a tanto ‖ *to — s.o. on the floor*, mandar qlcu. lungo e disteso sul pavimento **2.** estendersi: *this district stretches to the North*, questa regione si estende al nord **3.** forzare; sfruttare oltre il giusto limite; esagerare, abusare di: *don't — the truth!*, non esagerare!; *he stretches his power*, abusa del suo potere **4.** (*sl.*) impiccare **5.** *to — out*, allungare, allungarsi: *columns of people stretched out along the street*, una fiumana di gente si snoda lungo la strada; *he stretched out his hand*, allungò la mano.

stretcher ['stretʃə*], *s.* **1.** tenditore, stenditore **2.** lettiga, barella **3.** (*mec.*) tenditore; allargatore **4.** (*mar.*) traversino, puntapiedi, pedana **5.** (*edil.*) mattone per piano **6.** (*fam.*) frottola, esagerazione ☆ — *-bearer* (o — *man*), barelliere ‖ *boot* —, forma allungascarpe; *canvas* —, telaio (di dipinto).

stretching ['stretʃiŋ], *s.* **1.** stiramento; allungamento, allargamento **2.** (*mec.*) tensione.

to **strew** [stru:], *pass.* **strewed** [stru:d], *p.p.* **strewn** [stru:n], **strewed**, *v.t.* spargere, sparpagliare; cospargere, coprire: *he strewed the papers all over the place*, disseminò le carte un po' dappertutto; *the park was strewn with litter*, il parco era coperto di rifiuti; *to — flowers in s.o.'s path*, spargere fiori sul cammino di qlcu.

strewing ['struiŋ], *s.* sparpagliamento; cospargimento.

strewn [stru:n], *p.p.* di to **strew**.

stria ['straiə], *pl.* **striae** ['straii:], *s.* **1.** (*arch.*) stria (di colonna) **2.** (*anat.*) stria **3.** (*bot. geol.*) striatura.

striate ['straiit], *ag.* (*anat. bot. geol.*) striato.

to **striate** ['straieit], *v.t.* striare.

striately ['straiitli], *av.* a strie.

striation [strai'eiʃən], *s.* striatura.

stricken ['strikən], *p.p.* (*arc.*) di to **strike** ‖ *ag.* colpito, ferito (anche *fig.*): *the — deer*, il cervo ferito; — *heart*, cuore afflitto; — *with paralysis*, colpito da paralisi ☆ *panic-* —, atterrito, sgomento.

strickle ['strikl], *s.* **1.** rasiera (per cereali, ecc.) **2.** (*metal.*) sagoma, forma **3.** cote, pietra da affilare.

strict [strikt], *ag.* **1.** stretto; preciso, esatto: *in the strictest sense of the word*, nel senso più stretto della parola **2.** *fig.* severo, rigido, rigoroso; scrupoloso: *a — law*, una legge severa; — *morals*, morale rigida; — *parents*, genitori severi; *she told me so in — confidence*, me lo disse in gran segretezza; *to keep — watch over s.o.*, esercitare una rigorosa sorveglianza su qlcu.

strictly ['striktli], *av.* **1.** esattamente, con precisione: — *speaking*, a rigor di termini **2.** rigorosamente, severamente: — *prohibited*, rigorosamente proibito.

strictness ['striktnis], *s.* **1.** precisione, esattezza **2.** rigore, severità.

stricture ['striktʃə*], *s.* **1.** (*patol.*) stenosi, restringimento **2.** *gener. pl.* critica, biasimo: *to pass strictures on* (o *upon*) *sthg., s.o.*, far delle critiche a ql.co., qlcu.

stridden ['stridn], *p.p.* di to **stride**.

stride [straid], *s.* passo; andatura: *to make great strides*, avanzare a grandi passi; *fig.* fare grandi progressi; *to shorten, to lengthen the* —, (*spor.*) accorciare, allungare il passo ‖ *to get into one's* —, mettersi con zelo (a fare un lavoro) ‖ *to take an obstacle in one's* —, *fig.* superare un ostacolo facilmente, senza il minimo sforzo.

to **stride**, *pass.* **strode** [stroud], *p.p.* **stridden** ['stridn], *v.t.i.* **1.** camminare a grandi passi ‖ *to — away*, allontanarsi a grandi passi‖ *to — up to s.o.*, avanzare a gran passi verso qlcu. **2.** scavalcare con un passo (un fosso, un sentiero) **3.** inforcare, cavalcare.

strident ['straidnt], *ag.* stridente, stridulo.

stridently ['straidntli], *av.* con stridore.

stridor ['straidə*], *s.* **1.** stridore **2.** (*patol.*) stridore respiratorio.

stridulant ['stridjulənt], *ag.* stridulante (di cicala, ecc.).

to **stridulate** ['stridjuleit], *v.i.* stridulare (di cicala, ecc.).

stridulation [ˌstridju'leiʃən], *s.* stridulazione (di cicala, ecc.).

stridulous ['stridjuləs], *ag.* stridulo.

strife [straif], *s.* contesa, lotta, conflitto: *to be at — with s.o.*, essere in lotta con qlcu.; *to cease from —*, deporre le armi.

strig [strig], *s.* gambo (di foglia, frutto, fiore).

striga ['straigə], *pl.* **strigae** ['straidʒi:], *s.* (*bot.*) pelo ispido.

strigil ['stridʒil], *s.* strigile.

strigose ['straigous], **strigous** ['straigəs], *ag.* (*bot.*) ispido.

strike [straik], *s.* **1.** sciopero: *the men are out on —*, gli operai sono in sciopero; *to go on —*, scioperare **2.** scoperta (di giacimento); *fig.* colpo fortunato; fortunata speculazione finanziaria **3.** (*geol.*) direzione di giacimento **4.** rasiera ☆ *— -breaker*, crumiro; *— -fault*, (*geol.*) faglia conforme (alla stratificazione); *— -pay*, indennità di sciopero ‖ *major —*, scoperta di un giacimento importante; *sitdown —*, sciopero bianco; *sympathetic —*, sciopero di solidarietà.

to **strike**, *pass.* **struck** [strʌk], *p.p.* **struck**, (*arc.*) **stricken** ['strikən], *v.t.i.* **1.** battere, colpire, percuotere, picchiare: *he struck his fist on the table*, battè il pugno sul tavolo; *she struck her head against the door*, battè la testa contro la porta; *the ship struck on a rock*, la nave urtò uno scoglio; *to — the bottom*, (*mar.*) arenarsi; *to — one's foot against a stone*, inciampare in un sasso ‖ *— me dead (if)!*, (*sl.*) mi venga un accidente (se)! ‖ *to — an attitude*, assumere un atteggiamento ‖ *to — a bargain*, concludere un affare ‖ *to — a blow for freedom*, battersi per la libertà ‖ *to — home*, (*fam.*) colpire nel segno ‖ *to — upon a brilliant idea*, avere un'idea brillante ‖ *to be struck dead*, morire improvvisamente ‖ *— while the iron is hot*, *prov.* batti il ferro finché è caldo **2.** *fig.* colpire, impressionare: *how does it — you?*, che cosa ne pensi?; *it strikes me that such a thing may be wrong*, ho l'impressione che una cosa simile sia sbagliata; *a suspicion struck me*, mi venne un sospetto; *what struck me was his generosity*, ciò che mi colpì fu la sua generosità ‖ *to — all of a heap*, (*fam.*) sorprendere, sbigottire ‖ *to be struck on s.o.*, (*fam.*) essere innamorato di qualcuno **3.** battere, suonare; toccare (tasti di pianoforte); pizzicare (corde d'arpa): *the clock has just struck twelve*, l'orologio ha appena battuto le dodici **4.** accendere, accendersi: *this match will not —*, questo fiammifero non si accende; *to — a light* (o *a match*), accendere un fiammifero **5.** (*far*) penetrare; infiggere: *the cold is striking into my marrow*, il freddo mi penetra nelle ossa; *sun-rays striking through the mist*, raggi di sole fendono la nebbia; *the tree strikes its roots into the soil*, la pianta affonda le radici nella terra; *to — a knife into s.o.'s heart*, piantare un coltello nel cuore di qlcu. **6.** scioperare, fare sciopero: *they are striking for better working conditions*, scioperano per ottenere migliori condizioni di lavoro **7.** scoprire: *to — oil*, (*amer.*) scoprire un giacimento di petrolio; *fig.* fare un buon affare; *to — the right track*, trovare la pista buona (anche *fig.*) **8.** (*mar. mil.*) ammainare (le vele, la bandiera, ecc.); *fig.* arrendersi, cedere (di città, di nave, ecc.): *to — camp*, levare il campo; *to — tents*, smontare le tende **9.** rasare, livellare (una misura di grano, sabbia, ecc.) **10.** *to — back*, rispondere all'attacco (di) **11.** *to — down*, abbat-

tere, mandare a terra con un colpo: *he was struck down by a heart attack*, fu colpito da un attacco cardiaco **12.** *to — in*, frapporsi, intervenire, interrompere: *while I was talking he struck in with the remark that...*, mentre parlavo, intervenne facendo osservare che... **13.** *to — off*, far cadere, abbattere; tagliare; cancellare; radiare; (*comm.*) dedurre, scontare; (*tip.*) tirare (delle copie): *they struck off his head*, lo decapitarono; *they struck off 5%*, fecero uno sconto del 5%; *to — off a name from a list*, radiare un nome da una lista; *to — off 500 copies a minute*, tirare 500 copie al minuto **14.** *to — out*, progettare, inventare; allungare un pugno; cancellare; tracciare (un cammino), aprire (una strada): *he struck out at his enemy*, allungò un pugno all'avversario; *to — out a line for oneself*, seguire una linea originale **15.** *to — through*, cancellare con un tratto di penna **16.** *to — up*, intonare (un canto); cominciare (una danza); iniziare (rapporti amichevoli, conversazione, ecc.); fare, concludere (trattato, accordo, ecc.): *they struck up a conversation with the other passengers in the compartment*, intavolarono una conversazione con gli altri passeggeri dello scompartimento.

striker ['straikə*], *s.c.* scioperante ‖ *s.* **1.** battitore **2.** (*mec.*) percussore, batacchio.

striking ['straikiŋ], *ag.* sorprendente, straordinario, singolare, sensazionale, impressionante: *— news*, notizie sensazionali ‖ *s.* **1.** colpo, battitura **2.** (*elett.*) innesco ☆ *— clock*, orologio a suoneria; *— surface*, (*mec.*) piano di battuta.

strikingly ['straikiŋli], *av.* in modo sorprendente, sensazionale; in maniera straordinaria, notevole; straordinariamente, singolarmente.

strikingness ['straikiŋnis], *s.* carattere sorprendente; singolarità; cospicuità.

string [striŋ], *s.* **1.** spago, cordicella, corda: *a piece of paper and some —*, un pezzo di carta e dello spago ‖ *to have two strings to one's bow*, *fig.* avere due corde al proprio arco ‖ *to pull every — to obtain sthg.*, *fig.* giocare ogni carta per ottenere ql.co. ‖ *to pull the strings*, *fig.* tenere in mano le fila, agire dietro le quinte **2.** laccio, legaccio, stringa ‖ *to have a — on s.o.*, (*amer. fig.*) aver influenza su qlcu. **3.** (*strum. mus.*) corda: *the strings*, gli strumenti a corda; *the strings of a violin*, le corde di un violino; *to touch the strings*, suonare ‖ *to harp on the same —*, *fig.* insistere sullo stesso tasto ‖ *to touch a — (in s.o.'s heart)*, *fig.* far vibrare una corda (nel cuore di qlcu.) **4.** fibra, filamento: *there are plenty of strings in these beans*, ci sono molti fili in questi fagiolini **5.** fila, filza; rosario: *a — of beads*, una collana; *a — of pearls*, un filo di perle **6.** filza, successione (anche *fig.*): *a — of abuses*, una filza di ingiurie; *a long — of children*, una lunga fila di bambini **7.** (*anat.*) tendine, nervo, legamento **8.** (*amer. biliardo*) colpo preliminare per stabilire chi giuoca per primo **9.** (*equitazione*) scuderia di cavalli da corsa: *Mr. X's —*, la scuderia del signor X **10.** (*amer.*) squadre di giocatori, di atleti scelti secondo le loro capacità ☆ *— -alphabet*, alfabeto per i ciechi; *— -band*, orchestra d'archi; *— -bean*, fagiolino; *— -board*, staggio di scala a piuoli; *— -pea*, pisello; *— -quartet*, quartetto d'archi ‖ *apron strings*, legacci di grembiule; *catgut —*, minugia; *fiddle —*, corda di violino; *first —*, (*amer.*) la migliore squadra; *shoe-strings*, (*amer.*) stringhe per scarpe.

to **string**, *pass.p.p.* **strung** [strʌŋ], *v.t.i.* **1.** munire di, legare con corde: *to — a tennis racket*, mettere le corde a una racchetta da tennis **2.** accordare (uno strumento); tendere, rendere teso: *to — a bow*, tendere un arco **3.** infilare, congiungere con corda: *to — beads*, infilare perline; *to — lies*, *fig.* infilare frottole una dietro l'altra **4.** (*cuc.*) togliere i fili a (fagiolini) **5.** diventare filamentoso, viscoso (di colla) **6.** (*sl. amer.*) farsi giuoco di **7.** (*biliardo*) colpire la palla per vedere chi giuoca per primo **8.** *to — out*, disporsi in fila a intervalli **9.** *to — up*, impiccare; *fig.* tendere:

her nerves are strung up to the highest pitch, i suoi nervi sono tesi al massimo.

stringed [strind], *ag.* a corde, fornito di corde.

stringency ['strindʒənsi], *s.* **1.** rigore, severità (di regole, leggi, stipulazioni, ecc.) **2.** carenza, mancanza: *the — of money,* la scarsità di denaro.

stringent ['strindʒənt], *ag.* **1.** stretto, preciso; rigoroso, severo; incontestabile; impellente: *— argument,* argomento irrefutabile; *— rules,* leggi severe; *he has a — need of funds,* egli ha impellente bisogno di fondi **2.** scarso, mancante (di denaro): *— market,* (*comm.*) mercato difficile, teso.

stringently ['strindʒəntli], *av.* rigorosamente, severamente, rigidamente, strettamente.

stringer ['striŋə*], *s.c.* chi infila (perle, ecc.) ‖ *s.* **1.** accordatore (di strumento musicale) **2.** (*arch.*) longarina; (*aut. aer.*) longarone **3.** (*miner.*) vena; (*geol.*) cordone **4.** *pl.* (*sl.*) manette **5.** (*amer.*) corrispondente occasionale di giornale ☆ *deck —,* (*mar.*) trincarino di coperta; *plate —,* (*mar.*) lamiera-trincarino.

stringy ['striŋi], *ag.* **1.** fibroso; filoso; filamentoso (di vegetali, carni, ecc.) **2.** viscoso (di liquidi).

strip[1] [strip], *s.* striscia, nastro: *a — of paper, of garden, of land,* una striscia di carta, di giardino, una lingua di terra ☆ *— -iron,* ferro in sbarre ‖ *comic — (o — cartoon),* racconto a fumetti: *comic — bandits,* banditi da romanzo a fumetti; *loading —,* (*mil.*) caricatore (di fucile mitragliatore, ecc.); *metal —,* nastro metallico.

to **strip**[1], *pass.p.p.* **stripped** [stript], *v.t.* tagliare a strisce.

strip[2], *s.* foglia di tabacco privata del gambo e della nervatura mediana.

to **strip**[2], *v.t.i.* **1.** svestire, svestirsi; denudare, denudarsi; spogliare, spogliarsi; togliere, strappare: *stripped to the skin,* completamente spogliato; *to — a house,* asportare i mobili di una casa; *to — a tree of its bark,* scortecciare un albero; *to — a tree of its leaves,* spogliare un albero delle foglie; *to — a wall,* strappare la tappezzeria da un muro **2.** *fig.* privare (di titoli, di proprietà); (*mil.*) esautorare: [*he was stripped of all authority,* egli fu privato di ogni autorità; *to — s.o. of his money,* derubare qlcu. **3.** (*mec.*) spanare, spanarsi; togliere la filettatura a (una vite, un dado) **4.** (*mec.*) smontare, smantellare (una macchina, un'arma); disarmare (una nave) **5.** togliere i gambi e le nervature da (foglie di tabacco) **6.** (*metal.*) togliere (il deposito metallico) mediante elettrolisi.

to **strip**[3], *v.t.* mungere (una mucca) sino all'ultima goccia di latte.

stripe[1] [straip], *s.* **1.** striscia, lista; riga; banda; (*mil.*) gallone: *black with a white —,* nero a righe bianche; *to lose, to get one's stripes,* (*mil.*) essere degradato, essere promosso ‖ *to wear the stripes,* (*amer. sl.*) essere in galera **2.** *pl.* (*fam.*) tigre **3.** (*amer. fam.*) tipo, genere; partito: *to be of the same political —,* essere dello stesso colore, partito politico.

to **stripe**[1], *v.t.* rigare, listare, striare.

stripe[2], *s. gener. pl.* (*arc.*) sferzata, frustata, staffilata.

to **stripe**[2], *v.t.* (*rar.*) sferzare, staffilare.

striped [straipt], *ag.* **1.** a strisce, a righe; rigato, striato, zebrato; (*anat.*) striato **2.** gallonato.

striper ['straipə*], *s.* (*sl. mil. amer.*) graduato.

stripiness ['straipinis], *s.* rigatura; striatura.

striping ['straipiŋ], *s.* rigatura.

stripling ['stripliŋ], *s.* giovanetto, adolescente.

stripper ['stripə*], *s.* **1.** (*mec. chim.*) estrattore **2.** (*pitt.*) sverniciatore **3.** (*miner.*) pozzo quasi esaurito **4.** (*sl.*) artista di spogliarello ☆ *leaf—,* (*ind. serica*) sfrondatoio.

strip-tease ['strip,ti:z], *s.* «strip-tease», spogliarello.

stripy ['straipi], *ag.* rigato, striato; a strisce, a righe.

to **strive** [straiv], *pass.* **strove** [strouv], *p.p.* **striven** ['strivn], *v.i.* sforzarsi; ingegnarsi: *she is striving hard*

to succeed, ella fa ogni sforzo per riuscire; *to — for* (*o after*) *an end,* sforzarsi di raggiungere un fine; *to — with, against,* lottare, combattere con, contro: *to — against temptation,* lottare contro la tentazione.

striving ['straiviŋ], *s.* **1.** sforzo **2.** contesa, gara, lotta.

strivingly ['straiviŋli], *av.* **1.** con grande sforzo **2.** a gara.

strobile ['strobail], *s.* (*bot.*) strobilo; pigna.

stroboscope ['strobəskoup], *s.* (*scient.*) stroboscopio.

stroboscopic [,strobə'skɔpik], *ag.* (*scient.*) stroboscopico.

strode [stroud], *pass.* di to **stride**.

stroke[1] [strouk], *s.* **1.** colpo, percossa, botta: *with one — of one's sword,* con un sol colpo di spada; *he was killed by a — of lightning,* fu ucciso da un fulmine; *they received ten strokes of the birch,* ricevettero dieci frustate; *to give s.o. the finishing —,* dare il colpo di grazia (anche *fig.*) ‖ *at a —,* d'un sol colpo ‖ *little strokes fell great oaks,* prov. la goccia scava la pietra **2.** colpo; movimento; bracciata (al nuoto); vogata, remata (al cannottaggio); battuta (al tennis, ecc.): *a — of wing,* un colpo d'ala; *he invented a new — in golf,* ha inventato un nuovo tipo di colpo al golf; *to be off one's —,* (*spor.*) essere fuori tempo; (*fam.*) essere sconcertato; *to keep —,* tenere il tempo, vogare in cadenza; *to play a good —,* (*spor.*) fare un bel colpo; *to row a fast, slow —,* vogare velocemente, lentamente ‖ *a — of genius,* un lampo di genio ‖ *a — of good luck,* un colpo di fortuna ‖ *a — of wit,* un tratto di spirito ‖ *a good — of business,* un buon affare ‖ *not to do a — of work,* (*fam.*) non far nulla; non alzare un dito **3.** tratto (di penna, di matita); tocco: *with a — of the pen,* con un tratto di penna; *to give the finishing strokes to a work,* (*fam.*) dare gli ultimi ritocchi a un'opera; *to put a few strokes of colour on a canvas,* dare alcune pennellate a una tela **4.** rintocco (d'orologio): *it is on the — of six,* stanno per suonare le sei; *to arrive somewhere on the —,* arrivare in un luogo puntualmente **5.** (*patol.*) colpo, attacco: *a — of apoplexy,* un colpo apoplettico; *he had a bad —,* ebbe un serio attacco di paralisi **6.** (*spor.*) primo rematore: *to row* (*o to pull*) *—,* dare il tempo ai rematori **7.** (*mec.*) corsa; tempo ☆ *-engraving,* (*artig.*) incisione a bulino; *— -oar,* (*spor.*) remo del primo rematore; primo rematore; *— -side,* (*mar.*) babordo ‖ *back- —,* (*spor.*) nuoto sul dorso; contraccolpo; *backward* (*o return*) *—,* (*mec.*) corsa di ritorno; *breast- —,* (*spor.*) nuoto a rana; *side- —,* (*spor.*) nuoto alla marinara; *working —,* (*mec.*) corsa utile.

to **stroke**[1], *v.t.i.* (*mar.*) vogare in cadenza: *to — thirty per minute,* vogare a trenta colpi di remo al minuto ‖ *to — a boat,* fare da primo rematore, segnare il tempo agli altri rematori.

stroke[2], *s.* carezza: *to give the dog a —,* accarezzare il cane.

to **stroke**[2], *v.t.* **1.** accarezzare, lisciare, dare una lisciata a; *fig.* adulare: *he stroked his chin,* s'accarezzò il mento con la mano; *to — the dog the wrong way,* accarezzare il cane contropelo ‖ *to — s.o.* (*o s.o.'s hair*) *the wrong way, fig.* prendere qlcu. per il verso sbagliato, irritare qlcu. **2.** *to — down, fig.* calmare, placare l'ira di.

stroker ['stroukə*], *s.c.* chi accarezza; *fig.* adulatore, adulatrice.

strokesman, *pl.* **strokesmen** ['strouksmən], *s.* (*spor.*) primo rematore (che segna il tempo agli altri).

stroking ['stroukiŋ], *s.* carezza.

strokingly ['stroukiŋli], *av.* carezzevolmente.

stroll [stroul], *s.* passeggiata, quattro passi: *to go for a —,* andare a fare quattro passi; *to take a —,* fare quattro passi, fare un giretto.

to **stroll,** *v.t.i.* **1.** passeggiare; andare a zonzo **2.** girovagare, vagabondare; percorrere a brevi tappe: *to — the country,* andar girovagando per il paese.

stroller ['stroulə*], *s.c.* **1.** vagabondo, vagabonda **2.** attore girovago, attrice girovaga.

strolling ['strouliŋ], *ag.* errante, girovago, ambulante ☆ — *company*, compagnia ambulante; — *player*, attore girovago.

stroma ['stroumə], *pl.* **stromata** ['stroumətə], *s.* (*bot. fisiol.*) stroma.

stromb [strɔm], *s.* (*zool.*) strombo, strombolo.

strong [strɔŋ], *ag.* **1.** forte, robusto, resistente: — *china*, porcellana resistente; — *cloth*, stoffa resistente; — *town*, città ben difesa; *are you quite — again?*, (*fam.*) ti sei rimesso del tutto? || *as — as a horse*, forte come un toro || *by the — arm* (o *hand*), di forza || *this is — meat for you!*, (*sl.*) non è pane per i tuoi denti! **2.** forte; energico; potente; violento; impetuoso: — *advocate*, patrono potente, influente; — *candidate*, (*pol.*) candidato con molte probabilità di successo; *a — character*, un carattere forte; — *eyes*, vista buona; — *in Greek*, forte in greco; *a — literary style*, un efficace stile letterario; — *measures*, misure energiche; — *passion*, passione violenta; — *situation*, situazione altamente drammatica; *a — voice*, una voce forte, penetrante; — *wind*, vento impetuoso; *to have a — hold on s.o.*, avere un forte ascendente su qlcu.; *to have a — imagination*, avere una grande immaginazione **3.** forte, numeroso: *an army 800.000 —*, un esercito di 800.000 uomini; *how — are they?*, in quanti sono? **4.** deciso; ardente; zelante: *a — conservative*, un conservatore deciso; *to give — support to s.o.*, parteggiare ardentemente per qlcu. **5.** piccante, forte; carico: — *cheese*, formaggio piccante; — *tea*, tè carico, forte; *to have a — smell*, emanare un odore forte **6.** (*comm.*) in rialzo: *markets are —*, i mercati sono in rialzo **7.** (*gram.*) forte (di verbo) ☆ — *-backed*, robusto di schiena; — *-box*, cassaforte; — *drink*, bevanda alcoolica; — *-headed*, cocciuto; — *-limbed*, nerboruto; — *-minded*, risoluto, deciso; — *-mindedness*, risolutezza, forza di carattere; — *-room*, camera blindata; — *verb*, verbo forte.

strong, *av.* (*rar.*) fortemente.

stronghold ['strɔŋhould], *s.* roccaforte, fortezza; cittadella (anche *fig.*).

strongly ['strɔŋli], *av.* **1.** fortemente; vigorosamente **2.** violentemente; vivamente.

strontia ['strɔnʃiə], *s.* (*chim.*) stronziana.

strontian ['strɔnʃiən], *ag.* (*chim.*) stronzianico || *s.* stronziana.

strontium ['strɔnʃiəm], *s.* (*chim.*) stronzio.

strop [strɔp], *s.* **1.** coramella (per rasoio) **2.** (*mar.*) stroppo.

to strop, *pass.p.p.* **stropped** [strɔpt], *v.t.* affilare (un rasoio) sulla coramella.

strophanthin [strə'fænθin], *s.* (*chim. farm.*) strofantina.

strophanthus [strə'fænθəs], *s.* (*bot.*) strofanto.

strophe ['stroufi], *s.* strofa.

strophic ['strɔfik], *ag.* strofico.

strove [strouv], *pass.* di to **strive.**

to strow [strou], (*arc.*) per to **strew.**

struck [strʌk], *pass.p.p.* di to **strike.**

structural ['strʌktʃərəl], *ag.* **1.** strutturale, di struttura **2.** (*geol.*) tettonico ☆ — *steel*, acciaio per costruzioni.

structurally ['strʌktʃərəli], *av.* relativamente alla struttura.

structure ['strʌktʃə*], *s.* **1.** struttura: *rock of basaltic —*, (*geol.*) roccia a struttura basaltica; *the — of modern science*, la struttura della scienza moderna; *the — of a sentence*, la struttura di una frase **2.** costruzione; edificio: *a — made of stone*, un edificio di pietra.

structureless ['strʌktʃəlis], *ag.* privo di struttura; amorfo.

struggle ['strʌgl], *s.* **1.** lotta, combattimento: *the — for existence*, la lotta per l'esistenza; *he gave in without a —*, non oppose alcuna resistenza **2.** sforzo; serie di sforzi: *a desperate — to get one's work done*

in time, uno sforzo disperato per finire in tempo il proprio lavoro ☆ — *class*, lotta di classe; *hand-to -hand —*, lotta corpo a corpo.

to struggle, *v.i.* **1.** lottare; cercare di liberarsi; divincolarsi; dibattersi: *the little girl struggled and kicked*, la bimba si dibattè convulsamente e tirò calci **2.** *fig.* lottare; sforzarsi, fare sforzi, cercare di: *he struggled hard to control his feelings*, fece sforzi inumani per dominare i propri sentimenti; *he struggled with adversity*, lottò contro le avversità; *they struggled for the prize*, si contesero il premio; *to — against destiny*, lottare contro il destino **3.** *to — along*, avanzare a stento; *fig.* destreggiarsi a stento, sopravvivere: *I am struggling along*, vivo alla meno peggio, mi difendo **4.** *to — in, out, through*, aprirsi un varco, penetrare a fatica (anche *fig.*): *we succeeded in struggling through*, ce l'abbiamo fatta **5.** *to — up*, ascendere con difficoltà.

struggler ['strʌglə*], *s.c.* contendente; chi lotta, chi si dibatte: *the strugglers against fate*, coloro che si dibattono contro il fato.

strugglingly ['strʌgliŋli], *av.* lottando; con sforzi.

Struldbrug ['strʌldbrʌg], *s.* (*lett.*) « Struldbrug » (essere immaginario condannato all'immortalità nei « Viaggi di Gulliver » di Swift).

strum [strʌm], *s.* strimpellamento.

to strum, *pass.p.p.* **strummed** [strʌmd], *v.t.i.* strimpellare: *to — a tune*, accennare un motivo al pianoforte.

struma ['stru:mə], *pl.* **strumae** ['stru:mi:], *s.* **1.** (*patol.*) struma, gozzo, scrofola **2.** (*bot.*) piccolo rigonfiamento alla base di una foglia.

strumose ['stru:mous], **strumous** ['stru:məs], *ag.* (*patol.*) scrofoloso, strumoso; gozzuto.

strumpet ['strʌmpit], *s.* sgualdrina; prostituta.

strung [strʌŋ], *pass.p.p.* di to **string.**

strut[1] [strʌt], *s.* andatura solenne, affettata; incedere impettito.

to strut[1], *pass.p.p.* **strutted** ['strʌtid], *v.i.* incedere con sussiego, camminare impettito.

strut[2], *s.* **1.** (*edil. mec.*) puntone; contropalo **2.** (*aer.*) montante.

to strut[2], *v.t.* (*arch.*) irrigidire, sostenere con puntoni.

struthious ['stru:θiəs], *ag.* di, simile a struzzo.

strutter ['strʌtə*], *s.c.* chi si pavoneggia; chi cammina con aria boriosa, solenne.

struttingly ['strʌtiŋli], *ag.* con andatura solenne, affettata; in modo tronfio, impettito.

strychnia ['strikniə], **strychnine** ['strikni:n], *s.* (*farm.*) stricnina.

stub [stʌb], *s.* **1.** troncone; ceppo **2.** mozzicone (di sigaro, sigaretta, matita, ecc.); rimanenza **3.** radice (di dente); moncherino (di coda di cane) **4.** matrice (di registro, libretto d'assegni) ☆ — *-axle*, (*mec.*) fuso a snodo; — *-end*, (*mec.*) testa di biella; — *-plane*, (*mec.*) pianetto; — *-tenon*, (*artig.*) tenone corto; — *-tooth*, (*mec.*) dente ribassato.

to stub, *pass.p.p.* **stubbed** [stʌbd], *v.t.* **1.** sradicare, estirpare; liberare (il terreno) da radici, ceppi **2.** urtare: *he stubbed his toe against the step*, inciampò contro il gradino **3.** *to — out*, spegnere, estinguere: *to — out a cigarette*, spegnere una sigaretta.

stubbed [stʌbd], *ag.* tagliato alla base (di albero).

stubble ['stʌbl], *s.* **1.** stoppia **2.** barba corta e ispida **3.** capelli a spazzola.

stubbly ['stʌbli], *ag.* **1.** coperto di stoppie **2.** ispido.

stubborn ['stʌbən], *ag.* **1.** ostinato, cocciuto, caparbio, testardo: *as — as a mule*, ostinato come un mulo **2.** tenace, ribelle; refrattario: — *fever*, febbre ribelle; — *ore*, minerale refrattario; — *soil*, terreno ingrato.

stubbornly ['stʌbənli], *av.* **1.** ostinatamente, caparbiamente **2.** tenacemente; inflessibilmente.

stubbornness ['stʌbənnis], *s.* **1.** ostinazione, caparbietà **2.** tenacia; inflessibilità.

stubby ['stʌbi], *ag.* **1.** troncato (di pianta) **2.** tozzo; tarchiato (di persona) **3.** coperto di ceppi, di tronconi (di terreno) **4.** ispido (di barba, capelli).

stucco ['stʌkou], *pl.* **stucco(e)s** ['stʌkouz], *s.* stucco ☆ — *decorator*, stucchinaio; — *-worker*, stuccatore.

to stucco, *v.t.* stuccare; decorare a stucco.

stuccoer ['stʌkouə*], *s.* stuccatore.

stuck [stʌk], *pass.p.p.* di **to stick**.

stuck-up ['stʌk'ʌp], *ag.* **1.** tronfio; presuntuoso; borioso; arrogante **2.** (*sl.*) imbarazzato: *I am* —, sono nei pasticci, in imbarazzo.

stud[1] [stʌd], *s.* **1.** chiodo a capocchia larga; pomo; borchia **2.** bottoncino (da camicia) **3.** (*mec. mar.*) perno; traversino **4.** (*mec.*) colonnetta, perno sporgente ☆ — *bolt*, (*mec.*) prigioniero, vite prigioniera; — *chain*, (*mar.*) catena rinforzata; — *rivet*, (*mec.*) rivetto a maschio ‖ *collar* —, bottoncino da colletto.

to stud[1], *pass.p.p.* **studded** ['stʌdid], *v.t.* **1.** guarnire di borchie; imbullettare **2.** costellare, tempestare, ornare: *crown studded with diamonds*, corona tempestata di diamanti **3.** (*mec.*) fissare con viti prigioniere.

stud[2], *s.* scuderia; allevamento di cavalli (da corsa, ecc.) ☆ — *-book*, registro della genealogia dei purosangue; — *-farm*, campo di allevamento (di cavalli di razza); — *-horse*, stallone; — *-mare*, (cavalla) fattrice.

studding-sail ['stʌdiŋseil], *s.* (*mar.*) coltellaccio.

student ['stju:dənt], *s.c.* **1.** studente, studentessa: *a — of law*, uno studente in legge; *medical* —, studente in medicina **2.** studioso: *he is a — of psychic phenomena*, è uno studioso dei fenomeni psichici **3.** studente che gode di una borsa di studio (in Inghilterra) ☆ — *interpreter*, studente di lingue orientali qualificato per il servizio consolare; — *lamp*, lampada portatile (per studiare, leggere, ecc.).

studentship ['stju:dənt-ʃip], *s.* borsa di studio.

studied ['stʌdid], *ag.* **1.** studiato, ricercato: — *carelessness*, studiata negligenza; *a dress of — elegance*, un abito di eleganza ricercata **2.** premeditato, intenzionale: — *insult*, insulto premeditato **3.** colto; versato: *she is — in literature*, è versata nelle lettere.

studiedly ['stʌdidli], *av.* **1.** studiatamente, affettatamente **2.** con premeditazione, intenzionalmente.

studiedness ['stʌdidnis], *s.* **1.** ricercatezza **2.** premeditazione.

studio ['stju:diou], *pl.* **studios** ['stju:diouz], *s.* **1.** studio (d'artista, di fotografo) **2.** (*cine.*) teatro di posa **3.** (*rad.*) auditorio **4.** *pl.* (*cine.*) studi ☆ *broadcasting* —, (*rad.*) studio d'emissione; *sound film* —, (*cine.*) teatro di posa sonoro.

studious ['stju:djəs], *ag.* **1.** studioso **2.** diligente, attento; premuroso, sollecito: — *to do* (o *of doing*) *sthg.*, sollecito a fare ql.co.: *he is — to forestall all our wishes*, è sollecito nel prevenire i nostri desideri; *with — care*, con ansiosa sollecitudine **3.** deliberato, volontario.

studiously ['stju:djəsli], *av.* **1.** studiosamente **2.** diligentemente, premurosamente **3.** deliberatamente.

studiousness ['stju:djəsnis], *s.* **1.** amore dello studio, passione per lo studio **2.** diligenza, premura, zelo.

study ['stʌdi], *s.* **1.** studio; materia di studio: *the — of mathematics*, lo studio della matematica; *to continue one's studies at a University*, continuare gli studi presso un'università; *to finish one's studies*, finire gli studi **2.** esame attento; investigazione; studio: *the — of a document*, l'attento esame di un documento; *to make a — of sthg.*, indagare su ql.co. **3.** oggetto degno d'attenzione, d'interesse: *his face was a perfect* —, il suo volto era veramente degno d'attenzione **4.** cura, attenzione, premura: *it shall be my — to please you*, sarà mia premura l'accontentarvi; *she makes it her — to help them*, si sforza d'aiutarli **5.** riflessione, meditazione ‖ *he is in a brown* —, è immerso nei propri pensieri **6.** (*pitt. scult.*) studio, abbozzo: — *of a hand*, studio di (una) mano **7.** (*mus.*) studio: *he played a — by Chopin*, ha suonato uno studio di Chopin **8.** (*lett.*) studio, dissertazione, saggio **9.** *to be a good, slow* —, (*teat.*) imparare facilmente, con difficoltà la propria parte ☆ — *group*, comunità di lavoro, gruppo di studio.

to study, *v.t.i.* **1.** studiare, compiere degli studi; applicarsi: *to — at the University*, studiare all'università; *to — for an examination*, prepararsi a un esame; *to — hard*, sgobbare ‖ *to — for the bar*, studiare legge **2.** esaminare attentamente; investigare: *to — a person's character*, studiare il carattere di una persona **3.** studiarsi, sforzàrsi: *he studied to avoid any argument*, cercava di evitare ogni discussione **4.** (*arc.*) riflettere, meditare; essere assorto **5.** *to — out*, studiare profondamente, meditare lungamente (un problema, ecc.) **6.** *to — up*, prepararsi agli esami.

stuff [stʌf], *s.* **1.** sostanza; materia prima; essenza: *the — heroes are made of*, la stoffa di cui son fatti gli eroi; *he has good — in him*, è di buona stoffa, ha buone qualità; *tallow is the — of which candles are made*, il sego è la materia prima di cui son fatte le candele; *they are of same* —, *fig.* sono della stessa razza **2.** cosa, roba: *funny* —, roba da ridere, cosa buffa; *what* —!, che roba!; *he writes nasty* —, scrive porcherie; *I like the — you gave me for dinner*, mi piace il piatto che mi desti a pranzo; *some — they call coffee*, della roba che chiamano caffè; *this wine is good, sorry* —, questo vino è eccellente, è una porcheria ‖ *doctor's* —, (*fam.*) medicina ‖ *hurry up, do your* —!, (*sl. amer.*) su, fa il tuo lavoro! ‖ *that's the* —!, questa è roba buona! *to be short of* —, (*fam.*) essere in bolletta, essere al verde **3.** stoffa, tessuto (specialmente di lana) **4.** sciocchezza, cosa di nessun valore: — *and nonsense!*, sciocchezze!; *what — to write!*, che sciocchezze da scrivere! ☆ — *-gown*, toga (di avvocati); giovane avvocato ‖ *bread-* —, ingredienti per fare il pane; *garden-* —, (o *green-* —), verdura; *household-* —, (*arc.*) mobilia; articoli casalinghi.

to stuff, *v.t.i.* **1.** imbottire, riempire: *a head stuffed with romance*, una testa piena zeppa di romanticherie; *to — a cushion with feathers*, riempire di piuma un cuscino ‖ *a stuffed shirt*, (*fam.*) un pallone gonfiato ‖ *to — s.o. for an exam*, (*fam.*) imbottire (la testa di) qlcu. per un esame **2.** (*cuc.*) farcire: *to — a turkey*, farcire un tacchino **3.** rimpinzare, rimpinzarsi; ingozzare, ingozzarsi: *she stuffed the child with sweets*, rimpinzò il bambino di dolci; *to — a goose*, fare ingrassare un'oca **4.** impagliare; imbalsamare: *a stuffed lion*, un leone imbalsamato **5.** turare; ostruire: *his nose is stuffed up*, ha il naso chiuso; *to — up a hole*, turare un buco **6.** stivare, stipare: *to — one's clothes into a trunk*, stipare i propri vestiti in un baule **7.** (*sl.*) darla a bere, gabbare: *he is only stuffing*, sta dandola ad intendere **8.** (*amer.*) mettere voti fraudolenti in (urna).

stuffer ['stʌfə*], *s.* impagliatore (di animali); imbalsamatore.

stuffiness ['stʌfinis], *s.* **1.** mancanza d'aria; odore di chiuso, di stantio **2.** (*fam.*) vecchi pregiudizi **3.** l'avere il naso chiuso per il raffreddore.

stuffing ['stʌfiŋ], *s.* **1.** imbottitura: *the — of a cushion*, l'imbottitura di un cuscino **2.** (*cuc.*) ripieno **3.** imbalsamazione; impagliatura ‖ *to take the — out of s.o.*, (*fam.*) sgonfiare qlcu. **4.** ingrasso (di oche, ecc.) **5.** chiusura, otturamento ☆ — *-box*, (*mec.*) premistoppa; (*mar.*) premibaderna.

stuffy ['stʌfi], *ag.* **1.** senz'aria, mal ventilato: *it is very — in this room*, in questa stanza si soffoca **2.** afoso, soffocante (di tempo): — *air*, aria viziata **3.** (*amer.*) cocciuto; imbronciato, di cattivo umore **4.** (*fam.*) conservatore, rigido; noioso.

stuggy ['stʌgi], *ag.* (*dial.*) tarchiato; tracagnotto.

stull [stʌl], *s.* (*amer. miner.*) sbadacchio, palo di sostegno in una galleria di miniera.

stultification [ˌstʌltifi'keiʃən], *s.* **1.** il rendere ridicolo **2.** l'infirmare; il privare di dignità, di valore, d'efficacia.

to stultify ['stʌltifai], *v.t.* **1.** togliere valore a; infirmare; invalidare (argomento, testimonianza, ecc.) **2.** rendere ridicolo **3.** confondere; rendere vano (progetto, ecc.) ‖ *to — oneself*, (*dir.*) smentirsi; contraddirsi: *the witness stultified himself*, il testimonio si contraddisse **4.** (*dir.*) mettere in dubbio il pieno possesso delle facoltà mentali di.

stum [stʌm], *s.* mosto.

to **stum**, *pass.p.p.* **stummed** [stʌmd], *v.t.* **1.** arrestare la fermentazione di (mosto); conciare (il vino) **2.** (*amer.*) rinvigorire (il vino) aggiungendo del mosto che rinnovi la fermentazione.

stumble [ˈstʌmbl], *s.* passo falso; *fig.* errore.

to **stumble**, *v.t.i.* **1.** inciampare, incespicare: *to — against sthg.*, inciampare, dare contro ql.co. ‖ *he stumbled along*, avanzava inciampando continuamente **2.** *fig.* fare un passo falso, fare errori **3.** impaperarsi, impappinarsi: *he stumbles in his speech*, egli s'impapera nel parlare ‖ *he stumbled through the poem*, recitò la poesia incespicando ad ogni parola **4.** (*arc.*) sconcertare, confondere **5.** *to — across* (*s.o., sthg.*), imbattersi in, trovare per caso **6.** *to — at* (*sthg.*), provare scrupoli di fronte a **7.** *to — over* (*sthg.*), esitare, tentennare di fronte a **8.** *to — (up)on* (*s.o., sthg.*), imbattersi in, trovare per caso.

stumbler [ˈstʌmblə*], *s.c.* **1.** chi incespica **2.** chi s'impapera.

stumbling [ˈstʌmbliŋ], *s.* incespicamento; *fig.* errore ☆ *— -block*, scoglio, ostacolo.

stumblingly [ˈstʌmbliŋli], *av.* **1.** incespicando; con passo incerto **2.** in modo esitante.

stump[1] [stʌmp], *s.* **1.** ceppo, tronco (di albero) ‖ *to be up a —*, essere in difficoltà, essere perplesso **2.** radice (di dente); moncherino, moncone (di membro) **3.** mozzicone (di matita, sigaretta, ecc.) **4.** matrice (di assegno) **5.** piattaforma, podio, tribuna (specialmente per comizi): *to go on* (o *to take*) *the —*, salire sul podio per fare un discorso politico **6.** *pl.* (*scherz.*) gambe: *move your stumps*, sposta le gambe; *to stir one's stumps*, muovere le gambe; affrettarsi **7.** (*cricket*) paletto ☆ *— -oratory*, oratoria da comizio; *— -speech*, arringa, discorso all'aria aperta.

to **stump**[1], *v.t.i.* **1.** mozzare, ridurre a ceppi; estirpare ceppi da (un terreno) **2.** camminare pesantemente zoppicando ‖ *to — about*, muoversi zoppicando **3.** (*amer.*) imbarazzare; sfidare: *I am stumped*, sono imbarazzato, perplesso **4.** attraversare (un paese) tenendo discorsi politici **5.** (*amer. fam.*) urtare (il piede) contro una pietra, una protuberanza **6.** (*cricket*) mettere fuori gara (un battitore) **7.** *to — up*, (*sl.*) pagare in contanti.

stump[2], *s.* **1.** andatura pesante, zoppicante **2.** (*amer. fam.*) sfida.

stump[3], *s.* sfumino (per disegno).

to **stump**[3], *v.t.* sfumare (disegni).

stumpage [ˈstʌmpidʒ], *s.* tassa pagata per poter abbattere tronchi su terreni demaniali.

stumper [ˈstʌmpə*], *s.* problema, domanda imbarazzante.

stumpy [ˈstʌmpi], *ag.* **1.** tarchiato, tozzo: *— man*, uomo tarchiato **2.** pieno di ceppi (di terreno).

stun [stʌn], *s.* **1.** stordimento, assordamento **2.** scalfittura (su una pietra, ecc.).

to **stun**, *pass.p.p.* **stunned** [stʌnd], *v.t.i.* **1.** stordire; assordare; intronare **2.** far perdere i sensi a; tramortire **3.** sbalordire, far stupire: *the news stunned us*, la notizia ci fece restar di sasso **4.** scalfire (una pietra, un minerale, ecc.); sfaldarsi (di pietra).

stung [stʌŋ], *pass.p.p.* di to **sting**.

stunk [stʌŋk], *pass.p.p.* di to **stink**.

stunner [ˈstʌnə*], *s.c.* **1.** chi assorda **2.** chi fa sbalordire, stupire: *she is a —*, (*fam.*) è meravigliosa, fenomenale.

stunning [ˈstʌniŋ], *ag.* **1.** assordante: *— noise*, rumore assordante **2.** (*sl.*) sbalorditivo; meraviglioso; magnifico; fenomenale.

stunningly [ˈstʌniŋli], *av.* **1.** in modo assordante **2.** (*sl.*) meravigliosamente, magnificamente.

stunsail, stuns'l [ˈstʌnsl], *s.* (*mar.*) coltellaccio.

stunt[1] [stʌnt], *s.* **1.** (*sl.*) bravata; ostentazione, dimostrazione di forza, destrezza **2.** trovata pubblicitaria **3.** (*giornalismo*) montatura; notizia sensazionale: *a — article*, un articolo sensazionale; *that's a good —!*, questa sì che è una buona trovata! **4.** (*aer.*) acrobazia: *to perform stunts*, eseguire acrobazie ☆ *— flying*, volo acrobatico; *— -man*, (*cine.*) controfigura.

to **stunt**[1], *v.i.* (*spec. amer.*) fare delle acrobazie.

stunt[2], *s.* **1.** arresto della crescita, dello sviluppo **2.** animale rachitico, nano.

to **stunt**[2], *v.t.* impedire, arrestare la crescita, lo sviluppo di.

stunted [ˈstʌntid], *ag.* striminzito, stentato.

stuntedness [ˈstʌntidnis], *s.* l'essere stentato, striminzito.

stupe[1] [stjuːp], *s.* (*med.*) compressa per impacchi caldi, fomenta.

to **stupe**[1], *v.t.* applicare, fare impacchi caldi a.

stupe[2], *s.* (*sl.*) stupido, sciocco, babbeo.

stupefacient [ˌstjuːpiˈfeiʃənt], *ag.s.* (*med.*) stupefacente.

stupefaction [ˌstjuːpiˈfækʃən], *s.* **1.** torpore provocato da stupefacenti **2.** stupore.

stupefactive [ˈstjuːpiˌfæktiv], *V.* **stupefacient**.

stupefier [ˈstjuːpiˌfaiə*], *s.* persona, cosa che istupidisce.

to **stupefy** [ˈstjuːpifai], *v.t.i.* **1.** istupidire, istupidirsi: *she was stupefied by grief*, era inebetita dal dolore **2.** abbrutire, abbrutirsi: *he was stupefied with drinking*, era abbrutito dal bere **3.** stordire, sbalordire, far stupire.

stupendous [stjuˈ(ː)pendəs], *ag.* splendido, stupendo, magnifico, prodigioso, formidabile.

stupendously [stjuˈ(ː)pendəsli], *av.* splendidamente, stupendamente, magnificamente, prodigiosamente, formidabilmente.

stupendousness [stjuˈ(ː)pendəsnis], *s.* mirabilità, prodigiosità, magnificenza.

stupeous [ˈstjuːpiəs], *ag.* stopposo, lanuginoso.

stupid [ˈstjuːpid], *ag.* **1.** stupido, ottuso, tardo, stolto: *my pupils are very —*, i miei scolari sono tardi; *you are a — thing*, (*fam.*) sei uno stupido **2.** istupidito, intontito: *to drive s.o. —*, intontire qlcu.; *to grow — with opium*, intontirsi con l'oppio **3.** insignificante, scialbo: *a — place*, un luogo noioso ‖ *s.* (*fam.*) stupido.

stupidity [stjuˈ(ː)piditi], *s.* stupidità, ottusità; stolidità.

stupidly [ˈstjuːpidli], *av.* stupidamente, stoltamente.

stupor [ˈstjuːpə*], *s.* **1.** stupore, meraviglia **2.** (*med.*) torpore, incoscienza.

stuporous [ˈstjuːpərəs], *ag.* (*med.*) letargico.

to **stuprate** [ˈstjuːpreit], *v.t.* stuprare.

stupration [stjuˈpreiʃən], *s.* **stuprum** [ˈstjuːprəm], *s.* stupro.

sturdied [ˈstəːdid], *ag.* (*vet.*) affetto da capogatto, vertigine (di un ovino).

sturdily [ˈstəːdili], *av.* **1.** vigorosamente, con forza **2.** risolutamente.

sturdiness [ˈstəːdinis], *s.* **1.** vigoria, forza **2.** risolutezza, fermezza.

sturdy [ˈstəːdi], *ag.* **1.** vigoroso, forte, robusto: *— child*, bambino robusto; *— fellow*, giovane gagliardo **2.** risoluto, fermo: *— opponent*, rivale risoluto **3.** (*vet.*) affetto da capogatto (di ovini) ‖ *s.* (*vet.*) capogatto, vertigine ☆ *— beggar*, individuo sfaccendato che mendica (invece di lavorare).

sturgeon [ˈstəːdʒən], *s.* (*ittiol.*) storione.

stutter [ˈstʌtə*], *s.* balbuzie; tartagliamento: *to have a terrible —*, soffrire di balbuzie accentuata.

to **stutter**, *v.t.i.* balbettare, tartagliare; essere balbuziente: *to — (out) a few words*, balbettare alcune parole.

stutterer [ˈstʌtərə*], *s.c.* balbuziente; tartaglione, tartagliona.

stuttering ['stʌtəriŋ], *ag.* balbuziente ‖ *s.* balbuzie.
stutteringly ['stʌtəriŋli], *av.* balbettando; da balbuziente.
St. Vincent [snt'vinsənt], *no.pr.* (*geog.*) St. Vincent.
sty[1] [stai], *s.* **1.** porcile **2.** *fig.* luogo sudicio e misero; luogo di corruzione.
to **sty**[1], *v.t.i.* **1.** mettere, confinare in un porcile **2.** *fig.* vivere in un porcile.
sty[2], **stye** [stai], *s.* orzaiolo: *to have a — in one's eye,* avere un orzaiolo.
Stygian ['stidʒiən], *ag.* **1.** stigio, dello Stige **2.** *fig.* infernale, tetro.
style [stail], *s.* **1.** stile; modello; genere, tipo; modo, maniera: *business —,* stile commerciale; *castle in the Gothic —,* castello in stile gotico; *her — of playing,* la sua maniera di suonare; *a gentleman of the old —,* un gentiluomo di vecchio stampo; *in good —,* in perfetto stile; *the — of Shakespeare,* lo stile di Shakespeare; *our — of living,* il nostro tenore di vita; *writers lacking —,* scrittori senza stile; *she lived in great —,* visse lussuosamente; *what is your — of business?,* che cosa trattate? **2.** tono, distinzione; classe: *he is a person of considerable —,* è una persona di gran distinzione; *there is no — about her,* è una ragazza che manca di classe **3.** moda: *hat, dress in the latest —,* cappello, vestito all'ultima moda **4.** titolo, nome: *she is entitled to the — of Baroness X,* ha diritto al titolo di baronessa X **5.** stilo (per scrivere) **6.** (*bot. med.*) stilo **7.** gnomone (di meridiana) **8.** puntina del grammofono **9.** (*comm.*) nome, ragione sociale: *the new — of his company is X.Y.,* la nuova ragione sociale della sua società è X.Y. **10.** (*st.*) *old —* (*O.S.*), vecchio sistema (secondo il calendario Giuliano); *new —* (*N.S.*), sistema nuovo (secondo il calendario Gregoriano).
to **style,** *v.t.* chiamare; nominare; denominare; designare: *to — s.o. baron,* concedere a qlcu. il titolo di barone.
stylet ['stailit], *s.* **1.** stiletto **2.** (*med.*) specillo flessibile.
styliform ['stailifɔːm], *ag.* stiliforme.
stylishˌ ['stailiʃ], *ag.* che ha distinzione; di classe; elegante.
stylishly ['stailiʃli], *av.* con distinzione; elegantemente.
stylishness ['stailiʃnis], *s.* eleganza; buon gusto; distinzione; stile.
stylist ['stailist], *s.* stilista.
stylistic [stai'listik], *ag.* stilistico; di stile.
stylistically [stai'listikəli], *av.* stilisticamente.
stylite ['stailait], *s.* (*relig.*) stilita.
stylization [ˌstaili'zeiʃən], *s.* stilizzazione.
to **stylize** ['stailaiz], *v.t.* stilizzare.
stylo ['stailou], *abbr.* di **stylograph.**
stylobate ['stailəbeit], *s.* (*arch.*) stilobate.
stylograph ['stailəgrɑːf], *s.* penna stilografica.
stylographie [ˌstailə'græfik], *ag.* stilografico.
stylographically [ˌstailə'græfikəli], *av.* (*rar.*) con la stilografica.
stylography [stai'lɔgrəfi], *s.* (*rar.*) metodo per scrivere, disegnare, incidere con stilo.
stylus ['stailəs], *s.* **1.** stilo **2.** puntina per grammofono **3.** gnomone (di meridiana) **4.** (*bot.*) stilo.
stymie ['staimi], *s.* (*golf*) «stymie» (palla dell'avversario che ostacola l'entrata in buca della palla del giocatore).
to **stymie,** *v.t.i.* **1.** (*golf*) ostacolare buche a (un avversario) **2.** *fig.* essere nell'imbarazzo, avere le mani legate.
styptic ['stiptik], *ag.* (*med.*) **1.** astringente **2.** antiemorragico.
stypticity [stip'tisiti], *s.* capacità astringente.
styrax ['staiəræks], *s.* (*chim. bot.*) storace.
styrene ['stairiːn], *s.* (*chim.*) stirolo.
Styria ['stiriə], *no.pr.* (*geog.*) Stiria.
Styrian ['stiriən], *ag.* (*geog.*) stiriano ‖ *s.c.* (*geog.*) stiriano, stiriana.

Styx [stiks], *no.pr.* (*mit. greca*) Stige ‖ *as black as —,* nero come l'inferno ‖ *to cross the —,* morire.
suability [ˌsju(ː)ə'biliti], *s.* (*dir.*) passibilità di giudizio, di processo.
suable ['sju(ː)əbl], *ag.* (*dir.*) passibile di processo, di giudizio.
suasion ['sweiʒən], *s.* persuasione.
suasive ['sweisiv], *ag.* persuasivo.
suasively ['sweisivli], *av.* in modo persuasivo.
suave [swɑːv], *ag.* soave, dolce; gentile, affabile, cortese: *he has — manners,* ha maniere cortesi.
suavely ['swɑːvli], *av.* soavemente; gentilmente, affabilmente.
suavity ['swæviti], *s.* soavità; dolcezza; affabilità, cortesia, gentilezza.
sub [sʌb], *s.* (*fam.*) **1.** subalterno **2.** sottomarino **3.** sottoscrizione **4.** sostituto.
to **sub,** *pass.p.p.* **subbed** [sʌbd], *v.i.* fare da sostituto: *to — for s.o.,* sostituire qlcu.
subacid ['sʌb'æsid], *ag.* acidulo; agrodolce (anche *fig.*).
subacidity [ˌsʌbə'siditi], *s.* l'essere acidulo.
subacrid ['sʌb'ækrid], *ag.* agretto.
subacute ['sʌbə'kjuːt], *ag.* subacuto.
subaerial ['sʌb'ɛəriəl], *ag.* subaereo.
subagency ['sʌb'eidʒənsi], *s.* posizione, condizione di subagente.
subagent ['sʌb'eidʒənt], *s.* subagente.
subahdar [ˌsuːbə'dɑː*], *s.* (*ang.-in.*) comandante indigeno di una compagnia di «sepoys».
subalpine ['sʌb'ælpain], *ag.* subalpino.
subaltern ['sʌbltən], *ag.* **1.** inferiore, sottoposto **2.** (*log.*) specifico, particolare ‖ *s.* **1.** subalterno (anche *mil.*); sottoposto **2.** (*log.*) proposizione secondaria.
subalternation ['sʌb,ɔːltə'neiʃən], *s.* subordinazione.
subappennine ['sʌb'æpinain], *ag.* subappennino.
subaquatic ['sʌbə'kwætik], **subaqueous** ['sʌb'eikwiəs], *ag.* subacqueo.
subarctic ['sʌb'ɑːktik], *ag.* subartico.
subastral ['sʌb'æstrəl], *ag.* terrestre.
subaudition ['sʌbɔː'diʃən], *s.* comprensione dei sottintesi.
subaxillary ['sʌb'æksiləri], *ag.* subascellare.
subbrigadier ['sʌb,brigə'diə*], *s.* alfiere, sottotenente di cavalleria.
subcaudal ['sʌb'kɔːdl], *ag.* subcaudale.
subcelestial ['sʌbsi'lestjəl], *ag.s.* terrestre, mondano.
subcentral ['sʌb'sentrəl], *ag.* posto sotto il centro.
subchaser ['sʌb,tʃeisə*], *s.* cacciasommergibili.
subclass ['sʌbklɑːs], *s.* (*bot. zool.*) sottoclasse.
subclassification ['sʌb,klæsifi'keiʃən], *s.* sottoclassificazione.
to **subclassify** ['sʌb'klæsifai], *v.t.* dividere in sottoclassi.
subclavian ['sʌb'kleivjən], **subclavicular** ['sʌbklə'vikjulə*], *ag.* (*anat.*) succlavio.
subcommission ['sʌbkə'miʃən], *s.* sottocommissione.
subcommissioner ['sʌbkə'miʃənə*], *s.* vice-commissario.
subcommittee ['sʌbkə,miti], *s.* sottocomitato.
subconscious ['sʌb'kɔnʃəs], *ag.* subcosciente.
subconsciously ['sʌb'kɔnʃəsli], *av.* subcoscientemente.
subconsciousness ['sʌb'kɔnʃəsnis], *s.* subcoscienza.
subcontract ['sʌb'kɔntrækt], *s.* subappalto.
to **subcontract** ['sʌbkən'trækt], *v.t.i.* subappaltare.
subcontrary ['sʌb'kɔntrəri], *ag.* contrario solo in parte.
subcutaneous ['sʌbkju(ː)'teinjəs], *ag.* (*med.*) sottocutaneo.
subdeacon ['sʌb'diːkən], *s.* (*eccl.*) suddiacono.
subdeaconship ['sʌb'diːkənʃip], *s.* (*eccl.*) suddiaconato.
subdean ['sʌb'diːn], *s.* sottodecano.
subdelegate ['sʌb'deligit], *s.* vicedelegato.
to **subdelegate** ['sʌb'deligeit], *v.t.* suddelegare.

subdelirium ['sʌbdi'liriəm], *s.* (*patol.*) subdelirio.

to subdivide ['sʌbdi'vaid], *v.t.i.* suddividere, suddividersi.

subdivisible ['sʌbdi'vizəbl], *ag.* suddivisibile.

subdivision ['sʌbdi,viʒən], *s.* suddivisione, ripartizione; spezzettamento.

subdolous ['sʌbdələs], *ag.* (*arc.*) subdolo.

subdominant ['sʌb'dəminənt], *s.* (*mus.*) sottodominante.

subduable [səb'dju(:)əbl], *ag.* domabile, soggiogabile; reprimibile.

subdual [səb'dju(:)əl], *s.* soggiogamento, asservimento; repressione; attenuazione.

to subduce [səb'dju:s], **to subduct** [səb'dʌkt], *v.t.* (*rar.*) ritirare; dedurre; sottrarre.

subduction [səb'dʌkʃən], *s.* (*rar.*) deduzione; sottrazione.

to subdue [səb'dju:], *v.t.* 1. conquistare; soggiogare, sottomettere; domare; controllare: *he subdued his passion*, controllò la sua passione; *he was subdued by her kindness*, fu soggiogato dalla sua gentilezza; *those enemies were subdued*, quei nemici furono sottomessi, soggiogati 2. ridurre, attenuare; addolcire, mitigare: *she subdued her voice*, ella abbassò la voce; *the sound was subdued by the distance*, il suono era attenuato dalla distanza.

subdued [səb'dju:d], *ag.* 1. soggiogato, sottomesso; represso; controllato: — *passions*, passioni represse 2. sommesso; attenuato; addolcito: — *colour*, colore attenuato; — *conversation*, conversazione a voce bassa; *in a* — *voice*, sottovoce.

subduedness [səb'dju(:)dnis], *s.* 1. sottomissione, asservimento 2. attenuazione (di voce, colore, luce, ecc.).

subduer [səb'dju(:)ə*], *s.* soggiogatore; vincitore; conquistatore.

to subedit ['sʌb'edit], *v.t.* redigere (specialmente in giornalismo).

subediting ['sʌb'editiŋ], *s.* lavoro redazionale (specialmente in giornalismo).

subeditor ['sʌb'editə*], *s.* redattore aggiunto (specialmente in giornalismo).

suberic [sju'berik], *ag.* 1. di sughero 2. (*chim.*) suberico ☆ — *acid*, acido suberico.

suberin ['sju:bərin], *s.* (*chim.*) suberina.

suberose ['sju:bərous], **suberous** ['sju:bərəs], *ag.* di sughero; sugheroso.

subfamily ['sʌb,fæmili], *s.* (*bot. zool.*) sottofamiglia, sottogruppo.

subfuse ['sʌbfʌsk], *ag.* (*rar.*) fosco, scuro.

subgenus ['sʌb,dʒi:nəs], *pl.* **subgenera** ['sʌb,dʒenərə], *s.* sottospecie.

subgovernor ['sʌb'gʌvənə*], *s.* vicegovernatore.

subgroup ['sʌbgru:p], *s.* sottogruppo.

subheading ['sʌb,hediŋ], *s.* sottotitolo.

subhuman ['sʌb'hju:mən], *ag.* 1. al di sotto del genere umano 2. quasi umano.

subinspector ['sʌbin'spektə*], *s.* vice-ispettore.

subjacent [sʌb'dʒeisənt], *ag.* inferiore, che giace sotto, al di sotto.

subject ['sʌbdʒikt], *ag.* 1. soggetto, assoggettato, sottoposto: *a* — *nation*, una nazione soggetta, schiava; *all men are* — *to the laws of nature*, tutti gli uomini sono soggetti alle leggi naturali; *a country held* — *by another*, un paese assoggettato ad un altro 2. soggetto, esposto, suscettibile di: *prices* — *to 10% discount*, prezzi suscettibili di uno sconto del 10%; *the evils to which we might be* —, mali a cui potremmo essere esposti; *he is* — *to colds*, egli è soggetto al raffreddore ‖ — *to*, salvo, subordinatamente a: — *to your consent*, salvo la tua approvazione.

subject, *s.* 1. argomento, soggetto, tema; materia (di studio): *a* — *for ridicule*, un oggetto di scherno; *the* — *of a letter*, il contenuto d'una lettera; *the* — *of a painting*, il soggetto d'un dipinto; — *of meditation*, oggetto di meditazione; *enough on this* —, basta con questo argomento; *it is a* — *for rejoicing*, è un'occasione di gioia; *let's drop the* —, lasciamo cadere l'argomento; *what subjects do you teach?*, quali materie insegnate?; *to be the* — *of an experiment*, essere oggetto d'un esperimento; *to lead s.o. on to the* — *of...*, portare qlcu. sull'argomento di...; *to wander from the* —, uscire d'argomento 2. (*gram.*) soggetto: — *and predicate*, soggetto e predicato; *the* — *of a sentence*, il soggetto d'una proposizione 3. suddito: *British* —, cittadino britannico 4. (*med.*) soggetto: *hysterical* —, soggetto isterico ☆ — *-matter*, soggetto (di un libro, una discussione).

to subject [səb'dʒekt], *v.t.* 1. assoggettare, sottomettere, soggiogare 2. esporre, sottoporre: *to* — *oneself to criticism*, esporsi a critiche; *to* — *s.o., sthg. to an examination*, sottoporre qlcu., ql.co. ad un esame.

subjection [səb'dʒekʃən], *s.* 1. assoggettamento; conquista 2. dipendenza, sottomissione; cattività: *to bring a tribe into* —, soggiogare una tribù; *to bring one's passions under* —, controllare, dominare le proprie passioni.

subjective [sʌb'dʒektiv], *ag.* 1. soggettivo, individuale 2. (*gram.*) soggettivo: *the* — *case*, il nominativo.

subjectively [sʌb'dʒektivli], *av.* soggettivamente.

subjectiveness [sʌb'dʒektivnis], *s.* soggettività.

subjectivism [səb'dʒektivizəm], *s.* soggettivismo.

subjectless ['sʌbdʒiktlis], *ag.* 1. senza argomento 2. (*gram.*) senza soggetto.

to subjoin ['sʌb'dʒɔin], *v.t.* unire, aggiungere; soggiungere.

subjugable ['sʌbdʒugəbl], *ag.* soggiogabile; asservibile.

to subjugate ['sʌbdʒugeit], *v.t.* soggiogare; asservire; vincere; domare.

subjugation ['sʌbdʒu'geiʃən], *s.* soggiogamento; asservimento; conquista.

subjugator ['sʌbdʒugeitə*], *s.* soggiogatore; conquistatore.

subjunctive [səb'dʒʌŋktiv], *ag.* (*gram.*) congiuntivo, soggiuntivo: *the* — *mood*, il modo congiuntivo ‖ *s.* (*gram.*) modo congiuntivo, soggiuntivo.

sublease ['sʌb'li:s], *s.* subaffitto.

to sublease, *v.t.* subaffittare.

sublessee ['sʌble'si:], *s.* 1. subaffittuario 2. subappaltatore (di un lavoro in corso).

sublessor ['sʌble'so:*], *s.c.* subaffittante.

sublet ['sʌb'let], *s.* subaffitto.

to sublet, *pass.p.p.* **sublet**, *v.t.* 1. subaffittare 2. subappaltare (un lavoro in corso).

sublibrarian ['sʌblai'brɛəriən], *s.c.* vicebibliotecario, vicebibliotecaria.

sublieutenancy ['sʌble'tenənsi], *s.* (*mil.*) sottotenenza, grado di sottotenente; (*mar.*) grado di sottotenente di vascello.

sublieutenant ['sʌble'tenənt], *s.* (*mil.*) sottotenente; (*mar.*) sottotenente di vascello.

sublimable [sə'blaiməbl], *ag.* (*rar.*) sublimabile.

sublimate ['sʌblimit], *ag.s.* (*chim.*) sublimato ☆ *corrosive* —, (*chim.*) sublimato corrosivo.

to sublimate ['sʌblimeit], *v.t.* 1. (*chim.*) sublimare 2. *fig.* purificare; idealizzare, elevare.

sublimation [,sʌbli'meiʃən], *s.* 1. (*chim.*) sublimazione 2. *fig.* purificazione; idealizzazione, elevazione.

sublime [sə'blaim], *ag.* 1. sublime, eccelso: — *heroism*, eroismo sublime ‖ *the* —, il sublime ‖ *the Sublime Porte*, la Sublime Porta 2. (*fam. iron.*) supremo, perfetto, senza pari: *he spoke with* — *impudence*, parlò con un'impudenza senza pari; *she acted with* — *indifference*, agì con suprema indifferenza 3. (*anat.*) superficiale, a fior di pelle: — *muscles*, muscoli a fior di pelle 4. (*poet.*) altezzoso, orgoglioso.

to sublime, *v.t.i.* 1. (*chim.*) sublimare, sublimarsi 2. *fig.* rendere sublime, sublimarsi; elevare, elevarsi; idealizzare.

sublimely [sə'blaimli], *av.* 1. in modo sublime 2. (*fam. iron.*) completamente, assolutamente.

subliminal [sʌb'limin̩l], *ag.s.* (*psicologia*) subliminale; subconscio.

sublimity [sə'blimiti], *s.* **1.** sublimità **2.** (*anat.*) superficialità (di muscoli, ecc.).

sublingual ['sʌb'liŋgwəl], *ag.* sublinguale.

sublunar ['sʌb'lu:nə*], **sublunary** ['sʌblu:nəri], *ag.* (*poet.*) sublunare.

submachinegun ['sʌbmə'ʃi:ngʌn], *s.* fucile mitragliatore, mitra.

submarine ['sʌbməri:n], *ag.* subacqueo, sottomarino ‖ *s.* sommergibile ☆ — *cable*, cavo sottomarino; — *earthquake*, (*geol.*) maremoto; — *mine*, mina subacquea; — *plants*, piante subacquee; — *shooting*, (*cine.*) ripresa subacquea ‖ *atomic* —, sommergibile atomico; *mine laying* —, (*mar. mil.*) sommergibile posamine.

submariner ['sʌbmə,ri:nə*], *s.* (*mar. mil.*) sommergibilista.

submaxillary ['sʌbmæk'siləri], *ag.* sottomascellare.

submedian ['sʌb'mi:djən], *ag.* che si trova sotto la linea mediana.

submental ['sʌb'mentl], *ag.* che sta sotto il mento.

to **submerge** [səb'mə:dʒ], *v.t.i.* immergere, immergersi; sommergere, affondare (anche *fig.*); inondare, allagare: *the submarine submerged*, il sottomarino s'immerse ‖ *the submerged tenth*, *fig.* i miserabili.

submergence [səb'mə:dʒəns], *s.* sommersione.

to **submerse** [səb'mə:s], *v.t.* immergere, sommergere.

submersed [səb'mə:st], *ag.* (*bot.*) che cresce sotto l'acqua.

submersible [səb'mə:səbl], *ag.* sommergibile; affondabile ‖ *s.* (*rar.*) sottomarino, sommergibile.

submersion [səb'mə:ʃən], *s.* sommersione, immersione.

submission [səb'miʃən], *s.* **1.** sottomissione; rassegnazione: *I ask for complete* —, domando completa sottomissione **2.** rispetto, docilità, umiltà **3.** tesi, teoria (sottoposta a un giuria, a un esperto, ecc.).

submissive [səb'misiv], *ag.* **1.** remissivo; docile **2.** umile; sottomesso.

submissively [səb'misivli], *av.* **1.** in modo remissivo, docilmente **2.** umilmente; rispettosamente.

submissiveness [səb'misivnis], *s.* **1.** sottomissione; docilità **2.** umiltà.

to **submit** [səb'mit], *pass.p.p.* **submitted** [səb'mitid], *v.t.i.* **1.** sottomettersi, sottoporsi; cedere, piegarsi; rassegnarsi: *the enemy had to* — *to defeat*, il nemico dovette rassegnarsi alla sconfitta; *to* — *to God's will*, rassegnarsi, sottomettersi alla volontà di Dio **2.** sottoporre, rimettere (a un giudizio, approvazione, ispezione): *to* — *a difference to an arbitrator*, sottoporre una divergenza a un arbitro; *to* — *a case to a court*, deferire, rimettere un caso al tribunale.

submultiple ['sʌb'mʌltipl], *ag.s.* (*mat.*) sottomultiplo.

subnormal ['sʌb'nɔ:məl], *ag.* al di sotto della norma ‖ *s.* (*geom.*) sottonormale.

subnubilar ['sʌb'nju:bilə*], *ag.* che si trova sotto le nubi.

suboccipital ['sʌbɔk'sipitl], *ag.* che sta sotto l'occipite.

suboceanic ['sʌb,ouʃi'ænik], *ag.* suboceanico.

subocular ['sʌb'ɔkjulə*], *ag.* che sta sotto l'occhio.

subofficer ['sʌb'ɔfisə*], *s.* sottufficiale.

suborbital ['sʌb'ɔ:bitl], *ag.* che si trova sotto l'orbita.

suborder ['sʌb'ɔ:də*], *s.* (*bot. zool.*) sottordine.

subordinacy [sə'bɔ:dinəsi], *s.* subordinazione.

subordinate [sə'bɔ:dṇit], *ag.* **1.** subordinato; secondario: — *clause*, (*gram.*) proposizione subordinata **2.** di ordine inferiore; in sott'ordine ‖ *s.* subalterno, inferiore ☆ — *commander*, (*mar.*) comandante in seconda.

to **subordinate** [sə'bɔ:dineit], *v.t.* **1.** subordinare, considerare meno importante: *to* — *s.o. to s.o. else*, subordinare qlcu. a qlcu. altro **2.** far dipendere; assoggettare: *to* — *one's passions to reason*, assoggettare le passioni alla ragione.

subordinately [sə'bɔ:dṇitli], *av.* subordinatamente; in posizione inferiore, secondaria.

subordination [sə,bɔ:di'neiʃən], *s.* **1.** subordinazione; sottomissione **2.** inferiorità di rango, di posizione **3.** (*gram.*) subordinazione.

to **suborn** [sʌ'bɔ:n], *v.t.* subornare, corrompere; sobillare: *to* — *witnesses*, corrompere dei testimoni.

subornation [,sʌbɔ:'neiʃən], *s.* subornazione; corruzione.

suborner [sʌ'bɔ:nə*], *s.c.* chi suborna, corrompe.

subplot ['sʌb,plɔt], *s.* (*letter.*) intreccio secondario.

subpoena [səb'pi:nə], *s.* (*dir.*) citazione, mandato di comparizione.

to **subpoena**, *v.t.* (*dir.*) citare (un testimonio): *to* — *s.o.*, notificare l'ordine di comparizione in tribunale a qlcu.

subpolar ['sʌb'poulə*], *ag.* sottopolare.

subprefect ['sʌb'pri:fekt], *s.* sottoprefetto, viceprefetto.

subprefecture ['sʌb'pri:fektjuə*], *s.* sottoprefettura.

subprior ['sʌb'praiə*], *s.* (*eccl.*) sottopriore.

subreption [səb'repʃən], *s.* (*dir.*) surrezione.

subreptitious [,sʌbrep'tiʃəs], *ag.* furtivo; subdolo; (*dir.*) surrettizio.

subreptitiously [,sʌbrep'tiʃəsli], *av.* subdolamente; furtivamente.

subrogation [,sʌbrə'geiʃən], *s.* (*dir.*) surrogazione.

to **subscribe** [səb'skraib], *v.t.i.* **1.** sottoscrivere, sottoscriversi; firmare **2.** sottoscrivere, aderire a; impegnarsi: *to* — *a bond*, impegnarsi con un patto; (*comm.*) sottoscrivere a un titolo; *to* — *for a book*, aderire alla sottoscrizione di un libro; *to* — *to a charity*, versare denaro per una iniziativa benefica **3.** trovarsi d'accordo, approvare: *I cannot* — *to that*, non posso approvare ciò **4.** abbonarsi: *let's* — *to this paper*, abboniamoci a questo giornale.

subscriber [səb'skraibə*], *s.c.* **1.** chi sottoscrive, firma ‖ *the* —, il sottoscritto; (*comm.*) il contraente **2.** abbonato, abbonata.

subscript ['sʌbskript], *ag.* (*gram. greca*) sottoscritto: *iota* —, iota sottoscritto.

subscription [səb'skripʃən], *s.* **1.** sottoscrizione, firma; colletta: *monument erected by public* —, monumento eretto con pubblica sottoscrizione; *to raise a* —, iniziare una sottoscrizione **2.** abbonamento: *subscriptions to be paid in advance*, abbonamenti da pagarsi anticipatamente **3.** consenso, approvazione ☆ — *form*, modulo di abbonamento.

subsection ['sʌb,sekʃən], *s.* sottosezione.

subsensible ['sʌb'sensəbl], *ag.* non percepibile dai sensi.

subsequence ['sʌbsikwəns], *s.* susseguenza.

subsequent ['sʌbsikwənt], *ag.* successivo; ulteriore; seguente: *the* — *chapter*, il capitolo successivo; *in the* — *years*, negli anni seguenti.

subsequently ['sʌbsikwəntli], *av.* successivamente; in seguito; posteriormente.

to **subserve** [səb'sə:v], *v.t.* promuovere; servire; giovare a; favorire (uno scopo, una funzione).

subservience [səb'sə:vjəns], **subserviency** [səb'sə:vjənsi], *s.* subordinazione; remissività; servilismo.

subservient [səb'sə:vjənt], *ag.* **1.** dipendente; ossequente; servile; soggetto (a uno scopo) **2.** che serve a promuovere, utile.

subserviently [səb'sə:vjəntli], *av.* subordinatamente.

to **subside** [səb'said], *v.i.* **1.** calare, decrescere, abbassarsi; sprofondare; cedere: *the flood is subsiding*, la piena sta calando; *the ground has subsided*, il terreno ha ceduto **2.** *fig.* quietarsi, calmarsi: *his anger will* —, la sua collera si placherà; *the storm is subsiding*, la tempesta si sta calmando **3.** cadere sul fondo (di sedimenti); depositare (di liquidi); precipitare (di una soluzione) **4.** cadere; lasciarsi andare: *she subsided into an armchair*, (*fam.*) si lasciò cadere in una poltrona **5.** *to* — *into* (*sthg.*), trasformarsi in; diventare: *she subsided into a housewife*, si trasformò in una donna di casa.

subsidence [səb'saidəns], *s.* **1.** abbassamento; cedimento (di terreno); crollo **2.** il calmarsi (di elementi, passioni, ecc.).

subsidiarily [səb'sidjərili], *av.* sussidiariamente; in secondo luogo.

subsidiary [səb'sidjəri], *ag.* **1.** sussidiario; supplementare; di riserva **2.** ausiliario; accessorio; secondario: — *company*, (*comm.*) società consociata; *a* — *stream*, un fiume tributario **3.** mantenuto da sussidi ‖ *s.* **1.** (*rar.*) persona, cosa accessoria, ausiliaria **2.** (*comm.*) società consociata.

to **subsidize** ['sʌbsidaiz], *v.t.* sussidiare; sovvenzionare.

subsidy ['sʌbsidi], *s.* sussidio, sovvenzione.

to **subsist** [səb'sist], *v.t.i.* **1.** sussistere, continuare a esistere: *this custom still subsists*, questa usanza esiste tuttora **2.** provvedere al mantenimento di, mantenere; tenere in vita, tenersi in vita: *to* — *on other men's charity*, vivere d'elemosina.

subsistence [səb'sistəns], *s.* **1.** esistenza, sussistenza **2.** mantenimento: *means of* —, mezzi di sussistenza ☆ — *money*, acconto paga.

subsistent [səb'sistənt], *ag.* sussistente; esistente.

subsoil ['sʌbsɔil], *s.* (*agr.*) sottosuolo.

subspecies, *pl.* **subspecies** ['sʌb,spi:ʃi:z], *s.* sottospecie.

substance ['sʌbstəns], *s.* **1.** sostanza, essenza; materia: *look at the* — *not at the shadow*, bada alla sostanza e non all'apparenza; *the Son is of one* — *with the Father*, (*teol.*) il Figlio è consustanziale al Padre **2.** sostanza, contenuto, l'essenziale: *the* — *of that article*, la sostanza di quell'articolo **3.** solidità; nerbo; fondamento: *argument of little* —, argomentazione debole; *there is no* — *in him*, non c'è nerbo in lui **4.** sostanze, beni, ricchezze: *a man of* —, un uomo di larghi mezzi **5.** (*chim.*) sostanza; elemento.

substantial [səb'stænʃəl], *ag.* **1.** sostanzioso; solido; resistente: — *food*, cibo sostanzioso; *a man of* — *build*, un uomo di costituzione robusta **2.** importante; notevole; effettivo: *a* — *contribution*, un contributo effettivo; *a* — *proof*, una prova schiacciante **3.** ricco; finanziariamente solido: *the* — *middle class*, la grossa borghesia **4.** sostanziale; reale: *a* — *lie*, una grossa bugia.

substantialism [səb'stænʃəlizəm], *s.* (*fil.*) sostanzialismo.

substantialist [səb'stænʃəlist], *s.* (*fil.*) sostanzialista.

substantiality [səb,stænʃi'æliti], *s.* **1.** (*fil.*) sostanzialità; esistenza reale **2.** concretezza; solidità; corporeità **3.** autenticità.

to **substantialize** [səb'stænʃəlaiz], *v.t.i.* rendere sostanziale, concreto; acquistare sostanza, concretezza.

substantially [səb'stænʃəli], *av.* **1.** solidamente; sostanziosamente **2.** fortemente; notevolmente **3.** sostanzialmente; realmente, effettivamente.

substantialness [səb'stænʃəlnis], *s.* sostanzialità.

substantials [səb'stænʃəlz], *s.pl.* le cose essenziali.

to **substantiate** [səb'stænʃieit], *v.t.* **1.** dimostrare la verità di; provare; dare fondamento a; convalidare: *to* — *a charge*, dimostrare la fondatezza di un'accusa **2.** dare sostanza a; rendere sostanziale: *Faith substantiates things not yet seen*, la Fede prova cose non ancora conosciute.

substantiation [səb,stænʃi'eiʃən], *s.* **1.** prova; giustificazione **2.** materializzazione.

substantival [,sʌbstən'taivəl], *ag.* di sostantivo.

substantivally [,sʌbstən'taivəli], *av.* sostantivamente.

substantive ['sʌbstəntiv], *ag.* **1.** indipendente, autosufficiente **2.** considerevole: *a* — *share*, una parte considerevole **3.** reale; essenziale **4.** (*gram.*) sostantivato ‖ *s.* (*gram.*) sostantivo.

substantively ['sʌbstəntivli], *av.* **1.** sostantivamente **2.** realmente.

substation ['sʌb,steiʃən], *s.* stazione sussidiaria.

substernal ['sʌb'stə:nl], *ag.* che si trova sotto lo sterno.

substitute ['sʌbstitju:t], *s.* **1.** sostituto; rappresentante; delegato: *as a* — *for*, in sostituzione di, al posto di; *to be appointed s.o.'s* —, essere nominato rappresentante di qlcu. **2.** surrogato; imitazione: *as a* — *for sugar*, come surrogato dello zucchero; *beware of substitutes!*, attenti alle imitazioni! **3.** supplente.

to **substitute**, *v.t.i.* **1.** sostituire, agire come sostituto: *to* — *sulphur for oxygen*, sostituire lo zolfo all'ossigeno **2.** rimpiazzare, supplire: *Englishmen are being substituted by natives*, gli inglesi vengono rimpiazzati da gente del luogo.

substitution [,sʌbsti'tju:ʃən], *s.* **1.** sostituzione **2.** (*dir.*) surrogazione.

substitutional [,sʌbsti'tju:ʃənl], *ag.* sostitutivo.

substitutionally [,sʌbsti'tju:ʃnəli], *av.* sostitutivamente.

substitutionary [,sʌbsti'tju:ʃnəri], *ag.* sostitutivo.

substratum ['sʌb'strɑ:təm], *pl.* **substrata** ['sʌb'strɑ:tə], **substratums** ['sʌb'strɑ:təmz], *s.* **1.** strato, substrato **2.** *fig.* base, fondo: *a* — *of truth*, un fondo di verità **3.** sottosuolo.

substructure ['sʌb,strʌktʃə*], *s.* **1.** base (anche *fig.*): *the social* —, le basi della società **2.** piano di posa (di strade, ecc.); (*edil.*) fondamento, sottostruttura.

to **subsume** [səb'sju:m], *v.t.* includere in una regola, classe; classificare.

subsumption [səb'sʌmpʃən], *s.* inclusione in una regola, classe; classificazione.

subtangent ['sʌb'tændʒənt], *s.* (*geom.*) sottotangente.

subtenancy ['sʌb'tenənsi], *s.* subaffitto.

subtenant ['sʌb'tenənt], *s.* subaffittuario.

to **subtend** [səb'tend], *v.t.* (*geom.*) sottendere.

subtense [səb'tens], *s.* (*geom.*) sottesa.

subterfuge ['sʌbtəfju:dʒ], *s.* sotterfugio, pretesto; raggiro.

subterrane ['sʌbtərein], *s.* sotterraneo; scantinato.

subterranean [,sʌbtə'reinjən], *ag.* **1.** sotterraneo: — *springs*, sorgenti sotterranee **2.** nascosto; segreto.

subterraneously [,sʌbtə'reinjəsli], *av.* sotto terra.

subtil(e), *V.* **subtle**.

subtility [sʌb'tiliti], *V.* **subtlety**.

subtilization [,sʌbtilai'zeiʃən], *s.* **1.** cavillo; sottigliezza **2.** (*chim.*) sublimazione.

to **subtilize** ['sʌbtilaiz], *v.t.i.* **1.** affinare; rendere acuto (la mente, i sensi) **2.** analizzare; interpretare con finezza e precisione **3.** sottilizzare; cercar cavilli **4.** (*arc.*) assottigliare; rarefare; raffinare **5.** (*chim.*) sublimare.

subtilty ['sʌbtilti], *V.* **subtlety**.

sub-title ['sʌb,taitl], *s.* (*lett.*) sottotitolo; (*cine.*) didascalia.

subtle ['sʌtl], *ag.* **1.** indefinibile, elusivo, misterioso: *a* — *charm*, un fascino misterioso; *a* — *power*, un potere misterioso **2.** penetrante, acuto; ingegnoso, sottile: *a* — *argument*, un ragionamento sottile; *a* — *remark*, un'osservazione acuta; *he is a* — *observer*, è un osservatore acuto **3.** astuto, scaltro: *a* — *enemy*, un nemico astuto **4.** (*arc.*) tenue, sottile; rarefatto: *a* — *vapour*, un vapore tenue.

subtleness ['sʌtlnis], **subtlety** ['sʌtlti], *s.* **1.** carattere elusivo **2.** acutezza, sagacia, sottigliezza **3.** astuzia.

subtly ['sʌtli], *av.* **1.** elusivamente **2.** ingegnosamente, acutamente; sottilmente **3.** astutamente.

to **subtract** [səb'trækt], *v.t.* detrarre, dedurre, defalcare; (*arit.*) sottrarre: *to* — *a quantity from* (o out of) *another*, sottrarre una quantità da un'altra.

subtraction [səb'trækʃən], *s.* sottrazione.

subtractive [səb'træktiv], *ag.* sottrattivo ☆ — *process*, (*foto.*) processo sottrattivo.

subtrahend ['sʌbtrəhend], *s.* (*arit.*) sottraendo.

subtropic(al) ['sʌb'trɔpik(əl), *ag.* subtropicale.

subulate ['sju:bjulit], **subuliform** [sju:bju:lifɔ:m], *ag.* (*bot. zool.*) a forma di lesina.

subungulate ['sʌb'ʌŋgjulit], *ag.s.* (*zool.*) subungulato.

suburb ['sʌbə:b], *s.* sobborgo; *pl.* periferia: *the suburbs of London*, la periferia di Londra.

suburban [sə'bə:bən], *ag.* **1.** suburbano, della periferia **2.** (*spreg.*) limitato, ristretto (di mentalità).

subvariety ['sʌbvə,raiəti], *s.* sottovarietà.

subvention [səb'venʃən], *s.* sovvenzione, sussidio.

subversion [sʌb'və:ʃən], *s.* sovversione; mutamento, sconvolgimento radicale.

subversive [sʌb'və:siv], *ag.* sovversivo, sovvertitore: *examples — of morality*, esempi sovvertitori della morale.

to subvert [sʌb'və:t], *v.t.* sovvertire, rovesciare (sistemi, principi, governi, ecc.).

subverter [sʌb'və:tə*], *s.c.* sovvertitore, sovvertitrice; demolitore, demolitrice.

subvertebral [sʌb'və:tibrəl], *ag.* che sta sotto la vertebra.

subway ['sʌbwei], *s.* **1.** sottopassaggio, passaggio sotterraneo, tunnel **2.** (*amer.*) metropolitana.

succades [sʌ'keidz], *s. pl.* (*comm.*) frutti canditi e sciroppati.

succedaneous [,sʌksi'deiniəs], *ag.* succedaneo.

succedaneum [,sʌksi'deiniəm], *pl.* **succedanea** [,sʌksi'deiniə], *s.* succedaneo, surrogato.

to succeed [sək'si:d], *v.t.i.* **1.** aver successo, riuscire: *if you try often enough you will — at last*, se ti ci provi molte volte, ci riuscirai alla fine; *they succeeded in translating this difficult passage*, riuscirono a tradurre questo passo difficile; *to — in life as a doctor*, affermarsi nella vita come medico **2.** succedere a, prendere il posto di: *to — a minister*, succedere a un ministro; *to — oneself*, (*amer.*) essere rieletto (alla Camera, a una carica, ecc.); *to — to a business*, rilevare un'azienda; *to — to an estate*, ereditare una proprietà; *to — to an office*, subentrare in una carica; *to — to the throne* (o *to the Crown*), salire al trono **3.** succedersi, seguire in ordine: *the storm was succeeded by calm*, alla tempesta seguì la calma; *years — years*, gli anni si susseguono.

succeeding [sək'si:diŋ], *ag.* susseguente, seguente ‖ *s.* successo.

succentor [sək'sentə*], *s.* (*eccl.*) sostituto del maestro del coro.

success [sək'ses], *s.* **1.** successo, buon esito, buona riuscita: *from — to —*, di successo in successo; *— leans now this way, now that*, la fortuna favorisce or gli uni, or gli altri; *I wish you — in your undertaking*, ti auguro che la tua impresa abbia buon esito **2.** successo materiale, ricchezza, posizione: *those men have achieved —*, quegli uomini si sono fatti un'ottima posizione **3.** persona che ha buona riuscita in ql.co.: *she was a great — as Ophelia*, fu una grande Ofelia **4.** cosa ben riuscita: *that book was a great —*, quel libro ebbe un grande successo.

successful [sək'sesful], *ag.* che ha successo, buon esito: *— candidates*, candidati eletti; *a — transaction*, un affare riuscito; *the action was —*, (*mil.*) l'azione ebbe buon esito; *to be — at the polls*, essere eletto.

successfully [sək'sesfuli], *av.* con successo; felicemente; favorevolmente.

succession [sək'seʃən], *s.* **1.** successione; serie: *the — of crops*, la rotazione dei raccolti; *a — of losses*, una serie di perdite; *in close —*, a brevi intervalli **2.** (diritto di) successione (al trono, a una carica): *he is second in the —*, è secondo in successione ‖ *the war of the Spanish Succession*, la guerra di successione spagnola **3.** eredi; discendenti: *left to her and her —*, legato a lei ed ai suoi discendenti **4.** eredità: *apostolic —*, eredità apostolica ☆ *— duty*, tassa di successione.

successional [sək'seʃənl], *ag.* **1.** di successione **2.** consecutivo.

successive [sək'sesiv], *ag.* successivo, seguente; consecutivo.

successively [sək'sesivli], *av.* successivamente, in seguito; consecutivamente.

successiveness [sək'sesivnis], *s.* consecutività.

successor [sək'sesə*], *s.* successore: *to appoint a — to an ambassador*, nominare un nuovo ambasciatore.

succinct [sək'siŋkt], *ag.* **1.** succinto, conciso, terso **2.** (*arc. poet.*) succinto (di veste).

succinctly [sək'siŋktli], *av.* succintamente.

succinctness [sək'siŋktnis], *s.* concisione, brevità.

succory ['sʌkəri], *s.* (*bot.*) cicoria.

succose ['sʌkous], *ag.* succoso; pieno di linfa.

succotash ['sʌkətæʃ], *s.* (*amer. indiano*) « succotash » (piatto di fagioli, granoturco e carne di maiale).

succour ['sʌkə*], *s.* **1.** soccorso, aiuto, assistenza **2.** *pl.* (*arc. mil.*) aiuti, rinforzi.

to succour, *v.t.* soccorrere, aiutare, correre in aiuto di.

succourless ['sʌkəlis], *ag.* privo di soccorso.

succuba ['sʌkjubə], *pl.* **succubae** ['sʌkjubi:]; **succubus** ['sʌkjubəs], *pl.* **succubi** ['sʌkjubai], *s.* **1.** succubo **2.** demonio.

succulence ['sʌkjuləns], *s.* squisitezza; succosità.

succulent ['sʌkjulənt], *ag.* succulento; squisito.

succulently ['sʌkjuləntli], *av.* in modo succulento; squisitamente.

to succumb [sə'kʌm], *v.i.* soccombere; soggiacere, essere costretto a cedere: *he succumbed to his many enemies*, egli piegò davanti ai suoi molti nemici; *to — to pneumonia*, morire di polmonite; *to — to temptation*, cedere alla tentazione.

succursal [sʌ'kə:səl], *ag.* (*eccl.*) succursale, sussidiario ‖ *s.* (*comm.*) succursale.

to succuss [sə'kʌs], *v.t.* (*med.*) percuotere (il torace).

succussion [sə'kʌʃən], *s.* percussione (del torace).

such [sʌtʃ (*forma forte*), sətʃ (*forma debole*)], *ag.* **1.** tale, simile, siffatto: *— a man*, un uomo simile; *— people as you*, gente come te; *in — cases*, in casi del genere; *in — weather*, con un tempo simile; *— food is very heavy*, cibo di tal genere è molto pesante; *— newspapers as these are always gossipy*, giornali come questi sono sempre pettegoli; *there are no — things as witches*, le streghe non esistono; *they said no — thing*, non hanno detto niente del genere; *they sent me — a present as I would never have dreamt of*, mi hanno mandato un regalo che non mi sarei mai aspettato ‖ *— as*, come: *European nations — as Spain, France and Italy*, nazioni europee come Spagna, Francia e Italia; *you may use my typewriter, — as it is*, puoi usare la mia macchina da scrivere così com'è, anche se non vale un gran che, se così si può chiamare **2.** *— that*, *— as to* (*con inf.*), tale che, tale da: *he spoke in — a way that I went away*, parlò in modo tale che me ne andai; *her behaviour was — as to make us feel ashamed*, il suo comportamento fu tale da farci vergognare; *his pain was — that...*, il suo dolore era tale che... **3.** (*intensivo*) **così, tale, tanto:** *— a clever man*, un uomo così intelligente; *— large houses*, delle case così grandi; *it was — a long time ago*, fu tanto tempo fa; *it was — a pity!*, fu un tal peccato!; *we were in — a hurry!*, avevamo una tale fretta!.

such, *pron.* **1.** tale, tali; questo, questa, questi, queste; quello, quella, quelli, quelle: *— is not my plan*, questo non è il mio progetto; *— is our present position*, tale è la nostra situazione attuale; *— is the world*, così va il mondo; *— were his words*, quelle furono le sue parole **2.** *as —*, come tale: *geography —*, la geografia come tale; *he was a soldier and was judged as —*, era un soldato e fu giudicato come tale **3.** *all —*, gente simile: *down with traitors and all —*, abbasso i traditori e gente di tal risma **4.** *and —*, e simili: *she enjoys cakes, ices and —*, le piacciono i dolci, i gelati e simili **5.** (*volg. comm.*) per *it, they, them*: *we note your remarks and in reply to — ...*, prendiamo nota delle vostre osservazioni e in risposta ad esse... **6.** *— as*, (*arc. poet.*) coloro i quali: *— as are of my opinion*, tutti coloro che sono del mio parere.

such-and-such ['sʌtʃənsʌtʃ], *ag.* tale, così e così, tal dei tali: *I have met — a person*, ho incontrato un tale, uno così e così ‖ *pron.* il tale, la tale (dei tali).

suchlike ['sʌtʃlaik], *ag.* simile, dello stesso genere; di tal genere ‖ *pron. gener. pl.* cose, persone simili:

beggars, tramps, and —, mendicanti, vagabondi e gente di tal fatta.

suck [sʌk], *s.* **1.** succhiata, poppata: *child at* —, poppante, lattante; *to give* — *to*, allattare **2.** sorso: *have* (o *take*) *a* — *at it*, bevine un sorso **3.** risucchio (di gorgo) **4.** (*sl.*) fiasco, insuccesso **5.** *pl.* (*sl. scolastico*) dolci ☆ — *bottle*, poppatoio.

to **suck**, *v.t.i.* **1.** succhiare, poppare: *the baby is sucking his mother's breast*, il bambino sta poppando dalla madre; *to* — *a lollipop*, succhiare un lecca-lecca ‖ *to* — *dry*, succhiare completamente **2.** assorbire; sorbire (anche *fig.*): *plants* — *water from the ground*, le piante assorbono l'acqua dal suolo; *to* — *s.o.'s brain*, sfruttare le idee di qlcu.; *to* — (*in*) *s.o.'s words*, bere le parole di qlcu. **3.** (*sl.*) bere, succhiare dalla bottiglia **4.** *to* — *in*, assorbire; inghiottire; aspirare (di pompa); (*sl.*) imbrogliare **5.** *to* — *up*, assorbire; (*sl.*) fare il leccapiedi.

sucker [′sʌkə*], *s.c.* **1.** chi succhia **2.** persona sempliciotta: *don't be a* —!, non essere uno stupido! **3.** parassita ‖ *s.* **1.** (*mec.*) pistone, pistone valvolato **2.** (*bot.*) pollone, succhione **3.** ventosa.

sucking [′sʌkiŋ], *ag.* **1.** lattante, poppante **2.** (*mec.*) aspirante (di pompa) **3.** inesperto: *a* — *barrister*, un avvocatino alle prime armi ‖ *s.* succhiamento ☆ — *bottle*, poppatoio; *a* — *child*, un lattante; — *-pig*, porcellino da latte; — *-sands*, sabbie mobili.

to **suckle** [′sʌkl], *v.t.* allattare.

suckling [′sʌkliŋ], *s.* lattante; lattonzolo: *babes and sucklings*, gli innocenti; bambini innocenti.

sucrose [′sju:krous], *s.* zucchero di canna, saccarosio.

suction [′sʌkʃən], *s.* succhiamento; (*tec.*) aspirazione: *to adhere by* —, aderire a ventosa ☆ — *pipe*, espiratore; — *pump*, pompa aspirante.

suctorial [sʌk′tɔ:riəl], *ag.* (*zool.*) provvisto di ventose, succhiatoi.

sudamina [sju′dæminə], *s.pl.* (*patol.*) sudamina, miliaria cristallina.

Sudanese [ˌsu:də′ni:z], *ag.s.c.* sudanese.

sudarium [sju(:)′dɛəriəm], *pl.* **sudaria** [sju(:)′dɛəriə], *s.* sudario.

sudatorium [ˌsju:də′tɔ:riəm], *pl.* **sudatoria** [ˌsju:-də′tɔ:riə], *s.* sudatorio.

sudatory [′sju:dətəri], *ag.s.* (*arc.*) sudorifero.

sudden [′sʌdn], *ag.* improvviso, inaspettato, repentino: — *death*, morte improvvisa; *to take a* — *resolve*, prendere una decisione improvvisa ‖ *this is so* —!, (*scherz.*) non me l'aspettavo! (generalmente di proposta di matrimonio) ‖ *s.* evento improvviso ‖ *all of a* —, all'improvviso.

suddenly [′sʌdnli], *av.* improvvisamente, d'un tratto; bruscamente, di colpo.

suddenness [′sʌdnnis], *s.* subitaneità ‖ *with startling* —, con un colpo di scena.

sudoriferous [ˌsju:də′rifərəs], *ag.* (*fisiol.*) sudorifero.

sudorific [ˌsju:də′rifik], *ag.s.* sudorifero.

Sudra [′su:drə], *s.* (*ang.-in.*) membro della più bassa casta indiana.

suds [sʌdz], *s.pl.* **1.** schiuma di sapone, saponata ‖ *in the* —, (*sl.*) in imbarazzo; nei pasticci **2.** (*sl. amer.*) birra.

Sue[1] [sju:], *no.pr.f. dim.* di **Susan**.

to **sue**[2], *v.t.i.* **1.** ricorrere in giudizio; citare in giudizio; far processare: *liable to be sued*, perseguibile; *to* — *s.o. at law*, intentare un processo a qlcu.; *to* — *s.o. for damages*, far causa a qlcu. per danni **2.** presentare una supplica, una richiesta: *to* — *to s.o. for sthg.*, sollecitare qlcu. per ql.co ‖ *to* — *for peace*, chiedere la pace ‖ *to* — *for a woman's hand*, chiedere una donna in moglie **3.** (*arc.*) corteggiare **4.** *to* — *out*, (*dir.*) ottenere dietro richiesta fatta a un tribunale, impetrare: *to* — *out a pardon for s.o.*, impetrare la grazia per qlcu.

suede [sweid], *s.* pelle scamosciata.

suet [sjuit], *s.* sugna, grasso (di bue) ‖ — *face*, (*am.*) viso flaccido.

Suetonius [swi:′tounjəs], *no.pr.m.* (*st. lett.*) Svetonio.

suety [′sjuiti], *ag.* sugnoso, grasso.

Suevian [′swi:viən], *ag.* (*st.*) svevo ‖ *s.c.* (*st.*) svevo, sveva.

to **suffer** [′sʌfə*], *v.t.i.* **1.** subire; patire: *to* — *defeat*, subire una sconfitta; *to* — *hunger*, soffrire la fame **2.** tollerare: *she suffered him to speak*, ella tollerò ch'egli parlasse ‖ *she will not* — *fools gladly*, ella non tollera gli imbecilli **3.** soffrire, essere sofferente: *to* — *acutely*, soffrire atrocemente; *to* — *for one's misdeeds*, scontare i propri errori; *to* — *greatly from rheumatism*, essere afflitto dai reumatismi **4.** essere danneggiato; risentire le conseguenze: *if you act badly, your reputation will* —, se agisci male la tua reputazione ne soffrirà; *trade is suffering from the war*, il commercio risente della guerra **5.** essere giustiziato; essere messo a morte: *he was to* — *on the next day*, egli doveva essere giustiziato il giorno successivo.

sufferable [′sʌfərəbl], *ag.* sopportabile, tollerabile.

sufferably [′sʌfərəbli], *av.* in modo tollerabile, sopportabile.

sufferance [′sʌfərəns], *s.* **1.** (*arc.*) sofferenza, dolore **2.** tacito assenso, rassegnazione; tolleranza: *the* — *of evil*, la sopportazione del male; *he remains here on* (o *by* o *through*) —, rimane qui per tacita tolleranza ‖ *bill of* —, (*comm.*) bolletta di merce esente.

sufferer [′sʌfərə*], *s.c.* chi soffre, chi patisce: — *from a calamity*, vittima di un disastro ☆ *fellow* —, compagno di sventura.

suffering [′sʌfəriŋ], *s.* **1.** sofferenza; pena, dolore **2.** sopportazione, tolleranza.

sufferingly [′sʌfəriŋli], *av.* penosamente.

suffete [′sʌfi:t], *s.* (*st.*) suffete.

to **suffice** [sə′fais], *v.t.i.* **1.** bastare, essere sufficiente, adeguato: *your word will* —, basta la vostra parola ‖ — *it to say that...*, basti dire che... **2.** soddisfare i bisogni di: *enough food to* — *an army*, cibo bastante per un esercito.

sufficiency [sə′fiʃənsi], *s.* **1.** sufficienza, l'essere sufficiente: *we have a* — *of provisions*, abbiamo una quantità sufficiente di viveri **2.** (*arc.*) capacità, qualificazione, competenza; efficienza: *the* — *of the present administration to meet an emergency*, la capacità dell'attuale governo a fronteggiare un caso di emergenza.

sufficient [sə′fiʃənt], *ag.* **1.** sufficiente, bastevole: *have you got courage* — *for that?*, avete coraggio sufficiente per fare ciò?; *this is* — *to feed a whole family*, questo è sufficiente a nutrire un'intera famiglia **2.** (*arc.*) capace, competente ‖ *s.* quantità sufficiente: *have you had* —?, avete mangiato abbastanza? ☆ — *reason*, (*fil.*) ragione sufficiente ‖ *self-* —, autosufficiente.

sufficiently [sə′fiʃəntli], *av.* sufficientemente, a sufficienza, abbastanza.

sufficingness [sə′faisiŋnis], *s.* sufficienza.

suffix [′sʌfiks], *s.* (*gram.*) suffisso.

to **suffix**, *v.t.* (*gram.*) aggiungere un suffisso a.

to **suffocate** [′sʌfəkeit], *v.t.i.* soffocare; asfissiare (anche *fig.*): *suffocated by* (o *with*) *grief*, soffocato dal dolore; *this weed suffocates every kind of plant*, questa erbaccia soffoca tutte le piante; *to* — *with rage*, soffocare di collera.

suffocating [′sʌfəkeitiŋ], *ag.* soffocante; asfissiante.

suffocatingly [′sʌfəkeitiŋli], *av.* in modo soffocante, asfissiante.

suffocation [ˌsʌfə′keiʃən], *s.* soffocazione, soffocamento, asfissia: *it was hot to* —, faceva tanto caldo da soffocare.

suffocative [′sʌfəkeitiv], *ag.* che soffoca ☆ — *catarrh*, (*patol.*) bronchite capillare.

suffragan [′sʌfrəgən], *ag.s.* (*eccl.*) suffraganeo.

suffraganship [′sʌfrəgənʃip], *s.* (*eccl.*) carica, ufficio di suffraganeo.

suffrage [′sʌfridʒ], *s.* **1.** suffragio; diritto di voto **2.** preghiera, suffragio ☆ *universal* —, suffragio universale.

suffragette [ˌsʌfrə'dʒet], s. suffragetta.

suffragist ['sʌfrədʒist], s. suffragista.

suffrutex ['sʌfruteks], pl. **suffrutices** [sʌ'fru:tisi:z], s (bot.) sottofrutice, suffrutice.

to **suffumigate** [sʌ'fju:migeit], v.t. (rar.) suffumigare.

suffumigation [sʌˌfju:mi'geiʃən], s. suffumigio.

to **suffuse** [sə'fju:z], v.t. coprire; cospargere: a blush suffused her cheeks, le sue guance si soffusero di rossore; her eyes were suffused with tears, i suoi occhi erano inondati di lacrime.

suffusion [sə'fju:ʒən], s. 1. spargimento 2. (patol.) suffusione.

Sufi ['su:fi], s. (relig.) chi pratica il sufismo.

Sufism ['su:fizəm], s. (relig.) sufismo.

sugar ['ʃugə*], s. 1. zucchero: — and water, acqua zuccherata 2. fig. atteggiamento melliffluo; lusinghe; adulazione; parole melate, insinuanti: she was all —, era tutta zucchero 3. (sl. amer.) denaro, « grana » ☆ — almond, confetto; (o — -bowl), zuccheriera; — -beet, barbabietola da zucchero; — -candy, zucchero candito; — -cane, canna da zucchero; — house, zuccherificio; — -maple, acero da zucchero; — -mill, zuccherificio (per zucchero di canna); — -plums, fondenti, chicche; — -refinery, raffineria di zucchero; — test, (med.) prova dello zucchero; — -tongs, mollette per zucchero ‖ barley- —, zucchero d'orzo; brown — (o raw —), zucchero greggio; castor —, zucchero in polvere; granulated —, zucchero cristallizzato; loaf —, zucchero in pani; lump- —, zucchero in zollette; milk —, (chim.) lattosio.

to **sugar**, v.t.i. 1. inzuccherare; addolcire; coprire, spolverare di zucchero 2. raffinare lo zucchero 3. fig. addolcire; adulare ‖ to — the pill, indorare la pillola 4. (sl.) lavorare pigramente, battere la fiacca.

sugariness ['ʃugərinis], s. 1. dolcezza 2. fig. mellifluità.

sugary ['ʃugəri], ag. 1. zuccheroso, zuccherino 2. fig. melliffluo, insinuante.

to **suggest** [sə'dʒest], v.t. 1. (I) proporre; suggerire: a solution suggested itself to me, mi venne in mente una soluzione; can anybody — a better plan?, nessuno ha un progetto migliore da proporre? 2. (I) ispirare, far nascere (una idea, ecc.): his words suggested that thought to me, le sue parole mi ispirarono quell'idea 3. insinuare: he suggested that I was lying, insinuò che mentivo; I — that you were not there at that time, (dir.) contesto che Lei fosse là in quel momento 4. esprimere; richiamare alla mente: her features suggested a doll, i suoi lineamenti facevano pensare a una bambola; the look on her face suggested triumph, la sua espressione esprimeva trionfo.

suggester [sə'dʒestə*], s.c. 1. suggeritore, suggeritrice 2. ispiratore, ispiratrice.

suggestibility [səˌdʒesti'biliti], s. suggestionabilità.

suggestible [sə'dʒestibl], ag. 1. suggeribile 2. suggestionabile.

suggestion [sə'dʒestʃən], s. 1. suggerimento; consiglio; proposta; ispirazione: a practical —, un consiglio pratico; suggestions for improvement, proposte per migliorie; to make (o to offer) a —, dare, offrire un consiglio 2. associazione di idee 3. lieve traccia; una punta di: he speaks with just a — of a foreign accent, egli parla con un leggero accento straniero 4. suggestione: hypnotic —, suggestione ipnotica.

suggestive [sə'dʒestiv], ag. 1. stimolante, che ispira, che richiama alla mente: trees — of autumn, alberi che fanno pensare all'autunno 2. allusivo.

suggestively [sə'dʒestivli], av. in modo allusivo, indicativo.

suggestiveness [sə'dʒestivnis], s. carattere allusivo, indicativo.

suicidal [sjui'saidl], ag. 1. suicida; che ha tendenze al suicidio 2. fig. fatale, rovinoso: the attempt to fight the league was —, il tentativo di opporsi alla lega fu disastroso ☆ — mania, mania suicida.

suicidally [sjui'saidəli], av. da suicida.

suicide ['sjuisaid], s. 1. suicidio: to attempt —, tentare il suicidio; to commit —, suicidarsi 2. suicida ☆ race- —, volontaria estinzione della razza.

suilline ['sjuilain], ag. suino.

suing ['sju:iŋ], s. (dir.) citazione.

suit [sju:t], s. 1. domanda, richiesta; preghiera: at the — of s.o., su richiesta di qlcu.; to press one's —, insistere con la propria richiesta 2. domanda di matrimonio 3. (dir.) causa: to be a party in a —, essere parte in causa; to bring (o to institute) a — against s.o., intentar causa a qlcu. 4. abito completo (da uomo): « tailleur » ‖ — of armour, armatura completa 5. — (of sails), (mar.) velatura 6. (carte) seme, colore: the four suits, i quattro semi; to follow —, rispondere a colore; fig. seguire l'esempio, imitare ☆ — -case, valigia ‖ civil, criminal —, causa civile, penale ‖ dress- —, abito da sera, abito da società; three-piece —, abito a tre pezzi; travelling —, abito da viaggio.

to **suit**, v.t.i. 1. soddisfare, andar bene a, convenire a: he is hard to —, è difficile da accontentare; this job does not — me, questo lavoro non mi si confà; this train will —, questo treno va bene ‖ — yourself, fa' a tuo piacimento, fa' come ti pare 2. far bene a, giovare a (di cibo, clima, ecc.): this food does not — me, questo cibo non mi fa bene 3. addirsi, accordarsi, intonarsi: green does not — with her complexion, il verde non si addice alla sua carnagione; your shoes do not — with your bag, le tue scarpe non si intonano alla tua borsetta 4. adattare; essere adatto, appropriato: he is not suited to be a journalist (o for journalism), non è tagliato per il giornalismo; to — one's tastes to the company, accordare i propri gusti alla compagnia.

suitability [ˌsju:tə'biliti], s. convenienza; opportunità.

suitable ['sju:təbl], ag. adatto, idoneo; conveniente: — reply, risposta adeguata; — to the occasion, adatto all'occasione; as seems —, come sembra conveniente; is the show — for children?, lo spettacolo è adatto per bambini?; it would have been more — to say so at once, sarebbe stato meglio dirlo subito; wherever you think —, dove meglio credi.

suitableness ['sju:təblnis], V. suitability.

suitably ['sju:təbli], av. appropriatamente; opportunamente; convenientemente.

suite [swi:t], s. 1. seguito, corteo 2. serie: a — of rooms, una serie di stanze; appartamento; — of furniture, mobilia per una stanza 3. (mus.) suite; sequenza.

suitings ['sju:tiŋz], s.pl. tessuti per confezione.

suitor ['sju:tə*], s. 1. postulante 2. corteggiatore 3. (dir.) attore.

suitress ['sju:tris], s. 1. postulante 2. (dir.) attrice.

Sukey ['su:ki], no.pr.f. dim. di **Susan** ‖ s. (dial.) cuccuma, bricco.

sulcate ['sʌlkeit], ag. (bot. anat.) solcato.

sulcus ['sʌlkəs], pl. **sulci** ['sʌlsai], s. (anat.) solco.

sulk [sʌlk], s. gener. pl. malumore, broncio: to be in the sulks, tenere il broncio.

to **sulk**, v.i. fare il broncio, tenere il broncio, essere di malumore.

sulker ['sʌlkə*], s.c. persona imbronciata; persona di cattivo umore.

sulkily ['sʌlkili], av. con aria imbronciata; di malumore.

sulkiness ['sʌlkinis], s. malumore.

sulky[1] ['sʌlki], ag. 1. imbronciato; scontroso, poco socievole 2. tetro, cupo: a — day, una giornata tetra.

sulky[2], s. (ippica) «sulky», sediolo.

Sulla ['sʌlə], no.pr.m. (st.) Silla.

sullage ['sʌlidʒ], s. 1. sudiciume; rifiuti; scolatura 2. (metal.) scorie.

Sullan ['sʌlən], ag. (st.) sillano.

sullen ['sʌlən], ag. 1. accigliato, imbronciato; astioso 2. tetro, cupo, lugubre.

sullenly ['sʌlənli], *av.* con astio, con risentimento; dj malumore.

sullenness ['sʌlənnis], *s.* cattivo umore, tetraggine; isentimento.

sullens ['sʌlənz], *s.pl.* cattivo umore; depressione: *to have the sullens*, essere di cattivo umore, depresso.

sully ['sʌli], *s.* (*arc.*) macchia.

to sully, *v.t.* 1. (*poet.*) macchiare, sporcare 2. *fig.* offuscare, macchiare, disonorare: *to — one's reputation*, macchiare la propria reputazione.

sulphamide ['sʌlfəmaid], *s.* (*chim.farm.*) sulfamidico.

sulphate ['sʌlfeit], *s.* (*chim.*) solfato.

sulphide ['sʌlfaid], *s.* (*chim.*) solfuro.

sulphite ['sʌlfait], *s.* (*chim.*) solfito.

sulphur ['sʌlfə*], *s.* 1. (*chim.*) zolfo: *flowers of —*, fiori di zolfo; *milk of —*, latte di zolfo; *to treat with —*, solforare 2. farfalla gialla ☆ — *-bottom* (o — *-whale*), (*zool.*) balenottera sulfurea; — *-match*, zolfanello; — *-mine* (o — *-pit*), solfatara; — *-ore*, (*chim.*) pirite di ferro; — *-spring*, sorgente solforosa; — *-yellow*, color giallo zolfo ‖ *free- —*, zolfo libero; *roll- —*, zolfo in pani.

to sulphur, to sulphurate ['sʌlfjureit], *v.t.* (*ind. chim.*) solforare.

sulphuration [,sʌlfju'reiʃən], *s.* (*agr.*) solforazione.

sulphurator ['sʌlfjureitə*], *s.* solforatrice.

sulphureous [sʌl'fjuəriəs], *ag.* 1. sulfureo 2. (*bot.*) del colore dello zolfo.

sulphureousness [sʌl'fjuəriəsnis], *s.* proprietà sulfurea.

sulphuretted ['sʌlfjuretid], *ag.* (*chim.*) solforato ☆ — *hydrogen*, idrogeno solforato.

sulphuric [sʌl'fjuərik], *ag.* (*chim.*) solforico ☆ — *acid*, acido solforico.

sulphurization [,sʌlfjurai'zeiʃən], *s.* (*agr.*) solforazione.

to sulphurize ['sʌlfjuraiz], *v.t.* (*ind. chim.*) solforare.

sulphurous ['sʌlfjurəs], *ag.* 1. *V.* **sulphureous** 2. (*chim.*) solforoso 3. satanico; infernale 4. focoso, infiammabile: — *temperament*, temperamento focoso.

sulphurwort ['sʌlfəwə:t], *s.* (*bot.*) peucedano, finocchio porcino.

sulphury ['sʌlfəri], *ag.* sulfureo.

sulphydric [sʌl'faidrik], *ag.* (*chim.*) solfidrico.

sultan ['sʌltən], *s.* 1. sultano 2. pollo sultano 3. (*bot.*) centaurea ☆ *sweet —*, (*bot.*) ambretta.

sultana [sʌl'ta:nə], *s.* 1. sultana 2. uva sultanina 3. gallina sultana.

sultanate ['sʌltənit], *s.* sultanato.

sultaness ['sʌltənis], *s.* sultana.

sultanic [sʌl'tænik], *ag.* dispotico, tirannico.

sultrily ['sʌltrili], *av.* in modo afoso, soffocante.

sultriness ['sʌltrinis], *s.* afa, caldo soffocante.

sultry ['sʌltri], *ag.* 1. afoso, soffocante: — *heat*, caldo soffocante 2. *fig.* infocato, appassionato 3. (*sl.*) grossolano, volgare.

sum [sʌm], *s.* 1. somma, quantità (di denaro): *a good —*, una bella somma 2. (*arit.*) somma, addizione; operazione aritmetica: *the four sums*, le quattro operazioni; *he is good at sums*, è bravo a far somme; *to do sums*, far calcoli 3. somma, totale: *the — of human experience*, la somma delle esperienze umane; *history is not merely a — o events*, la storia non è soltanto un insieme di eventi ‖ *in —*, in breve ☆ — *total*, somma totale.

to sum, *pass.p.p.* **summed** [sʌmd], *v.t.i.* 1. sommare, addizionare; fare una somma 2. *to — up*, riassumere, ricapitolare; (*dir.*) ricapitolare i fatti.

summing ['sʌmiŋ], *s.* somma ☆ — *-up*, (*dir.*) ricapitolazione dei fatti.

sumach ['su:mæk], *s.* (*bot.*) sommacco.

sumless ['sʌmlis], *ag.* innumerevole, incalcolabile.

summarily ['sʌmərili], *av.* sommariamente.

to summarize ['sʌməraiz], *v.t.* riassumere, compendiare.

summary ['sʌməri], *ag.* sommario, conciso ‖ *s.* som-

mario, compendio, ricapitolazione ☆ — *procedure*, (*dir.* procedura sommaria.

summation [sʌ'meiʃən], *s.* (*mat.*) sommatoria.

summer[1] ['sʌmə*], *ag.* estivo ‖ *s.* 1. estate: *in —*, d'estate ‖ *Indian* (o *St. Martin's* o *St. Luke's*) —, l'estate di S. Martino 2. *pl.* (*poet.*) anni: *a child of ten summers*, un bambino di dieci anni ☆ — *-heat*, caldo estivo; — *-house*, bersò; — *-school*, corso estivo; — *time*, estate; ora legale.

to summer[1], *v.t.i.* 1. passare, trascorrere l'estate: *we summered in Switzerland*, passammo l'estate in Svizzera; *to — and winter abroad*, passare tutto l'anno all'estero 2. far pascolare in estate.

summer[2], *s.* (*arch.*) architrave.

summer[3], *s.c.* chi fa somme.

summerless ['sʌməlis], *ag.* senza estate.

summerlike ['sʌməlaik], *ag.* come d'estate; estivo.

summerly ['sʌməli], *ag.* estivo.

summersault, summerset, *V.* **somersault.**

summertime ['sʌmətaim], *s.* stagione estiva.

summery ['sʌməri], *ag.* estivo.

summing ['sʌmiŋ], *s.* somma ☆ — *-up*, (*dir.*) ricapitolazione dei fatti.

summit ['sʌmit], *s.* 1. cima, vetta: *on the — of that mountain*, sulla cima di quel monte 2. *fig.* culmine, apice: *the — of happiness*, il colmo della felicità; *to be at the — of*, essere all'apice di.

to summon ['sʌmən], *v.t.* 1. chiamare, mandare a chiamare 2. convocare; (*dir.*) citare, chiamare in giudizio: *to — Parliament*, convocare il Parlamento; *to — a witness*, citare un testimonio 3. intimare a: *to — a town to surrender*, intimare la resa a una città 4. raccogliere; fare appello a: *I — (up) all my courage to do this*, raccolgo tutto il mio coraggio per fare ciò; *to — all one's energy*, raccogliere tutte le proprie energie.

summoner ['sʌmənə*], *s.* chi convoca; (*dir.*) usciere.

summons ['sʌmənz], *pl.* **summonses** ['sʌmənziz], *s.* 1. (*dir.*) citazione, ingiunzione 2. convocazione; chiamata: — *to arms*, chiamata alle armi.

to summons, *v.t.* citare in giudizio.

sump [sʌmp], *s.* 1. pozzo nero 2. (*miner.*) bacino di pompaggio 3. (*fam.*) palude, stagno; pozzanghera 4. (*mec.*) coppa ☆ — *-breather*, (*aer. mec.*) sfiato del pozzetto ‖ *dry — lubrication*, (*mec.*) lubrificazione a coppa secca; *engine oil —*, (*mec.*) coppa dell'olio del motore.

sumpter ['sʌmptə*], *s.* 1. bestia da soma 2. (*arc.*) chi conduce bestie da soma.

sumption ['sʌmpʃən], *s.* (*log.*) premessa maggiore (di sillogismo).

sumptuary ['sʌmptjuəri], *ag.* suntuario: — *law*, legge suntuaria.

sumptuous ['sʌmptjuəs], *ag.* sontuoso, fastoso, imponente.

sumptuously ['sʌmptjuəsli], *av.* sontuosamente, fastosamente.

sumptuousness ['sʌmptjuəsnis], *s.* sontuosità, fasto, imponenza.

sun [sʌn], *s.* 1. sole; raggi solari: *the — is down*, il sole è tramontato; *the — is shining*, splende il sole, c'è il sole; *the — is up*, il sole è sorto; *the — rises*, il sole sorge; *the — sets*, il sole tramonta; *to get a touch of the —*, prendere un leggero colpo di sole; *to let in the —*, lasciare entrare il sole; *to sit in the —*, sedersi al sole; *to take the —*, prendere il sole ‖ *against the —*, in senso contrario all'orologio; *with the —*, in senso orario ‖ *full in the —*, in pieno sole ‖ *nothing new under the —*, nulla di nuovo sotto il sole ‖ *a place in the —*, stare al sole ‖ *the Empire of the Rising Sun*, l'Impero del Sol Levante ‖ *to have the — in one's eyes*, (*sl.*) essere ubriaco ‖ *to hold a candle to the —*, portare acqua al mare ‖ *to make hay while the — shines*, battere il ferro finchè è caldo ‖ *to rise with the —*, alzarsi di buon mattino ‖ *to see the —*, vivere ‖ *to take (o to shoot)* *the* —, (*mar.*) prendere l'altezza del sole ‖ *let not the — go down upon your wrath*, (*biblico*) non lasciare che il sole tramonti sulla tua collera 2. *fig.* astro: *his — is set*, il suo momento è passato; *to worship the rising* —, onorare l'astro nascente 3. (*astr.*) stella fissa 4. (*poet.*) anno; giorno.

to **sun**, *pass.p.p.* **sunned** [sʌnd], *v.t.i.* esporre al sole; prendere il sole: *to — oneself*, crogiolarsi al sole.

sun, (*nei composti*): — *-bath*, bagno di sole; — *-blind*, persiana, veneziana; — *-bonnet*, cappellino da sole; — *-bright*, chiaro come il sole; — *-crack*, fessura (nel terreno) causata dal sole; — *-dew*, (*bot.*) drosera; — *-dial*, meridiana; — *-dog*, parelio; — *-dried*, disseccato al sole (di argilla, ecc.); — *-fish*, (*ittiol.*) mola, pesce luna; — *-glasses*, occhiali da sole; — *-myth*, mito solare; — *-parlour*, veranda; — *-picture*, fotografia; — *-rays*, raggi solari; raggi ultravioletti; — *-worship*, culto del Sole ‖ *midnight* —, sole di mezzanotte.

to **sunbathe** ['sʌnbeið], *v.i.* fare i bagni di sole.

sunbeam ['sʌnbi:m], *s.* raggio di sole.

sunbow ['sʌnbou], *s.* arcobaleno (negli spruzzi di una cascata, ecc.).

sunburn ['sʌnbə:n], *s.* 1. abbronzatura 2. scottatura (solare).

sunburnt ['sʌnbə:nt], *ag.* 1. abbronzato 2. scottato (dal sole).

sunburst ['sʌnbə:st], *s.* sprazzo di sole.

sundae ['sʌndei], *s.* (*amer.*) porzione di gelato misto con frutta e nocciole.

sundawn ['sʌndɔ:n], *s.* alba.

Sunday ['sʌndi], *s.* domenica: *he comes on Sundays*, di solito viene la domenica ‖ *a month of Sundays*, (*fam.*) un lungo periodo ☆ — *best* (o — *-go-to-meeting clothes*), gli abiti della domenica; — *-school*, scuola domenicale di istruzione religiosa.

to **sunder** ['sʌndə*], *v.t.i.* (*arc. poet.*) separare, separarsi; dividere, dividersi.

sundown ['sʌndaun], *s.* 1. tramonto 2. (*amer.*) cappello a larghe tese (da donna) ☆ — *student*, studente che frequenta corsi serali.

sundowner ['sʌn,daunə*], *s.* 1. (*austral.*) vagabondo (che arriva al calar del sole ad una fattoria solo per scroccare cibo e letto) 2. (*fam.*) aperitivo serale.

sundries ['sʌndriz], *s.pl.* 1. generi diversi, cose diverse; cianfrusaglie 2. (*comm.*) (spese) varie.

sundry ['sʌndri], *ag.* parecchi, vari, diversi: *he showed us — samples*, ci mostrò diversi campioni ‖ *all and* —, ciascuno e tutti, tutti quanti.

sunflower ['sʌn,flauə*], *s.* (*bot.*) girasole.

sung [sʌŋ], *p.p.* di to **sing**.

sungod ['sʌngɔd], *s.* dio Sole.

sunhat ['sʌnhæt], *s.* cappello a larghe tese.

sunk [sʌŋk], *p.p.* di to **sink**.

sunken ['sʌŋkən], *p.p.* (*rar.*) di to **sink** ‖ *ag.* 1. affondato; sommerso: — *wreck*, relitto sommerso 2. cavo, incavato: — *cheeks*, guance incavate 3. sprofondato: — *road*, strada che ha ceduto.

sunless ['sʌnlis], *ag.* senza sole; tetro.

sunlight ['sʌnlait], *s.* luce del sole ☆ — *treatment*, elioterapia.

sunlike ['sʌnlaik], *ag.* splendente come il sole.

sunlit ['sʌnlit], *ag.* illuminato dal sole, soleggiato.

sunny ['sʌni], *ag.* 1. luminoso 2. esposto al sole, soleggiato: *the — side of the house*, la parte della casa esposta al sole 3. *fig.* ridente, allegro, gioioso: *a — temper*, un carattere allegro, ottimista ‖ *the — side of the matter*, il lato buono della faccenda ‖ *to be on the — side of forty*, essere sotto ai quaranta.

sunproof ['sʌn-pru:f], *ag.* inalterabile al sole.

sunrise ['sʌnraiz], *s.* il sorger del sole: *at* —, al sorger del sole, all'alba.

sunset ['sʌnset], *s.* tramonto (anche *fig.*): *at* —, al tramonto; *the — of the colonial system*, il declino del sistema coloniale; *the — of life*, il tramonto della vita.

sunshade ['sʌn-ʃeid], *s.* parasole.

sunshine ['sʌnʃain], *s.* 1. luce del sole, sole; bel tempo; splendore, calore del sole: *in the* —, al sole, in pieno sole 2. *fig.* gioia, gaiezza, felicità ‖ *to have been in the* —, (*sl.*) essere ubriaco ‖ *to take a — view of everything*, vedere tutto roseo ☆ — *-recorder*, registratore della durata della luce solare; — *roof*, (*aut.*) tetto scorrevole.

sunspot ['sʌn-spot], *s.* macchia solare.

sunstroke ['sʌn-strouk], *s.* colpo di sole, insolazione.

sunstruck ['sʌn-strʌk], *ag.* sofferente per un colpo di sole.

sunward ['sʌnwəd], *ag.av.* verso il sole, controsole.

sunwards ['sʌnwədz], *av.* verso il sole, controsole.

sunwise ['sʌnwaiz], *av.* col sole, nella direzione del moto apparente del sole.

sup¹ [sʌp], *s.* (*dial.*) sorso; (*fam.*) goccia: *to take a — of wine*, prendere un sorso, una goccia di vino.

to **sup¹**, *pass.p.p.* **supped** [sʌpt], *v.t.i.* 1. sorseggiare, bere 2. *fig.* provare, sperimentare: *to — sorrow*, sperimentare il dolore.

to **sup²**, *pass.p.p.* **supped**, *v.t.i.* 1. cenare; offrire la cena a: *we'll — on fruit*, ceneremo di sola frutta 2. (*caccia*) dare l'ultimo pasto del giorno a (cavalli, cani, falconi, ecc.).

supawn [sʌ'pɔ:n], *s.* (*amer.*) polenta molle.

super ['sju:pə*], *ag.* (*fam.*) 1. (*comm.*) sopraffino, finissimo 2. (*misure*) quadrato, di superficie: *20 feet* —, venti piedi quadrati ‖ *s.* (*fam.*) 1. (*comm.*) articolo finissimo 2. *abbr.* di **superficial**, **superfine**, **supernumerary**.

superable ['sju:pərəbl], *ag.* superabile.

superableness ['sju:pərəblnis], *s.* superabilità.

to **superabound** [,sju:pərə'baund], *v.i.* sovrabbondare.

superabundance [,sju:pərə'bʌndəns], *s.* sovrabbondanza.

superabundant [,sju:pərə'bʌndənt], *ag.* sovrabbondante, copioso.

superabundantly [,sju:pərə'bʌndəntli], *av.* sovrabbondantemente, con sovrabbondanza.

superacute [,sju:pərə'kju:t], *ag.* molto acuto.

to **superadd** ['sju:pər'æd], *v.t.* aggiungere in più.

superaddition [,sju:pərə'diʃən], *s.* sopraggiunta.

superaltar ['sju:pər,ɔ:ltə*], *s.* 1. pietra consacrata (usata come altare portatile) 2. dossale d'altare.

superangelic [,sju:pəræn'dʒelik], *ag.* più che angelico.

to **superannuate** [,sju:pə'rænjueit], *v.t.i.* 1. collocare a riposo per limiti di età; raggiungere i limiti di età; mandare in pensione 2. chiedere il ritiro da scuola di (alunni bocciati).

superannuated [,sju:pə'rænjueitid], *ag.* 1. inabile per età 2. che ha raggiunto il limite di età 3. passato di moda, sorpassato.

superannuation [,sju:pə,rænju'eiʃən], *s.* 1. inabilità per vecchiaia 2. collocamento a riposo 3. pensione per vecchiaia 4. (*a scuola*) limite di età.

superb [sju:(:)'pə:b], *ag.* superbo, eccellente, magnifico, splendido: *a — view*, una vista superba.

superbly [sju:(:)'pə:bli], *av.* superbamente, splendidamente.

superbness [sju:(:)'pə:bnis], *s.* magnificenza, splendore.

to **supercalender** [,sju:pə'kælində*], *v.t.* (*ind. cartaria*) calandrare.

supercargo ['sju:pə,kɑ:gou], *s.* 1. commissario di bordo 2. (*comm.*) agente marittimo.

supercelestial [,sju:pəsi'lestjəl], *ag.* sopraceleste.

supercharge ['sju:pətʃɑ:dʒ], *s.* sovraccarico.

to **supercharge**, *v.t.* 1. sovraccaricare, riempire a dismisura 2. (*mec.*) sovralimentare.

supercharger ['sju:pə,tʃɑ:dʒə*], *s.* (*mec.*) compressore; sovralimentatore.

superciliary [,sju:pə'siliəri], *ag.* sopracigliare.

supercilious [,sju:pə'siliəs], *ag.* altero, arrogante.

superciliously [,sju:pə'siliəsli], *av.* arrogantemente, con sussiego.

superciliousness [,sju:pə'siliəsnis], *s.* arroganza, sussiego.

supercivilized [ˌsju:pə'sivilaizd], *ag.* ultracivile.
supercolumnar [ˌsju:pəkə'lʌmnə*], *ag.* a doppio ordine di colonne.
supercolumniation [ˌsju:pəkəˌlʌmni'eiʃən], *s.* sovrapposizione di un ordine architettonico ad un altro.
superconductivity [ˌsju:pəˌkɔndʌk'tiviti], *s.* (*elett.*) superconduttività, superconduzione.
to **supercool** ['sju:pəku:l], *v.t.* soprafondere.
superdominant [ˌsju:pə'dɔminənt], *s.* (*mus.*) sopradominante.
superdreadnought [ˌsju:pə'drednɔ:t], *s.* (*mar.*) « superdreadnought », supercorazzata.
superelevation [ˌsju:pəˌeli'veiʃən], *s.* sopraelevazione.
supereminence [ˌsju:pər'eminəns], *s.* preminenza, sovreminenza.
supereminent [ˌsju:pər'eminənt], *ag.* preminente, sovreminente.
supereminently [ˌsju:pər'eminəntli], *av.* in modo sovreminente.
supererogation [ˌsju:pərˌerə'geiʃən], *s.* supererogazione.
supererogatory [ˌsju:pəre'rɔgətəri], *ag.* supererogatorio.
to **superexalt** [ˌsju:pərig'zɔ:lt], *v.t.* sopraesaltare.
superexaltation [ˌsju:pərˌegzɔ:l'teiʃən], *s.* sopraesaltazione.
superexcellence [ˌsju:pər'eksələns], *s.* sovreccellenza.
superexcellent [ˌsju:pər'eksələnt], *ag.* sovreccellente.
superexcitation [ˌsju:pərˌeksi'teiʃən], *s.* ipereccitazione.
superfatted [ˌsju:pə'fætid], *ag.* obeso.
superfecundation [ˌsju:pəˌfi:kən'deiʃən], *s.* soprafecondamento.
superfetation [ˌsju:pəfi:'teiʃən], *s.* superfetazione.
superficial [ˌsju:pə'fiʃəl], *ag.* **1.** di superficie: — *foot*, piede quadrato; — *measure*, misura di superficie **2.** superficiale, poco profondo: *a* — *man*, un uomo superficiale, che si ferma alle apparenze; *a* — *wound*, una ferita poco profonda; *to have a* — *knowledge of sthg.*, avere un'infarinatura di ql.co.
superficiality [ˌsju:pəˌfiʃi'æliti], *s.* superficialità.
superficially [ˌsju:pə'fiʃəli], *av.* superficialmente.
superficialness [ˌsju:pə'fiʃəlnis], *s.* superficialità.
superficies, *pl.* **superficies** [ˌsju:pə'fiʃi:z], *s.* superficie.
superfine ['sju:pə'fain], *ag.* **1.** sopraffino, eccellente **2.** molto fine, raffinato: — *tastes*, gusti raffinati.
superfines ['sju:pə'fainz], *s.pl.* merci di qualità sopraffina.
superfluidity [ˌsju:pəflu(:)'iditi], *s.* iperfluidità.
superfluity [ˌsju:pə'flu(:)iti], *s.* superfluità; eccesso, sovrabbondanza.
superfluous [sju(:)'pə:fluəs], *ag.* superfluo; inutile.
superfluously [sju(:)'pə:fluəsli], *av.* superfluamente.
superfluousness [sju(:)'pə:fluəsnis], *V.* **superfluity**.
superfortress [ˌsju:pə'fɔ:tris], *s.* (*aer.*) superfortezza volante.
superfrontal ['sju:pəfrʌntl], *s.* paliotto d'altare.
to **superfuse** [ˌsju:pə'fju:z], *v.t.* (*chim. fis.*) soprafondere.
superfusion [ˌsju:pə'fju:ʒən], *s.* (*chim. fis.*) soprafusione.
to **superheat** ['sju:pəhi:t], *v.t.* (*fis.*) surriscaldare.
superheater ['sju:pə'hi:tə*], *s.* (*fis.*) surriscaldatore.
superheterodyne ['sju:pə'hetərədain], *s.* (*rad.*) supereterodina.
superhuman [ˌsju:pə'hju:mən], *ag.* sovrumano.
superhumanity [ˌsju:pəhju(:)'mæniti], *s.* sovrumanità.
superhumanly [ˌsju:pə'hju:mənli], *av.* in modo sovrumano.
superhumeral [ˌsju:pə'hju:mərəl], *s.* **1.** efod (paramento del Gran Sacerdote ebreo) **2.** stola vescovile.
to **superimpose** ['sju:pərim'pouz], *v.t.* sovrimporre,

sovrapporre: *superimposed title*, (*cine.*) titolo sovrapposto; *to* — *sthg. on sthg. else*, sovrapporre qualcosa a qualcos'altro.
superincumbence [ˌsju:pərin'kʌmbəns], *s.* sovrastamento.
superincumbent [ˌsju:pərin'kʌmbənt], *ag.* sovrastante; incombente.
to **superinduce** [ˌsju:pərin'dju:s], *v.t.* introdurre in aggiunta; sviluppare in più.
to **superintend** [ˌsju:prin'tend], *v.t.i.* sovraintendere a, sorvegliare; controllare; fare il sovraintendente.
superintendence [ˌsju:prin'tendəns], *s.* sovrintendenza; sorveglianza, controllo.
superintendency [ˌsju:prin'tendənsi], *s.* sovrintendenza, ufficio di sovrintendente.
superintendent [ˌsju:prin'tendənt], *s.* sovrintendente; sorvegliante ☆ *police* —, sovrintendente di polizia; *railway* —, ispettore delle ferrovie.
superintendentship [ˌsju:prin'tendəntʃip], *s.* carica di sovrintendente, di ispettore.
superior [sju(:)'piəriə*], *ag.* **1.** superiore (in posizione, grado, ecc.): — *officer*, ufficiale superiore; — *rank*, grado superiore ‖ *Lake Superior*, (*geog.*) Lago Superiore **2.** superiore; migliore; maggiore: — *quality*, qualità superiore; — *wisdom*, saggezza superiore; *my doctor is a* — *man*, il mio dottore è un uomo fuori del comune; *to be overcome by* — *numbers*, essere sopraffatto da forze superiori ‖ — *to*, superiore a, migliore di: *he rises* (o *is*) — *to temptation*, egli è al di sopra delle tentazioni; *this apple is* — *to that*, questa mela è migliore di quella **3.** superiore, superbo, sprezzante ‖ *don't put up a* — *air!*, non darti tante arie! ‖ *s.* **1.** superiore: *he has no* — *in courage*, nessuno lo supera in coraggio **2.** *Superior*, Superiore, Superiora (di monastero, ecc.): *Mother Superior*, Madre Superiora ☆ — *limit*, (*comm.*) limite massimo, termine ultimo (di consegna, ecc.); — *number*, (*mat.*) esponente algebrico.
superiority [sju(:)ˌpiəri'ɔriti], *s.* superiorità.
superiorly [sju(:)'piəriəli], *av.* **1.** superiormente **2.** meglio; di più **3.** con aria di sufficienza.
superiorship [sju(:)'piəriəʃip], *s.* superiorato.
superjacent [ˌsju:pə'dʒeisənt], *ag.* che giace sopra.
superlative [sju(:)'pə:lətiv], *ag.* **1.** superlativo, eccellente **2.** (*gram.*) superlativo: — *degree*, grado superlativo ‖ *s.* superlativo (anche *gram.*): *adjective in the* —, aggettivo superlativo ‖ *to speak in superlatives*, lodare esageratamente.
superlatively [sju(:)'pə:lətivli], *av.* superlativamente.
superlativeness [sju(:)'pə:lətivnis], *s.* eccellenza, perfezione.
superlunar [ˌsju:pə'lu:nə*], **superlunary** [ˌsju:pə'lu:nəri], *ag.* che è al di là della luna; celestiale, ultraterreno.
superman ['sju:pəmæn], *pl.* **supermen** ['sju:pəmen], *s.* superuomo.
supermundane [ˌsju:pə'mʌndein], *ag.* ultraterreno.
supernaculum [ˌsju:pə'nækjuləm], *s.* (*sl.*) **1.** liquore, vino di ottima qualità **2.** bicchiere ricolmo.
supernaculum, *av.* fino all'ultima goccia, fino in fondo: *to drink* —, bere fino all'ultima goccia.
supernal [sju(:)'pə:nl], *ag.* (*poet.*) superno, sommo; celeste, divino: — *loveliness*, bellezza divina.
supernally [sju(:)'pə:nəli], *av.* (*poet.*) divinamente.
supernatant [ˌsju:pə'neitənt], *ag.* che galleggia alla superficie.
supernatural [ˌsju:pə'nætʃrəl], *ag.* soprannaturale, straordinario; miracoloso: *an angel is a* — *being*, un angelo è un essere soprannaturale ‖ *the* —, il soprannaturale.
supernaturalism [ˌsju:pə'nætʃrəlizəm], *s.* (*fil. relig.*) fede nel soprannaturale.
supernaturalist [ˌsju:pə'nætʃrəlist], *s.* (*fil. relig.*) chi crede nel soprannaturale.
to **supernaturalize** [ˌsju:pə'nætʃrəlaiz], *v.t.* elevare ad una sfera soprannaturale.

supernaturally [ˌsjuːpəˈnætʃrəli], *av.* soprannaturalmente, straordinariamente; miracolosamente.

supernaturalness [ˌsjuːpəˈnætʃrəlnis], *s.* carattere, natura soprannaturale.

supernumerary [ˌsjuːpəˈnjuːmərəri], *ag.* **1.** in soprannumero, superfluo **2.** aggiunto ‖ *s.* **1.** soprannumerario (di impiegato, ufficiale, ecc.) **2.** (*teat.*) comparsa.

supernutrition [ˌsjuːpənjuː(ː)ˈtriʃən], *s.* supernutrizione.

superphosphate [ˌsjuːpəˈfɔsfeit], *s.* (*chim.*) perfosfato.

to **superpose** [ˈsjuːpəˈpouz], *v.t.* **1.** sovrapporre; disporre a piani: *to — sthg. on sthg.*, sovrapporre una cosa a un'altra **2.** (*geom.*) sovrapporre, far coincidere: *to — two triangles*, sovrapporre due triangoli.

superposition [ˈsjuːpəpəˈziʃən], *s.* sovrapposizione.

superrealism [ˌsjuːpəˈriəlizəm], *s.* surrealismo.

supersalt [ˈsjuːpəsɔːlt], *s.* (*chim.*) soprasale.

to **supersaturate** [ˌsjuːpəˈsætʃəreit], *v.t.* (*chim.*) soprasaturare.

supersaturation [ˌsjuːpəˌsætʃəˈreiʃən], *s.* soprasaturazione.

to **superscribe** [ˈsjuːpəˈskraib], *v.t.* **1.** fare una iscrizione, una soprascritta su: *a packet superscribed "fragile"*, un pacco con l'indicazione «fragile». intestare (un documento, col proprio nome); scrivere l'indirizzo sopra (una lettera).

superscript [ˈsjuːpəskript], *ag.s.* soprascritto.

superscription [ˌsjuːpəˈskripʃən], *s.* **1.** soprascritta; iscrizione **2.** intestazione.

to **supersede** [ˌsjuːpəˈsiːd], *v.t.* **1.** rimpiazzare, sostituire; prendere il posto di: *a more liberal generation was superseding the old ruling class*, una generazione più liberale prendeva il posto della vecchia classe dirigente; *tractors — horses*, i trattori rimpiazzano i cavalli; *to — an official*, sostituire un funzionario **2.** (*arc.*) desistere da, astenersi da.

supersedeas [ˌsjuːpəˈsiːdiæs], *s.* (*dir.*) ordine di sospendere un procedimento legale.

supersensitive [ˌsjuːpəˈsensitiv], *ag.* ipersensibile; di una sensibilità morbosa.

supersensitiveness [ˌsjuːpəˈsensitivnis], *s.* ipersensibilità; sensibilità morbosa.

supersensual [ˌsjuːpəˈsensjuəl], *ag.* soprasensibile, spirituale.

supersession [ˌsjuːpəˈseʃən], *s.* **1.** sostituzione **2.** sospensione.

supersolar [ˌsjuːpəˈsoulə*], *ag.* che sta al disopra del sole.

supersonic [ˈsjuːpəˈsonik], *ag.* **1.** ultrasonoro **2.** (*aer.*) supersonico ☆ *— flight*, volo supersonico; *— plane*, aereo supersonico; *— speed*, velocità supersonica.

superstition [ˌsjuːpəˈstiʃən], *s.* superstizione.

superstitious [ˌsjuːpəˈstiʃəs], *ag.* superstizioso.

superstitiously [ˌsjuːpəˈstiʃəsli], *av.* superstiziosamente.

superstratum [ˈsjuːpəˈstrɑːtəm], *pl.* **superstrata** ˌsjuːpəˈstrɑːtə], *s.* (*geol.*) strato superiore.

superstructure [ˈsjuːpəˌstrʌktʃə*], *s.* **1.** sovrastruttura **2.** (*ferr.*) armamento.

supertax [ˈsjuːpətæks], *s.* soprattassa; imposta supplementare.

superterrestrial [ˌsjuːpətiˈrestriəl], *ag.* **1.** sulla crosta terrestre **2.** ultraterreno.

to **supervene** [ˌsjuːpəˈviːn], *v.i.* sopraggiungere; sopravvenire: *should death —...*, se dovesse sopraggiungere la morte....

supervenient [ˌsjuːpəˈviːnjənt], *ag.* sopravveniente.

supervention [ˌsjuːpəˈvenʃən], *s.* sopravvenienza.

to **supervise** [ˈsjuːpəvaiz], *v.t.* sovrintendere a; sorvegliare ☆ *supervising action*, azione di sorveglianza.

supervision [ˌsjuːpəˈviʒən], *s.* **1.** sorveglianza: *to be under police —*, essere sorvegliato dalla polizia **2.** sovrintendenza.

supervisor [ˈsjuːpəˌvaizə*], *s.* **1.** sovrintendente;

ispettore; sorvegliante **2.** (*amer.*) funzionario amministrativo.

supervisory [ˈsjuːpəvaizəri], *ag.* di sorveglianza, di controllo.

supervolute [ˌsjuːpəvəˈljuːt], *ag.* (*bot.*) convoluto.

to **supinate** [ˈsjuːpineit], *v.t.* volgere all'insù (la mano, il palmo della mano).

supination [ˌsjuːpiˈneiʃən], *s.* supinazione.

supine [sjuːˈpain], *come s.* [ˈsjuːpain], *ag.* **1.** supino, sdraiato **2.** passivo, indifferente; indolente ‖ *s.* (*gram. lat.*) supino.

supinely [sjuːˈpainli], *av.* supinamente.

supineness [sjuːˈpainnis], *s.* **1.** posizione supina **2.** inerzia; passività.

supper [ˈsʌpə*], *s.* cena: *to have —*, cenare ‖ *the Last Supper*, l'ultima Cena ‖ *the Lord's Supper*, l'Eucarestia ☆ *— -party*, cena (con invitati): *to have a — -party*, dare una cena; *— -time*, ora di cena.

to **supper**, *v.t.i.* **1.** cenare **2.** invitare a cena.

supperless [ˈsʌpəlis], *ag.* senza cena.

to **supplant** [səˈplɑːnt], *v.t.* soppiantare; dare lo sgambetto a; prendere il posto di, rimpiazzare.

supplantation [ˌsʌplænˈteiʃən], *s.* soppiantamento.

supplanter [səˈplɑːntə*], *s.c.* soppiantatore, soppiantatrice.

supple [ˈsʌpl], *ag.* **1.** pieghevole, flessibile **2.** agile, elastico (anche *fig.*) **3.** *fig.* docile, arrendevole, compiacente ☆ *— jack*, liana; bastone flessibile; (*amer.*) marionetta.

to **supple**, *v.t.i.* rendere, divenire flessibile, pieghevole, docile: *to — a horse*, rendere docile un cavallo.

supplement [ˈsʌplimənt], *s.* supplemento, appendice: *literary —*, supplemento letterario (di un giornale).

to **supplement** [ˈsʌpliment], *v.t.* fare aggiunte a, completare, integrare: *to — one's income by private lessons*, arrotondare i propri guadagni con lezioni private.

supplemental [ˌsʌpliˈmentl], *ag.* supplementare.

supplementally [ˌsʌpliˈmentəli], *av.* in modo supplementare.

supplementarily [ˌsʌpliˈmentərili], *av.* suppletivamente.

supplementary [ˌsʌpliˈmentəri], *ag.* supplementare.

supplementation [ˌsʌplimənˈteiʃən], *s.* integrazione, aggiunta.

suppleness [ˈsʌplnis], *s.* **1.** flessibilità **2.** agilità, elasticità (anche *fig.*) **3.** compiacenza, arrendevolezza.

suppletive [səˈpliːtiv], *ag.* suppletivo.

suppliant [ˈsʌpliənt], *ag.* supplichevole ‖ *s.c.* supplicante, chi implora.

suppliantly [ˈsʌpliəntli], *av.* supplichevolmente.

to **supplicate** [ˈsʌplikeit], *v.t.i.* **1.** supplicare, implorare: *to — s.o. for sthg., to do sthg.*, supplicare, implorare qlcu. per ql.co., di fare ql.co. **2.** presentare una petizione (nell'università di Oxford).

supplicatingly [ˈsʌplikeitiŋli], *av.* supplichevolmente.

supplication [ˌsʌpliˈkeiʃən], *s.* **1.** supplica **2.** petizione (nell'università di Oxford).

supplicatory [ˈsʌplikətəri], *ag.* supplicatorio.

supplier [səˈplaiə*], *s.c.* fornitore, fornitrice.

supply [səˈplai], *av.s.* **1.** rifornimento, approvvigionamento, fornitura; provvista, scorta: *fresh —*, rinforz (di truppe, ecc.); *that shop has a large — of hats*, que negozio ha una grande scelta di cappelli; *to take (o t lay) in a — of sthg.*, fare provvista di ql.co. **2.** (*comm.*) fornitura; offerta: *equilibrium between demand and —* equilibrio tra domanda e offerta; *free play of demand an —*, domanda e offerta in regime di concorrenza **3.** *pl* (*mil.*) approvvigionamenti: *to cut off the enemy's sup plies*, tagliare i viveri al nemico **4.** *pl.* (*pol.*) sussid fondi **5.** sostituto: *to arrange for a —*, farsi supplir ☆ *— -main*, (*elett.*) cavo di distribuzione; *— -powe* forza motrice; *— -reel*, bobina alimentatrice ‖ *ammu nition —*, (*mil.*) rifornimento di munizioni; *food —* vettovaglie.

to **supply**, *v.t.i.* **1.** fornire, provvedere, rifornir

I shall — him with equipment, gli fornirò l'equipaggiamento; *river that supplies an electric power station*, fiume che alimenta una centrale elettrica; *this supplies proof*, ciò fornisce la prova **2.** supplire a; soddisfare: *to — the demand*, (comm.) soddisfare la richiesta di merci; *to — s.o.'s needs*, soddisfare i bisogni di qlcu. **3.** supplire, fare supplenza: *to — for s.o.*, tenere una supplenza; *to — s.o.'s place*, occupare il posto di qlcu.

support [sə'pɔ:t], *s.* **1.** sostegno, appoggio: *moral —*, sostegno morale; *she is the — of her family*, è il sostegno della sua famiglia; *to give — to a roof*, puntellare un tetto **2.** aiuto; assistenza: *troops in —*, truppe di rinforzo; *they found a sure — in religion*, trovarono un conforto sicuro nella religione; *to get* (o *to obtain*) *—*, ottenere un aiuto ‖ *in — of*, in favore di **3.** mantenimento, sostentamento: *to be without means of —*, essere senza mezzi di sostentamento **4.** (*tec. mec.*) supporto; sostegno; sella (di caldaia); mensola; (*arch.*) sostegno (di una volta, ecc.).

to **support**, *v.t.* **1.** sostenere, reggere: *I supported him with my arm*, lo sostenevo col braccio; *pillars — the roof*, i pilastri sostengono il tetto **2.** sostenere, dare appoggio a, incoraggiare: *evidence supporting a charge*, prove che sostengono un'accusa; *his conscience supports him*, lo sostiene la sua coscienza; *theory supported by experience*, teoria convalidata dall'esperienza; *to — the leading actor*, fare da spalla al primo attore; *to — the motion*, appoggiare la mozione **3.** mantenere: *charity supported by voluntary contributions*, istituzione benefica che si regge su contributi volontari; *the first duty of a father is to — his children*, il primo dovere di un padre è di mantenere i propri figli **4.** tollerare; sopportare: *he could not — such insolence*, egli non potè tollerare tale insolenza **5.** (*teat.*) sostenere (una parte, un ruolo) adeguatamente **6.** (*mil.*) rincalzare; mandar rinforzi a.

supportable [sə'pɔ:təbl], *ag.* **1.** sostenibile **2.** sopportabile, tollerabile.

supportably [sə'pɔ:təbli], *av.* tollerabilmente.

supporter [sə'pɔ:tə*], *s.* **1.** sostegno, appoggio **2.** fautore, partigiano, sostenitore **3.** (*arald.*) sostegno, supporto.

supporting [sə'pɔ:tiŋ], *ag.* di sostegno ‖ *s.* sostegno, rinforzo ☆ *— -beam*, trave portante; *— -block*, blocco di sostegno; *— -rib*, nervatura di rinforzo; *— -shoe*, supporto della fune; *— -structure*, ossatura, struttura portante; *— -wall*, muro di sostegno.

supportless [sə'pɔ:tlis], *ag.* senza appoggio, senza sostegno.

supposable [sə'pouzəbl], *ag.* supponibile.

to **suppose** [sə'pouz], *v.t.i.* **1.** supporre, fare l'ipotesi; immaginare: *— A B C an equilateral triangle*, supponiamo che A B C sia un triangolo equilatero; *— your sister came what would she say?*, se venisse tua sorella che direbbe?; *— we change the subject*, e se parlassimo d'altro?; *— we leave at once*, e se partissimo subito? **2.** presupporre: *creation supposes a creator*, la creazione presuppone un creatore **3.** presumere, credere, pensare: *I — he will be back in an hour*, penso che sarà di ritorno tra un'ora; *I — so*, lo penso; *I'm not supposed to do it*, non dovrei farlo; *she is supposed to be very wealthy*, la si ritiene molto ricca; *you are not supposed to answer such a question*, non sei tenuto a rispondere a una domanda del genere.

supposed [sə'pouzd], *ag.* presunto, supposto: *the — culprit*, il presunto colpevole.

supposedly [sə'pouzidli], *av.* per supposizione.

supposition [ˌsʌpə'ziʃən], *s.* supposizione, ipotesi, congettura: *unfounded —*, supposizione gratuita ‖ *on —*, per supposizione.

suppositional [ˌsʌpə'ziʃənl], *ag.* ipotetico, immaginario.

suppositionally [ˌsʌpə'ziʃnəli], *av.* ipoteticamente, per supposizione.

suppositious [ˌsʌpə'ziʃəs], *ag.* (*rar.*) ipotetico.

supposititious [sə,pɔzi'tiʃəs], *ag.* **1.** falso, spurio: *— works*, opere spurie **2.** ipotetico.

supposititiously [sə,pɔzi'tiʃəsli], *av.* **1.** falsamente **2.** per sostituzione.

supposititiousness [sə,pɔzi'tiʃəsnis], *s.* falsità, carattere spurio.

suppository [sə'pɔzitəri], *s.* (*farm.*) supposta.

to **suppress** [sə'pres], *v.t.* **1.** sopprimere, reprimere, sedare, far cessare: *to — a publication*, sopprimere una pubblicazione; *to — a revolt*, sedare una rivolta **2.** *fig.* soffocare, trattenere: *to — a yawn*, soffocare uno sbadiglio **3.** nascondere, tener nascosto: *to — a rumour*, non divulgare una diceria; *to — the truth*, tener nascosta la verità.

suppressible [sə'presəbl], *ag.* che può essere represso, soffocato, soppresso.

suppression [sə'preʃən], *s.* **1.** soppressione, repressione **2.** il mettere a tacere, il soffocare (uno scandalo, ecc.).

suppressive [sə'presiv], *ag.* repressivo.

suppressor [sə'presə*], *s.* **1.** repressore **2.** chi nasconde, soffoca (uno scandalo, ecc.).

to **suppurate** ['sʌpjuəreit], *v.i.* suppurare, venire a suppurazione.

suppuration [ˌsʌpjuə'reiʃən], *s.* suppurazione.

suppurative ['sʌpjurətiv], *ag.s.* suppurativo.

supramaxillary ['sju:prəmæk'siləri], *ag.s.* (osso) della mascella superiore.

supranatural ['sju:prə'nætʃrəl], *V.* **supernatural**.

supraorbital ['sju:prə'ɔ:bitl], *ag.* (*anat.*) sopraorbitale.

supraprotest ['sju:prə'proutest], *s.* (*comm.*) accettazione per intervento.

suprarenal ['sju:prə'ri:nl], *ag.* (*anat.*) surrenale.

supremacy [sju'preməsi], *s.* supremazia ‖ *Act of Supremacy*, Atto di Supremazia (legge del 1534 con cui venne riconosciuta alla Corona inglese la supremazia religiosa).

supreme [sju(:)'pri:m], *ag.* **1.** sommo, supremo: *to assume the — command*, assumere il comando supremo ‖ *the Supreme*, l'Altissimo ‖ *the Supreme Being*, l'Ente Supremo ‖ *the Supreme Court*, (*amer.*) la Corte Suprema; *the Supreme Court of Judicature*, la Corte suprema di Giustizia ‖ *the Supreme Pontiff*, il Sommo Pontefice **2.** supremo, massimo, eccelso: *— sacrifice*, sacrificio supremo; *it was their — hour of glory*, era la loro suprema ora di gloria; *to hold s.o. in — contempt*, avere il massimo disprezzo per qlcu.

supremely [sju(:)'pri:mli], *av.* supremamente.

sura[1] ['suərə], *s.* sura (capitolo del Corano).

sura[2] ['surɑ:], *s.* (*ang.-in.*) «sura» (bevanda alcoolica).

surah ['sjuərə], *s.* «surah» (stoffa di seta).

sural ['sjuərəl], *ag.* (*anat.*) surale.

Surat ['suərət], *no.pr.* (*geog.*) Surat ‖ **surat** [su'ræt], *s.* cotone, tessuto di cotone indiano.

surbase ['sə:beis], *s.* (*arch.*) modanatura, cornice di basamento.

surcease [sə:'si:s], *s.* (*arc.*) cessazione.

to **surcease**, *v.t.i.* (*arc.*) arrestare; cessare.

surcharge ['sə:tʃɑ:dʒ], *s.* **1.** sovraccarico **2.** sopratassa: *— on goods*, soprattassa sulla merce **3.** penalità **4.** soprapprezzo.

to **surcharge** [sə:'tʃɑ:dʒ], *v.t.* **1.** sovraccaricare: *the captain did not — his ship*, il capitano non sovraccaricò la sua nave **2.** tassare, multare con una soprattassa: *he was surcharged a big sum because his income-tax statement was inaccurate*, fu multato con una forte soprattassa perchè la sua dichiarazione di reddito era inesatta.

surcingle ['sə:siŋgl], *s.* **1.** sopraccinghia (della sella) **2.** cintura (di veste talare).

to **surcingle**, *v.t.* mettere la sopraccinghia a (un cavallo), legare con la sopraccinghia.

surcoat ['sə:-kout], *s.* sopravveste (nel medioevo).

surd [sə:d], *ag.* **1.** (*mat.*) irrazionale **2.** (*fonet.*) sordo ‖ *s.* **1.** (*mat.*) numero irrazionale **2.** (*fonet.*) consonante sorda.

sure [ʃuə*], *ag.* **1.** sicuro, certo; inevitabile: *don't be too* —, non essere troppo sicuro; *he is* — *he will come*, è sicuro di venire; *he is trying to avert a* — *disaster*, sta cercando di stornare un disastro inevitabile; *to be* — *of oneself, of sthg.*, essere sicuro di sè, di ql.co. ‖ *well, I'm* —!, davvero?! ‖ *to be* —, senza dubbio, d'accordo: *she was not very clever, to be* —, *but she was pretty*, non era molto intelligente, d'accordo, ma era graziosa ‖ *to be* — *to*, non mancare di: *be* — *to come tomorrow*, non mancare di venire domani; *he is* — *to fail*, è destinato a fallire ‖ *to make* —, essere sicuro, accertarsi; *to make* — *of*, procurarsi, assicurarsi: *I make* — *of a seat*, mi assicuro un posto **2.** fidato; attendibile; indubbio: *a* — *friend*, un amico fidato; *a* — *remedy*, un rimedio sicuro **3.** saldo, fermo: *a* — *belief*, una ferma certezza; *a* — *foundation*, una salda base ☆ — *-footed*, dal piede fermo; *fig.* che non fa passi falsi.

sure, *av.* **1.** (*fam. amer.*) certamente, sicuramente, davvero: *you* — *have a good accent*, hai davvero un buon accento ‖ — *enough*, certamente; effettivamente, in realtà ‖ *as* — *as a gun* (o *as* — *as eggs is eggs*), sicuro come due e due fanno quattro **2.** (*fam. amer.*) senz'altro: " *Are you coming?* ", " *Sure!* ", « Vieni? », « Senz'altro! » **3.** d'accordo: *it is pleasant*, —, *to see one's name in print*, è piacevole, d'accordo, vedere il proprio nome sui giornali.

surely [ʃuəli], *av.* **1.** sicuramente, certamente; senza dubbio (anche enfatico): — *we have met before*, senza dubbio ci siamo già incontrati; — *you don't believe that!*, non è possibile che tu lo creda!; *he will* — *come*, verrà certamente ‖ — *to goodness!*, (*fam.*) perbacco! **2.** con sicurezza; bene: *my pupil is learning English slowly but* —, il mio allievo sta imparando l'inglese lentamente, ma bene; *to plant one's feet* — *on the ground*, piantare bene i piedi per terra.

sureness [ʃuənis], *s.* sicurezza; certezza.

surety [ʃuəti], *s.* **1.** (*arc.*) certezza ‖ *of a* —, sicuramente, certamente **2.** garanzia; pegno ‖ *s.c.* garante: *to stand* (o *to go*) — *for s.o.*, farsi garante per qlcu.

suretyship [ʃuətiʃip], *s.* garanzia.

surf [sə:f], *s.* **1.** frangente; spuma dei marosi **2.** risacca ☆ — *-bathing*, bagni tra i frangenti; — *-boat*, barca piatta per navigare tra i frangenti; — *-duck*, (*ornit.*) orchetto dagli occhiali; — *-man*, uomo abile a navigare tra i frangenti; (*amer.*) marinaio guardacoste; — *-riding*, sport dell'acquaplano.

to surf, *v.i.* (*spor.*) praticare l'acquaplano.

surface [sə:fis], *s.* **1.** superficie (anche *fig.*): *Italy presents a very rugged* —, l'Italia presenta una superficie molto accidentata; *you only look at the* — *of things*, voi guardate soltanto l'apparenza delle cose ‖ *to break* —, ritornare in superficie (di sottomarino) **2.** (*geom.*) superficie; faccia: *the surface of a solid*, la superficie di un solido; *plane* —, superficie piana **3.** piano stradale ☆ — *-plate*, (*mec.*) piano di riscontro; — *-tension*, (*fis.*) tensione superficiale; — *-water*, acqua di scolo ‖ *bearing* —, (*mec.*) superficie portante; *sliding* —, (*mec.*) piano di scorrimento; *water* —, pelo dell'acqua.

to surface, *v.t.i.* **1.** (far) salire alla superficie (di sottomarino, ecc.) **2.** rifinire, spianare la superficie di.

surfeit [sə:fit], *s.* **1.** eccesso, sovrabbondanza: *there is a* — *of corn in the market*, c'è eccesso di grano sul mercato **2.** rimpinzamento; sazietà (anche *fig.*): *we have had a* — *of classical music recently*, ultimamente abbiamo sentito musica classica a sazietà; *to eat sthg. to* —, mangiare ql.co. fino alla sazietà.

to surfeit, *v.t.i.* rimpinzare, rimpinzarsi; saziare, saziarsi (anche *fig.*): *he surfeited the audience with words*, sommerse gli ascoltatori con un fiume di parole.

surfeiter [sə:fitə*], *s.c.* ghiottone, ghiottona.

surfy [sə:fi], *ag.* spumoso, spumeggiante.

surge [sə:dʒ], *s.* **1.** ondata, maroso, cavallone, flutto: *the* — *of the sea*, i flutti del mare **2.** *fig.* impeto: *a* — *of anger*, un impeto di collera **3.** (*elett.*) colpo di corrente, sovracorrente momentanea.

to surge, *v.t.i.* **1.** ondeggiare, fluttuare; agitarsi **2.** montare, sollevarsi (come un'ondata): *anger surged* (*up*) *within her*, montò in collera; *the blood surged to his cheeks*, il sangue gli affluì al viso **3.** (*mar.*) lascare; mollare, allentare (un argano, ecc.) **4.** girare a vuoto (di ruota).

surgeon [sə:dʒən], *s.* **1.** chirurgo **2.** (*mar. mil.*) medico ☆ — *-bird*, (*ornit.*) parra; — *-fish*, (*ittiol.*) acanturo ‖ *dental* —, medico dentista.

surgery [sə:dʒəri], *s.* **1.** chirurgia **2.** gabinetto medico; dispensario; (*amer.*) sala operatoria ☆ — *hours*, ore di consultazione ‖ *plastic* —, chirurgia plastica.

surgical [sə:dʒikəl], *ag.* chirurgico ☆ — *case*, caso chirurgico; borsa dei ferri chirurgici.

surgically [sə:dʒikəli], *av.* chirurgicamente.

surgy [sə:dʒi], *ag.* ondoso; agitato.

surlily [sə:lili], *av.* sgarbatamente, rudemente.

surliness [sə:linis], *s.* scontrosità, sgarberia; umor nero.

surloin [sə:lɔin], *s.* lombo di manzo.

surly [sə:li], *ag.* arcigno, burbero; sgarbato ‖ *he is as* — *as a bear*, è un orso fatto e finito.

surmise [sə:maiz], *s.* supposizione, congettura: *to be right in one's surmises*, aver indovinato.

to surmise [sə:ˈmaiz], *v.t.i.* supporre, congetturare; sospettare.

to surmount [sə:ˈmaunt], *v.t.* **1.** sormontare, coprire: *peaks surmounted with snow*, vette coperte di neve **2.** superare, vincere: *to* — *a difficulty*, superare una difficoltà.

surmountable [sə:ˈmauntəbl], *ag.* sormontabile, superabile.

surmountableness [sə:ˈmauntəblnis], *s.* superabilità.

surmullet [sʌˈmʌlit], *s.* (*ittiol.*) triglia.

surname [sə:neim], *s.* **1.** soprannome **2.** cognome.

to surname, *v.t.* **1.** soprannominare, chiamare per soprannome: *King Richard was surnamed Lion-heart*, re Riccardo fu soprannominato Cuor di Leone **2.** dare il cognome a: *he is surnamed Smith*, il suo cognome è Smith.

to surpass [sə:ˈpɑ:s], *v.t.* sorpassare, superare; vincere: *the result surpassed my expectations*, il risultato superò le mie aspettative; *you have surpassed yourself*, hai superato te stesso; *to* — *s.o. in intelligence*, superare qlcu. in intelligenza.

surpassable [sə:ˈpɑ:səbl], *ag.* superabile, sorpassabile.

surpassing [sə:ˈpɑ:siŋ], *ag.* superiore, eccellente, incomparabile: *she was of* — *kindness*, era di una gentilezza senza uguale ‖ *av. V.* **surpassingly**.

surpassingly [sə:ˈpɑ:siŋli], *av.* straordinariamente, incomparabilmente: — *beautiful*, straordinariamente bello.

surplice [sə:pləs], *s.* (*eccl.*) cotta ☆ — *-fees*, diritti di parrocchia.

surpliced [sə:pləst], *ag.* in cotta.

surplus [sə:pləs], *s.* **1.** sovrappiù, eccedenza, avanzo (anche *comm.*): — *of assets*, (*comm.*) residuo attivo; *the load just comes within the permissible* — *weight*, il carico è giusto nei limiti di eccedenza di peso tollerabile; *to have a* — *of sthg.*, avere ql.co. in sovrappiù **2.** residuati (di guerra) ☆ — *account*, (*comm.*) conto eccedenze; — *fund*, (*comm.*) fondo residui; — *population*, eccesso di popolazione; — *stock*, (*comm.*) rimanenze; (*mec.*) sovrametallo ‖ *budget* —, (*comm.*) eccedenza di bilancio; *earned* —, (*comm.*) utile netto.

surplusage [sə:pləsidʒ], *s.* eccedenza; superfluità.

surprisal [sə:ˈpraizəl], *s.* sorpresa.

surprise [sə:ˈpraiz], *s.* **1.** sorpresa: *the town was taken by* —, la città fu occupata di sorpresa; *to give s.o. a* —

fare una sorpresa a qlcu.; *to take s.o. by* —, sorprendere qlcu. **2.** sorpresa, stupore, meraviglia: *much to my* — (o *to my great* —), con mia grande meraviglia; *I watched them in* —, meravigliato li guardai; *they started up in* —, sobbalzarono per lo stupore ☆ — *attack*, attacco di sorpresa; — *party*, ricevimento a sorpresa; — *visit*, visita inaspettata.

to **surprise**, *v.t.* **1.** sorprendere, cogliere all'improvviso: *she was surprised in the act of reading the letter she had found*, fu colta in flagrante mentre leggeva la lettera che aveva trovato **2.** sorprendere, stupire: *I am surprised at you!*, mi stupisco di te!; *I should not be surprised if...*, non mi stupirei se, che...; *she is not surprised at it*, ciò non la sorprende.

surprisedly [sə'praizidli], *av.* con sorpresa.

surprising [sə'praiziŋ], *ag.* sorprendente: *their energy is* —, la loro energia è sorprendente.

surprisingly [sə'praiziŋli], *av.* sorprendentemente; in modo straordinario.

surra ['suərə], *s.* (*vet.*) forma di anemia del bestiame nei paesi tropicali.

surrealism [sə'riəlizəm], *s.* (*st. art.*) surrealismo.

surrealist [sə'riəlist], *ag.s.* surrealista.

to **surrebut** [‚sʌri'bʌt], *pass.p.p.* **surrebutted** [‚sʌri'bʌtid], to **surrejoin** [‚sʌri'dʒɔin], *v.i.* (*dir.*) ribattere le argomentazioni della difesa (dopo che questa ha ribattuto a sua volta).

surrebutter [‚sʌri'bʌtə*], **surrejoinder** [‚sʌri'dʒɔində*], *s.* (*dir.*) confutazione delle argomentazioni della difesa.

surrender [sə'rendə*], *s.* **1.** (*mil.*) resa, capitolazione **2.** abbandono, cessione, consegna ‖ *to make a* — *of principle(s)*, (*fam.*) abdicare ai propri principi ☆ — *value*, (*comm.*) riscatto (di polizza di assicurazione) ‖ *compulsory* —, espropriazione.

to **surrender**, *v.t.i.* **1.** cedere, consegnare, abbandonare; arrendersi: *they surrendered the fortress to the enemy*, essi abbandonarono la fortezza al nemico; *to* — *an insurance policy*, (*comm.*) cedere una polizza di assicurazione; *to* — *oneself to justice*, consegnarsi alla giustizia **2.** *fig.* abbandonare, rinunciare a, arrendersi: *he surrendered all hope*, abbandonò ogni speranza; *I* —, mi do per vinto; *to* — *oneself to grief*, abbandonarsi al dolore.

surrenderer [sə'rendərə*], *s.c.* chi si arrende, chi cede.

surreptitious [‚sʌrəp'tiʃəs], *ag.* **1.** clandestino, furtivo, segreto: — *edition*, edizione clandestina (non autorizzata dall'autore) **2.** spurio: — *writing*, scritto spurio.

surreptitiously [‚sʌrəp'tiʃəsli], *av.* furtivamente.

surrey ['sʌri], *s.* (*amer.*) vettura leggera a quattro ruote e due posti.

surrogate ['sʌrəgit], *s.* **1.** sostituto; delegato (specialmente di vescovo o suo cancelliere) **2.** (*amer.*) giudice incaricato di omologare testamenti.

surrogateship ['sʌrəgitʃip], *s.* carica di sostituto.

surround [sə'raund], *s.* bordura, bordo.

to **surround**, *v.t.* **1.** circondare, cingere, attorniare: *a crowd surrounded him*, una folla lo circondò; *a moat surrounds the castle*, un fossato cinge il castello; *surrounded by* (o *with*) *dangers*, circondato da pericoli; *to* — *a garden with a wall*, cingere un giardino con un muro **2.** (*mil.*) accerchiare, assediare.

surrounding [sə'raundiŋ], *ag.* circostante, vicino: *the* — *plain*, la pianura circostante.

surroundings [sə'raundiŋz], *s.pl.* **1.** dintorni: *this town has interesting* —, questa città ha dei dintorni interessanti **2.** ambiente, condizioni ambientali (anche *fig.*): *unhealthy* —, ambiente malsano; *to live amid religious* —, vivere in ambiente religioso.

surtax ['sə:tæks], *s.* soprattassa; imposta complementare.

to **surtax** [sə:'tæks], *v.t.* imporre una soprattassa a.

surtout ['sə:tu:], *s.* (*rar.*) soprabito (da uomo).

surveillance [sə:'veiləns], *s.* sorveglianza; ispezione.

surveillant [sə:'veilənt], *ag.s.c.* sorvegliante.

survey ['sə:vei], *s.* **1.** esame, indagine; sguardo generale: *a* — *course of modern history*, un corso generale di storia moderna; *the lecturer will give a* — *of the subject*, il conferenziere esporrà un quadro generale della materia; *to make a* —, fare una perizia; *to take a* — *of*, esaminare (una questione) **2.** rapporto; perizia, valutazione; studio ufficiale: *a war-time social* —, indagine sistematica sulle condizioni sociali in tempo di guerra **3.** misurazioni topografiche, rilievo topografico ☆ — *map*, mappa catastale ‖ *poverty* —, indagini sistematiche sulla povertà.

to **survey** [sə:'vei], *v.t.i.* **1.** esaminare, ispezionare **2.** contemplare; guardare: *to* — *the landscape from the top of a hill*, contemplare il paesaggio dalla cima di una collina **3.** compiere uno studio generale su; preparare un rapporto su; fare una perizia di: *to* — *the situation in the Middle East*, esaminare la situazione nel Medio Oriente **4.** misurare, rilevare; fare rilevazioni.

surveying [sə:'veiiŋ], *s.* **1.** ispezione, esame; sorveglianza **2.** misurazione topografica **3.** agrimensura.

surveyor [sə(:)'veiə*], *s.* **1.** ispettore; sovraintendente; (*amer.*) doganiere: — *of roads*, ispettore stradale; — *of weights and measures*, controllore dei pesi e delle misure **2.** agrimensore; topografo ☆ *land-* —, geometra.

surveyorship [sə(:)'veiəʃip], *s.* ispettorato; carica di sorvegliante.

survival [sə'vaivəl], *s.* **1.** sopravvivenza ‖ *the* — *of the fittest*, la sopravvivenza del più adatto **2.** avanzo, reliquia: *a* — *of times past*, un vestigio di tempi andati; *the few survivals of this type of verse*, i pochi esempi rimasti di questo genere poetico ☆ — *rate*, percentuale di sopravvivenza.

to **survive** [sə'vaiv], *v.t.i.* **1.** sopravvivere, vivere più a lungo di: *he will* — *his son*, vivrà più a lungo di suo figlio; *he will* — *us all*, ci seppellirà tutti; *to* — *a disease, a shipwreck*, sopravvivere a una malattia, ad un naufragio **2.** (*dir.*) passare: *the estate survived to a distant relation*, il patrimonio passò ad un lontano parente.

survivor [sə'vaivə*], *s.c.* superstite.

survivorship [sə'vaivəʃip], *s.* sopravvivenza.

Susan ['su:zn], *no.pr.f.* Susanna.

susceptibility [sə‚septə'biliti], *s.* **1.** *gener. pl.* suscettibilità: *they have their susceptibilities*, hanno le loro suscettibilità **2.** sensibilità **3.** predisposizione: — *to a disease*, predisposizione a una malattia.

susceptible [sə'septəbl], *ag.* **1.** suscettibile: *subject* — *of being enlarged upon*, argomento che può venire approfondito; *this letter is* — *of a different interpretation*, questa lettera è suscettibile di diversa interpretazione **2.** sensibile; impressionabile: — *to cold*, sensibile al freddo, freddoloso; *she is very* — *to kindness*, ella è molto sensibile alla gentilezza **3.** permaloso: *a very* — *child*, un bimbo molto permaloso **4.** soggetto, predisposto: — *to bronchitis*, soggetto a bronchiti.

susceptibly [sə'septəbli], *av.* suscettibilmente.

susceptive [sə'septiv], *ag.* suscettivo.

susceptiveness [sə'septivnis], *s.* suscettibilità.

to **suscitate** ['sʌsiteit], *v.t.* agitare; eccitare.

susi ['su:si], *s.* cotonata fine a righe di seta.

suspect ['sʌspekt], *ag.* sospetto: *to hold s.o.* —, sospettare di qlcu.; *your statement is* —, la vostra dichiarazione è sospetta ‖ *s.* persona sospetta: *political suspects*, persone politicamente sospette; *the authorities detained all small-pox suspects*, le autorità trattennero tutti i casi sospetti di vaiuolo.

to **suspect** [səs'pekt], *v.t.i.* **1.** aver l'impressione che: *I suspected the presence of fire from the odour*, dall'odore avevo l'impressione che ci fosse del fuoco **2.** sospettare di, essere sospettoso; dubitare: *I strongly* — *the authenticity of that document*, dubito molto dell'autenticità di quel documento; *they suspect-*

ed him of stealing, of murder, lo sospettavano di furto, di assassinio.

suspectable [səs'pektəbl], *ag.* sospettabile

suspectedly [səs'pektidli], *av.* in modo sospetto.

suspectless [səs'pektlis], *ag.* insospettabile.

to **suspend** [səs'pend], *v.t.* **1.** appendere, tenere sospeso: *look at the red balloon suspended in the air*, guarda il pallone rosso sospeso in aria **2.** sospendere; posporre, differire: *to — a licence*, ritirare una licenza (patente, ecc.); *to — a newspaper*, sospendere la pubblicazione di un giornale; *to — payments*, *(comm.)* sospendere i pagamenti; *to — proceedings*, *(dir.)* sospendere un'azione legale; *to — a sentence of death*, differire l'esecuzione di una sentenza capitale **3.** sospendere; licenziare: *to — a professor*, sospendere un professore universitario.

suspender [səs'pendə*], *s.* **1.** giarrettiera **2.** *pl.* *(amer.)* bretelle.

suspense [səs'pens], *s.* **1.** sospensione d'animo; indecisione, incertezza; attesa ansiosa: *to keep* (o *to hold*) *s.o. in —*, tener qlcu. nell'incertezza **2.** *(dir.)* sospensione ☆ *— account*, *(comm.)* conto in sospeso.

suspensible [səs'pensəbl], *ag.* *(rar.)* che si può lasciare in sospeso.

suspension [səs'penʃən], *s.* **1.** sospensione, interruzione, dilazione: *a — of arms* (o *of hostilities*), armistizio; *a — of payment*, sospensione di pagamento; *points of —*, *(gram.)* puntini di sospensione **2.** sospensione temporanea (di funzionario, pubblicazione, ecc.): *— of a licence*, ritiro temporaneo di una licenza (patente, ecc.) **3.** *(mec.)* sospensione: *a cardanic —*, una sospensione cardanica; *points of —*, punti di sospensione **4.** *(chim.)* sospensione ☆ *— band*, *(aer.)* gualdrappa; *— -bridge*, ponte sospeso; *— cable*, *(mec.)* cavo di sospensione; *— -chain*, *(mec.)* catena di sospensione || *front —*, *(aut.)* sospensione anteriore; molleggio anteriore.

suspensive [səs'pensiv], *ag.* **1.** sospensivo: *a — veto*, un veto sospensivo **2.** dubbioso, incerto.

suspensively [səs'pensivli], *av.* dubbiosamente.

suspensor [səs'pensə*], *s.* bendaggio a sospensorio.

suspensorial [ˌsʌspen'sɔːriəl], *ag.* *(anat.)* sospensorio.

suspensory [səs'pensəri], *ag.* *(anat.)* sospensorio: *a — muscle*, un muscolo sospensorio || *s.* *(anat.)* sospensorio.

suspicion [səs'piʃən], *s.* **1.** sospetto, dubbio: *with —*, con diffidenza; *he was right in his suspicions*, i suoi sospetti erano fondati; *I had my suspicions about it*, lo dubitavo; *my — is that...*, ho il sospetto che...; *she is above —*, è al di sopra di ogni sospetto; *to arouse* (o *to awaken*) *s.o.'s —*, destare sospetto in qlcu.; *to arrest* (o *to detain*) *s.o. on —*, *(dir.)* arrestare, trattenere qlcu. come sospetto; *to cast — on s.o.'s good faith*, sospettare della lealtà di qlcu.; *to have suspicions about s.o.* (o *to attach suspicions to s.o.*), sospettare di qlcu.; *to hold s.o. in —*, diffidare di qlcu.; *to lull —*, far tacere i sospetti **2.** piccolissima quantità, pizzico: *a — of a smile*, un accenno di sorriso; *just a — of vanilla*, un pizzico di vaniglia; *he detected a — of irony in her voice*, notò una traccia di ironia nella sua voce.

suspicionless [səs'piʃənlis], *ag.* senza sospetti.

suspicious [səs'piʃəs], *ag.* **1.** sospettoso, diffidente: *a — look*, uno sguardo diffidente; *public opinion is — with regard to...*, l'opinione pubblica è sospettosa nei riguardi di... **2.** sospetto, losco, ambiguo: *— actions*, azioni sospette; *— character*, losco figuro; *to look —*, avere un aspetto losco.

suspiciously [səs'piʃəsli], *av.* **1.** sospettosamente **2.** sospettamente.

suspiciousness [səs'piʃəsnis], *s.* **1.** diffidenza, carattere sospettoso **2.** natura sospetta.

suspiration [ˌsʌspi'reiʃən], *s.* *(poet.)* sospiro.

to **suspire** [səs'paiə*], *v.i.* *(poet.)* sospirare.

to **sustain** [səs'tein], *v.t.* **1.** mantenere, provvedere

a: *enough provisions to — the whole household*, provviste sufficienti per tutti i familiari e i dipendenti **2.** sostenere, prolungare: *a sustained effort carried us through*, con uno sforzo prolungato ne venimmo a capo; *to — a note*, *(mus.)* sostenere una nota **3.** reggere, sopportare, sostenere: *pillars — the balcony*, dei pilastri sostengono il balcone; *to — comparison with sthg.*, reggere al confronto con ql.co. **4.** sorreggere, incoraggiare: *faith sustained them*, la fede li sostenva **5.** subire; soffrire: *to — a loss*, subire una perdita **6.** appoggiare, confermare, convalidare: *the court sustained his claim*, il tribunale confermò i suoi diritti.

sustainable [səs'teinəbl], *ag.* sostenibile: *a — opinion*, un'opinione sostenibile.

sustainer [səs'teinə*], *s.c.* sostenitore, sostenitrice.

sustenance ['sʌstinəns], *s.* **1.** mezzi di sussistenza **2.** vitto, sostentamento; mantenimento (anche *fig.*): *hope was their —*, si nutrivano di speranza.

sustentation [ˌsʌsten'teiʃən], *s.* *(rar.)* sostentamento ☆ *— fund*, fondo di soccorso per il clero presbiteriano.

sutler ['sʌtlə*], *s.* vivandiere; cantiniere.

sutlery ['sʌtləri], *s.* **1.** mestiere di vivandiere, di cantiniere **2.** bettolino.

sutra ['suːtrə], *s.* raccolta di aforismi dalla letteratura sanscrita.

suttee ['sʌti(ː)], *s.* **1.** vedova indiana che s'immola sul rogo del marito **2.** il sacrificio della vedova indiana sul rogo del marito.

suttle ['sʌtl], *ag.* *(comm.)* netto ☆ *— weight*, peso netto.

sutural ['sjuːtjurəl], *ag.* *(chir. anat.)* suturale.

suturation [ˌsjuːtju'reiʃən], *s.* *(chir.)* cucitura, sutura.

suture ['sjuːtjuə*], *s.* **1.** *(anat.)* sutura, sinartrosi fissa **2.** *(chir.)* sutura **3.** materiale usato per le suture.

to **suture**, *v.t.* *(chir.)* suturare.

suzerain ['suːzərein], *s.* **1.** sovrano feudatario **2.** sovrano, stato avente diritto di sovranità su un altro stato.

suzerainty ['suːzəreinti], *s.* sovranità.

svelte [svelt], *ag.* snello, sottile; agile.

swab [swɔb], *s.* **1.** strofinaccio; *(mar.)* radazza **2.** *(med.)* tampone, zaffo **3.** campione (di sangue, muco, ecc.) prelevato per esame batteriologico **4.** *(sl. mar.)* persona maldestra **5.** *(sl. mar.)* spallina da ufficiale; ufficiale.

to **swab**, *pass.p.p.* **swabbed** [swɔbd], *v.t.* **1.** passare lo strofinaccio su; *(mar.)* radazzare: *the sailor is swabbing the deck*, il marinaio sta radazzando il ponte **2.** *to — up*, detergere; spugnare.

swabber ['swɔbə*], *s.* *(mar.)* mozzo; marinaio maldestro.

Swabia ['sweibjə], *no.pr.* *(geog. st.)* Svevia.

Swabian ['sweibjən], *ag.* svevo || *s.c.* svevo, sveva || *s.* dialetto svevo.

to **swaddle** ['swɔdl], *v.t.* fasciare (un bambino); bendare.

swaddling ['swɔdliŋ], *s.* fasciatura: ☆ *— -clothes* (o *— -bands*), fasce per bambini; *fig.* restrizioni, impedimenti: *science is still in its — -clothes*, *fig.* la scienza è ancora in fasce, ai primordi.

swag [swæg], *s.* **1.** movimento ondeggiante **2.** *(arch.)* festone **3.** *(sl.)* bottino ladresco; guadagni illegali **4.** fagotto di minatore, di vagabondo (in Australia) ☆ *— -bellied*, panciuto.

swage [sweidʒ], *s.* **1.** *(metal.)* stampo (da fabbro) **2.** *(artig.)* bordatura, modanatura ☆ *— -block*, *(metal.)* chiodaia.

to **swage**, *v.t.* *(metal.)* forgiare entro stampo.

swagger ['swægə*], *ag.* **1.** vistoso; sgargiante **2.** elegante || *s.* fanfaronata; boria; spavalderia; andatura spavalda: *to walk with a —*, pavoneggiarsi, fare la ruota ☆ *— -stick* (o *— cane*), frustino da ufficiale.

to **swagger**, *v.t.i.* **1.** muoversi, camminare con sussiego; pavoneggiarsi **2.** vantarsi, gloriarsi; fare lo spavaldo: *he swaggers about his relations*, egli si vanta della sua parentela ‖ *to — s.o. into doing sthg.*, costringere con prepotenza qlcu. a fare ql.co.

swaggerer ['swægərə*], *s.c.* persona vanagloriosa, spavalda.

swaggering ['swægəriŋ], *ag.* spavaldo, vanaglorioso.

swaggeringly ['swægəriŋli], *av.* spavaldamente.

swain [swein], *s.* 1. contadinotto, villico 2. (*poet.*) pastore innamorato; (*scherz.*) innamorato, corteggiatore.

swale[1] [sweil], *s.* (*spec. amer.*) buca, depressione (specialmente di luogo paludoso).

to swale[2], *v.t.i.* (*sl.*) 1. bruciare, dar fuoco a (sterpi, erbacce, ecc.) 2. bruciarsi, bruciacchiarsi, scottarsi 3. sciogliersi (di candela).

swallet ['swɔlit], *s.* (*dial.*) 1. corso d'acqua sotterraneo 2. pozzo naturale; buca (in cui sprofonda un corso d'acqua).

swallow[1] ['swɔlou], *s.* rondine; rondone ‖ *one — does not make a summer*, *prov.* una rondine non fa primavera ☆ *— -dive*, tuffo a rondine; *— -tail* (o *— -tailed coat*), frac, marsina; *— -tailed*, a coda di rondine; *— -wort*, (*bot.*) vincetossico.

swallow[2], *s.* 1. pozzo naturale, baratro, abisso 2. gola, faringe, esofago 3. deglutizione; capacità d'inghiottire 4. appetito, voracità (anche *fig.*) 5. boccone; sorso 6. (*mar.*) scanalatura.

to swallow[2], *v.t.i.* 1. inghiottire, deglutire, ingoiare: *he swallowed a pill* (*down*), egli inghiottì una pillola ‖ *to — the bait*, *fig.* abboccare, lasciarsi prendere all'amo 2. *fig.* inghiottire, assorbire; esaurire; divorare: *the earth swallowed the rain* (*up*), la terra assorbì la pioggia; *he swallowed the whole book in one evening*, divorò il libro in una sola sera; *her expenses swallowed up my earnings*, le sue spese esaurirono i miei guadagni; *the sea swallowed the wreck*, il mare inghiottì il relitto 3. accettare, credere facilmente: *that's hard to —*, questa è dura da mandar giù 4. sopportare, subire: *he had to — their ill-usage*, dovette sopportare i loro maltrattamenti 5. ritrattare: *I hope you won't — your words*, spero che non ritratterai quanto hai detto 6. soffocare, reprimere: *to — laughter, tears*, trattenere il riso, le lacrime.

swallower ['swɔlouə*], *s.c.* 1. chi inghiotte 2. credulone, credulona.

swam [swæm], *pass.* di to **swim**.

swamp [swɔmp], *s.* palude; acquitrino, pantano ☆ *— -fever*, febbre malarica.

to swamp, *v.t.i.* 1. inondare; sommergere, essere sommerso (anche *fig.*): *men swamped in debts*, uomini che affogano nei debiti; *I am swamped with too many letters*, sono sommersa da una valanga di lettere; *the waves swamped their boat*, le onde sommersero la loro barca 2. mandare in rovina, schiacciare: *he was swamped by mortgages*, fu rovinato dalle ipoteche.

swampy ['swɔmpi], *ag.* paludoso, acquitrinoso.

swan [swɔn], *s.* 1. cigno ‖ *the Swan*, (*astr.*) il Cigno ‖ *black —*, *fig.* mosca bianca ‖ *to think one's geese all swans*, valutare troppo ciò che si possiede 2. poeta, cantore ‖ *the Swan of Avon*, il Cigno dell'Avon (Shakespeare) ☆ *— -neck*, (*mec.*) collo d'oca; *— -quill*, penna di cigno; *— -shot*, (*caccia*) pallettoni; *— -song*, *fig.* canto del cigno; *— -upping*, spedizione annuale (sul Tamigi) per contrassegnare i giovani cigni di proprietà della Corona inglese ‖ *mute —* (o *domestic —*), cigno domestico.

swang [swæŋ], *pass.* (*rar.*) di to **swing**.

swank [swæŋk], *ag.* 1. (*scoz.*) vivace, attivo; snello, agile, flessibile 2. (*sl.*) di eleganza vistosa ‖ *s.* (*sl.*) pretenziosità; eleganza vistosa; ostentazione, boria.

to swank, *v.i.* darsi delle arie.

swankily ['swæŋkili], *av.* con eleganza vistosa.

swankiness ['swæŋkinis]. *s.* eleganza vistosa.

swanky ['swæŋki], *ag.* 1. borioso 2. *V.* **swank** 2.

swannery ['swɔnəri], *s.* allevamento di cigni.

swap [swɔp], *s.* (*fam.*) scambio, baratto.

to swap, *V.* to **swop**.

Swaraj [swə'rɑːdʒ], *s.* (*st.*) governo autonomo richiesto dai nazionalisti indiani.

sward [swɔːd], *s.* zolla erbosa; terreno erboso.

to sward, *v.t.* piotare, ricoprire con zolle erbose.

swardy ['swɔːdi], *ag.* ricoperto d'erba; erboso.

sware [swɛə*], *pass.* (*arc.*) di to **swear**.

swarm[1] [swɔːm], *s.* sciame; folla, frotta: *a — of children*, uno sciame di bambini ☆ *— -cell* (o *— -spore*), (*biol.*) zoospora.

to swarm[1], *v.t.i.* 1. sciamare; muoversi in frotte 2. affollare, affollarsi; pullulare, brulicare: *the audience swarmed the theatre*, il pubblico affollò il teatro; *the crowd swarmed over the foot-ball ground*, la folla irruppe nel campo da foot-ball; *the place was swarming with soldiers*, il luogo era brulicante di soldati.

to swarm[2], *v.t.i.* arrampicarsi: *to — (up) a pole*, arrampicarsi su di un palo.

swart [swɔːt], **swarth** [swɔːθ], *ag.* (*arc.*) 1. bruno, scuro (di carnagione) 2. *fig.* fosco; maligno.

swarthily ['swɔːðili], *av.* con tinta scura.

swarthiness ['swɔːðinis], *s.* carnagione, colore scuro.

swarthy ['swɔːði], *ag.* dalla carnagione scura; scuro; bruno.

swash[1] [swɔʃ], *ag.* 1. che colpisce con forza 2. (*dial.*) sfarzoso, appariscente.

swash[1], *s.* 1. massa d'acqua che si frange contro ostacoli; risacca; sciabordio 2. rumore di acqua agitata 3. (*amer.*) canale che attraversa un banco di sabbia, canale che scorre fra il banco e la riva 4. pesante colpo 5. smargiasso, fanfarone 6. spacconata 7. risciacquatura di piatti (che si dà ai maiali).

to swash[1], *v.t.i.* 1. schizzare (acqua); sguazzare: *he was swashing in the bath*, sguazzava nel bagno 2. battere rumorosamente, infrangersi (di acqua): *a heavy rain swashed against the window*, una fitta pioggia scrosciava contro la finestra 3. far rumore con la spada; *fig.* fare il fanfarone 4. (*arc.*) colpire violentemente.

swash[2], *ag.* obliquo ☆ *— letters*, (*tip.*) lettere ornate del corsivo; *— plate*, (*mec.*) disco inclinato.

swashbuckler ['swɔʃˌbʌklə*], *s.* fanfarone, rodomonte.

swashbuckling ['swɔʃˌbʌkliŋ], *ag.* borioso, spavaldo.

swashing ['swɔʃiŋ], *ag.* 1. borioso, spavaldo 2. violento.

swashy ['swɔʃi], *ag.* acquoso; melmoso.

swastika ['swæstikə], *s.* svastica, croce uncinata.

to swat [swɔt], *pass.p.p.* **swatted** ['swɔtid], *v.t.* (*amer.*) colpire, schiacciare d'un colpo (una mosca una zanzara, ecc.).

swatch[1] [swɔtʃ], *s.* (*scoz.*) campione (di stoffa); *fig.* campione, modello.

swatch[2], *s.* canale (tra due banchi di sabbia).

swath [swɔːθ], **swathe**[1] [sweið], *s.* 1. falciata; superficie lasciata libera da una sola falciata 2. erba, grano falciato (giacente sul terreno) 3. striscia, sezione longitudinale.

swathe[2], *s.* 1. benda, fascia 2. *fig.* impedimento, pastoia.

to swathe[2], *v.t.* fasciare, bendare; avvolgere (anche *fig.*).

sway [swei], *s.* 1. oscillazione 2. spinta 3. preponderanza; impero, dominio: *he held — over Europe*, era il signore d'Europa; *to bear* (o *to hold*) *— over a people*, esercitare potere su un popolo; *to have great — in the House*, avere grande influenza alla Camera.

to sway, *v.t.i.* 1. oscillare, far oscillare; inclinare, inclinarsi, piegare: *to — in the wind*, oscillare al vento 2. brandire (una spada); impugnare (lo scettro) 3. governare, influenzare: *he swayed our ideas*, egli influenzò le nostre idee; *to — s.o. from his course*, stornare qlcu. dai suoi progetti; *to refuse to be swayed*, essere inflessibile 4. *— up*, (*mar.*) alare, issare.

Swaziland ['swɑːzilænd], *no.pr.* (*geog.*) Swaziland.

to sweal [swiːl], *V.* to **swale**[2].

swear [swɛə*], *s. —(-word)*, bestemmia, imprecazione.

to **swear**, *pass.* **swore** [swɔ:*], (*arc.*) **sware** [swɛə*], *p.p.* **sworn** [swo:n], *v.t.i.* **1.** giurare, far giurare; prestare giuramento, far prestare giuramento; promettere solennemente: *to — peace, hatred, revenge*, giurare pace, odio, vendetta; *to — a solemn oath*, fare giuramento solenne; *to — s.o. to secrecy*, far giurare segretezza a qlcu.; *to — to do sthg.* (o *that one will do sthg.*), giurare di fare ql.co. ‖ *to be sworn judge of the peace*, essere creato giudice di pace **2.** bestemmiare; imprecare: *he went into a fit of swearing*, bestemmiò per un quarto d'ora; *it's enough to make a saint —*, ce n'è abbastanza per far bestemmiare un santo; *to — like a trooper* (o *like blazes*), bestemmiare come un turco **3.** *to — at* (*s.o., sthg.*), maledire, ingiurare ‖ *those two colours — at each other*, (*fam.*) quei due colori fanno a pugni **4.** *to — by* (*s.o.*), *sthg.*), chiamare a testimonio; credere ciecamente in ‖ *he swears by whisky*, per lui non c'è niente di meglio del whisky **5.** *to — to* (*sthg.*), attestare, certificare sotto giuramento: *would you — to it?*, giureresti che è vero? **6.** *to — in*, insediare in una carica facendo prestare giuramento **7.** *to — off*, rinunciare solennemente a **8.** *to — out*, (*amer.*) far arrestare giurando sulla veridicità dell'atto di accusa.

swearer ['swɛərə*], *s.* **1.** chi giura; chi fa giurare: *false —*, spergiuro **2.** bestemmiatore.

sweat [swet], *s.* **1.** sudore; traspirazione: *a cold —*, (*fam.*) un sudore freddo; *dripping with —*, grondante di sudore; *in* (o *by*) *the — of one's brow* (o *face*), col sudore della propria fronte (anche *fig.*); *to be in a —*, (*fam.*) essere tutto un sudore; *fig.* essere molto agitato, emozionato; *to have a —*, fare una sudata ‖ *nightly sweats*, sudori notturni **2.** (*fig. fam.*) sudata, lavoro duro, fatica ‖ *an old —*, (*sl. mil.*) un veterano ☆ *— -band*, striscia di pelle nell'interno di un cappello; *— bath*, bagno di sudore; *— -duct*, (*anat.*) dotto sudorifero; *— gland*, (*anat.*) ghiandola sudoripara.

to **sweat**, *v.t.i.* **1.** traspirare, sudare; far sudare; trasudare (di cose): *those walls were sweating dampness*, quelle pareti trasudavano umidità; *to — profusely*, sudare abbondantemente **2.** bagnare di sudore: *he sweated his shirt*, bagnò la camicia di sudore **3.** penare, affaticarsi; sfacchinare: *to — up a staircase*, arrancare su per una scala ‖ *to — blood*, *fig.* sudar sangue **4.** sfruttare (dipendenti) **5.** sottoporre a fermentazione (tabacco, pelli) **6.** (*metal.*) saldare a stagno, unire per fusione parziale **7.** (*mar.*) tendere il più possibile (corda, vela) **8.** strigliare **9.** (*sl.*) derubare, salassare ‖ *to — a coin*, sottrarre parte del metallo a una moneta **10.** (*sl.*) spendere (denaro) **11.** (*sl. amer.*) applicare il « terzo grado » a, strappare una confessione a **12.** *to — out*, trasudare, far trasudare; curare (una infreddatura) con sudoriferi: *he is sweating out his cold*, cura il raffreddore con una sudata.

sweater ['swetə*], *s.* **1.** chi suda **2.** giacchetta, maglione di lana **3.** sfruttatore (di dipendenti) **4.** lavoratore infaticabile **5.** chi altera il peso delle monete **6.** medicamento sudorifero.

sweatily ['swetili], *av.* sudando, con sudore.

sweatiness ['swetinis], *s.* traspirazione; trasudamento.

sweating ['swetiŋ], *s.* **1.** sudore, traspirazione; trasudamento **2.** sfruttamento (di dipendenti) ☆ *— -bath*, bagno turco; *— -room*, stanza per il bagno turco; *— -sickness*, (*med. arc.*) sudore anglico.

sweatless ['swetlis], *ag.* **1.** senza sudore **2.** *fig.* senza fatica.

sweaty ['sweti], *ag.* **1.** sudato, coperto di sudore **2.** che fa sudare; *fig.* penoso, faticoso: *a — piece of work*, un lavoro faticoso.

Swede [swi:d], *s.c.* svedese ‖ **swede**, *s.* rapa svedese.

Sweden ['swi:dn], *no.pr.* (*geog.*) Svezia.

Swedish ['swi:diʃ], *ag.* svedese.

sweeny ['swi:ni], *s.* (*amer.*) atrofia di muscoli (di cavallo).

sweep [swi:p], *s.* **1.** scopata; spazzata (anche *fig.*): *to give a room a good —*, dare una bella spazzata ad una stanza; *to make a clean — of old furniture*, *fig.* sbarazzarsi dei vecchi mobili ‖ *at one —*, in un colpo solo **2.** movimento circolare: *— of the eye*, sguardo circolare; *with a wide — of the arm*, con un ampio movimento del braccio **3.** curva, linea curva; distesa: *the — of a hill*, la curva di una collina; *a fine — of grass*, una bella distesa di erba; *the car took a big —*, l'automobile fece un'ampia curva; *the river makes a —*, il fiume fa un'ansa **4.** raggio, cerchio (d'azione); portata (anche *fig.*): *within the — of the audience*, alla portata del pubblico; *within the — of the guns*, a portata di cannone **5.** movimento rapido; incedere maestoso **6.** (*chimney-*) *—*, spazzacamino **7.** (*mar.*) remo sensile **8.** (*mar.*) cavo di dragaggio **9.** mazzacavallo (di pozzo) **10.** vela, pala di mulino a vento.

to **sweep**, *pass.p.p.* **swept** [swept], *v.t.i.* **1.** spazzare, scopare, ramazzare: *the deck was swept by a wave*, il ponte fu spazzato da un'onda; *she swept the room*, scopò la stanza ‖ *to — the board*, raccogliere l'intera posta (al giuoco); (*fam.*) riportare un completo successo ‖ *to — the seas*, battere i mari ‖ *to be swept off one's feet*, (*fam.*) essere sopraffatto dall'emozione **2.** incedere maestosamente: *she swept into the room*, entrò maestosamente nella stanza **3.** muoversi rapidamente: *the pestilence swept over the land*, la pestilenza dilagò nel paese **4.** estendersi in linea continua, curva: *the coast sweeps northwards*, la costa si estende verso nord **5.** sfiorare, toccare leggermente: *her dress swept the ground*, l'abito le scendeva a terra; *her fingers — the strings of the harp*, le sue dita sfiorano le corde dell'arpa **6.** percorrere con lo sguardo: *to — the horizon*, percorrere l'orizzonte con lo sguardo **7.** (*artigl.*) battere (col tiro) **8.** (*mar.*) dragare **9.** *to — along*, trasportare (anche *fig.*): *speaker who sweeps his audience along with him*, oratore che trascina il pubblico **10.** *to — away*, spazzar via: *the avalanche may — away the village*, la valanga può spazzar via il villaggio; *the bridge was swept away by the flood*, il ponte fu spazzato via dalla piena; *to — away the snow*, spazzar via la neve **11.** *to — down*, trascinare; abbattersi: *the enemy swept down upon us*, il nemico si abbatté su di noi **12.** *to — off*, spazzar via, distruggere: *the plague swept off thousands*, la pestilenza spazzò via migliaia di persone **13.** *to — on*, avanzare regolarmente **14.** *to — up*, raccogliere scopando: *to — up dry leaves*, spazzare foglie secche.

sweep, (nei composti): *— -device*, (*rad.*) dispositivo di deflessione; *— -net*, rete a strascico; *— -stakes*, lotteria (abbinata a corse di cavalli, ecc.) ‖ *blade —*, (*aer.*) passo angolare della pala (dell'elica); *door- —*, apertura della porta; *horizontal —*, (*tv.*) movimento di scansione orizzontale; *leading —*, (*aer.*) passo angolare positivo; *trailing —*, (*aer.*) passo angolare negativo.

sweeper ['swi:pə*], *s.c.* chi scopa, spazza ‖ *s.* **1.** (*mec.*) spazzatrice meccanica **2.** (*mar.*) dragamine ☆ *carpet - —*, aspirapolvere per tappeti; *chimney- —*, spazzacamino; *street- —*, spazzino; spazzatrice stradale.

sweeping ['swi:piŋ], *ag.* **1.** vasto, illimitato: *a — curtsy*, una profonda riverenza; *a — plain*, una pianura sconfinata **2.** completo; assoluto: *— changes*, cambiamenti radicali; *a — reform*, una riforma completa **3.** rapido, impetuoso (di corrente) ‖ *s.* **1.** scopatura **2.** (*metal.*) formatura a sagoma, a bandiera **3.** *pl.* rifiuti (anche *fig.*): *the sweepings of society*, i rifiuti della società.

sweepingly ['swi:piŋli], *av.* **1.** completamente; in modo assoluto **2.** rapidamente.

sweepingness ['swi:piŋnis], *s.* completezza; assolutezza: *he enjoyed the — of his victory*, era felice che la sua vittoria fosse così completa.

sweepy ['swi:pi], *ag.* impetuoso, rapido.

sweet [swi:t], *ag.* **1.** dolce, zuccherino: *as — as honey*, dolce come il miele; *to taste —*, avere un sapore dolce ‖ *to have a — tooth*, avere un debole per i dolci **2.** fresco, non alterato; non rancido: *is the butter still —?*, è ancora fresco il burro?; *was the ham still —?*, era ancora buono il prosciutto? **3.** profumato, fragrante **4.** armonioso, musicale, soave: — *voice*, voce soave **5.** piacevole, gradevole; gentile, amabile, caro: *it is* — *to know that one is loved*, è piacevole sapere di essere amati; *they are all very* —, sono tutti molto cari; *this is very* — *of you*, questo è molto carino da parte vostra ‖ *to be* — *on* (o *upon*) *s.o.*, essere innamorato di qlcu. ‖ *to say* — *nothings to s.o.*, dire paroline dolci a qlcu. **6.** (*fam.*) carino, grazioso: *a* — *frock*, un abito grazioso ‖ *s.* **1.** dolcezza ‖ —*!*, *my* —*!*, cara!, mia cara! **2.** dolciume, caramella **3.** dolce, torta **4.** *pl.* piaceri, delizie: *the sweets of life*, i piaceri della vita **5.** *gener. pl.* profumo, fragranza.

sweet, *av.* dolcemente.

sweet, (*nei composti*): — *-bay*, alloro; (*amer.*) specie di magnolia (« Magnolia glauca »); — *-brier* (o — *-briar*), rosa selvatica; — *-oil*, olio d'oliva; — *-pea*, pisello odoroso; — *-potato*, patata americana, dolce; — *-toothed*, che ha un debole per i dolci; — *violet*, violetta odorosa; — *water*, acqua potabile; — *-william*, garofano dei poeti, dianto.

sweetbread ['swi:tbred], *s.* (*cuc.*) animella.

to **sweeten** ['swi:tn], *v.t.i.* **1.** zuccherare, aggiungere zucchero a **2.** addolcire, addolcirsi; rendere piacevole; mitigare, alleviare: *to* — *a toil*, rendere piacevole una fatica **3.** depurare, purificare (aria, acqua, ecc.) **4.** (*sl.*) aggiungere denaro (ad una posta di giuoco); fare un'offerta ad un'asta (per alzare il prezzo).

sweetener ['swi:tnə*], *s.c.* chi addolcisce ‖ *s.* ciò che addolcisce.

sweetening ['swi:tniŋ], *s.* **1.** sostanza che addolcisce **2.** addolcimento; alleviamento **3.** purificazione (di aria, acqua, ecc.).

sweetheart ['swi:thɑ:t], *s.c.* innamorato, innamorata: *they have been sweethearts since childhood*, si amano dall'infanzia ‖ —*!*, amore!.

to **sweetheart**, *v.t.i.* corteggiare; fare all'amore.

sweetie ['swi:ti], *s.c.* (*amer.*) innamorato, innamorata ‖ *s.* dolciume, confetto.

sweeting ['swi:tiŋ], *s.c.*(*arc.*) innamorato, innamorata ‖ *s.* mela dolce.

sweetish ['swi:tiʃ], *ag.* dolciastro, dolcigno.

sweetishness ['swi:tiʃnis], *s.* sapore dolciastro.

sweetly ['swi:tli], *av.* **1.** dolcemente, soavemente; amabilmente; gradevolmente **2.** (*mec.*) in modo regolare: *the engine runs* —, la macchina funziona regolarmente.

sweetmeat ['swi:tmi:t], *s.* **1.** *spec. pl.* dolciumi, frutta candita **2.** vernice usata nella preparazione del cuoio.

sweetness ['swi:tnis], *s.* **1.** sapore dolce **2.** fragranza (di aria, ecc.) **3.** dolcezza, soavità, amabilità.

sweety, *V.* **sweetie**.

swell [swel], *ag.* **1.** (*fam.*) elegante; alla moda: — *parties*, riunioni eleganti; *a* — *place*, ritrovo alla moda **2.** (*sl.*) magnifico: *that's* —*!*, va magnificamente!; *you'll make a* — *dad*, (*amer.*) sarai un padre bravissimo ‖ *s.* **1.** rigonfiamento; protuberanza **2.** il gonfiarsi del mare, di massa d'acqua **3.** (*mus.*) crescendo; crescendo seguito da diminuendo **4.** mantice (dell'organo) **5.** (*sl.*) elegantone: *what a* — *you are!*, che elegantone sei! **6.** (*sl.*) tipo in gamba; persona importante: *he is a* — *in politics*, è un pezzo grosso in politica ☆ — *-mob*, ladri in guanti gialli.

to **swell** [swel], *ag.* **1.** *pass.* **swelled** [sweld], *p.p.* **swollen** ['swoulən], (*rar.*) **swelled**, *v.t.i.* **1.** gonfiare, gonfiarsi; dilatare, dilatarsi; ingrossare, ingrossarsi: *the injured wrist began to* — (*up*), il polso colpito incominciò a gonfiarsi; *a river swollen by the rain*, un fiume gonfiato dalla pioggia; *the sea swells into waves*, il mare si ingrossa e forma ondate; *the wind swells the sails*, il vento gonfia le vele **2.** crescere, aumentare: *prices are swelling every day*, i prezzi aumentano ogni giorno; *to* — *the number*, accrescere il numero **3.** aumentare di intensità (di suono): *the organ swelled*, il suono dell'organo si fece più forte **4.** *fig.* gonfiarsi; inorgoglirsi; montare in

superbia: *her heart swelled with pride*, il cuore le si gonfiò d'orgoglio; *they swelled with their success*, sono montati in superbia per il loro successo.

swelldom ['sweldəm], *s.* (*sl.*) società elegante.

swelling ['sweliŋ], *ag.* **1.** ondulato **2.** curvo ‖ *s.* **1.** rigonfiamento; ingrossamento **2.** protuberanza **3.** tumefazione, edema.

swellish ['sweliʃ], *ag.* (*fam.*) ricercato, sofisticato.

swelter ['sweltə*], *s.* afa, caldo oppressivo.

to **swelter**, *v.t.i.* **1.** soffocare per l'afa; essere oppresso dal caldo **2.** trasudare.

sweltering ['sweltəriŋ], *ag.* **1.** soffocante; opprimente (di caldo) **2.** molle di sudore.

swelteringly ['sweltəriŋli], *av.* in modo soffocante, opprimente.

sweltry ['sweltri], *ag.* **1.** afoso, opprimente **2.** oppresso dal caldo.

swept [swept], *pass. p.p.* di to **sweep.**

swerve [swə:v], *s.* deviazione; scarto improvviso.

to **swerve**, *v.t.i.* **1.** deviare, far deviare; fare uno scarto: *the horse swerved*, il cavallo fece uno scarto; *to* — *a ball*, deviare una palla **2.** *fig.* allontanarsi, scostarsi: *to* — *from the straight path*, abbandonare la retta via.

swift [swift], *ag.* **1.** rapido, lesto, veloce; agile: — *movements*, movimenti rapidi; *as* — *as thought*, rapido come il pensiero **2.** svelto, pronto: *he has a* — *wit*, ha uno spirito vivace; *she is* — *to anger*, è irascibile, facile ad adirarsi ‖ *s.* **1.** (*ornit.*) rondone **2.** (*zool.*) salamandra acquaiola; piccola lucertola **3.** (*entom.*) epialo **4.** (*mec.*) rocchetto; aspo.

swift, *av.* **1.** rapidamente, velocemente **2.** prontamente.

swift, (*nei composti*): — *-foot*, piè veloce; — *-footed*, dal piede veloce; — *-handed*, dalle mani abili; — *-tongued*, dalla risposta pronta; — *-winged*, dal volo rapido.

swifter ['swiftə*], *s.* **1.** (*mar.*) cintura **2.** (*mec.*) cinghia.

swiftly ['swiftli], *av.* **1.** rapidamente, velocemente **2.** prontamente.

swiftness ['swiftnis], *s.* **1.** rapidità, velocità **2.** prontezza.

swig[1] [swig], *s.* (*sl.*) sorsata, sorso; bevuta: *a* — *of whisky*, una sorsata di whisky.

to **swig**[1], *pass.p.p.* **swigged** [swigd], *v.t.i.* (*sl.*) tracannare, bere a lunghi sorsi: *to* — *off a glass*, bere un bicchiere d'un sol fiato.

swig[2], *s.* (*mar.*) paranco.

to **swig**[2], *v.t.i.* **1.** (*mar.*) parancare; issare (vele) **2.** (*rar.*) castrare (arieti) **3.** barcollare; vacillare.

swill [swil], *s.* **1.** risciacquatura, rifiuti; intruglio (per i maiali) **2.** risciacquata: *give the pail a* —, da' una risciacquata al secchio **3.** (*rar.*) abbondante bevuta (di liquori).

to **swill**, *v.t.i.* **1.** lavare, sciacquare: *to* — (*out*) *a basin*, sciacquare un catino **2.** tracannare, trincare; sbevazzare.

swiller ['swilə*], *s.* ubriacone.

swilling ['swiliŋ], *s.* **1.** risciacquatura **2.** *pl.* acque di rifiuto.

swim [swim], *s.* **1.** nuotata: *to have* (o *to take*) *a* —, fare una nuotata **2.** zona d'acqua pescosa **3.** *fig.* corrente principale ‖ *to be in the* —, *fig.* essere al corrente, essere all'avanguardia **4.** (*fam.*) leggero capogiro **5.** — (*-bladder*), (*rar.*) vescica natatoria.

to **swim**, *pass.* **swam** [swæm], *p.p.* **swum** [swʌm], *v.t.i.* **1.** nuotare; far nuotare: *he swims on his back, on his side*, nuota sul dorso, sul fianco; *to* — *against the stream*, nuotare contro la corrente; *fig.* andar contro corrente; *to* — *for one's life*, salvarsi a nuoto; *to* — *a horse across a river*, far passare a nuoto un cavallo attraverso un fiume; *to* — *a race*, partecipare a una gara di nuoto; *to* — *a stroke*, fare una bracciata; *to* — *under water*, nuotare sott'acqua ‖ *he is swimming in money*, nuota nell'oro, è ricco sfondato ‖ *to* — *like a fish*, nuotare come un pesce; *to — like a millstone* (o *a stone* o *a tailor's goose*), (*scherz.*) nuotare come il piombo ‖ *to — with the tide*, *fig.* seguire la corrente, la maggioranza **2.** attraversare nuotando: *to — a river*, passare a nuoto un fiume **3.** galleggiare: *the fruit-salad swims in juice*, la macedonia nuota nello sciroppo; *the leaf is swimming down the river*, la foglia galleggia lungo il fiume **4.** essere inondato; traboccare (anche *fig.*): *the floor swims in blood*, il pavimento è inondato di sangue; *his eyes were swimming with tears*, i suoi occhi erano inondati di lacrime **5.** ondeggiare; vacillare, avere il capogiro: *his head was swimming round*, gli girava la testa **6.** (*poet.*) scivolare dolcemente: *the moon swims in the sky*, la luna scivola dolcemente nel cielo.

swimmer ['swimə*], *s.c.* nuotatore, nuotatrice ‖ *s.* **1.** uccello acquatico **2.** organo natatorio (dei crostacei) **3.** galleggiante.

swimmeret ['swiməret], *s.* organo natatorio (dei crostacei).

swimming ['swimiŋ], *ag.* **1.** che nuota **2.** pieno di lacrime (di occhio) **3.** affetto da capogiro ‖ *s.* **1.** nuoto **2.** leggero capogiro ☆ — *-bath*, piscina coperta; — *-bell*, ombrello (di medusa); — *-belt*, salvagente; — *-bladder*, vescica natatoria; — *-pool*, piscina all'aperto.

swimmingly ['swimiŋli], *av.* agevolmente, a meraviglia: *it goes on —*, procede a meraviglia.

swimwear ['swimwɛə*], *s.* indumenti da nuoto, da bagno.

swindle ['swindl], *s.* truffa, frode, raggiro.

to **swindle**, *v.t.i.* truffare, raggirare: *to — s.o. out of sthg.* (o *sthg. out of s.o.*), truffare ql.co. a qlcu.

swindler ['swindlə*], *s.c.* truffatore, truffatrice; imbroglione, imbrogliona.

swindling ['swindliŋ], *s.* truffa, imbroglio, raggiro.

swine, *pl.* **swine** [swain], *s.* maiale, porco (anche *fig.*): *to behave like a —*, comportarsi da animale ‖ *to throw pearls before —*, gettar perle ai porci ☆ — *-bread*, (*bot.*) tartufo; — *-fever*, colera dei suini; — *-fish*, (*ittiol.*) spigolo, pesce lupo; — *-herd*, porcaro; — *-snout*, (*bot.*) radicchiella; — *-sty*, porcile.

swing [swiŋ], *s.* **1.** oscillazione, movimento oscillatorio; dondolio; ampiezza dell'oscillazione: *to give a hammock a —*, far dondolare un'amaca; *to walk with a —*, camminare dondolandosi ‖ *the — of a pendulum*, *fig.* l'alternarsi di vicende, idee, ecc.; l'alternarsi dei partiti al potere ‖ *to be in full —*, essere in piena attività, essere molto animato **2.** libertà d'azione, libero corso: *the admiral was given full — in the conduct of the war*, all'ammiraglio fu lasciata piena libertà d'azione nel condurre la guerra **3.** altalena **4.** ritmo (di poesia, musica): *this ballad has an enthralling —*, questa ballata ha un ritmo affascinante; *to go with a —*, avere un ritmo scorrevole; *fig.* procedere bene, con successo di avvenimenti, trattenimenti) ‖ (*-music*), « swing » (tipo di jazz) **6.** (*sl. amer. comm.*) fluttuazione periodica ☆ — *-boat*, barca ad altalena (di giostre); — *-bridge*, ponte girevole; — *-cot*, zana; — *-door*, porta a vento; — *-plough*, aratro senza ruote.

to **swing**, *pass.* **swung** [swʌŋ], (*rar.*) **swang** [swæŋ], *p.p.* **swung**, *v.t.i.* **1.** dondolare, dondolarsi; oscillare, fare oscillare: *the door is swinging to and fro in the wind*, la porta sbatte al vento; *to — a child*, cullare un bambino ‖ *there is no room to — a cat in*, non c'è spazio per girarsi ‖ *to — the lead*, (*sl. mil.*) marcare visita **2.** ruotare, far ruotare, far girare: *the ship swung at anchor*, la nave girava sull'ancora; *to — the car round*, far fare una brusca curva all'automobile; *to — a propeller*, avviare un'elica ‖ *to — open*, *to — to*, spalancarsi, chiudersi (di porta) **3.** camminare dondolandosi **4.** brandire, agitare, vibrare: *to — a sword*, brandire una spada **5.** penzolare; essere appeso: *lamp swung from the ceiling*, lampada sospesa al soffitto **6.** (*sl.*) essere impiccato: *he was swung up to the nearest tree*, fu impiccato all'albero più vicino;

to — for a crime, essere impiccato per un delitto.

to **swinge**[1] [swindʒ], *v.t.* (*arc.*) battere, frustare.

to **swinge**[2], *v.t.* (*dial.*) bruciacchiare, scottare.

swingeing ['swindʒiŋ], *ag.* **1.** violento: *a — blow*, un colpo durissimo **2.** (*fam.*) enorme: *a — majority*, una maggioranza schiacciante.

swinging ['swiŋiŋ], *ag.* **1.** oscillante, dondolante **2.** ritmico, cadenzato ‖ *s.* **1.** dondolio, oscillamento **2.** (*rad.*) fluttuazione, affievolimento, evanescenza; fluttuazione di frequenza.

swingingly ['swiŋiŋli], *av.* oscillando, dondolandosi.

swingle ['swiŋgl], *s.* (*ind. tessile*) gramola, maciulla.

to **swingle**, *v.t.* battere (il lino, la canapa, ecc.).

swingletree ['swiŋgltri:], *s.* bilancino (di carrozza, aratro, ecc.).

swingling ['swiŋgliŋ], *s.* il battere (lino, canapa, ecc.) ☆ — *-tow*, stoppa.

swinish ['swainiʃ], *ag.* bestiale; sozzo, sudicio; schifoso.

swinishly ['swainiʃli], *av.* bestialmente; sozzamente; sudiciamente; schifosamente.

swinishness ['swainiʃnis], *s.* bestialità; sudiceria.

swipe[1] [swaip], *s.* mazzacavallo (per attingere acqua).

swipe[2], *s.* colpo violento (al cricket, ecc.).

to **swipe**[2], *v.t.i.* **1.** (*cricket*) dare un colpo violento (a): *to — (at) the ball*, colpire violentemente la palla **2.** tracannare, ingoiare in un sorso **3.** (*sl.*) rubacchiare.

swiper ['swaipə*], *s.c.* chi batte violentemente (al cricket, ecc.).

swipes [swaips], *s.pl.* (*sl.*) birra leggera, di qualità scadente.

swire ['swaiə*], *s.* (*rar.*) depressione (tra due alture).

swirl [swɔ:l], *s.* **1.** vortice, turbine (anche *fig.*): *a — of dust*, un turbine di polvere; *the — of modern life*, *fig.* il turbine della vita moderna **2.** ricciolo **3.** treccia (intorno al capo); striscia di stoffa attorcigliata (intorno a un cappello).

to **swirl**, *v.t.i.* turbinare, girare, far girare vorticosamente.

swish [swiʃ], *ag.* (*fam.*) elegante, alla moda ‖ *s.* **1.** sibilo; fruscio; mormorio (d'acqua) **2.** forte getto di acqua **3.** sferza **4.** sferzata.

to **swish**, *v.t.i.* **1.** fischiare, far fischiare; sibilare, far sibilare; frusciare **2.** frustare.

Swiss [swis], *ag.* svizzero.

switch [switʃ], *s.* **1.** verga; frustino, frusta **2.** colpo di frusta **3.** capelli posticci, treccia falsa **4.** (*elett.*) interruttore; commutatore **5.** (*ferr.*) scambio ☆ — *-back*, ferrovia a zig-zag; montagne russe; — *-block*, (*ferr.*) deviatoio; — *-board*, (*elett.*) quadro di controllo; (*tel.*) tavolo di commutazione; — *-plug*, spina con interruttore incorporato; — *-signal*, segnale di scambio ‖ *lever —*, interruttore a leva; *lighting —*, interruttore luce; *reversing —*, (*elett.*) invertitore.

to **switch**, *v.t.i.* **1.** colpire, battere, percuotere con un frustino, una verga **2.** muovere bruscamente, agitare: *the cow switched her tail*, la mucca agitò la coda; *to — one's head round*, voltare bruscamente la testa **3.** (*ferr.*) smistare, deviare, far deviare **4.** *fig.* mutare; sviare: *to — the conversation to a new subject*, cambiare discorso **5.** *to — off*, (*elett.*) disinserire, interrompere; (*tel.*) interrompere la comunicazione: *to — off the light*, spegnere la luce **6.** *to — on*, (*elett.*) inserire: *to — on the ignition*, inserire l'accensione; *to — on the light, the wireless*, accendere la luce, la radio **7.** *to — over*, (*elett.*) commutare.

switchman, *pl.* **switchmen** ['switʃmən], *s.* (*ferr.*) deviatore.

switchyard ['switʃja:d], *s.* (*amer.*) piazzale degli scambi (in una stazione ferroviaria).

to **swither** ['swiðə*], *v.i.* (*scoz.*) esitare.

Switzer ['switsə*], *s.* (*arc.*) **1.** svizzero **2.** *gener. pl.* soldati mercenari svizzeri; guardia pontificia.

Switzerland ['switsələnd], *no.pr.* (*geog.*) Svizzera.

swivel ['swivl], *s.* (*mec.*) **1.** perno; anello girevole (di catena) **2.** piattaforma girevole (di sedia, cannoncino, ecc.) **3.** piccola spola, navetta ☆ — *bridge*, ponte girevole; — *chair*, sedia girevole; — *-eyed*, strabico; — *-gun*, cannoncino girevole.

to **swivel**, *pass.p.p.* **swivelled** ['swivld], *v.t.i.* **1.** ruotare, far ruotare su un perno **2.** assicurare mediante parte girevole.

swizz [swiz], *s.* (*sl.*) inganno; frode.

swizzle ['swizl], *s.* (*sl.*) « cocktail ».

(to) **swob**, *V.* (to) **swab**.

swobber, *V.* **swabber**.

swollen ['swoulən], *p.p.* di to **swell** ‖ *ag.* gonfio; rigonfio; *fig.* gonfio; enfatico ☆ — (o *swelled*) *head*, (*sl.*) presunzione: *to suffer from* (o *to have*) — *head*, essere pieno di sè; — *-headed* (o *swelled-headed*), vanitoso, presuntuoso.

swoon [swu:n], *s.* **1.** svenimento, deliquio **2.** (*poet.*) sonno profondo.

to **swoon**, *v.i.* **1.** svenire, venir meno **2.** smorzarsi dolcemente (di musica, ecc.).

swoop [swu:p], *s.* il piombare sulla preda (di uccelli rapaci); *fig.* calata improvvisa; attacco: *influenza came down upon me with a* —, fui colpito improvvisamente dall'influenza ‖ *at one* (*fell*) —, in un sol colpo.

to **swoop**, *v.t.i.* **1.** *to* — **down**, piombare (sulla preda, di uccelli rapaci); *fig.* calare improvvisamente, abbattersi: *the aeroplanes swooped down on the enemy*, gli aerei si abbatterono sul nemico; *the falcon swooped down on its prey*, il falco piombò sulla preda **2.** *to* — **up**, (*fam.*) afferrare a volo.

swop [swɔp], *s.* (*fam.*) scambio; baratto.

to **swop**, *pass.p.p.* **swopped** [swɔpt], *v.t.i.* (*fam.*)**1.** barattare; scambiare: *to* — *places with s.o.*, cambiar posto con qlcu.; *to* — *sthg. for sthg. else*, barattare ql.co. ‖ *never* — *horses while crossing a stream*, *prov.* non cambiar cavallo arrivato al guado **2.** (*sl.*) licenziare **3.** (*sl.*) imbrogliare.

sword [sɔ:d], *s.* spada (anche *fig.*): *the* — *of justice*, la spada della giustizia; *to draw one's* —, sguainare la spada; *to wear* (o *to carry*) *a* —, portar la spada ‖ *the* — *of Damocles*, la spada di Damocle ‖ *at the point of the* —, sotto la minaccia della guerra ‖ *fire and* —, ferro e fuoco; distruzione completa ‖ *to draw the* —, dare inizio alle ostilità ‖ *to measure* (o *to cross*) *swords with s.o.*, misurarsi, battersi con qlcu. ‖ *to be put to the* —, essere passato a fil di spada, essere ucciso ☆ — *-arm*, braccio destro; — *-bayonet*, baionetta; — *-bearer*, portatore di spada (nelle cerimonie), spadaro; — *-belt*, cinturone che sorregge la spada; — *-bill*, (*ornit.*) colibrì dal becco a spada; — *-blade*, lama della spada; — *-cane* (o — *-stick*), stocco; — *-cut*, fendente, sciabolata; — *-dance*, danza della spada; — *-grass*, (*bot.*) gladiolo; — *-guard*, guardia della spada; — *-hand*, mano destra; — *-knot*, dragona; — *-law*, legge marziale; — *-tail*, (*zool.*) limulo ‖ *cavalry* —, spadone.

swordcraft ['sɔ:dkrɑ:ft], *V.* **swordsmanship**.

swordfish ['sɔ:dfiʃ], *s.* (*ittiol.*) pesce spada.

swordlike ['sɔ:dlaik], *ag.* spadiforme.

swordplay ['sɔ:dplei], *s.* scherma.

swordsman, *pl.* **swordsmen** ['sɔ:dzmən], *s.* spadaccino.

swordsmanship ['sɔ:dzmənʃip], *s.* arte di maneggiare la spada.

swore [swo:*], *pass.* di to **swear**.

sworn [swo:n], *p.p.* di to **swear** ‖ *ag.* **1.** giurato: *a* — *enemy*, un acerrimo nemico; *a* — *friend*, un amico fidato **2.** (*dir.*) che ha giurato; sotto giuramento: *a* — *jury*, giuria che ha prestato giuramento; *a* — *statement*, dichiarazione sotto giuramento.

swot [swɔt], *s.c.* (*sl. scolastico*) secchione, secchiona ‖ *s.* (*sl. scolastico*) studio accanito.

to **swot**, *pass.p.p.* **swotted** ['swɔtid], *v.t.i.* (*sl. scolastico*) **1.** sgobbare, secchiare **2.** *to* — **up**, sgobbare su: *to* — *a subject up*, sgobbare su una materia.

swum [swʌm], *p.p.* di to **swim**.

swung [swʌŋ], *pass.p.p.* di to **swing**.

Sybarite ['sibərait], *s.c.* (*geog. st.*) sibarita ‖ **sybarite**. *ag.* sibaritico ‖ *s.c.* sibarita, persona raffinata e dedita ai piaceri.

sybaritic(al) [,sibə'ritik(əl)], *ag.* sibaritico; molle, lussuoso.

sybaritically [,sibə'ritikəli], *av.* sibariticamente, da sibarita; mollemente; lussuosamente.

sybaritism ['sibəraitizəm], *s.* vita, mollezze da sibarita.

sybil¹ ['sibil], *s.* **1.**(*st.*) sibilla **2.** fattucchiera; strega.

Sybil², *no.pr.f.* Sibilla.

sycamine ['sikəmain], *s.* (*arc.*) gelso nero.

sycamore ['sikəmɔ:*], *s.* (*bot.*) sicomoro.

syce [sais], *s.* (*ang.-in.*) servo; mozzo di stalla.

sycee [sai'si:], *s.* « sycee » (pezzetto d'argento usato come moneta in Cina).

syconium [sai'kouniəm], *s.* (*bot.*) siconio.

sycophancy ['sikəfənsi], *s.* adulazione servile.

sycophant ['sikəfənt], *s.* sicofante ‖ *s.c.* adulatore, adulatrice; parassita.

sycophantic [,sikə'fæntik], *ag.* adulatorio, servile.

sycophantism ['sikəfəntizəm], *s.* adulazione servile.

sycosis [sai'kousis], *s.* (*patol.*) sicosi.

syenite ['saiinait], *s.* (*min.*) sienite.

syenitic [,saii'nitik], *ag.* di sienite, simile a sienite.

syllabary ['siləbəri], *s.* lista di caratteri rappresentanti sillabe.

syllabic(al) [si'læbik(əl)], *ag.* sillabico.

syllabically [si'læbikəli], *av.* sillaba per sillaba.

to **syllabicate** [si'læbikeit], *v.t.* sillabare, leggere sillabando.

syllabication [si,læbi'keiʃən], **syllabification** [si,læbifi'keiʃən], *s.* sillabazione.

to **syllabify** [si'læbifai], to **syllabize** ['siləbaiz], *v.t.* sillabare, leggere sillabando.

syllable ['siləbl], *s.* sillaba: *long, short* —, sillaba lunga, corta; *he did not utter a* —, non proferì sillaba.

to **syllable**, *v.t.* **1.** sillabare **2.** (*poet.*) proferire, dire.

syllabled ['siləbld], *ag.* composto di sillabe ☆ *two-* —, bisillabo; *three-* —, trisillabo.

syllabub, ['siləbʌb], *s.* quagliata con zucchero e vino.

syllabus ['siləbəs], *pl.* **syllabi** ['siləbai], **syllabuses** ['siləbəsiz], *s.* **1.** sommario; programma, prospetto **2.** (*eccl.*) sillabo.

syllepsis [si'lepsis], *pl.* **syllepses** [si'lepsi:z], *s.* (*gram.*) sillepsi.

sylleptic [si'leptik], *ag.* (*gram.*) di sillepsi.

sylleptically [si'leptikəli], *av.* (*gram.*) con sillepsi.

syllogism ['silədʒizəm], *s.* (*log.*) sillogismo.

syllogistic [silə'dʒistik], *ag.* (*log.*) sillogistico.

syllogistically [,silə'dʒistikəli], *av.* (*log.*) sillogisticamente.

syllogization [,silədʒai'zeiʃən], *s.* (*log.*) ragionamento sillogistico.

to **syllogize** ['silədʒaiz], *v.t.i.* (*log.*) sillogizzare.

sylph [silf], *s.c.* silfo, silfide (anche *fig.*) ‖ *s.* (*ornit.*) colibrì.

sylphid ['silfid], *s.c.* giovane silfo, silfide.

silphlike ['silflaik], *ag.* leggera e graziosa come una silfide.

sylvan ['silvən], *ag.* silvano, silvestre ‖ *s.* **1.** abitatore dei boschi **2.** (*mit.*) silvano, divinità dei boschi.

Sylvester [sil'vestə*], *no.pr.m.* Silvestro.

sylvestrian¹ [sil'vestriən], *ag.* silvano, rustico.

Sylvestrian², *ag.s.* (*st. eccl.*) Silvestrino.

Sylvia ['silviə], *no.pr.f.* Silvia.

sylvicultural [,silvi'kʌltʃərəl], *ag.* di silvicoltura.

sylviculture [silvi,kʌltʃə*], *s.* silvicoltura.

sylviculturist [,silvi'kʌltʃərist], *s.* silvicoltore.

Sylvius ['silviəs], *no.pr.m.* Silvio.

symbiosis [,simbi'ousis], *s.* simbiosi.

symbiotic [,simbi'ɔtik], *ag.* in stato di simbiosi.

symbiotically [,simbi'ɔtikəli], *av.* in stato di simbiosi.

symbol ['simbəl], *s.* **1.** simbolo, emblema: *white is the — of purity*, il bianco è il simbolo della purezza **2.** (*mat. chim.*) simbolo.

to **symbol**, *pass. p.p.* **symbolled** ['simbəld], *v.t.* (*rar.*) simbolizzare.

symbolic(al) [sim'bolik(əl)], *ag.* simbolico.

symbolically [sim'bolikəli], *av.* simbolicamente.

symbolicalness [sim'bolikəlnis], *s.* l'essere simbolico.

symbolics [sim'boliks], *s.* simbolica.

symbolism ['simbəlizəm], *s.* simbolismo.

symbolist ['simbəlist], *s.* simbolista.

symbolization [,simbəlai'zeiʃən], *s.* simbolizzazione.

to **symbolize** ['simbəlaiz], *v.t.* simboleggiare.

symbology [sim'bolədʒi], *s.* simbologia.

symmetric(al) [si'metrik(əl)], *ag.* simmetrico.

symmetrically [si'metrikəli], *av.* simmetricamente.

symmetricalness [si'metrikəlnis], *s.* simmetria.

symmetrization [,simitrai'zeiʃən], *s.* il rendere simmetrico.

to **symmetrize** ['simitraiz], *v.t.* rendere simmetrico.

symmetry ['simitri], *s.* simmetria.

sympathetic [,simpə'θetik], *ag.* **1.** sensibile, comprensivo; che mostra simpatia: — *heart*, cuore comprensivo; — *smile*, sorriso di simpatia; *a teacher is often — to(wards) his pupils*, un insegnante è spesso comprensivo nei riguardi dei suoi allievi **2.** congeniale, adatto: *I work better in a — atmosphere*, lavoro meglio in un'atmosfera adatta **3.** (*anat.*) simpatico, del gran simpatico **4.** (*gallicismo*) simpatico || *s.* **1.** (*anat.*) sistema del gran simpatico; nervo simpatico **2.** persona facilmente ipnotizzabile, influenzabile ☆ — *ink*, inchiostro simpatico; — *nerve*, (*anat.*) nervo simpatico; — *pain*, pena causata da dolore altrui; dolore fisico causato da affezione in altra parte del corpo; — *strike*, sciopero di solidarietà; — *string*, corda che vibra in simpatia.

sympathetically [,simpə'θetikəli], *av.* con simpatia, con comprensione.

to **sympathize** ['simpəθaiz], *v.i.* **1.** sentire, mostrare comprensione; condividere i sentimenti altrui; aver compassione: *he sympathized with the poor*, aveva compassione dei poveri; *I — with him in his feelings*, condivido i suoi sentimenti || *their neighbours called to —*, i vicini andarono a presentare le loro condoglianze **2.** essere d'accordo; considerare favorevolmente: *they seemed to — with our scheme*, sembrava che considerassero favorevolmente il nostro piano; *to — with s.o. in his point of view*, condividere il punto di vista di qlcu.

sympathizer ['simpəθaizə*], *s.c.* **1.** chi è comprensivo; chi condivide i sentimenti altrui **2.** fautore, fautrice; simpatizzante (di partito, movimento, ecc.).

sympathy ['simpəθi], *s.* **1.** comprensione; partecipazione a sentimenti altrui; compassione: *he has no — with* (o *for*) *beggars*, non ha alcuna compassione per i mendicanti; *she claims our —*, ha diritto alla nostra comprensione; *you will find that he is a man of wide sympathies*, troverai che è un uomo molto comprensivo **2.** condoglianze: *a letter of —*, una lettera di condoglianze **3.** armonia, accordo; comunità (di sentimenti, opinioni, ecc.); affinità: *in — with*, in accordo con; *out of — with*, in disaccordo con; *to feel a — for s.o.*, sentirsi attratto da qlcu. **4.** (*med.*) simpatia.

symphonic [sim'fonik], *ag.* (*mus.*) sinfonico.

symphonious [sim'founiəs], *ag.* (*rar.*) armonico.

symphony ['simfəni], *s.* **1.** (*mus.*) sinfonia **2.** (*arc.*) armonia ☆ — *concert*, concerto sinfonico; — *orchestra*, orchestra sinfonica.

symposiac [sim'pouzjək], **symposial** [sim'pouzjəl], *ag.* conviviale, di simposio.

symposiarch [sim'pouzja:k], *s.* simposiarca.

symposium [sim'pouzjəm], *pl.* **symposia** [sim'pouzjə], *s.* **1.** simposio **2.** conferenza, discussione accademica **3.** raccolta di articoli (di vari autori) sullo stesso soggetto.

symptom ['simptəm], *s.* sintomo (di malattia); indizio, segno: *the symptoms of pleurisy*, i sintomi della pleurite; *the age showed symptoms of social unrest*, l'epoca presentava indizi di inquietudine sociale.

symptomatic(al) [,simptə'mætik(əl)], *ag.* sintomatico.

symptomatically [,simptə'mætikəli], *av.* in modo sintomatico: *diseases — alike*, malattie che presentano sintomi analoghi.

symptomatology [,simptəmə'tolədʒi], *s.* sintomatologia.

syn(a)eresis [si'niərəsis], *pl.* **syn(a)ereses** [si'niərəsi:z], *s.* sineresi.

synagogical [,sinə'godʒikəl], *ag.* di sinagoga.

synagogue ['sinəgog], *s.* (*relig. ebraica*) sinagoga.

synchro-mesh ['siŋkrou'meʃ], *s.* (*aut. contr.* di *synchronized mesh*) cambio di velocità sincronizzato.

synchronal ['siŋkrənl], **synchronic(al)** [siŋ'kronik(əl)], *ag.* sincrono, simultaneo.

synchronically [siŋ'kronikəli], *av.* sincronicamente.

synchronism ['siŋkrənizəm], *s.* sincronismo: *in —*, sincronizzato; *out of —*, non sincronizzato.

synchronistic [,siŋkrə'nistik], *ag.* sincronistico.

synchronization [,siŋkrənai'zeiʃən], *s.* sincronizzazione.

to **synchronize** ['siŋkrənaiz], *v.t.i.* **1.** sincronizzare (orologi, movimenti, sonoro di film, eventi, ecc.); muoversi sincronicamente: *clocks that —*, orologi che segnano la stessa ora; *to — two generators*, (*elett.*) sincronizzare due generatori **2.** accadere nello stesso tempo (di eventi).

synchronized ['siŋkrənaizd], *ag.* sincronizzato ☆ — *shifting*, (*aut.*) cambio sincronizzato.

synchronizer ['siŋkrənaizə*], *s.* sincronizzatore.

synchronous ['siŋkrənəs], *ag.* **1.** sincrono, simultaneo **2.** contemporaneo (di eventi) ☆ — *alternator*, (*elett.*) alternatore sincrono; — *machine*, (*elett.*) macchina sincrona; — *motor*, (*elett.*) motore sincrono; — *speed*, (*elett.*) velocità di sincronismo.

synchronously ['siŋkrənəsli], *av.* **1.** in modo sincrono **2.** contemporaneamente.

synchronousness ['siŋkrənəsnis], *s.* sincronia.

synchrony ['siŋkrəni], *s.* sincronismo ☆ — *mark*, (*cine.*) contrassegno di sincronismo.

synchrotron ['siŋkroutrən], *s.* (*fis. nucleare*) sincrotrone.

syncopal ['siŋkəpəl], *ag.* (*med.*) sincopale.

to **syncopate** ['siŋkəpeit], *v.t.* (*gram. mus.*) sincopare.

syncopation [,siŋkə'peiʃən], *s.* (*gram. mus.*) sincopatura.

syncope ['siŋkəpi], *s.* (*gram. mus. med.*) sincope.

syncop(t)ic [sin'kəp(t)ik], *ag.* (*med.*) relativo a, affetto da sincope.

syndic ['sindik], *s.* **1.** sindaco, magistrato, alto funzionario **2.** rappresentante (di corporazione, società, ditta) **3.** membro di uno speciale comitato del senato (all'università di Cambridge) **4.** (*st. greca*) magistrato.

syndicalism ['sindikəlizəm], *s.* sindacalismo.

syndicalist ['sindikəlist], *s.* sindacalista.

syndicate ['sindikit], | *s.* **1.** (*comm.*) sindacato: *member of a —*, membro di un sindacato **2.** ufficio di sindaco **3.** (*giornalismo*) agenzia di stampa **4.** speciale comitato del senato (all'università di Cambridge).

to **syndicate** ['sindikeit], *v.t.i.* **1.** reggere, dirigere a mezzo di sindacato **2.** costituirsi, riunirsi in sindacato.

syndication [,sindi'keiʃən], *s.* costituzione in sindacato.

syne [sain], *av.* (*scoz.*) fin da: *auld lang —*, i vecchi tempi, i giorni lontani.

synecdoche [si'nekdəki], *s.* (*ret.*) sineddoche.

syneresis [si'niərəsis], *pl.* **synereses** [si'niərəsi:z], *s.* (*gram.*) sineresi.

synizesis [,sini'zi:sis], *pl.* **synizeses** [,sini'zi:si:z], *s.* (*patol. gram.*) sinizesi.

synod ['sinəd], *s.* **1.** (*eccl. astr.*) sinodo: *oecumenical* —, sinodo ecumenico **2.** riunione, convegno.

synodal ['sinədl], *ag.* (*eccl.*) sinodale.

synodic(al) [si'nɔdik(əl)], *ag.* **1.** (*eccl.*) sinodale **2.** (*astr.*) sinodico ☆ — *month*, (*astr.*) lunazione.

synodically [si'nɔdikəli], *av.* (*eccl.*) sinodalmente.

synonym ['sinənim], *s.* sinonimo.

synonymic(al) [,sinə'nimik(əl)], *ag.* di sinonimo, relativo a sinonimo.

synonymity [,sinə'nimiti], *s.* sinonimia.

to **synonymize** [si'nɔnimaiz], *v.t.i.* (*rar.*) **1.** dare i sinonimi di: *to — a word*, dare i sinonimi di una parola **2.** usare sinonimi.

synonymous [si'nɔniməs], *ag.* sinonimo: *his name is — with cowardice*, il suo nome è sinonimo di codardia.

synonymously [si'nɔniməsli], *av.* con sinonimia.

synonymy [si'nɔnimi], *s.* **1.** studio dei sinonimi **2.** uso dei sinonimi **3.** sinonimia.

synopsis [si'nɔpsis], *pl.* **synopses** [si'nɔpsi:z], *s.* sinossi.

synoptic(al) [si'nɔptik(əl)], *ag.* sinottico ‖ *the — Gospels*, i Vangeli sinottici.

synoptically [si'nɔptikəli], *av.* in maniera sinottica.

synovia [si'nouviə], *s.* (*fisiol.*) sinovia.

synovial [si'nouviəl], *ag.* (*fisiol.*) sinoviale.

synovitis [,sinə'vaitis], *s.* (*patol.*) sinovite.

syntactic(al) [sin'tæktik(əl)], *ag.* (*gram.*) sintattico.

syntactically [sin'tæktikəli], *av.* (*gram.*) sintatticamente.

syntax ['sintæks], *s.* (*gram.*) sintassi.

synthesis ['sinθisis], *pl.* **syntheses** ['sinθisi:z], *s.* sintesi.

to **synthesize** ['sinθisaiz], *v.t.* sintetizzare.

synthetic(al) [sin'θetik(əl)], *ag.* sintetico ☆ — *rubber*, gomma sintetica.

synthetically [sin'θetikəli], *av.* sinteticamente.

to **synthetize** ['sinθitaiz], *v.t.* sintetizzare.

to **syntonize** ['sintənaiz], *v.t.* (*rad.*) sintonizzare.

syntony ['sintəni], *s.* (*rad.*) sintonia.

to **sypher** ['saifə*], *v.t.* unire (due assi di legno) in modo da formare una superficie piana.

syphilis ['sifilis], *s.* (*patol.*) sifilide.

syphilitic [,sifi'litik], **syphilous** ['sifiləs], *ag.* (*patol.*) sifilitico.

syphon, *V.* **siphon.**

Syracuse ['saiərəkiu:z, *negli Stati Uniti* 'sirəkju:s], *no.pr.* (*geog.*) Siracusa.

syren, *V.* **siren.**

Syria ['siriə], *no.pr.* (*geog.*) Siria.

Syriac ['siriæk], *ag.* siriaco ‖ *s.* lingua siriaca.

Syrian ['siriən], *ag.* siriano ‖ *s.c.* abitante della Siria.

syringa [si'ringə], *s.* (*bot.*) siringa.

syringe ['sirindʒ], *s.* siringa ☆ *garden* —, (*agr.*) siringa nebulizzatrice (per fiori, piante); *hypodermic* —, (*med.*) siringa ipodermica.

to **syringe**, *v.t.* **1.** siringare, iniettare **2.** (*agr.*) spruzzare (piante, ecc.) con siringa.

syringotomy [,sirin'gɔtəmi], *s.* (*chir.*) siringotomia.

syrinx ['sirinks], *pl.* **syrinxes** ['sirinksiz], **syringes** ['sirindʒi:z], *s.* **1.** zampogna, siringa **2.** (*anat.*) tromba d'Eustachio **3.** (*archeol.*) stretta galleria (nelle tombe egiziane) **4.** siringe (di uccelli).

syrtic ['sə:tik], *ag.* sirtico.

Syrtis ['sə:tis], *pl.* **Syrtes** ['sə:ti:z], *no.pr.* (*geog.*) Sirte ‖ **syrtis**, *s.* sabbia mobile.

syrup ['sirəp], *s.* sciroppo ☆ *golden* —, melassa.

syrupy ['sirəpi], *ag.* sciropposo.

systaltic [sis'tæltik], *ag.* (*fisiol.*) sistaltico, pulsante.

system ['sistim], *s.* **1.** sistema: — *of philosophy*, sistema filosofico **2.** metodo, organizzazione: — *of government*, sistema di governo; — *is necessary to succeed in business of any kind*, è necessario avere metodo per riuscire in qualsiasi affare **3.** organismo: *bad for the* —, dannoso per l'organismo ‖ *to get sthg. out of one's* —, cercare di dimenticare qlco. **4.** (*mus.*) insieme di righi di partitura ☆ *decimal* —, sistema decimale; *nervous* —, sistema nervoso; *railway* —, rete ferroviaria; *river* —, rete fluviale; *solar* —, (*astr.*) sistema solare; *telegraph* —, rete telegrafica.

systematic [,sisti'mætik], *ag.* sistematico, metodico.

systematically [,sisti'mætikəli], *av.* sistematicamente, metodicamente.

systematization ['sistimətai'zeiʃən], *s.* sistemazione.

to **systematize** ['sistimətaiz], *v.t.* ridurre a sistema.

systematizer ['sistimətaizə*], *s.* sistematore, chi instaura un sistema.

systemic [sis'temik], *ag.* dell'organismo, di tutto il corpo ☆ — *circulation*, (*fisiol.*) grande circolazione.

systemless ['sistimlis], *ag.* **1.** senza sistema **2.** (*biol.*) senza struttura organica.

systole ['sistəli], *s.* (*fisiol.*) sistole.

systolic [sis'tɔlik], *ag.* (*fisiol.*) sistolico.

systyle ['sistail], *ag.s.* (*arch.*) (edificio) sistilo.

systylous ['sistiləs], *ag.* (*bot.*) sistilo, a stili riuniti.

syzygy ['sizidʒi], *s.* (*astr.*) sizigia.

T

t [ti:], *pl.* **ts, t's** [ti:z], *s.* **1.** (*ventesima lettera dell'alfabeto inglese*) t — *for Tommy*, (*tel.*) t come Torino ‖ *to a T*, perfettamente, a pennello: *it suits you to a T*, ti sta a pennello, è la cosa che fa per te; *the soup was done to a T*, la minestra era squisita ‖ *to cross one's t's*, *fig.* mettere i punti sugli i **2.** oggetto a forma di T ☆ *T -bar, T iron, T section*, sbarra, ferro, segmento a T; *T -cart*, calessino; *T shirt*, maglietta aperta a T; *T -square*, squadra a T.

't, *pron. n.* (*contr. di* it; *in unione con il v.* essere): *'tis*, è; *'twas*, era.

ta [tɑ:], *s.* (*abbr. fam. di* thank you) grazie.

Taal [tɑ:l], *s.* «taal» (dialetto Olandese del Sud-Africa).

tab [tæb], *s.* **1.** puntale (di stringa) **2.** linguetta; passante **3.** (*ear-*) —, copriorecchi (di berretto) **4.** (*mil.*) mostrine (di ufficiale di Stato Maggiore) ‖ *red* —, (*sl.*) ufficiale di Stato Maggiore **5.** (*fam. amer.*) registrazione; controllo; conto ‖ *to keep tab(s) on s.o., on sthg.*, (*fam.*) sorvegliare attentamente, controllare qlcu., ql.co. **6.** cartellino portaindirizzi (per valigie) **7.** (*aer.*) aletta di compensazione, compensatore ☆ *spring* —, (*aer.*) aletta compensatrice elastica; *trimming* —, (*aer.*) correttore di assetto.

to tab, *pass. p.p.* **tabbed** [tæbd], *v.t.* (*fam.*) disporre in tabelle.

tabard ['tæbəd], *s.* (*st.*) **1.** cotta d'arme **2.** tabarro.

tabaret ['tæbərit], *s.* stoffa a righe alternate di seta marezzata e raso (per tappezzeria).

tabasheer, tabashir [,tæbə'ʃiə*], *s.* tabascir (concrezioni silicee del bambù usate in medicina).

tabby ['tæbi], *ag.* chiazzato, marezzato, tigrato ‖ *s.* **1.** — (*-cat*), gatto soriano, gatto tigrato; gatta **2.** moerro **3.** vecchia zitella pettegola **4.** conglomerato di cemento, calcestruzzo.

to tabby, *pass. p.p.* **tabbied** ['tæbid], *v.t.* marezzare (stoffa).

tabefaction [,tæbi'fækʃən], *s.* (*patol.*) deperimento, consunzione

to tabefy ['tæbifai], *v.t.i.* (*rar.*) consumare, consumarsi; deperire.

tabellion [tə'beljən], *s.* (*arc.*) tabellione, notaro.

taberdar ['tæbə(:)dɑ:*], *s.* (*st.*) membro del Queen's College a Oxford.

tabernacle ['tæbə(:)nækl], *s.* **1.** tabernacolo, ciborio; (*st. ebraica*) tabernacolo ‖ *Feast of Tabernacles*, festa dei tabernacoli **2.** tempio, chiesa **3.** *fig.* corpo umano **4.** (*arch.*) nicchia, cappelletta (con immagine sacra) **5.** (*mar.*) supporto scatolato.

to tabernacle, *v.t.i.* **1.** mettere nel tabernacolo **2.** abitare temporaneamente.

tabernacular [,tæbə'nækjulə*], *ag.* di tabernacolo.

tabes ['teibi:z], *s.* (*patol.*) tabe ☆ *dorsal* —, atassia locomotrice, tabe dorsale.

tabescence [tə'besns], *s.* (*patol.*) consunzione, tabe.

tabescent [tə'besnt], **tabetic** [tə'betik], **tabid** ['tæbid], *ag.* (*patol.*) tabetico, affetto da tabe.

tabinet ['tæbinit], *s.* stoffa marezzata di lana e seta per tappezzeria.

tabitude ['tæbitju:d], *s.* (*patol.*) consunzione, tabe.

tablature ['tæblətʃə*], *s.* **1.** rappresentazione mentale **2.** (*mus.*) intavolatura.

table ['teibl], *s.* **1.** tavola, tavolino; mensa: *nest of tables*, serie di tavolini a incastro; *to clear, to lay the* —, sparecchiare, apparecchiare la tavola; *to wait at* —, ser-vire a tavola (di domestici) ‖ *the Round Table*, la Tavola Rotonda ‖ *to keep a good* —, avere una buona tavola, mangiare bene ‖ *to lay a measure, a plan on the* —, rimandare un provvedimento, un progetto a tempo indeterminato ‖ *to lay* (o *to put*) *one's cards on the* —, *fig.* mettere le carte in tavola, fare un giuoco scoperto, parlar chiaro **2.** tavolata, commensali: *the* — *was young and gay*, i commensali erano giovani e allegri; *he amused the* —, tenne allegri i commensali **3.** tabella, elenco: — *of contents*, indice di un libro; — *of weights and measures*, tavola dei pesi e delle misure **4.** tavola, tavoletta, lastra (di pietra, bronzo, avorio, ecc.) ‖ *the tables of the Law* (o *the Two Tables*), le tavole della Legge (Mosaica), i dieci comandamenti; *the Twelve Tables*, (*st.*) le Dodici Tavole (dei Decemviri) **5.** — (*-land*), (*geog.*) tavolato, altipiano **6.** (*tec.*) piano, tavola **7.** (*oreficeria*) gemma tagliata in quadrato; faccia superiore di tale gemma **8.** (*chiromanzia*) quadrilatero delle linee nel palmo della mano **9.** (*anat.*) piastra ossea **10.** *pl.* (*rar.*) tavola reale, tric-trac ‖ *to turn the tables on s.o.*, rovesciare le posizioni, ritornare in posizione di vantaggio ☆ — *-clamp*, bloccaggio della tavola, morsetto; — *-cloth*, tovaglia; — *-flap*, ribalta di tavola; — *-fork*, — *-knife*, — *-spoon*, forchetta, coltello, cucchiaio da tavola; — *-leaf*, allungo di tavola; — *-linen*, biancheria da tavola; — *-mat*, sottopiatto; — *-money*, (*mar. mil.*) indennità per spese di rappresentanza (agli ufficiali superiori); (*fam.*) quota pagata dai soci di un circolo per i servizi di mensa; — *-rapping*, il battere sul tavolino (alle sedute spiritiche); — *-talk*, conversazione familiare; — *-tennis*, ping-pong; — *-turning*, il muoversi del tavolino (alle sedute spiritiche); — *-ware*, vasellame, stoviglie da tavola; — *-water*, acqua minerale da tavola; — *-wine*, vino da pasto ‖ *card*— (o *gaming*- —), tavolino da giuoco; *collapsible* —, tavolino pieghevole; *draw*- — (o *extension* — o *telescope* —), tavola allungabile; *flap*- —, tavola a ribalta; *high* —, tavola dei professori universitari, tavola d'onore; *inspection* —, banco di controllo; *multiplication* —, tavola pitagorica; *synoptic* —, tavola sinottica; *tea*- —, tavolino da tè; *tide*- —, indicatore delle maree; *time* - —, orario (ferroviario, scolastico).

to table, *v.t.* **1.** porre sul tavolo ‖ *to* — *a bill*, depositare un progetto di legge; (*amer.*) aggiornare un progetto di legge **2.** incastrare (legni) **3.** giuocare, buttare (una carta) **4.** (*mar.*) rafforzare l'orlo di (una vela) **5.** (*rar.*) elencare, classificare.

tableau ['tæblou], *pl.* **tableaux** ['tæblouz], *s.* **1.** — (*vivant*), *pl.* *tableaux* (*vivants*), quadro plastico **2.** *fig.* situazione, scena drammatica **3.** elenco ufficiale ☆ — *curtains*, (*teat.*) velario.

table d'hôte ['tɑ:bl'dout], *s.* pasto a prezzo ed ora fissi.

tableful ['teiblful], *s.* tavolata: *a* — *of old people*, una tavolata di vecchi, di persone anziane.

tablespoonful ['teiblspu:n,ful], *s.* cucchiaiata: *a* — *three times a day*, un cucchiaio da tavola tre volte al dì

tablet ['tæblit], *s.* **1.** tavoletta; lapide **2.** (*farm.*) compressa, pastiglia **3.** (*arch.*) cornicione ☆ *bronze* — , targa di bronzo.

tabling ['teiblin], *s.* **1.** incastro, connessione (di legni) **2.** (*mar.*) guaina, orlo rinforzato (di vela).

tabloid ['tæbloid], *ag.* conciso, succinto ‖ *s.* **1.** (*farm.*) pastiglia, compressa **2.** (*amer.*) rotocalco in formato ridotto, in stile semplice e conciso.

taboo [tə'bu:], *ag.* **1.** tabù, proibito, interdetto **2.** sacro ‖ *s.* tabù, interdizione, proibizione: *there was a — attached to the word legs*, la parola gambe era tabù.

to taboo, *v.t.* interdire, dare l'ostracismo a; proibire: *he was tabooed*, fu messo al bando.

tabor ['teibə*], *s.* (*mus.*) tamburello.

to tabor, *v.i.* suonare il tamburello.

taborer ['teibərə*], *s.* suonatore di tamburello.

tabour ['teibə*], *s.* (*mus.*) tamburello.

to tabour, *v.i.* suonare il tamburello.

tabouret ['tæbərit], *s.* **1.** sgabello **2.** telaio da ricamo.

(to) tabu, *V.* (to) **taboo**.

tabular ['tæbjulə*], *ag.* **1.** a forma di tabella, di prospetto **2.** catalogato, classificato **3.** piatto, piano: *— surface*, superficie piana **4.** a strati sottili, laminato.

tabularly ['tæbjuləli], *av.* **1.** in modo sinottico **2.** in modo piatto.

tabulate ['tæbjulit], *ag.* di superficie piatta, piana.

to tabulate ['tæbjuleit], *v.t.* disporre in tabelle, tavole sinottiche; catalogare.

tabulation [,tæbju'leiʃən], *s.* ordinamento in tabelle; classificazione, catalogazione.

tabulator ['tæbjuleitə*], *s.* (*mec.*) tabulatore ☆ *— key*, (*mec.*) tasto incolonnatore; *— stops ruler*, (*mec.*) comando arresti del tabulatore.

tacamahac ['tækəmə,hæk], *s.* **1.** taccamacca (resina aromatica del Sud-America) **2.** (*bot.*) pioppo del balsamo.

tac-au-tac [,tækou'tæk], *s.* (*scherma*) battuta e controbattuta.

tache[1] [ta:ʃ], *s.* **1.** macchia **2.** (*dial.*) tratto, caratteristica.

tache[2], *s.* (*rar.*) fibbia; fermaglio; gancio.

tacheometer [,tæki'ɔmitə*], *V.* **tachymeter**.

tacheometry [,tæki'ɔmitri], *s.* (*geodesia*) tacheometria.

tachometer [tæ'kɔmitə*], *s.* (*mec.*) tachimetro, contagiri ☆ *— drive*, (*mec.*) presa del contagiri.

tachycardia [,tæki'ka:diə], *s.* (*patol.*) tachicardia.

tachygraph ['tækigra:f], **tachygrapher** [tæ'kigrəfə*], *s.* esperto in tachigrafia, tachigrafo.

tachygraphic(al) [,tæki'græfik(əl)], *ag.* tachigrafico.

tachigraphy [tæ'kigrəfi], *s.* (*st.*) tachigrafia.

tachymeter [tæ'kimitə*], *s.* **1.** (*geodesia*) tacheometro **2.** (*mec.*) tachimetro.

tachymetry [tæ'kimitri], *s.* (*geodesia*) tacheometria.

tacit ['tæsit], *ag.* **1.** tacito, implicito, sottinteso: *a — consent*, un tacito consenso **2.** silenzioso.

tacitly ['tæsitli], *av.* **1.** tacitamente, implicitamente **2.** silenziosamente.

taciturn ['tæsitə:n], *ag.* taciturno.

taciturnity [,tæsi'tə:niti], *s.* taciturnità.

taciturnly ['tæsitə:nli], *av.* taciturnamente.

Tacitus ['tæsitəs], *no.pr.m.* (*st. lett.*) Tacito.

tack[1] [tæk], *s.* **1.** bulletta, chiodo ‖ *let's get down to brass tacks*, veniamo ai fatti, vediamo il lato pratico della faccenda **2.** punto lungo, imbastitura: *take out the tacks*, togli l'imbastitura **3.** (*mar.*) mura, cavo per orientare la vela **4.** (*mar.*) bordata: *to make a —*, fare una bordata; *to make — and —*, bordeggiare **5.** *fig.* linea di condotta: *to be on the right, wrong —*, essere sulla strada giusta, sbagliata; *to try another —*, cambiare linea di condotta **6.** (*pol.*) codicillo, articolo aggiunto **7.** viscosità; adesività (di vernice, ecc.) ☆ *— -hammer*, martello da tappezziere; *— welding*, (*mec.*) puntatura ‖ *heel —*, bulletta per tacchi; *thumb —*, puntina da disegno; *tin- —*, chiodino di ferro stagnato.

to tack[1], *v.t.i.* **1.** imbullettare, inchiodare ‖ *to — down a carpet*, fermare un tappeto con bullette **2.** imbastire: *she tacked her dress*, imbastì l'abito **3.** aggiungere, attaccare: *to — a moral at the end of the story*, aggiungere la morale alla fine della storia **4.** (*mar.*) bordeggiare; virare di bordo **5.** *fig.* cambiare condotta, tattica **6.** (*dir.*) aggiungere (una terza

ipoteca) alla prima (acquistando in tal modo priorità sulla seconda).

tack[2], *s.* **1.** cibo, alimento **2.** (*spreg.*) roba, robaccia ☆ *soft- —*, pane.

tack[3], *s.* (*scoz. fam.*) **1.** possesso per contratto d'affitto; periodo di locazione **2.** pascoli dati in affitto.

tackiness ['tækinis], *s.* viscosità, adesività.

tacking ['tækiŋ], *s.* **1.** l'imbullettare **2.** imbastitura **3.** (*mar.*) bordeggio **4.** (*pol.*) articolo, comma, aggiunta **5.** (*dir.*) priorità di una terza ipoteca sulla seconda ☆ *— cotton*, cotone da imbastire.

tackle ['tækl], *s.* **1.** (*mec.*) taglia; (*mar.*) paranco **2.** arnesi, utensili; attrezzatura (di sport, ecc.) **3.** finimenti (di cavallo) **4.** (*rugby*) placcaggio **5.** (*sl.*) cibo; bevande ☆ *— -block*, bozzello del paranco; *— -fall*, cavo del paranco ‖ *double —*, paranco doppio; *fishing - —*, arnesi da pesca.

to tackle, *v.t.* **1.** afferrare, trattenere (un nemico, ecc.): *that man tackled the thief*, quell'uomo afferrò il ladro **2.** affrontare (difficoltà, lavoro, argomento, ecc.): *he seems to — the job with real competence*, sembra affrontare il lavoro con vera competenza ‖ *he tackled the cake with a will*, (*fam.*) si attaccò al dolce con entusiasmo ‖ *to — s.o. over a matter*, sondare qlcu. su un argomento **3.** mettere finimenti a (un cavallo) **4.** (*rugby*) placcare **5.** *to — to*, mettersi d'impegno al lavoro: *after the death of her husband she's had to — to*, dopo la morte del marito ha dovuto mettersi seriamente al lavoro.

tackling ['tækliŋ], *s.* **1.** (*rar. mar.*) paranco **2.** (*rugby*) placcaggio.

tacksman, *pl.* **tacksmen** ['tæksmən], *s.* (*scoz.*) affittuario di grande tenuta (che subaffitta).

tacky ['tæki], *ag.* **1.** appiccicaticcio, viscoso **2.** (*amer.*) trascurato, in disordine.

tact [tækt], *s.* **1.** (*arc.*) tatto **2.** *fig.* tatto, riguardo, garbo, maniera: *to be wanting in —*, mancare di tatto.

tactful ['tæktful], *ag.* pieno di tatto, di garbo.

tactfully ['tæktfuli], *av.* con tatto, garbatamente.

tactic[1] ['tæktik], *ag.* tattico ‖ *s. V.* **tactics**.

tactic[2], *ag.* tattile.

tactical ['tæktikəl], *ag.* **1.** (*mil. mar.*) tattico, relativo alla tattica: *— methods*, metodi tattici **2.** abile.

tactician [tæk'tiʃən], *s.* **1.** (*mil. mar.*) tattico **2.** (*amer.*) dirigente abile, esperto.

tactics ['tæktiks], *s.* **1.** (*mil.*) tattica: *the old — proved inefficient*, la vecchia tattica si rivelò inadeguata **2.** *fig.* espediente, procedimento abile.

tactile ['tæktail], *ag.* **1.** tattile **2.** tangibile.

tactility [tæk'tiliti], *s.* **1.** tattilità **2.** tangibilità.

taction ['tækʃən], *s.* contatto.

tactless ['tæktlis], *ag.* che manca di tatto, senza tatto; indiscreto: *— question*, domanda indiscreta.

tactlessly ['tæktlisli], *av.* senza tatto.

tactlessness ['tæktlisnis], *s.* mancanza di tatto.

tactual ['tæktjuəl], *ag.* tattile.

tactually ['tæktjuəli], *av.* col tatto.

tad [tæd], *s.* (*amer.*) bambinetto.

tadpole ['tædpoul], *s.* (*zool.*) girino.

taedium ['ti:djəm], *s.* tedio, noia, uggia.

tael [teil], *s.* **1.** « tæl » (unità di peso cinese = g. 37 circa) **2.** unità monetaria cinese.

ta'en [tein], *contr.* di **taken**.

taenia ['ti:niə], *pl.* **taeniae** ['ti:nii:], *s.* **1.** tenia, verme solitario **2.** (*anat.*) formazione a nastro **3.** (*arch.*) tenia, fascia (di architrave) **4.** benda, fascia.

tafferel ['tæfərəl], *s.* **1.** (*mar.*) coronamento **2.** (*mar.*) ringhiera di poppa **3.** complimento rozzo, volgare.

taffeta ['tæfitə], *s.* taffettà.

taffrail ['tæfreil], *s.* (*mar.*) ringhiera di poppa.

taffy[1] ['tæfi], *s.* **1.** caramella **2.** (*sl. amer.*) adulazione, lisciamento.

Taffy[2], *no.pr.m.* (*gallese*) Davide ‖ *s.* (*fam.*) un gallese.

tafia ['tæfiə], *s.* rum ricavato dalla melassa.

tag¹ [tæg], *s.* **1.** lembo (di stoffa, nastro, ecc.) che pende **2.** cartellino, etichetta mobile (per pacchi, valigie, ecc.) **3.** puntale, aghetto (di stringa) **4.** tirante (di stivale) **5.** estremità della coda di un animale **6.** aggiunta a un discorso, a uno scritto; (*teat.*) discorso di chiusura; pistolotto finale **7.** frase fatta, luogo comune: *moral* —, massima moraleggiante **8.** ritornello (di canzonetta) ☆ — *-day*, (*amer.*) giorno di questua per scopi benefici ‖ *dog-* —, (*sl. amer.*) medaglia d'identità di un soldato; *licence* —, (*aut.*) bollo di circolazione.

to **tag¹**, *pass.p.p.* **tagged** [tægd], *v.t.i.* **1.** mettere il puntale a **2.** mettere, attaccare cartellini (mobili) a **3.** aggiungere parole, frasi fatte, versi a: *he tagged (on) some lines of his own making*, vi aggiunse qualche verso fatto da lui **4.** (*fam.*) seguire da vicino, pedinare **5.** tosare (pecore) **6.** appiccicare insieme **7.** rimare: *those two words do not* —, quelle due parole non rimano.

tag², *s.* il giuocare a rincorrersi.

to **tag²**, *v.t.* toccare (giuocando a rincorrersi).

tag³, *s.* pecora di due anni.

tagger ['tægə*], *s.* lamierino sottilissimo.

Tagus ['teigəs], *no.pr.* (*geog.*) Tago.

Tahiti [tɑ:'hi:ti], *no.pr.* (*geog.*) Ta(h)iti.

Tahitian [tɑ:'hi:tiən], *ag. s.c.* (abitante) di Ta(h)iti.

tahr [tɑ:*], *s.* (*zool.*) emitrago.

to **taigle** ['teigl], *v.t.i.* (*scoz.*) ritardare, impedire; ndugiare.

tail¹ [teil], *s.* **1.** coda; parte terminale, estremità: *the* — *of a comet*, coda di una cometa; *the* — *of the procession*, la coda, la parte estrema della processione; *the* — *of the q*, la coda della q; *the dog wags its* — *when it is pleased*, il cane mena la coda quando è contento ‖ *the* — *of the eye*, la coda dell'occhio ‖ *with his* — *between his legs*, con la coda tra le gambe ‖ *I can't make head or* — *of this*, non ne capisco niente ‖ *we can't have the* — *wagging the dog*, non sta agli inferiori dirigere i superiori ‖ *to have one's* — *down, up*, essere di cattivo, buon umore ‖ *to turn* —, scappare, darsela a gambe **2.** coda, falda, strascico (di abito); *pl.* marsina, «tight»: *boys go into tails at sixteen*, i ragazzi indossano l'abito a coda, la marsina a sedici anni **3.** (*tip.*) piede **4.** *gener. pl.* rovescio (di moneta), croce: *heads or tails*, testa o croce **5.** treccia (di capelli) ☆ — *-block*, (*mec.*) contropunta; — *-board*, ribalta di un carro; — *-boom*, (*aer.*) trave di coda; — *-coat*, marsina, frac; «tight»; — *-gate*, (*aut.*) sponda posteriore; porta di una chiusa; — *-light*, (*aut.*) fanalino di coda; — *-pipe*, (*aer.*) tubo d'aspirazione; ugello d'uscita; (*aut.*) tubo di scappamento; — *-shaft*, (*mar.*) albero portaelica; (*mil.*) manico (di bomba aerea); — *-skid*, (*aer.*) pattino di coda; — *-surface*, (*aer.*) impennaggio; — *-wheel*, (*aer.*) ruotino di coda; — *-wind*, (*aer.*) vento di coda ‖ *mares' tails*, cirri.

to **tail¹**, *v.t.i.* **1.** munire di coda **2.** essere in coda a, trovarsi all'ultimo posto di: *he tails the procession*, è in coda, chiude il corteo; *to* — *the class*, essere fra gli ultimi della classe **3.** tagliare, mozzare la coda di (agnello, ecc.); tagliare, togliere il picciolo di (frutto, fiore, ecc.) **4.** *to* — *after* (*s.o., sthg.*), pedinare, seguire da vicino: *that man was tailed after by a policeman*, quell'uomo fu pedinato da un poliziotto **5.** *to* — *away, off*, diminuire gradualmente, assottigliarsi; affievolirsi; (*elett.*) disperdersi: *the noise tailed away*, il rumore si affievolì; *the procession will* — *away very soon*, il corteo si assottiglierà ben presto **6.** *to* — *on*, aggiungere, unire; mettersi in coda **7.** *to* — *up*, (*aer.*) impennarsi; (*amer.*) fare la coda, mettersi in fila.

tail², *ag.* (*dir.*) limitato, regolato (da condizioni fissate dal donatore) ‖ *s.* (*dir.*) proprietà limitata a una persona e ai suoi eredi diretti: *estate in* —, proprietà in vincolo.

to **tail²**, *v.t.* (*dir.*) assegnare con delle limitazioni.

tailed [teild], *ag.* fornito di coda; caudato ☆ *long-* —, dalla lunga coda; *swallow-* —, a coda di rondine.

tailing ['teiliŋ], *s.* **1.** accodamento, l'accodarsi **2.** (*edil.*) parte incastrata di pietra, di mattone, in aggetto **3.** (*ind. tessile*) macchia, difetto (nelle cotonerie stampate) **4.** *pl.* mondiglia, lolla; (*ind.*) residui di scarto.

tailless ['teillis], *ag.* **1.** senza coda **2.** (*aer.*) tutt'ala ☆ — *aeroplane*, apparecchio tutt'ala.

tailor ['teilə*], *s.* sarto ☆ — *-bird*, (*ornit.*) uccello sarto; — *-made*, fatto dal sarto, fatto su misura; — *-made costume*, «tailleur», abito a giacca; — *'s shop*, sartoria; — *'s twist*, cordonetto di seta per occhielli.

to **tailor**, *v.t.i.* **1.** fare il sarto **2.** confezionare un abito per, vestire (un cliente): *a carefully tailored gentleman*, un signore raffinatamente elegante; *who tailors him?*, chi lo veste?, da chi si fa fare i vestiti? **3.** (*sl.*) rovinare (la selvaggina, sparando male).

tailoress ['teiləris], *s.* sarta.

tailoring ['teiləriŋ], *s.* mestiere, arte del sarto.

tailpiece ['teil-pi:s], *s.* **1.** (*tip.*) piede, finalino tipografico **2.** (*mus.*) cordiera.

tain [tein], *s.* foglia (dello specchio).

taint [teint], *s.* **1.** contaminazionĕ, infezione **2.** tara, vizio organico: *there is a* — *of insanity in her as in her family*, c'è un ramo di pazzia in lei come nella sua famiglia **3.** *fig.* marchio, segno, traccia: *the* — *of sin*, il marchio del peccato; *the* — *of vanity in his actions*, il segno della vanità nelle sue azioni.

to **taint**, *v.t.i.* guastare, guastarsi; infettare, inquinare (anche *fig.*): *meat taints easily in hot countries*, la carne si guasta facilmente nei paesi caldi; *the smoke of factories taints the air*, il fumo delle fabbriche infetta, inquina l'aria; *such books may* — *the minds of young readers*, tali libri possono guastare la mente dei giovani lettori; *your mind is tainted*, la tua mente è bacata.

taintless ['teintlis], *ag.* incontaminato, immacolato.

taintlessly ['teintlisli], *av.* in modo incontaminato, senza macchia.

Taiwan [tai'wæn], *no.pr.* (*geog.*) Taiwan (Formosa).

take [teik], *s.* **1.** il prendere **2.** presa (di selvaggina, ecc.); pesca, retata (di pesce) **3.** incasso **4.** (*cine. tv.*) ripresa **5.** (*tip.*) tiratura.

to **take**, *pass.* **took** [tuk], *p.p.* **taken** ['teikən], *v.t.i.* **1.** prendere; afferrare; impadronirsi di; catturare; cogliere, sorprendere: *he took me at a disadvantage*, mi colse in posizione di svantaggio; *they took me by the arm*, mi presero per il braccio; *the town was taken by storm*, la città fu presa d'assalto; *to be taken in the act*, essere colto sul fatto; essere sorpreso in fallo ‖ *to* — *advantage of*, abusare di, approfittare di ‖ *to* — *breath*, prender fiato ‖ *to* — *the bull by the horns*, prendere il toro per le corna ‖ *to* — *fire*, prendere fuoco ‖ *to* — *hold of*, afferrare ‖ *to* — *leave*, prendere congedo ‖ *to* — *one's chance*, tentare la propria sorte ‖ *to* — *sthg. in hand*, intraprendere ql.co. ‖ *to* — *time by the forelock*, afferrare la fortuna per i capelli **2.** acquistare; acquisire; accettare; ricevere; contrarre (malattia): *I can't* — *money from you*, non posso accettare denaro da te; *she took the first prize*, ella vinse il primo premio; *to* — *a degree*, laurearsi; *to* — *holy orders*, ricevere gli ordini (sacri); *to* — *a seat*, prender posto, sedersi; *to* — *shape*, prendere forma ‖ *to* — *the chair*, assumere la presidenza (di un consiglio, congresso) ‖ *to* — *into account*, prendere in considerazione ‖ *to* — *(it) upon oneself*, incaricarsi di, impegnarsi a, assumersi di ‖ *to* — *s.o. into one's confidence*, confidarsi con qlcu.; *to* — *sthg. into one's head*, mettersi ql.co. in testa **3.** affittare; prendere, comprare regolarmente; abbonarsi a: *do you* — *"The Times"?*, prendi il «Times»?; *to* — *a house, a room*, affittare una casa, una camera **4.** accompagnare, condurre: *where did you* — *him?*, dove l'hai condotto?; *will you* — *the child for a walk?*, vuoi accompagnare il bambino a spasso? **5.** bere, mangiare; consumare (un pasto); prendere (un bagno); fare (una passeggiata, un viaggio); sostenere (un esame): *do you — sugar with your tea?*, metti zucchero nel tè?; *he takes his meals at a restaurant*, mangia al ristorante; *I — a bath every morning*, faccio il bagno tutte le mattine; *I took my exam but I failed*, ho dato l'esame ma non sono stato promosso **6.** prendere (mezzi di trasporto): *I shall — a taxi*, prenderò un tassì **7.** prendere (appunti); fare (una fotografia): *he took a photograph of my sister*, fece una fotografia a mia sorella **8.** riuscire in fotografia: *she doesn't — well*, non è fotogenica **9.** attecchire, attaccare: *if the new vaccine doesn't — we are in for a bad time*, se il nuovo vaccino non attacca ce la vedremo brutta; *roses — very well in this soil*, le rose attecchiscono molto bene in questo terreno **10.** attrarre; aver successo, piacere: *he was taken by her good looks*, fu conquistato dalla sua bellezza; *his book did not —*, il suo libro non ebbe successo **11.** scegliere: *he took a partner*, si scelse un socio; *which road did you —?*, che strada hai preso? **12.** prendere, assumere (determinati atteggiamenti psicologici): — *things coolly!*, calma e sangue freddo!; *to — care of*, aver cura di; *to — an interest*, prendere interesse; *to — the trouble*, prendersi la briga ‖ — *it easy*, prenditela con comodo; non prendertela ‖ *to — amiss*, aversela a male ‖ *to — a fancy to*, accogliere bene, prendere in simpatia **13.** presumere; intendere; considerare; interpretare; supporre: *as I — it*, secondo me; *how would you — this?*, come interpreteresti questo? **14.** portar via; rubare; (*arit.*) sottrarre: — *the knife from the baby*, porta via il coltello al bambino; *who has taken my bag?*, chi ha preso la mia borsa?; *to — 5 from 11*, togliere 5 da 11 **15.** necessitare, occorrere: *it takes a clever man to do that work*, ci vuole un uomo intelligente per fare quel lavoro; *she will — two hours to go to London*, le ci vorranno due ore per andare a Londra **16.** *to — after* (*s.o.*, *sthg.*), assomigliare a: *she takes after her father*, assomiglia a suo padre **17.** *to — from* (*sthg.*), diminuire, sminuire: *this will — from his reputation*, questo andrà a scapito della sua reputazione **18.** *to — to* (*sthg.*), darsi a, mettersi a, cominciare a; provare simpatia per, affezionarsi a: *he took to drinking, gambling*, si diede al bere, al giuoco; *she took to him at once*, provò simpatia per lui immediatamente ‖ *to — to one's heels*, darsela a gambe **19.** *to — about*, condurre intorno (turisti); portare a spasso (una ragazza), per farle la corte) **20.** *to — away*, togliere, sottrarre ‖ *not to be taken away*, da consultarsi sul posto **21.** *to — back*, riprendere; riportare; *fig.* disdire, ritrattare: — *back what you said*, ritira quel che hai detto **22.** *to — down*, tirar giù, abbassare; demolire (un edificio); smontare (una macchina); *fig.* umiliare; inghiottire a fatica; prender nota di, scrivere: *did you — down his address?*, hai preso nota del suo indirizzo? ‖ *he wants taking down* (*a peg or two*), bisogna fargli abbassare le arie **23.** *to — in*, introdurre; ricevere, ospitare; accettare (lavori) a domicilio; ricevere per abbonamento; ridurre, stringere (abiti); serrare (vele); capire; ingannare; (*fam.*) credere: *he seems to — everything in*, pare che capisca tutto; *he takes it all in*, crede a tutto; *was not taken in*, non ci sono cascato; *who is taking you in to dinner?*, chi sarà il tuo cavaliere a tavola?; *will you — my card in? perhaps he will see me*, vuol fare passare il mio biglietto da visita? forse mi riceverà **24.** *to — off*, togliere; staccare; condurre via; scontare, defalcare; inghiottire, tranguggiare; fare il verso a, fare la caricatura a; saltare; (*aer.*) decollare: — *off your coat*, togliti il soprabito; *she took off the receiver and dialled the number*, staccò il ricevitore e fece il numero; *we can't — more than one per cent of our price*, non possiamo defalcare più dell'uno per cento dal prezzo fissato ‖ *to — oneself off*, andarsene (alla chetichella) **25.** *to — on*, intraprendere; assumere (responsabilità, dipendenti); (*fam.*) prendersela, scalmanarsi; accettare la sfida di in una partita: *we can't — on any more workers,*

non possiamo assumere altri operai; *you shouldn't — it on so much!*, non dovresti prendertela tanto! **26.** *to — out*, portar fuori; togliere; prendere, ottenere (brevetto, licenza, ecc.); accettare in pagamento: *he took it out in cigarettes*, si fece pagare in sigarette; *I had a tooth taken out this morning*, mi son fatto togliere un dente stamane; *will you — me out to-night?*, mi porti fuori questa sera? ‖ *to — it out of s.o.*, (*fam.*) fiaccare, spossare qlcu.; farla pagar cara a qlcu. **27.** *to — over*, succedere in (direzione, comando, ecc.); rilevare (un negozio, una casa, ecc.); trasportare: *he said he would — us over in his car*, disse che ci avrebbe portati lui con la sua automobile; *he wants his son to — over the business*, vuole che suo figlio lo sostituisca nella direzione degli affari; *the new manager will — over immediately from the retiring one*, il nuovo direttore succederà immediatamente al direttore uscente **28.** *to — round*, far girare, far passare intorno **29.** *to — up*, prender su, raccogliere; assorbire; occupare (tempo, spazio, ecc.); cominciare (a fare, a trattare); chiudere (un'arteria); continuare; interrompere bruscamente (chi parla); arrestare: *the blotting-paper takes up ink*, la carta assorbente assorbe l'inchiostro; *the bus stops to — up passengers*, l'autobus si ferma a raccogliere passeggeri; *he has taken up French lately*, si è messo a studiare il francese da qualche tempo; *he took up the challenge*, raccolse la sfida; *I will — the matter up*, comincerò ad occuparmi della faccenda ‖ *to — up with s.o.*, legarsi (di amicizia, d'amore, ecc.) con qlcu. ‖ *to be taken up*, essere occupato.

take, (nei composti): — *-down*, (*fam.*) mortificazione, umiliazione; (*mec.*) smontaggio; — *-in*, frode, inganno, turlupinatura; — *-up*, (*mec.*) tenditore; (*cine.*) avvolgitore; avvolgimento.

taken ['teikən], *p.p.* di *to* **take**.

take-off ['teik-ɔːf], *s.* **1.** caricatura; parodia **2.** (*aer.*) decollo **3.** (*spor.*) linea di partenza (di corridore, saltatore, ecc.) ☆ — *power*, (*aer.*) potenza di decollo ‖ *power —*, (*mec.*) presa di forza.

taker ['teikə*], *s.c.* **1.** chi prende, riceve **2.** chi accetta una scommessa ‖ *s.* (*ind.*) dispositivo che prende, rileva, separa ☆ — *-in*, truffatore, ingannatore.

takin ['taːkin], *s.* budorcade (ruminante tibetano).

taking ['teikiŋ], *ag.* **1.** attraente, seducente **2.** contagioso ‖ *s.* **1.** presa, cattura **2.** presa (di selvaggina); pesca **3.** *pl.* (*comm.*) incasso, introito **4.** (*arc.*) agitazione, turbamento.

takingly ['teikiŋli], *av.* in modo attraente.

takingness ['teikiŋnis], *s.* attrattiva, fascino.

talapoin ['tæləpɔin], *s.* **1.** monaco buddista **2.** (*zool.*) cercopiteco dell'Africa occidentale.

talaria [tə'lɛəriə], *s.pl.* talari (calzari alati di Mercurio).

talc [tælk], *s.* (*min.*) talco ☆ — *-schist*, talcoschisto.

talcky ['tælki], *ag.* (*min.*) talcoso.

talcoid ['tælkoid], *ag.* (*min.*) simile a talco.

talcose ['tælkous], **talcous** ['tælkəs], *ag.* (*min.*) talcoso, simile a talco.

talcum ['tælkəm], *s.* (*min.*) talco ☆ — *powder*, talco in polvere.

tale [teil], *s.* **1.** racconto, storia; favola; novella: *a — of adventures*, un racconto di avventure; *to tell a —*, raccontare una favola ‖ — *of a tub*, racconto fantastico, senza capo nè coda ‖ *old wives' tales*, racconti fantastici, incredibili ‖ " *The Winter's Tale* ", (*lett.*) « Il racconto d'inverno » ‖ *she always tells her own —*, la racconta sempre a modo suo ‖ *the thing tells its own —*, la cosa parla da sè **2.** chiacchiera, maldicenza; diceria: *I have heard a — about you*, ho sentito una chiacchiera sul tuo conto ‖ *to tell tales (out of school)*, fare della maldicenza; propalare un segreto **3.** (*arc. poet.*) conto; totale: *the — of dead and wounded is eighty*, il totale dei morti e dei feriti è ottanta ☆ — *-teller*, narratore di storie; persona maldicente ‖ *fairy- —*, racconto di fate, fiaba.

talebearer ['teil,bɛərə*], s.c. persona maldicente.

talebearing ['teil,bɛəriŋ], ag. maldicente ‖ s. maldicenza.

talent ['tælənt], s. 1. talento, ingegno; attitudine: *a man of* —, un uomo d'ingegno, di gran talento; *he has a* — *for music*, ha attitudine alla musica ‖ *he has a* — *for doing the wrong thing*, sembra nato per sbagliare 2. persona di talento; *coll.* persone di talento: *the local* —, gli ingegni del luogo ‖ *the* —, (*sl. spor.*) gli assidui scommettitori 3. (*st.*) talento (moneta, unità di peso variabile).

talented ['tæləntid], ag. che ha talento, molto dotato.

talentless ['tæləntlis], ag. senza talento.

tales ['teili:z], s. (*dir.*) elenco, convocazione di giurati supplenti; giurati supplenti: *to pray a* —, richiedere che vengano convocati giurati supplenti.

talesman, *pl.* **talesmen** ['teili:zmən], s. (*dir.*) giurato supplente.

Taliacotian [,tæliə'kouʃən], ag. (*chir.*) del Tagliacozzi ☆ — *operation*, rinoplastica di Tagliacozzi.

talion ['tæliən], s. (*st.*) taglione, legge del taglione.

taliped ['tæliped], ag. (*med.*) dal piede talo ‖ s. (*med.*) persona, animale dal piede talo.

talipes ['tælipi:z], s. (*med.*) piede talo.

talipot ['tælipɔt], s. (*bot.*) corifa.

talisman ['tælizmən], s. talismano.

talismanic [,tæliz'mænik], ag. di talismano; magico.

talk [tɔ:k], s. 1. conversazione, discussione, discorso: *he is giving a* — *on modern art on the radio to-morrow*, terrà una conversazione sull'arte moderna domani alla radio; *to engage s.o. in* —, attaccar discorso con qlcu.; *to have a talk with s.o.*, intrattenersi con qlcu.‖ *small* —, conversazione frivola, di società 2. parole, chiacchiere: *he is all* — *and we want facts*, è tutto parole mentre noi vogliamo fatti 3. argomento di pettegolezzo, di conversazione: *it is the* — *of the town*, è la favola della città.

to **talk**, v.t.i. 1. parlare; discorrere, conversare: *my child is learning to* —, il mio bambino impara a parlare; *to* — *about* (o *of*) *sthg.*, parlare di ql.co.; *to* — *by signs, by looks*, parlare a segni, a sguardi; *to* — *for the sake of talking*, parlare per il gusto di parlare; *to* — *to oneself*, parlare tra sè e sè; *to* — *to* (o *with*) *s.o.*, parlare con qlcu. ‖ *to* — *big*, vantarsi ‖ *to* — *through one's hat*, (*sl.*) esagerare 2. chiacchierare; far pettegolezzi: *people will* —, la gente mormorerà 3. intrattenersi su, parlare di; dire: *to* — *business, politics*, parlare di affari, di politica; *to* — *shop*, parlare del proprio lavoro; *to* — *sense, nonsense*, parlare assennatamente, dire sciocchezze; *to* — *treason*, parlare di tradimento 4. parlare (una lingua): *to* — *French*, parlar francese 5. portare ad una determinata condizione parlando: *to* — *oneself hoarse*, parlare tanto da diventare rauco; *to* — *s.o. into doing sthg.*, persuadere qlcu. a fare ql.co.; *to* — *s.o. out of doing sthg.*, dissuadere qlcu. dal fare ql.co. ‖ *to* — *a donkey's hind-leg off*, chiacchierare incessantemente 6. *to* — *at* (*s.o.*), alludere a: *to* — *at s.o.*, fare allusioni velate a qlcu. (che è presente) 7. *to* — *about*, discutere; far pettegolezzo: *to be talked about*, essere oggetto di pettegolezzo 8. *to* — *back*, replicare 9. *to* — *down*, ridurre al silenzio (parlando più forte, in modo più efficace); adeguarsi parlando: *to* — *down to one's audience*, adeguarsi al proprio uditorio 10. *to* — *out*, discutere a fondo ‖ *to* — *a bill out*, (*pol.*) prolungare il dibattito di un progetto di legge (perchè venga aggiornato) 11. *to* — *over*, discutere; persuadere discutendo: *we can* — *it over after lunch*, ne parleremo dopo pranzo 12. *to* — *round*, discutere senza giungere a una conclusione; persuadere: *I talked them round at last*, li persuasi alla fine 13. *to* — *up*, elogiare parlando: *to* — *up a book*, far scalpore intorno a un libro.

talkative ['tɔ:kətiv], ag. loquace, chiacchierone, linguacciuto.

talkatively ['tɔ:kətivli], av. loquacemente.

talkativeness ['tɔ:kətivnis], s. loquacità.

talkee-talkee ['tɔ:ki'tɔ:ki], s. 1. inglese storpiato parlato dai negri, ecc. 2. cicalio; discorso sconclusionato.

talker ['tɔ:kə*], s.c. 1. chi conversa; parlatore, parlatrice: *he is a brilliant* —, egli è un conversatore brillante 2. chiacchierone, chiacchierona ‖ *great talkers are little doers, prov.* molto fumo, poco arrosto.

talkies ['tɔ:kiz], s.pl. (*sl.*) film sonoro.

talking ['tɔ:kiŋ], ag. che parla ‖ s. 1. conversazione, discorso 2. chiacchiere: *there was little* — *at breakfast*, si parlò poco a colazione ☆ — *doll*, bambola parlante; — -*to*, rimprovero, ramanzina.

talky ['tɔ:ki], ag. — (-*talky*), loquace, chiacchierone.

tall [tɔ:l], ag. 1. alto; grande: *a* — *chimney*, un alto fumaiuolo; *a* — *man*, un uomo alto; *he is six feet* —, è alto sei piedi 2. (*fam.*) straordinario, incredibile, impossibile: *a* — *order*, un affare impossibile; *a* — *story*, una storia incredibile, una panzana ☆ — *hat*, cappello a cilindro, tuba.

tall, av. (*sl.*) in modo esagerato, eccessivo ‖ *to talk* —, esagerare, sballarle grosse.

tallage ['tælidʒ], s. (*st.*) tassa, imposta, dazio.

tallboy ['tɔ:lbɔi], s. canterano, cassettone.

tallish ['tɔ:liʃ], ag. piuttosto alto.

tallness ['tɔ:lnis], s. altezza; statura: *the amazing* — *of some modern buildings*, l'altezza stupefacente di talune costruzioni moderne.

tallow ['tælou], ag. di sego, simile a sego, segoso ‖ s. sego ☆ — -*candle*, candela di sego; — -*chandler*, fabbricante, venditore di candele (di sego); — -*faced*, dal viso pallido, terreo; — -*tree*, albero che produce sego vegetale.

to **tallow**, v.t.i. 1. coprire di sego 2. produrre sego 3. ingrassare (bestiame).

tallowish ['tælouiʃ], **tallowy** ['tæloui], ag. 1. segoso 2. (*fam.*) smunto, pallido.

tally[1] ['tæli], s. 1. tacca; piastrina di contrassegno 2. cartellino, etichetta 3. (*comm.*) duplicato, controparte 4. (*topografia*) piastrina indicatrice ☆ — -*clerk*, chi controlla la consegna di merci; — -*sheet*, (*comm.*) registro vendite rateali; — -*system* (o — -*trade*), (*comm.*) sistema di commercio a vendite rateali.

to **tally**[1], v.t.i. 1. (*comm.*) registrare; riscontrare 2. corrispondere, combaciare (anche *fig.*): *this does not* — *with what he said*, questo non concorda con quello che ha detto; *your list tallies neither with ours nor with the goods*, il vostro elenco non corrisponde nè al nostro nè alla merce 3. mettere etichette, cartellini a 4. *to* — *up*, (*amer.*) calcolare, sommare.

to **tally**[2], v.t.i. (*mar.*) 1. tendere (la scotta) 2. *to* — *on*, iniziare una manovra.

tally-ho ['tæli'hou], s. 1. grido di incitamento a cani nella caccia alla volpe 2. (*arc.*) diligenza; vettura.

to **tally-ho**, v.t. incitare con la voce (i cani, nella caccia alla volpe).

tallyman, *pl.* **tallymen** ['tælimən], s. negoziante che pratica il sistema rateale.

tallyshop ['tæliʃɔp], s. negozio che pratica il sistema di vendita rateale.

talma ['tælmə], s. talma.

talmi-gold ['tɑ:lmi-gould], s. ottone placcato d'oro

Talmud ['tælmud], s. (*st. relig.*) Talmud.

Talmudic(al) [tæl'mudik(əl)], ag. (*st. relig.*) talmudico.

Talmudist ['tælmədist], s. talmudista.

Talmudistic [,tælmə'distik], ag. (*st. relig.*) talmudistico.

talon ['tælən], s. 1. artiglio 2. dente (di stanghetta di serratura) 3. (*arch.*) modanatura a S 4. (*comm.* matrice; talloncino 5. mazzo di carte da giuoco rimasto dopo la distribuzione.

taloned ['tælənd], ag. provvisto di artigli.

talpa ['tælpə], s. 1. (*zool.*) talpa 2. (*patol.*) natta.

talus[1] ['teiləs], s. 1. pendio, scarpata 2. (*geol.*) ammasso di detriti ai piedi di una parete rocciosa.

talus², *pl.* **tali** ['teilai], *s.* **1.** (*anat.*) astragalo **2.** (*med.*) piede talo.

Tam [tæm], *no.pr.m. dim.* (*scoz.*) di **Thomas**.

tamability [,teimə'biliti], *s.* docilità, domabilità.

tamable ['teiməbl], *ag.* addomesticabile, domabile.

tamableness ['teiməblnis], *s.* docilità, domabilità.

tamarack ['tæməræk], *s.* **1.** (*bot.*) larice americano **2.** legno di larice americano.

tamarin ['tæmərin], *s.* mida (piccola scimmia sudamericana).

tamarind ['tæmərind], *s.* (*bot.*) tamarindo.

tamarisk ['tæmərisk], *s.* (*bot.*) tamerice, tamarisco.

tambour ['tæmbuə*], *s.* **1.** (*mus. arch. mil.*) tamburo **2.** tamburo, telaio da ricamo **3.** pesce tamburo.

to **tambour**, *v.t.* ricamare a telaio, a tamburo.

tambourine [,tæmbə'ri:n], *s.* (*mus.*) tamburello.

tame [teim], *ag.* **1.** domestico, addomesticato: *animal that easily grows —*, animale che si addomestica con facilità **2.** coltivato (di pianta, terra) **3.** (*fam.*) mansueto, sottomesso, docile: *her husband was a — little man*, suo marito era un ometto docile || *to be a — cat*, (*fam.*) essere un tipo servizievole **4.** (*fam.*) sbiadito, insipido, monotono: *a — description*, una descrizione monotona.

to **tame**, *v.t.i.* **1.** domare, addomesticare; ammansire, ammansirsi; sottomettere, sottomettersi: *your wife is difficult to be tamed*, (*fam.*) tua moglie ha un carattere un po' forte **2.** (*fam.*) diventare insipido, incolore: *here the story begins to —*, qui la storia diventa banale.

tameability [,teimə'biliti], *s.* docilità, domabilità.

tameable ['teiməbl], *ag.* addomesticabile, domabile.

tameableness ['teiməblnis], *s.* docilità, domabilità.

tameless ['teimlis], *ag.* indomito, indomabile; inaddomesticabile.

tamely ['teimli], *av.* **1.** docilmente, senza opporre resistenza **2.** debolmente, mollemente; servilmente.

tameness ['teimnis], *s.* **1.** docilità, mansuetudine **2.** (*fam.*) pusillanimità, mancanza di coraggio **3.** (*fam.*) banalità, insipidità, mancanza di originalità: *the — of his ideas, of his style*, la banalità delle sue idee, del suo stile.

tamer ['teimə*], *s.c.* domatore, domatrice.

Tamerlane ['tæmə(:)lein], *no.pr.m.* (*st.*) Tamerlano.

Tamil ['tæmil], *ag.* tamil, tamulico || *s.* **1.** tamil, tamulo **2.** lingua tamulica.

tamine ['tæmin], *s.* stamigna, « étamine ».

taming ['teimiŋ], *s.* addomesticamento; ammansimento; soggiogamento || *"The Taming of the Shrew"*, (*lett.*) « La bisbetica domata ».

Tammany ['tæməni], *s.* **1.** — (*Society*), (*st. amer.*) organizzazione centrale del partito democratico || — -*Hall*, sede dell'organizzazione del partito democratico a New York **2.** (*fam.*) corruzione.

tammy¹ ['tæmi], *s.* filtro; buratto.

tammy², *s.* stamigna, « étamine ».

tammy, *abbr.* di **tam-o'-shanter**.

tam-o'-shanter [,tæmə'ʃæntə*], *s.* berretto scozzese.

to **tamp** [tæmp], *v.t.* **1.** (*edil.*) pigiare, calcare, comprimere **2.** intasare (il fornello di una mina) **3.** costipare (terreno).

tampan ['tæmpæn], *s.* (*entom.*) acaro velenoso del Sud-Africa.

tamper¹ ['tæmpə*], *s.* pestello; mazzeranga.

to **tamper**², *v.i.*: *to — with* (*sthg.*), manomettere, alterare (manoscritti, testamenti); corrompere; immischiarsi, intrufolarsi: *don't — with my things*, non immischiarti nelle cose mie; *he tampered with a witness*, tentò di corrompere un testimonio || *to — with a horse*, (*ippica*) drogare un cavallo.

tamperer ['tæmpərə*], *s.c.* **1.** falsificatore, falsificatrice; corruttore, corruttrice **2.** ficcanaso.

tampering ['tæmpəriŋ], *s.* **1.** manomissione, falsificazione, alterazione: *the postman was dismissed for — with the parcels*, il portalettere fu licenziato perchè

aveva manomesso dei pacchi **2.** subornazione, corruzione.

tamping ['tæmpiŋ], *s.* **1.** (*edil.*) pigiatura, battitura **2.** costipamento (di terreno) ☆ — *rollers*, rulli costipatori.

tampion ['tæmpiən], *s.* **1.** tappo (per canna d'organo) **2.** (*artigl.*) tappo di volata.

tampon ['tæmpon], *s.* **1.** (*chir.*) tampone, stuello **2.** tampone (di incisore) **3.** imbottitura (per capelli).

to **tampon**, *v.t.* **1.** (*chir.*) tamponare, stuellare **2.** imbottire (capelli).

tamponade [,tæmpə'neid], **tamponage** ['tæmpənidʒ], *s.* (*chir.*) tamponamento.

tamtam ['tʌmtʌm], *V.* **tomtom**.

tan [tæn], *ag.* marrone rossiccio || *s.* **1.** concia, corteccia di quercia (specialmente della varietà vallonea da cui si ricava il tannino) **2.** polvere di tale corteccia (usata per ricoprire piste, percorsi, ecc.) || *the —*, (*sl.*) circo equestre **3.** tané, color marrone rossiccio **4.** abbronzatura (della pelle) ☆ — -*balls*, formelle (di segatura) da ardere; — -*liquor* (o — -*ooze* o — -*pickle*), liquido da concia; — -*vat*, tino per concia; — -*yard*, conceria.

to **tan**, *pass.p.p.* **tanned** [tænd], *v.t.i.* **1.** conciare (pelli) **2.** abbronzare, abbronzarsi **3.** (*sl.*) picchiare, conciare per le feste.

tan, *abbr.* di **tangent**.

Tanagra ['tænəgrə], *no.pr.* (*geog. st.*) Tanagra ☆ — *statuette* (o — *figurine*), statuetta di terracotta di Tanagra.

Tancred ['tæŋkred], *no.pr.m.* (*st.*) Tancredi.

tandem ['tændəm], *s.* **1.** tandem (bicicletta a due posti) **2.** tandem (carrozza con due cavalli uno dietro l'altro) ☆ — *propellers*, (*aer.*) eliche a tandem; — *system*, (*elett.*) cascata.

tandem, *av.* uno dietro l'altro, in fila indiana: *horses driven —*, cavalli guidati a tandem.

tang¹ [tæŋ], *s.* **1.** punta **2.** (*dial.*) aculeo, pungiglione; lingua di serpente **3.** codolo **4.** sapore caratteristico; odore penetrante: — *of the sea*, odore di salsedine; — *of the soil*, l'aroma della terra **5.** *fig.* punta, traccia: *there was a — of irony in his words*, c'era una punta d'ironia nelle sue parole **6.** (*ittiol.*) teute.

to **tang**¹, *v.t.* **1.** munire di punta **2.** dare odore, sapore a.

tang², *s.* suono acuto; vibrazione sonora (di corda musicale); tintinnio: *the — of the bell*, il trillare del campanello; *there was a — of pride in his voice*, *fig.* si sentiva vibrare l'orgoglio nella sua voce.

to **tang**², *v.t.i.* **1.** (far) risuonare, (far) vibrare, (far) tintinnare || *to — bees*, far strepito vicino all'alveare per impedire che le api sciamino **2.** proferire con accento vibrante.

tang³, *s.* (*bot. pop.*) laminaria.

tang⁴, *s.* (*zool.*) riccio del Madagascar.

Tanganyika [,tæŋgə'nji:kə], *no.pr.* (*geog.*) Tanganica.

tangency ['tændʒənsi], *s.* (*geom.*) tangenza.

tangent ['tændʒənt], *ag.s.* (*geom.*) tangente || *to fly off at a —*, *fig.* cambiare improvvisamente pensiero, modo di agire ☆ — *scale*, (*geom.*) scala delle tangenti; (*artigl.*) alzo; — *wheel*, (*mec.*) ruota elicoidale.

tangential [tæn'dʒenʃəl], *ag.* (*geom.*) tangenziale ☆ — *screw*, (*mec.*) vite senza fine, vite micrometrica; — *strength*, (*scienza delle costruzioni*) resistenza di taglio; — -*stress*, (*scienza delle costruzioni*) sollecitazione di taglio.

tangentially [tæn'dʒenʃəli], *av.* (*geom.*) tangenzialmente.

Tangerine [,tændʒə'ri:n], *ag.* di Tangeri || *s.c.* tingitano, tingitana || *s.* mandarino (agrume).

tangibility [,tændʒi'biliti], *s.* tangibilità, palpabilità.

tangible ['tændʒəbl], *ag.* **1.** tangibile, palpabile **2.** *fig.* definito; manifesto; sensibile: — *advantages*, vantaggi sensibili; — *reasons for complaint*, fondati motivi per reclamare.

tangibleness ['tændʒəblnis], s. tangibilità, palpabilità.

tangibly ['tændʒəbli], av. **1.** tangibilmente, palpabilmente **2.** fig. chiaramente.

Tangier [tæn'dʒiə*], no.pr. (geog.) Tangeri.

tangle[1] ['tæŋgl], s. (bot.) laminaria ☆ — fish, (ittiol.) signato.

tangle[2], s. **1.** groviglio; garbuglio, viluppo: her hair was in a —, i suoi capelli erano ingarbugliati, arruffati **2.** fig. pasticcio, disordine, complicazione: it's a — if ever there was one, è un pasticcio come non se ne sono mai visti; to get into a —, cacciarsi in un impiccio.

to **tangle**[2], v.t.i. **1.** aggrovigliare, aggrovigliarsi; ingarbugliare, ingarbugliarsi: the cat tangled (up) the wool by playing with it, il gatto giuocando con la lana, la aggrovigliò **2.** fig. complicare, complicarsi; imbrogliarsi **3.** intrappolare.

tangle[3], s. (bot.) millefoglie acquatico, fellandrio.

tangled ['tæŋgld], ag. **1.** arruffato, ingarbugliate, aggrovigliato: — hair, capelli arruffati **2.** fig. complicato, intricato: a — affair, un affare complicato.

tanglefoot ['tæŋglfut], s. (sl. amer.) bevanda alcoolica (specialmente whisky).

tanglesome ['tæŋglsəm], ag. ingarbugliato, intricato.

tanglingly ['tæŋgliŋli], av. confusamente; intricatamente.

tangly[1] ['tæŋgli], ag. pieno, cosparso di laminarie.

tangly[2], ag. ingarbugliato, intricato.

tango ['tæŋgou], s. tango (musica, danza).

to **tango**, v.i. ballare il tango.

tangram ['tæŋgrəm], s. « tangram » (giuoco cinese formato da un quadrato diviso in sette parti, con le quali si compongono varie figure).

tangy ['tæŋi], ag. piccante (di sapore); penetrante (di odore).

tanist ['tænist], s. (st.) successore di capo celtico (già designato dal predecessore).

tanistry ['tænistri], s. (st.) sistema celtico di successione per l'elezione alla dignità di capo.

tank [tæŋk], s. **1.** vasca; serbatoio; cisterna **2.** (elett.) cassa (d'interruttore, di trasformatore) **3.** (mil.) carro armato ☆ — -buster, (sl. amer.) aèreo munito di armi anticarro; — -car (o — -wagon), (ferr.) carro-cisterna; — drama, (sl. teat.) dramma sensazionale in cui si rappresenta un salvataggio da annegamento; — -engine, locomotiva autonoma (con serbatoio per acqua e deposito di carbone); — farming, idroponica, coltivazione artificiale; — town, (amer.) cittadina dove i treni si fermano solo per riempire i serbatoi dell'acqua; — trailer, (aut.) rimorchio di autobotte; — truck (o — -wagon), (aut.) autobotte || antirolling —, (mar.) vasca antirollio; ballast —, (mar.) cassone per zavorra; crash-diving —, (mar.) cassone di rapida immersione; drop —, (aer.) serbatoio supplementare sganciabile; gauge —, (idraulica) serbatoio di livello; gravity —, (mec.) serbatoio a gravità; peak —, (mar.) cassa del gavone; petrol —, (aut.) serbatoio della benzina; setting —, (ind.) serbatoio di decantazione.

to **tank**, r.t. mettere in un serbatoio, in una cisterna.

tankage ['tæŋkidʒ], s. **1.** prezzo di noleggio di un serbatoio **2.** capacità di un serbatoio **3.** riempimento di serbatoio, di cisterna **4.** residui di grassi usati per concime.

tankard ['tæŋkəd], s. boccale ☆ cool- —, bevanda rinfrescante (a base di acqua, vino, spremuta di limone, spezie).

tanker ['tæŋkə*], s. nave cisterna ☆ air —, (aer.) aerocisterna; (fuel) oil —, (mar.) petroliera.

tankful ['tæŋkful], s. contenuto di un serbatoio.

tannable ['tænəbl], ag. conciabile.

tannage ['tænidʒ], s. **1.** conciatura, concia **2.** materiale conciato.

tannate ['tænit], s. (chim.) tannato.

tanned [tænd], ag. **1.** conciato: — leather, cuoio conciato **2.** (sun-) —, abbronzato.

tanner[1] ['tænə*], s. conciatore.

tanner[2], s. (sl.) moneta da 6 penny.

tannery ['tænəri], s. **1.** conceria **2.** conciatura.

tannic ['tænik], ag. (chim.) tannico.

tannin ['tænin], s. (chim.) tannino.

tanning ['tæniŋ], s. conciatura; concia ☆ chrome — (ind.) concia al cromo; oil —, scamosciatura, concia ad olio.

tanrec ['tænrek], s. (zool.) riccio del Madagascar.

tansy ['tænzi], s. (bot.) tanaceto.

tantalic [tæn'tælik], ag. (chim.) tantalico.

tantalite ['tæntəlait], s. (min.) tantalite, niobite.

tantalization [,tæntəlai'zeifən], s. supplizio di Tantalo; tentazione; tormento.

to **tantalize** ['tæntəlaiz], v.t. infliggere il supplizio di Tantalo a; tormentare; tentare, stuzzicare; lusingare (con vane promesse).

tantalizer ['tæntəlaizə*], s.c. chi infligge il supplizio di Tantalo, chi tormenta, tenta, stuzzica, lusinga (con vane promesse).

tantalizing ['tæntəlaiziŋ], ag. allettante; lusingante; provocante: a — smell of foods, un profumo allettante di cibi.

tantalizingly ['tæntəlaiziŋli], av. in modo allettante, lusingante, provocante.

tantalum ['tæntələm], s. (chim.) tantalio.

Tantalus[1] ['tæntələs], no.pr.m. (mit.) Tantalo ☆ Tantalus cup, (fis.) vaso di Tantalo.

tantalus[2], s. **1.** mobiletto-bar in cui le bottiglie sono visibili **2.** (ornit.) tantalo.

tantamount ['tæntəmaunt], ag. equivalente: this is — to saying that you do not believe me, questo è come dire che non mi credi.

tantivy [tæn'tivi], ag. (arc.) veloce; al galoppo || s. (arc.) galoppata; rapido movimento.

to **tantivy**, v.i. (arc.) cavalcare a briglia sciolta; precipitarsi, affrettarsi.

tantivy, av. (arc.) al galoppo; velocemente.

tantra ['tæntrə], s. tantra (testo religioso sanscrito).

tantrum ['tæntrəm], s. accesso d'ira, collera: to be in one's tantrums, avere i nervi, avere un diavolo per capello; to go (o to get) into tantrums (o a —), montare in collera, uscire dai gangheri.

tap[1] [tæp], s. **1.** spina, zipolo; rubinetto, chiavetta to turn on the —, aprire il rubinetto || on —, alla spina; fig. a disposizione: beer on —, birra alla spina he has excuses always on —, ha sempre una scusa pronta **2.** fig. qualità (di birra, liquore, ecc.): an excellent —, un'ottima qualità **3.** (mec.) maschio (per filettare) ☆ — bolt, (mec.) vite mordente; — hole, (metal. foro di spillatura; — -house, birreria; — -root (bot.) fittone, radice principale; — water, acqua di rubinetto || current —, (elett.) presa di corrente; exhaus drain —, (mec.) tappo di scarico; plug —, (mec. secondo maschio a filettare; steam —, (mec.) presa di vapore.

to **tap**[1], pass.p.p. **tapped** [tæpt], v.t. **1.** munir di spina, rubinetto (botte, serbatoio, ecc.) **2.** spillare forare, bucare; (chir.) drenare: to — the trees, incider le piante (per estrarne la linfa) **3.** fig. spillare: he know he can — his uncle for money whenever he needs it sa che può spillare quattrini dallo zio quando n ha bisogno **4.** iniziare attività, rapporti commercial con: we can still — some districts in the South, possiam ancora stabilire rapporti commerciali con alcune zon del Sud **5.** (tel.) intercettare: to — a telegraph wire, telephone, intercettare una comunicazione telegrafica telefonica **6.** (mec.) maschiare.

tap[2], s. **1.** colpetto, colpo leggero: the — of her heel on the pavement, il ticchettio dei suoi tacchi sul mar ciapiede; we heard a — at the door, udimmo bussar all'uscio **2.** pl. (mil.) rullo del tamburo che annunci l'ora del rancio; (amer.) silenzio **3.** ferretto (per proteg gere il tacco); (amer.) tacco, suola (applicati per ripa rare scarpe) ☆ — -dancing, « tip-tap » (danza).

to **tap**[2], *v.t.* **1.** battere leggermente; bussare: *the blind man was tapping his stick*, il cieco batteva piccoli colpi di bastone; *she was tapping on the keyboard of her typewriter*, stava battendo sulla tastiera della macchina per scrivere **2.** (*sl. amer.*) rifare (i tacchi a), mettere una pezza a (la suola di) **3.** *to —* **in**, conficcare a colpi secchi **4.** *to —* **off**, (*tel.*) inviare (un messaggio) in alfabeto Morse **5.** *to —* **out**, estrarre con piccoli colpi; (*tel.*) emettere (un messaggio) in alfabeto Morse: *to — one's pipe on one's heel*, svuotare la pipa battendola sul tacco.

tape [teip], *s.* **1.** nastro; fettuccia; passamano **2.** (*spor.*) nastro del traguardo: *to breast the —*, tagliare il traguardo **3.** nastro (del telegrafo) ☆ *— -recorder*, magnetofono ‖ *electric —* (o *friction —* o *insulating —*), nastro isolante; *masking —*, nastro adesivo protettivo; *measuring —*, metro a nastro, rotella metrica; *recording —*, nastro magnetico; *steel- —*, nastro d'acciaio; *ticker- —*, (*tel.*) nastro di zona.

to **tape**, *v.t.* **1.** cucire con un nastro; applicare una fettuccia a **2.** (*legatoria*) legare su nastro **3.** misurare con un nastro; (*fig. fam.*) giudicare: *I've got him taped*, l'ho giudicato.

taper ['teipə*], *ag.* **1.** che gradatamente diminuisce in larghezza; affusolato; a punta **2.** (*tec. mec.*) conico; (*arch.*) rastremato ‖ *s.* **1.** candela, stoppino, lumicino **2.** (*arch.*) rastremazione **3.** (*rate of*) —, (*tec. mec.*) conicità ☆ *— check*, (*mec.*) controllo della conicità; *— fit*, (*mec.*) accoppiamento conico; *— gauge*, (*mec.*) calibro per (verifica) conicità; *— pin*, (*mec.*) spina, perno conico; *— sleeve*, (*mec.*) manicotto conico.

to **taper**, *v.t.i.* affilare, affilarsi; assottigliare, assottigliarsi; (*arch.*) rastremare, rastremarsi: *the column tapers upwards*, la colonna si assottiglia verso l'alto; *to —* (*off*) *to a point*, finire a punta.

tapering ['teipəriŋ], *ag.* **1.** affusolato **2.** (*tec. mec.*) conico; (*arch.*) rastremato ‖ *s.* **1.** diminuzione graduale in larghezza **2.** (*tec. mec.*) conicità; (*arch.*) rastremazione.

taperness ['teipənis], *s.* forma appuntita.

taperwise ['teipəwaiz], *ag.* appuntito; conico.

tapestried ['tæpistrid], *ag.* tappezzato; addobbato.

tapestry ['tæpistri], *s.* arazzo; paramento; tappezzeria.

to **tapestry**, *v.t.* **1.** adornare, coprire (un muro) di arazzi **2.** ricamare, dipingere ad arazzo.

tapeworm ['teip-wə:m], *s.* tenia, verme solitario.

tapioca [,tæpi'oukə], *s.* tapioca.

tapir ['teipə*], *s.* (*zool.*) tapiro.

tapis ['tæpi:], *s.*: *on the —*, *fig.* sul tappeto, in discussione, in considerazione.

tapotement [tə'poutmənt], *s.* massaggio per percussione.

tapper ['tæpə*], *s.c.* chi batte, chi picchia ‖ *s.* (*tel.*) tasto Morse.

tappet ['tæpit], *s.* (*aut.*) punteria.

tapping[1] ['tæpiŋ], *s.* **1.** spillatura (di botte) **2.** (*chir.*) drenaggio **3.** (*elett.*) presa **4.** (*ind. della gomma*) incisione (della corteccia) **5.** (*mec.*) maschiatura.

tapping[2], *s.* colpetto.

taproom ['tæp-rum], *s.* osteria, birreria; bar.

tapster ['tæpstə*], *s.* garzone di osteria, birreria; barista.

tapu ['ta:pu:], *V.* **taboo**.

tar [ta:*], *s.* **1.** pece liquida; catrame **2.** (*Jack*) —, marinaio, lupo di mare ☆ *— -brush*, spazzola per catramare: *to have a touch of the — -brush*, *fig.* avere un po' di sangue negro, indiano; *— -macadam*, (*amer. ing.*) macadam al catrame; *— paper*, carta catramata; *— -water*, (*farm.*) catramina ‖ *coal —*, (*ind. chim.*) catrame minerale.

to **tar**, *pass.p.p.* **tarred** [ta:d], *v.t.* incatramare, impeciare ‖ *to — and feather*, (*st.*) spalmare di pece e coprire di penne (per punizione) ‖ *to be tarred with the same brush* (o *stick*), avere gli stessi difetti.

taradiddle ['tærədidl], *s.* (*fam.*) frottola, invenzione.

tarantella [,tærən'telə], *s.* tarantella (musica, danza).

tarantism ['tærəntizəm], *s.* (*patol.*) tarantolismo.

tarantula [tə'ræntjulə], *s.* (*entom.*) tarantola.

taratantara [,ta:rə'tæntərə], *s.* taratantara (suono di tromba).

taraxacum [tə'ræksəkəm], *s.* (*bot.*) tarassico.

tarboosh, **tarbush** [ta:'bu:ʃ], *s.* «tarbush» (copricapo dei musulmani).

tardigrade ['ta:digreid], *ag.s.* (*zool.*) tardigrado.

tardily ['ta:dili], *av.* **1.** lentamente **2.** controvoglia, malvolentieri **3.** in ritardo, tardivamente.

tardiness ['ta:dinis], *s.* **1.** lentezza; indolenza **2.** malavoglia, riluttanza **3.** ritardo.

tardy ['ta:di], *ag.* **1.** tardo, lento, pigro **2.** svogliato, riluttante **3.** tardivo, in ritardo: *— excuses*, scuse tardive.

tare[1] [tɛə*], *s.* **1.** (*bot.*) veccia **2.** *pl.* (*biblico*) zizzania (anche *fig.*).

tare[2], *s.* (*comm.*) tara ☆ *average —*, tara media.

to **tare**[2], *v.t.* (*comm.*) fare la tara a, tarare.

target ['ta:git], *s.* **1.** bersaglio (anche *fig.*): *he is always a — for scorn*, è sempre oggetto di scherno **2.** rotella (piccolo scudo rotondo) **3.** (*cuc.*) spalla di agnello **4.** (*ferr.*) semaforo, disco **5.** (*fis.*) anticatodo ☆ *— area*, (*mil.*) area di bombardamento, di bersaglio; *— -card*, disco che serba traccia dei colpi tirati; *— -practice*, (*mil.*) esercitazione di tiro al bersaglio.

targeted ['ta:gitid], *ag.* munito di scudo.

targeteer [,ta:gi'tiə*], *s.* soldato armato di scudo.

tariff ['tærif], *s.* tariffa ☆ *— -reform*, riforma delle tariffe doganali; riforma favorevole all'abolizione del protezionismo (negli Stati Uniti) ‖ *customs —*, tariffa doganale; *flat-rate —* (o *two-part —*), (*elett.*) tariffa promiscua; *preferential —*, (*comm.*) tariffa preferenziale.

to **tariff**, *v.t.* stabilire la tariffa di; sottoporre a tariffa.

tarlatan ['ta:lətən], *s.* tarlatana, mussolina leggera.

tarmac ['ta:mæk], *s.* (*ing.*) macadam al catrame ‖ *the —*, (*fam.*) le piste di decollo, di atterraggio (negli aeroporti).

tarn [ta:n], *s.* laghetto montano.

tarnal ['ta:nl], *ag.* (*sl. amer.*) **1.** eterno **2.** dannato.

tarnation [ta:'neiʃən], *s.* (*sl. amer.*) dannazione.

tarnish ['ta:niʃ], *s.* **1.** appannamento; offuscamento; ossidazione (di metalli) **2.** *fig.* macchia (sull'onore, ecc.).

to **tarnish**, *v.t.i.* **1.** appannarsi; offuscarsi; ossidare, ossidarsi (di metallo) **2.** *fig.* macchiare, macchiarsi (di onore, ecc.).

tarnishable ['ta:niʃəbl], *ag.* che può appannarsi, offuscarsi; *fig.* che può macchiarsi (di onore, ecc.).

tarnished ['ta:niʃt], *ag.* **1.** appannato; offuscato; ossidato (di metallo) **2.** *fig.* macchiato (di onore, ecc.).

taro ['ta:rou], *s.* (*bot.*) colocasia.

taroc ['tærək], **tarot** ['tærou], *s.* tarocchi.

tarpan ['ta:pən], *s.* «tarpan» (cavallo selvaggio dell'Asia).

tarpaulin [ta:'pɔ:lin], *s.* **1.** incerata; telone impermeabile **2.** cappello impermeabile dei marinai **3.** (*arc.*) marinaio.

Tarpeian [ta:'pi:(ə)n], *ag.*: *the — Rock*, (*st.*) la Rupe Tarpea.

Tarquin ['ta:kwin], **Tarquinius** [ta:'kwiniəs], *no.pr.m.* (*st.*) Tarquinio.

tarradiddle ['tærədidl], *s.* (*fam.*) frottola, invenzione.

tarragon ['tærəgən], *s.* (*bot.*) dragoncello ☆ *— vinegar*, (*cuc.*) aceto aromatico.

Tarragona [,tærə'gounə], *no.pr.* (*geog.*) Tarragona ‖ *s.* vino di Tarragona.

tarred [ta:d], *ag.* catramato.

tarriance ['tæriəns], *s.* (*arc.*) indugio; procrastinazione.

tarrier[1] ['tæriə*], *s.c.* (*arc.*) chi indugia, ritarda.

tarrier[2], *s.* (*mec.*) trivella.

tarring ['ta:riŋ], *s.* catramatura.

tarrock ['tærək], *s.* (*ornit.*) **1.** gabbiano larissa **2.** rondine di mare (nelle isole Shetland).

tarry[1] ['tɑ:ri], *ag.* **1.** di, simile a catrame, catramoso **2.** catramato; ricoperto, sporco, impregnato di catrame ☆ — *residue*, residuo catramoso.

to **tarry**[2] ['tæri], *v.i.* **1.** (*letter.*) indugiare; tardare; sostare: *to* — *at* (o *in*) *a place*, sostare in un luogo **2.** attendere: *to* — *for s.o.*, attendere qlcu.

tarrying ['tæriiŋ], *s.* (*letter.*) indugio; ritardo.

tarsal ['tɑ:səl], *ag.* (*anat.*) tarsale, tarsico.

tarsia ['tɑ:siə], *s.* tarsia, intarsio.

tarsier ['tɑ:siə*], *s.* (*zool.*) tarsio, spettro.

tarsus ['tɑ:səs], *pl.* **tarsi** ['tɑ:sai], *s.* (*anat.*) tarso.

tart[1] [tɑ:t], *ag.* **1.** brusco, agro, aspro **2.** *fig.* aspro, mordace: *a* — *answer*, una risposta tagliente.

tart[2], *s.* torta di frutta ☆ *jam* —, crostata.

tart[3], *s.* (*sl.*) sgualdrina, prostituta.

tartan[1] ['tɑ:tən], *s.* **1.** «tartan» (caratteristico tessuto scozzese di lana a quadri); tessuto a quadri (di disegno scozzese) **2.** (*rar.*) scozzese; truppe scozzesi.

tartan[2], *s.* (*mar.*) tartana.

Tartar[1] ['tɑ:tə*], *ag.* tartaro, della Tartaria ‖ *s.c.* **1.** tartaro, tartara **2.** persona violenta, irritabile; megera ‖ *to catch a* —, trovare pane per i propri denti.

tartar[2], *s.* **1.** (*chim.*) tartaro: *cream of* —, cremore di tartaro **2.** tartaro (dei denti) ☆ — *emetic*, (*farm.*) tartaro emetico, stibiato.

Tartarean [tɑ:'tɛəriən], *ag.* tartareo, infernale.

Tartarian[1] [tɑ:'tɛəriən], *ag.* tartaro, della Tartaria.

Tartarian[2], *ag.* tartareo, infernale.

tartaric [tɑ:'tærik], *ag.* (*chim.*) tartarico ☆ — *-acid*, acido tartarico.

to **tartarize** ['tɑ:təraiz], *v.t.* (*chim.*) tartarizzare.

tartarous ['tɑ:tərəs], *ag.* (*chim.*) tartaroso.

Tartarus ['tɑ:tərəs], *no.pr.* (*geog. mit.*) Tartaro.

tartish ['tɑ:tiʃ], *ag.* **1.** acidulo **2.** *fig.* piuttosto mordace: *a* — *reply*, una risposta piuttosto caustica.

tartlet ['tɑ:tlit], *s.* pasta dolce.

tartly ['tɑ:tli], *av.* **1.** in modo agro, acido **2.** *fig.* aspramente; mordacemente.

tartness ['tɑ:tnis], *s.* **1.** asprezza (di vino, ecc.) **2.** *fig.* umore bisbetico; mordacità.

tartrate ['tɑ:trit], *s.* (*chim.*) tartrato.

Tartuf(f)e [tɑ:'tuf], *no.pr.m.* (*lett.*) Tartufo ‖ *s.* bacchettone, baciapile; ipocrita.

tartufism [tɑ:'tufizəm], *s.* bacchettoneria, ipocrisia.

task [tɑ:sk], *s.* dovere; incarico; mansione; lavoro, compito: *it is an arduous* —, è un incarico difficile; *to apply oneself to a* —, dedicarsi ad un lavoro; *to set a boy a* —, assegnare un compito ad un ragazzo ‖ *to take s.o. to* — *for sthg.*, rimproverare qlcu. per ql.co. ☆ — *force*, (*mil.*) gruppo d'assalto in missione speciale; (*amer.*) gruppo di esperti addetti allo studio di problemi militari; — *work*, lavoro a cottimo.

to **task**, *v.t.* **1.** assegnare un compito a; imporre un lavoro a **2.** affaticare; mettere a dura prova: *it tasks my powers*, mi costa un grande sforzo **3.** (*mar.*) provare la solidità di (una nave).

tasker ['tɑ:skə*], *s.c.* **1.** chi assegna un compito; chi impone un lavoro **2.** (*dial.*) cottimista.

taskmaster ['tɑ:sk,mɑ:stə*], *s.* maestro; sorvegliante: *sorrow is a hard* —, *fig.* il dolore è un maestro inflessibile.

Tasmania [tæz'meinjə], *no.pr.* (*geog.*) Tasmania.

Tasmanian [tæz'meinjən], *ag.* tasmaniano ‖ *s.c.* abitante della Tasmania ☆ — *devil*, (*zool.*) sarcofilo; — *wolf*, (*zool.*) tilacino.

tass [tæs], *s.* (*scoz.*) **1.** tazza **2.** sorso.

tassel[1] ['tæsəl], *s.* **1.** nappa; nappina **2.** nastrino segnalibro **3.** (*amer.*) barba (della pannocchia).

to **tassel**[1], *pass.p.p.* **tasselled** ['tæsəld], *v.t.i.* **1.** adornare, guarnire di fiocchi, nappine **2.** (*amer.*) fiorire (di granturco, canna da zucchero).

tassel[2], *s.* (*edil.*) tassello.

tasselled ['tæsəld], *ag.* infiocchettato.

tassie ['tɑ:si], *s.* (*scoz. irl.*) tazza, coppa ‖ *the Silver Tassie*, la Coppa d'Argento.

taste [teist], *s.* **1.** gusto; sapore: *acid* —, gusto acido; *the sense of* —, il senso del gusto; *I don't like the* — *of milk*, non mi piace il sapore del latte ‖ *to leave a bad* — *in the mouth*, lasciar la bocca amara **2.** assaggio (anche *fig.*); bocconcino: *give me just a* — *of cheese*, dammi un pezzettino di formaggio; *he had a* — *of success before his downfall*, ebbe un momento di successo prima del crollo; *that boy must be given a* — *of the whip*, quel ragazzo dovrebbe assaggiare la frusta **3.** gusto, inclinazione, predilezione: *he has a* — *for horse-racing*, è un appassionato di corse di cavalli; *he has no* — *for arguments*, non ama le discussioni; *that girl is not to my* —, quella ragazza non è di mio gusto; *to acquire, to develop a* —, acquisire, sviluppare un gusto, un'inclinazione: *smoking and drinking are acquired tastes*, il fumo, il bere sono gusti acquisiti ‖ *tastes differ*, i gusti son gusti **4.** buon gusto, raffinatezza, eleganza: *a woman of* —, una donna raffinata; *she wore a dress in perfect* —, indossava un abito di gran gusto; *what you say is in bad* —, quello che dite è di cattivo gusto.

to **taste**, *v.t.i.* **1.** gustare; assaggiare: *he refused to* — *food in protest*, per protesta si rifiutò di toccar cibo; *I can't* — *on account of my bad cold*, col raffreddore che ho non sento nessun sapore; *will you* — *the soup please?*, vuoi assaggiare la minestra per favore? **2.** *fig.* provare, conoscere, sentire: *one must* — *sorrow to appreciate happiness*, si deve aver provato il dolore per apprezzare la felicità ‖ *he who tastes* (*of*) *everything tires of everything*, *prov.* il poco piace, il troppo sazia **3.** aver gusto, sentire, saper (di): *this milk tastes sour*, questo latte sa di acido; *this wine tastes of cork*, questo vino sa di tappo; *to* — *good*, avere un buon sapore; *to* — *like honey*, saper di miele.

tasteful ['teistful], *ag.* fine, raffinato; di buon gusto.

tastefully ['teistfuli], *av.* con buon gusto; squisitamente; elegantemente.

tastefulness ['teistfulnis], *s.* buongusto.

tasteless ['teistlis], *ag.* **1.** insipido **2.** di cattivo gusto.

tastelessly ['teistlisli], *av.* senza gusto.

tastelessness ['teistlisnis], *s.* **1.** scipitezza, insipidità **2.** *fig.* mancanza di gusto.

taster ['teistə*], *s.c.* assaggiatore, assaggiatrice ‖ *s.* tazzina usata dagli assaggiatori; provino per formaggi ☆ *book-* —, lettore (di casa editrice); *tea, wine* —, assaggiatore di tè, vino.

tastily ['teistili], *av.* con buongusto.

tasty ['teisti], *ag.* **1.** (*fam.*) saporito, gustoso **2.** (*pop.*) di buon gusto.

tat[1] [tæt], *s.* (*sl.*) dado (specialmente truccato).

tat[2], *V.* **tit**[2].

tat[3], *s.* (*abbr.* di *tattoo*[3]) pony nativo dell'India.

to **tat**[4], *pass.p.p.* **tatted** ['tætid], *v.t.i.* fare il chiacchierino; fare (il pizzo) con la navetta.

ta-ta ['tæ'tɑ:], *inter.* (*fam.*) ciao!, arrivederci!.

Tatar, *V.* **Tartar**[1].

tatler, *V.* **tattler**.

tatter ['tætə*], *s. gener. pl.* cencio, brandello, straccio.

to **tatter**, *v.t.i.* (*rar.*) stracciare, stracciarsi; cadere a pezzi, a brandelli.

tatterdemalion [,tætədə'meiljən], *s.* pezzente, straccione.

tattered ['tætəd], **tattery** ['tætəri], *ag.* stracciato, cencioso ‖ *all* — *and torn*, tutto cenci e brandelli ‖ *he has a* — *reputation*, *fig.* ha una pessima reputazione.

tatting ['tætiŋ], *s.* chiacchierino (merletto).

tattle ['tætl], *s.* chiacchiera, ciancia; pettegolezzo.

to **tattle**, *v.i.* chiacchierare, cianciare; spettegolare.

tattler ['tætlə*], *s.c.* chiacchierone, chiacchierona; pettegolo, pettegola ‖ *s.* (*ornit.*) totano.

tattlingly ['tætliŋli], *av.* in modo pettegolo, ciarliero.

tattoo[1] [tə'tu:], *s.* **1.** (*mil.*) suono della ritirata: *to sound the* —, suonare la ritirata **2.** carosello militare 3. *fig.* il tamburellare ‖ *his heart was beating a* —, il cuore gli batteva all'impazzata ‖ *to beat the devil's* —, tamburellare con le dita in segno di impazienza.

to **tattoo**[1], *v.t.i.* 1. suonare (il tamburo) 2. (*fam.*) tamburellare (con le dita).

tattoo[2], *s.* tatuaggio.

to **tattoo**[2], *v.t.* tatuare.

tattoo[3], *s.* pony nativo dell'India.

tattooing [tə'tu(:)iŋ], *s.* tatuaggio.

tatty ['tæti], *s.* (*ang.-in.*) «tatty» (stuoia in erba cuscus che viene inumidita e appesa a porte e finestre per rinfrescare e profumare l'aria).

tau [tɔ:], *s.* tau (lettera dell'alfabeto greco).

taught [tɔ:t], *pass.p.p.* di to **teach**.

taunt[1] [tɔ:nt], *ag.* (*mar.*) eccessivamente alto (di albero).

taunt[2], *s.* 1. sarcasmo; rimprovero sarcastico; insulto 2. oggetto di scherno: *to be the* — *of the public*, essere lo zimbello del pubblico.

to **taunt**[2], *v.t.* 1. rimproverare aspramente; ingiuriare; rinfacciare: *they taunted him with having lost his money*, lo rimproverarono aspramente per aver perso il denaro; *to* — *s.o. with cowardice*, dare del codardo a qlcu. 2. schernire, dileggiare.

taunter ['tɔ:ntə*], *s.c.* schernitore, schernitrice; motteggiatore, motteggiatrice.

taunting ['tɔ:ntiŋ], *ag.* beffardo, sarcastico ‖ *s.* 1. rimprovero sarcastico 2. motteggio; scherno.

tauntingly ['tɔ:ntiŋli], *av.* 1. in tono di rimprovero 2. in tono canzonatorio.

taurine ['tɔ:rain], *ag.* taurino.

Tauris ['tɔ:ris], *no.pr.* (*geog. st.*) Tauride.

tauromachy [tɔ:'rɔməki], *s.* tauromachia.

Taurus ['tɔ:rəs], *no.pr.* (*astr.*) Toro.

taut [tɔ:t], *ag.* (*mar.*) 1. teso (di gomena, cavo) ‖ *the situation is* —, (*fam.*) la situazione è tesa 2. in ordine (di nave) ‖ — *and trim*, in completo assetto (di nave); dall'aspetto curato, ordinato (di persona).

to **tauten** ['tɔ:tn], *v.t.i.* tendere, tendersi.

tautly ['tɔ:tli], *av.* rigidamente.

tautness ['tɔ:tnis], *s.* tensione, rigidità.

tautologic(al) [,tɔ:tə'lɔdʒik(əl)], *ag.* (*ret.*) tautologico.

tautologically [,tɔ:tə'lɔdʒikəli], *av.* (*ret.*) in modo tautologico.

to **tautologize** [tɔ:'tɔlədʒaiz], *v.i.* (*ret.*) tautologizzare.

tautology [tɔ:'tɔlədʒi], *s.* (*ret.*) tautologia.

tautophony [tɔ:'tɔfəni], *s.* ripetizione dello stesso suono.

tavern ['tævən], *s.* osteria; taverna; trattoria ☆ — -*keeper*, oste, trattore.

taw[1] [tɔ:], *s.* 1. pallina, biglia (con cui giocano i bambini) 2. giuoco delle palline 3. limite di partenza (al giuoco delle biglie).

to **taw**[2], *v.t.* conciare (pelli) con allume, allumare.

tawdrily ['tɔ:drili], *av.* 1. vistosamente; in modo sgargiante 2. con cattivo gusto.

tawdriness ['tɔ:drinis], *s.* 1. aspetto vistoso, appariscente 2. cattivo gusto.

tawdry ['tɔ:dri], *ag.* 1. vistoso, appariscente; sgargiante 2. di cattivo gusto ‖ *s.* 1. ornamento vistoso 2. ornamento di cattivo gusto.

tawer ['tɔ:ə*], *s.* conciatore (che usa l'allume).

tawery ['tɔ:əri], *s.* conceria (in cui si usa l'allume).

tawniness ['tɔ:ninis], *s.* color tanè; bruno fulvo.

tawny ['tɔ:ni], *ag.* tanè; bruno fulvo; bronzeo.

tax [tæks], *s.* 1. (*amm.*) tassa, imposta, balzello: *to levy a* — *on sthg.*, mettere un'imposta su ql.co. 2. *fig.* peso, onere: *that boy is* — *on his parents*, quel ragazzo è un peso per i suoi genitori; *this work is a heavy* — *on my time*, questo lavoro mi porta via molto tempo ☆ — -*collector* (o — -*gatherer*), esattore delle imposte; — -*dodger*, (*fam.*) evasore fiscale; — -*free*, esente da tasse; — -*payer*, contribuente ‖ *direct* —, imposta diretta; *income* —, imposta sul reddito; *indirect* —, imposta indiretta; *land* —, imposta fondiaria; *licence* —, tassa di licenza.

to **tax**, *v.t.* 1. (*amm.*) tassare; imporre una tassa su 2. (*fam.*) mettere alla prova: *their endurance was taxed to the limit*, furono provati sino all'estremo limite della resistenza 3. *to* — *s.o. with sthg.*, rimproverare, accusare qlcu. di ql.co.: *he was taxed with laziness* egli fu accusato di pigrizia.

taxability [,tæksə'biliti], *s.* (*amm.*) tassabilità, imponibilità.

taxable ['tæksəbl], *ag.* (*amm.*) tassabile, imponibile.

taxableness ['tæksəblnis], *s.* (*amm.*) tassabilità, imponibilità.

taxation [tæk'seiʃən], *s.* (*amm.*) tassazione; imposte; tributi: *excessive* —, fiscalità eccessiva; *supplementary* —, tasse supplementari.

taxi ['tæksi], *s.* — (-*cab*), tassì, auto pubblica ☆ — -*driver* (o — -*man*), tassista; — *track* (o — *way*), (*aer.*) pista di rullaggio.

to **taxi**, *v.i.* 1. andare in tassì 2. (*aer.*) rullare; flottare (di idrovolante).

taxidermal [,tæksi'də:məl], *ag.* tassidermico.

taxidermist ['tæksidə:mist], *s.* tassidermista, impagliatore (di animali).

taxidermy ['tæksidə:mi], *s.* tassidermia.

taximeter ['tæksi,mi:tə*], *s.* tassametro.

taxin ['tæksin], *s.* (*chim.*) tassina.

taxiplane ['tæksi,plein], *s.* (*neol.*) aerotassì.

taxis ['tæksis], *s.* 1. (*chir.*) taxis 2. (*biol.*) tattismo.

taxonomic(al) [,tæksə'nomik(əl)], *ag.* tassonomico.

taxonomy [tæk'sonəmi], *s.* tassonomia.

Taylorism ['teilərizəm], *s.* taylorismo (distribuzione scientifica del lavoro).

tchick [tʃik], *s.* schiocco (della lingua).

to **tchick**, *v.i.* far schioccare (la lingua).

tea [ti:], *s.* 1. tè (foglie, infuso): *a cup of* —, una tazza di tè; *strong* —, tè carico, forte; *weak* —, tè chiaro; *I want a pound of* —, desidero una libbra di tè 2. tè (ricevimento): *to ask s.o. to* —, invitare qlcu. a un tè ☆ — -*ball* (o — -*infuser*), uovo da tè; — -*blending*, miscela di tè; — -*caddy*, scatola per il tè; — -*cake*, pastina da tè; — -*cloth*, tovaglietta da tè; (*fam.*) canovaccio per stoviglie; — -*cosy*, copriteiera; — -*garden*, giardino dove si serve il tè; piantagioni di tè; — -*gown*, abito da pomeriggio; — -*kettle*, bollitore; — -*party*, ricevimento all'ora del tè; — -*pot*, teiera; — -*room*, sala da tè; — -*set*, servizio da tè; — -*strainer*, colino per il tè; — -*taster*, degustatore, degustatrice di tè; — -*urn*, samovar ‖ *afternoon* —, tè delle cinque; *black* —, tè nero; *brick* — (o *tile* —), tè compresso a forma di mattonella; *green* —, tè verde, cinese; *high* —, «high-tea» (cena fredda, tè delle sette); *plain* —, merenda.

to **tea**, *v.t.i.* (*fam.*) prendere il tè; offrire il tè a.

to **teach** [ti:tʃ], *pass.p.p.* **taught** [tɔ:t], *v.t.i.* (IV) insegnare, istruire; fare l'insegnante: *I will* — *my grandchild French*, insegnerò il francese a mio nipote; *I will* — *her to speak the truth!*, (*fam.*) le insegnerò io a dire la verità!; *I will* — *him how to do this*, gli insegnerò a farlo; *I will* — *myself French*, imparerò il francese da solo ‖ *I will* — *him a lesson*, gli darò una lezione ‖ *I will* — *him a thing or two*, gli dirò quel che si merita; gli insegnerò a stare al mondo ‖ *that will* — *him!*, così imparerà! ‖ *to* — *one's grandmother to suck eggs*, voler insegnare a volare agli uccelli ‖ *to* — *school*, (*dial. amer.*) insegnare a scuola: *she taught school for some time*, fece l'insegnante per qualche tempo.

teachable ['ti:tʃəbl], *ag.* 1. che apprende facilmente (di persona); dall'intelligenza pronta 2. che si insegna facilmente (di materia).

teachableness ['ti:tʃəblnis], *s.* 1. capacità di apprendimento 2. facilità di insegnamento (di una materia).

teacher ['ti:tʃə*], *s.c.* insegnante; docente; maestro, maestra; professore, professoressa: *she is a Latin* —, è professoressa di latino ☆ *student* —, studente che fa il tirocinio di insegnamento.

teachership ['ti:tʃəʃip], *s.* insegnamento; professorato.

teaching ['ti:tʃiŋ], *ag.* che insegna ‖ *s.* **1.** insegnamento: *to go in for* —, dedicarsi all'insegnamento **2.** *pl.* insegnamenti, ammaestramento; dottrina: *the teachings of experience*, l'ammaestramento dell'esperienza; *the teachings of Socrates*, la dottrina di Socrate.

teacup ['ti:kʌp], *s.* tazza da tè.

Teague [ti:g], *s.* (*fam. spreg.*) irlandese.

teak [ti:k], *s.* tek (albero, legno).

teal, *pl.* **teal** [ti:l], *s.* (*ornit.*) alzavola.

team [ti:m], *s.* **1.** pariglia, muta (di cavalli) **2.** squadra: *in my school there are three teams*, nella mia scuola ci sono tre squadre ☆ — *-work*, collaborazione; lavoro di squadra: *the actors' — -work was magnificent*, l'affiatamento fra gli attori era splendido ‖ *football* —, squadra di calciatori.

to team, *v.t.i.* **1.** attaccare (bestie da tiro); aggiogare **2.** trasportare (per mezzo di un tiro) **3.** (*amer.*) guidare un tiro **4.** distribuire (lavoro) a squadre di operai **5.** *to* — **up**, (*fam.*) unirsi.

teaming ['ti:miŋ], *s.* **1.** l'attaccare (bestie da tiro) **2.** trasporto (per mezzo di un tiro) **3.** distribuzione (di lavoro) a squadre di operai **4.** (*edil.*) rimozione del materiale di scavo.

teamster ['ti:mstə*], *s.* **1.** carrettiere **2.** caposquadra.

teapoy ['ti:-pɔi], *s.* (*ang.-in.*) tavolino a tre piedi; tavolino da tè.

tear[1] [tiə*], *s.* **1.** lacrima: *to burst into tears*, scoppiare in lacrime; *to shed tears*, versare lacrime; *to weep bitter tears*, versare lacrime amare **2.** goccia ☆ — *-bottle*, (*archeol.*) vaso lacrimale; — *-drop*, lacrima; goccia: — *-drop ear-ring*, orecchino a goccia; — *-duct*, (*anat.*) condotto lacrimale; — *-exciting*, lacrimogeno; — *-gas*, gas lacrimogeno; — *-sac*, (*anat.*) sacco lacrimale.

tear[2] [tεə*], *s.* **1.** strappo, spacco; lacerazione **2.** (*fam.*) impeto, corsa a precipizio: *to go full* —, andare a tutta velocità **3.** (*fam.*) impeto iracondo: *to be in a* —, essere sconvolto dall'ira.

to tear[2], *pass.* **tore** [tɔ:*], *p.p.* **torn** [tɔ:n], *v.t.i.* **1.** stracciare, strappare, strapparsi; fare uno strappo a: *that boy tore his trousers*, quel ragazzo si fece uno strappo nei calzoni; *this paper tears too easily*, questa carta si strappa troppo facilmente; *to — a confession from s.o.*, *fig.* strappare una confessione a qlcu.; *to — (out) one's hair*, strapparsi i capelli ‖ *that's torn it!*, è finita!, non ci mancava altro! ‖ *to — open*, aprire lacerando **2.** dividere; straziare, lacerare: *country torn by factions*, paese dilaniato dalle fazioni; *he was torn with remorse*, era straziato dal rimorso; *she could not — herself away from him*, non poteva staccarsi da lui **3.** (*fam.*) correre, andare di gran carriera: *I saw him tearing along the road*, l'ho visto correre all'impazzata per la strada; *on hearing his voice she tore downstairs*, all'udire la sua voce si precipitò giù dalle scale **4.** *to — at* (*sthg.*), strappare con tutte le proprie forze **5.** *to — down*, smontare, fare a pezzi **6.** *to — off*, strappar via **7.** *to — up*, portar via a pezzi; sradicare.

tearaway ['tεərə,wei], *ag.* impetuoso.

tearer ['tεərə*], *s.c.* chi lacera, strappa.

tearful ['tiəful], *ag.* **1.** lacrimoso, piangente: — *voice*, voce lacrimosa **2.** triste: — *news*, triste notizia.

tearfully ['tiəfuli], *av.* piangendo, lacrimosamente, con le lacrime agli occhi.

tearing ['tεəriŋ], *ag.* lacerante; violento: — *wind*, vento impetuoso; *to be in a — hurry*, avere una fretta terribile ‖ *s.* lacerazione; strappo: — *of a muscle*, strappo muscolare ☆ — *strength*, (*mec.*) resistenza allo strappo.

tearless ['tiəlis], *ag.* senza lacrime, a ciglio asciutto.

tear-off ['tεərɔ:f], *ag.* da staccarsi (di biglietto, ecc.) ‖ *s.* parte (di biglietto, ecc.) da staccarsi.

tease [ti:z], *s.c.* chi stuzzica, molesta.

to tease, *v.t.* stuzzicare, molestare, far dispetti a: *don't — your brother*, non far dispetti a tuo fratello **2.** (*ind. tessile*) pettinare, cardare.

teasel ['ti:zl], *s.* **1.** (*bot.*) cardo **2.** (*ind. tessile*) garzatrice.

to teasel, *pass.p.p.* **tease(l)led** ['ti:zld], *v.t.* (*ind. tessile*) garzare.

teaseler ['ti:zlə*], *s.c.* (*ind. tessile*) garzatore, garzatrice ‖ *s.* (*mec.*) garzatrice.

teaser ['ti:zə*], *s.c.* **1.** seccatore, seccatrice **2.** (*ind. tessile*) cardatore, cardatrice ‖ *s.* (*fam.*) questione, problema difficile; rompicapo; domanda imbarazzante.

teasing ['ti:ziŋ], *ag.* dispettoso; molesto; irritante ‖ *s.* (*fam.*) dispetto, seccatura ☆ — *machine*, (*ind. tessile*) lupo carda, cardatrice.

teasingly ['ti:ziŋli], *av.* molestamente.

teaspoon ['ti:spu:n], *s.* cucchiaino da tè.

teaspoonful ['ti:spu(:)n,ful], *s.* quantità contenuta in un cucchiaino da tè: *a — of the mixture*, un cucchiaino da tè della pozione.

teat [ti:t], *s.* **1.** capezzolo **2.** tettarella.

teated ['ti:tid], *ag.* fornito di capezzoli.

tec [tek], *abbr.* (*sl.*) di **detective**.

techily ['tetʃili], *av.* con irritazione, stizza.

techiness ['tetʃinis], *s.* irritabilità; irascibilità.

technic ['teknik], *ag.* (*rar.*) tecnico ‖ *s.* **1.** *V.* **technique 2.** *gener. pl.* tecnica **3.** *pl.* terminologia tecnica.

technical ['teknikəl], *ag.* tecnico ☆ — *chemistry*, chimica industriale; — *institute*, scuola professionale.

technicality [,tekni'kæliti], *s.* tecnicismo.

technically ['teknikəli], *av.* tecnicamente.

technician [tek'niʃən], **technicist** ['teknisist], *s.* tecnico, perito.

technique [tek'ni:k], *s.* tecnica (di un'arte, di un artista, ecc.): *the — of Leonardo*, la tecnica leonardesca.

technocracy [tek'nɔkrəsi], *s.* (*pol. econ.*) governo di tecnici, scienziati.

technological [,teknə'lɔdʒikəl], *ag.* tecnologico.

technologist [tek'nɔlədʒist], *s.* tecnico.

technology [tek'nɔlədʒi], *s.* tecnologia.

techy ['tetʃi], *ag.* stizzoso, irritabile.

tectonic [tek'tɔnik], *ag.* **1.** strutturale **2.** (*geol.*) tettonico.

tectonics [tek'tɔniks], *s.* **1.** edilizia **2.** (*geol.*) tettonica.

tectorial [tek'tɔ:riəl], *ag.* (*anat.*) tettorio, tegminale.

tectrices [tek'traisi:z], *s.pl.* penne tettrici (di uccelli).

to ted [ted], *pass.p.p.* **tedded** ['tedid], *v.t.* rivoltare (erba, fieno, ecc.).

tedder ['tedə*], *s.c.* chi rivolta (erba, fieno, ecc.) ‖ *s.* (*agr.*) voltafieno.

Teddy ['tedi], *no.pr.m. dim.* di **Edward, Edmund, Theodore** ☆ — *-bear*, orsacchiotto di pezza; — *-boy*, « Teddy-boy », teppista.

tedious ['ti:djəs], *ag.* tedioso, noioso.

tediously ['ti:djəsli], *av.* tediosamente, noiosamente.

tediousness ['ti:djəsnis], **tedium** ['ti:djəm], *s.* tedio, noia, uggia.

tee[1] [ti:], *s.* **1.** ti (la lettera *t*) **2.** oggetto, strumento, raccordo, a forma di T ‖ *to a* —, a puntino, con precisione ☆ — *square*, squadra a T.

tee[2], *s.* bersaglio (al giuoco delle bocce, del lancio degli anelli, ecc.).

tee[3], *s.* (*golf*) « tee » (supporto su cui si poggia la palla).

to tee[3], *v.t.i.* (*golf*) **1.** collocare (la palla) sul « tee » **2.** *to — off*, dare la mazzata iniziale; *fig.* iniziare.

tee[4], *s.* cupoletta coronante la sommità di una pagoda.

to teem[1] [ti:m], *v.t.i.* **1.** abbondare, formicolare, brulicare: *the poem teems with metaphors*, la poesia abbonda in metafore; *wild life teems in the forest*, gli animali selvaggi abbondano nella foresta **2.** (*arc.*) generare, prolificare.

to teem[2], *v.t.* **1.** versare, vuotare **2.** (*metal.*) colare.

teemer ['ti:mə*], *s.* (*ind.*) operaio addetto alla colata (dell'acciaio).

teeming[1] ['ti:miŋ], *ag.* formicolante, brulicante; fertile: — *brain*, mente fertile.

teeming[2], *s.* (*metal.*) colata.

teemless ['ti:mlis], *ag.* (*arc. poet.*) sterile, infecondo.

teen [ti:n], *s.* (*arc.*) **1.** dolore, afflizione, pena **2.** irritazione, stizza.

to teen, *v.t.i.* (*arc.*) **1.** provare dolore, pena **2.** stuzzicare, irritare; addolorare.

teen-ager ['ti:n‚eidʒə*], *s.c.* chi ha meno di vent'anni, adolescente.

teens [ti:nz], *s.pl.* età da tredici a diciannove anni: *he is just out of his* —, ha appena vent'anni; *to be in one's* —, aver meno di vent'anni.

teeny[1] ['ti:ni], *ag.* (*fam.*) piccolo, minuto ‖ — *weeny*, piccolissimo.

teeny[2], *ag.* (*arc.*) fastidioso; maligno.

teepee ['ti:pi:], *s.* tenda dei pellirosse.

teetee ['ti:ti:], *s.* (*zool.*) crisotrice.

teeth [ti:θ], *pl.* di **tooth**.

to teethe [ti:ð], *v.i.* mettere i denti: *my child is teething*, il mio bambino sta mettendo i denti.

teething ['ti:ðiŋ], *s.* dentizione ☆ — *ring*, dentaruolo; — *troubles*, disturbi di crescita (anche *fig.*).

teetotal [ti:'toutl], *ag.* **1.** astemio **2.** (*dial.*) intero, assoluto.

teetotaler [ti:'toutlə*], *s.c.* astemio, astemia.

teetotalism [ti:'toutlizəm], *s.* **1.** astinenza completa dalle bevande alcooliche **2.** lotta contro l'alcoolismo.

teetotaller [ti:'toutlə*], *s.c.* astemio, astemia.

teetotally [ti:'toutli], *av.* **1.** da astemio **2.** (*dial.*) completamente, interamente.

teetotum ['ti:tou'tam], *s.* trottola.

tef(f) [tef], *s.* (*bot.*) tef.

teg [teg], *s.* pecora di due anni.

tegular ['tegjulə*], *ag.* di tegola; simile a tegola.

tegularly ['tegjuləli], *av.* in forma di tegola.

tegument ['tegjumənt], *s.* (*anat.*) tegumento.

tegumental [‚tegju'mentl], **tegumentary** [‚tegju-'mentəri], *ag.* tegumentale, tegumentario.

tehee [ti:'hi:], *s.* risatina beffarda.

to tehee, *v.i.* ridacchiare.

teil [ti:l], *s.* (*rar. bot.*) tiglio.

teind [ti:nd], *s.* (*scoz.*) decima.

telaesthesia [‚telis'θi:ziə], *s.* telestesia.

Telamon[1] ['teləmən], *no.pr.m.* (*lett.*) Telamone.

telamon[2], *pl.* **telamones** [‚telə'mouni:z], *s.* telamone (figura maschile che sostiene un architrave, ecc.).

telautograph [te'lo:təgrɑ:f], *s.* telescrivente.

telecamera [‚teli'kæmərə], *s.* (*tv.*) telecamera.

telecast ['telika:st], *s.* trasmissione televisiva, teletrasmissione.

to telecast, *pass. p. p.* **telecast**, *v. t.* teletrasmettere: *the show was* —, lo spettacolo fu teletrasmesso ☆ — *news*, telegiornale.

telecaster ['teli‚ka:stə*], *s.* apparecchio teletrasmittente.

telecommunication ['teli-kə‚mju(:)ni'keiʃən], *s.* (*tel.*) telecomunicazione.

telecontrol [‚telikən'troul], *s.* (*mec. rad.*) telecomando.

teledu ['telidu:], *s.* (*zool.*) tasso fetido.

telefilm ['telifilm], *s.* telefilm.

telegenic [‚teli'dʒenik], *ag.* telegenico.

telegram ['teligræm], *s.* telegramma ☆ *radio* — (o *wireless* —), radiotelegramma.

telegraph ['teligrɑ:f], *s.* telegrafo ☆ — *operator*, telegrafista; — *printer*, telescrittore ‖ *Morse* —, telegrafo Morse; *printing* —, telegrafo stampante.

to telegraph, *v.t.i.* telegrafare: *his son was telegraphed for*, si telegrafò a suo figlio di venire.

telegrapher [ti'legrəfə*], *s.c.* **1.** chi spedisce un telegramma **2.** (*amer.*) telegrafista.

telegraphese ['teligra:'fi:z], *ag.* (*fam.*) in stile telegrafico ‖ *s.* **1.** (*fam.*) stile telegrafico **2.** (*scherz.*) linguaggio, stile ampolloso, simile a quello degli articoli di fondo del Daily Telegraph.

telegraphic [‚teli'græfik], *ag.* telegrafico ☆ — *money order*, vaglia telegrafico.

telegraphically [‚teli'græfikəli], *av.* **1.** telegraficamente **2.** in stile telegrafico.

telegraphist [ti'legrəfist], *s.c.* telegrafista.

telegraphy [ti'legrəfi], *s.* telegrafia.

telekinesis [‚telikai'ni:sis], *s.* telecinesi.

Telemachus [ti'leməkəs], *no.pr.m.* (*lett.*) Telemaco.

telemark ['telima:k], *s.* (*sci*) « telemark » (manovra d'arresto, di rallentamento).

telemechanics [‚telimi'kæniks], *s.* telemeccanica.

telemeter ['telimi:tə*], *s.* telemetro.

telemetry ['telimi:tri], *s.* telemetria.

teleobjective [‚teliəb'dʒektiv], *s.* (*foto.*) teleobiettivo.

teleologic(al) [‚teliou'lodʒik(əl)], *ag.* (*fil.*) teleologico.

teleologically [‚teliou'lodʒikəli], *av.* (*fil.*) in modo teleologico.

teleology [‚teli'olədʒi], *s.* (*fil.*) teleologia.

telepathic [‚teli'pæθik], *ag.* telepatico.

telepathically [‚teli'pæθikəli], *av.* telepaticamente.

to telepathize [ti'lepəθaiz], *v.t.i.* trasmettere, influenzare per telepatia.

telepathy [ti'lepəθi], *s.* telepatia.

telephone ['telifoun], *s.* telefono: *are you on the* —?, hai il telefono? ☆ — *-box* (o — *-booth*), cabina telefonica; — *directory* (o — *book*), elenco telefonico; — *exchange*, centrale telefonica; — *operator*, telefonista; — *receiver*, ricevitore ‖ *dial-* —, telefono automatico; *extension* —, apparecchio telefonico derivato, derivazione.

to telephone, *v.t.i.* telefonare.

telephonic [‚teli'fonik], *ag.* telefonico.

telephonically [‚teli'fonikəli], *av.* telefonicamente.

telephonist [ti'lefənist], *s.c.* telefonista; centralinista.

telephony [ti'lefəni], *s.* telefonia.

telephoto ['teli'foutou], *s.* telefoto.

telephotograph ['teli'foutəgra:f], *s.* telefotografia.

telephotographic ['teli‚foutə'græfik], *ag.* telefotografico.

telephotography ['telifə'togrəfi], *s.* telefotografia.

teleprinter ['teli‚printə*], *s.* telescrivente.

teleprompter ['teli‚promptə*], *s.* (*tv.*) « teleprompter » (meccanismo suggeritore).

teleran ['teliræn], *s.* (*aer.*) radar televisivo.

telescope ['teliskoup], *s.* **1.** (*astr.*) telescopio **2.** (*mar.*) cannocchiale ☆ — *-joint*, (*mec.*) giunto a telescopio ‖ *range-finder* —, cannocchiale telemetrico; *reflecting* —, (*astr.*) telescopio a riflessione; *refracting* —, (*astr.*) telescopio a rifrazione, rifrattore; *sighting* —, (*artigl.*) cannocchiale di traguardo.

to telescope, *v.t.i.* incastrare, incastrarsi; commettere, commettersi (di parti); chiudersi a telescopio; condensare: *the Express telescoped into the back of the goods train*, l'espresso si incastrò nella parte posteriore del treno merci; *the legs of this tripod* — *very easily*, le gambe di questo treppiedi rientrano molto facilmente; *parts made to* —, pezzi fatti per essere incastrati.

telescopic(al) [‚telis'kopik(əl)], *ag.* **1.** telescopico **2.** a telescopio, a incastro ☆ — *-finder*, (*foto.*) mirino telescopico; — *-funnel*, (*mar.*) fumaiolo a telescopio; — *ladder*, scala a incastro; — *lens*, (*foto.*) teleobiettivo; — *toolholder*, portautensili a telescopio.

telescopically [‚telis'kopikəli], *av.* telescopicamente.

telescopiform [‚telis'koupifo:m], *ag.* a forma di telescopio.

telescopy [ti'leskəpi], *s.* (*astr.*) telescopia.

telescreen ['teli-skri:n], *s.* video, schermo televisivo.

telespectroscope [‚teli'spektrəskoup], *s.* (*astr.*) telespettroscopio.

telethermometer [‚teliθə'momitə*], *s.* (*fis.*) teletermometro.

teletype ['telitaip], *s.* **1.** telescrivente **2.** messaggio trasmesso per telescrivente.

to teletype, *v.t.i.* telescrivere.

teletypesetter ['teli'taip‚setə*], *s.* (*tip.*) telecompositrice.

teletypewriter ['teli'taip‚raitə*], *s.* telescrivente.

teletyping ['teli,taipiŋ], *s.* (*tel.*) **1.** telescrittura **2.** impiego della telescrivente.

to **teleview** ['telivju:], *v.t.i.* assistere a uno spettacolo televisivo; guardare (uno spettacolo) televisivo.

televiewer ['teli,vju:ə*], *s.c.* telespettatore, telespettatrice.

to **televise** ['telivaiz], *v.t.* (*tv.*) teletrasmettere; televricevere: *to — an opera from the stage*, teletrasmettere un'opera dal teatro.

television ['teli,viʒən], *s.* televisione ☆ — *camera*, telecamera; — *receiver* (o — *set*), apparecchio televisivo, televisore; — *telephone*, telefonovisore ‖ *relay* —, (*tv.*) ritrasmissione, rimbalzo.

televisor ['telivaizə*], *s.* televisore.

to **tell** [tel], *pass.p.p.* **told** [tould], *v.t.i.* **1.** dire, riferire; informare; raccontare, narrare: — *me about it*, raccontamelo; *he told me his story*, mi raccontò la sua storia; *he told me that he had talked to him*, mi disse d'avergli parlato; *I told him so!*, glielo avevo detto!; *I was told that...*, venni a sapere che...; *to — the truth, a lie*, dire la verità, una bugia ‖ — *that to the marines*, contala ai gonzi ‖ *I'll — you what!*, senti!, ascolta! ‖ *you are telling me!*, (*sl.*) a me lo dici! **2.** render noto, divulgare; manifestare, esprimere: *his face tells much of his past*, il suo volto rivela il suo passato; *I cannot — you how glad I am*, non so dirti quanto io sia felice; *to — tales about s.o., sthg.*, spargere chiacchiere sul conto di qlcu., ql.co. **3.** (III, IV) ordinare, comandare, imporre, ingiungere: *do as you are told*, fai come ti si dice; *I was told to go away*, mi fu ingiunto di andarmene **4.** sapere, prevedere: *no man can — what the future has in store for him*, nessuno può prevedere che cosa gli riserberà il futuro; *who can —?*, chi lo può sapere? **5.** discernere, distinguere, riconoscere: *he cannot — right from wrong*, non sa distinguere il bene dal male; *I can — him by his voice*, lo riconosco dalla voce **6.** enumerare, contare: *there were thirty people all told*, c'erano in tutto trenta persone ‖ *to — one's beads*, dire il rosario **7.** aver effetto, incidere: *his years are beginning to —*, gli anni cominciano a pesargli **8.** *to — against* (*s.o.*), nuocere a: *that tells against him*, ciò gli nuoce **9.** *to — for* (*s.o.*), essere favorevole a: *that tells for him*, ciò depone a suo favore **10.** *to — on* (*s.o.*), pesare su; (*sl.*) denunciare: *the strain is beginning to — on them*, essi risentono dello sforzo **11.** *to — off*, designare; (*sl.*) fare una ramanzina a: *I was told off for speaking*, mi presi una sgridata per aver parlato; *I was told off to guard the horses*, mi fu dato il compito di sorvegliare i cavalli.

tellable ['teləbl], *ag.* raccontabile, narrabile.

teller ['telə*], *s.c.* chi riferisce, racconta ‖ *s.* **1.** (*pol.*) scrutatore **2.** (*comm.*) cassiere (di banca, ecc.) ☆ — *in* (o *receiving* —), (*comm.*) cassiere alle riscossioni; — *out* (o *paying* —), (*comm.*) cassiere ai pagamenti.

tellina [te'lai:nə], *s.* (*zool.*) tellina.

telling ['teliŋ], *ag.* efficace; espressivo: *a — argument*, un argomento efficace; *a — blow*, un colpo ben assestato, efficace; *a — look*, uno sguardo espressivo ‖ *s.* **1.** il raccontare, il narrare: *his — made us laugh*, il suo modo di raccontare ci fece ridere ‖ *there's no —*, non si sa mai **2.** divulgazione, rivelazione (di segreto, ecc.): *his — was the ruin of his friend*, la sua rivelazione fu la rovina del suo amico ‖ — *on s.o.*, il denunciare qlcu. ‖ *that's —!*, (*fam.*) ma questo sarebbe spifferare ogni cosa! **3.** — (*over*), conto, scrutinio (di voti, ecc.).

tellingly ['teliŋli], *av.* efficacemente, vividamente.

telltale ['tel-teil], *ag. attributivo* rivelatore: — *look*, sguardo rivelatore; — *signs*, segni rivelatori.

telltale, *s.c.* chiacchierone, chiacchierona; persona indiscreta, pettegola, spiona ‖ *s.* **1.** (*tec.*) controllore **2.** (*mar.*) assiometro **3.** (*ferr.*) segnale di pericolo ☆ — *light*, (*elett.*) lampada spia ‖ *rudder* —, (*mar.*) assiometro del timone.

tellural [te'ljuərəl], *ag.* tellurico.

tellurian [te'ljuəriən], *ag.* terrestre.

telluric[1] [te'ljuərik], *ag.* terrestre.

telluric[2], *ag.* (*chim.*) tellurico.

tellurium [te'ljuəriəm], *s.* (*chim.*) tellurio.

tellurous ['teljurəs], *ag.* (*chim.*) telluroso.

telly ['teli], *s.* (*fam.*) televisione ☆ — *-don*, (*fam.*) conferenziere alla televisione.

telpher ['telfə*], *ag.* teleferico ‖ *s.* cabina di funivia ☆ — *line*, teleferica, funivia.

to **telpher**, *v.t.* trasportare per mezzo di funivia.

telpherage ['telfəridʒ], *s.* trasporto per teleferica.

temenos ['teminɔs], *s.* (*st. greca*) recinto sacro.

temerarious [,temə'rɛəriəs], *ag.* (*letter.*) temerario.

temerariously [,temə'rɛəriəsli], *av.* (*letter.*) temerariamente.

temerity [ti'meriti], *s.* temerità.

Tempe ['tempi], *no.pr.* (*geog. st.*) Tempe.

Tempean [tem'pi:ən], *ag.* (*geog. st.*) di Tempe.

temper ['tempə*], *s.* **1.** indole, carattere: *she is of a placid —*, ella è di indole pacifica ‖ *to be out of —*, essere in collera **2.** umore, disposizione: *he was in a bad, in a good —*, egli era di cattivo, di buon umore **3.** stizza, collera: *a fit of —*, un impeto di collera; *to fly into* (o *to be in*) *a —*, andare, essere in collera; *to get s.o.'s — up*, far andare qlcu. in collera **4.** calma, sangue freddo: *to keep one's —*, mantenersi calmo; *to lose one's —*, irritarsi, andare in collera **5.** (*ind.*) tempra (del vetro); rinvenimento (dell'acciaio) **6.** (*metal.*) miscela legante; percentuale di carbonio (nella lega di acciaio, ecc.) **7.** (*arc.*) il giusto mezzo.

to **temper**, *v.t.i.* **1.** moderare; temperare, temperarsi ‖ *God tempers the wind to the shorn lamb*, prov. Dio manda il freddo secondo i panni **2.** (*ind.*) temperare (vetro); rinvenire (acciaio) **3.** (*mus.*) modulare, accordare.

tempera ['tempərə], *s.* (*pitt.*) tempera.

temperament ['tempərəmənt], *s.* **1.** temperamento, indole, carattere: *he has an artistic —*, ha un temperamento artistico; *that woman is lacking in —*, quella donna manca di carattere **2.** carattere impulsivo, capriccioso, instabile **3.** (*mus.*) temperamento.

temperamental [,tempərə'mentl], *ag.* capriccioso; instabile; suscettibile.

temperamentally [,tempərə'mentəli], *av.* per temperamento, per costituzione: *he is — averse to...*, egli è per natura contrario a....

temperance ['tempərəns], *s.* **1.** temperanza; pazienza; moderazione **2.** astinenza (dall'alcool) ☆ — *hotel*, albergo in cui è proibita la vendita di bevande alcooliche; — *society*, lega contro l'alcoolismo.

temperate ['tempərit], *ag.* **1.** temperato (di clima) **2.** temperante, moderato, sobrio; paziente.

temperately ['tempəritli], *av.* moderatamente, sobriamente.

temperateness ['tempəritnis], *s.* moderazione, temperanza, sobrietà.

temperature ['tempritʃə*], *s.* temperatura: *the — of the room was intolerably hot*, la temperatura della stanza era terribilmente calda ‖ *to have* (o *to run*) *a —*, avere la febbre ☆ — *gradient*, (*meteorologia*) gradiente termico ‖ *dew-point* —, (*chim. fis.*) temperatura del punto di rugiada; *dry-bulb* —, temperatura letta a termometro asciutto; *room* —, temperatura ambiente.

tempered ['tempəd], *ag.* **1.** temprato (di vetro); rinvenuto (di acciaio) **2.** moderato (di passo, andatura, ecc.) **3.** di indole, di natura; di umore ☆ *bad* —, di cattivo umore, di cattivo carattere; *even* —, di umore costante; *quick* —, irritabile; *short* —, impulsivo.

tempering ['tempəriŋ], *s.* **1.** moderazione; temperamento, dominio (delle passioni) **2.** miscuglio (di qualità) **3.** (*ind.*) tempra (di vetro); rinvenimento (di acciaio) ☆ — *-furnace*, forno di rinvenimento.

tempest ['tempist], *s.* **1.** tempesta, burrasca, procella **2.** *fig.* agitazione, commozione.

tempestuous [tem'pestjuəs], *ag.* tempestoso, burrascoso, procelloso (anche *fig.*).

tempestuously [tem'pestjuəsli], *av.* tempestosamente; violentemente (anche *fig.*).

tempestuousness [tem'pestjuəsnis], *s.* stato tempestoso; agitazione (anche *fig.*).

templar ['templə*], *s.* 1. studioso di diritto 2. *Templar*, (*st.*) Templare.

template, *V.* **templet**.

temple[1] ['templ], *s.* tempio ‖ *Inner, Middle Temple*, nome degli «Inns of Court» a Londra (antica sede dei Templari).

temple[2], *s.* 1. (*anat.*) tempia 2. (*amer.*) templale, stanghetta da occhiali.

temple[3], *s.* (*ind. tessile*) templale ☆ *mechanical* —, templale automatico.

templet[1] ['templit], *s.* 1. (*arch.*) architrave 2. (*mec.*) calibro sagomato, sagoma, mascherina 3. (*edil.*) cuscino d'appoggio, piastra di ripartizione del carico.

templet[2], *s.* (*ind. tessile*) templale.

tempo ['tempou], *pl.* **tempi** ['tempi:], *s.* 1. (*mus.*) tempo 2. andamento, movimento, ritmo ‖ *the* — *of industry increases*, (*fam.*) il ritmo dell'industria si accelera.

temporal[1] ['tempərəl], *ag.* temporale ‖ *lords spiritual and* —, vescovi e pari d'Inghilterra ‖ *s.* — (*power*), (*eccl.*) (potere) temporale.

temporal[2], *ag.* (*anat.*) temporale ☆ — *bones*, ossa temporali.

temporality [,tempə'ræliti], *s.* 1. *gener. pl.* (*eccl.*) reddito di un beneficio; beni temporali 2. (*dir.*) provvisorietà, temporaneità.

temporally ['tempərəli], *av.* temporalmente.

temporalness ['tempərəlnis], *s.* (*rar.*) temporaneità, caducità.

temporalty ['tempərəlti], *s.* (*eccl.*) 1. laicato 2. *V.* **temporality** 1.

temporarily ['tempərərili], *av.* temporaneamente, provvisoriamente.

temporariness ['tempərərinis], *s.* temporaneità.

temporary ['tempərəri], *ag.* temporaneo, provvisorio; momentaneo, passeggero.

temporization [,tempərai'zeiʃən], *s.* temporeggiamento.

to **temporize** ['tempəraiz], *v.i.* temporeggiare; indugiare; prender tempo.

temporizer ['tempəraizə*], *s.c.* temporeggiatore, temporeggiatrice.

temporizingly ['tempəraiziŋli], *av.* temporeggiando; differendo, procrastinando.

to **tempt** [tempt], *v.t.* (IV) 1. tentare, allettare, attrarre, indurre: *I was tempted to come*, fui tentato di venire; *to* — *s.o. to evil*, indurre qlcu. al male 2. (*arc.*) tentare, mettere alla prova; provocare, sfidare: *God tempted Isaac*, Dio mise alla prova Isacco; *to* — *God, fate*, tentare Dio, sfidare il destino.

temptable ['temptəbl], *ag.* che si lascia tentare.

temptation [temp'teiʃən], *s.* tentazione: *to fall into* —, cadere in tentazione; *to yield to* —, cedere alla tentazione.

tempter ['temptə*], *s.* tentatore ‖ *the Tempter*, il Tentatore, il diavolo.

tempting ['temptiŋ], *ag.* seducente, allettante: — *food*, cibo appetitoso ‖ *s.* tentazione.

temptingly ['temptiŋli], *av.* seducentemente.

temptress ['temptris], *s.* tentatrice.

temulence ['temjuləns], **temulency** ['temjulənsi], *s.* (*rar.*) ubriachezza.

temulent ['temjulənt], *ag.* (*rar.*) ubriaco.

ten [ten], *ag.num.card.s.* dieci: *one out of* —, uno su dieci; *to arrange in tens*, disporre a gruppi di dieci ‖ *a* —, (*aut.*) un'automobile da 10 H.P. ‖ *the upper* —, *'aristocrazia* ‖ — *to one he won't do it*, (scommetto) dieci contro uno che non ce la fa ☆ — *cent store*, (*amer.*) magazzino popolare (a catena); — *gallon hat*, (*amer.*) cappello a larga tesa (da cow-boy); — *pounder*, (*fam.*) che vale 10 sterline, che pesa 10 libbre; (*st.*) elettore

(proprietario di un fondo del valore locativo di almeno 10 sterline).

tenability [,tenə'biliti], *s.* possibilità di tenere, di difendere.

tenable ['tenəbl], *ag.* 1. sostenibile, difendibile (argomento, posizione, ecc.) 2. che si può tenere per un tempo determinato (impiego, ufficio, ecc.).

tenableness ['tenəblnis], *s.* possibilità di tenere, di difendere.

tenacious [ti'neiʃəs], *ag.* 1. tenace; ostinato: *a* — *grip*, una stretta tenace; *to be* — *of one's principles*, essere molto attaccato ai propri principi 2. viscoso; adesivo.

tenaciously [ti'neiʃəsli], *av.* tenacemente; ostinatamente.

tenaciousness [ti'neiʃəsnis], *s.* 1. tenacità; forza adesiva 2. tenacia; ostinazione.

tenacity [ti'næsiti], *s.* tenacia; ostinazione.

tenaculum [ti'nækjuləm], *pl.* **tenacula** [ti'nækjulə], *s.* (*chir.*) tenacolo.

tenail, tenaille [ti'neil], *s.* (*mil.*) tanaglia.

tenancy ['tenənsi], *s.* (*dir.*) locazione; affitto; usufrutto.

tenant ['tenənt], *s.* 1. (*dir.*) proprietario 2. locatario, affittuario, conduttore ☆ — *farmer*, (*agr.*) affittuario, fittaiuolo.

to **tenant**, *v.t.* 1. (*dir.*) essere proprietario di 2. tenere in affitto; occupare (come inquilino).

tenantable ['tenəntəbl], *ag.* affittabile.

tenantless ['tenəntlis], *ag.* sfitto; non abitato.

tenantry ['tenəntri], *s. coll.* (*dir.*) 1. proprietari 2. inquilini; (*agr.*) fittaiuoli.

tench [tenʃ], *s.* (*ittiol.*) tinca.

to **tend**[1] [tend], *v.t.i.* curare, attendere a, badare a; aver cura; custodire: *to* — *the children*, custodire i bambini; *to* — *the fire*, badare al fuoco ‖ *to* — *upon s.o.*, servire qlcu. (a tavola).

to **tend**[2], *v.i.* 1. tendere, essere diretto 2. *fig.* tendere, aver tendenza: *pink tending to red*, rosa che tende al rosso; *she tends to cruelty*, ha tendenza alla crudeltà 3. tendere, condurre, servire: *this may* — *to prove what I say*, questo può servire ad avvalorare quello che dico; *too much smoking tends to injure one's voice*, il troppo fumare tende a rovinar la voce.

tendance ['tendəns], *s. arc.* 1. cura, attenzione 2. *coll.* il seguito, i domestici, i famigli.

tendency ['tendənsi], *s.* tendenza, inclinazione: — *to corpulence*, tendenza all'obesità.

tendentious [ten'denʃəs], *ag.* tendenzioso.

tender[1] ['tendə*], *ag.* 1. tenero: *a* — *steak*, una bracciuola tenera 2. delicato, sensibile (anche *fig.*); scrupoloso, suscettibile: *a* — *heart*, un cuore sensibile; — *skin*, pelle delicata; *a* — *spot*, (*fam.*) un punto dolorante; *fig.* una questione delicata: *don't ask him anything, it's a* — *spot*, non chiedergli nulla, lo pungeresti sul vivo 3. giovane, immaturo: — *age*, giovane età 4. affettuoso 5. sollecito: *American law is* — *of women's rights*, la legge americana si prende molta cura dei diritti delle donne; *he is very* — *of his fame*, è molto geloso della sua reputazione ☆ — *-loin*, (*amer.*) filetto (di carne); (*sl. amer.*) quartiere di New York (dove ferveva una corrotta vita notturna).

to **tender**[1], *v.t.* (*arc. dial.*) trattare con tenerezza, riguardo.

tender[2], *s.* 1. (*spec. amer.*) guardiano, custode 2. (*ferr.*) «tender», carro scorta 3. (*mar.*) nave appoggio; lancia ☆ *aircraft* —, nave appoggio e rifornimento per aerei; *bar* —, barista.

tender[3], *s.* 1. (*dir.*) offerta, proposta; offerta reale 2. (*comm. dir.*) offerta; contratto; capitolato (di appalto): *to make* (o *to put in* o *to send in*) *a* — *for*, dare in appalto ☆ *legal* —, (*comm. dir.*) valuta legale.

to **tender**[3], *v.t.i.* 1. offrire, presentare: *to* — *one's resignation*, porgere, dare le dimissioni 2. (*dir.*) offrire;

proporre (un prezzo), fare un'offerta: *to — money in discharge of debt*, fare una offerta reale **3.** concorrere, fare offerte (per un appalto).

tenderer ['tendərə*], *s.c.* chi offre, chi concorre (per un appalto).

tenderfoot ['tendəfut], *pl.* **tenderfoots** ['tendəfuts], **tenderfeet** ['tendəfi:t], *s.* **1.** (*sl. spec. amer.*) novizio, novellino **2.** (*scoutismo*) « piede tenero » (nuovo membro che ha appena pronunciato la promessa).

tenderizer ['tendəraizə*], *s.* (*cuc.*) « tenderizer » (preparato che rende la carne tenera).

tenderling ['tendəliŋ], *s.* **1.** persona delicata; (*rar. spreg.*) persona effeminata **2.** bambinetto.

tenderly ['tendəli], *av.* teneramente, affettuosamente.

tenderness ['tendənis], *s.* **1.** l'esser tenero (di cibo) **2.** delicatezza; sensibilità; fragilità (anche *fig.*) **3.** tenerezza, affettuosità **4.** sollecitudine.

tending ['tendiŋ], *s.* cure; sorveglianza: *his — of the garden proved a success*, le cure che egli dedicò al giardino si rivelarono ottime.

tendinous ['tendinəs], *ag.* (*anat.*) tendinoso.

tendon ['tendən], *s.* (*anat.*) tendine ☆ — *grafting*, trapianto dell'inserzione di un tendine; — *spindle*, fuso tendineo.

tendril ['tendril], *s.* (*bot.*) viticcio.

tendrilled ['tendrild], *ag.* (*bot.*) fornito di viticci.

tenebrae ['tenibri:], *s. pl.* (*eccl.*) ufficio delle tenebre.

tenebrific [,teni'brifik], *ag.* che produce oscurità.

tenebrous ['tenibrəs], *ag.* (*arc.*) tenebroso, oscuro.

tenement ['tenimənt], *s.* **1.** (*dir.*) podere, tenuta **2.** (*dir.*) possesso **3.** abitazione, appartamento ☆ — *house*, casamento, casa operaia.

tenesmic [ti'nezmik], *ag.* (*patol.*) tenesmico.

tenesmus [ti'nezməs], *s.* (*patol.*) tenesmo.

tenet ['ti:net], *s.* **1.** dogma, dottrina **2.** (*fam.*) opinione, credenza.

tenfold ['ten-fould], *ag.* decuplo.

tenfold, *av.* dieci volte tanto, al decuplo: *I will repay you —*, vi ripagherò dieci volte tanto; *to increase —*, decuplicare.

tenner ['tenə*], *s.* (*fam.*) biglietto da dieci sterline; (*amer.*) biglietto da dieci dollari.

tennis ['tenis], *s.* tennis ☆ — *-ball*, palla da tennis; — *-court*, campo da tennis; — *-player*, giocatore di tennis; — *-racket*, racchetta da tennis.

tenon ['tenən], *s.* **1.** (*artig.*) tenone **2.** (*mar.*) maschio, miccia ☆ — *saw*, (*artig.*) sega per tenoni.

to tenon, *v.t.* (*artig.*) congiungere con, munire di tenone.

tenor ['tenə*], *s.* **1.** tenore, sistema, tono (di vita, discorso, ecc.) **2.** (*dir.*) copia esatta **3.** (*mus.*) tenore; musica per tenore **4.** (*comm.*) scadenza ☆ — *voice*, voce tenorile.

tenorist ['tenərist], *s.* (*mus.*) tenore.

tenotomy [ti'nɔtəmi], *s.* (*chir.*) tenotomia.

tenpins ['tenpinz], *s.pl.* (*amer.*) giuoco con dieci birilli.

tenree ['tenrek], *s.* (*zool.*) riccio del Madagascar.

tense[1] [tens], *ag.* teso, tirato (anche *fig.*): — *silence*, silenzio impressionante; — *situation*, situazione tesa; *to be — with expectancy*, esser teso nell'aspettativa.

to tense[1], *v.t.i.* tendere, tendersi (anche *fig.*).

tense[2], *s.* (*gram.*) tempo: *future, past, present —*, tempo futuro, passato, presente.

tensely ['tensli], *av.* in modo teso (anche *fig.*): *I was thinking —*, pensavo con grande concentrazione.

tenseness ['tensnis], *s.* rigidità; tensione (anche *fig.*).

tensibility [,tensi'biliti], *s.* elasticità.

tensile ['tensail], *ag.* **1.** estensibile, elastico; duttile (di metallo) **2.** (*mec. fis.*) relativo alla tensione, alla trazione: — *test*, prova a trazione.

tension ['tenʃən], *s.* **1.** tensione; rigidità; stato di tensione (anche *fig.*) **2.** (*fis.*) tensione; pressione (di gas, liquido, ecc.) **3.** (*elett.*) tensione, potenziale: *high, low —*, alta, bassa tensione ☆ — *-rod*, (*mec.*) tirante || *surface —*, (*fis.*) tensione superficiale.

tensity ['tensiti], *s.* tensione; rigidità.

tenson ['tensən], *s.* (*lett.*) tenzone, gara.

tensor ['tensə*], *s.* (*anat.*) (muscolo) tensore.

tent[1] [tent], *s.* tenda, padiglione: *to pitch tents*, piantare le tende; *to strike tents*, levare le tende ☆ — *-fly*, doppia porta; tetto di tenda; — *-peg*, picchetto per tenda || *bell —*, tenda circolare; *oxygen —*, (*med.*) tenda ad ossigeno.

to tent[1], *v.t.i.* **1.** attendarsi; vivere sotto una tenda **2.** coprire con una tenda.

tent[2], *s.* (*chir.*) tampone, stuello, zaffo.

to tent[2], *v.t.* (*chir.*) mettere uno zaffo, uno stuello a.

tent[3], *s.* « tinto » (vino rosso spagnolo).

tentacle ['tentəkl], *s.* **1.** tentacolo **2.** viticcio, cirro.

tentacled ['tentəkld], *ag.* tentacolato.

tentacular [ten'tækjulə*], *ag.* tentacolare.

tentaculate [ten'tækjulit], **tentaculated** [ten'tækjuleitid], *ag.* tentacolato.

tentaculiform [ten'tækjulifɔ:m], *ag.* che ha forma di tentacolo.

tentaculum [ten'tækjuləm], *pl.* **tentacula** [ten'tækiulə], *s.* **1.** tentacolo **2.** viticcio, cirro.

tentage ['tentidʒ], *s.* **1.** equipaggiamento di tende **2.** sistemazione in tende.

tentative ['tentətiv], *ag.* di prova, sperimentale: — *proposal, offer*, proposta, offerta in via di esperimento || *s.* tentativo, prova.

tentatively ['tentətivli], *av.* come tentativo; a titolo di prova, sperimentalmente.

tented ['tentid], *ag.* **1.** pieno di tende (di luogo) **2.** a forma di tenda **3.** che vive attendato (di persona).

tenter[1] ['tentə*], *s.* (*ind. tessile*) stenditoio ☆ — *-hook*, uncino (di stenditoio): *to be on — -hooks*, *fig.* essere sulle spine.

tenter[2], *s.* addetto (ad una macchina, ecc.).

tentering ['tentəriŋ], *s.* (*ind. tessile*) distendimento ☆ — *machine*, macchina distenditrice.

tenth [tenθ], *ag.num.ord.* decimo || *s.* **1.** decimo **2.** (*eccl.*) decima **3.** (*mus.*) (intervallo di) decima.

tenthly ['tenθli], *av.* in decimo luogo.

tenuis ['tenjuis], *pl.* **tenues** ['tenjui:z], *s.* (*fonet.*) tenue.

tenuity [te'nju:)iti], *s.* **1.** tenuità, sottigliezza **2.** fluidità (di liquido); rarefazione (di gas) **3.** semplicità (di stile).

tenuous ['tenjuəs], *ag.* **1.** tenue, sottile **2.** fluido, rarefatto **3.** semplice (di stile).

tenuously ['tenjuəsli], *av.* tenuemente.

tenure ['tenjuə*], *s.* (*dir.*) **1.** possesso, godimento **2.** diritto di possesso **3.** periodo di possesso.

tenzon ['tenzən], *s.* (*lett.*) tenzone, gara.

teocalli [,ti:ou'kæli], *s.* « teocalli » (tempio messicano).

tepee ['ti:pi:], *s.* tenda dei pellirosse.

tepefaction [,tepi'fækʃən], *s.* intiepidimento.

to tepefy ['tepifai], *v.t.i.* intiepidire, intiepidirsi.

tephrite ['tefrait], *s.* (*geol.*) tefrina.

tepid ['tepid], *ag.* tiepido.

tepidarium [,tepi'dɛəriəm], *pl.* **tepidaria** [,tepi-'dɛəriə], *s.* (*archeol.*) tepidario.

tepidity [te'piditi], *s.* tepidezza, tepidità.

tepidly ['tepidli], *av.* tiepidamente.

tepidness ['tepidnis], *s.* tepidezza, tepidità.

teratism ['terətizəm], *s.* (*med.*) teratismo.

teratological [,terətou'lɔdʒikəl], *ag.* (*med.*) teratologico.

teratology [,terə'tɔlədʒi], *s.* (*med.*) teratologia.

teratoma [,terə'toumə], *s.* (*patol.*) teratoma.

teratosis [,terə'tousis], *s.* (*med.*) teratosi.

terbium ['tə:biəm], *s.* (*chim.*) terbio.

terce [tə:s], *s.* (*eccl.*) terza.

tercel ['tə:səl], *s.* (*ornit.*) terzuolo, falcone maschio.

tercentenary [,tə:sen'ti:nəri], **tercentennial** [,tə:-sen'tenjəl], *ag.s.* trecentenario.

tercet ['tə:sit], *s.* (*poes.*) terzina.
terebene ['terəbi:n], *s.* (*chim.*) terebene.
terebinth ['terəbinθ], *s.* (*bot.*) terebinto.
terebinthine [,terə'binθain], *ag.* di terebinto.
terebrant ['teribrənt], *ag.* terebrante (di dolore).
terebration [,teri'breiʃən], *s.* perforazione.
teredo [tə'ri:dou], *pl.* **teredos** [tə'ri:douz], *s.* (*zool.*) teredine.
Terence ['terəns], *no.pr.m.* (*st. lett.*) Terenzio.
Teresa [tə'ri:zə], *no.pr.f.* Teresa.
tergal ['tə:gəl], *ag.* dorsale.
to **tergiversate** ['tə:dʒivə:seit], *v.i.* fare un voltafaccia; tergiversare.
tergiversation [,tə:dʒivə:'seiʃən], *s.* tergiversazione.
tergiversator ['tə:dʒivə:,seitə*], *s.c.* tergiversatore, tergiversatrice.
tergum ['tə:gəm], *pl.* **terga** ['tə:gə], *s.* dorso (di animale).
term [tə:m], *s.* **1.** termine; periodo di tempo; (*scuola*) trimestre; (*dir.*) sessione: *the — begins in September*, il trimestre comincia in settembre; *the agreement was for a — of three years*, l'accordo stabiliva un periodo di tre anni; *the case will come up next —*, (*dir.*) la causa sarà discussa la prossima sessione; *his — of office expired some time ago*, il suo periodo di carica è spirato qualche tempo fa; *the usual — of our policies is four years*, (*comm.*) la durata solita delle nostre polizze è di quattro anni **2.** termine; condizione; clausola: *terms and conditions of an issue*, condizioni e modalità di una emissione; *terms of delivery*, condizioni di consegna; *terms of sale*, (*comm.*) condizioni di vendita; *easy terms*, facilitazioni (di vendita); *under the terms*, secondo le clausole del contratto; *name your own terms*, stabilite voi le condizioni; *to come to* (o *to make*) *terms with*, venire a patti con; trovare un accordo con: *he has come to terms with his creditors*, è venuto ad un accomodamento con i suoi creditori **||** *inclusive terms*, tutto compreso **3.** *pl.* rapporti, relazioni: *to be on bad, good terms with s.o.*, essere in cattivi, buoni rapporti con qlcu.; *not to be on speaking terms with s.o.*, essere in rotta con qlcu. **4.** (*mat. log.*) termine: *in terms of c.g.s. units*, espresso in unità c.g.s.; *major, minor —*, (*log.*) termine maggiore, minore (di un sillogismo); *to reduce a fraction to its lowest terms*, ridurre una frazione ai minimi termini **5.** parola, termine: *he spoke of her work in flattering terms*, lodò il suo lavoro; *he used very strong terms*, usò parole molto energiche; *to use the proper —*, usare la parola giusta, parlare con proprietà **6.** (*scult.*) erma.
to **term**, *v.t.* chiamare, definire: *he terms himself a scientist*, egli si autodefinisce scienziato; *I — this a bad action*, io lo chiamo una cattiva azione.
termagancy ['tə:məgənsi], *s.* natura bisbetica.
termagant ['tə:məgənt], *ag.* violento; turbolento; rissoso **||** *s.* bisbetica, brontolona; megera.
terminable ['tə:minəbl], *ag.* terminabile; limitabile.
terminal ['tə:min], *ag.* **1.** estremo, terminale **2.** (*scuola*) trimestrale **||** *s.* **1.** estremità, parte estrema **2.** (*amer. ferr.*) stazione di testa **3.** (*elett.*) morsetto ☆ *— voltage*, (*elett.*) tensione ai morsetti **||** *air —*, (*aer.*) « air terminal », aerostazione.
terminally ['tə:minəli], *av.* all'estremità, alla fine.
terminate ['tə:minit], *ag.* limitato; che ha un termine ☆ *— decimal fraction*, (*mat.*) frazione decimale finita.
to **terminate** ['tə:mineit], *v.t.i.* **1.** limitare **2.** terminare; portare a termine; porre fine a: *this word terminates in h*, questa parola termina per h; *to — one's work*, terminare il proprio lavoro.
termination [,tə:mi'neiʃən], *s.* **1.** termine, limite **2.** fine, cessazione; conclusione: *the — of an agreement*, la conclusione di un accordo; *to put a — to sthg.* (o *to bring sthg. to a —*), porre fine a ql.co. **3.** (*gram.*) terminazione, desinenza.
terminational [,tə:mi'neiʃənl], *ag.* (*gram.*) di terminazione, di desinenza.

terminator ['tə:mineitə*], *s.* **1.** chi, che termina **2.** (*astr.*) contorno, limite.
terminer ['tə:minə*], *s.*: *oyer and —*, (*dir.*) incarico di decidere cause penali pendenti (conferito a giudici).
terminism ['tə:minizəm], *s.* **1.** (*teol.*) terminismo **2.** (*fil.*) nominalismo.
terminological [,tə:minə'lədʒikəl], *ag.* di terminologia: *inexactitude*, inesattezza di terminologia; (*iron.*) bugia.
terminologically [,tə:minə'lədʒikəli], *av.* terminologicamente.
terminology [,tə:mi'nələdʒi], *s.* terminologia.
terminus[1] ['tə:minəs], *pl.* **termini** ['tə:minai], **terminuses** ['tə:minəsiz], *s.* **1.** capolinea; (*ferr.*) stazione di testa **2.** pietra di confine (nei campi) **3.** fine, meta **||** *— ad quem, a quo*, estremi circa la durata del rischio (nelle polizze di assicurazione marittima).
Terminus[2], *no.pr.m.* (*mit.*) Termine.
termitarium [,tə:mi'tɛəriəm], **termitary** ['tə:mitəri], *s.* termitaio.
termite ['tə:mait], *s.* (*entom.*) termite.
termless ['tə:mlis], *ag.* (*letter.*) senza limite.
termly ['tə:mli], *ag.* (*rar.*) periodico; a termine fisso **||** *av.* (*rar.*) periodicamente; entro termini fissi.
termor ['tə:mə*], *s.* (*dir.*) usufruttuario.
tern[1] [tə:n], *ag.* terno (di fiori, foglie) **||** *s.* terno, gruppo di tre.
tern[2], *s.* (*ornit.*) sterna, rondine marina.
ternary ['tə:nəri], *ag.* ternario.
ternate ['tə:nit], *ag.* terno (di fiori, foglie).
terne [tə:n], *s. — (-plate)*, lamiera piombata.
terpene ['tə:pi:n], *s.* (*chim.*) terpene.
Terpsichore [tə:p'sikəri], *no.pr.f.* (*mit.*) Tersicore.
Terpsichorean [,tə:psikə'ri(:)ən], *ag.* di Tersicore; relativo alla danza.
terra ['terə], *s.* (*lat.*) terra ☆ *— -cotta*, terracotta; *— -firma*, terraferma.
terrace ['terəs], *s.* **1.** terrazzo, terrapieno **2.** (*edil.*) terrazza, tetto a terrazza **3.** fila di case (generalmente su terreno elevato).
to **terrace**, *v.t.* disporre a terrazza; fornire di (terrazze): *the terraced hills of the Italian coast*, le alture a terrazze delle coste italiane; *the terraced roofs of southern houses*, i tetti a terrazze delle case meridionali.
terrain ['terein], *s.* (*geog. mil.*) terreno.
terramycin [,terə'maisin], *s.* (*farm.*) terramicina.
terraneous [te'reiniəs], *ag.* terrestre (di piante).
terrapin ['terəpin], *s.* (*zool.*) tartaruga acquatica.
terraqueous [te'reikwiəs], *ag.* terracqueo.
terrazzo [te'rætsou], *s.* mosaico alla palladiana.
terrene [te'ri:n], *ag.* terrestre; terreno (anche *fig.*) **||** *s.* **1.** terreno, suolo **2.** la Terra, il mondo.
terrenely [tə'ri:nli], *av.* terrenamente.
terreplein ['tɛə-plein], *s.* (*mil.*) terrapieno.
terrestrial [ti'restriəl], *ag.* terrestre **||** *s.* abitante della Terra.
terrestrially [ti'restriəli], *av.* terrenamente.
terrible ['terəbl], *ag.* **1.** terribile, spaventoso **2.** (*fam.*) grande; notevole: *he is a — bore*, è un gran seccatore.
terribleness ['terəblnis], *s.* terribilità.
terribly ['terəbli], *av.* **1.** terribilmente, spaventosamente **2.** (*fam.*) molto; notevolmente: *I am — hungry*, ho una fame da lupi.
terricolous [te'rikələs], *ag.* terricolo.
terrier[1] ['teriə*], *s.* **1.** (*zool.*) terrier, fox-terrier **2.** (*fam. scherz.*) membro dell'esercito territoriale.
terrier[2], *s.* **1.** catasto **2.** inventario.
terrific [tə'rifik], *ag.* **1.** spaventoso, terrificante **2.** (*fam.*) straordinario, magnifico, grandioso.
terrifically [tə'rifikəli], *av.* **1.** in modo terrificante **2.** (*fam.*) straordinario, moltissimo.
to **terrify** ['terifai], *v.t.* atterrire, spaventare.
terrigenous [te'ridʒinəs], *ag.* terrigeno.
territorial [,teri'to:riəl], *ag.* territoriale; proprio di un territorio **||** *s.* membro della milizia territoriale

☆ — *aristocracy*, aristocrazia terriera; — *army*, milizia territoriale; — *system*, (*eccl.*) ordinamento che contempla il predominio dell'autorità civile su quella ecclesiastica; — *waters*, acque territoriali.

territorialism [ˌteriˈtɔːriəlizəm], *s.* **1.** organizzazione territoriale **2.** (*eccl.*) teoria che contempla il predominio dell'autorità civile su quella ecclesiastica.

territoriality [ˌteriˌtɔːriˈæliti], *s.* territorialità.

territorially [ˌteriˈtɔːriəli], *av.* territorialmente.

territory [ˈteritəri], *s.* territorio; distretto ‖ *Territory*, regione degli Stati Uniti esclusa dal godimento dei pieni diritti degli altri stati della Confederazione.

terror [ˈterə*], *s.* **1.** terrore: *to be in* —, essere terrorizzato; *to go in* — *of s.o.*, (*fam.*) avere una paura matta di qlcu.; *to have a holy* — *of sthg.*, (*fam.*) avere un sacro terrore di ql.co. ‖ *the (Reign of) Terror*, (*st. francese*) il Terrore **2.** terrore, persona che incute terrore **3.** (*fam.*) diavoletto, birbante (di bambino).

terrorism [ˈterərizəm], *s.* terrorismo.

terrorist [ˈterərist], *s.* terrorista.

terroristic [ˌterəˈristik], *ag.* terroristico.

to **terrorize** [ˈterəraiz], *v.t.* atterrire, incutere terrore a, terrorizzare.

terry[1] [ˈteri], *s.* — (*cloth*), (*ind. tessile*) tessuto a riccio, a spugna.

Terry[2], *no.pr.f. dim.* di **Teresa**.

terse [təːs], *ag.* conciso, preciso, incisivo (di stile).

tersely [ˈtəːsli], *av.* con stringatezza (di stile).

terseness [ˈtəːsnis], *s.* concisione, stringatezza (di stile).

tertial [ˈtəːʃəl], *s.* penna terziaria (di uccello).

tertian [ˈtəːʃən], *ag.s.* (*patol.*) terzana ☆ — *fever*, febbre terzana.

tertiary [ˈtəːʃəri], *ag.* terziario ‖ *the Tertiary period*, (*geol.*) l'era terziaria ‖ *s.* (*eccl.*) terziario.

tertius [ˈtəːʃjəs], *ag.* (*lat.*) terzo (di più alunni con lo stesso cognome nella stessa scuola): *Brown* —, Brown numero tre ‖ — *gaudens*, il terzo gode.

tervalent [təːˈveilənt], *ag.* (*chim.*) trivalente.

tessellar [ˈtesələ*], *ag.* tassellato.

to **tessellate** [ˈtesileit], *v.t.* tassellare, lavorare ad intarsio; decorare a mosaico.

tessellated [ˈtesileitid], *ag.* tassellato; decorato con mosaico a scacchiera.

tessellation [ˌtesiˈleiʃən], *s.* tassellatura; decorazione a mosaico.

tessera [ˈtesərə], *pl.* **tesserae** [ˈtesəriː], *s.* **1.** tessera (di mosaico) **2.** *fig.* segno distintivo; parola d'ordine.

tesseral [ˈtesərəl], *ag.* a tessera (di mosaico).

test[1] [test], *s.* **1.** prova; esperimento, saggio: *the crucial* —, la prova decisiva; *weekly*, *final* —, esame, esperimento settimanale, finale; *to fail to pass a* —, fallire una prova; *to put s.o. to* (o *through*) *the* —, mettere qlcu. alla prova; *to stand the* —, superare la prova; *to undergo* (o *to be put through*) *a* —, subire una prova **2.** (*psicologia*) « test », saggio reattivo, reattivo psicologico **3.** (*ind.*) prova, collaudo **4.** (*chim.*) reattivo, reagente **5.** (*metal.*) saggio; coppella **6.** — (*film*), (*cine.*) provino **7.** *the Test*, (*st. inglese*) professione di fede ☆ — *bar*, (*mec.*) provetta, barretta; — *-bed*, (*mec.*) banco di prova; — *driver*, collaudatore; — *-paper*, (*chim.*) carta reattiva; — *pilot*, (*aer.*) pilota collaudatore; — *run*, (*ferr.*) corsa di prova; — *track*, (*aut.*) pista di prova; — *-tube*, (*chim.*) provetta ‖ *achievement* —, (*psicologia*) reattivo di rendimento; *aptitude* —, (*psicologia*) reattivo attitudinale; *bench* —, (*mec.*) prova al banco; *brake* —, (*mec.*) prova al freno; *drop* —, (*aer.*) prova d'urto; *endurance* —, (*spor.*) prova di resistenza; (*mec.*) prova di durata; *flight* —, (*aer.*) prova in volo; *hardness* —, (*metal.*) prova di durezza; *instrumental* —, (*psicologia*) reattivo analogico; *intelligence* —, (*psicologia*) reattivo intelligenza; *laboratory* —, (*mec.*) prova di laboratorio; *tensile* —, (*scienza delle costruzioni*) prova di trazione.

to **test**[1], *v.t.* **1.** esaminare; collaudare, provare: *to* —

accounts, controllare i conti; *to* — *sthg. carefully*, esaminare ql.co. con cura **2.** *fig.* mettere alla prova, cimentare, saggiare **3.** (*chim.*) analizzare **4.** (*metal.*) sottoporre a coppellazione.

test[2], *s.* guscio, conchiglia.

to **test**[3], *v.t.i.* (*dir.*) **1.** vistare (un documento); (*scoz.*) autenticare (un documento) **2.** (*scoz.*) fare testamento.

testable [ˈtestəbl], *ag.* provabile; collaudabile.

testacean [tesˈteiʃən], *ag. s.* (*zool.*) testaceo.

testaceous [tesˈteiʃəs], *ag.* **1.** (*zool.*) testaceo **2.** color rosso mattone.

testacy [ˈtestəsi], *s.* (*dir.*) condizione dell'essere testatore.

testament [ˈtestəmənt], *s.* testamento ‖ *the Old*, *the New Testament*, il Vecchio, il Nuovo Testamento.

testamental [ˌtestəˈmentl], *ag.* testamentario.

testamentarily [ˌtestəˈmentərili], *av.* per testamento.

testamentary [ˌtestəˈmentəri], *ag.* testamentario.

testamur [tesˈteimə*], *s.* certificato di promozione (nelle università inglesi).

testate [ˈtestit], *ag.s.* (*dir.*) testante.

testation [tesˈteiʃən], *s.* (*dir.*) **1.** disposizione di proprietà per testamento **2.** testimonianza.

testator [tesˈteitə*], *s.* (*dir.*) testatore.

testatrix [tesˈteitriks], *pl.* **testatrices** [tesˈteitrisiːz], *s.* (*dir.*) testatrice.

tester[1] [ˈtestə*], *s.c.* chi collauda; saggiatore, saggiatrice ‖ *s.* apparecchio di misura, di prova ☆ *insulation* —, (*elett.*) verificatore di isolamento, megaohmmetro.

tester[2], *s.* baldacchino ☆ — *bed*, letto a baldacchino.

tester[3], *s.* **1.** (*st.*) scellino di Enrico VIII **2.** (*fam.*) moneta da sei pence.

testicle [ˈtestikl], *s.* (*anat.*) testicolo.

testicular [tesˈtikjulə*], *ag.* (*anat.*) testicolare.

testification [ˌtestifiˈkeiʃən], *s.* (*rar.*) testimonianza.

testifier [ˈtestifaiə*], *s.* testimone, attestatore.

to **testify** [ˈtestifai], *v.t.i.* **1.** testimoniare, attestare; dimostrare: *work that testifies his deep knowledge of the subject*, lavoro che attesta la sua profonda conoscenza dell'argomento **2.** (*dir.*) dichiarare sotto giuramento, deporre: *the witness testified that the accused bore a good character*, il testimone dichiarò che l'accusato era uomo di buoni costumi **3.** *to* — *to* (*sthg.*), affermare, dar prova di: *he testified to having met me*, affermò, diede prova di avermi incontrato.

testily [ˈtestili], *av.* stizzosamente, irascibilmente.

testimonial [ˌtestiˈmounjəl], *ag.* testimoniale ‖ *s.* **1.** benservito, certificato di servizio: *to give a* — *to an employee*, dare un certificato di servizio ad un impiegato **2.** segno di gratitudine, stima; dono: *the old teacher was given a gold watch and other testimonials*, al vecchio insegnante furono dati un orologio d'oro ed altri doni.

to **testimonialize** [ˌtestiˈmounjəlaiz], *v.t.* (*rar.*) **1.** rilasciare un benservito a **2.** fare un omaggio, un dono a.

testimony [ˈtestiməni], *s.* **1.** testimonianza, attestazione ‖ *to give* —, (*relig.*) affermare pubblicamente la propria fede **2.** (*dir.*) dichiarazione sotto giuramento, deposizione: *to produce* — *of* (o *to*) *a statement*, allegare prove testimoniali alla deposizione **3.** (*relig.*) il Decalogo, le tavole della Legge; *pl.* i precetti di Dio.

testiness [ˈtestinis], *s.* irritabilità, suscettibilità.

testis [ˈtestis], *pl.* **testes** [ˈtestiːz], *s.*(*anat.*) testicolo.

testoon [tesˈtuːn], *s.* (*arc.*) testone, moneta d'argento.

testudinal [tesˈtjuːdinl], *ag.* di testuggine.

testudinarious [tesˌtjuːdiˈnɛəriəs], *ag.* macchiato come la corazza di una testuggine.

testudinate [tesˈtjuːdinit], *ag.* **1.** di testuggine **2.** ad arco, a volta (di tetto).

testudineous [ˌtestjuˈdinəs], *ag.* **1.** simile a corazza di testuggine **2.** lento, tardivo.

testudo [tesˈtjuːdou], *pl.* **testudos** [tesˈtjuːdouz], **testudines** [tesˈtjuːdiniːz], *s.* (*zool. st. mil.*) testuggine.

testy ['testi], *ag.* **1.** irascibile, suscettibile; risentito: *he muttered a few — words and went out*, borbottò poche parole risentite e uscì **2.** impetuoso, aggressivo.

tetanic [ti'tænik], *ag.* (*patol.*) tetanico ☆ — *spasm*, (*patol.*) spasmo tetanico.

tetanus ['tetənəs], *s.* (*patol.*) tetano.

tetany ['tetəni], *s.* (*patol.*) tetania.

tetchily ['tetʃili], *av.* con irritazione, stizza.

tetchiness ['tetʃinis], *s.* irritabilità; irascibilità.

tetchy ['tetʃi], *ag.* stizzoso, irritabile.

tether ['teðə*], *s.* **1.** pastoia, catena: *the matrimonial —*, *fig.* il vincolo matrimoniale **2.** *fig.* limite, termine; campo: *to be at the end of one's —*, essere all'estremo delle proprie risorse.

to **tether**, *v.t.* impastoiare (anche *fig.*).

tetrachord ['tetrəkɔ:d], *s.* (*mus.*) tetracordo.

tetrachordal [,tetrə'kɔ:dl], *ag.* (*mus.*) a quattro corde.

tetrad ['tetræd], *s.* **1.** gruppo di quattro **2.** (*chim.*) elemento, atomo, radicale tetravalente.

tetragon ['tetrəgən], *s.* (*geom.*) tetragono.

tetragonal [ti'trægənl], *ag.* (*geom.*) tetragonale.

tetragram ['tetrəgræm], *s.* tetragramma.

tetrahedral ['tetrə'hedrəl], *ag.* (*geom.*) tetraedrico.

tetrahedron ['tetrə'hedrən], *s.* (*geom.*) tetraedro.

tetralogy [te'trælədʒi], *s.* (*lett. mus.*) tetralogia.

tetrameter [te'træmitə*], *s.* (*poes.*) tetrametro.

tetramorph ['tetrəmɔ:f], *s.* tetramorfo (raffigurazione simbolica dei quattro evangelisti in una sola figura).

tetrandrian [te'trændriən], **tetrandrous** [te'trændrəs], *ag.* (*bot.*) a quattro stami.

tetrapod ['tetrəpod], *ag.s.* (*poes.*) tetrapodo.

tetrapody [ti'træpədi], *s.* (*poes.*) tetrapodia.

tetrarch ['ti:trɑ:k], *s.* (*st.*) tetrarca.

tetrarchate ['ti:trɑ:kit], *s.* (*st.*) tetrarcato.

tetrarchy ['ti:trɑ:ki], *s.* (*st.*) tetrarchia.

tetraspore ['tetrəspɔ:*], *s.* (*bot.*) tetraspora.

tetrastich ['tetrəstik], *s.* (*poes.*) tetrastico.

tetrastyle ['tetrəstail], *ag.s.* (*arch.*) tetrastilo.

tetrasyllabic ['tetrəsi'læbik], *ag.* quadrisillabo.

tetrasyllable ['tetrə,siləbl], *s.* quadrisillabo.

tetter ['tetə*], *s.* (*patol.*) impetigine, volatica ☆ — -*wort*, (*bot.*) celidonia.

Teucrian ['tju:kriən], *ag.* teucro ‖ *s.c.* teucro, teucra.

Teuton ['tju:tən], *ag.s.c.* teutone.

Teutonic [tju:(:)'tonik], *ag.* teutonico ‖ *the Teutonic Order*, (*st.*) l'Ordine Teutonico.

Teutonicism [tju:(:)'tonisizəm], **Teutonism** ['tju:tənizəm], *s.* **1.** germanismo **2.** germanesimo.

Teutonization [,tju:tənai'zeiʃən], *s.* germanizzazione.

to **Teutonize** ['tju:tənaiz], *v.t.i.* germanizzare, germanizzarsi.

Texan ['teksən], *ag.s.c.* (abitante) del Texas.

text [tekst], *s.* **1.** testo: *to restore a —*, ricostruire un testo **2.** argomento: *that was the — of his speech*, questo era l'argomento del suo discorso **3.** verso, passo delle Sacre Scritture ☆ — *book*, trattato, manuale; libro di testo ‖ *German —*, (*tip.*) caratteri gotici.

textile ['tekstail], *ag.s.* tessile: *the — industry*, l'industria tessile ☆ — *fibre*, fibra tessile.

textual ['tekstjuəl], *ag.* testuale: — *quotation*, citazione testuale ☆ — *criticism*, critica di un testo.

textualism ['tekstjuəlizəm], *s.* aderenza al testo.

textually ['tekstjuəli], *av.* testualmente.

texture ['tekstʃə*], *s.* **1.** trama (di tessuti) **2.** (*biol.*) tessuto **3.** struttura (anche *fig.*): — *of a speech*, struttura di un discorso.

textured ['tekstʃəd], *ag.* dalla trama ☆ *close-* —, a trama fitta; *light-* —, a trama rada.

textureless ['tekstʃəlis], *ag.* senza struttura; amorfo.

thack [θæk], (*dial. scoz.*) per **thatch**.

Thad(d)eus [θæ'di(:)əs], *no.pr.m.* Taddeo.

Thai [tai], *ag.s.c.* tailandese.

Thailand ['tailænd], *no.pr.* (*geog.*) Tailandia.

Thais ['θeiis], *no.pr.f.* (*st.*) Taide.

thalamus ['θæləməs], *pl.* **thalami** ['θæləmai], *s.* (*anat. bot. archeol.*) talamo ☆ *optic —*, (*anat.*) talamo ottico.

thalassic [θə'læsik], *ag.* talassico.

thalassocracy [,θælə'sokrəsi], *s.* talassocrazia.

thalassographic [θə,læsou'græfik], *ag.* talassografico.

thalassography [,θælə'sogrəfi], *s.* talassografia.

thalassotherapy [θə,læsou'θerəpi], *s.* (*med.*) talassoterapia.

thaler ['tɑ:lə*], *s.* tallero (moneta tedesca).

Thales [θeili:z], *no.pr.m.* (*st. fil.*) Talete.

Thalia [θə'laiə], *no.pr.f.* (*mit.*) Talia.

Thalian [θə'laiən], *ag.* di Talia.

thalictrum [θə'liktrəm], *s.* (*bot.*) talittro, ruta.

thallic ['θælik], *ag.* (*chim.*) tallico.

thallium ['θæliəm], *s.* (*chim.*) tallio.

thallus ['θæləs], *pl.* **thalli** ['θælai], **thalluses** ['θæləsiz], *s.* (*bot.*) tallo.

Thames [temz], *no.pr.* (*geog.*) Tamigi ‖ *he never set the — on fire*, (*fam.*) non è un genio, non ha fatto nulla di straordinario.

than [ðæn (*forma forte*), ðən (*forma debole*)], *cong.* **1.** (*dopo un comp.*) **che, di, di quello che, di quello che non; di quanto, di quanto non:** *more — once*, più di una volta; *he is kinder — his sister*, egli è più gentile di sua sorella; *I know you better — he (does)*, ti conosco meglio di lui; *I know you better — him*, conosco meglio te di lui; *I would do anything rather — let him go*, farei qualsiasi cosa piuttosto che lasciarlo andare; *no dearer — I told you*, non più caro di quanto ti dissi; *no sooner had he spoken — she fainted*, non appena egli ebbe parlato ella svenne **2.** (*dopo other, else* e composti) **che:** *no other — himself*, nessun altro che lui **3.** (*dopo hardly, scarcely*) **quando:** *hardly had he spoken — they entered*, aveva appena finito di parlare quando essi entrarono ‖ *prep.* **paragonato a:** *a writer — whom none is more appreciated*, uno scrittore che è più apprezzato di qualsiasi altro.

thanage ['θeinidʒ], *s.* (*st.*) **1.** carica di «thane» **2.** territorio appartenete a un «thane».

thanatoid ['θænətoid], *ag.* **1.** simile alla morte **2.** apparentemente morto.

thanatophidia [,θænətə'fidiə], *s.pl.* (*zool.*) serpenti velenosi.

thane [θein], *s.* (*st.*) «thane» (presso Angli e Sassoni, persona di rango intermedio tra gli uomini liberi e la nobiltà ereditaria).

thanedom ['θeindəm], *s.* (*st.*) giurisdizione, dominio di un «thane» scozzese.

thanehood ['θeinhud], *s.* (*st.*) dignità di «thane».

thaneship ['θeinʃip], *s.* (*st.*) posizione, ufficio di «thane» (specialmente scozzese).

thank [θæŋk], *V.* **thanks.**

to **thank**, *v.t.* ringraziare, dire grazie a: (*I*) — *you!*, grazie!; — *you for coming alone*, ti ringrazio di esser venuto da solo; — *you for your letter*, grazie della lettera; *I will — you for that book*, per favore, passami quel libro; *I will — you to shut the window*, ti sarei grato se chiudessi la finestra; *no, — you!*, no, grazie!; *she has only herself to —*, deve ringraziare solo se stessa, è solo colpa sua.

thankful ['θæŋkful], *ag.* riconoscente, grato.

thankfully ['θæŋkfuli], *av.* con riconoscenza, con gratitudine.

thankfulness ['θæŋkfulnis], *s.* riconoscenza, gratitudine.

thankless ['θæŋklis], *ag.* ingrato: *a — task*, un lavoro ingrato, mal ricompensato.

thanklessly ['θæŋklisli], *av.* **1.** con ingratitudine, senza riconoscenza **2.** senza compenso, soddisfazione.

thanklessness ['θæŋklisnis], *s.* **1.** ingratitudine **2.** l'essere ingrato, mal ricompensato (di lavoro, ecc.).

thank-offering ['θæŋk,ɔfəriŋ], *s.* **1.** regalo (in segno di riconoscenza **2.** (*Bibbia*) sacrificio di ringraziamento.

thanks [θæŋks], *s.pl.* grazie, ringraziamenti: *many, a thousand* —, molte, mille grazie; *accept my best* —, gradisca i miei migliori ringraziamenti; *I owe him many* —, gli devo molta riconoscenza; *small — I got for it!*, bel ringraziamento ne ho avuto! ‖ *— to me, of God, to my endeavours*, grazie a me, a Dio, ai miei sforzi.

thanksgiving ['θæŋks,givin], *s.* ringraziamento (specialmente a Dio) ‖ *Thanksgiving Day*, (*amer.*) giorno del Ringraziamento (l'ultimo giovedì di novembre).

thankworthy ['θæŋk,wə:ði], *ag.* (*rar.*) meritevole di riconoscenza.

thank-you-ma'am ['θæŋkju,mæm], *s.* (*amer. fam.*) cunetta (nel fondo stradale, che fa sobbalzare i passeggeri di un veicolo).

that [ðæt], *pl.* **those** [ðouz], *ag.* dimostrativo **1. quello, quella;** *this and* —, questo e quello; *those people who,* quelli che; *give me — book and those magazines,* dammi quel libro e quelle riviste; *I don't like this cup, give me — one,* non mi piace questa tazza, datemi quella (là) ‖ *— once,* quella sola volta: *I spoke to her only — once,* le parlai solo quella volta **2.** (*fam. scherz. spreg.*): *I don't know what they will do with — brother of his,* non so cosa faranno con quel suo fratello; *it's — cat again!,* è ancora quel gattaccio!; *well, how's — leg of yours?,* allora, come va la tua gamba? ‖ *pron.* dimostrativo **1. quello, quella; questo, questa; ciò:** *after, before* —, dopo, prima di questo; *are those your children?,* sono quelli i tuoi bambini?; *is — all you have bought?,* è tutto quello che hai comperato?; *what do you mean by* —?, cosa intendi dire con ciò?; *" What is* — *? ", " That is my hat "*, « Che è questo? », « Il mio cappello »; *" Who is* — *? ", " That's my brother "*, « Chi è quello? », « Mio fratello » ‖ *— is,* cioè: *I'll do it, — is if you want me to,* lo farò io, cioè, se tu vuoi ‖ *—'s all,* ecco tutto ‖ *—'s how I got it,* ecco come l'ho avuto ‖ *at — she burst into tears,* al che scoppiò in lacrime; *with — he closed the book,* al che, dopo di che, chiuse il libro ‖ *but for — I would invite him,* se non fosse per quello lo inviterei ‖ *has it come to* —?, siamo a questo punto? ‖ *is — you, Mary?*, (*fam.*) sei tu, Maria? ‖ *why do you look at me like* —?, perchè mi guardi a quel modo? **2.** (*enfatico*): *—'s a dear!,* sei proprio un tesoro!; *—'s right, —'s it,* è proprio così; *Ann has only two dresses and those are shabby,* Anna ha solo due abiti e per di più lisi; *he is an artist, and a well-known one at* —, è un artista e assai noto, per di più; *if anything will cure him, — will,* se qualcosa gli può far bene, è quella; *it was a horrid place, — it was!,* era un posto orribile, ecco quello che era! ‖ *—'s* —, ecco fatto; così stanno le cose: *I told you you cannot go out and —'s* —!, ti ho detto che non puoi uscire, e basta! **3.** (*antecedente a pron. rel.*) **quello, quella, ciò:** *give me all those — you want to,* dammi tutti quelli che vuoi; *I want sthg. different from — which he gave me,* voglio ql.co. di diverso da quello che mi ha dato; *those who want to speak may do so,* quelli che desiderano parlare possono farlo.

that, *pron. rel.* **1. che; il quale, la quale; i quali, le quali:** *all — lives must die,* tutto ciò che vive deve morire; *the book — we are talking about,* il libro di cui parliamo; *the chain — you bought,* la catena che tu comprasti; *the man — spoke with you,* l'uomo che ti parlò; *the people — were there, accepted,* i presenti accettarono; *the woman — he used to go out with,* la donna con cui soleva uscire **2.** (*con espressioni di tempo*) **in cui, nel quale:** *the day — he arrived,* il giorno in cui arrivò.

that, *cong.* **1. che:** *I'm so tired — I cannot stand,* sono così stanco che non posso stare in piedi; *I hope — he will come,* spero che venga; *it is not — I don't want to do it, but rather — I can't,* non è che non voglia, ma è che non posso farlo; *it was for this — I told you,* è per questo che te l'ho detto; *you ought to do it now — you are free,* ora che sei libero, dovresti farlo ‖ *in* —, (*arc.*) poichè, dal momento che **2. affinchè, perchè:** *he said it — you should be warned,* lo disse perchè

tu fossi avvertito; *they died — we may live,* morirono perchè noi potessimo vivere **3. purchè, a patto che:** *I would do anything — she should not know,* farei qualunque cosa purchè non lo sappia **4.** (*esclamativo*): *— he could do such a thing!,* (dire) che egli abbia potuto fare una cosa simile!; *— it were true!,* fosse vero!.

that, *av.* **1.** (*fam.*) **così, tanto:** *he talks — much,* parla così tanto; *she couldn't walk — far,* non poteva andare così lontano **2.** (*fam.*) **talmente, così tanto:** *she was — foolish that she could have done anything,* era così pazza che avrebbe potuto fare qualsiasi cosa.

thatch [θætʃ], *s.* **1.** copertura di paglia, stoppie, ramaglia, ecc. (per tetti) **2.** (*fam.*) capigliatura folta.

to thatch, *v.t.* coprire (un tetto) con paglia, ecc.

thatcher ['θætʃə*], *s.* artigiano specializzato per la copertura di tetti con paglia, canne, ecc.

thatching ['θætʃiŋ], *s.* **1.** mestiere, arte di coprire tetti con paglia, ecc. **2.** paglia, stoppie, ecc. (per coperture di tetti).

thaumaturge ['θɔ:mətə:dʒ], *s.* taumaturgo.

thaumaturgic(al) [,θɔ:mə'tə:dʒik(əl)], *ag.* taumaturgico.

thaumaturgist ['θɔ:mətə:dʒist], **thaumaturgus** [,θɔ:mə'tə:gəs], *pl.* **thaumaturgi** [,θɔ:mə'tə:dʒai], *s.* taumaturgo.

thaumaturgy ['θɔ:mətə:dʒi], *s.* taumaturgia.

thaw [θɔ:], *s.* sgelo, disgelo: *the — has set in,* il disgelo è cominciato.

to thaw, *v.t.i.* disgelare, disgelarsi (anche *fig.*); fondere, fondersi; sciogliere, sciogliersi: *after dinner he began to* —, dopo cena divenne più cordiale; *the river began to* —, il fiume cominciò a disgelarsi; *to — out the radiator,* (*aut.*) disgelare il radiatore.

thawy ['θɔ:i], *ag.* tiepido, mite (di tempo).

the [ði: (*forma enfatica*), ði (*davanti a vocale e h muta*), ðə (*davanti a consonante*)], *art. definito* **il, lo, la; i, gli, le 1.** (*con valore determinativo*): *Edward — Seventh,* Edoardo settimo; *— father was a doctor, so is — son,* il padre era medico, e medico è il figlio; *— sun shines in — day time and — moon at night* (o *in — night*), il sole brilla di giorno e la luna di notte; *he went to — seaside, — cinema, — library, — theatre,* egli andò al mare, al cinema, alla biblioteca, a teatro; *I'll see you on — 24th,* ti vedrò il 24; *I want — largest one,* voglio il più grande; *translated from — French,* tradotto dal francese; *what is — time?,* che ora è? ‖ *— Smiths,* i signori, la famiglia Smith **2.** (*per indicare la specie, per sostantivare un ag.*): *— dog and — cat are domestic animals,* il cane e il gatto sono animali domestici; *always seek — good and — beautiful,* ricerca sempre il buono e il bello; *— poor and — weak,* i poveri e i deboli **3.** (*con alcuni nomi geografici, di malattie*): *— Alps,* le Alpi; *— Cape,* il Capo (di Buona Speranza); *— Crimea,* la Crimea; *— measles,* il morbillo; *— Thames,* il Tamigi; *— United States,* gli Stati Uniti **4.** (*distributivo*): *so much — pound,* tanto (al)la libbra **5.** (*con valore dimostrativo*): *unfortunately I did not know at — time,* a quel tempo sfortunatamente non lo sapevo; *I shall go skiing in — winter,* andrò a sciare quest'inverno; *look at — child!,* guarda quel bambino! **6.** (*enfatico*): *a certain Cromwell, not the Cromwell,* un certo Cromwell, non *il* famoso Cromwell; *Doctor B. is the doctor in this place,* il Dottor B. è considerato il miglior dottore del luogo; *he is not the Mr. Churchill, is he?,* non è il famoso Churchill, vero?; *X's whisky is the whisky,* il whisky X è unico! ‖ *av.* (*davanti a comparativi*): *all — worse,* tanto peggio; *none — better,* per nulla meglio; *so much — worse for him,* tanto peggio per lui; *— more he has — more he wants,* quanto più ha tanto più vuole; *— more we are — better,* più siamo meglio è; *— sooner — better,* più presto è, meglio è.

theandric [θi'ændrik], *ag.* (*teol.*) teandrico.

theanthropic(al) [,θi:ən'θrɔpik(əl)], *ag.* (*teol.*) teantropico.

theater, *(amer.)* per **theatre.**

theatre ['θiətə*], *s.* **1.** teatro: *I saw him at the — last night*, lo vidi a teatro ieri sera; *to go to the —*, andare a teatro **2.** *fig.* teatro, luogo d'azione: *the — of the war*, il teatro della guerra **3.** anfiteatro (universitario) **4.** teatro, arte drammatica: *play that is good —*, commedia che si regge bene; *he wrote for the —*, scrisse per il teatro; *that actor's activity is divided between the — and painting*, l'attività di quell'attore è divisa fra il teatro e la pittura **5.** complesso di opere teatrali: *the English —*, il teatro inglese ☆ — *-goer*, chi frequenta abitualmente il teatro ‖ *anatomical —* (o *operating —*), anfiteatro per lezioni d'anatomia; *news —*, cineattualità; *open-air —*, teatro all'aperto; *picture —*, *(amer.)* grande cinematografo.

theatrical [θi'ætrikəl], *ag.* **1.** teatrale **2.** affettato, ostentato, pomposo.

theatricalism [θi'ætrikəlizəm], **theatricality** [θi,ætri'kæliti], *s.* teatralità.

to theatricalize [θi'ætrikəlaiz], *v.t.* rendere teatrale; rappresentare a teatro.

theatrically [θi'ætrikəli], *av.* teatralmente.

theatricalness [θi'ætrikəlnis], *s.* teatralità.

theatricals [θi'ætrikəlz], *s.pl.* rappresentazioni teatrali ☆ *amateur —*, attività, spettacoli filodrammatici.

Thebaid ['θi:beiid], *no.pr.* *(geog. st.)* Tebaide.

thebaine ['θi:bəi:n], *s.* *(farm.)* tebaina.

Theban ['θi:bən], *ag.* tebano ‖ *s.c.* tebano, tebana.

Thebes [θi:bz], *no.pr.* *(geog. st.)* Tebe.

theca ['θi:kə], *pl.* **thecae** ['θi:si:], *s.* *(bot.)* teca.

Thecla ['θeklə], *no.pr.f.* Tecla.

thee [ði:], *pron. pers.* 2ª *persona sing.* *(arc. poet.)* **1.** *(caso obliquo di* thou*)* te, ti: *I'll tell —*, te lo dirò; *we beseech —*, ti imploriamo ‖ *get — gone!*, vattene! **2.** *(fam. per* thou, *usato con la* 3ª *persona sing.)* tu: *— does not understand*, *(rar.)* tu non capisci.

theft [θeft], *s.* furto ☆ — *proof*, antifurto.

thegn, *V.* **thane.**

theine ['θi:ain], *s.* *(chim.)* teina.

their [ðɛə*], *ag.poss.* **1.** il loro, la loro, i loro, le loro: — *brother*, (il) loro fratello; — *mother and father*, (la) loro madre e (il) loro padre; *they hurt — hands*, si fecero male alle mani **2.** *(fam. per* his) **suo, suoi:** *if everyone minded — (own) business*, se ciascuno si occupasse dei fatti propri; *nobody in — right mind*, nessuno sano di mente.

theirs [ðɛəz], *pron. poss.* **il loro, la loro, i loro, le loro:** *a friend of —*, un loro amico; *these papers are mine and those are —*, queste carte sono (le) mie e quelle sono (le) loro.

theism[1] ['θi:izəm], *s.* *(fil.)* teismo.

theism[2], *s.* *(patol.)* intossicazione da tè.

theist ['θi:ist], *s.* *(fil.)* teista.

theistic(al) [θi:'istik(əl)], *ag.* *(fil.)* teistico.

them [ðem], *pron. pers.* 3ª *persona pl.* **1.** *(caso obliquo di* they) li, le; loro; sè: *have you seen —?*, li hai visti?; *I will write — a beautiful letter*, scriverò loro una bella lettera; *look at these bottles, there's nothing in —*, guarda queste bottiglie, non c'è dentro nulla; *they took the keys away with —*, hanno portato le chiavi con sè; *what will you do with —?*, che cosa ne farai? ‖ *both of —*, entrambi; *every one of —*, tutti, nessuno escluso; *neither of —*, nè l'uno nè l'altro; *three of —*, tre di loro ‖ *if anyone comes, tell — that I am out*, *(fam.)* se viene qlcu. digli che non sono in casa; *when you like a person, you ought to show —*, *(fam.)* quando provi simpatia per qualcuno dovresti dimostrarglielo **2.** *(fam. per* they): *it's —*, sono loro; *we are as famous as —*, siamo celebri come loro.

thematic [θi'mætik], *ag.* *(gram. mus.)* tematico.

theme [θi:m], *s.* **1.** tema, argomento; *(mus.)* motivo, tema **2.** tema, composizione (scolastica) **3.** *(gram.)* tema, radice ☆ *signature —*, sigla musicale.

Themis ['θemis], *no.pr.f.* *(mit.)* Temi.

themselves [ðəm'selvz], *pron.* 3ª *persona pl.* **1.** *r.* se stessi, se stesse; sè; si: *they are masters of —*, sono padroni di se stessi; *they saw — in the mirror*, si videro nello specchio ‖ *they went (all) by —*, andarono da soli ‖ *God helps those who help —*, *prov.* chi si aiuta il ciel l'aiuta **2.** *(enfatico)* **essi stessi, esse stesse: proprio loro:** *they did it —*, l'hanno fatto proprio loro ‖ *s.* **essi stessi, esse stesse:** *they are not — to-day*, non sono in forma oggi.

then [ðen], *ag.* di allora, di quel tempo: *the — Duke*, l'allora duca; *the — professor of Greek*, il professore di greco di allora ‖ *s.* *(gener. preceduto da prep.)* quel tempo, quell'epoca: *from — on he has been very sad*, da allora è molto triste; *he was dead by —*, a quell'epoca era ormai morto; *he will be here before —*, sarà qui prima di allora; *she believed him till —*, gli credette fino allora; *they lived happily since —*, da allora vissero felici; *between now and —*, di qui ad allora: *I cannot tell you what I shall do between now and —*, non posso dirti cosa farò di qui ad allora ‖ *every now and —*, di tanto in tanto, ogni tanto.

then, *av.* **1.** allora, a quell'epoca, in quel tempo: *I was — too busy*, avevo troppo da fare allora ‖ *— and there* (o *there and —*), subito, senza indugio: *I took the plane to Paris there and —*, presi immediatamente l'aereo per Parigi ‖ *now and —*, ogni tanto, di tanto in tanto: *she comes to see us now and —*, viene a trovarci di tanto in tanto **2.** dopo, poi, in seguito: *he ate all the bread and — wanted some wine*, mangiò tutto il pane e poi volle del vino; *I went home and — went out again*, andai a casa e poi uscii di nuovo ‖ *what —?*, e poi?, e allora?; *he is very rich, what —?*, egli è ricchissimo, e allora?; *if you shouldn't do it, what —?*, se non lo facessi, che importa? **3.** inoltre, poi, anche: *he is not rich, and — not handsome*, non è ricco e nemmeno bello; *I have not the time, and — it is not my business*, non ho tempo, e poi non è affar mio.

then, *cong.* in questo caso, dunque, allora: *(but) — why did you go away?*, ma allora perchè te ne sei andato?; *he stayed all the week —*, dunque è rimasto per tutta la settimana; *if you must do it, — do it*, se lo devi fare, allora fallo; *you wrote it all by yourself —*, l'hai scritto tutto tu, allora ‖ *but —*, però, tuttavia: *she was pretty, but — poor*, era carina, ma povera.

thence [ðens], *av.* *(arc. letter.)* **1.** di là, da quel luogo: *he has just come from —*, è appena giunto di là; *we went to Rome and — to Naples*, andammo a Roma e di là a Napoli **2.** quindi, pertanto: *it — follows that...*, ne consegue pertanto che...; *she was there in the morning — she should have heard sthg.*, era là il mattino quindi avrebbe dovuto udire ql.co.

thenceforth ['ðens'fɔ:θ], **thenceforward** ['ðens'fɔ:wəd], *av.* da allora in poi.

Theo]'θi(:)ou], *no.pr.m. dim.* di **Theodore** ‖ *no.pr.f. dim.* di **Theodora.**

Theobald ['θiəbɔ:ld], *no.pr.m.* Teobaldo.

theobroma [,θi:ou'broumə], *s.* *(bot.)* teobroma.

theobromine [,θi:ou'broumain], *s.* *(chim.)* teobromina.

theocracy [θi'ɔkrəsi], *s.* teocrazia.

theocrat ['θiəkræt], *s.* teocrate.

theocratic(al) [θiə'krætik(əl)], *ag.* teocratico.

theocratically [θiə'krætikəli], *av.* teocraticamente.

theocritean [θi,ɔkri'ti:ən], *ag.* *(st. lett.)* di Teocrito.

Theocritus [θi'ɔkritəs], *no.pr.m.* *(st. lett.)* Teocrito.

theodicy [θi'ɔdisi], *s.* *(teol.)* teodicea.

theodolite [θi'ɔdəlait], *s.* *(topografia)* teodolite ☆ *transit —*, tacheometro.

Theodora [θiə'dɔ:rə], *no.pr.f.* Teodora.

Theodore ['θiədɔ:*], *no.pr.m.* Teodoro.

Theodoric [θi'ɔdərik], *no.pr.m.* *(st.)* Teodorico.

Theodosius [θiə'dousjəs], *no.pr.m.* *(st.)* Teodosio.

theogony [θi'ɔgəni], *s.* teogonia.

theologian [θiə'loudʒjən], *s.* teologo.

theologic(al) [θiə'lɔdʒik(əl)], *ag.* teologico ‖ *the —
virtues*, le virtù teologali.
theologically [θiə'lɔdʒikəli], *av.* teologicamente.
to **theologize** [θi'ɔlədʒaiz], *v.t.i.* teologizzare.
theology [θi'ɔlədʒi], *s.* teologia.
Theophilus [θi'ɔfiləs], *no.pr.m.* Teofilo.
Theophrastus [θiə'fræstəs], *no.pr.m.* (*st.fil.*) Teofrasto.
theorbo [θi'ɔ:bou], *s.* (*mus.*) tiorba.
theorem [θ'iərəm], *s.* (*mat.*) teorema.
theorematic(al) [,θiəri'mætik(əl)], *ag.* (*mat.*) teore-
matico.
theoretic(al) [θiə'retik(əl)], *ag.* teorico, teoretico;
(*fil.*) speculativo.
theoretically [θiə'retikəli], *av.* teoreticamente, teo-
ricamente; (*fil.*) speculativamente.
theoretician [,θiərə'tiʃən], *s.* teorico.
theoretics [θiə'retiks], *s.* teorica, parte teorica (di
una disciplina, una tecnica).
theoric ['θiərik], *ag.* teorico.
theorist ['θiərist], *s.* teorico, teoreta.
to **theorize** ['θiəraiz], *v.i.* teorizzare; stabilire, formulare delle teorie.
theory ['θiəri], *s.* **1.** teoria, dottrina: *it is all very well
in —...*, in teoria va bene... **2.** opinione, tesi, concetto:
he has a — that..., la sua opinione, la sua idea è che....
theosoph ['θiəsəf], **theosopher** [θi'ɔsəfə*], *s.* (*fil.
teol.*) teosofo.
theosophic(al) [θiə'sɔfik(əl)], *ag.* (*fil. teol.*) teosofico.
theosophism [θi'ɔsəfizəm], *s.* (*fil. teol.*) teosofismo.
theosophist [θi'ɔsəfist], *s.* (*fil. teol.*) teosofista.
theosophy [θi'ɔsəfi], *s.* (*fil. teol.*) teosofia.
therapeutic(al) [,θerə'pju:tik(əl)], *ag.* terapeutico.
therapeutics [,θerə'pju:tiks], *s.* terapeutica.
therapeutist [,θerə'pju:tist], **therapist** ['θerəpist], *s.*
terapeuta.
therapy ['θerəpi], *s.* terapia ☆ *educational —*,
terapia di rieducazione; *electro convulsive — (E.C.T.)*,
elettrochoc.
there [ðɛə], *av.* **1.** là, lì, colà: *hello!, you¯—!*, ehi! voi
laggiù!; *he was going —*, stava andando là; *I shall
go straight —*, ci andrò direttamente; *put it —*, mettilo
là; *who is —?*, chi è (là)? ‖ *— and —*, qua e là ‖ *— and
then*, subito ‖ *he is all —*, è un tipo sveglio, è uno
che la sa lunga; *he is not all —*, gli manca un venerdì ‖
it is about three miles — and back, sono circa tre miglia
fra andata e ritorno **2. vi, ci**: *— are many books on
the table*, ci sono molti libri sul tavolo; *— is a page
missing*, manca una pagina; *— is some*, ce n'è; *—
was eating and drinking*, c'era da mangiare e da bere;
— was no stopping him from going, non ci fu modo
di impedirgli di andare; *— were tears in her eyes*,
aveva le lacrime agli occhi; *once upon a time — was...*,
c'era una volta... **3.** (*enfatico*): *— he goes again*, eccolo che ricomincia; *— he is*, eccolo là; *—'s a dear,
close the window*, sii bravo, chiudi la finestra; *— they
are, — we are*, eccoli, eccoci; *add a drop of milk, and
— you are*, aggiungete una goccia di latte, ed ecco
fatto **4. in ciò, in quanto a questo**: *— I am not with
you*, su questo punto non sono d'accordo con voi; *—
I quite agree*, su questo sono d'accordo; *— is the rub!*,
qui sta il difficile!; *— you have got me*, (*fam.*) qui hai
ragione tu ‖ *there, inter. ecco!*, su!: *—, don't cry!*, su,
non piangere!; *—, now, see what you have done*, ecco,
guarda quel che hai fatto; *yes, I did go out last night,
so —*, sì, sono uscito ieri sera, ecco tutto ‖ **there**, *s.*
quel luogo, là: *he is in —*, è là dentro; *I left it on
—*, l'ho lasciato là sopra; *I shall go to Rome and from
— to Naples*, andrò a Roma e di là a Napoli; *it's
under —*, è là sotto.
thereabout(s) ['ðɛərəbaut(s)], *av.* **1.** là vicino, là accanto; nei dintorni, nelle vicinanze; *he has a house in
Kew or —*, ha una casa a Kew o da quelle parti **2.** circa,
all'incirca, pressappoco: *he must be fifty or —*, deve
avere cinquant'anni o giù di lì; *it should contain four
gallons or —*, dovrebbe contenere diciotto litri circa.

thereafter [ðɛər'ɑ:ftə*], *av.* (*arc.*) poscia, dopo di
ciò, indi; quindi.
thereat [ðɛər'æt], *av.* (*arc.*) **1.** a quel proposito **2.** in
quel luogo.
thereby ['ðɛə'bai], *av.* **1.** per mezzo, a causa di
ciò; perciò: *he wrote a letter — causing all the trouble*,
egli scrisse una lettera dando così origine al pastic-
cio **2.** (*dial.*) là accanto **3.** (*letter. arc.*) a questo proposito:
— hangs a tale, c'è tutta una storia connessa a questo.
therefore ['ðɛəfɔ:*], *av.* quindi, dunque, perciò:
living is dear, — we have to economize, la vita è cara,
perciò dobbiamo fare economia.
therefrom [ðɛə'frɔm], *av.* (*arc.*) da ciò, da quella
cosa: *it follows — that...*, ne consegue che....
therein [ðɛər'in], *av.* (*arc.*) **1.** riguardo a ciò, in ciò:
— you are right, in ciò avete ragione **2.** entro, dentro:
all those that lived —, tutti quelli che vi abitavano.
thereinafter [,ðɛərin'ɑ:ftə*], *av.* (*arc. dir.*) più oltre,
più avanti: *the parties — called A. and B.*, le parti
più avanti chiamate A. e B.
thereinbefore [,ðɛərinbi'fɔ:*], *av.* (*arc. dir.*) prima,
precedentemente.
thereinto [ðɛər'intu], *av.* (*arc.*) ivi.
thereof [ðɛər'ɔv], *av.* (*arc.*) di, da ciò.
thereon [ðɛər'ɔn], *av.* (*arc.*) su di ciò.
thereout [ðɛər'aut], *av.* (*arc.*) **1.** da quello, da quella fonte **2.** (*scoz.*) fuori.
Theresa [ti'ri:zə], *no.pr.f.* Teresa.
thereto [ðɛə'tu:], **thereunto** [ðɛr'ʌntu(:)], *av.* (*arc.*) **1.** a
ciò, vi **2.** inoltre, oltre a ciò: *the plant and the equipment
fitted —*, l'impianto e l'attrezzatura ivi installata.
thereupon ['ðɛərə'pɔn], *av.* **1.** al che, tosto **2.** su,
sopra **3.** (*letter.*) a quel proposito: *there is nothing to be
said —*, non c'è niente da dire a quel proposito.
therewith [ðɛə'wið], **therewithal** [,ðɛəwi'ðɔ:l], *av.*
(*arc.*) **1.** con ciò **2.** di più, inoltre **3.** subito dopo,
tosto.
theriac ['θiəriæk], *s.* (*arc. farm.*) teriaca.
theriacal [θi'raiəkəl], *ag.* (*farm.*) teriacale.
therm [θə:m], *s.* (*fis.*) caloria.
thermae ['θə:mi:], *s.pl.* (*st. romana*) terme.
thermal ['θə:məl], *ag.* **1.** termico **2.** termale, caldo:
— springs, sorgenti termali ☆ *— capacity*, capacità
termica; *— efficiency*, rendimento termico; *— station*,
(*elett.*) centrale termica; *— unit*, unità di misura del
calore ‖ *British — unit* (*abbr.* Btu), quantità di calore
necessaria per elevare di 1 grado Fahrenheit la temperatura di 1 libbra di acqua.
thermic ['θə:mik], *ag.* termico ☆ *— inertia*, inerzia
termica; *— treatment*, (*metal.*) trattamento termico;
— weight, (*fis.*) entropia.
Thermidor ['θə:mido:*], *s.* (*st. francese*) termidoro.
Thermidorian [,θə:mi'dɔ:riən], *ag.* (*st. francese*) ter-
midoriano ‖ *s.* (*st. francese*) termidorista.
thermion [θə'maiən], *s.* (*fis.*) termione.
thermionic [,θə:mi'ɔnik], *ag.* (*fis.*) termoionico ☆ *—
amplifier*, (*rad.*) valvola amplificatrice; *— current*,
(*fis. elett. rad.*) corrente termoionica; *— tube* (o *—
valve*), (*elett. rad.*) valvola termoionica.
thermit [θə'mit], **thermite** ['θə:mait], *s.* (*chim.*)
termite.
thermobarometer ['θə:moubə'rɔmitə*], *s.* (*fis.*) ter-
mobarometro.
thermodynamics ['θə:moudai'næmiks], *s.* termodi-
namica.
thermoelectricity ['θə:mou,elek'trisiti], *s.* termoelettricità.
thermogenesis [,θə:mou'dʒenisis], *s.* (*biol.*) termo-
genesi.
thermogenic [,θə:mou'dʒenik], *ag.* termogeno.
thermograph ['θə:məgrɑ:f], *s.* (*fis.*) termografo.
thermography [θə'mɔgrəfi], *s.* (*fis.*) termografia.
thermology [θə'mɔlədʒi], *s.* (*fis.*) termologia.
thermometer [θə'mɔmitə*], *s.* (*fis.*) termometro
☆ *centigrade —*, termometro centigrado; *differential*

—, termometro differenziale; *maximum* —, termometro a massima; *mercury* —, termometro a mercurio; *minimum* —, termometro a minima; *spirit* —, termometro ad alcool.

thermometric(al) [ˌθəːməˈmetrik(əl)], *ag.* (*fis.*) termometrico.

thermometry [θəˈmɔmitri], *s.* (*fis.*) termometria.

thermopile [ˈθəːmoupail], *s.* (*elett.*) termopila.

Thermopylae [θəːˈmɔpiliː], *no.pr.pl.* (*geog. st.*) Termopili.

thermos [ˈθəːmɔs], *s.* — (*bottle* o *flask*), termos (recipiente termostatico).

thermoscope [ˈθəːmouskoup], *s.* (*fis.*) termoscopio.

thermosetting [ˌθəːmouˈsetiŋ], *ag.* (*ind. chim.*) termoindurente ☆ — *compositions*, materie plastiche termoindurenti.

thermostat [ˈθəːməstæt], *s.* (*fis.*) termostato.

thermostatic [ˌθəːməˈstætik], *ag.* (*fis.*) termostatico.

Thersites [θəːˈsaitiːz], *no.pr.m.* (*lett.*) Tersite.

thesaurus [θi(ː)ˈsɔːrəs], *pl.* **thesauri** [θi(ː)ˈsɔːrai], *s.* **1.** tesoro **2.** repertorio lessicale; florilegio; antologia.

these [ðiːz], *pl.* di **this**.

thesis [ˈθiːsis], *pl.* **theses** [ˈθiːsiːz], *s.* tesi; dissertazione.

Thespian [ˈθespiən], *ag.* di Tespi; drammatico ‖ *the* — *art*, il dramma ‖ *s.c.* attore, attrice.

Thespis [ˈθespis], *no.pr.m.* (*st. lett.*) Tespi.

Thessalian [θeˈseiljən], *ag.* tessalico ‖ *s.* tessalo.

Thessaly [ˈθesəli], *no.pr.* (*geog. st.*) Tessaglia.

theta [ˈθiːtə], *s.* teta (lettera dell'alfabeto greco).

Thetis [ˈθetis], *no.pr.f.* (*mit.*) Tetide.

theurgic(al) [θi(ː)ˈəːdʒik(əl)], *ag.* teurgico.

theurgist [ˈθiːəːdʒist], *s.* teurgo.

theurgy [ˈθiːəːdʒi], *s.* teurgia.

thewed [θjuːd], *ag.* **1.** muscoloso **2.** *fig.* vigoroso.

thewless [ˈθjuːlis], *ag.* debole, senza vigore (anche *fig.*).

thews [θjuːz], *s.pl.* **1.** muscoli: *he is all* — *and sinews*, è tutto nervi e muscoli **2.** *fig.* forza, vigore mentale, morale.

thewy [ˈθjuːi], *ag.* **1.** muscoloso **2.** *fig.* vigoroso, forte.

they [ðei], *pron.pers.* 3ª *persona pl.* **1.** essi, esse; loro: — *are staying at the Grand Hotel*, sono al Grand Hotel; — *did it*, *not us*, l'hanno fatto loro, non noi; *here* — *are!* (o *here* — *come!*), eccoli!; *I wish I knew who* — *are*, vorrei proprio sapere chi sono; *it is* — *who told me*, sono stati loro a dirmelo **2.** si: — *have afternoon tea in England*, si beve tè al pomeriggio in Inghilterra; — *say that...*, si dice che...; — *told me that you had left*, mi si disse che eri partito **3.** (*riferito a nomi coll. sing.*): *the crowd was moving but*, — *didn't know where* — *were going*, la folla avanzava, ma non sapeva dove andava **4.** (*fam.*) (*dopo pron. indef. sing.*): *nobody admits that* — *are wrong*, nessuno ammette di aver torto **5.** (*letter.*) (*davanti al rel. invece del dimostrativo*): — *who are my friends are not always your friends*, coloro, quelli che sono amici miei non sono sempre amici tuoi ‖ — *do least who talk most*, *prov.* chi più chiacchiera meno fa.

they'd [ðeid], *contr.* di **they had**, **they would**.

they'll [ðeil], *contr.* di **they will**.

they're [ðɛə*], *contr.* di **they are**.

thick [θik], *ag.* **1.** spesso; grosso; pesante: *a* — *book*, un grosso libro; *a* — *material*, un tessuto pesante; *a board four inches* —, un'asse dello spessore di quattro pollici ‖ *that's a bit* —!, (*sl.*) questa è grossa!, questa è bella! ‖ *to have a* — *skin*, (*fam.*) essere insensibile, avere il pelo al cuore **2.** fitto, folto; serrato, compatto: *a* — *forest*, una foresta fitta; *the crowd was* —, la folla era fitta; *your hair is very* —, hai una folta capigliatura ‖ *as* — *as peas*, (*fam.*) fitto fitto: *the hail was falling as* — *as peas*, la grandine cadeva fitta fitta **3.** denso; torbido, melmoso; cupo: — *oil*, olio denso; — *sauce*, salsa densa; — *weather*, tempo coperto; — *wine*, vino torbido **4.** velato (di voce): *her voice was* —, aveva la voce rauca **5.** (*sl.*)

tonto, stupido **6.** (*fam.*) intimo, molto unito: *they are very* —, *those two*, vanno molto d'accordo, quei due ‖ *to be as* — *as thieves*, essere amici per la pelle ‖ *s.* spessore; il fitto, il folto: *in the* — *of the fight*, nel folto della mischia ‖ *through* — *and thin*, nella buona e nella cattiva sorte.

thick, *av.* **1.** a strati grossi, spessi: *don't cut the bread* —, non tagliare il pane a fette grosse; *snow lay* — *on the ground*, uno spesso strato di neve copriva il suolo **2.** fittamente, fitto fitto: *his blows fell* —, i suoi colpi cadevano fitti; *the shrubs grew* —, i cespugli crescevano fitti.

thick, (*nei composti*): — *-and-thin*, fedelissimo; — *-headed* (o — *-skulled*), babbeo, stupido: *the poor boy is* — *-headed*, quel povero ragazzo è un po' tonto; — *-lips*, (*arc. letter.*) negro; — *-skinned*, insensibile, indifferente; — *-registrer*, (*mus.*) registro dei toni bassi; — *-sown*, seminato folto.

to thicken [ˈθikən], *v.t.i.* **1.** ispessire, ispessirsi; addensare, addensarsi: *the crowd was thickening*, la folla si addensava; *this sauce wants thickening*, *add an egg to* — *it*, questa salsa va fatta più densa, mettici un uovo per legarla **2.** ingrossare, ingrossarsi; aumentare: *my waist is thickening*, sto ingrossando di vita **3.** intorbidarsi, oscurarsi: *the weather will* —, il tempo volge al brutto **4.** *fig.* animarsi, prendere vigore: *when fresh troops arrived*, *the battle thickened*, quando arrivarono i rinforzi, la battaglia si riaccese **5.** complicarsi: *after the first 100 pages the plot thickens*, dopo le prime 100 pagine la trama si complica.

thickener [ˈθiknə*], *s.* (*ind. chim.*) concentratore; condensatore.

thickening [ˈθikniŋ], *s.* **1.** ispessimento **2.** sostanza che serve a rendere più denso, spesso: *use flour as a* — *for your sauce*, aggiungi farina per legare la salsa.

thicket [ˈθikit], *s.* boschetto, folto d'alberi ☆ *thorn* —, prunaio, roveto.

thickhead [ˈθikhed], *s.c.* persona stupida, tonta, ignorante.

thickish [ˈθikiʃ], *ag.* piuttosto grosso, spesso, denso.

thickly [ˈθikli], *av.* **1.** fittamente, densamente; abbondantemente: *the child was* — *wrapped in woollens*, il bambino era imbacuccato in panni di lana; *snow fell* —, la neve cadeva fitta **2.** con voce roca, indistinta: *he spoke so* — *that I could not catch what he said*, parlò con voce così rauca che non afferrai ciò che diceva.

thickness [ˈθiknis], *s.* **1.** spessore, grossezza: *a* — *of three centimetres*, uno spessore di tre centimetri **2.** consistenza; densità; nebbiosità, oscurità (di tempo) **3.** strato ☆ — *gauge*, (*tec.*) spessimetro; — *ratio*, (*aer.*) spessore relativo.

thickset [ˈθikˈset], *ag.* **1.** fitto, spesso; folto: *a* — *hedge*, una siepe fitta **2.** tozzo, tarchiato.

thief [θiːf], *pl.* **thieves** [θiːvz], *s.c.* ladro, ladra: *he was a notorious* —, era un ladro matricolato ‖ *stop* —!, al ladro! ‖ *the impenitent*, *the penitent* —, (*Bibbia*) il cattivo, il buon ladrone ‖ *to be as thick as thieves*, essere amici per la pelle ‖ *set a* — *to catch a* —, *prov.* per conoscere un furbo ci vuole un furbo e mezzo ‖ *s.* ladro (frammento di lucignolo acceso che cade sulla candela e la strugge) ☆ — *tube*, (*chim.*) sonda per campionatura; *thieves' kitchen*, covo di ladri; *thieves' Latin*, gergo dei ladri; *thieves' vinegar*, (*fam.*) aceto dei sette ladri.

to thieve [θiːv], *v.t.i.* **1.** rubare; essere ladro; commettere un furto **2.** (*chim.*) prelevare un campione da.

thievery [ˈθiːvəri], *s.* **1.** furto, ruberia **2.** refurtiva.

thievish [ˈθiːviʃ], *ag.* ladro, ladresco: — *fingers*, *looks*, mani, sguardi ladri.

thievishly [ˈθiːviʃli], *av.* ladramente, ladrescamente.

thievishness [ˈθiːviʃnis], *s.* tendenza al furto.

thigh [θai], *s.* coscia ‖ *to be beaten hip and* —, essere bastonato di santa ragione ☆ — *-bone*, (*anat.*) femore; — *-piece*, cosciale (di armatura).

thill [θil], *s.* stanga, timone (di carro) ☆ — *horse,* cavallo alle stanghe.

thiller ['θilə*], *s.* cavallo alle stanghe.

thimble ['θimbl], *s.* **1.** ditale **2.** (*mec.*) manicotto, bussola **3.** (*mec.*) mandrino conico allargatubi **4.** (*chim.*) elemento filtrante in carta **5.** (*mar.*) radancia.

thimbleful['θimblful], *s.* quanto sta in un ditale; piccola quantità: *I'll have a — of wine,* berrò un dito di vino.

thimble-rig ['θimblrig], *s.* giuoco dei bussolotti.

to thimble-rig, *pass.p.p.* **thimble-rigged** ['θimblrigd], *v.t.i.* **1.** fare il giuoco dei bussolotti **2.** imbrogliare.

thimble-rigger ['θimbl,rigə*], *s.* **1.** giuocatore di bussolotti **2.** imbroglione, truffatore.

thin [θin], *ag.* **1.** sottile, fine: *a — sheet of paper,* un sottile foglio di carta; *the script was very —,* la calligrafia era molto sottile **2.** magro, snello: *she has (got) a — figure,* ella ha una figura snella; *to grow (o to become) thinner,* dimagrire **3.** rado, raro; scarsamente popolato, frequentato: *her hair is very —,* i suoi capelli sono molto radi; *the theatre was — last night,* c'era poca gente a teatro ieri sera **4.** fluido; rarefatto: *the air was very — up there,* l'aria era molto rarefatta lassù **5.** debole, fiacco; poco convincente: *his was a — excuse,* la sua era una magra scusa; *it is a very — argument,* è un ragionamento molto fiacco **6.** tenue, pallido (di colore); esile, fievole (di voce, suono): *we walked in the — sunlight,* camminammo alla pallida luce del sole **7.** (*sl.*) difficile, brutto, sgradevole: *he had a — time of it,* se l'è passata piuttosto brutta ☆ — *captain,* biscotto secco; *— -skinned,* dalla pelle fine; *fig.* suscettibile, sensibile; *— -walled* dalle pareti sottili.

to thin, *pass.p.p.* **thinned** [θind], *v.t.i.* **1.** assottigliare, assottigliarsi; dimagrire: *you have thinned since I saw you last,* sei dimagrito dall'ultima volta che ti vidi **2.** diradare, diradarsi; sfoltire; decimare: *his hair was thinning,* i suoi capelli si stavano diradando; *the population was thinned by the war,* la popolazione fu decimata dalla guerra; *to — (out) the branches of a tree,* sfrondare un albero.

thine [ðain], (*arc. poet. ora usato nelle preghiere e dai quaccheri*) *ag. poss.* (*dinanzi a vocale e h muta*) **tuo, tua; tuoi, tue:** *when I look into — eyes,* quando guardo nei tuoi occhi ‖ *pron. poss.* **il tuo, la tua; i tuoi, le tue:** *my book and —,* il mio libro e il tuo; *what is mine is —,* quel che è mio è tuo.

thing [θiŋ], *s.* **1.** cosa, oggetto materiale: *it is a very cheap —,* è una cosa da poco; *where did you put that —?,* dove hai messo quella cosa? **2.** *pl.* cose personali; utensili, arnesi: *bring your things when you come,* porta l'occorrente, quando vieni; *I don't like your wearing my things,* non mi piace che tu indossi le mie cose **3.** soggetto, argomento: *there's a — I want to talk to you about,* c'è una cosa di cui voglio parlarti ‖ *for one —...,* in primo luogo...; *for another —...,* d'altra parte... ‖ *to take one — with another,* considerare il pro e il contro **4.** circostanza, avvenimento; affare: *as things are, I can do nothing,* stando così le cose non posso fare nulla; *don't take the — so badly,* non prendertela tanto; *things are not too good,* le cose, gli affari non vanno troppo bene ‖ *too much of a good —,* troppo bello per essere vero ‖ *well, of all things!,* be', chi l'avrebbe mai detto! ‖ *to make a good — of sthg.,* trarre profitto da ql.co. **5.** (*fam. affettuoso*) creatura: *poor little —!,* povera creatura!; *she is a sweet little —,* è un tesoro **6.** *the —,* la cosa migliore; l'essenziale: *the — now is to find a way out,* l'essenziale ora è trovare una via d'uscita ‖ *quite the —,* alla moda: *this is quite the latest — in hats,* questo è l'ultimo grido in fatto di cappelli; *to feel quite the —,* sentirsi in forma: *I am not feeling quite the —,* non mi sento molto in forma **7.** *pl.* (*dir.*) proprietà ☆ *things personal,* (*dir.*) beni mobiliari; *things real,* (*dir.*) beni immobiliari.

thingamy ['θiŋəmi], **thingumajig** ['θiŋəmidʒig], **thin(g)gumbob** ['θiŋəmbɔb], **thingummy** ['θiŋəmi], *s.* (*fam.*) **1.** un tale, un tizio: *did you speak to that*

Mr. —?, hai parlato con quel tale? **2.** coso, affare, arnese: *give me that —,* dammi quel coso.

to think [θiŋk], *pass.p.p.* **thought** [θɔ:t], *v.t.i.* **1.** pensare, riflettere, ragionare: *— before acting, speaking,* pensa prima di agire, di parlare; *— twice, again,* pensaci due volte, ripensaci; *he thinks evil thoughts,* ha dei cattivi pensieri; *his name was, let me —...,* si chiamava, fammi pensare...; *that boy thinks too much,* quel ragazzo pensa troppo; *to — aloud,* pensare a voce alta; *to — hard,* pensare, riflettere a lungo; *to — no harm,* non pensare a niente di male, non pensare di fare male **2.** ritenere, considerare, giudicare: *do you — you could do it?,* pensi di poterlo fare?; *the doctor thought it was scarlet fever,* il dottore pensò trattarsi di scarlattina; *I — so, not,* penso di sì, di no; *I should hardly — so,* credo sia poco probabile; *I thought (that) I heard a cry,* mi era parso di udire un grido; *it is right, don't you —, to go there?,* è giusto andar là, non è vero?; *they thought he was mad,* lo giudicavano pazzo; *they were thought to be poor,* passavano per poveri; *to — s.o., sthg. interesting,* ritenere qlcu., ql.co. interessante ‖ *to — no small beer of oneself,* avere una grande opinione di sè, ritenersi chissà chi **3.** credere, aspettarsi; immaginare, immaginarsi; figurarsi: *I little thought to go to Berlin again,* non mi aspettavo certo di tornare a Berlino; *who'd have thought it!,* chi l'avrebbe detto!; *you can't — how sorry I am,* non puoi immaginare quanto sia spiacente; *you might —, you were in Japan,* si direbbe che siamo in Giappone; *to — that I believed him!,* e pensare che avevo fiducia in lui! **4.** pensare; venire, avere in mente di: *did you — to bring any bread?,* hai pensato a portare del pane? **5.** *to — about* (*s.o., sthg.*), pensare; considerare: *did you — about that offer?,* hai ripensato a quell'offerta?; *I have so much to — about,* ho tante cose a cui pensare; *it isn't worth thinking about it,* non vale la pena di pensarci **6.** *to — of* (*s.o., sthg.*), pensare, immaginare; tenere in considerazione; avere in animo di; ricordare: *— of her surprise when...,* immagina la sua sorpresa quando...; *— of the time it would take,* pensa al tempo che ci vorrebbe; *he only thought of helping him,* il suo unico pensiero fu di aiutarlo; *I can't — of her name,* non mi ricordo il suo nome; *I couldn't — of it,* non c'è nemmeno da pensarci! è impossibile!; *I shouldn't — of telling him that!,* non mi sogno certo di raccontarglielo!; *I — of doing it myself,* penso di farlo io stesso; *I was thinking of you,* pensavo a te; *what do you — of that picture?,* cosa ne pensi di quel quadro?; *when I least — of it,* quando meno ci penso; *to — ill (o badly) of s.o.,* avere una cattiva opinione di qlcu.; *pensar male di qlcu.; to — of a plan,* fare un progetto; *to — very little of s.o., sthg.,* ql.co.; *to — well of s.o.,* stimare, avere una buona opinione di qlcu. ‖ *to — better of,* cambiare idea, opinione; avere un'opinione migliore di **7.** *to — out,* meditare, riflettere; escogitare, trovare (un piano, ecc.): *can you — out a way out?,* puoi trovare un modo di venirne fuori?; *let me — out,* lascia che ci pensi **8.** *to — over,* riflettere, ripensare, ponderare: *after thinking it over I decided not to go,* dopo averci ripensato decisi di non andare; *I will — it over* ci rifletterò **9.** *to — up,* escogitare (un piano, ecc.).

thinkable ['θiŋkəbl], *ag.* concepibile; immaginabile; ammissibile: *is it — that...?,* è ammissibile che...?.

thinker ['θiŋkə*], *s.c.* pensatore, pensatrice: *he is a shallow —,* ha una mente superficiale ☆ *free —,* libero pensatore.

thinking ['θiŋkiŋ], *ag.* pensante, ragionevole: *man is a — animal,* l'uomo è un animale ragionevole ‖ *s.* **1.** pensiero; riflessione; meditazione: *deep —,* pensieri profondi; *you had better do a little hard —,* faresti meglio a riflettere un po' seriamente **2.** opinione, giudizio; avviso: *to my —,* a mio avviso; *that is my way of —,* questo è il mio modo di vedere.

thinly ['θinli], *av.* **1.** leggermente; insufficientemente; scarsamente, appena: — *veiled allusion*, allusione appena velata; *country* — *populated*, paese scarsamente popolato **2.** in modo rado: — *sown corn*, grano seminato rado.

thinner ['θinə*], *s.* solvente, diluente (per pitture, ecc.).

thinness ['θinnis], *s.* **1.** sottigliezza; tenuità, finezza; magrezza **2.** radezza **3.** fluidità; rarefazione **4.** debolezza, inconsistenza (di scusa, ecc.).

thinning ['θiniŋ], *s.* **1.** — (*down*), assottigliamento; dimagrimento **2.** — (*out*), sfoltimento, diradamento.

thinnish ['θiniʃ], *ag.* **1.** piuttosto sottile; magrolino, mingherlino **2.** piuttosto rado (di capelli).

thiocyanate [,θaiou'saiəneit], *s.* (*chim.*) solfocianato.

thiosulphate [,θaiou'sʌlfeit], *s.* (*chim.*) tiosolfato; iposolfito ☆ *sodium* —, iposolfito di sodio.

third [θə:d], *ag. num. ord.* terzo: *every* — *day, year*, ogni tre giorni, anni; *on the* — *of May*, il tre maggio ‖ *the* — *Estate*, (*st.*) il Terzo Stato ‖ *Henry the Third*, Enrico III ‖ *s.* **1.** terzo: *he was the* —, egli fu il terzo; *to make a* —, essere il terzo (in un giuoco, gruppo) **2.** terzo, terza parte: *two thirds*, due terzi **3.** (*mus.*) terza **4.** (*aut.*) terza (marcia) **5.** *pl.* (*comm.*) articoli, merce di qualità scadente **6.** — *of exchange*, (*comm.*) terza di cambio ☆ — *-class* (o — *-rate*), di terza classe, scadente, dozzinale: *a* — *-class* (o — *-rate*) *artist*, un artista da strapazzo; — *cousin*, cugino in terzo grado; — *degree*, (*dir.*) terzo grado, interrogatorio di terzo grado: *to give s.o. the* — *degree*, sottoporre qlcu. a un interrogatorio di terzo grado; — *dimension*, terza dimensione; — *-hand*, di terza mano: — *-hand news*, notizia di terza mano; — *order*, (*eccl.*) terzo ordine; — *party*, (*dir. comm.*) terzi, chi non è in causa: *to take action against a* — *party*, agire contro terzi; — *party insurance*, (*dir. comm.*) assicurazione per danni contro terzi; — *rail*, terza rotaia ‖ *major* —, (*mus.*) terza maggiore; *minor* —, (*mus.*) terza minore.

thirding ['θə:diŋ], *s.* terza parte.

thirdly ['θə:dli], *av.* in terzo luogo.

thirl [θə:l], *s.* (*dial.*) foro, buco.

to **thirl**, *v.t.i.* (*dial.*) bucare, perforare; fare una perforazione.

thirst [θə:st], *s.* **1.** sete, arsura **2.** *fig.* avidità, desiderio intenso, brama: *his* — *for novelty, for* (o *after*) *knowledge*, la sua smania di novità, la sua sete di sapere.

to **thirst**, *v.i.* (*arc. letter.*) **1.** aver sete, soffrir la sete **2.** *to* — *after, for* (*sthg.*), aver sete di, bramare, desiderare: *to* — *for a glass of beer*, aver voglia di bere un bicchiere di birra; *to* — *for glory*, aver sete di gloria.

thirstily ['θə:stili], *av.* avidamente.

thirstiness ['θə:stinis], *s.* arsura, sete.

thirsty ['θə:sti], *ag.* **1.** assetato: *to be* (o *to feel*) —, aver sete; *to be* — *for*, *fig.* bramare, essere assetato di **2.** arido, secco: — *land*, terra arida **3.** che provoca sete: — *food*, cibo che provoca sete.

thirteen ['θə:'ti:n], *ag. num. card. s.* tredici ‖ *to talk* — *to the dozen*, (*fam.*) parlare a vanvera.

thirteenth ['θə:'ti:nθ], *ag. num. ord. s.* tredicesimo, decimoterzo.

thirtieth ['θə:tiiθ], *ag. num. ord. s.* trentesimo.

thirty ['θə:ti], *ag. num. card. s.* trenta: *give me* —, dammene trenta, una trentina ‖ *the thirties*, gli anni dal trentesimo al quarantesimo (in un secolo, nella vita di un uomo): *he was famous in the thirties*, era celebre fra il '30 e il '40; *she must be in her early thirties*, dev'essere sulla trentina; *she was in her late thirties*, era sulla quarantina ‖ *the Thirty Years' War*, (*st.*) la guerra dei Trent'anni.

this [ðis], *pl.* **these** [ði:z], *ag. dimostrativo* **questo, questa**: — *book, these letters*, questo libro, queste lettere; *it is cold* — *morning*, fa freddo stamane; *let me do it for* — *once*, lasciamelo fare per questa volta; *one of these days I shall have a talk with him*, uno di questi giorni gli parlerò ‖ — *agreement, convention*, (*dir. comm.*) il presente contratto, la presente convenzione ‖ — *day two years ago*, due anni fa come oggi; — *day week*, oggi a otto ‖ — *here boy is Tom's son*, (*fam.*) questo ragazzo qui è il figlio di Tom ‖ *he's been at it* — (o *these*) *ten minutes*, (*fam.*) sono dieci minuti che ci lavora ‖ *to run* — *way and that*, correre di qua e di là ‖ *pron. dimostrativo* **questo, questa:** — *is what he wrote*, questo è ciò che scrisse; *he will be sorry for* —, se ne pentirà; *I knew all* — *before*, sapevo tutto ciò fin da prima; *what is* —?, *what are these*?, che è questo?, che sono questi?; *which is yours*, — *or that*?, qual è il tuo, questo o quello? ‖ *he should have learned by* —, questo avrebbe dovuto servirgli di lezione ‖ *it was like* —, *he bought this thing and then sold it*, è andata così, egli comperò questa cosa e poi la rivendette ‖ *we spoke of* — *and that*, parlammo del più e del meno ‖ *you needn't tell me, I can put* — *and that together*, non occorre che tu me lo dica, so trarre le conclusioni da me.

Thisbe ['θizbi], *no. pr. f.* (*mit.*) Tisbe.

thisness ['ðisnis], *s.* (*fil.*) individualità.

thistle ['θisl], *s.* (*bot.*) cardo selvatico ‖ *Thistle*, (*arald.*) Cardo (emblema della Scozia) ‖ *Knight of the Order of the Thistle*, (*abbr. K.T.*) cavaliere dell'Ordine del Cardo ‖ *to grasp the* — *firmly*, affrontare risolutamente una situazione critica ‖ *gather thistles, expect prickles*, *prov.* chi semina vento raccoglie tempesta ☆ — *-down*, (*bot.*) lanuggine (del cardo); — *finch*, (*ornit.*) cardellino.

thistled ['θisld], *ag.* **1.** coperto di cardi **2.** recante l'emblema del cardo.

thistly ['θisli], *ag.* **1.** pieno di cardi **2.** spinoso, pungente.

thither ['ðiðə*], *ag. attributivo* (*rar.*) ulteriore; che è più oltre, di là: *the* — *bank of the river*, la riva più lontana, la sponda di là del fiume ‖ *av.* (*letter.*) là, colà, in quella direzione ‖ *to run hither and* —, correr qua e là.

thitherward(s) ['ðiðəwəd(z)], *av.* (*arc. letter.*) laggiù, in quella direzione.

tho [ðou], *abbr.* di **though**.

thole[1] [θoul], *s.* — (*-pin*), (*mar.*) scalmo.

to **thole**[2], *v.t.i.* (*arc.*) sopportare, subire; soffrire; pazientare.

Thomas ['tɔməs], *no. pr. m.* Tommaso ‖ *St.* — *Aquinas*, S. Tommaso d'Aquino.

Thomism ['toumizəm], *s.* (*fil.*) tomismo.

Thomist ['toumist], *s.* (*fil.*) tomista.

Thomistic(al) [tou'mistik(əl)], *ag.* (*fil.*) tomistico.

thong [θɔŋ], *s.* correggia; cinghia; sferza.

to **thong**, *v.t.* **1.** fornire di correggia, cinghie, assicurare con cinghie **2.** sferzare, staffilare.

Thor [θɔ:*], *no. pr. m.* (*mit.*) Thor (divinità nordica) ‖ — *'s hammer*, (*archeol.*) martello di selce.

thoracentesis [,θɔ:rəsen'ti:sis], *s.* (*chir.*) toracentesi.

thoracic [θɔ:'ræsik], *ag.* (*anat.*) toracico.

thoracocentesis [θɔ:,reikousen'ti:sis], *s.* (*chir.*) toracentesi.

thorax ['θɔ:ræks], *pl.* **thoraxes** ['θɔ:ræksiz], **thoraces** [θɔ:'reisi:z], *s.* (*anat.*) torace.

thoria ['θɔ:riə], *s.* (*chim.*) ossido di torio.

thoric ['θɔrik], *ag.* (*chim.*) di torio.

thorite ['θɔ:rait], *s.* (*min.*) torite.

thorium ['θɔ:riəm], *s.* (*chim.*) torio.

thorn [θɔ:n], *s.* **1.** spina (anche *fig.*): *a* — *in one's flesh*, una spina nel cuore; *to sit on thorns*, essere sulle spine ‖ *no rose without a* —, *prov.* non c'è rosa senza spine **2.** spino, rovo, roveto ☆ — *-apple*, (*bot.*) stramonio; — *-bush*, cespuglio spinoso; biancospino; — *-hedge*, siepe di biancospino.

thornback ['θɔ:nbæk], *s.* (*ittiol.*) razza.

thornbill ['θɔ:nbil], *s.* (*ornit.*) colibrì.

thornless ['θɔ:nlis], *ag.* senza spine.

thornset ['θɔ:nset], *ag.* pieno di spine.

thorntree ['θɔ:ntri:], *s.* (*bot.*) biancospino; acacia.

thorny ['θɔːni], *ag.* **1.** spinoso, pieno di spine **2.** *fig.* spinoso; aspro, arduo, difficile; tormentoso: — *cares*, pensieri tormentosi; *a* — *question*, una questione spinosa; *a* — *way*, un cammino difficile.

thorough[1] ['θʌrə], *ag.* **1.** completo, compiuto; profondo; totale: *a* — *comprehension*, una comprensione totale; *I want a* — *change*, desidero un cambiamento radicale **2.** perfetto; esperto: *a* — *gentleman*, un gentiluomo perfetto; *a* — *poet*, un poeta consumato; *a* — *rascal*, un vero mascalzone **3.** attento, preciso, accurato: *a* — *investigation*, una investigazione minuziosa; *a* — *work*, un lavoro accurato; *he is very* —, egli è molto coscienzioso, preciso ☆ — -*bass*, (*mus.*) basso continuo; — -*going*, deciso, risoluto; completo; — -*paced*, perfettamente addestrato (di cavallo); completo, perfetto.

Thorough[2], *s.* (*st. inglese*) politica rigida e intransigente di Strafford e Laud sotto Carlo I.

thorough[3], *prep.av.* (*arc.*) per **through**.

thoroughbred ['θʌrə-bred], *ag.* **1.** purosangue (di cavallo) **2.** *fig.* di vecchio lignaggio, distinto, che ha stile (di persona) ‖ *s.* (cavallo) purosangue.

thoroughfare ['θʌrəfɛə*], *s.* via, arteria di grande traffico ‖ *no* —, divieto di transito.

thoroughly ['θʌrəli], *av.* interamente, pienamente, completamente: — *yours...*, vostro devotissimo...; *a* — *reliable machine*, macchina di assoluta fiducia; *I* — *understand*, capisco perfettamente; *he knows his job* —, conosce il suo lavoro a fondo.

thoroughness ['θʌrənis], *s.* accuratezza, perfezione, serietà.

thorp(e) [θɔːp], *s.* (*arc.*) villaggio.

those [ðouz], *pl.* di **that**.

thou[1] [ðau], *pron.pers.* **2ª** *persona sing. nom.* (*arc. poet. ora usato nelle preghiere e dai quaccheri*) tu.

to thou[1], *v.t.i.* dare del *thou* a; usare il *thou*.

thou[2], *s.* (*abbr. fam.* di *thousand pounds*) mille sterline.

though [ðou], *av.* **comunque**, **tuttavia**, **però**: *he wanted to go, he didn't* —, voleva andare, però non andò; *I wish you had told me* —, però, se me lo avessi detto ‖ *cong.* **benchè**, **quantunque**, **sebbene**, **nonostante**, **anche se**: — *he is poor he is happy*, benchè sia povero è felice; *he came* — *ill*, venne benchè ammalato; *strange* — *it may seem*, per quanto strano sembri ‖ *as* —, come se: *it is as* — *you killed him*, è come se l'uccidessi ‖ *even* —, anche se: *it is better to ask him, even* — *he refuses*, è meglio chiederglielo, anche se dovesse rifiutare ‖ *what* —, che importa se: *what* — *he is dead?*, che importa se è morto?.

thought[1] [θɔːt], *s.* **1.** pensiero; riflessione, meditazione: *capable of* —, capace di pensare; *want of* —, mancanza di riflessione; *have you ever given it one* —?, ci hai mai pensato per un solo istante?; *his books stimulate* —, i suoi libri inducono alla meditazione; *I can read his* —, posso leggere nel suo pensiero; *to take* — *how to do sthg.*, riflettere sul come fare ql.co. ‖ *modern* —, il pensiero moderno ‖ *on second thoughts*, ripensandoci ‖ *quick as* —, veloce come il pensiero ‖ *to sit lost in* —, starsene meditabondo ‖ *second thoughts are best*, è sempre meglio riflettere **2.** idea; parere, opinione: *a bright* —, un'idea brillante; *tell me your thoughts on the matter*, ditemi il vostro parere sulla faccenda; *to collect one's thoughts*, raccogliere le proprie idee; riprendersi ‖ *a penny for your thoughts*, (*fam.*) vorrei sapere a cosa pensi **3.** concezione; immaginazione: *a beauty beyond* —, una bellezza al di là di ogni immaginazione **4.** preoccupazione, cura: *she was full of* — *for her sick father*, era piena di cure per il padre ammalato; *to take no* — *for the morrow*, non preoccuparsi del domani **5.** intenzione: *I had a* — (o *thoughts*) *of leaving*, avevo intenzione di partire **6.** *a* —, (*fam.*) un poco, un tantino, un'idea: *just a* — *of milk*, solo un'idea di latte; *she seemed to me a* — *conceited*, mi sembrò un tantino vanitosa ☆ — -*reading*, lettura del pensiero; — -*sick*, ossessionato

da un pensiero, da pensieri; — -*transference*, telepatia.

thought[2], *pass.p.p.* di **to think**.

thoughtful ['θɔːtful], *ag.* **1.** pensoso, pensieroso, meditabondo; riflessivo **2.** sollecito, premuroso, riguardoso: *it was very* — *of you to...*, fu molto gentile da parte vostra di...; *she was a most* — *nurse*, era un'infermiera molto premurosa **3.** profondo, ricco di pensiero: *a* — *writer*, uno scrittore profondo, meditativo.

thoughtfully ['θɔːtfuli], *av.* **1.** pensosamente, pensierosamente **2.** sollecitamente, premurosamente.

thoughtfulness ['θɔːtfulnis], *s.* **1.** meditazione, riflessione, raccoglimento **2.** premura, sollecitudine, riguardo.

thoughtless ['θɔːtlis], *ag.* **1.** sconsiderato, sventato, irriflessivo; imprudente, avventato: — *acts*, atti sconsiderati; — *girl*, ragazza sventata; — *youth*, gioventù spensierata **2.** negligente, incurante, trascurato; senza riguardo: *he is* — *of you*, ti trascura.

thoughtlessly ['θɔːtlisli], *av.* **1.** sventatamente, stoltamente **2.** negligentemente, trascuratamente.

thoughtlessness ['θɔːtlisnis], *s.* **1.** sconsideratezza, sventatezza, irriflessione; imprudenza, avventatezza **2.** negligenza, trascuratezza; mancanza di riguardo.

thousand ['θauzənd], *ag.num.card.* mille: *a* — *men*, mille uomini; *a* — *thanks*, mille grazie; *two* — *years*, due millenni ‖ *a* — *and one*, (*fam.*) moltissimi: *I have got a* — *and one things to attend to*, ho moltissime cose da fare ‖ *s.* migliaio; molti; gran numero: *by the* —, *by thousands*, a migliaia; *two in* (o *among*) *a* —, due su mille ☆ — -*headed cabbage*, (*amr.*) cavolini di Bruxelles; — -*leaf*, (*bot.*) millefoglio; — -*legs*, (*entom.*) millepiedi.

thousandfold ['θauzəndfould], *ag.* moltiplicato per mille ‖ *av.* mille volte tanto.

thousandth ['θauznθ], *ag.num.ord.* millesimo ‖ *for the* — *time*, per l'ennesima volta ‖ *s.* millesima parte, millesimo.

Thrace [θreis], *no.pr.* (*geog. st.*) Tracia.

Thracian ['θreiʃjən], *ag.* tracio ‖ *s.c.* abitante della Tracia.

thraldom ['θrɔːldəm], *s.* (*arc.*) schiavitù, servaggio.

thrall [θrɔːl], *ag.* (*arc.*) asservito, schiavo ‖ *s.* (*arc.*) **1.** schiavo, servo (anche *fig.*) **2.** ostaggio, prigioniero **3.** schiavitù, servaggio.

to thrall, *v.t.* (*arc.*) rendere schiavo.

thralldom ['θrɔːldəm], *s.* (*arc.*) schiavitù, servaggio.

thrash [θræʃ], *s.* **1.** battito continuo (della pioggia, delle onde) **2.** vibrazione (di trapano, elica, ecc.) **3.** (*spor.*) battuta delle gambe (nel nuoto) **4.** *V.* **thresh 1.**.

to thrash, *v.t.i.* **1.** battere, percuotere, sferzare: *his father will* — *him soundly*, suo padre gliele darà di santa ragione; *to* — *the water in swimming*, battere l'acqua nuotando **2.** (*mec.*) vibrare **3.** (*mar.*) navigare contro vento **4.** trebbiare; battere il grano **5.** (*sl. spor.*) sconfiggere: *we thrashed the visiting team*, abbiamo battuto la squadra ospite **6.** *to* — *out*, *fig.* discutere a fondo; definire: *I shall have no rest till I* — *out the truth*, non avrò pace finchè non avrò scoperto la verità.

thrasher ['θræʃə*], *s.* **1.** chi batte, percuote **2.** (*ittiol.*) volpe di mare **3.** *V.* **thresher**.

thrashing ['θræʃiŋ], *s.* **1.** bastonatura: *he needs a sound* —, egli ha bisogno di un sacco di legnate **2.** (*spor.*) sconfitta, disfatta.

thrasonical [θri'sɔnikəl], *ag.* vanaglorioso, borioso.

thread [θred], *s.* **1.** filo (anche *fig.*): *the* — *of life*, il filo, la trama della vita; *a* — *of light*, un filo di luce; *the* — *of a discourse*, il filo di un discorso ‖ *a length of* —, una gugliata ‖ *to gather up the threads of...*, raccogliere le fila di... ‖ *not to have a* — *to wear*, (*fam.*) non avere nulla da indossare ‖ *not to have a dry* — *on*, (*fam.*) essere fradicio, essere inzuppato fino all'osso **2.** vena, filone (di minerale) **3.** (*tec. mec.*) filettatura, filetto, impanatura (di vite) **4.** (*ind. tessile*) fibra; filo ☆ — -*counter*, (*ind. tessile*) contafili; — *cutting lathe*, (*mec.*) tornio per filettare; — *gauge*, (*mec.*) calibro per filettature; — *guide*, (*ind. tessile*) guidafilo; — *-lace*, merletto di cotone; — *-mark*, (*ind. cartaria*) filigrana (delle banconote); — *miller*, (*mec.*) fresatrice per filetti; — *-worm*, (*zool.*) filaria ‖ *basting* —, filo da imbastire; *darning* —, filo da rammendo; *embroidery* —, filo da ricamo; *knitting* —, filo per lavorare a maglia; *lisle* —, filo di Scozia; *water* —, (*idraulica*) filetto fluido dell'acqua.

to **thread**, *v.t.* **1.** infilare: *to — a needle*, infilare un ago; *to — pearls*, infilare perle **2.** (far) passare attraverso, penetrare, infiltrarsi: *he succeeded in threading the ball through the players*, riuscì a far passare la palla fra i giocatori; *he threaded his way through the crowd*, si fece strada tra la folla **3.** striare: *her hair is threaded with white*, i suoi capelli sono striati di bianco **4.** (*foto. cine.*) caricare (una pellicola) **5.** (*mec.*) filettare (una vite) ‖ — *into*, avvitarsi dentro **6.** (*elett.*) produrre linee di forza attorno a (un conduttore).

threadbare ['θredbɛə*], *ag.* **1.** consumato, consunto, frusto; liso, logoro **2.** *fig.* vieto; trito, banale.

threadbareness ['θredbɛənis], *s.* **1.** l'essere frusto, logoro **2.** *fig.* l'essere vieto, trito, banale (di argomento).

threaded ['θredid], *ag.* **1.** infilato **2.** (*mec.*) filettato.

threader ['θredə*], *s.c.* chi infila aghi ‖ *s.* (*ind.*) filettatrice, macchina per filettare.

threading ['θrediŋ], *s.* **1.** infilatura **2.** (*mec.*) filettatura (di vite) **3.** — (*up*), (*cine.*) caricamento della pellicola (nel proiettore).

treadlike ['θredlaik], *ag.* filiforme.

thready ['θredi], *ag.* **1.** filamentoso, fibroso, filaccioso **2.** (*patol.*) filiforme: — *pulse*, polso filiforme **3.** esile: — *voice*, voce sottile.

threat [θret], *s.* minaccia: *a — of storm*, una minaccia di temporale; *your threats do not frighten me*, le tue minacce non mi spaventano; *to carry out a —*, mettere in atto una minaccia.

to **threaten** ['θretn], *v.t.i.* minacciare, fare delle minacce: *the disease threatens to spread*, la malattia minaccia di estendersi; *he threatened him with death*, lo minacciò di morte; *though the sea threatens, we shall sail*, benché il mare sia minaccioso, noi salperemo; *to — punishment to trespassers*, minacciare sanzioni per i trasgressori.

threatener ['θretnə*], *s.c.* chi minaccia.

threatening ['θretniŋ], *ag.* minaccioso: *he spoke in a — voice*, parlò con voce minacciosa ‖ *s.* (*dir.*) minaccia, intimidazione ☆ — *letter*, lettera minatoria.

threateningly ['θretniŋli], *av.* minacciosamente.

three [θri:], *ag.num.card.s.* tre: *the rule of —*, la regola del tre ‖ *Three in One*, la Trinità ‖ *the — per cent*, (*fam.*) titoli dello Stato al 3% di interesse ‖ *the — unities*, le tre unità (aristoteliche) ☆ — *-coloured*, a tre colori; — *-colour process*, (*foto.*) tricromia; — *-cornered*, triangolare: — *-cornered hat*, cappello a tre punte, tricorno; — *-decker*, (*mar.*) nave a tre ponti; — *-dimensional*, tridimensionale; — *handed game*, partita (a carte) giocata da tre persone; — *-legged*, a tre piedi; — *-master*, (*mar.*) trealberi; — *-phase*, (*elett.*) trifase; — *-piece*, di, a tre pezzi; — *-ply*, a tre spessori, fili: — *-ply wood*, legno compensato (a tre strati); — *-ply wool*, lana a tre capi; — *quarter*, (*rugby*) tre quarti; — *-sided*, trilaterale.

threefold ['θri:-fould], *ag.* triplo, triplice.

threefold, *av.* tre volte, in modo triplice.

threepence ['θrepəns], *s.* valore di tre penny; moneta da tre pence: *a three-penny stamp costs —*, un francobollo da tre penny costa tre pence.

threepenny ['θrepəni], *ag.* **1.** che vale tre pence **2.** *fig.* a buon mercato; di poco conto: *a — novel*, un romanzetto di nessun valore ‖ *s.* — (*bit*), una moneta da tre pence.

threescore ['θri:'skɔ:*], *ag.* (*letter.*) sessanta: *he was — and ten*, aveva 70 anni.

threesome ['θri:səm], *ag.* di tre persone ‖ *s.* (*golf*) partita a tre.

threnode ['θri:noud], *s.* trenodia.

threnodial [θri'noudiəl], *ag.* lamentevole; lamentoso; lugubre, funebre.

threnodist ['θri:nədist], *s.* autore di trenodie.

threnody ['θri:nədi], *s.* trenodia.

thresh [θreʃ], *s.* **1.** il battere, il trebbiare il grano **2.** battito continuo (della pioggia, delle onde).

to **thresh**, *v.t.i.* **1.** trebbiare; battere il grano **2.** *V.* to **thrash** 1..

thresher ['θreʃə*], *s.* **1.** chi batte il grano, battitore **2.** macchina per battere il grano; trebbiatrice.

threshing ['θreʃiŋ], *s.* il battere, il trebbiare il grano ☆ — *-floor*, aia; — *-machine*, trebbiatrice.

threshold ['θreʃhould], *s.* **1.** soglia, limitare, entrata: *he was waiting for me on the — of my house*, mi aspettava sulla soglia di casa mia **2.** *fig.* soglia, esordio, inizio: *on the — of life*, sulla soglia della vita; *on the — of war*, sull'orlo della guerra ‖ — *of audibility*, (*fisiol.*) soglia delle percezioni auditive; — *of consciousness*, (*psicologia*) soglia della coscienza.

threw [θru:], *pass.* di to **throw**.

thrice [θrais], *av.* (*arc. letter.*) tre volte; *fig.* molto, altamente ☆ — *-blessed!*, tre volte benedetto!; — *-honourable*, molto onorevole; — *-told story*, storia detta e ridetta.

to **thrid** [θrid], (*arc. dial.*) per to **thread**.

thridace ['θridis], **thridacium** [θri'deiʃiəm], *s.* (*farm.*) tridace.

thrift [θrift], *s.* **1.** economia, parsimonia, frugalità **2.** (*bot.*) staticea.

thriftily ['θriftili], *av.* **1.** economicamente, parsimoniosamente, frugalmente **2.** prosperosamente, rigogliosamente; vigorosamente.

thriftiness ['θriftinis], *s.* **1.** economia, parsimonia, frugalità **2.** rigoglio; prosperità.

thriftless ['θriftlis], *ag.* prodigo, scialacquatore.

thriftlessly ['θriftlisli], *av.* prodigamente, senza economia; con spreco.

thriftlessness ['θriftlisnis], *s.* prodigalità; spreco.

thrifty ['θrifti], *ag.* **1.** frugale, economo, parsimonioso, parco **2.** prospero, fiorente; vigoroso.

thrill [θril], *s.* **1.** brivido, palpito, fremito: *she had a — of joy*, ebbe un fremito di gioia **2.** palpitazione **3.** (*sl.*) racconto sensazionale.

to **thrill**, *v.t.i.* (far) fremere, vibrare, palpitare, trasalire; rabbrividire (di terrore); eccitare, elettrizzare: *he was thrilled over the whole thing*, egli era eccitatissimo per tutta la faccenda; *his voice thrilled with emotion*, gli tremava la voce per l'emozione; *horror thrilled through his veins*, l'orrore serpeggiò nelle sue vene; *the news will — him*, la notizia lo elettrizzerà.

thriller ['θrilə*], *s.* (*sl.*) racconto, dramma, film sensazionale, impressionante, poliziesco.

thrilling ['θriliŋ], *ag.* **1.** sensazionale, impressionante, emozionante: *a — story*, una storia sensazionale, molto interessante **2.** penetrante, acuto: *a — voice*, una voce squillante.

thrillingly ['θriliŋli], *av.* in modo sensazionale, emozionante.

thrips [θrips], *s.* (*entom.*) tripide.

to **thrive** [θraiv], *pass.* **throve** [θrouv], *p.p.* **thriven** ['θrivn], (*amer.*) *pass.p.p.* **thrived** [θraivd], *v.i.* **1.** prosperare, fiorire; aver successo, far fortuna; trar profitto: *he will — on his friend's misfortune*, trarrà profitto dalla disgrazia del suo amico **2.** crescere vigorosamente; svilupparsi rigogliosamente, lussureggiare: *children — on milk*, i bambini crescono vigorosi bevendo latte; *vegetation was thriving in that climate*, la vegetazione lussureggiava in quel clima.

thriving ['θraiviŋ], *ag.* **1.** prospero, fiorente, fortunato, florido (di affari) **2.** rigoglioso, vigoroso, robusto (di piante, ecc.).

thrivingly ['θraiviŋli], *av.* **1.** prosperamente, floridamente, con successo **2.** rigogliosamente.

thro', **thro**, *V.* **through**.

throat [θrout], *s.* **1.** gola, strozza; esofago, trachea: *to take by the* —, afferrare per la gola ‖ *to cut each other's throats*, *fig.* tagliarsi la gola a vicenda, rovinarsi; *to cut one's own* —, *fig.* tagliarsi la gola da sè, darsi la zappa sui piedi ‖ *to give a person the lie in his* —, accusare una persona di mentire sfacciatamente; *to lie in one's* —, mentire sfacciatamente ‖ *to moisten one's* —, bagnarsi il becco, bere **2.** strozzatura, gola: *the* — *of the chimney*, la gola del camino; *the* — *of a pipe*, la strozzatura di un tubo **3.** (*arch.*) gola **4.** (*mec.*) gola, scanalatura **5.** (*mar.*) gola, angolo superiore prodiero (di vela); collo (di ancora) ☆ — *-band* (o — *-strap*), soggolo; — *-full*, pieno fino alla gola; — *wash*, gargarismo ‖ *sore* —, mal di gola.

to **throat**, *v.t.* (*arch.*) scanalare.

throated ['θroutid], *ag.* con la gola, dalla gola ☆ *red* - —, dalla gola rossa; *white-* —, dalla gola bianca.

throatiness ['θroutinis], *s.* carattere gutturale (della voce).

throaty ['θrouti], *ag.* **1.** gutturale: — *laugh*, risata gutturale; risata di gola **2.** gozzuto.

throb [θrɔb], *s.* **1.** battito, pulsazione; pulsare (di motore) **2.** *fig.* palpito, fremito: *throbs of pleasure*, palpiti di gioia ☆ *heart-throbs*, pene d'amore; (*sl. giornalistico*) rubrica di corrispondenza femminile.

to **throb**, *pass.p.p.* **throbbed** [θrɔbd], *v.i.* **1.** battere, pulsare; vibrare; rombare (di motore) **2.** *fig.* palpitare, fremere: *his heart throbbed with joy*, il suo cuore fremette di gioia.

throbbing ['θrɔbiŋ], *ag.* palpitante, vibrante (anche *fig.*); rombante (di motori): — *pain*, dolore lancinante; *a village* — *with activity*, un villaggio pulsante di attività ‖ *s.* **1.** battito, pulsazione; rombo (di motore) **2.** vibrazione, fremito (anche *fig.*).

throbbingly ['θrɔbiŋli], *av.* in maniera palpitante, vibrante, pulsante.

throe [θrou], *s. gener. pl.* doglie; spasimo, dolore acuto: *the throes of death*, gli spasimi della morte, l'agonia ‖ *in the throes*, (*fam.*) nel travaglio; nel pieno: *he was in the throes of composition*, era nel travaglio della composizione; *she was in the throes of spring -cleaning*, era alle prese con le pulizie di primavera.

to **throe**, *v.i.* (*rar.*) spasimare; essere in agonia.

Throgmorton Street [θrɔg'mɔ:tn,stri:t], *s.* **1.** la Borsa Valori di Londra **2.** operazioni alla Borsa di Londra.

thrombosis [θrɔm'bousis], *s.* (*patol.*) trombosi.

thrombus ['θrɔmbəs], *pl.* **thrombi** ['θrɔmbai], *s.* (*patol.*) trombo.

throne [θroun], *s.* trono; (*eccl.*) cattedra: *to come to the* —, salire al trono ‖ *the Thrones*, (*relig.*) i Troni (ordine angelico).

to **throne**, *v.t.i.* (*letter.*) **1.** porre sul trono **2.** sedere sul trono; *fig.* troneggiare.

throneless ['θrounlis], *ag.* senza trono, spodestato.

throng [θrɔŋ], *ag.* (*scoz. dial.*) **1.** occupato, indaffarato **2.** affollato ☆ — *hours*, ore di punta.

throng, *s.* folla, moltitudine, calca, ressa.

to **throng**, *v.t.i.* **1.** affollare, affollarsi; stipare, ammassare, accalcarsi: *people will* — *when they hear the bell ring*, la gente si adunerà quando udrà la campana suonare; *we thronged into the room*, ci stipammo nella stanza **2.** spingere, sospingere, premere.

throstle ['θrɔsl], *s.* **1.** (*ornit.*) tordo; tordo beccaccio **2.** (*ind. tessile*) filatoio.

throttle ['θrɔtl], *s.* **1.** gola; trachea **2.** — (*valve*), valvola (a farfalla), valvola regolatrice di flusso ☆ — *lever*, (*aut. aer.*) leva, manetta (di controllo del flusso di gas, aria, ecc.).

to **throttle**, *v.t.i.* **1.** strozzare, strangolare; soffocare (anche *fig.*): *to* — *sedition*, soffocare la rivolta **2.** (*mec.*) controllare, regolare (flusso di vapore, gas, a mezzo di valvola) **3.** *to* — **down**, rallentare, ridurre la velocità (di motore).

through [θru:], *av.* **1.** attraverso; da una parte all'altra; da cima a fondo; sino alla fine: *he was wet* —,

era bagnato fino alle ossa; *I read the paper* —, lessi il giornale da cima a fondo; *it lasted all* —, continuò per tutto il tempo; *the roof is in bad repair, so the rain pours* —, il tetto è in cattivo stato, così passa l'acqua; *to carry a project* —, portare a termine un progetto ‖ — *and* —, ripetutamente; del tutto, completamente; fino alla fine, da cima a fondo; da parte a parte: *he is bad* — *and* —, è veramente un pessimo soggetto; *I read the letter* — *and* —, lessi e rilessi la lettera ‖ *to be* —, (*amer.*) aver finito; (*amer.*) essere consumato, bucato; *fig.* essere spacciato, finito: *his trousers are* — *at the knees*, i suoi pantaloni sono bucati alle ginocchia ‖ *to be* — *to s.o.*, (*tel.*) avere la comunicazione con qlcu.; *to put s.o.* — *to s.o.*, (*tel.*) mettere qlcu. in comunicazione con qlcu.: *put me* — *to Mr. Brown, please*, mi faccia parlare col Sig. Brown, per favore ‖ *to be* — *with s.o.*, averne abbastanza di qlcu.; *to be* — *with sthg.*, aver finito ql.co.; averne abbastanza di ql.co.; *to be half* — *with sthg.*, essere a metà di ql.co. ‖ *to let s.o.* —, lasciar passare qlcu. **2.** (*ferr.*) direttamente: *the goods were sent* — *to Paris*, la merce fu spedita direttamente a Parigi; *I booked my luggage* — *to London*, spedii i bagagli direttamente a Londra.

through, *prep.* **1.** attraverso; per: *a road* — *the jungle*, una strada attraverso la giungla; *she is on her way* — *Rome*, ella è di passaggio a Roma; *she likes to walk* — *the crowd*, le piace camminare tra la folla; *to advance* — *the fields*, avanzare fra i campi; *to walk* — *a gate*, passare attraverso un cancello; *to wander* — *a forest*, vagare per un bosco ‖ — *thick and thin*, in ogni circostanza ‖ *to be* — *sthg.*, (*fam.*) aver finito ql.co.; *to be half* — *sthg.*, (*fam.*) essere a metà di ql.co.: *I'm only half* — *this letter*, sono solo a metà di questa lettera; *to have been* — *it*, (*fam.*) averne passate di tutti i colori ‖ *to go* — *sthg.*, andare attraverso ql.co.; passare ql.co. da parte a parte; esaminare ql.co.: *go* — *your homework again*, riesamina il tuo compito; *he went* — *many trials*, *fig.* fu molto provato dalla vita; *to go* — *s.o.'s papers, pockets*, frugare fra le carte, nelle tasche di qlcu. ‖ *to pay* — *the nose*, pagare un occhio, pagar salato ‖ *to put s.o.* — *it*, (*sl. fam.*) mettere alle strette qlcu. ‖ *to see* — *s.o.*, indovinare i pensieri, i propositi di qlcu.; *to see* — *sthg.*, indovinare, capire ql.co.: *I could see* — *his little game*, capivo benissimo ciò che aveva in mente di fare **2.** durante, per tutta la durata di: *all* — *the year* (o *all the year* —), per tutto l'anno; *he works* — *the day* (o *the day* —), lavora da mattina a sera, per tutta la giornata; *he slept* — *the lecture*, dormì durante tutta la conferenza; *such things have been known* — *the ages*, sono cose risapute da sempre **3.** per; per mezzo di; a causa di: *absent* — *illness*, assente per malattia; *he hid* — *fear of arrest*, si nascose per paura di essere arrestato; *he spoke* — *an interpreter*, parlò per mezzo di un interprete; *it all happened* — *a misunderstanding*, tutto accadde per un malinteso; *it is* — *me that you missed your train*, è per causa mia che perdesti il treno.

through, (*nei composti*): — *carriage*, vettura diretta; — *coupling*, (*mec.*) (accoppiamento in) presa diretta, accoppiamento diretto; — *shaft*, (*mec.*) albero passante; — *street*, strada transitabile; — *-ticket*, biglietto cumulativo; — *train*, treno diretto; — *way*, passaggio libero, diretto.

throughly ['θru:li], (*arc.*) per **thoroughly**.

throughout [θru(:)'aut], *av.* da un capo all'altro; da ogni parte; dal principio alla fine; completamente: *he is wrong* —, ha torto su tutti i punti; *that old table is rotten* —, quel vecchio tavolo è completamente marcio ‖ *prep.* in ogni parte di; da un capo all'altro di; dal principio alla fine; durante tutto il: *he has been respected* — *his life*, è stato rispettato tutta la vita; *she had to travel* — *the country*, dovette viaggiare da un capo all'altro del paese; *she lived there* — *the year*, ci visse un anno intero.

throve [θrouv], *pass.* di to **thrive**.

throw[1] [θrou], *s.* **1.** lancio; colpo; tiro; gittata (di missile, ecc.): *a — of dice*, un colpo di dadi; *a long —*, un tiro lungo; *he caught a fish at the first —*, prese un pesce al primo colpo ‖ *at a stone's —*, a breve distanza, a un tiro di pietra ‖ *it is your —*, tocca a te **2.** (*boxe*) l'atterrare l'avversario **3.** (*geol.*) rigetto, rigetto verticale **4.** (*mec.*) corsa massima **5.** (*mec.*) gomito, manovella **6.** (*elett.*) luce, campata.

to **throw**[1], *pass.* **threw** [θru:], *p.p.* **thrown** [θroun], *v.t.i.* **1.** gettare; scagliare, lanciare; fare un lancio (anche *fig.*): *— the dog a piece of bread*, butta un pezzo di pane al cane; *he threw the ball ten yards*, scagliò la palla a dieci iarde; *to — the blame on s.o.*, *fig.* gettare la colpa su qlcu.; *to — a bridge over* (o *across*) *a river*, gettare un ponte attraverso un fiume; *to — a shawl over one's shoulders*, buttarsi uno scialle sulle spalle; *to — sthg. at s.o.*, scagliare ql.co. contro qlcu.; *to — stones*, scagliare sassi; *fig.* criticare, accusare ‖ *to — cold water on a plan*, *s.o.'s enthusiasm*, scoraggiare un piano, raffreddare gli entusiasmi di qlcu. ‖ *to — difficulties in s.o.'s way*, mettere il bastone fra le ruote a qlcu. ‖ *to — dust in the eyes of s.o.*, *fig.* gettare polvere negli occhi a qlcu. ‖ *to — a fit*, (*sl. amer.*) cadere in convulsione, avere una crisi isterica ‖ *to — a glance at sthg.*, *s.o.*, lanciare uno sguardo a ql.co., a qlcu. ‖ *to — oneself at s.o.'s head*, (*fam.*) buttarsi fra le braccia di qlcu. ‖ *to — oneself into sthg.*, intraprendere ql.co. con entusiasmo ‖ *to — oneself on*, affidarsi a: *to — oneself on s.o.'s generosity*, affidarsi alla generosità di qlcu.; *to be thrown on one's own resources*, essere abbandonato a se stesso ‖ *to — open the door*, spalancare la porta: *to — open one's doors to s.o.*, aprire la propria casa a qlcu. ‖ *to — a party*, (*fam.*) dare una festicciuola ‖ *to — s.o. a kiss*, gettare un bacio a qlcu. ‖ *to — two rooms into one*, ridurre due stanze a una ‖ *to be thrown together*, (*fam.*) incontrarsi spesso: *we were thrown together quite a lot last summer*, ci incontrammo molto spesso l'estate scorsa **2.** proiettare: *to — a picture on the screen*, proiettare un'immagine sullo schermo ‖ *to — light on sthg.*, *fig.* far luce su ql.co. **3.** atterrare, rovesciare: *he was thrown from his horse*, fu disarcionato; *the wrestler threw his opponent*, il pugile atterrò l'avversario **4.** partorire (di animali) **5.** (*ind. tessile*) torcere, avvolgere **6.** (*artig.*) tornire (vasi) **7.** (*fam. amer.*) perdere intenzionalmente (una competizione sportiva) **8.** *to — about*, disseminare, gettare qua e là: *he is throwing his money about*, spende a piene mani; *to — one's arms about*, agitare le braccia; *to be thrown about*, essere sballottato ‖ *to — one's weight about*, (*fam.*) darsi molte arie **9.** *to — away*, buttar via, sprecare; scartare: *advice is thrown away on him*, i buoni consigli sono sprecati con lui; *to — away a chance*, sprecare un'occasione **10.** *to — back*, ributtare, buttare di nuovo; riflettere (di specchio); (*biol.*) essere soggetto a reversione, regredire: *he wore his hat thrown back*, portava il cappello all'indietro ‖ *to be thrown back* (*up*)*on sthg.*, *s.o.*, doversi accontentare di ql.co., qlcu.: *I was thrown back on my own company*, mi ritrovai solo **11.** *to — down*, gettare; *fig.* abbandonare; (*amer.*) rifiutare: *his offer has been thrown down*, la sua offerta è stata rifiutata; *the workers will — down their tools tomorrow*, gli operai sciopereranno domani **12.** *to — in*, buttar dentro; aggiungere; dare in aggiunta: *he threw a few words in here and there*, buttò là ogni tanto qualche parola; *I bought this cutlery for a few pounds with the case thrown in*, ho comprato per poche sterline queste posate, astuccio compreso ‖ *to — in one's hand*, cessare di giuocare a carte; dare partita vinta (anche *fig.*) ‖ *to — one's lot in with s.o.* (o *amer. to — in with s.o.*), unire la propria sorte a quella di un altro **13.** *to — off*, buttar fuori, emettere; togliere; liberarsi; improvvisare: *he threw off his clothes and jumped into the river*, si spogliò rapidamente e si buttò nel fiume; *I have thrown off the bad cold I had*, mi sono liberato dal forte raffreddore che avevo; *she can*

— off a dinner, a poem, a party at any time, ella sa improvvisare un pranzo, una poesia, un ricevimento in qualsiasi momento; *the steam, the water thrown off by a machine*, il vapore, l'acqua emessi da una macchina; *to — off a bad habit*, liberarsi da una cattiva abitudine **14.** *to — out*, buttar fuori; respingere; espellere; erigere; far risaltare; sconcertare: *the green of her dress throws out the red of her hair*, il verde del vestito fa risaltare il rosso dei suoi capelli; *he has a way of throwing out unpleasant things about his friends*, ha il vizio di insinuare cose poco simpatiche sui suoi amici; *I was completely thrown out by his suggestion*, fui del tutto sconcertato dalla sua proposta; *they will — out a new wing to their house*, vogliono far costruire una nuova ala alla loro casa; *to — out one's chest*, (*sl.*) mettere il petto in fuori ‖ *now — out the clutch*, (*aut.*) disinnesta la frizione **15.** *to — over*, abbandonare **16.** *to — up*, alzare; rigettare, vomitare; abbandonare; rinunciare a: *he has thrown up his job*, ha abbandonato il lavoro; *the volcano threw up lava and stones*, il vulcano vomitò lava e pietre.

throw[2], (*arc.*) per **throe**.

throwaway ['θrouə,wei], *s.* (*amer.*) volantino, manifestino pubblicitario.

throw-back ['θroubæk], *s.* **1.** movimento brusco all'indietro (della testa) **2.** (*biol.*) regressione, ritorno atavico **3.** ostacolo, impedimento: *his last minute refusal was a — for us all*, il suo rifiuto all'ultimo momento ci ha bloccati tutti.

thrower ['θrouə*], *s.c.* lanciatore, lanciatrice ‖ *s.* vasaio.

thrown [θroun], *p.p.* di to **throw** ‖ *ag.* **1.** modellato (di vaso) **2.** ritorto (di seta) ☆ *— -silk*, organzino.

throw-off ['θrouɔ:f], *s.* **1.** inizio (specialmente di battuta di caccia, corsa di cavalli) **2.** (*mec.*) dispositivo automatico di arresto.

throw-out ['θrouaut], *s.* *pl.* scarti, articoli difettosi **2.** (*mec.*) disinnesto; dispositivo di disinnesto.

throwster ['θroustə*], *s.* **1.** torcitore (di seta) **2.** (*sl.*) giuocatore d'azzardo.

thrum[1] [θrʌm], *s.* **1.** (*ind. tessile*) sfilaccio, filaccia (che rimane sul telaio quando si toglie il tessuto); cascame ‖ *thread and —*, buono e cattivo **2.** (*mar.*) filacce; baderna.

to **thrum**[1], *pass.p.p.* **thrummed** [θrʌmd[, *v.t.* **1.** tessere con filacce, cascame **2.** (*mar.*) coprire con baderna; stoppare un filaccе.

thrum[2], *s.* **1.** strimpellata, strimpellio **2.** il tamburellare **3.** (*dial.*) il fare le fusa.

to **thrum**[2], *v.t.i.* **1.** strimpellare (strumento a corde): *to — (on) the guitar*, strimpellare la chitarra **2.** tamburellare: *to — (on) the table*, tamburellare con le dita sulla tavola.

thrummer ['θrʌmə*], *s.c.* chi strimpella.

thrummy ['θrʌmi], *ag.* fibroso; filaccioso (di tessuti).

thrush[1] [θrʌʃ], *s.* **1.** (*patol.*) afta, mughetto **2.** (*vet.*) irritazione della forchetta (nel piede del cavallo).

thrush[2], *s.* (*ornit.*) tordo.

thrust [θrʌst], *s.* **1.** colpo, botta; spinta: *with one — he broke the door in*, con una sola spinta forzò la porta **2.** colpo con arma appuntita, pugnalata **3.** (*mil.*) attacco, assalto **4.** battuta; osservazione; nota: *that was a shrewd —*, fu una osservazione acuta ‖ *— and parry*, botta e risposta **5.** (*mec. arch.*) spinta: *— of an arch*, spinta di un arco **6.** crollo (di galleria di miniera) ☆ *— -block*, (*mec.*) cuscinetto reggispinta; *— -collars*, (*mec.*) bordini reggispinta; *— meter*, (*strum.*) misuratore di spinta, statimetro; *— reverser*, (*aer.*) invertitore di spinta; *— -shaft*, (*mar.*) asse reggispinta; *— spoiler*, (*aer.*) variatore di spinta ‖ *horizontal —*, spinta orizzontale; *take-off —*, (*aer.*) spinta al decollo.

to **thrust**, *pass.p.p.* **thrust**, *v.t.i.* **1.** spingere; ficcare; cacciare, cacciarsi: *she — the letter into her pocket*, ella cacciò la lettera in tasca; *they — past me in a rude way*, per passare mi spinsero in malo modo ‖ *to*

— *one's nose into everything*, *fig.* ficcare il naso dappertutto ‖ *to — oneself*, *fig.* intromettersi, cacciarsi: *he always thrusts himself in other people's business*, si intromette sempre negli affari degli altri **2.** intercalare, frapporre: *to — a word now and then*, frapporre una parola ogni tanto **3.** forzare: *he — his way through the crowd*, si fece strada tra la folla **4.** estendere; spiegare; spingere: *the trees — their branches far and wide*, gli alberi estendevano i rami in ogni direzione **5.** (*arc.*) premere, accalcarsi: *people — there in mighty concourse*, la gente accorse in folla **6.** *to — at* (*s.o.*), (*mil.*) attaccare, lanciarsi: *the soldier — at the man with his dagger*, il soldato si lanciò sull'uomo con il pugnale **7.** *to — through* (*s.o.*), trafiggere: *the spike — through him*, la punta lo passò da parte a parte **8.** *to — upon* (*s.o.*), imporre, costringere: *they did not choose it, they had it — upon them*, essi non lo scelsero, fu loro imposto ‖ *to — oneself upon s.o.*, imporre la propria compagnia a qlcu. **9.** *to — aside, away*, respingere, allontanare **10.** *to — back*, respingere, cacciare indietro **11.** *to — down*, cacciar giù, spingere in basso **12.** *to — forward*, spingere avanti, incitare; mettere avanti ‖ *to — oneself forward*, farsi avanti, mettersi in vista **13.** *to — out*, cacciar fuori: *he — his head out*, cacciò fuori la testa **14.** *to — together*, comprimere **15.** *to — up*, spingere in alto rapidamente: *the firemen — up their ladders in no time*, in un attimo i pompieri drizzarono le scale.

thruster ['θrʌstə*], *s.c.* **1.** chi spinge, chi si spinge avanti **2.** (*fam.*) arrivista; ficcanaso.

thrustor ['θrʌstə*], *s.* (*mec.*) servomotore ☆ — *operated brake*, freno con comando di servomotore idraulico.

Thucydides [θju(:)'sididi:z], *no.pr.m.* (*st. lett.*) Tucidide.

thud [θʌd], *s.* colpo, rumore sordo; tonfo: *he fell with a dull —*, cadde con un tonfo sordo.

to **thud**, *pass.p.p.* **thudded** ['θʌdid], *v.i.* fare un rumore sordo; cadere con un rumore sordo: *a bullet thudded into the wall*, una pallottola si conficcò nella parete con un rumore sordo.

thug [θʌg], *s.* **1.** «thug» (membro di setta religiosa indiana di strangolatori) **2.** strangolatore, assassino.

thuggee [θʌ'gi:], **thuggery** ['θʌgəri], **thuggism** ['θʌgizəm], *s.* **1.** l'azione della setta «thug» (in India) **2.** (*fam.*) banditismo, malavita.

thuja ['θjuːdʒə], *s.* (*bot.*) tuia.

Thule ['θjuːli(ː)], *no.pr.* (*geog. st.*) Tule ‖ *ultima —*, ultima Tule, terra remota e sconosciuta.

thumb [θʌm], *s.* pollice: *he holds a pin between finger and —*, tiene uno spillo fra il pollice e l'indice ‖ *thumbs up!*, evviva!, benone! ‖ *rule of —*, regola basata sull'esperienza, sulla pratica ‖ *his fingers are all thumbs*, è goffo, maldestro ‖ *to be under the — of s.o.*, essere oppresso da qlcu., subire l'influenza di qlcu. ‖ *to bite one's — at s.o.*, fare uno sberleffo a qlcu. ☆ — *index*, indice a rubrica; — *-latch*, saliscendi; — *-mark*, impronta di pollice; — *-marked*, pieno di ditate; — *-nail*, unghia del pollice; *a — -nail sketch*, schizzo in miniatura; descrizione concisa; — *nut*, (*mec.*) dado ad alette; — *-tack*, (*amer.*) puntina da disegno.

to **thumb**, *v.t.* **1.** lasciare ditate su (un libro, ecc.); sporcare, sciupare **2.** suonare malamente, strimpellare **3.** (*sl. amer.*) chiedere (un passaggio) facendo l'autostop: *I thumbed my way through England*, attraversai l'Inghilterra col il sistema dell'autostop **4.** *to — one's nose at s.o.*, (*amer. fam.*) schernire qlcu., far marameo a qlcu.

thumbed [θʌmd], *ag.* **1.** fornito di pollice **2.** pieno di ditate; sporco, sciupato dall'uso (di libro, ecc.).

thumbless ['θʌmlis], *ag.* **1.** senza pollice **2.** goffo, maldestro.

thumbscrew ['θʌm-skruː], *s.* **1.** (*st.*) strumento di tortura, con cui venivano schiacciati i pollici del condannato **2.** vite con testa zigrinata, ad alette.

thump [θʌmp], *s.* colpo; rumore sordo: *his stick hit the pavement with a —*, il suo bastone faceva toc-toc sul selciato; *I heard a — at the door*, udii un colpo alla porta.

to **thump**, *v.t.i.* **1.** battere; percuotere; dar pugni a: *he thumps (on) the table all the time when he speaks*, batte continuamente gran pugni sul tavolo quando parla; *my heart is thumping*, mi batte il cuore tumultuosamente; *they began to — one another*, cominciarono a picchiarsi ‖ *to — (on) the big drum*, *fig.* suonare la grancassa; *to — knowledge into a thick head*, ficcare la sapienza in testa a qlcu. **2.** *to — out*, strimpellare: *to — out a tune on the piano*, strimpellare una melodia sul piano.

thumper ['θʌmpə*], *s.* **1.** chi batte; chi dà pugni, mena colpi **2.** (*fam.*) enormità, grossa bugia: *he tells thumpers!*, ne racconta di grosse!

thumping ['θʌmpiŋ], *ag.* (*fam.*) grosso, enorme.

thunder ['θʌndə*], *s.* **1.** tuono: *a peal of —*, un colpo di tuono **2.** scoppio, rombo: *the — of guns*, il rombo dei cannoni; *the play was received with thunders of applause*, la commedia fu accolta con uno scoppio di applausi ‖ *to steal s.o.'s —*, anticipare la storia sensazionale che qlcu. sta per raccontare, impadronirsi dell'idea, della trovata di qlcu. **3.** fulmine, saetta (anche *fig.*); minaccia: *Jove's thunders*, i fulmini di Giove; *the thunders of the Church*, i fulmini della Chiesa ☆ — *-clap*, improvviso scoppio di tuono; *fig.* improvvisa notizia; — *-cloud*, nube temporalesca; — *-god*, dio del tuono; — *-shower*, acquazzone accompagnato da tuoni; — *-storm*, temporale; — *-struck*, fulminato; *fig.* meravigliato, attonito ‖ *blood-and- —*, sensazionale (di romanzo, racconto, ecc.).

to **thunder**, *v.t.i.* **1.** *imp.* tuonare: *it thunders*, tuona **2.** rumoreggiare, rimbombare: *the tanks thundered through the streets*, i carri armati attraversarono rombando le vie **3.** minacciare, scagliare invettive: *the preacher thundered against the sinners*, il predicatore tuonò contro i peccatori **4.** pronunciare con voce tonante.

thunderbolt ['θʌndəbəult], *s.* **1.** fulmine, saetta (anche *fig.*): *the news came upon us like a —*, la notizia ci colpì come un fulmine **2.** (*arc.*) meteorite.

thunderer ['θʌndərə*], *s.* chi, che tuona ‖ *the Thunderer*, (*mit.*) Giove tonante; (*scherz.*) il giornale inglese «The Times».

thundering ['θʌndəriŋ], *ag.* **1.** tonante; fulminante ‖ *to be in a — rage*, (*fam.*) essere in preda al furore **2.** (*fam.*) straordinario, enorme; formidabile: *a — lie*, una grossa bugia ‖ *s.* **1.** tuono **2.** rumore fragoroso.

thundering, *av.* (*fam.*) notevolmente; straordinariamente, enormemente: *a — great fish*, un pesce straordinariamente grande; *I'm — glad to see you!*, sono estremamente felice di vederti!.

thunderingly ['θʌndəriŋli], *av.* **1.** con fragore di tuono **2.** (*fam.*) straordinariamente, enormemente.

thunderous ['θʌndərəs], *ag.* **1.** temporalesco, minaccioso (di tempo) **2.** tonante; fragoroso: — *applause*, applauso fragoroso; *a — voice*, una voce tonante.

thunderously ['θʌndərəsli], *av.* con fragore di tuono.

to **thunderstrike** ['θʌndə-straik], *pass.p.p.* **thunderstruck** ['θʌndə-strʌk], *v.t.* **1.** fulminare, folgorare **2.** atterrire, sbalordire.

thundery ['θʌndəri], *ag.* minaccioso; tempestoso.

thurible ['θjuəribl], *s.* turibolo, incensiere.

thurifer ['θjuərifə*], *s.* (*eccl.*) turiferario.

thuriferous [θjuə'rifərəs], *ag.* turifero.

thurification [,θjuərifi'keiʃən], *s.* incensamento.

to **thurify** ['θjuərifai], *v.t.* incensare.

Thuringia [θjuə'rindʒiə], *no.pr.* (*geog.*) Turingia.

Thuringian [θjuə'rindʒiən], *ag.* turingio ‖ *s.c.* abitante della Turingia.

Thursday ['θəːzdi], *s.* giovedì: *he comes every —*, viene tutti i giovedì ‖ *Holy —*, il giorno dell'Ascensione (per gli anglicani); *Holy (Week) —*, giovedì santo (per i cattolici) ‖ *Maundy —* (o — *before Easter* o — *in*

Holy Week), giovedì santo ‖ *on Thursdays*, il giovedì: *we usually go there on Thursdays*, ci andiamo di solito il giovedì ‖ *when three Thursdays come together*, il giorno di san mai.

thus [ðʌs], *av.* 1. così, in questo modo: *if he does it* —, se lo fa in questo modo ‖ — *and so*, (*amer.*) proprio così ‖ — *and* —, così e così 2. così, talmente: — *far*, sin qui, fino a tal punto; — *much*, tanto, fin là 3. così, di conseguenza, perciò: —, *when he comes we shall tell him*, così, quando verrà glielo diremo.

thusness [ˈðʌsnis], *s.* (*scherz.*) l'essere così.

(to) **thwack** [θwæk], *V.* (to) **whack**.

thwart [θwɔːt], *ag.* (*arc.*) trasversale, obliquo ‖ *s.* (*mar.*) traversino; banco (del rematore).

to **thwart**, *v.t.* opporsi a; contrastare, ostacolare; frustrare, impedire: *she thwarted him in all his wishes*, si opponeva a tutti i desideri di lui.

thwart, *av.* (*arc.*) trasversalmente, di traverso, obliquamente ‖ *prep.* attraverso, trasversalmente a ☆ — *-ship(s)*, (*mar.*) trasversale allo scafo.

thwarter [ˈθwɔːtə*], *s.c.* oppositore, oppositrice.

thwartingly [ˈθwɔːtiŋli], *av.* in maniera ostile.

thy [ðai], (*arc. poet.* ora usato nelle preghiere e dai quaccheri) *ag. poss.* tuo, tua; tuoi, tue ‖ *pron. poss.* il tuo, la tua; i tuoi, le tue.

Thyestean [θaiˈestiən], *ag.* (*mit.*) di Tieste: — *banquet*, banchetto di Tieste (al quale fu servita carne umana).

Thyestes [θaiˈestiːz], *no.pr.m.* (*mit.*) Tieste.

Thyestian, *V.* **Thyestean**.

thylacine [ˈθailəsain], *s.* (*zool.*) tilacino.

thyme [taim], *s.* (*bot.*) timo ☆ — *oil*, essenza di timo.

thymic[1] [ˈtaimik], *ag.* (*chim.*) timico, derivato dal timo ☆ — *acid*, acido timico, timolo.

thymic[2] [ˈθaimik], *ag.* (*anat.*) timico.

thymol [ˈθaiməl], *s.* (*chim.*) timolo, acido timico.

thymus [ˈθaiməs], *pl.* **thymi** [ˈθaimai], *s.* (*anat.*) timo.

thymy [ˈtaimi], *ag.* di timo; odoroso di timo.

thyroid [ˈθairɔid], *ag.* (*anat.*) tiroideo ‖ *s.* (*anat.*) tiroide ☆ — *extract*, (*chim.*) tiroidina.

thyroidism [ˈθairɔidizəm], *s.* (*patol.*) tiroidismo.

Thyrsis [ˈθəːsis], *no.pr.m.* (*lett.*) Tirsi.

thyrsus [ˈθəːsəs], *pl.* **thyrsi** [ˈθəːsai], *s.* tirso.

thyself [ðaiˈself], *pron. r.* 2ª *persona sing.* (*arc. poet.* ora usato nelle preghiere e dai quaccheri) **e stesso, te stessa** ‖ *know* —, conosci te stesso.

tiara [tiˈɑːrə], *s.* 1. tiara (copricapo frigio e persiano) 2. (*eccl.*) tiara, triregno; *fig.* dignità papale 3. diadema: *a* — *of pearls*, un diadema di perle.

Tiber [ˈtaibə*], *no.pr.* (*geog.*) Tevere.

Tiberias [taiˈbiəriæs], *no.pr.* (*geog.*) Tiberiade: *the Lake of* —, il Lago di Tiberiade.

Tiberius [taiˈbiəriəs], *no.pr.m.* (*st.*) Tiberio.

Tibet [tiˈbet], *no.pr.* (*geog.*) Tibet.

Tibetan [tiˈbetən], *ag.* tibetano ‖ *s.c.* tibetano, tibetana ‖ *s.* lingua tibetana.

tibia [ˈtibiə], *pl.* **tibiae** [ˈtibiiː], *s.* 1. (*anat.*) tibia, stinco 2. (*mus.*) tibia.

tibial [ˈtibiəl], *ag.* (*anat.*) tibiale.

Tibullus [tiˈbʌləs], *no.pr.m.* (*st. lett.*) Tibullo.

tic [tik], *s.* tic (nervoso) ☆ — *douloureux*, nevralgia spastica facciale.

ticca [ˈtikə], *ag.* (*ang.-in.*) noleggiato, affittato ☆ — *-gharry*, carrozza da noleggio.

tick[1] [tik], *s.* 1. tic-tac, ticchettio (di orologio); battito; scatto (di contatore) ‖ *on the* —, (*fam.*) puntuale, in perfetto orario: *I was here at five on* (o *to) the* —, ero qui alle cinque in punto 2. (*fam.*) momento, istante, attimo: *I'll be there in two ticks*, sarò là in due minuti 3. segno, visto (indicante l'avvenuto controllo di una lista, ecc.) 4. picchiettatura, macchiettatura (di piume d'uccello, mantello d'animale).

to **tick**[1], *v.t.i.* 1. ticchettare, far tic-tac (di orologio); scattare (di contatore): *the clock is ticking* (*away*), l'orologio fa tic-tac (senza posa) 2. *to* — **off**, spuntare, contrassegnare; rimproverare: *he will* — *off your*

name, segnerà il tuo nome; *you will get ticked off for that!*, non la passerai liscia! 3. *to* — **out**, segnare, registrare: *they will* — *out your message at once*, il vostro telegramma sarà trasmesso subito 4. *to* — **over**, (*mec.*) rallentare al massimo.

tick[2], *s.* (*entom.*) acaro, zecca ‖ *full as a* —, (*sl. amer.*) pieno come un uovo, rimpinzato.

tick[3], *s.* traliccio; fodera di materasso.

tick[4], *s.* (*fam.*) credito; fido: *to buy* (o *to go*) *on* —, comprare a credito; *to sell on* —, vendere a credito.

to **tick**[4], *v.t.i.* (*fam.*) fare credito; comprare, vendere a credito.

ticked [tikt], *ag.* picchiettato, macchiettato (di piume d'uccello, mantello d'animale).

ticker [ˈtikə*], *s.* 1. cosa che ticchetta (orologio, ecc.) 2. (*scherz.*) cuore ☆ — *-tape*, nastro di telescrivente ‖ *stock* —, telescrivente che trasmette i listini di Borsa.

ticket [ˈtikit], *s.* 1. biglietto; tessera; scontrino, tagliando; etichetta: *give me two tickets for to-night's concert, please*, mi dia due biglietti per il concerto di questa sera ‖ *that's the* —!, (*fam.*) ben fatto! 2. (*mil.*) congedo: *to get one's* —, essere congedato 3. (*amer.*) certificato, diploma: *he was very young when he got his pilot's* —, prese il brevetto di pilota in età giovanissima 4. (*amer.*) lista dei candidati di un partito; *fig.* programma elettorale ☆ — *agency*, agenzia per la vendita dei biglietti; — *-collector*, bigliettario; — *-day*, vigilia di liquidazione in Borsa; — *-inspector*, controllore; — *-of-leave man*, prigioniero a piede libero; — *-porter*, portabagagli autorizzato; — *-punch*, pinza perforatrice per biglietti ‖ *circular* —, biglietto circolare; *mileage* —, biglietto di chilometraggio; *return* — (o *round trip* —), biglietto di andata e ritorno; *season* —, abbonamento stagionale; *single* —, biglietto di andata; *yearly* —, biglietto di abbonamento annuale.

to **ticket**, *v.t.i.* 1. mettere l'etichetta, il cartellino del prezzo a; *fig.* definire, qualificare: *to* — *all reformers as fanatics*, definire fanatici tutti i riformatori 2. fornire di biglietto; (*amer.*) emettere biglietti; prenotare.

tickey [ˈtiki], *s.* (*Sud-Africa*) (*fam.*) moneta da 3 pence.

ticking [ˈtikiŋ], *s.* tela da materassi; traliccio.

tickle [ˈtikl], *s.* solletico.

to **tickle**, *v.t.i.* 1. solleticare, fare solletico: *my hand tickles*, sento solletico a una mano 2. *fig.* stuzzicare, stimolare piacevolmente, lusingare: *food that tickles the palate*, cibo che stuzzica il palato; *she was tickled by her success*, fu lusingata dal successo ‖ *to* — *s.o.'s funny bone*, (*fam.*) stuzzicare il senso dell'umorismo di qlcu. 3. divertire, eccitare: *I was immensely tickled at the idea*, l'idea mi ha immensamente divertito ‖ *I was tickled to death at the news*, (*amer.*) questa notizia mi ha colmato di gioia ‖ *to be tickled to death at* (o *by) sthg.*, torcersi dalle risa per ql.co. 4. pescare con le mani (trote, ecc.) 5. *to* — **up**, (*fam.*) risvegliare, eccitare, stimolare.

tickler [ˈtiklə*], *s.c.* chi solletica, stuzzica, diverte ‖ *s.* 1. questione delicata, imbarazzante 2. (*mec.*) scuotitore 3. (*amer. comm.*) scadenziario 4. (*aut.*) titillatore (di carburatore).

tickling [ˈtikliŋ], *ag.* solleticante; stuzzicante; stimolante: — *cough*, tosse per irritazione ‖ *s.* 1. solletico 2. pesca con le mani.

ticklingly [ˈtikliŋli], *av.* in modo stimolante.

ticklish [ˈtikliʃ], *ag.* 1. sensibile al solletico 2. difficile, delicato, scabroso: *a* — *problem*, un problema delicato 3. suscettibile, permaloso: *he is* — *on this point*, egli è suscettibile su questo punto 4. incerto, instabile, mutevole: — *weather*, tempo mutevole.

ticklishness [ˈtikliʃnis], *s.* 1. sensibilità al solletico 2. difficoltà, scabrosità 3. suscettibilità 4. instabilità, mutevolezza.

tick-tack [ˈtiktæk], *s.* 1. tic-tac (dell'orologio); (*linguaggio infantile*) l'orologio 2. tic-tac (battito de cuore) **3.** specie di alfabeto muto usato per trasmettere informazioni agli allibratori ☆ — *-man*, chi trasmette informazioni di scuderia a un allibratore con segnalazioni speciali.

to **tick-tack**, *v.t.i.* **1.** ticchettare (di orologio) **2.** comunicare (informazioni di scuderia) per mezzo di segni convenzionali.

tidal ['taidl], *ag.* della marea, dipendente dalla marea ☆ — *air*, (*fisiol.*) ritmica emissione del respiro; — *breeze*, brezza causata dalla marea; — *harbour*, porto accessibile solo con l'alta marea; — *motor*, motore azionato dalla marea; — *river*, fiume soggetto alla marea; — *steamer*, piroscafo la cui partenza dipende dall'ora della marea; — *wave*, onda di marea; cavallone, maroso; *fig.* impulso travolgente; impeto di entusiasmo o indignazione popolare.

tidally ['taidli], *av.* regolarmente; periodicamente.

tidbit ['tidbit], *s.* bocconcino, leccornia; *fig.* primizia.

tiddledywinks ['tidldiwiŋks], *s.* giuoco della pulce.

tiddly ['tidli], *ag.* (*sl.*) alticcio, brillo.

tiddlywinks ['tidliwiŋks], *s.* giuoco della pulce.

tide[1] [taid], *s.* **1.** marea: *to stem the* —, navigare contro la marea **2.** *fig.* ondata; corrente, corso; apice: *a* — *of enthusiasm*, un'ondata di entusiasmo; *he died in the* — *of his glory*, morì all'apice della gloria; *to go with the* —, andare con la corrente **3.** (*poet.*) corso d'acqua, fiume, torrente; acqua di mare, mare **4.** (*arc.*) tempo; stagione; epoca; periodo || *to work double tides*, lavorare giorno e notte **5.** (*arc.*) momento opportuno ☆ — *-gate*, cancello che si apre e si chiude a seconda delle maree; — *-gauge*, (*mar.*) mareografo; — *-table*, indicatore delle maree; — *-waiter*, doganiere del porto; *fig.* chi aspetta il momento propizio per agire; opportunista; — *-wave*, onda di marea || *Christmas-* —, (periodo di) Natale; *counter* —, marea contraria; *ebb* - —, riflusso; *flood-* —, flusso; *high-* —, alta marea; *low-* —, bassa marea; *spring* —, marea sigiziale.

to **tide**[1], *v.t.i.* **1.** salire, crescere (come la marea) **2.** essere trasportato dalla marea; (far) andare con la corrente; (*mar.*) entrare, uscire (da porto, fiume) con l'aiuto della marea **3.** *to* — *over*, superare, sormontare || *the gift tided us over through the winter*, il dono ci aiutò a superare l'inverno.

to **tide**[2], *v.i.* (*arc.*) capitare, succedere.

tideless ['taidlis], *ag.* senza marea.

tideway ['taidwei], *s.* corso, letto della marea.

tidily ['taidili], *av.* lindamente; ordinatamente.

tidiness ['taidinis], *s.* ordine, pulizia.

tidings ['taidiŋz], *s. pl.* (*spec. letter.*) notizia, notizie.

tidy ['taidi], *ag.* **1.** ordinato, preciso; pulito, lindo **2.** (*fam.*) considerevole: *he will leave a* — *sum*, egli lascerà una somma considerevole **3.** (*dial.*) in buona salute: *I am feeling pretty* —, mi sento abbastanza bene || *s.* **1.** poggiacapo; fodera per braccioli **2.** astuccio, busta (per piccoli oggetti, cianfrusaglie) ☆ *street* —, cestino dei rifiuti (nelle vie, ecc.).

to **tidy**, *v.t. to* — (*up*), riordinare, mettere in ordine, rassettare: *when the maid comes she will* — *up*, quando verrà la cameriera, metterà tutto in ordine.

tie [tai], *s.* **1.** laccio, legaccio; stringa; cravatta **2.** *fig.* legame, connessione, vincolo: *the ties of blood*, i vincoli del sangue **3.** (*mus.*) legatura **4.** (*ferr.*) traversina **5.** (*spor.*) spareggio; partita eliminatoria: *to play off a* —, giocare una partita di spareggio **6.** *pl.* (*amer.*) scarpe senza tacco allacciate ☆ — *-beam* (o *-rod*), (*edil.*) catena; — *-clip*, fermacravatta; — *-pin*, spillo per cravatta; — *-plate*, (*ferr.*) piastra di fissaggio; — *-rod*, (*mec.*) tirante; (*aut.*) barra di accoppiamento; — *-up*, arresto, blocco (di traffico, produzione, ecc.), inceppamento; (*amer.*) sospensione forzata del lavoro; (*sl. boxe*) colpo decisivo, colpo di grazia; (*spec. amer.*) associazione, unione (di imprese commerciali); — *-wig*, parrucca legata con un fiocco || *cup-* —, (*spor.*) eliminatoria di torneo; *family ties*, legami familiari; *neck* - —, cravatta.

to **tie**, *v.t.i.* **1.** legare; attaccare, unire, congiungere (anche *fig.*): *he tied the horse to the cart*, attaccò il cavallo al carretto; *to* — *s.o.'s hands*, legare le mani a qlcu. (anche *fig.*); *to* — *s.o.'s tongue*, costringere uno al silenzio || *to be tied to a woman's apron strings*, essere attaccato alle gonne di una donna **2.** allacciare, annodare: *to* — *one's shoes*, allacciarsi le scarpe **3.** costringere, obbligare; vincolare: *illness tied her to bed*, la malattia la costrinse a letto **4.** (*spor.*) avere lo stesso punteggio di, pareggiare; (*fam.*) uguagliare: *to* — *for first place* (*with s.o.*), essere primo ex-equo (con qlcu.) **5.** (*mus.*) legare (le note) **6.** *to* — *up*, legare sicuramente, legare (un pacco); bloccare; vincolare; investire: *he tied up his money in land*, investì il suo denaro in terreni; *the will tied up the estate*, il testamento vincolava la proprietà; *to* — *up one's hair*, annodarsi i capelli || *to* — *up to* (o *with*), (*amer.*) far lega, unirsi, collegarsi: *to* — *up to* (o *with*) *a business house*, associarsi a una casa di commercio.

tied [taid], *ag.* vincolato, legato, schiavo: *to be* — *for time*, essere vincolato, stretto dai termini di consegna ☆ — (*public-*)*house*, « public house » il cui esercente è tenuto a rifornirsi presso un determinato fabbricante (che spesso è lo stesso proprietario).

tier[1] ['tai-ə*], *s.c.* chi lega, annoda, congiunge.

tier[2] [tiə*], *s.* **1.** fila, serie, ordine (in struttura a più piani): *a* — (*of seats*), una fila (di posti di gradinata); *three tiers of arches*, (*arch.*) tre ordini di archi **2.** (*mar.*) spirale di fune **3.** (*mar.*) andana ☆ *first* — *box*, (*teat.*) palco di prima fila.

to **tier**[2], *v.t.* disporre in file sovrapposte.

tierce [tiəs], *nel senso* **2.** [tə:s], *s.* **1.** « tierce » (misura di capacità = 1. 159); fusto contenente tale misura **2.** (*a carte*) sequenza di tre carte dello stesso seme **3.** (*mus. eccl. scherma*) terza.

tiercel ['tə:səl], *s.* (*ornit.*) terzuolo, falcone maschio.

tiercet ['tə:set], *s.* (*poes.*) terzina.

tiered [tiəd], *ag.* a gradini, a ripiani: *ancient theatres were* —, i teatri antichi erano a gradinate ☆ *three* —, a tre ripiani.

tiff[1] [tif], *s.* (*rar.*) sorso.

tiff[2], *s.* stizza, collera improvvisa e passeggera; bizza; lieve diverbio: *to be in a* —, essere in collera, tenere il broncio; *to have a* — *with*, bisticciare con.

to **tiff**[2], *v.i.* essere stizzito, tenere il broncio.

tiffany ['tifəni], *s.* garza, mussola finissima.

tige [ti:ʒ], *s.* **1.** (*arch.*) fusto (di colonna) **2.** (*bot.*) stelo, gambo.

tiger ['taigə*], *s.* **1.** tigre; *fig.* persona feroce e crudele || *to rouse the* — *in s.o.*, risvegliare gli istinti crudeli in qlcu. || *to work like a* —, lavorare con grande energia **2.** (*arc.*) lacchè **3.** (*fam.*) avversario temibile **4.** (*sl. amer.*) urrah! (grido di incoraggiamento) ☆ — *-eye*, (*min.*) occhio di tigre; — *-flower*, (*bot.*) tigridia; — *-lily*, (*bot.*) giglio tigrino; — *'s milk*, (*sl.*) gin; liquore forte; — *-nut*, tubero commestibile del cipero; — *-wolf*, (*zool.*) iena maculata, tilacino || *American* —, (*zool.*) giaguaro; *red* —, (*zool.*) coguaro, puma.

tigerish ['taigəriʃ], *ag.* **1.** tigresco; feroce, crudele **2.** infestato da tigri.

tigerishness ['taigəriʃnis], *s.* ferocia, crudeltà.

tight [tait], *ag.* **1.** impermeabile, impenetrabile, ermetico, a perfetta tenuta: *a* — *drawer*, un cassetto che chiude bene; *a* — *soil*, un terreno impermeabile **2.** teso, tirato: *a* — *rope*, una corda tesa **3.** stretto, legato, fissato sicuramente: — *screw*, vite stretta, ben avvitata **4.** stretto, aderente, attillato: *a* — *dress*, un vestito attillato; — *shoes*, scarpe strette **5.** conciso, terso, condensato: — *language*, linguaggio serrato; — *style*, stile conciso **6.** severo, duro; difficile: — *squeeze*, passaggio difficile, difficoltà; *he needs a* — *hand over him*, ha bisogno di un trattamento severo || *to be in a* — *place*, (*fam.*) trovarsi in difficoltà **7.** grazioso, ben fatto **8.** (*comm.*) scarso: *money is* —, il denaro è scarso **9.** (*spor.*) stretto, chiuso, serrato; cauto, equilibrato: — *game*, partita equilibrata; — *match*, giuoco serrato **10**. (*fam.*) avaro, tirato, tirchio **11**. (*sl.*) ubriaco.

tight, *av.* **1**. ermeticamente; a perfetta tenuta: *close the door* —, chiudi la porta ermeticamente **2**. in maniera tesa: *to blow, to pump a ball, a tyre* —, gonfiare, pompare un pallone, un pneumatico, fino a renderli duri || *blow me* —*!*, (*pop.*) questa poi!, chi l'avrebbe mai detto! **3**. strettamente, in modo fisso: *to hold* —, stringere, tenere stretto **4**. in modo aderente, attillato: *this coat fits me too* —, questo cappotto mi sta troppo stretto **5**. immobilmente: *to sit* —, sedere immobile; *fig.* non darla vinta, non mollare.

tight, (*nei composti*): — *-meshing*, (*mec.*) ingrandimento senza giuoco; — *-fisted* (o *amer.* — *wad*), (*sl.*) taccagno; — *-rope*, corda tesa per funamboli: — *-rope dancer* (o *walker*), funambulo || *fire-* —, (*amer.*) a prova di fuoco; *gas-* —, a tenuta di gas; *water-* —, a tenuta d'acqua, stagno.

to **tighten** ['taitn], *v.t.i.* **1**. serrare, serrarsi; stringere, stringersi: *to* — *one's lips*, serrare le labbra || *to* — *one's belt*, tirar la cinghia, saltare il pasto **2**. tendere, tendersi: *to* — *the ropes*, (*mar.*) tirare le corde.

tightener ['taitnə*], *s.c.* chi stringe || *s.* **1**. (*mec.*) galoppino **2**. (*sl.*) scorpacciata; baldoria.

tightening ['taitniŋ], *s.* tensione.

tightly ['taitli], *av.* **1**. ermeticamente **2**. strettamente, fortemente: *they went with their hands* — *clasped*, andavano tenendosi stretti per mano.

tightness ['taitnis], *s.* **1**. impermeabilità, ermeticità, tenuta: *a boat must have a perfect* —, una barca deve avere una perfetta tenuta **2**. tensione: — *of the chest*, difficoltà di respiro; — *of a rope*, tensione di una corda **3**. (*econ.*) scarsità di denaro, di valuta; irrigidimento (del mercato finanziario) **4**. (*sl.*) ubriachezza.

tights [taits], *s.pl.* **1**. calzamaglia (di acrobati, ballerine, ecc.): *flesh-coloured* —, calza maglia color carne **2**. (*st.*) calzoni corti e aderenti, stretti sotto il ginocchio.

tigress ['taigris], *s.* **1**. tigre (femmina) **2**. *fig.* donna crudele.

tigrine ['taigrain], *ag.* (*rar.*) tigresco; tigrato.

Tigris ['taigris], *no.pr.* (*geog.*) Tigri.

tike [taik], *s.* **1**. cane bastardo **2**. uomo volgare.

til [til], *s.* (*bot.*) sesamo indiano.

tilbury ['tilbəri], *s.* «tilbury», tipo di carrozza a due ruote assai in voga nel XIX secolo.

tilde ['tild], *s.* tilde (segno ortografico).

tile [tail], *s.* **1**. tegola, mattonella, piastrella || *to be* (o *to go*) *on the tiles*, (*sl.*) darsi ai bagordi || *to have a* — *loose*, (*sl.*) avere una rotella fuori posto **2**. cappello a cilindro ☆ — *conduit*, (*edil.*) tubo in terracotta, grondaia; — *kiln*, fornace (per la cottura di tegole); — *-red*, rosso mattone; — *-stone*, pietra per lastre di pavimentazione || *paving* —, piastrella per pavimenti.

to **tile**, *v.t.* **1**. coprire di tegole (un tetto); pavimentare; rivestire con piastrelle **2**. proteggere (una loggia massonica) dall'intrusione di estranei; *fig.* costringere a serbare il segreto **3**. (*spec. amer.*) drenare (il terreno) con tubi di terracotta.

tilemaking ['tail,meikiŋ], *s.* fabbricazione di tegole ☆ — *machine*, (*mec.*) tegoliera.

tiler ['tailə*], *s.* **1**. fabbricante di tegole; conciatetti **2**. custode (di una loggia massonica).

tilery ['tailəri], *s.* fabbrica di tegole, piastrelle, mattonelle.

tiling ['tailiŋ], *s.* **1**. copertura in tegole; pavimento in mattonelle **2**. custodia (di una loggia massonica).

till[1] [til], *prep.* **fino a**: — *after four o'clock*, fin dopo le quattro; — *next week*, fino alla settimana prossima; — *now*, — *then*, fino ad ora, fino allora; *from morning* — *night*, da mattina a sera; *he waited* — *the end, his departure, his return*, attese fino alla fine, fino alla sua partenza, fino al suo ritorno; *he worked* — *late at night*, lavorò fino a tarda notte; *to live* — *ninety*, vivere fino a novant'anni || *not...* —, non prima di...: *the performance did not start* — *nine*, lo spettacolo

non cominciò che alle nove; *we shall not come* — *after lunch*, non verremo che dopo colazione || *they have never been there* — *now*, non sono mai stati là prima d'ora || *cong.* **finchè non, fino a che (non), fintanto che, fino al momento in cui**: *he ran and ran* — *he could run no more*, corse finchè non ne potè più; *he waited* — *she came*, aspettò fino a che ella non venne; *I will not go out* — *I have my books*, non uscirò finchè non avrò i miei libri.

till[2], *s.* cassetto in cui riporre il denaro (in negozio, ufficio) ☆ — *alarm*, antifurto (per cassetto); — *money*, (*comm.*) denaro in cassa.

to **till**[2], *v.t.* mettere (denaro) nell'apposito cassetto (in negozio, in ufficio).

till[3], *s.* (*geol.*) argilla morenica.

to **till**[4], *v.t.* **1**. dissodare; arare, lavorare, coltivare (terra) **2**. *fig.* coltivare (la mente, ecc.).

tillable ['tiləbl], *ag.* arabile, coltivabile.

tillage ['tilidʒ], *s.* **1**. dissodamento; aratura; coltivazione: *in* —, in coltivazione **2**. terreno coltivato; raccolto.

tiller[1] ['tilə*], *s.* aratore, coltivatore, agricoltore.

tiller[2], *s.* (*mar.*) barra ☆ *rudder* —, (*mar.*) barra del timone.

tiller[3], *s.* (*bot.*) pollone.

to **tiller**[3], *v.i.* mettere fuori polloni; germogliare, tallire.

tilling ['tiliŋ], *s.* dissodamento; coltivazione.

Tilly ['tili], *no.pr.f. dim.* di **Matilda**.

tilt[1] [tilt], *s.* **1**. tenda, tendone, copertura (specialmente di barca, carro, vagone) **2**. capanna (di boscaiuolo, pescatore) ☆ — *-boat*, barca con tendone; — *-roof*, tetto a volta.

to **tilt**[1], *v.t.* coprire con tendone.

tilt[2], *s.* **1**. torneo, giostra, carosello; *fig.* scontro; disputa || *full* —, a tutta velocità, a tutta forza: *to ride* (*at*) *full* —, cavalcare a briglia sciolta, di gran carriera **2**. inclinazione, pendenza; piano inclinato: (*up*)*on the* —, in posizione inclinata **3**. (*geol.*) sollevamento ☆ — *-cart*, carro ribaltabile; — *-hammer*, maglio meccanico; — *-yard*, campo da torneo.

to **tilt**[2], *v.t.i.* **1**. inclinare, inclinarsi; piegare, piegarsi: *the board tilted* (*up*) *as he stepped on it*, la tavola s'inclinò quando egli vi montò sopra; *to* — *one's hat over one's eyes*, calarsi il cappello sugli occhi **2**. rovesciare; scaricare: *they tilted coal from the cart*, scaricarono il carbone dal carro **3**. oscillare **4**. (*mar.*) beccheggiare **5**. (*aer.*) scivolare d'ala **6**. giostrare, torneare; lottare; attaccare (anche *fig.*) || *to* — *at windmills*, (*fam.*) combattere contro mulini a vento **7**. puntare, vibrare (una lancia) **8**. (*metal.*) martellare; forgiare.

tilter ['tiltə*], *s.* **1**. giostratore, giostrante **2**. forgiatore; chi aziona il maglio a leva **3**. (*mec.*) dispositivo d'inclinazione, di ribaltamento.

tilting ['tiltiŋ], *ag.* inclinato; inclinabile; ribaltabile || *s.* inclinazione, pendenza ☆ — *furnace*, forno rovesciabile; — *seat*, strapuntino; — *stand*, cavalletto girevole.

tilth [tilθ], *s.* **1**. coltivazione, coltura **2**. terreno coltivato, coltivabile **3**. strato di terreno coltivato.

Timaeus [tai'mi:əs], *no.pr.m.* (*st.*) Timeo.

timbal ['timbəl], *s.* (*mus.*) timballo, timpano.

timbale [tæn'ba:l], *s.* **1**. (*cuc.*) timballo **2**. membrana vibratile (di insetto) (che produce un suono caratteristico).

timber ['timbə*], *s.* **1**. legname da costruzione **2**. alberi, bosco da legname **3**. trave, tavola, asse **4**. *fig.* tempra, carattere: *there are few men of his* —, ci sono pochi uomini della sua tempra **5**. (*mar.*) ordinata, costola || *shiver my timbers!*, (*sl. mar.*) tuoni e fulmini! ☆ — *-cart*, carro per il trasporto del legname; — *-framing*, armatura in legno; — *-head*, (*mar.*) bitta; — *-jumper*, (*sl.*) buon saltatore (di cavallo); — *-man*, operaio addetto ai lavori in legno; — *mill*, segheria; — *-toe*, (*sl.*) gamba di legno: — *-toes*, persona con una gamba di legno; — *-tree*, albero d'alto fusto;

— -*work*, costruzione in legno; — -*yard*, deposito di legname ‖ *standing* —, bosco in piedi.

to **timber**, *v.t.i.* **1.** (*arc.*) fare, costruire in legno **2.** rivestire, rinforzare, armare di legno.

timbered ['timbəd], *ag.* **1.** di legno; costruito in legno; rivestito, rinforzato con legno **2.** alberato, coperto d'alberi.

timbering ['timbəriŋ], *s.* **1.** atto del costruire, rivestire, armare di legno **2.** materiale per costruzione (specialmente ligneo) **3.** (*miner.*) armamento.

timbre[1] ['timbə*], *s.* timbro (di voce, di strumento musicale).

timbre[2], *s.* **1.** cresta (di elmo) **2.** (*arald.*) corona (che sormonta uno stemma).

timbrel ['timbrəl], *s.* (*mus.*) tamburello, cembalo.

Timbuctoo [,timbʌk'tu:], *no.pr.* (*geog.*) Timbuctù.

time [taim], *s.* **1.** tempo: *with* —, col passare del tempo; — *crept on*, il tempo trascorse inavvertitamente; — *hangs heavy*, il tempo non passa mai; — *left its marks on her face*, il tempo ha lasciato tracce sul suo volto; *he has lost* (*all*) *count of* —, ha perso la nozione del tempo; *to race against* —, gareggiare col tempo ‖ *once upon a* —, c'era una volta ‖ *as* — *goes on*, col passare del tempo ‖ *lost in the mists of* —, perso nella notte dei tempi ‖ — *is money*, *prov.* il tempo è denaro **2.** tempo, periodo di tempo: *after a short* —, dopo qualche tempo; *between times*, negli intervalli; *for a long* — *to come*, per molto tempo ancora; *for some* — *past*, da qualche tempo; *from* — *to* —, di tanto in tanto; *in* (*o in less than*) *no* —, presto, in un batter d'occhio; *in a short* —, in breve, fra breve; *give me* — *and I'll pay*, dammi tempo e pagherò; *he is doing his* —, sta scontando il suo periodo di pena; *he is serving his* —, sta facendo il tirocinio; *she is far on her* —, è in stato di gravidanza avanzata; *this hat has done its* —, questo cappello ha fatto il suo tempo; *this soldier is near the end of his* —, questo soldato è ormai vicino al congedo; *to take one's* — *over sthg.*, impiegare del tempo a far ql.co. ‖ — *is up!*, è ora! ‖ *to fool away one's* —, sciupare, perdere del tempo ‖ *to have* — *on one's hands*, aver del tempo d'avanzo ‖ *to kill* —, ammazzare il tempo ‖ *to make up for lost* —, ricuperare il tempo perduto **3.** tempo, tempi, circostanze: *hard times*, tempi difficili; *to have a bad* (*o rough*) —, passarsela male, passare un brutto quarto d'ora; *to have an easy* —, passarsela bene; *to have a good* —, divertirsi ‖ *as times go*, coi tempi che corrono ‖ *to have the* — *of one's life* (*o to have a high old* —), far baldoria, divertirsi alla follia **4.** *gener. pl.* tempo, epoca, età: *at the* — *of Elizabeth*, all'epoca di Elisabetta; *behind times*, in arretrato coi tempi; *from* — *immemorial* (*o from* — *out of mind*), da tempi remotissimi; *in our times*, ai nostri tempi; *a superstition of old times*, una superstizione del tempo passato; *in times to come*, per l'avvenire; *to be ahead of one's times*, essere all'avanguardia del proprio tempo ‖ *at no* —, mai ‖ — *was when*, ci fu un tempo in cui **5.** volta: *after* —, ripetutamente; — *and again*, molto spesso; *at times*, a volte; *at various times*, a diverse riprese; *many a* —, molte volte; *some* — *or other*, una volta o l'altra; *ten at a* —, dieci alla volta; *times without number*, innumerevoli volte; *every* — *I come to you*, ogni volta che vengo da te; *it is ten times easier*, è dieci volte più facile; *this* — *I'll forgive you*, questa volta ti perdono; *twenty times running*, venti volte di seguito; *two times two makes four*, due volte due fa quattro ‖ *many times and oft*, (*letter.*) molte e molte volte **6.** tempo, momento: *at the* — *of delivery*, al momento della consegna; *at a given* —, a un dato momento; *it is* — *she came down*, sarebbe ora che scendesse; *it is high* — *to go*, bisogna proprio andare; *it is no* — *for trifling*, non è il momento di scherzare; *my* — *is drawing near*, il mio momento si avvicina; *now it is no* — *to buy shares*, non è questo il momento di

comperare azioni; *they must bide their* —, devono aspettare il loro momento ‖ *in the nick of* —, proprio al momento giusto ‖ *to take the* — *by the forelock*, cogliere il momento giusto **7.** tempo (suddiviso in ore, giorni, stagioni, ecc.): *behind* —, in ritardo; *in good* —, per tempo; *in a week's* —, fra una settimana; *on* —, puntualmente; (*amer. fam.*) *a rate*; *out of* —, fuori tempo; troppo tardi; fuori stagione; *this* — *next year*, l'anno prossimo, di questi giorni; *the* — *was midnight*, era mezzanotte; *rain is unusual at this* — *of the year*, non piove di solito in questa stagione; *what* — *is it?*, che ore sono?; *to look at the* —, guardare l'ora ‖ *to keep* (*good*) —, essere puntuale **8.** orario: *the times of the trains to London*, gli orari dei treni per Londra; *short* — *has been enforced in our factory*, nella nostra fabbrica è stato applicato l'orario ridotto ‖ *double* —, paga doppia ‖ *my* — *is my own*, non sono soggetto ad alcun orario **9.** tempo, ritmo; (*mus.*) tempo; (*mil.*) passo: *in* —, a tempo; *out of* —, fuori tempo; *to beat* —, battere il tempo; *to dance in quick* —, danzare a ritmo veloce; *to keep* —, tenere il tempo ☆ — -*bargain*, (*comm.*) contratto a termine; — -*belt*, fuso orario; (*comm.*) cambiale a termine; — -*bomb*, bomba a orologeria; — -*book*, orario ferroviario; registro di presenza; — -*card* (*o* — -*sheet*), cartellino di presenza; — -*charter*, (*mar.*) nolo a tempo; — -*charter party*, (*mar.*) contratto di noleggio a tempo; — -*clause*, (*gram.*) proposizione temporale; — -*clock*, orologio per controllo presenze; — -*exposure*, (*foto.*) posa, esposizione; — -*fuse*, spoletta a tempo; — -*honoured*, venerando (per età); — -*keeper*, marcatempo; (*spor.*) cronometrista; — -*killer*, perditempo; — -*lag*, intervallo di tempo, ritardo; — -*money*, prestito a termine; — -*policy*, polizza a termine; — -*saving*, che fa risparmiare tempo; — -*server*, opportunista; — -*signal*, segnale orario; — -*signature*, (*mus.*) segno di misura; — -*table*, orario; — -*value*, (*mus.*) valore (di una nota); — -*work*, lavoro a ore, giornata; — -*worn*, logorato dal tempo; — -*zone*, fuso orario ‖ *apparent* — (*o solar* —), ora solare; *departure* —, ora di partenza; *dinner* —, ora di pranzo; *Greenwich* —, ora di Greenwich; *record* —, tempo di record; *ship's* —, ora di bordo; *sideral* —, ora astronomica; *sowing* —, stagione della semina; *standard* —, ora legale.

to **time**, *v.t.i.* **1.** fissare l'orario di; scegliere il momento giusto per; regolare: *the arrival of the Queen was timed for two o'clock*, l'arrivo della regina fu fissato per le due; *she knew how to* — *her remarks*, sapeva scegliere il momento opportuno per fare le sue osservazioni; *they have timed their clock by the time* -*signal*, hanno regolato l'orologio col segnale orario **2.** eseguire in tempo; tenere il tempo, andare a tempo: *the conductor timed the performance admirably*, il direttore d'orchestra ha diretto magnificamente l'esecuzione; *to* — *one's steps to the music*, ritmare il passo secondo la musica **3.** (*foto.*) fissare; regolare la durata di: *to* — *the exposure*, regolare la posa **4.** calcolare il tempo, la durata, la velocità di; cronometrare: *he finished in half an hour, I timed it*, ha finito in mezz'ora, ho calcolato il tempo con esattezza; *to* — *the speed of horses*, calcolare la velocità dei cavalli **5.** (*mec.*) regolare, sincronizzare; mettere a punto; mettere in fase.

timeful ['taimful], *ag.* (*rar.*) tempestivo, opportuno, a proposito.

timefully ['taimfuli], *av.* tempestivamente, a proposito.

timekeeper ['taim,ki:pə*], *s.* **1.** cronometro **2.** chi tiene calcolo del tempo (specialmente delle ore di lavoro degli operai); (*spor.*) cronometrista **3.** (*mus.*) chi batte il tempo.

timekeeping ['taim,ki:piŋ], *s.* (*ind.*) rilevamento dei tempi.

timeless ['taimlis], *ag.* **1.** (*poet.*) infinito, eterno **2.** senza data, senza tempo **3.** (*arc. poet.*) inopportuno, intempestivo, prematuro ‖ *av.* fuori tempo.

timeliness ['taimlinis], *s.* opportunità, tempestività.

timely ['taimli], *ag.* **1.** opportuno, tempestivo, a proposito: *your arrival was* —, sei arrivato al momento giusto **2.** (*rar. arc.*) precoce, prematuro || *av.* (*arc. poet.*) presto, per tempo.

timepiece ['taim-pi:s], *s.* orologio (specialmente da tavolo).

timer ['taimə*], *s.* **1.** cronometrista **2.** cronometro **3.** (*mec. elett.*) distributore di accensione ☆ *full - —*, chi lavora ad orario completo; *half- —*, chi lavora a mezza giornata; *old- —*, anziano, vecchio (del mestiere), esperto.

timid ['timid], *ag.* timido, vergognoso; timoroso, pauroso.

timidity [ti'miditi], *s.* timidezza, soggezione; timore, paura.

timidly ['timidli], *av.* timidamente, timorosamente.

timidness ['timidnis], (*rar.*) per **timidity.**

timing ['taimiŋ], *s.* **1.** calcolo del tempo (di posa fotografica, ecc.) **2.** (*mec.*) messa in fase; regolazione; sincronizzazione **3.** (*tv.*) cadenza ☆ *— adjustment*, (*mec.*) registrazione della distribuzione; *— pulses*, (*radar, tv.*) impulsi di sincronizzazione.

timist ['taimist], *s.* (*mus.*) tempista, chi tiene il tempo.

timocracy [tai'mokrəsi], *s.* timocrazia.

timocratic(al) [,taimə'krætik(əl)], *ag.* timocratico.

Timon ['taimən], *no.pr.m.* (*lett.*) Timone || *s.* misantropo.

timorous ['timərəs], *ag.* timoroso; timido.

timorously ['timərəsli], *av.* timorosamente; timidamente.

timorousness ['timərəsnis], *s.* timidezza.

Timothy ['timəθi], *no.pr.m.* Timoteo.

timothy(-grass) ['timəθi(grɑ:s)], *s.* (*bot.*) coda di topo.

timpanist ['timpənist], *s.* (*mus.*) timpanista.

timpano ['timpənou], *pl.* **timpani** ['timpəni:], *s.* (*mus.*) timpano.

tin [tin], *s.* **1.** stagno; latta **2.** (recipiente di) latta: *a — of biscuits*, una latta di biscotti **3.** (*sl.*) denaro, monete ☆ *— -can*, latta; *— -cow*, (*sl. amer.*) scatola di latte condensato; *— fish*, (*sl. mar.*) torpedine; *— hat*, (*sl. mil.*) elmetto; *— -liquor*, soluzione di sali di stagno; *— -opener*, apriscatole; *— -pan*, stampo, tortiera di latta; *— -plate*, lamiera stagnata; *— soldier*, soldatino di stagno; (*scherz.*) soldato della riserva; *— -tack*, chiodo da tappezziere; *— wedding*, nozze di stagno; *— works*, fonderia di stagno || *bar —*, stagno in verghe; *cake —*, stampo per dolci; *drop —*, stagno granulare; *petrol —*, bidone per benzina.

to **tin**, *pass.p.p.* **tinned** [tind], *v.t.* **1.** stagnare **2.** conservare in scatola; inscatolare.

tineal ['tinkəl], *s.* (*min.*) borace greggio.

tinct [tiŋkt], *ag.* (*poet.*) tinto, colorito; imbevuto || *s.* (*poet.*) tintura, colore, tinta; sfumatura (anche *fig.*); tocco.

tinctorial [tiŋk'tɔ:riəl], *ag.* tintorio, colorante.

tincture ['tiŋktʃə*], *s.* **1.** (*rar.*) colore, tinta; sfumatura; *fig.* infarinatura: *a — of knowledge*, un'infarinatura di cultura; *the Saxon language received no — from the Welsh*, il sassone non ricevette nessuna impronta dal gallese **2.** (*chim.*) estratto; soluzione alcoolica; aroma **3.** (*arald.*) smalti.

to **tincture**, *v.t.* **1.** tingere, colorare **2.** *fig.* imbevere, impregnare; improntare **3.** (*arc.*) dare aroma, colore a.

to **tind** [tind], *v.t.i.* **1.** (*dial.*) accendere, accendersi; far fuoco, prendere fuoco **2.** *fig.* infiammare, eccitare.

tindal ['tindl], *s.* (*ang.-in.*) **1.** sottufficiale indieno **2.** attendente.

tinder ['tində*], *s.* esca (per fuoco) ☆ *— -agaric* (o *— -fungus*), fungo seccato usato come esca; *— -box*, scatola contenente l'esca e l'acciarino.

tindery ['tindəri], *ag.* infiammabile (anche *fig.*).

tine[1] [tain], *s.* **1.** dente (di ferro); rebbio (di forca, di forchetta, erpice) **2.** ramificazione di corna di cervo.

to **tine**[2], *v.t.* (*dial.*) chiudere; rinchiudere; cintare, cingere.

tinea ['tiniə], *s.* **1.** (*patol.*) tigna **2.** (*entom.*) tignuola.

tinfoil ['tin'fɔil], *s.* **1.** lamiera di stagno; lamina di stagno **2.** mercurio (per specchi) **3.** stagnola.

to **tinfoil**, *v.t.* **1.** coprire, rivestire con una lamina, con un lamiera di stagno **2.** avvolgere con stagnola.

ting [tiŋ], *s.* tintinnio ☆ *— -a-ling*, drin drin.

to **ting**, *v.i.* tintinnare, risonare.

tinge [tindʒ], *s.* **1.** sfumatura, tocco: *a — of red in the brown*, un marrone rossiccio **2.** *fig.* pizzico; sapore; traccia: *a — of envy*, una punta d'invidia; *there was not a — of partisanship in his policy*, non v'era traccia di partigianeria nella sua politica.

to **tinge**, *v.t.* dare una sfumatura a (anche *fig.*): *admiration tinged with envy*, ammirazione mista ad invidia; *clouds tinged with red*, nuvole sfumate di rosso; *voice tinged with anger*, voce velata d'ira.

tingent ['tindʒənt], *ag.* (*rar.*) colorante.

tingle ['tiŋgl], *s.* **1.** tintinnio; fischio, ronzio **2.** formicolio, prurito; bruciore, pizzicore.

to **tingle**, *v.t.i.* **1.** tintinnare, far tintinnare; fischiare, ronzare **2.** arrossire (di guance): *my cheeks tingled with shame*, mi bruciavano le guance per la vergogna **3.** pizzicare, prudere; vibrare, fremere: *the boy tingled with anticipation before the party*, il ragazzo fremeva di impazienza in attesa della festa **4.** eccitare, stimolare: *news that tingles all hearts*, notizia che eccita tutti i cuori.

tingler ['tiŋglə*], *s.* (*fam.*) schiaffone.

tinhorn ['tinhɔ:n], *ag.* (*sl. amer.*) che ostenta ricchezza, abilità; ordinario e vistoso.

tink[1] [tiŋk], *s.* tintinnio.

to **tink**[1], *v.t.i.* (*arc.*) tintinnare; far tintinnare.

to **tink**[2], *v.t.* (*arc.*) stagnare.

tinkal ['tiŋkəl], *s.* (*min.*) borace greggio.

tinker ['tiŋkə*], *s.* **1.** calderaio (ambulante); stagnino **2.** abborracciatore, rabberciatore, guastamestieri (anche *fig.*) **3.** rattoppo, rabberciatura, rappezzatura (anche *fig.*).

to **tinker**, *v.t.i.* **1.** riparare, rabberciare || *to — up*, riparare alla meglio: *I tinkered up the garden fence*, riparai alla meglio il recinto del giardino **2.** arrabattarsi, cincischiare, gingillarsi: *to — about the house*, gingillarsi per casa; *to — at* (o *with*) *the wireless set*, armeggiare con la radio.

tinkle ['tiŋkl], *s.* tintinnio, suono argentino (specialmente di campanella).

to **tinkle**, *v.t.i.* **1.** (*rar.*) fischiare, ronzare (di orecchie) **2.** tintinnare, far tintinnare (campanella, ecc.).

tinkler[1] ['tiŋklə*], *s.c.* chi fa tintinnare || *s.* (*fam.*) ciò che tintinna; piccolo campanello.

tinkler[2], *s.* (*scoz.*) **1.** stagnino; calderaio ambulante **2.** vagabondo.

tinkling ['tiŋkliŋ], *s.* tintinnio.

tinkly ['tiŋkli], *ag.* tintinnante.

tinman, *pl.* **tinmen** ['tinmən], *s.* lattoniere, stagnaio.

tinner ['tinə*], *s.* **1.** minatore (in miniere di stagno) **2.** lattoniere **3.** inscatolatore (di conserva, ecc.).

tinnery ['tinəri], *s.* **1.** estrazione dello stagno **2.** *pl.* miniera, fonderia di stagno.

tinning ['tiniŋ], *s.* **1.** estrazione dello stagno **2.** (*metal.*) stagnatura **3.** rivestimento di stagno, latta, stagnola **4.** inscatolamento (di conserve, ecc.).

tinnitus [ti'naitəs], *s.* (*med.*) ronzio auricolare.

tinny ['tini], *ag.* **1.** di stagno **2.** ricco di stagno (di terreno) **3.** dal sapore di latta (di cibo in scatola) **4.** metallico (di suono) **5.** (*sl.*) riccone.

tinsel ['tinsəl], *ag.* vistoso, sgargiante, appariscente || *s.* **1.** (*ind. tessile*) « lamè » **2.** *fig.* orpello.

to **tinsel**, *pass.p.p.* **tinselled** ['tinsəld], *v.t.* orpellare, inorpellare (anche *fig.*).

tinselly ['tinsəli], *ag.* sgargiante, vistoso.

tinselry ['tinsəlri], *s.* orpellatura, falsa apparenza.

tinsmith ['tinsmiθ], *s.* lattoniere, stagnaio.

tinstone ['tinstoun], *s.* (*min.*) cassiterite.

tint [tint], *s.* **1.** tinta, colore delicato; sfumatura, tono, gradazione || *spring tints*, i colori della prima-vera **2.** (*incisione*) retino ☆ — -*block*, (*incisione*) cliché a mezza tinta; — *tone*, colore in diluizione.

to tint, *v.t.* **1.** colorire, tinteggiare **2.** (*incisione*) ombreggiare.

Tintagel [tin'tædʒəl], *no.pr.* (*geog. mit.*) Tintagel (nella tradizione arturiana: luogo di nascita di re Artù).

tinter ['tintə*], *s.* **1.** coloritore; strumento per colorare (fotografie, ecc.) **2.** vetrino colorato per lanterna magica.

tintinnabulant [,tinti'næbjulənt], **tintinnabulary** [,tinti'næbjuləri], *ag.* tintinnante.

to tintinnabulate [,tinti'næbjuleit], *v.i.* tintinnare; scampanellare.

tintinnabulation ['tinti,næbju'leiʃən], *s.* tintinnio; scampanellio.

tintinnabulum [,tinti'næbjuləm], *pl.* **tintinnabula** [,tinti'næbjulə], *s.* campanella; tintinnabolo; sonaglio.

tintometer [tin'tɔmitə*], *s.* (*ind.*) colorimetro.

tinty ['tinti], *ag.* a tinte discordanti.

tinware ['tinwɛə*], *s.* utensili, articoli di latta.

tiny ['taini], *ag.* piccino, minuscolo: *a — bit*, un pochino, un tantino.

tip[1] [tip], *s.* **1.** punta; cima: *on the — of the steeple*, sulla cima del campanile; *with the — of the spear*, con la punta della lancia || *at the tips of one's fingers*, sulla punta delle dita || *from — to toe*, dalla testa ai piedi || *on the — of one's tongue*, sulla punta della lingua **2.** puntale, calzuolo, gorbia, ghiera **3.** spazzo-lino (di peli di scoiattolo, cammello) per indora-re **4.** (*mec.*) cresta; placchetta ☆ — -*curled*, arricciato in punta; — -*tilted*, all'insù (di naso).

to tip[1], *pass.p.p.* **tipped** [tipt], *v.t.* **1.** mettere un puntale a; coprire, ornare la punta di: *a staff tipped with gold*, un bastone con il puntale d'oro; *white flowers tipped with pink*, fiori bianchi con la punta rosa-ta **2.** (*mec.*) riportare la placchetta, la punta a.

tip[2], *s.* **1.** inclinazione **2.** deposito (di carbone, ri-fiuti) **3.** carro ribaltabile (per lo scarico) ☆ — -*cat*, (*giuoco*) lippa; —*car, waggon*, carro, carrello ribal-tabile; — -*up*, ribaltabile; — -*seat*, strapuntino.

to tip[2], *v.t.i.* **1.** *to — (over)*, rovesciare, rovesciarsi; ribaltare, ribaltarsi; capovolgere, capovolgersi; capi-tombolare: *he tipped his friend out of the boat*, buttò il suo amico fuori dalla barca; *the servant tipped over the lamp*, l'inserviente rovesciò la lampada; *the table tipped over*, la tavola si rovesciò || *to — over the perch*, (*sl.*) morire **2.** *to — (up)*, inclinare, inclinarsi; piegare, piegarsi; sollevare, sollevarsi: *he tipped up his hat*, egli sollevò il cappello (in segno di saluto); *the plank tipped up*, la tavola si inclinò; *to — a cask*, rovesciare un barile || *to — the scales (at a hundred pounds)*, pesare (cento libbre) **3.** vuotare, scaricare: *to — rubbish*, sca-ricare immondizie; *to — a waggon*, scaricare un carro.

tip[3], *s.* (*sl.*) informazione (di Borsa, cavalli); indi-screzione; avviso; avvertimento, suggerimento || *to miss one's —*, fallire il proprio scopo ☆ — -*off*, in-formazione; avviso tempestivo (dato a qlcu. di cui sia imminente l'incriminazione, l'arresto, ecc.).

to tip[3], *v.t.i.* (*sl.*) dare informazioni di (Borsa, ca-valli); fare indiscrezioni; avvisare, avvertire: *X is tipped for the next Prime Minister*, si fa il nome di X come prossimo Primo ministro || *to — s.o. off*, av-visare qlcu. tempestivamente (quando ne sia immi-nente l'incriminazione, l'arresto, ecc.).

tip[4], *s.* tocco; (*spec. baseball*) colpo leggero.

to tip[4], *v.t.i.* **1.** toccare, battere leggermente, dare un colpetto a; sfiorare: *to — s.o. on the shoulder*, bat-tere sulla spalla a qlcu. **2.** camminare a passi leggeri, in punta di piedi.

tip[5], *s.* mancia.

to tip[5], *v.t.i.* **1.** (*sl.*) dare; sganciare; passare: *— me over your pouch*, passami la tua borsa del tabacco; *— me your fin*, qua la mano; *— me a shilling*, sgan-ciami uno scellino || *to — s.o. a wink*, (*sl.*) fare un se-

gnale a qlcu. **2.** dare la mancia a, ricompensare: *to — a servant*, dare la mancia a un servitore.

tipper ['tipə*], *s.* **1.** meccanismo di ribaltamen-to **2.** operaio addetto allo scarico di carri ribaltabili ☆ — *truck*, autocarro (a cassone) ribaltabile.

Tipperary [,tipə'rɛəri], *no.pr.* (*geog.*) Tipperary (città dell'Irlanda divenuta celebre per una canzone diffusa nell'esercito inglese durante la prima guerra mondiale).

tippet ['tipit], *s.* **1.** mantellina; pellegrina; cap-pa **2.** (*eccl.*) stola **3.** collare (di animale).

tipple[1] ['tipl], *s.* (*fam.*) bevanda alcoolica.

to tipple[1], *v.t.i.* **1.** (*fam.*) alzare il gomito; darsi al bere **2.** (*arc. poet.*) sorseggiare; centellinare.

tipple[2], *s.* (*amer.*) **1.** deposito (di carbone, rifiu-ti) **2.** carro ribaltabile (per lo scarico).

to tipple[2], *v.t.i.* **1.** cadere, capitombolare **2.** rove-sciare, ribaltare.

tippler[1] ['tiplə*], *s.* (*fam.*) bevitore; beone.

tippler[2], *s.* scaricatore meccanico.

to tipsify ['tipsifai], *v.t.* ubriacare.

tipsily ['tipsili], *av.* da ubriaco.

tipsiness ['tipsinis], *s.* ebbrezza.

tipstaff ['tipstɑːf], *pl.* **tipstaffs** ['tipstɑːfs], **tipstaves** ['tipsteivz], *s.* usciere; aiutante di sceriffo (che ha per insegna un bastone con puntale).

tipster ['tipstə*], *s.* chi fornisce informazioni confi-denziali sulle corse, su altre manifestazioni oggetto di scommesse.

tipsy ['tipsi], *ag.* **1.** brillo, alticcio; ubriaco: *to be slightly —*, essere leggermente brillo **2.** da ubriaco: *a — voice*, voce da ubriaco ☆ — -*cake*, zuppa in-glese.

tiptoe ['tiptou], *ag.* **1.** che sta, cammina sulla punta dei piedi **2.** *fig.* silenzioso, furtivo || *s.* punta dei pie-di: *on — (o upon one's tiptoes)*, sulla punta dei piedi; *fig.* ansioso, anelante: *to stand on — with expectation*, bruciare d'impazienza; *to walk on —*, camminare sulla punta dei piedi.

to tiptoe, *v.i.* **1.** camminare in punta di piedi **2.** cam-minare furtivamente, silenziosamente.

tiptoe, *av.* **1.** in punta di piedi **2.** *fig.* ansiosamente.

tiptop ['tip'tɔp], *ag.* (*fam.*) superlativo, eccellente, di prim'ordine: *a — concert*, un concerto meraviglioso || *s.* apice, cima, vertice (anche *fig.*): *at the — of his profession*, all'apice della sua professione.

tiptop, *av.* (*fam.*) al massimo grado; superlativamente.

tirade [tai'reid], *s.* **1.** tirata, diatriba, filippica **2.** ti-rata, lunga declamazione **3.** (*poes.*) lassa; (*mus.*) tirata.

to tire[1] ['taiə*], *v.t.i.* **1.** stancare, stancarsi; an-noiare, annoiarsi: *I hope I have not tired you*, spero di non averti annoiato; *it tires me to ride a bicycle*, l'andare in bicicletta mi stanca; *to — of s.o., sthg.*, stancarsi di ql.co., di qlcu.; *to — to death*, stancare, stancarsi a morte **2.** consumare, esaurire (anche *fig.*) *she tired her husband's patience*, ha fatto scappare la pazienza a suo marito; *to — land with tillage*, esaurire la terra con (troppe) colture **3.** *to — down*, inseguire (animali) fino ad esaurirli.

tire[2], *s.* (*aut.*) **1.** cerchione (di ruota) **2.** pneumatico; gomma; copertone: *flat —*, gomma a terra ☆ — -*chains*, catene antineve; — *gauge*, manometro per pneumatici — *rim*, cerchione per pneumatico || *high-pressure —*, pneumatico ad alta pressione; *shrunk-on- —*, cerchione fissato a caldo; *studded —*, pneumatico scolpito; *tube less —*, pneumatico senza camera d'aria.

to tire[2], *v.t.* fornire di cerchione, di pneumatico.

tire[3], *s.* **1.** (*arc.*) abito, veste **2.** acconciatura (per capelli); diadema **3.** (*amer.*) grembiule ☆ — -*room* (*teat.*) camerino; — *woman*, (*arc.*) cameriera personale.

to tire[3], *v.t.* (*arc.*) acconciare (capelli).

tired ['taiəd], *ag.* stanco, affaticato; esausto; annoia-to, infastidito: — *face*, viso stanco; *I am — of you* sono stufo di te; *I am — of reading*, sono stanco di leggere; *I am too — to stand*, sono troppo stanco per stare in piedi; *to feel —*, sentirsi stanco || *to b*

— *out*, essere stanco morto ‖ *to talk oneself* —, chiacchierare fino a stancarsi.

tiredness ['taiədnis], *s.* stanchezza.

tireless[1] ['taiəlis], *ag.* instancabile, inesauribile.

tireless[2], *ag.* (*aut.*) senza pneumatici.

tirelessly ['taiəlisli], *av.* instancabilmente.

tirelessness ['taiəlisnis], *s.* instancabilità.

Tiresias [tai'ri:siæs], *no.pr.m.* (*mit.*) Tiresia.

tiresome ['taiəsəm], *ag.* faticoso, stancante; noioso, fastidioso; seccante, spiacevole: *how* —*!*, che noia!, che seccatura!; *how* — *you are!*, come sei noioso!.

tiresomely ['taiəsəmli], *av.* tediosamente; fastidiosamente, in modo seccante.

tiresomeness ['taiəsəmnis], *s.* l'essere stancante, tedioso, fastidioso.

tiro ['taiərou], *pl.* **tiros, tiroes** ['taiərouz], *s.c.* novizio, novizia; principiante; apprendista.

tirocinium [ˌtairou'siniəm], *s.* tirocinio, apprendistato.

Tironian [tai'rounjən], *ag.* tironiano ☆ — *notes*, note tironiane.

'tis [tiz], *contr.* di *it is*.

tisane [ti(:)'zæn], *s.* tisana, infuso.

tissue ['tisju:], *s.* **1.** tessuto; *fig.* tessuto, rete: *a* — *of lies*, un tessuto di menzogne **2.** (*biol.*) tessuto **3.** (*foto.*) carta al carbone ☆ — *paper*, carta velina ‖ *adipose* —, (*biol.*) tessuto adiposo; *connective* —, (*biol.*) tessuto connettivo; *nervous* —, (*biol.*) tessuto nervoso.

tissued ['tisju:d], *ag.* tessuto, intessuto.

tit[1] [tit], *s.* **1.** (*ornit.*) cincia **2.** (*arc.*) cavallino; ronzino **3.** (*sl.*) ragazza, giovane donna; (*spreg.*) fraschetta, sfacciatella.

tit[2], *s.* colpo di ritorno; rappresaglia ‖ — *for tat*, pan per focaccia, occhio per occhio: *to give s.o.* — *for tat*, rendere la pariglia a qlcu.

tit[3], *s.* **1.** capezzolo **2.** tettarella.

Titan ['taitən], *no.pr.m.* (*mit.*) Titano ‖ **titan**, *s.* titano, gigante ☆ — *crane*, (*ind. mec.*) gru a martello; — *strength*, forza titanica.

titanate ['taitəneit], *s.* (*chim.*) titanato.

titanesque [ˌtaitə'nesk], *ag.* titanico; colossale.

Titania [ti'tɑ:njə], *no.pr.f.* (*lett.*) Titania.

titanian [tai'teiniən], *ag.* titanico; colossale.

titanic[1] [tai'tænik], *ag.* titanico (anche *fig.*).

titanic[2], *ag.* (*chim.*) di titanio (nella valenza più alta) ☆ — *oxide*, (*pitt.*) bianco biossido di titanio.

titaniferous [ˌtaitə'nifərəs], *ag.* (*min.*) titanifero.

titanism ['taitənizəm], *s.* titanismo.

titanite ['taitənait], *s.* (*min.*) titanite.

titanium [tai'teinjəm], *s.* (*chim.*) titanio.

Titanomachy [ˌtaitə'nɔməki], *s.* (*mit. lett.*) titanomachia.

titanous ['taitənəs], *ag.* (*chim.*) di titanio (nella valenza più bassa).

titbit ['titbit], *s.* bocconcino, leccornia; *fig.* primizia.

titer, (*amer.*) per **titre**.

tithable ['taiðəbl], *ag.* soggetto a decime.

tithe [taið], *s.* **1.** *gener.* *pl.* (*st.*) decima **2.** tassa; tributo **3.** la decima parte, un decimo: *I cannot tell you a* — *of what he said*, non posso dirvi la decima parte di ciò che egli disse ☆ — *-collector*, esattore di decime; — *-free*, esente da decime ‖ *predial* —, prediale.

to tithe, *v.t.* (*st.*) **1.** pagare le decime su ‖ *to* — *mint and cummin*, (*Bibbia*) perdersi in minuzie e trascurare il proprio dovere **2.** imporre, riscuotere le decime su.

tither ['taiðə*], *s.* (*st.*) esattore di decime.

tithing ['taiðiŋ], *s.* (*st.*) **1.** pagamento, esazione delle decime **2.** «tithing» (divisione amministrativa rurale) ☆ — *-man*, capo di un «tithing»; esattore di decime.

Titian ['tiʃiən], *no.pr.m.* (*st. pitt.*) Tiziano (Vecellio) ‖ *s.* dipinto di Tiziano ‖ **titian**, *ag.s.* **1.** (color) rosso Tiziano **2.** (persona) dai capelli rosso Tiziano.

Titianesque [ˌtiʃiə'nesk], *ag.* tizianesco; nello stile di Tiziano.

to titillate ['titileit], *v.t.* titillare, vellicare; *fig.* stuzzicare, solleticare (appetito, ecc.).

titillation [ˌtiti'leiʃən], *s.* titillamento; solletico (anche *fig.*).

to titivate ['titiveit], *v.t.i.* (*fam.*) azzimare, azzimarsi; agghindare, agghindarsi; abbellire, abbellirsi.

titlark ['titlɑ:k], *s.* (*ornit.*) lodola, calandra ☆ *meadow* —, (*ornit.*) mattolina.

title ['taitl], *s.* **1.** titolo (di libro, poema, ecc.) **2.** titolo, grado (di nobiltà, carica); appellativo, qualifica **3.** (*dir.*) titolo, intestazione (di atto, statuto, voce di statuto) **4.** diritto di proprietà; atto di proprietà; titolo, diritto: *a clear* — *to an estate*, diritto incontestabile ad una proprietà; *he has a* — *to a place among the greatest poets*, ha diritto a un posto tra i poeti maggiori; *he has no* — *to do so*, non ha diritto di agire così **5.** (*eccl.*) titolo, benefizio di chierico **6.** (*chim.*) titolo (di oro, argento) ☆ — *-deed*, (*dir.*) documento che stabilisce il titolo di proprietà; — *-page*, frontespizio; — *-part* (o — *-role*), (*teat.*) ruolo del personaggio che dà il titolo all'opera.

to title, *v.t.* **1.** intitolare, intestare **2.** chiamare, denominare **3.** chiamare col titolo di; conferire il titolo di, nominare, designare.

titled ['taitld], *ag.* titolato, nobile.

titleless ['taitlis], *ag.* senza titolo.

titling ['taitliŋ], *s.* titolo; l'intitolare.

titmouse ['titmaus], *pl.* **titmice** ['titmais], *s.* (*ornit.*) cinciallegra.

to titrate ['titreit], *v.t.* (*chim.*) titolare.

titration [ti'treiʃən], *s.* (*chim.*) titolazione.

titre ['ti:tə*], *s.* (*chim. metal.*) titolo (dell'oro, di una soluzione, ecc.).

titrimetry [ti'trimitri], *s.* (*chim.*) titolazione.

titter[1] ['titə*], *s.* risolino, riso soffocato.

to titter[1], *v.i.* ridacchiare, ridere in modo sciocco.

to titter[2], *v.i.* (*dial.*) **1.** traballare, vacillare **2.** altalenare, dondolarsi.

titter-totter ['titə'tɔtə*], *s.* (*dial.*) altalena.

titter-totter, *av.* **1.** in modo traballante **2.** irresolutamente, con esitazione.

tittle[1] ['titl], *s.* **1.** puntino; segno d'interpunzione; segno diacritico; trattino di penna **2.** *fig.* particella; quantità minima, inezia ‖ *not one jot or* —, niente affatto ‖ *to a* —, con assoluta esattezza.

to tittle[2], *v.t.i.* (*fam.*) sussurrare, mormorare.

tittlebat ['titlbæt], *s.* (*ittiol.*) spinello; spinarello.

tittle-tattle ['titlˌtætl], *ag.* pettegolo ‖ *s.* pettegolezzo; ciarla.

to tittle-tattle, *v.i.* pettegolare; ciarlare.

tittle-tattler ['titlˌtætlə*], *s.c.* pettegolo, pettegola.

tittup ['titəp], *s.* (*fam.*) **1.** balzo, saltello **2.** contegno allegro, vivace.

to tittup, *pass.p.p.* **tittupped** ['titəpt], *v.i.* (*fam.*) **1.** saltellare, balzare **2.** comportarsi allegramente, vivacemente **3.** (*sl. amer.*) giocarsi le consumazioni (lanciando una moneta).

tittuppy ['titəpi], *ag.* **1.** saltellante; vacillante **2.** allegro, vivace.

titty ['titi], *s.* (*linguaggio infantile*) seno materno.

titubancy ['titjubənsi], *s.* (*rar.*) vacillamento, instabilità; *fig.* esitazione.

titubant ['titjubənt], *ag.* (*rar.*) **1.** instabile, vacillante; *fig.* esitante **2.** balbuziente.

to titubate ['titjubeit], *v.i.* (*rar.*) **1.** vacillare; *fig.* esitare **2.** balbettare.

titubation [ˌtitju'beiʃən], *s.* (*rar.*) **1.** vacillamento, barcollamento; *fig.* perplessità, esitazione **2.** (*patol.*) titubazione.

titular ['titjulə*], *ag.* **1.** titolare, nominale: — *sovereignty*, sovranità nominale **2.** titolare, di titolo, che ha un titolo **3.** (*eccl.*) titolare ‖ *s.* titolare ☆ — *bishop*, vescovo titolare in partibus; — *church*, chiesa titolare, titolo; — *head*, titolare (di ditta); — *honours*, onori che derivano, spettano al titolo; — *saint*, santo patrono.

titularity [ˌtitjuˈlæriti], s. (rar.) stato, qualità di titolare.

titularly [ˈtitjuləli], av. in virtù di un titolo, nominalmente.

Titus [ˈtaitəs], no.pr.m. Tito.

tiver [ˈtivə*], s. (dial.) ocra rossa (usata per contrassegnare le pecore).

to **tiver**, v.t. (dial.) marcare (le pecore) con ocra rossa.

tmesis [ˈtmi:sis], s. (gram.) tmesi.

to [tu: (forma forte), tu (forma debole)], prep. **1. a, ad, verso; per, riguardo a**: he gave it — me, me lo diede; she is kind — me, è gentile con me; she has been a mother — her, è stata per lei una madre; what do you say — my suggestion?, che ne dici della mia proposta?; what is that — you?, cosa te ne importa?; to lend, to sell, to take sthg. — s.o., prestare, vendere, portare ql.co. a qlcu. **2.** (di moto) **a, in, da; verso**: — the boat, all'imbarcadero; — the right, — the left, a destra, a sinistra; — the south, — the north, verso sud, nord; — the west, verso ovest; the road — Cardiff, la strada per Cardiff; the way — the station, la strada per la stazione; what school do you go —?, a che scuola vai?; to go — church, school, America, London, the dentist's, andare in chiesa, a scuola, in America, a Londra, dal dentista; to go — ruin, fig. andare in rovina ‖ to see s.o. — the door, accompagnare qlcu. alla porta **3.** (di spazio, tempo) **fino a**: — this day, fino ad oggi; from beginning — end, dal principio alla fine; from morning — night, dal mattino alla sera; from ten — twelve, dalle dieci alle dodici; from top — bottom, da cima a fondo; it is 50 miles — Edinburgh, ci sono 50 miglia da qui a Edimburgo; to count up — ten, contare fino a dieci ‖ twenty — nine, venti alle nove; it is only twenty — ten, sono solo le dieci meno venti **4.** (esprime paragone, rapporto) **a; contro**: compared —, paragonato a; nine votes — three, nove voti contro tre; one goal — nil, una rete a zero; superior —, superiore a;ʼtwelve inhabitants — the square miles, dodici abitanti per miglio quadrato; it is ten — one that…, scommetto dieci contro uno che…; that's nothing — what I have seen, non è niente in confronto a quello che ho visto; two is — four as four is — eight, due sta a quattro come quattro sta a otto; to prefer walking — cycling, preferire andare a piedi piuttosto che in bicicletta **5. (Fraseologia)**: all appearances, (stando) alle apparenze; — the general surprise, tra la sorpresa generale; — my despair, con mia disperazione; — my knowledge, a quanto mi risulta; — this end, a questo scopo; generous — a fault, generoso all'eccesso; killed — a man, uccisi fino all'ultimo uomo; moved — tears, commosso fino alle lacrime; wet — the skin, bagnato fino alle midolla; that's all there is — it, non c'è più niente da aggiungere, questo è tutto; to cut sthg. down — a minimum, ridurre ql.co. al minimo; to shake sthg. — the foundations, scuotere ql.co. dalle fondamenta; to sing — the violin, cantare con accompagnamento di violino; to write — s.o.'s dictation, scrivere sotto la dettatura di qlcu.

to, 1. (segno d'inf.): — do, fare **2.** (con lo stesso valore omettendosi l'inf.): I ought to call on them, but there is no time —, dovrei andare a trovarli, ma non c'è tempo **3.** (con inf. in proposizioni soggettive) il, lo (omissibili): — be or not — be, essere o non essere **4.** (con inf. in proposizione oggettiva): I want him — do it, voglio che egli lo faccia **5.** (con inf. in proposizione epesegetica): desire — do sthg., desiderio di fare ql.co.; happy — do it, felice di farlo; house — be sold, casa da vendere; to have much — do, avere molto da fare **6.** (con inf. in proposizione avverbiale): beautiful — look at, bello da guardare; the first — arrive, il primo ad arrivare; good — eat, buono da mangiare; he came — help me, è venuto per aiutarmi; he is not a man — forget his friends, non è uomo da dimenticare i suoi amici; he woke — find the lamp still burning, si svegliò e trovò la lampada ancora accesa; — look at him one would never imagine that…, a guardarlo non si imma-

ginerebbe che… ‖ so — speak, per così dire **7.** (esprime imminenza, necessità di azione futura, spec. nei titoli dei giornali): a hundred employees — go, licenziati cento impiegati.

to, av. (esprime aspirazione ad una determinata condizione, conseguimento d'essa): to come —, riprendere conoscenza; to leave the door —, lasciare la porta accostata; to pull the shutters —, accostare le imposte ‖ — and fro, avanti e indietro: two journeys — and fro, due viaggi d'andata e ritorno; to go — and fro, andare e venire.

to, (nei composti): — -be, l'avvenire; — -do, (fam.) rumore, chiasso: what a — -do!, che chiasso!.

toad [toud], s. **1.** rospo ‖ to eat s.o.'s toads, comportarsi servilmente verso qlcu. **2.** fig. persona repulsiva, odiosa ☆ — -eater, parassita, adulatore; — -eating, servilità, ossequiosità servile; — -in-the-hole, pasticcio di carne; — -spotted, macchiettato come un rospo; — -stone, bufonite (pietra che credevasi si trovasse nella testa del rospo).

toadfish [ˈtoudfiʃ], s. rana pescatrice, pesce rospo.

toadflax [ˈtoudflæks], s. (bot.) linaiola.

toadish [ˈtoudiʃ], ag. di rospo, simile a rospo.

toadstool [ˈtoudstu:l], s. fungo velenoso.

toady [ˈtoudi], s.c. adulatore, adulatrice.

to **toady**, v.t.i. adulare; comportarsi servilmente; lisciare, leccare i piedi a.

toadyish [ˈtoudiiʃ], ag. servile, adulatorio.

toadyism [ˈtoudiizəm], s. servilismo, adulazione.

toast[1] [toust], s. **1.** pane abbrustolito, crostino: anchovies on —, acciughe servite su crostini; two pieces (o slices) of —, due fette di pane abbrustolito ‖ to be as warm as a —, avere un gran caldo ‖ to have s.o. on —, (sl.) avere qlcu. in pugno; mettere qlcu. nel sacco ☆ — -rack, porta tosti.

to **toast**[1], v.t.i. **1.** abbrustolire, tostare **2.** riscaldare (al fuoco); riscaldarsi.

toast[2], s. **1.** brindisi: let us drink a — to him!, facciamogli un brindisi! **2.** persona, cosa a cui si brinda ‖ she was a great — in her day, era molto festeggiata ai suoi bei tempi ☆ — -master, chi annuncia brindisi (in un banchetto, ecc.).

to **toast**[2], v.t.i. fare un brindisi, bere alla salute di.

toaster [ˈtoustə*], s. **1.** chi tosta **2.** utensile per tostare; graticola; tostino; tostapane.

toasting [ˈtoustiŋ], s. l'abbrustolire, il tostare ☆ — -fork (o — -iron), forchettone per tostare il pane; (scherz.) spada.

tobacco [təˈbækou], s. tabacco: mild —, tabacco dolce; to snuff —, fiutare tabacco ☆ — -box, tabacchiera; — -heart, (patol.) cardionevrosi da nicotinismo; — -pipe, pipa; — -plant, pianta del tabacco; — -pouch, borsa da tabacco; — -stopper, passatabacco (per premere il tabacco nella pipa); — -worker, tabacchino, tabacchina ‖ chewing —, tabacco da masticare; cut —, trinciato; leaf- —, tabacco in foglie; mountain —, (bot.) arnica; roll- —, tabacco in rotoli; twist- —, tabacco in corda.

tobacconist [təˈbækənist], s. tabaccaio: — 's shop, tabaccheria, spaccio di tabacchi.

Tobago [təˈbeigou], no.pr. (geog.) Tobago.

Tobiah [təˈbaiə], **Tobias** [təˈbaiəs], no.pr.m. Tobia.

toboggan [təˈbɔgən], s. (spor.) toboga ☆ — -shoot (o — -slide), pista per toboga.

to **toboggan**, v.i. **1.** (spor.) andare in toboga **2.** (amer.) calare; diminuire: prices tobogganed, i prezzi calarono.

tobogganer [təˈbɔgənə*], s. (spor.) chi va in toboga.

tobogganing [təˈbɔgəniŋ], s. sport del toboga.

tobogganist [təˈbɔgənist], s. (spor.) chi pratica il toboga.

Toby [ˈtoubi], no.pr.m. **1.** dim. di Tobiah, Tobias **2.** « Toby » (cane sapiente, negli spettacoli di burattini) ‖ s. — (jug), boccale da birra (raffigurante un vecchio con tricorno) ☆ — collar (o — frill), collare increspato (simile a quello del cane « Toby »).

toccata [təˈkɑːtə], s. (mus.) toccata.

tocology [təˈkɔlədʒi], s. tocologia, ostetricia.

tocsin [ˈtɔksin], s. 1. segnale d'allarme 2. campana a martello.

tod [tɔd], s. 1. «tod» (antica misura di peso per lana = kg. 12,70) 2. carico (di lana, fieno, ecc.) 3. cespuglio.

today, to-day [təˈdei], s. 1. oggi, quest'oggi: —'s news, le notizie odierne; "What is —?", "Today is Sunday", «Che giorno è oggi?», «Oggi è domenica» 2. il giorno d'oggi: the young of —, i giovani del giorno d'oggi.

today, to-day, av. 1. oggi, quest'oggi: — week, oggi otto; a week ago —, otto giorni fa || —, to-morrow thee, oggi a me, domani a te 2. di questi tempi, oggigiorno, al giorno d'oggi, oggidì, al presente: it is not to be found —, non se ne trova al giorno d'oggi.

toddle [ˈtɔdl], s. 1. andatura incerta, vacillante 2. breve passeggiata 3. infante ai primi passi.

to toddle, v.t.i. 1. camminare a passi incerti, a piccoli passi, trotterellare: the child toddled in, il bambino entrò trotterellando 2. passeggiare, fare quattro passi: to — home, andare passo passo verso casa || to — along, fare una passeggiatina, andare a zonzo || to — round to s.o.'s house, andare, arrivare passo passo fino a casa di qlcu. 3. to — off, andarsene.

toddler [ˈtɔdlə*], s.c. 1. chi cammina a passi incerti 2. infante ai primi passi.

toddy [ˈtɔdi], s. 1. succo estratto da certe specie di palme 2. ponce, «grog».

tody [ˈtoudi], s. (ornit.) todo.

toe [tou], s. 1. dito del piede: on one's toes, sulla punta dei piedi; (sl.) attivo, indaffarato; pieno di vita; sveglio; to stand on the tips of one's toes, alzarsi sulla punta dei piedi || from top to —, dalla testa ai piedi || heel and —, a passi brevi e rapidi; heel and — dance, giga || to tread on s.o.'s toes, fig. pestare i piedi a qlcu. || to turn up one's toes, (sl.) morire 2. punta, puntale (specialmente di scarpa, calza): my shoes are worn out at the toe(s), le mie scarpe sono consumate in punta 3. (tec.) punta; (mec.) perno; (ferr.) punta 4. punta di mazza da golf 5. (arch.) imbasamento 6. parte anteriore dello zoccolo equino ☆ — -cap, mascherina (di scarpa); — -clip, fermapiede (di bicicletta); — -crack, (vet.) malattia dello zoccolo del cavallo; — -dance, danza sulle punte; — -dancer, ballerino, ballerina che danza sulle punte; — -nail, unghia di dito del piede || great- (o big —), alluce; little —, mignolo (del piede); timber- —, gamba di legno.

to toe, v.t.i. 1. mettere, fare, rifare la punta a: to — a stocking, rifare la punta ad una calza 2. toccare; colpire (con la punta del piede, con la mazza da golf, ecc.); (sl.) prendere a calci || to — the line, allinearsi, essere pronto (per la partenza); tenere il piede a segno; fig. conformarsi alle direttive, alla regola (di un partito, ecc.) 3. piantare (chiodi) trasversalmente; inchiodare con chiodi piantati trasversalmente 4. to — in, camminare coi piedi in dentro 5. to — out, camminare coi piedi in fuori.

toff [tɔf], s. (sl.) 1. elegantone, damerino, zerbinotto || to act (o to play) the —, darsi delle arie 2. persona distinta; gentiluomo.

toffee, toffy [ˈtɔfi], s. caramella || not for —, (sl.) a nessun costo || he cannot sing for —, non sa affatto cantare.

tog [tɔg], s. gener. pl. (fam.) abiti, abbigliamento ☆ golf togs, tenuta da golf; long togs, (mar.) abiti borghesi; riding togs, costume da cavallerizzo.

to tog, pass.p.p. **togged** [tɔgd], v.t. 1. vestire 2. to — out, up, farsi bello, mettersi in ghingheri: to be all togged up, essere in abito di gran parata.

toga [ˈtougə], s. toga.

toga'd, togaed [ˈtougəd], ag. togato.

together [təˈgeðə*], av. 1. insieme; unitamente, in compagnia: — with, insieme con; — we forced the door open, insieme riuscimmo a sfondare la porta; I folded all things —, piegai tutte le cose insieme; they acted —,

essi agivano d'accordo; we live —, viviamo insieme; we went —, andammo in compagnia || all —, tutto insieme, complessivamente || pull yourself —, raccogli le idee; ricomponiti || to stand or fall —, essere solidali 2. l'un l'altro, l'un contro l'altro: if we compare them—, se li paragoniamo l'uno all'altro; two flints struck — yield fire, due selci, sfregate l'una contro l'altra, danno fuoco 3. contemporaneamente, nello stesso tempo: both — exclaimed, entrambi esclamarono contemporaneamente 4. consecutivamente, di seguito: we worked for ten hours —, lavorammo per dieci ore consecutive.

togetherness [təˈgeðənis], s. (neol. amer.) lo stare insieme, il fare le cose insieme (sistema di vita familiare avente per presupposto il concetto della famiglia come unità sociale organica e a sè stante).

togger [ˈtɔgə*], s. (sl.) 1. «togger» (barca usata per le regate di primavera a Oxford) 2. pl. regate di primavera (a Oxford).

toggle [ˈtɔgl], s. 1. (mar.) cavigliotto, coccinello 2. — (-joint), (mec.) giunto a ginocchiera ☆ — -iron (o — -harpoon), arpione a testa mobile; — -lever, (mec.) leva articolata; — -press, (mec.) pressa a ginocchiera.

Togo(land) [ˈtougou(lænd)], no.pr. (geog.) Togo.

toil[1] [tɔil], s. 1. fatica, duro lavoro: the toils of war, le fatiche della guerra 2. (arc.) lite, disputa; lotta ☆ — -worn, sfinito dalla fatica, logorato dal lavoro.

to toil[1], v.i. 1. faticare, lavorare duramente; tribolare: to — at sthg., lavorare duramente a ql.co.; to — and moil, sfacchinare || to — on, continuare la propria fatica 2. avanzare faticosamente, muoversi con fatica: to — along the road, avanzare faticosamente lungo la strada; to — up a mountain, salire faticosamente una montagna.

toil[2], s. gener. pl. rete (da caccia); laccio, trappola, trabocchetto (anche fig.): to be taken (o to get caught) in the toils, essere preso al laccio, cadere nella trappola.

to toil[2], v.t. prendere in trappola (anche fig.).

toile [twɑːl], s. tela.

toiler [ˈtɔilə*], s.c. lavoratore, lavoratrice.

toilet [ˈtɔilit], (arc.) **toilette** [twɑːˈlet], s. 1. toletta, pulizia; (st.) ricevimento di dama all'ora della toletta: to make one's —, far toletta, far pulizia 2. toletta, abbigliamento, vestito: a — of red satin, un abito di raso rosso 3. toletta, gabinetto di toletta; bagno, gabinetto 4. — (-table), (arc.) toletta, tavolo da toletta 5. (med.) pulizia e medicazione di una ferita ☆ — -case, necessario da toletta; — -cloth (o — -cover), tovaglia da toletta; — -glass, specchio da toletta; — -paper, carta igienica; — -powder, borotalco; — -set, servizio da toletta; — -soap, sapone da toletta.

toilful [ˈtɔilful], ag. laborioso, faticoso, penoso.

toilfully [ˈtɔilfuli], av. faticosamente, penosamente.

toilless [ˈtɔillis], ag. senza fatica.

toilsome [ˈtɔilsəm], ag. laborioso, faticoso, penoso.

toilsomely [ˈtɔilsəmli], av. laboriosamente, faticosamente, penosamente.

toilsomeness [ˈtɔilsəmnis], s. laboriosità, fatica, pena.

Tokay [touˈkei], s. «tokay» (vino ungherese).

toke [touk], s. (sl.) cibo; pane; tozzo di pane.

token [ˈtoukən], s. 1. segno, simbolo, emblema, insegna: a white flag is a — of surrender, una bandiera bianca è simbolo di resa 2. segno, prova, pegno, ricordo: gifts were brought as tokens of peace, furono portati doni come segno di pace || by this (the same), allo stesso modo, per la stessa ragione 3. (eccl. st.) gettone per essere ammessi alla Comunione (nella Chiesa d'Inghilterra) 4. (st.) moneta emessa da privati con valore nominale superiore a quello intrinseco ☆ — -money, moneta circolante con valore nominale superiore a quello intrinseco; — payment, pagamento simbolico || love —, pegno d'amore.

Tokyo [ˈtoukjou], no.pr. (geog.) Tokio.

tolbooth [ˈtɔlbuːθ], s. (scoz.) 1. municipio, palazzo municipale 2. prigione municipale 3. esattoria, ufficio di dogana.

told [tould], *pass.p.p.* di to **tell**.

Toledan [tɔ'li:dən], *ag.s.* toledano.

Toledo [tɔ'leidou], *no.pr.* (*geog.*) Toledo ‖ **toledo** [tɔ'li:dou], *pl.* **toledos** [tɔ'li:douz], *s.* spada, lama di Toledo.

tolerability [,tɔlərə'biliti], *s.* tollerabilità.

tolerable ['tɔlərəbl], *ag.* **1.** tollerabile, sopportabile **2.** discreto, passabile; mediocre.

tolerable, *av.* **1.** tollerabilmente **2.** passabilmente, discretamente.

tolerableness ['tɔlərəblnis], *s.* **1.** tollerabilità **2.** mediocrità.

tolerably ['tɔlərəbli], *av.* **1.** tollerabilmente; sopportabilmente **2.** discretamente.

tolerance ['tɔlərəns], *s.* **1.** tolleranza, sopportazione, indulgenza **2.** (*mec.*) tolleranza (di lavorazione).

tolerant ['tɔlərənt], *ag.* tollerante, indulgente ‖ *s.* persona tollerante.

tolerantly ['tɔlərəntli], *av.* con tolleranza.

to tolerate ['tɔləreit], *v.t.* tollerare, sopportare, permettere: *I cannot — him,* non lo posso soffrire; *inability to — a drug,* intolleranza di un farmaco.

toleration [,tɔlə'reiʃən], *s.* tolleranza (specialmente politica, religiosa) ‖ *Act of Toleration,* (*st. relig.*) Atto di Tolleranza (1689).

toll[1] [toul], *s.* **1.** pedaggio; dazio; gabella; diritto di posteggio (in un mercato): *to pay the —,* pagare il pedaggio **2.** molenda ☆ *— -bar* (o *— -gate*), barriera (di pedaggio); *— -bridge,* ponte a pedaggio; *— -call,* telefonata interurbana (tra luoghi non molto distanti); *— -free,* esente da pedaggio; *— -gatherer,* gabelliere, daziere; *— -house,* casello del dazio; *— -traverse,* diritto di passaggio (per proprietà privata) ‖ *road —,* mortalità per incidenti stradali.

to toll[1], *v.t.i.* (*rar.*) **1.** imporre, riscuotere pedaggio, dazio, gabella **2.** far pagare come pedaggio, dazio, gabella; far pagare un dazio, un pedaggio a.

toll[2], *s.* rintocco (di campana).

to toll[2], *v.t.i.* **1.** rintoccare, suonare, battere, scandire: *the clock tolls the hours,* l'orologio batte le ore; *I heard the bell —,* udii suonare la campana **2.** annunciare con rintocchi; chiamare a raccolta: *to — the people in,* chiamare i fedeli in chiesa; *to — s.o.'s death,* suonare a morto per qlcu.

tollable ['touləbl], *ag.* soggetto a pedaggio, dazio, gabella.

tollage ['toulidʒ], *s.* pedaggio, dazio, gabella.

tollbooth, *V.* **tolbooth**.

tolldish ['tɔldiʃ], *s.* piatto per misurare la molenda.

toller[1] ['toulə*], *s.* (*rar.*) gabelliere, daziere.

toller[2], *s.* chi suona a rintocco.

tolling ['touliŋ], *s.* rintocco.

tollman, *pl.* **tollmen** ['toulmən], *s.* gabelliere, daziere.

tollol [,tɔl'lɔl], *ag.* (*sl.*) passabile, discreto, mediocre.

tolly ['tɔli], *s.* (*sl. scolastico*) candela.

Toltec ['tɔltek], *s.c.* tolteco, tolteca.

Toltecan ['tɔltekən], *ag.* tolteco.

tolu [tou'lu:], *s.* (*bot.*) tolù.

toluene ['tɔljui:n], *s.* (*chim.*) toluene, toluolo.

Tom [tɔm], *no.pr.m. dim.* di **Thomas** ‖ *—, Dick and Harry,* Tizio, Caio e Sempronio; *every —, Dick and Harry,* chiunque, qualsiasi persona ‖ *— and Jerry shop,* birreria, taverna di infimo ordine ‖ *— o' Bedlam,* accattone, mendicante ‖ *— Thumb,* Pollicino ‖ *— Thumb nasturtium,* (*bot.*) nasturzio nano ‖ *— Tiddler's ground,* terra di nessuno (dal nome di un giuoco di bambini) ‖ **tom,** *s. —* (*cat*), gatto ☆ *Tom long,* chi è sempre in ritardo; *Tom -noddy,* scimunito, imbecille; *Tom tiler,* uomo qualunque; *tom truth,* persona senza peli sulla lingua; *tom turkey,* tacchino ‖ *blind Tom,* (*giuoco*) mosca cieca; *great Tom,* campanone del Christ Church College (a Oxford); *Long Tom,* cannone a grande gettata; *Old Tom,* (*sl.*) gin; *peeping Tom,* persona curiosa.

tomahawk ['tɔməhɔ:k], *s.* « tomahawk », (ascia di guerra degli indiani del Nord America): *to bury* (o *to lay aside*) *the —,* seppellire l'ascia di guerra; *fig.* cessare le ostilità; *to dig up* (o *to raise* o *to take up*) *the —,* disseppellire l'ascia di guerra; *fig.* aprire le ostilità.

to tomahawk, *v.t.* **1.** uccidere, colpire con il « tomahawk » **2.** *fig.* criticare, attaccare aspramente (un'opera letteraria, ecc.).

toman [tou'mɑ:n], *s.* (*scoz.*) collina morenica.

tomato [tə'mɑ:tou], *pl.* **tomatoes** [tə'mɑ:touz], *s.* pomodoro ☆ *— juice,* succo di pomodoro; *— ketchup,* salsa rubra; *— sauce,* salsa di pomodoro.

tomb [tu:m], *s.* tomba, sepolcro: *to go down into the —,* scendere nella tomba; *to rifle a —,* violare una tomba ‖ *beyond the —,* *fig.* dopo la morte.

to tomb, *v.t.* seppellire; racchiudere in una tomba.

tombac ['tɔmbək], *s.* (*metal.*) tombacco.

tombless ['tu:mlis], *ag.* senza tomba, senza sepoltura.

tombola ['tɔmbələ], *s.* tombola.

tomboy ['tɔmbɔi], *s.* **1.** ragazza indiavolata, maschiaccio **2.** (*lett.*) ragazza immodesta.

tombstone ['tu:m-stoun], *s.* pietra sepolcrale, tombale.

tome [toum], *s.* **1.** tomo, volume **2.** lettera, epistola papale.

tomentose [tou'mentous], **tomentous** [tou'mentəs], *ag.* (*bot.*) tomentoso.

tomentum [tou'mentəm], *s.* (*bot.*) tomento.

tomfool ['tɔm'fu:l], *ag.s.* sciocco, stupido.

to tomfool, *v.i.* fare lo sciocco, lo stupido.

tomfoolery [tɔm'fu:ləri], *s.* scemenza, stupidaggine.

Tommy ['tɔmi], *no.pr.m. dim.* di **Thomas** ‖ *—* (*Atkins*), soldato semplice inglese ‖ **tommy,** *s.* **1.** pane, pagnotta; generi alimentari **2.** provviste (che l'operaio si porta da casa per la colazione) **3.** (*mec.*) spina, spezzone di ferro tondo ☆ *— -bar,* (*mec.*) spina; *— -gun,* fucile mitragliatore, mitra; *— -rot,* sciocchezze, assurdità ‖ *soft —,* (*sl. mar.*) pane fresco.

tomorrow, to-morrow [tə'mɔrou], *av.* domani: *— week,* domani a otto; *we shall meet —,* ci incontreremo domani ‖ *s.* domani: *—'s paper,* il giornale di domani; *the day after —,* dopodomani; *without a —,* senza un domani; *who knows what — holds!,* chi sa cosa ci riserba il domani! ‖ *— never comes, prov.* domani vuol dire mai; *never put off till — what you can do to-day, prov.* non rimandare mai a domani ciò che puoi fare oggi.

tompion ['tɔmpjən], *V.* **tampion**.

tomtit ['tɔm'tit], *s.* (*ornit.*) cinciazzurra; cincia.

tomtom ['tɔmtɔm], *s.* tam-tam (tamburo di popolo primitivo).

to tomtom, *v.i.* battere, suonare il tam-tam.

ton[1] [tʌn], *s.* **1.** (*long* o *gross* o *shipper's*) *—,* tonnellata (misura di peso = kg. 1·016); (*short*) *—,* tonnellata (= kg. 907,18 usata negli Stati Uniti, nel Canada, in Sud-Africa); *metric —,* tonnellata metrica (= 2,204.6 lb.) **2.** (*fam.*) gran quantità: *he knows tons o, people in London,* conosce moltissime persone a Londra; *he has tons of money,* ha un sacco di soldi **3.** (*mar.*) tonnellata di stazza.

ton[2] [tɔŋ], *s.* (*rar.*) **1.** moda; eleganza **2.** gente alla moda; mondo elegante.

tonal ['tounl], *ag.* (*mus.*) tonale.

tonality [tou'næliti], *s.* (*mus. pitt.*) tonalità.

tone [toun], *s.* **1.** tono; timbro; accento; intonazione; inflessione: *the deep — of a bell,* il timbro profondo di una campana; *a low — of voice,* un basso timbro di voce; *our letter had a friendly —,* la nostra lettera aveva un tono amichevole; *then he changed his —,* allora cambiò tono **2.** (*comm.*) tendenza, inclinazione: *the — of the market,* la tendenza del mercato **3.** (*med.*) tono (fisico): *want of —,* atonia ‖ *to los —,* deprimersi **4.** (*fonet.*) accento tonico **5.** (*pitt.*) tono sfumatura: *a light* — *of blue*, una lieve sfumatura d'azzurro ☆ — *-arm*, braccio di radiogrammofono; — *-poem*, (*mus.*) poema sinfonico ‖ *Gregorian tones*, canto gregoriano.

to **tone**, *v.t.i.* **1.** (*mus.*) dare il tono a, accordare (strumenti); intonare **2.** (*pitt.*) sfumare, modificare la tonalità di **3.** armonizzare, accordarsi, intonarsi: *the carpet does not* — (*in* with) *the curtains*, il tappeto non s'intona con le tende **4.** (*foto.*) virare **5.** *to* — **down**, addolcire, addolcirsi; attenuare, attenuarsi; sfumare **6.** *to* — **up**, tonificare, tonificarsi; ritemprare, ritemprarsi.

toned [tound], *ag.* **1.** intonato; con tono, con tonalità, con intonazione **2.** (*pitt.*) sfumato, colorato; (*foto.*) virato **3.** — (*up*), tonificato ☆ — *paper*, carta color avorio ‖ *high-* —, in tono elevato; *low-* —, a bassa voce, a bassa tonalità.

toneless [ˈtounlis], *ag.* **1.** senza tono; inespressivo **2.** privo di colore **3.** privo di vigore.

tonelessly [ˈtounlisli], *av.* **1.** senza tono; inespressivamente **2.** senza colore **3.** senza vigore.

tonelessness [ˈtounlisnis], *s.* **1.** mancanza di tono, di tonalità; inespressività **2.** mancanza di colore **3.** atonia.

tong [tɔŋ], *s.* società segreta (in Cina).

Tonga [ˈtɔŋə], *no.pr.* (*geog.*) Tonga.

tonga [ˈtɔŋgə], *s.* veicolo leggero a due ruote (in India).

tongs [tɔŋz], *s.pl.* pinza; molle; tenaglia: *a pair of* —, un paio di molle, di tenaglie ‖ *hammer and* —, con tutte le forze, con ogni energia ‖ *not to touch with a pair of* —, da non toccarsi nemmeno con le molle ☆ *curling* —, ferro da ricci; *fire* —, molle per il fuoco; *sugar* —, mollette per lo zucchero; *welder's* —, tenaglia da saldatore.

tongue [tʌŋ], *s.* **1.** lingua: *to have a dirty* —, avere la lingua sporca, patinosa; *to put out one's* —, tirar fuori, mostrare la lingua ‖ *to be on the tongues of men*, essere sulla bocca di tutti ‖ *to have sthg. on the tip of one's* —, aver ql.co. sulla punta della lingua **2.** lingua, favella, parola; discorso: *to have a glib* —, avere la lingua sciolta, lo scilinguagnolo sciolto; *to have a ready* —, avere la lingua pronta; *to have a sharp* —, avere la lingua tagliente; *to have a smooth* —, avere la parola facile ‖ *slip of the* —, lapsus linguae ‖ *to bridle one's* —, tenere la lingua a freno; *to guard one's* —, misurare le parole ‖ *to find one's* —, ritrovare, riacquistare la favella ‖ *to hold one's* —, mantenere il silenzio ‖ *to keep a civil* — *in one's head*, tenere un linguaggio educato ‖ *to lose one's* —, perdere la favella ‖ *to speak with one's* — *in one's cheek*, parlare ironicamente ‖ *to wag one's* —, parlare a vanvera ‖ *the* — *is sharper than any sword*, *prov.* ne uccide più la lingua che la spada **3.** lingua, linguaggio, idioma: *the English* —, la lingua inglese ‖ *the tongues*, le lingue straniere, le lingue classiche **4.** lingua (di terra, di fuoco); linguetta (di scarpa); battaglio (di campana); puntale (di fibbia); ago (di bilancia); timone (di carro); (*ferr.*) ago; (*mec.*) linguetta, aletta, flangia **5.** (*mus.*) linguetta, ancia ☆ — *-bone*, (*anat.*) ioide; — *-fish*, (*ittiol.*) sogliola; — *-shaped*, linguiforme, a forma di lingua; — *-tie*, (*patol.*) anchiloglossia; — *-tied*, bleso; muto, ammutolito; taciturno, reticente; — *-twister*, scioglilingua; — *-worm*, (*entom.*) linguatula ‖ *hart's* —, (*bot.*) lingua cervina; *hound's* —, (*bot.*) cinoglossa; *mother-* —, lingua materna; lingua madre; *smoked* —, (*cuc.*) lingua affumicata.

to **tongue**, *v.t.i.* **1.** toccare con la lingua; lambire; leccare **2.** protendersi, sporgersi (come una lingua); emettere lingue (di fuoco) **3.** dire; pronunciare; parlare, chiacchierare: *to* — (*it*) *incessantly*, parlare incessantemente **4.** rimproverare; sgridare **5.** (*mus.*) staccare (note); produrre effetto di staccato (servendosi di strumenti a fiato) **6.** (*tec.*) incastrare, tagliare a linguetta.

tongued [tʌŋd], *ag.* **1.** munito di lingua, linguet-

---

ta **2.** linguacciuto ☆ *close-* —, discreto, taciturno; *double-* —, falso; *two-* —, bilingue.

tongueless [ˈtʌŋlis], *ag.* **1.** senza lingua **2.** muto, ammutolito; silenzioso.

tonguelet [ˈtʌŋlit], *s.* linguetta.

tonguey [ˈtʌŋi], *ag.* linguale.

tonic [ˈtɔnik], *ag.* **1.** tonico, corroborante, energetico **2.** (*mus. fonet.*) tonico ‖ *s.* **1.** (*med.*) tonico **2.** (*mus.*) tonica ☆ — *chord*, (*mus.*) accordo naturale; — *spasm*, (*med.*) spasmo tonico.

tonically [ˈtɔnikəli], *av.* in modo tonico.

tonicity [touˈnisiti], *s.* tonicità.

tonight, to-night [təˈnait], *s.* questa notte; questa sera.

tonight, to-night, *av.* stanotte; stasera.

tonnage [ˈtʌnidʒ], *s.* **1.** (*mar.*) tonnellaggio, stazza, portata; *fig.* traffico marittimo **2.** tonnellaggio, tassa per tonnellata ‖ — *and poundage*, (*st.*) tassa imposta su ogni barile di vino e ogni libbra di merce esportata e importata **3.** (*rar.*) tonnellaggio, peso in tonnellate ☆ — *-deck*, (*mar.*) ponte di stazza ‖ *dead-weight* —, (*mar.*) portata lorda; *displacement* —, (*mar.*) tonnellaggio di dislocamento; *gross* —, (*mar.*) stazza lorda; *net-* — (o *registered* —), (*mar.*) stazza netta.

tonner [ˈtʌnə*], *s.* nave di determinato tonnellaggio: *a five thousand* —, una nave di 5·000 tonnellate.

tonometer [touˈnɔmitə*], *s.* (*fis.*) tonometro.

tonsil [ˈtɔnsl], *s.* (*anat.*) tonsilla.

tonsilar, tonsillar [ˈtɔnsilə*], **tonsillary** [ˈtɔnsiləri], *ag.* (*anat.*) tonsillare.

tonsillectomy [ˌtɔnsiˈlæktəmi], *s.* (*chir.*) tonsillectomia.

tonsillitic [ˌtɔnsiˈlitik], *ag.* tonsillare.

tonsillitis [ˌtɔnsiˈlaitis], *s.* (*patol.*) tonsillite.

tonsillotomy [ˌtɔnsiˈlɔtəmi], *s.* (*chir.*) tonsillectomia.

tonsor [ˈtɔnsə*], *s.* barbiere, barbitonsore.

tonsorial [tɔnˈsɔːriəl], *ag.* di barbiere.

tonsure [ˈtɔnʃə*], *s.* tonsura; chierica.

to **tonsure**, *v.t.* tonsurare.

tonsured [ˈtɔnʃəd], *ag.* tonsurato.

tontine [tɔnˈtiːn], *s.* (*dir.*) tontina.

tonus [ˈtounəs], *s.* **1.** (*med.*) tono, tonicità **2.** (*med.*) spasmo tonico.

Tony [ˈtouni], *no.pr.m. dim.* di **Antony**.

tony, *ag.* (*amer. iron.*) elegante, di stile.

too [tuː], *av.* **1.** troppo: — *many friends*, troppi amici; — *much work*, troppo lavoro; *he is* — *lazy*, è troppo pigro; *he is* — *kind a man*, è un uomo troppo gentile; *he studies* — *little*, studia troppo poco; *I gave him one pound* — *much*, gli diedi una sterlina di troppo; *I was one* — *many there*, ero di troppo là ‖ — *bad!*, che peccato! ‖ *this is* — *much* (*of a good thing*), (*fam.*) questo è troppo, è intollerabile ‖ — *much of a good thing is good for nothing*, *prov.* il troppo stroppia **2.** **anche, pure:** *I shall come* —, verrò anch'io; *I told him* —, lo dissi anche a lui; *she works much* —, anche lei lavora molto **3.** **inoltre, per di più:** *the woman*, —, *was big with child*, la donna, per di più, aspettava un bambino **4.** (*fam.*) **veramente, estremamente:** *I am* — *glad*, sono veramente contento.

took [tuk], *pass.* di to **take**.

too-too [ˈtuːtuː], *ag.* **1.** squisito **2.** esuberante, espansivo ‖ *av.* davvero, veramente troppo.

tool [tuːl], *s.* **1.** arnese, attrezzo, utensile, strumento; (*arc.*) arma: *the tools of one's trade*, i ferri del mestiere; *the tools of a shoemaker*, gli arnesi del calzolaio; *books are a scholar's tools*, i libri sono gli strumenti dello studioso **2.** rullo, timbro per decorazione (del rilegatore); pennello (per imbianchino, decoratore) **3.** *fig.* strumento; burattino, fantoccio: *he had become the tyrant's* —, era divenuto lo strumento del tiranno; *he was a mere* — *in their hands*, era solo un burattino nelle loro mani; *to make a* — *of s.o.*, servirsi di qlcu. **4.** (*machine*) —, macchina utensile ☆ — *-bag*, borsa attrezzi; — *-box* (o — *-case*), cassetta attrezzi; — *-car*, carro attrezzi; — *maker*, chi fabbrica utensili, attrezzista; fabbro; — -post (o — -rest), portautensile; — -roll, borsa, « trousse » per gli arnesi ‖ broad- —, scalpello da muratore; edge- —, utensili da taglio; gardening tools, attrezzi da giardimaggio.

to **tool**, v.t.i. 1. lavorare (con arnesi) 2. martellinare (pietra) 3. decorare (una rilegatura) 4. (sl.) guidare (carrozza, ecc.); scarrozzare; portare, andare (su veicoli): to — through the park, scarrozzare per il parco 5. fornire di arnesi, macchinario; attrezzare: to — a factory, attrezzare una fabbrica.

tooler['tu:lə*], s. 1. martellinatore 2. decoratore (di rilegature di libri) 3. martellina, scalpello da muratore.

tooling ['tu:liŋ], s. 1. martellinatura (di pietra) 2. decorazione (di rilegature) ☆ gold- —, doratura.

toom [tu:m], ag. (scoz.) vuoto.

to **toom**, v.t. (scoz.) vuotare.

toon [tu:n], s. (bot.) acagiù.

toot [tu:t], s. suono di corno, cornetta, tromba; colpo di clacson, fischio di sirena.

to **toot**, v.t.i. suonare; suonare il clacson; suonare uno strumento a fiato; emettere suoni (di strumento a fiato): to — the horn, dare un colpo di clacson.

tooth [tu:θ], pl. **teeth** [ti:θ], s. 1. dente; zanna: artificial (o false) —, dente finto; cutting of teeth, dentizione; set of false teeth, dentiera; you have a fine set of teeth, hai una bella dentatura; to cut one's teeth, mettere i denti; to have a — out, farsi cavare un dente; to lose a —, perdere un dente ‖ armed to the teeth, fig. armato fino ai denti ‖ from the teeth outwards, (arc.) insinceramente ‖ in the teeth of, a dispetto di; in opposizione a; in faccia a ‖ to be long in the —, non essere più giovane ‖ to cast (o to throw) sthg. in one's teeth, rinfacciare ql.co. a qlcu. ‖ to escape by the skin of one's teeth, cavarsela per il rotto della cuffia ‖ to fight — and nail, combattere con accanimento ‖ to grind one's teeth, digrignare i denti ‖ to set one's teeth, stringere i denti ‖ to set one's teeth on edge, far allegare i denti ‖ to show one's teeth, fig. mostrare i denti ‖ to take the bit between one's teeth, respingere ogni controllo, impennarsi ‖ an eye for an eye, a — for a —, occhio per occhio, dente per dente 2. dente (di forchetta, pettine, ecc.); dente d'ingranaggio 3. fig. gusto, appetito ‖ she has a sweet —, è ghiotta di dolci ‖ to lie in one's teeth, (arc.) mentire per la gola 4. (tec.) grana (di carta, superficie, ecc.) ☆ — -billed, dal becco dentellato (di uccello); — -chisel, (edil.) gradina; — -drawer, (sl.) dentista; — -like, dentiforme; — -ornament, (arch.) dentello; — -paste, dentifricio; — -pick, stuzzicadenti; — -powder, polvere dentifricia; — -rash, (patol.) strofulo; — -socket, alveolo dentario ‖ back- —, (dente) molare; buck- —, dente sporgente; canine — (o eye- —), (dente) canino; gullet —, (strum. artig.) dente a becco; incisive-, (dente) incisivo; milk- —, dente di latte; wisdom- —, dente del giudizio.

to **tooth**, v.t.i. 1. fornire di denti; dentellare 2. (mec.) ingranarsi 3. mordere, rosicchiare.

toothache ['tu:θ-eik], s. mal di denti.

toothbrush ['tu:θbrʌʃ], s. spazzolino da denti.

toothed [tu:θt], ag. 1. dentato, a denti 2. (bot.) dentellato ☆ — -bar, dentiera; — gearing, (mec.) trasmissione ad ingranaggi; — wheel, (mec.) ruota dentata.

toothful ['tu:θful], s. piccolo boccone (di cibo); sorso (di liquore, ecc.).

toothing ['tu:θiŋ], s. 1. dentatura; dentellatura 2. (edil.) addentellato ☆ — plane, (strum. artig.) pialla con ferro a denti; — -stone, (edil.) morsa di muro, addentellato.

toothless ['tu:θlis], ag. senza denti, sdentato.

toothlet ['tu:θlit], s. dentino.

toothsome ['tu:θsəm], ag. 1. gustoso, saporito (di cibo) 2. (arc.) ghiotto, goloso (di persona).

toothsomeness ['tu:θsəmnis], s. gustosità, sapore gradevole.

toothy ['tu:θi], ag. 1. dentato; dai denti sporgenti 2. gustoso, saporito.

tootle ['tu:tl], s. 1. modulazione 2. chiacchiere vane, senza senso.

to **tootle**, v.i. 1. modulare 2. scrivere parole senza senso.

tootsy(-wootsy) ['tutsi('wutsi)], s. piedino (nel linguaggio infantile).

top[1] [tɔp], s. 1. cima, sommità; fig. apice, apogeo: the — of the hill, la cima della collina; he was at the — of his profession, era all'apice della sua carriera ‖ — of the morning to you!, (irl.) buongiorno! ‖ at the — of the tree, fig. all'apice, al primo posto ‖ from — to bottom, da cima a fondo, completamente; from — to toe, dalla testa ai piedi ‖ on the — of it, inoltre ‖ to blow one's —, (sl.) andare fuori dai gangheri; dare i numeri ‖ to come to the —, ottenere fama, successo ‖ to run at the — of one's speed, correre a tutta velocità; to shout at the — of one's voice, gridare a squarciagola 2. superficie; piano, parte superiore; « capote » (di automobile); imperiale (di diligenza) 3. (mar.) coffa 4. (ind. tessile) nastro pettinato ☆ — -boot, stivale con risvolto; — -dog, (sl.) vincitore, capo; — -dressing, (agr.) concimazione in superficie; — -form, gran forma: to be in — -form, essere in gran forma; — gear, (aut.) presa diretta; — -hat, cappello a cilindro; — -heavy, sovraccarico; (sl.) brillo; — -hole, (sl.) di prima qualità; — -light, (mar.) fanale di gabbia; — -management, (comm.) direzione generale; — -secret, segreto di importanza vitale; — -side, la parte superiore; (mar.) opera morta ‖ turnip-tops, (cuc.) cime di rapa.

to **top**[1], pass.p.p. **topped** [tɔpt], v.t. 1. coprire: — that bottle, please, metti il tappo a quella bottiglia, per favore 2. raggiungere la sommità di; essere sulla cima di; fig. essere all'apice di 3. essere a capo di; superare; essere più alto, più importante di 4. svettare (alberi) 5. misurare (di altezza): that boy tops five feet, quel ragazzo è alto cinque piedi 6. to — off, terminare, concludere; dare il tocco finale a 7. to — up, riempire; terminare; dare il tocco finale a: — it up with water, riempilo fino all'orlo di acqua; she topped up her dinner with an ice-cream, concluse il pranzo con un gelato.

top[2], s. trottola ‖ to sleep like a —, dormire come un ghiro.

to **top**[3], v.t.i. 1. (mar.) imbroncare 2. inclinarsi.

topaz ['toupæz], s. topazio (anche ornit.).

topazolite [tou'pæzoulait], s. (min.) topazolite.

topcoat ['tɔp'kout], s. soprabito pesante.

tope[1] [toup], s. (ang.-in.) boschetto (di manghi).

tope[2], s. monumento buddista (in India).

tope[3], s. pescecane.

to **tope**[4], v.t.i. bere; sbevazzare; ubriacarsi.

toper ['toupə*], s. (fam.) beone, ubriacone.

topflight ['tɔp-flait], ag. (sl. amer.) migliore.

topgallant [tɔp'gælənt], ag. (mar.) sopra la linea di congiunzione ☆ — mast, alberello.

toph [touf], V. **tophus**.

tophaceous [tou'feiʃəs], ag. 1. (med.) tartareo 2. (min.) tufaceo.

Tophet ['toufet], no.pr. (geog. biblica) Tophet ‖ s. fig. inferno.

tophus ['toufəs], pl. **tophi** ['toufai], s. 1. (med.) tartaro 2. (min.) tufo.

topia ['toupiə], s. decorazione murale a paesaggi (presso gli antichi romani).

topiary ['toupjəri], ag. di taglio ornamentale (di piante, arbusti) ☆ — art, arte di tosare le piante.

topic ['tɔpik], s. 1. argomento, soggetto, tema: it's the — of the day, è l'argomento del giorno; (ret.) topica.

topical ['tɔpikəl], ag. 1. d'attualità: — allusion, allusione ai fatti del giorno; — film, film di attualità 2. (ret.) topico 3. (med.) topico, locale.

topknot ['tɔpnɔt], s. 1. nastro da capelli 2. ciuffo, cresta.

topless ['tɔplis], *ag.* **1.** senza cima, senza testa **2.** *fig.* altissimo, irraggiungibile.

toplofty ['tɔp'lɔfti], *ag.* (*scherz.*) vanitoso; borioso.

topman, *pl.* **topmen** ['tɔpmən], *s.* (*mar.*) gabbiere.

topmast ['tɔpmɑːst], *s.* (*mar.*) albero di gabbia.

topmost ['tɔpmoust], *ag.* il più alto, il più elevato.

topographer [tə'pɔgrəfə*], *s.* topografo.

topographie(al) [,tɔpə'græfik(əl)], *ag.* topografico.

topographically [,tɔpə'græfikəli], *av.* topograficamente.

topography [tə'pɔgrəfi], *s.* topografia.

toponymy [tə'pɔnimi], *s.* toponomastica.

topped [tɔpt], *ag.* **1.** fornito di cima, di punta **2.** (*bot.*) dalla cima troncata; svettato.

topper ['tɔpə*], *s.c.* (*fam.*) persona, cosa che eccelle ‖ *s.* (*sl.*) cappello a cilindro.

topping ['tɔpiŋ], *ag.* **1.** eminente; eccellente; di prima qualità; principale **2.** (*amer.*) presuntuoso; arrogante ‖ *s.* **1.** svettamento **2.** (*ind. chim.*) predistillazione **3.** cresta; ciuffo; (*scherz.*) testa **4.** *pl.* fronde tagliate.

toppingly ['tɔpiŋli], *av.* in maniera superiore, eccellentemente.

to topple ['tɔpl], *v.t.i.*: *to — down*, **over**, vacillare, far vacillare; traballare, far traballare; cadere, far cadere: *to — the building down*, far crollare l'edificio; *to bring the Government toppling down*, rovesciare il governo.

topsail ['tɔpsl], *s.* (*mar.*) vela di gabbia, seconda vela.

topsyturvily ['tɔpsi'tə:vili], *av.* sottosopra, disordinatamente.

topsyturviness ['tɔpsi'tə:vinis], *s.* disordine; scompiglio.

topsyturvy ['tɔpsi'tə:vi], *ag.* capovolto; sottosopra; disordinato, scompigliato: *to turn sthg.* —, rovesciare ql.co., mettere ql.co. sottosopra ‖ *s.* capovolgimento; scompiglio, soqquadro, confusione, disordine.

to topsyturvy, *v.t.* capovolgere; mettere sossopra, mettere a soqquadro.

topsyturvy, *av.* sottosopra, in disordine.

topsyturvydom ['tɔpsi'tə:vidəm], *s.* regno del disordine.

toque [touk], *s.* **1.** (*st.*) berretto **2.** « toque », tocco; cuffia **3.** specie di scimmia (« Macacus pileatus »).

tor [tɔ:*], *s.* picco, sommità rocciosa.

torch [tɔ:tʃ], *s.* torcia, fiaccola ‖ *to hand on the* —, *fig.* tener viva la fiaccola ☆ — *-bearer*, portatore di fiaccola; — *-fishing*, pesca notturna (con lampara); — *-igniter*, (*mec.*) accenditore; — *-race*, (*st.*) corsa tra portatori di fiaccole ‖ *electric* —, lampadina tascabile; *oxyhydrogen* —, cannello ossidrico.

torchlight ['tɔ:tʃ-lait], *s.* **1.** luce di fiaccole, torce **2.** illuminazione con fiaccole ☆ — *procession*, fiaccolata.

torchon ['tɔ:ʃən], *s.* strofinaccio ☆ — *lace*, varietà di pizzo a trama rada; — *paper*, carta ruvida per dipingere (specialmente acquerello).

tore[1] [tɔ:*], *s.* (*arch. geom.*) toro.

tore[2], *pass.* di to **tear**.

toreador ['tɔriədɔ:*], *s.* torero.

toreutic [tə'ru:tik], *ag.* di, della toreutica.

toreutics [tə'ru:tiks], *s.* toreutica.

torment ['tɔ:ment], *s.* **1.** tormento, tortura; supplizio; strazio: *the torments of jealousy*, il tormento della gelosia; *she suffered torments*, soffrì terribilmente; *to be in* —, essere torturato, patire la tortura **2.** causa di sofferenze, preoccupazioni: *that boy is a positive* —, quel ragazzo è un vero tormento.

to torment [tɔ:'ment], *v.t.* tormentare, torturare: *she is tormented with remorse*, è tormentata dal rimorso; *to be tormented by a disease*, essere tormentato da una malattia.

tormentil ['tɔ:məntil], *s.* (*bot.*) tormentilla.

tormentingly [tɔ:'mentiŋli], *av.* tormentosamente.

tormentor [tɔ:'mentə*], *s.* **1.** tormentatore, torturatore **2.** cosa che tormenta **3.** (*agr.*) erpice **4.** (*cine.*) schermo trasportabile usato nei teatri di posa per ridurre la riverberazione.

tormentress [tɔ:'mentris], *s.* tormentatrice.

tormentum [tɔ:'mentəm], *pl.* **tormenta** [tɔ:'mentə], *s.* (*mil. st.*) tormento, catapulta.

torn [tɔ:n], *p.p.* di to **tear**.

tornado [tɔ:'neidou], *s.* tornado, ciclone, uragano (anche *fig.*).

torose [tɔ:'rous], **torous** ['tɔurəs], *ag.* **1.** nodoso (di pianta) **2.** che ha protuberanze (di animale).

torpedo [tɔ:'pi:dou], *pl.* **torpedoes** [tɔ:'pi:douz], *s.* **1.** (*ittiol.*) torpedine **2.** (*mar.*) torpedine, siluro ☆ — *-boat*, torpediniera; — *-boat destroyer*, cacciatorpediniere; — *-net*, rete di protezione (contro i siluri); — *plane*, aerosilurante; — *-tube*, lanciasiluri.

to torpedo, *v.t.* **1.** colpire, distruggere con torpedini, silurare **2.** *fig.* paralizzare, silurare: *to — the negotiations*, far fallire i negoziati.

torpid ['tɔ:pid], *ag.* **1.** torpido; intorpidito **2.** apatico, inerte.

torpidity [tɔ:'piditi], *s.* **1.** torpore **2.** apatia, inerzia.

torpidly ['tɔ:pidli], *av.* **1.** torpidamente **2.** apaticamente, indifferentemente.

torpidness ['tɔ:pidnis], *s.* **1.** torpore **2.** apatia, inerzia.

to torpify [tɔ:'pifai], *v.t.* intorpidire.

torpor ['tɔ:pə*], *s.* **1.** torpore **2.** apatia, inerzia.

torquate(d) ['tɔ:kweit(id)], *ag.* con collare, dal collare (di animale).

torque[1] [tɔ:k], *s.* collana, monile (portato da Galli e Britanni).

torque[2], *s.* (*mec.*) coppia ☆ — *stress*, (*edil.*) sollecitazione di torsione ‖ *starting* —, (*elett. mec.*) coppia d'avviamento.

torrefaction [,tɔri'fækʃən], *s.* torrefazione.

to torrefy ['tɔrifai], *v.t.* torrefare, tostare.

torrent ['tɔrənt], *s.* torrente (anche *fig.*): *a — of tears*, un fiume di lacrime; *the rain fell in torrents*, la pioggia cadeva a torrenti.

torrential [tɔ'renʃəl], *ag.* **1.** torrenziale **2.** torrentizio.

torrentially [tɔ'renʃəli], *av.* torrenzialmente; a torrenti.

Torricellian [,tɔri'tʃeliən], *ag.* (*fis.*) di Torricelli, torricelliano.

torrid ['tɔrid], *ag.* torrido ☆ — *zone*, zona torrida.

torridity [tɔ'riditi], **torridness** ['tɔridnis], *s.* calore torrido.

torsel ['tɔ:səl], *s.* **1.** voluta, ornamento a spirale **2.** (*edil.*) tassello.

torsion ['tɔ:ʃən], *s.* torsione.

torsional ['tɔ:ʃən], *ag.* di torsione.

torsk [tɔ:sk], *s.* (*ittiol.*) brosmio (pesce dei Gadidi).

torso ['tɔ:sou], *pl.* **torsos** ['tɔ:souz], *s.* **1.** (*scult.*) torso **2.** opera mutilata, incompiuta.

tort [tɔ:t], *s.* (*dir.*) torto, danno.

torticollis [,tɔ:ti'kɔlis], *s.* torcicollo.

tortile [tɔ:'tail], *ag.* ritorto, a spire.

tortility [tɔ:'tiliti], *s.* tortezza.

tortilla [tə'ti:ljə], *s.* « tortilla » (focaccia messicana di granoturco).

tortious ['tɔ:ʃəs], *ag.* (*dir.*) dannoso, pregiudizievole.

tortiously ['tɔ:ʃəsli], *av.* (*dir.*) dannosamente, pregiudizievolmente.

tortoise ['tɔ:təs], *s.* **1.** tartaruga **2.** (*st. romana*) testuggine ☆ — *-shell*, guscio di tartaruga; tartaruga (lavorata); — *-shell cat*, gatto variegato ‖ *alligator* —, (*zool.*) chelidro.

tortrix ['tɔ:triks], *s.* (*zool.*) tortrice.

tortuosity [,tɔ:tju'ɔsiti], *s.* tortuosità.

tortuous ['tɔ:tjuəs], *ag.* tortuoso.

tortuously ['tɔ:tjuəsli], *av.* tortuosamente.

tortuousity [,tɔ:tju'ɔsiti], **tortuousness** ['tɔ:tjuəsnis], *s.* tortuosità.

torture ['tɔ:tʃə*], *s.* **1.** tortura, strumento di tortura: *he was put to the* —, fu sottoposto alla tortura **2.** tormento (anche *fig.*): *his life was one long* —, la sua vita è stata un lungo calvario; *toothache is a real* —, il mal di denti è un vero tormento.

to **torture**, *v.t.* **1.** torturare, porre alla tortura **2.** tormentare, affliggere: *he was tortured by fear*, era tormentato dalla paura **3.** *fig.* distorcere, sforzare il senso di: *that passage has been completely tortured*, il senso di quel brano è stato svisato completamente.

torturer ['tɔːtʃərə*], *s.* aguzzino.

torturingly ['tɔːtʃəriŋli], *av.* in modo torturante.

torturous ['tɔːtʃərəs], *ag.* tormentoso.

torus ['tɔːrəs], *pl.* **tori** ['tɔːrai], *s.* **1.** (*arch. geom.*) toro **2.** (*bot.*) ricettacolo.

Tory ['tɔːri], *ag.* (*pol.*) conservatore: *the* — *Party*, il partito conservatore ‖ *s.* (*pol.*) Tory, conservatore ☆ — *Democrat*, conservatore democratico.

Toryism ['tɔːriizəm], *s.* (*pol.*) conservatorismo.

tosh [tɔʃ], *s.* (*sl.*) sciocchezza, stupidaggine.

tosher ['tɔʃə*], *s.* (*sl.*) studente universitario che non appartiene a nessun collegio.

toss [tɔs], *s.* **1.** lancio ‖ *pitch and* —, testa e croce; *to win the* —, vincere a testa e croce **2.** movimento del capo: *a* — *of the head*, una scrollata del capo; *she threw up her head with a scornful* —, alzò la testa con un movimento sdegnoso **3.** agitazione (anche *fig.*) **4.** caduta da cavallo: *to take a* —, essere sbalzato di sella ☆ — *up*, lancio in aria (di moneta); questione incerta.

to **toss**, *pass.p.p.* **tossed** [tɔst], (*poet.*) **tost** [tɔst], *v.t.i.* **1.** gettare, lanciare (in aria): *to* — *sthg. to s.o.*, gettare ql.co. a qlcu. ‖ *to* — (*the*) *oars*, alzare i remi (in segno di saluto) ‖ *to* — *one's money about*, sperperare il proprio denaro **2.** scuotere: *he tossed his head*, scosse la testa **3.** agitare, agitarsi (anche *fig.*); sbattere; sballottare; dimenarsi: *a ship tossed by the waves*, una nave sballottata dalle onde; *to* — *in bed*, rivoltarsi nel letto ‖ *this plan has been tossed about for years*, si discute questo progetto da molti anni ‖ *to pitch and* —, (*mar.*) beccheggiare **4.** tirare a sorte: *they tossed who should begin*, tirarono a sorte chi dovesse incominciare **5.** sbalzare (di sella) **6.** *to* — **aside, away**, gettare da parte **7.** *to* — **off**, bere avidamente; scrivere in fretta, buttar giù (articolo, ecc.); fare affrettatamente **8.** *to* — **up**, gettare in aria (una moneta); preparare in fretta (pranzo, ecc.).

tot[1] [tɔt], *s.c.* bimbetto, bimbetta: *books for tiny tots*, libri per i più piccini ‖ *s.* **1.** (*spec. dial.*) bicchierino **2.** sorso (di liquore).

tot[2], *s.* cifre da sommare; totale (di un'addizione).

to **tot**[2], *pass.p.p.* **totted** ['tɔtid], *v.t.i.*: *to* — **up**, (*fam.*) addizionare, sommare; ammontare: *it tots up to seven pounds*, ammonta a sette sterline.

total ['toutl], *ag.* totale, completo; assoluto: *his* — *ignorance of the subject*, la sua ignoranza assoluta in materia; *the war brought about the* — *loss of his fortune*, la guerra gli ha fatto perdere l'intero patrimonio ‖ *s.* totale: *our weekly expenses reach a total of...*, le nostre spese settimanali ammontano a....

to **total**, *pass.p.p.* **totalled** ['toutld], *v.t.i.* sommare, fare il totale di; ammontare a: — *these amounts for me*, fammi l'addizione di queste cifre; *the guests* — *fifty*, gli ospiti sono cinquanta in tutto.

totalitarian [,toutæli'tɛəriən], *ag.* totalitario: *a* — *state*, uno stato totalitario.

totalitarianism [,toutæli'tɛəriənizəm], *s.* totalitarismo.

totality [tou'tæliti], *s.* totalità.

totalization [,toutəli'zeiʃən], *s.* totalizzazione.

totalizator ['toutəlaizeitə*], *s.* totalizzatore.

to **totalize** ['toutəlaiz], *v.t.i.* **1.** totalizzare; calcolare in totale **2.** usare il totalizzatore (nelle scommesse).

totalizer ['toutəlaizə*], *s.* totalizzatore.

totally ['toutli], *av.* totalmente; completamente; interamente.

tote [tout], (*sl. abbr.*) di **total, totalizator**.

to **tote**, *v.t.* (*amer.*) portare, trasportare ‖ *to* — *fair*, (*fam.*) agire lealmente.

totem ['toutəm], *s.* totem.

totemism ['toutəmizəm], *s.* totemismo.

t'other, tother ['tʌðə*], *ag., pron.* (*dial. abbr.*) di *the other*), l'altro, l'altra: *I can't tell tother from which*, non posso distinguerli l'uno dall'altro.

to **totter** ['totə*], *v.i.* **1.** oscillare, barcollare; camminare barcollando ‖ *to* — *in*, entrare barcollando **2.** essere pericolante (anche *fig.*): *the Roman empire was tottering to its fall*, l'impero romano andava verso la sua rovina.

totterer ['totərə*], *s.c.* chi vacilla, barcolla.

tottering ['totəriŋ], *ag.* barcollante, vacillante; incerto, malsicuro (anche *fig.*): — *steps*, passi malsicuri.

totteringly ['totəriŋli], *av.* in modo traballante, barcollando.

tottery ['totəri], *ag.* vacillante, barcollante, malfermo.

toucan ['tuːkən], *s.* (*ornit. astr.*) tucano.

touch [tʌtʃ], *s.* **1.** tocco, colpetto: *at a* —, con un lieve tocco; *he felt a* — *on his arm*, si sentì toccare il braccio ‖ *to have a light* —, (*mus.*) avere un tocco delicato ‖ *to have a near* —, (*sl.*) scamparla bella **2.** tatto: *the sense of* —, il senso del tatto; *to know sthg. by the* —, riconoscere ql.co. al tatto **3.** contatto; rapporto; relazione: *to be in* — *with s.o.*, essere in contatto con qlcu.; *to get into* — *with s.o.*, mettersi in contatto con qlcu.; *to lose* — *with s.o.*, perdere i contatti con qlcu. **4.** tocco, tratto: *to give the last* — *to a work*, dare l'ultimo tocco a un lavoro **5.** piccola quantità; pizzico; leggero attacco (di malattia): *a* — *of flu*, una leggera influenza; *a* — *of irony*, una punta d'ironia; *a* — *of madness*, un pizzico di follia **6.** (*arc.*) pietra di paragone **7.** (*rugby*) « touche ».

to **touch**, *v.t.i.* **1.** toccare, tastare, palpare: *don't* — *my papers!*, non toccate le mie carte!; *I have already touched these subjects*, *fig.* ho già sfiorato questi argomenti; *to* — *s.o.'s shoulder*, toccare qlcu. sulla spalla; *to* — *s.o. slightly*, sfiorare qlcu.; *to* — *sthg. with one's hand*, toccare ql.co. con la mano ‖ *we have not touched food for two days*, non tocchiamo cibo da due giorni ‖ *to* — *the bell*, suonare il campanello ‖ *to* — *the harp*, suonare l'arpa ‖ *to* — *one's hat*, portare la mano al cappello (per salutare) ‖ *to* — *one's horse with the spur*, spronare il cavallo **2.** *fig.* toccare, commuovere, colpire: *I was touched by his kindness*, fui commosso dalla sua gentilezza; *to* — *s.o.'s heart*, toccare il cuore di qlcu.; *to* — *s.o. to the quick*, toccare qlcu. sul vivo **3.** toccare, raggiungere (anche *fig.*): *the law can't* — *him*, *fig.* la legge non può nulla contro di lui; *no one can* — *him in comedy*, (*fam.*) non c'è nessuno che lo eguagli nella commedia; *the thermometer touched 40° yesterday*, ieri il termometro ha raggiunto i 40°; *this mountain seems to* — *the clouds*, questa montagna sembra toccare le nuvole; *to* — *land*, approdare ‖ *to* — *bottom*, toccare il fondo (anche *fig.*) ‖ *to* — *the spot*, (*fam.*) indovinare, fare ciò che è necessario **4.** essere in contatto; confinare: *his garden touches mine*, il suo giardino confina col mio; *point where the tangent touches the circle*, punto in cui la tangente incontra il cerchio **5.** concernere, riguardare: *this discussion touches us nearly*, questa discussione ci riguarda da vicino **6.** guastare, danneggiare: *these roses are touched by the frost*, queste rose sono guastate dal gelo **7.** (*sl.*) chiedere denaro in prestito: *to* — *s.o. for one pound*, chiedere una sterlina in prestito a qlcu. **8.** *to* — (*and reef*) *a sail*, (*mar.*) (fare) ammainare una vela **9.** *to* — *at* (*a place*), (*mar.*) fare scalo a, approdare: *the ship touched at Genoa*, la nave fece scalo a Genova **10.** *to* — **down**, (*aer.*) atterrare **11.** *to* — **in**, disegnare, aggiungere tratti a (un disegno, ecc.) **12.** *to* — **off**, abbozzare, schizzare; scaricare (un cannone); far esplodere (mine, ecc.) **13.** *to* — **up**, correggere, ritoccare; ravvivare (colori); rimettere a nuovo (mobili); frustare (un cavallo): *to* — *up a drawing*, ritoccare un disegno ‖ *to* — *up s.o.'s memory*, rinfrescare la memoria a qlcu.

touch, (*nei composti*): — *-and-go*, incerto, rischioso ‖ — *-down*, (*aer.*) appoggio; — *-hole*, (*artigl.*) focone

— -line, (geom.) tangente; (rugby) linea di « touche »; — -me-not, (bot.) balsamina; — -needle, ago d'assaggio; — -paper, (ind.) carta nitrata.

touchable ['tʌtʃəbl], ag. tangibile; palpabile.

touchableness ['tʌtʃəblnis], s. tangibilità; palpabilità.

touched [tʌtʃt], ag. (fam.) tocco, pazzerello: he is slightly —, è un po' pazzo.

toucher ['tʌtʃə*], s.c. chi tocca || s. (bocce) boccia a contatto col pallino || as near as a —, (sl.) vicinissimo, quasi sul punto di: he was as near as a — to falling into the stream, ci è mancato poco che cadesse nel fiume.

touchily ['tʌtʃili], av. con suscettibilità; con irascibilità.

touchiness ['tʌtʃinis], s. suscettibilità; irascibilità.

touching ['tʌtʃiŋ], ag. toccante (anche fig.), commovente; patetico: a — scene, una scena commovente || s. 1. tocco; contatto 2. fig. allusione: — upon sthg., allusione a ql.co.

touching, prep. (arc. letter.) circa, riguardo a: — the defence, per quanto riguarda la difesa.

touchingly ['tʌtʃiŋli], av. in modo commovente; pateticamente.

touchingness ['tʌtʃiŋnis], s. carattere commovente, patetico.

touchstone ['tʌtʃstoun], s. (gioielleria) pietra di paragone (anche fig.).

touchwood ['tʌtʃwud], s. esca (per accendere il fuoco).

touchy ['tʌtʃi], ag. suscettibile; permaloso; irascibile; puntiglioso: to be —, irritarsi, prendersela per nulla.

tough [tʌf], ag. 1. duro: — meat, carne dura, tigliosa 2. forte, robusto, resistente: a — person, una persona robusta, resistente 3. fig. inflessibile, tenace: a — will, una volontà tenace 4. duro, difficile: this is a — job, è un lavoro difficile 5. (amer.) brutale, violento; grossolano || — luck!, una bella disdetta! 3. (sl. amer.) malvivente, delinquente ☆ — pitch, (metal.) rame raffinato.

to **toughen** ['tʌfn], v.t.i. indurire, indurirsi.

toughish ['tʌfiʃ], ag. 1. piuttosto duro, resistente 2. piuttosto difficile.

toughly ['tʌfli], av. 1. tenacemente; inflessibilmente, ostinatamente 2. con difficoltà.

toughness ['tʌfnis], s. 1. durezza, solidità 2. tenacia; inflessibilità; ostinazione 3. difficoltà.

toupée, toupet ['tu:pei], s. tuppé.

tour [tuə*], s. 1. giro; viaggio; escursione || the Grand Tour, (st.) viaggio sul continente (complemento dell'educazione di un giovane inglese di un tempo) 2. (teat.) tournée 3. (mil.) turno.

to **tour**, v.t.i. 1. girare; viaggiare, fare un viaggio: to — through Europe, viaggiare attraverso l'Europa 2. (teat.) fare una tournée.

touraco ['tuərəkou], s. (ornit.) turaco.

tourbillon [tuə'biljən], s. girandola.

tourer ['tuərə*], s.c. turista || s. vettura da turismo.

touring ['tuəriŋ], ag. turistico; da turismo ☆ — -car, vettura da turismo.

tourism ['tuərizəm], s. turismo.

tourist ['tuərist], s.c. turista ☆ — office, agenzia turistica; — ticket, biglietto turistico.

tourmalin(e) ['tuəməli(:)n], s. (min.) tormalina.

tournament ['tuənəmənt], s. 1. (st.) torneo (di cavalieri) 2. (spor.) torneo ☆ tennis —, torneo di tennis.

tournay [tuə'nei], s. « tournay » (stoffa stampata per tappezzerie).

tourney ['tuəni], s. (st.) torneo (di cavalieri).

to **tourney**, v.i. (st.) torneare, partecipare a un torneo di cavalieri).

tourniquet ['tuənikei], s. (chir.) pinza emostatica.

tournure [tuə'nju:ə*], s. 1. contorno, forma 2. puf imbottitura ai fianchi di abito femminile).

to **tousle** ['tauzl], v.t.i. malmenare; scompigliare; mettere in disordine; agitarsi: tousled hair, capelli arruffati.

tousy ['tauzi], ag. spettinato; arruffato; disordinato.

tout [taut], s. 1. sollecitatore; chi procura clienti (ad alberghi, ecc.) 2. (racing) —, informatore (sul comportamento dei cavalli durante gli allenamenti).

to **tout**, v.i. 1. sollecitare ordinazioni commerciali; cercare clienti (per alberghi, ecc.) 2. cercare informazioni sul comportamento dei cavalli durante gli allenamenti.

touter ['tautə*], s. (rar.) per **tout**.

tow[1] [tou], s. 1. rimorchio: to have (o to take) in (o on) —, rimorchiare; fig. prendere sotto la propria guida 2. (cavo di) rimorchio ☆ — -boat, chiatta da rimorchio, rimorchiatore; — hook, (aut.) gancio per rimorchio; — -path, strada alzaia; — -rope, gomena per rimorchio || glider —, (aer.) dispositivo per il rimorchio di un aliante.

to **tow**[1], v.t.i. rimorchiare, essere rimorchiato; trainare; alare.

tow[2], s. stoppa (di lino, canapa).

towage ['touidʒ], s. 1. diritti di rimorchio 2. rimorchio; alaggio.

toward ['touəd], ag. (arc.) 1. promettente (di giovane); docile 2. propizio, favorevole 3. che si sta svolgendo: I went to see what was —, andai a vedere che cosa stesse accadendo || av. nella direzione voluta || prep. V. **towards**.

towardliness ['touədlinis], s. (arc.) docilità.

towardly ['touədli], av. (arc.) 1. docilmente 2. in modo propizio.

towardness ['touədnis], s. (arc.) docilità.

towards [tə'wo:dz], prep. 1. verso, in direzione di: my room looks — the mountains, la mia camera guarda verso i monti; we walked — the country, andavamo verso la campagna 2. verso, riguardo a: his attitude — me, il suo atteggiamento verso di me; I feel no animosity — you, non ho nessun rancore verso di te 3. (di tempo) verso, circa: — the end of the day, verso la fine della giornata; — noon, verso mezzogiorno 4. per, a favore di: to save — the children's education, risparmiare per far studiare i bambini.

towel ['tauəl], s. asciugamano || to throw in the —, (spor.) gettare la spugna (anche fig.) ☆ — -horse (o — -rack o — -rail), porta-asciugamano; — -roller, asciugamano a rullo || sanitary —, assorbente igienico.

to **towel**, pass.p.p. **towelled** ['tauəld], v.t.i. asciugare, asciugarsi.

towelling ['tauəliŋ], s. 1. tessuto per asciugamani 2. asciugatura.

tower ['tauə*], s. torre; pilone || the Tower of London, la Torre di Londra || — of strength, fig. campione, paladino ☆ — -crane, gru a torre; — -man, (ferr. amer.) segnalatore || church —, campanile; clock —, torre dell'orologio; control —, (aer.) torre di controllo; ivory —, fig. torre d'avorio; water —, torre serbatoio.

to **tower**, v.i. 1. torreggiare; dominare 2. elevarsi.

towered ['tauəd], ag. turrito; difeso da torri.

towering ['tauəriŋ], ag. 1. torreggiante; elevato, sublime 2. violento: a — rage, una collera violenta.

towery ['tauəri], ag. 1. turrito, munito di torri 2. torreggiante; elevato.

towing ['touiŋ], s. (aut. mar.) rimorchio ☆ — -path, strada alzaia; — -rope, cavo da rimorchio.

towline ['toulain], s. cavo da rimorchio.

town [taun], s. 1. città; centro importante: to be in —, essere in città; to be out of —, essere fuori città; to go into (o up to) —, andare in città || a man about —, un uomo di mondo || to paint the — red, fare baldoria 2. cittadinanza; i cittadini || — and gown, studenti e abitanti della città (specialmente a Oxford e Cambridge) || the talk of the —, i pettegolezzi della città ☆ — -clerk, segretario comunale; — -council, consiglio comunale; — -crier, banditore municipale; — life, vita di città; — -planning, piano regolatore; — -talk, diceria, pettegolezzo || border —, città di frontiera; chief —, capoluogo; country —, città di provincia; county —, capoluogo di contea.

townee [tau′ni:], *s.* (*sl. universitario*) abitante di città universitaria (non membro dell'università).

townhall [′taunhɔːl], *s.* municipio.

townhouse [′taunhaus], *s.* residenza di città.

townish [′tauniʃ], *ag.* cittadino.

townless [′taunlis], *ag.* senza città.

townlet [′taunlit], *s.* (*fam.*) cittadina, piccola città.

townscape [′taun-skeip], *s.* veduta (di città).

townsfolk [′taunzfouk], *s.* cittadini, abitanti di una città.

township [′taun-ʃip], *s.* **1.** territorio, giurisdizione di una città **2.** (*amer.*) suddivisione di contea **3.** (*austral.*) area destinata alla fondazione di una città **4.** borgata.

townsman, *pl.* **townsmen** [′taunzmən], *s.* cittadino; concittadino.

townspeople [′taunz‚piːpl], *s.* cittadini, cittadinanza.

townward(s) [′taunwəd(z)], *av.* verso la città.

towny [′tauni], *s.* (*sl.*) cittadino; concittadino.

towy [′toui], *ag.* stopposo.

toxaemia [tɔk′siːmiə], *s.* (*patol.*) tossiemia.

toxic(al) [′tɔksik(əl)], *ag.* tossico.

toxically [′tɔksikəli], *av.* in modo tossico.

toxicity [tɔk′sisiti], *s.* tossicità.

toxicological [‚tɔksikə′lɔdʒikəl], *ag.* tossicologico.

toxicologist [‚tɔksi′kɔlədʒist], *s.* tossicologo.

toxicology [‚tɔksi′kɔlədʒi], *s.* tossicologia.

toxin [′tɔksin], *s.* (*fisiol.*) tossina.

toxophilite [tɔk′sɔfilait], *s.c.* chi pratica il tiro con l'arco.

toy [tɔi], *s.* **1.** giocattolo; balocco, trastullo **2.** bagattella, bazzecola; inezia, nonnulla ☆ — *-man*, venditore di giocattoli; — *soldier*, soldatino di piombo; — *-woman*, venditrice di giocattoli.

to toy, *v.i.* **1.** giocherellare; trastullarsi; divertirsi: *to* — *with one's stick*, giocherellare col proprio bastone **2.** (*fam.*) amoreggiare, civettare, flirtare.

toyingly [′tɔiiŋli], *av.* per giuoco; in maniera scherzosa.

toyish [′tɔiiʃ], *ag.* **1.** simile a giocattolo **2.** insignificante, da nulla.

toyishness [′tɔiiʃnis], *s.* piccolezza.

toyshop [′tɔi-ʃɔp], *s.* negozio di giocattoli.

trabeate(d) [′treibieit(id)], *ag.* (*arch.*) con trabeazione.

trabeation [‚treibi′eiʃən], *s.* (*arch.*) trabeazione.

trabecula [trə′bekjulə], *pl.* **trabeculae** [trə′bekjuliː], *s.* (*anat.*) trabecola.

trace[1] [treis], *s.* **1.** *gener. pl.* traccia; orma; impronta **2.** residuo, piccola quantità: *this glass contains traces of wine*, in questo bicchiere ci sono tracce di vino **3.** resti; vestigia: *traces of Roman civilization*, tracce della civiltà romana **4.** tracciato (di disegno).

to trace[1], *v.t.* **1.** tracciare: *to* — *a line*, tracciare una linea **2.** seguire le tracce, le orme di: *to* — *an animal*, seguire le tracce di un animale **3.** trovare; scoprire; rintracciare **4.** ricalcare: *to* — *a copy*, fare una copia ricalcata **5.** *to* — **back**, risalire, far risalire: *he traces his origins back to the times of Queen Anne*, fa risalire le sue origini ai tempi della regina Anna.

trace[2], *s.* tirella ‖ *in the traces*, (*fig. letter.*) bardato ‖ *to kick over the traces*, *fig.* ribellarsi.

traceability [‚treisə′biliti], *s.* **1.** possibilità di essere tracciato **2.** l'essere ricalcabile **3.** rintracciabilità.

traceable [′treisəbl], *ag.* **1.** che si può tracciare **2.** ricalcabile **3.** rintracciabile.

traceableness [′treisəblnis], *V.* traceability.

traceless [′treislis], *ag.* senza traccia.

tracelessly [′treislisli], *av.* senza traccia.

tracer [′treisə*], *s.c.* **1.** chi traccia **2.** chi rintraccia: *the* — *of the crime*, chi ha scoperto l'autore del delitto **3.** chi ricalca ‖ *s.* — (*-bullet* o *-shell*), (*mil.*) proiettile tracciante ☆ — *element*, (*fis.*) elemento tracciante radioattivo.

tracery [′treisəri], *s.* **1.** disegno, decorazione: *the*

---

delicate — *of light and shade*, il delicato contrasto di luci ed ombre **2.** (*arch.*) decorazione ad intaglio: *the* — *of that Gothic window*, il traforo di quella finestra gotica **3.** nervatura (di ali di insetti, foglie, ecc.).

trachea [trə′kiː)ə], *pl.* **tracheae** [trə′kiː)iː], *s.* (*anat.*) trachea.

tracheal [trə′kiː)əl], **trachean** [trə′kiː)ən], *ag.* tracheale.

tracheitis [‚treiki′aitis], *s.* (*patol.*) tracheite.

tracheotomy [‚træki′ɔtəmi], *s.* (*chir.*) tracheotomia.

trachoma [trə′koumə], *s.* (*patol.*) tracoma.

trachyte [′treikait], *s.* (*min.*) trachite.

tracing [′treisiŋ], *s.* **1.** tracciamento; tracciato **2.** calco; ricalco ☆ — *-cloth*, tela da ricalco; — *-paper*, carta da ricalco.

track[1] [træk], *s.* **1.** traccia, impronta (anche *fig.*): *the ground was covered with wolves' tracks*, il suolo era solcato da numerose tracce di lupi; *he left his* — *everywhere in the organization of the firm*, lasciò la sua impronta in tutta l'organizzazione della ditta; *they were on the thief's* —, erano sulle piste del ladro; *to lose* — *of*, perdere le tracce di, *fig.* non essere più in relazione con ‖ *to make tracks*, (*fam.*) svignarsela; *to make tracks for a place*, (*fam.*) dirigersi rapidamente verso un luogo **2.** sentiero, via, corso (anche *fig.*): *he keeps* — *of all events*, segue il corso di tutti gli avvenimenti; *to be off the* —, essere fuori strada; *essere fuori argomento*; *to be on the good* —, essere sulla buona strada ‖ *the beaten* —, *fig.* il sentiero battuto: *she was not afraid to leave the beaten* —, non aveva paura di allontanarsi dalla norma **3.** (*spor.*) pista **4.** (*ferr.*) binario: *goods on* —, (*comm. amer.*) merce spedita per ferrovia **5.** (*astr.*) corso, orbita: *the* — *of a comet*, il corso di una cometa **6.** (*mar.*) rotta, scia; (*aer.*) rotta effettiva: *the* — *of a ship*, la scia di una nave **7.** (*mec.*) cingolo ☆ — *angle*, (*aer.*) angolo di rotta; — *boat*, chiatta; — *-walker*, (*ferr. amer.*) guardalinee ‖ *sound* —, (*cine.*) colonna sonora; *test* —, (*aut.*) pista di prova.

to track[1], *v.t.i.* **1.** inseguire, pedinare, seguire le tracce di: *the Police are tracking the murderer*, la polizia sta pedinando l'assassino **2.** tracciare un sentiero, tracciare una via **3.** posare binari; fornire di binari **4.** (*mec.*) avere lo scartamento di **5.** *to* — **down**, raggiungere, catturare: *he has been tracked down at last*, finalmente è stato catturato **6.** *to* — **out**, scoprire, scovare: *they were trying to* — *out the tiger*, cercavano di stanare la tigre.

to track[2], *v.t.* rimorchiare.

trackage[1] [′trækidʒ], *s.* (*amer.*) binari, rotaie.

trackage[2], *s.* **1.** rimorchiamento; rimorchio **2.** spesa di rimorchio.

tracker[1] [′trækə*], *s.* battitore, perlustratore.

tracker[2], *s.* **1.** chi rimorchia **2.** rimorchiatore.

tracklayer [′trækˌleiə*], *s.* (*ferr. amer.*) (operaio) posatore di binari.

trackless [′træklis], *ag.* **1.** senza traccia, sentiero, rotaie **2.** impraticabile.

tracklessly [′træklisli], *av.* senza traccia, sentiero, rotaie.

tracklessness [′træklisnis], *s.* assenza di tracce, di sentieri, di rotaie.

trackman, *pl.* **trackmen** [′trækmən], *s.* (*ferr. amer.*) guardalinee.

tract[1] [trækt], *s.* trattatello; opuscolo, libretto.

tract[2], *s.* **1.** (*arc.*) periodo: *a long* — *of time*, un lungo periodo di tempo **2.** zona; regione, distretto: *a large* — *of sand*, una vasta distesa di sabbia **3.** (*anat.*) apparato.

tractability [‚træktə′biliti], *s.* docilità, arrendevolezza.

tractable [′træktəbl], *ag.* **1.** docile, arrendevole **2.** facile da maneggiare, usare.

tractableness [′træktəblnis], *s.* docilità, arrendevolezza.

tractably [′træktəbli], *av.* docilmente, arrendevolmente.

Tractarian [træk'tɛəriən], *ag.* (*st. relig.*) del « Tractarianism » ‖ *s.* (*st. relig.*) seguace del « Tractarianism ».

Tractarianism [træk'tɛəriənizəm], *s.* (*st. relig.*) « Tractarianism » (Movimento di Oxford iniziato nel 1833).

tractate ['trækteit], *s.* trattato.

traction ['trækʃən], *s.* **1.** trazione **2.** contrazione: *the — of muscles*, la contrazione dei muscoli ☆ *— engine*, (*agr.*) trattrice; *— rope*, cavo di trazione; *— wheels*, ruote motrici ‖ *steam —*, (*ferr.*) trazione a vapore.

tractive ['træktiv], *ag.* trattivo ☆ *— force*, (*mec.*) forza di trazione; *— power*, (*mec.*) sforzo di trazione.

tractor ['træktə*], *s.* **1.** (*agr.*) trattrice **2.** aeroplano ad elica traente.

trade [treid], *s.* **1.** mestiere, occupazione: *these are the tricks of the —*, questi sono i trucchi del mestiere; *to carry on a —*, esercitare un mestiere ‖ *everyone to his —*, a ciascuno il suo mestiere **2.** commercio; traffico; affari: *to be in —*, essere in commercio, negli affari ‖ *Board of Trade*, Ministero del Commercio e dell'Industria **3.** commercianti: *the — will never submit to these conditions*, i commercianti non si sottometteranno mai a queste condizioni ‖ *the —*, (*fam.*) i rivenditori autorizzati di alcoolici; (*sl. mar.*) i sottomarini **4.** *pl. the trades* (*— -winds*), (venti) alisei ☆ *— allowance*, sconto ai rivenditori; *— bank*, banca commerciale; *— hall*, camera di commercio; *— -mark*, marchio di fabbrica ‖ *Board of Trade*, *— -name*, nome depositato; *— -price*, prezzo del fabbricante al rivenditore; *— -route*, rotta commerciale; *trades-folk* (o *trades-people*), commercianti, classe dei commercianti; *— -show*, (*cine.*) anteprima per distributori e critici; *— -union*, sindacato; *— -unionism*, sindacalismo; *— -unionist*, sindacalista ‖ *free- —*, commercio libero, libero scambio; *domestic —* (o *home —*), commercio interno; *retail —*, commercio al minuto; *wholesale —*, commercio all'ingrosso.

to **trade**, *v.t.i.* **1.** commerciare; negoziare; trafficare: *we — in carpets*, commerciamo in tappeti **2.** *fig.* commercio di (onore, ecc.) **3.** *to — on*, approfittare di; speculare su.

trader ['treidə*], *s.* **1.** commerciante; negoziante; mercante **2.** nave mercantile.

tradesman, *pl.* **tradesmen** ['treidzmən], *s.* **1.** commerciante; esercente **2.** artigiano.

trading ['treidiŋ], *ag.* commerciale ‖ *s.* commercio; traffico ☆ *— company*, società commerciale; *— stamp*, (*amer.*) buono premio; *— vessel*, nave mercantile.

tradition [trə'diʃən], *s.* **1.** tradizione: *this law is based on —*, questa legge è basata sulla tradizione **2.** (*dir.*) trapasso.

traditional [trə'diʃənl], *ag.* tradizionale.

traditionalism [trə'diʃnəlizəm], *s.* tradizionalismo.

traditionalist [trə'diʃnəlist], *s.* tradizionalista.

traditionalistic [trə,diʃnə'listik], *ag.* tradizionalistico.

traditionally [trə'diʃnəli], *av.* tradizionalmente.

traditionary [trə'diʃnəri], *ag.* tradizionale.

traditionist [trə'diʃnist], *s.* tradizionalista.

to **traduce** [trə'dju:s], *v.t.* calunniare, diffamare.

traducement [trə'dju:smənt], *s.* calunnia, diffamazione; maldicenza.

traducer [trə'dju:sə*], *s.c.* calunniatore, calunniatrice; diffamatore, diffamatrice.

traducian [trə'dju:siən], *s.* (*st. relig.*) traduciano.

traducianism [trə'dju:siənizəm], *s.* (*st. relig.*) traducianismo.

traducianist [trə'dju:siənist], *s.* (*st. relig.*) traduciano.

traducible [trə'dju:səbl], *ag.* calunniabile.

Trafalgar [trə'fælgə*], *no.pr.* (*geog.*) Trafalgar ‖ *— Square*, Trafalgar Square (una delle principali piazze di Londra).

traffic ['træfik], *s.* **1.** traffico, negozio, commercio: *— in arms*, commercio d'armi **2.** traffico, movimento, circolazione: *there is much — on this road*, su questa strada c'è molto traffico; *to direct the —*, dirigere il traffico; *to open a road for —*, aprire una strada al traffico ☆ *— beam*, (*aut.*) luce anabbagliante; *— density*, den-

sità di traffico; *— flow*, deflusso del traffico; *— jam*, ingorgo stradale; *— lights*, semaforo ‖ *air —*, traffico aereo; *drug —*, commercio di stupefacenti: *to be engaged in the drug —*, commerciare in stupefacenti; *ocean —*, navigazione di lungo corso; *railway —*, traffico ferroviario.

to **traffic**, *pass.p.p.* **trafficked** ['træfikt], *v.t.i.* trafficare, commerciare; fare commercio di (anche *fig.*): *to — in sthg.*, commerciare in ql.co.

trafficator ['træfikeitə*], *s.* (*aut.*) indicatore di direzione ☆ *— arm*, (*aut.*) freccia.

trafficker ['træfikə*], *s.c.* trafficante, negoziante, commerciante ☆ *drug- —*, trafficante in stupefacenti.

trafficless ['træfiklis], *ag.* senza traffico.

tragacanth ['trægəkænθ], *s.* (*farm.*) gomma dragante.

tragedian [trə'dʒi:djən], *s.* **1.** tragediografo **2.** attore tragico.

tragedienne [trə,dʒi:di'en], *s.* attrice tragica.

tragedy ['trædʒidi], *s.* tragedia: *"Othello" is a —*, l'« Otello » è una tragedia ‖ *to make a — out of nothing*, fare una tragedia per nulla.

tragic(al) ['trædʒik(əl)], *ag.* tragico.

tragically ['trædʒikəli], *av.* tragicamente.

tragicalness ['trædʒikəlnis], *s.* tragicità.

tragicomedy ['trædʒi'kɔmidi], *s.* tragicommedia.

tragicomic(al) ['trædʒi'kɔmik(əl)], *ag.* tragicomico.

tragicomically ['trædʒi'kɔmikəli], *av.* tragicomicamente.

tragopan ['trægoupæn], *s.* (*ornit.*) tragopa.

trail [treil], *s.* **1.** striscia: *the — of a meteor*, la traccia di una meteora; *a — of smoke*, un pennacchio di fumo **2.** pesta; pista; traccia; orma: *to lose the —*, perdere la traccia, la pista; *to be on the — of*, essere sulle tracce di **3.** cammino, sentiero **4.** (*artigl.*) coda d'affusto ‖ *at the —*, (*mil.*) bilanciarm ☆ *— -eye*, (*artigl.*) orecchione di traino; *— -net*, strascino; *— -rope*, (*aer.*) cavo moderatore; *— -spade*, (*artigl.*) vomero.

to **trail**, *v.t.i.* **1.** trascinare, trascinarsi; strascicare; strisciare: *her coat trails on the carpet*, il suo mantello strascica sul tappeto; *to — sthg. (along)*, trascinare ql.co. dietro di sé **2.** inseguire; seguire le tracce di **3.** strisciare, arrampicarsi (di piante) **4.** *to — arms*, (*mil.*) bilanciare i fucili **5.** *to — away, off*, andar via camminando faticosamente; *fig.* degenerare, mutare: *the discussion trailed off into a quarrel*, la discussione degenerò in alterco.

trailer ['treilə*], *s.c.* chi insegue ‖ *s.* **1.** rimorchio; (*amer.*) « roulotte » **2.** pianta rampicante **3.** (*cine.*) presentazione di scene di un film, il « prossimamente ».

trailing ['treiliŋ], *ag.* strisciante; rampicante (di pianta) ☆ *— axle*, (*aut.*) assale posteriore; *— edge*, (*aer.*) bordo d'uscita; *— wheel*, ruota portante, ruote posteriori.

train [trein], *s.* **1.** strascico; coda **2.** seguito, corteo, accompagnamento: *to be in the — of s.o.*, essere al seguito di qlcu. **3.** serie, successione, fila: *a long — of sightseers*, una lunga fila di visitatori; *a painful — of events*, una dolorosa serie di avvenimenti **4.** corso, svolgimento, sviluppo: *a — of thought*, il corso del pensiero; *I do not know what this event will bring in its —*, non so quali saranno gli sviluppi di questo avvenimento **5.** treno, convoglio: *to get into the —*, montare, salire in treno; *to go by —*, andare in treno; *to miss the —*, perdere il treno **6.** sistema d'ingranaggi **7.** miccia **8.** slitta (in Canada) ☆ *— -bearer*, paggio; *— boy*, venditore di bibite, giornali, ecc.; *— band*, (*st.*) milizia cittadina (di Londra); *— -ferry*, nave traghetto; *— jumper*, (*amer.*) viaggiatore clandestino; *— -sickness*, nausea, malessere (provocati dal treno) ‖ *armoured —*, treno blindato; *excursion —*, treno festivo; *express —* (o *fast —* o *through —*), rapido; *goods —*, treno merci; *passenger —*, treno viaggiatori; *slow —*, accelerato.

to **train**, *v.t.i.* **1.** allevare, far crescere, educare; istruire, formare: *to — a child*, allevare un bambino **2.** esercitare, esercitarsi; allenare, allenarsi; addestrare, ammaestrare: *a trained dog*, un cane ammaestrato; *they were training for the match*, si allenavano per l'incontro **3.** far crescere, far arrampicare (una pianta): *to — roses against a wall,* far crescere delle rose lungo un muro **4.** (*artigl.*) puntare, orientare: *to — guns on a fort,* puntare i cannoni contro un forte **5.** (*fam.*) viaggiare in treno **6.** *to — down,* (*spor.*) ridurre il peso con l'allenamento.

trainable ['treinəbl], *ag.* addestrabile, ammaestrabile, allenabile, esercitabile.

trainee [trei'ni:], *s.* **1.** chi, che viene ammaestrato, allenato **2.** (*amer. mil.*) recluta.

trainer ['treinə*], *s.* istruttore; allenatore; ammaestratore.

training ['treiniŋ], *s.* educazione; ammaestramento; addestramento; allenamento, esercitazione; apprendistato; tirocinio: *to be in —,* (*spor.*) essere in periodo di allenamento; essere in forma ☆ *— -college* (o *— -school*), scuola di tirocinio per insegnanti; *— -ship,* nave scuola ‖ *military —,* addestramento militare.

train-oil ['treinoil], *s.* olio di balena.

trait [treit], *s.* tratto; tocco; caratteristica.

traitor ['treitə*], *s.* traditore.

traitorous ['treitərəs], *ag.* traditore.

traitorously ['treitərəsli], *av.* a tradimento; slealmente.

traitress ['treitris], *s.* traditrice.

Trajan ['treidʒən], *no.pr.m.* (*st.*) Traiano.

to **traject** [trə'dʒekt], *v.t.i.* (*rar.*) **1.** traghettare, far attraversare **2.** proiettare (luce, colore, ombra) **3.** trasmettere.

trajection [trə'dʒekʃən], *s.***1.**traghetto **2.**trasmissione.

trajectory ['trædʒiktəri], *s.* traiettoria.

tram[1] [træm], *s.* **1.** (*-car*), tram, vettura tranviaria; *— (-line),* linea tranviaria **2.** carrello, vagoncino da miniera ☆ *— -conductor,* manovratore del tram; *— -road,* (*miner.*) linea di binari per vagoncini; *— -stop,* fermata del tram.

to **tram**[1], *pass.p.p.* **trammed** [træmd], *v.t.i.* **1.** andare in tram **2.** (*miner.*) trasportare in vagoncini.

tram[2], *s.* (*ind. tessile*) filo di seta per trama.

trammel ['træməl], *s.* **1.** (*-net*), tramaglio **2.** *gener. pl.* intoppo, ostacolo **3.** (*geom.*) ellissografo.

to **trammel,** *pass.p.p.* **trammelled** ['træməld], *v.t.* **1.** impedire, ostacolare **2.** irretire.

tramontane [trə'mɔntein] *ag.* **1.** oltremontano (specialmente riferito alle Alpi); straniero **2.** di tramontana (di vento) ‖ *s.* **1.** oltremontano; straniero; barbaro **2.** (vento di) tramontana.

tramp [træmp], *s.* **1.** calpestio, scalpiccio **2.** viaggio a piedi ‖ *to be on the —,* vagabondare **3.** vagabondo, barbone; disoccupato **4.** (*mar.*) carretta.

to **tramp,** *v.t.i.* **1.** camminare pesantemente **2.** viaggiare a piedi: *we had to — it,* dovemmo fare la strada a piedi **3.** vagabondare ‖ *to — the streets,* vagabondare in cerca di lavoro.

trample ['træmpl], *s.* calpestio.

to **trample,** *v.t.i.* **1.** calpestare, camminare su; *fig.* offendere; trattare con disprezzo: *the child trampled on the flowers in the garden,* il bambino calpestò i fiori in giardino; *to — on s.o. feelings,* offendere i sentimenti di qlcu. **2.** camminare pesantemente.

trampler ['træmplə*], *s.c.* chi calpesta.

tramway ['træmwei], *s.* tranvia, linea tranviaria.

trance [trɑ:ns], *s.* **1.** (*poet.*) estasi, rapimento **2.** (*patol.*) trance, catalessi ipnotica.

to **trance,** *v.t.* (*poet.*) estasiare; rapire, incantare.

trancedly ['trɑ:nsidli], *av.* (*poet.*) estaticamente.

tranquil ['træŋkwil], *ag.* tranquillo, quieto, calmo.

tranquillity [træŋ'kwiliti], *s.* tranquillità.

tranquillization [ˌtræŋkwilai'zeiʃən], *s.* il tranquillizzare.

to **tranquillize** ['træŋkwilaiz], *v.t.* tranquillizzare.

tranquillizer ['træŋkwilaizə*], *s.c.* chi tranquillizza ‖ *s.* (*farm.*) tranquillante.

tranquillizingly ['træŋkwilaiziŋli], *av.* in modo tranquillante.

tranquilly ['træŋkwili], *av.* tranquillamente.

tranquilness ['træŋkwilnis], *s.* tranquillità.

to **transact** [træn'zækt], *v.t.i.* compiere, negoziare, trattare (affari); fare, trattare affari.

transaction [træn'zækʃən], *s.* **1.** affare, operazione; condotta, trattativa (di un affare): *he left the — of the matter to his secretary,* lasciò al suo segretario il compito di sbrigare l'affare; *he effected some important banking transactions,* eseguì alcune importanti operazioni di banca **2.** (*dir.*) transazione **3.** *pl.* atti, memorie, verbali di una società.

transactor [træn'zæktə*], *s.c.* negoziatore, negoziatrice.

transalpine ['trænz'ælpain], *ag.s.* transalpino.

transatlantic ['trænzət'læntik], *ag.* transatlantico ☆ *— steamer,* (*mar.*) transatlantico.

transcalent [træns'keilənt], *ag.* (*fis.*) diatermano.

to **transcend** [træn'send], *v.t.i.* **1.** (*fil.*) trascendere **2.** superare, oltrepassare.

transcendence [træn'sendəns], **transcendency** [træn'sendənsi], *s.* (*fil.*) trascendenza.

transcendent [træn'sendənt], *ag.* **1.** superiore, preminente, straordinario **2.** (*fil.*) trascendente ‖ *s.* entità trascendente.

transcendental [ˌtrænsen'dentl], *ag.* (*fil.*) trascendentale.

transcendentalism [ˌtrænsen'dentəlizəm], *s.* (*fil.*) trascendentalismo.

transcendentalist [ˌtrænsen'dentəlist], *s.* (*fil.*) seguace del trascendentalismo.

transcendentally [ˌtrænsen'dentəli], *av.* trascendentalmente.

transcendently [træn'sendəntli], *av.* trascendentemente.

transcontinental ['trænz,kɔnti'nentl], *ag.* transcontinentale: *a — railway,* una ferrovia transcontinentale.

to **transcribe** [træns'kraib], *v.t.* trascrivere (anche *mus.*): *to — a manuscript,* trascrivere un manoscritto.

transcriber [træns'kraibə*], *s.c.* trascrittore, trascrittrice.

transcript ['trænskript], *s.* copia; riproduzione.

transcription [træns'kripʃən], *s.* trascrizione (anche *mus.*); copia.

transept ['trænsept], *s.* (*arch.*) transetto.

transfer [træns'fə(:)*], *s.* **1.** trasferimento; (*dir.*) cessione; trapasso; (*comm.*) storno **2.** decalcomania ☆ *— -book,* registro cessioni; *— -ink,* inchiostro litografico; *— -paper,* carta per copie riproducibili; *— -table,* (*ferr. ind.*) carrello trasbordatore; *— ticket,* biglietto cumulativo.

to **transfer** [træns'fə:*], *pass.p.p.* **transferred** [træns'fə:d], *v.t.* **1.** trasferire; cedere; eseguire il trapasso di; (*comm.*) stornare **2.** decalcare, ricalcare (disegni).

transferable [træns'fə:rəbl], *ag.* trasferibile.

transferibility [træns,fə:rə'biliti], *s.* trasferibilità.

transferee [ˌtrænsfə(:)'ri:], *s.* (*dir.*) cessionario.

transference ['trænsfərəns], *s.* trasferimento.

transferor [træns'fə:rə*], **transferrer** [træns'fə:rə*], *s.* (*dir.*) cedente.

transfiguration [ˌtrænsfigju'reiʃən], *s.* trasfigurazione.

to **transfigure** [træns'figə*], *v.t.* trasfigurare.

to **transfix** [træns'fiks], *v.t.* **1.** trafiggere, trapassare **2.** *fig.* immobilizzare, paralizzare, inchiodare: *transfixed with fear,* paralizzato dalla paura.

transfixion [træns'fikʃən], *s.* **1.** trafiggimento **2.** (*chir.*) trasfissione.

to **transform** [træns'fɔ:m], *v.t.* **1.** trasformare: *he was transformed into a stone,* fu trasformato in un sasso **2.** *— down, up,* (*elett.*) abbassare, elevare la tensione.

transformable [træns'fɔ:məbl], *ag.* trasformabile.

transformation [ˌtrænsfə'meiʃən], *s.* **1.** trasformazione **2.** (*zool. geol.*) metamorfosi **3.** parrucca **4.** (*patol.*

degenerazione ☆ — -range, (metal.) intervallo critico; intervallo termico di trasformazione; — -ratio, (elett.) rapporto di trasformazione.

transformative [træns'fɔ:mətiv], ag. trasformativo.

transformer [træns'fɔ:mə*], s. **1.** trasformatore, chi trasforma **2.** (elett. mec.) trasformatore ☆ current —, (elett.) trasformatore amperometrico; voltage —, (elett.) trasformatore voltometrico.

transformism [træns'fɔ:mizəm], s. (biol.) trasformismo.

transformist [træns'fɔ:mist], s. trasformista.

to **transfuse** [træns'fju:z] v.t. **1.** travasare; fig. trasfondere **2.** (med.) fare una trasfusione a.

transfusible [træns'fju:zəbl], ag. trasfondibile.

transfusion [træns'fju:ʒən], s. trasfusione ☆ blood —, trasfusione di sangue.

to **transgress** [træns'gres], v.t.i. **1.** trasgredire, violare; infrangere; contravvenire a; peccare **2.** oltrepassare.

transgression [træns'greʃən], s. trasgressione, violazione; colpa; infrazione.

transgressor [træns'gresə*], s. trasgressore; peccatore.

to **tranship** [træn'ʃip], pass.p.p. **transhipped** [træn'ʃipt], v.t.i. (mar.) trasbordare.

transhipment [træn'ʃipmənt], s. (mar.) trasbordo.

transhuman [træns'hju:mən], ag. sovrumano.

to **transhumanize** [træns'hju:mənaiz], v.t. rendere sovrumano.

transience ['trænziəns], **transiency** ['trænziənsi], s. transitorietà; brevità, fugacità.

transient ['trænziənt], ag. transitorio, passeggero; fugace: a — lodger, (amer.) un ospite di passaggio.

transiently ['trænziəntli], av. transitoriamente; fugacemente.

transientness ['trænziəntnis], V. **transience**.

transilience [træn'siliəns], **transiliency** [træn'siliənsl], s. (spec. miner.) passaggio repentino da una condizione all'altra.

transilient [træn'siliənt], ag. (spec. mincr. med.) che passa da una condizione ad un'altra.

transire [træns'aiəri], s. lasciapassare doganale.

transistor [træn'zistə*], s. (elett.) transistor.

transit ['trænsit], s. **1.** transito, passaggio: ships in —, navi in transito **2.** trasporto: this wine loses quality in —, questo vino si deteriora durante il trasporto **3.** (astr.) passaggio (di corpo celeste sul meridiano di un luogo) ☆ — -duty, dazio su merci di transito; — -instrument, (astr.) equatoriale.

to **transit**, v.t. (astr.) attraversare il disco di (sole, ecc.) (detto di corpo celeste).

transition [træn'siʒən], s. **1.** transizione, passaggio, cambiamento **2.** (mus.) transizione ☆ — style, (arch.) stile di transizione.

transitional [træn'siʒənl], **transitionary** [træn'siʒnəri], ag. di transizione.

transitive ['trænsitiv], ag. (gram.) transitivo ‖ s. (gram.) verbo transitivo.

transitively ['trænsitivli], av. (gram.) transitivamente.

transitiveness ['trænsitivnis], s. (gram.) carattere transitivo.

transitorily ['trænsitərili], av. transitoriamente.

transitoriness ['trænsitərinis], s. transitorietà.

transitory ['trænsitəri], ag. transitorio.

translatable [træns'leitəbl], ag. traducibile.

to **translate** [træns'leit], v.t.i. **1.** tradurre: I have to — a passage from Italian into English, devo tradurre un brano dall'italiano all'inglese; poetry does not — easily, la poesia non è facilmente traducibile **2.** convertire, far passare da uno stato ad un altro: to — sounds into phonetic symbols, rendere dei suoni con simboli fonetici **3.** fig. interpretare, spiegare: they translated this as a protest, l'interpretarono come una protesta **4.** trasferire, rimuovere (vescovi); far assurgere al cielo **5.** (tel.) trasmettere col ripetitore **6.** (mec.) imprimere un movimento di traslazione a.

translation [træns'leiʃən], s. **1.** traduzione, versione **2.** trasferimento, rimozione (di vescovo); trasporto, assunzione (al cielo) **3.** (tel.) trasmissione con ripetitore **4.** (mec. astr.) traslazione.

translational [træns'leiʃənl], ag. **1.** di traduzione **2.** (mec. astr.) di traslazione.

translator [træns'leitə*], s. **1.** traduttore **2.** (tel.) ripetitore.

translatress [træns'leitris], s. traduttrice.

to **transliterate** [trænz'litereit], v.t. traslitterare (trascrivere nei caratteri di un altro alfabeto).

transliteration [,trænzlitə'reiʃən], s. traslitterazione (trascrizione nei caratteri di un altro alfabeto).

translucence [trænz'lu:sns], **translucency** [trænz'lu:snsi], s. **1.** traslucidità **2.** (fam.) trasparenza.

translucent [trænz'lu:snt], **translucid** [trænz'lu:sid], ag. **1.** traslucido **2.** (fam.) trasparente.

translunary [trænz'lu:nəri], ag. translunare.

transmarine [,trænzmə'ri:n], ag. transmarino.

transmigrant ['trænzmigrənt], ag.s. trasmigrante; emigrante.

to **transmigrate** ['trænzmaigreit], v.i. trasmigrare; emigrare.

transmigration [,trænzmai'greiʃən], s. trasmigrazione; emigrazione ‖ — (of souls), trasmigrazione delle anime, metempsicosi.

transmigrator ['trænzmaigreitə*], s. trasmigrante; emigrante.

transmissibility [trænz,misə'biliti], s. trasmissibilità.

transmissible [trænz'misəbl], ag. trasmissibile.

transmission [trænz'miʃən], s. (fis. aut. rad. elett.) trasmissione, cambio ☆ — level, (elett.) livello di trasmissione ‖ all-round —, (rad.) trasmissione circolare.

transmissive [trænz'misiv], ag. **1.** trasmettitore **2.** trasmissibile.

to **transmit** [trænz'mit], pass.p.p. **transmitted** [trænz'mitid], v.t. **1.** trasmettere (ordini, malattie, ecc.) **2.** (mec. fis.) trasmettere, condurre (calore, ecc.).

transmittable [trænz'mitəbl], ag. trasmissibile.

transmitter [trænz'mitə*], s.c. chi trasmette ‖ s. (tel.) trasmettitore; (rad.) radiotrasmettitore; manipolatore (di telegrafo).

transmogrification [,trænzmogrifi'keiʃən], s. (scherz.) trasformazione magica, metamorfosi.

to **transmogrify** [trænz'mogrifai], v.t. (scherz.) trasformare magicamente.

transmontane [trænz'montein], ag. oltremontano.

transmutability [trænz,mju:tə'biliti], s. trasmutabilità.

transmutable [trænz'mju:təbl], ag. trasmutabile.

transmutableness [trænz'mju:təblnis], s. trasmutabilità.

transmutation [,trænzmju:'teiʃən], s. trasmutazione, trasformazione.

to **transmute** [trænz'mju:t], v.t. trasmutare, trasformare.

transnormal [trænz'nɔ:məl], ag. straordinario, fuori del normale.

transoceanic ['trænz,ouʃi'ænik], ag. transoceanico.

transom ['trænsom], s. **1.** (arch.) traversa **2.** (mar.) specchio di poppa; arcaccia; dragante **3.** — (-window), vasistas.

transonic [træn'sonik], ag. (aer.) transonico.

transpadane ['trænzpədein], ag. transpadano.

transparence [træns'pɛərəns], s. trasparenza.

transparency [træns'pɛərənsi], s. **1.** trasparenza; limpidezza **2.** trasparente **3.** (foto.) diapositiva.

transparent [træns'pɛərənt], ag. **1.** trasparente; limpido; diafano: — glass, vetro trasparente **2.** chiaro, evidente, franco: — allusion, allusione chiara **3.** chiaro, limpido, terso: a — style, uno stile chiaro.

transparently [træns'pɛərəntli], av. **1.** trasparentemente **2.** chiaramente, evidentemente **3.** chiaramente, limpidamente.

transparentness [træns'pɛərəntnis], s. trasparenza.

to **transpierce** [træns'piəs], *v.t.* trafiggere, trapassare.
transpirable [træns'paiərəbl], *ag.* traspirabile.
transpiration [ˌtrænspi'reiʃən], *s.* traspirazione.
to **transpire** [træns'paiə*], *v.t.i.* **1.** traspirare; esalare **2.** *fig.* trapelare: *nothing had transpired*, non era trapelato nulla **3.** *(volg.)* accadere.
transplant [træns'plɑ:nt], *s. (bot. chir.)* trapianto.
to **transplant**, *v.t. (bot. chir.)* trapiantare.
transplantable [træns'plɑ:ntəbl], *ag.* trapiantabile.
transplantation [ˌtrænsplɑ:n'teiʃən], *s. (bot. chir.)* trapianto.
transplanter [træns'plɑ:ntə*], *s. (bot. agr.)* **1.** trapiantatore **2.** trapiantatoio.
transpontine ['trænz'pɔntain], *ag.* **1.** al di là del ponte, d'oltreponte (specialmente di quella parte di Londra situata sulla riva destra del Tamigi) **2.** *(teat.)* melodrammatico (con riferimento ai drammi rappresentati nei teatri della riva destra nel XIX sec.).
transport ['trænspɔ:t], *s.* **1.** trasporto || *Minister of Transport*, Ministro dei Trasporti **2.** mezzo di trasporto; nave da trasporto; aereo di linea **3.** *fig.* trasporto, slancio, rapimento, estasi **4.** *(st.)* forzato, deportato ☆ — *charges*, spese di trasporto; — *service*, servizio di spedizione || *inland water* —, trasporto fluviale interno; *water-borne* —, trasporto per via d'acqua.
to **transport** [træns'pɔ:t], *v.t.* **1.** trasportare **2.** *fig.* trasportare, rapire: *he was transported with joy*, era fuori di sè dalla gioia **3.** *(st.)* deportare.
transportability [trænsˌpɔ:tə'biliti], *s.* capacità di essere trasportato.
transportable [træns'pɔ:təbl], *ag.* **1.** trasportabile **2.** *(st.)* punibile con deportazione.
transportation [ˌtrænspɔ:'teiʃən], *s.* **1.** trasportazione, trasporto **2.** *(st.)* deportazione, relegazione: — *for life*, relegazione a vita **3.** *(amer.)* mezzo di trasporto: *our* — *was a camel*, il nostro mezzo di trasporto era un cammello **4.** *(amer.)* biglietto.
transporter [træns'pɔ:tə*], *s.* **1.** trasportatore **2.** *(mec.)* gru scorrevole ☆ — *bridge*, ponte trasportatore.
transporting [træns'pɔ:tiŋ], *ag.* che rapisce, che incanta || *s.* **1.** atto del trasportare **2.** *(st.)* deportazione.
transportingly [træns'pɔ:tiŋli], *av.* con trasporto.
transposable [træns'pouzəbl], *ag.* trasponibi.e.
transposal [træns'pouzəl], *s.* trasposizione.
to **transpose** [træns'pouz], *v.t.* **1.** trasporre (parole, cifre, ecc.), spostare **2.** *(mus.)* trasportare da un tono a un altro: *to — a piece to a lower key*, abbassare il tono di un pezzo musicale.
transposition [ˌtrænspə'ziʃən], *s.* **1.** trasposizione (di parole, cifre, ecc.), spostamento **2.** *(mus.)* trasporto di tono **3.** *(med.)* trasposizione, inversione: — *of the heart and liver*, trasposizione del cuore e del fegato.
transpositive [træns'pouzitiv], *ag.* traspositivo.
to **trans-ship** [træns'ʃip], *pass.p.p.* **trans-shipped** [træns'ʃipt], *v.t. (mar.)* trasbordare.
trans-shipment [træns'ʃipmənt], *s. (mar.)* trasbordo.
Trans-siberian ['trænzsai'biəriən], *ag. (geog.)* transiberiano.
to **transubstantiate** [ˌtrænsəb'stænʃieit], *v.t. (teol.)* transustanziare.
transubstantiation ['trænsəbˌstænʃi'eiʃən], *s. (teol.)* transustanziazione.
transudation [ˌtrænsju'deiʃən], *s.* trasudamento, trasudazione.
to **transude** [træn'sju:d], *v.i.* trasudare, traspirare.
Transvaal ['trænzvɑ:l], *no.pr. (geog.)* Transvaal.
Transvaaler ['trænzˌvɑ:lə*], *s.c.* abitante, nativo, nativa del Transvaal.
transversal [trænz'və:səl], *ag.s.* trasversale.
transversally [trænz'və:sli], *av.* trasversalmente.
transverse ['trænzvə:s], *ag.* trasverso; trasversale || *s. (anat.)* (muscolo) trasverso.
transversely [trænz'və:sli], *av.* trasversalmente.
Transylvania [ˌtrænsil'veinjə], *no.pr. (geog.)* Transilvania.

to **trant** [trænt], *v.i. (dial.)* fare il venditore ambulante con carretto e cavallo.
tranter ['træntə*], *s. (dial.)* venditore ambulante con carretto e cavallo.
trap[1] [træp], *s.* **1.** trappola **2.** *fig.* tranello, insidia: *his question was a real* —, la sua domanda era una vera trappola **3.** botola **4.** calesse **5.** collo d'oca (di uno scarico, ecc.) **6.** *(sl.)* poliziotto **7.** *(spor.)* lancia piattelli (al tiro al piattello) ☆ — *-cellar*, spazio vuoto sotto il palcoscenico; — *-door*, botola; strappo a forma di sette; — *reaction*, *(chim.)* reazione di fissazione; — *shooting*, *(spor.)* tiro al piccione || *fly* —, acchiappamosche; *rat* —, dionea; *rat* —, trappola per topi.
to **trap**[1], *pass.p.p.* **trapped** [træpt], *v.t.i.* **1.** prendere in trappola, accalappiare (anche *fig.*) **2.** munire di sifone **3.** trovare un ostacolo in una conduttura (detto di vapore) **4.** fornire di botole (un palcoscenico).
trap[2], *s. (geol.)* trappo, trappio.
to **trap**[3], *v.t.* adornare, bardare (un cavallo).
trapeze [trə'pi:z], *s. (ginnastica)* trapezio.
trapezial [trə'pi:ziəl], *ag.* di trapezio.
trapeziform [trə'pi:zifɔ:m], *ag.* trapeziforme.
trapezium [trə'pi:zjəm], *s. (geom.)* trapezio.
trapezoid ['træpizɔid], *ag.s. (geom.)* trapezoide.
trapezoidal [ˌtræpi'zɔidəl], *ag.* trapezoidale.
trappean ['træpiən], *ag. (geol.)* di trappo, trappio.
trapper ['træpə*], *s.* chi tende trappole (specialmente ad animali da pelliccia); cacciatore.
trappings ['træpiŋz], *s. pl.* **1.** gualdrappa **2.** *fig.* ornamenti, decorazioni.
Trappist ['træpist], *s. (eccl.)* trappista.
Trappistine ['træpistin], *s.* monaca trappista || **trappistine**, *s.* liquore dei trappisti.
trappy ['træpi], *ag. (fam.)* maligno, insidioso.
traps [træps], *s.pl. (fam.)* oggetti personali, bagaglio: *pack up your* —, prepara il tuo bagaglio.
trash[1] [træʃ], *s.* **1.** rifiuto; robaccia; ciarpame **2.** sciocchezze; bubbole **3.** ramaglia, foglie della canna da zucchero usate come combustibile **4.** gente spregevole, abietta; *(amer.)* bianchi poveri **5.** letteratura dozzinale.
to **trash**[1], *v.t.* **1.** sfrondare, sfogliare **2.** scartare.
trash[2], *s.* guinzaglio.
to **trash**[2], *v.t.* **1.** tenere al guinzaglio **2.** *fig.* ostacolare.
trashery ['træʃəri], *s.* ciarpame; rifiuti, scarti.
trashily ['træʃili], *av.* in modo spregevole.
trashiness ['træʃinis], *s.* mancanza di valore; nullità.
trashy ['træʃi], *ag.* **1.** senza valore; di scarto **2.** spregevole.
Trasimene ['træzimi:n], *no.pr. (geog.)* Trasimeno.
trauma ['trɔ:mə], *s. (patol.)* trauma.
traumatic [trɔ:'mætik], *ag.* traumatico.
traumatism ['trɔ:mətizəm], *s. (patol.)* traumatismo.
travail ['træveil], *s.* **1.** sforzo penoso, faticoso; travaglio **2.** *(arc.)* doglie del parto.
to **travail**, *pass.p.p.* **travailled** ['træveild], *v.i.* **1.** affaticarsi **2.** *(arc.)* soffrire le doglie del parto.
travel ['trævl], *s.* **1.** viaggi: *to be fond of* —, amare i viaggi **2.** *(mec.)* corsa, spostamento ☆ — *agency*, agenzia di viaggi; — *shot*, *(cine.)* carrellata; — *-worn*, sfinito dal viaggio.
to **travel**, *pass.p.p.* **travelled** ['trævld], *v.t.i.* **1.** viaggiare, essere in viaggio: *he travels on business*, viaggia per affari; *she travelled the country*, viaggiò per tutto il paese; *to* — *by train*, viaggiare in treno; *to* — *on foot*, viaggiare a piedi || *his mind travelled over the events of the year*, con la mente riandò agli avvenimenti di quell'anno **2.** *(comm.)* fare il commesso viaggiatore: *he travels for Messrs. Lewis & Co.*, fa il commesso viaggiatore per la ditta Lewis & C.; *to* — *in furs*, fare il rappresentante di pellicce **3.** *(fis.)* propagarsi (di onde sonore, ecc.).
travelled ['trævld], *ag.* che ha viaggiato: *he is a well* (o *much*) — *man*, è un uomo che ha viaggiato molto, che conosce il mondo.

traveller ['trævlə*], *s.c.* viaggiatore, viaggiatrice ‖ *s.* **1.** (*mar.*) canestrello della randa **2.** (*ind. tessile*) anellino, cursore ☆ *travellers' cheque*, (*comm.*) assegno per viaggiatori; —*'s-joy*, (*bot.*) vitalba; —*'s-tale*, racconto inverosimile ‖ *commercial* —, commesso viaggiatore; *fellow-* —, compagno di viaggio, (*neol.*) criptocomunista.

travelling ['trævliŋ], *ag.* **1.** viaggiante, circolante **2.** di, da viaggio **3.** mobile ‖ *s.* il viaggiare ☆ — *bag*, borsa da viaggio; — *dress*, abito da viaggio; — *expenses*, spese di viaggio; — *preparations*, preparativi di viaggio; — *staircase* (o — *stairs*), scala mobile.

travelogue ['trævəloug], *s.* conferenza su un viaggio (illustrata da proiezioni).

traversable ['trævə(:)səbl], *ag.* **1.** attraversabile (di strada, ecc.) **2.** (*dir.*) contestabile.

traverse ['trævə(:)s], *ag.* trasversale, obliquo ‖ *s.* **1.** — (*road*), traversa, via trasversale **2.** (*arch.*) galleria trasversale (di chiesa, ecc.) **3.** (*mil.*) riparo trasversale, parascheggie **4.** (*geom.*) linea trasversale **5.** (*mec.*) spostamento laterale **6.** (*alpinismo*) traversata **7.** (*mar.*) navigazione a bordate **8.** (*artigl.*) brandeggio, spostamento di direzione **9.** (*dir.*) contestazione ‖ — (*survey*), (*topografia*) poligonale ☆ — *arc*, (*mil.*) arco di tiro; — *board*, (*mar.*) tavola della timoneria; — *motor*, (*mec.*) motore del movimento trasversale; — *station*, (*topografia*) vertice di poligonale; — *table*, (*ferr.*) carrello trasbordatore ‖ *hand* —, (*mec.*) spostamento a mano.

to traverse, *v.t.i.* **1.** traversare, attraversare: *district traversed by canals*, regione attraversata da canali **2.** spostarsi lateralmente **3.** (*alpinismo*) fare una traversata **4.** (*mar.*) mettere per lungo, per chiglia **5.** (*artigl.*) brandeggiare (cannoni) **6.** (*dir.*) contestare **7.** opporsi a, ostacolare **8.** *fig.* discutere, considerare a fondo **9.** girare su perno (di compasso, ecc.).

traverser ['trævə(:)sə*], *s.* (*ferr.*) piattaforma girevole; trasbordatore.

travertin(e) ['trævə:tin], *s.* (*min.*) travertino.

travesty ['trævisti], *s.* **1.** parodia **2.** travestimento; travisamento: *it is a — of the truth*, è un travisamento della verità.

to travesty, *v.t.* **1.** parodiare **2.** travestiire; travisare.

trawl [tro:l], *s.* (*mar.*) strascico, sciabica ☆ — *-anchor*, piccola ancora di palamite; — *-boat*, battello da pesca; — *-line*, palamite.

to trawl, *v.t.i.* pescare con strascico, sciabicare.

trawler ['tro:lə*], *s.* **1.** chi pesca con strascico **2.** motopeschereccio a strascico.

trawling ['tro:liŋ], *s.* pesca con strascico.

tray [trei], *s.* **1.** vassoio **2.** (*developing*) —, (*foto.*) bacinella per sviluppo **3.** scompartimento (di cassa, baule, ecc.) ☆ — *-cloth*, tovagliolino (per vassoio); — *-galley* (*tip.*) vantaggio; *ash-* —, portacenere; *tea-* —, vassoio da tè.

treacherous ['tretʃərəs], *ag.* traditore; sleale; perfido: — *blow*, colpo sleale; — *weather*, tempo traditore.

treacherously ['tretʃərəsli], *av.* proditoriamente; slealmente; perfidamente.

treacherousness ['tretʃərəsnis], **treachery** ['tretʃəri], *s.* tradimento; slealtà; perfidia: *to commit an act of — towards s.o.*, commettere un'azione perfida contro qlcu.

treacle ['tri:kl], *s.* melassa.

treacly ['tri:kli], *ag.* di melassa, simile a melassa ‖ — *words*, *fig.* parole melate.

tread [tred], *s.* **1.** passo, andatura: *heavy* —, passo pesante **2.** pedata (di scalino); piuolo (di scala) **3.** superficie di contatto (di scarpa, rotaia); battistrada (di ruota) **4.** atto dell'accoppiamento (detto di uccello maschio).

to tread, *pass.* **trod** [trod], *p.p.* **trodden** ['trodn], *v.t.i.* **1.** camminare: *to — lightly*, camminare con passo leggero; *fig.* trattare con prudenza soggetti delicati ‖ *to — in s.o.'s steps*, *fig.* seguire le orme di qlcu. ‖ *to — a measure*, fare un passo di danza **2.** calpestare; *fig.*

schiacciare, opprimere: *do not — on the flower-beds*, vietato calpestare le aiuole; *to — grapes*, pigiare l'uva; *to — on s.o.'s toes*, pestare i piedi a qlcu. (anche *fig.*) ‖ *to — the boards*, calcare le scene ‖ *to — under foot*, *fig.* mettere sotto i piedi **3.** accoppiarsi con (di uccello maschio) **4.** *to — down*, calpestare; distruggere **5.** *to — in*, calcare dentro, far entrare **6.** *to — out*, estinguere (incendio); reprimere (rivolta).

treadle ['tredl], *s.* pedale: *to work the* —, azionare il pedale ☆ — *-machine*, macchina a pedale.

to treadle, *v.i.* azionare un pedale.

treadmill ['tredmil], *s.* **1.** (*st.*) cilindro orizzontale azionante un mulino (era fatto girare da persone, specialmente carcerati, che camminavano su gradini disposti lungo di esso) **2.** *fig.* lavoro monotono, ingrato.

treason ['tri:zn], *s.* tradimento ☆ *high* —, alto tradimento; lesa maestà.

treasonable ['tri:znəbl], *ag.* proditorio, ingannevole; infido.

treasonableness ['tri:znəblnis], *s.* slealtà.

treasonably ['tri:znəbli], *av.* a tradimento, proditoriamente.

treasonous ['tri:znəs], *ag.* **1.** proditorio, infido **2.** sedizioso.

treasure ['treʒə*], *s.* tesoro (anche *fig.*) ☆ — *-house*, tesoreria; — *-trove*, (*dir.*) tesoro trovato.

to treasure, *v.t.* **1.** ammassare, accumulare: *to — up wealth*, accumulare ricchezze **2.** *fig.* custodire gelosamente; attribuire alto valore a: *she treasures the ring her husband gave her*, considera un tesoro l'anello che le diede suo marito; *to — (up) memories of one's childhood*, custodire gelosamente il ricordo della propria fanciullezza.

treasurer ['treʒərə*], *s.* tesoriere.

treasurership ['treʒərəʃip], *s.* dignità, ufficio di tesoriere.

treasury ['treʒəri], *s.* **1.** tesoreria, erario **2.** *Treasury*, Ministero del Tesoro ‖ *First Lord of the Treasury*, (titolo ufficiale del) Primo Ministro Britannico ‖ *Secretary of the Treasury*, (*amer.*) Ministro del Tesoro ☆ — *bench*, banchi ministeriali; — *bill*, Buono del Tesoro.

treat [tri:t], *s.* festa, trattenimento: *to give the school-children a* —, dare una festa agli scolari ‖ *to stand* —, (*fam.*) pagare le spese del ricevimento **2.** piacere: *to-day I'll give my students a* —, *I'll show them a film*, oggi farò qualcosa di piacevole per i miei allievi, proietterò loro un film ☆ *school* —, festa, trattenimento scolastico.

to treat, *v.t.i.* **1.** trattare, comportarsi con: — *her kindly*, trattala con gentilezza; *is that how you — him?*, è così che ti comporti con lui?; *to — s.o. as if he were a child*, trattare qlcun. come se fosse un bambino **2.** trattare, discutere: *a book treating of physics*, un libro che tratta di fisica; *to — of a subject*, discutere un argomento **3.** trattare, negoziare: *to — for peace*, venire a trattative di pace **4.** (*chim.*) trattare; (*med.*) curare: *he treated me for pneumonia*, mi curò la polmonite; *to — a substance with an acid*, trattare una sostanza con un acido **5.** offrire un trattenimento, pranzo, ecc. a: *to — a person to a good dinner*, offrire ad una persona un buon pranzo.

treater ['tri:tə*], *s.* **1.** negoziatore **2.** anfitrione **3.** chi tratta, discute un argomento.

treating ['tri:tiŋ], *s.* **1.** trattenimento, ricevimento **2.** pranzo offerto agli elettori per accaparrarsene i voti.

treatise ['tri:tiz], *s.* trattato, dissertazione: *a — on ethics*, dissertazione sull'etica; *Cicero's — on friendship*, la dissertazione di Cicerone sull'amicizia.

treatment ['tri:tmənt], *s.* **1.** trattamento **2.** (*med.*) cura: *to undergo — for rheumatism*, sottoporsi a una cura per i reumatismi.

treaty ['tri:ti], *s.* **1.** trattato; patto, convenzione: — *of peace*, trattato di pace **2.** contratto; trattativa ‖ *to be in — for sthg.*, essere in trattative per ql.co.

treble ['trebl], *ag.* **1.** triplo, triplice **2.** (*mus.*) di soprano ‖ *s.* **1.** triplo: *six is the — of two*, sei è il triplo di due **2.** (*mus.*) soprano ☆ — *clef*, (*mus.*) chiave di sol, di violino.

to **treble**, *v.t.i.* triplicare, triplicarsi.

treble, *av.* tre volte tanto: *he earns — my salary*, guadagna tre volte tanto me.

trebling ['treblɪŋ], *s.* moltiplicazione per tre.

trebly ['trebli], *av.* triplicemente, tre volte tanto.

trebuchet ['trebəʃet], **trebucket** ['triːbʌkit], *s.* **1.** (*st.*) trabucco, macchina per lanciare pietre **2.** trappola.

treck, *V.* **trek**.

trecentist [treiˈtʃentist], *s.* (*lett. pitt.*) trecentista.

trecento [trəˈtʃentə], *s.* (*art. lett. italiana*) trecento.

tree [triː], *s.* **1.** albero: *to climb a —*, arrampicarsi su un albero ‖ *to be at the top of the —*, *fig.* essere al culmine della carriera ‖ *to be up a —*, essere perplesso, nell'imbarazzo **2.** (*arc.*) croce (su cui fu crocifisso Gesù) **3.** (*arch.*) trave **4.** (*miner.*) puntello, appoggio ☆ — *-creeper*, (*ornit.*) rampichino; — *-fern*, (*bot.*) felce arborea; — *-frog*, (*zool.*) raganella ‖ *Christmas —*, albero di Natale; *family —*, albero genealogico; *gallows- —*, forca, patibolo.

to **tree**, *v.t.i.* **1.** far rifugiare, rifugiarsi su alberi **2.** mettere in forma (stivali).

treeless ['triːlis], *ag.* senza alberi.

treenail ['triːneil], *s.* (*mar.*) caviglia di legno.

to **treenail**, *v.t.* (*mar.*) assicurare con caviglie.

treetop ['triːtɔp], *s.* cima d'albero.

trefoil ['trefoil], *s.* **1.** (*bot.*) trifoglio **2.** (*arch.*) ornamento trilobato.

trefoiled ['trefoild], *ag.* a forma di trifoglio, trilobato.

trek [trek], *s.* **1.** viaggio in carro trainato da buoi (nel Sud Africa) **2.** migrazione, spedizione organizzata.

to **trek**, *pass.p.p.* **trekked** [trekt], *v.i.* **1.** viaggiare su carro trainato da buoi (nel Sud Africa) **2.** emigrare **3.** trainare un carro (detto di buoi).

trekker ['trekə*], *s.* **1.** chi viaggia su un carro trainato da buoi (nel Sud Africa) **2.** emigrante.

trellis ['trelis], *s.* traliccio, reticolato di legno, ferro; graticcio ☆ — *-work*, graticciata.

to **trellis**, *v.t.* ingraticciare; fornire di graticci.

tremble ['trembl], *s.* tremito, tremolio; fremito: *there was a — in his voice*, ci fu un tremolio nella sua voce ‖ *the trembles*, paralisi agitante, morbo di Parkinson ‖ *to be all of a —*, (*fam.*) tremare come una foglia.

to **tremble**, *v.i.* **1.** tremare (anche *fig.*) : *I — for his safety*, tremo per la sua salvezza; *I — to think what has become of him*, tremo al pensiero di ciò che gli è accaduto; *to — with fear, rage, cold*, tremar di paura, rabbia, freddo ‖ *to — like a leaf* (o *in every limb*), tremare come una foglia **2.** vibrare: *the bridge trembled but did not fall*, il ponte vibrò ma non cadde.

tremblement ['tremblmənt], *s.* (*poet.*) tremito.

trembler ['tremblə*], *s.c.* chi trema ‖ *s.* **1.** cosa che trema **2.** (*elett.*) ruttore; (*mec.*) vibratore.

trembling ['tremblɪŋ], *ag.* tremante, tremolante; fremente ‖ *s.* tremito; tremolio; fremito ‖ *in fear and —*, tutto tremante; in stato di nervosismo ☆ — *-poplar*, (*bot.*) tremolino, pioppo tremolo.

tremblingly ['tremblɪŋli], *av.* tremando; trepidando.

trembly ['trembli], *ag.* (*fam.*) tremante; tremulo.

tremella [triˈmelə], *s.* (*bot.*) tremella (specie di fungo).

tremellose ['treməlous], *ag.* (*bot.*) gelatinoso.

tremendous [triˈmendəs], *ag.* **1.** tremendo; terribile: *it was a — experience*, fu un'esperienza terribile **2.** (*fam.*) enorme; straordinario: *the play had a — success*, la commedia ebbe uno straordinario successo.

tremendously [triˈmendəsli], *av.* **1.** tremendamente **2.** (*fam.*) straordinariamente: — *wealthy*, arciricco.

tremendousness [triˈmendəsnis], *s.* **1.** terribilità **2.** carattere straordinario, singolare.

tremolant ['tremələnt], **tremolo** ['treməlou], *s.* (*mus.*) tremolo.

tremor ['tremə*], *s.* tremore; fremito; brivido.

tremorless ['treməlis], *ag.* senza tremito.

tremulant ['tremjulənt], *s.* (*mus.*) tremolo.

tremulous ['tremjuləs], *ag.* **1.** tremante; tremulo: — *voice*, voce tremula **2.** *fig.* timido: *a — smile*, un timido sorriso.

tremulously ['tremjuləsli], *av.* **1.** tremando, tremolando **2.** timidamente.

tremulousness ['tremjuləsnis], *s.* **1.** tremito, tremolio **2.** *fig.* timidezza.

(to) **trenail**, *V.* (to) **treenail**.

trench [trentʃ], *s.* **1.** fosso, canale **2.** (*mil.*) trincea ☆ — *-coat*, impermeabile militare; — *-mortar*, (*mil.*) mortaio; — *-plough*, aratro per solchi profondi; — *warfare*, guerra di trincea ‖ *front-line —*, trincea avanzata; *water —*, canale d'irrigazione; *zigzag —*, trincea a biscia.

to **trench**, *v.t.i.* **1.** scavare fossi, canali, trincee in **2.** aprirsi un varco **3.** solcare **4.** *to — (up)on* (*sthg.*), usurpare (diritti, ecc.); rasentare.

trenchancy ['trentʃənsi], *s.* mordacità, causticità; acutezza.

trenchant ['trentʃənt], *ag.* tagliente; acuto; penetrante, incisivo (anche *fig.*): — *style*, stile incisivo; *a — sword*, una spada affilata; — *words*, parole taglienti.

trenchantly ['trentʃəntli], *av.* in modo tagliente; acutamente; incisivamente.

trencher[1] ['trentʃə*], *s.* tagliere ☆ — *-cap*, tocco accademico quadrato; — *-friend*, (*letter.*) scroccone, parassita; — *-man*, mangiatore, buona forchetta.

trencher[2], *s.* scavatore di trincee.

trend [trend], *s.* direzione; *fig.* orientamento, tendenza: *the — of the coastline*, la direzione della costa; *the — of my thoughts*, il corso dei miei pensieri.

to **trend**, *v.i.* (*spec. fig.*) dirigersi, tendere: *public opinion is trending towards materialism*, l'opinione pubblica tende al materialismo; *the river trends southwards*, il fiume volge verso sud.

Trent [trent], *no.pr.* (*geog.*) Trento.

trental ['trentl], *s.* (*eccl.*) trigesimo.

trepan[1] [triˈpæn], *s.* **1.** (*chir.*) trapano **2.** (*mec.*) trivella.

to **trepan**[1], *pass.p.p.* **trepanned** [triˈpænd], *v.t.i.* **1.** (*chir.*) trapanare **2.** (*mec.*) tornire scanalature anulari in.

trepan[2], *s.c.* (*arc.*) chi insidia, inganna ‖ *s.* trucco, stratagemma; insidia.

to **trepan**[2], *pass.p.p.* **trepanned**, *v.t.* (*arc.*) prendere in trappola; ingannare; insidiare.

trepanation [,trepəˈneiʃən], *s.* (*chir.*) trapanazione.

trepang [triˈpæŋ], *s.* (*zool.*) oloturia.

trepanning [triˈpænɪŋ], *s.* **1.** (*chir.*) trapanazione **2.** (*metal.*) punzonatura cava.

trephine [triˈfiːn], *s.* (*chir.*) trapano.

to **trephine**, *v.t.* (*chir.*) trapanare.

trepid ['trepid], *ag.* (*rar.*) trepido.

trepidation [,trepiˈdeiʃən], *s.* **1.** trepidazione, ansietà **2.** (*med.*) tremito **3.** vibrazione, oscillazione.

trespass ['trespəs], *s.* **1.** trasgressione, infrazione; (*dir.*) violazione di proprietà: — *of frontier*, violazione di frontiera; *action for —*, causa per violazione di proprietà **2.** (*relig.*) peccato; offesa.

to **trespass**, *v.i.* **1.** violare; disobbedire; oltrepassare i confini: *to — (up)on s.o.'s rights*, violare i diritti di qlcu. ‖ *to — on s.o.'s preserves*, *fig.* invadere il campo d'attività di qlcu., occuparsi di cose che non ci riguardano **2.** (*fam.*) abusare: *to — (up)on s.o.'s kindness*, abusare della gentilezza di qlcu. **3.** (*letter. relig.*) peccare; offendere: *to — against the moral law*, offendere la legge morale ‖ *...as we forgive them that — against us*, ...come noi perdoniamo coloro che ci hanno offeso.

trespasser ['trespəsə*], *s.c.* **1.** trasgressore, trasgreditrice; contravventore, contravventrice ‖ *trespassers will be prosecuted*, vietato entrare, i trasgressori saranno puniti a termine di legge **2.** (*relig.*) peccatore, peccatrice.

tress [tres], *s.* **1.** treccia **2.** ricciolo **3.** *pl.* capigliatura.

to **tress**, *v.t.* intrecciare.

tressed [trest], *ag.* **1.** intrecciato **2.** con trecce ☆ *golden-* —, dalle trecce d'oro.

tressy ['tresi], *ag.* adorno di trecce.

trestle ['tresl], *s.* **1.** cavalletto, trespolo **2.** intelaiatura, traliccio **3.** (*edil.*) capra ☆ — *-bridge*, ponte a trespolo; — *-table*, tavolo da disegno su cavalletti; — *-tree*, (*mar.*) barra costiera.

trestlework ['treslwə:k], *s.* traliccio, travatura a traliccio.

tret [tret], *s.* (*comm. st.*) supplemento di merce (fornito talvolta agli acquirenti per risarcirli dei danni eventualmente derivati dal trasporto).

Treves [tri:vz], *no.pr.* (*geog. st.*) Treviri.

trevet, *V.* **trivet.**

trews [tru:z], *s.pl.* calzoni di stoffa scozzese (portati dai soldati di alcuni reggimenti).

trey [trei], *s.* tre (alle carte, ai dadi).

triable ['traiəbl], *ag.* **1.** tentabile **2.** (*dir.*) processabile; giudicabile.

triad ['traiəd], *s.* **1.** (*fil. teol. mus.*) triade **2.** (*chim.*) elemento trivalente.

triadie [trai'ædik], *ag.* triadico.

trial ['traiəl], *s.* **1.** (*dir.*) giudizio; processo: *to be sent for* —, essere rinviato a giudizio; *to bring s.o. to* —, portare qlcu. in giudizio; *to commit to* —, rinviare a giudizio; *to enter a case for* —, iscrivere a ruolo una causa; *to grant s.o. a new* —, accordare a qlcu. la revisione del processo; *to stand* (*o to undergo*) *a* —, essere processato **2.** prova, esperimento, tentativo: *on* (*o by way of*) —, in prova; a titolo di prova, di esperimento; *to be put to* —, essere messo alla prova; *to give s.o. a* —, prendere qlcu. in prova; *to give sthg. a* — (*o to make a* — *of sthg.*), provare ql.co.; *to make* — *of s.o.'s courage*, mettere alla prova il coraggio di qlcu.; *to stand the* —, reggere alla prova **3.** *fig.* prova: *his brother is a real* — *to him*, suo fratello è una vera croce per lui; *to meet with sad trials*, essere duramente provato ☆ — *balance*, (*comm.*) bilancio di verificazione; — *flight*, volo di prova; — *judge*, (*amer. dir.*) giudice di prima istanza; — *lawyer*, avvocato difensore; — *match*, (*spor.*) eliminatoria; — *trip*, viaggio di prova || *civil* —, (*dir.*) azione civile; *criminal* —, (*dir.*) azione penale.

triandria [trai'ændriə], *s.* (*bot.*) triandria.

triandrian [trai'ændriən], **triandr(i)ous** [trai'ændr(i)əs], *ag.* (*bot.*) triandrio.

triangle ['traiæŋgl], *s.* **1.** (*geom. mec. mus.*) triangolo || *the Triangle*, (*astr.*) il Triangolo **2.** (*amer.*) squadra (da disegno) ☆ *reaction* —, (*aut.*) triangolo di reazione; *right-angled* —, (*geom.*) triangolo rettangolo.

triangular [trai'æŋgjulə*], *ag.* triangolare.

triangularis [trai,æŋgju'lɛəris], *pl.* **triangulares** [trai,æŋgju'lɛəri:z], *s.* (*anat.*) triangolare.

triangularity [trai,æŋgju'læriti], *s.* triangolarità.

triangularly [trai'æŋgjuləli], *av.* triangolarmente.

triangulate [trai'æŋgjulit], *ag.* **1.** triangolato; a triangoli **2.** triangolare.

to triangulate [trai'æŋgjuleit], *v.t.* **1.** rendere triangolare **2.** dividere in triangoli **3.** (*geodesia*) fare la triangolazione di.

triangulation [trai,æŋgju'leiʃən], *s.* (*geodesia*) triangolazione.

triareh ['traiɑ:k], *s.* triarca.

triarchy ['traiɑ:ki], *s.* triarchia.

triassic [trai'æsik], *ag.* (*geol.*) triassico.

tribadism ['tribədizəm], *s.* tribadismo.

tribal ['traibəl], *ag.* tribale, di tribù.

tribalism ['traibəlizəm], *s.* organizzazione in tribù.

tribally ['traibəli], *av.* in tribù.

tribasic [trai'beisik], *ag.* (*chim.*) tribasico.

tribe [traib], *s.* tribù (anche *bot. zool.*).

tribesman, *pl.* **tribesmen** ['traibzmən], *s.* membro li tribù.

tribrach ['tribræk], *s.* (*poes.*) tribraco.

tribrachic [tri'brækik], *ag.* (*poes.*) tribrachico.

tribulation [,tribju'leiʃən], *s.* tribolazione.

tribunal [trai'bju:nl], *s.* tribunale (anche *fig.*).

tribunate ['tribjunit], *s.* (*st.*) tribunato.

tribune[1] ['tribju:n], *s.* **1.** (*st.*) tribuno: — *of the people*, tribuno della plebe **2.** (*fam.*) tribuno, demagogo.

tribune[2], *s.* **1.** tribuna (d'oratore); trono episcopale **2.** (*eccl. arch.*) tribuna.

tribuneship ['tribju:nʃip], *s.* (*st.*) tribunato.

tribunitial [,tribju'niʃəl], **tribunitian** [,tribju'niʃən], *ag.* (*st.*) tribunizio.

tributary ['tribjutəri], *ag.* tributario: — *states*, stati tributari || *s.* **1.** tributario: *they were tributaries of the Romans*, erano tributari dei Romani **2.** (*geog.*) affluente, tributario.

tribute ['tribju:t], *s.* **1.** tributo: *to lay a nation under* —, imporre un tributo a una nazione **2.** *fig.* tributo, omaggio: *the* — *of a tear*, il tributo di una lacrima; *floral tributes*, omaggi floreali; *to pay a* — *to s.o.*, rendere omaggio a qlcu. **3.** (*spec. miner.*) retribuzione in natura.

triear ['trai-kɑ:*], *s.* automobile a tre ruote.

trice [trais], *s.*: *in a* —, in un batter d'occhio.

to trice, *v.t.*: *to* — (**up**), (*mar.*) issare e legare.

tricentenary [trai'sentinəri], *ag.s.* trecentenario.

tricephalous [trai'sefələs], *ag.* tricipite, a tre teste.

tricephalus [trai'sefələs], *s.* (*mostro*) tricipite.

triceps ['traiseps], *ag.s.* (*anat.*) tricipite.

trichi ['tritʃi], *abbr.* di **trichinopoli.**

trichiasis [,triki'eisis], *s.* (*patol.*) trichiasi.

trichina [tri'kainə], *pl.* **trichinae** [tri'kaini:], *s.* (*zool.*) trichina.

trichinopoli [,tritʃi'nəpəli], *s.* «trichinipoli» (sigaro indiano).

trichinosis [,triki'nousis], *s.* (*patol.*) trichinosi.

trichoma [tri'koumə], *s.* (*patol.*) **1.** trichiasi **2.** tricoma.

trichome ['trikoum], *s.* (*bot.*) tricoma.

trichord ['trai-kɔ:d], *ag.* (*mus.*) tricorde || *s.* (*mus.*) tricordo.

trichosis [tri'kousis], *s.* (*patol.*) tricosi.

trichotomy [trai'kɔtəmi], *s.* tricotomia.

trichromatic [,traikrou'mætik], *ag.* (*foto.*) tricromico.

trick [trik], *s.* **1.** trucco; espediente; artificio: *the tricks of the trade*, i trucchi del mestiere; *the tricks of writing*, gli artifici dello stile || *he's up to every* —, la sa lunga || *to get the* —, mangiare la foglia **2.** tiro; imbroglio, inganno: *a nasty* (*o shabby*) — , un tiro mancino; *to play a* — *on s.o.*, giocare un tiro a qlcu. || *he has been up to his old tricks*, ne ha fatta una delle sue **3.** giuoco di abilità, di prestigio **4.** vezzo; mania; abitudine: *she has the* — *of repeating herself*, ha l'abitudine di ripetersi **5.** (*carte*) mano: *to lose*, *to win the* —, perdere, vincere la mano **6.** (*mar.*) turno al timone ☆ — *-cyclist*, ciclista acrobata; — *photography*, (*foto.*) fotografia truccata.

to trick, *v.t.i.* **1.** ingannare; gabbare; turlupinare; giocare brutti tiri a: *to* — *s.o. into doing sthg.*, indurre qlcu. con l'inganno a fare ql.co. || *to* — *s.o. out of sthg.*, scroccare ql.co. a qlcu. **2.** (*arald.*) decorare, dipingere (stemmi) **3.** *to* — **out, up,** (*fam.*) agghindare.

trickery ['trikəri], *s.* inganno, frode; stratagemma.

trickily ['trikili], *av.* **1.** astutamente; ingannevolmente **2.** (*fam.*) in modo rischioso, complicato.

trickiness ['trikinis], *s.* **1.** astuzia, furberia; malizia **2.** (*fam.*) natura complicata (di meccanismo, ecc.); difficoltà, natura rischiosa, delicata (di missione, ecc.).

trickish ['trikiʃ], *ag.* **1.** astuto, scaltro, furbo **2.** (*fam.*) rischioso, complicato.

trickishly ['trikiʃli], *av.* **1.** astutamente, da furbo **2.** (*fam.*) in modo rischioso, complicato.

trickishness ['trikiʃnis], *V.* **trickiness.**

trickle ['trikl], *s.* **1.** gocciolio, gocciolamento **2.** filo di acqua, ruscelletto ☆ — *charge*, (*elett.*) carica centellinare, carica di compensazione.

to trickle, *v.t.i.* **1.** (far) gocciolare; (far) stillare; colare: *blood was trickling from the wound*, il sangue colava dalla ferita **2.** *to* — **in**, infiltrarsi **3.** *to* — **out**, gocciolare, stillare (di liquidi); *fig.* trapelare (di notizie, ecc.).

tricklet ['triklit], s. filo d'acqua.

trickly ['trikli], ag. gocciolante.

tricksiness ['triksinis], s. **1.** furbizia, malizia **2.** giocosità, gaiezza.

trickster ['trikstə*], s. briccone; imbroglione.

tricksy ['triksi], ag. **1.** furbo, malizioso, birichino **2.** giocoso.

trick-track ['trik,træk], s. (giuoco) tric-trac.

tricky ['triki], ag. **1.** astuto, furbo, scaltro **2.** (fam.) complicato (di meccanismo, ecc.); rischioso, delicato (di missione, ecc.).

triclinic [trai'klinik], ag. (min.) triclino.

triclinium [trai'kliniəm], pl. **triclinia** [trai'kliniə], s. (st. romana) triclinio.

tricoline ['trikəlin], s. popeline setificato.

tricolor, (amer.) per **tricolour**.

tricolour ['trikələ*], ag. tricolore ‖ s. tricolore, bandiera tricolore.

tricoloured ['trai,kʌləd], ag. a tre colori, tricolore.

tricorn ['traikɔ:n], ag. tricorno, a tre punte ‖ s. tricorno.

tricorporal [trai'kɔ:pərəl], **tricorporate** [trai'kɔ:pərit], ag. tricorporeo.

tricot ['trikou], s. « tricot », tessuto a maglia.

tricuspid [trai'kʌspid], **tricuspidate** [trai'kʌspideit], ag. (anat.) tricuspide, tricuspidale ☆ — valve, (anat.) valvola tricuspide.

tricycle ['traisikl], s. triciclo ☆ landing gear —, (aer.) carrello triciclo; motor —, (mec.) mototriciclo.

to **tricycle**, v.i. andar in triciclo.

tricyclist ['traisiklist], s.c. chi va in triciclo.

tridactyl(ous) [trai'dæktil(əs)], ag. (zool.) tridattilo.

trident ['traidənt], s. tridente.

tridental [trai'dentl], **tridentate** [trai'denteit], ag. tridentato.

Tridentine [trai'dəntain], ag. **1.** trentino, di Trento **2.** tridentino, del Concilio di Trento ‖ s. cattolico romano.

tridimensional [,traidi'menʃən], ag. tridimensionale.

triduo ['tri:duou], **triduum** ['traidjuəm], s. (eccl.) triduo.

triennial [trai'enjəl], ag. triennale: — plants, piante triennali ‖ s. **1.** terzo anniversario **2.** avvenimento che ricorre ogni tre anni (specialmente visita episcopale).

triennially [trai'enjəli], av. ogni tre anni.

triennium [trai'enjəm], s. triennio.

trier ['trai-ə*], s. **1.** sperimentatore; saggiatore **2.** (fam.) persona tenace, che non si scoraggia **3.** (dir.) giudice; pl. arbitri **4.** prova; cosa difficile ☆ — on, chi prova gli abiti ai clienti in sartoria).

trierarch ['traiərɑ:k], s. (st. greca) trierarca.

trierarchy ['traiərɑ:ki], s. (st. greca) trierarchia.

trifid ['traifid], ag. (bot. zool.) trifido.

trifle ['traifl], s. **1.** bagattella, inezia, cosa di poca importanza: it's a mere —, è una sciocchezza; the merest — puts her out, la minima sciocchezza la innervosisce; to waste time on trifles, perdere il tempo in sciocchezze ‖ a —, un po': your coat is a — long, il tuo soprabito è un po' lungo **2.** piccola somma di denaro: give a — to the waiter, da' ql.co. al cameriere **3.** (lett. mus.) bagattella, opera leggera **4.** (cuc.) sorta di zuppa inglese **5.** peltro.

to **trifle**, v.t.i. **1.** baloccarsi, gingillarsi; scherzare: don't — with love, non scherzar con l'amore; he trifled with a pair of glasses, si gingillava con un paio d'occhiali; she was a girl not to be trifled with, era una ragazza con cui non si poteva scherzare; to — over one's food, gingillarsi col cibo che si ha nel piatto; to — with s.o., prendersi giuoco di qlcu. **2.** to — away, buttar via, sprecare: to — one's time, money away, sprecare il proprio tempo, il proprio denaro.

trifler ['traiflə*], s.c. persona frivola, leggera; chi si gingilla.

trifling ['traiflɪŋ], ag. **1.** insignificante; di poca importanza, trascurabile: a — error, un errore trascurabile; of — value, di valore insignificante **2.** frivolo, eggero (di persona).

triflingly ['traiflɪŋli], av. **1.** in maniera trascurabile **2.** frivolmente, futilmente.

triflingness ['traiflɪŋnis], s. **1.** trascurabilità, scarsa importanza **2.** frivolezza, leggerezza.

trifloral [trai'flɔ:rəl], **triflorous** [trai'flɔ:rəs], ag. (bot.) che ha tre fiori.

trifoliate [trai'fouliit], ag. trifogliato.

trifolium [trai'fouljəm], s. (bot.) trifoglio.

triforium [trai'fɔ:riəm], s. (arch.) triforio.

triform(ed) ['traifɔ:m(d)], ag. triforme.

trig[1] [trig], ag. ordinato; elegante, azzimato (di persona).

to **trig**[1], pass.p.p. **trigged** [trigd], v.t. (dial.) mettere in ordine; azzimare: to — oneself out, azzimarsi.

trig[2], s. bietta di puntello, zeppa (usata come freno).

to **trig**[2], pass.p.p. **trigged**, v.t. frenare con bietta, con zeppa (una ruota).

trig, abbr. di **trigonometry**.

trigamist ['trigəmist], s. trigamo.

trigamous ['trigəməs], ag. trigamo (anche bot.).

trigamy ['trigəmi], s. trigamia.

trigeminal [trai'dʒeminl], ag.s. (anat.) trigemino.

trigeminus [trai'dʒeminəs], s. (anat.) trigemino.

trigger ['trigə*], s. **1.** grilletto (di arma da fuoco): to pull the —, premere il grilletto **2.** (mec.) levetta di comando, di sgancio ☆ — -finger, indice (della mano destra); — -valve, (mec.) valvola di regolazione della pressione ‖ — release —, (foto.) scatto.

triglyph ['traiglif], s. (arch.) triglifo.

triglyphic(al) [trai'glifik(əl)], ag. (arch.) di triglifo.

trigness ['trignis], s. ordine; accuratezza; eleganza.

trigon ['traigən], s. **1.** (geom.) trigono; triangolo **2.** (astr. mus.) trigono.

trigonal ['trigənl], ag. (geom.) triangolare; trigonale.

trigone [tri'goun], s. (anat.) trigono.

trigonometric(al) [,trigənə'metrik(əl)], ag. trigonometrico.

trigonometrically [,trigənə'metrikəli], av. trigonometricamente.

trigonometry [,trigə'nɔmitri], s. trigonometria.

trihedral [trai'hi:drəl], ag. (geom.) triedro.

trihedron [trai'hi:drən], s. (geom.) triedro.

trike [traik], s. (fam.) triciclo.

to **trike**, v.i. (fam.) andare in triciclo.

trilabiate [trai'leibiit], ag. trilabiato.

trilateral [trai'lætərəl], ag. trilaterale, trilatero ‖ s. (geom.) triangolo.

trilby ['trilbi], s. **1.** — (hat), cappello floscio di feltro **2.** pl. (sl.) piedi.

trilinear [trai'liniə*], ag. (geom.) trilineare, trilineo.

trilingual [trai'liŋgwəl], ag. trilingue.

trill [tril], s. **1.** trillo (anche mus.) **2.** (fonet.) consonante vibrata.

to **trill**, v.t.i. **1.** trillare (anche mus.) **2.** (fonet.) far vibrare ☆ trilled consonant, consonante vibrata.

trilling ['trilɪŋ], s. **1.** nato da parto trigemino **2.** (min.) cristallo composto di tre elementi.

trillion ['triljən], s. trilione; (amer.) bilione.

trillionth ['triljənθ], ag. trilionesimo.

trilobate [trai'ləbeit], ag. (bot.) trilobato.

trilobite ['trailəbait], s. (paleont.) trilobite.

trilogy ['triləd
ʒi], s. (lett. mus.) trilogia.

trim [trim], ag. ordinato; lindo; azzimato; ben tenuto ‖ s. **1.** ordine; disposizione; condizione: everythin was in perfect —, tutto era in perfetto ordine ‖ to b in good —, essere di buon umore, in forma ‖ to be i no — for doing sthg., non sentirsi di fare ql.co. ‖ t be out of —, essere di cattivo umore **2.** (mar. aer. assetto: in fighting —, in assetto di guerra **3.** tagli (di capelli) **4.** (aut.) interno della carrozzeria; fin tura **5.** (cine.) taglio.

to **trim**, pass.p.p. **trimmed** [trimd], v.t.i. **1.** ordinar ripulire; assettare **2.** tagliare; spuntare; potare; cimar to — s.o.'s hair, spuntare i capelli a qlcu.; fi spogliare; pelare; to — a tree, potare un albero **3.** o nare, ornarsi; abbellire, abbellirsi 4. (*mar. aer.*) equilibrare; assettare; *to — the sails*, orientare le vele 5. (*pol.*) tergiversare, temporeggiare; barcamenarsi 6. (*fam.*) rimproverare; castigare; bastonare; sconfiggere ‖ *to — s.o.'s jacket*, bastonare qlcu. **7.** *to — away, off*, ritagliare, raffilare **8.** *to — up*, mettere in ordine; assettare; azzimare.

trimester [trai'mestə*], *s.* trimestre.

trimestrial [trai'mestriəl], *ag.* trimestrale.

trimeter ['trimitə*], *s.* (*poes.*) trimetro.

trimly ['trimli], *av.* ordinatamente; accuratamente; elegantemente.

trimmer ['trimə*], *s.c.* **1.** decoratore, decoratrice **2.** (*pol.*) opportunista ‖ *s.* **1.** (*mar.*) stivatore **2.** (*arch.*) trave principale che sopporta una trave secondaria **3.** (*mec.*) attrezzo sbavatore **4.** (*rad.*) compensatore.

trimming ['trimiŋ], *s.* **1.** guarnizione, rifinitura; ornamento, passamaneria **2.** equilibrazione **3.** (*mec.*) sbavatura **4.** (*pol.*) opportunismo **5.** (*fam.*) rimprovero; bastonata: *to give one a sound —*, picchiare uno di santa ragione **6.** *pl.* guarnizioni; contorno: *chicken and trimmings*, pollo con contorno.

trimness ['trimnis], *s.* ordine; accuratezza; eleganza.

trimorphism [trai'mɔ:fizəm], *s.* (*min.*) trimorfismo.

trinal ['trainl], *ag.* trino; triplice.

trinary ['trainəri], *ag.* ternario; triplice.

trine [train], *ag.* trino; triplice ‖ *s.* **1.** triade **2.** (*astr.*) aspetto trino (di due pianeti divergenti di 120°).

trinervate [train'nə:veit], *ag.* (*bot.*) a triplice nervatura.

tringle ['triŋgl], *s.* **1.** bacchetta per tendaggi **2.** (*arch.*) listello.

Trinidad ['trinidæd], *no.pr.* (*geog.*) Trinidad.

Trinitarian [,trini'tɛəriən], *ag.s.* (*teol.*) trinitario.

Trinitarianism [,trini'tɛəriənizəm], *s.* (*teol.*) **1.** dottrina della Trinità **2.** fede nella Trinità.

trinitrotoluene [trai'naitrou'tɔljui:n], *s.* (*chim.*) trinitrotoluene.

trinity ['triniti], *s.* **1.** triplicità **2.** *the Trinity*, (*teol.*) la SS. Trinità ‖ *Trinity Sunday*, festa della SS. Trinità **3.** *Trinity House*, ente competente incaricato della concessione di brevetti di piloti, permessi per la costruzione di fari, ecc.

trinket ['triŋkit], *s.* gingillo, ninnolo, ciondolo.

trinketry ['triŋkitri], *s. coll.* ninnoli, fronzoli, gingilli.

trinomial [trai'noumjəl], *ag.* (*alg.*) trinomiale ‖ *s.* (*alg.*) trinomio.

trio ['tri(:)ou], *pl.* **trios** ['tri(:)ouz], *s.* **1.** (*mus.*) trio **2.** terzetto.

triole ['tri(:)oul], *s.* (*mus.*) terzina.

triolet ['tri(:)oulet], *s.* (*poes.*) componimento poetico di otto versi.

triones [trai'ouni:z], *s.pl.* (*astr.*) trioni.

trior, *V.* **trier**.

trip [trip], *s.* **1.** gita; viaggio; escursione: *to go for to take*) *a —*, fare una gita, un viaggetto **2.** passo agile, veloce **3.** passo falso (anche *fig.*) **4.** sgambetto **5.** (*mec.*) disinnesto, rilascio ☆ *— -gear*, (*mec.*) dispositivo a scatto; *— -hammer*, (*mec.*) maglio meccanico a leva ‖ *round —*, viaggio di andata e ritorno.

to **trip**, *pass.p.p.* **tripped** [tript], *v.t.i.* **1.** camminare con passo agile e leggero; saltellare: *he tripped along*, avanzava saltellando **2.** (*mec.*) far scattare; liberare; (*mar.*) spedare (l'ancora) **3.** (*arc.*) fare una gita, un viaggio **4.** *to — over* (*sthg.*), inciampare; *fig.* fare un passo falso; sbagliare **5.** *to — (up)*, fare inciampare; *fig.* cogliere in fallo.

tripartite ['trai'pɑ:tait], *ag.* tripartito.

tripartitely ['trai'pɑ:taitli], *av.* tripartitamente.

tripartition [,traipɑ:'tiʃən], *s.* tripartizione.

tripe [traip], *s.* **1.** (*cuc.*) trippa **2.** *gener. pl.* (*volg.*) ventre, interiora **3.** (*sl.*) sciocchezze; robaccia ☆ *— de-roche*, sostanza nutritiva ricavata dai licheni.

tripedal ['traipidl], *ag.* che ha tre piedi.

tripeman, *pl.* **tripemen** ['traipmən], *s.* trippaio, ipparo.

tripery ['traipəri], *s.* tripperia.

tripetalous [trai'petələs], *ag.* (*bot.*) tripetalo.

triphthong ['trifθɔŋ], *s.* (*fonet.*) trittongo.

triplane [trai-plein], *s.* (*aer.*) triplano.

triple ['tripl], *ag.* triplo, triplice ☆ *— crown*, triregno, tiara pontificia.

to **triple**, *v.t.i.* triplicare, triplicarsi: *he tripled his efforts*, triplicò i suoi sforzi.

triplet ['triplit], *s.* **1.** (*poes. mus.*) terzina **2.** serie di tre cose **3.** (*fam.*) il nato da un parto trigemino **4.** (*fis.*) tripletto **5.** (*ott.*) sistema di tre lenti.

triplex ['tripleks], *ag.* triplice ‖ *s.* (*mus.*) ritmo in tre tempi; composizione in tre movimenti ☆ *— glass*, vetro infrangibile.

triplicate ['triplikit], *ag.* triplo; triplicato ‖ *s.* triplice copia: *to draw up documents in —*, redigere documenti in triplice copia.

to **triplicate** ['triplikeit], *v.t.* triplicare.

triplication [,tripli'keiʃən], **triplicature** ['triplikeitʃə*], *s.* triplicazione.

triplicity [tri'plisiti], *s.* triplicità.

triply ['tripli], *av.* triplicemente.

tripod ['traipɔd], *s.* **1.** treppiedi; tavolo, sedia con tre gambe **2.** (*archeol.*) tripode.

Tripoli ['tripəli], *no.pr.* (*geog.*) Tripoli ‖ **tripoli**, *s.* (*min.*) tripoli, tripolo.

tripos ['traipɔs], *s.* promozione con lode (all'università di Cambridge).

tripper ['tripə*], *s.c.* **1.** (*fam.*) gitante, escursionista: *I detest noisy trippers*, non posso soffrire i gitanti rumorosi **2.** chi si muove con passo agile **3.** chi inciampa; chi fa inciampare ‖ *s.* cosa che fa inciampare.

tripping ['tripiŋ], *ag.* **1.** agile, leggero; saltellante: *— step*, passo agile] **2.** che inciampa; *fig.* che sbaglia.

trippingly ['tripiŋli], *av.* agilmente.

triptych ['triptik], *s.* (*art.*) trittico.

to **tripudiate** [trai'pju:dieit], *v.i.* (*letter.*) tripudiare; danzare di gioia.

triquetra [trai'kwetrə], *pl.* **triquetrae** [trai'kwetri:], *s.* ornamento simmetrico a tre archi intrecciati.

triquetral [trai'kwetrəl], **triquetrous** [trai'kwetrəs], *ag.* (*spec. bot.*) triangolare.

triradial [trai'reidjəl], **tiradiate(d)** [trai'reidjeit(id)], *ag.* a tre raggi; a tre bracci.

trireme ['trairi:m], *s.* trireme.

to **trisect** [trai'sekt], *v.t.* tripartire, dividere in tre parti uguali.

trisection [trai'sekʃən], *s.* trisezione.

trisector [trai'sektə*], *s.* trisettore.

trisepalous [trai'sepələs], *ag.* (*bot.*) trisepalo.

triserial [trai'siəriəl], **triseriate** [trai'siəriit], *ag.* (*anat. bot.*) a tre, in serie di tre.

trismus ['trizməs], *s.* (*patol.*) trisma.

Tristan ['tristæn], *no.pr.m.* (*lett.*) Tristano.

tristful ['tristful], *ag.* (*arc.*) triste.

Tristram ['tristrəm], *no.pr.m.* (*lett.*) Tristano.

trisyllabic(al) ['trai-si'læbik(əl)], *ag.* trisillabo, trisillabico.

trisyllable ['trai'siləbl], *s.* trisillabo.

trite [trait], *ag.* trito, comune, banale.

tritely ['traitli], *av.* in modo trito, banalmente.

triteness ['traitnis], *s.* banalità.

tritheism ['traiθiizəm], *s.* (*st. relig.*) triteismo.

tritheist ['traiθiist], *s.* (*st. relig.*) triteista.

tritheistic(al) [,traiθi'istik(əl)], *ag.* (*st. relig.*) triteistico.

tritium ['tritiəm], *s.* (*chim.*) tritio.

Triton ['traitn], *no.pr.m.* (*mit.*) Tritone ‖ **triton**, *s.* (*zool.*) tritone.

tritone ['traitoun], *s.* (*mus.*) tritono.

triturable ['tritjurəbl], *ag.* triturabile.

to **triturate** ['tritjureit], *v.t.* triturare.

trituration [,tritju'reiʃən], *s.* triturazione.

triturator ['tritjureitə*], *s.* (*ind.*) trituratore.

triumph ['traiəmf], s. **1.** (st.) trionfo **2.** trionfo, successo: to achieve great triumphs, riportare grandi successi **3.** fig. esultanza, gioia; aria di trionfo: there was a note of — in his voice, c'era una nota di esultanza nella sua voce.

to **triumph**, v.t.i. **1.** (st.) celebrare il trionfo **2.** trionfare: to — over one's enemies, trionfare sui propri nemici **3.** esultare **4.** (rar.) vincere, sottomettere.

triumphal [trai'ʌmfəl], ag. trionfale ☆ — arch, arco di trionfo.

triumphant [trai'ʌmfənt], ag. trionfante; vittorioso.

triumphantly [trai'ʌmfəntli], av. trionfalmente.

triumpher ['traiəmfə*], s.c. trionfatore, trionfatrice.

triumphingly ['traiəmfiŋli], av. trionfalmente.

triumvir [trai'ʌmvə(:)*], pl. **triumvirs** [trai'ʌmvə(:)z], **triumviri** [trai'ʌmvirai], s. (st.) triumviro.

triumvirate [trai'ʌmvirit], s. (st.) triumvirato.

triune ['traiju:n], ag. (teol.) uno e trino.

trivalence [trai'veiləns], **trivalency** [trai'veilənsi], s. (chim.) trivalenza.

trivalent ['trivələnt], ag. (chim.) trivalente.

trivalve ['traivælv], **trivalvular** [trai'vælvjulə*], ag. (bot. zool.) trivalve.

trivet ['trivit], s. treppiedi ‖ as right as a —, (fam.) in ottime condizioni; benissimo, alla perfezione.

trivial ['triviəl], ag. **1.** insignificante, banale, futile (di argomento, ecc.) **2.** superficiale, leggero (di persona) **3.** (bot. zool.) popolare, non scientifico.

trivialism ['triviəlizəm], **triviality** [,trivi'æliti], s. **1.** banalità; futilità **2.** superficialità.

to **trivialize** ['triviəlaiz], v.t. (rar.) rendere meschino, banale.

trivially ['triviəli], av. **1.** banalmente **2.** leggermente, superficialmente.

trivialness ['triviəlnis], s. **1.** banalità, futilità **2.** superficialità.

trivium ['triviəm], s. (st.) trivio.

triweekly [trai'wi:kli], ag. trisettimanale.

trizonal ['trai'zounl], ag. a tre zone.

troat [trout], s. bramito (di cervo).

to **troat**, v.i. bramire (di cervo).

troear ['troukα:*], s. (chir.) trequarti.

trochaic [trou'keiik], ag. (poes.) trocaico.

trochal ['trɔkəl], ag. a forma di ruota (di rotiferi).

trochanter [trou'kæntə*], s. (anat.) trocantere.

troche [trouʃ], s. (farm.) pastiglia.

trochee ['trouki:], s. (poes.) trocheo.

trochilus¹ ['trɔkiləs], s. (ornit.) **1.** colibrì **2.** piviere dei coccodrilli.

trochilus², s. (arch.) trochilo.

trochlea ['trɔkliə], pl. **trochleae** ['trɔklii:], s. (anat.) troclea.

troclear ['trɔkliə*], ag. (anat.) trocleare.

trod [trɔd], pass. di to tread.

trodden ['trɔdn], p.p. di to tread.

troglodyte ['trɔglədait], s. troglodita.

troglodytic(al) [,trɔglou'ditik(əl)], ag. trogloditico.

troglodytism ['trɔglədaitizəm], s. trogloditismo.

troika ['trɔikə], s. « troika ».

Troilus ['trouiləs], no.pr.m. (lett.) Troilo.

Trojan ['troudʒən], ag. troiano ‖ — horse, « quinta colonna » ‖ s.c. troiano, troiana ‖ to work like a —, sgobbare come un negro.

troll¹ [troul], s. **1.** giro; ripetizione **2.** (mus.) canone **3.** mulinello (di canna da pesca); cucchiaino da pesca.

to **troll¹**, v.t.i. **1.** girare, far girare, far rotolare **2.** cantare (in un canone), cantare a voce spiegata **3.** pescare con il cucchiaino **4.** (arc.) far girare (la bottiglia) a tavola.

troll², s. (mit. scandinava) **1.** (arc.) gigante **2.** spiritello, gnomo, nano.

trolley ['trɔli], s. **1.** carrello; carretto **2.** (elett.) « trolley », rotella di presa ☆ — -bus (o — -coach), filobus; — -car, (amer.) vettura tranviaria; — -line, linea tranviaria; — -pole, (elett.) asta di presa; — -table, carrello, tavola a rotelle; — -wheel, (elett.) rotella di presa.

trollop ['trɔləp], s. **1.** sudiciona **2.** sgualdrina, prostituta.

trollopish ['trɔləpiʃ], **trollopy** ['trɔləpi], ag. sporco; disordinato.

trolly, V. **trolley.**

trombone [trɔm'boun], s. (mus.) trombone.

trombonist [trɔm'bounist], s. suonatore ditrombone.

trommel ['trɔməl], s. (miner.) vaglio a tamburo.

trompe [trɔmp], s. (mec.) tromba a vento.

trona ['trounə], s. (chim.) trona.

troop [tru:p], s. **1.** banda; frotta; gruppo; gregge, branco: in troops, a frotte **2.** pl. (mil.) truppe **3.** squadrone di cavalleria; comando di uno squadrone di cavalleria ‖ to get one's —, essere promosso capitano **4.** segnale di adunata delle truppe (dato col tamburo) **5.** « troupe », compagnia di attori ☆ — -carrier, aereo per trasporto di truppe; — -ship, nave per trasporto di truppe; — -train, tradotta.

to **troop**, v.t.i. **1.** radunare, radunarsi; raggruppare, raggrupparsi; raccogliersi; affollarsi **2.** camminare in folla, in gruppo: the children trooped along the sidewalk, i bambini camminavano in gruppo lungo il marciapiede **3.** sfilare ‖ to — the colours, (mil.) passare in rassegna.

trooper ['tru:pə*], s. **1.** soldato di cavalleria ‖ to swear like a —, bestemmiare come un turco **2.** cavallo di truppa **3.** nave per trasporto di truppe.

tropaeolum [trou'pi:ələm], pl. **tropaeolums** [trou-'pi:ələmz], **tropaeola** [trou'pi:ələ]. s. (bot.) tropeolo.

trope [troup], s. (ret.) tropo.

trophie ['trɔfik], ag. (anat.) trofico ☆ — nerves, nervi trofici.

trophied ['troufid], ag. ornato di trofei.

trophy ['troufi], s. trofeo.

tropic ['trɔpik], s. **1.** (astr. geog.) tropico ‖ — of Cancer, Tropico del Cancro; — of Capricorn, Tropico del Capricorno **2.** pl. regioni tropicali ☆ — -bird, (ornit.) fetonte.

tropical ['trɔpikəl], ag. **1.** tropicale; lussureggiante **2.** ardente; appassionato **3.** metaforico, figurato.

tropically ['trɔpikəli], av. **1.** in modo lussureggiante **2.** ardentemente; appassionatamente **3.** metaforicamente, in modo figurato.

tropological [,trɔpou'lɔdʒikəl], ag. (ret.) tropologico.

tropologically [,trɔpou'lɔdʒikəli], av. (ret.) tropologicamente.

tropology [trou'pɔlədʒi], s. (ret.) tropologia.

trot [trɔt], s. **1.** trotto; trottata: he went off for a short —, se ne andò per una trottatina; to break into a —, mettersi al trotto; to go at a slow —, andare al piccolo trotto ‖ to keep s.o. on the —, tener qlcu. in movimento; far sgobbare qlcu. **2.** bambino, trottolino **3.** (sl. scolastico amer.) bigino.

to **trot**, pass.p.p. **trotted** ['trɔtid], v.t.i. **1.** (far) trottare; andare al trotto; mettere al trotto: he trotted his horse to death, fece trottare il suo cavallo fino a sfinirlo **2.** to — along, trotterellare; andarsene in fretta: it is getting late so I must — along, si fa tardi, devo andarmene in fretta **3.** to — out, far trottare (un cavallo) per mostrare la sua andatura; fig. esibire, mostrare (persona, cosa, ecc.) per suscitare ammirazione.

troth [trouθ], s. (arc.) **1.** verità: in —; in verità **2.** parola: promessa: to plight one's —, dare la propria parola (specialmente nei fidanzamenti).

trotter ['trɔtə*], s. **1.** trottatore (cavallo) **2.** (scherz.) piede **3.** pl. (cuc.) zampetto.

troubadour ['tru:bəduə*], s. (st. lett.) trovatore.

trouble ['trʌbl], s. **1.** disturbo; pena; noia, fastidio, guaio: his troubles are over, i suoi guai sono finiti; le cose gli vanno meglio; I am putting you to a lot of —, Le sto procurando molto disturbo; it is not worth the —, non ne vale la pena; life is full of small troubles, la vita è piena di piccole noie; what shall I give you for the —?, che cosa Le debbo per il disturbo?; to take the — to do sthg., prendersi la pena di fare ql.co. **2.** difficoltà

intrigo; imbroglio, pasticcio: *the — is that...*, la difficoltà sta nel fatto che...; *you will have — with him*,
avrai delle seccature con lui; *to be in —*, essere nei
pasticci; *to get into —*, cacciarsi nei pasticci; *to get out
of —*, togliersi dai pasticci 3. (*patol.*) disturbo; malattia: *he had liver troubles*, ha avuto disturbi di fe-
gato; *to have heart —*, avere disturbi di cuore || *what
is the —?*, che disturbi hai? 4. disordine, conflitto
sociale: *there has been a good deal of — there during
recent years*, ci sono stati molti disordini là in questi
ultimi anni 5. (*mec.*) guasto, sregolazione ☆ —
shooting device, (*elett.*) apparecchio per la localizzazione dei guasti.

to **trouble**, *v.t.i.* 1. (IV) disturbare, disturbarsi; incomodare, incomodarsi; importunare: *don't — to write
to him*, non darti la pena di scrivergli; *I am sorry to —
you*, mi spiace disturbarti; *I shall not — you with
the details*, non ti importunerò con i particolari ||
may I — you for the bread?, vorresti passarmi il pane,
per favore?; *may I — you to shut the door?*, ti spiacerebbe chiudere la porta? 2. preoccuparsi: *don't — about
it*, non preoccupartene 3. affliggere, far soffrire: *how long
has this cough been troubling you?*, da quanto tempo ti
affligge questa tosse?; *I am troubled with neuralgia*,
sono tormentato dalla nevralgia.

troubled ['trʌbld], *ag.* agitato, turbato; inquieto,
ansioso: *a — sleep*, un sonno agitato; *a — soul*, un'ani-
ma inquieta || *to fish in — waters*, *fig.* pescare nel
torbido.

troubler ['trʌblə*], *s.c.* disturbatore, disturbatrice.

troublesome ['trʌblsəm], *ag.* 1. importuno; fastidioso; noioso, seccante 2. penoso, tormentoso, doloroso.

troublesomely ['trʌblsəmli], *av.* importunamente,
fastidiosamente.

troublesomeness ['trʌblsəmnis], *s.* fastidio; noia,
molestia, seccatura.

troublous ['trʌbləs], *ag.* (*arc.*) agitato, inquieto,
turbato || *— times*, tempi difficili.

trough [trɔf], *s.* 1. trogolo; tinozza, mastello 2. doccia (di grondaia); canale (per lo scolo delle acque) 3. (*conveying*) —, (*ind.*) canale trasportatore 4. cavo dell'onda: *in the — of the sea*, fra i marosi 5. (*meteorologia*) avvallamento, depressione a V ☆ *drinking
—*, abbeveratoio; *mercury —*, vaschetta del mercurio.

to **trounce** [trauns], *v.t.* 1. bastonare, picchiare 2. punire, castigare 3. sgridare, rimproverare.

trouncing ['traunsiŋ], *s.* 1. busse, percosse 2. punizione, castigo 3. rimprovero.

troupe [tru:p], *s.* «troupe» (compagnia di attori,
ecc.).

trouper ['tru:pə*], *s.* membro di una «troupe».

trousers ['trauzəz], *s.pl.* (*a pair of*) —, calzoni, pantaloni ☆ — *-clip*, molletta per calzoni; — *-press* (o
— *-stretcher*), stiracalzoni.

trousered ['trauzəd], *ag.* che porta, che ha i calzoni.

trousering ['trauzəriŋ], *s.* stoffa per calzoni.

trousseau ['tru:sou], *pl.* **trousseaus, trousseaux**
['tru:souz], *s.* corredo (da sposa).

trout [traut], *s.* (*invariato al pl.*) trota: *a river full
of —*, un fiume ricco di trote ☆ — *-coloured*, trotino
(di cavallo); — *-fishing*, pesca delle trote; — *-stream*,
vivaio di trote || *salmon- —* (o *sea- —*), trota salmonata.

to **trout**, *v.i.* pescare trote.

troutlet ['trautlit], **troutling** ['trautliŋ], *s.* (*ittiol.*)
rotella.

trouty ['trauti], *ag.* ricco di trote.

trouvère [tru:'vɛə*], *s.* (*st. lett.*) troviero.

trove [trouv], *s.* (*dir.*) tesoro trovato.

trover ['trouvə*], *s.* (*dir.*) 1. ricupero di proprietà
perduta 2. azione legale per ottenere la restituzione
di beni illegalmente perduti.

to **trow** [trou], *v.t.* (*arc.*) pensare, credere; domandarsi: *what ails him*, (*I*) —?, mi domando che cosa
lo affligga.

trowel ['trauəl], *s.* 1. (*strum. artig.*) mestola, caz-

zuola; fratazzo || *to lay it on with a —*, *fig.* adulare
grossolanamente 2. paletta da giardiniere; trapiantatoio.

to **trowel**, *pass.p.p.* **trowelled** ['trauəld], *v.t.* lisciare,
stendere con la cazzuola, la mestola (gesso, ecc.).

trowsers, *V.* **trousers**.

Troy [trɔi], *no.pr.* (*geog. st.*) Troia.

troy, *s.* —(*weight*), «troy» (sistema di pesi usato in
Gran Bretagna e negli Stati Uniti per pietre e metalli
preziosi, medicinali): *ounce —*, oncia troy (= g. 31,10).

truancy ['tru(:)ənsi], *s.* 1. svogliatezza, pigrizia, poltroneria 2. assenza ingiustificata (da scuola); il marinare la scuola.

truant ['tru(:)ənt], *ag.* svogliato, pigro, poltrone,
vagabondo, ozioso || *s.c.* 1. persona che trascura il
lavoro 2. ragazzo, ragazza che marina la scuola: *to
play —*, marinare la scuola.

to **truant**, *v.i.* 1. poltrire 2. marinare la scuola.

truantly ['tru(:)əntli], *av.* pigramente, oziosamente,
svogliatamente.

truantship ['tru(:)əntʃip], *s.* poltroneria.

truce [tru:s], *s.* 1. tregua, armistizio || *the — of God*,
(*st.*) la tregua di Dio || *flag of —*, bandiera bianca 2. ri-
poso; cessazione (di affanni, ecc.): *let there be a — to
that trouble*, date tregua a questo affanno ☆ — *-bearer*,
(*mil.*) parlamentario; — *breaker*, violatore della tregua.

truceless ['tru:slis], *ag.* senza tregua.

truck[1] [trʌk], *s.* 1. baratto, scambio; traffico 2. (*fam.*)
rapporti: *we have no — with him*, non abbiamo nulla
a che fare con lui 3. pagamento in natura || *Truck
Acts*, leggi vietanti il sistema di pagamento in natura 4. articoli vari 5. (*fam.*) merce scadente, robaccia;
fig. sciocchezze 6. (*amer.*) ortaggi ☆ — *-system*, sistema di pagamento in natura.

to **truck**[1], *v.t.i.* 1. barattare, scambiare; trafficare,
commerciare 2. (*fam.*) avere relazioni 3. pagare in
natura.

truck[2], *s.* 1. carro; carrello; (*amer.*) autocarro 2. (*ferr.*)
pianale; carrello 3. (*mar.*) formaggetta, pomo, galletta
☆ — *crane*, (*mec.*) carro gru; — *driver*, camionista;
— *trailer*, (*aut.*) rimorchio; — *wheel*, (*ferr.*) ruota del
carrello || *fire —*, (*aut.*) autopompa; *gasoline —*, auto-
cisterna per benzina; *hand —*, carrello a mano;
railroad —, carrello portabagagli; *refrigerator —*,
autofrigorifero.

to **truck**[2], *v.t.* trasportare (su carrello, carro, ecc.).

truckage ['trʌkidʒ], *s.* 1. trasporto (con autocarro) 2. costo di trasporto (con autocarro).

trucker[1] ['trʌkə*], *s.* (*amer.*) coltivatore, ortolano.

trucker[2], *s.* camionista.

truckle ['trʌkl], *s.* 1. puleggia, carrucola 2. — (*-bed*),
letto basso con rotelle; brandina.

to **truckle**, *v.i.* abbassarsi, avvilirsi, strisciare.

truckler ['trʌklə*], *s.c.* persona servile.

truculence ['trʌkjuləns], **truculency** ['trʌkjulənsi],
s. truculenza, ferocia.

truculent ['trʌkjulənt], *ag.* truculento; feroce; brutale.

truculently ['trʌkjuləntli], *av.* ferocemente; trucemente; brutalmente.

trudge [trʌdʒ], *s.* cammino faticoso.

to **trudge**, *v.t.i.* camminare faticosamente; percorrere (un cammino) a fatica.

Trudy ['tru:di], *no.pr.f.* dim. di **Gertrude**.

true [tru:], *ag.* 1. vero, conforme a verità; esatto:
the sad news was only too —, purtroppo la triste notizia era più che vera; *to come* (o *to prove*) —, realizzarsi, avverarsi 2. vero, reale; autentico; legittimo:
the — God, il vero Dio; *the — heir*, l'erede legittimo;
a — poet, un vero poeta 3. fedele; leale: *to be — to
s.o.*, essere fedele a qlcu. || *as — as steel*, a tutta pro-
va 4. intonato (di voce, strumento) 5. preciso, accurato 6. puro, non adulterato 7. centrato; diritto, al-
lineato: *the table isn't —*, il tavolo non è orizzontale;
to centre a wheel —, centrare perfettamente una ruota ||
s. (*mec.*) centratura, allineamento ☆ — *-blue*, (*fam.*)

(persona) fedele, leale; — -born, vero, autentico, genuino: a — -born gentleman, un vero gentiluomo; — -bred, di razza, purosangue: a — -bred horse, un cavallo purosangue; — copy, (comm.) copia conforme; — -hearted, sincero, fedele; — -heartedness, sincerità, fedeltà; — -love, innamorato, innamorata; (bot.) paride quadrifoglia; — -love(r's) knot, nodo d'amore.

to **true**, v.t. (mec.) centrare, allineare; rettificare: to — (up) a wheel, centrare una ruota.

true, av. (rar.) veramente, sinceramente.

trueness ['tru:-nis], s. (rar.) 1. verità 2. sincerità, fedeltà, lealtà 3. esattezza.

truffle ['trʌfl], s. tartufo ☆ — -dog, cane da tartufi.

truffled ['trʌfld], ag. tartufato.

trug [trʌg], s. 1. secchiello di legno (per il latte) 2. cestino di vimini; panierino.

truism ['tru(:)izm], s. truismo, verità lapalissiana.

trull [trʌl], s. (arc.) sgualdrina.

truly ['tru:li], av. 1. veramente, sinceramente; in verità, davvero ǁ yours (very) —, vostro devotissimo (nella chiusa di una lettera) 2. fedelmente, lealmente 3. esattamente; con precisione.

trump[1] [trʌmp], s. 1. (carte) trionfo, briscola ǁ to put s.o. to his trumps, fig. ridurre qlcu. agli estremi ǁ to turn up trumps, fig. riuscire, avere fortuna 2. (fam.) persona retta, onesta ☆ — card, (carte) trionfo, briscola.

to **trump**[1], v.t.i. 1. giocare una briscola; vincere (una carta) con una briscola 2. to — up, fig. inventare (scuse, pretesti).

trump[2], s. (arc. poet.) tromba: the — of doom, la tromba del Giudizio Universale.

trumpery ['trʌmpəri], ag. vistoso; illusorio; senza valore ǁ s. 1. chincaglieria 2. sciocchezza.

trumpet ['trʌmpit], s. 1. tromba: to blow a —, dar fiato alla tromba ǁ to blow one's own —, tessere le proprie lodi 2. (mil.) trombettiere; araldo 3. cornetto acustico; — -call, suono di tromba; — -flower, (bot.) gelsomino; — -major, (mil.) primo trombettiere ǁ ear- —, cornetto acustico; speaking —, portavoce, megafono.

to **trumpet**, v.t.i. 1. proclamare a suon di tromba; strombazzare 2. suonare la tromba 3. barrire.

trumpeter ['trʌmpitə*], s. 1. suonatore di tromba; (mil.) trombettiere 2. (ornit.) piccione trombettiere.

truncal ['trʌŋkəl], ag. di tronco.

truncate ['trʌŋkeit], ag. tronco, troncato ☆ — cone, (geom.) tronco di cono.

to **truncate**, v.t. troncare, mozzare.

truncately ['trʌŋkeitli], av. troncamente.

truncation [trʌŋ'keiʃən], **truncature** ['trʌŋkətʃə*], s. troncamento.

truncheon ['trʌntʃən], s. bastone; manganello.

to **truncheon**, v.t. bastonare; dare colpi di manganello a.

trundle ['trʌndl], s. 1. rotella orientabile 2. (mec.) rullo 3. carrello a ruote basse ☆ — bed, letto a rotelle.

to **trundle**, v.t.i. 1. (far) rotolare, correre, ruzzolare, scorrere: he trundled a hoop along the path, fece correre un cerchio lungo il sentiero 2. (sl.) lanciare (al cricket).

trundler ['trʌndlə*], s. (sl.) lanciatore (al cricket).

trunk [trʌŋk], s. 1. tronco 2. (arch.) fusto 3. baule; cassa 4. (mar.) cassa 5. (miner.) vasca per la purificazione di minerali 6. proboscide 7. pl. calzoni corti 8. pl. calzoncini (da bagno, da tennis, ecc.) ☆ — -call, (tel.) comunicazione interurbana; — -engine, (mec.) motore a pistoni cavi; — -exchange, (tel.) centrale interurbana; — -line, (tel.) linea principale; — -maker, valigiaio; — -nail, borchia; — -road, strada maestra ǁ railroad —, (ferr.) complesso di binari; sewer — (o drain —) line, collettore di fognatura.

to **trunk**, v.t. (miner.) separare (un minerale) da altre sostanze.

trunkful ['trʌŋkful], s. quanto è contenuto in un baule.

trunnion ['trʌnjən], s. (artigl.) orecchione.

trunnioned ['trʌnjənd], ag. (artigl.) munito di orecchioni.

trusion ['tru:ʒən], s. 1. (dir.) usurpazione 2. (rar.) spinta.

truss [trʌs], s. 1. fascio; fastello (di fieno, paglia); balla 2. (arch.) capriata; armatura in legno; travatura; puntello 3. (mar.) trozza 4. (med.) cinto erniario ☆ — -beam, (edil.) trave composta; — head screw, (mec.) vite con testa a goccia; — tackle, (mar.) paranco di stazza ǁ king-post —, (arch.) capriata semplice; scissors —, (arch.) capriata di tipo tedesco.

to **truss**, v.t. 1. legare le ali di (un capo di selvaggina, ecc., prima di cuocerlo); legare lungo il corpo (le braccia di una persona) ǁ to — a sail, (mar.) raccogliere una vela 2. (arch.) puntellare 3. to — (up), impiccare.

trust [trʌst], s. 1. fiducia, fede: — in God, fede in Dio; I put my — in her, ho fiducia in lei 2. speranza: that girl was our sole —, quella ragazza era la nostra unica speranza 3. (comm.) credito: to supply goods on —, fornire merci a credito 4. incarico di fiducia: to desert one's —, mancare al proprio dovere ǁ breach of —, abuso di fiducia 5. custodia: to hold sthg. in —, avere ql.co. in custodia 6. (dir.) fidecommisso 7. «trust», sindacato ǁ the Standard Oil Trust, il «trust» del petrolio (1879) ☆ — deed, atto di fidecommisso; — money, deposito di garanzia ǁ financial —, sindacato di capitali; manufacturing —, sindacato industriale.

to **trust**, v.t.i. 1. aver fiducia (in), confidare (in), fidarsi (di): he cannot be trusted with this transaction, non gli si può affidare questa operazione; he trusts in his luck, si fida della propria fortuna; she may be trusted to execute her task, si può esser sicuri che eseguirà il suo compito; to — s.o. with sthg., affidare ql.co. a qlcu.; to — to memory, fidarsi della memoria 2. sperare: I — you will soon be better, spero che presto starete meglio 3. (comm.) far credito.

trustee [trʌs'ti:], s. 1. (dir.) fidecommissario; fiduciario; curatore 2. amministratore ǁ board of trustees, consiglio di amministrazione.

trusteeship [trʌs'ti:-ʃip], s. 1. (dir.) fidecommisso; carica di curatore 2. amministrazione ǁ — territory, territorio sottoposto ad amministrazione fiduciaria.

truster ['trʌstə*], s.c. chi si fida; chi fa credito.

trustful ['trʌstful], ag. fiducioso, confidente.

trustfully ['trʌstfuli], av. fiduciosamente.

trustfulness ['trʌstfulnis], s. fiducia, confidenza.

trustification [,trʌstifi'keiʃən], s. (comm.) fusione in consorzio monopolistico.

to **trustify** ['trʌstifai], v.t. (comm.) fondere in consorzio monopolistico.

trustily ['trʌstili], av. fedelmente; lealmente.

trustiness ['trʌstinis], s. fedeltà; lealtà.

trustingly ['trʌstiŋli], av. fiduciosamente.

trustless ['trʌstlis], ag. 1. infedele, indegno di fiducia; sleale 2. diffidente, sospettoso.

trustworthiness ['trʌst,wə:ðinis], s. 1. lealtà, onestà; fedeltà 2. credibilità, veracità; esattezza (di testimonianza, ecc.).

trustworthy ['trʌst,wə:ði], ag. 1. fido, fidato, leale 2. degno di fede; esatto, attendibile: we have learnt from a — source that..., abbiamo appreso da fonte sicura che....

trusty ['trʌsti], ag. (arc.) fidato, leale: to our lieges, ai nostri fedeli sudditi ǁ s. (amer.) carcerato che si comporta bene.

truth [tru:θ], s. verità, vero: the honest (o real, plain o naked) —, la pura e semplice verità; there is some — in what he said, c'è del vero in ciò che disse; to tell (o to speak) the —, dire la verità; — to tell (o to say), (arc.) a dire il vero ǁ in — (o of a —), dire il vero, sinceramente ǁ — will out, prov. la verità viene sempre a galla ☆ — -serum, siero della verità; Gospel —, verità indiscussa: this is Gospel —!, questo è Vangelo! ǁ home truths, verità spiacevoli.

truthful ['tru:θful], *ag.* **1.** vero, veritiero, verace; sincero **2.** fedele, esatto (di riproduzioni artistiche).

truthfully ['tru:θfuli], *av.* **1.** veracemente, sinceramente **2.** fedelmente, esattamente.

truthfulness ['tru:θfulnis], *s.* **1.** veracità; sincerità **2.** fedeltà, esattezza (di riproduzioni artistiche).

truthless ['tru:θlis], *ag.* **1.** falso, menzognero **2.** sleale.

truthlessness ['tru:θlisnis], *s.* **1.** falsità, menzogna **2.** slealtà, malafede.

try [trai], *s.* (*fam.*) prova, tentativo: *to have a —at sthg.*, fare un tentativo, provare a fare ql.co.; *to have a — for sthg.*, concorrere a ql.co.

to try, *pass.p.p.* tried [traid], *v.t.i.* **1.** provare, tentare; sperimentare; cercare, sforzarsi: *he tried how far he could throw the ball*, provò a quale distanza riusciva a lanciare la palla; *she tried to smile*, si sforzò di sorridere; *she was trying hard to go on*, cercava con ogni mezzo di continuare; *why don't you — these pills?*, perchè non provi queste pillole?; *to — an experiment*, tentare un esperimento ‖ *it is worth trying*, vale la pena di tentare ‖ *to — one's best* (o *hardest*) *to do sthg.*, fare il possibile per fare ql.co. ‖ *to — one's hand at sthg.*, tentare di fare ql.co. ‖ *to — one's strength*, misurare le proprie forze **2.** provare, mettere alla prova: *he has been sorely tried by life*, è stato duramente provato dalla vita; *you are trying my patience*, stai mettendo alla prova la mia pazienza ‖ *to — one's eyes*, affaticarsi gli occhi **3.** verificare: *— the brakes of the car*, verifica i freni della macchina **4.** assaggiare: *to — a dish*, assaggiare un piatto **5.** (*dir.*) processare, giudicare; (*amer.*) difendere (una causa): *he was tried for murder*, fu processato per assassinio **6.** *to — for* (*sthg.*), cercare di ottenere; concorrere a, competere per ottenere **7.** *to — back*, (*caccia*) ritornare sui propri passi **8.** *to — down*, (*ind.*) fondere (il grasso) **9.** *to — on*, provare, misurare (abiti) ‖ *to — it on with s.o.*, (*fam.*) cercare di mettere qlcu. nel sacco **10.** *to — out*, sottoporre a dura, prolungata prova; raffinare (metalli); fondere (grasso di balena) **11.** *to — over*, provare (un pezzo di musica, ecc.) **12.** *to — up*, (*artig.*) piallare (una tavola).

try, (*nei composti*): *— -on*, prova (di abiti); (*fam.*) tentativo d'inganno; *— -out*, prova (di macchine, ecc.); (*teat.*) rappresentazione in provincia (per saggiare il giudizio del pubblico); *— -plane*, (*artig.*) pialla; *— -square*, (*tec.*) squadra a battente; *— -your-strength machine*, macchina per misurare la forza.

trying ['traiiŋ], *ag.* **1.** difficile, duro; penoso: *— times*, tempi difficili; *— winter*, inverno rigido **2.** che mette a dura prova; difficilmente sopportabile: *— light*, luce che affatica gli occhi; *she is very —*, è davvero insopportabile ‖ *s.* **1.** prova: *— of the engines*, (*mar.*) prova macchine **2.** (*dir.*) giudizio.

tryingly ['traiiŋli], *av.* duramente, penosamente; in modo da mettere a dura prova.

trypanosome ['tripənəsoum], *s.* (*biol.*) tripanosoma.

trypanosomiasis [,tripənousou'maiəsis], *s.* (*patol.*) tripanosomiasi.

trypsin ['tripsin], *s.* (*chim.*) tripsina.

tryst [traist], *s.* (*arc.*) appuntamento: *to break, to keep —*, mancare, andare a un appuntamento.

to tryst, *v.t.i.* (*arc.*) dare, fissare un appuntamento (a, in).

trysting ['traistiŋ], *s.* appuntamento ☆ *—day*, giorno dell'appuntamento; *— place*, luogo dell'appuntamento.

tsar [zɑ:*], *s.* zar.

tsarevitch ['zɑ:rəvitʃ], *s.* zarevic.

tsarina [zɑ:'ri:nə], *s.* zarina.

tsetse ['tsetsi], *s.* mosca tsè-tsè.

tub [tʌb], *s.* **1.** tino, tinozza; mastello; botte ‖ *a tale of a —*, una fantasticheria, un racconto fantastico **2.** vasca da bagno: *to have a —*, fare un bagno **3.** (*miner.*) vagonetto **4.** (*mar.*) barcaccia: *an old —*, una vecchia carcassa ☆ *— thumper*, oratore ampolloso.

to tub, *pass.p.p.* tubbed [tʌbd], *v.t.i.* **1.** prendere

un bagno (in una tinozza) **2.** mettere in un mastello, in una botte **3.** (*miner.*) rivestire con legno, lamiera (le pareti di un pozzo) **4.** (*spor.*) allenare (rematori); allenarsi (a remare).

tuba ['tju:bə], *s.* (*mus.*) tuba.

tubal ['tju:bəl], tubar ['tju:bə*], *ag.* (*anat.*) tubarico ☆ *— pregnancy*, gravidanza tubarica.

tubbish ['tʌbiʃ], tubby ['tʌbi], *ag.* **1.** a forma di tinozza **2.** grosso, obeso, corpulento **3.** senza risonanza (di strumenti musicali).

tube [tju:b], *s.* **1.** tubo, tubetto **2.** camera d'aria **3.** (*mil.*) anima (di fucile) **4.** (*mec.*) valvola, tubo **5.** (*fam.*) ferrovia sotterranea (a Londra) ☆ *— cast*, (*anat.*) cilindro renale; *— colour*, colore in tubetto; *— culture*, coltura di microbi in provetta; *— railway*, ferrovia sotterranea; *— rolling*, trafilature del tubo; *— socket*, (*rad.*) supporto della valvola; *— station*, stazione di ferrovia sotterranea (a Londra) ‖ *air —*, (*aut.*) camera d'aria; *choke —*, (*aut.*) diffusore; *electron —*, (*elett.*) valvola termoionica; *graduated —*, (*chim.*) provetta graduata; *outer —*, (*artigl.*) cerchio; *picture —*, (*tv.*) tubo a raggi catodici per televisione, cinescopio; *screen grid —*, (*rad.*) valvola con griglia di schermo; *still —*, (*chim.*) tubo di distillazione; *test —*, (*chim.*) provetta; *tracheotomy —*, (*chir.*) cannula tracheale.

to tube, *v.t.i.* **1.** fornire di tubo **2.** chiudere in un tubo **3.** (*fam.*) viaggiare in ferrovia sotterranea (a Londra) **4.** (*chir.*) drenare (una ferita).

tuber ['tju:bə*], *s.* **1.** (*bot.*) tubero **2.** (*patol.*) nodo, tumefazione.

tubercle ['tju:bə:kl], *s.* **1.** (*bot. med.*) tubercolo **2.** (*patol.*) tubercolosi.

tubercled ['tju:bə:kld], *V.* tuberculate(d).

tubercular [tju:(:)'bə:kjulə*], *ag.* **1.** (*bot. med.*) a tubercoli, tubercolare; *— root*, radice tubercolare **2.** (*patol.*) tubercoloso.

to tubercularize [tju:(:)'bə:kjuləraiz], *v.t.* (*patol.*) infettare di tubercolosi.

tuberculate [tju:(:)'bə:kjulit], tuberculated [tju:(:)'bə:kjuleitid], *ag.* (*bot. med.*) tubercolare, nodulare.

tuberculation [tju:(:),bə:kju'leiʃən], *s.* (*patol.*) formazione di tubercoli, noduli.

tuberculization [tju:(:),bə:kjulai'zeiʃən], *s.* (*patol.*) tubercolizzazione.

to tuberculize [tju:(:)'bə:kjulaiz], *v.t.* (*patol.*) infettare di tubercolosi.

tuberculoid [tju:(:)'bə:kjuloid], *ag.* tubercoloide, simile a tubercolo.

tuberculose [tju:(:)'bə:kjulous], *ag.* (*patol.*) tubercoloso.

tuberculosis [tju:(:),bə:kju'lousis], *s.* (*patol.*) tubercolosi: *— of the lungs*, tubercolosi polmonare.

tuberculous [tju:(:)'bə:kjuləs], *ag.* (*patol.*) tubercoloso.

tuberose ['tju:bərous], *come s.* ['tju:bərouz], *ag.* (*anat.*) tuberoso, nodulare ‖ *s.* (*bot.*) tuberosa.

tuberosity [tju:bə'rositi], *s.* (*anat. bot.*) tuberosità.

tuberous ['tju:bərəs], *ag.* (*anat. bot.*) tuberoso.

tuberousness ['tju:bərəsnis], *s.* (*anat. bot.*) tuberosità.

tubful ['tʌbful], *s.* quanto è contenuto in un tino.

tubiform ['tju:bifo:m], *ag.* tubiforme.

tubing ['tju:biŋ], *s.* **1.** tubatura, tubazione **2.** (*miner.*) tubaggio ☆ *— head*, (*miner.*) testa della tubazione; *— spider*, (*miner.*) clampa per tubazioni ‖ *oil well —*, tubi per pozzi petroliferi.

tubular ['tju:bjulə*], *ag.* tubolare ☆ *— boiler*, caldaia a tubi di fumo; *— rivet*, (*mec.*) rivetto tubolare.

to tubulate ['tju:bjuleit], *v.t.* munire di tubo; trasformare in tubo.

tubulated ['tju:bjuleitid], *ag.* munito di tubo.

tubule ['tju:bju:l], *s.* tubetto.

tubuliform ['tju:bjuli,fo:m], *ag.* a forma di tubetto.

tubulose ['tju:bjulous], tubulous ['tju:bjuləs], *ag.* tubolare.

tuck[1] [tʌk], *s.* **1.** piega; basta (di abito) **2.** (*mar.*) poppa **3.** (*sl.*) cibarie (specialmente dolciumi).

to **tuck**[1], *v.t.i.* **1.** fare pieghe a (un abito) **2.** ripiegare: *the little bird tucked its head under its wing*, l'uccellino ripiegò il capo sotto l'ala **3.** riporre; stipare, pigiare: *she managed to* — *her shoes in the suitcase*, riuscì a far entrare le scarpe nella valigia ‖ *to* — *(away) sthg. in a drawer*, chiudere ql.co in un cassetto **4.** *to* — **in**, ripiegare; piegare in dentro; (*fam.*) fare una scorpacciata **5.** *to* — **up**, rimboccare; (*sl.*) impiccare: — *up your shirt-sleeves*, rimboccati le maniche della camicia ‖ *to* — *s.o. up in bed*, rimboccare le coltri a qlcu.

tuck[1], (*nei composti*): — *-in* (o — *-out*), (*sl.*) scorpacciata; — *-shop*, (*sl.*) spaccio di generi alimentari, specialmente dolciumi (nelle scuole).

tuck[2], *s.* (*arc.*) squillo (di tromba); rullo (di tamburo).

tucker ['tʌkə*], *s.c.* chi fa pieghe ‖ *s.* **1.** pezzo di tessuto, pizzo (che copriva le spalle nell'abbigliamento femminile dei secc. XVII e XVIII) ‖ *to put on one's best bib and* —, (*fam.*) mettersi gli abiti migliori **2.** (*sl.*) cibo.

to **tucker**, *v.t.* (*fam. amer.*) stancare; affaticare: *tuckered out*, esausto.

tucket ['tʌkit], *s.* (*arc.*) fanfara.

tucum ['tu:kəm], *s.* palma del Brasile.

Tudor ['tju:də*], *ag. attributivo* dei Tudor, dell'epoca Tudor: — *style*, (*arch.*) stile Tudor, elisabettiano ‖ *s.* **1.** membro della dinastia dei Tudor (XVI sec.) **2.** inglese, specialmente poeta, dell'epoca dei Tudor.

Tuesday ['tju:zdi], *s.* martedì: *on* — *next*, martedì prossimo ☆ *Shrove* —, martedì grasso.

tufa ['tju:fə], *s.* tufo.

tufaceous [tu:'feifəs], *ag.* tufaceo.

tuff [tʌf], *s.* tufo vulcanico.

tuft [tʌft], *s.* **1.** ciuffo (d'erba, capelli, piume, ecc.) **2.** fiocco (di lana, seta); nappa **3.** barbetta, pizzo **4.** (*anat.*) glomerulo (di vasi sanguigni) **5.** (*sl. universitario*) studente universitario nobile ☆ — *-hunter*, chi ricerca la compagnia di nobili; parassita.

to **tuft**, *v.t.i.* **1.** ornare, guarnire di ciuffi, fiocchi, ecc. **2.** crescere in ciuffi (di piante) **3.** trapuntare **4.** (*caccia*) battere (i cespugli) per farne uscire la selvaggina.

tufty ['tʌfti], *ag.* **1.** ornato di fiocchi **2.** folto; fronzuto.

tug [tʌg], *s.* **1.** strappo, tirata: *to give a* —, dare uno strappo; sforzo; strazio: *it will be a* — *to leave them*, sarà uno strazio lasciarli **3.** — (*boat*), (*mar.*) rimorchiatore **4.** tirella (nei finimenti del cavallo) ☆ — *-of-war*, tiro alla fune.

to **tug**, *pass. p.p.* **tugged** [tʌgd], *v.t.i.* **1.** dare strattoni, tirare; strappare; trascinare: *the dog tugs at the leash*, il cane tira il guinzaglio **2.** tormentare: *the recollection tugged at his heart-strings*, (*fam.*) il ricordo gli tormentava il cuore **3.** (*mar.*) rimorchiare.

tugger ['tʌgə*], *s.c.* chi tira con forza.

tuition [tju(:)'ifən], *s.* istruzione, insegnamento.

tuitional [tju(:)'ifnl], **tuitionary** [tju(:)'ifnəri], *ag.* relativo all'insegnamento.

tula(-work) ['tu:lə(wə:k)], *s.* niello.

tulip ['tju:lip], *s.* (*bot.*) tulipano.

tulipomania [,tju:lipə'meiniə], *s.* mania per i tulipani (quale si diffuse in Olanda nel XVII sec.).

tulle [tju:l], *s.* tulle, velo.

Tullian ['tʌliən], *ag.* tulliano, ciceroniano.

Tully ['tʌli], *no.pr.m.* (*st. lett.*) Tullio (Cicerone).

tulwar ['tʌlwɑ:*], *s.* «tulwar» (sciabola usata nell'India settentrionale).

tum [tʌm], *s.* suono di banjo (e di simili strumenti).

tumble ['tʌmbl], *s.* **1.** caduta; capitombolo; capriola: *a nasty* —, un brutto capitombolo **2.** disordine, confusione: *it was all in a* —, era tutto in gran disordine ☆ — *-bug*, (*entom.*) scarabeo stercorario.

to **tumble**, *v.t.i.* **1.** cadere, far cadere; ruzzolare, far ruzzolare **2.** agitarsi: *to toss and* — *in bed*, rigirarsi nel letto **3.** precipitarsi, gettarsi: *to* — *into, out of bed*, gettarsi sul, giù dal letto; *to* — *upstairs, downstairs*, precipitarsi su, giù per le scale **4.** fare acrobazie **5.** mettere in disordine, scompigliare; rovesciare: *to* — *everything into a box*, rovesciare ogni cosa alla rinfusa

in una scatola; *to* — *one's skirt*, stazzonarsi la gonna; *to* — *s.o.'s hair*, scompigliare i capelli di qlcu. **6.** *to* — *on* (*sthg.*), imbattersi in **7.** *to* — *to* (*sthg.*), afferrare il significato di, rendersi conto di: *you've tumbled to it!*, ci sei arrivato finalmente! **8.** *to* — **down**, andare in rovina; abbattere: *building that is tumbling down*, edificio in rovina; *to* — *down a bird*, abbattere un uccello **9.** *to* — **in**, incastrare (travi, ecc.); (*sl.*) andare a letto: inclinarsi all'indentro (di fianco di nave).

tumbler ['tʌmblə*], *s.* **1.** acrobata **2.** (*ornit.*) piccione tomboliere **3.** misirizzi (giocattolo) **4.** bicchiere largo (senza piede) **5.** blocco (di arma da fuoco) **6.** (*metal.*) barilatrice (per pulire i getti) **7.** (*paddle-*) —, (*conceria*) bottale ☆ — *gear*, (*mec.*) cambio di velocità; invertitore; — *switch*, (*mec.*) commutatore oscillante.

tumblerful ['tʌmbləful], *s.* contenuto di un bicchiere.

tumbling ['tʌmbliŋ], *s.* **1.** caduta, capitombolo; crollo **2.** acrobazia **3.** (*metal.*) barilatura, pulitura al tamburo **4.** verniciatura a buratto, a tamburo ☆ — *-barrel* (o — *-box* o — *-drum*), (*metal.*) barilatrice, tamburo per pulire i getti; — *-shaft*, (*mec.*) albero a camme.

tumbly ['tʌmbli], *ag.* (*rar.*) cadente, crollante.

tumbrel ['tʌmbrəl], **tumbril** ['tʌmbril], *s.* **1.** (*st.*) sedia su cui venivano posti i condannati alla berlina; carretta per il trasporto dei condannati a morte (durante la Rivoluzione francese) **2.** carro ribaltabile; carro per trasporto di letame **3.** (*mil.*) carretta.

tumefacient [,tju:mi'feifənt], *ag.* tumefacente.

tumefaction [,tju:mi'fækfən], *s.* tumefazione, gonfiore.

to **tumefy** ['tju:mifai], *v.t.i.* tumefare, tumefarsi.

tumescence [tju:'mesns], *s.* tumescenza.

tumescent [tju:'mesnt], *ag.* **1.** tumescente **2.** gonfio, ampolloso (di stile, ecc.).

tumid ['tju:mid], *ag.* **1.** tumido, gonfio **2.** ampolloso (di stile, ecc.).

tumidity [tju:'miditi], *s.* **1.** tumidezza, gonfiore **2.** ampollosità (di stile, ecc.).

tumidly ['tju:midli], *av.* **1.** tumidamente, gonfiamente **2.** ampollosamente (di stile, ecc.).

tumidness ['tju:midnis], *V.* tumidity.

tummy ['tʌmi], *s.* (*fam.*) stomaco, ventre ‖ *to have a* —, soffrire di mal di stomaco.

tumorous ['tju:mərəs], *ag.* (*patol.*) **1.** che ha carattere di tumore maligno **2.** affetto da tumore.

tumour ['tju:mə*], *s.* (*patol.*) tumore.

to **tump** [tʌmp], *v.t.* (*amer.*) trascinare.

tumular ['tju:mjulə*], *ag.* tumulare.

tumult ['tju:mʌlt], *s.* tumulto, agitazione (anche *fig.*).

tumultuarily [tju(:)'mʌltjuərili], *av.* tumultuariamente.

tumultuariness [tju(:)'mʌltjuərinis], *s.* turbolenza.

tumultuary [tju(:)'mʌltjuəri], *ag.* tumultuario.

tumultuous [tju(:)'mʌltjuəs], *ag.* tumultuoso.

tumultuously [tju(:)'mʌltjuəsli], *av.* tumultuosamente.

tumultuousness [tju(:)'mʌltjuəsnis], *s.* carattere tumultuoso.

tumulus ['tju:mjuləs], *pl.* **tumuli** ['tju:mjulai], *s.* tumulo.

tun [tʌn], *s.* botte; barile per la fermentazione della birra.

to **tun**, *pass.p.p.* **tunned** [tʌnd], *v.t.* imbottare, mettere in botti.

tuna ['tu:nə], *s.* (*amer.*) tonno.

tunable ['tju:nəbl], *ag.* **1.** armonioso, musicale **2.** accordabile.

tunableness ['tju:nəblnis], *s.* **1.** armoniosità **2.** possibilità di essere accordato.

tunably ['tju:nəbli], *av.* armoniosamente.

tundish ['tʌndif], *s.* (*dial.*) grosso imbuto.

tundra ['tʌndrə], *s.* tundra.

tune [tju:n], *s.* **1.** (*mus.*) aria, motivo: *to play a*

—, suonare un'aria ‖ *to buy sthg. to the* — *of sixty pounds*, comperare ql.co. al prezzo esorbitante di sessanta sterline **2.** (*mus.*) tono; accordo, consonanza: *to be in* —, essere intonato; *to be out of* —, essere stonato **3.** *fig.* accordo, armonia: *I live in* — *with my relatives*, vivo in buona armonia con i miei parenti **4.** disposizione, vena; umore: *to be in* — *for sthg.*, essere propenso a ql.co.; *to be in bad* —, essere di cattivo umore ☆ — *up*, (*mec.*) messa a punto.

to **tune**, *v.t.i.* **1.** (*mus.*) accordare: *to* — *a piano*, accordare un piano **2.** *fig.* essere in armonia, accordo; adattare, adattarsi; armonizzare **3.** (*poet.*) produrre musica **4.** *to* — *in*, (*rad.*) sintonizzare **5.** *to* — *up*, (*mec.*) mettere a punto; (*mus.*) accordarsi (di orchestra); (*scherz.*) cominciare a piangere (di bambini).

tuneful ['tju:nful], *ag.* armonioso, melodioso.

tunefully ['tju:nfuli], *av.* armoniosamente, melodiosamente.

tunefulness ['tju:nfulnis], *s.* qualità melodica.

tuneless ['tju:nlis], *ag.* **1.** scordato, stonato **2.** che non emette suono, muto.

tuner ['tju:nə*], *s.* **1.** accordatore (di strumenti musicali) **2.** (*rad.*) sintonizzatore **3.** motorista.

tungstate ['tʌŋstit], *s.* (*chim.*) tungstato.

tungsten ['tʌŋstən], *s.* (*chim.*) tungsteno, wolframio ☆ — *lamp*, lampada al tungsteno.

tungstic ['tʌŋstik], *ag.* (*chim.*) tungstico.

tunic ['tju:nik], *s.* tunica.

Tunicata [,tju:ni'keitə], *s.pl.* (*zool.*) i tunicati.

tunicate(d) ['tju:nikeit(id)], *ag.* (*zool. bot.*) tunicato.

tunicate ['tju:nikeit], *s.* (*zool.*) tunicato.

tunicle ['tju:nikl], *s.* **1.** (*bot. zool.*) membrana, tunica **2.** (*eccl.*) tonacella; dalmatica.

tuning ['tju:niŋ], *s.* **1.** accordatura **2.** (*rad.*) sintonia **3.** (*mec.*) messa a punto (di motore) ☆ — *fork*, diapason; — *-hammer*, chiave di accordatore; — *indicator*, (*rad.*) indicatore di sintonia.

Tunis ['tju:nis], *no.pr.* (*geog.*) Tunisi.

Tunisia [tju(:)'niziə], *no.pr.* (*geog.*) Tunisia.

Tunisian [tju(:)'niziən], *ag.* tunisino ‖ *s.c.* tunisino, tunisina.

tunnage, *V.* **tonnage**.

tunnel ['tʌnl], *s.* tunnel, galleria; traforo ☆ — *-borer*, perforatrice; — *-net*, rete a imbuto; — *vault*, (*arch.*) volta a botte.

to **tunnel**, *pass.p.p.* **tunnelled** ['tʌnld], *v.t.i.* scavare una galleria; traforare: *to* — (*through, into*) *a hill*, traforare una collina.

tunning ['tʌniŋ], *s.* imbottitura.

tunny ['tʌni], *s.* (*ittiol.*) tonno.

tuny ['tju:ni], *ag.* melodioso, armonioso.

tup [tʌp], *s.* **1.** (*zool.*) ariete, montone **2.** (*mec.*) mazza battente.

to **tup**, *pass. p.p.* **tupped** [tʌpt], *v.t.* **1.** coprire, montare (di montone) **2.** (*mec.*) battere con un maglio.

tuppence, (*fam.*) per **twopence**.

tuppenny, (*fam.*) per **twopenny**.

turban ['tə:bən], *s.* turbante ☆ — *-shell*, (*zool.*) turbo.

turbaned ['tə:bənd], *ag.* fornito di turbante.

turbary ['tə:bəri], *s.* **1.** torbiera **2.** (*dir.*) diritto di estrarre torba da terreno altrui.

turbid ['tə:bid], *ag.* torbido; fangoso; *fig.* agitato, confuso.

turbidity [tə:'biditi], *s.* torbidità, torbidezza; *fig.* agitazione, confusione.

turbidly ['tə:bidli], *av.* torbidamente; *fig.* confusamente.

turbidness ['tə:bidnis], *s.* torbidità, torbidezza; *fig.* agitazione, confusione.

turbinate ['tə:binit], *ag.* turbinato, a forma di spira ☆ — *bones*, (*anat.*) turbinati.

turbination [,tə:bi'neifən], *s.* turbinazione.

turbine ['tə:bin], *s.* (*mec.*) turbina ☆ — *-engine*, motore a turbina; — *-generator*, turboalternatore; — *set*, (*mec.*) gruppo di turbine; — *starter*, avviatore a

turbina; — *steamship*, turbonave (a vapore); — *tanker*, turbocisterna ‖ *axial-flow* —, (*mec.*) turbina assiale; *exhaust steam* —, (*mec.*) turbina a bassa pressione, a vapore di scarico; *steam-* —, turbina a vapore; *water* —, turbina idraulica.

turbiniform [tə:'binifɔ:m], **turbinoid** ['tə:binɔid], *ag.* a forma di spirale.

turbit ['tə:bit], *s.* piccione dal becco corto.

turbo-dynamo ['tə:bou'dainəmou], *s.* (*elett.*) turbodinamo.

turbojet ['tə:bou'dʒet], *s.* (*aer.*) turbogetto ☆ — *engine*, turboreattore.

turbot ['tə:bət], *s.* (*ittiol.*) rombo.

turbulence ['tə:bjulens], **turbulency** ['tə:bjulensi], *s.* turbolenza, agitazione.

turbulent ['tə:bjulənt], *ag.* turbolento, tumultuoso.

turbulently ['tə:bjuləntli], *av.* turbolentemente.

Turco ['tə:kou], *pl.* **Turcos** ['tə:kouz], *s.* (*st.*) zuavo (fuciliere algerino dell'esercito francese).

turd [tə:d], *s.* (*volg.*) sterco, escrementi.

turdine ['tə:din], *ag.* simile a tordo.

turdus ['tə:dəs], *s.* (*ornit.*) tordo.

tureen [tə'ri:n], *s.* zuppiera, terrina.

turf [tə:f], *pl.* **turfs** [tə:fs], **turves** [tə:vz], *s.* **1.** piota, zolla erbosa; tappeto erboso **2.** torba (in Irlanda) **3.** *the* —, il campo delle corse; le corse; il mondo delle corse ☆ — *-accountant*, allibratore; — *-clad*, erboso; — *-man*, amatore di corse di cavalli; — *-spade*, tagliazolle.

to **turf**, *v.t.* **1.** coprire di zolle erbose **2.** *to* — *out*, (*sl.*) gettare fuori.

turfiness ['tə:finis], *s.* **1.** natura erbosa **2.** ricchezza, presenza di torba.

turfite ['tə:fait], *s.* (*sl.*) frequentatore, appassionato di corse (di cavalli).

turfy ['tə:fi], *ag.* **1.** erboso; coperto d'erba **2.** torboso; ricco di torba.

turgescence [tə:'dʒesns], *s.* **1.** (*med.*) turgescenza, turgidezza **2.** *fig.* pomposità, ampollosità, enfasi.

turgescent [tə:'dʒesnt], *ag.* **1.** (*med.*) turgescente, turgido **2.** *fig.* ampolloso, enfatico.

turgid ['tə:dʒid], *ag.* **1.** turgido **2.** *fig.* ampolloso enfatico.

turgidity [tə:'dʒiditi], *s.* **1.** turgidezza **2.** *fig.* pomposità, ampollosità, enfasi.

turgidly ['tə:dʒidli], *av.* **1.** turgidamente **2.** *fig.* ampollosamente, enfaticamente.

Turin [tju'rin], *no.pr.* (*geog.*) Torino.

Turinese [,tjuri'ni:z], *ag.s.c.* torinese.

turion ['tjuəriən], *pl.* (*arc.*) **turiones** ['tjuəriəni:z], *s* (*bot.*) getto, germoglio.

Turk [tə:k], *ag.* turco ‖ *s.c.* turco, turca ☆ —'*s cap*, (*bot.*) martagone; —'*s head*, testa di saracino (testa finta infilata su un palo e adoperata per esercitarsi all'uso della spada); nodo a turbante; tortiera con foro centrale.

Turkestan [,tə:kis'ta:n], *no.pr.* (*geog.*) Turkestan.

Turkey[1] ['tə:ki], *no.pr.* (*geog.*) Turchia ☆ — *carpet*, tappeto turco.

turkey[2], *s.* **1.** (*ornit.*) tacchino **2.** (*sl. teat. amer.*) fiasco ☆ — *-cock*, tacchino; *fig.* persona vanesia: *red as a* — *-cock*, *fig.* rosso come un tacchino; arrabbiato; — *-hen*, tacchina; — *-poult*, tacchinotto.

Turkish ['tə:kiʃ], *ag.* turco ‖ *s.* lingua turca ☆ — *bath*, bagno turco.

Turkman, *pl.* **Turkmen** ['tə:kmən], **Turkoman** ['tə:kəmən], *pl.* **Turkomans** ['tə:kəmənz], *s.* turcomanno.

turmalin(e) ['tə:məlin], *s.* (*min.*) tormalina.

turmeric ['tə:mərik], *s.* (*bot.*) curcuma ☆ — *paper*, carta alla curcuma.

turmoil ['tə:mɔil], *s.* agitazione; inquietudine; tumulto; scompiglio: *the whole town is in a* —, tutta la città è in agitazione.

to **turmoil**, *v.t.* (*arc.*) agitare; turbare; scompigliare.

turn [tə:n], *s.* **1.** giro, rotazione: *one* — *of the pro-*

peller, un giro d'elica ‖ *a — of Fortune's wheel*, un giro della ruota della fortuna ‖ *the meat is done to a —*, la carne è cotta a puntino ‖ *to give a — to the screw, fig.* dare un giro di vite **2.** giro, cambiamento di direzione; curva, svolta, piega; (*mar. aer.*) virata: *a road full of twists and turns*, una strada tutta a curve e svolte; *business is taking a bad —*, gli affari stanno prendendo una brutta piega; *he gave a new — to the conversation*, cambiò discorso; *she took a — to the right*, svoltò a destra; *things are taking a — for the better*, la situazione volge per il meglio ‖ *the milk is on the —*, il latte sta diventando acido ‖ *the tide is on the —*, la marea sta cambiando **3.** disposizione, inclinazione, attitudine; vena, gusto: *he has a — for foreign languages*, ha inclinazione per le lingue straniere; *she was of a humorous —*, era in vena d'allegria; *Tom has no great — for Latin*, Tom non è molto portato per il latino **4.** giro, forma (di frase): *French — of speech*, gallicismo; *do you like the — of this sentence?*, ti piace la forma di questa frase? **5.** volta, turno: *each one in his —*, uno alla volta; *I will speak to you all in —*, parlerò con ognuno di voi singolarmente; *whose — is it?*, a chi tocca?; *you must not speak out of —*, parla quando tocca a te; *to take turns*, fare turni ‖ *— and — about*, a turni: *we work — and — about*, lavoriamo a turni ‖ *— for —*, a buon rendere ‖ *in —* (o *by turns*), alternativamente: *she laughed and cried by turns*, ora rideva, ora piangeva **6.** servizio, favore: *don't do me a bad —*, non farmi un brutto scherzo ‖ *this serves my —*, ciò fa al caso mio ‖ *to owe s.o. a good —*, avere dei doveri verso qlcu. ‖ *one good — deserves another, prov.* chi semina raccoglie **7.** giretto, passeggiatina: *come for a — round the town*, vieni a fare un giretto per la città **8.** (*fam.*) colpo, sussulto; crisi: *it gave me quite a —*, mi ha fatto sussultare; *she had a — of her illness*, ha avuto una crisi del suo male **9.** (*tip.*) lettera rovesciata **10.** (*mec.*) giro (di spirale) **11.** (*mus.*) gruppetto.

to **turn**, *v.t.i.* **1.** girare, girarsi; voltare, voltarsi; dirigere, dirigersi; volgere, volgersi: *he turned towards me*, si voltò verso di me; *the stream turns to the right*, il torrente gira a destra; *this dress has been turned and now it looks new*, questo vestito è stato rivoltato ed ora sembra nuovo; *the wind is turning*, il vento cambia direzione; *to — the bed*, voltare il materasso; *to — a blow*, deviare un colpo; *to — the corner*, voltar l'angolo; *fig.* superare il momento critico; *to — for a landing*, (*aer.*) virare per l'atterraggio; *to — a key in its lock*, girare la chiave nella serratura; *to — the line*, (*mar.*) invertire la rotta; *to — one's steps homewards*, dirigere i propri passi verso casa; *to — the pages of a book*, sfogliare un libro; *to — a ship from its course*, invertire la rotta di una nave; *to — upside down*, capovolgersi (di imbarcazione); *to — capote* (di auto, ecc.); *to toss and — in bed*, rivoltarsi nel letto ‖ *he doesn't know which way to —, fig.* non sa che pesci pigliare ‖ *he is* (o *has*) *turned fifty*, ha cinquant'anni suonati ‖ *his luck has turned*, la fortuna gli ha voltato le spalle ‖ *I shall now — to another matter*, cambierò argomento ‖ *it has turned six o'clock*, sono le sei passate ‖ *it is turning to rain*, sta per piovere ‖ *my head turns*, mi gira la testa ‖ *she can — her hand to any kind of work*, può fare qualsiasi genere di lavoro ‖ *she didn't — a hair*, rimase impassibile ‖ *this smell turns my stomach*, questo odore mi dà la nausea ‖ *to — the flank of an army*, aggirare un esercito ‖ *to — the cold shoulder to s.o.*, trattare qlcu. con freddezza ‖ *to — a deaf ear*, far orecchi da mercante ‖ *to — an honest penny*, guadagnare denaro onestamente ‖ *to — a letter*, (*tip.*) bloccare una lettera ‖ *to — one's back on s.o., fig.* abbandonare qlcu. ‖ *to — one's coat*, (*fam.*) cambiar bandiera ‖ *to — the scale*, far traboccare la bilancia; decidere una questione in sospeso ‖ *to — sthg. to account*, trar vantaggio da ql.co. ‖ *to — tail*, fuggire ‖ *to — the tide of the battle*, mutare l'esito della battaglia **2.** rivolgere, rivolgersi; riferirsi: *to — (one's attention)*

to sthg., rivolgere la propria attenzione a ql.co.; *to — one's mind to sthg.*, applicarsi a ql.co.; *to — one's thoughts to God*, rivolgere i propri pensieri a Dio; *to — to the dictionary*, consultare il dizionario; *to — to a document*, riferirsi a un documento; *to — to s.o.*, ricorrere all'aiuto di qlcu. ‖ *to — to law as a profession*, intraprendere la professione di avvocato **3.** cambiare, cambiarsi; trasformare, trasformarsi; convertire, convertirsi; diventare; farsi: *the apricots are turning yellow*, le albicocche stanno maturando; *he turned everything he touched into gold*, trasformava in oro tutto ciò che toccava; *he turned mad*, impazzì; *the milk has turned sour*, il latte si è cagliato; *profit has turned into loss*, il guadagno si è tramutato in perdita; *to — Catholic*, farsi cattolico; *to — one's land into money*, convertire in denaro i propri possedimenti **4.** rendere, tradurre: *how would you — this sentence?*, come tradurresti questa frase?; *to — English into Italian*, tradurre dall'inglese in italiano **5.** tornire (anche *fig.*): *to — the legs of a chair*, tornire le gambe di una sedia **6.** (*edil.*) costruire **7.** *to — against* (*s.o., sthg.*), ribellarsi a **8.** *to — to* (*sthg.*), applicarsi, mettersi a: *to — to work, to doing sthg.*, mettersi al lavoro, a fare ql.co. **9.** *to — (up)on* (*s.o., sthg.*), dipendere da; rivolgersi contro, attaccare: *everything turns on your answer*, tutto dipende dalla tua risposta **10.** *to — about*, girare, girarsi; rigirarsi; agitarsi **11.** *to — away*, voltare (la testa, gli occhi, ecc.); cacciare; congedare; andar via **12.** *to — back*, (far) tornare sui propri passi; rialzare, rimboccare, ripiegare: *she turned back her skirt over her knees*, alzò la gonna fin sopra le ginocchia **13.** *to — down*, piegare; abbassare (luce, gas, ecc.); respingere (proposta, candidato) **14.** *to — in*, piegare, ripiegare; (*mar.*) mettere a bordo; (*fam.*) andare a letto ‖ *his toes — in*, ha i piedi vari **15.** *to — off*, spegnere (luce, gas, ecc.); chiudere (un rubinetto); licenziare, congedare; scrivere, comporre; cambiar strada, rotta; (*sl.*) impiccare; (*scherz.*) sposare **16.** *to — on*, aprire (rubinetto, ecc.); accendere (luce, ecc.); (*fam.*) dar libero sfogo a ‖ *to — s.o. on to do sthg.*, far fare ql.co. a qlcu. **17.** *to — out*, mettere alla porta, scacciare, licenziare; rovesciare (anche *fig.*); vuotare; pulire a fondo; produrre, fabbricare; spegnere (gas, ecc.); uscire, apparire in pubblico; alzarsi dal letto; risultare, accadere, verificarsi: *it turned out to be true*, risultò vero; *it turns out that...*, accade che..., risulta che...; *things have turned out badly*, le cose sono andate male; *to — out the government*, rovesciare il governo; *to — out (on strike)*, mettersi in sciopero; *to — out to s.o.'s advantage*, tornare a vantaggio di qlcu. ‖ *his toes — out*, ha i piedi valghi **18.** *to — over*, rovesciare; rivoltare; voltare (pagina); capovolgere; capotare (di automobile, ecc.); trasferire; trasbordare (equipaggio); *fig.* riconsiderare, rimuginare: *to — over and over*, voltare e rivoltare; *to — over a new leaf*, cambiar vita ‖ *they — over forty pounds a day*, hanno un giro d'affari di quaranta sterline al giorno ‖ *to — sthg. over to s.o.*, trasferire, rimettere ql.co. a qlcu. **19.** *to — round*, girare, voltare, voltarsi; *fig.* cambiar idea, bandiera; (*mar.*) virare di bordo ‖ *to — round on s.o.*, assalire improvvisamente qlcu. **20.** *to — to*, incominciare a lavorare **21.** *to — up*, alzare; rimboccare; scoprire (carta da giuoco); uscire (di carta da giuoco); riferirsi a; alzare (gas); arrivare all'improvviso; accadere, succedere; far vomitare (anche *fig.*); (*mar.*) radunare l'equipaggio sul ponte: *to — up at s.o.'s house*, capitare a casa di qlcu.; *to — up one's nose*, arricciare, torcere il naso; *to — up a word in the dictionary*, cercare una parola nel dizionario; *to — up one's heels*, (*sl.*) morire.

turn, (nei composti): — -*bridge*, ponte girevole; — -*indicator*, (*aer.*) indicatore di virata; — -*out*, sciopero; assemblea, adunanza; (*aut.*) binario laterale; (*aut.*) piazzuola; equipaggio (carrozza e cavalli); produzione fabbricazione; — -*plate*, (*ferr.*) piattaforma girevole; — -*round*, (*mar. aer.*) operazioni di carico e scarico;

cambiamento (di posizione, politica, ecc.); — *-screw* cacciavite; — *-table*, (*ferr.*) piattaforma girevole; piatto (di giradischi); — *-up*, piega, risvolto; colpo di fortuna.

turnabout ['tə:nəbaut], *s.* **1.** il volgersi nella direzione opposta **2.** — (*-face*), voltafaccia, cambiamento d'opinione **3.** (*rar.*) girella, voltagabbana **4.** (*amer.*) giostra **5.** (*mar.*) inversione di rotta.

turncoat ['tə:nkout], *s.* voltagabbana, girella; apostata; disertore.

turncock ['tə:nkɔk], *s.* fontaniere.

turner ['tə:nə*], *s.* **1.** tornitore **2.** tipo di piccione tomboliere.

turnery ['tə:nəri], *s.* **1.** arte del tornitore **2.** tornitura **3.** officina di tornitore.

turning ['tə:niŋ], *ag.* **1.** girevole, ruotante **2.** tortuoso, sinuoso; a svolte ‖ *s.* **1.** giro, rotazione **2.** svolta, curva; deviazione; (*aut.*) sterzata **3.** (*mec.*) tornitura **4.** *pl.* (*mec.*) trucioli ☆ — *-chisel*, scalpello da tornitore; — *-lathe*, (*mec.*) tornio; — *-point*, svolta decisiva, momento critico; (*topografia*) vertice; — *-radius*, (*aut.*) raggio di sterzo; — *-saw*, (*strum. artig.*) sega a volgere; — *-tool*, (*strum. artig.*) utensile per tornire.

turnip ['tə:nip], *s.* **1.** (*bot.*) rapa **2.** — (*watch*), (*sl.*) cipolla (orologio di poco valore) ☆ — *-cabbage*, cavolorapa; — *-moth*, (*entom.*) agrotide; — *-top*, cima di rapa.

turnkey ['tə:nki:], *s.* (*arc.*) carceriere, secondino (al quale sono affidate le chiavi).

turnover ['tə:n,ouvə*], *s.* **1.** rovesciamento; capovolgimento; ribaltamento **2.** (*comm.*) giro, movimento d'affari **3.** torta, pasticcio **4.** articolo di giornale che inizia in una pagina e continua nelle successive.

turnpike ['tə:npaik], *s.* (*st.*) **1.** barriera (per oltrepassare la quale si pagava un pedaggio) **2.** strada a pedaggio.

turnside ['tə:nsaid], *s.* vertigine, capogiro (nei cani).

turnsole ['tə:nsoul], *s.* **1.** (*bot.*) girasole, eliotropio **2.** (*chim.*) tornasole.

turnspit ['tə:nspit], *s.* girarrosto.

turnstile ['tə:n-stail], *s.* **1.** arganello, cancelletto girevole (per passaggi pedonali) **2.** torchietto (spesso azionato a gettone, all'ingresso di musei, esposizioni, ecc.).

turpentine ['tə:pəntain], *s.* (*chim.*) trementina: *oil of* —, (*chim.*) olio essenziale di trementina; acqua ragia ☆ — *tree*, (*bot.*) terebinto.

turpitude ['tə:pitju:d], *s.* turpitudine.

turps [tə:ps], *s.* (*chim. pop.*) essenza di trementina.

turquoise ['tə:kwɑ:z], *s.* **1.** (*min.*) turchese **2.** color turchese.

turret ['tʌrit], *s.* **1.** torretta, piccola torre **2.** (*mil. mar.*) torretta **3.** lanternino, lucernario (di tram, ecc.) ☆ — *-ship*, nave corazzata con torretta ‖ *disappearing*— —, (*mil.*) torretta eclissabile; *revolving*— —, (*mil. aer.*) torretta girevole.

turreted ['tʌritid], *ag.* turrito; fornito di torrette.

turriculate [tʌ'rikjulit], **turriculated** [tʌ'rikjuleitid], *ag.* **1.** turrito **2.** a lunga spirale (di conchiglia).

turtle[1] ['tə:tl], *s.* — (*-dove*), (*ornit.*) tortora.

turtle[2], *s.* (*zool.*) tartaruga ‖ *to turn* —, (*sl. mar.*) capovolgersi, ribaltarsi ☆ — *-shell*, guscio di tartaruga; — *-soup*, zuppa di tartaruga.

to **turtle**, *v.i.* cacciare tartarughe.

turtler ['tə:tlə*], *s.* cacciatore di tartarughe.

Tuscan ['tʌskən], *ag.* toscano ‖ *s.c.* toscano, toscana.

Tuscany ['tʌskəni], *no.pr.* (*geog.*) Toscana.

tush[1] [tʌʃ], *inter.* (*arc.*) oibò!.

tush[2], *s.* **1.** zanna **2.** dente canino (di cavallo).

tushery ['tʌʃəri], *s.* (*letter.*) abuso di arcaismi.

tusk [tʌsk], *s.* zanna.

to **tusk**, *v.t.* azzannare.

tusked [tʌskt], *ag.* zannuto.

tusker ['tʌskə*], *s.* animale zannuto (specialmente elefante, cinghiale).

tusky ['tʌski], *ag.* zannuto.

Tussaud's [tə'so:dz], *no. pr.* Tussaud (museo delle statue di cera a Londra).

tusser ['tʌsə*], *s.* **1.** tussorina (baco da seta selvatico) **2.** — (*- silk*), tussor (seta ricavata dalla tussorina).

tussive ['tʌsiv], *ag.* di tosse, causato da tosse.

tussle ['tʌsl], *s.* zuffa, rissa: *to have a*—, venire alle mani.

to **tussle**, *v.i.* azzuffarsi, lottare.

tussock ['tʌsək], *s.* ciuffo (d'erba, di capelli, ecc.).

tussocky ['tʌsəki], *ag.* fornito di ciuffi; a ciuffi.

tussore, *V.* tusser.

tut[1] [tʌt], *s.* cottimo; lavoro a cottimo.

to **tut**[1], *pass.p.p.* **tutted** ['tʌtid], *v.i.* lavorare a cottimo.

to **tut**[2], *pass. p.p.* **tutted**, *v.i.* esprimere impazienza, rimprovero.

tut[2], *inter.* via!, silenzio! (per indicare impazienza, rimprovero).

tutania [tju(:)'teiniə], *s.* (*metal.*) tutania.

tutelage ['tju:tilidʒ], *s.* (*dir.*) tutela.

tutelar ['tju:tilə*], **tutelary** ['tju:tiləri], *ag.* tutelare.

tutenag ['tju:tənæg], *s.* (*metal.*) **1.** zinco (importato dalla Cina, dalle Indie Orientali) **2.** alpacca.

tutor ['tju:tə*], *s.* (*dir. scoz.*) tutore **2.** precettore, istitutore; insegnante privato, ripetitore **3.** professore incaricato di seguire direttamente il lavoro degli studenti (nelle università inglesi e americane).

to **tutor**, *v.t.* **1.** istruire, ammaestrare **2.** controllare; disciplinare **3.** fare il precettore.

tutorage ['tju:təridʒ], *s.* **1.** (*dir.*) tutela **2.** mansione di precettore.

tutoress ['tju:təris], *s.* **1.** (*dir. scoz.*) tutrice **2.** istitutrice.

tutorial [tju(:)'tɔ:riəl], *ag.* **1** (*dir.*) tutorio **2.** di precettore ‖ *s.* esercitazione; lezione privata.

tutorially [tju(:)'tɔ:riəli], *av.* **1.** da tutore **2.** da precettore.

tutorship ['tju:təʃip], *s.* **1.** mansione di precettore, istitutore **2.** (*dir.*) tutela.

tutsan ['tʌtsən], *s.* (*bot.*) iperico.

tutti-frutti ['tu:ti'fru:ti], *s.* tutti frutti (gelato di frutta con gusti diversi).

tut-tut ['tʌt'tʌt], *V.* tut[2].

tutty ['tʌti:], *s.* (*chim.*) tuzia.

tutwork ['tʌtwə:k], *s.* (*dial.*) lavoro a cottimo.

tutworker ['tʌt,wə:kə*], *s.* (*dial.*) lavoratore a cottimo.

tu-whit [tu'wit], **tu-whoo** [tu'wu:], *s.* squittio (della civetta).

tuxedo [tʌk'si:dou], *s.* (*amer.*) « smoking ».

tuyère [twiə*], *s.* (*metal.*) ugello.

twa [twɑ:], (*scoz.*) per **two**.

twaddell ['twɔdl], *s.* (*chim.*) idrometro; scala idrometrica « Twaddell » (dal nome dell'inventore).

twaddle ['twɔdl], *s.* ciarle, chiacchiere; sciocchezze: *to talk* —, dir sciocchezze.

to **twaddle**, *v.i.* dire sciocchezze; parlare a vanvera.

twaddler ['twɔdlə*], *s.c.* chiacchierone, chiacchierona.

twaddly ['twɔdli], *ag.* chiacchierone, ciarliero.

twain [twein], *ag.* (*arc.*) due: (*to cut*) *in* —, (tagliare) in due ‖ *s.* (*arc.*) due persone, due cose.

twang[1] [twæŋ], *s.* **1.** stridore; suono acuto (di strumento a corde) **2.** suono nasale: *to speak with a* —, parlare con voce nasale.

to **twang**[1], *v.t.i.* **1.** (far) vibrare, (far) risuonare, (far) stridere, pizzicare le corde di **2.** parlare con voce nasale, pronunciare suoni nasali **3.** tendere la corda di un arco.

twang[2], *s.* sapore, odore sgradevole.

to **twangle** ['twæŋgl], *v.t.i.* **1.** tintinnare **2.** suonare (strumento a corde).

twangy ['twæŋi], *ag.* stridulo, vibrato.

'twas [twɔz], *contr.* di *it was*.

twayblade ['tweibleid], *s.* (*bot.*) pianta delle orchidacee (specialmente «Listera ovata», «Listera cordata»).

tweak [twi:k], *s.* pizzicotto.

to **tweak**, *v.t.* **1.** pizzicare **2.** tirare.

tweaker ['twi:kə*], *s.* (*sl.*) fionda.

tweed [twi:d], *s.* **1.** « tweed » (tessuto di lana ruvida generalmente a più colori) **2.** *pl.* abito di « tweed ».

tweedle ['twi:dl], *s.* suono acuto (come di violino).

to **tweedle**, *v.t.i.* **1.** emettere suoni acuti (di strumenti musicali) **2.** strimpellare **3.** adescare, lusingare.

tweedledum and tweedledee ['twi:dl'dʌmən'twi:d-l'di:], *s.* due persone, due cose simili (che differiscono solo per nome): *it is tweedledum and tweedledee*, *prov.* se non è zuppa è pan bagnato.

tweedy ['twi:di], *ag.* simile a « tweed » || *a — person*, (*fam.*) una persona che indossa abiti sportivi, che affetta l'aria del proprietario di campagna.

'tween [twi:n], (*arc. poet. contr.*) di **between**.

tweeny ['twi:ni], *s.* **1.** (*fam.*) sguattera **2.** sigaretto.

tweet [twi:t], *s.* cinguettio.

to **tweet**, *v.i.* cinguettare.

to **tweezer** ['twi:zə*], *v.t.i.* estrarre con pinzette; usare pinzette.

tweezers ['twi:zəz], *s.pl.* (*a pair of*) —, pinzette ☆ — -case, astuccio (per piccoli oggetti).

twelfth [twelfθ], *ag.num.ord.s.* dodicesimo: (*on*) *the — of June*, il dodici giugno; *he was the — in his class*, era il dodicesimo della classe || *Twelfth-day*, Epifania; *Twelfth-night*, la sera precedente l'Epifania.

twelve [twelv], *ag.num.card.* dodici: — *stockings*, una dozzina di calze || *s.* **1.** dodici: *a girl of —*, una ragazza di dodici anni; *it is half past —*, sono le dodici e mezzo || *the Twelve*, i Dodici Apostoli || *in twelves*, (*tip.*) in dodicesimo **2.** automobile a dodici cavalli.

twelvemo ['twelvmou], *s.* (*tip.*) dodicesimo.

twelvemonth ['twelvmʌnθ], *s.* anno: *this day —*, un anno fa; *fra un anno*.

twentieth ['twentiiθ], *ag.num.ord.s.* ventesimo.

twenty ['twenti], *ag.num.card.* venti: *about — people*, una ventina di persone || *s.* **1.** venti: *to be in the early twenties*, avere poco più di vent'anni; *to be in the late twenties*, essere vicino alla trentina || *the twenties*, gli anni dal '20 al '30 **2.** automobile a venti cavalli.

'twere, *contr.* di *it were*.

twibill ['twaibill], *s.* ascia a doppio taglio.

twice [twais], *av.* due volte; doppiamente: — *as big as*, due volte più grande di; *I am — as old as you* (*are*) (o *I am — your age*), ho il doppio della tua età || *in —*, (*fam.*) in due riprese || *to think — before doing sthg.*, pensarci su due volte prima di fare ql.co.

twicer ['twaisə*], *s.* (*tip.*) compositore e stampatore.

twiddle ['twidl], *s.* leggera rotazione.

to **twiddle**, *v.t.i.* (far) girare; (far) roteare || *to — one's moustache*, attorcigliarsi i baffi || *to — one's thumbs*, gingillarsi, girare i pollici.

twig [twig], *s.* **1.** ramoscello; verga || *to hop the —*, (*fam.*) morire **2.** (*anat.*) ramo terminale di arteria **3.** (*elett.*) piccolo conduttore di distribuzione **4.** bacchetta di rabdomante.

to **twig**, *pass.p.p.* **twigged** [twigd], *v.t.* **1.** (*fam.*) notare, osservare **2.** comprendere, afferrare: *I soon twigged his game*, ho capito subito il suo giuoco.

twiggy ['twigi], *ag.* ricco di ramoscelli.

twigless ['twiglis], *ag.* senza ramoscelli.

twilight ['twailait], *s.* **1.** crepuscolo || *the Twilight of the Gods*, (*mit. nordica*) il Crepuscolo degli Dei **2.** luce fioca, soffusa **3.** *fig.* conoscenza imperfetta, imprecisa ☆ — *sleep*, (*med.*) metodo per rendere il parto indolore.

to **twilight**, *v.t.* (*rar.*) illuminare debolmente.

twill [twil], *s.* (*ind. tessile*) tessuto diagonale ☆ *cross —*, spigato; *reversed —*, saia alla rovescia.

to **twill**, *v.t.* (*ind. tessile*) tessere in diagonale.

'twill, *contr.* di *it will*.

twin [twin], *ag.* gemello || *s.c.* gemello, gemella || *the Twins*, (*astr.*) i Gemelli ☆ — *-birth*, parto gemellare; *un gemello*; *una coppia di gemelli*; — *-brother*, fratello gemello; — *cylinder*, (*aut.*) (motore) a due cilindri; — *jet*, (*aer.*) bireattore; — *magneto*, (*aut.*) magnete gemello; — *-screw*, a due eliche; — *-set*, completo (di due golf per donna); — *-sister*, sorella gemella.

to **twin**, *pass.p.p.* **twinned** [twind], *v.t.i.* accoppiare, accoppiarsi; appaiare, appaiarsi; abbinare.

twine [twain], *s.* **1.** spago, corda **2.** intreccio; spira, voluta **3.** groviglio, garbuglio.

to **twine**, *v.t.i.* **1.** torcere, torcersi; attorcigliare, attorcigliarsi; intrecciare **2.** serpeggiare, procedere tortuosamente.

twinge [twindʒ], *s.* **1.** fitta; contrazione dolorosa **2.** dolore; rimorso: — *of conscience*, rimorso di coscienza.

to **twinge**, *v.t.* (*rar.*) causare dolore acuto a; tormentare.

twiningly ['twainiŋli], *av.* sinuosamente.

twinkle ['twiŋkl], *s.* **1.** scintillio, balenio **2.** emissione di luce balenante **3.** ammicco, strizzata d'occhio; rapido movimento in su e in giù (di palpebre, di piedi nella danza) || *in a —*, in un battere d'occhio.

to **twinkle**, *v.t.i.* **1.** scintillare; brillare; balenare **2.** emettere balenii di (luce) **3.** ammiccare, strizzar (l'occhio); muoversi rapidamente in su e in giù (di palpebre, piedi nella danza).

twinkler ['twiŋklə*], *s.* oggetto brillante, balenante.

twinkling ['twiŋkliŋ], *s.* scintillio; balenio || *in the — of an eye* (o *arc. of a bedpost*), in un baleno.

twinling ['twinliŋ], *s.c.* gemello, gemella.

to **twire** ['twaiə*], *v.i.* (*arc.*) sbirciare.

twirl [twə:l], *s.* **1.** giro; piroetta; mulinello **2.** svolazzo, ghirigoro.

to **twirl**, *v.t.i.* (far) girare; (far) roteare; attorcigliare.

twist [twist], *s.* **1.** filo ritorto; cordoncino; treccia (di pane, tabacco, ecc.) **2.** torsione, torcimento: *to give a — to s.o.'s arm*, torcere il braccio a qlcu. **3.** curva **4.** inclinazione, tendenza (di carattere) **5.** miscela di liquori **6.** (*fam.*) appetito **7.** (*neol.*) « twist » (danza).

to **twist**, *v.t.i.* **1.** intrecciare, intrecciarsi; attorcigliare, attorcigliarsi: *she twisted the flowers into a wreath*, intrecciò i fiori in una ghirlanda; *the woman kept twisting the thread round her fingers*, la donna continuò ad avvolgere il filo intorno alle dita **2.** torcere, torcersi; contorcere, contorcersi: *he twisted his ankle*, si slogò la caviglia; *the man twisted about in pain*, l'uomo si contorceva in preda al dolore **3.** *fig.* alterare, travisare: *he twisted what I had said so as to give a wrong impression*, travisò ciò che avevo detto in modo da dare un'impressione errata **4.** serpeggiare; insinuarsi: *the road twists through the fields*, la strada serpeggia tra i campi; *she twisted through the crowd*, si insinuò tra la folla **5.** *fig.* ingannare, abbindolare **6.** *to — off*, strappare (attorcigliando) **7.** *to — up*, attorcigliare a spirale.

twistable ['twistəbl], *ag.* che si può attorcigliare, intrecciare.

twisted ['twistid], *ag.* **1.** torto, ritorto, attorcigliato; intrecciato **2.** distorto; contorto **3.** alterato (di significato).

twister ['twistə*], *s.c.* **1.** chi torce **2.** (*sl.*) truffatore, truffatrice || *s.* **1.** parte interna della coscia (su cui ci si appoggia quando si è a cavallo) **2.** compito difficile, scabroso: *that's a — for you*, ecco ql.co. che ti darà del filo da torcere **3.** (*ind. tessile*) ritorcitoio.

twisting ['twistiŋ], *s.* **1.** torcitura, torcimento; contorcimento **2.** contrazione **3.** alterazione (di significato) **4.** (*mec.*) svergolamento.

twisty ['twisti], *ag.* **1.** pieno di pieghe **2.** tortuoso **3.** *fig.* disonesto.

twit [twit], *s.* rimprovero; biasimo.

to **twit**, *pass.p.p.* **twitted** ['twitid], *v.t.* rimproverare, rimbrottare; biasimare.

twitch [twitʃ], *s.* **1.** contrazione involontaria, spasmodica **2.** tirata; strappo; strattone.

to **twitch**, *v.t.i.* **1.** contrarre, contrarsi; contorcersi: *her face twitches*, ha un tic nervoso al viso **2.** tirare; dare uno strappo, uno strattone a: *to — s.o.'s sleeve*, tirare qlcu. per la manica.

twitching ['twitʃiŋ], *s.* **1.** contrazione **2.** strattone.

twite [twait], *s.* (*ornit.*) fanello.

twitter ['twitə*], s. **1.** cinguettio; pigolio **2.** (fam.) stato d'ansia, di agitazione.

to **twitter**, v.t.i. cinguettare (anche fig.); pigolare.

twitteringly ['twitəriŋli], av. con cinguettii; con pigolii.

twittingly ['twitiŋli], av. con biasimo.

'twixt [twikst], abbr. di **betwixt**.

two [tu:], ag.num.card.s. due: one or — pens, una penna o due; qualche penna; they came in by twos, entrarono a gruppi di due; to fold sthg. in —, piegare ql.co. in due; to walk in twos (o — and — o — by —), camminare a due a due ‖ — can play at that game!, non sei il solo a saperlo fare! ‖ to put — and — together, procedere a fil di logica; tirare le conclusioni ☆ — -colour(ed), bicolore; — -cycle, a due tempi (di motore); — -decker, nave a due ponti; vettura tranviaria, autobus a imperiale; — edged, a doppio taglio; (bot.) gladiato; — -eyed, con due occhi; binoculare (di microscopio, ecc.); — -faced, con due facce; fig. falso, doppio; — -footed (o — -legged), bipede; — -handed, con, per due mani; ambidestro; che si giuoca in due; — -headed, bicipite; — -horse, a due cavalli; — -masted, (mar.) a due alberi; — -phase, (elett.) bifase; — -piece, a due pezzi; — -ply, a due capi (di corda, ecc.); a due strati; — -sided, bilaterale; che ha due aspetti, due facce, due superfici, ecc.; fig. ambiguo; — -step, (danza) passo doppio; — -storied (o — -story), a due piani (di casa); — -stroke, (mec.) a due tempi; — -tongued, fig. falso; — -way, a due sensi (di strada); a due vie (di rubinetto); — -way switch, (elett.) interruttore bipolare; — -winged, (entom.) dittero; — -yearly, biennale; — -year-old, di due anni.

twofold ['tu:-fould], ag. doppio ‖ av. doppiamente.

twoness ['tu:nis], s. dualità.

twopence ['tʌpəns], s. **1.** valore di due pennies ‖ not to care —, (fam.) non importare nulla, un fico secco **2.** (sl.) moneta da due pennies **3.** cosa di poco valore.

twopenny ['tʌpni], ag. **1.** che vale due pennies **2.** a buon mercato; di poco valore: a — remedy, un medicamento da quattro soldi ‖ s. **1.** (sl.) quarto di birra (venduto a due pennies) **2.** (sl.) testa (al giuoco della cavallina): tuck in your —!, abbassa la testa! ☆ — -halfpenny, due penny e mezzo; insignificante; senza valore.

twosome ['tu:səm], ag. in coppia (di giuochi, danze) ‖ s. giuoco, danza in coppia.

'twould [twud], contr. di it would.

twyer ['twaiə*], s. (metal.) ugello.

Tyburn ['taibə:n], no.pr. (st. geog.) Tyburn (luogo in Londra dove avvenivano le esecuzioni capitali).

tycoon [tai'ku:n], s. **1.** (st. giapponese) « taicùn » (gran principe) **2.** (sl.) capitalista; magnate.

tyke [taik], s. **1.** cane bastardo **2.** uomo volgare.

tyler ['tailə*], s. custode (di una loggia massonica).

tylopod ['tailoupəd], ag.s. (zool.) tilopodo.

tylopodous [tai'lopədəs], ag. (zool.) tilopodo.

tylosis [tai'lousis], s. (patol.) tiloma, tilosi.

tymp [timp], s. (metal.) timpano (di altoforno).

tympan ['timpən], s. (anat. arch. tip.) timpano.

tympanic [tim'pænik], ag. (anat.) timpanico ☆ — membrane, membrana timpanica.

tympanism ['timpənizəm], s. (patol.) timpanite.

tympanist ['timpənist], s. (mus.) timpanista.

tympanites [,timpə'naiti:z], s. (patol.) timpanite.

tympanitis [,timpə'naitis], s. (patol.) otite media.

tympanum ['timpənəm], pl. **tympana** ['timpənə], s. (mus. arch. anat.) timpano.

Tynwald ['tinwɔ:ld], s. « Tynwald » (assemblea legislativa dell'isola di Man).

typal ['taipəl], ag. tipico.

type [taip], s. **1.** tipo; modello; simbolo: the King's sceptre is a — of royal authority, lo scettro del re è un simbolo dell'autorità regale **2.** tipo; classe; genere; gruppo: Australia has many types of animal life not found in other continents, l'Australia ha molti tipi di vita animale che non si trovano in altri continenti;

she has a special — of beauty, ha un tipo speciale di bellezza **3.** (tip.) carattere tipografico: to set up in —, comporre **4.** impronta (di monete, medaglie) **5.** (chim.) composto tipo ☆ — -bar, (tip.) riga di composizione; — -founder, (tip.) fonditore dei caratteri; — -foundry, (tip.) fonderia di caratteri; — -script, dattiloscritto; — -setter, (tip.) compositore di caratteri; — -setting, (tip.) composizione; — -setting machine, (tip.) compositrice.

to **type**, v.t. **1.** rappresentare, simboleggiare **2.** dattilografare **3.** (med.) determinare (il gruppo sanguigno).

to **typewrite** ['taip-rait], pass. **typewrote** ['taip-rout], p.p. **typewritten** ['taip,ritn], v.t. dattilografare.

typewriter ['taip,raitə*], s. macchina per scrivere ‖ s.c. dattilografo, dattilografa.

typewriting ['taip,raitiŋ], s. dattilografia.

typewritten ['taip,ritn], p.p. di to **typewrite**.

typewrote ['taip-rout], pass. di to **typewrite**.

typhlitis [ti'flaitis], s. (patol.) tiflite.

typhoid ['taifoid], ag. (patol.) tifoideo ‖ s. — (fever), febbre tifoidea.

typhomania [,taifou'meinjə], s. (patol.) tifomania.

typhoon [tai'fu:n], s. (mar.) tifone.

typhous ['taifəs], ag. (patol.) tifoso, del tifo.

typhus ['taifəs], s. (patol.) tifo.

typic(al) ['tipik(əl)], ag. tipico; caratteristico.

typically ['tipikəli], av. tipicamente.

typicalness ['tipikəlnis], s. caratteristica.

typification [,tipifi'keiʃən], s. **1.** rappresentazione simbolica **2.** esemplificazione.

to **typify** ['tipifai], v.t. **1.** rappresentare simbolicamente; incarnare **2.** esemplificare.

typist ['taipist], s.c. dattilografo, dattilografa.

typo ['taipou], abbr. di **typographer**.

typographer [tai'pɔgrəfə*], s. tipografo.

typographic(al) [,taipə'græfik(əl)], ag. tipografico.

typographically [,taipə'græfikəli], av. tipograficamente.

typography [tai'pɔgrəfi], s. tipografia.

typolithographic [,taipə,liθə'græfik], ag. tipolitografico.

typolithography [,taipəli'θɔgrəfi], s. tipolitografia.

typometer [tai'pɔmitə*], s. (tip.) tipometro.

typtology [tai'pɔlədʒi], s. (spiritismo) tiptologia.

tyrannic(al) [ti'rænik(əl)], ag. tirannico, dispotico.

tyrannically [ti'rænikəli], av. tirannicamente.

tyrannicalness [ti'rænikəlnis], s. tirannia.

tyrannicidal [ti,ræni'saidəl], ag. tirannicida.

tyrannicide [ti'rænisaid], s. **1.** tirannicida **2.** tirannicidio.

to **tyrannize** ['tirənaiz], v.t.i. tiranneggiare: to — (over) s.o., tiranneggiare qlcu.

tyrannous ['tirənəs], ag. tirannico.

tyrannously ['tirənəsli], av. tirannicamente.

tyranny ['tirəni], s. tirannia; tirannide.

tyrant ['taiərənt], s. **1.** tiranno: to play the —, fare il tiranno ‖ Thirty Tyrants, (st.) i Trenta Tiranni **2.** — (-bird o -flycatcher), (ornit.) tiranno.

to **tyrant**, v.i. fare il, comportarsi da tiranno.

tyre[1], V. **tire**[2].

Tyre[2] ['taiə*], no.pr. (geog. st.) Tiro.

tyriasis [ti'raiəsis], s. (patol.) elefantiasi.

tyro, V. **tiro**.

Tyrol ['tirɔl], no.pr. (geog.) Tirolo.

Tyrolean [ti'rouliən], **Tyrolese** [,tirə'li:z], ag.s.c. tirolese.

Tyrolienne [ti,rouli'en], s. (mus.) tirolese.

tyrosine ['taiərousi:n], s. (chim.) tirosina.

Tyrrhene [ti'ri:n], **Tyrrhenian** [ti'ri:njən], ag. s. tirreno ‖ the Tyrrhenian Sea, il Mar Tirreno.

Tyrtaeus [tə:'ti:əs], no.pr.m. (st. lett.) Tirteo.

tzar [tsɑ:*], s. zar.

tzarina [tsɑ:'ri:nə], s. zarina.

tzetze ['tsetsi], s. mosca tsè-tsè.

Tzigane [tsi'gɑ:n], ag. tzigano ‖ s.c. tzigano, tzigana.

U

u [ju:], *pl.* **us, u's** [ju:z], *s.* (*ventunesima lettera dell'alfabeto inglese*) u ‖ — *for uncle*, (*tel.*) u come Udine ☆ *U-boat*, sottomarino tedesco; *U-tube*, tubo ad U.

U, *ag.* (*abbr.* di *upper-class*) (tipico) delle classi superiori (di parole, ecc.) ☆ *non- —*, non (tipico) delle classi superiori (di parole, ecc.).

uberous ['ju:bərəs], *ag.* (*rar.*) 1. ricco di latte 2. fertile.

ubication [,ju:bi'keiʃən], **ubiety** [ju(:)'baiiti], *s.* ubicazione, collocazione.

ubiquitarian [ju(:),bikwi'tɛəriən], *ag.* (*st. relig.*) ubiquitario ‖ *s. gener. pl.* (*st. relig.*) ubiquitario, ubiquista.

ubiquitous [ju(:)'bikwitəs], *ag.* dotato di ubiquità.

ubiquitously [ju(:)'bikwitəsli], *av.* con ubiquità.

ubiquitousness [ju(:)'bikwitəsnis], **ubiquity** [ju(:)-'bikwiti], *s.* ubiquità.

udal ['ju:dəl], *ag.* (*dir.*) allodiale ‖ *s.* (*dir.*) allodio.

udaller ['ju:dələ*], **udalman,** *pl.* **udalmen** ['ju(:)dəlmən], *s.* (*dir.*) proprietario di beni allodiali.

udder ['ʌdə*], *s.* mammella (di animali da latte).

uddered ['ʌdəd], *ag.* con mammelle (di animali da latte).

udderless ['ʌdəlis], *ag.* privato del latte materno, privato della madre (di vitello, ecc.).

udometer [ju(:)'dɔmitə*], *s.* udometro, pluviometro.

Uganda [ju(:)'gændə], *no.pr.* (*geog.*) Uganda.

ugh [uh], *inter.* uh!.

uglification [,ʌglifi'keiʃən], *s.* imbruttimento.

to uglify ['ʌglifai], *v.t.* rendere brutto, imbruttire.

uglily ['ʌglili], *av.* 1. spiacevolmente 2. vilmente; in modo spregevole.

ugliness ['ʌglinis], *s.* 1. bruttezza; deformità 2. abiezione, bassezza.

ugly ['ʌgli], *ag.* 1. brutto; deforme; sgradevole: *I am not going to buy such an — house*, non ho nessuna intenzione di comprare una casa così brutta ‖ *the — duckling*, il brutto anatroccolo ‖ *as — as sin*, brutto come il peccato 2. vile, turpe, abietto: *— vices*, vizi turpi; *— rumours are spreading about him*, si diffondono delle calunnie sul suo conto 3. pericoloso; minaccioso; non promette bene: *business was taking an — look*, gli affari stavano prendendo una brutta piega; *the police got hold of that — man*, la polizia mise le mani su quell'uomo pericoloso.

Ugrian ['u:griən], **Ugric** ['u:grik], *ag.* finnico.

uhlan ['u:lɑ:n], *s.* (*st.*) ulano.

Uitlander ['eitlændə*], *s.* (*sud-africano*) straniero.

ukase [ju:'keiz], *s.* 1. ukase (editto dello zar di Russia) 2. ordine arbitrario; editto dittatoriale.

Ukraine [ju(:)'krein], *no.pr.* (*geog.*) Ucraina.

Ukrainian [ju(:)'kreinjən], *ag.* ucraino ‖ *s.c.* abitante dell'Ucraina ‖ *s.* lingua ucraina.

ukulele [,ju:kə'leili], *s.* «ukulele» (chitarra hawaiana).

ulcer ['ʌlsə*], *s.* 1. piaga; ulcera 2. *fig.* piaga morale ☆ *duodenal —*, ulcera duodenale.

to ulcerate ['ʌlsəreit], *v.t.i.* ulcerare, ulcerarsi; *fig.* irritare.

ulceration [,ʌlsə'reiʃən], *s.* (*patol.*) ulcerazione.

ulcered ['ʌlsəd], *ag.* (*patol.*) ulcerato.

ulcerous ['ʌlsərəs], *ag.* (*patol.*) ulceroso.

ulcerousness ['ʌlsərəsnis], *s.* (*patol.*) stato ulceroso.

ulema ['u:limə], *s.* ulema (teologo e giurista musulmano).

uliginose [ju(:)'lidʒinous], *ag.* 1. fangoso, melmoso 2. che cresce in luoghi umidi, paludosi (di pianta).

ullage ['ʌlidʒ], *s.* 1. quantità di liquido mancante (in una botte, ecc.); calo: *barrel on —*, barile scemo 2. deposito, rifiuto; merce di qualità inferiore.

to ullage, *v.t.* calcolare il calo di (un liquido).

ulmaceous [ʌl'meiʃəs], *ag.* (*bot.*) olmaceo.

ulmic ['ʌlmik], *ag.* (*chim.*) ulmico.

ulmin ['ʌlmin], *s.* (*chim.*) ulmina.

ulna ['ʌlnə], *pl.* **ulnae** ['ʌlni:], *s.* (*anat.*) ulna.

ulnar ['ʌlnə*], *ag.* (*anat.*) ulnare.

Ulrica ['ʌlrikə], *no.pr.f.* Ulrica.

Ulster ['ʌlstə*], *no.pr.* (*geog.*) Ulster ‖ **ulster,** *s.* « ulster » (cappotto ampio e pesante).

ulterior [ʌl'tiəriə*], *ag.* 1. ulteriore; più remoto, più lontano 2. segreto; nascosto: *without — motive*, senza secondi fini; *he had an — motive to do that*, aveva un motivo segreto per fare ciò.

ulteriorly [ʌl'tiəriəli], *av.* ulteriormente; più tardi.

ultimate ['ʌltimit], *ag.* 1. ultimo, finale; definitivo: *— results*, risultati definitivi 2. basilare, fondamentale: *— cause*, causa prima.

ultimately ['ʌltimitli], *av.* 1. alla fine; in definitiva 2. fondamentalmente.

ultimatum [,ʌlti'meitəm], *pl.* **ultimatums** [,ʌlti'meitəmz], **ultimata** [,ʌlti'meitə], *s.* 1. ultimatum 2. principio fondamentale 3. conclusione definitiva.

ultimo ['ʌltimou], *ag.* dello scorso mese, ultimo scorso: *on the third —*, il tre del mese scorso.

ultra ['ʌltrə], *ag.* ultra; estremo; eccessivo: *wearied by the — zeal of his friends*, stanco dello zelo eccessivo degli amici ‖ *s.* 1. estremista, oltranzista (in politica, in religione) 2. persona eccentrica nel vestire.

ultrafashionable ['ʌltrə'fæʃənəbl], *ag.* all'ultima moda.

ultraism ['ʌltrəizəm], *s.* (*pol.*) radicalismo; estremismo.

ultraist ['ʌltrəist], *s.* (*pol.*) oltranzista; radicalista estremista.

ultramarine [,ʌltrəmə'ri:n], *ag.* 1. oltremarino, d'oltremare 2. azzurro oltremare ‖ *s.* (colore) azzurro oltremare.

ultramicroscope ['ʌltrə'maikrəskoup], *s.* (*ott.*) ultramicroscopio.

ultramicroscopic(al) ['ʌltrə,maikrəs'kɔpik(əl)], *ag.* (*ott.*) ultramicroscopico.

ultramontane [,ʌltrə'mɔntein], *ag.s.* 1. oltremontano, subalpino; italiano 2. (*relig.*) oltremontano.

ultramontanism [,ʌltrə'mɔntinizəm], *s.* (*relig.*) oltremontanismo.

ultramontanist [,ʌltrə'mɔntinist], *s.* (*relig.*) sostenitore dell'oltremontanismo.

ultramundane [,ʌltrə'mʌndein], *ag.* 1. non compreso nel sistema solare 2. oltremondano.

ultra-red ['ʌltrə'red], *ag.* (*fis.*) infrarosso.

ultrasonic ['ʌltrə'sɔnik], *ag.* (*fis.*) ultrasonico.

ultrasonics ['ʌltrə'sɔniks], *s.* (*fis.*) scienza degli ultrasuoni.

ultra-short ['ʌltrə'ʃɔ:t], *ag.* ultracorto ☆ *— wave* (*rad.*) onde cortissime.

ultraviolet ['ʌltrə'vaiəlit], *ag.* (*fis.*) ultra-violetto *— rays*, raggi ultravioletti.

ultroneous [ʌl'trouniəs], *ag.* spontaneo, volontario

ultroneously [ʌl'trouniəsli], *av.* spontaneamente, volontariamente.

ululant ['ju:ljulənt], *ag.* che ulula.

to **ululate** ['ju:ljuleit], *v.i.* 1. ululare 2. lamentarsi (di persona).

ululation [,ju:lju'leifən], *s.* 1. ululato 2. lamento (di persona).

Ulyssean [ju(:)'lisiən], *ag.* 1. di, da Ulisse 2. *fig.* astuto, simulatore.

Ulysses [ju(:)'lisi:z], *no.pr.m.* (*lett.*) Ulisse.

umbel ['ʌmbəl], *s.* (*bot.*) ombrella.

umbellal [ʌm'beləl], **umbellar** ['ʌmbilə*], **umbellate** ['ʌmbilit], *ag.* (*bot.*) a forma di ombrella.

umbellet ['ʌmbilit], *s.* (*bot.*) ombrelletta.

umbelliferous [,ʌmbe'lifərəs], *ag.* (*bot.*) ombrellifero.

umbelliform [ʌm'belifɔ:m], *ag.* (*bot.*) a forma di ombrella.

umbellule [ʌm'belju:l], *s.* (*bot.*) piccola ombrella, ombrella secondaria.

umber[1] ['ʌmbə*], *s.* (*ittiol.*) temolo.

umber[2], *ag.* di color terra d'ombra; fosco, scuro ‖ *s.* (*pitt.*) terra d'ombra ☆ *burnt* —, terra d'ombra bruciata; *raw* —, terra d'ombra naturale.

to **umber**[2], *v.t.* (*pitt.*) colorare con terra d'ombra.

umbery ['ʌmbəri], *ag.* di color terra d'ombra; fosco, scuro.

umbilical [,ʌmbi'laikəl], *ag.* 1. (*anat.*) ombelicale 2. parente per parte di madre ☆ — *cord*, (*anat.*) cordone ombelicale.

umbilicate [ʌm'bilikit], *ag.* ombelicato; avente l'ombelico.

umbilicus [ʌm'bilikəs], *s.* (*anat.*) ombelico.

umbles ['ʌmblz], *s.pl.* interiora (specialmente di cervo).

umbo ['ʌmbou], *pl.* **umbones** [ʌm'bouni:z], **umbos** ['ʌmbouz], *s.* 1. umbone (di scudo) 2. (*bot. zool.*) protuberanza; nodo.

umbonal ['ʌmbounl], **umbonate** ['ʌmbounit], *ag.* umbonato (di scudo).

umbra ['ʌmbrə], *pl.* **umbrae** ['ʌmbri:], *s.* 1. ombra; spirito, fantasma 2. (*astr.*) cono d'ombra (in eclisse totale); parte centrale di macchia solare.

umbraculum [ʌm'brækjuləm], *s.* (*bot.*) appendice ombrelliforme.

umbrage ['ʌmbridʒ], *s.* 1. (*poet.*) ombra; ombria 2. sospetto, dubbio 3. protezione, rifugio 4. dispiacere; offesa; risentimento: *to give* — *to s.o.*, dare dispiacere a, offendere qlcu.; *to take* — *at sthg.*, adombrarsi, risentirsi per ql.co.

to **umbrage**, *v.t.* 1. dare ombra a, ombreggiare; *fig.* mettere in ombra 2. offendere.

umbrageous [ʌm'breidʒəs], *ag.* 1. ombroso; ombreggiato 2. (*rar. fig.*) ombroso, irascibile.

umbrella [ʌm'brelə], *s.* 1. ombrello: *to put up one's* —, aprire l'ombrello; *to take down* (o *to fold up*) *one's* —, chiudere l'ombrello 2. ombrello (di medusa, ecc.) 3. (*bot.*) ombrella ☆ — *-case*, fodero dell'ombrello; — *-stand*, portaombrelli; — *-tree*, (*bot.*) magnolia tripetala.

umbrellad, umbrellaed [ʌm'breləd], *ag.* munito di ombrello.

Umbria ['ʌmbriə], *no.pr.* (*geog.*) Umbria.

Umbrian ['ʌmbriən], *ag.* umbro ‖ *s.c.* umbro, umbra.

umbriferous [ʌm'brifərəs], *ag.* ombrifero.

umbrous ['ʌmbrəs], *ag.* ombroso.

umiak, umyak ['u:miæk], *s.* « umiak » (grossa barca squimese).

umpirage ['ʌmpaiəridʒ], *s.* (*spor.*) arbitraggio.

umpire ['ʌmpaiə*], *s.* (*dir. spor.*) arbitro.

to **umpire**, *v.t.i.* (*dir. spor.*) arbitrare.

umpireship ['ʌmpaiəfip], *s.* (*dir. spor.*) arbitrato; funzioni d'arbitro.

umpteen ['ʌmpti:n], *ag.* (*sl.*) molti; un gran numero, un numero imprecisato: *to have* — *reasons for doing sthg.*, avere mille ragioni per fare ql.co.

'un [ən], (*fam.*) per **one**.

unabashed ['ʌnə'bæʃt], *ag.* imperturbato, impassibile.

unabated ['ʌnə'beitid], *ag.* non diminuito, non scemato: *with* — *speed*, con velocità costante.

unabiding ['ʌnə'baidiŋ], *ag.* transitorio; effimero.

unable ['ʌn'eibl], *ag.* 1. incapace, inabile: *to be* — *to do sthg.*, non potere, non essere in grado di fare ql.co. 2. (*rar. poet.*) debole, impotente.

unabolished ['ʌnə'bɔliʃt], *ag.* non abolito, in vigore, vigente.

unabridged ['ʌnə'bridʒd], *ag.* non abbreviato; intero; completo: — *edition*, edizione integrale.

unabrogated ['ʌn'æbrougeitid], *ag.* (*dir.*) non abrogato.

unacademic ['ʌn,ækə'demik], *ag.* non accademico.

unaccented ['ʌnæk'sentid], *ag.* non accentato, atono ☆ — *beat*, (*mus.*) battuta debole.

unacceptable ['ʌnək'septəbl], *ag.* 1. inaccettabile 2. non accetto, sgradito: *a little help would not be* — *to him*, un po' di aiuto non gli sarebbe sgradito.

unaccomodating ['ʌnə'kɔmədeitiŋ], *ag.* poco condiscendente, poco accomodante; scortese.

unaccompanied ['ʌnə'kʌmpənid], *ag.* 1. non accompagnato, solo: *ladies* — *by a gentleman are not admitted*, non sono ammesse le signore non accompagnate 2. (*mus.*) senza accompagnamento.

unaccomplished ['ʌnə'kɔmpliʃt], *ag.* 1. incompleto, incompiuto 2. che manca di educazione; privo di talento (di persona).

unaccomplishment ['ʌnə'kɔmpliʃmənt], *s.* mancanza di compiutezza.

unaccordant ['ʌnə'kɔ:dənt], *ag.* in disaccordo.

unaccountability ['ʌnə,kauntə'biliti], *s.* 1. inesplicabilità; stranezza 2. irresponsabilità.

unaccountable ['ʌnə'kauntəbl], *ag.* 1. inesplicabile; strano, bizzarro: *an* — *person*, una persona strana, enigmatica 2. irresponsabile: *an odd* — *fellow*, uno strano tipo irresponsabile.

unaccountableness [,ʌnə'kauntəblnis], *s.* 1. inesplicabilità; stranezza 2. irresponsabilità.

unaccountably [,ʌnə'kauntəbli], *av.* 1. inesplicabilmente; stranamente 2. in modo irresponsabile.

unaccredited ['ʌnə'kreditid], *ag.* non accreditato, non autorizzato, senza poteri.

unaccustomed ['ʌnə'kʌstəmd], *ag.* 1. non abituale, insolito: *with* — *rudeness*, con insolita scortesia 2. non abituato, poco abituato: *I am* — *to being kept waiting*, non sono abituato ad aspettare.

unachievable ['ʌnə'tʃi:vəbl], *ag.* ineseguibile, irrealizzabile, irraggiungibile.

unachieved ['ʌnə'tʃi:vd], *ag.* non realizzato, non raggiunto.

unaching ['ʌn'eikiŋ], *ag.* che non duole.

unacknowledged ['ʌnək'nɔlidʒd], *ag.* 1. non riconosciuto; non confessato: — *crimes*, crimini non confessati 2. senza risposta (di lettere, ecc.) 3. non accreditato: — *agent*, agente non accreditato.

unacquaintance ['ʌnə'kweintəns], *s.* ignoranza, mancanza di conoscenza.

unacquainted ['ʌnə'kweintid], *ag.* 1. ignaro, non al corrente; poco esperto 2. sconosciuto, poco familiare; strano 3. non presentato, che non ha fatto la conoscenza: *I have often heard of Mr. X, but I am* — *with him*, ho spesso sentito parlare del Sig. X, ma non ne ho fatto la conoscenza.

unacquaintedness ['ʌnə'kweintidnis], *s.* 1. ignoranza, mancanza di conoscenza; inesperienza 2. l'essere sconosciuto.

unacquired ['ʌnə'kwaiəd], *ag.* non acquisito; innato, naturale.

unacquitted ['ʌnə'kwitid], *ag.* non assolto.

unacted ['ʌn'æktid], *ag.* 1. non fatto, non eseguito 2. (*teat.*) non rappresentato, non recitato.

unactive ['ʌn'æktiv], *ag.* inattivo.

unactuated ['ʌn'æktjueitid], *ag.* non influenzato, non spinto.

unadaptable [ˈʌnəˈdæptəbl], *ag.* inadattabile.
unadapted [ˈʌnəˈdæptid], *ag.* non adatto, inadatto, poco adatto.
unaddicted [ˈʌnəˈdiktid], *ag.* non dedito.
unaddressed [ˈʌnəˈdrest], *ag.* non indirizzato; senza indirizzo.
unadjudged [ˈʌnəˈdʒʌdʒd], *ag.* non aggiudicato; non attribuito.
unadmired [ˈʌnədˈmaid], *ag.* non ammirato.
unadmonished [ˈʌnədˈmɔniʃt], *ag.* non ammonito; non avvertito.
unadorned [ˈʌnəˈdɔ:nd], *ag.* disadorno.
unadulterated [ˌʌnəˈdʌltəreitid], *ag.* non adulterato, non sofisticato (anche *fig.*): — *praise*, lode sincera; *this oil is* —, questo olio non è adulterato.
unadvertised [ˈʌnˈædvətaizd], *ag.* non annunziato, non reso noto.
unadvisable [ˈʌnədˈvaizəbl], *ag.* 1. non consigliabile; inopportuno 2. che non vuole intender ragione (di persona).
unadvised [ˈʌnədˈvaizd], *ag.* 1. non consigliato; non avvertito 2. imprudente, irriflessivo.
unadvisedly [ˌʌnədˈvaizidli], *av.* 1. senza essere ben consigliato 2. imprudentemente, sconsideratamente.
unadvisedness [ˈʌnədˈvaizidnis], *s.* imprudenza, sconsideratezza.
unaffected [ˌʌnəˈfektid], *ag.* 1. senza affettazione, semplice; genuino, sincero: — *kindness of heart*, vera gentilezza d'animo; — *manners*, modi semplici, non affettati 2. impassibile; insensibile 3. inalterabile, inattaccabile: *stone* — *by the weather*, pietra che resiste al tempo.
unaffectedly [ˌʌnəˈfektidli], *av.* senza affettazione; con naturalezza.
unaffectedness [ˌʌnəˈfektidnis], *s.* schiettezza, franchezza; semplicità, naturalezza.
unaffecting [ˌʌnəˈfektiŋ], *ag.* che non causa emozione; che non turba.
unafraid [ˈʌnəˈfreid], *ag.* impavido.
unaided [ˈʌnˈeidid], *ag.* senza assistenza; senza aiuto: — *by a doctor*, senza l'assistenza di un medico.
unaired [ˈʌnˈɛəd], *ag.* 1. non ventilato, senza aria: — *room*, stanza non aereata 2. umido: — *sheets*, lenzuola umide.
unalarmed [ˈʌnəˈlɑ:md], *ag.* non allarmato, tranquillo.
unalarming [ˈʌnəˈlɑ:miŋ], *ag.* non allarmante.
unalienable [ˈʌnˈeiljənəbl], *ag.* inalienabile.
unalienably [ʌnˈeiljənəbli], *av.* in modo inalienabile.
unallayed [ˈʌnəˈleid], *ag.* 1. puro, non mescolato 2. non placato.
unallied [ˈʌnəˈlaid], *ag.* 1. senza relazione, senza connessione 2. senza alleati.
unallotted [ˈʌnəˈlɔtid], *ag.* non diviso, non ripartito.
unallowable [ˈʌnəˈlau-əbl], *ag.* inammissibile.
unalloyed [ˈʌnəˈlɔid], *ag.* senza lega; *fig.* puro.
unalluring [ˈʌnəˈljuəriŋ], *ag.* poco attraente.
unalterability [ʌnˌɔ:ltərəˈbiliti], *s.* inalterabilità.
unalterable [ʌnˈɔ:ltərəbl], *ag.* inalterabile; immutabile.
unalterableness [ʌnˈɔ:ltərəblnis], *s.* inalterabilità, immutabilità.
unalterably [ʌnˈɔ:ltərəbli], *av.* inalterabilmente, immutabilmente.
unaltered [ˈʌnˈɔ:ltəd], *ag.* inalterato, immutato; costante.
unamazed [ˈʌnəˈmeizd], *ag.* non meravigliato; impassibile; indifferente.
unambiguous [ˈʌnæmˈbigjuəs], *ag.* non ambiguo, non equivoco; chiaro, evidente: — *answer*, risposta chiara; — *terms*, termini precisi.
unambiguously [ˈʌnæmˈbigjuəsli], *av.* senza ambiguità; chiaramente, esplicitamente: *to speak* —, (*fam.*) mettere i puntini sugli i.

unambiguousness [ˈʌnæmˈbigjuəsnis], *s.* chiarezza, evidenza.
unambitious [ˈʌnæmˈbiʃəs], *ag.* senza ambizioni, poco ambizioso; modesto.
unambitiously [ˈʌnæmˈbiʃəsli], *av.* senza ambizioni; modestamente.
unambitiousness [ˈʌnæmˈbiʃəsnis], *s.* mancanza di ambizione; modestia.
unamenable [ˈʌnəˈmi:nəbl], *ag.* 1. refrattario, ribelle, indocile: *he is* — *to reason*, non vuole intendere ragione 2. (*dir.*) irresponsabile.
unamendable [ˈʌnəˈmendəbl], *ag.* incorreggibile.
unamended [ˈʌnəˈmendid], *ag.* non emendato, non corretto: *to pass a bill* —, adottare un progetto di legge senza emendamenti.
un-American [ˈʌnəˈmerikən], *ag.* poco americano; contrario ad usi, costumi e interessi americani.
unamiability [ˈʌnˌeimjəˈbiliti], *s.* mancanza di amabilità; inamabilità.
unamiable [ˈʌnˈeimjəbl], *ag.* poco amabile, poco affabile; burbero.
unamiableness [ˈʌnˈeimjəblnis], *s.* mancanza di amabilità; inamabilità.
unamiably [ˈʌnˈeimjəbli], *av.* in modo poco amabile, poco affabile.
unamused [ˈʌnəˈmju:zd], *ag.* non divertito; annoiato.
unamusing [ˈʌnəˈmju:ziŋ], *ag.* poco divertente; noioso.
unanalysable [ˈʌnˈænəlaizəbl], *ag.* non analizzabile.
unanalytical [ˈʌnˌænəˈlitikəl], *ag.* non analitico.
to **unanchor** [ˈʌnˈæŋkə*], *v.t.* togliere l'ancora a, disancorare.
unanchored [ˈʌnˈæŋkəd], *ag.* disancorato; senz'ancora.
to **unanimate** [juˈnænimeit], *v.t.* rendere unanime.
unanimated [ˈʌnˈænimeitid], *ag.* 1. inanimato, senza vita 2. non ispirato.
unanimity [ˌju:nəˈnimiti], *s.* unanimità.
unanimous [ju(:)ˈnæniməs], *ag.* unanime: *a* — *vote*, un voto unanime.
unanimously [ju(:)ˈnæniməsli], *av.* unanimemente, all'unanimità.
unanimousness [ju(:)ˈnæniməsnis], *s.* unanimità.
unannealed [ˈʌnəˈni:ld], *ag.* (*metal.*) non temperato.
unannexed [ˈʌnəˈnekst], *ag.* non annesso.
unannounced [ˈʌnəˈnaunst], *ag.* non annunciato; improvviso, imprevisto.
unannoyed [ˈʌnəˈnɔid], *ag.* non annoiato, non molestato.
unanointed [ˈʌnəˈnɔintid], *ag.* 1. non unto 2. non consacrato; che non ha ricevuto l'Estrema Unzione.
unanswerability [ˈʌnˌɑ:nsərəˈbiliti], *s.* 1. irrefutabilità, incontestabilità 2. irresponsabilità.
unanswerable [ʌnˈɑ:nsərəbl], *ag.* 1. a cui non si può rispondere 2. irrefutabile, incontestabile: *an* — *proof*, una prova irrefutabile 3. irresponsabile: *he committed the offence whilst* — *for his acts*, egli commise l'infrazione mentre era irresponsabile delle sue azioni.
unanswerableness [ʌnˈɑ:nsərəblnis], *s.* 1. irrefutabilità; incontestabilità 2. irresponsabilità.
unanswerably [ʌnˈɑ:nsərəbli], *av.* 1. irrefutabilmente 2. irresponsabilmente.
unanswered [ˈʌnˈɑ:nsəd], *ag.* senza risposta.
unapostolic [ˈʌnˌæpəsˈtɔlik], *ag.* non apostolico.
unappalled [ˈʌnəˈpɔ:ld], *ag.* non intimidito, senza timore, intrepido.
unappealable [ˈʌnəˈpi:ləbl], *ag.* inappellabile.
unappealably [ˈʌnəˈpi:ləbli], *av.* in modo inappellabile.
unappeasable [ˈʌnəˈpi:zəbl], *ag.* implacabile: — *hatred*, odio implacabile.
unappeased [ˈʌnəˈpi:zd], *ag.* insoddisfatto; non placato.
unappetizing [ˈʌnˈæpitaiziŋ], *ag.* poco appetitoso.

unapplied ['ʌnə'plaid], *ag.* non impiegato, inapplicato.

unappreciated ['ʌnə'pri:ʃieitid], *ag.* non apprezzato; incompreso.

unapprehended ['ʌn,æpri'hendid], *ag.* 1. non arrestato: *the criminal is still* —, il criminale è ancora latitante 2. non compreso, non capito.

unapprehensive ['ʌn,æpri'hensiv], *ag.* 1. lento nell'apprendere 2. non apprensivo; non ansioso.

unapprehensiveness ['ʌn,æpri'hensivnis], *s.* 1. lentezza nell'apprendere 2. assenza di apprensione, di sospetti, di ansia.

unapprised ['ʌnə'praizd], *ag.* non avvertito, non prevenuto.

unapproachable [,ʌnə'proutʃəbl], *ag.* inaccessibile; inavvicinabile (anche *fig.*).

unapproachableness [,ʌnə'proutʃəblnis], *s.* inaccessibilità (anche *fig.*).

unapproachably [,ʌnə'proutʃəbli], *av.* in modo inaccessibile (anche *fig.*).

unapproached ['ʌnə'proutʃt], *ag.* non avvicinato.

unappropriate [,ʌnə'proupriit], *ag.* non adatto, non appropriato.

unapproved ['ʌnə'pru:vd], *ag.* non approvato, disapprovato.

unapproving ['ʌnə'pru:viŋ], *ag.* che non approva, che disapprova.

unapprovingly ['ʌnə'pru:viŋli], *av.* con disapprovazione.

unapt ['ʌn'æpt], *ag.* 1. non adatto, non appropriato; sconveniente (di linguaggio): — *words*, parole non adatte, sconvenienti; *a ground* — *to receive seeds*, un terreno non adatto alla semina 2. inetto; poco portato; incapace: *she is* — *to learn*, è poco portata allo studio 2. poco disposto, poco incline.

unaptly ['ʌn'æptli], *av.* male a proposito, a sproposito; in modo non appropriato.

unaptness ['ʌn'æptnis], *s.* incapacità, inettitudine.

unarchitectural ['ʌn,ɑ:ki'tektʃərəl], *ag.* 1. non conforme alle leggi dell'architettura 2. non esperto in architettura.

unargued ['ʌn'ɑ:gju:d], *ag.* indiscusso.

to **unarm** ['ʌn'ɑ:m], *v.t.i.* 1. disarmare 2. (*arc.*) togliere, togliersi l'armatura.

unarmed ['ʌn'ɑ:md], *ag.* disarmato; inerme; innocuo.

unarmoured ['ʌn'ɑ:məd], *ag.* non protetto da armatura, da corazza.

unarraigned ['ʌnə'reind], *ag.* non chiamato in giudizio, non accusato.

unarrayed ['ʌnə'reid], *ag.* 1. disadorno 2. in disordine.

unarrested ['ʌnə'restid], *ag.* ininterrotto.

unartful ['ʌn'ɑ:tful], *ag.* 1. privo di artifici; ingenuo; spontaneo 2. goffo, impacciato 3. privo di abilità.

unartfully ['ʌn'ɑ:tfuli], *av.* 1. senza artifici; ingenuamente; spontaneamente 2. goffamente 3. senza abilità.

unarticulated ['ʌnɑ:'tikjuleitid], *ag.* 1. inarticolato, indistinto: — *language*, linguaggio inarticolato 2. disarticolato.

unartificial ['ʌn,ɑ:ti'fiʃəl], *ag.* (*rar.*) naturale; spontaneo.

unartistic ['ʌnɑ:'tistik], *ag.* non artistico.

unascendable ['ʌnə'sendəbl], **unascendible** ['ʌnə'sendibl], *ag.* inaccessibile, che non si può scalare.

unascertainable ['ʌnæsə'teinəbl], *ag.* non verificabile.

unascertained ['ʌnæsə'teind], *ag.* sconosciuto, non accertato.

unashamed ['ʌnə'ʃeimd], *ag.* spudorato.

unasked ['ʌn'ɑ:skt], *ag.* non richiesto.

unaspirated ['ʌn'æspəreitid], *ag.* (*fonet.*) non aspirato.

unaspiring ['ʌnəs'paiəriŋ], *ag.* senza ambizione.

unassailable [,ʌnə'seiləbl], *ag.* 1. inattaccabile 2. irrefutabile.

unassailed ['ʌnə'seild], *ag.* inattaccato.

unassayed ['ʌnə'seid], *ag.* non provato; non analizzato.

unasserted ['ʌnə'se:tid], *ag.* non asserito.

unassessed ['ʌnə'sest], *ag.* 1. non valutato 2. non gravato d'imposta.

unassignable ['ʌnə'sainəbl], *ag.* 1. non assegnabile 2. (*dir.*) non trasferibile.

unassimilated ['ʌnə'simileitid], *ag.* non assimilato.

unassisted ['ʌnə'sistid], *ag.* non aiutato; non assistito.

unassociated ['ʌnə'souʃieitid], *ag.* non associato.

unassuaged ['ʌnə'sweidʒd], *ag.* non calmato, non soddisfatto (di sete, ecc.).

unassuming ['ʌnə'sju:miŋ], *ag.* modesto, senza pretese.

unassured ['ʌnə'ʃuəd], *ag.* 1. incerto, dubbio 2. diffidente, malsicuro 3. (*comm.*) non assicurato.

unatonable ['ʌnə'tounəbl], *ag.* 1. inespiabile 2. (*arc.*) irreconciliabile.

unatoned ['ʌnə'tound], *ag.* inespiato.

unattached ['ʌnə'tætʃt], *ag.* 1. indipendente, libero 2. non fidanzato; non sposato 3. non appartenente (a collegio universitario, associazione, ecc.).

unattackable ['ʌnə'tækəbl], *ag.* inattaccabile.

unattainable ['ʌnə'teinəbl], *ag.* inaccessibile, irraggiungibile.

unattainableness ['ʌnə'teinəblnis], *s.* inaccessibilità, irraggiungibilità.

unattainted ['ʌnə'teintid], *ag.* senza macchia, puro.

unattempted ['ʌnə'temptid], *ag.* intentato.

unattended ['ʌnə'tendid], *ag.* 1. senza seguito, solo 2. senza guidatore (di veicoli); incustodito 3. — *to*, trascurato: *to leave sthg.* — *to*, trascurare ql.co.

unattending ['ʌnə'tendiŋ], *ag.* 1. disattento 2. che non assiste, non cura 3. che non è presente.

unattenuated ['ʌnə'tenjueitid], *ag.* 1. non attenuato 2. non assottigliato.

unattested ['ʌnə'testid], *ag.* non comprovato; senza conferma.

unattired ['ʌnə'taiəd], *ag.* senza ornamento.

unattractive [,ʌnə'træktiv], *ag.* che non attrae, poco attraente.

unattractively [,ʌnə'træktivli], *av.* in modo poco attraente.

unattractiveness [,ʌnə'træktivnis], *s.* mancanza di attrattive.

unau ['ju:nɔ:], *s.* (*zool.*) bradipo.

unaudited ['ʌn'ɔ:ditid], *ag.* incontrollato.

unaugmented ['ʌnɔ:g'mentid], *ag.* 1. non accresciuto 2. (*gram.*) senza aumento (di verbi greci).

unauspicious ['ʌnɔ:s'piʃəs], *ag.* di cattivo augurio.

unauthentic ['ʌnɔ:'θentik], *ag.* non autentico, apocrifo.

unauthenticated ['ʌnɔ:'θentikeitid], *ag.* non autenticato (di documenti).

unauthoritative ['ʌnɔ:'θɔritətiv], *ag.* senza autorità.

unauthorized ['ʌn'ɔ:θəraizd], *ag.* 1. non autorizzato 2. illecito, illegale, abusivo.

unavailable ['ʌnə'veiləbl], *ag.* 1. inutile, vano: — *lamentations*, lamenti inutili 2. non disponibile 3. inutilizzabile 4. non valido (di biglietto ferroviario).

unavailableness ['ʌnə'veiləblnis], *s.* 1. inefficacia; inutilità 2. indisponibilità 3. non validità (di biglietto ferroviario).

unavailing ['ʌnə'veiliŋ], *ag.* inutile; inefficace.

unavailingly [,ʌnə'veiliŋli], *av.* inutilmente; senza efficacia.

unavenged ['ʌnə'vendʒd], *ag.* inulto, impunito.

unaverted ['ʌnə'və:tid], *ag.* non allontanato; non distolto; non stornato.

unavoidable [,ʌnə'vɔidəbl], *ag.* inevitabile.

unavoidableness [,ʌnə'vɔidəblnis], *s.* inevitabilità, ineluttabilità; fatalità.

unavoidably [,ʌnə'vɔidəbli], *av.* inevitabilmente, ineluttabilmente.

unavoided ['ʌnə'vɔidid], *ag.* non evitato, non schivato.

unavowable ['ʌnə'vauəbl], *ag.* inconfessabile.

unavowed ['ʌnə'vaud], *ag.* non confessato.

unawakened ['ʌnə'weikənd], *ag.* non sveglio, non desto, dormiente; addormentato.

unaware ['ʌnə'wɛə*], *ag.* inconsapevole; inconscio; ignaro: *they were — of their danger*, erano ignari del pericolo.

unawareness ['ʌnə'wɛənis], *s.* inconsapevolezza.

unawares ['ʌnə'wɛəz], *av.* **1.** inconsapevolmente, inconsciamente, inavvertitamente **2.** inaspettatamente, di sorpresa: *age steals upon us —*, la vecchiaia ci coglie inaspettatamente; *I was taken* (o *caught*) *—*, fui colto di sorpresa.

unawed ['ʌn'ɔːd], *ag.* non intimidito, non intimorito.

unbacked ['ʌn'bækt], *ag.* **1.** senza appoggi, senza sostenitori **2.** mai montato; non allenato (di cavalli).

unbaffled ['ʌn'bæfld], *ag.* **1.** non sconcertato, non imbarazzato **2.** non frustrato.

to unbag ['ʌn'bæg], *pass.p.p.* **unbagged** ['ʌn'bægd], *v.t.* togliere, fare uscire da un sacco.

unbaked ['ʌn'beikt], *ag.* **1.** non cotto **2.** *fig.* immaturo.

unbalance ['ʌn'bæləns], *s.* **1.** squilibrio, mancanza di equilibrio **2.** (*comm.*) spareggio.

to unbalance, *v.t.* squilibrare, sbilanciare.

unbalanced ['ʌn'bælənst], *ag.* **1.** sbilanciato, non equilibrato, in equilibrio instabile **2.** squilibrato, instabile (di mente) **3.** (*comm.*) non pareggiato.

to unballast ['ʌn'bæləst], *v.t.* alleggerire della zavorra; liberare dalla zavorra.

unballasted ['ʌn'bæləstid], *ag.* **1.** senza zavorra **2.** *fig.* leggero; instabile.

to unbandage ['ʌn'bændidʒ], *v.t.* sbendare, togliere le bende a.

unbanded ['ʌn'bændid], *ag.* sbendato, slegato.

unbaptized ['ʌnbæp'taizd], *ag.* non battezzato.

to unbar ['ʌn'bɑ:*], *pass.p.p.* **unbarred** ['ʌn'bɑːd], *v.t.* levare le sbarre a; disserrare, aprire: *to — a gate*, aprire un cancello.

unbarbed[1] ['ʌn'bɑːbd], *ag.* non bardato (di cavallo).

unbarbed[2], *ag.* **1.** senza punte **2.** senza penne.

unbarred ['ʌn'bɑːd], *ag.* **1.** aperto; non sbarrato; non ostruito **2.** (*dir.*) non escluso **3.** (*mus.*) non diviso in battute.

unbashful ['ʌn'bæʃful], *ag.* ardito, senza vergogna; impudente.

to unbaste ['ʌn'beist], *v.t.* togliere l'imbastitura a.

unbated ['ʌn'beitid], *ag.* (*arc.*) non diminuito; non affievolito.

unbathed ['ʌn'beiðd], *ag.* non bagnato, non immerso; asciutto.

to unbe ['ʌn'bi:], *v.t.i.* **1.** distruggere, far ritornare al nulla **2.** cessare di esistere, non esistere.

unbearable [ʌn'bɛərəbl], *ag.* insopportabile, intollerabile.

unbearableness [ʌn'bɛərəblnis], *s.* insopportabilità, intollerabilità.

unbearably [ʌn'bɛərəbli], *av.* insopportabilmente, intollerabilmente: *it is — hot*, fa un caldo insopportabile.

unbearded ['ʌn'biədid], *ag.* imberbe; senza barba.

unbeaten ['ʌn'bi:tn], *ag.* **1.** insuperato; non battuto **2.** non frequentato, non battuto (di sentiero): *the — paths of science*, *fig.* i sentieri inesplorati della scienza.

unbecoming ['ʌnbi'kʌmiɳ], *ag.* **1.** disdicevole, sconveniente: *it is — of him to act in this manner*, è sconveniente da parte sua agire in tale modo **2.** inadatto; che non si addice (di abiti).

unbecomingly ['ʌnbi'kʌmiɳli], *av.* sconvenientemente, disdicevolmente; impropriamente.

unbecomingness ['ʌnbi'kʌmiɳnis], *s.* sconvenienza, disdicevolezza; indecorosità.

unbefitting ['ʌnbi'fitiɳ], *ag.* inadatto; disdicevole.

unbefriended ['ʌnbi'frendid], *ag.* senza amici; abbandonato.

unbegotten ['ʌnbi'gɔtn], *ag.* **1.** (*teol.*) non concepito; non generato **2.** eterno.

unbegun ['ʌnbi'gʌn], *ag.* non iniziato, senza principio; eterno.

unbeknown ['ʌnbi'noun], *ag.* sconosciuto.

unbeknown, *av.* (*fam.*) all'insaputa: *he went out — to me*, uscì a mia insaputa.

unbelief ['ʌnbi'li:f], *s.* incredulità; scetticismo; miscredenza.

unbelievable [,ʌnbi'li:vəbl], *ag.* incredibile.

unbeliever ['ʌnbi'li:və*], *s.c.* persona incredula; miscredente.

unbelieving ['ʌnbi'li:viɳ], *ag.* incredulo; miscredente.

unbelievingly ['ʌnbi'li:viɳli], *av.* con incredulità.

to unbend ['ʌn'bend], *pass.p.p.* **unbent** ['ʌn'bent], *v.t.i.* **1.** raddrizzare, raddrizzarsi **2.** allentare; slegare; (*mar.*) sciogliere, allentare (le vele, le gomene) **3.** *fig.* rilassare, rilassarsi; distendere, distendersi: *some people find the reading of detective stories unbends their minds*, per alcune persone il leggere storie poliziesche rappresenta un completo riposo della mente; *to — one's brow*, spianare la fronte **4.** *fig.* farsi affabile; perdere il sussiego.

unbending ['ʌn'bendiɳ], *ag.* **1.** rigido, non pieghevole **2.** *fig.* risoluto; inflessibile; ostinato.

unbendingly ['ʌn'bendiɳli], *av.* **1.** in modo rigido **2.** *fig.* risolutamente; inflessibilmente.

unbeneficed ['ʌn'benifist], *ag.* (*dir. eccl.*) senza benefici.

unbeneficial ['ʌn,beni'fiʃəl], *ag.* inefficace; poco vantaggioso: *— to health*, poco salutare.

unbenefited ['ʌn'benifitid], *ag.* non beneficato, non avvantaggiato.

unbent ['ʌn'bent], *pass. p.p.* di to **unbend**.

unbequeathed ['ʌnbi'kwi:ðd], *ag.* (*dir.*) non assegnato per testamento.

to unbeseem ['ʌnbi'si:m], *v.t.* non convenirsi a, non essere adatto a.

unbeseeming ['ʌnbi'si:miɳ], *ag.* sconveniente, disdicevole.

unbeseemingly ['ʌnbi'si:miɳli], *av.* sconvenientemente, disdicevolmente.

unbeseemingness ['ʌnbi'si:miɳnis], *s.* sconvenienza.

unbesought ['ʌnbi'sɔ:t], *ag.* non sollecitato; non richiesto.

unbespoken ['ʌnbi'spoukən], *ag.* non prenotato; non ordinato.

unbestowed ['ʌnbi'stoud], *ag.* non elargito, non concesso.

unbethought ['ʌnbi'θɔ:t], *ag.* non premeditato, non ponderato.

unbetrayed ['ʌnbi'treid], *ag.* non tradito.

unbewailed ['ʌnbi'weild], *ag.* non compianto, illacrimato; non deplorato.

unbias(s)ed ['ʌn'baiəst], *ag.* imparziale; senza preconcetti: *any — observer would admit it*, qualsiasi osservatore imparziale lo ammetterebbe.

unbias(s)edly ['ʌn'baiəstli], *av.* imparzialmente: senza pregiudizi.

unbias(s)edness ['ʌn'baiəstnis], *s.* imparzialità.

unbidden ['ʌn'bidn], *ag.* **1.** non comandato; spontaneo **2.** non invitato.

to unbind ['ʌn'baind], *pass.p.p.* **unbound** ['ʌn'baund], *v.t.* sciogliere, slegare: *he unbound the ropes that held him*, sciolse le corde che lo legavano; *she unbound her hair*, si sciolse i capelli.

unbishoped ['ʌn'biʃəpt], *ag.* (*eccl.*) privato del vescovato: *he was —*, il vescovo fu interdetto.

to unbit ['ʌn'bit], *pass.p.p.* **unbitted** ['ʌn'bitid], *v.t.* togliere il morso, il freno a.

to unbitt ['ʌn'bit], *v.t.* (*mar.*) sbittare.

unbitted ['ʌn'bitid], *ag.* **1.** senza freno, morso **2.** *fig.* sfrenato: *— lust*, lussuria sfrenata.

unblamable ['ʌn'bleiməbl], *ag.* non biasimevole, irreprensibile; senza macchia, innocente.

unblamableness [ˈʌnˈbleiməblnis], *s.* irreprensibilità; purezza, innocenza.

unblamably [ˈʌnˈbleiməbli], *av.* irreprensibilmente.

unblamed [ˈʌnˈbleimd], *ag.* senza biasimo.

unbleached [ˈʌnˈbliːtʃt], *ag.* non candeggiato; non ossigenato; al colore naturale.

unbleeding [ˈʌnˈbliːdiŋ], *ag.* che non sanguina.

unblemished [ʌnˈblemiʃt], *ag.* puro, senza macchia (anche *fig.*): *her skin is* —, ha una pelle perfetta; *his reputation is* —, ha una reputazione irreprensibile.

unblenching [ˈʌnˈblentʃiŋ], *ag.* intrepido; che non indietreggia.

unblended [ˈʌnˈblendid], *ag.* non mescolato, puro.

unblessed, unblest [ˈʌnˈblest], *ag.* **1.** non benedetto **2.** disgraziato, infelice.

unblighted [ˈʌnˈblaitid], *ag.* **1.** non colpito da golpe (di grano, ecc.) **2.** intatto (di affetto, speranza).

unblooded [ˈʌnˈblʌdid], *ag.* che non è di razza; che non è puro sangue (di cavallo).

unbloody [ˈʌnˈblʌdi], *ag.* **1.** incruento **2.** non assetato di sangue.

unblotted [ˈʌnˈblɔtid], *ag.* **1.** senza macchia, non macchiato **2.** non cancellato.

unblown[1] [ˈʌnˈbloun], *ag.* **1.** non battuto, spazzato dal vento **2.** non suonato (di strumento).

unblown[2], *ag.* non sbocciato, non fiorito.

unblushing [ʌnˈblʌʃiŋ], *ag.* che non arrossisce; sfacciato; sfrontato, impudente.

unblushingly [ʌnˈblʌʃiŋli], *av.* senza arrossire; sfacciatamente, impudentemente.

unblushingness [ʌnˈblʌʃiŋnis], *s.* sfacciataggine, sfrontatezza, impudenza.

unbodied [ˈʌnˈbɔdid], *ag.* incorporeo; immateriale; senza forma.

unboiled [ˈʌnˈbɔild], *ag.* non bollito.

to **unbolt** [ˈʌnˈboult], *v.t.* **1.** disserrare, aprire; togliere il chiavistello a **2.** (*mec.*) sbullonare.

unbolted[1] [ˈʌnˈboultid], *ag.* **1.** disserrato, aperto **2.** (*mec.*) non bullonato.

unbolted[2], *ag.* non abburattato, non stacciato (di farina).

to **unbonnet** [ˈʌnˈbɔnit], *v.t.i.* **1.** togliere il cappello a, togliersi il cappello ‖ *to* — *to a person*, salutare una persona (togliendosi il cappello) **2.** (*aut.*) aprire il cofano a.

unbonneted [ˈʌnˈbɔnitid], *ag.* **1.** senza cappello, a capo scoperto **2.** (*aut.*) senza cofano.

unbooked [ˈʌnˈbukt], *ag.* **1.** non registrato **2.** non prenotato **3.** non libresco.

to **unboot** [ˈʌnˈbuːt], *v.t.i.* togliere, togliersi gli stivali.

unbooted [ˈʌnˈbuːtid], *ag.* senza stivali.

unborn [ˈʌnˈbɔːn], *ag.* non nato, nascituro; futuro, che deve venire: *generations yet unborn*, generazioni future.

unborrowed [ˈʌnˈbɔroud], *ag.* non preso a prestito; non copiato; originale: *an* — *poem*, una poesia originale.

to **unbosom** [ʌnˈbuzəm], *v.t.i.* rivelare; confidare, confidarsi; sfogare, sfogarsi: *to* — *one's sorrows to s.o.*, rivelare, confidare i propri dispiaceri a qlcu.; *to* — *oneself to s.o.*, confidarsi, aprirsi con qlcu.

unbought [ˈʌnˈbɔːt], *ag.* **1.** non comprato; invenduto **2.** gratuito.

unbound [ʌnˈbaund], *pass.p.p.* di to **unbind** ‖ *ag.* **1.** slegato; sciolto: — *hair*, capelli sciolti **2.** libero ‖ "*Prometheus Unbound*",(*lett.*) «Prometeo liberato» **3.** non rilegato (di libro).

unbounded [ʌnˈbaundid], *ag.* sconfinato, illimitato, smisurato (anche *fig.*): — *ambition*, ambizione smisurata.

unboundedly [ˈʌnˈbaundidli], *av.* illimitatamente; smisuratamente (anche *fig.*).

unboundedness [ˈʌnˈbaundidnis], *s.* mancanza di limiti; sfrenatezza; dismisura.

unbowed [ˈʌnˈbaud], *ag.* **1.** non curvato; non piegato **2.** *fig.* indomito, fiero.

to **unbrace** [ˈʌnˈbreis], *v.t.* **1.** allentare; slacciare, sfibbiare: *to* — *the yards of a ship*, allentare i pennoni

di una nave **2.** distendere, rilassare (muscoli, ecc.): *to* — *one's mind*, rilassare la mente; *to* — *one's nerves*, distendere i nervi **3.** snervare, indebolire.

to **unbraid** [ˈʌnˈbreid], *v.t.* strecciare (corde, capelli, ecc.); stessere.

unbranched [ˈʌnˈbrɑːntʃt], *ag.* senza diramazioni.

unbranching [ˈʌnˈbrɑːntʃiŋ], *ag.* che non si dirama.

unbreakable [ˈʌnˈbreikəbl], *ag.* infrangibile ☆ — *glass*, (*ind.*) vetro infrangibile.

unbreathable [ˈʌnˈbriːðəbl], *ag.* irrespirabile.

unbreathed [ˈʌnˈbriːðd], *ag.* **1.** non esausto **2.** non sussurrato, non pronunciato **3.** *fig.* non contaminato, non offuscato.

unbred [ˈʌnˈbred], *ag.* **1.** allevato male; ineducato **2.** incolto; inesperto: *he was* — *in* (o *to*) *any trade*, era inesperto di qualsiasi mestiere.

to **unbreech** [ˈʌnˈbriːtʃ], *v.t.* **1.** togliere i calzoni a **2.** (*artigl.*) togliere la culatta a (un cannone).

unbribable [ˈʌnˈbraibəbl], *ag.* incorruttibile.

unbribed [ˈʌnˈbraibd], *ag.* incorrotto.

to **unbridle** [ˈʌnˈbraidl], *v.t.* sbrigliare, dare libero corso a (anche *fig.*): *to* — *one's tongue*, sfogare i propri sentimenti, la propria ira.

unbridled [ʌnˈbraidld], *ag.* **1.** senza briglia **2.** *fig.* sfrenato, scatenato, violento, sbrigliato, impetuoso: *the* — *passions of the crowd*, le passioni scatenate della folla.

unbroken [ˈʌnˈbroukən], *ag.* **1.** intatto, intero; inviolato, vergine: — *oath*, giuramento inviolato; — *soil*, terreno vergine, mai arato **2.** incessante, ininterrotto, continuo: — *peace*, pace ininterrotta **3.** indomito, invitto; non sorpassato, non infranto: *record still* —, record imbattuto; — *spirit*, spirito indomito.

unbrotherly [ˈʌnˈbrʌðəli], *ag.* non fraterno, indegno di un fratello; non amichevole.

unbruised [ˈʌnˈbruːzd], *ag.* non ammaccato; illeso; intatto, indenne.

to **unbuckle** [ˈʌnˈbʌkl], *v.t.i.* **1.** sfibbiare; slacciare **2.** *fig.* uscire dal riserbo.

unbudded [ˈʌnˈbʌdid], *ag.* (*poet.*) che non ha ancora messo le gemme (di pianta).

to **unbuild** [ˈʌnˈbild], *pass.p.p.* **unbuilt** [ˈʌnˈbilt], *v.t.* demolire.

unbuilt [ˈʌnˈbilt], *pass.p.p.* di to **unbuild** ‖ *ag.* non ancora costruito.

unbuoyed [ˈʌnˈbɔid], *ag.* (*mar.*) non sostenuto, non tenuto a galla.

to **unburden** [ʌnˈbəːdn], *v.t.* **1.** scaricare; alleggerire **2.** *fig.* sollevare (da preoccupazioni, ecc.); alleviare; scaricare; confessare: *to* — *oneself of a secret*, liberarsi del peso di un segreto; *to* — *oneself to s.o.*, confidarsi, sfogarsi con qlcu.

unburdened [ʌnˈbəːdnd], *ag.* **1.** alleggerito **2.** non oppresso (da preoccupazioni, segreti, ecc.).

unburied [ˈʌnˈberid], *ag.* insepolto.

unburned [ˈʌnˈbəːnd], **unburnt** [ˈʌnˈbəːnt], *ag.* non bruciato; non cotto.

to **unbury** [ˈʌnˈberi], *v.t.* disseppellire, esumare, dissotterrare.

unbusinesslike [ʌnˈbiznislaik], *ag.* poco pratico, senza metodo; non portato per gli affari; non commerciale: *to conduct one's affairs in an* — *way*, trattare i propri affari senza metodo.

to **unbutton** [ˈʌnˈbʌtn], *v.t.i.* sbottonare, sbottonarsi.

to **uncage** [ˈʌnˈkeidʒ], *v.t.* togliere dalla gabbia, mettere in libertà.

uncalled [ˈʌnˈkɔːld], *ag.* **1.** non chiamato, non invitato **2.** — *for*, non necessario, superfluo; non richiesto, gratuito; fuori di posto: — *for insult*, insulto gratuito; *his help was* — *for*, il suo aiuto non era necessario.

uncancelled [ˈʌnˈkænsəld], *ag.* non cancellato; non annullato.

uncandid [ˈʌnˈkændid], *ag.* non schietto, insincero.

uncandidly [ˈʌnˈkændidli], *av.* senza schiettezza, insinceramente.

uncanny [ʌnˈkæni], *ag.* misterioso, strano, irreale, fantastico; inquietante: — *sort of fear*, paura soprannaturale.

uncanonical [ˌʌnkəˈnɔnikəl], *ag.* non canonico; non conforme ai canoni.

uncanonically [ˌʌnkəˈnɔnikəli], *av.* in modo non conforme ai canoni.

uncanonicalness [ˌʌnkəˈnɔnikəlnis], *s.* mancanza di rispetto ai canoni.

uncanonized [ʌnˈkænənaizd], *ag.* non canonizzato.

uncanopied [ʌnˈkænəpid], *ag.* senza baldacchino.

to uncap [ʌnˈkæp], *pass.p.p.* **uncapped** [ʌnˈkæpt], *v.t.i.* scoprire, scoprirsi; togliere il cappello; scappellarsi.

uncared-for [ʌnˈkɛədfɔ:*], *ag.* negletto; abbandonato.

uncareful [ʌnˈkɛəful], *ag.* **1.** sbadato, disattento **2.** incurante: — *of* (o *for*) *him*, incurante di lui **3.** privo di preoccupazioni.

uncarpeted [ʌnˈkɑ:pitid], *ag.* senza tappeto.

to uncase [ʌnˈkeis], *v.t.* estrarre (da astuccio, scatola, fodero); *fig.* esporre; scoprire: *his hypocrisy should be uncased*, la sua ipocrisia dovrebbe esser messa a nudo.

uncased [ʌnˈkeist], *ag.* senza astuccio, senza scatola.

uncatalogued [ʌnˈkætəlɔgd], *ag.* non catalogato.

uncatechized [ʌnˈkætikaizd], *ag.* non catechizzato.

uncatholic [ʌnˈkæθəlik], *ag.s.* non cattolico.

uncaught [ʌnˈkɔ:t], *ag.* inafferrato, libero.

uncaused [ʌnˈkɔ:zd], *ag.* **1.** non causato; senza motivo **2.** senza causa prima.

unceasing [ʌnˈsi:siŋ], *ag.* incessante.

unceasingly [ʌnˈsi:siŋli], *av.* incessantemente.

unceded [ʌnˈsi:did], *ag.* non ceduto.

uncelebrated [ʌnˈselibreitid], *ag.* non celebrato; senza fama.

uncemented [ˌʌnsiˈmentid], *ag.* non cementato.

uncensurable [ʌnˈsenʃərəbl], *ag.* incensurabile.

uncensured [ʌnˈsenʃəd], *ag.* incensurato.

unceremonious [ˌʌnˌseriˈmounjəs], *ag.* non cerimonioso; semplice, alla buona.

unceremoniously [ˌʌnˌseriˈmounjəsli], *av.* senza cerimonie; alla buona.

unceremoniousness [ˌʌnˌseriˈmounjəsnis], *s.* semplicità; mancanza di cerimonie.

uncertain [ʌnˈsə:tn], *ag.* **1.** incerto; malsicuro; dubbio, aleatorio: *it is — who will win*, non si sa con sicurezza chi vincerà **2.** irresoluto; volubile; mutevole: — *weather*, tempo mutevole.

uncertainly [ʌnˈsə:tnli], *av.* **1.** in modo incerto, malsicuro **2.** irresolutamente; volubilmente.

uncertainty [ʌnˈsə:tnti], *s.* **1.** incertezza; ambiguità: *to prefer a certainty to an —*, preferire il certo all'incerto **2.** irresolutezza; volubilità.

to unchain [ʌnˈtʃein], *v.t.* sciogliere da catene; liberare.

unchallenged [ʌnˈtʃælindʒd], *ag.* **1.** non provocato, non sfidato **2.** non chiamato in questione; incontestato.

unchangeable [ʌnˈtʃeindʒəbl], *ag.* immutabile; invariabile.

unchangeableness [ʌnˈtʃeindʒəblnis], *s.* immutabilità; invariabilità.

unchangeably [ʌnˈtʃeindʒəbli], *av.* immutabilmente; invariabilmente.

unchanged [ʌnˈtʃeindʒd], *ag.* immutato; invariato.

unchanging [ʌnˈtʃeindʒiŋ], *ag.* immutabile; invariabile, costante.

uncharactered [ʌˈpˈkæriktəd], *ag.* **1.** che manca di carattere **2.** (*fonet.*) non rappresentato da simboli grafici (di suono).

uncharacteristic [ˈʌnˌkæriktəˈristik], *ag.* non caratteristico.

uncharged [ʌnˈtʃɑ:dʒd], *ag.* **1.** non carico, senza fardelli; scarico: *an — battery*, (*elett.*) una batteria scarica **2.** non incriminato **3.** non assalito **4.** — *for*, (*comm.*) gratuito, esente da spese.

uncharitable [ʌnˈtʃæritəbl], *ag.* poco caritatevole.

uncharitableness [ʌnˈtʃæritəblnis], *s.* mancanza di carità.

uncharitably [ʌnˈtʃæritəbli], *av.* senza carità; in modo poco caritatevole.

uncharity [ʌnˈtʃæriti], *s.* mancanza di carità.

to uncharm [ʌnˈtʃɑ:m], *v.t.* **1.** privare del potere magico **2.** liberare da un incantesimo **3.** privare del fascino.

uncharming [ʌnˈtʃɑ:miŋ], *ag.* senza fascino.

uncharted [ʌnˈtʃɑ:tid], *ag.* non segnato su carta geografica, marittima.

unchartered [ʌnˈtʃɑ:təd], *ag.* senza autorizzazione, senza licenza; irregolare.

unchary [ʌnˈtʃɛəri], *ag.* **1.** incauto, imprudente **2.** intemperante.

unchaste [ʌnˈtʃeist], *ag.* impuro; incontinente.

unchastely [ʌnˈtʃeistli], *av.* impudicamente; licenziosamente.

unchastised [ˌʌntʃæsˈtaizd], *ag.* non castigato; impunito.

unchastity [ʌnˈtʃæstiti], *s.* impudicizia; incontinenza; lussuria.

unchecked [ʌnˈtʃekt], *ag.* **1.** sfrenato, non represso; indisciplinato: — *anger*, collera sfrenata; — *child*, bambino indisciplinato **2.** non verificato; non controllato.

uncheered [ʌnˈtʃiəd], *ag.* non applaudito; non incoraggiato.

uncheerful [ʌnˈtʃiəful], *ag.* malinconico; triste.

uncheerfulness [ʌnˈtʃiəfulnis], *s.* malinconia; tristezza.

unchewed [ʌnˈtʃu:d], *ag.* **1.** non masticato; non ruminato **2.** *fig.* non ponderato; non meditato.

unchid [ʌnˈtʃid], *ag.* non rimproverato.

to unchild [ʌnˈtʃaild], *v.t.* **1.** privare dei figli **2.** privare delle caratteristiche infantili, del carattere infantile.

unchilled [ʌnˈtʃild], *ag.* non raffreddato.

unchivalrous [ʌnˈʃivəlrəs], *ag.* poco cavalleresco; poco leale; ingeneroso; scortese.

unchosen [ʌnˈtʃouzn], *ag.* non scelto.

to unchristen [ʌnˈkrisn], *v.t.* **1.** sciogliere il vincolo battesimale a **2.** privare del nome di battesimo.

unchristened [ʌnˈkrisnd], *ag.* **1.** non battezzato; non convertito al cristianesimo; pagano **2.** senza nome.

unchristian [ʌnˈkristjən], *ag.* **1.** non cristiano; non degno di un cristiano **2.** (*fam.*) irragionevole, assurdo: *at this — hour*, a quest'ora impossibile.

to unchristianize [ʌnˈkristjənaiz], *v.t.* (far) allontanare dal cristianesimo.

unchristianly [ʌnˈkristjənli], *av.* poco cristianamente; in modo non cristiano.

unchronicled [ʌnˈkrɔnikld], *ag.* non ricordato nelle cronache.

unchronological [ˌʌnˌkrɔnəˈlɔdʒikəl], *ag.* non cronologico.

to unchurch [ʌnˈtʃə:tʃ], *v.t.* **1.** espellere dalla Chiesa, scomunicare **2.** privare dei diritti ecclesiastici; sconsacrare.

unchurched [ʌnˈtʃə:tʃt], *ag.* **1.** scomunicato; sconsacrato **2.** che non appartiene ad alcuna Chiesa.

uncial [ˈʌnsiəl], *ag.* **1.** onciale **2.** duodecimale ‖ *s.* lettera, scrittura onciale.

unciform [ˈʌnsifɔ:m], *ag.* unciforme; uncinato ‖ *s.* (*anat.*) osso uncinato.

uncinate [ˈʌnsinit], *ag.* uncinato, unciforme ☆ — *attack*, (*patol.*) aura epilettica.

uncircumcised [ˈʌnˈsə:kəmsaizd], *ag.* (*relig.*) incirconciso.

uncircumscribed [ˈʌnˈsə:kəmskraibd], *ag.* non circoscritto.

uncircumspect [ʌnˈsə:kəmspekt], *ag.* imprudente, incauto.

uncircumspectly [ʌnˈsə:kəmspektli], *av.* senza circospezione, incautamente.

uneircumstantial [ˈʌn͵səːkəmˈstænʃəl], *ag.* non particolareggiato, sommario.

uneivil [ˈʌnˈsivil], *ag.* **1.** barbaro, incivile **2.** scortese, maleducato, incivile **3.** indecoroso.

uncivilized [ˈʌnˈsivilaizd], *ag.* non civilizzato, barbaro.

uncivilly [ˈʌnˈsivili], *av.* **1.** barbaramente **2.** scortesemente **3.** indecorosamente.

unelad [ˈʌnˈklæd], *ag.* (*letter.*) non vestito, nudo, spogliato; spoglio: — *with leaves*, spoglio di foglie.

unelaimed [ˈʌnˈkleimd], *ag.* non reclamato.

unelarified [ˈʌnˈklærifaid], *ag.* non chiarificato; torbido.

to **unclasp** [ˈʌnˈklɑːsp], *v.t.i.* **1.** slacciare, sfibbiare, aprire **2.** allentare la stretta, lasciare la presa.

unelasped [ˈʌnˈklɑːspt], *ag.* slacciato, allentato, aperto.

unelassable [ˈʌnˈklɑːsəbl], *ag.* non classificabile

unclassical [ˈʌnˈklæsikəl], *ag.* non classico.

unelassifiable [ˈʌnˈklæsifaiəbl], *ag.* non classificabile.

unclassified [ˈʌnˈklæsifaid], *ag.* non classificato.

unele [ˈʌŋkl], *s.* **1.** zio ‖ *Uncle Sam*, (*scherz.*) lo Zio Sam (personificazione degli Stati Uniti; il tipico cittadino degli Stati Uniti) ‖ *Welsh* —, cugino primo che gli genitori ‖ *to talk* (*to s.o.*) *like a Dutch* —, parlare a qlcu.) con bonaria severità **2.** (*sl.*) chi presta su pegno.

unclean [ˈʌnˈkliːn], *ag.* **1.** impuro, impudico ‖ — *spirit*, spirito immondo, demonio **2.** sporco, sudicio.

uncleanable [ˈʌnˈkliːnəbl], *ag.* che non può essere pulito.

uncleanliness [ˈʌnˈklenlinis], *s.* **1.** impurità, impudicizia **2.** sporcizia, sudiceria.

uneleanly [ˈʌnˈklenli], *ag.* **1.** impuro, sporco, impudico **2.** sporco, sudicio.

uncleanness [ˈʌnˈkliːnnis], *s.* **1.** impurità, impudicizia **2.** sporcizia, sudiceria.

uncleansed [ˈʌnˈklenzd], *ag.* **1.** non purificato **2.** non pulito.

unclear [ˈʌnˈkliə*], *ag.* non chiaro, oscuro; opaco.

uncleared [ˈʌnˈkliəd], *ag.* **1.** non chiarito, non spiegato **2.** non disboscato **3.** non liberato dall'accusa di colpa.

to **unclench** [ˈʌnˈklentʃ], *v.t.i.* schiudere, disserrare; aprire (il pugno).

unclerical [ˈʌnˈklerikəl], *ag.* non clericale; che non si addice al clero.

to **unclew** [ˈʌnˈkluː], *v.t.* **1.** disfare, srotolare **2.** *fig.* rovinare.

to **unclinch** [ˈʌnˈklintʃ], *V.* to **unclench**.

unclipped [ˈʌnˈklipt], *ag.* **1.** non tagliato; non tosato **2.** non forato (di biglietto).

to **uncloak** [ˈʌnˈklouk], *v.t.i.* **1.** togliere, togliersi il mantello **2.** *fig.* svelare, smascherare.

to **unclog** [ˈʌnˈklɔg], *pass.p.p.* **unclogged** [ˈʌnˈklɔgd], *v.t.* liberare da impedimenti.

to **unclose** [ˈʌnˈklouz], *v.t.i.* **1.** aprire, aprirsi; schiudere, schiudersi **2.** *fig.* rivelare.

unclosed [ˈʌnˈklouzd], *ag.* aperto: *an* — *controversy*, una questione non conchiusa.

to **unclothe** [ˈʌnˈklouð], *v.t.* svestire, denudare.

unclothed [ˈʌnˈklouðd], *ag.* svestito, nudo.

to **uncloud** [ˈʌnˈklaud], *v.t.* liberare (dalle nubi), rischiarare (anche *fig.*).

unclouded [ˈʌnˈklaudid], *ag.* senza nubi, sereno (anche *fig.*).

uncloudedness [ˈʌnˈklaudidnis], *s.* serenità (anche *fig.*).

uncloudy [ˈʌnˈklaudi], *ag.* senza nubi, sereno.

unco [ˈʌŋkou], *ag.* (*scoz.*) **1.** sconosciuto; strano, misterioso **2.** notevole, grande ‖ *s.* cosa, persona, notizia strana ‖ *av.* molto, esageratamente.

uncoagulable [ˈʌnkouˈægjuləbl], *ag.* non coagulabile.

uncoagulated [ˈʌnkouˈægjuleitid], *ag.* non coagulato.

to **uncock** [ˈʌnˈkɔk], *v.t.* **1.** abbassare il cane di un'arma da fuoco) **2.** sparpagliare (mucchi di fieno).

uncocked [ˈʌnˈkɔkt], *ag.* **1.** col cane abbassato (di arma da fuoco) **2.** sparpagliato, non più raccolto in mucchio (di fieno).

uncodified [ˈʌnˈkɔdifaid], *ag.* non codificato.

uncoffined [ˈʌnˈkɔfind], *ag.* senza bara.

to **uncoil** [ˈʌnˈkɔil], *v.t.i.* svolgere, svolgersi (di bobine, ecc.); sgomitolare.

uncoined [ˈʌnˈkɔind], *ag.* non coniato (di metallo).

uncollected [ˈʌnkəˈlektid], *ag.* **1.** non raccolto: — *poems*, poesie sparse **2.** non riscosso **3.** *fig.* agitato: — *mind*, mente agitata.

uncolonized [ˈʌnˈkɔlənaizd], *ag.* non colonizzato.

uncoloured [ˈʌnˈkʌləd], *ag.* non colorato; incolore (anche *fig.*): — *style*, stile incolore.

uncombed [ˈʌnˈkoumd], *ag.* spettinato; non pettinato (di lana).

to **uncombine** [ˈʌnkəmˈbain], *v.t.i.* separare, separarsi.

uncome-at-table [ˈʌnkʌmˈætəbl], *ag.* (*fam.*) inaccessibile; irraggiungibile.

uncomeliness [ˈʌnˈkʌmlinis], *s.* **1.** mancanza di grazia; bruttezza **2.** sconvenienza.

uncomely [ˈʌnˈkʌmli], *ag.* **1.** sgraziato; brutto **2.** sconveniente.

uncomfortable [ʌnˈkʌmfətəbl], *ag.* **1.** scomodo; a disagio: *to be* (o *to feel*) —, essere scomodo; sentirsi a disagio; *to be* (o *to feel*) — *about sthg.*, essere inquieti per ql.co.; *this chair is* —, questa sedia è scomoda **2.** spiacevole, fastidioso: *to make things* — *for s.o.*, procurare dei fastidi, delle noie a qlcu.

uncomfortableness [ʌnˈkʌmfətəblnis], *s.* **1.** scomodità; disagio **2.** inquietudine.

uncomfortably [ʌnˈkʌmfətəbli], *av.* **1.** senza comodità **2.** spiacevolmente; a disagio **3.** in ansia.

uncomforted [ˈʌnˈkʌmfətid], *ag.* sconsolato.

uncommendable [ʌnkəˈmendəbl], *ag.* non raccomandabile.

uncommended [ʌnkəˈmendid], *ag.* non raccomandato.

uncommercial [ˈʌnkəˈməːʃəl], *ag.* poco commerciale.

uncommitted [ˈʌnkəˈmitid], *ag.* **1.** non rimessa alla commissione (di legge) **2.** libero, non impegnato **3.** non commesso (di delitto, ecc.).

uncommon [ʌnˈkɔmən], *ag.* insolito; raro, eccezionale.

uncommonly [ʌnˈkɔmənli], *av.* insolitamente; stranamente; straordinariamente.

uncommonness [ʌnˈkɔmənnis], *s.* rarità, singolarità.

uncommunicable [ˈʌnkəˈmjuːnikəbl], *ag.* incomunicabile.

uncommunicative [ˈʌnkəˈmjuːnikətiv], *ag.* riservato, poco comunicativo; taciturno.

uncommunicatively [ˈʌnkəˈmjuːnikətivli], *av.* senza comunicativa, riservatamente; taciturnamente.

uncommunicativeness [ˈʌnkəˈmjuːnikətivnis], *s.* riservatezza; taciturnità.

uncompanionable [ˈʌnkəmˈpænjənəbl], *ag.* poco socievole.

uncompared [ˈʌnkəmˈpɛəd], *ag.* incomparato.

uncompassionate [ˈʌnkəmˈpæʃənit], *ag.* non compassionevole; senza compassione, senza pietà.

uncompassionately [ˈʌnkəmˈpæʃənitli], *av.* senza compassione, senza pietà.

uncompelled [ˈʌnkəmˈpeld], *ag.* non costretto; spontaneo, volontario.

uncompensated [ˈʌnˈkɔmpenseitid], *ag.* **1.** non compensato, non risarcito **2.** (*mec.*) non compensato, non (contro)bilanciato.

uncomplaining [ˈʌnkəmˈpleiniŋ], *ag.* che non si lamenta, che non si lagna; paziente, rassegnato: — *submission*, sottomissione rassegnata.

uncomplainingly [ˈʌnkəmˈpleiniŋli], *av.* senza lamentarsi, senza lagnarsi; rassegnatamente.

uncomplainingness [ˈʌnkəmˈpleiniŋnis], *s.* pazienza, rassegnazione.

uncomplaisant [ˈʌnkəmˈpleizənt], *ag.* scompiacente.

uncompleted ['ʌn-kəm'pli:tid], *ag.* incompleto; incompiuto.

uncompliant ['ʌn-kəm'plaiənt], *ag.* inflessibile; indocile.

uncomplicated ['ʌn'kɔmplikeitid], *ag.* non complicato; semplice.

uncomplimentary ['ʌn,kɔmpli'mentəri], *ag.* poco complimentoso.

uncomplying ['ʌn-kəm'plaiiŋ], *ag.* poco accomodante; intransigente, inflessibile.

uncomposed ['ʌn-kəm'pouzd], *ag.* 1. non composto, semplice 2. non composto, non unito 3. scomposto, disordinato; eccitato: *the — gestures of the drunkard*, i gesti scomposti dell'avvinazzato.

uncompounded ['ʌn-kəm'paundid], *ag.* non composto, semplice.

uncomprehended ['ʌn,kɔmpri'hendid], *ag.* incompreso.

uncomprehensive ['ʌn,kɔmpri'hensiv], *ag.* 1. non comprensivo, che non include 2. (*arc.*) non comprensivo, che manca di comprensione.

uncompressed ['ʌn-kəm'prest], *ag.* 1. non compresso 2. integrale (di edizione).

uncompressible ['ʌn-kəm'presəbl], *ag.* incomprimibile.

uncompromising [ʌn'kɔmprəmaiziŋ], *ag.* intransigente, inflessibile; che non scende a compromessi: *— sincerity*, sincerità assoluta.

uncompromisingly [ʌn'kɔmprəmaiziŋli], *av.* inflessibilmente; senza compromessi.

unconcealable ['ʌn-kən'si:ləbl], *ag.* che non si può nascondere.

unconcealed ['ʌn-kən'si:ld], *ag.* non celato, non dissimulato; manifesto: *— inclination*, manifesta simpatia.

unconceivable ['ʌn-kən'si:vəbl], *ag.* inconcepibile.

unconceived ['ʌn-kən'si:vd], *ag.* non concepito.

unconcern ['ʌn-kən'sə:n], *s.* indifferenza, noncuranza: *smile of —*, sorriso distaccato.

unconcerned ['ʌn-kən'sə:nd], *ag.* 1. indifferente, noncurante: *— air*, aria indifferente; *to be — about s.o.'s troubles*, essere indifferente alle pene di qlcu. 2. imparziale, neutrale; estraneo: *to be — in a business*, essere estraneo a un affare.

unconcernedly ['ʌn-kən'sə:nidli], *av.* 1. con aria indifferente, con noncuranza 2. con imparzialità, neutralità.

unconcernedness ['ʌn-kən'sə:nidnis], *s.* indifferenza, noncuranza.

unconcerning ['ʌn-kən'sə:niŋ], *ag.* irrilevante; che non interessa: *a subject — him*, un argomento che non lo interessa.

unconcerted ['ʌn-kən'sə:tid], *ag.* non concertato.

unconciliating ['ʌn-kən'silieitiŋ], *ag.* non conciliante.

unconciliatory ['ʌn-kən'siliətəri], *ag.* non conciliativo.

unconcluded ['ʌn-kən'klu:did], *ag.* inconcluso.

unconclusive ['ʌn-kən'klu:siv], *ag.* non conclusivo; non decisivo.

uncondemned ['ʌn-kən'demd], *ag.* non condannato: *to leave an abuse —*, passar sopra a, tollerare un abuso.

uncondensable ['ʌn-kən'densəbl], *ag.* che non si può condensare.

uncondensed ['ʌn-kən'denst], *ag.* non condensato.

unconditional ['ʌn-kən'diʃənl], *ag.* incondizionato, assoluto; senza riserve: *— approval*, approvazione senza riserve; *— refusal*, rifiuto categorico; *— surrender*, resa incondizionata.

unconditionally ['ʌn-kən'diʃnəli], *av.* incondizionatamente; senza riserve.

unconditioned ['ʌn-kən'diʃənd], *V.* **unconditional.**

unconfessed ['ʌn-kən'fest], *ag.* non confessato; senza confessione.

unconfinable ['ʌn-kən'fainəbl], *ag.* illimitabile.

unconfined ['ʌn-kən'faind], *ag.* sconfinato.

unconfirmed ['ʌn-kən'fə:md], *ag.* 1. non confermato: *— news*, notizia non confremata 2. (*eccl.*) non cresimato.

unconformable ['ʌn-kən'fɔ:məbl], *ag.* 1. non conformabile; incompatibile 2. (*relig.*) non conformista 3. (*geol.*) discordante (di strato).

unconformableness ['ʌn-kən'fɔ:məblnis], *s.* 1. incompatibilità 2. (*relig.*) non conformismo 3. (*geol.*) discordanza (di strati).

unconformably ['ʌn-kən'fɔ:məbli], *av.* 1. incompatibilmente 2. (*relig.*) non conformemente 3. (*geol.*) a strati discordanti.

unconfused ['ʌn-kən'fju:zd], *ag.* 1. non confuso, distinto 2. non turbato, non imbarazzato; disinvolto.

unconfutable ['ʌn-kən'fju:təbl], *ag.* inconfutabile.

unconfuted ['ʌn-kən'fju:tid], *ag.* inconfutato.

uncongealable ['ʌn-kən'dʒi:ləbl], *ag.* incongelabile, che non può essere congelato.

uncongealed ['ʌn-kən'dʒi:ld], *ag.* non congelato; non rappigliato.

uncongenial ['ʌn-kən'dʒi:njəl], *ag.* 1. antipatico; spiacevole, sgradito: *— atmosphere*, ambiente ostile; *— climate*, clima poco favorevole; *— job*, lavoro ingrato 2. non congeniale; incompatibile.

uncongenially ['ʌn-kən'dʒi:njəli], *av.* 1. in modo antipatico 2. senza affinità; in modo incompatibile.

unconnected ['ʌn-kə'nektid], *ag.* 1. non connesso, non collegato, disgiunto: *— railway lines*, linee ferroviarie non collegate 2. sconnesso, sconclusionato: *an — narrative*, una narrazione sconclusionata 3. senza parentele; privo di amicizie: *families bearing the same name, but —*, famiglie con lo stesso nome, ma senza legami di parentela.

unconnectedly ['ʌn-kə'nektidli], *av.* in modo sconnesso; senza legami.

unconquerable [ʌn'kɔŋkərəbl], *ag.* invincibile, insuperabile; indomabile; incontrollabile; irresistibile: *his — thirst of vengeance*, la sua insaziabile sete di vendetta.

unconquerably ['ʌn'kɔŋkərəbli], *av.* invincibilmente; indomabilmente.

unconquered ['ʌn'kɔŋkəd], *ag.* 1. invitto; indomito 2. insormontabile.

unconscientious ['ʌn,kɔnʃi'enʃəs], *ag.* poco coscienzioso; senza scrupoli.

unconscientiously ['ʌn,kɔnʃi'enʃəsli], *av.* poco coscienziosamente; in modo poco scrupoloso.

unconscientiousness ['ʌn,kɔnʃi'enʃəsnis], *s.* l'essere poco coscienzioso.

unconscionable [ʌn'kɔnʃnəbl], *ag.* 1. poco scrupoloso 2. inconcepibile; irragionevole; eccessivo: *to take an — time in doing sthg.*, impiegare un tempo eccessivo per fare ql.co.

unconscionableness [ʌn'kɔnʃnəblnis], *s.* 1. mancanza di scrupoli 2. irragionevolezza; enormità.

unconscionably [ʌn'kɔnʃnəbli], *av.* 1. senza scrupoli 2. irragionevolmente; eccessivamente.

unconscious [ʌn'kɔnʃəs], *ag.* 1. inconscio, ignaro, inconsapevole: *to be — of sthg.*, non accorgersi di ql.co.; *he is — of any danger*, è ignaro del pericolo; *she was — of exercising any ascendancy*, ella era inconsapevole di avere un certo ascendente ‖ *the —*, il subconscio 2. privo di sensi; insensibile (anche *fig.*): *the patient is still —*, il paziente è ancora privo di sensi.

unconsciously [ʌn'kɔnʃəsli], *av.* inconsciamente, inconsapevolmente.

unconsciousness [ʌn'kɔnʃəsnis], *s.* 1. inconsapevolezza 2. insensibilità; stato di incoscienza.

unconsecrated ['ʌn'kɔnsikreitid], *ag.* non consacrato; non benedetto.

unconsenting ['ʌn-kən'sentiŋ], *ag.* non consenziente.

unconsidered ['ʌn-kən'sidəd], *ag.* 1. inconsiderato, sconsiderato, avventato 2. non preso in considerazione; ignorato, trascurato.

unconsolable ['ʌn-kən'souləbl], *ag.* inconsolabile.

unconsoled ['ʌn-kən'sould], *ag.* inconsolato.

unconsolidated [ˈʌn-kənˈsɔlideitid], *ag.* non consolidato.

unconstitutional [ˈʌnˌkɔnstiˈtjuːʃən]], *ag.* (*dir.*) incostituzionale.

unconstitutionality [ˈʌnˌkɔnstiˌtjuːʃəˈnæliti], *s.* (*dir.*) incostituzionalità.

unconstitutionally [ˈʌnˌkɔnstiˈtjuːʃnəli], *av.* (*dir.*) incostituzionalmente.

unconstrained [ˈʌn-kənˈstreind], *ag.* 1. non costretto, senza costrizione, libero; spontaneo (di gesto, ecc.): — *freedom*, libertà completa 2. disinvolto, naturale: — *manner*, aria naturale, disinvolta 3. sfrenato: — *laughter*, risata sfrenata.

unconstrainedly [ˈʌn-kənˈstreinidli], *av.* 1. senza costrizione, liberamente; spontaneamente 2. senza impaccio; disinvoltamente 3. sfrenatamente.

unconstraint [ˈʌn-kənˈstreint], *s.* 1. assenza di costrizione, libertà 2. spontaneità, franchezza (di linguaggio) 3. scioltezza, facilità (di stile).

unconsumed [ˈʌn-kənˈsjuːmd], *ag.* non consumato; non distrutto (dal fuoco).

uncontaminated [ˈʌn-kənˈtæmineitid], *ag.* incontaminato.

uncontemplated [ˈʌnˈkɔntempleitid], *ag.* non contemplato, imprevisto.

uncontestable [ˌʌn-kənˈtestəbl], *ag.* incontestabile.

uncontested [ˈʌn-kənˈtestid], *ag.* incontestato.

uncontradicted [ˈʌnˌkɔntrəˈdiktid], *ag.* non contraddetto.

uncontrollable [ˌʌn-kənˈtrouləbl], *ag.* 1. incontrollabile; irrefrenabile; irresistibile, irreprimibile 2. assoluto (di potere).

uncontrollableness [ˌʌn-kənˈtrouləblnis], *s.* incontrollabilità; indocilità.

uncontrollably [ˌʌn-kənˈtrouləbli], *av.* senza controllo; in modo incontrollabile; irresistibilmente.

uncontrolled [ˈʌn-kənˈtrould], *ag.* senza controllo, senza ritegno, sfrenato.

uncontrolledly [ˈʌn-kənˈtroulidli], *av.* senza controllo, incontrollatamente.

uncontroverted [ˈʌnˈkɔntrəvəːtid], *ag.* incontestato, indiscusso.

unconventional [ˈʌn-kənˈvenʃən]], *ag.* non convenzionale, anticonformista; disinvolto.

unconventionality [ˈʌn-kənˌvenʃəˈnæliti], *s.* anticonvenzionalismo, anticonformismo.

unconventionally [ˈʌn-kənˈvenʃnəli], *av.* in modo non convenzionale, in modo anticonformista.

unconversable [ˈʌn-kənˈvəːsəbl], *ag.* poco socievole, riservato.

unconversant [ˈʌn-kənˈvəːsənt], *ag.* poco versato, poco pratico: *to be — with a question*, non essere al corrente di una questione.

unconverted [ˈʌn-kənˈvəːtid], *ag.* non convertito.

unconvertible [ˈʌn-kənˈvəːtəbl], *ag.* inconvertibile.

unconvicted [ˈʌn-kənˈviktid], *ag.* non riconosciuto colpevole; non condannato.

unconvinced [ˈʌn-kənˈvinst], *ag.* non convinto; scettico.

unconvincing [ˈʌn-kənˈvinsiŋ], *ag.* non convincente, poco verosimile, poco persuasivo.

uncookable [ˈʌnˈkukəbl], *ag.* che non si può cucinare.

uncooked [ˈʌnˈkukt], *ag.* non cucinato, non cotto; crudo.

to **uncord** [ˈʌnˈkɔːd], *v.t.* slegare, sciogliere.

to **uncork** [ˈʌnˈkɔːk], *v.t.* 1. sturare, stappare 2. *fig.* sfogare, dare libero corso a: *to — one's feelings*, dare libero corso ai propri sentimenti.

uncorrected [ˈʌn-kəˈrektid], *ag.* non corretto; non rettificato.

uncorrupted [ˈʌn-kəˈrʌptid], *ag.* incorrotto, integro, incontaminato.

uncorruptedness [ˈʌn-kəˈrʌptidnis], *s.* integrità, purezza.

uncorruptibility [ˈʌn-kəˌrʌptəˈbiliti], *s.* incorruttibilità.

uncorruptible [ˈʌn-kəˈrʌptəbll], *ag.* incorruttibile.

uncountable [ˈʌnˈkauntəbl], *ag.* innumerabile, innumerevole.

uncounted [ˈʌnˈkauntid], *ag.* 1. non contato 2. incalcolabile, innumerevole.

to **uncouple** [ˈʌnˈkʌpl], *v.t.* 1. sguinzagliare, lasciar liberi (cani) 2. staccare, sganciare, disgiungere.

uncoupled [ˈʌnˈkʌpld], *ag.* staccato, sganciato; non associato; libero.

uncourtly [ˈʌnˈkɔːtli], *ag.* scortese; ordinario, rozzo.

uncouth [ʌnˈkuːθ], *ag.* 1. ordinario, rozzo; goffo, sgraziato: *of — manners*, rozzo di modi 2. desolato, selvaggio (di luogo) 3. (*arc.*) strano, bizzarro.

uncouthly [ʌnˈkuːθli], *av.* 1. goffamente; grossolanamente 2. (*arc.*) stranamente, bizzarramente.

uncouthness [ʌnˈkuːθnis], *s.* 1. goffaggine; grossolanità 2. (*arc.*) stranezza, singolarità.

uncovenanted [ˈʌnˈkʌvinəntid], *ag.* non convenuto; non stipulato per contratto ‖ *the free — mercy of God*, (*teol.*) la misericordia incondizionata di Dio.

to **uncover** [ʌnˈkʌvə*], *v.t.i.* 1. scoprire 2. spogliare 3. scappellarsi, togliersi il cappello: *everyone uncovered when the bell rang*, tutti si tolsero il cappello quando suonò la campana 4. (*mil.*) esporre, mettere allo scoperto (le truppe, una posizione, ecc.) 5. *fig.* rivelare, palesare: *to — one's heart*, rivelare i propri sentimenti.

uncovered [ʌnˈkʌvəd], *ag.* 1. scoperto; senza riparo; senza tetto 2. spogliato, nudo 3. senza cappello, a capo scoperto 4. (*comm.*) (allo) scoperto.

uncramped [ˈʌnˈkræmpt], *ag.* libero; non impacciato.

to **uncreate** [ˈʌn-kri(ː)ˈeit], *v.t.* privare dell'esistenza; annientare.

uncreate(d) [ˈʌn-kri(ː)ˈeit(id)], *ag.* non creato, increato.

uncredited [ˈʌnˈkreditid], *ag.* non creduto; non stimato.

uncrippled [ˈʌnˈkripld], *ag.* 1. non storpiato 2. non impedito nei movimenti: *the ship remained — by the fire*, l'incendio non ostacolò i movimenti della nave.

uncritical [ˈʌnˈkritikəl], *ag.* 1. non critico; privo di senso critico: — *audience*, pubblico poco critico, poco esigente 2. non conforme ai principi della critica.

uncropped [ˈʌnˈkrɔpt], *ag.* 1. non mietuto; non falciato; non raccolto (di messi, ecc.) 2. non seminato, incolto (di terreno) 3. intonso, non accorciato (di capelli, ecc.).

to **uncross** [ˈʌnˈkrɔs], *v.t.* disincrociare (le braccia, ecc.).

uncrossed [ˈʌnˈkrɔst], *ag.* 1. non incrociato 2. (*comm.*) non sbarrato (di assegno) 3. non ostacolato: *a rapid rise to power — by any rivals*, una rapida ascesa al potere non ostacolata da rivali.

uncrowded [ˈʌnˈkraudid], *ag.* non affollato.

to **uncrown** [ˈʌnˈkraun], *v.t.* detronizzare, privare della corona.

uncrowned [ˈʌnˈkraund], *ag.* non coronato; senza corona: *some called Parnell the — King of Ireland*, alcuni chiamarono Parnell il re senza corona dell'Irlanda.

uncrystallizable [ˈʌnˈkristəlaizəbl], *ag.* non cristallizzabile.

uncrystallized [ˈʌnˈkristəlaizd], *ag.* non cristallizzato.

unction [ˈʌŋkʃən], *s.* 1. unzione (anche *eccl.*) ‖ *Extreme Unction*, Estrema Unzione 2. unguento; *fig.* balsamo 3. unzione, mellifuità, blandizie: — *is no longer admired in a preacher*, le blandizie non sono più ammirate in un predicatore 4. fervore, entusiasmo affettato 5. gusto, compiacimento: *she told the story with much —*, raccontò la storia compiacendosene molto.

unctuosity [ˈʌŋktjuˈɔsiti], *s.* untuosità (anche *fig.*).

unctuous [ˈʌŋktjuəs], *ag.* 1. untuoso, grasso, oleoso 2. *fig.* untuoso, mellifluo.

unctuously [ˈʌŋktjuəsli], *av.* untuosamente (anche *fig.*).

unctuousness [ˈʌŋktjuəsnis], s. untuosità (anche *fig.*).

uneulled [ˈʌnˈkʌld], *ag.* 1. non raccolto 2. non scelto.

uncultivable [ˈʌnˈkʌltivəbl], *ag.* non coltivabile.

uncultivated [ˈʌnˈkʌltiveitid], *ag.* incolto (anche *fig.*).

uncultured [ˈʌnˈkʌltʃəd], *ag.* incolto, senza cultura.

uncumbered [ˈʌnˈkʌmbəd], *ag.* non ingombrato, non gravato.

uncurbed [ˈʌnˈkəːbd], *ag.* sfrenato, sregolato.

uncured [ˈʌnˈkjuəd], *ag.* non guarito.

to **uncurl** [ˈʌnˈkəːl], *v.t.i.* disfare (i riccioli), disfarsi (di riccioli); sgomitolarsi, svolgersi.

uncurled [ˈʌnˈkəːld], *ag.* non arricciato, disfatto; sgomitolato, svolto.

uncurrent [ˈʌnˈkʌrənt], *ag.* non corrente, che non ha corso (di denaro).

uncurtailed [ˈʌnˈkəːˈteild], *ag.* 1. non abbreviato, non ridotto; per esteso 2. senza restrizione.

uneustomary [ˈʌnˈkʌstəməri], *ag.* insolito, inconsueto.

uncustomed [ˈʌnˈkʌstəmd], *ag.* non soggetto a dogana; che non ha pagato dogana.

uncut [ˈʌnˈkʌt], *ag.* intonso, non tagliato.

undamaged [ˈʌnˈdæmidʒd], *ag.* in buone condizioni; non guasto, non avariato; intatto: — *reputation*, reputazione intatta.

undamped [ˈʌnˈdæmpt], *ag.* 1. non umido; secco 2. non scoraggiato; sostenuto: *he is* — *by this failure*, non è per nulla scoraggiato da questo insuccesso 3. (*elett. fis.*) non smorzato, persistente ☆ — *waves*, (*rad.*) oscillazioni continue.

undarkened [ˈʌnˈdɑːkənd], *ag.* non oscurato.

undate(d) [ˈʌndeit(id)], *ag.* (*rar.*) ondulato, ondeggiante.

undated [ˈʌnˈdeitid], *ag.* non datato; senza data.

undaunted [ʌnˈdɔːntid], *ag.* intrepido, impavido; imperterrito.

undauntedly [ʌnˈdɔːntidli], *av.* intrepidamente; senza paura.

undauntedness [ʌnˈdɔːntidnis], s. intrepidezza.

undazzled [ʌnˈdæzld], *ag.* non abbagliato, che non si lascia abbagliare.

undebarred [ˈʌndiˈbɑːd], *ag.* non escluso; non ostacolato: — *from doing sthg.*, libero di fare ql.co.; *countries* — *from commerce*, paesi aperti al commercio.

undebased [ˈʌndiˈbeist], *ag.* 1. non degradato, non avvilito 2. inalterato, di buona lega (di monete, ecc.).

undebated [ˈʌn-diˈbeitid], *ag.* che non è ancora stato oggetto di discussione; indiscusso: *to accept a motion* —, accettare una mozione senza discussione.

undebauched [ˈʌndiˈbɔːtʃt], *ag.* incorrotto.

undecagon [ʌnˈdekəgən], s. (*geom.*) endecagono.

undecayed [ˈʌndiˈkeid], *ag.* non guasto; intatto; in buono stato.

undecaying [ˈʌndiˈkeiiŋ], *ag.* imperituro.

undeceitful [ˈʌndiˈsiːtful], *ag.* non ingannevole.

undeceivable [ˈʌn-diˈsiːvəbl], *ag.* 1. che non può essere ingannato 2. (*arc.*) che non può ingannare.

to **undeceive** [ˈʌn-diˈsiːv], *v.t.* disingannare, disilludere: *I have not the heart to* — *him*, non ho il coraggio di disilluderlo; *to* — *oneself*, disilludersi.

undeceived [ˈʌn-diˈsiːvd], *ag.* disingannato, disilluso.

undecennial [ˈʌndiˈsenjəl], *ag.* undecennale.

undeceptive [ˈʌndiˈseptiv], *ag.* non ingannevole.

undecided [ˈʌndiˈsaidid], *ag.* 1. indeciso; non risolto: *an* — *problem*, un problema non risolto 2. indefinito, incerto (di colore, forma, ecc.) 3. irresoluto, indeciso; esitante (di carattere): *he was* — *whether he would go or not*, era indeciso se andare o no; *to be* — *how to act*, essere indeciso sul da farsi.

undecidedly [ˈʌndiˈsaididli], *av.* in modo indeciso; irresolutamente.

undecipherable [ˈʌndiˈsaifərəbl], *ag.* indecifrabile.

undeciphered [ˈʌndiˈsaifəd], *ag.* indecifrato.

undecisive [ˈʌndiˈsaisiv], *ag.* 1. non decisivo 2. irresoluto, esitante.

to **undeek** [ˈʌnˈdek], *v.t.* (*rar.*) privare di ornamenti; sguarnire, spogliare.

undecked [ˈʌnˈdekt], *ag.* 1. privo di ornamenti; sguarnito 2. senza coperta (di nave).

undeclared [ˈʌndiˈkleəd], *ag.* non dichiarato.

undeclinable [ˈʌndiˈklainəbl], *ag.* indeclinabile.

undecomposable [ˈʌnˌdiːkəmˈpouzəbl], *ag.* indecomponibile.

undecomposed [ˈʌnˌdiːkəmˈpouzd], *ag.* indecomposto.

undecorated [ˈʌnˈdekəreitid], *ag.* non decorato.

undedicated [ˈʌnˈdedikeitid], *ag.* 1. senza dedica (di libro) 2. non dedicato, non consacrato (di chiesa).

undee [ˈʌndei], *ag.* (*arald.*) a onde, a forma di onda.

undefaced [ˈʌndiˈfeist], *ag.* non sfigurato, non mutilato; intatto (di monumenti, ecc.).

undefeated [ˈʌndiˈfiːtid], *ag.* invitto.

undefended [ˈʌndiˈfendid], *ag.* 1. indifeso; privo di protezione 2. (*dir.*) non assistito da difesa legale: — *suit*, causa in cui il difensore si astiene dal comparire 3. non proibito.

undefied [ˈʌndiˈfaid], *ag.* non sfidato.

undefiled [ˈʌndiˈfaild], *ag.* puro; senza macchia; intemerato.

undefinable [ˌʌndiˈfainəbl], *ag.* indefinibile; indeterminabile.

undefinableness [ˌʌndiˈfainəblnis], s. indefinibilità.

undefined [ˌʌndiˈfaind], *ag.* indefinito; indeterminato; vago.

undelegated [ˈʌnˈdeligeitid], *ag.* non delegato.

undeliberate [ˈʌndiˈlibərit], *ag.* indeliberato.

undelighted [ˈʌndiˈlaitid], *ag.* spiaciuto.

undelivered [ˈʌndiˈlivəd], *ag.* 1. (*comm.*) non recapitato, non consegnato: — *goods*, merce non consegnata 2. non liberato; non sgravato 3. non pronunciato (di discorso, sentenza).

undeluded [ˈʌndiˈluːdid], *ag.* disingannato.

undemanded [ˈʌndiˈmɑːndid], *ag.* non richiesto.

undemolished [ˈʌndiˈmɔliʃt], *ag.* non demolito.

undemonstrable [ˈʌnˈdemənstrəbl], *ag.* indimostrabile.

undemonstrative [ˈʌndiˈmɔnstrətiv], *ag.* poco espansivo; riservato, chiuso.

undeniable [ˌʌndiˈnaiəbl], *ag.* innegabile, irrefutabile.

undeniably [ˌʌndiˈnaiəbli], *av.* innegabilmente, irrefutabilmente.

undenominational [ˈʌndiˌnɔmiˈneiʃən], *ag.* non appartenente ad alcuna denominazione religiosa, laico: — *school*, scuola laica.

undepending [ˈʌndiˈpendiŋ], *ag.* (*arc.*) indipendente.

undeplored [ˈʌndiˈplɔːd], *ag.* non compianto; non deplorato.

undepraved [ˈʌndiˈpreivd], *ag.* non depravato; incorrotto; sano.

undepreciated [ˈʌndiˈpriːʃieitid], *ag.* non deprezzato.

undepressed [ˈʌndiˈprest], *ag.* 1. non abbassato; *fig.* non depresso 2. (*comm.*) fermo, stabile.

undeprived [ˈʌndiˈpraivd], *ag.* non privo, non privato.

under [ˈʌndə*], *prep.* 1. sotto, al di sotto di: — *the bed*, sotto il letto; — *ground*, sotto terra; — *the skin*, sotto la pelle; *the town lies* — *the mountain*, la città è situata ai piedi della montagna; *to grow sthg.* — *a wall*, far crescere ql.co. al riparo di un muro; *to look at sthg. from* — *one's spectacles*, guardare ql.co. da sotto gli occhiali; *to trample sthg.* — *one's feet*, schiacciare ql.co. sotto i piedi ‖ — *the circumstances*, in queste circostanze; stando così le cose ‖ — *a favourable light*, sotto una luce favorevole ‖ — *his father's will*, secondo la volontà, il testamento di suo padre ‖ — *lock and key*, sotto chiave ‖ — *the name of Brown*, col nome di Brown ‖ — *the necessity of*, nella necessità di ‖ — *our very eyes*, sotto i nostri stessi occhi; *he did it* — *my nose*, me l'ha fatta sotto il naso ‖ — *pain of death*, sotto pena di morte; *to be* — *sentence of death*, essere condannato a morte ‖ — *the Stuarts*, sotto gli Stuart ‖ — *the terms of the treaty*, in virtù del trattato; — *these conditions*, in queste condizioni ‖ *patient — observation, treatment*, paziente in osservazione, in cura ‖ *the question is — examination*, il problema è in esame ‖ *to be — a cloud*, essere in disgrazia ‖ *to be — a delusion*, soffrire per una delusione ‖ *to be — a terrible accusation*, essere sotto il peso di una grave accusa ‖ *to speak — one's breath*, parlare sottovoce ‖ *to take s.o. — one's wing*, prendere qlcu. sotto la propria protezione **2. in corso di, in via di:** — *construction*, in costruzione; — *repair*, in riparazione **3. meno di:** *he must be — fifty*, deve avere meno di cinquant'anni; *his income is — ten thousand pounds*, il suo reddito è inferiore alle diecimila sterline; *she will come in — two hours*, verrà in meno di due ore.

under, *av.* sotto, al di sotto: *the boat went —*, la barca affondò; *to keep s.o. —*, tenere qlcu. soggetto; *to stay — for two minutes*, rimanere sott'acqua due minuti.

under, *(nei composti):* — *-age*, minorenne; — *-driven*, *(mec.)* comandato dal basso; — *-jaw*, mascella inferiore, mandibola; — *-production*, sotto-produzione; — *-ripe*, immaturo, di non completa maturazione; — *-roof*, sottotetto; — *-school*, scuola inferiore; — *-secretary*, sottosegretario.

to **underact** ['ʌndər'ækt], *v.t.* *(teat.)* interpretare inadeguatamente: *he has underacted the part of Hamlet*, ha interpretato con scarsa efficacia la parte di Amleto.

underaction ['ʌndər'ækʃən], *s.* **1.** *(teat.)* azione subordinata, azione secondaria **2.** azione incompleta, insufficiente.

underagent ['ʌndər'eidʒənt], *s.* *(comm.)* subagente.

to **underbid** ['ʌndə'bid], *pass.p.p.* **underbid**, *v.t.* *(comm.)* offrire meno del giusto valore per.

underboard ['ʌndə'bɔ:d], *av.* *(rar.)* sotto banco; *fig.* segretamente, clandestinamente.

underbody ['ʌndə'bɔdi], *s.* *(aut.)* sottoscocca.

underbreath ['ʌndə'breθ], *ag.* sussurrato ‖ *s.* sussurro.

underbred ['ʌndə'bred], *ag.* **1.** maleducato; rozzo **2.** bastardo (di animali).

underbrush ['ʌndə-brʌʃ], *s.* sottobosco.

to **underbuy** ['ʌndə'bai], *pass.p.p.* **underbought** ['ʌndə'bɔ:t], *v.t.* acquistare a prezzo inferiore al normale, a prezzo di svendita.

undercarriage ['ʌndə,kæridʒ], *s.* **1.** *(aer.)* carrello d'atterraggio **2.** *(aut.)* telaio.

to **undercharge** ['ʌndə'tʃɑːdʒ], *v.t.* **1.** far pagare troppo poco a; far pagare meno del dovuto a **2.** caricare (arma da fuoco) in modo insufficiente.

underclay ['ʌndə-klei], *s.* *(geol.)* sottostrato argilloso.

underclothes ['ʌndə klouðz], *s. pl.* biancheria intima.

underclothing ['ʌndə,klouðiŋ], *s.* biancheria intima.

undercoat ['ʌndəkout], *s.* **1.** *(rar.)* sottoveste **2.** peluria (di animali); piumino (di uccelli).

undercook ['ʌndə'kuk], *s.* sottocuoco.

undercroft ['ʌndə-krɔft], *s.* *(arch.)* cripta.

undercurrent ['ʌndə,kʌrənt], *ag.* che scorre sotto; nascosto, segreto ‖ *s.* **1.** corrente sottomarina **2.** *fig.* attività, forza, tendenza nascosta.

undercut ['ʌndəkʌt], *s.* **1.** filetto di manzo; *(amer.)* arrosto disossato **2.** *(amer.)* taglio inferto in un tronco dalla parte in cui lo si vuol far cadere **3.** rientranza **4.** *(mec.)* sottosquadro **5.** *(fonderia)* canalino, incisione marginale.

to **undercut** ['ʌndə'kʌt], *pass.p.p.* **undercut**, *v.t.* **1.** colpire, tagliare dal basso verso l'alto; tagliare sotto **2.** *(comm.)* offrire a minor prezzo di; lavorare per salari più bassi di **3.** *(spor.)* tagliare (la palla).

underdealing ['ʌndə'di:liŋ], *s.* maneggio segreto.

underdeck ['ʌndə'dek], *s.* ponte inferiore (di nave).

to **underdevelop** ['ʌndədi've'ləp], *v.t.* **1.** sviluppare insufficientemente **2.** *(foto.)* sottosviluppare.

underdeveloped ['ʌndədi'veləpt], *ag.* **1.** poco sviluppato **2.** *(econ.)* sottosviluppato, depresso: — *countries*, paesi sottosviluppati **3.** *(foto.)* sottosviluppato.

to **underdo** ['ʌndə'du:], *pass.* **underdid** ['ʌndə'did],

p.p. **underdone** ['ʌndə'dʌn], *v.t.i.* **1.** fare, agire in modo insufficiente, inadeguato **2.** (far) cuocere poco.

underdog ['ʌndədɔg], *s.* **1.** cane sconfitto (in un combattimento) **2.** *fig.* chi ha la peggio; persona socialmente inferiore.

underdone ['ʌndədʌn], *p.p.* di to **underdo** ‖ *ag.* poco cotto, non abbastanza cotto: *I do like — meat*, mi piace molto la carne al sangue.

underdose ['ʌndədous], *s.* dose scarsa.

underdrain ['ʌndədrein], *s.* *(ing.)* drenaggio sotterraneo.

to **underdrain** ['ʌndə'drein], *v.t.* *(ing.)* drenare.

to **underdraw** ['ʌndə'drɔ:], *pass.* **underdrew** ['ʌndə'dru:], *p.p.* **underdrawn** ['ʌndə'drɔ:n], *v.t.* **1.** rappresentare, descrivere inadeguatamente **2.** coprire, rivestire di assi, listelli *(p.e.* interno di tetto) **3.** sottolineare.

underdress ['ʌndədres], *s.* sottoveste; biancheria.

to **underdress** ['ʌndə'dres], *v.t.i.* **1.** vestire, vestirsi dimessamente **2.** vestire, vestirsi con abiti leggeri.

underdressed ['ʌndə'drest], *ag.* non sufficientemente vestito.

underdrew ['ʌndə'dru:], *pass.* di to **underdraw**.

underearth ['ʌndərə:θ], *ag.* sotterraneo ‖ *s.* sottosuolo.

underestimate ['ʌndər'estimit], *s.* stima inferiore al valore.

to **underestimate** ['ʌndər'estimeit], *v.t.* sottovalutare.

underestimation ['ʌndər,esti'meiʃən], *s.* stima inferiore al valore.

to **underexpose** ['ʌndəriks'pouz], *v.t.* *(foto.)* sottoesporre.

underexposure ['ʌndəriks'pouʒə*], *s.* *(foto.)* sottoesposizione.

underfed ['ʌndə'fed], *ag.* denutrito.

to **underfeed** ['ʌndə'fi:d], *pass.p.p.* **underfed** ['ʌndə'fed], *v.t.i.* **1.** nutrire, nutrirsi insufficientemente **2.** stare a dieta: *the doctor advises me to — for a bit*, il medico mi consiglia di stare a dieta per qualche tempo.

underfired ['ʌndə'faiəd], *ag.* non abbastanza cotto (di ceramica).

underfoot [,ʌndə'fut], *av.* sotto i piedi; *fig.* in stato, in posizione di inferiorità.

to **underfurnish** ['ʌndə'fə:niʃ], *v.t.* fornire in modo insufficiente.

undergarment ['ʌndə,gɑ:mənt], *s.* indumento intimo.

to **undergo** [,ʌndə'gou], *pass.* **underwent** [,ʌndə'went], *p.p.* **undergone** [,ʌndə'gɔn], *v.t.* **1.** subire; essere sottoposto a: *he underwent a serious operation*, subì un grave intervento chirurgico; *to — a loss*, subire una perdita **2.** sopportare; soffrire, patire; *the explorers underwent much suffering*, gli esploratori patirono molte sofferenze.

undergown ['ʌndə-gaun], *s.* sottoveste.

undergraduate [,ʌndə'grædjuit], *s.c.* studente, studentessa (di università).

undergraduette ['ʌndə,grædju'et], *s.* *(sl.)* studentessa universitaria.

underground ['ʌndəgraund], *ag.* **1.** sotterraneo: *the — railway*, la ferrovia sotterranea **2.** *(pol.)* clandestino; partigiano: — *forces*, forze partigiane **3.** oscuro, segreto: — *intrigues*, intrighi segreti ‖ *s.* **1.** sottosuolo **2.** *(pol.)* movimento clandestino **3.** *(ferr.)* metropolitana.

underground [,ʌndə'graund], *av.* **1.** sottoterra **2.** *(pol.)* clandestinamente **3.** segretamente.

undergrove ['ʌndə-grouv], *s.* sottobosco.

undergrown ['ʌndə'groun], *ag.* gracile, esile, poco sviluppato.

undergrowth ['ʌndə-grouθ], *s.* sottobosco.

underhand ['ʌndəhænd], *ag.* **1.** clandestino, nascosto, segreto: — *dealings*, intrighi, mene segrete; — *methods*, vie traverse **2.** furbo, astuto **3.** *(cricket)* fatto con la mano al di sotto del gomito o della spalla (di servizio, ecc.).

underhand ['ʌndə'hænd], *av.* **1.** segretamente, clandestinamente; di soppiatto **2.** (*cricket*) con la mano al di sotto del gomito o della spalla.

underhanded [,ʌndə'hændid] *ag.* **1.** clandestino, segreto **2.** a corto di mano d'opera.

underhandedly [,ʌndə'hændidli], *av.* clandestinamente, segretamente; sottomano.

underhandedness [,ʌndə'hændidnis], *s.* l'agire segretamente, clandestinamente.

underhung ['ʌndə'hʌŋ], *ag.* sporgente (di mascella inferiore).

underived ['ʌndi'raivd], *ag.* originale; non derivato.

underlaid [,ʌndə'leid], *pass.p.p.* di to **underlay**.

underlain [,ʌndə'lein], *p.p.* di to **underlie**.

underlay[1] ['ʌndəlei], *s.* **1.** (*tip.*) tacco, alzo **2.** (*miner.*) inclinazione (di filone) **3.** feltro (posto sotto un tappeto, ecc.).

to **underlay**[1] [,ʌndə'lei], *pass.p.p.* **underlaid** [,ʌndə'leid], *v.t.* **1.** metter sotto **2.** (*tip.*) taccheggiare **3.** (*miner.*) essere in posizione inclinata (di filone).

underlay[2], *pass.* di to **underlie**.

underlease ['ʌndəli:s], *s.* subaffitto.

underlessee [,ʌndəle'si:], *s.* subaffittuario.

underlessor ['ʌndəle'sɔ:*], *s.* sublocatore.

to **underlet** [,ʌndə'let], *pass.p.p.* **underlet**, *v.t.* **1.** subaffittare **2.** affittare a prezzo troppo basso.

underletter ['ʌndə'letə*], *s.c.* chi subaffitta.

underletting ['ʌndə'letiŋ], *s.* subaffitto.

to **underlie** [,ʌndə'lai], *pass.* **underlay** [,ʌndə'lei], *p.p.* **underlain** [,ʌndə'lein], *v.t.* **1.** giacere sotto, essere al di sotto di **2.** essere alla base di: *the principles which — our policy*, i principi che sono alla base della nostra politica **3.** sottostare a, subire.

to **underline** [,ʌndə'lain], *v.t.* sottolineare.

underlinen ['ʌndə,linin], *s.coll.* biancheria personale.

underling ['ʌndəliŋ], *ag.* **1.** subordinato **2.** piccolo, debole **3.** poco importante ‖ *s.c.* subalterno, subalterna; dipendente; (*spreg.*) tirapiedi.

underlining[1] [,ʌndə'lainiŋ], *s.* sottolineatura.

underlining[2], *s.* sottofodera, imbottitura.

underlying [,ʌndə'laiiŋ], *ag.* che sta sotto, che giace sotto: *the — strata*, gli strati sottostanti.

to **underman** ['ʌndə'mæn], *pass.p.p.* **undermanned** ['ʌndə'mænd], *v.t.* **1.** fornire mano d'opera insufficiente a **2.** equipaggiare scarsamente.

undermanned ['ʌndə'mænd], *ag.* **1.** a corto di mano d'opera **2.** con equipaggio insufficiente.

undermasted ['ʌndə'mɑ:stid], *ag.* con alberatura insufficiente (di nave).

undermentioned ['ʌndə'menʃənd], *ag.* sottoindicato; menzionato in calce.

to **undermine** [,ʌndə'main], *v.t.* **1.** minare; scalzare: *the sea undermines the cliffs*, il mare scalza la scogliera **2.** *fig.* indebolire, insidiare: *drink is undermining his health*, il bere sta indebolendo la sua salute.

undermost ['ʌndəmoust], *ag.* il più basso; estremo; infimo.

underneath [,ʌndə'ni:θ], *ag.* più basso, inferiore ‖ *s.* la parte più bassa.

underneath, *av.* di sotto, al di sotto, in basso ‖ *prep.* sotto, al di sotto di.

undernote ['ʌndə'nout], *s.* (*mus.*) nota bassa.

underpaid ['ʌndə'peid], *pass.p.p.* di to **underpay** ‖ *ag.* mal pagato, insufficientemente retribuito.

underpart ['ʌndəpɑ:t], *s.* **1.** parte inferiore **2.** (*teat.*) ruolo secondario.

underpass ['ʌndəpɑ:s], *s.* sottopassaggio.

to **underpay** [,ʌndə'pei], *pass.p.p.* **underpaid** [,ʌndə'peid] *v.t.* pagare inadeguatamente.

underpeopled ['ʌndə'pi:pld], *ag.* poco popolato.

to **underpin** [,ʌndə'pin], *pass.p.p.* **underpinned** [,ʌndə'pind], *v.t.* sottomurare; puntellare.

to **underplay** ['ʌndə'plei], *v.t.* **1.** (*teat.*) recitare in maniera inferiore alle proprie capacità **2.** (*carte*) giocare una carta bassa avendone una più alta in mano.

underplot ['ʌndə-plɔt], *s.* **1.** intreccio secondario (di commedia, romanzo, ecc.) **2.** complotto, manovra.

underpopulated ['ʌndə'pɔpjuleitid], *ag.* sottopopolato.

to **underprop** [,ʌndə'prɔp], *pass.p.p.* **underpropped** [,ʌndə'prɔpt], *v.t.* puntellare; sostenere.

underran ['ʌndə'ræn], *pass.* di to **underrun**.

to **underrate** [,ʌndə'reit], *v.t.* sottovalutare, stimare troppo poco.

to **underrun** ['ʌndə'rʌn], *pass.* **underran** ['ʌndə'ræn], *p.p.* **underrun**, *v.t.i.* **1.** scorrere, passare sotto **2.** (*mar.*) ispezionare, esaminare (un cavo, ecc.) nella parte inferiore.

underrunner ['ʌndə'rʌnə*], *s.* (*tip.*) postilla marginale che continua in calce alla pagina.

to **underscore** [,ʌndə'skɔ:*], *v.t.* sottolineare.

underscoring [,ʌndə'skɔ:riŋ], *s.* sottolineatura.

underscriber ['ʌndə'skraibə*], *s.* sottoscrittore.

undersea [,ʌndə'si:], *ag.* sottomarino.

undersea(s) [,ʌndə'si:(z)], *av.* in fondo al mare.

underself ['ʌndə'self], *s.* subcosciente.

to **undersell** [,ʌndə'sel], *pass.p.p.* **undersold** ['ʌndə'sould], *v.t.* vendere a minor prezzo di; svendere.

underseller ['ʌndə'selə*], *s.c.* chi vende sottocosto.

underset ['ʌndə-set], *s.* **1.** vena profonda (di minerale) **2.** corrente marina profonda (contraria alla corrente di superficie).

to **underset** ['ʌndə'set], *pass.p.p.* **underset**, *v.t.i.* **1.** puntellare; *fig.* sostenere **2.** subaffittare **3.** porre sotto.

undershapen [,ʌndə'ʃeipn], *ag.* di forma imperfetta.

undersheriff ['ʌndə'ʃerif], *s.* vice-sceriffo.

undershirt ['ʌndəʃə:t], *s.* (*amer.*) maglia, camiciola.

undershot ['ʌndəʃɔt], *ag.* (*idraulica*) mosso dall'acqua che passa di sotto ☆ — *water wheel*, ruota per di sotto; ruota a pala.

undershrub ['ʌndəʃrʌb], *s.* sottobosco.

underside ['ʌndəsaid], *s.* parte inferiore.

to **undersign** [,ʌndə'sain], *v.t.* firmare in calce, sottoscrivere.

undersignature ['ʌndə'signitʃə*], *s.* firma in calce.

undersigned ['ʌndəsaind], *ag.* sottoscritto, firmato in calce.

undersized ['ʌndə'saizd], *ag.* **1.** di misura inferiore al normale **2.** (*mec.*) minorato.

underskirt ['ʌndə-skə:t], *s.* sottogonna.

undersleeve ['ʌndə-sli:v], *s.* sottomanica.

undersoil ['ʌndə'sɔil], *s.* sottosuolo.

undersold ['ʌndə'sould], *pass.p.p.* di to **undersell**.

understaffed ['ʌndə'stɑ:ft], *ag.* che ha personale in sufficiente.

to **understand** [,ʌndə'stænd], *pass.p.p.* **understoo**d [,ʌndə'stud], *v.t.i.* **1.** capire, comprendere, intendere; rendersi conto di: *I don't — mathematics at all*, non ca pisco niente di matematica; *I quite — his wanting t leave at once*, mi rendo perfettamente conto del su desiderio di partire subito; *she doesn't — her son well* non capisce a fondo suo figlio; *William and Mar; — each other*, vi è reciproca comprensione tra Willian e Mary; *in order to — what follows*, per poter capir ciò che segue ‖ *to make oneself understood*, farsi capire *to make s.o. — sthg.*, far capire ql.co. a qlcu. **2.** dedurre supporre; venire a conoscenza, sentir dire: *am I to — you have given up smoking?*, devo dunque supporre ch hai smesso di fumare?; *I — he will get here at seven* ho sentito dire, mi risulta che arriverà qui alle sette *to give s.o. to —*, far credere a qlcu., dar motivo qlcu. di credere: *I was given to — he would help us* mi era stato fatto capire che ci avrebbe aiutato **3.** sot tintendere: *it is understood you too are invited to th party*, è sottinteso che anche tu sei invitato alla festa *the verb may be understood in this case*, in questo cas il verbo può essere sottinteso.

understandable [,ʌndə'stændəbl], *ag.* comprensibil

understanding [,ʌndə'stændiŋ], *ag.* comprensivo sensibile; intelligente ‖ *s.* **1.** comprensione; conoscenz intelligenza; intelletto; ragione: *difficulties beyond our* —, difficoltà al di là della nostra comprensione; *lacking in* —, poco comprensivo; *a man of fine* —, un uomo di grande acutezza; *he has a good* — *of economics*, conosce bene il campo dell'economia **2.** accordo, patto, intesa; armonia: *he had a secret* — *with another firm*, aveva un accordo segreto con un'altra ditta; *we must come to an* —, dobbiamo venire ad un accordo ‖ *on this* —, a queste condizioni; *on the* — *that*, alla condizione che **3.** *pl.* (*sl.*) piedi; gambe; scarpe; stivali: *she has a sound pair of understandings*, ha un magnifico paio di gambe.

to **understate** [ˌʌndə'steit], *v.t.* attenuare; minimizzare.

understatement [ˌʌndə'steitmənt], *s.* **1.** attenuazione del vero **2.** affermazione inadeguata.

to **understock** [ˌʌndə'stɔk], *v.t.* fornire in modo insufficiente.

understood [ˌʌndə'stud], *pass.p.p.* di to **understand** ‖ *ag.* **1.** compreso; conosciuto **2.** convenuto, stabilito: *it was an* — *thing that...*, era ben inteso che...; *that is* —, ciò va da sè, è chiaro **3.** (*gram.*) sottinteso.

understrapper [ˈʌndəˌstræpə*], *s.* (*fam.*) subalterno; impiegato in sottordine; subordinato.

understratum [ˌʌndə'strɑ:təm], *pl.* **understrata** [ˌʌndə'strɑ:tə], *s.* sostrato.

to **understroke** [ˌʌndə'strouk]. *v.t.* (*amer.*) sottolineare.

understudy [ˈʌndəˌstʌdi], *s.* sostituto (di un attore).

to **understudy**, *v.t.* **1.** studiare (una parte) per sostituire un attore in caso di necessità **2.** sostituire (un attore, un'attrice).

undertakable [ˌʌndə'teikəbl], *ag.* che può essere intrapreso.

to **undertake** [ˌʌndə'teik], *pass.* **undertook** [ˌʌndə'tuk], *p.p.* **undertaken** [ˌʌndə'teikən], *v.t.i.* **1.** intraprendere, iniziare: *to* — *a journey*, intraprendere un viaggio; *to* — *a task*, intraprendere un lavoro **2.** incaricarsi di; impegnarsi a; assumersi (una responsabilità): *I can't* — *to do that*, non posso impegnarmi a far ciò **3.** prendere in appalto **4.** promettere; assicurare: *I can't* — *that you will make a profit*, non posso assicurare che farai un guadagno **5.** (*fam.*) fare l'imprenditore di pompe funebri **6.** garantire, rispondere: *she undertook for her brother's good behaviour*, si rese garante del buon comportamento di suo fratello **7.** (*arc.*) impegnare (un combattimento, ecc.).

undertaker [ˌʌndə'teikə*], *nel senso* **3.** [ˈʌndəˌteikə*], *.* **1.** chi intraprende un affare, ecc. **2.** impresario, appaltatore **3.** imprenditore di pompe funebri.

undertaking [ˌʌndə'teikiŋ], *nel senso* **3.** [ˈʌndəˌteikiŋ], *ag.* intraprendente ‖ *s.* **1.** l'intraprendere **2.** (*comm.*) impresa, intrapresa **3.** impresa di pompe funebri **4.** impegno; promessa: *a written* —, un impegno scritto.

to **undertax** [ˌʌndə'tæks], *v.t.* tassare troppo poco.

undertenancy [ˈʌndə'tenənsi], *s.* subaffitto.

undertenant [ˈʌndə'tenənt], *s.* subaffittuario.

undertimed [ˌʌndə'taimd], *ag.* (*foto.*) sottoesposto.

undertint [ˈʌndətint], *s.* colore smorzato, spento.

undertone [ˈʌndətoun], *s.* **1.** tono sommesso, bisbiglio: *to speak in an* —, parlare a voce bassa **2.** colore smorzato, spento.

undertook [ˌʌndə'tuk], *pass.* di to **undertake**.

undertreasurer [ˈʌndə'treʒərə*], *s.* vicetesoriere.

undervaluation [ˈʌndəˌvælju'eiʃən], *s.* **1.** valutazione inferiore al dovuto; scarsa stima **2.** svalutazione.

to **undervalue** [ˈʌndə'vælju:], *v.t.* **1.** sottovalutare **2.** deprezzare; svalutare: *the currency has been undervalued by the fraudulent issue*, la moneta corrente è stata svalutata dall'emissione fraudolenta.

undervaluer [ˈʌndə'væljuə*], *s.* deprezzatore; svalutatore.

underwear [ˈʌndəwɛə*], *s.* biancheria intima.

underweight [ˈʌndə'weit], *s.* peso insufficiente.

underwent [ˌʌndə'went], *pass.* di to **undergo**.

underwing [ˈʌndəwiŋ], *s.* **1.** ala inferiore **2.** (*entom.*) catocala.

underwood [ˈʌndəwud], *s.* **1.** sottobosco **2.** bosco ceduo.

underwork [ˈʌndəwə:k], *s.* **1.** struttura di sostegno **2.** lavoro di secondaria importanza **3.** lavoro clandestino.

to **underwork** [ˌʌndə'wə:k], *v.t.i.* **1.** minare (anche *fig.*) **2.** lavorare, far lavorare in modo inadeguato **3.** lavorare per un compenso inadeguato; lavorare a prezzi di concorrenza nei confronti di.

underworld [ˈʌndəwə:ld], *s.* **1.** terra **2.** oltretomba; Ade **3.** antipodi **4.** malavita.

to **underwrite** [ˌʌndərait], *pass.* **underwrote** [ˈʌndərout], *p.p.* **underwritten** [ˈʌndəˌritn], *v.t.i.* **1.** sottoscrivere; firmare **2.** (*comm.*) assicurare; far l'assicuratore.

underwriter [ˈʌndəˌraitə*], *s.* **1.** sottoscrittore; firmatario **2.** (*comm.*) assicuratore.

underwriting [ˈʌndəˌraitiŋ], *s.* **1.** sottoscrizione; firma **2.** (*comm.*) assicurazione.

underwritten [ˈʌndəˌritn], *p.p.* di to **underwrite**.

underwrote [ˈʌndərout], *pass.* di to **underwrite**.

undescribable [ˌʌndis'kraibəbl], *ag.* indescrivibile.

undescribed [ˌʌndis'kraibd], *ag.* non descritto.

undescried [ˌʌndis'kraid], *ag.* non visto; non scoperto.

undeserved [ˌʌndi'zə:vd], *ag.* immeritato.

undeservedly [ˌʌndi'zə:vidli], *av.* immeritatamente.

undeservedness [ˌʌndi'zə:vidnis], *s.* mancanza di merito.

undeserving [ˌʌndi'zə:viŋ], *ag.* immeritevole ‖ *s.* mancanza di merito.

underservingly [ˌʌndi'zə:viŋli], *av.* immeritevolmente.

undesigned [ˌʌndi'zaind], *ag.* non meditato; involontario; accidentale.

undesignedly [ˌʌndi'zainidli], *av.* senza intenzione; involontariamente; accidentalmente.

undesigning [ˌʌndi'zainiŋ], *ag.* innocente, schietto, sincero; leale.

undesirable [ˌʌndi'zaiərəbl], *ag.* indesiderabile.

undesirableness [ˌʌndi'zaiərəblnis], *s.* l'essere indesiderabile.

undesirably [ˌʌndi'zaiərəbli], *av.* in modo indesiderabile.

undesired [ˌʌndi'zaiəd], *ag.* indesiderato.

undesiring [ˌʌndi'zaiəriŋ], *ag.* indifferente.

undesirous [ˌʌndi'zaiərəs], *ag.* non desideroso.

undespairing [ˌʌndis'pɛəriŋ], *ag.* che non dispera.

undespoiled [ˌʌndis'pɔild], *ag.* non rovinato.

undestroyable [ˌʌndis'trɔiəbl], *ag.* indistruttibile.

undestroyed [ˌʌndis'trɔid], *ag.* non distrutto; intatto.

undetected [ˌʌndi'tektid], *ag.* non scoperto.

undeterminable [ˌʌndi'tə:minəbl], *ag.* indeterminabile.

undetermined [ˌʌndi'tə:mind], *ag.* **1.** indeterminato; indefinito: *the question was left* —, la questione fu lasciata insoluta **2.** indeciso; irresoluto: *he was* — *whether he would go or not*, era indeciso se andare o no.

undeterred [ˌʌndi'tə:d], *ag.* non scoraggiato; non distolto.

undeveloped [ˌʌndi'veləpt], *ag.* **1.** non sviluppato **2.** non sfruttato (di terreno).

undeviating [ʌn'di:vieitiŋ], *ag.* **1.** diritto, diretto, che non devia **2.** costante; che non si smentisce.

undeviatingly [ʌn'di:vieitiŋli], *ag.* **1.** direttamente, senza deviazioni **2.** costantemente; senza smentirsi.

undevout [ˌʌndi'vaut], *ag.* non devoto.

undevoutly [ˌʌndi'vautli], *av.* senza devozione.

undid [ʌn'did], *pass.* di to **undo**.

undies [ˈʌndiz], *s.pl.* (*fam. abbr.* di *underclothes*) biancheria intima (per donna).

undifferentiated [ˈʌnˌdifə'renʃieitid], *ag.* non differenziato.

undigested [ˌʌndi'dʒestid], *ag.* **1.** non digerito **2.** confuso, caotico.

undigestible [ˌʌndi'dʒestəbl], *ag.* non digeribile, poco digeribile.

undignified [ʌn'dignifaid], *ag.* poco dignitoso; senza dignità.

undiluted [ˌʌndai'lju:tid], *ag.* non diluito; non indebolito.

undiminished [ˌʌndi'miniʃt], *ag.* non diminuito.

undimmed ['ʌn'dimd], *ag.* non offuscato; chiaro; brillante.

undine ['ʌndi:n], *s.* (*mit.*) ondina.

undiplomatic ['ʌnˌdiplə'mætik], *ag.* non, poco diplomatico; poco abile.

undipped ['ʌn'dipt], *ag.* 1. non immerso 2. non battezzato.

undirected ['ʌndi'rektid], *ag.* 1. non diretto, non guidato; senza consiglio 2. senza indirizzo (di lettera).

undiscerned ['ʌndi'sə:nd], *av.* inosservato, non scorto; non percepito.

undiscernible ['ʌndi'sə:nəbl], *ag.* indiscernibile; impercettibile.

undiscernibleness ['ʌndi'sə:nəblnis], *s.* indiscernibilità; impercettibilità.

undiscernibly ['ʌndi'sə:nəbli], *av.* in modo indiscernibile; impercettibilmente.

undiscerning ['ʌndi'sə:niŋ], *ag.* senza discernimento; poco giudizioso.

undiscerningly ['ʌndi'sə:niŋli], *av.* senza discernimento; in modo poco giudizioso.

undischarged ['ʌndis'tʃɑ:dʒd], *ag.* 1. non scaricato 2. incompiuto 3. (*comm.*) non saldato, non liquidato: — *debt*, debito non saldato 4. non scarcerato.

undisciplinable ['ʌn'disiplinəbl], *ag.* indisciplinabile.

undisciplined [ʌn'disiplind], *ag.* indisciplinato.

undisclosed ['ʌndis'klouzd], *ag.* segreto, nascosto.

undiscouraged ['ʌndis'kʌridʒd], *ag.* non scoraggiato, non abbattuto.

undiscoverable ['ʌndis'kʌvərəbl], *ag.* introvabile.

undiscovered ['ʌndis'kʌvəd], *ag.* non scoperto; sconosciuto; *the murderer remains* —, l'assassino resta introvabile.

undiscriminating ['ʌndis'krimineitiŋ], *ag.* che non distingue, che non fa distinzioni: — *praise*, elogi indiscriminati.

undiscussed ['ʌndis'kʌst], *ag.* indiscusso.

undisgraced ['ʌndis'greist], *ag.* non disonorato.

undisguisable ['ʌndis'gaizəbl], *ag.* non mascherabile; evidente.

undisguised ['ʌndis'gaizd], *ag.* 1. non mascherato; evidente, manifesto: *with* — *pleasure*, con evidente piacere 2. *fig.* aperto, franco, schietto.

undisguisedly ['ʌndis'gaizidli], *av.* 1. manifestamente 2. *fig.* apertamente, francamente, sinceramente.

undishonoured ['ʌndis'ɔnəd], *ag.* non disonorato.

undisjoined ['ʌndis'dʒɔind], *ag.* non disgiunto, non separato.

undismayed ['ʌndis'meid], *ag.* senza paura, imperterrito, non spaventato: — *by difficulties*, non spaventato dalle difficoltà.

undispersed ['ʌndis'pə:st], *ag.* non disperso.

undisposed ['ʌndis'pouzd], *ag.* 1. non disposto: — *to do sthg.*, non disposto a fare ql.co. 2. non destinato, non assegnato; non venduto: *stock* — *of*, merci non vendute.

undisputed ['ʌndis'pju:tid], *ag.* incontestato, incontrastato, indiscusso.

undisputedly ['ʌndis'pju:tidli], *av.* incontestatamente, incontrastatamente.

undissembled ['ʌndi'sembld], *ag.* non dissimulato; aperto, palese.

undissembling ['ʌndi'sembliŋ], *ag.* che non dissimula; franco, aperto.

undissolvable ['ʌndi'zɔlvəbl], *ag.* indissolubile.

undissolved ['ʌndi'zɔlvd], *ag.* 1. non sciolto (di matrimonio, ecc.) 2. non disciolto, non fuso.

undistilled ['ʌndis'tild], *ag.* non distillato.

undistinctive ['ʌndis'tiŋktiv], *ag.* che non fa distinzioni.

undistinguishable ['ʌndis'tiŋgwiʃəbl], *ag.* non distinguibile.

undistinguishably ['ʌndis'tiŋgwiʃəbli], *av.* indistintamente, in modo non distinguibile.

undistinguished ['ʌndis'tiŋgwiʃt], *ag.* 1. indistinto, confuso 2. mediocre, comune: *an* — *set of people*, un ambiente mediocre.

undistinguishing ['ʌndis'tiŋgwiʃiŋ], *ag.* che non distingue, che non fa distinzioni.

undistracted ['ʌndis'træktid], *ag.* che non si distrae.

undistracting ['ʌndis'træktiŋ], *ag.* che non distrae.

undistributed ['ʌndis'tribjutid], *ag.* non distribuito.

undisturbed ['ʌndis'tə:bd], *ag.* 1. indisturbato 2. calmo, tranquillo, imperturbato.

undisturbedly ['ʌndis'tə:bidli], *av.* 1. senza disturbo 2. tranquillamente, pacificamente.

undiversified ['ʌndai'və:sifaid], *ag.* non variato, monotono.

undiverted ['ʌndai'və:tid], *ag.* 1. non deviato; non stornato; non distratto 2. non divertito.

undividable ['ʌndi'vaidəbl], *ag.* indivisibile.

undivided ['ʌndi'vaidid], *ag.* indiviso, intero.

undividedly ['ʌndi'vaididli], *av.* indivisibilmente.

undividedness ['ʌndi'vaididnis], *s.* indivisibilità.

undivine ['ʌndi'vain], *ag.* non divino.

undivorced ['ʌndi'vɔ:st], *ag.* non divorziato.

undivulged ['ʌndai'vʌldʒd], *ag.* non divulgato.

to undo ['ʌn'du:], *pass.* **undid** ['ʌn'did], *p.p.* **undone** ['ʌn'dʌn], *v.t.* 1. disfare, sciogliere, slacciare, slegare: — *the top button of your coat*, slaccia il primo bottone della tua giacca; *I cannot* — *this knot*, non riesco a disfare questo nodo ‖ *what is done cannot be undone*, *prov.* cosa fatta capo ha 2. annullare, rovinare, distruggere, mandare in rovina: *drink has undone him*, il bere l'ha rovinato; *he undid his father's good work*, rovinò tutto il lavoro di suo padre.

to undock ['ʌn'dɔk], *v.t.i.* (*mar.*) uscire, far uscire dal bacino.

undoer ['ʌn'du(:)ə*], *s.* 1. distruttore, rovinatore 2. (*arc.*) seduttore.

undogmatic ['ʌndɔg'mætik], *ag.* non dogmatico.

undoing ['ʌn'du(:)iŋ], *s.* 1. scioglimento, slegamento, disfacimento 2. rovina, distruzione; perdita; sfacelo.

undomestic ['ʌn-də'mestik], *ag.* 1. non domestico 2. poco amante della casa.

undomesticated ['ʌn-də'mestikeitid], *ag.* 1. non addomesticato 2. poco amante della casa.

undone[1] ['ʌn'dʌn], *p.p.* di **undo** ‖ *ag.* 1. disfatto, slegato, slacciato 2. rovinato: *I am* —!, (*letter.*) sono rovinato!.

undone[2], *ag.* incompiuto, non fatto: *to leave nothing* —, non lasciar nulla di intentato.

to undouble ['ʌn'dʌbl], *v.t.i.* sdoppiare, sdoppiarsi; svolgere.

undoubtable ['ʌn'dautəbl], *ag.* indubitabile.

undoubted [ʌn'dautid], *ag.* indubitato, indubbio; certo, incontestato.

undoubtedly [ʌn'dautidli], *av.* indubbiamente, certamente; incontestabilmente.

undoubting ['ʌn'dautiŋ], *ag.* che non dubita, sicuro, convinto.

undoubtingly ['ʌn'dautiŋli], *av.* senza dubbio, senza incertezza, sicuramente.

undrainable ['ʌn'dreinəbl], *ag.* non prosciugabile.

undramatic ['ʌndrə'mætik], *ag.* non drammatico; che manca di qualità drammatiche.

to undrape ['ʌn'dreip], *v.t.* scoprire, liberare dai drappi.

undraped ['ʌn'dreipt], *ag.* 1. non drappeggiato 2. scoperto, nudo.

undrawn ['ʌn'drɔ:n], *ag.* 1. non disegnato 2. non munto 3. non tirato, non teso.

undreaded ['ʌn'dredid], *ag.* non temuto.

undreamed(-of), undreamt(-of) [ʌn'dremt(ɔv)], *ag.* non sognato, impensato, inaudito: *an — success*, un successo impensato; *wonders still —*, meraviglie non ancora sognate.

undress ['ʌn'dres], *s.* 1. (*mil.*) uniforme, divisa ordinaria 2. veste da camera.

to undress, *v.t.i.* svestire, svestirsi; spogliare, spogliarsi (anche *fig.*).

undressed ['ʌn'drest], *ag.* 1. svestito, poco vestito; in veste da camera 2. spettinato, non acconciato 3. greggio, non levigato (di pietra, legno, ecc.) 4. non condito: — *salad*, insalata scondita 5. mal disposto (di vetrina, ecc.).

undried ['ʌn'draid], *ag.* non seccato.

undrilled ['ʌn'drild], *ag.* 1. non esercitato (di truppe) 2. (*mec.*) non perforato, non forato.

undrinkable ['ʌn'driŋkəbl], *ag.* imbevibile; non potabile.

undriven ['ʌn'drivn], *ag.* non spinto; non cacciato.

undrooping ['ʌn'dru:piŋ], *ag.* che non langue; che non avvizzisce; vigoroso.

undue ['ʌn'dju:], *ag.* 1. non dovuto, indebito 2. inadatto, non appropriato 3. illegale; ingiusto; immeritato: *use of — authority*, (*dir.*) abuso di autorità 4. sproporzionato, eccessivo: *with — tenderness*, con tenerezza eccessiva 5. (*comm.*) non scaduto.

undulant ['ʌndjulənt], *ag.* ondeggiante ☆ — *fever*, (*patol.*) febbre maltese.

undulate ['ʌndjulit], *ag.* 1. ondulato 2. ondeggiante, fluttuante.

to undulate ['ʌndjuleit], *v.i.* 1. ondeggiare, fluttuare 2. essere ondulato, avere una superficie ondulata.

undulately ['ʌndjulitli], *av.* a onda, in modo ondeggiante.

undulating ['ʌndjuleitiŋ], *ag.* 1. ondulato 2. ondeggiante.

undulatingly ['ʌndjuleitiŋli], *av.* in modo ondeggiante.

undulation [,ʌndju'leiʃən], *s.* 1. ondulazione 2. (*fis.*) movimento ondulatorio.

undulatory ['ʌndjulətəri], *ag.* 1. ondulatorio 2. ondulato.

unduly ['ʌn'dju:li], *av.* 1. indebitamente; ingiustamente 2. eccessivamente: *he has been — harsh with his son*, è stato eccessivamente duro con suo figlio.

undurable ['ʌn'djuərəbl], *ag.* non duraturo.

unduteous ['ʌn'dju:tjəs], **undutiful** ['ʌn'dju:tiful], *ag.* 1. che manca ai propri doveri 2. irriverente.

undutifully ['ʌn'dju:tifuli], *av.* 1. senza rispetto (ai propri doveri) 2. irriverentemente.

undutifulness ['ʌn'dju:tifulnis], *s.* 1. mancanza ai propri doveri 2. irriverenza.

undying [ʌn'daiiŋ], *ag.* imperituro, immortale.

undyingly [ʌn'daiiŋli], *av.* imperituramente.

unearned ['ʌn'ə:nd], *ag.* 1. non guadagnato col lavoro 2. immeritato.

to unearth ['ʌn'ə:θ], *v.t.* 1. dissotterrare, scoprire, portare alla luce 2. *fig.* rivelare 3. far uscire dalla tana (un animale).

unearthly [ʌn'ə:θli], *ag.* 1. ultraterreno; celeste; soprannaturale 2. lugubre, sinistro; mortale: — *pallor*, pallore mortale 3. (*fam.*) impossibile, assurdo, irragionevole: — *hour*, ora impossibile.

uneasily [ʌn'i:zili], *av.* 1. con difficoltà; a disagio 2. con inquietudine; ansiosamente: *to sleep —*, dormire un sonno agitato.

uneasiness [ʌn'i:zinis], *s.* 1. pena; fastidio; disagio 2. inquietudine; ansia.

uneasy [ʌn'i:zi], *ag.* 1. a disagio; inquieto, ansioso, agitato, penoso, travagliato: *they had an — suspicion*, avevano un sospetto inquietante; *to be —*, essere agitato, ansioso; *to feel — about the future*, essere inquieti per il futuro 2. (*rar.*) disagevole; scomodo.

uneatable ['ʌn'i:təbl], *ag.* immangiabile.

uneaten ['ʌn'i:tn], *ag.* non mangiato.

unecclesiastical ['ʌni,kli:zi'æstikəl], *ag.* non ecclesiastico; non clericale.

uneconomic(al) ['ʌn,i:kə'nɔmikl], *ag.* 1. non economico 2. non, poco economo.

to unedge ['ʌn'edʒ], *v.t.* spuntare; smussare.

unedible ['ʌn'edibl], *ag.* immangiabile.

unedifying ['ʌn'edifaiiŋ], *ag.* non, poco edificante.

unedited ['ʌn'editid], *ag.* inedito.

uneducated ['ʌn'edjukeitid], *ag.* 1. rozzo; non istruito, ignorante 2. dialettale (di accento).

uneffected ['ʌni'fektid], *ag.* non effettuato; non realizzato.

uneffectual ['ʌni'fektjuəl], *ag.* inefficace.

unelaborate ['ʌni'læbərit], *ag.* non elaborato, semplice.

unelastic ['ʌni'læstik], *ag.* non elastico; (*scienza delle costruzioni*) anelastico.

unelected ['ʌni'lektid], *ag.* non eletto (di candidato).

unelegant ['ʌn'eligənt], *ag.* inelegante.

unemancipated ['ʌni'mænsipeitid], *ag.* non emancipato (di minorenne, schiavo).

unembarrassed ['ʌnim'bærəst], *ag.* non imbarazzato, a proprio agio, disinvolto.

unembittered ['ʌnim'bitəd], *ag.* non amareggiato, non inasprito.

unembodied ['ʌnim'bɔdid], *ag.* incorporeo.

unemotional ['ʌni'mouʃən], *ag.* 1. indifferente, freddo, non emozionabile 2. non emozionante.

unemotionally ['ʌni'mouʃnəli], *av.* impassibilmente; con sangue freddo.

unemphatic ['ʌnim'fætik], *ag.* non enfatico.

unemphatically ['ʌnim'fætikəli], *av.* senza enfasi.

unemployable ['ʌnim'plɔiəbl], *ag.* non adatto ad assumere un impiego 2. che non può essere usato, sfruttato.

unemployed ['ʌnim'plɔid], *ag.* 1. disoccupato, non occupato ‖ *the —*, i disoccupati 2. non usato, non sfruttato: — *capital*, capitale giacente, infruttifero.

unemployment ['ʌnim'plɔimənt], *s.* disoccupazione ☆ — *benefit*, sussidio di disoccupazione; — *insurance*, assicurazione contro la disoccupazione.

unempowered ['ʌnim'pauəd], *ag.* non autorizzato.

unenclosed ['ʌnin'klouzd], *ag.* non cintato.

unencumbered ['ʌnin'kʌmbəd], *ag.* non ingombro; libero: — *estate*, proprietà non gravata da ipoteche.

unended ['ʌn'endid], *ag.* (*rar.*) incompiuto.

unending [ʌn'endiŋ], *ag.* interminabile, eterno, senza fine.

unendowed ['ʌnin'daud], *ag.* non, poco dotato.

unendurable ['ʌnin'djuərəbl], *ag.* insopportabile, intollerabile.

unendurably ['ʌnin'djuərəbli], *av.* insopportabilmente, intollerabilmente.

unenduring ['ʌnin'djuəriŋ], *ag.* 1. che non tollera 2. che non dura, che non resiste.

unenfranchised ['ʌnin'fræntʃaizd], *ag.* 1. non affrancato (di schiavo) 2. che non ha diritto di voto.

unengaged ['ʌnin'geidʒd], *ag.* 1. non impegnato, libero, non occupato 2. non fidanzato.

unengaging ['ʌnin'geidʒiŋ], *ag.* 1. non avvincente, non attraente 2. poco simpatico.

un-English ['ʌn'iŋgliʃ], *ag.* non tipicamente inglese (di carattere, abitudini, ecc.): *he is — in his ways*, non si comporta da inglese.

unenjoyed ['ʌnin'dʒɔid], *ag.* non goduto.

unenlightened ['ʌnin'laitnd], *ag.* non illuminato (di secolo); ignorante: *the — herd*, la massa ignorante.

to unentangle ['ʌnin'tæŋgl], *v.t.* districare.

unentangled ['ʌnin'tæŋgld], *ag.* 1. non inceppato; districato 2 *fig.* libero, senza legami (di persona, paese, ecc.): — *with alliances*, libero da qualsiasi alleanza.

unentered ['ʌn'entəd], *ag.* 1. impenetrabile; impenetrato 2. (*comm.*) non registrato.

unenterprising ['ʌn'entəpraiziŋ], *ag.* poco intraprendente; senza iniziativa.

unentertaining [ˌʌnˌentəˈteiniŋ], *ag.* poco divertente, noioso.

unentertainingness [ˌʌnˌenteˈteininnis], *s.* uggiosità.

unenthralled [ˈʌninˈθrɔːld], *ag.* **1.** non ammaliato **2.** (*arc.*) non ridotto in schiavitù.

unentombed [ˈʌninˈtuːmd], *ag.* insepolto.

unenviable [ˈʌnˈenviəbl], *ag.* non invidiabile.

unenvied [ˈʌnˈenvid], *ag.* non invidiato.

unenvious [ˈʌnˈenviəs], *ag.* non invidioso.

unequable [ˈʌnˈekwəbl], *ag.* ineguale; variabile, instabile.

unequal [ˈʌnˈiːkwəl], *ag.* **1.** ineguale, disuguale, irregolare: — *pulse*, polso irregolare; *a fine but — poem*, una poesia bella ma ineguale **2.** inadeguato; incapace: — *to the task*, non all'altezza del compito; *to be — to doing sthg.*, non essere all'altezza di fare ql.co. **3.** ingiusto; impari; non equamente distribuito: *so — a fight*, una lotta così impari.

unequalled [ˈʌnˈiːkwəld], *ag.* ineguagliato, senza pari, incomparabile.

unequally [ˈʌnˈiːkwəli], *av.* **1.** inegualmente, irregolarmente **2.** inadeguatamente.

unequalness [ˈʌnˈiːkwəlnis], *s.* ineguaglianza.

unequivocal [ˈʌniˈkwivəkəl], *ag.* non equivoco, inequivocabile; chiaro, schietto: *to give an — answer*, dare una risposta chiara.

unequivocally [ˈʌniˈkwivəkəli], *av.* inequivocabilmente; chiaramente.

unequivocalness [ˈʌniˈkwivəkəlnis], *s.* evidenza, chiarezza.

uneradicable [ˈʌniˈrædikəbl], *ag.* inestirpabile.

uneradicated [ˈʌniˈrædikeitid], *ag.* inestirpato.

unerased [ˈʌniˈreizd], *ag.* non cancellato.

unerring [ˈʌnˈəːriŋ], *ag.* infallibile; sicuro; esatto: — *aim*, mira esatta; — *judgement*, giudizio infallibile.

unerringly [ˈʌnˈəːriŋli], *av.* infallibilmente; sicuramente; con precisione.

unerringness [ˈʌnˈəːriŋnis], *s.* infallibilità; sicurezza; precisione.

unescapable [ˈʌnisˈkeipəbl], *ag.* inevitabile; ineluttabile.

unessayed [ˈʌneˈseid], *ag.* non provato, non sperimentato.

unessential [ˈʌniˈsenʃəl], *ag.* non essenziale, poco importante; accessorio.

unevangelical [ˈʌnˌiːvænˈdʒelikəl], *ag.* non evangelico.

uneven [ˈʌnˈiːvən], *ag.* **1.** ineguale, irregolare, non uniforme: *he is making — progress*, fa progressi saltuari; *she has an — character*, ha un carattere capriccioso **2.** ruvido; non livellato: *the road was all —*, la strada non era ben livellata **3.** (*mat.*) dispari: — *numbers*, numeri dispari.

unevenly [ˈʌnˈiːvənli], *av.* **1.** irregolarmente; in modo non uniforme **2.** (*mat.*) in modo dispari.

unevenness [ˈʌnˈiːvənnis], *s.* **1.** disuguaglianza, irregolarità, scarsa uniformità **2.** dislivello; anfrattuosità; scabrosità (di terreno, ecc.) **3.** (*mat.*) l'essere dispari.

uneventful [ˈʌniˈventful], *ag.* pacifico, calmo, tranquillo; senza avvenimenti importanti: *an — life*, una vita tranquilla.

uneventfully [ˈʌniˈventfuli], *av.* pacificamente, in modo tranquillo; senza avvenimenti importanti.

unevident [ˈʌnˈevidənt], *ag.* inevidente.

unevolved [ˈʌniˈvolvd], *ag.* non evoluto.

unexaminable [ˈʌnigˈzæminəbl], *ag.* non esaminabile; non verificabile.

unexamined [ˈʌnigˈzæmind], *ag.* non esaminato, non verificato, non controllato.

unexampled [ˈʌnigˈzɔːmpld], *ag.* senza esempio, senza precedenti; unico.

unexcelled [ˈʌnikˈseld], *ag.* insuperato, non sorpassato, senza pari.

unexceptionable [ˌʌnikˈsepʃnəbl], *ag.* **1.** ineccepibile; irreprensibile; perfetto, eccellente **2.** (*rar.*) che non ammette eccezioni.

unexceptionableness [ˌʌnikˈsepʃnəblnis], *s.* irreprensibilità.

unexceptionably [ˌʌnikˈsepʃnəbli], *av.* irreprensibilmente.

unexceptional [ˈʌnikˈsepʃənl], *ag.* **1.** senza eccezioni; che non ammette eccezioni **2.** ineccepibile, irreprensibile; eccellente.

unexceptionally [ˈʌnikˈsepʃnəli], *av.* senza eccezioni.

unexcited [ˈʌnikˈsaitid], *ag.* non eccitato; calmo, tranquillo: *to be — about sthg.*, restare indifferente a ql.co.

unexcluded [ˈʌniksˈkluːdid], *ag.* non escluso.

unexclusive [ˈʌniksˈkluːsiv], *ag.* che non esclude, non esclusivo.

unexecuted [ˈʌnˈeksikjuːtid], *ag.* **1.** non eseguito; non compiuto **2.** non giustiziato.

unexercised [ˈʌnˈeksəsaizd], *ag.* non esercitato.

unexerted [ˈʌnigˈzəːtid], *ag.* non esercitato; non adoperato; non messo in opera.

unexhausted [ˈʌnigˈzɔːstid], *ag.* inesausto; non completamente sfruttato.

unexpanded [ˈʌniksˈpændid], *ag.* **1.** non espanso, non disteso **2.** non sbocciato, non schiuso (di fiore).

unexpected [ˈʌniksˈpektid], *ag.* inatteso, imprevisto; inopinato: — *meeting*, incontro inatteso; *the — turns of conversation*, l'imprevisto della conversazione.

unexpectedly [ˈʌniksˈpektidli], *av.* inaspettatamente, improvvisamente.

unexpectedness [ˈʌniksˈpektidnis], *s.* l'essere inaspettato, inatteso, imprevisto.

unexpensive [ˈʌniksˈpensiv], *ag.* poco costoso, poco dispendioso; a buon prezzo.

unexperienced [ˈʌniksˈpiəriənst], *ag.* **1.** inesperto, privo di esperienza **2.** non sperimentato.

unexpired [ˈʌniksˈpaiəd], *ag.* non scaduto, non spirato.

unexplainable [ˈʌniksˈpleinəbl], *ag.* non spiegabile.

unexplained [ˈʌniksˈpleind], *ag.* non spiegato.

unexplored [ˈʌniksˈplɔːd], *ag.* inesplorato.

unexposed [ˈʌniksˈpouzd], *ag.* non esposto; celato; protetto.

unexpressed [ˈʌniksˈprest], *ag.* inespresso, sottinteso, tacito.

unexpressive [ˈʌniksˈpresiv], *ag.* inespressivo.

unexpurgated [ˈʌnˈekspəːgeitid], *ag.* non espurgato.

unextended [ˈʌniksˈtendid], *ag.* **1.** non esteso, non aperto **2.** che non ha estensione **3.** che non ha bisogno di impegnarsi al massimo (di atleta, di cavallo).

unextinguishable [ˈʌniksˈtiŋgwiʃəbl], *ag.* inestinguibile, perpetuo.

unextinguishably [ˈʌniksˈtiŋgwiʃəbli], *av.* inestinguibilmente, perpetuamente.

unextinguished [ˈʌniksˈtiŋgwiʃt], *ag.* inestinto, estinto.

unextirpated [ˈʌnˈekstəːpeitid], *ag.* non estirpato.

uneyed [ˈʌnˈaid], *ag.* non visto, non osservato.

to unface [ˈʌnˈfeis], *v.t.* smascherare; esporre.

unfadable [ˈʌnˈfeidəbl], *ag.* **1.** che non può appassire **2.** solido (di colore).

unfaded [ˈʌnˈfeidid], *ag.* **1.** non appassito, fresco **2.** non sbiadito.

unfading [ʌnˈfeidiŋ], *ag.* **1.** che non appassisce **2.** che non sbiadisce **3.** imperituro.

unfadingly [ˈʌnˈfeidiŋli], *av.* **1.** inalterabilmente **2.** imperituramente.

unfailing [ʌnˈfeiliŋ], *ag.* **1.** infallibile, sicuro: *an — friend*, un amico sicuro **2.** immancabile **3.** inesauribile.

unfailingly [ʌnˈfeiliŋli], *av.* **1.** infallibilmente **2.** immancabilmente **3.** inesauribilmente.

unfailingness [ʌnˈfeiliŋnis], *s.* **1.** infallibilità **2.** immancabilità **3.** inesauribilità.

unfair [ˈʌnˈfɛə*], *ag.* **1.** non equo, ingiusto; sleale; disonesto: — *wages*, salari non equi, inadeguati **2.** non favorevole (di vento).

unfairly [ʌn'fɛəli], *av.* non equamente; ingiustamente; slealmente.

unfairness [ʌn'fɛənis], *s.* ingiustizia; improbità; malafede; slealtà; disonestà.

unfaith [ʌn'feiθ], *s.* mancanza di fede, di fiducia.

unfaithful [ʌn'feiθful], *ag.* 1. infedele; sleale; disonesto: *a servant — to his master*, un servo sleale verso il suo padrone 2. inesatto, impreciso: *— quotations*, citazioni inesatte.

unfaithfully [ʌn'feiθfuli], *av.* infedelmente; slealmente.

unfaithfulness [ʌn'feiθfulnis], *s.* infedeltà; slealtà.

unfaltering [ʌn'fɔːltəriŋ], *ag.* fermo, non esitante; risoluto: *— voice*, voce ferma.

unfalteringly [ʌn'fɔːltəriŋli], *av.* senza esitazioni.

unfamiliar [ʌn-fə'miljə*], *ag.* 1. poco conosciuto: *— sentence*, frase poco abituale 2. che non conosce, poco pratico: *to be — with the customs of a place*, non conoscere le abitudini di un luogo.

unfamiliarity [ʌn-fə,mili'æriti], *s.* mancanza di familiarità.

unfamiliarly [ʌn-fə'miljəli], *av.* senza familiarità.

unfashionable [ʌn'fæʃnəbl], *ag.* 1. fuori moda, non alla moda 2. (*rar.*) che non può essere modellato.

unfashionableness [ʌn'fæʃnəblnis], *s.* l'essere fuori moda.

unfashionably [ʌn'fæʃnəbli], *av.* fuori moda.

unfashioned [ʌn'fæʃənd], *ag.* 1. inelegante; rozzo 2. (*rar.*) non modellato, senza forma.

to unfasten [ʌn'fɑːsn], *v.t.i.* slacciare, slacciarsi; slegare, slegarsi; sciogliere, sciogliersi; aprirsi: *she unfastened her dress*, si slacciò il vestito.

unfathered[1] [ʌn'fɑːðəd], *ag.* orfano di padre.

unfathered[2], *ag.* 1. illegittimo 2. di oscura origine.

unfatherly[ʌn'fɑːðəli], *ag.* poco paterno, non paterno.

unfathomable [ʌn'fæðəməbl], *ag.* 1. che non si può scandagliare, insondabile; impenetrabile: *her — face*, il suo viso impenetrabile 2. vasto; incommensurabile: *Thy goodness is —*, la Tua bontà è incommensurabile.

unfathomably [ʌn'fæðəməbli], *av.* 1. in modo impenetrabile 2. in modo incommensurabile.

unfathomed [ʌn'fæðəmd], *ag.* non scandagliato; non misurato (anche *fig.*).

unfaulty [ʌn'fɔːlti], *ag.* 1. senza colpa 2. senza difetto.

unfavourable [ʌn'feivərəbl], *ag.* sfavorevole, non propizio.

unfavourableness [ʌn'feivərəblnis], *s.* l'essere sfavorevole, contrario.

unfavourably [ʌn'feivərəbli], *av.* sfavorevolmente.

unfeared [ʌn'fiəd], *ag.* non temuto.

unfearing [ʌn'fiəriŋ], *ag.* che non teme; senza paura.

unfearingly [ʌn'fiəriŋli], *av.* senza paura.

unfeasible [ʌn'fiːzəbl], *ag.* ineseguibile, non fattibile, inattuabile.

to unfeather [ʌn'feðə*], *v.t.* spennare; spiumare.

unfeathered [ʌn'feðəd], *ag.* senza penne; senza piume; implume.

unfed [ʌn'fed], *ag.* non nutrito; non alimentato.

unfeed [ʌn'fiːd], *ag.* non pagato in anticipo; non pagato.

unfeeling [ʌn'fiːliŋ], *ag.* insensibile; arido; duro di cuore, spietato.

unfeelingly [ʌn'fiːliŋli], *av.* insensibilmente; duramente, spietatamente.

unfeelingness [ʌn'fiːliŋnis], *s.* insensibilità, aridità; spietatezza.

unfeigned [ʌn'feind], *ag.* sincero; genuino, vero.

unfeignedly [ʌn'feinidli], *av.* sinceramente, senza finzione.

unfeignedness [ʌn'feinidnis], *s.* sincerità, mancanza di finzione.

unfelt [ʌn'felt], *ag.* non sentito, non provato.

unfeminine [ʌn'feminin], *ag.* poco femminile.

unfenced[ʌn'fenst], *ag.* non cintato; senza palizzata; aperto; (*arc.*) indifeso.

unfermented [ʌn-fə(:)'mentid], *ag.* non fermentato.

unfertile [ʌn'fəːtail], *ag.* infruttifero; sterile.

unfertilized [ʌn'fəːtilaizd], *ag.* non fertilizzato.

to unfetter [ʌn'fetə*], *v.t.* liberare, sciogliere da catene (anche *fig.*).

unfettered [ʌn'fetəd], *ag.* libero, senza ceppi; *fig.* senza restrizioni, senza impacci.

unfiled[1] [ʌn'faild], *ag.* non limato; *fig.* rozzo, grossolano.

unfiled[2], *ag.* non archiviato; non schedato.

unfilial [ʌn'filjəl], *ag.* non filiale, poco filiale.

unfilially [ʌn'filjəli], *av.* in modo poco filiale.

unfilled [ʌn'fild], *ag.* 1. vuoto, non riempito 2. libero, vacante, non occupato.

unfiltered [ʌn'filtəd], *ag.* non filtrato.

unfinished [ʌn'finiʃt], *ag.* incompiuto, non terminato; incompleto, imperfetto; non rifinito: *an — house*, una casa non terminata; *an — style*, uno stile grezzo ☆ *— products*, (*ind.*) semilavorati.

unfit [ʌn'fit], *ag.* 1. inadatto, disadatto; incapace; indegno: *— to eat*, immangiabile; *— to rule*, indegno di regnare; *road — for motor traffic*, strada non automobilistica 2. di debole costituzione; inabile: *— for military service*, inabile al servizio militare; *to be — to take a journey*, non essere in condizioni di intraprendere un viaggio.

to unfit [ʌn'fit], *v.t.* rendere incapace, inabile, inadatto; squalificare: *drink unfits him for work*, il bere lo rende inabile al lavoro.

unfitly [ʌn'fitli], *av.* in modo inadatto, non appropriatamente.

unfitness [ʌn'fitnis], *s.* 1. inettitudine; inidoneità: *— for* (o *to do*) *sthg.*, incapacità di fare ql.co. 2. debole costituzione, salute delicata.

unfitted [ʌn'fitid], *ag.* disadatto; non idoneo.

unfitting [ʌn'fitiŋ], *ag.* poco adatto, inopportuno; sconveniente.

unfittingly [ʌn'fitiŋli], *av.* in modo inopportuno, a sproposito: *not —*, non ingiustamente.

to unfix [ʌn'fiks], *v.t.i.* 1. staccare, staccarsi; slegare, slegarsi: *to — bayonets*, (*mil.*) togliere le baionette 2. *fig.* sconvolgere, rendere dubbioso.

unfixed [ʌn'fikst], *ag.* 1. non fisso, non fissato; mobile: *to come —*, staccarsi, sciogliersi 2. irresoluto, incostante.

unflagging [ʌn'flægiŋ], *ag.* che non cede, costante; instancabile.

unflattering [ʌn'flætəriŋ], *ag.* poco lusinghiero.

unflatteringly [ʌn'flætəriŋli], *av.* in modo poco lusinghiero.

unflawed [ʌn'flɔːd], *ag.* senza difetti.

unfledged [ʌn'fledʒd], *ag.* 1. implume; *fig.* giovane, inesperto: *— youth*, prima giovinezza 2. poco sviluppato.

to unflesh [ʌn'fleʃ], *v.t.* scarnificare.

unfleshed [ʌn'fleʃt], *ag.* 1. scarnito 2. non ancora avvezzo al sangue (di animali) 3. *fig.* inesperto, non iniziato.

unflinching [ʌn'flintʃiŋ], *ag.* fermo; intrepido, che non indietreggia.

unflinchingly [ʌn'flintʃiŋli], *av.* senza indietreggiare, intrepidamente; fermamente.

unflinchingness [ʌn'flintʃinnis], *s.* intrepidezza; fermezza, saldezza.

to unfold[1] [ʌn'fould], *v.t.i.* 1. aprire, aprirsi; schiudere, schiudersi; spiegare, spiegarsi: *— your lips*, schiudi le labbra; *buds — in the summer*, i bocciuoli si schiudono in estate; (*the*) *landscape unfolds* (*itself*) *before us*, il paesaggio si spiega dinanzi a noi; *to — a newspaper*, spiegare un giornale 2. rivelare; svelare, svelarsi: *to — one's intentions*, rivelare le proprie intenzioni.

to unfold[2], *v.t.* far uscire dal chiuso (le pecore).

unfolded[1] [ʌn'fouldid], *ag.* 1. aperto; dischiuso; spiegato 2. rivelato, svelato.

unfolded[2], *ag.* fuori dal chiuso (di pecore).

unforbearing [ʌn-fɔː'bɛəriŋ], *ag.* insofferente; intollerante; impaziente.

unforbidden [ʌn-fə'bidn], *ag.* non proibito, lecito.

unforced [ˈʌnˈfɔːst], *ag.* **1.** non forzato, libero; spontaneo, naturale: — *mirth*, allegria spontanea; — *obedience*, obbedienza non forzata **2.** (*bot.*) non forzato (di coltivazione).

unfordable [ˈʌnˈfɔːdəbl], *ag.* inguadabile.

unforeknown [ˈʌn-fɔːˈnoun], *ag.* non conosciuto prima.

unforeseeing [ˈʌn-fɔːˈsiːiŋ], *ag.* imprevidente.

unforeseen [ˈʌn-fɔːˈsiːn], *ag.* imprevisto, inatteso: — *event*, evento inatteso.

unforetold [ˈʌn-fɔːˈtould], *ag.* non predetto.

unforewarned [ˈʌn-fɔːˈwɔːnd], *ag.* non preavvertito; non preammonito.

unforfeited [ˈʌnˈfɔːfitid], *ag.* non confiscato.

unforgetful [ˈʌn-fəˈgetful], *ag.* non immemore.

unforgettable [ˈʌn-fəˈgetəbl], *ag.* indimenticabile, inobliabile.

unforgivable [ˈʌn-fəˈgivəbl], *ag.* imperdonabile.

unforgiven [ˈʌn-fəˈgivn], *ag.* senza perdono, imperdonato.

unforgiving [ˈʌn-fəˈgiviŋ], *ag.* senza misericordia, inesorabile, implacabile.

unforgotten [ˈʌn-fəˈgɔtn], *ag.* inobliato: *he remained* —, non fu dimenticato.

unformal [ˈʌnˈfɔːməl], *ag.* senza formalità, senza cerimonie.

unformed [ˈʌnˈfɔːmd], *ag.* **1.** non (ancora) formato; *fig.* immaturo, incolto **2.** informe, amorfo.

unforsaken [ˈʌn-fəˈseikən], *ag.* non abbandonato.

unfortified [ˈʌnˈfɔːtifaid], *ag.* non fortificato.

unfortunate [ʌnˈfɔːtʃnit], *ag.* **1.** sfortunato; disgraziato **2.** sfavorevole, poco propizio ‖ *s.c.* infelice, disgraziato, disgraziata ‖ *s.* prostituta.

unfortunately [ʌnˈfɔːtʃnitli], *av.* sfortunatamente, per disgrazia.

unfostered [ˈʌnˈfɔstəd], *ag.* non protetto; non sostenuto.

unfought [ˈʌnˈfɔːt], *ag.* non combattuto.

unfouled [ˈʌnˈfauld], *ag.* incontaminato.

unfound [ˈʌnˈfaund], *ag.* non trovato.

unfounded [ˈʌnˈfaundid], *ag.* infondato, senza base: — *hopes*, speranze infondate, ingiustificate.

to **unframe** [ˈʌnˈfreim], *v.t.* togliere dalla cornice.

unfree [ˈʌnˈfriː], *ag.* **1.** non libero, privo di libertà **2.** (*comm.*) non gratuito; non esente da tasse, imposte, dogana.

unfreed [ˈʌnˈfriːd], *ag.* non liberato.

to **unfreeze** [ˈʌnˈfriːz], *pass.* **unfroze** [ˈʌnˈfrouz], *p.p.* **unfrozen** [ˈʌnˈfrouzn], *v.t.i.* disgelare, disgelarsi; scongelare, scongelarsi.

unfrequency [ˈʌnˈfriːkwənsi], *s.* (*rar.*) infrequenza.

unfrequent [ʌnˈfriːkwənt], *ag.* infrequente, raro.

unfrequented [ˈʌn-friˈkwentid], *ag.* poco frequentato, poco praticato.

unfrequently [ʌnˈfriːkwəntli], *av.* raramente, infrequentemente.

unfriended [ˈʌnˈfrendid], *ag.* senza amici.

unfriendliness [ˈʌnˈfrendlinis], *s.* inimicizia; ostilità; scortesia.

unfriendly [ˈʌnˈfrendli], *ag.* **1.** poco amichevole, mal disposto; ostile: *to be* — *towards s.o.*, essere mal disposto verso qlcu. **2.** sfavorevole, poco propizio.

unfriendly, *av.* (*rar.*) in modo poco gentile, poco amichevole.

to **unfrock** [ˈʌnˈfrɔk], *v.t.* (*eccl.*) spretare, sfratare.

unfrozen [ˈʌnˈfrouzn], *ag.* non gelato, disgelato.

unfrugal [ˈʌnˈfruːgəl], *ag.* poco parco; poco economo.

unfruitful [ˈʌnˈfruːtful], *ag.* infruttuoso, infruttifero; infecondo, sterile.

unfruitfully [ˈʌnˈfruːtfuli], *av.* infruttuosamente.

unfruitfulness [ˈʌnˈfruːtfulnis], *s.* infruttuosità; infecondità, sterilità.

unfulfilled [ˈʌn-fulˈfild], *ag.* mancato; inadempiuto; non esaudito.

unfunded [ˈʌnˈfʌndid], *ag.* (*comm.*) non consolidato, fluttuante ☆ — *debt*, debito fluttuante.

to **unfurl** [ʌnˈfəːl], *v.t.i.* spiegare, spiegarsi (di vele, bandiere, ecc.): *to* — *the sails*, far vela, partire.

unfurnished [ˈʌnˈfəːniʃt], *ag.* **1.** non ammobiliato, senza mobili **2.** sfornito, sprovvisto: — *with news*, sprovvisto di notizie.

unfurrowed [ˈʌnˈfʌroud], *ag.* non solcato, senza solchi; senza rughe.

unfused [ˈʌnˈfjuːzd], *ag.* non fuso.

ungained [ˈʌnˈgeind], *ag.* non guadagnato.

ungainful [ˈʌnˈgeinful], *ag.* che non procura guadagno, poco rimunerativo.

ungainliness [ʌnˈgeinlinis], *s.* **1.** goffaggine **2.** sgarbatezza, grossolanità.

ungainly [ʌnˈgeinli], *ag.* **1.** goffo, maldestro, sgraziato **2.** sgarbato, grossolano.

ungainly, *av.* **1.** goffamente **2.** sgarbatamente.

ungallant [ʌnˈgælənt], *ag.* poco galante; poco cavalleresco; scortese.

ungallantly [ʌnˈgæləntli], *av.* senza galanteria; poco cavallerescamente; in modo scortese.

ungalled [ʌnˈgɔːld], *ag.* (*arc.*) non irritato, non infastidito.

ungarbled [ʌnˈgaːbld], *ag.* **1.** non mutilo, integro (di testo, ecc.) **2.** vero, esatto: *the* — *truth*, la verità pura e semplice.

ungarnished [ʌnˈgaːniʃt], *ag.* privo di ornamenti, sguarnito; semplice.

ungarrisoned [ʌnˈgærisnd], *ag.* non presidiato, privo di guarnigione (di città, ecc.).

ungartered [ʌnˈgaːtəd], *ag.* senza giarrettiere.

ungathered [ʌnˈgæðəd], *ag.* non colto, non raccolto.

to **ungear** [ʌnˈgiə*], *v.t.* **1.** (*mec.*) disingranare **2.** (*dial.*) togliere i finimenti a (cavalli, ecc.).

ungeared [ʌnˈgiəd], *ag.* (*mec.*) **1.** disingranato **2.** senza ingranaggi.

ungenerous [ʌnˈdʒenərəs], *ag.* **1.** ingeneroso; meschino; gretto **2.** sterile (di terreno).

ungenerously [ʌnˈdʒenərəsli], *av.* ingenerosamente; meschinamente; grettamente.

ungenial [ʌnˈdʒiːnjəl], *ag.* **1.** antipatico; freddo, poco socievole **2.** inclemente, rigido (di tempo).

ungenteel [ˈʌndʒenˈtiːl], *ag.* **1.** sconveniente, disdicevole (di cosa) **2.** rozzo, volgare, plebeo (di persona).

ungenteelly [ˈʌndʒenˈtiːlli], *av.* **1.** in modo sconveniente, disdicevole **2.** con modi volgari, rozzamente.

ungentle [ʌnˈdʒentl], *ag.* duro, rude, aspro (di persona).

ungentlemanlike [ʌnˈdʒentlmənlaik], *ag.* **1.** indegno di un gentiluomo: — *conduct*, condotta indegna di un uomo dabbene **2.** maleducato.

ungentlemanliness [ʌnˈdʒentlmənlinis], *s.* **1.** slealtà **2.** mancanza di educazione, di distinzione.

ungentlemanly [ʌnˈdʒentlmənli], *V.* **ungentlemanlike**.

ungentleness [ʌnˈdʒentlnis], *s.* durezza, rudezza, asprezza (di modi).

ungently [ʌnˈdʒentli], *av.* duramente, rudemente, aspramente.

un-get-at-able [ˈʌngetˈætəbl], *ag.* difficile da raggiungere; inaccessibile.

ungifted [ˈʌnˈgiftid], *ag.* non dotato.

ungilded [ˈʌnˈgildid], **ungilt** [ˈʌnˈgilt], *ag.* non dorato, senza doratura.

to **ungird** [ˈʌnˈgəːd], *pass.p.p.* **ungirded** [ˈʌnˈgəːdid], **ungirt** [ˈʌnˈgəːt], *v.t.* togliere, slacciare la cintura a.

ungirt [ˈʌnˈgəːt], *ag.* **1.** senza cintura **2.** slacciato (di cintura).

to **ungirth** [ˈʌnˈgəːθ], *v.t.* togliere le cinghie a (un cavallo).

unglad [ˈʌnˈglæd], *ag.* scontento.

unglazed [ˈʌnˈgleizd], *ag.* **1.** senza vetri (di finestra) **2.** non lucido, opaco (di carta, ecc.).

unglorious [ʌn'glɔːriəs], *ag.* inglorioso.

to **unglove** [ʌn'glʌv], *v.t.* togliere i guanti a.

to **unglue** [ʌn'gluː], *v.t.i.* scollare, scollarsi.

ungodlily [ʌn'gɔdlili], *av.* empiamente.

ungodliness [ʌn'gɔdlinis], *s.* empietà; irreligiosità.

ungodly [ʌn'gɔdli], *ag.* empio; irreligioso.

ungored [ʌn'gɔːd], *ag.* non ferito, incolume, illeso.

ungorged [ʌn'gɔːdʒd], *ag.* non sazio.

ungot [ʌn'gɔt], **ungotten** [ʌn'gɔtn], *ag.* non ottenuto.

ungovernable [ʌn'gʌvənəbl], *ag.* **1.** incontrollabile, indisciplinato **2.** sfrenato, violento (di desideri, ecc.): — *passions*, passioni violente.

ungovernably [ʌn'gʌvənəbli], *av.* **1.** in modo incontrollabile, indisciplinatamente **2.** sfrenatamente, violentemente.

ungoverned [ʌn'gʌvənd], *ag.* **1.** senza governo **2.** incontrollato (di passioni, ecc.).

ungowned [ʌn'gaund], *ag.* **1.** senza toga **2.** stogato.

ungraced [ʌn'greist], *ag.* non dotato, non favorito.

ungraceful [ʌn'greisful], *ag.* sgraziato, goffo.

ungracefully [ʌn'greisfuli], *av.* senza grazia, sgraziatamente.

ungracefulness [ʌn'greisfulnis], *s.* mancanza di grazia, di garbo.

ungracious [ʌn'greiʃəs], *ag.* **1.** sgraziato, goffo **2.** poco gentile, offensivo.

ungraciously [ʌn'greiʃəsli], *av.* **1.** in modo sgraziato, goffo **2.** bruscamente; in modo offensivo.

ungraciousness [ʌn'greiʃəsnis], *s.* **1.** goffaggine **2.** malagrazia, asprezza.

ungrammatical [ʌngrə'mætikəl], *ag.* sgrammaticato, scorretto.

ungrammatically [ʌngrə'mætikəli], *av.* in modo sgrammaticato, scorretto.

ungrateful [ʌn'greitful], *ag.* **1.** ingrato: *to be — to s.o. for sthg.*, non essere grato a qlcu. per ql.co. **2.** spiacevole, ingrato: — *task*, compito ingrato.

ungratefully [ʌn'greitfuli], *av.* senza gratitudine, senza riconoscenza.

ungrounded [ʌn'graundid], *ag.* **1.** infondato **2.** senza preparazione: *to be — in a subject*, non avere preparazione su un argomento, su una materia.

ungrown [ʌn'groun], *ag.* immaturo.

ungrudging [ʌn'grʌdʒiŋ], *ag.* **1.** concesso di buon grado; generoso (di lodi, ecc.) **2.** generoso, liberale (di persona).

ungrudgingly [ʌn'grʌdʒiŋli], *av.* di buon grado, generosamente.

ungual [ʌŋgwəl], *ag.* (*anat.*) dell'unghia ‖ *s.* (*anat.*) falangetta.

to **unguard** [ʌn'gɑːd], *v.t.* sguarnire, lasciare senza difesa.

unguarded [ʌn'gɑːdid], *ag.* **1.** sguarnito, senza difesa, senza protezione **2.** *fig.* imprudente, sconsiderato, incauto.

unguardedly [ʌn'gɑːdidli], *av.* **1.** senza guardia **2.** sconsideratamente, imprudentemente, incautamente.

unguent [ʌŋgwənt], *s.* unguento.

unguessable [ʌn'gesəbl], *ag.* che non si può indovinare.

unguided [ʌn'gaidid], *ag.* senza guida.

ungula [ʌŋgjulə], *pl.* **ungulae** [ʌŋgjuliː], *s.* ungula, zoccolo (di animale).

ungulate [ʌŋgjuleit], *ag. s.* (*zool.*) ungulato.

unhabituated [ʌnhə'bitjueitid], *ag.* non abituato.

unhacked [ʌn'hækt], *ag.* non tritato, non tagliuzzato.

unhackneyed [ʌn'hæknid], *ag.* nuovo, originale, non trito: — *phrase*, frase originale.

unhailed [ʌn'heild], *ag.* non salutato, non acclamato.

to **unhair** [ʌn'hɛə*], *v.t.i.* **1.** strappare i capelli a; depilare **2.** perdere i capelli.

to **unhallow** [ʌn'hælou], *v.t.* profanare.

unhallowed [ʌn'hæloud], *ag.* **1.** non consacrato, profano **2.** empio, sacrilego.

unhampered [ʌn'hæmpəd], *ag.* non impedito, libero: — *by rules*, libero da regole.

to **unhand** [ʌn'hænd], *v.t.* (*arc.*) abbandonare la presa di, togliere le mani da: — *me!*, lasciami!.

unhandily [ʌn'hændili], *av.* in modo maldestro, goffo.

unhandiness [ʌn'hændinis], *s.* goffaggine; inettitudine.

unhandsome [ʌn'hænsəm], *ag.* **1.** non bello; malfatto **2.** scortese **3.** meschino, basso: — *behaviour*, comportamento meschino.

unhandsomely [ʌn'hænsəmli], *av.* **1.** in modo sgarbato **2.** meschinamente, bassamente.

unhandsomeness [ʌn'hænsəmnis], *s.* **1.** mancanza di bellezza **2.** indelicatezza; scortesia **3.** meschinità.

unhandy [ʌn'hændi], *ag.* **1.** maldestro, goffo; inetto **2.** poco maneggevole, scomodo.

to **unhang** [ʌn'hæŋ], *pass.p.p.* **unhung** [ʌn'hʌŋ], *v.t.* staccare, smontare: *he unhung the picture from the wall*, staccò il quadro dalla parete.

unhanged [ʌn'hæŋd], *ag.* non impiccato.

unhappily [ʌn'hæpili], *av.* **1.** infelicemente; sfortunatamente, disgraziatamente: — *he died*, disgraziatamente morì; *to live* —, vivere tristemente **2.** male, malamente: *thought — expressed*, pensiero mal espresso.

unhappiness [ʌn'hæpinis], *s.* **1.** infelicità **2.** (*arc.*) sfortuna.

unhappy [ʌn'hæpi], *ag.* **1.** infelice, triste; sfortunato: *an — creature*, una creatura sfortunata; *to be — at leaving s.o.*, rattristarsi nel lasciare qlcu.; *to look* —, aver l'aria triste **2.** poco felice, poco ispirato; poco opportuno: — *translation*, traduzione poco felice; *he arrived at an — moment*, arrivò in un momento inopportuno; *to be — in one's choice of words*, essere poco felice nella scelta delle parole.

unharboured [ʌn'hɑːbəd], *ag.* **1.** senza riparo **2.** stanato (di animale).

unhardened [ʌn'hɑːdnd], *ag.* non indurito; non temperato (di acciaio).

unhardy [ʌn'hɑːdi], *ag.* debole; irresoluto.

unharmed [ʌn'hɑːmd], *ag.* intatto; illeso, indenne.

unharmful [ʌn'hɑːmful], *ag.* innocuo.

unharmonious [ʌnhɑː'mounjəs], *ag.* non armonioso.

to **unharness** [ʌn'hɑːnis], *v.t.* **1.** staccare i finimenti a; togliere il giogo a; staccare (un cavallo) **2.** togliere l'armatura; disarmare.

unharvested [ʌn'hɑːvistid], *ag.* non mietuto (di campo, di grano, ecc.).

unhatched [ʌn'hætʃt], *ag.* **1.** non covato (di uovo) **2.** non schiuso (di uovo).

unhazarded [ʌn'hæzədid], *ag.* non azzardato.

unhazardous [ʌn'hæzədəs], *ag.* non rischioso, non pericoloso.

unhealable [ʌn'hiːləbl], *ag.* inguaribile.

unhealthily [ʌn'helθili], *av.* **1.** in modo malsano, poco igienico **2.** senza salute.

unhealthiness [ʌn'helθinis], *s.* **1.** insalubrità (di clima) **2.** salute malferma.

unhealthy [ʌn'helθi], *ag.* **1.** malsano, insalubre; *fig.* dannoso: — *books*, libri dannosi; — *curiosity*, curiosità morbosa; *the most — region*, la regione più insalubre **2.** malaticcio, non in buona salute: — *complexion*, colorito malsano **3.** (*sl. mil.*) pericoloso: *this place is rather* —, questo luogo è piuttosto pericoloso, esposto al fuoco.

unheard [ʌn'həːd], *ag.* **1.** non udito; non percepito: *the ship's S.O.S. was* —, l'S.O.S. della nave non fu udito **2.** non ascoltato: — *prayer*, preghiera non esaudita; *I will not condemn you* —, non ti condannerò senza averti ascoltato **3.** non menzionato; sconosciuto, strano ☆ — *-of*, inaudito; senza precedenti: *an — -of crime*, un delitto inaudito.

to **unheart** [ʌn'hɑːt], *v.t.* (*arc.*) scoraggiare.

unheated [ʌn'hiːtid], *ag.* non riscaldato: — *greenhouse*, serra fredda.

unheeded ['ʌn'hi:did], *ag.* non curato, negletto; inosservato: *to pass* —, passare inosservato.

unheedful ['ʌn'hi:dful], *ag.* disattento, sbadato.

unheeding ['ʌn'hi:diŋ], *ag.* **1.** distratto, disattento **2.** incurante: *I walk — of the rain*, cammino senza curarmi della pioggia.

to **unhelm** ['ʌn'helm], *v.t.* togliere l'elmo a.

unhelmed ['ʌn'helmd], *ag.* senza elmo.

to **unhelmet** ['ʌn'helmit], *v.t.* togliere l'elmo a.

unhelped ['ʌn'helpt], *ag.* **1.** non aiutato; senza aiuto **2.** non servito (a tavola).

unhelpful ['ʌn'helpful], *ag.* vano, inutile: — *advice*, consiglio vano.

unhelpfully ['ʌn'helpfuli], *av.* vanamente, inutilmente.

unhemmed ['ʌn'hemd], *ag.* **1.** senza orlo **2.** sconfinato.

unheroic [ʌnhi'rouik], *ag.* poco eroico; pusillanime.

unhesitating [ʌn'heziteitiŋ], *ag.* che non esita; fermo, risoluto: — *reply*, risposta pronta.

unhesitatingly [ʌn'heziteitiŋli], *av.* senza esitare, senza esitazioni: *I say — that*, non esito a dire che.

unhewn ['ʌn'hju:n], *ag.* non sbozzato, informe; *fig.* rozzo, grezzo: — *stone*, pietra grezza; — *style*, stile grossolano.

unhidden ['ʌn'hidn], *ag.* non celato; aperto, manifesto.

unhindered ['ʌn'hindəd], *ag.* non ostacolato, senza impedimento.

to **unhinge** [ʌn'hindʒ], *v.t.* **1.** scardinare; togliere dai cardini **2.** *fig.* sconvolgere: *his mind is unhinged*, la sua mente è sconvolta.

unhired ['ʌn'haiəd], *ag.* **1.** non noleggiato; non affittato **2.** (*amer.*) non assunto (di persona).

unhistoric(al) ['ʌnhis'tɔrik(əl)], *ag.* leggendario.

to **unhitch** ['ʌn'hitʃ], *v.t.* staccare, distaccare.

to **unhive** ['ʌn'haiv], *v.t.* fare uscire dall'alveare.

unholily ['ʌn'houlili], *av.* empiamente; profanamente.

unholiness [ʌn'houlinis], *s.* empietà; profanità.

unholy [ʌn'houli], *ag.* **1.** non santo, non sacro; profano **2.** empio, sacrilego **3.** (*fam.*) terribile: — *muddle*, disordine spaventoso ‖ *s.* persona empia.

unhonoured ['ʌn'ɔnəd], *ag.* inonorato; disdegnato.

to **unhood** ['ʌn'hud], *v.t.* (*caccia*) scappucciare (il falco).

unhooded ['ʌn'hudid], *ag.* scappucciato.

to **unhook** ['ʌn'huk], *v.t.i.* sganciare, sganciarsi; staccare, staccarsi: *to — the receiver*, staccare il ricevitore (del telefono).

to **unhoop** ['ʌn'hu:p], *v.t.* togliere i cerchi a (una botte, ecc.).

unhoped ['ʌn'houpt], *ag.* insperato, inatteso: *an — -for success*, un successo insperato.

unhopeful ['ʌn'houpful], *ag.* privo di speranza.

to **unhorse** ['ʌn'hɔ:s], *v.t.* **1.** disarcionare **2.** staccare i cavalli da.

unhospitable ['ʌn'hɔspitəbl], *ag.* (*rar.*) inospitale.

unhostile ['ʌn'hostail], *ag.* non ostile.

to **unhouse** ['ʌn'hauz], *v.t.* privare della casa, del rifugio.

unhoused ['ʌn'hauzd], *ag.* privato della casa; scacciato da un rifugio.

unhuman ['ʌn'hju:mən], *ag.* **1.** non umano; sovrumano **2.** (*rar.*) inumano, crudele, spietato.

unhung [ʌn'hʌŋ], *ag.* **1.** non esposto (di quadro) **2.** (*rar.*) senza tappezzerie **3.** (*rar.*) non impiccato.

unhunted ['ʌn'hʌntid], *ag.* non cacciato ☆ — *territory*, territorio con divieto di caccia.

unhurt ['ʌn'hə:t], *ag.* illeso, incolume; sano e salvo.

unhurtful ['ʌn'hə:tful], *ag.* non nocivo, innocuo.

unhusbanded ['ʌn'hʌzbəndid], *ag.* **1.** non curato, non coltivato **2.** senza marito.

to **unhusk** ['ʌn'hʌsk], *v.t.* togliere il guscio, la loppa.

Uniat ['ju:niæt], **Uniate** ['ju:niit], *s.* (*st. relig.*) uniate.

uniaxial [ju:ni'æksiəl], *ag.* (*ott.*) monoassiale.

unicameral ['ju:ni'kæmərəl], *ag.* (*pol.*) monocamerale.

unicapsular ['ju:ni'kæpsjulə*], *ag.* (*bot.*) che ha una sola capsula.

unicellular ['ju:ni'seljulə*], *ag.* (*biol.*) unicellulare.

unicity [ju'nisiti], *s.* unicità.

unicorn ['ju:nikɔ:n], *s.* **1.** (*mit.*) unicorno, liocorno **2.** (*zool.*) narvalo.

unideaed ['ʌnai'di:əd], *ag.* senza idee.

unideal ['ʌnai'diəl], *ag.* non ideale; prosaico.

unidentified ['ʌnai'dentifaid], *ag.* non identificato.

unidiomatic ['ʌn,idiə'mætik], *ag.* non idiomatico.

unification [,ju:nifi'keiʃən], *s.* unificazione.

unifier ['ju:nifaiə*], *s.c.* unificatore, unificatrice.

uniflorous ['ju:ni'flɔrəs], *ag.* (*bot.*) che dà un fiore solo.

unifoliate ['ju:ni'fouliit], *ag.* (*bot.*) avente una sola foglia.

uniform ['ju:nifɔ:m], *ag.* uniforme: — *life*, vita uniforme, grigia; — *temperature*, temperatura costante; — *velocity*, velocità costante; *body of — density*, corpo uniformemente compatto ‖ *s.* uniforme, divisa: *in* —, in uniforme; *out of* —, in borghese ☆ *drill* —, (*mil.*) tenuta da campo; *full (-dress)* —, (*mil.*) alta tenuta; *field-service* —, (*mil.*) tenuta da campagna; *undress* —, divisa ordinaria.

to **uniform**, *v.t.* **1.** uniformare **2.** far indossare l'uniforme a.

uniformed ['ju:nifɔ:md], *ag.* in uniforme.

uniformity [,ju:ni'fɔ:miti], *s.* **1.** uniformità; regolarità; costanza **2.** *Uniformity*, (*relig.*) conformismo ‖ *Act of Uniformity*, (*st. inglese*) legge per l'uniformità del culto.

uniformly ['ju:nifɔ:mli], *av.* uniformemente.

to **unify** ['ju:nifai], *v.t.* unificare.

unilabiate ['ju:ni'leibiit], *ag.* (*bot.*) unilabiato.

unilateral ['ju:ni'lætərəl], *ag.* unilaterale: — *contract*, (*dir.*) contratto unilaterale.

unilaterally ['ju:ni'lætərəli], *av.* unilateralmente.

unilluminated ['ʌni'lju:mineitid], *ag.* **1.** non illuminato; oscuro **2.** *fig.* poco ispirato.

unillumined ['ʌni'lju:mind], *ag.* non illuminato.

unillustrated ['ʌn'iləstreitid], *ag.* **1.** non illustrato, privo di illustrazioni **2.** privo di esempi.

unilocular ['ju:ni'lɔkjulə*], *ag.* (*bot.*) monoloculare.

unimaginable [,ʌni'mædʒinəbl], *ag.* inimmaginabile; inconcepibile.

unimaginableness [,ʌni'mædʒinəblnis], *s.* inimmaginabilità; inconcepibilità.

unimaginably [,ʌni'mædʒinəbli], *av.* inimmaginabilmente; inconcepibilmente.

unimaginative ['ʌni'mædʒinətiv], *ag.* privo di immaginazione; prosaico.

unimaginatively ['ʌni'mædʒinətivli], *av.* senza immaginazione; prosaicamente.

unimaginativeness ['ʌni'mædʒinətivnis], *s.* mancanza di immaginazione; prosaicità.

unimagined ['ʌni'mædʒind], *ag.* inimmaginato.

unimbued ['ʌnim'bju:d], *ag.* non imbevuto.

unimitated ['ʌn'imiteitid], *ag.* inimitato, non imitato.

unimpairable ['ʌnim'pɛərəbl], *ag.* che non può essere danneggiato, indebolito, alterato.

unimpaired ['ʌnim'pɛəd], *ag.* non danneggiato; inalterato, intatto; in tutto il suo vigore: *with faculties* —, in pieno possesso delle proprie facoltà; *his mind is* —, conserva ancora una mente lucidissima.

unimpassioned ['ʌnim'pæʃənd], *ag.* spassionato; calmo; freddo, distaccato: — *speech*, discorso misurato.

unimpeachable ['ʌnim'pi:tʃəbl], *ag.* **1.** incensurabile, irreprensibile, inattaccabile **2.** irrefutabile; incontestabile: *I have it from an — source*, lo so da fonte sicura.

unimpeachableness [,ʌnim'pi:tʃəblnis], *s.* **1.** incensurabilità **2.** incontestabilità.

unimpeded ['ʌnim'pi:did], *ag.* non impedito, non ostacolato; libero.

unimplied ['ʌnim'plaid], *ag.* non implicito.

unimportance ['ʌnim'pɔ:təns], *s.* scarsa importanza; mancanza d'importanza, di significato.

unimportant ['ʌnim'pɔ:tənt], *ag.* privo d'importanza;

insignificante, trascurabile: *this is quite — to me*, ciò non mi importa proprio nulla.

unimposed ['ʌnim'pouzd], *ag.* non imposto, spontaneo.

unimposing ['ʌnim'pouziŋ], *ag.* **1.** poco importante; che non fa soggezione **2.** insignificante.

unimpoverished ['ʌnim'pɔvəriʃt], *ag.* non impoverito.

unimpregnated ['ʌn'impregneitid], *ag.* non impregnato, non saturo.

unimpressed ['ʌnim'prest], *ag.* **1.** non impressionato **2.** non impresso (di moneta, ecc.).

unimpressionable ['ʌnim'preʃṇəbl], *ag.* non impressionabile, non emotivo.

unimpressive ['ʌnim'presiv], *ag.* che non impressiona, non colpisce; che non commuove.

unimpressively ['ʌnim'presivli], *av.* senza produrre impressione; senza commuovere.

unimprisoned ['ʌnim'priznd], *ag.* non imprigionato, libero.

unimprovable ['ʌnim'pru:vəbl], *ag.* **1.** incorreggibile **2.** non suscettibile di miglioramenti, perfetto.

unimproved ['ʌnim'pru:vd], *ag.* non migliorato, non valorizzato, senza migliorie ‖ *— site value*, (*agr.*) valore intrinseco di terreno (indipendente da migliorie).

unimproving ['ʌnim'pru:viŋ], *ag.* che non migliora.

unimpugned ['ʌnim'pju:nd], *ag.* non impugnato, non contestato.

unindebted ['ʌnin'detid], *ag.* non indebitato, senza debiti.

unindexed ['ʌn'indekst], *ag.* senza indice dei nomi; non registrato nell'indice dei nomi.

unindorsed ['ʌnin dɔ:st], *ag.* (*comm.*) non girato.

unindustrious ['ʌnin'dʌstriəs], *ag.* non industrioso, non laborioso.

uninfected ['ʌnin'fektid], *ag.* non infetto, non contaminato.

uninfectious ['ʌnin'fekʃəs], *ag.* non contagioso, non infettivo.

uninfested ['ʌnin'festid], *ag.* non infestato.

uninflamed ['ʌnin'fleimd], *ag.* non infiammato, non acceso.

uninflammable ['ʌnin'flæməbl], *ag.* non infiammabile.

uninfluenced ['ʌn'influənst], *ag.* non influenzato.

uninfluential ['ʌn,influ'enʃəl], *ag.* non influente, che non ha influenza, autorità.

uninformed ['ʌnin'fɔ:md], *ag.* **1.** non informato, ignaro **2.** ignorante **3.** senza vita, senza animazione.

uninhabitable ['ʌnin'hæbitəbl], *ag.* inabitabile.

uninhabitableness ['ʌnin'hæbitəblnis], *s.* inabitabilità.

uninhabited ['ʌnin'hæbitid], *ag.* disabitato, deserto.

uninitiated ['ʌni'niʃieitid], *ag.* non iniziato, non introdotto ‖ *the —*, i profani, i non iniziati.

uninjured ['ʌn'indʒəd], *ag.* incolume; indenne; intatto.

uninjurious ['ʌnin'dʒuəriəs], *ag.* innocuo.

uninominal [,ju:ni'nɔminl], *ag.* uninominale, individuale.

uninquiring ['ʌnin'kwaiəriŋ], *ag.* che non indaga, non curioso, che non chiede.

uninquisitive ['ʌnin'kwizitiv], *ag.* non curioso, che non indaga.

uninscribed ['ʌnin'skraibd], *ag.* non iscritto.

uninspired ['ʌnin'spaiəd], *ag.* non ispirato, senza ispirazione, prosaico.

uninstructed ['ʌnin'strʌktid], *ag.* **1.** non istruito, ignorante **2.** che non ha ricevuto istruzioni.

uninstructive ['ʌnin'strʌktiv], *ag.* non istruttivo.

uninsulated ['ʌn'insjuleitid], *ag.* non isolato, non staccato.

uninsured ['ʌnin'ʃuəd], *ag.* non assicurato.

unintellectual ['ʌn,inti'lektjuəl], *ag.* non intellettuale.

unintelligence ['ʌnin'telidʒəns], *s.* mancanza di intelligenza, ottusità.

unintelligent ['ʌnin'telidʒənt], *ag.* non intelligente, ottuso; stupido.

unintelligently ['ʌnin'telidʒəntli], *av.* senza intelligenza.

unintelligibility ['ʌnin,telidʒə'biliti], *s.* inintelligibilità, incomprensibilità.

unintelligible ['ʌnin'telidʒəbl], *ag.* inintelligibile, incomprensibile.

unintelligibly ['ʌnin'telidʒəbli], *av.* inintellegibilmente, incomprensibilmente.

unintended ['ʌnin'tendid], *ag.* involontario; non intenzionale; non prestabilito.

unintentional ['ʌnin'tenʃən], *ag.* non intenzionale, involontario.

unintentionally ['ʌnin'tenʃṇəli], *av.* inintenzionalmente, involontariamente.

uninterested ['ʌn'intristid], *ag.* non interessato, indifferente.

uninteresting ['ʌn'intristiŋ], *ag.* poco interessante; privo di interesse.

uninterestingly ['ʌn'intristiŋli], *av.* in modo poco interessante; senza interesse.

unintermitted ['ʌn,intə(:)'mitid], *ag.* ininterrotto.

unintermitting ['ʌn,intə(:)'mitiŋ], *ag.* incessante, ininterrotto, continuo.

unintermittingly ['ʌn,intə(:)'mitiŋli], *av.* incessantemente, ininterrottamente, continuamente.

uninterpreted ['ʌnin'tə:pritid], *ag.* non interpretato.

uninterred ['ʌnin'tə:d], *ag.* insepolto.

uninterrupted ['ʌn,intə'rʌptid], *ag.* ininterrotto, continuo: — *correspondence*, corrispondenza ininterrotta.

uninterruptedly ['ʌn,intə'rʌptidli], *av.* ininterrottamente, incessantemente.

unintoxicating ['ʌnin'tɔksikeitiŋ], *ag.* non inebriante; non eccitante; analcolico.

uninured ['ʌni'njuəd], *ag.* non abituato, non assuefatto, non avvezzo: — *to work*, non avvezzo al lavoro.

uninvaded ['ʌnin'veidid], *ag.* non invaso; non violato.

uninventive ['ʌnin'ventiv], *ag.* non inventivo; privo di immaginazione.

uninvested ['ʌnin'vestid], *ag.* **1.** non investito **2.** (*mil.*) non assediato.

uninvidious ['ʌnin'vidiəs], *ag.* **1.** non irritante; non odioso **2.** non invidiabile **3.** (*rar.*) non invidioso.

uninvidious ['ʌnin'vidiəs], *ag.* non invidioso, non maligno.

uninvited ['ʌnin'vaitid], *ag.* non invitato: *to come —*, venire senza essere invitato.

uninviting ['ʌnin'vaitiŋ], *ag.* poco attraente; poco allettante; poco appetitoso.

uninvoked ['ʌnin'voukt], *ag.* non invocato.

uninvolved ['ʌnin'vɔlvd], *ag.* **1.** non implicato, non coinvolto **2.** non involuto; semplice.

union ['ju:njən], *s.* **1.** unione: *the — of human nature with the divine*, l'unione della natura umana con quella divina; *to promote the — between two families*, incoraggiare l'unione tra due famiglie **2.** matrimonio, accoppiamento: *a lasting —*, un matrimonio durevole **3.** associazione, lega, società, confederazione ‖ *the Union*, gli Stati Uniti; l'unione della Gran Bretagna e dell'Irlanda ‖ *Union Flag* (o *Union Jack*), bandiera del Regno Unito di Gran Bretagna e Irlanda ‖ *Union of South Africa*, Unione del Sud-Africa **4.** (*trade-*) —, sindacato: *tramping from one — to another*, il passare da un sindacato all'altro **5.** concordia, accordo: *in perfect —*, in perfetta armonia **6.** (*mec.*) raccordo, bocchettone **7.** (*ind. tessile*) tela mista di lino e cotone **8.** — (*workhouse*), ospizio fondato da alcune parrocchie in collaborazione ☆ *— sleeve*, (*mec.*) manicotto di raccordo; *— suit*, (*amer.*) combinazione (capo di biancheria).

unionism ['ju:njənizəm], *s.* **1.** tendenza ad unirsi **2.** (*trade-*) —, sindacalismo.

unionist ['ju:njənist], *s.c.* **1.** unionista **2.** (*trade-*) —, sindacalista, membro di un sindacato.

to **unionize** ['ju:njənaiz], *v.t.* riunire (in associazioni, sindacati, ecc.).

uniparous [ju(:)'nipərəs], *ag.* (*biol.*) uniparo.

unipersonal ['ju:ni'pə:sn̩l], *ag.* **1.** (*teol.*) in una sola persona **2.** (*gram.*) impersonale.

unique [ju:'ni:k], *ag.* **1.** unico, solo, singolo: *there is perhaps a — opportunity*, c'è forse una sola opportunità **2.** senza eguale, eccezionale ‖ *s.* cosa unica; pezzo unico.

uniquely [ju:'ni:kli], *av.* unicamente.

uniqueness [ju:'ni:knis], *s.* **1.** unicità, l'essere unico **2.** l'essere senza pari.

unirritated ['ʌn'iriteitid], *ag.* non irritato.

unirritating ['ʌn'iriteitiŋ], *ag.* non irritante.

unisepalous ['ju:ni'sepələs], *ag.* (*bot.*) monosepalo.

uniserial ['ju:ni'siəriəl], *ag.* in una serie, in una fila.

unisexual ['ju:ni'seksjuəl], *ag.* (*biol.*) unisessuale.

unison ['ju:nizn], *ag.* unisono ‖ *s.* **1.** (*mus.*) unisono **2.** *fig.* accordo, concordia: *in — (with)*, all'unisono (con); in armonia, d'accordo (con); *they acted in perfect —*, agivano in accordo perfetto.

unisonance [ju(:)'nisənəns], *s.* **1.** (*mus.*) unisonanza **2.** *fig.* accordo, concordia.

unisonant [ju(:)'nisənənt], *ag.* all'unisono.

unisonous [ju(:)'nisənəs], *ag.* **1.** (*mus.*) unisono **2.** *fig.* d'accordo.

unissued ['ʌn'isju:d], *ag.* non emesso.

unit ['ju:nit], *s.* **1.** unità; unità di misura: *— of area*, unità di superficie: *— of heat*, unità di calore **2.** complesso, insieme, gruppo: *the lens — of a camera*, l'insieme di lenti di una macchina fotografica **3.** (*mil.*) unità, reparto ☆ *monetary —*, unità monetaria.

Unitarian [,ju:ni'tɛəriən], *ag.s.* (*st.relig.*) unitario.

Unitarianism [,ju:ni'tɛəriənizəm], *s.* (*st.relig.*) unitarismo.

unitary ['ju:nitəri], *ag.* unitario ☆ *— method*, (*mat.*) metodo di riduzione all'unità.

to **unite** [ju:'nait], *v.t.i.* **1.** unire, unirsi; congiungere, congiungersi; combinare, combinarsi: *England and Scotland united in 1707*, l'Inghilterra e la Scozia si unirono nel 1707; *they were bound to —*, erano destinati a unirsi (in matrimonio); *water will not — with oil*, l'acqua non si combina con l'olio **2.** mettersi d'accordo; allearsi; agire congiuntamente: *they united in their hate against him*, si allearono nel comune odio contro di lui.

united [ju:'naitid], *ag.* unito; collegato; combinato: *a — effort*, uno sforzo congiunto (per un comune proposito) ‖ *the United Kingdom*, il Regno Unito.

unitedly [ju:'naitidli], *av.* unitamente; congiuntamente.

United States [ju:'naitid'steits], *no.pr.pl.* (*geog.*) Stati Uniti (d'America).

unity ['ju:niti], *s.* **1.** unità: *that painting lacks —*, quel quadro manca di unità ‖ *the dramatic unities*, (*st. teat.*) le (tre) unità drammatiche **2.** armonia, accordo; concordia: *— is essential to a community*, la buona armonia è essenziale in una comunità; *they lived together in —*, vissero insieme in perfetto accordo ‖ *— is strength*, *prov.* l'unione fa la forza **3.** (*mat.*) unità; il numero uno.

univalence [ju(:)'nivələns], **univalency** [ju(:)'nivələnsi], *s.* (*chim.*) monovalenza.

univalent [ju(:)'nivələnt], *ag.* (*chim.*) monovalente.

univalve ['ju:nivælv], *ag.* (*zool.*) univalve ‖ *s.* mollusco univalve.

univalvular ['ju:ni'vælvjulə*], *ag.* (*bot.*) univalve.

universal [,ju:ni'və:səl], *ag.* universale; totale, generale: *they met with — applause*, ottennero il plauso universale; *to make —*, universalizzare ‖ *s.* (*fil.*) universale ☆ *— agent*, (*comm. dir.*) mandatario generale; *— coupling* (o *— joint*), (*mec.*) giunto cardanico, giunto universale; *— provider*, negoziante di generi vari.

universalism [,ju:ni'və:səlizəm], *s.* (*teol.*) universalismo.

universalist [,ju:ni'və:səlist], *s.* (*teol.*) universalista.

universality [,ju:nivə:'sæliti], *s.* universalità.

universalization ['ju:ni,və:səlai'zeiʃən], *s.* universalizzazione.

to **universalize** [,ju:ni'və:səlaiz], *v.t.* universalizzare.

universally [,ju:ni'və:səli], *av.* universalmente.

universe ['ju:nivə:s], *s.* universo.

university [,ju:ni'və:siti], *s.* **1.** università **2.** gli appartenenti ad una università (professori e studenti) **3.** associazione, squadra rappresentante l'università ☆ *— boat-race*, gara di canottaggio tra squadre universitarie; *— degree*, laurea; *— education*, istruzione universitaria; *— extension*, ammissione all'università di studenti esterni; *— professor*, docente universitario.

univocal [ju:ni'voukəl], *ag.* **1.** univoco, con un solo significato; non ambiguo **2.** (*arc.*) unanime.

univocally ['ju:ni'voukəli], *av.* univocamente.

unjaundiced ['ʌn'dʒɔ:ndist], *ag.* non invidioso; non geloso.

to **unjoin** ['ʌn'dʒɔin], *v.t.* (*rar.*) disgiungere, separare.

to **unjoint** ['ʌn'dʒɔint], *v.t.* disgiungere; smontare; disarticolare.

unjointed ['ʌn'dʒɔintid], *ag.* **1.** disgiunto: senza giunture **2.** *fig.* incoerente, scucito.

unjoyous ['ʌn'dʒɔiəs], *ag.* senza gioia, triste.

unjoyously ['ʌn'dʒɔiəsli], *av.* tristemente, senza gioia.

unjudged ['ʌn'dʒʌdʒd], *ag.* non giudicato.

unjust ['ʌn'dʒʌst], *ag.* ingiusto.

unjustifiable [ʌn'dʒʌstifaiəbl], *ag.* ingiustificabile.

unjustifiableness [ʌn'dʒʌstifaiəblnis], *s.* l'essere ingiustificabile.

unjustifiably [ʌn'dʒʌstifaiəbli], *av.* ingiustificabilmente.

unjustified ['ʌn'dʒʌstifaid], *ag.* ingiustificato.

unjustly ['ʌn'dʒʌstli], *av.* ingiustamente.

unjustness ['ʌn'dʒʌstnis], *s.* ingiustizia.

unkempt ['ʌn'kempt], *ag.* **1.** spettinato, scarmigliato **2.** trascurato, disordinato; sciatto.

unkenned ['ʌn'kend], *ag.* (*arc.*) sconosciuto, ignoto.

to **unkennel** ['ʌn'kenl], *pass.p.p.* **unkennelled** ['ʌn'kenld], *v.t.i.* **1.** stanare, uscire dalla tana **2.** far uscire dal canile.

unkept ['ʌn'kept], *ag.* **1.** non tenuto, non trattenuto **2.** trascurato, non curato **3.** non osservato, non rispettato.

unkind [ʌn'kaind], *ag.* **1.** sgarbato, scortese: *he was — to me*, fu scortese con me **2.** crudele, inesorabile.

unkindly [ʌn'kaindli], *ag.* **1.** sgarbato, scortese **2.** inclemente, duro, crudele.

unkindly, *av.* **1.** sgarbatamente ‖ *to take —*, risentirsi di **2.** crudelmente, duramente.

unkindness [ʌn'kaindnis], *s.* **1.** scortesia **2.** durezza, crudeltà.

to **unking** ['ʌn'kiŋ], *v.t.* (*rar.*) detronizzare, deporre dal trono.

unkingly ['ʌn'kiŋli], *ag.* non regale, indegno di un re.

unkissed ['ʌn'kist], *ag.* non baciato.

unknightly ['ʌn'naitli], *ag.* non cavalleresco, indegno di un cavaliere.

to **unknit** ['ʌn'nit], *pass.p.p.* **unknitted** ['ʌn'nitid], *v.t.* *spec. fig.* disfare, sciogliere ‖ *to — one's brows*, rasserenarsi in viso.

to **unknot** ['ʌn'nɔt], *pass.p.p.* **unknotted** ['ʌn'nɔtid], *v.t.* slegare, slacciare, disfare i nodi di.

unknowable ['ʌn'nouəbl], *ag.* che non si può sapere; inconoscibile.

unknowing ['ʌn'nouiŋ], *ag.* **1.** ignaro, inconsapevole **2.** ignorante.

unknowingly ['ʌn'nouiŋli], *av.* inconsapevolmente.

unknown ['ʌn'noun], *ag.* sconosciuto, non conosciuto, ignoto ‖ *— to me*, a mia insaputa ‖ *the Unknown Warrior*, il Milite Ignoto ‖ *s.* **1.** ignoto: *towards the —*, verso l'ignoto **2.** (*mat.*) incognita.

unlabelled ['ʌn'leibld], *ag.* senza etichetta.

unlaborious ['ʌnlə'bɔ:riəs], *ag.* non difficile a farsi.

unlaboured ['ʌn'leibəd], *ag.* **1.** non lavorato, incolto **2.** non elaborato, spontaneo, scorrevole (di stile).

to **unlace** ['ʌn'leis], *v.t.* slacciare, sciogliere.

to **unlade** ['ʌn'leid], *pass.* **unladed** ['ʌn'leidid], *p.p.* **unladen** ['ʌn'leidn], *v.t.* scaricare; togliere la soma da.

unladen ['ʌn'leidn], *ag.* non caricato; scaricato; scarico (anche *fig.*).

unlading ['ʌn'leidiŋ], *s.* scaricamento.

unladylike ['ʌn'leidilaik], *ag.* non adatto a una signora; indegno di una signora.

unlamented ['ʌnlə'mentid], *ag.* non rimpianto, illacrimato.

to **unlash** ['ʌn'læʃ], *v.t.* (*mar.*) allentare, sciogliere (gomene).

to **unlatch** ['ʌn'lætʃ], *v.t.* tirare il saliscendi a.

unlawful ['ʌn'lɔ:ful], *ag.* illegale; illecito; illegittimo.

unlawfully ['ʌn'lɔ:fuli], *av.* illegalmente; illecitamente; illegittimamente.

unlawfulness ['ʌn'lɔ:fulnis], *s.* illegalità; illegittimità.

to **unlay** ['ʌn'lei], *v.t.* (*mar.*) disfare, sciogliere i capi di (una fune).

to **unlead** ['ʌn'led], *v.t.* (*tip.*) sterlineare.

to **unlearn** ['ʌn'lə:n], *pass.p.p.* **unlearnt, unlearned** ['ʌn'lə:nt], *v.t.* disimparare, dimenticare.

unlearned ['ʌn'lə:nid], *ag.* non istruito; ignorante.

unlearnedly ['ʌn'lə:nidli], *av.* da ignorante, con ignoranza.

unlearnedness ['ʌn'lə:nidnis], *s.* ignoranza; mancanza di istruzione, di cultura.

unlearnt ['ʌn'lə:nt], *pass.p.p.* di to **unlearn** ‖ *ag.* disimparato; non imparato.

unleavened ['ʌn'levnd], *ag.* non lievitato; senza lievito; *fig.* senza fermento ☆ — *bread*, pane azzimo.

unled ['ʌn'led], *ag.* non guidato, senza guida.

unless [ən'les], *cong.* **a meno che, salvo che, se non, eccetto se:** — *you come*, a meno che tu non venga; *this baby seldom cries* — *he is tired*, questo bimbo piange raramente tranne quando è stanco.

unlessoned ['ʌn'lesnd], *ag.* incolto, non istruito.

unlettered ['ʌn'letəd], *ag.* **1.** illetterato, analfabeta, ignorante **2.** non espresso in lettere alfabetiche.

unlevelled ['ʌn'levld], *ag.* non livellato, non spianato; accidentato (di terreno).

unlicensed ['ʌn'laisənst], *ag.* non autorizzato, illecito; senza permesso, senza licenza: — *premises*, locale dove la vendita di alcoolici non è autorizzata.

unlicked ['ʌn'likt], *ag.* **1.** (*spec. fig.*) non leccato; non levigato **2.** rozzo, non manierato.

unlighted ['ʌn'laitid], *ag.* non illuminato; non acceso.

unlike ['ʌn'laik], *ag.* dissimile; diverso; poco somigliante: *this portrait is rather* —, questo ritratto è poco somigliante; *he is* — *your father*, non assomigli a tuo padre; *your plan is* — *mine*, il tuo progetto è diverso dal mio ‖ *s.* chi è dissimile; *pl.* persone, cose dissimili.

unlike, *prep.* diversamente da, a differenza di: *you play bridge* — *the people I have been playing with*, giocate a bridge diversamente dalle persone con cui ho giocato.

unlikelihood [ʌn'laiklihud], **unlikeliness** [ʌn'laiklinis], *s.* inverosimiglianza, improbabilità.

unlikely [ʌn'laikli], *ag.* inverosimile, improbabile: *an* — *story*, una storia inverosimile; *he is* — *to leave this evening*, è improbabile che parta questa sera.

unlikely, *av.* improbabilmente.

unlikeness ['ʌn'laiknis], *s.* dissomiglianza, differenza.

to **unlimber** [ʌn'limbə*], *v.t.* (*mil.*) staccare l'avantreno di (cannone); mettere in batteria.

unlimited [ʌn'limitid], *ag.* illimitato; sconfinato: — *liability*, (*comm.*) responsabilità illimitata.

unlimitedly [ʌn'limitidli], *av.* illimitatamente, senza limiti.

unlimitedness ['ʌn'limitidnis], *s.* l'essere illimitato; immensità.

to **unline** ['ʌn'lain], *v.t.* sfoderare, togliere la fodera a.

unlined[1] ['ʌn'laind], *ag.* senza fodera, sfoderato.

unlined[2], *ag.* senza rughe.

to **unlink** ['ʌn'liŋk], *v.t.* **1.** sciogliere, disfare, slegare **2.** disgiungere, staccare.

unliquidated ['ʌn'likwideitid], *ag.* non liquidato (di debito).

unlistened ['ʌn'lisnd], *ag.* inascoltato.

unlistening ['ʌn'lisniŋ], *ag.* che non ascolta, disattento.

unlit ['ʌn'lit], *ag.* non illuminato.

unliterary ['ʌn'litərəri], *ag.* non letterario.

to **unlive** ['ʌn'liv], *v.t.* cancellare (il passato).

unliveliness ['ʌn'laivlinis], *s.* mancanza di vivacità.

unlively ['ʌn'laivli], *ag.* non vivace.

to **unload** ['ʌn'loud], *v.t.* **1.** scaricare; *fig.* alleggerire, liberare da un peso: *they started unloading the ship*, incominciarono a scaricare la nave; *to* — *a gun*, scaricare un fucile **2.** (*Borsa*) liberarsi di (un pacchetto azionario), vendere (azioni).

unloaded ['ʌn'loudid], *ag.* non caricato; scaricato; *fig.* alleggerito.

unloading ['ʌn'loudiŋ], *s.* scaricamento; scarico.

unlocated ['ʌn'loukeitid], *ag.* non localizzato.

to **unlock** ['ʌn'lɔk], *v.t.* **1.** aprire (con chiave): far scattare (la serratura) **2.** *fig.* rivelare, scoprire (un segreto) **3.** sbloccare.

unlocked ['ʌn'lɔkt], *ag.* non chiuso a chiave.

unlooked-for [ʌn'luktfɔ:*], *ag.* imprevisto.

to **unloose** ['ʌn'lu:s], *to* **unloosen** [ʌn'lu:sn], *v.t.* slegare, sciogliere, slacciare.

unlorded ['ʌn'lɔ:did], *ag.* privato del titolo di «lord».

unlosable ['ʌn'lu:zəbl], *ag.* che non può essere perduto.

unlost ['ʌn'lɔst], *ag.* non perduto, non smarrito.

unlovable ['ʌn'lʌvəbl], *ag.* poco amabile; spiacevole, antipatico.

unloved ['ʌn'lʌvd], *ag.* non amato.

unloveliness ['ʌn'lʌvlinis], *s.* bruttezza.

unlovely ['ʌn'lʌvli], *ag.* poco attraente, brutto.

unloving ['ʌn'lʌviŋ], *ag.* poco affettuoso.

unluckily [ʌn'lʌkili], *av.* sfortunatamente, disgraziatamente, sventuratamente.

unluckiness [ʌn'lʌkinis], *s.* sfortuna.

unlucky [ʌn'lʌki], *ag.* **1.** sfortunato, disgraziato, sventurato: *a most* — *hour*, un'ora disgraziatissima **2.** di cattivo augurio, malaugurato, sinistro.

unmade [ʌn'meid], *pass.p.p.* di to **unmake** ‖ *ag.* **1.** non fatto; non confezionato; disfatto **2.** esistente senza essere stato creato.

to **unmaiden** [ʌn'meidn], *v.t.* deflorare.

unmaidenly [ʌn'meidnli], *ag.* che non si addice a una fanciulla.

unmailable ['ʌn'meiləbl], *ag.* che non può essere spedito per posta.

unmaimed ['ʌn'meimd], *ag.* non storpiato.

unmakable ['ʌn'meikəbl], *ag.* non fattibile.

to **unmake** ['ʌn'meik], *pass.p.p.* **unmade** [ʌn'meid], *v.t.* **1.** disfare **2.** *fig.* distruggere, annullare.

unmalleability ['ʌn,mæliə'biliti], *s.* mancanza di malleabilità.

unmalleable ['ʌn'mæliəbl], *ag.* non malleabile.

to **unman** ['ʌn'mæn], *pass.p.p.* **unmanned** ['ʌn'mænd], *v.t.* **1.** castrare, evirare **2.** abbrutire **3.** togliere forza, coraggio a; effeminare **4.** (*mar.*) disarmare, privare dell'equipaggio: *he could not venture to* — *his fleet*, non potè azzardarsi a disarmare la sua flotta.

unmanageable [ʌn'mænidʒəbl], *ag.* **1.** incontrollabile; intrattabile; indomabile **2.** poco maneggevole.

unmanliness ['ʌn'mænlinis], *s.* mancanza di virilità; debolezza.

unmanly ['ʌn'mænli], *ag.* **1.** indegno di un uomo **2.** non virile, effeminato; pusillanime.

unmanned ['ʌn'mænd], *ag.* **1.** evirato **2.** senza uomini (di nave, forte, ecc.) **3.** senza abitanti.

unmannered [ˈʌnˈmænəd], *ag.* maleducato, rozzo.

unmannerliness [ʌnˈmænəlinis], *s.* scortesia.

unmannerly [ʌnˈmænəli], *ag.* scortese, villano ‖ *av.* scortesemente.

to **unmantle** [ˈʌnˈmæntl], *v.t.* togliere il mantello a; scoprire.

unmanufactured [ˈʌnˌmænjuˈfæktʃəd], *ag.* grezzo; non lavorato, non finito.

unmanured [ˈʌnməˈnjuəd], *ag.* non fertilizzato.

unmarked [ˈʌnˈmɑːkt], *ag.* **1.** non marcato, non segnato **2.** inosservato.

unmarketable [ˈʌnˈmɑːkitəbl], *ag.* invendibile.

unmarred [ˈʌnˈmɑːd], *ag.* non sciupato, non danneggiato.

unmarriageable [ˈʌnˈmæridʒəbl], *ag.* non adatto al matrimonio.

unmarriageableness [ˈʌnˈmæridʒəblnis], *s.* inidoneità al matrimonio.

unmarried [ˈʌnˈmærid], *ag.* non coniugato, non sposato.

to **unmarry** [ˈʌnˈmæri], *v.t.i.* sciogliere il vincolo matrimoniale di; divorziare.

to **unmask** [ˈʌnˈmɑːsk], *v.t.i.* **1.** togliere, togliersi la maschera **2.** *fig.* smascherare, smascherarsi: *to — a conspiracy*, smascherare una cospirazione.

unmasked [ˈʌnˈmɑːskt], *ag.* **1.** senza maschera **2.** *fig.* smascherato.

unmastered [ˈʌnˈmɑːstəd], *ag.* indomato, incontrollato (di passione, ecc.); non superato (di difficoltà).

unmatched [ˈʌnˈmætʃt], *ag.* **1.** senza rivali, impareggiabile **2.** scompagnato: *two old — chairs*, due vecchie sedie scompagnate.

unmated [ˈʌnˈmeitid], *ag.* senza compagno.

unmeaning [ʌnˈmiːniŋ], *ag.* **1.** senza significato, privo di senso **2.** inespressivo (di viso).

unmeaningly [ʌnˈmiːniŋli], *av.* senza significato.

unmeaningness [ʌnˈmiːniŋnis], *s.* **1.** mancanza di significato **2.** inespressività (di viso).

unmeant [ʌnˈment], *ag.* involontario, fatto senza intenzione.

unmeasurable [ʌnˈmeʒərəbl], *ag.* incommensurabile; illimitato; smisurato: *the — eulogies he bestows upon her*, gli elogi esagerati che riversa su di lei.

unmeasurableness [ˈʌnˈmeʒərəblnis], *s.* incommensurabilità.

unmeasurably [ʌnˈmeʒərəbli], *av.* incommensurabilmente.

unmeasured [ʌnˈmeʒəd], *ag.* **1.** non misurato **2.** smisurato, immenso; sconfinato **3.** non controllato (di linguaggio).

unmechanical [ˈʌnmiˈkænikəl], *ag.* non meccanico; non conforme ai principi della meccanica.

unmechanically [ˈʌnmiˈkænikəli], *av.* in modo non meccanico; in modo non conforme ai principi della meccanica.

unmeddling [ˈʌnˈmedliŋ], *ag.* che non si immischia negli affari altrui.

unmeditated [ʌnˈmediteitid], *ag.* non meditato; non ponderato.

unmeet [ˈʌnˈmiːt], *ag.* inadatto, improprio; sconveniente: *— to do sthg.*, inadatto a fare ql.co.; *sight — for a girl*, vista poco adatta per una ragazza.

unmeetly [ˈʌnˈmiːtli], *av.* impropriamente; sconvenientemente.

unmeetness [ˈʌnˈmiːtnis], *s.* inattitudine, improprietà; sconvenienza.

unmellowed [ˈʌnˈmeloud], *ag.* non maturato, acerbo.

unmelodious [ˈʌnmiˈloudjəs], *ag.* non melodioso, non armonioso; discordante.

unmelodiously [ˈʌnmiˈloudjəsli], *av.* poco armoniosamente, poco melodiosamente.

unmelted [ˈʌnˈmeltid], *ag.* non fuso, non sciolto.

unmendable [ˈʌnˈmendəbl], *ag.* irreparabile.

unmentionable [ʌnˈmenʃnəbl], *ag.* innominabile; irripetibile.

unmentionables [ʌnˈmenʃnəblz], *s.pl.* (*scherz.*) calzoni.

unmentioned [ˈʌnˈmenʃənd], *ag.* non menzionato: *to leave sthg. —*, far passare ql.co. sotto silenzio.

unmercenary [ˈʌnˈməːsinəri], *ag.* non mercenario, disinteressato.

unmerchantable [ˈʌnˈməːtʃəntəbl], *ag.* (*comm.*) invendibile, non commerciabile.

unmerciful [ʌnˈməːsiful], *ag.* spietato; inumano.

unmercifully [ʌnˈməːsifuli], *av.* spietatamente; senza misericordia, senza indulgenza.

unmercifulness [ʌnˈməːsifulnis], *s.* mancanza di misericordia; crudeltà, durezza.

unmerited [ˈʌnˈmeritid], *ag.* immeritato.

unmeriting [ˈʌnˈmeritiŋ], *ag.* immeritevole.

unmethodical [ˈʌnmiˈθɔdikəl], *ag.* non metodico, non sistematico.

unmilitary [ˈʌnˈmilitəri], *ag.* **1.** non militare; civile, borghese **2.** antimilitarista.

unmilked [ˈʌnˈmilkt], *ag.* non munto.

unmilled [ˈʌnˈmild], *ag.* non macinato.

unminded [ˈʌnˈmaindid], *ag.* negletto, non curato.

unmindful [ʌnˈmaindful], *ag.* **1.** immemore, dimentico: *— of his duty*, immemore del suo dovere **2.** incurante: *— of the warnings*, incurante degli avvertimenti.

unmindfully [ʌnˈmaindfuli], *av.* **1.** senza pensare **2.** senza curarsi, senza preoccuparsi.

unmindfulness [ʌnˈmaindfulnis], *s.* **1.** oblio **2.** incuria; negligenza.

unmingled [ʌnˈmiŋgld], *ag.* non mescolato; puro, scevro: *joy — with regret*, gioia scevra da rimpianto.

unministerial [ˈʌnˌministiˈəriəl], *ag.* **1.** non ministeriale **2.** non esecutivo.

unmissed [ˈʌnˈmist], *ag.* di cui non si sente la mancanza: *he will be —*, la sua assenza non sarà sentita.

unmistakable [ˈʌnmisˈteikəbl], *ag.* chiaro, evidente; indubbio; inequivocabile: *black clouds are an — sign of coming rain*, le nuvole nere sono un segno indubbio che sta per piovere.

unmistakably [ˈʌnmisˈteikəbli], *av.* chiaramente, evidentemente; senza alcun dubbio, indubbiamente.

unmitigated [ʌnˈmitigeitid], *ag.* **1.** non mitigato, non attenuato **2.** vero, assoluto: *he is an — ass*, è un perfetto imbecille, un imbecille nel vero senso della parola.

unmixed [ˈʌnˈmikst], *ag.* puro, genuino, non mescolato: *— joy*, gioia pura, perfetta.

unmodernized [ˈʌnˈmɔdə(ː)naizd], *ag.* non modernizzato, antiquato.

unmodifiable [ˈʌnˈmɔdifaiəbl], *ag.* non modificabile.

unmodified [ˈʌnˈmɔdifaid], *ag.* non modificato.

unmodulated [ˈʌnˈmɔdjuleitid], *ag.* non modulato.

unmoistened [ˈʌnˈmɔisnd], *ag.* non inumidito; secco.

unmolested [ˈʌnmouˈlestid], *ag.* non molestato; indisturbato.

unmoneyed [ˈʌnˈmʌnid], *ag.* privo di denaro.

to **unmoor** [ˈʌnˈmuə*], *v.t.* (*mar.*) **1.** disormeggiare, togliere gli ormeggi a **2.** disafforcare.

unmoral [ˈʌnˈmɔrəl], *ag.* amorale.

unmorality [ˈʌnməˈræliti], *s.* amoralità.

unmortgaged [ˈʌnˈmɔːgidʒd], *ag.* (*comm.*) non ipotecato, libero da ipoteca.

unmotherly [ˈʌnˈmʌðəli], *ag.* indegno di una madre, poco materno.

to **unmould** [ˈʌnˈmould], *v.t.* sformare; cambiare la forma a.

unmoulded [ˈʌnˈmouldid], *ag.* non modellato, sformato.

to **unmount** [ˈʌnˈmaunt], *v.t.i.* smontare.

unmounted [ˈʌnˈmauntid], *ag.* **1.** non montato (di fotografia, ecc.); non incastonato (di gemma, ecc.) **2.** non a cavallo; a piedi (di soldato).

unmourned [ˈʌnˈmɔːnd], *ag.* non pianto, non compianto: *to die —*, morire illacrimato, incompianto.

unmov(e)able [ˈʌnˈmuːvəbl], *ag.* **1.** saldo, che non può essere mosso **2.** che non si commuove.

unmov(e)ably [ˈʌnˈmuːvəbli], *av.* saldamente.

unmoved [ˈʌnˈmuːvd], *ag.* **1.** non rimosso; fisso, immobile: *we found everything* —, trovammo ogni cosa al suo posto **2.** impassabile, insensibile; inflessibile: *he remained — by all entreaties*, rimase insensibile a tutte le preghiere; *to hear sthg.* —, ascoltare ql.co. senza alcuna emozione.

unmoving [ˈʌnˈmuːviŋ], *ag.* non commovente, che non commuove.

unmown [ˈʌnˈmoun], *ag.* non mietuto.

to **unmuffle** [ˈʌnˈmʌfl], *v.t.i.* scoprire, scoprirsi; liberare dai ripari, dagli impedimenti.

unmunitioned [ˈʌnmju(ː)ˈnifənd], *ag.* sprovvisto di munizioni.

unmurmuring [ˈʌnˈməːməriŋ], *ag.* **1.** che non mormora, non sussurra **2.** che non si lagna, non borbotta.

unmurmuringly [ˈʌnˈməːməriŋli], *av.* **1.** senza mormorare **2.** senza lagnarsi.

unmusical [ˈʌnˈmjuːzikəl], *ag.* **1.** non armonioso (di suono) **2.** non musicale (di orecchio) **3.** che non ama la musica.

unmusically [ˈʌnˈmjuːzikəli], *av.* senza armonia.

unmutilated [ˈʌnˈmjuːtileitid], *ag.* non mutilato.

to **unmuzzle** [ˈʌnˈmʌzl], *v.t.* **1.** togliere la museruola a **2.** *fig.* liberare, dare libero sfogo a.

unmuzzled [ˈʌnˈmʌzld], *ag.* privo di museruola; *fig.* libero di parlare: *the Press is — at last*, la stampa è finalmente libera.

to **unnail** [ˈʌnˈneil], *v.t.* schiodare, sbullettare.

unnamed [ˈʌnˈneimd], *ag.* **1.** innominato, non nominato **2.** senza nome; anonimo.

unnatural [ʌnˈnætʃrəl], *ag.* **1.** innaturale, non naturale; artificiale; *he is rather stiff and* —, è piuttosto rigido e artificioso **2.** contro natura, anormale; disumano; mostruoso: *a mother cruel to her children is* —, una madre crudele coi propri figli è contro natura.

to **unnaturalize** [ˈʌnˈnætʃrəlaiz], *v.t.* **1.** rendere innaturale, artificiale **2.** snaturare; disumanare.

unnaturally [ʌnˈnætʃrəli], *av.* **1.** in modo poco naturale; artificialmente **2.** disumanamente, snaturatamente.

unnaturalness [ʌnˈnætʃrəlnis], *s.* **1.** mancanza di naturalezza; artificiosità **2.** snaturatezza; disumanazione.

unnavigable [ˈʌnˈnævigəbl], *ag.* non navigabile.

unnavigated [ˈʌnˈnævigeitid], *ag.* non (ancora) navigato: *— river*, fiume su cui non si è ancora navigato.

unnecessaries [ˈʌnˈnesisəriz], *s.pl.* cose inutili.

unnecessarily [ʌnˈnesisərili], *av.* senza necessità, inutilmente: *to be — fussy*, agitarsi inutilmente.

unnecessariness [ʌnˈnesisərinis], *s.* inutilità.

unnecessary [ʌnˈnesisəri], *ag.* non necessario, inutile; superfluo: *to do without — things*, far a meno del superfluo.

unnecessitated [ˈʌnniˈsesiteitid], *ag.* non richiesto dalle necessità.

unneeded [ˈʌnˈniːdid], *ag.* non necessario, inutile.

unnegotiable [ˈʌnniˈgoufjəbl], *ag.* (*comm.*) non negoziabile; non commerciabile.

unneighbourly [ˈʌnˈneibəli], *ag.* non amichevole, da cattivo vicino: *to behave in an — manner*, comportarsi scortesemente.

unneighbourly, *av.* in modo poco amichevole, scortesemente.

to **unnerve** [ˈʌnˈnəːv], *v.t.* snervare; indebolire, fiaccare.

unnoted [ˈʌnˈnoutid], *ag.* inosservato, non notato.

unnoticeable [ˈʌnˈnoutisəbl], *ag.* che passa inosservato, impercettibile.

unnoticed [ˈʌnˈnoutist], *ag.* inosservato.

unnumbered [ˈʌnˈnʌmbəd], *ag.* **1.** non numerato **2.** innumerevole.

unnurtured [ˈʌnˈnəːtʃəd], *ag.* **1.** non nutrito **2.** non educato.

unobjectionable [ˈʌnəbˈdʒekʃnəbl], *ag.* ineccepibile, irreprensibile.

unobjectionableness [ˈʌnəbˈdʒekʃnəblnis], *s.* ineccepibilità, irreprensibilità.

unobjectionably [ˈʌnəbˈdʒekʃnəbli], *av.* irreprensibilmente, ineccepibilmente.

unobliging [ˈʌnəˈblaidʒiŋ], *ag.* poco compiacente, non servizievole, poco gentile.

unobnoxious [ˈʌnəbˈnɔkʃəs], *ag.* **1.** non sgradevole; non molesto **2.** (*dir.*) irresponsabile **3.** non ossequiente (ad una autorità).

unobscured [ˈʌnəbˈskjuəd], *ag.* non oscurato.

unobservable [ˈʌnəbˈzəːvəbl], *ag.* inosservabile; non percepibile, impercettibile.

unobservance [ˈʌnəbˈzəːvəns], *s.* **1.** inosservanza **2.** disattenzione.

unobservant [ˈʌnəbˈzəːvənt], *ag.* **1.** inosservante **2.** disattento, distratto.

unobserved [ˈʌnəbˈzəːvd], *ag.* inosservato.

unobserving [ˈʌnəbˈzəːviŋ], *ag.* **1.** disattento; trascurato **2.** inosservante.

unobstructed [ˈʌnəbˈstrʌktid], *ag.* non ostruito, non impedito; libero.

unobtainable [ˈʌnəbˈteinəbl], *ag.* non ottenibile, irraggiungibile.

unobtained [ˈʌnəbˈteind], *ag.* non ottenuto.

unobtrusive [ˈʌnəbˈtruːsiv], *ag.* non importuno; discreto; modesto; riservato: *— watch*, sorveglianza discreta.

unobtrusively [ˈʌnəbˈtruːsivli], *av.* con discrezione; modestamente; riservatamente.

unobtrusiveness [ˈʌnəbˈtruːsivnis], *s.* discrezione; riserbo; modestia.

unobvious [ˈʌnˈɔbviəs], *ag.* non evidente, non manifesto.

unoccupied [ˈʌnˈɔkjupaid], *ag.* **1.** disoccupato; libero; vacante, vuoto **2.** ozioso: — *life*, vita oziosa.

unoffended [ˈʌnəˈfendid], *ag.* non offeso.

unoffending [ˈʌnəˈfendiŋ], *ag.* inoffensivo, innocuo; innocente.

unoffensive [ˈʌnəˈfensiv], *ag.* inoffensivo, innocuo.

unoffered [ˈʌnˈɔfəd], *ag.* non offerto.

unofficial [ˈʌnəˈfiʃəl], *ag.* non ufficiale, ufficioso, non confermato.

unofficially [ˈʌnəˈfiʃəli], *av.* ufficiosamente.

unopened [ˈʌnˈoupənd], *ag.* chiuso, non aperto, non dissuggellato.

unopening [ˈʌnˈoupniŋ], *ag.* che non (si) apre.

unopposed [ˈʌnəˈpouzd], *ag.* senza opposizione, incontrastato: *to be* —, non incontrare opposizione.

unoppressive [ˈʌnəˈpresiv], *ag.* non oppressivo.

unoppressively [ˈʌnəˈpresivli], *av.* in modo non oppressivo.

unordained [ˈʌnɔːˈdeind], *ag.* **1.** (*eccl.*) non ordinato; non designato **2.** non decretato.

unordered [ˈʌnˈɔːdəd], *ag.* **1.** non ordinato, non comandato **2.** non messo in ordine, disordinato.

unorderly [ˈʌnˈɔːdəli], *av.* disordinatamente.

unorganized [ˈʌnˈɔːgənaizd], *ag.* non organizzato, disorganizzato.

unoriginal [ˈʌnəˈridʒənl], *ag.* non originale.

unornamental [ˈʌnˌɔːnəˈmentl], *ag.* non ornamentale.

unornamented [ˈʌnˈɔːnəmentid], *ag.* senza ornamenti; semplice.

unorthodox [ˈʌnˈɔːθədɔks], *ag.* non ortodosso.

unostentatious [ˈʌnˌɔstenˈteiʃəs], *ag.* modesto, non vistoso.

unostentatiously [ˈʌnˌɔstenˈteiʃəsli], *av.* senza ostentazione, modestamente.

unostentatiousness [ˈʌnˌɔstenˈteiʃəsnis], *s.* modestia, mancanza di ostentazione.

unowned [ˈʌnˈound], *ag.* **1.** non posseduto; senza possessore **2.** non riconosciuto; sconfessato.

unoxygenated [ˈʌnˈɔkˈsidʒineitid], *ag.* non ossigenato.

unpacified [ˈʌnˈpæsifaid], *ag.* non pacificato.

to **unpack** [ˈʌnˈpæk], *v.t.i.* **1.** disfare (le valige) **2.** togliere da; disimballare.

unpacked ['ʌn'pækt], *ag.* **1.** non imballato; non impacchettato **2.** sballato, tolto dalla balla.

unpaid ['ʌn'peid], *ag.* non pagato, non saldato ‖ *the (Great) Unpaid*, *(letter.)* i giudici di pace.

unpainful ['ʌn'peinful], *ag.* non doloroso.

to **unpaint** ['ʌn'peint], *v.t.* togliere, cassare la pittura, la vernice da.

unpainted ['ʌn'peintid], *ag.* non dipinto; non imbellettato.

unpaired ['ʌn'pɛəd], *ag.* spaiato, non accoppiato.

unpalatable ['ʌn'pælətəbl], *ag.* **1.** di gusto sgradevole **2.** *fig.* spiacevole.

to **unparadise** ['ʌn'pærədais], *v.t.* **1.** espellere dal Paradiso **2.** privare di una felicità suprema.

unparelleled [ʌn'pærəleld], *ag.* senza pari, impareggiabile, incomparabile.

unpardonable [ʌn'pɑ:dŋəbl], *ag.* imperdonabile.

unpardonableness [ʌn'pɑ:dŋəblnis], *s.* imperdonabilità.

unpardonably [ʌn'pɑ:dŋəbli], *av.* imperdonabilmente.

unparliamentary ['ʌn,pɑ:lə'mentəri], *ag.* non parlamentare; contrario al sistema parlamentare.

unparted ['ʌn'pɑ:tid], *ag.* indiviso, non separato.

unpassionate ['ʌn'pæʃənit], *ag.* **1.** senza passioni **2.** spassionato, imparziale.

unpatented ['ʌn'peitəntid], *ag.* non brevettato.

unpathed ['ʌn'pɑ:θt], *ag.* senza sentieri.

unpathetic ['ʌnpə'θetik], *ag.* non patetico.

unpatriotic ['ʌn,pætri'ɔtik], *ag.* non patriottico, poco patriottico.

unpatriotically ['ʌn,pætri'ɔtikəli], *av.* in modo non patriottico.

unpatronized ['ʌn'pætrənaizd], *ag.* **1.** senza protettore; senza protezione **2.** senza clientela abituale.

unpatterned ['ʌn'pætənd], *ag.* **1.** non decorato con disegni **2.** *(arc.)* ineguagliato; senza precedenti.

unpaved ['ʌn'peivd], *ag.* non selciato, non lastricato.

unpawned ['ʌn'pɔ:nd], *ag.* non impegnato, non pignorato.

unpeaceable ['ʌn'pi:səbl], **unpeaceful** ['ʌn'pi:sful], *ag.* agitato, senza pace; litigioso: — *world*, mondo senza pace.

unpedantic ['ʌnpi'dæntik], *ag.* non pedantesco.

unpedigreed ['ʌn'pedigri:d], *ag.* senza « pedigree », bastardo (di animale).

unpeeled ['ʌn'pi:ld], *ag.* non pelato, non sbucciato.

unpeerable ['ʌn'piərəbl], *ag.* impareggiabile.

unpeered ['ʌn'piəd], *ag.* ineguagliato.

to **unpeg** ['ʌn'peg], *pass.p.p.* **unpegged** ['ʌn'pegd], *v.t.* togliere le caviglie, i piuoli da.

to **unpen** ['ʌn'pen], *pass.p.p.* **unpenned** ['ʌn'pend], *v.t.* far uscire dal chiuso, dall'ovile.

unpensioned ['ʌn'penʃənd], *ag.* senza pensione.

to **unpeople** ['ʌn'pi:pl], *v.t.* spopolare.

unperceivable ['ʌnpə'si:vəbl], *ag.* impercettibile.

unperceived ['ʌnpə'si:vd], *ag.* non percepito, anavvertito.

unperfect ['ʌn'pə:fikt], *ag.* imperfetto; difettoso.

unperfected ['ʌn-pə'fektid], *ag.* non perfezionato.

unperformed ['ʌn-pə'fɔ:md], *ag.* **1.** ineseguito, non fatto **2.** *(teat.)* non rappresentato.

unperishable ['ʌn'periʃəbl], *ag.* **1.** duraturo, imperituro **2.** non deperibile, che non si deteriora.

unperishing ['ʌn'periʃiŋ], *ag.* imperituro.

unperjured ['ʌn'pə:dʒəd], *ag.* non spergiuro.

unpermitted ['ʌn-pə'mitid], *ag.* non permesso, non concesso.

unperplexed ['ʌn-pə'plekst], *ag.* **1.** non perplesso; non incerto, deciso **2.** non complicato, non involuto.

unpersuadable ['ʌn-pə'sweidəbl], *ag.* impersuadibile.

unpersuaded ['ʌn-pə'sweidid], *ag.* non persuaso.

unpersuasive ['ʌn-pə'sweisiv], *ag.* non persuasivo, poco convincente.

unperturbed ['ʌn-pə(:)'tə:bd], *ag.* imperturbato; impassibile; calmo, sereno.

unperturbedness ['ʌn-pə(:)'tə:bidnis], *s.* imperturbabilità; calma.

unperverted ['ʌn-pə(:)'və:tid], *ag.* non pervertito.

unphilosophic(al) ['ʌn,filə'sɔfik(əl)], *ag.* non filosofico, poco filosofico.

unphilosophically ['ʌn,filə'sɔfikəli], *av.* non filosoficamente; in modo poco filosofico.

unphilosophicalness ['ʌn,filə'sɔfikəlnis], *s.* mancanza di carattere filosofico.

to **unpick** ['ʌn'pik], *v.t.* scucire.

unpickable ['ʌn'pikəbl], *ag.* a prova di scasso.

unpicked[1] ['ʌn'pikt], *ag.* **1.** non scelto **2.** non raccolto: *the fruit was still* —, la frutta non era ancora stata raccolta.

unpicked[2], *ag.* non cernito (di lana).

unpierced ['ʌn'piəst], *ag.* non forato, non bucato.

unpillowed ['ʌn'piloud], *ag.* senza guanciale.

unpiloted ['ʌn'pailətid], *ag.* senza pilota; *fig.* senza guida.

to **unpin** ['ʌn'pin], *pass.p.p.* **unpinned** ['ʌn'pind], *v.t.* togliere gli spilli a, spuntare; togliere i cavicchi da.

unpiteous ['ʌn'pitiəs], *ag.* *(arc.)* spietato, crudele.

unpiteously ['ʌn'pitiəsli], *av.* *(arc.)* spietatamente.

unpitied ['ʌn'pitid], *ag.* non compianto, non commiserato.

unpitiful ['ʌn'pitiful], *ag.* che non ha pietà, che non ha compassione; spietato.

unpitifully ['ʌn'pitifuli], *av.* senza pietà, senza compassione; spietatamente.

unpitying [ʌn'pitiiŋ], *ag.* che non ha pietà, che non ha compassione; spietato.

unpityingly ['ʌn'pitiiŋli], *av.* senza pietà, senza compassione; spietatamente.

unplaced ['ʌn'pleist], *ag.* **1.** privo di posto; non messo a posto **2.** privo d'impiego (di persona) **3.** *(ippica)* non piazzato.

unplagued ['ʌn'pleigd], *ag.* non tormentato.

to **unplait** ['ʌn'plæt], *v.t.* disfare, sciogliere trecce (di capelli, ecc.).

unplanted ['ʌn'plɑ:ntid], *ag.* **1.** non piantato, non coltivato **2.** disboscato; privato di ogni vegetazione.

unplausible ['ʌn'plɔ:zəbl], *ag.* poco plausibile, poco convincente.

unplausibly ['ʌn'plɔ:zəbli], *av.* in modo poco plausibile, poco convincente.

unplayable ['ʌn'pleiəbl], *ag.* **1.** che non si può giocare (di partita, ecc.) **2.** non rappresentabile (di lavoro teatrale) **3.** ineseguibile (di musica).

unpleadable ['ʌn'pli:dəbl], *ag.* che non può essere difeso.

unpleaded ['ʌn'pli:did], *ag.* non difeso.

unpleasant [ʌn'pleznt], *ag.* spiacevole; sgradevole: *an* — *sight*, una vista spiacevole; *an* — *voice*, una voce sgradevole; — *weather*, brutto tempo.

unpleasantly [ʌn'plezntli], *av.* spiacevolmente; sgradevolmente.

unpleasantness [ʌn'plezntnis], *s.* **1.** spiacevolezza; carattere sgradevole: *you can imagine the* — *of my position*, puoi immaginare quanto fosse spiacevole la mia situazione **2.** dissenso, disaccordo: *we have had a slight* — *with our landlady*, abbiamo avuto una piccola discussione con la padrona di casa ‖ *the late* —, *(amer. scherz.)* la guerra di Secessione.

unpleased ['ʌn'pli:zd], *ag.* scontento; insoddisfatto.

unpleasing ['ʌn'pli:ziŋ], *ag.* spiacevole; sgradevole.

unpledged ['ʌn'pledʒd], *ag.* non impegnato; libero: *to be* — *to any party*, non appartenere ad alcun partito.

unpliable ['ʌn'plaiəbl], **unpliant** ['ʌn'plaiənt], *ag.* poco arrendevole; poco compiacente; inflessibile.

unploughed ['ʌn'plaud], *ag.* **1.** inarato, incolto (di terreno) **2.** non rifilato (di orlo di libro).

unplucked ['ʌn'plʌkt], *ag.* **1.** non colto, non raccolto (di fiore, ecc.) **2.** non spennato (di pollame).

to **unplumb** [ˌʌn'plʌm], *v.t.* spiombare, levare il piombo a.

unplumbed [ˌʌn'plʌmd], *ag.* 1. spiombato; privo di piombatura 2. non scandagliato; inesplorato (anche *fig.*): — *depths*, (*letter.*) profondità inesplorate.

to **unplume** [ˌʌn'plu:m], *v.t.* privare delle piume; *fig.* spennare.

unplundered [ˌʌn'plʌndəd], *ag.* non saccheggiato.

unpoetic(al) [ˌʌn-pou'etik(əl)], *ag.* poco poetico.

unpoetically [ˌʌn-pou'etikəli], *av.* senza poesia, non poeticamente; prosaicamente.

unpoeticalness [ˌʌn-pou'etikəlnis], *s.* mancanza di poesia; prosaicità.

unpointed [ˌʌn'pointid], *ag.* 1. senza punteggiatura; (*filologia*) senza segni diacritici 2. spuntato, smussato.

unpoised [ˌʌn'poizd], *ag.* non equilibrato.

to **unpoison** [ˌʌn'poizn], *v.t.* svelenare, liberare dal veleno.

unpolarized [ˌʌn'pouləraizd], *ag.* non polarizzato (di luce, ecc.).

unpolished [ˌʌn'poliʃt], *ag.* 1. non pulito; non lucidato 2. non levigato, grezzo 3. *fig.* grossolano, rozzo: — *style*, stile rozzo.

unpolite [ˌʌn-pə'lait], *ag.* rozzo; villano; screanzato.

unpolitely [ˌʌn-pə'laitli], *av.* rozzamente; villanamente; screanzatamente.

unpoliteness [ˌʌn-pə'laitnis], *s.* rozzezza, villania.

unpolitic(al) [ˌʌn'politik(əl)], *ag.* non politico, impolitico.

unpolled [ˌʌn'pould], *ag.* 1. che non ha votato: *an — elector*, elettore che non ha votato 2. non registrato, non ottenuto (di voto).

unpolluted [ˌʌn-pə'lu:tid], *ag.* incontaminato; puro.

unpopular [ˌʌn'popjulə*], *ag.* impopolare ‖ *to make oneself — with everybody*, farsi malvolere da tutti.

unpopularity [ˌʌn,popju'læriti], *s.* impopolarità.

unpopularly [ˌʌn'popjuləli], *av.* impopolarmente.

unportable [ˌʌn'po:təbl], *ag.* (*arc.*) non portabile.

unportioned [ˌʌn'po:ʃənd], *ag.* senza dote.

unpossessed [ˌʌn-pə'zest], *ag.* 1. non posseduto 2. che non possiede.

unpotable [ˌʌn'poutəbl], *ag.* non potabile.

unpractical [ˌʌn'præktikəl], *ag.* 1. non pratico 2. inattuabile (di progetto, ecc.).

unpracticality [ˌʌn,prækti'kæliti], *s.* mancanza di praticità.

unpractically [ˌʌn'præktikəli], *av.* in modo non pratico.

unpractised [ˌʌn'præktist], *ag.* inesperto; novellino: — *in business*, privo di esperienza negli affari.

unpraised [ˌʌn'preizd], *ag.* non lodato.

unprecarious [ˌʌn-pri'kɛəriəs], *ag.* non precario, sicuro; stabile, duraturo.

unpreceded [ˌʌn-pri(:)'si:did], *ag.* non preceduto.

unprecedented [ˌʌn'presidəntid], *ag.* senza precedenti.

unprecedentedly [ˌʌn'presidəntidli], *av.* senza precedenti.

unprecise [ˌʌn-pri'sais], *ag.* impreciso, inesatto.

unpredestined [ˌʌn-pri(:)'destind], *ag.* non predestinato.

unprejudiced [ˌʌn'predʒudist], *ag.* 1. spregiudicato, senza prevenzioni 2. imparziale.

unpremeditated [ˌʌn pri'mediteitid], *ag.* impremeditato.

unpremeditatedly [ˌʌn-pri'mediteitidli], *av.* senza premeditazione.

unpremeditatedness [ˌʌn-pri'mediteitidnis], *s.* mancanza di premeditazione.

unprepared [ˌʌn-pri'pɛəd], *ag.* impreparato; senza preparazione: — *speech*, discorso improvvisato ‖ *to catch s.o. —*, prendere qlcu. alla sprovvista ☆ — *translation*, traduzione estemporanea.

unpreparedly [ˌʌn-pri'pɛəridli], *av.* senza preparazione.

unpreparedness [ˌʌn-pri'pɛəridnis], *s.* impreparazione.

unprepossessed [ˌʌn,pri:pə'zest], *ag.* 1. non posseduto precedentemente 2. senza prevenzioni, spregiudicato.

unprepossessing [ˌʌn,pri:pə'zesiŋ], *ag.* senza attrattive; antipatico; che predispone sfavorevomente.

unprescribed [ˌʌn-pris'kraibd], *ag.* non prescritto.

unpresentable [ˌʌn-pri'zentəbl], *ag.* impresentabile: *not —*, passabile.

unpresuming [ˌʌn-pri'zju:miŋ], **unpresumptuous** [ˌʌn-pri'zʌmptjuəs], *ag.* modesto, senza presunzione.

unpretending [ˌʌn-pri'tendiŋ], *ag.* modesto, semplice, senza pretese.

unpretendingly [ˌʌn-pri'tendiŋli], *av.* modestamente, semplicemente, senza pretese.

unpretentious [ˌʌn-pri'tenʃəs], *ag.* modesto, semplice, senza pretese.

unpretentiously [ˌʌn-pri'tenʃəsli], *av.* modestamente, semplicemente, senza pretese.

unpretentiousness [ˌʌn-pri'tenʃəsnis], *s.* modestia, semplicità, mancanza di pretese.

unprevailing [ˌʌn-pri'veiliŋ], *ag.* inefficace, senza forza.

unpreventable [ˌʌn-pri'ventəbl], *ag.* che non si può impedire, inevitabile.

unprevented [ˌʌn-pri'ventid], *ag.* non impedito; non evitato.

unpriced [ʌn'praist], *ag.* 1. senza indicazione di prezzo 2. senza prezzo, inestimabile.

unpriestly [ʌn'pri:stli], *ag.* che non si addice a un prete.

unprincely [ʌn'prinsli], *ag.* che non si addice a un principe.

unprincipled [ʌn'prinsəpld], *ag.* senza principi, amorale: — *conduct*, condotta senza scrupoli.

unprintable [ʌn'printəbl], *ag.* non adatto ad essere stampato; non pubblicabile (perchè osceno).

unprinted [ʌn'printid], *ag.* non stampato; esistente solo in manoscritto.

to **unprison** [ʌn'prizn], *v.t.* liberare dalla prigione.

unprivileged [ʌn'privilidʒd], *ag.* senza privilegi.

unprized [ʌn'praizd], *ag.* non apprezzato.

unproclaimed [ʌn-prə'kleimd], *ag.* non proclamato; non reso noto pubblicamente.

unprocurable [ʌn-prə'kjuərəbl], *ag.* non procurabile.

unproductive [ʌn-prə'dʌktiv], *ag.* improduttivo; sterile: — *capital*, (*comm.*) capitale infruttifero; — *land*, terreno sterile; *the remedy was — of any improvement*, il rimedio non sortì alcun effetto.

unproductively [ʌn-prə'dʌktivli], *av.* improduttivamente; sterilmente.

unproductiveness [ʌn-prə'dʌktivnis], *s.* improduttività; sterilità.

unprofaned [ʌn-prə'feind], *ag.* non profanato; non violato.

unprofessional [ʌn-prə'feʃənl], *ag.* 1. non professionale: — *conduct*, scorrettezza professionale, condotta contraria agli usi della professione 2. non professionista: — *medical man*, medicastro 3. (*spor.*) dilettante.

unprofessionally [ʌn-prə'feʃnəli], *av.* in modo non professionale.

unprofitable [ʌn'profitəbl], *ag.* poco vantaggioso; inutile, vano.

unprofitableness [ʌn'profitəblnis], *s.* inutilità, infruttuosità.

unprofitably [ʌn'profitəbli], *av.* inutilmente, senza profitto.

unprogressive [ʌn-prə'gresiv], *ag.* retrogrado; conservatore (anche *pol.*).

unprohibited [ʌn-prə'hibitid], *ag.* non proibito; lecito.

unprojected [ʌn-prə'dʒektid], *ag.* 1. non progettato 2. che non sporge.

unprolific [ʌn-prə'lifik], *ag.* sterile, infecondo.

unpromised [ʌn'promist], *ag.* non promesso.

unpromising [ˈʌnˈprɔmisiŋ], *ag.* non promettente: *the weather looked —*, il tempo non prometteva niente di buono.

unprompted [ˈʌnˈprɔmptid], *ag.* spontaneo: *to say sthg. —*, dire ql.co. spontaneamente, senza farsi pregare.

unpronounceable [ˈʌn-prəˈnaunsəbl], *ag.* impronunciabile.

unpronounced [ˈʌn-prəˈnaunst], *ag.* non pronunciato.

to **unprop** [ˈʌnˈprɔp], *pass.p.p.* **unpropped** [ˈʌnˈprɔpt], *v.t.* togliere il sostegno a.

unprophetic [ˈʌn-prəˈfetik], *ag.* non profetico.

unpropitious [ˈʌn-prəˈpiʃəs], *ag.* non propizio, sfavorevole; sinistro; infausto.

unpropitiously [ˈʌn-prəˈpiʃəsli], *av.* sfavorevolmente; sinistramente, infaustamente.

unpropitiousness [ˈʌn-prəˈpiʃəsnis], *s.* sfavore; l'essere non propizio, infausto, sinistro.

unproportionate [ˈʌn-prəˈpɔːʃnit], *ag.* sproporzionato.

unproportioned [ˈʌn-prəˈpɔːʃənd], *ag.* non proporzionato.

unproposed [ˈʌn-prəˈpouzd], *ag.* non proposto.

unprosperous [ˈʌnˈprɔspərəs], *ag.* **1.** non prospero; poco fiorente: *— trade*, commercio poco fiorente **2.** poco propizio; sfavorevole: *— winds*, venti sfavorevoli.

unprosperously [ˈʌnˈprɔspərəsli], *av.* senza successo.

unprosperousness [ˈʌnˈprɔspərəsnis], *s.* **1.** mancanza di prosperità **2.** sfavore; mancanza di successo.

unprotected [ˈʌnprəˈtektid], *ag.* non protetto, senza protezione.

to **unprotestantize** [ˈʌnˈprɔtistəntaiz], *v.t.* togliere il carattere protestante a.

unprovable [ˈʌnˈpruːvəbl], *ag.* che non si può provare, indimostrabile.

unprovided [ˈʌn-prəˈvaidid], *ag.* **1.** sfornito, sprovvisto: *to be — with*, essere sprovvisto di **2.** impreparato: *if they die —*, se muoiono impreparati **3.** imprevisto: *the — expenses of the year*, le spese impreviste dell'annata; *contingencies — for*, casi imprevisti.

unprovoked [ˈʌn-prəˈvoukt], *ag.* non provocato: *— abuse*, insulti immeritati, ingiustificati ‖ *to remain —*, mantenere la calma, non prendersela.

unpruned [ˈʌnˈpruːnd], *ag.* non potato.

unpublished [ˈʌnˈpʌbliʃt], *ag.* **1.** inedito, non pubblicato **2.** non reso pubblico.

unpunctual [ˈʌnˈpʌŋktjuəl], *ag.* non puntuale, in ritardo.

unpunctuality [ˈʌnˌpʌŋktjuˈæliti], *s.* mancanza di puntualità.

unpunctually [ˈʌnˈpʌŋktjuəli], *av.* in ritardo.

unpunctuated [ˈʌnˈpʌŋktjueitid], *ag.* non punteggiato, senza punteggiatura.

unpunishable [ˈʌnˈpʌniʃəbl], *ag.* impunibile.

unpunished [ˈʌnˈpʌniʃt], *ag.* impunito.

unpurchasable [ˈʌnˈpəːtʃəsəbl], *ag.* non acquistabile.

unpurchased [ˈʌnˈpəːtʃəst], *ag.* non comprato.

unpure [ˈʌnˈpjuə*], *ag.* impuro.

unpurged [ˈʌnˈpəːdʒd], *ag. fig.* non purgato.

unpurified [ˈʌnˈpjuərifaid], *ag.* non purificato.

unpurposed [ˈʌnˈpəːpəst], *ag.* non intenzionale.

unpursued [ˈʌnpəˈsjuːd], *ag.* **1.** non inseguito **2.** non perseguito.

unputrefied [ˈʌnˈpjuːtrifaid], *ag.* non putrefatto.

unquailing [ˈʌnˈkweiliŋ], *ag.* che non (si) scoraggia; fermo, risoluto.

unqualified [ˈʌnˈkwɔlifaid], *ag.* **1.** incompetente; incapace, inabile: *— to do sthg.*, incompetente a fare ql.co. **2.** non qualificato; non abilitato; non autorizzato (di medico, ecc.): *— to vote*, privo dei diritti di voto **3.** assoluto, categorico: *— denial*, diniego categorico; *— praise*, elogio senza riserve.

to **unqualify** [ˈʌnˈkwɔlifai], *v.t.* **1.** inabilitare **2.** squalificare.

to **unqueen** [ˈʌnˈkwiːn], *v.t.* detronizzare (una regina).

unquenchable [ʌnˈkwentʃəbl], *ag.* inestinguibile; insaziabile (anche *fig.*).

unquenched [ˈʌnˈkwentʃt], *ag.* inestinto; insaziato (anche *fig.*).

unquestionable [ʌnˈkwestʃənəbl], *ag.* **1.** incontestabile; indiscutibile; indubitabile: *— evidence*, evidenza incontestabile **2.** (*rar.*) contrario ad essere interrogato.

unquestionableness [ʌnˈkwestʃənəblnis], *s.* incontestabilità; indiscutibiltà.

unquestionably [ʌnˈkwestʃənəbli], *av.* indiscutibilmente; incontestabilmente.

unquestioned [ʌnˈkwestʃənd], *ag.* **1.** indiscusso; incontestato **2.** non esaminato.

unquestioning [ʌnˈkwestʃəniŋ], *ag.* che non fa domande: *— obedience*, obbedienza cieca.

unquestioningly [ʌnˈkwestʃəniŋli], *av.* ciecamente, senza fare domande.

unquickened [ˈʌnˈkwikənd], *ag.* **1.** non ravvivato; non rinvigorito **2.** non accelerato.

unquiet [ˈʌnˈkwaiət], *ag.* inquieto, agitato; irrequieto: *— soul*, anima inquieta; *— times*, tempi agitati.

unquietly [ˈʌnˈkwaiətli], *av.* inquietamente; irrequietamente.

unquietness [ˈʌnˈkwaiətnis], *s.* inquietudine; irrequietezza.

unraised [ˈʌnˈreizd], *ag.* **1.** non alzato, non sollevato **2.** *fig.* non elevato.

unransomed [ˈʌnˈrænsəmd], *ag.* non riscattato.

unravaged [ˈʌnˈrævidʒd], *ag.* non devastato.

to **unravel** [ˈʌnˈrævəl], *pass.p.p.* **unravelled** [ʌnˈrævəld], *v.t.i.* **1.** districare, districarsi; sbrogliare, sciogliere; disfare, disfarsi (di corda, nodo, tessuto, ecc.); dipanare **2.** *fig.* districare, districarsi; chiarire, chiarirsi: *to — a situation*, mettere in chiaro una situazione.

unravelling [ʌnˈrævliŋ], *s.* **1.** scioglimento, districamento **2.** (*teat.*) scioglimento (dell'azione).

unravelment [ʌnˈrævlmənt], *s.* scioglimento; districamento.

unravished [ˈʌnˈræviʃt], *ag.* inviolato.

unrazored [ˈʌnˈreizəd], *ag.* non raso, non sbarbato.

unreached [ˈʌnˈriːtʃt], *ag.* non raggiunto.

unread [ˈʌnˈred], *ag.* **1.** non letto; senza lettori (di libro) **2.** illetterato, ignorante.

unreadable [ˈʌnˈriːdəbl], *ag.* **1.** noioso, spiacevole a leggersi **2.** illeggibile, non chiaro (di scrittura).

unreadily [ˈʌnˈredili], *av.* senza prontezza; lentamente.

unready [ˈʌnˈredi], *ag.* **1.** impreparato: *to be — for sthg.*, essere impreparato a ql.co., non essere pronto a ql.co.; *to be — to do sthg.*, non essere pronto a fare ql.co., non essere disposto a fare ql.co. **2.** tardo, lento; irresoluto **3.** (*arc.*) non vestito, in abito succinto.

unreal [ˈʌnˈriəl], *ag.* **1.** irreale, illusorio, immaginario **2.** menzognero.

unreality [ˈʌnriˈæliti], *s.* **1.** irrealtà, carattere illusorio **2.** illusione, chimera.

unrealizable [ˈʌnˈriəlaizəbl], *ag.* irrealizzabile.

unrealized [ˈʌnˈriəlaizd], *ag.* **1.** non realizzato **2.** non capito, di cui non ci si è resi conto.

unreaped [ˈʌnˈriːpt], *ag.* non mietuto, non raccolto.

unreason [ˈʌnˈriːzn], *s.* **1.** irrazionalità; assurdità, sciocchezza **2.** (*arc.*) ingiustizia.

unreasonable [ʌnˈriːznəbl], *ag.* **1.** irragionevole; stravagante: *— demand*, richiesta assurda; *don't be —*, sii ragionevole **2.** assurdo, eccessivo.

unreasonableness [ʌnˈriːznəblnis], *s.* **1.** irragionevolezza; stravaganza **2.** assurdità; eccesso.

unreasonably [ʌnˈriːznəbli], *av.* in modo irragionevole.

unreasoned [ˈʌnˈriːznd], *ag.* non ragionato, non ponderato.

unreasoning [ʌnˈriːzniŋ], *ag.* che sragiona; irragionevole.

unrebuked [ˈʌnriˈbjuːkt], *ag.* non rimproverato; non biasimato.

unrecalled [ˈʌnriˈkɔːld], *ag.* non richiamato.

unreceipted [ˈʌnriˈsiːtid], *ag.* (*comm.*) senza ricevuta.

unreceived [ˈʌnriˈsiːvd], *ag.* non ricevuto.

unreciprocated [ˈʌnriˈsiprəkeitid], *ag.* non ricambiato.

unreckoned [ˈʌnˈrekənd], *ag.* non calcolato, non contato, non stimato.

unreclaimed [ˈʌnriˈkleimd], *ag.* **1.** non redento (di peccatore) **2.** non civilizzato (di selvaggio) **3.** incolto; non bonificato (di terreno).

unrecognizable [ˈʌnˈrekəgnaizəbl], *ag.* irriconoscibile.

unrecognized [ˈʌnˈrekəgnaizd], *ag.* non riconosciuto.

unrecommended [ˈʌnˌrekəˈmendid], *ag.* non raccomandato; senza raccomandazioni.

unrecompensed [ˈʌnˈrekəmpenst], *ag.* non ricompensato.

unreconcilable [ˈʌnˈrekənsailəbl], *ag.* irriconciliabile.

unreconciled [ˈʌnˈrekənsaild], *ag.* non riconciliato.

unrecorded [ˈʌnriˈkɔːdid], *ag.* **1.** non registrato; non segnalato **2.** non registrato (di musica).

unrecoverable [ˈʌnriˈkʌvərəbl], *ag.* **1.** irrecuperabile; senza rimedio **2.** inguaribile.

unrecovered [ˈʌnriˈkʌvəd], *ag.* non ricuperato.

unrectified [ˈʌnˈrektifaid], *ag.* **1.** non rettificato; non corretto **2.** (*elett. rad.*) non raddrizzato.

unredeemed [ˈʌnriˈdiːmd], *ag.* **1.** irredento **2.** non compensato, non controbilanciato **3.** (*comm.*) non disimpegnato, non estinto, non riscattato, non ammortizzato.

unreduced [ˈʌnriˈdjuːst], *ag.* non ridotto.

unreducible [ˈʌnriˈdjuːsəbl], *ag.* irriducibile.

to **unreel** [ˈʌnˈriːl], *v.t.i.* svolgere, svolgersi (di rotolo, ecc.).

unrefined [ˈʌnriˈfaind], *ag.* **1.** non raffinato; grezzo; impuro (di metallo, ecc.): — *sugar*, zucchero non raffinato **2.** *fig.* poco raffinato, grossolano; volgare.

unreflecting [ˈʌnriˈflektiŋ], *ag.* irriflessivo.

unreformable [ˈʌnriˈfɔːməbl], *ag.* irriformabile.

unreformed [ˈʌnriˈfɔːmd], *ag.* non riformato; non corretto ☆ — *characters*, gli incorreggibili.

unrefracted [ˈʌnriˈfræktid], *ag.* (*ott.*) non rifratto.

unrefreshed [ˈʌnriˈfreʃt], *ag.* **1.** non rinfrescato **2.** non ristorato; non riposato: *to awake* —, svegliarsi poco riposato.

unrefreshing [ˈʌnriˈfreʃiŋ], *ag.* **1.** che non rinfresca **2.** che non ristora, che non riposa.

unrefuted [ˈʌnriˈfjuːtid], *ag.* inconfutato.

unregarded [ˈʌnriˈgɑːdid], *ag.* trascurato, negletto.

unregardful [ˈʌnriˈgɑːdful], *ag.* **1.** incurante, negligente: — *of sthg.*, incurante di ql.co. **2.** irrispettoso.

unregenerate [ˈʌnriˈdʒenərit], *ag.* **1.** non rigenerato **2.** (*teol.*) non redento.

unregretful [ˈʌnriˈgretful], *ag.* che non ha rimpianti.

unregretted [ˈʌnriˈgretid], *ag.* non rimpianto.

unregulated [ˈʌnˈregjuleitid], *ag.* non regolato.

unrehearsed [ˈʌnriˈhəːst], *ag.* **1.** non preparato, improvvisato; (*teat.*) non provato: — *play*, recita senza prove preliminari; — *speech*, discorso improvvisato **2.** impremeditato, improvviso: — *effect*, effetto impremeditato.

unreined [ˈʌnˈreind], *ag.* sfrenato, incontrollato.

unrejoicing [ˈʌnriˈdʒɔisiŋ], *ag.* senza gioia, triste.

unrelatable [ˈʌnriˈleitəbl], *ag.* non raccontabile, non riferibile.

unrelated [ˈʌnriˈleitid], *ag.* **1.** senza rapporti; senza legami: *they are entirely* —, tra loro non esiste alcun legame di parentela **2.** non raccontato, passato sotto silenzio: *to leave a fact* —, non raccontare, passare sotto silenzio un fatto.

unrelenting [ˌʌnriˈlentiŋ], *ag.* inesorabile, implacabile; irremovibile, inflessibile: *he was* —, fu inflessibile.

unrelentingly [ˌʌnriˈlentiŋli], *av.* inesorabilmente, implacabilmente; inflessibilmente.

unrelentingness [ˌʌnriˈlentiŋnis], *s.* inesorabilità, implacabilità; inflessibilità.

unreliability [ˈʌnriˌlaiəˈbiliti], *s.* **1.** inattendibilità; inesattezza; incertezza **2.** instabilità (di persona).

unreliable [ˈʌnriˈlaiəbl], *ag.* **1.** non fidato; su cui non si può fare affidamento; instabile, incostante **2.** inattendibile; inesatto; incerto: — *clock*, orologio inesatto; *to have sthg. from an* — *source*, sapere ql.co. da fonte poco attendibile.

unreliableness [ˈʌnriˈlaiəblnis], *V.* unreliability.

unrelieved [ˈʌnriˈliːvd], *ag.* **1.** non soccorso, privo di soccorso; non alleviato; non confortato, privo di conforto **2.** invariato, uniforme; monotono: *plain* — *by any hillock*, pianura non interrotta da alcuna collina; *news of* — *gloom*, notizie uniformemente rattristanti.

unremarkable [ˈʌnriˈmɑːkəbl], *ag.* irrilevante.

unremarked [ˈʌnriˈmɑːkt], *ag.* inosservato, non visto ‖ — *on*, passato sotto silenzio.

unremedied [ˈʌnˈremidid], *ag.* non rimediato.

unremembered [ˈʌnriˈmembəd], *ag.* obliato, non ricordato.

unremembering [ˈʌnriˈmembəriŋ], *ag.* dimentico.

unremitted [ˈʌnriˈmitid], *ag.* **1.** non rimesso, non perdonato: *an* — *sin*, peccato non perdonato **2.** incessante, ininterrotto **3.** perseverante (di persona).

unremittedly [ˈʌnriˈmitidli], *av.* incessantemente, ininterrottamente, senza posa.

unremitting [ˌʌnriˈmitiŋ], *ag.* **1.** incessante, ininterrotto: — *rain*, pioggia incessante **2.** assiduo, instancabile: *he was* — *in courting her*, la corteggiava assiduamente.

unremittingly [ˌʌnriˈmitiŋli], *av.* incessantemente, ininterrottamente; senza posa.

unremorseful [ˈʌnriˈmɔːsful], *ag.* senza rimorsi.

unremovable [ˈʌnriˈmuːvəbl], *ag.* (*rar.*) **1.** inamovibile **2.** irremovibile.

unremoved [ˈʌnriˈmuːvd], *ag.* (*rar.*) **1.** non rimosso **2.** fisso, fermo.

unremunerative [ˈʌnriˈmjuːnərətiv], *ag.* non rimunerativo, poco rimunerativo; infruttifero.

unrepaid [ˈʌnriˈpeid], *ag.* non ripagato; non ricompensato.

unrepaired [ˈʌnriˈpɛəd], *ag.* non riparato (anche *fig.*).

unrepealed [ˈʌnriˈpiːld], *ag.* non abrogato, irrevocato.

unrepeatable [ˈʌnriˈpiːtəbl], *ag.* irripetibile.

unrepeated [ˈʌnriˈpiːtid], *ag.* non ripetuto.

unrepentant [ˈʌnriˈpentənt], *ag.* impenitente, incorreggibile: *he died* —, morì senza essersi pentito.

unrepining [ˈʌnriˈpainiŋ], *ag.* che non si lagna.

unrepiningly [ˈʌnriˈpainiŋli], *av.* senza lagnanze.

unreplenished [ˈʌnriˈpleniʃt], *ag.* non riempito.

unreported [ˈʌnriˈpɔːtid], *ag.* non riferito, non segnalato: — *to the police*, non denunziato alla polizia.

unreposing [ˈʌnriˈpouziŋ], *ag.* che non riposa; che non dà riposo.

unrepresented [ˈʌnˌrepriˈzentid], *ag.* non rappresentato.

unrepressed [ˈʌnriˈprest], *ag.* non represso.

unreprievable [ˈʌnriˈpriːvəbl], *ag.* indilazionabile.

unreprieved [ˈʌnriˈpriːvd], *ag.* non dilazionato, senza dilazione.

unreproached [ˈʌnriˈproutʃt], *ag.* non rimproverato.

unreprovable [ˈʌnriˈpruːvəbl], *ag.* irriprovevole; irreprensibile.

unreproved [ˈʌnriˈpruːvd], *ag.* non ripreso, non biasimato.

unrequested [ˈʌnriˈkwestid], *ag.* non richiesto; non invitato: *to speak* —, parlare senza essere stato invitato.

unrequired [ˈʌnriˈkwaiəd], *ag.* non richiesto; facoltativo.

unrequitable [ˈʌnriˈkwaitəbl], *ag.* **1.** che non si può ricambiare **2.** che non si può ricompensare.

unrequited [ˈʌnriˈkwaitid], *ag.* **1.** non ricambiato: — *love*, amore non corrisposto **2.** non ricompensato: — *labours*, lavori non compensati **3.** invendicato, impunito.

unrescued [ˈʌnˈreskjuːd], *ag.* non liberato; non salvato.

unresented [ˌʌnriˈzentid], *ag.* senza risentimento; non risentito: — *criticism*, critica accolta di buon grado.

unreserve [ˈʌnriˈzəːv], *s.* 1. mancanza di riserbo 2. franchezza, schiettezza.

unreserved [ˈʌnriˈzəːvd], *ag.* 1. franco, schietto 2. illimitato, incondizionato: — *confidence*, fiducia illimitata 3. non prenotato: — *seats*, posti non prenotati.

unreservedly [ˌʌnriˈzəːvidli], *av.* 1. francamente 2. illimitatamente, incondizionatamente.

unreservedness [ˈʌnriˈzəːvidnis], *s.* 1. mancanza di riserbo 2. franchezza, schiettezza.

unresigned [ˈʌnriˈzaind], *ag.* non rassegnato.

unresisted [ˈʌnriˈzistid], *ag.* 1. irresistibile (di tentazione, ecc.) 2. che non ha incontrato opposizione: *to do sthg.* —, fare ql.co. senza incontrare opposizione.

unresisting [ˈʌnriˈzistiŋ], *ag.* senza resistenza; sottomesso, docile.

unresistingly [ˈʌnriˈzistiŋli], *av.* senza resistenza; docilmente.

unresolvable [ˈʌnriˈzɔlvəbl], *ag.* insolubile; non risolvibile.

unresolved [ˈʌnriˈzɔlvd], *ag.* 1. irresoluto, indeciso: *I was — whether I should go or not*, ero incerto se andare o no 2. insoluto, non risolto; senza soluzione: *my doubts are still* —, i miei dubbi sono ancora insoluti.

unrespected [ˈʌnrisˈpektid], *ag.* non rispettato.

unrespirable [ˈʌnˈrespirəbl], *ag.* irrespirabile.

unresponsible [ˈʌnrisˈpɔnsəbl], *ag.* 1. irresponsabile; non responsabile 2. senza, che non comporta responsabilità.

unresponsibleness [ˈʌnrisˈpɔnsəblnis], *s.* irresponsabilità; mancanza di responsabilità.

unrest [ˈʌnˈrest], *s.* inquietudine, agitazione: *poverty causes social* —, la povertà è causa di fermento sociale.

unrestful [ˈʌnˈrestful], *ag.* inquieto, irrequieto.

unrestfully [ˈʌnˈrestfuli], *av.* con inquietudine, con irrequietezza.

unrestfulness [ˈʌnˈrestfulnis], *s.* inquietudine, irrequietezza.

unresting [ˈʌnˈrestiŋ], *ag.* 1. inquieto, irrequieto 2. che non si stanca 3. incessante: — *activity*, attività incessante.

unrestingly [ʌnˈrestiŋli], *av.* 1. con inquietudine 2. incessantemente.

unrestored [ˈʌnrisˈtɔːd], *ag.* 1. non reso, non restituito 2. non restaurato, non riparato 3. non ripristinato, non reintegrato (nelle funzioni, ecc.).

unrestrained [ˈʌnrisˈtreind], *ag.* non represso, senza freni; sfrenato; libero: — *by our presence, he went on talking*, per nulla impacciato dalla nostra presenza continuò a parlare.

unrestrainedly [ˈʌnrisˈtreinidli], *av.* senza freno.

unrestricted [ˈʌnrisˈtriktid], *ag.* senza restrizioni ☆ — *race, (spor.)* gara di corsa a formula libera; — *road*, strada senza limitazioni di velocità.

unrestrictedly [ˈʌnrisˈtriktidli], *av.* senza restrizioni.

unretentive [ˈʌnriˈtentiv], *ag.* che non ritiene: — *memory*, memoria labile.

unretracted [ˈʌnriˈtræktid], *ag.* non ritrattato.

unreturned [ˈʌnriˈtəːnd], *ag.* 1. non ritornato 2. non contraccambiato.

unrevealed [ˈʌnriˈviːld], *ag.* non rivelato; non divulgato: *to leave a secret* —, mantenere un segreto.

unrevenged [ˈʌnriˈvendʒd], *ag.* non vendicato, invendicato.

unrevengeful [ˈʌnriˈvendʒful], *ag.* non vendicativo.

unreversed [ˈʌnriˈvəːst], *ag.* non annullato; non revocato.

unrevised [ˈʌnriˈvaizd], *ag.* non riveduto.

unrevoked [ˈʌnriˈvoukt], *ag.* non revocato; non abrogato.

unrewarded [ˈʌnriˈwɔːdid], *ag.* non rimunerato, non ricompensato.

unrhymed [ˈʌnˈraimd], *ag.* non rimato.

unrhythmical [ˈʌnˈriðmikəl], *ag.* non ritmico, senza ritmo.

unridable [ˈʌnˈraidəbl], *ag.* non cavalcabile.

to unriddle [ˈʌnˈridl], *v.t.* risolvere; spiegare.

unrifled [ˈʌnˈraifld], *ag.* non saccheggiato.

to unrig [ˈʌnˈrig], *pass.p.p.* **unrigged** [ˈʌnˈrigd], *v.t. (mar.)* disarmare.

unrighteous [ʌnˈraitʃəs], *ag.* ingiusto, iniquo; cattivo.

unrighteously [ʌnˈraitʃəsli], *av.* ingiustamente.

unrighteousness [ʌnˈraitʃəsnis], *s.* ingiustizia, iniquità; disonestà.

unrightful [ˈʌnˈraitful], *ag.* ingiusto.

unrightfully [ˈʌnˈraitfuli], *av.* ingiustamente.

unrightfulness [ˈʌnˈraitfulnis], *s.* ingiustizia.

to unrip [ˈʌnˈrip], *pass.p.p.* **unripped** [ˈʌnˈript], *v.t.* scucire; strappare, lacerare.

unripe [ˈʌnˈraip], **unripened** [ˈʌnˈraipənd], *ag.* immaturo, acerbo (anche *fig.*): — *death*, morte prematura.

unripeness [ˈʌnˈraipnis], *s.* immaturità.

unrivalled [ʌnˈraivəld], *ag.* impareggiabile; senza rivali: *our goods are* —, la nostra merce non teme concorrenza.

to unrivet [ˈʌnˈrivit], *v.t.* schiodare; *fig.* rimuovere, distogliere: *I unriveted my gaze*, distolsi lo sguardo.

unroasted [ˈʌnˈroustid], *ag.* non arrostito; non abbrustolito, non tostato.

to unrobe [ˈʌnˈroub], *v.t.i.* svestire, svestirsi; spogliare, spogliarsi.

to unroll [ˈʌnˈroul], *v.t.i.* svolgere, svolgersi; spiegare, spiegarsi; aprire.

unromantic [ˈʌnrəˈmæntik], *ag.* poco romantico; senza fantasia.

unromantically [ˈʌnrəˈmæntikəli], *av.* in modo poco romantico, senza romanticherie; senza fantasia.

to unroof [ˈʌnˈruːf], *v.t.* togliere il tetto a; distruggere il tetto di.

to unroot [ˈʌnˈruːt], *v.t.* sradicare, estirpare, svellere.

unrounded [ˈʌnˈraundid], *ag.* non arrotondato.

unroyal [ˈʌnˈrɔiəl], *ag.* poco regale; indegno di un re.

unroyally [ˈʌnˈrɔiəli], *av.* poco regalmente; in modo indegno di un re.

unruffled [ˈʌnˈrʌfld], *ag.* calmo; sereno; imperturbabile.

unruled [ˈʌnˈruːld], *ag.* 1. non regolato; non controllato 2. non governato 3. non rigato.

unruliness [ʌnˈruːlinis], *s.* 1. sregolatezza 2. indisciplinatezza, insubordinazione, turbolenza.

unruly [ʌnˈruːli], *ag.* 1. sregolato 2. indisciplinato, insubordinato; turbolento.

to unrumple [ˈʌnˈrʌmpl], *v.t.* levare le pieghe a; distendere; spianare.

to unsaddle [ˈʌnˈsædl], *v.t.* 1. dissellare, levare la sella a 2. disarcionare.

unsaddled [ˈʌnˈsædld], *ag.* 1. senza sella 2. disarcionato.

unsafe [ˈʌnˈseif], *ag.* malsicuro, pericoloso.

unsafely [ˈʌnˈseifli], *av.* in modo malsicuro, in modo pericoloso, pericolosamente.

unsafeness [ˈʌnˈseifnis], *s.* mancanza di sicurezza; rischio, pericolo.

unsaid [ˈʌnˈsed], *ag.* non detto, taciuto: *things better left* —, cose che è meglio passare sotto silenzio.

unsalability [ˈʌnˌseiləˈbiliti], *s.* invendibilità.

unsalable [ˈʌnˈseiləbl], *ag.* invendibile.

unsalaried [ˈʌnˈsælərid], *ag.* non stipendiato.

unsalted [ˈʌnˈsɔːltid], *ag.* non salato, scipito.

unsaluted [ˈʌnsəˈluːtid], *ag.* insalutato.

unsanctified [ˈʌnˈsæŋktifaid], *ag.* non santificato; profano.

unsanctioned [ˈʌnˈsæŋkʃənd], *ag.* non sanzionato, non autorizzato.

unsanitary [ˈʌnˈsænitəri], *ag.* insalubre, malsano; poco igienico.

unsated [ˈʌnˈseitid], *ag.* insaziato.

unsatiable [ˈʌnˈseiʃjəbl], *ag.* insaziabile.

unsatisfactorily [ˈʌnˌsætisˈfæktərili], *av.* in modo insoddisfacente, manchevole.

unsatisfactoriness [ˈʌnˌsætisˈfæktərinis], *s.* carattere non soddisfacente, manchevolezza.

unsatisfactory [ˈʌnˌsætisˈfæktəri], *ag.* non soddisfacente; non sufficiente, manchevole.

unsatisfied [ˈʌnˈsætisfaid], *ag.* 1. non soddisfatto; non sazio 2. non convinto 3. non saldato (di debito).

unsatisfying [ˈʌnˈsætisfaiiŋ], *ag.* 1. che non soddisfa, non soddisfacente 2. non convincente.

unsaturated [ˈʌnˈsætʃəreitid], *ag.* non saturato.

unsaved [ˈʌnˈseivd], *ag.* 1. non salvato; perduto 2. non risparmiato.

unsavourily [ˈʌnˈseivərili], *av.* 1. insipidamente 2. disgustosamente; *fig.* spiacevolmente.

unsavouriness [ˈʌnˈseivərinis], *s.* 1. scipitezza 2. disgustosità; *fig.* spiacevolezza.

unsavoury [ˈʌnˈseivəri], *ag.* 1. insipido, scipito 2. disgustoso; *fig.* spiacevole, molesto; ripugnante.

to **unsay** [ˈʌnˈsei], *pass.p.p.* **unsaid** [ˈʌnˈsed], *v.t.* disdire, ritrattare; negare.

unscalable [ˈʌnˈskeiləbl], *ag.* che non si può scalare.

unscarred [ˈʌnˈskɑːd], *ag.* senza cicatrici; illeso.

unscathed [ˈʌnˈskeiðd], *ag.* illeso, indenne.

unscented [ˈʌnˈsentid], *ag.* non profumato.

unscheduled [ˈʌnˈʃedjuːld], *ag.* 1. non schedato 2. non incluso nell'orario (di treno).

unscholarly [ˈʌnˈskɔləli], *ag.* 1. indegno di un letterato 2. non erudito.

unschooled [ˈʌnˈskuːld], *ag.* 1. senza istruzione; illetterato 2. indisciplinato 3. spontaneo, naturale (di sentimento, ecc.) 4. non esercitato, non avvezzo; inesperto: — *to patience,* non avvezzo a pazientare.

unscientific [ˈʌnˌsaiənˈtifik], *ag.* non scientifico, poco scientifico.

unscientifically [ˈʌnˌsaiənˈtifikəli], *av.* non scientificamente.

unscorched [ˈʌnˈskɔːtʃt], *ag.* non bruciato, non bruciacchiato: *he escaped* —, uscì indenne dall'incendio.

unscoured [ˈʌnˈskauəd], *ag.* non lavato, non sgrassato; non fregato; non strigliato (di cavallo).

unscratched [ˈʌnˈskrætʃt], *ag.* non graffiato, senza un graffio.

unscreened [ˈʌnˈskriːnd], *ag.* 1. esposto; non riparato (di luogo) 2. senza schermo 3. non vagliato.

to **unscrew** [ˈʌnˈskruː], *v.t.i.* svitare, svitarsi; allentare, allentarsi.

unscriptural [ˈʌnˈskriptʃərəl], *ag.* non conforme alle Sacre Scritture.

unscripturally [ˈʌnˈskriptərəli], *av.* non in conformità alle Sacre Scritture.

unscrupulous [ʌnˈskruːpjuləs], *ag.* senza scrupoli, poco scrupoloso: *man of* — *ambition,* uomo che ha un'ambizione senza scrupoli.

unscrupulously [ʌnˈskruːpjuləsli], *av.* senza scrupoli; poco scrupolosamente.

unscrupulousness [ʌnˈskruːpjuləsnis], *s.* mancanza di scrupoli, di scrupolosità.

to **unseal** [ˈʌnˈsiːl], *v.t.* dissigillare, dissuggellare; rivelare, aprire: *to* — *a letter,* aprire una lettera ‖ *to* — *the future,* rivelare il futuro ‖ *to* — *s.o.'s eyes, fig.* aprire gli occhi a qlcu. ‖ *to* — *s.o.'s lips, fig.* rendere a qlcu. la libertà di parola.

unsealed [ˈʌnˈsiːld], *ag.* 1. dissuggellato 2. senza sigillo.

unsearchable [ʌnˈsəːtʃəbl], *ag.* imperscrutabile; misterioso.

unsearchableness [ʌnˈsəːtʃəblnis], *s.* imperscrutabilità.

unsearchably [ʌnˈsəːtʃəbli], *av.* imperscrutabilmente.

unsearched [ʌnˈsəːtʃt], *ag.* non perquisito.

unseasonable [ʌnˈsiːznəbl], *ag.* fuori stagione; *fig.* intempestivo, inopportuno: — *fruit,* frutta fuori stagione; — *joke,* scherzo inopportuno; — *request,* domanda intempestiva.

unseasonableness [ʌnˈsiːznəblnis], *s.* l'essere fuori stagione; *fig.* intempestività, inopportunità.

unseasonably [ʌnˈsiːznəbli], *av.* fuori stagione; *fig.* intempestivamente; inopportunamente.

unseasoned [ˈʌnˈsiːznd], *ag.* 1. immaturo; *fig.* inesperto 2. (*cuc.*) non condito 3. non stagionato.

to **unseat** [ˈʌnˈsiːt], *v.t.* 1. disarcionare; far cadere: *to* — *a rider,* disarcionare un cavaliere 2. (*pol.*) defenestrare 3. (*pol.*) privare del seggio: *to* — *a member of Parliament,* deporre un membro del Parlamento.

unseated [ˈʌnˈsiːtid], *ag.* 1. non seduto 2. disarcionato 3. (*pol.*) deposto; non rieletto.

unseaworthiness [ˈʌnˈsiːˌwəːðinis], *s.* (*mar.*) mancanza di idoneità alla navigazione.

unseaworthy [ˈʌnˈsiːˌwəːði], *ag.* (*mar.*) non idoneo alla navigazione.

unseconded [ˈʌnˈsekəndid], *ag.* non assecondato; non appoggiato.

unsectarian [ˈʌnˈsekˈtɛəriən], *ag.* non settario; non partigiano.

unsecured [ˈʌnˈsiˈkjuəd], *ag.* 1. malsicuro 2. (*comm.*) scoperto, non garantito: — *creditor,* creditore non garantito 3. non assicurato, non fissato.

unseduced [ˈʌnˈsiˈdjuːst], *ag.* non sedotto; non attratto.

unseeded [ˈʌnˈsiːdid], *ag.* privo di semi; non seminato.

unseeing [ˈʌnˈsiːiŋ], *ag.* cieco; che non vede: *to look at s.o., sthg. with* — *eyes,* guardare ql.co., qlcu. senza vederlo.

unseeming [ˈʌnˈsiːmiŋ], *ag.* (*rar.*) non apparente.

unseemliness [ʌnˈsiːmlinis], *s.* indecenza, sconvenienza.

unseemly [ʌnˈsiːmli], *ag.* indecente, sconveniente.

unseen [ˈʌnˈsiːn], *ag.* non visto, inosservato ‖ *s.* 1. — (*translation*), traduzione a prima vista 2. *the* —, l'altro mondo, l'al di là.

unseizable [ˈʌnˈsiːzəbl], *ag.* inafferrabile.

unseized [ˈʌnˈsiːzd], *ag.* 1. non preso, non afferrato: — *opportunity, fig.* occasione mancata 2. (*dir.*) non confiscato.

unselected [ˈʌn siˈlektid], *ag.* non scelto, non selezionato.

unselfish [ˈʌnˈselfiʃ], *ag.* disinteressato, altruista.

unselfishly [ˈʌnˈselfiʃli], *av.* altruisticamente, disinteressatamente.

unselfishness [ˈʌnˈselfiʃnis], *s.* disinteresse, altruismo.

unsensational [ˈʌnˈsenˈseiʃənl], *ag.* non sensazionale.

unsent [ˈʌnˈsent], *ag.* 1. non mandato, non spedito 2. — *for,* senza essere stato chiamato, non convocato.

unserved [ˈʌnˈsəːvd], *ag.* non servito.

unserviceable [ˈʌnˈsəːviˈsəbl], *ag.* 1. inservibile, inutilizzabile; poco pratico (di abito, ecc.) 2. (*mil.*) inabile 3. non servizievole.

unserviceableness [ˈʌnˈsəːviˈsəblnis], *s.* inserviibilità, inutilità.

unset [ˈʌnˈset], *ag.* fuori posto, non sistemato.

to **unsettle** [ˈʌnˈsetl], *v.t.i.* 1. mettere in disordine 2. disturbare; sconvolgere, sconvolgersi; turbare, turbarsi: *to* — *a person's opinions,* turbare le opinioni di una persona.

unsettled [ˈʌnˈsetld], *ag.* 1. disordinato 2. sconvolto, turbato; agitato 3. mutevole, instabile; indeciso, incerto: — *weather,* tempo instabile; *this point is* —, questa questione è ancora indecisa 4. (*comm.*) non pagato, non saldato: — *debts,* debiti non saldati 5. senza fissa dimora 6. non popolato, disabitato: — *lands,* terre disabitate.

unsettledness [ˈʌnˈsetldnis], *s.* 1. disordine; turbamento; agitazione 2. instabilità; incertezza, indecisione.

unsevered [ˈʌnˈsevəd], *ag.* indiviso, inseparato.

to **unsew** [ˈʌnˈsou], *pass.* **unsewed** [ˈʌnˈsoud], *p.p.* **unsewn** [ˈʌnˈsoun], *v.t.* scucire.

unsewed, unsewn, *ag.* non cucito, scucito: *this hem has come* —, quest'orlo si è scucito.

to **unsex** [ˈʌnˈseks], *v.t.* rendere asessuato (specialmente donna); mascolinizzare.

unsexed [ˈʌnˈsekst], *ag.* asessuato.

to **unshackle** ['ʌn'ʃækl], *v.t.* togliere dai ceppi; liberare.

unshackled ['ʌn'ʃækld], *ag.* liberato dai ceppi; libero: — *by conventions*, libero dalle convenzioni.

unshaded ['ʌn'ʃeidid], *ag.* senz'ombra, non ombreggiato, senza ombreggiatura (di luogo, disegno, ecc.).

unshadowed ['ʌn'ʃædoud], *ag.* 1. non ombreggiato 2. *fig.* non offuscato, non rattristato: *a life — by any calamity*, una vita non rattristata da alcuna sventura.

unshakable [ʌn'ʃeikəbl], *ag.* incrollabile, fermo: — *devotion*, affetto costante.

unshakably ['ʌn'ʃeikəbli], *av.* incrollabilmente, fermamente.

unshaken ['ʌn'ʃeikən], *ag.* non scosso, fermo, irremovibile, incrollabile.

to **unshape** ['ʌn'ʃeip], *v.t.* guastare; deformare.

unshapely ['ʌn'ʃeipli], *ag.* 1. senza forma, informe 2. deforme; sgraziato, malfatto.

unshapen ['ʌn'ʃeipn], *ag.* 1. senza forma 2. deforme, malfatto.

unshared ['ʌn'ʃɛəd], *ag.* non condiviso.

unshattered ['ʌn'ʃætəd], *ag.* saldo, equilibrato: *with nerves —*, coi nervi a posto.

unshaven ['ʌn'ʃeivn], *ag.* non rasato, non sbarbato.

to **unsheathe** ['ʌn'ʃi:ð], *v.t.* sguainare: *to — the sword*, sguainare la spada; *fig.* dichiarare guerra, cominciare le ostilità.

unshed ['ʌn'ʃed], *ag.* non sparso, non versato: — *tears*, lacrime non versate.

unshelled ['ʌn'ʃeld], *ag.* non sgusciato; non sgranato.

unsheltered ['ʌn'ʃeltəd], *ag.* non riparato, non protetto, esposto.

unshielded ['ʌn'ʃi:ldid], *ag.* non protetto, esposto.

unshifted ['ʌn'ʃiftid], *ag.* immutato, invariato.

unshifting ['ʌn'ʃiftiŋ], *ag.* immutabile, invariabile.

to **unship** ['ʌn'ʃip], *pass.p.p.* **unshipped** ['ʌn'ʃipt], *v.t.* (*mar.*) sbarcare; scaricare; smontare; disarmare.

unshocked ['ʌn'ʃɔkt], *ag.* non scosso, non impressionato; non scandalizzato.

unshod ['ʌn'ʃɔd], *pass.p.p.* di to **unshoe** ‖ *ag.* 1. senza scarpe, scalzo 2. non ferrato (di cavalli).

to **unshoe** ['ʌn'ʃu:], *pass.p.p.* **unshod** ['ʌn'ʃɔd], *v.t.* 1. togliere le scarpe a 2. togliere i ferri a (un cavallo).

unshorn ['ʌn'ʃɔ:n], *ag.* non tosato, intonso.

unshortened ['ʌn'ʃɔ:tnd], *ag.* non accorciato.

unshot ['ʌn'ʃɔt], *ag.* 1. non scaricato (di arma) 2. non colpito: *he escaped —*, fuggì incolume.

to **unshot**, *v.t.* scaricare (un'arma).

unshrinkable ['ʌn'ʃriŋkəbl], *ag.* irrestringibile.

unshrinking ['ʌn'ʃriŋkiŋ], *ag.* intrepido, impavido, ardito; fermo: — *eyes*, occhi arditi.

unshrinkingly [ʌn'ʃriŋkiŋli], *av.* intrepidamente, arditamente; fermamente.

unshrunken ['ʌn'ʃrʌŋkən], *ag.* non ritirato, non ristretto.

unshunned ['ʌn'ʃʌnd], *ag.* non evitato.

unshut ['ʌn'ʃʌt], *ag.* non chiuso, aperto.

unsifted ['ʌn'siftid], *ag.* 1.non setacciato, non passato al setaccio 2. *fig.* non vagliato, non esaminato a fondo.

unsighted ['ʌn'saitid], *ag.* non visto, invisibile.

unsightliness ['ʌn'saitlinis], *s.* bruttezza.

unsightly [ʌn'saitli], *ag.* brutto, spiacevole a vedersi.

unsigned ['ʌn'saind], *ag.* non firmato, senza firma.

to **unsinew** ['ʌn'sinju:], *v.t.* togliere le forze a, indebolire.

unsinged ['ʌn'sindʒd], *ag.* non abbruciacchiato, non strinato.

unsinning ['ʌn'siniŋ], *ag.* senza peccato; innocente.

unsistered ['ʌn'sistəd], *ag.* che non ha sorella.

unsisterly ['ʌn'sistəli], *ag.* indegno di una sorella.

unsizeable ['ʌn'saizəbl], *ag.*: — *fish*, pesce di misura inferiore a quella regolamentare per la pesca.

unsized[1] ['ʌn'saizd], *ag.* 1. non fatto su misura 2. non diviso secondo la misura.

unsized[2], *ag.* senza colla; senza appretto.

unskilful ['ʌn'skilful], *ag.* inabile; inetto; inesperto; maldestro.

unskilfully ['ʌn'skilfuli], *av.* senza abilità; malamente; in modo maldestro.

unskilfulness ['ʌn'skilfulnis], *s.* incapacità; inabilità; imperizia.

unskilled ['ʌn'skild], *ag.* inesperto; inabile ☆ — *labour*, lavoro manuale; manovalanza; — *worker*, operaio non specializzato; manovale.

unskimmed ['ʌn'skimd], *ag.* non scremato.

unslackened ['ʌn'slækənd], *ag.* non allentato; non rilassato.

unslaked ['ʌn'sleikt], *ag.* non smorzato, non spento; non estinto ☆ — *lime*, calce viva.

unsleeping ['ʌn'sli:piŋ], *ag.* che non dorme, desto; vigilante.

to **unsling** ['ʌn'sliŋ], *pass.p.p.* **unslung** ['ʌn'slʌŋ], *v.t.* (*mar.*) togliere l'imbracatura a.

unslumbering ['ʌn'slʌmbəriŋ], *ag.* desto, che non sonnecchia; all'erta.

unsmirched ['ʌn'smə:tʃt], *ag.* non sporcato, non lordato; *fig.* non macchiato.

unsmoked ['ʌn'smoukt], *ag.* 1. non fumato 2. non affumicato.

unsober ['ʌn'soubə*], *ag.* 1. sregolato, intemperante 2. dedito al bere.

unsoberly ['ʌn'soubəli], *av.* smoderatamente.

unsociable [ʌn'souʃəbl], *ag.* poco socievole; scontroso.

unsociableness [ʌn'souʃəblnis], *s.* insocievolezza; scontrosità.

unsociably [ʌn'souʃəbli], *av.* in modo poco socievole.

unsocial ['ʌn'souʃəl], *ag.* 1. non socievole 2. asociale.

unsoftened ['ʌn'sɔfnd], *ag.* non mitigato; non addolcito; non placato.

unsoiled ['ʌn'sɔild], *ag.* non insudiciato; incontaminato; puro.

unsold ['ʌn'sould], *ag.* invenduto.

to **unsolder** ['ʌn'sɔldə*], *v.t.* (*mec.*) dissaldare.

unsoldierlike ['ʌn'souldʒəlaik], **unsoldierly** ['ʌn'souldʒəli], *ag.* indegno di un soldato.

unsolicited ['ʌn-sə'lisitid], *ag.* non sollecitato, non richiesto.

unsolicitous ['ʌn-sə'lisitəs], *ag.* incurante di; non preoccupato.

unsolid ['ʌn'sɔlid], *ag.* poco solido.

unsolved ['ʌn'sɔlvd], *ag.* insoluto, non risolto.

unsonlike ['ʌn'sʌnlaik], *ag.* indegno di un figlio.

unsophisticated ['ʌn-sə'fistikeitid], *ag.* 1. non sofisticato, non adulterato; genuino 2. semplice; naturale.

unsorted ['ʌn'sɔ:tid], *ag.* non scelto, non assortito.

unsought ['ʌn'sɔ:t], *ag.* 1. non cercato, non ricercato; non richiesto; spontaneo 2. non esaminato.

unsouled ['ʌn'sould], *ag.* privo dell'anima; senza anima.

unsound ['ʌn'saund], *ag.* 1. malsano, malato; insano: — *of mind*, insano di mente, pazzo 2. guasto, rovinato, avariato (di merce); *fig.* vizioso, corrotto 3. erroneo, fallace, falso: — *doctrine*, dottrina fallace; — *judgment*, giudizio erroneo 4. poco solido; instabile; pericolante 5. agitato: *an — sleep*, un sonno agitato.

unsounded[1] ['ʌn'saundid], *ag.* non scandagliato, non sondato.

unsounded[2], *ag.* non pronunciato (di sillaba).

unsoundly ['ʌn'saundli], *av.* 1. in modo malsano 2. erroneamente 3. instabilmente 4. agitatamente.

unsoundness ['ʌn'saundnis], *s.* 1. insalubrità; infermità; cattiva salute 2. difettosità; cattivo stato (di merce) 3. erroneità; fallacia 4. instabilità, incertezza.

unsoured ['ʌn'sauəd], *ag.* non inacidito; *fig.* non inasprito.

unsown ['ʌn'soun], *ag.* non seminato.

unspared ['ʌn'spɛəd], *ag.* 1. non risparmiato 2. senza economia; abbondante.

unsparing [ʌn'spɛəriŋ], *ag.* **1.** inesorabile, spietato **2.** zelante, che non si risparmia **3.** prodigo, generoso, liberale.

unsparingly [ʌn'spɛəriŋli], *av.* **1.** inesorabilmente, spietatamente **2.** senza economia, prodigalmente.

unsparingness [ʌn'spɛəriŋnis], *s.* **1.** inesorabilità, spietatezza **2.** prodigalità, generosità, liberalità.

to **unspeak** ['ʌn'spi:k], *pass.* **unspoke** ['ʌn'spouk], *p.p.* **unspoken** ['ʌn'spoukən], *v.t.* ritrattare, disdire.

unspeakable [ʌn'spi:kəbl], *ag.* **1.** inesprimibile, indicibile: — *joy*, gioia ineffabile; — *torments*, tormenti inenarrabili; — *wickedness*, cattiveria indicibile **2.** detestabile, inqualificabile: *his manners are* —, ha un modo di fare odioso.

unspeakably [ʌn'spi:kəbli], *av.* **1.** indicibilmente, in modo inesprimibile **2.** in modo inqualificabile.

unspecified ['ʌn'spesifaid], *ag.* non specificato.

unspeculative ['ʌn'spekjulətiv], *ag.* non speculativo, poco speculativo.

to **unspell**[1] ['ʌn'spel], *v.t.* disincantare.

to **unspell**[2], *v.t.* (*tip.*) spaziare lettera da lettera in (una parola).

unspent ['ʌn'spent], *ag.* **1.** non speso **2.** inesausto.

to **unsphere** ['ʌn'sfiə*], *v.t. fig.* rimuovere dalla sua sfera (un corpo celeste, uno spirito celeste).

unspilt ['ʌn'spilt], *ag.* non versato, non sparso.

unspiritual ['ʌn'spiritjuəl], *ag.* non spirituale; materiale; mondano.

unsplit ['ʌn'split], *ag.* non spaccato.

unspoiled ['ʌn'spoilt], *ag.* **1.** non deteriorato, ben conservato **2.** non viziato, ben allevato **3.** non sciupato, non rovinato: — *countryside*, campagna non contaminata dal progresso **4.** non saccheggiato, non devastato.

unspoken ['ʌn'spoukən], *ag.* non profferito, non detto.

unsportsmanlike ['ʌn'spo:tsmənlaik], *ag.* antisportivo; sleale.

unspotted ['ʌn'spotid], *ag.* **1.** non macchiato **2.** *fig.* senza macchia, immacolato; incorrotto **3.** (*bot. zool.*) non maculato, non screziato, non chiazzato.

unsprung ['ʌn'sprʌŋ], *ag.* non molleggiato, senza molle.

unsquared ['ʌn'skwɛəd], *ag.* non squadrato.

unstable ['ʌn'steibl], *ag.* instabile; *fig.* mutevole, incostante: — *equilibrium*, (*mec.*) equilibrio instabile.

unstableness ['ʌn'steiblnis], *s.* instabilità; *fig.* incostanza.

unstably [ʌn'steibli], *av.* instabilmente, incostantemente.

unstaid ['ʌn'steid], *ag.* incostante, volubile, leggero.

unstaidness ['ʌn'steidnis], *s.* incostanza, volubilità, leggerezza.

unstained ['ʌn'steind], *ag.* **1.** non macchiato, non tinto **2.** *fig.* immacolato, puro, illibato: — *reputation*, riputazione intatta, incensurabile.

unstamped ['ʌn'stæmpt], *ag.* **1.** non timbrato; non affrancato; non munito di marca da bollo: — *document*, documento non timbrato; — *letter*, lettera non affrancata; *agreement on* — *paper*, contratto in carta libera **2.** non coniato (di moneta, ecc.).

unstanched ['ʌn'sta:ntʃt], *ag.* **1.** ancora sanguinante (di ferita) **2.** (*arc.*) non sazio; non soddisfatto **3.** (*arc.*) non reso impermeabile (all'acqua).

unstarched ['ʌn'sta:tʃt], *ag.* **1.** non inamidato **2.** (*fam.*) cordiale, non rigido (di maniere, ecc.).

unstatesmanlike ['ʌn'steitsmənlaik], *ag.* non confacente a uno statista.

unstatutable ['ʌn'stætju:təbl], *ag.* contrario allo statuto, non statutario.

unsteadfast ['ʌn'stedfəst], *ag.* incostante, instabile: *he has an* — *character*, è di carattere volubile.

unsteadfastly ['ʌn'stedfəstli], *av.* incostantemente, instabilmente.

unsteadfastness ['ʌn'stedfəstnis], *s.* instabilità, incostanza.

unsteadily ['ʌn'stedili], *av.* **1.** in modo vacillante **2.** con indecisione, irresolutamente **3.** instabilmente, incostantemente; irregolarmente; variabilmente.

unsteadiness ['ʌn'stedinis], *s.* **1.** instabilità, incostanza; irregolarità; variabilità **2.** indecisione, irresolutezza.

unsteady ['ʌn'stedi], *ag.* **1.** vacillante, barcollante, malsicuro: — *light*, luce traballante; *he is* — *on his legs*, ha un'andatura barcollante **2.** indeciso, irresoluto **3.** instabile, incostante; irregolare; variabile: *an* — *wind*, un vento variabile; *the market is* —, il mercato è instabile; *these goods are sold at an* — *price*, questa merce si vende a prezzo variabile.

to **unstick** ['ʌn'stik]. *pass.p.p.* **unstuck** ['ʌn'stʌk], *v.t.* staccare; scollare.

unstimulated [ʌn'stimjuleitid], *ag.* non stimolato.

unstinted [ʌn'stintid], *ag.* **1.** abbondante, copioso; illimitato, senza riserve: *to excite* — *admiration*, suscitare ammirazione senza limiti **2.** generoso, liberale.

unstirred ['ʌn'stə:d], *ag.* **1.** calmo, tranquillo: — *by these events*, calmo di fronte a questi avvenimenti **2.** non mosso, non spostato.

to **unstitch** ['ʌn'stitʃ], *v.t.* scucire; togliere i punti da.

to **unstock** ['ʌn'stok], *v.t.* **1.** privare di rifornimenti, ridurre i rifornimenti a **2.** (*mar.*) liberare dalle taccate, rimuovere dal cantiere (una nave).

unstocked ['ʌn'stokt], *ag.* sfornito, sprovvisto: *an* — *larder*, una dispensa sprovvista.

to **unstop** ['ʌn'stop], *pass.p.p.* **unstopped** ['ʌn'stopt], *v.t.* sturare, stasare, aprire.

unstored ['ʌn'stɔ:d], *ag.* **1.** non messo in serbo, non immagazzinato **2.** sprovvisto.

to **unstow** ['ʌn'stou], *v.t.* (*mar.*) distivare, liberare (la stiva) dal carico.

unstrained ['ʌn'streind], *ag.* **1.** non filtrato **2.** non forzato; non costretto; spontaneo, naturale.

unstraitened ['ʌn'streitnd], *ag.* non ristretto.

unstratified ['ʌn'strætifaid], *ag.* (*geol.*) non stratificato.

unstrengthened ['ʌn'streŋθənd], *ag.* non rinforzato; non fortificato.

unstressed ['ʌn'strest], *ag.* (*gram.*) non accentato, atono.

to **unstring** ['ʌn'striŋ], *pass.p.p.* **unstrung** ['ʌn'strʌŋ], *v.t.* **1.** sciogliere, slegare **2.** allentare, togliere le corde a (uno strumento): *to* — *a violin*, allentare le corde di un violino **3.** sfilare (perle) **4.** snervare.

unstrung, *ag.* **1.** allentato; sciolto; sfilato: — *beads*, perle sfilate; *an* — *bow*, arco allentato; *an* — *instrument*, strumento a corde allentate, senza corde **2.** snervato.

unstuck ['ʌn'stʌk], *pass.p.p.* di to **unstick**.

unstudied ['ʌn'stʌdid], *ag.* **1.** non studiato: *an* — *subject*, una materia non studiata **2.** ignorante: *he is* — *in Latin*, è ignorante in latino **3.** improvvisato; naturale, spontaneo: — *style*, stile improvvisato, spontaneo.

unstuffed ['ʌn'stʌft], *ag.* non imbottito.

unsubduable ['ʌn-səb'dju(:)əbl], *ag.* che non si può soggiogare, sottomettere; indomabile.

unsubdued ['ʌn-səb'dju:d], *ag.* non soggiogato, non sottomesso; indomito: *an* — *horse*, un cavallo non domato; *an* — *passion*, una passione indomita.

unsubmissive ['ʌn-səb'misiv], *ag.* non sottomesso; indocile, ribelle.

unsubmissively ['ʌn-səb'misivli], *av.* indocilmente, insubordinatamente.

unsubmitting ['ʌn-səb'mitiŋ], *ag.* che non si sottomette.

unsubstantial ['ʌn-səb'stænʃəl], *ag.* **1.** non sostanziale, poco importante; inconsistente: — *arguments*, argomenti vuoti, privi di fondamento **2.** immaginario, chimerico **3.** immateriale; poco solido **4.** poco sostanzioso; leggero: — *food*, cibo poco sostanzioso.

unsubstantiality ['ʌn-səb,stænʃi'æliti], *s.* **1.** mancanza di sostanza **2.** irrealtà **3.** incorporeità, immaterialità; mancanza di solidità.

unsubverted [ˈʌn-sʌbˈvəːtid], *ag.* non sovvertito; non distrutto.

unsuccess [ˈʌn-səkˈses], *s.* insuccesso; cattiva riuscita.

unsuccessful [ˈʌn-səkˈsesful], *ag.* mal riuscito; vano, infruttuoso; sfortunato: — *attempt*, tentativo mal riuscito; *(fam.)* colpo mancato; — *efforts*, sforzi vani; — *print*, *(foto.)* stampa, copia mal riuscita; *to be* —, non riuscire, fallire ‖ *the* — *party*, *(dir.)* la parte soccombente (in una causa).

unsuccessfully [ˈʌn-səkˈsesfuli], *av.* senza successo; invano, infruttuosamente.

unsuccessfulness [ˈʌn-səkˈsesfulnis], *s.* insuccesso; cattiva riuscita.

unsugared [ˈʌnˈʃugəd], *ag.* senza zucchero, non zuccherato.

unsuitable [ˈʌnˈsjuːtəbl], *ag.* **1.** inadatto, non idoneo: *he is* — *for this work*, è inadatto a questo lavoro **2.** non appropriato; inopportuno, incongruo: *an* — *marriage*, un matrimonio mal assortito; — *to the occasion*, non appropriato alla circostanza **3.** sconveniente; svantaggioso: *this proposal is* — *to us*, questa proposta non ci conviene.

unsuitableness [ˈʌnˈsjuːtəblnis], *s.* **1.** inadeguatezza **2.** improprietà; inopportunità **3.** sconvenienza.

unsuitably [ˈʌnˈsjuːtəbli], *av.* impropriamente; sconvenientemente.

unsuited [ˈʌnˈsjuːtid], *ag.* **1.** inadatto, non idoneo: *a person* — *for (o to) sthg.*, persona inadatta a qualcosa **2.** non appropriato; inopportuno; incongruo: *a slovenliness quite* — *to a man in his position*, una sciatteria incompatibile in un uomo del suo rango **3.** non soddisfatto, non accontentato: *we wish nobody to leave our shop* —, desideriamo che nessuno lasci il nostro negozio senza aver trovato ciò che desidera.

unsullied [ˈʌnˈsʌlid], *ag.* pulito; senza macchia (anche *fig.*): — *conscience*, coscienza immacolata.

unsung [ˈʌnˈsʌŋ], *ag.* **1.** non cantato **2.** non celebrato: — *victory*, vittoria non celebrata.

unsupplied [ˈʌn-səˈplaid], *ag.* **1.** non approvvigionato; sprovvisto, sfornito: *they were* — *with horses*, erano sprovvisti di cavalli **2.** non fornito, non consegnato (di merce, ecc.).

unsupportable [ˈʌn-səˈpoːtəbl], *ag.* insopportabile, intollerabile.

unsupported [ˈʌn-səˈpoːtid], *ag.* **1.** non confermato, non comprovato **2.** non appoggiato, non sostenuto, non aiutato; non incoraggiato **3.** *(edil.)* non puntellato, senza sostegno ☆ — *amendment*, *(pol.)* emendamento che non è stato appoggiato; — *battalion*, *(mil.)* battaglione scoperto.

unsure [ˈʌnˈʃuə*], *ag.* **1.** malsicuro; precario; poco solido, poco consistente: — *construction*, costruzione poco solida; — *position*, posizione precaria; *he is an* — *person*, *fig.* è una persona che dà poco affidamento **2.** incerto, indeterminato: — *fact*, fatto incerto **3.** incerto, poco sicuro, dubbioso: *he is* — *of the date*, è incerto sulla data.

unsurmountable [ˈʌn-sə(ː)ˈmauntəbl], *ag.* insormontabile.

unsurpassable [ˈʌn-sə(ː)ˈpɑːsəbl], *ag.* insorpassabile.

unsurpassed [ˈʌn-sə(ː)ˈpɑːst], *ag.* insorpassato.

unsusceptible [ˈʌn-səˈseptəbl], *ag.* non suscettibile.

unsuspectable [ˈʌn-səsˈpektəbl], *ag.* insospettabile.

unsuspected [ˈʌn-səsˈpektid], *ag.* insospettato; non sospetto.

unsuspecting [ˈʌn-səsˈpektiŋ], *ag.* non sospettoso, senza diffidenza.

unsuspectingly [ˈʌn-səsˈpektiŋli], *av.* senza sospetti, senza diffidenza.

unsuspended [ˈʌn-səsˈpendid], *ag.* non appeso; non sospeso.

unsuspicious [ˈʌn-səsˈpiʃəs], *ag.* **1.** non sospettoso, senza diffidenza **2.** che non desta sospetti.

unsuspiciously [ˈʌn-səsˈpiʃəsli], *av.* senza sospetti, senza diffidenza.

unsustainable [ˈʌn-səsˈteinəbl], *ag.* insostenibile.

unsustained [ˈʌn-səˈsteind], *ag.* non sostenuto.

to unswathe [ˈʌnˈsweið], *v.t.* sfasciare, sbendare.

unswayed [ˈʌnˈsweid], *ag.* non influenzato, non dominato, senza pregiudizi.

unsweet [ˈʌnˈswiːt], *ag.* sgradevole; sgradito.

unsweetened [ˈʌnˈswiːtnd], *ag.* non zuccherato, non addolcito.

unswept [ˈʌnˈswept], *ag.* non spazzato, non scopato.

unswerving [ʌnˈswəːviŋ], *ag.* **1.** costante, fermo: *an* — *purpose*, un proposito fermo **2.** diritto, rettilineo: *an* — *flight*, volo rettilineo.

unswervingly [ʌnˈswəːviŋli], *av.* **1.** costantemente, fermamente **2.** senza scarti, in linea retta.

unworn [ˈʌnˈswɔːn], *ag.* **1.** non legato da giuramento **2.** non confermato con giuramento (di testimonianza).

unsymmetrical [ˈʌn-siˈmetrikəl], *ag.* asimmetrico, senza simmetria.

unsymmetrically [ˈʌn-siˈmetrikəli], *av.* in maniera asimmetrica.

unsymmetry [ˈʌnˈsimitri], *s.* asimmetria.

unsympathetic [ˈʌnˌsimpəˈθetik], *ag.* indifferente; non comprensivo.

unsympathetically [ˈʌnˌsimpəˈθetikəli], *av.* con indifferenza; senza comprensione.

unsympathizing [ˈʌnˈsimpəθaiziŋ], *ag.* indifferente; che non mostra comprensione.

unsystematic [ˈʌnˌsistiˈmætik], *ag.* non sistematico.

unsystematically [ˈʌnˌsistiˈmætikəli], *av.* non sistematicamente.

to untack [ˈʌnˈtæk], *v.t.* **1.** staccare, disgiungere **2.** levare l'imbastitura a.

untainted [ˈʌnˈteintid], *ag.* incorrotto, non guasto; incontaminato; puro.

untaken [ˈʌnˈteikən], *ag.* non preso; libero.

untalented [ˈʌnˈtæləntid], *ag.* poco dotato, senza talento.

untamable [ˈʌnˈteiməbl], *ag.* indomabile; riottoso.

untame [ˈʌnˈteim], *ag.* selvaggio, non addomesticato.

untamed [ˈʌnˈteimd], *ag.* **1.** selvaggio, non addomesticato **2.** ribelle, indomito: — *passions*, indomite passioni.

to untangle [ˈʌnˈtæŋgl], *v.t.* districare.

untanned [ˈʌnˈtænd], *ag.* **1.** non abbronzato **2.** non conciato (di cuoio).

untarnished [ˈʌnˈtɑːniʃt], *ag.* **1.** non appannato; non ossidato **2.** *fig.* non macchiato, immacolato: — *reputation*, reputazione irreprensibile.

untasked [ˈʌnˈtɑːskt], *ag.* **1.** senza occupazione **2.** non messo alla prova.

untasted [ˈʌnˈteistid], *ag.* **1.** non assaggiato **2.** *fig.* non gustato.

untaught [ˈʌnˈtɔːt], *ag.* **1.** poco istruito, ignorante **2.** appreso senza insegnamento, spontaneo: *those* — *graces of style*, quelle innate grazie dello stile.

untaxed [ˈʌnˈtækst], *ag.* non tassato; esente da imposte.

unteachable [ˈʌnˈtiːtʃəbl], *ag.* **1.** non educabile, incapace di imparare **2.** difficile da insegnare.

unteachableness [ˈʌnˈtiːtʃəblnis], *ag.* **1.** incapacità di imparare **2.** difficoltà d'insegnamento.

untearable [ˈʌnˈtɛərəbl], *ag.* non lacerabile.

untempered [ˈʌnˈtempəd], *ag.* **1.** smoderato, sfrenato **2.** non temprato (di vetro); non rinvenuto (di acciaio).

untempted [ˈʌnˈtemptid], *ag.* non tentato; non allettato.

untempting [ˈʌnˈtemptiŋ], *ag.* che non tenta, poco attraente, poco appetitoso.

untenable [ˈʌnˈtenəbl], *ag.* non tenibile; indifendibile: *an* — *position*, una posizione indifendibile.

untenantable [ˈʌnˈtenəntəbl], *ag.* **1.** non affittabile **2.** inabitabile.

untenanted [ʌn'tenəntid], *ag.* **1.** non affittato **2.** disabitato.

untended [ʌn'tendid], *ag.* non curato, trascurato; incustodito.

untender [ʌn'tendə*], *ag.* non tenero; *fig.* duro, insensibile.

untenderly [ʌn'tendəli], *av.* duramente.

unterrified [ʌn'terifaid], *ag.* non atterrito; imperterrito.

untested [ʌn'testid], *ag.* non provato, non sperimentato; non verificato.

unthankful [ʌn'θæŋkful], *ag.* ingrato.

unthankfully [ʌn'θæŋkfuli], *av.* senza gratitudine; senza riconoscenza.

unthankfulness [ʌn'θæŋkfulnis], *s.* ingratitudine.

unthawed [ʌn'θɔːd], *ag.* non disgelato; non fuso, non sciolto.

unthinkable [ʌn'θiŋkəbl], *ag.* inimmaginabile, inconcepibile; inammissibile: *it would be — that hostilities should be renewed*, sarebbe inammissibile che riprendessero le ostilità.

unthinking [ʌn'θiŋkiŋ], *ag.* irriflessivo; sconsiderato; sventato; leggero: *in an — moment*, in un momento di distrazione, per sventatezza.

unthinkingly [ʌn'θiŋkiŋli], *av.* irriflessivamente; inconsideratamente; sventatamente, alla leggera.

unthought [ʌn'θɔːt], *ag.* **1.** impensato; inatteso, imprevisto: *an — circumstance*, circostanza imprevista **2.** dimenticato ☆ *— of*, a cui non si pensa, a cui non si è pensato, imprevisto.

unthoughtful [ʌn'θɔːtful], *ag.* **1.** spensierato; sconsiderato; imprudente; sventato **2.** privo di riguardi, di attenzioni.

to **unthread** [ʌn'θred], *v.t.* **1.** sfilare, togliere il filo a **2.** sciogliere, sbrogliare (anche *fig.*): *to — a mystery*, sciogliere un mistero **3.** trovare una via d'uscita da: *to — a maze*, trovare l'uscita di un labirinto.

unthreatened [ʌn'θretnd], *ag.* non minacciato.

unthriftily [ʌn'θriftili], *av.* prodigamente.

unthriftiness [ʌn'θriftinis], *s.* mancanza di parsimonia; prodigalità.

unthrifty [ʌn'θrifti], *ag.* **1.** prodigo; dissipatore, scialacquatore: *to be — of one's goods*, essere prodigo dei propri beni **2.** che cresce male, che non frutta (di pianta).

unthriving [ʌn'θraiviŋ], *ag.* che non prospera.

to **unthrone** [ʌn'θroun], *v.t.* detronizzare.

untidily [ʌn'taidili], *av.* disordinatamente; trascuratamente; sciattamente.

untidiness [ʌn'taidinis], *s.* disordine; trascuratezza; sciatteria.

untidy [ʌn'taidi], *ag.* disordinato; trascurato, trasandato; sciatto: *the — appearance of the room*, l'aspetto disordinato della stanza; *— hair*, capelli arruffati; *an — person*, una persona trasandata ‖ *his playing is —*, (mus.) la sua esecuzione non è accurata.

to **untie** [ʌn'tai], *v.t.i.* sciogliere, sciogliersi; snodare, snodarsi; slegare, slegarsi.

until [ən'til], *V.* till[1].

to **untile** [ʌn'tail], *v.t.* togliere le tegole di (un tetto): *to — a roof*, scoprire un tetto.

untiled [ʌn'taild], *ag.* senza tegole, non coperto da tegole.

untillable [ʌn'tiləbl], *ag.* incoltivabile, non lavorabile, non arabile.

untilled [ʌn'tild], *ag.* incolto, non coltivato.

untimeliness [ʌn'taimlinis], *s.* **1.** l'essere prematuro **2.** inopportunità, intempestività.

untimely [ʌn'taimli], *ag.* **1.** prematuro: *his father's — death*, la morte prematura di suo padre **2.** inopportuno, intempestivo: *an — call*, una visita inopportuna.

untimely, *av.* **1.** prematuramente **2.** inopportunamente, intempestivamente.

untinged [ʌn'tindʒd], *ag.* non tinto, non colorato;

fig. senz'ombra, senza traccia: *speech — with pedantry*, discorso senza ombra di pedanteria.

untirable [ʌn'taiərəbl], *ag.* instancabile, infaticabile.

untired [ʌn'taiəd], *ag.* non stanco.

untiring [ʌn'taiəriŋ], *ag.* instancabile, infaticabile; assiduo: *he gave me — assistance*, mi diede un'assistenza assidua.

untiringly [ʌn'taiəriŋli], *av.* instancabilmente.

untithed [ʌn'taiðd], *ag.* (*eccl.*) non soggetto a decime.

untitled [ʌn'taitld], *ag.* senza titolo.

unto ['ʌntu], *prep.* (*arc. letter. spec. biblico*) **1. a:** *— you is born this day in the city of David a Saviour*, oggi, nella città di David, vi è nato il Salvatore; *and I say — you...*, e io vi dico...; *known — few*, noto a pochi; *to liken s.o., sthg., — s.o., sthg.*, paragonare qlcu., ql.co. a, con qlcu., ql.co. **2. a, verso:** *suffer the little children to come — me*, lasciate che i pargoli vengano a me; *to come nigh — sthg.*, avvicinarsi a ql.co.; *to turn — s.o.*, girarsi verso qlcu. **3. fino a:** *— this day*, fino ad oggi; *path which runs — the hills*, sentiero che va alle colline.

untold [ʌn'tould], *ag.* **1.** innumerevole, incalcolabile; immenso: *his — riches*, le sue ricchezze incalcolabili; *it cost us — suffering*, ci costò immense sofferenze **2.** non detto, non raccontato; taciuto.

to **untomb** [ʌn'tuːm], *v.t.* dissotterrare, esumare.

untorn [ʌn'tɔːn], *ag.* non lacerato.

untouchable [ʌn'tʌtʃəbl], *ag.* **1.** intoccabile **2.** *fig.* irraggiungibile ‖ *s.* intoccabile (in India).

untouched [ʌn'tʌtʃt], *ag.* **1.** non toccato, intatto, inviolato: *he left the food —*, lasciò il cibo intatto; *his reputation is —*, *fig.* la sua reputazione è immacolata **2.** illeso, indenne **3.** non menzionato, non discusso: *the question remains — upon*, la questione non è stata toccata **4.** indifferente, insensibile **5.** senza uguale, ineguagliato.

untoward [ʌn'touəd], *ag.* **1.** restio, caparbio, indocile **2.** scomodo, difficile **3.** infausto, funesto, sinistro: *I hope nothing — has happened*, spero che non sia accaduta una disgrazia **4.** sconveniente, disdicevole.

untowardly [ʌn'touədli], *av.* **1.** indocilmente **2.** funestamente, sinistramente **3.** sconvenientemente.

untowardness [ʌn'touədnis], *s.* **1.** caparbietà, indocilità **2.** scomodità, difficoltà.

untraceable [ʌn'treisəbl], *ag.* introvabile, irreperibile.

untraced [ʌn'treist], *ag.* non rintracciato.

untracked [ʌn'trækt], *ag.* **1.** non battuto (di sentiero, ecc.) **2.** non seguito, non rintracciato.

untractable [ʌn'træktəbl], *ag.* (*rar.*) intrattabile.

untragic [ʌn'trædʒik], *ag.* non tragico.

untrained [ʌn'treind], *ag.* **1.** inesperto, impreparato **2.** non allenato, non esercitato; non istruito.

untrammelled [ʌn'træməld], *ag.* non impastoiato, non inceppato; sciolto, libero.

untransferable ['ʌn-trænsˈfəːrəbl], *ag.* non trasferibile.

untranslatable ['ʌntrænsˈleitəbl], *ag.* intraducibile.

untranslatableness ['ʌntrænsˈleitəblnis], *s.* intraducibilità.

untranslated ['ʌntrænsˈleitid], *ag.* non tradotto.

untransparent ['ʌntrænsˈpɛərənt], *ag.* non trasparente, opaco.

untransportable ['ʌntrænsˈpɔːtəbl], *ag.* intrasportabile, che non si può trasportare.

untravelled [ʌn'trævld], *ag.* **1.** che non ha viaggiato **2.** inesplorato, poco conosciuto: *an — corner of Devon*, un angolino poco frequentato del Devon.

untraversable [ʌn'trævə(ː)səbl], *ag.* non attraversabile.

untraversed [ʌn'trævə(ː)st], *ag.* non attraversato.

untried [ʌn'traid], *ag.* **1.** non provato, non sperimentato: *we have left no remedy —*, non abbiamo lasciato intentato nessun rimedio **2.** (*dir.*) non processato.

untrimmed [ʌn'trimd], *ag.* **1.** disordinato, non regolato **2.** non guarnito, non ornato.

untrodden [ʌn'trɔdn], *ag.* non calpestato; non battuto, non frequentato: — *snow*, neve immacolata; *to go by* — *paths*, camminare per sentieri poco battuti.

untroubled ['ʌn'trʌbld], *ag.* imperturbato; tranquillo, calmo; limpido, sereno: *the* — *surface of the lake*, la calma superficie del lago.

untrue ['ʌn'tru:], *ag.* **1.** falso, menzognero; erroneo: *it is absolutely* —, è completamente falso **2.** infedele; (*rar.*) sleale; disonesto: *she had been* — *to him*, non gli era stata fedele **3.** (*mec.*) difettoso; inesatto; non centrato.

untrueness ['ʌn'tru:nis], *s.* **1.** falsità, menzogna **2.** inesattezza **3.** infedeltà, slealtà.

untruly ['ʌn'tru:li], *av.* **1.** falsamente, contrariamente alla verità **2.** erroneamente, inesattamente **3.** infedelmente.

to untruss ['ʌn'trʌs], *v.t.i.* **1.** disfare; sciogliere, slegare **2.** slacciarsi gli abiti.

untrustworthily ['ʌn'trʌst,wə:ðili], *av.* **1.** in modo indegno di fiducia **2.** in modo inattendibile.

untrustworthiness ['ʌn'trʌst,wə:ðinis], *s.* **1.** slealtà; falsità **2.** inattendibilità.

untrustworthy ['ʌn'trʌst,wə:ði], *ag.* **1.** indegno di fiducia, falso, sleale **2.** poco sicuro, poco attendibile: — *memory*, memoria labile.

untruth ['ʌn'tru:θ], *s.* falsità, menzogna.

untruthful ['ʌn'tru:θful], *ag.* falso, menzognero, mentitore.

untruthfully ['ʌn'tru:θfuli], *av.* falsamente, poco veridicamente.

untruthfulness ['ʌn'tru:θfulnis], *s.* falsità; mancanza di veridicità.

to untuck ['ʌn'tʌk], *v.t.* **1.** tirar giù (maniche rimboccate, coperte da un letto rincalzato) **2.** (*fam.*) allungare (le gambe): *he untucked his legs from under him*, egli allungò le gambe.

untunable ['ʌn'tju:nəbl], *ag.* **1.** non musicale, non melodioso **2.** che non tiene l'accordatura (di strumento musicale).

to untune ['ʌn'tju:n], *v.t.* **1.** scordare (strumento musicale) **2.** *fig.* turbare (armonia).

untuned ['ʌn'tju:nd], *ag.* scordato, stonato.

unturned ['ʌn'tə:nd], *ag.* non rovesciato, non rivoltato ‖ *to leave no stone* —, non lasciare nulla di intentato; far fuoco e fiamme; fare l'impossibile.

untutored ['ʌn'tju:təd], *ag.* **1.** senza istruzione, ignorante, poco istruito **2.** naturale, spontaneo.

to untwine ['ʌn'twain], *v.t.i.* svolgere, svolgersi; sciogliere, sciogliersi; districare, districarsi.

to untwist ['ʌn'twist], *v.t.i.* sbrogliare, sbrogliarsi; districare, districarsi; sciogliere, sciogliersi.

unurged ['ʌn'ə:dʒd], *ag.* non sollecitato; spontaneo: *to do sthg.* —, fare ql.co. spontaneamente.

unusable ['ʌn'ju:zəbl], *ag.* inutilizzabile.

unused ['ʌn'ju:zd], *nel senso* **3.** ['ʌn'ju:st], *ag.* **1.** non usato, non utilizzato **2.** fuori uso **3.** non abituato: *to be* — *to* (*doing*) *sthg.*, non essere abituato a (fare) ql.co.

unusual [ʌn'ju:ʒuəl], *ag.* insolito, inusitato, raro, fuori del comune, eccezionale: *it is* —, è insolito, non si usa.

unusually [ʌn'ju:ʒuəli], *av.* insolitamente, raramente, eccezionalmente.

unusualness [ʌn'ju:ʒuəlnis], *s.* stranezza, rarità; natura eccezionale.

unutilized ['ʌn'ju:tilaizd], *ag.* inutilizzato.

unutterable [ʌn'ʌtərəbl], *ag.* **1.** indescrivibile, indicibile **2.** impronunciabile.

unutterably [ʌn'ʌtərəbli], *av.* in modo indescrivibile, indicibilmente.

unuttered ['ʌn'ʌtəd], *ag.* **1.** non pronunciato **2.** inespresso.

unvaccinated ['ʌn'væksineitid], *ag.* non vaccinato.

unvalued ['ʌn'vælju:d], *ag.* **1.** non valutato, non stimato (di proprietà) **2.** poco stimato; disprezzato.

unvanquished ['ʌn'væŋkwiʃt], *ag.* invitto.

unvaried [ʌn'vɛərid], *ag.* invariato; uniforme, monotono: — *food*, cibo che manca di varietà.

unvarnished ['ʌn'vɑ:niʃt], *nel senso* **2.** [ʌn'vɑ:niʃt], *ag.* **1.** non verniciato **2.** (*fam.*) semplice, genuino; senza abbellimenti.

unvarying [ʌn'vɛəriiŋ], *ag.* invariabile, uniforme, costante.

unvaryingly ['ʌn'vɛəriiŋli], *av.* invariabilmente.

to unveil [ʌn'veil], *v.t.i.* **1.** togliere il velo a; togliersi il velo: *to* — *a statue*, scoprire una statua **2.** *fig.* rivelare, svelare.

unvenomous ['ʌn'venəməs], *ag.* non velenoso.

unventilated ['ʌn'ventileitid], *ag.* **1.** non ventilato, non aerato **2.** *fig.* non ventilato, non posto in discussione.

unverifiable ['ʌn'verifaiəbl], *ag.* non verificabile, non controllabile.

unverified ['ʌn'verifaid], *ag.* non verificato.

unversed ['ʌn'və:st], *ag.* non versato; poco pratico, poco abile: — *in*, inesperto di.

unvictualled ['ʌn'vitld], *ag.* **1.** non fornito di vettovaglie; senza vettovaglie.

unvindicated ['ʌn'vindikeitid], *ag.* invendicato.

unviolated ['ʌn'vaiəleitid], *ag.* inviolato.

unvisited ['ʌn'vizitid], *ag.* non visitato; non frequentato.

unvitiated ['ʌn'viʃieitid], *ag.* non viziato; non corrotto.

unvoiced ['ʌn'vɔist], *ag.* **1.** non espresso, non pronunciato **2.** (*fonet.*) sordo.

unvouched ['ʌn'vautʃt], *ag.* non attestato; non confermato.

unwaked ['ʌn'weikt], **unwakened** ['ʌn'weikənd], *ag.* non sveglio, addormentato; non risvegliato.

unwalled ['ʌn'wɔ:ld], *ag.* senza muri; senza mura.

unwanted ['ʌn'wɔntid], *ag.* non desiderato, non richiesto; non necessario.

unwarily [ʌn'wɛərili], *av.* senza precauzioni, imprudentemente; sconsideratamente.

unwariness [ʌn'wɛərinis], *s.* imprudenza; sconsideratezza.

unwarlike ['ʌn'wɔ:laik], *ag.* poco bellicoso, pacifico.

unwarmed ['ʌn'wɔ:md], *ag.* non riscaldato.

unwarned ['ʌn'wɔ:nd], *ag.* non avvertito; non preavvisato; non ammonito.

unwarped ['ʌn'wɔ:pt], *ag.* **1.** non curvato; non deformato (di legno, ecc.) **2.** *fig.* libero da pregiudizi.

unwarrantable [ʌn'wɔrəntəbl], *ag.* **1.** che non può essere garantito **2.** che non può essere autorizzato **3.** ingiustificabile.

unwarrantableness [ʌn'wɔrəntəblnis], *s.* ingiustificabilità.

unwarrantably [ʌn'wɔrəntəbli], *av.* ingiustificabilmente.

unwarranted ['ʌn'wɔrəntid], *nel senso* **3.** [ʌn'wɔrəntid], *ag.* **1.** non autorizzato **2.** non garantito **3.** ingiustificato, infondato.

unwary [ʌn'wɛəri], *ag.* imprudente, incauto; sconsiderato.

unwashed ['ʌn'wɔʃt], *ag.* non lavato; sudicio, sporco ‖ *the* (*Great*) *Unwashed*, la plebaglia.

unwasted ['ʌn'weistid], *ag.* non sciupato, non sprecato; non consumato.

unwatched ['ʌn'wɔtʃt], *ag.* non sorvegliato, incustodito.

unwatchful ['ʌn'wɔtʃful], *ag.* non vigilante; disattento.

unwatchfulness ['ʌn'wɔtʃfulnis], *s.* mancanza di vigilanza; disattenzione, sbadataggine.

unwatered ['ʌn'wɔ:təd], *ag.* **1.** senz'acqua; non bagnato; non annacquato, non innaffiato; non irrigato; non diluito **2.** (*comm.*) non diluito (di capitale).

unwavering [ʌn'weivəriŋ], *ag.* che non vacilla; incrollabile, fermo, deciso.

unwaveringly [ʌn'weivəriŋli], *av.* senza esitare, fermamente.

unweaned [ˈʌnˈwiːnd], *ag.* non svezzato.

unwearable [ˈʌnˈwɛərəbl], *ag.* non indossabile.

unwearied [ˈʌnˈwiərid], *ag.* **1.** non stanco, non affaticato **2.** instancabile.

unweariedly [ˈʌnˈwiəridli], *av.* instancabilmente, infaticabilmente.

unweariedness [ˈʌnˈwiəridnis], *s.* instancabilità, infaticabilità.

unweary [ˈʌnˈwiəri], *ag.* non stanco; indefesso, infaticabile.

unwearying [ʌnˈwiəriiŋ], *ag.* instancabile; persistente, tenace.

unwearyingly [ˈʌnˈwiəriiŋli], *av.* instancabilmente, tenacemente.

to unweave [ˈʌnˈwiːv], *pass.* **unwove** [ˈʌnˈwouv], *p.p.* **unwoven** [ˈʌnˈwouvən], *v.t.* disfare (un tessuto), stessere.

unwebbed [ˈʌnˈwebd], *ag.* non fornito di membrana.

unwedded [ˈʌnˈwedid], *ag.* non sposato; celibe; nubile.

unweeded [ˈʌnˈwiːdid], *ag.* non sarchiato; non liberato dalle erbacce.

unweighed [ˈʌnˈweid], *ag.* **1.** non pesato **2.** *fig.* non ponderato; non esaminato.

unwelcome(d) [ʌnˈwelkəm(d)], *ag.* male accolto; sgradito; importuno.

unwell [ˈʌnˈwel], *ag.* indisposto; ammalato.

unwept [ˈʌnˈwept], *ag.* (*poet.*) non rimpianto; illacrimato.

unwet(ted) [ˈʌnˈwet(id)], *ag.* non inumidito, non bagnato.

unwhipped [ˈʌnˈwipt], *ag.* **1.** non frustato **2.** non sbattuto.

unwhitened [ˈʌnˈwaitnd], *ag.* non imbiancato.

unwholesome [ˈʌnˈhoulsəm], *ag.* **1.** malsano, insalubre **2.** *fig.* nocivo; guasto, corrotto.

unwholesomely [ˈʌnˈhoulsəmli], *av.* in modo malsano; corrottamente.

unwholesomeness [ˈʌnˈhoulsəmnis], *s.* **1.** insalubrità **2.** *fig.* l'essere nocivo, corrotto; morbosità.

unwieldily [ʌnˈwiːldili], *av.* pesantemente; in modo ingombrante; con difficoltà.

unwieldiness [ʌnˈwiːldinis], *s.* **1.** pesantezza; impaccio; difficoltà di movimento **2.** l'essere ingombrante.

unwieldy [ʌnˈwiːldi], *ag.* **1.** pesante; lento; impacciato **2.** ingombrante; poco maneggevole **3.** (*rar.*) *fig.* indocile, ribelle.

unwilling [ʌnˈwiliŋ], *ag.* **1.** riluttante, poco propenso: *he is — to give up everything,* è poco propenso a rinunciare a tutto **2.** involontario; non voluto, fatto controvoglia.

unwillingly [ʌnˈwiliŋli], *av.* malvolentieri; controvoglia.

unwillingness [ʌnˈwiliŋnis], *s.* **1.** riluttanza; avversione **2.** cattiva volontà, malavoglia.

to unwind [ˈʌnˈwaind], *pass.p.p.* **unwound** [ˈʌnˈwaund], *v.t.i.* srotolare, srotolarsi; svolgere, svolgersi; dipanare, dipanarsi.

unwinged [ˈʌnˈwiŋd], *ag.* privo di ali, senz'ali.

unwiped [ˈʌnˈwaipt], *ag.* non asciugato; non pulito.

unwisdom [ˈʌnˈwizdəm], *s.* mancanza di saggezza, di buon senso; imprudenza.

unwise [ˈʌnˈwaiz], *ag.* malaccorto, privo di buon senso; imprudente.

unwisely [ˈʌnˈwaizli], *av.* insensatamente; imprudentemente.

unwished [ʌnˈwiʃt], *ag.*: *— -for,* non desiderato, non voluto.

unwithered [ˈʌnˈwiðəd], *ag.* non appassito; ancora fresco.

unwithering [ˈʌnˈwiðəriŋ], *ag.* che non appassisce.

unwitnessed [ˈʌnˈwitnist], *ag.* senza testimoni; non testimoniato.

unwittily [ˈʌnˈwitili], *av.* **1.** scioccamente **2.** senza spirito.

unwitting [ʌnˈwitiŋ], *ag.* inconsapevole; involontario.

unwittingly [ʌnˈwitiŋli], *av.* inconsapevolmente; involontariamente.

unwitty [ˈʌnˈwiti], *ag.* **1.** sciocco **2.** poco spiritoso; senza spirito.

unwomanly [ʌnˈwumənli], *ag.* poco femminile.

unwon [ˈʌnˈwʌn], *ag.* non vinto.

unwonted [ʌnˈwountid], *ag.* non abituale, insolito; raro.

unwontedly [ʌnˈwountidli], *av.* insolitamente; raramente.

unwontedness [ʌnˈwountidnis], *s.* rarità; singolarità.

unwooed [ˈʌnˈwuːd], *ag.* non corteggiato.

unworkable [ˈʌnˈwəːkəbl], *ag.* **1.** ineseguibile **2.** che non può funzionare.

unworked [ˈʌnˈwəːkt], *ag.* non lavorato; non eseguito.

unworking [ˈʌnˈwəːkiŋ], *ag.* che non lavora.

unworkmanlike [ˈʌnˈwəːkmənlaik], *ag.* **1.** inetto, inesperto **2.** male eseguito.

unworldliness [ˈʌnˈwəːldlinis], *s.* spiritualità; disinteresse nelle cose terrene.

unworldly [ˈʌnˈwəːldli], *ag.* spirituale; non terreno.

unworn [ˈʌnˈwɔːn], *ag.* **1.** non indossato **2.** non logoro, non sciupato.

unworried [ˈʌnˈwʌrid], *ag.* **1.** indisturbato **2.** non preoccupato; sereno.

unworshipped [ˈʌnˈwəːʃipt], *ag.* non adorato, non venerato.

unworthily [ʌnˈwəːðili], *av.* indegnamente.

unworthiness [ʌnˈwəːðinis], *s.* indegnità.

unworthy [ʌnˈwəːði], *ag.* **1.** indegno: *— of notice,* indegno di considerazione; *this is — of him,* questo è indegno di lui **2.** spregevole: *an — person,* una persona indegna **3.** poco meritevole (di lavoro, ecc.).

unwound [ˈʌnˈwaund], *pass.p.p.* di to **unwind.**

unwounded [ˈʌnˈwuːndid], *ag.* illeso, incolume, non ferito.

unwove [ˈʌnˈwouv], *pass.* di to **unweave.**

unwoven [ˈʌnˈwouvən], *p.p.* di to **unweave.**

to unwrap [ˈʌnˈræp], *pass. p.p.* **unwrapped** [ˈʌnˈræpt], *v.t.* disfare, svolgere, aprire.

to unwreathe [ˈʌnˈriːð], *v.t.* sciogliere, disfare (una ghirlanda).

unwrinkled [ˈʌnˈriŋkld], *ag.* senza rughe, liscio.

unwritable [ˈʌnˈraitəbl], *ag.* che non può essere scritto.

unwritten [ˈʌnˈritn], *ag.* **1.** non scritto; orale; tradizionale: *— law,* legge tramandata oralmente ‖ *the — law,* legge d'onore (specialmente legge per cui un delitto di gelosia non dovrebbe essere punito) **2.** bianco (di carta).

unwrought [ˈʌnˈrɔːt], *ag.* **1.** non lavorato; non operato **2.** grezzo **3.** (*miner.*) non sfruttato (di giacimento).

unwrung [ˈʌnˈrʌŋ], *ag.* **1.** non torto; non strizzato **2.** *fig.* non colpito.

unyielded [ˈʌnˈjiːldid], *ag.* **1.** non prodotto **2.** non ceduto, non concesso.

unyielding [ʌnˈjiːldiŋ], *ag.* **1.** inflessibile; ostinato; rigido: *she is — in her opinions,* è inflessibile nelle sue opinioni **2.** che offre resistenza (di sostanza).

unyieldingly [ʌnˈjiːldiŋli], *av.* inflessibilmente; ostinatamente; rigidamente.

to unyoke [ˈʌnˈjouk], *v.t.i.* **1.** staccare, togliere il giogo a (buoi, ecc.); staccarsi dal giogo **2.** (*fam.*) cessare di lavorare **3.** *fig.* liberare, liberarsi dal giogo: *he unyoked his countrymen,* egli liberò i suoi compatrioti dal giogo.

up [ʌp], *av.* **1.** su, in su; in alto: *from five pounds —,* da cinque sterline in su; *from my youth —,* fin dalla mia giovinezza; *the curtains are —,* le tende sono alzate; *the moon is —,* la luna è alta; *the plane is —,* l'aeroplano è in volo; *the river is —,* il fiume è in piena; *the road goes sharply —,* la strada sale bruscamente; *the thermometer has gone —,* il termometro è salito;

what are you doing — there?, che cosa stai facendo lassù?; *to go — in price*, aumentare di prezzo; *to throw sthg. — in the air*, gettare ql.co. in aria ‖ *— above*, in alto; *— above sthg.*, al di sopra di ql.co. ‖ *— to windward*, (*mar.*) controvento ‖ *all the way —*, fino in cima ‖ *further —*, più in su, più oltre: *she lives two miles further —*, abita due miglia più in su ‖ *hands —*, mani in alto ‖ *road —*, strada interrotta, lavori in corso ‖ *this side* (o *end*) *—*, non capovolgere ‖ *to be —*, (*ippica*) essere in sella ‖ *to be one goal —*, (*spor.*) condurre per un punto ‖ *to be* (*well*) *— in a subject*, conoscere una materia a fondo ‖ *to give s.o. a leg —*, aiutare qlcu. a montare in sella; (*fam.*) dare una mano a qlcu. **2.** (*verso città, luogo importante, università, luogo più a nord*): *they came — from the country*, vennero su (a Londra) dalla campagna; *you have to go — to Cambridge for the examinations*, devi andare a Cambridge per gli esami; *to go — north*, andare al nord; *to go — to town*, andare in città **3.** (*verso il luogo in questione o in cui si trova chi parla*): *come — for dinner*, vieni da me a pranzo **4. in piedi:** *he sprang — from his seat*, si alzò in piedi di scatto; *she is not — yet*, non è ancora alzata; *to be — all night*, star su tutta notte; *to be — till late*, vegliare fino a tardi; *to get —*, alzarsi (in piedi, dal letto) ‖ *—* (*with*) *the Conservatives!*, evviva i conservatori! ‖ *as if nothing were —*, come se niente fosse ‖ *the beer is —*, la birra fa la schiuma ‖ *his blood is —*, gli è montato il sangue alla testa, gli ribolle il sangue ‖ *let us be — and doing*, mettiamoci all'opera ‖ *Parliament is —*, il Parlamento è in vacanza ‖ *what's —?*, cosa sta succedendo?; *what's — with you*, cosa ti prende? ‖ *to be — against sthg.*, essere alle prese con ql.co. ‖ *to be — in arms*, essere in armi; essere in rivolta **5.** (*unito a verbi: con uso intensivo, per indicare completamento, compiutezza, risultato, vicinanza*): *everything was burnt —*, era bruciato tutto; *the game is —*, tutto è perduto; *hurry —!*, spicciati!; muovetevi!; *it's all — with him*, è spacciato; è finita per lui; *time is —*, si chiude; è l'ora (di chiudere, di finire); *to follow s.o. —*, seguire qlcu. da vicino; *to praise s.o. —*, esaltare, portare alle stelle qlcu.; *to save — money*, risparmiare denaro; *to screw —*, avvitare; *to speak —*, parlare più forte; parlare liberamente ‖ **up to, 1.** fino a: *— now, then*, fino ad ora, fino ad allora; *from ten — twelve*, da dieci a dodici; *he went straight — the door*, andò dritto alla porta; *to blush — the ears*, arrossire fino alla radice dei capelli ‖ *to live — one's income*, spendere tutto quello che si guadagna, spendere tutto il proprio reddito ‖ *he is — his job*, è all'altezza del proprio lavoro ‖ *I don't feel — going out*, non me la sento di uscire; *I don't feel — it*, non me la sento ‖ *this book is not — much*, questo libro non vale un gran che ‖ *to be — anything*, essere capace di tutto ‖ *to be — one's neck in sthg.*, essere dentro fino al collo in ql.co. ‖ *to be — s.o.*, essere all'altezza di qlcu. **2.** *he is — sthg.*, sta tramando ql.co.; *what are the children —?*, che cosa stanno combinando i bambini? **3.** *it is — him to help them*, tocca a lui aiutarli; *it isn't — me*, non tocca a me, non è affar mio.

up, *prep.* **1. su, su per, in cima a:** *the cat is — the ladder*, il gatto è in cima alla scala; *to climb — a hill*, salire su una collina **2. verso il fondo** (di strada, ecc.), **verso l'interno** (di paese), **verso la sorgente** (di fiume): *— the lane*, in fondo al vicolo; *— the river*, verso la sorgente; risalendo il fiume; *— a monte* (di strada); *— the street*, più in là sulla strada; *to sail — a river*, risalire un fiume; *to travel — Africa*, viaggiare nell'interno dell'Africa.

up, *ag. attributivo* ascendente, che va verso l'alto; (*ferr.*) diretto verso la capitale (specialmente Londra): *— line*, la linea di Londra; *— train*, treno di Londra ‖ *s.: on the — and —*, (*fam. amer.*) leale, franco, onesto.

to **up,** *pass.p.p.* **upped** [ʌpt], *v.t.i.* **1.** (*fam.*) cominciare all'improvviso; balzar su (a fare, dire):

she upped and threw the tea-pot at him, balzò su e gli lanciò contro la teiera **2.** (*amer.*) aumentare: *they have upped the production*, hanno aumentato la produzione **3.** *to — with* (*sthg.*), sollevare, alzare: *he upped with his stick*, alzò il bastone.

up-a-daisy ['ʌpə‚deizi], *inter.* oplà!.

to **up-anchor** [ʌp'æŋkə*], *v.i.* (*mar.*) levare l'ancora.

up-and-coming ['ʌpən'kʌmiŋ], *ag.* (*amer.*) sveglio, intraprendente.

up-and-down ['ʌpən'daun], *ag. attributivo* **1.** che va in su e in giù; verticale **2.** variabile, oscillante.

up and down, *s. spec. pl.* ondulazioni (del terreno, ecc.), su e giù; *fig.* vicissitudini, alti e bassi: *the ups and downs of life*, gli alti e bassi della vita; *the ups and downs of the market*, le oscillazioni del mercato ‖ *av.* su e giù; avanti e indietro; da ogni parte: *to look for s.o. —*, cercare qlcu. dappertutto; *to walk —*, andare avanti e indietro ‖ *prep.* su e giù, avanti e indietro per: *to walk — the street*, andare avanti e indietro per una strada.

Upanishad [u'pʌniʃəd], *s.* (*lett.*) Upanishad.

upas ['ju:pəs], *s.* **1.** (*bot. farm.*) «upas» **2.** *fig.* influsso malefico.

to **upbear** [ʌp'bɛə*], *pass.* **upbore** [ʌp'bɔ:*], *p.p.* **upborne** [ʌp'bɔ:n], *v.t.* **1.** sollevare **2.** sorreggere, sostenere.

upbeat ['ʌpbi:t], *s.* **1.** (*mus.*) battuta in levare **2.** (*poes.*) anacrusi.

to **upbraid** [ʌp'breid], *v.t.* sgridare, rimproverare: *to — s.o. with* (o *for*) *sthg.*, rimproverare qlcu. per ql.co.

upbraider [ʌp'breidə*], *s.c.* chi rimprovera, biasima.

upbraiding [ʌp'breidiŋ], *s.* rimprovero.

upbraidingly [ʌp'breidiŋli], *av.* in tono di rimprovero.

upbringing ['ʌp‚briŋiŋ], *s.* educazione; allevamento: *this is the result of his bad —!*, questo è il risultato della sua cattiva educazione!.

upburst ['ʌpbə:st], *s.* scoppio, esplosione.

upcast ['ʌpka:st], *ag.* lanciato in alto *s.* **1.** lancio in alto **2.** (*min.*) pozzo di ventilazione.

to **upcast** [ʌp'ka:st], *pass.p.p.* **upcast**, *v.t.* gettare, lanciare in alto.

up-country ['ʌp'kʌntri], *ag.* situato all'interno di una regione ‖ *s.* regione interna, lontana dalla costa: *the — is barren*, l'interno del paese è sterile.

up-country, *av.* all'interno: *the explorers travelled — for a hundred miles*, gli esploratori si addentrarono nella regione per un centinaio di miglia.

to **up-end** [ʌp'end], *v.t.i.* (*dial.*) mettere, mettersi dritto; alzare, alzarsi in piedi.

to **upfill** [ʌp'fil], *v.t.* riempire.

upgrade ['ʌpgreid], *ag.* in salita, ascendente ‖ *s.* inclinazione; salita ‖ *on the —*, in ascesa; che cresce; *fig.* che migliora, in progresso.

upgrade, *av.* in salita.

to **upgrade** [ʌp'greid], *v.t.* (*amer.*) **1.** promuovere (un impiegato, ecc.) a un grado superiore **2.** aumentare il salario di.

upgrowth ['ʌpgrouθ], *s.* crescita; sviluppo.

upheaval [ʌp'hi:vəl], *s.* **1.** (*spec. geol.*) sollevamento, rigonfiamento **2.** *fig.* agitazione, sconvolgimento: *the general —*, lo scompiglio generale.

to **upheave** [ʌp'hi:v], *v.t.i.* (*spec. geol.*) sollevare, sollevarsi.

upheld [ʌp'held], *pass.p.p.* di to **uphold**.

uphill ['ʌp'hil], *ag.* **1.** erto, scosceso, ripido **2.** *fig.* arduo, difficile, faticoso ‖ *s.* salita, rampa, erta.

uphill, *av.* in salita, in su.

to **uphold** [ʌp'hould], *pass.p.p.* **upheld** [ʌp'held], *v.t.* **1.** sostenere, sorreggere **2.** *fig.* sostenere, appoggiare, patrocinare: *opinion that cannot be upheld*, opinione insostenibile; *to — s.o. in an action*, sostenere qlcu. in un'azione **3.** *fig.* mantenere, confermare: *to — a decision*, mantenere una decisione.

upholder [ʌp'houldə*], *s.* **1.** sostegno, appoggio **2.** *fig.* difensore, sostenitore, partigiano, propugnatore.

to **upholster** [ʌp'houlstə*], v.t. tappezzare; imbottire; ricoprire: *upholstered in* (o *with*) *velvet*, ricoperto di velluto.

upholsterer [ʌp'houlstərə*], s. tappezziere; decoratore.

upholstery [ʌp'houlstəri], s. **1.** tappezzeria; imbottitura **2.** mestiere del tappezziere.

upkeep ['ʌpki:p], s. mantenimento; manutenzione: *the — and the rent cost £ 150 a year*, il mantenimento e l'affitto costano 150 sterline all'anno.

upland ['ʌplənd], ag. alto, elevato; montano ‖ s. gener. pl. regione montagnosa (dell'interno), altipiano ☆ — *cotton*, cotone a fibra corta.

uplander ['ʌpləndə*], s. montanaro; abitante di un altipiano.

uplift ['ʌplift], s. **1.** sollevamento, innalzamento (specialmente di terreno) **2.** fig. elevatezza.

to **uplift** [ʌp'lift], v.t. **1.** sollevare, alzare **2.** fig. elevare, innalzare (fig.): *his soul was uplifted by music*, la musica elevò il suo spirito.

upon [ə'pɔn], prep. V. on (meno usato di on, generalmente preferito in fine di frase e in alcune espressioni: — *my word*, sulla mia parola; *not a chair to sit —*, non una sedia dove sedersi; *very little to live —*, molto poco per viverci).

upper ['ʌpə*], ag. **1.** superiore, più alto, più elevato (anche fig.): — *jaw, lip*, mascella, labbro superiore; *the — rooms of a house*, le stanze superiori di una casa; *the — stor(e)y*, il piano superiore (di una casa); (fam.) il cervello ‖ *the — crust*, (fam.) l'aristocrazia, la crema; *the — ten (thousand)*, « le trecento famiglie », la classe più potente, più ricca ‖ *the Upper House*, la Camera dei Lords, la Camera Alta ‖ *to have* (o *to get*) *the — hand*, avere la prevalenza, il predominio: *to have* (o *to get*) *the — hand of s.o.*, of a horse, soggiogare, aver ragione di qlcu., domare un cavallo **2.** più lontano (dall'ingresso, dalla foce, ecc.): *the — end of a church*, il fondo di una chiesa; *the — part of a river*, la parte a monte di un fiume ‖ *Upper Egypt*, Alto Egitto; *Upper Rhine*, Alto Reno **3.** (mus.) a destra (di tastiera); acuto (di registro) ‖ s. **1.** tomaia; gambale ‖ *to be on one's uppers*, (fam.) essere al verde **2.** pl. ghette.

uppercut ['ʌpəkʌt], s. (boxe) « uppercut » (colpo dal basso in alto).

uppermost ['ʌpəmoust], ag. **1.** il più alto, il più elevato **2.** il più importante; principale, predominante: *the — subject of conversation*, il principale argomento di conversazione.

uppermost, av. al di sopra, più in alto di tutto ‖ *she said whatever came —*, diceva la prima cosa che le veniva in mente.

upperworks ['ʌpəwə:ks], s. (mar.) opera morta.

uppish ['ʌpiʃ], ag. presuntuoso; arrogante, altezzoso.

uppishly ['ʌpiʃli], av. presuntuosamente; arrogantemente, in tono altezzoso.

uppishness ['ʌpiʃnis], s. presunzione; arroganza, altezzosità, boria: *the — of modern youth*, la presunzione dei giovani d'oggi.

to **upraise** [ʌp'reiz], v.t. sollevare, alzare; elevare, innalzare.

to **uprear** [ʌp'riə*], v.t. **1.** sollevare, innalzare **2.** esaltare.

upright ['ʌp'rait], nel senso **2.** e come s. ['ʌp-rait], ag. **1.** ritto, diritto, eretto; verticale; perpendicolare: *he has an — a[h]letic figure*, ha una figura diritta, atletica; *to take an t— position*, assumere una posizione eretta **2.** retto, integro, giusto, onesto: *an — judge*, un magistrato integro; *an — man*, un uomo onesto, per bene ‖ s. (edil. mec.) palo verticale, montante ☆ — *boiler*, caldaia verticale; — *piano*, piano verticale.

upright, av. dritto, retto, in piedi; perpendicolarmente; verticalmente: *to hold oneself —*, tenersi dritto; *to set sthg. —*, raddrizzare ql.co.; *to stand —*, stare in posizione eretta.

uprightly ['ʌp,raitli], av. **1.** (arc.) in piedi, in posizione verticale, eretta **2.** rettamente, onestamente.

uprightness ['ʌp,raitnis], s. **1.** perpendicolarità, verticalità **2.** rettitudine, integrità.

uprise ['ʌpraiz], s. **1.** (rar.) sorgere (del sole) **2.** ascesa.

to **uprise** [ʌp'raiz], pass. **uprose** [ʌp'rouz], p.p. **uprisen** [ʌp'rizn], v.i. (poet.) alzarsi, sorgere, levarsi.

uprising [ʌp'raiziŋ], s. **1.** il sorgere, l'alzarsi: *the — of a new social class*, il sorgere, l'apparizione di una nuova classe sociale **2.** rivolta, insurrezione.

upriver ['ʌp,rivə*], ag. a monte, verso la sorgente.

uproar ['ʌp,rɔ:*], s. tumulto; chiasso; trambusto: *the town was in an —*, la città era in tumulto; *to make an —*, far baraonda.

to **uproar** [ʌp'rɔ:*], v.i. (rar.) tumultuare.

uproarious [ʌp'rɔ:riəs], ag. tumultuoso; chiassoso: *an — meeting*, un'adunanza burrascosa; *she burst into — laughter*, scoppiò in una risata sonora; *there was — applause*, gli applausi scrosciarono.

uproariously [ʌp'rɔ:riəsli], av. tumultuosamente; rumorosamente.

uproariousness [ʌp'rɔ:riəsnis], s. tumulto; chiasso, baraonda.

to **uproot** [ʌp'ru:t], v.t. sradicare, svellere, estirpare (anche fig.): *they were uprooted from their homes*, furono strappati alle loro case; *we must — this evil from our life*, dobbiamo sradicare questo male dalla nostra vita; *the wind has uprooted a few trees*, il vento ha sradicato qualche albero.

uprooting [ʌp'ru:tiŋ], s. sradicamento, estirpazione.

uprose [ʌp'rouz], pass. di to **uprise**.

ups-a-daisy ['ʌpsə,deizi], inter. oplà!.

to **upsaddle** [ʌp'sædl], v.i. (sud-africano) sellare un cavallo.

upset [ʌp'set], nel senso **3.** ['ʌpset], ag. **1.** rovesciato, capovolto, ribaltato **2.** fig. sconvolto, turbato **3.** iniziale, d'apertura (di prezzo di un oggetto all'asta) ‖ s. **1.** ribaltamento, rovesciamento **2.** fig. confusione, disordine; turbamento.

to **upset**, pass.p.p. **upset**, v.t.i. **1.** rovesciare, rovesciarsi; ribaltare, ribaltarsi; capovolgere, capovolgersi: *the boy has — a bottle of wine*, il ragazzo ha rovesciato una bottiglia di vino; *the wind — the boat*, il vento capovolse la barca **2.** disturbare, sconvolgere, sventare: *to — a plot*, sventare un complotto **3.** turbare, sconvolgere, emozionare: *the news — her*, la notizia la sconvolse **4.** disturbare (lo stomaco) **5.** (mec.) ricalcare, battere il metallo.

upshot ['ʌpʃɔt], s. esito, conclusione, risultato: *the — of it all was that he resigned*, alla fine egli dovette dare le dimissioni.

upside ['ʌpsaid], s. lato, parte superiore ‖ av. sulla parte superiore.

upside-down ['ʌpsaid'daun], ag. disordinato, messo sottosopra ‖ av. **1.** capovolto **2.** sottosopra, in disordine, alla rinfusa.

upsides ['ʌpsaidz], av. (fam.) pari a ‖ *to get — with*, (dial.) rovesciare le posizioni, tornare in posizione di vantaggio; vendicarsi.

upsilon [ju:p'sailən], s. ipsilon (ventesima lettera dell'alfabeto greco).

to **upspring** [ʌp'spriŋ], pass. **upsprang** [ʌp'spræŋ], p.p. **upsprung** [ʌp'sprʌŋ], v.i. **1.** crescere (di piante) **2.** balzare in piedi; saltare in alto **3.** fig. nascere.

upstair ['ʌp'stɛə*], **upstairs** ['ʌp'stɛəz], ag. situato, relativo al piano superiore: *an — room*, una stanza al piano superiore.

upstairs, av. al piano superiore; di sopra: *the bedrooms are —*, le camere da letto sono al piano superiore; *he looked — and downstairs for you*, vi ha cercato dappertutto.

upstanding ['ʌp'stændiŋ], ag. **1.** eretto, dritto **2.** fig. franco, leale, onesto **3.** fisso, stabile (di salario).

upstart ['ʌp,stɑ:t], ag. divenuto improvvisamente importante ‖ s. nuovo ricco; persona venuta dal nulla.

upstream [ˈʌpˈstriːm], *ag.* a monte ‖ *av.* controcorrente.

upstroke [ˈʌp-strouk], *s.* **1.** tratto ascendente (nella scrittura) **2.** *(mec.)* corsa ascendente.

uptake [ˈʌpteik], *s.* **1.** *(rar.)* sollevamento **2.** comprensione: *he is very slow in the —,* è molto duro di comprendonio **3.** tiraggio (di ventilazione).

upthrow [ˈʌpθrou], *s.* **1.** lancio verso l'alto **2.** *(geol.)* sollevamento (di strati vulcanici).

upthrust [ˈʌpθrʌst], *s.* **1.** *(geol.)* sollevamento **2.** *(fis.)* pressione idrostatica.

up-to-date [ˈʌptəˈdeit], *ag. attributivo* **1.** aggiornato, informato **2.** alla moda, moderno.

uptown [ˈʌpˈtaun], *ag.* dei quartieri alti ‖ *av.* nei quartieri alti, verso i quartieri alti.

to **upturn** [ʌpˈtəːn], *v.t.i.* **1.** voltare, voltarsi verso l'alto; volgere, volgersi verso l'alto: *the children stood with upturned faces,* i bimbi stavano con la faccia volta verso l'alto **2.** rivoltare (le zolle, ecc.).

upward [ˈʌpwəd], *ag.* ascendente; ascensionale; diretto, rivolto (dal basso) verso l'alto; in salita (di strada): *— glance,* sguardo rivolto verso l'alto; *— movement,* movimento ascensionale; fase ascendente: *the constant — movement of prices,* la costante ascesa dei prezzi ☆ *— exhaust pipe,* *(mec.)* tubo di scarico rialzato; *— flowing current,* *(elett.)* corrente ascendente; *— gradient,* rampa; *— motion,* *(aer.)* cabrata; *— -sloping,* ascendente (di curva).

upward, *av.* **1.** in su, in alto; verso l'alto; in salita (di strada, ecc.); all'insù: *face —,* col viso all'insù; dalla parte diritta (di libro, ecc.); *the road runs —,* la strada sale; *we followed the river —,* risalimmo il corso del fiume; *to look —,* guardare in su **2.** al di sopra, oltre: *from twenty years —,* dai vent'anni in su; *soldiers of ten years' service and —,* soldati con dieci anni di servizio e più ‖ *— of,* più di, al di sopra di: *we have no pupils — of sixteen,* non abbiamo allievi al di sopra dei sedici anni.

upwardly [ˈʌpwədli], *av.* verso l'alto; all'insù.

upwards [ˈʌpwədz], *V.* **upward.**

uraemia [juəˈriːmjə], *s.* *(patol.)* uremia.

Urania [juəˈreinjə], *no.pr.f.* *(mit.)* Urania ‖ *no.pr.* *(astr.)* Urania.

uranie [juəˈrænik], *ag.* uranico.

uranium [juəˈreinjəm], *s.* *(min.)* uranio.

uranographie [ˌjuərənouˈgræfik], *ag.* uranografico.

uranographist [ˌjuərəˈnɔgrəfist], *s.* uranografo.

uranography [ˌjuərəˈnɔgrəfi], *s.* uranografia.

Uranus [ˈjuərənəs], *no.pr.m.* *(mit.)* Urano ‖ *no.pr.* *(astr.)* Urano.

urao [uːˈrɑːou], *s.* *(min.)* trona, urao.

urate [ˈjuəreit], *s.* *(chim.)* urato.

urban[1] [ˈəːbən], *ag.* urbano, di città.

Urban[2], *no.pr.m.* Urbano.

urbane [əːˈbein], *ag.* urbano, cortese.

urbanely [əːˈbeinli], *av.* urbanamente, cortesemente.

urbanity [əːˈbæniti], *s.* urbanità, cortesia.

to **urbanize** [ˈəːbənaiz], *v.t.* urbanizzare.

urchin [ˈəːtʃin], *s.* **1.** monello, moccioso; ragazzo **2.** *(zool.)* riccio, porcospino **3.** gobbo ☆ *sea —,* *(zool.)* riccio di mare.

Urdu [əːˈduː], *ag. s.* indostano (lingua).

urea [ˈjuəriə], *s.* *(chim.)* urea.

ureter [juəˈriːtə*], *s.* *(anat.)* uretere.

urethra [juəˈriːθrə], *s.* *(anat.)* uretra.

urethral [juəˈriːθrəl], *ag.* *(anat.)* uretrale.

urethritis [ˌjuəriˈθraitis], *s.* *(patol.)* uretrite.

urethrotomy [ˌjuəriˈθrɔtəmi], *s.* *(chir.)* uretrotomia.

uretie [juəˈretik], *ag.s.* *(med.)* diuretico.

urge [əːdʒ], *s.* **1.** impulso, stimolo, bisogno imperioso: *to feel the — of ambition,* sentire lo stimolo dell'ambizione **2.** spinta, sprone, incitamento.

to **urge,** *v.t.i.* **1.** (IV) spingere; incalzare; stimolare; incitare; incoraggiare; esortare: *he urged me to action,* mi spinse ad agire **2.** consigliare; raccomandare: *he urged*

that they should come, raccomandò che venissero **3.** insistere, addurre, far valere: *let me — upon you the importance of this measure,* permetti che insista con te sull'importanza di questo provvedimento.

urgency [ˈəːdʒənsi], *s.* **1.** urgenza; premura: *a matter of great —,* una questione di grande urgenza **2.** bisogno urgente, necessità pressante **3.** *(pol.)* istanza d'urgenza.

urgent [ˈəːdʒənt], *ag.* **1.** urgente, pressante, incalzante: *at their — requests,* alle loro richieste pressanti **2.** insistente: *they were — for him to start at once,* insistettero perchè partisse subito.

urgently [ˈəːdʒəntli], *av.* urgentemente; insistentemente.

Uriah [juəˈraiə], *no.pr.m.* *(Bibbia)* Uria.

uric [ˈjuərik], *ag.* urico ☆ *— acid,* acido urico.

Uriel [ˈjuəriəl], *no.pr.m.* *(lett.)* Uriel.

urinal [ˈjuərinl], *s.* orinale, pitale; orinatoio.

urinary [ˈjuərinəri], *ag.* orinario ‖ *s.* **1.** *(mil.)* baracca contenente gli orinatoi **2.** serbatoio per urine da usare come concime.

to **urinate** [ˈjuərineit], *v.i.* orinare.

urination [ˌjuəriˈneiʃən], *s.* orinazione.

urine [ˈjuərin], *s.* orina.

uriniferous [ˌjuəriˈnifərəs], *ag.* *(fisiol.)* urinifero.

urinometer [ˌjuəriˈnɔmitə*], *s.* *(med.)* urometro.

urinous [ˈjuərinəs], *ag.* orinoso.

urn [əːn], *s.* **1.** urna ‖ *Urn,* *(astr.)* Acquario **2.** sepolcro **3.** sorgente di fiume **4.** samovar ☆ *— burial,* seppellimento in urne.

to **urn,** *v.t.* chiudere in un'urna.

uroscopy [juəˈrɔskəpi], *s.* *(med.)* uroscopia.

Ursa [ˈəːsə], *no.pr.* *(astr.)* Orsa ‖ *— Major,* Orsa Maggiore; *— Minor,* Orsa Minore.

ursine [ˈəːsain], *ag.* di, simile a orso.

urson [ˈəːsən], *s.* *(zool.)* ursone.

Ursula [ˈəːsjulə], *no.pr.f.* Orsola.

Ursuline [ˈəːsjulain], *ag.s.* *(eccl.)* (di) Orsolina.

Uruguay [ˈurugwai], *no.pr.* *(geog.)* Uruguay.

us [ʌs], *pron.pers.* 1ª persona *pl.* *(caso obliquo di* we) **1.** noi, ci: *three of —,* tre di noi; *he did not tell —,* non ce lo disse; *he stayed with — a month,* rimase con noi un mese; *let — (o let's) go!,* andiamo!; *she gave — a present,* ci diede un regalo; *they will not see —,* non ci vedranno; *you cannot deceive — engineers,* non potete ingannarci, noi altri ingegneri **2.** *(fam.* per *we*): *it's —,* siamo noi **3.** (sta per *me* nel *pl.* di *maestà* e nell'uso *fam.*): *let's have a look,* *(fam.)* fammi vedere **4.** *(arc. poet.* per *ourselves*): *we sat — down,* ci sedemmo.

usable [ˈjuːzəbl], *ag.* usabile; servibile.

usage [ˈjuːzidʒ], *s.* **1.** uso, trattamento: *the good — of a machine,* il buon uso di una macchina **2.** usanza, consuetudine; tradizione: *the — and customs of a country,* gli usi e costumi di un paese **3.** uso, impiego: *wide — of a word,* largo impiego di una parola.

usance [ˈjuːzəns], *s.* *(comm.)* usanza: *bill at —,* cambiale pagabile secondo la consuetudine.

use [juːs], *s.* **1.** uso, impiego; applicazione: *for all uses,* per tutte le applicazioni; *I'll show you the — of the microscope,* ti farò vedere come si usa il microscopio; *they make — of the most modern machines,* fanno uso dei più moderni macchinari; *to put sthg. to a good —,* impiegare bene ql.co. ‖ *directions for —,* istruzioni per l'uso ‖ *in —,* in uso: *book in —,* libro in lettura; *word in everyday —,* parola d'uso corrente ‖ *out of —,* non usato, in disuso: *to fall (o to go) out of —,* cadere in disuso ‖ *with —,* con l'uso, usando: *to improve with —,* migliorare con l'uso ‖ *to come into —,* venire in uso: *this word came into — long ago,* questa parola è in uso da molto tempo **2.** utilità, vantaggio: *it is no — going there,* è inutile andarci; *what is the — of it?,* a che serve? ‖ *I have no — for it,* *(fam.)* non mi serve, non so che farmene ‖ *misfortune has its uses,* *prov.* non tutto il male vien per nuocere **3.** usanza, abitudine; costume: *— and wont,* uso e costume; *long — has taught me that,* la lunga consuetudine mi ha insegnato ciò **4.** (*eccl.*) rito; liturgia: *the Anglican* —, il rito anglicano **5.** (*dir.*) godimento, usufrutto, interesse.

to **use** [ju:z], *v.t.i.* **1.** usare, adoperare, servirsi di: *you may* — *my dictionary*, puoi usare il mio dizionario; *you must* — *your common sense*, devi usare il tuo buon senso **2.** trattare: *he used her like a servant*, la trattò come una serva; *he used me ill*, mi trattò male **3.** (*solo al pass. seguito da inf. equivalente all'imperfetto indic.*) solere, usare, avere l'abitudine di: *he often used to go there*, vi andava spesso; *it used to be said that...*, si soleva dire che... **4.** *to* — *up*, consumare, esaurire; *they will certainly* — *up the whole sum*, spenderanno certamente l'intera somma.

used [ju:zd], *nel senso* **2.** [ju:st], *ag.* **1.** usato, adoperato; logorato; di seconda mano: — *cars*, automobili usate || *hardly* —, quasi nuovo **2.** abituato: *to be* — *to sthg.*, *to doing sthg.*, essere abituato a ql.co., a fare ql.co.; *to get* — *to sthg.*, *to doing sthg.*, abituarsi a ql.co., a fare ql.co. ☆ — *-up*, finito, esaurito, consumato (di provviste, ecc.); stanco, snervato, estenuato.

useful [´ju:sful], *ag.* utile; pratico; vantaggioso: *this book was very* — *to me*, questo libro mi è stato molto utile; *to give* — *advice*, dare utili consigli || *it will come in very* —, (*fam.*) ciò sarà di grande utilità || *to be pretty* —, segnalarsi; intendersene; sapersi servire: *he is pretty* — *with his fists*, sa servirsi dei pugni || *to make oneself generally* —, rendersi utile ☆ — *life*, (*elett.*) durata utile (di una lampadina); — *load*, (*aer.*) carico utile.

usefully [´ju:sfuli], *av.* utilmente; vantaggiosamente.

usefulness [´ju:sfulnis], *s.* utilità; vantaggio || *institution that has survived its* —, istituzione che ha perduto la sua ragione d'essere.

useless [´ju:slis], *ag.* inutile, vano; infruttuoso: — *regrets*, rimpianti superflui; — *remedy*, rimedio inefficace; *to be* —, non servire a nulla: *it would be* — *to produce further proofs*, sarebbe inutile produrre altre prove; *to make sthg.* —, mettere ql.co. fuori uso || *a* — *person*, (*fam.*) un incapace || *to feel* —, sentirsi abbattuto

uselessly [´ju:slisli], *av.* inutilmente, invano; infruttuosamente.

uselessness [´ju:slisnis], *s.* inutilità.

user[1] [´ju:zə*], *s.c.* **1.** chi usa; utente **2.** (*dir.*) usufrutturaria, usufruttuaria.

user[2], *s.* (*dir.*) diritto di uso continuato; godimento di diritto: *right of* —, diritto di uso; *to reserve the* — *of sthg.*, riservarsi l'uso di ql.co.

usher [´ʌʃə*], *s.* **1.** usciere **2.** (*rar.*) maestro assistente (di scuola, collegio, ecc.).

to **usher**, *v.t.* **1.** precedere (in qualità di usciere); introdurre: *to* — *s.o. in(to) the presence of s.o.*, introdurre qlcu. alla presenza di qlcu. **2.** *to* — *in*, annunciare; inaugurare, introdurre: *the spring ushered itself in warm and mild*, la primavera si annunciò tiepida e dolce; *to* — *in a new epoch*, inaugurare un'epoca **3.** *to* — *out*, ricondurre alla porta: *to* — *s.o. out*, ricondurre qlcu. alla porta.

usherette [ˌʌʃə´ret], *s.* maschera (donna) (inserviente di cinema, ecc.).

ushership [´ʌʃəʃip], *s.* **1.** funzioni di usciere **2.** (*rar.*) ufficio di maestro, di assistente (di scuola, ecc.).

usquebaugh [´ʌskwibɔ:], *s.* (*irl.*) whisky; acquavite.

ustion [´ʌstʃən], *s.* ustione.

usual [´ju:zuəl], *ag.* usuale, consueto, abituale: *at the* — *time*, alla solita ora; *he said the* — *things*, disse le solite cose; *to come earlier, later than* —, venire più presto, più tardi del solito || *as* —, come al solito: *everything is going on as* —, tutto procede come al solito.

usually [´ju:zuəli], *av.* di solito, abitualmente, ordinariamente.

usualness [´ju:zuəlnis], *s.* **1.** abitudine, consuetudine **2.** frequenza **3.** mancanza di originalità.

usucapion [ˌju:zju(:)´keipiən], **usucaption** [ˌju:zju(:)´kæpʃən], *s.* (*dir.*) usucapione.

usufruct [´ju:sju(:)frʌkt], *s.* (*dir.*) usufrutto.

usufructuary [ˌju:sju(:)´frʌktjuəri], *ag.* (*dir.*) usufruttuario || *s.c.* (*dir.*) usufruttuario, usufruttuaria.

usurer [´ju:ʒərə*], *s.c.* usuraio, usuraia.

usurious [ju:´ʒuəriəs], *ag.* usurario, da usuraio: *a* — *transaction*, una transazione da usuraio.

usuriously [ju:´ʒjuəriəsli], *av.* da usuraio.

usuriousness [ju:´ʒjuəriəsnis], *s.* esosità; l'essere usuraio.

to **usurp** [ju:´zə:p], *v.t.i.* usurpare: *he usurped the power*, usurpò il potere || *to* — *on* (o *upon*) *s.o.'s rights*, usurpare i diritti di qlcu.

usurpation [ˌju:zə:´peiʃən], *s.* usurpazione: *the* — *of a throne*, l'usurpazione di un trono.

usurpatory [ju:´zə:pətəri], *ag.* usurpatorio.

usurper [ju:´zə:pə*], *s.c.* usurpatore, usurpatrice.

usurpingly [ju:´zə:piŋli], *av.* da usurpatore.

usury [´ju:ʒuri], *s.* usura || *with* —, *fig.* ad usura: *she returned his love with* —, ricambiò il suo amore ad usura.

ut [ʌt], *s.* (*mus.*) do.

utensil [ju:(:)´tensl], *s.* utensile; arnese; strumento: *set of kitchen utensils*, batteria da cucina.

uterine [´ju:tərain], *ag.* uterino.

uterus [´ju:tərəs], *pl.* **uteri** [´ju:tərai], *s.* (*anat.*) utero.

utilitarian [ˌju:tili´tɛəriən], *ag.* utilitario || *s.* (*fil.*) utilitarista.

utilitarianism [ˌju:tili´tɛəriənizəm], *s.* (*fil.*) utilitarismo.

utility [ju:(:)´tiliti], *s.* **1.** utilità; vantaggio, profitto: *to be of great, no* —, essere di grande, di nessuna utilità **2.** cosa, persona utile **3.** (*public*) — *service*, servizio pubblico **4.** — (*-man* o *actor*), (*teat.*) generico **5.** (*fil.*) utilitarismo **6.** (*econ. pol.*) utile ☆ — *coach*, autofurgone; — *company*, (*amer.*) compagnia di elettricità; — *passenger car*, (*aut.*) utilitaria; — *wagon*, (*aut.*) giardiniera.

utilizable [´ju:tilaizəbl], *ag.* utilizzabile.

utilization [ˌju:tilai´zeiʃən], *s.* utilizzazione ☆ *thermal* — *factor*, (*fis.*) coefficiente di utilizzazione termica.

to **utilize** [´ju:tilaiz], *v.t.* utilizzare.

utmost [´ʌtmoust], *ag.* **1.** estremo, ultimo: *the* — *ends of the earth*, gli estremi confini della Terra **2.** massimo, sommo: *with the* — *care*, con la massima cura; *they lived in the* — *poverty*, vivevano nella miseria più nera; *we made the* — *efforts to*, abbiamo fatto i massimi sforzi per || *s.* il massimo, il limite estremo, il possibile: *he tried his* — *to succeed*, fece tutto il possibile per riuscire; *I shall do my* — *to help you*, farò del mio meglio per aiutarti; *she trusted him to the* —, aveva la massima fiducia in lui.

Utopia [ju:´toupjə], *no.pr.* (*lett.*) Utopia (isola ideata da T. More come sede di un sistema politico-sociale ideale) || *s.* utopia.

Utopian [ju:´toupjən], *ag.s.c.* **1.** (*lett.*) (abitante) di Utopia **2.** *fig.* (di, da) utopista.

utopianism [ju:´toupjənizəm], *s.* (*fil.*) idealismo utopistico.

utopist [´ju:təpist], *s.c.* utopista.

utricle [´ju:trikl], *s.* (*anat. bot.*) otricolo.

utricular [ju:´trikjulə*], *ag.* (*anat. bot.*) otricolare.

utter[1] [´ʌtə*], *ag.* **1.** completo, totale, assoluto; estremo: *to my* — *horror*, con mio grande orrore; *he is an* — *stranger to me*, mi è completamente estraneo; *the room was in* — *darkness*, la stanza era immersa nell'oscurità più completa; *we think he is an* — *scoundrel*, lo consideriamo un perfetto mascalzone **2.** (*arc.*) esterno ☆ — *barrister*, praticante penalista.

to **utter**[2], *v.t.* **1.** emettere: *he did not* — *a sound*, non articolò suono; *she keeps on uttering sighs*, continua a sospirare; *she uttered a groan*, emise un gemito **2.** esprimere, pronunciare: *the last words he uttered*, le ultime parole che pronunciò; *she uttered her thoughts*, espresse i suoi pensieri; *you must never* — *his name again*, non devi mai più pronunciare il suo nome **3.** emettere, mettere in circolazione: *he uttered a libel*, mise in circolazione un libello; *to — false coins*, spacciare monete false.

utterable ['ʌtərəbl], *ag.* esprimibile.

utterance[1] ['ʌtərəns], *s.* (*letter.*) limite, punto estremo: *fight to the —*, combattimento ad oltranza, fino all'ultimo.

utterance[2], *s.* **1.** espressione; sfogo: *he gave — to his rage*, diede sfogo alla sua ira; *she gave — to her feelings*, espresse liberamente i propri sentimenti **2.** pronuncia; modo di parlare: *he has a defective —*, ha una pronuncia difettosa **3.** (*rar.*) emissione, il mettere in circolazione.

utterer ['ʌtərə*], *s.c.* **1.** chi esprime; chi pronunzia **2.** chi mette in circolazione: *an — of slander*, un diffamatore, una diffamatrice.

uttering ['ʌtəriŋ], *s.* **1.** espressione; pronuncia **2.** emissione: *forging and — a cheque is punished by law*,

il contraffare e spacciare un assegno è punito dalla legge.

utterly ['ʌtəli], *av.* completamente, totalmente: *I am — exhausted*, sono stanco morto; *the war has — ruined that family*, la guerra ha rovinato completamente quella famiglia.

uttermost ['ʌtəmoust], *ag.* **1.** estremo, ultimo **2.** sommo ‖ *s.* estremo grado, limite: *the — of his patience*, il limite della sua pazienza.

uvea ['juːviə], *s.* (*anat.*) uvea.

uvula ['juːvjulə], *pl.* **uvulae** ['juːvjuliː], **uvulas** ['juːvjuləz], *s.* (*anat.*) ugola.

uvular ['juːvjulə*], *ag.* (*anat.*) dell'ugola.

uxorial [ʌk'sɔːriəl], *ag.* di moglie.

uxoricide[1] [ʌk'sɔːrisaid], *s.* uxoricida.

uxoricide[2], *s.* uxoricidio.

uxorious [ʌk'sɔːriəs], *ag.* eccessivamente innamorato della moglie; dominato dalla moglie.

V

v [vi:], *pl.* **vees, v's** [vi:z], *s.* **1.** (*ventiduesima lettera dell'alfabeto inglese*) v ‖ — *for Victor*, (*tel.*) v come Venezia **2.** V, (*cifra romana*) 5 ☆ V-*block*, (*mec. elett.*) blocco a V; V-*gear*, ingranaggio elicoidale doppio; V-*neck*, scollatura a punta; V-*note*, (*amer.*) biglietto da cinque dollari; V-*shaped*, a forma di V; V-*sign*, segno di vittoria; V-*thread*, passo triangolare (di vite).

vacancy ['veikənsi], *s.* **1.** vacanza, l'essere vacante **2.** posto vacante: *to fill a* —, coprire un posto vacante **3.** vuoto, lacuna ‖ *to look into* —, guardare nel vuoto **4.** *fig.* mancanza d'intelligenza; vacuità.

vacant ['veikənt], *ag.* **1.** vacante, vuoto, non occupato, libero: *a* — *house*, una casa non occupata; — *possession*, immobile libero subito; *to apply for a* — *post*, fare domanda per un posto libero **2.** vacuo, vuoto; distratto, indifferente: — *stare*, sguardo vacuo.

vacantly ['veikəntli], *av.* in modo vacuo; in modo distratto, indifferente.

to **vacate** [və'keit], *v.t.* **1.** lasciare vacante; dare le dimissioni da; sgomberare: *all civilians must be vacated from the city*, tutti i civili devono essere fatti evacuare dalla città; *to* — *a flat*, lasciare libero un appartamento; *to* — *a position*, ritirarsi da un posto **2.** (*dir.*) annullare, rendere inoperante: *this omission will not* — *the contract*, questa omissione non invaliderà il contratto.

vacation [və'keifən], *s.* **1.** abbandono; il ritirarsi; il lasciare libero (un posto, una casa): *his* — *of such a good position was a foolish act*, il suo ritiro da un posto così buono è stato una sciocchezza **2.** vacanza, vacanze ☆ *long* (o *summer*) —, vacanze estive.

to **vacation**, *v.i.* (*amer.*) **1.** trascorrere le vacanze **2.** prendere le vacanze.

vacationist [və'keifənist], *s.c.* (*amer.*) villeggiante; chi è in vacanza.

vaccinal ['væksinl], *ag.* vaccinico.

to **vaccinate** ['væksineit], *v.t.i.* vaccinare.

vaccination [,væksi'neifən], *s.* vaccinazione.

vaccinationist [,væksi'neifənist], *s.c.* sostenitore, sostenitrice della vaccinazione.

vaccinator ['væksineitə*], *s.* **1.** vaccinatore **2.** lancetta per vaccinazione.

vaccine ['væksi:n], *ag.* **1.** vaccino, di vacca **2.** vaccinico; pertinente alla vaccinazione ‖ *s.* vaccino ☆ — *farm*, centro di produzione dei vaccini; — *inoculation*, vaccinazione; — *rash*, (*patol.*) eritema, rash vaccinico; — *virus*, virus del vaiolo, vaccinico.

vaccinia [væk'siniə], *s.* (*vet.*) vaccino, vaiolo bovino.

vaccinic [væk'sinik], *ag.* vaccinico.

to **vacillate** ['væsileit], *v.i.* **1.** vacillare, barcollare **2.** *fig.* esitare; essere incostante.

vacillating ['væsileitiŋ], *ag.* **1.** vacillante **2.** *fig.* incostante; irresoluto.

vacillatingly ['væsileitiŋli], *av.* **1.** barcollando **2.** in modo esitante; incostantemente.

vacillation [,væsi'leifən], *s.* **1.** vacillamento **2.** *fig.* esitazione, irresolutezza.

vacillatory ['væsilətəri], *ag.* **1.** ondeggiante; vacillante **2.** *fig.* esitante, irresoluto.

vacuity [væ'kju(:)iti], *s.* **1.** vacuità; vuoto; spazio vuoto **2.** *fig.* vacuità, mancanza di idee.

vacuolar ['vækjuələ*], *ag.* (*biol.*) vacuolare, di vacuolo.

vacuolate(d) ['vækjuəleit(id)], *ag.* (*biol.*) contenente vacuoli, alterato da vacuoli.

vacuole ['vækjuoul], *s.* (*biol.*) vacuolo.

vacuous ['vækjuəs], *ag.* **1.** vacuo, vuoto **2.** *fig.* vuoto, privo di espressione, sciocco; ozioso, inutile: *a* — *life*, una vita vuota, oziosa; — *remark*, osservazione senza senso; — *stare*, sguardo privo di espressione.

vacuousness ['vækjuəsnis], *V.* **vacuity**.

vacuum ['vækjuəm], *pl.* **vacuums** ['vækjuəmz], **vacua** ['vækjuə], *s.* (*fis.*) vuoto, vuoto pneumatico ☆ — -*brake*, (*ferr.*) freno a depressione; — -*cleaner*, aspirapolvere; — -*flask* (o — -*bottle*), (bottiglia) thermos; — -*gauge*, (*fis.*) vacuometro; — -*pump*, (*mec.*) pulsometro; (*aer.*) depressore; — -*tube*, tubo a vuoto; — -*valve*, valvola termoionica ‖ *absolute* —, (*fis.*) vuoto assoluto.

vade-mecum ['veidi'mi:kəm], *s.* vademecum; prontuario; manuale.

vagabond ['vægəbɔnd], *ag.* vagabondo; nomade, errabondo ‖ *s.c.* **1.** vagabondo, vagabonda **2.** lazzarone, lazzarona; buono a nulla, buona a nulla.

to **vagabond**, *v.i.* vagare, vagabondare.

vagabondage ['vægəbɔndidʒ], **vagabondism** ['vægəbɔndizəm], *s.* vagabondaggio.

to **vagabondize** ['vægəbɔndaiz], *v.i.* vagabondare.

vagal ['veigəl], *ag.* (*anat.*) vagale ☆ — *nerve*, (*anat.*) nervo vago.

vagarious [və'gɛəriəs], *ag.* **1.** errante, vagante **2.** capriccioso, bizzarro.

vagary ['veigəri], *s.* capriccio; ghiribizzo; idea stravagante.

vagina [və'dʒainə], *pl.* **vaginae** [və'dʒaini:], **vaginas** [və'dʒainəz], *s.* **1.** (*anat.*) vagina **2.** (*bot.*) guaina.

vaginal [və'dʒainəl], *ag.* (*anat.*) vaginale.

vaginate ['vædʒinit], **vaginated** ['vædʒineitid], *ag.* **1.** (*anat.*) invaginato **2.** (*bot.*) chiuso in una guaina.

vaginitis [,vædʒi'naitis], *s.* (*patol.*) vaginite.

vagrancy ['veigrənsi], *s.* **1.** vagabondaggio **2.** accattonaggio.

vagrant ['veigrənt], *ag.* vagabondo, nomade: — *musicians*, suonatori ambulanti; — *tribes*, tribù nomadi ‖ *s.c.* **1.** vagabondo, vagabonda **2.** mendicante; accattone, accattona.

vagrantly ['veigrəntli], *av.* da vagabondo.

vagrom ['veigrəm], *ag.* (*letter.*) vagabondo; errante.

vague [veig], *ag.* vago; impreciso; indistinto; indeterminato: *a* — *analogy*, una vaga analogia; — *terms*, termini vaghi ‖ *in the* —, nell'incertezza.

vaguely ['veigli], *av.* vagamente; in modo impreciso, indistinto.

vagueness ['veignis], *s.* indeterminatezza.

vail[1] [veil], *s. gener. pl.* (*arc.*) mancia; donativo; gratificazione.

to **vail**[2], *v.t.i.* (*arc. poet.*) **1.** abbassare (le armi); abbassare in segno di rispetto (gli occhi, la testa) **2.** abbassarsi; inchinarsi; togliersi il cappello **3.** *fig.* manifestare sottomissione.

vain [vein], *ag.* **1.** vano, inutile, infruttuoso: — *boasting*, inutili vanterie; — *efforts*, sforzi vani; *my hopes were* —, le mie speranze furono vane; *to speak was* —, parlare fu inutile ‖ *in* —, invano; inutilmente: *you speak in* —, parli invano ‖ *to take the name of God in* —, pronunziare il nome di Dio invano **2.** vano, vanitoso; orgoglioso: *he is as* — *as a peacock*, è vanitoso come un pavone; *he was — of his success*, era orgoglioso del suo successo.

vainglorious [vein'glɔ:riəs], *ag.* vanaglorioso.

vaingloriously [vein'glɔ:riəsli], *av.* vanagloriosamente.

vainglory [vein'glɔ:ri], *s.* vanagloria.

to **vainglory**, *v.i.* vanagloriarsi, vantarsi a vuoto.

vainly ['veinli], *av.* **1.** inutilmente, infruttuosamente **2.** vanitosamente; orgogliosamente.

vainness ['veinnis], *s.* **1.** inutilità, infruttuosità **2.** vanità; orgoglio.

vair [veə*], *s.* (*arald.*) vaio.

vairy ['veəri], *ag.* (*arald.*) di vaio; del colore del vaio; variegato (come il vaio).

valance ['væləns], *s.* **1.** mantovana (drappeggio per finestra) **2.** cortina (attorno ad un letto).

valanced ['vælənst], *ag.* **1.** ornato di mantovana (di finestra) **2.** provvisto di cortina (di letto).

vale[1] [veil], *s.* (*poet.*) valle: *this — of tears*, questa valle di lacrime.

vale[2] ['veili], *s.* addio; lettera di addio.

vale[2], *inter.* addio!.

valediction [,væli'dikʃən], *s.* **1.** addio; commiato **2.** parole, discorso di commiato.

valedictorian [,vælidik'tɔuriən], *s.* (*amer.*) studente incaricato di tenere il discorso di commiato nel giorno della laurea.

valedictory [,væli'diktəri], *ag.* di saluto; d'addio || *s.* (*amer.*) discorso di commiato (di studente nel giorno della laurea) ☆ *a — address*, parole di saluto, parole di commiato; *a — speech*, un discorso d'addio.

valence ['veiləns], *s.* (*chim.*) valenza.

Valencia [və'lenʃiə], *no.pr.* (*geog.*) Valencia || *s.* **1.** tessuto misto in lana e seta, lana e cotone, a righe (per panciotti) **2.** *pl.* uva passa; mandorle di Valencia.

Valencian [və'lenʃiən], *ag.* di Valencia.

Valenciennes [,vælənsi'en], *s.* Valenciennes (pizzo).

valency ['veilənsi], *s.* (*chim.*) valenza.

Valentine ['væləntain], *no.pr.m.* Valentino || *St. —'s day*, giorno di San Valentino (14 febbraio) || **valentine**, *s.c.* fidanzato, fidanzata; innamorato, innamorata (scelti nel giorno di S. Valentino) || *s.* biglietto amoroso, scherzoso (che si invia a persona di sesso diverso il giorno di S. Valentino).

valerian [və'liəriən], *s.* (*bot. farm.*) valeriana.

valerianic [və,liəri'ænik], **valeric** [və'liərik], *ag.* (*bot. arm.*) di valeriana; valerianico.

valet ['vælit], *s.* valletto, cameriere.

to **valet**, *v.t.i.* servire come valletto, cameriere.

valetudinarian ['væli,tju:di'nɛəriən], *ag.* **1.** valetudinario, malaticcio **2.** eccessivamente preoccupato per la propria salute || *s.c.* **1.** persona di salute cagionevole; infermo; inferma **2.** malato immaginario, malata immaginaria.

valetudinarianism ['væli,tju:di'nɛəriənizəm], *s.* **1.** salute malferma **2.** il temere continuamente di essere malato.

valetudinary [,væli'tju:dinəri], *V.* **valetudinarian**.

Valhalla [væl'hælə], *s.* **1.** (*mit.*) Valalla **2.** *fig.* luogo che accoglie le tombe di persone illustri; panteon.

valiance ['væliəns], **valiancy** ['væliənsi], *s.* **1.** valore **2.** (*arc.*) atto di valore; prodezza.

valiant ['væljənt], *ag.* valoroso, prode; animoso.

valiantly ['væljəntli], *av.* valorosamente; animosamente.

valiantness ['væljəntnis], *s.* valore, prodezza.

valid ['vælid], *ag.* **1.** valido; valevole; legittimo: *a — objection*, una obiezione valida; *the marriage was not —*, il matrimonio non era valido; *the only — method of investigation*, l'unico metodo valido di investigazione **2.** valido, robusto: *his — health*, la sua salute robusta.

to **validate** ['vælideit], *v.t.* rendere valido, legittimo; confermare; convalidare; ratificare.

validation [,væli'deiʃən], *s.* convalidazione; ratificazione.

validity [və'liditi], *s.* validità; legittimità.

validly ['vælidli], *av.* validamente; legittimamente.

validness ['vælidnis], *s.* validità; legittimità.

valise [və'li:z], *s.* **1.** valigia; borsa da viaggio **2.** zaino, sacco militare.

Valkyr ['vælkiə*], *s.* (*mit. nordica*) Valchiria.

Valkyrian [væl'kiriən], *ag.*|(*mit. nordica*) di Valchiria.

Valkyrie ['vælkiri], *s.* (*mit. nordica*) Valchiria.

vallecula [væ'lekjulə], *pl.* **valleculae** [væ'lekjuli:], *s.* (*anat. bot.*) vallecola.

valley ['væli], *s.* **1.** valle, vallata: *the Red River —*, la vallata del Fiume Rosso || *the — of the shadow of death*, (*Bibbia*) la valle dell'ombra della morte **2.** (*edil.*) compluvio **3.** (*edil.*) conversa.

vallum ['væləm], *s.* (*st. romana*) vallo.

valonia [və'louniə], *s.* (*bot.*) vallonea, cupola della vallonea.

valorization [,vælərai'zeiʃən], *s.* (*comm.*) avvaloramento, valorizzazione.

to **valorize** ['væləraiz], *v.t.* (*comm.*) dare valore a, valorizzare.

valorous ['vælərəs], *ag.* (*lett.*) valoroso, prode.

valorously ['vælərəsli], *av.* valorosamente.

valour ['vælə*], *s.* (*lett.*) valore, prodezza, coraggio.

valse [vɑ:ls], *s.* valzer.

to **valse**, *v.i.* ballare il valzer.

valuable ['væljuəbl], *ag.* **1.** costoso; prezioso, di gran valore **2.** valutabile: *her services are not — in money*, le sue prestazioni non sono valutabili in denaro || *s. gener. pl.* oggetto, oggetti di valore, preziosi: *I sent all my valuables to the bank*, ho mandato tutti i miei valori in banca.

valuableness ['væljuəblnis], *s.* **1.** valore, preziosità **2.** valutabilità.

valuation [,vælju'eiʃən], *s.* **1.** valutazione, stima; perizia: *they made a — of the goods*, fecero la stima della merce **2.** stima, considerazione.

valuator ['væljueitə*], *s.* perito, stimatore.

value ['vælju:], *s.* **1.** (*comm.*) valore, prezzo, costo; *fig.* valore, pregio: *a book of great —*, un libro di grande valore; *a person of little —*, una persona di poco valore; *it is nothing of any —*, non è cosa che valga; *this book is quite good — for five shillings*, questo libro vale certamente cinque scellini; *to confer* (o *to set*) *— on* (o *to attach — to*), attribuire valore a; *to declare* (o *to state*) *the —*, dichiarare il valore; *to go down in —*, perdere di valore; *to lose* (o *to fall in*) *—*, svalutarsi, deprezzarsi; *to pay the — of sthg.*, rimborsare il prezzo di ql.co.; pagare ql.co. per quello che vale; *to raise* (o *to increase*) *the —*, aumentare il valore; *to rise in —*, aumentare di valore; *to set a low, a high — (up)on sthg.*, attribuire poco, grande valore a ql.co. || *— in exchange* (o *exchangeable —*), valore di scambio; *— on account*, valuta in conto || *— received in goods*, valuta in merci || *for —, received —*, valore ricevuto || *loss of* (o *fall in*) *—*, svalutazione **2.** valore, utilità, importanza: *the — of education*, l'importanza dell'educazione; *that book has been of great — to me*, quel libro mi è stato prezioso, di grande aiuto; *to set little — on sthg.*, attribuire scarsa importanza a ql.co. **3.** (*rar.*) stima, considerazione: *my — for him is great*, la mia stima per lui è grande **4.** valore, significato (di parole) **5.** (*mus.*) valore, lunghezza, quantità, durata (di una nota) **6.** (*mat.*) valore: *to give X a —*, attribuire ad X un valore **7.** (*chim.*) valore, numero **8.** (*fis.*) potere **9.** (*pitt.*) armonia di luci ed ombre **10.** *pl.* valori morali ☆ *— agreed*, valuta intesa || *aggregate —*, valore complessivo; *calorific —* (o *heating —*), (*fis.*) potere calorifico; *commercial —*, valore commerciale; *iodine —*, (*chim.*) indice iodico; *nominal —*, valore nominale; *rateable —*, valore imponibile; *real* (o *true*) *—*, valore effettivo; *selling* (o *saleable*) *—*, valore venale.

to **value**, *v.t.* **1.** (*comm.*) valutare, stimare, periziare, computare: *he valued the house* (*at*) *£ 5,000*, stimò la casa 5000 sterline; *to — a loss*, computare, calcolare una perdita **2.** dare importanza a; tenere in grande considerazione; stimare, apprezzare: *I shall always — your riendship*, terrò sempre in gran conto la tua amicizia; *to — one's life*, aver cara la propria vita ‖ *he valued himself on his actions*, si vantava delle sue azioni **3.** *to — upon* (*s.o.*), emettere tratta su.

valued ['væljuːd], *ag.* **1.** (*comm.*) valutato; apprezzato: — *policy*, polizza valutata; *a — possession*, una proprietà di valore; *your — orders*, i vostri stimati ordini **2.** stimato: *my — friend Mr. Smith*, il mio stimato amico Mr. Smith.

valueless ['væljulis], *ag.* di nessun valore.

valuelessness ['væljulisnis], *s.* mancanza di valore.

valuer ['væljuə*], *s.* stimatore, perito.

valvar ['vælvə*], *ag.* (*bot. zool.*) valvare.

valvate ['vælvit], *ag.* (*bot. zool.*) **1.** a forma di valva **2.** munito di valva.

valve [vælv], *s.* **1.** (*anat. mec.*) valvola: *the valves of the heart*, le valvole del cuore **2.** (*bot. zool.*) valva **3.** valva, battente (di porta) ☆ — *body*, corpo della valvola; — *bonnet* (o — *cap*), coperchio della valvola, — *chamber*, cassa della valvola; — *cock*, rubinetto a valvola; — *face* (o — *seat*), sede della valvola; — *gear*, (*mec.*) distribuzione, meccanismo della distribuzione; — *guide*, guida valvola; — *lifter*, alzavalvole; — *set*, (*rad.*) apparecchio a valvole ‖ *air* —, valvola di sfiato; *amplifying* —, (*rad.*) valvola amplificatrice; *ball* —, valvola a sfera; *butterfly* —, valvola a farfalla; *check* — (o *non-return* —), valvola di ritegno; *exhaust* — (o *outlet* —), valvola di scarico; *flap* —, (*mec.*) valvola a cerniera; *float* —, valvola galleggiante; *foot* — (o *suction* —), valvola di fondo; *gate* —, (valvola a) saracinesca; *globe* — (o *stop* —), valvola di arresto; *inlet* — (o *intake* —), valvola di ammissione, di aspirazione; *light* —, (*cine.*) fotovalvola, valvola a bagliore; *magnetic* —, valvola elettromagnetica; *pressure-reducing* —, valvola di riduzione della pressione; *rectifying* →, (*rad.*) valvola rettificatrice; *safety* —, (*mec.*) valvola di sicurezza.

valved [vælvd], *ag.* **1.** (*anat. mec.*) munito di valvole **2.** (*bot. zool.*) munito di valva **3.** (*bot. zool.*) a forma di valva.

valveless ['vælvlis], *ag.* **1.** (*anat. mec.*) privo di valvole **2.** (*bot. zool.*) privo di valva.

valvelet ['vælvlit], *s.* **1.** (*anat. mec.*) valvoletta **2.** (*bot. zool.*) piccola valva.

valvular ['vælvjulə*], *ag.* **1.** (*anat. mec.*) valvolare **2.** (*bot. zool.*) di valva.

to vamoose [və'muːs], **to vamose** [və'mous], *v.t.i.* (*sl. amer.*) andarsene, filarsela; levare le tende da, lasciare.

vamp[1] [væmp], *s.* **1.** tomaia (di scarpa) **2.** rabberciamento, rappezzamento **3.** (*mus.*) improvvisazione.

to vamp[1], *v.t.i.* **1.** rappezzare, mettere la tomaia a (scarpe) **2.** raffazzonare, rabberciare: *to — (up) an article out of old notes*, mettere insieme un articolo basandosi su vecchi appunti **3.** (*mus.*) improvvisare **4.** (*dial.*) camminare faticosamente.

vamp[2], *s.* (*sl. amer. abbr.* di *vampire*) maliarda, donna fatale.

to vamp[2], *v.t.i.* (*sl. amer.*) ammaliare, adescare, sedurre; atteggiarsi a donna fatale.

vamper ['væmpə*], *s.c.* **1.** (*mus.*) improvvisatore, improvvisatrice **2.** rappezzatore, rappezzatrice.

vampire ['væmpaiə*], *s.* **1.** vampiro; *fig.* persona malvagia e crudele; sfruttatore, succhiasangue **2.** (— *bat*), (*zool.*) vampiro **3.** (*teat.*) botola a molla (per far scomparire gli attori dalla scena).

vampiric [væm'pirik], *ag.* vampirico.

vampirism ['væmpaiərizəm], *s.* **1.** credenza nell'esistenza dei vampiri **2.** *fig.* sfruttamento vergognoso.

van[1] [væn], *s.* (*abbr.* di *caravan*) **1.** furgone, carrozzone **2.** vagone ferroviario ☆ *luggage* —, (*ferr.*) bagagliaio.

to **van**[1], *pass.p.p.* **vanned** [vænd], *v.t.* mandare a mezzo di carro, di vagone.

van[2], *s.* **1.** vaglio, crivello **2.** vela di mulino a vento **3.** (*poet.*) ventaglio.

to **van**[2], *v.t.* vagliare (un minerale).

van[3], *s.* (*abbr.* di *vanguard*) avanguardia (anche *fig.*): *to form the — of scientific progress*, formare l'avanguardia del progresso scientifico; *to lead the —*, essere in testa ‖ *in the — of*, a capo di, alla testa di.

van[4], *abbr.* di **vantage**.

vanadium [və'neidjəm], *s.* (*chim.*) vanadio ☆ — *steel*, acciaio al vanadio.

Vandal ['vændəl], *ag.s.* (*st.*) vandalo ‖ **vandal**, *ag.* barbaro, vandalico ‖ *s. fig.* vandalo.

Vandalic [væn'dælik], *ag.* (*st.*) vandalo, vandalico ‖ **vandalic**, *ag.* vandalico, da devastatore: — *fury*, furia vandalica.

vandalism ['vændəlizəm], *s.* vandalismo, brutale devastazione.

Vandyke [væn'daik], *ag.* (*pitt.*) alla Van Dyck: *a — beard*, un pizzo alla Van Dyck; *a — collar*, un colletto alla Van Dyck.

Vandyke, *no.pr.* (*st. pitt.*) Van Dyck ‖ *s.* **1.** (quadro di) Van Dyck **2.** smerlo (sul tipo di quelli che appaiono nei quadri del pittore).

to **vandyke**, *v.t.* **1.** ornare con smerli alla Van Dyck **2.** tagliare con delle dentellature.

vane [vein], *s.* **1.** banderuola; mostravento **2.** (*mec.*) pala (di mulino a vento, turbina) **3.** (*mar. aer.*) manica a vento **4.** (*mil.*) governale (di bomba aerea) **5.** traguardo; mirino (di strumento per rilievi topografici) ☆ — *wheel*, (*mec.*) ruota a palette ‖ *deflector* —, (*mec.*) paletta direttrice (di turbina).

vaneless ['veinlis], *ag.* **1.** privo di banderuola **2.** senza pala.

Vanessa[1] [və'nesə], *no.pr.f.* (*lett.*) Vanessa.

vanessa[2], *s.* (*entom.*) vanessa.

vang [væŋ], *s.* (*mar.*) ostino.

vanguard ['vænɡɑːd], *s.* avanguardia (anche *fig.*).

vanilla [və'nilə], *s.* (*bot.*) vaniglia ☆ — -*bean*, baccello di vaniglia; — *essence*, (*cuc.*) essenza di vaniglia; — *ice-cream*, gelato alla vaniglia.

vanillate ['vænileit], *s.* (*chim.*) vanigliato.

vanille [və'nil], *V.* **vanilla**.

vanillic [və'nilik], *ag.* di vaniglia.

vanillin ['vænilin], *s.* (*chim.*) vaniglina.

vanish ['væniʃ], *s.* (*fonet.*) suono terminale di vocale, dittongo pronunciato debolmente.

to **vanish**, *v.t.i.* **1.** svanire, sparire, far sparire; perdersi; dileguarsi: *the charm will — into air*, l'incantesimo svanirà nell'aria; *several species have vanished without leaving trace*, parecchie specie sono svanite senza lasciar traccia **2.** (*mat.*) diventar zero.

vanishing ['væniʃiŋ], *s.* il dileguarsi, lo sparire ☆ — *point*, punto di fuga in una prospettiva; (*fam. scherz.*) zero assoluto: *profits have dwindled to the — point*, i profitti hanno raggiunto lo zero assoluto.

vanishingly ['væniʃiŋli], *av.* in maniera evanescente.

vanity ['væniti], *s.* **1.** vanità, futilità; inutilità: *the — of wordly wealth*, la vanità delle ricchezze del mondo; *all is —*, tutto è vanità ‖ *" Vanity Fair "*, (*lett.*) «La fiera delle vanità» **2.** vanità, vanagloria: *injured —*, vanità offesa ☆ — -*bag* (o — -*case*), borsetta da signora contenente il necessario per il trucco.

to **vanquish** ['væŋkwiʃ], *v.t.* (*letter.*) vincere, conquistare: *love vanquished pride*, l'amore vinse l'orgoglio.

vanquishable ['væŋkwiʃəbl], *ag.* (*letter.*) vincibile, conquistabile.

vanquisher ['væŋkwiʃə*], *s.* (*letter.*) conquistatore, vincitore.

vanquishment ['væŋkwiʃmənt], *s.* (*letter.*) il vincere, il trionfare.

vantage ['vɑːntidʒ], *s.* **1.** (*tennis*) vantaggio **2.** (*arc.*) vantaggio, profitto ☆ — -*ground*, terreno favorevole; — *in*, *out*, (*tennis*) vantaggio interno, esterno.

to **vantage**, v.t. (arc.) avvantaggiarsi, profittare di.

vapid ['væpid], ag. **1.** svaporato, insignificante, insulso: a — conversation, una conversazione insulsa **2.** (rar.) insipido: — food, cibo insipido.

vapidity [væ'piditi], s. insipidezza (anche fig.); insulsaggine, futilità.

vapidly ['væpidli], av. in modo insipido, insulso.

vapidness ['væpidnis], V. **vapidity.**

(to) **vapor**, (amer.) per (to) **vapour.**

vaporability [,veipərə'biliti], s. l'essere evaporabile.

vaporable ['veipərəbl], ag. evaporabile.

vaporiferous [,veipə'rifərəs], ag. che porta vapori.

vaporific [,veipə'rifik], ag. **1.** che produce vapori **2.** V. **vaporous.**

vaporiform ['veipərifɔ:m], ag. allo stato di vapore.

vaporization [,veipərai'zeifən], s. **1.** evaporazione **2.** (med.) vaporizzazione.

to **vaporize** ['veipəraiz], v.t.i. far evaporare, evaporare, svaporare (anche fig.): money seems to have vaporized away, fig. il denaro sembra essersi volatilizzato.

vaporizer ['veipəraizə*], s. vaporizzatore ☆ — injector, (mec.) iniettore.

vaporosity [,veipə'rositi], s. (rar.) vaporosità.

vaporous ['veipərəs], ag. **1.**vaporoso; nebbioso **2.**(fig. arc.) chimerico, fantastico.

vaporously ['veipərəsli], av. **1.** in modo vaporoso **2.** fig. in modo fantastico.

vaporousness ['veipərəsnis], s. vaporosità.

vapour ['veipə*], s. **1.** vapore; esalazione; nebbia **2.**fig. chimera, creazione fantasiosa: the vapours of a disordered mind, le fantasie di una mente malata **3.** pl. (arc.) depressione; irritabilità; isterismo: she had a fit of vapours, ebbe un attacco di isterismo ☆ — -bath, bagno di vapore; — -density, densità di una sostanza allo stato di vapore; — -engine, macchina a vapore || water —, vapor acqueo.

to **vapour**, v.i. **1.** trasformarsi in vapore; evaporare: his life has vapoured away in hopes, fig. la sua vita è svanita in speranze (non realizzate) **2.** vantarsi, gloriarsi; dir sciocchezze, straparlare.

vapourer ['veipərə*], s.c. persona vanagloriosa.

vapouring ['veipəriŋ], ag. **1.** che evapora **2.** vanaglorioso || s. millanteria: the vapourings of that fellow, le spacconate di quell'individuo.

vapourish ['veipəriʃ], ag. **1.** vaporoso, pieno di vapori **2.** ipocondriaco, nevrastenico.

vapourishness ['veipəriʃnis], s. **1.** vaporosità, l'esser pieno di vapori **2.** ipocondria; nevrastenia.

vapoury ['veipəri], ag. **1.** vaporoso, di consistenza simile al vapore **2.** fig. vago, indefinito.

vapulation [,væpju'leiʃən], s. (rar.) fustigazione.

varan ['væərən], s. (zool.) varano.

varec, varech ['væərek], s. **1.** (bot.) varecchi **2.** soda greggia (ottenuta bruciando varecchi).

variability [,veəriə'biliti], s. variabilità, mutevolezza; incostanza: the — of the weather, la variabilità del tempo.

variable ['veəriəbl], ag. variabile, mutevole; incostante: — mood, umore instabile; the weather is — in March, in marzo il tempo è mutevole || s. **1.** (mat.) quantità variabile **2.** (mar.) vento variabile **3.** pl. la regione dei venti variabili ☆ — motion, (mec.) moto vario; — quantity, (mat.) quantità variabile.

variableness ['veəriəblnis], s. variabilità.

variably ['veəriəbli], av. variabilmente, mutevolmente; incostantemente.

variance ['veəriəns], s. **1.** variazione, variabilità, mutevolezza: variances in temperature, variazioni della temperatura **2.** disaccordo, disputa: he was at — with his father, era in disaccordo con suo padre; historians are at — on this point, gli storici sono in disaccordo su questo punto **3.** (dir.) discordanza.

variant ['veəriənt], ag. variante; differente: the — forms of a word, le varie forme di una parola || s. variante: a — in the spelling, una variante nella grafia;

two variants of the same story, due varianti, versioni, della medesima storia.

variation [,veəri'eiʃən], s. **1.** variazione, oscillazione; modificazione, mutamento: variations in public opinion, oscillazioni dell'opinione pubblica; — of pressure, oscillazione di pressione; — of speed, variazione di velocità; — of temperature, oscillazione di temperatura **2.** (mat. mus. biol.) variazione: — of species, (biol.) variazione delle specie; calculus of variations, (mat.) il calcolo delle variazioni **3.** (astr.) declinazione ☆ — compass, bussola di declinazione, declinometro || annual —, (astr.) declinazione, ascensione annuale di una stella; magnetic —, declinazione magnetica.

variational [,veəri'eiʃənl], ag. soggetto a variazioni, variabile.

varicated ['væərikeitid], ag. che ha varici (di conchiglia).

varicella [,væəri'selə], s. (patol.) varicella.

varicocele ['væərikou,si:l], s. (patol.) varicocele.

varicoloured ['veəri,kʌləd], ag. variopinto; variegato.

varicose ['væərikous], ag. (patol.) varicoso ☆ — veins, vene varicose.

varicosed ['væərikoust], ag. (patol.) affetto da varici.

varicosity [,væəri'kositi], s. (patol.) varice, varicosità.

varied ['veərid], ag. **1.** vario, variato; mutevole: a — experience, una esperienza varia; — interests, interessi svariati **2.** variopinto, variegato.

to **variegate** ['veərigeit], v.t. variegare, screziare.

variegated ['veərigeitid], ag. **1.** variegato: white petals — with pink, petali bianchi screziati di rosa **2.** fig. vario, multiforme.

variegation [,veəri'geiʃən], s. screziatura, varietà di colori.

varietal [və'raiitl], ag. (bot. zool.) appartenente a varietà distinta.

variety [və'raiəti], s. **1.** varietà, diversità: a — of opinions, una diversità di opinioni || — is the mother of enjoyment, il mondo è bello perché è vario **2.** varietà, assortimento; molteplicità: a — of fabrics, un assortimento di tessuti; I did it for a — of reasons, lo feci per ragioni varie **3.** (bot. zool.) varietà (di una specie): there are now several varieties of roses, vi sono ora parecchie varietà di rose **4.** (teat.) varietà ☆ — artist, artista di varietà; — entertainment (o — show), spettacolo di varietà; — theatre, teatro di varietà.

variform ['veərifɔ:m], ag. di varie forme; multiforme.

variola [və'raiələ], s. (patol.) vaiolo.

to **variolate** ['veəriəleit], v.t. vaccinare contro il vaiolo.

variolation [,veəriə'leiʃən], s. inoculazione di vaiolo; vaccinazione antivaiolosa.

variole ['veərioul], s. buttero (segno del vaiolo).

variolite ['veəriəlait], s. (min.) variolite.

varioloid ['veəriələid], ag. (patol.) vaioloso; caratteristico del vaiolo || s. (patol.) vaioloide.

variolous [və'raiələs], ag. (patol.) vaioloso.

variometer [,veəri'ɔmitə*], s. (elett.) variometro.

variorum [,veəri'ɔ:rəm], ag. con note di vari commentatori || A New Variorum Edition of Shakespeare, una nuova edizione delle opere di Shakespeare con note di diversi commentatori.

various ['veəriəs], ag. **1.** alcuni; parecchi: — books vari, parecchi libri; — occupations, occupazioni varie; for — reasons, per parecchie ragioni **2.** (arc.) vario; di verso; mutevole; versatile; instabile: the — character of Nero, il carattere mutevole di Nerone; his conversation was easy and —, la sua conversazione era scorrevole e varia.

variously ['veəriəsli], av. variamente; diversamente.

variousness ['veəriəsnis], s. (rar.) varietà; diversità.

varix ['veəriks], pl. **varices** ['væərisi:z], s. (patol.) varice.

varlet ['vɑ:lit], s. **1.** paggio; valletto **2.** (arc. scherz.) furfante, briccone.

varletry ['vɑ:litri], *s. coll.* (*arc.*) **1.** i paggi; i valletti **2.** (*spreg.*) servitorame.

varment, varmint ['vɑ:mint], *s.* (*volg. scherz.*) **1.** insetto parassita; animale nocivo **2.** (*caccia*) la volpe **3.** furfante; briccone.

varnish ['vɑ:niʃ], *s.* **1.** vernice; lacca **2.** *fig.* verniciatura; apparenza, aspetto esteriore: *to put a — of legality upon one's actions*, (*fam.*) mascherare le proprie azioni sotto un'apparenza di legalità ☆ — *filter*, (*ind.*) filtro per vernici; — *remover*, (*ind.*) sverniciatore; — *tree*, albero da cui si estrae una sostanza resinosa (per vernici) ‖ *nail* —, smalto (per unghie); *oil* —, (*ind.*) vernice grassa.

to **varnish**, *v.t.* **1.** verniciare; laccare **2.** *fig.* mascherare, velare (difetti, colpe); abbellire, adornare.

varnisher ['vɑ:niʃə*], *s.* verniciatore.

varnishing ['vɑ:niʃiŋ], *s.* verniciatura; laccatura ☆ — *-day*, vernice, « vernissage » (di mostra, esposizione di dipinti).

varsal ['vɑ:səl], (*fam. rar.*) per **universal**.

varsity ['vɑ:siti], (*fam.*) per **university**.

varus ['vɛərəs], *s.* (*patol.*) piede varo.

to **vary** ['vɛəri], *v.t.i.* **1.** variare, cambiare; mutare, mutarsi; modificare, modificarsi: *to — the menu, the programme*, variare il « menu », il programma; *to — one's methods*, cambiare metodo; *to — one's plans*, modificare i propri piani ‖ *y varies inversely as x*, (*mat.*) *y* è inversamente proporzionale a *x* **2.** differire, essere differente: *opinions — on this point*, i pareri differiscono a questo riguardo; *to — from*, differire da: *this edition varies very little from its predecessor*, questa edizione differisce pochissimo dalla precedente **3.** (*mus.*) fare variazioni a (un tema).

varyingly ['vɛəriŋli], *av.* in vari modi, variamente.

vas [væs], *pl.* **vasa** ['veisə], *s.* (*anat. bot.*) vaso ☆ — *aberrans*, vaso aberrante; — *deferens*, dotto deferente.

vasal ['veisəl], *ag.* (*anat. bot.*) vasale.

vascular ['væskjulə*], *ag.* (*fisiol. bot.*) vascolare ☆— *bundle*, (*bot.*) fascio vascolare; — *system*, (*fisiol.*) sistema vascolare; — *tissue*, (*bot.*) tessuto vascolare.

vascularization [,væskjulərai'zeiʃən], *s.* (*fisiol.*) vascolarizzazione.

to **vascularize** ['væskjuləraiz], *v.t.* (*fisiol.*) vascolarizzare.

vasculose ['væskjulous], *ag.* (*bot.*) vascoloso ‖ *s.* (*bot.*) tessuto vascoloso.

vase [vɑ:z], *s.* **1.** vaso **2.** (*arch.*) vaso (di capitello corinzio) ☆ — *-painting*, (*art. greca*) arte di decorare vasi; — *-shaped*, a forma di vaso ‖ *flower-* —, vaso da fiori.

vaseline ['væsili:n], *s.* (*chim.*) vaselina.

vasoconstrictor ['veizoukən'striktə*], *ag. s.* (*anat. farm.*) vasocostrittore.

vasodilator ['veizoudai'leitə*], *ag.s.* (*anat. farm.*) vasodilatatore.

vasomotor ['veizou'moutə*], *ag.s.* (*anat. farm.*) vasomotore.

vassal ['væsəl], *ag.* **1.** di vassallo **2.** servile ‖ *s.* **1.** (*st.*) vassallo **2.** servo; (*rar.*) schiavo.

vassalage ['væsəlidʒ], *s.* **1.** (*st.*) vassallaggio **2.** *fig.* condizione servile.

vast [vɑ:st], *ag.* vasto; immenso; esteso; ampio; grande; enorme: *a — expanse of water*, una vasta distesa d'acqua; *a — knowledge*, una vasta cultura; *a scheme of — scope*, un progetto d'ampia portata; *I saw a — number*, ne vidi un numero enorme; *to spend a — amount of money*, spendere una grande quantità di denaro ‖ *s.* (*poet.*) estensione; vastità: *the — of heaven*, l'immensità del cielo.

vastitude ['vɑ:stitju:d], *s.* vastità; immensità; ampiezza.

vastity ['vɑ:stiti], *s.* (*rar.*) vastità; l'essere vasto, immenso.

vastly ['vɑ:stli], *av.* vastamente; ampiamente; immensamente, enormemente: *you are — mistaken*, vi sbagliate di grosso.

vastness ['vɑ:stnis], *s.* vastità; immensità.

vasty ['vɑ:sti], *ag.* (*poet.*) vasto; immenso: *the — deep*, il vasto mare.

vat [væt], *s.* tino; tinozza ☆ — *dyeing*, (*ind. tessile*) tintura al tino ‖ *bleaching* —, (*ind. tessile*) vasca per il candeggio; *soaking* —, (*ind.*) vasca di macerazione; *tan* —, (*ind.*) tino per concia.

to **vat**, *pass.p.p.* **vatted** ['vætid], *v.t.* mettere in un tino, in una tinozza; far fermentare, conciare (in un tino).

vatful ['vætful], *s.* quantità contenuta in un tino.

Vatican ['vætikən], *no.pr.* (*geog.*) Vaticano ‖ *the* —, *City*, la Città del Vaticano ‖ *the* — *Council*, (*st.*) il Concilio Vaticano ‖ *the* — *State*, (*st.*) lo Stato Pontificio.

Vaticanist ['vætikənist], *s.* vaticanista.

to **vaticinate** [væ'tisineit], *v.t.* vaticinare, profetizzare.

vaticination [,vætisi'neiʃən], *s.* vaticinio, profezia.

vaticinator [væ'tisineitə*], *s.* vaticinatore, profeta.

vaudeville ['voudəvil], *s.* **1.** « vaudeville », commedia musicale; operetta **2.** (*amer.*) spettacolo di varietà.

vault[1] [vɔ:lt], *s.* **1.** (*arch.*) volta; volta a cantina; sotterraneo a volte **3.** sepolcro **4.** *fig.* volta celeste, cielo: *the blue — of heaven*, la volta azzurra del cielo **5.** (*anat.*) volta ☆ *barrel-* —, (*arch.*) volta a botte; *cranial* —, (*anat.*) volta cranica; *family* —, tomba, cripta di famiglia; *safety* —, camera di sicurezza (di banca); *wine* —, cantina per vino.

to **vault**[1], *v.t.i.* coprire con una volta; costruire a forma di volta; curvarsi a volta.

vault[2], *s.* **1.** volteggio, salto (eseguito appoggiandosi con le mani ad un sostegno); salto con l'asta **2.** falcata (di cavallo).

to **vault**[2], *v.t.i.* saltare (appoggiandosi sulle mani, su un'asta); volteggiare: *to — a fence* (o *over a fence*), saltare uno steccato; *to — into the saddle*, balzare in sella.

vaulted ['vɔ:ltid], *ag.* (*arch.*) a volta.

vaulter ['vɔ:ltə*], *s.c.* saltatore, saltatrice; volteggiatore, volteggiatrice.

vaulting[1] ['vɔ:ltiŋ], *s.* **1.** il costruire volte **2.** costruzione a volta **3.** *coll.* volte ☆ *cross-* —, (*arch.*) volta a crociera.

vaulting[2], *ag.* che salta; che supera gli ostacoli (anche *fig.*): — *ambition*, ambizione che non conosce ostacoli ‖ *s.* salto; volteggio ☆ — *-horse*, (*ginnastica*) cavalletto, cavallo.

vaunt [vɔ:nt], *s.* vanto; vanteria, millanteria.

to **vaunt**, *v.t.i.* **1.** vantare, vantarsi; gloriarsi: *to — (of) one's skill*, vantarsi della propria abilità **2.** lodare, decantare: *he vaunted the beauties of London*, decantava le bellezze di Londra.

vaunt-courier ['vɔ:nt,kuəriə*], *s.* precursore.

vaunter ['vɔ:ntə*], *s.c.* millantatore, millantatrice.

vaunting ['vɔ:ntiŋ], *ag.* vanitoso, vanaglorioso ‖ *s.* vanto; millanteria.

vauntingly ['vɔ:ntiŋli], *av.* in modo vanaglorioso; da gradasso.

vavasour ['vævəsuə*], *s.* (*st.*) valvassore.

've [v], *contr.* di **have**.

veal [vi:l], *s.* (*cuc.*) vitello ☆ — *cutlet*, costoletta di vitello.

vealy ['vi:li], *ag.* **1.** simile a vitello **2.** *fig.* immaturo.

vector ['vektə*], *s.* **1.** vettore **2.** (*med.*) portatore **3.** (*radius*) —, (*astr.*) raggio vettore.

vectorial [vek'tɔ:riəl], *ag.* vettoriale.

Veda ['veidə], *s.* Veda (libri sacri dell'antica India).

Vedanta [ve'dɑ:ntə], *s.* Vedanta (filosofia indù basata sui Veda).

Vedantist [ve'dɑ:ntist], *s.* seguace del Vedanta.

vedette [vi'det], *s.* (*mil.*) vedetta ☆ — *boat*, (*mar.*) vedetta.

Vedic ['veidik], *ag.* vedico, riguardante i Veda ‖ *s.* lingua vedica.

Vedism ['veidizəm], *s.* dottrina dei Veda.

veer[1] [viə*], s. **1.** cambiamento di direzione; (*mar.*) virata **2.** *fig.* cambiamento di opinione, condotta.

to **veer**[1], *v.i.* **1.** cambiar direzione; (*mar.*) virare, cambiare rotta: *the wind veered to the west*, il vento girò ad ovest **2.** *fig.* cambiare opinione, condotta.

to **veer**[2], *v.t.* (*mar.*) filare, mollare (gomena, cavo, ecc.) ‖ *to — and haul*, tesare e filare (alternativamente).

veeringly ['viərinli], *av.* **1.** cambiando direzione; (*mar.*) virando **2.** *fig.* cambiando opinione, condotta.

Vega ['vi:gə], *no.pr.* (*astr.*) Vega.

vegetable ['vedʒitəbl], *ag.* vegetale ‖ *s.* **1.** vegetale, pianta **2.** ortaggio; *pl.* verdura, verdure ☆ *— butter*, burro vegetale; *— diet*, dieta vegetariana; *— hair*, crine vegetale; *— kingdom*, regno vegetale; *— marrow*, zucca; *— mould*, terra vegetale; *— soup*, minestra di verdura.

vegetal ['vedʒitl], *ag.* **1.** vegetale: *phenomena of animal and — life*, fenomeni della vita animale e vegetale **2.** vegetativo: *the — functions*, le funzioni vegetative ‖ *s.* (*rar.*) vegetale, pianta.

vegetarian [,vedʒi'tɛəriən], *ag.* vegetariano: *— diet*, dieta vegetariana ‖ *s.c.* vegetariano, vegetariana.

vegetarianism [,vedʒi'tɛəriənizəm], *s.* vegetarianismo.

to **vegetate** ['vedʒiteit], *v.i.* vegetare (anche *fig.*): *they — rather than live*, più che vivere vegetano.

vegetation [,vedʒi'teiʃən], *s.* **1.** vegetazione: *the luxuriant — of your park*, la vegetazione lussureggiante del tuo parco; *— almost ceases in autumn*, la vegetazione cessa quasi totalmente in autunno **2.** *fig.* il vegetare, il vivere in modo piatto ed insignificante **3.** (*patol.*) vegetazione; fungosità.

vegetative ['vedʒitətiv], *ag.* vegetativo (anche *med.*) ☆ *— nervous system*, (*fisiol.*) sistema neuro-vegetativo.

vegetatively ['vedʒitətivli], *av.* in modo vegetativo.

vegetativeness ['vedʒitətivnis], *s.* natura vegetativa.

vehemence ['vi:iməns], *s.* veemenza; impeto; ardore.

vehement ['vi:imənt], *ag.* veemente; impetuoso; ardente; violento: *a — desire*, un desiderio violento; *a — wind*, un vento impetuoso.

vehemently ['vi:iməntli], *av.* con veemenza; impetuosamente; ardentemente.

vehicle ['vi:ikl], *s.* **1.** veicolo, mezzo di trasporto: *bicycles, motor-cars and other vehicles*, biciclette, automobili e altri veicoli; *the jolling — stopped at our door*, il veicolo traballante si fermò alla nostra porta **2.** veicolo; mezzo di trasmissione, di propagazione: *air is the — of sound*, l'aria è il mezzo di propagazione del suono; *art is sometimes a — for propaganda*, l'arte è talvolta un mezzo di propaganda **3.** (*med.*) veicolo: *water is the — of this disease*, l'acqua è il veicolo di questa malattia **4.** (*farm.*) eccipiente **5.** (*pitt.*) veicolo (legante) ☆ *— battery*, (*mec.*) accumulatore per trazione ‖ *street watering —*, innaffiatrice stradale; *track-laying —*, (*aut.*) veicolo cingolato.

vehicular [vi'hikjulə*], *ag.* di veicolo, relativo a veicolo.

veil [veil], *s.* **1.** velo: *she raised, dropped her —*, alzò, abbassò il velo ‖ *to take the —*, prendere il velo, farsi monaca **2.** velo, cortina: *a — of mist*, un velo di nebbia; *to draw* (o *to throw* o *to cast*) *a — over sthg.*, *fig.* stendere un velo su ql.co., non parlarne più ‖ *beyond the —*, *fig.* nell'aldilà **3.** *fig.* maschera; apparenza, pretesto: *under the — of patriotism, of religion*, sotto la maschera del patriottismo, della religione **4.** (*anat. zool. bot.*) velo; membrana **5.** raucedine **6.** (*foto.*) velo ☆ *eye —* (o *hat —*), veletta.

to **veil**, *v.t.* **1.** velare; coprire: *she veiled her face with her hand*, si coprì il volto con la mano **2.** *fig.* nascondere; mascherare; dissimulare: *she could not — her resentment*, non poteva nascondere il suo risentimento.

veiled [veild], *ag.* **1.** velato, coperto da un velo **2.** *fig.* nascosto; mascherato; dissimulato: *with hardly — hostility*, con mal dissimulata ostilità **3.** velato (di voce); indistinto (di suono).

veiling ['veiliŋ], *s.* **1.** il velare, il coprire con un velo **2.** velo; schermo **3.** velo (tessuto).

veilless ['veillis], *ag.* **1.** senza velo **2.** *fig.* non nascosto; non dissimulato.

vein [vein], *s.* **1.** (*anat.*) vena **2.** (*bot. entom.*) venatura, nervatura; (*min.*) venatura: *a fine diamond free of veins*, un bel diamante immune da venature **3.** (*miner.*) vena; filone: *a — of gold*, un filone d'oro **4.** (*solo sing.*) vena, disposizione; umore: *he is not in the — for a joke*, non è in vena di scherzare; *she is of an imaginative —*, ella ha molta fantasia; *we are not in the — for doing that*, non siamo in vena di far ciò ☆ *coronary —*, vena coronaria; *hypogastric —*, vena ipogastrica; *jugular —*, vena giugulare; *portal —*, vena porta; *pulmonary —*, vena polmonare; *Saphenous veins*, vene safene; *varicose —*, vena varicosa.

to **vein**, *v.t.* **1.** venare, coprire di vene, venature **2.** *fig.* venare: *all the gold that veins the world*, tutto l'oro che è sparso per il mondo.

veined [veind], *ag.* **1.** venato **2.** (*bot. entom.*) con venature, nervature.

veining ['veiniŋ], *s.* **1.** venatura **2.** (*bot. entom.*) venatura, nervatura.

veinless ['veinlis], *ag.* **1.** (*bot. entom.*) senza venature, nervature; (*min.*) senza venature **2.** (*miner.*) senza filoni.

veinlet ['veinlit], *s.* (*anat.*) venuzza, piccola vena.

veinlike ['veinlaik], *ag.* **1.** (*anat.*) simile a vena **2.** (*bot. entom. min.*) simile a venatura.

veinous ['veinəs], *ag.* **1.** (*anat.*) venoso; di vena **2.** attraversato da vene **3.** dalle vene grandi, prominenti: *the old man had knotted and — hands*, il vecchio aveva mani nodose e coperte di vene.

veiny ['veini], *ag.* **1.** (*anat.*) ricco di vene; attraversato da vene **2.** (*bot. entom. min.*) attraversato da venature.

velar ['vi:lə*], *ag.* (*fonet.*) velare.

veld(t) [velt], *s.* « veldt » (terreno aperto privo di alberi in Sud-Africa).

velite ['vi:lait], *s.* (*st. romana*) velite.

velleity [ve'li:iti], *s.* velleità.

to **vellicate** ['velikeit], *v.t.i.* (*rar.*) **1.** vellicare; solleticare; stimolare **2.** contrarsi; contorcersi.

vellication [,veli'keiʃən], *s.* (*rar.*) **1.** vellicamento, vellicazione **2.** contorsione.

vellum ['veləm], *s.* pergamena (materia e manoscritto su essa vergato) ☆ *— paper*, carta pergamena.

velocimeter [,velə'simitə*], *s.* (*tec.*) tachimetro.

velocipede [vi'ləsipi:d], *s.* **1.** velocipede **2.** (*amer.*) triciclo per bambini.

velocipedist [vi'ləsipi:dist], *s.* velocipedista.

velocity [vi'ləsiti], *s.* velocità: *— of light*, (*fis.*) velocità della luce; *— of sound*, (*fis.*) velocità del suono ☆ *— head*, (*fis.*) altezza cinetica; *— pressure*, (*fis.*) pressione dinamica; *— ratio*, (*mec.*) rapporto di trasmissione; *— stage*, (*mec.*) salto di velocità ‖ *mass —*, (*fis.*) velocità di massa; *phase —*, (*fis.*) velocità di propagazione di un'onda; *terminal —*, (*aer.*) velocità limite assoluta.

velours [və'luə*], *s.* **1.** « velours », velluto; felpa (per cappelli) **2.** cuscinetto di velluto per spazzolare cappelli.

velum ['vi:ləm], *pl.* **vela** ['vi:lə], *s.* (*anat. bot. zool.*) velo, membrana.

velure [vi'ljuə*], *s.* **1.** tessuto simile al velluto **2.** cuscinetto di velluto per spazzolare cappelli.

velutinous [vi'lju:tinəs], *ag.* (*bot. entom.*) vellutato.

velveret [,velvə'ret], *s.* velluto di qualità scadente.

velvet ['velvit], *ag.* **1.** di velluto: *a — gown*, un abito di velluto ‖ *an iron hand in a — glove*, *fig.* pugno di ferro in guanto di velluto **2.** vellutato: *a — paw*, una zampa vellutata; *fig.* crudeltà mascherata da dolcezza; *with — tread*, con passo felpato ‖ *s.* **1.** velluto ‖ *to be on —*, riposare sul velluto, trovarsi in una posizione favorevole **2.** *fig.* guadagno, profitto ☆ — *-pile*, tessuto peloso ‖ *cotton-* —, velluto di cotone; *fancy* —, velluto operato; *silk-* —, velluto di seta.

velveted ['velvitid], *ag.* **1.** vestito di velluto **2.** vellutato.

velveteen ['velvi'ti:n], *s.* **1.** velluto di cotone; velluto a coste **2.** *pl.* calzoni di velluto alla cacciatora **3.** *pl.* (*fam.*) guardacaccia.

velvetings ['velvitiŋz], *s. pl.* (*comm.*) velluti.

velvety ['velviti], *ag.* vellutato, morbido; *fig.* gentile.

venal[1] ['vi:nl], *ag.* venale, che si può comperare, corruttibile: *a — judge*, un giudice corruttibile.

venal[2], *ag.* (*rar. anat.*) di vena; venoso (di sangue).

venality [vi:'næliti], *s.* venalità, corruttibilità.

venally ['vi:nəli], *av.* venalmente.

venatic [vi'nætik], *ag.* venatorio, della caccia.

venation[1] [vi'neiʃən], *s.* (*rar.*) caccia.

venation[2], *s.* (*bot. entom.*) nervatura.

vend [vend], *s.* **1.** vendita **2.** vendita di carbone (da parte di una miniera).

to **vend**, *v.t.i.* **1.** (*dir.*) vendere; vendersi facilmente (di merce) **2.** *fig.* esporre, formulare (un'opinione).

vendee [ven'di:], *s.* compratore, acquirente.

Vendémiaire [,va:ŋdei'mjεə*], *s.* (*st. francese*) vendemmiaio.

vender ['vendə*], *s.* venditore; venditore ambulante.

vendetta [ven'detə], *s.* vendetta (tra membri di famiglie nemiche).

vendible ['vendəbl], *ag.* **1.** vendibile; *fig.* accettabile **2.** mercenario; venale ‖ *s.* articolo in vendita.

vendition [ven'diʃən], *s.* vendita.

vendor ['vendo:*], *s.* venditore; venditore ambulante.

veneer [vi'niə*], *s.* **1.** impiallacciatura; foglio per impiallacciatura **2.** *fig.* vernice, maschera: *under a superficial — of politeness*, sotto una vernice di cortesia ☆ — *-cutting machine*, piallatrice da impiallacciatura; — *-saw*, sega per impiallacciatura.

to **veneer**, *v.t.* **1.** impiallacciare **2.** *fig.* mascherare, nascondere sotto una apparenza attraente.

veneering [vi'niəriŋ], *s.* **1.** impiallacciatura **2.** *fig.* vernice; maschera.

venerability [,venərə'biliti], *s.* venerabilità.

venerable ['venərəbl], *ag.* **1.** venerabile (anche *eccl.*) **2.** venerando: — *ruins*, rovine venerande; *a — scholar*, un autorevole uomo di cultura.

venerableness ['venərəblnis], *s.* venerabilità.

venerably ['venərəbli], *av.* in modo venerando, che incute rispetto.

to **venerate** ['venəreit], *v.t.* venerare; riverire.

veneration [,venə'reiʃən], *s.* venerazione; adorazione: *to have* (o *to hold*) *in* —, venerare.

venerator ['venəreitə*], *s.c.* veneratore, veneratrice.

venereal [vi'niəriəl], *ag.* venereo.

venery[1] ['venəri], *s.* (*arc.*) caccia.

venery[2], *s.* (*arc.*) lussuria.

venesection [,veni'sekʃən], *s.* (*med.*) salasso, flebotomia.

Venetian [vi'ni:ʃən], *ag.* veneziano ‖ *s.c.* veneziano, veneziana; ☆ — *blind*, persiana alla veneziana; — *glass*, vetro, vetri di Murano; cristalli di Venezia; — *window*, (*arch.*) trifora.

Venezuela [,vene'zweilə], *no.pr.* (*geog.*) Venezuela.

to **venge** [vendʒ], *v.t.* (*arc. ret.*) vendicare.

vengeance ['vendʒəns], *s.* vendetta: *to take — on s.o.*, vendicarsi di qlcu. ‖ *with a —*, (*fam.*) abbondantemente; ad oltranza: *the rain comes down with a —*, la pioggia cade a più non posso.

vengeful ['vendʒful], *ag.* (*ret.*) vendicativo, vendicatore: — *fire falling from heaven*, fuoco vendicatore che cade dal cielo.

vengefully ['vendʒfuli], *av.* in modo vendicativo; a scopo di vendetta.

vengefulness ['vendʒfulnis], *s.* carattere vendicativo; spirito di vendetta.

venger ['vendʒə*], *s.* (*arc. ret.*) vendicatore.

venial ['vi:njəl], *ag.* veniale; perdonabile.

veniality [,vi:ni'æliti], *s.* venialità.

venially ['vi:njəli], *av.* venialmente; in modo perdonabile.

venialness ['vi:njəlnis], *s.* venialità.

Venice ['venis], *no.pr.* (*geog.*) Venezia ☆ — *glass*, vetro, vetri di Murano; — *talc*, (*min.*) steatite; — *treacle*, (*arc. farm.*) triaca.

venison ['venzn], *s.* **1.** carne di cervo, di daino (usata come alimento) **2.** (*arc.*) selvaggina.

Venite [vi'naiti], *s.* salmo XCV della liturgia anglicana e XCIV della Vulgata, cantato al mattino.

venom ['venəm], *s.* **1.** veleno (di serpenti, di insetti) **2.** *fig.* cattiveria, malignità.

venomed ['venəmd], **venomous** ['venəməs], *ag.* **1.** velenoso **2.** *fig.* cattivo, maligno.

venomously ['venəməsli], *av.* **1.** velenosamente **2.** *fig.* malignamente.

venomousness ['venəməsnis], *s.* **1.** velenosità **2.** *fig.* malignità.

venose ['vi:nous], *ag.* (*bot. zool.*) con nervature.

venosity [vi'nositi], *s.* (*anat.*) venosità.

venous ['vi:nəs], *ag.* **1.** (*anat.*) venoso **2.** (*bot. zool.*) con nervature ☆ — *system*, sistema venoso.

vent[1] [vent], *s.* spacco, apertura in un abito (specialmente nella parte posteriore di una giacca).

vent[2], *s.* **1.** sbocco, apertura; orifizio; foro, buco: *the — of a cask*, il forellino di un barile (da cui entra l'aria mentre si spilla il vino); *the — of a chimney*, la conduttura di un camino; *the — of a flute*, il foro di un flauto; *the — of a volcano*, il camino di un vulcano; *the waters found a — through the dykes*, le acque trovarono uno sfogo attraverso le dighe **2.** *fig.* sfogo; espressione: *laughter is a — of any sudden joy*, il riso è la manifestazione di qualsiasi gioia improvvisa; *to find —*, trovare sfogo; *to give — to sthg.*, dare libero corso a ql.co.: *to give — to one's indignation*, sfogare la propria indignazione **3.** (*anat.*) podice (specialmente di pesci, uccelli, rettili) **4.** il venire alla superficie per respirare (di lontra, castoro) ☆ — *hole*, apertura di sfogo; — *peg* (o — *plug*), zipolo; — *pipe*, tubo di sfiato; — *wire*, (*fonderia*), ago, spillo, spillone (per stampo) ‖ *bleeder* —, (*mec.*) foro di spurgo dell'aria; *tank — pipe*, (*mec.*) tubo di sfiato del serbatoio.

to **vent**[2], *v.t.i.* **1.** scaricare, svuotare, evacuare, esalare: *the chimney vents well*, il camino tira bene; *new wine often bursts the bottle by venting*, il vino nuovo spesso fa scoppiare la bottiglia per le sue esalazioni **2.** *fig.* sfogare, dare libero corso a (sentimenti, pensieri); esprimere: *I must — my griefs or my heart will burst*, devo dar sfogo alle mie pene altrimenti mi scoppierà il cuore; *the Presidency vented the most bitter complaints*, la presidenza espresse le più amare lamentele **3.** (*mil.*) fornire (un'arma da fuoco) di ventola **4.** venire alla superficie per respirare (di lontra, castoro).

vent[3], *s.* **1.** vendita **2.** spaccio.

to **vent**[3], *v.t.* (*dial.*) vendere.

ventage ['ventidʒ], *s.* **1.** foro, spiraglio **2.** (*mus.*) foro, apertura (di strumento a fiato).

venter ['ventə*], *s.* (*anat.*) **1.** ventre; utero; grembo ‖ *his sons by first —*, (*dir.*) i suoi figli di primo letto **2.** parte concava di un osso; ventre: — *of the scapula*, parte concava della scapola.

ventiduct ['ventidΛkt], *s.* (*edil.*) sfiatatoio; condotto dell'aria.

ventil ['ventil], *s.* (*mus.*) valvola che regola l'immissione dell'aria in un organo e altri strumenti consimili; ventilabro.

to **ventilate** ['ventileit], *v.t.* **1.** ventilare, far passare l'aria in; ossigenare (il sangue): *lungs — the blood*, i polmoni apportano ossigeno al sangue **2.** *fig.* esaminare, discutere, mettere in discussione; rendere manifesto: *the matter should not be hushed but freely ventilated*, la questione non dovrebbe essere messa a tacere, ma essere discussa liberamente.

ventilation [ˌventiˈleiʃən], s. **1.** ventilazione, aerazione; ossigenazione: *the — should be improved*, la ventilazione dovrebbe essere migliorata **2.** *fig.* discussione ☆ *course —*, (*miner.*) ventilazione in serie; *plenum —*, (*miner.*) ventilazione in pressione; *vacuum —*, (*miner.*) ventilazione in depressione.

ventilator [ˈventileitə*], s. **1.** ventilatore **2.** persona incaricata della ventilazione (di un edificio, ecc.) ☆ *unit —*, gruppo autonomo per ventilazione.

ventose [ˈventous], ag. (*arc.*) **1.** ventoso; flatulento **2.** vanaglorioso; presuntuoso.

Ventôse [ˌvɑːˈn̩touz], s. (*st. francese*) ventoso.

ventosity [venˈtositi], s. (*patol.*) flatulenza; ventosità.

ventral [ˈventrəl], ag. (*anat.*) ventrale, addominale ‖ s. — (*fin*), pinna ventrale.

ventricle [ˈventrikl], s. **1.** (*anat.*) ventricolo **2.** cavità addominale, ventre **3.** ventriglio (di animale).

ventricose [ˈventrikous], ag. panciuto; protuberante.

ventricoseness [ˈventrikousnis], **ventricosity** [ˌventriˈkositi], s. l'essere panciuto, rigonfio; gonfiezza; convessità.

ventricous [ˈventrikəs], ag. panciuto; protuberante.

ventricular [venˈtrikjulə*], ag. **1.** ventricolare **2.** addominale.

ventriloquial [ˌventriˈloukwiəl], ag. ventriloquo.

ventriloquially [ˌventriˈloukwiəli], av. da ventriloquo.

ventriloquism [venˈtriləkwizəm], s. ventriloquio.

ventriloquist [venˈtriləkwist], s. ventriloquo.

to **ventriloquize** [venˈtriləkwaiz], v.t.i. parlare, dire come un ventriloquo; praticare il ventriloquio.

ventriloquous [venˈtriləkwəs], ag. ventriloquo.

ventriloquy [venˈtriləkwi], s. ventriloquio.

venture [ˈventʃə*], s. **1.** avventura; azzardo: *he declined the —*, rinunciò all'avventura; *he was ready for any —*, era pronto a qualsiasi azzardo; *to make a desperate —*, fare un tentativo disperato **2.** (*comm.*) speculazione: *a mining —*, una speculazione mineraria; *ventures in the East*, speculazioni in Oriente **3.** (*arc.*) caso: *at a —*, a casaccio, a caso: *to answer at a —*, rispondere a caso.

to **venture**, v.t.i. avventurare, avventurarsi; arrischiare, arrischiarsi; osare: *he ventured a few words*, si arrischiò a dire alcune parole; *I — to say that...*, oso dire che...; *I'll — that experiment*, tenterò quell'esperimento; *I would not — on ice, if I were you*, se fossi te non mi avventurerei sul ghiaccio; *to — money upon sthg.*, arrischiare denaro su ql.co. ‖ *nothing —, nothing have*, prov. chi non risica, non rosica.

venturer [ˈventʃərə*], s. **1.** avventuriero **2.** (*merchant-*) —, (*st.*) mercante che investiva il suo denaro in speculazioni commerciali in terre lontane.

venturesome [ˈventʃəsəm], ag. **1.** ardito; temerario: *he was most — in his actions*, era molto ardito nelle sue azioni **2.** rischioso, arrischiato: — *act*, atto rischioso.

venturesomely [ˈventʃəsəmli], av. **1.** arditamente, audacemente **2.** in modo arrischiato.

venturesomeness [ˈventʃəsəmnis], s. **1.** ardimento, audacia **2.** rischio.

venturous [ˈventʃərəs], V. **venturesome**.

venturously [ˈventʃərəsli], V. **venturesomely**.

venturousness [ˈventʃərəsnis], s. **1.** ardimento, audacia **2.** rischio.

venue [ˈvenjuː], s. **1.** (*dir.*) giurisdizione; sede di un processo: *to change the —*, rinviare la causa davanti ad altra corte **2.** (*pop.*) luogo di ritrovo.

Venus [ˈviːnəs], no.pr.f. (*mit.*) Venere ‖ no.pr. (*astr.*) Venere ☆ s. **1.** amore; voluttà **2.** donna molto bella ☆ —*'s fly-trap*, (*bot.*) dionea; —*'s hair*, (*bot.*) capelvenere; —*'s navelwort*, (*bot.*) ombelico di Venere.

Vera [ˈviərə], no.pr.f. Vera.

veracious [veˈreiʃəs], ag. verace; veritiero.

veraciously [veˈreiʃəsli], av. veracemente; con sincerità.

veracity [veˈræsiti], s. veracità.

veranda(h) [vəˈrændə], s. veranda.

verb [vəːb], s. (*gram.*) verbo: *active —*, verbo attivo; *auxiliary —*, verbo ausiliare.

verbal [ˈvəːbəl], ag. **1.** verbale; testuale; letterale: *a — copy*, una copia testuale; *a — memory*, una memoria testuale; *a — translation*, una traduzione letterale **2.** orale; verbale, a parole: *a — explanation*, una spiegazione orale; *by — order*, per ordine verbale; *the opposition is rather — than real*, l'opposizione è più a parole che a fatti **3.** (*gram.*) verbale, relativo ai verbi: *a — ending*, una terminazione verbale ‖ s. — (*noun*), nome verbale.

verbalism [ˈvəːbəlizəm], s. **1.** verbalismo; eccessiva ricercatezza nel parlare **2.** vocabolo; locuzione, espressione verbale.

verbalist [ˈvəːbəlist], s. **1.** persona esperta nella scelta delle parole **2.** chi dà importanza solo alle parole.

verbalization [ˌvəːbəlaiˈzeiʃən] s. il trasformare (un nome) in verbo.

to **verbalize** [ˈvəːbəlaiz], v.t.i. **1.** trasformare (un nome) in verbo **2.** essere verboso, prolisso.

verbally [ˈvəːbəli], av. **1.** verbalmente; oralmente **2.** letteralmente.

verbatim [vəːˈbeitim], ag. letterale; testuale ‖ av. parola per parola; testualmente: *a speech reported —*, un discorso riportato testualmente.

verbena [və(ː)ˈbiːnə], s. (*bot.*) verbena.

verberation [ˌvəːbəˈreiʃən], s. **1.** ripercussione; il ripercuotere **2.** colpo.

verbiage [ˈvəːbiidʒ], s. **1.** verbosità **2.** dizione.

to **verbify** [ˈvəːbifai], v.t. trasformare (un nome) in verbo.

verbose [vəːˈbous], ag. verboso, prolisso.

verbosely [vəːˈbousli], av. verbosamente, prolissamente.

verboseness [vəːˈbousnis], **verbosity** [vəːˈbositi], s. verbosità, prolissità.

verdancy [ˈvəːdənsi], s. **1.** il verde; il verdeggiare: *the — of the fields and woods*, il verdeggiare dei campi e dei boschi **2.** *fig.* inesperienza; immaturità; ingenuità: *with the rashness typical of his youthful —*, con la tipica impetuosità della sua giovanile inesperienza.

verdant [ˈvəːdənt], ag. **1.** verdeggiante; verde: *the — fields*, i campi verdeggianti **2.** *fig.* inesperto; immaturo; ingenuo: — *youth*, gioventù inesperta.

verd-antique [ˈvəːdænˈtiːk], s. **1.** (marmo) verde antico **2.** (patina di) verderame.

verderer, verderor [ˈvəːdərə*], s. (*st.*) soprintendente alle foreste reali.

verdict [ˈvəːdikt], s. **1.** (*dir.*) verdetto: *a — of not guilty*, un verdetto di non colpevolezza **2.** giudizio; parere, opinione: *the popular —*, l'opinione popolare.

verdigris [ˈvəːdigris], s. (*chim.*) verderame.

verditer [ˈvəːditə*], s. (*chim.*) verdeterra; carbonato basico di rame.

verdure [ˈvəːdʒə*], s. **1.** verzura; vegetazione **2.** il verde: *the perennial — of cypress*, il verde perenne del cipresso **3.** *fig.* freschezza; giovinezza.

verdured [ˈvəːdʒəd], ag. coperto di vegetazione; verdeggiante.

verdureless [ˈvəːdʒəlis], ag. brullo.

verdurous [ˈvəːdʒərəs], ag. verdeggiante; verde; coperto di vegetazione.

verge[1] [vəːdʒ], s. **1.** orlo; limite; estremità (anche *fig.*): *they drew near to the very — of the river*, si spinsero fin sulla sponda del fiume ‖ *on the — of*, sull'orlo di, sul punto di: *my father is on the — of forty*, mio padre è sulla soglia dei quaranta; *they were on the — of succeeding*, erano sul punto di riuscire ‖ *to the — of*, vicino a: *he was driven to the very — of despair*, fu trascinato sull'orlo della disperazione **2.** bordo (di un'aiuola) **3.** verga, bacchetta; mazza **4.** (*st.*) area di giurisdizione: *within the —*, entro l'area di giurisdizione **5.** (*mec.*) asse del bilanciere **6.** (*arch.*) fusto, stele ☆ — -*board*, (*arch.*) cornice di frontone.

to **verge**[1], *v.i.* confinare; essere contiguo, adiacente, essere vicino (anche *fig.*): *his generosity verges on extravagance*, la sua generosità rasenta la stravaganza; *the path verges on the edge of the precipice*, il senticro costeggia l'orlo del precipizio.

to **verge**[2], *v.i.* tendere, volgere; piegare, piegarsi; declinare: *the sun was verging towards the horizon*, il sole declinava verso l'orizzonte; *to — towards old age*, avvicinarsi alla vecchiaia.

verger ['və:dʒə*], *s.* **1.** mazziere (anche *eccl.*) **2.** sagrestano, scaccino **3.** bidello.

Vergil ['və:dʒil], *no.pr.m.* Virgilio.

veridical [ve'ridikəl], *ag.* (*spec. iron.*) veridico, veritiero.

veridically [ve'ridikəli], *av.* veridicamente.

veridicous [ve'ridikəs], *ag.* veridico, veritiero.

verifiability [‚verifaiə'biliti], *s.* verificabilità.

verifiable ['verifaiəbl], *ag.* verificabile, constatabile.

verifiableness ['verifaiəblnis], *s.* verificabilità.

verifiably ['verifaiəbli], *av.* in modo verificabile.

verification [‚verifi'keiʃən], *s.* verificazione; verifica, controllo.

verifier ['verifaiə*], *s.c.* verificatore, verificatrice.

to **verify** ['verifai], *v.t.* **1.** verificare, controllare: *to — accounts*, verificare i conti **2.** attuare, adempiere **3.** (*dir.*) provare, autenticare; dimostrare con prove: *to — documents*, autenticare documenti.

verily ['verili], *av.* (*letter.*) in verità; veramente, realmente: *he — believes him honest*, lo crede realmente onesto; — *I say unto you*, (*Bibbia*) in verità vi dico....

verisimilar [‚veri'similə*], *ag.* verosimile.

verisimilarly [‚veri'siməli], *av.* verosimilmente.

verisimilitude [‚verisi'militju:d], *s.* verosimiglianza: *beyond the bounds of —*, al di là del verosimile.

verism ['viərizəm], *s.* (*art.*) verismo.

verist ['viərist], *s.* (*art.*) verista.

veritable ['veritəbl], *ag.* vero; genuino, autentico: *a — heroine*, un'autentica eroina; *we had a — deluge*, fu un vero diluvio.

veritably ['veritəbli], *av.* veramente; in effetti, in verità.

verity ['veriti], *s.* **1.** verità, realtà: *to challenge the — of sthg.*, mettere in dubbio la verità di ql.co. ‖ *the eternal verities*, le verità eterne ‖ *of a —*, (*arc.*) in verità **2.** fatto reale: *unquestionable verities*, fatti indiscutibili.

verjuice ['və:dʒu:s], *s.* agresto, succo di frutta acerba ‖ *she looked vinegar and —*, *fig.* aveva un'aria terribilmente acida.

to **verjuice**, *v.t.* inacidire; rendere acido; rendere aspro.

vermeil ['və:meil], *ag.s.* **1.** « vermeil » (argento dorato) **2.** (*poet.*) vermiglio.

to **vermeil**, *v.t.* colorire di vermiglio.

vermian ['və:miən], *ag.* di verme; simile a verme.

vermicelli [‚və:mi'seli], *s.* (*cuc.*) vermicelli.

vermicide ['və:misaid], *s.* (*farm.*) vermifugo.

vermicular [və:'mikjulə*], **vermiculate** [və:'mikjulit], *ag.* **1.** vermicolare; vermiforme: *a — appendix*, un'appendice vermiforme **2.** (*fisiol.*) peristaltico: *the — motion of the intestine*, i movimenti peristaltici dell'intestino.

vermiculated [və:'mikjuleitid], *ag.* **1.** mangiato dai vermi **2.** (*arch.*) vermicolato.

vermiculation [və:‚mikju'leiʃən], *s.* **1.** l'essere infestato dai vermi **2.** (*arch.*) disegno vermicolato **3.** (*fisiol.*) peristalsi.

vermicule ['və:mikju:l], *s.* vermiciattolo; baco; larva.

vermiculite [və:'mikjulait], *s.* (*min.*) vermiculite.

vermiform ['və:mifo:m], *s.* vermiforme ☆ — *appendix*, appendice vermiforme.

vermifugal [və:'mifjugəl], *ag.* vermifugo.

vermifuge ['və:mifju:dʒ], *ag.s.* vermifugo.

vermilion [və'miljən], *ag.* vermiglio ‖ *s.* **1.** vermiglione, cinabro **2.** (color) vermiglio.

to **vermilion**, *v.t.* tingere di vermiglio.

vermin ['və:min], *s. coll.* **1.** animali nocivi; insetti parassiti **2.** *fig.* persone nocive; feccia della società.

vermination [‚və:mi'neiʃən], *s.* (*patol.*) verminazione.

verminous ['və:minəs], *ag.* **1.** infestato da parassiti, da animali nocivi: *a — cellar*, una cantina infestata da topi; — *children*, bambini infestati da parassiti **2.** (*patol.*) verminoso: — *disease*, malattia causata da parassiti **3.** *fig.* vile; degradante; offensivo.

verminously ['və:minəsli], *av.* **1.** con parassiti **2.** *fig.* nocivamente; vilmente.

vermivorous [və:'mivərəs], *ag.* vermivoro.

vermouth ['və:məθ], *s.* vermouth, vermut.

vernacular [və'nækjulə*], *ag.* **1.** vernacolo; nativo; paesano; indigeno: *the — languages of India*, le lingue indigene dell'India; *a — poet*, un poeta dialettale **2.** (*patol.*) endemico ‖ *s.* **1.** vernacolo; dialetto nativo: *in the —*, nel dialetto (di un paese) **2.** gergo: *the — of the stage*, il gergo del teatro; *to use the — of engineers*, usare il linguaggio (tecnico) degli ingegneri.

vernacularism [və'nækjulərizəm], *s.* (*gram.*) idiotismo.

vernacularity [və‚nækju'læriti], *s.* caratteristica del vernacolo.

vernacularization [və‚nækjulərai'zeiʃən], *s.* il tradurre in vernacolo.

to **vernacularize** [və'nækjuləraiz], *v.t.* tradurre in vernacolo.

vernacularly [və'nækjuləli], *av.* secondo il vernacolo; in dialetto.

vernal ['və:nl], *ag.* (*poet. astr.*) primaverile: *a — shower*, un acquazzone primaverile ☆ — *equinox*, equinozio di primavera.

vernation [və'neiʃən], *s.* (*bot.*) vernazione.

vernicle ['və:nikl], *s.* (*eccl.*) veronica.

vernier ['və:njə*], *s.* (*tec.*) verniero; nonio ☆ — *calipers*, calibro a corsoio; — *scale*, scala del nonio.

Verona [vi'rounə], *no.pr.* (*geog.*) Verona.

Veronal ['verənl], *s.* (*farm.*) Veronal.

Veronese [‚verə'ni:z] *ag.s.c.* veronese.

Veronica [vi'ronikə], *no.pr.f.* Veronica ‖ *s.* (*eccl.*) veronica **2.** (*bot.*) veronica.

verruca [ve'ru:kə], *pl.* **verrucae** [ve'ru:si:], *s.* verruca.

verruciform [ve'ru:sifo:m], *ag.* simile a verruca.

verrucose [ve'ru:kous], **verrucous** [ve'ru:kəs], **verruculose** [ve'ru:kjulous], *ag.* verrucoso.

versant ['və:sənt], *s.* versante, declivio.

versatile ['və:sətail], *ag.* **1.** versatile; multiforme: *a — inventor*, un inventore versatile **2.** girevole: — *spindle*, fuso girevole **3.** (*bot. zool.*) mobile **4.** incostante, volubile.

versatilely ['və:sətailli], *av.* in modo versatile.

versatility [‚və:sə'tiliti], *s.* **1.** versatilità **2.** (*bot. zool.*) mobilità **3.** incostanza, volubilità.

verse[1] [və:s], *s.* **1.** verso: *iambic —*, verso giambico ‖ *in —*, in versi **2.** strofa; stanza **3.** componimento in versi; poesia: *he wrote very good —*, scrisse ottime poesie **4.** versetto (della Bibbia).

to **verse**[1], *v.t.i.* **1.** comporre versi, versificare **2.** narrare in versi **3.** (*bot. zool.*)

to **verse**[2], *v.t.i.* istruire, istruirsi; impraticarsi.

versed[1] [və:st], *ag.* istruito; versato; abile: *he is well — in mathematics*, è molto versato in matematica.

versed[2], *ag.*: — *sine*, (*mat.*) seno verso; (*arch.*) monta, rigoglio di arco.

verselet ['və:slit], *s.* breve poesia.

versemonger ['və:s‚mʌŋgə*], *s.* poetastro.

verset ['və:set], *s.* versetto.

versicle ['və:sikl], *s.* (*liturgia*) versetto (di salmo, ecc.).

versicoloured ['və:si‚kʌləd], *ag.* variegato, iridescente.

versicular [və:'sikjulə*], *ag.* di versi: — *division*, divisione in versi.

versification [,və:sifi'keiʃən], *s.* **1.** versificazione **2.** stile poetico, metrica **3.** riduzione in versi.

versificator ['və:sifikeitə*], **versifier** ['və:sifaiə*], *s.c.* versificatore, versificatrice; poeta, poetessa.

to **versify** ['və:sifai], *v.t.i.* **1.** versificare, comporre versi **2.** narrare in versi **3.** volgere in versi.

version ['və:ʃən], *s.* **1.** versione, traduzione ‖ *the Authorized Version of the Bible*, la versione anglicana della Bibbia (1611) **2.** versione; descrizione; racconto: *she gave quite a different — of the matter*, diede una versione del tutto differente della faccenda; *this painting is a larger — of the one at Windsor Castle*, questo dipinto è una versione più grande di quello al Castello di Windsor **3.** (*med.*) versione (del feto).

to **version**, *v.t.* tradurre.

versional ['və:ʃənl], *ag.* di versione; riguardante una versione.

vers libre [,vɛə'li:br], *s.* (*poes.*) verso libero.

verslibrist [,vɛə'li:brist], *s.* autore di versi liberi.

verso ['və:sou], *pl.* **versos** ['və:souz], *s.* verso, rovescio (di pagina, medaglia, ecc.).

versor ['və:sə*], *s.* (*mat.*) versore.

verst [və:st], *s.* versta.

versus ['və:səs], *prep.* (*abbr. v., vs.*) (*spor. dir.*) contro: *Smith — Brown*, Smith contro Brown.

vert[1] [və:t], *s.* **1.** verde, vegetazione (di bosco) **2.** (*dir. arc.*) diritto di tagliare piante verdi **3.** (*arald.*) colore verde.

vert[2], *s.c.* (*fam. abbr.* di *convert, pervert*) convertito, convertita; apostata.

to **vert**[2], *v.i.* (*fam.*) convertirsi.

to **vert**[3], *v.t.* (*anat. patol.*) volgere; piegare in posizione innaturale.

vertebra ['və:tibrə], *pl.* **vertebrae** ['və:tibri:], *s.* (*anat.*) vertebra ‖ *the vertebrae*, la colonna vertebrale; la spina dorsale.

vertebral ['və:tibrəl], *ag.* (*anat.*) vertebrale ‖ *s.* vena, arteria vertebrale ☆ — *column*, colonna vertebrale; — *foramen*, foro vertebrale; — *ribs*, coste fluttuanti.

Vertebrata [,və:ti'bra:tə], *s.pl.* (*zool.*) i vertebrati.

vertebrate ['və:tibrit], *ag.s.* (*zool.*) vertebrato.

vertebrated ['və:tibreitid] *ag.* (*zool.*) vertebrato.

vertebration [,və:ti'breiʃən], *s.* **1.** (*zool.*) formazione di vertebre; divisione in segmenti simili a vertebre **2.** *fig.* nerbo, spina dorsale.

vertex ['və:teks], *pl.* **vertices** ['və:tisi:z], *s.* **1.** vertice; apice; sommità **2.** (*anat.*) vertice; sommità del capo **3.** (*geom.*) vertice: — *of an angle*, vertice di un angolo; — *of a polygon*, vertice di un poligono **4.** (*astr.*) zenit ☆ — *presentation*, (*fisiol.*) presentazione di vertice.

vertical ['və:tikəl], *ag.* **1.** verticale; perpendicolare **2.** situato al vertice, allo zenit **3.** (*anat. zool.*) situato al vertice del capo ‖ *s.* verticale; piano verticale ☆ — *circle*, (*astr.*) azimut; — *engine*, (*tec.*) motore verticale; — *line*, linea perpendicolare all'orizzonte; — *milling machine*, (*mec.*) fresatrice verticale; — *rudder*, (*aer.*) timone di direzione; — *section*, (*arch.*) sciografia; spaccato; — *shaft*, (*tec.*) albero verticale.

verticality [,və:ti'kæliti], *s.* posizione verticale; perpendicolarità.

vertically ['və:tikəli], *av.* verticalmente; a perpendicolo.

verticalness ['və:tikəlnis], *s.* posizione verticale; perpendicolarità.

verticil ['və:tisil], *s.* (*bot.*) verticillo.

verticillate [və:'tisilit], *ag.* (*bot.*) verticillato.

verticillation [və:,tisi'leiʃən], *s.* (*bot.*) verticillo; a forma di verticillo.

vertiginous [və:'tidʒinəs], *ag.* **1.** vertiginoso, vorticoso: *a — motion*, moto vertiginoso; *a — wind*, vento vorticoso **2.** che soffre di vertigini: *to feel* (o *to grow*) —, avere le vertigini **3.** che dà le vertigini: *a — height*, un'altezza che dà le vertigini.

vertiginously [və:'tidʒinəsli], *av.* vertiginosamente; vorticosamente.

vertiginousness [və:'tidʒinəsnis], *s.* vorticosità.

vertigo ['və:tigou], *s.* **1.** (*med.*) vertigine; capogiro **2.** *fig.* stordimento.

vertu, *V.* **virtu**.

Verulamian [,veru'leimjən], *ag.* (*geog.*) di, da Verulamio.

Verulamium [,veru'leimjəm], *no.pr.* (*geog. st.*) Verulamio (l'odierna St. Albans).

vervain ['və:vein], *s.* (*bot.*) verbena.

verve [vɛəv], *s.* « verve », vigore, energia; brio, entusiasmo: *to play with* —, recitare con brio, con calore.

vervet ['və:vit], *s.* (*zool.*) cercopiteco.

very ['veri], *ag.* **1.** **vero e proprio, autentico; perfetto**: *he has proved (to be) a — gentleman*, si è dimostrato un vero gentiluomo; *this is my — son*, questo è veramente mio figlio; *the veriest fool knows that*, lo sa anche il più gran cretino ‖ — *God of* — *God*, Dio vero da Dio vero ‖ *in — deed*, in realtà, di fatto ‖ *in — truth*, sinceramente **2.** (*uso enfatico, intensivo*) **proprio, esatto, stesso, medesimo:** *at that — moment*, in quel preciso istante; *from this — day*, a partire esattamente da oggi; *the — children knew of it*, perfino i bambini lo sapevano; *the — thought makes me shiver*, il solo pensiero mi fa rabbrividire; *he died a year ago to the — day*, morì proprio un anno fa; *it grieves me to the — heart*, mi addolora nel più profondo del cuore; *she saw him in the — act of stealing it*, lo vide proprio nell'atto di rubarlo; *sitting in this — room*, seduti in questa stessa stanza; *that's the — thing!*, questo è proprio quello che ci vuole!; *they live at the — end of the town*, vivono all'estremo limite della città; *those were his — words*, quelle furono le sue precise parole.

very, *av.* **1.** **molto, assai:** — *amusing*, molto divertente; — *difficult*, molto difficile, difficilissimo; — *far*, molto lontano, lontanissimo; — *good*, buonissimo; benissimo; — *much*, moltissimo; — *pleased*, molto lieto, lietissimo; *he is — well known in London*, è molto conosciuto a Londra; *that's — nice of you*, è molto gentile da parte tua; *they took only a — little*, ne presero pochissimo; *"Were you happy?", "Yes, —"*, « Eri felice? », « Sì, molto » ‖ — *well*, molto bene, benissimo, va bene **2.** (*uso enfatico*): *the — first*, il primissimo; *the — last*, proprio l'ultimo; *the — next day*, il giorno immediatamente successivo; *the — same*, proprio lo stesso; *I did the — best I could*, ho fatto tutto il possibile; *you may keep it for your — own*, puoi tenerlo per te ‖ *at the — most*, tutt'al più; *at the — latest*, al più tardi **3.** (*in frasi negative dà luogo a litote*): *I am not — keen on going there*, non ho alcuna voglia di andare là; *I don't sing — well*, canto piuttosto male.

vesica ['vesikə], *s.* **1.** (*anat. bot.*) vescica **2.** — *piscis*, (*art.*) mandorla mistica.

vesical ['vesikəl], *ag.* (*anat. bot.*) vescicale ☆ — *calculus*, (*patol.*) calcolo vescicale.

vesicant ['vesikənt], *ag. s.* (*farm.*) vescicante.

to **vesicate** ['vesikeit], *v.t.i.* produrre vescicole a; coprirsi di vescicole.

vesication [,vesi'keiʃən], *s.* vescicazione, formazione di vescicole.

vesicatory ['vesikeitəri], *ag.s.* (*farm.*) vescicatorio.

vesicle ['vesikl], *s.* **1.** vescichetta, vescicola **2.** (*geol.*) cavità vescicolare (di rocce vulcaniche).

vesicular [vi'sikjulə*], *ag.* (*anat. med. geol.*) vescicolare.

vesiculate [vi'sikjulit], **vesiculated** [vi'sikjuleitid], *ag.* **1.** a forma di vescichetta, di vescicola **2.** (*patol.*) coperto di vescichette, di vesciche.

vesiculation [vi,sikju'leiʃən], *s.* (*patol.*) vescicolazione.

vesiculiform [vi'sikjulifo:m], *ag.* vescicoliforme.

Vespasian [ves'peizjən], *no.pr.m.* (*st.*) Vespasiano.

vesper ['vespə*], *s.* **1.** (*poet.*) sera, vespro ‖ *Vesper*, (*astr.*) Vespero **2.** *pl.* (*eccl.*) i vespri ‖ *the Sicilian Vespers*, (*st.*) i Vespri Siciliani ☆ — *-bell*, campana che chiama ai vespri.

vesperal ['vespərəl], *ag.* (*rar.*) vesperale, vespertino ‖ *s.* (*eccl.*) libro dei vespri.

vespertilio [,vespə'tiliou], *s.* (*zool.*) vespertillo.

vespertine ['vespətain], *ag.* **1.** vespertino: — *star*, stella vespertina **2.** notturno (di animale, fiore).

vespiary ['vespiəri], *s.* vespaio.

vespine ['vespain], *ag.* di vespa, di vespe.

vessel ['vesl], *s.* **1.** vaso, recipiente **2.** *fig.* (*Bibbia*) vaso, ricettacolo: *a chosen* —, vaso d'elezione, anima eletta ‖ *the weaker* —, il sesso debole **3.** (*anat. bot.*) vaso **4.** (*mar.*) nave, vascello **5.** aeroplano ☆ *air* —, (*mar.*) serbatoio d'aria (compressa); *blood-* —, (*anat.*) vaso sanguigno; *crystallization* —, (*chim.*) cristallizzatore; *full-deck* —, (*mar.*) nave a struttura normale; *shade-deck* —, (*mar.*) nave a ponte tenda.

vesselful ['veslful], *s.* contenuto di un recipiente.

vest [vest], *s.* **1.** panciotto **2.** maglia (di cotone; camiciola **3.** davantino, pettorina **4.** (*arc.*) vestito, abbigliamento ☆ — *-pocket camera*, macchina fotografica tascabile.

to **vest**, *v.t.i.* **1.** investire; conferire: *he was vested with great authority*, gli fu conferita grande autorità **2.** (*dir.*) assegnare, dare in possesso a; passare a: *to* — *a person with rights in an estate*, conferire ad una persona diritti su un patrimonio; *to* — *property in s.o.*, assegnare dei beni a qlcu.; *this estate vests in the heir*, il patrimonio passa all'erede **3.** (*poet. eccl.*) vestire; indossare la veste: *the Bishop vested himself to say Mass*, il vescovo indossò i paramenti per dire messa.

Vesta ['vestə], *no.pr.f.* (*mit.*) Vesta ‖ *no.pr.* (*astr.*) Vesta ‖ **vesta**, *s.* fiammifero; cerino.

vestal ['vestl], *ag.* **1.** vestale, di Vesta **2.** *fig.* verginale ‖ *s.* **1.** (*st.*) vestale **2.** *fig.* donna casta; vergine; suora.

vested ['vestid], *ag.* **1.** vestito con paramenti ecclesiastici **2.** (*dir.*) assegnato; acquisito: — *rights, interests*, diritti, interessi acquisiti.

vestiarian [,vesti'eəriən], *ag.* (*rar.*) concernente, relativo ai paramenti ecclesiastici.

vestiary ['vestiəri], *ag.* (*rar.*) relativo a vestiario ‖ *s.* (*st.*) guardaroba (di monastero, ecc.).

vestibular [ves'tibjulə*], *ag.* (*anat.*) vestibolare, relativo al vestibolo.

vestibule ['vestibju:l], *s.* **1.** vestibolo, entrata, anticamera **2.** portico (di chiesa) **3.** (*anat.*) vestibolo **4.** (*mec.*) passaggio **5.** (*amer. ferr.*) passaggio a mantice ☆ — *car*, (*ferr.*) carrozza intercomunicante; — *ganglion*, (*anat.*) ganglio vestibolare.

vestige ['vestidʒ], *s.* **1.** *fig.* vestigio, traccia, orma: *the last vestiges of prehistoric life*, gli ultimi vestigi della vita preistorica; *not a* — *of the old abbey remains*, non rimane una sola traccia della vecchia abbazia; *she has not a* — *of evidence for this assertion*, non ha la minima prova per affermare ciò **2.** (*biol.*) residuo (di organo scomparso).

vestigial [ves'tidʒiəl], *ag.* **1.** (*biol.*) rudimentale, rudimentario **2.** residuale ☆ — *fold*, plica vestigiale; — *muscle*, muscolo rudimentario.

vesting ['vestiŋ], *s. spec. pl.* tessuto per panciotti.

vesture ['vestʃə*], *s.* **1.** (*zool.*) rivestimento (di peli, scaglie, ecc.) **2.** (*arc.*) vesti.

vestment ['vestmənt], *s.* **1.** abito (da cerimonia) **2.** (*eccl.*) pianeta **3.** tovaglia (d'altare).

vestry ['vestri], *s.* **1.** sagrestia **2.** cappella (annessa alle chiese anglicane, dove si prega e si tengono riunioni religiose) **3.** consiglio di amministrazione di una parrocchia **4.** assemblea parrocchiale ☆ — *-clerk*, segretario del consiglio di amministrazione di una parrocchia.

vestryman, *pl.* **vestrymen** ['vestrimən], *s.* membro di assemblea parrocchiale.

vesture ['vestʃə*], *s.* **1.** (*poet.*) vestimento, veste **2.** (*dir.*) tutto ciò che cresce sul suolo (eccettuato gli alberi).

to **vesture**, *v.t.* (*poet.*) vestire, rivestire.

vesturer ['vestʃərə*], *s.* sagrestano, custode di arredi sacri.

Vesuvian [vi'su:vjən], *ag.* vesuviano ‖ **vesuvian**, *s.* **1.** fiammifero controvento **2.** (*min.*) vesuvianite.

vesuvianite [vi'su:vjənait], *s.* (*min.*) vesuvianite.

Vesuvius [vi'su:vjəs], *no.pr.* (*geog.*) Vesuvio.

vet[1] [vet], *s.* (*fam. abbr.* di *veterinary*) veterinario.

to **vet**[1], *pass.p.p.* **vetted** ['vetid], *v.t.* (*fam.*) **1.** curare, visitare (un animale) **2.** (*scherz.*) curare (un essere umano) **3.** (*fam. fig.*) esaminare; criticare (manoscritti, ecc.).

vet[2], *s.* (*amer. abbr.* di *veteran*) reduce, ex-combattente.

vetch [vetʃ], *s.* (*bot.*) veccia ☆ *milk* —, (*bot.*) astragalo.

vetchling ['vetʃliŋ], *s.* (*bot.*) latiro.

vetchy ['vetʃi], *ag.* veccioso.

veteran ['vetərən], *ag.* **1.** veterano, vecchio, esperto: *a* — *golfer*, un veterano del golf **2.** di veterano, di veterani: *a* — *army*, un esercito di veterani ‖ *s.* **1.** veterano (anche *fig.*): *a* — *of many campaigns*, veterano di molte campagne **2.** (*amer.*) reduce.

to **veteranize** ['vetərənaiz], *v.t.i.* **1.** (*amer.*) rendere veterano **2.** arruolarsi nuovamente.

veterinarian [,vetəri'neəriən], *s.* veterinario.

veterinary ['vetərinəri], *ag.s.* veterinario.

veto ['vi:tou], *pl.* **vetoes** ['vi:touz], *s.* **1.** veto; proibizione: *father has put his* — *on our going out to-night*, papà ci ha proibito di uscire questa sera; *to put* (o *to set*) *one's* — (*up*)*on sthg.*, porre il proprio veto a ql.co. **2.** diritto di veto: *the Lords exercised their* —, i Lord esercitarono il loro diritto di veto.

to **veto**, *v.t.* mettere il veto a; proibire: *the Crown may* — *a bill that both Houses have passed*, la Corona può porre il veto a un progetto di legge approvato da tutte e due le Camere; *the Police vetoed the meeting*, la polizia vietò l'assemblea.

to **vex** [veks], *v.t.* **1.** vessare, opprimere **2.** irritare, stizzire: *her continuous whining vexes me*, mi irritano i suoi piagnistei continui **3.** (*arc.*) affliggere, addolorare: *gout vexed him*, lo tormentava la gotta **4.** (*poet.*) agitare, sconvolgere (il mare): *the storms vexing the ocean*, le tempeste che agitano l'oceano.

vexation [vek'seiʃən], *s.* **1.** vessazione, oppressione **2.** irritazione; noia, fastidio, contrarietà, seccatura: *all the trifling vexations one has to put up with*, tutte le piccole seccature che si devono sopportare; *much to my* — *I just missed my train*, con mia grande rabbia persi il treno.

vexatious [vek'seiʃəs], *ag.* **1.** irritante, spiacevole, fastidioso: — *neighbours*, vicini di casa noiosi; — *rules*, regolamenti seccanti; *moving house is always a* — *business*, un trasloco è sempre un grosso fastidio **2.** (*dir.*) vessatorio.

vexatiously [vek'seiʃəsli], *av.* in modo seccante, irritante.

vexatiousness [vek'seiʃəsnis], *s.* **1.** l'essere irritante, noioso, fastidioso **2.** (*dir.*) l'essere vessatorio.

vexed [vekst], *ag.* **1.** vessato (anche *fig.*); oppresso ‖ — *question*, questione dibattuta **2.** irritato, contrariato, seccato: *to be* — *at sthg.*, essere contrariato da ql.co.; *to be* — *with s.o.*, essere seccato con qlcu.; *to get* — *at sthg.*, seccarsi di ql.co. **3.** (*poet.*) agitato (di mare).

vexedly ['veksidli], *av.* in modo irritato, seccato.

vexillary ['veksiləri], *s.* (*st. romana*) vessillario.

vexillum [vek'siləm], *pl.* **vexilla** [vek'silə], *s.* **1.** vessillo, stendardo **2.** (*eccl.*) stendardo **3.** (*bot.*) stendardo **4.** vessillo, barba (di penna di uccello).

vexingly ['veksiŋli], *av.* in modo irritante.

via ['vaiə], *prep.* per, via, attraverso: — *air mail*, per via aerea; *Milan to Rome* — *Florence*, Milano-Roma via Firenze.

viability [,vaiə'biliti], *s.* vitalità; capacità di vivere.

viable ['vaiəbl], *ag.* **1.** vitale **2.** germinabile.

viaduct ['vaiədʌkt], *s.* viadotto.

vial ['vaiəl], *s.* fiala ‖ *to pour out vials of wrath,* dar libero sfogo alla propria collera.

to **vial,** *pass.p.p.* **vialled** ['vaiəld], *v.t.* mettere, tenere in fiala.

viand ['vai-ənd], *s. gener.pl.* vivanda, cibo.

viaticum [vai'ætikəm], *s.* **1.** (*relig.*) viatico **2.** viatico; denaro, provviste per un viaggio.

viator [vai'eitə*], *pl.* **viatores** [,vaiə'touri:z], *s.* viandante.

vibrant ['vaibrənt], *ag.* vibrante; tremante; risonante: *the — notes of his voice,* le note vibranti della sua voce; — *with enthusiasm,* vibrante di entusiasmo.

to **vibrate** [vai'breit], *v.t.i.* **1.** vibrare, far vibrare (anche *fig.*); risuonare: *a voice vibrating with anger,* una voce vibrante d'ira; *your voice vibrates in* (o *on*) *my ear,* la tua voce mi risuona all'orecchio **2.** oscillare, far oscillare: *long pendulums — more slowly than short ones,* i pendoli lunghi oscillano più lentamente di quelli corti **3.** misurare oscillando: *a pendulum vibrating seconds,* un pendolo che misura i secondi oscillando.

vibratile ['vaibrətail], *ag.* vibratile.

vibratility [,vaibrə'tiliti], *s.* vibratilità.

vibration [vai'breiʃən], *s.* **1.** vibrazione; tremolio **2.** oscillazione: — *due to bending stress,* oscillazione di flessione; — *of a pendulum,* oscillazione di un pendolo **3.** (*fis.*) vibrazione ☆ — *damper,* (*mec.*) ammortizzatore di vibrazioni.

vibrational [vai'breiʃənl], *ag.* vibratorio, di vibrazione.

vibrative [vai'breitiv], *ag.* (*rar.*) **1.** vibratorio **2.** vibrante.

vibrator [vai'breitə*], *s.* (*fis. elett.*) vibratore.

vibratory ['vaibrətəri], *ag.* **1.** vibratorio: *the — motion of the nerves,* il movimento vibratorio dei nervi **2.** oscillatorio **3.** vibrante: *a voice — with excitement,* una voce vibrante per l'eccitazione.

vibrissae [vai'brisi:], *s.pl.* vibrisse.

viburnum [vai'bə:nəm], *s.* (*bot.*) viburno.

vicar ['vikə*], *s.* **1.** curato, parroco (nella Chiesa d'Inghilterra) ‖ — *of Bray,* opportunista (allusione all'omonima canzone) **2.** vicario (nella Chiesa Cattolica) ‖ *the Vicar of Christ,* il Vicario di Cristo, il Papa ☆ — *-apostolic,* vicario apostolico.

vicarage ['vikəridʒ], *s.* **1.** canonica, casa del parroco **2.** carica, dignità di parroco.

vicaress ['vikəris], *s.* **1.** (madre) vicaria **2.** moglie di parroco.

vicarial [vai'kɛəriəl], *ag.* **1.** vicariale, di vicario **2.** delegato.

vicarian [vai'kɛəriən], *ag.* concernente un sostituto, un rappresentante.

vicariate [vai'kɛəriit], *s.* vicariato.

vicarious [vai'kɛəriəs], *ag.* **1.** delegato; rappresentante **2.** fatto, subìto in sostituzione di un'altra persona: — *punishment,* punizione subita da una persona al posto di un'altra **3.** vicariante, vicario, sostituto ☆ — *hypertrophy,* (*fisiol.*) ipertrofia vicariante, compensatoria; — *respiration,* (*fisiol.*) respirazione vicariante.

vicariously [vai'kɛəriəsli], *av.* **1.** in qualità di vicario, come vicario **2.** in luogo di un altro.

vicariousness [vai'kɛəriəsnis], *s.* autorità di vicario, di parroco.

vicarship ['vikəʃip], **vicary** ['vikəri], *s.* vicariato.

vice¹ [vais], *s.* **1.** immoralità, depravazione: *when — prevails,* quando l'immoralità trionfa **2.** vizio: *avarice is a —,* l'avarizia è un vizio **3.** difetto, vizio (di cavalli): *this horse has the — of kicking,* questo cavallo ha il vizio di scalciare **4.** difetto, imperfezione, pecca: *vices of style,* imperfezioni stilistiche.

vice², *s.* (*mec.*) morsa: *as firm as a —,* fermamente fissato; *fig.* irremovibile ‖ — *cheek* (o — *jaw*), ganascia di una morsa ‖ *bench —,* morsa da banco.

to **vice²,** *v.t.* chiudere in una morsa (anche *fig.*).

vice³, *s.* **1.** sostituto, vice **2.** (*fam. abbr.* di *vice-president*) vicepresidente.

vice⁴ ['vaisi], *prep.* in luogo di.

vicegerency ['vais'dʒerənsi], *s.* vicegerenza.

vicegerent ['vais'dʒerənt], *ag.* rappresentante; delegato ‖ *s.* vicegerente.

vicennial [vai'senjəl], *ag.* ventennale.

viceregal ['vais'ri:gəl], *ag.* di vicerè, concernente il vicerè.

vicereine ['vais'rein], *s.* viceregina.

viceroy ['vais-roi], *s.* vicerè.

viceroyalty ['vais-roiəlti], **viceroyship** ['vais-roi,ʃip], *s.* **1.** carica di vicerè **2.** vicereame.

vice-versa ['vaisi'və:sə], *av.* viceversa.

vicinage ['visinidʒ], *s.* **1.** territori vicini, confinanti: *the metropolis and its —,* la metropoli e i territori limitrofi **2.** vicinato, i vicini.

vicinal ['visinəl], *ag.* **1.** vicinale: — *road* (o *way*), strada vicinale **2.** (*mat. min.*) adiacente.

vicinity [vi'siniti], *s.* **1.** vicinanza, prossimità: *the — of Mars to the Earth,* la vicinanza di Marte alla Terra **2.** affinità: *a— of disposition,* una affinità di carattere **3.** vicinanze, dintorni.

vicious ['viʃəs], *ag.* **1.** vizioso, immorale, depravato: *a — life,* una vita immorale **2.** maligno, cattivo, dispettoso: *a — look,* uno sguardo maligno; *a — remark,* un'osservazione cattiva; *a — temper,* un temperamento dispettoso **3.** bizzarro, balzano (di cane, cavallo): *a — animal that has injured many persons,* un animale bizzarro che ha fatto male a molte persone **4.** guasto, difettoso; imperfetto; impuro: *a — manuscript,* un manoscritto scorretto; *a — style,* uno stile scorretto ‖ — *circle,* (*log.*) circolo vizioso.

viciously ['viʃəsli], *av.* **1.** viziosamente, depravatamente **2.** malignamente, con cattiveria **3.** imperfettamente.

viciousness ['viʃəsnis], *s.* **1.** viziosità **2.** malignità, cattiveria **3.** imperfezione.

vicissitude [vi'sisitju:d], *s.* **1.** vicissitudine, vicenda: *the vicissitudes of life,* le vicissitudini della vita **2.** (*arc. poet.*) avvicendamento.

vicissitudinous [vi,sisi'tju:dinəs], *ag.* caratterizzato da vicissitudini.

Vicky ['viki], *no.pr.f. dim.* di **Victoria.**

victim ['viktim], *s.* **1.** vittima: *he fell a — to his own ambition,* fu vittima della sua ambizione; *he fell a — to malaria,* cadde vittima della malaria **2.** preda: *the — of dishonest shopkeepers,* la preda di negozianti disonesti **3.** vittima (sacrificata ad una divinità).

victimization [,viktimai'zeiʃən], *s.* sacrificio; martirio.

to **victimize** ['viktimaiz], *v.t.* **1.** ingannare; truffare: *he was victimized by swindlers,* fu truffato da imbroglioni **2.** sacrificare, offrire come vittima.

victor¹ ['viktə*], *s.* vincitore, conquistatore ‖ — *sword,* spada vincitrice ‖ *the —,* truppe vittoriose.

Victor², *no.pr.m.* Vittorio.

Victoria [vik'tɔ:riə], *no.pr.f.* Vittoria ‖ — *Cross,* Croce della Regina Vittoria (massima onorificenza per merito di guerra) ‖ — *Day,* anniversario della nascita della Regina Vittoria (24 maggio) ‖ *no.pr.* (*astr.*) Vittoria ‖ **victoria,** *s.* **1.** vittoria (tipo di carrozza) **2.** (*bot.*) vittoria regia.

Victorian¹ [vik'tɔ:riən], *ag.* vittoriano, del periodo della regina Vittoria; *fig.* antiquato: — *morals,* morale vittoriana ‖ *s.* persona, scrittore del tempo della regina Vittoria.

Victorian², *ag.* della colonia di Vittoria (in Australia) ‖ *s.* colono, abitante di Vittoria (in Australia).

Victorianism [vik'tɔ:riənizəm], *s.* gusto, spirito, tendenze caratteristiche del regno della regina Vittoria.

victorine ['viktəri:n], *s.* «victorine» (mantellina di pelo per signora).

victorious [vik'tɔ:riəs], *ag.* vittorioso.

victoriously [vik'tɔ:riəsli], *av.* vittoriosamente.

victory ['viktəri], s. vittoria: *to gain* (o *to get* o *to win*) *a — over the enemy*, ottenere una vittoria sul nemico ‖ *a Pyrrhic —*, una vittoria di Pirro.

victress ['viktris], s. vincitrice.

victual ['vitl], s. *gener. pl.* vettovaglie, viveri, provvigioni.

to victual, *pass. p.p.* **victualled** ['vitld], *v.t.i.* vettovagliare; approvvigionare, approvvigionarsi: *the ship victualled at New York*, la nave si approvvigionò a Nuova York; *to — a ship*, vettovagliare una nave.

victualler ['vitlə*], s. **1.** incaricato dei rifornimenti, vivandiere **2.** nave di rifornimento ☆ *licensed —*, gestore di locale pubblico autorizzato anche alla vendita di alcoolici ai consumatori sul posto.

victualling ['vitliŋ], s. vettovagliamento, approvvigionamento ☆ *-house*, taverna; *— -note*, (*mar.*) autorizzazione a distribuire i viveri a un nuovo marinaio; *— -office*, (*mar.*) ufficio che provvede al vettovagliamento della Marina.

vicuna, **vicuña** [vi'kju:nə], s. (*zool.*) vigogna ☆ *— cloth*, stoffa di vigogna.

vide ['vaidi(:)], 2ª *persona sing. pres. imperat. del v. lat. videre* (*abbr.* v.) vedi: *— supra*, vedi sopra.

videlicet [vi'di:liset], *av. lat.* (*abbr.* viz.) cioè: *two subjects must be taken*, viz., *English and mathematics*, sono obbligatorie due materie, e cioè inglese e matematica.

video ['vidiou], *ag.* (*tv.*) video, di immagine ‖ s. (*amer.*) televisione ☆ *— amplifier*, amplificatore video; *— frequency*, video frequenza; *— signal*, segnale d'immagine.

viduage ['vidjuidʒ], s. **1.** vedovanza **2.** *coll.* le vedove.

vidual ['vidjuəl], *ag.* vedovile.

viduity [vi'dju:iti], s. (*rar.*) vedovanza.

to vie [vai], *v.i.* gareggiare, rivaleggiare, entrare in lizza: *to — with s.o. for first place*, gareggiare con qlcu. per il primo posto.

Vienna [vi'enə], *no.pr.* (*geog.*) Vienna.

Viennese [,vie'ni:z], *ag.s.c.* viennese ‖ *the —*, i viennesi.

Vietnam ['vjet'næm], *no.pr.* (*geog.*) Vietnam.

Vietnamese [,vjetnə'mi:z], *ag.s.c.* (abitante) del Vietnam.

view [vju:], s. **1.** vista; sguardo; *fig.* visione: *he went away from our —*, si allontanò dalla nostra vista; *to offer a general — of the problem*, offrire una visione generale del problema ‖ *at first —*, a prima vista ‖ *in —*, in vista: *we came in — of the church*, giungemmo in vista della chiesa; *to have sthg. in —*, *fig.* avere ql.co. in vista; *to stand in full — of s.o.*, essere sotto lo sguardo di qlcu. ‖ *out of —*, fuori di vista **2.** mostra; esposizione: *on —*, in mostra: *the latest styles were on —*, si esponevano gli ultimi modelli **3.** veduta, vista; panorama: *I want some postcards with views of the town*, voglio delle cartoline con vedute della città; *the mist spoilt the —*, la nebbia offuscò il panorama **4.** opinione, giudizio: *I should like to know his views on politics*, mi piacerebbe conoscere le sue opinioni politiche; *that's taking an extreme — of his conduct*, questo è formulare un giudizio definitivo sulla sua condotta ‖ *in — of*, considerato che ‖ *point of —*, punto di vista **5.** intento, scopo, mira: *with the — of* (o *with a — to*), allo scopo di, col proposito di: *he has bought land with a — to building a house*, ha comperato del terreno allo scopo di costruirvi una casa; *to have other views for s.o., sthg.*, avere altre mire per qlcu., ql.co. ‖ *to fall in with a person's views*, condividere gli scopi di una persona ‖ *to meet a person's views*, andare incontro ai desideri di una persona **6.** (*dir.*) sopralluogo ☆ *— -finder*, mirino (di macchina fotografica); *— -hallo(o)!*, grido di cacciatori di volpi che avvistano la preda ‖ *first —*, (*cine.*) prima visione; *private —*, mostra, esposizione personale.

to view, *v.t.* **1.** guardare attentamente; osservare; *fig.* considerare: *the surgeon viewed the wound*, il chi-

rurgo esaminò la ferita; *we must — the matter in a different light*, dobbiamo considerare la faccenda sotto una luce diversa ‖ *an order to —* (*a house*), permesso di visitare (una casa) **2.** (*dir.*) fare un sopralluogo.

viewer ['vju:ə*], *s.c.* **1.** chi guarda **2.** spettatore, spettatrice; telespettatore, telespettatrice ‖ *s.* **1.** ispettore; (*dir.*) chi deve compiere i sopralluoghi **2.** sovraintendente in una miniera di carbone.

viewless ['vju:lis], *ag.* **1.** (*poet.*) invisibile **2.** (*amer.*) privo di opinioni **3.** senza vista (di casa, ecc.).

viewpoint ['vju:point], s. **1.** punto di vista **2.** belvedere.

viewy ['vju:i], *ag.* **1.** fantasioso; visionario; capriccioso **2.** (*fam.*) vistoso; allettante.

vigesimal [vai'dʒesiml], *ag. num. ord.* vigesimo.

vigil ['vidʒil], *s.* **1.** veglia: *to keep —*, vegliare **2.** vigilia; giorno di digiuno **3.** *gener.pl.* preghiere notturne.

vigilance ['vidʒiləns], s. **1.** vigilanza: *to exercise —*, esercitare la vigilanza **2.** insonnia ☆ *— committee*, comitato di vigilanza.

vigilant ['vidʒilənt], *ag.* vigilante, vigile.

vigilante [,vidʒi'lænti], s. (*amer.*) membro del comitato di vigilanza.

vigilantly ['vidʒiləntli], *av.* vigilantemente.

vignette [vi'njet], s. **1.** vignetta; illustrazione **2.** fotografia, ritratto (a mezzo busto con fondo sfumato).

to vignette, *v.t.* **1.** fare una vignetta di **2.** ritrarre (a mezzo busto con fondo sfumato).

vignettist [vi'njetist], s. vignettista.

vigorous ['vigərəs], *ag.* vigoroso, forte.

vigorously ['vigərəsli], *av.* vigorosamente.

vigorousness ['vigərəsnis], s. vigorosità.

vigour ['vigə*], s. vigore, energia, vitalità.

viking ['vaikiŋ], s. (*st.*) vichingo.

vile [vail], *ag.* **1.** vile, spregevole; abietto: *a — calumny*, una vile calunnia; *a — language*, un linguaggio spregevole **2.** (*fam.*) orribile, pessimo: *— weather*, tempo pessimo.

vilely ['vailli], *av.* vilmente; in modo abietto.

vileness ['vailnis], s. viltà; bassezza; abiezione; indegnità.

vilification [,vilifi'keifən], s. **1.** diffamazione **2.** avvilimento, degradazione.

vilifier ['vilifaiə*], *s.c.* diffamatore, diffamatrice.

to vilify ['vilifai], *v.t.* **1.** diffamare; vilipendere **2.** (*rar.*) avvilire; degradare.

to vilipend ['vilipend], *v.t.* (*letter.*) vilipendere.

vill [vil], s. **1.** (*st.*) distretto territoriale feudale **2.** (*poet.*) villaggio.

villa ['vilə], s. villa.

villadom ['vilədəm], s. insieme di ville e dei loro abitanti.

village ['vilidʒ], s. villaggio; paese; borgata.

to village, *v.i.* stabilirsi in un villaggio.

villager ['vilidʒə*], *s.c.* abitante di villaggio.

villain ['vilən], *ag.* furfantesco; malvagio ‖ s. **1.** scellerato; furfante, anima nera (in un romanzo, ecc.); infame: *in this drama he plays the —*, in questo dramma fa la parte del cattivo **2.** (*fam. scherz.*) mascalzoncello **3.** (*st.*) vassallo; servo feudale **4.** (*arc.*) villano; zoticone.

villainage ['vilinidʒ], s. (*st.*) condizione di vassallo, di servo.

villainous ['vilənəs], *ag.* **1.** scellerato; infame **2.** (*fam.*) abominevole; pessimo: *a — restaurant*, un pessimo ristorante; *what — weather!*, che tempo spaventoso!.

villainously ['vilənəsli], *av.* indegnamente; scelleratamente; malvagiamente.

villainousness ['vilənəsnis], s. indegnità; scellerataggine; malvagità.

villainy ['vileni], s. scelleratezza; infamia: *he made all kinds of villainies*, commise ogni sorta di atrocità.

villanelle [,vilə'nell, s. (*poes.*) villanella.

villein ['vilin], s. (*st.*) vassallo; servo feudale.

villeinage, *V.* villainage.

villiform ['vilifɔ:m], *ag.* (*anat. bot.*) villiforme.

villose ['vilous], *ag.* (*anat. bot.*) villoso.

villosity [vi'lɔsiti], *s.* (*anat. bot.*) villosità.

villous ['viləs], *ag.* (*anat. bot.*) villoso.

villus ['viləs], *pl.* **villi** ['vilai], *s. gener. pl.* (*anat. bot.*) villo.

vim [vim], *s.* (*fam.*) forza, vigore; energia.

vina ['vi:nə], *s.* (*mus.*) vina (liuto indiano).

vinaceous [vai'neiʃəs], *ag.* vinoso.

vinaigrette [,vinei'gret], *s.* 1. boccetta per sali aromatici 2. — (*sauce*), salsa verde.

Vincent ['vinsənt], *no.pr.m.* Vincenzo.

Vincentian [vin'senʃən], *ag.* di San Vincenzo de' Paoli || *s.* membro della Congregazione fondata da S. Vincenzo de' Paoli.

vincible ['vinsibl], *ag.* vincibile; conquistabile; superabile.

vincibly ['vinsibli], *av.* in modo conquistabile, non invincibile, non insormontabile.

vinculum ['viŋkjuləm], *pl.* **vincula** ['viŋkjulə], *s.* 1. vincolo, legame 2. (*mat.*) linea tracciata sopra due o più termini di una espressione algebrica (equivalente a parentesi) 3. (*anat.*) frenulo.

vindemial [vin'di:miəl], *ag.* vendemmiale.

vindemiation [vin,di:mi'eiʃən], *s.* vendemmia.

vindicability [,vindikə'biliti], *s.* rivendicabilità.

vindicable ['vindikəbl], *ag.* 1. difendibile; giustificabile 2. sostenibile; rivendicabile.

to vindicate ['vindikeit], *v.t.* 1. rivendicare; sostenere: *to — one's rights*, far valere i propri diritti; *to — a privilege*, rivendicare un privilegio 2. difendere, giustificare: *his success vindicated their belief in him*, il suo successo giustificava la loro fede in lui; *to — one's acts*, giustificare le proprie azioni.

vindication [,vindi'keiʃən], *s.* 1. rivendicazione; asserzione (di un diritto, ecc.) 2. difesa; giustificazione: *his last — of English liberty*, la sua ultima apologia della libertà inglese.

vindicative ['vindikətiv], *ag.* 1. rivendicatore 2. difensore.

vindicator ['vindikeitə*], *s.* 1. rivendicatore 2. difensore.

vindicatory ['vindikeitəri], *ag.* 1. che difende; che giustifica 2. (*rar. dir.*) punitivo.

vindicatress ['vindikeitris], *s.* 1. rivendicatrice 2. difenditrice.

vindictive [vin'diktiv], *ag.* 1. vendicativo 2. (*rar. dir.*) punitivo || — *damages*, (*dir.*) risarcimento danni imposto per punizione all'imputato.

vindictively [vin'diktivli], *av.* per vendetta; in modo vendicativo.

vindictiveness [vin'diktivnis], *s.* carattere vendicativo; spirito di vendetta.

vine [vain], *s.* 1. (*grape-*) —, vite || *under one's — and fig-tree, fig.* a casa propria 2. (*amer.*) pianta rampicante ☆ — *-branch*, tralcio, sarmento; — *-clad*, coperto di viti; — *-dresser*, vignaiuolo; — *-grower*, viticoltore; — *-growing*, viticoltura; — *-leaf*, pampino; — *-louse* (o — *-pest*), (*entom.*) fillossera; — *-mildew*, (*bot.*) oidio; — *-rod*, bastone di centurione romano; — *-shot*, sarmento, tralcio || *honeysuckle-* —, pianta di caprifoglio.

vinegar ['vinigə*], *s.* 1. aceto: *aromatic* —, aceto aromatico || *mother of* —, madre dell'aceto 2. *fig.* carattere acido.

to vinegar, *v.t.* acetare; rendere acido (anche *fig.*).

vinegarish ['vinigəriʃ], **vinegary** ['vinigəri], *ag.* agro; acido.

vinery ['vainəri], *s.* serra per viti.

vineyard ['vinjəd], *s.* vigna, vigneto.

vinic ['vainik], *ag.* di vino, vinoso.

viniculture ['viniˌkʌltʃə*], *s.* vinicoltura.

viniculturist [,vini'kʌltʃərist], *s.* vinicoltore.

viniferous [vi'nifərəs], *ag.* vinifero.

vinification [,vainifi'keiʃən], *s.* trasformazione del mosto in vino.

vinolent ['vainələnt], *ag.* dedito al bere.

vinometer [vai'nomitə*], *s.* alcoolometro.

vinous ['vainəs], *ag.* 1. di vino; vinoso: — *flavour*, sapore vinoso 2. color vino 3. dedito al vino || — *eloquence*, l'eloquenza dell'ubriaco.

to vint [vint], *v.t.* fare (vino, liquori).

vintage ['vintidʒ], *s.* 1. vendemmia; prodotto della vendemmia: *the — of 1906*, la produzione vinicola del 1906; *time of* —, tempo di vendemmia 2. annata, raccolto: *wine of the — 1917*, vino del 1917 || *car of ancient* —, automobile di vecchio modello, tipo; *car of the 1930* —, automobile del 1930 3. (*poet.*) vino ☆ — *wine*, vino di marca; vino di una buona annata; — *year*, buona annata (per il raccolto del vino).

to vintage, *v.t.* 1. vendemmiare 2. fare (il vino).

vintager ['vintidʒə*] *s.c.* vendemmiatore, vendemmiatrice.

vintner ['vintnə*], *s.* vinaio; commerciante di vini.

vintnery ['vintnəri], *s.* (*rar.*) commercio dei vini.

vintry ['vintri], *s.* (*arc.*) negozio di vini, cantina.

viny ['vaini], *ag.* 1. ricco, coperto di viti 2. (caratteristico) della vite; simile alla vite.

vinyl ['vainil], *s.* (*chim.*) vinile ☆ — *resin*, (*ind. chim.*) resina vinilica.

viol ['vaiəl], *s.* (*mus.*) viola (antica).

viola[1] ['vaiələ], *s.* (*bot.*) viola.

Viola[2], *no. pr. f.* Viola.

viola[3] [vi'oulə], *s.* (*mus.*) 1. viola moderna 2. viola antica ☆ — *d'amore*, viola d'amore; — *da gamba*, viola da gamba.

violable ['vaiələbl], *ag.* violabile.

violaceous [,vaiə'leiʃəs], *ag.* 1. violaceo 2. (*bot.*) delle violacee.

to violate ['vaiəleit], *v.t.* 1. violare; trasgredire; infrangere: *to — the law*, violare la legge 2. profanare; oltraggiare 3. violentare 4. *fig.* violare, turbare: *to — s.o.'s privacy*, violare l'intimità di qlcu.

violation [,vaiə'leiʃən], *s.* 1. violazione, infrazione, trasgressione: — *of the principles of the constitution*, violazione dei principi della costituzione 2. profanazione; oltraggio: *the — of a sacred place by a murderer*, la profanazione di un luogo sacro da parte di un assassino 3. violenza, stupro 4. interruzione (di sonno, di quiete).

violator ['vaiəleitə*], *s.* 1. violatore; trasgressore: — *of the law*, trasgressore della legge 2. profanatore 3. violentatore 4. perturbatore.

violence ['vaiələns], *s.* 1. violenza; veemenza: *the — of his passions*, la violenza delle sue passioni; *the — of the wind*, la violenza del vento; *an outburst of* —, una esplosione di violenza; *he knocked with* —, bussò con violenza 2. oltraggio; uso illegale di forza: *to do — to s.o.*, usare violenza contro qlcu. || *robbery with* —, (*dir.*) rapina a mano armata.

violent ['vaiələnt], *ag.* 1. violento; impetuoso: *a — temper*, un carattere violento; *he died a — death*, morì di morte violenta 2. violento, intenso; acuto: *a — toothache*, un acuto mal di denti.

violently ['vaiələntli], *av.* in modo violento.

violer ['vaiələ*], *s.* (*arc.*) suonatore di viola.

violet ['vaiəlit], *ag.* violetto; di color viola || *s.* 1. (*bot.*) violetta; viola mammola 2. colore viola ☆ (*ultra-*) *-ray*, raggio ultravioletto.

to violet, *v.t.i.* 1. tingere di violetto 2. raccogliere violette.

violin [,vaiə'lin], *s.* (*mus.*) violino: *to play first* —, suonare da primo violino (anche *fig.*).

violin(e) ['vaiəlin], *s.* (*farm.*) violina.

violinist ['vaiəlinist], *s.* violinista.

violist [vi'oulist], *s.* 1. (*nel sens* 2.) ['vaiəlist], *s.* 1. suonatore di viola 2. suonatore di viola antica.

violoncellist [,vaiələn'tʃelist], *s.* violoncellista.

violoncello [,vaiələn'tʃelou], *s.* (*mus.*) violoncello.

viper ['vaipə*], *s.* vipera (anche *fig.*) || *to nourish a — in one's bosom*, nutrire una serpe in seno.

viperine ['vaipərain], *ag.* viperino (anche *fig.*).

viperous ['vaipərəs], *ag.* di vipera; vipereo (anche *fig.*): — *brood* (o — *generation*), *fig.* generazione di vipere; *a* — *tongue*, una lingua velenosa.

viperously ['vaipərəsli], *av.* malignamente, velenosamente.

virago [vi'rɑːgou], *s.* **1.** (*arc.*) virago **2.** donna violenta, sfacciata.

virelay ['virəlei], *s.* (*st. poes.*) « virelai » (componimento poetico francese).

virescence [vi'resəns], *s.* **1.** (*bot.*) virescenza **2.** verdezza.

virescent [vi'resənt], *ag.* **1.** (*poet.*) virescente **2.** verdeggiante.

virgate[1] ['vəːgit], *ag.* dritto e sottile (di vegetale).

virgate[2], *s.* (*st.*) « virgate » (misura di superficie = are 1214).

Virgil ['vəːdʒil], *no.pr.m.* (*st. lett.*) Virgilio.

Virgilian [vəː'dʒiliən], *ag.* virgiliano; di Virgilio.

virgin ['vəːdʒin], *ag.* **1.** vergine, virgineo, puro, casto: *a* — *life*, una vita casta; — *modesty*, modestia virginea ‖ *the Virgin Queen*, la regina vergine (Elisabetta I d'Inghilterra) **2.** non coltivato; non toccato da alcuno: — *forest*, foresta vergine; *a* — *peak*, vetta inviolata; — *snow*, neve vergine; — *soil*, terreno vergine ‖ *s.* vergine, donna casta ‖ *the (Blessed) Virgin*, la Beata Vergine ‖ *Virgin*, (*astr.*) Vergine ☆ — *bower*, (*bot.*) vitalba; — *gold*, oro puro; — *-tree*, (*bot.*) sassafrasso orientale; — *-wax*, cera vergine.

virginal[1] ['vəːdʒinl], *ag.* verginale, puro, casto.

virginal[2], *s. gener. pl.* (*st. mus.*) virginale.

virginhood ['vəːdʒinhud], *s.* verginità.

Virginia[1] [vəː'dʒinjə], *no.pr.f.* Virginia.

Virginia[2], *no.pr.* (*geog.*) Virginia ‖ *s.* — (*tobacco*), tabacco della Virginia ☆ — *creeper*, vite vergine; — *reel*, contraddanza.

Virginian [vəː'dʒinjən], *ag.s.c.* (abitante) della Virginia.

Virgin Islands (the) ['vəːdʒin'ailəndz], *no.pr.pl.* (*geog.*) Isole Vergini.

virginity [vəː'dʒiniti], *s.* verginità.

Virgo ['vəːgou], *no.pr.* (*astr.*) Vergine.

virid ['virid], *ag.* (*poet.*) verde, verdeggiante.

viridescence [‚viri'desns], *s.* (*rar.*) l'essere verde, verdeggiante.

viridescent [‚viri'desnt], *ag.* (*rar.*) verde, verdeggiante.

viridian [vi'ridiən], *ag.s.* verde veronese.

viridity [vi'riditi], *s.* (*rar.*) verdezza.

virile ['virail], *ag.* virile, maschio.

virility [vi'riliti], *s.* virilità.

virose ['vairous], *ag.* (*rar.*) **1.** velenoso **2.** fetido.

virtu [vəː'tuː], *s.* gusto per l'arte, per gli oggetti d'arte ‖ *articles* (o *objects* o *pieces*) *of* —, articoli, oggetti, pezzi d'arte.

virtual ['vəːtjuəl], *ag.* virtuale, effettivo, di fatto: — *confession*, confessione virtuale; *he is the* — *head of the business*, è il capo effettivo dell'azienda ☆ — *focus*, (*fis.*) fuoco virtuale; — *image*, (*fis.*) immagine virtuale; — *velocity*, velocità virtuale.

virtuality [‚vəːtju'æliti], *s.* potenzialità; virtualità.

virtually ['vəːtjuəli], *av.* virtualmente, in effetto, praticamente.

virtue ['vəːtjuː], *s.* **1.** virtù; castità; moralità; forza d'animo, valore: *a woman of easy* —, una donna di facili costumi; — *is its own reward*, la virtù è premio a se stessa; *patience is a* —, la pazienza è una virtù; (*to make a* — *of necessity*, fare di necessità virtù ‖ *in* (o *by*) — *of*: in virtù di, in forza di: *he was elected in* — *of his honesty*, fu eletto in virtù della sua onestà **2.** qualità, vantaggio, merito: *it has the* — *of being unbreakable*, ha il vantaggio di essere infrangibile **3.** potere, efficacia, virtù: *the* — *of herbs to heal sickness*, la virtù delle erbe per curare le malattie: *this medicine is of great* —, questa medicina è di gran-

de efficacia **4.** *pl.* (*relig.*) virtù (quinta gerarchia degli angeli) ☆ *cardinal* —, (*teol.*) virtù cardinale: *the seven cardinal virtues*, le sette virtù cardinali.

virtueless ['vəːtjuːlis], *ag.* **1.** privo di ogni virtù; immorale **2.** inefficace.

virtuosity [‚vəːtju'ositi], *s.* virtuosismo.

virtuoso [‚vəːtju'ouzou], *pl.* **virtuosos** [‚vəːtju'ouzouz], **virtuosi** [‚vəːtju'ouzi], *s.* **1.** (*mus.*) virtuoso **2.** amatore, conoscitore.

virtuous ['vəːtjuəs], *ag.* **1.** virtuoso, morale, casto **2.** (*arc.*) efficace, potente, salutare.

virtuously ['vəːtjuəsli], *av.* virtuosamente; in modo morale, retto.

virtuousness ['vəːtjuəsnis], *s.* virtuosità.

virulence ['virulans], *s.* virulenza.

virulent ['virulənt], *ag.* **1.** virulento: — *disease*, malattia virulenta **2.** *fig.* virulento, velenoso, maligno: — *speech*, discorso virulento.

virulently ['viruləntli], *av.* in modo virulento.

virus ['vaiərəs], *s.* **1.** (*patol.*) virus **2.** *fig.* influenza nefanda ☆ *filterable* —, ultravirus, virus filtrabile.

visa ['viːzə], *s.* visto consolare.

to **visa**, *v.t.* vistare (un passaporto).

visage ['vizidʒ], *s.* (*letter.*) volto, faccia, sembiante.

visaged ['vizidʒd], *ag.* dal viso, dall'aspetto ☆ *gloomy* —, dall'aspetto triste, tetro; *grim-* — *war*, la guerra dall'orrendo viso.

visard ['vizɑːd], *V.* **visor**.

vis-à-vis ['viːzɑːviː], *s.* **1.** persona che sta di fronte **2.** « vis à vis » (vettura per due che ha i sedili opposti) ‖ *av.* di faccia, dirimpetto, di fronte.

viscacha [vis'kɑːtʃə], *s.* (*zool.*) viscaccia.

viscera ['visərə], *s.pl.* (*anat.*) visceri, viscere.

visceral ['visərəl], *ag.* (*anat.*) viscerale ☆ — *cavity*, cavità viscerale.

to **viscerate** ['visəreit], *v.t.* (*rar.*) sbudellare.

viscid ['visid], *ag.* viscido; viscoso.

viscidity [vi'siditi], *s.* viscidità; viscosità.

viscin ['visin], *s.* (*chim.*) viscina.

viscose ['viskous], *s.* viscosa (fibra tessile).

viscosimeter [‚viskou'simitə*], *s.* viscosimetro.

viscosity [vis'kositi], *s.* viscosità.

viscount ['vaikaunt], *s.* visconte.

viscountcy ['vaikauntsi], *s.* titolo, dignità di visconte.

viscountess ['vaikauntis], *s.* viscontessa.

viscous ['viskəs], *ag.* viscoso.

viscousness ['viskəsnis], *s.* viscosità.

vise, (*amer.*) per **vice**[2].

visé ['viːzei], *s.* visto consolare.

to **visé**, *v.t.* vistare (un passaporto).

Vishnu ['viʃnuː], *no.pr.m.* (*relig. indù*) Visnù.

visibility [‚vizi'biliti], *s.* visibilità.

visible ['vizəbl], *ag.* **1.** visibile; evidente, manifesto: *he spoke with* — *satisfaction*, parlò con evidente soddisfazione; *pneumonia may arise without any* — *cause*, la polmonite può insorgere senza alcuna causa manifesta **2.** visibile, accessibile, che può esser visto: *is she* —?, la si può vedere? **3.** (*comm.*) sottomano, pronto: — *stock*, merce che può essere vista subito ‖ *s.* entità visibile ‖ *the* —, il mondo visibile ☆ — *direction*, direzione apparente; — *horizon*, orizzonte visibile; — *signal*, segnale ottico.

visibleness ['vizəblnis], *s.* visibilità.

visibly ['vizəbli], *av.* visibilmente, palesemente.

Visigoth ['vizigəθ], *s.* (*st.*) visigoto.

Visigothic [‚vizi'gəθik], *ag.* (*st.*) visigotico.

vision ['viʒən], *s.* **1.** vista; capacità visiva: *beyond our* —, al di là della nostra capacità visiva; *the field of* —, il campo visivo **2.** visione, intuizione; immagine: *he had a* — *of the future*, ebbe una visione, una intuizione del futuro **3.** allucinazione; apparizione: *to see visions*, avere delle allucinazioni.

to **vision**, *v.t.* **1.** mostrare come in una visione **2.** vedere come in una visione.

visional ['viʒənl], *ag.* irreale, immaginario.

visionally ['viʒnəli], *av.* come in una visione, in modo irreale.

visionariness ['viʒənərinis], *s.* **1.** carattere sognatore (di persona) **2.** irrealtà.

visionary ['viʒnəri], *ag.* **1.** visionario; sognatore: *a — mind*, una mente sognatrice **2.** immaginario, chimerico ‖ *s.c.* visionario, visionaria; utopista.

visionist ['viʒənist], *s.c.* visionario, visionaria.

visionless ['viʒənlis], *ag.* **1.** privo delle capacità visive **2.** privo di intuizione, di immaginazione.

visit ['vizit], *s.* **1.** visita: *doctor's round of visits*, giro di visite di un medico; *to be on a — to s.o.*, essere in visita da qlcu.; *to pay s.o. a —*, fare una visita a qlcu.; *to receive s.o.'s —*, ricevere qlcu.; *to return s.o.'s —*, restituire una visita a qlcu. **2.** *(fam. amer.)* chiacchierata amichevole ☆ *courtesy —*, visita di cortesia.

to visit, *v.t.i.* **1.** visitare; fare una visita; andare a trovare: *I must — my friends*, devo andare a trovare i miei amici; *spot visited by few*, luogo poco frequentato; *they visited the British Museum*, visitarono il Museo Britannico; *to — the poor*, fare visite di carità **2.** colpire, attaccare, assalire (di malattia, ecc.): *the poet Burns was visited by fits of gloom*, il poeta Burns era frequentemente colpito da eccessi di malinconia **3.** ispezionare, esaminare: *to — the scene*, *(dir.)* fare un sopralluogo **4.** *(arc.)* punire; vendicare: *to — the sins of the fathers upon the children*, far ricadere sui figli le colpe dei padri **5.** *(fam. amer.)* far conversazione, chiacchierare (in visita).

visitable ['vizitəbl], *ag.* che può essere visitato.

visitant ['vizitənt], *ag.* che visita ‖ *s.c. (poet.)* visitatore, visitatrice ‖ *s.* **1.** uccello di passo **2.** apparizione soprannaturale **3.** *Visitant*, (suora) visitandina.

visitation [ˌviziˈteiʃən], *s.* **1.** visita ufficiale; *(eccl.)* visita pastorale **2.** *(fam.)* visita troppo lunga **3.** *(comm.)* visita; ispezione, esame ‖ *right of —*, *(mar.)* diritto di visita **4.** visita del Signore (con allusione ad un lutto familiare) **5.** *Visitation*, *(relig.)* Visitazione (della Vergine a Elisabetta); festa della Visitazione (2 luglio) ‖ *Visitation*, *(eccl.)* (Ordine della) Visitazione: *Nuns of the Visitation*, (suore) visitandine **6.** migrazione anormale (di animali).

visitatorial [ˌvizitəˈtɔːrjəl], *ag.* **1.** di visita ufficiale **2.** di ispezione ☆ *— board*, commissione di ispezione.

visiting ['vizitiŋ], *s.* il far visite ☆ *—-card*, biglietto da visita; *— hours*, orario delle visite; *— list*, lista degli amici, conoscenti: *he is not on my — list*, *(fam.)* non è un mio amico; *— terms*, termini di amicizia: *to be on — terms*, essere in termini di amicizia tali da scambiarsi visite.

visitor ['vizitə*], *s.c.* visitatore, visitatrice; ospite ‖ *s.* **1.** ispettore, verificatore **2.** uccello di passo ☆ *visitors' book*, registro degli ospiti ‖ *summer —*, visitatore, villeggiante estivo.

visor ['vaizə*], *s.* **1.** visiera **2.** maschera (per nascondere il volto) ☆ *—-mask*, domino.

visored ['vaizəd], *ag.* **1.** fornito di visiera **2.** con visiera abbassata; mascherato, travestito.

vista ['vistə], *s.* **1.** prospettiva; scorcio (panoramico): *a — of the house from between the trees*, una prospettiva della casa di tra gli alberi **2.** viale d'alberi (inquadranti una prospettiva) **3.** galleria panoramica **4.** visione (del passato, del futuro): *the vistas of bygone times*, i ricordi dei tempi andati; *new vistas*, nuovi orizzonti ☆ *—-dome car*, *(ferr. amer.)* carrozza panoramica.

visual ['vizjuəl], *ag.* **1.** visuale, visivo **2.** visibile ‖ *s.c.* persona dotata di memoria, immaginazione visiva ☆ *— angle*, angolo visivo; *— field*, campo visivo; *— nerve*, *(anat.)* nervo ottico; *— organ*, organo visivo; *— ray*, raggio visivo; *— tuning indicator*, *(rad.)* indicatore ottico di sintonia, occhio magico.

visuality [ˌvizjuˈæliti], *s.* visione mentale.

visualization [ˌvizjuəlaiˈzeiʃən], *s.* **1.** chiarezza di vedute **2.** immagine mentale **3.** il rendere chiaro, visibile.

to visualize ['vizjuəlaiz], *v.t.i.* **1.** vedere con chiarezza **2.** rendere chiaro, visibile.

visually ['vizjuəli], *av.* in modo visivo.

vital ['vaitl], *ag.* **1.** vitale, essenziale, capitale: *a — necessity*, una necessità vitale; *of — importance*, di importanza capitale **2.** fatale (alla vita, alla riuscita, ecc.): *a — error*, un errore fatale; *a — wound*, una ferita mortale ☆ *— centre*, centro vitale; *— energy*, energia vitale; *— organs*, organi vitali; *— statistics*, statistiche anagrafiche; *(fam.)* misure femminili (busto, vita, fianchi).

vitalism ['vaitəlizəm], *s. (biol.)* vitalismo.

vitalist ['vaitəlist], *s.* sostenitore del vitalismo.

vitalistic [ˌvaitəˈlistik], *ag. (biol.)* vitalistico.

vitality [vaiˈtæliti], *s.* **1.** vitalità, forza, vigore **2.** *fig.* vigore; vivacità.

to vitalize ['vaitəlaiz], *v.t.* infondere vita a; animare.

vitally ['vaitəli], *av.* vitalmente; in modo essenziale.

vitals ['vaitlz], *s.pl.* **1.** organi vitali **2.** *fig.* parti essenziali.

vitamin(e) ['vitəmin], *s.* vitamina.

vitellin [viˈtelin], *s. (chim.)* vitellina.

vitelline [viˈtelain], *ag.* **1.** del colore del tuorlo d'uovo **2.** *(biol.)* vitellino, del vitello dell'uovo ☆ *— membrane*, *(biol.)* membrana vitellina.

vitellus [viˈteləs], *pl.* **vitelli** [viˈtelai], *s.* vitello, tuorlo d'uovo.

to vitiate ['viʃieit], *v.t.* **1.** viziare; corrompere; guastare: *vitiated air*, aria viziata **2.** *(dir.)* invalidare, viziare: *this clause may — the contract*, questa clausola può invalidare il contratto.

vitiation [ˌviʃiˈeiʃən], *s.* **1.** lo sciupare; il guastare, il corrompere **2.** *(dir.)* l'invalidare.

viticulture ['vitikʌltʃə*], *s.* viticoltura.

vitreosity [ˌvitriˈositi], *s.* qualità vitrea, vetrosità.

vitreous ['vitriəs], *ag.* vitreo; vetroso ☆ *— electricity*, elettricità positiva; *— humour*, *(anat.)* umore vitreo.

vitrifiability [ˌvitriˌfaiəˈbiliti], *s.* vetrificabilità.

vitrifiable ['vitrifaiəbl], *ag.* vetrificabile.

vitrification [ˌvitrifiˈkeiʃən], *s.* vetrificazione.

to vitrify ['vitrifai], *v.t.i.* vetrificare, vetrificarsi.

vitriol ['vitriəl], *s.* **1.** *(chim.)* vetriolo **2.** *fig.* sarcasmo pungente ☆ *blue —*, vetriolo azzurro (di rame); *green —*, vetriolo verde (di ferro); *oil of —*, acido solforico concentrato; *white —*, vetriolo bianco (di zinco).

to vitriolate ['vitrioleit], *v.t.* *(chim.)* **1.** convertire in vetriolo **2.** trattare con vetriolo.

vitriolation [ˌvitrioˈleiʃən], *V.* vitriolization.

vitriolic [ˌvitriˈolik], *ag.* **1.** *(chim.)* vetriolico **2.** *fig.* maligno, sarcastico.

vitriolizable ['vitriəlaizəbl], *ag.* **1.** trasformabile in vetriolo **2.** che può essere sottoposto all'azione del vetriolo.

vitriolization [ˌvitriəlaiˈzeiʃən], *s.* **1.** il trasformare in vetriolo **2.** il sottoporre all'azione del vetriolo; il vetrioleggiare.

to vitriolize ['vitriəlaiz], *v.t.i.* **1.** *(chim.)* convertire in vetriolo **2.** sottoporre all'azione del vetriolo; vetrioleggiare.

vitriolizer ['vitriəlaizə*], *s.c.* chi vetrioleggia.

Vitruvian [viˈtruːvjən], *ag.* di Vitruvio, secondo lo stile di Vitruvio ☆ *— scroll*, *(arch.)* cartoccio.

Vitruvius [viˈtruːvjəs], *no.pr.m. (st. arch.)* Vitruvio.

vitta ['vitə], *pl.* **vittae** [ˈviti], *s.* **1.** vitta (benda del capo presso gli antichi romani) **2.** infula della mitria **3.** stria, striscia di colore (di animale) **4.** canalino oleoso (di frutto).

vittate ['viteit], *ag.* **1.** contenente canalini oleosi (di frutto) **2.** striato, con striature (di animale).

to vituperate [viˈtjuːpəreit], *v.t.* vituperare; biasimare.

vituperation [viˌtjuːpəˈreiʃən], *s.* invettiva; rimprovero, biasimo.

vituperative [viˈtjuːpərətiv], *ag.* vituperativo.

vituperatively [vi'tju:pərətivli], *av.* vituperevolmente.

vituperator [vi'tju:pəreitə*], *s.c.* vituperatore, vituperatrice.

viva[1] ['vi:və], *s. inter.* evviva!.

viva[2] ['vaivə], (*fam.*) per **viva-voce**.

vivacious [vi'veiʃəs], *ag.* 1. vivace, vispo, pieno di vita 2. (*bot.*) perenne.

vivaciously [vi'veiʃəsli], *av.* vivacemente.

vivacity [vi'væsiti], *s.* vivacità; brio; animazione.

vivarium [vai'vɛəriəm], *pl.* **vivaria** [vai'vɛəriə], **vivariums** [vai'vɛəriəmz], *s.* 1. vivaio, acquario 2. giardino zoologico.

viva-voce ['vaivə'vousi], *ag.* orale || *s.* esame orale || *av.* a viva voce, oralmente.

to viva-voce, *v.t.* esaminare oralmente.

vivers ['vaivəz], *s.pl.* (*spec. scoz.*) viveri; vettovaglie.

Vivian ['viviən], *no.pr.m.* Viviano || *no.pr.f.* Viviana.

vivid ['vivid], *ag.* 1. vivace, vivo, vigoroso: *a — imagination,* una immaginazione vivace 2. vivido; colorito; intenso; brillante: *a deep — blue,* un blu scuro intenso.

vividly ['vividli], *av.* 1. vivacemente, vigorosamente 2. vividamente; brillantemente.

vividness ['vividnis], *s.* vivezza; vivacità.

Vivienne ['viviən], *no.pr.f.* Viviana.

vivification [,vivifi'keiʃən], *s.* vivificazione.

to vivify ['vivifai], *v.t.* vivificare; animare; rinvigorire.

viviparity [,vivi'pæriti], *s.* (*zool. bot.*) l'essere viviparo; qualità di viviparo.

viviparous [vi'vipərəs], *ag.* (*zool. bot.*) viviparo.

viviparously [vi'vipərəsli], *av.* (*zool. bot.*) da viviparo; come i vivipari.

viviparousness [vi'vipərəsnis], *V.* **viviparity**.

to vivisect [,vivi'sekt], *v.t.i.* vivisezionare; praticare la vivisezione.

vivisection [,vivi'sekʃən], *s.* vivisezione.

vivisectional [,vivi'sekʃənl], *ag.* relativo alla vivisezione.

vivisectionist [,vivi'sekʃnist], **vivisector** [,vivi'sektə*], *s.* chi pratica o approva la vivisezione.

vixen ['viksn], *s.* 1. volpe femmina 2. megera; donna litigiosa e brontolona.

vixenish ['viksniʃ], **vixenly** ['viksnli], *ag.* 1. volpino 2. maligno; litigioso.

viz. [vi'di:liset], *V.* **videlicet**.

vizard ['vizɑ:d], *V.* **visor**.

vizcacha [viz'kɑ:tʃə], *s.* (*zool.*) viscaccia.

vizier [vi'ziə*], *s.* visir || *Grand Vizier,* gran visir.

vizierate [vi'ziərit], *s.* visirato.

vocable ['voukəbl], *s.* vocabolo; parola.

vocabulary [və'kæbjuləri], *s.* 1. vocabolario: *a word not found in the Chaucerian —,* una parola che non figura nel vocabolario di Chaucer; *his — is limited,* il suo vocabolario è limitato 2. elenco di voci, nomenclatura; glossario: *this French grammar has a — at the back,* questa grammatica francese reca in appendice un dizionarietto.

vocal ['voukəl], *ag.* 1. vocale; di voce; espresso con la voce 2. (*fonet.*) avente carattere di vocale; sonante 3. (*mus.*) cantato; vocale || *s.* vocale ☆ — *concert,* concerto vocale; — *cords,* (*anat.*) corde vocali; — *music,* musica vocale; — *organs,* (*anat.*) organi vocali.

vocalic [vou'kælik], *ag.* vocalico; di vocale.

vocalism ['voukəlizəm], *s.* 1. (*mus.*) vocalizzo, gorgheggio 2. (*fonet.*) vocalismo.

vocalist ['voukəlist], *s.c.* cantante.

vocalization [,voukəlai'zeiʃən], *s.* vocalizzazione.

to vocalize ['voukəlaiz], *v.t.i.* 1. (*mus.*) far vocalizzi 2. vocalizzare 3. (*scherz.*) dire; cantare.

vocally ['voukəli], *av.* 1. a voce; oralmente 2. cantando.

vocation [vou'keiʃən], *s.* 1. vocazione; chiamata divina 2. inclinazione; attitudine: *to have no — for teaching,* non avere attitudine all'insegnamento 3. professione; impiego: *to change one's —,* cambiare la propria professione; *to mistake one's —,* scegliere la carriera sbagliata.

vocational [vou'keiʃən], *ag.* professionale ☆ *a — school,* una scuola professionale; — *training,* istruzione professionale.

vocationally [vou'keiʃnəli], *av.* 1. secondo vocazione 2. professionalmente.

vocative ['vokətiv], *ag.s.* (*gram.*) vocativo.

to vociferate [vou'sifəreit], *v.t.i.* gridare; vociferare; vociare.

vociferation [vou,sifə'reiʃən], *s.* clamore; vociferazione.

vociferator [vou'sifəreitə*], *s.c.* vociferatore, vociferatrice.

vociferous [vou'sifərəs], *ag.* rumoroso; vociferante.

vociferously [vou'sifərəsli], *av.* rumorosamente.

vociferousness [vou'sifərəsnis], *s.* clamore, rumore; vocio.

vodka ['vodkə], *s.* vodka.

voe [vou], *s.* (*dial. scoz.*) piccola insenatura.

vogue [voug], *s.* voga, moda: *war novels have a great —,* i romanzi di guerra sono in gran voga; *to be in —,* essere in voga, essere di moda.

voice [vɔis], *s.* 1. voce; verso, grido (di animali): *a thick —,* una voce grossa; *a thin —,* una voce sottile; *don't you recognize my —?,* non riconosci la mia voce?; *he is not in good —,* è giù di voce; *hear the — of the cuckoo,* ascolta il verso del cuculo; *to lose one's —,* perdere la voce || *to lift up one's —,* esprimersi, parlare 2. *fig.* voce: *the — of Nature,* la voce della Natura; *the voices of the night,* i suoni della notte; *to find — to express oneself,* trovare modo di esprimersi; *to give — to,* esprimere || *the — of the people is the — of God, prov.* voce di popolo, voce di Dio 3. opinione, giudizio: *with one —,* all'unanimità 4. (*gram.*) voce (di verbo): *passive —,* voce passiva 5. suffragio; voto; appoggio: *his — is for peace,* egli è favorevole alla pace; *I count on your —,* conto sul vostro appoggio || *I have no — in the matter,* non ho voce in capitolo.

to voice, *v.t.* 1. esprimere, dire; essere il portavoce di: *to — the general feelings,* esprimere i sentimenti della massa; *to — the Opposition,* essere il portavoce dell'opposizione 2. (*mus.*) intonare: *to — the pipes of an organ,* intonare le canne di un organo 3. (*fonet.*) rendere sonoro.

voiced [vɔist], *ag.* 1. dalla voce 2. (*fonet.*) sonoro ☆ *deep- —,* dalla voce profonda; *sweet- —,* dalla voce dolce.

voiceful ['vɔisful], *ag.* (*poet.*) sonoro; risonante; dalle molte voci: *the — sea,* il mare risonante.

voiceless ['vɔislis], *ag.* 1. senza voce, muto; silenzioso: — *prayer,* preghiera muta; — *woe,* dolore senza parole 2. (*fonet.*) muto; sordo.

voicelessly ['vɔislisli], *av.* silenziosamente; senza voce.

voicelessness ['vɔislisnis], *s.* mancanza di voce; silenzio; mutismo.

void [vɔid], *ag.* 1. vuoto; vacante: *a — space,* uno spazio vuoto 2. privo: — *of common sense,* privo di senso comune 3. (*dir.*) non valido, nullo; illegale: *the agreement, not having been signed, was —,* l'accordo, non essendo stato firmato, era nullo 4. (*poet.*) inutile || *s.* 1. vuoto: *to disappear into the —,* sparire nel vuoto 2. *fig.* vuoto; mancanza: *an aching —,* un vuoto doloroso.

to void, *v.t.* 1. vuotare, liberare (un luogo) 2. (*fisiol.*) scaricare, evacuare 3. (*dir.*) annullare, abrogare 4. (*arc.*) lasciare, abbandonare.

voidable ['vɔidəbl], *ag.* (*dir.*) annullabile.

voidance ['vɔidəns], *s.* 1. svuotamento 2. (*dir.*) annullamento 3. (*eccl.*) vacanza (di un beneficio).

voided ['vɔidid], *ag.* 1. reso vuoto, vacante 2. invalidato, reso nullo 3. (*arald.*) vuoto (di figura).

voidee ['vɔidi:], *s.* (*st.*) spuntino a base di vino con spezie e di dolci (consumato prima di andare a letto o prima che gli ospiti si congedino).

voider ['vɔidə*], *s.* **1.** (*st.*) servo che ha l'incarico di sparecchiare **2.** (*dial.*) vassoio per portar via dalla mensa piatti sporchi, avanzi.

vol [vɔl], *abbr.* di **volume.**

vol, *s.* (*arald.*) volo.

volant ['voulənt], *ag.* **1.** (*zool.*) che vola, capace di volare **2.** (*poet.*) agile; rapido **3.** (*arald.*) volante.

volar ['voulə*], *ag.* (*anat.*) **1.** palmare, del palmo della mano **2.** della pianta del piede.

volary ['vouləri], *s.* **1.** (*rar.*) voliera, uccelliera **2.** *coll.* uccelli in una voliera.

volatile ['vɔlətail], *ag.* **1.** volatile, alato **2.** *fig.* volubile, capriccioso; incostante; mutevole; instabile: *the fickle, inconstant, — temper of the people,* il carattere capriccioso, incostante e volubile del popolo **3.** (*chim.*) volatile ‖ *s.* **1.** (*ornit.*) volatile **2.** (*chim.*) sostanza volatile ☆ *— alkali,* ammoniaca; *— oil,* olio essenziale; *— salt,* sale volatile.

volatileness ['vɔlətailnis], **volatility** [,vɔlə'tiliti], *s.* **1.** (*chim.*) volatilità **2.** *fig.* volubilità; stoltezza.

volatilizable ['vɔlətilaizəbl], *ag.* (*chim.*) volatizzabile.

volatilization [vɔ,lætilai'zeiʃən], *s.* (*chim.*) volatizzazione; il volatizzare.

to **volatilize** [vɔ'lætilaiz], *v.t.i.* (*chim.*) volatizzare, volatizzarsi.

vol-au-vent ['vɔlou'vɑːŋ], *s.* « vol-au-vent » (pasticcio di pasta sfoglia).

volcanic [vɔl'kænik], *ag.* **1.** (*geol.*) vulcanico: *— cinders,* ceneri vulcaniche **2.** *fig.* ardente, esplosivo ☆ *— glass,* ossidiana; *— tufa,* tufo vulcanico.

volcanicity [,vɔlkə'nisiti], **volcanism** ['vɔlkənizəm], *s.* stato vulcanico, fenomeni vulcanici.

volcano [vɔl'keinou], *pl.* **volcanoes** [vɔl'keinouz], *s.* vulcano: *active —,* vulcano in attività; *dormant —,* vulcano inattivo; *extinct —,* vulcano estinto ☆ *mud —,* vulcano di fango, salsa.

volcanology [,vɔlkə'nɔlədʒi], *s.* (*geol.*) vulcanologia.

vole[1] [voul], *s.* cappotto (in certi giuochi di carte).

vole[2], *s.* (*zool.*) arvicola ☆ *field- —,* topo campagnolo; *water- —,* topo d'acqua.

volet ['vɔlei], *s.* antina, tavola di trittico.

volitant ['vɔlitənt], *ag.* svolazzante; volteggiante.

volition [vou'liʃən], *s.* volizione.

volitional [vou'liʃənl], *ag.* volitivo.

volitionally [vou'liʃnəli], *av.* in modo volitivo.

volitionary [vou'liʃnəri], *ag.* volitivo.

volitive ['vɔlitiv], *ag.* **1.** volitivo **2.** (*gram.*) desiderativo ‖ *s.* (*gram.*) verbo desiderativo.

volley ['vɔli], *s.* **1.** scarica, raffica; salva (anche *fig.*): *a — of bullets,* una raffica di proiettili; *a — of oaths,* un profluvio di bestemmie; *a — of stones,* una scarica di pietre **2.** (*poet.*) rovescio di pioggia; tempesta di grandine **3.** (*tennis*) volata ☆ *—-ball,* palla a volo.

to **volley,** *v.t.i.* **1.** scaricare (proiettili, ecc.), sparare a raffiche; lanciare una salva **2.** investire con un profluvio di parole **3.** (*tennis*) colpire la palla al volo.

volplane ['vɔl-plein], *s.* (*aer.*) volo planato.

to **volplane,** *v.i.* (*aer.*) planare.

volt[1] [vɔlt], *s.* (*equitazione, scherma*) volta.

to **volt**[1], *v.i.* (*equitazione*) volteggiare; (*scherma*) fare una volta.

volt[2] [voult], *s.* (*elett.*) volt.

voltage ['voultidʒ], *s.* (*elett.*) voltaggio, tensione elettrica: *high —,* alta tensione ☆ *— -drop,* caduta di tensione; *— -regulator,* regolatore di tensione ‖ *terminal —,* tensione ai morsetti.

voltaic [vɔl'teiik], *ag.* voltaico ☆ *— pile,* pila voltaica.

Voltairean, Voltairian [vɔl'tɛəriən], *ag.* volterriano, di Voltaire ‖ *s.* seguace di Voltaire.

voltameter [vɔl'tæmitə*], *s.* (*elett.*) voltametro.

volte ['vɔlti], *s.* (*equitazione, scherma*) volta.

volte-face ['vɔlt'fɑːs], *s.* (*spec. fig.*) voltafaccia.

voltmeter ['voult,miːtə*], *s.* (*elett.*) voltometro.

volubility [,vɔlju'biliti], *s.* scioltezza, speditezza (di eloquio); loquacità (di persona).

voluble ['vɔljubl], *ag.* **1.** spedito (di eloquio); loquace (di persona) **2.** (*bot.*) volubile **3.** (*rar.*) incostante.

volubleness ['vɔljublnis], *s.* speditezza; loquacità.

volubly ['vɔljubli], *av.* speditamente; loquacemente.

volume ['vɔljum], *s.* **1.** volume; tomo; libro: *work in two volumes,* opera in due volumi ‖ *the Christian —,* il Nuovo Testamento ‖ *the sacred —,* la Bibbia ‖ *to speak volumes for,* dare ampia dimostrazione; porre in luce favorevole: *it speaks volumes for his generosity,* ciò è una chiara dimostrazione della sua generosità **2.** (*st.*) documento, papiro **3.** volume; mole; massa: *the — of the earth,* il volume della Terra; *— of water,* massa d'acqua; *increase of —,* (*fis.*) aumento di volume, dilatazione **4.** (*mus.*) volume: *a voice of great —,* una voce di grande volume.

to **volume,** *v.t.i.* **1.** raccogliere in volume **2.** dilatarsi, formarsi in una massa.

volumed ['vɔljumd], *ag.* **1.** in volume, in volumi **2.** che forma una massa ☆ *three- —,* in tre volumi.

volumetric(al) [,vɔlju'metrik(əl)], *ag.* volumetrico ☆ *— analysis,* (*chim.*) analisi volumetrica; *— efficiency,* (*mec.*) rendimento volumetrico; *— expansion,* (*fis.*) espansione volumetrica.

voluminosity [və,lju:mi'nɔsiti], *s.* **1.** voluminosità **2.** l'avvolgersi in spire.

voluminous [və'lju:minəs], *ag.* **1.** in molti volumi, tomi: *a — history,* una storia in molti volumi **2.** *fig.* fecondo (di scrittore) **3.** di grande mole: *a — correspondence,* una corrispondenza voluminosa; *— hair,* capigliatura folta **4.** a spirale; a volute.

voluminously [və'lju:minəsli], *av.* **1.** in molti volumi **2.** voluminosamente **3.** a spire.

voluminousness [və'lju:minəsnis], *s.* **1.** voluminosità **2.** l'avvolgersi in spire.

voluntarily ['vɔləntərili], *av.* volontariamente; spontaneamente, liberamente.

voluntariness ['vɔləntərinis], *s.* spontaneità; volontarietà.

voluntarism ['vɔləntərizəm], *V.* **voluntaryism.**

voluntarist ['vɔləntərist], *V.* **voluntaryist.**

voluntary ['vɔləntəri], *ag.* **1.** volontario; spontaneo; libero: *a — confession,* una confessione spontanea; *a — contribution,* un contributo volontario; *— service,* servizio volontario **2.** mantenuto da contributi privati, non statale **3.** voluto; fatto di proposito: *— waste,* distruzione perpetrata di proposito **4.** (*fisiol.*) volontario ‖ *s.* (*mus. eccl.*) assolo (di organo) ☆ *— muscle,* (*fisiol.*) muscolo volontario; *— school,* scuola privata sovvenzionata, mantenuta da contribuenti volontari.

voluntaryism ['vɔləntəriizəm], *s.* indirizzo di pensiero secondo il quale la Chiesa e le Scuole dovrebbero essere sovvenzionate dai privati e non dallo Stato.

voluntaryist ['vɔləntəriist], *s.* seguace del « voluntaryism ».

volunteer [,vɔlən'tiə*], *ag.* **1.** volontario **2.** che cresce spontaneamente (di pianta) ‖ *s.* **1.** soldato volontario: *to call for volunteers,* chiedere volontari **2.** (*dir.*) beneficiario di una cessione a titolo gratuito ☆ *— army,* (*mil.*) esercito di volontari; *— plants,* (*bot.*) piante spontanee; *— service,* (*mil.*) servizio volontario.

to **volunteer,** *v.t.i.* **1.** offrire, offrirsi volontariamente: *to — some information,* dare spontaneamente delle informazioni; *to — to do sthg.,* offrirsi volontariamente di fare ql.co. **2.** (*mil.*) arruolarsi come volontario: *to — for a campaign,* arruolarsi come volontario in una campagna.

voluptuary [və'lʌptjuəri], *ag.* voluttuario; voluttuoso, sensuale ‖ *s.c.* epicureo, epicurea; libertino, libertina; persona sensuale.

voluptuous [və'lʌptjuəs], *ag.* voluttuoso; sensuale.

voluptuously [və'lʌptjuəsli], *av.* voluttuosamente; sensualmente.

voluptuousness [və'lʌptjuəsnis], *s.* voluttà; sensualità.

volute [və'lju:t], *ag.* a voluta, a spira ‖ *s.* 1. voluta; spira, spirale 2. (*arch. zool.*) voluta ☆ — *chamber*, (*mec.*) canale collettore (di pompa centrifuga); — *spring*, (*mec.*) molla a spirale conica.

voluted [və'lju:tid], *ag.* 1. avvolto a spirale 2. (*arch.*) provvisto di voluta.

volution [və'lju:ʃən], *s.* 1. attorcigliamento; avvolgimento a spirale 2. (*anat.*) circonvoluzione 3. spira (di conchiglia).

vomer ['voumə*], *s.* (*anat.*) vomere.

vomit ['vɔmit], *s.* 1. vomito 2. ciò che è stato vomitato 3. (*farm.*) emetico ☆ — *-nut*, noce vomica ‖ *black —*, (*patol.*) vomito nero, febbre gialla.

to **vomit**, *v.t.i.* 1. vomitare (anche *fig.*) 2. eruttare (di vulcano, ecc.).

vomiting ['vɔmitiŋ], *s.* vomito ☆ — *boiler*, (*ind.*) bollitore a tubi di circolazione.

vomition [vou'miʃən], *s.* vomito.

vomitive ['vɔmitiv], *ag. s.* (*farm.*) emetico.

vomito ['vɔmitou], *s.* (*patol.*) ematemesi da febbre gialla.

vomitory ['vɔmitəri], *ag.* emetico ‖ *s.* 1. (*arc. farm.*) emetico 2. (*st. romana*) vomitorio.

vomiturition [ˌvɔmitju'riʃən], *s.* conato di vomito.

voodoo ['vu:du:], *s.* 1. « voodoo » (pratiche superstiziose di origine africana) 2. seguace del « voodoo » ☆ — *doctor* (o — *priest*), stregone « voodoo ».

to **voodoo**, *v.t.* praticare stregoneria « voodoo » a.

voodooism ['vu:du:izəm], *s.* riti, credenze « voodoo ».

voracious [və'reiʃəs], *ag.* ingordo, vorace (anche *fig.*): *a — dog*, un cane vorace; *a — reader*, un lettore insaziabile.

voraciously [və'reiʃəsli], *av.* voracemente.

voraciousness [və'reiʃəsnis], **voracity** [vɔ'ræsiti], *s.* voracità.

vortex ['vɔ:teks], *pl.* **vortices** ['vɔ:tisi:z], **vortexes** ['vɔ:teksiz], *s.* vortice, turbine, gorgo (anche *fig.*): *the — of war*, il vortice della guerra ☆ — *cordis*, (*anat.*) vortice cardiaco; — *-ring*, spira; — *sheet*, (*fis.*) strato vorticoso; — *street*, (*fis.*) nastro vorticoso, coppia di piani vorticosi ‖ *line —*, (*fis.*) vortice lineare; *trailing —*, (*fis.*) vortice di uscita.

vortical ['vɔ:tikəl], *ag.* vorticoso, turbinoso.

vortically ['vɔ:tikəli], *av.* in modo vorticoso.

vorticel(la) [ˌvɔ:ti'sel(ə)], *s.* (*zool.*) vorticella.

vorticism ['vɔ:tisizəm], *s.* (*vitt.*) vorticismo.

vorticist ['vɔ:tisist], *s.* (*pitt.*) vorticista.

vorticose ['vɔ:tikous], **vortiginous** [vɔ'tidʒinəs], *ag.* vorticoso, turbinoso.

votal ['voutl], *ag.* votivo.

votaress ['voutəris], *s.* donna legata da voti religiosi.

votary ['voutəri], *s.* 1. chi è legato da un voto 2. chi è devoto, fedele; appassionato seguace: *a — of art*, un amante dell'arte.

vote [vout], *s.* voto, suffragio, votazione: *a — of censure*, un voto di opposizione; *a — of confidence*, voto di fiducia; *to put to the —*, mettere ai voti ‖ *to cast a —*, votare ‖ *to take the —*, procedere allo scrutinio ‖ *to take a — by calling over the names of the members*, votare per appello nominativo.

to **vote**, *v.t.i.* 1. votare: *to — against*, votare contro; *to — a bill through*, far passare una legge: *to — for*, votare in favore di 2. stanziare (una somma): *to — a sum for the sufferers*, stanziare una somma per i sofferenti 3. dichiarare: *they voted that he was the best singer of the season*, dichiararono che era il miglior cantante della stagione 4. (*fam.*) proporre, suggerire: *I — that we go*, propongo di andare 5. *to — down*, sconfiggere (mediante votazione): *to — down a proposal*, respingere una proposta 6. *to — in*, eleggere (con votazione).

voteless ['voutlis], *ag.* senza voto; privo del diritto di voto.

voter ['voutə*], *s.c.* chi vota; elettore, elettrice.

voting ['voutiŋ], *s.* il votare, votazione ☆ — *-paper*, scheda elettorale; — *station*, seggio elettorale.

votive ['voutiv], *ag.* votivo: — *offerings*, offerte votive.

vouch [vautʃ], *s.* (*fam.*) asserzione, attestazione.

to **vouch**, *v.t.i.* 1. (*dir. arc.*) citare come garante 2. *to — for* (*s.o., sthg.*), attestare, garantire: *I — for his ability to pay*, rispondo io della sua solvibilità; *to — for s.o.*, rendersi garante per qlcu.: *I am ready to — for him*, sono pronto a garantire per lui.

vouchee [vau'tʃi:], *s.c.* testimone garante.

voucher ['vautʃə*], *s.c.* testimone ‖ *s.* 1. documento giustificativo, pezza d'appoggio; fideiussione 2. buono, tagliando; (*comm.*) ricevuta.

to **vouchsafe** [vautʃ'seif], *v.t.* concedere, accordare.

vow[1] [vau], *s.* voto, promessa solenne, giuramento: *he was under a — to smoke no more*, aveva fatto voto di non fumare più; *to take the vows*, (*eccl.*) pronunciare i voti ☆ *baptismal vows*, voti battesimali.

to **vow**[1], *v.t.* fare voto di, promettere, giurare: *to — a pilgrimage to the Holy Land*, fare voto di compiere un pellegrinaggio in Terra Santa.

to **vow**[2], *v.t.* (*arc.*) dichiarare, affermare solennemente: *I — you are very obliging*, riconosco che sei molto gentile ‖ —, (*amer.*) davvero: *I —, child, you are pretty!*, davvero, bambina, sei graziosa!.

vowel ['vauəl], *s.* vocale.

to **vowelize** ['vauəlaiz], *v.t.* inserire vocali in.

vowelled ['vauəld], *ag.* che ha molte vocali.

vowelless ['vauəlis], *ag.* senza vocali.

vowelly ['vauəli], *av.* per mezzo di vocali; con vocali.

voyage ['vɔidʒ], *s.* viaggio (specialmente per via d'acqua), traversata: *to go for a —*, intraprendere un viaggio (per mare); *to make a —*, fare un viaggio (per mare).

to **voyage**, *v.t.i.* fare una traversata, navigare, viaggiare (per via d'acqua).

voyageable ['vɔidʒəbl], *ag.* navigabile.

voyager ['vɔidʒə*], *s.c.* viaggiatore, viaggiatrice; passeggero, passeggera (di nave, battello) ‖ *s.* navigatore.

Vulcan ['vʌlkən], *no.pr.m.* (*mit.*) Vulcano ‖ **vulcan**, *s. fig.* fabbro.

vulcanic [vʌl'kænik], **vulcanicity** [ˌvʌlkə'nisiti], *V.* **volcanic, volcanicity**.

vulcanite ['vʌlkənait], *s.* vulcanite, ebanite.

vulcanizable ['vʌlkənaizəbl], *ag.* (*ind.*) vulcanizzabile.

vulcanization [ˌvʌlkənai'zeiʃən], *s.* (*ind.*) vulcanizzazione ☆ — *coefficient*, coefficiente di vulcanizzazione; — *heat*, calore di vulcanizzazione ‖ *moulding —*, vulcanizzazione in stampo; *open* (o *free*) *steam —*, vulcanizzazione in vapore libero; *press —*, vulcanizzazione sotto pressa.

to **vulcanize** ['vʌlkənaiz], *v.t.* (*ind.*) vulcanizzare.

vulcanizer ['vʌlkənaizə*], *s.* (*ind.*) vulcanizzatore.

vulgar ['vʌlgə*], *ag.* 1. volgare, triviale, plebeo; ordinario, grossolano: — *display of wealth*, volgare sfoggio di ricchezza; — *expression*, espressione triviale ‖ *the — herd*, il popolino 2. volgare, popolare, comune ‖ *the — era*, l'era volgare ‖ *the — tongue*, il volgare ☆ — *fraction*, (*arit.*) frazione ordinaria, comune.

vulgarian [vʌl'gɛəriən], *s.c.* 1. persona volgare, triviale 2. persona del volgo.

vulgarism ['vʌlgərizəm], *s.* 1. volgarità, trivialità 2. espressione popolare, volgarismo.

vulgarity [vʌl'gæriti], *s.* volgarità, cattivo gusto: *to lapse into —*, cadere nel cattivo gusto, nella volgarità.

vulgarization [ˌvʌlgərai'zeiʃən], *s.* 1. il rendere volgare, triviale 2. divulgazione.

to **vulgarize** ['vʌlgəraiz], *v.t.* 1. rendere volgare, triviale 2. volgarizzare, divulgare.

vulgarly ['vʌlgəli], *av.* volgarmente.

Vulgate [ˈvʌlgit] *s.* Volgata (traduzione latina della Bibbia).

vulgus [ˈvʌlgəs], *s.* (*sl. scolastico*) esercizio di versificazione greca, latina.

vulnerability [ˌvʌlnərəˈbiliti], *s.* vulnerabilità.

vulnerable [ˈvʌlnərəbl], *ag.* vulnerabile ‖ *that is his — spot*, è il suo tallone d'Achille.

vulnerableness [ˈvʌlnərəblnis], *s.* vulnerabilità.

vulnerary [ˈvʌlnərəri], *ag.* (*farm.*) vulnerario, cicatrizzante ‖ *s.* (*bot. farm.*) vulneraria.

vulpicide [ˈvʌlpisaid], *s.* **1.** uccisore di volpe (non durante una caccia) **2.** uccisione di volpe (non durante una caccia).

vulpine [ˈvʌlpain], *ag.* volpino, di volpe; *fig.* astuto.

vulture [ˈvʌltʃə*], *s.* **1.** (*ornit.*) avvoltoio **2.** *fig.* individuo rapace, avido.

vulturine [ˈvʌltʃurain], **vulturish** [ˈvʌltʃuriʃ], **vulturous** [ˈvʌltʃurəs], *ag.* di avvoltoio; caratteristico dell'avvoltoio; rapace.

vulva [ˈvʌlvə], *s.* (*anat.*) vulva.

vulvar [ˈvʌlvə*], *ag.* (*anat.*) di vulva, vulvare.

vulvitis [vʌlˈvaitis], *s.* (*patol.*) vulvite.

W

w ['dʌblju(:)], *pl.* **ws, w's** ['dʌblju(:)z], *s.* **1.** (*ventitreesima lettera dell'alfabeto inglese*) w ǁ — *for William,* (*tel.*) w come Washington **2.** *W, abbr.* di **West 3.** *W,* (*chim.*) W (simbolo del tungsteno).

Waac [wæk], *s.* (*fam.*) membro del «Women's Army Auxiliary Corps» (corpo ausiliario militare femminile, nella 1ª guerra mondiale).

Waaf [wæf], *s.* (*fam.*) membro del «Women's Auxiliary Air Force» (corpo ausiliario femminile dell'aeronautica, nella 2ª guerra mondiale).

(to) **wabble,** *V.* (to) **wobble.**

wacke ['wækə], *s.* (*geol.*) varietà di argilla grigia o bruna di origine vulcanica.

wad[1] [wɔd], *s.* **1.** batuffolo, tampone **2.** stoppaccio; borra **3.** (*dial.*) covone **4.** (*sl. amer.*) rotolo: a — *of dollar bills,* un rotolo di biglietti da un dollaro.

to **wad**[1], *pass.p.p.* **wadded** ['wɔdid], *v.t.* **1.** comprimere in batuffolo **2.** tappare, tamponare **3.** imbottire; foderare (un abito) **4.** (*dial.*) legare, sistemare in piccoli covoni **5.** (*sl. amer.*) arrotolare.

wad[2], *s.* (*min.*) idrossido di manganese.

wadable ['weidəbl], *ag.* guadabile.

wadding ['wɔdiŋ], *s.* **1.** ovatta, ovattina (per sarti) **2.** bambagia **3.** feltro per borre, stoppaccio.

waddle ['wɔdl], *s.* **1.** ondeggiamento **2.** andatura ondeggiante (a mo' di anitra).

to **waddle,** *v.i.* camminare ondeggiando (a mo' di anitra).

to **wade** [weid], *v.t.i.* **1.** guadare, passare a guado **2.** avanzare faticosamente, procedere a stento (anche *fig.*): to — *through a book,* procedere lentamente nella lettura di un libro **3.** to — *in,* attaccare vigorosamente l'avversario; accingersi con energia a un lavoro.

wader ['weidə*], *s.c.* chi passa a guado ǁ *s.* **1.** (*ornit.*) trampoliere **2.** *pl.* stivaloni impermeabili.

wadi ['wɔdi], *s.* uadi (letto petroso di fiume asciutto).

wading ['weidiŋ], *ag.* che guada ǁ *s.* il guadare ☆ — *bird,* trampoliere; — *place,* (*amer.*) guado.

wady ['wɔdi], *s.* uadi (letto petroso di fiume asciutto).

wafer ['weifə*], *s.* **1.** cialda, wafer ǁ *as thin as a* —, magro come un chiodo **2.** (*eccl. farm.*) ostia **3.** disco adesivo di carta per sigilli ☆ — *core,* (*mec.*) anima per fusioni in conchiglie.

to **wafer,** *v.t.* sigillare (con disco adesivo).

wafery ['weifəri], *ag.* sottilissimo; fragilissimo.

to **waff** [wɑːf], *v.t.i.* **1.** agitare, agitarsi; ondeggiare; fluttuare (al vento) **2.** far vento.

waffle ['wɔfl], *s.* (*cuc.*) cialda (in America consumata calda con burro e melassa).

waft [wɑːft], *s.* **1.** soffio di vento; corrente d'aria **2.** alito, soffio, zaffata (di odore) **3.** soffio, ondata (di musica) **4.** ondeggiamento **5.** (*mar.*) segnalazione (per chiedere aiuto).

to **waft,** *v.t.i.* **1.** (*poet.*) sospingere (sull'acqua, attraverso l'aria); diffondere, spandere: *the music was wafted through the garden,* la musica si diffondeva nel giardino ǁ to — *a kiss,* mandare un bacio (sulla punta delle dita) **2.** fluttuare; soffiare blandamente (di brezza).

wag[1] [wæg], *s.* **1.** bontempone, burlone, capo ameno **2.** (*sl. scolastico*) ragazzo che marina la scuola: *to play (the)* —, salare, marinare la scuola.

wag[2], *s.* movimento, cenno (del capo); scodinzolamento (di cane): *he answered with a — of his head,* rispose scuotendo la testa; *the vase was knocked down by a — of the dog's tail,* scodinzolando il cane ha fatto cadere il vaso.

to **wag**[2], *pass.p.p.* **wagged** [wægd], *v.t.i.* scuotere, scuotersi; agitare, agitarsi; dimenare: *the dog wagged its tail,* il cane scodinzolava; *he wagged his finger at her,* la ammonì (scherzosamente) col dito; *to — one's head,* scuotere la testa (con aria canzonatoria o divertita) ǁ *he set chins wagging, fig.* suscitò dei pettegolezzi ǁ *he wags his beard too much, when he is drunk, fig.* quando è brillo chiacchiera troppo ǁ *none of your wagging!, fig.* basta con le tue chiacchiere!, basta con le tue malignità! ǁ *she lets the world —, fig.* lascia che la gente chiacchieri ǁ *tongues are wagging, fig.* le male lingue si sono messe in moto ǁ *not to — a finger,* non muovere un dito.

wage [weidʒ], *s. gener. pl.* salario, paga: *do you get good wages?,* hai una buona paga?; *he takes all his wages home to his mother,* porta a casa a sua madre la paga intera; *when wages are high, prices are high,* i prezzi salgono quando aumentano i salari ǁ *the wages of sin is death,* (*arc.*) il prezzo del peccato è la morte ☆ — *-earner,* salariato; (*fam.*) il sostegno della famiglia: *the — -earner is the wife, not he,* chi tira avanti la baracca è la moglie, non lui; — *-fund,* (*econ.*) la parte del capitale destinata al pagamento delle retribuzioni; — *scale,* tabella base delle paghe; — *-sheet,* foglio paga; — *sliding scale,* scala mobile dei salari ǁ *living* —, salario sufficiente per vivere.

to **wage,** *v.t.* **1.** intraprendere, ingaggiare: to — *war,* muover guerra **2.** (*arc.*) retribuire, ricompensare.

wager ['weidʒə*], *s.* **1.** scommessa: *to lay a* —, fare una scommessa; *to win a* —, vincere una scommessa **2.** (*rar.*) posta (di una scommessa).

to **wager,** *v.t.i.* scommettere; fare una scommessa: *I'll — five shillings on that horse,* punterò cinque scellini su quel cavallo; *she wagered that...,* ha scommesso che....

wagerer ['weidʒərə*], *s.c.* scommettitore, scommettitrice.

waggery ['wægəri], *s.* buon umore; amenità; comicità: *he is full of fun and* —, è molto arguto e divertente.

waggish ['wægiʃ], *ag.* faceto, arguto; brioso; comico.

waggishly ['wægiʃli], *av.* scherzosamente, per celia.

waggishness ['wægiʃnis], *s.* gusto per le facezie, per le burle piacevoli: *there was a sort of — about him,* c'era un che di faceto in lui.

waggle ['wægl], *s.* dondolamento; oscillazione.

to **waggle,** *v.t.i.* **1.** (*fam.*) scuotere, dondolare, agitare, dimenare: *the dog waggled its tail,* il cane dimenava la coda; *she waggled her head at my laughing,* scosse la testa quando mi misi a ridere **2.** (*golf*) dondolare la mazza (prima di colpire la palla).

waggly ['wægli], *ag.* dondolante; malfermo.

wag(g)on ['wægən], *s.* **1.** carro; (*amer.*) carro coperto (dei pionieri) ǁ *the Wagon,* (*astr.*) l'Orsa Maggiore ǁ *to hitch one's — to a star, fig.* appoggiarsi a una persona influente **2.** vagone, vagone merci ☆ — *-load,* (*comm.*) (carico di) un vagone; — *roof,* tetto a botte; — *-wright,* costruttore di carri ǁ *band- —,* (*amer.*) carro della banda musicale (che precede una parata, specialmente durante le elezioni): *to climb the band- —,* (*fig. amer.*) sostenere il candidato più forte; seguire l'opinione prevalente ‖ *cask* —, carro botte; *crane* —, carro gru; *snow-plough* —, carro spazzaneve; *tank* —, carro cisterna; *tipping* —, vagonetto ribaltabile.

wag(g)onage ['wægənidʒ], *s.* **1.** trasporto a mezzo di carri **2.** prezzo per trasporto a mezzo di carri.

wag(g)oner ['wægənə*], *s.* carrettiere ‖ *the Wagoner*, (*astr.*) l'Auriga.

wag(g)onette [,wægə'net], *s.* « wagonette » (carrozza con sedili laterali).

Wagnerian [vɑ:g'niəriən], *ag.* (*st. mus.*) wagneriano.

Wagnerianism [vɑ:g'niəriənizəm], **Wagnerism** ['vɑ:gnərizəm], *s.* (*st. mus.*) wagnerismo.

Wagnerist ['vɑ:gnərist], *s.* (*st. mus.*) wagneriano.

wagtail ['wægteil], *s.* **1.** (*ornit.*) cutrettola; coditremola **2.** persona ossequiosa **3.** (*arc.*) prostituta.

Wahabi [wə'hɑ:bi], *s.* Wahabita (appartenente ad una setta rigorista musulmana fondata nel XVIII secolo).

waif [weif], *s.* **1.** trovatello ‖ *waifs and strays*, infanzia abbandonata **2.** oggetto, animale smarrito **3.** relitto.

wail [weil], *s.* **1.** gemito, lamento **2.** (*rar.*) vagito.

to wail, *v.t.i.* gemere, lamentarsi ‖ *to — out a song,* straziare una canzone.

wailer ['weilə*], *s.c.* chi si lamenta.

wailful ['weilful], *ag.* (*poet.*) lamentoso; piagnucoloso; doloroso.

wailingly ['weiliŋli], *av.* lamentosamente.

wain [wein], *s.* (*poet. agr.*) carro ‖ *the Wain* (o *Charles's Wain*), (*astr.*) l'Orsa Maggiore.

wainage ['weinidʒ], *s.* **1.** coppia di buoi **2.** attrezzi agricoli **3.** terra coltivata.

wainscot ['weinskət], *s.* **1.** rivestimento a pannelli di legno **2.** zoccolo (di muro).

to wainscot, *v.t.* coprire, rivestire con pannelli.

wainscoting ['weinskətiŋ], *s.* **1.** rivestimento in legno (di pareti) **2.** legno per rivestimenti.

waist [weist], *s.* **1.** cintola, vita, cintura: *down to the* —, fino alla cintola: *from the shoulder down to the* —, dalla spalla alla cintola; *up from the* —, dalla cintola in giù; *she has no* —, non ha la vita segnata; *she is very small round the* —, ha la vita sottile; *the tall grass reached up to his* —, l'erba alta gli arrivava fino alla cintola **2.** strozzatura, restringimento **3.** (*amer.*) camicetta, corpetto **4.** (*mar.*) parte centrale (di nave) ☆ *— -anchor,* (*mar.*) ancora riposta al centro della nave; *— -deep* (o *— -high*), che arriva fino alla cintola.

waistband ['weistbænd], *s.* cintura, fascia.

waistbelt ['weistbelt], *s.* cintura.

waistboat ['weistbout], *s.* (*mar.*) scialuppa collocata al centro della nave.

waistcloth ['weistklɔθ], *s.* perizoma.

waistcoat ['weiskout], *s.* panciotto.

waistcoating ['weiskoutiŋ], *s.* tessuto per panciotti.

waister ['weistə*], *s.* (*mar.*) mozzo di baleniera.

waistline ['weistlain], *s.* **1.** (*sartoria*) vita, altezza della vita: *natural* —, vita normale; *long* —, vita bassa; *short* —, vita alta **2.** (*aut.*) linea della cintura.

wait [weit], *s.* **1.** attesa: *we had a long — at the station*, attendemmo a lungo alla stazione **2.** agguato, imboscata ‖ *to lay — for s.o.*, tendere un'imboscata a qlcu.; *to lie in —*, stare in agguato **3.** *pl.* cantori che, nel periodo natalizio, passano di casa in casa cantando inni.

to wait, *v.t.i.* **1.** aspettare, attendere: *— for me*, aspettami; *whom are you waiting for?*, chi stai aspettando? ‖ *— a minute, please,* attendi un attimo, per piacere ‖ *he is waiting his opportunity*, è in attesa del suo momento ‖ *I won't keep you waiting*, non ti farò aspettare; *— and see!*, non essere impaziente, aspetta e vedrai! ‖ *he didn't — to be told twice*, non se lo fece dire due volte **2.** ritardare (un pasto): *they waited dinner for him*, ritardarono il pranzo per lui **3.** servire: *our young maid was not accustomed to waiting at table*, la nostra giovane domestica non era abituata a servire a tavola **4.** *to — (up)on (s.o.)*, servire, essere al servizio di; (*comm.*) visitare: *our traveller will — on you at your earliest convenience*, (*comm.*) il nostro viaggiatore passerà da voi a vostro comodo; *we used to be waited upon by servants*, eravamo abituati ad essere serviti da domestici ‖ *to — on s.o. hand and foot*, essere schiavi di qlcu. **5.** *to — up*, restare alzati: *we waited up for him*, lo aspettammo alzati.

wait-a-bit, *ag.s.* « wait-a-bit » (nome dato a diverse piante e cespugli spinosi del Sud Africa).

waiter ['weitə*], *s.c.* chi aspetta ‖ *s.* **1.** cameriere (di caffè, albergo) **2.** vassoio **3.** (*arc.*) doganiere ☆ *dumb —*, «servo muto», carrello portavivande; (*amer.*) montacarico (per vivande); *head- —*, capo cameriere.

waitering ['weitəriŋ], *s.* (*rar.*) impiego di cameriere.

waiting ['weitiŋ], *s.* **1.** attesa ‖ *no —*, divieto di sosta **2.** servizio ☆ *— -maid* (o *— -woman*), cameriera personale; *— -room*, sala d'aspetto ‖ *lady-in- —,* dama d'onore.

waitress ['weitris], *s.* cameriera (di caffè, albergo).

to waive [weiv], *v.t.* rinunciare a; desistere da; derogare a; tralasciare: *waiving aside all other considerations*, tralasciando ogni altra considerazione; *to — one's rights*, rinunciare ai propri diritti.

waiver ['weivə*], *s.* (*dir.*) rinuncia; deroga.

waiving ['weiviŋ], *s.* abbandono, rinuncia; deroga.

wake[1] [weik], *s.* **1.** veglia **2.** (*dial.*) vigilia **3.** *gener. pl.* (*dial.*) festa del patrono (di una parrocchia) **4.** (*spec. irl.*) veglia funebre.

to wake[1], *pass.* **waked** [weikt], **woke** [wouk], *p.p.* **waked, woke, woken** ['woukən], *v.t.i.* **1.** svegliare, svegliarsi (anche *fig.*): *the alarm woke me (up) at six*, la sveglia mi destò alle sei; *I said I was not to be woken*, dissi che non dovevo essere svegliato; *I woke (up) with a start*, mi svegliai di soprassalto; *the news will — him (up)*, quella notizia lo sveglierà, distruggerà i suoi sogni, gli darà nuova energia; *to — up to sthg.*, divenir conscio di qlco.: *at last he woke up to the truth*, finalmente aprì gli occhi e si rese conto della verità ‖ *— up!*, svegliati! ; *fig.* sta' attento, non dormire! **2.** risvegliare, ridestare; animare, animarsi (conversazione, immagini, ecc.) **3.** vegliare; (*irl.*) vegliare un morto: *to — a sick person*, vegliare un malato **4.** provocare, risvegliare: *they woke echoes in the valley*, fecero risuonare la vallata di echi.

wake[2], *s.* **1.** scia (anche *fig.*): *the daughter is in the — of her mother*, la figlia segue le orme della madre; *wars bring misery in their —*, le guerre son seguite dalla miseria **2.** (*mar.*) rotta.

wakeful ['weikful], *ag.* **1.** sveglio; desto; insonne: *a — night*, una notte insonne **2.** vigile, attento: *he appeared — and suspicious*, sembrava guardingo e sospettoso.

wakefully ['weikfuli], *av.* **1.** senza dormire **2.** in modo vigile, guardingo.

wakefulness ['weikfulnis], *s.* **1.** insonnia **2.** vigilanza.

to waken ['weikən], *v.t.i.* svegliare, svegliarsi; risvegliare, risvegliarsi; ridestare: *don't — him*, non svegliarlo; *the noise was fit to — the dead*, (*fam.*) c'era tanto rumore da ridestare i morti.

wakener ['weikənə*], *s.c.* persona, cosa che sveglia.

wakening ['weikniŋ], *s.* risveglio.

waker ['weikə*], *s.c.* chi sveglia; chi si sveglia ☆ *early —*, mattiniero.

wakerife ['weikraif], *ag.* (*scoz.*) guardingo; vigile.

waking ['weikiŋ], *ag.* **1.** sveglio; desto; insonne: *am I — or sleeping?*, sogno o son desto? **2.** vigilante ‖ *s.* **1.** risveglio: *on my —*, al mio risveglio **2.** veglia: *between sleeping and —*, tra il sonno e la veglia **3.** (*irl.*) il vegliare un morto.

Walach ['wɔlək], *s.* valacco.

Waldemar ['vældəma:*], *no.pr.m.* Valdemaro.

Waldenses [wɔl'densi:z], *s. pl.* (*st. relig.*) valdesi.

Waldensian [wɔl'densiən], *ag.s.c.* (*st. relig.*) valdese.

waldhorn ['wɔ:ldhɔ:n], *s.* corno da caccia.

wale[1] [weil], *s.* **1.** segno, marchio lasciato da una frustata **2.** costa (di tessuto) **3.** (*edil.*) trave orizzontale in legno **4.** *pl.* (*mar.*) corsi di tavolame del fasciame.

to wale[1], *v.t.* **1.** segnare, striare (con frustate) **2.** unire, legare con assi orizzontali.

wale[2], *s.* (*scoz.*) scelta; selezione.

to wale[2], *v.t.* (*scoz.*) scegliere; selezionare.

Waler ['weilə*], *s.* « Waler » (cavallo importato in India dalla Nuova Galles del Sud).

Wales [weilz], *no.pr.* (*geog.*) Galles || *New South* —, Nuova Galles del Sud || *Prince of* —, Principe di Galles (titolo conferito al principe ereditario di Gran Bretagna).

Walhalla, *V.* **Valhalla**.

walk [wɔːk], *s.* **1.** passeggiata; giro; marcia; camminata; percorso: *an hour's* —, una passeggiata, un percorso di un'ora; *it is half an hour's* — *from here*, è a mezz'ora di cammino da qui; *this house is not on the postman's* —, questa casa non è compresa nel giro del portalettere; *to go for* (o *to take*) *a* —, fare una passeggiata; *to take s.o. for a* —, accompagnare qlcu. a fare una passeggiata **2.** viale, passeggiata; ambulacro: *a* — *bordered with a yew-hedge*, un viale fiancheggiato da una siepe di tassi **3.** andatura, passo: *a dignified* —, un'andatura altera; *one can often recognize a person by his* —, si può spesso riconoscere una persona dalla sua andatura; *to go at a* —, andare al passo (di cavallo) **4.** *fig.* sfera, dominio; rango: — *of* (o *in*) *life*, livello sociale; professione, mestiere: *people in the humbler walks of life*, gente dei ceti più bassi, di umile condizione **5.** (*side-*) —, (*amer.*) marciapiede ☆ — *-over*, (*spor.*) vittoria facile (alle corse); *fig.* successo sicuro; — *-out*, (*fam.*) sciopero || *cat-* —, passerella; *sheep-* —, pascolo; *stern-* —, (*mar.*) galleria di poppa.

to walk, *v.t.i.* **1.** (far) camminare, passeggiare, condurre a spasso; percorrere: *she walked herself tired*, camminò fino a stancarsi; *we walked a few miles*, percorremmo alcune miglia a piedi || *to* — *the boards*, (*teat.*) calcare le scene || *to* — *the chalk*, camminare su una linea segnata col gesso (per dimostrare di non essere ubriachi) || *to* — *a horse*, mettere un cavallo al passo || *to* — *the hospitals*, essere studente in medicina || *to* — *in one's sleep*, essere sonnambulo || *to* — *on all fours*, camminare a quattro zampe || *to* — *s.o. off his legs*, far stancare qlcu. camminando || *to* — *the plank*, (*arc.*) essere condannato a morte dai pirati || *to* — *a puppy*, addestrare un cucciolo **2.** andare a piedi: *I* — *to the office*, vado in ufficio a piedi; *you can* — *it* (o *there*) *in a few minutes*, ci si va a piedi in pochi minuti || *to* — *the streets*, vagare per le strade, gironzolare; (*sl.*) battere i marciapiedi **3.** (*arc.*) comportarsi: *to* — *in darkness*, vivere nell'errore, nel peccato; *to* — *in His laws*, seguire le leggi del Signore **4.** apparire (di spettri) || *the ghost walks*, (*sl. teat.*) è il giorno di paga **5.** *to* — *into* (*s.o., sthg.*), entrare in, penetrare in; (*fam.*) trovarsi faccia a faccia con; dire il fatto suo a || *to* — *into a cake, a sum of money*, far piazza pulita di una torta, di una somma di danaro **6.** *to* — *about*, passeggiare, bighellonare **7.** *to* — *away*, andarsene: *to* — *away from s.o.*, (*spor.*) distanziare un avversario **8.** *to* — *back*, ritornare a piedi: *I had to* — *all the way back*, dovetti ritornare a piedi **9.** *to* — *down*, discendere **10.** *to* — *in*, entrare: *please* — *in*, entrate senza bussare || — *in!*, avanti! **11.** *to* — *off*, andarsene, partire; (*fam.*) andarsene alla chetichella || *to* — *off one's anger*, far sbollire l'ira camminando || *to* — *off one's dinner*, camminare per digerire || *to* — *off with sthg.*, rubare, portar via ql.co. **12.** *to* — *on*, avanzare; (*teat.*) fare la comparsa: *he just only walks on* (o *has a walking on part*) *in that play*, fa soltanto la comparsa in quella commedia **13.** *to* — *out*, uscire; (*amer.*) scioperare: *to* — *one's girl out*, uscire con la propria ragazza || *to* — *out on*, piantare in asso, abbandonare || *to* — *out with*, corteggiare **14.** *to* — *over*, stravincere; vincere per mancanza di validi concor-

renti **15.** *to* — *through*, attraversare **16.** *to* — *up*, salire: *to* — *up and down*, camminare su e giù, avanti e indietro; *to* — *up to s.o.*, avvicinarsi a qlcu.

walkable ['wɔːkəbl], *ag.* che si può percorrere a piedi, praticabile.

walker ['wɔːkə*], *s.c.* camminatore, camminatrice; pedone: *to be a bad, a slow, a fast* —, essere un cattivo, un lento, un veloce camminatore ☆ — *-on*, (*teat.*) comparsa || *shop-* —, direttore di reparto (di un grande negozio); *sleep-* —, sonnambulo; *street* —, donna da marciapiede, peripatetica.

walkie-talkie ['wɔːki,tɔːki], *s.* (*rad.*) trasmettitore-ricevitore portatile.

walking ['wɔːkiŋ], *ag.* **1.** che cammina; (*scherz.*) ambulante: *he is a* — *encyclopaedia*, è una enciclopedia ambulante **2.** a trazione animale; (*mec.*) oscillante, mobile || *s.* il camminare: *are you fond of* —*?*, ti piace camminare?; *it is a matter of ten minutes'* —, si tratta di dieci minuti di cammino; *it is within* — *distance*, ci si può andare a piedi ☆ — *beam*, (*miner.*) bilanciere; — *gentleman*, — *lady*, (*teat.*) comparsa; — *leaf*, (*entom.*) fillio fogliasecca; — *pace*, passo d'uomo: *all cars to drive in at* — *pace*, tutte le automobili devono entrare a passo d'uomo; — *-papers* (o — *-ticket*), (*sl. spec. amer.*) licenziamento; — *stick*, bastone da passeggio; — *tour*, escursione a piedi.

walkway ['wɔːkweiʲ], *s.* (*neol.*) passaggio pedonale.

Walkyrie ['vɔɛlkiri], *s.* (*mit. nordica*) Valchiria.

walky-talky, *V.* **walkie-talkie**.

wall [wɔːl], *s.* **1.** muro, parete (anche *fig.*): *blank* —, parete nuda; *the garden is surrounded by a* —, il giardino è circondato da un muro || *be careful, walls have ears*, sta' attento, i muri hanno orecchie || *to be with one's back to the* —, *fig.* essere con le spalle al muro || *to drive to the* —, ridurre all'estremo || *to give s.o. the* —, cedere il passo a qlcu. || *to go to the* —, fallire, avere la peggio || *to leave by the* —, lasciare in disparte || *to run one's head against a* —, arrampicarsi sui vetri || *to see through a brick* —, avere un grande intuito **2.** *pl.* mura, fortificazioni: *within, without the walls*, entro, fuori le mura **3.** spalliera (per piante rampicanti) **4.** (*miner.*) parete, muro **5.** (*anat.*) parete ☆ — *bed*, letto ribaltabile; — *bracket*, mensola a muro; — *chase*, incassatura per tubazioni; — *fruit*, frutti da spalliera; — *gillyflower*, violacciocca; — *hook*, gancio a muro; — *lamp*, lampada a muro; — *lizard*, (*zool.*) lucertola muraiuola; — *moss*, (*bot.*) sedum; — *painting*, affresco; — *paper*, carta da parato; — *plate*, (*mec.*) piastra a muro per fissaggio; — *socket*, (*elett.*) presa a muro; — *spacers*, (*edil.*) distanziatori per casseforme; — *tree*, pianta da spalliera || *blind* —, muro pieno; *decorating* —, muro di rivestimento; *header* —, muratura di punta, muro di rivestimento; *hanging* —, *main* —, muro maestro; *party* —, muro comune, di confine, divisorio; *sea* —, muro frangiflutti; *stretcher* —, muratura di coltello; *town walls*, mura (di città).

to wall, *v.t.* **1.** circondare di mura || *we had to* — *off the chicken run*, dovemmo cintare il pollaio **2.** *to* — *up*, murare, ostruire: *he had two windows walled up*, fece murare due finestre.

wallaby ['wɔləbi], *s.* **1.** (*zool.*) piccolo canguro australiano || *to be on the* —, (*fam.*) vagabondare in cerca di lavoro **2.** *pl.* (*fam.*) gli Australiani.

wallah ['wɔlə], *s.* (*ang.-in.*) impiegato; fattorino ☆ *competition* —, impiegato statale (nominato per concorso).

wallaroo ['wɔləruː], *s.* (*zool.*) canguro gigante.

wallet ['wɔlit], *s.* **1.** portafogli **2.** borsetta per attrezzi **3.** (*arc.*) bisaccia; sacca.

wall-eye ['wɔːlai], *s.* (*med. vet.*) glaucoma; leucoma corneale; strabismo divergente.

walleyed ['wɔːlaid], *ag.* (*med. vet.*) affetto da glaucoma; strabico.

wallflower ['wɔːl,flauə*], *s.* **1.** (*bot.*) violacciocca **2.** (*fam.*) ragazza che « fa da tappezzeria » ad un ballo.

walling ['wɔ:liŋ], s. **1.** muro di cinta; mura (di città) **2.** opera in muratura.

Walloon [wɔ'lu:n], ag. vallone, dei valloni ‖ s. vallone (abitante, lingua).

wallop ['wɔləp], s. **1.** (fam.) percossa; colpo violento **2.** (sl.) movimento brusco e maldestro.

to **wallop**, pass.p.p. **wallopped** ['wɔləpt], v.t.i. **1.** (fam.) percuotere **2.** (sl.) muoversi maldestramente, pesantemente.

wallop(p)ing ['wɔləpiŋ], ag. (sl.) grande; enorme ‖ s. (sl.) bastonatura, legnata.

wallow ['wɔlou], s. pantano, brago.

to **wallow**, v.i. **1.** rotolarsi, guazzare nel brago (di animali) **2.** fig. voltolarsi; sguazzare: to — in wealth, nuotare nell'abbondanza **3.** (mar.) rollare.

Wallsend ['wɔ:lzənd], no.pr. (geog.) Wallsend.

walnut ['wɔ:lnət], s. (bot.) **1.** noce (frutto) ‖ over the walnuts and wine, (fam.) al dessert **2.** — (tree), noce (albero, legno): — suite (of furniture), mobilio in noce ☆ — shell, guscio di noce.

Walpurgis night [væl'puəgis,nait], s. notte di Valpurga (la vigilia del 1° maggio).

walrus ['wɔ:lrəs], s. (zool.) tricheco ☆ — moustache, (fam.) baffi spioventi.

Walter ['wɔ:ltə*], no.pr.m. Walter, Gualtiero.

waltz [wɔ:ls], s. (mus.) valzer.

to **waltz**, v.t.i. ballare il valzer; far ballare il valzer a: he waltzed her round the room, le fece fare un giro di valzer.

waltzer ['wɔ:lsə*], s.c. ballerino, ballerina di valzer.

wampum ['wɔmpəm], s. « wampum » (conchiglie infilate, usate dai pellirosse per ornamento e come moneta).

wan [wɔn], ag. **1.** esangue, smorto, smunto; languido: to grow —, impallidire **2.** debole, pallido (di luce, ecc.): a — smile, un debole sorriso **3.** (arc.) oscuro, nero, livido: — waters, acque livide.

to **wan**, pass.p.p. **wanned** [wɔnd], v.t.i. (rar.) impallidire, far impallidire.

wand [wɔnd], s. **1.** bacchetta: conductor's —, bacchetta di direttore d'orchestra; conjurer's —, bacchetta di prestigiatore ‖ Mercury's —, (mit.) caduceo **2.** bastone di comando; mazza (d'usciere) ☆ hazel —, bacchetta divinatoria.

wander ['wɔndə*], s. passeggiata senza meta; vagabondaggio.

to **wander**, v.t.i. **1.** vagare, errare, vagabondare; percorrere senza meta: he wandered for miles and miles, vagò per molte miglia; his eyes wandered over the familiar landscape, il suo sguardo percorse il paesaggio familiare; his thoughts wandered back to the past, egli riandava col pensiero al passato; to — through the woods, errare attraverso i boschi; to let one's thoughts —, lasciar vagare i propri pensieri ‖ to — about, andare alla ventura: to — about the world, andare per il mondo **2.** deviare, uscire dalla retta via; smarrirsi (anche fig.): some of the sheep have wandered away, alcune pecore si sono smarrite ‖ to — (away) from the point (o from the subject). sviare l'argomento, fare una digressione **3.** vaneggiare; delirare: he is wandering (in his mind), egli vaneggia.

wanderer ['wɔndərə*], s.c. **1.** vagabondo, vagabonda; (fam.) girandolone, girandolona **2.** chi devia, chi esce dalla retta via, chi si smarrisce (anche fig.) ‖ a — from the fold, fig. una pecorella smarrita.

wandering ['wɔndəriŋ], ag. **1.** errante, vagante; vagabondo; nomade: — life, vita vagabonda; — tribes, tribù nomadi ‖ the — Jew, l'Ebreo errante **2.** distratto: — eyes, occhi distratti **3.** (med.) migrante, aberrante: — kidney, rene migrante **4.** che vaneggia, che delira ‖ s. **1.** vagabondaggio (anche fig.); nomadismo **2.** deviamento; distrazione; smarrimento (anche fig.) **3.** pl. vaneggiamento; (patol.) delirio.

wanderingly ['wɔndəriŋli], av. **1.** errando; da vagabondo; alla ventura **2.** in modo distratto, incoerente **3.** vaneggiando, delirando.

wane [wein], s. declino: on the —, in declino (anche fig.): his fame is on the —, la sua fama è in declino; the moon is on the —, la luna è calante, è in fase decrescente.

to **wane**, v.i. **1.** decrescere, calare (della luna) **2.** declinare; indebolirsi; decadere; deperire: his strength is slowly waning, sta perdendo lentamente le forze.

wangle ['wæŋgl], s. (sl.) maneggio, traffico, intrigo.

to **wangle**, v.t.i. (sl.) **1.** brigare, darsi da fare: he wangled the money out of his father, tanto fece che riuscì a far allentare i cordoni della borsa paterna **2.** presentare sotto la luce desiderata; accomodare, falsificare (fatti, ecc.).

wanion ['wɔnjən], s.: a — to, (arc.) un malanno a; with a (wild) —, con vendetta.

wanly ['wɔnli], av. pallidamente.

wanna ['wɔnə], (sl. amer.) per want to: I — go, voglio andare.

wanness ['wɔnnis], s. pallidezza, pallore.

wannish ['wɔniʃ], ag. piuttosto pallido, palliduccio.

want [wɔnt], s. **1.** mancanza, difetto; deficienza, scarsezza: — of imagination, mancanza d'immaginazione; his behaviour shows a — of tact, il suo comportamento rivela mancanza di tatto ‖ for — of a nail the shoe was lost, for — of a shoe the horse was lost, prov. per un punto Martin perdè la cappa **2.** bisogno, necessità; esigenza: they have but few wants, hanno poche esigenze; to be in — of sthg., avere bisogno di ql.co. **3.** povertà: to live in —, vivere nel bisogno, nell'indigenza ‖ to come to —, cadere in povertà.

to **want**, v.t.i. **1.** mancare (di); essere privo di, essere sprovvisto di: his book wants a page, al suo libro manca una pagina; it wants five minutes to twelve, mancano cinque minuti alle dodici; they — judgment, mancano di giudizio **2.** (II) aver bisogno di, richiedere: he badly wants rest, ha assoluto bisogno di riposo; this matter wants careful handling, questa faccenda richiede una certa delicatezza; will you — your car to-morrow?, ti occorrerà l'automobile domani?; you are wanted in the kitchen, c'è bisogno di te in cucina; your dress wants ironing (o to be ironed), il tuo vestito ha bisogno di essere stirato **3.** (IV, VI) volere, desiderare: I — him to come here at once, voglio che venga qui subito; I don't — her to do it, non voglio che lo faccia; she wants some tea, desidera del tè; we wanted it done without delay, volevamo che fosse fatto senza indugio; you — me to go there, but I don't — to, tu vuoi che io ci vada, ma io no; to — sthg. of s.o. (o from s.o.), voler ql.co. da qlcu. ‖ the more a man gets, the more he wants, prov. l'appetito vien mangiando **4.** abbisognare, essere nel bisogno: he must not be allowed to — in his old age, non bisogna lasciarlo in condizioni disagiate nella vecchiaia; he wants for nothing, non gli manca nulla **5.** essere necessario, dovere (al condiz.): it wants to be looked into with great care, dovrebbe essere esaminato con molta attenzione; you — to cut the bread thinner, il pane dovrebbe essere tagliato più sottile; you — to have your teeth seen to, dovresti farti curare i denti; you — to see a doctor at once, dovresti consultare il medico immediatamente.

wantage ['wɔntidʒ], s. (sl. comm. amer.) mancanza; deficit.

wanted ['wɔntid], ag. **1.** ricercato: — for murder, ricercato per omicidio **2.** richiesto: these goods are not — nowadays, non c'è richiesta di questi articoli oggigiorno ‖ —, cercasi (negli annunci economici).

wanter ['wɔntə*], s.c. **1.** chi manca di ql.co.; indigente **2.** (dial.) chi cerca moglie, marito.

wanting ['wɔntiŋ], ag. che manca, mancante: five pounds are — to make up the sum, mancano cinque sterline per completare la somma ‖ to be —, essere mancante; (fam.) essere povero di spirito: he is — in patience, manca di pazienza; his exam results were —, il risultato del suo esame deluse le aspettative.

wanting, prep. senza, in mancanza di: — money, everything becomes difficult, senza soldi tutto diventa difficile.

wantless ['wɔntlis], *ag.* senza bisogno; senza desideri.

wanton ['wɔntən], *ag.* **1.** licenzioso, sfrenato; impudico: — *thoughts*, pensieri impudichi; — *woman*, donna dissoluta **2.** pazzerello; gaio; capriccioso; irresponsabile: — *loves*, amori passeggeri; — *winds*, brezze capricciose **3.** vano; arbitrario: — *destruction*, distruzione inutile, senza scopo; — *insult*, insulto gratuito, arbitrario **4.** lussureggiante; selvatico: — *vegetation*, vegetazione lussureggiante || *s.c.* persona (specialmente donna) dissoluta || *to play the* —, folleggiare; (*arc.*) essere dissoluto.

to **wanton**, *v.i.* **1.** (*letter.*) scherzare, folleggiare: *the wind wantoned with the leaves*, il vento scherzava con le foglie **2.** (*rar.*) agire licenziosamente.

wantonly ['wɔntənli], *av.* **1.** lascivamente; impudicamente **2.** scherzosamente, capricciosamente **3.** senza scopo, inutilmente: *he did it* —, lo fece così per fare, senza motivo.

wantonness ['wɔntənnis], *s.* **1.** dissolutezza, libertinaggio **2.** leggerezza, allegria sfrenata; capriccio: *he did it out of sheer* —, lo fece senza riflettere, per leggerezza.

wap, *V.* whop.

wapiti ['wɔpiti], *s.* (*zool.*) vapiti.

war [wɔ:*], *s.* guerra (anche *fig.*): — *of the elements*, la furia degli elementi; — *of mines*, guerra con mine; — *of nerves*, guerra dei nervi; — *to the knife*, *fig.* lotta a coltello; *to be at* — *with a country*, essere in guerra con una nazione; *to be on a* — *footing*, essere sul piede di guerra; *to carry the* — *into the enemy's country*, portare la guerra in territorio nemico; passare all'attacco (anche *fig.*); *to declare* — (*up*)*on s.o.*, dichiarare guerra a qlcu. (anche *fig.*); *to go to* —, entrare in guerra, in conflitto; *to make* (o *to wage*) — (*on*, *against s.o.*), fare guerra (a qlcu.), guerreggiare (con qlcu.) || *War Department*, (*negli Stati Uniti*) Ministero della Guerra; *War Office*, (*in Gran Bretagna*) Ministero della Guerra; *War Secretary*, (*in Gran Bretagna*) Ministro della Guerra || *civil* —, guerra civile; *cold* —, guerra fredda; *holy* —, guerra santa; *hot* —, guerra guerreggiata; '*private* —, faida; (*pol.*) guerra privata || *the First World War*, la prima guerra mondiale, la grande guerra (1914-1918) || *trade of* —, professione del soldato || *you look as if you had been in the wars*, *fig.* hai l'aria malconcia || *to go to the wars*, (*arc.*) fare il soldato || *all's fair in love and* —, *prov.* tutto è lecito in amore e in guerra ☆ —*baby*, figlio di guerra; — —*balloon*, (*mil.*) pallone d'osservazione; — —*cloud*, nube, minaccia di guerra; — —*correspondent*, corrispondente di guerra; — —*cry*, grido di guerra; — —*dance*, danza di guerra; — — *fever*, psicosi di guerra; — —*gas*, (*mil.*) aggressivo chimico; — —*game*, « kriegspiel » (esercitazione tattica su mappa); — —*god*, dio della guerra; — —*horse*, (*arc.*) cavallo da battaglia: *he is an old* — —*horse*, *fig.* è un veterano; è un uomo che vanta molte battaglie politiche; — —*loan*, prestito di guerra; — —*lord*, (*gener. spreg.*) generalissimo; — —*memorial*, monumento ai caduti; — —*paint*, pitture di guerra (dei pellirosse); (*fam.*) abito di gala, alta tenuta; — —*song*, canzone di guerra; — —*whoop*, grido di guerra (dei pellirosse); — —*widow*, vedova di guerra; — —*worn*, danneggiato, devastato dalla guerra (di un paese); logorato dalla guerra (di una persona); — *zone*, zona militare.

to **war**, *pass. p.p.* **warred** [wɔ:d], *v.i.* far guerra, guerreggiare; lottare: *to* — *against*, lottare contro.

warble[1] ['wɔ:bl], *s.* **1.** trillo, gorgheggio, modulazione **2.** mormorio (di acque, voci).

to **warble**[1], *v.t.i.* **1.** trillare, gorgheggiare; modulare **2.** mormorare (di acque, voci).

warble[2], *s.* **1.** *gener. pl.* indurimento (prodotto sul dorso del cavallo dalla sella) **2.** (*vet.*) tumore (prodotto dalla larva del tafano) ☆ — *fly*, (*entom.*) larva di tafano.

warbler ['wɔ:blə*], *s.c.* chi emette trilli, gorgheggi || *s.* uccello canoro.

warbling ['wɔ:bliŋ], *ag.* melodioso || *s.* **1.** gorgheggio, canto **2.** mormorio (di acque, voci).

ward [wɔ:d], *s.c.* (*dir.*) minorenne; pupillo, pupilla || *s.* **1.** guardia, difesa: *to keep watch and* —, vigilare **2.** (*scherma*) guardia, parata **3.** sala, corsia (di ospedale); reparto, cella (di prigione) **4.** rione, circoscrizione comunale **5.** (*dir.*) tutela **6.** *pl.* seghettature di serratura (per il funzionamento di una determinata chiave) ☆ —*room*, (*mar.*) quadrato (degli ufficiali) || *condemned* —, cella della morte; *electoral* —, circoscrizione elettorale.

to **ward**, *v.t.i.* **1.** (*arc.*) proteggere; vigilare; stare in guardia **2.** *to* — *off*, parare (un colpo); schivare, evitare, parare, respingere.

warden[1] ['wɔ:dn], *s.c.* custode; guardiano, guardiana || *s.* **1.** (*rar.*) sentinella **2.** reggente; governatore; sovrintendente; rettore (di università); direttore (di scuola; prigione); superiore (di convento).

warden[2], *s.* pera (da cuocere) ☆ — *pie*, torta di pere.

wardenship ['wɔ:dnʃip], *s.* carica, ufficio di guardiano, di custode, di governatore, di rettore (di università), di direttore (di scuola, prigione), di superiore (di convento).

warder ['wɔ:də*], *s.* **1.** (*arc.*) sentinella **2.** carceriere, guardiano **3.** (*st.*) bastone del comando.

wardmote ['wɔ:dmout], *s.* giunta di circoscrizione (della City di Londra).

wardog ['wɔ:dɔg], *s.* **1.** cane usato in guerra **2.** *fig.* veterano **3.** (*amer.*) guerrafondaio.

Wardour Street ['wɔ:də,stri:t], *s.* Wardour Street (via di Londra già famosa per i negozi di antichità e ora per le sedi di compagnie cinematografiche) || *English*, inglese affettatamente arcaico.

wardress ['wɔ:dris], *s.* carceriera.

wardrobe ['wɔ:droub], *s.* **1.** armadio, guardaroba **2.** vestiti: *she has a very rich* —, ha molti vestiti ☆ — *dealer*, rivenditore di abiti usati; — *keeper*, guardarobiera (in collegi, ecc.); (*teat.*) costumista; — *trunk*, baule armadio.

wardship ['wɔ:dʃip], *s.* (*dir.*) tutela: *to be under* —, essere sotto tutela.

ware[1] [wɛə*], *ag.* (*arc.*) conscio; vigile, prudente.

to **ware**[1], *v.t. gener. all'imperat.* evitare, fare attenzione a: — *wire!*, attenti al filo spinato! || — *hawks!*, (*sl. malavita*) attenti alle guardie!.

ware[2], *s.* **1.** manufatto; vasellame **2.** merce, articoli **3.** *pl.* merci, mercanzie (anche *fig.*): *he can puff his wares*, sa vendere bene la sua merce ☆ *basket*, *china* —, articoli di vimini, di porcellana; *silver* —, argenteria; *Wedgwood* —, vasellame di Wedgwood.

ware[3], *s.* (*scoz. dial.*) alga marina (usata come concime).

to **ware**[4], *v.t.* (*scoz. dial.*) spendere, investire (denaro).

warehouse ['wɛəhaus], *s.* **1.** magazzino, deposito **2.** negozio ☆ *bonded* —, magazzino doganale.

to **warehouse** ['wɛəhauz], *v.t.* immagazzinare; depositare (in magazzino).

warehouseman, *pl.* **warehousemen** ['wɛəhausmən], *s.* **1.** magazziniere **2.** commerciante all'ingrosso.

warehousing ['wɛəhauziŋ], *s.* l'immagazzinare; il depositare in dogana ☆ — *charges*, spese di magazzinaggio.

wareless ['wɛəlis], *ag.* (*arc.*) incauto, imprudente.

warfare ['wɔ:fɛə*], *s.* guerra, stato di guerra ☆ *biological* —, guerra biologica; *ideological* —, guerra ideologica; *trench* —, guerra di trincea.

warfarer ['wɔ:,fɛərə*], *s.* combattente.

warfaring ['wɔ:,fɛəriŋ], *ag.* guerriero, bellicoso, aggressivo: *a* — *nation*, una nazione bellicosa, aggressiva.

warily ['wɛərili], *av.* avvedutamente, cautamente.

wariness ['wɛərinis], *s.* cautela, avvedutezza, circospezione.

warlike ['wɔ:laik], *ag.* guerriero, bellicoso, marziale; militare: *a* — *people*, un popolo guerriero; — *temper*, umore battagliero.

warlock ['wɔːlɔk], *s.* (*arc.*) stregone.

warlockry ['wɔːlɔkri], *s.* (*arc.*) stregoneria.

warm [wɔːm], *ag.* **1.** caldo; che tien caldo: — *clothes*, abiti caldi, che tengono caldo; *our room is rather —*, la nostra stanza è piuttosto calda; *this water is barely —*, quest'acqua è tiepida **2.** *fig.* cordiale, affettuoso; ardente: *a — heart*, un cuore caldo, ardente; *a — reception*, un'accoglienza calorosa; (*scherz.*) una accanita resistenza ‖ *he still has a — place in his heart for her*, le vuole ancora bene **3.** *fig.* animato, appassionato; eccitato, violento: *he always grows — in discussion*, si infiamma sempre nella discussione **4.** *fig.* difficile, pericoloso: *a — work*, una pericolosa occupazione ‖ *they'll make it — for you*, ti ostacoleranno, ti renderanno la vita difficile **5.** caldo (di colore): — *tints*, tinte calde **6.** (*fam.*) ricco, benestante: *he is quite —*, sta benone, non gli manca nulla **7.** fresco, recente (di traccia di selvaggina) ‖ *you're getting —*, (*fam.*) ci sei vicino, fuoco!, fuochino! (nei giuochi dei bambini) ☆ — *-blooded*, che ha sangue caldo; impulsivo, impetuoso; — *-hearted*, che ha cuore caldo; affettuoso, espansivo; — *-heartedly*, cordialmente, affettuosamente; — *-heartedness*, cordialità, affettuosità.

warm, *s.* (*fam.*) l'atto di scaldare, di scaldarsi: *I wish I could have a proper —*, come vorrei potermi scaldare una buona volta; *sit by the fire and have a —*, siedi accanto al fuoco e scaldati; *to give sthg. a —*, scaldare ql.co. (al fuoco).

to **warm**, *v.t.i.* **1.** scaldare, scaldarsi; riscaldare, riscaldarsi: *the sun has warmed the air*, il sole ha scaldato l'aria; *to — oneself at the fire, in the sun*, scaldarsi al fuoco, al sole; *to — one's hands*, scaldarsi le mani **2.** eccitare, eccitarsi; animare, animarsi; entusiasmare, entusiasmarsi: *he warmed as he got into the subject*, si animava man mano che si addentrava nell'argomento; *my heart warmed as I read of his success*, il mio cuore si entusiasmò leggendo del suo successo; *to — to one's work*, appassionarsi, entusiasmarsi al proprio lavoro ‖ *to — to s.o.*, aver simpatia per qlcu. **3.** (*sl.*) bastonare, picchiare ‖ *to — s.o.'s jacket*, prendere a bastonate qlcu. **4.** *to — up*, riscaldare, riscaldarsi; animare, animarsi: *the game was warming up*, la partita si animava; *the wine will — him up*, il vino lo riscalderà ‖ *to — up over a game*, entusiasmarsi a un giuoco.

warman, *pl.* **warmen** ['wɔːmən], *s.* (*rar.*) guerriero.

warmer ['wɔːmə*], *s.c.* (*poet.*) chi riscalda, chi accende ‖ *s.* riscaldatore ☆ *dish- —*, scaldapiatti; *foot —*, scaldapiedi.

warming ['wɔːmiŋ], *s.* **1.** riscaldamento: *let's have a good — before we go out*, scaldiamoci per bene prima di uscire **2.** (*sl.*) bastonatura: *to get a —*, essere bastonato ☆ — *pad*, (*elett.*) termoforo; — *pan*, scaldaletto; *fig.* sostituto (in ufficio, carica, ecc.) ‖ *house- —*, festa per l'inaugurazione di una casa.

warmly ['wɔːmli], *av.* **1.** in modo da riscaldare: *the child is — dressed*, il bambino è ben coperto **2.** *fig.* caldamente, con calore, cordialmente: *he spoke — of it*, mi parlò con entusiasmo della cosa; *we were — received*, fummo accolti con cordialità.

warmness ['wɔːmnis], *s.* **1.** caldo, calore (di fuoco, sole, ecc.) **2.** *fig.* calore; ardore; zelo; cordialità; calorosità: *in the — of the debate*, nel calore della discussione **3.** *fig.* risentimento, ira: *he replied with —*, rispose con risentimento **4.** (*pitt.*) intensità di colore.

warmonger ['wɔːˌmʌŋgə*], *s.* guerrafondaio.

warmongering ['wɔːˌmʌŋgəriŋ], *s.* propaganda di guerra.

warmth [wɔːmθ], *V.* **warmness**.

to **warn** [wɔːn], *v.t.* **1.** (IV) avvertire, mettere in guardia, ammonire: *he warned her not to do it again*, l'ammonì di non farlo un'altra volta; *I warned him against smoking so many cigarettes*, lo misi in guardia sul pericolo di fumar tanto; *they warned me of the danger*, mi avvertirono del pericolo **2.** dar l'allarme;

informare: *you should — the police*, dovresti informare la polizia **3.** (*mil.*) designare: *to — s.o. for guard*, designare qlcu. per la guardia **4.** (*dir. comm.*) diffidare **5.** *to — off*, intimare di allontanarsi a, invitare a tenersi lontano: *he has been warned off*, è stato invitato ad allontanarsi.

warner ['wɔːnə*], *s.c.* chi avverte ‖ *s.* (*mec.*) segnale d'allarme.

warning ['wɔːniŋ], *ag.* che avverte, ammonisce: *a — look*, uno sguardo di avvertimento ‖ *s.* **1.** ammonimento, avvertimento: *he gave — of danger*, avvertì del pericolo; *let this be a — to them*, che questo serva loro di lezione **2.** avviso, notifica: *to send a — to the police*, avvisare la polizia **3.** (*dir. comm.*) diffida **4.** preavviso di licenziamento: *I'll give the servant a week's —*, darò gli otto giorni al domestico ☆ — *light*, spia luminosa ‖ *air-raid —*, allarme aereo.

warningly ['wɔːniŋli], *av.* in tono premonitore, di ammonimento, di avvertimento.

warp [wɔːp], *s.* **1.** (*ind. tessile*) ordito **2.** deformazione, curvatura (di legname) **3.** *fig.* alterazione (della mente); inclinazione viziosa **4.** (*mar.*) (cavo da) tonneggio **5.** deposito alluvionale ☆ — *beam*, (*ind. tessile*) subbio dell'ordito; — *chain*, (*ind. tessile*) catena d'ordito ‖ *full —*, (*ind. tessile*) catena piena; *half —*, (*ind. tessile*) mezza catena.

to **warp**, *v.t.i.* **1.** (*ind. tessile*) ordire **2.** piegare, piegarsi; curvare, curvarsi (di legname) **3.** *fig.* deformare, deformarsi; guastare, guastarsi; alterare, alterarsi (di mente, ecc.): *don't — the meaning of what I have said*, non falsare il senso di ciò che ho detto; *his life had been warped by his unhappy childhood*, la sua vita era stata rovinata da un'infanzia infelice **4.** (*mar.*) tonneggiare, tonneggiarsi; rimorchiare **5.** bonificare (terre) coprendole di depositi alluvionali **6.** (*aer.*) svergolare.

warpath ['wɔːpɑːθ], *s.* sentiero di guerra (dei pellirosse): *to be on the —*, *fig.* essere sul sentiero di guerra.

warped [wɔːpt], *ag.* **1.** curvato, piegato (di legno) **2.** *fig.* deformato, alterato, corrotto: *everything seemed evil to his — mind*, tutto sembrava peccaminoso alla sua mente alterata **3.** bonificato con deposito alluvionale (di terreno) **4.** (*aer.*) svergolato.

warper ['wɔːpə*], *s.c.* orditore, orditrice.

warping ['wɔːpiŋ], *s.* **1.** (*ind. tessile*) orditura **2.** curvatura (del legname); (*metal.*) deformazione **3.** *fig.* deformazione, alterazione; perversione **4.** (*mar.*) tonneggio **5.** bonifica per mezzo di deposito alluvionale **6.** (*aer.*) svergolamento ☆ — *engine*, (*mar.*) macchina di tonneggio; — *machine* (o — *mill*), (*ind. tessile*) orditoio.

warrant ['wɔrənt], *s.* **1.** garanzia; garante: *I will your —*, io vi sarò garante; *you have no — for such a statement*, non hai garanzia per una tale affermazione **2.** (*dir.*) mandato, autorizzazione, ordine: *a — is out against this man*, vi è un mandato di cattura per quest'uomo ‖ — *of attorney*, procura **3.** diritto, autorizzazione: *what — have you to say that?*, che diritto avete di dire ciò? **4.** (*comm.*) certificato, ordine: — *for delivery*, ordine di consegna ☆ — *officer*, (*mar.*) capocarico; (*mil.*) sergente maggiore ‖ *death —*, ordine di esecuzione; *distress —*, ordine di sequestro; *dock —*, (*comm.*) certificato di deposito; *search —*, ordine di perquisizione; *stock —*, certificato di azione al portatore.

to **warrant**, *v.t.* **1.** garantire, assicurare, attestare: *I — him a perfectly honest man*, garantisco che è un uomo onestissimo; *she won't do it again, I'll — you!*, non lo farà più, ve lo garantisco io! **2.** (*dir.*) autorizzare **3.** giustificare: *this could — his behaviour*, questo potrebbe giustificare il suo comportamento.

warrantable ['wɔrəntəbl], *ag.* **1.** giustificabile **2.** legittimo **3.** autorizzato, permesso.

warrantableness ['wɔrəntəblnis], *s.* **1.** giustificabilità **2.** legittimità.

warrantably ['worəntəbli], *av.* **1.** legittimamente **2.** in modo giustificabile.

warranted ['worəntid], *ag.* **1.** garantito: — *real silk*, (*comm.*) seta pura garantita **2.** (*dir.*) autorizzato: *I am — in assuming that...*, sono autorizzato a pensare che....

warrantee [,worən'ti:], *s.c.* (*dir.*) **1.** chi riceve una garanzia **2.** persona colpita da mandato di cattura.

warranter ['worəntə*], **warrantor** ['worənto:*], *s.* mallevadore; garante.

warranty ['worənti], *s.* **1.** (*comm.*) garanzia **2.** autorizzazione; giustificazione.

warren ['worin], *s.* conigliera; gabbia, recinto (per conigli) || *as thick as rabbits in a —*, *fig.* moltissimi, fitti come formiche in un formicaio.

warring ['wo:riŋ], *ag.* in stato di guerra; contendente; contrastante: — *nations*, nazioni contendenti; — *interests*, *principles*, interessi, principi contrastanti, in opposizione.

warrior ['woriə*], *s.* (*letter.*) guerriero || *the Unknown Warrior*, il Milite Ignoto ☆ — *ants*, (*entom.*) formiche guerriere.

Warsaw ['wo:so:], *no.pr.* (*geog.*) Varsavia.

warship ['wo:-ʃip], *s.* nave da guerra.

wart [wo:t], *s.* **1.** escrescenza, porro, verruca; bitorzolo || *to paint s.o. with his warts*, (*fam.*) fare il ritratto fedele di qlcu. **2.** protuberanza (di un tronco) ☆ — *-hog*, (*zool.*) facocero.

wartime ['wo:taim], *s.* tempo di guerra.

warty ['wo:ti], *ag.* **1.** pieno di escrescenze, verrucoso; bitorzoluto **2.** simile a porro, verruca.

wary ['wεəri], *ag.* prudente, cauto, circospetto; diffidente: *they are — of strangers*, diffidano dei forestieri; *you ought to be —*, dovresti essere cauto, usar prudenza || *to keep a — eye on*, diffidare di.

was [woz (*forma forte*), wəz, wz (*forme deboli*)], 1ª, 3ª *persona sing. pass.* di to **be**.

wash[1] [woʃ], *s.* **1.** lavatura, lavaggio; abluzione: *give him a good —*, dagli una bella lavata; *I'd like to have a —*, vorrei darmi una lavatina || *to have a — and brush-up*, farsi un po' di toilette **2.** bucato || *the —*, bucato in lavanderia: *has the — come in?*, hanno riportato il bucato?; *send it to the —*, mandalo in lavanderia || *it will all come out in the —*, (*fam.*) alla fine tutto si aggiusterà **3.** lozione; liquido cosmetico **4.** sciabordio, sciacquio: *the — of the waves*, lo sciacquio delle onde **5.** depositi alluvionali; limo, detriti **6.** broda, brodaglia (per maiali); risciacquatura di piatti: *this coffee is a mere —*, questo caffè è acqua sporca **7.** mano di colore, coloritura (per pareti, metalli, ecc.); (*pitt.*) acquarello, guazzo **8.** pala di remo **9.** scia (di nave, aereo).

to **wash**[1], *v.t.i.* **1.** lavare, lavarsi: — *your face*, lavati la faccia; *you have not washed before lunch*, non ti sei lavato prima di colazione; *to — (oneself)*, lavarsi || *to — one's hands of sthg.*, *fig.* lavarsi le mani, declinare ogni responsabilità riguardo a ql.co. **2.** fare il bucato: *to — a few articles*, fare un bucatino || *to — for s.o.*, fare la lavandaia: *she washes for a living*, fa la lavandaia di mestiere **3.** essere lavabile: *this fabric won't —*, questo tessuto non è lavabile; *"Will this material —?"*, *"It washes very well"*, « Questa stoffa è lavabile? », « Resiste benissimo alla lavatura » || *that story won't —*, (*fam.*) questa non la bevo, non ci credo **4.** lavare (metalli); depurare (gas) **5.** tinteggiare (pareti) **6.** galvanizzare, metallizzare **7.** bagnare, lambire; spazzare (di mare, fiume, ecc.): *the cliff is washed by the sea*, la scogliera è lambita dal mare; *the waves were washing the pier*, le onde spazzavano il molo **8.** gettare, trasportare: *a wave washed him ashore*, un'ondata lo gettò sulla riva **9.** (*poet.*) bagnare, inumidire, umettare: *flowers washed with dew*, fiori imperlati di rugiada **10.** *to — away*, lavar via, eliminare (una macchia); *fig.* purificare; corrodere; trascinar via: *the bank had been washed away in places*, la sponda era stata qua e là erosa dalle acque; *the tide will*

— *your boat away if you leave it there*, la marea trascinerà via la tua barca se la lasci là **11.** *to — down*, lavare con getti d'acqua; (*fam.*) annaffiare cibo: *he washed down the walls of his house, his car, the kitchen floor*, ha dato una energica lavata ai muri della casa, alla sua auto, al pavimento di cucina; *to — down one's dinner with a glass of wine*, annaffiare il proprio pranzo con un bicchiere di vino **12.** *to — off*, togliere, eliminare lavando: *I'll — it off*, laverò via la macchia **13.** *to — out*, eliminare una macchia (anche *fig.*); sbiadire: *to — out an insult in blood*, lavare un affronto col sangue **14.** *to — up*, rigovernare (stoviglie).

wash[1], (*nei composti*): — *-ball*, saponetta; — *-basin* (o — *-stand*), lavabo, lavandino; — *-board*, asse per lavare; (*mar.*) battente di boccaporto; (*edil.*) zoccolo di legno; (*chim.*) spruzzetta; — *-bottle*, (*chim.*) spruzzetta; — *-cloth*, panno per lavare i piatti; (*amer.*) pezzuola per lavarsi; — *-day*, (*amer.*) giorno di bucato; — *-drawing*, (*pitt.*) tempera; — *-fountain*, lavabo, lavatoio circolare; — *-house*, lavanderia, lavatoio; — *-in*, (*aer.*) svergolamento positivo; — *-leather*, pelle scamosciata lavabile, per lavare; — *-gloves*, guanti lavabili; — *-out*, (*geol.*) erosione; smagnetizzazione di nastro magnetico; (*aer.*) svergolamento negativo; *fig.* completo fallimento; — *sale*, (*sl. amer.*) vendita fittizia (in Borsa); — *-trough*, truogolo; bacino di lavaggio (di sabbie aurifere); — *-tub*, mastello, tinozza per bucato; — *-up*, lavaggio; — *-water*, acqua di lavaggio || *colour —*, tinteggiatura per pareti; *eye- —*, (*farm.*) collirio; *fig.* polvere negli occhi; sciocchezza; *hair- —*, lozione per capelli; *mouth- —* (o *throat- —*), colluttorio, sciacquo, gargarismo; *stomach —*, lavanda gastrica.

Wash[2] **(the)**, *no.pr.* (*geog.*) il Wash (grande baia lagunare che divide il Lincolnshire dal Norfolk).

washable ['woʃəbl], *ag.* lavabile.

washed [woʃt], *ag.* **1.** lavato **2.** laminato, ricoperto di lamine ☆ — *-out*, scialbo, sbiadito, slavato; (*fam.*) privo di energia: — *-out complexion*, colorito scialbo; — *-out red*, rossastro, rosso sbiadito.

washer ['woʃə*], *s.c.* lavandaio, lavandaia || *s.1.* (*mec.*) lavatrice **2.** (*mec.*) rondella, ranella, rosetta **3.** (*chim.*) gorgogliatore di lavaggio ☆ — *lock*, (*mec.*) bloccaggio mediante rondella || *air- —*, (*ind.*) depuratore d'aria; *dish —*, lavastoviglie; *distance —*, (*mec.*) spessore; *gold —*, addetto al lavaggio di sabbie aurifere; *open —*, (*mec.*) rondella spaccata; *round —*, (*mec.*) rondella circolare; *screw —*, (*miner.*) lavatrice a spirale; *tab —*, (*mec.*) rondella di sicurezza.

washerman, *pl.* **washermen** ['woʃəmən], *s.* **1.** lavandaio **2.** (*miner.*) addetto al lavaggio di minerali.

washerwoman ['woʃə,wumən], *pl.* **washerwomen** ['woʃə,wimin], *s.* lavandaia.

washily ['woʃili], *av.* **1.** insipidamente (di cibo) **2.** fiaccamente (di stile) **3.** slavatamente (di colore).

washiness ['woʃinis], *s.* **1.** scipitezza (di cibo) **2.** fiacchezza (di stile) **3.** smortezza (di colore).

washing ['woʃiŋ], *ag.* **1.** che lava, usato per lavare **2.** lavabile || *s.* **1.** lavatura, lavaggio; bucato: *children need frequent —*, i bambini hanno spesso bisogno di essere lavati; *to hang out the — to dry*, stendere il bucato ad asciugare **2.** risciacquatura: — *of dishes*, risciacquatura di piatti **3.** (*ind.*) depurazione **4.** (*miner.*) lavaggio ☆ — *-board*, asse per lavare; — *boiler*, (*ind. tessile*) caldaia per lavaggio; — *-day*, giorno di bucato; — *flask*, (*chim.*) spruzzetta; — *-machine*, lavatrice: *stone —machine*, (*edil.*) lavatrice per pietrame; — *-mill*, (*ind.*) depuratore; — *pan*, (*miner.*) vaschetta di lavaggio; — *-powder*, detersivo; — *room*, (*ind.*) sala di depurazione; — *-soda*, soda per lavare; — *tub*, mastello; — *-up*, rigovernatura (di piatti) || *immersion —*, (*ind.*) lavaggio ad immersione.

washroom ['woʃru:m], *s.* (*amer.*) **1.** lavanderia **2.** gabinetto.

washy ['woʃi], *ag.* **1.** insipido, acquoso (di cibo) **2.** fiacco (di stile) **3.** scialbo, smorto (di colore).

wasn't ['wɔznt], *contr.* di *was not*.

wasp [wɔsp], *s.* vespa (anche *fig.*) ☆ — *-bee*, (*entom.*) nomada; — ('*s*) *nest*, vespaio (anche *fig.*); — *-waisted*, dal vitino di vespa.

waspish ['wɔspiʃ], *ag.* pungente, stizzoso, bisbetico.

waspishly ['wɔspiʃli], *av.* in modo irascibile, irritabile.

waspishness ['wɔspiʃnis], *s.* irascibilità, irritabilità.

wassail ['wɔseil], *s.* (*arc.*) **1.** brindisi: —*!*, alla tua salute! **2.** festa, gozzoviglia **3.** « wassail » (bevanda di birra con spezie, zucchero, ecc. che si beveva a Natale, Epifania) ☆ — *-bowl*, — *-cup*, — *-horn*, recipiente, coppa, corno usati per il « wassail ».

to wassail, *v.i.* (*arc.*) gozzovigliare, fare baldoria.

wast [wɔst (*forma forte*), wəst (*forma debole*)], 2ª *persona sing. pass.* (*arc. poet.*) di **to be**.

waste [weist], *ag.* **1.** deserto, desolato, arido, incolto, sterile (di terreno): *to lie* —, rimanere incolto ‖ *to lay* —, (*arc.*) devastare, saccheggiare **2.** inutile, di scarto ‖ *s.* **1.** sciupio, spreco: *the* — *was terrific*, lo sciupio era spaventoso; *it was a sheer* — *of energy*, non era altro che uno spreco di energia; *so much water going to* —*!*, tanta acqua sprecata!; *what a* — *of time!*, quanto tempo sprecato!; *to cut cloth to* —, sciupare della stoffa (nel tagliare) ‖ *wilful* — *makes woeful want*, *prov.* chi spreca deliberatamente finisce nella miseria più nera **2.** scarto, rifiuto: *we throw all the* — *away*, eliminiamo tutto lo scarto; *with the new processing there isn't so much* —, con il nuovo sistema di lavorazione non c'è molto scarto **3.** deserto, distesa sterile; terreno incolto: *the wastes of Africa*, il deserto africano; *they have let their garden go to* —, hanno lasciato inselvatichire il giardino ‖ *a* — *of waters*, una immensa distesa di acqua ☆ — *-basket*, — *-paper basket*, cestino per la carta straccia, cestino per rifiuti; — *-book*, (*comm.*) brogliaccio; — *-paper*, carta straccia; — *-pipe*, tubazione di scarico; — *product*, rifiuti, (prodotti di) scarto; — *water*, acque di scolo ‖ *cotton* —, cascame di cotone; *silk* —, cascame di seta; *top* —, cascame di pettinato; *wool* —, cascame di lana.

to waste, *v.t.i.* **1.** sciupare, sprecare; sperperare scialacquare: *don't* — *any money on that business*, non sprecare denaro in quell'affare; *he is wasted in that job*, è sprecato in quell'impiego, fa un lavoro inferiore alle sue capacità; *he wasted his life on that useless research*, sciupò, sprecò la vita in quell'inutile ricerca; *the joke was wasted on them*, non capirono lo scherzo; *she is wasting her chance*, si lascia sfuggire una buona occasione; *you are wasting your breath*, sprechi il fiato ‖ — *not, want not*, *prov.* chi risparmia guadagna **2.** logorarsi, sciuparsi, consumarsi: *he was wasting away for lack of food*, deperiva sempre più per mancanza di cibo ‖ *to* — *away to skin and bone*, (*fam.*) ridursi a pelle e ossa **3.** (*dir.*) lasciar deteriorare (proprietà, ecc.): *he was fined for letting the estate* —, dovette pagare una grossa multa per aver trascurato la proprietà.

wasteful ['weistful], *ag.* **1.** rovinoso, funesto **2.** prodigo, dissipatore, spendereccio: *the* — *administration of past governments*, la rovinosa amministrazione dei passati governi; *all* — *expenditure must be avoided*, bisogna eliminare tutte le spese superflue; *he is a* — *man*, spende e spande; *she has* — *habits*, ha delle abitudini piuttosto costose, è una sciupona; ha le mani bucate.

wastefully ['weistfuli], *av.* **1.** prodigalmente, da dissipatore **2.** rovinosamente.

wastefulness ['weistfulnis], *s.* sciupio; sperpero.

waster ['weistə*], *s.c.* **1.** dissipatore, dissipatrice **2.** (*sl.*) persona incapace, buono a nulla, buona a nulla ‖ *s.* (*metal.*) pezzo di scarto.

wasting ['weistiŋ], *ag.* **1.** logorante, che consuma; rovinoso: — *care*, preoccupazione assillante; — *disease*, malattia che mina l'organismo; (*arc.*) mal sottile; tisi **2.** che diminuisce: *a* — *fortune*, un patrimonio che va in fumo ‖ *s.* **1.** sciupio, spreco **2.** devastazione **3.** deperimento, consunzione.

wastrel ['weistrəl], *s.* **1.** buono a nulla; fannullone; discolo **2.** sprecone **3.** fanciullo abbandonato, trovatello **4.** (*ind.*) pezzo di scarto.

watch [wɔtʃ], *s.* **1.** orologio a molla (da polso, tasca): *to use a* — *as a compass*, orientarsi con un orologio **2.** (*rar.*) veglia: *in the watches of the night*, nelle veglie della notte, nelle ore di veglia ‖ *to pass as a* — *in the night*, (*fam.*) essere ben presto dimenticato **3.** guardia, vigilanza; sorveglianza, attenzione: *a good* —, una buona guardia ‖ *to be on the* —, stare in guardia, all'erta; essere in attesa: *be on the* —*!*, apri l'occhio! ‖ *to keep* —, montare la guardia; *to keep* (*a*) *good* (o *close*) —, fare buona guardia; *to keep a close* — *on* (o *over*) *s.o.*, sorvegliare qlcu. da vicino ‖ *to set a* — *on s.o.*, far sorvegliare qlcu. **4.** (*st.*) guardia, sentinella, scolta: *the constables of the* —, la ronda notturna **5.** (*st.*) vigilia (uno dei periodi in cui era divisa la notte) **6.** (*mar.*) quarto: *the officer of the* —, l'ufficiale di quarto; *to be on* —, essere di quarto; *to set the watches*, regolare i quarti ☆ — *chain*, catena di orologio; — *-committee*, comitato addetto alla supervisione dei servizi di polizia e illuminazione; — *-dog*, cane da guardia; — *-fire*, fuoco di bivacco; — *-glass*, vetro di orologio; — *-key*, chiave da orologio; rimontorio; — *-night*, (*eccl.*) ufficio (dell'ultima notte dell'anno); — *-post*, (*mil.*) posto di guardia; corpo di guardia; — *spring*, molla d'orologio; — *-tower*, torre d'osservazione; garitta ‖ *first* —, (*mar.*) primo turno di guardia; *middle* —, (*mar.*) secondo turno di guardia; *port* —, (*mar.*) guardia di babordo; *starboard* —, (*mar.*) guardia di tribordo; *stop-* —, cronometro.

to watch, *v.t.i.* **1.** vegliare, stare svegli: *I watched with him all night*, ho vegliato tutta la notte al suo capezzale **2.** stare in guardia, all'erta; vigilare su, sorvegliare ‖ — *for the opportunity to occur*, non lasciarti sfuggire l'occasione ‖ — *out*, (*fam.*) state attento ‖ *to* — *over s.o., sthg.*, badare a, vigilare su qlcu., ql.co. **3.** (I, V) osservare, guardare; tenere d'occhio: *we shall have to* — *the expenses*, dovremo badare a non spendere troppo; *to* — *the course of events*, osservare il corso degli avvenimenti; *to have s.o. watched*, far tenere d'occhio, far sorvegliare qlcu. ‖ — *your step!*, (*fam. amer.*) siate prudenti! agite con circospezione! ‖ *to* — *after s.o.*, (*rar.*) seguire qlcu. con lo sguardo ‖ *to* — *a case*, (*dir.*) difendere gli interessi di qlcu. (in una causa) ‖ *watched pot never boils*, *prov.* il desiderio rende lunga l'attesa **4.** aspettare, attendere ‖ *to* — *one's time*, aspettare il momento opportuno.

watcher ['wɔtʃə*], *s.c.* **1.** chi veglia **2.** spettatore, spettatrice **3.** sorvegliante; sentinella ☆ *bird* —, ornitologo; *night* —, guardiano notturno.

watchful ['wɔtʃful], *ag.* **1.** vigilante, attento ‖ *to keep a* — *eye on sthg., s.o.*, sorvegliare con attenzione ql.co., qlcu. **2.** cauto, guardingo **3.** (*arc.*) insonne: — *nights*, notti insonni.

watchfulness ['wɔtʃfulnis], *s.* **1.** vigilanza, sorveglianza **2.** circospezione, cautela.

watching ['wɔtʃiŋ], *s.* **1.** osservazione: *bird* — *is very popular in England*, molti si dedicano all'osservazione degli uccelli in Inghilterra **2.** vigilanza, sorveglianza: *that child needs* — (*over*), quel bambino va sorvegliato **3.** veglia ☆ — *candle*, cero acceso a una veglia funebre.

watchman, *pl.* **watchmen** ['wɔtʃmən], *s.* **1.** (*arc.*) sentinella **2.** guardia notturna; guardiano; sorvegliante ☆ *track* —, (*ferr.*) guardalinee, cantoniere.

watchword ['wɔtʃwə:d], *s.* parola d'ordine.

water ['wɔ:tə*], *s.* **1.** acqua: *cold* —, acqua fredda; *hot* —, acqua bollente; *running hot and cold* —, acqua corrente calda e fredda ‖ *to get into hot* —, (*fam.*) cacciarsi nei guai ‖ *to hold* —, *fig.* essere logico, dimostrabile (di teoria, ecc.) ‖ *to spend money like* —, scialacquare, sperperare denaro ‖ *to take in* —, (*mar.*) fare acqua; imbarcare un colpo di mare ‖ *to throw cold* — *on s.o.*, (*fam.*) scoraggiare qlcu. **2.** distesa d'acqua;

acque (di mare, fiume, lago, ecc.): *the waters of the Danube*, le acque del Danubio ‖ *by* —, per via d'acqua ‖ *in smooth* —, *fig.* in acque tranquille ‖ *like a fish ou of* —, come un pesce fuor d'acqua ‖ *on the* —, in mare ‖ *under* —, sott'acqua ‖ *written in* —, scritto sull'acqua, inconsistente ‖ *to be in deep waters, fig.* essere in cattive acque ‖ *to cast one's bread upon the waters, fig.* far del bene senza aspettarsi ricompensa ‖ *to keep one's head above* —, tenersi a galla (anche *fig.*) ‖ *to make a hole in the* —, (*sl.*) annegarsi ‖ *to take the* —, gettarsi a nuoto; imbarcarsi; (*amer. fig.*) abbandonare le proprie posizioni; essere varato (di nave) ‖ *still waters run deep, prov.* le acque chete rovinano i ponti 3. *gener. pl.* acque termali: *to drink the waters*, far la cura di, bere acque termali 4. acqua (umore di corpo animale): — *on the brain*, (*patol.*) idrocefalia; — *on the knee*, (*patol.*) sinovite ‖ *to bring the* — *to one's eyes*, far venire le lacrime agli occhi; *to bring the* — *to one's mouth*, far venire l'acquolina in bocca ‖ *to make* —, orinare 5. trasparenza; acqua (di diamante, ecc.): *the* — *of a pearl*, la trasparenza di una perla ‖ *of the first* —, della più bell'acqua (anche *fig.*).

to water, *v.t.i.* **1.** innaffiare; irrigare, bagnare, (contrade, campi, regioni): *the Lombard plain is watered by the Po*, la pianura lombarda è bagnata dal Po **2.** annacquare (vino, latte, ecc.); diluire: *to* — *one's wine*, mettere acqua nel vino; *to* — *a solution*, (*chim.*) diluire una soluzione **3.** abbeverare, abbeverarsi **4.** rifornire, rifornirsi, approvvigionarsi d'acqua **5.** secernere (lacrime, saliva, ecc.): *my left eye is watering*, mi lacrima l'occhio sinistro ‖ *it makes one's mouth* —, fa venire l'acquolina in bocca **6.** *to* — *the capital*, (*comm.*) emettere nuove azioni (aumentando il capitale nominale) **7.** (*ind. tessile*) marezzare (seta) **8.** *to* — **down**, diluire; *fig.* attenuare (fatti, ecc.): *to* — *down a statement*, attenuare un'affermazione.

water, (*nei composti*): — -*bag*, otre; — -*bailiff*, guardapesca; — -*bath*, (*ind. chim.*) bagnomaria; — -*bearer*, portatore d'acqua; — -*bed*, materasso di gomma contenente acqua (per ammalati); — -*bird*, uccello acquatico; — -*biscuit* (o — -*cracker*), « cracker », galletta; — -*boa*, (*zool.*) anaconda; — -*boatman*, (*entom.*) idrometra; — -*borne*, trasportato via acqua (di merci); propagato da acqua inquinata (di malattia); — -*bottle*, bottiglia per acqua; borraccia; — -*buffalo*, bufalo indiano; — -*butt*, botte per acqua piovana; — -*carriage*, trasporto di merci via acqua; — -*cart*, (*mec.*) annaffiatrice; — -*cell*, cella acquifera (di stomaco di cammello); — -*chestnut*, (*bot.*) trapa, castagna d'acqua; — -*clarification*, (*ind.*) decantazione dell'acqua; — -*clock*, clessidra ad acqua; — -*closet*, gabinetto a serbatoio d'acqua; — -*colour*, acquerello (colore, dipinto); — -*colourist*, acquerellista; — -*cooler*, raffreddatore di acqua; — -*craft*, imbarcazione, imbarcazioni; — -*crane*, gru idraulica; — -*cress*, (*bot.*) crescione; — -*cure*, idroterapia; — -*diviner* (o — -*finder*), rabdomante; — -*dog*, cane addestrato alla caccia in canneto, in palude; *fig.* bravo nuotatore; marinaio; — -*drain*, scarico d'acqua; — -*drinker*, astemio; — -*drop*, goccia d'acqua; lacrima; — -*engine*, macchina idraulica; motore ad acqua; — -*equivalent*, (*fis.*) equivalente in acqua; capacità termica; — -*flood*, inondazione; — -*fly*, insetto acquatico; — -*fowl*, uccelli acquatici; — -*front*, banchina; fronte del porto; — -*gate*, cateratta, chiusa; — -*gauge*, idrometro; — -*glass*, livello (di boiler); idroscopio; (*chim.*) tetrasilicato di sodio; — -*hammer*, colpo d'ariete; — -*jacket*, (*mec.*) camicia d'acqua; — -*jug* (o — -*pot*), brocca per acqua; — -*level*, livello dell'acqua; (*mec.*) livella ad acqua; (*mar.*) linea di galleggiamento, di immersione; — -*lily*, (*bot.*) ninfea; — -*line*, (*mar.*) livello, linea di galleggiamento, linea di immersione; (*ind. cartaria*) linea di filigrana; — -*logged*, non governabile (di imbarcazione, per aver imbarcato troppa acqua): saturo di acqua; — -*main*, conduttura d'acqua, acquedotto; — -*meadow*, (*agr.*) marcita; — -*melon*,

cocomero, anguria; — -*mill*, mulino ad acqua; — -*motor*, motore ad acqua, turbina; — -*nymph*, (*mit.*) naiade; — -*pipe*, conduttura d'acqua; — -*plane*, piano di galleggiamento, pelo d'acqua; (*aer.*) idrovolante; — -*polo*, (*spor.*) pallanuoto; — -*power*, forza idrica, energia idraulica; carbone bianco: — -*power station*, centrale idroelettrica; — -*pox*, varicella; — -*pump*, pompa ad acqua; — -*rat*, topo di fogna; marinaio; pirata; — -*rate*, tariffa per il consumo dell'acqua; — -*rights*, diritto di attingere acqua; — -*seal*, chiusura idraulica; — -*skiing*, (*spor.*) sci nautico; — -*skin*, otre; — -*softener*, (*chim.*) depuratore d'acqua; — -*spout*, tromba marina; (*edil.*) pluviale; — -*stained*, macchiato dall'umidità; tinteggiato ad acqua; — -*supply*, provvista, approvvigionamento d'acqua; — -*surface*, superficie dell'acqua; — -*system*, impianto idrico; — -*table*, (*arch.*) marcapiano sporgente; (*geol.*) superficie freatica; — -*tower*, torre serbatoio; — -*waving*, (*ind. tessile*) marezzatura; messa in piega (dei capelli); — -*wheel*, (*mec.*) turbina idraulica; — -*wings*, salvagente (per imparare a nuotare); — -*worn*, liscio, levigato; eroso dall'acqua ‖ *barley-* —, orzata; *drinking-* —, acqua potabile; *fresh-* —, acqua dolce; *hard* —, acqua dura; *heavy* —, (*fis.*) acqua pesante; *high-* —, alta marea; *hot* — *bottle*, borsa dell'acqua calda; *lavender -* —, (acqua di) lavanda; *low-* —, bassa marea; *mineral* —, acqua minerale; bibita gassata; *salt-* —, acqua di mare; *soda-* —, acqua di seltz; *soft* —, acqua leggera; *strong waters*, acquavite; *table-* —, acqua da tavola; *tonic* —, acqua brillante.

waterage ['wɔːtəridʒ], *s.* **1.** trasporto via acqua **2.** costo, prezzo di trasporto via acqua.

watercourse ['wɔːtəkɔːs], *s.* **1.** corso d'acqua; fiume; ruscello **2.** canale.

watered ['wɔːtəd], *ag.* **1.** innaffiato; irrigato, bagnato **2.** annacquato; diluito (anche *fig.*) **3.** (*ind. tessile*) marezzato.

waterer ['wɔːtərə*], *s.c.* annaffiatore, annaffiatrice ‖ *s.* chi conduce le bestie all'abbeverata.

waterfall ['wɔːtəfɔːl], *s.* cascata; cateratta.

wateriness ['wɔːtərinis], *s.* **1.** acquosità; (*med.*) sierosità **2.** (*fam.*) scipitezza (di cibo, stile, argomento): *the* — *of his style*, il suo stile scipito.

watering ['wɔːtəriŋ], *s.* **1.** annaffiamento; bagnatura; irrigazione **2.** annacquamento; diluizione **3.** l'abbeverare, l'abbeverarsi **4.** rifornimento d'acqua (di navi, ecc.) **5.** secrezione (di lacrime, saliva, ecc.) **6.** (*ind. tessile*) marezzatura; marezzo ☆ — -*can* (o — -*pot*), annaffiatoio; — -*cart*, carro irrigatore; — -*place*, abbeveratoio; luogo di rifornimento d'acqua; stazione termale, balneare; — -*trough*, abbeveratoio.

waterish ['wɔːtəriʃ], *ag.* **1.** acquoso, acqueo, umido **2.** acquoso, insipido, scipito.

waterless ['wɔːtəlis], *ag.* senz'acqua; arido.

to waterlog ['wɔːtəlɔg], *pass.p.p.* **waterlogged** ['wɔːtəlɔgd], *v.t.* **1.** saturare, imbevere (terreno, legname, imbarcazione, ecc.) **2.** rendere ingovernabile (un'imbarcazione, riempiendola d'acqua).

Waterloo [ˌwɔːtəˈluː], *come attributivo* ['wɔːtəluː], *no.pr.* (*geog.*) Waterloo ‖ — *Bridge*, il ponte di Waterloo ‖ *to meet one's* —, subire una disfatta, uno scacco decisivo.

waterman, *pl.* **watermen** ['wɔːtəmən], *s.* **1.** barcaiolo; traghettatore; battelliere **2.** esperto rematore.

watermark ['wɔːtəmɑːk], *s.* **1.** filigrana (nella carta) **2.** indicatore di livello **3.** livello d'acqua **4.** (*mar.*) linea d'immersione.

to watermark, *v.t.* (*ind. cartaria*) filigranare.

waterproof ['wɔːtəpruːf], *ag.s.* impermeabile.

to waterproof, *v.t.* impermeabilizzare.

waterquake ['wɔːtəkweik], *s.* maremoto.

watershed ['wɔːtəʃed], *s.* **1.** spartiacque **2.** bacino idrografico.

watertight ['wɔːtətait], *ag.* stagno, impermeabile, a

tenuta d'acqua ☆ — *compartment*, compartimento stagno.

waterworks ['wɔ:təwə:ks], *s.pl.* **1.** impianto idrico, acquedotto **2.** giochi, scherzi d'acqua (di fontana) ‖ *to turn on the* —, (*sl.*) piangere come una fontana; far pipì.

watery ['wɔ:təri], *ag.* **1.** acquoso, umido, acquitrinoso **2.** pieno d'acqua; annunciante pioggia: — *clouds*, nuvole gonfie di pioggia; — *moon*, luna offuscata, annunciante pioggia **3.** lacrimoso, pieno di lacrime: — *eyes*, occhi pieni di lacrime **4.** (*poet.*) fatto d'acqua ‖ *the* — *plains*, i mari ‖ *to have a* — *grave*, morire annegato **5.** acquoso, insipido (di cibo, stile); stinto, slavato (di colore).

Watling Street ['wɔtliŋ‚stri:t], *s.* (*st.*) Watling Street (grande strada romana che dalla Manica portava a Wroxeter, passando per Londra e St. Albans).

watt [wɔt], *s.* (*fis. elett.*) watt ☆ — *-hour*, wattora: — *-hour meter*, contatore elettrico, wattorametro.

wattle[1] ['wɔtl], *s.* **1.** canniccio, graticcio; graticciata: — *and daub wall*, muro a cannicciata ricoperto di fango, argilla **2.** canne, vimini, rami **3.** (*bot.*) acacia australiana.

to **wattle**[1], *v.t.* **1.** intrecciare, ingraticciare **2.** circondare, chiudere con graticciata.

wattle[2], *s.* bargiglio; caruncola; barbetta (di pesci).

wattled ['wɔtld], *ag.* munito di bargigli.

wattling ['wɔtliŋ], *s.* graticciata, cannicciata.

to **waul** [wɔ:l], *v.i.* urlare, gemere come un gatto.

wave [weiv], *s.* **1.** onda, flutto, maroso; ondata (anche *fig.*): *a* — *of anger*, un impeto d'ira; — *of enthusiasm*, ondata di entusiasmo ‖ *to attack in waves*, (*mil.*) attaccare a ondate successive **2.** cenno, gesto (con la mano, ecc.): *he greeted her from afar with a* — *of his hat*, la salutò da lontano agitando il cappello; *she dismissed the subject with a* — *of her hand*, pose fine al discorso con un gesto della mano **3.** ondulazione (di capelli, ecc.): *I have a natural* —, i miei capelli sono ondulati naturalmente **4.** (*fis.*) onda **5.** *pl.* (*poet.*) mare ☆ — *-band*, (*rad.*) gamma di lunghezza d'onda; — *-front*, (*elett. fis.*) fronte d'onda; — *-guide*, (*rad.*) guida d'onda, guida cava; — *-meter*, (*elett. rad.*) ondametro; — *-motion*, movimento ondulatorio; — *-set*, messa in piega ‖ *cold*— —, ondata di freddo; *heat*- —, ondata di caldo; *ground* —, (*amer. rad.*) onda diretta; *sky* —, (*amer. rad.*) onda indiretta; *tidal* —, onda di marea; maremoto.

to **wave**, *v.t.i.* **1.** ondeggiare, fluttuare: *flags* — *in the breeze*, le bandiere ondeggiano al vento; *seaweeds* — *below the surface of the water*, le alghe fluttuano sotto la superficie dell'acqua **2.** agitare; far segni, cenni: *I waved to him to stop*, gli feci segno di fermarsi; *to* — *good-bye to s.o.*, fare un cenno d'addio a qlcu. ‖ *to* — *s.o. aside*, far scostare qlcu. con un gesto della mano ‖ *to* — *s.o. away*, fare segno a qlcu. di allontanarsi ‖ *to* — *s.o. on*, far segno a qlcu. di continuare, proseguire ‖ *to* — *away a proposal*, *fig.* scartare una proposta **3.** ondulare, rendere ondulato; essere ondulato (di capelli, ecc.): *her hair waves naturally*, i suoi capelli hanno onde naturali **4.** brandire (spada, ecc.).

waved [weivd], *ag.* ondulato; increspato.

wavelength ['weivleŋθ], *s.* (*rad.*) lunghezza d'onda.

waveless ['weivlis], *ag.* **1.** senz'onde **2.** *fig.* calmo, liscio.

wavelet ['weivlit], *s.* piccola onda, ondicina.

wavelike ['weivlaik], *ag.* simile ad onda; ondulato.

to **waver** ['weivə*], *v.i.* **1.** oscillare, ondeggiare; vacillare; guizzare (di fiamma): *the flame wavered*, la fiamma guizzò; *the line wavered and broke before the shock of the cavalry*, la linea ondeggiò e si sbandò sotto l'urto della cavalleria **2.** *fig.* titubare, tentennare: *inflexible in his resolve, he never wavers*, inflessibile nella sua decisione, non esita mai.

waverer ['weivərə*], *s.c.* chi è vacillante, irresoluto.

wavering ['weivəriŋ], *ag.* **1.** ondeggiante; vacillante; guizzante **2.** titubante, irresoluto ‖ *s.* **1.** oscillazione, ondeggiamento; guizzo **2.** esitazione.

waveringly ['weivəriŋli], *av.* **1.** oscillando, vacillando **2.** irresolutamente.

wavily ['weivili], *av.* a onde, in modo ondeggiante.

waviness ['weivinis], *s.* ondulazione; ondosità.

waving ['weiviŋ], *ag.* **1.** ondeggiante, fluttuante **2.** che si agita; che fa cenni ‖ *s.* **1.** ondeggiamento; sventolio **2.** cenno (della mano, ecc.) **3.** ondulazione (dì capelli) ☆ — *-iron*, ferro per ondulare i capelli.

wavy ['weivi], *ag.* **1.** ondulato; ondoso: — *hair*, capelli ondulati **2.** ondeggiante.

to **wawl** [wɔ:l], *v.i.* urlare, gemere come un gatto.

wax[1] [wæks], *s.* **1.** cera ‖ *to mould s.o. like* —, plasmare il carattere di qlcu. **2.** cera vegetale; pece; ceralacca; paraffina; ozocerite **3.** prima registrazione (su disco) ☆ — *-chandler*, fabbricante di candele; — *-cloth*, tela cerata; — *-doll*, bambola di cera; *fig.* donna bella ma inespressiva; — *-end*, spago impeciato (da calzolaio); — *-light*, candela di cera; — *-palm*, (*bot.*) cerossilo; — *-paper*, carta paraffinata; — *-red*, rosso ceralacca ‖ *cobbler's* —, pece; *finishing* —, cera per lucidare; *sealing* —, ceralacca.

to **wax**[1], *v.t.* **1.** dare la cera a; incerare: *to* — *the floor*, dar la cera al pavimento **2.** registrare (su disco).

wax[2], *s.* (*fam.*) collera, scoppio d'ira: *to be in a* —, essere in collera; *to put s.o. in a* —, far montare qlcu. in collera.

to **wax**[3], *pass.* **waxed** [wækst], *p.p.* **waxed**, (*poet.*) **waxen** ['wæksən], *v.i.* (*spec. letter.*) **1.** crescere (della luna): *to* — *and wane*, crescere e calare (specialmente della luna) **2.** divenire, farsi: *to* — *fat*, ingrassare; *to* — *old*, diventar vecchio; *to* — *sentimental*, cadere nel sentimentalismo **3.** (*poet.*) crescere, aumentare.

waxen ['wæksən], *ag.* **1.** di cera, come cera, cereo: — *complexion*, colorito cereo **2.** plasmabile (come cera).

waxer ['wæksə*], *s.c.* chi dà la cera (ai pavimenti).

waxily ['wæksili], *av.* come cera.

waxiness ['wæksinis], *s.* aspetto cereo.

waxing[1] ['wæksiŋ], *s.* inceratura, lucidatura a cera: *give it a good* —, lucidalo bene con la cera.

waxing[2], *s.* **1.** il crescere, l'ingrandirsi **2.** quarto (di luna).

waxwork ['wæks-wə:k], *s.* **1.** modellamento in cera **2.** modello, statuetta, figura di cera **3.** *pl.* museo di riproduzioni in cera: *Madame Tussaud's Waxworks*, il museo delle statue di cera di Madame Tussaud (a Londra).

waxy[1] ['wæksi], *ag.* **1.** di cera; simile a cera; cereo **2.** plasmabile.

waxy[2], *ag.* (*fam.*) in collera, rabbioso.

way [wei], *s.* **1.** via, strada, cammino, passaggio, sentiero (anche *fig.*): *the* — *to the station*, la strada della stazione; *across* (o *over*) *the* —, dall'altro lato della strada; di faccia; *the right* —; la strada giusta; la retta via; *to ask one's* (o *the*) —, chiedere la strada; *to be on the* — *to doing* (o *to do*) *sthg.*, essere in via, sulla buona via di fare ql.co.; *to find* (o *to know*) *one's* — *about*, sapersi orientare; *fig.* sapersi cavare d'impiccio; *to find one's* — *back*, trovare la strada del ritorno; *to find one's* — *into*, riuscire a introdursi in (anche *fig.*); *to find one's* — *to a place*, trovare la strada per arrivare in un luogo; *to get* (o *to go*) *out of s.o.'s* —, far posto, cedere il passo a qlcu.; *to go the longest*, *the shortest* —, andare per, prendere la via più lunga, più breve; *to go one's* —, andare per la propria strada: *to go one's own* —, (*fam.*) andare per la propria strada; *fare di testa propria*; non seguire gli altri; *to go out of one's* —, allontanarsi dalla propria strada; fare una deviazione; *to go the wrong* —, sbagliare strada; *to lead the* —, far strada, fare da guida; *to light the* — *for s.o.*, far luce a qlcu.; *to lose one's* (o *the*) —, perdere la strada, smarrirsi; *to make* —, avanzare,

progredire; far posto; *to make a — for oneself, fig.*
farsi strada; *to make — for s.o.*, far posto, far largo
a qlcu.; *to make one's — back*, ritornare; *to make one's
— in the world, fig.* farsi strada nel mondo; *to make
one's — out of, into*, uscire da, penetrare in; *to make one's
— towards a place, s.o.*, dirigersi verso un luogo, verso
qlcu.; riuscire a raggiungere un luogo, qlcu.; *to make
(o to work) one's — through the crowd*, farsi largo, aprirsi
un varco tra la folla; *to pave (o to prepare) the — for*,
preparare la via per; *to show s.o. the —*, mostrare la
strada a qlcu.; *to start on one's —*, mettersi in cammino;
to work one's — up, fig. farsi strada, farsi una posizione,
venire dalla gavetta; *to work one's — westward*, dirigersi verso ovest ‖ *— in*, entrata; *— out*, uscita;
— through, strada transitabile: *there is no — through*,
non si può passare, la strada è sbarrata ‖ *the Way of the
Cross*, la Via Crucis ‖ *the Milky —, (astr.)* la Via Lattea ‖ *on the —*, strada facendo; *on my — home*, andando
a casa; *on one's — to...*, andando a...; sulla strada
di... ‖ *out of the —*, fuori mano; *fig.* fuori del comune:
he lives in a little house out of the —, abita in una casetta
fuori mano; *it was nothing out of the —*, non era nulla di
eccezionale; *that boy is always out of the — when he is
wanted*, quel ragazzo non c'è mai quando si ha bisogno
di lui ‖ *right of —, (dir.)* servitù (di passaggio); passaggio privato ‖ *to be in s.o.'s —*, intralciare, ostacolare
qlcu.: *he is always in my —*, mi sta sempre fra i piedi ‖
to get in one another's —, intralciarsi a vicenda ‖ *to
get out of the —*, togliersi di mezzo; *(mar.)* allontanarsi
dalla rotta; *to get s.o., sthg. out of the —*, sbarazzarsi
di, allontanare qlcu., ql.co. ‖ *to go out of one's — to
hurt s.o.*, fare di tutto per ferire qlcu.; *to go out of
one's — to oblige s.o.*, far di tutto per far piacere a
qlcu. ‖ *to pay one's —*, bastare a se stessi ‖ *to put
oneself out of the —*, scomodarsi; *to put s.o. out of
the —, (fam.)* sbarazzarsi di, far fuori, uccidere qualcuno **2.** distanza, tragitto, percorso: *he has gone a
long —*, è andato molto lontano (anche *fig.*); *it's
a long · — from here*, è molto lontano da qui; *it's a
long, short — off*, è molto lontano, vicino; *it's a long
— to London*, Londra è molto distante ‖ *all the —*,
per tutto il cammino, tragitto: *we have suits all the
— from five dollars to fifty, (fam. amer.)* abbiamo vestiti da cinque a cinquanta dollari ‖ *by a long —*,
di gran lunga, di molto; *his name goes a long —*, il
suo nome apre tutte le porte; *a smile goes a long —*,
con un sorriso si ottengono molte cose; *to make a penny
go a long —*, fare buon uso del proprio denaro **3.** lato,
direzione: *in the wrong —*, in senso contrario; *this —*,
per di qua; *he lives Hampstead —, (fam.)* abita dalle
parti di Hampstead; *I am going your —*, vado nella
tua stessa direzione; *I didn't know which — to look*,
non sapevo da che parte guardare; ero imbarazzato;
which — did you come?, da che parte sei venuto?;
the wind was blowing the other —, il vento soffiava
in senso contrario ‖ *I have nothing to say one — or
the other*, non ho niente da dire pro o contro ‖ *such
people have not often come my —*, raramente ho avuto
a che fare con gente simile ‖ *they would do anything
that came their —*, farebbero qualunque cosa capitasse
loro **4.** via, modo, maniera; linea di condotta: *the —
of doing sthg.*, il modo di fare ql.co.; *the — of living*,
il sistema di vita; *the good old ways*, le usanze del buon
tempo antico; *in no —*, in nessun modo; affatto; *in one
— or another*, in un modo o nell'altro; *in such — that*,
di modo che; *to my — of thinking*, secondo la mia opinione; *the — things are going*, l'andamento delle cose;
in its — it is really lovely, è molto bello nel suo genere;
in which — is it to be taken, to be understood?, in che
modo si deve prendere, si deve intendere ciò?; *is that
the — it strikes you?*, è questa l'impressione che ti
fa?; *she gets what she wants with her pretty ways*, ottiene
quello che vuole con le sue moine; *that's not my — (of
doing things)*, non è il mio modo di fare; *that's the
— the money goes!*, ecco come se ne va il denaro!; *without*

in any — wishing to criticize, senza voler in alcun modo
criticare; *to find the — (o one's —)*, trovare la via,
il modo, la maniera ‖ *she has a — with old people*,
sa come trattare i vecchi ‖ *there are no two ways
about it*, non c'è da discutere ‖ *you are going the right
— to work to make him angry, (fam.)* sei sulla strada
giusta per farlo arrabbiare ‖ *you must find a — out*,
devi trovare una soluzione ‖ *to be in the — of doing
sthg.*, avere l'abitudine di fare ql.co.; *to get (o to fall)
into the — of doing sthg.*, prendere l'abitudine di, abituarsi a fare ql.co. ‖ *to have (o to get) one's (own) —*,
fare a modo proprio, di testa propria ‖ *to learn sthg.
the hard —*, imparare ql.co. a proprie spese ‖ *where
there's a will there's a —*, *prov.* volere è potere **5.** aspetto, punto di vista: *in a —*, in un certo senso; *in many
ways*, sotto molti punti di vista; *she is a lady in every
—*, sotto ogni aspetto è una vera signora **6.** stato,
condizione; tenore di vita; grado: *she was in a terrible
—*, era agitatissima; *the crops are in a bad —*, il raccolto si preannunzia male; *things seem in a bad —*,
le cose hanno l'aria di andar male; *to be in a bad, in a
good —*, essere in cattive, in buone condizioni; *to put
s.o. in a — to do (o in the — of doing) sthg.*, mettere qlcu. nelle condizioni di fare ql.co. ‖ *he lives in
a small —*, vive modestamente ‖ *he makes furniture
in a small —*, fabbrica mobili su piccola scala **7.** sfera,
campo d'attività: *this is not in my —*, questo esula
dalla mia competenza ‖ *— of business*, mestiere; *he
is in the grocery —*, fa il droghiere; *his father is in a
large — of business*, suo padre commercia in grande;
they work in a small — of their own, hanno un piccolo
commercio in proprio **8.** *by the —*, strada facendo;
fig. incidentalmente, tra parentesi; a (questo) proposito **9.** *by — of*, via; a titolo di; in luogo, in sostituzione
di; con l'intenzione di: *by — of introduction*, a titolo
di introduzione; *I'm going to Rome by — of Florence*,
vado a Roma via Firenze; *they use cups by — of
(o in the — of) glasses*, adoperano tazze in luogo di
bicchieri ‖ *he is by — of being an actor, (fam.)* ha una
certa fama di attore **10.** *once in a —*, ogni tanto:
I play golf only once in a —, giuoco al golf solo ogni
tanto **11.** *(mec.)* guida, superficie di scorrimento **12.** *pl.
(costruzioni navali)* scalo di costruzione; invasatura
☆ *— -bill, (comm.)* nota di spedizione; lettera di
vettura; lista di passeggeri, merci; *— -gate, (idraulica)*
canale di scarico; *— -leave, (miner. aer.)* diritto di
passaggio; *— -station, (amer.)* stazione secondaria;
— -train, (amer.) treno locale; omnibus ‖ *one- —*,
senso unico.

way, *av. (fam. amer. per away)*: *it was — back
in 1890*, questo risale al 1890; *it was — back since 1940
that...*, era fin dal 1940 che... ‖ *— down, — up*, laggiù,
lassù.

to wayfare ['weifɛə*], *v.i. (arc.)* viaggiare (specialmente a piedi).

wayfarer ['wei,fɛərə*], *s.c. (arc.)* viandante.

wayfaring ['wei,fɛəriŋ], *ag. (arc.)* viaggiante ‖ *s.
(arc.)* chi viaggia (specialmente a piedi).

to waylay [wei'lei], *pass.p.p.* **waylaid** [wei'leid],
v.t. **1.** tendere un agguato a, appostare **2.** attendere
al varco, abbordare.

wayside ['wei-said], *s. (generalmente usato come att.)*
margine della strada: *a — inn*, un'osteria al margine
della strada; *a — poster*, un cartellone stradale.

wayward ['weiwəd], *ag.* **1.** indocile, ribelle, ostinato **2.** capriccioso.

waywardly ['weiwədli], *av.* **1.** ostinatamente, caparbiamente **2.** capricciosamente.

waywardness ['weiwədnis], *s.* **1.** ostinazione, caparbietà **2.** carattere capriccioso.

we [wi:], *pron.pers.* 1ª *persona pl.* **1.** noi: *— all
thought so*, l'abbiamo pensato tutti; *— doctors and
teachers know that...*, noi medici e insegnanti sappiamo che...; *— love them*, noi li amiamo; *it is — who
did it*, siamo noi che l'abbiamo fatto; *let's do it — two*,

(*fam.*) facciamolo noi due; *they are not so active as — are*, non sono così attivi come noi ‖ *here — are!*, eccoci! **2.** (*indefinito*) si: *he was what — call a tramp*, era quel che si dice un barbone; *— drink much wine in Italy*, si beve molto vino in Italia **3.** (*pl. di maestà*) **noi** (di re, autore, ecc.): *— have seldom read a book that — liked so much*, raramente abbiamo letto un libro che ci sia piaciuto tanto; *— thank our people*, ringraziamo il nostro popolo.

weak [wi:k], *ag.* **1.** debole (anche *fig.*); gracile; fragile: *— eyes*, occhi delicati; *— health*, salute malferma, cagionevole; *— voice*, voce fievole; *he has a — character*, ha un carattere debole; *I am too — to walk*, sono troppo fiacco per camminare ‖ *— vessel* (*fam.*), persona di cui non ci si può fidare ‖ *the weaker sex*, il sesso debole; *the weaker vessel*, (*fam.*) la donna **2.** inefficace, fiacco; inconsistente: *the — point* (o *side*) *of an argument*, il punto, il lato debole di un argomento; *a — style*, uno stile fiacco; *the measures proved —*, le misure si rivelarono inefficaci **3.** acquoso, diluito: *— coffee, tea*, caffè, tè leggero; *— mixture*, (*aut.*) miscela povera **4.** (*gram.*) debole: *— verb*, verbo debole ☆ *— -eyed*, dagli occhi delicati; *— -handed*, senza forza; *— -headed*, di scarsa intelligenza; *— -hearted*, poco coraggioso; *— -kneed*, fiacco (anche *fig.*); *— -minded*, poco intelligente; irresoluto, facilmente influenzabile; *— -sighted*, dalla vista debole; *— -spirited*, codardo.

to **weaken** ['wi:kən], *v.t.i.* indebolire, indebolirsi; infiacchire, infiacchirsi (anche *fig.*): *the market is weakening*, (*comm.*) il mercato si fa fiacco; *the mixture has weakened*, (*aut.*) la miscela si è impoverita; *voice weakened by illness*, voce resa fievole dalla malattia.

weakish ['wi:kiʃ], *ag.* piuttosto debole, fiacco.

weakling ['wi:k-liŋ], *s.* creatura debole, gracile; *fig.* persona debole di carattere.

weakly ['wi:kli], *ag.* debole; gracile, malaticcio ‖ *av.* debolmente.

weakness ['wi:knis], *s.* **1.** debolezza (anche *fig.*); fiacchezza: *he was in a state of extreme —*, era in uno stato di estrema debolezza **2.** lato debole: *his one — is his love for his daughter*, il suo unico lato debole è l'amore per la figlia; *she has a — for dogs*, ha un debole per i cani.

weal¹ [wi:l], *s.* (*letter.*) benessere; felicità; prosperità: *the common —*, il bene comune ‖ *in — and woe*, nella buona e nella cattiva sorte ☆ *— -public*, il bene pubblico.

weal², *V.* **wale¹**.

to **weal²**, *V.* to **wale¹**.

weald [wi:ld], *s.* (*poet.*) campagna aperta; regione boscosa ‖ *the Weald*, il Weald (regione nel Sud dell'Inghilterra).

wealth [welθ], *s.* (*solo sing.*) **1.** ricchezza, ricchezze; opulenza: *all the — of Asia*, tutte le ricchezze dell'Asia; *the — of that man is enormous*, la ricchezza di quell'uomo è enorme; *to achieve —*, fare fortuna ‖ *to be rolling in —*, (*fam.*) nuotare nell'abbondanza **2.** abbondanza, profusione, gran numero di: *a — of illustrations, of fruit, of knowledge*, una grande abbondanza, una profusione di illustrazioni, di frutta, di cognizioni **3.** (*arc.*) benessere, prosperità.

wealthily ['welθili], *av.* riccamente; doviziosamente.

wealthiness ['welθinis], *s.* ricchezza; opulenza.

wealthy ['welθi], *ag.* ricco, opulento; dovizioso.

wean¹ [wi:n], *s.* (*scoz.*) bimbo.

to **wean²**, *v.t.* **1.** slattare, svezzare **2.** togliere il vezzo, l'abitudine a: *his last illness weaned him from drinking*, l'ultima malattia gli ha tolto il vizio del bere.

weaning ['wi:niŋ], *ag.* che si va svezzando ‖ *s.* svezzamento: *I had no trouble with the — of the baby*, lo svezzamento del bambino non mi diede pensiero ☆ *— eye*, (*patol.*) pterigio; *— feeding*, dieta svezzante.

weanling ['wi:nliŋ], *s.* bambino, animale appena svezzato.

weapon ['wepən], *s.* arma (anche *fig.*): *the — of fear*, l'arma del terrore; *he took up the stick as a —*,

afferrò il bastone come un'arma ‖ *to beat s.o. with his own weapons*, controbattere qlcu. con le sue stesse armi.

weaponed ['wepənd], *ag.* armato.

weaponless ['wepənlis], *ag.* disarmato; inerme.

wear¹ [wɛə*], *s.* **1.** il portare (abiti, ecc.); uso: *a carpet which has been many years in —*, un tappeto in uso da molti anni; *to be the worse for —*, essere sgualcito, impresentabile (di abito) ‖ *in —*, in uso, di moda; *out of —*, fuori uso, fuori moda **2.** logorio, consumo, usura ‖ *— and tear*, logoramento; *fair — and tear*, (*dir.*) usura normale, legittima; *you must account for the — and tear of time*, bisogna tener conto del logorio del tempo **3.** durata: *stuff of very good —*, tessuto di ottima durata **4.** abbigliamento; articolo di vestiario ☆ *— resistance*, resistenza all'usura ‖ *children's, lady's —*, articoli d'abbigliamento per bambini, per signora; *evening —*, abito da sera; *foot —*, calzature; *negligible —*, (*mec.*) usura trascurabile.

to **wear¹**, *pass.* **wore** [wo:*], *p.p.* **worn** [wo:n], *v.t.i.* **1.** portare; indossare; calzare: *she likes to — black*, le piace vestire di nero; *she was wearing a splendid gown*, indossava un abito magnifico; *she wears her hair very long*, porta i capelli molto lunghi; *she wears small size shoes*, calza scarpe piccolissime ‖ *to — the breeches*, *fig.* portare i calzoni **2.** *fig.* avere, mostrare: *she wore a sad look*, aveva un'aria triste; *you — your years well*, porti bene i tuoi anni ‖ *to — one's heart upon one's sleeve*, non saper nascondere i propri sentimenti; essere troppo emozionabile **3.** logorare, logorarsi; consumare, consumarsi; stancare; esaurirsi: *holes had been worn in the carpet*, nel tappeto si erano formati dei buchi per il lungo uso; *a path had been worn across the field*, era stato battuto un sentiero attraverso il campo; *she will — herself to death*, finirà con l'esaurirsi; *sorrow and anxiety — one more than hard work*, il dolore e l'ansia logorano più della fatica; *steps worn by the feet of thousands*, scalini consumati da migliaia di piedi; *your child's whining wore him weary*, il piagnucolio del tuo piccino lo stancò fino all'esasperazione **4.** durare, resistere (anche *fig.*): *this cloth will — well for years*, questa stoffa durerà anni; *we seldom meet, but our friendship wears through the years*, ci incontriamo di rado, ma la nostra amicizia resiste al passare degli anni **5.** *to — away*, consumare, consumarsi; logorare, logorarsi; passare lentamente: *the long winter wore away*, il lungo inverno trascorse lentamente; *she wore away her best time*, ha sciupato i suoi anni migliori **6.** *to — down*, logorare, logorarsi; *fig.* abbattere: *his heels are worn down*, ha le scarpe scalcagnate; *to — down every opposition*, abbattere ogni opposizione **7.** *to — off*, consumare, consumarsi; cancellarsi; *fig.* svanire: *his grief wore off*, il suo dolore svanì lentamente; *the novelty will soon — off*, la novità perderà presto il suo fascino; *the paint is worn off*, la vernice si è consumata **8.** *to — on*, passare lentamente: *time wore on*, il tempo passò tediosamente **9.** *to — out*, logorare, logorarsi; stancare, stancarsi; esaurirsi: *her dress is worn out*, il suo vestito si è logorato; *my patience was worn out*, la mia pazienza era giunta al limite ‖ *to feel worn out*, sentirsi sfinito, essere esausto.

to **wear²**, *pass. p.p.* **wore**, *v.t.i.* (*mar.*) (far) virare.

wearable ['wɛərəbl], *ag.* portabile, che si può indossare ‖ *s. gener. pl.* indumento.

wearer ['wɛərə*], *s.c.* chi porta, chi indossa: *the coat was too large for the —*, la giacca era troppo larga per chi la indossava.

wearied ['wiərid], *ag.* stanco, affaticato.

weariful ['wiəriful], *ag.* **1.** stanchevole **2.** tedioso **3.** annoiato.

wearifully ['wiərifuli], *av.* **1.** in modo stanchevole **2.** tediosamente.

weariless ['wiərilis], *ag.* instancabile, incessante.

wearily ['wiərili], *av.* **1.** stancamente; faticosamente **2.** tediosamente.

weariness ['wiərinis], *s.* 1. stanchezza, fatica 2. noia; tedio.

wearing ['wɛəriŋ], *ag.* 1. da indossare, da portare 2. che logora, che si logora; che consuma, che si consuma: *the — action of time*, l'azione logorante del tempo 3. che dura, durevole: *hard — material*, stoffa resistente, di lunga durata ☆ — *-apparel*, abbigliamento; — *course*, manto superficiale (di strada); — *depth*, (*ferr.*) entità di logoramento; — *plate*, lastra di protezione; — *surface*, superficie di usura.

wearing, *s.* 1. l'indossare; l'usare: *your shoes will stretch in the —*, le scarpe ti si allargheranno con l'uso 2. logorio, usura ‖ *the — of time*, il passare del tempo.

wearisome ['wiərisəm], *ag.* 1. faticoso, pesante 2. tedioso; fastidioso.

wearisomely ['wiərisəmli], *av.* 1. faticosamente 2. tediosamente.

wearisomeness ['wiərisəmnis], *s.* 1. fatica 2. tedio.

weary ['wiəri], *ag.* 1. stanco, affaticato: *my hand was — with writing*, avevo la mano stanca per lo scrivere ‖ *a — Willie*, (*fam.*) un fannullone, un Michelaccio 2. stanco, disgustato, annoiato: *she says she is — of life*, dice di essere stanca della vita; *to be — of sthg.*, essere annoiato, seccato di ql.co. 3. fastidioso, noioso: *a — day*, una giornata terribilmente lunga, lunga come la fame; *a — work*, un lavoro noioso; *to have a — time*, annoiarsi a morte.

to **weary**, *v.t.i.* 1. affaticare, affaticarsi; stancare, stancarsi: *to — of sthg.*, stancarsi di ql.co. ‖ *to — for sthg.*, desiderare ardentemente ql.co. 2. annoiare, annoiarsi: *she wearied us to death with her stories*, ella ci annoiò a morte con le sue storie.

wearying ['wiəriiŋ], *ag.* 1. faticoso, gravoso 2. molesto, tedioso.

weasand ['wi:zənd], *s.* (*arc. dial.*) gola: *to slit s.o.'s —*, tagliar la gola a qlcu.

weasel ['wi:zl], *s.* (*zool.*) donnola ‖ *to catch a — asleep*, (*fam.*) ingannare una persona molto furba ☆ — *-faced*, faccia da furbo; — *word*, (*spec. amer.*) parola ambigua, trabocchetto (in un contratto, ecc.).

weather ['wɛðə*], *s.* tempo (atmosferico): *bad* (o *dirty* o *foul*) —, brutto tempo; *fine —*, bel tempo; *under stress of —*, (*mar.*) a causa del mal tempo; *how is the —?*, che tempo fa? ‖ *heavy —*, (*mar.*) mare grosso ‖ *to be under the —*, (*fam.*) essere indisposto ‖ *to keep one's — eye open*, (*scherz.*) stare in guardia, stare all'erta ‖ *to make good, bad —*, (*mar.*) affrontare bene, male una tempesta ☆ — *-beaten*, esposto alle intemperie, rovinato dalle intemperie; — *-bound*, confinato dal cattivo tempo; — *-box*, igrometro; — *-chart*, carta meteorologica; — *conditions*, condizioni atmosferiche; — *-forecast*, previsione del tempo; — *-gauge*, (*mar.*) sopravvento: *to get the — -gauge of a ship*, prendere il sopravvento di una nave; *to have the — -gauge of a ship*, navigare in sopravvento; — *-glass*, barometro; — *lore*, tradizioni popolari sulle previsioni del tempo: *that old man is a mine of — lore, ask him*, quel vecchio sa tutto sul tempo che farà, chiedi a lui; — *moulding*, (*arch.*) cornicione, gocciolatoio, gronda; — *-proof*, che resiste alle intemperie; — *-report*, bollettino meteorologico; — *resisting*, a prova di intemperie (di vernice, ecc.); — *-ship*, nave attrezzata per l'osservazione meteorologica; — *-side*, lato esposto al vento; — *-stained*, macchiato dalle intemperie; — *station*, osservatorio meteorologico; — *-strip*, guarnizione per serramenti; — *-wise*, che sa prevedere il tempo; — *-worn*, logorato dalle intemperie.

to **weather**, *v.t.i.* 1. esporre all'aria 2. alterare, alterarsi; scolorire, scolorirsi; patinare, patinarsi (per esposizione alle intemperie) 3. (*mar.*) doppiare: *to — a headland*, doppiare un capo 4. superare, resistere a: *to — a storm*, resistere a una tempesta ‖ *to — through*, *fig.* cavarsela 5. (*edil.*) inclinare (un piano) per lo scolo della pioggia.

weatherboard ['wɛðəbɔ:d], *s.* 1. (*edil.*) asse a sgrondo (sulla battuta esterna di finestra, ecc.) 2. asse per rivestimento esterno di pareti 3. (*mar.*) lato di sopravvento; tavola di copertura.

to **weatherboard**, *v.t.* rivestire con assi, tavole, pareti esterne.

weatherboarding ['wɛðəˌbɔ:diŋ], *s.* 1. rivestimento esterno di pareti con assi sovrapposte orizzontalmente: — *is typical of many country-houses in U.S.A.*, il rivestimento esterno in legno è la caratteristica di molte case di campagna negli Stati Uniti 2. assi che servono per rivestimenti.

weathercock ['wɛðəkɔk], *s.* ventaruola; banderuola (anche *fig.*).

weathering ['wɛðəriŋ], *s.* 1. (*arch.*) pendenza a sgrondo 2. (*geol.*) deterioramento, sgretolamento, erosione (causati da agenti atmosferici).

weave[1] [wi:v], *s.* (*ind. tessile*) 1. tessuto; tessitura 2. armatura ☆ *plain —*, armatura semplice.

to **weave**[1], *pass.* **wove** [wouv], *p.p.* **woven** ['wouvən], *v.t.i.* 1. tessere; fare il tessitore; lavorare a telaio: *to — thread into cloth*, trasformare il filo in tessuto 2. intrecciare, imbastire, ordire (anche *fig.*): *to — facts into a story*, inserire fatti in una storia; costruire una storia su dei fatti; *to — a plot*, ordire un complotto; *to — wreaths*, intrecciare ghirlande 3. insinuarsi, serpeggiare: *the road weaves through the valley*, la strada serpeggia nella valle; *to — through the traffic*, aprirsi un varco in mezzo al traffico.

to **weave**[2], *v.t.i.* 1. muoversi ripetutamente da un punto all'altro; sgusciare 2. (*boxe*) schivare 3. (*mar.*) fare segnalazioni a (una nave).

weaver ['wi:və*], *s.c.* (*ind. tessile*) tessitore, tessitrice ‖ *s.* — (*-bird*), (*ornit.*) tessitore.

weaving ['wi:viŋ], *s.* 1. (*ind. tessile*) tessitura 2. intrecciamento; orditura 3. serpeggiamento, tortuosità.

weazen ['wi:zn], *ag.* avvizzito, raggrinzito; rugoso.

web [web], *s.* 1. tela, tessuto; velo 2. *fig.* trama, rete: *a — of lies*, un tessuto di menzogne; *the — of life*, la trama della vita 3. (*cob w spider's*) — ragnatela 4. membrana connettiva (di palmipede) 5. barba (di piuma) 6. (*mar.*) braccio (di remo) 7. (*ferr.*) anima, gambo (di rotaia) 8. (*mec.*) ingegno; spalla, braccio (di manovella), maschetta ☆ — *-eye*, (*patol.*) cateratta; — *finger*, — *toe*, (*anat.*) sindattilia (della mano, del piede); — *footed*, dal piede palmato, palmipede; — *press*, rotativa ‖ *card —*, velo di carda; *cotton —*, *silk —*, *wool —*, tessuto di cotone, di seta, di lana.

webbed [webd], *ag.* palmato: — *feet*, piedi palmati.

webbing ['webiŋ], *s.* 1. (*ind. tessile*) tessuto ritorto 2. (*ind.*) cinghia; tela da cinghia (per letti, ecc.) 3. membrana connettiva (di palmipede).

webby ['webi], *ag.* membranoso; provvisto di membrana (di palmipede).

to **wed** [wed], *pass.p.p.* **wedded** ['wedid], (*rar.*) **wed**, *v.t.i.* 1. sposare, sposarsi; unire, unirsi in matrimonio: *to — one's daughter to s.o.*, sposare la figlia a qlcu. ‖ *to be wedded to a habit*, essere attaccato a un'abitudine 2. unire, accoppiare, combinare: *in this book simplicity and art are happily wedded*, in questo libro semplicità ed arte si combinano felicemente.

wedded ['wedid], *ag.* 1. sposato, unito in matrimonio: *a — pair*, una coppia di sposi ‖ *my — wife*, la mia legittima sposa 2. coniugale: — *life*, vita coniugale 3. attaccato, devoto: — *to one's profession*, attaccato al proprio lavoro 4. unito, combinato, accoppiato.

wedding ['wediŋ], *s.* nozze, sposalizio, sponsali: *to attend a —*, assistere a un matrimonio ☆ — *-breakfast*, rinfresco (per uno sposalizio); — *-cake*, torta nuziale; — *-card*, partecipazione di nozze; — *-day*, giorno, anniversario di nozze; — *-ring*, fede nuziale ‖ *diamond —*, nozze di diamante; *golden —*, nozze d'oro; *silver —*, nozze d'argento.

wedge [wedʒ], *s.* 1. cuneo, conio; bietta, zeppa ‖ *the thin end of the —*, *fig.* azione di scarsa importanza destinata a successivo sviluppo **2.** oggetto cuneiforme; (*tv.*) angolo di definizione ☆ — *bar,* (*edil.*) barretta triangolare a cuneo; — *gear,* (*mec.*) ruota di frizione (con gola a cuneo); — *hook,* (*elett.*) gancio a cuneo; — *-shaped,* a forma di cuneo; — *-tailed,* (*ornit.*) a coda cuneiforme ‖ *sliding* —, (*mec.*) chiavistello, saliscendi; *wooden* —, (*artig.*) cuneo di legno.

to **wedge,** *v.t.* **1.** incuneare, imbiettare; rincalzare (con zeppa): *to* — (*up*) *a piece of furniture,* rincalzare un mobile **2.** incastrare; serrare, conficcare (fra due cose): *to* — *oneself into the crowd,* inserirsi tra la folla ‖ *a small garden wedged in between two buildings,* un giardinetto incuneato fra due edifici **3.** (*rar.*) fendere per mezzo di cunei **4.** *to* — **away, off,** spingere fuori.

wedgewise ['wedʒwaiz], *av.* a guisa di cuneo.

wedging ['wedʒiŋ], *s.* **1.** fissaggio mediante cuneo **2.** (*ind.*) zeppe (di legno) impiegate come cunei.

Wedgwood ['wedʒwud], *s.* **1.** « Wedgwood » (varietà di ceramica semivetrificata con decorazioni in rilievo, così chiamata dal nome dell'inventore) **2.** oggetto in tale ceramica.

wedlock ['wedlɔk], *s.* (*dir.*) vincolo matrimoniale; stato coniugale: *born in, out of* —, (figlio) legittimo, illegittimo.

Wednesday ['wenzdi], *s.* mercoledì: *I see him on* —, lo vedo mercoledì ‖ *Ash* —, le Ceneri.

wee [wi:], *ag.* piccolissimo, minuscolo, minuto: *a* — *drop of whisky,* un goccio di whisky ‖ *a* — (*little*) *bit,* un tantino: *she is a* — *bit jealous,* è un tantino gelosa ‖ *Wee Frees,* (*st. relig.*) minoranza indipendente della Chiesa Scozzese ‖ *s.* breve distanza; breve tempo.

weed[1] [wi:d], *s.* **1.** malerba, erbaccia ‖ *ill weeds grow apace,* prov. la mal'erba cresce **2.** *the* (*Indian*) —, il tabacco **3.** (*fam.*) sigaro, sigaretta **4.** *fig.* persona sparuta, magra, allampanata **5.** *fig.* ronzino, cavallo bolso ☆ — *-grown,* coperto di erbacce.

to **weed**[1], *v.t.i.* **1.** (*agr.*) sarchiare **2.** *to* — **out,** estirpare, sradicare; *fig.* eliminare, epurare: *to* — *out undesirable persons from a community,* eliminare persone indesiderabili da una comunità.

weed[2], *s.* **1.** (*arc.*) abito; abbigliamento **2.** *pl.* (*widow's*) *weeds,* gramaglie (di vedova).

weeder ['wi:də*], *s.c.* (*agr.*) sarchiatore, sarchiatrice ‖ *s.* (*agr.*) sarchiatura, sarchio.

weediness ['wi:dinis], *s.* **1.** abbondanza di erbacce, di male erbe **2.** *fig.* magrezza, gracilità.

weeding ['wi:diŋ], *s.* (*agr.*) sarchiatura ☆ — *-hook,* (*agr.*) sarchio, sarchiello; — *-machine,* (*agr.*) sarchiatrice.

weedless ['wi:dlis], *ag.* **1.** privo di erbacce **2.** (*mar.*) antialga.

weedy[1] ['wi:di], *ag.* **1.** coperto di erbacce **2.** *fig.* sparuto, magro, allampanato **3.** *fig.* sfiancato, bolso (di cavallo).

weedy[2], *ag.* vestito a lutto; in gramaglie.

week [wi:k], *s.* settimana: *a* — *ago to-day,* otto giorni fa; *last, next* —, la settimana scorsa, la settimana prossima; *to-day* —, oggi a otto; *to-morrow* —, otto giorni domani; *I have not seen her for weeks,* sono settimane che non la vedo; *what day of the* — *is it?,* che giorno della settimana è oggi?; *what I can't get done in the* — *I do on Sundays,* quello che non riesco a fare durante la settimana lo faccio la domenica; *to be paid by the* —, essere pagato a settimana ‖ — *in* — *out,* una settimana dopo l'altra, continuamente ‖ *a* — *of Sundays* (o *of weeks*), sette settimane; (*fam.*) un'eternità ‖ *Holy Week,* la Settimana Santa ‖ *to knock s.o. into the middle of next* —, dare a qlcu. una lezione da ricordarsene per un pezzo; *fig.* stupire qlcu. fortemente ☆ — *-end,* vacanza di fine settimana; — *-ender,* gitante, turista di fine settimana.

weekday ['wi:kdei], *s.* giorno feriale, giorno lavorativo.

weekend ['wi:k'end], *s.* « weekend », vacanza di fine settimana: *I stayed with them over the* —, sono stato da loro durante la vacanza di fine settimana ☆ — *ticket,* biglietto (a riduzione) domenicale.

to **weekend,** *v.i.* passare la fine settimana: *to* — *at Brighton,* passare la vacanza di fine settimana a Brighton.

weekly ['wi:kli], *ag.* settimanale, ebdomadario ‖ *s.* settimanale, rivista settimanale.

weekly, *av.* settimanalmente: *twice* —, due volte alla settimana.

to **ween** [wi:n], *v.t.* (*poet.*) pensare, immaginare, credere; aspettarsi: *I* —, io immagino.

weeny ['wi:ni], *ag.* (*fam.*) piccolino.

weep [wi:p], *s.* pianto; sfogo di pianto: *I had a good* —, *then I felt better,* piansi a calde lacrime e poi mi sentii meglio; *she had a little* —, *and that was all,* versò qualche lacrimuccia e fu tutto.

to **weep,** *pass.p.p.* **wept** [wept], *v.t.i.* **1.** piangere; versare lacrime: *she wept over the heroine of the novel,* pianse sulla sorte dell'eroina del romanzo; *that's nothing to* — *over* (o *about*), non c'è di che piangere, non c'è ragione di piangere; *to* — *for joy, pain,* piangere di gioia, di dolore; *to* — *over one's sad fate,* piangere sulla propria triste sorte; *to* — *tears of blood,* piangere lacrime di sangue ‖ *to* — *away the time,* passare il tempo a piangere ‖ *to* — *oneself blind,* consumarsi gli occhi piangendo ‖ *to* — *oneself to sleep,* addormentarsi piangendo ‖ *to* — *one's eyes* (o *heart*) *out,* piangere tutte le lacrime dei propri occhi, piangere fino a spezzarsi il cuore **2.** stillare; trasudare; colare: *the wall seems to* —, sembra che il muro trasudi **3.** *to* — **out,** parlare piangendo: *she wept out an excuse,* mormorò una scusa tra le lacrime.

weeper ['wi:pə*], *s.c.* **1.** chi piange, geme **2.** lamentatore, lamentatrice ‖ *s.* **1.** prefica **2.** velo di crespo delle vedove **3.** nastro di crespo annodato sul cappello degli uomini in segno di lutto **4.** *pl.* (*st.*) polsini bianchi delle vedove **5.** scolatoio (di acque).

weeping ['wi:piŋ], *ag.* **1.** piangente; (*bot.*) pendulo **2.** trasudante; — *wound,* piaga in suppurazione ‖ *s.* **1.** pianto, lacrime: *a fit of* —, una crisi di lacrime **2.** trasudamento ☆ — *-ash,* frassino pendulo; *weeping cross,* (*st.*) croce penitenziale collocata ai crocicchi: *to come home by the* — *cross,* provare una grande delusione, soffrire per un insuccesso; — *-willow,* salice piangente.

weepy ['wi:pi], *ag.* **1.** (*fam.*) lagrimoso **2.** (*dial.*) che trasuda.

weever ['wi:və*], *s.* (*ittiol.*) ragana, trachino dragone.

weevil ['wi:vil], *s.* (*entom.*) curculionide.

weevilled ['wi:vild], **weevily** ['wi:vili], *ag.* infestato, danneggiato da insetti.

weft [weft], *s.* (*ind. tessile*) trama: — *and warp,* la trama e l'ordito ☆ — *backed fabric,* tessuto a doppia faccia; — *insertion,* inserzione della trama; — *stop,* rompitrama; — *winding machine* (o — *winder*), incannatoio, spolettiera.

weigh[1] [wei], *s.:* *under* —, (*mar.* per *under way*) in moto.

weigh[2], *s.* il pesare, il soppesare.

to **weigh**[2], *v.t.i.* **1.** pesare, aver peso; soppesare (anche *fig.*); calcolare, considerare: *can you* — *this parcel for me, please?,* puoi pesarmi questo pacco per favore?; *he weighed one argument with* (o *against*) *the other,* confrontò una tesi con l'altra; *he weighed the thing in his hand,* con la mano soppesava l'oggetto; *he will never* — *the consequences,* non riflette mai sulle conseguenze; *I weighed the matter in my mind,* ho riflettuto su quella faccenda; *it weighs heavy, light,* pesa molto, poco; *personal considerations ought not to* — *at all upon this decision,* le considerazioni personali non dovrebbero avere alcun peso su questa decisione; *the secret weighed on his conscience,* il segreto gli pesava sulla coscienza; *selfish interests don't* — *with him at all,* non tiene alcun conto dei tuoi interessi personali;

when did you — last?, quando ti sei pesato l'ultima volta?; *you should — your words*, dovresti soppesare le tue parole 2. *to — anchor*, (*mar.*) salpare, levare l'ancora 3. *to — down*, piegare; *fig.* opprimere: *the apple trees were weighed down with fruit*, i meli si piegavano sotto il peso dei frutti; *I felt weighed down with grief*, mi sentivo oppresso dal dolore 4. *to — in*, pesarsi (di fantini, boxeurs, prima della competizione) || *to — in* (*with an argument*), intervenire con un argomento determinante in una discussione 5. *to — out*, pesarsi (di fantini, boxeurs, dopo la competizione); misurare pesando: *the cook weighed out the flour for the cake*, il cuoco pesò la farina per la torta.

weigh[2], (*nei composti*): — *-bar*, (*mec.*) albero oscillante; — *-beam*, stadera; braccio di stadera; — *-bridge*, pesatrice a ponte; — *-house*, pesa pubblica; — *-out*, peso (di fantini).

weighable ['weiəbl], *ag.* che si può pesare.

weigher ['weiə*], *s.* pesatore; impiegato addetto alla verifica di pesi.

weighing ['weiiŋ], *s.* pesatura, pesata ☆ — *bottle*, (*chim.*) pesafiltri; — *enclosure*, (*spor.*) recinto del peso; — *-machine*, pesa, pesatrice: *automatic — -machine*, bilancia automatica.

weight [weit], *s.* 1. peso: *weights of a clock*, pesi di un orologio; *a set of weights*, una serie di pesi (di bilancia); *vapours and gases appear to have hardly any —*, si direbbe che gas e vapori non abbiano quasi peso; *to be over, under —*, avere peso superiore, inferiore al dovuto; *to gain* (o *to put on*) —, aumentare di peso, ingrassare (di persona); *to put — into a blow*, colpire a tutta forza; *to sell by —*, vendere a peso || *to be worth one's — in gold*, valere tanto oro quanto si pesa || *to carry —*, (*spor.*) essere handicappato (di cavallo) || *to hang a — round one's own neck*, mettersi la corda al collo; darsi la zappa sui piedi || *to pull one's —*, mettercela tutta || *to throw one's — about*, darsi delle arie 2. *fig.* peso, responsabilità: *he couldn't bear the — of sorrow*, non poteva sopportare il peso del dolore; *I feel the — of my position*, sento la responsabilità della mia posizione; *that is a great — off my mind!*, mi sono levato un bel peso!; *to feel the — of years*, sentire il peso degli anni 3. peso, influenza, importanza: *an argument of great —*, un argomento di grande importanza; *he did not realize the — of her words*, non si rese conto dell'importanza delle sue parole; *he is a person of —*, *of no —*, è una persona importante, di nessuna importanza; *his word carries —*, la sua parola ha del peso ☆ — *lifting*, sollevamento pesi || *balance —*, (*mec.*) contrappeso; *dead —*, peso morto; *delivery —*, peso di consegna; *gross —* (o *total —*), peso lordo; *net —*, peso netto.

to weight, *v.t.* 1. caricare con un peso: appesantire (anche *fig.*): *a stick weighted with lead*, un bastone appesantito con piombo; *eyelids weighted with sleep*, palpebre appesantite dal sonno 2. (*ind. tessile*) caricare.

weighted ['weitid], *ag.* 1. appesantito (anche *fig.*) 2. (*ind. tessile*) caricato ☆ — *average* (o *— mean*), media ponderata (in statistica); — *safety-valve*, valvola di sicurezza a contrappeso.

weightily ['weitili], *av.* 1. pesantemente 2. *fig.* gravemente 3. in modo influente.

weightiness ['weitinis], *s.* 1. pesantezza 2. *fig.* gravità, ponderatezza, importanza 3. influenza, autorità.

weighting ['weitiŋ], *s.* (*ind. tessile*) carica.

weightless ['weitlis], *ag.* 1. senza peso: — *condition*, (*astronautica*) perdita di gravità 2. *fig.* senza importanza.

weightlessness ['weitlisnis], *s.* (*astronautica*) perdita di gravità.

weighty ['weiti], *ag.* 1. pesante; gravoso 2. *fig.* grave; importante; ponderato 3. influente (di persona).

weir [wiə*], *s.* sbarramento, chiusa (di corso d'acqua).

weird [wiəd], *ag.* 1. fatidico; fatale || *the — sisters*, le Parche; le streghe (nel «Macbeth» di Shakespeare) 2. magico, misterioso; soprannaturale 3. (*fam.*) strano, bizzarro: *he wore a — costume*, indossava un

costume bizzarro || *s.* (*scoz.*) 1. fato, destino: *to dree one's —*, accettare, sottomettersi al proprio destino 2. malia, incantesimo.

to weird, *v.t.* (*scoz.*) destinare, predestinare; avvertire.

weirdly ['wiədli], *av.* 1. (*rar.*) fatalmente 2. (*fam.*) stranamente, in modo bizzarro.

weirdness ['wiədnis], *s.* 1. carattere soprannaturale, misterioso 2. (*fam.*) stranezza, bizzarria.

Weismannism ['vaismənizəm], *s.* teoria del Weismann (sull'ereditarietà).

Welch, *V.* Welsh.

to welch, *V.* to welsh.

welcome ['welkəm], *ag.* grato, gradito: *a — guest*, un ospite gradito || *you're —*, (*amer.*) prego, non c'è di che || *you are — to do what you like*, sei libero di fare ciò che vuoi || *you are — to my books*, i miei libri sono a tua disposizione || *s.* buona accoglienza; benvenuto: *to bid s.o. —*, dare il benvenuto a qlcu.; *to find a kind —*, essere bene accolto; *to meet with a cold —*, essere male accolto; *to outstay* (o *to overstay* o *to wear out*) *s.o.'s —*, abusare dell'ospitalità altrui.

to welcome, *v.t.* 1. dare il benvenuto a, fare buona accoglienza a 2. accettare, gradire: *I'll — your suggestions*, gradirò i tuoi suggerimenti || *discussion is welcomed*, tutti sono invitati a intervenire nella discussione.

welcome, *inter.* benvenuto: — *to Milan Fair!*, benvenuti alla Fiera di Milano!.

welcomeness ['welkəmnis], *s.* l'essere benvenuto, gradito.

welcomer ['welkəmə*], *s.c.* chi dà il benvenuto.

weld[1] [weld], *s.* (*mec.*) saldatura ☆ — *line*, linea di saldatura; — *time*, tempo di saldatura || *arc —*, saldatura ad arco; *electric spot —*, saldatura elettrica a punti.

to weld[1], *v.t.i.* (*mec.*) saldare, saldarsi.

weld[2], *s.* (*bot.*) guaderella.

weldability [,weldə'biliti], *s.* (*mec.*) possibilità di essere saldato.

weldable ['weldəbl], *ag.* (*mec.*) saldabile.

welder ['weldə*], *s.* 1. saldatore 2. (*mec.*) saldatrice ☆ *flash —*, (*mec.*) saldatrice elettrica a scintillio.

welding ['weldiŋ], *s.* (*mec.*) saldatura ☆ — *machine*, saldatrice; — *set*, saldatrice ad arco; — *torch*, cannello per saldatura autogena || *arc —*, saldatura ad arco; *backhand —*, saldatura a destra, saldatura indietro; *butt —*, saldatura di testa, a combaciamento; *circular seam —*, saldatura continua circolare; *cold —*, saldatura a freddo; *forehand —*, saldatura a sinistra, saldatura avanti; *lap —*, saldatura a sovrapposizione; *seam —*, saldatura continua; *spot —*, saldatura a punti; *tack —*, saldatura provvisoria.

weldless ['weldlis], *ag.* (*mec.*) senza saldatura.

welfare ['welfeə*], *s.* prosperità, benessere: *the state —*, il benessere della nazione ☆ — *contributions*, oneri previdenziali; — *institution*, opera di assistenza, opera pia; — *state*, stato assistenziale; — *work*, servizi di assistenza sociale; — *worker*, assistente sociale.

welk [welk], *s.* (*patol.*) 1. acne rosacea 2. nodulo cutaneo d'origine infiammatoria.

to welk, *v.t.i.* (*arc.*) (far) appassire; (fare) avvizzire.

welkin ['welkin], *s.* (*poet.*) cielo, volta celeste: *to make the — ring*, far risuonare la volta celeste.

we'll [wi:l], *contr.* di we will.

well[1] [wel], *s.* 1. pozzo; fontana, fonte (anche *fig.*): *the — of knowledge*, la fonte del sapere; *a — of learning*, un pozzo di scienza; *to drive* (o *to sink*) *a —*, scavare, perforare un pozzo 2. tromba delle scale; vano dell'ascensore 3. (*mar.*) condotto delle pompe; (*aer.*) carlinga || — *of a blast furnace*, crogiuolo di altoforno 4. spazio riservato agli avvocati in tribunale ☆ — *-beam*, carrucola; — *-bucket*, secchia del pozzo; — *-curb*, vera da pozzo; — *-deck*, (*mar.*) ponte a pozzo; — *dish*, piatto di portata con incavo per il sugo; — *-room*, locale delle terme dove si distribuisce l'acqua; — *-spring*, (*poet.*) fonte perenne; — *sweep*, mazzacavallo; — *water*, acqua di pozzo || *artesian —*, pozzo artesiano; *drain* —, pozzo di drenaggio; *hot* —, sorgente d'acqua calda; *ink-* —, calamaio (per banchi di scuola, ecc.); *oil-* —, pozzo di petrolio; *open* —, pozzo a cielo scoperto; *periscope* —, (*mar.*) tubo (di rientro) del periscopio; *stair-* —, tromba delle scale.

to **well**[1], *v.i.* sgorgare, scaturire, zampillare: *tears welled from her eyes*, le sgorgarono le lacrime dagli occhi ‖ *water began to* — *up out of that rusty fountain*, l'acqua incominciò a zampillare da quella fontana arrugginita.

well[2], *comp.* **better** ['betə*], *superl.* **best** [best], *av.* **1. bene**; **attentamente**, **con cura**; **completamente**, **a fondo**: *can you speak English* —?, parli bene l'inglese?; *everything is going* — *with him*, tutto gli va bene; *how did she take it?*, *not very* —, come l'ha presa?, non troppo bene; *she was sleeping* —, dormiva bene, sodo; *that boy will do* —, quel ragazzo farà bene, si farà strada; *this is remarkably* — *done*, questo è fatto a meraviglia; *to come off* —, cavarsela bene, aver fortuna; riuscire bene (di avvenimento, ecc.); *to do* — *to...*, far bene a...: *you would do* — *to be silent*, faresti bene a tacere; *to examine sthg.* —, esaminare ql.co. attentamente, a fondo; *to know s.o., sthg.* —, conoscere qlcu., ql.co. bene, a fondo; *to live* (o *to do oneself*) —, viver bene, passarsela bene; *to receive s.o.* —, fare buona accoglienza a qlcu.; *to speak* — *of s.o.*, parlar bene di qlcu. ‖ — *done!*, ben fatto! bravo! *to be* — *out of sthg.*, cavarsela a buon mercato, venirne fuori felicemente ‖ *to deserve* — *of s.o.*, ben meritare la gratitudine di qlcu. ‖ *to speak* — *for s.o.*, far onore a qlcu.: *it speaks* — *for him that he refused*, gli fa onore l'aver rifiutato ‖ *to stand* — *with s.o.*, essere nelle buone grazie di qlcu. ‖ — *begun is half done*, *prov.* chi ben comincia è alla metà dell'opera **2. bene, a ragione**: *you can't very* — *refuse to help him*, non puoi a ragione rifiutarti di aiutarlo; *you might* — *say so*, potresti ben dirlo **3.** (*rafforzativo*): *he is* — *up in mathematics*, è ferrato in matematica; *I am* — *on in life*, sono bene in là con gli anni; *it is* — *worth trying*, val bene la pena di provare; *it was* — *on midnight*, era già quasi mezzanotte; *she is* — *past thirty*, ha passato la trentina da un bel po' **4. as** —, pure, anche: *I shall come as* —, verrò io pure; *take it as* —, prendi anche questo; *you might (just) as* — *do it by yourself*, tanto vale che tu lo faccia da solo, potresti anche farlo da solo ‖ *as* — *as*, come pure; tanto quanto: *I gave him my books as* — *as my pen*, gli diedi sia i miei libri che la mia penna; *you can come in the morning as* — *as at night*, puoi venire tanto di mattina che di sera.

well[2], *comp.* **better**, *superl.* **best**, *ag. predicativo* **1. sano, in buona salute**: *are you feeling* — *to-day?*, ti senti bene oggi?; *he is not very* —, non sta bene; *I'm* — *enough*, sto benino, me la cavo; *I am quite* —, sto benone; *to get* —, guarire, ristabilirsi ‖ — *and strong*, forte e robusto **2. opportuno, utile, consigliabile**: *it would be* — *to ask him once more*, sarebbe opportuno domandarglielo di nuovo **3. bello; buono; giusto; soddisfacente**: —*and good!*, d'accordo! sta bene!: *if he does it himself*, — *and good*, se lo fa lui, va benissimo; *all's* —!, (*mil.*) tutto bene!; *he is all very* — (*in his way*), *but don't ask him for money*, non c'è niente da ridire su di lui, ma non chiedergli denaro; *it is all very* — *for you to say so*, (*iron.*) sei libero di dire così, puoi ben dirlo; *it was* — *for him that you were there*, è stata una fortuna per lui che tu fossi là; *that's all very* —, *but...*, sta bene, ma... ‖ *all's* — *that ends* —, *prov.* tutto è bene ciò che finisce bene ‖ *ag. attributivo* (*rar. gener. amer.* o *arc.*) **sano**: *the sick and the* —, i malati e i sani; *he was not a* — *man*, non era un uomo sano ‖ *s.* **bene**: *to wish s.o.* —, augurare del bene a qlcu. ‖ *let* (o *leave*) — *alone*, *prov.* il meglio è nemico del bene.

well[2], *inter.* **bene**; **ebbene**, **dunque**; **allora**; **ma**: —!, *very* —!, bene!, benone!; — *I never!*, (*fam.*) ma no!, davvero?, chi l'avrebbe mai detto!; —, *as night came*

they went out, dunque, come fu notte uscirono; —, *I see*, bene, bene, capisco; —, *it may be true*, be', può essere vero; — *then*, *are you coming?*, e allora, vieni?; —, *who could have imagined it?*, ebbene, ma chi l'avrebbe potuto immaginare?.

well[2], (*nei composti*): —*-advised*, saggio, prudente; — *-affected*, ben disposto; ben pensante; leale; — *-balanced*, equilibrato; — *-behaved*, (bene) educato; — *-being*, benessere; prosperità; — *-beloved*, amatissimo; — *-born*, di buona famiglia; — *-bred*, educato, cortese; purosangue (di cavallo); — *-connected*, che ha buone relazioni (sociali); di buon parentado; — *-disposed*, ben disposto, benevolo; — *-done*, ben fatto; ben cotto (di carne); — *-earned*, (ben) meritato; — *-found*, (*arc.*) ben provvisto; equipaggiato; — *-grounded*, ben fondato; competente; — *-informed*, ben informato; istruito; — *-intentioned*, bene intenzionato; — *-knit*, compatto; robusto; ben piantato (di persona); — *-known*, rinomato, noto; — *-made*, ben fatto; — *-mannered*, cortese, educato; — *-marked*, chiaro, evidente; ben marcato; — *-meaning*, ben intenzionato; — *-meant*, detto, fatto a fin di bene; — *-nigh*, (*arc.*) quasi; — *-off*, agiato, benestante: *to be* — *-off for sthg.*, essere ben fornito di ql.co.; — *-oiled*, ben lubrificato; *fig.* mellifluo; (*sl.*) sbronzo; — *-ordered* (o — *-regulated*), ben regolato, ben diretto; — *-pleasing*, molto piacevole; — *-read*, colto, istruito; — *-rounded*, ben finito; completo; ben tornito (di frase); — *-set*, compatto, solido; — *-set up*, ben fatto, ben piantato (di persona); — *-spoken*, raffinato nel parlare; — *-timed*, opportuno; — *-to-do*, prospero, agiato: *the* — *-to-do*, i benestanti; — *-tried*, provato, sperimentato (con successo); — *-trodden*, molto frequentato; *fig.* comune, trito; — *-turned*, ben tornito (di frase, ecc.); — *-wisher*, amico, sostenitore (di cause, ecc.); — *-wishing*, bene augurante; — *-worn*, liso, consunto *fig.* comune, trito.

welladay ['welə'dei], *inter.* (*arc. dial.*) ahimè!.

well-doing ['wel'du(:)iŋ], *ag.* che agisce bene ‖ *s.* buona condotta: *he found his pleasure in* —, trovava piacere nell'agire bene.

wellingtonia [,weliŋ'tounjə], *s.* (*bot.*) albero del mammut, sequoia.

wellingtons ['weliŋtənz], *s.pl.* **1.** stivaloni; soprascarpe di gomma a gambale **2.** (*bot.*) varietà di mele.

Welsh [welʃ], *ag.* gallese ‖ *the Welsh*, i gallesi ‖ *s.* gallese (lingua) ☆ — *mile*, (*fam.*) distanza lunga e noiosa da percorrere; — *mutton*, pecora gallese di montagna dalla carne delicata; — *niece*, cugina di primo grado; — *rabbit* (o *rarebit*), pane tostato con formaggio fuso.

to **welsh**, *v.t.i.* **1.** (*sl.*) andarsene senza pagare (il vincitore di una scommessa) alle corse **2.** andarsene alla chetichella senza pagare i debiti (specialmente di giuoco).

welsher ['welʃə*], *s.* **1.** allibratore che non paga una scommessa **2.** chi se la squaglia senza pagare i debiti.

Welshman, *pl.* **Welshmen** ['welʃmən], *s.* (uomo) gallese.

Welshwoman ['welʃ,wumən], *pl.* **Welshwomen** ['welʃ,wimin], *s.* (donna) gallese.

welt [welt], *s.* **1.** (*calzoleria*) guardone; tramezza **2.** cordone (per tappezzeria) **3.** rinforzo (di calze) **4.** (*mec.*) coprigiunto **5.** (*aut. amer.*) paraspruzzi **6.** riga, striscia (causata da sferzata); lividore **7.** colpo; sferzata.

to **welt**, *v.t.* **1.** mettere la tramezza, il guardone a (scarpe); il rinforzo a (calze) **2.** cucire il cordone (di tappezzeria) **3.** (*mec.*) mettere il coprigiunto a **4.** staffilare; colpire.

welter[1] ['weltə*], *s.* **1.** confusione, tumulto **2.** rullio, sballottamento.

to **welter**[1], *v.i.* **1.** (*poet.*) avvoltolarsi, guazzare; essere immerso: *he weltered in his blood*, era immerso nel proprio sangue **2.** essere in tumulto, accavallarsi; ondeggiare.

welter[2], *s.* **1.** (*spor.*) fantino, pugile di peso « welter » **2.** oggetto, persona grande e pesante ☆ — *-race,* corsa ippica per fantini welter; — *-weight,* peso welter; *light* — *-weight,* peso medio-leggero.

weltering ['weltəriŋ], *ag.* (*lett.*) ribollente: *the — seas,* le acque tumultuose ‖ *s.* ribollimento, tumulto (di acque).

wen [wen], *s.* (*patol.*) **1.** cisti sebacea **2.** porro **3.** gozzo.

Wenceslaus ['wensislo:s], *no.pr.m.* Venceslao.

wench [wentʃ], *s.* **1.** (*arc. dial.*) ragazza, giovane donna **2.** ragazza di campagna; popolana **3.** (*fam.*) donna di servizio; (*fam. amer.*) serva negra **4.** (*arc.*) prostituta.

Wend [wend], *s.c.* abitante della Sassonia orientale.

to wend, *v.t.i.* **1.** (*arc.*) andare, viaggiare **2.** (*letter.*) dirigere (il cammino); proseguire: *to — one's way,* proseguire la propria strada; incamminarsi.

wennish ['weniʃ], **wenny**['weni], *ag.* (*patol.*) **1.** che ha natte **2.** gozzuto.

went [went], **1.** *pass.* di to **go 2.** (*arc.*) *pass.* di to **wend.**

wentletrap ['wentltræp], *s.* (*zool.*) scalaria.

wept [wept], *pass.p.p.* di to **weep.**

were [wə:* (*forma forte*), wə* (*forma debole*)], 2ª persona sing., 1ª, 2ª, 3ª persona pl. pass. di to **be.**

we're [wiə*], *contr.* di we **are.**

weren't [wə:nt], *contr.* di *were not.*

wer(e)wolf ['wə:wulf], *pl.* **wer(e)wolves** ['wə:wulvz], *s.* lupo mannaro; licantropo.

wert [wə:t (*forma forte*), wət (*forma debole*)], 2ª persona sing. pass. (*arc.*) di to **be.**

Wertherism ['və:tərizəm], *s.* (*st. lett.*) romanticismo esagerato.

Wesleyan ['wezliən], *ag.s.* (*st. relig.*) chi, che appartiene alla setta metodista fondata da John Wesley (1703-91).

Wesleyanism ['wezliənizəm], *s.* (*st. relig.*) dottrina di John Wesley; metodismo.

Wessex ['wesiks], *no.pr.* (*geog. st.*) Wessex (uno dei regni della eptarchia anglosassone).

west [west], *ag.* occidentale, a ovest, dell'ovest: *the — wind,* il vento dell'ovest ‖ *the West End,* il " West End " (quartiere elegante di Londra) ‖ *West Indies,* le Indie Occidentali ‖ *West Point,* " West Point " (accademia militare degli Stati Uniti) ‖ *West Side,* " West Side " (quartieri occidentali di New York) ‖ *s.* l'ovest, l'occidente ‖ *the West,* (*amer.*) la regione a ovest del Mississippi ‖ *the Far West,* (*amer.*) la regione a ovest delle Montagne Rocciose ‖ *the Middle West,* (*amer.*) la regione tra gli Allegani e le Montagne Rocciose.

west, *av.* verso ovest, a occidente: *to go —,* andare all'ovest; (*sl. pop.*) crepare; *to sail due —,* (*mar.*) fare rotta verso ovest; *to travel —,* viaggiare verso ovest.

to wester ['westə*], *v.i.* dirigersi all'ovest (di astri); passare bruscamente ad ovest (di vento).

westering ['westəriŋ], *ag.* **1.** che muove verso ovest **2.** che volge al tramonto ‖ *s.* (*mar.*) rotta verso ovest.

westerly ['westəli], *ag.* verso ovest; dall'ovest (di vento) ‖ *av.* verso ovest.

western ['westən], *ag.* occidentale: — *civilization,* la civiltà occidentale ‖ *the Western Church,* la Chiesa Romana ‖ *the Western Empire,* (*st.*) l'Impero Romano d'Occidente ‖ *the Western Powers,* le potenze occidentali ‖ *s.c.* abitante dell'occidente ‖ *s.* « western » (racconto, film di avventure di cow-boy, sceriffi, ecc.).

westerner ['westənə*], *s.c.* occidentale.

to westernize ['westənaiz], *v.t.i.* occidentalizzare, occidentalizzarsi; apportare, adottare la civiltà dell'occidente.

westernmost ['westənmoust], *ag.* il più occidentale; all'estremo occidente.

westing ['westiŋ], *s.* distanza percorsa verso ovest.

Westminster ['westminstə*], *no.pr.* **1.** Westminster (distretto di Londra) ‖ — (*Abbey*), Abbazia di West-

minster; — *Cathedral,* Cattedrale di Westminster (cattedrale cattolica di Londra) **2.** Westminster (Palazzo del Parlamento) **3.** Westminster (scuola di Londra; membro di tale scuola).

Westphalia [west'feiljə], *no.pr.* (*geog.*) Vestfalia.

Westralian [wes'treiljən], *ag.* dell'Australia occidentale ‖ *s.c.* abitante dell'Australia occidentale.

westward ['westwəd], *ag.* volto a occidente ‖ *s.* regione occidentale ‖ *av.* verso occidente, a ponente.

westwards ['westwədz], *av.* verso occidente, a ponente.

wet [wet], *ag.* **1.** umido; bagnato; fradicio, zuppo: *her eyes were —,* aveva gli occhi umidi; *to get one's feet —,* bagnarsi i piedi ‖ *as — as a drowned rat,* bagnato come un pulcino; *to be — through* (o *to the skin*), essere bagnato fradicio; *to be soaking* (o *sopping* o *wringing*) —, essere bagnato da torcere (di indumento); essere bagnato fino all'osso (di persona) **2.** piovoso, umido: *a — day,* un giorno piovoso; — *weather,* tempo umido, piovoso; — *wind,* vento umido; *it is going to be —,* sta per piovere **3.** non asciutto, fresco: — *paint,* vernice fresca **4.** (*sl.*) brillo; dedito al bere **5.** (*fam.*) antiproibizionista: — *America,* l'America antiproibizionista.

wet, *s.* **1.** umidità; pioggia; tempo piovoso **2.** (*sl.*) bevanda alcoolica: *to have a —,* bagnarsi l'ugola **3.** antiproibizionista **4.** (*sl.*) persona incompetente, insignificante.

to wet, *pass.p.p.* **wet, wetted** ['wetid], *v.t.i.* **1.** bagnare, bagnarsi; inumidire, inumidirsi; inzuppare, inzupparsi: *to — oneself,* bagnarsi; *to — a sponge,* inzuppare una spugna ‖ *to — one's whistle,* bagnarsi l'ugola, bere **2.** bagnare, celebrare bevendo: *to — a bargain,* bagnare la conclusione di un affare **3.** (*mar.*) imbarcare acqua.

wet, (*nei composti*): — *blanket,* persona noiosa; guastafeste; — *-dock,* (*mar.*) darsena; — *nurse,* balia; — *plate,* (*foto.*) lastra al collodio umido; — *pleurisy,* (*patol.*) pleurite essudativa; — *-shod,* con scarpe, piedi bagnati.

wether ['weðə*], *s.* castrato, montone castrato ☆ *bell* —, montone che guida il gregge; *fig.* capobanda.

wetness ['wetnis], *s.* umidità.

wetting ['wetiŋ], *ag.* che bagna, inumidisce ‖ *s.* bagnatura; l'essere bagnato: *to get a —,* bagnarsi fino all'osso ☆ — *agent,* (*foto.*) agente inumidente.

wettish ['wetiʃ], *ag.* umidiccio.

we've [wi:v], *contr.* di we **have.**

wey [wei], *s.* « wey » (unità di peso variabile).

whack [wæk], *s.* **1.** percossa, bastonata **2.** (*sl.*) parte, porzione: *she had her — of joy,* ebbe la sua parte di gioia.

to whack, *v.t.* **1.** percuotere, battere, picchiare **2.** dividere, spartire.

whacker ['wækə*], *s.* **1.** (*amer.*) conducente di muli **2.** (*sl.*) enormità; grossa bugia, frottola.

whacking ['wækiŋ], *ag.* (*sl.*) enorme, colossale: *a — lie,* una colossale bugia ‖ *s.* percossa.

whale[1] [weil], *s.* **1.** balena ‖ *I had a — of a time,* (*sl. amer.*) mi sono divertito un pozzo ‖ *the result is a — of a book,* il risultato è un libro formidabile ☆ — *-boat,* baleniera; — *-calf,* (*zool.*) balenottero; — *-fishery* (o — *-fishing*), caccia alla balena; — *-man,* baleniere; — *-oil,* olio di balena ‖ *bull —,* balena maschio; *cow —,* balena femmina; *sperm —,* (*zool.*) capodoglio.

to whale[1], *v.i.* andare alla caccia della balena.

to whale[2], *v.t.* (*fam. amer.*) colpire duramente.

whalebone ['weilboun], *s.* **1.** fanone **2.** stecca di balena.

whaler ['weilə*], *s.* **1.** baleniere **2.** (*mar.*) baleniera.

whaling ['weiliŋ], *s.* caccia alla balena ☆ — *-master,* capitano di una baleniera; — *-ship,* (*mar.*) baleniera.

whang [wæŋ], *s.* (*fam.*) **1.** colpo rumoroso; scoppio **2.** rimbombo.

to whang, *v.t.i.* (*fam.*) **1.** colpire con forza **2.** rimbombare.

whangee [wæŋ'gi:], *s.* bastone da passeggio di bambù.

(to) **whap**, *V.* (to) **whop**.

wharf [wɔ:f], *pl.* **wharfs** [wɔ:fs], **wharves** [wɔ:vz], *s.* (*mar.*) pontile, banchina, molo ☆ *discharging* —, banchina di scarico; *loading* —, banchina di carico; *unloading* —, banchina di scarico.

to wharf, *v.t.* 1. attraccare, ormeggiare (una nave) alla banchina 2. scaricare a un molo.

wharfage ['wɔ:fdʒ], *s.* 1. (*comm.*) diritto di banchina 2. carico, scarico a un molo.

wharfinger ['wɔ:fndʒə*], *s.* 1. proprietario di banchina 2. guardiano di banchina.

what [wɔt], *ag.* 1. *interr.* quale?, quali?, che?: — *car do you prefer?*, che macchina preferisci?; — *girl is she?*, che ragazza è?, che tipo di ragazza è?; — *time is it?*, che ore sono?; *I don't know by* — *train I am leaving*, non so con che treno partirò; *I know* — *difficulties there were*, so quali difficoltà ci fossero; *tell me* — *books you want*, dimmi che libri vuoi ‖ — *good is it?* (o — *use is it?*), a che pro?, a che serve? 2. *rel.* quello che, quella che, quelli che, quelle che: *he saved* — *little money he could*, risparmiava quel poco denaro che poteva; *he will give you* — *books he can*, ti darà i libri che potrà; *wear* — *shoes you like*, metti le scarpe che vuoi 3. (*esclamativo*) che!: — *fun!*, che spasso!; — *an idea!*, che idea!; — *a pity!*, che peccato!; — *a shame!*, che vergogna!.

what, *pron.* 1. *interr.* che?, che cosa?: — *can I do for you?*, in che cosa posso esserti utile?; — *happened?*, che cosa è successo?; — *is it all about?*, di che cosa si tratta?; *let me know* — *is going on*, fammi sapere che cosa succede ‖ — *about a cup of tea?*, che cosa ne dici di una tazza di tè? ‖ — *else?*, che altro?: — *else did you buy?*, che cos'altro hai comprato? ‖ — *for?*, perchè?, a che scopo?: — *is that for?*, a che serve quello? ‖ — *if...?*, che importa se...?, che succederebbe se...?: — *if it is true?*, ebbene, e se fosse vero?; — *if she doesn't come?*, e se non viene? ‖ — *next?*, che ci può essere ancora? ‖ — *of it?*, che importa?, e con ciò? ‖ — *on earth for?*, e perchè mai? ‖ *so* —?, (*sl.*) e chi se ne infischia? ‖ — *d' you call it?*, (*fam.*) come si dice?: *pass me* — *d' you call it?*, passami quell'affare lì ‖ — *is he?*, che cosa fa?, che mestiere fa? ‖ — *is he like?*, che tipo è? ‖ *God knows* — *he is doing*, Dio solo sa che cosa sta facendo ‖ *he knows* —*'s* —, la sa lunga: *I don't know* —*'s* —, ho le idee confuse in materia ‖ *I'll tell you* —, ti dirò io che cosa fare; ascolta ‖ *she bought apples, pears, plums and* — *not*, comperò mele, pere, prugne e dell'altro ancora 2. *rel.* **ciò che, la cosa che**: — *he thinks, doesn't matter*, non ha importanza ciò che pensa; — *this school needs is a good headmaster*, quello che occorre a questa scuola è un buon direttore; *it is a lovely house and* — *is more, not very expensive*, è una bella casa e, quel che più conta, non costa molto; *say* — *you will*, di' quel che ti pare ‖ — *with studying and working he had a breakdown*, tra lo studiare e il lavorare si prese un esaurimento ‖ *there wasn't a day but* — *it rained*, non c'era giorno che non piovesse 3. (*esclamativo*) **quanto!**, **come!**: — *he has suffered!*, quanto ha sofferto!; — *she smokes!*, come fuma!.

what, *inter.* come!, ma come!: —, *here already?*, come, già qui?!.

whate'er [wɔt'ɛə*], *contr.* di **whatever**.

whatever [wɔt'evə*], *ag.* 1. qualunque, qualsiasi: — *excuses she may make, I'll not believe her*, qualsiasi scusa adduca, non la crederò; — *thing you may do...*, qualsiasi cosa tu faccia... 2. (*enfatico, in frasi negative*): *there was no doubt* —, non c'era dubbio alcuno; *they can see nothing* —, non possono vedere assolutamente niente ‖ *pron. indef. rel.* **qualunque cosa, qualsiasi cosa**; **quello che**: — *you do, you are always wrong*, qualsiasi cosa tu faccia, hai sempre torto; *do* — *you like*, fa' quel che vuoi.

whatnot ['wɔtnɔt], *s.* 1. nonnulla, cosa di poca importanza 2. scaffaletto, scansia.

whatsoever [,wɔtsou'evə*], *enfatico* per **whatever**.

wheal[1] [wi:l], *s.* miniera (specialmente di stagno).

(to) **wheal**[2], *V.* (to) **weal**[2].

wheat [wi:t], *s.* grano, frumento.

wheatear ['wi:tiə*], *s.* (*ornit.*) sassicola.

wheaten ['wi:tn], *ag.* di grano; fatto con frumento.

to wheedle ['wi:dl], *v.t.i.* adulare, lusingare; persuadere, ingannare con lusinghe; ottenere con lusinghe: *don't try to* — *it out of me!*, non adularmi perchè te lo regali!; *he wheedled money out of his father*, con le moine riuscì a farsi dare del denaro da suo padre; *she wheedles anything out of me*, ottiene qualsiasi cosa da me con le lusinghe; *to* — *s.o. into doing sthg.*, persuadere qlcu. a fare ql.co. lusingandolo.

wheedler ['wi:dlə*], *s.c.* adulatore, adulatrice.

wheedlesome ['wi:dlsəm], *ag.* pieno di lusinghe.

wheedling ['wi:dliŋ], *ag.* lusinghiero; carezzevole: *a* — *voice*, una voce carezzevole ‖ *s.* lusinga, blandizia.

wheedlingly ['wi:dliŋli], *av.* per mezzo di adulazioni, lusinghe; in modo lusinghiero, carezzevole.

wheel [wi:l], *s.* 1. ruota (di veicolo): *the wheels of a car*, le ruote di un carro ‖ *there are wheels within wheels*, (*fam.*) è un affare complicato, è un gran pasticcio ‖ *to go on wheels*, *fig.* progredire con successo ‖ *to put one's shoulder to the* —, aiutare una causa 2. (*mec.*) ingranaggio, ruota dentata 3. ruota del timone; volante: *don't speak to the man at the* —, non parlare all'uomo al volante 4. ruota di tortura: *to break a person upon the* —, infliggere a una persona il supplizio della ruota 5. (*fam.*) bicicletta, triciclo 6. movimento circolare; evoluzione in cerchio: *the wheels of the swallows in the air*, i cerchi delle rondini nell'aria; *a left* —, (*mil.*) una conversione a sinistra ☆ — *balancing*, (*aut.*) equilibratura ruote; — *body*, (*mec.*) corpo della ruota; — *-box*, (*aut.*) vano passaruote; — *-chair*, sedia a rotelle per invalidi; — *-control*, (*aer.*) comando a volante; — *-guard*, (*mec.*) protezione della mola; — *landing*, (*aer.*) atterraggio sulle ruote; — *-pen*, tiralinee; — *-set*, (*ferr.*) sala montata, asse montato; — *-window*, (*arch.*) rosone ‖ *bull* —, (*miner.*) tamburo di trivellazione; *calf* —, (*miner.*) tamburo di elevazione; *chain-* —, (*mec.*) puleggia per catena; *cog* —, (*mec.*) ruota a denti; *driving* —, (*mec. aut.*) ruota motrice; *faired* —, (*aer.*) ruota carenata; *Fortune's* —, la ruota della fortuna; *front* —, (*aut.*) ruota anteriore; *grinding* —, (*mec.*) mola; *hand* —, (*mec.*) volantino; *mirror scanning* —, (*tv.*) ruota (esploratrice) a specchi; *nose* —, (*aer.*) ruota anteriore; *spare* —, (*aut.*) ruota di scorta; *spoke* —, (*mar.*) ruota a caviglie; *sprocket* —, (*mec.*) ruota a denti, ruota di catena; *steering-* —, (*aut.*) volante; (*mar.*) ruota del timone; *wire* —, (*aut.*) ruota a raggi; *worm* —, (*mec.*) ingranaggio elicoidale.

to wheel, *v.t.i.* 1. (far) ruotare, (far) girare; roteare; turbinare: *the sea-gulls wheeled in the air above me*, i gabbiani roteavano nell'aria sul mio capo 2. spingere, tirare (un veicolo a ruote): *the invalid was wheeled into the garden*, portarono l'infermo in giardino sulla poltrona a rotelle 3. (*mil.*) fare una conversione 4. (*fam.*) andare in bicicletta, pedalare.

wheelbarrow ['wi:l,bærou], *s.* carriuola.

wheeled [wi:ld], *ag.* con ruote, a ruote.

wheeler ['wi:lə*], *s.* 1. conducente di veicolo a ruote 2. cavallo del timone 3. carraio ☆ *four-* —, veicolo a quattro ruote.

wheelless ['wi:llis], *ag.* senza ruote.

wheelman, *pl.* **wheelmen** ['wi:lmən], *s.* 1. timoniere 2. (*fam.*) ciclista.

wheelwright ['wi:lrait], *s.* carradore, carraio.

wheeze [wi:z], *s.* 1. respiro affannoso; sibilo 2. (*sl. teat.*) battuta comica 3. (*sl.*) aneddoto.

to wheeze, *v.t.i.* 1. ansare, ansimare 2. *to* — *out*, parlare affannosamente: *he wheezed out a few words*, profferì alcune parole ansimando.

wheezily ['wi:zili], *av.* affannosamente.

wheeziness ['wi:zinis], *s.* respiro affannoso; l'ansare.

wheezing ['wi:ziŋ], *s.* (*patol.*) dispnea, asma.

wheezy ['wi:zi], *ag.* affannoso, ansante, asimante.

whelk[1] [welk], *s.* (*patol.*) pustola; acne rosacea.

whelk[2], *s.* (*zool.*) buccino.

to **whelm** [welm], *v.t.* 1. (*ret.poet.*) sommergere, inghiottire; sopraffare 2. distruggere, rovinare.

whelp [welp], *s.* 1. cucciolo (di cane, di animale feroce) 2. bambino, ragazzo maleducato.

to **whelp**, *v.t.i.* 1. figliare; (*spreg.*) partorire (di donna) 2. (*fig. spec. spreg.*) partorire, produrre: *he whelped a prologue with great pains*, partorì un prologo con grandi difficoltà.

when [wen], *av.* 1. *interr.* **quando?**: — *did you tell him?*, quando glielo dicesti?; — *is the party?*, quand'è il ricevimento? 2. *rel.* **in cui, nel quale**: *the day* — *I met you*, il giorno in cui ti incontrai; *I was watching for the moment* — *he would be free*, aspettavo il momento in cui sarebbe stato libero || *cong.* 1. **quando, nel momento in cui**: — *spring came they got married*, quando venne la primavera si sposarono; — *young, she was very pretty*, da giovane era molto carina; *I wonder* — *they are arriving*, mi chiedo quando arriveranno; *ring them up* — *you are ready*, telefona loro appena sei pronto; *that was just* — *we were going out*, fu proprio mentre stavamo uscendo 2. (*concessivo*) **quando; sebbene**: *he walks* — *he might ride*, va a piedi mentre potrebbe andare a cavallo 3. (*ipotetico*) **qualora**: — *you translate from English into Italian, make use of a good dictionary*, qualora tu traduca dall'inglese all'italiano, usa un buon dizionario || *pron.* 1. *interr.* **quando?**: *till* — *will you be there?*, fino a quando sarai là? 2. *rel.* **quando**: *that was years ago, since* — *things have improved*, così era anni fa, da allora le cose sono migliorate.

when, *s.* il quando: *he wanted to know the* — *and the how of it*, volle sapere tutto per filo e per segno.

whenas [wen'æz], *av. cong.* (*arc.*) 1. quando 2. mentre 3. qualora.

whence [wens], *av.* (*letter.*) 1. *interr.* **donde?, da dove?; da che cosa?**: — *all this confusion?*, da che tutta questa confusione?; — *are we and why are we?*, donde veniamo e perchè siamo? 2. *rel.* **da dove, da cui**: *the source* — *these things sprung*, la fonte da cui provennero queste cose || *cong.* **donde, da dove, da cui, da che cosa**: *I don't know* — *he started*, non so da dove partì.

whence, *s.* origine, causa, fonte: *we do not know our* —, non conosciamo la nostra origine.

whene'er [wen'εə*], *contr.* di **whenever**.

whenever [wen'evə*], *av. rel. indef.* ogni volta che, tutte le volte che: — *I meet him, he is with her*, ogni volta che lo incontro è con lei.

whensoever [,wensou'evə*], *enfatico* per **whenever**.

where [wεə*], *av.* 1. *interr.* **dove?**: — *are they now?*, dove sono ora?; — *does the river rise?*, dove nasce il fiume?; — *should I be, if I had followed your advice?*, dove sarei se avessi seguito il tuo consiglio? || — *is the use of your being obstinate?*, dove credi di arrivare con la tua ostinazione? 2. *rel.* **dove, nel luogo in cui**: *I will stay* — *I am*, rimarrò dove sono; *that is* — *you are mistaken*, è qui che ti sbagli; *we ran to* — *the car lay overturned*, accorremmo nel luogo in cui l'automobile giaceva rovesciata; *you will find your pipe* — *you left it*, troverai la pipa dove l'hai lasciata || *cong.* **dove**: *I wonder* — *you have been all this time*, mi chiedo dove tu sia stato tutto questo tempo; *she doesn't know* — *he lives*, non sa dove egli abiti; *we didn't know* — *to begin*, non sapevamo da che parte incominciare || *I don't know* — *to have him*, non so da che parte prenderlo.

where, *s.* luogo: *the wheres and the whens*, il dove e il quando.

whereabout(s) ['wεərə'baut(s)], *come cong. e s.* ['wεərəbaut(s)], *av. interr.* **dove?, in che luogo?** (*non assolutamente determinato*): — *did you find it?*, dove l'hai trovato? || *cong.* **dove, in che luogo**: *I asked him* — *he lived*, gli chiesi dove abitava || *s.* **luogo, zona, paraggi**: *her present* — *is unknown*, non si sa dove si trovi attualmente.

whereas [wεər'æz], *cong.* 1. (*spec. dir.*) **poichè, siccome, dal momento che**: — *it has seemed good to the Queen's Majesty...*, poichè Sua Maestà la Regina ha ritenuto opportuno... 2. (*con valore avversativo*) **mentre, laddove**: — *in her youth she was slim, in later years she became very fat*, mentre da giovane era snella, invecchiando diventò molto grassa.

whereat [wεər'æt], *av.* (*letter.*) 1. *interr.* **perchè?, di che?**: — *did he get so angry?*, perchè si è tanto arrabbiato? 2. *rel.* **a cui, per cui**: *he said sthg.* — *everyone laughed*, disse ql.co. di cui tutti risero; *the table* — *he was sitting*, la tavola a cui sedeva.

whereby [wεə'bai], *av.* 1. *interr.* **come?, in che modo?, con quale mezzo?**: — *shall we know him?*, da che cosa lo riconosceremo? 2. *rel.* **per mezzo di cui; a causa di cui**: *reason* —, ragione per la quale.

where'er [wεər'εə*], *contr.* di **wherever**.

wherefore ['wεəfo:*], *av.* 1. *interr.* **perchè?, per quale ragione?**: — *do you cry?*, perchè piangi? 2. *rel.* **perciò, quindi, per la qual cosa**: *he was angry,* — *he could not think of it*, egli era in collera, perciò non poteva pensarci || *s.* causa, motivo || *the why's and the wherefore's*, i perchè ed i percome.

wherein [wεər'in], *av.* (*letter.*) 1. *interr.* **in che cosa?**: — *am I mistaken?*, in che cosa mi sbaglio? 2. *rel.* **in cui, nel quale**: *the garden* — *they played*, il giardino in cui giocavano.

whereof [wεər'ov], *av.* (*letter.*) 1. *interr.* **di che?, di che cosa?**: — *is it made?*, di che cosa è fatto? 2. *rel.* **di che, di che cosa; da che, da che cosa**: *materials* — *clothes are made*, stoffe di cui sono fatti i vestiti.

whereon [wεər'on], *av.* (*letter.*) 1. *interr.* **su che?, su che cosa?**: — *did she sit?*, su che cosa si è seduta? 2. *rel.* **su cui**: *the ground* — *the house will be built*, il terreno su cui si costruirà la casa.

wheresoever [,wεəsou'evə*], *enfatico* per **wherever**.

wherethrough [wεə'θru:], *av. rel.* (*letter.*) **attraverso cui; per mezzo di cui; a causa di cui**.

whereto [wεə'tu:], *av.* (*letter.*) 1. *interr.* **a che cosa?; verso dove?; a che scopo?**: — *serves mercy?*, a che serve la clemenza? 2. *rel.* **a cui**: *there was a party* — *many guests were invited*, ci fu una festa con molti invitati.

whereunder [wεər'ʌndə*], *av.rel.* (*letter.*) **sotto cui**.

whereupon [,wεərə'pon], *av.* 1. *interr.* **su che cosa?** 2. **dopo di che; in conseguenza di che**: — *he left*, dopo di che partì.

wherever [wεər'evə*], *av.* 1. *interr.* (*fam.*) **dove?** 2. *rel.* **dovunque**: *I shall remember it* — *I go*, me ne ricorderò dovunque io vada || *cong.* **dovunque, in qualunque luogo**: *sit* — *you like*, siediti dove vuoi; *he will get lost* — *he goes*, si perderà dovunque vada.

wherewith [wεə'wiθ], *av.* (*letter.*) 1. *interr.* **con che?, con che cosa?**: — *shall they be fed?*, con che cosa si devono nutrire? 2. *rel.* **con cui**: *we have nothing* — *to feed them*, non abbiamo nulla con cui sfamarli.

wherewithal ['wεəwiðo:l], *av.* (*arc.*) per **wherewith** || *s.* denaro, mezzi: *have you the* — *to do that?*, hai i mezzi per fare ciò?.

wherry ['weri], *s.* (*mar.*) leggera imbarcazione a remi (per traghetto di passeggeri).

whet [wet], *s.* 1. affilatura 2. *fig.* incitamento, allettamento (ad un'azione) 3. stimolante; aperitivo: *to take a* —, prendere un aperitivo.

to **whet**, *pass.p.p.* **whetted** ['wetid], *v.t.* 1. affilare, appuntare 2. *fig.* aguzzare, stimolare: *drink that whets the appetite*, bevanda che stimola l'appetito.

whether ['weðə*], *cong.* 1. (*nelle interr. indirette, dubitative*) **se**: *I don't know* — *he will come*, non so se verrà; *it depends upon* — *you are in a hurry or not*, dipende dalla fretta che hai; *it is doubtful* — *we may remain here*, è dubbio che si possa rimanere qui;

she was not interested — you approved or not, non le interessava il fatto che tu approvassi o meno **2.** (*correlativa, avversativa*) — *... or*, o ... o: — *he is guilty or not, you must speak to him*, sia egli colpevole o no, devi parlargli; — *to-day or to-morrow it is bound to happen*, oggi o domani, accadrà sicuramente ‖ — *or not*, in ogni caso: *I'll write to them — or not*, scriverò loro in ogni caso ‖ — *it rains or blows*, piova o tiri vento.

whetstone ['wetstoun], *s.* **1.** (*strum. artig.*) cote ad acqua, pietra per affilare a umido **2.** *fig.* chi, che stimola l'attività mentale.

whetter ['wetə*] *s.* bevitore abituale (di aperitivi).

whey [wei], *s.* siero (del latte) ☆ — *-faced*, (*arc.*) pallido (specialmente per la paura).

wheyey ['weii], **wheyish** ['weiiʃ], *ag.* sieroso.

which [witʃ], *ag.* **1.** *interr.* **quale?, quali?:** — *book have you already read?*, quale libro hai già letto?; — *way are you going*, da che parte vai?; — *way is the wind?*, da che parte spira il vento?; — *way shall we do it?*, come dobbiamo farlo?; *"Here's my brother with his friends!"*, *"Which one of them is he?"*, « Ecco mio fratello coi suoi amici! », « Qual è di loro? » **2.** *rel.* **il quale, la quale, i quali, le quali:** *I came with the Smiths and the Bowers, — latter are my intimate friends*, venni con gli Smith e i Bower, i quali ultimi sono miei intimi amici; *I stayed there three days, during — time it kept raining*, rimasi là tre giorni, durante i quali piovve di continuo ‖ — *look — way you wish...*, da qualunque punto di vista si consideri il problema... ‖ *pron.* **1.** *interr.* **chi?, quale?, quali?:** — *is that?*, qual è quello?; — *of the two books is the more interesting?*, quale dei due libri è il più interessante?; — *of you is going to play with us?*, chi di voi ha intenzione di giocare con noi?; — *will you take, tea or coffee?*, cosa prendi, tè o caffè?; *of — are you speaking?*, di quale stai parlando? ‖ — *is —?*, qual è l'uno e qual è l'altro?; *they are so alike I can never tell — is —*, si assomigliano talmente che non riesco mai a distinguerli ‖ *I don't mind —*, per me è lo stesso **2.** *rel.* (di animali e cose; di *s. coll.* di persona) **il quale, la quale, i quali, le quali; che; il che, la qual cosa:** *after — she went out*, dopo di che uscì; *the book — we bought together is rather interesting*, il libro che comprammo insieme è piuttosto interessante; *the countries — I am going to*, i paesi in cui andrò; *he drinks too much, — is bad for his health*, egli beve troppo, il che nuoce alla sua salute; *the house from — I have come is not far*, la casa da cui vengo non è lontana.

whichever [witʃ'evə*], *ag. indef.* **qualunque, qualsiasi:** — *way he turned, he saw nothing but sea*, da qualunque parte si voltasse, non vedeva che mare; *take — book you like*, prendi qualsiasi libro ti piaccia ‖ *pron. indef.* **chiunque, qualunque cosa:** — *comes will be received*, chiunque venga sarà ricevuto; — *he chooses he will make a mistake*, qualunque cosa sceglierà sbaglierà.

whichsoever [,witʃsou'evə*], *enfatico* per **whichever**.

whidah-bird ['widə'bə:d], *s.* (*ornit.*) vedova.

whiff[1] [wif], *s.* **1.** soffio, alito; sbuffo (di aria, fumo, ecc.); zaffata (di cattivo odore): *there wasn't a — of wind*, non c'era un alito di vento; *to go out for a — of fresh air*, uscire a prendere una boccata d'aria **2.** leggera imbarcazione a remi **3.** piccolo sigaro.

to whiff[1], *v.t.i.* soffiare; emettere sbuffi (di fumo).

whiff[2], *s.* (*ittiol.*) pleuronettide.

to whiff[2], *v.i.* pescare con la lenza a fior d'acqua.

whiffet ['wifit], *s.* **1.** piccolo sbuffo **2.** cagnolino ‖ *s.c.* (*fam. amer. spreg.*) persona insignificante.

whiffle ['wifl], *s.* leggero movimento d'aria.

to whiffle, *v.t.i.* **1.** alitare, spirare (del vento) **2.** oscillare, ondeggiare (anche *fig.*) **3.** cambiare direzione, far deviare (del vento)

whiffler ['wiflə*], *s.c.* persona mutevole, incostante.

Whig [wig], *ag.* (*st. pol.*) liberale: — *member*, deputato liberale ‖ *s.* (*st. pol.*) liberale ‖ *the Whigs and the Tories*, i liberali e i conservatori.

Whiggery ['wigəri], *s.* (*st. pol.*) liberalismo.

Whiggish ['wigiʃ], *ag.* (*st. pol.*) di, relativo a liberale.

Whiggishly ['wigiʃli], *av.* (*st. pol.*) da liberale.

Whiggishness ['wigiʃnis], *s.* (*st. pol.*) l'essere di idee liberali.

Whiggism ['wigizəm], *s.* (*st. pol.*) liberalismo.

while [wail], *cong.* **1.** **mentre, nello stesso tempo in cui; finchè:** — *eating, he reads*, mentre mangia legge ‖ — *there is life there is hope*, *prov.* finchè c'è vita c'è speranza **2.** (*concessivo*) **sebbene, quantunque:** — *I admit* (o — *admitting*) *the thing is difficult, I don't think it impossible*, pure ammettendo che la cosa sia difficile, non la credo impossibile **3.** (*avversativo*) **mentre:** — *I have nothing to do you are even too busy*, mentre io non ho nulla da fare tu sei perfino troppo occupato.

while, *s.* momento, tempo: *in a little —*, in breve tempo, tra un momento; *once in a —*, una volta ogni tanto; *to rest a —*, riposarsi un momento; *to stay for a —*, fermarsi per un momento ‖ *it is worth — doing*, vale la pena di farlo ‖ *the —*, (*poet.*) nel frattempo.

to while, *v.t.* far passare (il tempo) piacevolmente ‖ *to — away the time*, ammazzare il tempo.

whiles [wailz], *cong.* (*arc.*) mentre.

whilom ['wailəm], *ag.* (*arc.*) antico, di altri tempi ‖ *av.* (*arc.*) anticamente, in altri tempi, una volta.

whilst [wailst], *cong.* mentre ‖ *s.* (*arc.*): *the —*, nel frattempo.

whim [wim], *s.* **1.** capriccio, fantasia, ghiribizzo **2.** (*miner.*) argano.

to whim, *pass.p.p.* **whimmed** [wimd], *v.t.i.* **1.** desiderare (ql.co.) per capriccio; (*arc.*) essere mutevole, capriccioso **2.** (*arc.*) essere in preda alle vertigini.

whimbrel ['wimbrəl], *s.* (*ornit.*) chiurlo piccolo.

whimmy ['wimi], *ag.* capriccioso.

whimper ['wimpə*], *s.* **1.** piagnisteo, piagnucolio **2.** uggiolio.

to whimper, *v.t.i.* **1.** piagnucolare; gemere; lagnarsi; esprimere piagnucolando **2.** uggiolare **3.** mormorare, gemere (di acqua, vento).

whimperer ['wimpərə*], *s.c.* piagnucolone, piagnucolona; persona lagnosa.

whimpy ['wimpi], *s.* (*cuc.*) polpetta di carne di manzo tritata e cipolla.

whimsical ['wimzikəl], *ag.* fantastico, stravagante, eccentrico, bizzarro, capriccioso.

whimsicality [,wimzi'kæliti], *s.* fantasticheria; stravaganza; bizzarria; capriccio.

whimsically ['wimzikəli], *av.* fantasticamente; in modo bizzarro; stranamente; a capriccio.

whimsicalness ['wimzikəlnis], *s.* fantasticheria; stravaganza; eccentricità; capriccio.

whimsy ['wimzi], *ag.* capriccioso; variabile ‖ *s.* capriccio; fantasia; condotta capricciosa.

whin [win], *s.* (*bot.*) ginestra spinosa, ginestrone.

whinchat ['win-tʃæt], *s.* (*ornit.*) saltimpalo.

whine [wain], *s.* **1.** uggiolio **2.** piagnucolio, lamento.

to whine, *v.t.i.* uggiolare; piagnucolare, lamentarsi; esprimere piagnucolando: *you have nothing to — about*, non avete nulla di cui lamentarvi.

whiner ['wainə*], *s.c.* piagnucolone, piagnucolona.

whiningly ['waininli], *av.* **1.** uggiolando **2.** in modo piagnucoloso.

whinny[1] ['wini], *ag.* coperto, ricco di ginestroni.

whinny[2], *s.* nitrito.

to whinny[2], *v.i.* nitrire.

whinstone ['winstoun], *s.* (*geol.*) basalto; diopside.

whip [wip], *s.* **1.** frusta, scudiscio, staffile, sferza **2.** (*fam.*) cocchiere **3.** bracchiere **4.** (*pol.*) organizzatore (incaricato di mantenere la disciplina nel suo partito) **5.** (*pol.*) convocazione (ad intervenire a una seduta parlamentare) **6.** (*mar.*) ghia ☆ — *-and-derry*, (*mar.*) ghia; — *-hand*, vantaggio: *to have the — -hand of*, essere in posizione di vantaggio su; — *-handle* (o — *-staff*), manico della frusta; — *-round*, colletta;

— *and spur*, a spron battuto; — *-stitch*, sopraggitto; (*fam.*) sarto; — *-tail*, dalla coda lunga e sottile.

to **whip**, *pass.p.p.* **whipped** [wipt], *v.t.i.* **1.** frustare, battere, sferzare; *fig.* criticare aspramente: *to — the wheat*, battere il grano ‖ *to — the cat*, (*fam.*) essere molto parsimonioso; lavorare a giornata come sarto; bighellonare ‖ *to — the devil round the post*, (*fam.*) riuscire nel proprio intento per vie traverse **2.** sbattere; montare; frullare: *to — the cream*, montare la panna; *to — the eggs*, sbattere le uova **3.** precipitarsi; slanciarsi: *the little girl whipped under the table*, la bambina si precipitò sotto il tavolo **4.** (*sl. amer.*) vincere, superare: *to — a rival*, abbattere un rivale **5.** cucire a sopraggitto **6.** avvolgere strettamente con corda, spago **7.** (*mar.*) issare **8.** *to — away*, portar via bruscamente; andarsene di punto in bianco: *he whipped away to France*, partì improvvisamente per la Francia **9.** *to — in*, cacciar dentro; entrare all'improvviso **10.** *to — off*, togliere bruscamente, carpire; andarsene di punto in bianco: *the thief whipped the jewels off*, il ladro carpì i gioielli **11.** *to — on*, costringere a proseguire: *he whipped the horse on*, incitò il cavallo con la frusta **12.** *to — out*, cacciar fuori; esclamare con violenza; uscire all'improvviso: *he whipped out an oath*, profferì una bestemmia; *the warrior whipped out his sword*, il guerriero sguainò la spada **13.** *to — round*, girarsi bruscamente: *he whipped round and fired at his enemy*, si girò bruscamente e sparò sul nemico.

whipcat ['wipkæt], *s.* sarto, falegname a giornata.

whipcord ['wipkɔ:d], *s.* **1.** corda per fruste **2.** (*ind. tessile*) saia a diagonali marcate.

whipper ['wipə*], *s.c.* frustatore, frustatrice; sferzatore, sferzatrice ☆ — *-in*, bracchiere; (*pol.*) persona incaricata di mantenere la disciplina nel suo partito; (*ippica*) cavallo all'ultimo posto (durante la corsa).

whippersnapper ['wipə,snæpə*], *s.* farfallino; vanerello.

whippet ['wipit], *s.* **1.** « whippet » (razza canina, incrocio fra un levriero e uno « spaniel » o « terrier »); cane da corsa **2.** (*mil.*) carro armato leggero e veloce.

whipping ['wipiŋ], *s.* **1.** il frustare; il battere **2.** frustata, scudisciata **3.** (*dir.*) (pena della) flagellazione **4.** (*cuc.*) il frullare ☆ — *-boy*, (*st.*) fanciullo allevato insieme ad un principino e castigato in sua vece; capro espiatorio; — *-post*, palo, colonna dove si legavano i condannati alla flagellazione; — *-top*, trottola.

whip-poor-will ['wippuə,wil], *s.* (*pop. amer.*) (*ornit.*) caprimulgo.

whip-saw ['wipsɔ:], *s.* segaccio a mano; sega per tronchi.

to **whip-saw**, *v.t.* **1.** segare **2.** (*sl. amer.*) vincere (qlcu.) su tutta la linea.

whipster ['wipstə*], *s.* (*spreg.*) **1.** bambinetto **2.** individuo insignificante, presuntuoso e irritante.

(to) **whir**, *V.* (to) **whirr.**

whirl [wə:l], *s.* **1.** rotazione rapida **2.** turbine; vortice; mulinello: *a — of dust*, un turbine di polvere **3.** *fig.* attività frenetica: *the — of modern life*, il dinamismo della vita moderna **4.** *fig.* confusione, smarrimento: *my head is in a —*, ho una gran confusione in testa ☆ — *-blast*, turbine di vento.

to **whirl**, *v.t.i.* **1.** (far) girare rapidamente; (far) roteare; turbinare; volteggiare; piroettare: *the dancers whirled round the room*, i ballerini piroettavano intorno alla stanza; *the wind whirled the dead leaves*, il vento faceva turbinare le foglie morte **2.** correre via (di veicoli); trascinare, essere trascinato via rapidamente: *the carriage whirled out of sight*, la carrozza scomparve rapidamente alla nostra vista **3.** *fig.* turbinare (di pensieri); girare (di testa); essere confuso, smarrito: *my head whirls*, mi gira la testa.

whirligig ['wə:ligig], *s.* **1.** giostra; carosello; girandola; trottola **2.** *fig.* l'avvicendarsi degli avvenimenti: *the — of history*, l'avvicendarsi degli eventi storici **3.** (*entom.*) girinide (« Gyrinus natator »).

whirlpool ['wə:l-pu:l], *s.* vortice, gorgo (anche *fig.*).

whirlwind ['wə:lwind], *s.* turbine, vortice (di vento); tromba d'aria ‖ *to sow the wind and reap the —*, *prov.* seminar vento e raccogliere tempesta.

whirr [wə:*], *s.* ronzio; frullio (d'ali); rombo (di motore).

to **whirr**, *v.i.* ronzare; frullare (d'ali); rombare (di motore): *the birds whirred past*, gli uccelli passarono via con un frullo d'ali.

to **whirry** ['wə:ri], *v.t.i.* (*scoz.*) muovere, muoversi rapidamente.

whish [wiʃ], *s.* sibilio; fruscio.

to **whish**, *v.i.* muoversi sibilando, frusciando.

whisk [wisk], *s.* **1.** piumino per la polvere; scopino **2.** (*cuc.*) frusta; frullino **3.** movimento rapido: *a — of the tail*, uno scodinzolio ‖ *in* (o *with*) *a —*, in un lampo, in un baleno.

to **whisk**, *v.t.i.* **1.** spolverare; spazzolare: *she whisked off the crumbs*, spazzò via le briciole **2.** sbattere (uova, crema) **3.** agitare, agitarsi; guizzare (via); muovere, muoversi rapidamente: *the cow whisked her tail*, la mucca agitò la coda; *the lizard whisked into a hole*, la lucertola guizzò dentro un buco.

whisker ['wiskə*], *s. gener pl.* **1.** fedine, basette; favoriti **2.** vibrisse; baffi (di gatto, ecc.) **3.** (*mar.*) pennoni di civada.

whiskered ['wiskəd], **whiskery** ['wiskəri], *ag.* **1.** fornito di basette, di favoriti **2.** baffuto.

whiskey[1] ['wiski], *s.* whisky (irlandese).

whiskey[2], *s.* baroccino, calesse.

whiskified ['wiskifaid], *ag.* intossicato dall'alcool; ubriaco.

whisky[1] ['wiski], *s.* whisky (scozzese).

whisky[2], *s.* baroccino, calesse.

whisper ['wispə*], *s.* **1.** bisbiglio, sussurro; mormorio; lo stormire (di foglie): *in a —*, sottovoce, a bassa voce **2.** diceria, insinuazione: *a — of the scandal had come to his ears*, un'eco dello scandalo gli era giunta alle orecchie.

to **whisper**, *v.t.i.* **1.** bisbigliare, sussurrare; parlare a bassa voce: *whispered conversation*, conversazione a voce bassa **2.** mormorare; riferire; dir male: *it is whispered that*, si mormora che; corre voce che **3.** stormire (di foglie).

whisperer ['wispərə*], *s.c.* **1.** chi bisbiglia, sussurra **2.** maldicente ‖ *s.* informatore segreto.

whispering ['wispəriŋ], *ag.* **1.** che bisbiglia, sussurra; che parla sottovoce; mormorante **2.** maldicente ‖ *s.* **1.** bisbiglio, sussurrio, mormorio; lo stormire **2.** diceria; maldicenza ☆ — *-dome*, volta acustica; — *-gallery*, galleria acustica.

whisperingly ['wispəriŋli], *av.* bisbigliando, sussurrando.

whist[1] [wist], *ag.* (*arc. dial.*) silenzioso, muto ‖ *s.* (*irl.*) silenzio.

to **whist**[1], *v.t.i.* (*arc. dial.*) essere silenzioso; stare in silenzio; mettere a silenzio.

whist[1], *inter.* (*dial.*) zitto!, silenzio!.

whist[2], *s.* « whist » (giuoco di carte) ☆ — *-drive*, torneo di whist.

whistle ['wisl], *s.* **1.** fischio, sibilo **2.** fischietto, zufolo: *to blow a —*, dare un colpo di fischietto ‖ *to pay for one's —*, *fig.* pagare caro un capriccio **3.** (*fam.*) ugola: *to wet one's —*, bagnarsi l'ugola, il becco.

to **whistle**, *v.t.i.* **1.** fischiare, zufolare: *to — one's time away*, passar il tempo fischiettando **2.** chiamare con un fischio: *the boy whistled his dog back*, il ragazzo richiamò il cane con un fischio; *to — for a taxi*, chiamare un taxi con un fischio ‖ *you may — for your money!*, (*fam.*) aspetta pure il tuo denaro!.

whistler ['wislə*], *s.c.* chi fischia, zufola ‖ *s.* **1.** (*zool.*) marmotta canadese **2.** (*ornit.*) uccello fischiatore **3.** cavallo bolso.

whistling ['wisliŋ], *s.* il fischiare; fischio.

whit[1] [wit], *s.* particella infinitesimale; nulla: *every —*, completamente; *not a —*, niente affatto.

Whit², *ag.* (*eccl.*) di Pentecoste: — *Monday, Tuesday, etc.*, lunedì, martedì, ecc., di Pentecoste.

white [wait], *ag.* **1.** bianco, candido; pallido, smorto: *a — dress*, un abito bianco; *he was — with terror*, era pallido per il terrore ‖ *the White House*, (*st. amer.*) la Casa Bianca ‖ *as — as a sheet*, bianco come un lenzuolo **2.** chiaro, incolore: — *wine*, vino bianco **3.** *fig.* innocente, puro **4.** di razza bianca ‖ *s.* **1.** colore bianco: *she was dressed in —*, era vestita di bianco ‖ *to call — black*, cambiare le carte in tavola **2.** uomo di razza bianca: *poor whites*, (*amer.*) i poveri bianchi del sud **3.** albume: — *of egg*, chiara d'uovo, albume **4.** (*anat.*) cornea: *to turn up the whites of one's eyes*, mostrare il bianco degli occhi **5.** *pl.* (*patol.*) leucorrea.

white, (*nei composti*): — *alloy*, lega metallica di poco pregio imitante l'argento; — *-ant*, formica bianca; — *-bear*, orso bianco; — *-beard*, vecchio uomo; — *-bearded*, dalla barba bianca; — *-bonnet*, falso offerente a un'asta; — *-coffee*, cappuccino; — *-collar*, impiegato; — *-corpuscle*, globulo bianco; — *-faced*, dal volto pallido; — *-feather*, viltà; — *-friar*, frate carmelitano; — *frost*, brina; — *-handed*, dalle mani bianche; *fig.* dalle mani pure; — *-heat*, (*metal.*) calore bianco; — *-horse*, cavallone, ondata; — *-iron*, (*metal.*) ghisa bianca; — *-lead*, (*chim.*) biacca di piombo; — *lie*, bugia innocente, detta a fin di bene; — *-light*, (*fis.*) luce bianca; — *-lipped*, che ha le labbra esangui; — *-livered*, codardo; — *magic*, magia bianca; — *maple*, (*bot.*) acero bianco; — *paper*, relazione governativa; — *pine*, (*bot.*) pino bianco americano; — *rope*, (*mar.*) fune non incatramata; — *sale*, fiera del bianco, vendita di biancheria; — *sapphire*, (*min.*) corindone bianco; *scourge*, (*patol.*) tubercolosi; — *sheet*, veste del penitente; — *slave*, schiava bianca; — *slavery*, tratta delle bianche; — *-squall*, tempesta tropicale che scoppia improvvisamente a cielo sereno; — *-vitriol*, (*chim.*) vetriolo bianco (di zinco); — *witch*, strega che pratica la magia bianca.

to white, *v.t.* (*rar.*) imbiancare ‖ *whited sepulchre*, *fig.* sepolcro imbiancato.

whitebait ['waitbeit], *s.* bianchetti (frittura di pesci piccolissimi).

whitecap ['waitkæp], *s.* **1.** qualunque uccello dalla testa bianca **2.** cavallone, onda spumeggiante **3.** *Whitecap*, (*st. amer.*) « Whitecap » (membro di una setta che commetteva violenze col pretesto di regolare la morale pubblica).

Whitechapel ['wait‚tʃæpl], *s.* Whitechapel (quartiere di Londra) ‖ *ag. attributivo* basso, volgare ☆ *cart*, carretto a due ruote (per trasportare merci).

Whitehall ['wait'hɔ:l], *s.* Whitehall (strada di Londra dove hanno sede alcuni ministeri importanti) ‖ *s. fig.* la politica, il governo britannico.

to whiten ['waitn], *v.t.i.* **1.** imbiancare; sbiancare, sbiancarsi; impallidire **2.** assolvere da una colpa; far apparire senza colpa.

whitener ['waitnə*], *s.* **1.** imbianchino **2.** candeggiante.

whiteness ['waitnis], *s.* **1.** bianchezza; *fig.* purezza **2.** pallore.

whitening ['waitniŋ], *s.* **1.** imbiancamento; candeggiamento **2.** biacca, gesso (per imbiancare).

whitesmith¹ ['waitsmiθ], *s.* lattoniere, stagnaio.

whitesmith², *s.* (*bot.*) uva spina (bianca).

whitethorn ['waitθɔ:n], *s.* (*bot.*) biancospino.

whitethroat ['waitθrout], *s.* (*ornit.*) silvia.

whitewash ['wait-wɔʃ], *s.* **1.** calce (per imbiancare), intonaco **2.** *fig.* aspetto esteriore, vernice: *the — of diplomacy*, le forme esteriori della diplomazia **3.** (*fam.*) bicchiere di « sherry » a fine pasto **4.** (*amer. spor.*) vittoria schiacciante (senza che l'avversario segni punti).

to whitewash, *v.t.* **1.** imbiancare; intonacare **2.** *fig.* nascondere, coprire le pecche di; riabilitare: *to — a person*, riabilitare una persona **3.** (*amer. spor.*) vincere senza permettere all'avversario di segnare punti.

whitewasher ['wait-wɔʃə*], *s.* imbianchino.

whitewashing ['wait-wɔʃiŋ], *s.* **1.** imbiancatura **2.** *fig.* riabilitazione.

whither ['wiðə*], *av.* (*arc.*) **1.** *interr.* verso che luogo?, dove? **2.** *rel.* dove: *you shall go — you will*, andrai dove vuoi.

whithersoever [‚wiðəsou'evə*], *av.* (*arc.*) in qualunque luogo.

whitherward ['wiðəwəd], *av.* (*arc.*) **1.** dove?, verso quale direzione? **2.** in qualsiasi direzione.

whiting¹ ['waitiŋ], *s.* bianco di Spagna; gesso in polvere (per imbiancare).

whiting², *s.* (*ittiol.*) merlano.

whitish ['waitiʃ], *ag.* biancastro, bianchiccio.

whitishness ['waitiʃnis], *s.* colore bianchiccio.

whitleather ['wit‚leðə*], *s.* cuoio bianco.

whitlow ['witlou], *s.* (*patol.*) patereccio.

Whitsun ['witsn], *ag.* (*eccl.*) di Pentecoste.

Whitsunday ['wit'sʌndi], *s.* (*eccl.*) Pentecoste.

Whitsuntide ['witsntaid], *s.* (*eccl.*) settimana della Pentecoste.

whittle¹ ['witl], *s.* (*dial.*) lungo coltello.

to whittle¹, *v.t.i.* **1.** tagliare, tagliuzzare; aguzzare (legno) **2.** *to — away, down*, ridurre, ridurre tagliuzzando.

whittle², *s.* (*dial.*) **1.** camiciola di flanella per bambino **2.** scialle.

whity ['waiti], *ag.* biancastro.

whiz(z) [wiz], *s.* **1.** ronzio, sibilo **2.** (*sl. amer.*) accordo, affare.

to whiz(z), *v.t.i.* **1.** (*dial.*) ronzare, sibilare **2.** passare sibilando: *an arrow whizzed past*, una freccia passò sibilando **3.** (*mec.*) asciugare con una macchina centrifuga.

whizzer ['wizə*], *s.* **1.** trottola **2.** (*mec.*) centrifuga (per asciugare i panni).

whizzing ['wiziŋ], *s.* sibilo, ronzio.

who [hu:], *pron.sogg.* (*riferito a persona*) **1.** *interr.* chi?: — *am I that...?*, chi sono mai io da...?; — *are ready to follow me?*, chi è pronto a seguirmi?; — *does he think he is?*, cosa si crede di essere?; — *is it?*, chi è?; — *is that?*, chi è quello?; —*'s there?*, chi è là?; — *of us can understand it?*, chi di noi può capirlo?; *" I met Mr. Brown ", " Who? "*, « Ho incontrato il signor Brown », « Chi? »; *" Look at John ", " Who (did you say?) "*, « Guarda John », « Chi (hai detto)? »; *would you mind asking — that man is?*, ti dispiacerebbe chiedere chi è quell'uomo? ‖ — *knows*, chissà ‖ *" Who's Who "*, « Chi è » (annuario delle personalità) ‖ *she knows —'—*, conosce (vita, morte e miracoli di) tutti **2.** *interr.* (*fam. per whom*) chi?: — *did you speak to?*, con chi parlasti?; — *does he come from?*, da parte di chi viene? **3.** *rel.* **chi, che, il quale, la quale, i quali, le quali;** (*arc.*) **colui che, colei che, coloro che:** *anybody — says that, is a liar*, chiunque dice ciò, mente; *the boy, the girl, those — came yesterday*, il ragazzo, la ragazza, coloro che vennero ieri; *it is I — have done it*, sono io che l'ho fatto; *the person — came here yesterday is my doctor*, la persona che venne qui ieri è il mio dottore ‖ *as — should say that...*, come a dire che... ‖ — *breaks pays*, *prov.* chi rompe paga.

whoa [wou], *inter.* ferma!.

whodun(n)it [hu:'dʌnit], *s.* (*sl. contr.* di *who done it?*) racconto giallo, poliziesco.

whoever [hu:(:)'evə*], *pron.sogg.rel.indef.* (*riferito a persona*) **1.** chiunque: — *finds it may keep it*, chiunque lo trova può tenerlo; — *he may be*, chiunque egli sia; — *may object, I shall approve*, anche se qualcuno obietterà, io approverò; — *wrote that letter is a fool*, chiunque abbia scritto quella lettera è un pazzo **2.** (*fam. per whomever*) **chiunque:** — *she marries will be lucky*, chiunque ella sposerà, sarà fortunato.

whole [houl], *ag.* **1.** tutto; intero; completo: *the — day*, tutto il giorno; *the — town is talking about it*, l'intera città ne parla; *he swallowed it —*, l'ha ingoiato intero; *I want to know the — truth*, voglio sapere tutta la verità || *to do sthg. with one's — heart*, fare ql.co. di tutto cuore || *to go the — hog*, andare fino in fondo || *to fabricate a pack of lies out of — cloth*, inventare un cumulo di bugie di sana pianta **2.** intatto; integro; incolume: *there is not a plate left —*, non è rimasto intatto un solo piatto || *with a — skin*, sano e salvo **3.** (*arc.*) sano, in buona salute || *as — as a fish*, sano come un pesce.

whole, *s.* il tutto, l'intero; il complesso, il totale, somma: *the — of my family*, tutta la mia famiglia; *a harmonic —*, un complesso armonico; *the — amounts to...*, il totale ammonta a...; *the — we call civilization*, il complesso che chiamiamo civiltà; *he spent the — of that year in London*, passò tutto quell'anno a Londra; *two halves make a —*, due metà fanno un intero || *as a —*, nell'insieme || *on (o upon) the —*, nel complesso, tutto considerato.

whole, (*nei composti*): *— -footed*, (*fam.*) aperto, schietto; *— -hearted*, generoso, espansivo; *— -heartedly*, di tutto cuore; *— -hoofed*, (*zool.*) solidungolo; *— -length*, (*pitt.*) a tutta figura (di ritratto); *— -meal*, farina integrale; *— -milk*, latte intero; *— -note*, (*amer. mus.*) semibreve; *— -number*, (*mat.*) numero intero; *— -saler*, grossista; *— -time job*, lavoro a tutta giornata.

wholeness ['houlnis], *s.* **1.** totalità; interezza **2.** integrità.

wholesale ['houl-seil], *ag.* all'ingrosso; su vasta scala: *a — slaughter*, un'uccisione in massa, uno sterminio || *s.* vendita all'ingrosso || *— and retail*, (*comm.*) all'ingrosso e al minuto ☆ *— business*, affari all'ingrosso; *— dealer*, grossista; *— goods*, merce all'ingrosso; *— manufacture*, fabbricazione all'ingrosso; *— price*, prezzo all'ingrosso.

wholesale, *av.* all'ingrosso: *to buy, to sell —*, comprare, vendere all'ingrosso.

wholesome ['houlsəm], *ag.* **1.** salutare, salubre: *— air*, aria salubre **2.** (*arc.*) sano: *a — appearance*, un aspetto sano **3.** morale: *— reading matter*, letture morali, sane.

wholesomely ['houlsəmli], *av.* **1.** sanamente; salubremente **2.** moralmente.

wholesomeness ['houlsəmnis], *s.* **1.** sanità; salubrità **2.** moralità.

wholly ['houlli], *av.* totalmente, interamente; completamente, del tutto: *I don't — agree*, non sono del tutto d'accordo.

whom [hu:m], *pron.* (*caso diretto e obliquo di* who) **1.** *interr.* chi?: *— else?*, chi altro?; *— did you ask to dinner?*, chi invitasti a pranzo?; *— did you speak to?*, a chi parlasti? **2.** *rel.* che, il quale, i quali, le quali, cui; (*arc.*) colui che, colei che, coloro che: *the boy — I saw*, il ragazzo che io vidi; *the girl, the children — I played with*, la ragazza, i bambini con cui io giocai; *this is the man about — I was speaking*, questo è l'uomo del quale stavo parlando || *— the gods love die young*, muor giovane chi al cielo è caro.

whomever [hu:m'evə*], *pron.rel.indef.* (*caso diretto e obliquo di* whoever) **chiunque:** *— they choose will have the right...*, chiunque verrà scelto, avrà il diritto di...; *she smiled at — she met*, sorrideva a chiunque incontrasse.

whomsoever [,hu:msou'evə*], *enfatico per* **whomever.**

whoop [hu:p], *s.* **1.** urlo, grido **2.** grido di guerra (degli indiani del Nord-America) **3.** urlo della pertosse.

to whoop, *v.t.i.* **1.** gridare forte, urlare; schiamazzare, mandare un grido; incalzare con grida **2.** fare l'urlo caratteristico della pertosse.

whoopee ['wupi:], *s.* (*fam.*) allegria rumorosa, baldoria sfrenata: *to make —*, divertirsi in modo chiassoso; far baldoria.

whooper ['hu:pə*], *s.c.* chi grida, chi schiamazza || *s.* (*zool.*) cigno canoro.

whooping-cough ['hu:piŋkɔf], *s.* (*patol.*) pertosse.

whop [wɔp], *s.* colpo, botta; percossa.

to whop, *pass.p.p.* **whopped** [wɔpt], *v.t.* (*sl.*) **1.** batte-

re, fustigare, flagellare, frustare **2.** sconfiggere; superare.

whopper ['wɔpə*], *s.* (*sl.*) **1.** chi batte, fustiga **2.** cosa enorme, enormità: *twenty millions is a —!*, venti milioni sono un'enormità! **3.** fandonia, bugia solenne.

whopping ['wɔpiŋ], *ag.* (*sl.*) enorme: *a — lie*, una enormità, una fanfaronata.

whore [hɔ:*], *s.* (*volg.*) puttana; prostituta, meretrice ☆ *— -house*, bordello, casa di malaffare.

to whore, *v.t.i.* (*volg.*) **1.** fornicare; bazzicare donne di malaffare **2.** fare la prostituta; prostituire.

whoredom ['hɔ:dəm], *s.* (*arc.*) **1.** prostituzione; fornicazione **2.** idolatria.

whoremonger ['hɔ:,mʌŋgə*], *s.* mezzano, ruffiano; libertino.

whoreson ['hɔ:sʌn], *s.* (*spreg.*) bastardo.

whorish ['hɔ:riʃ], *ag.* (*rar.*) **1.** di prostituta; lascivo, impudico **2.** (*arc.*) idolatra.

whorl [wə:l], *s.* **1.** spira, giro di spirale **2.** (*bot.*) verticillo **3.** disco che regola il movimento di un fuso.

whorled [wə:ld], *ag.* **1.** disposto a spirale **2.** (*bot.*) verticillato.

whortleberry ['wə:tl,beri], *s.* (*bot.*) mirtillo.

whose [hu:z], *pron.* (*genitivo possessivo di* who) **1.** *interr.* di chi?: *— are these leather gloves?*, di chi sono questi guanti di pelle?; *— is this?*, di chi è?; *— seat is this?*, di chi è questo posto? **2.** *rel.* di chi, del quale, della quale, dei quali, delle quali, il cui, la cui, i cui, le cui: *the author — works you dislike*, l'autore di cui non apprezzi le opere; *the lady — dress was much admired*, la signora il cui vestito fu molto ammirato; *the person for — sake he did it*, la persona per cui fece ciò; *the young man to — sister I am writing*, il giovanotto, alla cui sorella sto scrivendo.

whosever [hu:z'evə*], *pron.rel.indef.* (*genitivo possessivo di* whoever) **di chiunque:** *burn this bad book — it is*, brucia questo libraccio, di chiunque esso sia.

whosesoever [,hu:zsou'evə*], *enfatico per* **whosever.**

whoso ['hu:sou], (*arc.*) *per* **whoever.**

whosoever [,hu:sou'evə*], *enfatico per* **whoever.**

why [wai], *av.* **1.** *interr.* perchè?, per quale causa?, per quale ragione?: *— didn't you say so?*, perchè non l'hai detto?; *— has he come?*, perchè è venuto? || *— not?*, perchè no?; *— not let him do as he likes?*, perchè non lasciargli fare ciò che preferisce? || *— so?*, perchè, per quale ragione? || *— the deuce does he meddle?*, di che diavolo si immischia? **2.** *rel.* per cui: *the reason — I want to go*, la ragione per la quale voglio andare || *cong.* perchè, per quale ragione: *I don't know — she is not here*, non so perchè non sia qui; *this is — I did so*, ecco perchè feci così.

why, *s.* il perchè, la causa, il motivo, la ragione || *the whys and the wherefores*, i perchè e i percome.

why, *inter.* ebbene!; per Bacco!, diamine!: *— I should say so!*, diamine, direi!.

wick[1] [wik], *s.* **1.** lucignolo, stoppino **2.** (*chir.*) stuello.

wick[2], *s.* (*arc.*) villaggio, paese, frazione; fattoria.

wicked ['wikid], *ag.* **1.** malvagio, maligno, perverso **2.** peccaminoso, vizioso.

wickedly ['wikidli], *av.* malvagiamente, perversamente; con cattiveria.

wickedness ['wikidnis], *s.* malvagità, malignità; cattiveria, perversità.

wicker ['wikə*], *s.* vimine ☆ *— -work*, lavoro in vimini.

wickered ['wikəd], *ag.* di vimini, in vimini.

wicket ['wikit], *s.* **1.** sportello **2.** (*edil.*) porta pedonale, portello; cancellino **3.** (*cricket*) porta ☆ *— -door* (o *— -gate*), portello, cancellino.

wide [waid], *ag.* **1.** largo, vasto; immenso; spazioso: *the — Atlantic*, l'immenso Atlantico; *it was one foot —*, era largo un piede **2.** *fig.* ampio, esteso: *to have — interests*, avere vasti interessi **3.** alto (di tessuto) **4.** spalancato: *to stare with — eyes*, fissare ad occhi spalancati **5.** lontano; fuori posto: *a — ball*, (*cricket*) una palla lontana dalla porta; *— of the truth*, lontano dalla verità; *an answer — of the mark*, una risposta non azzeccata ‖ *to give a — berth to*, stare alla larga da.

wide, *s.* **1.** (*cricket*) palla caduta lontano dal battitore **2.** (*poet.*) ampiezza, estensione: *the waste — of that abyss*, la desolata vastità di quell'abisso ‖ *the —*, (*arc.*) il mare aperto ‖ *to be broken to the —*, (*fam.*) essere completamente rovinato ‖ *done* (o *whacked*) *to the —*, (*sl.*) essere a terra, esausto.

wide, *av.* **1.** largamente, con ampiezza: *to search far and —*, cercare in lungo e in largo **2.** completamente, del tutto: *open your eyes —*, spalanca gli occhi **3.** a vuoto: *the blow went —*, il colpo andò a vuoto.

wide, (*nei composti*): *— -angle*, (*foto. ott.*) grandangolare; *— -open*, spalancato.

wide-awake ['waidə'weik], *come s.* ['waidəweik], *ag.* completamente sveglio; *fig.* vigilante ‖ *s.* cappello floscio ad ala larga.

widely ['waidli], *av.* largamente; molto: *a — known subject*, un argomento largamente conosciuto; *a — read author*, un autore molto letto; *a — travelled lady*, una signora che ha viaggiato molto.

to widen ['waidn], *v.t.i.* **1.** allargare, allargarsi; ampliarsi, ampliarsi: *to — a ditch*, allargare un fossato; *to — one's intellectual horizon*, *fig.* ampliare il proprio orizzonte intellettuale **2.** *to — out*, estendersi.

wideness ['waidnis], *s.* larghezza; estensione.

widespread ['waidspred], *ag.* esteso, diffuso.

widgeon ['widʒən], *pl.* **widgeon**, **widgeons** ['widʒənz], *s.* (*ornit.*) fischione.

widish ['waidiʃ], *ag.* piuttosto ampio; abbastanza largo.

widow ['widou], *s.* **1.** vedova **2.** (*ornit.*) vedova **3.** (*fam.*) (*a carte*) distribuzione di mano supplementare **4.** *the —*, (*fam.*) champagne ☆ *— -hunter*, (*fam.*) cacciatore di vedove; *— -'sweeds*, abiti vedovili ‖ *grass- —*, donna il cui marito è momentaneamente assente.

to widow, *v.t.* **1.** rendere vedovo, vedova; privare del compagno, della compagna **2.** (*poet.*) privare di un amico.

widower ['widouə*], *s.* vedovo.

widowhood ['widouhud], *s.* vedovanza (specialmente di donna).

width [widθ], *s.* **1.** larghezza, ampiezza (anche *fig.*): *— of mind*, larghezza di vedute; *— of resonance*, (*rad.*) ampiezza di risonanza; *— of wings*, ampiezza d'ala (di uccello, di aereo) **2.** altezza (di stoffa): *I want to know the — of this cloth*, voglio sapere l'altezza di questo tessuto.

to wield [wi:ld], *v.t.* **1.** tenere, brandire; maneggiare: *he wielded his sword*, brandì la spada **2.** controllare; dirigere, governare: *to — power*, esercitare il potere.

wieldable ['wi:ldəbl], *ag.* controllabile; maneggevole.

wieldy ['wi:ldi], *ag.* **1.** controllabile; dominabile; maneggevole **2.** (*dial.*) agile, vigoroso.

wife [waif], *pl.* **wives** [waivz], *s.* **1.** moglie, sposa: *a lawful —*, una moglie legittima; *to make a good —*, essere una buona moglie; *to take a girl to —*, prendere una ragazza in moglie ‖ *all the world and his —*, (*scherz. fam.*) uomini e donne, tutti quanti **2.** (*arc.*) comare: *the old wives*, le vecchie comari ‖ *" The Merry Wives of Windsor "*, (*lett.*) « Le allegre comari di Windsor ».

wifehood ['waifhud], *s.* condizione di moglie.

wifeless ['waiflis], *ag.* celibe, senza moglie.

wifelike ['waiflaik], **wifely** ['waifli], *ag.* da, di moglie; che si addice a una moglie.

wifie ['waifi], *s.* moglïettina.

wig [wig], *s.* **1.** parrucca ‖ *the —, the scalpel and the cloth*, il Diritto, la Medicina e la Chiesa **2.** (*fam.*) dignitario **3.** (*scherz.*) capigliatura: *curly —*, capelli ricciuti **4.** (*fam.*) sgridata, rimprovero ‖ *wigs on the green*, (*sl. irl.*) botte da orbi.

to wig, *pass.pp.* **wigged** [wigd], *v.t.* **1.** imparruccare **2.** (*fam.*) rimproverare, sgridare, rimbrottare.

wigan ['wigən], *s.* (*ind. tessile*) tela da fusto.

wigeon, *V.* **widgeon**.

wigged [wigd], *ag.* imparruccato.

wiggery ['wigəri], *s.* **1.** parrucca; insieme di parrucche **2.** (*rar.*) formalità inutile; burocrazia (nei procedimenti legali).

wigging ['wigiŋ], *s.* (*fam.*) sgridata; lavata di capo: *to give s.o. a good —*, dare una bella lavata di capo a qlcu.

to wiggle ['wigl], *v.t.i.* **1.** (*fam.*) (far) muovere da una parte all'altra; dimenarsi **2.** spingere: *to — a boat*, spingere una barca con un sol remo a poppa.

wight¹ [wait], *ag.* **1.** coraggioso; valoroso; forte **2.** attivo; agile; veloce.

wight², *s.* (*arc. dial. scherz.*) individuo; persona: *a luckless —*, un tipo sfortunato.

wigless ['wiglis], *ag.* senza parrucca.

wigwag ['wigwæg], *s.* (*mar. mil.*) segnalazione con bandiera.

to wigwag, *pass.p.p.* **wigwagged** ['wigwægd], *v.t.i.* **1.** agitare, agitarsi **2.** (*mar. mil.*) fare segnalazioni con bandiera.

wigwam ['wigwæm], *s.* « wigwam » (capanna, tenda dei pellirosse).

wild [waild], *ag.* **1.** selvaggio, feroce; barbaro: *— tribes*, tribù barbare **2.** selvatico, incolto, deserto: *a — and mountainous country*, una regione deserta e montagnosa ‖ *to run —*, inselvatichire (di pianta); diventare sfrenato (di persona) ‖ *to sow one's — oats*, *fig.* correre la cavallina **3.** incontrollato, sregolato, sfrenato: *a — young man*, un giovanotto sfrenato **4.** tempestoso, tumultuoso, agitato: *a — sea*, un mare in tempesta **5.** eccitato; furibondo, pazzo: *anxiety almost drove her —*, l'ansietà la rese quasi pazza; *he has a — look*, ha uno sguardo folle; *he was in — spirits*, era eccitatissimo; *to be — with anger*, essere fuori di sè dalla rabbia **6.** timido, pauroso: *the deer are very —*, i cervi sono molto paurosi **7.** malaccorto; imprudente, avventato; fatto a caso: *— shooting*, sparatoria a casaccio (scaricando il fucile senza puntare); *— talk*, discorso imprudente **8.** disordinato, confuso: *— hair*, capelli in disordine ‖ *s.* (*poet.*) deserto; regione non coltivata; *fig.* solitudine: *the wilds of Africa*, le regioni selvagge dell'Africa ‖ *the call of the —*, il richiamo della foresta (della vita libera e selvaggia).

wild, *av.* selvaggiamente; impulsivamente; senza freno: *to shoot —*, sparare all'impazzata, a casaccio; *to talk —*, parlare sconsideratamente.

wild, (*nei composti*): *— animals*, animali feroci; *— -ass*, (*zool.*) onagro; *— -boar*, (*zool.*) cinghiale; *— -cherry*, ciliegio selvatico; *— -dog*, (*zool.*) dingo; *— -duck*, anatra selvatica; *— -flowers*, fiori di campo; *— -fowl*, selvaggina alata; *— -goose*, oca selvatica; *fig.* persona sciocca; *— -honey*, miele selvatico; *— -olive*, (*bot.*) oleastro; *— plants*, piante selvatiche; *— shot*, (*artigl.*) colpo anomalo; *— steel*, (*metal.*) acciaio effervescente; *— -wood*, bosco selvaggio, inaccessibile.

wildcat ['waildkæt], *ag. attributivo* **1.** (*amer.*) arrischiato, rischioso (di impresa commerciale) **2.** illegale, immorale ‖ *s.* **1.** gatto selvatico; (*amer.*) lince **2.** persona impulsiva, focosa (specialmente donna) **3.** affare rischioso **4.** (*sl. amer.*) sondaggio per ricerche petrolifere in zona ritenuta improduttiva ☆ *— gambler*, speculatore su pozzi dove si presume ci sia petrolio; *— well*, pozzo in cui si presume ci sia petrolio.

to wildcat, *pass.p.p.* **wildcatted** ['waild,kætid], *v.t.* (*sl. amer.*) perforare, trivellare (una zona ritenuta improduttiva) per la ricerca del petrolio: *to — for oil*, compiere una trivellazione esplorativa (per il petrolio).

wildcatter ['waild,kætə*], *s.* **1.** speculatore in imprese commerciali **2.** (*sl. amer.*) scopritore, proprietario di pozzi petroliferi **3.** (*sl. amer.*) chi compie trivellazioni esplorative (per il petrolio).

wildcatting ['waild,kætiŋ], *s.* **1.** l'avventurarsi in operazioni commerciali rischiose **2.** (*sl. amer.*) trivellazione sperimentale (per il petrolio).

wildebeest ['wildibi:st], *s.* (*zool.*) gnu.

to wilder ['waildə*], *v.t.i.* (*poet. arc.*) **1.** errare, smarrirsi; sviare, condurre su una falsa strada **2.** rendere perplesso; confondere.

wilderness ['wildənis], *s.* **1.** deserto, solitudine, landa: *the voice of one crying in the* —, (*Bibbia*) la voce di uno che grida nel deserto **2.** distesa desolata: *a* — *of waters,* una distesa desolata di acqua.

wildfire ['waild,faiə*], *s.* **1.** fuoco greco || *to spread like* —, diffondersi assai rapidamente **2.** lampo (senza tuono) **3.** (*patol.*) erisipela.

wilding ['waildiŋ], *ag.* selvatico, non coltivato || *s.* pianta, frutto selvatico.

wildish ['waildiʃ], *ag.* piuttosto selvaggio.

wildly ['waildli], *av.* **1.** selvaggiamente; selvaticamente **2.** ferocemente, violentemente.

wildness ['waildnis], *s.* **1.** selvatichezza, stato selvatico, selvaggio **2.** ferocia, furore; impetuosità.

wile[1], [wail], *s. gener. pl.* stratagemma; astuzia; inganno: *the wiles of the devil,* le astuzie del diavolo; *to fall a victim to the wiles of s.o.,* cader vittima delle seduzioni di qlcu.

to wile[1], *v.t.* allettare; ingannare; adescare: *to* — *s.o. into a place,* attirare qlcu. in un luogo.

to wile[2], *V.* to while.

Wilfred ['wilfrid], *no.pr.m.* Vilfredo.

wilful ['wilful], *ag.* **1.** ostinato, caparbio; volitivo **2.** volontario, intenzionale, premeditato: *a* — *murder,* un assassinio premeditato.

wilfully ['wilfuli], *av.* **1.** ostinatamente **2.** volontariamente; con premeditazione.

wilfulness ['wilfulnis], *s.* **1.** ostinazione, caparbietà **2.** premeditazione.

Wilhelmina [,wilhel'mi:nə], *no.pr.f.* Guglielmina.

wilily ['wailili], *av.* astutamente.

wiliness ['wailinis], *s.* astuzia, scaltrezza.

will[1] [wil (*forma forte*), wəl, əl (*forme deboli*)], *v.* difettivo (V); (2ª *persona sing. pres. arc.*) **wilt** [wilt (*forma forte,* əlt, lt (*forme deboli*)]; *forma negativa* **will not** [wil nət]; *forma contratta* **won't** [wount]; *per il pass.* **would** *V.* a questa voce) **1.** (*ausiliare per la* 1ª *persona sing. pl. del futuro volitivo*): *I* — *speak,* parlerò, ho intenzione di parlare; *we* — *help him,* lo aiuteremo **2.** (*ausiliare per la* 2ª, 3ª *persona sing. pl. del futuro predicente*): *he* — *be a wiser man by then,* allora sarà più saggio; *I shall think and you* — *write,* io detterò e tu scriverai; *if she rings up, you* — *let her know...,* se telefona, le farai sapere...; *they* — *go there,* essi si recheranno là || *I* — *be happy to meet you,* (*amer.* per *I shall be happy...*) sarò felice di incontrarti || *murder* — *out, prov.* ogni nodo viene al pettine **3.** (*nel senso di* volere, desiderare): *do as you* —, fa' come vuoi; *he* — *not study even if I help him,* non vuole assolutamente studiare nemmeno se lo aiuto; *in spite of what I tell him he* — *not obey his parents,* nonostante ciò che gli dico, non vuole ubbidire ai suoi genitori; *say what you* —, *you* — *not be believed,* qualunque cosa tu dica, non sarai creduto || — *you have a cup of tea?,* desideri una tazza di tè? || *won't you sit down?,* non vuoi accomodarti? || *he that* — *not when he may, when he* — *he shall have nay, prov.* ogni lasciata è persa **4.** (*nel senso di* acconsentire, permettere): *I* — *not have it said,* non permetto che si dica questo || *he* — *have none of it,* non vuole sentirne parlare **5.** (*enfatico*): *he* — *have it that my watch is fast,* persiste nell'affermare che il mio orologio va avanti; *he* — *insist on coming every day,* vuole assolutamente venire ogni giorno; *things* — *happen,* non si può cambiare il corso degli eventi || *he* — *have* (*it*) *his way,* vuol fare di testa sua **6.** (*esprimente supposizione*): *this* — *be the Art Gallery no doubt,* credo proprio che questa sia la galleria d'arte.

will[2], *s.* (*solo sing.*) **1.** volontà, volere, determinazione; desiderio: *good, ill* —, buona, cattiva volontà; *lack of* —, mancanza di volontà; *strong, weak* —, volontà forte, debole; *God's* — *be done,* sia fatta la volontà di Dio; *he has always had his* —, ha sempre fatto ciò che ha voluto; *she married him against the* — *of her parents,* ella lo sposò contro il volere dei genitori; *what is your* —?, cosa desiderate (che sia fatto)? || *to take the* — *for the deed,* tener conto delle intenzioni || *where there's a* — *there's a way, prov.* volere è potere **2.** energia, entusiasmo: *to work with a* —, lavorare di buona lena **3.** (*gener.* con *at*) consenso, beneplacito: *you may come and go at* —, puoi andare e venire a tuo piacimento || *tenant at* —, usufruttuario a tempo indeterminato **4.** testamento: *to make one's* —, fare testamento ☆ — *-power,* forza di volontà || *free* —, libero arbitrio; *ill-* —, malanimo, rancore, livore, astio: *bear me no ill-* —, non avercela con me; *iron* —, volontà di ferro.

to will[2], *v.t.i.* **1.** desiderare intensamente, volere; disporre: *God willed that we should be happy,* Dio dispose che fossimo felici; *if he wills success he is likely to achieve it,* se desidera intensamente il successo probabilmente lo raggiungerà; *it must be as God wills,* deve essere come Dio vuole **2.** costringere; dominare con la forza di volontà: *to* — *s.o. to do* (o *into doing*) *sthg.,* costringere qlcu. a fare ql.co.: *can you* — *yourself to study?,* riesci a importi di studiare? **3.** lasciare per testamento: *he willed most of his money to a hospital,* lasciò la maggior parte del suo denaro a un ospedale.

Will[3], *no.pr.m. dim.* di **William.**

willed [wild], *ag.* **1.** testamentario, lasciato per testamento **2.** dominato, controllato dall'altrui volontà **3.** che ha volontà ☆ *ill* —, che serba rancore, astioso; *strong* —, di forte volontà.

willemite ['wiləmait], *s.* (*min.*) silicato di zinco.

willet ['wilit], *s.* (*ornit.*) beccaccino dell'America Settentrionale.

willful, *V.* wilful.

William ['wiljəm], *no.pr.m.* Guglielmo || — *the Conqueror,* (*st.*) Guglielmo il Conquistatore.

Willie ['wili], *no.pr.m. dim.* di **William.**

willing ['wiliŋ], *ag.* **1.** volenteroso; di buon cuore, compiacente: *a* — *horse,* un cavallo generoso; *a* — *worker,* un lavoratore volenteroso; *he is* — *to do what you ask,* è disposto a fare ciò che chiedi || — *or not,* volente o nolente **2.** spontaneo, volontario ☆ — *-minded,* compiacente.

willingly ['wiliŋli], *av.* volentieri, di buon grado, prontamente.

willingness ['wiliŋnis], *s.* buona volontà; compiacenza; propensione (ad agire).

will-less ['wil-lis], *ag.* senza volontà, privo di volontà.

will-o'-the-wisp ['wiləðwisp], *s.* **1.** fuoco fatuo **2.** *fig.* persona inafferrabile.

willow ['wilou], *s.* **1.** — (*-tree*), (*bot.*) salice || *to wear the green* —, piangere l'assenza, la perdita dell'amato **2.** (*ind. tessile*) battitoio, lupo **3.** (*spor.*) bastone per il giuoco del cricket ☆ — *pattern,* disegno convenzionale di tipo cinese; — *ware,* porcellana con disegno di salici || *weeping* —, salice piangente.

to willow, *v.t.* (*ind. tessile*) battere con il lupo.

willowing-machine ['wilouiŋməʃi:n], *V.* willow 2.

willowy ['wiloui], *ag.* **1.** fiancheggiato da salici, ombreggiato da molti salici **2.** sottile, grazioso, pieghevole: *a girl with a* — *figure,* una ragazza sottile come un giunco.

willy[1] ['wili], *s.* **1.** cestino di vimini **2.** (*ind. tessile*) battitoio, lupo.

Willy[2], *no.pr.m. dim.* di **William.**

willy-nilly ['wili'nili], *ag.* volente o nolente.

willy-nilly, *av.* per amore o per forza.

willy-willy ['wili,wili], *s.* (*austral.*) ciclone, uragano.

Wilma ['wilmə], *no.pr.f.* Vilma.

to wilt [wilt], *v.t.i.* (far) appassire, avvizzire: *the flowers soon wilted in the over-heated room,* i fiori appassirono presto nella stanza surriscaldata.

Wilton ['wiltən], *no.pr.* (*geog.*) Wilton ‖ *s.* — (*carpet*), tappeto fabbricato a Wilton.

wily ['waili], *ag.* astuto, scaltro.

wimble ['wimbl], *ag.* (*dial.*) attivo, agile ‖ *s.* **1.** (*miner.*) trivella, succhiello **2.** (*mec.*) menaruola.

to **wimble**, *v.t.i.* **1.** trivellare, fare buchi con un succhiello **2.** *fig.* insinuarsi: *to — into sthg.*, insinuarsi in ql.co.

wimple ['wimpl], *s.* **1.** soggolo **2.** piega, arricciatura **3.** meandro (di fiume).

to **wimple**, *v.t.i.* **1.** mettere il soggolo a **2.** velare (anche *fig.*) **3.** pieghettare, arricciare; cadere in pieghe **4.** andare a zig-zag; descrivere meandri (di fiume).

wimpled ['wimpld], *ag.* **1.** avviluppato in un velo, soggolo **2.** pieghettato, arricciato **3.** *fig.* intricato.

win[1] [win], *s.* (*fam.*) ` vittoria, successo: *our team had six wins last summer*, la nostra squadra ottenne sei vittorie l'estate scorsa.

to **win**[1], *pass.p.p.* **won** [wʌn], *v.t.i.* **1.** vincere, conquistare (anche *fig.*); essere vittorioso (anche *fig.*): *I am glad I have won your confidence*, sono lieto di aver ottenuto la tua fiducia; *I won one pound from* (o *off*) *him at cards*, gli vinsi una sterlina a carte; *which team won?*, che squadra vinse?; *to — a battle*, vincere una battaglia; *to — fame*, conquistare la fama; *to — a fortress*, conquistare una fortezza; *to — a lady's hand*, ottenere la mano di una donna; *to — one's spurs*, guadagnarsi gli speroni, essere fatto cavaliere; *fig.* ottenere il riconoscimento dei propri meriti ‖ *to — the day* (o *the field*), essere vittorioso; *to — free*, riuscire a fuggire con successo; riuscire nei propri sforzi; *to — hands down*, (*fam.*) vincere senza fatica **2.** persuadere; ottenere il favore di: *he won us to come*, ci persuase a venire; *to — all hearts*, ottenere il favore di tutti **3.** raggiungere (con sforzo): *to — the summit*, raggiungere la cima.

win[2], *s.* (*sl.*) un penny.

wince[1] [wins], *s.* **1.** sussulto, sobbalzo, trasalimento **2.** (*dial.*) calcio.

to **wince**[1], *v.i.* **1.** sussultare, sobbalzare, ritrarsi trasalendo: *he winced at the insult*, egli trasalì all'insulto **2.** (*dial.*) scalciare d'impazienza, di dolore.

wince[2], *s.* (*mec.*) verricello.

to **wince**[2], *v.t.* immergere, calare a mezzo di un verricello, rullo.

wincey ['winsi], *s.* flanella di lana, di lana e cotone.

winch [wintʃ], *s.* **1.** argano **2.** manovella **3.** *V.* **wince**[2].

Winchester ['wintʃistə*], *no.pr.* (*geog.*) Winchester ‖ *s.* **1.** — (*rifle*), « Winchester » (fucile da caccia) **2.** — (*quart*), mezzo gallone.

wind[1] [wind], *s.* **1.** vento: *contrary —*, vento contrario; *fair —*, vento favorevole; *a gust of —*, una raffica di vento; *a slant of —*, (*mar.*) una brezza favorevole; *the — is rising, falling*, il vento si sta alzando, sta cessando; *he ran like the —*, corse come il vento; *my papers were blown to the four winds*, le mie carte furono sparse ai quattro venti; *strange sounds came on the —*, giunsero strani suoni portati dal vento ‖ *before* (o *down*) *the —*, col vento in poppa ‖ *in the —*, preparato, discusso in segreto ‖ *in the —'s eye* (o *in the teeth of the —*), (*mar.*) contro vento ‖ *off the —*, fuori vento ‖ *they cast prudence to the winds*, *fig.* abbandonarono ogni prudenza ‖ *to find out how the — blows*, *fig.* sentire da che parte tira il vento ‖ *to get the — up*, (*sl.*) aver fifa ‖ *to put the — upon s.o.*, (*sl.*) spaventare qlcu. ‖ *to raise the —*, (*sl.*) ottenere il denaro necessario ‖ *to sail close to the —*, (*mar.*) andare all'orza; *fig.* sfiorare l'indecenza, la disonestà ‖ *to sow the — and reap the whirlwind*, *prov.* chi semina vento raccoglie tempesta **2.** respiro, fiato: *the runner soon lost his —*, al corridore mancò presto il fiato ‖ *sound in — and limbs*, in eccellenti condizioni fisiche **3.** sentore; odore portato dal vento: *the deer got — of the hunter*, il cervo fiutò l'odore del cacciatore; *to get — of a plot*, *fig.* aver sentore di un com-

plotto **4.** flatulenza **5.** parole vuote, vacue, senza significato: *his poems are mere —*, le sue poesie sono del tutto insignificanti ☆ — *-bound*, (*mar.*) immobilizzato dal vento; — *-break*, frangivento; — *-broken*, bolso; — *-egg*, uovo non fecondato; — *-fanner*, (*ornit.*) falchetto; — *-flower*, (*poet.*) anemone; — *-gall*, (*vet.*) tumore (nelle giunture dei cavalli); — *-instruments*, strumenti a fiato; — *-jammer*, (*sl. mar.*) nave mercantile, veliero; — *-screen*, (*aut.*) parabrezza: — *-screen wiper*, (*aut.*) tergicristallo; — *-tight*, che non lascia passare l'aria.

to **wind**[1] [wind; *nel senso* **1.** waind], *v.t.* **1.** suonare (strumenti a fiato): *to — the horn*, suonare il corno **2.** fiutare: *the hounds had winded the hare*, i cani avevano fiutato la lepre **3.** sfiatare, far perdere il fiato a: *he was winded by the run*, era rimasto senza fiato per la corsa **4.** far riprendere fiato a: *I stopped to — the horse*, mi fermai per far prender fiato al cavallo.

wind[2] [waind], *s.* **1.** giro (di carica, manovella) **2.** avvolgimento **3.** curva, svolta ☆ — *-up*, fine, conclusione; (*teat.*) scioglimento.

to **wind**[2], *pass.p.p.* **wound** [waund], *v.t.i.* **1.** serpeggiare; salire a spirale, a chiocciola (di scala): *the path winds round the lawn*, il sentiero gira attorno al prato; *the river winds its way to the sea*, il fiume scorre serpeggiando verso il mare; *the road winds up, down the hill*, la strada sale, scende serpeggiando; *to — oneself* (o *one's way*) *into s.o.'s heart*, *fig.* insinuarsi nel cuore di qlcu. **2.** avvolgere, circondare, cingere: *the plant winds round the pole*, la pianta si attorciglia attorno al palo; *she wound a blanket round him*, lo avvolse in una coperta; *she wound her arms round her child* (o *she wound the child in her arms*), cinse il bambino con le braccia; *the snake winds itself round its prey*, il serpente si attorciglia attorno alla preda; *to — a bobbin*, avvolgere il filo su bobina; *to — cotton on a reel*, avvolgere cotone su bobina; *to — the wool into a ball*, avvolgere la lana in gomitolo ‖ *to — s.o. round one's little finger*, *fig.* far fare a, fare di qlcu. ciò che si vuole **3.** caricare (molla, orologio); girare, far girare: *to — a handle*, girare, azionare una manovella; *to — the ship*, (*mar.*) virare di bordo **4.** sollevare (peso), portare in superficie per mezzo di argano: *to — water from a well*, estrarre acqua da un pozzo **5.** incurvarsi (di tavola, albero) **6.** *to — off*, svolgere, svolgersi; dipanare, dipanarsi **7.** *to — up*, avvolgere, arrotolare; caricare (molla, orologio); tendere al massimo (anche *fig.*); finire, terminare; (*comm.*) liquidare, chiudere (società, conti): *the company wound up*, (*comm.*) la società fu messa in liquidazione; *he is winding himself up for the effort, to do his best*, *fig.* sta raccogliendo tutte le sue forze per lo sforzo, per fare del suo meglio; *he was wound up to a fury*, *fig.* era al parossismo della collera; *how does the story — up?*, come si conclude la storia?; *to — up a meeting, a debate*, sciogliere una seduta, chiudere un dibattito; *to — up the shutter*, (*foto.*) caricare l'otturatore; *to — up the strings of a fiddle*, tendere al massimo le corde di un violino; *to — up wool*, aggomitolare la lana.

windage ['windidʒ], *s.* **1.** differenza tra il diametro di un proiettile e quello interno della canna dell'arma da fuoco **2.** influenza del vento nella deviazione di un proiettile **3.** (*mar.*) superficie della nave esposta al vento; superficie esterna dell'opera morta.

windbag ['windbæg], *s.* **1.** otre (di cornamusa) **2.** (*fig. fam.*) parolaio.

winded ['windid], *ag.* sfiatato ☆ *long —*, dal fiato lungo; *fig.* verboso; *short —*, dal respiro corto.

winder[1] ['waində*], *nel senso* **2.** ['wində*], *s.* **1.** suonatore di strumento a fiato **2.** colpo, corsa che toglie il fiato.

winder[2], *s.* **1.** operaio addetto all'argano, all'incannatoio **2.** (*miner.*) apparecchio di sollevamento **3.** chiave per caricare l'orologio; manovella (di argano, ecc.) **4.** (*ind. tessile*) incannatoio, rocchettiera **5.** (*edil.*) gradino di scala a chiocciola **6.** (*cine.*) bobinatrice **7.** (*bot.*) (pianta) volubile.

windfall ['windfɔ:l], *s.* **1.** frutto fatto cadere dal vento **2.** fortuna inaspettata.

windily ['windili], *av.* **1.** in modo ventoso **2.** *fig.* vanamente; verbosamente.

windiness ['windinis], *s.* **1.** clima ventoso **2.** *fig.* vuotaggine; verbosità **3.** (*arc.*) flatulenza, ventosità.

winding ['waindiŋ], *ag.* sinuoso, tortuoso, a zigzag; a chiocciola (di scala) || *s.* **1.** movimento, corso sinuoso; serpeggiamento; tortuosità (anche *fig.*); sinuosità **2.** curva, svolta, tornante, zig-zag; spira; meandro, anfratto **3.** incurvatura (di tavola, asse) **4.** caricamento, avvitamento (di orologio, molla, ecc.) **5.** (*elett.*) avvolgimento, bobinaggio; spira **6.** (*ind. tessile*) bobinatura, avvolgimento; incannatura; matassa, ritorcitura **7.** (*miner.*) estrazione; sollevamento ☆ — *drum*, (*mec.*) tamburo di avvolgimento; — *engine*, (*miner.*) apparecchio di sollevamento; — *frame* (o — *machine*), (*ind. tessile*) spolatrice, incannatoio; — *machine*, (*elett.*) bobinatrice; — *ratio*, (*elett.*) rapporto di trasformazione, di spire; — *-sheet*, sudario; — *stairs*, scala in curva; — *tackle*, (*mar.*) caliorna, grosso paranco || *coil* —, (*elett.*) avvolgimento a bobina; *cross* —, (*ind. tessile*) incannatura a filo incrociato; *parallel* —, (*ind. tessile*) incannatura parallela; *shunt* —, (*elett.*) avvolgimento in parallelo.

windingly ['waindiŋli], *av.* sinuosamente, tortuosamente; a meandri; a zig-zag; a chiocciola, a spirale.

windlass ['windləs], *s.* argano, verricello.

to **windlass**, *v.t.* sollevare, issare con un argano.

windless ['windlis], *ag.* **1.** senza vento **2.** (*rar.*) trafelato, senza fiato.

windmill ['winmil], *s.* **1.** mulino a vento || *to fight windmills*, *fig.* combattere contro i mulini a vento **2.** (*aer.*) mulinello **3.** mulinello, girandola (giocattolo) **4.** (*comm.*) cambiale di comodo.

window ['windou], *s.* finestra; finestrino; sportello; apertura, vano: *he looked out of the* —, guardò fuori della finestra || *to have all one's goods in the* —, aver tutte le merci in mostra; *fig.* essere superficiale ☆ — *-box*, cassetta per i fiori (per davanzali); — *-dresser*, vetrinista; — *-dressing*, l'arte di comporre una vetrina; *fig.* l'arte di presentare una situazione sotto una luce favorevole; — *-envelope*, busta a finestra; — *-pane*, vetro di finestra; — *-pull*, maniglia di finestra; — *-sash*, telaio di finestra; — *-shutter*, imposta; — *-sill*, davanzale || *French-* —, porta finestra; *shop-* —, vetrina (di negozio).

windowed ['windoud], *ag.* munito di finestre.

windpipe ['windpaip], *s.* (*anat.*) trachea.

windshield ['windʃi:ld], *s.* (*amer. aut.*) parabrezza ☆ — *vizor*, visiera parasole; — *wiper*, tergicristallo: — *wiper blade*, spazzola del tergicristallo.

Windsor ['winzə*], *no.pr.* (*geog.*) Windsor || *the House of* —, la dinastia dei Windsor ☆ — *-chair*, sedia in legno con lo schienale ricurvo e braccioli; — *-soap*, sapone di Windsor (profumato e di colore scuro).

windward ['windwəd], *ag.* **1.** che si muove contro vento **2.** situato verso la parte da cui soffia il vento; con la faccia rivolta verso il vento || *s.* sopravvento.

Windward Islands (the) ['windwəd'ailəndz], *no.pr. pl.* (*geog.*) le Isole Sopravvento.

windy ['windi], *ag.* **1.** ventoso, esposto al vento: *it is very* — *to-day*, oggi c'è molto vento **2.** verboso; ampolloso, vacuo: *a* — *lecturer*, un conferenziere verboso **3.** flatulento **4.** (*sl.*) spaventato.

wine [wain], *s.* **1.** vino || *Adam's* —, l'acqua || *new* — *in old bottles*, *fig.* principi troppo originali per essere confinati in vecchie istituzioni || *to be in* —, essere brillo **2.** succo fermentato (di frutti, distillato dal grano, ecc.) **3.** festa universitaria in cui si beve vino ☆ — *-bag* (o — *-bibber*), ubriacone, beone; — *-bottle*, bottiglia per il vino; — *-card*, lista dei vini; — *-cellar* (o — *-vault*), cantina per vini; — *-cooler*, secchiello

per ghiaccio; — *-glass*, bicchiere da vino; — *-grower*, viticultore; — *-press*, torchio da vino; — *-skin*, otre || *currant* —, succo fermentato di ribes; *dry* —, vino secco; *sparkling* —, spumante; *sweet* —, vino dolce.

to **wine**, *v.t.i.* (*fam.*) **1.** (far) bere vino; offrire vino a **2.** partecipare a una festa di studenti in cui si beve vino.

wing [wiŋ], *s.* **1.** ala (di uccelli, insetti) (anche *fig.*): *the wings of a bird*, le ali di un uccello; *on the wings of the wind*, sulle ali del vento; velocemente || *fear lent him wings*, la paura gli dava le ali || *to clip s.o.'s wings*, tarpare le ali a qlcu., limitare l'attività di qlcu. || *to take s.o. under one's* —, prendere qlcu. sotto la propria protezione **2.** volo: *on the* —, in volo; *to take* —, prendere il volo **3.** ala: *the left* — *of this palace is new*, l'ala sinistra di questo palazzo è nuova; *the right* — *of the army is ready to attack*, l'ala destra dell'esercito è pronta all'attacco; *the right* — *of that football team is very swift*, l'ala destra di quella squadra di calcio è molto veloce **4.** battente (di porta) **5.** *pl.* (*teat.*) quinte: *before entering the stage the actors were in the wings*, prima di entrare in scena, gli attori stavano tra le quinte **6.** *pl.* distintivo di pilota (della R.A.F., ecc.) ☆ — *-commander*, (*mil.*) tenente colonnello della R.A.F.; — *flap*, (*aer.*) ipersostentatore; — *-footed*, con le ali ai piedi; — *-loading*, (*aer.*) carico alare; — *nut* (*mec.*) dado a alette; — *over*, (*aer.*) virata sghemba; — *section*, (*aer.*) sezione alare; — *-shell*, (*zool.*) strombo; — *span*, (*aer.*) apertura alare || *center* —, (*aer.*) tronco centrale; *slotted* —, ala a fessura.

to **wing**, *v.t.i.* **1.** dare ali a (anche *fig.*); accelerare: *hate winged his vengeance*, l'odio diede ali alla sua vendetta **2.** (*poet.*) volare: *their planes winged over the Alps*, i loro aeroplani sorvolarono le Alpi; *the swallow winged (its way) to its nest*, la rondine volò al nido **3.** ferire alle ali (uccelli); ferire alle braccia (persone).

winged [wiŋd], *ag.* alato (anche *fig.*): — *words*, parole alate || *the* — *god*, (*mit. poet.*) Mercurio; *the* — *horse*, (*mit. poet.*) Pegaso.

wingless ['wiŋlis], *ag.* senza ali, aptero.

winglet ['wiŋlit], *s.* aletta.

wink [wiŋk], *s.* **1.** lo sbattere delle palpebre; ammicco, strizzatina d'occhi: *without a* — *of the eyelid*, senza batter ciglio || *to tip s.o. the* —, (*sl.*) ammiccare, far cenno con gli occhi a qlcu. **2.** *fig.* istante: *I have not slept a* —, non ho chiuso occhio || *in a* —, in un istante **3.** breve sonno || *forty winks*, (*fam.*) un sonnellino.

to **wink**, *v.t.i.* **1.** sbattere (le palpebre), sbattere (delle palpebre); strizzare l'occhio **2.** brillare, scintillare (di luce, stelle, ecc.) **3.** *to* — *at* (*s.o., sthg.*), ammiccare a; fingere di non vedere: *to* — *at an abuse*, passar sopra a un abuso; *to* — *at s.o.*, ammiccare a qlcu.

winking ['wiŋkiŋ], *s.* **1.** lo sbatter le palpebre; l'ammiccare, lo strizzare l'occhio || *like* —, molto rapidamente; in un batter d'occhio **2.** il brillare, lo scintillare (di luce, stelle, ecc.).

winkingly ['wiŋkiŋli], *av.* battendo le palpebre; ammiccando.

winkle ['wiŋkl], *s.* (*zool. abbr.* di *periwinkle*) chiocciola di mare.

winner ['winə*], *s.c.* vincitore, vincitrice ☆ *bread* —, sostegno economico della famiglia.

winning ['winiŋ], *ag.* **1.** vincente, vincitore: *the* — *horse*, il cavallo vincente **2.** attraente, avvincente: *a* — *smile*, un sorriso simpatico, attraente; — *ways*, modi seducenti || *s.* **1.** vittoria, conquista **2.** (*miner.*) estrazione **3.** *pl.* vincite (al giuoco) ☆ *the* — *game*, (*giuoco*) la bella; — *post*, traguardo.

winningly ['winiŋli], *av.* in modo avvincente, attraente, affascinante.

to **winnow** ['winou], *v.t.i.* **1.** vagliare, spulare, ventilare || *to* — *out the chaff from the grain*, separare la loppa dal grano **2.** *fig.* vagliare; separare; esaminare, discutere, ponderare: *to — the true from the false*, separare il vero dal falso **3.** (*poet.*) sbattere (le ali); agitare (l'aria con le ali); sparpagliare (di vento).

winnower ['winouə*], *s.c.* chi vaglia.

winnowing ['winouiŋ], *s.* vagliatura; spulatura; scelta ☆ — *-fan* (o — *-machine*), (*agr.*) macchina vagliatrice.

winsome ['winsəm], *ag.* attraente; amabile; seducente; cattivante.

winsomely ['winsəmli], *av.* in modo attraente; amabilmente.

winsomeness ['winsəmnis], *s.* amabilità, grazia.

winter ['wintə*], *ag.* d'inverno, invernale ‖ *s.* **1.** inverno: *a hard —*, un inverno rigido; *a mild —*, un inverno mite **2.** anno: *a man of eighty winters*, un uomo di ottant'anni **3.** *fig.* vecchiaia; periodo di difficoltà e tristezza ☆ — *-bourne*, torrente, fiume che scorre solo d'inverno; — *-cherry*, (*bot.*) palloncini, alchechengi; — *-clothing*, abiti pesanti; — *-crops*, messi tagliate in tardo autunno; — *-garden*, giardino d'inverno; — *-quarters*, (*mil.*) quartieri d'inverno; — *-sleep*, ibernazione; — *solstice*, (*astr.*) solstizio d'inverno; — *sports*, sport invernali; — *-tide*, (*poet.*) inverno.

to winter, *v.t.i.* **1.** passare l'inverno; svernare: *he wintered in Italy*, trascorse l'inverno in Italia **2.** mantenere, nutrire (piante, animali) durante l'inverno.

wintered ['wintəd], *ag.* **1.** esposto all'influenza dell'inverno, gelato, inaridito dall'inverno **2.** (*arc.*) vecchio.

wintergreen ['wintəgri:n], *s.* (*bot.*) gaultheria.

to winter-ground ['wintəgraund], *v.t.* proteggere (piante) durante i rigori invernali.

winterless ['wintəlis], *ag.* senza inverno.

winterly ['wintəli], *ag.* invernale.

wintriness ['wintrinis], *s.* rigore invernale; aspetto invernale.

wintry ['wintri], *ag.* **1.** invernale; rigido, freddo: *a — sky*, un cielo invernale **2.** *fig.* triste; senza calore, senza vivacità: *a — smile*, un sorriso freddo, forzato.

winy ['waini], *ag.* vinoso: *a — nose*, un naso da avvinazzato.

wipe [waip], *s.* **1.** asciugatura; strofinata; spolverata: *to give sthg. a —*, dare una spolverata a ql.co. **2.** sferzata; fendente **3.** (*sl.*) fazzoletto.

to wipe, *v.t.i.* **1.** asciugare; pulire; strofinare: *to — the dishes*, asciugare i piatti; *to — one's eyes*, asciugarsi gli occhi; *to — one's nose*, soffiarsi il naso ‖ *to — the floor with s.o.*, (*sl.*) infliggere una umiliazione, una sconfitta, ecc. a qlcu. ‖ *to — s.o.'s eyes*, (*sl.*) aver la meglio su qlcu., bagnare il naso a qlcu. **2.** *to — at* (*s.o.*), (*sl.*) colpire, sferzare, allungare un colpo a **3.** *to — off*, togliere strofinando, cancellare: *to — off a debt*, regolare, liquidare un debito **4.** *to — out*, cancellare; distruggere, annientare: *to — out an army*, annientare un esercito; *to — out an insult*, vendicare un insulto.

wiper ['waipə*], *s.c.* chi è addetto alle pulizie ‖ *s.* **1.** strofinaccio **2.** (*sl.*) fazzoletto **3.** (*mec.*) eccentrico, elemento sporgente ☆ *screen- —*, (*aut.*) tergicristallo.

wire ['waiə*], *s.* **1.** filo metallico ‖ *to be on wires*, *fig.* avere i nervi tesi ‖ *to pull the wires*, manovrare i fili (di marionette); *fig.* tenere le fila (di una situazione) **2.** (*fam.*) telegramma: *by —*, per telegrafo; *he will send me a —*, mi manderà un telegramma ☆ — *bar*, (*mec.*) sbozzato per trafile; — *brush*, (*mec.*) spazzola metallica; — *cutter*, pinza tagliafili; — *drawing*, (*mec.*) trafilatura; — *entanglement*, (*mil.*) reticolato di filo spinato; — *glass*, vetro retinato; — *-haired*, a pelo ruvido (di cane); — *netting*, (*ind.*) rete metallica; — *puller*, burattinaio; *fig.* chi regge segretamente le fila di ql.co.; — *recorder*, magnetofono; — *recording*, registrazione su filo; — *-tapping*, intercettazione di messaggi telegrafici; — *walker*, funambolo; — *-worm*, (*entom.*) enteride; millepiedi; — *wove*, di qualità superiore (di carta) ‖ *barbed —*, filo spinato; *copper —*, filo di rame; *live —*, filo carico di elettricità; *fig.* persona attiva ed energica.

to wire, *v.t.i.* **1.** legare, assicurare con filo metallico: *he wired the cork of the bottle*, assicurò il tappo della bottiglia con un filo metallico; *to — two things together*, legare due cose con filo metallico **2.** (*elett.*) installare fili elettrici in (una casa) **3.** prendere in trappola (animali) **4.** telegrafare, spedire un telegramma **5.** *to — in*, (*sl.*) mettersi di lena al lavoro: *you had better — in and finish your job*, faresti meglio a metterti di lena per finire il lavoro.

wired ['waiəd], *ag.* **1.** sostenuto, rinforzato con filo metallico; legato con filo metallico **2.** munito di, recintato con grate, inferriate.

to wiredraw ['waiə-dro:], *pass.* **wiredrew** ['waiə-dru:], *p.p.* **wiredrawn** ['waiə-dro:n], *v.t.* **1.** (*mec.*) trafilare in fili **2.** decomprimere (vapore, ecc.) **3.** *fig.* allungare, tirare in lungo; sforzare: *a wiredrawn lecture*, una conferenza prolissa.

wireless ['waiəlis], *ag.* senza fili ‖ *s.* radio: *to talk*, *to sing on the —*, parlare, cantare alla radio ☆ — *commentator*, radiocronista; — *message*, radiomessaggio; — *operator*, radiotelegrafista; — *telegraphy*, radiotelegrafia, telegrafia senza fili; — *telephony*, radiotelefonia.

to wireless, *v.t.i.* radiotelegrafare.

wirily ['waiərili], *av.* tenacemente; instancabilmente.

wiriness ['waiərinis], *s.* tenacia; instancabilità.

wiring ['waiəriŋ], *s.* **1.** (*elett. tel.*) impianto, complesso delle linee **2.** (*elett.*) cablaggio, fascio dei conduttori ☆ *surface —*, (*elett.*) impianto non incassato.

wiry ['waiəri], *ag.* **1.** di, simile a filo metallico ‖ *-hair*, capelli ispidi **2.** flessibile; sottile e resistente; *fig.* tenace; instancabile: *a — person*, una persona instancabile **3.** (*med.*) filiforme: — *pulse*, polso filiforme.

to wis [wis], *v.t.:* *I —*, (*arc.*) so bene.

wisdom ['wizdəm], *s.* **1.** saggezza; sapienza; giudizio, senno; discernimento, buon senso **2.** (*arc.*) scienza, erudizione ☆ — *-tooth*, dente del giudizio: *to cut one's — -teeth*, mettere giudizio.

wise[1] [waiz], *ag.* **1.** saggio, savio, assennato; prudente, circospetto: *it would not be — to do it*, non sarebbe prudente farlo; *to hide one's ignorance by assuming a — look*, nascondere la propria ignoranza dietro un'aria di sicurezza ‖ *the Wise Men of the East*, i Re Magi **2.** (*arc.*) sapiente, erudito **3.** (*amer.*) ben informato: *he went away none the wiser*, se ne andò via senza saperne più di prima; *to put s.o. — to sthg.*, informare qlcu., mettere qlcu. al corrente di ql.co. **4.** (*arc.*) abile, esperto **5.** (*dial.*) sano di mente **6.** (*arc.*) esperto nelle arti magiche ☆ — *man*, stregone; — *woman*, strega, indovina; (*scoz.*) levatrice.

to wise[1], *v.t.i.:* *to — up*, (*sl. amer.*) informare; venire a sapere.

wise[2], *s.* modo, maniera; sorta, guisa: *in no —*, in nessun modo; *in some —*, in qualche modo.

to wise[2], *v.t.* (*rar.*) guidare; mostrare (la strada).

wiseacre ['waiz,eikə*], *s.* persona saccente, sapientone.

wise-crack ['waizkræk], *s.* (*sl. amer.*) spiritosaggine, detto arguto.

to wise-crack, *v.i.* (*sl. amer.*) dire, fare spiritosaggini.

wisehead ['waizhed], *s.* (*iron.*) saccentone.

wisely ['waizli], *av.* saggiamente; giudiziosamente, con senno.

wish [wiʃ], *s.* **1.** desiderio, voglia: *he has no — to go to school*, non ha alcun desiderio di andare a scuola ‖ *the — is father to the thought*, *prov.* i desideri guidano i pensieri **2.** desiderio, richiesta: *to carry out s.o.'s wishes*, realizzare i desideri di qlcu. **3.** augurio, voto: *my best wishes!*, i miei migliori auguri! **4.** desiderio, cosa desiderata: *you have got your — at last*, hai finalmente ottenuto quello che volevi.

to wish, *v.t.i.* **1.** desiderare; volere; augurare, augurarsi: *to — for sthg.*, desiderare ql.co.: *to have everything one can —for*, avere tutto ciò che si può desiderare **2.** (IV;

VI) volere; desiderare: *do you — me to go?*, vuoi che me ne vada?; *to — to do sthg.*, voler fare ql.co.; *I — it (to be) done*, voglio che ciò sia fatto; *I — you to do so*, voglio che tu faccia ciò **3.** (*seguito dal pass. congiunt.*) volere (al condizionale): *I — I could go*, vorrei poter andare; *I — I had a car*, vorrei avere un'automobile; *she wishes she were younger*, vorrebbe essere più giovane **4.** augurare, augurarsi: *I — you may succeed*, mi auguro che tu possa riuscire; *to — s.o. joy, luck*, augurare a qlcu. gioia, buona fortuna; *to — well, ill*, augurare ogni bene, male ‖ *I — myself dead*, vorrei essere morto ‖ *it is to be wished that...*, ci si deve augurare che... ‖ *to — s.o. good-night*, augurare la buona notte a qlcu.

wisher ['wiʃə*], *s.c.* **1.** chi desidera **2.** chi augura.

wishful ['wiʃful], *ag.* desideroso, bramoso: *to be — of sthg.*, *to do sthg.*, essere desideroso di ql.co., di fare ql.co. ‖ *— thinking*, il credere vero ql.co. perchè lo si desidera intensamente.

wishfully ['wiʃfuli], *av.* con desiderio.

wishfulness ['wiʃfulnis], *s.* desiderio; brama.

wishing ['wiʃiŋ], *ag.* desideroso, bramoso ‖ *s.* il desiderare ☆ *— -bone*, forchetta dello sterno di volatile (se spezzata, la parte più lunga porta fortuna a chi la ottiene); *— -cap*, berretto magico (chi lo porta ottiene ciò che desidera).

wish-wash ['wiʃwɔʃ], *s.* **1.** brodaglia **2.** *fig.* discorso insipido.

wishy-washy ['wiʃi,wɔʃi], *ag.* **1.** annacquato **2.** *fig.* di poco spirito.

wisp [wisp], *s.* **1.** manciata; piccolo fascio, ciuffo (di paglia, erba, ecc.): *a — of hair*, una ciocca, un ciuffo di capelli ‖ *a — of smoke*, un filo di fumo **2.** stormo (di beccaccini) **3.** (*will-o'-the*) —, fuoco fatuo; *fig.* persona inafferrabile.

to wisp, *v.t.i.* **1.** legare in piccoli fasci, attorcigliare **2.** strigliare (un cavallo) **3.** *to — away*, svanire, disperdersi: *to — away as a wisp of vapour*, disperdersi come una nuvola di vapore.

wispy ['wispi], *ag.* a mazzi; a ciuffi.

wist [wist], *pass.* di to **wit**.

wistaria [wis'tɛəriə], **wisteria** [wis'tiəriə], *s.* (*bot.*) glicine.

wistful ['wistful], *ag.* **1.** pieno di desiderio; ansioso: *— look*, sguardo ansioso; *— voice*, voce ansiosa **2.** pensoso, meditabondo, intento: *he grew silent and —*, si fece taciturno e assorto.

wistfully ['wistfuli], *av.* **1.** con desiderio; con ansia **2.** con aria pensosa, meditabonda, intenta.

wistfulness ['wistfulnis], *s.* **1.** desiderio; ansia **2.** pensosità; malinconia.

wit [wit], *s.* **1.** (*arc.*) intelligenza, ingegno; intuito, buon senso: *the — of man*, l'intelletto umano; *he has not the — to see it*, non ha l'intelligenza di vedere ciò **2.** *pl.* facoltà mentali: *to have quick wits*, essere d'ingegno vivace ‖ *to be at one's wits' end*, essere perplesso, non sapere più cosa fare; *to be out of one's wits*, essere pazzo; essere sconvolto; *to have one's wits about oneself*, essere nel pieno possesso delle poprie facoltà; avere prontezza di spirito ‖ *to live by one's wits*, vivere di espedienti **3.** spirito, brio, arguzia: *flash of —*, tratto di spirito; *a man of —*, un uomo di spirito **4.** persona arguta, spiritosa; bello spirito ‖ *the university wits*, (*st. lett.*) i begli ingegni universitari.

to wit (usato nel *pres. I*, *he* **wot** [wɔt], *pass.* **wist** [wist], *p.pr.* **witting** ['witiŋ]), *v.t.i.* (*arc.*) sapere: *God wot*, Dio lo sa ‖ *to —*, (*dir.*) vale a dire, cioè.

Witan ['witən], *s.* (*st.*) « Witan », i membri dell'assemblea nazionale Anglo-Sassone; l'assemblea stessa.

witch[1] [witʃ], *s.* (*dial.*) stregone, mago ☆ *— -doctor*, stregone.

witch[2], *s.* **1.** strega, maga, fattucchiera ‖ *as nervous as a —*, (*fam. amer.*) nervoso e agitato ‖ *white —*, maga benefica **2.** megera **3.** giovane donna affascinante; maliarda ☆ *— -finder*, chi individuava le

streghe; *— -hunter*, cacciatore di streghe; (*sl. amer.*) chi accusa presunti sovversivi; *—'s bells*, (*bot.*) digitale; *witches' butter*, (*bot.*) nostoc; *witches' Sabbath*, sabba delle streghe.

to witch[2], *v.t.* **1.** stregare **2.** affascinare, ammaliare.

witch[3], *s.* (*bot.*) olmo riccio.

witchcraft ['witʃkra:ft], *s.* **1.** stregoneria; arti magiche **2.** malia, incantesimo; *fig.* fascino.

witchery ['witʃəri], *s.* **1.** stregoneria, incantesimo **2.** fascino; incanto.

witching ['witʃiŋ], *ag.* **1.** che ha potere magico **2.** affascinante; incantevole, malioso.

witchingly ['witʃiŋli], *av.* **1.** magicamente **2.** incantevolmente.

Witenagemot ['witinəgi'mout], *s.* (*st.*) assemblea nazionale degli anglo-sassoni.

with [wið], *prep.* **1.** con, insieme a; presso: *come for a walk — me*, vieni a fare una passeggiata con me; *I had dinner — a friend*, pranzai con un amico; *I have been — this firm two years*, lavoro presso questa ditta da due anni; *I have no money — me*, non ho denaro con me; *I have no one to go out —*, non ho nessuno con cui uscire; *I sympathized — him at once*, simpatizzai subito con lui; *this colour does not go — my hair*, questo colore non sta bene coi miei capelli ‖ *— child*, incinta; *— young*, gravido, pregno (di animale) ‖ *— God*, defunto **2.** con, per mezzo di: *I'll cut it — a knife*, lo taglierò con un coltello; *we see — our eyes*, vediamo per mezzo degli occhi **3.** da, a causa di: *bent — age*, curvo per gli anni; *she shivered — fear*, tremava dalla paura **4.** con, munito di; provvisto di; dotato di: *a coat — three pockets*, una giacca con tre tasche; *a knife — a wooden handle*, un coltello con un manico di legno; *a woman — grey hair*, una donna dai capelli grigi **5.** con, contro: *to fight — s.o.*, lottare contro qlcu.; *to quarrel — s.o.*, litigare con qlcu. **6.** con, nonostante: *— all his faults I like him*, nonostante tutti i suoi difetti mi piace **7.** nel caso di, per, riguardo a: *— him, knowledge is important only for making money*, nel suo caso il sapere è importante solo per far denaro; *— me, it is the same*, per me fa lo stesso **8.** (Fraseologia): *— ease*, facilmente ‖ *— an eye to*, non trascurando, tenendo d'occhio ‖ *— one accord*, unanimente ‖ *— reference to*, in riferimento a ‖ *— regard* (o *respect*) *to*, a proposito di ‖ *— this* (o *that*), con ciò, pertanto ‖ *— your leave*, col vostro permesso ‖ *away — him!*, portatelo via! ‖ *down — traitors!*, morte ai traditori! ‖ *endowed —*, dotato di: *endowed — great sensibility*, dotato di grande sensibilità ‖ *be off — you!*, (*fam.*) vattene! ‖ *bear — me*, scusatemi ‖ *the decision lies* (o *rests*) *— you*, sta a te decidere ‖ *get along — you!*, muoviti! ‖ *I am — you there*, ne convengo ‖ *I could do — a cup of tea*, (*fam.*) gradirei una tazza di tè ‖ *I have done — it*, non ne voglio più sentire parlare ‖ *I have nothing to do — him*, non ho niente in comune con lui ‖ *I think — you*, la penso come te ‖ *it is a habit — me*, è una mia abitudine ‖ *it is pouring — rain*, piove a catinelle ‖ *this book deals — the life of the natives*, questo libro tratta della vita degli indigeni ‖ *you must part — your friends*, devi separarti dai tuoi amici ‖ *to begin —*, per cominciare.

to withdraw [wið'drɔ:], *pass.* **withdrew** [wið'dru:], *p.p.* **withdrawn** [wið'drɔ:n], *v.t.i.* **1.** tirare indietro, levare: *he withdrew his hand from the hot stove*, ritirò la mano dalla stufa ardente **2.** ritirare, ritirarsi, allontanare, allontanarsi: *the ladies withdrew*, le signore si ritirarono; *those coins were withdrawn from circulation*, quelle monete furono ritirate dalla circolazione; *you ought to — your daughter from that school*, dovresti ritirare tua figlia da quella scuola.

withdrawal [wið'drɔ:əl], *s.* **1.** ritirata; ritiro **2.** (*comm.*) prelevamento di fondi **3.** ritrattazione.

withdrawn [wið'drɔ:n], *p.p.* di to **withdraw**.

withdrew [wið'dru:], *pass.* di to **withdraw**.

withe [wiθ], *s*. vimine, vinco.

wither ['wiðə*], *s*. (*ind*.) essiccazione (delle foglie di tè).

to **wither**, *v.t.i.* **1.** (far) appassire; avvizzire; disseccare; inaridire (anche *fig*.): *her affections withered*, i suoi sentimenti si inaridirono; *your roses have withered (up)*, le vostre rose sono appassite **2.** deperire, languire: *age has withered (away) her beauty*, l'età ha fatto sfiorire la sua bellezza **3.** (*scherz*.) agghiacciare; fulminare: *she withered him with a look*, lo fulminò con una occhiata.

withered ['wiðəd], *ag*. appassito, sfiorito; avvizzito; disseccato; inaridito.

withering ['wiðəriŋ], *ag*. **1.** che inaridisce, che appassisce; che fa appassire **2.** languente **3.** (*scherz*.) sprezzante; fulminante: — *contempt*, disprezzo che annienta.

witheringly ['wiðəriŋli], *av*. **1.** in modo da fare appassire **2.** in modo sprezzante.

witherite ['wiðərait], *s*. (*min*.) witherite.

withers ['wiðəz], *s.pl.* garrese ‖ *my — are unwrung*, *fig*. l'accusa, l'argomento non mi tocca.

to **withhold** [wið'hould], *pass.p.p.* **withheld** [wið'held], *v.t.* trattenere; ritirare; rifiutare: *I will — my consent*, negherò il mio consenso; *to — the truth from s.o.*, nascondere la verità a qlcu.

within [wi'ðin], *prep*. **1.** dentro, entro, in; al di qua di: — *the frontier*, al di qua della frontiera; — *the house*, in casa; — *a radius of two miles*, in un raggio di due miglia; — (*the*) *walls*, entro le mura; *dissentions* — *the Church*, dissensi in seno alla Chiesa; *to keep* — *the laws*, mantenersi nella legalità; *to live* (o *to keep*) — *one's income*, vivere secondo le proprie possibilità ‖ — *board*, (*mar*.) a bordo ‖ — *call*, a portata di voce ‖ — *doors*, in casa ‖ — *hearing*, fin dove si può udire ‖ — *limits*, moderatamente ‖ — *oneself*, tra sè, mentalmente: *he thought — himself that...*, pensò tra sè che ... ‖ — *s.o.'s reach*, a portata di qlcu. ‖ — *sight*, in vista, visibile **2.** (*in espressioni di tempo*) **in meno di, non oltre:** — *a week*, entro una settimana, in meno di una settimana; — *the week*, entro la (fine della) settimana; *delivery* — *a month*, (*comm*.) consegna a un mese.

within, *av*. **1.** all'interno, dentro: *from* — *terno; to decorate a house* — *and without*, decorare una casa all'interno e all'esterno **2. in casa, a casa:** *is the doctor* —?, è in casa il dottore? **3.** *fig*. in sè, **nell'animo 4.** (*teat*.) **dietro alle quinte.**

without [wi'ðaut], *prep*. **1. senza, senza di:** — *delay*, senza indugio; — *doubt*, senza dubbio; — *fail*, senza fallo; — *me*, senza di me; — *speaking*, senza parlare; — *your saying so*, senza che tu lo dica; *times* — *number*, innumerevoli volte; *he went out* — *an umbrella*, uscì senza ombrello; *I was* — *money*, non avevo danaro ‖ — *so much as apologizing*, senza nemmeno scusarsi ‖ *it goes* — *saying*, va da sè, è ovvio ‖ *to do* —, fare a meno di: *you'll have to do* — *a servant*, dovrai fare a meno della cameriera ‖ *to go* —, fare a meno di, sopportare la mancanza di: *to go* — *food*, digiunare **2.** (*letter*.) **fuori, fuori di, al di fuori di:** — *bounds*, — *limits*, fuori confine, al di fuori dei limiti ‖ *cong*. (*arc*.) **senza che, a meno che:** *you will not succeed — you work hard*, non riuscirai senza lavorare molto.

without, *av*. (*letter*.) **fuori, al di fuori** (anche *fig*.): *he listened to the noise* —, ascoltò il rumore fuori; *you will be at ease — and at peace within*, starai bene di dentro e di fuori.

without, *s*. **esterno, parte esterna:** *to look at sthg. from* —, guardare ql.co. dall'esterno.

to **withstand** [wið'stænd], *pass.p.p.* **withstood** [wið'stud], *v.t.i.* resistere, opporsi, opporre resistenza (a); sostenere: *to — a siege*, sostenere un assedio; *a cloth that can — hard wear*, una stoffa che resiste all'usura.

withstander [wið'stændə*], *s.c.* oppositore, oppositrice; antagonista, avversario, avversaria.

withstood [wið'stud], *pass.p.p.* di to **withstand.**

withy ['wiði], *s*. vimine, vinco.

witless ['witlis], *ag*. senza intelligenza, senza spirito; sciocco, stupido.

witlessly ['witlisli], *av*. senza spirito; scioccamente.

witlessness ['witlisnis], *s*. mancanza di intelligenza, di spirito; stupidità.

witling ['witliŋ], *s.c.* chi si reputa spiritoso.

witness ['witnis], *s.c.* testimone, teste: *hostile* —, teste avverso; *God is my* —, Dio mi è testimone ‖ *s*. testimonianza; prova, dimostrazione: *the empty cupboard was a — of his poverty*, la credenza vuota testimoniava la sua povertà; *to bear* — *to* (o *of*) *sthg*., testimoniare ql.co.; *to call to* —, chiamare a testimonianza; *to give* — *on behalf of*, testimoniare a favore di ☆ — -*box*, banco dei testimoni ‖ *eye*- —, testimone oculare.

to **witness**, *v.t.i.* **1.** testimoniare, fare da testimone: *none could — that he was present*, nessuno potè testimoniare la sua presenza; *to — against*, testimoniare contro; *to — for*, testimoniare a favore di **2.** mostrare, tradire: *his pale face witnessed his agitation*, il suo volto pallido tradiva l'agitazione che provava **3.** essere presente a, vedere: *to — an accident*, essere presente a un incidente **4.** firmare (un documento) come testimone.

witticism ['witisizəm], *s*. **1.** frizzo, arguzia, motto di spirito **2.** (*arc. spreg*.) dileggio, beffa.

wittily ['witili], *av*. spiritosamente; argutamente.

wittiness ['witinis], *s*. spirito; argutezza.

wittingly ['witiŋli], *av*. consapevolmente; di proposito.

wittol ['witəl], *s*. (*arc*.) marito tradito e compiacente; uno sciocco.

witty ['witi], *ag*. **1.** spiritoso; brillante; arguto: *a — remark*, un'osservazione arguta **2.** (*dial*.) intelligente; abile.

to **wive** [waiv], *v.t.i.* (*arc*.) **1.** prendere moglie **2.** dare moglie a **3.** divenire la moglie di.

wives, *pl*. di **wife**.

wizard ['wizəd], *ag*. **1.** stregato, incantato, magico **2.** che ha poteri magici ‖ *s*. stregone; mago (anche *fig*.): *he is a financial* —, è un mago della finanza.

wizardry ['wizədri], *s*. stregoneria (anche *fig*.).

wizen ['wizn], **wizened** ['wiznd], *ag*. avvizzito, raggrinzito; rugoso.

to **wizen**, *v.t.i.* avvizzire, avvizzirsi; disseccare, disseccarsi; raggrinzire, raggrinzirsi.

wo, woa [wou], *inter*. (*per fermare i cavalli*) oh!.

woad [woud], *s*. **1.** (*bot*.) guado **2.** guado (tintura).

to **woad**, *v.t.* tingere col guado.

wobble ['wobl], *s*. **1.** dondolio, oscillazione **2.** *fig*. incertezza, esitazione, ondeggiamento **3.** (*mec*.) rotazione fuori piano **4.** (*aut*.) sfarfallamento ☆ — *plate*, (*mec*.) rotore a disco inclinato; — *pump*, (*aer*.) pompa ausiliaria a mano.

to **wobble**, *v.t.i.* **1.** (far) dondolare, oscillare, vacillare; tremolare **2.** *fig*. tentennare, esitare; ondeggiare: *to — between two opinions*, esitare fra due opinioni **3.** (*mec*.) girare fuori piano.

wobbler ['woblə*], *s.c.* chi vacilla; *fig*. chi esita, tentenna ‖ *s*. (*mec*.) trefolo (di cilindro di laminatoio).

wobbly ['wobli], *ag*. **1.** vacillante, barcollante **2.** *fig*. esitante, titubante.

Woden ['woudn], *no.pr.m.* (*mit*.) Odino.

woe [wou], *s*. (*arc*.) dolore, pena, male; calamità, sventura: *a tale of* —, un racconto di sventure; *in weal and* —, nella prosperità e nella miseria; *to tell all one's woes*, raccontare tutte le proprie sventure ‖ — *is me!*, ahimè! ‖ — (*be*) *to him!*, sia maledetto! ‖ — *worth the day!*, (*arc*.) sia maledetto il giorno!.

woebegone ['woubi,gon], *ag*. triste, desolato, abbattuto: *to have a — look*, avere un'espressione addolorata.

woeful ['wouful], *ag*. doloroso; triste; afflitto: — *day*, un triste giorno.

woefully ['woufuli], *av.* in modo triste, miserando; disgraziatamente.

woefulness ['woufulnis], *s.* tristezza; miseria.

woke [wouk], *pass. p.p.* di to **wake**.

woken ['woukǝn], *p.p.* di to **wake**.

wold [would], *s.* terra non coltivata; landa; brughiera.

wolf [wulf], *pl.* **wolves** [wulvz], *s.* **1.** lupo: *the wolves howled from the prairies*, i lupi ululavano nelle praterie ‖ *to be a — in sheep's clothing*, essere un lupo in veste d'agnello ‖ *to be as hungry as a —*, avere una fame da lupo ‖ *to cry —*, gridare al lupo; dare falsi allarmi ‖ *to hold the — by the ears*, *fig.* essere in una situazione difficile ‖ *to keep the — from the door*, tener lontana la miseria **2.** persona avida, rapace **3.** (*mus.*) dissonanza ☆ *—'s-bane*, (*bot.*) aconito; *— -cub*, lupacchiotto; lupetto (nell'ordinamento scoutistico); *— -dog*, cane lupo; *— -fish*, (*ittiol.*) lupo di mare; *— shot*, lupara ‖ *she- —*, lupa.

to wolf, *v.t.* **1.** divorare avidamente ‖ *to — down food*, divorare il cibo in modo ingordo **2.** ingannare con falsi allarmi.

wolfish ['wulfiʃ], *ag.* da lupo, simile a un lupo; *fig.* selvaggio; crudele; vorace: *a — appetite*, un appetito da lupo.

wolfishly ['wulfiʃli], *av.* come un lupo; *fig.* crudelmente; avidamente.

wolfishness ['wulfiʃnis], *s.* carattere da lupo; *fig.* crudeltà; avidità.

wolfling ['wulfliŋ], *s.* lupacchiotto.

wolfram ['wulfrǝm], *s.* (*chim.*) wolframio; tungsteno ☆ *— steel*, (*metal.*) acciaio al tungsteno.

to wolve [wulv], *v.i.* **1.** agire da lupo **2.** emettere un suono lamentoso simile ad un ululato (di organo).

wolverene, wolverine ['wulvǝri:n], *s.* **1.** (*zool.*) ghiottone **2.** (*fam. amer.*) soprannome degli abitanti del Michigan ‖ *— State*, il Michigan.

wolves, *pl.* di **wolf**.

woman ['wumǝn], *pl.* **women** ['wimin], *s.* **1.** donna, femmina; (*fam.*) moglie: *a — of the world*, una donna di mondo; *a — with a past*, una donna con un passato; *born of —*, nato da donna, mortale; *a single —*, una donna nubile ‖ *there's a — in it!*, c'è di mezzo una donna! ‖ *to be tied to a —'s apron strings*, stare attaccato alla gonna di qlcu. **2.** femminuccia, donnicciuola: *there is sthg. of the — in his character*, c'è un cho di femmineo nel suo carattere; *to play the —*, fare la donnicciuola **3.** (*arc.*) dama di compagnia; cameriera ☆ *— doctor*, dottoressa; *— friend*, amica; *— hater*, misogino; *—'s man*, uomo galante; *women's movement*, movimento femminista; *women's rights*, i diritti della donna; *— servant*, cameriera; *— suffrage*, suffragio femminile; *—'s wit*, intuito femminile.

to woman, *v.t.* **1.** (*arc.*) spingere a comportarsi come una donna **2.** (*spreg.*) apostrofare col nome « donna » **3.** rifornire di personale femminile.

womanhood ['wumǝnhud], *s.* **1.** qualità, condizione, stato di donna; maturità fisica della donna **2.** *coll.* le donne.

womanish ['wumǝniʃ], *ag.* **1.** effeminato **2.** femminile; donnesco.

womanishly ['wumǝniʃli], *av.* **1.** effeminatamente **2.** femminilmente.

womanishness ['wumǝniʃnis], *s.* **1.** effeminatezza **2.** femminilità.

to womanize ['wumǝnaiz], *v.t.i.* **1.** effeminare; rendere effeminato **2.** frequentare prostitute.

womankind ['wumǝnkaind], *s.* le donne; il sesso femminile.

womanlike ['wumǝnlaik], *ag.* femminile; femmineo ‖ *av.* da donna.

womanliness ['wumǝnlinis], *s.* femminilità; qualità femminile.

womanly ['wumǝnli], *ag.* femminile, di donna; de-

gno di donna: *— modesty*, pudore femminile; *a truly — woman*, una vera donna.

womb [wu:m], *s.* ventre; grembo; seno; (*anat.*) utero: *fruit of the —*, (*letter.*) i figli; *in the — of time*, *fig.* nel grembo del tempo, nel futuro.

wombat ['wombǝt], *s.* (*zool.*) vombato.

women, *pl.* di **woman**.

won [wʌn], *pass.p.p.* di to **win**.

wonder ['wʌndǝ*], *s.* **1.** prodigio, portento; miracolo; oggetto, persona, avvenimento che suscita meraviglia: *a nine days' —*, un fuoco di paglia; *no — (that)*, non fa meraviglia che; *the seven wonders of the world*, le sette meraviglie del mondo; *what a —!*, che miracolo!; *this child is a —*, questo bambino è un prodigio; *to do* (o *to perform* o *to work*) *wonders*, far miracoli; fare grandi cose ‖ *for a —*, strano a dirsi: *he is punctual to-day for a —*, che miracolo! oggi è puntuale ‖ *signs and wonders*, miracoli e prodigi **2.** meraviglia, stupore; sorpresa; ammirazione: *I listened to him in —*, lo ascoltavo con stupore; *to be filled with —*, essere pieno di meraviglia ☆ *— -struck* (o *— -stricken*), stupefatto, trasecolato; *— -work*, lavoro, atto miracoloso; *— -worker*, operatore di miracoli; taumaturgo.

to wonder, *v.t.i.* **1.** meravigliarsi; stupirsi; ammirare: *I — at you*, mi meraviglio di te; *I — to see you here*, mi stupisco di trovarti qui; *we — that he did not come with you*, ci meravigliamo che non sia venuto con voi **2.** fantasticare; essere curioso di sapere; domandarsi: *I —*, vorrei sapere, mi domando, chissà: *I — what the time is*, mi domando che ora sia; *I — who he is*, mi chiedo chi sia; *I — why she has not arrived*, mi chiedo perchè non sia arrivata.

wonderful ['wʌndǝful], *ag.* meraviglioso; stupendo; prodigioso; portentoso; sorprendente: *— courage*, coraggio prodigioso; *a — escape*, una fuga portentosa; *a — sight*, una vista stupenda.

wonderfully ['wʌndǝfli], *av.* in modo meraviglioso, stupendo, prodigioso, stupefacente.

wonderfulness ['wʌndǝfulnis], *s.* l'essere meraviglioso, sorprendente.

wonderingly ['wʌndǝriŋli], *av.* con meraviglia, con stupore; con aria stupefatta.

wonderland ['wʌndǝlænd], *s.* **1.** paese delle meraviglie, regno delle fate **2.** paese ricco di risorse naturali.

wonderment ['wʌndǝmǝnt], *s.* **1.** meraviglia; stupore **2.** fatto, cosa meravigliosa.

wondrous ['wʌndrǝs], *ag.* (*letter.*) meraviglioso, mirabile, stupendo ‖ *av.* (*letter.*) mirabilmente; straordinariamente: *— kind*, straordinariamente gentile; *— pretty*, infinitamente grazioso.

wondrously ['wʌndrǝsli], *av.* mirabilmente; straordinariamente.

wondrousness ['wʌndrǝsnis], *s.* l'essere meraviglioso, stupendo.

wonky ['woŋki], *ag.* (*sl.*) vacillante, traballante; storto; instabile; debole; malfermo: *— chair*, sedia traballante.

wont [wount], *ag.* abituato, solito, avvezzo: *to be —*, essere abituato: *she was — to go for a walk every morning*, usava fare una passeggiata ogni mattina ‖ *s.* uso, abitudine; costume: *it was his — to say so*, era sua abitudine dire così ‖ *use and —*, uso e costume.

to wont, *pass.* **wont**, *p.p.* **wont, wonted** ['wountid], *v.i.* (*arc.*) usare, solere, essere solito.

won't [wount], *contr.* di **will not**.

wonted ['wountid], *ag.* (*amer.*) solito, avvezzo, abituato; (*arc.*) abituale.

to woo [wu:], *v.t.i.* (*letter.*) **1.** amoreggiare; corteggiare; chiedere in matrimonio **2.** cercare di ottenere; sollecitare; allettare: *to — fame*, cercare di ottenere la fama.

wood [wud], *s.* **1.** bosco, foresta; selva (anche *fig.*): *a — of beech-trees*, un bosco di faggi; *a — of words*, una selva di parole; *to ride through the woods*, andare a cavallo per i boschi ‖ *man of the woods*, orang-utan ‖ *out of the* —, fuori dei guai: *don't halloo till you are out of the* —, non dir quattro se non l'hai nel sacco ‖ *not to see the* — *for the trees*, perdersi nei dettagli 2. legno; legname; legna: *a table made of* —, un tavolo di legno; *put some* — *on the fire*, metti della legna sul fuoco ‖ *touch* —*!*, (*fam.*) tocca ferro! 3. *fig.* sostanza, stoffa: *I know of what* — *that man is made*, so di che stoffa è fatto quell'uomo 4. botte, barile: *whisky aged in* —, whisky invecchiato in fusto 5. *gener. pl.* strumenti a fiato (un tempo in legno) 6. (*spor.*) boccia 7. (*sl.*) pulpito ☆ — *-alcohol* (o — *-spirit*), (*chim.*) alcool metilico; — *-carver*, intagliatore; — *-carving*, scultura in legno; — *-coal*, carbone di legna; — *-cutter*, boscaiolo, legnaiolo; — *-engraver*, incisore; — *-engraving*, l'incidere su legno; incisione in legno; — *-house*, legnaia; — *-lily*, (*bot.*) mughetto; — *-louse*, (*zool.*) onisco; — *-monger*, commerciante in legname; — *-note*, poesia, canzone spontanea; — *-nymph*, (*mit.*) ninfa dei boschi, driade; — *-pigeon*, colombo selvatico; — *-pulp*, (*ind. cartaria*) cellulosa, pasta di legno; — *-screw*, (*tec.*) vite a legno; — *-seasoning*, stagionatura del legno; — *-tar*, (*chim.*) catrame di legno; — *-turner*, tornitore in legno; — *-turning*, tornitura del legno; — *-vinegar*, (*chim.*) acido pirolegnoso, acido acetico grezzo; — *-wind*, strumento musicale a fiato; — *-wool*, lana di legno.

to wood, *v.t.i.* 1. rimboschire 2. rifornire, rifornirsi di legna da ardere 3. caricare di legname.

woodbind ['wudbaind], **woodbine** ['wudbain], *s.* (*bot.*) caprifoglio; (*amer.*) vite del Canada.

woodblock ['wudblɔk], *s.* 1. (*tip.*) matrice in legno 2. blocchetto di legno.

woodchuck ['wudtʃʌk], *s.* (*zool.*) marmotta dell'America Settentrionale.

woodcock ['wudkɔk], *s.* 1. (*ornit.*) beccaccia 2. (*arc.*) persona sciocca; semplicïotto.

woodcraft ['wudkrɑ:ft], *s.* 1. conoscenza dei boschi 2. abilità nel lavorare il legno.

woodcut ['wudkʌt], *s.* 1. incisione su legno 2. xilografia.

wooded ['wudid], *ag.* boscoso, coperto di alberi.

wooden ['wudn], *ag.* 1. di legno, legnoso: — *steps*, scalini di legno 2. rigido; impacciato; inespressivo: *a* — *smile*, un sorriso stereotipato; *a* — *stare*, sguardo inespressivo ☆ — *-head*, testa di legno; stupido; — *-headed*, stupido, testone; — *-headedness*, stupidità; — *horse*, cavallo di Troia; (*ginnastica*) cavalletto; (*arc.*) nave; — *leg*, gamba di legno; — *-shoes*, zoccoli; — *walls*, (*st.*) navi da guerra.

woodenly ['wudnli], *av.* in modo legnoso, rigido.

woodenness ['wudnis], *s.* 1. legnosità 2. *fig.* rigidità; stupidità.

woodiness ['wudinis], *s.* 1. boscosità 2. legnosità.

woodland ['wudlənd], *s.* terreno boscoso; luogo boschivo, silvestre.

woodless ['wudlis], *ag.* privo di boschi.

woodman, *pl.* **woodmen** ['wudmən], *s.* 1. guardaboschi; guardia forestale 2. taglialegna 3. (*arc.*) cacciatore.

woodpecker ['wud,pekə*], *s.* (*ornit.*) picchio.

woodsman, *pl.* **woodsmen** ['wudzmən], *s.* abitatore dei boschi.

woodsy ['wudzi], *ag.* (*amer.*) boschivo, silvano.

woodward ['wudwəd], *s.* (*st.*) guardaboschi; guardia forestale.

woodwork ['wudwə:k], *s.* lavoro in legno.

woody ['wudi], *ag.* 1. boscoso: *a* — *hill*, un colle coperto di boschi 2. legnoso, ligneo: *the* — *parts of a plant*, le parti legnose di una pianta.

wooer ['wu:ə*], *s.* (*letter.*) corteggiatore, spasimante.

woof [wu:f], *s.* (*ind. tessile*) trama; tessuto; tessitura.

wooing ['wu:iŋ], *ag.* (*letter.*) che corteggia ‖ *s.* corteggiamento.

wooingly ['wu:iŋli], *av.* amorosamente; in modo suadente.

wool [wul], *s.* 1. lana; filato, tessuto di lana; vello: *he wears* — *next to his skin*, porta indumenti di lana sulla pelle ‖ *against the* —, contropelo; *fig.* in direzione sbagliata ‖ *dyed in the* —, lana tinta (prima della filatura, della tessitura); *fig.* da una parte all'altra, completamente ‖ *much cry and little* —, *fig.* molto fumo e poco arrosto ‖ *they went for* — *and came home shorn*, andarono per suonare e furono suonati ‖ *to pull the* — *over a person's eyes*, gettar fumo negli occhi di, imbrogliare una persona 2. peluria (di animale) 3. capigliatura riccia e lanosa; (*scherz.*) capigliatura ‖ *to lose one's* —, (*sl.*) arrabbiarsi ☆ — *-carding*, cardatura della lana; — *-cloth*, panno di lana; — *-hall*, mercato della lana; — *-shed*, recinto per la tosatura delle pecore, imballaggio della lana; — *waste*, cascame di lana ‖ *cotton* —, bambagia, ovatta; *long-stapled* —, lana a fibra lunga.

woolfat ['wulfæt], *s.* (*chim.*) lanolina.

woolfell ['wulfel], *s.* vello.

wool-gathering ['wul,gæðəriŋ], *ag.* distratto, sbadato ‖ *s.* distrazione, sbadataggine; sogno ad occhi aperti: *to go* —, perdersi in fantasticherie.

wool(l)en ['wulin], *ag.* di lana, lanoso: *she was wearing a* — *dress*, portava un abito di lana ‖ *s.* stoffa, articolo di lana; — *draper*, venditore di articoli di lana; — *yarn*, filato di lana.

woolliness ['wulinis], *s.* 1. lanosità 2. *fig.* confusione mentale.

woolly ['wuli], *ag.* 1. di lana, lanoso; lanuto; lanuginoso: — *clouds*, *fig.* (cielo a) pecorelle; — *hair*, capelli lanosi 2. *fig.* indistinto, impreciso; confuso; annebbiato: *a* — *mind*, una mente annebbiata; — *voice*, voce indistinta ‖ *s.* indumento di lana.

woolsack ['wul-sæk], *s.* 1. cuscino del seggio del Lord Cancelliere di Inghilterra 2. carica, dignità di Lord Cancelliere.

wootz [wu:ts], *s.* acciaio speciale fabbricato anticamente in India.

woozy ['wu:zi], *ag.* (*sl. amer.*) brillo, ubriaco.

wop [wɔp], *s.* (*sl. amer.*) immigrato negli U.S.A. dal Centro, Sud-Europa (specialmente dall'Italia).

word [wə:d], *s.* 1. parola, termine, vocabolo: " *beautiful* " *is not the* — *for her*, « bella » non è il termine esatto per lei ‖ — *for* —, alla lettera, letteralmente ‖ *in a* —, in una parola, in breve ‖ *a play upon words*, un giuoco di parole 2. *gener. pl.* parola, discorso: *big words*, parole grosse, vanterie; *fair words*, belle parole, complimenti; *good words*, parole incoraggianti; *hard words*, parole dure; *he is a man of few words*, è un uomo di poche parole; *he never says a* —, non parla mai; *I am repeating his very words*, ripeto esattamente le sue parole; *when we speak, we express our thoughts into words*, quando parliamo traduciamo i nostri pensieri in parole ‖ *a* — *in, out of season*, un consiglio, un'osservazione opportuna, fuori luogo ‖ *beyond words*, che non può essere espresso in parole ‖ *by* — *of mouth*, oralmente ‖ *the last* — *in*, l'ultima novità (in un campo) ‖ *on* (o *with*) *the* —, subito dopo aver detto ‖ *it is a* — *and a blow with him*, passa facilmente dalle parole ai fatti ‖ *to be too kind for words*, essere gentile oltre ogni dire ‖ *to come to high words*, arrivare alle ingiurie ‖ *to eat one's words*, ritrattare le proprie parole, scusarsi ‖ *to have the last* — (*on a subject*), avere l'ultima parola (su un argomento) ‖ *to have a* — *with s.o.*, avere un breve colloquio con qlcu. ‖ *to have words* (*with s.o.*), litigare (con qlcu.) ‖ *to put in, to say a good* — *for s.o.*, mettere, dire una buona parola per qlcu. ‖ *to say a few words*, far quattro chiacchiere ‖ *to suit the action to the* —, passare dalle parole ai fatti ‖ *to take s.o. at his* —, prendere qlcu. in parola ‖ *to waste words*, sprecare il fiato ‖ *a* — *to the wise* (*is sufficient*), prov. a buon intenditor poche parole 3. parola (d'onore); promessa: *I give you my* — *for* *it,* vi do la mia parola; *you must never break your* —, non devi mai mancare alla parola data ‖ *my* — *upon it,* vi do la mia parola; *upon my* —, sulla mia parola ‖ *he is a man of his* —, è un uomo di parola ‖ *he is as good as his* —, mantiene tutto ciò che promette **4.** ordine, comando; parola d'ordine; motto: *to give the* — (*to do sthg.*), dare ordine (di fare ql.co.); *they must give the* — *before they can pass,* devono dare la parola d'ordine prima di passare **5.** notizia, informazione: — *came that I was to leave at once,* giunse notizia che dovevo partire immediatamente; *to send s.o.* — *of sthg.,* far sapere ql.co. a qlcu. **6.** *the Word of God,* il Vangelo; *the Word (of God),* il Verbo (di Dio) ☆ — -*book,* lessico; libretto d'opera; — -*bound,* impacciato nel discorso; vincolato da una promessa; — -*building,* costruzione della parola; — -*memory,* memoria uditiva; — -*painting,* descrizione pittoresca, vivace; — -*perfect,* (*teat.*) chi sa a memoria la parte; — -*picture,* descrizione vivida e accurata; — -*splitter,* pedante, meticoloso nell'uso dei vocaboli; — -*square,* quadrato delle parole incrociate.

to word, *v.t.* esprimere; mettere in parole; formulare: *I should* — *it rather differently,* lo esprimerei con parole diverse; *telegram worded as follows,* telegramma del seguente tenore.

wordily ['wə:dili], *av.* **1.** verbosamente **2.** a parole.

wordiness ['wə:dinis], *s.* verbosità; prolissità.

wording ['wə:diŋ], *s.* **1.** espressione, enunciazione: *a different* — *might make the meaning clearer,* una espressione diversa potrebbe rendere più chiaro il significato; *the meaning is clear, though the* — *is involved,* il significato è chiaro benchè l'enunciazione sia involuta **2.** dicitura: *rubber stamp bearing the* —..., timbro recante la dicitura....

wordless ['wə:dlis], *ag.* senza parole.

wordy ['wə:di], *ag.* **1.** verboso, prolisso (di discorso, persona, ecc.) **2.** verbale: — *warfare,* guerra di parole.

wore [wo:*], *pass.* di to **wear.**

work [wə:k], *s.* **1.** lavoro, fatica: *factory at* —, fabbrica in pieno lavoro; *it was hard* — *rowing, for the wind was against us,* fu una dura fatica remare perchè avevamo il vento contrario; *to be at* — *upon sthg.,* essere occupato a far ql.co.; *to convert heat into* —, (*fis.*) trasformare il calore in lavoro; *to set* (o to *get*) *to* —, cominciare a lavorare; *to set* (o to *go*) *about one's* —, iniziare il proprio lavoro ‖ *all in the day's* —, tutto regolare ‖ *dry* (o *thirsty*) —, lavoro che mette sete ‖ *to have one's* — *cut out,* (*fam.*) aver di che lavorare ‖ *all* — *and no play makes Jack a dull boy,* prov. chi troppo studia matto diventa **2.** attività, occupazione; impiego: *our father is at* — *now,* nostro padre è al lavoro; *a teacher does his* — *at school,* un insegnante svolge la sua attività a scuola; *what is your* —?, che lavoro fai? ‖ *of all* —, che svolge ogni genere di lavori: *a maid of all* —, una domestica tutto fare ‖ *to be out of* —, essere disoccupato ‖ *to have a hand in the* — *oneself,* avere le mani in pasta ‖ *to make* —, fare confusione ‖ *to make* — *for s.o.,* trovare un'occupazione a qlcu. ‖ *to make short* — *of it,* sbrigarsela in fretta **3.** lavoro; oggetto lavorato: *the villagers sell their works to the tourists,* gli abitanti del villaggio vendono oggettini ricordo ai turisti; *what a beautiful piece of* —!, che bell'oggetto! **4.** opera; prodotto dell'ingegno: — *of art,* opera d'arte; *the works of Coleridge,* le opere di Coleridge; *historical* —, opera storica; *this is your best* —, è la tua opera migliore **5.** *pl.* lavori di costruzione, di ingegneria; (*mil.*) fortificazioni: *defensive works,* opere di difesa ‖ *the Office of Works,* Ministero dei Lavori Pubblici **6.** *pl.* meccanismo; macchinario; parti mobili di una macchina: *the works of a clock,* il meccanismo di un orologio **7.** *pl.* officina; fabbrica, stabilimento: *the engineer has gone to the works,* l'ingegnere si è recato in officina; *the works closed for the summer holidays,* la fabbrica chiuse per le vacanze estive.

to work, *pass.p.p.* **worked** [wə:kt], (*rar.*) **wrought** [rɔ:t], *v.t.i.* **1.** lavorare, far lavorare: *I have been working hard all day,* ho lavorato sodo tutto il giorno; *she works her servants unmercifully,* fa lavorare i suoi servitori senza misericordia; *they always* — *overtime,* fanno sempre lavoro straordinario ‖ *to* — *oneself to death,* ammazzarsi di lavoro **2.** funzionare, far funzionare (anche *fig.*); azionare, manovrare; muovere, far muovere; mettere in moto: *the electric bell doesn't* —, il campanello elettrico non funziona; *his heart is working badly,* il suo cuore funziona male; *the millwheel is worked by the stream,* la ruota del mulino è azionata dalla corrente; *that plan worked well,* quel piano ha funzionato bene; *we do not think your idea will* —, non crediamo che la tua idea sia attuabile; *to* — *a crane,* azionare una gru **3.** amministrare, dirigere, controllare: *he works the scheme,* ha il controllo del progetto; *to* — *a farm,* dirigere una fattoria **4.** attuare, ottenere con fatica: *he worked his way through the jungle,* si aprì un cammino attraverso la giungla; *the roots worked down between the stones,* le radici riuscirono a penetrare fra le pietre; *to* — *a nail into a hole,* introdurre a poco a poco un chiodo in un buco ‖ *to* — *southwards,* (*mar.*) navigare verso sud, controvento; *to* — *up stream,* risalire la corrente **5.** divenire lentamente: *he worked his hands free,* a poco a poco si è liberato le mani; *the screw has worked loose,* la vite si è allentata a poco a poco **6.** produrre, causare, esercitare, operare, compiere: *his words wrought a great impression on me,* le sue parole produssero una grande impressione su di me; *time works many changes,* il tempo opera molti cambiamenti; *to* — *the ruin of s.o.,* causare la rovina di qlcu.; *to* — *wonders,* far miracoli **7.** (*mat.*) risolvere; calcolare: *to* — *a problem in algebra,* risolvere un problema algebrico **8.** pagare, ottenere col lavoro: *to* — *one's passage on a ship,* pagarsi la traversata su una nave lavorando **9.** agitare, agitarsi; contrarsi: *his features worked with excitement,* i suoi lineamenti si contraevano per l'eccitazione **10.** fermentare, far fermentare (anche *fig.*): *just drop a judicious hint and let it* — *in his mind,* insinuagli nella mente un saggio suggerimento e lascia che germogli in lui; *the yeast is beginning to* —, il lievito comincia a fermentare **11.** sfruttare: *the silver-mines are no longer worked,* le miniere d'argento non sono più sfruttate **12.** plasmare, forgiare; lavorare (pasta, burro, ecc.): *easily wrought iron,* ferro malleabile; *to* — *clay into a statuette,* modellare una statuetta con l'argilla ‖ *to* — *an audience into enthusiasm,* sollevare l'entusiasmo di un uditorio; *to* — *oneself into a rage,* montare a poco a poco in collera **13.** ricamare: *the flowers are worked in silk;* i fiori sono ricamati in seta **14.** *to* — *at* (*sthg.*), applicarsi a; studiare: *he is working at a new novel,* sta lavorando ad un nuovo romanzo; *to* — *at history,* studiare la storia **15.** *to* — *against* (*s.o., sthg.*), opporsi a; complottare: *to* — *against time,* lottare col tempo **16.** *to* — *in,* introdurre, introdursi; far penetrare: *the lecture would be improved if you could* — *in a few jokes,* la conferenza sarebbe migliore se vi si potessero introdurre alcune frasi scherzose ‖ *to* — *in with,* combaciare con; adattarsi a: *his plan will not* — *in with ours,* il suo piano non si adatterà al nostro **17.** *to* — *off,* liberarsi di; sfogare; (*comm.*) svendere: *she worked off her anger,* sfogò la sua collera **18.** *to* — *out,* calcolare; risolvere; progettare; elaborare; esaurire; ottenere a fatica: *the mine was worked out long ago,* la miniera si esaurì tempo fa; *the plan is being worked out,* il progetto è allo studio; *we have worked out our share of the expenses,* abbiamo calcolato la nostra quota di spese **19.** *to* — *up,* preparare, prepararsi; elaborare; eccitare, fomentare, istigare: *he worked up the feelings of the audience,* eccitò i sentimenti del pubblico; *she worked up the sketch into a picture,* sviluppò lo schizzo in un quadro; *to* — *up a rebellion,* fomentare una rivolta.

work, (*nei composti*): — *-bag*, borsa da lavoro; — *-box*, scatola, cassetta contenente gli arnesi da lavoro; — *-day*, giorno lavorativo, giorno feriale; — *-fellow*, collega, compagno di lavoro; — *-people*, operai, manovali; — *-shy*, persona che detesta lavorare, fannullone; — *-table*, tavolo da lavoro; — *-woman*, operaia ‖ *fancy-* —, decorazione a ricamo; *glass-works*, vetreria; *road works*, lavori stradali; *stone-* —, costruzione, lavoro in pietra.

workable ['wə:kəbl], *ag.* **1.** eseguibile; lavorabile; sfruttabile; praticabile **2.** realizzabile (di piano, schema).

workaday ['wə:kədei], *ag.* di ogni giorno; pratico; comune: — *clothes*, abiti ordinari, da lavoro; *this* — *world*, questo mondo prosaico e noioso.

worker ['wə:kə*], *s.c.* lavoratore, lavoratrice; operaio, operaia; lavorante; bracciante ‖ *the workers*, il proletariato ‖ *workers of evil*, i cattivi; i malfattori ☆ — *-bee*, ape operaia ‖ *fellow-* —, compagno di lavoro; *unskilled* —, manovale; *welfare* —, assistente sociale.

workhouse ['wə:khaus], *s.* **1.** ospizio di mendicità **2.** (*amer.*) casa di lavoro per condannati per reati minori **3.** (*arc.*) laboratorio.

working ['wə:kiŋ], *ag.* **1.** che lavora, laborioso, attivo; operante: *a* — *theory*, una teoria operante **2.** che funziona, funzionante: *the* — *parts of a machine*, le parti funzionanti di una macchina ‖ *s.* **1.** lavoro; lavorio; attività; processo: *the* — *of conscience*, il lavorio della coscienza **2.** (*mec.*) funzionamento; operazione: *the* — *of an engine*, il funzionamento di un motore; *to put a machine in* — *order*, mettere una macchina in stato di funzionare ‖ — *at full load*, andatura a pieno carico **3.** (*ind.*) lavorazione **4.** contrazione (del viso) **5.** *gener. pl.* (*miner.*) galleria: *he was found in a disused* —, fu trovato in una galleria abbandonata **6.** (*mat.*) calcolo ☆ — *capital*, capitale liquido; — *-class*, classi operaie, proletariato; — *clothes*, abiti di fatica, da lavoro; — *cost*, costo di lavorazione; — *cylinder*, (*tec.*) cilindro motore; — *-day*, giornata lavorativa; — *-drawing*, disegno costruttivo; — *expenses*, spese d'esercizio; — *hours*, ore di lavoro; — *load*, carico di lavoro; — *man*, operaio; — *out*, elaborazione, sviluppo; risoluzione (di problema); — *speed*, velocità di lavoro; — *woman*, operaia ‖ *cold* —, (*metal.*) lavorazione a freddo; *hot* —, (*metal.*) lavorazione a caldo.

workless ['wə:klis], *ag.* senza lavoro, disoccupato.

workman, *pl.* **workmen** ['wə:kmən], *s.* operaio, lavoratore; salariato; artigiano ☆ *workmen staff*, maestranza; — *-like*, ben fatto, eseguito; abile, competente ‖ *skilled* —, operaio specializzato.

workmanship ['wə:kmənʃip], *s.* **1.** abilità; abilità tecnica **2.** fattura, esecuzione, lavorazione, lavoro: *articles of excellent* —, articoli di eccellente fattura.

workroom ['wə:k-rum], *s.* officina; laboratorio; stanza da lavoro.

workshop ['wə:kʃop], *s.* officina; laboratorio; bottega.

world [wə:ld], *s.* **1.** mondo, universo: *the creation of the* —, la creazione del mondo; *the end of the* —, la fine del mondo; *in this* —, in questo mondo; *he is not long for this* —, non ha molto da vivere ‖ — *-without end*, per sempre ‖ *the other* —, l'altro mondo, l'oltretomba; *the lower* —, l'inferno ‖ *for all the* — *like*, sotto ogni rispetto, esattamente; *not for all the* — (o *not for worlds*), per nulla al mondo ‖ *to the* —, (*sl.*) completamente: *tired to the* —, stanco morto ‖ *to carry the* — *before one*, diventare famoso, aver successo ‖ *to make the best of both worlds*, conciliare i piaceri del mondo con la salute spirituale **2.** mondo, terra; pianeta: *to go round the* —, fare il giro del mondo; *there are other worlds beside ours*, ci sono altri pianeti oltre al nostro ‖ *the New World*, il Nuovo Mondo; *the Old World*, il Vecchio Mondo ‖ *all over the* — (o *all the* — *over*), dappertutto **3.** mondo, vita:

she is all the — *to me*, ella è tutta la mia vita; *to bring a child into the* —, mettere al mondo un bambino ‖ *how goes the* — *with you?*, (*fam.*) come va la vita? ‖ *to take the* — *as it is*, prendere il mondo come viene **4.** mondo, vita sociale; vita mondana: *a man of the* —, un uomo di mondo; *to forsake the* —, abbandonare il mondo, i piaceri mondani; *to live out of the* —, vivere fuori del mondo ‖ *the great* —, il bel mondo ‖ *so the* — *wags*, così va il mondo ‖ *to begin the* —, iniziare la carriera ‖ *to have gone down in the* —, aver conosciuto giorni migliori ‖ *to have the* — *before one*, aver tutto il mondo davanti a sè ‖ *to let the* — *slide*, lasciar che gli eventi corrano; lasciar che il mondo parli ‖ *to make a noise in the* —, far parlare molto di sè **5.** mondo, gente: *the* — *of letters*, il mondo delle lettere; *the* — *of sport*, il mondo dello sport; *what will the* — *think of it?*, che cosa ne penserà la gente? ‖ *the English speaking* —, i popoli di lingua inglese **6.** *a* — *of*, una gran quantità di: *a* — *of trouble*, un mare di guai ☆ — *-history*, storia universale; — *-old*, vecchio come il mondo; — *-politics*, politica mondiale; — *-weary*, stanco della vita; — *-wide*, diffuso e conosciuto in tutto il mondo; mondiale ‖ *animal* —, regno animale.

worldliness ['wə:ldlinis], *s.* **1.** temporalità; condizione terrena **2.** mondanità.

worldling ['wə:ldliŋ], *s.c.* persona mondana, persona amante dei piaceri della vita.

worldly ['wə:ldli], *ag.* **1.** di questo mondo, terreno: — *goods*, beni temporali ‖ *all one's* — *goods*, (*fam.*) tutta la propria roba **2.** mondano: — *life*, vita mondana, dedicata ai piaceri materiali ☆ — *-minded*, attaccato alle cose terrene; — *-wise*, esperto delle cose del mondo.

worm [wə:m], *s.* **1.** verme; baco; bruco; larva; tarlo: *to be food for worms*, essere cibo per i vermi, essere morto; *to have worms*, avere i vermi ‖ *the* — *of conscience*, il tarlo della coscienza, il rimorso ‖ *even a* — *will turn*, anche la pazienza ha un limite **2.** *fig.* persona vile, spregevole **3.** (*mec.*) vite senza fine **4.** (*mec.*) serpentino **5.** filetto della lingua (di cane) ☆ — *-cast*, terra sollevata dal lombrico; — *-eaten*, mangiato dai vermi; — *-eating*, che si nutre di vermi; — *-gear*, (*mec.*) ingranaggio elicoidale; — *-hob*, (*mec.*) fresa a vite senza fine; — *-holed*, bucherellato, tarlato; — *-powder*, vermifugo; — *-screw*, vite senza fine; — *-wheel*, (*mec.*) ruota, ingranaggio elicoidale ‖ *glow-* —, lucciola; *silk-* —, baco da seta.

to worm, *v.t.i.* **1.** muoversi lentamente, strisciare (come un verme); *fig.* insinuarsi: *he wormed his way through the bushes*, avanzò strisciando tra i cespugli; *she wormed her way into my heart*, si insinuò nel mio cuore **2.** liberare dai vermi; estrarre i vermi da **3.** spiare, carpire (un segreto): *they wormed the secret out of him*, riuscirono a carpirgli il segreto **4.** tagliare il filetto della lingua a (un cane) **5.** (*mar.*) intregnare.

wormwood ['wə:mwud], *s.* **1.** (*bot.*) assenzio **2.** *fig.* mortificazione; amarezza: *life to him was* —, la vita gli era molto amara.

worn [wɔ:n], *p.p.* di to *wear* ‖ *ag.* **1.** portato; consumato; sciupato **2.** esausto; indebolito ☆ — *-out*, logoro; *fig.* esausto, sfinito ‖ *care-* —, consumato dagli affanni; *love-* —, consumato dall'amore; *time-* —, logorato dal tempo; *way-* —, esaurito dal lungo cammino.

worried ['wʌrid], *ag.* preoccupato; inquieto; tormentato.

worriedly ['wʌridli], *av.* ansiosamente; con inquietudine.

worrier ['wʌriə*], *s.c.* seccatore, seccatrice; tormentatore, tormentatrice ‖ *s.* animale da preda.

worriment ['wʌrimənt], *s.* preoccupazione; inquietudine; affanno.

worrisome ['wʌrisəm], *ag.* (*dial. fam.*) **1.** noioso; che causa preoccupazione **2.** preoccupato; inquieto.

(to) **worrit** ['wʌrit], (*volg.*) per (to) **worry**.

worry ['wʌri], *s.* **1.** ansia; inquietudine: *to show signs of* —, dar segni di inquietudine **2.** *gener. pl.* preoccupazioni, fastidi, dispiaceri, guai: *little domestic worries*, piccole preoccupazioni familiari; *what a* — *this boy is!*, che assillo è questo ragazzo! **3.** l'azzannare la preda (di cane, gatto).

to **worry**, *v.t.i.* **1.** infastidire, importunare; seccare; annoiare: *don't* — *him!*, lasciatelo tranquillo! **2.** preoccupare, preoccuparsi; tormentare, tormentarsi; essere in ansia: *don't* — *about me*, non preoccuparti per me; *he is very worried*, è molto preoccupato **3.** azzannare, dilaniare, lacerare a morsi, tormentare (la preda): *the dog was worrying an old shoe*, il cane stava lacerando una vecchia scarpa **4.** *to* — **along**, sbrigarsela, tirarsi d'impaccio **5.** *to* — **out**, affrontare fino a risolvere: *to* — *out a problem*, affrontare un problema da tutti i lati fino a risolverlo.

worrying ['wʌriiŋ], *ag.* **1.** preoccupante **2.** tormentoso; molesto.

worryingly ['wʌriiŋli], *av.* in modo tormentoso, preoccupante, assillante.

worse [wə:s], *ag.* (*comp.* di *bad, ill*) **1.** peggiore: *he is bad, but his brother is* —, egli è cattivo ma suo fratello è peggiore; *she is a* — *player than he*, giuoca peggio di lui; *they couldn't have had* — *weather*, non avrebbero potuto avere un tempo peggiore ‖ *the* — *for wear*, logoro, consumato dall'uso: *this dress is certainly the* — *for wear*, questo abito si è certamente logorato a forza di portarlo **2.** (*predicativo*): *he is getting* — *and* —, sta sempre peggio; *she is none the* — *for the accident*, ella non ha risentito per nulla dell'incidente ‖ *s.* **peggio**: — *could not happen*, peggio non poteva capitare; *his son was emprisoned, but* — *was yet to follow* (*o to come*), suo figlio fu imprigionato, ma il peggio doveva ancora venire; *I had* — *to tell*, non avevo ancora detto il peggio; *things were going from bad to* —, le cose andavano di male in peggio ‖ *to change for the* —, peggiorare; alterarsi ‖ *to have the* —, avere la peggio ‖ *to put to the* —, sconfiggere.

worse, *av.* (*comp.* di *badly, ill*) **peggio**: *he has been taken* —, è peggiorato; *he sang* — *than ever*, cantò peggio che mai; *to make things* (*o matters*) —, il *train was late*, per peggiorare la situazione, il treno era in ritardo ‖ — *off*, in situazione peggiore: *she has lost her job and is* — *off than ever*, ha perso il posto e sta peggio che mai ‖ *none the* —, per nulla meno; ugualmente: *I shall love you none the* — *if you go away*, ti vorrò bene lo stesso anche se te ne andrai; *to think none the* — *of s.o.*, avere sempre stima di qlcu.

worsement ['wə:smənt], *s.* (*dir.*) deterioramento di una proprietà a causa di terzi.

to **worsen** ['wə:sn], *v.t.i.* peggiorare; aggravare, aggravarsi: *the situation has worsened*, la situazione si è aggravata.

worship ['wə:ʃip], *s.* **1.** adorazione, venerazione, culto: *the* — *of success*, il culto del successo; *place of* —, luogo sacro; *to do a person* —, fare omaggio, onorare una persona **2.** (*titolo*) eminenza; eccellenza; signoria: *Your Worships*, le Signorie Vostre **3.** (*arc.*) merito, virtù: *to win* —, acquistare vasta fama ☆ *hero* - —, culto degli eroi; *image-* —, iconolatria; *public* —, servizio religioso in una chiesa.

to **worship**, *pass.p.p.* **worshipped** ['wə:ʃipt], *v.t.i.* **1.** adorare, venerare: *the Greeks worshipped many gods*, i greci adoravano molti dei; *I worshipped the very ground she walked on*, veneravo il suolo su cui camminava **2.** venerare, avere un culto per, idolatrare: *to* — *one's mother*, idolatrare la propria madre **3.** prender parte a servizi religiosi; essere praticante.

worshipful ['wə:ʃipful], *ag.* (*titolo onorifico*) eccellente, eccellentissimo; onorevole, venerabile: *the Right Worshipful the Mayor of Bath*, il molto onorevole sindaco di Bath.

worshipfully ['wə:ʃipfuli], *av.* (*rar.*) onorevolmente, rispettabilmente.

worshipfulness ['wə:ʃipfulnis], *s.* (*rar.*) onorabilità:

worshipper ['wə:ʃipə*], *s.c.* chi venera; chi adora. *the worshippers*, i fedeli.

worshipping ['wə:ʃipiŋ], *s.* culto, adorazione.

worst [wə:st], *ag.* (*superl.* di *bad, ill*) (**il**) **peggiore**: *the* — *picture I ever saw*, il peggior film che io abbia mai visto ‖ *s.* (**il**) **peggio**: *the* — *of it is that...*, il peggio è che...; *the* — *of the winter has passed now*, il peggio dell'inverno è ormai passato; *I am prepared for the* —, sono preparato al peggio ‖ *at the* —, nella peggiore delle ipotesi ‖ *if the* — *comes to the* —, nel peggiore dei casi ‖ *to be at one's* —, essere, trovarsi nel peggior stato possibile ‖ *to do one's* —, fare il peggior male possibile; (*fam.*) agire come si vuole: *let her do her* —, (*fam.*) può ben fare ciò che vuole ‖ *to have the* —, avere la peggio ‖ *to put to the* —, sconfiggere.

to **worst**, *v.t.* sconfiggere, avere la meglio su: *to be worsted*, soccombere, avere la peggio.

worst, *av.* (*superl.* di *badly*) **nel modo peggiore**: *Charles played* (*the*) —, Carlo fu il peggior giocatore; *that frightened him* — *of all*, questo fu ciò che lo spaventò maggiormente.

worsted ['wə:stid], *ag.*: — *fabric*, (*ind. tessile*) tessuto di lana pettinata.

wort[1] [wə:t], *s.* (*rar.*) pianta, erba.

wort[2], *s.* mosto di malto.

worth[1] [wə:θ], *ag. gener. predicativo* **1.** che vale, di valore; equivalente al valore di: *how much is it* —?, quanto vale?; *I sell you this for what it is* —, (*fam.*) te la vendo per quello che vale; *it is nothing* —, non vale niente; *it is not* — *the trouble*, non ne vale la pena; *the rarer a thing is the more it is* —, quanto più una cosa è rara tanto più vale; *she is* — *a lot of money*, è molto ricca ‖ *the game is not* — *the candle*, il giuoco non vale la candela ‖ — *while attempt*, un tentativo che vale la pena di fare; *is it* — *while?*, ne vale la pena? ‖ *to die* — *a million*, morire lasciando un milione ‖ *a bird in the hand is* — *two in the bush*, *prov.* meglio un uovo oggi che una gallina domani **2.** degno, meritevole: *the book is not* — *reading*, il libro non merita di esser letto; *is it* — *going there?*, vale la pena di andare là? ‖ *s.* **1.** prezzo, valore: *a ring of great* —, un anello di grande valore; *I bought a pound's* — *of stamps*, ho comperato francobolli per una sterlina **2.** *fig.* valore, merito: *a person of great* —, una persona di gran merito ☆ *penny* —, del valore di un penny.

worth[2], *s.* (*st.*) cascina, fattoria.

to **worth**[3], *v.i.* (*poet. arc.*) accadere: *well* — *the hour!*, benedetta l'ora!; ben venga l'ora!; *woe* — *the day!*, maledetto sia il giorno!.

worthful ['wə:θful] *ag.* degno di rispetto; meritevole.

worthily ['wə:ðili], *av.* degnamente; meritatamente: *a life* — *spent*, una vita trascorsa degnamente.

worthiness ['wə:ðinis] *s.* **1.** merito, valore **2.** rispettabilità; dignità.

worthless ['wə:θlis], *ag.* **1.** senza valore, di nessun valore **2.** immeritevole, indegno: *a* — *woman*, una donna indegna.

worthlessly ['wə:θlisli], *av.* indegnamente.

worthlessness ['wə:θlisnis], *s.* **1.** poco valore, mancanza di valore **2.** bassezza; indegnità.

worthy ['wə:ði], *ag.* **1.** meritevole, degno: *behaviour* — *of great respect*, comportamento degno di grande rispetto; *he found an enemy* — *of him*, trovò un nemico degno di lui; *to be* — *to do sthg.*, essere degno di fare ql.co.; *to receive a* — *reward*, ricevere una degna ricompensa **2.** (*rar. scherz.*) rispettabile, onorevole: *who is that* — *gentleman?*, chi è quel degno signore? ‖ *s.* **1.** persona illustre, celebrità; notabile: *an Elizabethan* —, una personalità dell'epoca elisabettiana; *the village worthies*, i maggiorenti del paese **2.** (*scherz.*) personaggio, tipo: *who is the* — *with the bald head?*, chi è quel tipo con la testa calva?.

wot [wɔt], *pres.* di to **wit**.

would [wud (*forma forte*); wəd, əd (*forme deboli*)], *v. difettivo* (V), *pass.* di **will**; (2ᵃ *persona sing. pass.* (*arc.*) **wouldst** [wudst]; *forma negativa* **would not** [wud not]; *forma contratta* **wouldn't** [ˈwudnt]) **1.** (*ausiliare per la* 2ᵃ, 3ᵃ *persona sing. pl. del condiz.*): had she warned him, he — have done sthg. about it, se ella lo avesse avvertito, egli vi avrebbe provveduto in qualche modo; he told me he — come, mi disse che sarebbe venuto **2.** (*enfatico per* should *nella* 1ᵃ *persona sing. pl.*): if I were rich, I — buy a car, se fossi ricco, comprerei l'automobile **3.** (*nel senso di* volere, avere l'intenzione di, in tutte le persone sing. pl. del pass. e del condiz.*): he continue though he was warned to stop, volle continuare nonostante lo consigliassero di fermarsi; I — go to England next summer, avrei l'intenzione di andare in Inghilterra l'estate prossima; (I) — (that) I were a poet, vorrei essere poeta; the man I — meet, l'uomo che vorrei incontrare; what — you have him do?, che cosa vorresti che egli facesse? || — you kindly pass me the salt?, vorresti per favore passarmi il sale? || he — have none of it, non ne voleva sentir parlare || he — rather go than stay with her, preferirebbe andare piuttosto che stare con lei **4.** (*nel senso di* volere, in tutte le persone sing. pl. dell'imperfetto congiunt.*): he could leave if he —, potrebbe partire se volesse || — it were not so!, volesse il cielo che non fosse così!; — to God!, to heaven!, piacesse a Dio!, volesse il cielo! **5.** (*nel senso di* solere, usare, in tutte le persone dell'imperfetto indic.*): the cat — come every day for its milk, il gatto veniva tutti i giorni per il suo latte; he — come to see us twice in a week in those days, allora soleva venire a trovarci un paio di volte alla settimana **6.** (*esprimente supposizione*): I was a young man then, it — be during the First World War, ero un giovanotto allora, deve essere stato durante la prima guerra mondiale.

would-be [ˈwudbiː], *ag.* sedicente; preteso: the — king, il sedicente re; my daughter's — husband, l'aspirante alla mano di mia figlia.

wouldn't [ˈwudnt], *contr.* di would not.

wound[1] [wuːnd], *s.* **1.** ferita, piaga: he had a knife — in the leg, aveva una ferita da coltello nella gamba || the Five Wounds, le Cinque Piaghe (di Cristo) **2.** *fig.* offesa, ingiuria: to inflict a — upon s.o.'s vanity, offendere la vanità di qlcu. **3.** (*poet.*) pena d'amore.

to wound[1], *v.t.* **1.** ferire: thirty soldiers were wounded in the action, trenta soldati furono feriti nell'azione **2.** *fig.* offendere: I was wounded in my affections, fui ferito nei miei affetti; to — s.o.'s feelings, urtare la suscettibilità di qlcu.

wound[2] [waund], *pass.p.p.* di to **wind**[1].

wounded [ˈwuːndid], *ag.* ferito: seriously —, gravemente ferito.

woundless [ˈwuːndlis], *ag.* senza ferite; illeso.

woundwort [ˈwuːndwəːt], *s.* (*bot.*) vulneraria.

wove [wouv], *pass.* di to **weave**.

woven [ˈwouvən], *p.p.* di to **weave**.

wow [wau], *s.* (*sl. amer.*) successo clamoroso, sensazionale: it was a —, fu un successo clamoroso.

to wow, *v.t.* (*sl. amer.*) aver successo presso, entusiasmare: the speech wowed the citizens, il discorso entusiasmò i cittadini.

wow, *inter.* oh!.

wrack[1] [ræk], *s.* **1.** danno, oltraggio (a persona) **2.** rovina: to go to — and ruin, andare in completa rovina.

wrack[2], *s.* **1.** relitti **2.** alghe, rifiuti di mare (usati come concime).

wraith [reiθ], *s.* spettro, fantasma.

wrangle [ˈræŋgl], *s.* alterco; baruffa, rissa.

to wrangle, *v.i.* discutere; disputare; azzuffarsi.

wrangler [ˈræŋglə*], *s.* **1.** attaccabrighe **2.** (*a Cambridge*) studente classificato tra i primi all'esame di matematica **3.** (*amer.*) guardiano di cavalli.

wrap [ræp], *s. gener.pl.* scialle, sciarpa; mantello; coperta (da viaggio).

to wrap, *pass.p.p.* **wrapped** [ræpt], *v.t.i.* **1.** avvolgere, coprire (anche *fig.*): his life was wrapped in mystery, la sua vita era avvolta nel mistero; they wrapped the child in a shawl, avvolsero il bimbo in uno scialle || to — oneself up, avvolgersi, coprirsi: she wrapped herself up and went out, si coprì bene ed uscì; to — sthg. in paper, incartare ql.co. || to be wrapped up in s.o., sthg., essere completamente preso da qlcu., ql.co.; vivere per qlcu., ql.co.: she is wrapped up in her child, ella vive per il suo bambino; they are wrapped up in their work, sono completamente assorbiti dal lavoro **2.** sovrapporsi: the edges do not —, gli orli non si sovrappongono.

wrappage [ˈræpidʒ], *s.* involucro; copertina; busta; carta da imballo.

wrapper [ˈræpə*], *s.* **1.** imballatore **2.** carta da imballo; involucro, copertina; fascetta (di giornale) **3.** (*amer.*) veste da camera **4.** (*fam. amer.*) foglia esterna di tabacco di un sigaro.

wrapping [ˈræpiŋ], *s.* **1.** l'avvolgere; il fare pacchi **2.** involucro, copertura ☆ — -paper, carta da imballo.

wrasse [ræs], *s.* (*ittiol.*) labro.

wrath [rɔːθ], *s.* collera, ira; indignazione: my brother is slow to —, mio fratello non è facile alla collera.

wrathful [ˈrɔːθful], *ag.* adirato, sdegnato; indignato.

wrathfully [ˈrɔːθfuli], *av.* con ira, sdegnosamente.

wrathfulness [ˈrɔːθfulnis], *s.* collera, ira; furore.

to wreak [riːk], *v.t.* **1.** dar libero corso a; sfogare: he wreaked his anger upon the poor child, sfogò la sua ira sul povero bambino; he wreaked his grief with tears, diede sfogo al suo dolore piangendo; resolved to — his vengeance, deciso a mettere in atto la sua vendetta **2.** (*arc.*) vendicare.

wreakful [ˈriːkful], *ag.* vendicativo.

wreath [riːθ], *pl.* **wreaths** [riːðz], *s.* **1.** ghirlanda, serto, corona (di fiori, foglie) **2.** anello, cerchio; spirale: a — of smoke, un anello di fumo.

to wreathe [riːð], *v.t.i.* **1.** intrecciare: to — a garland, intrecciare una ghirlanda **2.** inghirlandare; incoronare **3.** attorcigliare, attorcigliarsi; avvolgersi: I saw a snake wreathing itself round a branch, vidi un serpente che si attorcigliava attorno ad un ramo **4.** innalzarsi in spire, in volute (di fumo) **5.** alterare (i lineamenti): their faces were wreathed with fear, i loro volti erano alterati dalla paura.

wreathed [riːðd], *ag.* (*arc.*) intrecciato; attorcigliato; contorto.

wreathy [ˈriːθi], *ag.* **1.** inghirlandato **2.** a forma di ghirlanda, di cerchio.

wreck [rek], *s.* **1.** naufragio, rovina, distruzione (anche *fig.*): the — of the "Deutschland", il naufragio del «Deutschland»; his father's death is the — of his plans, la morte del padre rappresenta il naufragio dei suoi progetti **2.** nave che ha subito un naufragio; relitto, rottame, rudere (anche *fig.*): after the crash the car was reduced to a —, dopo lo scontro l'automobile era ridotta ad un rottame; she was but a — of her former self, non era più che l'ombra di se stessa.

to wreck, *v.t.i.* **1.** naufragare, far naufragare: the ship was wrecked by the storm, la tempesta fece naufragare la nave **2.** rovinare, distruggere, andare in pezzi (anche *fig.*): the car wrecked the tree, l'automobile abbattè l'albero; he will — my hopes and plans, rovinerà, manderà in fumo le mie speranze e i miei piani; my nervous system has been completely wrecked, il mio sistema nervoso è stato completamente rovinato, è andato in pezzi.

wreckage [ˈrekidʒ], *s.* **1.** naufragio (anche *fig.*): the — of his hopes, il naufragio delle sue speranze **2.** relitti (anche *fig.*); rottami.

wrecked [rekt], *ag.* naufragato, rovinato, distrutto

(anche *fig.*):— *building*, edificio rovinato; *a* — *life*, una vita distrutta; — *sailors*, marinai naufraghi.

wrecker ['rekə*], *s.* **1.** saccheggiatore; persona che causa naufragi a scopo di saccheggio **2.** (*amer.*) nave, persona addetta al recupero di navi, di oggetti naufragati **3.** ostruzionista.

wren [ren], *s.* (*ornit.*) scricciolo, troglodita.

wrench [rentʃ], *s.* **1.** strappo, spinta; torsione; tirata **2.** strappo muscolare; storta; slogatura: *to give one's knee a* —, slogarsi un ginocchio **3.** *fig.* strazio, dolore: *it was a terrible* — *to leave our old home*, fu uno strazio lasciare la nostra vecchia casa **4.** (*mec.*) chiave (fissa) ☆ *double-ended* —, chiave (fissa) doppia; *monkey* —, chiave inglese, chiave a rollino; *stillson* —, chiave stringitubi; *tap* —, giramaschi.

to wrench, *v.t.* **1.** strappare; torcere, storcere, slogare: *to* — *a plant out of the ground*, strappare una pianta dal terreno; *to* — *one's foot*, slogarsi un piede **2.** *fig.* alterare, svisare: *he wrenched the meaning of my words*, alterò il significato delle mie parole.

wrest [rest], *s.* **1.** (*mus.*) chiave per accordare strumenti musicali **2.** strappo; tirata; torsione.

to wrest, *v.t.* **1.** strappare, togliere con violenza; torcere (anche *fig.*); estorcere: *to* — *a confession*, strappare una confessione; *to* — *a weapon from s.o.'s grasp*, strappare un'arma di mano a qlcu. **2.** svisare, travisare: *you must not* — *the facts*, non devi svisare i fatti.

wrestle ['resl], *s.* **1.** lotta; (*spor.*) incontro di lotta libera **2.** *fig.* sforzo, fatica; dura lotta.

to wrestle, *v.t.i.* lottare; fare la lotta; combattere (anche *fig.*): *he wrestled with difficulties*, egli lottò contro le difficoltà; *you must* — *with temptations*, devi combattere le tentazioni ‖ *to* — *in prayer* (o *to* — *with God*), pregare con fervore.

wrestler ['reslə*], *s.* lottatore.

wrestling ['reslin], *s.* lotta, combattimento; (*spor.*) lotta libera ☆ — *match*, incontro di lotta libera.

wretch [retʃ], *s.* **1.** persona miserabile, infelice, disgraziata: *poor* —, poveretto, povero disgraziato **2.** persona spregevole, indegna, vile **3.** (*scherz.*) incosciente.

wretched ['retʃid], *ag.* **1.** miserabile; infelice, disgraziato, sfortunato: *a* — *life*, una vita infelice, disgraziata; *the* — *woman had lost all her money*, la povera donna aveva perso tutto il suo denaro **2.** vile, spregevole **3.** di cattiva qualità; non soddisfacente: — *food*, cibo di cattiva qualità; — *health*, salute malferma; — *weather*, brutto tempo **4.** preoccupante; serio; grave: *the* — *state of things*, il preoccupante stato delle cose **5.** squallido, deprimente: *what a* — *place to live in!*, che luogo squallido per viverci! **6.** (*spreg.*) enorme; spaventoso: — *ignorance*, ignoranza crassa; *his* — *stupidity*, la sua enorme stupidità.

wretchedly ['retʃidli], *av.* miseramente; spregevolmente; infelicemente; disgraziatamente; sfortunatamente.

wretchedness ['retʃidnis], *s.* **1.** miserabilità; infelicità, disgrazia, sfortuna **2.** l'essere poco soddisfacente, di cattiva qualità **3.** gravità; squallore **4.** (*spreg.*) enormità.

wrick [rik], *s.* strappo; storta; slogatura: *she has a* — *in her neck*, ha il torcicollo.

to wrick, *v.t.* storcere, slogare leggermente: *to* — *one's ankle*, slogare una caviglia.

wriggle ['rigl], *s.* contorsione; contorcimento.

to wriggle, *v.t.i.* **1.** contorcere, contorcersi; dimenare, dimenarsi: *the dog wriggled his tail*, il cane dimenò la coda **2.** *fig.* dare risposte evasive; equivocare **3.** *to* — **along**, procedere con contorsioni: *the worm wriggled along*, il verme avanzava contorcendosi **4.** *to* — **out**, sgusciar fuori; *fig.* cavarsi d'impaccio per mezzo di espedienti.

wright [rait], *s.* **1.** (*rar.*) artigiano; operaio **2.** falegname, carpentiere.

wring [rin], *s.* **1.** torsione; stretta: *he gave my hand a* —, mi serrò calorosamente la mano; *she gave the sheets a* —, strizzò le lenzuola **2.** dolore acuto.

to wring, *pass.p.p.* **wrung** [rʌŋ], *v.t.i.* **1.** torcere, contorcere, contorcersi; attorcere; stringere, serrare (anche *fig.*): *he wrung my hand*, mi serrò forte la mano; *her sad story wrung my heart*, la sua triste storia mi strinse il cuore; *I'll* — *your neck!*, (*scherz.*) ti torcerò il collo!; *it wrings my heart to...*, mi si stringe il cuore a...; *to* — *a bird's neck*, tirare il collo a un volatile; *to* — *one's hands in despair*, torcersi le mani dalla disperazione; *to* — (*out*) *the linen*, torcere, strizzare la biancheria; *to* — *with pain*, contorcersi dal dolore ‖ *to know where the shoe wrings one*, (*fam.*) conoscere per esperienza le cause di una afflizione **2.** estorcere, strappare: *they wrung a confession out of* (o *from*) *the prisoner*, strapparono una confessione al prigioniero; *to* — *money out of s.o.*, estorcere denaro a qlcu. **3.** (*arc.*) alterare, travisare: *to* — *the truth*, alterare la verità **4.** *to* — **out**, spremere (torcendo); *fig.* strappare, estorcere: — *the water out of the sheets*, strizza le lenzuola; *he managed to* — *out a tear*, riuscì a spremere una lacrimuccia.

wringer ['riŋə*], *s.* asciugatrice meccanica; (*ind.*) torcitoio ‖ *s.c.* **1.** torcitore, torcitrice **2.** chi ricorre ad estorsione.

wringing ['riŋiŋ], *ag.* lacerante (di dolore) ‖ *s.* torcitura; asciugatura meccanica (dei panni) ☆ — *-machine*, asciugatrice meccanica; (*ind.*) torcitoio; — *wet*, bagnato fradicio.

wrinkle ['riŋkl], *s.* **1.** ruga; grinza; piega: *the wrinkles of a dress*, le grinze di un vestito; *she has many wrinkles on her face*, ha il viso tutto rughe **2.** *fig.* macchia, colpa **3.** (*fam.*) espediente, trovata astuta; suggerimento; consiglio utile ☆ — *finish*, (*ind.*) verniciatura vetrificata.

to wrinkle, *v.t.i.* corrugare, corrugarsi; raggrinzire, raggrinzirsi; increspare; spiegazzare: *to* — (*up*) *one's forehead*, corrugare la fronte.

wrinkled ['riŋkld], **wrinkly** ['riŋkli], *ag.* corrugato; rugoso; raggrinzito: — *with age*, rugoso per l'età.

wrist [rist], *s.* **1.** polso **2.** — (*-pin*), (*mec.*) spinotto ☆ — *-drop*, (*patol.*) paralisi dei muscoli estensori del carpo; — *-joint*, (*anat.*) articolazione radio-carpica; — *-watch*, orologio da polso.

wristband ['ristbænd], *s.* polsino (di camicia).

wristlet ['ristlit], *s.* **1.** braccialetto (come ornamento, per protezione del polso) **2.** manetta ☆ — *-watch*, orologio da polso.

writ [rit], *s.* **1.** (*dir.*) mandato; ordine; mandato esecutivo: *to serve a* — *on*, consegnare un mandato a ‖ — *of sequestration*, sequestro giudiziario **2.** (*arc.*) scritto; documento ‖ *the Holy Writ*, la Sacra Scrittura.

writable ['raitəbl], *ag.* **1.** scrivibile **2.** adatto per scrivere.

to write [rait], *pass.* **wrote** [rout], (*arc.*) **writ** [rit], *p.p.* **written** ['ritn], (*arc.*) **writ**, *v.t.i.* **1.** scrivere (anche *fig.*): *a page written all over*, una pagina scritta fitta fitta; — *in pencil*, scrivi a matita; *he writes to me every week*, mi scrive ogni settimana; *pain was written on her face*, il dolore era dipinto sul suo volto; *she writes a good hand*, ha una bella calligrafia; *she wrote two sheets*, riempì due fogli; *to* — *in one's own hand*, scrivere di proprio pugno ‖ *writ large*, a caratteri cubitali ‖ *written in the dust* (o *in sand* o *in water*), effimero ‖ *that's nothing to* — *home about*, non è niente di straordinario, di speciale **2.** scrivere, comporre; fare lo scrittore di professione: *he makes a living by writing*, vive facendo lo scrittore; *to* — *for the papers*, fare il giornalista **3.** qualificare, designare: *he writes himself a doctor*, si qualifica dottore ‖ *to* — *oneself man*, raggiungere la maggiore età **4.** *to* — **back**, rispondere (per iscritto) **5.** *to* — **down**, annotare, registrare; descrivere; denigrare; ridurre (romanzo, capitale, ecc.): *I could* — *her down as a beauty*, potrei definirla una bellezza **6.** *to* — **in**, inserire **7.** *to* — **off**, scrivere con facilità; cancellare: *to* — *off the description of a character*, buttar giù rapidamente la descrizione di un personaggio; *to — off a debt*, cancellare un debito **8.** *to —* **out**, copiare, trascrivere: *to — out the copy of a contract*, trascrivere la copia di un contratto ‖ *to — oneself out*, esaurirsi: *that novelist has written himself out*, quel romanziere ha esaurito la sua vena **9.** *to —* **up**, aggiornare (diario, contabilità, ecc.); redigere, scrivere (rendiconto, elogio, ecc.).

writer ['raitə*], *s.c.* **1.** chi scrive; scrittore, scrittrice; autore, autrice: *the —* (*of this letter*), lo scrivente **2.** copista ‖ *s.* **1.** (*scoz.*) avvocato, procuratore ‖ *Writer to the Signet*, alto funzionario dei tribunali scozzesi **2.** manuale che insegna a scrivere in una lingua ☆ *—'s cramp*, crampo degli scrivani.

writership ['raitəʃip], *s.* ufficio, mestiere di scrivano, di copista.

writhe [raið], *s.* contorcimento; convulsione.

to writhe, *v.t.i.* **1.** contorcere, contorcersi; dimenarsi (convulsamente): *to — in agony*, contorcersi nell'agonia **2.** *fig.* fremere; risentirsi: *he writhed with hatred*, fremeva d'odio; *to — at* (o *under*) *an insult*, fremere sotto un insulto; *to — with shame*, fremere di vergogna.

writhen ['riðn], *ag.* contorto; attorcigliato; intrecciato.

writing ['raitiŋ], *s.* **1.** lo scrivere: *she was busy with her —*, era occupata a scrivere **2.** scrittura, calligrafia: *I cannot understand his —*, non capisco la sua calligrafia **3.** scritto, documento scritto; scritta: *that leading article is a fine piece of —*, quell'articolo di fondo è un pezzo buono ‖ *the — on the wall*, *fig.* presagio infausto ‖ *in —*, per iscritto: *evidence in —*, (*dir.*) prova scritta **4.** *pl.* scritti, opere letterarie: *the writings of John Henry Newman*, gli scritti di John Henry Newman ☆ *— -book*, quaderno; *— -case*, astuccio con il necessario per scrivere; *— -desk*, scrivania; *— -master*, insegnante di calligrafia; *— -paper*, carta da lettera, carta da scrivere; *— -table*, scrittoio, scrivania.

written ['ritn], *p.p.* di *to* **write** ‖ *ag.* **1.** messo per iscritto: *I want a — apology*, voglio delle scuse per iscritto **2.** (*dir.*) formulato nei codici, in documenti **3.** iscritto, scolpito.

wrong [rɔŋ], *ag.* **1.** sbagliato; erroneo; inesatto; scorretto; ingiusto: *we got into the — train*, salimmo sul treno sbagliato; *you always do the — thing*, fai sempre quello che non dovresti fare ‖ *what is — with you?*, (*fam.*) che cos'è che non va?; *what is — with her?*, (*fam.*) che trovate da ridire sul suo conto? ‖ *to be —*, avere torto: *it is — of me to think so*, ho torto a pensare così; *it is — of you to help her*, fai male ad aiutarla ‖ *to be born on the — side of the blanket*, essere figlio illegittimo ‖ *to be in the — box*, essere in una situazione imbarazzante, difficile, in condizioni di inferiorità ‖ *to be on the — side of thirty*, aver oltrepassato la trentina ‖ *to get out of bed on the — side*, alzarsi di cattivo umore ‖ *to have hold of the — end of the stick*, avere una idea, una teoria completamente sbagliata **2.** peccaminoso; cattivo, immorale; illegale: *it is — to steal*, rubare è peccato.

wrong, *s.* **1.** ingiustizia; torto; danno: *the wrongs of time*, le ingiurie del tempo; *he complained of the wrongs he had suffered*, si lamentò dei torti subiti; *to be in the —*, essere dalla parte del torto; *to put s.o. in the —*, fare apparire colpevole qlcu.; (*dir.*) dimostrare la colpevolezza di qlcu. ‖ *the king can do no —*, il re non è responsabile ‖ *two wrongs do not make a right*, due neri non fanno un bianco ‖ *the dead are always in the —*, *prov.* il torto è degli assenti **2.** male, peccato; ingiustizia morale: *to know right from —*, distinguere il bene dal male **3.** (*dir.*) danno ☆ *private*

—, violazione del diritto privato; *public —*, violazione del diritto pubblico.

to wrong, *v.t.* **1.** far torto a, offendere; trattare ingiustamente; maltrattare; giudicare male: *he wrongs me when he says I am jealous*, mi fa torto quando dice che sono gelosa **2.** imbrogliare; nuocere a **3.** (*mar.*) superare nel navigare; navigare più velocemente di; *fig.* oltrepassare.

wrong, *av.* **1.** erroneamente; impropriamente; in modo inesatto; ingiustamente; male, malamente; a torto: *all your plans went —*, tutti i tuoi piani andarono a monte; *you have got it —*, vi siete sbagliati, non avete capito bene; *to guess —*, capire male, fraintendere ‖ *to get in — with s.o.*, (*fam.*) diventare antipatico a qlcu. **2.** in modo peccaminoso, immorale; illegale: *to go —*, peccare, cadere in peccato; deviare dal retto cammino.

wrong, (*nei composti*): *— -doer*, peccatore; offensore; trasgressore; *— -doing*, peccato, offesa; trasgressione, infrazione; *— end up*, capovolto, a rovescio; *— fount*, (*tip.*) refuso; *— -headed*, ostinato nell'errore; *— side out*, a rovescio.

wrongful ['rɔŋful], *ag.* **1.** ingiusto; iniquo; sleale **2.** illegale **3.** ingiustificato.

wrongfully ['rɔŋfuli], *av.* ingiustamente; a torto.

wrongfulness ['rɔŋfulnis], *s.* ingiustizia; iniquità; colpevolezza.

wrongly ['rɔŋli], *av.* **1.** a torto; ingiustamente **2.** male, erroneamente: *I was — informed*, fui informato male.

wrote [rout], *pass.* di *to* **write**.

wroth [rouθ], *ag. predicativo* (*poet. scherz.*) irritato, adirato, sdegnato; furente: *to wax —*, irritarsi, adirarsi, divenire furibondo.

wrought [rɔːt], *pass.p.p.* (*rar.*) di *to* **work** ‖ *ag.* lavorato; elaborato; lavorato, battuto, fucinato (di metallo) ☆ *— -iron*, ferro battuto; (*metal.*) saldato; *— -silver*, argento battuto; *— -steel*, (*metal.*) acciaio saldato; *— -up*, teso, agitato; perturbato: *his face was — up with pain*, il suo viso era contratto dal dolore; *nowadays everyone has — -up nerves*, al giorno d'oggi tutti hanno i nervi tesi.

wrung [rʌŋ], *pass.p.p.* di *to* **wring**.

wry [rai], *comp.* **wryer**, **wrier** ['rai-ə*], *superl.* **wryest**, **wriest** ['raiist], *ag.* **1.** storto; obliquo, sbieco: *on hearing that, he made a — mouth*, udendo ciò, storse la bocca ‖ *to make a — face*, fare una smorfia (di disgusto, di disappunto, ecc.) **2.** svisato, falso (di parola, pensiero, ecc.) ☆ *— -neck*, torcicollo.

to wry, *v.t.* contorcere, torcere.

wryly ['rai-li], *av.* per traverso; di sbieco; obliquamente.

wryneck ['rainek], *s.* (*ornit.*) torcicollo.

wryness ['rai-nis], *s.* l'essere contorto, storto; mancanza di regolarità, di simmetria.

wulfenite ['wulfənait], *s.* (*min.*) wulfenite, molibdato di piombo.

wych-elm ['witʃ'elm], *s.* (*bot.*) olmo riccio.

Wyclif(f)ism ['wiklifizəm], *s.* (*st. relig.*) wycliffismo.

Wyclif(f)ite ['wiklif-ait], *ag.* (*st. relig.*) di, appartenente a Wycliffe ‖ *s.* (*st. relig.*) seguace di Wycliffe.

Wykehamical [wi'kæmikəl], *ag.* del collegio di Winchester.

Wykehamist ['wikəmist], *ag.s.* studente, ex-studente del collegio di Winchester.

wynd [waind], *s.* (*scoz.*) strada secondaria; vicolo; viuzza.

wyvern ['waivə(ː)n], *s.* (*arald.*) dragone alato a due zampe.

X

x [eks], *pl.* **xs, x's** [ˈeksiz], *s.* **1.** *(ventiquattresima lettera dell'alfabeto inglese)* x ‖ — *for Xmas, (tel.)* x come Xanthia **2.** *(mat.)* x, prima incognita **3.** X, *(cifra romana)* 10.

Xanadu [ˈzænədu], *no.pr.* *(lett.)* Xanadu.

Xanthian [ˈzænθiən], *ag.* di Zante.

xanthic [ˈzænθik], *ag.*: — *acid, (chim.)* acido xantico.

xanthin [ˈzænθin], *s. (chim.)* xantina.

Xanthippe [zænˈθipi], *no.pr.f. (st. greca)* Santippe ‖ *s.* Santippe, moglie bisbetica.

xanthoma [zænˈθoumə], *s. (patol.)* xantoma: — *multiplex,* xantoma multiplo.

xanthous [ˈzænθəs], *ag.* giallo; mongoloide.

Xanthus [ˈzænθəs], *no.pr. (geog.)* Zante.

Xantippe [zænˈtipi], *no.pr.f. (st. greca)* Santippe ‖ *s.* Santippe, moglie bisbetica.

xebec [ˈziːbek], *s. (mar.)* sciabecco.

xenial [ˈziːniəl], *ag.* di ospitalità.

Xenocrates [ziˈnɔkrətiːz], *no.pr.m. (st. fil.)* Senocrate.

xenogamy [ziˈ(ː)ˈnɔgəmi], *s. (bot.)* fecondazione incrociata.

xenon [ˈzenɔn], *s. (chim.)* xeno.

xenophobe [ˈzenəfoub], *s.* xenofobo.

xenophobia [ˌzenəˈfoubjə], *s.* xenofobia.

Xenophon [ˈzenəfən], *no.pr.m. (st. lett.)* Senofonte.

xeroderma [ˌziərəˈdəːmə], *s. (patol.)* xeroderma.

xerophilous [ziˈrɔfiləs], *ag. (bot.)* xerofilo.

Xerxes [ˈzəːksiːz], *no.pr.m. (st.)* Serse.

xi [gsai], *s.* ksi (lettera dell'alfabeto greco).

xiphoid [ˈzifoid], *ag. (anat.)* xifoideo ‖ *s. (anat.)* xifoide.

Xmas, *V.* **Christmas.**

xoanon [ˈzouənɔn], *s.* immagine primitiva greca scolpita in legno, specialmente di divinità.

X-ray [ˈeksˈrei], *ag. attributivo* a, di raggi X ☆ — *photograph, (med.)* radiografia; — *spectrograph, (fis.)* spettrografo per raggi X; — *tube, (fis.)* lampada, tubo a vuoto per raggi X.

to X-ray, *v.t.* sottoporre a raggi X; radiografare ☆ — *-rayed*, sottoposto a raggi X.

X-rays [ˈeksˈreiz], *s. pl.* raggi X; radiografia.

xylem [ˈzailem], *s. (bot.)* xilema.

xylobalsamum [ˌzailouˈbɔːˌbəmem], *s. (bot.)* silobalsamo.

xylograph [ˈzailəgrɑːf], *s.* xilografia.

xylographer [zaiˈlɔgrəfə*], *s.* xilografo.

xylography [zaiˈlɔgrəfi], *s.* xilografia.

xylophagan [zaiˈlɔfəgən], *s. (zool.)* silofago.

xylophagous [zaiˈlɔfəgəs], *ag.* che mangia il legno.

xylophone [ˈzailəfoun], *s. (mus.)* xilofono.

xylophonist [zaiˈlɔfənist], *s.* xilofonista.

xyster [ˈzistə*], *s. (chir.)* raschiatoio.

xystus [ˈzistəs], *pl.* **xysti** [ˈzistai], *s.* **1.** *(arch. greca)* sisto **2.** sisto; viale di giardino.

Y

y [wai], *pl.* **ys, y's** [waiz], *s.* **1.** (*venticinquesima lettera dell'alfabeto inglese*) y ‖ — *for yellow*, (*tel.*) y come York **2.** (*mat.*) y, seconda incognita.

yabber ['jæbə*], *s.* **1.** (*austral.*) discorso, conversazione **2.** linguaggio parlato dagli indigeni in Australia.

to yabber, *v.t.i.* (*austral.*) chiacchierare; parlare.

yacht [jɔt], *s.* (*mar.*) yacht, panfilo.

to yacht, *v.i.* viaggiare su panfilo; prender parte a gare di panfili.

yachter ['jɔtə*], *s.* comandante di panfilo.

yachting ['jɔtiŋ], *s.* il viaggiare su panfilo; il prendere parte a gare di panfili ☆ — *cruise*, crociera in panfilo.

yachtsman, *pl.* **yachtsmen** ['jɔtsmən], *s.* proprietario, comandante di panfilo.

yaffil, yaffle ['jæfl], *s.* (*ornit.*) picchio verde.

yah [jɑː], *inter.* puah!.

Yahoo [jə'huː], *no.pr.* (*lett.*) Yahoo (bruto in forma umana) ‖ **yahoo**, *s.* **1.** bruto; persona irragionevole e violenta **2.** (*amer.*) zoticone, ignorante.

Yahveh ['jɑːvei], *no.pr.m.* (*Bibbia*) Geova.

yak [jæk], *s.* (*zool.*) yak (bue tibetano).

Yale [jeil], *no.pr.* Yale (famosa università americana).

yam [jæm], *s.* **1.** (*bot.*) igname **2.** (*amer.*) patata dolce.

to yammer ['jæmə*], *v.i.* piangere, lamentarsi.

yank¹ [jæŋk], *s.* (*fam.*) strattone; scossa.

to yank¹, *v.t.i.* (*fam.*) dare uno strattone; tirare con violenza.

Yank², *abbr.* di **Yankee**.

Yankee ['jæŋki], *s.* **1.** (*fam.*) « Yankee », americano (degli Stati Uniti) **2.** (*amer.*) nativo della Nuova Inghilterra.

Yankeedom ['jæŋkidəm], *s.* **1.** gli Yankee **2.** il paese degli Yankee.

Yankeefied ['jæŋkifaid], *ag.* americanizzato.

Yankeeism ['jæŋkiizəm], *s.* americanismo.

yaourt ['jɑːəːt], *s.* yogurt.

yap [jæp], *s.* **1.** guaito, l'uggiolare di un cucciolo **2.** (*fam.*) chiacchierio.

to yap, *pass.p.p.* **yapped** [jæpt], *v.i.* **1.** guaire, abbaiare **2.** (*fam.*) parlare a vanvera **3.** parlare in modo brusco.

yard¹ [jɑːd], *s.* **1.** (*abbr.* yd.) iarda (misura di lunghezza = 91,4399 cm) **2.** (*mar.*) pennone ‖ *a — of ale*, (*sl.*) un boccale di birra; *a — of satin*, (*sl.*) un bicchiere di gin ☆ — *-measure*, strumento di misura di una iarda ‖ *crossjack —*, (*mar.*) pennone di mezzana; *cubic —*, iarda cubica (misura di volume = 0,7645 m³); *main —*, (*mar.*) pennone di maestra; *square —*, iarda quadrata (misura di superficie = 0,8361 m²).

yard², *s.* cortile; recinto; terreno cintato ‖ *Scotland Yard* (o *the Yard*), Scotland Yard (sede centrale della polizia londinese) ☆ *brick- —*, cortile di una fabbrica di mattoni; mattonaia; *ship- —*, cantiere navale; *stock- —*, recinto per il bestiame; *tan- —*, conceria.

to yard², *v.t.* (*amer.*) rinchiudere (bestiame) in un recinto.

yardage¹ ['jɑːdidʒ], *s.* **1.** misurazione in iarde **2.** (*edil.*) materiale di sterro in iarde cubiche.

yardage², *s.* (prezzo per) uso di recinto.

yard-stick ['jɑːdstik], *s.* **1.** stecca di una iarda di lunghezza **2.** *fig.* pietra di paragone.

yarn [jɑːn], *s.* **1.** filo, filato (di lana, cotone, ecc.) **2.** *fig.* racconto, storia, aneddoto: *to spin a —*, raccontare una storia; *to spin yarns*, (*fam.*) raccontar storie, spararle grosse ☆ — *lever*, (*ind. tessile*) leva di alimentazione del filo; — *reel*, aspo (per filato) ‖ *carded —*, filato cardato; *dyed —*, filato tinto; *mercerized —*, filo mercerizzato; *weft —*, filo di trama; *woollen —*, filato di lana.

to yarn, *v.i.* (*fam.*) raccontare storie.

yarrow ['jærou], *s.* (*bot.*) millefoglie.

yashmak ['jæʃmæk], *s.* velo delle donne arabe.

yataghan ['jætəgən], *s.* yatagàn (spada turca).

yaw [jɔː], *s.* **1.** (*aer.*) imbardata **2.** (*mar.*) straorzata.

to yaw, *v.i.* **1.** (*aer.*) imbardare **2.** (*mar.*) straorzare.

yawl¹ [jɔːl], *s.* (*mar.*) iole.

(to) yawl², *V.* **(to) yowl**.

yawn [jɔːn], *s.* **1.** sbadiglio **2.** apertura; voragine.

to yawn, *v.t.i.* **1.** sbadigliare; parlare sbadigliando: *she yawned sthg.*, disse ql.co. sbadigliando **2.** aprirsi, spalancarsi: *the gulf yawned at his feet*, l'abisso si spalancava sotto i suoi piedi.

yawning ['jɔːniŋ], *ag.* **1.** sonnolento **2.** spalancato.

yawningly ['jɔːniŋli], *av.* con sbadigli, sbadigliando.

yaws [jɔːz], *s.pl.* (*patol.*) frambesia.

yclept [i'klept], *ag.* (*arc. scherz.*) chiamato; nominato.

ye [jiː], *pron.pers.* **1.** (*arc.* 2ᵃ *persona pl. caso diretto e obliquo*) voi: *I do beseech —*, vi prego; *where were —?*, dove eravate? **2.** (*poet. scherz.* 2ᵃ *persona sing.pl. caso diretto e obliquo*) tu, voi: *how d' — do?*, come stai?, come state?; *thank —*, grazie.

yea [jei], *s.* (*arc.*) affermazione, certezza; voto favorevole: *yeas and nays*, voti favorevoli e voti sfavorevoli.

yea, *av.* sì.

to yean [jiːn], *v.t.i.* partorire (agnelli, capretti); figliare (di pecore, capre).

yeanling ['jiːnliŋ], *s.* agnellino; capretto.

year [jəː*], *s.* **1.** anno, annata ‖ — *by —* (o *from — to —*), di anno in anno ‖ — *in — out*, un anno dopo l'altro ‖ *all the — round*, per tutto l'anno ‖ *New Year's Day*, Capodanno ‖ *New Year's Eve*, San Silvestro **2.** *pl.* età: *young for his years*, giovane per la sua età ‖ *in years*, vecchio ☆ — *-book*, annuario ‖ *calendar —* (o *civil —* o *legal —*), anno civile; *fiscal —*, anno fiscale; *leap —* (o *bisextile —*), anno bisestile; *lunar —*, anno lunare; *solar —*, anno solare; *school —*, anno scolastico.

yearling ['jəːliŋ], *ag.s.* (animale) di un anno di età.

yearlong ['jəːlɔŋ], *ag.* che dura un anno.

yearly ['jəːli], *ag.* annuale ‖ *av.* annualmente.

to yearn [jəːn], *v.t.i.* languire, struggersi; angustiare: *it yearns me*, (*arc.*) sono angustiato; *to — for sthg.*, agognare, bramare, desiderare ardentemente ql.co.

yearning ['jəːniŋ], *ag.* desideroso, bramoso ‖ *s.* desiderio ardente, brama, smania, struggimento.

yearningly ['jəːniŋli], *av.* ardentemente, bramosamente.

yeast [jiːst], *s.* lievito; fermento ☆ — *-powder*, lievito in polvere (per il pane).

to yeast, *v.i.* fermentare (anche *fig.*).

yeastiness ['jiːstinis], *s.* fermentazione.

yeasty ['jiːsti], *ag.* **1.** spumoso, schiumante, spumeggiante: — *waves*, onde spumeggianti **2.** in fermento (anche *fig.*): — *conscience*, coscienza agitata **3.** superficiale; verboso; frivolo: — *speech*, discorso frivolo.

yegg [jeg], *s.* (*sl. amer.*) scassinatore; svaligiatore (che cambia continuamente località).

yelk [jelk], (*arc.*) per **yolk**[1].

yell [jel], *s.* 1. urlo, strillo, grido 2. (*amer.*) grido d'incitamento (di studenti) 3. (*sl. amer.*) persona, cosa molto buffa.

to yell, *v.t.i.* urlare, strillare, gridare: *he yelled (out) his anger*, sfogò la sua collera gridando; *that makes one — with pain*, fa urlare dal dolore.

yellow ['jelou], *ag.* 1. giallo ‖ *Yellow Book*, rivista letteraria inglese dal 1894 al 1897; Libro Giallo (pubblicazione ufficiale del governo francese) ‖ *Yellow Sea*, Mar Giallo 2. di pelle gialla: — *men*, uomini di razza gialla; — *race*, razza gialla 3. *fig.* geloso, sospettoso; invidioso; (*fam.*) vile, codardo ‖ *s.* 1. (colore) giallo 2. (*fam.*) viltà, codardia 3. *the yellows*, (*patol. vet.*) itterizia; ingiallimento delle piante; (*arc.*) gelosia ☆ — -*boy*, (*sl.*) moneta d'oro; — *earth*, ocra gialla; — -*fever*, (*patol.*) febbre gialla; — -*flag*, bandiera di quarantena ‖ — -*gum*, (*patol.*) itterizia di neonato; — -(*h*)*ammer*, (*ornit.*) zigolo giallo; — *jack*, (*sl.*) febbre gialla; — *jacket*, (*amer. fam.*) vespa, calabrone; — *journalism*, giornalismo scandalistico; — *peril*, pericolo giallo; — *press*, stampa scandalistica; — *sickness*, (*patol.*) itterizia; — -*spot*, (*anat.*) macula lutea.

to yellow, *v.t.i.* ingiallire, rendere giallo: *we found some books yellowed with age*, trovammo dei libri ingialliti dal tempo.

yellowback ['jeloubæk], *s.* romanzo (francese) in edizione economica, dalla copertina gialla.

yellowish ['jelouiʃ], *ag.* giallastro, giallognolo.

yellowishness ['jelouiʃnis], **yellowness** ['jelounis], *s.* colore giallastro.

yellowy ['jeloui], *ag.* giallastro.

yelp [jelp], *s.* guaito.

to yelp, *v.i.* guaire.

yelper ['jelpə*], *s.* 1. chi guaisce 2. cucciolo.

yen[1], *pl.* **yen** [jen], *s.* « yen » (unità monetaria giapponese).

yen[2], *s.* (*sl. amer.*) intenso desiderio: *to have a — for a whisky*, desiderare ardentemente un whisky.

yeoman, *pl.* **yeomen** ['joumən], *s.* 1. piccolo proprietario terriero; agricoltore 2. (*mil.*) volontario di corpo di cavalleria composto da agricoltori ‖ *Yeoman of the Guard*, (*st.*) guardia del corpo reale ‖ —('*s*) *service*, aiuto utile, efficiente 3. (*st.*) proprietario di terre (che avendo una rendita annua di 40 scellini, poteva far parte di giurie, votare per i cavalieri della contea, ecc.) 4. (*mar.*) sottufficiale.

yeomanly ['joumənli], *ag.* 1. di piccolo proprietario terriero, di agricoltore 2. vigoroso 3. semplice.

yeomanry ['joumənri], *s.* 1. classe dei piccoli proprietari terrieri 2. guardia nazionale a cavallo composta di agricoltori volontari.

yes [jes], *av.* 1. sì (nelle risposte): *"Are you ready?"*, *"Yes"*, « Sei pronto? », « Sì » 2. *interr.* davvero?; d'accordo?; è chiaro?; e allora?: *"He is a very unscrupulous fellow"*, *"Yes?"*, « È un tipo di pochi scrupoli », « Davvero? »; *we must take to the right*, —?, dobbiamo andare a destra, d'accordo?; *when I came in, he said: "Yes?"*, quando entrai egli disse: « E allora? » ‖ *inter.* non solo; e per di più: *he will insult you*, —, *and cheat you as well*, ti insulterà e, per di più, ti ingannerà ‖ *s.* (*pl.* **yeses** ['jesiz]) sì: *confine yourself to yeses and noes*, lìmitati ai sì e ai no ☆ — -*man*, (*fam.*) persona accondiscendente; uomo senza carattere.

yesterday ['jestədi], *av.* ieri: — *week*, ieri a otto ‖ *the day before* —, l'altro ieri ‖ *s.* 1. ieri: — *was the tenth*, ieri era il dieci ‖ — *afternoon*, ieri pomeriggio; — *evening*, ieri sera; — *morning*, ieri mattina 2. *pl.* il passato: *all our yesterdays*, il nostro passato.

yestereve(ning) [,jestə'i:v(niŋ)], *av.s.* (*arc. poet.*) ieri sera.

yestermorn(ing) [,jestə'mɔ:n(iŋ)], *av.s.* (*arc. poet.*) ieri mattina.

yesternight [,jestə'nait], *av.s.* (*arc. poet.*) ieri sera; ieri notte.

yesteryear [,jestə'jə:*], *av.* (*poet.*) l'anno scorso.

yestreen [jes'tri:n], *av.s.* (*poet.scoz.*) iersera.

yet [jet], *av.* 1. (*gener. letter.*) ancora, tuttora: *he is — alive*, è tuttora vivo; *I can see her* —, la vedo ancora 2. ancora, in più: *much work is — to be done*, c'è ancora molto lavoro da fare; *we have — much to say*, abbiamo ancora molto da dire ‖ — *again* (o — *once more*), ancora una volta ‖ — *more*, ancor più: *a — more interesting lecture*, una conferenza ancora più interessante ‖ — *one more*, ancora un altro 3. ancora, già; finora: *he has not — arrived*, non è ancora arrivato; *I have never found a fault in them* —, finora non sono riuscito a trovare in loro alcun difetto; *"Need you go —?"*, *"Not —"*, « Devi già andare? », « Non ancora » ‖ *as* —, fino ad ora: *as — nothing has been done*, fino ad ora niente è stato fatto 4. eppure, malgrado tutto, ciononostante: *he will win* —, malgrado tutto vincerà; *she is poor* —, *honest*, è povera, ma onesta 5. nor —, neppure: *they won't talk to me nor — to you*, non vogliono parlare con me e neppure con te ‖ *cong.* ma, però, tuttavia: *he seems honest*, — *I don't trust him*, sembra onesto, tuttavia non mi fido di lui.

yew [ju:], *s.*: — (-*tree*), (*bot.*) tasso.

Yg(g)drasil ['ig,dræsl], *no.pr.* (*mit. scandinava*) « Yggdrasil » (albero che collega cielo, terra e inferno e che ricopre coi suoi rami la terra).

Yiddish ['jidiʃ], *ag.s.* « Yiddish » (tedesco arcaico, frammisto a parole slave e ebraiche, parlato attualmente da ebrei americani).

yield [ji:ld], *s.* 1. prodotto; raccolto: *there is a good — of wheat this year*, il raccolto del grano è buono quest'anno 2. (*ind.*) resa, rendimento; produzione 3. (*comm.*) rendita, reddito, frutto: — *on securities*, reddito su azioni.

to yield, *v.t.i.* 1. produrre, fruttare, rendere: *does it — well?*, rende bene? 2. cedere, arrendersi, sottomettersi: *to — to force*, cedere alla forza ‖ *to — oneself prisoner*, darsi prigioniero 3. cedere, concedere, acconsentire; dare: *I — to none*, non sono secondo a nessuno; *I won't — to their requests*, non cederò alle loro pretese ‖ *to — up the ghost* (o *one's soul*), rendere l'anima.

yieldable ['ji:ldəbl], *ag.* cedibile; arrendevole.

yielder ['ji:ldə*], *s.c.* chi si arrende, chi cede.

yielding ['ji:ldiŋ], *ag.* 1. docile; condiscendente; compiacente; remissivo 2. pieghevole, flessibile.

yieldingly ['ji:ldiŋli], *av.* in modo arrendevole, condiscendente, compiacente.

yieldingness ['ji:ldiŋnis], *s.* 1. sottomissione; compiacenza, arrendevolezza 2. pieghevolezza, flessibilità.

yill [jil], *s.* (*scoz.*) birra.

yodel ['joudl], *s.* « jodler » (canto in falsetto dei montanari tirolesi).

to yodel, *pass.p.p.* **yodel(l)ed** ['joudld], *v.t.i.* cantare alla maniera dei montanari tirolesi.

yoga ['jougə], *s.* (*fil. indiana*) yoga.

yogi ['jougi], *s.* seguace dello yoga.

yogurt ['jougə:t], *s.* yogurt.

yo-heave-ho ['jou'hi:v'hou], **yoho** [jou'hou], *inter.* (*mar.*) issa! (grido dei marinai quando compiono uno sforzo simultaneo).

to yoick [joik], *v.t.i.* gridare « yoicks »; aizzare (cani) gridando « yoicks ».

yoicks [joiks], *inter.* « yoicks » (grido dei cacciatori durante la caccia alla volpe).

yoke [jouk], *s.* 1. giogo (anche *st.*); *fig.* giogo, schiavitù: *the — of convention*, il giogo delle convenzioni; *to pass under the* —, passare sotto il giogo; *to throw* (o *to cast*) *off the* —, liberarsi dal giogo 2. *fig.* legame, vincolo; vincolo matrimoniale 3. (*invariato al pl.*) (generalmente dopo numerali) paio, coppia: *a — of oxen*, una coppia di buoi; *four — of oxen*, quattro coppie di buoi 4. giogo da acquaiolo 5. (*sartoria*) sprone 6. (*mar.*)

barra del timone ☆ — -bone, (anat.) osso zigomatico; — -fellow (o — -mate), coniuge; collega.

to **yoke**, v.t.i. **1.** aggiogare, mettere il giogo a (anche fig.) **2.** fig. accoppiare, accoppiarsi; (fam.) unire, unirsi (in matrimonio, ecc.) **3.** accordarsi, lavorare insieme.

yokel ['joukəl], s. contadino; campagnolo; bifolco.

yolk[1] [jouk], s. tuorlo, rosso d'uovo ☆ — -bag (o — -sac), (biol.) sacco vitellino.

yolk[2], s. lanolina.

yolky ['jouki], ag. con lanolina.

yon [jon], ag. (arc. poet.) lontano, distante ‖ av. (arc. poet.) laggiù; lassù; là ‖ pron. (arc. poet.) quello là, quella cosa là.

yonder ['jondə*], ag. situato lassù; situato laggiù ‖ av. lassù; laggiù.

yore [jo:*], s. (arc.) tempo antico ‖ of —, antico, di un tempo.

York [jo:k], no.pr. (geog.) York ‖ House of —, (st.) Casa di York.

Yorkish ['jo:kiʃ], ag. **1.** di York **2.** che parteggia per la Casa di York.

Yorkshire ['jo:kʃiə*], no.pr. (geog.) Yorkshire ‖ to put — on (s.o.), (fam.) ingannare (qlcu.) ☆ — pudding, pasticcio al forno cotto con sugo di manzo che si mangia con il roast-beef.

Yorkist ['jo:kist], ag.s. (st.) partigiano della Casa di York.

you [ju:], pron.pers. 2ª persona sing.pl. (caso diretto e obliquo) **1.** voi, ve, vi; tu, te, ti; Ella, Lei, Loro: — and I will go by train, tu ed io andremo in treno; — are very kind, Sir, Lei è molto gentile, Signore; — are wrong, my children, avete torto, figli miei; all of — who entered first, tutti voi che siete entrati per primi; all of — were there, tutti voi eravate là; how are —?, come stai?; come state?; I'll come with —, verrò con te; I love — all, vi amo tutti; if I were —, se fossi in te; it's — I'm speaking to, è a te che parlo; Ladies and Gentlemen, — will excuse my broken English, Signore e Signori, mi scuseranno se il mio inglese non è perfetto ‖ — lawyers, voi altri avvocati ‖ away with —!, vattene!; andatevene! **2.** (talvolta espresso nell'imperat.): — sit down and eat your breakfast, siediti e fa' colazione; now — make a speech, ora tocca a voi parlare **3.** (esclamativo): — darling!, cara!; — silly boy!, sciocchino che sei!; — there! why don't — answer?, ehi, tu laggiù!, perchè non rispondi? **4.** (indefinito) si: — never can tell, non si sa mai, non si può mai dire; the joy — feel when — meet a friend, la gioia che si prova quando si incontra un amico **5.** (arc. per yourself): sit — down, siediti.

young [jʌŋ], ag. giovane; fig. inesperto: a man still —, un uomo ancora giovane; he is — in swimming, è inesperto del nuoto; which is — Smith?, qual è il giovane Smith? ‖ Young Italy, (st.) la Giovine Italia ‖ — lady, signorina; — man, giovanotto; the — ones, i bambini; — people, i giovani (matrimoniabili) ‖ in my — days, nei miei verdi anni; to be in one's — days, essere giovane ‖ to be — for one's years, portare bene gli anni ‖ s. coll. piccolo, piccoli, prole (di animale) ‖ to be with —, essere gravido (di animale).

youngish ['jʌŋiʃ], ag. piuttosto giovane.

youngling ['jʌŋliŋ], ag. (poet.) giovane ‖ s. (poet.) bimbo; piccolo (di animale).

youngly ['jʌŋli], av. (rar.) da giovane; in gioventù.

youngness ['jʌŋnis], s. giovinezza.

youngster ['jʌŋstə*], s. ragazzo, giovincello, giovane.

younker ['jʌŋkə*], s. (arc. fam.) ragazzo.

your [jo:*], ag.poss. 2ª persona sing. pl. **1.** vostro, vostra, vostri, vostre; tuo, tua, tuoi, tue; Suo, Sua, Suoi, Sue; Loro: — father and mother, tuo padre e tua madre; — friends, i tuoi amici; — house, la vostra casa; have — children come back?, i Loro figlioli sono ritornati?; have you hurt — hand?, ti sei fatto male alla mano?; how is — father, Miss Brown?, come sta Suo padre, Signorina Brown? ‖ Your Majesty, Vostra Maestà ‖ — turn!, tocca a te! **2.** (indefinito) proprio: you cannot alter — nature, non si può cambiare il proprio carattere **3.** (enfatico, gener. spreg.): — true savage can never be thoroughly civilized, (arc. fam.) il vero selvaggio non può mai essere completamente civilizzato; this is — cricket, is it?, è tutto qui il tuo famoso cricket?

you're [juə*], contr. di you are.

yours [jo:z], pron.poss. 2ª persona sing. pl. il vostro, la vostra, i vostri, le vostre; il tuo, la tua, i tuoi, le tue; il Suo, la Sua, i Suoi, le Sue; il Loro, la Loro, i Loro, le Loro: my children and —, i miei bimbi e i vostri; you and —, tu e i tuoi, tu e la tua famiglia; give me some books of —, dammi qualche tuo libro; isn't this a book of —, Mr. Smith?, non è un Suo libro questo, Signor Smith?; that is no business of —, non ti riguarda, non è affar tuo ‖ — of the 15th inst., (comm.) la vostra pregiata del 15 c. m. ‖ — truly (o faithfully), (nella chiusa delle lettere) sinceramente vostro; (comm.) distinti saluti.

yourself [jo:'self], pl. **yourselves** [jo:'selvz], pron. 2ª persona **1.** r. voi stessi, vi; te stesso, te stessa, ti; Lei stesso, Lei stessa, Si: wash —, lavati ‖ (all) by —, da solo: you must do this work (all) by —, devi fare questo lavoro da solo **2.** (enfatico) voi stessi, tu stesso, tu stessa; Lei stesso, Lei stessa: won't you go —?, non vuoi andare tu stesso?; you saw it —, didn't you, Mr. Brown?, lo ha visto Lei stesso, non è vero, Signor Brown? ‖ s. voi stessi; tu stesso, tu stessa; Lei stesso, Lei stessa: you were not quite yourselves yesterday, non eravate voi ieri (eravate di umore diverso dal solito) ‖ be —!, (sl. amer.) cerca di ricomporti!.

youth [ju:θ], s. **1.** gioventù, giovinezza, adolescenza: the days of —, gli anni della gioventù **2.** adolescente, giovane, giovanetto **3.** coll. i giovani, gioventù: the — of the town, la gioventù della città ☆ — hostel, ostello della gioventù.

youthful ['ju:θful], ag. **1.** giovane, giovanile: a — bride, una giovane sposa **2.** giovanile, di gioventù: — ambitions, ambizioni giovanili; her hat was too — for her face, il cappello era troppo giovanile per il suo viso.

youthfully ['ju:θfuli], av. giovanilmente, da giovane.

youthfulness ['ju:θtfulnis], s. giovanilità; aspetto giovanile.

youthsome ['ju:θsəm], ag. giovane; giovanile.

yowl [jaul], s. ululato; miagolio.

to **yowl**, v.i. ululare; miagolare.

ytterbium [i'tə:biəm], s. (chim.) itterbio.

yttrium ['itriəm], s. (chim.) ittrio.

yucca ['jʌkə], s. (bot.) iucca.

Yugoslav ['ju:gou'sla:v], ag. iugoslavo ‖ s.c. iugoslavo, iugoslava.

Yugoslavia ['ju:gou'sla:vjə], no.pr. (geog.) Jugoslavia.

yulan ['ju:lən], s. (bot.) magnolia cinese.

yule [ju:l], s. (scoz.) feste natalizie ☆ — log, ceppo di Natale; — -tide, periodo natalizio.

Z

z [zed, *amer.* zi:], *pl.* **zs, z's** [zedz, *amer.* zi:z], *s.* **1.** (*ventiseiesima lettera dell'alfabeto inglese*) z ‖ — *for zebra*, (*tel.*) z come Zara **2.** oggetto a forma di Z **3.** (*mat.*) z, terza incognita.

Zachariah [ˌzækəˈraiə], **Zacharias** [ˌzækəˈraiəs], **Zachary** [ˈzækəri], *no.pr.m.* (*Bibbia*) Zaccaria.

zaffer, zaffre [ˈzæfə*], *s.* (*min.*) zaffera.

Zagreb [ˈzɑːgreb], *no.pr.* (*geog.*) Zagabria.

Zambesi [zæmˈbiːzi], *no.pr.* (*geog.*) Zambesi.

zamia [ˈzeimiə], *s.* (*bot.*) zamia.

zamindar, *V.* **zemindar**.

zany [ˈzeini], *s.* **1.** zanni, buffone **2.** (*dial.*) semplicione.

to zany, *v.t.* mimare, imitare goffamente.

Zanzibar [ˌzænziˈbɑː*], *no.pr.* (*geog.*) Zanzibar.

Zanzibari [ˌzænziˈbɑːri], *ag.s.* (nativo) di Zanzibar.

Zarathustrian [ˌzærəˈθuːstriən], *V.* **Zoroastrian**.

zareba, zariba [zəˈriːbə], *s.* siepe, palizzata (attorno a un accampamento, a un villaggio nel Sudan).

zeal [ziːl], *s.* zelo, ardore.

Zealand [ˈziːlənd], *no.pr.* (*geog.*) Zelanda.

Zealander [ˈziːləndə*], *s.c.* zelandese.

zealot [ˈzelət], *s.* zelatore, partigiano, fanatico.

zealotry [ˈzelətri], *s.* zelo; fanatismo.

zealous [ˈzeləs], *ag.* zelante, premuroso, sollecito.

zealously [ˈzeləsli], *av.* zelantemente, sollecitamente, premurosamente.

zealousness [ˈzeləsnis], *s.* zelo, ardore, premura.

zebra, *pl.* **zebra** [ˈziːbrə], **zebras** [ˈziːbrəz], *s.* (*zool.*) zebra ☆ — *crossing*, passaggio pedonale zebrato.

zebrine [ˈziːbrain], *ag.* simile a zebra, di zebra.

zebu, *pl.* **zebu** [ˈziːbuː], **zebus** [ˈziːbuːz], *s.* (*zool.*) zebù.

zed [zed], *s.* zeta (la lettera *z*).

zedoary [ˈzedouəri], *s.* (*bot.*) zedoaria.

zee [ziː], *s.* (*amer.*) zeta (la lettera *z*).

zemindar [ˈzemindɑː*], *s.* **1.** (*st. ang.-in.*) proprietario di terre che pagava l'imposta fondiaria al governo britannico **2.** esattore di imposte fondiarie.

zemstvo [ˈzemstvou], *s.* assemblea elettiva che regolava gli affari di un distretto (in Russia).

Zen [zen], *s.* (*fil. relig.*) Zen.

zenana [zeˈnɑːnə], *s.* gineceo (in India).

zend [zend], *s.* zend (lingua persiana in cui è scritto lo Zend-Avesta).

zenith [ˈzeniθ], *s.* **1.** (*astr.*) zenit **2.** *fig.* culmine, apice: *in those days she was at her* —, in quel tempo ella era all'apice del suo splendore ☆ — -*distance*, distanza zenitale.

zenithal [ˈzeniθəl], *ag.* zenitale.

Zeno [ˈziːnou], *no.pr.m.* (*st. fil.*) Zenone.

Zenobia [ziˈnoubjə], *no.pr.f.* Zenobia.

zephyr [ˈzefə*], *s.* **1.** zeffiro, favonio **2.** «zephyr» (tessuto leggerissimo di lino, di cotone).

Zepp [zep], *abbr.* (*fam.*) di **Zeppelin**.

Zeppelin [ˈzepəlin], *s.* Zeppelin (grande dirigibile tedesco).

zero [ˈziərou], *pl.* **zeros** [ˈziərouz], *s.* zero: *above, below* —, sopra zero, sotto zero ‖ *at* —, (*aer.*) sotto i 1000 piedi (riferito a volo) ☆ — *hour*, ora zero; — *potential*, (*elett.*) potenziale nullo.

zest [zest], *s.* **1.** aroma, gusto, sapore piccante **2.** *fig.* godimento; interesse; entusiasmo; nota piccante: *to add a — to the story*, aggiungere una nota piccante alla storia; *to give — to sthg.*, accrescere il piacere di ql.co.

zeta [ˈziːtə], *s.* zeta (lettera greca).

zeugma [ˈzjuːgmə], *s.* (*gram.*) zeugma.

Zeus [zjuːs], *no.pr.m.* (*mit.*) Zeus.

zibeline [ˈzibəlin], *s.* (*zool.*) zibellino.

zigzag [ˈzigzæg], *ag.* a zigzag ‖ *s.* zigzag; strada a zigzag; (*mil.*) trincea a zigzag ‖ *av.* a zigzag.

to zigzag, *pass.p.p.* **zigzagged** [ˈzigzægd], *v.t.i.* **1.** andare a zigzag **2.** percorrere a zigzag.

zigzaggy [ˈzigˌzægi], *ag.* a zigzag.

zillah [ˈzilə], *s.* (*ang.-in.*) distretto amministrativo.

zimocca [ziˈmɔkə], *s.* (*zool.*) zimmoca.

zinc [ziŋk], *s.* (*chim.*) zinco ☆ — *blende*, (*min.*) blenda; — *oxide*, (*chim.*) ossido di zinco.

to zinc, *pass.p.p.* **zin(c)ked** [ziŋkt], *v.t.* zincare.

zincification [ˌziŋkifiˈkeiʃn], *s.* zincatura.

to zincify [ˈziŋkifai], *v.t.* zincare.

zin(c)king [ˈziŋkiŋ], *s.* zincatura.

zincograph [ˈziŋkougrɑːf], *s.* (*tip.*) zincografia.

to zincograph, *v.t.* imprimere su lastre di zinco.

zincographer [ziŋˈkɔgrəfə*], *s.* zincografo.

zincographic [ˌziŋkouˈgræfik], *ag.* zincografico.

zincography [ziŋˈkɔgrəfi], *s.* (*tip.*) zincografia.

zincoid [ˈziŋkɔid], *s.* (*elett.*) anodo di zinco.

zincotype [ˈziŋkoutaip], *s.* (*tip.*) zincotipia.

zincous [ˈziŋkəs], *ag.* di zinco.

zingaro [ˈziŋgərou], *pl.* **zingari** [ˈziŋgəri(ː)], *s.* zingaro.

zinky [ˈziŋki], *ag.* di zinco; contenente zinco.

zinnia [ˈziniə], *s.* (*bot.*) zinnia.

Zion [ˈzaiən], *no.pr.* (*geog.*) Sion (la collina sacra di Gerusalemme) ‖ *s.* **1.** teocrazia israelita **2.** regno dei cieli **3.** Chiesa Cristiana.

Zionism [ˈzaiənizəm], *s.* (*st.*) sionismo.

Zionist [ˈzaiənist], *ag.s.c.* (*st.*) sionista.

zip [zip], *s.* **1.** sibilo, fischio **2.** *fig.* energia, vigore, attività ☆ — -*fastener*, cerniera, chiusura lampo.

zipper [ˈzipə*], *s.* cerniera, chiusura lampo.

zircon [ˈzəːkən], *s.* (*min.*) zircone.

zirconium [zəˈkounjəm], *s.* (*chim.*) zirconio.

zither [ˈziθə], **zithern** [ˈziθən], *s.* (*mus.*) cetra tirolese.

zizania [ziˈzeiniə], *s.* (*bot.*) zizzania acquatica.

zloty [ˈzloti], *s.* zloti (moneta polacca).

zodiac [ˈzoudiæk], *s.* (*astr.*) zodiaco: *the signs of the* —, i segni dello zodiaco.

zodiacal [zouˈdaiəkəl], *ag.* zodiacale.

zoiatria [zouˌaiəˈtraiə], *s.* zooiatria.

zoic [ˈzouik], *ag.* **1.** degli animali **2.** (*geol.*) contenente tracce di vita animale.

Zolaism [ˈzouləizəm], *s.* (*st. lett.*) verismo zoliano.

Zolaist [ˈzouləist], *s.* (*st. lett.*) chi segue il verismo zoliano.

zombie [ˈzɔmbi], *s.* **1.** pitone (divinità) **2.** morto resuscitato (per magia) **3.** (*sl. amer.*) persona sciocca.

zonal [ˈzounl], *ag.* zonale.

zonally [ˈzounəli], *av.* a zone.

zonate [ˈzouneit], *ag.* a zone.

zone [zoun], *s.* **1.** (*geog.*) zona **2.** (*poet.*) fascia, cintura ☆ — *time*, ora locale ‖ *frigid, temperate, torrid* —, (*geog.*) zona glaciale, temperata, torrida.

to zone, *v.t.* **1.** circondare; fasciare **2.** dividere in zone.

zoned [zound], *ag.* **1.** a zone **2.** diviso in zone, in regioni **3.** che indossa una cintura; *fig.* vergine, casto.

zoo [zuː], *s.* (*fam.*) giardino zoologico, zoo.

zoography [zou'ɔgrəfi], *s.* zoografia.
zooid ['zouɔid], *ag.s.* (*biol.*) zooide.
zoolatry [zou'ɔlətri], *s.* zoolatria.
zoolite ['zouəlait], *s.* (*paleont.*) zoolito.
zoological [,zouə'lɔdʒikəl], *ag.* zoologico ☆ — *garden*, giardino zoologico.
zoologist [zou'ɔlədʒist], *s.* zoologo.
to **zoologize** [zou'ɔlədʒaiz], *v.t.i.* **1.** studiare zoologia **2.** esaminare dal punto di vista zoologico.
zoology [zou'ɔlədʒi], *s.* zoologia.
zoom [zu:m], *s.* **1.** rombo **2.** (*sl. aer.*) salita in candela.
to **zoom**, *v.i.* **1.** rombare **2.** (*sl. aer.*) salire in candela.
zoomagnetism [,zouou'mægnitizəm], *s.* zoomagnetismo.
zoomorph ['zououmɔ:f], *s.* figura, disegno zoomorfo.
zoomorphic [,zouou'mɔ:fik], *ag.* zoomorfo.
zoomorphism [,zouou'mɔ:fizəm], *s.* zoomorfismo.
zoophagous [zou'ɔfəgəs], *ag.* carnivoro.
zoophilist [zou'ɔfilist], *s.* zoofilo.
zoophilous [zou'ɔfiləs], *ag.* zoofilo.
zoophily [zou'ɔfili], *s.* zoofilia.
zoophyte ['zouəfait], *s.* (*biol.*) zoofito.
zooplasty ['zouou,plæsti], *s.* (*chir.*) trapianto di tessuto da animale a uomo.
zoosperm ['zouəspə:m], *s.* **1.** (*fisiol.*) spermatozoo **2.** (*fisiol.*) zoospora.
zootechnics [,zouou'tekniks], **zootechny** ['zouou,tekni], *s.* zootecnia.
zootomic(al) [,zouou'tɔmik(əl)], *ag.* zootomico.

zootomy [zou'ɔtəmi], *s.* zootomia.
zoril(le) ['zɔril], **zorilla** [zə'rilə], *s.* (*zool.*) zorilla.
Zoroaster [,zɔrou'æstə*], *no.pr.m.* (*st. relig.*) Zoroastro.
Zoroastrian [,zɔrou'æstriən], *ag.* di Zoroastro ‖ *s.* seguace di Zoroastro.
Zoroastrianism [,zɔrou'æstriənizəm], *s.* (*st. relig.*) zoroastrismo, dottrina di Zoroastro.
zouave [zu(:)'ɑ:v], *s.* **1.** (*mil.*) zuavo **2.** zuava (giacchetta corta da donna).
zounds [zaundz], *inter.* (*arc.*) caspita!, perbacco!.
Zulu ['zu:lu:], *ag.* zulù ‖ *s.* **1.** zulù; lingua degli zulù **2.** cappello di paglia conico.
Zurich ['zjuərik], *no.pr.* (*geog.*) Zurigo.
Zwingli ['zwiŋli], *no.pr.* (*st. relig.*) Zwinglio.
Zwinglian ['zwiŋliən], *ag.* (*st. relig.*) di Zwinglio.
zygodactyl [,zaigou'dæktil], *s.* (*ornit.*) zigodattilo.
zygoma [zai'goumə], *pl.* **zygomata** [zai'goumətə], *s.* zigomo.
zygomatic [,zaigou'mætik], *ag.* zigomatico.
zygomorphous [,zaigou'mɔ:fəs], *ag.* (*bot.*) zigomorfo.
zygosis [zai'gousis], *s.* (*biol.*) zigosi.
zygospore ['zaigouspɔ:*], *s.* (*biol.*) zigospora.
zygote ['zaigout], *s.* (*biol.*) zigote.
zyme [saim], *s.* enzima (fermento, virus che produce malattie enzimatiche).
zymosis [zai'mousis], *s.* **1.** zimosi, fermentazione **2.** malattia infettiva.
zymotic [zai'mɔtik], *ag.* enzimatico, fermentativo; soggetto a fermentazione; infettivo.

APPENDIX

PROPER NAMES WITH THE SAME FORM IN BOTH LANGUAGES

GEOGRAPHICAL NAMES *

A

Aberdeen [ˌæbə'di:n].
Aberystwyth [ˌæbə'ristwiθ].
Adelaide ['ædəlid].
Agra ['ɑ:grə].
Airedale ['ɛədeil].
Akron ['ækrɔn].
Alabama [ˌælə'bæmə].
Alaska [ə'læskə].
Albany ['ɔ:lbəni].
Alberta [æl'bə:tə].
Albury ['ɔ:lbəri].
Alderney ['ɔ:ldəni].
Aldershot ['ɔ:ldəʃɔt].
Allentown ['ælintaun].
Alloa ['ælouə].
Altrincham ['ɔ:ltriŋəm].
Anglesey ['æŋglsi].
Angus ['æŋgəs].
Annapolis [ə'næpəlis].
Antrim ['æntrim].
Appleby ['æplbi].
Argyll [ɑ:'gail].
Arizona [ˌæri'zounə].
Arkansas ['ɑ:kənsɔ:].
Armagh [ɑ:'mɑ:].
Arran ['ærən].
Ashb(o)urne ['æʃbə:n].
Assam ['æsæm].
Athabasca [ˌæθə'bæskə].
Athlone [æθ'loun].
Atlanta [ət'læntə].
Auckland ['ɔ:klənd].
Augusta [ɔ:'gʌstə].
Austin ['ɔstin].
Avon ['eivən].
Ayer [ɛə*].
Aylesbury ['eilzbəri].
Ayr [ɛə*].

B

Banff [bæmf].
Bangor ['bæŋgə*].
Banks [bæŋks].
Baroda [bə'roudə].
Bath [bɑ:θ].
Bathurst ['bæθə(:)st].
Baton Rouge ['bætən'ru:ʒ].
Beaumaris [bou'mæris].
Bedford(shire) ['bedfəd(ʃiə*)].
Belfast [bel'fɑ:st].
Belize [be'li:z].

B

Benares [bi'nɑ:riz].
Ben Nevis [ben'nevis].
Berkeley ['bɑ:kli, amer. 'bə:kli].
Berkshire ['bɑ:kʃiə*].
Berwick ['berik].
Beverley ['bevəli].
Bhutan [bu'tɑ:n].
Birkenhead ['bə:kənhed].
Birmingham ['bə:miŋəm].
Bismarck ['bizmɑ:k].
Blackburn ['blækbə:n].
Blackpool ['blækpu:l].
Bodmin ['bɔdmin].
Boise [ˈbɔizi].
Bolton ['boultən].
Bombay [bɔm'bei].
Boston ['bɔstən].
Bougainville ['bu:gənvil].
Bournemouth ['bɔ:nməθ].
Boyne [bɔin].
Bradford ['brædfəd].
Brecknock(shire) ['breknɔk(ʃiə*)].
Brentford ['brentfəd].
Bridgeport ['bridʒpout].
Brighton ['braitn].
Brisbane ['brizbən].
Bristol ['bristl].
Brunei [bru:'nai].
Buckinghamshire ['bʌkiŋəmʃiə*].
Buffalo ['bʌfəlou].
Bute [bju:t].

C

Ca(e)rnarvon(shire) [kə'nɑ:vən-
(ʃiə*)].
Caithness ['keiθnes].
Calcutta [kæl'kʌtə].
California [ˌkæli'fɔ:njə].
Cam [kæm].
Cambridge(shire) ['keimbridʒ-
(ʃiə*)].
Camden ['kæmdən].
Canberra ['kænbərə].
Canton ['kæntn].
Cardiff ['kɑ:dif].
Cardiganshire ['kɑ:digənʃiə*].
Carlisle [kɑ:'lail].
Carmarthen(shire) [kə'mɑ:ðən-
(ʃiə*)].
Carson City ['kɑ:sn'siti].
Cawnpore [kɔ:n'pɔ:*].
Charleston ['tʃɑ:lstən].
Charlotte ['ʃɑ:lət].

C

Chattanooga [ˌtʃætə'nu:gə].
Che(a)sapeake ['tʃesəpi:k].
Chelmsford ['tʃelmsfəd].
Cheshire ['tʃeʃə*].
Chester ['tʃestə*].
Cheviot ['tʃeviət].
Cheyenne [ʃai'æn].
Chicago [ʃi'kɑ:gou].
Chichester ['tʃitʃistə*].
Chiltern ['tʃiltə(:)n].
Christchurch ['kraist-tʃə:tʃ].
Cincinnati [ˌsinsi'næti].
Cirencester ['saiərənsestə*].
Clackmannan [klæk'mænən].
Cleveland ['kli:vlənd].
Clifton ['kliftən].
Clyde [klaid].
Colchester ['koultʃistə*].
Colombo [kə'lʌmbou].
Colorado [ˌkɔlə'rɑ:dou].
Columbia [kə'lʌmbiə].
Columbus [kə'lʌmbəs].
Concord ['kɔŋkɔ:d].
Connaught ['kɔnɔ:t].
Connecticut [kə'netikət].
Cook [kuk].
Cork [kɔ:k].
Cotswold ['kɔtswould].
Coventry ['kɔvəntri].
Croydon ['krɔidn].
Culloden [kə'lɔdn].
Cumberland ['kʌmbələnd].
Cupar ['ku:pə*].

D

Dalhousie [dæl'hauzi].
Dalkeith [dæl'ki:θ].
Dallas ['dæləs].
Dar es Salaam ['dɑ:ressə'lɑ:m].
Dartmoor ['dɑ:tmuə*].
Darwin ['dɑ:win].
Dayton ['deitn].
Delaware ['deləwɛə*].
Delhi ['deli].
Denbigh(shire) ['denbi(ʃiə*)].
Denver ['denvə*].
Derby(shire) ['dɑ:bi(ʃiə*)].
Derwent ['də:wənt].
Des Moines [di'mɔin].
Detroit [də'trɔit].
Devonshire ['devnʃiə*].
Dingwall ['diŋwɔ:l].
Dolgelley [dɔl'geθli].

* The names in this list are taken from the United States of America, the British Isles and the British Commonwealth. Other geographical names may be found in the dictionary.

2069

Donegal ['donigo:l].
Dorchester ['do:tʃistə*].
Dornoch ['do:nɔk].
Dorsetshire ['do:sit-ʃiə*].
Douglas ['dʌgləs].
Dover ['douvə*].
Down [daun].
Downpatrick [daun'pætrik].
Drogheda ['droiidə].
Duluth [dju:'lu:θ].
Dumbarton [dʌm'ba:tn].
Dumfries [dʌm'fri:s].
Dundee [dʌn'di:].
Dunedin [dʌ'ni:din].
Dungeness [,dʌndʒi nes].
Duns [dʌnz].
Durban ['do:bən].
Durham ['dʌrəm].

E

Ealing ['i:liŋ].
Ebbw ['ebu:].
Eddystone ['edistən].
Edmonton ['edməntən].
Elgin ['elgin].
Elizabeth [i'lizəbəθ].
El Paso [el'pæsou].
Ely ['i:li].
Enniskillen [,enis'kilin].
Erie ['iəri].
Essex ['esiks].
Evansville ['evənzvil].
Exeter ['eksətə*].
Eyre [ɛə*].

F

Fall River ['fo:l'rivə*].
Fenwick ['fenik].
Fermanagh [fə(:)'mænə].
Fife [faif].
Fitzroy ['fitsrɔi].
Flint [flint].
Flintshire ['flint-ʃiə*].
Florida ['flɔridə].
Folkestone ['foukstən].
Forfar ['fo:fə*].
Forres ['fɔris].
Forth [fo:θ].
Fort Wayne [fo:t'wein].
Fort Worth [fo:t'wə:θ].
Frankfort ['fræŋkfət].
Freetown ['fri:-taun].
Fresno ['freznou].

G

Galvestone ['gælvistən].
Galway ['gɔ:lwei].
Gary ['gɛəri].
Gateshead ['geitshed].
Georgetown ['dʒo:dʒtaun].
Georgia ['dʒo:dʒjə].
Glamorgan(shire) [glə'mo:gən-(ʃiə*)].
Glasgow ['gla:sgou].
Glencoe [glen'kou].
Glenmore [glen'mo:*].
Gloucester ['glɔstə*].
Gloucestershire ['glɔstəʃiə*].
Grand Rapids [grænd'ræpidz].
Grasmere ['gra:s-miə*].
Greenwich ['grinidʒ].

Grimsby ['grimzbi].
Guernsey ['gə:nzi].
Guildford ['gilfəd].

H

Haddington ['hædiŋtən].
Halifax ['hælifæks].
Ham [hæm].
Hamilton ['hæmiltən].
Hampshire ['hæmpʃiə*].
Hampton ['hæmptən].
Harrisburg ['hærisbə:g].
Hartford ['ha:tfəd].
Harwell ['ha:wəl].
Harwich ['hæridʒ].
Haverfordwest ['hævəfəd'west].
Hawaii [ha:'waʃi:].
Hecla ['heklə].
Hekla ['heklə].
Helena ['helinə].
Heligoland ['heligoulænd].
Hendon ['hendən].
Hereford(shire) ['herifəd(ʃiə*)].
Hertford(shire) ['ha:fəd(ʃiə*)].
Hobart ['houba:t].
Holland ['hɔlənd].
Hollywood ['hɔliwud].
Honolulu [,hɔnə'lu:lu:].
Houston ['hju:stən].
Huddersfield ['hʌdəzfi:ld].
Hudson ['hʌdsn].
Hull [hʌl].
Humber ['hʌmbə*].
Hunter ['hʌntə*].
Huntingdon(shire) ['hʌntiŋdən-(ʃiə*)].
Huron ['hjuərən].
Hyderabad ['haidərəba:d].

I

Idaho ['aidəhou].
Ilford ['ilfəd].
Illinois [,ili'nɔi].
Indiana [,indi'ænə].
Indianapolis ['indiə'næpəlis].
Inverary [,invə'rɛəri].
Inverness [,invə'nes].
Iowa ['aiouə].
Ipswich ['ipswitʃ].
Islington ['izliŋtən].

J

Jackson ['dʒæksn].
Jacksonville ['dʒæksnvil].
Jamestown ['dʒeimztaun].
Jedburgh ['dʒedbərə].
Jefferson City ['dʒefəsn'siti].
Jersey City ['dʒə:zi'siti].
Jesselton ['dʒesltən].
Johannesburg [dʒou'hænisbə:g].
Juneau ['dʒu:nou].

K

Kalahari [,ka:la:'ha:ri].
Kansas ['kænzəs].
Kansas City ['kænzəs'siti].
Karachi [kə'ra:tʃi].
Katrine (Loch) ['kætrin(lɔk)].
Kendall ['kendl].

Kenilworth ['kenilwə:θ].
Kent [kent].
Kentucky [ken'tʌki].
Kerry ['keri].
Kesteven [kes'ti:vən].
Keswick ['kezik].
Kew [kju:].
Kildare [kil'dɛə*].
Kilkenny [kil'keni].
Kilmarnock [kil'ma:nək].
Kimberley ['kimbəli].
Kincardine [kin'ka:din].
Kingston upon Hull ['kiŋstən əpən'hʌl].
Kinross [kin'rɔs].
Kirkcudbright [kə:'ku:bri].
Kirkwall ['kə:k-wo:l].
Knoxville ['nɔksvil].
Kosciusko [,kɔzi'ʌskou].

L

Labrador ['læbrədo:*].
Lahore [lə'hɔ:*].
Lambeth ['læmbəθ].
Lanark ['lænək].
Lancashire ['læŋkəʃiə*].
Lancaster ['læŋkəstə*].
Land's End ['lændz'end].
Lansing ['lænsiŋ].
Launceston ['lo:nstən].
Leeds [li:dz].
Leicester ['lestə*].
Leicestershire ['lestəʃiə*].
Leinster ['lenstə*].
Lerwick ['lə:wik].
Lewes ['lu(:)is].
Lewis ['lu(:)is].
Leyton ['leitn].
Liffey ['lifi].
Limpopo [lim'poupou].
Lincoln(shire) ['liŋkən(ʃiə*)].
Lindisfarne ['lindisfa:n].
Lindsey ['lindzi].
Linlithgow [lin'liθgou].
Little Rock ['litl'rɔk].
Liverpool ['livəpu:l].
Llandudno [læn'didnou].
Lomond ['loumənd].
Londonderry [,lʌndən'deri].
Long Beach ['lɔŋ'bi:tʃ].
Longford ['lɔŋfəd].
Los Angeles [lɔs'ændʒili:z].
Lothian ['louðjən].
Louisiana [lu(:),i:zi'ænə].
Lousville ['lu:ivil].
Louth [lauð].
Lucknow ['lʌknau].
Ludlow ['lʌdlou].
Lusaka [lu:'sa:kə].
Luton ['lu:tn].

M

Mackenzie [mə'kenzi].
Madison ['mædisn].
Madras [mə'dra:s].
Mafeking ['mæfikiŋ].
Maidstone ['meidstən].
Maine [mein].
Malmesbury ['ma:mzbəri].
Malvern ['mɔ:lvə(:)n].
Man [mæn].
Manchester ['mæntʃistə*].

Manitoba [ˌmæniˈtoubə].
March [mɑːtʃ].
Marlborough [ˈmɔːlbərə].
Maryland [ˈmɛərilænd, amer. ˈmerilənd].
Massachusetts [ˌmæsəˈtʃuːsets].
Mayo [ˈmeiou].
Mbabane [mbaːˈbaːn].
Meath [miːð].
Medway [ˈmedwei].
Melbourne [ˈmelbən].
Melrose [ˈmelrouz].
Memphis [ˈmemfis].
Menai [ˈmenai].
Merioneth(shire) [ˌmeriˈɔniθ(ʃiə*)].
Mersey [ˈməːzi].
Miami [maiˈæmi].
Michigan [ˈmiʃigən].
Middlesbrough [ˈmidlzbrə].
Middlesex [ˈmidlseks].
Midlothian [midˈlouðjən].
Midway [ˈmidwei].
Milwaukee [milˈwɔːki(ː)].
Minneapolis [ˌminiˈæpəlis].
Minnesota [ˌminiˈsoutə].
Mississippi [ˌmisiˈsipi].
Missouri [miˈzuəri].
Mobile [məˈbiːl].
Moffat [ˈmɔfət].
Mold [mould].
Monaghan [ˈmɔnəhən].
Monmouth(shire) [ˈmʌnməθ(ʃiə*)].
Montana [mɔnˈtænə].
Montgomery(shire) [məntˈgʌməri(ʃiə*)].
Montpelier [mɔntˈpiːljə*].
Montreal [ˌmɔntriˈɔːl].
Moray [ˈmʌri].
Morecambe [ˈmɔːkəm].
Munster [ˈmʌnstə*].
Mysore [maiˈsɔː*].

N

Nairn [nɛən].
Nairobi [ˌnaiəˈroubi].
Nantucket [nænˈtʌkit].
Naseby [ˈneizbi].
Nashville [ˈnæʃvil].
Nassau [ˈnæsɔː].
Natal [nəˈtæl].
Neagh [nei].
Nebraska [niˈbræskə].
Nelson [ˈnelsn].
Nevada [neˈvaːdə].
Newark [ˈnjuː(ː)ək].
New Bedford [njuːˈbedfəd].
Newbury [ˈnjuːbəri].
Newcastle [ˈnjuːˌkaːsl].
New Hampshire [njuːˈhæmpʃiə*].
New Haven [njuː(ː)ˈheivn].
New Jersey [njuːˈdʒəːzi].
New Mexico [njuːˈmeksikou].
New Orleans [njuːˈɔːliənz].
Newport [ˈnjuːpɔːt].
New York [njuːˈjɔːk].
Norfolk [ˈnɔːfək].
Northallerton [nɔːˈθælətn].
Northampton(shire) [nɔːˈθæmptən(ʃiə*)].
Northanger [nɔːˈθæŋgə*].
North Carolina [ˈnɔːθˌkærəˈlainə].
North Dakota [ˈnɔːθdəˈkoutə].
Northumberland [nɔːˈθʌmbələnd].

Norwick [ˈnɔridʒ, amer. ˈnɔːwitʃ].
Nottingham(shire) [ˈnɔtiŋəm(ʃiə*)].
Nyasa [ˈnjæsə].
Nyasaland [ˈnjæsəlænd].

O

Oakham [ˈoukəm].
Oakland [ˈoukˌlənd].
Offaly [ˈɔfəli].
Ohio [ouˈhaiou].
Oklahoma [ˌoukləˈhoumə].
Oklahoma City [ˌoukləˈhouməˈsiti].
Oldham [ˈouldəm].
Olympia [ouˈlimpiə].
Omagh [ˈoumə].
Omaha [ˈouməhaː].
Onslow [ˈɔnzlou].
Ontario [ɔnˈtɛəriou].
Orange [ˈɔrindʒ].
Oregon [ˈɔrigən].
Orkney [ˈɔːkni].
Otsego [ɔtˈsiːgou].
Ottawa [ˈɔtəwə].
Ouse [uːz].
Oxford(shire) [ˈɔksfəd(ʃiə*)].

P

Paddington [ˈpædiŋtən].
Palomar [ˈpæləmɑː*].
Pasadena [ˌpæsəˈdiːnə].
Paterson [ˈpætəsn].
Peebles [ˈpiːblz].
Pemba [ˈpembə].
Pembroke(shire) [ˈpembruk(ʃiə*)].
Pennine [ˈpenain].
Pennsylvania [ˌpensilˈveinjə].
Penrith [ˈpenriθ].
Penzance [penˈzæns].
Peoria [piˈouriə].
Perth [pəːθ].
Peterborough [ˈpiːtəbrə].
Phoenix [ˈfiːniks].
Pierre [piə*].
Pitlochry [pitˈlɔkri].
Pittsburgh [ˈpitsbəːg].
Plymouth [ˈpliməθ].
Poona [ˈpuːnə].
Portland [ˈpɔːtlənd].
Port Louis [pɔːtˈluː(ː)i(s)].
Portobello [ˌpɔːtouˈbelou].
Portsmouth [ˈpɔːtsməθ].
Potomac [pəˈtoumæk].
Presteign [presˈtiːn].
Preston [ˈprestən].
Pretoria [priˈtɔːriə].
Providence [ˈprɔvidəns].
Punjab [pʌnˈdʒaːb].
Purbeck [ˈpəːbek].

Q

Quebec [kwiˈbek].
Queensland [ˈkwiːnzlənd].

R

Radnor [ˈrædnə*].
Radnorshire [ˈrædnəʃiə*].
Raleigh [ˈrɔːli].
Rawalpindi [rɔːlˈpindi].

Reading [ˈrediŋ].
Renfrew [ˈrenfruː].
Rhode Island [roudˈailənd].
Rhondda [ˈrɔndə].
Richmond [ˈritʃmənd].
Rochester [ˈrɔtʃistə*].
Roscommon [rɔsˈkɔmən].
Ross-Cromarty [rɔsˈkrɔməti].
Rothesay [ˈrɔθsi].
Roxburgh(e) [ˈrɔksbərə].
Rutland(shire) [ˈrʌtlənd(ʃiə*)].
Rye [rai].

S

Sacramento [ˌsækrəˈmentou].
Salem [ˈseilem].
Salford [ˈsɔːlfəd].
Salisbury [ˈsɔːlzbəri].
Salt Lake City [ˈsɔːltˈleikˈsiti].
San Antonio [ˌsænænˈtounjou].
San Diego [ˌsændiˈeigou].
Sandringham [ˈsændriŋəm].
San Francisco [ˌsænfrənˈsiskou].
Santa Fé [ˌsæntəˈfei].
Sarawak [səˈraːwək].
Saskatchewan [səsˈkætʃiwən].
Savannah [səˈvænə].
Seafell [ˈskɔːˈfel].
Scarb(o)rough [ˈskaːbrə].
Seilly [ˈsili].
Scranton [ˈskræntn].
Seattle [siˈætl].
Selkirk [ˈselkəːk].
Severn [ˈsevə(ː)n].
Shaftesbury [ˈʃaːftsbəri].
Shannon [ˈʃænən].
Sheffield [ˈʃefiːld].
Shetland [ˈʃetlənd].
Shreveport [ˈʃriːvpɔːt].
Shrewsbury [ˈʃrouzbəri].
Shropshire [ˈʃrɔpʃiə*].
Skiddaw [ˈskidɔː].
Skye [skai].
Sleaford [ˈsliːfəd].
Sligo [ˈslaigou].
Snowdon [ˈsnoudn].
Solent [ˈsoulənt].
Solway [ˈsɔlwei].
Somerset(shire) [ˈsʌməsit(ʃiə*)].
Somerville [ˈsʌməvil].
Southampton [sauθˈæmptən].
South Bend [ˈsauθˈbend].
South Carolina [ˈsauθˌkærəˈlainə]
South Dakota [ˈsauθdəˈkoutə].
Southend on Sea [ˈsauθendənˈsiː].
South Shields [ˈsauθˈʃiːldz].
Spokane [spəˈkæn].
Springfield [ˈspriŋfiːld].
Stafford(shire) [ˈstæfəd(ʃiə*)].
St. Albans [sntˈɔːlbənz].
St. Andrews [sntˈændruːz].
St. George's [sntˈdʒɔːdʒiz].
St. Helens [sntˈhelinz].
St. John's [sntˈdʒɔnz].
St. Lawrence [sntˈlɔrəns].
St. Louis [sntˈluis].
St. Paul [sntˈpɔːl].
Stirling [ˈstəːliŋ].
Stockport [ˈstɔkpɔːt].
Stoke on Trent [ˈstoukənˌtrent].
Stonehaven [stounˈheivn].
Stranraer [strænˈraːə*].
Suffolk [ˈsʌfək].

2071

Sunderland ['sʌndələnd].
Surrey ['sʌri].
Susquehanna [,sʌskwə'hænə].
Sussex ['sʌsiks].
Sutherland ['sʌðələnd].
Suva ['su:və].
Swansea ['swɔnzi].
Sydney ['sidni].

T

Tacoma [tə'koumə].
Tallahassee [,tælə'hæsi].
Tampa ['tæmpə].
Tarawa [tə'rɑ:wə].
Taunton ['tɔ:ntən].
Tavistock ['tævistɔk].
Tay [tei].
Tees [ti:z].
Tennessee [,tene'si:].
Teviot ['ti:vjət].
Texas ['teksəs].
Toledo [tə'leidou].
Topeka [tou'pi:kə].
Toronto [tə'rɔntou].
Tottenham ['tɔtnəm].
Trent [trent].
Trenton ['trentn].
Trossachs ['trɔsəks].
Tueson [tu:'sɔn].
Tulsa ['tʌlsə].
Tweed [twi:d].
Tweedsmuir ['twi:dzmjuə*].
Tyne [tain].
Tyrone [ti'roun].

U

Ullswater ['ʌlz,wɔ:tə*].
Utah ['ju:tɑ:].
Utica ['ju:tikə].
Uttar Pradesh ['utəprə'deiʃ].

V

Vaal [vɑ:l].
Valletta [və'letə].
Vancouver [væn'ku:və*].
Vermont [və'mɔnt].
Victoria [vik'tɔ:riə].
Virginia [və'dʒinjə].

W

Wakefield ['weikfi:ld].
Wallasey ['wɔləsi].
Walsall ['wɔ:lsɔ:l].
Walthamstow ['wɔ:lθəmstou].
Wapping ['wɔpiŋ].
Warwick(shire) ['wɔrik(ʃiə*)].
Washington ['wɔʃiŋtən].
Waterbury ['wɔ:təbəri].
Waterford ['wɔ:təfəd].
Waverley ['weivəli].
Wellington ['weliŋtən].
Westmor(e)land ['westmələnd].
West Virginia ['westvə'dʒinjə].
Wexford ['weksfəd].
Wichita ['witʃitɔ:].
Wick [wik].

Y

Yarmouth ['jɑ:məθ].
Yellowstone ['jelou-stoun].
Yonkers ['jɔŋkəz].
York(shire) ['jɔ:k(ʃiə*)].
Yosemite [jou'semiti].
Youngstown ['jʌŋztaun].
Yukon ['ju:kɔn].

Wicklow ['wiklou].
Wight [wait].
Wigtown ['wigtən].
Willesden ['wilzdən].
Wilmington ['wilmiŋtən].
Wiltshire ['wilt-ʃiə*].
Wimbledon ['wimbldən].
Winchester ['wintʃistə*].
Windermere ['windəmiə*].
Winnipeg ['winipeg].
Wisconsin [wis'kɔnsin].
Witwatersrand [wit'wɔ:təzrænd].
Woburn ['wu:bə:n].
Wolverhampton ['wulvə,hæmptən].
Woolwich ['wulidʒ].
Worcester ['wustə*].
Worcestershire ['wustəʃiə*].
Wyoming [wai'oumiŋ].

Z

Zomba ['zɔmbə].
Zululand ['zu:lu(:)lænd].

SURNAMES

A

Abbott ['æbət].
Abercrombie ['æbəkrʌmbi].
Acheson ['ætʃisn].
Acton ['æktən].
Adams ['ædəmz].
Addison ['ædisn].
Aiken ['eikin].
Ainsworth ['einzwə:θ].
Akenside ['eikinsaid].
Albermarle ['ælbimɑ:l].
Alcock ['ælkɔk].
Alcott ['ɔ:lkət].
Aldington ['ɔ:ldiŋtən].
Aldrich ['ɔ:ldritʃ].
Allein(e) ['ælin].
Allen ['ælin].
Allenby ['ælənbi].
Alleyn ['ælin].
Allingham ['æliŋəm].
Allsop(p) ['ɔ:lsəp].
Althorp ['ɔ:lθɔ:p].
Amery ['eiməri].
Amory ['eiməri].
Ampthill ['æmpθil].
Anderson ['ændəsn].
Andrade ['ændreid].
Andrew(e)s ['ændru:z].
Anstey ['ænsti].

Appleby ['æplbi].
Appleton ['æpltən].
Aram ['ɛərəm].
Arbuthnot(t) [ɑ:'bʌθnət].
Archer ['ɑ:tʃə*].
Arkwright ['ɑ:krait].
Armitage ['ɑ:mitidʒ].
Armstrong ['ɑ:mstrɔŋ].
Arnold ['ɑ:nld].
Arrowsmith ['ærou-smiθ].
Arundel(l) ['ærəndl].
Asbury ['æzbəri].
Ascham ['æskəm].
Asquith ['æskwiθ].
Astor ['æstə*].
Atkins ['ætkinz].
Atkinson ['ætkinsn].
Attlee ['ætli].
Auchinleck [,ɔ:kin'lek].
Auden ['ɔ:dn].
Austen ['ɔstin].
Austin ['ɔstin].
Avebury ['eivbəri].
Aylmer ['eilmə*].

B

Babbitt ['bæbit].
Babington ['bæbiŋtən].
Baden-Powell ['beidn'pouel].

Bagehot ['bædʒət].
Bailey ['beili].
Baillie ['beili].
Baker ['beikə*].
Balch [bɔ:ltʃ].
Baldwin ['bɔ:ldwin].
Balfour ['bælfuə*].
Ballantyne ['bæləntain].
Bal(l)iol ['beiljəl].
Bancroft ['bænkrɔft].
Barbour ['bɑ:bə*].
Barclay ['bɑ:kli].
Baring ['bɛəriŋ].
Barker ['bɑ:kə*].
Barlow ['bɑ:lou].
Barnes [bɑ:nz].
Barnfield ['bɑ:nfi:ld].
Barnum ['bɑ:nəm].
Barrett ['bærət].
Barrie ['bæri].
Barrow ['bærou].
Barrymore ['bærimɔ:*].
Bartlett ['bɑ:tlit].
Barton ['bɑ:tn].
Baruch [bə'ru:k].
Baskervill(e) ['bæskəvil].
Basset(t) ['bæsit].
Bates [beits].
Bathurst ['bæθə(:)st].
Baxter ['bækstə*].

2072

Beaconsfield ['bi:kənzfi:ld].
Beardsley ['biədzli].
Beattie ['bi:ti].
Beauchamp ['bi:tʃəm].
Beaufort ['boufət].
Beaumont ['boumənt].
Beauregard ['bourəga:d].
Beaverbrook ['bi:vəbruk].
Becket(t) ['bekit].
Beckford ['bekfəd].
Beddoes ['bedouz].
Beecham ['bi:tʃəm].
Beerbohm ['biəboum].
Behn [bein].
Behrman ['bɛəmən].
Bell [bel].
Bellamy ['beləmi].
Belloc [be'lɔk].
Benét [be'nei].
Bennet(t) ['benit].
Benson ['bensn].
Bentham ['bentəm].
Bentinck ['bentiŋk].
Bentley ['bentli].
Beresford ['berizfəd].
Bering ['beriŋ].
Berkeley ['ba:kli, amer. 'bə:kli].
Berners ['bə:nəz].
Besant ['besənt].
Bessborough ['bezbrə].
Betterton ['betətən].
Bevan ['bevən].
Beveridge ['bevəridʒ].
Bevin ['bevin].
Bickerstaff ['bikəsta:f].
Biddle ['bidl].
Bierce [biəs].
Bigelow ['bigilou].
Billings ['biliŋz].
Binyon ['binjən].
Birkbeck ['bə:kbek].
Birrell ['birəl].
Blackmore ['blækmɔ:*].
Blackwell ['blækwəl].
Blackwood ['blækwud].
Blaine [blein].
Blair [blɛə*].
Blake [bleik].
Bligh [blai].
Blo(o)mfield ['blu:mfi:ld].
Blount [blʌnt].
Blunden [blʌndn].
Blunt [blʌnt].
Boas ['bouæz].
Bodley ['bodli].
Bolingbroke ['boliŋbruk].
Bolinger ['boulindʒə*].
Bollinger ['bolindʒə*].
Bonar ['bonə*].
Boone [bu:n].
Boots [bu:ts].
Borrow ['borou].
Boswell ['bozwəl].
Bosworth ['bozwə(:)θ].
Bothwell ['boθwəl].
Bourne [buən].
Bowater ['bou,wo:tə*].
Bowden ['boudn].
Bowdler ['baudlə*].
Bowen ['bouin].
Bowes [bouz].
Bowes-Lyon ['bouz'laiən].
Bowra ['baurə].
Bowring ['bauriŋ].
Boyd [boid].

Boyle [boil].
Bradford ['brædfəd].
Bradlaugh ['brædlo:].
Bradley ['brædli].
Bradshaw ['brædʃo:].
Bradstreet ['brædstri:t].
Bragg [bræg].
Brailsford ['breilsfəd].
Braun [bro:n].
Brawne [bro:n].
Bridges ['bridʒiz].
Bridg(e)water ['bridʒ,wo:tə*].
Briggs [brigz].
Brinsley ['brinzli].
Britten ['britn].
Brixton ['brikstən].
Brome [bru:m].
Bromfield ['bromfi:ld].
Brontë ['bronti].
Brook(e) [bruk].
Brooks [bruks].
Brougham [brum].
Broughton ['brautn].
Brown(e) [braun].
Browning ['brauniŋ].
Bruce [bru:s].
Bryant ['braiənt].
Bryce [brais].
Buchan ['bʌkən].
Buchanan [bju(:)'kænən].
Buck [bʌk].
Buckle ['bʌkl].
Buckley ['bʌkli].
Buell ['bju:əl].
Buick ['bju(:)ik].
Bullough ['bulou].
Bulwer ['bulwə*].
Bunyan ['bʌnjən].
Burbage ['bə:bidʒ].
Burdett Coutts ['bə:det'ku:ts].
Burgess ['bə:dʒis].
Burgh [bə:g, 'bʌrə].
Burghley ['bə:li].
Burgoyne ['bə:goin].
Burke [bə:k].
Burleigh ['bə:li].
Burlington ['bə:liŋtən].
Burnaby ['bə:nəbi].
Burne-Jones ['bə:n'dʒounz].
Burnet ['bə:nit].
Burney ['bə:ni].
Burns [bə:nz].
Burnside ['bə:nsaid].
Burroughs ['bʌrouz].
Burton ['bə:tn].
Bury ['beri].
Butler ['bʌtlə*].
Butterick ['bʌtərik].
Buxton ['bʌkstən].
Byrd [bə:d].
Byrom ['baiərəm].
Byron ['baiərən].

C

Cabell ['kæbəl].
Cable ['keibl].
Cabot ['kæbət].
Cadillac ['kædilæk].
Cadogan [kə'dʌgən].
Caird [kɛəd].
Calder ['kɔ:ldə*].
Caldwell ['kɔ:ldwəl].
Calhoun [kæl'houn].

Callaghan ['kæləhən].
Calvert ['kælvə(:)t].
Camden ['kæmdən].
Campbell ['kæmbl].
Campion ['kæmpjən].
Canning ['kæniŋ].
Carew [kə'ru:].
Carey ['kɛəri].
Carl(e)ton ['ka:ltən].
Carlyle [ka:'lail].
Carmichael [ka:'maikəl].
Carnegie [ka:'negi].
Carpenter ['ka:pintə*].
Carrington ['kæriŋtən].
Carroll ['kærəl].
Carson ['ka:sn].
Carteret ['ka:təret].
Cassel(l) ['kæsl].
Castlereagh ['ka:slrei].
Cather ['kæðə*].
Cavendish ['kævəndiʃ].
Caxton ['kækstən].
Chadwick ['tʃædwik].
Chamberlain ['tʃeimbəlin].
Chambers ['tʃeimbəz].
Chandler ['tʃa:ndlə*].
Channing ['tʃæniŋ].
Chantrey ['tʃa:ntri].
Chaplin ['tʃæplin].
Chapman ['tʃæpmən].
Chappell ['tʃæpəl].
Charrington ['tʃæriŋtən].
Chase [tʃeis].
Chatham ['tʃætəm].
Chatterton ['tʃætətən].
Chatto ['tʃætou].
Chaucer ['tʃo:sə*].
Cheke [tʃi:k].
Chesterfield ['tʃestəfi:ld].
Chesterton ['tʃestətən].
Chettle ['tʃetl].
Cheyne ['tʃeini].
Chillingworth ['tʃiliŋwə:θ].
Chorley ['tʃo:li].
Chrysler ['kraizlə*].
Church [tʃə:tʃ].
Churchill ['tʃə:tʃil].
Churchyard ['tʃə:tʃəd].
Chuzzlewit ['tʃʌzlwit].
Cibber ['sibə*].
Clare [klɛə*].
Claridge ['klæridʒ].
Clark(e) [kla:k].
Claverhouse [kleivəhaus].
Clay [klei].
Clemens ['klemənz].
Clifford ['klifəd].
Clinton ['klintən].
Clive [klaiv].
Clough [klʌf].
Cobb(e) [kob].
Cobbett ['kobit].
Cobden ['kobdən].
Cody ['koudi].
Cohen ['kouin].
Coke [kouk].
Cole [koul].
Col(e)man ['koulmən].
Coleridge ['koulridʒ].
Collier ['koliə*].
Collins ['kolinz].
Colman ['koulmən].
Colquhoun [kə'hu:n].
Combe [ku:m].
Compton ['kʌmptən].

2073

Conant ['kɔnənt].
Congreve ['kɔŋgriːv].
Conrad ['kɔnræd].
Constable ['kʌnstəbl].
Conway ['kɔnwei].
Cook(e) [kuk].
Coolidge ['kuːlidʒ].
Cooper ['kuːpə*].
Cop(e)land ['kouplənd].
Cornell [kɔːˈnel].
Cornwallis [kɔːnˈwɔlis].
Coryate ['kɔriət].
Cotton ['kɔtn].
Coverdale ['kʌvədeil].
Coward ['kauəd].
Cowley ['kauli].
Cowper ['kuːpə*].
Cox [kɔks].
Crabb(e) [kræb].
Craigavon [kreigˈævən].
Crane [krein].
Cranford ['krænfəd].
Cranmer ['krænmə*].
Crashaw ['kræʃɔː].
Crawford ['krɔːfəd].
Creighton ['kraitn].
Crichton ['kraitn].
Crockett ['krɔkit].
Croker ['kroukə*].
Cromwell ['krɔmwəl].
Cronin ['krounin].
Cruickshank ['krukʃæŋk].
Crusoe ['kruːsou].
Cudworth ['kʌdwə(ː)θ].
Cummings ['kʌmiŋz].
Cunningham ['kʌniŋəm].
Curtis ['kəːtis].
Curzon ['kəːzn].
Custer ['kʌstə*].

D

Daimler ['deimlə*].
Dale [deil].
Dalrymple [dælˈrimpl].
Dalton ['dɔːltən].
Daniel ['dænjəl].
D'Arcy, Darcy ['dɑːsi].
Darnley ['dɑːnli].
Darwin ['dɑːwin].
Davenant ['dævinənt].
Davenport ['dævnpɔːt].
Davidson ['deividsn].
Davies ['deivis].
Davis ['deivis].
Day [dei].
Dayton ['deitn].
De Bourgh, De Burgh [dəˈbəːg].
Defoe [dəˈfou].
Dekker ['dekə*].
De la Mare [ˌdeləˈmɛə*].
Delany [dəˈleini].
De Morgan [dəˈmɔːgən].
Denham ['denəm].
Dennis ['denis].
De Quincey [dəˈkwinsi].
Deronda [dəˈrɔndə].
de Selincourt [dəˈselinkɔːt].
De Valera [dəvəˈlɛərə].
De Vere [dəˈviə*].
Devereux ['devəruː].
Dewey ['djuː(ː)i].
Dickens ['dikinz].
Dickinson ['dikinsn].
Digby ['digbi].

Dilke(s) [dilk(s)].
Dillon ['dilən].
Disney ['dizni].
Disraeli [dizˈreili].
Dix [diks].
Dixon ['diksn].
Dobell [douˈbel].
Dobson ['dɔbsn].
Doddrige ['dɔdridʒ].
Dodge [dɔdʒ].
Dodgson ['dɔdʒsn].
Dombey ['dɔmbi].
Donald(son) ['dɔnld(sn)].
Donne [dʌn].
Doolittle ['duːlitl].
Dos Passos [dɔsˈpæsəs].
Doughty ['dauti].
Douglas ['dʌgləs].
Dowden ['daudn].
Dowland ['daulənd].
Dowson ['dausn].
Doyle [dɔil].
Drake [dreik].
Drayton ['dreitn].
Dreiser ['draizə*].
Drew [druː].
Dreyfus ['dreifəs].
Drinkwater ['driŋk,wɔːtə*].
Drummond ['drʌmənd].
Dryden ['draidn].
Duchesne [djuːˈʃein].
Duckworth ['dʌkwəːθ].
Duff [dʌf].
Duffy ['dʌfi].
Dulles ['dʌlis].
Du Maurier [dju(ː)ˈmɔːriei].
Dunbar ['dʌnbɑː*].
Dundas [dʌnˈdæs].
Dunsany [dʌnˈseini].
Dupont, Du Pont ['djuːpɔnt].
Dwight [dwait].
Dyce [dais].
Dyer ['dai-ə*].

E

Earle [əːl].
Eastman ['iːstmən].
Eaton ['iːtn].
Eccles ['eklz].
Eddington ['ediŋtən].
Eden ['iːdn].
Edgeworth ['edʒwəːθ].
Edison ['edisn].
Edward(e)s ['edwədz].
Eggleston ['eglstən].
Einstein ['ainstain].
Eisenhower ['aizən,hauə*].
Elgar ['elgɑː*].
El(l)iot(t) ['eljət].
Ellwood ['elwud].
Ellis ['elis].
Elyot ['eljət].
Emerson ['eməsn].
Erskine ['əːskin].
Etherege ['eθəridʒ].
Evans ['evənz].
Everett ['evərit].

F

Faber ['feibə*].
Fagin ['feigin].
Fahrenheit ['færənhait].
Fairclough ['fɛə-klʌf].

Fairfax ['fɛə-fæks].
Fairle(i)gh ['fɛəli].
Falkenbridge ['fɔːkənbridʒ].
Falstaff ['fɔːlstɑːf].
Fanshawe ['fænʃɔː].
Faraday ['færədi].
Farjeon ['fɑːdʒən].
Farquhar ['fɑːkwə*].
Farrell ['færəl].
Faulkes [fɔːks].
Faulks [fouks].
Faulkner ['fɔːknə*].
Faweett ['fɔːsit].
Fawkes [fɔːks].
Featherston(e) ['feðəstən].
Fenton ['fentən].
Fergus(s)on ['fəːgəsn].
Ferrier ['feriə*].
Field [fiːld].
Fielding ['fiːldiŋ].
Finlay ['finlei].
Finn [fin].
Fisher ['fiʃə*].
Fitzgerald [fitsˈdʒerəld].
Fitzherbert [fitsˈhəːbət].
Fitzjames [fitsˈdʒeimz].
Fitzpatrick [fitsˈpætrik].
Fitzroy [fitsˈrɔi].
Flaherty ['flɛəti].
Flanagan ['flænəgən].
Flaxman ['flæksmən].
Fleeker ['flekə*].
Fleming ['flemiŋ].
Fletcher ['fletʃə*].
Flint [flint].
Florio ['flɔːriou].
Foerster ['fəːstə*].
Foote [fut].
Forbes [fɔːbz].
Ford [fɔːd].
Forester ['fɔristə*].
Forster ['fɔːstə*].
Forsyte ['fɔːsait].
Forsyth [fɔːˈsaiθ].
Fortescue ['fɔːtiskjuː].
Foster ['fɔstə*].
Fowler ['faulə*].
Fowles [faulz].
Fox(e) [fɔks].
Foyle [fɔil].
Franklin ['fræŋklin].
Fraser ['freizə*].
Freeman ['friːmən].
Fremantle ['friːmæntl].
Frémont ['friːmɔnt].
Freneau ['friːnou].
Frere [friə*].
Frost [frɔst].
Froude [fruːd].
Fry(e) [frai].
Fuller ['fulə*].
Fulton ['fultən].
Fyfield ['faifiːld].

G

Gadsby ['gædzbi].
Gage [geidʒ].
Gager ['geidʒə*].
Gainsborough ['geinzbərə].
Gaitskell ['geitskəl].
Gallup ['gæləp].
Galsworthy ['gɔːlzwəːði].
Galt [gɔːlt].
Gandhi ['gændiː].

2074

Gard(i)ner ['gɑ:dnə*].
Garland ['gɑ:lənd].
Garner ['gɑ:nə*].
Garnet(t) ['gɑ:nit].
Garrick ['gærik].
Garth [gɑ:θ].
Gascoigne ['gæskoin].
Gascoyne ['gæskoin].
Gaskell ['gæskəl].
Gates [geits].
Gatling ['gætliŋ].
Gauden ['gɔ:dn].
Gaunt [gɔ:nt].
Gay [gei].
Geddes ['gedis].
Geiger ['gaigə*].
Geikie [gi:ki].
George [dʒɔ:dʒ].
Gerould ['dʒerəld].
Gershwin ['gəːʃwin].
Gibbon(s) ['gibən(z)].
Gibbs [gibz].
Gibson ['gibsn].
Gielgud ['gilgud].
Gifford ['gifəd].
Gilder ['gildə*].
Gillette [dʒi'let].
Gil(l)man ['gilmən].
Gilpin ['gilpin].
Gissing ['gisiŋ].
Gladstone ['glædstən].
Glanvill ['glænvil].
Glover ['glʌvə*].
Glyn [glin].
Goddard ['gɔdəd].
Godolphin [gə'dɔlfin].
Godwin ['gɔdwin].
Gogarty ['gougəti].
Golding ['gouldiŋ].
Goldsmith ['gouldsmiθ].
Gollancz [gə'lænts].
Gooch [gu:tʃ].
Googe [gudʒ].
Gosson ['gɔsn].
Gough [gɔf].
Gower ['gauə*].
Grafton ['grɑ:ftən].
Graham(e) ['greiəm].
Grainger ['greindʒə*].
Grand [grænd].
Grandison ['grændisn].
Grant [grɑ:nt].
Granville ['grænvil].
Graves [greivz].
Gray [grei].
Green(e) [gri:n].
Greensleeves ['gri:n-sli:vz].
Gregory ['gregəri].
Gresham ['greʃəm].
Grey [grei].
Grierson ['griəsn].
Griffin ['grifin].
Grimes [graimz].
Grocyn ['grousin].
Grosvenor ['grouvnə*].
Guedalla [gwi'dælə].
Guggenheim ['gugənhaim].
Guildenstern ['gildənstə:n].
Guinness ['ginis].
Gwyn(ne) [gwin].

H

Habington ['hæbiŋtən].
Hadley ['hædli].

Haggard ['hægəd].
Haig(h) [heig].
Hakluyt ['hæklu:t].
Haldane ['hɔ:ldein].
Hales [heilz].
Hall [hɔ:l].
Hallam ['hæləm].
Halleck ['hælək].
Hamilton ['hæmiltən].
Hammond ['hæmənd].
Hannay ['hænei].
Harcourt ['hɑ:kət].
Harding(e) ['hɑ:diŋ].
Hardy ['hɑ:di].
Harewood ['hɛəwud].
Hargreaves ['hɑ:gri:vz].
Harlow(e) ['hɑ:lou].
Harnack ['hɑ:næk].
Harper ['hɑ:pə*].
Harrap ['hærəp].
Har(r)ington ['hæriŋtən].
Harris ['hæris].
Harrison ['hærisn].
Harrow ['hærou].
Hart(e) [hɑ:t].
Hartley ['hɑ:tli].
Harvey ['hɑ:vi].
Haslett ['heizlit].
Haughton ['hɔ:tn].
Havelo(c)k ['hævlɔk].
Hawes [hɔ:z].
Hawkesworth ['hɔ:kswəθ].
Hawkins ['hɔ:kinz].
Hawkwood ['hɔ:k-wud].
Hawthorne ['hɔ:θɔ:n].
Hay [hei].
Haydn ['haidn].
Haydon ['heidn].
Hayes [heiz].
Haynes [heinz].
Hazlitt ['hæzlit].
Heal(e)y ['hi:li].
Hearn(e) [hə:n].
Hearst [hə:st].
Heathfield ['hi:θfi:ld].
Heinemann ['hainəmən].
Hemingway ['hemiŋwei].
Henderson ['hendəsn].
Henryson ['henrisn].
Henslowe ['henzlou].
Hepburn ['hebə(:)n].
Herbert ['hə:bət].
Herrick ['herik].
Herschel(l) ['hə:ʃəl].
Hervey ['hɑ:vi].
Hewlett ['hju:lit].
Heywood ['heiwud].
Hichens ['hitʃinz].
Higgins ['higinz].
Hill [hil].
Hilliard ['hiliəd].
Hillman ['hilmæn].
Hillyard ['hiljəd].
Hilton ['hiltn].
Hitchcock ['hitʃkɔk].
Hoare [hɔ:*].
Hobbes [hɔbz].
Hobhouse ['hɔbhaus].
Hoby ['houbi].
Hoccleve ['hɔkli:v].
Hogarth ['hougɑ:θ].
Hogg [hɔg].
Holcroft ['houlkrɔft].
Holinshed ['hɔlinʃed].
Holland ['hɔlənd].

Holmes [houmz].
Home [houm, hju:m].
Hood [hud].
Hook [huk].
Hooker ['hukə*].
Hoover ['hu:və*].
Hope [houp].
Hopkins ['hɔpkinz].
Horne [hɔ:n].
Horton ['hɔ:tn].
Hough [hʌf].
Houghton ['hɔ:tn].
Housman ['hausmən].
Houston ['hu:stən].
Howard ['hau-əd].
Howe [hau].
Howells ['hauəlz].
Hubbard ['hʌbəd].
Hughes [hju:z].
Hull [hʌl].
Hume [hju:m].
Hunt [hʌnt].
Hunter ['hʌntə*].
Hurd [hə:d].
Hutcheson ['hʌtʃisn].
Hutchinson ['hʌtʃinsn].
Hutton ['hʌtn].
Huxley ['hʌksli].
Hyde [haid].

I

Ingoldsby ['iŋgəldzbi].
Irving ['ə:viŋ].
Irwin ['ə:win].
Isaacs ['aizəks].
Isherwood ['iʃə(:)wud].

J

Jackson ['dʒæksn].
Jacob(s) ['dʒeikəb(z)].
James [dʒeimz].
Jameson ['dʒeimsn].
Jansen ['dʒænsn].
Jefferies ['dʒefriz].
Jeffers ['dʒefəz].
Jefferson ['dʒefəsn].
Jekyll ['dʒi:kil].
Jenner ['dʒenə*].
Jerome [dʒə'roum].
Johnson ['dʒɔnsn].
Johnston ['dʒɔnstən].
Jones [dʒounz].
Jonson ['dʒɔnsn].
Jowett ['dʒauit].
Jowitt ['dʒauit].
Joyce [dʒɔis].

K

Kay [kei].
Kean [ki:n].
Keats [ki:ts].
Keble ['ki:bl].
Keith [ki:θ].
Kellogg ['kelɔg].
Kemble ['kembl].
Kennan ['kenən].
Kennedy ['kenidi].
Key [ki:].
Keyes [ki:z].
Keynes [keinz].
Kidd [kid].

Killigrew ['kiligru:].
Kinglake ['kiŋleik].
Kingsley ['kiŋzli].
Kipling ['kipliŋ].
Kirkpatrick [kə:k'pætrik].
Kneller ['nelə*].
Knickerbocker ['nikəbəkə*].
Knox [nɔks].
Kronin ['krounin].
Kyd [kid].

L

Lafayette [,la:fai'et].
Landor ['lændɔ:*].
Lang [læŋ].
Langland ['læŋlənd].
Langton ['læŋtən].
Lansdowne ['lænzdaun].
Lascelles ['læsəlz].
Latimer ['lætimə*].
Laughton ['lɔ:tn].
Law [lɔ:].
Lawrence ['lorəns].
Lecky ['leki].
Lee [li:].
Legge [leg].
Legros [lə'grou].
Lehmann ['leimən].
Leigh [li:].
Leighton ['leitn].
Lely ['li:li].
Len(n)ox ['lenəks].
L'Estrange [ləs'treindʒ].
Lever ['li:və*].
Leverhulme ['li:vəhju:m].
Leveson ['levisn].
Leveson-Gower ['lu:sn'gɔ:*].
Levy ['li:vi].
Lewes ['lu(:)is].
Lewis ['lu(:)is].
Liddell ['lidl].
Liebig ['li:big].
Lillo ['lilou].
Linacre ['linəkə*].
Lincoln ['liŋkən].
Lindsay ['lindzi].
Linklater ['liŋk,leitə*].
Lipton ['liptən].
Littleton ['litltən].
Livingston(e) ['liviŋstən].
Lloyd [loid].
Locke [lɔk].
Lockhart ['lɔkət].
Locksley ['lɔksli].
Lodge [lɔdʒ].
London ['lʌndən].
Longfellow ['lɔŋ,felou].
Longman ['lɔŋmən].
Longstreet ['lɔŋ,stri:t].
Lonsdale ['lɔnzdeil].
Lough [lʌf].
Loughborough ['lʌfbərə].
Loughton ['lautn].
Lovat ['lʌvət].
Lovelace ['lʌvleis].
Lowell ['louəl].
Lowes [louz].
Lubbock ['lʌbək].
Lundy ['lʌndi].
Lydgate ['lidgeit].
Lyly ['lili].
Lynch [lintʃ].
Lyndsay ['lindzi].

Lyons ['laiənz].
Lytton ['litn].

M

MacArthur [mə'ka:θə*].
Macaulay [mə'kɔ:li].
McCallum [mə'kæləm].
M'Carthy [mə'ka:θi].
McCormack [mə'kɔ:mək].
Macdonald [mək'dɔnəld].
MacDuff [mək'dʌf].
MacFarlane [mək'fa:lin].
Macintosh ['mækintɔʃ].
Mackay [mə'kai].
Mackaye [mə'kai].
McKenna [mə'kenə].
Mackenzie [mə'kenzi].
McKinley [mə'kinli].
Mackintosh ['mækintɔʃ].
Macleane [mə'klein].
MacLeish [mə'kli:ʃ].
Macleod [mə'klaud].
MacManus [mək'mænəs].
Macmillan [mək'milən].
Macmorran [mək'mɔrən].
MacNeice [mək'ni:s].
MacPherson [mək'fə:sn].
Macready [mə'kri:di].
Madison ['mædisn].
Malan ['mælən].
Mal(l)ory ['mæləri].
Malthus ['mælθəs].
Mandeville ['mændəvil].
Manley ['mænli].
Manning ['mæniŋ].
Mansfield ['mænsfi:ld].
Map [mæp].
Markham ['ma:kəm].
Marlow(e) ['ma:lou].
Marquand ['ma:kwənd].
Marryat ['mæriət].
Marshall ['ma:ʃəl].
Marston ['ma:stən].
Martineau ['ma:tinou].
Masefield ['meisfi:ld].
Mason ['meisn].
Massinger ['mæsindʒə*].
Masters ['ma:stəz].
Mather ['meiðə*].
Ma(t)thews ['mæθju:z].
Matthiessen ['mæθisn].
Maturin ['mætjurin].
Maugham [mɔ:m].
Maxwell ['mækswəl].
Meade [mi:d].
Melville ['melvil].
Mencken ['meŋkən].
Menzies ['menziz].
Meredith ['merədiθ].
Meres [miəz].
Mer(r)ivale ['meriveil].
Merton ['mə:tn].
Methuen ['meθjuin].
Meyer [maiə*].
Meynell ['menl].
Micawber [mi'kɔ:bə*].
Middleton ['midltən].
Milford ['milfəd].
Millais ['milei].
Millay [mi'lei].
Miller ['milə*].
Mills [milz].
Milne [miln].

Milton ['miltən].
Minot ['mainət].
Minto ['mintou].
Mitchell ['mitʃəl].
Mitford ['mitfəd].
Monro(e) [mən'rou].
Montagu ['mɔntəgju:].
Montaigne [mɔn'tein].
Moody ['mu:di].
Moore [muə*].
Moran ['mɔ:rən].
More [mɔ:*].
Morgan ['mɔ:gən].
Morison ['mɔrisn].
Morrell ['mʌrəl].
Morris ['mɔris].
Morton ['mɔ:tn].
Motley ['mɔtli].
Mountbatten [maunt'bætn].
Muir [mjuə*].
Muirhead ['mjuəhed].
Munday ['mʌndi].
Munro [mʌn'rou].
Murphy ['mə:fi].
Murr(a)y ['mʌri].
Myers ['maiəz].

N

Napier ['neipiə*].
Nash [næʃ].
Nelson ['nelsn].
Newbolt ['nju:boult].
Newman ['nju:mən].
Newton ['nju:tn].
Nichols ['nikəlz].
Nicholson ['nikəlsn].
Nickleby ['niklbi].
Nicolls ['nikəlz].
Nicolson ['nikəlsn].
Nixon ['niksn].
Norris ['nɔris].
Norton ['nɔ:tn].
Noyes [nɔiz].
Nye [nai].

O

O' Brien [ou'braiən].
O' Callaghan [ou'kæləhən].
O' Casey [ou'keisi].
Occam ['ɔkəm].
Occleve ['ɔkli:v].
O' Connell [ou'kɔnl].
O' Con(n)or [ou'kɔnə*].
O' Donnell [ou'dɔnl].
O' Flaherty [ou'flɛəti].
Ogilvie ['ouglvi].
O' Hara [ou'ha:rə].
O' Kelly [ou'keli].
Oldham ['ouldəm].
O' Neil(l) [ou'ni:l].
Orczy ['ɔ:ksi].
Orwell ['ɔ:wəl].
Osborn(e) ['ɔzbən].
O' Sullivan [ou'sʌlivən].
Otis ['outis].
Otway ['ɔtwei].
Overbury ['ouvəbəri].

P

Packard ['pæka:d].
Paget ['pædʒit].

Pain(e) [pein].
Painter ['peintə*].
Palgrave ['po:lgreiv].
Palmer ['pɑ:mə*].
Palmerston(e) ['pɑ:məstən].
Palsgrave ['po:lzgreiv].
Pankhurst ['pæŋkhə:st].
Parker ['pɑ:kə*].
Parkinson ['pɑ:kinsn].
Parnell [pɑ:'nel].
Parsons ['pɑ:snz].
Paston ['pæstən].
Pater ['peitə*].
Pat(t)erson ['pætəsn].
Patmore ['pætmɔ:*].
Peabody ['pi:ˌbodi].
Peacock ['pi:kok].
Pears [piəz].
Pearson ['piəsn].
Peel(e) [pi:l].
Penn [pen].
Pepys [pi:ps].
Perkins ['pə:kinz].
Pershing ['pə:ʃiŋ].
Peters ['pi:təz].
Pettie ['peti].
Phelps [felps].
Philips ['filips].
Phillpotts ['filpots].
Phipps [fips].
Pickering ['pikəriŋ].
Pickford ['pikfəd].
Pickwick ['pikwik].
Pierce [piəs].
Pinero [pi'niərou].
Pitman ['pitmən].
Pitt [pit].
Plunket(t) ['plʌŋkit].
Poe [pou].
Polk [pouk].
Pollard ['poləd].
Pollock ['polək].
Pomfret ['pʌmfrit].
Ponsonby ['pʌnsnbi].
Poole [pu:l].
Pope [poup].
Pound [paund].
Powell ['pouel].
Praed [preid].
Pratt [præt].
Price [prais].
Priestley ['pri:stli].
Pringle ['priŋgl].
Prior ['praiə*].
Pritchard ['pritʃəd].
Procter ['proktə*].
Prowse [praus].
Prynne [prin].
Pugin ['pju:dʒin].
Pulitzer ['pulitsə*].
Pullman ['pulmən].
Purcell ['pə:sl].
Pusey ['pju:zil].
Putnam ['pʌtnəm].

Q

Quiller-Couch ['kwilə'ku:tʃ].
Quinault ['kwinlt].
Quine(e)y ['kwinsi].

R

Radcliffe ['rædklif].
Raeburn ['reibə:n].

Rale(i)gh ['ro:li].
Ramsay ['ræmzi].
Ramsey ['ræmzi].
Rank [ræŋk].
Ransom(e) ['rænsəm].
Rathbone ['ræθboun].
Rawlings ['ro:liŋz].
Rawlinson ['ro:linsn].
Read(e) [ri:d].
Reading ['rediŋ].
Reed [ri:d].
Rees(e) [ri:s].
Reeve [ri:v].
Reid [ri:d].
Remington ['remiŋtən].
Reynolds ['renldz].
Rhodes [roudz].
Ricardo [ri'kɑ:dou].
Rice [rais].
Rich [ritʃ].
Richardson ['ritʃədsn].
Ridgway ['ridʒwei].
Riley ['raili].
Roberts ['robəts].
Robertson ['robətsn].
Robins ['robinz].
Robinson ['robinsn].
Rockefeller ['rokifelə*].
Rockingham ['rokiŋəm].
Rodgers ['rodʒəz].
Rogers ['rodʒəz].
Rolle [roul].
Romney ['romni].
Roosevelt ['rouzəvelt].
Roper ['roupə*].
Roscoe ['roskou].
Ross [ros].
Rossetti [ro'seti].
Rothermere ['roðəmiə*].
Rothschild ['roθtʃaild].
Routledge ['rautlidʒ].
Rowe [rou].
Rowley ['rouli].
Rowse [raus].
Rush [rʌʃ].
Ruskin ['rʌskin].
Russell ['rʌsl].
Rutherford ['rʌðəfəd].
Ryan ['raiən].
Rymer ['raimə*].

S

Sacheverell [sə'ʃevərəl].
Sackville ['sækvil].
Saintsbury ['seintsbəri].
Sandburg ['sændbə:g].
Sandys [sændz].
Sarge(a)nt ['sɑ:dʒənt].
Saroyan [sə'roiən].
Sassoon [sə'su:n].
Savile ['sævil].
Sawyer ['so:jə*].
Scott [skot].
Scribner ['skribnə*].
Sedgwick ['sedʒwik].
Sedley ['sedli].
Selden ['seldən].
Selfridge ['selfridʒ].
Seward ['si:wəd].
Seymour ['si:mɔ:*].
Shackleton ['ʃækltən].
Shadwell ['ʃædwəl].
Shak(e)spear(e) ['ʃeikspiə*].
Shandy ['ʃændi].

Shaw [ʃo:].
Shelley ['ʃeli].
Sheridan ['ʃeridn].
Sherman ['ʃə:mən].
Sherwood ['ʃə:wud].
Shirley ['ʃə:li].
Siddons ['sidnz].
Sidgwick ['sidʒwik].
Sidney ['sidni].
Simpson ['simpsn].
Sinclair ['siŋkleə*].
Singer ['siŋə*].
Singleton ['siŋltən].
Sitwell ['sitwəl].
Skelton ['skeltn].
Skinner ['skinə*].
Sloan(e) [sloun].
Smith [smiθ].
Smollett ['smolit].
Smyth [smiθ].
Soane [soun].
Somerville ['sʌməvil].
Southerne ['sʌðən].
Southey ['sauði].
Southwell ['sauθwəl].
Spencer ['spensə*].
Spender ['spendə*].
Spenser ['spensə*].
Spurgeon ['spə:dʒən].
Stanford ['stænfəd].
Stanhope ['stænəp].
Stanley ['stænli].
Stanyhurst ['stænihə:st].
Steel(e) [sti:l].
Stein [stain].
Steinbeck ['stainbek].
Stephens ['sti:vnz].
Stephenson ['sti:vnsn].
Sterne [stə:n].
Stevens ['sti:vnz].
Stevenson ['sti:vnsn].
Stewart [stjuət].
Stillingfleet ['stiliŋˌfli:t].
Stokes [stouks].
Stowe [stou].
Strachey ['streitʃi].
Stuart ['stjuət].
Studebaker ['stu:dəbeikə*]
Suckling ['sʌkliŋ].
Sullivan ['sʌlivən].
Sumner ['sʌmnə*].
Surtees ['sə:ti:z].
Swift [swift].
Swinburne ['swinbə:n].
Swinnerton ['swinətn].
Sykes [saiks].
Sylvester [sil'vestə*].
Symond ['saimənd].
Symonds ['saimndz].
Symons ['saimənz].
Synge [siŋ].

T

Taft [tæft].
Tagore [tə'gɔ:*].
Talfourd ['tælfəd].
Tanner ['tænə*].
Tarkington ['tɑ:kiŋtən].
Tate [teit].
Taylor ['teilə*].
Temple ['templ].
Tennyson ['tenisn].
Thackeray ['θækəri].

Thomas ['tɔməs].
Thompson ['tɔmpsn].
Thomson ['tɔmsn].
Thoreau ['θɔːrou].
Tornhill ['θɔːnhil].
Thornton ['θɔːntən].
Thorp(e) [θɔːp].
Ticknor ['tiknə*].
Tillotson ['tilətsn].
Tindal(e) ['tindl].
Todd [tɔd].
Toland ['toulənd].
Tompkins ['tɔmpkinz].
Tottel ['tɔtl].
Tourneur ['təːnə*].
Tovey ['tʌvi].
Townsend ['taunzənd].
Townshend ['taunzənd].
Toynbee ['tɔinbi].
Traherne [trə'həːn].
Trelawn(e)y [tri'lɔːni].
Trenchard ['trentʃɑːd].
Trevelyan [tri'viljən].
Trevithick ['treviθik].
Trollope ['trɔləp].
Truman ['truːmən].
Tucker ['tʌkə*].
Turner ['təːnə*].
Twain [twein].
Tyler ['tailə*].
Tyndale ['tindl].

U

Udall ['juːdəl].
Unwin ['ʌnwin].
Upton ['ʌptən].
Urquhart ['əːkət].

V

Valera [və'lɛərə].
Vanbrugh ['vænbrə].
Van Buren [væn'bjuːrən].
Vandenberg ['vændənbəːg].

Vanderbilt ['vændəbilt].
Vansittart [væn'sitət].
Vaughan [vɔːn].
Vere [viə*].
Vickers ['vikəz].
Villiers ['viləz].

W

Wainwright ['weinrait].
Walford ['wɔːlfəd].
Walker ['wɔːkə*].
Wallace ['wɔlis].
Waller ['wɔlə*].
Walpole ['wɔːlpoul].
Walsh [wɔːlʃ].
Walsingham ['wɔːlsiŋəm].
Walton ['wɔːltən].
Warbeck ['wɔːbek].
Warburton ['wɔːbətn].
Ward [wɔːd].
Warner ['wɔːnə*].
Warren ['wɔrin].
Warton ['wɔːtn].
Watson ['wɔtsn].
Watts [wɔts].
Waugh [wɔː].
Wavell ['weivəl].
Webb [web].
Webster ['webstə*].
Welle(s) [welz].
Wellesley ['welzli].
Wellington ['weliŋtən].
Wendell ['wendl].
Wesley ['wesli].
West [west].
Wharton ['wɔːtn].
Wheeler ['wiːlə*].
Whistler ['wislə*].
Whiston ['wistən].
Whit(t)aker ['witikə*].
White [wait].
Whitehead ['waithed].
Whitman ['witmən].
Whittier ['witiə*].
Whittington ['witiŋtən].

Wicklif(fe) ['wiklif].
Wilberforce ['wilbəfɔːs].
Wilde [waild].
Wilder ['waildə*].
Wilk(e)s [wilks].
Wilkie ['wilki].
Wilkins ['wilkinz].
Wilkinson ['wilkinsn].
Williams ['wiljəmz].
Williamson ['wiljəmsn].
Willoughby ['wiləbi].
Wilmot ['wilmət].
Wilson ['wilsn].
Windsor ['winzə*].
Wiseman ['waizmən].
Wither ['wiðə*].
Wodehouse ['wudhaus].
Wolf [wulf].
Wollstonecraft ['wulstənkrɑːft].
Wolsey ['wulzi].
Woods [wudz].
Woodward ['wudwəd].
Woolf [wulf].
Woolner ['wulnə*].
Woolsey ['wulzi].
Woolworth ['wulwəːθ].
Wordsworth ['wəːdzwə(ː)θ].
Wotton ['wɔtn].
Wren [ren].
Wright [rait].
Wriothesley ['raiəθsli].
Wyat(t) ['waiət].
Wycherley ['witʃəli].
Wyclif(fe) ['wiklif].
Wyndham ['windəm].
Wythe [wiθ].

Y

Yeat(e)s [jeits].
Yonge [jʌŋ].
Young [jʌŋ].

Z

Zangwill ['zæŋgwil].
Zilliacus [ˌzili'ɑːkəs].

FIRST NAMES

A

Adlai ['ædlei].
Adonais [ˌædou'neiis].
Aelfric ['ælfrik].
Aileen ['eiliːn].
Alastair ['æləstə*].
Alastor [ə'læstɔː*].
Aldhelm ['ældhelm].
Aldred ['ɔːldrid].
Alfric ['ælfrik].
Algernon ['ældʒənən].
Alison ['ælisn].
Amabel ['æməbel].
Amy ['eimi].
Amyas ['eimjəs].
Aneurin [ə'naiərin].

Angus ['æŋgəs].
Anth(a)ea [æn'θiə].
Arabella [ˌærə'belə].
Arden ['ɑːdn].
Asa ['eisə].
Astrophel ['æstrəfel].
Athelstan ['æθəlstən].
Audrey ['ɔːdri].
Ava ['ɑːvə].
Aylwin ['eilwin].

B

Bell [bel].
Bella ['belə].
Beowulf ['beiəwulf].

Beryl ['beril].
Bevis ['biːvis].
Boadicea [ˌbouədi'siə].
Boris ['bɔris].
Brenda ['brendɑː].
Brian ['briːən].
Bruce [bruːs].
Bysshe [biʃ].

C

Caedmon ['kædmən].
Caleb ['keileb].
Cary ['kɛəri].
Cedric ['siːdrik].
Celia ['siːljə].

2078

Chloris ['klɔːris].
Christabel ['kristəbel].
Clarence ['klærəns].
Clarissa [klə'risə].
Clifton ['kliftən].
Clive [klaiv].
Colleen ['kɔliːn].
Comus ['kouməs].
Conan ['kounən].
Connor ['kɔnə*].
Cophetua [kou'fetjuə].
Cuthbert ['kʌθbət].
Cynewulf ['kiniwulf].

D

Deirdre ['diədri].
Derek ['derik].
Derrik ['derik].
Desmond ['dezmənd].
Diggory ['digəri].
Dilys ['dilis].
Donalbain ['dɔnlbein].
Dorcas ['dɔːkəs].
Dorian ['dɔːriən].
Dougal ['duːgəl].
Douglas ['dʌgləs].
Drapier ['dreipiə*].
Dudley ['dʌdli].
Dugald ['duːgəld].
Dulcie ['dʌlsi].
Duncan ['dʌŋkən].
Dunstan ['dʌnstən].
Dwight [dwait].
Dylan ['dilən].

E

Eamon ['eimən].
Edna ['ednə].
Edwin ['edwin].
Eirene [ai'riːni].
Eldred ['eldrid].
Elfreda [el'friːdə].
Elfrida [el'friːdə].
Eli ['iːlai].
Elspeth ['elspeθ].
Emmeline ['emiliːn].
Enid ['iːnid].
Eric ['erik].
Errol ['erəl].
Erwin ['əːwin].
Esmé ['ezmi].
Ethel ['eθəl].
Ethelbert ['eθəlbəːt].
Ethelred ['eθəlred].
Euphues ['juːfju(ː)iːz].
Evelyn ['iːvlin].
Ewan ['juː(ː)in].
Ewen ['juː(ː)in].

F

Farquhar ['fɑːkwə*].
Fay [fei].
Fergus ['fəːgəs].
Fidelia [fi'diːljə].
Fingal ['fiŋgəl].
Fiona [fi'ounə].
Fleance ['fliːəns].
Fulke [fulk].

G

Gareth ['gæreθ].
Geraint ['geraint].
Godwin ['gɔdwin].
Gorboduc ['gɔːbədʌk].
Gordon ['gɔːdn].
Grendel ['grendl].
Griffith ['grifiθ].
Gwyneth ['gwiniθ].

H

Hamish ['heimiʃ].
Hartley ['hɑːtli].
Hazel ['heizl].
Hiawatha [,haiə'wɔθə].
Hiram ['haiərəm].
Hodge [hɔdʒ].
Honor ['ɔnə*].
Huckleberry ['hʌklbəri].
Humphr(e)y ['hʌmfri].

I

Ianthe [ai'ænθi].
Ifor ['aivə*].
Igor ['iːgɔː*].
Ina ['ainə].
Inge [iŋ].
Ingram ['iŋrəm].
Iolanthe [,aiə'lænθi].
Ira ['aiərə].
Ivor ['aivə*].
Ivy ['aivi].
Iza ['aizə].

J

Jabez ['dʒeibez].
Jan [dʒæn].
Jedidiah [,dʒedi'daiə].
Jemima [dʒi'maimə].
Jennifer ['dʒenifə*].
Jervis ['dʒɑːvis].
Jessica ['dʒesikə].
Jethro ['dʒeθrou].
Jill [dʒil].
Joel ['dʒouel].
Joyce [dʒɔis].
June [dʒuːn].

K

Keith [kiːθ].
Kenelm ['kenelm].
Kenneth ['keniθ].
Kezia [ki'zaiə].
Kynewulf ['kiniwulf].

L

Lachlan ['læklən].
Lafcadio [læf'kɑːdiou].
Lance [lɑːns].
Laurie ['lɔːri].
Layamon ['laiəmən].
Lear [liə*].
Lemuel ['lemjuəl].

Lesley ['lesli].
Leslie ['lezli, *amer.* 'lesli].
Llewellyn [lu(ː)'elin].
Lloyd [lɔid].
Logan ['lougən].
Lorna ['lɔːnə].

M

Mabel ['meibəl].
Macbeth [mək'beθ].
Madoc ['mædək].
Magnus ['mægnəs].
Maida ['meidə].
Malcolm ['mælkəm].
Malvolio [mæl'vouljou].
Marigold ['mærigould].
Marilyn ['mærilin].
Marmaduke ['mɑːmədjuːk].
Marmion ['mɑːmjən].
Maureen ['mɔːriːn].
Mavis ['meivis].
Mildred ['mildrid].
Miles [mailz].
Millicent ['milisnt].
Minnie ['mini].
Moira ['mɔiərə].
Mona ['mounə].
Montagu(e) ['mɔntəgjuː].
Morag ['mɔːræg].
Moreen [mɔː'riːn].
Morgan ['mɔːgən].
Morgana [mɔː'gɑːnɑː].
Mortimer ['mɔːtimə*].
Murdoch ['məːdɔk].
Muriel ['mjuəriəl].
Myrtle ['məːtl].
Mysia ['misiə].

N

Nahum ['neihəm].
Nigel ['naidʒəl].
Norman ['nɔːmən].

O

Odo ['oudou].
Olaf ['oulæf].
Orson ['ɔːsn].
Osbert ['ɔzbəːt].
Osmund ['ɔzmənd].
Oulda ['wiːdə].
Owen ['ouin].

P

Parnel [pɑː'nel].
Patience ['peiʃəns].
Perceval ['pəːsivəl].
Percival ['pəːsivəl].
Percy ['pəːsi].
Perdita ['pəːditə].
Perry ['peri].
Phebe ['fiːbi].
Phineas ['finiæs].
Primrose ['primrouz].

Q

Queenie ['kwiːni].

R

Rasselas ['ræsiləs].
Reuben ['ru:bin].
Rhoda ['roudə].
Rhys [ri:s].
Rodney ['rɔdni].
Rowena [rou'i:nə].
Roy [rɔi].
Ruby ['ru:bi].
Rudyard ['rʌdjəd].
Rufus ['ru:fəs].
Rupert ['ru:pət].

S

Seamas ['ʃeiməs].
Seamus ['ʃeiməs].
Sean [ʃɔ:n].
Seth [seθ].
Shane [ʃɑ:n].
Sheila ['ʃi:lə].

Shirley

Shirley ['ʃə:li].
Shylock ['ʃailɔk].
Silas ['sailəs].
Stanley ['stænli].
Sydney ['sidni].

T

Tabitha ['tæbiθə].
Talbot ['tɔ:lbət].
Thorold ['θɔrəld].
Tib [tib].
Tracy ['treisi].
Trevor ['trevə*].

U

Ughtred ['u:trid].
Ulick ['ju:lik].
Una ['ju:nə].
Uther ['ju:θə*].

V

Vathek ['væθek].
Venetia [vi'ni:ʃə].
Vere [viə*].
Vernon ['və:nən].

W

Wace [weis].
Waldo ['wɔ:ldou].
Wendy ['wendi].
Wilfred ['wilfrid].
Winifred ['winifrid].
Winnie ['wini].
Winston ['winstən].
Woodrow ['wudrou].

Y

Yehudi [je'hu:di].

2080

ABBREVIATIONS IN COMMON USE
IN THE ENGLISH-SPEAKING COUNTRIES

a, *are*, a, ara.

a., 1. *acre(s)* 2. *active*, (*gram.*) att., attivo 3. *adjective*, ag., aggettivo 4. *afternoon*, pomeriggio 5. *anode*, anodo.

A, 1. *adult*, per adulti (di pellicola cinematografica) 2. *ampere*, A, ampere 3. *argon* (*chim.*) Ar, argo.

Å, A, *angstrom* (*unit*), (*fis.*) Å, angstrom.

A.A., 1. *antiaircraft*, autiaereo 2. *Automobile Association*, Automobile Club.

A.A.E., *American Association of Engineers*, Ordine Americano degli Ingegneri.

A.A. of A., *Automobile Association of America*, Automobile Club d'America.

A.A.R., *against all risks*, (*formula assicurativa*) contro tutti i rischi.

A.B., (*lat.: Artium Baccalaureus*) *Bachelor of Arts*, Diplomato in Lettere.

abbr., abbrev., 1. *abbreviated*, abbreviato 2. *abbreviation*, abbr., abbreviazione.

A.B.C., 1. *Aerated Bread Company*, nome di una catena di ristoranti economici in Gran Bretagna 2. *American Broadcasting Company*, Radio Audizioni Americane 3. *A.B.C. Railway Guide*, orario ferroviario per ordine alfabetico.

ab iuit., (*lat.: ab initio*) *from the beginning*, dal principio.

abl., *ablative*, abl., ablativo.

Abp., *Archbishop*, Arcivescovo.

abr., 1. *abridged*, ridotto (di libro) 2. *abridgment*, riduzione (di libro).

abs., 1. *absolute*, assoluto (di temperatura) 2. *abstract*, astratto.

abt., *about*, circa.

ac., *account*, c.to, conto.

a.c., *alternating current*, c.a., corrente alternata.

a/c, *account*, c.to, conto.

Ac, *actinium*, (*chim.*) Ac, attinio.

A.C., 1. *Air Corps*, Forze Aeree 2. *Alpine Club*, Club Alpino 3. *alternating current*, c.a., corrente alternata 4. *Army Corps*, C. d'A., Corpo d'Armata.

A/C, *account current*, c.c., c/c, conto corrente.

acc., 1. *acceptance*, accettazione 2. *accepted*, accettato 3. *account*, conto 4. *accusative*, acc., accusativo.

act, *active*, (*gram.*) att., attivo.

ad., *adverb*, av., avv., avverbio.

A.D., (*lat.: Anno Domini*) *in the year of the Lord*, A.D., Anno Domini; d. C., dopo Cristo.

A.D.C., A.-D.-C., *Aide-de-Camp*, aiutante di campo.

ad int., (*lat.: ad interim*) *in the meantime*, ad interim.

adj., *adjective*, ag., aggettivo.

Adj., Adjt., *Adjutant*, Aiutante.

ad lib., ad libit., (*lat.: ad libitum*) *at one's pleasure*, ad libitum, a volontà.

Adm., 1. *Admiral*, Ammiraglio 2. *Admiralty*, Ammiragliato.

adv., 1. *adverb*, av., avv., avverbio 2. *advertisement*, annuncio pubblicitario.

A.E.A., *Atomic Energy Anthority*, Commissione per l'Energia Atomica (in Gran Bretagna).

A.E.C., *Atomic Energy Commission*, Commissione per l'Energia Atomica (negli Stati Uniti).

A.F., 1. *Admiral of the Fleet*, Ammiraglio 2. *Air Force*, Aeronautica 3. *Audio Frequency*, (*rad.*) audiofrequenza.

A.F.H.Q., *Air Force Head Quarters*, Quartier Generale dell'Aeronautica.

A.F.L., *American Federation of Labor*, Federazione Americana del Lavoro.

A.F.M., *Air Force Medal*, medaglia al valore aeronautico.

Afr., 1. *Africa*, Africa 2. *African*, africano.

aft., *afternoon*, pomeriggio.

Ag, *silver*, (*chim.*) Ag, argento.

A.G., *Attorney General*, P.G., Proc. Gen., Procuratore Generale.

agcy., *agency*, agenzia.

agr., agric., *agriculture*, agricoltura.

Ah, *ampere-hour*, Ah, amperora.

A.I., *artificial insemination*, fecondazione artificiale.

A.I.P.O., *American Institute of Public Opinion*, ente scientifico per il sondaggio dell'opinione pubblica.

Al, *aluminium*, (*chim.*) Al, alluminio.

A.L., *American Legion*, Legione Americana (associazione di ex-combattenti).

Ala., (*geog.*) *Alabama*.

Alas., (*geog.*) *Alaska*.

ale., *alcohol*, alcool.

alg., *algebra*, alg., algebra.

alt., 1. *alternate*, alternato 2. *altitude*, alt., altitudine.

a.m., (*lat.: ante meridiem*) (*before midday*, a.m., ant., antimeridiano.

Am, *americium*, (*chim.*) Am, americio.

Am., 1. *America*, America 2. *American*, amer., americano.

A.M., 1. *Air Mail*, Posta Aerea 2. *Air Ministry*, Ministero dell'Aeronautica 3. *amplitude modulation*, (*rad.*) modulazione di ampiezza 4. (*lat.: Artium Magister*) *Master of Arts*, Laureato in Lettere.

A.M.A., *American Medical Association*, Ordine Americano dei Medici.

Amer., 1. *America*, America 2. *American*, amer., americano.

amt., *amount*, ammontare.

Angl., *Anglican*, anglicano.

Ang.-Sax., *Anglo-Saxon*, anglosassone.

anon., *anonymous*, anonimo.

ap., *apothecary*.

Ap., *April*, apr., aprile.

A.P., *Associated Press*, Stampa Associata.

app., *appendix*, appendice.

approx., 1. *approximate*, approssimato 2. *approximately*, approssimativamente.

Apr., *April*, apr., aprile.

Apt., *apartment*, appartamento.

apx., *appendix*, appendice.

ar., *arrival*, arrivo.

a.r., (*lat.: anno regni*) *in the year of the reign*, sotto il regno (di).

A.R.A., *Associate of the Royal Academy,* Membro dell'Accademia Reale.

A.R.C., *American Red Cross,* Croce Rossa Americana.

arch., *architect,* arch., architetto.

Arch., Archbp., *Archbishop,* Arc., arcivescovo.

Archd., 1. *Archdeacon,* Arcidiacono 2. *Archduke,* Arciduca.

archt., *architect,* arch., architetto.

Ariz., *(geog.) Arizona.*

Ark., *(geog.) Arkansas.*

A.R.P., *Air Raid Precautions,* Difesa Antiaerea.

arr., *arrival,* arrivo.

art., 1. *article, (gram.)* art., articolo 2. *artillery,* artiglieria.

As, *arsenic, (chim.)* As, arsenico.

As., 1. *Asia,* Asia 2. *Asian, Asiatic,* Asiatico.

A.S., 1. *Academy of Science,* Accademia Scientifica 2. *Anglo-Saxon,* anglosassone 3. *Assistant Secretary,* vice-segretario.

ass., 1. *assistant,* assistente 2. *association,* associazione.

assn., assoc., *association,* associazione.

Asst., *assistant,* assistente.

at, *(metric) atmosphere,* at, atmosfera (metrica).

at., *atomic,* atomico.

At, *astatine, (chim.)* At, astato.

Atl., *Atlantic,* Atlantico.

atm., *atmospheric,* atmosferico.

Atm, *(standard) atmosphere,* Atm, atmosfera (fisica).

atm. press., *atmospheric pressure,* pressione atmosferica.

at. no., *atomic number,* numero atomico.

Att., *Attorney,* Procuratore Legale.

Att.-Gen., *Attorney-General,* P. G., Proc. Gen., Procuratore Generale; *(negli Stati Uniti)* Ministro della Giustizia.

attrib., *attribute, (gram.)* attr., attributo.

Atty., *Attorney,* Procuratore Legale.

at.vol., *atomic volume,* volume atomico.

at.wt., *atomic weight,* peso atomico.

Au, *gold, (chim.)* Au, oro.

Aug., *August,* ag., ago., agosto.

Aus., 1. *Austria,* Austria 2. *Austrian,* austriaco.

Austral., 1. *Australia,* Australia 2. *Australian,* australiano.

auth., 1. *author,* A., autore 2. *authorized,* autorizzato.

Auth. Ver., *Authorized Version,* Versione Autorizzata (traduzione ufficiale, anglicana della Bibbia, 1611).

av., 1. *avenue,* V.le, viale 2. *average,* medio 3. *avoirdupois.*

A.V., *Authorized Version,* Versione Autorizzata (traduzione ufficiale, anglicana della Bibbia, 1611).

avdp., *avoirdupois.*

ave., *avenue,* V.le, viale.

avoir., *avoirdupois.*

B

b., 1. *book,* libro 2. *born,* n., nato

B, *boron, (chim.)* B, boro.

B., 1. *Baron,* bar., Barone 2. *Bible,* Bibbia 3. *British,* britannico.

Ba, *barium,* (chim.) Ba, bario.

B.A., 1. *(lat.: Baccalaureus Artium) Bachelor of Arts,* Diplomato in Lettere 2. *British Association (for the Advancement of Science),* Associazione Britannica (per il Progresso della Scienza).

bap., bapt., *baptised,* battezzato.

Bap., Bapt., *Baptist, (relig.)* Battista.

bar., barr., *barrister,* avv., avvocato.

Bart., *Baronet,* Baronetto.

B.B.C., *British Broadcasting Corporation,* Ente Radiofonico Britannico.

bbl., *barrel(s).*

B.C., 1. *before Christ,* a.C., avanti Cristo 2. *British Columbia,* Colombia Britannica.

B.D., *Bachelor of Divinity,* Diplomato in Teologia.

B/D, *bank draft,* tratta bancaria.

b.e., *bill of exchange,* cambiale.

Be, *beryllium, (chim.)* Be, berillio.

B.E., 1. *Bachelor of Engineering,* Ingegnere Diplomato 2. *bill of exchange,* cambiale 3. *Board of Education,* Ministero dell'Istruzione.

B.E.A., 1. *British East Africa,* Africa Orientale Britannica 2. *British European Airways,* Compagnia Britannica delle Linee Europee.

Beds., *(geog.) Bedfordshire.*

bef., *before,* prima.

Bel., Belg., 1. *Belgian, Belgic,* belga 2. *Belgium,* Belgio.

Benelux, *Belgium, Netherlands, Luxemburg,* Benelux, BE.NE.LUX., Belgio, Olanda, Lussemburgo.

BEPO, *British Experimental Pile O,* reattore sperimentale (costruito a Harwell nel 1948).

Berks., *(geog.) Berkshire.*

bet., *between,* fra.

b. h. p., B. H. P., *brake horsepower, (mec.)* potenza al freno.

Bi, *bismuth, (chim.)* Bi, bismuto.

B.I., 1. *Board of Investigation,* Comitato di Investigazione 2. *British India,* India Britannica.

Bib., *Bible,* Bibbia.

bibl., *bibliography,* bibl., bibliografia.

Bibl., *Biblical,* biblico.

B.I.F., *British Industries Fair,* Fiera dell'Industria Britannica.

Bk, *berkelium, (chim.)* Bk, berkelio.

b.l., *bill of lading,* polizza di carico.

Bl., *Blessed,* B., Beato.

bldg., *building,* edificio.

blvd., *boulevard,* V.le, viale.

B.M., *British Museum,* Museo Britannico.

B.M.A., *British Medical Association,* Ordine Britannico dei Medici.

Bn., *Baron,* bar., Barone.

b.o., *branch office,* succursale, filiale.

B.O.A.C., *British Overseas Airways Corporation,* Compagnia Britannica delle Linee Transoceaniche.

B. of A., *Bank of America,* Banca d'America.

B. of E., *Bank of England,* Banca d'Inghilterra.

B. of T., *Board of Trade,* Ministero del Commercio e dell'Industria.

Boul., *Boulevard,* V.le, viale.

b. p., *boiling point,* punto di ebollizione.

Bp., *Bishop,* Vescovo.

B.P.C., *British Petroleum Company,* Compagnia Petrolifera Britannica.

Br, *bromine, (chim.)* Br, bromo.

B.R., *British Railways,* Ferrovie Britanniche.

B.R.C.S., *British Red Cross Society,* Croce Rossa Britannica.

Brecon, *(geog.) Brecknockshire.*

brev., 1. *brevet,* brev., brevetto 2. *breveted,* brevettato.

Brit., 1. *Britain,* (Gran) Bretagna 2. *British,* britannico.

Brit. Mus., *British Museum,* Museo Britannico.

Bros., *Brothers, (comm.)* F.lli, Fratelli.

B.R.S., *British Road Services,* Servizio Stradale Britannico.

b.s., 1. *balance sheet,* bilancio 2. *bill of sale,* nota di vendita, fattura.

B.S., 1. *Bachelor of Science,* Diplomato in Scienze 2. *Boy Scout,* Giovane Esploratore.

B.S.T., *British Summer Time,* Ora Legale Britannica.

Bt., *Baronet,* Baronetto.

B.T.C., *British Transport Commission,* Commissione Britannica per i Trasporti.

Btu, B. T. U., *British thermal unit.*

bu., *bushel(s).*
Bucks., *(geog.) Buckinghamshire.*
bul., *bulletin,* bollettino.
Bulg., **1.** *Bulgaria,* Bulgaria **2.** *Bulgarian,* Bulgaro.
B.U.P., *British United Press,* Stampa Unita Britannica.
bur., *bureau,* ufficio.
bus., *business,* affari.
B.V.M., *(lat.: Beata Virgo Maria) Blessed Virgin Mary,* B.V.M., Beata Vergine Maria.
B.W., *Biological Warfare,* Guerra Biologica.
B.W.I., *British West Indies,* Indie Occidentali Britanniche.

C

c., **1.** *capacity,* (*elett.*) capacità **2.** *cent,* cèntesimo (di moneta) **3.** *century,* sec., secolo **4.** *(lat.: caput) chapter,* c., Cap., capitolo.
C, **1.** *carbon,* (*chim.*) C, carbonio **2.** *Celsius,* C, Celsius **3.** *coulomb,* C, coulomb.
ca., **1.** *(lat.: circa) about,* c., circa **2.** *cathod,* catodo.
Ca, *calcium,* (*chim.*) Ca, calcio.
C.A., **1.** *Central America,* America Centrale **2.** *Chartered Accountant,* Ragioniere Diplomato.
Ca/C, *current account,* c.c., c/c, conto corrente.
cal., *small calorie,* cal, piccola caloria.
Cal., **1.** *(geog.) California* **2.** *large calorie,* Cal, grande caloria.
Calif., *(geog.) California.*
Cam., Camb., *Cambridge.*
Cambs., *(geog.) Cambridgeshire.*
can., **1.** *canon,* canone **2.** *canto,* canto.
Can., **1.** *Canada,* Canada **2.** *Canadian,* canadese.
Cant., *Canterbury.*
Cantab., *(lat.: Cantabrigiensis) of Cambridge,* cantabrigense.
Cantuar., **1.** *(lat.: Cantuaria) Canterbury* **2.** *(lat.: Cantuariensis) of Canterbury,* di Canterbury.
cap., **1.** *capital,* capitale **2.** *(lat.: caput) chapter,* c., Cap., capitolo.
caps., *capital letters,* lettere maiuscole.
Capt., *Captain,* Cap., capitano.
Card., *Cardinal,* Card., Cardinale.
Cardig., *(geog.) Cardiganshire.*
Carmarths., *(geog.) Carmarthenshire.*
Cath., *Catholic,* cattolico.
C.B.C., *Canadian Broadcasting Corporation,* Ente Radiofonico Canadese.
C.B.E., *Commander (of the Order) of the British Empire,* Comandante dell'Ordine dell'Impero Britannico.
cc., *(lat.: capita) chapters,* Capp., capitoli.
C.C., **1.** *Cape Colony,* Colonia del Capo **2.** *Code Civil,* C.C., Codice Civile **3.** *County Council,* Consiglio Municipale.
C.C.C., *Corpus Christi College.*
C.C.P., *Code of Civil Procedure,* C.P.C., Codice di Procedura Civile.
C. Cr. P., *Code of Criminal Procedure,* C.P.P., Codice di Procedura Penale.
C.C.U.S., *Chamber of Commerce of the United States,* Camera di Commercio degli Stati Uniti.
c.d., *cash discount,* sconto cassa.
Cd, *cadmium,* (*chim.*) Cd, cadmio.
C.D., **1.** *Civil Defence,* Difesa Civile **2.** *Corps Diplomatique,* C.D., Corpo Diplomatico.
Ce, *cerium,* (*chim.*) Ce, cerio.
CE, *Council of Europe,* C.E., Consiglio Europeo.
C.E., **1.** *Church of England,* Chiesa d'Inghilterra **2.** *Civil Engineer,* Ingegnere Civile.
C.E.D., *Community for European Defense,* C.E.D., Comunità Europea di Difesa.
Celt., *Celtic,* celtico.
cent., **1.** *centigrade,* centigrado **2.** *centimetre,* cm, centimetro **3.** *central,* centrale **4.** *century,* sec., secolo **5.** *(lat.: centum) a hundred,* cento.

CERN, *(francese: Centre Européen des Recherches Nucléaires) European Council for Nuclear Research,* C.E.R.N., Consiglio Europeo per le Ricerche Nucleari.
cf., *(lat.: confer) compare,* cfr., confronta.
c.f., *cost and freight,* costo e nolo.
Cf, *californium,* (*chim.*) Cf, californio.
C.F., *Chaplain to the Forces,* Cappellano Militare.
c.f.i., *cost, freight, and insurance,* costo, nolo e assicurazione.
cg, *centigram(me),* cg, centigrammo.
C.G., **1.** *Coast Guard,* Guardia Costiera **2.** *Consul General,* C.G., Console Generale.
C.G.H., *Cape of Good Hope,* Capo di Buona Speranza.
C.G.S., *centimetre-gram(me)-second (unit, system),* C.G.S., (unità, sistema) centimetro-grammo massa-secondo.
ch., **1.** *chapter,* c., Cap., capitolo **2.** *child,* bambino.
Ch., **1.** *Chief,* Capo **2.** *China,* Cina **3.** *Chinese,* cinese **4.** *Church,* Chiesa.
chal., *chaldron.*
Chanc., **1.** *Chancellor,* Cancelliere **2.** *Chancery,* Cancelleria.
chap., *chapter,* c., Cap., capitolo.
Chap., *Chaplain,* Cappellano.
Ches., *(geog.) Cheshire.*
Ch.J., *Chief-Justice,* Presidente della Corte.
Ch. M., *(lat.: Chirurgiae Magister) Master of Surgery,* Medico Chirurgo.
chn., *chain.*
Chr., **1.** *Christ,* Cristo **2.** *Christian,* cristiano.
chron., **1.** *chronicle,* cronaca **2.** *chronology,* cronologia **3.** *chronological,* cronologico.
c.i., *cost and insurance,* costo e assicurazione.
C.I., *Channel Islands,* Isole Normanne.
c.i.f., *cost, insurance, freight,* c.i.f., costo compreso il nolo e l'assicurazione.
C.-in-C., *Commander-in-Chief,* Comandante in Capo.
cit., **1.** *citation,* citazione **2.** *citizen,* cittadino.
cl, **1.** *centilitre,* cl, centilitro **2.** *class,* classe **3.** *clause,* clausola.
Cl, *chlorine,* (*chim.*) Cl, cloro.
cm, *centimetre,* cm, centimetro.
Cm, *curium,* (*chim.*) Cm, curio.
c/o, **1.** *care of,* presso (negli indirizzi) **2.** *cash order,* tratta a vista.
Co, *cobalt,* (*chim.*) Co, cobalto.
Co., **1.** *Company,* C.ia, Compagnia **2.** *County,* Contea.
C.O., **1.** *Colonial Office,* Ufficio Coloniale **2.** *Commanding Officer,* Ufficiale Comandante **3.** *conscientious objector,* obiettore di coscienza.
cod., *codex,* cod., codice.
c.o.d., C.O.D., *cash on delivery,* pagamento alla consegna.
coeff., *coefficient,* coeff., coefficiente.
C. of E., *Church of England,* Chiesa d'Inghilterra.
Col., **1.** *Colonel,* Col., Colonnello **2.** *(geog.) Colorado.*
coll., **1.** *colleague,* collega **2.** *collection,* collezione **3.** *collective,* coll., collettivo **4.** *college,* collegio **5.** *colloquial,* colloquiale.
Colo., *(geog.) Colorado.*
com., **1.** *comedy,* commedia **2.** *commerce,* commercio **3.** *commission,* commissione **4.** *common,* comune **5.** *community,* comunità.
Com., **1.** *Commander,* com., Comandante **2.** *Committee,* Comitato **3.** *Commodore,* Commodoro **4.** *Commonwealth.*
comp., *comparative,* comp., comparativo.
compar., **1.** *comparative,* comp., comparativo **2.** *comparison,* paragone.
Con., *Consul,* Console.
conj., *conjunction,* cong., congiunzione.
Conn., *(geog.) Connecticut.*
Consols., *Consolidated Funds,* Fondi Consolidati.
const., *constant,* (*mat.*) cost., costante.
cont., contd., *continued,* continua.

contr., 1. *contracted,* contratto **2.** *contraction,* contr., contrazione.

co-op., *co-operative,* cooperativo.

Corn., 1. *Cornish,* dialetto, abitante della Cornovaglia **2.** *Cornwall,* Cornovaglia.

corp., 1. *corporal,* cap., caporale **2.** *corporation,* ente, corporazione.

corr., 1. *corrupted,* (*bibliografia*) corrotto **2.** *corruption,* (*bibliografia*) corruzione.

cos, *cosine,* cos, coseno.

c.o.s., *cash on shipment,* pagamento alla spedizione.

cosec, *cosecant,* cosec, cosecante.

cosh, *hyperbolic cosine,* Ch, coseno iperbolico.

cot, *cotangent,* ctg, cotangente.

ep., *compare,* cfr., confronta.

c.p., *carriage paid,* franco di porto.

C.P., 1. *Cape Province,* Provincia del Capo **2.** *Code of Procedure,* Codice di Procedura **3.** *Communist Party,* Partito Comunista.

C.P.R., *Canadian Pacific Railway,* Ferrovia Canadese del Pacifico.

C.P.S., (*lat.: Custos Privati Sigilli*) *Keeper of the Privy Seal,* Custode del Sigillo Privato.

cr., 1. *credit,* credito **2.** *creditor,* creditore **3.** *crown,* corona.

Cr, *chromium,* (*chim.*) Cr, cromo.

c/s, *cycles per second,* per/sec, periodi al secondo.

Cs, *caesium,* (*chim.*) Cs, cesio.

C.S, *Civil Service,* impiego di Stato.

C.S.A., *Confederate States of America,* Stati Confederati Americani (gli undici Stati secessionisti del Sud, 1861).

C.T.C., *Cyclists' Touring Club,* Consociazione Turistica dei Ciclisti.

etf., *certificate,* certificato.

etl., *cental(s).*

etr., *centre,* centro.

eu., *cubic,* cubico, cubo.

Cu, *copper,* (*chim.*) Cu, rame.

Cumb., (*geog.*) *Cumberland.*

C.U.P., *Cambridge University Press,* Edizioni dell'Università di Cambridge.

eur., *currency,* val., valuta.

CV, *cheval-vapeur,* CV, cavallo vapore.

CW, *continuous wave,* (*rad.*) onda persistente.

ewt., *hundredweight(s).*

ey., 1. *capacity,* capacità **2.** *county,* contea **3.** *currency,* val., valuta.

Cyclo., *Cyclopaedia,* Enciclopedia.

C.Z., *Canal Zone,* Zona del Canale (di Panama).

D

d., 1. *day,* g., giorno **2.** *dead,* m., morto **3.** (*lat.: dele*) *delete,* (*tip.*) cassa **4.** *duke,* duca **5.** (*lat.: denarius, denarii*) *penny, pence.*

D., 1. *December,* dic., dicembre **2.** *Duchess,* d.ssa, duc.sa, Duchessa **3.** *Duke,* Duca **4.** *Dutch,* olandese.

D/A, *Deposit Account,* conto vincolato.

D.A.B., *Dictionary of American Biography,* Dizionario Biografico Americano.

dal, *decalitre,* dal, decalitro.

Dan., *Danish,* danese.

dat., *dative,* dat., dativo.

dau., *daughter,* figlia.

d.c., *direct current,* c.c., corrente continua.

D.C., 1. *direct current,* c.c., corrente continua **2.** *District of Columbia,* Distretto Federale della Columbia (nel quale si trova la capitale federale degli U.S.A., Washington).

D.C.L., *Doctor of Civil Law,* Dottore in Diritto Civile.

dd., d/d, *delivered,* consegnato.

d—d, *damned,* dannazione!; acc., accidenti!.

D.D., (*lat.: Divinitatis Doctor*) *Doctor of Divinity,* Dottore in Teologia.

DDT, *dichlorodiphenyltrichloroethane,* D.D.T., diclorodifeniltricloroetano.

dec., 1. *decimetre,* dm, decimetro **2.** *declaration,* dichiarazione **3.** *declension,* (*gram.*) declinazione.

Dec., *December,* dic., dicembre.

decl., 1. *declaration,* dichiarazione **2.** *declension,* (*gram.*) declinazione.

deg., *degree(s),* grado, gradi.

Del., (*geog.*) *Delaware.*

Dem., *Democrat, Democratic,* democratico.

Den., *Denmark,* Danimarca.

dep., dept., *department,* reparto.

Dev., (*geog.*) *Devonshire.*

D.F.C., *Distinguished Flying Cross,* Croce al Valore Aeronautico.

D.F.M., *Distinguished Flying Medal,* Medaglia al Valore Aeronautico.

dft., 1. *defendant,* difensore **2.** *draft,* tr., tratta.

dg, *decigram(me),* dg, decigrammo.

dict., 1. *dictator,* dittatore **2.** *dictionary,* dizionario.

Dir., *Director,* Direttore.

disc., 1. *discount,* sconto **2.** *discoverer,* scopritore.

dkg, *decagram(me),* dag, decagrammo.

dkl, *decalitre,* dal, decalitro.

dkm, *decametre,* dam, decametro.

dl, *decilitre,* dl, decilitro.

D. Lit., D. Litt., 1. (*lat.: Doctor Litterarum*) *Doctor of Letters,* Dottore in Lettere **2.** (*lat.: Doctor Litteraturae*) *Doctor of Literature,* Dottore in Letteratura.

dm, *decimetre,* dm, decimetro.

D.N.B., *Dictionary of National Biography,* Dizionario Biografico Nazionale.

do., *ditto, the same,* suddetto.

dol., *dollar,* dollaro.

dols., *dollars,* dollari.

Dom., *Dominion.*

doz., *dozen,* dozzina, dozzine.

D.P., *Displaced Person,* profugo, rifugiato politico; deportato.

D. Ph., D. Phil., (*lat.: Doctor Philosophiae*) *Doctor of Philosophy,* Dottore in Filosofia.

dpt., 1. *department,* reparto **2.** *deponent,* (*gram.*) deponente.

dr., 1. *debtor,* debitore **2.** *dram(s).*

Dr., *Doctor,* dott., Dottore; dr.ssa, Dottoressa.

dram. pers., *dramatis personae,* (*teat.*) personaggi.

D.Sc., *Doctor of Science,* Dottore in Scienze.

D.S.I.R., *Department of Scientific and Industrial Research,* Reparto per le Ricerche Scientifiche e Industriali.

Dub., *Dublin,* Dublino.

Dur., Durh., (*geog.*) *Durham.*

dwt., *pennyweight.*

Dy, *dysprosium,* (*chim.*) Dy, disprosio.

E

E., 1. *Earl,* Conte (in Gran Bretagna) **2.** *East,* E., Est **3.** *Easter,* Pasqua **4.** *Eastern,* orientale; (zona) Orientale (di una città) **5.** *England,* Inghilterra **6.** *English,* inglese.

ea., *each,* ogni; cad., cadauno.

E. & O.E., *errors and omissions excepted,* (*comm.*) S.E.O., salvo errori ed omissioni.

E.B., *Encyclopaedia Britannica,* Enciclopedia Britannica.

E.B.R., *experimental breeder reactor,* pila atomica autorigeneratrice sperimentale.

E.C., *East Central,* (zona) Centro-orientale (di una città).

E.C.M., *European Common Market,* M.E.C., Mercato Europeo Comune.

ECSC, *European Coal and Steel Community,* C.E.C.A., Comunità Europea per il Carbone e l'Acciaio.

E.C.T., *electroconvulsive therapy,* elettroshock.

ed., 1. *edited*, pubblicato **2.** *edition*, edizione.

Ed., *Editor*, Redattore Capo.

E.D.C., *European Defense Community*, C.E.D., Comunità Europea di Difesa.

Edin., *Edinburgh*, Edimburgo.

edit., 1. *edited*, pubblicato **2.** *edition*, edizione.

E.E., 1. *Early English*, (*filologia*) Antico Inglese **2.** *Electrical Engineer*, Ingegnere Elettrotecnico **3.** *errors excepted*, salvo errori.

E.F.T.A., *European Free Trade Association*, Associazione europea di libero scambio.

e.g., (*lat.*: *exempli gratia*) *for instance*, p.e., p. es., per esempio.

E.I., *East Indies*, Indie Orientali.

Emp., *Emperor*, Imperatore.

encl., *enclosure*, all., allegato.

Ency., Encyc., *Encyclopaedia*, Enciclopedia.

eng., *engineer*, ing., ingegnere.

Eng., 1. *England*, Inghilterra **2.** *English*, inglese.

e.o.d., *every other day*, un giorno sì e un giorno no.

E.P., *extended play*.

Epis., *Episcopal*, episcopale.

eq., 1. *equal*, uguale **2.** *equation*, equazione.

Er, *erbium*, (*chim.*) Er, erbio.

E.R.P., *European Recovery Programme*, Programma di Ricostruzione Europea.

esp., espec., *especially*, spec., specialmente.

Esq., Esqr., *Esquire* (titolo di cortesia usato negli indirizzi).

Ess., (*geog.*) *Essex*.

etc., (*lat.*: *et cetera*) *and so on*, ecc., eccetera.

Eu, *europium*, (*chim.*) Eu, europio.

Eur., 1. *Europe*, Europa **2.** *European*, europeo.

Eurovision, *European Television*, Eurovision, Televisione Europea.

ex., 1. *example*, es., esempio **2.** *exception*, eccezione **3.** *export*, esportazione.

exc., 1. *excellent*, eccellente **2.** *excepted*, eccettuato **3.** *exception*, eccezione.

Exc., *Excellency*, Ecc., Eccellenza (per ambasciatore, ministro, ecc.).

F

f., 1. *farthing* (un quarto di penny) **2.** *feminine*, f., fem., femminile **3.** *following*, seg., seguente.

F, 1. *Fahrenheit*, F, Fahrenheit **2.** *farad*, F, farad **3.** *fluorine*, (*chim.*) F, fluoro.

F.A., *Football Association*, Associazione Calcistica.

f.a.q., *free at quay*, franco banchina.

F.B.A., *Fellow of the British Academy*, Membro dell'Accademia Britannica.

F.B.I., 1. *Federal Bureau of Investigation*, Polizia Federale Statunitense **2.** *Federation of British Industries*, Federazione delle Industrie Britanniche.

F.D., (*lat.*: *Fidei Defensor*) *Defender of the Faith*, Difensore della Fede.

f.e., *for example*, p.e., p. es., per esempio.

Fe, *iron*, (*chim.*) Fe, ferro.

Feb., *February*, feb., febbraio.

Fed., *Federal*, Federale.

fem., *feminine*, f., fem., femminile.

F.I., *Falkland Islands*, Isole Falkland.

Fin., 1. *Finland*, Finlandia **2.** *Finnish*, finlandese.

fl., *florin*(s), fiorino, fiorini.

Fla., Flor., (*geog.*) *Florida*.

fm., *fathom*.

Fm, *fermium*, (*chim.*) Fm, fermio.

F.M., 1. *Field-Marshal*, Feldmaresciallo **2.** *frequency modulation*, (*rad.*) M.F., modulazione di frequenza.

fo., *folio*, (*bibliografia*) in-fol., in folio; c., carta.

F.O., *Foreign Office*, Ministero degli Affari Esteri.

f.o.b., *free on board*, f.o.b., franco a bordo.

fol., 1. *folio*, (*bibliografia*) in-fol., in folio; c., carta **2.** *following*, seg., seguente.

f.o.r., *free on rail*, franco rotaie.

f.p., *freezing point*, punto di congelamento.

F.P., *fire plug*, bocca da incendio.

f.p.m., *feet per minute*, piedi al minuto.

f.p.s., *feet per second*, piedi al secondo.

Fr, *francium*, (*chim.*) Fr, francio.

Fr., 1. *Father*, (*eccl.*) P., Padre **2.** *France*, Francia **3.** *French*, francese **4.** *Friar*, Fra, Frate **5.** *Friday*, v., ven., venerdì.

F.R.A.M., *Fellow of the Royal Academy of Music*, Membro della Reale Accademia di Musica.

F.R.C.S., *Fellow of the Royal College of Surgeons*, Membro del Reale Collegio dei Chirurghi.

Fri., *Friday*, v., ven., venerdì.

F.R.S., *Fellow of the Royal Society*, Membro della « Royal Society ».

ft., *foot*, *feet*, piede, piedi.

fur., *furlong*.

fut., *future*, (*gram.*) fut., futuro.

G

g, 1. *gram*(me), g, grammo **2.** (*acceleration of*) *gravity*, g, (accelerazione di) gravità.

g., *gender*, (*gram.*) genere.

Ga, *gallium*, (*chim.*) Ga, gallio.

Ga., (*geog.*) *Georgia*.

G.A., *General Assembly*, Assemblea Generale.

Gael., *Gaelic*, Gaelico.

gaz., *gazette*, gazzetta.

G.B., *Great Britain*, G.B., Gran Bretagna.

G.B. and I., *Great Britain and Ireland*, Gran Bretagna e Irlanda.

G.B.S., *George Bernard Shaw*.

G.C.V.O., (*Knight*) *Grand Cross of the* (*Royal*) *Victorian Order*, (Cavaliere) Gran Croce del (Reale) Ordine di Vittoria.

Gd, *gadolinium*, (*chim.*) Gd, gadolino.

G.D., *Grand Duke*, G.D., Granduca.

Ge., *germanium*, (*chim.*) Ge, germanio.

gen., 1. *gender*, (*gram.*) genere **2.** *generally*, gener., generalmente **3.** *genitive*, gen., genitivo **4.** *genus*, (*scient.*) genere.

Gen., *General*, Gen., Generale.

genit., *genitive*, gen., genitivo.

gent., *gentleman*, signore.

Geo., (*geog.*) *Georgia*.

ger., *gerund*, ger., gerundio.

Ger., 1. *German*, tedesco **2.** *Germany*, Germania.

Gestapo, (*tedesco*: *Geheime Staatliche Polizei*) *Nazi secret police*, Ge.sta.po. (Polizia segreta politica).

G.H.Q., *General Headquarters*, Q.G., Quartier Generale.

gi., *gill*(s).

G.I., *General Issue*, (*mil. amer.*) soldato semplice.

Gib., *Gibraltar*, Gibilterra.

Gk., *Greek*, greco.

Glam., (*geog.*) *Glamorganshire*.

Glos., (*geog.*) *Gloucestershire*.

G.M., 1. *General Manager*, Direttore Generale **2.** *General Motors*.

G.M.T., *Greenwich Mean Time*, Ora di Greenwich.

gn., *guinea*(s), ghinea, ghinee.

G.P., *general practitioner*, medico generico.

G.P.O., *General Post Office*, Posta Centrale.

gr., 1. *grain*(s) **2.** *grammar*, grammatica **3.** *group*, gruppo.

Gr., 1. *Greece*, Grecia **2.** *Greek*, greco.

grad., 1. *graduate*, laureato **2.** *graduated*, graduato.

G.S., *General Staff*, S.M.G., Stato Maggiore Generale.

Gt. Br., Gt. Brit., *Great Britain*, Gran Bretagna.

gu., *guinea*(s), ghinea, ghinee.

guar., *guaranteed*, garantito.

G.W.(R.), *Great Western* (*Railway*), Grande (Ferrovia) Occidentale.

H

h., *hour,* h, ora.
H, 1. *henry,* (*elett.*) H, henry **2.** *horrific,* dell'orrore (di pellicola cinematografica) **3.** *hydrogen,* (*chim.*) H, idrogeno.
ha, *hectare,* ha, ettaro.
Hauts, (*geog.*) *Hampshire.*
Haw., (*geog.*) *Hawaii.*
H.B.M., *His, Her Britannic Majesty,* Sua Maestà Britannica.
H.C., *House of Commons,* Camera dei Comuni.
h.c.f., *highest common factor,* M.C.D., massimo comun divisore.
He, *helium,* (*chim.*) He, elio.
H.E., 1. *His Eminence,* S. Em., Sua Eminenza **2.** *His Excellency,* S.E., Sua Eccellenza.
Heref., (*geog.*) *Herefordshire.*
Herts., (*geog.*) *Hertfordshire.*
hf., *half,* mezzo, metà.
Hf, *hafnium,* (*chim.*) Hf, afnio.
H.F., *high frequency,* (*rad. tv.*) H.F., alta frequenza.
hg, *hectogram(me),* hg, ettogrammo.
Hg, *mercury,* (*chim.*) Hg, mercurio.
H.G., 1. *High German,* (*filologia*), Alto Tedesco **2.** *His, Her Grace,* S.G., Sua Grazia.
H.H., 1. *His, Her Highness,* S.A., Sua Altezza **2.** *His Holiness,* S.S., Sua Santità.
hhd., *hogshead.*
H.I., *Hawaian Islands,* Isole Hawaii.
H.I.M., *His, Her Imperial Majesty,* Sua Maestà Imperiale.
hl, *hectolitre,* hl, ettolitro.
H.L., *House of Lords,* Camera dei Lord.
hm, *hectometre,* hm, ettometro.
H.M., *His, Her Majesty,* S.M., Sua Maestà.
H.M.S.O., *His, Her Majesty's Stationery Office,* Istituto Poligrafico dello Stato.
Ho, *holmium,* (*chim.*) Ho, olmio.
H.O., *head office,* S.C., Sede Centrale.
hon., *honorary,* onorario.
Hon., *Honourable,* Onorevole.
h.p., H.P., *high pressure,* A.P., alta pressione.
h.p., HP, H.P., *horsepower.*
h.p.-hr., *horsepower-hour,* horsepower-ora.
H.Q., *headquarters,* Q.G., Quartier Generale.
hr., *hour,* h, ora.
H.R., 1. *Home Rule,* autodeterminazione **2.** *House of Representatives,* Camera dei Deputati (negli Stati Uniti) **3.** *Human Relations,* Relazioni Umane.
H.R.H., *His, Her Royal Highness,* S.A.R., Sua Altezza Reale.
H.S.H., *His, Her Serene Highness,* Sua Altezza Serenissima.
ht., 1. *heat,* calore **2.** *height,* alt., altezza.
Hun., 1. *Hungarian,* Ungherese **2.** *Hungary,* Ungheria.
Hunts., (*geog.*) *Huntingdonshire.*
H.V., *high voltage,* A.T., alta tensione.
Hz., *hertz,* Hz, hertz.

I

i., *intransitive,* intr., intrans., intransitivo.
I, *iodine,* (*chim.*) I, iodio.
I., 1. (*geog.*) *Idaho* **2.** (*geog.*) *Iowa.*
Ia., (*geog.*) *Iowa.*
ib., ibid., (*lat.*: *ibidem*) *in the same place,* ibid., nello stesso luogo.
I.C.B.M., *Intercontinental Ballistic Missile,* missile balistico intercontinentale.
Ice., *Iceland,* Islanda.
id., (*lat.*: *idem*) *the same,* id., lo stesso.
Id., (*geog.*) *Idaho.*
I.D., *Intelligence Department,* Ufficio Informazioni.
Ida., (*geog.*) *Idaho.*

i.e., (*lat.*: *id est*) *that is,* cioè.
I.F.S., *Irish Free State,* Stato Libero d'Irlanda.
Ill., (*geog.*) *Illinois.*
I.L.O., *International Labour Organization,* O.I.L., Organizzazione Internazionale del Lavoro.
I.M., *Isle of Man,* Isola di Man.
imp., 1. *imperative,* imp., imper., imperativo **2.** *imperfect,* imperf., impf., imperfetto.
imper., *imperative,* imp., imper., imperativo.
imperf., imp., *imperfect,* imperf., impf., imperfetto.
imp. gal., *imperial gallon(s),* gallone imperiale, galloni imperiali.
impv., *imperative,* imp., imper., imperativo.
in., *inch(es),* pollice, pollici.
In., *indium,* (*chim.*) In, indio.
inc., 1. *including,* compreso **2.** *incorporated,* incorporato.
ind., *indicative,* indic., indicativo.
Ind., 1. *India,* India **2.** (*geog.*) *Indiana.*
indic., *indicative,* indic., indicativo.
inf., infin., *infinitive,* inf., infinito.
I.N.S., *International News Service,* Agenzia Stampa Internazionale.
inst., *instant, the present month,* c.m., corrente mese; m.c., mese corrente.
int., 1. *interjection,* int., inter., interiezione **2.** *intransitive,* intr., intrans., intransitivo.
interj., *interjection,* int., inter., interiezione.
INTER.POL., *International Police,* INTER.POL., Polizia Internazionale.
intr., intrans., *intransitive,* intr., intrans., intransitivo.
inv., *invoice,* fatt., fattura.
Io., (*geog.*) *Iowa.*
I.O.M., *Isle of Man,* Isola di Man.
I.O.U., *I owe you,* (*comm.*) pagherò.
I.O.W., *Isle of Wight,* Isola di Wight.
I.P.A., *International Phonetic Association,* Associazione Fonetica Internazionale.
I.Q., *intelligence quotient,* coefficiente di intelligenza.
Ir, *iridium,* (*chim.*) Ir, iridio.
Ir., 1. *Ireland,* Irlanda **2.** *Irish,* irlandese.
I.R., *Inland Revenue,* fisco.
I.R.C., *International Red Cross,* C.R.I., Croce Rossa Internazionale.
It., 1. *Italian,* Italiano **2.** *Italy,* Italia.

J

J, *joule,* J, joule.
Jam., *Jamaica,* Giamaica.
Jan., *January,* gen., gennaio.
J.C., *Jesus Christ,* G.C., Gesù Cristo.
J.P., *Justice of the Peace,* Giudice di Pace.
jr., *junior.*
Ju., *June,* giu., giugno.
Jul., *July,* lu., lug., luglio.
Jun., *June,* giu., giugno.

K

k., *knot,* (*mar.*) nodo.
K, 1. *Kelvin,* K, Kelvin **2.** (*geog.*) *Kent* **3.** *potassium,* (*chim.*) K, potassio.
Kan., Kans., Kas., (*geog.*) *Kansas.*
K.B., *Knight of the Bath,* Cavaliere dell'Ordine del Bagno.
K.B.E., *Knight (Commander of the Order) of the British Empire,* Cavaliere (Maestro dell'Ordine) dell'Impero Britannico.
kc, kc., (*rad.*) **1.** *kilocycle(s),* kc, chilociclo, chilocicli **2.** *kilocycles per second,* kc/s, chilocicli al secondo.
K.C., *King's Council,* Consiglio della Corona.
Ken., (*geog.*) *Kentucky.*
K.G., *Knight (of the Order) of the Garter,* Cavaliere (dell'Ordine) della Giarrettiera.
kg, *kilogram(me),* kg, chilogrammo.

kg-cal, *kilogram-calorie,* kcal, chilocaloria.
kg-m, *kilogram-metre,* kgm, chilogrammetro.
K.K.K., *Ku-Klux-Klan.*
kl, *kilolitre,* kl, chilolitro.
K.L.H., *Knight of the Legion of Honour,* Cavaliere della Legion d'Onore.
km, *kilometre,* km, chilometro.
Km., *Kingdom,* Regno.
kmph., *kilometres per hour,* km/h, chilometri all'ora.
kmps., *kilometres per second,* km/sec, chilometri al secondo.
Knt., *Knight,* Cavaliere.
K.O., *knock out,* k.o., fuori combattimento.
Kr, *krypton,* (*chim.*) Kr, cripto.
Kt., *Knight,* Cavaliere.
K.T., *Knight of the Thistle,* Cavaliere dell'Ordine del Cardo.
kts., *knots,* (*mar.*) nodi.
kv., *kilovolt,* kV, chilovolt.
kw., *kilowatt,* kW, chilowatt.
kw-h, kw-hr, K.W.K., *kilowatt-hour,* kWh, chilowattora.
Ky., (*geog.*) *Kentucky.*

L

l, *litre,* l, litro.
l., **1.** *latitude,* lat., latitudine **2.** *league,* lega **3.** *length,* lunghezza **4.** *line(s)* **5.** *long,* lungo.
L., **1.** *Lake,* Lago **2.** *Latin,* Latino **3.** *Liberal,* Liberale.
£, *pound (sterling),* L.st., lira sterlina.
La, *lanthanum,* (*chim.*) La, lantanio.
La., (*geog.*) *Louisiana.*
Lancs., (*geog.*) *Lancashire.*
lang., *language,* lingua, linguaggio.
lat., *latitude,* lat., latitudine.
Lat., *Latin,* Latino.
law., *lawyer,* avv., avvocato.
lb., *pound(s),* libbra, libbre.
l.c., (*lat.: loco citato*) *in the place cited,* l.c., loc.cit., luogo citato.
L.C., *Lord Chancellor,* Lord Cancelliere.
L.C.C., *London County Council,* Consiglio della Contea di Londra.
l.c.m., *lowest (o least) common multiple,* m.c.m., minimo comune multiplo.
Ld., *Lord.*
Ldp., *Lordship,* Signoria; (*per vescovo*) Ecc., Eccellenza.
lea., *league.*
leg., **1.** *legal,* legale **2.** *legate,* (*dir.*) legato.
Leics., (*geog.*) *Leicestershire.*
L.F., *bassa frequenza,* (*rad.tv.*) L.F., low frequency.
L.H.D., *Left Hand Drive,* Guida a Sinistra (targa posteriore sulle automobili con guida a sinistra circolanti in Gran Bretagna).
Li, *lithium,* (*chim.*) Li, litio.
lib., *library,* bibl., biblioteca.
Lieut., *Lieutenant,* Ten., Tenente.
Lincs., (*geog.*) *Lincolnshire.*
lit., **1.** *literally,* letteralmente **2.** *literary,* lett., letterario **3.** *literature,* lett., letteratura.
LL.B., (*lat.: Legum Baccalaureus*) *Bachelor of Laws,* Diplomato in Legge.
LL.D., (*lat.: Legum Doctor*) *Doctor of Laws,* Dottore in Legge.
lm, *lumen,* (*fis.*) lm, lumen.
L.M.T., *local mean time,* ora locale.
ln, *natural logarithm,* ln, logaritmo naturale.
loc. cit., (*lat.: loco citato*) *in the place cited,* l.c., loc. cit., luogo citato.
log, log., *logarithm,* log., logaritmo.
lon., *longitude,* long., longitudine.
Lon., Lond., *London,* Londra.
long., *longitude,* long., longitudine.
l.p., *low pressure,* B.P., bassa pressione.

Lp., *Lordship,* Signoria; (*per vescovo*) Ecc., Eccellenza.
L.P., **1.** *Labour Party,* Partito Laburista **2.** *long playing.*
L.P.T.B., *London Passenger Trasport Board,* Compagnia Londinese Trasporto Passeggeri.
L.R., *Lloyd's Register,* Registro del Lloyd.
L.S.D., (*lat.: librae, solidi, denarii*) *pounds shillings, pence,* sterline, scellini, pence.
l.t., *long ton.*
Ltd. (Co.), *Limited (Company),* S.r.l., Società a responsabilità limitata.
Lu, *lutetium,* (*chim.*) Lu, lutezio.
Lux., *Luxemburg,* Lussemburgo.
L.V., *low voltage,* B.T., bassa tensione.
lx, *lux,* (*fis.*) lx, lux.

M

m, *metre,* m, metro.
m., **1.** *male,* maschio **2.** *married,* sposato **3.** *masculine,* m., maschile **4.** (*lat.: meridiem*) *noon,* mezzogiorno **5.** *mile,* miglio **6.** *minute,* min, minuto **7.** *month,* mese.
μ, *micron,* μ, micron.
M., **1.** *March,* mar., marzo **2.** *Monday,* l., lun., lunedì.
μA, *microampere,* μA, microampere.
Ma., *milliampere,* mA, milliampere.
M.A., **1.** *Master of Arts,* Dottore in Lettere **2.** *Military Academy,* Accademia Militare **3.** *milliampere,* mA, milliampere.
Maj., *Major,* Magg., Maggiore.
Mar., *March,* mar., marzo.
March, *Marchioness,* M.sa, Marchesa.
Marq., *Marquis,* march., M.se, Marchese.
masc., *masculine,* m., maschile.
Mass., (*geog.*) *Massachusetts.*
max., *maximum,* max., massimo.
M.C., **1.** *Master of Ceremonies,* Cerimoniere **2.** *Member of Congress,* Membro del Congresso (negli Stati Uniti) **3.** *metric carat,* carato metrico **4.** *Military Cross,* Croce di Guerra.
Md., (*geog.*) *Maryland.*
M.D., (*lat.: Medicinae Doctor*) *Doctor of Medicine,* Dottore in Medicina.
Mdx., (*geog.*) *Middlesex.*
Me., (*geog.*) *Maine.*
M.E., **1.** *Middle East,* Medio Oriente **2.** *Middle English* (inglese parlato fra il 1200 e il 1500 circa) **3.** *Most Excellent,* Eccellentissimo.
Messrs., *Messieurs,* Sigg., Signori.
met., **1.** *metaphor,* metafora **2.** *metaphysical,* metafisico **3.** *metropolitan,* metropolitano.
Mex., **1.** *Mexican,* messicano **2.** *Mexico,* Messico.
μF, *microfarad,* μF, microfarad.
M.F., *medium frequency,* (*rad. tv.*) M.F., media frequenza.
mfd., *manufactured,* fabbricato.
mg, *milligram(me),* mg, milligrammo.
Mg, *magnesium,* (*chim.*) Mg, magnesio.
Mgr., **1.** *Manager,* Direttore **2.** *Monseigneur,* Monsignore **3.** *Monsignor,* (*eccl.*) mons., monsignore.
Mich., (*geog.*) *Michigan.*
min., **1.** *minim(um),* min., minimo **2.** *minute,* min, minuto.
Minn., (*geog.*) *Minnesota.*
Miss., (*geog.*) *Mississippi.*
ml, *millilitre,* ml, millilitro.
mm, *millimetre,* mm, millimetro.
mμ, *millimicron,* mμ, millimicron.
Mn, *manganese,* (*chim.*) Mn, manganese.
Mo, *molybdenum,* (*chim.*) Mo, molibdeno.
Mo., (*geog.*) *Missouri.*
M.O., *Medical Officer,* Ufficiale Medico.
Mon., **1.** *Monday,* l., lun., lunedì **2.** (*geog.*) *Monmouthshire.*

Mons., (*geog.*) *Monmouthshire.*

Mont., (*geog.*) *Montana.*

m.p., *melting point,* punto di fusione.

M.P., 1. *melting point,* punto di fusione **2.** *Member of Parliament,* deputato; on., onorevole **3.** *Metropolitan Police,* Polizia Metropolitana **4.** *Military Police,* P.M., Polizia Militare.

mph, m.p.h., MPH, *miles per hour,* miglia all'ora.

mpm., *metres per minute,* m/min, metri al minuto.

mps., *metres per second,* m/sec, metri al secondo.

Mr., *Mister,* Sig., Signore.

M.R.C.S., *Member of the Royal College of Surgeons,* Membro del Reale Collegio dei Chirurghi.

Mrs., *Mistress,* Sig.a, Signora.

ms., MS., *manuscript,* ms., MS., manoscritto.

M.S., 1. *Master of Science,* Dottore in Scienze **2.** *Master of Surgery,* Dottore in Chirurgia.

M/S, *motorship,* M/N, motonave.

m.s.l., M.S.L., *mean sea level,* livello medio del mare.

Mt., *Mount,* M., Monte.

M.T.B., *motor torpedo-boat,* MAS, motoscafo antisommergibile.

mus., 1. *museum,* museo **2.** *music,* mus., musica **3.** *musical,* mus., musicale.

Mx., (*geog.*) *Middlesex.*

myg., *myriagram(me),* Mg, miriagrammo.

myl., *myrialitre,* Ml, mirialitro.

mym., *myriametre,* Mm, miriametro.

N

n., 1. (*lat.:* *natus*) *born,* n., nato **2.** *neuter,* n., neutro **3.** *nominative,* (*gram.*) nom., nominativo **4.** *noun,* s., sost., sostantivo.

N, *nitrogen,* (*chim.*) N, azoto.

N., 1. *North,* N., Nord **2.** *Northern,* settentrionale; (zona) Settentrionale (di una città).

Na, *sodium,* (*chim.*) Na, sodio.

N.A., 1. *North America,* Nord America **2.** *North Atlantic,* Nord Atlantico.

nat., 1. *national,* naz., nazionale **2.** *natural,* naturale.

N.A.T.O., *North Atlantic Treaty Organization,* N.A.T.O., Organizzazione del Trattato Nord-Atlantico.

naut. mi., *nautical mile(s),* miglio marittimo, miglia marittime.

Nb, *niobium,* (*chim.*) Nb, niobio.

N.B., (*lat.:* *nota bene*) *note well,* N.B., nota bene.

N.B.C., *National Broadcasting Company,* Ente Radiofonico Nazionale (negli Stati Uniti).

N.C., (*geog.*) *North Carolina.*

n.d., *no date, not dated,* (*bibliografia*) s.d., senza data, non datato.

Nd, *neodymium,* (*chim.*) Nd, neodimio.

N.D., N. Dak., (*geog.*) *North Dakota.*

Ne, *neon,* (*chim.*) Ne, neo.

N.E., 1. *Naval Engineer,* Ingegnere Navale **2.** *New England,* Nuova Inghilterra **3.** *North-East,* N.E., Nord-Est **4.** *North-Eastern,* (zona) Nord-Orientale (di una città).

Neb., Nebr., (*geog.*) *Nebraska.*

N. Eng., *New England,* Nuova Inghilterra.

Neth., *Netherlands,* Paesi Bassi.

neut., *neuter,* n., neutro.

Nev., (*geog.*) *Nevada.*

New M., (*geog.*) *New Mexico.*

N.F., 1. *Newfoundland,* Terranova **2.** *Norman French,* Franco-Normanno.

N.H., (*geog.*) *New Hampshire.*

N. Heb., *New Hebrides,* Nuove Ebridi.

Ni, *nickel,* (*chim.*) Ni, nichel.

N.J., (*geog.*) *New Jersey.*

N.M., N. Mex., (*geog.*) *New Mexico.*

No., 1. *North,* N., Nord **2.** *Northern,* Settentrionale **3.** *number,* N°, No., numero.

nom., *nominative,* (*gram.*) nom., nominativo.

Nor., 1. *Norway,* Norvegia **2.** *Norwegian,* Norvegese.

Norf., (*geog.*) *Norfolk.*

Northants., (*geog.*) *Northamptonshire.*

Northumb., (*geog.*) *Northumberland.*

Notts., (*geog.*) *Nottinghamshire.*

Nov., *November,* nov., novembre.

n.p., *new paragraph,* a.c., a capo; d.c., da capo.

Np, *neptunium,* (*chim.*) Np, nettunio.

N.P., *North Pole,* Polo Nord.

n.p. or d., *no place or date,* (*bibliografia*), s.d.l., senza data o luogo.

N.S., *Nova Scotia,* Nuova Scozia.

N.S.P.C.A., *National Society for the Prevention of Cruelty to Animals,* Società Nazionale per la Protezione degli Animali.

N.T., *New Testament,* N.T., Nuovo Testamento.

N.W., 1. *North Wales,* Galles del Nord **2.** *North-West,* N.O., Nord-Ovest **3.** *North-Western,* (zona) Nord-Occidentale (di una città).

N.Y., (*geog.*) *New York.*

N.Z., N.Zeal., *New Zealand,* Nuova Zelanda.

Ω, *ohm,* Ω, ohm.

O

O, *oxygen,* (*chim.*) O, ossigeno.

O., 1. *October,* ott., ottobre **2.** (*geog.*) *Ohio* **3.** (*geog.*) *Oregon.*

O.B.E., *Officer (of the Order) of the British Empire,* Ufficiale (dell'Ordine) dell'Impero Britannico.

obs., 1. *observation,* osservazione **2.** *obsolete,* obsoleto, disusato.

Oc., *Ocean,* Oceano.

Oct., *October,* ott., ottobre.

O.E., *Old English,* (*filologia*) Antico Inglese.

O.E.D., *Oxford English Dictionary,* Dizionario Inglese di Oxford.

O.E.E.C., *Organization for European Economic Co-operation,* O.E.C.E., Organizzazione Economica per la Cooperazione Europea.

O.F.M., *Order of Friars Minor,* O.F.M., Ordine dei Frati Minori.

Ogpu, (*russo: Obedinennoe Gossudarstvennoe Politicheskoe Upravlenie*) *Unified State Political Directorate,* Ghe.Pe.U., Polizia Segreta Russa (1922-34).

O.H.M.S., *On His, Her Majesty's Service,* al servizio di Sua Maestà.

O.K., *all correct,* O.K., tutto bene.

Okla., (*geog.*) *Oklahoma.*

Ont., (*geog.*) *Ontario.*

o.p., *out of print,* esaurito (di libro).

O.P., (*lat.:* *Ordinis Praedicatorum*) *of the Order of Preachers,* dell'Ordine dei Predicatori (Domenicani).

op. cit., (*lat.:* *opere citato*) *in the work cited,* op. cit., opera citata.

Or., Ore., Oreg., (*geog.*) *Oregon.*

Os, *osmium,* (*chim.*) Os, osmio.

O.T., *Old Testament,* A.T., Antico Testamento.

O.U.P., *Oxford University Press,* Edizioni dell'Università di Oxford.

Ox., Oxf., *Oxford.*

Oxon., 1. (*lat.:* *Oxonia*) *Oxford* **2.** (*lat.:* *Oxonia*) (*geog.*) *Oxfordshire* **3.** (*lat.:* *Oxoniensis*) *Oxonian, of Oxford,* ossoniano, di Oxford.

oz., *ounce(s),* oncia, once.

P

p., 1. *page,* p., pag., pagina **2.** *participle,* part., participio **3.** *past,* (*gram.*) pass., passato.

P, 1. *Parking,* P, Posteggio **2.** *phosphorus,* (*chim.*) P, fosforo.

P., 1. *President,* Presidente **2.** *Prince,* Principe.

Pa, *protoactinium,* (*chim.*) Pa, protoattinio.

Pa., (*geog.*) *Pennsylvania.*

P.A., *Press Association,* Associazione della Stampa.

P.A.A., *Pan American Airways,* Linee Aeree Pan-Americane.

Pac., Pacif., *Pacific,* Pacifico.

Pak., *Pakistan.*

Pal., *Palestine,* Palestina.

Pan., *Panama.*

par., 1. *paragraph,* par., paragrafo 2. *parallel,* parallelo 3. *parenthesis,* parentesi 4. *parish,* parrocchia.

part., *participle,* part., participio.

pass., 1. *(lat.: passim) passim, in every part, (nelle citazioni)* pass., passim, in diversi luoghi 2. *passive, (gram.)* pass., passivo.

pat., 1. *patent,* patente; brev., brevetto 2. *patented,* patentato, brevettato.

Pat. Off., *Patent Office,* Ufficio Brevetti.

P.A.Y.E., *pay as you earn,* trattenuta delle imposte sulle paghe dei dipendenti da parte dell'imprenditore.

payt, *payment,* ver., versamento.

Pb, *lead,* *(chim.)* Pb, piombo.

p.c., *postcard,* c.p., cartolina postale.

p/c, 1. *per cent,* per cento 2. *petty cash,* piccole spese e piccole entrate 3. *prices current,* prezzi correnti.

P.C., 1. *Police Constable,* agente di polizia 2. *postcard,* c.p., cartolina postale 3. *Privy Council,* Consiglio Privato (di Sovrano).

P/C, 1. *per cent,* per cento 2. *petty cash,* piccole spese e piccole entrate 3. *prices current,* prezzi correnti.

pd., *paid,* pagato.

Pd, *palladium,* *(chim.)* Pd, palladio.

Penn., Penna., *(geog.) Pennsylvania.*

per pro., *(lat.: per procurationem) by the agency (of),* p.p., per procura (di).

Pg., 1. *Portugal,* Portogallo 2. *Portuguese,* Portoghese.

Ph. B., *(lat.: Philosophiae Baccalaureus) Bachelor of Philosophy,* Diplomato in Filosofia.

Ph. D., *(lat.: Philosophiae Doctor) Doctor of Philosophy,* Dottore in Filosofia.

phon., phonet., *phonetics,* fonet., fonetica.

phot., *photography,* foto., fotografia.

pk., *peck.*

pl., plu., plur., *plural,* pl., plurale.

P.L.U.T.O., *Pipeline Under the Ocean,* Oleodotto Sotto l'Oceano (1944).

p.m., 1. *(lat.: post meridiem) after midday,* p.m., pomeridiano 2. *(lat.: post mortem) after death,* post mortem.

Pm, *promethium,* *(chim.)* Pm, prometeo.

P.M., *Prime Minister,* Primo Ministro.

po., *pole.*

Po, *polonium,* *(chim.)* Po, polonio.

P.O., 1. *Postal Order,* vaglia postale 2. *Post Office,* Ufficio Postale.

p.o.b., *post-office box,* casella postale.

p.o.d., *pay on delivery,* pagamento alla consegna.

pol., 1. *political,* pol., politico 2. *politics,* pol., politica.

Pol., 1. *Poland,* Polonia 2. *Polish,* polacco.

pop., *population,* pop., popolazione; ab., abitanti.

P.O.W., *prisoner of war,* prigioniero di guerra.

p.p., 1. *(lat.: per procurationem) by proxy,* p.p., per procura 2. *parcel post,* p.p., pacco postale.

pr., 1. *power,* *(fis.)* potenza 2. *present,* pres., presente 3. *pronoun,* pr., pron., pronome.

Pr, *praseodymium,* *(chim.)* Pr, praseodimio.

Pr., 1. *priest,* prete 2. *Prince,* Principe 3. *Provençal,* Provenzale.

P.R.A., *President of the Royal Academy,* Presidente dell'Accademia Reale.

P.R.B., *Pre-Raphaelite Brotherhood,* Confraternita dei Pre-Raffaelliti.

pred., *predicate,* pred., predicato.

pref., 1. *preface,* pref., prefazione 2. *prefix,* pref., prefisso.

prep., 1. *preparation,* preparazione 2. *preposition,* pr., prep., preposizione.

pres., *present,* *(gram.)* pres., presente.

Pres., *President,* Presidente.

press., *pressure,* pressione.

Prof., *Professor,* prof., professore.

pron., *pronoun,* pr., pron., pronome.

prox., *(lat.: proximo mense) next (month),* p.v., prossimo venturo.

P.S., *(lat.: post scriptum) postscript,* P.S., post scriptum.

p.s.f., *pounds per square foot,* libbre per piede quadrato.

p.s.i., *pounds per square inch,* libbre per pollice quadrato.

pt., *pint(s),* pinta, pinte.

Pt, *platinum,* *(chim.)* Pt, platino.

Pte., *Private,* soldato (semplice).

Ptg., 1. *Portugal,* Portogallo 2. *Portuguese,* Portoghese.

P.T.O., *please turn over,* t.s.v.p., tournez s'il vous plaît; v.r., vedi retro.

Pu, *plutonium,* *(chim.)* Pu, plutonio.

pun., *puncheon.*

Q

q, *quintal,* q, quintale.

Q, *queue,* mettersi in coda.

Q., 1. *Quebec* 2. *Queensland* 3. *query,* quesito 4. *question,* domanda.

Q.B., *Queen's Bench,* Regia Corte (tribunale inglese).

Q. C., 1. *Queen's Council,* Consiglio della Regina 2. *Queen's College.*

q.e.d., *(lat.: quod erat demonstrandum) which was to be demonstrated,* q.e.d., c.d.d., come dovevasi dimostrare.

qr., *quarter.*

qrs., *quarters.*

q.s., *(lat.: quantum sufficit) a sufficient quantity,* q.b., quanto basta (nelle ricette).

qt., 1. *quantity,* quantità 2. *quart.*

qto, *quarto,* *(bibliografia)* in quarto.

qts., *quarts.*

Qu., 1. *Queen,* Regina 2. *query,* quesito 3. *question,* domanda.

Que., 1. *Quebec* 2. *Queensland.*

q.v., 1. *(lat.: quantum vis) as much as you will,* a volontà 2. *(lat.: quod vide) which see,* v., vedi.

R

r., 1. *recto,* *(bibliografia)* r., recto 2. *river,* fiume 3. *road,* strada.

R, *radius,* *(geom.)* r, raggio.

R., 1. *(lat.: Rex) King,* R., Re 2. *(lat.: Regina) Queen,* R., Regina.

Ra, *radium,* *(chim.)* Ra, radio.

R.A., *Royal Academy,* Accademia Reale.

R.A.A.F., *Royal Australian Air Force,* Regia Aeronautica Australiana.

R.A.C., *Royal Automobile Club,* Real Automobile Club.

R.A.D.I.A.C., *Radioactivity Detection Identification and Computation,* rivelazione, identificazione e computo della radioattività.

R.A.F., *Royal Air Force,* Regia Aeronautica.

R.A.M., *Royal Academy of Music,* Regia Accademia di Musica.

Rb, *rubidium,* *(chim.)* Rb, rubidio.

R.C., 1. *Red Cross,* Croce Rossa 2. *Roman Catholic,* Cattolico Apostolico Romano.

R.C.A., *Radio Corporation of America,* Ente Radiofonico Americano.

R.C.A.F., *Royal Canadian Air Force,* Regia Aeronautica Canadese.

rd., *rod.*

Rd., *Road,* C.so, Corso.

Re, *rhenium,* *(chim.)* Re, renio.

rec., *receipt*, ric., ricevuta.

ref., *reference*, riferimento.

Ref. Ch., *Reformed Church*, Chiesa Riformata.

refl., *reflexive*, rifl., riflessivo.

reg., 1. *region*, regione 2. *register*, registro 3. *registered*, registrato.

Reg. Prof., *Regius Professor*, Professore (universitario) titolare.

rel., 1. *relating*, riferentesi (a) 2. *relation*, relazione 3. *religion*, religione.

rem., *remittance*, ver., versamento.

rep., *republic*, Rep., repubblica.

Rep., 1. *report*, rapporto 2. *reporter*, cronista, corrispondente (di giornale) 3. *representative*, rappresentante.

Repub., *Republic*, R., Repubblica.

retd., 1. *retired*, in pensione 2. *returned*, restituito.

Rev., 1. *Revelation*, Rivelazione 2. *Reverend*, (*eccl.*) R., Rev., Reverendo 3. *revision*, revisione.

Rev. Ver., *Revised Version*, Versione Riveduta della Bibbia Anglicana (1870-84).

R.G.S., *Royal Geographical Society*, Regia Società Geografica.

Rgt., *Regiment*, Reggimento.

Rh, *rhodium*, (*chim.*) Rh, rodio.

R.H., *Royal Highness*, A.R., Altezza Reale.

R.H.A., *Royal Horse Artillery*, Regia Artiglieria a Cavallo.

R.I., (*geog.*) *Rhode Island*.

R.I.B.A., *Royal Institute of British Architects*, Regio Collegio Britannico degli Architetti.

Rn, *radon*, (*chim.*) Rn, rado.

R.N., 1. *registered nurse*, infermiera diplomata 2. *Royal Navy*, Regia Marina.

ro., *rood*.

Rom. Cath., *Roman Catholic*, Cattolico Apostolico Romano.

Roum., 1. *Roumania*, Romania 2. *Roumanian*, Rumeno.

rpm, **r.p.m.**, *revolutions per minute*, giri/min, giri al minuto.

rps, **r.p.s.**, *revolutions per second*, giri/sec, giri al secondo.

rpt., *report*, rapporto.

R.R., *Right Reverend*, (*eccl.*) M.R., Molto Reverendo.

R.S., *Royal Society*.

RSFSR, **R.S.F.S.R.**, *Russian Soviet Federated Socialist Republic*, U.R.S.S., Unione Repubbliche Socialiste Sovietiche.

R.S.P.C.A., *Royal Society for the Prevention of Cruelty to Animals*, Regia Società per la Protezione degli Animali.

R.S.V.P., (*francese: répondez s'il vous plaît*) si prega rispondere, R.S.V.P., reply if you please.

Rt. Hon., *Right Honourable*, Molto Onorevole.

Rt. Rev., *Right Reverend*, (*eccl.*) Rev.mo, Reverendissimo.

Ru, *ruthenium*, (*chim.*) Ru, rutenio.

Rutd., **Rutl.**, (*geog.*) *Rutlandshire*.

Ry., *railway*, ferr., ferrovia.

S

s., 1. *second*, s, sec, secondo 2. *shilling*, scellino 3. *signed*, f.to, firmato 4. *singular*, sing., singolare.

S, 1. *siemens*, S, siemens 2. *sulphur*, (*chim.*) S, solfo.

S., 1. *Saint*, S., Santo 2. *Shelter*, R., Rifugio (antiaereo) 3. *South*, S., Sud 4. *Southern*, meridionale; (zona) Meridionale (di una città).

Sa., *Saturday*, s., sab., sabato.

S.A., 1. *Salvation Army*, Esercito della Salvezza 2. *South Africa*, Sud-Africa 3. *South Australia*, Australia del Sud.

Salop, (*geog.*) *Shropshire*.

Sask., (*geog.*) *Saskatchewan*.

Sat., *Saturday*, s., sab., sabato.

Sb, *antimony*, (*chim.*) Sb, antimonio.

sc., *science*, scienza.

Sc, *scandium*, (*chim.*) Sc, scandio.

Sc., 1. *Scotch*, Scozzese 2. *Scots*, gli Scozzesi 3. *Scottish*, scozzese.

S.C., 1. (*geog.*) *South Carolina* 2. *Supreme Court*, S.C., Suprema Corte.

sch., 1. *school*, scuola 2. *schooner*, (*mar.*) goletta.

Scot., 1. *Scotland*, Scozia 2. *Scottish*, scozzese.

scr., *scruple*.

Script., *Scripture*, (Sacra) Scrittura.

S.D., **S. Dak.**, (*geog.*) *South Dakota*.

Se, *selenium*, (*chim.*) Se, selenio.

S.E., 1. *South-East*, S.E., Sud-Est 2. *South-Eastern*, (zona) Sud-Orientale (di una città).

S.E.A.T.O., *South-East Asia Treaty Organization*, S.E.A.T.O., Organizzazione del Trattato relativo al Sud-Est Asiatico.

sec, *secant*, sec, secante.

sec., 1. *second*, s, sec, secondo 2. *secretary*, segretario 3. *section*, sezione.

sen., *senator*, sen., senatore.

Sep., **Sept.**, *September*, sett., settembre.

sergt., *sergeant*, serg., sergente.

s.g., *specific gravity*, peso specifico.

sh., *shilling*, scellino.

Shak., *Shakespeare*.

SHAPE, **S.H.A.P.E.**, *Supreme Headquarters Allied Powers Europe*, Supremo Quartier Generale delle Truppe Alleate in Europa.

Shrops., (*geog.*) *Shropshire*.

Si, *silicon*, (*chim.*) Si, silicio.

S.I., *Sandwich Islands*, Isole Sandwich.

sin, *sine*, (*trigonometria*) sen, seno.

sing., *singular*, sing., singolare.

sinh, *hyperbolic sine*, (*trigonometria*) Sh, seno iperbolico.

S.J., *Society of Jesus*, C.d.G., Compagnia di Gesù.

Skr., *Sanskrit*, Sanscrito.

s.l., *sea level*, l.m., livello del mare.

Sm, *samarium*, (*chim.*) Sm, samario.

Sn, *tin*, (*chim.*) Sn, stagno.

So., 1. *South*, S., Sud 2. *Southern*, meridionale.

Sol., *solicitor*, avv., avvocato.

Soc., *Society*, Soc., Società.

Sol. Gen., *Solicitor General*, avvocato erariale.

Som., (*geog.*) *Somersetshire*.

S.O.S., (*Save Our Souls*) *appeal for help or rescue*, S.O.S., segnale internazionale di richiesta di soccorso.

sp., 1. *special*, speciale 2. *species*, specie 3. *specific*, specifico 4. *specimen*, saggio, campione.

Sp., 1. *Spain*, Spagna 2. *Spaniard*, Spagnolo 3. *Spanish*, spagnolo.

S.P.C.A., *Society for the Prevention of Cruelty to Animals*, S.P.A., Società Protettrice degli Animali.

S.P.C.C., *Society for the Prevention of Cruelty to Children*, Società per la Protezione dell'Infanzia.

sp. gr., *specific gravity*, peso specifico.

sp. ht., *specific heat*, calore specifico.

S.P.Q.R., (*lat.: Senatus Populusque Romanus*) *the Senate and People of Rome*, S.P.Q.R., Senato e Popolo Romano.

sq., *square*, q., quadrato; P.za, piazza.

Sr, *strontium*, (*chim.*) Sr, stronzio.

Sr., 1. *senior* 2. *Sir*.

S.R.E., (*lat.: Sancta Romana Ecclesia*) *Holy Roman Church*, S.R.C., Santa Romana Chiesa.

S.R.I., (*lat.: Sacrum Romanum Imperium*) *Holy Roman Empire*, S.R.I., Sacro Romano Impero.

SS., 1. (*tedesco: Schutzstaffel*) *Hitler bodyguard*, SS., milizia di protezione nazista 2. (*lat.: Sanctissimus*) *Most Holy*, SS., Santissimo 3. *Saints*, SS., Santi.

S/S, *steamship*, piroscafo.

st., *stone*.

s.t., *short ton.*
St., 1. *Saint,* S., Santo 2. *Strait,* Stretto 3. *Street,* strada; V., via.
Staffs., *(geog.) Staffordshire.*
sta. mi., *statute mile(s),* miglio, miglia.
Stdy., *Saturday,* s., sab., sabato.
st. Ex., *Stock Exchange,* Borsa Valori.
Su., *Sunday,* dom., domenica.
Subj., *subjunctive,* cong., congiuntivo.
Suff., *(geog.) Suffolk.*
Sun., Sund., *Sunday,* dom., domenica.
sup., *superlative,* sup., superlativo.
Sup. Ct., *Supreme Court,* Corte Suprema.
superl., *superlative,* sup., superlativo.
supp., *supplement,* supplemento.
Sur., *(geog.) Surrey.*
surg., 1. *surgeon,* chirurgo 2. *surgery,* chir., chirurgia.
Sus., *(geog.) Sussex.*
S.V.P., *(francese: s'il vous plaît) please,* S.V.P., per favore.
Sw., 1. *Sweden,* Svezia 2. *Swedish,* svedese.
S.W., 1. *South Wales,* Galles del Sud 2. *South-West,* S.O., Sud-Ovest 3. *South-Western,* (zona) Sud-Occidentale (di una città).
Swit., Swtz., *Switzerland,* Svizzera.

T

t, *ton(s),* t, tonnellata, tonnellate.
t., 1. *time,* tempo 2. *tome,* (*bibliografia*) tom., tomo 3. *transitive,* trans., transitivo 4. *troy.*
T., 1. *Testament,* Testamento 2. *Tuesday,* mar., mart., martedì 3. *Turkish,* turco.
Ta, *tantalum,* (*chim.*) Ta, tantalio.
tan, *tangent,* tg, tangente.
tanh, *hyperbolic tangent,* Th, tangente iperbolica.
Tb, *terbium,* (*chim.*) Tb, terbio.
T.B., *tuberculosis,* tbc, TBC, tubercolosi.
T.B.D., *torpedo-boat destroyer,* cacciatorpediniere.
tbs., *tablespoon,* cucchiaio da tavola.
tc., *tierce(s).*
Tc, *technetium,* (*chim.*) Tc, tecnezio.
Te, *tellurium,* (*chim.*) Te, tellurio.
techn., 1. *technical,* tec., tecnico 2. *technology,* tec., tecnologia, tecnica.
tel., 1. *telegram,* telegramma 2. *telegraph,* telegrafo 3. *telephone,* tel., telefono.
Tenn., *(geog.) Tennessee.*
Test., *Testament,* Testamento.
Teut., *Teutonic,* teutonico.
Tex., *(geog.) Texas.*
Th, *thorium,* (*chim.*) Th, torio.
theor., *theorem,* teorema.
3-D, *three-dimension picture,* film a tre dimensioni.
Thur., Thurs., *Thursday,* gio., giov., giovedì.
Ti, *titanium,* (*chim.*) Ti, titanio.
Tl, *thalium,* (*chim.*) Tl, tallio.
Tm, *thulium,* (*chim.*) Tm, tulio.
TNT, *trinitrotoluene,* (*chim.*) trinitrotoluolo.
t.o., *turn over,* volta pagina.
T.O., *Telegraph-Office,* Ufficio del Telegrafo.
tr., 1. *transactions,* transazioni 2. *transitive,* trans., transitivo 3. *translator,* traduttore 4. *trustee,* fiduciario, amministratore.
trag., 1. *tragedy,* trag., tragedia 2. *tragic,* tragico.
trans., 1. *transitive,* trans., transitivo 2. *translated,* tradotto 3. *translator,* traduttore.
treas., *treasurer,* tesoriere.
Trin., *Trinity,* Trinità.
T.T., *telegraphic transfer,* versamento telegrafico.
Tu., *Tuesday,* mar., mart., martedì.
T.U., *Trade-Union,* Sindacato.
T.U.C., *Trades Union Congress,* Congresso dei Sindacati.
Tues., *Tuesday,* mar., mart., martedì.
Turk., 1. *Turkey,* Turchia 2. *Turkish,* turco.

TV, *television,* TV, televisione.
TVA, T.V.A., *Tennessee Valley Authority,* Ente per la Vallata del Tennessee.
T.W.A., *Trans World Airlines,* Linee Aeree Intercontinentali.

U

u., *uncle,* zio.
U, *uranium,* (*chim.*) U, uranio.
U., 1. *Union,* Unione 2. *universal,* per tutti (di pellicola cinematografica) 3. *(geog.) Utah.*
U.A.R., *United Arab Republic,* R.A.U., Repubblica Araba Unita.
U.H.F., *ultrahigh frequency,* (*rad. tv.*) U.H.F., frequenza ultraelevata.
U.K., *United Kingdom,* R.U., Regno Unito (Gran Bretagna e Irlanda del Nord).
U.K.A.E.A., *United Kingdom Atomic Energy Authority,* Ente Britannico per l'Energia Atomica.
ult., (*lat.: ultimo) last* (*month*), u.s., ultimo scorso.
UN, U.N., *United Nations,* N.U., Nazioni Unite.
UNESCO, *United Nations Educational, Scientific, and Cultural Organization,* UNESCO, Organizzazione educativa, scientifica e culturale delle Nazioni Unite.
U.N.I.C.E.F., *United Nations International Children's Emergency Fund,* fondo di emergenza delle Nazioni Unite per l'infanzia.
Univ., 1. *Universalist,* universalista 2. *University,* Università.
U.N.O., *United Nations Organization,* O.N.U., Organizzazione delle Nazioni Unite.
UNRRA, *United Nations Relief and Rehabilitation Administration,* U.N.R.R.A., Soccorso per i territori europei danneggiati dalla guerra.
U. of S.A., U. of S.Afr., *Union of South Africa,* Unione del Sud-Africa.
U.P., 1. *United Press,* Stampe Associate 2. *United Provinces,* Province Riunite.
U.P.U., *Universal Postal Union,* U.P.U., Unione Postale Universale.
U.S., *United States,* S.U., Stati Uniti.
USA, U.S.A., 1. *United States of America,* S.U.A., U.S.A., Stati Uniti d'America 2. *United States Army,* Esercito Statunitense.
U.S.A.F., *United States Air Force,* Aeronautica Statunitense.
U.S.I.S., *United States Information Service,* Ufficio Informazioni per gli Stati Uniti d'America.
U.S.N., *United States Navy,* Marina Statunitense.
USSR, U.S.S.R., *Union of Soviet Socialist Republics,* U.R.S.S., Unione delle Repubbliche Socialiste Sovietiche.
usu., 1. *usual,* usuale 2. *usually,* usualmente, di solito.
Ut., *(geog.) Utah.*

V

v, 1. *volt,* V, volt 2. *volume,* vol., volume.
v., 1. *verb,* v., vb., verbo 2. *verse,* (*poes.*) v., verso 3. *verso,* (*bibliografia*) v., verso 4. *versus,* (*spor. dir.*) contro 5. *volume,* vol., volume.
V, 1. *vanadium,* (*chim.*) V, vanadio 2. *velocity,* (*fis.*) velocità 3. *volt,* V, volt 4. *volume,* vol., volume.
V., 1. *Vicar,* Vicario 2. *Viscount,* Visconte 3. *vocative,* voc., vocativo.
Va., *(geog.) Virginia.*
V.A., 1. *Vicar Apostolic,* Vicario Apostolico 2. *Vice Admiral,* Vice-Ammiraglio 3. (*Royal Order of) Victoria and Albert,* Reale Ordine di Vittoria e Alberto.
Vat., *Vatican,* Vat., Vaticano.
vb., *verb,* v., vb., verbo.
V.C., 1. *Vice Chancellor,* Vice-Cancelliere 2. *Vice-Consul,* V.C., Vice-Console 3. *Victoria Cross,* Croce della Regina Vittoria.

Ven., *Venerable,* Ven., Venerabile.

vet., 1. *veteran,* veterano **2.** *veterinary,* vet., veterinario.

V.H.F., *very high frequency,* (*rad. tv.*) V.H.F., altissima frequenza.

vic., 1. *vicar,* vicario **2.** *vicarage,* vicariato.

Vict., *Victoria.*

V.I.P., *Very Important Person,* (*sl.*) pezzo grosso, persona molto importante.

Virg., (*geog.*) *Virginia.*

Vis., Visc., Visct., 1. *Viscount,* Visconte **2.** *Viscountess,* Viscontessa.

viz., (*lat.: videlicet*) *namely,* vale a dire.

V.L.F., *very low frequency,* (*rad. tv.*) V.L.F., bassissima frequenza.

V.O., *Victorian Order,* Ordine della Regina Vittoria.

voc., *vocative,* voc., vocativo.

vol., 1. *volcano,* vulcano **2.** *volume,* vol., volume **3.** *volunteer,* volontario.

V.P., *Vice-President,* Vice-Presidente.

vs., *versus,* (*spor. dir.*) contro.

V.S., *Veterinary Surgeon,* Chirurgo Veterinario.

Vt., (*geog.*) *Vermont.*

vul., vulg., *vulgar,* volgare.

Vul., Vulg., *Vulgate,* Vulgata.

W

w., 1. *watt,* W, watt **2.** *week(s),* settimana, settimane **3.** *wife,* moglie **4.** *with,* con **5.** *work,* (*fis.*) lavoro.

W, *tungsten,* (*chim.*) W, volframio.

W., 1. (*geog.*) *Washington* **2.** *Welsh,* gallese **3.** *West,* O., Ovest **4.** *Western,* occidentale; (zona) Occidentale (di una città).

W.A.A.C., *Women's Army Auxiliary Corps,* Corpo Ausiliario Femminile dell'Esercito.

W.A.A.F., *Women's Auxiliary Air Force,* Corpo Ausiliario Femminile dell'Aeronautica.

War., (*geog.*) *Warwickshire.*

Wash., (*geog.*) *Washington.*

W.C., 1. *War Council,* Consiglio di Guerra **2.** *water-closet,* W.C., gabinetto di decenza **3.** *Western Central,* (zona) Centro-Occidentale (di una città).

W.C.A., *Women's Christian Association,* Unione Cristiana Femminile.

W.D., *War Department,* Ministero della Guerra (negli Stati Uniti).

We., Wed., *Wednesday,* mer., merc., mercoledì.

Westm., (*geog.*) *Westmorland.*

wh., whr., *watt-hour,* Wh, wattora.

W.I., *West Indies,* Indie Occidentali.

Wilts., (*geog.*) *Wiltshire.*

Wis., Wisc., (*geog.*) *Wisconsin.*

wk., *week,* settimana.

w.l., *wave length,* (*fis. rad.*) lunghezza d'onda.

W.L., *water line,* linea di galleggiamento.

W.O., *War Office,* Ministero della Guerra (in Gran Bretagna).

Worcs., (*geog.*) *Worcestershire.*

W.R.A.C., *Women's Royal Army Corps,* Corpo Femminile del Regio Esercito.

wt., *weight,* peso.

W.T., *wireless telegraphy,* R.T., radiotelegrafia.

W. Va., (*geog.*) *West Virginia.*

W.V.S., *Women's Voluntary Service,* Servizio Volontario Femminile.

Wy., Wyo., (*geog.*) *Wyoming.*

X

X, 1. *excluded,* vietato ai minori di 16 anni (di pellicola cinematografica) **2.** *xenon,* (*chim.*) X, xeno.

X., *Christ,* X., Cristo.

Xe, *xenon,* (*chim.*) X, xeno.

Xm., Xmas., *Christmas,* Natale.

Xnty., *Christianity,* Cristianità.

Xt., *Christ,* X., Cristo.

Xtian., *Christian,* Cristiano.

Y

Y, *yttrium,* (*chim.*) Y, ittrio.

Yb, *ytterbium,* (*chim.*) Yb, itterbio.

Y.B., *Yearbook,* Annuario.

yd., *yard(s),* iarda, iarde.

Y.H.A., *Youth Hostels Association,* Associazione degli Ostelli della Gioventù.

Y.M.C.A., *Young Men's Christian Association,* A.C.D.G., Associazione Cristiana dei Giovani.

Yorks., (*geog.*) *Yorkshire.*

yr., 1. *year,* anno **2.** *younger,* più giovane **3.** *your,* vs., vostro.

yrs., *yours,* vs., vostro.

Y.W.C.A., *Young Women's Christian Association,* U.C.D.G., Unione Cristiana delle Giovani.

Z

z., *zero,* zero.

Z, *atomic number,* z, numero atomico.

Z.G., *Zoological Garden(s),* Giardino Zoologico.

Zn, *zinc,* (*chim.*) Zn, zinco.

Zr, *zirconium,* (*chim.*) Zr, zirconio.

&

&, (*lat.: et*) *and,* &, e.

&c., (*lat.: et cetera*) *and so on,* ecc., eccetera.

WEIGHTS AND MEASURES (*)]

Measures of Length - Misure di lunghezza

IN GREAT BRITAIN AND IN
THE UNITED STATES
line (*abbr.* l.), 1 l. = 2,12 mm
inch (*abbr.* in.), 1 in. = 12 l. = 2,54 cm
foot (*abbr.* ft.), 1 ft. = 12 in. = 30,48 cm
yard (*abbr.* yd.), 1 yd. = 3 ft. = 91,44 cm
fathom (*abbr.* fm.), 1 fm. = 2 yd. = 1,83 m
rod (*abbr.* rd.), **pole** (*abbr.* po.), **perch,** 1 rd. = 1 po. =

= 1 perch = 5,5 yd. = 5,03 m
chain (*abbr.* chn.), 1 chn. = 4 rd. = 20,11 m
furlong (*abbr.* fur.), 1 fur. = 10 chn. = 201,17 m
(statute) mile (*abbr.* (sta.) mi.), 1 sta.mi. = 8 fur. =
= 1,61 km
(nautical) mile (*abbr.* (naut.) mi.), **knot** (*abbr.* k.),
1 naut.mi. = 1 k. = 1,15 sta.mi. = 1,853 km
league (*abbr.* lea.), 1 lea. = 3 naut.mi. = 5.559,78 m

Square Measures - Misure di superficie

IN GREAT BRITAIN AND IN
THE UNITED STATES

square inch (*abbr.* sq. in.), 1 sq. in. = 6,45 cm²
square foot (*abbr.* sq. ft.), 1 sq. ft. = 144 sq. in. =
9,29 dm²
square yard (*abbr.* sq. yd.), 1 sq. yd. = 9 sq. ft. =
0,83 m²
square rod (*abbr.* sq. rd.), **square pole** (*abbr.* sq. po.),

square perch, 1 sq. rd. = 1 sq. po. = 1 sq. perch =
30,25 sq. yd. = 25,29 m²
rood (*abbr.* ro.), 1 ro. = 40 sq. rd. = 10,11 a =
10,11 dam²
acre (*abbr.* a.), 1 a. = 4 ro. = 40,46 a = 0,40 ha
square chain (*abbr.* sq. chn.), 1 sq. chn. = 16 sq.
rd. = 4,04 a = 4,04 dam²
square mile (*abbr.* sq. mi.), 1 sq. mi. = 6.400 sq.
chn. = 640 a. = 2,59 km²

Cubic Measures - Misure di volume

IN GREAT BRITAIN AND IN
THE UNITED STATES

cubic inch (*abbr.* cu. in.), 1 cu. in. = 16,38 cm³

cubic foot (*abbr.* cu. ft.), 1 cu. ft. = 1.728 cu. in. =
28,31 dm³
cubic yard (*abbr.* cu. yd.), 1 cu. yd. = 27 cu. ft. =
0,76 m³

Measures of Capacity - Misure di capacità
for liquid commodities   *per liquidi*

IN GREAT BRITAIN

gill (*abbr.* gi.), 1 gi. = 0,14 l
pint (*abbr.* pt.), 1 pt. = 4 gi. = 0,57 l
quart (*abbr.* qt.), 1 qt. = 2 pt. = 1,13 l
(imperial) gallon (*abbr.* (imp.) gal.), 1 imp. gal. =
4 qts. = 4,54 l
barrel (*abbr.* bbl.), 1 bbl. = 36 imp. gal. = 163,65 l
hogshead (*abbr.* hhd.), 1 hhd. = 52,5 imp. gal. =
238,66 l
pipe, 1 pipe = 2 hhd. = 105 imp. gal. = 477 l
butt, 1 butt = 108 imp. gal. = 491 l
(wine) gallon (*abbr.* gal.) (*arc.*), 1 gal. = 3,78 l
tierce (*abbr.* tc.) (*arc.*), 1 tc. = 42 wine gal. = 159 l
puncheon (*abbr.* pun.) (*arc.*), 1 pun. = 2 tc. = 318 l

tun (*arc.*), 1 tun = 252 wine gal. = 953,9 l

IN THE UNITED STATES

U.S. gill (*abbr.* gi.), 1 U.S. gi. = 0,12 l
U.S. pint (*abbr.* pt.), 1 U.S. pt. = 4 U.S. gi. = 0,47 l
U.S. quart (*abbr.* qt.), 1 U.S. qt. = 2 U.S. pt. = 0,94 l
U.S. gallon (*abbr.* gal.), 1 U.S. gal. = 4 U.S. qts. =
3,78 l
U.S. barrel (*abbr.* bbl.), 1 U.S. bbl. = 31,5 U.S.
gal. = 119,24 l
U.S. hogshead (*abbr.* hhd.), 1 U.S. hhd. = 63 U.S.
gal. = 238,47 l
pipe, 1 pipe = 2 U.S. hhd. = 126 U.S. gal. = 477 l
butt, 1 butt = 129,7 U.S. gal. = 491 l

Measures of Capacity - Misure di capacità
for dry commodities   *per aridi*

IN GREAT BRITAIN

(dry) pint (*abbr.* pt.), 1 pt. = 0,56 l
(dry) quart (*abbr.* qt.), 1 qt. = 2 pt. = 1,13 l
(dry) gallon (*abbr.* gal.), 1 gal. = 4 qts. = 4,54 l
peck (*abbr.* pk.), 1 pk. = 8 qts. = 9,09 l
(imperial) bushel (*abbr.* (imp.) bu.), 1 imp. bu. =
4 pk. = 36,36 l

quarter (*abbr.* qr.), 1 qr. = 8 imp. bu. = 2,91 hl
chaldron (*abbr.* chal.), 1 chal. = 36 imp. bu. = 13,09 hl

IN THE UNITED STATES

U.S. (dry) pint (*abbr.* pt.), 1 U.S. pt. = 0,55 l
U.S. (dry) quart (*abbr.* qt.), 1 U.S. qt. = 2 U.S. pt. =
1,10 l

U.S. peck (*abbr.* pk.), 1 U.S. pk. = 8 U.S. qts. = 8,81 l

U.S. (standard) bushel (*abbr.* (std.) bu.), 1 U.S. bu. = 4 U.S. pk. = 35,24 l

Avoirdupois Weights - Pesi avoirdupois

IN GREAT BRITAIN

grain (avoirdupois) (*abbr.* gr. av.), 1 gr. av. = 0,064 g
dram (*abbr.* dr.), 1 dr. = 27,34 gr. av. = 1,77 g
ounce (avoirdupois) (*abbr.* oz. av.), 1 oz. av. = 16 dr. = 28,35 g
pound (avoirdupois) (*abbr.* lb. av.), 1 lb. av. = 16 oz. av. = 453,60 g
stone (*abbr.* st.), 1 st. = 14 lb. av. = 6,35 kg
quarter (*abbr.* qr.), 1 qr. = 28 lb. av. = 12,70 kg
cental (*abbr.* ctl.), 1 ctl. = 100 lb. av. = 45,36 kg
hundredweight (*abbr.* cwt.), 1 cwt. = 112 lb. av. = 50,80 kg
ton (*abbr.* t.), 1 t. = 2.240 lb. av. = 1,016 t

IN THE UNITED STATES

grain (avoirdupois) (*abbr.* gr. av.), 1 gr. av. = 0,065 g
dram (*abbr.* dr.), 1 dr. = 27,34 gr. av. = 1,77 g

ounce (avoirdupois) (*abbr.* oz. av.), 1 oz. av. = 16 dr. = 28,35 g
pound (avoirdupois) (*abbr.* lb. av.), 1 lb. av. = 16 oz. av. = 453,60 g
U.S. quarter (*abbr.* qr.), 1 U.S. qr. = ¼ short cwt. = 25 lb. av. = 11,34 kg
U.S. quarter (*abbr.* qr.), 1 U.S. qr. = ¼ long cwt. = 28 lb. av. = 12,70 kg
U.S. quarter (*abbr.* qr.), 1 U.S. qr. = ¼ s.t. = 500 lb. av. = 226,79 kg
U.S. quarter (*abbr.* qr.), 1 U.S. qr. = ¼ l.t. = 560 lb. av. = 254 kg
short hundredweight (*abbr.* cwt.), 1 short cwt. = 100 lb. av. = 45,36 kg
long hundredweight (*abbr.* cwt.), 1 long cwt. = 112 lb. av. = 50,80 kg
short ton (*abbr.* s.t.), 1 s.t. = 2.000 lb. av. = 907,18 kg
long ton (*abbr.* l.t.), 1 l.t. = 2.240 lb. av. = 1,016 t

Troy Weights - Pesi troy
for precious stones   per preziosi

IN GREAT BRITAIN AND IN
THE UNITED STATES
grain (troy) (*abbr.* gr. t.), 1 gr. t. = 0,064 g
(carat) grain, (pearl) grain (*abbr.* gr.), 1 gr. = ¼ M.C. = 0,77 gr. t. = 50 mg
metric carat (*abbr.* M.C.), 1 M.C. = 3,08 gr. t. =

200 mg
pennyweight (*abbr.* dwt.), 1 dwt. = 24 gr. t. = 1,55 g
ounce (troy) (*abbr.* oz. t.), 1 oz. t. = 20 dwt. = 31,10 g
pound (troy) (*abbr.* lb. t.), 1 lb. t. = 12 oz. t. = 373,24 g

CONVERSION TABLE (*)

	to convert per trasformare	into in	multiply by below moltiplicare per i valori sotto indicati
0,3937	*inches*, pollici	*centimetres*, centimetri	2,54
3,2808	*feet*, piedi	*metres*, metri	0,3048
1,0933	*yards*, iarde	*metres*, metri	0,9144
0,6214	*statute miles*, miglia	*kilometres*, chilometri	1,6093
0,5396	*nautical miles*, miglia marine	*kilometres*, chilometri	1,85315
0,1550	*square inches*, pollici quadrati	*square centimetres*, centimetri quadrati	6,4516
10,7639	*square feet*, piedi quadrati	*square metres*, metri quadrati	0,09290
1,1960	*square yards*, iarde quadrate	*square metres*, metri quadrati	0,8361
0,3861	*square miles*, miglia quadrate	*square kilometres*, chilometri quadrati	2,590
0,06102	*cubic inches*, pollici cubici	*cubic centimetres*, centimetri cubici	16,3870
35,3148	*cubic feet*, piedi cubici	*cubic metres*, metri cubici	0,02831
1,3080	*cubic yards*, iarde cubiche	*cubic metres*, metri cubici	0,7646
2,20462	*pounds avoirdupois*, libbre avoirdupois	*kilogrammes*, chilogrammi	0,4536
0,03527	*ounces avoirdupois*, once avoirdupois	*grammes*, grammi	28,3495
15,3846	*grains*, grani	*grammes*, grammi	0,064
0,01968	*hundredweights*	*kilogrammes*, chilogrammi	50,80
0,984	*(long) tons*, tonnellate (inglesi)	*tons*, tonnellate (metriche)	1,016
0,220	*(imperial) gallons*, galloni	*litres*, litri	4,546
0,9863	*horsepowers*	*chevaux-vapeurs*, cavalli-vapore	1,0139
multiply by above moltiplicare per i valori sopra indicati	**to obtain** per ottenere	**from** da	

(*) The punctuation signs appearing in the above figures are those used in Italy and other Continental countries, namely a comma instead of the decimal point and a full stop instead of a comma to mark off the thousands: e.g. 2.5 = 2,5 ; 2,500 = 2.500.

MONETARY SYSTEMS OF THE ANGLO-SAXON COUNTRIES

GREAT BRITAIN
(basic unit = *pound*, sterlin)

coins, monete
bronze, bronzo
farthing (1/4d.), un quarto di penny (soppresso dal gennaio 1961).
halfpenny (1/2d.), mezzo penny.
penny (1d.), penny, dodicesima parte dello scellino.
silver, argento
threepence, threepenny (bit) (3d.), tre penny.
sixpence (6d.), sei pence, mezzo scellino.
shilling (1s., 1/-), scellino, ventesima parte della sterlina.
florin, two-shilling piece (2s., 2/-), due scellini.
half-crown (2s. 6d., 2/6), mezza corona, due scellini e sei pence.
crown (5s., 5/-), corona, cinque scellini (*).

gold, oro
half-sovereign (10s.), mezza sovrana, dieci scellini oro (*).
sovereign, pound sterling (£1), sovrana, sterlina oro (*).
bank-notes, banconote
ten-shilling note (10s), mezza sterlina, dieci scellini.
pound note (£1), sterlina carta.
five-pound note (£5), cinque sterline.
nominal coins, (**) monete nominali
half-guinea (10s. 6d., 10/6), mezza ghinea, dieci scellini e sei pence.
guinea (£1.1s., 21s.), ghinea, ventun scellini.

(*) Moneta non circolante.
(**) Si usano nelle parcelle dei professionisti, quote di associazioni, prezzi di libri e di oggetti di l····›, ecc.

COMMONWEALTH

Australia (*Commonwealth of Australia*): *Australian pound* (£ *A*), lira australiana.
Canada (*Dominion of Canada*): *Canadian dollar* ($ *Can.*), dollaro canadese.
Ceylon (*Dominion of Ceylon*): *rupee* (*R.*), rupia.
Federazione Centro-africana (*Central African Federation: Northern and Southern Rhodesia and Nyasaland*): *Rhodesian pound* (£ *Rh.*), lira della Rhodesia.
Federazione Malese (*Federation of Malaya*): *Malay dollar* ($ *Mal.*), dollaro malese.
Ghana (*Republic of Ghana*): *Ghanaian pound*, lira del Ghana.

India (*Indian Union, Bharat*): *rupee* (*R.*), rupia.
Indie Occidentali (*Caribbean Federation*): *West Indies dollar* ($ *W.I.*), dollaro delle Indie Occidentali.
Nigeria (*Federation of Nigeria*): *Nigerian pound*, lira della Nigeria.
Nuova Zelanda (*New Zealand*): *New Zealand pound* (£ *NZ.*), lira neozelandese.
Pakistan (*Islamic Republic of Pakistan*): *Pakistani rupee* (*Pak. R.*), rupia del Pakistan.
Singapore (*State of Singapore*): *Singapore dollar*, dollaro di Singapore.

UNITED STATES OF AMERICA
(basic unit = *dollar*, dollaro)

coins, monete
bronze, bronzo
cent (1c.), un centesimo di dollaro.
copper and nickel alloy, lega di rame e nickel
nickel, five cents (5c.), cinque centesimi di dollaro.
silver, argento
dime (10c.), dieci centesimi di dollaro.
quarter (25c.), venticinque centesimi di dollaro.
half-dollar (50c.), mezzo dollaro, cinquanta centesimi di dollaro.
dollar ($1), dollaro.

gold, (*) oro
dollar ($1), dollaro.
quarter-eagle ($2.5), due dollari e mezzo.
half-eagle ($5), cinque dollari.
eagle ($10), dieci dollari.
double-eagle ($20), venti dollari.
bills, banconote
Si hanno tagli da $ *1, 2, 5, 10, 20, 50, 100, 500, 1000, 5000, 10000* (i tre ultimi non sono in circolazione normale).

(*) Gold coins are no longer in circulation.

MOST IMPORTANT ENGLISH IRREGULAR VERBS

INFINITIVE	PAST	PAST PARTICIPLE
to **abide** [ə'baid]	**abode** [ə'boud], **abided** [ə'baidid]	**abode** [ə'boud], **abided** [ə'baidid]
to **arise** [ə'raiz]	**arose** [ə'rouz]	**arisen** [ə'rizn]
to **awake** [ə'weik]	**awoke** [ə'wouk]	**awaked** [ə'weikt], **awoke** [ə'wouk]
to **backbite** ['bækbait]	**backbit** ['bækbit]	**backbitten** ['bæk,bitn], **backbit** ['bækbit]
to **backslide** ['bæk'slaid]	**backslid** ['bæk'slid]	**backslid** ['bæk'slid]
to **be** [bi:]	**was** [wɔz]	**been** [bi:n]
to **bear** [bɛə*]	**bore** [bɔ:*], (arc.) **bare** [bɛə*]	**borne, born** [bɔ:n]
to **beat** [bi:t]	**beat** [bi:t]	**beaten** ['bi:tn], **beat** [bi:t]
to **become** [bi'kʌm]	**became** [bi'keim]	**become** [bi'kʌm]
to **befall** [bi'fɔ:l]	**befell** [bi'fel]	**befallen** [bi'fɔ:lən]
to **beget** [bi'get]	**begot** [bi'gɔt]	**begot** [bi'gɔt], **begotten** [bi'gɔtn]
to **begin** [bi'gin]	**began** [bi'gæn]	**begun** [bi'gʌn]
to **behold** [bi'hould]	**beheld** [bi'held]	**beheld** [bi'held]
to **bend** [bend]	**bent** [bent]	**bent** [bent]
to **bereave** [bi'ri:v]	**bereaved** [bi'ri:vd], **bereft** [bi'reft]	**bereaved** [bi'ri:vd], **bereft** [bi'reft]
to **beseech** [bi'si:tʃ]	**besought** [bi'sɔ:t]	**besought** [bi'sɔ:t]
to **beset** [bi'set]	**beset** [bi'set]	**beset** [bi'set]
to **bespeak** [bi'spi:k]	**bespoke** [bi'spouk]	**bespoken** [bi'spoukən]
to **bestride** [bi'straid]	**bestrode** [bi'stroud]	**bestriden** [bi'stridn]
to **bet** [bet]	**bet** [bet]	**bet** [bet]
to **betake** [bi'teik]	**betook** [bi'tuk]	**betaken** [bi'teikən]
to **bethink** [bi'θiŋk]	**bethought** [bi'θɔ:t]	**bethought** [bi'θɔ:t]
to **bid** [bid]	**bade** [beid], **bad** [bæd], **bid** [bid]	**bidden** [bidn], **bid** [bid]
to **bide** [baid]	**bode** [boud]	**bided** ['baidid]
to **bind** [baind]	**bound** [baund]	**bound** [baund]
to **bite** [bait]	**bit** [bit]	**bit** [bit], **bitten** ['bitn]
to **bleed** [bli:d]	**bled** [bled]	**bled** [bled]
to **blend** [blend]	**blended** ['blendid], **blent** [blent]	**blended** ['blendid], **blent** [blent]
to **bless** [bles]	**blessed**, (poet.) **blest** [blest]	**blessed**, (poet.) **blest** [blest]
to **blow** [blou]	**blew** [blu:]	**blown** [bloun]
to **break** [breik]	**broke** [brouk], (arc.) **brake** [breik]	**broken** ['broukən], (fam.) **broke** [brouk]
to **breed** [bri:d]	**bred** [bred]	**bred** [bred]
to **bring** [briŋ]	**brought** [brɔ:t]	**brought** [brɔ:t]
to **broadcast** ['brɔ:dkɑ:st]	**broadcast** ['brɔ:dkɑ:st], **broadcasted** ['brɔ:d,kɑ:stid]	**broadcast** ['brɔ:dkɑ:st], **broadcasted** ['brɔ:d,kɑ:stid]
to **browbeat** ['braubi:t]	**browbeat** ['braubi:t]	**browbeaten** ['braubi:tn]
to **build** [bild]	**built** [bilt]	**built** [bilt]
to **burn** [bə:n]	**burnt** [bə:nt], **burned** [bə:nd]	**burnt** [bə:nt], **burned** [bə:nd]
to **burst** [bə:st]	**burst** [bə:st]	**burst** [bə:st]
to **buy** [bai]	**bought** [bɔ:t]	**bought** [bɔ:t]
to **cast** [kɑ:st]	**cast** [kɑ:st]	**cast** [kɑ:st]
to **catch** [kætʃ]	**caught** [kɔ:t]	**caught** [kɔ:t]
to **chide** [tʃaid]	**chid** [tʃid], **chided** ['tʃaidid]	**chidden** ['tʃidn], **chid** [tʃid], **chided** ['tʃaidid]
to **choose** [tʃu:z]	**chose** [tʃouz]	**chosen** ['tʃouzn]
to **cleave** [kli:v]	**cleaved** [kli:vd], **cleft** [kleft], (letter.) **clove** [klouv], (arc.) **clave** [kleiv]	**cleaved** [kli:vd], **cleft** [kleft], (letter.) **cloven** ['klouvn], **clove** [klouv]
to **climb** [klaim]	**climbed** [klaimd], (arc. dial.) **clomb** [kloum]	**climbed** [klaimd], (arc. dial.) **clomb** [kloum]
to **cling** [kliŋ]	**clung** [klʌŋ]	**clung** [klʌŋ]
to **clothe** [klouð]	**clothed** [klouðd], **clad** [klæd]	**clothed** [klouðd], **clad** [klæd]
to **come** [kʌm]	**came** [keim]	**come** [kʌm]
to **cost** [kɔst]	**cost** [kɔst]	**cost** [kɔst]
to **creep** [kri:p]	**crept** [krept]	**crept** [krept]
to **crow** [krou]	**crowed** [kroud], **crew** [kru:]	**crowed** [kroud]
to **cut** [kʌt]	**cut** [kʌt]	**cut** [kʌt]
to **dare** [dɛə*]	**dared** [dɛəd], (rar.) **durst** [də:st]	**dared** [dɛəd]
to **deal** [di:l]	**dealt** [delt]	**dealt** [delt]
to **dig** [dig]	**dug** [dʌg]	**dug** [dʌg]
to **do** [du:]	**did** [did]	**done** [dʌn]

INFINITIVE	PAST	PAST PARTICIPLE
to draw [drɔ:]	drew [dru:]	drawn [drɔ:n]
to dream [dri:m]	dreamed [dri:md], dreamt [dremt]	dreamed [dri:md], dreamt [dremt]
to drink [driŋk]	drank [dræŋk]	drunk [drʌŋk], (arc.) drunken ['drʌŋkən]
to drive [draiv]	drove [drouv]	driven ['drivn]
to dwell [dwel]	dwelt [dwelt], (amer.) dwelled [dweld]	dwelt [dwelt], (amer.) dwelled [dweld]
to eat [i:t]	ate [et], (arc.) eat [i:t]	eaten ['i:tn]
to fall [fɔ:l]	fell [fel]	fallen ['fɔ:lən]
to feed [fi:d]	fed [fed]	fed [fed]
to feel [fi:l]	felt [felt]	felt [felt]
to fight [fait]	fought [fɔ:t]	fought [fɔ:t]
to find [faind]	found [faund]	found [faund]
to flee [fli:]	fled [fled]	fled [fled]
to fling [fliŋ]	flung [flʌŋ]	flung [flʌŋ]
to fly [flai]	flew [flu:]	flown [floun]
to forbear [fɔ:'bɛə*]	forbore [fɔ:'bɔ:*]	forborne [fɔ:'bɔ:n]
to forbid [fə'bid]	forbade [fə'beid]	forbidden [fə'bidn]
to forecast ['fɔ:-ka:st]	forecast ['fɔ:-ka:st]	forecast ['fɔ:-ka:st]
to forego [fɔ:'gou]	forewent [fɔ:'went]	foregone [fɔ:'gɔn]
to foreknow [fɔ:'nou]	foreknew [fɔ:'nju:]	foreknown [fɔ:'noun]
to foresee [fɔ:'si:]	foresaw [fɔ:'sɔ:]	foreseen [fɔ:'si:n]
to foretell [fɔ:'tel]	foretold [fɔ:'tould]	foretold [fɔ:'tould]
to forget [fə'get]	forgot [fə'gɔt]	forgotten [fə'gɔtn]
to forgive [fə'giv]	forgave [fə'geiv]	forgiven [fə'givn]
to forsake [fə'seik]	forsook [fə'suk]	forsaken [fə'seikən]
to forswear [fɔ:'swɛə*]	forswore [fɔ:'swɔ:*]	forsworn [fɔ:'swɔ:n]
to freeze [fri:z]	froze [frouz]	frozen ['frouzn]
to gainsay [gein'sei]	gainsaid [gein'seid]	gainsaid [gein'seid]
to get [get]	got [gɔt]	got [gɔt], (arc. o talvolta amer.) gotten ['gɔtn]
to gird [gə:d]	girded ['gə:did], girt [gə:t]	girded ['gə:did], girt [gə:t]
to give [giv]	gave [geiv]	given ['givn]
to go [gou]	went [went]	gone [gɔn]
to grave [greiv]	graved [greivd]	graved [greivd], graven ['greivən]
to grind [graind]	ground [graund]	ground [graund]
to grow [grou]	grew [gru:]	grown [groun]
to hang [hæŋ]	hung [hʌŋ], hanged [hæŋd]	hung [hʌŋ], hanged [hæŋd]
to have [hæv]	had [hæd]	had [hæd]
to hear [hiə*]	heard [hə:d]	heard [hə:d]
to heave [hi:v]	heaved [hi:vd], hove [houv]	heaved [hi:vd]
to hew [hju:]	hewed [hju:d]	hewed [hju:d], hewn [hju:n]
to hide [haid]	hid [hid]	hid [hid], hidden ['hidn]
to hit [hit]	hit [hit]	hit [hit]
to hold [hould]	held [held]	held [held], (arc.) holden ['houldən]
to hurt [hə:t]	hurt [hə:t]	hurt [hə:t]
to inlay ['in'lei]	inlaid ['in'leid]	inlaid ['in'leid]
to keep [ki:p]	kept [kept]	kept [kept]
to kneel [ni:l]	knelt [nelt]	knelt [nelt]
to knit [nit]	knitted ['nitid], knit [nit]	knitted ['nitid], knit [nit]
to know [nou]	knew [nju:]	known [noun]
to lade [leid]	laded ['leidid]	laden ['leidn]
to lay [lei]	laid [leid]	laid [leid]
to lead [li:d]	led [led]	led [led]
to lean [li:n]	leaned, leant [lent]	leaned, leant [lent]
to leap [li:p]	leaped, leapt [lept]	leaped, leapt [lept]
to learn [lə:n]	learnt [lə:nt], learned [lə:nd]	learnt [lə:nt], learned [lə:nd]
to leave [li:v]	left [left]	left [left]
to lend [lend]	lent [lent]	lent [lent]
to let [let]	let [let]	let [let]
to lie [lai]	lay [lei]	lain [lein]
to light [lait]	lighted ['laitid], lit [lit]	lighted ['laitid], lit [lit]
to lose [lu:z]	lost [lɔst]	lost [lɔst]
to make [meik]	made [meid]	made [meid]
to mean [mi:n]	meant [ment]	meant [ment]
to meet [mi:t]	met [met]	met [met]
to melt [melt]	melted ['meltid]	melted ['meltid], (arc.) molten ['moultən]
to misdeal ['mis'di:l]	misdealt ['mis'delt]	misdealt ['mis'delt]
to misgive [mis'giv]	misgave [mis'geiv]	misgiven [mis'givn]
to mislay [mis'lei]	mislaid [mis'leid]	mislaid [mis'leid]
to mislead [mis'li:d]	misled [mis'led]	misled [mis'led]
to mistake [mis'teik]	mistook [mis'tuk]	mistaken [mis'teikən]

INFINITIVE	PAST	PAST PARTICIPLE
to **misunderstand** ['misʌndə'stænd[	**misunderstood** ['misʌndə'stud]	**misunderstood** ['misʌndə'stud]
to **mow** [mou]	**mowed** [moud]	**mown** [moun]
to **outbid** [aut'bid]	**outbade** [aut'beid]	**outbidden** [aut'bidn]
to **outdo** [aut'du:]	**outdid** [aut'did]	**outdone** [aut'dʌn]
to **outgo** [aut'gou]	**outwent** [aut'went]	**outgone** [aut'gon]
to **outgrow** [aut'grou]	**outgrew** [aut'gru:]	**outgrown** [aut'groun]
to **outride** [aut'raid]	**outrode** [aut'roud]	**outridden** [aut'ridn]
to **outrun** [aut'rʌn]	**outran** [aut'ræn]	**outrun** [aut'rʌn]
to **outshine** [aut'ʃain]	**outshone** [aut'ʃon]	**outshone** [aut'ʃon]
to **outspread** [aut'spred]	**outspread** [aut'spred]	**outspread** [aut'spred]
to **outwear** [aut'wɛə*]	**outwore** [aut'wɔ:*]	**outworn** [aut'wɔ:n]
to **overbear** [,ouvə'bɛə*]	**overbore** [,ouvə'bɔ:*]	**overborne** [,ouvə'bɔ:n]
to **overcast** ['ouvə-kɑ:st]	**overcast** ['ouvə-kɑ:st]	**overcast** ['ouvə-kɑ:st]
to **overcome** [,ouvə'kʌm]	**overcame** [,ouvə'keim]	**overcome** [,ouvə'kʌm]
to **overdo** [,ouvə'du:]	**overdid** [,ouvə'did]	**overdone** [,ouvə'dʌn]
to **overdraw** ['ouvə'drɔ:]	**overdrew** ['ouvə'dru:]	**overdrawn** ['ouvə'drɔ:n]
to **overeat** ['ouvər'i:t]	**overate** ['ouvər'et]	**overeaten** ['ouvər'i:tn]
to **overfeed** ['ouvə'fi:d]	**overfed** ['ouvə'fed]	**overfed** ['ouvə'fed]
to **overgrow** ['ouvə'grou]	**overgrew** ['ouvə'gru:]	**overgrown** ['ouvə'groun]
to **overhang** ['ouvəhæŋ]	**overhung** ['ouvəhʌŋ]	**overhung** ['ouvəhʌŋ]
to **overhear** [,ouvə'hiə*]	**overheard** [,ouvə'hɔ:d]	**overheard** [,ouvə'hə:d]
to **overlay** [,ouvə'lei]	**overlaid** [,ouvə'leid]	**overlaid** [,ouvə'leid]
to **overleap** [,ouvə'li:p]	**overleaped, overleapt** [,ouvə'lept]	**overleaped, overleapt** [,ouvə'lept]
to **overlie** [,ouvə'lai]	**overlay** [,ouvə'lei]	**overlain** [,ouvə'lein]
to **override** [,ouvə'raid]	**overrode** [,ouvə'roud]	**overridden** [,ouvə'ridn]
to **overrun** [,ouvvə'rʌn]	**overran** [,ouvə'ræn]	**overrun** [,ouvə'rʌn]
to **oversee** ['ouvə'si:]	**oversaw** ['ouvə'sɔ:]	**overseen** ['ouvə'si:n]
to **overset** ['ouvə'set]	**overset** ['ouvə'set]	**overset** ['ouvə'set]
to **overshoot** ['ouvə'ʃu:t]	**overshot** ['ouvə'ʃot]	**overshot** ['ouvə'ʃot]
to **oversleep** ['ouvə'sli:p]	**overslept** ['ouvə'slept]	**overslept** ['ouvə'slept]
to **overspread** [,ouvə'spred]	**overspread** [,ouvə'spred]	**overspread** [,ouvə'spred]
to **overtaake** [,ouvə'teik]	**overtook** [,ouvə'tuk]	**overtaken** [,ouvə'teikən]
to **overthrow** [,ouvə'θrou]	**overthrew** [,ouvə'θru:]	**overthrown** [,ouvə'θroun]
to **partake** [pɑ:'teik]	**partook** [pɑ:'tuk]	**partaken** [pɑ:'teikən]
to **pay** [pei]	**paid** [peid]	**paid** [peid]
to **put** ['put]	**put** [put]	**put** [put]
to **read** [ri:d]	**read** [red]	**read** [red]
to **rebuild** ['ri:'bild]	**rebuilt** ['ri:'bilt]	**rebuilt** ['ri:'bilt]
to **recast** ['ri:'kɑ:st]	**recast** ['ri:'kɑ:st]	**recast** ['ri:'kɑ:st]
to **relay** ['ri:'lei]	**relaid** ['ri:'leid]	**relaid** ['ri:'leid]
to **rend** [rend]	**rent** [rent]	**rent** [rent]
to **repay** [ri:'pei]	**repaid** [ri:'peid]	**repaid** [ri:'peid]
to **reset** ['ri:'set]	**reset** ['ri:'set]	**reset** ['ri:'set]
to **retell** ['ri:'tel]	**retold** ['ri:'tould]	**retold** ['ri:'tould]
to **rid** [rid]	**rid** [rid], **ridded** ['ridid]	**rid** [rid]
to **ride** [raid]	**rode** [roud], (*arc.*) **rid** [rid]	**ridden** ['ridn], (*arc.*) **rid** [rid]
to **ring** [riŋ]	**rang** [ræŋ]	**rung** [rʌŋ]
to **rise** [raiz]	**rose** [rouz]	**risen** ['rizn]
to **rive** [raiv]	**rived** [raivd]	**rived** [raivd], **riven** ['rivən]
to **run** [rʌn]	**ran** [ræn]	**run** [rʌn]
to **saw** [sɔ:]	**sawed** [sɔ:d]	**sawn** [sɔ:n], (*rar.*) **sawed** [sɔ:d]
to **say** [sei]	**said** [sed]	**said** [sed]
to **see** [si:	**saw** [sɔ:]	**seen** [si:n]
to **seek** [si:k]	**sought** [sɔ:t]	**sought** [sɔ:t]
to **seethe** [si:ð]	**seethed** [si:ðd], (*arc.*) **sod** [sod]	**seethed** [si:ðd], (*arc.*) **sodden** ['sodn]
to **sell** [sel]	**sold** [sould]	**sold** [sould]
to **send** [send]	**sent** [sent]	**sent** [sent]
to **set** [set]	**set** [set]	**set** [set]
to **sew** [sou]	**sewed** [soud]	**sewn** [soun]
to **shake** [ʃeik]	**shook** [ʃuk]	**shaken** ['ʃeikən]
to **shear** [ʃiə*]	**sheared** [ʃiəd], (*arc.*) **shore** [ʃɔ:*]	**shorn** [ʃɔ:n], (*rar.*) **sheared** [ʃiəd]
to **shed** [ʃed]	**shed** [ʃed]	**shed** [ʃed]
to **shine** [ʃain]	**shone** [ʃon], **shined** [ʃaind]	**shone** [ʃon], **shined** [ʃaind]
to **shoe** [ʃu:]	**shod** [ʃod], (*rar.*) **shoed** [ʃu:d]	**shod** [ʃod], (*rar.*) **shoed** [ʃu:d]
to **shoot** [ʃu:t]	**shot** [ʃot]	**shot** [ʃot]
to **show** [ʃou]	**showed** [ʃoud]	**shown** [ʃoun]
to **shrink** [ʃriŋk]	**shrank** [ʃræŋk]	**shrunk** [ʃrʌŋk]
to **shrive** [ʃraiv]	**shrove** [ʃrouv]	**shriven** ['ʃrivn]
to **shut** [ʃʌt]	**shut** [ʃʌt]	**shut** [ʃʌt]
to **sing** [siŋ]	**sang** [sæŋ]	**sung** [sʌŋ]
to **sink** [siŋk]	**sank** [sæŋk], (*rar.*) **sunk** [sʌŋk]	**sunk** [sʌŋk]
to **sit** [sit]	**sat** [sæt]	**sat** [sæt]